MARTINDALE-HUBBELL® LAW DIRECTORY

VOLUME 9

NORTH CAROLINA
NORTH DAKOTA, OHIO
OKLAHOMA, OREGON

LexisNexis®

121 Chanlon Road, New Providence, NJ 07974 • Phone: 1-800-526-4902
Email: info@martindale.com • www.martindale.com • www.lawyers.com

Published by LexisNexis® Martindale-Hubbell®

John Roney, Senior Vice President, Operations, Customer Support, & Technology
Marty Falle, Vice President, Sales
Joe Douress, Vice President, Business Development
Philip Evans, Vice President, Chief Financial Officer
Dean Hollister, Vice President, Database Production
Carlton Dyce, Senior Director, Customer Experience

For additional help or explanation, please call Martindale-Hubbell Customer Service at 1-800-526-4902, or in New Jersey at 908-464-6800.

International Standard Book Number: 1-56160-690-1 (Set)

Printed and bound in the United States of America
by R.R. Donnelley
Chicago, Illinois and Willard, Ohio

ISBN 1-56160-690-1

9 781561 606900

IMPORTANT NOTICES

Martindale-Hubbell® has used its best efforts in collecting and preparing material for inclusion in the **Martindale-Hubbell Law Directory** but cannot warrant that the information herein is complete or accurate, and does not assume, and hereby disclaims, any liability to any person for any loss or damage caused by errors or omissions in the **Martindale-Hubbell Law Directory** whether such errors or omissions result from negligence, accident or any other cause.

Lawyers providing information regarding themselves and their law firms for inclusion in the **Martindale-Hubbell Law Directory** are responsible for both the accuracy of the information submitted and compliance with local law and bar regulations.

Some lawyers and law firms are omitted from the **Martindale-Hubbell Law Directory** by request while others are omitted because adequate information is not available.

The Martindale-Hubbell Peer Review Ratings contained in this Directory are intended primarily for the use of lawyers and law firms in the practice of their profession. They may not be used in any advertisement or for any commercial, political or other purpose. Peer Review Ratings may be referenced in printed lawyer-to-lawyer communications (such as law firm brochures), professional announcements, and legal directories targeted to lawyers and law firms. For more information on requirements for acknowledgements, please see Guidelines for Using Your Martindale-Hubbell Peer Review Rating on page XV, or visit www.martindale.com/ratings.

Omission of individual lawyer Peer Review Ratings should not be construed as unfavorable since Martindale-Hubbell does not undertake to develop ratings for every lawyer. In addition, certain lawyers have requested their Peer Review Ratings not be published while in other instances, definitive information has yet to be developed.

FOREWORD

We are pleased to present the 2006 edition of the **Martindale-Hubbell® Law Directory**, the world's leading guide to the legal profession since 1868.

What began as a two-volume register of recommended lawyers has evolved into a global network of over one million legal practitioners, firms, alliances, and services. Today Martindale-Hubbell's 17 volumes offer uniquely authoritative practice profiles and professional biographies of virtually every lawyer and law firm in the United States, along with extensive coverage of the international legal community in over 165 countries — from Albania to Zimbabwe.

The classic print edition represents but a single component of the Martindale-Hubbell Legal Network, a multimedia legal research and networking tool. Spanning the full array of fast-access digital formats, the **Law Directory** is also available via the *Martindale-Hubbell Lawyer Locator* at *martindale.com*® and *lawyers.com*SM, on CD-ROM, and online through LexisNexis®.

To help the lawyers and firms represented in our database unlock new opportunities for practice development, our growing network of strategic alliance partners within the legal, business, and consumer spheres offers prominent access to *martindale.com* and its consumer-facing counterpart, *lawyers.com*. Our Internet partners range from professional sites such as CNN.com and law.com to high-traffic consumer destinations including Google, Yahoo!, SuperPages and MSN, which reach over 85% of Internet users. Together, these alliance partners attract over 100 million unique visitors each month, delivering a vast universe of potential clients.

To ensure the most up-to-date information on lawyers and law firms is made available in our directories, we recently launched the *Client Service Center*. This online updating tool allows law firms to securely make changes to their Martindale-Hubbell listing whenever they have new information to share, including staff changes, new practice areas, updated contact information and recent awards.

We are also continuing to enhance and expand our Web marketing tools, designed to help law firms grow their practices via the Internet. *Custom Web Sites* and *Search Placement Pro* maximize a firm's Internet presence through sophisticated graphics, creative content, and improved ranking in the results of major search engines. City, county, state and nationwide *Sponsorships* on *lawyers.com* are also available in specific practice areas to increase visibility and drive targeted prospects to a firm's credentials.

Another initiative, *The Advantage Program*, is a unique portfolio of client development opportunities that includes speaking engagements at well-respected conferences; publication in *Counsel to Counsel* magazine and in *Legal Articles* on *martindale.com*; the opportunity to co-host a Counsel to Counsel forum; expanded practice area and industry *Group Profiles* and *Diversity Profiles* on our proprietary Web sites.

In addition, we are pleased to announce that we've re-launched *Experts & Services* on *martindale.com*. The new *Experts & Services* — available from links via *martindale.com's* home page or directly at www.martindale.com/resources — is the Internet's most comprehensive directory of resources available to attorneys. It includes extensive information on experts, consultants, investigators, court reporters, and many other legal-service providers.

While technological advances will no doubt further enhance the practice of law and our own offering of services, nothing will change Martindale-Hubbell's fundamental partnership with the legal profession: a commitment to enhance the visibility and working efficiency of every firm and individual attorney.

Carlton Dyce
Senior Director, Customer Experience

TABLE OF CONTENTS

TABLE OF CONTENTS — *continued*

LEGAL ADVISORY BOARD

The Advisory Board's mission is to ensure that LexisNexis and Martindale-Hubbell are responsive to the constantly changing needs of the legal profession. In response to these needs, the Board entertains new strategies and concepts developed by the company, and provides impartial and candid points of view. The following lawyers selected from the private, corporate, academic and international sectors of the profession comprise the 2005-2006 Board.

DENNIS W. ARCHER of Dickinson Wright PLLC; Detroit, Michigan. Mr. Archer is the former Mayor of the City of Detroit, (1994-2001) and a former Associate Justice of the Michigan Supreme Court (1986-1990). He is the past President of the Wolverine Bar Association, the National Bar Association and the State Bar of Michigan. Mr. Archer is the past President of the National League of Cities, past President of the National Conference of Democratic Mayors and a past member of the Board of Trustees of the United States Conference of Mayors and Board of Directors of the National Conference of Black Mayors. He currently serves on the American Bar Association's Board of Governors. He was President of the American Bar Association-August 2002 to August 2003, the first person of color to be so honored. He also serves as Chairman of Dickinson Wright PLLC.

MARTHA W. BARNETT of Holland & Knight, Tallahassee, Florida. Ms. Barnett is a former Chair of the House of Delegates of the American Bar Association, the first woman lawyer to be so honored, and has served on the ABA's Board of Governors. She was elected President of the American Bar Association, serving as such from July 2000 to August 2001. Ms. Barnett now serves as Chair of Holland & Knight.

ROBERT H. BERNSTEIN joined Reed Smith in January 2005. Mr. Bernstein heads the Firm's Labor & Employment Global Marketing Team, strengthening the Firm's offering to its national and international corporate clients. During the past 23 years, Mr. Bernstein has developed an extensive labor and employment practice, exclusively representing multinational and domestic corporations nationwide, with an emphasis in employment litigation. Mr. Bernstein lectures and writes extensively throughout the United States and overseas concerning a wide array of employment law issues. In 1982, Mr. Bernstein earned his J.D. from Georgetown University Law Center; in 1979, he received his B.S.F.S., with distinction, from the Georgetown University School of Foreign Service. Mr. Bernstein is admitted to the New Jersey Bar, the U.S. Court of Appeals for the Third Circuit, and the U.S. District Court for the District of New Jersey. He is a member of the Labor Law Section and Litigation Section of the American Bar Association.

BENJAMIN R. CIVILETTI of Venable, Baetjer, Howard & Civiletti, Washington, D.C. and Baltimore, Maryland. Mr. Civiletti is a former Attorney General of the United States under President Carter, 1979-1981. He is the former Chairman of the ABA Litigation Section and has been a member of the ABA House of Delegates since 1991. He also serves as the ABA Representative to the United Nations. He is the former Chairman of Venable. Mr. Civiletti is a Fellow of the American College of Trial Lawyers and the American Law Institute.

THOMAS R. CURTIN of Graham, Curtin & Sheridan, A Professional Association, Morristown, New Jersey. Mr. Curtin is a Life Fellow of the American Bar Foundation. He is a past President of the Morris County Bar Association (1978-1979), the New Jersey State Bar Foundation (1986-1988), the New Jersey State Bar Association (1993-1994), and the Notre Dame Law Foundation (2000-2001). He is a former Chairman of the New Jersey Commission on Professionalism in the Law (1996-1998). He is a member of the American Bar Association House of Delegates, serving as the New Jersey State Delegate, and the Sports Lawyers Association. He is currently a member of the Notre Dame Law School Advisory Council and has been on the Board of Directors for the National Football Foundation and College Hall of Fame since 2002.

THOMAS G. HEINTZMAN, O.C., Q.C., is a trial and appellant counsel practicing with the law firm of McCarthy Tétrault, Toronto, Ontario. He is a Bencher of the Law Society of Upper Canada and an Officer of the Order of Canada. Mr. Heintzman is a Fellow of the International Academy of Trial Lawyers, and the American College of Trial Lawyers and the Chair of its Canadian Competitions Committee.

DOUGLAS B. HENDERSON is the Founding and Senior Partner of Finnegan, Henderson, Farabow, Garrett & Dunner, Washington, D.C. Mr. Henderson is a Member of the Advisory Council of the United States Court of Federal Claims, and a Member of the Board of the Federal Circuit Bar Association. He was formerly Chairman of the Patent Division and Member of Council of the Section of Intellectual Property Law of the American Bar Association. He was the Founder of the Federal Circuit Bar Association, a co-founder of the U.S. Court of Federal Claims Bar Association, and a co-founder of the ITC Trial Lawyers Association.

PATRICK E. HOBBS, Dean of Seton Hall University School of Law, first joined the faculty of Seton Hall in 1990. He teaches in the area of taxation and has taught Federal Income Taxation, Corporate Taxation and Business Planning, and Law and Literature. In 1995, he became the Associate Dean for Finance. In 1999, he became the Law School's seventh Dean. Dean Hobbs graduated magna cum laude from Seton Hall University with a B.S. in Accounting. He received his J.D. from the University of North Carolina at Chapel Hill, and earned his LL.M. from New York University. Dean Hobbs was recently appointed a Commissioner on the New Jersey State Commission of Investigation by former Governor James McGreevy. He has chaired the American Bar Association, Section of Legal Education and Admissions to the Bar, Law School Development Committee since 2002, and was also recently appointed to serve on the American Bar Association Standards Review Committee. He also serves as a member of the boards of the Newark Alliance, LexisNexis, Newark Beth Israel Medical Center, the New Jersey Commission of Professionalism, and the New Jersey Institute for Continuing Legal Education. In 2004, he served as Chair of the Newark, New Jersey Mayor's Blue Ribbon Commission on the Downtown Core Redevelopment.

THOMAS J. KLITGAARD, formerly Senior Vice President and General Counsel of Sega of America, Inc., is now a partner with Dillingham & Murphy, San Francisco. He is a former Chairman of the California State Bar's Committee on the Maintenance of Professional Competence. He is a member of the panel of technology arbitrators of the American Arbitration Association in New York and a member of the Advisory Board of the Southwestern Legal Foundation in Dallas. He is currently the chairman of a graduate business management program in Shanghai, China.

RALPH I. LANCASTER, JR. of Pierce Atwood, Portland, Maine has served as Independent Counsel, In Re Herman, by appointment of the Special Division of the D.C. Court of Appeals. He previously served as Counsel for the United States before the International Court of Justice in a case concerning delimitation of the Maritime Boundary in the Gulf of Maine and as Special Master by appointment of the United States Supreme Court in State of New Jersey vs. State of Nebraska and again as Special Master in State of Virginia vs. State of Maryland. Mr. Lancaster began his legal career as a law clerk to the Honorable Edward T. Gignoux. He is a Past-President of the Maine State Bar Association and a former member of the House of Delegates of the American Bar Association. He served as Chair of the Standing Committee on Federal Judiciary of the ABA. He is a Fellow of the American College of Trial Lawyers and served as its President, 1989-1990. He is engaged in civil and criminal trial practice.

JUDY PERRY MARTINEZ of Northrop Grumman Corp., New Orleans, Louisiana. Ms. Martinez has been on the Board of Directors of the American Judicature Society, (1991-1998) and the Elmo B. Hunter Center for Judicial Excellence, (1994-1997). She is a Lifetime Fellow of the Louisiana Bar Foundation and a Fellow of the American Bar Foundation. She is a Member of the New Orleans, Louisiana State (Chairperson of the Minority Involvement and Professionalism and Quality of Life Committee, 1992-1993) and American (Member of the Executive Committee, 1998-1999; Board of Governors, 1996-1999; Standing Committee on Federal Judiciary (2000-2003); Commission on Women in the Profession, 1991-1994; ABA Nominating Committee, 1993-1996;

Chair: Young Lawyers Division, 1990-1991; Chair Commission on Domestic Violence, 1999—; Member: Executive Council, Young Lawyers Division, 1986-1996; Special Advisor, Standing Committee on the Federal Judiciary, 1994-1995; Division Delegate, 1991-1996 and Delegate-at-Large, 1999—, ABA House of Delegates; Young Lawyers Division Liason to the ABA Section of Litigation, 1991-1993); Bar Associations and also the Association for Women Attorneys.

JERALYN E. MERRITT is a criminal defense lawyer in private practice in Colorado. Her practice is limited to criminal defense and related forfeitures, with an emphasis on complex federal drug and white collar crimes. Ms. Merritt served as Treasurer and Secretary and on the Board of Directors of the National Association of Criminal Defense Lawyers, from 1996 through 2004. She was a member of the governing council of the American Bar Association's Criminal Justice Section from 2000 through 2004. She is an elected fellow of the American Board of Criminal Lawyers and a past member of its Board of Governors. Ms. Merritt has testified before both Congress and the United States Sentencing Commission on drug sentencing laws. She is the co-author of a text on the Patriot Act, published by Lexis Publishing. She lectures nationally on a variety of criminal defense topics, and since 1996, has provided insightful legal analysis for MSNBC, Fox News, CNN, Court TV and other television and radio networks. From 2000 to 2003, she was a Lecturer-In-Law at Denver University's College of Law teaching "Wrongful Convictions" and "Criminal Defense." In 1996 and 1997, she served as one of the principal trial lawyers for Timothy McVeigh in the Oklahoma City Bombing Case. She is the founder and creator of two award winning websites, CrimeLynx.com, and TalkLeft: The Politics of Crime (TalkLeft.com), a weblog for legal professionals, journalists and the public.

PAUL F. MICKEY, JR. is a partner in Steptoe & Johnson LLP of Washington, D.C. Prior to joining Steptoe & Johnson LLP, Mr. Mickey was with Pillsbury Winthrop Shaw Pittman LLP where he founded the firm's employment law practice and led it for a decade prior to assuming a full-time management role. He has served as Chair of the D.C. Bar's Subcommittee on Individual Employment Rights, handled several noted employment cases, and argued successfully before the U.S. Supreme Court. Mr. Mickey often serves as an arbitrator in cases involving contract, commercial, workplace, and environmental disputes, and is a member of the CPR Panels of Distinguished Neutrals. He received his A.B. degree, summa cum laude, from Princeton University in 1971, and in 1974 he was awarded his J.D. degree from the University of Virginia Law School, where he served as Articles Editor of the Virginia Law Review. His professional background includes serving as law clerk to the Hon. George E. MacKininnon, U.S. Court of Appeals for the District of Columbia Circuit, 1974-1977; as Attorney-Advisor in the Office of Legal Advisor, U.S. Department of State, 1975-1977; and as Vice President-General Counsel, 1979-1983, and Executive Vice President - Law and Public Affairs, 1983-1985, of the National Railroad Passenger Corp. ("Amtrak"). He is a Fellow of the College of Law Practice Management.

WILLIAM G. PAUL of Crowe & Dunlevy, Oklahoma City, Oklahoma. Mr. Paul is the former Senior Vice President & General Counsel, Phillips Petroleum Company, Bartlesville, Oklahoma. In 1999, he was elected President of the American Bar Association, to serve as such from August 1999 to July 2000. He has served as President for both the Oklahoma State Bar Association and National Conference of Bar Presidents. Mr. Paul has been a Member of the American Bar Association, House of Delegates since 1975 and is a Fellow in the American College of Trial Lawyers.

FERNANDO POMBO, Founder and Senior Partner of Gomez-Acebo & Pombo, Madrid, Spain, has contributed to and authored several publications in the field of international business law. Currently, he is Vice-President of the International Bar Association. Mr. Pombo has been a visiting professor at the Institute on International Legal Studies in Salzburg, Austria since 1985. He is also a former President of LES International and a member of the Spanish Arbitration Court. He is fluent in Spanish, English, French and German.

WM. REECE SMITH, JR. of Tampa, Florida, is the senior member of Carlton, Fields, Ward, Emmanuel, Smith & Cutler, P.A. A Rhodes Scholar at Oxford University, England, he was later President of The Florida Bar (1972-73), the American Bar Association (1980-81), and the International Bar Association (1988-90). He is a Fellow of the American College of Trial Lawyers and the International Academy of Trial Lawyers and serves on the Council of the American Law Institute. He received the American Bar Association's Gold Medal for "exceptionally distinguished service to the cause of American Jurisprudence."

STEVEN T. WALTHER of Walther, Key, Maupin, Oats, Cox & LeGoy of Reno, Nevada, is a Trustee of The National Judicial College, former President of the Boalt Hall Alumni Association, University of California, Berkeley, Immediate past Chair of The Fellows of the American Bar Foundation, and a member of the Executive Board of the ABA Central and East European Law Initiative. Mr. Walther previously served as a member of the Board of Governors of the ABA, President of the State Bar of Nevada, Chair of the Board of Trustees of The Nevada Law Foundation, Chair of the ABA Standing Committee on World Order Under Law, and Chair of the ABA Section on International Activities. Mr. Walther has also served as the ABA representative to the United Nations. Mr. Walther has a degree in Russian and has lectured extensively on rule of law, international and human rights issues, both in the United States and Russia.

WALTER H. WHITE, JR. is a Founding Partner of White, Savelieva, LLP London, England. Mr. White previously has served as a Partner of Steptoe & Johnson L.L.P. in Washington, D.C. and as the Managing Director of its Moscow office. Mr. White is a former Commissioner of Securities for the State of Wisconsin 1988-1991. He has served as a member of the ABA House of Delegates, as the Chair of the Section of Individual Rights and Responsibilities and as chair of the Young Lawyers Division. Mr. White has also been a member of the State Bar of Wisconsin Board of Governors, on the Board of the Milwaukee Foundation and is currently a Board member of the Central-Asian-American Enterprise Fund by appointment of former President Clinton. He also currently serves as a member of the American Bar Association Board of Governors.

LONNIE J. WILLIAMS, JR. is a Partner of Quarles & Brady LLP, Phoenix, Arizona. Mr. Williams has served as Past President of the Maricopa County Bar Association and as a Past Delegate of the American Bar Association. He is also a Member of the National Bar Association and the Arizona Women Lawyers Association and currently serves as President for the National Conference of Bar Presidents. Mr. Williams was inducted as a Fellow into the American College of Trial Lawyers and the American Bar Foundation. He has been listed in the *Best Lawyers in America* since 1995.

USER GUIDE

The **Martindale-Hubbell® Law Directory** now consists of:

- twelve numbered U.S. volumes (burgundy spine accent). Each volume consists of three main sections, which have been separated for easy access: Practice Profiles on blue pages, Professional Biographies on white pages and Experts & Services on white pages following the divider tab. Included in Volume 1 are listings for the Corporate Law Departments and in Volume 12 are Law School listings. In each Section, headings are provided at the top of each page to indicate the section being referenced and to provide a guide to the listings on that page.
- two volumes of the **Martindale-Hubbell International Law Directory** (blue spine accent), containing listings for lawyers and firms in over 165 countries (including sections for Canada and U.S. lawyers with international interests).
- one **Martindale-Hubbell Law Digest** for the U.S. (black spine accent).
- one **Martindale-Hubbell International Law Digest** (black spine accent).
- one **Martindale-Hubbell Directory of Experts & Legal Services** (Buyer's Guide), a national directory of service providers to the legal industry.

Guam, Northern Mariana Islands, Puerto Rico, U.S. Pacific Territories and the U.S. Virgin Islands can be found both at the end of the U.S. volumes (Volume 12) and in the appropriate sections of the **Martindale-Hubbell International Law Directory** (see Table of Contents).

EXPLANATORY NOTES AND SYMBOLS

Dates following a name, i.e., "'31 '57," indicate the year of birth and the year of first admission to the Bar.

"C." or "L." followed by a numeral indicates the college or law school attended; first degree, if known, is shown following the number. See Index of Colleges, Universities and Law Schools in prefatory section.

Individual alphabetical listings, which are published without charge or other obligation, include lawyers admitted and located at a particular place, as well as others who are not admitted to the Bar of that jurisdiction. In the case of the latter, nonadmission is shown, as is the state of first admission. *It is always possible that a lawyer has been admitted subsequent to the insertion of a listing.* Confirmation of individual state admission can be obtained by writing the admitting authority of the jurisdiction or the lawyer.

"*" following the name of a place in the United States or Canada indicates a county seat. *Population* figures following the name of the place are the most recent available.

"[Lobe,B.&R.]" indicates a lawyer is in the primary firm management of Lobe, Bryant & Rogers; such as member, partner, managing partner, principal, shareholder, senior partner, marketing partner, hiring partner or director; or is an employee of an office operating as a legal professional association, company, corporation or other legal entity, unless otherwise disclosed.

"[A Hane,M.&H.]" indicates a lawyer is employed as a junior partner, senior attorney, senior associate or similar position by the office shown.

"[C Shipley&S.]" indicates a lawyer has the relationship of Counsel or Of Counsel, senior or special counsel with the office shown.

"[S Snell,S.C.&B.]" indicates a lawyer is employed as a staff or contract attorney by the office shown.

"***PRACTICE AREAS***" appearing near the end of a lawyer's professional biography indicates the area(s) of practice to which he or she devotes a significant portion of professional time. In each case, the information has been supplied by the attorney and constitutes a "representation" by the lawyer and does not imply official approval or certification by any state authority.

All "officially recognized" specialties are indicated with language that identifies the approving or certifying authority. Such programs are now in existence in Arizona, Arkansas, California, Connecticut, Florida, Georgia, Idaho, Indiana, Louisiana, Michigan, Minnesota, New Jersey, New Mexico, North Carolina, Ohio, Pennslyvania, South Carolina, Tennessee, Texas and Ontario, Canada.

Title of public office, *company name*, *government agency*, *educational institution*, *etc.*, with which a lawyer is connected is shown in his or her listing.

Professional Companies, Corporations or Associations: Chartered, Associated, P.C., P.A., S.C., Inc., Ltd., etc. following the name of an individual lawyer or law firm means that such office is operating as a Professional Company, Corporation or Association under the laws of that jurisdiction.

"‡" indicates one who devotes all or the greater part of one's time to the affairs of a single client, or is retired, semi-retired or semi-active, or principally engaged in activities other than the practice of law.

"⊙" indicates a lawyer maintains law offices at more than one place.

"★" indicates a lawyer is with the Armed Forces.

"(Pat.)" indicates lawyers who are registered to practice before the U.S. Patent and Trademark Office and who devote a considerable portion of time or duties to Patent, Trademark and other related matters.

"Ⓣ" indicates the Peer Review Rating was established in an admitting jurisdiction other than where the attorney is currently listed.

"BR" indicates a subscriber to the **Martindale-Hubbell® Bar Register of Preeminent Lawyers™**.

SECTION DESCRIPTIONS

PRACTICE PROFILES (BLUE PAGES)

This section contains rosters for the Bars of the United States. Listings of United States Government Lawyers located in Washington, D.C. are grouped by departments, agencies and commissions, etc. and follow the regular listings for that city in Volume 3.

This Section is alphabetically arranged by state, by city or town, and then by name of attorney or law firm. Contact information for state bar associations appears on the first page of each state.

Listings for individual attorneys include the following information, when available: name, Peer Review Rating (if any), year of birth, first year of admission to the Bar, college attended, first degree received, law school attended, first degree received, and where the attorney practices.

A typical individual attorney listing follows:

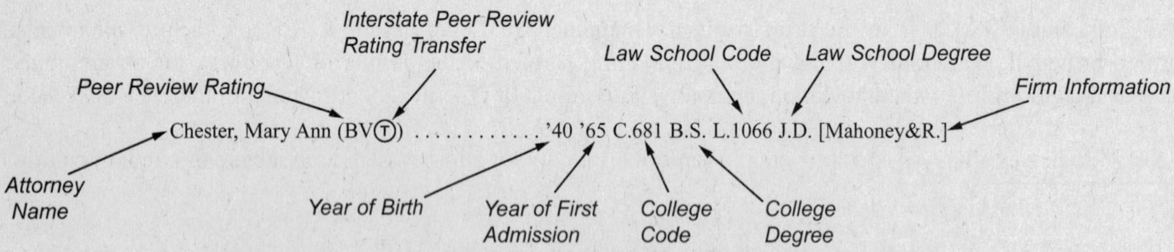

Law firm listings provide name, address and rating information, where available.

A typical law firm listing will appear as follows:

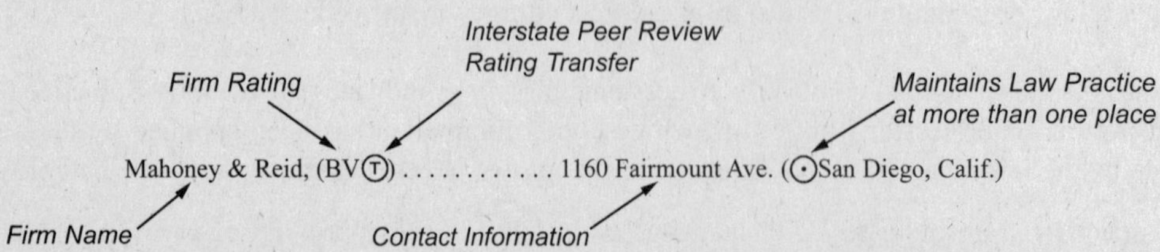

Practice Profiles listings for subscribing attorneys and law firms appear in boldface type and include name, Peer Review Rating (if available), address, firm personnel, statement of practice, representative clients, references, and language proficiency as well as other pertinent information.

Typical Subscriber Full Practice Profiles follow:

Firm Subscriber:

Firm Rating · *Interstate Peer Review Rating Transfer* · *Bar Register Listing Indicator* · *Firm Name* · *Contact Information* · *Statement of Practice* · *Clients* · *Biographical Listing Reference*

Letterman & Lewis, (AVⓉ) BR
713 Shady Lane, 94111⊙
Telephone: 415-555-1313
Email: lawinfo@lettlew.com URL: http://www.lettlew.com
Members of Firm: Michelle J. Letterman; Marvin Lewis;—Edgar Catello.
General Practice, Trials, Banking Estate Planning and Probate Law.
Representative Clients: California Home Security, Inc.; American Flight School, Inc.; West Coast Recycling Co.; American Fire Insurance Corp.
Reference: Pacific National Bank.
Berkeley, California Office: Suite 3500, Johnson Place. Telephone: 510-555-4563.

See Professional Biographies, SAN FRANCISCO, CALIFORNIA

Firm — members, associates, etc.:

Year of First Admission · *College Degree* · *Peer Review Rating* · *Year of Birth* · *College Code* · *Law School Code* · *Attorney Name* · *Number of Cases* · *Law School Degree* · *Firm Information*

Bershad, Abe M., (AV) . . . . '35 '60 C.681 B.S. L.1066 J.D. [Davis&J.]
*PRACTICE AREAS: Insurance Law (68).

Individual subscriber:

Year of First Admission · *College Degree* · *College Code* · *Peer Review Rating* · *Law School Code* · *Year of Birth* · *Law School Degree* · *Attorney Name* · *Bar Register Indicator* · *Contact Information* · *Additional Firm Information* · *Biographical Listing Reference* · *Number of Cases*

Schetlick, Robert M., (AV) '41 '65 C.816 B.S. L.705 J.D. BR
Suite 3500, Johnson Place, 07974⊙
Telephone: 908-555-4563 FAX: 908-555-4972
Email: schetlick@netadd.com URL: http://netadd.com/schetlick
(Also Of Counsel to Aiello & Smertick)
***PRACTICE AREAS: Insurance Law (125).**
Representative Client: East Coast Recycling Corp.
Approved Attorney For: SMAD Title Insurance Co.
Summit, New Jersey Office: 713 Shady Lane. Telephone: 908-555-1313.

See Professional Biographies, FLANDERS, NEW JERSEY

PATENT AND TRADEMARK PRACTICE PROFILES (BLUE PAGES)

This Section contains the names of subscribing lawyers registered to practice Patent Law and those who practice Trademark Law before the United States Patent and Trademark Office and who devote a considerable portion of their practice or duties to this field of law. It is arranged in the same manner as the Practice Profiles Section.

USER GUIDE: SECTION DESCRIPTIONS — *continued*

PROFESSIONAL BIOGRAPHIES (WHITE PAGES)

The Professional Biographies Section is arranged alphabetically by state, by city or town, and then by name of attorney or law firm. It provides substantial biographical information on individual attorneys within law firms. Entries in this section include the firm name, contact information, statement of practice, firm profile, individual biographical information, representative clients and references. A typical entry appears as follows:

Firm Name	***LETTERMAN & LEWIS***
Firm Descriptor	A Partnership including A Professional Corporation
Year Established	*Established in 1990*
Formerly	Formerly Letterman and Rosta
Contact Information	*731 SHADY LANE* ***SAN FRANCISCO, CALIFORNIA 94111*** *Telephone: 415-555-1313* *FAX: 415-555-7351* *Email: lawinfo@lettlew.com* *URL: http://www.lettlew.com*
Branch Office Information	*Berkeley, California Office:* Suite 3500, 110 Johnson Place. Telephone: 510-555-4563. Fax: 510-555-4972.
Statement of Practice	*General Practice, Trials, Banking, Finance, Wills, Trusts, Estate Planning and Probate Law.*
Firm Profile	*FIRM PROFILE: Letterman & Lewis was founded in 1990. The firm encourages continuing professional development and all partners and associates participate in continuing legal education seminars, professional association activities and civic affairs.*
Firm Associations	*LAW FIRM ALLIANCES/ASSOCIATIONS:* ***AmeriLaw:*** *Founded in 1981, AmeriLaw is an ever-expanding network of independent law firms organized to assist and support its firms in the development and improvement of their practices through a variety of programs so they can better serve their clients.*
	MEMBERS OF FIRM
Individual Biographical Information; *Military*	***MICHELLE J. LETTERMAN, (P.C.),*** born Summit, New Jersey, January 14, 1939; admitted to bar 1968, California. *Education:* United States Naval Academy (B.S., 1960); Harvard University (J.D., summa cum laude, 1968). Private Pilots License, 1960. *Member:* State Bar of California. [Lt., U.S. Navy, 1961-1964]. ***PRACTICE AREAS:*** Banking Law; Finance; Wills and Trusts. ***Email:*** mjletter@lettlew.com
Number of Cases	***MARVIN LEWIS,*** born Jeanette, Pennsylvania, October 7, 1940; admitted to bar, 1965, California. *Education:* University of California at Berkeley (B.A., summa cum laude, 1962); Hastings College of the Law, University of California (J.D., summa cum laude, 1965). *Member:* State Bar of California. (Also Of Counsel, Rudy & Catello). ***LANGUAGES:*** Spanish and French. ***SPECIAL AGENCIES:*** Goodman Zoning Board. ***REPORTED CASES:*** Bilko Inc. v. Zotser Trucking Co. ***TRANSACTIONS:*** Aiello Packing merger with Alboum Paper Products. ***PRACTICE AREAS:*** Estate Planning Law (78); Probate Law. ***Email:*** mlewis@lettlew.com
Associate Indicator	———————
Pending Admission Indicator; *Individual Email Address*	***EDGAR CATELLO,*** born San Mateo, California, January 11, 1972; (admission pending). *Education:* Radcliffe College (B.S., cum laude, 1994); Boalt Hall School of Law, University of California (J.D. summa cum laude, 1998). ***Email:*** ecatello@lettlew.com
	LEGAL SUPPORT PERSONNEL
	KATHLEEN VEGA, born Summit, New Jersey, August 22, 1962. *Education:* Rutgers University (B.A., 1984). Certified Paralegal, New Jersey, 1984. *Member:* National Association of Paralegals. (Paralegal). ***PRACTICE AREAS:*** Estates.
Clients	REPRESENTATIVE CLIENTS: California Home Security, Inc.; American Flight School, Inc.; West Coast Recycling Co.; American Fire Insurance Corp. REFERENCE: Pacific National Bank.

CORPORATE LAW DEPARTMENTS (WHITE PAGES)

Corporate Law Department representations reside in Volume 1. They are arranged alphabetically by name and present information about corporations and corporate attorneys. Typical information supplied includes name, company profile, office location(s) and type of business.

LAW SCHOOLS (WHITE PAGES)

The Law School Section, in Volume 12, profiles the academic programs, special course offerings and teaching staff of participating schools. Non-participating schools are also identified.

For each school, the data may include: school name, address, telephone and fax numbers; a substantial profile including ABA approval information, history, academic character, resources, special programs and activities of the institution; the names, titles and direct dial numbers of key contacts; and a roster of full-time faculty with biographical summary information. This Section is arranged alphabetically by law school name.

School Name →

JOHN A. JAMES SCHOOL OF LAW

Contact Information →

214 HOYT AVENUE
HONOLULU, HAWAII 98621
Telephone: (808) 555-9038
Fax: (808) 555-0983
Email: law@jaj.edu
URL: http://www.jaj.law.edu

ABA Approval Information →

ABA Approved Since 1994

School Profile →

The John A. James School of Law is a privately funded institution with a highly diversified student body, representing over 40 countries. Founded in 1988, it quickly achieved a reputation as one of the top universities specializing in the area of environmental law. With close connections to several firms on the North American and Asian continents, the School of Law provides its students with the opportunity to experience law as practiced on both sides of the Pacific. Sixty full-time faculty members represent 35 law schools across the globe; holding a total of 40 advanced degrees in law and 18 Ph.D. degrees.

Key Contacts →

Dean: John Posta (808) 555-5649
Admissions Officer: Tracey Hutchinson (808) 555-6218
Director of Library Services: Robert Berry (808) 555-6214
Placement Officer: Harriett Ko (808) 555-8281

FULL TIME FACULTY

Faculty Sketch →

ARTHUR JAMES, born Newark, New Jersey, June 30, 1957; admitted to bar 1982, New Jersey. Education: Drew University (B.A., 1978; M.A. 1984); Harvard University (J.D., 1982); Yale University (LL.M., 1985; J.S.D. 1989). Professor and a Director of the Environmental Law Center. *Courses:* Environmental Liability, Water Rights, Torts.

STATE BAR ASSOCIATION PROFILES

State Bar Association Profiles can now be found at *www.martindale.com*. These profiles include a bar profile, mission statements of the association, names of officers, directors, and key staff personnel, as well as membership and program information.

EXPERTS & SERVICES (WHITE PAGES)

Experts & Services provides information on businesses and professionals serving the legal community. This section is arranged alphabetically by state, city or town, category of service provided, and company name. Typical information in the company listing includes contact information, company profile, office locations and services provided.

DIRECTORY OF EXPERTS & SERVICES (BUYER'S GUIDE)

The Directory of Experts & Services (Buyer's Guide) is a print directory that's provided (at no additional cost) as part of each Martindale-Hubbell subscription. This directory is a national consolidation of the thousands of Experts & Services listings contained in the Martindale-Hubbell Law Directories (see above) and places them in one, easy to use desk reference.

USER AIDS

In the front matter, sections are provided to aid in the use of the Directory. "Explanatory Notes and Symbols," found on page IX, provides a guide to the various symbols and notations which are utilized in the individual entries. The "Index of Colleges, Universities, and Law Schools," found on page XVII, provides a comprehensive guide to numeric codes which are used in Practice Profiles listings to indicate academic institutions and law schools attended by individual attorneys.

Page numbers in the 2006 **Martindale-Hubbell® Law Directory** are constructed in the format XXYYYZ, where XX is the state, province or international grouping, YYY is a consecutive page numbering, and Z is a code denoting section.

Pages listing attorneys under the U.S. Government use the abbreviation "GV", the Law School Section uses the abbreviation "LS", and the Corporate Section uses the abbreviation "C". For International Volumes, the following group abbreviations are used:

EU	Europe	NA	North America
AS	Asia	CB	The Caribbean
AU	Australasia	CS	Central & South America
AF	Middle East & Africa		

Z may be one of the following:

P	Practice Profiles	T	Patent & Trademark
B	Professional Biographies	S	Experts and Services

For additional help or explanation, please call Martindale-Hubbell Customer Service at 1-800-526-4902, or in New Jersey at 908-464-6800.

LEXISNEXIS MARTINDALE-HUBBELL PEER REVIEW RATINGS

The first Martindale books were published in 1868, the principal one being *Martindale's United States Law Directory* and later *Martindale's American Law Directory*.

In 1930, the publishing rights to *Hubbell's Legal Directory* were purchased by the Martindale Company and ever since has been known as the **Martindale-Hubbell® Law Directory**.

Legal Ability and General Ethical Standards Ratings have appeared in the Directory for over 100 years. Martindale-Hubbell strives to publish fair and accurate Peer Review Ratings for as many lawyers as possible, subscribers and non-subscribers alike. While the vast majority of rating reviews are initiated by the Company, an inquiry will be undertaken upon request. When forwarding legal matters, lawyers in private practice and in corporate law departments rely with confidence on the accuracy of the Peer Review Ratings published.

Legal Ability Ratings are: "C" (from Good to High), "B" (from High to Very High), "A" (from Very High to Preeminent).

General Ethical Standards Rating is: "V" (Very High).

Unless a Peer Review Rating is established in both categories, no rating will be published.

Over 115,000 rating reviews are undertaken each year. Of those, approximately 80% are done at our own initiative. An additional 20% are conducted by request and through the efforts of our Field Staff.

Martindale-Hubbell develops its Peer Review Ratings for individual lawyers by soliciting confidential opinions from members of the Bar, including those who themselves have ratings and those who do not. In addition, members of the U.S. Judiciary are queried. We encourage all lawyers to participate in the process. Greater participation assures the continued accuracy of the system. Respondents to written questionnaires and personal interviews are asked to base their opinions on the following:

LEGAL ABILITY RATING

Based on the standard of ability for the area where the lawyer practices, it takes into consideration experience, nature of practice and qualifications relevant to the profession. Where a lawyer's practice is limited or specialized, rating opinions are made on the basis of performance in those Fields of Law.

GENERAL ETHICAL STANDARDS RATING

Embraces faithful adherence to professional standards of conduct and ethics of the legal profession, professional reliability and diligence, and standards relevant to the attorney's discharge of his or her professional responsibilities.

Legal Ability and General Ethical Standards Ratings appearing in the Directory reflect strictly confidential opinions and responses to professionally developed surveys and adhere to meticulously monitored research principles and practices. Martindale-Hubbell does not make any independent evaluation of lawyers. Rather, it depends exclusively upon the opinions of its confidential sources.

FIRM RATING

Generally, a law firm will be accorded the rating of its highest-rated principal.

In some instances, lawyers may be asked to submit names of lawyers and judges with whom they have had professional experience. Inquiries are then directed to those sources in addition to sources developed by Martindale-Hubbell.

Field Representatives of Martindale-Hubbell visit tens of thousands of law offices on an annual basis. They make oral rating inquiries during these calls and submit written reports. However, a formal rating review must occur before any Peer Review Rating is established, advanced, lowered or withdrawn.

Martindale-Hubbell does not undertake developing ratings for every listed lawyer. The absence of a rating should not be construed as unfavorable since some lawyers have requested their Peer Review Ratings not be published while in other instances definitive information has not yet been completely developed.

LEXISNEXIS MARTINDALE-HUBBELL PEER REVIEW RATINGS — *continued*

Peer Review Ratings are published for lawyers in the United States, the U.S. Virgin Islands, Northern Mariana Islands and Canada.

No subscription or listing in the **Martindale-Hubbell® Law Directory** is ever solicited or accepted on the promise of publication of a particular Peer Review Rating. No preferential consideration is ever given to any lawyer or law firm.

As a general rule, Peer Review Ratings are transferable within state boundaries. Ratings may be transferred inter-state/inter-province, with the Ⓣ symbol indicating the rating was established in another jurisdiction.

It is our policy to conduct regular periodic reviews of all Peer Review Ratings to insure their accuracy. Where supporting opinions dictate, appropriate action (such as deleting, raising or lowering a rating) is taken.

There is never any payment made to lawyers and judges who participate in rating reviews. The process is a cooperative service to the Bar. It has always been Martindale-Hubbell policy to treat all phases of the rating review process as absolutely confidential. Sources contacted participate with that understanding, and under no circumstances will any review materials ever be released.

Peer Review Ratings are intended primarily for the use of lawyers in the practice of their profession. Specific guidelines for particular uses of a Peer Review Rating or the Peer Review Rated icon can be found on the Martindale-Hubbell Peer Review Ratings website at www.martindale.com/ratings or can be requested in writing from:

LexisNexis Martindale-Hubbell
Peer Review Rating Services
121 Chanlon Road
New Providence, NJ 07974

Or via Email: ratings@martindale.com

In addition to the previously permitted uses of the Peer Review Ratings, rated lawyers are now also permitted to more widely and prominently display the Peer Review Rated icon:

LexisNexis®
Martindale-Hubbell®
Peer Review Rated
For Ethical Standards and Legal Ability

Peer Review Rated attorneys can display the icon in multiple media consistent with the original purpose of facilitating lawyer-to-lawyer referrals and also to announce to a wider audience that they have been rated by their peers. As with the other permitted uses of the Peer Review Ratings, lawyers must use the icon in compliance with the requirements of their local and state bars.

If you would like to publish your Peer Review Rating in a format not mentioned in the detailed Usage Guidelines, prior written permission from LexisNexis Martindale-Hubbell Peer Review Rating Services must be obtained.

Note: Please review Important Notices located on page III.

Index of Colleges, Universities and Law Schools

This list is a guide to the numeric school codes found in Practice Profiles Section entries. Institutions which no longer exist, junior colleges, correspondence schools or colleges with very small enrollments are not included. Such unlisted schools are indicated by the numeric code "999".

01. Acadia University
Wolfville, NS
02. Alberta, University of
Edmonton, AB
03. Bishop's University
Lennoxville, QU
04. British Columbia, Law Society of
Vancouver, BC
05. British Columbia, University of
Vancouver, BC
06. Dalhousie University
Halifax, NS
07. King's College, University of
Halifax, NS
08. Laval University
Quebec, QU
09. Concordia University
Formerly Loyola College
Montreal, QU
010. MacDonald College
Ste. A. de Bellevue, QU
011. Manitoba, University of
Winnipeg, MB
012. McGill University
Montreal, QU
013. McMaster University
Hamilton, ON
014. Montreal, University of
Montreal, QU
015. Mount Allison University
Sackville, NB
016. New Brunswick, University of
Fredericton, NB
017. Nova Scotia College of Agriculture
Truro, NS
018. Ottawa, University of
Ottawa, ON
019. Queen's University
Kingston, ON
020. St. Dunstan's University
Charlottetown, PE
021. St. Francis Xavier University
Antigonish, NS
022. St. Joseph's University
St. Joseph, NB
023. Ste. Marie, College of
Montreal, QU
024. Saskatchewan, University of
Saskatoon, SK
025. Toronto, University of
Toronto, ON
026. Upper Canada, Law Society of
Toronto, ON
027. Victoria University
Toronto, ON
028. Western Ontario, University of
London, ON
029. Osgoode Hall
Toronto, ON
030. Assumption University
Windsor, ON
031. Windsor, University of
Windsor, ON
032. Royal Military College
Kingston, ON
033. Wilfrid Laurier University
Formerly Waterloo Lutheran University
Waterloo, ON
034. Carleton University
Ottawa, ON
035. York University
Toronto, ON
036. Memorial University of Newfoundland
St. John's, NF
037. Calgary, University of
Calgary, AB
038. Waterloo, University of
Formerly Waterloo University
Waterloo, ON
039. Victoria, University of
Victoria, BC
040. Guelph, University of
Guelph, ON
041. Concordia University
Formerly (Sir) George Williams University
Montreal, QU
042. St. Marys University
Halifax, NS
043. Simon Fraser University
Burnaby, BC
044. Lethbridge, University of
Lethbridge, AB
045. Winnipeg, University of
Winnipeg, MB
046. Moncton, University of
Moncton, NB
047. St. Thomas University
Fredericton, NB
048. Regina, University of
Regina, SK
049. Brandon University
Brandon, MB
050. Cambridge University
Cambridge, England
051. Oxford University
Oxford, England
052. Heidelberg University
Baden, Germany
054. London, University of
London, England
055. Paris, University of
Formerly Sorbonne University
Paris, France
056. Rome, University of
Rome, Italy
057. Vienna, University of
Vienna, Austria
058. Trinity College, University of Dublin
Dublin, Ireland
059. Edinburgh University
Edinburgh, Scotland
060. Munich, University of
Munich, Germany
062. National University of Ireland, Dublin
Dublin, Ireland
063. Royal Military Academy
Sandhurst, England
064. Santo Thomas, University of
Manila, Philippines
065. Durham, University of
Durham, England
066. Manuel L. Quezon University
Manila, Philippines
067. Stockholm, University of
Stockholm, Sweden
068. Queen's University, The
Belfast, Northern Ireland
080. Lakehead University
Thunder Bay, ON
081. Brock University
St. Catharines, ON
082. Prince Edward Island, University of
Charlottetown, PE
083. Laurentian University of Sudbury
Sudbury, ON
084. Trent University
Peterborough, ON
085. Quebec, University of
Sainte Foy, Montreal, Trois-Rivieres, Chicoutimi, Hull and Rimouski, QU
086. Sherbrooke, University of
Sherbrooke, QU
087. Quebec Bar Law School
Montreal, QU
1. Abilene Christian University
Abilene, TX
3. Adams State College
Alamosa, CO
4. Adelphi University
Garden City, NY
5. Adrian College
Adrian, MI
6. Agnes Scott College
Decatur, GA
7. Akron University Law School
Akron, OH
8. Akron, University of
Formerly Buchtel College
Akron, OH
9. Montevallo, University of
Formerly Alabama College
Montevallo, AL
10. Auburn University
Formerly Alabama Polytechnic Institute
Auburn and Montgomery, AL
11. North Alabama, University of
Formerly Alabama State Teachers College
Florence, AL
12. Jacksonville State University
Formerly Alabama State Teachers College
Jacksonville, AL
13. West Alabama, The University of
Formerly Livingston University
Livingston, AL
14. Alabama State University
Formerly Montgomery State College
Montgomery, AL
15. Troy State University
Formerly Alabama State Teachers CollegeTroy, AL
16. Alabama, University of
Birmingham, Huntsville and Tuscaloosa, AL
17. Alaska, University of
Fairbanks, Anchorage and Juneau, AK
18. Albany College
Portland, OR
19. Albertus Magnus College
New Haven, CT
20. Albion College
Albion, MI
21. Albright College
Reading, PA
22. Alcorn A. & M. College
Alcorn, MS
23. Alderson-Broaddus College
Philippi, WV
24. Alfred University
Alfred, NY
25. Allegheny College
Meadville, PA
26. Allen University
Columbia, SC
27. Alma College
Alma, MI
28. American International College
Springfield, MA
29. American University
Los Angeles, CA
30. American University
Washington, DC
See Also No. 904
31. Amherst College
Amherst, MA
32. Andrew Jackson University
Nashville, TN

142. Chattanooga College of Law
Chattanooga, TN
143. Tennessee at Chattanooga, University of
Formerly Chattanooga, University of
Chattanooga, TN
144. Chicago Law School
Formerly Midland University
Chicago, IL
145. Chicago, University of
Chicago, IL
146. Chicago-Kent College of Law, Illinois
Institute of Technology
Chicago, IL
147. California State University, Chico
Formerly Chico State College
Chico, CA
148. Chicora College
Columbia, SC
149. Chowan College
Murfreesboro, NC
150. Cincinnati, University of
Cincinnati, OH
151. Cincinnati Y.M.C.A. Schools
Cincinnati, OH
152. Citadel, The
Charleston, SC
153. Claflin College
Orangeburg, SC
154. Claremont McKenna College
Claremont, CA
155. Clark Atlanta University
Atlanta, GA
156. Clark University
Worcester, MA
157. Clarke College
Dubuque, IA
158. Clarkson University
Formerly Clarkson College of
Technology
Potsdam, NY
159. Cleary College
Ypsilanti, MI
160. Clemson University
Clemson, SC
161. Cleveland State University
Cleveland, OH
162. Coe College
Formerly Western College
Cedar Rapids, IA
163. Coker College
Hartsville, SC
164. Colby College
Waterville, ME
165. Colgate University
Hamilton, NY
166. Holy Names College
Formerly College of the Holy Names
Oakland, CA
167. College Misericordia
Dallas, PA
168. College of the Ozarks
Clarksville, AR
169. Pacific, University of the
Formerly College of the Pacific
Stockton, CA
See Also No. 464
170. Colorado College
Colorado Springs, CO
171. Colorado School of Mines
Golden, CO
172. Colorado State University
Formerly Colorado A. & M. College
Fort Collins, CO
173. Northern Colorado, University of
Formerly Colorado State College
Greeley, CO
174. Colorado at Boulder, University of
Boulder, CO
176. Columbia College
Columbia, SC
177. Loras College
Formerly Columbia College of
Dubuque
Dubuque, IA
178. Columbia University
New York, NY
179. Capital University
Formerly Columbus College of Law
Columbus, OH
See Also No. 117
180. Columbus School of Law of The Catholic
University of America
Washington, DC
See Also No. 128
181. Concord College
Athens, WV
182. Concordia College
Moorehead, MN
183. Connecticut College
New London, CT
184. Connecticut, University of
Storrs and Hartford, CT
185. Converse College
Spartanburg, SC
186. Cooper Union
New York, NY
187. Cornell College
Mount Vernon, IA
188. Cornell University
Ithaca, NY
189. Cotner College
Lincoln, NE
190. Creighton University
Omaha, NE
191. Culver-Stockton College
Canton, MO
192. Cumberland School of Law of Samford
University
Formerly part of Cumberland
University (now Cumberland College
of Tennessee, at Lebanon, TN)
Birmingham, AL
193. Dakota Wesleyan University
Mitchell, SD
194. Dana College
Blair, NE
195. Daniel Baker College
Brownwood, TX
196. Daniel W. Voorhees Law School
Terre Haute, IN
197. Dartmouth College
Hanover, NH
198. Davidson College
Davidson, NC
199. Davis & Elkins College
Elkins, WV
200. Dayton Law School
Dayton, OH
201. Dayton, University of
Dayton, OH
202. Decorah College for Women
Decorah, IA
203. Defiance College
Defiance, OH
204. Delaware State College
Dover, DE
205. Delaware, University of
Newark, DE
206. Delta State College
Cleveland, MS
207. Denison University
Granville, OH
208. Denver, University of
Denver, CO
209. DePaul University
Chicago, IL
210. DePauw University
Greencastle, IN
211. Des Moines College of Law
Des Moines, IA
212. Wayne University
Formerly Detroit City Law School
Detroit, MI
213. Michigan State University College of
Law
Formerly Michigan State University
Detroit College of Law
Detroit, MI
214. Detroit Institute of Technology
Detroit, MI
215. Detroit Mercy, University of
Formerly University of Detroit
Detroit, MI
216. Dickinson College
Carlisle, PA
217. Dillard University
New Orleans, LA
218. Doane College
Crete, NE
219. Dominican College of San Rafael
San Rafael, CA
220. St. Mary's Dominican College
Formerly Dominican College
New Orleans, LA
221. Drake University
Des Moines, IA
222. Drew University
Formerly Brothers College
Madison, NJ
223. Drexel University
Philadelphia, PA
224. Dropsie University
Philadelphia, PA
225. Drury College
Springfield, MO
226. Dubuque, University of
Dubuque, IA
227. Duchesne College
Omaha, NE
228. Duke University
Durham, NC
229. Duquesne University
Pittsburgh, PA
230. D'Youville College
Buffalo, NY
231. Earlham College
Richmond, IN
232. East Carolina University
Greenville, NC
233. Texas A&M University-Commerce
Formerly East Texas State University
Commerce, TX
234. Eastern Illinois University
Charleston, IL
235. Eastern Kentucky University
Formerly Kentucky Normal College
Richmond, KY
236. Eastern Nazarene College
Quincy, MA
237. Elizabethtown College
Elizabethtown, PA
238. Elmhurst College
Elmhurst, IL
239. Elmira College
Elmira, NY
240. Elon College
Elon College, NC
241. Emerson College
Boston, MA
242. Emmanuel College
Boston, MA
243. Andrews University
Formerly Emmanuel Missionary
College
Berrien Springs, MI
244. Emory and Henry College
Emory, VA
245. Emory University School of Law
Formerly Lamar School of Law
Atlanta, GA
246. Emporia, College of
Emporia, KS
247. Erskine College
Due West, SC
248. Eureka College
Eureka, IL
249. Evansville, University of
Evansville, IN
250. Fairmont State College
Fairmont, WV

362. Stetson University
Formerly John B. Stetson University
De Land and St. Petersburg, FL
363. John Carroll University
Formerly St. Ignatius College
Cleveland, OH
364. Kletzing College
Formerly John Fletcher College
University Park, IA
365. John Marshall Law School
Chicago, IL
366. John Randolph Neal College of Law
Knoxville, TN
367. Johns Hopkins University
Baltimore, MD
368. Johnson Bible College
Kimberlin Heights, TN
369. Johnson C. Smith University
Formerly Biddle University
Charlotte, NC
370. Jones Law School
Montgomery, AL
371. Judson College
Marion, AL
372. Juniata College
Huntingdon, PA
373. Kalamazoo College
Kalamazoo, MI
374. Kansas City School of Law
Part of University of Missouri at Kansas City
Kansas City, MO
375. Kansas State University
Formerly Kansas State College of Agriculture and Applied Science
Manhattan, KS
376. Emporia State University
Formerly Kansas State College
Emporia, KS
377. Pittsburg State University
Formerly Kansas State College
Pittsburg, KS
378. Kansas, University of
Lawrence, KS
379. Kansas Wesleyan University
Salina, KS
380. Keene State College
Keene, NH
381. Kent State University
Kent, OH
382. Kentucky State University
Frankfort, KY
383. Kentucky, University of
Lexington, KY
384. Kentucky Wesleyan College
Owensboro, KY
385. Kenyon College
Gambier, OH
386. Keuka College
Keuka Park, NY
387. King College
Bristol, TN
388. Knox College
Galesburg, IL
389. Knoxville College
Knoxville, TN
390. Lafayette College
Easton, PA
391. LaGrange College
LaGrange, GA
392. Lake Erie College
Painesville, OH
393. Lake Forest College
Lake Forest, IL
394. Lambuth College
Jackson, TN
395. Lander College
Greenwood, SC
396. Lane College
Jackson, TN
397. LaSalle University
Philadelphia, PA
398. La Verne, University of
La Verne, CA
399. Lawrence University
Appleton, WI
400. Lebanon Valley College
Annville, PA
401. Lehigh University
Bethlehem, PA
402. Leland College
Baker, LA
403. Le Moyne-Owen College
Memphis, TN
404. Lenoir-Rhyne College
Hickory, NC
405. Illinois Institute of Technology
Formerly Lewis Institute
Chicago, IL
See Also No. 46
406. Limestone College
Gaffney, SC
407. Lincoln College of Indiana
Indianapolis, IN
408. Lincoln College of Law
Bakersfield, CA
409. Lincoln Memorial University
Harrogate, TN
410. Lincoln University
Jefferson City, MO
411. Lincoln University
Lincoln University, PA
412. Lindenwood University
Formerly The Lindenwood Colleges
St. Charles, MO
413. Linfield College
McMinnville, OR
414. Livingstone College
Salisbury, NC
415. Long Island University, C.W. Post Campus of
Brookville, NY
416. Loretto Heights College
Denver, CO
417. Louisiana College
Pineville, LA
418. Louisiana Tech University
Formerly Louisiana Polytechnic Institute
Ruston, LA
419. Northwestern State University
Formerly Louisiana State Normal College
Natchitoches, LA
420. Louisiana State University
Baton Rouge, LA
421. Louisville, University of
Louisville, KY
422. Lowell Technological Institute
Part of University of Lowell
Lowell, MA
423. Loyola College
Baltimore, MD
424. Loyola University
Chicago, IL
425. Loyola University
New Orleans, LA
426. Loyola Marymount University
Los Angeles, CA
427. Luther College
Decorah, IA
428. Lynchburg College
Lynchburg, VA
429. Macalester College
St. Paul, MN
430. MacMurray College
Jacksonville, IL
431. Maine, University of
Orono, Farmington, Fort Kent, Machias and Presque Isle, ME
432. Manchester College
N. Manchester, IN
433. Manhattan College
Riverdale, NY
434. Marietta College
Marietta, OH
435. Marion College
Marion, IN
436. Marquette University
Milwaukee, WI
437. Marshall University
Huntington, WV
438. Mary Baldwin College
Staunton, VA
439. Mary Hardin-Baylor College
Belton, TX
440. Mary Manse College
Toledo, OH
441. Marygrove College
Detroit, MI
442. Maryland College for Women
Lutherville, MD
443. Frostburg State College
Formerly Maryland State Teachers College
Frostburg, MD
444. Salisbury State University
Formerly Maryland State Teachers College
Salisbury, MD
445. Towson State University
Formerly Maryland State Teachers College
Towson, MD
446. Maryland, University of
Baltimore and College Park, MD
447. Marylhurst College
Oswego, OR
448. Marymount College of Kansas
Salina, KS
449. Marymount College
Tarrytown, NY
450. Maryville College
St. Louis, MO
451. Maryville College
Maryville, TN
452. Marywood College
Scranton, PA
453. Massachusetts Institute of Technology
Cambridge, MA
454. Massachusetts, University of
Amherst and Boston, MA
455. Bridgewater State College
Formerly Massachusetts State College
Bridgewater, MA
456. Fitchburg State College
Formerly Massachusetts State College
Fitchburg, MA
457. Framingham State College
Formerly Massachusetts State College
Framingham, MA
458. Hyannis State College
Formerly Massachusetts State College
Hyannis, MA
459. Massachusetts Lowell, University of
Formerly Massachusetts State College
Lowell, MA
460. North Adams State College
Formerly Massachusetts State College
North Adams, MA
461. Salem State College
Formerly Massachusetts State College
Salem, MA
462. Westfield State College
Formerly Massachusetts State College
Westfield, MA
463. Worcester State College
Formerly Massachusetts State College
Worcester, MA
464. McGeorge School of Law
Part of University of the Pacific
Sacramento, CA
465. McKendree College
Lebanon, IL
466. McMurry College
Abilene, TX
467. McPherson College
McPherson, KS
468. Rutgers University
Formerly Mercer Beasley School of Law
Newark, NJ
See Also No. 705

469. Mercer University
Macon, GA
470. Mercyhurst College
Erie, PA
471. Meredith College
Raleigh, NC
472. Miami, University of
Coral Gables, FL
473. Miami University
Oxford, OH
474. Michigan Technological University
Houghton, MI
475. Michigan State University
East Lansing, MI
476. Eastern Michigan University
Formerly Michigan State Normal College
Ypsilanti, MI
477. Michigan, University of
Ann Arbor, Dearborn and Flint, MI
478. Middlebury College
Middlebury, VT
479. Middlesex University
Waltham, MA
480. Midland Lutheran College
Formerly Fremont College
Fremont, NE
481. Miles College
Birmingham, AL
482. Milligan College
Milligan College, TN
483. Mills College
Oakland, CA
484. Millsaps College
Jackson, MS
485. Milton College
Milton, WI
486. Milwaukee-Downer College
Milwaukee, WI
487. William Mitchell College of Law
Formerly Minnesota College of Law
Minneapolis, MN
See Also No. 1035
488. Bemidji State University
Bemidji, MN
489. Minnesota Duluth, University of
Duluth, MN
490. Mankato State University
Formerly Minnesota State Teachers College
Mankato, MN
491. Moorhead State University
Formerly Minnesota State Teachers College
Moorhead, MN
492. St. Cloud State University
Formerly Minnesota State Teachers College
St. Cloud, MN
493. Winona State University
Formerly Minnesota State Teachers College
Winona, MN
494. Minnesota, University of
Minneapolis and St. Paul, MN
495. Mission House College & Theological Seminary
Plymouth, WI
496. Mississippi College
Clinton, MS
497. Mississippi State University
State College, MS
498. Mississippi University for Women
Columbus, MS
499. Mississippi, University of Southern
Hattiesburg, MS
500. Mississippi, University of
University, MS
(Also maintains branch campuses at Oxford, Jackson, Southaven and Tupelo, MS)
501. William Carey College
Formerly Mississippi Woman's College
Hattiesburg, MS
502. Missouri, University of
Columbia, Rolla, St. Louis and Kansas City, MO
503. Missouri Valley College
Marshall, MO
504. Monmouth College
Monmouth, IL
505. Montana College of Mineral Science and Technology
Butte, MT
506. Montana State University
Bozeman, MT
507. Western Montana College
Formerly Montana State Normal College
Dillon, MT
508. Montana, University of
Formerly Montana State University
Missoula, MT
509. Moravian College & Theological Seminary
Bethlehem, PA
510. Morehead State University
Morehead, KY
511. Morehouse College
Atlanta, GA
512. Morgan State University
Baltimore, MD
513. Morningside College
Formerly University of Northwest
Sioux City, IA
514. Morris Brown College
Atlanta, GA
515. Morris College
Sumter, SC
516. Charleston, University of
Formerly Morris Harvey College
Charleston, WV
517. Mount Angel Seminary
St. Benedict, OR
518. Mount Holyoke College
South Hadley, MA
519. Mount Mary College
Milwaukee, WI
520. Mount Mercy College
Grand Rapids, MI
521. Carlow College
Formerly Mount Mercy College
Pittsburgh, PA
522. Chestnut Hill College
Formerly Mount St. Joseph College
Chestnut Hill, PA
523. Mount St. Joseph-on the Ohio, College of
Mount St. Joseph, OH
524. Mount St. Mary's College
Emmitsburg, MD
525. Mount St. Mary's College
Los Angeles, CA
526. Mount St. Scholastica College
Atchison, KS
527. Mount St. Vincent, College of
Riverdale, NY
528. Mount Union College
Alliance, OH
529. Muhlenberg College
Allentown, PA
530. Mundelein College
Chicago, IL
531. Murray State University
Murray, KY
532. Muskingum College
New Concord, OH
533. Tennessee State University
Formerly Nashville Agricultural Normal Institute
Nashville, TN
See Also No. 1220
534. Nassau College
Hempstead, NY
535. Nasson College
Springvale, ME
536. National College of Education
Formerly Pestalozzi Froebel Teachers College
Evanston, IL
537. George Washington University
Formerly National University
Washington, DC
See Also No. 273
538. Nazareth College
Louisville, KY
539. Nazareth College
Nazareth, MI
540. Nazareth College of Rochester
Rochester, NY
541. Nebraska Central College
Central City, NE
542. Chadron State College
Formerly Nebraska State Teachers College
Chadron, NE
543. Nebraska at Kearney, University of
Formerly Nebraska State Teachers College
Kearney, NE
544. Peru State College
Formerly Nebraska State Teachers College
Peru, NE
545. Wayne State College
Formerly Nebraska State Teachers College
Wayne, NE
546. Nebraska at Lincoln, University of
Lincoln, NE
547. Nebraska Wesleyan University
Lincoln, NE
549. Nevada, University of
Reno and Las Vegas, NV
550. New Hampshire, University of
Durham, NH
551. Douglass College of Rutgers University
Formerly New Jersey College for Women
New Brunswick, NJ
See Also No. 705
552. Rutgers University
Formerly New Jersey Law School
Newark, NJ
See Also No. 705
553. Kean College of New Jersey
Formerly New Jersey State College
Union, NJ
555. Montclair State University
Formerly New Jersey State College
Upper Montclair, NJ
556. New Mexico State University
Formerly New Mexico College of A. & M. Arts
University Park, NM
557. New Mexico Highlands University
Las Vegas, NM
558. New Mexico Institute of Mining & Technology
Socorro, NM
559. Western New Mexico University
Formerly New Mexico Western College
Silver City, NM
560. New Mexico, University of
Albuquerque, NM
561. West Virginia Institute of Technology
Formerly New River State College
Montgomery, WV
562. New Rochelle, College of
New Rochelle, NY
563. New York, City College of the City University of
New York, NY
564. New York Law School
New York, NY
565. New York College of Environmental Science & Forestry, State University of
Formerly New York State College of Forestry
Syracuse, NY
566. New York State College for Teachers
Albany, NY

567. New York at Buffalo, State University of
Formerly New York State Teachers College
Buffalo, NY
See Also No. 107
568. New York Teachers College
New York, NY
569. New York University
New York, NY
570. New Jersey Institute of Technology
Formerly Newark College of Engineering
Newark, NJ
571. Rutgers University
Formerly Newark, University of
Newark, NJ
See Also No. 705
572. Newberry College
Newberry, SC
573. Niagara University
Niagara University, NY
574. North Carolina Central University
Durham, NC
575. North Carolina at Chapel Hill, University of
Chapel Hill, NC
576. North Carolina State University
Raleigh, NC
577. North Carolina, University of, Greensboro, N.C.
Greensboro, NC
578. North Central College
Naperville, IL
579. North Dakota State University
Formerly North Dakota Agricultural College
Fargo, ND
580. North Dakota State Normal & Industrial College
Part of University of North Dakota
Ellendale, ND
581. Dickinson State College
Formerly North Dakota State College
Dickinson, ND
582. Mayville State College
Formerly North Dakota State College
Mayville, ND
583. Valley City State University
Formerly North Dakota State College
Valley City, ND
584. Minot State University
Formerly Dakota Northwestern University
Minot, ND
585. North Dakota, University of
Grand Forks, ND
586. North Texas, University of
Formerly North Texas State University
Denton, TX
587. Truman State University
Formerly Northeast Missouri State University
Kirksville, MO
588. Northeastern University
Boston, MA
589. Northern Illinois University
DeKalb and Glen Ellyn, IL
590. Northern State College
Aberdeen, SD
591. Northern Michigan University
Marquette, MI
592. Northland College
Ashland, WI
593. Northwest Missouri State University
Maryville, MO
594. Northwest Nazarene College
Nampa, ID
595. Northwestern College
Watertown, WI
596. Lewis & Clark Law School
Formerly Northwestern School of Law
Portland, OR
597. Northwestern University
Evanston, IL
598. Norwich University
Northfield, VT
599. Notre Dame College
South Euclid, OH
600. Notre Dame of Maryland, College of
Baltimore, MD
601. Notre Dame College of Staten Island
Part of St. Johns University
Staten Island, NY
See Also No. 724
602. Notre Dame, University of
Notre Dame, IN
603. Oakland City College
Oakland City, IN
604. Oberlin College
Oberlin, OH
605. Occidental College
Los Angeles, CA
606. Oglethorpe University
Atlanta, GA
607. Ohio Northern University
Ada, OH
608. Ohio State University, The
Columbus, OH
609. Athenaeum of Ohio, The
Formerly Ohio Teachers College
Cincinnati, OH
610. Ohio University
Athens, OH
611. Ohio Wesleyan University
Delaware, OH
612. Oklahoma State University
Formerly Oklahoma A. & M. College
Stillwater, OK
613. Oklahoma Baptist University
Shawnee, OK
614. Central State University
Formerly Oklahoma Central State Teachers College
Edmond, OK
See Also No. 1147
615. Oklahoma City University School of Law
Formerly Oklahoma City College of Law
Oklahoma City, OK
616. Oklahoma City University
Formerly Epworth University
Oklahoma City, OK
617. Science and Arts of Oklahoma, University of
Formerly Oklahoma College of Liberal Arts
Chickasha, OK
618. East Central Oklahoma State University
Formerly Oklahoma East Central State College
Ada, OK
619. Northeastern State University
Tahlequah, OK
620. Northwestern Oklahoma State University
Formerly Oklahoma Northwestern State College
Alva, OK
621. Southeastern Oklahoma State University
Formerly Oklahoma Southeastern State College
Durant, OK
622. Southwestern Oklahoma State University
Formerly Oklahoma Southwestern Institute of Technology
Weatherford, OK
623. Oklahoma, University of
Norman, OK
624. Olivet Nazarene College
Kankakee, IL
625. Olivet College
Olivet, MI
626. Omaha Law School, Inc., University of
Omaha, NE
627. Nebraska at Omaha, University of
Formerly Omaha, Municipal University of
Omaha, NE
628. Oregon State University
Corvallis, OR
629. Oregon, University of
Eugene, OR
630. Ottawa University
Ottawa, KS
631. Otterbein College
Westerville, OH
632. Ouachita Baptist University
Arkadelphia, AR
633. Elms College
Formerly Our Lady of the Elms, College of
Chicopee, MA
634. Our Lady of the Lake University
San Antonio, TX
635. George Fox College
Formerly Pacific College
Newberg, OR
636. Pacific Union College
Angwin, CA
637. Pacific University
Forest Grove, OR
638. Paine College
Augusta, GA
639. Oklahoma Panhandle State University of Agriculture and Applied Sciences
Formerly Panhandle State College
Goodwell, OK
640. Park College
Parkville, MO
641. Parsons College
Fairfield, IA
642. Pasadena College
Pasadena, CA
643. Chatham College
Formerly Pennsylvania College for Women
Pittsburgh, PA
644. Widener University
Formerly Pennsylvania Military College
Chester, PA and Wilmington, DE
See Also No. 1338
645. Pennsylvania State University
University Park, PA
646. Bloomsburg University of Pennsylvania
Formerly Pennsylvania State Teachers College
Bloomsburg, PA
647. California University of Pennsylvania
Formerly Pennsylvania State Teachers College
California, PA
648. Clarion University of Pennsylvania
Formerly Pennsylvania State Teachers College
Clarion, PA
649. East Stroudsburg University
Formerly Pennsylvania State Teachers College
E. Stroudsburg, PA
650. Edinboro University of Pennsylvania
Formerly Pennsylvania State Teachers College
Edinboro, PA
651. Indiana University of Pennsylvania
Formerly Pennsylvania State Teachers College
Indiana, PA
652. Kutztown University
Formerly Pennsylvania State Teachers College
Kutztown, PA
653. Lock Haven University of Pennsylvania
Formerly Pennsylvania State Teachers College
Lock Haven, PA
654. Mansfield University
Formerly Pennsylvania State Teachers College
Mansfield, PA
655. Millersville University of Pennsylvania
Formerly Pennsylvania State Teachers College
Millersville, PA

762. San Antonio Public School of Law
San Antonio, TX
763. San Diego State University
San Diego, CA
764. Lone Mountain College
Formerly San Francisco College for Women
San Francisco, CA
765. San Francisco Law School
San Francisco, CA
766. San Francisco State University
Formerly California State University
San Francisco, CA
767. San Francisco, University of
Formerly St. Ignatius College
San Francisco, CA
768. San Jose State University
San Jose, CA
769. California at Santa Barbara, University of
Formerly Santa Barbara State College
Santa Barbara, CA
770. Santa Clara University
Formerly Santa Clara, University of
Santa Clara, CA
771. Sarah Lawrence College
Bronxville, NY
772. Scarritt College for Christian Workers
Nashville, TN
773. Scripps College
Claremont, CA
774. Seattle Pacific University
Seattle, WA
775. Selma University
Selma, AL
776. Seton Hall University
South Orange & Newark, NJ
777. Seton Hill College
Greensburg, PA
778. Shaw University
Raleigh, NC
779. Shepherd College
Shepherdstown, WV
780. Shorter College
Formerly Shorter-Flipper-Curry College
N. Little Rock, AR
781. Shorter College
Rome, GA
782. Shurtleff College
Alton, IL
783. Simmons College
Boston, MA
784. Simpson College
Indianola, IA
785. Sioux Falls College
Sioux Falls, SD
786. Sisters' College of Cleveland
Cleveland, OH
787. Skidmore College
Saratoga Springs, NY
788. Smith College
Northampton, MA
789. South Carolina State College
Orangeburg, SC
790. South Carolina, University of
Columbia, SC
791. South Dakota State University
Brookings, SD
792. South Dakota School of Mines and Technology
Rapid City, SD
793. South Dakota, University of
Vermillion, SD
794. Georgia Teachers College
Formerly South Georgia Teachers College
Collegeboro, GA
795. Rutgers University
Formerly South Jersey, College of
Camden, NJ
See Also No. 1292
796. South Texas College of Law
Houston, TX
797. South, University of the
Sewanee, TN
798. Southeast Missouri State University
Cape Girardeau, MO
799. Southeastern University
Washington, DC
800. Southern California, University of
Los Angeles, CA
801. Southern Illinois University
Carbondale and Edwardsville, IL
802. Southern Methodist University
Dallas, TX
803. Southern University
Baton Rouge, LA
804. Missouri State University
Formerly Southwest Missouri State University
Springfield, MO
805. Texas State University-San Marcos
Formerly Southwest Texas State University
San Marcos, TX
806. Rhodes College
Formerly Southwestern at Memphis
Memphis, TN
807. Southwestern College
Winfield, KS
808. Southwestern Louisiana, University of
Lafayette, LA
809. Southwestern University School of Law
Los Angeles, CA
810. Southwestern University
Georgetown, TX
811. Spelman College
Atlanta, GA
812. Spring Hill College
Spring Hill, AL
813. Stanford University
Stanford, CA
814. Stephen F. Austin State University
Nacogdoches, TX
815. Sterling College
Sterling, KS
816. Stevens Institute of Technology
Hoboken, NJ
817. Wisconsin-Stout, University of
Formerly Stout State College
Menomonie, WI
818. Suffolk University
Boston, MA
819. Sul Ross State University
Alpine, TX
820. Susquehanna University
Selinsgrove, PA
821. Swarthmore College
Swarthmore, PA
822. Sweet Briar College
Sweet Briar, VA
823. Syracuse University
Syracuse, NY
824. Talladega College
Talladega, AL
825. Tampa, University of
Tampa, FL
826. Tarkio College
Tarkio, MO
827. Taylor University
Upland, IN
828. Teachers College of the City of Boston
Boston, MA
829. Central Connecticut State College
Formerly Teachers College of Connecticut, The
New Britain, CT
830. Teachers College of Kansas City
Kansas City, MO
831. Temple University
Philadelphia, PA
832. Tennessee State University
Formerly Tennessee A. & I. State University
Nashville, TN
833. Tennessee College for Women
Murfreesboro, TN
834. Tennessee Technological University
Formerly Tennessee Polytechnic Institute
Cookeville, TN
835. East Tennessee State University
Formerly Tennessee State Teachers College
Johnson City, TN
836. Memphis, University of
Formerly Memphis State University
Memphis, TN
See Also No. 1015
837. Middle Tennessee State University
Formerly Tennessee State Teachers College
Murfreesboro, TN
838. Tennessee at Knoxville, University of
Knoxville, TN
839. Texas A & M University
College Station, TX
840. Texas Christian University
Fort Worth, TX
841. Texas College
Tyler, TX
842. Texas Arts & Industries University
Kingsville, TX
843. Texas at El Paso, University of
Formerly Texas, College of Mines & Metallurgy
El Paso, TX
844. Texas Woman's University
Formerly Texas State College for Women
Denton, TX
845. Texas Tech University
Lubbock, TX
846. Texas at Austin, University of
Austin, TX
847. Texas Wesleyan University
Fort Worth, TX
848. Thiel College
Greenville, PA
849. Huston-Tillotson College
Formerly Tillotson College
Austin, TX
See Also No. 1037
850. Toledo Teachers College
Toledo, OH
851. Toledo, University of
Toledo, OH
852. Tougaloo College
Tougaloo, MS
853. Transylvania University
Lexington, KY
854. Tri-State University
Angola, IN
855. Trinity College
Hartford, CT
856. Trinity College
Washington, DC
857. Trinity College
Sioux City, IA
858. Trinity College
Burlington, VT
859. Trinity University
San Antonio, TX
860. Tufts University
Medford, MA
861. Tulane University
New Orleans, LA
862. Tulsa, University of
Tulsa, OK
863. Tusculum College
Greeneville, TN
864. Tuskegee University
Tuskegee, AL
865. Union College
Barbourville, KY
866. Union College
Lincoln, NE
867. Union College
Schenectady, NY
868. Union University
Jackson, TN

869. United States Coast Guard Academy
New London, CT
870. United States Military Academy
West Point, NY
871. United States Naval Academy
Annapolis, MD
872. Upper Iowa University
Fayette, IA
873. Upsala College
East Orange, NJ
874. Ursinus College
Collegeville, PA
875. Ursuline College
New Orleans, LA
876. Ursuline College
Cleveland, OH
877. Utah State University
Formerly Utah State Agricultural College
Logan, UT
878. Utah, University of
Salt Lake City, UT
879. Valparaiso University
Formerly Northern Indiana Law School
Valparaiso, IN
880. Vanderbilt University
Nashville, TN
881. Vassar College
Poughkeepsie, NY
882. Vermont, University of
Burlington, VT
883. Villa Maria College
Erie, PA
884. Villanova University
Villanova, PA
885. Virginia Military Institute
Lexington, VA
886. Virginia Polytechnic Institute and State University
Blacksburg, VA
887. Virginia State University
Petersburg (Ettrick), VA
888. Radford University
Formerly Virginia State Teachers College
East Radford, VA
889. Longwood College
Formerly Virginia State Teachers College
Farmville, VA
890. Mary Washington College
Formerly Virginia State Teachers College
Fredericksburg, VA
892. Virginia Union University
Richmond, VA
893. Virginia, University of
Charlottesville, VA
894. Wabash College
Crawfordsville, IN
895. Wagner College
Staten Island, NY
896. Wake Forest University
Winston-Salem, NC
897. Walla Walla College
College Place, WA
898. Wartburg College
Waverly, IA
899. Wartburg Theological Seminary
Dubuque, IA
900. Washburn University of Topeka
Topeka, KS
901. Washington & Jefferson College
Washington, PA
902. Washington & Lee University
Lexington, VA
903. Washington College
Chestertown, MD
904. Washington College of Law
(of American University)
Washington, DC
See Also No. 30
905. Columbia Union College
Formerly Washington Missionary College
Takoma Park, DC
906. Washington State University
Pullman, WA
907. Western Washington University
Formerly Washington State Normal School
Bellingham, WA
908. Eastern Washington University
Formerly Washington State Normal School
Cheney, WA
909. Central Washington University
Formerly Washington State Normal School
Ellensburg, WA
910. Washington University
St. Louis, MO
911. Washington, University of
Seattle, WA
912. Wayne State University
Detroit, MI
913. Waynesburg College
Waynesburg, PA
914. Wellesley College
Wellesley, MA
915. Wells College
Aurora, NY
916. Wesley College
Grand Forks, ND
917. Wesleyan College
Macon, GA
918. Wesleyan University
Middletown, CT
919. West Baden College
West Baden, IN
920. West Liberty State College
W. Liberty, WV
921. West Texas State University
Canyon, TX
922. West Virginia State College
Institute, WV
923. West Virginia University
Morgantown, WV
924. West Virginia Wesleyan College
Buckhannon, WV
925. Western Carolina University
Cullowhee, NC
926. Western College
Oxford, OH
927. Western Illinois University
Macomb, IL
928. McDaniel College
Formerly Western Maryland College
Westminster, MD
929. Western Kentucky University
Formerly Western Kentucky State College
Bowling Green, KY
930. Case Western Reserve University
Formerly Western Reserve University
Cleveland, OH
931. Western State College of Colorado
Gunnison, CO
932. Western Michigan University
Kalamazoo, MI
933. Westmar College
Formerly Western Union College
Le Mars, IA
934. Westminster College
Fulton, MO
935. Westminster College
New Wilmington, PA
937. Wheaton College
Wheaton, IL
938. Wheaton College
Norton, MA
939. Whitman College
Walla Walla, WA
940. Whittier College
Whittier, CA
941. Whitworth College
Spokane, WA
942. Wichita State University
Wichita, KS
943. Wilberforce University
Wilberforce, OH
944. Wiley College
Marshall, TX
945. William & Mary, College of
Williamsburg, VA
946. William Jennings Bryan College
Dayton, TN
947. William Jewell College
Liberty, MO
948. William McKinley School of Law
Canton, OH
949. William Penn College
Oskaloosa, IA
950. Willamette University
Salem, OR
951. Williams College
Williamstown, MA
952. Wilmington College
Wilmington, OH
953. North Carolina at Wilmington, University of
Formerly Wilmington College
Wilmington, NC
954. Wilson College
Chambersburg, PA
955. Winston-Salem State University
Winston-Salem, NC
956. Winthrop College
Rock Hill, SC
957. Wisconsin-Eau Claire, University of
Eau Claire, WI
958. Wisconsin-La Crosse, University of
La Crosse, WI
959. Wisconsin-Milwaukee, University of
Milwaukee, WI
960. Wisconsin-Oshkosh, University of
Oshkosh, WI
961. Wisconsin-Platteville, University of
Platteville, WI
962. Wisconsin-River Falls, University of
River Falls, WI
963. Wisconsin-Stevens Point, University of
Stevens Point, WI
964. Wisconsin-Superior, University of
Superior, WI
965. Wisconsin-Whitewater, University of
Whitewater, WI
966. Wisconsin-Madison, University of
Madison, WI
967. Wittenberg University
Springfield, OH
968. Wofford College
Spartanburg, SC
969. Woodrow Wilson College of Law
Formerly Kilbride Law School
Atlanta, GA
970. Wooster, College of
Wooster, OH
971. Worcester Polytechnic Institute
Worcester, MA
972. Wyoming, University of
Laramie, WY
973. Xavier University
Cincinnati, OH
974. Xavier University of Louisiana
New Orleans, LA
975. Y.M.C.A. Schools
Houston, TX
976. Yale University
New Haven, CT
977. Yankton College
Yankton, SD
978. Yeshiva University
New York, NY
979. York College
York, NE
980. Youngstown State University
Youngstown, OH
981. LaSalle Extension University
Chicago, IL
982. Albany Law School of Union University
Albany, NY

983. San Antonio, University of
San Antonio, TX
984. Blue Ridge College
New Windsor, MD
985. Briar Cliff College
Sioux City, IA
986. Missouri at Kansas City, University of
Formerly University of Kansas City
Kansas City, MO
987. Sulpician Seminary of the Northwest
Formerly St. Edward's Seminary
Seattle, WA
988. Seattle University
Seattle, WA
989. Cleveland-Marshall College of Law
Formerly John Marshall Law School
Cleveland, OH
See Also No. 1003
990. Pepperdine University
Los Angeles, Malibu, Anaheim and Santa Ana, CA
991. Barat College
Lake Forest, IL
992. Anderson College
Anderson, IN
993. St. Mary's College
Orchard Lake, MI
994. Queens College of the City University of New York
Flushing, NY
995. Alfred Holbrook College
Manchester, OH
996. Lincoln College of Law
Springfield, IL
997. Seton Hall University
Formerly John Marshall Law School
Jersey City, NJ
See Also No. 776
998. Houston Law School
Houston, TX
999. Unlisted colleges, etc., see prefatory notice
1000. John Marshall Law School
Atlanta, GA
1001. Pacific Coast University
Los Angeles, CA
1002. Baltimore School of Law, University of
Formerly Mt. Vernon School of Law
Baltimore, MD
1003. Cleveland-Marshall College of Law
Part of Cleveland State University
Cleveland, OH
1004. St. Mary of the Plains College
Dodge City, KS
1005. Southern Law University
Part of Memphis State University
Memphis, TN
1006. College of St. Francis Xavier
New York, NY
1007. American Extension School of Law
Chicago, IL
1008. Blackstone School of Law
Carrollton, TX
1009. Brooklyn Law School
Brooklyn, NY
1010. Alabama Agricultural & Mechanical University
Formerly State Agricultural and Mechanical Institute
Normal, AL
1011. Fayetteville State University
Fayetteville, NC
1012. Eastern New Mexico University
Portales, NM
1014. Robert H. Terrell Law School
Washington, DC
1015. Memphis State University
Memphis, TN
1016. Roosevelt University
Chicago, IL
1017. Dickinson School of Law of the Pennsylvania State University
Carlisle, PA
1018. William Mitchell College of Law
Formerly Minneapolis-Minnesota College of Law
Minneapolis, MN
See Also No. 1035
1019. Hofstra University
Hempstead, NY
1020. Portland University Law School
part of University of Maine
Portland, ME
See Also No. 431
1021. Siena College
Formerly St. Bernardine of Siena College
Loudonville, NY
1022. New England School of Law
Formerly Calvin Coolidge College
Boston, MA
See Also No. 1202
1023. Central State University
Wilberforce, OH
1024. St. Joseph's College
Rensselaer, IN
1025. Jersey City State College
Formerly New Jersey State College
Jersey City, NJ
1026. Lincoln University
San Francisco, San Jose and Sacramento, CA
1027. United States Merchant Marine Academy
Kings Point, NY
1028. Wilkes University
Wilkes-Barre, PA
1029. Bridgeport, University of
Bridgeport, CT
1030. Fairfield University
Fairfield, CT
1031. Le Moyne College
Syracuse, NY
1032. Idaho State University
Formerly Idaho State College
Pocatello, ID
1033. Hartford, University of
Formerly Hillyer College
Hartford, CT
1034. Christian Brothers College
Memphis, TN
1035. William Mitchell College of Law
St. Paul, MN
1036. Brandeis University
Waltham, MA
1037. Huston-Tillotson College
Austin, TX
1038. Jacksonville University
Jacksonville, FL
1039. North Georgia College
Dahlonega, GA
1040. Pace University
New York, Pleasantville and White Plains, NY
1041. Iona College
New Rochelle, NY
1042. California State University, Long Beach
Formerly Long Beach State University
Long Beach, CA
1043. California State University, Los Angeles
Formerly Los Angeles State College of Applied Arts and Sciences
Los Angeles, CA
See Also No. 1097
1044. New York at Albany, State University of
Albany, NY
1045. Nashville School of Law
Nashville, TN
1046. Fairleigh Dickinson University
Madison, Rutherford and Teaneck, NJ
1047. Lycoming College
Williamsport, PA
1048. Western New England College
Springfield, MA
1049. San Diego, University of
San Diego, CA
1050. Midwestern State University
Wichita Falls, TX
1051. Lewis and Clark College
Portland, OR
1052. Houston Baptist University
Houston, TX
1053. Messiah College
Grantham, PA
1054. Tennessee Wesleyan College
Athens, TN
1055. Southeastern Louisiana College
Hammond, LA
1056. Portland State University
Portland, OR
1057. Merrimack College
North Andover, MA
1058. Pacific Lutheran University
Tacoma, WA
1059. Georgia State University
Atlanta, GA
1060. California State University, Sacramento
Formerly Sacramento State College
Sacramento, CA
1061. Lamar University
Beaumont, TX
1062. Gannon University
Erie, PA
1063. Georgia Southern College
Statesboro, GA
1064. Lipscomb University
Formerly David Lipscomb College
Nashville, TN
1065. Hastings College of the Law, University of California
San Francisco, CA
1066. Boalt Hall School of Law, University of California
Berkeley, CA
1067. California School of Law, Davis, University of
Davis, CA
1068. California School of Law, Los Angeles, University of
Los Angeles, CA
1069. Chaminade University of Honolulu
Honolulu, HI
1070. United States Air Force Academy
Colorado Springs, CO
1071. Southern Oregon State College
Ashland, OR
1072. Alliance College
Cambridge Springs, PA
1073. California State University, Hayward
Hayward, CA
1074. California Polytechnic State University
San Luis Obispo, CA
1075. California State Polytechnic University
Pomona, CA
1076. Orange State College
Fullerton, CA
1077. California State University, Northridge
Formerly San Fernando Valley State College
Northridge, CA
1078. Sonoma State University
Rohnert Park, CA
1079. California State University, Stanislaus
Formerly Stanislaus State College
Turlock, CA
1080. Northeast Louisiana University
Monroe, LA
1081. Austin Peay State University
Clarksville, TN
1082. Quincy University
Quincy, IL
1083. Old Dominion University
Norfolk, VA
1084. Northern Montana College
Havre, MT
1085. Weber State College
Ogden, UT
1086. Florida Atlantic University
Boca Raton, FL
1087. Catholic University of Puerto Rico
Ponce, PR
1088. Inter-American University of Puerto Rico
San Juan, PR

1089. McNeese State University
Lake Charles, LA
1090. Virginia Commonwealth University
Formerly Richmond Professional Institute
Richmond, VA
1091. South Alabama, University of
Mobile, AL
1092. Princess Anne State College
Princess Anne, MD
1093. Utica College of Syracuse University
Utica, NY
1094. Southern Arkansas University
Formerly Southern State College
Magnolia, AR
1095. La Verne College of Law, University of
Formerly San Fernando Valley, University of
Sepulveda, CA
1096. Angelo State University
Formerly San Angelo State University
San Angelo, TX
1097. California State University, Los Angeles
Formerly Los Angeles State College
Los Angeles, CA
1098. Louisiana State University at Alexandria
Alexandria, LA
1099. New Orleans, University of
Formerly Louisiana State University of New Orleans
New Orleans, LA
1100. Shimer College
Waukegan, IL
1101. Blackburn College
Carlinville, IL
1102. Southern Connecticut State College
New Haven, CT
1103. Western Connecticut State University
Danbury, CT
1104. Eastern Oregon College
La Grande, OR
1105. Dallas, University of
Irving, TX
1106. North Park College
Chicago, IL
1107. Assumption College
Worcester, MA
1108. Monmouth University
West Long Branch, NJ
1109. California State University, Fullerton
Fullerton, CA
1110. California State University, San Bernardino
San Bernardino, CA
1111. South Florida, University of
Tampa, FL
1112. Urbana College
Urbana, OH
1113. King's College
Wilkes Barre, PA
1114. Van Norman University
Los Angeles, CA
1115. Wheeling Jesuit University
Formerly Wheeling Jesuit College
Wheeling, WV
1116. Rowan University
Formerly Glassboro State College
Glassboro, NJ
1117. Pepperdine University School of Law
Formerly Orange University College of Law
Malibu, CA
1118. Thomas More College
Formerly Villa Madonna College
Covington, KY
1119. Indiana University School of Law - Bloomington
Bloomington, IN
1120. Westminster College
Salt Lake City, UT
1121. Aquinas College
Grand Rapids, MI
1122. St. John Fisher College
Rochester, NY
1123. Goddard College
Plainfield, VT
1124. Eastern Mennonite College
Harrisonburg, VA
1125. Arkansas Tech University
Formerly Arkansas Polytechnic University
Russellville, AR
1126. Belmont Abbey College
Belmont, NC
1127. California College of Law
Hollywood and West Covina, CA
1128. North Carolina at Charlotte, University of
Charlotte, NC
1129. Mars Hill College
Mars Hill, NC
1130. St. Andrews Presbyterian College
Laurinburg, NC
1131. California State University, Dominguez Hills
Dominguez Hills, CA
1132. Humphreys College
Stockton, CA
1133. New York Institute of Technology
New York, NY
1134. Bentley College
Waltham, MA
1135. Marymount-Manhattan College
New York, NY
1136. West Los Angeles, University of
Culver City, CA
1137. Western State University
Fullerton, CA
1138. Baruch College of the City University of New York
New York, NY
1139. John Jay College of Criminal Justice of the City University of New York
New York, NY
1140. College of Staten Island of the City University of New York
Formerly Richmond College of the City University of New York
Staten Island, NY
1141. York College of the City University of New York
Queens, NY
1142. Texas at Arlington, University of
Arlington, TX
1143. Albuquerque, University of
Albuquerque, NM
1144. Bethel College
St. Paul, MN
1145. Bryant College
Smithfield, RI
1146. Santa Fe, College of
Santa Fe, NM
1147. Central Oklahoma, University of
Formerly Central State University
Edmond, OK
1148. Whittier College School of Law
Formerly Beverly College of Law
Los Angeles, CA
1149. Boston State College
Boston, MA
1150. Bellarmine College
Formerly Bellarmine Ursuline College
Louisville, KY
1151. Lewis University
Lockport, IL
1152. South Bay University
Harbor City, CA
1153. John F. Kennedy University
Walnut Creek, CA
1154. Oakland University
Rochester, MI
1155. Babson College
Babson Park, MA
1156. New Haven, University of
West Haven, CT
1157. St. Joseph College
East Chicago, IN
1158. St. Thomas University
Formerly Biscayne College
Miami, FL
1159. Indiana Institute of Technology
Fort Wayne, IN
1160. Herbert H. Lehman College of the City University of New York
Bronx, NY
1161. Northern Kentucky University
Highland Heights, KY
1162. Antioch School of Law
Washington, DC
1163. Loma Linda University
Formerly La Sierra College
Loma Linda, CA
1164. Colorado at Colorado Springs, University of
Colorado Springs, CO
1165. Colorado at Denver, University of
Denver, CO
1166. Nicholls State University
Thibodaux, LA
1167. Harvey Mudd College
Claremont, CA
1168. Pitzer College
Claremont, CA
1169. California at Santa Cruz, University of
Santa Cruz, CA
1170. Franklin Pierce College
Rindge, NH
1171. Wisconsin-Green Bay, University of
Green Bay, WI
1172. Wisconsin-Parkside, University of
Kenosha, WI
1173. Southeastern Massachusetts University
North Dartmouth, MA
1174. William Paterson College of New Jersey
Wayne, NJ
1175. Central Florida, University of
Formerly Florida Technological University
Orlando, FL
1176. West Florida, University of
Pensacola, FL
1177. Grambling State University
Grambling, LA
1178. City University of New York School of Law, Queens College
Flushing, NY
1179. Northrop University
Inglewood, CA
1180. Bloomfield College
Bloomfield, NJ
1181. Western Oregon State College
Formerly Oregon College of Education
Monmouth, OR
1182. Benedictine College
Atchison, KS
1183. Northeastern Illinois University
Chicago, IL
1185. Southern College of Seventh-Day Adventists
Formerly Southern Missionary College
Collegedale, TN
1186. Ventura College of Law
Ventura, CA
1187. Thomas M. Cooley Law School
Lansing, MI
1188. United States International University
Formerly California Western University
San Diego, CA
1189. San Joaquin, College of Law
Fresno, CA
1190. Glendale University
Glendale, CA
1191. Chicago State University
Chicago, IL
1192. Dowling College
Oakdale, NY
1193. Boise State University
Boise, ID
1194. Vermont Law School
South Royalton, VT
1195. Covenant College
Lookout Mountain, TN

1313. New School for Social Research
New York, NY
1314. Ozarks, School of the
Point Lookout, MO
1315. Oklahoma Christian College
Oklahoma City, OK
1316. Philadelphia College of Textiles and Science
Philadelphia, PA
1317. Pembroke State University
Pembroke, NC
1318. Pfeiffer College
Misenheimer, NC
1319. Pikeville College
Pikeville, KY
1320. St. Johns College
Santa Fe, NM
1321. Southwest Baptist University
Bolivar, MO
1322. Stephens College
Columbia, MO
1323. Steubenville, University of
Steubenville, OH
1324. Southern Utah University
Formerly Southern Utah State College
Cedar City, UT
1325. Touro College Jacob D. Fuchsberg Law Center
New York, NY
1326. York College of Pennsylvania
York, PA
1327. Trevecca Nazarene College
Nashville, TN
1328. Baptist College at Charleston
Charleston, SC
1329. Christopher Newport College
Formerly Christopher Newport College of the College of William and Mary
Newport News, VA
1330. Castleton State College
Castleton, VT
1331. Evergreen State College, The
Olympia, WA
1332. Tarleton State University
Stephenville, TX
1333. Embry-Riddle Aeronautical University
Daytona Beach, FL
1334. Guam, University of
Agana, GU
1335. Brigham Young University
Laie, HI
1336. Southern California Institute of Law
Santa Barbara and Ventura, CA
1337. Texas at Galveston, University of
Galveston, TX
1338. Widener University
Including Widener University School of Law, formerly Delaware Law School
Chester, PA and Wilmington, DE
1339. Regent University
Formerly CBN University
Virginia Beach, VA
1340. Salmon P. Chase College of Law
Highland Heights, KY
1341. Texas at Houston, University of
Houston, TX
1342. Southwest State University
Marshall, MN
1343. Caldwell College
Caldwell, NJ
1344. Oakland College of Law
Oakland, CA
1345. Wiggins, Norman A., School of Law
Formerly Campbell University School of Law
Buies Creek, NC
1346. Prescott College
Prescott, AZ
1347. Missouri at St. Louis, University of
St. Louis, MO
1348. Northwestern College
Orange City, IA
1349. New York at Binghamton, State University of
Binghamton, NY
1350. New York at Stony Brook, State University of
Stony Brook, NY
1351. Simon Greenleaf School of Law
Anaheim, CA
1352. Alverno College
Milwaukee, WI
1353. Long Island University, Brooklyn Campus of
Brooklyn, NY
1354. Monterey Institute of International Studies
Monterey, CA
1355. San Francisco Law School, University of
San Francisco, CA
1356. George Mason University
Formerly George Mason College of The University of Virginia
Fairfax, VA
1537. Istanbul University
Istanbul, Turkey
1357. Touro College
New York, NY
1358. Seattle University School of Law
Formerly University of Puget Sound School of Law
Tacoma, WA
1359. Evangel College
Springfield, MO
1360. Roger Williams University School of Law
Bristol, RI
1362. Langston University
Langston, OK
1363. Texas Wesleyan University School of Law
Irving, TX
1364. District of Columbia School of Law
Washington, DC
1365. Emory University
Atlanta, GA
1366. California Southern Law School
Riverside, CA
1367. Siena Heights College
Adrian, MI
1369. James Madison University
Harrisonburg, VA
1370. Thomas Jefferson School of Law
San Diego, CA
1371. New York College at Cortland, State University of
Cortland, NY
1372. New York College at Geneseo, State University of
Geneseo, NY
1373. New York College at New Paltz, State University of
New Paltz, NY
1374. New York College at Oneonta, State University of
Oneonta, NY
1375. California, Berkeley, University of
Berkeley, CA
1376. College of New Jersey, The
Formerly Trenton State College
Trenton, NJ
1377. Valdosta State University
Valdosta, GA
1378. North Carolina Agricultural & Technical State University
Greensboro, NC
1379. Chapman University School of Law
Anaheim, CA
1380. New York College at Purchase, State University of
Purchase, NY
1381. New York College at Brockport, State University of
Brockport, NY
1382. Queensland, University of
Brisbane, Australia
1383. Madras, University of
Chennai, India
1384. National University of Ireland, Galway
Galway, Ireland
1385. New York College at Potsdam, State University of
Potsdam, NY
1386. Appalachian School of Law
Grundy, VA
1387. National Law School of India
Bangalore, India
1388. Virginia Wesleyan College
Norfolk, VA
1389. Massachusetts School of Law
Andover, MA
1390. Alfred Adler Institute of San Francisco
San Francisco, CA
1391. Franciscan University of Steubenville
Steubenville, OH
1392. Francaise Alliance USA
Paris, France
1393. Thunderbird American Graduate School of International Management
Glendale, AZ
1394. American University in Cairo
Cairo, Egypt
1395. Anna Maria College
Paxton, MA
1396. Associated Mennonite Biblical Seminary
Elkhart, IN
1397. Bangalore University
Bangalore, India
1398. Benjamin N. Cardozo School of Law, Yeshiva University
New York, NY
1399. Cairo University
Cairo, Egypt
1400. Concordia University
Irvine, CA
1401. Canadian Mennonite University
Winnipeg, Manitoba
1402. Catholic University of Argentina
Buenos Aires, Argentina
1403. Central Bible College
Springfield, MO
1404. Chadwick University
Birmingham, AL
1405. City Colleges of Chicago
Chicago, IL
1406. City College of San Francisco
San Francisco, CA
1407. College for Financial Planning
Denver, CO
1408. College of Law, London, The
London, England
1409. College of Saint Mary
Omaha, NE
1410. Denver, College of Law, University of
Denver, CO
1411. Columbia Pacific University
Novato, CA
1412. Curtis Institute of Music, The
Philadelphia, PA
1413. Czech Technical University
Prague, Czechlovakia
1414. Daemen College
Amherst, NY
1415. Delft University of Technology
Delft, Netherlands
1416. Delhi, The University of
Delhi, India
1417. Finch University of Health Sciences/The Chicago Medical School
1418. Flagler College
St. Augustine, FL
1419. Francis Marion University
Florence, SC
1420. Freed-Hardeman University
Henderson, TN
1421. Fresno Pacific College
Fresno, CA
1422. Fuller Theological Seminary
Pasadena, CA
1423. Frankfurt, University of
Frankfurt, Germany

1424. Institute of Political Studies, Paris
Paris, France
1425. Institute for Advanced Studies
Geneva, Switzerland
1426. Sophia University
Tokyo, Japan
1427. Johannes Gutenberg University
Mainz, Germany
1428. Johnson State College
Westbury, VT
1429. Kemper Military School & College
Boonville, MO
1430. Kennesaw State University
Kennesaw, GA
1431. Kennedy-Western University
Cheyenne, WY
1432. Lehman College of the City University of New York
Bronx, NY
1433. Lesley College
Cambridge, MA
1434. Lourdes College
Sylvania, OH
1435. Catholic University of Louvain
Louvain-la-Neuve, Belgium
1436. Manhattan School of Music
New York, NY
1437. Massachusetts College of Pharmacy & Health Sciences
Boston, MA
1438. Mennonite Brethren Biblical Seminary
Fresno, CA
1439. Missouri at Columbia, School of Law, University of
Columbia, MO
1440. Molloy College
Rockville, NY
1441. National Chung Hsing University
Taiwan, China
1442. National Law Center for Inter-American Free Trade
Tucson, AZ
1443. National University of Mexico
Mexico City, Mexico
1444. National War College
Washington, DC
1445. New York Medical College
Valhalla, NY
1446. Pacific School of Religion
Berkeley, CA
1447. Parsons School of Design
New York, NY
1448. Polytechnic School of Engineering
Milan, Italy
1449. Rivier College
Nashua, NH
1450. Royal Academy of Arts
London, England
1451. Seoul National University
Seoul, Korea
1452. Shenandoah University
Winchester, VA
1453. Smith Institute
London, England
1454. Southwestern Michigan College
Dowagaic, MI
1455. Spring Garden College
Philadelphia, PA
1456. St. Petersburg State Institute of Technology
St. Petersburg, Russia
1457. New York at Fredonia, State University of
Fredonia, NY
1458. New York at Oswego, State University of
Oswego, NY
1459. New York, Brooklyn College of Medicine, State University of
Brooklyn, NY
1460. New York, Institute of Technology at Utica/Rome, State University of
Utica/Rome, NY
1461. Teheran, University of
Teheran, Iran
1462. National Judicial College, The
Reno, NV
1463. Texas Southern University, Thurgood Marshall School of Law
Houston, TX
1464. Defense Language Institute, The
Monterey, CA
1465. Union Theological Seminary
New York, NY
1466. Bordeaux, University of
Bordeaux, France
1467. Universidad Iberoamericana
La Cruz, Mexico
1468. Amsterdam, University of
Amsterdam, Netherlands
1469. Birmingham, University of
Birmingham, England
1470. Bristol, University of
Bristol, England
1471. Catholic University of Brussels
Brussels, Belgium
1472. Canterbury, University of
Canterbury, New Zealand
1473. Costa Rica, University of
Moravia, Costa Rica
1474. East Anglia, University of
East Anglia, England
1475. Exeter, University of
Exeter, England
1476. Geneva, University of
Geneva, Switzerland
1477. Grenoble, University of
Grenoble, France
1478. Hannover, University of
Hannover, Germany
1479. Keele, University of
Keele, England
1480. Kent at Canterbury, University of
Canterbury, England
1481. Manchester, University of
Manchester, England
1482. New South Wales, University of
New South Wales, Australia
1483. Newcastle-upon-Tyne, University of
Newcastle-upon-Tyne, England
1484. Northern California, University of
Petaluma, CA
1485. Panama, University of
Panama, Rep. of Panama
1486. San Carlos, University of
University City, Guatemala
1487. Santa Monica College
Santa Monica, CA
1488. Sheffield, University of
Sheffield, England
1489. National University of Singapore
Singapore, Singapore
1490. Sydney, University of
Sydney, Australia
1491. Vrije Universiteit
Amsterdam, Netherlands
1492. Valley Forge Military Academy and College
Wayne, PA
1493. Zurich, University of
Zurich, Switzerland
1494. California at Los Angeles, University of
Los Angeles, CA
1495. Henry W. Bloch School of Business & Public Administration, University of Missouri
Los Angeles, CA
1496. European University
Amsterdam, Netherlands
1497. Nevada Mackay School of Mines, University of
Reno, NV
1498. Havana, University of
Havana, Cuba
1499. Rio Grande University
Rio Grande, OH
1500. Rhode Island School of Design
Providence, RI
1502. Ryerson Polytechnic University
Toronto, Canada
1503. Paul H. Nitze School of Advanced International Studies
Washington, DC
1504. California at Sacramento, University of
Sacramento, CA
1505. New York at Stony Brook, State University of
Stony Brook, NY
1506. Thayer School of Engineering at Darmouth College
Hanover, NH
1507. New York at Brockport, State University of
Brockport, NY
1508. Denver, Graduate School of International Studies, University of
Denver, CO
1509. Richmond, T.C. Williams School of Law, University of
Richmond, VA
1510. Long Island University, Southampton College
Southampton, NY
1511. St. Paul's College
Lawrenceville, VA
1512. Strayer University
Washington, DC
1513. Hague Academy of International Law, The
The Hague, Netherlands
1514. Naval Justice School
Newport, RI
1515. Glasgow, University of
Glasgow, Scotland
1516. Madrid, University of
Madrid, Spain
1517. Americas, University of the
Mexico City, Mexico
1518. Witwatersrand, University of the
Johannesburg, South Africa
1519. Webb Institute
Glen Cove, NY
1520. Southern New England School of Law
North Dartmouth, MA
1521. Leicester, University of
Leicester, England
1522. Loyola Law School
Los Angeles, CA
1523. Katholieke Universiteit Leuven
Leuven, Belgium
1524. Belmont University
Nashville, TN
1525. Universidad Nacional de Mexico
Mexico City, Mexico
1526. Florida Coastal School of Law
Jacksonville, FL
1527. British-American University School of Law
Santa Ana, CA
1528. Florida Metropolitan University
Tampa, FL
1529. New York College at Buffalo, State University of
Buffalo, NY
1530. Hebrew University of Jerusalem, The
Jerusalem, Israel
1531. Southern New Hampshire University
Manchester, NH
1532. Thomas Aquinas College
Santa Paula, CA
1533. Copenhagen, University of
Copenhagen, Denmark
1534. Basel, University of
Basel, Switzerland
1535. Bern, University of
Bern, Switzerland
1536. Tokyo, The University of
Tokyo, Japan
1538. Athens, University of
Athens, Greece
1539. Ner Israel Rabbinical College
Baltimore, MD
1540. London School of Economics and Political Science
London, England

1541. Pittsburgh School of Law, University of
Pittsburgh, PA
1542. Buenos Aires, University of
Buenos Aires, Argentina
1543. Hamburg, University of
Hamburg, Germany
1544. Malaya, University of
Kuala Lumpur, Malaysia
1545. Uppsala University
Uppsala, Sweden
1546. Lund University
Lund, Sweden
1547. Leeds Metropolitan University
Leeds, England
1548. Ghana, University of
Accra, Ghana
1549. Waseda University
Tokyo, Japan
1550. Buckingham, University of
Buckingham, England
1551. Monash University
Melbourne, Victoria, Australia
1552. Mount Mercy College
Cedar Rapids, IA
1553. William S. Boyd School of Law
Las Vegas, NV
1554. Salve Regina University
Newport, RI
1555. Eastern Oregon University
La Grande, OR
1556. Cornell University Law School
Ithaca, NY
1557. Rutgers College
New Brunswick, NJ
1558. Ave Maria School of Law
Ann Arbor, MI
1559. Philadelphia Biblical University
Langhorne, PA
1560. Barry University School of Law
Orlando, FL
1561. Lancaster University
Lancaster, England
1562. Paul Tulane College
New Orleans, LA
1563. St. Francis University
Loretto, PA
1564. Point Park University
Pittsburgh, PA
1565. Harvard Law School
Cambridge, MA
1566. William Howard Taft University
Santa Ana, CA
1567. Trinity Law School
Santa Ana, CA
1568. Liberty University
Formerly Lynchburg Baptist College
Lynchburg, VA
1569. New York at Plattsburgh, State
University of
Plattsburgh, NY
1570. Moody Bible Institute
Chicago, IL
1571. St. Thomas School of Law
Minneapolis, MN
1572. Charleston Southern University
Charleston, SC
1573. Grand Canyon University
Phoenix, AZ
1574. California State University, Bakersfield
Bakersfield, CA
1575. Tel Aviv University
Ramat Aviv, Tel Aviv, Israel
1576. Colby-Sawyer College
New London, NH
1577. Mercy College
Bronx, Dobbs Ferry, Manhattan,
White Plains and Yorktown, NY
1578. Charter Oak State College
New Britain, CT
1579. New York College at Old Westbury,
State University of
Old Westbury, NY
1580. New York, Maritime College, State
University of
Throggs Neck, NY
1581. Florida Memorial University
Miami Gardens, FL
1582. Albany State University
Albany, GA
4210. Louis D. Brandeis School of Law,
University of Louisville
Louisville, KY

PRACTICE PROFILES BAR ROSTER

NORTH CAROLINA
NORTH DAKOTA, OHIO
OKLAHOMA, OREGON

NORTH CAROLINA

CAPITAL: RALEIGH

North Carolina State Bar
P.O. Box 25908
Raleigh, North Carolina 27611-5908
Telephone: 919-828-4620
Fax: 919-821-9168

Index of Towns and Cities Listed by County

*Indicates County Seat

Alamance County
Burlington
Elon College
Gibsonville
* Graham
Mebane

Alexander County
Stony Point
* Taylorsville

Alleghany County
Glade Valley
* Sparta

Anson County
* Wadesboro

Ashe County
* Jefferson
West Jefferson

Avery County
Banner Elk
Linville
* Newland

Beaufort County
Aurora
Belhaven
* Washington

Bertie County
* Windsor

Bladen County
Clarkton
* Elizabethtown
White Lake

Brunswick County
Bald Head Island
* Bolivia
Calabash
Holden Beach
Leland
Oak Island
Ocean Isle Beach
Shallotte
Southport
Sunset Beach
Supply

Buncombe County
Arden
* Asheville
Black Mountain
Candler
Enka
Fairview
Skyland
Swannanoa
Weaverville

Burke County
Drexel
Hickory
* Morganton
Valdese

Cabarrus County
* Concord
Harrisburg
Kannapolis
Midland
Mount Pleasant

Caldwell County
Blowing Rock
Granite Falls
Hickory
* Lenoir

Camden County
* Camden

Carteret County
Atlantic
Atlantic Beach
Bath
* Beaufort
Cedar Point
Emerald Isle
Morehead City
Newport
Pine Knoll Shores

Caswell County
* Yanceyville

Catawba County
Claremont
Conover
Hickory
* Newton
Terrell

Chatham County
* Pittsboro
Siler City

Cherokee County
Andrews
Marble
* Murphy

Chowan County
* Edenton

Clay County
* Hayesville

Cleveland County
Kings Mountain
* Shelby

Columbus County
Tabor City
* Whiteville

Craven County
Havelock
* New Bern
Trent Woods

Cumberland County
* Fayetteville
Fort Bragg
Hope Mills
Spring Lake

Currituck County
Corolla
* Currituck
Harbinger
Moyock
Point Harbor

Dare County
Avon
Duck
Kill Devil Hills
Kitty Hawk
Manns Harbor
* Manteo
Nags Head
Southern Shores
Wanchese

Davidson County
Denton
High Point
* Lexington
Thomasville

Davie County
Advance
* Mocksville

Duplin County
Beulaville
* Kenansville
Rose Hill
Wallace
Warsaw

Durham County
Bahama
Chapel Hill
* Durham
Morrisville
Research Triangle Park

Edgecombe County
Conetoe
Pinetops
Rocky Mount
* Tarboro

Forsyth County
Clemmons
High Point
Kernersville
King
Lewisville
Pfafftown
Walkertown
* Winston-Salem

Franklin County
Franklinton
* Louisburg
Youngsville

Gaston County
Belmont
Cherryville
Dallas
* Gastonia
Kings Mountain
Lowell

Gaston Co.—*Continued*
Mount Holly
Stanley

Gates County
* Gatesville

Graham County
* Robbinsville

Granville County
Butner
Creedmoor
* Oxford

Greene County
* Snow Hill

Guilford County
Archdale
Brown Summit
Gibsonville
* Greensboro
High Point
Jamestown
Oak Ridge
Summerfield
Whitsett

Halifax County
Enfield
* Halifax
Littleton
Roanoke Rapids
Scotland Neck
Weldon

Harnett County
Angier
Buies Creek
Coats
Dunn
Erwin
* Lillington

Haywood County
Canton
Clyde
Maggie Valley
* Waynesville

Henderson County
Flat Rock
Fletcher
* Hendersonville
Horse Shoe
Laurel Park
Mountain Home
Tuxedo

Hertford County
Ahoskie
Harrellsville
Murfreesboro
Winton

Hoke County
* Raeford

Hyde County
Engelhard
Ocracoke
* Swanquarter

Iredell County
Mooresville
* Statesville
Stony Point
Troutman

Jackson County
Balsam
Cashiers
Cullowhee
Sapphire Valley
* Sylva
Whittier

Johnston County
Benson
Clayton
Four Oaks
Kenly
Selma
* Smithfield

Jones County
* Trenton

Lee County
* Sanford

Lenoir County
Grifton
* Kinston
La Grange

Lincoln County
Denver
* Lincolnton

Macon County
* Franklin
Highlands
Otto

Madison County
Hot Springs
* Marshall
Mars Hill

Martin County
* Williamston

McDowell County
Little Switzeland
* Marion
Nebo

Mecklenburg County
* Charlotte
Cornelius
Davidson
Huntersville
Matthews
Paw Creek
Pineville
Weddington

Mitchell County
Spruce Pine

Montgomery County
Mount Gilead
* Troy

Moore County
Aberdeen
* Carthage
Jackson Springs
Pinehurst
Robbins
Southern Pines
West End
Whispering Pines

Nash County
* Nashville
Rocky Mount
Spring Hope

New Hanover County
Carolina Beach
Castle Hayne
Kure Beach
* Wilmington
Wrightsville Beach

Northampton County
* Jackson
Rich Square
Woodland

Onslow County
Holly Ridge
Hubert
* Jacksonville
Richlands
Sneads Ferry
Surf City
Swansboro

Orange County
Carrboro
Chapel Hill
Efland
* Hillsborough
Mebane

Pamlico County
* Bayboro
Oriental

Pasquotank County
* Elizabeth City

Pender County
* Burgaw
Hampstead
Surf City

Perquimans County
* Hertford

Person County
* Roxboro

Pitt County
Ayden
Farmville
* Greenville
Grifton
Winterville

Polk County
* Columbus
Saluda
Tryon

Randolph County
Archdale
* Asheboro
High Point

Randolph Co.—*Continued*
Liberty
Ramseur
Trinity

Richmond County
Hamlet
* Rockingham

Robeson County
Fairmont
* Lumberton
Maxton
Pembroke
Red Springs
Rowland
St. Pauls

Rockingham County
Eden
Madison
Reidsville
Stoneville
* Wentworth

Rowan County
China Grove
Granite Quarry
Kannapolis
Landis
Mount Ulla
Rockwell
* Salisbury
Spencer

Rutherford County
Forest City
Lake Lure
* Rutherfordton
Spindale

Sampson County
* Clinton
Newton Grove
Roseboro
Salemburg

Scotland County
* Laurinburg
Maxton
Wagram

Stanly County
* Albemarle
Badin
Norwood

Stokes County
* Danbury
King
Pinnacle
Walnut Cove

Surry County
* Dobson
Elkin
Mount Airy
Pilot Mountain

Swain County
* Bryson City
Cherokee

Transylvania County
Balsam Grove
* Brevard
Cedar Mountain
Lake Toxaway
Pisgah Forest

Tyrrell County
* Columbia

Union County
Indian Trail
* Monroe
Waxhaw
Weddington

Vance County
* Henderson

Wake County
Apex
Cary
Fuquay-Varina
Garner
Holly Springs
Knightdale
Morrisville
* Raleigh
Wake Forest
Wendell
Zebulon

Warren County
* Warrenton

Washington County
* Plymouth

Watauga County
Blowing Rock
* Boone
Sugar Grove
Vilas

Wayne County
Fremont
* Goldsboro
Mount Olive

Wilkes County
Elkin
North Wilkesboro
* Wilkesboro

Wilson County
Elm City
Kenly
* Wilson

Yadkin County
Jonesville
* Yadkinville

Yancey County
* Burnsville

*Indicates County Seat

ABERDEEN, 3,400, *Moore Co.*

Adams, Matthew D. .... '75 '05 C.575 B.S. L.574 J.D. [Ⓐ Webb&G.]
Craven, Richard C. '52 '76 C.896 B.S. L.574 J.D.
910 N. Sandhills Blvd., U.S. Hwy. 1 N.
Dedmond, Heath K. .... '72 '01 C.575 B.S. L.574 J.D. [Ⓐ Webb&G.]
Lantz, Elizabeth .... '67 '01 C.339 B.S. L.424 J.D. 1407 Churchill Downs Dr.
McCrann, Michael Johnathan, (CV) .... '43 '76 Aberdeen Legal Clinic
Parker, Robbie B. .... '— '03 C.232 B.S. L.1228 J.D. [Ⓐ Webb&G.] ⊙

Van Camp, Meacham & Newman, PLLC
(See Pinehurst)

Webb, W. Y. Alex, (BV) .... '48 '73 C.925 B.A. L.575 J.D. [Webb&G.]
Webb & Graves, P.L.L.C., (BV)
910 N. Sandhills Boulevard, U.S. Highway 1 N. (⊙Wilmington)
Webster, W. Terrell, Jr. .... '22 '48 C&L.575 B.S., LL.B. P.O. Box 1125‡

ADVANCE, 200, *Davie Co.*

Hairston, Peter W. .... '13 '35 C&L.575 A.B., LL.B. 415 Peter Hairston Rd.‡
Ketner, J. Laross .... '56 '96 C.576 B.S. L.896 J.D. 522 N. Hiddenbrooke Dr.
Riden, Thomas K., (AVⓉ) '43 '68 C&L.362 B.A., J.D.
(adm. in FL; not adm. in NC) V.F. Knitwear, Inc.

AHOSKIE, 4,523, *Hertford Co.*

Asbell, Valerie Mitchell, (BV) '67 '92
C.1365 B.A. L.861 J.D. Dist. Atty., The Dist. Atty. Off.
Baker, Ronald G., (AV) .... '49 '75 C&L.575 B.S., J.D. [Baker,J.D.M.&D.] ⊙

Baker, Jones, Daly, Murray, Carter & Daughtry, P.A., (AV) BR
304 West Sunset Street, P.O. Box 986, 27910-0986 ⊙
Telephone: 252-332-2181 Fax: 252-332-8354 Real Estate Fax: 252-209-0046
Email: ahoskie@bjjlawoffices.com
Ronald G. Baker; Robert C. Jenkins (1943-2002); W. Hugh Jones, Jr.; Roswald B. Daly, Jr.; Ernie K. Murray (Resident, Rocky Mount Office); Ernest R. Carter, Jr.; Kevin Neil Lewis (Resident, Rocky Mount Office); Bruce L. Daughtry (Resident, Rocky Mount Office);—Amy Lorrelle Elliott.
General Insurance Defense Civil Practice. Trials. Real Estate, Estate Planning, Probate, Business, Personal Injury Defense, Professional Liability, Insurance, Workers Compensation and Collections.
Representative Clients: North Carolina Farm Bureau Mutual Insurance Co.; Nationwide Mutual Insurance Co.; Great American Insurance Cos.; Integon Insurance Corporation; Lawyers Mutual Insurance Company of North Carolina; Travelers Insurance Company; Employers Mutual Insurance Group; Universal Insurance Company; Travelers Property Casualty.
Rocky Mount, North Carolina Office: 140 North Franklin Street, P.O. Box 68. Telephone: 252-442-1977. Facsimile: 252-442-5175.
See Professional Biographies, AHOSKIE, NORTH CAROLINA

Ballance Moody, Vershenia M., (BV) .... '70 '96 C.575 B.A. L.574 J.D. 418 Everett Street
Carter, Ernest R., Jr., (BV) .... '59 '84 C.575 B.S.B.A. L.1228 J.D. [Baker,J.D.M.&D.] ⊙
Cherry, Thomas L. .... '28 '58 C&L.896 B.S., LL.B. 119 W. Main St.‡
Curtis, Stuart A. .... '20 '51 C&L.896 B.S., J.D. 106 Railroad St.‡
Daly, Roswald B., Jr., (BV) .... '51 '76 C&L.575 A.B., J.D. [Baker,J.D.M.&D.] ⊙
Daughtry, Bruce L., (BV) .... '66 '93 C.1228 B.B.A. L.1345 J.D. [Baker,J.D.M.&D.] ⊙
Earp, Anita C. .... '60 '86 C.34 B.A. L.574 J.D. Legal Servs. of the Costal Plains
Elliott, Amy Lorrelle .... '75 '00 C.945 B.A. L.884 J.D. [Ⓐ Baker,J.D.M.&D.]
Evans, Ernest L. .... '44 '69 C&L.896 B.A., J.D. Pres., ELE, Inc.
Gragson, John D. .... '71 '97 C&L.575 B.A., J.D. P.O. Box 564
Grant, Rosiland T., & Associates, (CV) .... '56 '82 C.801 B.S. L.574 J.D. P.O. Box 129
Jones, W. Hugh, Jr., (BV) .... '54 '80 C.198 A.B. L.575 J.D. [Baker,J.D.M.&D.] ⊙
Lewis, Kevin Neil, (BV) .... '65 '92 C.1228 B.A. L.1345 J.D. [Baker,J.D.M.&D.] ⊙
Lewis, W. Rob, (CV) .... '55 '81 C.1044 B.S. L.150 J.D. P.O. Box 129
Martin, Perry W. .... '28 '50 C&L.896 LL.B. 419-A Peachtree St.
McLean, Mitchell S., (BV) .... '54 '79 C.232 B.A. L.896 J.D. [Taylor&M.]
Montague, Marlene W. '52 '81
C.1378 B.S.E. L.574 J.D. Legal Servs. of the Coastal Plains
Moore, Charles A., (CV) .... '54 '81 C.232 B.A. L.896 J.D. 217 W. Main St.
Murray, Ernie K., (BV) .... '52 '80 C.575 B.A. L.896 J.D. [Baker,J.D.M.&D.] ⊙
Overton, Larry S., (BV) .... '52 '77 C&L.896 B.A., J.D. 101 N. Railroad St.
Taylor, Donnie R., (BV) .... '50 '78 C.576 B.A. L.896 J.D. [Taylor&M.]
Taylor & McLean, (BV) .... 616 East Church Street
Whitaker, Sonya Lakesha .... '74 '99 C&L.574 B.A., J.D. 144 Forest Drive
Whitehead-Taylor, Lynda, (CV) '50 '91 C.232 B.A. L.574 J.D.
Staff Atty., Legal Services of the Coastal Plains

ALBEMARLE, * 15,680, *Stanly Co.*

Bahner, John M., Jr., (BV) .... '45 '74 C.896 B.A. L.879 J.D. P.O. Box 1210
Beaver, David A., (BV) .... '51 '77 C.575 B.A. L.896 J.D. [Doby&B.]
Blalock, Steven F., (AV) .... '52 '78 C.228 A.B. L.575 J.D. 219 W. Main St.
Bridges, Kevin M. .... '65 '90 C&L.575 B.A., J.D. Dist. J.
Brown, Charles P., (AV) .... '42 '66 C&L.575 B.S., J.D. [Brown,B.&B.]

Brown, Brown & Brown, P.L.L.C., (AV)
101 South Second Street, P.O. Drawer 400, 28002
Telephone: 704-982-2141 Telecopier: 704-982-0902
Email: brownlaw28001@ctc.net URL: http://www.brownbrownandbrown.com
Members of Firm: James Milton Brown (1851-1923); Richard L. Brown, Sr. (1887-1938); Richard L. Brown, Jr. (1910-1998); Charles P. Brown; G. Crawford Rippy, III;—Connie E. Josey.
General Civil and Criminal Trial Practice in all State Courts. Business, Insurance, Personal Injury and Wrongful Death, Real Estate, Probate, Estate Administration, Municipal Corporation.
Representative Clients: Aluminum Company of America; Norfolk Southern Railway.
Approved Attorneys for: Lawyers Title Insurance Corp.; Chicago Title Insurance Co.; Wachovia Bank & Trust Co.
See Professional Biographies, ALBEMARLE, NORTH CAROLINA

Burris, Ronald W., (BV) '50 '75 C.1128 B.A. L.575 LL.B.
Gen. Coun., Stanly Memorial Hospital Hospital
Chandler, Gerald R., (AV) .... '29 '54 C&L.896 B.A., J.D. P.O. Box 704
Coble, Warren L., (AV) .... '22 '49 C&L.896 B.A., LL.B. 117 W. North St.‡
Currie, Patrick Wade, (BV) .... '68 '93 C.198 B.A. L.1228 J.D. 214 E. North Street
Doby, Henry C., Jr., (AV) .... '20 '50 C.575 L.896 LL.B. City Atty. [Doby&B.]
Doby & Beaver, (AV) .... 117 West South Street
Grigg, David L., (AV) .... '39 '64 C.575 A.B. L.228 LL.B. [Morton,G.&P.]

Hartsell & Williams, P.A.
(See Concord)

Josey, Connie E. .... '79 '03 C.576 B.S. L.575 J.D. [Ⓐ Brown,B.&B.]
Lefler, Charles B., Jr. .... '48 '74 C.576 B.A. L.575 J.D. 1000 Lafayette Dr.‡
Lowder, Mark T., (BV) .... '56 '83 C.94 B.S.B.A. L.472 J.D. [M.T.Lowder&Assoc.]
Lowder, M.T., & Associates, (BV) .... 115 South Second Street
Mabry, Clegg W., Jr. .... '58 '83 C&L.896 B.A., J.D. 125 N. 4th St.‡
Medlin, R. Ward, (BV) .... '52 '77 C.925 B.A. L.1206 J.D. P.O. Box 1210
Morton, Ernest H., Jr., (AV) .... '26 '53 C&L.896 B.S., LL.B. [Morton,G.&P.]
Morton, Joshua J., Jr., (BV) .... '40 '66 C&L.896 B.A., LL.B. 120 King Ave.
Morton, Grigg and Phillips, L.L.P., (AV) .... 117 West North Street
Odom, Robert W., (BV) .... '45 '70 C.575 A.B. L.896 J.D. [R.W.Odom]
Odom, Robert W., P.A., (BV) .... 125 N. 4th St.
Parnell, Charles W., Jr., (BV) .... '67 '93 C.577 B.S. L.1228 J.D. P.O. Box 700
Pastorini, Vita A. .... '58 '93 C.415 B.S. L.201 J.D. 809 Mcgill Street
Phillips, James A., Jr., (BV) .... '52 '77 C.575 B.S. L.1206 J.D. [Morton,G.&P.]
Rippy, G. Crawford, III, (BV) .... '56 '83 C.269 B.A. L.192 J.D. [Brown,B.&B.]
Singletary, Howard E., Jr., (BV) .... '56 '81 C.152 B.A. L.1228 J.D. [Tucker&S.]
Tucker, William C., (AV) .... '48 '74 C.925 B.A. L.896 J.D. [Tucker&S.]
Tucker & Singletary, P.A., (AV) .... P.O. Box 1518
Webster, John W., (CV) .... '70 '96 C.712 B.A. L.1202 J.D. 307 N. 1st. St.

ANDREWS, 1,602, *Cherokee Co.*

Galardi, Wm. L. '20 '55 C.262 B.S. L.969 LL.B.
(adm. in GA; not adm. in NC) P.O. Box 1033‡

ANGIER, 3,419, *Harnett Co.*

Hales & Conaway, PLLC, The Law Offices of
(See Clinton)

Sauls, S. Vann .... '70 '97 C.575 B.S. L.1228 J.D. [S.V.Sauls]
Sauls, S. Vann, PA .... 10596 NC 50 Hwy. N.
Sparkman, Richard D., (BV) .... '50 '75 C.1129 B.A. L.896 J.D. [R.D.Sparkman&Assoc.]
Sparkman, Richard D., P.A. & Associates, (BV) .... 32 W. Williams St.

APEX, 20,212, *Wake Co.*

Bickford, Barbara Jean '60 '97 C.1172 B.A. L.93 J.D.
(adm. in MA; not adm. in NC) 102 Northcote Drive
Burt, Marianna R. .... '40 '90 C.145 M.A. L.575 J.D. P.O. Box 768
Ciulla, Ann H. .... '61 '87 C.896 B.A. L.273 J.D. 201 Briardale Ave.
Coomes, Donald Louis .... '48 '01 C.999 B.F.A. L.574 J.D. 405 Brierridge Drive
Danchi, Theodore S., (BV) .... '50 '87 C&L.879 B.S., J.D. [Stam,F.&D.]
Donaldson, Dorothy L. .... '63 '89 C.831 B.A. L.356 J.D. P.O. Box 1401
Fordham, Henry C., Jr., (AV) .... '54 '85 C.575 B.A. L.896 J.D. [Stam,F.&D.]
Frasco, William A., Jr., (BVⓉ) .... '52 '89 C&L.1048 B.S., J.D. 311 Chanticlair Drive

Gibbs, Benita Walker
(See Cary)

Godfrey, David R., (AV) .... '52 '78 C.576 B.A. L.896 J.D. 315 S. Salem St.
Higginbotham, Susan D. .... '59 '97 C.1090 B.A. L.1228 J.D. 405 Brierridge Dr.
Malone, G. Michael, (BV) .... '65 '90 C.228 B.A. L.1228 J.D. 1705 Bullfinch Ln.
McBlief, William, (BV) .... '50 '82 C&L.575 B.A., J.D. 1318 Park Summit Blvd.
McGrew, Gregory .... '63 '94 C.1060 B.S. L.464 J.D. 1412 Willow Leaf Way
Percival, Arlen R. .... '— '97 C.67 B.A. L.94 J.D. P.O. Box 1435

Richardson, Jonathan, The Law Office of
(See Cary)

Ruger, William G., (AVⓉ) '32 '61 C.354 B.A. L.188 J.D.
(adm. in NY; not adm. in NC) 1502 Pink Cherokee Court
Savage, Robert L., Jr., (AV) .... '30 '53 C&L.896 B.A., J.D. 315 S. Salem St., Suite 100
Shaffer, Leonard B. .... '39 '65 C.232 B.A. L.575 LL.B. 3532 Friendship Rd.
Stam, Paul, (AV) .... '50 '75 C.475 B.S. L.575 J.D. [Stam,F.&D.]

Stam, Fordham & Danchi, P.A., (AV)
(Successor to Holleman & Stam)
510 West Williams Street, P.O. Box 1600, 27502
Telephone: 919-362-8873 Fax: 919-387-1171
Email: paulstam@bellsouth.net URL: http://www.lawyers.com/sfdlaw
Carl P. Holleman (1921-1992); Paul Stam; Henry C. Fordham, Jr.; Theodore S. Danchi.
General Civil Practice in all State and Federal Courts. Corporation, Real Estate, Probate, Land Condemnation, Municipal Government, Personal Injury and Litigation. Workers Compensation.
See Professional Biographies, APEX, NORTH CAROLINA

Sudbury-Haydel, Leslie D. .... '66 '92 C.974 B.A. L.602 J.D. 1603 Patterson Grove Rd.

Toms, Frederic E., & Associates, PLLC
(See Cary)

ARCHDALE, 9,014, *Guilford & Randolph Cos.*

Haworth, William B., (AV) .... '35 '60 C.296 A.B. L.575 LL.B. 306 D Eden Terrace
Miller, Don G., (AV) '40 '64
C&L.575 A.B., LL.B. 11246 N. Main St., Ste. 310 Southern Center

ARDEN, —, *Buncombe Co.*

Kelley, Phillip G., (BV) .... '48 '74 C.835 B.S.W. L.838 J.D. 36 Old Shoals Rd.‡
Martin, Wyatt T. '46 '75 C&L.259 B.S., J.D.
(adm. in FL; not adm. in NC) 2 Oak Grove Rd.‡
Sigman, Lloyd M., (BV) .... '45 '75 C.855 B.S. L.477 J.D. 414 Long Shoals Rd.
Stewart, Robert P. .... '16 '40 C.228 A.B. L.477 J.D. 250 Rocky Mountain Way‡

ASHEBORO, * 21,672, *Randolph Co.*

Adams, J. Jane, (BV) .... '46 '76 C.296 B.A. L.616 J.D. 131 Lawyers Row
Alexander, J. Wilson, Jr., (AV) .... '50 '76 C.576 B.A. L.896 J.D. [Smith&A.]
Bell, Clark R., (AV) .... '58 '83 C.575 B.A. L.574 J.D. P.O. Box 4060
Bell and Browne, P.A., (BV) .... 151 North Fayetteville Street

Berman, Jeffrey S.
(Greensboro)

Bradley, Tanji L. .... '— '96 C.576 B.A. L.1228 J.D. P.O. Box 2024
Browne, Charles T., (BV) .... '46 '76 C.316 A.B. L.575 J.D. [Bell&B.]
Bunch, W. Edward .... '55 '80 C.575 B.A. L.896 J.D. [Bunch,R.&S.]

Bunch, Robins & Stubblefield, LLP, (BV)
117 Sunset Avenue, 27203-5607
Telephone: 336-629-2121 Fax: 336-626-5736
Email: asheborolawyers@triad.rr.com
Members of Firm: W. Edward Bunch; Thomas D. Robins; Julie H. Stubblefield.
Criminal and Traffic, Family Law, Real Estate, Personal Injury, Mediation, Workers Compensation, Social Security, Civil, Business, Bankruptcy, Wills and Estates.
Representative Clients: Duke Power Co.; First National Bank & Trust Co.; Triad Heating and Cooling, Inc.; Allen Precision Industries, Inc.; Laurven, Inc.; The Timken Co.; Kearns and McDowell Developers, LLC.
See Professional Biographies, ASHEBORO, NORTH CAROLINA

Burton, Ottway .... '18 '45 C&L.575 B.S., J.D. [O.Burton]
Burton, Ottway, P.A. .... 838 Westmont Drive

Chapman, Heidi G., P.L.L.C.
(See Chapel Hill)

Cox, Richard L., (BV) .... '54 '81 C.896 B.S. L.1228 J.D. [Gavin,C.P.&W.]

Dail & Linton
(See High Point)

Davis, Andrew W., Attorney at Law '74 '01 C.232 B.A. L.615 J.D.
200 Worth St., Ste. E

Deuterman Law Group, The, P.A.
(See Greensboro)

Dunn, Scott N., (BV) '60 '90 C.1236 B.A. L.362 J.D.
162 E. Ward Street, 27203-5517
Telephone: 336-629-1650 Fax: 336-629-0043
Email: sndunn@earthlink.net URL: http://www.scottdunnlaw.com
Family Law, Divorce, Child Custody and Support, Juvenile Law, Criminal Law, DWI, Traffic Violations, Social Security Disability.
See Professional Biographies, ASHEBORO, NORTH CAROLINA

Etheridge, Scott C. .... '68 '94 C.1083 Cr.Jus. L.1228 J.D. Dist. J.

Flowe, William H., Jr., Law Offices of
(See Liberty)

French, Jodi Michelle .... '75 '00 C.1228 B.S. L.575 J.D. Dist. Atty. Off.
Gavin, Lee W. .... '62 '89 C&L.896 B.A., J.D. Dist. Ct. J.
Gavin, W. Ed, (AV) .... '21 '48 C&L.896 B.S., LL.B. [Gavin,C.P.&W.] ‡

Gavin, Cox, Pugh and Wilhoit, L.L.P., (AV)
119 Worth Street, 27203
Telephone: 336-629-2600 Facsimile: 336-629-4734
W. Ed Gavin (Retired); Richard L. Cox; Alan V. Pugh; Robert E. Wilhoit.
General Civil and Criminal Practice, Federal and State Courts. Estate Planning, Personal Injury. Trials, Probate and Real Estate Law. State and Local Government Law, Appellate Practice, Traffic.
Representative Clients: American Television & Communications Corp. (Cablevision); Dan Thomas Pontiac Inc.; Hedgecock Home Builders, Inc.; J.J. Chretien Co. (Commercial Real Estate); M.C. Whitley Construction Co.; McMillion-Eubanks (Real Estate); Nationwide Mutual Insurance Co.; Pugh Oil Co.; Randolph Community College; Randolph County.
See Professional Biographies, ASHEBORO, NORTH CAROLINA

Goode, William S. .... '14 '40 C.886 B.S. L.692 LL.B. 514 Vision Dr.‡
Hammond, L. T., Sr., (AV) .... '10 '32 C&L.575 B.A., LL.B. 345 Lindley Avenue‡
Hayes, Shaun L. .... '78 '03 C.34 B.S. L.575 J.D. [Hayes]
Hayes Law Firm .... 138-A Scarboro St.
Heafner, William H., (BV) .... '47 '73 C.575 A.B. L.896 J.D. 127 Worth St.
Hole, Sonja M., (BV) .... '53 '86 C.296 B.A. L.574 J.D. Asst. Dist. Atty.
Ingram, John Randolph, Law Offices of '29 '54
C&L.575 B.S. in B.A., J.D. 618 Sunset Ave.
Ivey, William W., (BV) .... '40 '66 C&L.575 B.S., LL.B. 111 Worth St.
Little, Jeffrey L., (CV) .... '69 '99 C.577 B.A. L.574 .D. 170 Worth Street
Long, Vance Bradford .... '58 '83 C&L.1228 B.S., J.D. Dist. J.
Mason, Robert A., (AV) .... '52 '88 C.597 B.S. L.469 J.D. [MasonLaw]
MasonLaw, PLLC, (AV) .... 350 N. Cox Street, Suite 9
Mathers, William E., (BV) .... '52 '79 C.896 B.A. L.1228 J.D. 135 Worth St.
Megerian, Jonathan L., (AV) .... '53 '81 C.262 B.A. L.575 J.D. [Megerian&W.]

Megerian & Wells, (AV)
175 East Salisbury Street, 27203
Telephone: 336-625-1436 Fax: 336-625-0553
Email: mandwlaw@triad.rr.com
Members of Firm: Jonathan L. Megerian; Franklin E. Wells, Jr.
Civil and Criminal Trials in State and Federal Courts. Criminal Defense, Civil Litigation, Family Law.
Reference: Randolph Bank and Trust Co.
See Professional Biographies, ASHEBORO, NORTH CAROLINA

Miller, Michael C. '51 '78 C.575 B.A. L.896 J.D.
Pres. & CEO, First Nat'l Bk. & Tr. Co.
Morgan, Benjamin Cranford .... '73 '99 C.34 B.A. L.838 J.D. [Smith&A.]

Morgan, Herring, Morgan, Green, Rosenblutt & Gill, LLP
(See High Point)

Morris, Anthony Hal .... '71 '97 C.232 B.A. L.862 J.D. Asst. Dist. Atty.
Moser, D. Wescott, (AV) .... '24 '50 C&L.575 A.B., J.D. [Ⓐ Moser,S.&R.] ‡
Moser, Schmidly & Roose, (BV) .... 115 S. Fayetteville St.
Neely, William M. .... '49 '76 C.140 B.S. L.790 J.D. Chf. Dist. J.
Newman, Robert T., Sr., (BV) .... '40 '85 C.259 B.S. L.1228 J.D. 200 Worth St.
O'Briant, Lillian B. .... '39 '79 C.296 A.B. L.896 J.D. Dist. J.‡
Oldham, Pierre, (AV) .... '47 '71 C&L.575 B.A., J.D. 129 Lawrence Row
Pugh, Alan V., (AV) .... '52 '76 C&L.575 A.B., J.D. [Gavin,C.P.&W.]

Quinn Law Firm, The
(See Greensboro)

Redding, Scott J., (CV) .... '62 '96 C.198 A.B. L.575 J.D. 173 Scarboro St.
Robins, Thomas D. .... '56 '81 C.575 A.B. L.896 J.D. [Bunch,R.&S.]
Roose, Richard G., (BV) .... '47 '76 C.806 B.A. L.838 J.D. [Moser,S.&R.]

Schell Bray Aycock Abel & Livingston P.L.L.C.
(See Greensboro)

Schmidly, Stephen S., (P.A.), (BV) .... '49 '77 C.845 B.A. L.896 J.D. [Moser,S.&R.]
Smith, Archie L., Jr., (BV) .... '45 '69 C&L.896 B.A., J.D. [Smith&A.]
Smith & Alexander, L.L.P., (AV) .... 141 Worth St.

Stockdale, Matt A., PLLC, Law Office of
(See Greensboro)

Stubblefield, Julie H., (BV) .... '68 '93 C.1228 B.A. L.1345 J.D. [Bunch,R.&S.]
Sugg, Jeffrey C., (CV) .... '67 '98 C&L.575 B.S., J.D. 146 N. Church St.

Tuggle Duggins & Meschan, P.A.
(See Greensboro)

Vaughan, Donald R., and Associates
(See Greensboro)

Walker, Russell G., Jr. .... '43 '69 C&L.896 B.B.A., J.D. Supr. Ct. J.
Warburton, Raymond J., (BV) .... '60 '95 C.576 B.S. L.1338 J.D. Off. of Dist. Atty.
Wells, Franklin E., Jr., (BV) .... '60 '86 C&L.575 B.A., J.D. [Megerian&W.]
Whatley, L. McKay .... '55 '88 C.309 B.A. L.574 J.D. 19 South Fayetteville Street
White, Brenda B. .... '51 '91 C.999 B.S. L.575 J.D. Randolph Co. Div. of Social Serv.'s
Wilhoit, Robert E., (BV) .... '53 '81 C.896 B.A. L.1228 J.D. [Gavin,C.P.&W.]
Wilkins, Robert M. .... '56 '93 C.575 B.S. L.472 J.D. Commanding Officer
Williams, Robert Pate, (CV) .... '47 '73 C.316 A.B. L.575 J.D. 111-C Davis St.
Yates, H. Wade, (AV) .... '22 '43 L.896 LL.B. 179 Salisbury St. E.‡
Young, James W., (BV) .... '68 '94 C.928 B.A. L.30 J.D. 103 Worth St.

ASHEVILLE, * 68,889, *Buncombe Co.*

Abrams, Frank A., (AV Ⓣ) '59 '86 C&L.260 B.A., J.D.
(adm. in FL; not adm. in NC) 804 River Ridge Dr.
Aceto, Steven T., (BV) .... '56 '83 C.575 B.A. L.896 J.D. [S.T.Aceto]
Aceto, Steven T., P.A., (BV) .... 181 Charlotte St.
Adams, Joe G., Jr., (BV) .... '55 '86 C.48 B.A. L.896 J.D. [Adams]
Adams, Marla Tugwell, (AV) .... '54 '80 C.471 B.A. L.896 J.D. [VanWinkle,B.W.S.&D.]

Adams, Hendon, Carson, Crow & Saenger, P.A., (AV)
72 Patton Avenue, P.O. Box 2714, 28802
Telephone: 828-252-7381 Fax: 828-252-5018
URL: http://www.adamsfirm.com
Junius G. Adams, Jr. (1908-1991); George Ward Hendon; Philip G. Carson; Samuel J. Crow; George W. Saenger; Martin K. Reidinger; Gregory S. Hilderbran; E. Thomison Holman;—Susan Taylor Rash; Joy Gragg McIver; Daniel E. Hitchcock; Matthew S. Roberson.
General Civil Trial Practice in State and Federal Courts. Administrative, Corporation, Taxation, Business, Real Estate and Construction Law, Litigation, Wills, Probate, Trusts and Estates, Estate Planning, Contracts, Family Law, Divorce, Child Custody, Child Support.
Representative Clients: Asheville School, Inc.; Avondale Mills, Inc.; Belk Stores of Asheville, Inc.; General Electric Corp.; General Motors Corp.; Merrill, Lynch, Pierce, Fenner & Smith, Inc.; NCNB National Bank of North Carolina; Universal Underwriters Insurance Co.; Westinghouse Electric Corp.
Local Counsel for: Norfolk Southern Corp.
See Professional Biographies, ASHEVILLE, NORTH CAROLINA

Adams Law Firm, The, (BV) .... 81-B Central Ave.
Allen, C. Walter .... '27 '57 C&L.575 B.S., LL.B. Supr. Ct. J.‡
Allen, Robert E., Jr., (CV) .... '67 '95 C&L.383 B.A., J.D. 123 Biltmore Ave.
Anderson, Philip Scott, (BV) .... '69 '95 C.277 B.E.E. L.575 J.D. [Long,P.W.&J.]
Anderson, Scott M., (BV Ⓣ) '63 '89
C.575 B.A. L.790 J.D. [Grimes&T.] (ⓒGreenville, SC)

Anderson, William E., (AV) '43 '68 C.673 B.A. L.575 J.D. BB
17 North Market Street, Suite 201, 28801
Telephone: 828-252-3861 Fax: 828-251-5840
General Criminal Trial Practice in all Courts, Drug Crimes, DWI, Traffic Violations.
See Professional Biographies, ASHEVILLE, NORTH CAROLINA

Andres, Carol B., (CV) .... '40 '90 C.1206 B.S. L.574 J.D. 120 College St.
Arcuri, Patricia L., (BV) .... '50 '84 C.140 B.A. L.1292 J.D. [Ⓐ Cogburn,G.B.&R.]
Atherton, Andrew D. .... '73 '00 C.929 B.S. L.1161 J.D. 29 N. Market St.
Auman, William D., (BV) .... '61 '86 C.576 B.A. L.1345 J.D. Sr. Asst. Pub. Def.
Bailey, Derrick R., (BV) .... '57 '88 C.140 B.S. L.1345 J.D. [Northup&M.]
Baldwin, Garza, Jr. .... '21 '48 C.347 B.S. L.1119 J.D. 1745 Hendersonville Rd.‡
Baley, James M., III, (BV) .... '44 '68 C&L.575 B.S., J.D. [Baley&B.]
Baley, James M., Jr., (AV) .... '12 '33 C&L.575 A.B., LL.B. 5 Red Oak Rd.‡
Baley & Baley, P.A., (BV) .... 17 N. Market St., Ste. 201
Baliles, Janese McGiboney, (CV) '58 '82 C.925 B.S.B.A. L.575 J.D.
206 E. Chestnut St.
Ball, Ervin L., Jr., (AV) .... '45 '70 C&L.838 B.S., J.D. [Ball,B.&B.]

Ball, Barden & Bell, P.A., (AV)
18-20 North Spruce Street, 28801
Mailing Address: P.O. Box 7157, Asheville, NC 28802
Telephone: 828-252-0682 Fax: 828-252-6774
Email: BalBarBel@aol.com
Ervin L. Ball, Jr.; Stephen L. Barden, III (1945-2005); Thomas R. Bell, Jr.
Trials and Appeals in State and Federal Courts. Insurance Defense, Workers Compensation, Personal Injury, Commercial Law, Automobile Accidents, Wrongful Death.
Representative Clients: Bituminous Casualty Co.; The Concord Group Insurance Co.
See Professional Biographies, ASHEVILLE, NORTH CAROLINA

Bamberger, Elizabeth W., (BV) '72 '98
C.575 B.A. L.30 J.D. Staff Atty., Pisgah Legal Services, Inc.
Banzhoff, Andrew Brady, (CV) .... '72 '99 C.825 B.A. L.896 J.D. 22 South Pack Square
Barbour, Frederick S., (AV) .... '57 '84 C&L.575 B.A., J.D. [McGuire,W.&B.]
Barbour, Susan Strayhorn, (AV) .... '59 '84 C&L.575 B.A., J.D. [McGuire,W.&B.]
Barrett, James A., (BV) '56 '83
C.968 B.A. L.575 J.D. Exec. Dir., Pisgah Legal Services, Inc.
Barrett, Sandra J., Attorney at Law, (CV) .... '48 '83 C.48 B.A. L.259 J.D. 1 Tampa Ave.
Barrett, Sharon Tracey, (BV) .... '61 '86 C.93 B.A. L.276 J.D. [Patla,S.R.&M.]
Barton, Susan Chitwood .... '44 '81 C&L.347 A.B., J.D. [Ⓐ Ganly&R.]
Belcher Reynolds, Emily A. .... '78 '03 C&L.902 B.A., J.D. [Ⓐ VanWinkle,B.W.S.&D.]
Bell, Thomas R., Jr., (BV) .... '47 '72 C.797 A.B. L.575 J.D. [Ball,B.&B.]
Belser, David G., (AV) .... '50 '79 C.309 B.A. L.790 J.D. 17 North Market Street, Suite 1
Bennett, Gregory E., (CV) .... '57 '84 C&L.469 B.A., J.D. 501 College St.
Bennett, Harold K., (AV) .... '14 '36 C&L.575 A.B., LL.B. 47 Windsor Rd.‡
Bergoffen, Martin J. '62 '96 C.816 B.S. L.629 J.D.
(adm. in AZ; not adm. in NC) Southern Appalachian Biodiversity Proj.
Best, Peter Farquhard, (AV) .... '44 '69 C.797 B.A. L.575 J.D. [Best&B.P.]
Best, Scott Campbell, (BV) .... '71 '99 C.945 B.A. L.192 J.D. [Best&B.P.]

Best & Best PLLC, (AV)
138 Charlotte Street, Suite 200, 28801
Telephone: 828-255-7772 Fax: 828-255-9232
Email: info@bestpllc.com
Peter Farquhard Best; Scott Campbell Best; Jason M. Peltz.
Residential, Commercial and Investment Real Estate, Condominium Law, Creditor's Rights, Foreclosures, Estate Administration, Commercial Litigation, Tax Deferred Exchanges, Construction Law.
See Professional Biographies, ASHEVILLE, NORTH CAROLINA

Bidwell, Paul Louis, (AV) .... '58 '85 C&L.896 B.A., J.D. 29 N. Market St.
Biggers, William T., (AV) .... '46 '73 C.925 B.A. L.896 J.D. [Biggers&H.]

Biggers & Hunter, PLLC, (AV) BB
79 Woodfin Place, Suite 211, 28801
Telephone: 828-258-0576 Fax: 828-258-9857
URL: http://www.lawyers.com/biggers&hunter
William T. Biggers; John C. Hunter; Jeffrey K. Stahl.
Real Estate, Business Law, Wills and Probate, Trusts and Estates, Elder Law, Traffic Violations, Driving While Intoxicated (DWI), Personal Injury, Labor and Employment Law, Wage and Hour Law, Criminal Law, Environmental Law, Real Estate Closings, Real Estate Litigation, Foreclosures, Boundary Disputes, Title Examinations.
See Professional Biographies, ASHEVILLE, NORTH CAROLINA

Bissette, W. Louis, Jr., (BV) .... '43 '68 C.896 B.A. L.575 J.D. [McGuire,W.&B.]

Blanchard, Newman & Hayes
(See Hendersonville)

Bleynat, Edward L., Jr., (BV) .... '63 '89 C.160 B.S. L.575 J.D. [Ferikes&B.]
Boatwright, Robert Scott .... '66 '92 C.575 A.B. L.228 J.D. 24 Pheasant Dr.
Boone, Stephen T., (CV) .... '62 '92 C.34 B.S. L.1228 J.D. Asst. Dist. Atty.
Boyum, William, (BV) '59 '86
C&L.575 A.B., J.D. Asst. Dist. Atty., Spec. Asst. U.S. Atty.
Brazil, W. O., III, (BV) .... '64 '89 C.69 B.A. L.896 J.D. [Cogburn,G.B.&R.]
Brewer, Charles R., (BV) .... '48 '74 C&L.896 B.A., J.D. 530 Merrimon Avenue
Brison, Sarah Patterson .... '50 '83 C.577 B.A. L.1345 J.D. [Roberts&S.]
Broker, Leah M., (BV) .... '67 '92 C.436 B.A. L.575 J.D. [Broker&H.]
Broker & Hamrick, P.A., (BV) .... 56 College St., Ste. 201

Brondyke, Ronald Dale, (BV) .... '47 '73 C.625 B.A. L.575 J.D. [Long,P.W.&J.]
Brown, Bruce J., (CV) .... '27 '54 C.362 A.B. L.575 J.D. 70 Woodfin Pl.
Brown, Shirley Hastings .... '50 '79 C&L.575 B.A., J.D. Dist. J.
Bruce, Gary T. '73 '00 C.628 B.A. L.902 J.D.
Staff Atty., Mission - St. Joseph's Health Sys., Inc.
Brunner, Major O. '28 '56 C.900 A.B. L.862 LL.B.
(adm. in OK; not adm. in NC) 67 Forest Rd.‡
Buchanan, Victor W., (BV) .... '42 '68 C&L.575 B.A., J.D. [Patla,S.R.&M.]
Bull, Adam William, (BV) .... '67 '92 C.576 B.A. L.575 J.D. [Firm of A.W.Bull]
Bull, Adam W., The Law Firm of, (BV) .... 64 Broadway, Ste. 100
Burner, Faye A., (BV) .... '55 '80 C.917 A.B. L.260 J.D. Off. of Pub. Def.

Byers, Martelle & Williams, P.L.L.C.
(See Rutherfordton, North Carolina)

Byrd, Jones Pharr, (AV) .... '46 '71 C&L.896 B.A., J.D. [VanWinkle,B.W.S.&D.]
Cady, Michele M. .... '71 '94 L.575 J.D. [Worley&C.]
Cagle, William B., (BV) .... '37 '63 C.575 B.S. L.910 J.D. [Shuford,C.&M.]
Campbell, Christopher Z., (CV) .... '69 '96 C&L.575 B.A., J.D. [Roberts&S.]
Carson, Philip G., (AV) .... '38 '67 C&L.575 A.B., J.D. [Adams,H.C.C.&S.]
Carter, David M., (AV) .... '46 '73 C.929 B.S. L.273 J.D. [Carter S.&M.] (See Pat. Sect.)
Carter, Scott, (BV) .... '49 '74 C.198 B.A. L.575 J.D. 181 Charlotte St.

Carter Schnedler & Monteith, P.A., (AV)
56 Central Avenue, Suite 101, P.O. Box 2985, 28802
Telephone: 828-252-6225 FAX: 828-252-6316
Email: mail@ashevillepatent.com URL: http://www.ashevillepatent.com
David M. Carter; Steven C. Schnedler; J. Derel Monteith, Jr.
Patents, Trademarks, Copyrights.
See Professional Biographies, ASHEVILLE, NORTH CAROLINA

Cartner, David W., (BV) .... '52 '81 C.575 B.S. L.796 J.D. 29 N. Market St.
Cash, Gary S. .... '49 '76 C.198 A.B. L.575 J.D. Dist. J.
Casterline, Michael E., (CV) .... '61 '91 C.475 B.A. L.838 J.D. [M.E.Casterline]
Casterline, Michael E., P.A., (CV) .... 68 North Market Street
Chidnese, Patrick N. '40 '68 C&L.472 B.A., J.D.
(adm. in FL; not adm. in NC) P.O. Box 18419‡
Childress, Vincent D., Jr., (BV) .... '56 '83 C&L.575 B.A., J.D. [Roberts&S.]
Chitwood-Barton, Susan .... '44 '81 C&L.347 A.B., J.D. 61 N. Market
Christy, Robert H., Jr. .... '54 '81 C.34 B.A. L.574 J.D. Law Clk., Supm. Ct.
Ciochina, Michael E., (CV) .... '62 '92 C.347 B.A. L.362 J.D. 120 College Street
Clarke, William, (BV) .... '56 '82 C.674 A.B. L.575 J.D. [Roberts&S.]
Claxton, Douglas A., (BV) .... '69 '95 C.575 B.A. L.1228 J.D. [Claxton]

Claxton Law Firm, P.A., (BV)
22 South Pack Square, Suite 1200, 28801
Telephone: 828-253-8818 Fax: 828-253-8812 URL: http://www.claxtonlawfirm.com
Email: doug@claxtonlawfirm.com URL: http://www.lawyers.com/claxtonlawfirm
Douglas A. Claxton.
Real Estate, Wills, Trusts, Estates, Business.
See Professional Biographies, ASHEVILLE, NORTH CAROLINA

Clerici, Guy F. .... '59 '84 C.577 B.S. L.607 J.D. [VanWinkle,B.W.S.&D.] ‡
Cloninger, John C., (AV) .... '56 '81 C.1128 B.A. L.575 J.D. [Cloninger,L.H.&S.]
Cloninger, M. Charles, (BV) .... '55 '82 C&L.575 B.A., J.D. [McGuire,W.&B.]
Cloninger, Lindsay, Hensley & Searson, P.L.L.C., (AV) .... 366 Merrimon Avenue
Clontz, Stanford K., (BV) .... '50 '80 C.925 B.A. L.838 J.D. [S.K.Clontz]
Clontz, Stanford K., P.A., (BV) .... One Oak Plaza, Suite 306
Cogburn, Julia C. .... '55 '83 C.228 A.B. L.575 J.D. City Planning Dir.
Cogburn, Max O., Jr., (AV) .... '51 '76 C.575 A.B. L.192 J.D. [Cogburn,G.B.&R.]
Cogburn, Steven Douglas, (AV) .... '56 '82 C&L.575 A.B., J.D. [Cogburn,G.B.&R.]

Cogburn, Goosmann, Brazil & Rose, P.A., (AV)
77 Central Avenue, Suite H, 28801
Mailing Address: P.O. Box 7436, Asheville, NC 28802
Telephone: 828-258-0150 Fax: 828-258-1305
Email: info@cgbrlawfirm.com URL: http://www.cgbrlawfirm.com
Max O. Cogburn, Sr. (1927-2003); Steven Douglas Cogburn; George F. Goosmann, Jr.; W. O. Brazil, III; John R. Rose (Board Certified Specialist in Real Property Law - Residential Transactions, North Carolina State Board of Legal Specialization); Max O. Cogburn, Jr.;—William Kennon Reed; Phillip C. Price; Patricia L. Arcuri; Frank J. Contrivo, Jr.
General Civil Practice before all Courts. Business Torts, Commercial Litigation, Commercial Torts, Commercial Real Estate, Real Estate Acquisition, Contract Litigation, Corporate Litigation, Criminal Law, Drug Crimes, Civil Litigation, Insurance Law, Insurance Defense, Torts, Real Estate, Construction, Eminent Domain, Zoning and Land Use.
See Professional Biographies, ASHEVILLE, NORTH CAROLINA

Collins, Gale Forman .... '53 '89 C.454 B.A. L.1206 J.D. 330 Vanderbilt Rd.
Connolly, Joseph A., (BV) .... '48 '73 C.34 B.S. L.575 J.D. [Westall,G.C.&D.]
Conroy, David J. .... '18 '47 C&L.309 B.S., LL.B. 36 Sunset Summit‡

Constangy, Brooks & Smith, LLC, (AV)
80 Peachtree Road, Suite 208, 28803 ⊙
Telephone: 828-277-5137 Fax: 828-277-5138
URL: http://www.constangy.com
Member: Jonathan W. Yarbrough.
Labor Relations, Employment Litigation, Employee Benefits Law, Wage and Hour, OSHA Law, Business Immigration, Affirmative Action.
Atlanta, Georgia Office: 230 Peachtree Street, N.W., Suite 2400. Telephone: 404-525-8622. Fax: 404-525-6955.
Austin, Texas Office: 111 Congress Avenue, Fourth Floor. Telephone: 512-391-4989. Fax: 512-391-6821.
Birmingham, Alabama Office: 1901 Sixth Avenue North, Suite 1410. Telephone: 205-252-9321. Fax: 205-323-7674.
Columbia, South Carolina Office: 1301 Gervais Street, Suite 810. Telephone: 803-256-3200. Fax: 803-256-6277.
Fairfax, Virginia Office: 4100 Monument Corner Drive, Suite 520. Telephone: 571-522-6100. Fax: 571-522-6101.
Jacksonville, Florida Office: 200 West Forsyth Street, Suite 1610. Telephone: 904-356-8900. Fax: 904-356-8200.
Kansas City, Missouri Office: 2600 Grand Avenue, Suite 300. Telephone: 816-472-6400. Fax: 816-472-6401.
Macon, Georgia Office: 577 Mulberry Street, Suite 710. Telephone: 478-750-8600. Fax: 478-750-8686.
Nashville, Tennessee Office: Vanderbilt Plaza, Suite 925, 2100 West End Avenue. Telephone: 615-320-5200. Fax: 615-321-5891.
San Antonio, Texas Office: The Forum, 8000 IH 10 West, Suite 600. Telephone: 210-525-7977. Fax: 210-525-7978.
Tampa, Florida Office: 100 North Tampa Street, Suite 3350. Telephone: 813-223-7166. Fax: 813-223-2515.
Winston-Salem, North Carolina Office: 100 North Cherry Street, Suite 300. Telephone: 336-721-1001. Charlotte: 704-344-1040.
See Professional Biographies, ASHEVILLE, NORTH CAROLINA

Contrivo, Frank J., Jr. .... '76 '02 C.48 B.A. L.575 J.D. [Cogburn,G.B.&R.]
Cooke, Cynthia L., (BV) .... '68 '94 C.340 B.A. L.575 J.D. 75 Church St.
Coward, Carolyn Lloyd .... '52 '99 C.838 B.S. L.575 J.D. [VanWinkle,B.W.S.&D.]
Cox, D. Lynn .... '56 '81 C.10 B.A. L.192 J.D. 34 Wall Street, Suite 706
Coxe, Wm. F. P., Jr., (BV) .... '27 '52 C&L.575 A.B., LL.B. 517 Flat Iron Bldg.
Coxie, Anthony Alan .... '65 '00 C.999 B.S. L.896 J.D. [A.A.Coxie]

Coxie, Anthony Alan, PA Attorney at Law
Bank of Asheville Building, Suite 203-B, 79 Woodfin Place, 28801
Mailing Address: P.O. Box 1262, Asheville, NC 28802
Telephone: 828-252-8808 Fax: 828-252-8188
Email: acoxie@bellsouth.net URL: http://www.lawyers.com/coxielaw
Anthony Alan Coxie.
Workers Compensation, Employment Law, Wrongful Termination, Personal Injury, Automobile Accidents, Wrongful Death, Slip and Fall, Civil Litigation, General Practice, Health Law, White Collar Crime, Criminal Law, Traffic Violations, DWI, Juvenile Law, Parole and Probation, Administrative Law, Insurance.
See Professional Biographies, ASHEVILLE, NORTH CAROLINA

Craig, Bernard D., (AVⓉ) '39 '64 C.602 B.B.A. L.276 J.D.
(adm. in MO; not adm. in NC) [Craig&Assoc.]
Craig, Christopher M. .... '70 '01 C.296 B.A. L.574 J.D. [Craig&Assoc.]
Craig Associates, PC .... 20 Battery Park Avenue
Crow, Samuel J., (AV) .... '37 '62 C.1365 A.B. L.896 LL.B. [Adams,H.C.C.&S.]
Curriden, Dale A. .... '69 '97 C.101 B.A. L.575 J.D. [VanWinkle,B.W.S.&D.]
Currie, Walter L., (AV) .... '40 '68 C.228 B.A. L.575 J.D. [Roberts&S.]

Curry, John S., Law Offices of '43 '70 C.198 B.A. L.575 J.D.
Suite 515 BB&T Building, One West Pack Square, 28802
Mailing Address: P.O. Box 2091, Asheville, NC 28802
Telephone: 828-255-8195 Cell: 828-215-4512 Fax: 828-255-8195
Email: jscattorney@bellsouth.net
Environment Law.
See Professional Biographies, ASHEVILLE, NORTH CAROLINA

Daniels, Richard S., (AV) .... '52 '79 C&L.575 B.A., J.D. [Patla,S.R.&M.]
Daniels, Walter E., III .... '72 '00 C&L.16 B.A., J.D. [Daniels]
Daniels Law Firm .... 191 Merriman Ave.
Davis, Barbara Ann .... '52 '77 C&L.260 B.A., J.D. 14 Clayton St.
Davis, David K., (BV) .... '63 '88 C.575 B.A. L.1228 J.D. Staff Atty., U.S. Dist. Ct.
Davis, Roy W., Jr., (AV) .... '30 '55 C.198 B.S. L.575 J.D. [VanWinkle,B.W.S.&D.]
Davis, Sara H., (AV) .... '47 '80 C.48 B.A. L.575 J.D. [Westall,G.C.&D.]
Dembo, Barry S. '47 '75 C.30 B.A. L.945 J.D.
(adm. in NY; not adm. in NC) F.B.I.
Deutsch, Robert J., (BV) .... '47 '73 C.477 B.A. L.309 J.D. [R.J.Deutsch]

Deutsch, Robert J., P.A., (BV)
75 North Market Street, 28801
Telephone: 828-251-0600 Fax: 828-251-5508
Email: deutsch@charter.net URL: http://www.bobdeutschlaw.com
Robert J. Deutsch (Member of Powell & Deutsch).
General Civil Trial Practice, Wills and Probate, Business, Family Law, Equitable Distribution, Real Estate, Corporate Law, Zoning, Personal Injury, Products Liability, Wrongful Death, Computer Law.
Approved Attorneys for: Lawyers Title Insurance Corp.; Chicago Title Insurance Corp.
References: First Federal Savings & Loan Assn.; First Commercial Bank.
See Professional Biographies, ASHEVILLE, NORTH CAROLINA

Devereux, Sean Patrick, (AV) '47 '77
C.228 B.A. L.575 J.D. 22 South Pack Square, Suite 1100
DeYoe, John M., (AVⓉ) '13 '40 C.674 A.B. L.976 J.D.
(adm. in NJ; not adm. in NC) 357 Rose Hill Rd.‡
Diefenbach, Tracy Kreider ...... '68 '96 C.645 B.A. L.245 J.D. [VanWinkle,B.W.S.&D.]
Dillard, John R., (BV) '55 '80
C.925 B.S.B.A. L.192 J.D. Pres. &Gen. Coun., Stewart Title of N.C.
Dodd, Gary A., (BV) .... '38 '72 C.968 B.A. L.838 J.D. 530 Merrimon Ave.
Dorsey, Angeleigh E. .... '— '93 C&L.1119 B.A., J.D. Legal Aid of NC
Dotson-Smith, Susan M., (BV) .... '66 '91 C.228 A.B. L.896 J.D. P.O. Box 2866‡
Douglas, Donna .... '56 '84 C.471 B.S. L.574 J.D. [Patla,S.R.&M.]
Dray, Andrea F., (CV) .... '58 '94 C.823 B.A. L.1029 J.D. [R.E.Riddle]
Drye, Michael W., (BV) .... '51 '76 C.1128 B.A. L.896 J.D. [M.W.Drye]

Drye, Michael W., P.C., (BV)
12 1/2 Wall Street, Suite C, 28801
Telephone: 828-258-1384 Fax: 828-258-1871
Email: michaelwdrye@aol.com URL: http://www.michaeldryelawfirm.com
Michael W. Drye.
Family Law, Children, Divorce.
See Professional Biographies, ASHEVILLE, NORTH CAROLINA

DuMont, Harry .... '14 '41 C.293 B.A. L.597 J.D. 606 Northwestern Plaza
Dungan, Robert E., (BV) .... '46 '82 C.576 B.S. L.280 J.D. [Dungan&Assoc.]
Dungan & Associates PA, (BV) .... 1 Rankin Ave., 3rd Fl.
Eaton, Marie L. '— '79 C.420 B.A. L.425 J.D.
(adm. in LA; not adm. in NC) 16 Reynolds Pl.‡
Edwards, Richard Lee .... '56 '81 C.228 A.B. L.188 J.D. U.S. Atty.'s Off.

Ehrmann, Jacob C. '73 '00 C&L.575 B.A., J.D.
68 North Market Street, 28801
Mailing Address: 825-C Merriman Avenue, Suite 362, Asheville, NC 28804
Telephone: 828-582-2768 Fax: 828-255-8693
Email: jacobehrmann@earthlink.net URL: http://www.jacobehrmann.com
Domestic Violence, Family Law, Divorce, Child Custody, Child Support, Entertainment Law, Copyrights, Contracts.
See Professional Biographies, ASHEVILLE, NORTH CAROLINA

Elkins & Elkins
(See Hendersonville)

Eller, Cynthia W., (BV) .... '51 '83 C.576 B.A. L.575 J.D. [VanWinkle,B.W.S.&D.]
Ellison, Eugene W., Law Office of, (BV) '56 '84
C.892 B.A. L.574 J.D. 185 Biltmore Ave.
Elmore, Bruce A., (AV) .... '20 '47 C&L.575 A.B., J.D. [Elmore]
Elmore, Bruce A., Jr., (AV) .... '52 '76 C&L.575 B.A., J.D. [Elmore]

Elmore Law Firm, The, P.A., (AV)
53 North Market Street, 28801
Telephone: 828-253-1492 Fax: 828-253-9648 URL: http://www.theelmorelawfirm.com
Email: info@theelmorelawfirm.com URL: http://www.theelmorelawoffice.com
Bruce A. Elmore; Bruce A. Elmore, Jr.
Catastrophic Injury, Medical Malpractice, Toxic Torts, Pharmaceutical Litigation, Personal Injury, Wrongful Death, Automobile Accidents, Sexual Abuse, Slip and Fall, Construction Accidents, Aviation, Airplane Crashes, Nursing Home Negligence, Products Liability, Birth Trauma, Spinal Injury, Brain Injury, Workers Compensation, Federal Criminal Law and State Criminal Law, Driving While Intoxicated, Drug Crimes, Parole and Probation, Traffic Violations, White Collar Crime, Murder, Social Security Disability.
See Professional Biographies, ASHEVILLE, NORTH CAROLINA

English, David L. .... '67 '98 C.160 B.S. L.192 J.D. [Roberts&S.]
Erickson, Paul L., (BV) '55 '83 C&L.838 B.S., J.D.
1998 Hendersonville Road Building 1, Suite 3
Erwin, James P., Jr., (AV) .... '37 '63 C&L.575 A.B., LL.B. 10 Stonebridge Drive‡

Eubank, Carol, (BV) .... '49 '75 C&L.383 B.A., J.D. [Patla,S.R.&M.]
Euler, Mary E., (BV) .... '67 '94 C.16 B.A. L.902 J.D. [A McGuire,W.&B.]
Evans, Susan L. .... '— '00 C.680 B.A. L.1228 J.D. [A Ferikes&B.]
Fairbairn, Holly J. '67 '97 C.296 B.A. L.574 J.D.
Staff Atty., Pisgah Legal Services, Inc.
Ferguson, David L., (CV) '57 '82
C.260 B.A. L.469 J.D. Sr. V.P., Rankin Pa Herson Oil Co., Inc.
Ferikes, Joseph A., (BV) .... '49 '74 C.576 B.A. L.16 J.D. [Ferikes&B.]

Ferikes & Bleynat, PLLC, (BV)
21 Broad Street, 28801
Telephone: 828-251-1588 Telecopier: 828-251-2214
URL: http://www.lawyers.com/ferikes&bleynat
Joseph A. Ferikes; Edward L. Bleynat, Jr.;—Susan L. Evans.
Business Litigation, Business Torts, Construction Litigation, Appellate Practice, Property Law and Litigation; Personal Injury and Medical Malpractice, Automobile Accidents, Wrongful Death, Brain Injury, Torts, Commercial Liability, Commercial Real Estate Litigation, Construction Defects and Liens, Contract Litigation, Corporate Litigation, Workers Compensation.
See Professional Biographies, ASHEVILLE, NORTH CAROLINA

Fetterman, Adam C. .... '70 '98 [A Strauss&Assoc.]
Finkelstein, Johanna, (CV) .... '62 '94 C.94 B.A. L.574 J.D. 62 Clayton St.
Fisher, William Perry, II, (AV) '61 '87 C.575 B.A. L.896 J.D.
[VanWinkle,B.W.S.&D.]
Fleming, John N., (BV) .... '62 '87 C.659 B.S. L.880 J.D. [McGuire,W.&B.]
Flynn, Michael L., (BV) .... '64 '90 C.880 B.A. L.228 J.D. 265 Charlotte St., Apt. 36
Freeman, Robert A., III, (AV) .... '40 '69 C&L.896 B.A., J.D. [Patla,S.R.&M.]
Friedman, Jessica E. .... '75 '01 C&L.575 B.A., J.D. [A Adams]
Friedman, Kerry A., (AV) .... '54 '80 C&L.575 B.A., J.D. [Patla,S.R.&M.]
Friesen, Ingrid K., (BV) .... '53 '82 C.011 B.A. L.161 J.D. 77 Church Street
Frue, John Calhoun .... '60 '86 C.575 A.B. L.469 J.D. [Frue,P.]
Frue, Michael Calhoun, (BV) .... '61 '88 C.575 A.B. L.1228 J.D. 3 Woodcrest Pl.
Frue, William C., Jr., (AV) .... '34 '60 C.902 A.B. L.575 LL.B. [Frue,P.]

Frue Law Firm, The, PLLC, (AV) BB
16 Church Street, P.O. Box 7627, 28802-7627
Telephone: 828-258-0570 Fax: 828-258-0591
Email: law@frue.net
Members of Firm: William C. Frue, Jr.; John Calhoun Frue.
General Civil Practice, Real Estate, Probate, Corporate Law, Business Law.
Reference: Asheville Savings Bank.
See Professional Biographies, ASHEVILLE, NORTH CAROLINA

Ganly, David M. .... '37 '80 C.976 B.A. L.574 J.D. [Ganly&R.] ‡
Ganly & Ramer, (AV) .... 61 N. Market St.

Gantt, David, Law Office, (BV) '56 '81 C.575 B.A. L.1228 J.D.
82 Church Street, 28801
Telephone: 828-252-2852 Toll Free: 1-800-273-4002 Fax: 828-254-4539
Email: lawyer@davidgantt.com URL: http://www.davidgantt.com
Insurance Claims, Personal Injury, Automobile, Social Security Claims, Workers' Compensation.
A List of Representative Clients will be furnished upon request.
See Professional Biographies, ASHEVILLE, NORTH CAROLINA

Gerber, Ronette Alesia .... '67 '98 C.1317 B.A. L.575 J.D. Appalachian Legal Servs.
Going, Michael P., (AV Ⓣ) '61 '87 C.893 B.A. L.896 J.D.
(adm. in PA; not adm. in NC)
V.P. & Gen. Coun., Volvo Construction Equipment N. Amer., Inc.
Goins, Carol L., (CV) .... '— '89 C&L.574 B.A., J.D. [A Gudger&G.]
Goldstein, Steven I., (AV) .... '43 '67 C&L.575 A.B., J.D. [Patla,S.R.&M.]
Goosmann, George F., Jr., (BV) '62 '88 C.575 B.S.B.A. L.472 J.D.
[Cogburn,G.B.&R.]
Grabenstein, Stephen J., (BV) .... '57 '82 C&L.838 B.A., J.D. [VanWinkle,B.W.S.&D.]
Grady, Cynthia S. .... '49 '87 C.608 B.A. L.326 J.D. [Roberts&S.]
Grant, Jacqueline D., (BV) .... '70 '95 C.925 B.S. L.575 J.D. [Roberts&S.]
Gray, David G., (AV) .... '46 '72 C&L.575 B.A., J.D. [Westall,G.C.&D.]
Gregory, Lyman J. .... '67 '98 C.925 B.A. L.575 J.D. [Marshall&R.]
Grella, Thomas C., (BV) .... '60 '85 C.1369 B.B.A. L.896 J.D. [McGuire,W.&B.]
Grimes, S. Janson, (BV) .... '46 '72 C&L.575 B.A., J.D. [Grimes&T.] ⊙

Grimes & Teich, (BV)
535 College Street, P.O. Box 7074, 28801-2412 ⊙
Telephone: 800-533-6845; 828-251-0800 Fax: 828-252-4678 URL: http://www.grimesandteich.com
Email: teich@grimesandteich.com URL: http://www.lawyers.com/grimesandteich
S. Janson Grimes; Henry E. Teich (Board Certified Specialist in Workers Compensation, North Carolina State Board of Legal Specialization); Ruth C. Smith; Scott M. Anderson; Thomas W. Henson, Jr.; Sarah Lockett.
Personal Injury, Automobile Accidents, Trucking Accidents, Motorcycle Accidents, Boating Accidents, Brain and Head Injuries, Dog Bites, Products Liability, Catastrophic Injury, Pedestrian Injuries, Slip and Fall Injuries, Workers Compensation, Social Security Law, Social Security Disability, Medical Malpractice, Nursing Home Negligence, Nursing Home Abuse, Wrongful Death, Fire Injuries.
Waynesville Office: 385 N. Haywood Street, 28786. Telephone: 828-452-7888.
Rutherfordton Office: 365 Charlotte Road, 28139. Telephone: 828-286-1033.
Greenville, South Carolina Office: 111 East North Street, 29601. Telephone: 800-533-6845.
See Professional Biographies, ASHEVILLE, NORTH CAROLINA

Gudger, Lamar, (AV) .... '19 '42 C&L.575 A.B., LL.B. [Gudger&G.] (⊙Hendersonville)
Gudger, Sally Tickle, (CV) .... '58 '85 C&L.896 B.A., J.D. 1 Oak Plaza, Suite 306
Gudger, Vonno Lamar, III, (BV) .... '55 '85 C.575 B.A. L.1228 J.D. [Gudger&G.]
Gudger & Gudger, (AV) .... One Oak Plaza, Suite 306
Gum, Howard L., (AV) .... '51 '76 C.98 B.A. L.339 J.D. [Gum,H.&M.]

Gum, Hillier & McCroskey, P.A., (AV) BB
47 N. Market Street, P.O. Box 3235, 28802
Telephone: 828-258-3368 Fax: 828-252-6721
Email: info@gumandhillier.com URL: http://www.gumandhillier.com
Howard L. Gum (Board Certified Specialist in Family Law, North Carolina State Board of Legal Specialization); David R. Hillier (Board Certified Specialist in Bankruptcy Law); Patrick S. McCroskey (Board Certified Specialist in Family Law, North Carolina State Board of Legal Specialization).
Family Law, Bankruptcy, Real Estate, Wills and Corporate Law.
Representative Client: Shoney's Restaurants.
References: Asheville Savings Bank; Wachovia Bank and Trust Co.
See Professional Biographies, ASHEVILLE, NORTH CAROLINA

Habel, Robert W. '32 '58 C&L.208 B.S., LL.B.
(adm. in CO; not adm. in NC; Pat.) 102 Big Spring Dr.‡
Hall, Frank W. .... '31 '56 C&L.575 B.A., LL.B. 233 S. Liberty St.
Hamilton, Jackson D., (BV) .... '49 '74 C.165 B.A. L.659 J.D. [Roberts&S.]
Hamrick, Anna R., (BV) .... '68 '94 C.575 B.A. L.273 J.D. [Broker&H.]
Hamrick, W. Samuel, Jr. .... '56 '88 C.1128 B.A. L.1228 J.D. Law Clk., U.S. Dist. Ct.
Harbin, Cynthia C. '65 '91 C.758 B.A. L.575 J.D.
Assoc. Coun. Eastern Band, Cherokee Indians
Harris, Larry C., Jr., (BV) .... '53 '83 C.575 B.A. L.1228 J.D. [VanWinkle,B.W.S.&D.]
Hartley, Larry S. .... '60 '96 C.502 B.S. L.260 J.D. [A Strauss&Assoc.]
Harvey, Patricia W., (BV) .... '62 '91 C.575 B.A. L.208 J.D. 46 Orchard St., Ste. C
Hasty, Rodney G., (BV) .... '69 '95 C.576 B.A. L.896 J.D. Off. of Dist. Atty.
Hay, Edward C., Jr., (BV) .... '49 '74 C.198 B.A. L.280 J.D. [Pitts,H.&H.]

Hedrick Eatman Gardner & Kincheloe, L.L.P.
(See Charlotte)

Hendon, George Ward, (AV) .... '41 '67 C.838 B.S. L.575 J.D. [Adams,H.C.C.&S.]
Hensley, John C., Jr., (BV) .... '64 '89 C.1129 B.A. L.575 J.D. [Cloninger,L.H.&S.]
Henson, Thomas W., Jr., (BV) '65 '89
C&L.575 B.S.B.A., J.D. [Grimes&T.] (⊙Raleigh, Rocky Mount)
Hilderbran, Gregory S., (AV) .... '63 '89 C.575 B.S. L.280 J.D. [Adams,H.C.C.&S.]
Hill, G. Edison, (BV) .... '25 '52 C.232 L.692 29 N. Market St.
Hill, Tammera S. .... '71 '96 C&L.575 B.A., B.A. Atty. Gen.
Hiller, Aleece M., Law Office of .... '63 '92 C.347 B.A. L.836 J.D. P.O. Box 231
Hillier, David R., (BV) .... '48 '74 C.797 B.A. L.228 J.D. [Gum,H.&M.]
Himelein, Levant M., Jr., (BV Ⓣ) '23 '48 C.645 L.107 LL.B.
(adm. in NY; not adm. in NC) 1617 Hendersonvile Rd., Apt. 1318
Hitchcock, Daniel E. .... '66 '93 C.207 B.A. L.1051 J.D. [A Adams,H.C.C.&S.]
Holman, E. Thomison, (BV) .... '66 '92 C.575 B.S. L.192 J.D. [Adams,H.C.C.&S.]
Horton & Horton, P.A., (BV) .... 1407 BB&T Bldg.
Howell, Dennis L. .... '51 '76 C.925 B.S. L.575 J.D. U.S. Mag.
Hufstader, John R. .... '41 '67 C&L.575 B.A., J.D. Off. of Pub. Def.
Hugenschmidt, James J., (BV) .... '44 '73 C&L.575 A.B., J.D. [Pitts,H.&H.]
Hunt, Kenneth R. .... '73 '99 C.890 B.A. L.896 J.D. [A Roberts&S.]
Hunt, Ronald F. .... '43 '68 C&L.575 A.B., J.D. 15 Cedar Hill Dr.‡
Hunter, John C., (AV) .... '59 '85 C&L.896 B.A., J.D. [Biggers&H.]
Hutchins, Gregory D., (BV) .... '62 '87 C.896 B.S. L.1228 J.D. [Roberts&S.]
Hyde, Herbert L., (AV) .... '25 '54 C.925 A.B. L.569 J.D. [H.L.Hyde]
Hyde, Herbert L., P.A., (AV) .... 29 N. Market
Hyldburg, Carl A. .... '23 '48 C.550 A.B. L.228 J.D. 29 N. Market St., Suite 410
Hyler, George B., Jr., (BV) .... '48 '73 C.576 B.A. L.896 J.D. [Hyler&L.]
Hyler & Lopez, P.A., (BV) .... 38 Orange St.
Ikbal, Farruk, Law Office of .... '54 '98 C.1080 B.S.Ph. L.734 J.D. 1 Oak Plz., Ste. 306
Iovacchini, Eric V. '47 '73 C.282 B.A. L.546 J.D.
(adm. in NE; not adm. in NC) Vice Chanc. for Student Affs., Univ. of N.C. at Asheville
Jackson, Cecil C., Jr. .... '34 '60 C&L.896 B.A., J.D. 17 Arlington St.
Jackson, Steven Andrew, (BV) '56 '81 C.1365 B.A. L.990 J.D.
79 Woodfin Pl., Ste. 303
Jacobs, Robin L. .... '69 '95 C.896 B.A. L.990 J.D. Staff Atty., Pisgah Legal Services, Inc.
Johnson, Cecilia, (CV) .... '67 '92 C&L.280 B.A., J.D. 127 W. Chestnut St.
Johnson, William James .... '73 '00 C.968 B.A. L.790 J.D. [A VanWinkle,B.W.S.&D.]
Johnston, John D., Jr. '32 '56 C&L.228 A.B., LL.B.
Prof. of Law, Emeritus, New York University‡
Jones, Stephen H., Jr. '46 '71 C.269 B.A. L.790 J.D.
Sr. V.P., The Title Company of North Carolina, Inc.
Jones, W. Scott, (BV) .... '65 '91 C.575 A.B. L.893 J.D. [Long,P.W.&J.]
Joyner, John C., Jr. .... '33 '59 C&L.896 B.S., LL.B. 100 Sheridan Rd.‡
Justus, Craig D., (BV) .... '65 '91 C&L.575 B.A., J.D. [VanWinkle,B.W.S.&D.]
Karriker, Robert G., (BV) .... '51 '84 C.404 B.A. L.192 J.D. 31 College Pl., Ste. D307
Kelly, E. Glenn, (AV) .... '38 '63 C&L.575 A.B., LL.B. [Kelly&R.]

Kelly & Rowe, P.A., (AV)
50 Merrimon Avenue, 28801
Mailing Address: P.O. Box 2865, Asheville, NC 28802
Telephone: 828-251-9310 FAX: 828-251-9320
Email: kelly_rowe@bellsouth.net URL: http://www.kellyrowelaw.com
E. Glenn Kelly; James Gary Rowe.
Asset Protection, Arbitration and Mediation, Automobile Accidents, Banking and Financial Law, Building and Construction Law, Civil Practice in all Federal and State Courts, Commercial Litigation, Condemnation, Contract, Corporate Law, Equitable Distribution, Divorce, Employment, Estate Planning and Administration, Insurance Law, Personal Injury, Products Liability, Medical Malpractice, Negligence, Real Estate Litigation, Eminent Domain, Wrongful Death.
See Professional Biographies, ASHEVILLE, NORTH CAROLINA

Kelso, John G., (BV) .... '70 '96 C.198 B.A. L.575 J.D. [VanWinkle,B.W.S.&D.]
Kempson, Barry B., (AV) .... '43 '69 C.259 B.A. L.260 J.D. [VanWinkle,B.W.S.&D.]
Kepple, Julie Matthiessen .... '— '99 C.838 B.A. L.1015 J.D. Asst. Dist. Atty.
Kimel, Larry S., (BV) .... '47 '72 C&L.280 A.B.J., J.D. 14 Clayton Street
King, Sandra M., (AV) .... '43 '69 C&L.575 B.A., J.D. [Russell&K.]
Knight, Joseph Carroll '58 '00
C.1129 B.A. L.574 J.D. Staff Atty., Pisgah Legal Services, Inc.
Knight, Rebecca B. .... '55 '82 C.34 B.S. L.1228 J.D. Dist. J.
Kopp, Kevin P. .... '72 '98 C.34 B.S. L.776 J.D. [A Roberts&S.]
Kort, Richard A., (BV) .... '64 '91 C.1365 B.B.A. L.575 J.D. [McGuire,W.&B.]
Krause, Edward B., (BV) .... '47 '73 C.860 B.S. L.276 J.D. 96 Central Avenue
Kropelnicki, Steven, Jr., (BV) .... '46 '75 C&L.575 B.A., J.D. 181 Charlotte St.
Kumar, Jeri L. .... '58 '94 C.477 B.A. L.215 J.D. One West Pack Square
Kuniholm, Elizabeth F., (AV) .... '47 '81 C&L.228 A.B., J.D. [Kuniholm] ⊙
Kuniholm Law Firm, (AV) .... 46 Haywood St., Ste. 250 (⊙Raleigh)
Kurdys, Mark C., (AV) .... '56 '80 C.477 B.G.S. L.851 J.D. [Roberts&S.]
Lambert, Sheila M., (BV) .... '49 '82 C.280 A.B. L.861 J.D. 1 W. Pack Sq.
Lamm, Riddick M., Jr. '44 '81 C.55 A.B. L.1228 J.D.
V.P. & Tr. Offr., Wachovia Bk. of N.C., N.A.
Lassiter, Lauren F. .... '61 '88 C.593 B.A. L.896 J.D. [L.F.Lassiter]
Lassiter, L. F. .... 50 Riceville Rd., Ste. C304
Lavelle, Brian F. D., (AV) .... '41 '66 C.893 B.A. L.880 J.D. [VanWinkle,B.W.S.&D.]
Lawrence, Betty Tenn, (CV) .... '49 '84 C.699 A.B. L.228 J.D. [B.T.Lawrence]
Lawrence, Betty T., (CV) .... 142 Hillside St.
Leake, Larry B., (AV) .... '50 '74 C&L.575 B.A., J.D. [Leake&S.] ⊙

Leake & Scott, (AV) BB
501 BB&T Building, 28801 ⊙
Telephone: 828-253-3661 Fax: 828-258-8754
Email: leakeandscott@bellsouth.net
Members of Firm: A. E. Leake (1911-1992); Robert E. Harrell (1925-2000); Larry B. Leake; Ward D. Scott; Christopher B. Reinhardt.
General Practice and Trial in all Courts. Interstate Commerce, Insurance, Corporation, Real Estate, Governmental, Medical Malpractice, Personal Injury, Taxation Law, Family Law.
Reference: Branch Banking and Trust, Asheville, North Carolina.
Marshall, North Carolina Office: Mashburn Building, P.O. Box 451. Telephone: 828-649-3883.
See Professional Biographies, ASHEVILLE, NORTH CAROLINA

Ledbetter, Jeffrey Taylor .... '46 '92 C.48 B.A. L.574 J.D. Dept. of Correction
Lee, Charles G., III, (BV) .... '26 '52 C.152 A.B. L.896 J.D. 15 Church St.
Legal Aid of North Carolina, Inc. .... 184 E. Chestnut Street
Leicht, Gene T., (BV) .... '64 '91 C.260 B.A. L.999 J.D. 62 Clayton Street
Lentz, Bryan Todd .... '66 '01 C.1129 B.A. L.1526 J.D. 17 N. Market St., Ste. 4
Lentz, DeVere C., Jr., (BV) .... '29 '54 C&L.575 B.A., LL.B. [DeVere L.&Assoc.]
Lentz, DeVere & Associates, P.A., (BV) .... 17-19 N. Market St.
Leonard, T. Bentley, (BV) .... '47 '73 C&L.577 A.B., J.D. [Leonard,T.B.]
Leonard, T. Bentley, PLLC, (BV) .... 274 Merrimon Avenue

Lewis, Robert D. ... '29 '56 C.228 A.B. L.575 LL.B. Supr. Ct. J.

Lewis, Susan C., Law Office, (BV) ... '59 '84 C&L.575 B.A., J.D. 1 Oak Plz., Ste. 306

Lindsay, Stephen P., (BV) ... '58 '85 C.296 B.A.S. L.575 J.D. [Cloninger,L.H.&S.]

Little, Jennifer Louise ... '71 '01 C.893 B.A. L.260 J.D. 89 Montford Avenue

Litzenberger, Virginia P. ... '46 '81 C.880 B.A. L.383 J.D. [Patla,S.R.&M.] ‡

Livingstain, Harris M. ... '57 '85 C.273 B.A. L.329 J.D. [Ⓐ McGuire,W.&B.]

Lloyd, James M. ... '66 '92 C&L.575 B.S., J.D. [J.M.Lloyd]

Lloyd, James Michael, P.A.
75 Church Street, P.O. Box 948, 28802
Telephone: 828-350-1765 Fax: 828-350-1766
Email: lloydlaw@att.net URL: http://www.jameslloydpa.com
James M. Lloyd.
Construction Law, Condominium/Homeowner Association Law, Litigation, Corporate and Business Law.

See Professional Biographies, ASHEVILLE, NORTH CAROLINA

Lockett, Sarah ... '— '04 C.945 B.A. L.575 J.D. [Grimes&T.]

Loftin, Carl W., (AV) ... '36 '61 C.198 A.B. L.575 LL.B. [Roberts&S.]

Long, Robert B., Jr., (AV) ... '42 '65 C&L.575 A.B., LL.B. [Long,P.W.&J.]

Long, Parker, Warren & Jones, P.A., (AV) BR
Suite 600, 14 South Pack Square, P.O. Box 7216, 28802
Telephone: 828-258-2296 Fax: 828-253-1073
URL: http://www.longparker.com
Robert B. Long, Jr.; William A. Parker; Steve Ray Warren; W. Scott Jones; Philip Scott Anderson;—Ronald Dale Brondyke (Board Certified Specialist in Real Property Law-Residential Transactions, North Carolina State Board of Legal Specialization); Andrew B. Parker.
General Trial Practice. Civil Litigation, Commercial Litigation, Personal Injury Litigation, Federal Litigation, Eminent Domain, Medical Malpractice, Family Law, Business Litigation.

See Professional Biographies, ASHEVILLE, NORTH CAROLINA

Loomis, Doris Phillips, (BV) ... '56 '81 C.198 B.S. L.896 J.D. [McGuire,W.&B.]

Loose, William E. ... '60 '88 C.260 B.A. L.861 J.D. 68 N. Market St.

Lopez, Robert J., (BV) ... '50 '86 C.260 B.S. L.575 J.D. [Hyler&L.]

Lovins, Shannon Michele, (CV) ... '72 '98 C&L.838 B.S., J.D. [Ⓐ Dungan&Assoc.]

Lyman, Christopher B. ... '— '93 C.893 B.A. L.861 J.D. [Ⓐ McGuire,W.&B.]

Maccorkle, Eleanor, (BV) ... '53 '78 C.575 B.A. L.280 J.D. 138 E. Chestnut St.

Manheimer, Esther E. ... '71 '98 C.174 B.A. L.575 J.D. [Ⓐ VanWinkle,B.W.S.&D.]

Mann, Marjorie Rowe, (BV) ... '60 '85 C.27 B.A. L.896 J.D. [Roberts&S.]

Mann-Stadt, Rendi, (BV) ... '55 '94 C.93 B.S. L.339 J.D. [Ⓐ McGuire,W.&B.]

Marshall, Clifford C., Jr., (BV) ... '57 '82 C&L.575 B.A., J.D. [Marshall&R.]

Marshall & Roth, Professional Corporation, (BV)
90 Southside Avenue, Suite 150, 28801
Telephone: 828-281-2100 Fax: 828-281-2120
Clifford C. Marshall, Jr.; Philip J. Roth, Jr.; Lyman J. Gregory.
Federal and State Court Litigation, Personal Injury, Auto Accidents, Wrongful Death, Medical Malpractice, Civil Litigation, Corporate and Business Transactions, Employment Law, Contract Law, Physician/Patient Confidentiality Matters, Healthcare Litigation, Real Estate Litigation, Real Estate, Probate, Environmental Law, Zoning and Land Use.

See Professional Biographies, ASHEVILLE, NORTH CAROLINA

Martin, Dennis L., Jr. ... '73 '01 C.968 B.A. L.1228 J.D. [Ⓐ Roberts&S.]

Martin, Harry C., (AV) ... '20 '48 C.575 A.B. L.309 LL.B. [Martin] ⊙

Martin, J. Matthew, (BV) ... '60 '86 C&L.575 B.A., J.D. [Ⓒ Martin]

Martin, Mark C., (BV) ... '65 '91 C.575 B.A. L.692 J.D. [Patla,S.R.&M.]

Martin Law Firm, The, PA, (AV) ... 1 Hilltop Road (⊙Hillsborough)

Mason, John W., (AV) ... '44 '73 C.198 B.A. L.575 J.D. [Roberts&S.]

Matney, David E., III, (BV) ... '52 '78 C&L.575 B.A., J.D. [Matney&Assoc.]

Matney & Associates, P.A., (BV) ... 22 South Pack Square, Suite 402

McClellan, Thomas K., (BV) ... '54 '79 C.902 B.A. L.896 J.D. [Shuford,C.&M.]

McConnell, Elizabeth Ellen, (BV) ... '59 '85 C.576 B.A. L.896 J.D. [Northup&M.]

McCroskey, Patrick S., (BV) ... '70 '95 C.228 B.A. L.575 J.D. [Gum,H.&M.]

McDevitt, Larry S., (AV) ... '42 '68 C&L.575 B.A., J.D. [VanWinkle,B.W.S.&D.]

McDonald, Diane K., (BV) ... '46 '79 C&L.546 B.A., J.D. [McDonald]

McDonald Law Office, The, P.A., (BV) ... 22 South Pack Square, Suite 1000

McDowall, William D., Jr., (BV) ... '46 '80 C.1128 B.A. L.1228 J.D. 168 S. Liberty St.

McGlohon, Howard C., (BV) '— '77
C&L.574 B.Sc., J.D. 22 South Pack Square, Suite 800

McGuire, Joseph P., (AV) ... '50 '75 C.575 B.A. L.309 J.D. [McGuire,W.&B.]

McGuire, Peter B. ... '73 '02 C.198 B.A. L.508 J.D. [Ⓐ Roberts&S.]

McGuire, Walter R., (AV) ... '13 '37 C&L.575 A.B., LL.B. [McGuire,W.&B.] ‡

McGuire, Wood & Bissette, P.A., (AV) BR
Drhumor Building, 48 Patton Avenue, P.O. Box 3180, 28802
Telephone: 828-254-8800 Fax: 828-252-2438
Email: mwb@mwbavl.com URL: http://www.mwbavl.com
W. Louis Bissette, Jr.; Douglas O. Thigpen (Board Certified Specialist in Real Property Law, Residential Transactions, Business, Commercial and Industrial Transactions, North Carolina State Board of Legal Specialization); Joseph P. McGuire; Doris Phillips Loomis (Board Certified Specialist in Estate Planning and Probate Law, North Carolina State Board of Legal Specialization); M. Charles Cloninger; Thomas C. Grella; Grant B. Osborne; T. Douglas Wilson, Jr.; Richard A. Kort (Board Certified Specialist in Estate Planning and Probate Law, North Carolina State Board of Legal Specialization); Frederick S. Barbour; John N. Fleming; Susan Strayhorn Barbour;—Sarah Sparboe Thornburg; Douglas J. Tate; Mary E. Euler; Jeffrey J. Owen; Rendi Mann-Stadt; Harris M. Livingstain (Board Certified Specialist in Estate Planning and Probate Law, North Carolina State Board of Legal Specialization); Adam H. Reynolds; Christopher B. Lyman. Of Counsel: Richard A. Wood, Jr. Retired: Walter R. McGuire.
General Civil Practice in State and Federal Courts, Bankruptcy (Creditors Representation), Commercial Law, Corporate Law, Construction Law, Condominium Law, Estate Planning, Probate, Health Care, Insurance, Labor and Employment Law, Labor Relations, Litigation, Media, Personal Injury, Product Liability, Wrongful Death, Real Estate, Taxation, Securities Law, Appellate Advocacy, Alternative Dispute Resolution, and Mediation.
Representative Clients: Dave Steel Company, Inc. (Steel Fabricating); First Union Corporation (Banking); The Givens Estates, Inc. (Methodist Retirement Community); Grove Arcade Public Market Foundation; Hayes & Lunsford Electrical Contractors, Inc.; Home Depot; Progress Energy, Inc. (formerly Carolina Power & Light Company); Sisters of Mercy Services Corporation; Wellco Enterprises, Inc.; WLOS-TV.

See Professional Biographies, ASHEVILLE, NORTH CAROLINA

McIver, Joy Gragg, (BV) ... '66 '96 C.275 B.A. L.575 J.D. [Ⓐ Adams,H.C.C.&S.]

McKinney, J. Bruce ... '43 '74 C.77 B.S. L.421 J.D. Asst. Atty. Gen.

McLaughlin, W. Kevin, Jr., (BV) '71 '98
C.575 B.A. L.896 J.D. [VanWinkle,B.W.S.&D.]

McMinn, Eileen M., (BV) ... '51 '90 C.66 B.A. L.184 J.D. [Patla,S.R.&M.]

Merrell, Robin L., (BV) '75 '00
C.896 B.A. L.577 J.D. Staff Atty., Pisgah Legal Services, Inc.

Messer, Albert M., (BV) ... '69 '97 C.790 B.S. L.45 J.D. [Messer]

Messer Law Firm, (BV) ... 22 South Pack Sq., Ste. 700

Metcalf, W. Carleton, (BV) ... '72 '97 C&L.575 B.A., J.D. [VanWinkle,B.W.S.&D.]

Miller, Bonnie E. ... '64 '89 C&L.576 B.A., J.D. [Miller,M.L.]

Miller, Jerry W., (AV) ... '48 '76 C.576 B.S. L.192 J.D. Asst. U. S. Atty.

Miller, Michael L., (AV) ... '52 '78 C&L.208 B.A., J.D. [Miller,M.L.]

Miller, Michael L., P.A., (AV) ... 537 College Street

Mills, Anna S. ... '70 '97 C&L.575 B.A., J.D. [VanWinkle,B.W.S.&D.]

Minton, Blan V. ... '39 '86 C.896 B.A. L.574 J.D. [Legal A.N.C.]

Monroe, Vaughn S. ... '76 '03 C.232 B.S. L.574 J.D. [Ⓐ VanWinkle,B.W.S.&D.]

Monteith, J. Derel, Jr. ... '68 '98 C.472 B.M. L.575 J.D. [Carter S.&M.] (See Pat. Sect.)

Moore, George W., (BV) ... '43 '71 C.896 B.A. L.575 J.D. [Moore]

Moore, Jennifer Wayland, (BV) ... '72 '97 C&L.896 B.A., J.D. [Moore]

Moore, Ronald L., (BV) ... '52 '80 C.48 B.A. L.192 J.D. [R.L.Moore]

Moore, Stephen C. ... '75 '01 C.968 B.S. L.1194 J.D. [Ⓐ Leonard,T.B.]

Moore, William C. ... '31 '59 C&L.896 B.S., LL.B. [Patla,S.R.&M.] ‡

Moore Law Firm, The, (BV)
One Oak Plaza, Suite 303, 28801
Mailing Address: P.O. Box 7602, Asheville, NC 28802
Telephone: 828-258-8053 Fax: 828-251-0972
Email: gmoorelaw@charter.net URL: http://www.georgemoorelawyer.com
George W. Moore; Jennifer Wayland Moore.
Personal Injury, Medical Malpractice, Family Law, Child Custody, Child Support, Adoptions, Automobile Accidents, Divorce, Equitable Distribution, Workers' Compensation, Labor and Employment, Nursing Home Litigation..

See Professional Biographies, ASHEVILLE, NORTH CAROLINA

Moore, Ron L., P.A., (BV) ... One W. Pack Square, Suite 1509

Morley, E.K., PLLC, Law Offices of
(See Hendersonville)

Morris, William C., III, (BV) ... '54 '83 C.48 B.A. L.575 J.D. 700 Biltmore Ave.

Morris York Williams Surles & Barringer, L.L.P.
(See Charlotte)

Morrison, Lisa M., (CV) ... '— '92 C.1128 B.A. L.896 J.D. [Ⓐ Worley&C.]

Morrison, Robert Torrence ... '58 '86 C.309 A.B. L.94 J.D. 5 Brad Street

Mullen Holland & Cooper P.A.
(See Gastonia)

Mulligan, Paulette C. ... '48 '78 C.569 B.A. L.564 J.D. [Ⓐ Strauss&Assoc.]

Myers, Gloria J., (BV) '52 '85 C.475 B.A. L.128 J.D.
Assoc. Gen. Coun., Mission - St. Joseph's Health Sys., Inc.

Neill, D. Samuel
(See Hendersonville)

Neumann, Scott D.
(See Brevard)

Newton, Heather, (BV) ... '63 '89 C.119 B.A. L.575 J.D. 12 Lawyers Walk

Newton, Patrick D. ... '73 '00 C.577 B.S. L.896 J.D. [Ⓐ Strauss&Assoc.]

Northup, Isaac Noyes, Jr., (AV) ... '53 '80 C&L.575 A.B., J.D. [Northup&M.]

Northup & McConnell, PLLC, (AV)
123 Biltmore Avenue, 28801
Telephone: 828-232-4481 Facsimile: 828-232-4489
URL: http://www.northupmcconnell.com
Isaac Noyes Northup, Jr.; Elizabeth Ellen McConnell; Steven Weir Sizemore; Derrick R. Bailey.
Medical Malpractice, Professional Malpractice, Personal Injury, Automobile Accidents, Litigation, Products Liability, Employment Law, Commercial Litigation.

See Professional Biographies, ASHEVILLE, NORTH CAROLINA

Oakes, Jane M. ... '63 '96 C.457 B.A. L.94 J.D. Staff Atty., Pisgah Legal Services, Inc.

Olesiuk, John M., (BV) ... '50 '86 C.228 B.A. L.896 J.D. 17-19 N. Market St.

Olinger, Benjamin R., (BV) ... '63 '95 C.575 B.A. L.607 J.D. 168 South Liberty St.

Orr, William W. ... '13 '54 40 Gertrude Pl. Annex‡

Osborne, Grant B., (BV) ... '59 '86 C&L.228 B.A., J.D. [McGuire,W.&B.]

Owen, Jeffrey J. ... '74 '02 C&L.896 B.A., J.D. [Ⓐ McGuire,W.&B.]

Parker, Andrew B. ... '77 '02 C.896 B.A. L.575 J.D. [Ⓐ Long,P.W.&J.]

Parker, William A., (AV) ... '47 '74 C.896 B.A. L.575 J.D. [Long,P.W.&J.]

Patla, Straus, Robinson & Moore, P.A., (AV)
Suite 300, 29 North Market, P.O. Box 7625, 28802
Telephone: 828-255-7641 Fax: 828-258-9222
Email: info@psrmlaw.com
Joseph A. Patla (1881-1979); Robert J. Robinson; William C. Moore (Retired, 1987); Steven I. Goldstein (Board Certified Specialist in Real Property Law-Residential, Business, Commercial and Industrial Transactions, North Carolina State Board of Legal Specialization); Victor W. Buchanan; Robert A. Freeman, III; Richard S. Daniels; Kerry A. Friedman; Virginia P. Litzenberger (Retired, 2002); Sharon Tracey Barrett; Mark C. Martin; Carol Eubank; Eileen M. McMinn; Donna Douglas; Cindy M. Rice. Of Counsel: Karl H. Straus.
Business Organizations, Tax, Planning and Administration of Estates, Employee Benefit Planning, Real Estate, Construction, Health Care, Labor and Employment, Condemnation, General Civil Trial and Appellate Practice before State and Federal Courts and Administrative Agencies.
Representative Clients: Asheville Regional Airport Authority; Asheville Waste Paper Co.; Giles Chemical Corp.; Grove Park Inn Resort, Inc.; Harry's Cadillac-Pontiac-GMC Truck Co., Inc.; Matthews Ford, Inc.; Mission Hospitals, Inc.; H. Putsch & Co., a Division of H. Putsch & Co. (Germany); Royal Crown Cola Bottling Co.

See Professional Biographies, ASHEVILLE, NORTH CAROLINA

Patton, Frank C., III ... '60 '87 C.228 B.A. L.575 J.D. District Attorney's Office

Payne, Ronald K. ... '51 '77 C.576 B.A. L.896 J.D. Supr. Ct. J.

Peltz, Jason M. ... '76 '02 C.910 B.A. L.896 J.D. [Ⓐ Best&B.P.]

Penland, Talmage N., (BV) ... '30 '71 C.34 B.S. L.575 J.D. 207 One Oak Plz.

Peterson, Brian L., (CV) ... '63 '94 C.902 B.A. L.575 J.D. [B.Peterson]

Peterson, David E., (BVⓉ) ... '38 '70 C.813 A.B. L.1065 J.D. P.O. Box 7668

Peterson, Brian, The Law Offices of, (CV) ... P.O. Box 2868

Phillips, Ann Holsonback, (AV) ... '18 '65 C.232 B.S. L.575 LL.B. 14 N. Kensington Rd.‡

Pinkston, Mark A., (AV) ... '63 '89 C.576 B.S. L.838 J.D. [VanWinkle,B.W.S.&D.]

Pitts, Robert M., (AV) ... '44 '73 C&L.575 A.B., J.D. [Pitts,H.&H.]

Pitts, Hay & Hugenschmidt, PA, (AV) ... 137 Biltmore Ave.

Poisson, Jack, (BV) '43 '70 C.576 B.S. L.575 J.D.
29 North Market Street The Seventh Floor, 28801-2983
Telephone: 828-252-9889 Toll Free: 800-366-0076 Cell Phone: 828-275-7577 Fax: 828-252-0511
URL: http://www.jackpoisson-law.com URL: http://www.jackpoissonlaw.com
Email: higherlaw@bellsouth.net URL: http://www.jpoissonlaw.com
Family Law, Civil Litigation, Personal Injury, Automobile Accidents, Criminal Traffic, Defense, DUI, Divorce, Child Support, Child Custody, Equitable Distribution.

See Professional Biographies, ASHEVILLE, NORTH CAROLINA

Pope, Marvin P., Jr., (BV) ... '49 '73 C.404 A.B. L.896 J.D. Dist. J.

Poston, Met R. ... '20 '52 C.143 B.S. L.273 LL.B. P.O. Box 8408

Powell, John A., (BV) ... '46 '73 C.645 B.A. L.477 J.D. [Powell&D.]

Powell, Sidney K., (AVⓉ) '55 '78 C&L.575 B.A., J.D.
(adm. in TX; not adm. in NC) [S.Powell] ⊙

Powell & Deutsch, (BV) ... 75 N. Market St.

Powell, Sidney, Law Offices of, (AVⓉ)
1854A Hendersonville Road, Suite 228, 28803 ⊙
Telephone: 828-651-9543 Fax: 828-684-5343
Email: sidneypowell@federalappeals.com

(This Listing Continued)

Powell, Sidney, Law Offices of (Continued)
Sidney K. Powell (Not admitted in NC).
Federal Appeals, Consulting in Complex Federal Litigation.
Dallas, Texas Office: 1920 Abrams Parkway, Suite 369, 75214. Telephone: 214-653-3933. Fax: 214-319-2502.
See Professional Biographies, ASHEVILLE, NORTH CAROLINA

Price, Phillip C. .... '73 '01 C.34 B.S. L.1228 J.D. [A Cogburn,G.B.&R.]
Prince, Youngblood & Massagee
(See Hendersonville)

Radford, Michael Eugene .... '53 '97 C.925 B.S.N. L.574 J.D. 89 Hickory Tree Rd.
Ramer, Thomas F., (AV) .... '59 '84 C.8 B.S. L.607 J.D. [Ganly&R.]
Rash, Susan Taylor, (BV) .... '61 '89 C.160 B.A. L.280 J.D. [A Adams,H.C.C.&S.]
Ray, David Kilburn '67 '94 C.198 B.A. L.280 J.D.
(adm. in FL; not adm. in NC) So. Appalachian Highlands Conservancy
Reed, William Kennon ....'71 '98 C.1458 B.A. L.904 J.D. [A Cogburn,G.B.&R.]
Reidinger, Martin K., (AV) ....'58 '84 C&L.575 B.A., J.D. [Adams,H.C.C.&S.]
Reinhardt, Christopher B. .... '77 '03 C.999 B.A. L.575 J.D. [Leake&S.]
Reinhardt, Rebecca Johnston .... '74 '03 C.48 B.S. L.575 J.D. [A Roberts&S.]
Religa, Stanley F. '21 '50 C.960 L.365 J.D.
(adm. in IL; not adm. in NC) 164 Skyview Circle‡
Reynolds, Adam H. .... '— '03 C.880 B.S. L.902 J.D. [A McGuire,W.&B.]
Rice, Cindy M. ....'78 '03 C&L.575 B.S., J.D. [A Patla,S.R.&M.]
Riddle, Robert E., (AV) ....'36 '58 C&L.896 B.S., J.D. [R.E.Riddle]
Riddle, Robert E., P.A., (AV) .... P.O. Box 7406
Rifkin, Paul L. ....'42 '69 C.280 B.A. L.896 J.D. [P.L.Rifkin]
Rifkin, Paul L., P.A. ....21 Page Ave.
Rippon, Michelle, (AV) ....'44 '81 C.06 B.A. L.574 J.D. [VanWinkle,B.W.S.&D.]
Ritzen, James F. .... '45 '86 C.225 A.B. L.502 J.D. 90 Lanvale Ave.
Roberson, Matthew S. .... '79 '04 C.575 B.A. L.1345 J.D. [A Adams,H.C.C.&S.]
Roberson, Peggie Lewis ....'43 '78 C.16 B.A. L.192 J.D. Coun., Mills Mfg. Corp.
Roberts, Landon, (AV) ....'21 '48 C&L.575 A.B., J.D. [C Roberts&S.]
Roberts, Thomas DuBose, (CV) ....'54 '85 C.228 A.B. L.861 J.D. 20 Battery Park Avenue

Roberts & Stevens, P.A., (AV) BR
BB&T Building, One West Pack Square, Suite 1100, P.O. Box 7647, 28802
Telephone: 828-252-6600 Facsimile: 828-253-7200
Email: info@roberts-stevens.com URL: http://www.roberts-stevens.com
John Shorter Stevens; James Walker Williams; Carl W. Loftin; Walter L. Currie; John W. Mason; Marc Rudow; Sheryl Howell Williams (Board Certified Specialist in Real Property Law-Residential Transactions); William Clarke; Vincent D. Childress, Jr.; Marjorie Rowe Mann; Gregory D. Hutchins; Jackson D. Hamilton; Wyatt Shorter Stevens; Mark C. Kurdys; Jacqueline D. Grant; Christopher Z. Campbell; Sarah Patterson Brison; David L. English; Cynthia S. Grady; F. Lachicotte Zemp, Jr.;—Kenneth R. Hunt; Dennis L. Martin, Jr.; Peter B. McGuire; Kevin P. Kopp; Rebecca Johnston Reinhardt; K. Dean Shatley, II. Of Counsel: Landon Roberts.
General Civil and Trial Practice Before all Courts, Administrative Law, Bankruptcy, Civil Litigation, Construction, Corporation, Education, Employment, Environmental, Health Care, Hospital, Insurance, Estate Planning, Probate, Public Sector, Real Estate, Taxation.
Representative Clients: Blue Ridge Paper Products; Medical Mutual Insurance Co. of North Carolina; The Biltmore Co.; Buncombe County Board of Education; Cigna Insurance Co.; Scottsdale Insurance Co.; St. Joseph's Health System, Inc.; Wal-Mart, Inc.
See Professional Biographies, ASHEVILLE, NORTH CAROLINA

Robinson, Robert J., (AV) .... '36 '60 C&L.896 A.B., LL.B. [Patla,S.R.&M.]
Roda, Peter L. ....'35 '62 C.31 B.A. L.228 LL.B. Dist. J.
Rollman, Tony E., (CV) .... '69 '94 C.48 B.S. L.362 J.D. P.O. Box 8088
Rose, John R., (BV) .... '62 '88 C.575 B.S. L.1228 J.D. [Cogburn,G.B.&R.]
Roth, Katherine Langley .... '64 '92 C.276 B.S. L.966 J.D. 11 N Market St.
Roth, Philip J., Jr., (CV) ....'58 '92 C&L.966 B.A., J.D. [Marshall&R.]
Rowe, James Gary, (AV) ....'46 '72 C&L.575 B.A., J.D. [Kelly&R.]
Rudow, Marc, (AV) .... '53 '79 C.1275 B.A. L.575 J.D. [Roberts&S.]
Ruley, Douglas A. .... '61 '87 C.575 B.A. L.309 J.D. Southern Environ. Law Ctr.
Russell, J. William, (AV) ....'23 '50 C&L.575 B.A., J.D. [Russell&K.]
Russell, Raymond W., (AV Ⓣ) '39 '67 C&L.575 B.A., J.D.
(adm. in FL; not adm. in NC) 307 Vanderbilt Rd.

Russell & King, P.A., (AV)
17 North Market Street, P.O. Box 7668, 28802
Telephone: 910-252-7651 Fax: 910-258-0648
J. William Russell; Sandra M. King.
Civil Trials and Appeals in all Courts. Insurance Law, Insurance Defense, Casualty Insurance, General Liability Insurance, Bad Faith, Nursing Home Liability, Medical Negligence, Civil Litigation, Labor and Employment and Workers Compensation Law.
See Professional Biographies, ASHEVILLE, NORTH CAROLINA

Saenger, George W., (AV) ....'46 '76 C&L.575 A.B., J.D. [Adams,H.C.C.&S.]
St. John-Ritzen, Cathie, (CV) '44 '00 C&L.502 B.G.S., J.D.
188 Charlotte Highway, P.O. Box 6318, 28816-6318
Telephone: 828-255-8813 Fax: 828-255-8823
Email: cathie@asheville-elderlaw.com
Elder Law, Nursing Home Litigation, Probate, Estate Administration, Guardianship, Wills, Trust Law.
See Professional Biographies, ASHEVILLE, NORTH CAROLINA

Schlanger, Joanne M. .... '65 '91 C.260 B.S. L.569 J.D. 75 Church St.
Schnedler, Steven C., (AV) '48 '74
C.475 B.S.E.E. L.213 J.D. [Carter S.&M.] (See Pat. Sect.)
Schumacher, Richard ....'48 '82 C&L.801 B.S., J.D. Asst. Clk. of Superior Ct.
Scott, Ward D., (BV) ....'66 '97 C.48 B.A. L.575 J.D. [Leake&S.]
Searson, W. Bradford, (BV) ....'61 '86 C.790 B.A. L.245 J.D. [Cloninger,L.H.&S.]
Shackelford, John E., (BV) ....'30 '59 C.966 B.S. L.575 J.D. 120 College St.
Shatley, K. Dean, II .... '74 '03 C.34 B.M. L.575 J.D. [A Roberts&S.]
Shoaf, Ryan Douglas ....'75 '01 C.575 B.A. L.472 J.D. 80 Peachtree Road
Shuford, John F., (AV) ....'20 '44 C&L.575 A.B., LL.B. [C Shuford,C.&M.] ‡

Shuford, Cagle & McClellan, P.A., (BV)
53 Asheland Avenue, Suite 104, 28801
Mailing Address: P.O. Box 1530, Ashville, NC 28802
Telephone: 828-258-2211 Fax: 828-252-8309
Email: scmlaw@att.net URL: http://www.lawyers.com/scmlaw
George H. Wright (1884-1958); William B. Cagle; Thomas K. McClellan. Retired Of Counsel: John F. Shuford.
General Civil Practice. Real Property, Probate Law and Business Law.
Counsel for: First Federal Savings & Loan Assn.
Reference: Wachovia Bank & Trust Co., N.A., Asheville, North Carolina.
See Professional Biographies, ASHEVILLE, NORTH CAROLINA

Shults, Glen C., Law Offices of '55 '81 C.188 B.A. L.273 J.D.
14 South Pack Square Suite 360, P.O. Box 1384, 28802
Telephone: 828-251-9676 Fax: 828-251-0648
Email: shults.law@worldnet.att.net
Labor and Employment Law, Wrongful Termination, Employer Defense, Employee Rights, Discrimination, Labor Management Relations, Wage and Hour Law, Employee Benefits.
See Professional Biographies, ASHEVILLE, NORTH CAROLINA

Siemens, A. James, (CV) .... '67 '94 C.575 B.A. L.861 J.D. [Siemens]
Siemens Law Office, P.A., (CV)
22 South Pack Square, Suite 700, 28801
Telephone: 828-252-5080
Email: jim@wnclaw.com URL: http://www.wnclaw.com
A. James Siemens.
Family Law, Divorce, Child Custody, Child Support, Domestic Violence, Adoptions, Criminal Law, Traffic Offenses, DWI, Traffic Violations, Personal Injury, Automobile Accidents, Wrongful Death, Medical Malpractice.
See Professional Biographies, ASHEVILLE, NORTH CAROLINA

Sizemore, Steven Weir, (BV) .... '65 '91 C.925 B.S.B.A. L.1228 J.D. [Northup&M.]
Sklar, Catherine A. '47 '83 C.355 B.A. L.1040 J.D.
(adm. in NY; not adm. in NC) 86 Edgemont Rd.
Slawter, William F., (BV) ....'45 '73 C&L.575 A.B., J.D. [W.F.Slawter]
Slawter, William F., PLLC, (BV) ....1 Oak Plz., Ste. 208

Sluder, Curtis Alan '68 '98 C.999 B.A. L.575 J.D.
124 College Street, Suite 105, 28801
Telephone: 828-254-9505 Fax: 828-254-9514
Email: curtis@sluderlaw.com URL: http://www.sluderlawoffice.com
Criminal Law, Traffic Violations, Driving While Intoxicated, Expunction.
See Professional Biographies, ASHEVILLE, NORTH CAROLINA

Smith, Philip J., (AV) ....'46 '72 C.896 B.A. L.831 J.D. [VanWinkle,B.W.S.&D.]
Smith, Roger T., (BV) '54 '79 C.575 B.A. L.990 J.D.
70 North Market Street, P.O. Box 7172, 28801
Telephone: 828-254-4658 Fax: 828-254-0787
Email: rogertsmithatty@aol.com URL: http://www.rogertsmithatty.com
Criminal Law, Divorce, Family Law, Child Custody, Child Support, Spousal Support, Palimony, Equitable Distribution, Domestic Violence, Driving While Impaired, Traffic Violations, DMV Hearings, Drug Crimes, Sexual Offenses, Felonies and Misdemeanors, Mediations.
See Professional Biographies, ASHEVILLE, NORTH CAROLINA

Smith, Russell A. .... '56 '86 C.705 B.A. L.178 J.D. [Smith D.&D.] ⊙
Smith, Ruth C., (CV) ....'72 '99 C&L.575 B.A., J.D. [Grimes&T.]
Smith Dornan & Dehn PC ....670 Runaway Ridge Clyde (⊙New York, NY)
Snead, Samuel A., (CV) ....'64 '96 C.575 B.A. L.1364 J.D. Off. of Pub. Def.
Sneed, Albert L., Jr., (AV) ...... '43 '73 C.575 B.S. L.228 J.D. [VanWinkle,B.W.S.&D.]
Snyder, Keith S., (AV) ....'33 '58 C&L.575 A.B., LL.B. 12 Allesarn Rd.‡
Spradlin, J. Elizabeth, (CV) .... '59 '93 C.937 B.A. L.1228 J.D. 120 College St.
Stahl, Jeffrey K. .... '76 '04 C.925 B.S. L.1386 J.D. [Biggers&H.]
Starnes, O. E., (AV) .... '24 '50 C.198 B.S. L.575 LL.B. [VanWinkle,B.W.S.&D.]
Stevens, John Shorter, (AV) ....'33 '61 C&L.575 A.B., J.D. [Roberts&S.]
Stevens, Leslie E. ....'— '88 C.232 B.S. L.574 J.D. P.O. Box 18356
Stevens, Wyatt Shorter, (BV) ....'69 '94 C&L.48 B.A., J.D. [Roberts&S.]
Stevenson, Joel B., (BV) .... '42 '70 C.925 B.A. L.575 J.D. [J.B.Stevenson]
Stevenson, Joel B., P.L.L.C., (BV) ....One West Pack Square
Stewart, Jack W., Jr., (AV) .... '55 '81 C.34 B.A. L.192 J.D. [J.W.Stewart]

Stewart, Jack W., P.A., (AV)
61 North Market Street, P.O. Box 1920, 28802
Telephone: 828-253-5673 Fax: 828-253-7100 URL: http://www.ashevillecriminallawyer.com
Email: jack@jackstewartlaw.com URL: http://www.jackstewartlaw.com
Jack W. Stewart, Jr.
Criminal and Civil Trial Practice in all State and Federal Courts. Criminal Defense, DWI Law, Traffic Citations, Family Law, Divorce, Child Custody, Child Support, Equitable Distribution.
See Professional Biographies, ASHEVILLE, NORTH CAROLINA

Stoker, Lawrence C. .... '26 '52 C.316 A.B. L.575 LL.B. P.O. Box 5291
Stone & Christy, P.A.
(See Black Mountain)

Straus, Karl H., (AV) ....'21 '51 C&L.569 LL.B. [C Patla,S.R.&M.]
Strauss, Andrew A., (AV) ....'53 '78 C.659 B.S. L.276 J.D. [Strauss&Assoc.]
Strauss & Associates, P.A., (AV) ....77 Central Ave., Suite F
Streitwieser, Jary V. '47 '77 C.627 B.A. L.190 J.D.
(adm. in NE; not adm. in NC) 74 Crabapple Ln.
Strobel, Daniel L. ....'63 '91 L.790 J.D. P.O. Box 5302
Stubbs, Donald F. '30 '55 C&L.477 A.B., LL.B.
V.P. & Tr. Coun., Fiduciary Trust Company International
Swearingen, Ann Logan Spurlock ....'54 '84 C.174 B.S. L.420 J.D. [A Hyler&L.]
Tarleton, Allan R., (AV) ....'52 '80 C&L.896 B.A., J.D. [VanWinkle,B.W.S.&D.]
Tate, Douglas J., (BV) ....'63 '89 C.575 A.B. L.245 J.D. [A McGuire,W.&B.]
Taylor, Paul B., (AV) ....'55 '81 C.575 B.A. L.128 J.D. Asst. U.S. Atty.
Teich, Henry E., (BV) ....'50 '78 C.1044 B.A. L.767 J.D. [Grimes&T.]
Thatcher, Karen J. ....'54 '82 C.1264 B.A. L.208 J.D. [A W.F.Slawter]
Thigpen, Douglas O., (AV) ....'51 '76 C&L.575 A.B., J.D. [McGuire,W.&B.]
Thomas, Robt. F. ....'15 '38 C.896 L.904 LL.B. 165 Elkwood Ave.‡
Thornburg, Lacy H. ....'29 '54 C&L.575 B.A., LL.B. U.S. Dist. J.
Thornburg, Sarah Sparboe, (BV) ....'69 '96 C.228 A.B. L.896 J.D. [A McGuire,W.&B.]
Thornton, David B., (BV) ....'54 '86 C.48 B.A. L.574 J.D. 17-19 N. Market St., Ste. 1
Trilling, Joel S. ....'67 '96 C.48 B.A. L.1292 J.D. [J.Trilling]
Trilling, Joel, Attorney at Law ...., 56 College St., Ste. 301
True, Ronald C., (BV) ....'59 '85 C.296 B.S. L.1228 J.D. One Oak Plaza
Trull, William J., Jr., (BV) ....'50 '75 C.838 B.S. L.228 J.D. [W.J.Trull,Jr.]
Trull, William J., Jr., P.A., (BV) ....31 Clayton Street
Tucker, Robert P., II ....'62 '88 C.48 B.A. L.575 J.D. P.O. Box 1511

Van Winkle, Buck, Wall, Starnes and Davis, P.A., (AV) BR
11 North Market Street, P.O. Box 7376, 28802-7376 ⊙
Telephone: 828-258-2991 FAX: 828-255-0255; 257-2767; 257-2773
Email: vw@vwlawfirm.com URL: http://www.vwlawfirm.com
Robertson Wall (1913-1996); O. E. Starnes; Roy W. Davis, Jr.; Brian F. D. Lavelle (Board Certified Specialist in Estate Planning and Probate Law, North Carolina State Board of Legal Specialization); Larry S. McDevitt; Philip J. Smith; Barry B. Kempson; Albert L. Sneed, Jr.; Robert H. Haggard (Board Certified Specialist in Estate Planning and Probate Law, North Carolina State Board of Legal Specialization) (Resident, Hendersonville Office); Marla Tugwell Adams; Jones Pharr Byrd; Allan R. Tarleton; Larry C. Harris, Jr.; Michelle Rippon; William Perry Fisher, II; Michael M. Thompson (Resident, Hendersonville Office); Mark A. Pinkston; Stephen J. Grabenstein; Craig D. Justus; Cynthia W. Eller (Board Certified Specialist, Real Property Law, Residential Transactions, North Carolina State Board of Legal Specialization); Stephen B. Williamson; Adam L. Shealy (Board Certified Specialist in Estate Planning and Probate Law, North Carolina State Board of Legal Specialization) (Resident, Hendersonville Office); John G. Kelso (Board Certified Specialist in Estate Planning and Probate Law, North Carolina State Board of Legal Specialization); Dale A. Curriden; W. Carleton Metcalf; W. Kevin McLaughlin, Jr.; Caroline T. Knox (Resident, Hendersonville Office); Carolyn Lloyd Coward; Anna S. Mills; Guy F. Clerici; Tracy Kreider Diefenbach;—Esther E. Manheimer; William James Johnson; Vaughn S. Monroe; Emily A. Belcher Reynolds.
Language: Spanish.
Corporate and Commercial, Tax Litigation, Commercial Real Estate, Business and Succession Planning, Employee Benefits, Intellectual Property, Securities, Banking, Environmental, Construction, Trusts and Estates, Health Care, Civil Litigation, Commercial Litigation, Professional Malpractice, Fiduciary Litigation, Personal Injury, Wrongful Death, Products Liability, Bankruptcy, Creditors Rights, Public Finance, Governmental Regulation.

(This Listing Continued)

Van Winkle, Buck, Wall, Starnes and Davis, P.A. (Continued)

Representative Clients: Asheville Cardiology Associates; Carolina Power and Light Co., a Progress Energy Company; Central Carolina Restaurants, Inc.; Champion Hills Associates; Charles D. Owen Mfg. Co.; Chicago Title Insurance Co.; Chrysler Corp.; Columbia Carolina Corp.;CVS/Revco Drug Centers; EchoStar Communications Companies.
Hendersonville, North Carolina Office: 422 South Main Street. Telephone: 828-697-6196. Fax: 828-693-3999.

See Professional Biographies, ASHEVILLE, NORTH CAROLINA

Vardiman, Cynthia G. .... '64 '92 C.896 B.A. L.575 J.D. 366 Merrimon Ave.
Venable, Curtis B., (BV) '59 '83
C.575 B.A. L.574 J.D. Sr. Staff Atty., Pisgah Legal Services, Inc.
Vinson, Gay Paisley ....'53 '78 C.228 B.A. L.893 J.D. 22 Buena Vista Rd.
Viot, Van H. '14 '39 C.502 A.B. L.477 LL.B.
(adm. in MO; not adm. in NC) CC6 Crowfield Dr.‡
Walker-Mcglohon, Martha Ann .... '58 '88 C.577 B.A. L.575 J.D. Asst. City Atty.
Walton, Michele M., (CV) ....'70 '94 C.48 B.A. L.575 J.D. 38 Orange St.
Walton, S. Thomas, (CV) ....'25 '51 C.152 L.790 LL.B. BB&T Bldg.
Waltz, Julie A. ....'53 '78 C.25 B.A. L.575 J.D. 138 E. Chestnut St.
Warren, Steve Ray, (AV) .... '57 '83 C.925 B.S.B.A. L.575 J.D. [Long,P.W.&J.]
Wells, Reeves H. ....'10 '37 C.575 A.B. L.999 17 19 N. Market St.
Westall, Jack W., Jr., (BV) ....'44 '68 C&L.575 B.A., J.D. [Westall,G.C.&D.]
Westall, Gray, Connolly & Davis, P.A., (AV) ....81 Central Ave.
Whalen, William J., (AV) '49 '74
C&L.575 B.S., J.D. Sr. Staff Atty., Pisgah Legal Services, Inc.
Whatley, Michael J. ....'56 '81 C.896 B.A. L.575 J.D. 5 Oak Street

Whitmire Beeker & Townsend
(See Hendersonville)

Williams, Albert L., II, (BV) ....'56 '81 C.34 B.A. L.692 J.D. Dist. Atty. Off.
Williams, James Walker, (AV) .... '46 '70 C&L.575 B.S., J.D. [Roberts&S.]
Williams, Martha ....'53 '80 C.575 B.A. L.107 J.D. Law Clk.
Williams, Reed G., (BV) ....'53 '81 C.696 B.A. L.285 J.D. 17 N. Market St., Ste. 204
Williams, Sheryl Howell, (AV) .... '50 '80 C.1208 B.A. L.575 J.D. [Roberts&S.]
Williams, Todd Mckinnon ......'69 '99 C.575 B.A. L.588 J.D. Staff Atty., 20 A Jud. Dist.
Williamson, Stephen B. ....'63 '93 C.760 B.S. L.1228 J.D. [VanWinkle,B.W.S.&D.]
Wilson, Jennifer R. ....'76 '03 C.576 B.A. L.574 J.D. [Ⓐ R.E.Riddle]
Wilson, Susan E. ....'— '91 C.1365 B.A. L.280 J.D. Child Support Enforce.
Wilson, T. Douglas, Jr., (AVⓉ) .... '46 '73 C&L.575 A.B., J.D. [McGuire,W.&B.]
Winner, Dennis J. ....'42 '66 C&L.575 A.B., J.D. Supr. J.
Wittstruck, Clarke K., (CV) ....'55 '86 C.59 B.A. L.846 J.D. 24 Cornell St.
Wood, Richard A., Jr., (AV) .... '37 '62 C&L.228 A.B., LL.B. [Ⓒ McGuire,W.&B.]
Worley, Charles R., (BV) ....'45 '70 C&L.575 A.B., J.D. [Worley&C.]
Worley & Cady, (BV) ....109 Central Avenue
Yarbrough, Jonathan W., (BV) .... '67 '94 C.896 B.A. L.421 J.D. [Constangy,B.&S.]
Young, Ann Yaeger, (BV) '50 '75 C&L.575 A.B., J.D.
Gen. Coun., Mission - St. Joseph's Health Sys., Inc.
Young, Francis W. ....'27 '56 C.16 B.S.M.E. L.273 LL.B. 175 Robinhood Rd.‡

Young, Stanley D., (BV) '56 '84 C.48 L.574 J.D.
68 North Market Street, P.O. Box 3176, 28802
Telephone: 828-255-0569 Fax: 828-255-8693
Civil and Criminal Litigation in all State and Federal Courts. Personal Injury, Auto Accidents, Wrongful Death, DWI, Criminal Traffic Offenses, Family Law, Divorce, Child Support and Custody, Adoptions, Equitable Distribution.

See Professional Biographies, ASHEVILLE, NORTH CAROLINA

Zemp, F. Lachicotte, Jr., (BVⓉ) .... '60 '90 C.198 B.A. L.1218 J.D. [Roberts&S.]

ATLANTIC, —, *Carteret Co.*

Winborne, Saml. P. ....'23 '51 C&L.575 B.S., LL.B. P.O. Box 194‡

ATLANTIC BEACH, 1,781, *Carteret Co.*

Hooks, C. Dock, Jr. ....'54 '97 C.1083 B.A. L.574 J.D. P.O. Box 474
Swain, Ray F. ....'22 '49 C&L.896 J.D. 108 Bogue Sound Dr. E.‡

AURORA, 654, *Beaufort Co.*

Thompson, T. R., Jr., (BV) .... '38 '63 C&L.575 B.A., LL.B. Hwy. 33

AVON, —, *Dare Co.*

Ames, Robin L. ....'53 '83 C.967 B.A. L.200 J.D. P.O. Box 945
Dixon, David R., (CV) ....'65 '93 C.575 B.A. L.1345 J.D. Askins Creek Dr.
Dixon, Jean Louise C., (CV) '64 '89
C.692 B.A. L.1202 J.D. Highway 12 & Askins Creek Dr.
Jones, Ralph V. '24 '54 C&L.659 J.D.
(adm. in DC; not adm. in NC) P.O. Box 37‡

AYDEN, 4,622, *Pitt Co.*

Bawtinhimer, Stacey B., (BV) .... '61 '90 C.945 B.A. L.1059 J.D. [S.Bawtinhimer]
Bawtinhimer, Stacey, Law Office of, (BV) ......................................P.O. Box 9
Evans, DeLyle M., (BV) ....'47 '73 C.575 A.B. L.896 J.D. 467 Second St.

BADIN, 1,154, *Stanly Co.*

Michael, Jeffrey D. .... '65 '92 C&L.575 B.S.B.A., J.D. P.O. Box 707‡

BAHAMA, —, *Durham Co.*

Paul, Janice Perrin .... '54 '85 C&L.575 B.A., J.D. 9509 S. Lowell Road‡

BALD HEAD ISLAND, 173, *Brunswick Co.*

Farmer, R. Lee, (AV) ....'48 '73 C.240 B.A. L.896 J.D. [R.L.Farmer] (⊙Yanceyville)
Farmer, R. Lee, P.L.L.C. Law Offices of
19 Ibis Roost (⊙Granite City, IL; Yanceyville, NC)

BALSAM, —, *Jackson Co.*

Donlin, R. David '42 '76 C.999 B.S.E. L.472 J.D.
(adm. in FL; not adm. in NC) P.O. Box 488‡
Schiess, Frederick E. ....'28 '52 C&L.472 A.B., J.D. General Delivery‡

BALSAM GROVE, —, *Transylvania Co.*

Clayton, Ralph R. '22 '49 C&L.362 A.B., LL.B.
(adm. in FL; not adm. in NC) P.O. Box 101‡

BANNER ELK, 811, *Avery Co.*

Alderson, Thomas G. '23 '53 C&L.472 LL.B.
(adm. in FL; not adm. in NC) C-106 Rte. 2‡

Angle, Robert B., Jr., Attorney P.A.
(See Boone)

Hardin, Edward R., (BV) .... '36 '60 C&L.228 A.B., J.D. 2922 SugarTop Dr.
Holcomb, Gregory F. .... '40 '76 C.280 B.B.A. L.51 J.D. 800 Raven Ridge Road
Jones, Nancy Byerly ....'49 '88 C.1128 B.A. L.575 J.D. [N.B.Jones]
Jones, Nancy Byerly, PLLC, Law Office of, The ....44 Shawneehaw Avenue
Kaufman, Samuel L. '07 '30
(adm. in NY; not adm. in NC) 152 Swiss Lane‡
Lyerly, R. A., II .... '44 '75 C.34 B.A. L.796 J.D. Chf. Dist. Ct. J.
Pfaff, J. Lawrence, (BV) ....'49 '81 C.1129 B.A. L.575 J.D. 1 Banner St.
Wright, John M., (BV) ....'50 '79 C.575 B.A. L.896 J.D. [J.M.Wright]
Wright, John Maffitt, (BV) .... 139 Main Street

BATH, 275, *Carteret Co.*

Crampton, George W. '30 '55 C.188 B.A. L.597 J.D.
(adm. in IL; not adm. in NC) Rt. 1‡

BAYBORO, * 733, *Pamlico Co.*

Hollowell, Bernard B. .... '22 '48 C&L.896 LL.B. [Ⓒ Hollowell&H.]
Hollowell, Bernard B., Jr., (BV) .... '52 '79 C.575 B.A. L.574 J.D. [Hollowell&H.]
Hollowell, Steven Earl, (BV) .... '64 '90 C.575 B.A. L.896 J.D. [Hollowell&H.]
Hollowell & Hollowell, (BV) .... 203 Main Street

BEAUFORT, * 3,808, *Carteret Co.*

Crowe, Roger L., Jr., (BV) .... '58 '82 C.576 L.1228 J.D. [R.L.Crowe,Jr.]
Crowe, Roger L., Jr., P.A., (BV) ....402 Turner St.
Davis, Warren J., (AV) .... '37 '65 C.886 B.S. L.893 J.D. [Ⓒ Davis,M.&L.]

Davis, Murrelle & Lyles, P.A., (AV) BB
412 Front Street, P.O. Box 819, 28516
Telephone: 252-728-4080 Fax: 252-728-3235
Email: dml.law@bizec.rr.com URL: http://www.lawyers.com/dmlpalaw
Edward L. Murrelle; Janet M. Lyles (Board Certified Specialist in Workers Compensation, North Carolina State Board of Legal Specialization);—Amie M. Huber. Of Counsel: Warren J. Davis.
Personal Injury, Automobile Accidents, Professional Liability, Products Liability, Arbitration, Premises Liability, Workers' Compensation, Social Security, Business Litigation, Admiralty and Maritime Law.
Representative Clients: Cooperative Bank for Savings; International Longshoreman's Association Local 1807; Morehead City Export Terminal, Inc.; Crow Hill Farms, Inc.; Phoenix Foods, Inc.; Core Sound Waterfowl Museum, Inc.; Northland Ins. Co.

See Professional Biographies, BEAUFORT, NORTH CAROLINA

Dodge, Robert C., (BV) ....'60 '88 C.575 B.A. L.896 J.D. 402 Turner Street
Fulcher, Rodney Gray .... '72 '99 C.575 B.A. L.1339 J.D. 300 Campen Road, Unit D-2

Garner, Margaret Ann
(See Morehead City)

Goodwin, Debra Jeanne ....'72 '99 C.316 B.S. L.201 J.D. Dist. Atty. Off.
Gordon, Richard F. ....'32 '56 C&L.896 B.S., J.D. 241 Rudolph Dr.‡
Huber, Amie M. ....'73 '01 C.125 B.A. L.1338 J.D. [Ⓐ Davis,M.&L.]
Lupton, James M., (BV) .... '65 '92 C.896 B.S. L.575 J.D. [Wheatly,W.W.V.&L.]
Lyles, Janet M., (BV) .... '49 '84 C&L.575 A.B., J.D. [Davis,M.&L.]
Maroules, J. Christy, (CV) ....'60 '88 C.232 B.A. L.1345 J.D. 613 Cedar St.

Mason & Mason, P.A.
(See Morehead City)

Massie, Debra L., (BV) ....'58 '90 C.896 B.A. L.1345 J.D. Off. of Pub. Def.
Murrelle, Edward L., (AV) .... '38 '64 C.296 A.B. L.896 J.D. [Davis,M.&L.]
Newton, J. Jefferson, (BV) .... '58 '83 C&L.1228 B.S., J.D. [Newton]

Newton Law Firm, (BV)
814 Cedar Street (U.S. Highway 70), P.O. Drawer 630, 28516-0630
Telephone: 252-728-4000 Fax: 252-728-3900
Email: info@newtonlaw.com URL: http://www.newtonlaw.com
J. Jefferson Newton (Board Certified Specialist in Workers Compensation Law, North Carolina State Board of Legal Specialization).
Civil Litigation including Personal Injury and Workers' Compensation. Mediation and Arbitration.

See Professional Biographies, BEAUFORT, NORTH CAROLINA

Stanley, Richard L., (BV) .... '46 '70 C&L.896 B.A., J.D. P.O. Box 150

Sumrell, Sugg, Carmichael, Hicks & Hart, P.A.
(See New Bern)

Talton, Hugh C., Jr., (CV) .... '51 '79 C&L.1228 B.S., J.D. [Talton&T.]
Talton & Taylor, (CV) ....416 Live Oak Street
Taylor, Katherine S. ....'67 '98 C.953 B.S. L.575 J.D. [Talton&T.]
Tilghman, Carl L. ....'44 '69 C&L.896 B.A., J.D. Spec. Supr. Ct. J.
Valentine, Stephen M., (BV) .... '55 '80 C.575 B.S. L.896 J.D. [Wheatly,W.W.V.&L.]
Wainwright, George L., Jr. .... '43 '85 C.575 A.B. L.896 J.D. Supr. Ct. J.

Wallace, Morris, Barwick, Landis & Stroud, P.A.
(See Kinston)

Ward, Hallett S., III, (CV) ....'61 '88 C.232 B.A. L.896 J.D. [H.S.Ward]
Ward, Hallett S., P.A., (CV) ....503 Cedar St.
Weeks, Stevenson L., (AV) ....'52 '80 C.232 B.A. L.1228 J.D. [Wheatly,W.W.V.&L.]
Wheatly, Claud R., III, (BV) ......'47 '72 C.152 B.A. L.790 J.D. [Wheatly,W.W.V.&L.]
Wheatly, Claud R., Jr., (AV) ..... '18 '41 C&L.575 A.B., LL.B. [Wheatly,W.W.V.&L.]

Wheatly, Wheatly, Weeks, Valentine & Lupton, P.A., (AV)
710 Cedar Street, P.O. Box 360, 28516
Telephone: 252-728-3158 Fax: 252-728-5282
Email: firm@wwnwpa.com URL: http://www.wwnwpa.com
Claud R. Wheatly, Jr.; Claud R. Wheatly, III; Stevenson L. Weeks; Stephen M. Valentine; James M. Lupton.
General Civil and Criminal Trial Practice. Admiralty, Probate, Corporation and Real Estate Law, Domestic, Family Law, Personal Injury, Criminal, Traffic, DWI, Felonies.
Reference: First Citizens Bank.

See Professional Biographies, BEAUFORT, NORTH CAROLINA

Whitley, John B., (BV) ....'38 '63 C&L.575 A.B., J.D. 913 Ann St.
Williams, James W., Jr. '30 '63 C.885 B.S. L.64 LL.B.
(adm. in MD; not adm. in NC) 2211 Front St.‡

BELHAVEN, 1,968, *Beaufort Co.*

Leiken, Jerome, (AV) '28 '52 C.608 L.607 J.D.
(adm. in OH; not adm. in NC) 204 Shoreline Dr.‡
Raynor, Harvey W., III, (CV) .... '50 '81 C.575 A.B. L.574 J.D. [Raynor]
Raynor Firm, The, (CV) ....P.O. Box 9

BELMONT, 8,705, *Gaston Co.*

Gaeng, Paul E. '12 '57 L.1002 LL.B.
(adm. in MD; not adm. in NC) 329 Southfork Dr.‡
Rhodes, Susan E., (BV) ....'51 '87 C&L.575 A.B., J.D. [S.E.Rhodes]
Rhodes, Susan E., P.A., (BV) ....8320 Catawba Cove Dr.
Robinson & Wilson, L.L.P., (AV) .... 32 North Main St. (⊙Gastonia)
Schmitz, Ann Marie S. .... '68 '95 C.475 B.A. L.1187 J.D. 5018 Graystone Estate Dr.

Wilson, Parks H., Jr., (AV) ....'53 '79 C.198 B.A. L.192 J.D. [Robinson&W.]

BENSON, 2,923, *Johnston Co.*

Canaday, C. C., Jr., (AV) ....'18 '48 C&L.575 A.B., J.D. [Canaday&C.]
Canaday, Claude C., III, (BV) ....'51 '76 C&L.575 B.A., J.D. [Canaday&C.]
Canaday, Harry E. ....'25 '50 C.575 L.896 LL.B. Ret. Supr. Ct. J.
Canaday & Canaday, P.A., (AV) ....2031 N.C. 50 North

Hales & Conaway, PLLC, The Law Offices of
(See Clinton)

Hatch, Jonathan Lee, (BV) ....'68 '94 C.576 B.S. L.1228 J.D. 106 W. Main St.
Hodges, Thomas E., (BV) ....'52 '79 C.53 B.S. L.329 J.D. 100 N. Market St.
Levinson, James R., (BV) ....'44 '74 C.871 B.A./B.S. L.575 J.D. [Levinson&L.] ⊙
Levinson, Joseph Lee ....'— '04 C.575 B.A. L.115 J.D. [Levinson&L.]
Levinson & Levinson, (BV) ....124 E. Main Street (⊙Smithfield)
McLamb, Jack E., III ....'69 '96 C.575 B.A. L.115 J.D. 500 A South Market Street
Murphy, George R., (BV) ....'46 '73 C.1228 B.S. L.896 J.D. 202 N. Market St.

Narron, O'Hale & Whittington, P.A., (AV)
207 East Main Street, P.O. Box 457, 27504 ⊙
Telephone: 919-894-8565 Fax: 919-894-1198
O. Hampton Whittington, Jr.;—E. Scott Tart.
General Practice. Civil, Criminal Trials and Appeals in State and Federal Courts. DWI, Corporate, Administrative and Real Property Law. Taxation, Probate, Estate Planning and Stock and Asset Acquisitions and Mergers, Personal Injury, Automobile Accidents and Injuries, Wrongful Death, Workers Compensation, Mediation.
Representative Clients: T. E. Johnson Lumber Co., Inc.
Approved Attorneys for: Lawyers Title Insurance Corp.; Federal Land Bank of Columbia; First Title Insurance Co.; Chicago Title Insurance Co.; AMI Title Insurance Co.
Smithfield, North Carolina Office: 102 South Third Street, P.O. Box 1567. Telephone: 919-934-6021. Fax: 919-934-6280.
See Professional Biographies, BENSON, NORTH CAROLINA

Simmons, Barry Keith ......'54 '83 C.232 B.S.B.A. L.469 J.D. 4909-D, NC 50 Hwy., N.‡

Stewart Law Firm
(See Dunn)

Tart, E. Scott ....'76 '01 C.1228 B.A. L.577 J.D. [⊠ Narron,O.&W.] ⊙
Whittington, O. Hampton, Jr., (AV) .....'49 '75 C.198 B.A. L.575 J.D. [Narron,O.&W.]

BEULAVILLE, 1,067, *Duplin Co.*

Harrell, Katie Quinn ....'61 '94 C.953 B.A. L.574 J.D. Mag.

BLACK MOUNTAIN, 7,511, *Buncombe Co.*

Begley, Wm. Michael, (BV) ....'52 '77 C&L.575 B.S., J.D. [Begley]

Begley Law Firm, P.A., (BV)
103 Richardson Boulevard, 28711
Telephone: 828-669-4000 Fax: 828-669-9619
Email: mike@begleylaw.net
Wm. Michael Begley.
Estate Planning, Estate Administration, Real Estate, Business Law and Non-Profit Administration.
References: Central Carolina Bank; Community Foundation of WNC; Mountain Retreat Association; Black Mountain Savings Bank; Montreat Development Council; Black Mountain Community Endowment Fund; Black Mountain Center for the Arts.
See Professional Biographies, BLACK MOUNTAIN, NORTH CAROLINA

Christy, William H., (BV) ....'56 '89 C.999 B.A. L.260 LL.M. [Stone&C.]
Craig, Wendy A. ....'65 '90 C.896 B.A. L.880 J.D. [W.A.Craig]
Craig, Wendy A., P.A. ....207 E. State St.
Davis, R. Walton, III, (BV) ....'56 '85 C.575 A.B. L.893 J.D. [Stone&C.]
Ellis, James M. ....'34 '58 C&L.575 A.B., LL.B. 110 N. Dougherty Street‡
Ellis, James M. ....'70 '96 C.999 B.A. L.790 J.D. [Stone&C.]
Le Van, Gerald, (AVⓣ) '34 '62 C.802 B.A. L.420 J.D.
(adm. in LA; not adm. in NC) [LeVan] (⊙Shreveport, LA)
Le Van Company, The, LLC, (AVⓣ) ....P.O. Box 10
Nicholson, Robert H. '23 '50 C&L.838 B.S., J.D.
(adm. in GA; not adm. in NC) 2517 N.C. 9‡
Schaich, Norman V., (BV) ....'53 '84 C.34 B.S. L.421 J.D. 208 Sutton Ave.
Sneed, Ronald E., (BV) ....'50 '78 C.1038 B.A. L.575 J.D. [R.E.Sneed]
Sneed, Ronald E., PA, (BV) ....104 Church St.

Stone & Christy, P.A., (BV)
110 N. Dougherty Street, 28711
Telephone: 828-669-7642 Fax: 828-669-5678
URL: http://www.stoneandchristy.com
Members of Firm: Richard B. Stone (1925-1998); William H. Christy; Bryant D. Webster; James M. Ellis; R. Walton Davis, III.
Corporate and Commercial Litigation, Real Estate Litigation, Buying and Selling a Home, Tax Litigation, Fiduciary Litigation, Civil Litigation, Commercial Real Estate, Residential Real Estate, Workers Compensation, Personal Injury, Wrongful Death, Trusts and Estates, Business and Succession Planning, Commercial Collections.
See Professional Biographies, BLACK MOUNTAIN, NORTH CAROLINA

Warren, Robert W. ....'44 '73 C.673 B.A. L.790 J.D. [B.Warren]
Warren, Bob, PA, Law Offices of ......................................P.O. Box 1367
Webster, Bryant D., (CV) ....'69 '94 C&L.575 B.A., J.D. [Stone&C.]

BLOWING ROCK, 1,418, *Caldwell & Watauga Cos.*

Canaday, Arthur C. '32 '60 C.674 A.B. L.260 J.D.
(adm. in FL; not adm. in NC) P.O. Box 1028
Claiborne, Robert C. '11 '34 C&L.16 J.D.
(adm. in AL; not adm. in NC) P.O. Box 1325‡

Di Santi Watson Capua & Wilson
(See Boone)

Kime, Robt. C. '18 '46 C&L.260 A.B., J.D.
(adm. in FL; not adm. in NC) P.O. Box 1253‡
Mattar, Richard E., (BV) ....'48 '74 C.576 B.S. L.575 J.D. P.O. Box 447
Murray, Charles O., III '44 '74 C.575 B.A. L.893 J.D.
(adm. in CA; not adm. in NC) P.O. Box 2308‡
Young, William L., (AV) ....'51 '76 C.575 A.B. L.896 J.D. 129 Valley View Road

BOLIVIA, * 228, *Brunswick Co.*

Austin & Cooke, PLLC
(See Wilmington)

Godwin Law Firm
(See Wilmington)

Hankins, Pauline ....'68 '94 C.576 EE L.574 J.D. [P.Hankins]

Hankins, Pauline, P.A., Law Office of
3029 Old Ocean Highway, P.O. Box 157, 28422
Telephone: 910-253-7400 Fax: 910-253-7403
Email: phankins@2khiway.net

(This Listing Continued)

Hankins, Pauline, P.A., Law Office of (Continued)
Pauline Hankins.
Juvenile Law, Traffic Violations, Divorce, Family Law, Child Custody, Child Support, Spousal Support, Criminal Misdemeanors, Domestic Violence
See Professional Biographies, BOLIVIA, NORTH CAROLINA

Salcines, Lillian ....'59 '85 C.575 B.A. L.93 J.D. Off. of Dist. Atty.
Seagle, James M. ....'70 '98 C.953 B.A. L.1228 J.D. Asst. Co. Atty., Brunswick Co.

BOONE, * 13,472, *Watauga Co.*

Angle, Robert B., Jr., (BV) ....'56 '86 C.575 B.A. L.896 J.D. [R.B.Angle,Jr.]

Angle, Robert B., Jr., Attorney P.A., (BV)
910 W. King Street, 28607
Telephone: 828-265-0016 Fax: 828-265-3651
Email: robangle@charter.net
Robert B. Angle, Jr.
Real Estate, Wills, Trusts and Estates, Business Law, Traffic Violations.
See Professional Biographies, BOONE, NORTH CAROLINA

Berndt, Stephen R., (BV) ....'52 '77 C&L.259 B.A., J.D. 869 Highway 105 Ext., Ste. 7
Blake, Charlotte Gail, (BV) '60 '85
C.893 B.A. L.575 J.D. Prog. Dir., Legal Servs. of the Blue Ridge
Capua, Andrea N., (BV) ....'62 '88 C.1222 B.S. L.796 J.D. [DiSanti W.C.&W.] ⊙
Carlson, Steven M., (CV) ....'62 '95 C.77 B.A. L.896 J.D. P.O. Box 73
Cherry, Robert L., Jr. '45 '79 C.575 A.B. L.896 J.D.
Prof. of Bus. Law & Real Estate, Appalachian State Univ.
Clement, Charles E., (AV) ....'39 '64 C.575 B.A. L.896 J.D. [Clement]

Clement Law Office, (AV)
756 West King Street, Drawer 32, 28607
Telephone: 828-264-6411 Fax: 828-264-5424
Email: attorneys@clementlawoffice.com URL: http://www.clementlawoffice.com
Members of Firm: Charles E. Clement; Donald D. Howard.
General Civil Practice in all Courts. Real Estate, Civil Litigation, Corporate and Business, Wills and Estates, Public Utilities, Employment, Municipal and Land Use Law, Condemnation and Eminent Domain, Administrative, Regulatory and Governmental Law.
See Professional Biographies, BOONE, NORTH CAROLINA

Cole, Dayton T. .....'54 '81 C.805 B.B.A. L.796 J.D. Univ. Atty., Appalachian State Univ.
Deal, James M., Jr., (BV) ....'49 '74 C.34 B.A. L.575 J.D. [Deal,M.&S.]
Deal, Moseley & Smith, LLP, (BV) ....770 West King Street
Dillard, Margaret S. ....'62 '92 C.575 B.A. L.880 J.D. 400 Shadowline Dr., Ste. 101
Di Santi, Anthony S., (AV) ....'47 '75 C.575 B.S. L.896 J.D. [DiSanti W.C.&W.] ⊙

Di Santi Watson Capua & Wilson, (AV)
642 West King Street, P.O. Box 193, 28607-4040 ⊙
Telephone: 828-264-6126 Telefax: 828-264-7743
URL: http://www.lawyers.com/disantiwatson&capua
Members of Firm: Anthony S. Di Santi; Donald M. Watson, Jr.; Andrea N. Capua; Frank C. Wilson, III. Of Counsel: W. Kelly Johnson (Not admitted in NC).
General Civil Practice and in all State and Federal Courts. Corporation, Real Property, Insurance, Family, Municipal, Personal Injury, Automobile Accidents and Injuries, Estate Planning, Probate, Real Estate Development and Interstate Land Sales.
Reference: NCNB National Bank of North Carolina, Boone, North Carolina.
Newland, North Carolina Office: 102 Elk Street, 28657. Telephone: 828-733-9273.
See Professional Biographies, BOONE, NORTH CAROLINA

Eggers, Kimberly Mcguire ....'78 '01 C.34 B.A. L.1228 J.D. 659 W. King Street
Eggers, Stacy C., IV ....'76 '01 C.34 B.A. L.1228 J.D. [Eggers,E.E.&E.]
Eggers, Stacy C., Jr., (AV) ....'24 '50 C.34 L.896 [Eggers,E.E.&E.]

Eggers, Eggers, Eggers & Eggers, (AV)
737 West King Street, P.O. Box 248, 28607
Telephone: 828-264-3601 Fax: 828-262-5229
Email: four.eggers@eggers-law.com URL: http://www.eggers-law.com
Members of Firm: Stacy C. Eggers, Jr.; Stacy C. Eggers, III (1948-1990); Rebecca Eggers-Gryder; Stacy C. Eggers, IV.
Real Estate, General Civil Practice, Domestic Law, Elder Law, Probate, Juvenile Law, Personal Injury, Criminal, Condemnation, Corporate, Commercial, Traffic, Social Security Disability.
Representative Clients: NCNB; First Union National Bank; Watanga County, Town of Seven Devils.
Approved Attorneys for: Lawyers Title Insurance Corp.; Farm Credit Assn.; Jefferson-Pilot Title Insurance Co.
References: First Union National Bank; BB&T-Branch Banking and Trust; Centura Bank.
See Professional Biographies, BOONE, NORTH CAROLINA

Eggers-Gryder, Rebecca, (BV) ....'60 '86 C.34 B.S. L.1228 J.D. [Eggers,E.E.&E.]
Elkins, Nathaniel B. ....'14 '37 C.188 B.A. L.569 J.D. 580 Green Knob Mountain Rd.‡
Eller, Eric F., (CV) ....'65 '95 C.34 B.S. L.896 J.D. 161 Howard St., Ste. MN
Furgiuele, Samuel F., Jr., (BV) ....'51 '77 C.216 B.A. L.884 J.D. 659 W. King St.
Gates, Paul H., Jr. '53 '86 C.319 B.A. L.61 J.D.
(adm. in LA; not adm. in NC) 222 Wey Hall‡
Geary, John P. '41 '67 C.16 A.B. L.192 J.D.
(adm. in AL; not adm. in NC) Prof. of Bus. Law, Appalachian State Univ.
Ginn, C. Philip, (BV) ....'53 '77 C.34 B.A. L.575 J.D. 842 W. King St., Ste. 16
Greene, Douglas W., (CV) ....'43 '71 C.575 A.B. L.836 J.D. P.O. Box 100
Hedrick, Jeffery M., (BV) ....'56 '82 C&L.575 B.A., J.D. 659 W. King St.
Howard, Donald D., (AVⓣ) ....'44 '69 C.378 B.A. L.813 LL.B. [Clement]
Huffman, Paul F. '— '97 C.34 B.Mus., B.Ed. L.896 J.D.
805 State Farm Road, Suite 202
Johnson, Linda L., (BV) ....'51 '76 C.945 B.A. L.893 J.D. [Miller&J.]
Johnson, W. Kelly, (AVⓣ) '61 '86 C.347 B.A. L.150 J.D.
(adm. in OH; not adm. in NC) [⊠ DiSanti W.C.&W.] ⊙
Kaplan, Bruce L., (BV) ....'49 '74 C.112 A.B. L.1068 J.D. P.O. Box 455
Kepley, Michael P. ....'77 '05 C.34 B.A. L.1228 J.D. 136 N. Water St.
Lamm, Charles C., Jr. ....'44 '69 C&L.896 B.A., J.D. Supr. Ct. J.
Larry, David H., (AVⓣ) '41 '76 C.951 B.A. L.629 J.D.
Asst. Univ. Atty., Appalachian State University
Mangum, R. Worth, (BV) ....'42 '68 C&L.575 A.B., J.D. 114 N. Depot St.
McGee, Linda Mace ....'49 '73 C&L.575 B.A., J.D. Ct. of App. J.
Miller, Paul E., Jr., (BV) ....'50 '76 C.575 B.A. L.893 J.D. [Miller&J.]
Miller and Johnson, PLLC, (BV) ....766 West King Street

Morley, E.K., PLLC, Law Offices of
(See Hendersonville)

Moseley, Allen C., (BV) ....'54 '80 C.69 B.A. L.896 J.D. [Deal,M.&S.]
Norris, Charlene D., (CV) ....'60 '88 C.34 B.S.C.J. L.1228 J.D. Asst. Dist. Atty.
Ortmayer, Russell A. '17 '40 C.56 L.793 LL.B.
(adm. in SD; not adm. in NC) P.O. Box RR2, Box 355‡
Paletta, David R., (BV) ....'54 '80 C.228 B.A. L.575 J.D. 910 W. King St.
Robson, Charles B., Jr., (AV) ....'38 '66 C.976 B.A. L.575 J.D. 180 Pat Robson Rd.
Rogers, Chilton ....'56 '84 C&L.575 A.B., J.D. 176 Ravens View
Rusher, James T., (BV) ....'42 '67 C&L.575 A.B., J.D. Dist. Atty.

Seegers, Joseph W.
(See Newland)

Smith, Claude D., Jr. ....'52 '82 C&L.469 B.A., J.D. [Deal,M.&S.] ‡
Spainhour, Carole, (CV) ....'51 '93 C&L.575 B.A., J.D. 400 Shadowline Dr., Ste. 206
Speed, Robert T., Law Offices of, (BV) ....'51 '83 C&L.34 B.S., J.D. P.O. Box 432
Stacy, Dustin Neely ....'75 '01 C.575 B.A. L.1339 J.D. P.O. Box 569
Tarrier, Richard T. ....'50 '86 C.602 B.A. L.896 J.D. 184 N. Water St.‡
Turlington, David J., III ....'58 '87 C.232 B.A. L.574 J.D. [D.J.Turlington,III]

Turlington, David J., III, Attorney at Law, PC
756 West King Street, 28607
Telephone: 828-263-8860 Fax: 828-263-8862 URL: http://www.turlingtonlaw.com
Email: info@turlingtonlaw.com URL: http://www.lawyers.com/davidjturlington
David J. Turlington, III.
Family Law, Custody, Divorce, Equitable Distribution, Adoptions, Construction Law, Business Law, Corporate Law, Criminal Law, Traffic, DWI, Drug Offenses.
See Professional Biographies, BOONE, NORTH CAROLINA

Turner, John A., (BV) ....'57 '83 C.673 B.A. L.575 J.D. [Turner&Y.]

Turner & Yates, P.A., (BV)
136 North Water Street, 28607
Telephone: 828-264-5900 Fax: 828-264-9767 Real Estate Fax: 828-264-5969
URL: http://www.lawyers.com/turnerandyates
John A. Turner; David W. Yates. Of Counsel: Patricia L. Wilson.
Real Estate, Residential and Commercial Real Estate Development, Civil Litigation, Construction Law, Banking Law, Business Law, Corporate Law, Municipal Law, Employment Law, Personal Injury, Wills, Trusts and Estates, Utility Law.
See Professional Biographies, BOONE, NORTH CAROLINA

Watson, Donald M., Jr., (BV) ....'49 '74 C&L.575 B.S., J.D. [DiSanti W.C.&W.] ⊙
Weeks, Christopher J. '68 '93 C.10 B.A. L.245 J.D.
(adm. in SC; not adm. in NC) Asst. Gen. Coun., Samaritan's Purse
West, Robert H., (CV) ....'24 '73 C.228 A.B. L.472 J.D. 815 W. King St.
Whittle, Chester E., Jr., (BV) ....'43 '68 C.198 B.A. L.260 J.D. 756 West King Street
Wilson, Frank C., III, (BV) ....'54 '83 C.16 B.A. L.192 J.D. [DiSanti W.C.&W.] ⊙
Wilson, Gerald W., (BV) ....'50 '76 C.835 B.S. L.896 J.D. Asst. Dist. Atty.
Wilson, Patricia L. ....'53 '89 C.575 B.A. L.228 J.D. [Ⓡ Turner&Y.]
Yates, David W., (BV) ....'62 '87 C.34 B.A. L.831 J.D. [Turner&Y.]

BREVARD, * 6,789, *Transylvania Co.*

Adams, Richard N., (BV) ....'55 '86 C.290 B.A. L.192 J.D. Water Oak Suites
Averette, H. Paul, Jr., (BV) ....'45 '74 C.576 B.A. L.192 J.D. 6 N. Rice St.
Barton, Donald H., (BV) ....'51 '77 C.77 A.B. L.192 J.D. [D.H.Barton]
Barton, Donald H., P.C., (BV) ....205 E. Main St.

Blanchard, Newman & Hayes
(See Hendersonville)

Brown, Charles R. '14 '39 C.210 A.B. L.477 J.D.
(adm. in OH; not adm. in NC) 17 Tsalagi Dr.‡
Cagney, Joseph B. '45 '75 C.966 B.B.A. L.424 J.D.
(adm. in IL; not adm. in NC) 192 Connestee Trail
Dalton, Tony C., (BV) ....'56 '81 C.34 B.S. L.1228 J.D. [White&D.]
Desmond, Timothy P. '45 '76 C.1055 B.S. L.861 J.D.
(adm. in LA; not adm. in NC) 8 Quinn Dr.‡
Domonkos, Michael ....'34 '61 C&L.912 B.A., J.D. 506 Stone Dr.

Elkins & Elkins
(See Hendersonville)

Eubanks, Michael C., (BV Ⓣ) '46 '75 C&L.280 A.B., J.D.
52-A West Main Street, P.O. Box 588, 28712
Telephone: 828-884-7900 Fax: 828-884-7905
Email: insyt@citcom.net
Languages: French.
Family Law, Divorce, Child Custody, Equitable Distribution, Personal Injury, Wrongful Death, Automobile Accidents, Business, Estate and Real Property Litigation.
See Professional Biographies, BREVARD, NORTH CAROLINA

Ferikes & Bleynat, PLLC
(See Asheville)

Gardo, William L., II
(See Henderson)

Gash, Robert T. ....'24 '50 C&L.575 A.B., J.D. Ret. Dist. J.‡
Hall, Jeanne P. ....'59 '86 C.198 B.A. L.1040 J.D. [Neumann,P.]
Hart, Ladson F., (BV) ....'43 '68 C.576 B.A. L.896 J.D. 218 S. Broad
Henson, David A., (BV) ....'55 '81 C&L.260 B.A., J.D. 4 West Main Street, Suite 9
Himes, Anne L., (AV Ⓣ) ....'48 '77 C.577 B.A. L.178 J.D. P.O. Box 1629
Howard, Samuel A. ....'12 '35 C&L.896 LL.B. 1 College Row‡
Hudson, John R., Jr. ....'31 '58 C&L.575 A.B., J.D. 124 Frazier Rd.‡
Hunt, Jeffrey P., (BV) ....'50 '75 C&L.896 B.A., J.D. Dist. Atty.
Hunt, Margaret McDermott, (BV) ....'45 '75 C.446 B.A. L.896 J.D. 52 W. Main St.

Jackson, Frank B., Law Offices of
(See Hendersonville)

Jones, Shelton, (AV Ⓣ) ....'42 '71 C&L.575 B.S., J.D. [Jones,G.&L.] ⊙
Jones, Gillaspia & Loyd, L.L.P., (AV Ⓣ) ....5 Park Place, Straus Park (⊙Hous., TX)

Jordan, Donald E., (BV) '53 '78 C.208 B.A. L.174 J.D.
McMinn Building, 4 West Main Street, Suite 5, 28712
Telephone: 828-862-8735 Fax: 828-966-9556
Email: jordanlaw@infoave.net
Estate Planning, Trusts and Estates, Wills, Estate Administration, Probate Law, Real Estate Law, Business Law, Corporations.
See Professional Biographies, BREVARD, NORTH CAROLINA

Kimzey, James M., (AV) ....'36 '64 C&L.575 B.S., LL.B. P.O. Box 506
McConnell, Joseph H. '06 '31 C.198 B.S. L.893 LL.B.
(adm. in NY; not adm. in NC) R.R. 4, Box 211A‡
Neumann, David C., (BV) ....'40 '86 C.870 B.S. L.280 J.D. [Neumann,P.]

Neumann, Scott D., (CV) '66 '93 C.280 B.B.A. L.362 J.D.
10 South Broad Street, 28712
Telephone: 828-884-9899 Fax: 828-862-3334
Email: sneumann@citcom.net URL: http://www.scottneumannlaw.com
Family Law, Divorce, Child Custody and Support, Adoptions, Domestic Violence, Visitation Rights, Civil Practice, Criminal Law, Driving While Intoxicated, Traffic Violations, Drug Crimes, Juvenile Crimes, Parole and Probation, White Collar Crime, Real Estate, Buying or Selling a Home, Construction, Commercial Real Estate, Bankruptcy, Business Law, Buying or Selling a Business, Immigration and Naturalization, Visas, Trusts and Estates, Estate Planning, Wills and Probate.
See Professional Biographies, BREVARD, NORTH CAROLINA

Neumann Law Firm, The, PLLC, (BV)
46 East Main Street, 28712
Telephone: 828-884-6575 Fax: 828-884-6636 URL: http://www.neumann-law.com
Email: dneumann@citcom.net URL: http://www.neu-hall-law.com

(This Listing Continued)

Neumann Law Firm, The, PLLC (Continued)

Member of the Firm: David C. Neumann; Jeanne P. Hall.
Business Law, Corporate Law, Business Formation, Business Litigation, Commercial Finance Transactions, Small Business Planning, Family Limited Partnerships, Civil Litigation, Conflict Management Systems, Business Negotiations and Strategic Business Planning, Mediation and Arbitration, Estate Planning, Wills, Trusts, Powers of Attorney, Estate Administration, Probate, Guardianship, Real Estate, Residential and Commercial Real Estate Transactions, IRC 1031 Exchange Planning, Construction Contracts, Transactional Legal Opinions, Tax and Corporate Compliance, Income Tax Planning.
See Professional Biographies, BREVARD, NORTH CAROLINA

Philips, Brian P., (BV) ....'55 '81 C.362 B.A. L.192 J.D. 520 Country Club Road
Potts, Jack H. ....'18 '53 C&L.575 A.B., LL.B. Williamson Creek Rd.‡
Pratt, Michael K., (BV) ....'56 '81 C.577 B.A. L.896 J.D. [Ramsey&P.]

Prince, Youngblood & Massagee
(See Hendersonville)

Ramsey, Gayle E., (AV) ....'38 '69 C.896 B.A. L.575 J.D. [Ramsey&P.]

Ramsey & Pratt, P.A., (AV)
Legal Building, One North Gaston Street, 28712
Telephone: 828-884-4113 Telecopier: 828-885-2494
URL: HTTP://WWW.RAMSEY-PRATT.COM
Ralph H. Ramsey, Jr. (1900-1984); John K. Smart, Jr. (1935-1995); Cecil J. Hill (1919-2002); Gayle E. Ramsey; Michael K. Pratt.
General Practice, State and Federal Courts. Wills and Trusts, Probate and Estates, Estate Planning, Estate Administration, Real Estate, Municipal Law, Administrative Law, Personal Injury, Civil Litigation, Corporation Law, Business Law.
Attorneys for: Duke Power Co.; City of Brevard; Glen Cannon Country Club; Brevard College; Brevard Music Center; Citizens Telephone Co.; Sylvan Valley CATV Co.; Wachovia Bank; Lake Toxaway Co.; Outdoor Resort of N.C., Inc.
See Professional Biographies, BREVARD, NORTH CAROLINA

Skerrett, Cassandra D., (CV) ....'64 '90 C&L.1228 B.S., J.D. 412 S. Caldwell St.
Tener, Albert J. '12 '37 C.640 A.B. L.477 J.D.
(adm. in NY; not adm. in NC) 41 Grouse Lane‡
Warwick, George W., Jr. '20 '49 C.383 A.B. L.421 LL.B.
(adm. in KY; not adm. in NC) Drawer 1649‡
Welch, Paul B., III, (BV) ....'55 '80 C.198 A.B. L.575 J.D. 412 S. Caldwell St.
White, William R., (BV) ....'35 '64 C&L.896 B.S., LL.B. [White&D.]
White & Dalton, (BV) ....602 South Caldwell Street
Young, Malcolm D. ....'51 '96 C&L.813 B.A., J.D. 151 Las Praderas Cir.

BROWN SUMMIT, —, *Guilford Co.*

Doss, Marion Kenneth, Sr. ....'39 '65 C.277 B.S. L.280 LL.B. 7902 Southerland Dr.

BRYSON CITY, * 1,411, *Swain Co.*

Bell, Felicia G. '61 '93 C.260 B.S. L.472 J.D.
(adm. in FL; not adm. in NC) [Greene&B.]
Brigham, Elizabeth J., (BV) ....'56 '87 C.383 B.S. L.1228 J.D. [McKeever,E.D.&H.]
Graham, Curtiss A., (BV) ....'48 '91 L.259 J.D. 601 Donnie Cochran Rd.
Greene, Alan Douglas, (AV Ⓣ) '32 '59 C.128 A.B. L.276 J.D.
(adm. in FL; not adm. in NC) [Greene&B.]
Greene & Bell, P.A., (AV Ⓣ) ....75 Bacon Dr.
Macon, Nathaniel, Jr., (CV Ⓣ) ....'60 '89 C.999 B.A. L.838 J.D. P.O. Box 754
McKeever, Edwards, Davis & Hays, P.A., (AV)
28 Everett Street (⊙Hayesville, Murphy)
Moody, Fred H., Jr., (AV) ....'48 '72 C&L.575 B.A., J.D. [McKeever,E.D.&H.]
Porter, Carolyn '63 '88 C.282 B.A. L.846 J.D.
(adm. in TX; not adm. in NC) 13077 US Hwy 19 West‡
Richards, William L. '52 '80 C.1059 B.A. L.280 J.D.
(adm. in GA; not adm. in NC) #7 River St.
Toms, Margaret L. '50 '76 C.260 B.A. L.228 J.D.
(adm. in FL; not adm. in NC) P.O. Box 68‡

BUIES CREEK, 2,215, *Harnett Co.*

Anderson, Thomas P. '48 '75 C.16 B.A. L.192 J.D.
(adm. in AL; not adm. in NC) Prof. of Law, Campbell Univ.
Bowser, Richard Thomas '61 '91 C.294 B.A. L.1345 J.D.
(adm. in PA; not adm. in NC) Assoc. Prof., Campbell Univ.
Button, Alan L. '54 '82 C.188 A.B. L.902 J.D.
(adm. in NY; not adm. in NC) Assoc. Prof., Campbell Univ. Sch. of Law
Buzzard, Lynn Robert '40 '84 C.228 B.A. L.209 J.D.
(adm. in IL; not adm. in NC) Prof and Dir., Campbell Univ.
Cary, Jean M. ....'49 '75 C.228 B.A. L.276 J.D. Assoc. Prof., Campbell Univ. Sch. of Law
Cogswell, Robert C., Jr., (BV) '44 '70
C.260 B.S.B.A. L.259 J.D. Gen Coun., Campbell University
Davis, F. Leary, Jr. ....'41 '67 C.896 A.B. L.178 LL.M. Prof. of Law, Campbell Univ.
Dunham, Catherine Ross ....'62 '96 C.575 B.A. L.1228 J.D. Campbell Univ. Sch. of Law
Gupton, Willis F. ....'22 '48 C.316 B.S. L.896 LL.B. P.O. Box 103
Hetrick, Patrick K. '45 '71 C.966 B.S. L.436 J.D.
(adm. in WI; not adm. in NC) Campbell U. Law Sch.
Lewis, Charles C. '46 '71 C&L.902 B.A., J.D.
(adm. in VA; not adm. in NC) Prof. of Law, Campbell Univ. School of Law
Loftis, Robert O., Jr. '42 '73 C.1086 B.S. L.245 J.D.
(adm. in TN; not adm. in NC) Prof., Campbell Univ.
Lord, Richard A. '51 '75 C.24 B.A. L.836 J.D.
(adm. in TN; not adm. in NC) Campbell Univ. Sch. of Law
McLaughlin, James B., Jr. '46 '73 C.1063 B.S. L.469 J.D.
(adm. in GA; not adm. in NC) Assoc. Dean, Campbell Univ. Law Sch.
Schilpp, E. Allen '10 '35 C.311 A.B. L.446 LL.B.
(adm. in MD; not adm. in NC) Campbell Univ., Sch. of Law
Sorvari, Karen C. '43 '85
C.1086 B.A. L.1228 J.D. Assoc. Prof., Campbell Univ. Sch. of Law
Wallace, E. Gregory '53 '90 C&L.45 B.A., J.D.
(adm. in AR; not adm. in NC) Asst. Prof., Campbell Univ. Sch. of Law
Weeks, Olivia Leigh '47 '91 C.471 B.A. L.1345 J.D.
Assoc. Law Libr., Campbell Univ. Sch. of Law
Wiggins, Norman A. ....'24 '52 C&L.896 B.S., LL.B. Pres., Campbell Univ.
Woodruff, William A. '48 '78 C.16 B.A. L.790 J.D.
(adm. in SC; not adm. in NC) Prof., Campbell Univ. Sch. of Law

BURGAW, * 3,337, *Pender Co.*

Biberstein, Richard von, Jr., (AV) ....'35 '60 C&L.575 B.S., J.D. [Biberstein&N.]

Biberstein & Nunalee, L.L.P., (AV)
102 South Walker Street, P.O. Box 428, 28425-0428 ⊙
Telephone: 910-259-2175 Fax: 910-259-6823
Email: bnlaw@bellsouth.net
Richard von Biberstein, Jr.; Mark I. Nunalee.

(This Listing Continued)

Biberstein & Nunalee, L.L.P. (Continued)

General Practice. Trials. Real Estate, Personal Injury, Automobile Accidents, Wrongful Death, Wills, Probate and Estate Planning, Corporate and Commercial Law, Taxation.
Counsel for: Hedgecock Builders Supply Co.; Pender Memorial Hospital.
Representative Clients: Black River Health Services; Pres-Tige Label Corp.; Martin-Marietta Corp.; Robbins Nursery, Inc.; H.W. Williams Lumber Co., Inc.
Hampstead, North Carolina Office: 16191 Highway 17. Telephone: 910-270-4347. Fax: 910-270-2293.

See Professional Biographies, BURGAW, NORTH CAROLINA

Boyette Law Firm, The
(See Wilmington)

Culbreth Law Firm, L.L.P.
(See Wilmington)

Hale & Harrell, (CV)
107 E. Fremont, 28425
Telephone: 910-259-7772 Fax: 910-259-7796
Members of Firm: Catherine Hewlett-Hale; R. Kent Harrell.
Family Law, Criminal Law, Civil Litigation, Driving While Intoxicated, Traffic Offenses.

See Professional Biographies, BURGAW, NORTH CAROLINA

Harrell, R. Kent ... '70 '96 C.1128 B.A. L.574 J.D. [Hale&H.]
Hewlett-Hale, Catherine, (CV) ... '— '95 C.953 B.S. L.1228 J.D. [Hale&H.]
Kenan, Robert C., Jr. ... '68 '97 C.575 B.A. L.574 J.D. P.O. Box 957

Mako & Associates, P.A.
(See Wilmington)

Moore, Clifton L., Jr., (AV) ... '36 '61 C&L.575 A.B., J.D. 105 N. Wright St.
Nunalee, Mark I., (BV) ... '55 '81 C&L.575 B.S., J.D. [Biberstein&N.] ⊙
Pollock, Harold Lee, (BV) ... '50 '78 C.576 B.A. L.896 J.D. [H.Pollock]
Pollock, Harold, (BV) ... 105 E. Fremont St.
Trawick, Gary E., (AV) ... '44 '69 C&L.575 B.S., J.D. Special Supr. Ct. J.

BURLINGTON, 44,917, *Alamance Co.*

Adams, Donald L. ... '37 '72 205 Rolling Rd.
Adams, Nathan R. ... '74 '99 C.575 B.A. L.896 J.D. [Ⓐ Wishart,N.H.&P.]
Allen, Dawn D. ... '68 '02 C.240 B.A. L.574 J.D. [Ⓐ Wishart,N.H.&P.]
Allen, Jasper B., Jr. ... '38 '71 C.240 B.A. L.575 J.D. Supr. Ct. J.
Allen, Louis C., Jr., (AV) ... '25 '49 C&L.228 A.B., J.D. Drawer 29
Andrews, Jeffrey A., (AV) ... '49 '76 C&L.893 B.S.C.E., J.D. [Vernon,V.W.B.A.&G.]
Ayotte, Tiana Gibson, (CV) ... '64 '90 C&L.575 B.A., J.D. 430 South Spring Street
Bateman, Charles L., (AV) ... '37 '65 C.240 A.B. L.228 LL.B. [Bateman,O.&K.]
Bateman, Oertel & Koonts, (AV) ... 3061 South Church Street
Bennett, John R., (CV) ... '49 '92 C.797 B.A. L.896 J.D. [Bennett&D.]
Bennett & Deal, PLLC, (CV) ... 3017 S. Church St.
Berry, Amy S. ... '67 '98 C.577 B.A. L.1345 J.D. 2501 S. Mebane St.
Blaetz, Peter T., (BV) ... '59 '85 C.294 B.A. L.896 J.D. [Holt,L.W.&B.]
Blevins, James R. ... '49 '78 C&L.896 B.A., J.D. First Financial Ins. Co.

Brenman, Lisa R.
(See Chapel Hill)

Britt, Jill S., (CV) ... '68 '93 C.758 B.A. L.575 J.D. [Ⓐ Wishart,N.H.&P.]
Brown, Charlie D. ... '70 '97 C&L.896 B.A., J.D. [Ⓐ Wishart,N.H.&P.]
Brown, E. Lawson, Jr., (AV) ... '50 '75 C.232 B.A. L.896 J.D. [Vernon,V.W.B.A.&G.]
Champion, Ricky W., (BV) ... '58 '84 C.575 B.S. L.574 J.D. [Hemric,L.C.&M.]
Coleman, Julian B., (CV) ... '65 '93 C.575 B.A. L.574 J.D. [Patterson&C.]
Conner, Christopher Lee ... '74 '02 C&L.575 A.B., J.D. [Ⓐ Vernon,V.W.B.A.&G.]
Dalton, William Reid, III ... '53 '78 C&L.575 A.B., J.D. 420 Tarpley Street
Dameron, E. S. W., Jr. ... '20 '48 C&L.575 A.B., LL.B. 2511 Pineway Dr.‡
Deal, J. Ray, (CV) ... '54 '92 C.240 B.A. L.1228 J.D. [Bennett&D.]
Doyle, John A., Jr. ... '67 '94 C.705 B.A. L.425 J.D. Lab. Corp. America
Drew, Glenn A. ... '61 '85 C.446 B.S. L.472 J.D. Assoc. Coun., Fortress Re, Inc.
Duffy, Pamela S., (BV) ... '67 '91 C.93 B.A. L.945 J.D. [Wishart,N.H.&P.]
Edelman, Charles D. ... '42 '68 C.659 B.S. L.309 J.D. Fortress RE, Inc.

Farmer, R. Lee, P.L.L.C. Law Offices of
(See Yanceyville)

Garrett, Ruby Joyce B., (AV) ... '46 '82 C.838 B.S. L.575 J.D. [Vernon,V.W.B.A.&G.]
Gavigan, Brian P., (BV) ... '59 '84 C&L.446 B.A., J.D. [Wishart,N.H.&P.]
Giles, Robert C., II ... '— '02 C.575 B.M. L.574 J.D. [Ⓐ Wishart,N.H.&P.]
Hall, Ronald L., (CV) ... '48 '88 C.296 B.A.S. L.574 J.D. Legal Adv. to Police Dept.
Hallstrom, Frank W. ... '45 '87 C.550 B.A. L.896 J.D. 2501 S. Melbane St.
Harrison, Wade, (AV) ... '54 '79 C&L.575 B.A., J.D. [Wishart,N.H.&P.]
Hemric, H. Clay, Jr., (AV) ... '45 '71 C&L.896 B.A., J.D. [Hemric,L.C.&M.]
Hemric, Nancy G., (BV) ... '51 '83 C&L.896 B.S., J.D. 445 S. Spring St.
Hemric, Lambeth, Champion & Moseley, P.A., (AV) ... 445 South Spring Street

Holt, Longest, Wall & Blaetz, P.L.L.C., (AV) BB
407 South Broad Street, P.O. Drawer 59, 27216
Telephone: 336-227-7461 FAX: 336-227-9716
W. Clary Holt (1913-2003); Frank A. Longest, Jr.; N. Madison Wall, II; Peter T. Blaetz (Board Certified Specialist in Estate Planning and Probate Law, North Carolina State Board of Legal Specialization).
General Practice in all State and Federal Courts. Trials, Corporation, Insurance, Taxation, Administrative, Real Estate and Probate Law.
Counsel for: NationsBank, N.A.; Burlington Industries; AT&T Technologies; Burlington - Alamance County Association of Realtors; Nationwide Mutual Insurance Co.; The Times-News Publishing Co., Inc.; United States Fidelity and Guaranty Co.

See Professional Biographies, BURLINGTON, NORTH CAROLINA

Horton, Donald E., Jr. '63 '89 C&L.575 B.A., J.D.
Dir., Public Policy & Advocacy, Lab. Corp. of Amer. Holdings
Hoy, Douglas Richard, (BV) ... '46 '86 C.1129 B.A. L.1228 J.D. 1205 Maple Ave #A
Johnson, Barbara Ackerman '48 '79 C.880 B.A. L.1045 J.D.
(adm. in TN; not adm. in NC) 2728 Bedford Street
Johnson, James Hunt ... '71 '98 C.575 B.A. L.896 J.D. [Ⓐ Vernon,V.W.B.A.&G.]
Jones, Mark A., (BV) ... '54 '88 C.347 B.A. L.879 J.D. [Vernon,V.W.B.A.&G.]
Kalo, Joseph J., IV, (CV) ... '68 '94 C.880 B.A. L.575 J.D. [Wishart,N.H.&P.]
Koonts, F. Paul, (BV) ... '66 '95 C.925 B.A. L.575 J.D. [Bateman,O.&K.]
Kyle, Kathryn Wright '71 '97 C.788 B.A. L.245 J.D.
(adm. in MA; not adm. in NC) Coun., Laboratory Corp. of America
Lambeth, D. Thomas, Jr., (AV) ... '59 '85 C&L.575 A.B., J.D. [Hemric,L.C.&M.]
Latham, James F., (AV) ... '20 '42 C&L.228 A.B., J.D. [Latham,W.&D.] ⊙
Latham, Wood & Dorrestein, L.L.P., (AV) ... 2859 S. Fairway Dr. (⊙Graham)
Liles, G. Kemp, (BV) ... '56 '87 C.240 B.A. L.1345 J.D. P.O. Box 5068
Longest, Frank A., Jr., (AV) ... '45 '71 C&L.575 B.S.B.A., J.D. [Holt,L.W.&B.]

McEntire & DiLello
(See Graham)

McLelland, D. Marsh ... '21 '48 C&L.575 A.B., J.D. 2018 Nottingham Lane‡
McRae, G. Steven Clay ... '72 '00 C.575 B.A. L.896 J.D. [Ⓐ Vernon,V.W.B.A.&G.]
Messick, Steven H., (BV) ... '54 '79 C.232 B.A. L.1228 J.D. [Messick,M.&M.]
Messick, T. Paul ... '20 '52 C.240 A.B. L.228 LL.B. 3009 E. Church St.‡
Messick, T. Paul, Jr., (AV) ... '48 '74 C&L.575 A.B., J.D. [Messick,M.&M.]
Messick, Messick & Messick, (AV) ... 3009 S. Church St.
Miller, Carol Vincent, (BV) ... '58 '83 C.577 B.S.W. L.1345 J.D. [Vernon,V.W.B.A.&G.]
Morgan, Zachary D. ... '78 '04 C.269 B.A. L.1228 J.D. [Ⓐ Vernon,V.W.B.A.&G.]
Moseley, W. Phillip, (BV) ... '47 '73 C&L.575 A.B., J.D. [Hemric,L.C.&M.]
Oertel, Geoffrey K. ... '72 '00 C.446 B.A. L.1002 J.D. [Bateman,O.&K.]
Oertel, Paul L., III, (CV) ... '69 '93 C.477 B.S. L.896 J.D. [Bateman,O.&K.]
O'Neal, Christopher Marc ... '75 '00 C.575 B.A. L.1228 J.D. [O'Neal]
O'Neal Law Office, PLLC ... 338 Holly Hill Lane
Orndorff, Molly A. ... '76 '05 C.240 B.A. L.896 J.D. [Ⓐ Wishart,N.H.&P.]
Overby, Benjamin D. ... '74 '99 C.575 B.A. L.1228 J.D. [Ⓐ Vernon,V.W.B.A.&G.]
Patterson, John K., (BV) ... '36 '63 C.240 A.B. L.575 LL.B. [Patterson&C.]
Patterson & Coleman, (BV) ... 344 Maple Avenue
Pittman, Dorn C., Jr., (BV) ... '48 '77 C&L.896 B.B.A., J.D. [Wishart,N.H.&P.]

Quinn Law Firm, The
(See Greensboro)

Raiford, R. Chase, (BV) ... '36 '66 C.1228 A.B. L.896 LL.B. 1116 S. Church St.
Risher, Julie Ann ... '61 '90 C.759 B.A. L.1128 J.D. 3120 S. Church St.
Royster, Charles F., III ... '55 '82 C&L.575 B.S., J.D. [Tuggle&R.]

Schell Bray Aycock Abel & Livingston P.L.L.C.
(See Greensboro)

Simpson, Christine B. ... '52 '80 C.128 B.A. L.945 J.D. 3120 S. Church St.
Smith, David I. ... '39 '64 C&L.575 A.B., LL.B. 1147 S. Church St.
Stedman, Charles Norman "Chuck", (AV) ... '45 '71 C.575 B.S. L.838 J.D. [Stedman]

Stedman Law Firm, (AV)
330 Holly Hill Lane, 27215
Telephone: 336-584-6472 Fax: 336-584-6479
Email: cnstedman@triadbiz.rr.com URL: http://www.stedmanlaw.com
Charles Norman "Chuck" Stedman.
Personal Injury, Workers Compensation Injuries, Commercial & Residential Real Estate, Trusts, Estates & Wills, Business & Corporate Law.

See Professional Biographies, BURLINGTON, NORTH CAROLINA

Steed, Derek B. ... '72 '97 C.924 B.A. L.575 J.D. [Wishart,N.H.&P.]
Steele, C. Thomas, Jr., (BV) ... '62 '87 C.48 B.S. L.575 J.D. [Wishart,N.H.&P.]
Tuggle, Richard J., Jr., (AV) ... '53 '79 C.925 B.S.B.A. L.575 J.D. [Tuggle&R.]

Tuggle Duggins & Meschan, P.A.
(See Greensboro)

Tuggle & Royster, (AV) ... 3011 S. Church St.
Van Der Vaart, Sandra D., (BV) '59 '93 C.575 B.S. L.893 J.D.
Asst. Gen. Coun., Labcorp
Vernon, John H., III, (AV) ... '42 '67 C&L.896 B.A., J.D. [Vernon,V.W.B.A.&G.]
Vernon, Vernon, Wooten, Brown, Andrews & Garrett, P.A., (AV)
522 S. Lexington Ave.
Wall, N. Madison, II, (BV) ... '56 '81 C.198 B.A. L.575 J.D. [Holt,L.W.&B.]
Ward, Robert M., (BV) ... '42 '70 C&L.575 A.B., J.D. City Atty.
Washburn, James Kent ... '39 '73 C.999 B.A. L.575 J.D. Dist. J.

Watlington, Stuart N.
(See Yanceyville)

Weld, Konstantine H. H. '62 '89 C.577 B.S.N. L.734 J.D.
(adm. in MO; not adm. in NC) 2521 Hickory Ave.★
Whitaker, Hillary Davis, (CV) ... '70 '95 C.198 B.A. L.896 J.D. [Ⓐ Wishart,N.H.&P.]
Whitney, N. Morgan, Jr. ... '69 '00 C.575 B.A. L.574 J.D. 445 S. Spring St.
Wishart, Robert J., (AV) ... '44 '73 C.478 B.A. L.575 J.D. [Wishart,N.H.&P.]

Wishart, Norris, Henninger & Pittman, P.A., (AV)
3120 South Church Street, P.O. Box 1998, 27215-9114 ⊙
Telephone: 336-584-3388 FAX: 336-584-3994
Email: derek.steed@wnhplaw.com URL: http://www.wnhplaw.com
Robert J. Wishart; Dorn C. Pittman, Jr.; Wade Harrison (Board Certified Specialist in Family Law, North Carolina State Board of Legal Specialization); Brian P. Gavigan; C. Thomas Steele, Jr. (Board Certified Specialist in Real Property Law-Residential, Business, Commercial and Industrial Transactions); Pamela S. Duffy; Joseph J. Kalo, IV (Board Certified Specialist in Real Property Law-Residential, Commercial, Business and Industrial Transactions, North Carolina State Board of Legal Specialization); Derek B. Steed. Associates: Dawn D. Allen; Jill S. Britt; Hillary Davis Whitaker; Charlie D. Brown; Robert C. Giles, II; Nathan R. Adams; Molly A. Orndorff.
Arbitration, Appellate Practice, Business Law, Civil Litigation, Commercial and Residential Real Estate, Contracts, Corporate and Commercial Law, Creditor Bankruptcy, Employment Law, Environmental Law, Estate Administration, Estate Planning, Family Law, Federal and State Taxation, Financial Transactions, Franchise Matters, Investments, Joint Ventures and Partnerships, Limited Liability Companies, Mediation, Mergers and Acquisitions, Securities, Succession Planning, Tax Controversy, Wills and Trusts, Zoning, Planning and Land Use, Criminal and Traffic Matters, Elder Law.
Charlotte, North Carolina Office: 6832 Morrison Boulevard. Telephone: 704-364-0010. FAX: 704-365-5945; 704-364-0569.
Mebane, North Carolina Office: 111 East Center Street. Telephone: 919-304-4200. FAX: 919-304-4207.

See Professional Biographies, BURLINGTON, NORTH CAROLINA

Wooten, Wiley P., (AV) ... '43 '68 C&L.896 B.B.A., J.D. [Vernon,V.W.B.A.&G.]

BURNSVILLE, * 1,623, *Yancey Co.*

Bailey, Garrett D., (AV) ... '27 '51 C.77 A.B. L.896 J.D. [Ⓒ Bailey&B.]
Bailey, J. Todd, (BV) ... '58 '83 C.198 B.A. L.575 J.D. [Bailey&B.]
Bailey and Bailey, (BV) ... One Town Square
Buker, Charles E., Jr. '26 '51 C&L.472 B.B.A., J.D.
(adm. in FL; not adm. in NC) P.O. Box 1103‡
Howell, Ronald W., (AV) ... '41 '66 C&L.575 A.B., J.D. [R.W.Howell]
Howell, Ronald W., P.A., (AV) ... 715 East Main Street
Hughes, Farrell W. ... '56 '81 C.925 B.A. L.574 J.D. Law Clk., Supr. Ct.
Laws, Donny Joel, (BV) ... '58 '85 C&L.575 B.A., J.D. P.O. Box 397
Phillips, Robert A. ... '44 '69 C&L.16 B.S., J.D. 109 W. Main
Poe, Leonard, (CV) ... '59 '83 C&L.260 B.S., J.D. 4 Town Sq.
Wilson, Jack L., Jr., (BV) ... '63 '91 C.34 B.S. L.574 J.D. Briggs Bldg., Town Sq.

BUTNER, 5,792, *Granville Co.*

Bulluck, Yvonne E. '69 '95 C.329 B.A. L.575 J.D.
NC Gov. Advocacy Coun. for Persons with Disab.
Burlington, Bill '48 '80 C.112 B.A. L.770 J.D.
(adm. in CA; not adm. in NC) U.S. Bur. of Prisons
Preddy, Laurie Bradsher, (CV) ... '61 '86 C&L.575 A.B., J.D. 410 Central Ave.

CALABASH, 711, *Brunswick Co.*

Anzich, Methodius J. '15 '45 C.966 Ph.B. L.436 LL.B.
(adm. in WI; not adm. in NC) 40 Carolina Shores Pkwy.‡

Baxley, Douglas W., (AV) '46 '75
C&L.575 A.B., J.D. 10164 Beach Drive, SW (⊙Shallotte)
Corbin, Robert D. '17 '46 C.705 A.B. L.997
(adm. in NJ; not adm. in NC) 24 Carolina Shores Dr.‡
Jeffcoat, Otis Allen, III, (AVⓉ) ...... '48 '73 C.674 B.A. L.790 J.D. [Jeffcoat,P.&N.] ⊙

Jeffcoat, Pike & Nappier, LLC, (AVⓉ)
10150 Beach Drive SW, Unit 1, P.O. Box 44000, 28467 ⊙
Telephone: 910-579-4050 Telecopier: 910-579-2770
Email: info@jeffcoatlaw.com URL: http://www.jeffcoatlaw.com
Partners: Otis Allen Jeffcoat, III; Mark A. Nappier. Associates: Amie Sloane; J. Harrison Rushton (Resident).
Real Estate, Estate Planning and Probate, Construction Law, Corporate/Business Law, Auto Accidents, Personal Injury and Homeowners Association Law, Elder Law, Wrongful Death, Real Estate, Commercial real Estate, Real Estate Development, Residential Real Estate Business Law, Contracts, Construction Law, Leases and Leasing, Trusts and Estates, Probate, Wills, Guardianship and Conservatorship, Personal Injury, Wrongful Death, Collections, Homeowners Association Law, foreclosures, Auto Accidents and Injuries, Estate Planning.
Myrtle Beach, South Carolina Office: 2024 Corporate Centre Drive, Suite 206, 29577. Telephone: 843-626-9000. Telecopier: 843-448-1914. Email: info@jeffcoatlaw.com.
North Myrtle Beach, South Carolina Office: 110 Ye Olde Kings Highway, P.O. Box 4360, 29597-4360. Telephone: 843-249-3581. Telecopier: 843-249-6231. Email: info@jeffcoatlaw.com.
Pawleys Island, South Carolina Office: True Blue Executive Center, 9841 Ocean Highway, Suite D, 29585. Telephone: 843-235-0300. Telecopier: 843-235-2056. Email: info@jeffcoatlaw.com.
See Professional Biographies, CALABASH, NORTH CAROLINA

Nappier, Mark A., (BVⓉ) .... '66 '91 C&L.790 B.S., J.D. [Jeffcoat,P.&N.] ⊙
Rushton, J. Harrison '— '02
C.160 B.A. L.790 J.D. [⊠ Jeffcoat,P.&N.] (⊙Myrtle Beach, SC)
Sloane, Amie '74 '03 C.999 B.A. L.1386 J.D.
[⊠ Jeffcoat,P.&N.] (⊙North Myrtle Beach, Pawleys Island, SC)
Trest, Roy D., (AV) .... '48 '77 C.575 B.S. L.500 J.D. [Trest&T.] ⊙

Trest & Twigg, (AV)
9580 Ocean Highway West, 28467
Telephone: 910-575-7337 Fax: 910-575-7338
Email: TrestTwigg@atmc.net
Members of Firm: Roy D. Trest; Tonia Trest Twigg.
General Litigation Practice, Probate, Personal Injury, Wrongful Death, Civil Litigation, Criminal Law, Traffic Violations, DWI.
See Professional Biographies, CALABASH, NORTH CAROLINA

Twigg, Tonia Trest .... '73 '02 C.575 B.A. L.574 J.D. [Trest&T.]

CAMDEN, * 5,904, *Camden Co.*

Hammond, Roy J. '29 '59 C.597 B.S. L.209 J.D.
(adm. in IL; not adm. in NC) Pres. & CEO, Whitehall Consultants, Ltd.‡
Person, Jean F. .... '43 '95 C.232 A.B. L.1339 J.D. 100 Hwy. 343, N.

Vincent Law Firm, The, PC
(See Southern Shores)

CANDLER, —, *Buncombe Co.*

Blanchard, Newman & Hayes
(See Hendersonville)

Contrivo, Frank J., P.A, (BV) ..... '51 '83 C.1175 B.A. L.259 J.D. 111 Camp Creek Drive
Edmonds, James M., (BV) .... '49 '77 C.893 B.A. L.896 J.D. [Sutton&E.]
Neal, Albert M., Jr., (CV) .... '49 '73 C&L.575 B.A., J.D. P.O. Box 1455
Sease, John M. .... '44 '72 C.925 B.S. L.896 J.D. Canton Svgs. & Loan Assn.
Sutton, April Burt .... '70 '00 C.259 B.S. L.1158 J.D. [⊠ Sutton&E.]
Sutton, John R., (BV) .... '43 '71 C.575 B.S. L.273 J.D. [Sutton&E.]
Sutton, John Richard, Jr. .... '74 '00 L.1158 J.D. [⊠ Sutton&E.]
Sutton & Edmonds, (BV) .... 70 Pisgah Highway

CANTON, 4,029, *Haywood Co.*

Burris, Charles L. '19 '49 C.999 L.192 LL.B.
(adm. in GA; not adm. in NC) Rte 5, Box 482B‡
Clark, Walter C., (BV) .... '23 '51 C&L.575 B.S., J.D. Town Atty.
Furci, Frank C. '37 '79 C.1155 B.S.B.A. L.472 J.D.
(adm. in FL; not adm. in NC) Rte. 2, Box 350A‡
Hensley, Robert Edward, Jr. .... '60 '00 C.1111 B.A. L.69 J.D. 94 Main St.
Hensley, Robert J., Jr., (BV) .... '47 '77 2 Church Street
Kuykendall, Janna Dale Allison .... '68 '99 C.925 B.S.B.A. L.616 J.D. P.O. Box 1166
Norwood, Gina L., (CV) .... '69 '96 C.896 B.A. L.421 J.D. 118 Main St., Ste. B
Smathers, Patrick U., (BV) .... '54 '79 C.228 B.A. L.896 J.D. 2 Church St.
Stanley, Patricia Sue '50 '87 C.1223 B.B.A. L.1059 J.D.
(adm. in GA; not adm. in NC) RR 2, Box 270‡

CAROLINA BEACH, 4,701, *New Hanover Co.*

Barnes, Ned M., (BV) .... '55 '81 C.576 B.A. L.1228 J.D. A-3 Pleasure Island Plz.
Calder, Robert, Jr., (BV) .... '50 '84 C.953 B.A. L.575 J.D. [Calder&C.] ⊙
Calder & Calder, (BV) .... 1025-A Lake Park Boulevard (⊙Wilmington)
Ito, Chiaki .... '69 '98 C.575 B.A. L.790 J.D. 200 Wilson Ave.
Jaski, Thomas P., (CV) .... '69 '94 C.228 B.A. L.1228 J.D. A-3 Pleasure Island Plz.
Lewis, James H. '22 '50 C.282 B.A. L.178 LL.B.
(adm. in NY; not adm. in NC) P.O. Box 2227‡
Shilling, William R. .... '61 '04 C.1044 B.S. L.260 J.D. [W.R.Shilling]
Shilling, William R., PLLC .... 503-B South 4th St.

CARRBORO, 16,782, *Orange Co.*

Bircher, Richard .... '46 '74 [Bircher&C.]
Bircher & Connerat .... 216 Carr Mill Mall

Brenman, Lisa R.
(See Carrboro)

Connerat, Jean H. .... '48 '74 C.280 A.B. L.575 J.D. [Bircher&C.]
Danek, Richard Bland .... '66 '94 C&L.575 B.A., J.D. 210 Cedarwood Lane
DeWitt, Gregory .... '72 '03 C.575 B.S. L.574 J.D. [DeWitt L.]
DeWitt Law, PLLC .... 118 E. Main St., Ste. A
Dorosin, Mark Edward .... '65 '94 C.228 B.A. L.575 J.D. P.O. Box 555
Hay, Jennifer Allen .... '63 '01 C.586 B.M. L.575 J.D. 107 Pine St.
Hollers, Russell J., III, (BV) .... '65 '92 C&L.575 B.A., J.D. P.O. Box 1131
Howard, Jeffrey A., (AVⓉ) '60 '85 C&L.846 B.B.A., J.D.
(adm. in TX; not adm. in NC) 133 Friar Ln.
Julian, Alexander, III .... '47 '96 C.790 L.575 J.D. P.O. Box 265
Lee, Victor S. .... '63 '91 C.674 A.B. L.880 J.D. 202 Westbrook Dr
Riek, Jeanne Lanese '63 '89 C.475 B.A. L.215 J.D.
(adm. in IL; not adm. in NC) 103 Wild Oak Lane‡
Seahorn, Susan K., (BV) .... '57 '81 C&L.838 B.A., J.D. Off. of Pub. Def.
Stewman, G. Kevin .... '59 '91 C&L.575 B.S., J.D. [G.K.Stewman]
Stewman, G. Kevin, P.L.L.C. .... P.O. Box 1014

Vira, Lisa Khim .... '70 '00 C.10 B.S. L.574 J.D. [Vira] ⊙

Vira Law Firm, The, PA
205 W. Main Street, Suite 207, 27510 ⊙
Telephone: 919-918-8000 Fax: 919-918-7887
Email: lisa_vira@nc.rr.com URL: http://www.lisakvira.com
Lisa Khim Vira.
Trusts and Estates, Probate, Wills, Real Estate, Taxation, Business Law.
Durham Office: 133 Celeste Circle, 27517. Telephone: 919-918-8000. Fax: 919-918-7887.
See Professional Biographies, CARRBORO, NORTH CAROLINA

Woodson, John W., (BV) .... '42 '69 C&L.575 B.S., J.D. P.O. Box 28

CARTHAGE, * 1,871, *Moore Co.*

Alford, Joy K. .... '74 '03 [⊠ Krueger L.&Assoc.]
Bibey, Stephen A., (CV) .... '58 '97 C.999 B.S. L.574 J.D. 107 S. McNeill St.
Blue, Arthur M., (BV) .... '65 '90 C&L.1228 B.B.A., J.D. 406 Monroe St.
Boyette, Mosley G., Jr., (BV) .... '40 '65 C&L.575 A.B., LL.B. [Boyette&B.]
Boyette & Boyette, (BV) .... P.O. Box 1282
Krueger, Maureen H., (CV) '70 '99
C.1161 B.A. L.150 J.D. Asst. Dist. Atty. [Krueger L.&Assoc.]
Krueger & Associates, Attorneys at Law, (CV) .... 208 Monroe St., 2nd Fl.
Lapping, Stephan F., (CV) .... '56 '86 C.577 B.A. L.575 J.D. 105 E. Barrett St.
Mcsweeney, Warren .... '76 '01 C.673 B.A. L.1228 J.D. Dist. Atty. Off.

Morris Law Office
(See Whispering Pines)

Motta, Stephen F. .... '57 '02 C.1030 B.S. L.574 J.D. Asst. Dist. Atty.
Rothbeind, Matthew, (CV) .... '53 '82 C.24 B.A. L.1398 J.D. [M.Rothbeind]
Rothbeind, Matthew, P.C., (CV) .... 1044 Carriage Oaks
Rowland, Michael C., Jr., (CV) .... '70 '97 C&L.575 B.A., J.D. P.O. Box 637
Stryker, Joseph M. '22 '50 C&L.378 B.S., LL.B.
(adm. in OK; not adm. in NC) P.O. Box 883

Thompson, Hurley E., Jr., (BV) '46 '73 C&L.575 A.B., J.D.
208 Monroe Street, P.O. Box 1300, 28327
Telephone: 910-947-5141; 1-800-756-5943 Facsimile: 910-947-2709
Email: hurthom@mindspring.com
Residential Real Property, Foreclosure, Traffic Offenses, Wills, Estates, Personal Injury.
See Professional Biographies, CARTHAGE, NORTH CAROLINA

Van Camp, Meacham & Newman, PLLC
(See Pinehurst)

Yauger, Brett S., (CV) .... '69 '96 C.576 B.A. L.190 J.D. 406 Monroe St.

CARY, 94,536, *Wake Co.*

Agapion, Stephen .... '32 '56 C&L.575 A.B., LL.B. P.O. Box 309
Alexander, Ann-Margaret, (BV) .... '66 '95 C.790 B.A. L.574 J.D. [Alexander&D.]

Alexander & Doyle, P.A., (BV)
523 Keisler Drive, Suite 102, 27511
Telephone: 919-380-1001 Fax: 919-380-4099
Email: info@alexanderdoylelaw.com URL: http://www.alexander-doylelaw.com
Ann-Margaret Alexander; Andrea S. Nyren Doyle.
Family Law, Child Custody, Child Support, Spousal Support, Domestic Violence, Adoptions, Termination of Parental Rights, Wills, Trusts and Estates, Probate Law, Criminal Law (Misdemeanors), Traffic Law.
See Professional Biographies, CARY, NORTH CAROLINA

Allen, Reynold S. .... '53 '83 C.576 B.A., B.S. L.574 J.D. 824 Chip Cir. (Pat.)
Anderson, Charles N., Jr., (BV) ...'56 '86 C.576 B.A. L.575 J.D. [Ellis&W.] (⊙Raleigh)
Anderson, Elizabeth Terry ....'61 '86 C.896 B.A. L.280 J.D. 100 Regency Forest Drive
Aranda, Andrew R. .... '69 '04 C.846 B.S.M.E. L.326 J.D. [⊠ Coats&B.]

Araneda Law Firm, P.C.
(See Raleigh)

Arnold, Deirdre M. ....'— '94 C.575 B.A. L.1228 J.D. Sr. Corp. Coun., SAS Institute Inc.

Bailey & Dixon, L.L.P.
(See Raleigh)

Baloch, Omar, The Law Offices of
(See Raleigh)

Barish, Jay E. '60 '91 C.145 A.B. L.174 J.D.
(adm. in CO; not adm. in NC) 509 Hearthridge Lane‡
Barringer, Brent D., (AV) .... '59 '84 C&L.575 B.S.B.A., J.D. [Barringer]
Barringer, Tamara, (AV) .... '58 '85 C&L.575 B.S., J.D. [Barringer]

Barringer Law Firm, LLP, (AV)
111 Commonwealth Court, Suite 101, P.O. Box 5566, 27511
Telephone: 919-467-6700 Telecopier: 919-481-9190
Email: admin@barringerlaw.com
Members of Firm: Brent D. Barringer; Tamara Barringer. Associate: Thomas J. Schuettpelz.
Corporate and Business, Estate Planning and Administration. Real Estate, Development and Construction Law, Community Associations, Tax.
References: Branch Banking & Trust Co.; Southern National Bank.
See Professional Biographies, CARY, NORTH CAROLINA

Bayard, David B. .... '62 '00 C.693 B.S. L.575 J.D. [D.B.Bayard]
Bayard, David B., PLLC .... 913 Tanglewood Dr.
Baysinger, Diane .... '73 '04 C.576 B.A. L.190 J.D. [Baysinger&B.]
Baysinger & Bruno, PLLC .... P.O. Box 1604
Begun, Arthur Daniel .... '53 '83 C.696 B.A. L.575 J.D. [A.D.Begun]
Begun, Arthur D. .... 104 Aberson Ct.
Bennett, David E., (BV) .... '59 '85 C.1128 B.A. L.575 J.D. [Coats&B.] (Pat.)
Berger, Erik O. '56 '98 C.453 B.S.E.E. L.487 J.D.
(adm. in MN; not adm. in NC) Infineon Technologies North America Corp.
Biller, Anthony J., (BV) .... '68 '97 C.679 B.A. L.1345 J.D. [Coats&B.]
Blake, Bambee B. .... '70 '95 C.575 B.A. L.1228 J.D. [⊠ Brooks,S.&P.]
Blake, Matthew P. .... '72 '98 C.896 B.A. L.1228 J.D. [Brooks,S.&P.]
Blue, Thomas D., Jr. .... '60 '97 C.48 B.A. L.575 J.D. [Ellis&W.] (⊙Raleigh)
Blumberg, Donna K., (BV) .... '59 '85 C&L.575 B.A., J.D. [⊠ Ellis&W.] (⊙Raleigh)
Boswell, John G. .... '— '85 C&L.790 B.A., J.D. V.P. & Gen. Coun., SAS Institute Inc.
Brewer, Joy H. .... '71 '96 C.575 B.A. L.1228 J.D. [Brooks,S.&P.]

Brewer Law Firm, The
(See Raleigh)

Bridges, Ulmer "Zeke", III .... '77 '03 C.280 B.A. L.1228 J.D. [Bridges]
Bridges Law Firm, PLLC .... 1616 Evans Rd., Ste. 201
Bridgman, David A. .... '72 '98 C.575 B.A. L.896 J.D. [⊠ F.E.Toms&Assoc.]
Brigham, Ronald M. .... '50 '75 C.575 B.S L.347 J.D. 301 Creek Park Dr.

Brinkley, Dewey P.
(See Raleigh)

Brooks, David Victor, (AV) .... '48 '77 C.576 B.A. L.575 J.D. [Brooks,S.&P.] ‡

Brooks, Stevens & Pope, P.A., (AV) BV
11000 Regency Parkway, Suite 401, P.O. Box 1870, 27512-1870
Telephone: 919-481-9103 Fax: 919-481-9137
URL: http://www.bsp-pa.com
David Victor Brooks (Retired); Robert H. Stevens, Jr. (Retired); Daniel Carter Pope, Jr.; Michael C. Sigmon; Kathlyn Corbett Hobbs; Robert S. Welch; Joy H. Brewer; Matthew P. Blake;—Cathy H. Elkins; Bambee B. Blake; Kimberley A. D'Arruda; Leslie Sudbury Haydel; Joel J. Hardison; Rebecca J. Livert; Ginny P. Lanier. Of Counsel: Archie W. Futrell, III.
General Civil and Appellate Practice, Employment Law, OSHA, Workers' Compensation, Insurance, Self-Insurance, Municipal and Family Law.
See Professional Biographies, CARY, NORTH CAROLINA

Brown, Jay M. ....'56 '83 C.197 B.A. L.276 J.D. 123 Barnes Spring Ct. (Pat.)
Brown, Patricia L. '54 '86 C.376 B.M.E. L.575 J.D.
Asst. Gen. Coun., SAS Institute Inc.
Browne, H. Howard, III, (BV) '— '85
C.198 A.B. L.896 J.D. Sr. Corp. Coun., SAS Institute Inc.
Brown-Sumrell, Leah E. ....'63 '92 C.1090 L.383 J.D. Tensky Solutions
Bruno, Danielle I. ....'74 '04 C.754 B.S. L.190 J.D. [Baysinger&B.]

Bumgardner & Rose, P.A.
(See Raleigh)

Bunn, Kevin B., (BV) ...... '63 '93 C&L.575 B.A., J.D. 1125 Kildaire Farm Rd., Ste. 202

Burns, Day & Presnell, P.A.
(See Raleigh)

Bush, Robert J. '66 '93 C.602 B.B.A. L.597 J.D.
(adm. in NY; not adm. in NC) V.P., Gen. Coun. & Corp. Secy., R. H. Donnelley, Inc.
Carlyle, JoAnne L. ....'60 '89 C.1128 B.A. L.1345 J.D. 590 New Waverly Pl.
Carr, Susan Waters, (BV) '69 '94 C.575 B.A. L.1228 J.D.
Sr. Contracts Negotiation Specialist, SAS Institute Inc.
Catalini, Jason Christopher '70 '97 C.454 B.A. L.128 J.D.
(adm. in FL; not adm. in NC) Spectrasite Communications, Inc.
Chamberlin, Andrew S., (AV) ... '64 '90 C&L.280 B.A., J.D. [Ellis&W.] (⊙Greensboro)
Chambers, Jeffrey B. '62 '88 C.105 B.A. L.884 J.D.
Dir. Human Res., SAS Institute, Inc.

Chambers, David R.
(See Raleigh)

Chen, Derek O. ....'72 '98 C.367 B.A. L.575 J.D. 115 Bright Angel Dr.
Chilson, John A. .... '69 '99 C.871 B.S. L.477 J.D. [Ⓐ Ellis&W.] ⊙

Chocklett, Gregory P., Law Offices of
(See Raleigh)

Clifford, Carrie Blythe .... '— '01 C.576 B.A. L.575 J.D. 202 Mackenan Court

Clifton & Singer, L.L.P.
(See Raleigh)

Coats, Larry L., (AV) ....'45 '71 C.576 B.S. L.575 J.D. [Coats&B.] (Pat.)

Coats & Bennett, PLLC, (AV)
1400 Crescent Green, Suite 300, 27511
Telephone: 919-854-1844 Fax: 919-854-2084
URL: http://www.coatsandbennett.com
Larry L. Coats (Resident); David E. Bennett (Resident); John R. Owen (Resident); David D. Kalish; Anthony J. Biller; Michael D. Murphy;—Edward H. Green, III; Andrew R. Aranda; Rebecca Crandall.
Patent, Trademark, Copyright and Unfair Competition Practice before all Courts.
See Professional Biographies, CARY, NORTH CAROLINA

Coleman, Gledhill, Hargrave & Peek, P.C.
(See Hillsborough)

Collier, William H., (BV) .... '58 '83 C.232 B.A. L.1228 J.D. 1150-3 Executive Circle
Cooke, Kim Daniel, (BVⓉ) '55 '81 C.1086 B.A. L.213 J.D.
(adm. in MI; not adm. in NC)
Chairman, General Counsel, Consolidated Mortgage & Financial Services Corporation
Cooper, Lisa I., (AV) '61 '86 C&L.823 B.S., J.D.
Dir. of Envir. Health & Safety Compl., Progress Ventures, Inc.
Corey, Joseph J., Jr. ....'40 '88 C.870 B.S. L.574 J.D. 804 Prince St.
Crandall, Rebecca ....'78 '04 C.185 B.A./B.S. L.575 J.D. [Ⓐ Coats&B.]

Creech, Paul P., Attorney at Law, PLLC
(See Raleigh)

Criner, Sherman Lee, (BV) ....'66 '94 C.576 B.A. L.1228 J.D. [WorkersCompensation] ⊙
Cromer, Charles L., (CV) .... '39 '75 C.575 B.A. L.896 J.D. 503 Center Pointe Drive‡
Curran, Catherine M. '48 '78 C.705 B.A. L.776 J.D.
(adm. in NJ; not adm. in NC) Div. Coun., SAS Institute Inc.‡

Dalton Law Firm, The, P.A.
(See Raleigh)

D'Arruda, Kimberley A. ....'72 '98 C.575 B.S.B.A. L.1228 J.D. [Ⓐ Brooks,S.&P.]
Davenport, Taylor M. .... '72 '97 C&L.228 B.S.E., J.D. [Ⓐ Withrow&T.]
Davis, Randall A. ....'59 '84 C&L.575 B.S., J.D. Bus. Dev. Mgr., SAS Institute Inc.

Davis, Adrian J., Attorney at Law
(See Raleigh)

De Jongh, J. Paul '50 '75 C.855 B.A. L.569 J.D.
(adm. in MA; not adm. in NC) Mktg. Coun., SAS Institute Inc.
DeJongh, John Paul ....'50 '75 C.858 B.A. L.569 J.D. Mktg. Coun., SAS Institute
DelGiorno, John F. ....'52 '90 C.589 B.S. L.365 J.D. 318 Schubauer Dr.
Derrick, Paul H., (BVⓉ) .... '57 '89 C.572 B.A. L.790 J.D. [Jackson L.]
Devine, Julie Z. .... '— '03 C.228 B.A. L.1565 J.D. 2500 Regency Pkwy., Ste. 236
Dick, Geoffrey C. '66 '91 C.1365 B.S. L.790 J.D.
(adm. in GA; not adm. in NC) 11000 Regency Pkwy
Dillon, Mary M., (AV) ....'66 '93 C.575 A.B. L.893 J.D. [Ellis&W.]
Doyle, Andrea S. Nyren, (BV) .... '68 '95 C.232 B.S. L.574 J.D. [Alexander&D.]

Eads, Wayne Buchanan
(See Raleigh)

Earls, Thomas A., (BV) ....'48 '74 C.319 B.A. L.228 J.D. 102-A Commonwealth Ct.
Early, Stephanie Barr ....'67 '94 C.1044 B.A. L.994 J.D. 109 Dagenham Lane
Edwards, Debra Cole ....'61 '91 C.577 B.A. L.574 J.D. P.O. Box 1358
Elkins, Cathy H. ....'59 '87 C.162 B.A. L.575 J.D. [Ⓐ Brooks,S.&P.]
Ellis, Richard W., (AV) ....'42 '69 C&L.575 A.B., J.D. [Ellis&W.] (⊙Raleigh)

Ellis & Winters LLP, (AV)
1100 Crescent Green, Suite 200, 27511-8105 ⊙
Telephone: 919-865-7000 Facsimile: 919-865-7010
URL: http://www.elliswinters.com
Richard W. Ellis; Michael G. Winters; Jonathan D. Sasser; Leslie C. O'Toole; Charles N. Anderson, Jr.; Paul K. Sun, Jr.; Matthew W. Sawchak; Andrew S. Chamberlin; Alex J. Hagan; Julia F. Youngman; Thomas D. Blue, Jr.; Curtis J. Shipley; Mary M. Dillon. Associates: Suzanne Collins

(This Listing Continued)

Ellis & Winters LLP (Continued)
Lagerholm; Wendy I. Sexton; George F. Sanderson, III; Danielle Eng Rose; Thomas H. Segars; Brian C. Vick; Stephen C. Keadey; John A. Chilson. Of Counsel: Donna K. Blumberg.
Trial and Appellate Practice in all State and Federal Courts. Commercial Litigation, Administrative Litigation, Medical Malpractice, Products Liability, Antitrust, Corporate, Real Estate and Finance.
Raleigh, North Carolina Office: P.O. Box 33550, 27636. Telephone: 919-865-7000. Facsimile: 919-865-7010.
Greensboro, North Carolina Office: 100 N. Greene Street, Suite 102, 27401. Telephone: 336-217-4193. Facsimile: 336-217-4198.
See Professional Biographies, CARY, NORTH CAROLINA

Everett, Gaskins, Hancock & Stevens, LLP
(See Raleigh)

Exum, Carol Wooten .... '70 '95 C.228 B.A. L.893 J.D. 304 Camden Branch Dr.
Fleming, Robert David '60 '99 C.69 B.A. L.192 J.D.
(adm. in TN; not adm. in NC) Sr. Contracts Negotiation Specialist, SAS Institute Inc.

Flexner Law Firm, The, P.A.
(See Raleigh)

Ford, Jeanne B., (BV) .... '46 '98 C.822 B.A. L.574 J.D. [Ⓐ C.H.Montgomery]
Forehand, Karen .... '64 '93 C.1059 B.A. L.228 J.D. Ste. 150, 2000 Regency Pkwy.
French, James C., Jr. '53 '80 C&L.575 B.A., J.D.
Chief Exec. Off., The DreamCatcher Co. of N.C., LLC
Frick, Amy J. '68 '99 C&L.805 B.A., J.D.
(adm. in DC; not adm. in NC) The Dialog Corporation
Futrell, Archie W., III, (AV) ....'54 '78 C&L.575 A.B., J.D. [Ⓒ Brooks,S.&P.]

Gailor, Wallis & Hunt, PLLC
(See Raleigh)

Gibbs, Benita Walker '60 '90 C.575 B.A. L.1228 J.D.
209 South Academy Street Main Level, 27511
Telephone: 919-481-0903 Fax: 919-481-0882
Email: bgibbslaw@hotmail.com URL: http://www.caryrealestatesclosing.com
Residential Real Estate, Commercial Real Estate, Mortgages, Construction Loans, Equity Finance, Reverse Mortgages.
See Professional Biographies, CARY, NORTH CAROLINA

Graebe, William Siegfried ....'63 '92 C.362 B.B.A. L.896 J.D. P.O. Box 1929
Grantmyre, William E. '45 '70
C.576 B.A. L.575 J.D. V.P. & Gen. Coun., Heater Utilities, Inc.
Graves, Wm. Griffin, III, (AV) .....'50 '76 C.575 A.B. L.896 J.D. [Higgins,F.G.&M.] ⊙
Gray, Philip T. .... '69 '97 C.576 B.S. L.1228 J.D. [Stephenson&S.]
Green, Edward H., III ....'61 '99 C.834 B.S.E.E. L.574 J.D. [Ⓐ Coats&B.]
Green, Jay B. ....'70 '97 C.1111 B.S. L.615 J.D. 103-A Kilmayne Dr.
Gregg, William J. '15 '42 C.299 L.564 LL.B.
(adm. in NY; not adm. in NC) 216 Excalibur Ct.‡
Grimes, Donald W. .... '44 '71 C&L.575 A.B., J.D. 903 Kildaire Farm Rd.
Haddon, M. Leigh '54 '83 C.94 B.S. L.1137 J.D.
(adm. in CA; not adm. in NC) SAS Campus Dr.
Hagan, Alex J., (AV) ....'65 '92 C&L.575 B.A., J.D. [Ellis&W.] (⊙Raleigh)
Hall, John H., Jr., (BV) ....'63 '90 C&L.896 B.A., J.D. King Pharmaceuticals
Hall, Jonathan E., (BV) ....'67 '93 C.575 B.A. L.896 J.D. [Hall&M.]

Hall, Kyle S.
(See Raleigh)

Hall & Messick, LLP, (BV) ....1225 Crescent Green
Hardison, Joel J. ....'76 '04 C&L.575 B.A., J.D. [Ⓐ Brooks,S.&P.]
Hatch, Richard C. .... '28 '53 C.95 A.B. L.178 J.D. 217 Beachers Brook Lane
Haydel, Leslie Sudbury ....'66 '92 C.974 B.A. L.602 J.D. [Ⓐ Brooks,S.&P.]

Haynsworth Baldwin Johnson & Greaves LLC
(See Ogletree, Deakins, Nash, Smoak & Stewart, P.C., Raleigh)

Heath, Charlotte A. '56 '80 C.269 B.A. L.790 J.D.
(adm. in SC; not adm. in NC) First V.P. & Tr. Offr., Central Carolina Bk. & Tr. Co.

Hedspeth Law Firm, PLLC
(See Raleigh)

Hemphill, Nancy H., (BV) ....'56 '81 C.95 A.B. L.575 J.D. 106 Dorchester Pines Ct.
Henderson, Mark, Law Offices of '57 '86
C.886 B.S. L.280 J.D. 531 Keisler Drive, Suite 201
Hepburn, Kari L. ....'67 '97 C&L.260 B.S., J.D. [Ⓐ Vining&Assoc.]

Herring McBennett Mills & Finkelstein, PLLC
(See Raleigh)

Hester, John F. ....'49 '75 C.576 B.A. L.574 J.D. Lawyers Mutual Liability Ins. Co.

Higgins, Frankstone, Graves & Morris, P.A., (AV)
14600 Weston Parkway, Suite 300, 27513-2259 ⊙
Telephone: 919-968-8880 Fax: 919-678-8885
Email: info@hfgmcary.com URL: http://www.hfgmlaw.com
Wm. Griffin Graves, III.
Estate Planning, Probate, Corporate, Real Estate, Civil Litigation, Taxation and Business Law.
Chapel Hill, North Carolina Office: 1414 Raleigh Road, Suite 320. Telephone: 919-968-4717. Fax: 919-929-1415.
See Professional Biographies, CARY, NORTH CAROLINA

Hilbert Law Firm, The, PLLC
(See Raleigh)

Hobbs, Kathlyn Corbett ....'62 '91 C.550 B.A. L.1338 J.D. [Brooks,S.&P.]
Holland, Brian G. '63 '90 C.1109 B.A. L.276 J.D.
(adm. in TX; not adm. in NC) General Counsel, Global Knowledge, Inc.

Hollowell Law Offices, P.A.
(See Cary)

Holmes, Kenneth H. '36 '62 C&L.494 B.S.L., LL.B.
(adm. in NY; not adm. in NC) 105 Weeping Beach Way‡
Holmsen, Lisa Wright ....'56 '88 C.475 B.A. L.574 J.D. 411 New Rail Dr.

Holt York McDarris & High, LLP
(See Raleigh)

Hough, Joseph Mark ....'— '95 C.154 B.A. L.880 J.D. Sr. Corp. Coun., SAS Institute Inc.

Howard, Stallings, From & Hutson, P.A.
(See Raleigh)

Hubbard, Brett A. '54 '88 C.575 B.A. L.1228 J.D.
1220 S. E. Maynard Road, Suite 203, 27511
Telephone: 919-460-6883 Fax: 919-460-8932
Email: hubbard3@bellsouth.net URL: http://www.bretthubbardlaw.com
Family Law, Separation Agreements, Child Custody, Child Support, Divorce, Bankruptcy, Bankruptcy Chapter 7, Bankruptcy Chapter 13, Wills, Estate Planning, Probate, Estate Administration, Traffic Violations, Criminal Law, Driving While Intoxicated, Real Estate, Employment Law, Small Business Law, Personal Injury.
See Professional Biographies, CARY, NORTH CAROLINA

Jackson Lewis LLP, (BVⓉ)
1400 Crescent Green, Suite 320, 27511 ⊙
Telephone: 919-854-0044 Facsimile: 919-854-0908
URL: http://www.jacksonlewis.com
Partners: Paul H. Derrick; Richard S. McAtee (Not admitted in NC; Managing Partner, Raleigh-Durham Office).
Employment, Labor, Benefits, Immigration Law, and Other Related Litigation, On Behalf of Management Exclusively.
Other offices located in: Atlanta, GA; Boston, MA; Chicago, IL; Dallas, TX; Greenville, SC; Hartford, CT; Long Island, NY; Los Angeles, CA; Miami, FL; Minneapolis, MN; Morristown, NJ; New York, NY; Orlando, FL; Pittsburgh, PA; Sacramento, CA; San Francisco, CA; Seattle, WA; Stamford, CT; Vienna, VA; White Plains, NY.
Satellite Offices: 127 Dorrance Street, Providence, Rhode Island 02903. Phone: 401-490-3444. Fax: 401-454-8855.
1225 Market Street, Wheeling, West Virginia 26003. Phone: 304-230-1461. Fax: 304-230-1462.
11 Federal Plaza, Suite 300, Youngstown, OH 44503. Phone: 330-746-2324. Fax: 330-746-7023.

See Professional Biographies, CARY, NORTH CAROLINA

Janak Law Firm, P.A.
(See Raleigh)

Jernigan, Miriam K. .... '55 '81 C.228 B.S.N. L.893 J.D. 735 Preston Grove Ave.
Johanson Berenson LLP, (AVⓉ)
201 Shannon Oaks Circle, Suite 200 (⊙Napa, CA; Wash., DC; Great Falls, VA)

Jordan Price Wall Gray Jones & Carlton
(See Raleigh)

Kalish, David D. .... '67 '97 C.576 B.S. L.1218 J.D. [Coats&B.] (Pat.)
Keadey, Stephen C. .... '69 '03 C&L.575 A.B., J.D. [🄰 Ellis&W.] (⊙Raleigh)
Keim, David Brent '— '91 C.999 B.A. L.1339 J.D.
(adm. in VA; not adm. in NC) Sr. Corp. Coun., SAS Institute Inc.

Kirby & Holt, L.L.P.
(See Raleigh)

Kirkhart, H C. .... '43 '91 C.768 B.S. L.574 J.D. 1350 SE Maynard Rd.
Klemm, Brian W. '— '81 C.555 B.S. L.776 J.D.
(adm. in NJ; not adm. in NC) Mktg. Coun., SAS Institute Inc.

Knott, Clark & Berger, L.L.P.
(See Raleigh)

Kuruc, Joan W. .... '50 '94 C.575 B.A. L.424 J.D. [🄰 F.E.Toms&Assoc.]
Lagerholm, Suzanne Collins .... '67 '99 C&L.575 B.A., J.D. [🄰 Ellis&W.] (⊙Raleigh)
Lanier, Ginny P. .... '76 '03 C.34 B.S.B.A. L.1228 J.D. [🄰 Brooks,S.&P.]
Ledbetter, Joel R. .... '68 '94 C.575 B.A. L.1228 J.D. [Ledbetter&T.]

Ledbetter & Titsworth, P.A.
1135 Kildaire Farm Road, 27511
Telephone: 919-460-9798; Toll Free: 888-222-9656 Fax: 919-460-9631
URL: http://www.ledbetterandtitsworth.com
Joel R. Ledbetter; Daniel B. Titsworth.
Workers Compensation, Personal Injury, Automobile Accidents, Trucking Accidents, Medical Malpractice.

See Professional Biographies, CARY, NORTH CAROLINA

Liggin, Susan Anne .... '59 '99 C.576 B.A. L.574 J.D. P.O. Box 4081
Livert, Rebecca J. .... '78 '05 C.575 B.A. L.1228 J.D. [🄰 Brooks,S.&P.]
Lynch, John H. '58 '84 C.611 B.A. L.608 J.D.
(adm. in OH; not adm. in NC)
Vice President & General Counsel, SpectraSite Communications, Inc.
Malone, Lois L. .... '45 '75 C&L.705 B.A., J.D. 963 N. Harrison Ave.

Manning & Crouch
(See Raleigh)

Manning, Fulton & Skinner, P.A.
(See Raleigh)

Maple, Marie-Claire B. '64 '92 C.475 B.S.E.E. L.818 J.D.
(adm. in MA; not adm. in NC; Pat.) Infineon Technologies North America Corp.
Maready, Ken .... '69 '97 C&L.896 B.A., J.D. [Venture]
Markle, Suzanne .... '55 '92 C.36 B.A. L.228 J.D. Level 8 Systems, Inc.
Massarelli, Matthew S. .... '66 '91 C.473 B.S. L.930 J.D. TowerCo, Inc.
McAtee, Richard S. '69 '95 C.188 B.S.I.L.R L.229 J.D.
(adm. in PA; not adm. in NC) [Jackson L.] (⊙Pitts., PA)
McCoppin, Andrew, (BV) .... '— '95 C.112 B.A. L.1065 J.D. [A.McCoppin]

McCoppin, Andrew, P.A., The Law Office of, (BV)
1320 S.E. Maynard Road, Suite 102, 27511
Mailing Address: P.O. Box 2884, Raleigh, NC 27602
Telephone: 919-516-3622 Toll Free: 888-516-3622 Fax: 919-462-8089 URL: http://www.amccoppinlaw.com
Email: andrewmccoppin@nc.rr.com URL: http://www.andrewmccoppin.com
Andrew McCoppin.
Driving While Intoxicated, Traffic Violations, Violent Crimes, Drug Crimes, White Collar Crimes, Domestic Violence and Federal Criminal Law.

See Professional Biographies, CARY, NORTH CAROLINA

McCuiston, W. Thomas .... '66 '98 C&L.575 B.S., J.D. [McCuiston]
McCuiston Law Offices, PLLC .... 3750 NW Cary Parkway, Suite 105
McKinnie, Dennis '57 '83 C.868 B.A. L.192 J.D.
(adm. in AL; not adm. in NC)
Sr. V.P., Chf. Legal and Admin. Offr., Level 8 Systems, Inc.

Mediratta Law Firm
(See Raleigh)

Messick, William Curtis .... '65 '00 C.575 B.A. L.574 J.D. [Hall&M.]
Meyer, Jaye Powell, (AV) .... '61 '90 C.896 B.A. L.575 J.D. [Tharrington S.] ⊙
Miller, Marty E. .... '58 '95 C.232 B.S. L.1339 J.D. [Miller&S.]

Miller & Shedor, PLLC
Cooper Building, Suite 100, 315 N. Academy Street, P.O. Box 3525, 27519-3525
Telephone: 919-462-1640 Fax: 919-462-1641
Members of the Firm: Marty E. Miller; Peter R. Shedor. Associate: Solomon B. Weiner.
Criminal Law, Driving While Intoxicated, Juvenile Crimes, Traffic Violations, Bankruptcy, Foreclosures, Family Law, Adoptions, Child Support, Child Custody, Divorce, Visitation Rights, Real Estate, Landlord and Tenant Law, Wills, Probate, Collections, Personal Injury, Automobile Accidents, Slip and Fall, Wrongful Death, Workers Compensation, Discrimination, Sexual Harassment, Wrongful Termination.

See Professional Biographies, CARY, NORTH CAROLINA

Millikan, Kathleen M., (BV) .... '62 '91 C&L.575 B.S.N., J.D. [Hall&M.]
Mills, Allen .... '64 '89 C.383 B.A. L.494 J.D. [🄰 F.E.Toms&Assoc.]
Monaco, Michael A. .... '73 '00 C&L.576 B.S.C.E., J.D. 2500 Regency Parkway
Monteith, Charles E. .... '55 '80 C&L.575 B.A., J.D. 105 Joust Ct.

Montgomery, Charles H., Law Offices of, (AV) '49 '74 C.228 B.A. L.880 J.D.
590 New Waverly Place, Suite 110, P.O. Box 1325, 27512-1325
Mailing Address: P.O. Box 1325, Cary, NC 27512-1325
Telephone: 919-816-9002 919-816-9003
Email: charles@montylaw.com URL: http://www.montylaw.com
Board Certified Specialist in Family Law, North Carolina State Board of Legal Specialization.

(This Listing Continued)

Montgomery, Charles H., Law Offices of (Continued)

Associate: Jeanne B. Ford.
Family Law, Civil Litigation, Civil Appeals, Mediation, Arbitration, Divorce, Separation Agreements, Child Custody, Spousal Support, Marital Property Distribution, Premarital Agreements.

See Professional Biographies, CARY, NORTH CAROLINA

Moreau, David S. .... '70 '98 C&L.575 B.A., J.D. Corp. Coun., Konover Property Trust
Murphy, Dean F., (BV) ... '59 '86 C.896 B.S. L.575 J.D. 1140 Kildaire Farm Rd., Ste. 307
Murphy, Michael D. .... '— '04 C.561 B.S.E.E. L.574 J.D. [Coats&B.] (Pat.)
Musacchia, Mary U., (AV) '— '77
C.502 B.S. L.734 J.D. Coun. to the Pres., SAS Institute Inc.
Nanney, Elaine R. .... '58 '86 C.896 B.S. L.575 J.D. Asst. Exec. Dir., N.C. Bar Assn.
Nesbitt, Stephanie A., (BV) .... '56 '84 C&L.477 B.B.A., J.D. 101 Lochwood E. Dr.
Osborne, Amy Whinery .... '72 '97 C&L.862 B.S.B.A., J.D. [A.W.Osborne]
Osborne, Amy Whinery, P.C., The Law Offices of .... 1135 Kildaire Farm Road, Suite 200
O'Toole, Leslie C., (AV) .... '61 '86 C.103 A.B. L.575 J.D. [Ellis&W.] (⊙Raleigh)
Owen, John R. .... '60 '96 C.228 B.S.E. L.575 J.D. [Coats&B.] (Pat.)
Padovano, Robert K. .... '66 '92 C.576 B.A. L.1187 J.D. [Padovano&Z.]
Padovano & Zillioux .... 1330 SE Maynard Rd.
Pardue, James H. .... '52 '81 C.34 B.S.B.A. L.575 J.D. 1140 Kildaire Farm Road

Patterson, Dilthey, Clay, Bryson & Anderson, L.L.P.
(See Raleigh)

Payne, John Abb ...... '69 '98 C.575 B.A. L.910 J.D. 11000 Regency Parkway, Suite 401
Peaslee, William W., (BV) .... '66 '91 C.575 B.A. L.1345 J.D. 102-K Commonwealth Ct.
Phillips, Michael C. .... '53 '96 C.576 E.E. L.574 J.D. P.O. Box 1245

Pinna Johnston & Burwell, P.A.
(See Raleigh)

Pope, Daniel Carter, Jr., (AV) .... '64 '88 C.576 B.A. L.575 J.D. [Brooks,S.&P.]
Porter, Karen Meyer '52 '83
C.846 B.A. L.190 J.D. Gen. Coun., Relativity Technologies, Inc.
Powell, Clabron Ann, (BVⓉ) '41 '78 C.471 A.B. L.969 J.D.
(adm. in GA; not adm. in NC) 200 New Londondale Drive
Powell, Dillard M. .... '25 '70 C.576 B.S. L.577 J.D. 203 New Edition Court
Pratt, Claire B. .... '— '80 C.682 A.B. L.575 J.D. Mktg. Coun., SAS Institute Inc.

Ragsdale Liggett PLLC
(See Raleigh)

Rebeor, Daniel E. '68 '94 C.1044 B.S. L.201 J.D.
(adm. in OH; not adm. in NC) Director, Real Estate Operations, SpectraSite Comm., Inc.
Reed, J. George '49 '78 C.259 B.A. L.893 J.D.
Baptist State Convention of North Carolina
Reinhard, Steven I., (AV) '61 '85 C&L.575 B.S., J.D.
100 Regency Forest Dr., Suite 400

Richardson, Jonathan, The Law Office of '68 '04 C.575 B.A. L.201 J.D.
1140 Kildaire Farm Road, Suite 305, 27511
Telephone: 919-469-9904 Fax: 919-469-9905
Email: realestateattorney@earthlink.net URL: http://www.richardsonlaw-firm.com
Personal Injury, Real Estate, Closings, Workers Compensation, Injuries, Traffic Violations, Tickets, Wrongful Death.

See Professional Biographies, CARY, NORTH CAROLINA

Riggsbee, Renee C., (AV) .... '51 '86 C.471 B.A. L.575 J.D. Lawyers Mutual
Rives, Elizabeth C. '67 '00
C&L.575 B.A., J.D. Title Mgr., SpectraSite Communications, Inc.
Rodgers, Dwight G., Jr. .... '66 '98 C.383 B.A. L.546 J.D. [Hall&M.]
Rose, Danielle Eng .... '72 '00 C.945 B.A. L.228 J.D. [🄰 Ellis&W.] (⊙Raleigh)
Roy, Melissa M. .... '— '91 C.31 B.A. L.93 J.D. Sr. Mktg. Coun., SAS Institute, Inc.
Rubel, Douglas A., (AVⓉ) .... '59 '86 C.494 B.S. L.904 J.D. [Johanson B.]
Sanderson, George F., III .... '73 '00 C.276 A.B. L.569 J.D. [🄰 Ellis&W.] (⊙Raleigh)
Sargent, Dennis J., Jr. '65 '96 C.239 B.S. L.1338 J.D.
(adm. in DE; not adm. in NC) Lead Title Manager, SpectraSite Communication, Inc.
Sasser, Jonathan D., (AV) .... '56 '81 C&L.575 B.A., J.D. [Ellis&W.] (⊙Raleigh)

Sasser, Travis, (BV) '74 '99 C.576 B.A. L.280 J.D.
875 Walnut Street, Suite 342, 27511
Telephone: 919-319-7400 Fax: 919-657-7400 URL: http://www.carybankruptcy.com
Email: tsasser@carybankruptcy.com URL: http://www.lawyers.com/carybankruptcy
(Board Certified Specialist in Consumer Bankruptcy Law by North Carolina State Board of Legal Specialization).
Bankruptcy, Consumer Bankruptcy, Commercial Bankruptcy, Foreclosures.

See Professional Biographies, CARY, NORTH CAROLINA

Sawchak, Matthew W., (AV) ...... '62 '89 C.309 A.B. L.228 J.D. [Ellis&W.] (⊙Raleigh)
Schuettpelz, Thomas J. .... '73 '98 C.436 B.A. L.896 J.D. [🄰 Barringer]
Segars, Thomas H. .... '75 '00 C.896 B.A. L.575 J.D. [🄰 Ellis&W.] (⊙Raleigh)
Sexton, Wendy I. .... '73 '99 C.575 B.A. L.896 J.D. [🄰 Ellis&W.] (⊙Raleigh)
Shedor, Peter R. .... '55 '88 C.999 B.S. L.1228 J.D. [Miller&S.]
Shipley, Curtis J. .... '63 '90 C.597 B.S. L.352 J.D. [Ellis&W.] ⊙
Shuster, Barry K., Law Offices of ..... '57 '00 C.112 B.A. L.574 J.D. 103-A Kilmayne Dr.
Sigmon, Michael C., (BV) .... '61 '86 C.576 B.A. L.575 J.D. [Brooks,S.&P.]

Simmons, Stephen Russell, Attorney and Counsellor at Law
(See Raleigh)

Sloane, Jay R. .... '— '86 C.1044 B.A. L.1009 J.D. Sr. Mktg. Coun., SAS Institute Inc.
Smith, Shannon H. .... '74 '00 C.576 B.A. L.124 J.D. [🄲 B.E.Wood]

Sokol McLamb Schilawski Oliver Ladd PLLC
(See Raleigh)

Sours, Paula Barnes .... '53 '99 C.296 B.S. L.575 J.D. Corp. Coun., SAS Institute Inc.
Southerland, Marcia N. .... '66 '94 C.576 B.A. L.1228 J.D. [Stephenson&S.]
Stephenson, James B., II, (BV) .... '58 '84 C.240 B.A. L.1228 J.D. [Stephenson&S.]
Stephenson, Neil W., Jr. .... '58 '85 C&L.1228 B.S., J.D. 8000 Weston Pkwy., Ste. 340
Stephenson, Richard C. .... '64 '92 C.34 B.S.B.A. L.1228 J.D. [Stephenson&S.]★

Stephenson & Stephenson, LLP, (BV)
580 New Waverly Place Suite 240, 27511
Telephone: 919-858-7008 Fax: 919-858-8414
URL: http://www.stephensonandstephenson.com
Members of Firm: James B. Stephenson II; Richard C. Stephenson. Associates: Marcia N. Southerland; Philip T. Gray; Dena White Waters.
Insurance Defense, Construction Litigation, Condemnation, Personal Injury, Health Care Law, Corporate Law, Estate Planning, Estate Administration, Commercial and Residential Real Estate, Foreclosures, Civil Litigation, Collections, Contract Litigation.

See Professional Biographies, CARY, NORTH CAROLINA

Stevens, Rebecca L., (BV) .... '53 '86 C.575 B.A. L.1228 J.D. 547 Keisler Dr., Ste. 204
Stevens, Robert H., Jr., (AV) .... '41 '71 C.835 B.S. L.838 J.D. [Brooks,S.&P.] ‡
Stewart, Stephen P. .... '66 '92 C&L.790 B.S., J.D. [Stewart]

Stewart Law Office, PLLC
201 Shannon Oaks Circle, Suite 200, 27511
Telephone: 919-654-4583 Fax: 919-654-4584
Email: sstewart@carylawoffice.com URL: http://www.stewartlawoffice.com

(This Listing Continued)

Stewart Law Office, PLLC (Continued)

Stephen P. Stewart.
Estate Planning, Trusts, Living Trusts, Trusts and Estates, Wills, Business Law, Contracts, Corporate Law.
See Professional Biographies, CARY, NORTH CAROLINA

Stroud, W. Randall, (BV) .... '62 '94 C.198 A.B. L.575 J.D. [Waller,S.&S.]
Sullivan, John D. .... '61 '93 C.602 B.A. L.1187 J.D. 206 Crickentree Drive

Sullivan & Grace, P.A.
(See Raleigh)

Sun, Paul K., Jr., (AV) ....'57 '89 C.967 B.A. L.228 J.D. [Ellis&W.] (⊙Raleigh)
Taylor, Marvin E., Jr. ....'37 '66 C&L.575 A.B., J.D. 119 S.W. Maynard Rd.

Tenney & Tenney, LLP
(See Raleigh)

Terranova, Steven N. ....'70 '99 C.576 B.S. L.574 J.D. [Withrow&T.]
Tharrington Smith, (AV) ....106 B Fountain Brook Cir. (⊙Raleigh)
Thorstad, J. Cheryl .... '62 '87 C.886 B.S. L.945 J.D. 102 Kettlebridge Dr.
Tilson, Hugh H., Jr., (AV) '63 '94
C&L.575 B.A., J.D. V.P. Cust Rel. & Assoc. Gen. Coun.
Titsworth, Daniel B. ....'62 '94 C.339 B.A. L.1228 J.D. [Ledbetter&T.]
Toms, Frederic E., (BV) ....'41 '70 C&L.575 B.A., J.D. [F.E.Toms&Assoc.]

Toms, Frederic E., & Associates, PLLC, (BV)
103-A Kilmayne Drive, 27511
Telephone: 919-467-3294 Fax: 919-467-3296
URL: http://www.frederictomslaw.com
Frederic E. Toms;—David A. Bridgman; Allen Mills; Joan W. Kuruc.
Personal Injury, Medical Malpractice, Creditor, Traffic Violations, Nursing Home Litigation, Automobile Accidents, Wrongful Death.
See Professional Biographies, CARY, NORTH CAROLINA

Tower, Daniel T., P.A.
(See Raleigh)

Twiggs, Beskind, Strickland & Rabenau, P.A.
(See Raleigh)

Twomey, Richard J. ......'70 '96 C.575 B.S. L.1228 J.D. 1320 S.E. Maynard Rd., Ste. 101

Venture Counsel
408 Legault Drive, 27513
Telephone: 919-463-5500 Fax: 919-463-5600
Email: ken@venture-counsel.com URL: http://www.venture-counsel.com
Ken Maready.
Venture Capital, Entrepreneurial Law; Corporate Law; Securities Law; Technology and Science.
See Professional Biographies, CARY, NORTH CAROLINA

Vick, Brian C. ....'72 '02 C.881 B.A. L.280 J.D. [🄰 Ellis&W.] (⊙Raleigh)
Vining, Julia Baughman ....'60 '88 C.914 B.A. L.800 J.D. [🄰 Vining&Assoc.]
Vining, Steven J., (BV) ....'57 '85 C.454 B.A. L.800 J.D. [Vining&Assoc.]
Vining & Associates, PLLC, (BV) ....1003 High House Road, Suite 106
Vohlers, Richard J. '55 '79 C&L.37 B.A., J.D.
(adm. in AZ; not adm. in NC) 110 Livingstone Dr.‡
Waller, Betty S., (BV) ....'46 '82 C.576 B.A. L.1228 J.D. [Waller,S.&S.]
Waller, Stroud & Stewart, LLP, (BV) ....201 Shannon Oaks Circle, Suite 200
Ward, J. Randolph, (AV) ....'53 '78 C&L.896 B.A., J.D. 311 Fairfield Lane
Ward, Linda K., Law Office of, (CV) '70 '98
C.999 B.A. L.574 J.D. 201 Shannon Oaks Circle, Ste. 200

Washburn, Jeanne H.
(See Raleigh)

Waters, Dena White ....'74 '01 C.471 B.A. L.1228 J.D. [Stephenson&S.]
Way, Mark J., (BVⓉ) '55 '79 C.1062 B.A. L.930 J.D.
(adm. in PA; not adm. in NC) Senior Attorney & Senior Secretary, Lord Corp.
Weiner, Solomon B. ....'51 '02 C.576 B.A. L.575 J.D. [🄰 Miller&S.]
Weiss, Jennifer, (BV) ....'59 '86 C.575 A.B. L.893 J.D. 303 Tibbetts Rock Dr.
Welch, Robert S., (BV) ....'58 '88 C.923 B.A. L.1228 J.D. [Brooks,S.&P.]

Wellons Law Firm, The
(See Raleigh)

White, H. Glenn, III '53 '79 C&L.575 B.A., J.D.
V.P. & Gen. Coun., White Oil Co., Inc.

Williams, Edward V., Attorney at Law
(See Raleigh)

Wilson, Timothy K. '— '92 C.645 B.S. L.823 J.D.
(adm. in PA; not adm. in NC) Sr. Corp. Coun., SAS Institute Inc.
Winters, Michael G., (AV) ....'53 '78 C&L.575 B.S., J.D. [Ellis&W.] (⊙Raleigh)
Withrow, Benjamin S. ....'68 '95 C.561 B.S.E.E. L.1218 J.D. [Withrow&T.] (Pat.)
Withrow & Terranova, PLLC ....201 Shannon Oaks Circle, Suite 200 (Pat.)
Wood, Brent E., (BV) ....'62 '89 C&L.896 B.A., J.D. [B.E.Wood]
Wood, Brent E., P.L.L.C., (BV) ....3750 N.W. Cary Pkwy., Ste. 111
Workers Compensation Law Firm, The, (BV)
1120 Southeast Cary Parkway Suite 201 (⊙Wilmington)
Wright, James W. '40 '67 C&L.838 B.S., J.D.
(adm. in TN; not adm. in NC; Pat.) V.P., Legal Affs. & Secy., Lord Corp.
Yeager, James B., Law Office of '50 '85 C.531 B.A. L.1209 J.D.
1220 S.E. Maynard Road
Younger, T. Carlton, Jr., (AV) '48 '75 C&L.575 B.A., J.D.
Lawyers Mutual Liability Insurance Co. of NC
Youngman, Julia F., (AV) .... '65 '94 C&L.228 B.S., J.D. [Ellis&W.] (⊙Raleigh)
Zillioux, Kristen Laurenti .... '69 '94 C.1044 B.A. L.982 J.D. [Padovano&Z.]
Zuercher, Brian K. .... '— '89 C.494 B.A. L.575 J.D. Sr. Mngt. Atty., SAS Institute Inc.

CASHIERS, 196, *Jackson Co.*

Alexander, John R. '32 '63 C&L.575 B.A., LL.B.
(adm. in FL; not adm. in NC) P.O. Box 9
Andrews, William Robert '21 '70 C.610 B.S.C.E. L.472 J.D.
(adm. in FL; not adm. in NC) P.O. Box 2382‡
Black, Lynda M. ....'42 '93 C.1222 B.S. L.1158 J.D. [Henson&B.]
Coward, Kimberly R., (BV) ....'62 '88 C.350 B.A. L.575 J.D. [Coward,H.&S.]
Coward, William H., (BV) ....'58 '87 C.198 B.A. L.575 J.D. [Coward,H.&S.]

Coward, Hicks & Siler, P.A., (AV)
211 Cashiers School Road, P.O. Box 1918, 28717 ⊙
Telephone: 828-743-2401 Fax: 828-743-2403
Ralph L. Hicks; Kimberly R. Coward; William H. Coward.
General Practice in all Courts. Trials, Eminent Domain, Personal Injury and Workers Compensation, Probate, Estate Planning, Real Estate, Corporations, Family Law.
Sylva, North Carolina Office: 705 West Main Street, 28779. Telephone: 828-586-2147. Fax: 828-586-2605.

(This Listing Continued)

Coward, Hicks & Siler, P.A. (Continued)

Franklin, North Carolina Office: 43 West Main Street, 28734. Telephone: 828-524-6475. Fax: 828-524-9833.
See Professional Biographies, CASHIERS, NORTH CAROLINA

Culpepper, L. Polk '48 '74 C&L.420 B.A., J.D.
(adm. in KY; not adm. in NC) P.O. Box 32‡
Ellis, Benjamin D. ....'69 '97 C.893 B.A. L.1059 J.D. P.O. Box 1918
Foster, David S., III, (BVⓉ) '27 '64 C.893 B.A. L.861 J.D.
(adm. in LA; not adm. in NC) P.O. Box 467‡
Foster, William A., (AV) '27 '52 C.1365 L.260 J.D.
(adm. in FL; not adm. in NC) Rt. 2, Box 217E
Freeman, William M. '27 '51 C&L.424 J.D.
(adm. in IL; not adm. in NC) P.O. Box 417‡
Henson, J. Edwin, (BV) ....'49 '74 C&L.575 A.B., J.D. [Henson&B.]
Henson & Black, PLLC, (BV) ....Ten Chestnut Square
Hicks, Ralph L., (BV) ....'24 '81 C.497 B.S. L.896 J.D. [Coward,H.&S.]
Paul, Peter A., (CV) ....'48 '82 C.259 B.A. L.192 J.D. [P.A.Paul]

Paul, Peter A., P.C., (CV)
872 U.S. Highway 64 West, P.O. Box 3049, 28717
Telephone: 828-743-5200 Fax: 828-743-5224
Peter A. Paul.
Real Estate Law, General Civil Practice, Corporation Law, Business Law, Estate Planning, Wills, Probate, Personal Injury, Automobile Accidents and Injuries.
See Professional Biographies, CASHIERS, NORTH CAROLINA

CASTLE HAYNE, 1,182, *New Hanover Co.*

Higgins, Edward B., Jr. '48 '73
C.125 B.S. L.896 J.D. Instructor, Cape Fear Community Coll.

CEDAR MOUNTAIN, —, *Transylvania Co.*

Tate, John E., Jr. ....'55 '80 C.249 B.A. L.575 J.D. P.O. Box 659

CEDAR POINT, 929, *Carteret Co.*

Erwin, Frank W., (BV) ....'52 '77 C.198 A.B. L.228 J.D. [Erwin,S.&S.] ⊙
Erwin, Simpson & Stroud, P.L.L.C., (BV) ....708 Cedar Point Blvd. (⊙Jacksonville)
Hume, Robert J., III, Law Office of '47 '75
C.178 B.A. L.930 J.D. 604 Cedar Point Boulevard
Simpson, John P., (BV) ....'45 '72 C&L.896 B.A., J.D. [Erwin,S.&S.] ⊙
Stroud, Joseph E., Jr., (BV) ....'51 '77 C.232 B.A. L.896 J.D. [Erwin,S.&S.] ⊙

CHAPEL HILL, 48,715, *Durham & Orange Cos.*

Adler, Robert S. ....'44 '69 C.659 A.B. L.477 J.D. 506 Bayberry Dr.
Agrawal, Gail Bopp '51 '86 C.1099 B.A. L.861 J.D.
Prof. & Sr. Asooc. Dean, Univ. of NC Law Sch.
Aiken, Michael W. ....'69 '98 C.36 B.S. L.190 J.D. Investors Title Ins. Co.
Albert, Lynne Townsend, (BV) .... '59 '84 C.260 B.S.B.A. L.880 J.D. 207 Longwood Dr.
Alexander, Sydenham B., Jr., (BV) ....'50 '75 C&L.575 A.B., J.D. [Alexander&M.]
Alexander & Miller, LLP., (BV) ....1526 Franklin St., Suite 202
Alpert, Robert L., (AV) '43 '69 C.321 B.S. L.262 J.D.
(adm. in NY; not adm. in NC) Pres., ICALM Grp.
Anders, Patrick Maxwell, (CV) ....'68 '93 C&L.575 B.A., J.D. [🄰 Edgar&P.]
Anderson, Barbara D., (CV) ....'36 '81 C.821 B.A. L.228 J.D. [🄲 Lewis,A.P.G.&H.]
Athey, Carol J. '47 '95 C.446 B.A. L.574 J.D.
(adm. in AL; not adm. in NC) Corp. Coun., Rho, Inc.
Averett, D. Melissa ....'64 '98 C.575 B.A. L.574 J.D. [Averett]
Averett Law Offices, P.L.L.C. ....P.O. Box 2866
Awalt, Francis G., Jr. '21 '53 C.575 A.B. L.276 J.D.
(adm. in DC; not adm. in NC) 1 St. James Pl.‡
Aycock, Wm. B. ....'15 '48 C.576 B.S. L.575 J.D. 6 Carolina Meadows‡
Baddour, Richard Allen, Jr. ....'71 '97 C&L.575 B.A., J.D. [Baddour&M.]
Baddour & Milner, PLLC ....P.O. Box 9011
Bagwell, O. Kenneth, Jr., (AV) ....'50 '79 C&L.575 B.A., J.D. [🄲 Bagwell,H.&S.]

Bagwell, Holt & Smith, P.A., (BV)
111 Cloister Court, Suite 200, 27517
Telephone: 919-401-0062 Fax: 919-403-0063
Email: info@bhspa.com URL: http://www.bhspa.com
Thomas R. Holt; Nathaniel C. Smith;—Christopher A. Crowson. Of Counsel: Beth Tillman Logan; O. Kenneth Bagwell, Jr.
Commercial and Residential Real Estate, Business, Civil Litigation, Estate Planning, Creditor's Rights, Collections, Workers Compensation, Automobile Accidents, Personal Injury, Wrongful Death, Wills, Probate.
See Professional Biographies, CHAPEL HILL, NORTH CAROLINA

Barley, Tracy Hicks, & Associates, P.A.
(See Durham)

Barry, Jeffery W. '38 '64 C.20 B.A. L.477 J.D.
(adm. in MI; not adm. in NC) 116 Rhododendron Ct.‡
Battle, F. Gordon ....'32 '58 C&L.575 B.S., J.D. 501 Redbud Rd.
Bayliss, William H., (AV) .....'23 '72 C.309 M.B.A. L.228 J.D. 137 East Franklin Street‡

Bayliss, Hudson & Merritt, (AV)
Bank of America Plaza, Suite 31, 137 East Franklin Street, P.O. Drawer 389, 27514
Telephone: 919-942-5191 Fax: 919-967-9089
Email: bhmnc@bellsouth.net
Members of Firm: Marcus Hudson (Board Certified Specialist in Estate Planning and Probate Law, North Carolina State Board of Legal Specialization); Ronald W. Merritt. Associate: Candace A. Wehr. General Practice. Trials and Appeals in all State and Federal Courts, Trusts and Estates, Estate Planning, Probate, Wills, Contracts, Corporate, Business Law, Real Estate, Tax, Criminal, Traffic Violations, Driving While Intoxicated.
See Professional Biographies, CHAPEL HILL, NORTH CAROLINA

Beemer, Charles G., (BV) ....'40 '74 C.170 B.A. L.575 J.D. 1829 E. Franklin St.
Bell, A. Fleming, II ....'54 '82 C&L.228 A.B., J.D. Univ. of N.C. at Chapel Hill
Bennick, Donna E., (BVⓉ) ....'59 '85 C&L.575 B.A., J.D. [D.E.Bennick]

Bennick, Donna E., P.C., (BVⓉ)
1829 East Franklin Street Building 600, 27514
Telephone: 919-968-6883 Fax: 919-968-6884
Email: donnabennick@yahoo.com URL: http://www.donnabennickpc.com
Donna E. Bennick.
Family Law, Divorce, Separation, Child Custody, Alimony, Property Settlements, Prenuptial Agreements, Certified Guardian Ad Litem and Parent Coordinator, Collaborative Law.
See Professional Biographies, CHAPEL HILL, NORTH CAROLINA

Benninger, Sheila R. ....'48 '78 C.629 B.A. L.976 J.D. [🄰 Snider&R.]
Bennington, David A., (AV) '49 '78
C&L.575 B.A., J.D. V.P. & Title Atty., Investors Title Ins. Co.
Bernard, William D., (BV) ....'56 '82 C&L.575 B.A., J.D. [Brown&B.]

Bernholz, Dorothy C. '41 '75
C.575 B.A. L.574 J.D. Dir., Carolina Student Legal Services, Inc.
Bernholz, Roger B., (BV) ....'49 '73 C&L.575 A.B., J.D. 1202 Roosevelt Drive
Bernholz, Steven A., (AV) ....'40 '67 C&L.575 A.B., LL.B. [▣ Rudolf W.&F.]
Bilionis, Louis D. ....'57 '83 C.575 A.B. L.309 J.D. Univ. N. Carolina Law School
Birchfield, Judith L. ....'57 '86 C.475 B.A. L.884 J.D. 104 Concord Dr.
Blakey, Walker J. '40 '67 C.309 A.B. L.608 J.D.
(adm. in OH; not adm. in NC) Univ. of N. C. School of Law
Blue, J. William, Jr., (AV) ....'50 '75 C&L.575 A.B., J.D. [Northen B.]
Boger, John Charles '46 '75 C.228 B.A. L.575 J.D.
(adm. in NY; not adm. in NC) Prof. of Law, Univ. of N.C. Sch. of Law
Boyarsky, Saul, (BVⓉ) '23 '83 C.882 M.D. L.910 J.D.
(adm. in MO; not adm. in NC) 6412 Mimosa Dr.‡
Boyette, Heidi S. .... '— '00 C.705 B.A. L.309 J.D. Legal Coun., All Kinds of Minds

Brenman, Lisa R. '57 '95 C.330 B.S. L.878 J.D.
Building 600, 1829 E. Franklin Street, 27514
Telephone: 919-932-4593 Fax: 919-942-8674
Email: attorney@visas-us.com URL: http://www.visas-us.com
Family Immigration, Business Immigration, Labor Certification, Asylum, Student Visas, Citizenship.
See Professional Biographies, CHAPEL HILL, NORTH CAROLINA

Brenner, Jason A. ....'75 '01 C.296 B.A. L.93 J.D. 400 Market St., Ste. 103
Brenner, Lawrence H. .... '46 '71 C.912 B.A. L.93 J.D. 400 Market St., Ste. 103
Britt, Margurete R. .... '58 '85 C.198 A.B. L.896 J.D. 4033 Duck Pond Trl.
Broadfoot, Winston ....'18 '43 C&L.575 A.B., LL.B. 2001 Lake Shore Dr.
Broome, Lissa Lamkin '57 '82
C.339 B.S. L.309 J.D. Prof. of Law, Univ. of NC Sch. of Law
Brower, David J. '30 '60 C&L.477 B.A., J.D.
(adm. in MI; not adm. in NC) Resch. Prof., Univ. of N.C.
Brown, Caroline N. ....'47 '76 C.112 B.A. L.472 J.D. Prof., Univ of N. C. Law Sch.
Brown, Charles Gordon, (AV) ....'50 '75 C.575 A.B. L.893 J.D. [Brown&B.]
Brown, LeAnn Nease, (AV) ....'55 '84 C&L.575 B.A., J.D. [Brown&B.] (⊙Chapel Hill)
Brown, Susan M. ....'57 '94 C.815 B.A. L.575 J.D. [S.M.Brown]

Brown & Bunch, PLLC, (AV)
101 North Columbia Street, 27514 ⊙
Telephone: 919-968-1111 Fax: 919-968-1444
Members of Firm: Charles Gordon Brown (Resident); William W. Bunch, III (Resident, Raleigh Office); William D. Bernard (Resident); A. Vann Irvin (Board Certified Specialist in Estate Planning and Probate Law, North Carolina State Board of Legal Specialization) (Resident, Durham Office); LeAnn Nease Brown (Resident); Scott D. Zimmerman (Resident).
General Practice in all State and Federal Courts, Administrative Law, Antitrust Litigation, Appeals, Collections, Commercial Litigation, Commercial Transactions, Construction, Corporate Practice, Creditors' Rights, Employment Law, Estates and Trusts, Health Law, Lender Liability Defense, Mediation, Municipal and Land Use Law, Real Estate, State and Federal Taxation, Trade Regulation and Trials.
Counsel for: NationsBank; First Union National Bank; Centura Bank; The Chase Manhattan Bank; Mellon Bank, N.A.; Branch Banking and Trust Co.; Central Carolina Bank and Trust Co., N.A.; Triangle East Bank; Ameribanc Savings Bank.
Raleigh, North Carolina Office: 4900 Falls of Neuse Road, Suite 210, Post Office Box 19409. Telephone: 919-878-8060. Fax: 919-878-8062.
Durham, North Carolina Office: 21 West Colony Place, Suite 250, 27705. Telephone: 919-490-9700. Fax: 919-419-9736.
See Professional Biographies, CHAPEL HILL, NORTH CAROLINA

Brown, Susan M., Law Offices of, P.A. ....1829 E. Franklin Street, Suite 600
Brown-Graham, Anita R. ...... '67 '91 C.420 B.A. L.575 J.D. Unc Chapel Hill Cb # 3330
Browning, Jennifer J. ....'46 '88 C.604 A.B. L.678 J.D. Law Clk. to Ct. of App.
Bryan, James T., III, (BV) ....'48 '77 C.976 B.A. L.574 J.D. Town Council
Bunting, Elizabeth C. '49 '74 C&L.575 A.B., J.D.
Assoc. V.P. for Legal Affrs., University of North Carolina, The
Burton, William R. ....'54 '87 C.999 B.S. L.575 J.D. 132 Willow Way
Butler, Elvira O. '48 '77 C.1046 B.A. L.776 J.D.
(adm. in NJ; not adm. in NC) 8807 Galax Ct.‡
Cabe, Samantha Hyatt ....'75 '02 C.925 B.S.B.A. L.575 J.D. [▣ Northen B.]
Cannon, Ashley '73 '01 C.896 B.A. L.575 J.D.
Dir. of Develop., Univ. of NC-Chapel Hill, Dept. of Allied Health Sciences
Caplan, Lee A. '55 '85 C.443 B.S. L.64 J.D.
(adm. in MD; not adm. in NC) 112 Graylyn Drive
Carey, Moses, Jr. .... '45 '81 C.999 B.S. L.574 J.D. Univ. of N.C.
Carroll, Kathryn G. .... '54 '91 C.1090 B.S.N. L.273 J.D. 2012 S. Lakeshore Dr.
Carter, Derb S., Jr. ......'53 '81 C.575 B.A. L.629 J.D. Sr. Atty., Southern Envir. Law Ctr.
Chapman, Heidi G., (BV) ....'53 '83 C.228 B.A. L.575 J.D. [H.G.Chapman]

Chapman, Heidi G., P.L.L.C., (BV)
100 Europa Drive, Suite 560, 27517
Telephone: 919-968-6116 Fax: 919-968-6166
Email: heidi@heidichapmanlaw.com URL: http://www.lawyers.com/heidichapmanlaw
Heidi G. Chapman.
Workers Compensation, Auto Accidents, Wrongful Death, Personal Injury, Social Security Disability.
See Professional Biographies, CHAPEL HILL, NORTH CAROLINA

Chastain, Margaret E. ....'— '78 C.569 B.A. L.790 J.D. [M.E.Chastain]
Chastain, M. Elizabeth .... 152 Cedar Hills Circle
Clement, Nathaniel E., & Associates ....'— '82 C.902 L.692 100 Europa Dr., Ste. 403
Clifford, Donald F., Jr. '35 '63 C.128 A.B. L.174 LL.B.
(adm. in CO; not adm. in NC) Prof. of Law, Univ. of N.C. School of Law
Cole, Roy M. ....'17 '53 C&L.575 A.B., J.D. 7016 Old Greensboro Hwy.

Coleman, Gledhill, Hargrave & Peek, P.C.
(See Hillsborough)

Congleton, W. Russell ....'57 '82 C.63 B.S. L.285 J.D. [▣ Stark]
Conti, Sara A., (AV) ....'50 '81 C.577 B.A. L.896 J.D. P.O. Box 3463
Cooper, Robert E. .... '31 '56 C.309 A.B. L.575 J.D. [Cooper&W.]
Cooper and Williams, P.A. ....121 South Estes Drive
Copeley, Leto, (AV) ....'54 '84 C.331 B.A. L.309 J.D. [Patterson H.] (⊙Raleigh)
Corrado, Michael L. '40 '85 C.645 B.A. L.145 J.D.
(adm. in IL; not adm. in NC) Prof. of Law, Univ. of N.C.
Costley, Margaret V., (BV) ....'61 '86 C.228 A.B. L.896 J.D. Drawer 2687
Cowan, Spencer M. '49 '77 C.178 A.B. L.94 J.D.
(adm. in MA; not adm. in NC) Univ. of N.C. at Chapel Hill
Coyne, Jeffrey C., (AVⓉ) '54 '79 C.112 A.B. L.228 J.D.
(adm. in CA; not adm. in NC) 1054 Burning Tree Drive
Craige, Burton, (AV) ....'49 '80 C.309 B.A. L.575 J.D. [Patterson H.] (⊙Raleigh)
Crane, Shelly D. ....'69 '94 C.924 B.A. L.923 J.D. 141 Providence Road
Crescenzo, David E. ....'54 '81 C.945 B.A. L.896 J.D. P.O. Box 1224
Crocker, Geoerge-Ann P. ....'76 '01 C.575 B.A. L.1228 J.D. [▣ Higgins,F.G.&M.]
Crowson, Christopher A. ....'72 '04 C.575 B.A. L.1228 J.D. [▣ Bagwell,H.&S.]
Darter, O. Lloyd, Jr. .... '23 '51 C.387 B.A. L.880 LL.B. 20 Vauxhall Pl.‡
Davidson, Karen P., (BV) ....'50 '81 C.813 B.A. L.575 J.D. [Epting&H.]
Davis, Donna Ambler, (BV) ....'59 '88 C.555 B.A. L.902 J.D. [D.A.Davis]
Davis, Nancy Worth, (CVⓉ) '45 '82 C.1278 B.A. L.472 J.D.
(adm. in FL; not adm. in NC) 117 Donegal Dr.
Davis, Donna Ambler, P.C., (BV) ....740 East Franklin Street
Daye, Charles E. ....'44 '70 C.574 B.A. L.178 J.D. Prof., Univ. of NC Sch. of Law
Dean, Margaret G. ....'— '80 C.331 B.A. L.184 J.D. [Mediation]
Denton, Desiree P. ....'55 '81 C&L.838 B.A., J.D. Law Instructor, Univ. of NC
Derian, Cathryn Blue '54 '81 C.880 B.A. L.16 J.D.
(adm. in AL; not adm. in NC) 411 Westwood Dr.‡
Doyle, George P., Law Offices of, (CV) '50 '81
C.575 B.A. L.589 J.D. 210 N. Columbia St.
Drake, David A. ....'45 '72 C.352 B.A. L.228 J.D. P.O. Box 904‡
Ducker, Richard D. '44 '76 C.174 B.A. L.1068 J.D.
(adm. in CA; not adm. in NC) Univ. of NC
Edgar, Karl F., (BV) ....'59 '85 C.1349 B.A. L.564 J.D. [Edgar&P.]
Edgar & Paul, (BV) ....1777 Durham-Chapel Hill Road, Suite 204
Edwards, David N., Jr. '39 '67 C.198 B.A. L.228 LL.B.
Assoc. V.P. for Legal Affrs., University of North Carolina, The

Edwards & Trenkle, PLLC
(See Durham)

Ehringhaus, Susan H. ....'44 '68 C&L.575 B.A., J.D. Univ. of N. C.
Eifort, Joseph D., (BV) ....'39 '73 C.198 A.B. L.575 J.D. 1607 Old Oxford Rd.

Ekstrand & Ekstrand, LLP
(See Durham)

Emmerson, Fred B., Jr. '45 '72
C.575 A.B. L.421 J.D. V.P. & Gen. Coun., The Davis Group
Epting, Robert, (AV) ....'45 '70 C&L.575 A.B., J.D. [Epting&H.]

Epting & Hackney, (AV) ▣
410 Martin Luther King, Jr. Blvd., P.O. Box 1329, 27514
Telephone: 919-929-0323 Fax: 919-929-3960
Members of Firm: Robert Epting; Joe Hackney; Elizabeth Lackey Jacobs; Karen P. Davidson; Steve Lackey.
General Civil and Criminal Practice, Trials, Family Law, Real Estate, Business and Corporations, Wills, Probate, Estate Planning.
See Professional Biographies, CHAPEL HILL, NORTH CAROLINA

Esser, George H. ....'21 '50 C.885 B.S. L.309 LL.B. 211 N. Elliott Rd.‡
Evans, Melinda Melhorn, (BV) .... '55 '81 C.125 B.A. L.896 J.D. 111 MacRae Court
Everett, Wesley H. S. ....'64 '01 C.575 B.S. L.574 J.D. [Everett]
Everett Law Firm, P.A. .... 1829 E. Franklin St., Ste. 700D
Farb, Robert L. '47 '73 C.575 A.B. L.309 J.D.
Prof. of Pub. Law & Govt., Univ. of N. C.
Farren, J. David, (BV) ....'55 '82 C.659 B.A. L.575 J.D. Southern Envir. Law Ctr.
Farrow, Richard S., (AVⓉ) '25 '50 C&L.309 S.B., LL.B.
(adm. in NY; not adm. in NC) 104 Overlake Dr.

Ferguson, Stein, Chambers, Gresham & Sumter, P.A., (AV)
Suite 2, 312 West Franklin Street, 27516 ⊙
Telephone: 919-933-5300 Fax: 919-967-4953 Email: astein@fswags.com
Email: wsimpson@law.fswags.com
Adam Stein; William G. Simpson, Jr.
General Civil, Employment and Labor, Criminal, Trial and Appellate Practice. Specializes in Medical Negligence, Civil Rights, Education and Personal Injury Law.
Charlotte, North Carolina Office: 741 Kenilworth Avenue, Suite 300 Telephone: 704-375-8461. Fax: 704-334-5654.
See Professional Biographies, CHAPEL HILL, NORTH CAROLINA

Ferrell, Joseph S. '38 '64 C&L.575 B.S., LL.B.
Prof. of Pub. Law & Govt., Univ. of N. C.

Fitzpatrick, John C., P.C., Law Office of
(See Durham)

Fox, Carl R., (AV) .... '53 '78 C&L.575 B.A., J.D. Dist. Atty.
Foy, Kevin C., (CV) ....'56 '94 C.385 B.A. L.574 J.D. [Foy&L.]
Foy & Lavelle, (CV) ....891 Willow Drive, Suite 8
Franklin, Susan R. .... '49 '79 C.999 B.A. L.146 J.D. [Franklin] ⊙

Franklin Law Center, PLLC
Exchange West at Meadowmont, 1414 Raleigh Road, Suite 290, 27517-8834 ⊙
Telephone: 919-942-0800 Fax: 919-942-0607
Email: sfranklin@franklinlawcenter.com URL: http://www.franklinlawcenter.com
Susan R. Franklin.
Divorce, Alimony, Spousal Support, Separation Agreements, Marital Property Settlements, Equitable Distribution of Assets, Cohabitation Agreements, Community Property Law, Non-Traditional Family Law, Divorce Mediation, Divorce Arbitration, Collaborative Family Law, Adoption, International Family Law, Child Custody, Military Divorce, Military Family Law, Trial Practice in all Courts.
Pittsboro Office: 60 West Street, P.O. Box 685, 27312. Telephone: 919-942-0800. Fax: 919-942-0607.
See Professional Biographies, CHAPEL HILL, NORTH CAROLINA

Frankstone, David R., (AV) ....'48 '75 C.902 B.S. L.575 J.D. [Higgins,F.G.&M.]
Freedman, Irving M. .... '28 '58 C.588 B.S.E.E. L.273 J.D. 33 Wedgewood Rd. (Pat.)
French, Thomas R. '48 '87 C.1044 B.A. L.1340 J.D.
(adm. in KY; not adm. in NC)
Assoc. Dir., & Clinical Assoc. Prof., Univ. of NC Law Libr.
Froehling, Elizabeth A. .... '65 '92 C.34 B.S.B.A. L.575 J.D. 800 Eastowne Dr.
Fuierer, Marianne '46 '95 C.1381 B.S. L.107 J.D.
[▣ Intellectual/ T.L.] (See Pat. Sect.)
Fuierer, Tristan A. '68 '03 C.1122 B.S. L.575 J.D.
[▣ Intellectual/ T.L.] (See Pat. Sect.)
Fuller, L. Lynnette ....'67 '91 C&L.575 B.A., J.D. Asst. Prof., Univ. of NC
Fuller, Virginia Hudson '66 '94 C.228 B.A. L.575 J.D.
Assoc. Dir. for Pub. Interest Law, Univ. of N. Carolina Sch. of Law
Gale, Terrie Jean ....'45 '77 C.788 B.A. L.30 J.D. Chapel Hill Police Atty.
Gamber, Christopher R. .... '71 '98 C.705 B.S. L.1209 J.D. 1525 E. Franklin St., Ste. 5B
Gasaway, Laura N. '45 '74 C.844 B.A. L.326 J.D.
(adm. in TX; not adm. in NC) Prof. of Law & Dir. Law Libr., Univ. of N.C.
Gibson, S. Elizabeth '50 '76 C.228 B.A. L.575 J.D. Univ. of NC Sch. of Law
Gilbert, Benjamin, (CV) '51 '81
C.477 B.G.S. L.575 J.D. Sr. V.P., Gen. Cnsl, Univ. of N.C. Hospitals
Ginter, Fiona Valerie ....'76 '02 C.576 B.S. L.1345 J.D. [▣ Stark]
Glenn, David R. .... '67 '94 C&L.575 B.A., J.D. P.O. Box 4323
Glover, James R., (AV) .... '42 '70 C.121 B.A. L.966 J.D. [Glover&P.]
Glover & Petersen, P.A., (AV) ....1506 E. Franklin St., Ste. 100
Graham, T. D. .... '45 '73 C&L.575 A.B., J.D. 231 Forest Hill Rd.
Graves, Wm. Griffin, III, (AV) .....'50 '76 C.575 A.B. L.896 J.D. [Higgins,F.G.&M.] ⊙
Green, Philip P., Jr. ....'22 '49 C.674 A.B. L.309 J.D. 602 Emory Dr.‡
Greene, Herman F., (AV) ....'45 '80 C.260 B.A. L.575 J.D. [▣ Lewis,A.P.G.&H.]
Groninger, Ann Elizabeth, (AV) '69 '95
C.475 B.S. L.861 J.D. [Patterson H.] (⊙Raleigh)
Groves, Harry E. ....'21 '51 C.174 A.B. L.145 J.D. Villa 276, Carolina Meadows‡

Gustafson, Vincent K. '70 '98 C.112 B.S.M.E. L.1522 J.D.
(adm. in CA; not adm. in NC) [Intellectual/ T.L.]
Hackney, Joe, (AV) .... '45 '70 C&L.575 A.B., J.D. [Epting&H.]
Hall, Janet Gayer .... '47 '01 C.477 B.Mus. L.575 J.D. P.O. Box 4825
Halpern, Adrian .... '60 '89 C&L.575 B.A., J.D. 219 McCauley St.
Hart, David J., (CV) .... '61 '91 C.763 B.S. L.575 J.D. [Higgins,F.G.&M.]
Hayes, Deborah Lark ....'49 '77 C.880 B.A. L.94 J.D. Sr. Atty., Southern Envir. Law Ctr.
Hazen, Thomas L. '47 '73 C&L.178 B.A., J.D.
(adm. in NY; not adm. in NC) Univ. of N.C. Sch. of Law
Heafner, Gregory A., (CV) '63 '95 C.446 B.A. L.575 J.D.
308 W. Rosemary St., Ste. 303
Herman, G. Nicholas, (BV) .... '54 '83 C.575 B.A. L.228 J.D. 1829 E. Franklin St.
Herman-Giddens, Gregory, (BV) '61 '88 C.575 B.A. L.861 J.D.
[G.T.Herman-Giddens]

Herman-Giddens, Gregory, TrustCounsel, P.A., (BV)
205 Providence Road, 27514
Telephone: 919-493-6351 Toll Free: 800-201-0413 Facsimile: 919-493-6355
Email: ghgiddens@trustcounselpa.com URL: http://www.trustcounselpa.com
Gregory Herman-Giddens (Board Certified Specialist in Estate Planning and Probate Law, North Carolina State Bar Board of Legal Specialization).
Trusts and Estates, Wills, Probate, Taxation, Business Law, Guardianships, Charitable Trusts and Foundations, Elder Law, Estate Planning, Asset Protection.
See Professional Biographies, CHAPEL HILL, NORTH CAROLINA

Higgins, Thomas D., III, (AV) .... '46 '71 C&L.575 B.A., J.D. [Higgins,F.G.&M.]

Higgins, Frankstone, Graves & Morris, P.A., (AV)
The Exchange West at Meadowmont, 1414 Raleigh Road, Suite 320, 27517-8834 ⊙
Mailing Address: P.O. Box 2869, Chapel Hill, NC 27514
Telephone: 919-968-4717 Fax: 919-929-1415
URL: http://www.hfgmlaw.com
Thomas D. Higgins, III; David R. Frankstone (Board Certified Specialist in Estate Planning and Probate Law, North Carolina State Board of Legal Specialization); Wm. Griffin Graves, III; David S. Morris (Resident, Cary Office); Kenneth L. Eagle (Resident, Cary Office);—David J. Hart; Robert Kendrick Rice; Geoerge-Ann P. Crocker.
Estate Planning, Probate, Corporate, Real Estate, Civil Litigation, Taxation and General Business Law.
References: Central Carolina Bank & Trust Co.; NCNB National Bank of North Carolina; Investors Title Insurance Co.; First Union National Bank; First Title Insurance Co.; Lawyers Title Insurance Co.
Cary, North Carolina Office: 14600 Weston Parkway, Suite 300, 27513-2259. Telephone: 919-678-8880. Fax: 919-678-8885.
See Professional Biographies, CHAPEL HILL, NORTH CAROLINA

Hinkle, Christina Goshaw .... '69 '93 C.228 B.S. L.575 J.D. [Lewis,A.P.G.&H.]
Hinson, Eric W., (BV) .... '63 '92 C&L.575 B.A., J.D. [E.W.Hinson]
Hinson, Eric W., P.A., (BV) .... 1526 E. Franklin Street, Suite 105
Hodach, Albertina E. .... '45 '86 C.054 B.Sc. L.966 J.D. 101 Derby Lane
Hodson, Charles B. .... '25 '53 C&L.575 B.A., LL.B. 301 Severin St.‡
Holcomb, Carol J., (BV) .... '49 '89 C.12 B.S. L.575 J.D. [Northen B.]
Holman, J. Blanding, IV ....'69 '96 C.575 B.A. L.893 J.D. Southern Envir. Law Ctr.
Holmes, Douglas M., CPA ....'43 '71 C.1083 B.S.B.A. L.575 J.D. 2 Elmstead Place
Holt, Thomas R., (BV) .... '58 '90 C.199 B.A. L.575 J.D. [Bagwell,H.&S.]
Holtkamp, Lynne, (BV) .... '59 '89 C.210 B.A. L.574 J.D. 312 W. Franklin St.
Hornik, Nancy Friel, (BV⊕) '60 '86
C.923 B.A. L.902 J.D. Town of Carrboro Planning Dept.
Hornik, Robert E., Jr., (BV⊕) .... '59 '85 C.1031 B.A. L.902 J.D. 1829 E. Franklin Street
Hostetler, David R. '60 '90 C.935 B.A. L.228 J.D.
Dir., Legal Servs., Principals Exec. Prog., Univ. of NC

Howard, Stallings, From & Hutson, P.A.
(See Raleigh)

Howes, Margaret M. K. .... '66 '92 C&L.128 B.A., J.D. 219 Stratford Dr.
Hudson, Marcus, (AV) ....'40 '65 C.198 A.B. L.575 LL.B. [Bayliss,H.&M.]
Hultquist, Steven J., (BV) '49 '80
C.910 B.S.Ch.E. L.262 J.D. [Intellectual/ T.L.] (See Pat. Sect.)
Hunt, Douglass '24 '52 C.575 A.B. L.976 LL.B.
(adm. in DC; not adm. in NC) Adviser to the Chancellor, Univ. of N. C. at Chapel Hill
Igou, Richard James .... '54 '89 C.145 B.A. L.575 J.D. P.O. Box 491

Intellectual Property/ Technology Law, (BV)
1414 Raleigh Road, Suite 201, 27517
Mailing Address: P.O. Box 14329, Research Triangle Park, NC 27709
Telephone: 919-419-9350 Fax: 919-419-9354
Email: Info@iptl.com URL: http://www.iptl.com
Steven J. Hultquist. Senior Associate: Marianne Fuierer. Associates: Tristan A. Fuierer; Vincent K. Gustafson (Not admitted in NC).
Intellectual Property, Technology and Biotechnology, Patents, Trademarks, Licensing and Copyright Law.
See Professional Biographies, CHAPEL HILL, NORTH CAROLINA

Jacobs, Elizabeth Lackey, (BV) .... '52 '81 C.790 B.A. L.575 J.D. [Epting&H.]
James, Karen L. '57 '90 C&L.575 B.A., J.D.
Kenan-Flagler Bus. Sch., UNC Chapel Hill
Jamison, W. Richard ....'52 '84 C.896 B.A. L.245 J.D. 6110 Falconbridge Rd.
Johnson, Valerie Alston .... '64 '94 C&L.575 B.A., J.D. [Patterson H.] (⊙Raleigh)
Joines, Chellie Martin ....'51 '04 C.575 B.A. L.574 J.D. [Lewis,A.P.G.&H.]
Jones, Daniel C. '25 '68 C.999 M.S. L.980 J.D.
(adm. in OH; not adm. in NC) 1106 Burning Tree Dr.‡
Joyce, Robert P. .... '51 '76 C.575 B.A. L.309 J.D. Univ. of NC
Kalo, Joseph J. ....'44 '68 C.475 B.A. L.477 J.D. Prof. of Law, Univ. of N. C.
Karpinos, Carolyn A., (BV) .... '48 '95 C.228 B.A. L.574 J.D. 112 Braswell Road
Karpinos, Ralph D., (BV) .... '50 '78 C.228 A.B. L.790 J.D. Town Atty.
Kelley, Michael J., (BV⊕) '64 '89
C.607 B.S. L.851 J.D. Sr. Claims Coun., Investors Title Ins. Co.
Kelley, Thomas A., III ....'61 '91 C.309 B.A. L.588 J.D. Prof., Univ. of NC
Kelly, Dayna J. ....'61 '91 C.475 B.A. L.477 J.D. [D.Kelly]
Kelly, Dayna, PC, Law Offices of .... P.O. Box 17297
Kempter, Bryan C. ....'52 '77 C.228 B.A. L.575 J.D. 2700 Winningham Rd.
Kennedy, Maria Savasta '62 '88 C.112 B.A. L.1068 J.D.
(adm. in CA; not adm. in NC) 404 Hogan Woods Cir.
Kern, Robert G. ....'57 '85 C.896 B.S. L.575 J.D. 1200 Cra-Mer Lane
Kiziah, Brent D., (BV) .... '60 '85 C&L.575 A.B., J.D. Asst. Atty. Gen.
Koeze, Jeffrey Scott ....'60 '88 C.575 B.A. L.893 J.D. Assoc. Prof., Univ. of N.C.

Kornbluth Law Firm, The, P.A.
(See Durham)

Lackey, Steve .... '57 '96 C&L.575 B.A., J.D. [Epting&H.]
Lamb, Gwendolyn H. ....'34 '88 C.880 A.B. L.575 J.D. 2 Wysteria Way
Landever, Carolyn M. ....'64 '89 C.976 B.A. L.569 J.D. 712 Kenmore Rd.
Larsen, Robert A., Esquire ....'67 '94 C.529 B.A. L.705 J.D. 205 Parkside Circle
Lata, Celia Grasty ....'46 '91 C.577 B.M. L.228 J.D. Spec. Deputy Atty. Gen.

Lavelle, Lydia E. ....'61 '93 C.1130 B.A. L.574 J.D. [Foy&L.]
Lawrence, David M. ....'43 '69 C.674 A.B. L.309 J.D. Institute of Government
Lederman, Sema E. .... '47 '83 C.477 B.A. L.629 J.D. 204 Glenview Place
Lee, Raine ....'52 '86 C.320 B.A. L.692 J.D. 411 Overland Dr.
Levi, Emma Jean Hemby, (CV) ...... '40 '77 C.369 B.A. L.574 J.D. 2007 Billabong Lane
Levine, Michael D., (BV) .... '40 '69 C.659 B.A. L.575 J.D. [Levine&S.] ‡

Levine & Stewart, (BV)
Suite 202, University Square, 143 West Franklin Street, 27516-2517
Telephone: 919-929-0386 Fax: 919-968-4601
Email: info@levineandstewart.com URL: http://www.levineandstewart.com
Members of Firm: Michael D. Levine (Retired); John T. Stewart.
Real Estate, Civil, Domestic, Criminal, Corporate and Estate Planning, Personal Injury, Mediation, Arbitration.
See Professional Biographies, CHAPEL HILL, NORTH CAROLINA

Lewis, Susan H. .... '45 '71 C.683 B.A. L.846 J.D. [Lewis,A.P.G.&H.]

Lewis, Anderson, Phillips, Greene & Hinkle, PLLC, (AV)
141 Providence Road, Suite 200, 27514
Mailing Address: P.O. Drawer 4825, Chapel Hill, NC 27515-4825
Telephone: 919-967-8989 Fax: 919-419-1429
URL: http://www.lapgh.com
Susan H. Lewis; J. Dickson Phillips, III; Christina Goshaw Hinkle; Anthony D. Nicholson; Chellie Martin Joines. Of Counsel: Barbara D. Anderson; Herman F. Greene.
Business Law, Commercial Litigation, Family Law, Divorce, Estate Planning and Administration, Probate, Wills, Civil Litigation, Intellectual Property Litigation, Copyright, Trademark, Personal Injury, Real Estate Litigation, Construction, Condemnation, Employment Contracts, Corporate Taxation, Corporate Finance, Partnership Taxation, Mediation, Arbitration, Computer Law.
See Professional Biographies, CHAPEL HILL, NORTH CAROLINA

Link, Ronald C. .... '40 '65 C&L.339 B.A., J.D. Prof. of Law, Univ. of N. C.
Loeb, Ben F., Jr. '32 '60 C&L.880 B.A., J.D.
Prof. of Pub. Law & Govt., Univ. of N. C. at Chapel Hill
Logan, Beth Tillman .... '63 '93 C.880 B.A. L.575 J.D. [Bagwell,H.&S.]
Logan, Sarah E. Tillman ....'63 '93 C.880 B.A. L.575 J.D. 210 N. Columbia St.
Long, Florence J., (BV) ....'— '84 C&L.575 A.B., J.D. [Long&L.]
Long, Lunsford, (AV) ....'45 '72 C&L.575 A.B., J.D. [Long&L.]

Long & Long, (AV)
127 TimberHill Place, 27514
Telephone: 919-929-0408 Fax: 919-929-6819
Members of Firm: Lunsford Long; Florence J. Long;—Dannette D. Toth.
Family Law, Custody, Support, Property Division, Mediation, Arbitration, Collaborative Law.
See Professional Biographies, CHAPEL HILL, NORTH CAROLINA

Louis, Martin B. '34 '60 C.674 A.B. L.309 LL.B.
(adm. in PA; not adm. in NC) Prof. of Law, Univ. of N.C.
Lowing, Wayne E. ....'57 '90 C.381 B.A. L.575 J.D. P.O. Box 3087
Ludington, Richard P. ....'46 '78 C&L.575 B.A., LL.B. Conserv. Off.
Ludwig, Britt B. '64 '92 C.645 B.A. L.174 J.D.
(adm. in CO; not adm. in NC) 209 Commons Way
Macklin, Karen G. Z. .... '53 '89 C.373 B.A. L.184 J.D. P.O. Box 2052
Maguire, W. Terry '48 '75 C.103 B.A. L.273 J.D.
(adm. in DC; not adm. in NC) Coun., Mediterranean Media Ctr.
Maher, Thomas K., (AV) .... '57 '82 C.597 B.A. L.575 J.D. [Winston&M.]
Maitland, Robert N., II ....'62 '97 C.112 B.A. L.575 J.D. [Maitland&M.]
Maitland, Scott .... '66 '97 C.870 B.S. L.575 J.D. [Maitland&M.]

Maitland & Maitland, PLLC
Maitland Law Building, 2 Couch Road, 27514
Mailing Address: P.O. Box 2525, Chapel Hill, NC 27515-2525
Telephone: 919-265-0800 Fax: 919-960-9554
Email: Info@MaitlandLaw.com URL: http://www.MaitlandLaw.com
Robert N. Maitland, II; Scott Maitland.
Language: Spanish.
Real Estate, Closings, Residential, Commercial, Business Law, Entrepreneurial, Partnerships, Small Business, Entrepreneur, Business Formation, Immigration, Naturalization, Citizenship, Permanent Resident, Investor, Teacher Visas, H1B, J1, Visa Petitions, Litigation, Banking, Contracts, Foreclosure, Mortgages, Personal Injury, Traffic Violations, DWI, DUI, Liquor License, Alcohol Permit, Wills, Banking, Collection, Sports, Entertainment Law.
See Professional Biographies, CHAPEL HILL, NORTH CAROLINA

Malizia, Deborah A., Law Office of '54 '86 C.174 B.A. L.575 J.D.
105 Dartmouth Court
Mandell, Rachel B. '70 '94 C.228 B.A. L.446 J.D.
(adm. in MD; not adm. in NC) Life Sciences Law PLLC
Mann, Richard A. .... '46 '75 C.575 B.S. L.976 J.D. Univ. of N.C.

Manning & Crouch
(See Raleigh)

Marshall, Sally J. ....'44 '80 C.55 B.A. L.284 J.D. 1058 Canterbury Ln.
Massengale, William F.W., (BV) ....'49 '84 C.951 A.B. L.575 J.D. [Massengale&O.]

Massengale & Ozer, (BV)
211 North Columbia Street, 27514
Telephone: 919-967-8555 Fax: 919-967-9835
Email: redwood@nc.rr.com URL: http://www.lawyers.com/massengale&ozer
Members of Firm: William F.W. Massengale; Marilyn G. Ozer.
Criminal Law, Traffic Violations, Driving While Intoxicated (DWI), Felonies, Drug Crimes, Misdemeanors, Sexual Assault, Criminal Appeals, Personal Injury, Motor Vehicle Law, Auto Accidents, Wrongful Death, Wills.
See Professional Biographies, CHAPEL HILL, NORTH CAROLINA

McCain, Grover C., Jr., (AV) ..... '46 '71 C&L.575 A.B., J.D. 1414 Raleigh Rd., Ste. 330
McCormick, John G., (BV) .... '48 '76 C&L.575 B.S., J.D. [J.G.McCormick]
McCormick, John G., P.A., (BV) ....976 Airport Road, Suite 150
McLamb, Janet H. ....'52 '96 C.575 B.A. L.574 J.D. 1414 Raleigh Rd., Ste. 290
McNeill, Paschall Hancock .... '42 '72 C&L.575 A.B., J.D. 1268 White Cross Rd.‡
McSurely, Alan, (BV) .... '36 '88 C.575 B.A. L.574 J.D. P.O. Box 1290
McUsic, Molly '62 '91 C.602 B.A. L.309 J.D.
(adm. in AZ; not adm. in NC) Assoc. Prof., Univ. of N.C. Sch. Of Law
Mediation Services .... P.O. Box 4886
Melamut, Steven J. '51 '97 C.690 B.S. L.575 J.D.
Law Libr., Univ. of N. C. - Chapel Hill
Merritt, Ronald W., (BV) .... '53 '78 C&L.575 A.B., J.D. [Bayliss,H.&M.]
Miller, Stephen B., (BV) ....'53 '85 C&L.575 B.A., J.D. [Alexander&M.]
Milliken, James B. '57 '84 C.546 B.A. L.569 J.D.
(adm. in NY; not adm. in NC)
V.P. for Pub. Affrs & Univ. Advancement, University of North Carolina, The
Milner, Robert Terrell .... '66 '97 C.500 B.F.A. L.575 J.D. [Baddour&M.]
Morgan, William C., Jr. '63 '88 C.34 B.S.B.A. L.575 J.D.
1829 E. Franklin St., Ste. 800-A
Morphis, Thomas C., Jr. ..... '76 '02 C&L.575 B.A., J.D. 1829 E. Franklin St., Ste. 800-A
Mount, Lillard H., (AV) ....'14 '47 C.1318 L.228 J.D. Gen. Coun., Investors Title Ins. Co.

Muller, Eric L. '62 '87 C.103 A.B. L.976 J.D.
(adm. in NJ; not adm. in NC) Prof. of Law, Univ. of NC Sch. of Law
Murphy, Janine McPeters .... '52 '85 C&L.575 B.A., J.D. UNC-Chapel Hill
Murphy, Karen Krajci, (BV) .... '49 '75 C.589 B.A. L.209 J.D. 1829 E. Franklin St.
Murrell, Sherrill T. .... '64 '93 C&L.575 B.A., J.D. 210 N. Columbia St., 2nd Fl.
Nakell, Barry, Law Offices of .... '42 '66 C.112 L.339 LL.B. 149 Dixie Drive
Nease, Martha LeAnn, (AV) '55 '84
C&L.575 B.A., J.D. 101 North Columbia Street (⊙Chapel Hill)
Nicholson, Anthony D. .... '68 '98 C.150 B.U.P. L.575 J.D. [Lewis,A.P.G.&H.]
Norman, Wilfred H. '22 '78 C.011 B.S. L.724 J.D.
(adm. in NJ; not adm. in NC) 255 Carolina Meadows Villa
Northen, John A., (AV) .... '50 '75 C&L.575 A.B., J.D. [Northen B.]

Northen Blue, L.L.P., (AV) BB
1414 Raleigh Road Suite 435, P.O. Box 2208, 27515-2208
Telephone: 919-968-4441 Facsimile: 919-942-6603
Email: jla@nbfirm.com
Members of Firm: John A. Northen; J. William Blue, Jr.; David M. Rooks, III; Charles H. Thibaut; Carol J. Holcomb; Vicki L. Parrott. Associates: Emily Curto Weatherford; Stephanie Osborne-Rodgers; Samantha Hyatt Cabe.
Personal Injury, Professional Liability, Trials, Bankruptcy, Business Law, Real Property, Land Use, Family Law, Wills, Estate Planning, Estate Administration, Trusts, Juvenile Law.
References: SunTrust Bank; Investors Title Insurance Co.; First Union National Bank; Centura Bank; BB&T; Balbirer & Coleman, CPA's.
See Professional Biographies, CHAPEL HILL, NORTH CAROLINA

Nowlin, Michelle B. ....'65 '92 C.260 B.A. L.228 J.D. Sr. Atty., Southern Envir. Law Ctr.
Oettinger, Elmer R., Jr. ...... '13 '40 C&L.575 A.B., LL.B. Prof. Emeritus, Univ. of N.C.‡
Oglesby, David W. ....'51 '84 C.576 B.S. L.575 J.D. Kenan Institute of Private Enterprise
Oglesby, H. Patrick .... '47 '77 C.198 B.A. L.575 J.D. [P.Oglesby]
Oglesby, Patrick .... 1830 N. Lakeshore Dr.
Okun, Michael G., (AV) .... '47 '80 C.33 B.A. L.575 J.D. [Patterson H.] (⊙Raleigh)

Osborn, J. Kirk, (AV) '42 '74 C.174 B.A. L.575 J.D.
1829 East Franklin Street 600 Franklin Square, 27514
Telephone: 919-929-0987 Fax: 919-929-2740
Email: kirkosborn@aol.com URL: http://www.kirkosborn.com
General Civil and Criminal Litigation in State and Federal Courts. Criminal, Drug Crimes, Driving While Intoxicated (DWI), White Collar Crimes, Homicide, Traffic Violations, Premises Liability, Personal Injury and Nursing Home Litigation, Wrongful Death, Civil Rights.
See Professional Biographies, CHAPEL HILL, NORTH CAROLINA

Osborne-Rodgers, Stephanie .... '67 '00 C.383 B.A. L.896 J.D. [Ⓐ Northen B.]
Owens, David W. '50 '75 C&L.575 A.B., J.D.
Prof. of Pub. Law & Govt., Univ. of NC at Chapel Hill
Ozer, Marilyn G., (BV) ....'48 '91 C.881 A.B. L.575 J.D. [Massengale&O.]
Parrott, Vicki L. .... '68 '98 C.575 B.A. L.1228 J.D. [Northen B.]

Patrick, Michael W., (AV) '50 '77 C.228 A.B. L.575 J.D.
312 West Franklin Street, P.O. Box 16848, 27516-6848
Mailing Address: P.O. Box 16848, Chapel Hill, NC 27516-6848
Telephone: 919-960-5848 Fax: 919-967-4953
Email: mpatrick@ncproductslaw.com URL: http://www.ncproductslaw.com
Products Liability, Malpractice, Environmental, Toxic Torts, Asbestos, Federal Criminal Law.
See Professional Biographies, CHAPEL HILL, NORTH CAROLINA

Patterson, Henry N., Jr., (AV) '40 '66 C&L.575 A.B., LL.B.
[Patterson H.] (⊙Raleigh)

Patterson Harkavy LLP, (AV) BB
100 Europa Drive, Suite 250, 27517 ⊙
Telephone: 919-942-5200 Toll Free: 800-458-2541 Facsimile: 919-942-5256
URL: http://www.pathlaw.com
Henry N. Patterson, Jr.; Leto Copeley; Valerie Alston Johnson; Burton Craige (Resident, Raleigh, North Carolina Office); Ann Elizabeth Groninger (Resident, Raleigh, North Carolina Office); Michael G. Okun (Resident, Raleigh, North Carolina Office).
Trial, Appellate and Dispute Resolution Practice in all State and Federal Courts. Personal Injury, Wrongful Death, Medical Malpractice, Workers' Compensation, Labor, Employment, Civil Rights, and Criminal.
Greensboro, North Carolina Office: 101 South Elm Street, P.O. Box 29269, 27429-9269. Telephone: 336-370-4200. Facsimile: 336-274-8490.
Raleigh, North Carolina Office: 414 West Jones Street, P.O. Box 27927, 27611. Telephone: 919-755-1812. Facsimile: 919-755-0124.
See Professional Biographies, CHAPEL HILL, NORTH CAROLINA

Paul, Stephen R. .... '57 '86 C.103 B.A. L.809 J.D. [Edgar&P.]
Peele, Stanley .... '32 '59 C&L.575 LL.B. 1709 Michaux Rd.
Petersen, Ann Bach, (AV) .... '48 '78 C&L.966 J.D. [Glover&P.]
Phay, Robert E. .... '38 '64 C.500 B.A. L.976 J.D. Univ. of N.C.
Phillips, J. Dickson, III .... '54 '79 C.198 A.B. L.575 J.D. [Lewis,A.P.G.&H.]
Phillips, J. Dickson, Jr. .... '22 '48 C.198 B.S. L.575 J.D. Sr. U.S. Cir. J.
Phillips, James D., Jr. .... '22 '49 C.198 B.S. L.575 J.D. P.O. Box 4691‡
Pickering, Sandra J. .... '52 '81 C.429 B.A. L.767 J.D. 1829 E. Franklin St., Ste. 600
Pieroni, Mario J. '14 '40 C.63 L.602 LL.B.
(adm. in IN; not adm. in NC) 9 Rogerson Dr.‡
Pipkin, R. Michael, (BV) .... '36 '72 C.968 B.A. L.575 J.D. [R.M.Pipkin]
Pipkin, R. Michael, P.A., (BV) .... 100 Europa Dr.
Poole, Gary R., (BV) .... '60 '85 C&L.575 B.A., J.D. [G.R.Poole]
Poole, Gary R., P.A., Law Office of, (BV) .... 124 Timberhill Place
Potter, Michael R. .... '49 '78 C.674 A.B. L.923 J.D. 75 Cedar Hills Circle
Reynolds, Lisa Anne Wagner .... '66 '00 C.1130 B.A. L.575 J.D. [Ⓐ D.A.Davis]
Rice, Robert Kendrick .... '73 '02 C.34 B.S., B.A. L.472 J.D. [Ⓐ Higgins,F.G.&M.]
Richardson, Dexter '— '02 C.1163 B.A. L.577 J.D.
1829 E. Franklin Street, Building 600
Riddle, Helen C. .... '53 '88 C.575 B.A. L.276 J.D. 8210 Reynard Rd.
Robbins, Orrin R. ....'51 '88 C.575 B.A. L.1345 J.D. 431 W. Franklin Street
Roberson, Antony Derek ....'70 '96 C&L.575 B.S.B.A., J.D. [Snider&R.]
Roberts, Barry S. ....'48 '73 C.645 B.A. L.659 J.D. Campus Box 3490 Mccall Bldg
Robertson, Michelle F. .... '51 '83 C.228 B.A. L.575 J.D. Univ. of N. C.
Rogers, Cynthia D. .... '59 '95 C.147 B.A. L.940 J.D. 101 Forest Ridge Dr.
Rooks, David M., III, (AV) .... '49 '76 C.575 A.B. L.228 J.D. [Northen B.]
Rosenberg, Martin A., (BV) ...'47 '89 C.24 B.A. L.574 J.D. 1829 E. Franklin St., Ste. 500
Rudolf, David S., (AV) .... '49 '75 C.705 A.B. L.569 J.D. [Rudolf W.&F.] ⊙
Rudolf Widenhouse & Fialko, (AV) .... 312 West Franklin Street (⊙Charlotte)
Rundell, Margaret Dube .... '51 '79 C.867 B.A. L.575 J.D. P.O. Box 1194
Sacco, James S., (CV) ....'63 '91 C.415 B.S. L.1019 J.D. 25307 Ludwell
Sanders, John L. .... '27 '55 C&L.575 B.A., J.D. Univ. of N. C. at Chapel Hill
Saunders, Melissa L. .... '60 '88 C.976 B.A. L.893 J.D. UNC Law School
Savery, Rex T., Jr. .... '41 '69 C&L.575 B.A., J.D. 1829 E. Franklin St.
Schmitt, Anne Luper ....'48 '80 C.228 B.A. L.215 J.D. 1926 Overland Dr.
Schwab, Anna Katherine ....'61 '90 C&L.575 B.A., J.D. 1011 Highland Woods Rd.
Schwarcz, Susan K. '54 '80 C.66 B.A. L.978 J.D.
(adm. in NY; not adm. in NC) 109 Boxwood Pl.‡
Sechriest, Mary P. ....'51 '76 C&L.575 A.B., J.D. Univ. of N. Carolina at Chapel Hill
Seidel, Robert Raymond, (CV) '62 '88
C.746 B.A. L.300 J.D. 1525 E. Franklin St., Ste. 5B

Sessoms & Rogers, P.A.
(See Durham)

Shangler, Dean A., (BV) .... '— '83 C.112 B.A. L.575 J.D. 1829 E. Franklin St., Ste. 600
Sharpless, Richard Kennedy '11 '36 C.94 A.B. L.309 J.D.
(adm. in PA; not adm. in NC) 750 Weaver Dairy Rd.‡
Sheldon, James E. .... '47 '72 C.197 B.A. L.1065 J.D. 3 Sedgewood Rd.
Shivers, David O. '67 '92 C.880 B.A. L.744 J.D.
V.P. & Tr. Off., Central Carolina Bk. & Tr. Co.
Simmons, Jan S. '55 '85 C.383 B.S. L.790 J.D.
The U of NC At Chapel Hill, Cb # 3330
Simpson, William G., Jr. .... '60 '86 C&L.575 B.A., J.D. [Ferguson,S.C.G.&S.]
Smith, Joanna Carey '70 '95 C&L.575 B.A., J.D.
Asst. Univ. Coun., UNC-Chapel Hill, Off. of Univ. Coun.
Smith, Nathaniel C., (BV) ....'61 '93 C&L.575 B.A., J.D. [Bagwell,H.&S.]
Smith, Virginia D. .... '52 '93 C.575 B.A. L.1228 J.D. 108 Hampshire Pl.
Snider, Richard J., Jr., (BV) .... '49 '79 C.363 B.A. L.161 J.D. [Snider&R.]
Snider & Roberson, P.A., (BV) ....1829 E. Franklin St., Ste. 800-C
Sobocinski, Eric J. .... '69 '96 C&L.884 B.A., J.D. 100 Europa Dr., Ste. 300
Stackhouse, Alexis N. .... '— '99 C.160 B.A. L.575 J.D. U.S. Air Force JAG Offr.
Stancill, Susan A., (BV) ....'62 '88 C&L.575 B.A., J.D. Univ. of N.C. Sch. of Law
Stanford, Donald M., Jr. .... '51 '78 C.103 A.B. L.1162 J.D. P.O. Box 495
Stanford, Lewis '— '91 C&L.575 B.S., J.D.
Gen. Legal Coun., Chf. Legal Offr., Divi Resorts
Stark, Thomas H., (BV) ....'55 '81 C&L.228 B.A., J.D. [Stark]

Stark Law Group, PLLC, (BV)
5925 Farrington Road, Suite 200, 27517
Telephone: 919-490-5550 Fax: 919-490-5551
Email: tom@starklawgroup.com URL: http://www.lawyers.com/thomasstark
Thomas H. Stark. Associates: Fiona Valerie Ginter; W. Russell Congleton.
Construction, Commercial and Corporate Litigation. Personal Injury Litigation, Environmental Law, Computer and Intellectual Property Law, Corporate Acquisitions and Real Property Law, Real Estate Closings, Business Law.
See Professional Biographies, CHAPEL HILL, NORTH CAROLINA

Stave, Gregg M. .... '57 '84 C.453 S.B. L.228 J.D. 6407 Stoneridge Pl.
Stein, Adam, (AV) ....'37 '68 C.569 B.A. L.273 J.D. [Ferguson,S.C.G.&S.]
Stein, Kimberly P. .... '68 '96 C&L.575 B.A., J.D. 207 Short Street
Stewart, John T., (BV) .... '46 '75 C.575 B.A. L.574 J.D. [Levine&S.]
Stewart, Judith G. ....'30 '89 C.881 B.A. L.574 J.D. 101 Mossbark Ln
Stewart, Richard E. '33 '60 C.923 B.A. L.309 LL.B.
(adm. in NY; not adm. in NC) Stewart Economics, Inc.
Stewart, William S., (AV) .... '25 '48 C.277 B.S. L.309 LL.B. 449 Lake Shore Ln.‡
Strohm, Leslie Chambers '56 '81
(adm. in MO; not adm. in NC) Gen. Coun., Univ. of N.C.
Suddarth, Thomas H., Jr. .... '23 '51 C&L.575 B.A., J.D. 209 1/2 N. Columbia St.‡
Sussman, Oscar '17 '88 L.776 J.D.
(adm. in FL; not adm. in NC) 750 Weaver Dairy Rd., Apt. 6102‡
Taylor, Nelson F. ....'21 '49 C.575 B.A. L.309 LL.B. Univ. of NC Sch. of Law‡

Tharrington Smith
(See Raleigh)

Thibaut, Charles H., (BV) .... '53 '81 C.296 B.A. L.574 J.D. [Northen B.]
Thomas, Kathryn J. .... '56 '86 C.881 A.B. L.575 J.D. 1415 Tallyho Tr.
Thornburg, Thomas H. .... '62 '90 C.231 B.A. L.477 J.D. Prof., Univ. of North Carolina
Thorp, William L., (AV) .... '25 '51 C&L.575 LL.B. 214 A McCauley St.
Toth, Dannette D. ....'46 '03 C.112 A.B. L.577 J.D. [Ⓐ Long&L.]

Twiggs, Beskind, Strickland & Rabenau, P.A.
(See Raleigh)

Tyndall, Amos G. .... '65 '92 C.575 B.A. L.574 J.D. [A.Tyndall]
Tyndall, Amos .... 312 W. Franklin St.
Vancil, Paul, (AVⓉ) .... '51 '86 C.502 B.J. L.575 J.D. [P.Vancil] ⊙
Vancil, Paul, P.C., Law Office of, (AVⓉ) .... 7621 Justin Place (⊙Atlanta, GA)
Van Noppen, Donnell, III, (AV) '52 '80
C.976 B.A. L.575 J.D. Sr. Atty., Southern Envir. Law Ctr.

Vira Law Firm, The, PA
(See Carrboro)

Wahl, Kenneth John ....'40 '81 128 Forsyth Drive, Suite A
Waldrup, J. Charles .... '51 '76 C.838 B.S. L.575 J.D. P.O. Box 2688
Walker, Patrice .... '— '76 C&L.575 A.B., J.D. P.O. Box 16157
Wallace, Carl E., Jr. '44 '70
C&L.575 A.B., J.D. V.P. & Corp. Coun., Investors Title Ins. Co.
Weatherford, Emily Curto ....'73 '00 C.575 B.A. L.1228 J.D. [Ⓐ Northen B.]
Wegner, Judith W. '50 '76 C.966 B.A. L.1068 J.D.
(adm. in CA; not adm. in NC) Dean, Univ. of N.C. Sch. of Law
Wehr, Candace A. .... '78 '03 C.575 B.A. L.574 J.D. [Ⓐ Bayliss,H.&M.]
Weissman, Deborah M., (BVⓉ) .... '51 '75 C&L.823 B.A., J.D. U. of NC School of Law
West, David A. .... '73 '98 C.659 B.A. L.309 J.D. 95131 Vance Knls.
Whaley, Gary M., (AV) '52 '84 C.575 B.A. L.117 J.D.
Investors Title Insurance Company
Widenhouse, M. Gordon, Jr., (AV) ....'54 '81 C.198 A.B. L.896 J.D. [Rudolf W.&F.]
Willett, Christopher M. ....'73 '00 C&L.575 B.A., J.D. [Ⓐ J.G.McCormick]
Williams, Donald A. .... '23 '51 C&L.575 LL.B. [Ⓒ Alexander&M.]
Wilson, Peter S., Jr., (AVⓉ) ....'58 '84 C.1031 B.S. L.982 J.D. 106 Hillspring Ln.‡
Winer, David M. .... '44 '68 C.696 B.A. L.93 LL.B. 111 Stoneridge Dr.‡
Winfrey, Carolyn B., (BV) ......'61 '91 C.575 B.S. L.574 J.D. Kenneth R. Embree PLLC
Winner, Leslie J., (AV) '50 '76 C.103 A.B. L.588 J.D.
V.P. & Gen. Coun., University of North Carolina, The
Winston, Barry T., (AV) .... '34 '61 C&L.575 A.B., J.D. [Winston&M.]

Winston & Maher, (AV) BB
312 W. Franklin Street, 27516
Telephone: 919-929-1043 Fax: 919-967-4953
Email: winstonandmaher.com URL: http://www.winstonandmaher.com
Members of Firm: Barry T. Winston (Board Certified Specialist in Criminal Law, North Carolina State Board of Legal Specialization); Thomas K. Maher.
General Civil, Criminal Trial Practice in all State and Federal Courts, Felonies, Misdemeanors, Drugs and Narcotics, White Collar Crime, Traffic Violations, Driving While Intoxicated.
Reference: Village Bank.
See Professional Biographies, CHAPEL HILL, NORTH CAROLINA

Wolfenden, Betsy J., Law Office of '55 '00
C.296 B.S. L.575 J.D. 99 S. Elliott Road, Suite 11
Wright, Katherine Settle, (BV) .... '26 '48 C.945 A.B. L.575 LL.B. 201A E. Rosemary St.

Yarborough, Jan E., (AV) ... '57 '87 C.577 B.S.N. L.896 J.D. [Yarborough]

Yarborough Law Office, (AV)
P.O. Box 2635, 27515-2635
Telephone: 919-401-5399 Fax: 919-402-9339
Email: jyarborough@jyarborough.com URL: http://www.lawyers.com/yarboroughlaw
Jan E. Yarborough.
Health Care Law, Hospital Law, Managed Care Contracting and Regulatory Compliance.
See Professional Biographies, CHAPEL HILL, NORTH CAROLINA

Yarbrough, Marilyn V. '45 '73 C.887 B.A. L.1068 J.D.
(adm. in CA; not adm. in NC) Univ. of N.C. College of Law

Zaman, Karen, & Associates
(See Charlotte)

Zeiger, Errol ... '39 '91 C.563 B.S. L.574 J.D. 800 Indian Springs Rd‡
Zimmerman, Scott D., (BV) ... '63 '89 C&L.575 B.A., J.D. [Brown&B.]
Zoffer, David B., (AV) ... '47 '73 C.1019 B.A. L.262 J.D. Exec. V.P., ICALM Grp.

CHARLOTTE, * 540,828, *Mecklenburg Co.*

Abbott, Claudia Hahn ... '59 '84 C.475 B.A. L.838 J.D. 5601 Red Osier Ct.
Abel, Robert M. ... '42 '71 C&L.339 B.S., J.D. 121 West Trade Street, Suite 3000
Abel, Shelley K. ... '80 '05 C&L.575 A.B., J.D. [🄰 Rayburn C.&D.]
Aberman, J. Mitchell, (AV) ... '56 '84 C&L.893 B.S., J.D. [James,M.&D.]
Abernethy, W. Miller, Jr., (AV) ... '61 '87 C.575 B.A. L.309 J.D. [Moore&V.P.]
Aberra, Adam E. ... '77 '02 C&L.575 B.A., J.D. [🄰 Moore&V.P.]
Abner, Kenneth J., (BV) ... '69 '95 C.575 B.S. L.276 J.D. Gen. Coun., The Boulevard Co.
Achenberg, Arden Lynn, (CVⓉ) '67 '92
C.696 B.A. L.201 J.D. Corp. Coun., Compass Group, U.S.A. Inc.
Acker, Sheila E. '62 '88 C.867 B.A. L.978 J.D.
(adm. in NY; not adm. in NC) Of Coun., J. Richards Gallery
Ackermann, Stacy G. ... '76 '01 C.269 B.A. L.790 J.D. [🄰 Alston&B.]
Ackermann, Steven T. ... '— '02 C.801 B.S. L.1119 J.D. [🄰 McGuireWoods]
Acton, William D., Jr., (BV) ... '52 '77 C.576 B.A. L.574 J.D. [DeVore A.&S.]
Adams, Alice Pinckney ... '— '97 C&L.838 B.A., J.D. [Robinson,B.&H.]
Adams, Carmen R. '60 '92 C.161 B.Ch.E. L.1003 J.D.
V.P. & Asst. Gen. Coun., Wachovia Corporation (Pat.)
Adams, G. Bryan, III, (AV) ... '65 '90 C.968 B.A. L.896 J.D. [VanHoy,R.A.&D.]
Adams, Michael G., (BV) ... '62 '89 C.893 B.A. L.846 J.D. [Parker,P.A.&B.]
Adams, Norris A., II ... '79 '04 C.1228 B.A. L.896 J.D. [🄰 Essex R.]

Adams, Robert C. '61 '95 C.1128 B.A. L.790 J.D.
6425 Idlewild Road, Suite 212-A, 28212
Telephone: 704-566-9898 Fax: 704-566-9899
Email: adamslaw@carolina.rr.com URL: http://www.robertcadamslaw.com
Wills, Living Wills, Trust Law, Trusts and Estates, Estate Planning, Estate Administration, Trust Administration, Probate, Taxation, Tax Law, Income Tax, Business Law, Corporate Law, Business Formation, Incorporation, Contracts Breach of Contract, Contract Litigation.
See Professional Biographies, CHARLOTTE, NORTH CAROLINA

Adams, T. Jonathan ... '63 '95 C.383 B.B.A. L.575 J.D. [Hamilton F.M.S.S.&M.]
Adams, T.V., (AV) ... '39 '70 C.198 A.B. L.575 J.D. 6201 Fairview Rd.
Adams, W. Thad, III, (AV) ... '46 '71 C.576 B.S. L.575 J.D. [Adams E.] (See Pat. Sect.)

Adams Evans P.A., (AV)
2180 Two Wachovia Center, 301 South Tryon Street, 28282
Telephone: 704-375-9249 Fax: 704-375-0729 URL: http://www.adamsevans.com
URL: http://www.adamspat.com
W. Thad Adams, III; J. Scott Evans;—Stephen S. Ashley, Jr.; Matthew Jacob Ladenheim; Jonathan M. Hines; Brandon C. Trego; Kathryn A. Gromlovits; Seth L. Hudson.
Patent, Trademark, Copyright and Unfair Competition Law.
Representative Clients: Aplix, S.A.; B/E Aerospace, Inc.; Armstrong World Industries, Inc.; Belmont Textile Machinery Co.; BSN Medical, Inc.; Britax Child Safety, Inc.; Nissan Motors; Royal Doulton (UK) Limited.
Reference: Wachovia Bank.
See Professional Biographies, CHARLOTTE, NORTH CAROLINA

Adamy, Ansley M. ... '72 '98 C&L.362 B.A., J.D. P.O. Box 79197
Adcock, A. Mark, (AV) ... '57 '83 C.896 B.A. L.575 J.D. [Moore&V.P.]
Adden, Robert S., Jr., (BV) ... '57 '82 C.152 B.S. L.575 J.D. [Ruff,B.C.W.&B.]
Additon, Richard L. ... '66 '96 C.431 B.S. L.893 J.D. [Summa&A.] (See Pat. Sect.)
Adkins, Karl ... '46 '71 C.575 A.B. L.477 J.D. Supr. Ct. J.
Agisim, Keith D. '69 '96 C.477 B.S. L.178 J.D.
Gen. Coun., IP Innovations Financial Services, Inc. (Pat.)
Agosto, Lou M. ... '67 '97 C.575 B.S.B.A. L.880 J.D. [Moore&V.P.]
Ahlum, Greg C., (BV) ... '62 '87 C&L.896 B.S., J.D. [Johnston,A.&H.]
Ainsworth, Jenny S. ... '60 '86 C.896 B.A. L.1228 J.D. E.E.O.C.
Aitken, P.C. ... 345 E. Woodlawn Road
Aitken, Margaret A. ... '48 '74 C.838 B.A. L.880 J.D. [Aitken]
Akers, James E. ... '71 '97 C.880 B.A. L.845 J.D. [Moore&V.P.]
Albanese, Marna M. ... '— '98 C.890 B.A. L.564 J.D. [🄰 McNair]
Albee, Christopher Jay ... '66 '00 C.886 B.A. L.574 J.D. [🄰 McMillan&T.]
Aldrich, Jeffrey W., Jr. '70 '02 C.976 B.A. L.945 J.D.
(adm. in OH; not adm. in NC) [🄰 Cadwalader,W.&T.]
Alexander, Dennis W. '46 '72 C.401 B.S. L.884 J.D.
(adm. in PA; not adm. in NC) Group Sr. V.P. & Gen. Coun., Cogentrix Energy, Inc.
Alexander, H. Heath, (AV) ... '54 '79 C&L.575 B.S., J.D. [Moore&V.P.]
Alexander, Mason G., (AVⓉ) ... '59 '85 C.797 B.A. L.790 J.D. [Fisher&P.]
Alexander, Rodney E. ... '60 '88 C.760 B.S. L.326 J.D. [Mayer,B.R.&M.]
Alexander, Thais M. '74 '02 C.116 B.A. L.107 J.D.
(adm. in NY; not adm. in NC) [🄰 Mayer,B.R.&M.]
Allan, Albert P. ... '57 '92 C.472 B.S. L.602 J.D. [Summa&A.] (See Pat. Sect.)
Allen, David Neal, (AV) ... '55 '80 C&L.575 A.B., J.D. [Parker,P.A.&B.]
Allen, James, Jr., (AV) ... '33 '64 C.260 B.S.B.A. L.575 LL.B. 123 Wonderwood Drive
Allen, R. Michael, (AV) ... '59 '84 C&L.575 B.S., J.D. [Cranford,S.&T.]
Allen, Robert W., (BV) ... '— '85 C&L.575 A.B., J.D. [🄲 Robinson,B.&H.]
Allen, Wm. A. ... '21 '43 C&L.893 B.A., LL.B. 200 Colville Rd.‡
Alley, Wade H., Jr. ... '43 '68 C.608 B.A. L.575 J.D. Sr. V.P., Bank of America, N.A.
Allison, Courtney D. '67 '92 C.838 B.A. L.245 J.D.
(adm. in AL; not adm. in NC) First Union
Allison, F. Eugene, (BV) ... '59 '88 C.886 B.S. L.575 J.D. [Kirk P.&T.]
Allison, James W., (AV) ... '44 '69 C.198 A.B. L.575 J.D. [Johnston,A.&H.]
Allison, John D., (BV) ... '— '92 C.198 B.A. L.245 J.D. [Kennedy C.L.&H.]
Allison, June K., (BV) ... '54 '81 C&L.575 B.A., J.D. [Wishart,N.H.&P.]
Allred, John T., (AV) ... '— '59 C&L.575 B.S., J.D. [Kilpatrick S.]
Allred, Stephen David ... '63 '92 C.1320 B.A. L.893 J.D. [Helms M.&W.]
Almond, Michael A., (AV) ... '49 '75 C&L.575 B.A., J.D. [🄲 Parker,P.A.&B.]
Alridge, Carl Spencer, II ... '66 '92 C.339 B.A. L.273 J.D. Transamerica Reinsurance
Alridge, Spencer '66 '92 C.339 B.A. L.273 J.D.
V.P. & Assoc. Gen. Coun., Transamerica Reinsurance
Alston, Charles L., Jr. ... '68 '93 C&L.575 B.A., J.D. [Alston]
Alston, Simone F. ... '— '93 C.659 B.A. L.575 J.D. [Alston]

Alston & Bird LLP, (AV) BR
Bank of America Plaza, 101 South Tryon Street, Suite 4000, 28280-4000 ⊙
Telephone: 704-444-1000 Telecopier: 704-444-1111
Email: info@alston.com URL: http://www.alston.com
Members of Firm: Blas P. Arroyo; William M. Atkinson; Martha Gayle Barber; John J. Barnhardt, III; John F. Baron; Mark T. Calloway; Michael S. Connor; Jason P. Cooper; James A.L. Daniel, Jr.; Brian M. Davis; Paul S. Donohue; Charles B. Elderkin; Guy R. Gosnell; Donald M. Hill, Jr.; H. Bryan Ives III; Gary C. Ivey; Larry C. Jones; C. Mark Kelly; Lance A. Lawson; Raymond O. Linker, Jr.; Ernest B. Lipscomb, III; Dickson M. Lupo; Michael D. McCoy; Richard M. McDermott; Catherine Amspacher Meeker; William Kevin Ransom; Bruce J. Rose; Charles B. Simmons, Jr.; John L. Sullivan, Jr.; George M. Taulbee; Anne M. Tompkins; Henry B. Ward, III. Of Counsel: Paul B. Bell. Counsel: Michelle J. Cole; Meredith S. Jeffries; Samuel G. Layton, Jr.; Leigh M. Levine; Lee R. Rimler; Robert J. Sullivan (Not admitted in NC); Thomas G. Walker. Associates: Stacy G. Ackermann; Timothy Balts; Joseph E. Bracken; Kirk T. Bradley; Nachael L. Bright; Gregory J. Carlin; Michael T. Cecka; Glen R. Drysdale; Brian Ellsworth; Alexis W. Finniss; Nicholas F. Gallo; Christopher J. Gegg; Theodore C. George; David L. Gildernew (Not admitted in NC); Heather Gregg; Catherine L. Hess; Hannah H. Kim; Trent A. Kirk; Jonathan E. Kutner; Clay A. Littlefield; Beth R. MacDonald; Jitendra Malik, Ph.D.; Ashley B. Menser; Michael G. Mosier; Kevin O'Brien; Katharine F. Pierce; S. Benjamin Pleune; Anne J. Randall; Keith Roberson; Benjamin F. Sidbury; Jason M. Sneed; Jason J. Solomon; Andrew T. Spence; R. Flynt Strean; Brian J. Teague; Chad Thorson; Christian C. Warpula; John Mark Wilson.
Languages: Bangla, Bulgarian, Croatian, French, German, Gujarati, Hindi, Italian, Japanese, Korean, Portuguese, Russian, Spanish, Tamil, Thai, Turkish, Urdu.
Administrative Law, Alternative Dispute Resolution, Antitrust and Trade Regulation, Appellate Practice, Bankruptcy, Banks and Banking, Biotechnology, Business Law, Class Actions, Commercial Real Estate, FCC Licensing, FCC Regulation, Wireless Communications, Complex and Multi-District Litigation, Computers and Software, Constitutional Law, Construction Law, Copyrights, Corporate Ethics, Corporate Governance, Corporate Law, Criminal Law, Debtor and Creditor, Electronic Commerce, Emerging Growth Companies, Employee Benefits, Employment Law, Entertainment Law, ERISA, ERISA Litigation, Energy, Environmental Law, Environmental Litigation, Executive Compensation; Finance, Franchises and Franchising, Government Investigations; Health Care Corporate Law, Health Care Regulation, Immigration Law, Insurance Defense, Intellectual Property, International Finance, International Law, International Taxation, International Trade, Internet Law, Labor Law, Labor and Employment, Land Use, Legislative Practice, Life Sciences, Litigation, Local Taxation, Medical Malpractice, Mergers, Acquisitions and Divestitures, Multimedia Law, Municipal Law, Nonprofit and Charitable Organizations, Occupational Safety and Health, Partnership Law, Patents, Privacy Law, Products Liability, Professional Liability, Public Finance, Public Policy, Real Estate Finance, Regulatory Law, RICO, Securities, Securities Litigation, State Taxation, Taxation, Tax Litigation, Technology and Science, Telecommunications Law, Trademarks, Trusts and Estates, Utility Law, Venture Capital, White Collar Crime, Zoning.
Atlanta, Georgia Office: One Atlantic Center, 1201 West Peachtree Street 30309-3424. Telephone: 404-881-7000. Telecopier: 404-881-7777.
Washington, D.C. Office: 601 Pennsylvania Avenue, N.W., North Building, 10th Floor, 20004-2601. Telephone: 202-756-3300. Telecopier: 202-756-3333.
Raleigh, North Carolina Office (Research Triangle Area): 3201 Beechleaf Court, Suite 600, 27604-1062. Telephone: 919-862-2200. Telecopier: 919-862-2260.
New York, New York Office: 90 Park Avenue, 10016-1387. Telephone: 212-210-9400. Fax: 212-210-9444.
(Liaison Office) Munich, Germany Office: Brienner Strasse 11/V, 80333 Munich. Telephone: (49) (89) 238-0-70. Telecopier: (49) (89) 238-0-7110.
See Professional Biographies, CHARLOTTE, NORTH CAROLINA

Alston Law Firm, PLLC ... 801 Baxter Street, Suite 404
Altamura, Vincent '60 '87 C.569 B.A. L.813 J.D.
(adm. in NY; not adm. in NC) Wachovia Corp.
Altman, Adam P. ... '72 '98 C.446 B.A. L.575 J.D. [🄰 Cozen O.]
Alwan, Suzanne V. '65 '99 C.36 B.A. L.228 J.D.
(adm. in NY; not adm. in NC) [🄰 Mayer,B.R.&M.]
Amann, William A. ... '47 '84 C.776 B.S. L.1206 J.D. 2613 Winding Oak Dr.
Ames, Scott K. '53 '93 C.36 B.S. L.1051 J.D.
(adm. in AZ; not adm. in NC) [Moore&V.P.]
Anders, Amanda Brantley, (BV) ... '53 '78 C&L.575 B.A., J.D. 219 Greenwich Rd.
Anderson, Corby Cochran ... '54 '94 C.945 B.A. L.893 J.D. [Helms M.&W.]
Anderson, Jennifer S. ... '— '02 C.1552 B.A. L.1228 J.D. [🄰 Hedrick E.G.&K.]
Anderson, John B. ... '71 '96 C&L.896 B.A., J.D. Wachovia Corp., Legal Div. NC0630
Anderson, John R. ... '65 '92 C.902 B.S. L.575 J.D. 2120 Scott Ave.
Anderson, L. Mark, IV ... '68 '93 C&L.838 B.S., J.D. Mng. Dir.
Anderson, Marcus L. ... '78 '04 C.846 B.A. L.896 J.D. [🄰 Hunton&W.]
Anderson, Peter C., (AV) ... '63 '92 C.705 B.S. L.893 J.D. [Shumaker,L.&K.]
Anderson, Richard Lee ... '68 '93 C.575 B.A. L.896 J.D. [Price,S.H.P.&A.]
Andolino, Joseph F. '53 '78 C&L.776 B.A., J.D.
(adm. in NY; not adm. in NC) V.P., Bus. Dev. & Tax, Goodrich Corporation
Andresen, Kenneth P., (BV) ... '50 '80 C.732 B.A. L.896 J.D. [Andresen&Assoc.]

Andresen & Associates, (BV)
2319 Crescent Avenue, 28207
Telephone: 704-377-8881 Fax: 704-377-8880
Email: ken@charlottelawyer.com URL: http://www.charlottelawyer.com
Kenneth P. Andresen.
Business Law, Business Litigation, Contracts, Corporate Law, Criminal Defense, Traffic Violations, DUI, Whit Collar Crimes, Drug Crimes.
See Professional Biographies, CHARLOTTE, NORTH CAROLINA

Andrews, Neil P. ... '— '95 C.184 B.S. L.1048 J.D. [Hedrick E.G.&K.]
Andry, Allain C., IV, (AV) ... '— '86 C.228 A.B. L.813 J.D. [Robinson,B.&H.]
Aniel, Jan H. '— '82 C.112 B.A. L.800 J.D.
(adm. in CA; not adm. in NC) Asst. Gen. Coun., Bank of America
Annas, Katherine R. ... '— '03 C.968 B.A. L.575 J.D. [🄰 Kennedy C.L.&H.]
Antrim, Patrick S. ... '— '74 C&L.575 B.A., J.D. Asst. Gen. Coun., Bank of America
Aperans, Gundars '— '72 C.197 A.B. L.893 J.D.
(adm. in NY; not adm. in NC) [🄲 Robinson,B.&H.]
Archibald, C. Murphy ... '44 '80 C.88 B.A. L.588 J.D. P.O. Box 35605
Archie, Carla N. ... '— '95 C.302 B.S. L.945 J.D. Dist. Atty.'s Off.
Ardizzone, Dale S. '63 '90 C.888 B.S. L.1338 J.D.
(adm. in DC; not adm. in NC)
V.P., Bus. Affrs. & Gen. Coun., The Inspirational Network, Inc.
Arey, A. Carter ... '— '03 C&L.575 B.A., J.D. [🄰 Helms M.&W.]
Arfa, Richard S. ... '45 '71 C.331 B.A. L.273 J.D. [🄰 Carroll&C.]
Arnholt Kahn, Raizel ... '77 '02 C&L.575 B.A., J.D. [🄰 Bishop,C.&M.]
Arnot, Justin T. ... '69 '98 C.506 B.S. L.300 J.D. Billy Graham Evangelistic Assoc.
Arrowood, John S., (BV) ... '56 '82 C.125 B.A. L.575 J.D. [James,M.&D.]
Arroyo, Blas P., (AV) ... '56 '81 C.576 B.S. L.902 J.D. [Alston&B.] (See Pat. Sect.)
Asbill, Craig O. ... '74 '00 C.576 B.A. L.469 J.D. [🄲 C.G.Monnett,III&Assoc.]
Ashburg, Ray ... '71 '03 C.1128 B.S. L.896 J.D. [Hammer,A.&H.]

Ashcraft, Thomas J., (AV) '51 '78 C.575 B.A. L.896 J.D.
Suite 120, 521 E. Morehead Street, 28202-2631
Telephone: 704-333-2300 Fax: 704-333-2352
Litigation in Federal and State Courts.
See Professional Biographies, CHARLOTTE, NORTH CAROLINA

Ashe, Jesse B., III, (CV) '63 '98 C.1070 B.S. L.831 J.D.
11610 North Community House Road, Suite 200 (Pat.) (⊙Charlotte)

Ashe, Jesse B., III, (CV) '63 '98
C.1070 B.S. L.831 J.D. [Summa&A.] (See Pat. Sect.) (⊙Charlotte)
Ashley, Debra A. '67 '94 C.66 B.A. L.276 J.D.
(adm. in NY; not adm. in NC) Asst. Gen. Coun., Lending Tree, Inc.
Ashley, Stephen S., Jr. ....'71 '97 C.230 B.A. L.356 J.D. [Ⓐ Adams E.] (See Pat. Sect.)
Ashton, Abraham M. ....'— '05 C.779 B.S. L.923 J.D. [Ⓐ Kennedy C.L.&H.]
Askins-Sullivan, Myra T. ....'— '94 C.838 B.S. L.896 J.D. [Ⓐ Kennedy C.L.&H.]
Asmar, Thomas M. '74 '01 C&L.339 B.S., J.D.
(adm. in IL; not adm. in NC) [Ⓐ Poyner&S.]
Asmer, Peter F., Jr., (BV) .... '65 '91 C.968 B.A. L.790 J.D. [Cozen O.]
Atkins, Gay Rousseau ....'49 '76 C.290 A.B. L.192 J.D. 720 E. 4th St.
Atkinson, Brian Thomas, (BV) ....'65 '92 C.1128 B.S. L.575 J.D. [Moore&V.P.]
Atkinson, Terra K. ....'77 '02 C.699 B.A. L.893 J.D. [Ⓐ Katten M.R.]
Atkinson, William M., (AV) '58 '88 C.632 B.S. L.1209 J.D.
[Alston&B.] (See Pat. Sect.)
Atta, Maureen C. ....'71 '01 C.269 B.A. L.574 J.D. Legal Aid of North Carolina, Inc.
Auger, Arlene Patricia ....'65 '92 C.1019 B.B.A. L.1325 J.D. [Auger&A.]
Auger, Herbert W.........................'65 '90 C.1353 B.S. L.1325 J.D. [Auger&A.]

Auger & Auger
6425 Idlewild Road, Suite 212, 28212
Telephone: 704-567-7571 Toll Free: 1-800-977-7396 Fax: 704-568-4062
Email: hwa@augerlaw.com URL: http://www.lawyers.com/augerlaw
Herbert W. Auger; Arlene Patricia Auger.
Automobile and Truck Accidents, Wrongful Death Claims, Workers' Compensation, Dog Bites, Injuries to Children, Daycare Accidents, Construction Site Accidents, Nursing Home Negligence and Medical Malpractice.
See Professional Biographies, CHARLOTTE, NORTH CAROLINA

Augliera, Anthony R. '65 '91 C.1041 B.B.A. L.262 J.D.
(adm. in NY; not adm. in NC) First Union Corp.
Austin, Patricia J. '— '87 C.881 B.A. L.823 J.D.
(adm. in PA; not adm. in NC) Wachovia Corporation
Avram, M. Andrew, (BV) .... '60 '90 C&L.896 B.A., J.D. [Cranfill,S.&H.]
Ayers, John F., III, (BV) .... '60 '86 C.575 B.S. L.1228 J.D. [Sellers,H.A.D.&L.]
Ayers, Kristen Ness .... '73 '00 C.228 B.A. L.790 J.D. [Ⓑ Moore&V.P.]
Aylward, Ilonka .... '67 '02 C.145 Ph.D. L.893 J.D. 414 Fenton Pl., Ste. D
Aylward, Robert J. .... '61 '93 C.1374 B.A. L.1325 J.D. [Ⓐ Golding H.&P.]
Ayscue, E. Osborne, Jr., (AV) ....'33 '60 C&L.575 A.B., J.D. [Ⓑ Helms M.&W.]
Aziz, Cynthia A., (BV) .... '— '87 C.518 B.A. L.1202 J.D. [C.A.Aziz]
Aziz, C. A., P.A., (BV) .... 1804 East Boulevard
Azzariti, Deborah S. '72 '97 C.896 B.A. L.245 J.D.
(adm. in GA; not adm. in NC) [Ⓐ Morris,M.&M.]

Bach, Eric A. '66 '93 C.198 A.B. L.692 J.D.
900 Baxter Street, Suite 109, P.O. Box 33566, 28204
Telephone: 704-376-3980 Fax: 704-331-9636
Email: ebach@mindspring.com URL: http://www.ericbachlaw.com
Criminal Law in State and Federal Courts, Drug Offences, Driving While Impaired, Traffic Violations, Speeding, Assault and Battery, Capital Offenses, Criminal Appeals, Extradition, Felonies, Parole and Probation, Sexual Assault, Personal Injury, Automobile Accidents.
See Professional Biographies, CHARLOTTE, NORTH CAROLINA

Badger, David R., (AV) ....'47 '72 C&L.575 A.B., J.D. [D.R.Badger]
Badger, David R., P.A., (AV) .... 2108 South Boulevard
Baehman, Schuyler J. ....'75 '00 C.966 B.A. L.436 J.D. 120 W. Morehead St.
Baer, Arthur J., Jr. ....'27 '51 C&L.145 Ph.B., J.D. 2026 Pinewood Cir.‡
Bailey, Allen A., (AV) ....'24 '50 C&L.896 A.B., LL.B. [Bailey]
Bailey, Brad Allen .... '64 '00 C.575 B.A. L.1338 J.D. [Ⓐ McMillan&T.]
Bailey, Dianne Chipps ....'— '96 C.1375 B.A. L.276 J.D. [Ⓐ Robinson,B.&H.]
Bailey, Michael A., (BV) ....'51 '77 C.1228 B.B.A. L.896 J.D. [Bailey]
Bailey, Virginia L. ....'— '03 C.797 B.A. L.896 J.D. [Ⓐ Kilpatrick S.]
Bailey Law Firm, The, P.A., (AV) ....1341 East Morehead Street, Suite 102
Bain, Brian T. ....'76 '01 C.925 B.S.B.A. L.1228 J.D. [Ⓐ Lutzel,G.&Assoc.]
Baird, H. Elizabeth '62 '87 C.914 B.A. L.245 J.D.
(adm. in GA; not adm. in NC) Assoc. Gen Coun., Bank of America
Baker, Anna D.........................'78 '03 C.758 B.A. L.575 J.D. [Ⓑ Conrad T.&K.]
Baker, Gilbert (Trey) ....'77 '05 C.352 B.S. L.945 J.D. [Ⓐ Wishart,N.H.&P.]
Baker, Lawrence M., (AV) ....'— '90 C.27 B.A. L.896 J.D. [Cranfill,S.&H.]
Baker, Robert V., (AV) ....'54 '82 C.496 B.S. L.500 J.D. [Moore&V.P.]
Baker, Tyyawdi M. ....'73 '99 C.955 B.A. L.575 J.D. [Baker&B.]

Baker and Blake L.L.P.
106-1 Providence Road, 28207
Telephone: 704-332-2959 Fax: 704-332-2357
URL: http://www.bakerblakelaw.com
Tyyawdi M. Baker; Aretha V. Blake.
Personal Injury, Automobile Accidents, Wrongful Death, Nursing Home Abuse, Workers Compensation, Criminal Law, Drug Crimes, DUI/DWI, Traffic Violations, Wills, Estates, Probate, Estate Planning, Estate Administration, Civil Litigation, Business Law, Business Formation, Non-Profit Organization Representation.
See Professional Biographies, CHARLOTTE, NORTH CAROLINA

Baldauf, Craig R., (BV) '— '97 C.886 B.S. L.896 J.D.
(adm. in VA; not adm. in NC) Asst. Gen. Coun., Bank of America
Baldwin, Benjamin W., (AV) .... '— '88 C&L.575 B.A., J.D. [Robinson,B.&H.]
Baldwin, Garza, III, (AV) ....'51 '78 C.575 A.B. L.896 J.D. [Womble C.S.&R.]
Balent, Lisa '— '87 C&L.831 B.A., J.D.
(adm. in PA; not adm. in NC) Bank of America
Ballenger, B. Garrison, Jr., (BV) .... '55 '80 C.94 B.A. L.575 J.D. 6213 Deveron Drive
Balsamo, Salvatore, (BV) .... '68 '93 C.436 B.A. L.896 J.D. [S.Balsamo]

Balsamo, Salvatore, P.C., The Law Office of, (BV)
2100 Crescent Avenue, Suite 201, 28207
Telephone: 704-343-2815 Fax: 704-342-3987
Email: sal@salbalsamo.com URL: http://www.salbalsamo.com
Salvatore Balsamo.
Real Estate, Residential and Commercial Real Estate, Trust and Estates, Estate Planning and Administration, Wills, Probate, Small Business Law.
See Professional Biographies, CHARLOTTE, NORTH CAROLINA

Balts, Timothy .... '71 '02 C.628 B.S. L.823 J.D. [Ⓐ Alston&B.] (See Pat. Sect.)
Banks, Douglas ....'— '93 C.34 B.S. L.896 J.D. [Cozen O.]
Banks, James E., Jr. '56 '87 C.378 B.S. L.1068 J.D.
(adm. in TX; not adm. in NC) 1 NationsBank Plaza
Barber, Martha Gayle, (BV) .... '53 '82 C.228 B.A. L.896 J.D. [Alston&B.]
Barber, Stephen Richard ....'68 '94 C.790 B.A. L.896 J.D. 100 N. Tryon St.‡
Barber, Timothy G., (AV) ....'55 '85 C.385 B.A. L.896 J.D. [Womble C.S.&R.]
Bares, Jacqueline C. .... '— '90 C.436 B.A. L.597 J.D. [Ⓑ Kennedy C.L.&H.]
Barger, Brian D., (BV) ....'65 '90 C&L.893 B.A., J.D. [Helms M.&W.]
Barker, Samuel E. ....'— '04 C&L.923 B.S., J.D. [Ⓐ Hedrick E.G.&K.]
Barkley, Jane S., (BV) ....'55 '81 C.296 B.A. L.575 J.D. Stewart Title of the Carolinas
Barksdale, Holland L...................'— '05 C.228 B.A. L.472 J.D. [Cranfill,S.&H.]

Barnard, Christopher S. '50 '74 C.880 B.A. L.245 J.D.
(adm. in GA; not adm. in NC) Sr. V.P.-Legal, Secy. & Gen. Coun., Clariant Corp.
Barnes, Catherine Allen ....'62 '95 C.461 B.A. L.575 J.D. [James,M.&D.]
Barnes, Edwin L., Jr. ....'— '00 C.902 B.S. L.790 J.D. [Ⓐ Kennedy C.L.&H.]
Barnes, Haywood A. .... '64 '94 C.953 B.S. L.896 J.D. [Hunton&W.]
Barnes, Jeffrey D., (CV) ....'67 '95 C.259 B.S. L.575 J.D. [Ⓐ Culp E.&C.]
Barnes, Kevin M. ....'72 '04 C.1070 B.S. L.945 J.D. [Ⓐ Moore&V.P.]
Barnes, Michael D. ....'71 '99 C.575 B.A. L.574 J.D. [Barnes]
Barnes, W. Faison, (BV) ....'23 '48 C&L.575 B.S., J.D. 325 Queens Rd.
Barnes Law Office, PLLC .... 1909 J.N. Pease Place
Barnett, James E., Jr. '52 '79 C&L.1019 B.A., J.D.
(adm. in MA; not adm. in NC) F.B.I.
Barnett, Kevin L., (AV) .... '58 '84 C.228 B.S. L.469 J.D. [Barnett&F.]

Barnett & Falls, P.A., (AV)
130 North McDowell Street, Suite C, 28204-2268
Telephone: 704-334-2044 Fax: 704-334-2095
Email: kb@barnettfalls.com URL: http://www.barnettfalls.com
Kevin L. Barnett; R. Deke Falls.
Trials and Appeals in Federal and State Courts, Criminal Defense, Driving While Intoxicated, Drug Crimes, White Collar Crimes, Felonies, Misdemeanors, Probation Violations, Traffic Violations, Civil Rights Litigation.
See Professional Biographies, CHARLOTTE, NORTH CAROLINA

Barnette, Joseph K. ....'— '03 C.575 B.S.B.A. L.1565 J.D. [Ⓐ Hunton&W.]
Barnhardt, John J., III, (AV) '45 '72 C.198 B.S. L.893 J.D.
[Alston&B.] (See Pat. Sect.)
Barnhardt, W. Doak, (AV) .... '57 '84 C.896 B.A. L.575 J.D. [Moore&V.P.]
Barnhill, G. Michael, (AV) ....'56 '81 C.198 B.A. L.896 J.D. [Womble C.S.&R.]
Baron, John F., (AV) .... '62 '87 C.205 B.A. L.776 J.D. [Alston&B.]
Barrett, Jonathan A., (AV) ....'49 '78 C&L.575 B.A., J.D. [Mayer,B.R.&M.]
Barrett, Sybil Helena '74 '00 C.575 B.A. L.910 J.D.
(adm. in MA; not adm. in NC) P.O. Box 11429
Barrier, Joseph L., (BV) .... '24 '57 C&L.575 B.A., LL.B. 4322 Country Lane
Barringer, John P., (BV) .... '59 '86 C.48 B.S. L.1335 J.D. [Morris Y.W.S.&B.]
Barrow, Ayanna ....'— '02 C.228 A.B. L.276 J.D. [Ⓐ Kilpatrick S.]
Bartok, Michael F. '59 '85 C.860 B.A. L.228 J.D.
(adm. in NY; not adm. in NC)
Executive Vice President & General Counsel, Paramount Parks, Inc.
Barton, Grandon D., Jr. ....'32 '57 C&L.575 B.S., LL.B. P.O. Box 11722
Barwick, Peter S. ....'— '01 C.31 B.A. L.228 J.D. [Ⓐ Kennedy C.L.&H.]
Bashford, David H. ....'— '02 C.198 B.A. L.575 J.D. [Ⓑ Bradley A.R.&W.]
Basile Edwards, Zipporah Marie ....'69 '94 C&L.896 B.A., J.D. [Horack,T.P.&L.]

Basinger, A. Marshall, II, (AV) '39 '65 C&L.575 B.A., LL.B. ⒷⒷ
831 East Morehead Street, Suite 850, 28202
Telephone: 704-377-2984 Fax: 704-377-4721 Email: marshall@bellsouth.net
Email: ambii@bellsouth.net URL: http://www.mbasingerlaw.com
(Board Certified Specialist in Family Law, North Carolina State Board of Legal Specialization).
Family Law, Separation, Child Custody, Alimony, Equitable Distribution, Divorce, Trial and Appellate Practice, Civil and Domestic Trial Mediator.
See Professional Biographies, CHARLOTTE, NORTH CAROLINA

Basnight, Daniel F. ....'— '98 C&L.893 B.A., J.D. [Ⓐ Robinson,B.&H.]
Bass, Evan M. ....'79 '05 C.340 B.S. L.896 J.D. [Ⓐ Moore&V.P.]
Bass, Samuel Eric ....'70 '02 C.586 B.B.A. L.896 J.D. [Ⓐ Wishart,N.H.&P.]
Bates, Richard B. '53 '77 C&L.623 B.A., J.D.
(adm. in OK; not adm. in NC) Duke Energy Corp.
Battle, George E., III '73 '99 C&L.575 B.A., J.D.
Assoc. Corp. Coun., Charlotte-Mecklenburg Hosp. Auth.
Batty, David L., (AV) ....'— '91 C.273 B.A. L.93 J.D. [Kennedy C.L.&H.]
Baucom, Lloyd F., (AV) ....'34 '61 C&L.896 B.A., J.D. [Baucom,C.B.M.&W.]

Baucom, Claytor, Benton, Morgan & Wood, P.A., (AV)
1351 East Morehead Street, Suite 201, P.O. Box 35246, 28235
Telephone: 704-376-6527 Fax: 704-376-6207
Lloyd F. Baucom; William M. Claytor; Kenneth R. Benton; Rex C. Morgan; James F. Wood, III; Richard F. Kronk;—Timothy R. Moore.
General and Trial Practice in all State and Federal Courts. Probate, Real Estate, Condemnation, Labor, Corporation, Commercial, Negligence and Insurance Law.
Representative Clients: America Security Insurance Co.; Nationwide Mutual Insurance Co.
See Professional Biographies, CHARLOTTE, NORTH CAROLINA

Bauermeister, Herman O. '14 '47 C.46 M.S. L.209 J.D.
(adm. in MO; not adm. in NC; Pat.) 7413 Truelight Church Rd.
Baxter, Lawrence G. '52 '88 C.999 B.Com. L.050 LL.B.
Chief eCommerce Officer, Wachovia Corporation (legal Department)
Baynard, Mary Kay, (BV) ....'61 '86 C&L.575 B.A., J.D. [Ⓑ James,M.&D.]
Baynard, Paul R., (BV) ....'61 '88 C.198 B.A. L.575 J.D. [Rayburn C.&D.]
Bayne, J. Scott, (CVⓣ) ....'63 '88 C.547 B.A. L.546 J.D. [Ⓐ Golding H.&P.]
Baynes, Abbie G. '— '91 C.228 A.B. L.273 J.D.
(adm. in MD; not adm. in NC) [Ⓐ Katten M.R.]
Beachum, P. B., Jr. ....'10 '39 C.198 B.S. L.273 J.D. Ret. Dist. J.
Beaty, Rufus F., (BV) ....'58 '83 C.228 A.B. L.575 J.D. Chapman Associates
Beck, C. Vance ....'60 '86 C.198 B.A. L.575 J.D. Staff Atty., First Union Corporation
Becton, Taurus E. .... '— '04 C.302 B.A. L.575 J.D. [Ⓐ Hedrick E.G.&K.]
Beddow, John W., (AV) .... '52 '77 C&L.575 B.S., J.D. [James,M.&D.]
Bednarik, Michael J., (BV) .... '55 '81 C.896 B.A. L.809 J.D. 2004 Park Drive (⊙Shelby)
Bedrick, Richard E. '55 '80 C.575 A.B. L.705 J.D.
(adm. in NJ; not adm. in NC) 819 Edgehill Rd.‡
Beers, William M. '40 '69 C.950 L.596 J.D.
(adm. in OR; not adm. in NC) Asst. Gen. Coun., Royal & SunAlliance
Behning, Lawrence E., (AV) ....'— '92 C.820 B.S. L.776 J.D. [Ⓑ Kennedy C.L.&H.]
Belcher, William T., (AVⓣ) ....'50 '75 C.181 B.S. L.923 J.D. [Poyner&S.]
Belk, Claudia W. ....'37 '63 C.320 B.A. L.575 LL.B. Ret. Dist. J.
Bell, Kenneth D. ....'58 '83 C&L.896 B.A., J.D. [Mayer,B.R.&M.]
Bell, Lisa C., (BV) .... '66 '91 C.896 B.A. L.575 J.D. Dist. J.
Bell, Paul B., (AV) .... '22 '48 C&L.896 B.S., J.D. [Ⓑ Alston&B.] (See Pat. Sect.)
Bell, William R. .... '53 '85 C.228 B.A. L.896 J.D. Supr. Ct. J.

Bell, Davis & Pitt, P.A., (AV)
Carillon Building, Suite 2160, 227 West Trade Street, 28202 ⊙
Mailing Address: P.O. Box 21029, Winston-Salem, NC 27120
Telephone: 704-227-0400 Fax: 704-227-0178
URL: http://www.belldavispitt.com
—Edward B. Davis.
General Practice in State and Federal Court Trials. Banking and Commercial Law. Corporation and Labor Law, Federal, State and Local Taxation, Estate Planning, Probate and Real Estate Law.
Winston-Salem, North Carolina Office: Century Plaza, Suite 600, 100 North Cherry Street, 27101.
Telephone: 336-722-3700. Fax: 336-748-5890.
See Professional Biographies, CHARLOTTE, NORTH CAROLINA

Bellar, Lila G. ....'28 '52 C.102 L.569 LL.B. 1901 Park Dr.

Belthoff, Richard C., Jr., (BV) '58 '84 C.232 B.S.P. L.575 J.D.
V.P & Asst. Gen. Coun., Wachovia Corporation (Legal Department)
Beltz, John E. .... '64 '91 C.401 B.S. L.188 J.D. [Moore&V.P.]

Bender, Harold J., The Law Offices of, (AV) '42 '69 C.290 A.B. L.575 J.D. BB
200 North McDowell Street, 28204
Telephone: 704-333-2169 Fax: 704-333-0837
Email: hjblaw@bellsouth.net URL: http://www.hbenderlaw.com
(Board Certified Specialist in Criminal Law, North Carolina Board of Legal Specialization).
Criminal Law, State and Federal Courts, Drug Crimes, DWI, Assault, Traffic Violations.
See Professional Biographies, CHARLOTTE, NORTH CAROLINA

Bennett, Jason E. .... '74 '04 C.576 B.S.M.E. L.1341 J.D. [Ⓐ Moore&V.P.]
Bennett, Jennifer E., (AV) '— '92
C&L.575 B.S., J.D. Assoc. Gen. Coun., Bank of America
Benson, Christopher A. '53 '80
C.147 B.A. L.1019 J.D. Asst. Gen. Coun., Royal & SunAlliance
Benson, Douglas W. .... '74 '00 C.696 B.A. L.228 J.D. [Ⓐ Moore&V.P.]
Benson, Frederick R. .... '50 '77 C.228 B.A. L.575 J.D. P.O. Box 32696
Benton, Jason R. .... '76 '01 C&L.896 B.A., J.D. [Ⓐ Parker,P.A.&B.]
Benton, Kenneth R., (AV) .... '49 '74 C&L.896 B.A., J.D. [Baucom,C.B.M.&W.]

Bentsi-Enchill, Kofi '62 '91 C.454 B.A. L.112 J.D.
5222 Monroe Road, Suite 126, 28205
Telephone: 704-537-8466 Fax: 704-537-1142
Email: kenchill@bellsouth.net URL: http://www.kofilaw.com
Immigration and Naturalization, Labor Certifications, Citizenship, Visas, Business Visas, Personal Injury, Automobile Accidents, Slip and Fall, Workers Compensation.
See Professional Biographies, CHARLOTTE, NORTH CAROLINA

Beres, Melinda R. .... '— '99 C.673 B.A. L.790 J.D. [Ⓐ Hunton&W.]
Berger, Hal .... '62 '98 C.1083 B.A. L.1187 J.D. [H.Berger]

Berger, Hal, P.A., A Professional Law Corporation
5950 Fairview Road, Suite 808, 28210
Telephone: 704-553-7614 Facsimile: 704-553-7824
Email: halberger@earthlink.net URL: http://www.halbergerlaw.com
Hal Berger. Associate: Jaimée L. Bond.
Real Estate Closings, Residential Real Estate, Commercial Real Estate, Estate Planning, Trusts and Estates, Business Law, Corporate Law.
See Professional Biographies, CHARLOTTE, NORTH CAROLINA

Berkeley, Arthur Eliot '43 '68 C.188 B.S. L.569 J.D.
(adm. in NY; not adm. in NC) Assoc. Prof., Johnson C. Smith Univ.
Bernanke, Seth M., (BV) .... '58 '85 C.1036 B.A. L.228 J.D. P.O. Box 36295
Bernard, Christopher L. '71 '96
C.477 B.S.E. L.597 J.D. [Dougherty,C.H.&B.] (See Pat. Sect.)
Bernardini, Andrew N. .... '74 '00 C.999 B.A. L.982 J.D. [Ⓐ W.F.Porter]
Bernhardt, Robert J., (AV) .... '43 '68 C.347 B.S. L.477 J.D. [Bernhardt&S.]

Bernhardt and Strawser, P.A., (AV)
5821 Fairview Road, Suite 550, 28209
Telephone: 704-335-0444 Facsimile: 704-335-0551
URL: http://www.bernhardtandstrawser.com
Robert J. Bernhardt; Amy B. Strawser; Charles C. Euripides; Tonya L. Urps.
Commercial and Retail Collections, Debtor and Creditor Law, Creditor Rights, Collections.
See Professional Biographies, CHARLOTTE, NORTH CAROLINA

Bernstein, Mark R., (AV) .... '30 '57 C.659 A.B. L.976 LL.B. [Ⓒ Parker,P.A.&B.]
Berry, Brandy D. .... '75 '01 C.1228 B.A. L.790 J.D. [Ⓐ Womble C.S.&R.]
Bertram-Timm, Beverly, (AV) '62 '91 C.1128 B.A. L.896 J.D.
VP & Gen Coun., HLM Design, Inc. (⊙Knoxville, TN)
Bethune, Marvin A., (AV) .... '48 '73 C.198 B.A. L.575 J.D. [Ruff,B.C.W.&B.]
Betler, Christy-Anne V. .... '— '01 C.893 B.A. L.575 J.D. [Ⓐ Mayer,B.R.&M.]
Betz, Kimberly A. .... '71 '99 C.896 B.S. L.575 J.D. [Ⓐ Parker,P.A.&B.]
Beyer, John H., (CV) .... '70 '97 C.198 B.A. L.575 J.D. [Parker,P.A.&B.]
Bierman, Jeffrey B. '— '81 C.818 B.S. L.990 J.D.
(adm. in PA; not adm. in NC) Assoc. Gen. Coun., Bank of America
Bigger, Richard A., Jr., (AV) .... '37 '64 C.674 A.B. L.893 LL.B. [Wishart,N.H.&P.]
Biggers, James Larry "Chip", Jr. .... '62 '00 C.277 B.S. L.790 J.D. [Ⓐ Foodman,H.&K.]
Bilas, Jay S., (BV) .... '63 '92 C&L.228 A.B., J.D. [Ⓒ Moore&V.P.]
Bingham, Debra B. .... '— '00 C.577 B.A. L.896 J.D. [Ⓐ Robinson,B.&H.]
Bingham, James H., Jr. .... '— '00 C.309 A.B. L.228 J.D. [Ⓐ Robinson,B.&H.]
Bisanar, Robert M., (AV) '50 '75
C.198 A.B. L.575 J.D. Assoc. Gen. Coun., Duke Energy Corp.
Bisanar, Sandra Tindall, (BV) .... '51 '75 C.956 B.A. L.790 J.D. Asst. Co. Atty.
Bishop, J. Daniel, (BV) .... '64 '90 C&L.575 B.S., J.D. [Bishop,C.&M.]
Bishop, Lynn, (BV) .... '50 '75 C.691 B.A. L.228 J.D. [L.Bishop]
Bishop, Marlene Y. '49 '80 C.645 B.S. L.1065 J.D.
(adm. in CA; not adm. in NC) 2663 Oakmeade Dr.‡

Bishop, Capitano & Moss, P.A., (BV)
4521 Sharon Road, Suite 350, 28211
Telephone: 704-716-1200 Fax: 704-716-1201
URL: http://www.bcandm.com
J. Daniel Bishop; A. Todd Capitano; Joseph W. Moss, Jr.;—Raizel Arnholt Kahn.
Business Law, Limited Liability Company Law, Partnerships, Corporate, Contracts, Commercial Litigation, Construction Law, Labor and Employment, Securities Law.
See Professional Biographies, CHARLOTTE, NORTH CAROLINA

Bishop, Lynn, P.A., (BV) .... Ste 206, 101 N. McDowell St.
Bissell, Marilyn R. .... '27 '80 C.294 B.S. L.574 J.D. Dist. J.
Bisulca, Anthony A. .... '67 '94 C.160 B.S. L.790 J.D. Clariant Corporation (Pat.)
Bivens, Harry R. .... '54 '90 C.838 B.S.C.E. L.464 J.D. [Ⓒ Smith,C.&H.]
Bjorklund, Kurt W. '53 '90 C.429 B.A. L.309 J.D.
(adm. in DC; not adm. in NC) [Ⓒ Cadwalader,W.&T.]
Black, Russell M. .... '62 '88 C.838 B.S. L.880 J.D. [Ⓒ Katten M.R.]
Blackmon, Daniel M., (CVⓉ) .... '47 '72 C&L.588 B.A., J.D. Certified Supr. Ct. Med.
Blackwelder, Anna K. .... '68 '95 C.34 B.A. L.469 J.D. SGL Carbon, LLC
Blackwood, Thomas J., II .... '54 '87 C.198 B.A. L.615 J.D. 700-A Lexington Ave.
Blair, Dalton G. .... '— '02 C.575 B.A. L.896 J.D. [Ⓐ Hedrick E.G.&K.]
Blair, Robert S., Jr., (AV) .... '65 '91 C.968 B.A. L.896 J.D. [Horack,T.P.&L.]

Blair Conaway Bograd & Martin, P.A.
(See Shumaker, Loop & Kendrick, LLP)

Blake, Aretha V. .... '78 '02 C.259 B.S. L.280 J.D. [Baker&B.]
Blake, Elizabeth K., Law Office of .... '— '93 C.347 B.S. L.574 J.D. 6715 Fairview Road
Blake, Mark T. '54 '83 C.260 B.A. L.1206 J.D.
(adm. in FL; not adm. in NC) Gen. Coun., Swisher International, Inc.
Blake, Robert A., Jr., (BV) .... '69 '94 C.575 B.S. L.896 J.D. [Wyatt&B.]
Blanchfield, Francis J., Jr., (AV) ...... '45 '70 C.321 A.B. L.569 J.D. [Mayer,B.R.&M.]
Blanco, Jeanette Hait, (AVⓉ) '— '84 C.260 B.S. L.245 J.D.
(adm. in GA; not adm. in NC) Sr. Coun., Bank of America
Blane, James L., (AV) .... '51 '76 C.575 B.S. L.893 J.D. [J.L.Blane]

Blane, James L., PLLC, (AV) BB
1057 East Morehead Street, 28204
Mailing Address: P.O. Box 31551, Charlotte, NC 28231
Telephone: 704-331-0030 Facsimile: 704-372-1677
Email: JBLANELAW@BELLSOUTH.NET URL: http://www.james-blanelaw.com
James L. Blane.
Mediation, Creditor Law, Bankruptcy, Business Law, Corporate Law, Contract, Estate and Probate, Real Estate, Civil Litigation.
Representative Clients: Moss Supply Company; Beech Mountain Resort, Inc.; R&G Construction Company; Oceanside Village, LLC.; Rowells, Inc.; Horizon CSA, LLC; Andrew Roby, Inc.
Approved Attorney for: Lawyers Title Insurance Corp.
See Professional Biographies, CHARLOTTE, NORTH CAROLINA

Blanton, John R. .... '67 '97 C.705 B.A. L.574 J.D. 720 E. 4th St., Ste. 308
Bledsoe, Louis A., III, (AV) .... '— '85 C.575 A.B. L.309 J.D. [Robinson,B.&H.]
Bledsoe, Louis A., Jr., (AV) .... '27 '55 C&L.575 B.S.B.A., LL.B. [Bledsoe&B.]

Bledsoe & Bledsoe, P.L.L.C., (AV)
1057 East Morehead Street, P.O. Box 36779, 28236-6779
Telephone: 704-372-1676 Fax: 704-372-1677
Email: labjrbled@aol.com URL: http://www.louisabledsoe.com
Louis A. Bledsoe, Jr.—Margaret M. Bledsoe (1966-1996).
General Civil Practice in State and Federal Courts. Litigation, Arbitration and Mediation.
See Professional Biographies, CHARLOTTE, NORTH CAROLINA

Blowers, Erik B. '65 '89 C.1044 B.S. L.117 J.D.
(adm. in OH; not adm. in NC) Chf. Div. Coun., FBI
Blue, Lacy W., (CV) .... '25 '50 C.673 L.896 LL.B. 801 E. Morehead St.
Blundell, Melinda S. .... '77 '02 C.612 B.S. L.893 J.D. [Ⓐ Moore&V.P.]
Blythe, Robert B., (AV) .... '35 '61 C.198 A.B. L.575 LL.B. [Parham,H.H.B.&M.]
Bochicchio, Paul '— '74 C.93 B.A. L.262 J.D.
(adm. in NY; not adm. in NC) Bank of America (⊙Boston, MA)
Boehm, Carl R. .... '— '99 C.992 B.A. L.228 J.D. [Ⓐ Robinson,B.&H.]
Boggs, David C., (BV) .... '53 '78 C.198 B.A. L.896 J.D. [Wishart,N.H.&P.]

Bogle, Anthony & Leach, P.A.
(See Gastonia)

Boglovits, Suzanne M. .... '63 '92 C&L.575 B.A., J.D. Wachovia Corp., Legal Div.
Bohm, David A. .... '72 '98 C&L.900 B.A., J.D. [Ⓐ Johnston,A.&H.]
Boland, Brian P., (AVⓉ) '54 '82 C.188 B.A. L.262 J.D.
(adm. in NY; not adm. in NC)
V,P, & Asst. Gen. Coun., Wachovia Corp. (Legal Department)
Bolduc, Darryll .... '60 '03 C.103 B.A. L.1228 J.D. [Bolduc,P.]

Bolduc Law Firm, The, PLLC
401 North Tryon Street, 10th Floor, 28202
Telephone: 704-998-5188 Fax: 704-998-5704 URL: http://www.bolduclawfirm.com
URL: http://www.bolduclaw.com
Darryll Bolduc.
NASD Arbitration, Business Litigation, Securities Fraud, Corporate Malfeasance, Mutual Fund Disputes, Wrongful Termination, Banking and Finance Law, and Accounting.
See Professional Biographies, CHARLOTTE, NORTH CAROLINA

Bolick, Ryan D. .... '— '99 C.575 B.A. L.1228 J.D. [Cranfill,S.&H.]
Bolinger, Maureen Connolly ...... '66 '97 C.454 B.S. L.1003 J.D. [Ⓐ Cadwalader,W.&T.]
Bollinger, Bobby L., Jr., (AV) .... '58 '88 C.575 B.A. L.1228 J.D. [Bollinger&P.]

Bollinger & Piemonte, PC, (AV)
601 E. Fifth Street, Suite 250, 28202
Telephone: 704-373-1777 Fax: 704-373-1977
URL: http://www.bollingerandpiemonte.com
Bobby L. Bollinger, Jr. (Board Certified Specialist in Workers' Compensation, North Carolina State Board of Legal Specialization); George C. Piemonte.
Workers Compensation, Social Security Disability, Personal Injury, Disability Insurance, General Civil Litigation, Wrongful Death, Railroad Disability.
See Professional Biographies, CHARLOTTE, NORTH CAROLINA

Bolster, Jeffrey S., (BV) .... '68 '94 C.575 B.A. L.896 J.D. [Bolster]

Bolster Law Firm, The, P.A., (BV)
1043 East Morehead Street, Suite 111, 28204
Telephone: 704-347-4884 Facsimile: 704-347-1087
Email: jbolster@bolsterlawfirm.com URL: http://www.bolsterlawfirm.com
Jeffrey S. Bolster; Alec D. Rogers;—Amy Fitzgerald.
Insurance Defense Litigation, Insurance Coverage Disputes and General Civil Litigation.
See Professional Biographies, CHARLOTTE, NORTH CAROLINA

Bond, Jaimée L. .... '75 '02 C.1091 B.A. L.117 J.D. [Ⓐ H.Berger]
Bond, John D., III .... '54 '87 C.15 B.S. L.192 J.D. [Bradley A.R.&W.]
Bond, Lyn, Jr., (AV) .... '27 '54 C&L.575 A.B., J.D. [Ruff,B.C.W.&B.]
Boner, Richard D. .... '49 '75 C&L.575 A.B., J.D. Supr. J.
Boney, N. Bruce, Jr. .... '24 '51 C&L.575 A.B., LL.B. 1530 Queens Rd.
Booe, J. Michael, (AV) .... '— '71 C.198 B.A. L.575 J.D. [Kennedy C.L.&H.]
Booher, Edward S., Jr. .... '51 '82 C&L.896 B.A., J.D. [Moore&V.P.]
Booth, Ralph H. '29 '52 C.1059 B.A. L.969 J.D.
(adm. in SC; not adm. in NC) 3200 Rea Rd.‡

Booth Harrington & Johns, LLP
(See Greensboro)

Borch, Frederic L., III .... '54 '79 C.198 B.A. L.575 J.D. 1326 Lynbrook Dr.★
Bos, Gerard Alford, (AV) .... '50 '76 C.903 B.A. L.861 J.D. [Wilson&B.]
Boswell, Sally G. .... '76 '01 C.886 B.A. L.823 J.D. [Ⓐ McAngus G.&C.]
Bosworth, David B., (BV) .... '46 '74 C.805 B.S. L.744 J.D. Financial Charting Ltd.
Bouknight, Whitney G. .... '— '04 C.269 B.A. L.902 J.D. [Ⓐ Kennedy C.L.&H.]
Bourget, Nicole E. .... '75 '00 C.945 B.A. L.893 J.D. [Ⓐ Littler M.]
Boutwell, John D., (BV) .... '68 '93 C.69 B.A. L.575 J.D. [Thurman,W.&B.]
Bowen, Carol Ewald, (AV) .... '57 '85 C.228 A.B. L.880 J.D. [Moore&V.P.]
Bowen, Krista R. .... '— '98 C.923 B.S.B.Ad. L.902 J.D. [Robinson,B.&H.]
Bowers, Alicia Almeida '72 '98 C&L.575 B.A., J.D.
Charlotte-Mecklenburg Hospital Authority, The
Bowers, John W. .... '71 '97 C&L.575 B.A., J.D. [Ⓐ Horack,T.P.&L.]
Bowers, Robert C., (BV) .... '71 '96 C.198 A.B. L.228 J.D. [Moore&V.P.]
Bowman, Everett J., (AV) .... '— '79 C&L.309 A.B., J.D. [Robinson,B.&H.]
Bowman, William J., Jr., (BV) '50 '76 C.228 B.A. L.472 J.D.
Assoc. Gen. Coun., Duke Energy Corporation
Boyce, Timothy J., (BVⓉ) '54 '79 C.276 B.S.F.S. L.659 J.D.
(adm. in CT; not adm. in NC) [Dechert]
Boyd, H. Michael, (AV) .... '48 '72 C&L.228 A.B., J.D. Sr. Dep. City Atty.
Boyd, Sheena Jones, (CV) .... '65 '94 C&L.577 B.S., J.D. Dir. of Employee Rel.
Boyer, Allen W. .... '30 '58 C.103 A.B. L.930 J.D. 1409 East Blvd.
Boyer, Karen L. '64 '93 C.575 B.S.B.A. L.1128 J.D.
Tax Mgr., Belk Stores Services, Inc. (Legal Department)
Boyle, B. Irvin, (AV) .... '12 '36 C&L.575 A.B., LL.B. [Ⓒ Johnston,A.&H.]
Boyle, Margaret N. .... '78 '04 C.665 B.A. L.1509 J.D. [Ⓐ McGuireWoods]

Bracken, Joseph E. .... '75 '04 C.674 B.S.E.E. L.569 J.D. [A Alston&B.] (See Pat. Sect.)
Brackett, Douglas A., (BV) .... '43 '70 C.576 B.S. L.575 J.D. 9407 Providence Rd.
Brackett, Martin L., Jr., (AV) .... '— '72 C.198 B.A. L.575 J.D. [Robinson,B.&H.]
Bradley, J. Curtis, III, (BVⓉ) '45 '74 C.893 B.A. L.273 J.D.
(adm. in VA; not adm. in NC) 4530 Rosecliff Dr.
Bradley, Kirk T. .... '74 '99 C.160 B.S. L.790 J.D. [A Alston&B.] (See Pat. Sect.)
Bradley, Laura L., Esq. .... '67 '92 C&L.228 B.A., J.D. 7804C Fairview Road

Bradley Arant Rose & White LLP
Bank of America Corporate Center, 100 N. Tryon Street Suite 2690, 28202 ⊙
Telephone: 704-332-8842 Facsimile: 704-332-8858
Email: info@bradleyarant.com URL: http://www.bradleyarant.com
Members of Firm: John D. Bond, III; Michael W. Knapp. Associates: David H. Bashford; Colin R. Stockton (Not admitted in NC).
Alternative Dispute Resolution; Antitrust and Trade Regulation; Appellate Practice; Banking and Financial Services; Bankruptcy; Business Law; Complex and Multi-District Litigation; Compliance; Computers and Software; Construction and Procurement; Corporate Law; Corporate Governance; Energy; Environmental Law; Environmental Litigation; ERISA; ERISA Litigation; Government Contracts; Governmental Affairs; Health Care Fraud; Health Care Law; Intellectual Property; Copyrights; Patents; Trademarks; Trade Secrets; International Law; International Transactions; Labor and Employment; Land Use; Leasing; Life Sciences; Litigation; Media Law; Mergers and Acquisitions; Partnership Law; Private Equity and Investment Funds; Products Liability; Public Finance; Public Utility Law; Real Estate Finance and Development; Real Estate Law; Reorganization Restructuring and Insolvency; Securities; Securities Litigation; State and Local Taxation; Tax Exempt Facilities; Tax Litigation; Taxation; Technology and Science; Trusts and Estates; Venture Capital; White Collar Crime; Workouts.
Counsel for: SouthTrust Bank of Alabama, National Association; Energen Corporation; Blount, Inc.; Torchmark Corp.; Russell Corp.; Coca-Cola Bottling Company United, Inc.; Ford Motor Co.; Walter Industries, Inc.; The Birmingham Post Co. (Post-Herald); The New York Times Co.
Birmingham, Alabama Office: One Federal Place, 1819 5th Avenue North, 35203-2119. Telephone: 205-521-8000. Facsimile: 205-521-8800.
Huntsville, Alabama Office: 200 Clinton Avenue West, Suite 900, 35801. Telephone: 256-517-5100. Facsimile: 256-517-5200.
Montgomery, Alabama Office: Alabama Center for Commerce, 401 Adams Avenue, Suite 780, 36104. Telephone: 334-956-7700. Facsimile: 334-956-7701.
Washington, D.C. Office: 1133 Connecticut Avenue, N.W., 12th Floor, 20036. Telephone: 202-393-7150. Facsimile: 202-347-1684.
Jackson, Mississippi Office: 188 East Capitol Street, Suite 450, 39201. Telephone: 601-948-8000. Facsimile: 601-948-3000.
Reviser of the Alabama Law Digest for this Directory.
See Professional Biographies, CHARLOTTE, NORTH CAROLINA

Bradley, Guthery, Turner & Curry
(See Horack, Talley, Pharr & Lowndes)

Bradlow, Julie M. '63 '88 C.976 B.A. L.145 J.D.
(adm. in IL; not adm. in NC) Goodrich Corp.
Bradshaw, Robert W., Jr., (AV) ..... '— '57 C&L.228 A.B., LL.B. [G Robinson,B.&H.]
Brady, Christopher J. .... '61 '93 C.1128 B.S. L.575 J.D. [Mayer,B.R.&M.]
Brady, Sarah M. .... '78 '04 C.575 B.A. L.1556 J.D. [A James,M.&D.]
Bragg, Ellis M., Jr., (BV) .... '47 '73 C.387 B.A. L.896 J.D. 500 E. Morehead St.
Bramlett, Ken R., Jr., (AV) .... '— '84 C.896 B.A. L.575 J.D. [Kennedy C.L.&H.]
Branham, Phaedra R. '67 '91 C&L.69 B.B.A., J.D.
(adm. in TX; not adm. in NC) Sr. Corp. Coun., Compass Group, U.S.A. Inc.

Brannon Strickland, PLLC
(See Raleigh)

Braun, Nancy E. '61 '89 C.188 B.S. L.107 J.D.
(adm. in NY; not adm. in NC) 4109 Rutherford Dr.‡
Bray, William Parks .... '67 '93 C.198 B.A. L.790 J.D. [Bray,P.]

Bray Law Firm, The, PLLC
4701 Hedgemore Drive, Suite 816, 28209
Telephone: 704-523-7777 Fax: 704-523-7780
Email: wbray@braylaw.com URL: http://www.braylaw.com
William Parks Bray;—Milton H. Gilbert, Jr.
Business and Litigation Practice including Business Litigation, Contracts, Construction, Employment, Entertainment Law, General Corporate, Incorporation, Intellectual Property, Limited Liability Companies, Mergers and Acquisitions, Partnerships, Products Liability, Professional Liability, Sports Law, Tax, Technology and Emerging Business, and Tort Litigation.
Representative Clients: MoRisen Records; Golf Scotland; Longhorn Transportation; AlvaCor Construction; Anglerschannel.com; Digital Intersect; America's Carpet Gallery; InterCerve; Myles Julian Apparel; RT Ross Foods.
See Professional Biographies, CHARLOTTE, NORTH CAROLINA

Brearley, Jennifer S., (BV) .... '62 '87 C.198 B.A. L.575 J.D. 4610 Messian Court
Brendle, Wayne M., (BV) .... '29 '57 C&L.896 B.S., J.D. Cameron Brown Bldg.
Brennan, James N., IV .... '58 '86 C.682 B.S. L.209 J.D. [Parker,P.A.&B.]

Brennan Law Firm, PLLC
(See Cornelius)

Brenner, Irving M., (AV) .... '60 '86 C&L.893 B.S., J.D. [Helms M.&W.]
Brenner, Teresa M., (AV) '— '87
C.27 B.A. L.896 J.D. Assoc. Gen. Coun., Bank of America
Breunig, Erin Lang ....'— '97 C.198 B.S. L.893 J.D. Asst. Gen. Coun., Bank of America
Brewer, Daniel Josev .... '75 '01 C.269 B.A. L.790 J.D. [A Hunton&W.]
Bricker, Ross B., (AVⓉ) '56 '80 C.393 B.A. L.910 J.D.
(adm. in IL; not adm. in NC) SPX Corp.
Briggs, Susan Hunt .... '68 '94 C&L.575 B.A., J.D. [Morris Y.W.S.&B.]
Bright, Nachael L. .... '71 '01 C&L.575 B.A., J.D. [A Alston&B.]
Brighton, Jo Ann, (AVⓉ) .... '— '89 C.205 B.S. L.564 J.D. [G Kennedy C.L.&H.]
Brim, Thomas P., (BV) .... '44 '71 C.228 B.A. L.575 J.D. 122 N. McDowell St.
Brinson, Russ A. .... '73 '99 C.575 B.S. L.896 J.D. [Cozen O.]
Briotte, Kristin E. '66 '91 C.321 B.A. L.1019 J.D.
(adm. in CT; not adm. in NC) V.P. & Assoc. Gen. Coun., Compass Group, U.S.A. Inc.
Britts, George M. '45 '72 C.893 B.A. L.309 J.D.
(adm. in MA; not adm. in NC) 2300 Archdale Dr.
Brock, E. Casey, II '61 '89 C&L.16 B.S.M.E., J.D.
(adm. in GA; not adm. in NC) 3833 Selwyn Ave.‡
Brock, Stuart A. '67 '00 C.896 B.S. L.574 J.D.
[A Womble C.S.&R.] (⊙Winston-Salem)
Brockmann, Todd C. .... '69 '95 C.587 B.S. L.589 J.D. [Brockmann]
Brockmann Law Firm, The, P.C. .... 8058 Corporate Center Drive, Suite 100
Brodhag, Jonathan D. .... '79 '05 C.577 B.S. L.477 J.D. [A Moore&V.P.]
Brooks, Alicia D., (BV) .... '66 '92 C&L.575 B.S., J.D. [Brooks]
Brooks, Tamara W. .... '66 '97 C.1369 B.A. L.356 J.D. [Brooks]

Brooks Law Firm, The, P.C., (BV)
401 East Second Street, Suite 101, 28202
Telephone: 704-332-1618 Fax: 704-332-1624 Cell: 704-488-4343
Email: ABROOKS@THEBROOKSLAWFIRM.COM URL: http://www.abrookslawfirm.com
Alicia D. Brooks.
Criminal Defense, Driving While Intoxicated, Drug Crimes, Parole and Probation, Misdemeanor and Felony, Traffic Violations, License Reinstatements, Expungements, Name Changes.
See Professional Biographies, CHARLOTTE, NORTH CAROLINA

Brooks Law Office
5120 Monroe Road, 28205
Telephone: 704-567-5297 Fax: 704-567-5389
Email: lawbrooks@bellsouth.net URL: http://www.tjbbulldog.com
Member: Tamara W. Brooks.
Medical Malpractice, Wrongful Death, Personal Injury, Automobile Accidents, Slip and Fall, Employment Law, Employment Discrimination, Wrongful Termination, Sexual Harassment, Contracts, Employment Contracts, Sports, Entertainment.
See Professional Biographies, CHARLOTTE, NORTH CAROLINA

Brose, R. Christian '— '95 C.902 B.A. L.802 J.D.
(adm. in TX; not adm. in NC) [A Helms M.&W.]
Brotherton, Allen C., (BV) .... '60 '85 C&L.575 B.A., J.D. [Knox B.K.&G.]
Brower, Nancy C. .... '62 '89 C.418 B.S. L.575 J.D. [Poyner&S.]
Brown, A. Todd .... '60 '86 C&L.790 B.S., J.D. [Hunton&W.]
Brown, Caroline .... '— '05 C.160 B.S. L.790 J.D. [A Kennedy C.L.&H.]
Brown, Collin W. .... '77 '03 C.500 B.A. L.896 J.D. [A Horack,T.P.&L.]
Brown, David A. '54 '79 C.651 B.A. L.161 J.D.
(adm. in OH; not adm. in NC) 227 W. Trade St.‡
Brown, David W., Jr. .... '66 '91 C.575 B.A. L.880 J.D. [G Parker,P.A.&B.]
Brown, Donald M., Jr. '60 '87
C.575 B.A. L.1228 J.D. 10701 Mcmullen Creek Pkwy., Ste. B
Brown, Frank C. '50 '84 C&L.502 A.B., J.D.
(adm. in IL; not adm. in NC) Vice President & General Counsel, Rexam Inc.
Brown, Hayden D., (AV) .... '58 '84 C.174 B.A. L.596 J.D. [Mayer,B.R.&M.]
Brown, Jefferson W., (AV) .... '— '84 C.575 B.S. L.880 J.D. [Kennedy C.L.&H.]
Brown, Patrick F., (AV) .... '— '87 C.931 B.A. L.128 J.D. [Nexsen P.A.K.]
Brown, R. Kent, (AV) .... '49 '75 C.575 B.A. L.896 J.D. [Brown,M.&Assoc.]
Brown, Richard K. .... '— '87 C.882 B.S. L.1029 J.D. [G Kennedy C.L.&H.]
Brown, Thomas Daniel, (BV) .... '59 '85 C.968 B.A. L.273 J.D. [Shuford,H.&B.]

Brown, Moore & Associates, PLLC, (AV)
200 Queens Road, Suite 200, 28204
Telephone: 704-335-1500 Fax: 704-333-1636
URL: http://www.brownandmoorelaw.com
R. Kent Brown; Jon R. Moore. Associate: Marie C. Shea.
Catastrophic Injury, Personal Injury, Automobile Accidents, Brain Injury, Spinal Cord Injury, Professional Liability, Wrongful Death, Products Liability, Truck Accidents, Medical Malpractice, Legal Malpractice, Construction Accidents, Nursing Home Negligence and Insurance Law.
See Professional Biographies, CHARLOTTE, NORTH CAROLINA

Browne, Herbert H., Jr., (AV) .... '33 '58 C.575 A.B. L.309 LL.B. [G Helms M.&W.]
Browne, Flebotte, Wilson & Webb, PLLC, (BV)
301 South McDowell Street, Suite 1201 (⊙Creedmoor, Durham, Fayetteville, Greensboro)
Broyles, D. Scott, (BVⓉ) '58 '91 C.896 B.A. L.902 J.D.
(adm. in GA; not adm. in NC) Asst. U.S. Atty.
Brumley, A. Neal, (BV) .... '37 '63 C&L.575 A.B., LL.B. 2245 W. Sugar Creek Rd.
Bruner, Taber C. .... '72 '02 C&L.790 B.A., J.D. [A Moore&V.P.]
Brunson, N. Deane .... '43 '73 C&L.575 A.B., J.D. [Griffin,B.&P.]
Bruny, Roger H., (BV) .... '42 '68 C&L.145 B.S., J.D. [Newitt&B.]
Bryan, Robert M., (AV) .... '— '76 C&L.893 B.A., J.D. [Robinson,B.&H.]
Bryan, Robert P., III .... '71 '98 C.575 B.A. L.228 J.D. [G Parker,P.A.&B.]
Bryant, Frank L., (AV) .... '47 '72 C&L.575 B.A., J.D. [Poyner&S.]
Bryant, James R., III, (AV) .... '44 '69 C.198 A.B. L.575 J.D. [Dechert]
Bryant, Patrick S., (BV) .... '— '90 C&L.880 B.A., J.D. [Robinson,B.&H.]
Bryant, Tamille W. ....'— '90 C.575 B.S. L.896 J.D. Asst. Gen. Coun., Bank of America
Bryant, Victor Alexander .... '65 '96 C.902 B.A. L.575 J.D. Barnhardt Mfg. Co.
Buben, John R., Jr., (BV) .... '65 '91 C.260 B.S. L.259 J.D. [Johnston,A.&H.]
Buchan, Jonathan E., Jr., (AV) .... '50 '78 C.674 A.B. L.228 J.D. [Helms M.&W.]
Buchanan, Christopher T. .... '71 '98 C.806 B.A. L.896 J.D. [A Moore&V.P.]
Buck, Peter C., (AV) .... '— '76 C&L.228 A.B., J.D. [Robinson,B.&H.]
Buckley, Bruce A., (AV) .... '55 '81 C&L.575 A.B., J.D. [G Womble C.S.&R.]
Buckley, Charles R., III, (BV) .... '42 '69 C&L.575 B.S., J.D. [Buckley,M.&B.]
Buckley, McMullen & Buie, P.A., (BV) .... 4421 Sharon Road, Suite 200
Budzichowski, Laura Considine .....'— '02 C.602 B.A. L.477 J.D. [A Robinson,B.&H.]
Buie, Craig Pennington, (BV) .... '59 '84 C.575 B.S. L.896 J.D. [Buckley,M.&B.]

Bumgardner, Don H.
(See Gastonia)

Bunting, William C., Jr. .... '75 '01 C.34 B.S. L.575 J.D. [A Shumaker,L.&K.]
Buonanno, Joseph B. '63 '90 C.696 B.M. L.188 J.D.
(adm. in NY; not adm. in NC) [Hunton&W.]
Burbank, C. Todd .... '70 '98 C.575 B.A. L.260 J.D. [Helms M.&W.]
Burbank, Meredith P. .... '75 '99 C.575 B.A. L.893 J.D. [A Womble C.S.&R.]
Burch, Cynthia B. '61 '86 C&L.861 B.A., J.D.
(adm. in LA; not adm. in NC) Fair Housing Coun. City of Charlotte
Burchette, Robert L., (AV) .... '49 '76 C.296 B.A. L.896 J.D. [Johnston,A.&H.]
Buric, John Robert .... '64 '96 C.576 B.S.C.E. L.94 J.D. [James,M.&D.]
Burk, Eric L. .... '— '97 C.160 B.S. L.923 J.D. [Kennedy C.L.&H.]
Burke, Barry S., (BV) .... '55 '83 C&L.896 B.A., J.D. 225 Marsh Road
Burke, Eloise W. .... '38 '75 C&L.575 B.A., J.D. 1204 Cameron Brown Bldg.
Burke, Erin E. .... '70 '95 C.645 B.A. L.602 J.D. [A Womble C.S.&R.]
Burke, Raymond A. .... '64 '96 [Burke&Assoc.]
Burke & Associates, (BV) .... 4731 Hedgemore Drive (⊙Jackson, MS; Ripley, TN)
Burkholder, David S. .... '70 '00 C.94 B.A. L.124 J.D. [A Cadwalader,W.&T.]
Burnette, Amelia Y. .... '— '05 C.48 B.A. L.575 J.D. [A Kennedy C.L.&H.]
Burns, B. Bernard, Jr., (AV) .... '48 '73 C.269 B.A. L.228 J.D. [G McGuireWoods]
Burns, Melissa G. .... '63 '90 C.880 B.A. L.910 J.D. [G Moore&V.P.]
Burns, William F., Jr., (BV) '46 '72
C.1126 A.B. L.575 J.D. 319 S. Sharon Amity Rd., Ste. 230
Burris, Margery A., (BV) .... '67 '92 C.880 B.A. L.575 J.D. [Burris,M.P.&B.]
Burris, Robert N., (AV) .... '40 '70 C.790 A.B. L.575 J.D. [Burris,M.P.&B.]

Burris, MacMillan, Pearce & Burris, PLLC, (AV) BR
6857 Fairview Road, 28210
Telephone: 704-365-2600 Fax: 704-364-2637
Robert N. Burris; Douglas P. MacMillan; Hugo A. Pearce, III; Margery A. Burris.
General Civil Practice, Real Estate, Residential Real Estate, Commercial Real Estate, Real Estate Litigation, Estate Planning, Administration, Wills and Probate.
See Professional Biographies, CHARLOTTE, NORTH CAROLINA

Burroughs, R. Alexander, (BV) .... '69 '94 C.1365 B.A. L.831 J.D. [Moore&V.P.]
Burt, Laura B., (BV) .... '66 '91 C.575 B.A. L.896 J.D. [G Gilpin&H.]
Burt, Michael L., (BV) .... '64 '91 C.821 B.A. L.896 J.D. First American Title Ins. Co.
Burtis, John M., (AV) '45 '70 C.602 B.A. L.880 J.D.
Dir., Claims & Litig., United Dominion Industries, Inc. (Legal Department)
Busch, Mark R. .... '— '95 C.112 B.A. L.228 J.D. [Kennedy C.L.&H.]
Bush, Tom, (AV) .... '48 '73 C.259 B.A. L.838 J.D. [Bush&P.]

Bush & Powers, Law Offices of, (AV) BR
A Partnership of Professional Associations
821 East Boulevard, 28203
Telephone: 704-342-4357; 347-0110 704-358-9074 (Espanol) Fax: 704-347-8840 URL: http://www.CharlotteLegalHelp.com
URL: http://www.bushandpowers.com
Tom Bush; Bill Powers.
Language: Spanish.
Driving While Impaired, Traffic and Criminal Defense, Personal Injury, Bankruptcy, Medical Malpractice, Civil Litigation, Family Law, Immigration.
See Professional Biographies, CHARLOTTE, NORTH CAROLINA

Business Law Advisors, The, (BV)
1900 South Boulevard, Suite 304, 28203
Telephone: 980-297-7900 Fax: 888-463-0097
Email: ddulaney@tbladvisors.com URL: http://www.tbladvisors.com
Partners: Dain J. Dulaney, Jr.; Michael J. Miller; Michael S. Marr; Scott S. Mehler.
Mergers and Acquisitions, Financing, Corporate, Business, Intellectual Property Protection, Contracts, Closely Held Businesses, Limited Liability Company Law, Partnerships, Tax Planning.
See Professional Biographies, CHARLOTTE, NORTH CAROLINA

Butler, Norman, (BV) .... '52 '81 C&L.574 B.A., J.D. 725 E. Trade St., Ste. 115
Butler & Hosch, P.A.
4421 Stuart Andrew Boulevard, Suite 604 (⊙Ft Laud., Orlando, FL; Baton Rouge, LA; Columbia, SC; Dallas, TX)
Butrus, John J., Jr. '61 '87 C.1019 B.B.A. L.910 J.D.
(adm. in TX; not adm. in NC) [Butrus K.W.V.] ⊙

Butrus Khoshbin Wilson Vogt, LLP, (AVⓉ)
11520 North Community House Road, Suite 175, 28277 ⊙
Telephone: 704-759-0529 Fax: 704-759-0623
URL: http://www.bkwvlaw.com
John J. Butrus, Jr. (Not admitted in NC); S. A. Khoshbin (Not admitted in NC); Michael C. Wilson (Not admitted in NC); Peter W. Vogt; Mark W. Moran (Not admitted in NC);—Jennifer Driscoll Jasper (Not admitted in NC); Laura L. Reed.
Litigation, Trials and Appeals.
Dallas, Texas Office: 740 Park Creek Place, 3625 North Hall Street, 75219. Telephone: 214-219-1170. Facsimile: 214-219-1173.
See Professional Biographies, CHARLOTTE, NORTH CAROLINA

Butterworth, Amy E. .... '78 '04 C.446 B.A. L.896 J.D. [Ⓐ Horack,T.P.&L.]
Byers-Bailey, Thelma, Law Office of '43 '78
C.254 B.A. L.734 J.D. 1816 Beatties Ford Road
Byrne, G. Bland, III, (AVⓉ) .... '52 '78 C.575 A.B. L.309 J.D. [Byrne,D.&H.] ⊙
Byrne, Davis & Hicks, P.C., (AVⓉ) .... 1235-E East Boulevard 50 (⊙Atlanta, GA)
Byrnes, Kevin P., (CV) '55 '81
C.209 B.A. L.607 J.D. 1229 Greenwood Cliff Dr., Suite 210
Byrum, David E. .... '18 '60 C&L.896 B.S., LL.B. 5124 Tarrywood Lane‡
Byrum, Henry C., Jr., (AV) .... '53 '81 C.1128 B.A. L.469 J.D. [Stiles B.&H.]
Byrum, Porter B., (AV) .... '20 '42 C&L.896 LL.B. 4201-A Park Rd.‡
Cabaniss, Thomas E., (AVⓉ) .... '49 '75 C.576 B.S. L.893 J.D. [McGuireWoods]
Cacheris, John J., (BV) .... '66 '94 C.893 B.A. L.896 J.D. 435 E. Morehead St.
Cacheris, Kimberly Q. .... '68 '93 C.477 B.A. L.896 J.D. [McGuireWoods]

Caddell, H. Morris, Jr., (BV) '54 '79 C.575 B.A. L.896 J.D.
Cameron Brown Building, Suite 1210, 301 South McDowell Street, 28204
Telephone: 704-333-3700 Fax: 704-373-1308
Email: lawhmc@aol.com URL: http://www.lawyers.com/lawhmc
Civil Litigation, Family/Domestic Law, Equitable Distribution, Child Custody, Child Support, Alimony, Divorce, Visitation Rights, Commercial Law, Trusts and Estates, Condemnation.
See Professional Biographies, CHARLOTTE, NORTH CAROLINA

Cadwalader, Wickersham & Taft LLP, (AVⓉ)
227 West Trade Street Suite 2400, 28202 ⊙
Telephone: 704-348-5100 Fax: 704-348-5200
Email: cwtinfo@cwt.com URL: http://www.cadwalader.com
Members of Firm: James P. Carroll; Steven N. Cohen; Stuart N. Goldstein (Not admitted in NC); Henry A. LaBrun; Jeffrey J. Lee (Not admitted in NC); Richard Madden, Jr. (Not admitted in NC); Christopher M. McDermott; Robert L. Ughetta (Not admitted in NC). Special Counsel: Kurt W. Bjorklund (Not admitted in NC); James S. Hassan; Francisco J. Linares; John Robert White (Not admitted in NC); Alexander Zolfaghari (Not admitted in NC). Senior Attorneys: Patrick M. McNeely; Robert W. Watson, Jr. Associates: Jeffrey W. Aldrich, Jr. (Not admitted in NC); Maureen Connolly Bolinger; David S. Burkholder; Anderson Drew Caperton; Marc Daniels (Not admitted in NC); John Domby; Julie Ann Durham; Daniel J. Ellowitch (Not admitted in NC); Nicholas R. Finn; Kristen Froelich; Brad W. Funk; Annie R. George; J. Eric Holland; David A. Iacuzio; Starr S. Ilzhoefer (Not admitted in NC); Gregg L. Klingenberg (Not admitted in NC); Alexander T. Lin; Bruce G. Luna, II; Donal A. Luna; Patricia J. Luna; Geoffrey R. Maibohm; Holly S. Marcille; Bryon J. Mulligan (Not admitted in NC); Jeffrey Nagle; Kathleen Pearson (Not admitted in NC); Tia S. Phillips (Not admitted in NC); Matthew H. Robertson; Connie W. Sawyer, III; Harry B. Shadoan; Joshua M. Smith (Not admitted in NC); Richard Spooner; Venus Yvette Springs; John A. Teer; Ezell H. Underdown (Not admitted in NC); Jian Wang; Amy McNutt Woltman; Joshua J. Yablonski.
Banks and Banking, Bankruptcy, Capital Markets, Corporate Law, Finance, Litigation, Mergers, Acquisitions and Divestitures, Real Estate, Securities, Securitization and Taxation.
New York, N.Y. Office: One World Financial Center, 10281-0006. Telephone: 212-504-6000. Fax: 212-504-6666.
Washington, D.C. Office: 1201 F Street, N.W., Suite 1100, 20004. Telephone: 202-862-2200. Fax: 202-862-2400.
London, England Office: 265 Strand, WC2R 1BH. Telephone: +44 (0) 20 7170 8700. Fax: +44 (0) 20 7170 8600.
See Professional Biographies, CHARLOTTE, NORTH CAROLINA

Cagnina, Christine D. '— '95 C.37 B.S. L.597 J.D.
(adm. in IL; not adm. in NC) [Ⓐ Mayer,B.R.&M.]
Calame, Parmele Price .... '70 '95 C.797 B.A. L.790 J.D. [Poyner&S.]
Caldarelli, Paul A. '— '94 C.966 B.B.A. L.1206 J.D.
(adm. in FL; not adm. in NC) Asst. Gen. Coun., Bank of America
Caldwell, Stokely G., Jr., (AV) ....'— '86 C.301 B.A. L.902 J.D. [Robinson,B.&H.]
Calloway, Mark T., (AV) .... '58 '83 C.576 B.A. L.1228 J.D. [Alston&B.]
Cammarn, Scott A. '— '87 C.608 B.S. L.228 J.D.
Assoc. Gen. Coun., Bank of America
Cammarota, Michael J. '60 '86 C&L.724 B.A., J.D.
(adm. in NY; not adm. in NC) Site Coun., IBM North Amer.-Industry Sol. Unit
Camp, Lewis F., Jr. .... '28 '55 C&L.575 B.S., J.D. 10200 Shopton Rd., W.‡
Campbell, Boyd C., Jr., (AV) .... '41 '66 C.198 A.B. L.893 J.D. [Helms M.&W.]
Campbell, Carlyle, Jr. .... '28 '58 C&L.575 B.S., LL.B. 4221 Blacktree Lane
Campbell, Clair G., (BV) .... '61 '85 C.16 B.A. L.192 J.D. [Campbell&Assoc.]
Campbell, Hugh B., Jr., (AV) '37 '63 C.198 A.B. L.309 LL.B.
700 E. Fourth St., Ste. 3304
Campbell, Jack William, IV .... '— '98 C.575 B.S. L.880 J.D. [Ⓐ Helms M.&W.]
Campbell, John R., (AV) .... '38 '63 C&L.923 B.S., J.D. 3401 Gresham Pl.
Campbell, Justice Harrison ... '69 '99 C.34 B.S. L.469 J.D. 301 S. McDowell St., Ste. 204
Campbell, Sarah W. '57 '86 C.207 B.S. L.273 J.D.
V.P. & Dep. Gen. Coun., Transamerica Reinsurance

Campbell & Associates, PLC, (BV)
717 East Boulevard, 28203 ⊙
Telephone: 704-333-0885 Fax: 704-372-7718 URL: http://www.campbellandtaylorlaw.com
URL: http://www.lawyers.com/campbellandassoc
Member: Clair G. Campbell.
Auto Accidents, Personal Injury, Wrongful Death, Head Trauma, Motorcycle Accidents, Spinal Cord Injuries, Civil Litigation, Industrial Accidents, Slip and Fall, Workers Compensation, Medical Malpractice.
Hickory, North Carolina Office: 104 3rd Street. N.E., Suite 400, 28601. Telephone: 828-324-9191. Fax: 828-324-9592.
Gastonia, North Carolina Office: 603 Cox Road, Suite D, 28054. Telephone: 704-866-9191. Fax: 704-830-0104.
See Professional Biographies, CHARLOTTE, NORTH CAROLINA

Canepa, Mark B., (BVⓉ) .... '59 '89 C.766 B.A. L.1065 J.D. [Ⓐ Morris Y.W.S.&B.]
Canipe, Jeremy T. .... '— '02 C.575 B.A. L.790 J.D. [Ⓐ Hedrick E.G.&K.]
Cannaday, Kenneth S., (AV) .... '46 '74 C&L.575 A.B., J.D. 1929 Ewing Ave.‡
Cannon, David Rees, (AV) .... '— '77 C.269 B.A. L.790 J.D. [Nexsen P.A.K.]
Cannon, Thomas R., (AV) .... '40 '65 C&L.575 A.B., LL.B. [Horack,T.P.&L.]
Cannon, William B. .... '80 '05 C.198 B.S. L.575 J.D. [Ⓐ Parker,P.A.&B.]
Cannon, William H., (AV) .... '39 '66 C.198 B.A. L.575 LL.B. [W.H.Cannon] ⊙

Cannon, William H., P.A., (AV)
1900 Abbott Street, Suite 102, 28203 ⊙
Telephone: 704-376-7963 Telecopier: 704-335-0921
Email: WCANNONLAW@Aol.com URL: http://www.wcannonlaw.com
William H. Cannon.
Commercial Real Estate, particularly Golf Course and Resort Law. Acquisitions, Dispositions, Development and Lending. Zoning and Land Use.
References: Branch Banking and Trust Company; Nations Bank.
Manteo Office: 207 Queen Elizabeth Avenue, Suite 1, 27954. Telephone: 252-475-1624. Telecopier: 252-475-1625.
See Professional Biographies, CHARLOTTE, NORTH CAROLINA

Cantrell, Daphene L. .... '30 '54 C&L.575 A.B., LL.B. Dist. J.‡
Cantrell, Jeffrey P. .... '61 '88 C.259 B.A. L.260 J.D. [Mayer,B.R.&M.]
Cantu, Nicole Brovet .... '— '00 C.37 B.A. L.477 J.D. [Ⓐ Kilpatrick S.]
Canty, F. Douglas, (BV) .... '42 '75 C&L.575 B.S., J.D. Asst. City Atty.
Caperton, Anderson Drew .... '69 '97 C.893 B.A. L.575 J.D. [Ⓐ Cadwalader,W.&T.]
Capitano, A. Todd, (BV) .... '66 '94 C&L.575 B.A., J.D. [Bishop,C.&M.]
Capitano, John H., (BV) .... '— '95 C.198 B.A. L.1228 J.D. [Ⓐ Kennedy C.L.&H.]
Capwell, Jeffrey R., (AVⓉ) .... '63 '90 C.197 A.B. L.823 J.D. [McGuireWoods]
Caraway, Todd A. .... '62 '93 C.966 B.B.A. L.665 J.D. [Moore&V.P.]
Cardinal, Roger S. .... '58 '84 C.575 B.A. L.469 J.D. 2100 Crescent Avenue, Suite 202
Cardwell, Charlita C. '73 '00 C.896 B.A. L.659 J.D.
(adm. in NY; not adm. in NC) Compass Group, U.S.A. Inc.
Carles, Robert S. .... '41 '69 C.363 B.S. L.930 J.D. Secy. & Atty., Lance, Inc.
Carley, Linde H. .... '53 '85 C.813 B.A. L.426 J.D. Sr. V.P., Bank of America
Carley, Stephen R., (BV) .... '46 '75 C.197 A.B. L.893 J.D. [Carley&R.]
Carley & Rabon, PLLC, (BV) .... 300 Providence Road, Suite 105
Carlin, Gregory J. ...... '70 '00 C.665 B.S.M.E. L.273 J.D. [Ⓐ Alston&B.] (See Pat. Sect.)
Carlino, Peter N. .... '70 '95 C&L.896 B.A., J.D. 6743 Fairview Rd.
Carlson, Mark E. .... '76 '02 C.575 B.A. L.1228 J.D. [Carlson P.]
Carlson Law Firm, PLLC .... 1015 Falls Creek Ln., Apt. 10
Carlsten, Lars A., (BVⓉ) '55 '80 C.367 B.A. L.446 J.D.
(adm. in MD; not adm. in NC)
V.P. & Asst. Gen. Coun., Legal Div., First Union Corporation
Carlton, JoAnn P. '— '91 C.282 B.A. L.117 J.D.
(adm. in PA; not adm. in NC) Asst. Gen. Coun., Bank of AMerica
Carlton, Robert W. ... '55 '81 C.198 A.B. L.575 J.D. Off. of Hearings & App, Dept. HHS
Carmichael, John H., (BV) .... '— '93 C&L.575 B.A., J.D. [Kennedy C.L.&H.]
Carmody, Brendan P. '38 '70 C.1041 B.A. L.724 J.D.
(adm. in NY; not adm. in NC) V.P., Newton & Assocs., Inc.
Carpenter, John Joseph, (AV) .... '58 '84 C&L.896 B.S., J.D. [Culp E.&C.]
Carpenter, Mark E., (AV) .... '60 '85 C.575 A.B. L.893 J.D. [Moore&V.P.]
Carr, Michael P., (BV) .... '44 '69 C.524 B.S. L.896 J.D. [Goodman,C.L.L.&M.]

Carrigan, Mary V., (BV) '45 '84 C.840 B.A. L.575 J.D.
435 East Moorehead Street, 28202
Telephone: 704-333-8855 Fax: 704-331-0773 URL: http://maryvcarriganlaw.com
URL: http://www.maryvcarrigan.com
(Board Certified Specialist in Family Law, North Carolina State Board of Legal Specialization).
Domestic Relations, Family Law, Divorce, Equitable Distribution, Child Custody and Child Support, Alimony, Premarital Agreements.
See Professional Biographies, CHARLOTTE, NORTH CAROLINA

Carroll, Beverly A., (AVⓉ) '— '81
C.956 B.A. L.790 J.D. [Kennedy C.L.&H.] (⊙Rock Hill, SC)
Carroll, James P., (AVⓉ) '52 '77
C.276 B.A. L.128 J.D. [Cadwalader,W.&T.] (⊙Wash., DC)
Carroll, Karen K. '60 '85 C.112 B.A. L.1068 J.D.
(adm. in CA; not adm. in NC) [Carroll&C.]
Carroll, Scott P. .... '60 '85 C.631 B.A. L.809 J.D. [Carroll&C.]
Carroll & Carroll, P.L.L.C. .... 831 East Morehead Street, Suite 440
Carson, B. David, (BV) .... '62 '88 C.602 B.A. L.575 J.D. [Erwin&E.]
Carson, James H., Jr., (AV) .... '35 '63 C&L.575 A.B., LL.B. 1521 Elizabeth Ave.‡
Carter, Amy F. .... '71 '96 C.893 B.A. L.896 J.D. Bk. of America

Carter, James H.
(See Matthews)

Cary, Brian K. .... '62 '93 C.575 B.A. L.692 J.D. [Moore&V.P.]

Casey, Deborah G., (BV) '54 '91 C.925 B.S. L.192 J.D.
6525 Morrison Boulevard, Suite 314, 28211
Telephone: 704-362-1660 Fax: 704-362-1499 URL: http://www.dgcaseylaw.com
Email: deborah@dgcaseylaw.com URL: http://www.lawyers.com/deborahcasey
Serious Personal Injury, Medical Malpractice, Auto Accidents, Wrongful Death, Mediation.
See Professional Biographies, CHARLOTTE, NORTH CAROLINA

Cassada, Garland S., (AV) .... '— '84 C&L.893 B.A., J.D. [Robinson,B.&H.]
Casstevens, Nelson M., Jr., (AV) '41 '65 C.125 B.A. L.896 LL.B.
[Casstevens,H.G.&R.]

Casstevens, Hanner, Gunter & Riopel, P.A., (AV) BR
602 East Morehead Street, P.O. Box 34607, 28234
Telephone: 704-372-2140 Fax: 704-372-1150
URL: http://www.chgrlaw.com
Nelson M. Casstevens, Jr.; Robert P. Hanner, II (Board Certified Specialist in Family Law, North Carolina State Board of Legal Specialization); Dorian H. Gunter; Mark D. Riopel;—J. Huntington Wofford.
General Civil, Trial and Appellate Practice for all State and Federal Courts. Personal Injury, Domestic Relations, Family Law, Alimony, Equitable Distribution, Separation Agreements, Child Custody, Divorce, Child Support, Collaborative Law.
Approved Attorneys for: Lawyers Title Insurance Corp.; Old Republic Title Co.; Fidelity National Title Co.; First American Title Co.; Investors Title Co.; Stewart Title Co.

(This Listing Continued)

Casstevens, Hanner, Gunter & Riopel, P.A. (Continued)
Reference: Central Carolina Bank.
See Professional Biographies, CHARLOTTE, NORTH CAROLINA

Castagna, Edward C., Jr., (AV🅃) '48 '75 C.1176 B.A. L.260 J.D. (adm. in FL; not adm. in NC) 129 W. Trade St.‡
Caudill, J. Gentry .... '42 '72 C&L.575 A.B., J.D. Resident Supr. Ct. J.
Caudle, L. Cameron, Jr., (AV) .... '60 '87 C.228 A.B. L.1228 J.D. [Caudle&S.]

Caudle & Spears, P.A., (AV) BR
2600 Interstate Tower, 121 West Trade Street, 28202
Telephone: 704-377-1200 Telecopier: 704-338-5858
Email: caudlespears@caudlespears.com URL: http://www.caudlespears.com
Harold C. Spears; L. Cameron Caudle, Jr.; Jeffrey L. Helms; Christopher J. Loebsack; Michael J. Selle; Eric Allen Rogers;—C. Grainger Pierce, Jr.; Joseph R. Marek.
General Civil and Trial Practice. Real Estate, Business Associations, Bankruptcy, Personal Injury, Insurance Defense, Probate and Trusts, Taxation, Employee Benefits, Environmental Law; Estate Planning.
Counsel for: Bituminous Casualty Corp.; Baumann Springs A.G.; Boone Sales and Service Co.; Capitol Funds, Inc.; Employers Mutual Casualty Co.; Mark Oil Company, Inc.; Metromont Materials; Otis Elevator Co.; N.C. Farm Bureau Mutual Insurance Co.
See Professional Biographies, CHARLOTTE, NORTH CAROLINA

Cayer, David S. '54 '79 C.902 B.A. L.30 J.D. Resident Supr. Ct. J., Mecklnberg Co. Courthouse
Cecka, Michael T. .... '74 '03 C.712 B.A. L.469 J.D. [🄰 Alston&B.]
Chadd, Alan J. .... '69 '97 C&L.228 B.A., J.D. [Moore&V.P.]
Chaffin, Rebecca S. .... '64 '89 C.228 B.A. L.893 J.D. [Helms M.&W.]
Chambers, Julius LeVonne .... '36 '62 C.574 A.B. L.575 J.D. [Ferguson,S.C.G.&S.]
Chambers, Rolly L., (AV) .... '53 '84 C.575 A.B. L.945 J.D. [Smith,C.&H.]
Chamblee, Gary D., (AV) .... '52 '78 C&L.575 A.B., J.D. [Womble C.S.&R.]
Champion, Michael T. .... '73 '04 C.1128 B.A. L.575 J.D. [🄰 Moore&V.P.]
Chandler, Lynn F., (AV) .... '55 '88 C.575 B.S.B.A. L.190 J.D. [Morris,M.&M.]
Chandler, R. Michael .... '72 '99 C.240 B.S. L.896 J.D. [Hull&C.]
Chandler, Theodore G., Jr. .... '57 '83 C&L.575 B.A., J.D. Sr. Coun., Royal & Sunalliance
Chandler, William J., Jr., (AV) .... '42 '66 C&L.575 A.B., LL.B. 1508 E. 4th
Chapman, Ronald L., (BV) .... '47 '78 C.69 B.A. L.776 J.D. [Murphy&C.]

Chastain, Peter, & Associates, P.A.
(See Greensboro)

Cheatwood, David L. .... '— '04 C&L.575 B.S., J.D. [🄰 Kilpatrick S.]
Cheek, Joseph A. .... '67 '94 C&L.575 B.A., J.D. 821 East Boulevard
Cheney, Charles D. .... '64 '95 C&L.575 B.A., J.D. [🄰 McAngus G.&C.]
Chesson, Calvin W. .... '36 '62 C.232 A.B. L.575 J.D. 101 N. McDowell St., Ste. 114
Chew, Elizabeth C. .... '71 '97 C.184 B.A. L.306 J.D. Coun., Royal & SunAlliance
Childers, C. J. .... '— '99 C.100 B.S. L.923 J.D. [🄰 Hedrick E.G.&K.]
Chinuntdet, John S. .... '66 '92 C.896 B.A. L.802 J.D. [Moore&V.P.]
Chiu, Julie C., (AV) .... '— '89 C.575 B.A. L.309 J.D. [Robinson,B.&H.]
Chomakos, Andrea C. .... '71 '97 C.477 B.A. L.215 J.D. [🄰 Moore&V.P.]
Christ, Cindy, (BV) .... '59 '89 C.790 B.A. L.1345 J.D. [Christ]
Christ Law Firm, The, PA, (BV) .... 5500 Strawberry Hill Dr., Apt. B.
Christensen, Aaron M., (AV) .... '67 '93 C.896 B.A. L.893 J.D. [Smith&C.]
Christman, Susan, (AV) .... '51 '76 C.45 B.A. L.880 J.D. [Horack,T.P.&L.]
Chromy, David M. .... '— '03 C.93 B.S. L.1522 J.D. [🄰 Helms M.&W.]
Chubb, Philip S., (BV) .... '56 '82 C.473 A.B. L.851 J.D. [Shumaker,L.&K.]
Churchill, Matthew S. .... '— '94 C.228 A.B. L.813 J.D. [Robinson,B.&H.]
Citrano, Lauren M. .... '66 '91 C.1292 B.A. L.896 J.D. [🄰 McAngus G.&C.]
Clardy, Carlton S., Jr. .... '56 '82 C.893 B.A. L.862 J.D. 13024 Idlewild Rd.
Clark, Alan B. '65 '91 C.893 B.S. L.945 J.D. (adm. in VA; not adm. in NC) Asst. Gen. Coun. & Compl. Offr., Lending Tree, Inc.
Clark, Bernard B., (AV) .... '47 '72 C.790 B.A. L.228 J.D. [Moore&V.P.]
Clark, C. Christopher .... '71 '01 C.888 B.M. L.577 J.D. [🄰 Shumaker,L.&K.]
Clark, David J. .... '— '77 C.197 A.B. L.846 J.D. [Robinson,B.&H.]
Clark, Deborah R. .... '56 '81 C.112 B.A. L.309 J.D. P.O. Box 5274
Clark, Francis C., (AV) '51 '76 C.575 A.B. L.902 J.D. Sr. V.P. & Dep. Gen. Coun., First Union Corp.
Clarke, Dumont, IV, (AV) .... '52 '78 C.881 B.A. L.575 J.D. [Moore&V.P.]
Clarke, T. Hal, Jr., (AV🅃) '52 '76 C&L.902 A.B., J.D. Sr. V.P., Dep. Gen. Coun., First Union Corp.
Clarke, Timothy A., (AV🅃) '— '81 C.732 B.A. L.1048 J.D. (adm. in MA; not adm. in NC) Bank of America (⊙Glastonbury, CT)
Clary, Robert Allen, II .... '— '05 C.34 B.A. L.472 J.D. [🄰 Kennedy C.L.&H.]
Clawson, Samuel R., (AV🅃) .... '48 '80 C.968 B.A. L.1228 J.D. [Clawson&S.] ⊙

Clawson & Staubes, LLC, (AV) BR
756 Tyvola Road, Suite 130, 28217 ⊙
Telephone: 704-940-9128 Fax: 704-522-9033
Email: rcraig@clawson&staubes.com
Samuel R. Clawson; Ronnie F. Craig; J. Ronald Jones, Jr. (Certified Specialist, Bankruptcy Law, The Supreme Court of South Carolina). Associates: Michael J. Kitson; Andrew J. Santaniello.
Bankruptcy, Commercial Collections, Creditors Rights and Subrogations, Civil Litigation.
Representative Clients: Allstate Insurance Co.; Blue Cross Blue Shield of South Carolina; City of Charleston; CNA Insurance Co.; First Federal Savings & Loan Association of Charleston; Maryland Casualty Co.; NationsBank; Nationwide Mutual Insurance Co.; State Farm Mutual Insurance Companies; United Carolina Bank.
Charleston, South Carolina Office: 126 Seven Farms Road, Suite 200, 29492-7595. Telephone: 803-577-2026. Facsimile: 803-722-2867.
See Professional Biographies, CHARLOTTE, NORTH CAROLINA

Claypoole, Theodore F. .... '63 '88 C.228 A.B. L.608 J.D. [Womble C.S.&R.]
Claytor, William M., (AV) .... '41 '69 L.836 J.D. [Baucom,C.B.M.&W.]
Clements, Gregory N. '51 '81 C.150 B.S.Ch.E. L.1209 J.D. [Dougherty,C.H.&B.] (See Pat. Sect.)
Clifton, Daniel J. ... '50 '83 C.232 B.A. L.284 J.D. 301 South McDowell Street, Suite 604
Cline, Todd W., (BV) .... '64 '89 C.968 B.A. L.790 J.D. [T.W.Cline]
Cline, Todd W., P.A., (BV) .... 101 N. McDowell Street, Suite 220
Clodfelter, Daniel G., (AV) .... '50 '77 C.198 B.A. L.976 J.D. [Moore&V.P.]
Clontz, Ralph C., III, (AV) .... '50 '76 C.576 B.S. L.575 J.D. [Clontz&C.P.]

Clontz & Clontz PLLC, (AV)
The Justice Building, 225 South McDowell Street, 28204-2294
Telephone: 704-376-0045 Fax: 704-376-2746
URL: http://www.lawyers.com/clontzlegal
Ralph C. Clontz, Jr. (1922-2001); Ralph C. Clontz III;—Claudia L. Reisch.
Collections, Bankruptcy, Creditor's Rights, Banking, and General Trial and Appellate Practice. Community Law.
Representative Client: First Union National Bank of North Carolina.
See Professional Biographies, CHARLOTTE, NORTH CAROLINA

Coale, Elizabeth Chase .... '71 '98 C&L.896 B.A., J.D. [🄰 Helms M.&W.]
Cobb, James O., (AV) .... '27 '55 C.198 B.S. L.575 LL.B. [Ruff,B.C.W.&B.]
Cobb, John H. .... '62 '89 C.198 B.A. L.893 J.D. [Helms M.&W.]
Coble, Debbie Q. .... '65 '91 C&L.1128 B.A., J.D. Fed. Law Clk.
Coble, E. Kenneth .... '77 '03 C&L.575 B.A., J.D. [Dozier,M.P.&M.]
Cocklin, Kim R. .... '51 '81 C.942 B.S. L.900 J.D. Piedmont Natural Gas Company, Inc.
Coe, Kenneth S., (AV) .... '50 '76 C.575 A.B. L.228 J.D. [Moore&V.P.]
Cogdell, Harold W., Jr. .... '69 '97 C.577 B.S. L.574 J.D. 310 Arlington Ave., Ste. 218
Cogdell, Joe B., Jr., (AV) .... '53 '78 C&L.45 B.A., J.D. [Womble C.S.&R.]
Coggin, Gerry C., II .... '72 '03 C.575 B.S. L.896 J.D. [🄰 Gilpin&H.]
Coghill, Cornelius W., III, (AV) .... '51 '78 C.198 A.B. L.575 J.D. [Womble C.S.&R.]
Cohan, Richard A., (BV) .... '23 '60 C.575 A.B. L.30 J.D. 1515 Mockingbird Lane

Cohen, Howard M., (BV) '50 '76 C.273 B.A. L.161 J.D.
Suite 952 Johnston Building, 212 South Tryon Street, 28281
Telephone: 704-335-8139 Fax: 704-335-8130
Email: hcohen@bellsouth.net URL: http://www.lawyers.com/howardcohen
Labor and Employment Law, Personal Injury and Workers Compensation and Civil Litigation before State and Federal Courts and Agencies. Mediation and Arbitration.
See Professional Biographies, CHARLOTTE, NORTH CAROLINA

Cohen, Jack V. '42 '67 C&L.273 B.A., LL.B. Sr. V.P. & Asst. Gen. Coun., First Union Corporation
Cohen, Jeffrey E. .... '61 '87 C.867 B.A. L.904 J.D. Sr. Coun., KoSa
Cohen, Steven N. '53 '82 C.918 B.A. L.569 J.D. [Cadwalader,W.&T.] (⊙New York, NY)
Colas, Arthur H., Jr. '— '73 C.188 B.A. L.208 J.D. (adm. in CO; not adm. in NC) Bank of America (⊙San Fran., CA)
Cole, Claire Pierce .... '36 '86 C.1128 B.A. L.574 J.D. 301 S. McDowell St.‡
Cole, Glenn, III .... '68 '94 C.575 B.A. L.500 J.D. Asst. Dist. Atty.
Cole, John D. .... '62 '91 C.902 B.A. L.280 J.D. [Ogletree,D.N.S.&S.]
Cole, Michelle J. .... '70 '96 C.188 B.A. L.880 J.D. [🄲 Alston&B.]
Coleman, S. Walt, IV '69 '96 C.893 B.A. L.902 J.D. Asst. Gen. Coun., Duke Energy Corp.
Coleman, Shelley W. .... '— '96 C.16 B.A. L.902 J.D. [Hedrick E.G.&K.]
Colgate, Adrianne Huffman .... '— '03 C&L.575 B.A., J.D. [🄰 Hamilton F.M.S.S.&M.]
Coman, Francis X., (AV) '48 '75 C.776 A.B. L.896 J.D. Sr. V.P. & Coun., Lawyers Title of N.C.
Combs, Karen Craft, (BV) .... '53 '78 C.683 B.A. L.692 J.D. [Combs&Assoc.]
Combs & Associates, (BV) .... P.O. Box 32185
Conard, Spencer D., (AV🅃) '60 '86 C&L.378 B.S.Ch.E., J.D. SPX Corporation (Law Department) (Pat.)
Conaway, David Harris, (BV) .... '58 '83 C.575 B.A. L.16 J.D. [Shumaker,L.&K.]
Concha, David Alexander .... '73 '98 C.576 B.S. L.347 J.D. 1101 Tyvola Rd., Ste. 214
Conley, John M., (AV) .... '— '77 C.309 A.B. L.228 J.D. [🄲 Robinson,B.&H.]
Connelly, Charles W., Jr. .... '43 '69 C.269 B.A. L.790 J.D. McGuire Properties
Connelly, Christopher A., (CV) '62 '87 C.262 B.A. L.1325 J.D. 101 N. McDowell St., Ste. 104
Conner, Richard Horace, III .... '— '02 C&L.575 B.A., J.D. [🄰 Helms M.&W.]
Connette, Edward G., III, (AV) .... '52 '77 C.198 B.A. L.575 J.D. [Essex R.]
Connor, Heather Graham, (BV) ... '73 '98 C.420 B.A. L.861 J.D. [🄰 Morris Y.W.S.&B.]
Connor, Michael S., (AV) '62 '88 C.871 B.S.M.E. L.575 J.D. [Alston&B.] (See Pat. Sect.)
Conrad, James T. .... '49 '80 C.235 B.S. L.436 J.D. [J.T.Conrad]
Conrad, Robert J., Jr. .... '58 '83 C.160 B.A. L.893 J.D. Dist. J.
Conrad, James T., PA .... P.O. Box 620120

Conrad Trosch & Kemmy, P.A., (AV)
Cameron Brown Building, 301 South McDowell Street, Suite 809, 28204
Telephone: 704-553-8221 Fax: 704-331-0595
Email: troschbill@ctklawyers.com URL: http://www.ctklawyers.net
Louis A. Trosch; Michael J. Kemmy; William Conrad Trosch; Minette C. Trosch; Kristin L. Smith;—Anna D. Baker; Eric C. Trosch.
Family Law, Real Estate, Wills, Probate, Estate Planning, Trusts, Business Law, Criminal Law, Divorce, Personal Injury, Wrongful Death.
Other Charlotte, North Carolina Office: Park View Building, 5821 Fairview Road, Suite 405, 28209. Telephone: 704-553-8221. Fax: 704-553-7689.
See Professional Biographies, CHARLOTTE, NORTH CAROLINA

Constangy, H. William (Bill) .... '42 '68 C.896 B.A. L.228 J.D. Dist. Ct. J.
Constitution Law Associates, LLC 11525 Carmel Commons Boulevard (⊙Huntersville, Monroe, NC; Fort Mill, Lake Wylie, Rock Hill, SC)
Cook, Barry A., (BV) .... '48 '73 C.97 B.A. L.7 J.D. Dist. Atty. Off.
Cook, Christopher W. .... '— '04 C.1053 B.A. L.896 J.D. [🄰 Dean&G.]
Cook, Elise A. .... '71 '96 C.280 B.B.A. L.469 J.D. Asst. Gen. Coun., Bank of America
Cook, P. Neal .... '69 '95 C.575 B.A. L.896 J.D. [Parker,P.A.&B.]
Cook, Thaddeus W. .... '— '98 C.1128 B.S. L.1187 J.D. Coun., Bank of America
Cooksey, Neil C., (AV) .... '61 '86 C.198 A.B. L.477 J.D. [Smith,C.&V.]
Cooley, Amanda Harmon .... '78 '03 C.575 B.A. L.577 J.D. [🄰 Parker,P.A.&B.]
Cooley, Jim D., (AV) .... '46 '73 C.198 B.A. L.575 J.D. [Womble C.S.&R.]
Cooney, James P., III, (AV) .... '57 '84 C.228 A.B. L.893 J.D. [Womble C.S.&R.]
Cooper, Jason P., (AV) '66 '92 C.679 B.S.M.E. L.347 J.D. [Alston&B.] (See Pat. Sect.)
Cooper, Susan Hager, (BV) .... '— '93 C&L.575 B.A., J.D. [Kilpatrick S.]
Cooper, W. Scott, (AV) .... '52 '77 C.228 B.A. L.945 J.D. [Rayburn C.&D.]
Cooper, William R. '38 '64 C&L.893 B.S., LL.B. Sr. V.P., Interstate/Johnson Lane Corporation
Corbett, K. Stacie .... '77 '02 C.577 B.A. L.893 J.D. [🄰 Hunton&W.]
Cordell, Stephen L., (BV) .... '57 '83 C.576 B.A. L.896 J.D. [Helms M.&W.]
Cordes, David C., (BV) .... '63 '92 C.976 B.A. L.896 J.D. [Koehler&C.]
Cordle, Robert B., (AV) .... '41 '66 C.198 A.B. L.569 LL.B. [Mayer,B.R.&M.]
Cornell, Carolyn C. '62 '91 C.699 B.A. L.724 J.D. (adm. in NY; not adm. in NC) 2508 Whitney Hill Road
Corrigan, Timothy W. .... '68 '94 C.347 B.S. L.575 J.D. [Moore&V.P.]
Cory, G. Lee, Jr. .... '— '93 C.575 B.A. L.893 J.D. [Kennedy C.L.&H.]
Cory, Jennifer L. '69 '95 C.320 B.A. L.362 J.D. (adm. in FL; not adm. in NC) [🄰 Garfinkel]
Cosper, Harvey L., Jr., (AV) .... '48 '75 C.575 B.A. L.896 J.D. [Parker,P.A.&B.]
Cosper, Harvey L., Sr. '21 '47 C.1365 B.Ph. L.245 LL.B. (adm. in GA; not adm. in NC) 6735 Burlwood Dr.‡
Coss, Elizabeth C. .... '65 '90 C.575 B.S. L.896 J.D. [🄲 Womble C.S.&R.]
Coss, Stephen K. '69 '94 C.228 B.A. L.893 J.D. Sr. V.P., Gen. Coun. & Secy., Sonic Auto., Inc.
Cottingham, T. Thomas, III, (AV🅃) .... '47 '76 C.198 A.B. L.188 J.D. [Hunton&W.]
Cottrell, Eric H. .... '70 '95 C.896 B.A. L.575 J.D. [🄰 Mayer,B.R.&M.]
Coviello, Maria T. '75 '00 C.262 B.A. L.1040 J.D. (adm. in CT; not adm. in NC) Sr. Corp. Coun., Compass Group, U.S.A. Inc.
Covington, George C., (AV) .... '— '84 C.198 B.A. L.575 J.D. [Kennedy C.L.&H.]
Covington, Peter J., (AV) .... '53 '80 C.575 B.A. L.861 J.D. [Helms M.&W.]
Cowell, Marion A., Jr., (AV) .... '— '64 C&L.575 B.S., LL.B. [🄲 Kilpatrick S.]

Cox, Berkeley C. '67 '91 L.999 LL.B.
(adm. in NY; not adm. in NC) 227 W. Trade St., Suite 2400
Cox, Brian C. .... '— '99 C.228 A.B. L.893 J.D. [[A] Kennedy C.L.&H.]
Cox, Christa E. .... '73 '98 C&L.790 B.A., J.D. Dist. Atty. Off.
Cox, David M. .... '47 '72 C&L.575 B.S., J.D. 3901 Flowerfield Rd.
Cox, John N. .... '— '92 C.576 B.S. L.665 J.D. [[A] Dickie,M.&C.] (Pat.)
Cox, Marie Gibbs .... '— '96 C.575 B.A. L.893 J.D. [[A] Kennedy C.L.&H.]
Cox, Matthew E., (BVⓉ) '71 '99 C.101 B.S. L.790 J.D.
(adm. in SC; not adm. in NC) [[A] Smith,C.&H.]
Cox, Robert A., Jr., (BV) .... '69 '95 C.575 B.A. L.896 J.D. [[A] McGuireWoods]
Cox, Shelia June, (BV) .... '69 '94 C.362 B.A. L.896 J.D. [Poyner&S.]
Coyne, Rachel Worlds .... '72 '99 C.198 B.A. L.896 J.D. [[A] Moore&V.P.]

Cozen O'Connor, A Professional Corporation, (AV) [BB]
One First Union Center, Suite 2100, 301 South College Street, 28202 ⊙
Telephone: 704-376-3400; 800-762-3575 Fax: 704-334-3351
URL: http://www.cozen.com
Firm Members in Charlotte: Peter F. Asmer, Jr.; Douglas Banks; Russ A. Brinson; Tracy L. Eggleston; B. Elizabeth Gast; Joshua R. Goodman; T. David Higgins, Jr.; Garrett J. McAvoy; Albert S. Nalibotsky; Hunter C. Quick; Paul A. Reichs; Kimberly Sullivan; John W. Reis. Firm Associates in Charlotte: Adam P. Altman; Michael Durr; Megan A. Lammon.
Advertising Liability/Personal Injury, Alternative Dispute Resolution, Agent/Broker Liability, Antitrust and Unfair Competition, Appellate Practice, Arbitration and Alternative Dispute Resolution, Arson and Fraud, Aviation Litigation, Bad Faith Litigation, Bankruptcy, Insolvency and Restructuring, Business Torts, Cargo Losses, Class Actions, Multi-District Litigation and Other Consolidated Claims, Commercial General Liability, Commercial Litigaion, Construction Law and Litigation, Construction Liability, Corporate and Partnership Law, Corporate Planning, Crisis Management, Cross Border Transactions, Directors' and Officers' Liability, E-Commerce, Internet and Cyber-Peril Insurance, Emerging Business and Venture Capital, Employee Benefits and Executive Compensation, Employment, Labor and Employee Benefits, Environmental Coverage, Environmental Litigation, Estate Planning and Administration, Excess and Surplus Lines, Family Law, Fidelity and Surety, Financial Services, Health Law, Health Care Malpractice, Insurance Corporate and Regulatory Law, Intellectual Property, Intellectual Property Litigation, International Tax and Estate Planning, Labor and Employment, Life, Health and Disability Maritime Law, Medical Device and Drug Litigation, Mergers and Acquisitions, Personal Lines, Privacy Law and Regulation, Private Wealth Services, Products Liability, Professional Liability, Property Insurance, Public and Project Finance, Public Utilities and Energy, Punitive Damages, Real Estate, Real Estate Litigation, Reinsurance, Securities, Securities Litigation and Civil RICO, Security and Premises Liability, Tax, Tax Litigation, Toxic and Other Mass Torts, White Collar Crime.
Dallas, Texas Office: 2300 BankOne Center, 1717 Main Street, 75201. Telephones: 214-462-3000; 800-448-1207. Fax: 214-462-3299.
New York, N.Y. Offices: 45 Broadway Atrium, 16th Floor, 10006. Telephones: 212-509-9400; 800-437-7040. Fax: 212-509-9492. Midtown Office: 909 Third Avenue, 17th Floor, 10022. Telephones: 212-509-9400; 800-437-7040. Fax: 212-207-4938.
Philadelphia, Pennsylvania Office: 1900 Market Street, 19103. Telephones: 215-665-2000; 800-523-2900. Fax: 215-665-2013.
West Conshohocken, Pennsylvania Office: 200 Four Falls Corporate Center, Suite 400, P.O. Box 800, 19428. Telephone: 610-941-5400; 800-379-0695. Fax: 610-941-0711.
San Diego, California Office: Suite 1610, 501 West Broadway, 92101. Telephones: 619-234-1700; 800-782-3366. Fax: 619-234-7831.
Los Angeles, California Office: 777 South Figueroa Street, Suite 2850, 90017. Telephones: 213-892-7900; 800-563-1027. Fax: 213-892-7999.
Seattle, Washington Office: Suite 5200, Washington Mutual Tower, 1201 Third Avenue, 98101. Telephones: 206-340-1000; 800-423-1950. Fax: 206-621-8783.
Newark, New Jersey Office: One Newark Center, Suite 1900, 07102. Telephone: 973-286-1200; 888-200-9521. Fax: 973-242-2121.
Atlanta, Georgia Office: Suite 2200, SunTrust Plaza, 303 Peachtree Street, N.E., 30308. Telephones: 404-572-2000; 800-890-1393. Fax: 404-572-2199.
London, England Office: Fountain House, 130 Fenchurch Street, London EC3M 5DJ. Telephone: 011-44-20-7864-2000. Fax: 011-44-20-7864-2013.
Wilmington, Delaware Office: Chase Manhattan Centre, 1201 North Market Street, Suite 1400, 19801. Telephone: 302-295-2000; 888-207-2440. Fax: 302-295-2013.
Las Vegas, Nevada Office (Affiliated with the Law Offices of J. Goldberg & D. Grossman): 601 South Rancho, Suite 20, 89106. Telephone: 800-782-3366.
San Francisco, California Office: 425 California Street, Suite 2400, 94104-2203. Telephone: 415-617-6100; 800-818-0165. Fax: 415-617-6101.
Chicago, Illinois Office: 222 South Riverside, Suite 1500, 60606. Telephone: 312-382-3100; 877-992-6036. Fax: 312-382-8910.
Washington, D.C. Office: 1667 K Street, NW, 20006. Telephone: 202-912-4800; 800-540-1355. Fax: 202-912-4830.
Cherry Hill, New Jersey Office: LibertyView, Suite 300, 457 Haddonfield Road, P.O. Box 5459, 08002-2220. Telephone: 856-910-5000; 800-989-0499. Fax: 856-910-5075.
Wichita, Kansas Office: 8415 E. 21st Street, Suite 220, 67206. Telephone: 316-609-3380. Fax: 316-634-3837.
Denver, Colorado Office: 707 17th Street, Suite 3100, 80202. Telephone: 303-292-9080. Fax: 303-292-9650.
Trenton, New Jersey Office: 144-B West State Street, 08608. Telephone: 609-989-8620.
Houston, Texas Office: 1 Houston Center, 1221 McKinney Street, Suite 2900, 77010. Telephone: 800-448-8502; 832-214-3900. Fax: 832-214-3905.
Toronto, Ontario Office: One Queen Street East, Suite 2000, M5C 2W5. Telephone: 416-361-2000. Fax: 416-361-1405.
Santa Fe, New Mexico Office: 125 Lincoln Avenue, Suite 400, 87501. Telephones: 505-820-3346; 866-231-0144. Fax: 505-820-3347.
See Professional Biographies, CHARLOTTE, NORTH CAROLINA

Crabtree, Hillary B. .... '69 '99 C.198 B.A. L.575 J.D. [[A] Moore&V.P.]
Crabtree, Michelle S. .... '66 '92 C&L.923 B.S., J.D. [[A] McMillan&T.]
Craig, Ronnie F., (BVⓉ) .... '59 '86 C.1130 B.A. L.45 J.D. [Clawson&S.]
Craig, William R. .... '52 '80 C.478 A.B. L.923 J.D. 125 Huntley Place‡
Cramer, Mark C. .... '54 '79 C.575 A.B. L.893 J.D. 1201 Greenwood Cliff, Ste. 310
Cramer, Robert W., (AV) .... '57 '84 C&L.575 A.B., J.D. [Helms M.&W.]
Cranfill, W. T., Jr., (AV) .... '41 '68 C&L.896 B.A., J.D. [McGuireWoods]

Cranfill, Sumner & Hartzog, L.L.P., (AV) [BB]
227 West Trade Street, Suite 600, P.O. Box 30787, 28230 ⊙
Telephone: 704-332-8300 Fax: 704-332-9994
URL: http://www.cshlaw.com
Members Of The Firm: Samuel H. Poole, Jr.; M. Andrew Avram; Patrick H. Flanagan; Emerson M. Thompson III; Nicholas Peter Valaoras; J. Shannon Harris; Lawrence M. Baker; Nicole Dolph Viele; Jeffrey A. Howle; Todd Alexander King; Robert Marc Rubin; Julie L. Kerr; Victoria A. Street; Ryan D. Bolick; Holland L. Barksdale; Bradley P. Kline.
General Trial and Appellate Practice before all State and Federal Courts. Litigation of Insurance Law, Personal Injury, Medical Malpractice, Nursing Home Negligence, Professional Malpractice, Products Liability, Premises Liability, Municipal and Police Liability, Intentional Torts, Commercial Litigation, Worker's Compensation, Employment, Construction and Land Condemnation Law.
Raleigh, North Carolina Office: Hillsborough Place, 225 Hillsborough Street, Suite 300, P.O. Box 27808. Telephone: 919-828-5100. Fax: 919-828-2277.
Wilmington, North Carolina Office: 1209 Culbreth Drive, Suite 200, 28405. Telephone: 910-509-9778. Fax: 910-509-9676.
See Professional Biographies, CHARLOTTE, NORTH CAROLINA

Cranford, Charles H., (BV) .... '46 '73 C&L.575 A.B., J.D. [Cranford,S.&T.]

Cranford, Schultze and Tomchin, P.A., (AV)
2813 Coltsgate Road, Suite 200, 28211
Telephone: 704-442-1010 Fax: 704-442-1020
URL: http://www.cstpa.com
Charles H. Cranford; Michael F. Schultze; R. Gregory Tomchin; R. Michael Allen.

(This Listing Continued)

Cranford, Schultze and Tomchin, P.A. (Continued)
General Civil and limited Criminal Trials in all Courts. Residential and Commercial Real Estate Law; General Business Law; Collections and Foreclosures; Debtor and Creditors Rights Law; Bankruptcy; Personal Injury and Wrongful Death Litigation; Estate Planning and Administration.
See Professional Biographies, CHARLOTTE, NORTH CAROLINA

Crawford, Michelle V. .... '— '03 C.893 B.A. L.896 J.D. [[A] Hedrick E.G.&K.]
Crews, Alfred, Jr. '62 '89 C.1070 B.S. L.945 J.D.
(adm. in VA; not adm. in NC)
General Dynamics Armament and Technical Products Inc.★
Crisp, C. Michael .... '73 '98 C&L.575 B.S., J.D. [Grier F.&C.]
Crock, Jane E., Law Office of .. '58 '91 C.352 B.B.A. L.221 J.D. 3216 French Woods Rd.
Crocker, Gary B. .... '71 '96 C.575 B.A. L.861 J.D. Off. of Pub. Def.
Cromartie, Martha A. '57 '88
C.174 B.A. L.575 J.D. 101 N. Tryon St., 1900 Independence Ctr.
Cromwell, Brian S., (CV) .... '64 '96 C.1046 B.S. L.262 J.D. [[A] Mayer,B.R.&M.]
Cronin, Michael T. .... '71 '96 C.608 B.A. L.930 J.D. [[C] Moore&V.P.]
Cross, J. Emory '14 '45 C&L.260 B.S., J.D.
(adm. in FL; not adm. in NC) 5114 Dunes Ct.‡
Crotty, Jonathan M., (AV) .... '63 '88 C&L.228 B.A., J.D. [Parker,P.A.&B.]
Crowder, Kirk R., (AVⓉ) '62 '87
C.900 B.B.A. L.734 J.D. Asst. Gen. Coun., Clariant Corp.
Crowther, Mark O., (BV) .... '66 '93 C.198 B.A. L.1228 J.D. [Stiles B.&H.]
Crumpacker, Jack R. '59 '85 C&L.900 B.B.A., J.D.
(adm. in KS; not adm. in NC) 8310 Technology Dr.‡
Culbreth, James H., Jr. .... '53 '81 C.896 B.A. L.273 J.D. [Helms M.&W.]
Culicerto, Andrew S. .... '— '03 C&L.923 B.S.B.A., J.D. [[A] Hedrick E.G.&K.]
Culler, Jena P., (BV) .... '64 '89 C.575 B.S. L.1228 J.D. [Culler&C.]
Culler, Richard Andrew, (BV) .... '62 '87 C.896 B.A. L.1228 J.D. [Culler&C.]
Culler & Culler, P.A., (BV) .... 301 South McDowell Street, Suite 807
Culp, Christopher J., (BV) .... '61 '86 C.198 A.B. L.575 J.D. [[A] Mitchell,R.&T.]
Culp, Heather W. .... '73 '97 C.472 B.A. L.383 J.D. [[A] Mitchell,R.&T.]
Culp, Marylin E., (AVⓉ) .... '49 '86 C.352 B.A. L.362 J.D. [Littler M.]
Culp, William R., Jr., (P.A.), (AV) .... '53 '78 C&L.575 B.S., J.D. [Culp E.&C.]

Culp Elliott & Carpenter, P.L.L.C., (AV) [BB]
A Professional Limited Liability Company
4401 Barclay Downs Drive Suite 200, 28209
Telephone: 704-372-6322 Fax: 704-551-5700
URL: http://www.ceandc.com
William R. Culp, Jr., (P.A.) (Board Certified Specialist in Estate Planning and Probate Law, North Carolina State Board of Legal Specialization); W. Curtis Elliott, Jr.; John Joseph Carpenter (Board Certified Specialist in Estate Planning and Probate Law, North Carolina State Board of Legal Specialization); Paul M. Hattenhauer (Board Certified Specialist in Estate Planning and Probate Law, North Carolina State Board of Legal Specialization); Christopher E. Hannum; Mark Louis Richardson (Board Certified Specialist in Estate Planning and Probate Law, North Carolina State Board of Legal Specialization). Senior Associate: Jeffrey D. Barnes. Associates: Paul J. Smith; Holly B. Norvell; Stanton P. Geller; Benjamin H. Ellis; Carl L. King; Richard A. Pelak; Deborah H. King.
Federal, State, Local and International Taxation, Real Estate and Commercial Law, International Business Negotiations and Planning, Securities, Partnership and Corporate Law, Employee Benefits, Estate Planning and Tax Litigation and Controversies.
See Professional Biographies, CHARLOTTE, NORTH CAROLINA

Culver, John H., III, (AV) .... '— '85 C.893 B.A. L.446 J.D. [Kennedy C.L.&H.]
Cummings, Angela B. .... '72 '99 C&L.575 B.A., J.D. [[A] Littler M.]
Cummings, Humphrey S. .... '45 '77 C.1128 B.A. L.575 J.D. [Cummings]
Cummings, Rachel R., (AV) .... '— '82 C.259 B.S. L.896 J.D. Mgr., Bank of America
Cummings, Sandra U. .... '51 '77 C.977 B.A. L.575 J.D. [Cummings]
Cummings, Thomas E., (AV) .... '41 '66 C&L.575 A.B., J.D. 2220 Selwyn Ave.

Cummings Law Firm, The, P.A.
1230 West Morehead, Suite 404, 28208-5210
Telephone: 704-376-2853 Fax: 704-376-3334
Email: Cummingslawfirm@aol.com URL: http://www.thecummingslawfirm.com
Sandra U. Cummings; Humphrey S. Cummings.
Consumer Bankruptcy, Commercial Bankruptcy, Collections, Debtor Rights, Employment Discrimination, Sexual Harassment, Social Security Disability, Federal Workers Compensation, Wrongful Termination, Civil Rights.
See Professional Biographies, CHARLOTTE, NORTH CAROLINA

Curran, Martha Hawkins .... '51 '79 C.575 B.A. L.790 J.D. Law Clk., Supr. Ct.
Curry, Clayton S., Jr., (BV) .... '48 '72 C.575 B.S. L.838 J.D. [Horack,T.P.&L.]
Dabbs, David W., (AV) .... '— '90 C.896 B.S. L.228 J.D. [Robinson,B.&H.]
D'Agata, Michael C. .... '60 '86 C.301 B.A. L.896 J.D. P.O. Box 35312
Dagenhart, Larry J., (AV) .... '32 '58 C.198 B.S. L.569 LL.B. [[C] Helms M.&W.]
Daisley, Michel C., (BV) .... '55 '85 C.198 B.A. L.575 J.D. [Wells&D.]
Dalton, Kevin Joseph .... '71 '96 C.896 B.A. L.64 J.D. [[A] Fisher&P.]
Daly, George, (AV) .... '37 '65 C.674 A.B. L.309 LL.B. 139 Altondale Avenue
Daly, Virginia "Ginger" Theis '— '99 C.893 B.A. L.273 J.D.
(adm. in OH; not adm. in NC) [[A] Nelson M.R.&S.]
Danello, Timothy F. '56 '81
C.197 A.B. L.930 J.D. Wachovia Corporation (Legal Department)
Daniel, James A.L., Jr. .... '67 '96 C.198 A.B. L.896 J.D. [Alston&B.]
Daniel, James E., (AV) .... '55 '82 C.575 B.S. L.245 J.D. [Womble C.S.&R.]

Daniel, John T., (AV) '54 '83 C.806 B.A. L.904 J.D.
216 N. McDowell Street, Suite 208, 28204-2260
Telephone: 704-333-0900 Fax: 704-333-0993
Email: jtdaniel@bellsouth.net URL: http://www.lawyers.com/johndaniel
Civil Litigation. Concentration in Business Litigation, Contracts, Construction Claims, Collections, Commercial Litigation, Construction Litigation, Contracts Litigation, Negligence.
See Professional Biographies, CHARLOTTE, NORTH CAROLINA

Daniels, Marc '— '95 C.453 S.B. L.477 J.D.
(adm. in NY; not adm. in NC) [[A] Cadwalader,W.&T.]
Daugherty, Harry K., Jr. .... '60 '89 C.228 B.S. L.910 J.D. 1245 Wareham Ct.
Daugherty, Leslee K. .... '— '88 C&L.575 B.S., J.D. [[C] Kennedy C.L.&H.]
Dautel, Timothy P. .... '45 '72 C.207 B.A. L.124 J.D. 3146 Ingelow Lane
Davidson, Camille M. .... '67 '93 C.484 B.B.A. L.276 J.D. Asst. Coun.
Davidson, Lawrence U., III, (CV) .... '51 '83 C.1378 B.A. L.896 J.D. P.O. Box 16426
Davies, Janice L. .... '66 '99 C.1318 B.S. L.1228 J.D. [[A] Morris,M.&M.]
Davies, Kenneth T., (BV) .... '53 '80 C.575 B.A. L.1051 J.D. [Davies&G.]

Davies & Grist, LLP, (BV)
15720 John J. Delaney Drive, Suite 445, 28277
Telephone: 704-731-0600 Fax: 704-731-0606
Kenneth T. Davies; Daniel W. Grist.
Real Estate, Buying and Selling, Zoning, Planning and Land Use, Homeowners Association Law, Family Law, Divorce, Child Custody, Child Support.
Other Charlotte Office: 310 Arlington Avenue, 28203. Telephone: 704-376-2059. Fax: 702-335-8161.
See Professional Biographies, CHARLOTTE, NORTH CAROLINA

Davis, Brian M. .... '68 '96 C.923 B.A. L.910 J.D. [Alston&B.]
Davis, Edward B. .... '72 '99 C.198 B.A. L.575 J.D. [[A] Bell,D.&P.]

Davis, Egbert L., IV .... '66 '93 C.674 A.B. L.575 J.D. S. Shore Partners, Inc.
Davis, James C., Jr. .... '70 '97 C.896 B.A. L.228 J.D. [Ⓒ Parker,P.A.&B.]
Davis, Jeffrey Allen .... '65 '01 C.925 B.S. L.356 J.D. Dist. Atty. Off.
Davis, Jeffrey J., (AV) .... '47 '75 C&L.339 B.S., J.D. [Moore&V.P.]
Davis, K. Neal, (AV) .... '48 '73 C.925 B.S. L.327 J.D. [Guthrie,D.H.&S.]
Davis, Lyonnette M. .... '56 '91 C.496 B.S.B.A. L.1059 J.D. [Byrne,D.&H.] ⊙
Davis, Matthew J. .... '73 '98 C.477 B.A. L.893 J.D. [Ⓐ McGuireWoods]
Davis, Patricia K. '50 '86 C&L.776 B.A., J.D.
(adm. in NJ; not adm. in NC) 7736 Arboretum Dr.‡
Davis, Ronald H., (CV) ....'40 '65 C.228 A.B. L.575 LL.B. 347-A N. Caswell Rd.
Davis, W. Leon ....'37 '67 C.871 B.S. L.896 J.D. [W.L.Davis]
Davis, William M., Jr. ....'32 '86 C.627 B.G.E. L.574 J.D. Asst. Pub. Def.
Davis, W. Leon, P.C. .... 6425 Idlewild Rd., Ste 212
Day, Isabel Scott, (AV) ....'49 '79 C.953 B.A. L.575 J.D. Pub. Def. Off.
Dean, Barbara J., (BV) .... '46 '73 C.207 B.A. L.477 J.D. [Ⓒ Dean&G.]
Dean, Karen A. .... '57 '95 C.820 B.A. L.705 J.D. [Ⓒ Moore&V.P.]
Dean, Rodney A., (AV) .... '— '73 C.475 B.A. L.477 J.D. [Dean&G.]
Dean, Stuart '— '96 C.861 B.A. L.188 J.D.
(adm. in NY; not adm. in NC) Bank of America (⊙New York, NY)

Dean & Gibson, L.L.P., (AV)
Suite 900, Cameron Brown Building, 301 South McDowell Street, 28204-2686
Telephone: 704-372-2700 Facsimile: 704-372-1804
Email: info@deanandgibson.com URL: http://www.deanandgibson.com
Rodney A. Dean; Michael G. Gibson; John Whitelaw Ong; Susan L. Hofer; Isidore T. Zarsadias. Associates: Colin E. Scott; Thomas G. Nance, II; Christopher W. Cook; Amy E. Drayton. Of Counsel: Barbara J. Dean.
General Corporate and Insurance Litigation, Products Liability, Professional Malpractice, Construction, First Party, Aviation, Defense and Subrogation, Municipal, Bankruptcy.
See Professional Biographies, CHARLOTTE, NORTH CAROLINA

de Bernardo, John Paul .... '51 '80 C.93 B.A. L.733 J.D. [deBernardo]
de Bernardo Law Firm .... 212 S. Tryon Street
DeBlasis, Abigail Loftus .... '— '04 C.473 B.S. L.896 J.D. [Ⓐ Kennedy C.L.&H.]

Dechert LLP, (AV) BB
Bank of America Corporate Center, 100 North Tryon Street, Suite 4000, 28202 ⊙
Telephone: 704.339.3100 Telefax: 704.339.3101
URL: http://www.dechert.com
Partners: Timothy J. Boyce (Not admitted in NC); James R. Bryant, III; John M. Timperio. Associates: Kerri DeRuyter (Not admitted in NC); Christopher Paul Duerden; Victoria S. Durham (Not admitted in NC); David Graham Fine; Gerald F. Keefe; Donald L. Lancaster (Not admitted in NC); W. Todd Stillerman. Counsel: Frederick H. Sherley (Not admitted in NC).
Antitrust, Bankruptcy and Reorganization, Business and Technology, Commercial Litigation, Copyrights, Corporate Finance, Competition, Criminal and Civil Fraud, Defamation, Domestic Taxation, Employee Benefits and Executive Compensation, Employment, Environmental, Estate Planning, Financial Services, First Amendment, Government Affairs, Health Care, Intellectual Property, Information Technology, International Business, International Taxation, International Trade, Investment Management, Labor, Life Sciences, Mass Torts, Media, Mergers and Acquisitions, Patent Law and Litigation, Privacy, Private Equity, Products Liability, Real Estate and Mortgage Finance, Retail, Securities Litigation and Enforcement, Securitization, State and Local Taxation, Tax-Exempt Organizations, Trademarks, Venture Capital, White Collar Litigation.
Philadelphia, Pennsylvania: 4000 Bell Atlantic Tower, 1717 Arch Street, 19103-2793. Telephone: 215.994.4000.
New York, New York: 30 Rockefeller Plaza, 10112. Telephone: 212.698.3500.
Washington, D.C.: 1775 I Street, N.W., 20006-2401. Telephone: 202.261.3300.
Harrisburg, Pennsylvania: Thirty North Third Street, 17101-1603. Telephone: 717.237.2000.
Princeton, New Jersey: Princeton Pike Corporate Center, P.O. Box 5218, 08543-5218. Telephone: 609.620.3200.
Boston, Massachusetts: 200 Clarendon Street, 27th Floor, 02116-5021. Telephone: 617.728.7100.
Hartford, Connecticut Office: 90 State House Square, 06103-3702. Telephone: 860.524.3999.
Newport Beach, California Office: 4675 MacArthur Court, Suite 1400, 92660-8842. Telephone: 949.442.6000.
San Francisco, California Office: Spear Tower, 1 Market Street, 16th Floor, 94105. Telephone: 415.262.4500.
London, England: 2 Serjeants' Inn, EC4Y 1LT. Telephone: +44.20.7583.5353.
Brussels, Belgium: 13th Floor, Avenue Louise 480, 1050. Telephone: +32.2.535.5411.
Paris, France: 55, avenue Kléber, 75116. Telephone: +33.1.53.65.05.00.
Luxembourg: Brucher & Seimetz in association with Dechert, Avocats a la Cour, 10 rue de Vianden, B.P. 709, L-2017. Telephone: +352.45.62.62.
Frankfurt/Main, Germany Office: Mainzer Landstrasse 16, 60325. Telephone: +49.69.971.68.245.
Palo Alto, California Office: 1117 California Avenue, 94304. Telephone: 650.813.4800. Telefax: 650.813.4848.
Munich, Germany Office: Theresienstrasse 6, 830333. Telephone: +49.0.89.21.21.63.0.
See Professional Biographies, CHARLOTTE, NORTH CAROLINA

DeCurtins, Robert J., (BV) .....'54 '84 C.235 B.S. L.201 J.D. 301 South McDowell Street
DeGeorge, R. Steven, (AV) .... '— '86 C&L.966 B.A., J.D. [Robinson,B.&H.]
Dekle, Donne R. .... '39 '68 C.576 B.S. L.575 J.D. 5522 Chedworth Dr.
DeKoster, Paul Ronald '— '74 C.114 B.A. L.800 J.D.
(adm. in CA; not adm. in NC) Asst. Gen. Coun., Bank of America
DeLaney, Barbara H. .... '48 '73 C.956 B.A. L.575 J.D. 7601 Baltusrol Ln.‡
DeLaney, Ernest S., Jr. .... '20 '52 C.228 A.B. L.575 J.D. 301 S. McDowell St.
DeLaney, Ernest S. (Mike), III, (AV) ...... '48 '73 C.228 B.A. L.575 J.D. [Moore&V.P.]
Dellinger, Stephen D. .... '64 '89 C.34 B.A. L.896 J.D. [Ogletree,D.N.S.&S.]
DeMaere, Christine .... '— '05 C.576 B.A. L.259 J.D. [Ⓐ Kennedy C.L.&H.]
DeMayo, Michael A., (BV) ....'65 '91 C.896 B.A. L.575 J.D. [M.A.DeMayo] ⊙

DeMayo, Michael A., L.L.P., Law Offices of, (BV)
741 Kenilworth (Park Plaza), Suite 100, P.O. Box 34426, 28204 ⊙
Telephone: 704-333-1000 Fax: 704-333-6677 URL: http://www.demayolaw.com
URL: http://www.michaeldemayo.com
Michael A. DeMayo; Frank F. Voler.
Personal Injury, Automobile Accidents, Motorcycle Accidents, Wrongful Death, Brain Injury, Medical Malpractice, Worker's Compensation, Pharmaceutical Litigation, Nursing Home Litigation.
Hickory, North Carolina Office: 321 Third Avenue, N.W., 28601. Telephone: 828-345-1111. Fax: 828-345-1112.
Monroe, North Carolina Office: 406 South Sutherland Avenue, 28112. Telephone: 704-291-9200. Fax: 704-291-9292.
See Professional Biographies, CHARLOTTE, NORTH CAROLINA

DeMoss, Douglas P., (BVⓉ) '56 '86 C.870 B.S. L.945 J.D.
(adm. in VA; not adm. in NC)
V.P. & Gen'l Coun., General Dynamics Armament and Technical Products
DeNio, Jeffery R. ....'64 '94 C.494 B.A. L.880 J.D. P.O. Box 38114
Denny, Michael J. ....'— '02 C.160 B.S. L.1119 J.D. [Ⓐ Kennedy C.L.&H.]
Dent, Sharon E. ....'— '98 C.329 B.A. L.574 J.D. [Ⓐ Hedrick E.G.&K.]
Denton, Brett J., (BV) '68 '93 C.953 B.S.B.A. L.575 J.D.
V.P. & Dep. Gen. Coun., Charlotte-Mecklenburg Hosp. Auth.
Derr, Tricia Morvan, (BV) .... '72 '97 C&L.575 B.A., J.D. [Ⓐ Womble C.S.&R.]
DeRuyter, Kerri '— '03 C.1349 B.A. L.188 J.D.
(adm. in NY; not adm. in NC) [Ⓐ Dechert]
Devin, William J., III .... '76 '01 C.575 B.A. L.472 J.D. 3800 Monroe Street, Suite B
De Vore, Bradford A., (AV) .... '60 '86 C.475 B.A. L.790 J.D. [Womble C.S.&R.]
DeVore, Fred W., III, (AV) ....'53 '82 C.575 B.A. L.896 J.D. [DeVore A.&S.]

DeVore Acton & Stafford, P.A., (AV)
831 East Morehead Street, Suite 245, 28202-2773
Telephone: 704-377-5242 Facsimile: 704-332-2825
Email: firm@devact.com URL: http://www.devact.com
Fred W. DeVore, III; William D. Acton, Jr. (Board Certified Specialist in Workers' Compensation, North Carolina State Board of Legal Specialization); Troy J. Stafford.
General Civil Trial Practice in State and Federal Courts. Personal Injury, Wrongful Death, Automobile Accidents, Workers Compensation, Medical Malpractice, Insurance Bad Faith, Construction Law, Commercial Litigation, Products Liability Litigation.
See Professional Biographies, CHARLOTTE, NORTH CAROLINA

DeVries, Margaret B., (BV) .... '46 '97 C.1236 B.A. L.575 J.D. [Ⓐ Sasser]
Dewey, Robert J., (BVⓉ) '45 '74 C.475 B.A. L.838 J.D.
(adm. in MI; not adm. in NC) 2629 Central Avenue
Dexter, Alan G., (AV) ....'60 '85 C.188 B.A. L.228 J.D. [Parker,P.A.&B.]
Diaz, Albert .... '60 '89 C.659 B.S. L.569 J.D. Supr. Ct. J., 26th Jud. Dist.

Dickie, McCamey & Chilcote, P.C., (AVⓉ)
212 South Tryon Street Suite 465, 28281-0007 ⊙
Telephone: 704-334-1108 Fax: 704-334-1163
URL: http://www.dmclaw.com
Shareholder: Thomas P. Lutz. Associate: John N. Cox.
General Practice including Alternative Dispute Resolution; Appellate Advocacy; Antitrust; Asbestos; Bad Faith; Bankruptcy; Business Law; Business Torts; Civil Litigation; Class Actions; Commercial Agreements; Commercial Litigation; Commercial Transactions; Compliance Programs; Construction Law; Contract Disputes; Contract Drafting; Corporate Compliance; Computer Law; Corporate Finance; Corporate Governance; Corporate Law; Corporate Services; Creditors' Rights; Education Law; Employment Law; Environmental Law; Estate Planning and Administration; Estates and Trusts; Family Law; First Amendment/Defamation; Finance Law and Financial Institutions; Food and Beverage; General Liability; Health Law Business; Insurance Defense; Insurance Law and Litigation; Insurance and Risk Management; Intellectual Property; Labor Law; Lender Liability; Licenses; Litigation; Medical Malpractice Defense; Mergers and Acquisitions; Product Liability; Professional Liability; Real Estate Transactions; Securities; Silica; Surety; Technology Law; Technology Transfer; Telecommunications; Toxic Tort; Transportation Law; White Collar Crime; Workers' Compensation.
Pittsburgh, Pennsylvania Office: Two PPG Place, Suite 400, 15222-5402. Telephone: 412-281-7272. Fax: 412-392-5367.
Camp Hill, Pennsylvania Office: 1200 Camp Hill Bypass, Suite 205, 17011-3700. Telephone: 717-731-4800. Fax: 717-731-4803.
Philadelphia, Pennsylvania Office: Public Ledger Building, Suite 901, 150 South Independence Mall, West, 19106-3409. Telephone: 215-925-2289. Fax: 215-925-0307.
Washington, D.C. Office: 1301 Pennsylvania Avenue, N.W., Suite 1000, 20004-1707. Telephone: 1-888-434-5566.
Haddonfield, New Jersey Office: 30 N. Haddon Avenue, Suite 100, 08033-2429. Telephone: 856-354-0192. Fax: 856-354-8164.
Steubenville, Ohio Office: Dickie, McCamey & Chilcote, A Professional Corporation, 401 Market Street, Suite 401, 43952-2846. Telephone: 740-284-1682. Fax: 740-284-1692.
Wheeling, West Virginia Office: Dickie, McCamey & Chilcote, L.C., 1233 Main Street, Suite 2002, 26003-2839. Telephone: 304-233-1022. Fax: 304-233-1026.
See Professional Biographies, CHARLOTTE, NORTH CAROLINA

Dickinson, Paul R., Jr., (BV) ....'60 '90 C.1111 B.A. L.796 J.D. [Lewis&R.]
Dickinson, Thomas W., (AV) .... '49 '75 C&L.575 B.A., J.D. [Rawls,D.&S.]
Diehl, William K., Jr., (AV) ....'44 '69 C.575 A.B. L.893 LL.B. [James,M.&D.]
Dillashaw, Brendan G. .... '— '04 C.575 B.A. L.790 J.D. [Ⓐ Hedrick E.G.&K.]
Dingfelder, Jessica '71 '96 C.1369 B.A. L.273 J.D.
(adm. in VA; not adm. in NC) Off. of Hearings & App.
Dingle, Randall T. .... '77 '02 C.381 B.B.A. L.228 J.D. [Ⓐ Moore&V.P.]
Dion, Jonathan W. ....'73 '99 C.550 B.A. L.896 J.D. [Ⓐ Parker,P.A.&B.]
Dion, Susan Pyle ....'— '01 C.576 B.A. L.896 J.D. [Ⓐ McGuireWoods]
Di Piero, Frank A., (AVⓉ) '56 '82 C.980 B.A. L.851 J.D.
(adm. in OH; not adm. in NC) Segment Coun., Goodrich Corporation
Dittner, Derek E. .... '68 '95 C.160 B.S. L.64 J.D. [Gorman&D.]
Dixon, Jessica L. '77 '03 C&L.966 B.A., J.D.
Trial Atty., U.S. Equal Employ. Opportunities Comm.
Dixon, Mary Alice, (BV) ....'51 '92 C.881 B.A. L.896 J.D. Ste 300, 4600 Park Rd
Dixon, Miriam Ann, (AV) .... '62 '87 C.228 B.A. L.309 J.D. [Moore&V.P.]
Dobbins, Jo H. ....'44 '81 C.896 B.A. L.574 J.D. 101 N. Mcdowell St., Ste. 114
Dodge, Courtney L. '67 '92 C.838 B.A. L.245 J.D.
(adm. in AL; not adm. in NC) 2734 Normandy Rd.‡
Dohan, John W., (AVⓉ) '58 '83 C.477 B.A. L.215 J.D.
(adm. in MI; not adm. in NC) [J.W.Dohan]
Dohan, John W., P.C., (AVⓉ) ....2054 Queens Rd. E.
Domby, John .... '79 '04 C.575 B.A. L.893 J.D. [Ⓐ Cadwalader,W.&T.]
Donaldson, Walter T., III ....'77 '03 C.576 B.A. L.884 J.D. [Ⓐ McGuireWoods]
Donat, Robert A. '53 '80
C.932 B.S. L.1187 J.D. 7810 Ballantyne Commons Pkwy., Ste. 300
Donlon, Robert M., (AV) .... '57 '83 C.93 B.A. L.982 J.D. [Womble C.S.&R.]
Donohue, Paul S., (AV) .... '64 '90 C.321 B.A. L.724 J.D. [Alston&B.]
Dooley, Kathleen H. ....'59 '88 C&L.776 B.A., J.D. [Helms M.&W.]
Dorsett, Ann Terrell ....'60 '89 C&L.575 A.B., J.D. [Ⓒ Helms M.&W.]
Dortch, Robert C., Jr., (AV) .... '58 '83 C.896 B.S.B.A. L.1228 J.D. [Sellers,H.A.D.&L.]
Dougherty, Ralph H., (AV) '35 '69
C.171 Met.E. L.229 J.D. [Dougherty,C.H.&B.] (See Pat. Sect.)

Dougherty, Clements, Hofer & Bernard, (AV)
1901 Roxborough Road, Suite 300, 28211
Telephone: 704-366-6642 Fax: 704-366-9744 URL: http://www.lawyers.com/dougherty&clements
Email: patlaw@worldpatents.com URL: http://www.worldpatents.com
Members of Firm: Ralph H. Dougherty; Gregory N. Clements; Ronald L. Hofer; Christopher L. Bernard. Associates: Brandon G. Williams (Not admitted in NC); Russell Racine (Not admitted in NC).
Intellectual Property Matters including Patent, Trademark, Copyright, Trade Secret, Licensing, Litigation and Computer Law.
Reference: First Commerce Bank.
See Professional Biographies, CHARLOTTE, NORTH CAROLINA

Douglas-Gershowitz, Melissa Ann '68 '94 C.107 B.A. L.564 J.D.
(adm. in NY; not adm. in NC) 8617 Brookstead Dr.
Dove, W. Scott ....'— '99 C.896 B.A. L.569 J.D. [Robinson,B.&H.]
Dowd, Willis F., IV '55 '83 C.575 B.S. L.893 J.D.
Sr. V.P., Charlotte Pipe & Foundry Co.
Downer, Joseph Henry ....'56 '00 C.232 B.A. L.1228 J.D. 2 Wachovia Ctr., Ste. 1760
Downer, Thomas T. ....'37 '67 C&L.575 A.B., J.D. Two First Union Ctr.
Dozier, W. Joseph, Jr., (AV) ....'48 '73 C.902 B.A. L.575 J.D. [Dozier,M.P.&M.]

Dozier, Miller, Pollard & Murphy, LLP, (AV) BB
Cameron Brown Building, 301 South McDowell Street, Suite 700, 28204
Telephone: 704-372-6373 Fax: 704-347-0674
URL: http://www.lawcharlotte.com
Members of Firm: W. Joseph Dozier, Jr.; R. Craig Miller, Jr.; Scott T. Pollard; Gary L. Murphy (Board Certified Specialist in Criminal Law, North Carolina State Board of Legal Specialization); Timothy H. Graham; George N. Miller (Board Certified Specialist in Immigration and Nationality Law, North Carolina State Board of Legal Specialization); Richard S. Gordon; Thomas J. Falish; John C. Nipp; Anne Dunton Lam; E. Kenneth Coble. Of Counsel: William Patrick Hobson.
General Civil and Criminal Trial Practice in all State and Federal Courts. Plaintiffs Personal Injury and Wrongful Death, Hazardous Products Liability (Aviation, Motor Vehicles), Medical Malpractice,

(This Listing Continued)

Dozier, Miller, Pollard & Murphy, LLP (Continued)
Domestic Relations, Immigration and Naturalization Law, Business and Corporate Law, Sales and Acquisitions, Banking Litigation, Collections., Bankruptcy, Estate Planning and Probate.
See Professional Biographies, CHARLOTTE, NORTH CAROLINA

Drake, Richard N. ... '61 '86 C.228 A.B. L.477 J.D. [Morris,M.&M.]
Drayton, Amy E. ... '— '04 C.122 B.A. L.1187 J.D. [Ⓐ Dean&G.]
Drew, William F., Jr., (AV) ... '— '70 C.228 A.B. L.893 LL.B. [Kennedy C.L.&H.] ‡
Drummond, P. Wayne, Jr. ... '65 '91 C&L.575 B.A., J.D. P.O. Box 242425
Drysdale, Glen R. ... '— '04 C.474 B.S. L.966 J.D. [Ⓐ Alston&B.]
DuBose, Charles O., (AV) ... '— '68 C.198 B.A. L.575 J.D. [Kennedy C.L.&H.]
Duerden, Christopher Paul ... '80 '04 C&L.575 B.A., J.D. [Ⓐ Dechert]
Duffy, Robert T., (AV) ... '45 '71 C.1208 B.A. L.309 J.D. [Mayer,B.R.&M.]
Dulaney, Dain J., Jr. ... '63 '89 C.902 B.A. L.896 J.D. [BusinessAdvisors]
Dunklin, Garth K., (AV) ... '62 '88 C&L.575 B.A., J.D. [Wishart,N.H.&P.]
Dunn, J. Thomas, Jr., (AV) ... '43 '68 C.1126 A.B. L.575 J.D. [Moore&V.P.]
Dunn, Landon A., (BV) ... '56 '81 C.683 A.B. L.469 J.D. [L.A.Dunn]
Dunn, Richard C. ... '— '02 C.228 B.A. L.945 J.D. [Ⓐ Robinson,B.&H.]
Dunn, Stephen J. ... '73 '98 C.228 B.A. L.575 J.D. [VanHoy,R.A.&D.]
Dunn, Landon A., P.A., (BV) ... 7417 Matthews-Mint Hill Road
DuPré, Daniel F. '— '90 C&L.902 B.A., J.D.
(adm. in GA; not adm. in NC) Bank of America
DuPuy, James D. ... '73 '99 C.198 B.A. L.575 J.D. [Ruff,B.C.W.&B.]
DuPuy, John S. '72 '97 C.276 B.S. L.575 J.D.
Corp. Coun., The Charloatte-Mecklenburg Hosp. Auth.
Durham, Albert F., (AV) ... '47 '75 C&L.575 B.A., J.D. [Rayburn C.&D.]
Durham, Brett A. ... '— '00 C.692 B.S. L.893 J.D. [Ⓐ Kennedy C.L.&H.]
Durham, J. Porter, Jr., (AVⓉ) '61 '85 C&L.228 A.B., J.D.
(adm. in TN; not adm. in NC) Staff Counsel, Duke Endowment
Durham, Joshua Blake ... '71 '98 C.576 B.A. L.1345 J.D. [Ⓐ Poyner&S.]
Durham, Julie Ann ... '76 '00 C.473 B.A. L.893 J.D. [Ⓐ Cadwalader,W.&T.]
Durham, Victoria S. '— '96 C.269 B.A. L.838 J.D.
(adm. in TN; not adm. in NC) [Ⓐ Dechert]
Durr, Michael ... '69 '97 C.696 B.A. L.326 J.D. [Ⓐ Cozen O.]
Durrett, Bryan P. ... '59 '96 C.228 B.A. L.665 J.D. [Moore&V.P.]
Dwiggins, George Albert '52 '95 C.575 B.S. L.790 J.D.
(adm. in SC; not adm. in NC) First Union Corp.
Eades, David L., (AV) ... '60 '86 C.806 B.A. L.880 J.D. [Moore&V.P.]
Eady, Karen E., (BV) ... '68 '92 C.945 B.A. L.896 J.D. Asst. U.S. Atty.
Earle, James E., (BV) ... '— '91 C.198 B.A. L.813 J.D. [Kennedy C.L.&H.]
Earthman, J. Benjamin '76 '02 C.1034 B.A. L.836 J.D.
(adm. in NY; not adm. in NC) [Ⓐ Mayer,B.R.&M.]
Eatman, Edward L., Jr., (AV) ... '— '69 C&L.575 A.B., J.D. [Hedrick E.G.&K.]
Eatman, Thomas D., Jr., (AV) ... '58 '83 C&L.575 B.A., J.D. [Poyner&S.]
Echols, William R., (BV) ... '42 '66 C&L.575 A.B., J.D. 7301 Carmel Executive Park Dr.
Edgar, Allison B. ... '76 '01 C&L.893 B.A., J.D. [Ⓐ Parker,P.A.&B.]
Edgar, Jonathan Harlan ... '74 '00 C.674 A.B. L.273 J.D. [Ⓐ McGuireWoods]
Edmonds, Alan B., (BV) ... '55 '80 C.198 A.B. L.575 J.D. Assoc. Co. Atty.
Edmondson, Patricia B., (BV) ... '42 '85 C.1050 B.A. L.896 J.D. [Rayburn C.&D.]
Edney, Deborah L. ... '67 '97 C.418 B.A., B.S. L.575 J.D. [Ⓒ Parker,P.A.&B.]
Edwards, Bartina L. ... '— '04 C.140 B.A. L.574 J.D. [B.Edwards]
Edwards, Christopher '72 '01 C.198 B.A. L.1565 J.D.
Asst. Gen. Coun., Bank of America, Global Corp. & Invest. Bk.
Edwards, David L. ... '69 '02 C&L.896 B.A., J.D. [Ⓐ Horack,T.P.&L.]
Edwards, David L., (BV) ... '55 '90 C.1128 B.S. L.192 J.D. [Justice,E.&E.]
Edwards, Deborah A. '— '83 C.347 B.S. L.910 J.D.
(adm. in IL; not adm. in NC) Asst. Gen. Coun., Bank of America
Edwards, Deborah L. '57 '88
C.956 B.S. L.896 J.D. Assoc. Gen. Coun., Duke Energy Corp.
Edwards, Douglas R., (AVⓉ) '57 '86 C.893 B.A. L.107 J.D.
Sr. V.P. & Dep. Gen. Coun., First Union Corp.
Edwards, Elizabeth R. ... '— '95 C.896 B.A. L.575 J.D. [Ⓐ C.A.Aziz]
Edwards, Harold M., (BV) ... '30 '59 C&L.896 B.S., J.D. P.O. Box 668604
Edwards, Mark B., (AV) ... '39 '63 C&L.228 A.B., J.D. [Ⓒ Poyner&S.]
Edwards, Regina O. ... '74 '99 C.1378 B.S. L.574 J.D. 301 S. McDowell St., Suite 1201
Edwards, Bartina, The Law Office of ... 10925 David Taylor Drive, Suite 100
Efird, Paul H., III ... '44 '69 C.198 B.A. L.575 J.D. [Horack,T.P.&L.]
Egan, Judith E., (BV) ... '56 '85 C.734 B.S.N. L.575 J.D. 600 S. College St.
Eggert, Elizabeth P. '— '78 C.309 B.A. L.94 J.D.
(adm. in MA; not adm. in NC) Bank of America (○Boston, MA)
Eggleston, Tracy L., (BV) ... '57 '82 C.269 B.A. L.790 J.D. [Cozen O.]
Elam, William H., (AV) ... '46 '72 C.232 B.A. L.790 J.D. [Elam&R.]
Elam & Rousseaux, P.A., (AV)
128-A N. McDowell Street (28204), P.O. Box 30457, 28230
Mailing Address: P.O. Box 30457, Charlotte, NC 28230
Telephone: 704-343-0000 Facsimile: 704-343-9992
URL: http://www.er-lawfirm.com
William H. Elam; Michael J. Rousseaux.
Medical Malpractice, Nursing Home Abuse and Neglect, Professional Malpractice, Wrongful Death.
See Professional Biographies, CHARLOTTE, NORTH CAROLINA
Elderkin, Charles B., (BV) '38 '64
C.679 B.S.M.E. L.273 LL.B. [Alston&B.] (See Pat. Sect.)
Eleazer, L. Holmes, Jr., (AV) ... '46 '76 C.198 B.A. L.575 J.D. [Erwin&E.]
El-Khouri, Catherine M., (AV) ... '61 '86 C.34 B.A. L.1228 J.D. Asst. Pub. Def.
Elkins, Richard A., (AV) ... '51 '76 C&L.575 B.A., J.D. [James,M.&D.]
Ellerbe, Billie R. ... '54 '80 C.575 B.A. L.574 J.D. 301 South McDowell Street, Suite 806
Elliott, W. Curtis, Jr., (AV) ... '55 '80 C&L.790 B.S., J.D. [Culp E.&C.]
Elliott Law Firm, P.C.
(See Huntersville)
Ellis, Benjamin H. ... '78 '05 C.197 B.A. L.896 J.D. [Ⓐ Culp E.&C.]
Ellowitch, Daniel J. '74 '02 C.174 B.A. L.94 J.D.
(adm. in NJ; not adm. in NC) [Ⓐ Cadwalader,W.&T.]
Ellsworth, Brian ... '75 '02 C.477 B.S.M.E. L.896 J.D. [Ⓐ Alston&B.] (See Pat. Sect.)
Ellzey & Brooks, LLC
(See Fisher & Phillips LLP)
Emehel, Johneric C. ... '68 '93 C.1378 B.A. L.790 J.D. [Sherrill&E.]
Emken, Judith C., (BV) ... '58 '83 C.575 B.A. L.245 J.D. 601 E. Trade St.
Emory, C Randolph ... '63 '91 C.575 B.A. L.574 J.D. [Emory]
Emory, Frank E., Jr., (AV) ... '57 '82 C.228 A.B. L.575 J.D. [Hunton&W.]
Emory Law Firm, The, P.C. ... 401 N. Tryon Street, 10th Floor
England, Margaret C. '50 '83
C.801 B.S. L.796 J.D. V.P. & Coun., First Union Mortgage Corp.
Epstein, David M. '38 '64 C.645 B.A. L.659 LL.B.
(adm. in PA; not adm. in NC) 5701 Challisford Lane‡

Erdman, David W., (BV) ... '49 '75 C.228 B.S.E. L.276 J.D. [Erdman&H.]
Erdman and Hockfield, LLP, (AV)
2300 East Seventh Street, Suite 100, 28204-4366
Telephone: 704-333-7800 Fax: 704-343-2886
URL: http://www.lawyers.com/charlotte-nc-law
David W. Erdman; Steven A. Hockfield. Associate: Lina E. James.
General Civil Practice. Business Law, Corporate Law, Personal Injury, Family, Marital, Domestic and Matrimonial Law, Commercial Real Estate, Land Use and Zoning. Trial Practice in all State and Federal Courts.
Reference: Bank of Mecklenburg.
See Professional Biographies, CHARLOTTE, NORTH CAROLINA
Errington, C. Margaret, (AV) ... '54 '85 C.918 B.A. L.588 J.D. [Ferguson,S.C.G.&S.]
Ervin, Winfred R., (AV) ... '27 '52 C&L.575 B.S., LL.B. 225 E. Kingston Ave.
Ervin, Winfred R., Jr., (BV) '50 '76 C.575 B.A. L.245 J.D.
128-A North McDowell Street
Erwin, Fenton T., Jr., (AV) ... '41 '66 C.232 A.B. L.575 J.D. [Erwin&E.]
Erwin and Eleazer, P.A., (AV)
831 East Morehead Street 840, 28202
Telephone: 704-369-7900 Facsimile: 704-335-5433
Email: ferwin@eelaw.net URL: http://www.lawyers.com/eelaw
Fenton T. Erwin, Jr.; L. Holmes Eleazer, Jr.; B. David Carson; Peter F. Morgan.
General Civil Law, Corporate and Commercial Litigation, Construction, Negligence and Personal Injury Litigation, Bankruptcy.
See Professional Biographies, CHARLOTTE, NORTH CAROLINA
Esser, William L., IV, (CV) ... '74 '99 C.1126 B.A. L.602 J.D. [Ⓐ Parker,P.A.&B.]
Essex, Kenneth F., (AV) ... '43 '70 C.198 B.A. L.575 J.D. [Essex R.]
Essex Richards, P.A., (AV)
1701 South Boulevard, 28203
Telephone: 704-377-4300 Telecopier: 704-372-1357
URL: http://www.essexrichards.com
Edward G. Connette, III; Kenneth F. Essex; Debra L. Foster (Board Certified Specialist in Estate Planning and Probate Law, North Carolina State Board of Legal Specialization); G. Miller Jordan; Lisa T. Kelly (Board Certified Specialist in Estate Planning and Probate, North Carolina State Board of Legal Specialization); Louis L. Lesesne, Jr.; T. Patrick Matus, II; Stephen H. Morris; Channing O. Richards;—Norris A. Adams, II.
Business and Personal Matters: including formation and general representation of Business Entities, Estate Planning and Probate, Employment, Labor, Commercial Real Estate, Mergers and Acquisitions, Health Care, Guardianship, Tax.
Litigation Matters: including Personal Injury, Wrongful Death, Condemnation, Employment, Business, Domestic Relations and Equitable Distribution, Constitutional, ERISA, Class Action, Mental Health, Criminal and General Civil.
Arbitration and Mediation.
See Professional Biographies, CHARLOTTE, NORTH CAROLINA
Euripides, Charles C. ... '61 '91 C.893 B.A. L.692 J.D. [Bernhardt&S.]
Evans, Brian P., (AV) ... '— '75 C.198 B.A. L.575 J.D. [Kennedy C.L.&H.]
Evans, J. Scott, (AV) ... '62 '92 C.69 B.F.A. L.421 J.D. [Adams E.]
Evans, Jason Doughton ... '76 '01 C&L.575 B.A., J.D. [Ⓐ Helms M.&W.]
Evans, John R. ... '73 '99 C.228 B.A. L.597 J.D. [Ⓐ Moore&V.P.]
Evans, Stephanie K. Briggs, (BV) ... '72 '98 C.575 B.A. L.896 J.D. [Ⓐ Helms M.&W.]
Evans, Yvonne Mims ... '51 '76 C.914 B.A. L.228 J.D. Dist. Ct. J.
Eve, R. Michael, Jr., (AV) ... '53 '78 C.575 B.A. L.192 J.D. [Justice,E.&E.]
Everett, Kerry B. '68 '99 C.16 B.S. L.988 J.D.
5120 Monroe Road, 28205
Telephone: 704-567-5297 Fax: 704-567-5389
Email: kbeverett@earthlink.net URL: http://www.kbeverettlaw.com
Adoptions, Real Estate, Buying or Selling a Home, Buying or Selling a Business, State and Federal Appellate and Civil Practice, Wills and Probate.
See Professional Biographies, CHARLOTTE, NORTH CAROLINA
Everman, Gregory R. ... '66 '99 C&L.851 B.S.M.E., J.D. [Everman] (Pat.)
Everman Law Firm, PA
6000 Fairview Road Suite 1200, 28210
Telephone: 704-552-3999 Fax: 704-552-3705
URL: http://www.evermanlawfirm.com
Gregory R. Everman.
Intellectual Property, Trademarks, Patents, Copyrights, Copyrights, Buying or Selling a Home.
See Professional Biographies, CHARLOTTE, NORTH CAROLINA
Ewald, Stephen P. ... '— '94 C&L.150 B.A., J.D. Asst. Gen. Coun., Bank of America
Ewing, B. Chad ... '— '02 C.269 B.A. L.893 J.D. [Ⓐ Robinson,B.&H.]
Exum, James J. ... '— '89 C&L.575 B.A., J.D. 301 S. McDowell St., Ste. 310
Ey, Douglas W., Jr., (AV) ... '55 '79 C.198 A.B. L.880 J.D. [Helms M.&W.]
Fagan, Gail G., (BVⓉ) '52 '78 C&L.260 B.A., J.D.
(adm. in FL; not adm. in NC) V.P. & Asst. Gen. Coun., First Union Corporation
Faircloth, Frederick W., IV ... '— '03 C.160 B.S. L.790 J.D. [Ⓐ Kennedy C.L.&H.]
Fairley, John W., Jr. ... '42 '67 C.1318 A.B. L.575 J.D. [J.Fairley]
Fairley, John, Law Office of ... 1721 Norland Road
Faison, Yates W., III, (BV) '47 '72 C.198 A.B. L.575 J.D.
8401 University Executive Park Drive, Suite 112, 28262
Telephone: 704-717-0663 Fax: 704-717-0744
Email: faisony@bellsouth.net
Residential and Commercial Real Estate, Mortgages, Real Property Closings.
See Professional Biographies, CHARLOTTE, NORTH CAROLINA
Falish, Thomas J. ... '63 '89 C.575 B.S. L.228 J.D. [Dozier,M.P.&M.]
Falls, Charity Babington ... '— '03 C.1128 B.A. L.1049 J.D. [Ⓐ McNair]
Falls, R. Deke, (BV) ... '70 '97 C.1128 B.S. L.575 J.D. [Barnett&F.]
Farbman, Mark I., Law Office of '62 '94
C.576 B.S. L.861 J.D. 301 S. McDowell, Ste. 912
Faris, Douglas McGruder '54 '81
C.902 B.S. L.896 J.D. Sr. V.P., Indus. Div., Binswanger Co.
Farley, Richard L., (BV) ... '57 '87 C.790 B.A. L.575 J.D. [Katten M.R.]
Farmer, B. D., III, (AV) ... '— '68 C.976 B.A. L.893 LL.B. [Kennedy C.L.&H.]
Farmer, Woodard E., Jr., (AV) ... '48 '73 C.861 B.A. L.880 J.D. [Parker,P.A.&B.]
Farris, Jami Jackson ... '71 '99 C.945 B.A. L.575 J.D. [Ⓐ Parker,P.A.&B.]
Farris, Ray S., (AV) ... '40 '67 C&L.575 A.B., J.D. [Johnston,A.&H.]
Farthing, William P., Jr., (AV) ... '48 '74 C&L.575 A.B., J.D. [Parker,P.A.&B.]
Faulk, Thomas H., Jr., (BVⓉ) ... '58 '92 C.575 B.S. L.259 J.D. P.O. Box 49433
Fay, Richard E., (AV) ... '56 '81 C.198 A.B. L.893 J.D. [Hamilton F.M.S.S.&M.]
Feeken, Karen R. ... '77 '03 C.218 B.A. L.1439 J.D. [Ⓐ R.L.Robertson&Assoc.]
Feit, Jonathan D. ... '74 '01 C.10 B.A. L.838 J.D. [James,M.&D.]
Feleke, Bethelehem '68 '99 C.999 L.1339 J.D.
(adm. in MD; not adm. in NC) [Ⓐ Tin F.G.&O.]
Fennebresque, John C., (AV) ... '47 '73 C.575 B.A. L.880 J.D. [McGuireWoods]
Fennell, Richard B., (BV) ... '63 '90 C&L.575 A.B., J.D. [James,M.&D.]
Fennimore, C. Thomas ... '47 '73 C.679 B.S. L.347 J.D. V.P., First Union Corporation
Fenninger, Cynthia T., (BV) ... '67 '93 C&L.575 B.A., J.D. [Orsbon&F.]
Ferguson, George W., Jr., (AV) ... '33 '56 C&L.575 A.B., LL.B. Coun., Duke Power Co.
Ferguson, James E., II, (AV) ... '42 '67 C.574 B.A. L.178 LL.B. [Ferguson,S.C.G.&S.]
Ferguson, Jocelyn ... '78 '03 C.260 B.S.B.A. L.575 J.D. [Ⓐ Morris Y.W.S.&B.]

Ferguson, Stein, Chambers, Gresham & Sumter, P.A., (AV)
741 Kenilworth Avenue, Suite 300, 28204-2828
Mailing Address: P.O. Box 36486, Charlotte, NC 28236-6486
Telephone: 704-375-8461 Fax: 704-334-5654
Email: Fergietwo@aol.com URL: http://www.fergusonstein.com
James E. Ferguson, II; Adam Stein (Resident, Chapel Hill Office); Julius LeVonne Chambers; John W. Gresham; Geraldine Sumter; Henderson Hill; C. Margaret Errington; Stephen Luke Largess; William G. Simpson, Jr. (Resident, Chapel Hill Office). Of Counsel: Jonathan P. Wallas;—Jacob H. Sussman; Brandon M. Lofton.
Civil Rights, Employment and Labor, General Civil, Criminal, Plaintiff's Medical Malpractice, Trial and Appellate Practice. Probate and Real Estate Law.
Chapel Hill, North Carolina Office: Suite 2, 312 West Franklin Street. Telephone: 919-933-5300. Fax: 919-967-4953.

See Professional Biographies, CHARLOTTE, NORTH CAROLINA

Fernandez, Christopher J. '68 '01 C.846 B.S.Chem. Eng L.902 J.D. [Ⓐ Parker,P.A.&B.]
Fernandez, Joseph A. ... '72 '97 C.575 B.A. L.896 J.D. [Moore&V.P.]
Fialko, Christopher C., (BV) ... '66 '92 C.813 B.A. L.575 J.D. [Rudolf W.&F.]
Fiel, Patrick V., Jr. '— '04 C.945 B.S. L.838 J.D. (adm. in TN; not adm. in NC) [Ⓐ Hunton&W.]
Fillette, Theodore ... '45 '73 C.228 B.A. L.94 J.D Legal Servs. of Southern Piedmont
Fine, David Graham ... '78 '03 C.976 B.A. L.896 J.D. [Ⓐ Dechert]
Finn, Nicholas R. ... '78 '04 C.840 B.B.A. L.880 J.D. [Ⓐ Cadwalader,W.&T.]
Finniss, Alexis W. ... '78 '03 C.280 B.S. L.896 J.D. [Ⓐ Alston&B.]
Finniss, Matthew W. ... '— '01 C.696 B.A. L.896 J.D. [Ⓐ Kilpatrick S.]
Fisher, Carrie S. ... '75 '01 C.88 B.A. L.896 J.D. [Ⓐ Parker,P.A.&B.]
Fisher, Edgar B., III ... '69 '98 C&L.575 B.A., J.D. [Ⓐ Moore&V.P.]
Fisher, Neal W. ... '55 '85 C.893 B.S. L.896 J.D. 1125 E. Morehead St., Ste. 304
Fisher, Robert A. ... '67 '01 C.845 B.B.A. L.945 J.D. [Ⓐ Moore&V.P.]
Fisher, Walter D., Jr., (AV) ... '— '86 C.160 B.A. L.575 J.D. [Kennedy C.L.&H.]

Fisher & Phillips LLP, (AV Ⓣ)
Suite 2020, 227 West Trade Street, 28202
Telephone: 704-334-4565 Fax: 704-334-9774
Email: fp@laborlawyers.com URL: http://www.laborlawyers.com
Member of Firm: Mason G. Alexander (Certified Specialist, Employment and Labor Law, The Supreme Court of South Carolina). Associates: Kevin Joseph Dalton; James Michael Honeycutt; Shannon (Missy) Sumerell Spainhour.
Labor and Employment, Alternative Dispute Resolution, Arbitration, Business Immigration, Collective Bargaining, Employment Discrimination, Labor Relations, Mergers, Acquisitions and Divestitures, Occupational Safety and Health, Pension and Benefits, Sexual Harassment, Wage and Hour, Whistleblower Litigation, Wrongful Termination.
Atlanta, Georgia Office: 1500 Resurgens Plaza, 945 East Paces Ferry Road, 30326. Telephone: 404-231-1400. Fax: 404-240-4249.
Chicago, Illinois Office: 1000 Marquette Building, 140 South Dearborn Street, 60603. Telephone: 312-346-8061. Fax: 312-346-3179.
Columbia, South Carolina Office: Suite 1400, 1901 Main Street, 29201. Telephone: 803-255-0000. Fax: 803-255-0202.
Dallas, Texas Office: 4343 Thanksgiving Tower, 1601 Elm Street, 75201. Telephone: 214-220-9100. Fax: 214-220-9122.
Fort Lauderdale, Florida Office: Suite 800, 450 East Las Olas Boulevard, 33301. Telephone: 954-525-4800. Fax: 954-525-8739.
Irvine, California Office: Suite 400, 18400 Von Karman Avenue, 92612. Telephone: 949-851-2424. Fax: 949-851-0152.
Kansas City, Missouri Office: Suite 400, 104 West Ninth Street, 64105. Telephone: 816-842-8770. Fax: 816-842-8767.
Las Vegas, Nevada Office: Suite 650, 3993 Howard Hughes Parkway, 89109. Telephone: 702-252-3131. Fax: 702-252-7411.
New Orleans, Louisiana Office: Suite 3710, 201 St. Charles Avenue, 70170. Telephone: 504-522-3303. Fax: 504-529-3850.
Oakland, California Office: City Center, Suite 200, 501 Fourteenth Street, 94612. Telephone: 510-763-4411. Fax: 510-763-4418.
Orlando, Florida Office: 1250 Lincoln Plaza, 300 South Orange Avenue, 32801. Telephone: 407-541-0888. Fax: 407-541-0887.
Portland, Oregon Office: Suite 1600, 1001 S.W. Fifth Avenue, 97204. Telephone: 503-242-4262. Fax: 503-242-4263.
San Diego, California Office: 4225 Executive Square, Suite 950, La Jolla, California, 92037. Telephone: 858-597-9600. Fax: 858-597-9601.
Somerset, New Jersey Office: Corporate Park III, Third Floor, 580 Howard Avenue, 08873. Telephone: 732-560-7100. Fax: 732-560-0788.
Tampa, Florida Office: Suite 2525, 401 East Jackson Street, 33602. Telephone: 813-769-7500. Fax: 813-769-7501.

See Professional Biographies, CHARLOTTE, NORTH CAROLINA

Fitzgerald, Amy ... '77 '02 C.651 B.A. L.645 J.D. [Ⓐ Bolster]
Fitzgerald, Erin L. ... '78 '04 C.198 B.A. L.790 J.D. [Ⓐ Moore&V.P.]
Fitzgerald, Geo. L. ... '26 '55 C&L.823 LL.B. 101 N. McDowell
Fitzgerald, Melanie ... '73 '02 C.838 B.A. L.790 J.D. [Ⓐ Hunton&W.]
Flanagan, Patrick H., (BV) ... '65 '90 C.732 B.S. L.896 J.D. [Cranfill,S.&H.]
Flanary, Walker G., (BV) ... '54 '81 C.383 B.A. L.796 J.D. [W.Flanary]
Flanary, Walker, PA, (BV) ... 1125 E. Morehead St., Ste. 207
Fleming, J. Carlton, (AV) ... '28 '51 C&L.228 A.B., J.D. [Womble C.S.&R.]
Flemma, Robert J., Jr., (AV Ⓣ) '60 '86 C.198 A.B. L.436 J.D. (adm. in WI; not adm. in NC) Gen. Coun., Lending Tree, Inc.
Flemming, Timothy E. '57 '82 C.221 B.A. L.424 J.D. (adm. in IL; not adm. in NC) Compass Group USA
Fletcher, Deborah L., (BV) ... '— '82 C.1090 B.A. L.692 J.D. [Kilpatrick S.]
Fletcher, John Walter, III, (BV) ... '58 '88 C.160 B.S. L.896 J.D. [Fletcher&R.]

Fletcher & Rhoton, P.A., (BV)
316 East Worthington Avenue, 28203
Telephone: 704-334-3400 Facsimile: 704-334-3001
Email: jfletcher@fletcherrhoton.com URL: http://www.fletcherrhoton.com
John Walter Fletcher, III; W. Porter Rhoton, III;—Bryan W. Stone.
Commercial Bankruptcy and Litigation, Motor Vehicle and Leasing Equipment, Foreclosures, Business Law, Buying and Selling Businesses, Limited Liability Company Law, Small Business, Breach of Contracts, Collections, Creditors Rights, Automobile Insurance, Condominium Law, Wills, Estates, Guardianships.

See Professional Biographies, CHARLOTTE, NORTH CAROLINA

Flint, Henry W., (AV) ... '— '80 C&L.893 B.A., J.D. [Ⓒ Kennedy C.L.&H.]
Flynn, Ana M. ... '48 '93 C.788 B.A. L.146 J.D. [Moore&V.P.]
Flynn, W. James ... '— '98 C.269 B.A. L.790 J.D. [Ⓐ Hedrick E.G.&K.]
Fogarty, Patrick J., (AV) ... '60 '86 C.188 B.A. L.262 J.D. [Poyner&S.]
Foodman, Adam Will, (AV) ... '68 '94 C.575 B.A. L.469 J.D. [Foodman,H.&K.]

Foodman, Hunter & Karres, PLLC, (AV)
1001 Morehead Square Drive, Suite 610, 28203
Telephone: 704-333-3323 Fax: 704-358-1808
Members: Adam Will Foodman; Catherine C. Hunter; Andrew T. Karres; Benjamin A. Yarbrough. Associates: Toni K. Grove; James Larry "Chip" Biggers, Jr.; Elizabeth D. Mullis.
Business Law, Commercial and Residential Real Estate, Contracts, Corporate Law, Debt and Equity Finance, E-Commerce, Emerging Growth Companies, Entrepreneurial Business Law, Estate Planning, Franchise Law, Intellectual Property, Land Sales, Land Use Regulation, Limited Liability Companies and Partnerships, Mergers and Acquisitions, Private Equity, Real Estate Development, Real Estate Finance, Real Estate Leasing, Technology Law, Traffic Violations, Trust and Estates, Venture Capital.

(This Listing Continued)

Foodman, Hunter & Karres, PLLC (Continued)
Representative Clients: Lewis Homes; Dan Moser Co.; Grubb Properties; Bravo Development Partners, LLC; Lennar Communities of Carolina, Inc.; MDC Homes, Inc.
Other Charlotte, North Carolina Office: 10710 Sikes Place, Suite 300, 28277. Telephone: 704-849-8649. Fax: 704-849-9278.

See Professional Biographies, CHARLOTTE, NORTH CAROLINA

Ford, Andrea Shaffer ... '62 '89 C.999 B.S. L.692 J.D. [A.S.Ford]
Ford, Kiah T., IV, (AV) ... '69 '94 C.893 B.A. L.902 J.D. [Parker,P.A.&B.]
Ford, Patrick V. ... '48 '75 C.475 B.A. L.912 J.D. [P.V.Ford]
Ford, Andrea Shaffer, P.A. ... 6715-D Fairview Road

Ford, Patrick V., LLC
1401 East Seventh Street, 28204
Telephone: 704-333-3456 Fax: 704-376-9330
Email: ford@lawyer.com URL: http://www.patrickfordlaw.com
Patrick V. Ford.
Criminal Law, Assault and Battery, Burglary, Criminal Defense, Criminal Fraud, Domestic Violence, Drivers License Suspension, Driving While Intoxicated, Drug Crimes, Felonies, Misdemeanors, Theft, Traffic Violations, Weapons Charges.

See Professional Biographies, CHARLOTTE, NORTH CAROLINA

Forquer, Robert A. ... '66 '93 C.1185 B.A. L.1209 J.D. 4801 E. Independence Blvd.
Forrester, Denzil H. ... '65 '95 C.1102 B.S. L.1048 J.D. 3325 Washburn Ave., Ste. 103

Fosbinder, Julie H., Law Office of, (BV) '56 '85 C.399 B.A. L.564 J.D.
1515 Mockingbird Lane, Suite 218, 28209
Telephone: 704-522-7500 Fax: 704-522-7509
URL: http://www.lawyers.com/jfosbinder
Associate: Joshua Reed Van Kampen.
Labor and Employment Law, Employment Discrimination Sexual Harassment, Wrongful Termination, Long Term Disability, Personal Injury.

See Professional Biographies, CHARLOTTE, NORTH CAROLINA

Foster, Debra L., (AV) ... '56 '82 C.577 B.A. L.575 J.D. [Essex R.]
Foster, Mark P., Jr., (BV) '56 '81 C.800 A.B. L.1068 J.D. 1800 Camden Road, Suite 105
Fountain, John E., (BV Ⓣ) '50 '77 C.16 B.A. L.192 J.D. (adm. in AL; not adm. in NC) V.P. & Gen. Coun., Compass Group, U.S.A. Inc.
Fox, Anthony, (AV) ... '55 '83 C.1378 B.A. L.574 J.D. [Parker,P.A.&B.]
Fox, Elyse H. '50 '75 C&L.477 B.A., J.D. (adm. in IL; not adm. in NC) Principal, Legal Info. Servs.
Foxx, Anthony ... '71 '97 C.198 A.B. L.569 J.D. [Ⓐ Hunton&W.]
Foy, Mary L. ... '61 '86 C.185 B.A. L.575 J.D. Bank of Amer., NA.
Franchina, David A. ... '— '88 C.367 B.A. L.262 J.D. [Kennedy C.L.&H.]
Francis, Arthur W. ... '42 '74 C.112 B.A. L.564 J.D. Sr. Coun., Royal& Sunalliance
Francis, Sheldon M. ... '73 '98 C.228 B.A. L.575 J.D. [Ⓐ Helms M.&W.]
Francisco, John W., (AV) ... '68 '93 C.893 B.A. L.902 J.D. [Parker,P.A.&B.]
Frank, Jonathan S. ... '47 '75 C.966 B.B.A. L.209 J.D. [J.S.Frank]
Frank, Jonathan S., P.C., The Law Offices of ... 6000 Fairview Road, Suite 1200
Franklin, Benjamin, Jr., (BV) '64 '90 C.575 B.A. L.1228 J.D. 800 Briar Creek Road, Suite DD 517
Franklin, Robert Wier, (AV) ... '65 '92 C.160 B.S. L.896 J.D. Sr. Coun., CIT Group Inc.
Franklin, Ron D. '65 '94 C.605 A.B. L.477 J.D. (adm. in NY; not adm. in NC) [Mayer,B.R.&M.]
Fravel, Charlene A. ... '73 '98 C.820 B.A. L.1338 J.D. [Ⓐ Kellam&P.]
Freeman, Claude Q., Jr., (AV) ... '— '68 C&L.575 A.B., J.D. [Robinson,B.&H.]
Freeman, John S., (AV) ... '44 '70 C&L.575 B.S., J.D. 2228-D East Seventh St.
Freeman, Katherine ... '59 '85 C.352 B.A. L.879 J.D. [Klein&F.]
Fretwell, James L., (BV) ... '57 '82 C.918 B.A. L.823 J.D. [Ⓐ Mitchell,R.&T.]
Froelich, Kristen ... '— '03 C.579 B.S. L.945 J.D. [Ⓐ Cadwalader,W.&T.]
Frost, Branon R., Jr. ... '42 '67 C&L.575 A.B., J.D. 1235 E. East Blvd.
Frumkin, Brian E. '— '80 C.966 B.A. L.477 J.D. (adm. in CA; not adm. in NC) Assoc. Gen. Coun./Grp. Head, Bank of America
Fulcher, Stacy D. ... '72 '98 C.1019 B.B.A. L.564 J.D. 8520 Cliff Cameron Dr.
Fulcher, Stephanie ... '— '05 C.1128 B.A. L.896 J.D. [Ⓐ Kennedy C.L.&H.]
Fuller, Nathan C. ... '72 '98 C.608 B.S.B.A. L.790 J.D. [Ⓐ Nelson M.R.&S.]
Fuller, Robert W., (AV) ... '— '83 C.575 B.S. L.228 J.D. [Robinson,B.&H.]
Fuller, Trevor M., (CV) ... '67 '93 C.299 A.B. L.276 J.D. [Fuller]
Fuller, William H., III, (BV) ... '66 '93 C.1128 B.A. L.893 J.D. [Moore&V.P.]
Fuller Law Firm, The, P.C., (CV) ... 212 South Tryon Street, Suite 1640
Fulton, Ross R. ... '— '03 C.1372 B.A. L.945 J.D. [Ⓐ Rayburn C.&D.]
Fulton, Shirley L. ... '— '81 C.1378 B.S. L.228 J.D. [Tin F.G.&O.]
Funck, Elizabeth F. ... '62 '88 C.347 B.A. L.896 J.D. 150 Osprey Point Drive
Funk, Brad W. ... '74 '03 C.867 B.S. L.896 J.D. [Ⓐ Cadwalader,W.&T.]
Furr, Diane P. ... '57 '82 C.47 B.A. L.896 J.D. [Poyner&S.]
Furr, J. Cameron, Jr., (BV) ... '64 '89 C&L.575 B.A., J.D. [Grier F.&C.]
Gach, Gregory H., (AV) ... '59 '85 C.473 B.S. L.477 J.D. [Gach]

Gach Law Firm, PLLC, (AV)
6000 Monroe Road Suite 350, 28212
Telephone: 704-531-9355 FAX: 704-531-9354
Email: greg.gach@gachlaw.com URL: http://www.lawyers.com/gregoryhgach
Gregory H. Gach;—Brian H. Nolen.
Corporate, Contract, Corporate Finance, Partnership and Commercial Real Estate. Federal, State and Local Taxation. Sports and Entertainment Law. Motorsports Law and Automobile Dealership Law.

See Professional Biographies, CHARLOTTE, NORTH CAROLINA

Gage, Gaston H., (AV) ... '30 '58 C.228 B.A. L.575 LL.B. [Ⓒ Parker,P.A.&B.]
Gallant, Robert M. ... '— '97 C.1105 B.A. L.1228 J.D. [Ⓐ Butler&H.]
Gallo, Nicholas F. ... '75 '01 C.980 B.E. L.1066 J.D. [Ⓐ Alston&B.]
Gan, Murray Ian ... '66 '90 C.999 B.S. 100 North Tryon Street NC1-007-20-01
Gardner, Jared E. ... '70 '99 C.763 B.S. L.1066 J.D. [Ⓐ James,M.&D.]
Gardner, John ... '— '04 C.575 B.A. L.896 J.D. [Ⓐ Kennedy C.L.&H.]
Gardner, John A., III, (AV) ... '— '74 C.576 B.S. L.575 J.D. [Hedrick E.G.&K.]
Gardner, Nicole L. ... '72 '99 C.645 B.A. L.1066 J.D. [Ⓐ Moore&V.P.]
Gardner, Steven D. ... '61 '92 C.228 B.A. L.608 J.D. Distribution Properties, LLC
Garfinkel, Steven H., (AV) ... '59 '84 C&L.896 B.A., J.D. [Garfinkel]

Garfinkel Immigration Law Firm, (AV)
6230 Fairview Road, Suite 105, 28210
Telephone: 704-442-8000 Fax: 704-442-8080
Email: shg@gilfusa.com URL: http://www.gilfusa.com
Steven H. Garfinkel (Board Certified Specialist in Immigration Law, North Carolina State Board of Legal Specialization). Associates: Jennifer L. Cory (Not admitted in NC); Susan W. Ramos.
Immigration and Naturalization Law, primarily Employment-Based Immigration.

See Professional Biographies, CHARLOTTE, NORTH CAROLINA

Garis, Jeffrey I. ... '54 '90 C.667 B.S.E.E. L.1040 J.D. [Garis]

Garis Law Firm
4929 Monroe Road, 28205
Telephone: 704-536-3336 Fax: 704-536-3316
Email: jeff@garislaw.com URL: http://www.garislaw.com

(This Listing Continued)

Garis Law Firm (Continued)

Jeffrey I. Garis.
Corporate Law, Business Law, Contracts, Collections, Employment, Real Estate, Foreclosure, Trusts and Estates, Wills, Bankruptcy, Debtor and Creditor, Personal Injury, Automobile Accidents, Workers Compensation, Uncontested Divorces, Family Law, Construction, Litigation.
See Professional Biographies, CHARLOTTE, NORTH CAROLINA

Garlitz, Thomas D., (AV) '53 '78 C&L.575 A.B., J.D. [Garlitz&W.]

Garlitz & Williamson, PLLC, (AV)
212 South Tryon Street, Suite 930, The Johnston Building, 28281
Telephone: 704-372-1282 Fax: 704-372-1621
URL: http://www.lawyers.com/garlitzwilliamson
Thomas D. Garlitz; F. Lane Williamson. Of Counsel: Thomas Ashe Lockhart.
General Civil Practice in all Courts. Litigation, Appellate Practice, Insurance, Commercial Litigation, Employment Litigation, Transportation, Personal Injury, Creditors Rights, Environmental Litigation, Professional Liability, Governmental Liability, ERISA Litigation, Mediation and Arbitration.
See Professional Biographies, CHARLOTTE, NORTH CAROLINA

Garner, Christina M. '73 '99 C.665 B.A. L.300 J.D.
(adm. in MN; not adm. in NC) Assoc. Lic. Coun., NASCAR, Inc.
Garofalo, Mel J., (AV) '— '78 C.201 B.A. L.896 J.D. [Hedrick E.G.&K.]
Garrett, Shawna R. '— '04 C.925 B.S. L.575 J.D. [Ⓐ Rayburn C.&D.]
Garrity, William J., (BV) '60 '85 C.902 B.S. L.896 J.D. [Ⓐ P.M.Goodson]
Garver, John B., III, (AV) '— '83 C.870 B.S. L.228 J.D. [Robinson,B.&H.]
Garza & Trotman, PLLC 3547 North Sharon Amity Road, Suite 203
Gaskins, Charlotte Cooper '65 '94 C.806 B.A. L.575 J.D.
Instructor, Central Piedmont Community Coll.
Gaskins, Richard C., Jr., (AV) '58 '84 C.228 B.S.M.E. L.309 J.D. [Moore&V.P.]
Gast, B. Elizabeth, (BV) '63 '92 C.1164 B.A. L.990 J.D. [Cozen O.]
Gatehouse, James B., (BV) '66 '92 C.923 B.A. L.893 J.D. [Rayburn C.&D.]
Gates, Christine Calbert, (CV) '— '89 C.741 B.A. L.1187 J.D. 225 E. Kingston Ave.
Gates, Tilman Thomas '— '98 C&L.228 A.B., J.D. [Robinson,B.&H.]
Gathings, John T., Jr. '65 '91 C.198 A.B. L.192 J.D. [Moore&V.P.]
Gatrell, M. Bryant '70 '97 C.502 B.A. L.477 J.D. [Moore&V.P.]
Gavigan, Timothy B. '62 '89 C.577 B.S. L.1338 J.D. 6832 Morrison Blvd.
Gaylord, Scott W. '— '99 C.165 B.A. L.602 J.D. [Ⓐ Robinson,B.&H.]
Gegg, Christopher J. '77 '02 C.894 B.A. L.896 J.D. [Ⓐ Alston&B.] (See Pat. Sect.)
Geib, Sally L. '56 '80 C.477 B.A. L.309 J.D.
(adm. in MI; not adm. in NC) V.P., Assoc. Gen. Coun. & Secy., Goodrich Corp.
Geller, Stanton P. '78 '05 C.994 B.A. L.260 J.D. [Ⓐ Culp E.&C.]
Gemmiti, Nathan V. '70 '98 C.708 B.A. L.93 J.D.
(adm. in ME; not adm. in NC) Principal, Scottish Re (U.S.), Inc.
Genay, Michael J. '65 '01 C.999 B.S. L.893 J.D. [Ⓐ Hunton&W.]
Gennett, Stephen P., II, (BV) '65 '91 C.276 B.S. L.575 J.D. [Johnston,A.&H.]
Gentile, Marc S., (BV) '71 '96 C.446 B.A. L.1202 J.D.
Coun., USPS, Eastern Area Law Office-Charlotte
George, Angela S. '71 '97 C.329 B.B.A. L.665 J.D. Asst. Dist. Atty.
George, Annie R. '72 '99 C.188 B.S. L.818 J.D. [Ⓐ Cadwalader,W.&T.]
George, Theodore C. '72 '00 C.280 B.S.Ed. L.94 J.D. [Ⓐ Alston&B.]
George, Twyla H. '71 '96 C.8 B.A. L.500 J.D. Assoc. Co. Atty., Mecklenburg Co.
Georgiade, Carolyn R. '75 '03 C.806 B.A. L.228 J.D. [Ⓐ Mayer,B.R.&M.]
Gerber, Andrew A. '67 '93 C&L.446 B.S., J.D. [Hunton&W.]
Gerdes, Phillip E., (AV) '38 '64 C&L.575 B.A., J.D. [Gerdes,M.&S.]

Gerdes, Mason & Simpson, L.L.P., (AV)
216 North McDowell Street, Suite 110, P.O. Box 30068, 28230
Telephone: 704-372-3180 Fax: 704-343-2942
Email: gmsl@gmsllaw.com URL: http://www.gmsllaw.com
Members of Firm: Phillip E. Gerdes; James L. Mason, Jr.; David T. Simpson, Jr.; Benjamin D. Williams.
General Civil and Criminal Trial Practice before all State and Federal Courts. Personal Injury, Wrongful Death, Social Security Disability, Corporation, Real Estate, Bankruptcy, Domestic Relations, Estate Planning and Probate Law.
Approved Attorneys for: Lawyers Title Insurance Corp.; First Title Insurance Co.; A.M.I. Title Insurance Co.
Reference: Central Carolina Bank and Trust Co.
See Professional Biographies, CHARLOTTE, NORTH CAROLINA

Gerhold, Timothy A. G., (AVⓉ) '— '74 C.118 B.A. L.976 J.D.
(adm. in MA; not adm. in NC) Bank of America (ⓄBoston, MA)
Gerock, Julie Curran '72 '99 C.472 B.A. L.93 J.D. [Whitesides&W.]
Ghartey-Tagoe, Kodwo '63 '88
C.012 B.A. L.228 J.D. Assoc. Gen. Coun., Duke Energy Corp.
Ghidina, Douglas R., (AV) '62 '87 C.917 B.A. L.477 J.D. [Moore&V.P.]
Gibson, Michael G., (BV) '54 '79 C.198 B.A. L.896 J.D. [Dean&G.]
Gibson, Richard W., Jr., (AV) '— '83 C&L.575 B.A., J.D. [Robinson,B.&H.]
Gibson, Ronald L., (BV) '51 '78 C.198 A.B. L.575 J.D. [Ⓒ Tin F.G.&O.]
Gieryn, Richard T. '20 '49 L.215 LL.B.
(adm. in MI; not adm. in NC) 7404 Red Oak Lane‡
Gilardi, David, (CVⓉ) '— '85 C.1057 B.S. L.1252 J.D. [Ⓐ Gorman&D.]
Gilbert, Milton H., Jr '71 '01 C.1128 B.A. L.8 J.D. [Ⓐ Bray,P.]
Gilbert, Timothy W., (BV) '— '81 C&L.896 B.A., J.D. [Ⓒ Moore&V.P.]
Gilchrist, Peter Spence, III, (AV) '39 '65 C.575 A.B. L.228 LL.B. Dist. Atty.
Gildernew, David L. '71 '97 C&L.229 B.S.B.A., J.D.
(adm. in PA; not adm. in NC) [Ⓐ Alston&B.]

Gillespie, Donald S., Jr., (AV) '45 '71 C.198 A.B. L.575 J.D.
122 North McDowell Street, 28204
Telephone: 704-375-8750 Fax: 704-375-8759
Email: Donald-Gillespie@hbm-attys.com
General Civil and Trial Practice in all Courts, Family Law, Real Property, Guardianships, Decedent's Estates and Probate.
References: Bank of America; First Trust Bank; Wachovia Bank; The Scottish Bank.
See Professional Biographies, CHARLOTTE, NORTH CAROLINA

Gilpin, David W., (BV) '64 '92 C.34 B.S. L.575 J.D. [Gilpin&H.]
Gilpin & Hatcher, P.C., (BV) 801 East Trade Street, Suite 100
Ginsburg, Matthew J. '71 '98 C.1365 B.A. L.93 J.D. [Ⓐ Shumaker,L.&K.]
Giovannelli, T. Richard '— '96 C.893 B.A. L.945 J.D. [Kennedy C.L.&H.]
Gledhill, Karen A., (AV) '— '88 C.790 B.A. L.178 J.D. [Robinson,B.&H.]
Glenn, W. Lewis, III '68 '98 C.871 B.S. L.945 J.D. [Ⓐ Parker,P.A.&B.]
Glenney, Jeffrey W., (AV) '63 '89 C.228 B.A. L.800 J.D. [Moore&V.P.]
Glidewell, Matthew D. '— '00 C.327 B.A. L.896 J.D. [Ⓐ Hedrick E.G.&K.]
Glosson, Brad Cameron '74 '95 C.198 B.A. L.896 J.D. Eagle Ltd.
Gmyrek, Elizabeth M. '70 '96 C.381 B.B.A. L.1040 J.D. [Ⓐ Templeton&R.]
Godfrey, Lisa G., (BV) '56 '80 C.446 B.S. L.128 J.D. [Knox B.K.&G.]
Godwin, Jeremy H., (BV) '71 '96 C.198 B.A. L.896 J.D. [Moore&V.P.]
Gohil, Sanjay R., Law Offices of '72 '97
C.228 B.A. L.575 J.D. 6201 Fairview Road, Suite 200
Gold, Norman '50 '81 C.102 B.S. L.1009 J.D. 5606 Oak Crest Green Drive
Goldberg, Jon '— '05 C&L.575 B.A., J.D. [Ⓐ Kennedy C.L.&H.]
Goldenberg, Grant D. '— '02 C.347 B.A. L.896 J.D. [Ⓐ Helms M.&W.]
Golding, John G., (AV) '28 '53 C.951 B.A. L.575 J.D. [Golding H.&P.]

Golding Holden & Pope, L.L.P., (AV) 🅑🅑
3325 Springbank Lane, Suite 304, 28226
Telephone: 704-374-1600 Fax: 704-759-8966
Members of Firm: John G. Golding; C. Byron Holden; James W. Pope. Associates: Robert J. Aylward; Elizabeth Sprenger; J. Scott Bayne.
General Insurance and Civil Defense Practice in State and Federal Courts, Professional Malpractice, Fire, Casualty and Life Insurance, Surety Practice, Workers Compensation, Construction, Premises and Products Liability.
Representative Clients: State Farm Insurance Companies; Allstate Insurance Company; Nationwide Mutual Insurance Companies; GMAC; Builders Mutual Insurance Co.
See Professional Biographies, CHARLOTTE, NORTH CAROLINA

Goldman, Lawrence J., (BV) '61 '88 C.1237 B.S. L.420 J.D. [Jones,H.&W.]
Goldstein, Meg D., (AV) '54 '79 C.910 B.A. L.575 J.D. [Hamilton F.M.S.S.&M.]
Goldstein, Stuart N. '67 '92 C.188 B.S. L.1066 J.D.
(adm. in CA; not adm. in NC) [Cadwalader,W.&T.]
Gonzalez, Victoria S., (BV) '67 '94 C.184 B.A. L.306 J.D. [Gonzalez&Assoc.]
Gonzalez & Associates, (BV) 4448 Central Avenue
Goode, Elizabeth Whitener, (AV) '60 '85 C.575 B.A. L.178 J.D. [Helms M.&W.]
Goodenow, Marsha L., (BV) '59 '84 C.680 B.A. L.8 J.D. Asst. Dist. Atty.
Goodman, Joshua R. '72 '98 C.152 B.A. L.1206 J.D. [Cozen O.]
Goodman, Robert W. '27 '58 C.893 B.S. L.245 LL.B.
(adm. in GA; not adm. in NC) P.O. Box 34331‡
Goodman, W. Clark, (BV) '67 '93 C.228 A.B. L.309 J.D. [Womble C.S.&R.]
Goodman, Carr, Laughrun, Levine and Murray, (AV) 301 S. McDowell St.

Goodson, Paul M. '68 '95 C.575 B.S. L.896 J.D.
Midtown Plaza, Suite 425, 1300 Baxter Street, P.O. Box 35341, 28235 ⊙
Telephone: 704-331-8014 Toll Free 1-866-NC HURT 1 (866-624-8781) Fax: 704-331-8017
URL: http://www.lawyers.com/goodson
Email: potentialclient@pgoodsonlaw.com URL: http://www.pgoodson.com
Associate: William J. Garrity.
Civil Litigation, Personal Injury, Auto Accidents, Slip & Fall, Social Security Disability, Wrongful Death and Workers Compensation, Class Action, Pharmaceutical Class Action.
Durham, North Carolina Office: 3101 Guess Road, F-106, 27705. Telephone: 919-471-5000; 877-298-3634.
Raleigh, North Carolina Office: 422 St. Mary's Street, Suite 1, 27605. Telephone: 919-834-6360; 877-298-3634.
See Professional Biographies, CHARLOTTE, NORTH CAROLINA

Gordon, Alan, (AV) '— '77 C.645 B.A. L.472 J.D. [A.Gordon]
Gordon, David Stott '51 '77 C&L.280 A.B., J.D.
Sr. V.P. & Gen. Coun., Caldwell Aircraft Trading Company, Inc.
Gordon, Marc R., (BV) '55 '80 C&L.575 A.B., J.D. 319 S. Sharon Amity, Ste. 230
Gordon, Richard S., (BV) '45 '70 C&L.896 B.A., J.D. [Dozier,M.P.&M.]

Gordon, Alan, Immigration Law, (AV)
1018 East Boulevard, Suite 7, 28203
Telephone: 704-332-2555 Fax: 704-377-1172
Email: asgordon@greencards.com URL: http://www.greencards.com
Member of Firm: Alan Gordon (Approved Areas of Practice under the Florida Designation Plan; Immigration and Naturalization; Board Certified Specialist in Immigration, North Carolina State Board of Legal Specialization). Associate: Miguel Manna.
Languages: Spanish.
Concentrating in Immigration Law including Employment Visas, Visas for Healthcare Professionals, Investor Visas, Consular Processing, Citizenship Law, Employment Verification (Form I-9) Law, Due Diligence during Mergers and Acquisitions; and Immigration and Citizenship Matters for Foreign Nationals, and their families.
See Professional Biographies, CHARLOTTE, NORTH CAROLINA

Gorelick, Scott R., (BV) '58 '85 C.893 B.S. L.575 J.D. [Gorelick,S.R.]
Gorelick, Scott R., PC, (BV) 6000 Fairview Rd., Ste. 1415
Gorman, Anna Shedden, (BV) '67 '94 C.575 B.S. L.1228 J.D. [Poyner&S.]
Gorman, Thomas J., (BV) '— '85 C.93 B.A. L.228 J.D. [Gorman&D.]

Gorman & Dittner, (BV)
13925 Ballantyne Corporate Place, Suite 200, 28277
Telephone: 704-544-2500 Facsimile: 704-544-2596
URL: http://www.gormlaw.com
Thomas J. Gorman; Derek E. Dittner. Associates: David Gilardi; Jessica E. Thurbee; Mary Lee E. Mrochek.
Trusts and Estates, Asset Protection, Estate Planning, Wills and Probate, Real Estate, Buying or Selling, Commercial Leasing, Construction, Corporate, Business Law, Franchises, Limited Liability Companies, Partnership, Contracts, Lawsuits, Mergers, Personal Injury, Automobile Accidents, Criminal Law, Shopping Center Development.
See Professional Biographies, CHARLOTTE, NORTH CAROLINA

Gorman Law Firm, El Centro Hispano
3410 Central Avenue, 28205
Telephone: 704-537-1400 Toll Free: 1-888-523-6876 Fax: 704-537-3727 URL: http://www.elcentrohispano.com
URL: http://www.lawyers.com/ruthgorman
Ruth Gorman-Vega.
Language: Spanish.
Immigration and Naturalization, Business Immigration, Citizenship, Employment Authorizations, Employment Immigration, Employment Visas, Family Immigration, Labor Certificates, Visas, General Business Practice, Contracts, Corporations, International Law, Criminal Law, Misdemeanors.
See Professional Biographies, CHARLOTTE, NORTH CAROLINA

Gorman-Vega, Ruth '65 '94 C.69 B.B.A. L.990 J.D. [Gorman]
Gosnell, Guy R., (AV) '65 '92 C.502 B.S.E.E. L.734 J.D. [Alston&B.] (See Pat. Sect.)
Gossage, Kimberly A., (BV) '64 '98 C.1128 B.A. L.896 J.D. [Ⓐ Morris Y.W.S.&B.]
Gott, Mark D. '68 '95 C.999 B.A. L.1339 J.D. [Sellers,H.A.D.&L.]
Gottehrer, Kevin B. '75 '01 C.103 B.A. L.94 J.D. [Ⓐ Parker,P.A.&B.]
Grady, Jeffrey C. '— '04 C.911 B.A. L.896 J.D. [Ⓐ Katten M.R.]
Graham, David A. '46 '77 C&L.575 B.A., J.D. Dist. Atty. Off.
Graham, Thomas E., (AV) '57 '84 C.608 B.S. L.273 J.D. [Moore&V.P.]
Graham, Timothy H., (BV) '61 '86 C.34 B.S. L.1228 J.D. [Dozier,M.P.&M.]
Graham, William M., (BV) '60 '91
C.125 B.A. L.33 J.D. [Ⓒ Jackson,P.] & [Wallace&G.] (ⓄSalisbury)
Grainger, Allyson '72 '97 C.36 B.S. L.228 J.D. [Ⓐ McGuireWoods]
Grandy, C. William, (BV) '58 '83 C.575 B.A. L.896 J.D. [Grandy&M.]
Grandy & Martin, (BV) 115-G E. Park Avenue
Gray, Marvin K. '31 '60 C&L.896 B.A., J.D. Supr. Ct. J.
Grayson, Lawrence P., II '69 '00 C.446 B.A. L.597 J.D. [Ⓐ Moore&V.P.]
Greci, Marcia T. '74 '04 C.247 B.S. L.989 J.D. [Ⓐ Summa&A.] (See Pat. Sect.)
Greeley, Tanya D. '73 '99 C.645 B.S. L.446 J.D. [Ⓒ Moore&V.P.]
Green, Keith S., (Mrs.) '25 '51 C.320 A.B. L.575 LL.B. 1911 Cassamia Pl.‡
Green, Larry Ray '45 '71 C&L.575 B.S., J.D. P.O. Box 11289
Green, Maurice O., (BV) '67 '91 C&L.228 B.A., J.D. P.O. Box 30035
Green, Stanley B. '70 '98
C.575 B.A. L.1194 J.D. [Ⓐ Womble C.S.&R.] (ⓄWinston-Salem)
Greene, Christopher E. '68 '98 C.577 B.A. L.472 J.D. [Tin F.G.&O.]

Greene, James N., III ... '71 '99 C.1128 B.S. L.575 J.D. [Parker,P.A.&B.]
Greene, Michael J. ... '73 '00 C.197 B.A. L.896 J.D. [🄰 Goodman,C.L.L.&M.]
Greene, Robert J., Jr., (BV) ... '46 '79 C&L.878 B.A., J.D. [Smith,C.&H.]
Gregg, Heather ... '77 '02 C.577 B.S. L.896 J.D. [🄰 Alston&B.] (See Pat. Sect.)
Gregory, W. Wallace, Jr., (AV) ... '42 '68 C&L.790 B.S., J.D. 717 Hungerford Pl.
Gresham, John W., (AV) ... '45 '75 C.198 A.B. L.94 J.D. [Ferguson,S.C.G.&S.]
Greve, Theodore A., (CV) ... '57 '93 C.280 B.B.A. L.574 J.D. 1201 N. Tryon St.
Grier, Joseph W., III, (AV) ... '51 '77 C&L.575 B.A., J.D. [Grier F.&C.]
Grier, Joseph W., Jr., (AV) ... '15 '40 C.575 A.B. L.309 LL.B. [🄲 Grier F.&C.]
Grier, Raymond L. '53 '88 C.789 B.A. L.329 J.D.
(adm. in PA; not adm. in NC) 2582 Hemphill St.‡

Grier Furr & Crisp, (AV)
101 North Tryon Street, Suite 1240, 28246
Telephone: 704-375-3720 FAX: 704-332-0215
URL: http://www.grierlaw.com
Members of Firm: Joseph W. Grier, III (Board Certified Specialist in Bankruptcy Law, North Carolina State Board of Legal Specialization); J. Cameron Furr, Jr.; C. Michael Crisp. Associates: Alan M. Presel; A. Cotten Wright. Of Counsel: Joseph W. Grier, Jr.
General Civil Trial and Business Practice. Business, Bankruptcy, Corporations, Municipal, Real Estate and Land Use Regulation, Trusts, Wills, and Estates.
Approved Attorneys for: Lawyers Title Insurance Corp.
See Professional Biographies, CHARLOTTE, NORTH CAROLINA

Griffin, Barbara M. L. '62 '87 C.477 A.B. L.309 J.D.
(adm. in NY; not adm. in NC) Collins & Aikman Corp.
Griffin, Joseph M., (AV) ... '35 '61 C&L.228 A.B., J.D. [Griffin,B.&P.]
Griffin, Martha W., (BV) ... '67 '91 C.228 A.B. L.309 J.D. Sr. Coun., Clariant Corp.
Griffin, Michael C. ... '69 '00 C.152 B.A. L.273 J.D. [🄰 McGuireWoods]
Griffin, Richard L. ... '25 '52 C&L.575 B.S., J.D. Asst. U.S. Atty.
Griffin, Robert G., (AV) ... '— '78 C&L.575 A.B., J.D. [Robinson,B.&H.]
Griffin, Thomas N., III, (AV) ... '58 '83 C.896 B.A. L.893 J.D. [Parker,P.A.&B.]
Griffin, Timothy W., (AV) ... '54 '80 C&L.575 B.A., J.D. [Poyner&S.]
Griffin, Brunson & Perle, L.L.P., (AV) ... 301 S. McDowell St.
Griffith, Cynthia J. '— '91 C.276 B.A. L.145 J.D.
(adm. in CA; not adm. in NC) Bk. of America
Griffith, Steve C., Jr., (AV) ... '33 '59 C.160 B.S. L.790 LL.B. 422 S. Church St.
Griffith, W. Mark ... '71 '96 C&L.575 B.A., J.D. [🄰 Poyner&S.]
Grigg, David L., Jr., (CV) ... '66 '92 C&L.575 B.S., J.D. Jud. Law Clk., U.S. Dist. Ct.
Grigg, William H., (AV) '32 '58 C&L.228 A.B., LL.B.
Chmn. & CEO, Duke Power Co.
Griggs, Eugene S., (AV) ... '61 '87 C.198 A.B. L.575 J.D. [Poyner&S.]
Griggs, Julie Zydron, (AV) ... '62 '87 C.945 B.A. L.893 J.D. [Robinson,B.&H.]
Grim, Harry J., (AVⓉ) ... '30 '59 C&L.902 A.B., LL.B. [🄲 Moore&V.P.]
Grimes, Beth Yount ... '72 '99 C.34 B.A. L.575 J.D. [🄰 Moore&V.P.]
Grimes, J. Douglas ... '— '04 C.953 B.S. L.1228 J.D. [🄰 Hedrick E.G.&K.]
Griset, Jill Crawley, (BV) ... '71 '97 C.575 B.A. L.893 J.D. [🄰 Helms M.&W.]
Grist, Daniel W. ... '74 '02 C.232 B.S. L.1187 J.D. [Davies&G.]
Grist, William T. ... '20 '51 C.404 L.228 LL.B. Ret. Supr. Ct. J.
Griswold, Thomas H. '52 '77 C.9 B.S. L.16 J.D.
V.P., Legal & Asst. Secy., John Deere Consumer Products (Pat.)
Grogan, David M., (BV) ... '49 '84 C.259 B.S. L.228 J.D. [Shumaker,L.&K.]
Gromlovits, Kathryn A. ... '76 '04 C.575 B.S. L.790 J.D. [🄰 Adams E.] (See Pat. Sect.)
Gronquist, James E., (BV) ... '41 '81 C.260 B.A. L.1162 J.D. [Nixon,P.&G.]
Grove, Ann W. '66 '93 C.165 B.A. L.880 J.D.
(adm. in CA; not adm. in NC) 2901 Sunset Dr.‡
Grove, Toni K., (BV) ... '55 '93 C.1128 B.A. L.1228 J.D. 10710 Sikes Place, Suite 300
Grover, James P. '53 '79 C.24 B.A. L.1202 J.D.
V.P. & Assoc. Gen. Coun., Transamerica Reinsurance
Groves, J. Randall, (AV) ... '39 '64 C.152 B.A. L.861 LL.B. [Groves,D.&B.] ‡
Groves, Dunklin & Boggs, P.C., (AV) ... P.O. Box 78826
Gruendel, Stephen E. ... '72 '98 C.976 B.A. L.93 J.D. [🄰 Moore&V.P.]
Grupp, John E., (BV) ... '70 '95 C.228 B.S.E. L.893 J.D. [Parker,P.A.&B.]
Gsell, Scott, Attorney at Law '59 '86 C.223 B.S. L.809 J.D.
3325 Washburn Ave., Ste. 104
Guarnieri, Albert E., (BV) ... '60 '86 C.477 B.A. L.893 J.D. [Parker,P.A.&B.]
Gudzy, Lillian N. '57 '84 C.705 B.A. L.1068 J.D.
(adm. in NY; not adm. in NC) Elite Info. Grp., Inc.
Guinan, Richard C., Jr., (AV) '42 '69 C.846 B.B.A. L.802 J.D.
(adm. in TX; not adm. in NC) V.P. & Asst. Gen. Coun., First Union Corporation
Gulley, Jack Marshall '24 '50 C&L.945 A.B., J.D.
(adm. in VA; not adm. in NC) 7015 Quail Hill Rd.‡
Gundel, Norman L., (AV) '52 '79 C.277 B.I.E. L.260 J.D.
(adm. in TX; not adm. in NC; Pat.) Atty., Intell. Prop. Law, IBM Corp.
Gunson, Douglas R. ... '61 '90 C&L.101 B.A., J.D. Corp. Coun., Nucor Corp.
Gunst, Cyril C., Jr. ... '24 '51 C.228 B.A. L.1541 J.D. [Gunst&G.] ‡
Gunst, Robert C. ... '55 '80 C.896 B.A. L.990 J.D. [Gunst&G.]
Gunst & Gunst ... 5950 Fairview Road, Suite 706
Gunter, D. Shane '— '00 C.999 B.S. L.1017 J.D.
(adm. in DE; not adm. in NC) [🄰 Kilpatrick S.]
Gunter, Dorian H., (AV) ... '53 '79 C&L.896 B.A., J.D. [Casstevens,H.G.&R.]
Gustafson, Marc '— '02 C.575 A.B. L.347 J.D.
(adm. in GA; not adm. in NC) [🄰 Kennedy C.L.&H.]
Guterman, James H., (AV) ... '52 '78 C.881 A.B. L.575 J.D. [Helms M.&W.]
Guthery, Paul B., Jr., (AV) ... '29 '56 C.198 B.S. L.575 J.D. [Horack,T.P.&L.] ‡
Guthrie, Dennis L., (AV) ... '44 '69 C.968 A.B. L.469 J.D. [Guthrie,D.H.&S.]

Guthrie, Davis, Henderson & Staton, P.L.L.C., (AV)
719 East Boulevard, 28203
Telephone: 704-372-5600; 375-1431; 332-6141 Fax: 704-372-4601
Email: firm@gdhs.com URL: http://www.firm@gdhs.com
Members of Firm: Dennis L. Guthrie; K. Neal Davis; Robert E. Henderson; Kevin W. Tydings. Retired Member: John S. Staton (Retired). Associate: Benjamin R. Hardwick. Of Counsel: John H. Hasty; James D. Monteith; William J. Waggoner; S. Dean Hamrick; Kimberly R. Matthews.
Trial Practice in State and Federal Court. Litigation of Personal Injury, Premises Liability, Products Liability, and Criminal Law, General Civil Practice, Business Representation, Commercial Real Estate, Taxation, Estate Planning, Corporate and Securities Law, Zoning and Land Use, Creditor's Rights, Bankruptcy (creditors), Alcoholic Beverage Control, Media, Communications, Libel, Defamation, Banking, Probate and Construction.
Representative Clients: Associates Commercial Corp.; Winn-Dixie Charlotte, Inc.; The Great Atlantic & Pacific Tea Co.; Navistar, Inc.; Empire Distributors of North Carolina, Inc.; Kinder-Care Learning Centers, Inc.; Pep Boys-Manny, Moe & Jack; Genuine Parts, Inc.; Ind-Com Electric Co., Inc.
Reference: Bank of Mecklenburg.
See Professional Biographies, CHARLOTTE, NORTH CAROLINA

Gwaltney, Alton Larue, III ... '68 '93 C.301 B.A. L.692 J.D. [🄰 Moore&V.P.]
Ha, Jennifer T. '— '02 C.1494 B.S. L.1066 J.D.
(adm. in NY; not adm. in NC) [🄰 Mayer,B.R.&M.]
Habenicht, Andrew M. ... '— '04 C.301 B.A. L.1209 J.D. [🄰 Kennedy C.L.&H.]
Haden, Kara L. Gibbon ... '68 '96 C.683 B.A. L.692 J.D. Sr. Tr. Atty.
Hader, Stephen M. ... '62 '87 C.567 B.A. L.705 J.D. [Moore&V.P.]
Haenni, Scott Alan '— '99 C.575 B.S.B.A. L.276 J.D.
Dir., Corp. and Legal Affairs, The Lash Group, Inc.
Hagerman, Michael C. '— '81 C.352 B.A. L.221 J.D.
(adm. in IA; not adm. in NC) Bank of America
Hahn, Cynthia A. '— '94 C.540 B.S. L.818 J.D.
(adm. in MA; not adm. in NC) Bank of America
Hahn, Robert J., (BV) ... '56 '85 C&L.724 B.A., J.D. [Hunton&W.]
Hairr, John R., III, (AV) ... '65 '90 C.575 B.A. L.228 J.D. [Parker,P.A.&B.]
Haldin, James W. ... '74 '00 C.260 B.A. L.902 J.D. [🄰 Moore&V.P.]
Haley, Charles F. '45 '73 C&L.665 B.A., J.D.
(adm. in PA; not adm. in NC) 2001 Rexford Rd.
Hall, C. Wells, III, (AV) ... '47 '73 C.575 B.S. L.228 J.D. [Mayer,B.R.&M.]
Hall, Dana C. ... '56 '82 C.575 B.A. L.1228 J.D. [Miller&H.]
Hall, J. Andre, (BV) ... '65 '90 C.269 B.A. L.575 J.D. Segment Coun., Goodrich Corp.
Hall, Katherine ... '— '04 C&L.896 B.A., J.D. [🄰 McAngus G.&C.]
Hall, Rachel B., (AV) '— '87 C.198 A.B. L.575 J.D.
Asst. Gen. Coun., Bank of America
Ham, Edwin C., (BV) ... '60 '86 C&L.232 B.S.B.A., J.D. [E.C.Ham]
Ham, Edwin C., P.C., (BV) ... 508 East Boulevard
Hamel, Reginald S., (AV) ... '33 '62 C.228 A.B. L.896 J.D. [Hamel]
Hamel, William B., Sr., (BV) ... '65 '90 C.896 B.A. L.1228 J.D. [Horack,T.P.&L.]
Hamel, William F., (AV) ... '39 '69 C.1126 B.S. L.836 J.D. [Hamel]

Hamel Law Firm, The, P.A., (AV)
Woodfield Corporate Center, Suite 208, 8008 Corporate Center Drive, 28226
Telephone: 704-542-1648 Telecopier: 704-542-8616
Email: thehamellawfirm.com URL: http://www.lawyers.com/hamellawfirm
Reginald S. Hamel; William F. Hamel;—Paul G. Wamsley.
General Practice, Civil Litigation, Commercial Law, Business Law, Corporate Law, Immigration Law, Personal Injury, Estate Planning, Trust Law, Probate, Insurance, Real Estate.
See Professional Biographies, CHARLOTTE, NORTH CAROLINA

Hamilton, David B., (AV) ... '52 '77 C.276 B.S.F.S. L.575 J.D. [Hamilton F.M.S.S.&M.]
Hamilton, Edward J., Jr., (AVⓉ) '47 '74 C.968 B.A. L.790 J.D.
(adm. in SC; not adm. in NC) Asst. Gen. Coun. & V.P., Wachovia Corp., Legal Div.
Hamilton, Sarah R. '— '04 C&L.259 B.S., J.D.
(adm. in FL; not adm. in NC) [🄰 Kilpatrick S.]

Hamilton Fay Moon Stephens Steele & Martin, PLLC, (AV) BR
201 South College Street, Suite 2020, 28244-2020
Telephone: 704-344-1117 Facsimile: 704-344-1483
URL: http://www.lawHFM.com
T. Jonathan Adams; Richard E. Fay; Meg D. Goldstein; David B. Hamilton; Margaret Behringer Maloney; Bentford E. Martin; Keith J. Merritt; Travis W. Moon; David G. Redding; Jackson N. Steele; Robert C. Stephens; George W. Sistrunk, III; Allen L. West;—Adrianne Huffman Colgate; Kevin M. Profit; Mark R. Kutny; Roxanne Matthews Lucy; Erik M. Rosenwood.
Litigation, including Civil, Trial and Appellate Practice in all State and Federal Courts in North Carolina, and all Areas of Law, including Construction, Debtor/Creditor, Environmental, General Business, Intellectual Property, Labor and Employment, Land Use, Securities, Telecommunications, and Unfair Competition. Alternative Dispute Resolution, Arbitration and Mediation. Probate and Trusts and Estates, Business Litigation.
See Professional Biographies, CHARLOTTE, NORTH CAROLINA

Hammer, Robert H., III, (BV) '55 '85
C.688 B.S.Ch.E. L.831 J.D. [Hammer,A.&H.] (Pat.)

Hammer, Ashburg & Hanf, P.C., (BV)
3125 Springbank Lane Suite G, 28226
Telephone: 704-927-0400 Fax: 704-927-0485
Email: bhammer@hammerpatent.com URL: http://www.hammerpatent.com
Robert H. Hammer, III; Scott E. Hanf; Ray Ashburg.
Patent, Trademark, Copyright, Trade Secret, Unfair Competition, Intellectual Property, Antitrust Law.
See Professional Biographies, CHARLOTTE, NORTH CAROLINA

Hamner Inman, E. Diana ... '63 '89 C.896 B.S. L.999 J.D. 5418 Dunedin Lane
Hamrick, Joseph N. ... '— '01 C.1228 B.S. L.896 J.D. [🄰 McAngus G.&C.]
Hamrick, S. Dean, (AV) ... '28 '52 C.896 B.S. L.575 J.D. [🄲 Guthrie,D.H.&S.]
Hands, David W. ... '70 '02 C.1011 B.S. L.574 J.D. [Hands]
Hands Law Office, PLLC ... 800 Briar Creek Rd., Ste. DD-518
Hanes, Heather R. ... '71 '99 C&L.896 B.A., J.D. [🄰 Sasser]
Hanf, Scott E. ... '61 '94 C.62 B.S. L.1003 J.D. [Hammer,A.&H.] (Pat.)
Hankins, Irvin W., III, (AV) ... '46 '75 C&L.575 A.B., J.D. [Parker,P.A.&B.]
Hankins, Wendy J. '50 '92 C.454 B.S. L.1218 J.D.
(adm. in NH; not adm. in NC) P.O. Box 667695‡
Hanna, George V., III, (AV) ... '43 '68 C&L.575 A.B., J.D. [Moore&V.P.]
Hanner, Robert P., II, (AV) ... '44 '69 C.152 B.S. L.896 J.D. [Casstevens,H.G.&R.]
Hannum, Christopher E. ... '66 '92 C.25 B.A. L.260 J.D. [Culp E.&C.]
Hansen, Daniel R. ... '67 '95 C.97 B.A. L.930 J.D. [Shumaker,L.&K.]
Harden, Debbie Weston, (AV) ... '57 '82 C&L.575 B.A., J.D. [Womble C.S.&R.]
Harden, Jill D. '65 '90 C.573 B.S. L.1048 J.D.
(adm. in CT; not adm. in NC) First Union Corp. (Contract Servs. Grp.)
Hardin, James C., III, (AVⓉ) ... '— '74 C.968 A.B. L.228 J.D. [J.C.Hardin,III] ⊙

Hardin, James C., III, PLLC, (AVⓉ)
6201 Fairview Road, Suite 200, 28210 ⊙
Telephone: 704-944-4286 Fax: 704-552-6332
Email: jhardin@jimhardinlaw.com URL: http://www.jimchardinlaw.com
James C. Hardin III (Board Certified Specialist in Estate Planning and Probate Law, North Carolina State Board of Legal Specialization); (Certified Specialist, Estate Planning and Probate Law, The Supreme Court of South Carolina).
Estate Planning, Wills and Probate, Trust Law, Elder Law, Tax Planning, Asset Protection, Guardianship, IRS Audits.
Rock Hill, South Carolina Office: 113 East Main Street, Suite 330, 29730. Telephone: 803-329-7601. Fax: 803-329-8121
See Professional Biographies, CHARLOTTE, NORTH CAROLINA

Hardison, Kenneth L., (BV) ... '56 '82 C&L.1228 B.S., J.D. [Hardison&L.] ⊙
Hardison & Leone, L.L.P., (AV)
6047 Tyvola Glen Circle (⊙Dunn, Fayetteville, Greensboro, Raleigh, Southern Pines, NC; Myrtle Beach, SC)
Hardwick, Benjamin R. ... '72 '97 C.575 B.A. L.896 J.D. [🄰 Guthrie,D.H.&S.]
Hardymon, G. Kirkland, (BV) ... '64 '92 C.34 B.S.B.A. L.896 J.D. [Rayburn C.&D.]
Hardymon, Glen B., (AV) ... '— '63 C.228 A.B. L.575 LL.B. [Kennedy C.L.&H.]
Hargett, Jeffrey B., (BV) ... '64 '90 C&L.575 B.A., J.D. [Price,S.H.P.&A.]
Hargrove, Donna L. ... '68 '98 C.838 B.S.N. L.790 J.D. [🄰 Womble C.S.&R.]
Harkey, Averill C., (AV) ... '52 '79 C.902 B.A. L.896 J.D. [Harkey L.]
Harkey, Henry A., (AV) ... '49 '75 C.902 B.A. L.896 J.D. [Harkey L.]
Harkey Lambeth LLP, (AV) ... 1043 East Morehead Street
Harmon, Louise F. ... '71 '96 C.160 B.A. L.896 J.D. [Horack,T.P.&L.]
Harmon, R. Douglas, (AV) ... '58 '83 C.861 B.A. L.228 J.D. [Parker,P.A.&B.]
Harper, Jack L. ... '56 '98 C&L.574 B.S., J.D. 17211 Belllhaven Walk Ct.
Harper, Jane V. ... '40 '80 C.790 B.A. L.575 J.D. Dist. J.

Harrell, J. Hayden, (AV) .... '— '85 C&L.896 B.A., J.D. [Nexsen P.A.K.]
Harrington, James M. .... '75 '01 C.45 B.A. L.276 J.D. [J.M.Harrington]
Harrington, Robert E., (AVⓉ) .... '— '89 C&L.228 A.B., J.D. [Robinson,B.&H.]

Harrington, James M., P.A.
P.O. Box 481095, 28269
Telephone: 704-625-0282 Fax: 704-625-0284
Email: jim@jimharrington.net URL: http://www.lawyers.com/jimharrington
James M. Harrington.
Patent Law, Patent Applications, Patent Litigation, Patent Licensing, Trademark Registration, Trademark Litigation, Copyright Litigation, Intellectual Property, Internet Law, E-Commerce, Licensing Agreements, Domain Name Disputes, Trade Secrets, Slander, Libel, Defamation, and Invasion of Privacy.
See Professional Biographies, CHARLOTTE, NORTH CAROLINA

Harris, C. Marcus, (AV) .... '43 '72 C&L.228 A.B., J.D. [Poyner&S.]
Harris, Charles J. .... '76 '02 C.577 B.A. L.893 J.D. [Ⓐ Moore&V.P.]
Harris, Fred Damon ...... '45 '73 C.339 B.S. L.146 J.D. Pres., F.D. Harris Consulting, Inc.
Harris, H. Stanley, Jr., (BV) .... '57 '83 C.280 A.B. L.838 J.D. [H.S.Harris]
Harris, J. Shannon .... '75 '00 C.577 B.A. L.472 J.D. [Cranfill,S.&H.]
Harris, Janna D. .... '50 '87 C.925 B.S. L.940 J.D. Soc. Sec. Admn.
Harris, Julie E., (BV) '58 '90 C.59 B.A. L.802 J.D.
Assoc. Gen. Coun., Cameron M. Harris & Co.
Harris, Kenneth R., Jr. .... '72 '02 C&L.228 B.A., J.D. [Ⓐ Parker,P.A.&B.]
Harris, Ralph C., Jr., (BV) .... '44 '69 C&L.575 B.S., J.D. [Parham,H.H.B.&M.]
Harris, William N., (AV) .... '— '89 C&L.575 B.A., J.D. [Kennedy C.L.&H.]
Harris, H. Stanley, (BV) .... 130-A N. McDowell St.
Hart, Hollie H. .... '72 '97 C.893 B.A. L.228 J.D. [Moore&V.P.]
Hart, Jeffrey C. .... '— '97 C.198 B.A. L.228 J.D. [Robinson,B.&H.]
Hartley, Tia G. .... '73 '00 C.471 B.A. L.1187 J.D. [Ⓐ Browne,F.W.&W.]
Hartman, Fred W. '73 '99 C.645 B.A. L.1541 J.D.
(adm. in PA; not adm. in NC) [Ⓐ Mayer,B.R.&M.]
Hartman, Miriam L. .... '63 '91 C.771 B.A. L.1040 J.D. P.O. Box 480231
Harvell, Charlena Alise .... '74 '00 C.125 B.A. L.201 J.D. Pub. Def. Off.
Haselkorn, Zev '61 '88 C.1044 B.A. L.107 J.D.
In-house Counsel, Rehab Solutions of America
Hassan, James S. .... '68 '94 C&L.880 B.A., J.D. [Ⓒ Cadwalader,W.&T.]
Hasty, John H., (AV) .... '35 '60 C&L.896 B.A., LL.B. [Ⓒ Guthrie,D.H.&S.]
Hatcher, J. Gregory, (BV) .... '68 '93 C.880 B.A. L.896 J.D. [Gilpin&H.]
Hatcher, Julia Kate Harris .... '70 '95 C.893 B.A. L.896 J.D. [Ⓒ Helms M.&W.]
Hattendorf, Richard L. .... '— '75 C.347 B.A. L.146 J.D. 3508 F Colony Rd.
Hattenhauer, Paul M., (AV) .... '66 '91 C.723 B.S. L.494 J.D. [Culp E.&C.]
Hausler, Kurt F., (BV) .... '64 '95 C.575 B.S.B.A. L.1228 J.D. [Jackson,P.]
Haver, Dennis T. '51 '77 C.1350 B.A. L.724 J.D.
Dep. Gen. Coun., Royal & SunAlliance
Hawfield, W. B., Jr., (AV) .... '47 '72 C.575 A.B. L.813 J.D. [Moore&V.P.]
Hawley, Michael S., (AV) .... '— '80 C&L.260 B.S.B.A., J.D. [Kennedy C.L.&H.]
Hay, Dana Handy .... '63 '92 C.575 B.A. L.893 J.D. P.O. Box 1017
Hay, Jeffrey S., (BV) .... '60 '83 C.247 B.A. L.790 J.D. [Womble C.S.&R.]
Hayden, J. Patrick .... '— '95 C.575 B.A. L.178 J.D. [Kennedy C.L.&H.]
Hayes, Joeie .... '78 '02 C.999 B.S. L.201 J.D. [Tippens&Z.]
Hayles, Bryan A. .... '77 '05 C.576 B.S. L.896 J.D. [Ⓐ Poyner&S.]
Haynes, A. Myles, (AV) .... '27 '52 C.575 A.B. L.273 J.D. 3900 Stoney Ridge Trail
Haynes, Alton M., Jr. .... '27 '52 C.577 B.A. L.273 J.D. 1508 E. 4th St.

Haynsworth Baldwin Johnson & Greaves LLC
(See Ogletree, Deakins, Nash, Smoak & Stewart, P.C.)

Hazlehurst, John L., (BV) .... '56 '80 C.575 B.A. L.976 J.D. [Ⓒ Parham,H.H.B.&M.]
Hazlett, J. Richard, (AV) .... '55 '80 C.896 B.A. L.575 J.D. [Helms M.&W.]
Hearn, Michael D., (AV) .... '— '76 C&L.575 B.S.B.A., J.D. Bank of America

Heasley, C. Wayne, (CV) '— '83 C.829 B.S. L.900 J.D.
Merchandise Mart Office Building, 800 Briar Creek Road, Suite DD-518, 28205
Telephone: 704-338-1322 Fax: 704-338-1338
URL: http://www.cwayneleasleylaw.com
Family Law, Divorce, Alimony, Equitable Distribution, Expungements, Child Support, Child Custody, Visitation Rights, Criminal, Driving While Intoxicated (DWI), Traffic Violations.
See Professional Biographies, CHARLOTTE, NORTH CAROLINA

Heath, Jennifer R., (BV) '— '87
C.228 A.B. L.245 J.D. Asst. Gen. Coun., Bank of America
Hebert, Michael P. .... '76 '02 C.588 B.A. L.896 J.D. [Ⓐ Moore&V.P.]
Hebner, David A. '58 '84 C.401 B.A. L.273 J.D.
(adm. in DC; not adm. in NC) V.P. & Asst. Gen. Coun., First Union Corporation
Hedrick, James T., Jr. .... '— '94 C.575 A.B. L.228 J.D. [Kennedy C.L.&H.]
Hedrick, Patricia P. .... '61 '86 C&L.575 B.A. [Hedrick,P.P.]

Hedrick Eatman Gardner & Kincheloe, L.L.P., (AV)
6000 Fairview Road, Suite 1000, 28210 ⊙
Mailing Address: P.O. Box 30397, Charlotte, NC 28230
Telephone: 704-366-1101 Fax: 704-366-6181
URL: http://www.hedrickeatman.com
Partners: Philip R. Hedrick (1919-1999); Edward L. Eatman, Jr.; John A. Gardner, III; Hatcher B. Kincheloe; Mel J. Garofalo; Thomas W. Page; L. Kristin King; Paul C. Lawrence; Allen C. Smith; Jeffrey A. Doyle (Resident, Raleigh Office); Jeffrey A. Kadis; Jennifer I. Mitchell; Erica B. Lewis (Resident, Wilmington Office); Jeffrey H. Blackwell (Resident, Wilmington Office); Shelley W. Coleman; Thomas M. Morrow (Resident, Raleigh Office); Donald J. Vicini; Neil P. Andrews; Edwin P. Martin, Jr. (Resident, Columbia, South Carolina Office); R. Daniel Addison (Resident, Columbia, South Carolina Office). Of Counsel: Mark A. Michael (Certified as a Civil Trial Advocacy Specialist by the National Board of Trial Advocacy). Associates: Elizabeth A. Martineau; Jessica C. Smythe (Resident, Raleigh Office); Melissa L. McDonald; Kimberly P. Reaves; Sharon E. Dent; C. J. Childers; Erin Dancy Eveson (Resident, Raleigh Office); Matthew D. Glidewell; Jennifer S. Jerzak (Resident, Raleigh Office); Shannon Metcalf; Harmony Whalen Taylor; Hope Fisher Smelcer; W. James Flynn; Heidi L. Maske; Tracie H. Brisson (Resident, Wilmington Office); Tonya D. Davis (Resident, Raleigh Office); Jennifer Vega Ruiz (Resident, Raleigh Office); Michael Duane Jones; Jeremy T. Canipe; Heather Teale Twiddy; Michelle V. Crawford; Andrew S. Culicerto; Barry C. Jennings (Resident, Raleigh Office); Joel K. Turner; Adam E. Whitten; Meredith T. Everhart (Resident, Wilmington Office); Bettina Mumme (Resident, Raleigh Office); Luke Sbarra; Dalton G. Blair; Ryan W. Keevan; Samuel E. Barker; Taurus E. Becton; Brendan G. Dillashaw; William B. Dulaney (Resident, Wilmington Office); Erika D. Taylor (Resident, Raleigh Office); J. Douglas Grimes; Edward A. Sweeney; Vachelle D. Willis; Benton L. Toups (Resident, Wilmington Office); Stacy M. Race (Resident, Raleigh Office); Jennifer S. Anderson; Leah L. Rudd; Jennifer P. Pulley; M. Kathleen Short; Deepa Tungare; J. Philip Murphy (Resident, Columbia, South Carolina Office); Dana C. Moody (Resident, Raleigh Office); Keri A. Rose (Resident, Columbia, South Carolina Office); Susan J. VanDerweert (Resident, Raleigh Office); Joseph S. Murray IV; Marc A. Metcalf; Megan V. Johnson.
General Civil Litigation and Insurance Defense, Legal and Professional Malpractice, Motor Vehicle Negligence, Premises Liability, Product Liability, Construction, Insurance Coverage Disputes, Arson and Fraud, Employment Law, Trucking and Transportation and Worker's Compensation.
Representative Clients: Ace-USA; Carolinas Healthcare Systems; Chubb Group; Continental Tire; Liberty Mutual; Medical Mutual Insurance; PMA Group; St. Paul Travelers Insurance Co.; United Parcel Service; USAA; Wal-Mart Corp.
Raleigh, North Carolina Office: 4011 Westchase Boulevard, Suite 300, 27607. Telephone: 919-832-9424. Fax: 919-832-9425.
Wilmington, North Carolina Office: 1508 Military Cutoff Road, Suite 202, 28403. Telephone: 910-509-9664. Fax: 910-509-9630.

(This Listing Continued)

Hedrick Eatman Gardner & Kincheloe, L.L.P. (Continued)
Columbia, South Carolina Office: 1201 Main Street, Suite 1200, 29201. Mailing Address: P.O. Box 11267, 29211. Telephone: 803-727-1200. Fax: 803-727-1259.
See Professional Biographies, CHARLOTTE, NORTH CAROLINA

Hedrick, Pat Padgett .... 3414 Foxcroft Rd.
Hefferon, Paul, (BV) .... '54 '83 C.1128 B.A. L.575 J.D. [Hefferon&H.]
Hefferon, Thomas J., (AV) .... '52 '81 C&L.575 B.A., J.D. [Hefferon&H.]

Hefferon & Hefferon, (AV) BR
Cameron Brown Building, 301 South McDowell Street, Suite 130, 28204
Telephone: 704-376-3700 888-200-7977 Fax: 704-376-6090 URL: http://www.hefferonlaw.com
Email: firm@hefferonlaw.com URL: http://www.hefferonandhefferon.com
Thomas J. Hefferon; Paul Hefferon.
Catastrophic Injury, Wrongful Death, Products Liability, Inadequate Security, Insurance Claims, Business Torts, Truck Accidents, Medical Malpractice, Legal Malpractice, Construction Accidents, Automobile Accidents, Nursing Home Negligence, Commercial Litigation.
See Professional Biographies, CHARLOTTE, NORTH CAROLINA

Hegg, Phillip W. .... '47 '81 C.941 B.A. L.678 J.D. 301 S. McDowell St.
Heiden, Nicole L. .... '75 '01 C.140 B.A. L.192 J.D. [Ⓐ Gilpin&H.]
Heim, Barbara E., (BV) .... '66 '91 C.699 B.A. L.880 J.D. Sunbelt Rentals, Inc.
Heiser, Kevin J. .... '72 '98 C.1369 B.S. L.790 J.D. [Ⓐ Nelson M.R.&S.]
Helfing, Kenneth I., Law Offices of '68 '99
C.999 B.A. L.1370 J.D. 205 Regency Executive Park Drive
Helms, H. Parks, (AV) .... '35 '61 C&L.575 B.A., J.D. [Helms,H.&Assoc.]
Helms, Jeffrey L., (BV) .... '67 '93 C.576 B.S. L.575 J.D. [Caudle&S.]
Helms, Neal G., (BV) .... '34 '63 C&L.575 LL.B. [Parham,H.H.B.&M.]

Helms, Henderson & Associates, P.A., (AV)
Suite 340, Morehead Place, 521 East Morehead Street, 28202
Telephone: 704-372-4884 Fax: 704-332-0585
Email: nreid@helmshenderson.com URL: http://www.lawyers.com/helmshenderson
H. Parks Helms; David L. Henderson;—Charles J. Henderson (1920-1999).
General, Civil and Criminal Trial Practice in State and Federal Courts and Agencies, Corporation, Real Estate, Probate, Insurance, Bankruptcy, Commercial, Personal Injury, Collections and Tax.
See Professional Biographies, CHARLOTTE, NORTH CAROLINA

Helms Mulliss & Wicker, PLLC, (AV) BR
201 North Tryon Street, P.O. Box 31247 (28231), 28202 ⊙
Telephone: 704-343-2000 Fax: 704-343-2300. Telex: 572460
URL: http://www.hmw.com
William F. Mulliss (1911-1987); Fred B. Helms (1896-1998). Members of Firm: Stephen David Allred; Corby Cochran Anderson; Brian D. Barger; Irving M. Brenner; Jonathan E. Buchan, Jr.; C. Todd Burbank; Boyd C. Campbell, Jr.; Rebecca S. Chaffin; John H. Cobb; Stephen L. Cordell; Peter J. Covington; Robert W. Cramer; James H. Culbreth, Jr.; Kathleen H. Dooley; Douglas W. Ey, Jr.; Elizabeth Whitener Goode; James H. Guterman; J. Richard Hazlett; Benne C. Hutson; Bradley R. Kutrow; Harrison L. Marshall, Jr.; William C. Mayberry; John G. McDonald; E. Graham McGoogan, Jr. (Board Certified Specialist in Estate Planning and Probate Law, North Carolina State Board of Legal Specialization); James G. Middlebrooks; Robert A. Muckenfuss; Christopher S. M. Nesbit; Kathy L. Pilkington; William F. Potts, Jr.; Robert H. Pryor; Manley W. Roberts; P. Christian Scheurer; L. D. Simmons, II; Robert W. Simmons; William DeVane Tidwell; Scott P. Vaughn; Richard W. Viola; H. Landis Wade, Jr.; W. Kent Walker; John B. Yorke. Of Counsel: E. Osborne Ayscue, Jr.; Herbert H. Browne, Jr. (Board Certified Specialist in Estate Planning and Probate Law, North Carolina State Board of Legal Specialization); Larry J. Dagenhart; Ann Terrell Dorsett; Julia Kate Harris Hatcher; Anne Team Kelly; R. Malloy McKeithen; Thomas W. Murrell, III; Catherine E. Thompson. Associates: A. Carter Arey; R. Christian Brose (Not admitted in NC); Jack William Campbell IV; David M. Chromy; Elizabeth Chase Coale; Richard Horace Conner, III; Jason Doughton Evans; Stephanie K. Briggs Evans; Sheldon M. Francis; Grant D. Goldenberg; Jill Crawley Griset; Matthew Hoefling; James S. Humphrey; Mark Weston Johnson; J. Trevor Johnston; Brian A. Kahn; Melissa M. Kidd; Gregory R. Kilpatrick; Mark W. Kinghorn; C. Andrew Konia; Kevin Landmesser; Amy Rickner Langdon; Tony Lauro; Jennifer Rouse Leahy; Marcus S. Lee; Julianna P. Lowe; Ingrid McClintock; Kevin A. McGinnis; Robynn E. Moraites; Paul M. Navarro; Lowndes C. Quinlan; Amanda K. Short; Tracy E. Strickland; Benjamin R. Thomas; Clay B. Tousey III; Mayleng F. Watson; Mary Lindsay Weatherly; Danielle E. Webb; Brett G. Weber; H. Ramsey White III; Amy R. Worley.
Banking, Finance, Corporate, Government Relations, Business Litigation, Tax, Securities, Real Property and Finance, Labor and Employment (Management) Law, Employee Benefits, International, Technology, Insurance Coverage, Media, Commercial Bankruptcy, Environmental, Public Finance, ERISA, Estate Planning and Administration, Education, Venture Capital, Intellectual Property.
Raleigh, North Carolina Office: 2600 Two Hannover Square (27601), P.O. Box 27507 (27611). Telephone: 919-755-6600. Fax: 919-755-6699.
Wilmington, North Carolina Office: 127 Grace Street (28401), P.O. Box 599 (28402). Telephone: 910-254-3800. Fax: 910-254-3900.
See Professional Biographies, CHARLOTTE, NORTH CAROLINA

Helweg, Joseph E., III, (AV) '69 '94
C.197 B.A. L.896 J.D. 200 S. College Street, NC1-014-10-02
Helweg, Sally G., (BV) .... '67 '93 C.575 B.A. L.896 J.D. 1427 Baltimore Dr.
Hemric, Gary S., (AV) .... '48 '74 C.198 B.A. L.575 J.D. [James,M.&D.]
Henderson, Darryl K. '60 '86 C.1365 B.A. L.280 J.D.
(adm. in GA; not adm. in NC) 8337 Beardsley Dr.
Henderson, David H., (AV) .... '14 '37 C&L.228 B.A., J.D. 5100 Sharon Rd.‡
Henderson, David L., (AV) .... '50 '77 C.576 B.A. L.192 J.D. [Helms,H.&Assoc.]
Henderson, Gary L. .... '70 '99 C.34 B.A. L.574 J.D. P.O. Box 26584
Henderson, James H., (BV) .... '61 '86 C.228 A.B. L.896 J.D. [J.H.Henderson]
Henderson, Rebecca Sofley, (AV) '57 '85
C.34 B.S. L.575 J.D. Dep. Gen. Coun., Wachovia Corp.
Henderson, Robert E., (AV) .... '54 '79 C&L.228 B.A., J.D. [Guthrie,D.H.&S.]
Henderson, James H., P.C., (BV) .... 1201 Harding Place
Hennessey, Edward F., IV, (AV) .... '— '88 C.197 A.B. L.188 J.D. [Robinson,B.&H.]
Henninger, Joseph B., Jr., (BV) ..... '50 '79 C.575 B.A. L.1358 J.D. [Wishart,N.H.&P.]
Henriques, Mark P., (AV) .... '64 '92 C&L.893 B.A., J.D. [Womble C.S.&R.]
Henry, Mark O. .... '— '00 C.608 B.S.B.A. L.575 J.D. [Ⓐ Robinson,B.&H.]
Henson, Jeffrey A. .... '— '92 C.871 B.S. L.228 J.D. [Robinson,B.&H.]

Henson, Thomas B., (AV) '55 '80 C.880 B.A. L.902 J.D.
6100 Fairview Road, Suite 650, 28210
Telephone: 704-643-4148 Fax: 704-643-4482
Email: tom.henson@mailsouth.net URL: http://www.lawyers.com/thomasbhenson
Mergers and Acquisitions, Corporate Law, Executive Compensation.
See Professional Biographies, CHARLOTTE, NORTH CAROLINA

Herald, Alice A. .... '— '76 Dep. Gen. Coun., Global Commercial Banking
Herbert, W.C. Turner .... '76 '04 C.198 B.A. L.577 J.D. [Ⓐ Mayer,B.R.&M.]
Hernandez, Cesar E. '64 '87 L.904 LL.M.
(adm. in GA; not adm. in NC) Coun., Fluor Corp.
Herring, John M., (BV) .... '— '94 C&L.575 B.S., J.D. [Robinson,B.&H.]
Heslin, Brian S. .... '70 '97 C.800 B.A. L.1356 J.D. [Ⓐ Moore&V.P.]
Hess, Catherine L. .... '73 '00 C.1128 B.S.W. L.124 J.D. [Ⓐ Alston&B.]
Hester, Ann L. .... '68 '92 C.576 B.A. L.575 J.D. 1714 Redcoat Dr.
Hewitt, Lawrence W., (AV) .... '44 '69 C&L.896 B.A., J.D. [James,M.&D.]
Hey, Peggy Howard .... '70 '96 C.540 B.A. L.823 J.D. [Poyner&S.]
Hickman, Marcus T., (AV) .... '— '48 C&L.228 A.B., LL.B. [Kennedy C.L.&H.] ‡
Hickmon, James Edward .... '— '01 C.953 B.S.B.A. L.896 J.D. [Ⓐ McGuireWoods]
Hicks, Christopher A. .... '69 '99 C.575 B.A. L.896 J.D. [Ⓐ Katten M.R.]
Hicks, Eugene C., III, (BV) .... '32 '55 C&L.575 B.S., J.D. 725 E. Trade

Hicks, Fred A., (AV) '42 '68 C&L.575 A.B., J.D. [Katten M.R.]
Hicks, Josephine H., (AV) '61 '86 C.797 B.A. L.880 J.D. [Parker,P.A.&B.]
Hicks, R. Thomas '61 '85 C.228 A.B. L.575 J.D. [Byrne,D.&H.] ⊙
Higdon, Robert J., Jr. '63 '89 C&L.896 B.A., J.D. Asst. U.S. Atty.
Higgins, David R. '— '04 C.576 B.S. L.896 J.D. [🄰 Kennedy C.L.&H.]
Higgins, Sara W., (BV) '— '95 C.228 A.B. L.575 J.D. [Kennedy C.L.&H.]
Higgins, T. David, Jr. '59 '87 C&L.923 B.S., J.D. [Cozen O.]
Higley, Janet J. '72 '01 C.893 B.S. L.896 J.D. [🄰 Parks,C.&W.]
Hill, Donald M., Jr. '59 '95 C.679 B.S. L.150 J.D. [Alston&B.] (See Pat. Sect.)
Hill, Henderson, (BV) '56 '81 C.1160 B.A. L.309 J.D. [Ferguson,S.C.G.&S.]
Hinds, R. Gates '— '02 C.228 B.A. L.16 J.D. [🄰 Kennedy C.L.&H.]
Hines, Jonathan M. '72 '98 C.576 B.S.M.E. L.150 J.D. [🄰 Adams E.] (See Pat. Sect.)
Hingst, Marcy Conte '73 '00 C.860 B.A. L.608 J.D.
Asst. Gen. Coun., Bank of America Corp., Litig.
Hinshaw, Garl Edward (Eddie), Jr., (AV) '55 '83
C.34 B.S.B.A. L.896 J.D. [Sellers,H.A.D.&L.]
Hinson, Bobby D., (AV) '62 '87 C.228 A.B. L.893 J.D. [Womble C.S.&R.]
Hinson, Edward T., Jr., (AV) '52 '77 C.968 B.A. L.228 J.D. [James,M.&D.]
Hinson, Robin L., (AV) '— '58 C.198 B.S. L.575 J.D. [Robinson,B.&H.]
Hirata, William L., (BVⓉ) '57 '86 C.674 A.B. L.790 J.D.
[Parker,P.A.&B.] (⊙Columbia, Spartanburg, SC)
Hixson, William R. '74 '03 C.999 B.A. L.879 J.D. 10016 Janiero Dr.
Hobson, William Patrick, (BV) '41 '71 C&L.575 A.B., J.D. [🄴 Dozier,M.P.&M.]
Hockfield, Steven A., (AV) '45 '70 C&L.575 B.S., J.D. [Erdman&H.]
Hockman, Brian Randall '66 '92 C.896 B.A. L.884 J.D. [🄰 M.J.Bednarik]

Hodge, John E., Jr., (BV) '44 '72 C&L.575 B.S., J.D.
6725-D Fairview Road, 28210
Telephone: 704-442-9422 Telecopier: 704-442-1033
Email: hodgelaw@jehodgelaw.com URL: http://www.lawyers.com/johnehodgelaw
General and Civil Trial, Civil Appeals, Commercial Litigation, Contracts, Collection, Business Litigation, Insurance Litigation, Complex Litigation, Real Estate Litigation, Construction Defects, Unfair Trade Practice, Fraud.
See Professional Biographies, CHARLOTTE, NORTH CAROLINA

Hodges, Elizabeth T., (AV) '54 '79 C&L.575 A.B., J.D. [Horack,T.P.&L.]
Hodges, George R. '46 '73 C.893 B.S. L.575 J.D. U.S. Bkrptcy. J.
Hoefling, Matthew '74 '00 C&L.602 B.A., J.D. [🄰 Helms M.&W.]
Hofer, Ronald L., (AVⓉ) '44 '72
C.309 A.B. L.352 J.D. [Dougherty,C.H.&B.] (See Pat. Sect.)
Hofer, Susan L. '52 '88 C.128 B.A. L.446 J.D. [Dean&G.]
Hoffman, Carol Ann '54 '80 C.473 B.S. L.607 J.D.
(adm. in OH; not adm. in NC) Wachovia Bank
Hogewood, Ashley L., Jr., (AV) '40 '63 C&L.896 B.A., J.D. [Parker,P.A.&B.]
Hohnbaum, Cory, (AV) '— '90 C.1120 B.A. L.880 J.D. [Kennedy C.L.&H.]
Holcomb, Rick J. '58 '87 C.1267 B.A. L.1059 J.D.
(adm. in GA; not adm. in NC) Sr. Coun., Continental Tire North America, Inc.
Holden, C. Byron, (AV) '50 '75 C.976 B.A. L.896 J.D. [Golding H.&P.]
Holderness, Sara S. '65 '90 C&L.575 B.S., J.D. City Atty.'s Off.
Holderness, Thomas P., (BV) '— '90 C&L.575 B.S., J.D. [Robinson,B.&H.]
Holding, Graham D., Jr., (AV) '— '64 C.575 A.B. L.893 LL.B. [Robinson,B.&H.]
Holladay, Durand A. '25 '49 C.277 B.S. L.472 J.D.
(adm. in FL; not adm. in NC) 4312 Cameron Oaks Dr.‡
Holland, Benjamin R. '— '02 C.385 B.A. L.124 J.D. [🄰 Ogletree,D.N.S.&S.]
Holland, J. Eric '79 '04 C.273 B.A. L.880 J.D. [🄰 Cadwalader,W.&T.]
Holland, Michael Wade '71 '98 C.63 B.S. L.879 J.D.
(adm. in TN; not adm. in NC) Dir. of Bus. & Legal Affairs, Jeff Gordon, Inc.
Holliday, Katherine S., (AV) '48 '80 C.896 B.A. L.228 J.D. [James,M.&D.]
Hollnagel, Daryl L., (BVⓉ) '54 '80 C.27 B.A. L.8 J.D.
(adm. in OH; not adm. in NC) V.P. & Secy., Continental Tire North America, Inc.
Holloman, Connelia Z. '70 '96 C.198 B.A. L.861 J.D. Assoc. Co. Atty.
Hollowell, Thomas P. '43 '68 C&L.945 A.B., J.D.
(adm. in IA; not adm. in NC) Mng. Dir., Bowles, Hollowell, Conner & Co.
Holmes, Bret P., (AV) '70 '94 C.259 B.S. L.575 J.D. 301 S. College St.
Holmes, Harold D. "Chip", Jr., (BV) '68 '93 C.575 B.A. L.896 J.D. [Parker,P.A.&B.]
Holmquist, Michael G. '— '95 C.473 B.S. L.930 J.D.
(adm. in PA; not adm. in NC) Assoc. Gen Coun., Bank of America
Holofchak, Brian D. '— '02 C.577 B.A. L.499 J.D. [🄰 Kennedy C.L.&H.]
Holsenbeck, Mary Elizabeth '80 '05 C&L.575 B.A., J.D. [🄰 Parker,P.A.&B.]
Holt, C. Corley '— '90 C.228 B.S. L.976 J.D. [Kennedy C.L.&H.]
Homan, Matthew B. '72 '01 C.893 B.A L.896 J.D. [🄰 Womble C.S.&R.]
Honeycutt, James Michael '64 '01 C.577 B.A. L.213 J.D. [🄰 Fisher&P.]
Honeycutt, John B., Jr., (AV) '50 '78 C.999 B.A. L.425 J.D. [Smith D.N.W.S.&M.]
Honnold, Bradley B. '61 '95 C.158 B.S. L.823 J.D. [Honnold]

Honnold Law Firm, The, P.A.
6000 Fairview Road, Suite 1200, 28210
Telephone: 704-552-3707
Email: bhonnold@honnoldlaw.com
Bradley B. Honnold.
Family Law, Domestic Relations, Civil Litigation, Separation Agreements, Divorce, Child Custody, Child Support, Alimony, Post Separation Support, Property Division, Domestic Violence, Premarital Agreements.
See Professional Biographies, CHARLOTTE, NORTH CAROLINA

Hood, James R., Jr., (BV) '61 '86 C&L.896 B.A., J.D. [J.R.Hood,Jr.]
Hood, Roscoe C., Jr. '52 '91 C&L.575 A.B., J.D. 1912 Lombardy Cir.
Hood, James R., Jr., PC, (BV) 508 East Boulevard
Hooper, Thomas G. '72 '98 C.198 A.B. L.575 J.D. [🄰 Nelson M.R.&S.]
Hooper, Todd James '68 '93 C.896 B.S. L.945 J.D. First Union Corp.
Hoover, Donnie, (BV) '49 '74 C.575 B.A. L.574 J.D. [Hoover&W.]
Hoover & Williams, P.A., (BV) 301 S. McDowell St.
Hope, Stephen D., (AV) '47 '74 C.575 A.B. L.178 J.D. [Moore&V.P.]
Horack, Benj. S., (AV) '17 '41 C&L.228 A.B., LL.B. [Horack,T.P.&L.] ‡

Horack, Talley, Pharr & Lowndes, A Professional Association, (AV)
2600 One Wachovia Center, 301 South College Street, 28202-6038 ⊙
Telephone: 704-377-2500 Fax: 704-372-2619
URL: http://www.horacktalley.com
Paul R. Ervin (1908-1970); Ray W. Bradley, Jr. (1922-2000); James M. Talley, Jr.; Henry N. Pharr, II; William S. Lowndes (Retired); Thomas R. Cannon (Board Certified Specialist in Family Law, North Carolina State Bar, Board of Legal Specialization); Neil C. Williams; Paul H. Efird, III; G. Robert Turner, III; Clayton S. Curry, Jr.; Tate K. Sterrett (Board Certified Specialist in Family Law, North Carolina State Board of Legal Specialization); Susan Christman; Stephen L. Smith; Elizabeth T. Hodges (Board Certified Specialist in Family Law, North Carolina State Bar, Board of Legal Specialization); H. David Powell; Robert B. McNeill; Cheryl D. Steele; Michael S. Hunter; Henry N. Pharr, III; Gena Graham Morris (Board Certified Specialist in Family Law, North Carolina State Board of Legal Specialization); Kristin Decker Ogburn; William B. Hamel, Sr.; Robert S. Blair, Jr. (Board Certified Specialist in Family Law, North Carolina State Board of Legal Specialization); Zipporah Marie Basile Edwards; D. Christopher Osborn; Louise F. Harmon; John W. Bowers; Kathryn Mitchell Kelling (Board Certified Specialist in Family Law, North Carolina State Board of

(This Listing Continued)

Horack, Talley, Pharr & Lowndes, A Professional Association (Continued)
Legal Specialization); Kary C. Watson; Robyn M. Saye; Jonathan Charles Windham; Collin W. Brown; Katherine M. LeBar; Phillip E. Lewis (Also at Hedgemore Drive Office); David L. Edwards; Heather E. Lewis; Amy E. Butterworth; John T. Maheras. Of Counsel: Russell J. Schwartz. Retired: Benj. S. Horack (Retired); Paul B. Guthery, Jr. (Retired).
General Trial and Appellate Practice in all State and Federal Courts, Family Law, Business and Corporate Law for Small and Closely Held Businesses, Taxation, Securities, Commercial and Residential Real Estate Development, Administrative Law, Creditors Rights and Bankruptcy, Real Estate Title Disputes, Homebuilders, Personal and Business Asset Preservation, Estate Administration, Governments and Municipalities, Employer's Rights, Construction Litigation.
Representative Clients: Wachovia Bank; Queens College.
Reference: Wachovia Bank.
Other Charlotte, North Carolina Office: 4701 Hedgemore Drive, Suite 812, 28209. Telephone: 704-522-1575. Fax: 704-522-1736.
See Professional Biographies, CHARLOTTE, NORTH CAROLINA

Horack, Talley, Pharr & Lowndes, A Professional Association, (AV)
4701 Hedgemore Drive Suite 812 (⊙Charlotte)
Hord, James C. '43 '75 C.232 A.B. L.838 J.D. 5501 Exec. Ctr. Dr.
Hord, Joy M., (BV) '70 '95 C.198 A.B. L.880 J.D. [Parker,P.A.&B.]
Hord, Robert C., Jr., (AV) '40 '65 C.198 A.B. L.575 LL.B. [Johnston,A.&H.]
Horn, Carl, III '51 '76 C.893 B.A. L.790 J.D. Chief U.S. Mag. J.
Horn, Mark R. A. '71 '97 C.575 B.A. L.893 J.D. [Moore&V.P.]
Horne, Terry D., (AV) '59 '85 C.575 B.A. L.896 J.D. [Stiles B.&H.]
Horner, Adam L. '78 '04 C.575 B.A. L.1228 J.D. [🄰 James,M.&D.]
Horoschak, Mark J., (BV) '51 '77 C.30 B.A. L.945 J.D. [Womble C.S.&R.]
Horowitz, Steve C., (AV) '40 '65 C&L.260 B.S.B.A., J.D. [Wishart,N.H.&P.]
Horton, Rebecca J. '73 '99 C.269 B.A. L.790 J.D. [🄰 Katten M.R.]
Hosmer, Patricia F. '69 '94 C.575 B.A. L.976 J.D. [McGuireWoods]
Hovis, James W., (AV) '54 '80 C&L.575 B.S., J.D. [Moore&V.P.]
Howard, Amy R., (BV) '70 '95 C.645 B.A. L.1048 J.D. 821 East Blvd.
Howard, Deborah J. '— '86 C.143 B.S. L.150 J.D.
(adm. in OH; not adm. in NC) Asst. Gen. Coun., Bank of America
Howard, Joshua B. '74 '99 C.228 A.B. L.575 J.D. Asst. U.S. Atty.
Howle, Jeffrey A. '— '97 C.575 B.A. L.259 J.D. [Cranfill,S.&H.]
Hubbard, Angela R. '64 '90 C.811 B.A. L.280 J.D.
(adm. in GA; not adm. in NC) Nations Bk. Tr.
Hubbell, L. Caroline '77 '04 C.198 B.A. L.93 J.D. [🄰 Moore&V.P.]
Huckabee, Sherry L. '66 '93 C.846 B.A. L.472 J.D. 1517 Ideal Way
Huckel, Wayne P., (AV) '— '72 C.198 B.A. L.569 J.D. [Kennedy C.L.&H.]
Hudson, Seth L. '75 '02 C.576 B.S. L.692 J.D. [🄰 Adams E.] (See Pat. Sect.)
Huff, Jason P. '68 '99 C.945 B.A. L.896 J.D. [🄰 Moore&V.P.]
Huffenus, Daniel S. '— '94 C.390 A.B. L.569 J.D. [Katten M.R.]
Huffstetler, Seth '77 '03 C&L.228 B.A., J.D. [🄰 Womble C.S.&R.]
Huffstutler, John Haven '— '76 C.674 A.B. L.1026 J.D.
(adm. in CA; not adm. in NC) Assoc. Gen. Coun., Bank of America
Hughes, Kelly S. '— '03 C.880 B.M. L.472 J.D. [🄰 Ogletree,D.N.S.&S.]
Hughes, N. Renee '69 '02 C.896 B.S. L.574 J.D. [🄰 Moore&V.P.]
Hull, Nathan M., (AV) '73 '99 C.210 B.A. L.896 J.D. [Hull&C.]
Hull, Robert H., Jr., (AV) '— '80 C.1128 B.A. L.896 J.D. [Nexsen P.A.K.]

Hull & Chandler, P.A., (AV)
521 East Morehead Street, Suite 101, 28202
Telephone: 704-375-8488 Fax: 704-375-8487 URL: http://www.lawyercarolina.com
Email: nmhull@lawyercarolina.com URL: http://www.nathanhulllaw.com
Shareholders: Nathan M. Hull; R. Michael Chandler. Associate: Christopher S. Shumate.
Language: Spanish.
Business Law, Limited Liability Law Companies, Corporate Law, Partnership Law, Joint Ventures, Licensing Agreements, Mergers and Acquisitions, Contracts, Non Profit and Charitable Organizations, Lawsuits, Commercial Litigation, Transactions, Collections, Franchise Law, Tax Law, Estate Planning, Trusts and Estates, Wills, Probate, Intellectual Property, Patents, Copyrights, Trademarks, Personal Injury, Automobile Accidents, Automobile Insurance, Dog Bites, Construction Accidents and Workers Compensation.
See Professional Biographies, CHARLOTTE, NORTH CAROLINA

Hulse, William F., (BV) '42 '68 C&L.575 B.S., J.D. [Myers&H.]
Humphrey, G. Scott, (AV) '— '89 C.575 B.A. L.896 J.D. [Kilpatrick S.]
Humphrey, James S. '— '04 C.124 B.S. L.575 J.D. [🄰 Helms M.&W.]
Hunt, Michelle C. '— '01 C.813 B.A. L.767 J.D. [🄰 Poyner&S.]
Hunt, Seton Blake '— '99 C.112 B.A. L.1494 J.D. [🄰 Kennedy C.L.&H.]
Hunter, Catherine C., (BV) '54 '86 C.280 B.A.J. L.1228 J.D. [Foodman,H.&K.]
Hunter, Elaine M. '— '90 C.790 B.A. L.734 J.D. Asst. Gen. Coun., Bank of America
Hunter, G. Martin, (AV) '59 '86 C.198 A.B. L.896 J.D. [Shuford,H.&B.]
Hunter, G. Patrick, III, (BV) '60 '87 C.575 B.S. L.1187 J.D. [G.P.Hunter,III]
Hunter, G. Patrick, Jr., (AV) '35 '63 C&L.575 B.S., LL.B. Atty., Sheriff's Dept.
Hunter, Harold R., Jr. '70 '01 C&L.575 B.S., J.D. [Hunter]
Hunter, Jayne C. '— '90 C&L.575 B.A., J.D. [🄰 Robinson,B.&H.]
Hunter, John N. '65 '93 C.228 A.B. L.575 J.D. [🄴 Womble C.S.&R.]
Hunter, Mary Lynn Roberts '54 '89 C.575 B.A. L.838 J.D. Off. of Hearings & App.
Hunter, Michael S., (BV) '62 '87 C.575 B.S. L.896 J.D. [Horack,T.P.&L.]
Hunter, Pamela A. '54 '78 C.1378 B.S. L.574 J.D. 715 East Fifth Street, Suite 106
Hunter, G. Patrick, III, PA, (BV) 290 Meacham St., Ste. 201
Hunter Law Office, PLLC 464 East Way Drive
Hunting, Stephen R., (AV) '59 '84 C&L.575 B.A., J.D. [Parker,P.A.&B.]

Hunton & Williams LLP, (AV)
Bank of America Plaza Suite 3500, 101 South Tryon Street, 28280 ⊙
Telephone: 704-378-4700 Fax: 704-378-4890
URL: http://www.hunton.com
Partners: Haywood A. Barnes; A. Todd Brown; Joseph B. Buonanno (Not admitted in NC); T. Thomas Cottingham, III; Frank E. Emory, Jr.; Andrew A. Gerber; Robert J. Hahn; Michael C. Kerrigan; Wood W. Lay; Nash E. Long, III; Charles R. Monroe, Jr.; Frank J. Murphy, Jr.; Michael Nedzbala. Associates: Marcus L. Anderson; Joseph K. Barnette; Melinda R. Beres; Daniel Josev Brewer; K. Stacie Corbett; Patrick V. Fiel, Jr. (Not admitted in NC); Melanie Fitzgerald; Anthony Foxx; Michael J. Genay; Andrew M. Johnson; Hyun "Jonathan" S. Kim; Stephen D. Leasure; Brent A. Rosser; Wendy L. Spanbauer; Craig W. Walker; K. Cameron Walton; Valerie B. Wright; Jacqueline M. Yount.
General Practice. Administrative/Regulatory Law, Admiralty, Antitrust, Unfair Trade Practices, Bankruptcy, Business, Corporation, Environmental, Insurance, International, Labor, Municipal Bond and Finance Law, Non-Criminal Trials and Appeals, Real Property, Condemnation, Securities Regulation, Taxation, Trademarks, Copyright, Utilities, Probate and Estate Planning.
Washington, D.C. Office: 1900 K Street, N.W., 20006-1109. Telephone: 202-955-1500. Fax: 202-778-2201.
Miami, Florida Office: 1111 Brickell Avenue, Suite 2500, 33131. Telephone: 305-810-2500. Fax: 305-810-2460.
Atlanta, Georgia Office: Bank of America Plaza, 600 Peachtree Street, N.E., Suite 4100, 30308-2216. Telephone: 404-888-4000. Fax: 404-888-4190 and Georgia-Hill Office: Southside Legal Center, 250 Georgia Avenue, S.E., Suite 211, 30312. Telephone: 404-688-5512; 404-688-5513.
New York, New York Office: 200 Park Avenue, 43rd Floor, 10166-0136. Telephone: 212-309-1000. Fax: 212-309-1100.
Raleigh, North Carolina Office: One Bank of America Plaza, 421 Fayetteville Street Mall, Suite 1400, 27601. Telephone: 919-899-3000. Fax: 919-833-6352.
Knoxville, Tennessee Office: 2000 Riverview Tower, 900 South Gay Street, 37902. Telephone: 865-549-7700. Fax: 865-549-7704.

(This Listing Continued)

Hunton & Williams LLP (Continued)

Dallas, Texas Office: Energy Plaza, 30th Floor, 1601 Bryan Street, 75201-3402. Telephone: 214-979-3000. Fax: 214-880-0011.
Richmond, Virginia Office: Riverfront Plaza, East Tower, 951 East Byrd Street, 23219-4074. Telephone: 804-788-8200. Fax: 804-788-8218; 804-788-8219 and Church Hill Office: 2300 East Marshall Street, 23223. Telephone: 804-775-2248.
McLean, Virginia Office: 1751 Pinnacle Drive, Suite 1700, Tysons Corner, 22102. Telephone: 703-714-7400. Fax: 703-714-7410.
Norfolk, Virginia Office: 500 East Main Street, Suite 1000, 23510-3889. Telephone: 757-640-5300. Fax: 757-625-7720.
Brussels, Belgium Office: Ave Louise 326, B6, 1050 Brussels, Belgium. Telephone: +32 0-2-643-5800. Fax: +32 0-2-643-5822.
Bangkok, Thailand Office: 34/F Abdulrahim Place, 990 Rama IV Road, Bangkok, Thailand, 1050. Telephone: +011 662 636-2366. Fax: +011 662 636-2377.
London, England Office: Fleetway House, 25 Farringdon Street, London EC4A 4AB, England. Telephone: +44 (0)20 7246 5700. Fax: +44 (0)20 7246 5772.
Singapore, Singapore Office: 6 Battery Road, #24-01, Singapore, 049909. Telephone: +65 6534-5608. Fax: +65 6534-5532.
Beijing, China Office: 517-520 South Office Tower, Beijing Kerry Centre, No. 1 Guanghua Road, Chaoyang District, Beijing, PRC 100020, China. Telephone: +86 10 5863 7500. Fax: +86 10 5863 7591.

See Professional Biographies, CHARLOTTE, NORTH CAROLINA

Hurst, Gerald P. '— '79 C.383 B.S. L.128 J.D. (adm. in DC; not adm. in NC) Mgr., Bank of America
Huske, I. Manning, (BV) .... '42 '73 C.575 A.B. L.896 J.D. [M.Huske]
Huske, Manning, (BV) .... 1500 E. 4th St.
Hutchinson, William O. .... '— '04 C&L.902 B.S., J.D. [Ⓐ Kennedy C.L.&H.]
Hutson, Benne C., (AV) .... '57 '82 C.317 B.A. L.309 J.D. [Helms M.&W.]
Hutson, L. A., Jr. .... '23 '49 C&L.790 A.B., LL.B. 3336 Ferncliff Rd.‡
Hutson, Mary Lou '62 '87 C.1064 B.A. L.880 J.D. (adm. in TN; not adm. in NC) MCU Specialist, Envir. Claim Dept., Royal & Sunalliance
Iacuzio, David A. .... '70 '97 C.156 B.A. L.818 J.D. [Ⓐ Cadwalader,W.&T.]
Ilzhoefer, Starr S. '77 '03 C.911 B.A. L.94 J.D. (adm. in NY; not adm. in NC) [Ⓐ Cadwalader,W.&T.]
Inman, Diana Hamner .... '63 '89 C.896 B.S. L.945 J.D. Banc of Amer.
Isenhour, William C. .... '— '03 C.198 B.A. L.575 J.D. [Ⓐ Johnston,A.&H.]
Ives, H. Bryan, III, (AV) .... '55 '80 C&L.575 B.S.B.A., J.D. [Alston&B.]
Ivey, Gary C., (AV) .... '55 '81 C.575 B.S. L.813 J.D. [Alston&B.]
Ivsan, John V. .... '69 '94 C.112 B.A. L.607 J.D. 7400 Carmel Exec. Pk., Ste. 120
Jackson, Edward K. .... '57 '82 C.968 B.A. L.16 J.D. [Jackson,P.]
Jackson, Gary W., (AV) .... '54 '79 C&L.228 A.B., J.D. [Jackson,P.]
Jackson, Karen C. .... '65 '92 C&L.623 B.A., J.D. 711 Hempstead Place
Jackson, Susan Serad .... '— '97 C.160 B.S. L.896 J.D. [Kennedy C.L.&H.]

Jackson Law Firm, The, PLLC
6201 Fairview Road, Suite 200, 28210
Telephone: 704-944-3151 Fax: 704-944-3164
Email: EdJackson@carolina.rr.com URL: http://www.thejacksonlawfirm.com
Edward K. Jackson.
Business Law, Limited Liability, Trusts and Estates, Company Law, Contracts, Estate Planning, Tax-Estate and Gift, Asset Protection, Tax Planning, Wills and Probate.

See Professional Biographies, CHARLOTTE, NORTH CAROLINA

Jackson Law Group, The, PLLC, (AV)
831 East Morehead Street, Suite 550, 28202
Telephone: 704-377-6680 Toll Free: 866-377-6680 Fax: 704-337-6690
URL: http://www.thejacksonlawgroup.com
Gary W. Jackson; Kurt F. Hausler. Of Counsel: Mona Lisa Wallace; William M. Graham.
Personal Injury, Products Liability, Construction Defects, Class Actions, Consumer Fraud, Environmental, Toxic Torts, Pharmaceutical Litigation, Professional Negligence, Business Torts, FELA.

See Professional Biographies, CHARLOTTE, NORTH CAROLINA

Jacobsohn, Bruce J. .... '43 '68 C&L.659 B.S., LL.B. 600 Cedar Rose Ln.
Jacuzzo, Christina M. K. .... '67 '00 C&L.790 B.S., J.D. [Ⓐ Nelson M.R.&S.]
Jaffa, Michael I. .... '56 '82 C.280 B.B.A. L.1228 J.D. Pres., Graham Investment Co.
Jaffa, Sol A. .... '28 '50 C&L.575 B.S., LL.B. Asst. Secy., Graham Investment Co.
James, Henry, Jr., (BV) .... '30 '57 C.951 A.B. L.893 J.D. [Ⓒ James,M.&D.]
James, Jason Burke .... '74 '01 C.896 B.A. L.1228 J.D. [Ⓐ Poyner&S.]
James, Lina E. .... '71 '98 C.575 B.A. L.425 J.D. [Ⓐ Erdman&H.]
James, Mollie T. .... '69 '95 C&L.575 B.A., J.D. [Ⓐ J.H.Henderson]

James, Bruce L.
(See Huntersville)

James, McElroy & Diehl, P.A., (AV)
600 South College Street, Suite 3000, 28202
Telephone: 704-372-9870; 800-247-9870 Fax: 704-333-5508
URL: http://www.jmdlaw.com
J. Mitchell Aberman; John S. Arrowood; Catherine Allen Barnes; John W. Beddow; Sarah M. Brady; John Robert Buric; William K. Diehl, Jr.; Richard A. Elkins; Jonathan D. Feit; Richard B. Fennell; Jared E. Gardner; Gary S. Hemric; Lawrence W. Hewitt; Edward T. Hinson, Jr.; Katherine S. Holliday; Adam L. Horner; David M. Kern (Board Certified Specialist in Family Law, North Carolina State Board of Legal Specialization); Irene P. King; G. Russell Kornegay, III; Jeffrey A. Long; Pender R. McElroy; Fred B. Monroe; Preston O. Odom, III; Adam L. Ross; Robert H. Sheppard; Bruce M. Simpson; Patra Sinner; Charles Malcolm Viser; M. Neya Warren; Richard S. Wright. Of Counsel: Mary Kay Baynard; Henry James, Jr.; B Frederick Williams.
Civil Litigation, Appellate Practice, Family Law, Real Estate, Corporate Law, Professional Liability, Personal Injury, Criminal Law, Estate Planning, Estate Administration, Products Liability, Taxation, Securities, Environmental Law, Commercial Law.

See Professional Biographies, CHARLOTTE, NORTH CAROLINA

Jarrell, Douglas M., (BV) .... '— '94 C&L.575 B.A., J.D. [Robinson,B.&H.]
Jarrell, F. Fincher, (AV) .... '— '71 C&L.575 A.B., J.D. [Kennedy C.L.&H.]
Jarrett, Clifford R., (BV) .... '— '91 C.296 A.B. L.902 J.D. [Kennedy C.L.&H.]
Jarvis, Lisa F. .... '63 '88 C.48 B.A. L.838 J.D. [L.F.Jarvis]

Jarvis, Lisa F., SC, PC, Law Offices of
7825 Ballantyne Commons Parkway, Suite 230, 28277 ⊙
Telephone: 704-544-6303 Fax: 866-209-3745
Lisa F. Jarvis.
Real Estate, Wills, Probate, Business Law, Corporate Law.
Rock Hill, South Carolina Office: 1373 Ebenezer Road, 29732. Telephone: 803-980-2765. Fax: 803-980-2796.

See Professional Biographies, CHARLOTTE, NORTH CAROLINA

Jasper, Jennifer Driscoll '71 '00 C.846 B.S. L.326 J.D. (adm. in TX; not adm. in NC) [Ⓐ Butrus K.W.V.]
Jeffcoat, Brenton D., (AVⓉ) .... '47 '74 C&L.790 B.A., J.D. [McGuireWoods]
Jeffers-Nelson, Mekka D. .... '74 '99 C.575 B.A. L.329 J.D. [M.Jeffers-Nelson]
Jeffers-Nelson, Mekka, The Law Office of .... 212 S. Tyron St., Ste. 1600
Jeffries, James H., IV, (AV) .... '58 '88 C.228 B.A. L.575 J.D. [Moore&V.P.]
Jeffries, John T. .... '69 '95 C&L.575 B.A., J.D. [McAngus G.&C.]
Jeffries, Meredith S., (BV) .... '68 '94 C&L.893 B.A., J.D. [Ⓒ Alston&B.]
Jeffries, Ross E., Jr. '63 '89 C&L.896 B.A., J.D. V.P. & Asst. Gen. Coun., First Union Corporation
Jeffries Jones, Jane, (BV) .... '60 '86 C&L.896 B.A., J.D. [Womble C.S.&R.]

Jenkins, Patrick, (AV) .... '55 '80 C.216 B.A. L.228 J.D. 301 South McDowell Street
Jenkins, T. Patrick, (AV) .... '55 '80 C.216 B.A. L.228 J.D. [Sellers,H.A.D.&L.]
Jenkins, Wallace A., Jr. .... '28 '57 C.607 L.1003 J.D. 3825 Lovett Circle
Jernigan, Jerry W., (AV) .... '46 '74 C&L.228 B.A., J.D. [J.W.Jernigan]

Jernigan, Jerry W., P.A., (AV)
1801 East Boulevard, 28203
Telephone: 704-375-1008 Mobile: 704-458-6400 Fax: 704-375-3240
Email: jerry@jerrywjernigan.com URL: http://www.jerrywjernigan.com
Jerry W. Jernigan.
Business Law, Commercial Lending, Employment Law, Entertainment Law, Estate Planning, Estate Administration, International Law, Leases, Licensing, Mergers and Acquisitions, Private Placements.

See Professional Biographies, CHARLOTTE, NORTH CAROLINA

Jetton, William W. .... '67 '95 C.269 B.A. L.893 J.D. [Ⓐ Moore&V.P.]
Johnson, Amy K., (BV) .... '— '94 C.477 B.A. L.575 J.D. [Robinson,B.&H.]
Johnson, Andrew M. .... '74 '99 C.473 B.A. L.893 J.D. [Ⓐ Hunton&W.]
Johnson, Bradley H. .... '— '95 C.160 B.S. L.790 J.D. [Kennedy C.L.&H.]
Johnson, Brian '66 '96 C.228 B.S.E.E. L.790 J.D. 11610 North Community House Road, Suite 200 (Pat.) (⊙Charlotte)
Johnson, Brian '66 '96 C.228 B.S.E.E. L.790 J.D. [Ⓐ Summa&A.] (See Pat. Sect.) (⊙Charlotte)
Johnson, Carl E., Jr., (AV) .... '— '68 C.604 A.B. L.228 J.D. [Ⓒ Robinson,B.&H.]
Johnson, Charles E., (AV) .... '— '81 C.896 B.A. L.309 J.D. [Robinson,B.&H.]
Johnson, Clifton E. .... '41 '67 C&L.574 B.A., LL.B. 6024 Craftsbury Dr.
Johnson, Cyrus M., Jr., (AV) .... '54 '82 C&L.575 B.A., J.D. [Womble C.S.&R.]
Johnson, Daniel L., Jr., (BV) .... '60 '85 C&L.575 B.S.B.A., J.D. [Moore&V.P.]
Johnson, David L. .... '56 '86 C.1257 B.A. L.502 J.D. Systems Mgr., U.S. Dist. Ct.
Johnson, Heather N. .... '76 '02 C.610 B.A. L.1541 J.D. [Smith D.N.W.S.&M.]
Johnson, Janis W. '— '94 C&L.790 B.S.B.A., J.D. (adm. in SC; not adm. in NC) Asst. Gen. Coun., Bank of America
Johnson, Lea Stromire, (AV) .... '60 '85 C.138 L.880 J.D. [Moore&V.P.]
Johnson, Leslie Gandy .... '74 '98 C.240 B.A. L.1228 J.D. [Lutzel,G.&Assoc.] ⊙
Johnson, Mark R. .... '70 '98 C.198 B.A. L.1339 J.D. 821 East Boulevard
Johnson, Mark Weston .... '76 '02 C.302 B.S. L.477 J.D. [Ⓐ Helms M.&W.]
Johnson, Megan V. .... '— '05 C.902 B.A. L.896 J.D. [Ⓐ Hedrick E.G.&K.]
Johnson, R. Keith, (AV) .... '53 '79 C.198 A.B. L.575 J.D. [R.K.Johnson]
Johnson, Richard B. .... '61 '00 C.1376 B.A. L.1292 J.D. 301 S. McDowell St., Ste. 802
Johnson, Stuart H., (AV) .... '— '89 C.118 B.A. L.575 J.D. [Robinson,B.&H.]
Johnson, R. Keith, P.A., (AV) .... 312 W. Trade St.
Johnston, David E., (AVⓉ) .... '48 '74 C.385 B.A. L.1119 J.D. [Ⓒ Poyner&S.]
Johnston, H. Morrison, Jr., (AV) .... '37 '62 C&L.575 A.B., LL.B. [Johnston,A.&H.]
Johnston, J. Trevor .... '— '03 C.886 B.S. L.893 J.D. [Ⓐ Helms M.&W.]
Johnston, John W., (AV) .... '18 '49 C.269 B.S. L.309 LL.B. 214 N. Church St.‡
Johnston, Robert P. .... '47 '74 C.118 B.A. L.813 J.D. Supr. Ct. J.

Johnston, Allison & Hord, P.A., (AV)
610 East Morehead Street, P.O. Box 36469, 28236
Telephone: 704-332-1181 Fax: 704-376-1628
Email: jahlaw.com URL: http://www.jahlaw.com
Claude A. Cochran (1884-1958); Frank A. McCleneghan (1901-1970); F. Thomas Miller, Jr. (1917-1985); H. Morrison Johnston, Jr.; James W. Allison; Robert C. Hord, Jr.; Ray S. Farris; Robert L. Burchette; Paul A. Kohut; John A. Morrice; J. Darrell Shealy; Greg C. Ahlum; Patrick E. Kelly; Stephen P. Gennett, II; John R. Buben, Jr.; Alice K. Moore; Gary J. Welch; Wanda C. Townsend; Brian J. Schoeck; Michael L. Wilson; Kenneth T. Lautenschlager;—Martin L. White (Resident); N. Lucille Siler; Joe Franklin Teague, Jr.; Robert G. Lindauer, Jr.; Jennifer M. Patterson; Cameron T. Ware; David A. Bohm; Laura Pleicones; Ashley Davidson Tison; J. Nicholas Kendall; John C. Lindley, III; William C. Isenhour. Of Counsel: Lelia M. Alexander (Miss) (1911-1991); B. Irvin Boyle.
Administrative, Banking and Finance, Business, Bankruptcy, Commercial, Construction, Corporate Law and Business Planning, Creditors' Rights and Collections, Employee Benefit Plans, Employment Discrimination, Estate and Trust, Estate Planning and Administration, Health Care, Litigation, International Transactions, Mediation, Mergers and Acquisitions, OSHA, Real Estate Development and Zoning, Taxation, Trial and Appellate Practice in State and Federal Courts.
Attorneys for: Presbyterian Hospital; F.N. Thompson, Co.; Pharr Yarns; SouthTrust; Centura Bank; American Truetzschler; Carolinas Associated General Contractors; Eastern Federal Corp.; Novant Health, Inc.; Crowder Construction Co.

See Professional Biographies, CHARLOTTE, NORTH CAROLINA

Jolly, Raymond A., Jr., (AV) '36 '61 C&L.575 B.A., J.D. Sr. V.P., Assoc. Enterprise Group, Duke Power Co.
Jonas, Eric A., Sr., (AV) '34 '63 C.575 A.B. L.309 J.D. 101 North McDowell Street, Suite 214
Jones, Beverly J. '55 '82 C.863 B.A. L.836 J.D. (adm. in TN; not adm. in NC) 9300 Arrowpoint
Jones, Christopher J.C. .... '72 '97 C.893 B.A. L.1206 J.D. [Ⓐ Moore&V.P.]
Jones, Clayton L. .... '53 '85 C.34 B.S. L.574 LL.M. Dist. Atty. Off.
Jones, David H., (AV) .... '— '80 C.1081 B.S. L.896 J.D. [Kennedy C.L.&H.]
Jones, Diana B. .... '73 '98 C&L.577 B.A., J.D. [Ⓐ Moore&V.P.]
Jones, J. Charles .... '37 '76 C.369 B.S. L.329 J.D. 2014 West Trade St.
Jones, J. Keith .... '— '97 C.680 B.A. L.896 J.D. [Ⓒ Kilpatrick S.]
Jones, J. Ronald, Jr., (AV) .... '56 '88 C.575 A.B. L.1228 J.D. [Clawson&S.] ⊙
Jones, Jacqueline Jarvis '— '90 C.575 B.A. L.228 J.D. Assoc. Gen. Coun., Bank of America
Jones, Kent D. .... '68 '95 C.797 B.A. L.192 J.D. [Ⓐ G.W.Swindell]
Jones, Larry C., (AVⓉ) '48 '92 C.838 B.S.E.E. L.836 J.D. [Alston&B.] (See Pat. Sect.)
Jones, Laurence B. '50 '76 C.659 B.S. L.273 J.D. (adm. in NY; not adm. in NC) V.P., Gen. Coun & Sec., Compass Group, U.S.A. Inc. (⊙New York, NY)
Jones, Mary Ulmer .... '— '86 C&L.383 B.A., J.D. Bank of America
Jones, Michael Duane .... '— '01 C.301 B.A. L.575 J.D. [Ⓐ Hedrick E.G.&K.]
Jones, R. Bradley '77 '05 C.953 B.A. L.1338 J.D. 205 Regency Executive Park Dr., Ste. 450
Jones, Sean M., (BV) .... '— '90 C&L.838 B.A., J.D. [Kennedy C.L.&H.]
Jones, William G. .... '45 '71 C.198 B.A. L.575 J.D. Dist. J.

Jones, Greg, & Associates, P.A.
(See Wilmington)

Jones, Hewson & Woolard, (AV) BR
831 E. Morehead Street Suite 560, 28202
Telephone: 704-372-6541 FAX: 704-331-9068
Members of Firm: Hunter M. Jones (1902-1996); Harry C. Hewson (1922-1999); Robert Gilroy Spratt, III; Lawrence J. Goldman; William L. Woolard (1931-2005).
General Civil Litigation, Insurance Defense, Automobile Negligence, Premises Liability, Product Liability, Professional Liability, Workers' Compensation.
Representative Clients: Norfolk Southern Corp.; Norfolk Southern Railway Co. (Assistant Division Counsel); Cincinnati Insurance Co.; CNA Insurance; Zurich Insurance Co.; The Hartford; Crum & Forster; City of Charlotte.

See Professional Biographies, CHARLOTTE, NORTH CAROLINA

Jordan, Clark '— '95 C.244 B.S. L.602 J.D. Sr. V.P., Chf. Legal Offr. & Gen. Coun., End II End Communications, Inc.

Jordan, G. Miller, (AV) .... '46 '72 C&L.896 B.A., J.D. [Essex R.]
Jordan, Jon R. .... '— '04 C&L.896 B.A., J.D. [A Robinson,B.&H.]
Jordan, Kristin M. '69 '98
C.198 B.A. L.790 J.D. The McDowell St. Ctr. for Fam. Law, Inc.
Jordan, W. Clark .... '64 '95 C.244 B.S. L.602 J.D. [W.C.Jordan]
Jordan, W. Clark, PLLC .... 3428 Maryhurst Lane
Joyner, Matthew R., (BV) .... '59 '85 C.197 A.B. L.659 J.D. [M.R.Joyner]

Joyner, Matthew R., PLLC, (BV)
708 East Boulevard, Suite 300, 28203
Telephone: 704-295-0226 Fax: 704-295-0228
Email: mrjesq@prodigy.net URL: http://www.mattjoyner.net
Matthew R. Joyner.
General Counsel and Administration Services, Business Law, Contracts, Commercial, Employment Law, Mergers and Acquisitions.
See Professional Biographies, CHARLOTTE, NORTH CAROLINA

Juby, P. Michael .... '78 '05 C.576 B.S. L.575 J.D. [A Parker,P.A.&B.]
Jurs, Stephen Andrew, (BV) .... '70 '94 C.228 B.A. L.245 J.D. [Poyner&S.]
Justice, Max Edward, (AV) .... '45 '70 C.575 A.B. L.896 J.D. [Parker,P.A.&B.]

Justice, Eve & Edwards, P.A., (AV) BR
1801 East Boulevard, 28203
Telephone: 704-333-5176 Fax: 704-333-5443
URL: http://www.lawyers.com/jee
James F. Justice (1922-1998); R. Michael Eve, Jr.; David L. Edwards.
Civil Trials in State Courts. Construction, Eminent Domain, Land Condemnation, Family Law, Equitable Distribution, Alimony, Divorce, Workers Compensation, Personal Injury.
See Professional Biographies, CHARLOTTE, NORTH CAROLINA

Kadis, Jeffrey A., (BV) .... '— '94 C.575 B.S. L.896 J.D. [Hedrick E.G.&K.]
Kahn, Brian A. .... '— '00 C.575 B.A. L.893 J.D. [A Helms M.&W.]
Kallianos, Chris M., (BV) .... '62 '87 C&L.575 B.A., J.D. [Warren&K.]
Kane, McHenry J. .... '76 '02 C.896 B.A. L.790 J.D. [A Moore&V.P.]
Kane, Richard F., (AV) .... '44 '73 C.93 B.S. L.260 J.D. [McGuireWoods]
Kane, Terry Richard, (AV) .... '47 '80 C.228 A.B. L.880 J.D. [Poyner&S.]
Kaplan, Andrew D. .... '68 '01 C.354 B.A. L.1202 J.D. [Rudisill,W.&K.]
Kaplan, Ted .... '— '05 C.198 B.A. L.575 J.D. [A Kennedy C.L.&H.]
Karacaova, Rona .... '71 '98 C.860 B.A. L.575 J.D. Legal Aid of NC
Karney, Robert A., (BV) .... '49 '75 C.469 B.A. L.192 J.D. [Karney&K.]
Karney, William M., (BV) .... '52 '77 C.259 B.S. L.469 J.D. [Karney&K.]
Karney and Karney, (BV) .... 1208 S. Tryon St.
Karolyi, Ronald W. .... '48 '73 C.54 B.A. L.851 J.D. V.P., United Carolina Bk.
Karrenstein, Chris .... '— '97 C&L.575 B.A., J.D. 3719 Latrobe Drive, Suite 840
Karres, Andrew T., (BV) .... '64 '93 C.576 B.A. L.607 J.D. [Foodman,H.&K.]
Karro, Marshall H., (AV) .... '46 '73 C.575 B.A. L.276 J.D. [Karro,S.&L.]
Karro, Sellers & Langson, (AV) .... 428 E. 4th St.

Katten Muchin Rosenman LLP, (AV)
A Partnership including Professional Corporations
401 South Tryon Street, Suite 2600, 28202-1935 ⊙
Telephone: 704-444-2000 Fax: 704-444-2050
URL: http://www.kattenlaw.com
Partners: Richard L. Farley; Fred A. Hicks (Board Certified Specialist in Family Law, North Carolina State Board of Legal Specialization); Daniel S. Huffenus; William P. McMillan; Bradley E. Pearce (Board Certified Specialist in Bankruptcy Law, North Carolina State Board of Legal Specialization); Peter J. Shea; William L. Sitton, Jr.; Robert B. Tucker, Jr.; David R. Vines (Board Certified Specialist in Estate Planning and Probate Law, North Carolina State Board of Legal Specialization); A. Victor Wray. Associates: Terra K. Atkinson; Abbie G. Baynes (Not admitted in NC); Jeffrey C. Grady; Christopher A. Hicks; Rebecca J. Horton; Barrett C. Mallos; Charles A. Pettigrew; G. Laurence Plaisted; Nina Shor; Amy Simpson; Jennifer M. Stokley; Susan M. Walker. Special Counsel: Russell M. Black; Charles D. Lansden; Carlton A. Shannon, Jr. Of Counsel: William E. Underwood, Jr.
Advertising, Anti-Fraud Counseling and Litigation, Antitrust, Apparel and Fashion, Aviation, Bankruptcy, Reorganization and Creditors' Rights, Corporate and Securities, Corporate Governance, Customs and International Trade, Employee Benefits and Executive Compensation, Entertainment and Media, Entertainment and Media Finance, Entertainment and Media Litigation, Environmental, FCC and Telecommunications, Finance and Structured Finance, Financial Institutions, Financial Markets and Products, Financial Services, Health Care, Health Care Compliance, Health Care Insolvency, Health Information and HIPAA Compliance, Hotel and Hospitality, Intellectual Property, Intellectual Property Litigation, Investment Management, Labor and Employment, Licensing and Distribution, Life Sciences, Litigation and Dispute Resolution, Matrimonial and Family Law, Mergers and Acquisitions, Music Law, Private Client Services, Private Equity, Public Finance, Publishing, Real Estate, Real Estate Development, Real Estate Finance, Real Estate Litigation, Real Estate Taxation, Securities, Securities Litigation, Shopping Center and Retail Law, Sports Law and Sports Facilities, Tax Planning and Litigation, Taxation of Financial Products, Technology, Trusts and Estates, White Collar Criminal and Civil Litigation.
Chicago, Illinois Office: 525 West Monroe Street, Suite 1600, 60661-3693. Telephone: 312-902-5200. Fax: 312-902-1061.
New York, New York Office: 575 Madison Avenue, 10022-2585. Telephone: 212-940-8800. Fax: 212-940-8776.
Los Angeles, California Office: 2029 Century Park East, Suite 2600, 90067-3012. Telephone: 310-788-4400. Fax: 310-788-4471.
Washington, D.C. Office: 1025 Thomas Jefferson Street, N.W., East Lobby, Suite 700, 20007-5201. Telephone: 202-625-3500. Fax: 202-298-7570.
Palo Alto, California Office: 260 Sheridan Avenue, Suite 450, 94306-2047. Telephone: 650-330-3652. Fax: 650-321-4746.
Irving, Texas Office: 5215 N. O'Connor Boulevard, Suite 200, 75039-3732. Telephone: 972-868-9058. Fax: 972-868-9068.
See Professional Biographies, CHARLOTTE, NORTH CAROLINA

Katz, Eugene M., (AVⓉ) '48 '72 C&L.861 B.A., J.D.
Sr. V.P. & Asst. Gen. Coun., Wachovia Corp.
Kauders, A. Eric, Jr. '— '94 C.945 B.A. L.893 J.D.
(adm. in VA; not adm. in NC) Asst. Gen. Coun., Bank of America
Kaufman, Cheryl, Attorney at Law .... '72 '97 C.575 B.A. L.896 J.D. P.O. Box 36352
Kayne, Daniel J., (AVⓉ) '51 '76 C.659 B.A. L.150 J.D.
(adm. in OH; not adm. in NC) [Kayne] ⊙
Kayne Law Group, Co., P.A., (AVⓉ)
521 E. Morehead Street, Suite 100 (⊙Columbus, OH)
Kean, Warren P., (AV) .... '— '85 C.902 B.A. L.420 J.D. [Kennedy C.L.&H.]
Kearney, Stephen W., (CV) .... '59 '89 C.576 B.A. L.574 J.D. 2 First Union Center
Keefe, Gerald F. .... '71 '00 C.861 B.A. L.273 J.D. [A Dechert]
Keeling, Amie R. .... '79 '04 C.575 B.A. L.896 J.D. [A Gilpin&H.]
Keesler, David C., (AV) .... '62 '87 C.575 B.A. L.893 J.D. 401 West Trade Street
Keeton, Lori R. .... '73 '98 C.362 B.A. L.260 J.D. [A Parker,P.A.&B.]
Keevan, Ryan W. .... '— '04 C.923 B.A. L.347 J.D. [A Hedrick E.G.&K.]
Keister, Jeffrey D. "J.D." .... '76 '02 C.97 B.A. L.607 J.D. [A McAngus G.&C.]
Keith, Gary .... '62 '91 C.1130 B.A. L.790 J.D. [G.Keith]

Keith, Gary, P.A.
1230 West Morehead Street, Suite 410, 28208
Telephone: 704-333-4411 Fax: 704-333-2555 URL: http://www.garykeithpa.com
Email: garykeithpa@hotmail.com URL: http://www.lawyers.com/garykeithpa
Gary Keith.
Personal Injury, Wrongful Death, Automobile Accidents and Injuries, Motorcycle Accidents, Trucking Accidents, Head Injury, Spinal Injury.
See Professional Biographies, CHARLOTTE, NORTH CAROLINA

Kellam, W. J., Jr., (AV) .... '37 '63 C&L.575 A.B., LL.B. [Kellam&P.]

Kellam & Pettit, P.A., (AV)
2701 Coltsgate Road, Suite 300, 28211
Telephone: 704-442-9500 Telecopier: 704-442-8595 URL: http://kellampettit.com
URL: http://www.lawyers.com/kellam&pettit
W. J. Kellam, Jr.; William Walt Pettit; Michael Barry Stein. Associates: Matthew Thor McKee; W. Chris Parnell; Charlene A. Fravel.
Corporation, Bankruptcy, Creditors Rights, Foreclosure, Collections, Commercial Law. State and Federal Trial Practice.
References: Cabarrus Bank of North Carolina; First Charter National Bank.
See Professional Biographies, CHARLOTTE, NORTH CAROLINA

Keller, Kathy A. '72 '99 C.112 B.A. L.893 J.D.
(adm. in CA; not adm. in NC) Corp. Coun., Compass Group, U.S.A. Inc.
Kelligrew, Elizabeth .... '62 '91 C.576 B.A. L.575 J.D. Dist. J., Dist. Ct. J. Chambers
Kelling, Kathryn Mitchell, (BV) .... '72 '98 C.309 B.A. L.896 J.D. [Horack,T.P.&L.]
Kelly, Anne Team, (BV) .... '62 '87 C&L.575 B.S., J.D. [C Helms M.&W.]
Kelly, C. Mark, (BV) .... '61 '86 C.301 B.A. L.902 J.D. [Alston&B.]
Kelly, Lisa T., (BV) .... '58 '85 C&L.896 B.A., J.D. [Essex R.]
Kelly, Patrick E., (BV) .... '59 '89 C.870 B.S. L.575 J.D. [Johnston,A.&H.]
Kelly, W. Richard, Jr. '29 '54
C&L.228 A.B., LL.B. Sr. V.P. & Tr. Offr., Bank of America, N.A.
Kelso, Amy S. '65 '95 C&L.575 B.A., J.D.
Assoc. Atty., University of North Carolina at Charlotte
Kelso, David Mark '46 '74 C&L.902 B.S., J.D.
(adm. in OH; not adm. in NC) Assoc. Gen. Coun., Duke Energy Corp.
Kemmer, Melissa M. .... '69 '97 C.1075 B.A. L.861 J.D. [A McGuireWoods]
Kemmy, Michael J., (BV) .... '55 '80 C.190 B.S.B.A. L.900 J.D. [Conrad T.&K.]
Kemper, Michael B. .... '73 '02 C.797 B.A. L.1509 J.D. [A Whitesides&W.]
Kendall, J. Nicholas .... '78 '03 C.1128 B.A. L.575 J.D. [A Johnston,A.&H.]
Kennedy, Marsha C. .... '61 '88 C.575 B.A. L.280 J.D. Royal Insurance
Kennedy, Wade M., (BV) .... '63 '89 C.732 B.A. L.477 J.D. [McGuireWoods]

Kennedy Covington Lobdell & Hickman, L.L.P., (AV)
Hearst Tower, 214 North Tryon Street, 47th Floor, 28202 ⊙
Telephone: 704-331-7400 Fax: 704-331-7598
URL: http://www.kennedycovington.com
Partners: Frank H. Kennedy (1893-1975); Hugh L. Lobdell (1908-1982); William T. Covington, Jr. (1907-2001); John D. Allison; Stanford D. Baird (Resident, Raleigh, North Carolina Office); David L. Batty; F. Daniel Bell, III (Resident, Raleigh, North Carolina Office); J. Michael Booe; Ken R. Bramlett, Jr.; Curtis C. Brewer, IV (Resident, Raleigh, North Carolina Office); William J. Brian (Raleigh and Research Triangle Park, North Carolina Offices); Jefferson W. Brown; Eric L. Burk; Mark R. Busch; Amie F. Carmack (Resident, Raleigh, North Carolina Office); John H. Carmichael; Beverly A. Carroll; Kent F. Christison (Resident, Raleigh, North Carolina Office); G. Lee Cory, Jr.; George C. Covington; David Scott Coward (Resident, Raleigh, North Carolina Office); John H. Culver III; Charles O. DuBose (Co-Managing Partner); James E. Earle; Brian P. Evans; B. D. Farmer, III; Walter D. Fisher, Jr.; David A. Franchina; T. Richard Giovannelli; Glen B. Hardymon; William N. Harris; Michael S. Hawley; J. Patrick Hayden; James T. Hedrick, Jr.; Sara W. Higgins; James H. Hodges (Resident, Columbia, South Carolina Office); A. Lee Hogewood III (Resident Raleigh, North Carolina Office); Cory Hohnbaum; C. Corley Holt; Wayne P. Huckel; Susan Serad Jackson; F. Fincher Jarrell; Clifford R. Jarrett; Bradley H. Johnson; Mary Beth Johnston (Resident, Research Triangle Park, North Carolina Office); David H. Jones; Sean M. Jones; Warren P. Kean; Joseph B. C. Kluttz; Raymond S. Koloski; William C. Livingston; Felicia Washington Mauney; Stephen R. McCrae, Jr. (Resident, Rock Hill, South Carolina Office); Peter McLean III; Patricia T. Meador (Resident, Research Triangle Park, North Carolina Office); Kiran H. Mehta; Roy H. Michaux, Jr.; Lee West Movius; Raymond E. Owens, Jr.; Bailey Patrick, Jr.; Alan H. Peterson (Resident, Raleigh, North Carolina Office); E. Allen Prichard; Eugene C. Pridgen; J. Norfleet Pruden III; Gary S. Qualls (Resident, Research Triangle Park, North Carolina Office); Lacy H. Reaves (Resident, Raleigh, North Carolina Office); Stephen K. Rhyne; Alice Carmichael Richey; Michael E. Robbe; John L. Sarratt (Resident, Raleigh, North Carolina Office); Karl S. Sawyer, Jr.; William G. Scoggin (Resident, Raleigh, North Carolina Office); Raleigh A. Shoemaker; Russell F. Sizemore; A. Zachary Smith III; Paul A. Steffens; Richard D. Stephens; Kevin P. Stichter; Michael R. Thornton (Resident, Raleigh, North Carolina Office); Maynard E. Tipps; Michael A. Tobin; Mary Turk-Meena; Carol A. Jones Van Buren; Michel P. Vanesse (Not admitted in NC); Dean A. Warren; Amy Pritchard Williams; J. Michael Wilson; Robert B. Womble (Resident, Raleigh, North Carolina Office); Scott Yarbrough (Not admitted in NC). Of Counsel: Henry W. Flint; J. Donnell Lassiter; John M. Murchison, Jr.; Francis M. Pinckney; Dalbert U. Shefte; Charles V. Tompkins, Jr.; Clarence W. Walker. Special Counsel: Jacqueline C. Bares; Lawrence E. Behning; Eric M. Braun (Resident, Research Triangle Park and Raleigh, North Carolina Offices); Jo Ann Brighton; Richard K. Brown; Patrick L. Byker (Raleigh and Research Triangle Park, North Carolina Offices); Leslee K. Daugherty; Brett T. Hanna (Resident, Raleigh, North Carolina Office); Thomas I. Lyon (Resident, Raleigh, North Carolina Office); John E. (Jack) Markham, Jr. (Raleigh and Research Triangle Park, North Carolina Offices); Jeanne A. Pearson; Carolyn Gilmer Shaw; Neal B. Wolgin (Resident, Raleigh, North Carolina Office). Retired: William F. Drew, Jr.; Marcus T. Hickman; Henry C. Lomax; Edgar Love III; Ross J. Smyth. Associates: Ann M. Anderson (Resident, Raleigh, North Carolina Office); Katherine R. Annas; Abraham M. Ashton; Myra T. Askins-Sullivan; Edwin L. Barnes, Jr.; Jason L. Barron (Resident, Raleigh, North Carolina Office); Peter S. Barwick; Gina Louise Bertolini (Resident, Research Triangle Park, North Carolina Office); Whitney G. Bouknight; Caroline Brown; Amelia Y. Burnette; John H. Capitano; Robert Allen Clary, II; Brian C. Cox; Marie Gibbs Cox; Colleen M. Crowley (Resident, Research Triangle Park, North Carolina Office); Abigail Loftus DeBlasis; Christine DeMaere; Michael J. Denny; Brett A. Durham; James Ewing (Resident, Raleigh, North Carolina Office); Frederick W. Faircloth, IV; Brian Fork (Resident, Raleigh, North Carolina Office); Stephanie Fulcher; John Gardner; Jon Goldberg; Marc Gustafson (Not admitted in NC); Andrew M. Habenicht; Grayson S. Hale (Resident, Raleigh, North Carolina Office); David R. Higgins; R. Gates Hinds; Brian D. Holofchak; Seton Blake Hunt; William O. Hutchinson; David N. Jonson (Member, Raleigh, North Carolina Office); Ted Kaplan; Michael F. King (Resident, Raleigh, North Carolina Office); Christopher C. Lam; David R. Lapp; Allyson Bryant Lavins; René J. LeBlanc-Allman; Anne S. Leggett; Tracey Mitchell LeRoy; William B. Macurda; Donald E. Martin; Stephanie E. Mascia; Christopher D. McCoy; Katherine Stukes McKenzie (Resident, Raleigh, North Carolina Office); Shawn A. McMillan (Resident, Research Triangle Park, North Carolina Office); Carolyn Fixel Merritt (Resident, Research Triangle Park, North Carolina Office); Charlotte Mitchell (Resident, Raleigh, North Carolina Office); Jared D. Mobley; Candice M. Murphy-Farmer (Resident, Research Triangle Park, North Carolina Office); Erika Olson; Daniel J. Palmieri (Resident, Raleigh, North Carolina Office); Jonathan B. Polking; Samuel T. Reaves; Russell M. Reed; Allyn Burchfield Rhodes; Patrick L. Ridinger; Thomas D. Rivers; Kimberly Raymer Robertson; Allison G. Runge; Cecilia E. Rutherford (Not admitted in NC); Matthew G. St. Amand (Not admitted in NC); Craigie D. Sanders (Raleigh and Research Triangle Park, North Carolina Offices); Adam Smith; Virginia Leggett Stevenson; Mark V. Thigpen; Michael F. Tomlinson; J. Garrett Van Osdell; Ruben M. Veliz; David E. Wagner (Resident, Raleigh, North Carolina Office); Alexander F. Watson; Margaret Rose Westbrook (Resident, Raleigh, North Carolina Office); Suzanne Cress Williams; Evan N. Wolkofsky; Julianne G. Wood; James D. Wright; James R. Wyche; C. Allen York (Resident, Raleigh, North Carolina Office).
Administrative Law, Alternative Dispute Resolution, Antitrust and Trade Regulation, Bankruptcy, Banks and Banking, Business Law, Commercial Law, Commercial Real Estate Development, Construction Law, Corporate Law, Debt and Equity Finance, Emerging Growth Companies, Employee Benefits, Employment Law, Entrepreneurial Business Law, Environmental Law, Family Law, Finance, Governmental, Health Care, Immigration and Naturalization, Intellectual Property, International Law, Labor and Employment, Land Sales, Land Use Regulation, Limited Liability Companies and Partnerships, Litigation, Medical Malpractice, Mergers, Acquisitions and Divestitures, Non-Profit and Charitable Organizations, Patents, Private Equity, Products Liability, Professional Liability, Public Utility Law, Real Estate Development, Real Estate Leasing, Real Estate Finance, Securities, Taxation, Technology Law, Trademarks, Trial Practice, Trusts and Estates, Utility Law, Venture Capital, Zoning, Planning and Land Use.
Representative Clients: Bank of America and Subsidiaries; Crescent Resources, Inc.; Duke Energy Corporation; First Union Corporation and Subsidiaries; Fluor Daniel; Lance, Inc.; Piedmont Health Care System; Summit Properties, Inc.
Raleigh, North Carolina Office: 434 Fayetteville Street Mall, 19th Floor, P.O. Box 1070, 27602-1070. Telephone: 919-743-7300. Fax: 919-743-7358.
Research Triangle Park, North Carolina Office: P.O. Box 14210, Research Triangle Park, 27709-4210, 2801 Slater Road, Suite 120, Morrisville, 27560. Telephone: 919-466-1190. Fax: 919-831-7040.

(This Listing Continued)

Kennedy Covington Lobdell & Hickman, L.L.P. (Continued)
Columbia, South Carolina Office: NBSC Building, Suite 850, 1122 Lady Street, 29201. Telephone: 803-251-2300. Fax: 803-251-2315.
Rock Hill, South Carolina Office: 140 East Main Street, Suite 220, P.O. Box 11429, 29731-1429. Telephone: 803-329-7600. Fax: 803-329-7677.
See Professional Biographies, CHARLOTTE, NORTH CAROLINA

Kennon, Tolly Albert, III ....'73 '98 C.302 B.S. L.472 J.D. [Kennon&Assoc.]
Kennon & Associates, PA .... 1028 West 5th Street Suite B
Kenny, Robert I. ....'65 '91 C&L.339 B.A., J.D. [Moore&V.P.]
Kern, David M., (AV) ....'52 '78 C.575 A.B. L.893 J.D. [James,M.&D.]
Kerr, Julie L. ....'— '04 C.1228 B.S. L.896 J.D. [Cranfill,S.&H.]
Kerr, Kenneth P. ....'64 '90 C.651 B.A. L.1017 J.D. [Moore&V.P.]
Kerrigan, Devin S. ....'— '96 C.597 B.S. L.893 J.D. 1947 Ferncliff Road
Kerrigan, Michael C. ....'71 '96 C&L.893 B.A., J.D. [Hunton&W.]
Ketcham, Platt V. '10 '33 L.732 LL.B.
(adm. in NY; not adm. in NC) 5800 Old Providence Rd.‡
Ketron, Anthony S. ....'— '99 C.870 B.S. L.893 J.D. [[A] Robinson,B.&H.]
Khoshbin, S. A. '65 '90 C.429 B.A. L.209 J.D.
(adm. in TX; not adm. in NC) [Butrus K.W.V.] ⊙
Kidd, Melissa M. ....'— '01 C.1369 B.S. L.893 J.D. [[A] Helms M.&W.]
Killough, John C. ....'52 '76 C&L.790 A.B., J.D. 5300 Wilkinson Blvd.‡
Kilpatrick, Gregory R. ....'74 '99 C.302 B.A. L.575 J.D. [[A] Helms M.&W.]

Kilpatrick Stockton LLP, (AV)
Suite 2500, 214 North Tryon Street, 28202 ⊙
Telephone: 704-338-5000 Facsimile: 704-338-5125
Email: info@KilpatrickStockton.com URL: http://www.KilpatrickStockton.com
Members of Firm:
John T. Allred (Resident); Susan Hager Cooper; Deborah L. Fletcher; G. Scott Humphrey; E. Lynwood Mallard (Resident); Jonathan J. Nugent; Mark C. Prybylski; John Nicholas Suhr, Jr.; David B. Whelpley, Jr. (Resident); Noelle E. Wooten (Resident); Elizabeth G. Wren (Resident). Resident Counsel: Marion A. Cowell, Jr.; J. Keith Jones. Resident Associates: Virginia L. Bailey; Ayanna Barrow; Nicole Brovet Cantu; David L. Cheatwood; Matthew W. Finniss; D. Shane Gunter (Not admitted in NC); Sarah R. Hamilton (Not admitted in NC); Jill Klements; Paul J. McNamara; John W. Oakes; James M. Tucker.
Civil Trial and Appellate Practice in all State and Federal Courts, Federal State and Local Taxation, Probate, Trust and Estate Planning, Real Estate, Environmental, Corporate, Corporate Reorganization, Securities, Banking Commercial, Antitrust, Labor, Employment, Administrative, Bankruptcy, Construction, Healthcare, Intellectual Property, Professional Malpractice, Products Liability and Negligence Law, Domestic Law and Equitable Distribution, Employee Benefits and Executive Compensation, Entrepreneurial Development, Franchising, Insurance Defense, Sports and Entertainment, State Agency and Lobbying Practice.
Atlanta, Georgia Office: Suite 2800, 1100 Peachtree Street. Telephone: 404-815-6500. Facsimile: 404-815-6555. Telex: 54-2307.
Augusta, Georgia Office: 699 Broad Street, Suite 1400, 30903-2043. Telephone: 706-724-2622. Facsimile: 706-722-0219.
London, England Office: 39th Floor, One Canada Square, London E145 NZ. Telephone: 44 (0)20 7154 6000. Facsimile: 44 (0)20 7154 6100.
New York, New York Office: 805 Third Avenue, 20th Floor, 10022. Telephone: 212-912-3527.
Raleigh, North Carolina Office: Suite 400, 3737 Glenwood Avenue, 27612. Telephone: 919-420-1700. Facsimile: 919-420-1800.
Stockholm, Sweden Office: Box 5421, SE-114 84. Telephone: 46-8-505-646-00. Facsimile: 46-8-505-646-99.
Washington, D.C. Office: Suite 900, 607 14th Street, N.W., 20005-2018. Telephone: 202-508-5800. Facsimile: 202-508-5858.
Winston-Salem, North Carolina Office: 1001 West Fourth Street, 27101-2400. Telephone: 336-607-7300. Facsimile: 336-607-7500.
See Professional Biographies, CHARLOTTE, NORTH CAROLINA

Kim, Hannah H. ....'— '04 C&L.838 B.S.B.A., J.D. [[A] Alston&B.]
Kim, Hyun "Jonathan" S. ....'74 '04 C.576 B.A. L.896 J.D. [[A] Hunton&W.]
Kincheloe, Hatcher B., (AV) ....'—'75 C&L.575 A.B., J.D. [Hedrick E.G.&K.]
King, Amy R. ....'74 '02 C.692 B.S.B.A. L.902 J.D. [[A] Moore&V.P.]
King, Carl L. ....'70 '98 C.937 B.A. L.878 J.D. [[A] Culp E.&C.]
King, Deborah H. ....'— '01 C.550 B.A. L.1065 J.D. [[A] Culp E.&C.]
King, Irene P. ....'79 '04 C.473 B.A. L.575 J.D. [[A] James,M.&D.]
King, Jeffrey B. ....'71 '96 C.801 B.A. L.326 J.D. [[A] Moore&V.P.]
King, L. Kristin, (BV) ....'— '91 C.1128 B.S. L.575 J.D. [Hedrick E.G.&K.]
King, Patricia E. ....'43 '71 C.369 B.S. L.574 J.D. 4000 Beatties Ford Rd.
King, Robert W., Jr., (AV) ....'30 '59 C.301 B.S. L.575 J.D. [[C] Moore&V.P.]
King, Todd Alexander ....'76 '02 C&L.896 B.S., J.D. [Cranfill,S.&H.]

King Law Firm, The, PLLC
(See Huntersville)

Kinghorn, Mark W. ....'— '02 C.269 B.A. L.228 J.D. [[A] Helms M.&W.]
Kinny, Paul R., (BVⓉ) '56 '84 C.383 B.A. L.1065 J.D.
(adm. in KY; not adm. in NC) Assoc. Gen. Coun., Duke Solutions, Duke Energy Corp.
Kinsey, C. Ralph, Jr., (AV) ....'42 '67 C.232 B.A. L.575 J.D. [McGuireWoods]
Kirk, Kimberly S., (BV) ....'— '94 C.198 A.B. L.880 J.D. [[C] Moore&V.P.]
Kirk, Trent A. ....'76 '03 C.160 B.S. L.790 J.D. [[A] Alston&B.]
Kirk, William B., Jr., (BV) ....'62 '87 C&L.383 B.S., J.D. [Kirk P.&T.]
Kirk Palmer & Thigpen, P.A., (AV) ....1045 Providence Rd.
Kirkley, Joel L., Jr. ....'36 '65 C&L.896 B.A., LL.B. 4900 Unaka Ave.
Kirkley, Joel L. (Josh), III, (BV) ....'60 '87 C.1128 B.A. L.615 J.D. [Kirkley]
Kirkley Law Offices, P.L.L.C., (BV) ....101 North McDowell Street, Suite 222
Kirschbaum, Nanney, Keenan & Griffin, P.A., (AV) ...... 2429 Red Fox Trail (⊙Raleigh)
Kiser, James L., (BV) ....'64 '91 C.198 B.A. L.575 J.D. Sr. Corp. Coun., Rexam Inc.
Kite, Leigh A. ....'79 '05 C.575 B.A. L.902 J.D. [[A] Parker,P.A.&B.]
Kitson, Michael J. ....'60 '96 C.795 B.S. L.1338 J.D. [[A] Clawson&S.]
Klein, Jeffrey M. ....'54 '79 C.569 B.A. L.1009 J.D. V.P., Royal & SunAlliance
Klein, Linda S., (AV) ....'54 '83 C.1128 B.A. L.575 J.D. [L.S.Klein]
Klein, Paul I., (AV) ....'48 '75 C.705 A.B. L.724 J.D. [Klein&F.]

Klein & Freeman, PLLC, (AV) [BB]
4521 Sharon Road, Suite 150, P.O. Box 221648, 28222-1648
Telephone: 704-442-0660 Facsimile: 704-364-2295
URL: http://www.kleinfreeman.com
James P. Crews (1933-1999). Partners: Paul I. Klein; Katherine Freeman. Associate: Mindy B. Newman.
General Civil Trial Practice in all State and Federal Courts, Professional Liability and Personal Injury Law, Commercial Litigation, Products Liability, Wrongful Death, Head Injury.
See Professional Biographies, CHARLOTTE, NORTH CAROLINA

Klein, Linda S., P.A., (AV) ....1419 E. Seventh St.
Klements, Jill ....'— '02 C.446 B.A. L.273 J.D. [[A] Kilpatrick S.]
Kline, Bradley P. ....'— '05 C.575 B.A. L.896 J.D. [Cranfill,S.&H.]
Klingenberg, Gregg L. '69 '99 C.540 B.A. L.208 J.D.
(adm. in CO; not adm. in NC) [[A] Cadwalader,W.&T.]
Kluttz, Joseph B. C., (AV) ....'— '77 C.674 B.A. L.893 J.D. [Kennedy C.L.&H.]
Knapp, Michael W. ....'70 '95 C.1369 B.A. L.896 J.D. [Bradley A.R.&W.]
Knight, Jack M., Jr., (BV) ....'— '94 C.575 B.A. L.904 J.D. [[A] Mayer,B.R.&M.]
Knight, Raymond Allen ....'49 '81 C.326 B.S. L.896 J.D. Ernst & Young LLP
Knight, W. Ronald ....'59 '89 C&L.896 B.S., J.D. Sr. V.P., Bk. of America

Knox, Frances S., (BV) ....'46 '91 C.1128 B.A. L.896 J.D. [Knox B.K.&G.]
Knox, H. Edward, (AV) ....'37 '63 C.576 B.S. L.896 LL.B. [Knox B.K.&G.]

Knox Brotherton Knox & Godfrey, (AV)
817 E. Trade Street, 28230
Telephone: 704-372-1360 Fax: 704-372-7402
Email: eknox@knoxlawcenter.com URL: http://www.knoxlawcenter.com
Members of Firm: H. Edward Knox; Allen C. Brotherton; Frances S. Knox; Lisa G. Godfrey; Peter E. McArdle; Kara F. McIvor; Charles Ashley Lamm.
General Trial Practice including Criminal, Civil, Personal Injury, Medical Malpractice, Worker Compensation, Corporate and Criminal Litigation, Condemnation, Construction Law, Domestic and Traffic Offenses.
Representative Clients: Beck Mercedes; Century 21 of the Carolinas; Magla Products; United States Tire Disposal.
Cornelius, North Carolina Office: 104 Torrence Commons. Telephone: 704-892-0199.
See Professional Biographies, CHARLOTTE, NORTH CAROLINA

Knox, Sandra L., P.C.
(See Cornelius)

Knuth, Richard L. '58 '84 C.1229 B.S. L.608 J.D.
(adm. in OH; not adm. in NC) 2001 Rexford Rd.
Koch, Richard M., (BV) ....'53 '78 C.902 B.S. L.896 J.D. 8801 J.M. Keynes Drive
Kocher, John D. ....'68 '93 C.645 B.A. L.1017 J.D. [[A] Shumaker,L.&K.]
Koehler, Stephen D., (BV) ....'63 '91 C.1350 B.S. L.896 J.D. [Koehler&C.]
Koehler & Cordes, PLLC, (BV) ....6425 Idlewild Rd.
Koenig, Jeffrey Grant, (BV) ....'67 '93 C.198 B.A. L.1228 J.D. 831 E. Morehead St.
Kohler, Kathryn D. '— '82 C.25 B.S. L.945 J.D.
(adm. in FL; not adm. in NC) Bank of America
Kohler, William W. ....'57 '82 C.966 B.B.A. L.945 J.D. 9300 Arrowpoint Blvd.
Kohut, Paul A., (BV) ....'58 '83 C.112 B.A. L.896 J.D. [Johnston,A.&H.]
Kolb, Michael A., (CV) ....'68 '93 C&L.575 B.A., J.D. P.O. Box 481619
Koloski, Raymond S. ....'— '95 C.861 B.A. L.930 J.D. [Kennedy C.L.&H.]
Konia, C. Andrew ....'— '99 C.276 B.S.F.S. L.893 J.D. [[A] Helms M.&W.]
Korenchuk, Keith M., (AVⓉ) ....'53 '82 C.228 B.A. L.893 J.D. [McGuireWoods]
Kornberg, Leonard G. ....'70 '97 C.1128 B.A. L.192 J.D. [L.G.Kornberg]
Kornberg, Leonard G., P.A. ....1801 East Boulevard
Kornegay, G. Russell, III, (AV) ....'59 '84 C.575 B.S. L.1228 J.D. [James,M.&D.]
Kornfeld, Stanley D., (BV) ....'38 '64 C.575 B.S. L.30 LL.B. 412 East Blvd.
Kortan-Sampson, Maria A., (AVⓉ) '48 '94 C.999 B.A. L.1003 J.D.
(adm. in OH; not adm. in NC) Sr. Coun., Goodrich Corporation
Koulpasis, Deborah A. '70 '99 C.1211 L.1252
(adm. in SC; not adm. in NC) Zurich Ins. Group
Kratt, Emil F., (AV) ....'35 '61 C&L.896 B.S., LL.B. 3328 Providence Plan Ln
Krisko, Jonathan C. ....'— '02 C.228 B.A. L.575 J.D. [[A] Robinson,B.&H.]
Kroboth, Timothy R. ....'45 '76 C.575 B.S. L.378 J.D. [Kroboth] (Pat.)
Kroboth Law Office ....5501 Providence County Club Drive (Pat.)
Kronk, Richard F., (BV) ....'62 '92 C.260 B.S. L.1206 J.D. [Baucom,C.B.M.&W.]
Kronovet, Alan B. ....'59 '97 C.30 B.S.B.A. L.575 J.D. 1025 Laurel Park Lane
Krusch, Alan R., (AV) ....'52 '77 C.705 B.A. L.472 J.D. [A.R.Krusch]

Krusch, Alan R., P.A., (AV)
5950 Fairview Road, Suite 808, 28210
Telephone: 704-556-0707 Fax: 704-553-7824
Email: kruschlaw@earthlink.net URL: http://www.akruschlaw.com
Alan R. Krusch (Board Certified Specialist in Family Law, North Carolina State Board of Legal Specialization);—Leigh Ballenger Sellers.
Family Law, Domestic Relations, Divorce, Child Custody, Child Support, Equitable Distribution, Alimony, Post Separation Support.
See Professional Biographies, CHARLOTTE, NORTH CAROLINA

Kucy, Lawrence J. '50 '75 C.93 A.B. L.659 J.D.
Sr. V.P. & Asst. Gen. Couns., Wachovia Corp.
Kullmann, Sandra C. ....'47 '91 C.658 B.A. L.1035 J.D. 6407 Idlewild Rd.
Kunkleman, Gregory L., (BV) ....'55 '80 C.198 B.S. L.575 J.D. [Wishart,N.H.&P.]
Kupec, Christopher C., (AV) ....'53 '80 C&L.575 B.A., J.D. [Mayer,B.R.&M.]
Kurani, H. George, (BV) ....'69 '93 C.198 A.B. L.575 J.D. [McAngus G.&C.]
Kurzeja, Paul E. ..... '— '92 C.509 B.A. L.1252 J.D. Asst. Gen. Coun., Bank of America
Kushner, Howard L. ....'40 '64 C.188 B.A. L.276 J.D. [Kushner&K.]
Kushner, L. Stephen, (BV) ....'74 '98 C.228 B.A. L.575 J.D. [Morris Y.W.S.&B.]
Kushner, Laya R. ....'69 '95 C.1507 B.A. L.64 J.D. [Kushner&K.]
Kushner, Mathew B. ....'73 '99 C.823 B.A. L.564 J.D. [Kushner&K.]
Kushner & Kushner, P.C. ....6739 Fairview Road, 2nd Floor
Kutner, Jonathan E. ....'— '04 C.896 B.A. L.94 J.D. [[A] Alston&B.]
Kutny, Mark R. ....'75 '00 C.197 B.A. L.893 J.D. [[A] Hamilton F.M.S.S.&M.]
Kutrow, Bradley R., (AV) ....'59 '86 C.575 A.B. L.893 J.D. [Helms M.&W.]
LaBrun, Henry A. ....'65 '93 C.813 B.A. L.602 J.D. [Cadwalader,W.&T.]
Lacy, Robyn M. ....'73 '00 C&L.923 B.S.J., J.D. [[A] Morris Y.W.S.&B.]
Ladenheim, Matthew Jacob ....'73 '00 C.890 B.A. L.1017 J.D. [[A] Adams E.]
Lafferty, Richard Q. '— '87 C.575 B.A. L.896 J.D.
Asst. Gen. Coun., Bank of America
Lail, Rick D., (BV) ....'60 '88 C.1128 B.S. L.1187 J.D. 725 E. Trade St., Ste. 120
Lam, Anne Dunton ....'76 '02 C.228 B.A. L.575 J.D. [Dozier,M.P.&M.]
Lam, Christopher C. ....'— '02 C.228 B.A. L.577 J.D. [[A] Kennedy C.L.&H.]
Lamb, Christine M. ....'66 '93 C.339 B.S. L.575 J.D. P.O. Box 31366
Lamb, Robert J., Jr. ....'58 '84 C.968 B.A. L.790 J.D. [Lamb&Assoc.]
Lamb, Stephen A. ....'61 '87 C.576 B.A. L.790 J.D. [Lamb]
Lamb & Associates .... 10800 Sikes Pl., Ste. 300
Lamb Firm, The .... P.O. Box 36158
Lamberson, Kevin J. '63 '90 C.178 B.A. L.724 J.D.
(adm. in NY; not adm. in NC) 2409 Summerlake Rd.
Lambeth, Philip D., (AV) ....'46 '72 C&L.575 A.B., J.D. [Harkey L.]
Lambright, Patricia A. ....'52 '82 C.569 B.A. L.724 J.D. 8201 Trail View Drive
Lamm, Charles Ashley ....'72 '02 C.576 B.S. L.1228 J.D. [Knox B.K.&G.]
Lamm, Daniel K. ....'62 '87 C.575 B.S. L.178 J.D. 2427 Hassell Pl.
Lammon, Megan A. ....'74 '00 C.93 B.A. L.896 J.D. [[A] Cozen O.]
Lamothe, David ......'— '96 C.976 B.A. L.575 J.D. Asst. Gen. Coun., Bank of America
Lampe, Donald C., (AV) '57 '82
C.453 B.S. L.228 J.D. [Womble C.S.&R.] (⊙Greensboro)
Lancaster, Donald L. '— '96 C.058 B.B.S. L.94 J.D.
(adm. in MA; not adm. in NC) [[A] Dechert]
Landers, Michelle C. ....'61 '87 C&L.383 B.A., J.D. Hoechst Celanese Corp.
Landess, C. Barton ....'59 '86 C.198 B.A. L.893 J.D. Carolinas Found.
Landgraff, Donald N. '45 '72 C.645 B.A. L.30 J.D.
(adm. in NJ; not adm. in NC) 7436 Newmans Ridge Ct.‡
Landmesser, Kevin ....'— '00 C.932 B.B.A. L.477 J.D. [[A] Helms M.&W.]
Lane, Craig B. ....'69 '99 C.575 B.A. L.902 J.D. 1701 Scott Avenue
Lane, Maryl A. '58 '82 C.643 B.A. L.665 J.D.
(adm. in PA; not adm. in NC) Greater Charlotte Biz‡
Lane, Rosalind L. ....'70 '01 C.502 B.S.B.A. L.228 J.D. [[A] Moore&V.P.]

Langdon, Amy Rickner '71 '96 C.477 B.A. L.896 J.D. [Ⓐ Helms M.&W.]
Langdon, J. Mark '65 '92 C.893 B.A. L.259 J.D. [McGuireWoods]
Langdon, James R., (BV) '70 '96 C.112 B.A. L.896 J.D. [Ⓐ Moore&V.P.]
Langdon, Michelle Sain, (BV) '65 '90 C&L.575 B.A., J.D. [Morris Y.W.S.&B.]
Lange, David R., (BV) '61 '86
C.575 B.A. L.1228 J.D. 301 South McDowell Street, Suite 801
Lange, Katherine Thompson, (BV) '63 '91 C.575 B.S. L.896 J.D.
[Ⓒ Womble C.S.&R.]
Langson, Seth H., (AV) '51 '77 C.319 B.A. L.93 J.D. [Karro,S.&L.]
Lanning, James E. '39 '67 C.140 B.S. L.575 J.D. Dist. J.
Lanois, Jill Ramirez '— '91 C.893 B.A. L.692 J.D.
Asst. Gen. Coun., Bank of America
Lansche, John E., (BV) '44 '69 C&L.575 A.B., J.D. Wachovia Corp.
Lansden, Charles D. '60 '87 C&L.575 B.A., J.D. [Ⓒ Katten M.R.]
La Penta, John '63 '96 C.790 B.A. L.61 J.D.
(adm. in VA; not adm. in NC) 521 E. Morehead St., Ste. 250
Lapham, Stephen F. '69 '95
C&L.575 B.A., J.D. Assoc. Gen. Coun., Sonic Automotive, Inc.
Lapp, David R. '— '00 C.1369 B.S. L.945 J.D. [Ⓐ Kennedy C.L.&H.]
Largess, Stephen Luke, (AV) '56 '90 C.228 B.A. L.575 J.D. [Ferguson,S.C.G.&S.]
Lassiter, J. Donnell, (AV) '— '63 C&L.575 A.B., J.D. [Ⓒ Kennedy C.L.&H.]
Lassiter, John Wells '54 '80 C&L.896 B.A., J.D.
Senior V. P., Belk Brothers Company
Lassiter, Robert, Jr., (AV) '12 '39 C.976 A.B. L.309 LL.B. 726 Hempstead Pl.‡
Lathrop, Anthony T., (AV) '61 '88 C&L.575 B.A., J.D. [Moore&V.P.]
Latona, Christine '74 '00 C.665 B.A., B.S. L.896 J.D. [Ⓐ McAngus G.&C.]
Latorre, Stefan R., (CV) '64 '91 C.1222 B.A. L.259 J.D. [S.R.Latorre]
Latorre, Stefan R., P.A., Law Offices of, (CV) 2629 Central Ave.
Laughrun, George V., II, (AV) '55 '80 C.34 B.A. L.192 J.D. [Goodman,C.L.L.&M.]
Lauro, Tony '— '05 C.597 B.A. L.896 J.D. [Ⓐ Helms M.&W.]
Lautenschlager, Kenneth T., (BV) '71 '96 C.680 B.A. L.575 J.D. [Johnston,A.&H.]
Lavins, Allyson Bryant '— '05 C.197 B.A. L.93 J.D. [Ⓐ Kennedy C.L.&H.]
Lawing, Linda E. '63 '89 C&L.575 B.S., J.D. P.O. Box 31247
Lawrence, Corey A., (BV) '68 '97 C.329 B.B.A. L.245 J.D. [C.A.Lawrence]
Lawrence, Jennifer D. '74 '03 C.93 B.A. L.569 J.D.
(adm. in NY; not adm. in NC) [Ⓐ Mayer,B.R.&M.]
Lawrence, Kimberly A. '69 '95 C.473 B.A. L.665 J.D.
Asst. Gen. Coun., Bank of America
Lawrence, Laura S. '— '95 C.835 B.A. L.1017 J.D.
Vice President, Chief Managing Attorney, Royal & SunAlliance Co.
Lawrence, Paul C. '— '86 C.754 B.S. L.884 J.D. [Hedrick E.G.&K.]

Lawrence, Corey A., P.A., (BV)
Cameron Brown Building, 301 South McDowell Street, Suite 305, 28204
Telephone: 704-342-1444 Fax: 704-372-4477
Email: lawrence4law@juno.com URL: http://www.lawyers.com/coreylawrence
Corey A. Lawrence.
Criminal Law, Federal and State, Traffic Law, DWI, Drug Crimes, Felonies, Sexual Assault, Family Law, Personal Injury.
See Professional Biographies, CHARLOTTE, NORTH CAROLINA

Lawson, Lance A. '61 '97 C.870 B.S. L.602 J.D. [Alston&B.] (See Pat. Sect.)
Lax, Andrew W., (AV) '— '85 C.945 B.A. L.896 J.D. [McNair]
Lay, Wood W. '65 '91 C.893 B.A. L.902 J.D. [Hunton&W.]
Layton, Jason P. '74 '01 C.228 B.S. L.861 J.D.
Corp. Coun., Compass Group, U.S.A. Inc.
Layton, Samuel G., Jr., (AV) '36 '65 C.790 B.S. L.30 J.D.
[Ⓒ Alston&B.] (See Pat. Sect.)
Lazorcheck, Sandra M. '71 '97 C.823 B.A. L.564 J.D. [Moore&V.P.]
Lea, Haynes P., (AV) '— '82 C&L.575 B.A., J.D. [Robinson,B.&H.]
Leahy, Jennifer Rouse '75 '01 C.602 B.A. L.896 J.D. [Ⓐ Helms M.&W.]
Leasure, Stephen D. '71 '00 C&L.893 B.S., J.D. [Ⓐ Hunton&W.]
LeBar, Katherine M. '73 '03 C.145 A.B. L.910 J.D. [Ⓐ Horack,T.P.&L.]
LeBlanc-Allman, René J. '— '00 C&L.790 B.A., J.D. [Ⓐ Kennedy C.L.&H.]
Ledford, Joseph L., (AV) '57 '82 C.1128 B.A. L.1228 J.D.
130-A North McDowell Street
Le Donne, Nancy W. '— '87 C.228 A.B. L.128 J.D.
(adm. in NY; not adm. in NC) Asst. Gen. Coun., Bank of America
Lee, Charles B., Jr., (AV) '57 '83 C.228 B.A. L.893 J.D. [Parker,P.A.&B.]
Lee, Jeffrey J. '49 '73 C&L.94 B.A., J.D.
(adm. in NJ; not adm. in NC) [Cadwalader,W.&T.]
Lee, Marcus S. '71 '98 C&L.896 B.A., J.D. [Ⓐ Helms M.&W.]
Lee, Randall W., (BV) '53 '78 C.575 B.A. L.896 J.D. Stuart Title Company
Lee, Randolph Marshall, (BV) '55 '80 C&L.896 B.A., J.D. P.O. Box 77005
Lee-Stevens, Kathleen Gay '51 '87 C.316 B.A. L.575 J.D.
Mgr.-Risk Management, Piedmont Natural Gas
Leetzow, Karen B. '65 '91 C.882 B.A. L.30 J.D.
(adm. in MD; not adm. in NC)
Asst. Gen. Coun., Intell. Prop. & Competition, NASCAR, Inc.
Leggett, Anne S. '56 '83 C.228 B.A. L.178 J.D. [Ⓐ Kennedy C.L.&H.]
Lembo, Barbara Howie, (BV) '49 '76 C.747 B.A. L.347 J.D. [Ⓐ Wishart,N.H.&P.]
Leo, Scott E. '68 '97 C.576 B.A. L.575 J.D. [Parker,P.A.&B.]
Leon, Tania L., (P.A.), (CV) '41 '82 C.185 B.A. L.1228 J.D. 725 E. Trade St.
Leonard, C. Jerome, Jr. '36 '66 C&L.575 A.B., J.D. Dist. J.

Leone, Cindy Pauley, (AV) '52 '80 C.228 B.A. L.896 J.D.
Suite 1106 Cameron Brown Building, 301 South McDowell Street, P.O. Box 34546, 28204
Telephone: 704-332-5297 Fax: 704-372-5001
URL: http://www.cynthiapauleyleone.com
(Board Certified Specialist in Family Law, North Carolina State Board of Legal Specialization).
Practice limited to Family/Domestic Law. Equitable Distribution, Divorce, Child Custody, Child Support, Alimony and Separation Agreements.
Reference: Bank of Granite.
See Professional Biographies, CHARLOTTE, NORTH CAROLINA

Lerner, Mark S., (BV) '63 '89 C.276 B.A. L.575 J.D. Gen. Coun., Lerner & Co.
LeRoy, Tracey Mitchell '— '01 C.72 B.A. L.790 J.D. [Ⓐ Kennedy C.L.&H.]
Lesesne, Louis L., Jr., (AV) '45 '73 C.198 B.A. L.94 J.D. [Essex R.]
Lester, Matthew J. '73 '00 C.575 B.S.B.A. L.790 J.D [M.J.Lester]

Lester, Matthew J., PLLC
6100 Fairview Road, Suite 1200, 28210
Telephone: 704-556-1101 Fax: 704-556-1044
Email: m_j_lester@hotmail.com URL: http://www.mjlesterlaw.com
Matthew J. Lester.
Residential Real Estate, Commercial Real Estate, Mortgages, Trusts and Estates, Estate Planning, Wills, Probate, Business Law, Corporate Law, Limited Liability Companies, Contracts.
See Professional Biographies, CHARLOTTE, NORTH CAROLINA

Levine, Eric D., (BV) '57 '83 C.339 B.S. L.862 J.D.
Suite 602 Cameron-Brown Building, 301 South McDowell Street, 28204
Telephone: 704-372-2800 FAX: 704-372-6337
Email: ericlevine@cs.com URL: http://www.lawyers.com/ericdlevine
Civil Trial Practice, Personal Injury, Family, Domestic, Child Custody, Real Estate, Corporations, Business, Landlord Tenant Law.
See Professional Biographies, CHARLOTTE, NORTH CAROLINA

Levine, Lawrence P. '52 '77 C.659 B.A. L.930 J.D. [Ⓒ Moore&V.P.]
Levine, Leigh M. '69 '95 C.674 B.A. L.880 J.D. [Ⓒ Alston&B.]
Levine, Miles S., (BV) '54 '78 C&L.575 B.A., J.D. [Goodman,C.L.L.&M.]
Levine, Nicki F., (BV) '54 '82 C&L.575 B.A., J.D. 6832 Morrison Blvd.
Levine, Sol, (AV) '21 '48 C.339 L.228 LL.B. 301 South McDowell Street
Levinson, Hal A., (AV) '56 '82 C.575 A.B. L.477 J.D. [Moore&V.P.]
Levinson, Holly Hickman '61 '87 C.575 B.A. L.477 J.D. 2544 Hampton Ave.‡
Levinson, Peter A. '55 '80 C.228 A.B. L.790 J.D. 6337 Morrison Blvd.
Lewis, Charles R. '— '99 C.576 B.S.A.E. L.575 J.D. [Ⓐ Robinson,B.&H.]
Lewis, David T., (AV) '65 '93 C.692 B.S. L.192 J.D. [Moore&V.P.]
Lewis, Georgia J. '33 '89 C.556 B.A. L.574 J.D. 719 Sandridge Rd.
Lewis, Heather E. '76 '04 C&L.896 B.S., J.D. [Ⓐ Horack,T.P.&L.]
Lewis, Julie R. '62 '87 C.125 B.A. L.575 J.D.
Off. of Mecklenburg County Pub. Defender
Lewis, Laura Leigh '— '93 C.498 B.S. L.192 J.D.
(adm. in VA; not adm. in NC) Asst. Gen. Coun., Bank of America
Lewis, Phillip E. '71 '01 C.575 B.A. L.1228 J.D. [Ⓐ Horack,T.P.&L.]
Lewis, Robert Gregory, (BV) '64 '90 C.575 B.S. L.574 J.D. [Morris Y.W.S.&B.]

Lewis & Roberts, P.L.L.C., (AV)
128 South Tryon Street, Suite 1100, 28202-5012 ⊙
Telephone: 704-347-8990 Facsimile: 704-347-8929
URL: http://www.lewis-roberts.com
Gary Vance Mauney; Paul R. Dickinson, Jr.
Workers' Compensation Law, Commercial Litigation, Construction Law, Surety Law, Civil Trial Practice.
Raleigh Office: 1305 Navaho Drive, Suite 400. Telephone: 919-981-0191. Facsimile: 919-981-0199.
See Professional Biographies, CHARLOTTE, NORTH CAROLINA

Lewisohn, Brandon K. '70 '97 C.692 B.A. L.896 J.D.
[Parker,P.A.&B.] (⊙Columbia, Spartanburg, SC)
Lezman, Jack G. '70 '95 C.475 B.A. L.201 J.D. [J.G.Lezman]

Lezman, Jack G., P.A.
4801 E. Independence Boulevard Suite 616, 28212
Telephone: 704-536-7669 Toll Free: 888-693-7669 Fax: 704-536-0179 URL: http://www.lawyers.com/jlezman
Email: jlezman@dasia.net URL: http://www.jlezman.com
Jack G. Lezman.
Consumer Bankruptcy, Bankruptcy, Debtor Rights, Personal Injury, Auto Accidents, Workers Compensation and Social Security Disability Law.
See Professional Biographies, CHARLOTTE, NORTH CAROLINA

Li, Benjamin M. '56 '92 C.999 B.A. L.900 J.D. 4912 Park Road
Lilien, Robert S., (AV) '— '75 C.228 A.B. L.575 J.D. [Robinson,B.&H.] ‡
Lilly, James E., (BV) '60 '85 C.88 B.A. L.228 J.D. [Womble C.S.&R.]
Lin, Alexander T. '70 '98 C.111 B.S. L.178 J.D. [Ⓐ Cadwalader,W.&T.]
Linares, Francisco J. '58 '93 C.870 B.S. L.569 J.D. [Ⓒ Cadwalader,W.&T.]
Lincoln, Sara R., (BV) '68 '93 C.938 B.A. L.8 J.D. [Ⓐ Womble C.S.&R.]
Lindauer, Kerry M. F. '74 '00 C.790 B.S. L.575 J.D. [Ⓐ Moore&V.P.]
Lindauer, Robert G., Jr. '70 '00 C.680 B.A. L.575 J.D. [Ⓐ Johnston,A.&H.]
Lindley, John C., III '77 '03 C&L.575 B.A, J.D. [Ⓐ Johnston,A.&H.]
Lindquist, Kurt E., II, (AV) '— '83 C.228 A.B. L.896 J.D. [Nelson M.R.&S.]
Lindsay, C. Marshall, (BV) '72 '98 C.575 B.A. L.790 J.D. [Ⓐ Nelson M.R.&S.]
Lindsey, Robert L., Jr., (BV) '36 '60 C&L.575 B.S., J.D. [Lindsey&S.]
Lindsey and Schrimsher, P.A., (AV) 2316 Randolph Road
Linker, Raymond O., Jr., (AV) '46 '72
C.576 B.S. L.276 J.D. [Alston&B.] (See Pat. Sect.)
Linn, Shirley J., (AV) '50 '75 C.351 B.A. L.352 J.D.
V.P. & Gen. Coun., Fair Point Communications
Linnert, Terrence G. '46 '75 C.602 B.S.E.E. L.1003 J.D.
(adm. in OH; not adm. in NC) Exec. V.P., Adm. & Gen. Coun., Goodrich Corp.
Linnstaedter, J. Susan '— '82
(adm. in TX; not adm. in NC) Bank of America
Lipscomb, Ernest B., III, (AV) '41 '65 C&L.500 B.S., J.D.
[Alston&B.] (See Pat. Sect.)
Little, Danica L. '73 '04 C.1111 B.A. L.259 J.D. [Ⓐ Wishart,N.H.&P.]
Littlefield, Clay A. '73 '98 C.1059 B.A. L.500 j.d. [Ⓐ Alston&B.]

Littler Mendelson, A Professional Corporation, (AVⓉ)
Bank of America Corporate Center, 100 North Tryon Street, Suite 4150, 28202 ⊙
Telephone: 704-972-7000 Facsimile: 704-333-4005
Email: info@littler.com URL: http://www.littler.com
Marylin E. Culp (Resident); Corie D. Pauling; L. Stanford Sherrill, Jr.; J. René Toadvine;—Nicole E. Bourget; Angela B. Cummings; Jason McConnell; Aaron Menser; Jerry H. Walters, Jr.
Employment and Labor Law; Affirmative Action; Age Discrimination in Employment Civil Service; Collective Bargaining; Confidentiality Agreements; Covenants Not To Compete; Employee Drug Testing; Employee Privacy; Employer Liability; Employment Arbitration; Employment Breach of Contract; Employment Civil Rights; Employment Class Actions; Employment Discrimination; Employment Litigation; Equal Employment Opportunity Law; Fair Labor Standards; Family and Medical Leave Act; Harassment; Labor Relations; Labor Strikes; National Labor Relations Act; Noncompete Litigation; Noncompetition and Non-Solicitation Agreements; Personnel Policies; Prevailing Wage Litigation; Reductions in Force; Restrictive Covenants; Sexual Harassment; Title VII Discrimination; Unfair Labor Practices; Union Contract Negotiations; Union Elections; Union Organization; Wage and Hour Law; WARN Act; Whistleblower Litigation; Workplace Violence; Wrongful Termination; Wrongful Termination Defense.
Offices located in: Phoenix, Arizona; California — Fresno, Los Angeles, Sacramento, San Diego, San Francisco, San Jose, Santa Maria, Stockton and Walnut Creek; Denver, Colorado; Washington, D.C.; Miami, Florida; Atlanta, Georgia; Chicago, Illinois; Boston, Massachusetts; Minneapolis, Minnesota; Reno and Las Vegas, Nevada; Newark, New Jersey; New York, New York; Columbus, Ohio; Philadelphia and Pittsburgh, Pennsylvania; Dallas and Houston, Texas; Seattle, Washington.
See Professional Biographies, CHARLOTTE, NORTH CAROLINA

Livingston, William C., (AV) '— '74 C&L.575 A.B., J.D. [Kennedy C.L.&H.]
Lockhart, Thomas Ashe, (AV) '28 '51 C&L.575 B.A., J.D. [Ⓒ Garlitz&W.]
Loeb, Christopher W., (AV) '— '84 C.198 B.A. L.228 J.D. [Robinson,B.&H.]
Loebsack, Christopher J., (BV) '71 '96 C.160 B.S. L.228 J.D. [Caudle&S.]
Loepp, Kimberly S. '— '00 C.691 B.A. L.659 J.D.
(adm. in NY; not adm. in NC) Asst. Gen. Coun., Bank of America
Loftis, Brett Alan '75 '00
C.269 B.A. L.896 J.D. Dir. of Advocacy, Council for Children, Inc.
Lofton, Brandon M. '78 '04 C.575 B.A. L.569 J.D. [Ⓐ Ferguson,S.C.G.&S.]
Lokken, Rachel N. '71 '97 C.604 B.A. L.477 J.D. [Ⓐ Womble C.S.&R.]
Lomax, Henry C., (AV) '— '58 C&L.575 A.B., LL.B. [Kennedy C.L.&H.] ‡
Long, Arthur S., III, (BV) '46 '73 C&L.575 B.S.B.A., J.D. 101 N. McDowall St.
Long, Ashley M. '80 '05 C.160 B.S. L.896 J.D. [Ⓐ Parker,P.A.&B.]

Long, Jeffrey A. ....'70 '02 C.576 B.A. L.790 J.D. [[A] James,M.&D.]
Long, Joe O. ....'54 '80 C.575 B.A. L.896 J.D. Wachovia Corporation
Long, Maria G.B., (BV) ....'61 '91 C&L.575 B.S., J.D. Asst. Dist. Atty.
Long, Nash E., III, (BV) ....'71 '97 C.802 B.S. L.309 J.D. [Hunton&W.]
Long, Phyllis W. ....'51 '80 C.575 B.A. L.902 J.D. [P.W.Long]
Long, Phyllis W., P.C. ....6425 Idlewild Road, Suite 212
Longo, Aaron J. ....'75 '03 C.276 B.A. L.893 J.D. [[A] McGuireWoods]
Loughridge, John H., Jr., (AV) ......'45 '70 C.198 A.B. L.896 J.D. Wachovia Corporation
Love, Edgar, III, (AV) ....'— '59 C.575 B.S. L.309 J.D. [Kennedy C.L.&H.] ‡
Lovelace, Ronald S. ....'78 '02 C&L.575 B.S.B.A., J.D. [[A] Moore&V.P.]
Lovell, Peter H. '58 '85 C.902 B.A. L.1202 J.D.
(adm. in MA; not adm. in NC) Sr. Coun., Royal & SunAlliance
Loven, Dean P. ....'56 '96 L.575 J.D. [[A] Morris Y.W.S.&B.]
Loving, Kelly Luongo .....'— '98 C.228 B.A. L.893 J.D. [Robinson,B.&H.] (⊙Charlotte)
Lowe, Julianna P. ....'— '02 C&L.896 B.A., J.D. [[A] Helms M.&W.]
Lowndes, William S., (AV) ....'32 '66 C.228 A.B. L.575 J.D. [Horack,T.P.&L.] ‡
Lowrance, Fred T., (AV) ....'47 '72 C.198 A.B. L.893 J.D. [Parker,P.A.&B.]
Lucas, Edwin F., III, (AV) ....'— '78 C.575 B.A. L.893 J.D. [Robinson,B.&H.]
Lucas, Josiah C. T., (BV) ....'63 '88 C.575 B.A. L.228 J.D. [McGuireWoods]
Lucas, Robert T., III, (AV) '59 '86
C.228 B.A. L.896 J.D. Assoc. Gen. Coun., Duke Energy Corp.
Lucchesi, Kathleen K., (BV) ....'68 '97 C.344 B.S. L.500 J.D. [[A] Shumaker,L.&K.]
Lucey, Richard A. ....'41 '70 C.1030 B.S. L.262 J.D. 1123 S. Church St.
Lucy, Roxanne Matthews ....'75 '01 C.478 B.A. L.93 J.D. [[A] Hamilton F.M.S.S.&M.]
Luna, Bruce G., II ....'72 '01 C.446 B.A. L.846 J.D. [[A] Cadwalader,W.&T.]
Luna, Donal A. ....'72 '04 C.188 B.A. L.228 J.D. [[A] Cadwalader,W.&T.]
Luna, Patricia J. ....'— '02 C.280 B.A. L.846 J.D. [[A] Cadwalader,W.&T.]
Luongo, Kelly Ann '71 '98 C.228 B.A. L.893 J.D.
101 North Tryon Street, Suite 1900 (⊙Charlotte)
Lupo, Dickson M., (AV) '57 '85 C.576 B.S.M.E. L.896 J.D.
[Alston&B.] (See Pat. Sect.)
Luski, Moses, (AV) ....'53 '78 C.178 B.A. L.575 J.D. [Shumaker,L.&K.]
Lutz, Thomas P., (AVⓣ) ....'— '74 C.401 B.S. L.665 J.D. [Dickie,M.&C.] (⊙Pitts., PA)
Lutzel, Richard J., (BV) ....'66 '92 C.567 B.A. L.823 J.D. [Lutzel,G.&Assoc.] ⊙
Lutzel, Gandy & Associates, PLLC, (BV)
3420 Toringdon Way, Suite 210 (⊙Mooresville)
Lymberis, Robin S., (BV) '55 '83 C.575 B.A. L.192 J.D.
101 N. McDowell St., Ste. 226
Lynch, Craig T., (AV) ....'59 '86 C.259 B.S. L.575 J.D. [Parker,P.A.&B.]
Lynch, Stephen M., (AV) ....'— '86 C.24 B.S. L.228 J.D. [Robinson,B.&H.]
Lyons, Charles E. (Ed), II, (AV) ....'60 '85 C.1288 B.A. L.896 J.D. [Sellers,H.A.D.&L.]
Ma, Amy L. ....'59 '84 C.860 B.A. L.575 J.D. Central Piedmont Community Coll.
Mabon, James M. '48 '73 C.25 B.A. L.665 J.D.
Gen Coun. & V.P., Human Res., Asahi Glass Amer., Inc.
MacDonald, Beth R. ....'75 '00 C.443 B.A. L.276 J.D. [[A] Alston&B.]
Machen, Ernest W., Jr., (AV) ......'22 '49 C.362 A.B. L.575 J.D. 2501 High Bridge Road
Mack, Karol Page ...'61 '86 C&L.228 B.A., J.D. Assoc. Gen. Coun., Duke Energy Corp.
Mack, Richard L., (AV) ....'— '89 C.575 B.A. L.893 J.D. [Robinson,B.&H.]
Mack, Susan E. '57 '82 C.197 B.A. L.93 J.D.
(adm. in SC; not adm. in NC) Sr. V.P. & Gen. Coun., Transamerica Reinsurance
Mackey, Nick ....'67 '03 C.999 B.A. L.8 J.D. [Mackey&Assoc.]
Mackey & Associates, PLLC ....101 North McDowell Street, Suite 114
MacLatchie, Scott D., (AVⓣ) ....'57 '84 C.800 B.S. L.426 J.D. [Womble C.S.&R.]
MacMillan, Douglas P., (AV) ....'47 '72 C&L.575 A.B., J.D. [Burris,M.P.&B.]
Macurda, William B. ....'— '97 C.937 B.A. L.930 J.D. [[A] Kennedy C.L.&H.]
Madden, Richard, Jr. '57 '83 C&L.260 B.S., J.D.
(adm. in FL; not adm. in NC) [Cadwalader,W.&T.]
Maduro, Adrian C. ....'— '80 C.994 B.A. L.564 J.D. 9034 Pickering Grove Lane
Magee, Patricia Wilson ....'78 '03 C.575 B.A. L.1228 J.D. [[A] Shumaker,L.&K.]
Maheras, John T., (CV) ....'68 '94 C.198 B.A. L.575 J.D. [[A] Horack,T.P.&L.]
Mahoney, Valerie Paige ....'63 '01 C.659 B.S.Ec. L.1398 J.D. [[A] Nelson M.R.&S.]
Maibohm, Geoffrey R. ....'72 '99 C.1372 B.A. L.823 J.D. [[A] Cadwalader,W.&T.]
Major, Christopher B. ....'78 '03 C&L.790 B.A., J.D. [[A] Moore&V.P.]
Major, Joe S., III ....'44 '71 C&L.790 B.A., J.D. 1301 Harding Place (28204)
Malickson, Jeffrey W. ....'45 '70 C.446 B.S. L.128 J.D. 6407 Idlewild Rd.
Malik, Jitendra, Ph.D. .....'74 '04 C.575 B.S. L.896 J.D. [[A] Alston&B.] (See Pat. Sect.)
Mallard, E. Lynwood, (AV) ....'— '65 C.198 A.B. L.575 J.D. [Kilpatrick S.]
Mallard, Michelle V. ....'67 '04 C.161 B.B.A. L.1059 J.D. [Mallard P.]
Mallard Law Firm, PLLC, The ....106 Providence Rd., Ste. 2
Mallos, Barrett C. ....'— '04 C.198 B.A. L.575 J.D. [[A] Katten M.R.]
Malone, Melody Y. ....'— '97 C&L.575 B.A., J.D. [[A] Moore&V.P.]
Maloney, David P., (AV) ....'52 '77 C.970 B.A. L.575 J.D. Asst. Dist. Atty.
Maloney, Margaret Behringer, (BV) '59 '86
C.597 B.A. L.228 J.D. [Hamilton F.M.S.S.&M.]
Maloney, Theodore A. ....'75 '00 C&L.575 B.A., J.D. [Maloney&M.]
Maloney & Meier ....2333 Randolph Rd., Ste. 125
Mandeville, Mary K., (BV) ....'63 '88 C.790 B.S. L.228 J.D. [Mayer,B.R.&M.]
Mangum, M. Carrington ......'70 '96 C.198 B.A. L.575 J.D. Tr. Off., Wachoria Bk., N.A.
Manion, James Robert, III '56 '81 C.901 B.A. L.229 J.D.
(adm. in PA; not adm. in NC) Sr. V.P., Secy. & Gen. Coun., GreenPoint Mortgage
Mann, Christy Townley, (AV) '60 '85
C.499 B.S. L.500 J.D. 423 S. Sharon Amity Rd Ste C
Mann, Tamara Devon '71 '97 C.788 B.A. L.904 J.D.
(adm. in MD; not adm. in NC)
Vice Pres. & Asst. Gen. Coun., Wachovia Corporation (Legal Div.)

Mann Bracken, LLC
227 West Trade Street, Suite 1610, Carillon, 28202 ⊙
Telephone: 678-801-2352 Facsimile: 678-801-2355
Email: cbracken@mannbracken.com URL: http://www.mannbracken.com
—Karen D. Washington (Not admitted in NC); Ahmad S. Washington.
Creditors Rights, Arbitration.
Approved Attorneys for: American Title Insurance Co.
Reference: Wachovia Bank of Georgia, N.A.
Vienna, Virginia Office: 1953 Gallows Road, Suite 240, 22182. Telephone: 703-245-0580. Facsimile: 703-288-4070.
Nashville, Tennessee Office: 209 10th Avenue South, Suite 542, Cummins Station, 37203. Telephone: 678-801-2352. Fax: 678-801-2355.
Atlanta, Georgia Office: One Paces West, Suite 1400, 30339. Telephone: 678-801-2352. Fax: 678-801-2355.
See Professional Biographies, CHARLOTTE, NORTH CAROLINA

Manna, Miguel ....'74 '04 C.1128 B.A. L.744 J.D. [[A] A.Gordon]
Manzano, Kristin Pernoll, (BV) ....'65 '92 C.802 B.A. L.861 J.D. [Mayer,B.R.&M.]
Manzi, David A. ....'50 '90 C.1252 B.S. L.1049 J.D. [[A] R.A.Peniston&Assoc.]
Marcille, Holly S. ....'70 '98 C.1349 B.A. L.564 J.D. [[A] Cadwalader,W.&T.]
Marek, Joseph R. ....'71 '01 C.454 B.A. L.896 J.D. [[A] Caudle&S.]
Marino, Kenneth J. '— '82 C.452 B.S. L.1338 J.D.
(adm. in PA; not adm. in NC) Asst. Gen. Coun., Bank of America
Marks, Daniel C., (BV) ....'67 '92 C&L.575 B.S., J.D. [Moreau&M.]
Marr, Michael S., (BV) ....'60 '86 C.575 B.S.B.A. L.1228 J.D. [BusinessAdvisors]
Marsh, Edward M., Jr., (AV) '47 '74 C.575 B.S.B.A. L.896 J.D.
Dep. Gen. Coun. & Asst. Secy., Duke Energy Corp.
Marsh, Richard E., Jr., (AVⓣ) ....'— '81 C.105 B.A. L.575 J.D. [Marsh]

Marsh Law Firm, (AVⓣ)
828 East Boulevard, 28203
Telephone: 704-372-1112 Fax: 704-372-0133
Email: rmarsh@marshlawfirm.com
Richard E. Marsh, Jr.
Taxation, Estate Planning, International Business Law, Business Planning.
See Professional Biographies, CHARLOTTE, NORTH CAROLINA

Marshall, Andrea R. '71 '96 C&L.347 B.A., J.D.
2nd V.P. & Asst. Gen. Coun., Transamerica Reinsurance
Marshall, Harrison L., Jr., (AV) ....'57 '82 C.198 A.B. L.880 J.D. [Helms M.&W.]
Marshall, Robert B. ....'51 '76 C.228 A.B. L.896 J.D. Exec. V.P., Aston Properties, Inc.
Marshall, S. Aaron ....'77 '04 C.886 B.S. L.846 J.D. [[A] Yurko&Assoc.]
Martin, Bentford E., (AV) ....'53 '78 C.896 B.A. L.575 J.D. [Hamilton F.M.S.S.&M.]
Martin, Donald E. ....'— '01 C.853 B.A. L.383 J.D. [[A] Kennedy C.L.&H.]
Martin, Douglas M., (AV) ....'48 '74 C.1365 B.A. L.575 J.D. [Poyner&S.]

Martin, James E., Jr., (AV) '34 '64 C&L.575 A.B., J.D.
122 North McDowell Street, P.O. Box 36331, 28236
Telephone: 704-333-4711 Fax: 704-333-2884
Email: jem@hbm-attys.com
Estate Planning, Wills, Trusts, Probate, Corporate and Real Estate Law.
See Professional Biographies, CHARLOTTE, NORTH CAROLINA

Martin, Kathy King, (BV) ....'55 '83 C.896 B.A. L.575 J.D. P.O. Box 240239
Martin, Kenneth C., (BV) ....'58 '83 C.1248 B.A. L.896 J.D. [Grandy&M.]
Martineau, Elizabeth A. ....'— '94 C.550 B.A. L.1048 J.D. [[A] Hedrick E.G.&K.]
Mascia, Michael C. ....'71 '98 C&L.575 B.A., J.D. [[A] Mayer,B.R.&M.]
Mascia, Stephanie E. ....'— '99 C.945 B.A. L.896 J.D. [[A] Kennedy C.L.&H.]
Maske, Heidi L. ....'— '01 C.576 B.A. L.607 J.D. [[A] Hedrick E.G.&K.]
Mason, James L., Jr., (AV) ....'45 '72 C.198 B.A. L.575 J.D. [Gerdes,M.&S.]
Mason-Watson, S. Y., (CV) '58 '92
C.576 B.S. L.574 J.D. 801 East Morehead Street, Suite 103
Mast, Kerri L. ....'76 '03 C.896 B.A. L.245 J.D. [[A] Moore&V.P.]
Matheny, Stephen C. '— '99 C.174 B.S. L.209 J.D.
(adm. in IL; not adm. in NC) [[A] McGuireWoods]
Matsik, Bradley W. ....'67 '94 C&L.790 B.S., J.D. 6832 Morrison Blvd.
Matthews, Christie S. ....'— '00 C.574 B.A. L.976 J.D. [[A] Nexsen P.A.K.]
Matthews, D. Lane, (BV) ....'65 '92 C.575 B.A. L.838 J.D. [Stiles B.&H.]
Matthews, David A. ....'68 '98 C.1232 B.A. L.464 J.D. [[A] Shumaker,L.&K.]
Matthews, Kimberly R. ....'66 '92 C.198 B.A. L.896 J.D. [[G] Guthrie,D.H.&S.]
Matus, T. Patrick, II, (AV) ....'47 '73 C&L.575 A.B., J.D. [Essex R.]
Mauney, Felicia Washington, (BV) ...'— '90 C.575 B.A. L.893 J.D. [Kennedy C.L.&H.]
Mauney, Gary Vance, (AV) ....'65 '95 C.576 B.A. L.29 J.D. [Lewis&R.]
May, Christopher T. ....'67 '00 C.576 B.A. L.1526 J.D. 301 S. Tryon St., Ste. 1760
Mayberry, William C., (AV) ....'66 '91 C.228 A.B. L.902 J.D. [Helms M.&W.]

Mayer, Brown, Rowe & Maw LLP, (AV) [BB]
214 N. Tryon Street, Suite 3800, 28202 ⊙
Telephone: 704-444-3500 Fax: 704-377-2033
URL: http://www.mayerbrownrowe.com
Members of Firm: Rodney E. Alexander; Jonathan A. Barrett; Kenneth D. Bell; Francis J. Blanchfield, Jr.; Christopher J. Brady; Hayden D. Brown; Jeffrey P. Cantrell; Robert B. Cordle; Robert T. Duffy; Ron D. Franklin (Not admitted in NC); C. Wells Hall III; Christopher C. Kupec; Mary K. Mandeville; Kristin Pernoll Manzano; Kathleen A. McGill; Robert L. Mendenhall; Jay Parry Monge; Keith F. Oberkell. Associates: Thais M. Alexander (Not admitted in NC); Suzanne V. Alwan (Not admitted in NC); Christy-Anne V. Betler; Christine D. Cagnina (Not admitted in NC); Eric H. Cottrell; Brian S. Cromwell; J. Benjamin Earthman (Not admitted in NC); Carolyn R. Georgiade; Jennifer T. Ha (Not admitted in NC); Fred W. Hartman (Not admitted in NC); W.C. Turner Herbert; Jack M. Knight, Jr.; Jennifer D. Lawrence (Not admitted in NC); Michael C. Mascia; Thomas D. Ricks; Daniel L. Tedrick; Margaret J. Thompson.
Antitrust, Appellate, Asia, Bankruptcy, Biotech, Pharma & Life Science, Chemicals, Collateralized Debt Obligation, Company Secretarial, Construction & Engineering, Corporate & Securities, Corporate Governance, Derivatives, E-commerce, Emerging Companies, Employee Benefits & Executive Compensation, Employee Share Incentives, Employment & Labour, Energy, Environment, Finance, Financial Services, Global Trade, Government, Government Contracts, Health Care, Information Technology, Insurance & Reinsurance, Intellectual Property, International Arbitration, Investment Management, Latin America, Legislative, Litigation & Dispute Resolution, Natural Resources, Outsourcing, Pensions, PPP/PFI & Infrastructure, Private Equity, Private Investment Fund, Pro Bono, Professional Practices, Project Finance, Property Rights, Public Law, Rail, Real Estate, Regulated Industries, Restructuring & Insolvency, Securitisation, Tax Controversy & Transfer Pricing, Tax Transactions & Consulting, Telecommunications & Media, Venture & Technology, Wealth Management.
Brussels, Belgium Office: Square de Meeûs 35, B-1000. Telephone: +011-32 2 502 55 17. Facsimile: +011-32 2 502 54 21.
Chicago, Illinois Office: 71 S. Wacker, 60606-4637. Telephone: (312) 782-0600. Facsimile: (312) 701-7711. Telex: 190404. Cable Address: LEMAY.
Cologne, Germany Office: Kaiser-Wilhelm-Ring 27-29, 50672. Telephone: +49-221-5771-100. Facsimile: +49-221-5771-199.
Frankfurt am Main, Germany Office: Bockenheimer Landstraße 98-100, D-60323. Telephone: 011-49-69 79 41-0. Facsimile: 011-49-69 79 41-100.
Houston, Texas Office: 700 Louisiana Street, Suite 3600, 77002-2730. Telephone: (713) 221-1651. Facsimile: (713) 224-6410. Telex: 775809. Cable: LEMAYHOU.
London, England Office: 11 Pilgrim Street, London EC4V 6RW. Telephone: 011-44-207-248-4282. Facsimile: 011-44-207-248-2009.
Los Angeles, California Office: 350 South Grand Avenue, 25th Floor, 90071-1503. Telephone: (213) 229-9500. Facsimile: (213) 625-0248. Telex: 188089. Cable: LEMAYLA.
New York, New York Office: 1675 Broadway, 10019-5820. Telephone: (212) 506-2500. Facsimile: (212) 262-1910. Telex: 701842. Cable: LEMAYEN.
Palo Alto, California Office: Two Palo Alto Square, Suite 300, 94306. Telephone: (650) 331-2000. Facsimile: (650) 331-2060.
Paris, France Office: 41 Avenue Hoche, 75008. Telephone: 011-33-1-53-53-43-43. Facsimile: 011-33-1-53-96-03-83.
Washington, D.C. Office: 1909 K Street, N.W., 20006-1101. Telephone: (202) 263-3000. Facsimile: (202) 263-3300. Telex: 892603. Cable: LEMAYDC.
Representative Offices:
Beijing, People's Republic of China: 7-1-31, Qijayuanr, 9 Jianguomen Wai Avenue, Chaoyang District, 100600. Telephone: 011-86-10-85322221. Facsimile: 011-86-10-85322156.
Shanghai, People's Republic of China: 2805 Plaza 66, 1266 Nanjing Road West. Telephone: 011-86-21-6288-1250. Facsimile: 011-86-21-6288-1255.
Mexico City, Mexico, D.F., Independent Mexico Correspondent: Jáuregui, Navarrete, Nader y Rojas, S.C., Abogados Torre Arcos, Paseo de los Tamarindos No. 400-B. Col. Bosques de las Lomas, 05120. Telephone: 011-5255-5-267-45-00. Facsimile: 011-5255-5-267-45-98.
See Professional Biographies, CHARLOTTE, NORTH CAROLINA

Maynard, Katherine Gordon ....'— '99 C.896 B.A. L.4210 J.D. [[A] Robinson,B.&H.]
Mayo, Judy Zecchin '64 '90
C.659 B.A. L.145 J.D. Assoc. Gen. Coun., Duke Energy Corp.

Mayo, Stephen A., (BV) '— '90
C.896 B.A. L.902 J.D. Assoc. Gen. Coun., Bank of America
Mayopoulos, Timothy J. '— '85 C.188 B.A. L.569 J.D.
(adm. in NY; not adm. in NC) Exec. VP & Gen. Coun., Bank of America
McAllister, Lawana M. . . . . . '59 '83 C.30 B.S. L.831 J.D. 6517 Stonehill Ct.

McAngus Goudelock & Courie, P.L.L.C., (BV)
6302 Fairview Road, Suite 700, P.O. Box 30307, 28230 ⊙
Telephone: 704-643-6303 Telecopier: 704-643-2376
Email: mgc@mgclaw.com URL: http://www.mgclaw.com
H. George Kurani; John T. Jeffries; Andrew R. Ussery;—Trula R. Mitchell; Charles D. Cheney (Resident); Louis A. Waple; Christine Latona; Robert B. Starnes; Sally G. Boswell; Jeffrey D. "J.D." Keister; Lauren M. Citrano; John E. Spainhour; Kara L. Sharrard; Terry L. Wallace; Katherine Hall; Katherine L. McCarthy; Joseph N. Hamrick (Resident, Charlotte, North Carolina Office); Janiere Taylor; Rod Sherman.
General Civil Litigation Practice, Administrative, Insurance Defense, Workers Compensation, Employment Law, Bankruptcy, Banking and Consumer Law; Government, Construction, Product Liability, Premises Liability, Environmental, Commercial Law, Health Care, Administration and Litigation.
Columbia, South Carolina Office: 700 Gervais Street, Suite 300, P.O. Box 12519, Capitol Station, 29211-2519. Telephone: 803-779-2300. Telecopier: 803-748-0526.
Charleston, South Carolina Office: 78 Wentworth Street, Suite 200, P.O. Box 877, 29402. Telephone: 843-534-0101. Telecopier: 843-534-0605.
Greenville, South Carolina Office: 420 Park Avenue, Suite 301, P.O. Box 2980, 29602. Telephone: 864-239-4000. Telecopier: 864-242-3199.
See Professional Biographies, CHARLOTTE, NORTH CAROLINA

McArdle, Peter E., (BV) . . . . . '69 '95 C.575 B.A. L.1228 J.D. [Knox B.K.&G.]
McArthur, B. Palmer, Jr., (AV) . . . . . '54 '82 C.893 B.S. L.846 J.D. [Moore&V.P.]
McAvoy, Garrett J. . . . . . '63 '93 C.870 B.S. L.923 J.D. [Cozen O.]
McBryde, Neill G., (AV) . . . . . '44 '69 C.198 A.B. L.575 J.D. [Moore&V.P.]
McCachren, Jon H., (BV) . . . . . '57 '86 C.577 B.M. L.575 J.D. [Olive]
McCall, William G. . . . . . '51 '80 C.198 B.A. L.469 J.D. Asst. Dist. Atty.
McCarley, DeWitt F., (AV) . . . . . '52 '77 C&L.575 B.A., J.D. City Atty.
McCarthy, Katherine L. . . . . . '79 '04 C.577 B.A. L.575 J.D. [Ⓐ McAngus G.&C.]
McClerin, Richard Leon . . . . . '41 '94 C.801 B.A. L.790 J.D. 428 East 4th Street, Suite 428
McClintock, Ingrid . . . . . '68 '97 C&L.893 B.A., J.D. [Ⓐ Helms M.&W.]
McClure, M. DeVondria '— '98 C.813 B.A. L.575 J.D.
3325 Washburn Avenue, Suite 212
McConnell, David M., (AV) . . . . . '12 '36 C.198 B.S. L.276 J.D. 3518 Cypress Club Dr.
McConnell, Jason . . . . . '— '00 C.577 B.A. L.424 J.D. [Ⓐ Littler M.]
McConnell, Jennifer L. '72 '01 C.420 B.A. L.424 J.D.
Sr. Corp. Coun., Compass Group, U.S.A. Inc.
McCormack, J. Parrish '— '93 C.228 A.B. L.930 J.D.
VP & Asst. Gen. Coun., Wachovia Corporation (Legal Department)
McCoy, Christopher D. . . . . . '— '01 C.575 A.B. L.692 J.D. [Ⓐ Kennedy C.L.&H.]
McCoy, Leonard H. '18 '51 C.901 L.923 LL.B.
(adm. in WV; not adm. in NC) 3242 Mountainbrook Rd.‡
McCoy, Michael D., (AV) '50 '75 C.339 B.S.E.E. L.146 J.D.
[Alston&B.] (See Pat. Sect.)
McCready, Kent J., (AV) . . . . . '— '84 C.205 B.A. L.575 J.D. [Robinson,B.&H.]
McCrory, Susan I., (AV) . . . . . '— '81 C&L.500 B.A., J.D. [Ⓐ Robinson,B.&H.]
McCullough, Andrew M. . . . . . '79 '04 C&L.575 B.A., J.D. [Ⓐ Wishart,N.H.&P.]
McCullough, Joseph D., (AV) . . . . . '— '83 C&L.896 B.A., J.D. [Nexsen P.A.K.]
McCutcheon, R. Scott, (BV) . . . . . '46 '72 C.608 B.A. L.8 J.D. [McKaig&M.]
McDermott, Christopher M. . . . . . '60 '87 C.951 B.A. L.228 J.D. [Cadwalader,W.&T.]
McDermott, Gary T. . . . . . '75 '05 C.1458 B.A. L.280 J.D. [Ⓐ Parker,P.A.&B.]
McDermott, Richard M. . . . . '69 '94 C&L.436 B.S.E.E., J.D. [Alston&B.] (See Pat. Sect.)
McDonald, J. Bruce, (BV) . . . . . '55 '81 C.1195 B.A. L.575 J.D. 601 East Trade St.
McDonald, John G. . . . . . '66 '93 C.1031 B.S. L.823 J.D. [Helms M.&W.]
McDonald, Melissa L. . . . . . '— '97 C.574 B.A. L.1345 J.D. [Ⓐ Hedrick E.G.&K.]
McDonnell, Robert D., (BV) . . . . . '45 '70 C.1126 A.B. L.602 J.D. 212 South Tryon Street
McDonough, Stephen F. '65 '04 C.462 B.S. L.818 J.D.
10925 David Taylor Dr., Ste. 100
McDowell, Valecia M. . . . . . '73 '98 C&L.228 A.B., J.D. [Ⓐ Moore&V.P.]
McElroy, Heather Marie . . . . . '69 '99 C.643 B.A. L.744 J.D. 10802 Tradition View Dr.
McElroy, Pender R., (AV) . . . . . '40 '68 C&L.575 B.S., J.D. [James,M.&D.]
McGill, John K., (BV) . . . . '56 '83 C.247 B.S. L.575 J.D. 2810 Coliseum Ctr. Dr., Ste. 370
McGill, Kathleen A. . . . . . '— '86 C.174 B.A. L.276 J.D. [Mayer,B.R.&M.]
McGinley, Michael J. '49 '86 C.107 B.A. L.564 J.D.
(adm. in NY; not adm. in NC) V.P., Royal Ins. Co.
McGinnis, Karin M., (BV) . . . . . '67 '92 C.232 B.A. L.575 J.D. [Moore&V.P.]
McGinnis, Kevin A. . . . . . '74 '99 C.228 B.A. L.602 J.D. [Ⓐ Helms M.&W.]
McGirt, Sherri L., (AV) . . . . . '— '74 C&L.575 A.B., J.D. [McNair]
McGoogan, E. Graham, Jr., (AV) . . . . . '49 '74 C.198 B.A. L.575 J.D. [Helms M.&W.]
McGrath, Peter J., Jr., (AV) . . . . . '61 '86 C.976 B.A. L.575 J.D. [Moore&V.P.]

McGuireWoods LLP, (AV)
Bank of America Corporate Center, 100 North Tryon Street, Suite 2900, 28202-4011 ⊙
Telephone: 704-373-8999 Fax: 704-373-8935
Email: info@mcguirewoods.com URL: http://www.mcguirewoods.com
Partners: Thomas E. Cabaniss; Kimberly Q. Cacheris; Jeffrey R. Capwell; W. T. Cranfill, Jr.; John C. Fennebresque; Patricia F. Hosmer; Brenton D. Jeffcoat; Richard F. Kane; Wade M. Kennedy; C. Ralph Kinsey, Jr.; Keith M. Korenchuk; J. Mark Langdon; Josiah C. T. Lucas; John O. Pollard; Paul G. Porter; Marvin L. Rogers; Jason H. Scott; James C. Smith; Bruce M. Steen; Thomas E. Taylor. Of Counsel: B. Bernard Burns, Jr. Associates: Steven T. Ackermann; Margaret N. Boyle; Robert A. Cox, Jr.; Matthew J. Davis; Susan Pyle Dion; Walter T. Donaldson, III; Jonathan Harlan Edgar; Allyson Grainger; Michael C. Griffin; James Edward Hickmon; Melissa M. Kemmer; Aaron J. Longo; Stephen C. Matheny (Not admitted in NC); Staci E. Rosche; Miranda M. Zolot (Not admitted in NC).
Accountants Liability, Administrative Law, Advertising Law, Affordable Housing, Alternative Dispute Resolution, Americans with Disabilities Act, Antitrust, Appellate Practice, Asbestos Litigation, Asset Based Finance, Automotive Products Liability, Bankruptcy, Banks and Banking, Business Acquisitions, Business Divestitures, Business Law, Business Litigation, Buying and Selling of Businesses, Capital Markets, Charitable Giving, Class Actions, Coal Mining, Cogeneration; College and University Law, Commercial Litigation, Commercial Real Estate, Communications and Media, Complex Commercial Litigation, Computer Contracts, Confidentiality Agreements, Construction Equipment Liability, Construction Litigation, Consumer Finance, Content Licensing, Contracts, Copyright Licensing, Corporate Control Contests, Corporate Finance, Corporate Governance, Corporate Investigations, Corporate Law, Corporate Reorganization, Covenants Not to Compete, Creditors Rights, Criminal Taxation, Digital Signatures, Domain Name Infringement, Domain Names, Drug and Medical Device Defense, Drug and Medical Device Litigation, E-Commerce, Education Law, Electric Utilities, Emerging Growth Companies, Employee Benefits, Employee Benefits Litigation, Employment Breach of Contract, Employment Contracts, Employment Discrimination, Energy, Energy Acquisitions, Energy Project Development, Energy Regulation, Entertainment Law, Environmental Administrative Law, Environmental Compliance, Environmental Land Use, Environmental Law, Environmental Litigation, Environmental Real Estate, ERISA, Executive Compensation, False Advertising, Family Business Law, Fiduciary Litigation, Finance, First Amendment Law, Franchises and Franchising, Gas Utilities, Government Investigations, Government Relations, Health Care, High Technology Contracts, Hospital Administration, Hospital Law, Hostile Takeovers, Immigration Law, Independent Power, Insurance Litigation, Intellectual Property, Intellectual Property Licensing, Intellectual Property Litigation, Intellectual Property Portfolio Management, Intellectual Property Procurement, Intellectual Property Rights, International Arbitration, International Mergers and Acquisitions, International Taxation, International Trade, Internet Licensing, Joint Venture Litiga-

(This Listing Continued)

McGuireWoods LLP (Continued)
tion, Joint Ventures, Labor and Employment, Labor Relations, Land Use, Latex Allergy Litigation, Lead Poisoning, Leasing, Legal Ethics and Professional Responsibility, Leveraged Buyouts, Litigation, Litigation Management, Lobbying, Local Taxation, Marketing Law, Media Law, Merger Reorganization, Mergers and Acquisitions Finance, Mergers, Acquisitions and Divestitures, Motorcycle Products Liability, Municipal Law, Music Law, Natural Gas, North American Energy Trade, Oil and Gas Law, Partnership Law, Partnership Litigation, Partnership Taxation, Patent Litigation, Patent Prosecution, Patents, Petroleum Trading, Products Liability, Products Liability Insurance Coverage, Project Finance, Promotion Law, Proprietary Rights, Proxy Contests, Public Finance, Public Utility Law, Railroad Law, Real Estate, Real Estate Acquisitions, Real Estate Development, Real Estate Investment Trusts, Real Estate Leasing, Regulatory Law, Resorts and Leisure, Securities, Securities Litigation, Securities Regulation, Securitization, Software Copyright, Software Licensing, Software Protection, Spin-Offs, Sponsorship Law, Sports Law, Sports Licensing, Sports Marketing Law, State Taxation, Structured Finance, Sweepstakes, Takeovers, Tax Audits, Tax Credits, Tax Exempt Organizations, Tax Litigation, Taxation, Technology Licensing, Telephone Utility Regulation, Toxic Tort Class Actions, Toxic Torts, Trade Regulation, Trade Secrets, Trademark Registration, Trademarks, Transportation, Trusts and Estates, Trusts and Estates Taxation, Union Labor Law, Utility Law, Utility Regulation, Vaccine Injury, Web Site Development, White Collar Crime, Wrongful Termination.
Atlanta, Georgia Office: The Proscenium, 1170 Peachtree Street, N.E., Suite 2100, 30309-7649. Telephone: 404-443-5500. Fax: 404-443-5599.
Baltimore, Maryland Office: 7 Saint Paul Street, Suite 1000, 21202-1671. Telephone: 410-659-4400. Fax: 410-659-4599.
Charlottesville, Virginia Office: Court Square Building, 310 Fourth Street N.E., Suite 300, P.O. Box 1288, 22902-1288. Telephone: 434-977-2500. Fax: 434-980-2222.
Chicago, Illinois Office: 77 West Wacker Drive, Suite 4100, 60601-1815. Telephone: 312-849-8100. Fax: 312-849-3690.
Jacksonville, Florida Office: Bank of America Tower, 50 North Laura Street, Suite 3300, 32202-3661. Telephone: 904-798-3200. Fax: 904-798-3207.
Los Angeles, California Office: 11601 Wilshire Boulevard, 90025. Telephone: 310-575-1848.
McLean, (Tysons Corner) Virginia Office: 1750 Tysons Boulevard, Suite 1800, 22102-4215. Telephone: 703-712-5000. Fax: 703-712-5050.
New York, New York Office: 1345 Avenue of the Americas, 10105-0106. Telephone: 212-548-2100. Fax: 212-548-2150.
Norfolk, Virginia Office: World Trade Center, 101 West Main Street, Suite 9000, 23510-1655. Telephone: 757-640-3700. Fax: 757-640-3701.
Pittsburgh, Pennsylvania Office: Dominion Tower, 23rd Floor, 625 Liberty Avenue, 15222-3142. Telephone: 412-667-6000. Fax: 412-667-6050.
Richmond, Virginia Office: One James Center, 901 East Cary Street, 23219-4030. Telephone: 804-775-1000. Fax: 804-775-1061.
Washington, D.C. Office: Washington Square, 1050 Connecticut Avenue, N.W., Suite 1200, 20036-5317. Telephone: 202-857-1700. Fax: 202-857-1737.
Almaty, Republic of Kazakhstan Office: McGuireWoods Kazakhstan LLP, 41B, Kazibek Bi Street, 5th Floor, 480100. Telephone: +7-3272-596-100. Fax: +7-3272-596-116.
Brussels, Belgium Office: Avenue Louise 250, bte 64, 1050. Telephone: +32-(0)2-629-42-11. Fax: +32 (0)2 629 42 22.
Reviser of the Virginia Law Digest for this Directory.
See Professional Biographies, CHARLOTTE, NORTH CAROLINA

McIntosh, John V., (AV) . . . . . '54 '79 C&L.575 B.A., J.D. [Moore&V.P.]

McIntosh Law Firm, The, P.C.
(See Davidson)

McIntyre, D. Baker, III . . . . . '64 '92 C.576 B.S.M.E. L.1228 J.D. 1 Woodlawn Green
McIvor, Kara F. . . . . . '71 '98 C.880 B.A. L.902 J.D. [Knox B.K.&G.]
McKaig, A. Stuart, III, (AV) . . . . . '45 '74 C.228 A.B. L.880 J.D. [McKaig&M.]

McKaig & McCutcheon, P.A., (AV)
219 Greenwich Road, 28211
Telephone: 704-365-0390 Fax: 704-365-0652
URL: http://www.mckaigandmccutcheonlaw.com
—A. Stuart McKaig, III; R. Scott McCutcheon; Heather McKaig Tillman.
Business Law, Buying and Selling of Businesses, Limited Liability Law, Family Business, Partnership Law, Corporate Law, Business Litigation, Collections, Contracts, Estate Planning, Trusts and Estates, Real Estate, Condominium Law, Landlord and Tenant Law, Wills and Probate.
See Professional Biographies, CHARLOTTE, NORTH CAROLINA

McKee, Matthew Thor . . . . . '67 '02 C.925 B.S. L.469 J.D. [Ⓐ Kellam&P.]
McKee, Meredith '77 '02 C.597 B.S. L.1565 J.D.
(adm. in CA; not adm. in NC) [Ⓐ Womble C.S.&R.]
McKeithen, A. Ward, (AV) . . . . . '— '63 C.198 A.B. L.228 LL.B. [Robinson,B.&H.]
McKeithen, R. Malloy, (AV) . . . . . '39 '66 C.198 A.B. L.575 J.D. [Ⓒ Helms M.&W.]
McKinzie, C. Wayne . . . . . '67 '93 C.674 B.A. L.893 J.D. [Moore&V.P.]
McKnight, Reggie E. . . . . . '70 '97 C.790 B.A. L.574 J.D. 200 N. McDowell St.
McLain, Kevin G. '55 '80 C.529 B.A. L.809 J.D.
Transamerica Life Ins. and Annuity Co.
McLean, H. Randolph . . . . . '46 '71 C.838 A.B. L.893 J.D. Internal Revenue Service
McLean, John T., (BV) '67 '93 C.576 B.A. L.575 J.D.
NC State Counsel, LandAmerica Financial Group, Inc.
McLean, L. Thomas, Jr. '— '97
C&L.575 B.S.B.A., J.D. LendingTree, Inc. (Legal Department)
McLean, Peter, III, (AV) . . . . . '— '81 C.197 A.B. L.896 J.D. [Kennedy C.L.&H.]
McLean, Robert S., (BV) . . . . . '— '91 C.198 B.A. L.575 J.D. [Robinson,B.&H.]
McLoughlin, James P., Jr., (AV) . . . . . '56 '84 C.321 B.A. L.228 J.D. [Moore&V.P.]
McMahan, J. Kenneth . . . . . '11 '34 L.981 LL.B. 4527 Gaynor Rd.‡
McMahon, Arthur J. '46 '76 C.576 B.S. L.818 J.D.
(adm. in MA; not adm. in NC) Exec. V.P., Egret Holdings Inc.
McMahon, John P., (AVⓉ) . . . . . '42 '67 C.749 A.B. L.569 J.D. [McMahon&C.]
McMahon & Connell, P.C., (AVⓉ) . . . . . 428 East 4th Street, Suite 404 (⊙New York, NY)
McMillan, Ralph R., (AV) . . . . . '49 '77 C.968 A.B. L.575 J.D. [McMillan&T.]
McMillan, William P. . . . . . '60 '85 C.893 B.A. L.228 J.D. [Katten M.R.]

McMillan & Terry, P.A., (AV)
6101 Carnegie Boulevard, Suite 310, 28209
Telephone: 704-552-9997 Facsimile: 704-552-0540
Email: mailbox@mcmillan-terry.com URL: http://www.lawyers.com/mcmillanandterry
Ralph R. McMillan; Daniel A. Terry;—Brad Allen Bailey; Michelle S. Crabtree; Christopher Jay Albee.
Residential and Commercial Real Estate, Corporate, Estate Planning.
See Professional Biographies, CHARLOTTE, NORTH CAROLINA

McMillian, Alfonso, Jr. . . . . . '— '93 C.896 B.A. L.893 J.D. Bank of America
McMullen, William H., Jr., (BV) . . . . . '39 '69 C.228 A.B. L.500 J.D. [Buckley,M.&B.]
McNair, William H., (AV) . . . . . '34 '61 C.198 B.S. L.575 J.D. [Shumaker,L.&K.]

McNair Law Firm, P.A., (AV)
Two Wachovia Center, 301 South Tryon Street, Suite 1615, 28282 ⊙
Telephone: 704-347-1170 Facsimile: 704-347-4467
Email: cfort@mcnair.net URL: http://www.mcnair.net
Andrew W. Lax; Sherri L. McGirt; Allan W. Singer. Special Counsel: Chase B. Saunders;—Marna M. Albanese; Charity Babington Falls.
Administrative, Admiralty, Antitrust, Banking, Bankruptcy, Civil and Criminal Practice in all State and Federal Courts of Record, Corporate, Environmental, ERISA, Estate Planning, Health Care, Intellectual Property, Immigration, International, Interstate Land Sales, Labor and Employment Relations, Legislative/Governmental (National and State), Mergers and Acquisitions, Municipal Finance, Probate, Real Estate, Regulatory, Securities, Tax, Telecommunications, and Utility Law.
Columbia, South Carolina Office: 1301 Gervais Street, P.O. Box 11390, 29211. Telephone: 803-799-9800. Facsimile: 803-799-9804.

(This Listing Continued)

McNair Law Firm, P.A. (Continued)

Anderson, South Carolina Office: 500 South McDuffie Street, P.O. Box 4086, 29621. Telephone: 864-226-1688. Facsimile: 864-225-6456.
Bluffton, South Carolina Office: 5 Belfair Village Drive, 29910-2605. Telephone: 843-815-2171. Facsimile: 843-815-5991.
Charleston, South Carolina Office: 100 Calhoun Street, Suite 400, 29401. Telephone: 843-723-7831. Facsimile: 843-722-3227.
Georgetown, South Carolina Office: 121 Screven Street, P.O. Drawer 418, 29442. Telephone: 843-546-6102. Facsimile: 843-546-0096.
Greenville, South Carolina Office: Bank of America Plaza, 7 North Laurens Street-Suite 600, P.O. Box 447. 29602. Telephone: 864-271-4940. Facsimile: 864-233-0423; 864-271-4015.
Hilton Head Island, South Carolina Office: Shelter Cove Executive Park, 23-B Shelter Cove Lane, Suite 400, P.O. Drawer 3, 29938-0003. Telephone: 843-785-2171. Facsimile: 843-686-5991.
Myrtle Beach, South Carolina Office: Founders Centre, 2411 Oak Street, Suite 206, 29577. Telephone: 843-444-1107. Facsimile: 843-444-4729.
Raleigh, North Carolina Office: Landmark Center, Suite 500, 4601 Six Forks Road, 27609. Telephone: 919-786-4061. Fax: 919-786-4076.

See Professional Biographies, CHARLOTTE, NORTH CAROLINA

McNamara, Paul J. .... ’— ’03 C.575 B.A. L.896 J.D. [Ⓐ Kilpatrick S.]
McNaull, W. D., Jr. .... ’37 ’63 C&L.575 B.S., LL.B. P.O. Box 9235
McNeely, Patrick M., (AV) .... ’46 ’73 C&L.575 B.A., J.D. [Ⓒ Cadwalader,W.&T.]
McNeely, Richard P., (BV) .... ’37 ’63 C&L.575 B.A., LL.B. P.O. Box 21129

McNeely, Thomas A., (AV) ’40 ’70 C.790 A.B. L.575 J.D.
1011 East Morehead Street, Suite 300, 28204
Telephone: 704-376-6114 Fax: 704-332-2716
Email: tam@tmcneelylaw.com URL: http://www.lawyers.com/thomasmcneelylaw
Catastrophic Injury, Professional Liability, Wrongful Death, Products Liability, Inadequate Security, Bad Faith, Insurance Claims.

See Professional Biographies, CHARLOTTE, NORTH CAROLINA

McNeill, Robert B., (AV) .... ’60 ’85 C&L.575 B.S.B.A., J.D. [Horack,T.P.&L.]
McNeill, Thomas E., (BV) .... ’— ’88 C.575 B.S.B.A. L.896 J.D. [Ⓒ Robinson,B.&H.]
McPhail, E. Fred, Jr., (BV) .... ’47 ’72 C.880 B.A. L.575 J.D. 3300 Ferncliff
McPhee, Joel Elisha, Jr. ’65 ’93 C.999 B.A. L.117 J.D.
(adm. in OH; not adm. in NC) Dir. for Global Capabality Sourcing, Wachovia Corp.
McTammany, Heather Ann ’76 ’02 C&L.575 B.A., J.D.
227 West Trade Street, Suite 1200
Meacham, L. Hunter, Jr. ’48 ’73 C&L.575 B.S., J.D.
Fidelity National Title Insurance Co.
Meade, Carolyn P. .... ’72 ’01 C&L.893 B.A., J.D. [Ⓐ Moore&V.P.]
Meckler, Steven A., (BV) .... ’70 ’99 C.381 B.A. L.930 J.D. [Ⓐ Shumaker,L.&K.]
Meek, Richard T., (BV) .... ’31 ’54 C&L.838 LL.B. 101 N. McDowell St.
Meeker, Catherine Amspacher .... ’62 ’90 C.94 B.S. L.945 J.D. [Alston&B.]
Meekins, Frederick C., (AV) .... ’29 ’59 C&L.575 A.B., J.D. 301 S. McDowell St.‡
Mehler, Scott S. .... ’72 ’97 C.169 B.A. L.464 J.D. [BusinessAdvisors]
Mehta, Kiran H., (AV) .... ’— ’83 C.188 A.B. L.309 J.D. [Kennedy C.L.&H.]
Meier, Steven T. .... ’71 ’97 C.207 B.S. L.879 J.D. [Maloney&M.]
Melin, David S. .... ’75 ’00 C.966 B.A. L.575 J.D. [Ⓐ Rayburn C.&D.]
Mendenhall, Robert L., (AV) .... ’54 ’83 C.198 B.A. L.575 J.D. [Mayer,B.R.&M.]
Mendini, Jon .... ’65 ’91 C.1128 B.A. L.790 J.D. [Mendini]
Mendini Law Firm, The .... 201 Manning Dr.
Menser, Aaron .... ’— ’04 C.240 B.A. L.245 J.D. [Ⓐ Littler M.]
Menser, Ashley B. .... ’— ’04 C.260 B.A. L.245 J.D. [Ⓐ Alston&B.]
Menser, Barton M., (AV) .... ’50 ’78 C&L.575 A.B., J.D. Dep. Dist. Atty.
Mercer, Fritz Y., Jr. .... ’43 ’74 C.1126 B.S. L.421 J.D. Dist. J.
Merriam, Dennis C. ’55 ’81 C.188 B.S. L.259 J.D.
(adm. in FL; not adm. in NC) 2001 Rexford Rd.
Merrill, Heloise C., (AV) .... ’50 ’77 C&L.228 B.A., J.D. [Parker,P.A.&B.]
Merritt, Keith J., (AV) .... ’65 ’90 C&L.575 B.A., J.D. [Hamilton F.M.S.S.&M.]
Merritt, Mark W., (AV) .... ’— ’84 C.575 B.A. L.893 J.D. [Robinson,B.&H.]
Mesibov, Brian D. .... ’72 ’98 C.813 A.B. L.1066 J.D. [Ⓐ Moore&V.P.]
Messana, Frank S. .... ’57 ’85 C.1154 B.A. L.213 J.D. 12225 Bridge Creek Way
Metcalf, Marc A. .... ’— ’05 C.1128 B.A. L.575 J.D. [Ⓐ Hedrick E.G.&K.]
Metcalf, Shannon .... ’— ’00 C.34 B.S. L.574 J.D. [Ⓐ Hedrick E.G.&K.]
Metz, Mark K. ’59 ’87 C.188 B.S. L.107 J.D.
Sr. V.P. & Dep. Gen. Coun., First Union Corp.
Meyer, Robert B. .... ’63 ’94 C.797 B.A. L.192 J.D. Fam. Dollar Stores
Michael, Mark A., (BV) .... ’— ’75 C.676 B.S. L.228 J.D. [Ⓒ Hedrick E.G.&K.]
Michaux, Roy H., Jr., (AV) .... ’— ’65 C&L.575 B.S., LL.B. [Kennedy C.L.&H.]

Michel, Aaron E., (BV) ’— ’81 C.608 B.S. L.117 J.D.
3736 Surry Ridge Court, 28210-6921
Telephone: 704-451-8351 Fax: 704-643-1004
Email: mail@aaronmichel.com URL: http://www.aaronmichel.com
Litigation: Federal and State Practice.

See Professional Biographies, CHARLOTTE, NORTH CAROLINA

Middlebrooks, James G., (AV) .... ’58 ’83 C.1365 B.A. L.280 J.D. [Helms M.&W.]
Milgrom, Brent M., Jr., (AV) ’67 ’92 C.575 B.A. L.893 J.D.
[Parker,P.A.&B.] (⊙Columbia, Spartanburg, SC)
Miller, Connie J., (BV) ’— ’84 C.375 B.A. L.802 J.D.
(adm. in TX; not adm. in NC) Asst. Gen. Coun., Bank of America
Miller, George J., (AV) .... ’26 ’53 C&L.575 B.S., LL.B. [Ⓒ Wishart,N.H.&P.]
Miller, George N., (BV) .... ’60 ’86 C.575 B.S. L.1228 J.D. [Dozier,M.P.&M.]
Miller, J. Jerome .... ’38 ’75 C.645 B.S. L.327 J.D. 723 S. Sharon Amity Road, Suite 105
Miller, John R., (AV) .... ’— ’75 C&L.228 A.B., J.D. [Robinson,B.&H.]
Miller, John R., Jr. .... ’75 ’02 C.893 B.A. L.896 J.D. [Ⓐ Rayburn C.&D.]
Miller, Joseph J. .... ’38 ’75 C.945 B.S. L.327 J.D. 723 S. Sharon Amity Rd., Ste. 105
Miller, K. Matthew .... ’75 ’01 C.198 B.A. L.861 J.D. [Ⓐ Womble C.S.&R.]
Miller, Leslie H., (AV) .... ’54 ’79 C.232 B.A. L.692 J.D. [Miller&H.]
Miller, Mary Catherine ’60 ’85 C.300 B.A. L.276 J.D.
(adm. in DC; not adm. in NC) Assoc. Pastor, Amity Presbyterian Church
Miller, Michael J. .... ’67 ’93 C.477 B.A. L.146 J.D. [BusinessAdvisors]
Miller, Nick J., (AV) ’30 ’59 C&L.575 B.A., J.D.
725 East Trade Street, Suite 125 (⊙Matthews)
Miller, R. Craig, Jr., (AV) .... ’48 ’75 C&L.575 A.B., J.D. [Dozier,M.P.&M.]
Miller, Regan A., (BV) .... ’52 ’78 C.951 B.A. L.575 J.D. Dist. J.

Miller & Hall, P.A., (AV)
216 N. McDowell Street, Suite 106, 28204
Mailing Address: P.O. Box 36957, Charlotte, NC 28236-6957
Telephone: 704-375-8007 Fax: 704-375-1374
URL: http://www.millerandhallpa.com
Leslie H. Miller; Dana C. Hall.
General Civil Trial Practice, Real Estate, Corporate, Wills, Trust, Probate, Estate Planning and Collection Law.

See Professional Biographies, CHARLOTTE, NORTH CAROLINA

Millette, Samuel M., (AV) .... ’23 ’51 C&L.896 J.D. 101 N. McDowell St.

Mills, Victoria Aiken ’68 ’92
C&L.790 B.A., J.D. Real Estate Atty., Family Dollar Stores, Inc.
Millsap, Steven M. ’67 ’98
C.699 B.A. L.259 J.D. Atty., Continental Tire North America, Inc.

Millsaps, Joe T., (AV) ’34 ’61 C&L.896 A.B., LL.B.
404 Charlotte National Building, 428 East Fourth Street, 28202
Telephone: 704-358-8524 Fax: 704-358-8405; Toll Free: 800-500-8524
Email: attyjtm@bellsouth.net URL: http://www.lawyers.com/joemillsapslaw
Civil Trial Practice, Negligence, Personal Injury, Wills and Probate, Trusts, Estates, Estate Planning and Administration.
Reference: Central Carolina Bank and Trust Company.

See Professional Biographies, CHARLOTTE, NORTH CAROLINA

Mingo, Amanda A. .... ’— ’97 C.48 B.A. L.576 J.D. [Ⓐ Rawls,D.&S.]
Mistretta, Dawn T. .... ’73 ’03 C.1237 B.A. L.1228 J.D. [Ⓐ Womble C.S.&R.]
Mitchell, David P. .... ’— ’92 C.228 A.B. L.880 J.D. Asst. Gen. Coun., Bank of America
Mitchell, Jennifer I. .... ’— ’92 C.198 B.A. L.896 J.D. [Hedrick E.G.&K.]
Mitchell, Mcarthur D. .... ’51 ’89 C&L.574 B.S., B.S. 4733 Hanging Ivy Dr.
Mitchell, Richard M., (AV) .... ’40 ’72 C.1128 B.A. L.575 J.D. [Mitchell,R.&T.]
Mitchell, Rickye McKoy .... ’59 ’84 C&L.575 B.A., J.D. Dist. J.
Mitchell, Thomas L. .... ’64 ’93 C.339 B.S. L.902 J.D. [Moore&V.P.]
Mitchell, Trula R. .... ’72 ’98 C.923 B.A. L.790 J.D. [Ⓐ McAngus G.&C.]

Mitchell, Rallings & Tissue, PLLC, (AV)
1800 Carillon, 227 West Trade Street, 28202
Telephone: 704-376-6574 FAX: 704-342-1531
Members of Firm: Richard M. Mitchell (Board Certified Specialist in Bankruptcy Law, North Carolina State Board of Legal Specialization); Thomas B. Rallings, Jr.; Joseph N. Tissue. Associates: James L. Fretwell; Heather W. Culp; Christopher J. Culp.
General Civil and Trial Practice in all State and Federal Courts. Bankruptcy, Real Estate, Commercial Law, Corporate, Negligence, Banking, Business Law, Construction Law, Debtor and Creditor, Employment.
Representative Clients: Bonitz Contracting Co.; Captain D's. Inc.; Dyke Industries, Inc.; Edgcomb Metals; Titan Building Products, Inc.
References: Bank of Mecklenburg; Central Carolina Bank ; N.C.N.B.

See Professional Biographies, CHARLOTTE, NORTH CAROLINA

Mobley, Jared D. .... ’— ’98 C&L.790 B.S., J.D. [Ⓐ Kennedy C.L.&H.]
Moffett, M. Ellen, (BV) ’47 ’82 C.569 B.A. L.705 J.D.
(adm. in PA; not adm. in NC) Gen. Coun. & Sec., Compass Group, U.S.A. Inc.
Molony, Thomas J. .... ’— ’98 C&L.902 B.S., J.D. [Robinson,B.&H.]
Monaghan, Anthony F. .... ’72 ’98 C&L.575 B.A., J.D. 720 E 4th St., Ste. 308
Monge, Jay Parry, (AVⓉ) .... ’43 ’69 C.309 A.B. L.893 LL.B. [Mayer,B.R.&M.]

Monnett, Charles G., III, & Associates, (AV) ’57 ’83 C.34 B.A. L.575 J.D.
200 Queens Road, Suite 300, 28204
Mailing Address: P.O. Box 37206, Charlotte, NC 28237
Telephone: 704-376-1911 Fax: 704-376-1921
Email: cmonnett@carolinalaw.com URL: http://www.carolinalaw.com
Of Counsel: Craig O. Asbill.
Catastrophic Injury, Personal Injury, Brain Injury, Medical Malpractice, Birth Trauma, Spinal Cord Injury, Professional Liability, Wrongful Death, Products Liability, Inadequate Security, Insurance Bad Faith, Insurance Claims and Business Torts, Truck Accidents, Legal Malpractice, Construction Accidents, Automobile Accidents and Injuries, Nursing Home Negligence and Insurance Law.

See Professional Biographies, CHARLOTTE, NORTH CAROLINA

Monroe, Charles R., Jr. .... ’58 ’89 C.575 B.S. L.273 J.D. [Hunton&W.]
Monroe, Fred B. .... ’68 ’97 C.575 A.B. L.469 J.D. [James,M.&D.]
Monteith, James D., (AV) .... ’31 ’60 C.575 A.B. L.309 LL.B. [Ⓒ Guthrie,D.H.&S.]
Montgomery, Eric A., (BVⓉ) ’— ’91 C.574 B.A. L.436 J.D.
(adm. in MI; not adm. in NC) Bk. of America
Montgomery, Linda Konerding .... ’— ’02 C.276 A.B. L.893 J.D. [Ⓐ Robinson,B.&H.]
Moon, Travis W., (AV) .... ’45 ’71 C.797 B.A. L.575 J.D. [Hamilton F.M.S.S.&M.]
Moore, Alice K., (BV) .... ’64 ’92 C&L.896 B.A., J.D. [Johnston,A.&H.]
Moore, Brent Delynn .... ’73 ’01 C.575 B.S. L.893 J.D. Bank of America Securities, LLC
Moore, Gideon C. .... ’75 ’02 C.575 B.A. L.228 J.D. [Ⓐ Morris,M.&M.]
Moore, Jon R. .... ’76 ’02 C.597 B.A. L.276 J.D. [Brown,M.&Assoc.]
Moore, Lacey M. .... ’— ’03 C.280 B.A. L.327 J.D. [Ⓐ Nexsen P.A.K.]
Moore, Lawrence C., III .... ’— ’95 C.228 B.A. L.309 J.D. [Robinson,B.&H.]
Moore, Luther T., (AV) ’47 ’72 C.198 A.B. L.575 J.D.
Sr. V.P. & Asst. Gen. Coun., Belk Stores Servs., Inc.
Moore, Melony L. ’68 ’95 C.1286 B.A. L.201 J.D.
(adm. in SC; not adm. in NC) 2439 Finchley Dr.‡
Moore, Timothy R. .... ’71 ’97 C.575 B.A. L.902 J.D. [Ⓐ Baucom,C.B.M.&W.]
Moore, William H., Jr., (AV) .... ’57 ’83 C&L.790 B.S., J.D. [Moore&V.P.]

Moore & Van Allen PLLC, (AV) BR
100 North Tryon Street, Suite 4700, 28202-4003 ⊙
Telephone: 704-331-1000 Fax: 704-331-1159
URL: http://www.mvalaw.com
Resident Members: W. Miller Abernethy, Jr.; A. Mark Adcock; Lou M. Agosto; James E. Akers; H. Heath Alexander; Scott K. Ames (Not admitted in NC); Brian Thomas Atkinson; Robert V. Baker; W. Doak Barnhardt; John E. Beltz; Edward S. Booher, Jr.; Carol Ewald Bowen; Robert C. Bowers; R. Alexander Burroughs; Todd A. Caraway; Mark E. Carpenter; Brian K. Cary; Alan J. Chadd; John S. Chinuntdet; Bernard B. Clark; Dumont Clarke, IV; Daniel G. Clodfelter; Kenneth S. Coe; Timothy W. Corrigan; Jeffrey J. Davis; Ernest S. (Mike) DeLaney III; Miriam Ann Dixon; J. Thomas Dunn, Jr.; Bryan P. Durrett; David L. Eades; Joseph A. Fernandez; Ana M. Flynn; William H. Fuller, III; Richard C. Gaskins, Jr.; John T. Gathings, Jr.; M. Bryant Gatrell; Douglas R. Ghidina; Jeffrey W. Glenney; Jeremy H. Godwin; Thomas E. Graham; Stephen M. Hader; George V. Hanna III; Hollie H. Hart; W. B. Hawfield, Jr.; Stephen D. Hope; Mark R. A. Horn (Board Certified Specialist in Estate Planning and Probate Law, North Carolina State Board of Legal Specialization); James W. Hovis; James H. Jeffries, IV; Daniel L. Johnson, Jr.; Lea Stromire Johnson; Robert I. Kenny; Kenneth P. Kerr; Anthony T. Lathrop; Sandra M. Lazorcheck; Hal A. Levinson; David T. Lewis; B. Palmer McArthur, Jr.; Neill G. McBryde; Karin M. McGinnis; Peter J. McGrath, Jr.; John V. McIntosh; C. Wayne McKinzie; James P. McLoughlin, Jr.; Thomas L. Mitchell; William H. Moore, Jr.; Thomas S. Mullikin (Not admitted in NC); Gregory J. Murphy; Paul G. Murphy; Thomas D. Myrick; J. Christopher Oates; Thomas C. O'Bannon; Edward K. Oden; Thomas H. O'Donnell, Jr.; Kurt T. Oosterhouse; T. Randolph Perkins; Randel E. Phillips; M. Matthew Plyler; Alan W. Pope; Stephen G. Porter, Jr.; David J. Quattlebaum; Ernest W. Reigel; Skottowe W. Smith, Jr.; Ryan M. Smith; Barney Stewart, III; Scott D. Syfert; Beth A. Turner; Scott M. Tyler; David S. Walls; Victoria S. Windell; Michael E. Zeller. Resident Of Counsel: Jay S. Bilas; Harry J. Grim; Robert W. King, Jr.; Kimberly S. Kirk; T. Edmund Rast; William K. Van Allen. Resident Counsel: Kristen Ness Ayers; Melissa G. Burns; Michael T. Cronin; Karen A. Dean; Timothy W. Gilbert; Tanya D. Greeley; Lawrence P. Levine; David L. Ralls; Richard S. Sweet (Not admitted in NC); Ann P. West; William A. White. Resident Associates: Adam E. Aberra; Kevin M. Barnes; Evan M. Bass; Jason E. Bennett; Douglas W. Benson; Melinda S. Blundell; Jonathan D. Brodhag; Taber C. Bruner; Christopher T. Buchanan; Michael T. Champion; Andrea C. Chomakos; Rachel Worlds Coyne; Hillary B. Crabtree; Randall T. Dingle; John R. Evans; Edgar B. Fisher III; Robert A. Fisher; Erin L. Fitzgerald; Nicole L. Gardner; Lawrence P. Grayson II; Beth Yount Grimes; Stephen E. Gruendel; Alton Larue Gwaltney, III; James W. Haldin; Charles J. Harris; Michael P. Hebert; Brian S. Heslin; L. Caroline Hubbell; Jason P. Huff; N. Renee Hughes; William W. Jetton; Christopher J.C. Jones; Diana B. Jones; McHenry J. Kane; Amy R. King; Jeffrey B. King; Rosalind L. Lane; James R. Langdon; Kerry M. F. Lindauer; Ronald S. Lovelace; Christopher B. Major; Melody Y. Malone; Kerri L. Mast; Valecia M. McDowell; Carolyn P. Meade; Brian D. Mesibov; William R. Morton; Keith A. Mrochek; Todd H. Muldrew; Jonathan K. Murray; Mark A. Nebrig; Andrew L. Nesbitt; Lindsay M. Peed; Christian L. Polking; Jared W. Poplin; Justin M. Riess; Robert N. Rust IV; John C. Saydlowski; Nancy F. Smith;

(This Listing Continued)

Moore & Van Allen PLLC (Continued)

Robert R. Smith, II (Not admitted in NC); Noelle Hicks Sproul; Alyson R. Spurlock; Maranda W. Stevens; Wesley D. Thornton; Bradley T. Van Hoy; Suzanne Wentzel; McNeill Y. Wester.
Admiralty, Banking, Bankruptcy, Commercial Finance, Conduit Lending, Construction, Corporate, Distressed Debt Trading, Employee Benefits, Employment, Energy, Environmental, ERISA, Estate Planning and Administration, Government Contracts, Health Care, Immigration, Information Technology and E-Commerce, Insurance, Intellectual Property, International, Leasing, Litigation, Lobbying and Legislative Representation, Patent and Copyright, Real Estate, Securities, Surety, Taxation, Tax Incentives, Trusts, Utilities and Venture Capital.
Charleston, South Carolina Office: 40 Calhoun Street, Suite 300. Telephone: 843-579-7000. Fax: 843-579-7099.
Research Triangle Park, North Carolina Office: 430 Davis Drive, Suite 500, P.O. Box 13706. Telephone: 919-286-8000. Fax: 919-286-8199.

See Professional Biographies, CHARLOTTE, NORTH CAROLINA

Moraites, Robynn E. .... '— '04 C.259 B.S. L.575 J.D. [A Helms M.&W.]
Moran, Mark W., (AVⓅ) '65 '93 C.839 B.B.A. L.744 J.D.
(adm. in TX; not adm. in NC) [Butrus K.W.V.] ⊙
Moreau, W. Timothy .... '62 '89 C&L.420 B.A., J.D. [Moreau&M.]
Moreau & Marks, (BV) .... 419 S. Sharon Amity Road
Morehead, Arthur E., IV .... '— '96 C.198 B.A. L.790 J.D. [A Robinson,B.&H.]
Morgan, Charles L., Jr., Law Offices of, (BV) '56 '81
C.575 B.A. L.896 J.D. 101 North McDowell Street, Suite 200
Morgan, Peter F., (BV) .... '70 '95 C.30 B.A. L.902 J.D. [Erwin&E.]
Morgan, Rex C., (AV) .... '56 '81 C.1128 B.A. L.575 J.D. [Baucom,C.B.M.&W.]
Morrice, John A., (AV) .... '58 '83 C&L.896 B.A., J.D. [Johnston,A.&H.]
Morris, Gena Graham, (BV) .... '65 '92 C.575 B.A. L.1228 J.D. [Horack,T.P.&L.]
Morris, John F., (AV) .... '56 '81 C.228 A.B. L.575 J.D. [Morris Y.W.S.&B.]
Morris, Stephen H., (AV) .... '51 '76 C&L.575 B.S.B.A., J.D. [Essex R.]

Morris, Manning & Martin, LLP, (AV)
201 South College Street, Suite 2300, 28244 ⊙
Telephone: 704-554-7070 Fax: 704-554-5050
URL: http://www.mmmlaw.com
Members of Firm: Lynn F. Chandler (Board Certified Specialist in Estate Planning and Probate Law, North Carolina State Board of Legal Specialization); Richard N. Drake; John H. Northey III (Resident). Associates: Janice L. Davies; Gideon C. Moore. Of Counsel: Joseph Warren III.
Benefits and Compensation, Commercial Lending, Construction, Corporate, Corporate Technology, Creditor's Rights and Bankruptcy, Emerging Companies, Employment, Environmental, Healthcare, Hospitality, Insurance and Reinsurance, Insurance and Reinsurance Dispute Resolution, Intellectual Property, International, Life Sciences, Litigation, Medical Device, Mergers and Acquisitions, Privacy and Security, Products Liability and Toxic Torts, Real Estate Capital Markets, Real Estate Development and Finance, Residential Real Estate, Securities, Taxation, Technology, Technology Litigation, Telecommunications, Wealth Planning.
Other State Office Address:
Charlotte, NC Office: 10150 Mallard Creek Drive, Suite 105, 28262. Telephone: 704-369-7012. Fax: 704-369-7071.
Durham, NC Office: 1000 Park 40 Plaza, Suite 300. Telephone: 704-369-7012. Fax: 704-369-7071.
Washington, D.C. Office: City Center Building, 1401 H Street, N.W., Suite 760, 20005. Telephone: 202-408-5153. Fax: 202-408-5146.
Princeton, NJ Office: 601 Ewing Street, Suite C-8, 08540. Telephone: 609-430-1414. Fax: 609-430-1411.
Georgia Office Addresses:
Atlanta (Buckhead) Office: 1600 Atlanta Financial Center, 3343 Peachtree Road, N.E., Atlanta, GA 30326. Telephone: 404-233-7000.
Peachtree Dunwoody Office: 5775-C Peachtree Dunwoody Road, Suite 150, Atlanta, GA 30342. Telephone: 404-255-6900. Fax: 404-843-2317.
Cumming Office: 307 Atlanta Highway, Cumming, GA 30040. Telephone: 770-781-3000. Fax: 770-781-3007.
Duluth Office: 2180 Satellite Boulevard, Suite 180, Duluth, GA 30097. Telephone: 678-987-2800. Fax: 678-417-0056.
Alpharetta Office: 5780 Windward Parkway, Suite 225, Alpharetta, GA 30005. Telephone: 770-781-3000. Fax: 770-781-3007.

See Professional Biographies, CHARLOTTE, NORTH CAROLINA

Morris, Manning & Martin, LLP, (AV)
A Limited Liability Partnership
10150 Mallard Creek Drive Suite 105, 28262 ⊙
Telephone: 704-369-7012 Fax: 704-369-7071
URL: http://www.mmmlaw.com
Associate: Deborah S. Azzariti (Not admitted in NC).
Benefits and Compensation, Commercial Lending, Construction, Corporate, Corporate Technology, Creditor's Rights and Bankruptcy, Emerging Companies, Employment, Environmental, Healthcare, Hospitality, Insurance and Reinsurance, Insurance and Reinsurance Dispute Resolution, Intellectual Property, International, Life Sciences, Litigation, Medical Device, Mergers and Acquisitions, Privacy and Security, Products Liability and Toxic Torts, Real Estate Capital Markets, Real Estate Development and Finance, Residential Real Estate, Securities, Taxation, Technology, Technology Litigation, Telecommunications, Wealth Planning.
Other State Office Addresses:
Charlotte, NC Office: 201 South College Street, Suite 2300, 28244. Telephone: 704-554-7070. Fax: 704-556-5050.
Durham, NC Office: 1000 Park 40 Plaza, Suite 300. Telephone: 704-369-7012. Fax: 704-369-7071.
Washington, D.C. Office: City Center Building, 1401 H Street, N.W., Suite 760, 20005. Telephone: 202-408-5153. Fax: 202-408-5146.
Princeton, NJ Office: 601 Ewing Street, Suite C-8, 08540. Telephone: 609-430-1414. Fax: 609-430-1411.
Other Georgia Office Addresses:
Atlanta (Buckhead) Office: 1600 Atlanta Financial Center, 3343 Peachtree Road, N.E., Atlanta, GA 30326. Telephone: 404-233-7000.
Peachtree Dunwoody Office: 5775-C Peachtree Dunwoody Road, Suite 150, Atlanta, GA 30342. Telephone: 404-255-6900. Fax: 404-843-2317.
Duluth Office: 2180 Satellite Boulevard, Suite 180, Duluth, GA 30097. Telephone: 678-987-2800. Fax: 678-417-0056.
Cumming Office: 307 Atlanta Highway, Cumming, GA 30040. Telephone: 770-781-3000. Fax: 770-781-3007.
Alpharetta Office: 5780 Windward Parkway, Suite 225, Alpharetta, GA 30005. Telephone: 770-781-3000. Fax: 770-781-3007.

See Professional Biographies, CHARLOTTE, NORTH CAROLINA

Morris York Williams Surles & Barringer, L.L.P., (AV) BB
525 North Tryon Street, Suite 1400, 28202
Telephone: 704-375-4480 Facsimile: 704-375-6895
Email: firm@morrisyork.com URL: http://www.morrisyork.com
John F. Morris; Gregory C. York; Thomas E. Williams; Martha W. Surles; John P. Barringer; Robert Gregory Lewis; Michelle Sain Langdon; Susan Hunt Briggs; L. Stephen Kushner;—Keith B. Nichols; Kimberly A. Gossage; Roberta S. Sperry; Jocelyn Ferguson; Heather Graham Connor; Christopher B. Rawls; Robyn M. Lacy; Dean P. Loven; Mark B. Canepa.
Civil, Business and Commercial Litigation. Insurance Defense Litigation, Insurance Coverage and Workers Compensation. Medical and Professional Malpractice Defense. Land Condemnation and Alternative Dispute Resolution Services.

See Professional Biographies, CHARLOTTE, NORTH CAROLINA

Morrison, Dale S., Law Offices of, (BV) '46 '78 C.240 A.B. L.893 J.D.
1043 East Morehead Street, Suite 200, 28204
Telephone: 704-375-6788 Fax: 704-335-0853 URL: http://www.morrisonfiorella.com
Email: dsm@dalesmorrisonlaw.com URL: http://www.dalemorrisonlaw.com
Business Enterprises, Contracts, Corporate, Complex Civil Litigation, Estate Litigation, Personal Injury, Products Liability, White Collar Crime.

See Professional Biographies, CHARLOTTE, NORTH CAROLINA

Morrow, Elizabeth Randall, (BV) '55 '80
C.951 B.A. L.896 J.D. V.P., Bank of America, N.A.
Mortimer, James R., Jr. .... '68 '96 C.575 B.A. L.280 J.D. Sr. Coun., CIT Group Inc.
Morton, James H., (AV) .... '35 '66 C.576 L.575 LL.B. [Parham,H.H.B.&M.]
Morton, Richard E., (AV) .... '57 '90 C.296 B.S. L.790 J.D. [Womble C.S.&R.]
Morton, William R. .... '76 '05 C.575 B.A. L.280 J.D. [A Moore&V.P.]
Moser, John Kenneth .... '74 '00 C&L.896 B.A., J.D. Asst. Dist. Atty.
Mosier, Michael G. .... '— '02 C.299 B.A. L.228 J.D. [A Alston&B.]
Moss, Joseph W., Jr., (BV) .... '66 '93 C.198 B.A. L.896 J.D. [Bishop,C.&M.]
Movius, Lee West, (AV) .... '— '73 C.309 B.A. L.145 J.D. [Kennedy C.L.&H.]
Mrochek, Keith A. .... '73 '99 C.294 B.A. L.902 J.D. [A Moore&V.P.]
Mrochek, Mary Lee E. .... '— '98 C.16 B.A. L.902 J.D. [A Gorman&D.]
Muckenfuss, Robert A. .... '71 '97 C.893 B.A. L.790 J.D. [Helms M.&W.]
Mueller, Julie R. .... '— '01 C.575 B.A. L.1228 J.D. [A Nelson M.R.&S.]
Muldrew, Todd H. .... '74 '04 C.838 B.A. L.945 J.D. [A Moore&V.P.]
Mullen, Graham C. .... '40 '69 C&L.228 A.B., J.D. Chf. U.S. Dist. J.

Mullen Holland & Cooper P.A.
(See Gastonia)

Mulligan, Bryon J. '67 '98 C.763 B.S. L.1370 J.D.
(adm. in CA; not adm. in NC) [A Cadwalader,W.&T.]
Mullikin, Thomas S. '60 '86 C&L.790 B.A., J.D.
(adm. in SC; not adm. in NC) [Moore&V.P.]
Mullis, Elizabeth D., (CV) .... '61 '97 C.925 B.S. L.930 J.D. [A Foodman,H.&K.]
Murchison, Bradley D., (AV) '57 '83 C.575 A.B. L.273 J.D.
Sr. VP., Gen. Coun. & Secy., Baker & Taylor Corp.
Murchison, John M., Jr., (AV) ..... '— '71 C.198 A.B. L.575 J.D. [C Kennedy C.L.&H.]
Murdock, Sharon R., (BV) .... '43 '81 C&L.1015 B.A., J.D. P.O. Box 30306
Murphy, Calvin E., (AV) .... '48 '77 C.198 B.A. L.574 J.D. [Murphy&C.]
Murphy, Frank J., Jr., (AV) .... '47 '75 C.749 B.S. L.262 J.D. [Hunton&W.]
Murphy, Gary L., (AV) .... '48 '74 C.902 B.A. L.575 J.D. [Dozier,M.P.&M.]
Murphy, Gregory J., (AV) .... '64 '89 C.116 B.A. L.477 J.D. [Moore&V.P.]
Murphy, Kevin P. '56 '82 C&L.851 B.B.A., J.D.
(adm. in OH; not adm. in NC) V.P., Goodrich Corp.
Murphy, Paul G. .... '64 '92 C.893 B.S. L.575 J.D. [Moore&V.P.]
Murphy & Chapman, P.A., (AV) .... 101 North McDowell Street, Suite 210
Murray, Jonathan K. .... '73 '00 C.302 B.A. L.896 J.D. [A Moore&V.P.]
Murray, Joseph S., IV .... '— '05 C.886 B.S. L.790 J.D. [A Hedrick E.G.&K.]
Murray, R. Andrew, (AV) .... '62 '92 C.1128 B.A. L.575 J.D. [Goodman,C.L.L.&M.]
Murrell, Thomas W., III, (AVⓅ) ...... '48 '74 C.976 B.A. L.893 J.D. [C Helms M.&W.]
Myers, J. Patrick .... '61 '91 C.575 B.A. L.1228 J.D. Asst. Gen. Coun., Bank of America
Myers, R. Lee, (BV) .... '51 '76 C.232 B.A. L.616 J.D. [Myers&H.]
Myers and Hulse, (BV) .... 122 N. McDowell Street
Myrick, Thomas D., (AV) .... '54 '84 C&L.575 B.S.B.A., J.D. [Moore&V.P.]
Nachimson, Steven G., (BVⓅ) '60 '86 C.881 B.A. L.107 J.D.
Sr. Corp. Coun., Contracts, Compass Group, U.S.A. Inc.
Nagle, Jeffrey .... '76 '04 C.1044 B.A. L.569 J.D. [A Cadwalader,W.&T.]
Nail, Lester C. '60 '85 C.232 B.A. L.575 J.D.
(adm. in AR; not adm. in NC) Paramount Parks, Inc.
Nalibotsky, Albert S. .... '64 '91 C.260 B.S. L.362 J.D. [Cozen O.]
Nance, Deborah A. ..... '59 '85 C.574 B.A. L.575 J.D. Legal Servs. of Sou. Piedmont,Inc.
Nance, Thomas G., II .... '72 '97 C.232 B.A. L.896 J.D. [A Dean&G.]
Nason, Allen M. '72 '99 C.956 B.S. L.1358 J.D.
[Constitution&Assoc.] (⊙Huntersville, Monroe, NC; Rock Hill, SC)
Navarro, Paul M. .... '72 '98 C.896 B.A. L.893 J.D. [A Helms M.&W.]
Navarro, William A., (BV) .... '61 '87 C.588 B.S. L.93 J.D. [Wishart,N.H.&P.]
Neal, Charles S. '68 '94
C.838 B.S.B.A. L.69 J.D. V.P. & Asst. Gen. Coun., Wachovia Corp.
Neal, Nina Michelle '63 '93 C.575 B.S. L.574 J.D.
(adm. in SC; not adm. in NC) Central Piedmont Comm. Coll.
Nebrig, Mark A. .... '69 '02 C.575 B.A. L.831 J.D. [A Moore&V.P.]
Nedzbala, Michael, (AV) .... '62 '87 C.893 B.A. L.575 J.D. [Hunton&W.]
Neely, Stephanie Davis .... '57 '94 C.576 B.S. L.575 J.D. 7000 Abbotswood Dr.
Neill, Ann Mason .... '62 '87 C.575 A.B. L.896 J.D. 100 N. Tryon St.‡

Nelson Mullins Riley & Scarborough LLP, (AV)
Bank of America Corporate Center, Suite 2400, 100 North Tryon Street, 28202-4007 ⊙
Telephone: 704-417-3000 Telecopy: 704-377-4814
URL: http://www.nelsonmullins.com
Partners: Kurt E. Lindquist, II; Paul J. Osowski; Francis C. Pray, Jr.; Lawrence J. Scott; Tracy E. Tomlin; Mark Vasco; Raboteau T. Wilder, Jr.; Fred M. Wood, Jr. Associates: Virginia "Ginger" Theis Daly (Not admitted in NC); Nathan C. Fuller; Kevin J. Heiser; Thomas G. Hooper; Christina M. K. Jacuzzo; C. Marshall Lindsay; Valerie Paige Mahoney; Julie R. Mueller; Christopher M. Olds; PollyBeth Proctor; Caroline H. "Carrie" Ryan; Evan M. Sauda; Erik A. Schwanz; William M. Starr; Kerry L. Traynum; Clark C. Walton; Megan K. Watkins.
Business Litigation, Corporate, Government Relations and Administrative Law, Health Care, Labor and Employment Litigation, Product Liability, Securities Litigation, Taxation, Technology, Telecommunications, Utility Regulation.
Atlanta, Georgia Office: 999 Peachtree Street, N.E., Suite 1400, 30309-3964, P.O. Box 77707, 30357-0707. Telephone: 404-817-6000. Telecopy: 404-817-6050.
Charleston, South Carolina Office: Liberty Center, Suite 600, 151 Meeting Street, 29401-2239. P.O. Box 1806, 29402-1806. Telephone: 843-853-5200. Telecopy: 843-722-8700.
Columbia, South Carolina Office: Meridian, 17th Floor, 1320 Main Street, 29201, P.O. Box 11070, 29211-1070. Telephone: 803-799-2000. Telecopy: 803-256-7500.
Greenville, South Carolina Office: Poinsett Plaza, 104 South Main Street, Suite 900, 29601. P.O. Box 10084, 29603-0084. Telephone: 864-250-2300. Telecopy: 864-232-2925.
Myrtle Beach, South Carolina Office: Founders Centre, Suite 301, 2411 North Oak Street, 29577-3165. P.O. Box 3939, 29578-3939. Telephone: 843-448-3500. Telecopy: 843-448-3437.
Raleigh, North Carolina Office: GlenLake One, Suite 200, 4140 Parklake Avenue, 27612. Telephone: 919-877-3800. Telecopy: 919-877-3799.
Washington, D.C. Office: 101 Constitution Avenue, NW, Suite 900, 20001. Telephone: 202-712-2800. Fax: 202-712-2860.
Winston-Salem, North Carolina Office: The Knollwood, 380 Knollwood Street, Suite 530, 27103. Telephone: 336-774-3300. Fax: 336-774-3299.

See Professional Biographies, CHARLOTTE, NORTH CAROLINA

Nesbit, Christopher S. M. .... '63 '92 C.893 B.A. L.575 J.D. [Helms M.&W.]
Nesbitt, Andrew L. .... '77 '02 C&L.575 B.A., J.D. [A Moore&V.P.]
Newitt, John G., Jr., (AV) .... '41 '65 C&L.896 B.A., J.D. [Newitt&B.]

Newitt & Bruny, (AV)
Suite 104, 417 East Boulevard, 28203
Telephone: 704-372-6181 Facsimile: 704-377-0535
Email: NEWITTBRU@CS.COM
Members of Firm: John G. Newitt, Sr. (1897-1973); John G. Newitt, Jr.; Roger H. Bruny.
Business, Construction and Commercial, Civil Litigation, Mergers, Acquisitions and Divestitures, Commercial Real Estate, Collections.

See Professional Biographies, CHARLOTTE, NORTH CAROLINA

Newman, Eric M. '52 '77 C.1128 B.A. L.575 J.D.
Exec. V.P. & Gen. Coun., Bojangles' Restaurants, Inc.

Newman, Mindy B. ....'— '03 C.705 B.S. L.1228 J.D. [Ⓐ Klein&F.]
Newmark, Steven D. ....'— '96 C.945 B.A. L.893 J.D. [Robinson,B.&H.]
Newton, Frank C., Jr. ....'42 '81 C.1128 B.S. L.472 J.D. 1806 Rocky River Rd.
Newton, Paul R. '60 '85 C&L.575 B.S./B.A., J.D.
Vice Pres. & Gen. Coun., Duke Energy Corp.

Nexsen Pruet Adams Kleemeier, PLLC, (AV)
201 South Tryon Street Suite 1200, 28202 ⊙
Telephone: 704-339-0304 Facsimile: 704-338-5377
URL: http://www.npaklaw.com
William J. Adams, Jr. (1908-1993); Wilburn Brewer, Jr. (1939-2003); C. Alvin Brown (1940-1978); Paul A. Cooper (1889-1956); Daniel W. Fouts (1932-2003); Frank B. Gary (1900-1971); John A. Kleemeier, Jr. (1911-1973); Elizabeth Dunn White (1954-1995). Members of Firm: Patrick F. Brown; David Rees Cannon; David W. Gossett (Resident, Greenville, SC Office); J. Hayden Harrell; Robert H. Hull, Jr.; Marcus A. Manos (Resident, Columbia, SC Office); Joseph D. McCullough; Sean M. Phelan; James H. Pulliam; Matthew B. Roberts (Resident, Columbia, SC Office); Peter A. Santos; Marguerite Smith Willis (Resident, Columbia, SC Office); Richard W. Wilson. Associates: Laurie A. Becker (Resident, Columbia, SC Office); Christie S. Matthews; Nikole Setzler Mergo (Resident, Columbia, SC Office); Lacey M. Moore; Andrea B. Ricks; Patrick D. Sarsfield II; Melinda Fox Staley.
Acquisitions, Administrative Law, Alternative Dispute Resolution, Antitrust Law, Appellate Practice, Arbitration, Bankruptcy Law, Business Law, Collections Law, Construction Law, Commercial Law, Commercial Real Estate, Computers, Contracts, Copyrights, Corporate Law, Creditor-Debtor Rights, Disabilities, Domestic Relations Law, Economic Development Law, Education Law, Election, Eminent Domain Employee Benefits Law, Employment Law, Environmental Law, Estate Planning, Family Law, Fidelity Law, Finance Law, Governmental Representation, Health Care Law, Hospital Law, Immigration Law, Insurance Law, Insurance Defense, Intellectual Property Law, International Law, Internet Law, Investments, Labor Law, Land Use, Leasing Law, Litigation, Maritime Law, Mediation, Mergers, Naturalization Law, Partnership Law, Patents, Personal Injury, Probate, Products Liability Law, Professional Liability, Public Contracts, Public Finance, Real Estate Law, Real Estate Planning, Regulatory Law, Securities, Surety Law, Taxation Law, Technology Law, Torts, Trade Regulation, Trade Secrets, Trademarks, Transportation, Trusts, Utility Law, Wills, Workers' Compensation and Zoning Law.
See Professional Biographies, CHARLOTTE, NORTH CAROLINA

Nichols, Keith B. ....'75 '00 C.880 B.A. L.472 J.D. [Ⓐ Morris Y.W.S.&B.]
Nichols, Lara Simmons, (BV) '67 '93
C.659 B.A. L.575 J.D. Asst. Gen. Coun., Duke Energy Corp.
Nickerson, John ....'68 '99 C.140 L.115 J.D. [Nickerson]

Nickerson Law Firm, The
200 N. McDowell Street, 28204
Telephone: 704-370-7741 Fax: 704-370-0447
URL: http://www.nickersonlawfirm.com
John Nickerson.
Criminal, Drugs, Fraud, Burglary, Appeals, Traffic, Speeding, Forfeiture, Felonies, Federal Criminal, Forgery, Homicide, Murder, Search and Seizures.
See Professional Biographies, CHARLOTTE, NORTH CAROLINA

Nicopoulos, John V. ....'51 '79 C.34 B.A. L.575 J.D. 225 E. Kingston Ave.
Nipp, John C. ....'70 '96 C&L.575 B.A., J.D. [Dozier,M.P.&M.]
Nipp, Tracy B. '70 '96 C.806 B.A. L.575 J.D.
Asst. Gen. Coun., Lic. & Mktg. & Dir. of Bus. Affs, NASCAR, Inc.
Nixon, Theo X., (AV) ....'52 '77 C.576 B.A. L.790 J.D. [Nixon,P.&G.]
Nixon, Park & Gronquist, P.L.L.C., (AV) ....101 North McDowell Street, Suite 126
Noblitt, John H. ....'48 '76 C.228 B.A. L.896 J.D. 1106 Scotland Avenue‡
Nolen, Brian H. ....'76 '02 C.234 B.S. L.365 J.D. [Gach]
Norelli, Nancy Black ....'49 '77 C.914 B.A. L.588 J.D. Mecklenburg Co. Dist. Ct.
Norman, John Anderson, II '66 '94
C.797 B.A. L.616 J.D. Tax Consultant, Ernst & Young, L.L.P.
Norris, Robert B., (AV) ....'50 '76 C.198 A.B. L.575 J.D. [Wishart,N.H.&P.]
Northey, John H., III, (BV) ....'49 '75 C.575 A.B. L.188 J.D. [Morris,M.&M.]
Norton, John M., II '75 '00 C.269 B.A. L.362 J.D.
V.P., Regulatory Compl. Officer, Banc of America Investment Services, Inc.
Norvell, Holly B. ....'— '02 C&L.846 B.B.A., J.D. [Ⓐ Culp E.&C.]
Norwood, H. Vernon, Jr., (BV) ....'39 '64 C&L.575 A.B., LL.B. 1515 Mockingbird Lane
Nugent, Jonathan J., (BV) ....'— '96 C.062 B.C.L. L.575 J.D. [Kilpatrick S.]
Nwauwa, U. Wilfred ....'57 '93 C.395 B.S. L.838 J.D. 3325 Washburn Avenue, Suite 112
Nystrom, Patricia Wiggins, (AV) ....'56 '82 C&L.575 B.A., J.D. [Harkey L.]
Oakes, John W. ....'— '00 C.48 B.A. L.213 J.D. [Ⓐ Kilpatrick S.]
Oates, J. Christopher, (AV) ....'54 '84 C.951 A.B. L.575 J.D. [Moore&V.P.]
O'Bannon, Thomas C. ....'60 '88 C.623 B.B.A. L.846 J.D. [Moore&V.P.]
Oberkfell, Keith F. ....'68 '93 C.893 B.A. L.309 J.D. [Mayer,B.R.&M.]
O'Brien, Carrie Hailman, (CV) ....'75 '00 C.140 B.A. L.790 J.D. 1800 East Blvd.
O'Brien, Kevin ....'65 '00 C.277 B.S.M.E. L.790 J.D. [Ⓐ Alston&B.] (See Pat. Sect.)
Ockerbloom, John P. '66 '92 C.462 B.A. L.588 J.D.
(adm. in MA; not adm. in NC) NationsBank Corp. Ctr.
Ockerman, Steven B. ....'60 '92 C.871 B.S. L.910 J.D. [Ⓐ Wishart,N.H.&P.]
Oden, Edward K. ....'61 '86 C.802 B.A. L.902 J.D. [Moore&V.P.]
Odom, Brian J. ....'71 '96 C.140 B.A. L.790 J.D. 212 South Tryon Street, Suite 980
Odom, Martha C., (BV) ....'66 '93 C.296 B.S. L.790 J.D. [Odom]
Odom, Preston O., III ....'71 '97 C&L.259 B.A., J.D. [Ⓐ James,M.&D.]
Odom, T. LaFontine, Sr., (AV) ....'38 '62 C&L.575 A.B., LL.B. [Odom] ⊙
Odom, Thomas L., Jr., (BV) ....'61 '88 C.575 B.A. L.896 J.D. [Odom]

Odom Firm, The, PLLC, (AV)
1109 Greenwood Cliff, 28204 ⊙
Telephone: 704-377-7333 Fax: 704-377-5747
Email: theodomfirm@mecklaw.com URL: http://www.mecklaw.com
T. LaFontine Odom, Sr.; Thomas L. Odom, Jr.; Martha C. Odom.
Civil Litigation, Condemnation, Personal Injury, Legal Malpractice, Products Liability, Construction Law, Environmental Law, Disability Law, Guardianship, Competency Proceedings, Employment Law, Zoning and Land Use.
Raleigh, North Carolina Office: 1046 Washington Street, 27605.
See Professional Biographies, CHARLOTTE, NORTH CAROLINA

O'Donnell, Shannon Parry '72 '97
C.575 B.S. L.1194 J.D. Gen. Coun., American Asset Corp.
O'Donnell, Thomas H., Jr. ....'69 '97 C.776 B.A. L.1194 J.D. [Moore&V.P.]
Oettinger, Kenneth B., Jr., (BV) ......'66 '93 C&L.575 B.A., J.D. [Ⓒ Womble C.S.&R.]
Offerdahl, Charlotte L. ....'52 '88 C.401 B.A. L.575 J.D. [Parker,P.A.&B.]
Ogburn, Kristin Decker ....'67 '94 C.893 B.A. L.790 J.D. [Horack,T.P.&L.]
Ogburn, Thomas L., III ....'69 '96 C.575 B.A. L.896 J.D. [Poyner&S.]

Ogletree, Deakins, Nash, Smoak & Stewart, P.C., (AV) BR
400 West Trade Street, 28202-1627 ⊙
Telephone: 704-342-2588 Facsimile: 704-342-4379
Email: clientservices@ogletreedeakins.com URL: http://www.ogletreedeakins.com
James B. Spears, Jr. (Certified Specialist, Employment and Labor Law, South Carolina Supreme Court); Robert S. Phifer; Stephen D. Dellinger; John D. Cole;—Kelly S. Hughes; Benjamin R. Holland; Jeremy A. Stephenson (Not admitted in NC).
Labor Relations, Employment Litigation, Workers' Compensation. Civil Litigation in all State and Federal Courts and Administrative Agencies.
Atlanta, Georgia Office: 600 Peachtree Street, N.E., Suite 2100. Telephone: 404-881-1300.
Austin, Texas Office: 301 Congress Avenue, Suite 1250. Telephone: 512-344-4700.
Birmingham, Alabama Office: One Federal Place, Suite 1000, 1819 Fifth Avenue North. Telephone: 205-328-1900.

(This Listing Continued)

Ogletree, Deakins, Nash, Smoak & Stewart, P.C. (Continued)
Charleston, South Carolina Office: 134 Meeting Street, Suite 160, P.O. Box 1808. Telephone: 843-853-1300.
Chicago, Illinois Office: Twenty-Fifth Floor, Two First National Plaza, 20 South Clark Street. Telephone: 312-558-1220.
Columbia, South Carolina Office: 1320 Main Street, Suite 600. Telephone: 803-252-1300.
Dallas, Texas Office: 700 Preston Commons, 8117 Preston Road. Telephone: 214-987-3800.
Greensboro, North Carolina Office: 2725 Horse Pen Creek Road, Suite 101. Telephone: 336-375-9737.
Greenville, South Carolina Office: The Ogletree Building, 300 North Main Street, P.O. Box 2757. Telephone: 864-271-1300.
Houston, Texas Office: One Allen Center, 500 Dallas Street, Suite 3000. Telephone: 713-655-0855.
Kansas City, Missouri Office: 4717 Grand Avenue, Suite 300. Telephone: 816-471-1301.
Los Angeles, California Office: 633 West Fifth Street, Suite 5300. Telephone: 213-239-9800.
Indianapolis, Indiana Office: Suite 4600, 111 Monument Circle. Telephone: 317-916-1300.
Miami, Florida Office: 80 S.W. 8th Street, Suite 1830. Telephone: 305-374-0506.
Morristown, New Jersey Office: 10 Madison Avenue, Suite 402. Telephone: 973-656-1600.
Nashville, Tennessee Office: SunTrust Center, Suite 800, 424 Church Street. Telephone: 615-254-1900.
Phoenix, Arizona Office: 2415 East Camelback Road, Suite 800. Telephone: 602-778-3700.
Raleigh, North Carolina Office: 2301 Sugar Bush Road, Suite 600, P.O. Box 31608. Telephone: 919-787-9700.
San Antonio, Texas Office: 2600 Weston Centre, 112 East Pecan Street. Telephone: 210-354-1300.
St. Thomas, U.S. Virgin Islands Office: The Tunick Building, 1336 Beltjen Road, Suite 202. Telephone: 340-714-1235.
Tampa, Florida Office: 100 North Tampa Street, Suite 3600. Telephone: 813-289-1247.
Washington, D.C. Office: Fifth Floor, 2400 N Street, N.W. Telephone: 202-887-0855.
See Professional Biographies, CHARLOTTE, NORTH CAROLINA

O'Keefe, Donald E. '36 '60 C&L.724 B.A., LL.B.
(adm. in NY; not adm. in NC) 2550 W. Tyvola Rd.
O'Keefe, Edward P., (AVⓉ) '— '81 C.690 B.S. L.262 J.D.
(adm. in NJ; not adm. in NC) Deputy Gen. Coun., Bank of America
Olah, Nancy Lynne, (AV) ....'55 '79 C.604 B.A. L.477 J.D. [Ⓒ Parker,P.A.&B.]
Olds, Christopher M. ....'71 '02 C.886 B.S.Ch.E. L.790 J.D. [Ⓐ Nelson M.R.&S.]
Olive, Lee, (BV) ....'61 '89 C.575 B.S. L.421 J.D. [Olive]
Olive, Leon ....'24 '54 C.16 B.S. L.228 J.D. [Olive]
Olive Law Firm, P.A., The, (BV) ....200 Queens Rd., Suite 200
Olsen, John M., (CV) .....'53 '78 C.1222 B.A. L.472 J.D. 301 S. McDowell St., Ste. 306
Olson, Erika ....'— '05 C.93 B.A. L.896 J.D. [Ⓐ Kennedy C.L.&H.]
O'Marra, Lynn Burlingame ....'65 '94 C.971 B.S. L.184 J.D. KPMG, L.L.P.
Ong, John Whitelaw, (BV) ....'66 '91 C.183 B.A. L.245 J.D. [Dean&G.]
Onorato, David J., (AVⓉ) '— '87 C&L.276 B.S.B.A., J.D.
(adm. in MA; not adm. in NC) Mgr., Litigation, Bank of America
Oosterhouse, Kurt T. ....'68 '93 C.323 B.A. L.494 J.D. [Moore&V.P.]

Orbock Ruark & Dillard, PC
(See Winston Salem)

Orr, John R. '— '95 C.277 B.M.E. L.326 J.D.
(adm. in TX; not adm. in NC) Duke Energy Trading & Mktg., LLC
Orsbon, R. Anthony, (AV) ....'47 '72 C.198 B.A. L.880 J.D. [Orsbon&F.]

Orsbon & Fenninger LLP, (AV)
4201 Congress Street Suite 110, 28209
Telephone: 704-556-9600 Fax: 704-556-9601
Email: oandflaw.com URL: http://www.orsbonandfenninger.com
R. Anthony Orsbon (Board Certified Specialist in Estate Planning and Probate Law, North Carolina State Board of Legal Specialization); Cynthia T. Fenninger (Board Certified Specialist in Estate Planning and Probate Law, North Carolina State Board of Legal Specialization).
Estate Planning, Probate, Trusts and Estates, Taxation, Business Law.
See Professional Biographies, CHARLOTTE, NORTH CAROLINA

Osborn, D. Christopher, (AV) ....'70 '95 C.575 B.A. L.893 J.D. [Horack,T.P.&L.]
Osborne, Wallace S., (AV) ....'23 '50 C.160 L.228 LL.B. 347 N. Caswell Rd.
Osho, Lucky T. ....'55 '88 C.574 B.A. L.575 J.D. [L.Osho]
Osho, Lucky, P.C., Law Office of ....5533 Monroe Rd.
Osowski, Paul J., (BV) ....'68 '96 C.896 B.S. L.1228 J.D. [Nelson M.R.&S.]
O'Toole, John J. '— '81 C.273 B.A. L.128 J.D.
(adm. in NY; not adm. in NC) Assoc. Gen. Coun., Bank of America
Ott, Michael K. ....'64 '89 C.160 B.S. L.790 J.D. Sr. Coun., Royal & SunAlliance
Owen, C. Melissa ....'74 '99 C.473 B.A. L.229 J.D. [Tin F.G.&O.]
Owens, N. Todd ....'67 '94 C.575 B.A. L.280 J.D. Dist. J.
Owens, Raymond E., Jr., (AV) ....'— '78 C&L.575 A.B., J.D. [Kennedy C.L.&H.]
Owensby, Charlton Norman ....'59 '00 C&L.896 B.S., J.D. 3700 Moorland Dr.
Packard, William K. ....'— '99 C.228 A.B. L.575 J.D. [Ⓐ Robinson,B.&H.]
Page, Thomas W. ....'— '90 C.383 B.B.A. L.421 J.D. [Hedrick E.G.&K.]
Pak, Ashley Edward ....'74 '01 C.576 B.A. L.124 J.D. 5821 Fairview Road, Suite 107
Pallenik, Christine M. ....'57 '83 Sr. Assoc. Gen. Coun., Duke Energy Corp.
Palmer, Erin G. ....'— '04 C.597 B.A. L.575 J.D. [Ⓐ Robinson,B.&H.]
Palmer, H. William, Jr., (BV) ....'56 '84 C.575 B.S. L.1228 J.D. [Kirk P.&T.]

Pantazis, Annemarie, Law Office of, (CV) '73 '99 C.945 B.A. L.896 J.D.
1419 E. 7th Street, 28204
Mailing Address: P.O. Box 34278, Charlotte, NC 28234
Telephone: 704-342-2243 Fax: 704-342-3266
Email: pantazisa@carolina.rr.com URL: http://www.pantazislaw.com
Workers' Compensation, Personal Injury, Traffic Violations.
See Professional Biographies, CHARLOTTE, NORTH CAROLINA

Parham, Lewis H., Jr., (AV) ....'32 '57 C&L.575 B.S., J.D. [Parham,H.H.B.&M.]

Parham, Helms, Harris, Blythe & Morton, (AV)
6100 Fairview Road, Suite 1200, 28210
Telephone: 704-556-1101 Fax: 704-556-1044
Email: phhbmlaw@aol.com
Members of Firm: Lewis H. Parham, Jr.; Neal G. Helms; Ralph C. Harris, Jr.; Robert B. Blythe; James H. Morton. Of Counsel: John L. Hazlehurst.
General Civil Practice. Probate, Real Estate, Foreclosures, Corporation, Banking and Bankruptcy Law.
See Professional Biographies, CHARLOTTE, NORTH CAROLINA

Parise, William C. ....'69 '01 C.1349 B.A. L.893 J.D. [Ⓐ Poyner&S.]
Park, Charles B., III, (AV) .....'31 '57 C.576 B.S. L.477 J.D. 1211 E. Morehead St. (Pat.)
Park, G. Bruce, (AV) ....'59 '88 C.34 B.S.C.J. L.1228 J.D. [Nixon,P.&G.]
Park, Vera Goudes, (BV) ....'64 '89 C.34 B.A. L.575 J.D. P.O. Box 34396
Parker, Francis I., (AV) ....'23 '49 C&L.575 A.B., LL.B. [Ⓒ Parker,P.A.&B.]

Parker, John J., III, (AV) '51 '76 C.575 B.A. L.896 J.D.
212 South Tryon Street, Suite 1660, 28281
Telephone: 704-375-2100 Fax: 704-375-8770
Email: jparker@jjparkeriii.com URL: http://www.lawyers.com/jjparkeriii
General Civil Litigation including Business, Commercial, Contract, Employment and Real Estate Litigation.
See Professional Biographies, CHARLOTTE, NORTH CAROLINA

Parker, Thomas D. ....'27 '53 C&L.575 A.B., LL.B. 401 McCullough Dr.‡

Parker, Poe, Adams & Bernstein L.L.P., (AV)
Three Wachovia Center, 401 South Tryon Street, Suite 3000, 28202 ⊙
Telephone: 704-372-9000 Facsimile: 704-334-4706
Email: info@parkerpoe.com URL: http://www.parkerpoe.com
Partners: Michael G. Adams; David Neal Allen; John H. Beyer; James N. Brennan IV; P. Neal Cook; Harvey L. Cosper, Jr.; Jonathan M. Crotty; Alan G. Dexter; Woodard E. Farmer, Jr.; William P. Farthing, Jr.; Kiah T. Ford, IV; Anthony Fox; John W. Francisco; James N. Greene III; Thomas N. Griffin III; John E. Grupp; Albert E. Guarnieri; John R. Hairr III; Irvin W. Hankins III; R. Douglas Harmon; Josephine H. Hicks; William L. Hirata; Ashley L. Hogewood, Jr.; Harold D. "Chip" Holmes, Jr.; Joy M. Hord; Stephen R. Hunting; Max Edward Justice; Charles B. Lee, Jr.; Scott E. Leo; Brandon K. Lewisohn; Fred T. Lowrance; Craig T. Lynch; Heloise C. Merrill; Brent M. Milgrom, Jr.; Charlotte L. Offerdahl; W. Edward Poe, Jr.; J. William Porter; George H. Pretty II; William L. Rikard, Jr.; Richard K. Schell; Roy L. Smart III; Fred C. Thompson, Jr.; Donald P. Ubell; S. Rogers Warner, Jr.; Steven D. Weber; Keith M. Weddington; Edward W. Wellman, Jr.; Eric D. Welsh; A. Grant Whitney, Jr.; Stacy K. Wood; W. Samuel Woodard. Of Counsel: Michael A. Almond; Mark R. Bernstein; Gaston H. Gage; Francis I. Parker; James Y. Preston; Michael W. Taylor; Sydnor Thompson. Special Counsel: David W. Brown Jr.; Robert P. Bryan III; James C. Davis, Jr.; Deborah L. Edney; Nancy Lynne Olah; Regina Wheeler Swinea. Senior Counsel: Rose Marie Weber. Associates: Jason R. Benton; Kimberly A. Betz; William B. Cannon; Amanda Harmon Cooley; Jonathan W. Dion; Allison B. Edgar; William L. Esser, IV; Jami Jackson Farris; Christopher J. Fernandez; Carrie S. Fisher; W. Lewis Glenn, III; Kevin B. Gottehrer; Kenneth R. Harris, Jr.; Mary Elizabeth Holsenbeck; P. Michael Juby; Lori R. Keeton; Leigh A. Kite; Ashley M. Long; Gary T. McDermott; Kristin R. Poolos; Thomas M. Quirk; Richard J. Rivera; Adam C. Shearer; Shannon N. Stokes; Benjamin R. Sullivan, Jr.; F. Scott Thomas; Kendra W. Thornton; Kristi K. Walters; Amy L. Walton; Jason P. Walton; L. Kent Workman.
Administrative and Regulatory, Antitrust and Trade Regulation, Arbitration, Banking, Bankruptcy, Insolvency and Reorganization, Biotechnology, Capital Markets, Computer, Construction, Copyright, Corporate, Corporate Finance, Education, Employee Benefits and Compensation Plans, Employment, Environmental, Estate Planning and Administration, Governmental Contracts and Procurement, Governmental Relations, Health Care, Immigration, Insurance, Intellectual Property, International Trade and Investment, Joint Ventures, Lending and Finance, Limited Liability Companies and Partnerships, Litigation, Malpractice Defense, Mergers and Acquisitions, Municipal, Products Liability, Project Development, Project Finance, Public Finance, Commercial Real Estate, Securities, Tax Exempt Organizations, Taxation, Technology Management and Licensing, Telecommunications, Trademark, Transportation, Utilities Regulation, Zoning.
Representative Clients: Board of Governors of the University of North Carolina; Charlotte Mecklenburg Hospital Authority; Crescent Resources LLC, Duke Energy; Laboratory Corporation of America Holdings; North Carolina Biotechnology Center; Sonic Automotive; Speedway Motorsports; Sunbelt Rentals, Inc.; Wachovia.
Raleigh, North Carolina Office: Wachovia Capitol Center, 150 Fayetteville Street Mall, Suite 1400, P.O. Box 389, 27602-0389. Telephone: 919-828-0564. Facsimile: 919-834-4564.
Columbia, South Carolina Office: 1201 Main Street, Suite 1450, 29201. Telephone: 803-255-8000. Facsimile: 803-255-8017.
Spartanburg, South Carolina Office: 101 W. St. John Street, Suite 203, 29306. Telephone: 803-591-2030. Facsimile: 803-591-2050.
Charleston, South Carolina Office: 200 Meeting Street, Suite 301, 29401. Telephone: 843-727-2650. Facsimile: 843-727-2680.
See Professional Biographies, CHARLOTTE, NORTH CAROLINA

Parks, Chesin & Walbert, P.C., (AV)
521 East Morehead Street, Suite 120, 28202 ⊙
Telephone: 704-377-2770 Facsimile: 704-377-2703
Email: firm@pcwlawfirm.com URL: http://www.pcwlawfirm.com
Kevin V. Parsons (Resident). Associate: Janet J. Higley.
General Civil, Trial and Appellate Practice in all State and Federal Courts and Administrative Agencies. Antitrust, Arbitration, Bankruptcy, Commercial, Constitutional, Construction, Corporate, Employment Discrimination, Environmental, Family, Health Care, Labor, Professional Liability, Insurance, Intellectual Properties, Libel and Slander, Malpractice, Negligence, Personal Injury, Probate, Products Liability and Voting Rights.
Atlanta, Georgia Office: 26th Floor, 75 Fourteenth Street. 30309. Telephone: 404-873-8000. Facsimile: 404-873-8050.
See Professional Biographies, CHARLOTTE, NORTH CAROLINA

Parnell, E. Fitzgerald, III, (AV) ....'47 '73 C.576 B.S. L.575 J.D. [Poyner&S.]
Parnell, W. Chris, (BV) ....'49 '75 C.575 A.B. L.192 J.D. [Ⓐ Kellam&P.]
Parr, Ross H. ....'72 '99 C.475 B.A. L.945 J.D. [Ⓐ Womble C.S.&R.]
Parsons, Kevin V., (AV) ....'64 '92 C.546 B.A. L.602 J.D. [Parks,C.&W.]
Parsons, Pamela G., (BVⓉ) '58 '89 C.1090 B.S. L.945 J.D.
(adm. in VA; not adm. in NC) Sr. Coun., Goodrich Corp.
Paschall, Michael Alexander ....'64 '95 C.575 B.A. L.896 J.D. Banister Financial, Inc.
Passenant, Sheila G. ....'63 '89 C.754 B.A. L.1009 J.D. 5219 Winding Brook Rd.
Pastryk, John R. '56 '82 C.880 B.A. L.692 J.D.
Sr. Coun., John Deere Consumer Products
Patel, Sanjay S. ....'68 '96 L.365 J.D. 6419A Bannington Rd
Patrick, Bailey, Jr., (AV) ....'— '60 C&L.575 B.S. J.D. [Kennedy C.L.&H.]
Patterson, Jennifer M. ....'69 '00 C.575 B.A. L.896 J.D. [Ⓐ Johnston,A.&H.]
Patterson, William J., (BV) ....'42 '67 C&L.912 Ph.B., J.D. 6701 Carmel Road
Patteson, John H., Jr. ....'63 '89 C&L.575 A.B., J.D. [Ⓐ Byrne,D.&H.] ⊙
Patton, Cindy M. .....'56 '92 C.1128 B.A. L.575 J.D. Legal Servs. of Sou. Piedmont, Inc.
Patton, Lori Reese ....'68 '93 C.917 B.A. L.469 J.D. [Ⓒ Womble C.S.&R.]
Pauling, Corie D. ....'71 '98 C.477 B.Sc. L.597 J.D. [Littler M.]

Pawlowski, Paul L., (BV) '44 '72 C.959 B.S. L.575 J.D.
1001 Elizabeth Avenue, Suite 2-A, 28204
Telephone: 704-333-0312 Fax: 704-333-0313
Email: pawlowskilaw@yahoo.com URL: http://www.paulpawlowskilaw.com
Family Law, Child Custody, Child Support, Divorce, Equitable Distribution, Domestic Violence, Collaborative Law, Criminal Law, Traffic Violations, Driving While Impaired, Personal Injury, Automobile Accidents and Injuries, Wrongful Death.
See Professional Biographies, CHARLOTTE, NORTH CAROLINA

Payne, Philip S. '51 '78 C&L.945 B.S., J.D.
(adm. in VA; not adm. in NC) Exec. V.P., BNP Residential Properties, Inc.
Pearce, Bradley E., (AV) ....'60 '91 C.838 B.A. L.309 J.D. [Katten M.R.]
Pearce, Hugo A., III, (BV) ....'45 '73 C.572 A.B. L.790 J.D. [Burris,M.P.&B.]
Pearce, Theodore P. '49 '78 C.893 B.A. L.823 J.D.
V.P. & Gen. Coun., Meineke Car Care Centers, Inc.
Pearce, William Ruffin, Jr. ....'69 '96 C&L.896 B.S., J.D. [Womble C.S.&R.]
Pearlman, Joseph D. ....'57 '82 C.198 B.A. L.896 J.D. State Employ. Sec. Comm
Pearson, Jeanne A. ....'— '96 C.160 B.A. L.862 J.D. [Ⓒ Kennedy C.L.&H.]
Pearson, Kathleen '63 '00 C.945 B.A. L.1017 J.D.
(adm. in NY; not adm. in NC) [Ⓐ Cadwalader,W.&T.]
Pearson, Pamela M. '— '82 C.881 A.B. L.188 J.D.
Sr. V.P. & Asst. Gen. Coun., Wachovia Corporation (Legal Department)
Peed, Lindsay M. ....'76 '02 C.893 B.A. L.902 J.D. [Ⓐ Moore&V.P.]
Pelak, Richard A. ....'70 '95 C.1349 B.S. L.575 J.D. [Ⓐ Culp E.&C.]
Pender, William L. '36 '61 C&L.575 A.B., LL.B.
V.P. & Tr. Offr., Bank of America, N.A.
Pendergrass, Samantha D. '71 '96 C&L.575 B.A., J.D.
Asst. Dist. Atty., Dist. Attys. Off.
Pendleton, Melissa B. ....'65 '90 C.576 B.A. L.575 J.D. [Summa&A.] (See Pat. Sect.)
Pendry, Reita P. ....'45 '73 C.680 A.B. L.575 J.D. P.O. Box 42249
Peniston, Richard A., (BV) ....'49 '77 C.1128 B.A. L.575 J.D. [R.A.Peniston&Assoc.] ⊙

Peniston, Richard A., & Associates, P.A., (BV)
1901 Central Avenue, 28205 ⊙
Telephone: 704-373-0203; 800-279-2889 Facsimile: 704-373-2858
URL: http://www.lawyers.com/rpenistonlaw
Richard A. Peniston;—David A. Manzi; Adam M. Seifer.
Personal Injury, Automobile Accidents, Workers Compensation, Wrongful Death, Medical Malpractice, Social Security Disability, Criminal Law, Traffic, DWI, Wills and Estates, Business Law, General Practice.
Raleigh, North Carolina Office: 811 W. Morgan Street, 27603. Telephone: 919-834-2889. Facsimile: 919-834-1533.
Monroe, North Carolina Office: 211 Lancaster Avenue, 28112. Telephone: 704-225-8700. Facsimile: 704-238-0317.
See Professional Biographies, CHARLOTTE, NORTH CAROLINA

Penn, Philip J. ....'55 '81 C.228 A.B. L.574 J.D. Staff Atty., Children's Law Ctr.
Perkins, T. Randolph ....'55 '82 C.575 A.B. L.976 J.D. [Moore&V.P.]
Perle, Scott Ian ....'73 '97 C.472 B.A. L.575 J.D. [Griffin,B.&P.]
Perrin, Ellen A. ....'— '95 C.228 B.A. L.575 J.D. Asst. Gen. Coun., Bank of America
Perrin, Sean F. ....'70 '95 C.1369 B.A. L.575 J.D. [Ⓐ Womble C.S.&R.]
Peterson, Drew H. ....'77 '03 C.294 B.A. L.1209 J.D. [Ⓐ P.L.Whitfield&Assoc.]
Petho, Douglas A., (BV) ....'66 '91 C&L.575 B.S., J.D. [Price,S.H.P.&A.] ⊙
Pettigrew, Charles A. ....'— '04 C&L.575 B.A., J.D. [Ⓐ Katten M.R.]
Pettit, William Walt, (BV) ....'55 '80 C.576 B.A. L.469 J.D. [Kellam&P.]
Pharr, Henry N., II, (AV) ....'39 '64 C.198 A.B. L.575 J.D. [Horack,T.P.&L.]
Pharr, Henry N., III ....'66 '93 C&L.575 B.A., J.D. [Horack,T.P.&L.]
Phelan, Sean M., (BV) ....'— '92 C&L.575 B.A., J.D. [Nexsen P.A.K.]
Phifer, Robert S., (AV) ....'52 '77 C&L.790 B.A., J.D. [Ogletree,D.N.S.&S.]
Phillips, Don H. ....'34 '63 C.108 B.CH.E. L.262 LL.B. 4105 Sharon Common Lane
Phillips, Mark W. '63 '90 C.999 B.A. L.895 J.D.
(adm. in GA; not adm. in NC) Sr. Atty., Compass Group, U.S.A. Inc.
Phillips, Randel E., (AV) ....'47 '80 C.198 B.A. L.309 J.D. [Moore&V.P.]
Phillips, Tia S. '— '01 C&L.575 B.A., J.D.
(adm. in GA; not adm. in NC) [Ⓐ Cadwalader,W.&T.]
Phocas, Robert John ....'70 '98 C.881 B.A. L.228 J.D. [Ⓐ Womble C.S.&R.]
Piemonte, George C., (BV) ....'59 '87 C.260 B.S. L.1206 J.D. [Bollinger&P.]
Pierce, C. Grainger, Jr. ....'74 '00 C.228 A.B. L.575 J.D. [Ⓐ Caudle&S.]
Pierce, Katharine F. ....'— '05 C.228 A.B. L.575 J.D. [Ⓐ Alston&B.]
Piervincenti, Arthur H. ....'72 '04 C.1353 B.A. L.1019 J.D. [Ⓐ Yurko&Assoc.]
Pietropaolo, Vincent P. '— '96 C.461 B.S. L.1252 J.D.
(adm. in MA; not adm. in NC) Bank of America (⊙Boston, MA)
Pifer, Deni C. ....'68 '97 C.956 M.B.A. L.790 J.D. 3719 Latrobe Drive, Suite 840
Pilkington, Kathy L., (BV) ....'51 '89 C&L.575 B.S., J.D. [Helms M.&W.]
Pinckney, Francis M., (AV) ....'— '65 C.790 B.S. L.273 J.D. [Ⓒ Kennedy C.L.&H.]
Pitesa, Cynthia G. ......'61 '92 C.71 B.B.A. L.500 J.D. Sr. Coun., Goodrich Corporation
Pittman, Bryan W., (BV) ....'46 '73 C.198 A.B. L.575 J.D. [Wallace,P.&W.]
Pitts, Ralph A., (AVⓉ) '53 '78 C.575 A.B. L.309 J.D.
Exec. V.P. & Gen. Coun., Belk Stores Servs., Inc.
Plaisted, G. Laurence ....'71 '96 C&L.378 B.S., J.D. [Ⓐ Katten M.R.]
Platter, Lawrence ....'44 '73 C.390 B.S.E.E. L.665 J.D. [Ⓒ Gilpin&H.]
Pleicones, Laura ....'72 '00 C.280 A.B. L.790 J.D. [Ⓐ Johnston,A.&H.]
Pleune, S. Benjamin ....'77 '02 C.966 B.S. L.339 J.D. [Ⓐ Alston&B.] (See Pat. Sect.)
Plumides, Gregory John '68 '97 C.280 B.A. L.327 J.D.
301 S. McDowell Street, Suite 604
Plyler, Joyce E. ....'— '84 C.956 B.A. L.245 J.D. [Ⓒ Womble C.S.&R.]
Plyler, M. Matthew ....'71 '96 C&L.575 B.S., J.D. [Moore&V.P.]
Poe, W. Edward, Jr., (AV) ....'49 '74 C&L.896 B.A., J.D. [Parker,P.A.&B.]
Poelke, Mark J. .....'71 '97 C.160 B.S. L.280 J.D. First Union Corp. (Contract Servs. Grp.)
Poku-Kankam, O. Akomen ....'74 '00 C&L.477 B.A., J.D. [Ⓐ Womble C.S.&R.]
Polking, Christian L. ....'72 '04 C.128 B.A. L.1128 J.D. [Ⓐ Moore&V.P.]
Polking, Jonathan B. ....'— '05 C&L.602 B.B.A., J.D. [Ⓐ Kennedy C.L.&H.]
Pollard, John O., (AV) ....'37 '73 C.904 B.A. L.575 J.D. [McGuireWoods]
Pollard, Scott T., (AV) ....'49 '74 C&L.575 B.S., J.D. [Dozier,M.P.&M.]
Pollicino, Kristine '72 '98 C.93 B.A. L.262 J.D.
(adm. in NY; not adm. in NC) Asst. Coun., Compass Group, U.S.A. Inc.
(⊙New York, NY)
Ponder, Pamela R. ....'58 '83 C.122 B.A. L.575 J.D. Police Atty.
Poole, Samuel H., Jr., (BV) ....'60 '86 C&L.575 B.A., J.D. [Cranfill,S.&H.]
Poolos, Kristin R. ....'— '03 C.228 B.A. L.1565 J.D. [Ⓐ Parker,P.A.&B.]
Poolos, Stephen P. ....'— '04 C&L.228 B.A., J.D. 2319 Crescent Avenue
Pope, Alan W. ....'66 '94 C.160 B.S. L.245 J.D. [Moore&V.P.]
Pope, James W., (BV) ....'52 '81 C.575 B.A. L.790 J.D. [Golding H.&P.]
Pope, Lynn Ipock '55 '82 C.140 B.A. L.790 J.D.
(adm. in SC; not adm. in NC) 5012 Talmadge Ct.
Poplin, Jared W. ....'77 '02 C.327 B.A. L.575 J.D. [Ⓐ Moore&V.P.]
Porter, Charles W. ....'50 '76 C.323 B.S. L.209 J.D. [C.W.Porter]
Porter, J. William, (AV) ....'51 '77 C&L.575 A.B., J.D. [Parker,P.A.&B.]
Porter, Paul G. ....'64 '89 C.45 B.S.B.A. L.602 J.D. [McGuireWoods]
Porter, Stephen G., Jr. ....'70 '96 C&L.575 B.A., J.D. [Moore&V.P.]
Porter, Thomas C., (BV) ....'65 '92 C.803 B.A. L.831 J.D. [T.C.Porter]
Porter, W. Frank, (BV) ....'62 '90 C.1129 B.A. L.1228 J.D. [W.F.Porter]
Porter, Charles W., P.C. ....600 S. College St.
Porter, Thomas C., P.A., (BV) .... Suite 305 301 South McDowell Street

Porter, W. Frank, P.A., (BV)
8625 Crown Crescent Court, Suite 110, 28227
Telephone: 704-708-5176 Fax: 704-845-9629
Email: frankporter@wfrankporter.com URL: http://www.frankporterlaw.com
W. Frank Porter;—Benjamin D. Schwartz; Andrew N. Bernardini; Brian S. Rudolph.
Commercial Law, Commercial Litigation, Creditors Rights.
See Professional Biographies, CHARLOTTE, NORTH CAROLINA

Potter, C. Ann ....'64 '90 C.522 B.S.B.A. L.896 J.D. Dist. Atty's. Off.
Potter, Robert D. ....'23 '51 C&L.228 A.B., LL.B. Sr. U.S. Dist. J.

Potter, Robert D., Jr., (AV) '57 '90 C.871 B.S. L.896 J.D.
5821 Fairview Road, Suite 207, 28209
Telephone: 704-552-7742 Fax: 704-552-9287
URL: http://www.lawyers.com/robertdpotter
Language: French.
Aviation Law, General Practice, Commercial Litigation, Construction Law, Contracts, Qui Tam Litigation.
See Professional Biographies, CHARLOTTE, NORTH CAROLINA

Potts, William F., Jr., (AV) ....'53 '78 C.893 B.A. L.575 J.D. [Helms M.&W.]
Povall, Allie S., Jr. '41 '78 C&L.500 B.A., J.D.
(adm. in MS; not adm. in NC) 300 S. Brevard St.
Powell, H. David, (BV) ....'59 '85 C.575 B.S. L.896 J.D. [Horack,T.P.&L.]
Powers, Bill, (BV) ....'65 '92 C.576 B.A. L.1345 J.D. [Bush&P.]
Powers, James F. '59 '84 C.1031 B.A. L.902 J.D.
(adm. in VA; not adm. in NC) Sr. V.P. & Dep. Gen. Coun., First Union Corp.

Poyner & Spruill LLP, (AV)
One Wachovia Center, 301 South College Street Suite 2300, 28202 ⊙
Telephone: 704-342-5250 Telecopier: 704-342-5264
URL: http://www.poynerspruill.com
Members: C. Marcus Harris; Lee A. Spinks; Douglas M. Martin; Timothy W. Griffin; Judy D. Thompson; Terry Richard Kane; E. Fitzgerald Parnell, III; Nancy C. Brower; P. Marshall Yoder; Thomas D. Eatman, Jr.; Cynthia L. Van Horne; Constance L. Young; Frank L. Bryant; David L. Terry; Patrick J. Fogarty; Shelia June Cox; William T. Belcher; Parmele Price Calame; Anna Shedden Gorman; Thomas L. Ogburn, III; Stephen Andrew Jurs (Board Certified Specialist in Consumer Bankruptcy Law and Business Bankruptcy Law, North Carolina State Board of Legal Specialization); Diane P. Furr; Peggy Howard Hey; Eugene S. Griggs. Resident Associates: Joshua Blake Durham; Rebecca B. Wofford; Courtauld McBryde Young; Deborah M. Tyson; W. Mark Griffith; William C. Parise; Jason Burke James; Michelle C. Hunt; Thomas M. Asmar (Not admitted in NC); Bryan A. Hayles. Resident Of Counsel: Mark B. Edwards; David E. Johnston; Jason T. Sherwood.
Comprehensive business and litigation practice including: Appellate, Arbitration, Banking, Bankruptcy/Creditors' Rights, Complex Business Litigation, Construction, Credit and Financial Services, Eminent Domain/Condemnation, Employment Benefits, Employment Practices, Entertainment Law, Environmental, Estate, Exempt Organizations, General Corporate, Governmental Relations, Health Care, Intellectual Property Law, International, Land Use and Zoning, Limited Liability Companies, Local Government, Mediation, Partnerships, Personal and Financial Planning, Probate, Product Liability, Professional Liability, Railroad, Real Estate, Regulatory and Municipal, Securities, Sports Law, Tax, Technology and Emerging Business, Tort Litigation and Insurance Defense, Transactional including Mergers and Acquisitions, Transportation, Utilities, White Collar Criminal Defense.
Raleigh, North Carolina Office: 3600 Glenwood Avenue, P.O. Box 10096, 27605-0096. Telephone: 919-783-6400. Telecopier: 919-783-1075.
Rocky Mount, North Carolina Office: 130 S. Franklin Street, P.O. Box 353, 27802-0353. Telephone: 252-446-2341. Telecopier: 252-972-7045.
Southern Pines, North Carolina Office: 135 West New Hampshire Avenue, 28388-0371. Telephone: 910-692-6866. Telecopier: 910-695-3036.
See Professional Biographies, CHARLOTTE, NORTH CAROLINA

Pray, Francis C., Jr. .... '64 '89 C&L.893 B.A., J.D. [Nelson M.R.&S.]
Presel, Alan M. .... '72 '97 C.860 B.S. L.575 J.D. [A Grier F.&C.]
Preston, James Y., (AV) .... '37 '61 C&L.575 A.B., J.D. [C Parker,P.A.&B.]
Pretty, George H., II, (AV) '51 '77 C.228 B.A. L.790 J.D.
[Parker,P.A.&B.] (⊙Columbia, Spartanburg, SC)
Price, Glenn F. .... '33 '61 C&L.575 A.B., LL.B. State Farm Ins. Cos.
Price, Larry E., (P.A.), (BV) .... '42 '72 C.1130 B.S. L.896 J.D. [Price,S.H.P.&A.]
Price, Thomas A. .... '71 '98 C.198 B.A. L.896 J.D. [C Womble C.S.&R.]
Price Massingale, Michelle, (BV T) .... '70 '94 C&L.923 B.A., J.D. [Sellers,H.A.D.&L.]

Price, Smith, Hargett, Petho & Anderson, (AV) BB
A Partnership including a Professional Corporation
1430 Elizabeth Avenue, 28204 ⊙
Telephone: 704-372-2160 800-737-2160 Facsimile: 704-372-6516
Email: priceatty@aol.com URL: http://www.pshpanda.com
Larry E. Price (P.A.); Wm. Benjamin Smith; Jeffrey B. Hargett; Douglas A. Petho; Richard Lee Anderson.
Plaintiffs Catastrophic Personal Injury, Medical Malpractice, Brain Injury, Wrongful Death, Workers Compensation, Insurance Litigation for Plaintiff, Motor Vehicle Accidents .
Forest City, North Carolina Office: 552 Oak Street, 28043. Telephone: 828-248-1448. Fax: 828-248-4405.
See Professional Biographies, CHARLOTTE, NORTH CAROLINA

Prichard, Daniel K. .... '56 '83 C.12 B.S. L.280 J.D. 8929 J. M.Keynes Dr., Ste. 310
Prichard, E. Allen, (AV) .... '— '75 C.575 B.A. L.276 J.D. [Kennedy C.L.&H.]
Pridgen, Eugene C., (AV) .... '— '78 C.576 B.S. L.896 J.D. [Kennedy C.L.&H.]
Proctor, Nathaniel P. .... '56 '88 C.136 B.A.A. L.896 J.D. 700 East Fourth Street
Proctor, PollyBeth .... '76 '03 C.198 B.A. L.280 J.D. [A Nelson M.R.&S.]
Profit, Kevin M. .... '75 '02 C.477 B.A. L.665 J.D. [A Hamilton F.M.S.S.&M.]
Pruden, J. Norfleet, III, (AV) .... '— '73 C.575 A.B. L.893 J.D. [Kennedy C.L.&H.]
Pruden, Matthew G. .... '75 '04 C.296 B.S. L.896 J.D. [A Tin F.G.&O.]

Pruett, Ronnie A., (AV) '38 '66 C.575 A.B. L.178 LL.B. BB
744 Tyvola Road, Suite C, 28217
Telephone: 704-523-6020 Fax: 704-527-7711
Email: pruett@sprintmail.com
Immigration, International Trade, U.S. Customs and Antitrust Law.
See Professional Biographies, CHARLOTTE, NORTH CAROLINA

Prybylski, Mark C. .... '— '94 C.732 B.A. L.893 J.D. [Kilpatrick S.]
Pryor, Robert H., (AV) .... '57 '82 C&L.896 B.A., J.D. [Helms M.&W.]
Pulley, Jennifer P. .... '— '03 C.586 B.S. L.124 J.D. [A Hedrick E.G.&K.]
Pulliam, James H., (AV) .... '— '89 C&L.383 B.A., J.D. [Nexsen P.A.K.]
Purser, Rodney L., (BV) .... '38 '70 C.1128 B.A. L.575 J.D. 2730 E. W.T. Harris Blvd.
Pusey, N. Woodrow '39 '64 C.1083 B.A. L.945 J.D.
(adm. in VA; not adm. in NC) Sr. Coun., BASF Corp.
Quattlebaum, David J., (AV) .... '60 '86 C.197 A.B. L.228 J.D. [Moore&V.P.]
Quick, Hunter C. .... '49 '81 C.968 A.B. L.923 J.D. [Cozen O.]
Quinlan, Lowndes C. .... '67 '94 C.970 B.A. L.180 J.D. [A Helms M.&W.]
Quirk, Thomas M. .... '70 '98 C.893 B.A. L.896 J.D. [A Parker,P.A.&B.]
Rabon, Charles H., Jr., (BV) .... '62 '90 C.269 B.A. L.880 J.D. [Carley&R.]
Racine, Russell '71 '99 C.529 B.S. L.208 J.D.
(adm. in CO; not adm. in NC) [A Dougherty,C.H.&B.]
Radey, Kevin J. .... '75 '00 C.575 B.S. L.896 J.D. 1001 East Boulevard

Ragan & Ragan PLLC
(See Gastonia)

Rainey, Richard L., (AV) .... '62 '87 C.205 B.A. L.575 J.D. [Womble C.S.&R.]
Raley, Michael R. '72 '97 C&L.790 B.S., J.D.
(adm. in SC; not adm. in NC) Mng., KPMG, LLP
Rallings, Thomas B., Jr., (AV) .... '52 '77 C&L.575 B.S., J.D. [Mitchell,R.&T.]
Ralls, David L. .... '48 '75 C.112 B.A. L.767 J.D. [C Moore&V.P.]
Ralston, Henry H., (AV) .... '— '83 C&L.575 B.A., J.D. [Robinson,B.&H.]
Ramos, Susan W. .... '71 '99 C.245 B.A. L.742 J.D. [A Garfinkel]
Ramsay, Martha L. .... '67 '93 C.1385 B.A. L.107 J.D. [Ramsay]
Ramsay Law Firm .... P.O. Box 481210
Randall, Anne J. .... '— '03 C.896 B.A. L.276 J.D. [A Alston&B.]
Randolph, Denise L. '56 '89 C.112 B.A. L.769 J.D.
(adm. in CA; not adm. in NC) 5790 Linda Vista Ln.‡
Rankin, Edward L., III, (BV) '56 '82 C.575 A.B. L.192 J.D.
Gen. Coun., BellSouth Corp., Regulatory, North Carolina
Rankin, Wilton, (BV) .... '27 '59 C&L.575 A.B., J.D. 200 Hempstead Pl. (Pat.)
Ransom, William Kevin ..... '70 '97 C&L.838 B.S.E.E., J.D. [Alston&B.] (See Pat. Sect.)
Raper, William C., (AV) .... '46 '72 C.575 A.B. L.880 J.D. [Womble C.S.&R.]
Rash, Eugene F. .... '62 '95 C.576 B.S. L.896 J.D. [Taylor,P.R.&R.]
Rash, James Dennis '39 '65 C.575 A.B. L.893 J.D.
Sr. V.P., NationsBank Community Develop. Corp.
Rashid, James M. '56 '84 C.966 B.S.E.Met. L.184 J.D.
(adm. in CT; not adm. in NC; Pat.) Princ. Coun., Intell. Prop., Goodrich Corporation
Rast, T. Edmund, (AV) .... '47 '74 C.976 B.A. L.659 J.D. [C Moore&V.P.]
Ratteree, Jane S., (AV) .... '— '86 C.198 A.B. L.575 J.D. [Robinson,B.&H.]

Rauscher, Claire J., (AV) .... '55 '83 C.659 B.A. L.831 J.D. 435 East Morehead Street
Rawls, Christopher B. .... '79 '04 C.576 B.S. L.575 J.D. [A Morris Y.W.S.&B.]
Rawls, Eben T., III, (AV) .... '49 '78 C.228 B.A. L.575 J.D. [Rawls,D.&S.]
Rawls, Leslie C., (BV) .... '54 '83 C&L.575 B.A., J.D. P.O. Box 38325

Rawls, Dickinson & Scheer, P.A., (AV) BB
1011 East Morehead Street Suite 300, 28204
Telephone: 704-376-3200 Facsimile: 704-332-2716 URL: http://www.rdslaw.com
URL: http://www.rawlsdickinsonandscheer.com
Eben T. Rawls III (Board Certified Specialist in Criminal Law, North Carolina State Board of Legal Specialization); Thomas W. Dickinson; Anthony G. Scheer;—Sheena M. West; Amanda A. Mingo.
General Civil and Criminal Trial Practice in State and Federal Courts. Appellate Practice, Criminal Law, Driving While Intoxicated (DWI), Drug Crimes, Parole and Probation, Traffic Violations, White Collar Crimes, Personal Injury, Wrongful Death, Automobile Accidents, Products Liability, Medical Malpractice, Consumer Law.
See Professional Biographies, CHARLOTTE, NORTH CAROLINA

Rayburn, C. Richard, Jr., (AV) .... '47 '74 C.838 B.S. L.228 J.D. [Rayburn C.&D.]

Rayburn Cooper & Durham, P.A., (AV) BB
The Carillon, 227 West Trade Street, Suite 1200, 28202-1675
Telephone: 704-334-0891 Fax: 704-377-1897; 704-377-0395
Email: info@rcdlaw.net URL: http://www.rcdlaw.net
C. Richard Rayburn, Jr.; W. Scott Cooper; Albert F. Durham (Board Certified Specialist in Bankruptcy, North Carolina State Board of Legal Specialization); Paul R. Baynard; James B. Gatehouse; G. Kirkland Hardymon; Patricia B. Edmondson. Associates: David S. Melin; John R. Miller, Jr.; Ross R. Fulton; Tasha Leigh Winebarger; Shawna R. Garrett; Shelley K. Abel; Peter T. Reynolds.
General Civil Practice including Corporate, Business Organizations, Securities and Business Bankruptcy. Trial and Appellate Practice in all State and Federal Courts.
See Professional Biographies, CHARLOTTE, NORTH CAROLINA

Raynor, Kenneth R., (AV) .... '56 '82 C&L.575 B.S., J.D. [Templeton&R.]
Reaves, Kimberly P. .... '— '96 C.575 B.A. L.574 J.D. [A Hedrick E.G.&K.]
Reaves, Samuel T. .... '— '98 C&L.16 B.A., J.D. [A Kennedy C.L.&H.]
Reavis, David L. .... '20 '47 C&L.896 A.B., LL.B. Maryland Cas. Co.
Redding, David G. .... '63 '97 C.93 B.A. L.896 J.D. [Hamilton F.M.S.S.&M.]
Redding, Marjorie C. '68 '97 C.575 B.A. L.896 J.D.
Assoc. Atty., University of North Carolina at Charlotte
Redmond, Phillip H., Jr. '64 '89 C.575 A.B. L.1228 J.D.
Exec. Dir., Children's Law Ctr.
Reece, James W. '38 '66 C.197 A.B. L.347 LL.B.
(adm. in IN; not adm. in NC) 6924 N. Baltusrol Lane‡
Reed, Jerry D. .... '43 '72 C.347 B.S. L.345 J.D. 4011 Chevington Rd.
Reed, Laura L. .... '70 '97 C.401 B.A. L.1338 J.D. [A Butrus K.W.V.] ⊙
Reed, Russell M., (BV) .... '— '95 C.500 B.A. L.896 J.D. [A Kennedy C.L.&H.]
Reeder, Alton, Jr., (BV) ...... '64 '95 C.1288 B.A. L.1339 J.D. [A D.K.Simmons&Assoc.]
Reese, Jerry Alan, (AV) .... '52 '77 C&L.575 A.B., J.D. [J.A.Reese]

Reese, Jerry Alan, P.C., (AV)
411 Lansdowne Road, P.O. Box 32066, 28270
Telephone: 704-347-1044 Telecopier: 704-347-1045
Email: jreese@tryonlg.com URL: http://www.tryonlegalgroup.com
Jerry Alan Reese.
Residential and Commercial Real Estate, Commercial and Real Estate Lending and Business Law.
See Professional Biographies, CHARLOTTE, NORTH CAROLINA

Reichs, Paul A., (AV) .... '42 '67 C.293 B.A. L.339 LL.B. [Cozen O.]
Reid, Christy Eve, (AV) .... '— '76 C.788 B.A. L.575 J.D. [Robinson,B.&H.]
Reid, Cynthia Cline, (BV) .... '61 '85 C.680 B.A. L.896 J.D. City Atty.'s Office
Reid, Glenn J., (BV) .... '54 '83 C.1044 B.A. L.575 J.D. Bk of America
Reigel, Ernest W., (AV) .... '57 '83 C.198 A.B. L.945 J.D. [Moore&V.P.]
Reiner, Barry P. .... '61 '86 C.415 B.A. L.1009 J.D. Mng. Dir., First Union Secs.
Reis, John W. .... '66 '92 C.228 A.B. L.472 J.D. [Cozen O.]
Reisch, Claudia L. .... '62 '88 C.1019 B.A. L.724 J.D. [A Clontz&C.P.]
Renaud, Ronald K. '58 '83 C.705 B.A. L.990 J.D.
(adm. in NJ; not adm. in NC) 100 North Tryon Street NC1-007-20-01
Resen, W. Patrick .... '46 '74 C.843 B.A. L.502 J.D. P.O. Box 37244‡
Reutlinger, Craig A., (AV) .... '47 '73 C&L.259 B.A., J.D. [VanHoy,R.A.&D.]
Reveley, Elizabeth F. .... '52 '77 C.471 A.B. L.575 J.D. 2400 Yorkmont Road
Revelle, Jennifer Fisher .... '— '04 C.902 B.A. L.976 J.D. [A Robinson,B.&H.]
Reymann, Lucille E. '— '86 C.16 B.S. L.880 J.D.
(adm. in TX; not adm. in NC) Dep. Gen. Coun., Bank of America
Reynolds, Amy K. .... '69 '94 C.228 A.B. L.896 J.D. Meineke Car Care Centers, Inc.
Reynolds, Peter T. .... '79 '05 C.597 B.A. L.575 J.D. [A Rayburn C.&D.]
Rhodes, Allyn Burchfield .... '— '03 C.497 B.S. L.861 J.D. [A Kennedy C.L.&H.]
Rhoton, W. Porter, III .... '60 '87 C.198 B.A. L.896 J.D. [Fletcher&R.]
Rhyne, Stephen K., (AV) .... '— '77 C.870 B.S. L.273 J.D. [Kennedy C.L.&H.]
Rice, Garry Stephen, (AV) '61 '86
C&L.575 B.A.Ec., J.D. Assoc. Gen. Coun., Duke Energy Corp.
Rich, David B., III .... '— '95 C.938 A.B. L.692 J.D. Asst. Gen. Coun., Bank of America
Richards, Channing O., (AV) .... '41 '66 C.575 A.B. L.228 LL.B. [Essex R.]
Richardson, Greg .... '70 '99 C.790 B.A. L.861 J.D. Sr. Corp. Coun., Inspiration Networks
Richardson, Mark Louis .... '68 '95 C.893 B.S. L.790 J.D. [Culp E.&C.]
Richardson, O. Leonard, Jr. '40 '65 C.198 A.B. L.575 LL.B.
V.P., Bank of America, N.A.
Richburg, Sonya C. '71 '96 C.705 B.A. L.659 J.D.
(adm. in PA; not adm. in NC)
Ombudsman-Morrison Mgmt. Spec. & Crothall Servs., Compass Group, U.S.A. Inc.
Richey, Alice Carmichael, (AV) .... '— '86 C&L.575 B.A., J.D. [Kennedy C.L.&H.]
Richmond, Beth Alpha .... '67 '94 C.896 B.A. L.893 J.D. Law Clk., U.S. Dist. Ct.
Ricks, Andrea B. .... '— '02 C.575 B.A. L.896 J.D. [A Nexsen P.A.K.]
Ricks, Thomas D. .... '— '02 C&L.896 B.S., J.D. [A Mayer,B.R.&M.]
Ridenhour, Monroe H., III .... '44 '69 C&L.575 B.S., J.D. 3900 Churchill Rd.‡
Ridinger, Patrick L. .... '— '98 C.968 B.S. L.790 J.D. [A Kennedy C.L.&H.]
Riess, Justin M. .... '74 '01 C&L.880 B.S., J.D. [A Moore&V.P.]
Rikard, William L., Jr., (AV) .... '45 '70 C.198 B.A. L.880 J.D. [Parker,P.A.&B.]
Riley, James A. '69 '98 C.575 B.A. L.1345 J.D.
Tax Advsr., Charitable & Private Found., First Union Bank
Rimler, Lee R. .... '67 '94 C.1090 B.S. L.945 J.D. [C Alston&B.]
Riopel, Mark D., (BV) .... '66 '94 C.165 B.A. L.896 J.D. [Casstevens,H.G.&R.]
Rivera, Richard J. .... '72 '97 C.198 B.A. L.896 J.D. [A Parker,P.A.&B.]
Rivers, Thomas D. .... '— '05 C.806 B.A. L.880 J.D. [A Kennedy C.L.&H.]
Rizer, Michael P. '59 '85 C.201 B.A. L.150 J.D.
(adm. in OH; not adm. in NC) First Union Cooporation
Rizzo, Carl M. '— '77 C.198 B.A. L.692 J.D.
(adm. in VA; not adm. in NC) Asst. Gen. Coun., Bank of America
Robason, Donna K.S. '52 '77 C.1 B.S. L.845 J.D.
(adm. in TX; not adm. in NC) Estate & Gift Tax Atty.,Internal Rev. Serv.
Robason, Randy D. .... '53 '77 C.846 B.B.A. L.845 J.D. 100 N. Tryon St.‡
Robbe, Michael E. .... '— '95 C.473 B.S. L.880 J.D. [Kennedy C.L.&H.]
Roberson, Keith .... '76 '02 C.160 B.S. L.790 J.D. [A Alston&B.] (See Pat. Sect.)

Roberts, Manley W., (AV) ....'58 '84 C.575 A.B. L.976 J.D. [Helms M.&W.]
Roberts, Marcos .... '57 '97 C.1128 L.273 J.D. [M.Roberts]

Roberts Law Firm, The, P.A.
(See Gastonia)

Roberts, Marcos, P.A.
728 Central Avenue, 28204
Telephone: 704-335-7272 Espanol: 704-333-3676 Fax: 704-335-7277
URL: http://www.marcosroberts.com
Marcos Roberts.
Language: Spanish.
State and Federal Criminal Defense, Driving While Intoxicated (DWI), Drug Crimes, Felonies, Misdemeanors, Assault, Rape, Traffic Violations, White Collar Crimes.
See Professional Biographies, CHARLOTTE, NORTH CAROLINA

Robertson, Allen K., (AV) ....'— '88 C.575 B.A. L.309 J.D. [Robinson,B.&H.]
Robertson, Kimberly Raymer, (BV) '— '88 C&L.575 B.S., J.D. [[A] Kennedy C.L.&H.]
Robertson, Matthew H. .... '70 '95 C.205 B.A. L.228 J.D. [[A] Cadwalader,W.&T.]
Robertson, Richard H., (BV) ....'36 '63 C&L.575 A.B., LL.B. 1301 Harding Pl.
Robertson, Richard L., (AV) ...... '52 '77 C&L.575 B.A., J.D. [R.L.Robertson&Assoc.]

Robertson, Richard L., & Associates, P.A., (AV)
2730 East Harris Boulevard Suite 101, 28213-4108
Telephone: 704-597-5774 Facsimile: 704-599-5603 URL: http://www.rlrobertson.com
Email: rlrobertson@rlrobertson.com URL: http://www.rlrobertsonpa.com
Member of Firm: Richard L. Robertson;—Karen R. Feeken.
General Civil Trial and Business Practice, Commercial Litigation, Insurance Defense, Personal Injury, Bankruptcy, Commercial Real Estate, Estate Planning, Estate Administration, Collections and Corporations.
See Professional Biographies, CHARLOTTE, NORTH CAROLINA

Robicsek, Susanne M., (BV) '60 '87 C.576 B.E.D. L.896 J.D.
1701 Scott Avenue, 28203
Telephone: 704-377-0776 Fax: 704-377-0775 URL: http://www.robicsek.com
URL: http://www.lawyers.com/robicseklaw
Bankruptcy Law, Consumer, Bankruptcy, Commercial Bankruptcy, Foreclosures.
See Professional Biographies, CHARLOTTE, NORTH CAROLINA

Robinson, J. Neil, (AV) ....'58 '83 C&L.575 B.A., J.D. [Robinson]

Robinson, Robert Nelson, (AV) '— '55 C.1365 B.A. L.893 LL.B. [BB]
P.O. Box 220104, 28222
Telephone: 704-332-4833
URL: http://www.lawyers.com/robertnelsonrobinson
General and Trial Practice before State and Federal Courts. Corporation, Probate, Real Estate, Bankruptcy and Reorganization Law.
Approved Attorney For: Lawyers Title Insurance Corp.; Commonwealth Land Title Insurance Co.; Chicago Title Insurance Co.; The Title Insurance Company of Minnesota.
Reference: Bank of America.
See Professional Biographies, CHARLOTTE, NORTH CAROLINA

Robinson, Russell M., II, (AV) ....'— '56 C.674 L.228 LL.B. [Robinson,B.&H.]
Robinson, S. Graham ....'— '93 C.953 B.A. L.575 J.D. [Robinson,B.&H.]
Robinson, Waverly H. ....'32 '66 C.923 B.S.C.E. L.575 J.D. Ship to Shore, Inc.‡

Robinson, Bradshaw & Hinson, P.A., (AV) [BB]
101 North Tryon Street, Suite 1900, 28246-1900 ⊙
Telephone: 704-377-2536 Fax: 704-378-4000
Email: ylevine@rbh.com URL: http://www.rbh.com
Shareholders: Russell M. Robinson II; Robin L. Hinson; Robert C. Sink; A. Ward McKeithen; Graham D. Holding, Jr. (Board Certified Specialist in Estate Planning and Probate Law, North Carolina State Board of Legal Specialization); Richard A. Vinroot; Claude Q. Freeman, Jr.; John R. Wester; Martin L. Brackett, Jr.; John R. Miller; Robert S. Lilien; Peter C. Buck; Robert M. Bryan; Christy Eve Reid (Board Certified Specialist in Estate Planning and Probate Law, North Carolina State Board of Legal Specialization); Robert G. Griffin; Edwin F. Lucas III; Everett J. Bowman; Charles E. Johnson; Haynes P. Lea; Caroline Wannamaker Sink; Henry H. Ralston; Herman Spence III; Brent A. Torstrick (Board Certified Specialist in Real Property Law - Business, Commercial and Industrial Transactions, North Carolina State Board of Legal Specialization); Mark W. Merritt; Garland S. Cassada; Robert W. Fuller; Kent J. McCready; David C. Wright III; Louis A. Bledsoe III; Christopher W. Loeb; D. Blaine Sanders; Richard W. Gibson, Jr.; Stokely G. Caldwell, Jr.; Stephen M. Lynch; R. Steven DeGeorge; Jane S. Ratteree; Robert E. Harrington; Julie Zydron Griggs (Board Certified Specialist in Estate Planning and Probate Law, North Carolina State Board of Legal Specialization); Benjamin W. Baldwin; John B. Garver, III; Edward F. Hennessey, IV; Richard L. Mack; Allen K. Robertson; Stuart H. Johnson; Karen A. Gledhill; Allain C. Andry, IV; Patrick S. Bryant; David W. Dabbs; Julie C. Chiu; David M. Schilli; William W. Toole; Robert S. McLean; S. Graham Robinson; Julian H. Wright, Jr.; Stephan J. Willen; Matthew S. Churchill; John M. Herring; Lawrence C. Moore, III; Thomas P. Holderness; Douglas M. Jarrell; Amy K. Johnson; Laura C. Smith; Alice Pinckney Adams; David J. Clark; Jeffrey C. Hart; Jeffrey A. Henson; Richard S. Starling; Krista R. Bowen; Thomas J. Molony; Steven D. Newmark; W. Scott Dove; Tilman Thomas Gates; Kelly Luongo Loving. Associates: Susan I. McCrory; Arthur E. Morehead, IV; Daniel F. Basnight; Carl R. Boehm; Anthony S. Ketron; William K. Packard; Dianne Chipps Bailey; Katherine Gordon Maynard; Scott W. Gaylord; Charles R. Lewis; Blake W. Thomas; Angelique R. Vincent; Debra B. Bingham; James H. Bingham, Jr.; Laura Considine Budzichowski; Mark O. Henry; Richard C. Dunn; B. Chad Ewing; Linda Konerding Montgomery; Jonathan C. Krisko; Kristoffer B. Shepard; Andrew W.J. Tarr; Erin G. Palmer; Jennifer Fisher Revelle; Jon R. Jordan; Heidi E. Royal; Jayne C. Hunter. Of Counsel: Robert W. Bradshaw, Jr.; John M. Conley; Gundars Aperans (Not admitted in NC); Robert W. Allen; Thomas E. McNeill; Carl E. Johnson, Jr.
Antitrust and Trade Regulation, Banking and Finance, Bankruptcy, Business Law, Civil and Commercial Litigation, Class Action Litigation, Construction, Corporate and Commercial Law, Criminal Matters, E-Commerce, Employee Benefits, Employment and Labor Law, Energy Law, Environmental Law, Federal and State Taxation, Health Care, Insurance Coverage, Intellectual Property and Technology, International Law, Mergers and Acquisitions, Not-for-Profit Organizations and Foundations, Public Finance, Real Estate, Securities Regulation and Litigation, Sports and Entertainment Law, Tort and Product Liability Litigation, Trusts and Estates, and Venture Capital and Private Equity.
Rock Hill, South Carolina Office: 140 East Main Street, Suite 420, Post Office Drawer 12070. Telephone: 803-325-2900. FAX: 803-325-2929.
See Professional Biographies, CHARLOTTE, NORTH CAROLINA

Robinson Law Office, (AV)
1125 East Morehead Street, Suite 207, 28204
Telephone: 704-373-0077 Fax: 704-332-1261 URL: http://www.jnrobinsonlaw.com
Email: jnrlaw@bellsouth.net URL: http://www.jnrobinsonlawfirm.com
J. Neil Robinson.
Civil Practice, Appellate Practice, Commercial Litigation, Complex Litigation, Business Litigation, Products Liability, Estate Litigation, Trust Litigation, Personal Injury, Construction Litigation, Professional Liability, Banking Litigation, Insurance Litigation, Federal Indian Law.
See Professional Biographies, CHARLOTTE, NORTH CAROLINA

Rodenbeck, Frederick L., Jr. ....'18 '50 C.546 B.A. L.273 LL.B. 4023 Foxcroft Rd.‡
Rodgers, J. Neal, (BV) ....'53 '93 C.632 B.A. L.1341 J.D. [J.N.Rodgers]

Rodgers, J. Neal, PLLC, Law Offices of, (BV)
(Formerly, Tim L. Harris and Associates).
4000 Tuckaseegee Road, 28208
Telephone: 704-392-4111 Fax: 704-391-1905
Email: neal@jnrodgerslaw.com
J. Neal Rodgers (Resident).
Personal Injury, Wrongful Death, Automobile Accidents, Medical Malpractice, Jail Injury Cases, Employment Law, Civil Rights.

(This Listing Continued)

Rodgers, J. Neal, PLLC, Law Offices of (Continued)
Gastonia, North Carolina Office: 616 Cox Road. P.O. Box 249. Telephone: 704-864-3409. Fax: 704-853-1040.
Concord, North Carolina Office: 435 Church Street. Telephone: 704-795-9317. Fax: 704-795-5738
See Professional Biographies, CHARLOTTE, NORTH CAROLINA

Rogers, Alec D., (BV) ....'70 '96 C.160 B.A. L.896 J.D. [Bolster]
Rogers, Eric Allen ....'66 '92 C.446 B.A. L.890 J.D. [Caudle&S.]
Rogers, Marvin L., (AV) ....'60 '86 C.198 B.S. L.790 J.D. [McGuireWoods]
Rogers, Mary L., Law Office of, (CV) ....'— '99 C.198 B.A. L.575 J.D. 1719 Euclid Ave.
Rohe, George W. '42 '69 C.502 B.S. L.260 J.D.
(adm. in FL; not adm. in NC) 4101 Black Sycamore Dr
Rohm, Eric S. ....'— '94 C.276 A.B. L.608 J.D. BNP Residential Properties
Root, Hope A. ....'62 '87 C.232 B.S.B.A. L.896 J.D. Off. of City Atty.
Rosche, Staci E. ....'— '00 C.575 B.A. L.262 J.D. [[A] McGuireWoods]
Rose, Bruce J., (AV) ..... '63 '93 C.474 B.S.C.E. L.884 J.D. [Alston&B.] (See Pat. Sect.)
Rosen, Edith S., (BVⓉ) '56 '82 C.184 B.A. L.280 J.D.
(adm. in CT; not adm. in NC) Sr. Litig. Coun., U.S. Postal Serv. Eastern Area Law Dept.
Rosenberg, Robert E. '67 '92 C.823 B.A. L.178 J.D.
(adm. in NJ; not adm. in NC) First Union Securities
Rosenblatt, Edward G. '69 '94
C.577 B.S L.1209 J.D. V.P. & Asst. Gen. Coun., Wachovia Corp.
Rosensteel, Corey G. ....'76 '02 C.665 B.A. L.228 J.D. 122 N. McDowell St.
Rosenwood, Erik M. ....'74 '01 C.999 B.A. L.902 J.D. [[A] Hamilton F.M.S.S.&M.]
Ross, Adam L. ....'78 '03 C&L.575 B.A., J.D [[A] James,M.&D.]
Ross, John H. ....'70 '96 C.232 B.S. L.1228 J.D. Co. Dist. Aty.'s Off.
Rosser, Brent A. ....'77 '02 C.269 B.A. L.124 J.D. [[A] Hunton&W.]
Rossitch, Richard J. '70 '96 C&L.575 B.S., J.D.
Asst. Gen. Coun., Compass Group, U.S.A. Inc.
Roth, Robert J. ...... '— '88 C.433 B.S. L.1009 J.D. Asst. Gen. Coun., Bank of America
Rousseaux, Michael J., (BV) ....'65 '90 C.999 B.S. L.1345 J.D. [Elam&R.]

Rowan, Vicki Brown, (AV) '48 '87 C.834 B.S. L.846 J.D.
1515 Mockingbird Lane, Suite 400, 28209
Telephone: 704-525-4110 Fax: 704-525-4301
Email: VBRowan@bellsouth.net URL: http://www.vickibrowan.com
Concentrating in Employment Law, and General Civil Litigation in State and Federal Courts. Employment Discrimination, Sexual Harassment, Wage and Hours, Fair Labor Standards, Non-Compete Disputes, Family and Medical Leave, Severance Agreements, Americans with Disabilities Act, Wrongful Termination.
See Professional Biographies, CHARLOTTE, NORTH CAROLINA

Rowe, R. Leonard, Jr., (AV) '66 '92
C.575 B.S. L.790 J.D. Sr. Coun., Goodrich Corporation
Royal, Heidi E. ....'— '04 C.806 B.S. L.280 J.D. [[A] Robinson,B.&H.]
Rubin, Robert Marc, (CV) ....'— '95 C.790 B.A. L.472 J.D. [Cranfill,S.&H.]
Ruby, Jack E. ....'45 '76 C.1176 B.S. L.896 J.D. Sr. Trial Atty., E.E.O.C.
Rudd, Leah L. ....'— '02 C.575 B.A. L.1228 J.D. [[A] Hedrick E.G.&K.]
Rudisill, John F., (BV) ....'54 '79 C.228 A.B. L.575 J.D. 428 E. 4th Street
Rudisill, Steven M., (BVⓉ) ....'56 '84 C.575 B.S. L.790 J.D. [Rudisill,W.&K.]
Rudisill, White & Kaplan, P.L.L.C., (BVⓉ) .... 128 S. Tryon Street, Suite 1100
Rudnicki, Robert M. '— '81 C.1044 B.A. L.1068 J.D.
(adm. in CA; not adm. in NC) Assoc. Coun., Bank of America
Rudolf, David S., (AV) ....'49 '75 C.705 A.B. L.569 J.D. [Rudolf W.&F.] ⊙
Rudolf Widenhouse & Fialko, (AV) ....1800 Camden Road, Suite 105 (⊙Chapel Hill)
Rudolph, Brian S. ....'71 '99 C.1161 B.A. L.1340 J.D. [[A] W.F.Porter]
Ruegsegger, Martin C. '50 '76 C.375 B.S. L.802 J.D.
(adm. in TX; not adm. in NC; Pat.) V.P., Corp. Coun. & Secy., Piedmont Natural Gas
Ruff, Thomas C., (AV) ....'19 '48 C.301 A.B. L.893 LL.B. [Ruff,B.C.W.&B.]
Ruff, Thomas C., (AV) ....'48 '74 C&L.575 A.B., J.D. [T.C.Ruff,Jr.&Assoc.]

Ruff, Bond, Cobb, Wade & Bethune, L.L.P., (AV)
The Addison Building, 831 East Morehead Street, Suite 860, 28202
Telephone: 704-377-1634 FAX: 704-342-3308
Members of Firm: Thomas C. Ruff; Lyn Bond, Jr.; James O. Cobb; Hamlin L. Wade; Marvin A. Bethune; Robert S. Adden, Jr.; James D. DuPuy.
General Civil and Trial Practice.
See Professional Biographies, CHARLOTTE, NORTH CAROLINA

Ruff, Thomas C., Jr. & Associates, (AV)
201 McCullough Drive, Suite 130, 28262
Telephone: 704-549-9200 Facsimile: 704-549-0970
Email: truff@rufflaw.com URL: http://www.trufflaw.com
Thomas C. Ruff.
Real Estate, Commercial Real Estate, Condominium Law, Mortgages, Trust and Estates, Estate Planning, Wills, Probate, Zoning, Planning and Land Use, Business Law, Buying and Selling of Businesses, Limited Liability Company Law, Partnership Law, Contracts, Corporate Law, Elder Law, Health Care Law, Medicare and Medicaid.
See Professional Biographies, CHARLOTTE, NORTH CAROLINA

Runge, Allison G. ....'— '01 C.198 B.A. L.790 J.D. [[A] Kennedy C.L.&H.]
Runkel, Philip S. ....'64 '95 C.893 B.A. L.945 J.D. [[A] Womble C.S.&R.]
Russ, John E., III ....'64 '97 C.871 B.S. L.893 J.D. Sonic Automotive, Inc.
Russell, Erin Shubert ....'64 '93 C.896 B.S. L.575 J.D. Sr. Coun., Clariant Corp.
Rust, Robert, IV '— '03 C.797 B.A. L.880 J.D.
(adm. in GA; not adm. in NC) 100 North Tryon Street, Suite 4700
Rust, Robert N., IV ....'78 '03 C.797 B.A. L.880 J.D. [[A] Moore&V.P.]
Rutherford, Cecilia E. '— '00 C.118 B.A. L.94 J.D.
(adm. in NY; not adm. in NC) [[A] Kennedy C.L.&H.]
Ryan, Caroline H. "Carrie" ....'78 '05 C.951 B.A. L.228 J.D. [[A] Nelson M.R.&S.]
Ryan, Timothy R. ... '— '97 C.1369 B.S. L.893 J.D. Asst. Gen. Coun., Bank of America
Sadler, Megan ....'— '05 C.923 B.A. L.896 J.D. [[A] Wishart,N.H.&P.]
Sadow, Eric S., (BVⓉ) '— '83 C.790 B.A. L.851 J.D.
(adm. in OH; not adm. in NC) Asst. Gen. Coun., Bank of America
Sage, Russell R. '31 '55 C&L.494 B.S.L., LL.B.
(adm. in MN; not adm. in NC) U.S. Admin. Law J.
St. Amand, Matthew G. '— '00 C.890 B.A. L.575 J.D.
(adm. in FL; not adm. in NC) [[A] Kennedy C.L.&H.]
Salisbury, J. Alexander, (AV) ....'52 '80 C.893 B.A. L.575 J.D. [Womble C.S.&R.]
Sams, L. Wayne '44 '74 C&L.836 B.B.A., J.D.
Sr. V.P. & Asst. Gen. Coun., First Union Corp.
Sanchez, Joseph A. '— '94 C.37 B.A. L.36 J.D.
(adm. in AZ; not adm. in NC) Asst. Gen. Coun., Bank of America
Sanchez, Juan Antonio ....'69 '95 C.1222 B.A. L.259 J.D. [Olive]
Sanders, Ann Morgan, (BV) ....'57 '85 C&L.880 B.A., J.D. Children's Law Center
Sanders, Christopher C., (CV) ....'63 '94 C.575 B.A. L.192 J.D. P.O. Box 9492
Sanders, D. Blaine, (AV) ....'— '84 C.198 A.B. L.880 J.D. [Robinson,B.&H.]
Sanders, Robert G., (AV) '23 '48 C.152 L.260 J.D.
101 North McDowell Street, Suite 216
Santaniello, Andrew J., (CV) ....'70 '96 C.575 B.A. L.896 J.D. [[A] Clawson&S.]

Santaniello, Joseph J. ....'72 '97 C&L.575 B.A., J.D. [🄰 Shumaker,L.&K.]
Santos, Peter A., (AV) ....'— '89 C&L.229 B.A., J.D. [Nexsen P.A.K.]
Sarsfield, Patrick D., II, (BV) ....'— '93 C&L.575 B.A., J.D. [🄰 Nexsen P.A.K.]
Sasser, Charles McBrayer, (BV) ....'53 '81 C&L.575 B.A., J.D. [Sasser]

Sasser Law Firm, The, (BV)
1011 East Morehead Street Suite 350, 28204
Telephone: 704-342-4200 800-669-9529 Fax: 704-342-0798
Charles McBrayer Sasser. Associates: Margaret B. DeVries; Heather R. Hanes. Of Counsel: J. David Tolbert; Michael Weinberger.
Litigation, Personal Injury, Products Liability, Serious Injury, Class Action Litigation, Complex Litigation, Medical Negligence, Business, Workers Compensation, Social Security Disability and Employment Law.

See Professional Biographies, CHARLOTTE, NORTH CAROLINA

Satterwhite, Allison A. ... '64 '89 C&L.575 B.A., J.D. Staff Atty., First Union Corporation
Sauda, Evan M. ....'79 '04 C.575 B.A. L.902 J.D. [🄰 Nelson M.R.&S.]
Saunders, Chase B., (AV) ....'— '72 C&L.575 A.B., J.D. [🄲 McNair]
Sawyer, Connie W., III .... '78 '03 C.575 B.A. L.178 J.D. [🄰 Cadwalader,W.&T.]
Sawyer, Daniel W. ....'14 '36 L.896 LL.B. 4532 Bradbury Dr.‡
Sawyer, Karl S., Jr., (AV) ....'— '77 C.576 B.S. L.896 J.D. [Kennedy C.L.&H.]
Saydlowski, John C. ....'71 '97 C&L.896 B.A., J.D. [🄰 Moore&V.P.]
Saye, David B. ....'76 '02 C.228 A.B. L.896 J.D. [🄰 Womble C.S.&R.]
Saye, Robyn M. ....'77 '02 C.228 A.B. L.575 J.D. [Horack,T.P.&L.]
Sbarra, Luke ....'— '00 C.890 B.A. L.896 J.D. [🄰 Hedrick E.G.&K.]
Schattenfield, Scott W., (AV) ....'58 '88 C.446 B.A. L.273 J.D. [Schattenfield,P.]

Schattenfield Law Firm, The, PLLC, (AV)
6000 Fairview Road, Suite 1200, 28210
Telephone: 704-552-4004 Cell: 704-293-1405 Fax: 704-552-4005
Scott W. Schattenfield.
Trust and Estates, Estate Planning, Asset Protection, Estate and Trust Administration, Fiduciary Law, Business, Family Business, Limited Liability, Wills and Probate, Taxation.

See Professional Biographies, CHARLOTTE, NORTH CAROLINA

Scheer, Anthony G., (BV) ....'57 '92 C.228 B.A. L.575 J.D. [Rawls,D.&S.]
Schell, Paul ....'67 '00 C.956 B.A. L.575 J.D. 800 Briar Creek Road, Suite DD 518
Schell, Richard K., (AV) ....'59 '85 C&L.575 B.A., J.D. [Parker,P.A.&B.]
Schenk, Jennifer L. '72 '97 C.397 B.A. L.446 J.D.
Corp. Coun., Charlotte-Mecklenburg Hosp. Auth.
Scheurer, P. Christian ....'67 '92 C&L.838 B.S., J.D. [Helms M.&W.]
Schiffman, Samuel A., (AV) '50 '75 C&L.575 B.S., J.D.
V.P., Gen. Coun. & Secy., National Gypsum Co.
Schilli, David M., (AV) ....'— '88 C.269 B.A. L.902 J.D. [Robinson,B.&H.]
Schleunes, Anna F. ....'69 '98 C.902 B.A. L.575 J.D. City Atty. Off.
Schmidt, Joseph J. '56 '95 C.1069 B.B.A. L.1003 J.D.
(adm. in OH; not adm. in NC) KPMG Peat Marwick L.L.P.
Schmidt, Peter B. ...... '43 '75 C.33 B.A. L.365 J.D. Admin. Law J., U.S. Soc. Sec. Adm.
Schoeck, Brian J., (BV) ....'66 '97 C&L.260 B.S., J.D. [Johnston,A.&H.]
Schrimsher, B. Scott, (BV) ....'63 '94 C.575 B.a. L.1228 J.D. [Lindsey&S.]
Schrimsher, Frank L., (AV) ....'35 '60 C&L.575 B.S., J.D. [Lindsey&S.]
Schroeder, Thomas E. ....'50 '88 C&L.575 B.A., J.D. 9134 Stoney Corner Ln.
Schuber, John, Jr. ....'22 '49 C&L.902 B.S., LL.B. 2222 Selwyn Ave.‡
Schultz, Phyllis J. ....'47 '82 C.860 B.A. L.818 J.D. 2441 Sedley Rd.
Schultze, Michael F., (BV) ....'59 '84 C&L.575 B.S., J.D. [Cranford,S.&T.]
Schwanz, Erik A., (BV) ....'73 '98 C&L.896 B.A., J.D. [🄰 Nelson M.R.&S.]
Schwarting, Katrina H. '— '98
C.228 B.A. L.575 J.D. 8739 Research Drive, URP4-NC1075
Schwartz, Benjamin D. ....'73 '99 C.1292 B.S. L.896 J.D. [🄰 W.F.Porter]
Schwartz, Jeffrey J., (BV) ....'66 '92 C.160 B.S.C.E. L.790 J.D. [Schwartz] (Pat.)
Schwartz, Russell J., (AV) ....'58 '82 C.790 B.A. L.228 J.D. [🄲 Horack,T.P.&L.]
Schwartz, William Erskine '— '97 C.951 B.A. L.575 J.D.
(adm. in NY; not adm. in NC) Asst. Gen. Coun., Bank of America

Schwartz Law Firm, P.C., (BV)
South Park Towers, 6100 Fairview Road, Suite 530, 28210
Telephone: 704-552-1889 Fax: 704-552-1866 URL: http://www.schwartz-iplaw.com
Email: jjs@schwartz-iplaw.com URL: http://www.schwartz-ip.com
Jeffrey J. Schwartz.
Patents, Trademarks, Copyrights, Intellectual Property.

See Professional Biographies, CHARLOTTE, NORTH CAROLINA

Scofield, Michael S., Law Offices of, (AV) '43 '69
C.576 B.A. L.228 J.D. 212 S. Tryon St., Ste. 1680
Scott, Colin E., (BV) ....'68 '97 C.823 B.A. L.426 J.D. [🄰 Dean&G.]
Scott, Emma G. '— '82 C.1141 B.A. L.623 J.D.
(adm. in TX; not adm. in NC) Asst. Gen. Coun., Bank of America
Scott, Jason H. ....'71 '96 C.188 B.A. L.923 J.D. [McGuireWoods]
Scott, Jeffrey G. ....'61 '89 C.575 B.S. L.574 J.D. 1309 Harding Pl.
Scott, Lawrence J., (AV) ....'59 '84 C.269 B.A. L.790 J.D. [Nelson M.R.&S.]
Scott, Tamla Tymus .... '70 '96 C.1286 B.S. L.574 J.D. 700 East Boulevard, Suite 3
Seaford, Rodney W., (BV) ....'47 '77 C.34 B.S. L.945 J.D. 128 McDowell Ct.
Seifer, Adam M. .... '74 '00 C.860 B.A. L.339 J.D. [🄰 R.A.Peniston&Assoc.]
Selle, Michael J., (BV) ....'69 '94 C.280 B.A. L.469 J.D. [Caudle&S.]
Sellers, Carey A., (BV) ....'52 '77 C.575 A.B. L.790 J.D. [Karro,S.&L.]
Sellers, Leigh Ballenger ....'63 '90 C.880 B.A. L.790 J.D. [🄰 A.R.Krusch]
Sellers, Timothy G., (AV) .... '54 '80 C.198 B.A. L.575 J.D. [Sellers,H.A.D.&L.]

Sellers, Hinshaw, Ayers, Dortch & Lyons, P.A., (AV)
Suite 410 Cameron-Brown Building, 301 South McDowell Street, 28204-2686
Telephone: 704-377-5050 Fax: 704-339-0172
URL: http://www.lawyers.com/shadl
John F. Ayers III; Robert C. Dortch, Jr.; Mark D. Gott; Garl Edward (Eddie) Hinshaw, Jr.; T. Patrick Jenkins; Charles E. (Ed) Lyons II; Michelle Price Massingale; Timothy G. Sellers; Robert A. Whitlow.
Arbitration, Bankruptcy, Civil Litigation in all State, Federal and Tax Courts, Commercial Real Estate, Community Associations, Condemnation, Construction, Corporate and Commercial Law, Corporate and Municipal Finance, Employment, Foreclosures, Personal Injury, Estate Planning and Probate, Taxation, UCC and Workers' Compensation.
Representative Client: B & B Contracting Co.

See Professional Biographies, CHARLOTTE, NORTH CAROLINA

Seltzer, Donald M., (AV) .....'24 '55 C.576 B.S. L.537 LL.B. 1211 E. Morehead St. (Pat.)
Seltzer, Edward D. ....'53 '80 C.575 B.A. L.1228 J.D. 128 N. McDowell St., Ste. C
Serralles-Russell, Marjorie '58 '95 C.276 B.S.B.A. L.472 J.D.
(adm. in FL; not adm. in NC) 14275 Nolen Lane
Seth, Lynn S. '65 '91 C.205 B.A. L.1338 J.D.
(adm. in DE; not adm. in NC) 4100 Coca Cola Plz
Shadoan, Harry B. ....'43 '69 C.235 B.A. L.64 J.D. [🄰 Cadwalader,W.&T.]
Shafeek-Horton, Timika '— '93
C&L.575 B.S.B.A., J.D. Asst. Gen. Coun., Duke Energy Corp.
Shaffer, Harold W., Jr. '36 '80 C.980 B.S.B.A. L.8 J.D.
(adm. in OH; not adm. in NC) B.F. Goodrich Co.
Shah-Khan, S. Mujeeb, (BV) ....'68 '94 C.228 A.B. L.469 J.D. 600 E. Fourth St.
Shaia, William H., Jr. .... '49 '77 C.228 B.S. L.575 J.D. 212 N. McDowell St.
Shannon, Carlton A., Jr., (BV) .... '60 '85 C&L.575 B.A., J.D. [🄲 Katten M.R.]
Shapack, Claire K., (BV) ....'61 '86 C.185 B.A. L.861 J.D. [Shapack&S.]
Shapack, Edward S., (BV) ....'48 '85 C.705 B.A. L.861 J.D. [Shapack&S.]
Shapack & Shapack, P.A., (BV) .... 301 S. McDowell St., Ste. 802
Shappert, Gretchen C. F., (AV) .... '56 '80 C.228 A.B. L.902 J.D. Asst. U.S. Atty.
Sharpe, Jenny L., (BV) ....'60 '86 C.896 B.A. L.1228 J.D. [🄲 Murphy&C.]
Sharrard, Kara L. ....'71 '00 C.575 B.A. L.896 J.D. [🄰 McAngus G.&C.]
Shaver, Thomas S. .... '64 '95 C&L.575 B.A., J.D. 10120 Forest Landing Drive
Shaw, Carolyn Gilmer, (AV) ...... '— '77 C.438 B.A. L.575 J.D. [🄲 Kennedy C.L.&H.]
Shea, Marie C. .... '44 '97 C.230 B.S. L.567 J.D. [🄰 Brown,M.&Assoc.]
Shea, Peter J., (AV) ....'60 '88 C.945 B.A. L.659 J.D. [Katten M.R.]
Shealy, J. Darrell, (BV) ....'55 '83 C&L.575 B.S., J.D. [Johnston,A.&H.]
Shearer, Adam C. ....'75 '02 C.576 B.A. L.896 J.D. [🄰 Parker,P.A.&B.]
Shearin, Ronald V., (BV) '43 '68
C&L.228 A.B., J.D. First Union Corp. (Contract Servs. Grp.)
Sheehey, Christopher B. '63 '89 C&L.276 B.A., J.D.
(adm. in CT; not adm. in NC) Sr. Coun. & Dir., Goodrich Corp., Envir. Health & Safety
Shefte, Dalbert U., (AV) .... '— '52 C&L.597 B.S., J.D. [🄲 Kennedy C.L.&H.]
Shehan, George A. '40 '67 C.367 B.S. L.446 LL.B.
(adm. in MD; not adm. in NC) 1916 Charleston Pl. Lane‡

Shelley, Mark E.
(See Concord)

Shelton, Gregory L. ....'69 '95 C&L.259 B.S., J.D. [🄰 Smith,C.&H.]
Shepard, Kristoffer B. ....'— '03 C.575 B.A. L.893 J.D. [🄰 Robinson,B.&H.]
Sheppard, Robert H., (BV) ....'48 '79 C.893 B.A. L.744 J.D. [James,M.&D.]
Sherley, Frederick H. '— '96 C.659 B.A. L.228 J.D.
(adm. in NY; not adm. in NC) [🄲 Dechert]
Sherman, Lisa C. '67 '94 C.20 B.A. L.896 J.D.
Sr. Corp. Coun., Employment., Compass Group, U.S.A. Inc.
Sherman, Rod ....'74 '01 C.610 B.S. L.851 J.D. [🄰 McAngus G.&C.]
Sherrill, L. Stanford, Jr. .... '71 '95 C.1128 B.A. L.575 J.D. [Littler M.] (⊙Atlanta, GA)
Sherrill, W. Terry ....'55 '80 C&L.575 A.B., J.D. [Sherrill&E.]
Sherrill and Emehel, P.A. ....525 N. Tryon Street
Sherwood, Jason T. ....'68 '93 C.93 B.A. L.309 J.D. [🄲 Poyner&S.]
Shields, Randal D. '— '83 C.97 B.F.A. L.8 J.D.
(adm. in OH; not adm. in NC) Assoc. Gen. Coun., Bank of America
Shoemaker, Raleigh A., (AV) .... '— '70 C.228 A.B. L.575 J.D. [Kennedy C.L.&H.]
Shor, Nina ....'60 '86 C.025 B.A. L.564 J.D. [🄰 Katten M.R.]
Short, Amanda K. ....'75 '01 C&L.575 B.A., J.D. [🄰 Helms M.&W.]
Short, H. Milton ....'19 '46 C&L.575 A.B., J.D. 520 Providence Rd.
Short, M. Kathleen ....'— '05 C.575 B.S. L.896 J.D. [🄰 Hedrick E.G.&K.]
Shuford, A. Burton, (BV) ....'56 '81 C.896 B.S. L.575 J.D. [Shuford,H.&B.]

Shuford, Hunter & Brown, P.A., (AV)
301 South McDowell Street, Suite 1012, 28204
Telephone: 704-377-0280 Fax: 704-377-8666
Email: katelliott@shblawyers.com URL: http://www.shblawyers.com
A. Burton Shuford; G. Martin Hunter (Board Certified Specialist in Business and Consumer Bankruptcy Law, North Carolina State Bar Board of Legal Specialization); Thomas Daniel Brown.
General Practice in State and Federal Courts.

See Professional Biographies, CHARLOTTE, NORTH CAROLINA

Shumaker, Loop & Kendrick, LLP, (AV) BR
128 South Tryon Street Suite 1800, 28202 ⊙
Telephone: 704-375-0057 Fax: 704-332-1197
URL: http://www.slk-law.com
Resident Partners: Peter C. Anderson; Philip S. Chubb; David Harris Conaway; David M. Grogan; Daniel R. Hansen; Moses Luski; William H. McNair; Scott M. Stevenson; William H. Sturges; Frederick M. Thurman, Jr. Resident Associates: William C. Bunting, Jr.; C. Christopher Clark; Matthew J. Ginsburg; John D. Kocher; Kathleen K. Lucchesi; Patricia Wilson Magee; David A. Matthews; Steven A. Meckler; Joseph J. Santaniello; Karen H. Stiles; Robert Ernest Sumner, IV; S. Frederick Winiker, III.
Administrative Law; Advertising and Marketing; Agency and Distributorships; Agricultural Law; Alternative Dispute Resolution; Antitrust and Trade Regulation; Appellate Practice; Bankruptcy; Banks and Banking; Business Law; Business Crimes; Business Torts; Civil Rights; Commercial Law; Commercial Litigation; Commercial Real Estate; Communications and Media; Complex and Multi-District Litigation; Computers and Software; Construction Law; Contracts; Copyrights; Corporate Law; Federal Criminal Law; Debtor and Creditor; Domestic Relations; Education Law; Employee Benefits; Entertainment Law; Environmental Law; Fidelity and Surety; Finance; Franchises and Franchising; Health Care; Hospital Law; Immigration and Naturalization; Intellectual Property; International Law; Labor and Employment; Leases and Leasing; Litigation; Media Law; Medicare and Medicaid; Mergers, Acquisitions and Divestitures; Nonprofit and Charitable Organizations; Patent Litigation; Personal Injury; Probate; Products Liability; Professional Liability; Public Finance; Real Estate; Securities; Sports Law; Taxation; Torts; Trade Secrets; Trademarks; Trusts and Estates; Unfair Competition; Wills; Zoning, Planning and Land Use.
Representative Clients: AVAILABLE UPON REQUEST.
Toledo, Ohio Office: North Courthouse Square, 1000 Jackson, 43624-1573. Telephone: 419-241-9000. Fax: 419-241-6894.
Tampa, Florida Office: 101 East Kennedy Boulevard, Suite 2800, 33602-5151. Telephone: 813-229-7600. Fax: 813-229-1660.
Columbus, Ohio Office: Huntington Center, 41 South High Street, Suite 2400, 43215. Telephone: 614-463-9441. Fax: 614-463-1108.

See Professional Biographies, CHARLOTTE, NORTH CAROLINA

Shumate, Christopher S. ....'78 '03 C&L.790 B.A., J.D. [🄰 Hull&C.]
Sidbury, Benjamin F. ......'76 '01 C.999 B.A. L.823 J.D. [🄰 Alston&B.] (See Pat. Sect.)
Siler, N. Lucille ....'69 '97 C.198 B.S. L.575 J.D. [🄰 Johnston,A.&H.]
Simmons, Charles B., Jr., (BV) .... '61 '87 C.976 B.A. L.893 J.D. [Alston&B.]
Simmons, Douglas K., & Associates '55 '83 C.496 B.S.B.A. L.420 J.D.
8210 University Executive Park Drive, Suite 160
Simmons, L. D., II, (AV) ....'59 '84 C.198 A.B. L.880 J.D. [Helms M.&W.]
Simmons, Robert W., (AV) ....'— '84 C.575 A.B. L.893 J.D. [Helms M.&W.]
Simpson, Amy ....'70 '96 C.228 B.A. L.575 J.D. [🄰 Katten M.R.]
Simpson, Bruce M., (AV) ....'52 '78 C.198 A.B. L.575 J.D. [James,M.&D.]
Simpson, David A., (BV) ....'61 '86 C.198 A.B. L.575 J.D. 2901 Coltsgate Rd.
Simpson, David T., Jr., (BV) ....'59 '84 C&L.575 B.S., J.D. [Gerdes,M.&S.]
Simpson, Linda W. '59 '84 C.935 B.S. L.575 J.D.
Bkrpty. Admr. for Western Dist. of N.C.
Simpson, Mark L., (CVⓉ) .... '64 '94 C.1083 B.S. L.1339 J.D. 1201 N. Tyron St.
Sims, Algie W., III '— '77 C&L.790 B.A., J.D.
(adm. in SC; not adm. in NC) Asst. Gen. Coun., Bank of America
Sims, Shari L., Law Office of '63 '01
C.1128 B.S. L.575 J.D. 8035 Providence Rd., Ste. 320
Sims, Wendell M., (CVⓉ) '55 '87 C.560 B.A. L.37 J.D.
(adm. in NM; not adm. in NC) 129 W. Trade St. #400
Singer, Allan W., (AV) ....'— '69 C.197 A.B. L.228 J.D. [McNair]
Sink, Caroline Wannamaker, (AV) ....'— '82 C.758 B.A. L.902 J.D. [Robinson,B.&H.]
Sink, Robert C., (AV) ....'65 C&L.228 A.B., LL.B. [Robinson,B.&H.]
Sinner, Patra ....'73 '03 C&L.790 B.S, J.D. [🄰 James,M.&D.]
Sistrunk, George W., III ....'73 '98 C.945 B.A. L.896 J.D. [Hamilton F.M.S.S.&M.]

Sistrunk, Patricia (Tricia) C.608 B.A. L.896 J.D.
Meineke Car Care Centers, Inc. (Legal Department)
Sito, Jason E. '77 '03 C.575 B.A. L.893 J.D.
(adm. in VA; not adm. in NC) [Ⓐ Womble C.S.&R.]
Sitton, William L., Jr., (AV) .... '53 '78 C&L.575 A.B., J.D. [Katten M.R.]
Sizemore, Russell F., (AV) ....'— '96 C.31 A.B. L.976 J.D. [Kennedy C.L.&H.]
Skelton, Heather, Attorney at Law '71 '96
C.575 B.S. L.861 J.D. 401 N. Tyron St., 10th Fl.
Skufca, Ronald A. ....'70 '98 C.893 B.S. L.896 J.D. 501 E. Morehead St., Ste. 6
Sloan, Cheryl Leigh Thornton '56 '84
C.577 B.S.N. L.575 J.D. Dist. Off. Atty. & Spec. Asst. U.S. Atty.
Sloan, Price A., (BV) '— '88 C&L.502 B.S.B.A., J.D.
(adm. in MO; not adm. in NC) Asst. Gen. Coun., Bank of America
Smart, Roy L., III, (AV) ....'53 '80 C.309 B.A. L.893 J.D. [Parker,P.A.&B.]
Smedley, Kristen ....'70 '97 C.575 B.A. L.1228 J.D. [Tippens&Z.]
Smelcer, Hope Fisher ....'— '97 C.917 B.A. L.1365 J.D. [Ⓐ Hedrick E.G.&K.]
Smith, A. Zachary, III, (AV) ....'— '66 C.198 A.B. L.893 LL.B. [Kennedy C.L.&H.]
Smith, Aaron A. '49 '76 C.835 B.S. L.836 J.D.
(adm. in TN; not adm. in NC) 6000 Monroe Road
Smith, Adam ....'— '05 C.101 B.A. L.902 J.D. [Ⓐ Kennedy C.L.&H.]
Smith, Allen C., (BV) ....'— '92 C.198 B.A. L.575 J.D. [Hedrick E.G.&K.]
Smith, Bradley H. ....'74 '03 C.575 B.A. L.836 J.D. [Rudisill,W.&K.]
Smith, Briayn G. ....'79 '04 C.575 B.A. L.896 J.D. [Stiles B.&H.]
Smith, Chadwick D. ....'— '00 C.1228 B.S. L.575 J.D. [Ⓐ Browne,F.W.&W.]
Smith, Gary W. ....'73 '98 C.500 B.A. L.575 J.D. [Wishart,N.H.&P.]
Smith, Jacquelyn A., (BV) ....'64 '93 C.884 B.S. L.574 J.D. [Smith&S.]
Smith, James C., (AV) ....'46 '76 C.197 A.B. L.880 J.D. [McGuireWoods] (Pat.)
Smith, Jeffrey D., Law Office of, (BV) '55 '82
C.575 B.A. L.327 J.D. 1125 E. Morehead St., Ste. 304
Smith, Jill Anderson, (AVⓉ) '— '82 C.221 B.S.Ed. L.608 J.D.
(adm. in OH; not adm. in NC) Asst. Gen. Coun., Bank of America
Smith, John Brem, (BV) ....'61 '86 C.198 A.B. L.896 J.D. [Smith]
Smith, Joshua M. '— '02 C.276 B.S. L.477 J.D.
(adm. in NY; not adm. in NC) [Ⓐ Cadwalader,W.&T.]
Smith, Keith A., (BV) '68 '93 C&L.228 B.A., J.D.
Sr. V.P. & Gen. Coun., Charlotte-Mecklenburg Hospital Authority, The
Smith, Keith Strickland ....'63 '01 C.575 B.S.B.A. L.574 J.D. Asst. Dist. Atty.
Smith, Kenneth M., (BV) ....'65 '91 C.575 B.A. L.309 J.D. Asst. U.S. Atty.
Smith, Kristin L., (BV) ....'68 '93 C.228 B.A. L.280 J.D. [Conrad T.&K.]
Smith, Laura C., (AV) ....'— '95 C.575 A.B. L.976 J.D. [Robinson,B.&H.]
Smith, Nancy F. ....'73 '98 C&L.575 B.A., J.D. [Ⓐ Moore&V.P.]
Smith, Norman A., (BV) ....'44 '74 C&L.228 A.B., J.D. [N.A.Smith]
Smith, Paul J. ....'74 '99 C.232 B.S. L.575 J.D. [Ⓐ Culp E.&C.]
Smith, Robert R., II '73 '01 C&L.790 B.A., J.D.
(adm. in SC; not adm. in NC) [Ⓐ Moore&V.P.]
Smith, Ryan M. ....'71 '96 C&L.575 B.A., J.D. [Moore&V.P.]
Smith, Skottowe W., Jr., (AV) ....'69 '94 C&L.896 B.S., J.D. [Moore&V.P.]
Smith, Stephen L., (BV) ....'52 '76 C.575 A.B. L.893 J.D. [Horack,T.P.&L.]
Smith, Steven L. ....'68 '94 C.692 B.A. L.280 J.D. [Smith,C.&V.]

Smith, Timothy D., Law Office of '67 '93 C.575 B.A. L.61 J.D.
122 North McDowell Street, 28204
Telephone: 704-334-9909 Fax: 704-714-1451
Email: timsmith8615@hotmail.com URL: http://www.timsmithlawfirm.com
Immigration Law, Criminal Law, Driving While Intoxicated (DWI), Drug Crimes, Traffic Violations, Family Law/Divorce.
See Professional Biographies, CHARLOTTE, NORTH CAROLINA

Smith, Timothy M. ....'63 '91 C.1128 B.A. L.574 J.D. [Smith&S.]
Smith, W. Britton, Jr., (AV) ....'42 '67 C&L.575 B.S., J.D. [Smith&C.]
Smith, W. Lewis, Jr., (BV) ....'54 '80 C.575 B.A. L.425 J.D. 1125 E. Morehead Street
Smith, Wm. Benjamin, (AV) ....'50 '79 C&L.575 B.A., J.D. [Price,S.H.P.&A.]

Smith and Christensen, L.L.P., (AV)
One Fairview Center, 6302 Fairview Road, Suite 309, 28210-2226
Telephone: 704-522-1616 Fax: 704-522-7111
Email: attorneys@smithchrist.com URL: http://www.smithchrist.com
Members of Firm: W. Britton Smith, Jr.; Aaron M. Christensen.
Labor and Employment, Corporate Transactions.
See Professional Biographies, CHARLOTTE, NORTH CAROLINA

Smith, Cooksey & Vickstrom, PLLC, (AV)
6060 J.A. Jones Drive, Suite 208, 28287
Telephone: 704-557-9929 Fax: 704-557-9932
URL: http://www.scvlawfirm.com
Steven L. Smith; Neil C. Cooksey; Dwane E. Vickstrom.
Litigation, Corporate Counseling, Contract Drafting and Negotiation, Dispute Prevention, Alternative Dispute Resolution, Construction Litigation, Federal Procurement Litigation, State Procurement Litigation, Business Formation, Corporate Transactions, Manufacturing and Service Issues.
See Professional Biographies, CHARLOTTE, NORTH CAROLINA

Smith, Currie & Hancock LLP, (AV) BR
Suite 301, 1023 West Morehead Street, 28208 ⊙
Telephone: 704-334-3459 Telecopier: 704-334-7850
URL: http://www.smithcurrie.com
Partners of the Firm: Rolly L. Chambers; Robert J. Greene, Jr.; Steele B. ("Al") Windle, III. Of Counsel: Harry R. Bivens. Associates: Matthew E. Cox (Not admitted in NC); Gregory L. Shelton (Board Certified Construction Law Lawyer, Florida Bar Board of Legal Specialization and Education).
Construction, Government Contracts, Surety, Commercial, Environmental, International and related Mediations, Arbitration, Labor and Litigation.
Atlanta, Georgia Office: 2600 Harris Tower-Peachtree Center, 233 Peachtree Street, N.E. Telephone: 404-521-3800. Fax: 404-688-0671.
Tallahassee, Florida Office: 1004 DeSoto Park Drive, P.O. Box 589. Telephone: 850-878-3700. Fax: 850-656-0329.
Fort Lauderdale, Florida Office: Suit 620, One East Broward Boulevard. Telephone: 954-761-8700. Fax: 954-524-6927.
See Professional Biographies, CHARLOTTE, NORTH CAROLINA

Smith Debnam Narron Wyche Saintsing & Myers, L.L.P., (AV)
4201 Congress Street, Suite 460, 28209 ⊙
Telephone: 704-643-3220 Facsimile: 704-643-3898
Email: mail@smithdebnamlaw.com URL: http://www.smithdebnamlaw.com
John B. Honeycutt, Jr.; Heather N. Johnson.
General and Appellate Practice in all State and Federal Courts. Corporation, Bankruptcy, Non-Judicial Workouts and Reorganizations, Corporate Reorganization, Construction, Equipment Leasing and Finance, Estate Planning and Administration, Commercial and Retail Collections and Litigation. Administrative and Regulatory, Government Contracts and Procurement, Health Care, Land Use and Zoning, Limited Liability Companies and Partnerships, Public Finance, Residential and Commercial Real Estate, Family Law and Equitable Distribution, Telecommunications, Plaintiff's Personal Injury.
Raleigh, North Carolina Office: 4601 Six Forks Road, Suite 400, 27609. Telephone: 919-250-2000. Fax: 919-250-2211.
See Professional Biographies, CHARLOTTE, NORTH CAROLINA

Smith Law Firm, P.C., (BV)
5950 Fairview Road, Suite 710, 28210
Telephone: 704-643-6650 Telecopier: 704-643-6651
Email: jsmith@smithlawfirm.biz URL: http://www.smith-lawfirm.net
John Brem Smith.
Employment Law, Workers' Compensation, Litigation, Mediation.
See Professional Biographies, CHARLOTTE, NORTH CAROLINA

Smith, Norman A., P.A., (BV) ....2101 Sardis Rd., N.
Smith & Smith, P.A., (BV) ....900 Baxter Street, Suite 109
Smolen, Wendy Miller, (BV) ....'52 '82 C.228 B.A. L.896 J.D. 2142 Edenton Rd.
Smyth, Ross J., (AV) ....'36 '65 C.198 A.B. L.228 LL.B. [Kennedy C.L.&H.] ‡
Sneed, Jason M. ....'71 '97 C.840 B.A. L.893 J.D. [Ⓐ Alston&B.]
Snover, Beth Murphy, (AV) ....'61 '86 C&L.896 B.A., J.D. 227 N. Tryon St.
Snyder, Patricia ....'63 '95 C.1059 B.S. L.245 J.D. [Womble C.S.&R.]
Solomon, Jason J. ....'74 '00 C.575 B.S.B.A. L.902 J.D. [Ⓐ Alston&B.]
Somers, Lawrence B., (BV) '69 '95
C.575 B.A. L.228 J.D. Asst. Gen. Coun., Duke Energy Corp.
Sowell, Susan L., (BV) '56 '81 C&L.896 B.A., J.D.
Asst. Gen. Coun., Fair Point Communications, Inc.
Spado, James A. ....'67 '94 C&L.575 B.A., J.D. 4007 Mozart Ct.
Spainhour, John E. ....'74 '01 C.198 B.A. L.790 J.D. [Ⓐ McAngus G.&C.]
Spainhour, Shannon (Missy) Sumerell .....'75 '01 C.797 B.A. L.896 J.D. [Ⓐ Fisher&P.]
Spainhour, Sterling A., (AV) '45 '70
C.302 B.A. L.602 J.D. Sr. Dep. Gen. Coun., Wachovia Corp.
Spanbauer, Wendy L. ....'71 '98 C.228 B.A. L.575 J.D. [Ⓐ Hunton&W.]
Sparks, J. Timothy, (BV) ....'68 '95 C.198 B.A. L.1228 J.D. Coun., Royal & Sun Alliance
Sparks, M. Randolph '— '95 C.934 B.A. L.209 J.D.
(adm. in IL; not adm. in NC) Assoc. Gen. Coun., Bank of America
Spears, Harold C., (AV) ....'54 '79 C&L.228 A.B., J.D. [Caudle&S.]
Spears, James B., Jr., (AV) ....'48 '73 C&L.896 B.S., J.D. [Ogletree,D.N.S.&S.]
Spence, Andrew T. ......'75 '00 C.502 B.S.E.E. L.910 J.D. [Ⓐ Alston&B.] (See Pat. Sect.)
Spence, Herman, III, (AV) ....'— '82 C&L.575 B.S., J.D. [Robinson,B.&H.]
Sperry, Roberta S. ....'74 '99 C.198 B.A. L.575 J.D. [Ⓐ Morris Y.W.S.&B.]
Sperry & Tyson, PLLC
(See Matthews)
Spinks, Lee A., (AV) ....'55 '80 C.269 B.A. L.575 J.D. [Poyner&S.]
Spisich, Sarah B. ....'80 '05 C.902 B.A. L.896 J.D. [Stiles B.&H.]
Spooner, Richard ....'75 '02 C.896 B.S. L.575 J.D. [Ⓐ Cadwalader,W.&T.]
Spratt, Robert Gilroy, III, (AV) ....'48 '73 C&L.575 A.B., J.D. [Jones,H.&W.]
Sprenger, Elizabeth ....'75 '01 C.896 B.A. L.180 J.D. [Ⓐ Golding H.&P.]
Springer, John W., (BVⓉ) ....'53 '78 C.893 B.A. L.16 J.D. [Ⓒ Womble C.S.&R.]
Springs, Michael A. '— '97
C.789 B.S.E.E.T. L.574 J.D. Asst. Gen. Coun., Bank of America (Pat.)
Springs, Venus Yvette ....'— '02 C.1128 B.S. L.228 J.D. [Ⓐ Cadwalader,W.&T.]
Sproul, Noelle Hicks ....'76 '03 C.880 B.S. L.692 J.D. [Ⓐ Moore&V.P.]
Spurlock, Alyson R. ....'79 '04 C.383 B.S. L.896 J.D. [Ⓐ Moore&V.P.]
Stafford, Troy J., (BV) ....'66 '91 C.420 B.S. L.1228 J.D. [DeVore A.&S.]
Stagg, William L., (BV).................'30 '60 C.152 A.B. L.575 LL.B. 725 E. Trade St.
Staley, Melinda Fox ....'— '99 C.475 B.A. L.1187 J.D. [Ⓐ Nexsen P.A.K.]
Stanley, Timothy M. ....'65 '92 C.446 B.A. L.692 J.D. [Kirkley]
Starling, Richard S., (BV) ....'— '96 C&L.893 B.A., J.D. [Robinson,B.&H.]
Starnes, Robert B. ....'75 '01 C.576 B.S. L.790 J.D. [Ⓐ McAngus G.&C.]
Starr, William M. ....'78 '03 C.1372 B.A. L.575 J.D. [Ⓐ Nelson M.R.&S.]
Starrett, Judith A., (BV) ....'58 '86 C.546 B.S. L.245 J.D. Asst. City Atty.
Stathopoulos, Harry J. ....'62 '88 C.1128 B.A. L.790 J.D. [H.Stathopoulos]
Stathopoulos, Harry ....10700 Sikes Place, Ste. 300
Staton, John S., (BV) ....'53 '80 C.228 B.A. L.896 J.D. [Guthrie,D.H.&S.] ‡
Steele, Cheryl D., (BV) ....'61 '87 C.471 B.S. L.575 J.D. [Horack,T.P.&L.]
Steele, Deborah Brewer '63 '89
C.838 B.A. L.575 J.D. Cent. Piedmont Community College
Steele, Jackson N., (AV) ....'49 '75 C.198 B.A. L.880 J.D. [Hamilton F.M.S.S.&M.]
Steen, Bruce M., (BV) ....'61 '90 C.475 B.A. L.893 J.D. [McGuireWoods]
Steffens, Paul A. ....'— '96 C.228 B.S.E. L.575 J.D. [Kennedy C.L.&H.]
Steimer, William M., (AV) '44 '76 C.63 B.A. L.575 J.D.
Off. of Univ. Atty., University of North Carolina at Charlotte
Stein, Michael Barry ....'70 '95 C.575 B.A. L.896 J.D. [Kellam&P.]
Stephens, Richard D., (AV) ....'— '70 C.575 A.B. L.178 J.D. [Kennedy C.L.&H.]
Stephens, Robert C., (AV) ....'45 '70 C&L.896 B.A., J.D. [Hamilton F.M.S.S.&M.]
Stephenson, Jeremy A. '— '99 C.893 B.A. L.424 J.D.
(adm. in IL; not adm. in NC) [Ⓐ Ogletree,D.N.S.&S.]
Sterrett, Tate K., (AV) ....'46 '73 C.198 B.A. L.893 J.D. [Horack,T.P.&L.]
Stevens, G. Sefton, (BV) ....'51 '76 C.198 B.A. L.575 J.D. NationsBank Corp. Ctr.
Stevens, Maranda W. ....'78 '03 C&L.228 A.B., J.D. [Ⓐ Moore&V.P.]
Stevenson, Scott M., (BV) ....'54 '79 C.902 B.A. L.896 J.D. [Shumaker,L.&K.]
Stevenson, Virginia Leggett .... '— '96 C.945 B.A. L.902 J.D. [Ⓐ Kennedy C.L.&H.]
Stewart, Barney, III, (AV) ....'38 '67 C.976 B.A. L.623 J.D. [Moore&V.P.]
Stewart, Todd A. ....'65 '90 C.924 B.S. L.896 J.D. [T.A.Stewart]
Stewart, William Gerald ....'51 '80 C&L.790 B.S., J.D. Natl. Diagnostics, Inc.
Stewart, Todd A., J.D., C.P.A., P.A. ....6100 Fairview Rd.
Stichter, Kevin P. ....'— '93 C.103 A.B. L.880 J.D. [Kennedy C.L.&H.]
Stiles, Karen H. ....'72 '02 C.575 B.A. L.1345 J.D. [Ⓐ Shumaker,L.&K.]
Stiles, Ned A., (AV) ....'52 '79 C.575 B.S. L.896 J.D. [Stiles B.&H.]

Stiles Byrum & Horne, L.L.P., (AV) BR
The Arlington, Suite 650, 325 Arlington Avenue, 28203
Telephone: 704-332-2830 Facsimile: 704-332-3281 Email: kvalentine@sbhlaw.net
Email: sbh@sbhlaw.net URL: http://www.sbh-lawfirm.com
Ned A. Stiles; Henry C. Byrum, Jr.; Terry D. Horne; D. Lane Matthews; Mark O. Crowther; Briayn G. Smith; Sarah B. Spisich.
General Civil Practice. Employment, Workers Compensation and Insurance Law. Trials, State and Federal Courts.
See Professional Biographies, CHARLOTTE, NORTH CAROLINA

Stillerman, W. Todd ....'71 '97 C.896 B.A. L.309 J.D. [Ⓐ Dechert]
Stockman, Brien D., (BV) ......'61 '90 C.623 B.S. L.896 J.D. 301 South McDowell Street
Stockton, Colin R. '74 '00 C.1115 B.A. L.575 J.D.
(adm. in AL; not adm. in NC) [Ⓐ Bradley A.R.&W.]
Stokes, Shannon N. ....'77 '04 C.845 B.A. L.494 J.D. [Ⓐ Parker,P.A.&B.]
Stokes, Timothy M., (BV) .....'48 '76 C.576 B.A. L.575 J.D. 122 North McDowell Street
Stokley, Jennifer M. ....'69 '95 C.332 B.A. L.585 J.D. [Ⓐ Katten M.R.]
Stone, Bryan W. ....'78 '04 C.280 B.B.A. L.896 J.D. [Ⓐ Fletcher&R.]
Storick, Barry M., (BV) ....'35 '66 C&L.902 B.A., LL.B. P.O. Box 36898
Stott, Hollowell, Palmer & Windham, L.L.P.
(See Gastonia)
Stout, John J. ....'62 '92 C.321 A.B. L.94 J.D. [Stout L.]
Stout Law, P.C. ....P.O. Box 473334

Strader, Richard H. .... '59 '86 C.198 B.A. L.575 J.D. V.P., Prologis Trust
Stratakos, Marion D. .... '47 '84 C.471 B.A. L.575 J.D. First Union Nat. Bank
Strauss Scheer, Julia .... '69 '95 C.347 B.A. L.588 J.D. 428 East Fourth Street - Suite 101
Strawn, David V., (BV) .....'49 '74 C.269 B.A. L.790 J.D. 2115 Rexford Road, Suite 101
Strawser, Amy B., (BV) ....'69 '93 C.228 A.B. L.575 J.D. [Bernhardt&S.]
Strean, R. Flynt ....'— '04 C.886 B.S. L.383 J.D. [A Alston&B.]
Street, Victoria A. ....'— '04 C&L.575 B.S., J.D. [Cranfill,S.&H.]
Strickland, David H. .... '76 '02 C.896 B.A. L.1228 J.D. [D.H.Strickland]
Strickland, Tracy E. ....'— '05 C&L.896 B.A., J.D. [A Helms M.&W.]

Strickland, David H., PLLC., Law Office of
1409 East Boulevard, Suite 117, 28220
Telephone: 704-373-6077 Fax: 704-373-6306
URL: http://www.davidstricklandlaw.com
David H. Strickland.
Criminal Law, Driving While Intoxicated (DWI), Juvenile Crimes, Parole and Probation, Traffic Violations, Speeding, Felonies, Automobile Accidents, Medical Malpractice, Slip and Fall, Construction.

See Professional Biographies, CHARLOTTE, NORTH CAROLINA

Stringer, Tamara J. '62 '87 C.150 B.A. L.904 J.D.
(adm. in OH; not adm. in NC) Asst. Gen. Coun., Royal & SunAlliance
Stroud, Keith M., (BV) .... '43 '72 C.34 B.S. L.790 J.D. 1521 Elizabeth Ave.
Stuff, Ronald R., (AV) .... '59 '89 C.277 B.C.E. L.309 J.D. Sr. Coun., Fluor Corp.
Sturges, Francis W., (BV) .... '55 '80 C&L.893 B.A., J.D. [F.W.Sturges]
Sturges, William H., (AV) ....'53 '78 C.902 B.A. L.896 J.D. [Shumaker,L.&K.]
Sturges, William W., (AV) ....'23 '51 C.976 B.A. L.178 LL.B. 1100 S. Tryon St.‡
Sturges, Francis W., P.A., (BV) ....6000 Fairview Road, Suite 1200
Suhr, John Nicholas, Jr., (AV) .... '— '92 C.893 B.A. L.904 J.D. [Kilpatrick S.]
Sullivan, Benjamin R., Jr. .... '— '02 C.692 B.S. L.309 J.D. [A Parker,P.A.&B.]
Sullivan, James M., (BV) ...... '55 '79 C.317 B.A. L.276 J.D. 227 W. Trade St., Ste. 1700
Sullivan, John L., Jr., (AV) '44 '69
C.576 B.S.M.E. L.575 J.D. [Alston&B.] (See Pat. Sect.)
Sullivan, Kimberly ....'64 '90 C.205 B.S. L.1292 J.D. [Cozen O.]
Sullivan, Robert J. '63 '89 C.569 B.S. L.1009 J.D.
(adm. in NY; not adm. in NC) [⊡ Alston&B.]
Summa, Philip, (AV) ....'51 '83 C.282 B.A. L.1228 J.D. [Summa&A.] (See Pat. Sect.)

Summa & Allan, P.A., (AV) BB
Ballantyne Corporate Park, 11610 North Community House Road Suite 200, 28277-2162
Telephone: 704-945-6700 Fax: 704-945-6735
Email: phil@psumma.com URL: http://www.psumma.com
Members of Firm: Philip Summa; Albert P. Allan; Richard L. Additon; Jesse B. Ashe III; Melissa B. Pendleton. Associates: Brian Johnson; Marcia T. Greci.
Intellectual Property Law: Patents, Trademarks, Copyrights and Trade Secret Protection. Trials and Appeals in all Federal and State Courts and Proceedings before the United States Patent and Trademark Office.

See Professional Biographies, CHARLOTTE, NORTH CAROLINA

Sumner, Robert Ernest, IV ....'77 '02 C.575 B.A. L.790 J.D. [A Shumaker,L.&K.]
Sumter, Geraldine, (AV) ....'56 '81 C.329 B.A. L.228 J.D. [Ferguson,S.C.G.&S.]
Sumwalt, Mark T., (AV) ....'56 '81 C.198 B.A. L.790 J.D. [M.T.Sumwalt]
Sumwalt, Vernon R., (BV) ....'71 '98 C.472 B.A. L.790 J.D. [M.T.Sumwalt]
Sumwalt, Mark T., P.A., (AV) .... 1341 East Morehead Street Suite 101
Surles, John C., (BV) .... '55 '82 C&L.575 B.A., J.D. Colonial Title Co. Inc.
Surles, Martha W., (AV) .... '57 '82 C&L.575 B.A., J.D. [Morris Y.W.S.&B.]
Surles, Susan N., (AV) '55 '81 C.228 B.A. L.896 J.D.
Delinq. Atty., Children's Law Ctr.
Sussman, Jacob H. ....'— '03 C.918 B.A. L.569 J.D. [A Ferguson,S.C.G.&S.]
Swann, Marshall A. .... '52 '78 C.892 B.A. L.574 J.D. 6201 Fairview Road, Suite 200
Swearingen, E.S., (BVⓣ) '38 '64 C&L.790 B.S., J.D.
(adm. in SC; not adm. in NC) Mag. J.
Swecker, Christophe E. .... '56 '81 C.34 B.A. L.896 J.D. 400 S. Tryon St.‡
Sweeney, Edward A. .... '— '04 C.1430 B.S. L.896 J.D. [A Hedrick E.G.&K.]
Sweet, Lizabeth L. '53 '80 C.846 B.J. L.744 J.D.
(adm. in TX; not adm. in NC) 2341 Castlecomer Dr.‡
Sweet, Richard S. '41 '69 C.401 B.A. L.893 J.D.
(adm. in DC; not adm. in NC) [⊡ Moore&V.P.]
Swenson, Kenneth W. '— '87 C.378 B.A. L.800 J.D.
(adm. in CA; not adm. in NC) Asst. Gen. Coun., Bank of America

Swindell, Gary W., The Law Offices of, (AV) '54 '79 C.205 B.A. L.276 J.D.
227 West Trade Street, Suite 2030, 28202
Telephone: 704-376-1390 Fax: 704-376-1391
Email: gary@swindelllaw.com URL: http://www.lawyers.com/swindelllaw
Associate: Kent D. Jones.
Commercial Real Estate, Commercial Leasing, Zoning Planning and Land Use, Corporate, Capital Markets.

See Professional Biographies, CHARLOTTE, NORTH CAROLINA

Swinea, Regina Wheeler, (BV) .... '61 '86 C&L.575 B.A., J.D. [⊡ Parker,P.A.&B.]
Syfert, Scott D. ....'69 '97 C&L.575 B.A., J.D. [Moore&V.P.]
Sylvester, Christine J. ....'68 '93 C.953 L.574 J.D. [C.J.Sylvester]
Sylvester, Christine J., PA .... 2720 E. WT Harris Blvd., Ste. 100
Szeker, Julie Konneker '70 '98 C.575 B.A. L.477 J.D.
Corp. Coun., Charlotte-Mecklenburg Hospital Authority
Sztarkman, Helen S. '56 '82 C&L.912 B.A., J.D.
(adm. in MI; not adm. in NC) 10936 Wild Dove Lane‡
Tadlock, Warren L. ....'51 '79 C&L.575 A.B., J.D. Chapter 13 Standing Trustee
Talley, James M., Jr., (AV) .... '37 '64 C&L.575 B.S., J.D. [Horack,T.P.&L.]
Tallmadge, Jennifer .... '— '97 C&L.823 B.A., J.D. Bank of America
Taraska, Heather Lynne ....'74 '01 C.259 B.S. L.575 J.D. Co. Dist. Atty.'s Off.
Tarr, Andrew W.J. .... '— '03 C&L.575 B.A., J.D. [A Robinson,B.&H.]
Tate, Tshneka T. '71 '98 C.659 B.A. L.259 J.D.
(adm. in MD; not adm. in NC) Assoc. Gen. Coun., Lic. & Mktg., NASCAR, Inc.
Taulbee, George M., (AV) .... '62 '88 C.886 B.S. L.665 J.D. [Alston&B.] (See Pat. Sect.)

Taylor, Andrew D., Jr. & Associates, (AV) '44 '69 C.896 B.A. L.575 J.D.
The Arnold Palmer Corporate Center Calcutta Condominiums On The Lakes, 3701 Latrobe Drive, Suite 130, P.O. Box 221255, 28222-1255
Telephone: 704-366-6210 Telecopier: 704-366-4654
Email: adtaylor@vnet.net URL: http://www.lawyers.com/taylor&associates
Associate: Melissa D. Wright.
General, Civil Trial and Appellate Practice in all State and Federal Courts. Commercial, Corporate, Real Estate, Probate, Wills and Trusts, Domestic Relations, Family Law, Child Custody, Child Support, Divorce, Personal Injury, Auto Accidents, Slip and Fall, Wrongful Death, Credit Union, Collections, Product Liability, Business Law, Partnership.

See Professional Biographies, CHARLOTTE, NORTH CAROLINA

Taylor, Harmony Whalen .... '— '99 C&L.575 B.A., J.D. [A Hedrick E.G.&K.]
Taylor, Janiere .... '74 '00 C.1157 B.A. L.1187 [A McAngus G.&C.]

Taylor, Jason E., Law Offices of, (BV) '67 '93
C.319 B.A. L.904 J.D. 200 North McDowell St. (⊙Hickory)
Taylor, John B., (AV) ....'37 '65 C.576 B.S.E. L.575 LL.B. [Taylor,P.R.&R.]
Taylor, John W., (BV) '69 '94
C.269 B.A. L.260 J.D. 7421 Carmel Executive Pkwy., Ste. 226
Taylor, Michael W., (AV) .... '47 '78 C&L.575 B.A., J.D. [⊡ Parker,P.A.&B.]
Taylor, Thomas E. ....'46 '72 C.659 B.A. L.309 J.D. [McGuireWoods]
Taylor, Todd C. .... '71 '95 C.576 B.A. L.575 J.D. [⊡ Womble C.S.&R.]

Taylor, Penry, Rash & Riemann, PLLC, (AV)
2359 Perimeter Pointe Parkway, Suite 360, 28208 ⊙
Telephone: 704-424-2900 Fax: 704-424-2999
URL: http://www.tprr.com
John B. Taylor; Eugene F. Rash.
Construction Law, Construction Litigation, Commercial Litigation, Securities Litigation, Mediation, Arbitration, Intellectual Property Litigation, Insurance Coverage Litigation, Government Relations and Administrative Litigation.
Raleigh, North Carolina Office: 510 Glenwood Avenue, Suite 319, 27603. Telephone: 919-833-9449. Fax: 919-833-9448.

See Professional Biographies, CHARLOTTE, NORTH CAROLINA

Taylor-Brill, Barry '54 '83 C.339 A.B. L.597 J.D.
Sr. V.P. & Dep. Gen. Coun., First Union Corp.
Teague, Brian J. ...... '— '04 C.971 B.S.E.E. L.1509 J.D. [A Alston&B.] (See Pat. Sect.)
Teague, Dennard Lindsey, (BV) ..... '60 '85 C.198 A.B. L.280 J.D. 2036 Valencia Terrace
Teague, Franklin L. ....'24 '53 C&L.575 A.B. 601 BrackenburyLn.
Teague, Joe Franklin, Jr. .... '69 '98 C.404 A.B. L.575 J.D. [A Johnston,A.&H.]
Tedrick, Daniel L. .... '75 '00 C.198 B.A. L.896 J.D. [A Mayer,B.R.&M.]
Teer, John A. .... '73 '01 C&L.575 B.A, J.D. [A Cadwalader,W.&T.]

Temple Law Firm, PLLC
(See Raleigh)

Templeton, Thomas B., (BV) .... '57 '84 C.575 B.S. L.896 J.D. [Templeton&R.]
Templeton & Raynor, P.A., (AV) .... 1800 East Blvd.
Tenholder, Jolie Amie .... '75 '00 C.587 B.A. L.896 J.D. [A Womble C.S.&R.]
Tepper, Roberta L., (BV) .... '56 '87 C.102 B.A. L.37 J.D. Asst. Dist. Atty.
Terry, Daniel A. .... '62 '89 C.301 B.A. L.896 J.D. [McMillan&T.]
Terry, David L., (AV) ....'58 '83 C&L.896 B.S., J.D. [Poyner&S.]
Thalheimer, Ben S. ....'52 '86 C.679 B.S.B.M. L.893 J.D. Dist. J.
Tharrington, J. Cary, IV, (BV) '— '92 C.575 B.S. L.1228 J.D.
Assoc. Gen. Coun. & Litig. Dir., Sonic Auto., Inc.
Tharrington, Nicole L. '69 '94 C.576 B.A. L.1228 J.D.
Asst. Gen. Coun., Compass Group, U.S.A. Inc.
Thigpen, Mark V., (BV) ....'— '99 C.301 B.S. L.790 J.D. [A Kennedy C.L.&H.]
Thigpen, Richard E., Jr., (AV) .... '30 '56 C.228 A.B. L.575 LL.B. [Kirk P.&T.]
Thigpen, Richard M., (AV) .... '55 '83 C.228 B.A. L.1228 J.D. 800 S. Mint St.
Thomas, Benjamin R. ....'— '05 C.602 B.B.A. L.902 J.D. [A Helms M.&W.]
Thomas, Blake W. ....'— '00 C.951 B.A. L.309 J.D. [A Robinson,B.&H.]
Thomas, Diane D. '69 '99 C.759 B.A. L.245 J.D.
(adm. in GA; not adm. in NC) 2521 Hampton Ave.
Thomas, F. Scott ....'71 '99 C.575 B.A. L.192 J.D. [A Parker,P.A.&B.]
Thomas, Kelly S. ....'58 '83 C&L.145 B.A., J.D. Wachovia Corp. Legal Div.
Thomas, Susan Jesson ....'42 '86 C.62 B.A. L.215 J.D. [A M.J.Bednarik]

Thomas, Susan V.
(See Cornelius)

Thompson, Catherine E., (AV) ....'54 '80 C.228 B.A. L.976 J.D. [⊡ Helms M.&W.]
Thompson, Charles Sydnor, Jr. '24 '52 C.823 A.B. L.309 LL.B.
Ste 3000, 401 S Tryon St
Thompson, Emerson M., III, (BV) .... '64 '89 C&L.896 B.A., J.D. [Cranfill,S.&H.]
Thompson, Fred C., Jr., (AV) .... '42 '74 C&L.575 A.B., J.D. [Parker,P.A.&B.]
Thompson, Jeffrey C. '64 '89 C&L.280 A.B., J.D.
4801 E. Independence Blvd., Ste. 501
Thompson, Judy D., (AV) ....'47 '85 C.260 B.A. L.326 J.D. [Poyner&S.]
Thompson, Margaret J. .... '— '02 C.228 B.A. L.880 J.D. [A Mayer,B.R.&M.]
Thompson, Michelle '58 '91
C.369 B.A. L.910 J.D. First Union Corp. (Contract Servs. Grp.)
Thompson, Peter K., (BV) ....'48 '74 C.674 A.B. L.575 J.D. 214 Cherokee Rd.
Thompson, Sydnor, (AV) ....'24 '52 C.823 B.A. L.309 LL.B. [⊡ Parker,P.A.&B.]
Thornton, Kendra W. ....'77 '04 C.160 B.A. L.790 J.D. [A Parker,P.A.&B.]
Thornton, Wesley D. ....'77 '04 C.198 B.A. L.790 J.D. [A Moore&V.P.]
Thorsen, Haakon ... '59 '92 C.118 B.A. L.352 J.D. 1001 E.W.T. Harris Boulevard, Suite P
Thorson, Chad .... '73 '05 C.871 B.S. L.184 J.D. [A Alston&B.] (See Pat. Sect.)
Throneburg, Patricia B., (BV) .... '58 '82 C.264 B.A. L.575 J.D. 901 Mt. Vernon Ave.
Thurbee, Jessica E. ....'— '97 C.198 B.A. L.607 J.D. [A Gorman&D.]
Thurman, Frederick M., Jr. ....'70 '95 C.160 B.S. L.192 J.D. [Shumaker,L.&K.]
Thurman, W. David, (BV) .... '59 '83 C&L.575 B.A., J.D. [Thurman,W.&B.]
Thurman, Wilson & Boutwell, P.A., (AV) ....301 South McDowell Street
Tidwell, William DeVane ....'71 '97 C.198 B.A. L.575 J.D. [Helms M.&W.]
Tillman, Chad D., (BV) ....'70 '94 C.976 B.S. L.575 J.D. [Tillman I.] (Pat.)
Tillman, Heather McKaig ....'72 '96 C.228 A.B. L.692 J.D. [McKaig&M.]
Tillman Ivsan, PLLC, (BV) ....7400 Carmel Executive Park, Ste. 250 (Pat.)
Timothy, Marjory J. .... '56 '89 C.575 B.A. L.1228 J.D. Staff Atty., Children's Law Ctr.
Timperio, John M. ....'66 '91 C.659 B.A. L.276 J.D. [Dechert]
Tin, Noell P., (AV) ....'68 '94 C.473 B.A. L.588 J.D. [Tin F.G.&O.]

Tin Fulton Greene & Owen, PLLC, (AV) BB
212 South Tryon Street Suite 1200, 28281
Telephone: 704-338-1220 Fax: 704-338-1312
URL: http://www.tfgolawfirm.com
Members of Firm: Noell P. Tin; Shirley L. Fulton; Christopher E. Greene; C. Melissa Owen. Of Counsel: Ronald L. Gibson;—Matthew G. Pruden; Bethelehem Feleke (Not admitted in NC).
Immigration, Criminal Defense Trial and Appellate Practice, Drug Crimes, Felonies, Misdemeanors, White Collar Crime, Criminal Conspiracy.

See Professional Biographies, CHARLOTTE, NORTH CAROLINA

Tinkler, David K. '56 '82 C.198 A.B. L.575 J.D.
(adm. in AL; not adm. in NC) First Union Corporation, Legal Division
Tippens, Andre L. ....'70 '95 C&L.575 B.S., J.D. [Tippens&Z.]
Tippens & Zurosky, L.L.P., (CV) .... 301 S. McDowell Street, Suite 610
Tipps, Maynard E., (AV) .... '— '71 C.659 B.S. L.880 J.D. [Kennedy C.L.&H.]
Tison, Ashley Davidson .... '75 '00 C.1128 B.S.B.A. L.575 J.D. [A Johnston,A.&H.]
Tissue, Joseph N., (BV) .... '54 '80 C.659 B.A. L.665 J.D. [Mitchell,R.&T.]
Toadvine, J. René .... '— '93 C.1161 B.S. L.347 J.D. [Littler M.]
Tobin, Michael A., (AV) .... '— '97 C.871 B.A. L.896 J.D. [Kennedy C.L.&H.]
Todd, Steven O. '61 '88 C&L.575 B.S., J.D.
Vice President & General Counsel, Elite Information Group, Inc.
Tolbert, J. David, (AV) .... '56 '82 C.269 B.A. L.575 J.D. [⊡ Sasser]

Tomberlin, Richard H., Law Offices of, (BV) '46 '75
C.1042 B.A. L.990 J.D. 301 S. McDowell St., Ste. 510
Tomchin, R. Gregory, (BV) ....'60 '85 C.896 B.A. L.923 J.D. [Cranford,S.&T.]
Tomits, Bret, The Law Offices '75 '01
C.608 B.A. L.201 J.D. 301 S. McDowell Street, Suite 1104
Tomlin, Tracy E., (AVⓉ) ....'55 '85 C.228 B.S. L.472 J.D. [Nelson M.R.&S.]
Tomlinson, Michael F. ....'— '00 C.188 B.A. L.659 J.D. [🄰 Kennedy C.L.&H.]
Tompkins, Anne M. ....'62 '92 C.1128 B.A. L.575 J.D. [Alston&B.]
Tompkins, Charles V., Jr., (AV) '— '61 C.575 A.B. L.309 LL.B.
[🄲 Kennedy C.L.&H.]
Toney, Keenya ....'66 '97 C.454 B.B.A. L.575 J.D. Bk. of Amer.
Tool, H. Warren, Jr. '17 '49 C&L.546 B.S.
(adm. in MS; not adm. in NC) FBI.Spec. Agent, Retired‡
Toole, William W., (AV) ....'— '89 C.311 B.A. L.896 J.D. [Robinson,B.&H.]
Torning, Anders K. '64 '92
C.472 B.B.A. L.178 J.D. Assoc. Gen. Coun., Duke Energy Corp.
Torstrick, Brent A., (AV) ....'— '83 C.228 A.B. L.893 J.D. [Robinson,B.&H.]
Tourangeau, Paul R. '62 '89 C.112 B.A. L.1065 J.D.
(adm. in CA; not adm. in NC) Assoc. Gen. Coun., Duke Energy Corp.
Tousey, Clay B., III ....'05 C.309 A.B. L.893 J.D. [🄰 Helms M.&W.]
Towler, Marc D. ....'50 '80 C.337 A.B. L.339 J.D. Pub. Def., Off. of Pub. Def.
Townsend, Wanda C., (BV) ....'64 '91 C&L.575 B.A., J.D. [Johnston,A.&H.]
Tracey, Patricia A. ....'57 '81 C.1128 B.A. L.896 J.D. 1400 Dilworth Rd.
Travis, Jos. C., (BV) ....'23 '48 C&L.575 B.S., J.D. 1630 Mockingbird Lane
Travis, Susan T., (BVⓉ) '— '76 C.645 B.S. L.823 J.D.
(adm. in NY; not adm. in NC) V.P., Gen. Coun. & Sec., J.M. Huber Corp.
Traynum, Kerry L. ....'— '04 C.999 B.A. L.577 J.D. [🄰 Nelson M.R.&S.]
Treanor, Claire M. '57 '86 C.426 B.A. L.64 J.D.
(adm. in MD; not adm. in NC) 7115 Baltusrol Ln.‡
Treanor, Mark C., (AVⓉ) '46 '76 C.871 B.S. L.446 J.D.
(adm. in MD; not adm. in NC) Sr. Exec. V.P., Gen. Coun. & Secy., First Union Corp.
Treeter, David R. ....'51 '85 C.344 B.A. L.345 J.D. Equal Employ. Opportunity Comm.
Trego, Brandon C. ....'73 '03 C&L.923 B.S.M.E., J.D. [🄰 Adams E.] (See Pat. Sect.)
Trent, B. Keith, (AVⓉ) '59 '87 C.802 B.S.E.E. L.846 J.D.
(adm. in TX; not adm. in NC) Grp. V.P., Gen. Coun. & Secy., Duke Energy Corp.
Trepel, Jeffrey M., (AV) '51 '78
C.705 B.A. L.575 J.D. Assoc. Gen. Coun., Duke Energy Corp.
Treviño-Lane, Lucia '65 '92 C.93 B.A. L.575 J.D.
(adm. in GA; not adm. in NC) 3324 Rhett Butler Place
Trobich, Robert K., (BV) '60 '88
C.198 A.B. L.1292 J.D. 301 South McDowell Street, Suite 412
Troiano, Joann P. '57 '91 C.999 B.S. L.1029 J.D.
(adm. in CT; not adm. in NC) Coun., Royal & SunAlliance
Trosch, Eric C. ....'74 '02 C.575 B.A. L.896 J.D. [🄰 Conrad T.&K.]
Trosch, Louis A., (AV) ....'39 '65 C.81 B.A. L.923 J.D. [Conrad T.&K.]
Trosch, Minette C., (BV) ....'42 '95 C.210 B.A. L.575 J.D. [Conrad T.&K.]
Trosch, William Conrad, (BV) ....'68 '93 C&L.575 B.A., J.D. [Conrad T.&K.]
Trotman, Yolanda M. ....'74 '02 C.1128 B.A. L.665 J.D. [Garza&T.]
Tsai, Caroline '69 '00 C.477 B.A. L.904 J.D.
Asst. Gen. Coun., Bank of America Corp., Global Corp. & Invest. Bkg.
Tucci, Christopher J. '64 '94 C.573 B.S. L.117 J.D.
(adm. in OH; not adm. in NC) V.P. & Chief Legal Coun., EquiFirst Corporation
Tucker, James M. ....'— '99 C.260 B.A. L.352 J.D. [🄰 Kilpatrick S.]
Tucker, Larry D., (BV) ....'54 '79 C.34 B.S. L.201 J.D. 101 N. McDowell St., Ste. 114
Tucker, Leslie A., (CV) ....'61 '94 C.676 B.A. L.1345 J.D. Asst. Dist. Atty.
Tucker, Robert B., Jr., (AV) ....'43 '72 C.576 B.S. L.575 J.D. [Katten M.R.]
Tucker Moore, Wanda ....'66 '94 C.575 B.S., B.A. L.574 J.D. Mag. Off.
Tungare, Deepa ....'— '05 C&L.575 B.A., J.D. [🄰 Hedrick E.G.&K.]
Turk-Meena, Mary ....'— '79 C.62 B.M. L.831 J.D. [Kennedy C.L.&H.]
Turley, S. Shane '68 '96 C.482 B.S. L.1338 J.D.
(adm. in VA; not adm. in NC) Dep. Sr. Coun., U.S. LEC Corp.
Turner, Beth A. ....'68 '96 C.444 B.S. L.831 J.D. [Moore&V.P.]
Turner, Betty R. ....'51 '84 C&L.880 B.A., J.D. Guilford College
Turner, G. Robert, III, (BV) ....'44 '69 C.228 A.B. L.575 J.D. [Horack,T.P.&L.]
Turner, Joel K. ....'— '03 C&L.575 B.A., J.D. [🄰 Hedrick E.G.&K.]
Turtletaub, Philip A. ....'58 '88 C.260 B.S.B.A. L.61 J.D. 1101 Tyvola Rd., Ste. 102
Twaddell, James S. '64 '90 C.776 B.A. L.273 J.D.
(adm. in CT; not adm. in NC)
Coun., The Goodman-Gable-Gould Company/Adjusters International
Twiddy, Heather Teale ....'— '02 C.97 B.A. L.896 J.D. [🄰 Hedrick E.G.&K.]
Tydings, Kevin W. ....'67 '92 C.893 B.A. L.692 J.D. [Guthrie,D.H.&S.]
Tyler, Scott M., (AV) ....'70 '96 C.299 B.A. L.228 J.D. [Moore&V.P.]
Tyson, Bryan L. ....'— '96 C&L.575 B.A., J.D. [🄰 Womble C.S.&R.]
Tyson, Deborah M. ....'75 '01 C&L.896 B.A., J.D. [🄰 Poyner&S.]
Ubell, Donald P., (AV) ....'45 '70 C.575 A.B. L.477 J.D. [Parker,P.A.&B.]
Ughetta, Robert L. '66 '94 C.674 A.B. L.982 J.D.
(adm. in NY; not adm. in NC) [Cadwalader,W.&T.]
Uhler-Lewis, Emily Beth '73 '00
C.473 B.A. L.201 J.D. Atty. Advocate, Guard. Ad Litem Off.
Underdown, Ezell H. '66 '98 C.477 A.B. L.659 J.D.
(adm. in OH; not adm. in NC) [🄰 Cadwalader,W.&T.]

Underhill, Peter J. '46 '74 C&L.575 B.A., J.D.
4701 Hedgemore Drive, Suite 740, 28209
Telephone: 704-561-0090 Fax: 704-561-0905
Email: punderhill@carolina.rr.com URL: http://www.underhill-law.com
Consumer Bankruptcy, Bankruptcy Law, Foreclosures, Debtor and Creditor, Collections, Creditor Rights, Residential Real Estate, Mortgages, Business Law, Limited Liability Law, Wills and Probate.
See Professional Biographies, CHARLOTTE, NORTH CAROLINA

Underwood, William E., Jr., (AV) ....'37 '64 C&L.575 A.B., J.D. [🄲 Katten M.R.]
Urban, Edmund T., (AV) ....'47 '72 C&L.896 B.A., J.D. The Title Co. of NC
Urps, Tonya L. ....'67 '93 C.923 B.A. L.896 J.D. [Bernhardt&S.]
Ussery, Andrew R., (BV) '70 '98
C.896 B.A. L.575 J.D. [McAngus G.&C.] (⊙Columbia, SC)
Valaoras, Nicholas Peter, (BV) ....'67 '93 C&L.896 B.A., J.D. [Cranfill,S.&H.]
Van Allen, William K., (AV) ....'14 '38 C.299 B.A. L.309 LL.B. [🄲 Moore&V.P.]
Van Buren, Carol A. Jones, (BV) ....'— '91 C&L.896 B.S., J.D. [Kennedy C.L.&H.]

Vandiver & Bryan, Estate & Elder Law Firm of
(See Cornelius)

Vanesse, Michel P. '— '95 L.145 J.D.
(adm. in IL; not adm. in NC) [Kennedy C.L.&H.]
Van Hatten, Scott G. '70 '96
C.1350 B.S. L.564 J.D. V.P. & Asst. Gen. Coun., Wachovia Corp.
Van Horne, Cynthia L., (AV) ....'59 '91 C.575 B.A. L.1128 J.D. [Poyner&S.]
Van Hoy, Bradley T. ....'75 '00 C&L.577 B.A., J.D. [🄰 Moore&V.P.]
Van Hoy, Philip M., (AV) ....'47 '73 C.228 A.B. L.575 J.D. [VanHoy,R.A.&D.]

Van Hoy, Reutlinger, Adams & Dunn, (AV) 🄱🄱
737 East Boulevard, 28203
Telephone: 704-375-6022 Fax: 704-375-6024
URL: http://www.lawyers.com/vradlawfirm
Members of Firm: Philip M. Van Hoy; Craig A. Reutlinger; G. Bryan Adams, III; Stephen J. Dunn.
Labor Relations, Employment Discrimination, Employment Litigation, Employer Rights and Management Employment Law, OSHA and Wage and Hour (Employers only). Business Law, Health Law representing Health Care Providers.
Representative Clients: Duke Power Co.; Sunstrand Corp.; Pic 'N Pay Stores, Inc.; Parsons Main, Inc.; City of Fayetteville, North Carolina; McDowell Hospital; New York Life Insurance; Revlon Consumer Products.
See Professional Biographies, CHARLOTTE, NORTH CAROLINA

Van Kampen, Joshua Reed ....'71 '98 C.679 B.A. L.339 J.D. [🄰 J.H.Fosbinder]

Vann Law Firm, P.A.
(See Matthews)

Vano, Ann L. '58 '89 C.651 B.S. L.705 J.D.
(adm. in NJ; not adm. in NC) Corporate Counsel, Centurion Development Corp.
Van Osdell, J. Garrett ....'— '99 C.260 B.A. L.790 J.D. [🄰 Kennedy C.L.&H.]
Vasco, Mark ....'68 '94 C.823 B.A. L.575 J.D. [Nelson M.R.&S.]
Vaughan, Michel Denise '52 '78 C.254 B.A. L.329 J.D.
(adm. in DC; not adm. in NC) Equal Employ. Opportunity Comm.
Vaughn, Lisa Finger, (BV) '62 '87
C&L.1228 B.A., J.D. Assoc. Gen. Coun., Duke Energy Corp.
Vaughn, Scott P., (AV) ....'61 '86 C&L.575 B.S., J.D. [Helms M.&W.]
Veilleux, Jean Wright '60 '85 C.575 B.A. L.273 J.D.
(adm. in MD; not adm. in NC) V.P. & Corp. Coun., Novant Health, Inc.
Veliz, Ruben M. ....'— '01 C.276 B.A. L.569 J.D. [🄰 Kennedy C.L.&H.]
Venturelli, Lisa A. ....'68 '95 C.1345 B.S. L.1228 J.D. [L.Venturelli]
Venturelli, Lisa .... P.O. Box 32392
Vereckey, Michelle L. ....'73 '01 C.34 BSCJ L.645 J.D. First Natl. Fin. Title Services
Vetter, Connie J. ....'64 '94 C.608 B.A. L.588 J.D. 4037 E. Independence Blvd., Ste. 565
Vicini, Donald J., (CVⓉ) ....'— '91 C.477 B.A. L.796 J.D. [Hedrick E.G.&K.]
Vickers, David R. ....'61 '90 C.420 B.S. L.1059 J.D. GreenPoint Mortgage
Vickstrom, Dwane E. ....'46 '77 C&L.546 B.S., J.D. [Smith,C.&V.]
Viele, Nicole Dolph ....'70 '01 C.1128 B.A. L.575 J.D. [Cranfill,S.&H.]
Vincent, Angelique R. ....'— '00 C.228 B.A. L.309 J.D. [🄰 Robinson,B.&H.]
Vines, David R. ....'66 '94 C.1080 B.B.A. L.575 J.D. [Katten M.R.]
Vinroot, Richard A., (AV) ....'— '66 C&L.575 B.S., LL.B. [Robinson,B.&H.]
Viola, Richard W. ....'68 '94 C.884 B.S. L.724 J.D. [Helms M.&W.]
Viser, Charles Malcolm, (BV) ....'— '00 C.301 B.A. L.1228 J.D. [🄰 James,M.&D.]
Vogt, Peter W. ....'61 '89 C.216 B.A. L.180 J.D. [Butrus K.W.V.] ⊙
Voler, Frank F., (BV) ....'59 '90 C.871 B.S.M.E. L.575 J.D. [M.A.DeMayo]
Vong-Spillan, Demetria E. '— '92 C&L.477 B.A., J.D.
(adm. in MO; not adm. in NC) Asst. Gen. Coun., Bank of America
Voorhees, Richard L. ....'41 '68 C.198 A.B. L.575 J.D. U.S. Dist. J.
Wade, H. Landis, Jr., (AV) ....'57 '83 C.198 A.B. L.896 J.D. [Helms M.&W.]
Wade, Hamlin L., (AV) ....'30 '57 C.198 B.S. L.575 J.D. [Ruff,B.C.W.&B.]
Wade, Tyrone C., (BV) ....'53 '89 C.994 B.A. L.1325 J.D. Assoc. Co. Atty.
Wagers, Margaret H. '52 '78 C.575 B.A. L.846 J.D.
(adm. in GA; not adm. in NC) 226 Huntley Pl.‡
Waggoner, William J., (AV) ....'28 '54 C&L.575 A.B., LL.B. [🄲 Guthrie,D.H.&S.]
Wagner, Kenneth L., (AV) '56 '83 C&L.378 B.S., J.D.
(adm. in MO; not adm. in NC) Princ. Coun., Goodrich Corp.
Walker, Clarence W., (AV) ....'— '55 C&L.228 A.B., LL.B. [🄲 Kennedy C.L.&H.]
Walker, Craig W. ....'78 '04 C.228 A.B. L.893 J.D. [🄰 Hunton&W.]
Walker, David J. ....'54 '82 C.880 B.A. L.421 J.D. Sr. V.P., Bk. of America
Walker, Frank H., Jr., (BV) ....'39 '64 C&L.575 B.S., LL.B. [Burke&Assoc.]

Walker, James S., (AV) '57 '88 C.576 B.A. L.574 J.D.
6109 Rosecrest Drive, P.O. Box 240057, 28224-0057
Telephone: 704-552-7276 Fax: 704-552-5324
Email: js-walker@mindspring.com
Workers Compensation, Workers Compensation Mediation.
See Professional Biographies, CHARLOTTE, NORTH CAROLINA

Walker, John G., (BV) ....'43 '69 C&L.575 B.S., J.D. [Burke&Assoc.]
Walker, Judith C., (BV) ....'43 '85 C.683 B.A. L.896 J.D. 710 Hungerford Pl.
Walker, Nancy E., (BV) ....'62 '88 C&L.896 B.A., J.D. [Whitesides&W.]
Walker, R. Brent, Law Office of '70 '99
C.576 B.A. L.574 J.D. 212 S. Tryon St., Ste. 1360
Walker, Steven Williams ("Will") ...'74 '00 C.896 B.A L.228 J.D. [🄰 Womble C.S.&R.]
Walker, Susan M. ....'— '00 C.890 B.A. L.309 J.D. [🄰 Katten M.R.]
Walker, Thomas G., (AV) ....'— '90 C.69 B.A. L.1228 J.D. [🄲 Alston&B.]
Walker, W. Kent ....'68 '94 C.575 B.S.B.A. L.309 J.D. [Helms M.&W.]
Wallace, James G., (AV) ....'49 '75 C.575 B.S. L.896 J.D. [Wallace,P.&W.]
Wallace, Mona Lisa, (BV) '54 '79
C.575 B.A. L.896 J.D. [🄲 Jackson,P.] & [Wallace&G.] (⊙Salisbury)
Wallace, R. David, (BV) ....'55 '81 C.1128 B.A. L.192 J.D. Asst. Dist. Atty.
Wallace, Terry L. ....'74 '99 C.575 B.A. L.574 J.D. [🄰 McAngus G.&C.]

Wallace, Pittman & Webb, PLLC, (AV)
2101 Rexford Road, Suite 100E, 28211
Telephone: 704-365-5566 Facsimile: 704-364-9698; 365-6735
James G. Wallace; Bryan W. Pittman; Leslie Miller Webb (Board Certified Specialist in Residential, Business, Commercial and Industrial Transactions, North Carolina State Board of Legal Specialization).
Commercial and Residential Real Estate, Real Estate Development, Condominium Law.
See Professional Biographies, CHARLOTTE, NORTH CAROLINA

Wallas, Jonathan P., (AV) ....'45 '70 C.228 B.A. L.178 J.D. [🄲 Ferguson,S.C.G.&S.]
Waller, Susan E. ....'71 '99 C.1365 B.A. L.744 J.D. 821 East Boulevard
Walls, David S., (BV) ....'59 '84 C.198 B.A. L.309 J.D. [Moore&V.P.]
Walls, George R. '— '71 C&L.446 B.A., J.D.
(adm. in DC; not adm. in NC) Asst. Gen. Coun., Bank of America
Walters, Jerry H., Jr. ....'70 '96 C.575 B.A. L.1345 J.D. [🄰 Littler M.]
Walters, Kristi K. ....'— '99 C.198 B.A. L.575 J.D. [🄰 Parker,P.A.&B.]
Walton, Amy L. ....'74 '01 C.103 B.A. L.902 J.D. [🄰 Parker,P.A.&B.]
Walton, Clark C. ....'78 '05 C.575 B.S. L.276 J.D. [🄰 Nelson M.R.&S.]
Walton, Jason P. ....'75 '01 C.812 B.S. L.902 J.D. [🄰 Parker,P.A.&B.]
Walton, K. Cameron ....'— '99 C.680 B.A. L.575 J.D. [🄰 Hunton&W.]
Wamsley, Paul G. ....'62 '90 C.128 B.A. L.201 J.D. [🄰 Hamel]
Wang, Jian ....'76 '03 C.999 B.S. L.228 J.D. [🄰 Cadwalader,W.&T.]
Waple, Louis A. ....'71 '99 C.575 B.A. L.1228 J.D. [🄰 McAngus G.&C.]
Ward, Henry B., III ....'70 '96 C.277 B.S.M.E. L.245 J.D. [Alston&B.] (See Pat. Sect.)
Ward, Robert L., (BV) ....'57 '82 C.477 A.B. L.862 J.D. Asst. Pub. Def.
Ward, Stephen W., (AV) ....'55 '80 C.576 B.A. L.469 J.D. Asst. Dist. Atty.
Ware, Cameron T. ....'75 '00 C.1128 B.A. L.575 J.D. [🄰 Johnston,A.&H.]

Warlick, J. Thomas, IV, (AV) '65 '91
C.575 B.A. L.245 J.D. Asst. Gen. Coun., Media, NASCAR, Inc.
Warnement, Pamela Pearson, (AV) '57 '82 C.881 A.B. L.188 J.D.
Deputy General Counsel, Wachovia Securities, Inc.
Warner, S. Rogers, Jr., (AV) .... '64 '91 C&L.575 B.A., J.D. [Parker,P.A.&B.]
Warpula, Christian C. .... '73 '98 C.305 B.S. L.896 J.D. [A Alston&B.]
Warren, C. Jeff, (BV) .... '58 '91 C.445 B.S. L.575 J.D. [Warren&K.]
Warren, David P. '54 '78 C.1109 B.A. L.1137 J.D.
(adm. in CA; not adm. in NC) [A Carroll&C.]
Warren, Dean A., (AV) .... '— '85 C&L.575 B.S., J.D. [Kennedy C.L.&H.]
Warren, James A., Jr., (BV) .... '54 '79 C.576 B.A. L.1128 J.D. [J.A.Warren,Jr.]
Warren, John D., (BV) .... '22 '53 C&L.174 B.A., J.D. 1515 Elizabeth Ave.
Warren, Joseph, III, (AV) .... '39 '65 C&L.228 A.B., LL.B. [C Morris,M.&M.]
Warren, M. Neya .... '75 '02 C.575 B.A. L.1228 J.D. [James,M.&D.]
Warren, J. A., Jr., Law Office of, (BV) .... 1001 Elizabeth Ave., Ste. 2A

Warren & Kallianos, (BV)
301 South McDowell Street, Suite 130, 28204
Telephone: 704-377-7777 Fax: 704-376-6090
Email: warkal@bellsouth.net URL: http://www.attorneysfortheinjured.net
Members of Firm: C. Jeff Warren; Chris M. Kallianos.
Plaintiff's Personal Injury, Litigation, Medical Malpractice, Nursing Home Neglect, Business Torts.
See Professional Biographies, CHARLOTTE, NORTH CAROLINA

Washington, Ahmad S. ...... '75 '00 C.511 B.A. L.896 J.D. [A Mann B.] (⊙Atlanta, GA)
Washington, Karen D. '74 '03 L.575 J.D.
(adm. in SC; not adm. in NC) [A Mann B.] (⊙Atlanta, GA)
Wasser, Steven '64 '93 C.165 B.A. L.724 J.D.
(adm. in NY; not adm. in NC) Vice President, Deutsche Banc Mortgage Capital
Watkins, Megan K. .... '— '02 C&L.280 B.A., J.D. [A Nelson M.R.&S.]
Watson, Alexander F. .... '— '01 C.160 B.S. L.575 J.D. [A Kennedy C.L.&H.]
Watson, Carlos D. .... '70 '02 C.574 B.A. L.607 J.D. [Watson]
Watson, Kary C. .... '74 '01 C.575 B.A. L.896 J.D. [A Horack,T.P.&L.]
Watson, Leticia M. '— '92 C.329 B.A. L.446 J.D.
(adm. in MD; not adm. in NC) Asst. Gen. Coun., Bank of America
Watson, Mayleng F. .... '76 '01 C.968 B.A. L.1128 J.D. [A Helms M.&W.]
Watson, Robert W., Jr. .... '44 '73 C.885 B.A. L.893 J.D. [A Cadwalader,W.&T.]
Watson, Romulus S. .... '20 '53 C.576 B.S. L.575 LL.B. 2349 Thetford Ct.‡
Watson, Rush Price .... '75 '00 C.160 B.A. L.896 J.D. Asst. Dist. Atty.

Watson Law Firm, PLLC
212 South Tryon Street, Suite 480, 28281
Telephone: 704-333-4663 Fax: 704-333-7727
Email: cdwatson@watsonlawpllc.com URL: http://www.cdwatsonlaw.com
Carlos D. Watson.
Personal Injury, Automobile Accidents, Slip and Fall, Wrongful Death, Business Law, Joint Ventures, Limited Liability Company Law, Contracts, Criminal Law, Driving While Intoxicated, DWI, Traffic Violations.
See Professional Biographies, CHARLOTTE, NORTH CAROLINA

Watts, Peggy C. .... '48 '82 C.420 B.S. L.45 J.D. Coun., Belk Stores Servs., Inc.
Watts, William A. .... '18 '50 C.575 A.B. L.878 LL.B. Dep. City Atty.‡
Wayne, Kenneth R., (CV) .... '54 '81 C.1228 B.A. L.575 J.D. [K.Wayne&Assoc.]
Wayne, Ken, & Associates, (CV) .... 301 S. McDowell St., Ste. 1103
Weatherly, Karen Culbreth, (CV) .... '62 '88 C&L.575 B.S., J.D. [A Kirschbaum,N.K.&G.]
Weatherly, Mary Lindsay .... '— '04 C.575 B.A. L.893 J.D. [A Helms M.&W.]
Webb, Danielle E. .... '73 '98 C.478 B.A. L.945 J.D. [A Helms M.&W.]
Webb, Leslie Miller, (BV) .... '59 '85 C.198 A.B. L.896 J.D. [Wallace,P.&W.]
Webb, William B., Jr. '51 '77 C.968 A.B. L.896 J.D.
First American Title of the Carolinas
Weber, Brett G. .... '73 '99 C&L.896 B.A., J.D. [A Helms M.&W.]
Weber, Cameron Bader .... '76 '01 C.232 B.S. L.896 J.D. 5710 Bellechasse St.
Weber, Rose Marie .... '— '94 C.801 B.A. L.64 J.D. [C Parker,P.A.&B.]
Weber, Steven D., (BV) '69 '93 C.812 B.A. L.464 J.D.
[Parker,P.A.&B.] (⊙Columbia, Spartanburg, SC)
Weddington, Keith M., (AV) .... '61 '87 C&L.575 B.A., J.D. [Parker,P.A.&B.]
Weidner, James S., Jr., Law Office of '49 '76
C.1055 B.A. L.425 J.D. 200 E. Woodlawn Rd. Bldg., Ste. 118
Weilbacher, Tara Steinberg '— '99 C.880 B.S. L.802 J.D.
(adm. in TX; not adm. in NC) Asst. Gen. Coun., Bank of America
Weinberger, Michael, (AVⓉ) '54 '79
C.102 B.A. L.1009 J.D. [C Sasser] (⊙New York, NY)
Weiner, Ronald M. .... '54 '79 C.94 B.A. L.861 J.D. Radiator Specialty Co.
Weinstein, Maurice A., (AV) .... '15 '40 C&L.228 A.B., LL.B. 1100 S. Tryon St.‡
Weiss, Spencer C. '59 '84
C&L.893 B.S.C.E., J.D. Asst. Gen. Coun., Fluor Enterprises, Inc.
Welch, Gary J., (BV) .... '69 '94 C&L.575 B.S., J.D. [Johnston,A.&H.]
Welling, Alfred F., Jr., (BV) .... '41 '67 C&L.575 B.S., J.D. 325 Rensselaer Ave.
Welling, Charles M., (AV) .... '24 '52 C.893 L.575 LL.B. 404 Jefferson Dr.
Wellman, Edward W., Jr., (AVⓉ) ...... '45 '73 C.976 B.A. L.893 J.D. [Parker,P.A.&B.]
Wells, C. Phillip, (BV) '60 '92 C.575 B.A. L.809 J.D.
Dep. Gen. Coun. & Secy., Compass Group, U.S.A. Inc.
Wells, Jameson P., (BV) .... '56 '84 C.575 B.A. L.982 J.D. [Wells&D.]
Wells & Daisley, P.A., (BV) .... 1616 Cleveland Ave.
Welsh, Eric D., (AV) .... '62 '88 C&L.228 A.B., J.D. [Parker,P.A.&B.]
Welti, Belinda '— '84 C.67 B.A. L.1202 J.D.
(adm. in CT; not adm. in NC) Bank of America (⊙Boston, MA)
Wentzel, Suzanne .... '71 '96 C.473 B.A. L.8 J.D. [A Moore&V.P.]
Wertz, Phillip A. ...... '— '97 C.575 B.A. L.228 J.D. Asst. Gen. Coun., Bank of America
West, Allen L., (BV) .... '— '98 C&L.790 B.A., J.D. [Hamilton F.M.S.S.&M.]
West, Ann P. .... '61 '91 C&L.896 B.A., J.D. [C Moore&V.P.]
West, Sheena M. .... '72 '98 C.1128 B.A. L.574 J.D. [A Rawls,D.&S.]
West, Sherryl R. '62 '97 C.34 B.S. L.574 J.D.
Asst. Dist. Atty., Mecklenburg Co. Dist. Atty. Off.
Wester, John R., (AV) .... '— '72 C.575 A.B. L.228 J.D. [Robinson,B.&H.]
Wester, McNeill Y. .... '74 '02 C&L.575 B.A., J.D. [A Moore&V.P.]

Westmoreland, Anna N., Law Office of '— '04 C.1128 B.A. L.1202 J.D.
5120 Monroe Road, 28205
Telephone: 704-567-5297 Fax: 704-567-5389
Email: anw@westmorelandlawfirm.com URL: http://www.westmorelandlawfirm.com
Family Law, Divorce, Child Support, Employment Law, Employment Contracts, Wrongful Termination, Severance, Employment Benefits, Bankruptcy, Wills, Probate, Trusts and Estates.
See Professional Biographies, CHARLOTTE, NORTH CAROLINA

Whedon, Parker, (BV) .... '25 '51 C&L.575 LL.B. 519 Fenton Pl.
Wheeler, Joyce W., (AV) '51 '80 C.21 B.A. L.326 J.D.
Chf. Corp. Offr. & Gen. Coun., Royal & Sunalliance
Whelchel, Christopher Miles ..... '76 '03 C&L.790 B.A., J.D. Coun., Duke Energy Corp.
Whelpley, David B., Jr., (AV) .... '— '89 C.160 B.S. L.245 J.D. [Kilpatrick S.]

White, Barbara L., (CV) .... '54 '81 C.347 B.S. L.345 J.D. 500 E. Morehead St.
White, Cynthia Lewis, (BV) .... '58 '86 C.454 B.B.A. L.893 J.D. Asst. City Atty.
White, Garth H. .... '71 '97 C.1128 B.A. L.436 J.D. [Rudisill,W.&K.]
White, H. Ramsey, III .... '70 '99 C&L.896 B.S., J.D. [A Helms M.&W.]
White, John Robert '62 '98 C.865 B.S. L.383 J.D.
(adm. in NY; not adm. in NC) [C Cadwalader,W.&T.]
White, Joseph G. '74 '00
C.140 B.S. L.790 J.D. Corp. Coun., Compass Group, U.S.A. Inc.
White, Martin L., (BV) .... '71 '96 C.999 B.A. L.575 J.D. [A Johnston,A.&H.]
White, William A. .... '45 '72 C&L.966 B.A., J.D. [C Moore&V.P.]
Whitehurst, William R., (AV) '56 '82
C.896 B.A. L.575 J.D. [Womble C.S.&R.] (⊙Winston-Salem)
Whitesides, H. Monroe, Jr., (BV) ...... '59 '85 C.968 B.A. L.1228 J.D. [Whitesides&W.]

Whitesides & Walker, L.L.P., (BV)
212 South Tryon Street, Suite 980, 28281
Telephone: 704-376-6455 Fax: 704-332-5010
URL: http://www.whitesideswalker.com
Members of the Firm: H. Monroe Whitesides, Jr. (Board Certified Specialist, Federal and State Criminal Law); Nancy E. Walker; Julie Curran Gerock. Associate: Michael B. Kemper.
General Civil and Criminal Litigation, Appellate Practice, Personal Injury, Wrongful Death, Automobile Accidents and Injuries, Trucking and Transportation Defense, Asset Forfeiture, Insurance Defense, Sports Law, Entertainment Law, Employment, Violations, Collections, Environmental Law, Family Law, Domestic Relations, Divorce, Child Custody, Child Support, Traffic Violations.
See Professional Biographies, CHARLOTTE, NORTH CAROLINA

Whitfield, Michael G. .... '36 '63 C&L.575 A.B., LL.B. 1500 E. Fourth St.
Whitfield, Paul L., (BV) .... '36 '63 C&L.575 A.B., J.D. [P.L.Whitfield&Assoc.]
Whitfield, Paul L., & Associates, P.A., (BV) .... 1600 E. Fourth St.
Whitley, J. Craig .... '59 '84 C.198 B.A. L.896 J.D. Chf. J.
Whitley, Jerry W., (BV) .... '40 '65 C&L.896 B.A., LL.B. P.O. Box 6001
Whitlow, Robert A., (AVⓉ) .... '54 '79 C.269 B.A. L.280 J.D. [Sellers,H.A.D.&L.]
Whitman, Andrew '38 '69
(adm. in MN; not adm. in NC) Immigration Mgmt.
Whitman, Scott '66 '98
(adm. in WI; not adm. in NC) Immigration Mgmt.
Whitney, A. Grant, Jr., (AV) .... '54 '79 C&L.896 B.A., J.D. [Parker,P.A.&B.]
Whitten, Adam E. .... '— '03 C.101 B.A. L.575 J.D. [A Hedrick E.G.&K.]
Widis, Howard M. .... '51 '77 C&L.575 A.B., J.D. 222 N. Sharon Amity Rd.
Wiggins, Barrie Little, (BV) .... '52 '85 C&L.575 B.S., J.D. 6417 Seton House Lane

Wiggins, Roy H., (BV) '61 '88 C.232 B.S. L.1228 J.D.
122 North McDowell Street, 28204
Mailing Address: P.O. Box 36291, Charlotte, NC 28236-6291
Telephone: 704-332-6500 Fax: 704-332-6258
Email: rhwiggins@hbm-attys.com URL: http://www.lawyers.com/royhwiggins
Criminal Defense in all State and Federal Courts. Driving While Intoxicated, (DWI), Assault, Drug Crimes, Traffic Violations, Personal Injury, Automobile Accidents, Wrongful Death, Workers Compensation and Commercial Litigation Lawsuits.
See Professional Biographies, CHARLOTTE, NORTH CAROLINA

Wilcox, Staten L., Jr., (BV) .... '46 '78 C.575 B.A. L.896 J.D. [S.L.Wilcox]

Wilcox, Staten L., P.A., (BV)
1208 S. Tryon Street, 28203
Telephone: 704-342-2266 Fax: 704-342-9856
Email: rexatty@aol.com URL: http://www.statenwilcoxpa.com
Staten L. Wilcox, Jr.
Securities Arbitration Litigation, NASD Arbitration, Personal Injury, Automobile Accidents, Wrongful Death.
See Professional Biographies, CHARLOTTE, NORTH CAROLINA

Wilder, Raboteau T., Jr., (AV) .... '48 '73 C.896 B.A. L.228 J.D. [Nelson M.R.&S.]
Wiles, David R., (BV) '— '89
C.790 B.A. L.309 J.D. Assoc. Gen. Coun., Bank of America
Wilkerson, Douglas G. '50 '86 C.160 B.A. L.790 J.D.
(adm. in SC; not adm. in NC) I.R.S.
Willen, Stephan J. .... '— '91 C.477 B.A. L.228 J.D. [Robinson,B.&H.]
Williams, Algernon, The Law Office of '69 '00
C.999 B.A. L.608 J.D. 6425 Idlewild Rd., Ste. 212
Williams, Althea Johnson '62 '88
C&L.575 B.A., J.D. Asst. Gen. Coun., Lending Tree, Inc.
Williams, Amy Pritchard, (BV) ...... '— '92 C.575 B.A. L.893 J.D. [Kennedy C.L.&H.]
Williams, B Frederick .... '44 '78 C.228 A.B. L.128 J.D. [C James,M.&D.]
Williams, Benjamin D. .... '78 '03 C&L.575 B.A., J.D. [Gerdes,M.&S.]
Williams, Brandon G. '73 '02 C.846 B.S. L.1363 J.D.
(adm. in TX; not adm. in NC; See Pat. Sect.) [A Dougherty,C.H.&B.]
Williams, David F., (BV) .... '53 '85 C.970 B.A. L.574 J.B. [Hoover&W.]
Williams, Jane A. '58 '83 C.346 B.S. L.345 J.D.
(adm. in IN; not adm. in NC) 3809 Laxton Ct.
Williams, Karen S., (AV) '— '87
C.923 B.A. L.896 J.D. Asst. Gen. Coun., Bank of America
Williams, Neil C., (AV) .... '41 '66 C&L.228 A.B., LL.B. [Horack,T.P.&L.]
Williams, Ronald, (P.A.) .... '37 '62 C&L.280 A.B., LL.B. 2101 Marryat Ct.
Williams, Samuel S., (AV) .... '35 '61 C.674 A.B. L.575 J.D. [S.S.Williams]
Williams, Shantrell G. .... '73 '98 C.575 B.A. L.1228 J.D. P.O. Box 481893
Williams, Suzanne Cress .... '— '03 C.575 B.A. L.1509 J.D. [A Kennedy C.L.&H.]
Williams, Thomas E., (AV) .... '57 '82 C.34 B.A. L.896 J.D. [Morris Y.W.S.&B.]
Williams, Samuel S., P.A., (AV) .... 212 N. McDowell St., Suite 112
Williamson, Catherine C. .... '51 '76 C.758 A.B. L.575 J.D. 3210 Foxcroft Rd.
Williamson, F. Lane, (AV) .... '53 '78 C.1275 B.A. L.575 J.D. [Garlitz&W.]
Williams-Tracy, Jeffrey Scott, (BV) .... '69 '94 L.896 J.D. [Harkey L.]
Willis, Vachelle D. .... '— '04 C&L.575 B.A., J.D. [A Hedrick E.G.&K.]
Wilson, C. Michael, (AV) .... '— '76 C.576 B.S. L.228 J.D. [C.M.Wilson]
Wilson, Caroline T., (BV) '56 '87 C&L.575 B.A., J.D.
Corp. Coun., Charlotte-Mecklenburg Hosp. Auth.
Wilson, G. Gray, (AV) .... '51 '76 C.198 B.A. L.228 J.D. [Wilson&I.] ⊙
Wilson, Henry Hall, III, (AV) .... '51 '78 C.309 B.A. L.228 J.D. [Wilson&B.]
Wilson, Isvara M.A. ... '— '97 C.659 B.S. L.861 J.D. Asst. Gen. Coun., Bank of America
Wilson, J. Michael, (BV) .... '— '90 C&L.575 B.S.B.A., J.D. [Kennedy C.L.&H.]
Wilson, John Mark .... '72 '98 C.160 B.S.M.E. L.150 J.D. [A Alston&B.] (See Pat. Sect.)
Wilson, Michael C. '66 '91 C&L.846 B.B.A., J.D.
(adm. in TX; not adm. in NC) [Butrus K.W.V.] ⊙
Wilson, Michael L., (BV) .... '69 '96 C.1128 B.A. L.575 J.D. [Johnston,A.&H.]
Wilson, Richard W., (AV) .... '— '74 C&L.575 B.A., J.D. [Nexsen P.A.K.]
Wilson, Samuel A., III, (AV) .... '51 '75 C&L.575 A.B., J.D. [Thurman,W.&B.]

Wilson & Bos, (AV)
521 East Morehead Street, Suite 510, 28202
Telephone: 704-376-2225 Fax: 704-376-0703 URL: http://www.wilsboslaw.com
Email: hhwilson@wilsonbos.com URL: http://www.wilsonbos.com
Members of Firm: Henry Hall Wilson, III; Gerard Alford Bos.

(This Listing Continued)

Wilson & Bos (Continued)

General Civil and Commercial Litigation in all State and Federal Courts. Labor and Employment, Employment Discrimination, Wrongful Termination, Discrimination, Construction Law, Product Liability, Landlord and Tenant Law.

See Professional Biographies, CHARLOTTE, NORTH CAROLINA

Wilson, C. Michael, Attorney At Law, P.L.L.C., (AV) 216 North McDowell St., Suite 110

Wilson & Iseman, L.L.P., (AV)
435 E. Morehead Street, 28202 ⊙
Telephone: 704-331-9585 Fax: 704-331-0773
G. Gray Wilson.
General Civil Practice, including Civil Trial and Appellate Work in all State and Federal Courts, Administrative, Aviation, Commercial, Construction, Corporate, Employee Benefits and Executive Compensation, Employment, Criminal, Federal, State and Local Taxation, Insurance Defense, Personal Injury, Probate, Wills, Trusts and Estate Planning, Products Liability and Negligence Law, Professional Malpractice and Real Estate.
Winston-Salem Office: 110 Oakwood Drive, Suite 400, 27103. Telephone: 336-631-8866. Fax: 336-631-9770. URL: http://www.wilsonandiseman.com.

See Professional Biographies, CHARLOTTE, NORTH CAROLINA

Windell, Victoria S., (AV) '67 '93 C.896 B.S. L.1228 J.D. [Moore&V.P.]
Windham, Jonathan Charles '75 '03 C&L.575 B.S.B.A., J.D. [Horack,T.P.&L.]
Windle, Steele B. ("Al"), III, (AV) '56 '81 C.893 B.S. L.896 J.D. [Smith,C.&H.]
Winebarger, Tasha Leigh '79 '04 C.228 B.S. L.575 J.D. [Ⓐ Rayburn C.&D.]
Winiker, S. Frederick, III '66 '95 C.896 B.A. L.285 J.D. [Ⓐ Shumaker,L.&K.]
Winston, Ryland Addison, Jr. '62 '87 C.228 A.B. L.893 J.D. 1228 E. Moorehead St., Ste. 200

Wishart, Norris, Henninger & Pittman, P.A., (AV)
6832 Morrison Boulevard, 28211 ⊙
Telephone: 704-364-0010 FAX: 704-364-0569; 704-365-5945
Email: gary.smith@wnhplaw.com URL: http://www.wnhplaw.com
Robert B. Norris; Joseph B. Henninger, Jr. (Board Certified Specialist in Estate Planning and Probate Law, North Carolina State Board of Legal Specialization); Gregory L. Kunkleman; Steve C. Horowitz; June K. Allison; Garth K. Dunklin (Board Certified Specialist in Real Property Law - Residential, Commercial, Business and Industrial Transactions, North Carolina State Bar Board of Legal Specialization); William A. Navarro; David C. Boggs; Gary W. Smith. Associates: Megan Sadler; Richard A. Bigger, Jr. (Board Certified Specialist in Estate Planning and Probate Law, North Carolina State Board of Legal Specialization); Barbara Howie Lembo; Samuel Eric Bass; Steven B. Ockerman; Danica L. Little; Andrew M. McCullough; Gilbert (Trey) Baker. Of Counsel: George J. Miller.
Arbitration, Appellate Practice, Business Law, Civil Litigation, Commercial and Residential Real Estate, Contracts, Corporate and Commercial Law, Creditor Bankruptcy, Employment Law, Environmental Law, Estate Administration, Estate Planning, Family Law, Federal and State Taxation, Financial Transactions, Franchise Matters, Investments, Joint Ventures and Partnerships, Limited Liability Companies, Mediation, Mergers and Acquisitions, Securities, Succession Planning, Tax Controversy, Wills and Trusts, Zoning, Planning and Land Use, Criminal and Traffic Matters, Elder Law.
Burlington, North Carolina Office: 3120 South Church Street, P.O. Box 1998. Telephone: 336-584-3388. FAX: 336-584-3994.
Mebane, North Carolina Office: 111 East Center Street. Telephone: 919-304-4200. FAX: 919-304-4207.

See Professional Biographies, CHARLOTTE, NORTH CAROLINA

Witherspoon, James A. '64 '95 C.576 B.S.M.E. L.1059 J.D. [Ⓒ Womble C.S.&R.] (Pat.)
Wittenauer, Kenneth L., (BVⓉ) '55 '82 C.967 B.A. L.7 J.D. (adm. in OH; not adm. in NC) Sr. Coun., Continental Tire North America, Inc.
Wofford, J. Huntington, (CV) '71 '96 C.968 B.A. L.896 J.D. [Ⓐ Casstevens,H.G.&R.]
Wofford, Rebecca B. '72 '97 C.888 B.S. L.896 J.D. [Ⓐ Poyner&S.]
Wolkofsky, Evan N. '— '98 C.645 B.S. L.896 J.D. [Ⓐ Kennedy C.L.&H.]
Woltman, Amy McNutt '73 '04 C.951 B.A. L.1565 J.D. [Ⓐ Cadwalader,W.&T.]

Womble Carlyle Sandridge & Rice, (AV) BB
A Professional Limited Liability Company
3500 One Wachovia Center, 301 South College Street, 28202-6025 ⊙
Telephone: 704-331-4900 Fax: 704-331-4955
Email: lawyers@wcsr.com URL: http://www.wcsr.com
Resident Members: Garza Baldwin, III; Timothy G. Barber; G. Michael Barnhill; Gary D. Chamblee; Theodore F. Claypoole; Joe B. Cogdell, Jr.; Cornelius W. Coghill, III; Jim D. Cooley; James P. Cooney III; James E. Daniel; Bradford A. De Vore; Robert M. Donlon; J. Carlton Fleming; W. Clark Goodman; Debbie Weston Harden; Jeffrey S. Hay; Mark P. Henriques; Bobby D. Hinson; Mark J. Horoschak; Cyrus M. Johnson, Jr.; Jane Jeffries Jones; Donald C. Lampe (Also at Greensboro, North Carolina Office); James E. Lilly; Scott D. MacLatchie; Richard E. Morton; William Ruffin Pearce, Jr.; Richard L. Rainey; William C. Raper; J. Alexander Salisbury; Patricia Snyder; William R. Whitehurst (Also at Winston-Salem, North Carolina Office). Resident Associates: Brandy D. Berry; Stuart A. Brock (Also at Charlotte, North Carolina Office); Meredith P. Burbank; Erin E. Burke; Tricia Morvan Derr; Stanley B. Green (Also at Winston-Salem, North Carolina Office); Donna L. Hargrove; Matthew B. Homan; Seth Huffstetler; Sara R. Lincoln; Rachel N. Lokken; Meredith McKee (Not admitted in NC); K. Matthew Miller; Dawn T. Mistretta; Ross H. Parr; Sean F. Perrin; Robert John Phocas; O. Akomen Poku-Kankam; Philip S. Runkel; David B. Saye; Jason E. Sito (Not admitted in NC); Jolie Amie Tenholder; Bryan L. Tyson; Steven Williams ("Will") Walker; James B. Young, Jr.; Eric M.D. Zion. Senior Counsel: John N. Hunter; Katherine Thompson Lange. Resident Of Counsel: Bruce A. Buckley; Elizabeth C. Coss; Kenneth B. Oettinger, Jr.; Lori Reese Patton; Joyce E. Plyler; Thomas A. Price; John W. Springer; Todd C. Taylor; James A. Witherspoon.
General Civil Practice, Trial and Appellate Litigation. Administrative, Antitrust, Aviation, Banking, Bankruptcy and Creditor's Rights, Bond Financing, Civil Rights, Commercial, Construction, Consumer Lending, Corporate, E-Commerce, Employee Benefits, Environmental, Estate Planning, Family, Government Relations, Health Care, Insurance, Intellectual Property, International, Labor and Employment, Municipal, Negligence, Probate, Product Liability, Real Estate, Retirement Plans, Securities, Taxation, Toxic Tort, Wills and Trusts Law.
Representative Clients: Childress Klein Properties, Inc.; Food Lion, Inc.; J.A. Jones Construction Co.; Parkdale Mills, Inc.; Duke Power Co.; Bowles Hollowell Conner & Co.; ALLTEL Carolina, Inc.; Belk Store Services, Inc.; Philip Holzmann A.G.
Winston-Salem, North Carolina Office: One West Fourth Street, 27101. Telephone: 336-721-3600. Fax: 336-721-3660.
Raleigh, North Carolina Office: 2100 First Union Capitol Center, 150 Fayetteville Street Mall, P.O. Box 831. Telephone: 919-755-2100. Fax: 919-755-2150.
Research Triangle Park, North Carolina Office: 2530 Meridian Parkway, Suite 400 (Durham), 27713, P.O. Box 13069, Research Triangle Park, 27709. Telephone: 919-484-2300. Fax: 919-484-2340.
Greensboro, North Carolina Office: 300 North Greene Street. Telephone: 336-574-8030. Fax: 336-574-4520.
Atlanta, Georgia Office: One Atlantic Center, 1201 West Peachtree Street, Suite 3500. Telephone: 404-872-7000. Fax: 404-888-7490.
Other Atlanta, Georgia Office: Suite 404, 2296 Henderson Mill Road, N.E. Telephone: 770-492-9030. Fax: 770-492-9609.
Washington, D.C. Office: Suite 700, 1401 Eye Street. Telephone: 202-857-4400. Fax: 202-467-6910.
Greenville, South Carolina Office: 700 Poinsett Plaza, 104 South Main Street, P.O. Box 10208. Telephone: 864-255-5400. Fax: 864-255-5440.
Tysons Corner, Virginia Office: 8065 Leesburg Pike, Fourth Floor. Telephone: 703-790-3310. Fax: 703-790-2623.
Reviser of the North Carolina Law Digest for this Directory.

See Professional Biographies, CHARLOTTE, NORTH CAROLINA

Wood, Fred M., Jr., (AV) '63 '91 C.575 B.A. L.896 J.D. [Nelson M.R.&S.]
Wood, Gregory James '69 '02 C.1128 B.A. L.575 J.D. [Ⓐ Griffin,B.&P.]
Wood, James F., III, (BV) '56 '81 C.198 B.A. L.896 J.D. [Baucom,C.B.M.&W.]
Wood, Julianne G. '— '04 C.576 B.A. L.577 J.D. [Ⓐ Kennedy C.L.&H.]
Wood, Stacy K., (BV) '66 '91 C.575 B.S. L.659 J.D. [Parker,P.A.&B.] (ⓄColumbia, Spartanburg, SC)
Woodard, W. Samuel, (AV) '44 '69 C&L.575 B.S., J.D. [Parker,P.A.&B.]
Woodside, Michele '70 '97 C.454 B.S. L.1228 J.D. First Union Corp. (Contract Servs. Grp.)
Woodward, Danae Christina '66 '92 C.846 B.A. L.245 J.D. Asst. Gen. Coun., Duke Energy Corp.
Wooten, Marvin R. '28 '50 C&L.896 LL.B. U.S. Bkrptcy. Ct.
Wooten, Noelle E., (BV) '— '92 C.886 B.A. L.893 J.D. [Kilpatrick S.]
Workman, L. Kent '69 '00 C.152 B.S.E.E. L.893 J.D. [Ⓐ Parker,P.A.&B.]
Workman, William M. '— '97 1508 E. 4th St.
Worley, Amy R. '75 '00 C&L.469 B.A., J.D. [Ⓐ Helms M.&W.]
Wray, A. Victor, (AV) '43 '68 C.228 A.B. L.575 J.D. [Katten M.R.]
Wren, Elizabeth G., (AV) '— '80 C.1365 B.A. L.575 J.D. [Kilpatrick S.]
Wright, A. Cotten '51 '01 C.1038 B.A. L.575 J.D. [Ⓐ Grier F.&C.]
Wright, Barbara H., (BV) '61 '86 C.540 B.A. L.1128 J.D. V.P. & Asst. Gen. Coun., First Union Corp.
Wright, David C., III, (AV) '— '83 C.575 B.A. L.893 J.D. [Robinson,B.&H.]
Wright, James D., (BV) '— '97 C.576 B.S.E.E. L.575 J.D. [Ⓐ Kennedy C.L.&H.]
Wright, Julian H., Jr., (AV) '— '92 C.198 B.A. L.880 J.D. [Robinson,B.&H.]
Wright, L. Martin, III '53 '79 C&L.575 B.A., J.D. 2108 McLean Rd.‡
Wright, Melanie J. '62 '87 C&L.846 B.B.A., J.D. [Ⓐ Kirk P.&T.]
Wright, Melissa D. '74 '03 C.1318 B.A. L.192 J.D. [Ⓐ A.D.Taylor,Jr.]
Wright, Richard S. '71 '97 C&L.896 B.A., J.D. [James,M.&D.]
Wright, Roderick M., Jr. '72 '97 C.1378 B.S. L.575 J.D. [Wright]
Wright, Valerie B. '78 '03 C.597 B.S. L.145 J.D. [Ⓐ Hunton&W.]
Wright Law Firm, The 525 N. Tryon Street, 17th Floor
Wyatt, James F., III, (AV) '58 '82 C.880 B.S. L.228 J.D. [Wyatt&B.]

Wyatt & Blake, L.L.P., (AV) BB
435 East Morehead Street, 28202-2609
Telephone: 704-331-0767 Fax: 704-331-0773 URL: http://www.wyattandblakelaw.com
Email: jfw@wyattlaw.net URL: http://www.wyattandblake.com
James F. Wyatt, III; Robert A. Blake, Jr.
Criminal and Civil Trial Practice in all State and Federal Courts.

See Professional Biographies, CHARLOTTE, NORTH CAROLINA

Wyche, James R. '— '03 C.160 B.S. L.228 J.D. [Ⓐ Kennedy C.L.&H.]
Wyche, Paul B., Jr., (BV) '45 '71 C&L.575 A.B., J.D. Sr. V.P. & Assoc. Coun., Belk Stores Servs., Inc.
Wyrsch, Martha B., (AVⓉ) '58 '86 C.972 B.A. L.273 J.D. (adm. in CO; not adm. in NC) Pres. & CEO, Duke Energy Corp.
Yablonski, Joshua J. '72 '99 C.1372 B.A. L.823 J.D. [Ⓐ Cadwalader,W.&T.]

Yaeger, Laura L., (AV) '52 '77 C&L.575 B.A., J.D.
401 North Tryon Street, 10th Floor, 28202-2108
Telephone: 704-358-4984 Facsimile: 704-334-1785
Email: laura@lyaeger.com URL: http://www.lyaegerlaw.com
Business, Family Business, Limited Liability, Corporate Law, Trust and Estates, Estate Planning, Wills and Probate, Taxation.

See Professional Biographies, CHARLOTTE, NORTH CAROLINA

Yarbrough, Benjamin A. '67 '94 C.198 A.B. L.893 J.D. [Foodman,H.&K.]
Yarbrough, Scott '— '96 C.846 B.A. L.569 J.D. (adm. in NY; not adm. in NC) [Kennedy C.L.&H.]
Yates, Reginald L., (BV) '42 '73 C.1128 B.A. L.421 J.D. [R.L.Yates]
Yates, Reginald L., P.A., (BV) 1815 E. 7th St.
Yeager, J. Edward, Jr. '66 '93 C&L.575 B.A., J.D. 720 E. Fourth Street
Yoder, P. Marshall, (AV) '58 '87 C.575 B.A. L.1325 J.D. [Poyner&S.]
York, Gregory C., (BV) '56 '81 C&L.575 B.A., J.D. [Morris Y.W.S.&B.]
Yorke, John B., (AV) '54 '79 C.968 B.A. L.896 J.D. [Helms M.&W.]
Young, Anthony G. '54 '90 C.102 A.B. L.564 J.D. [A.G.Young]
Young, Constance L., (AV) '52 '88 C.612 B.A. L.862 J.D. [Poyner&S.]
Young, Courtauld McBryde '73 '01 C.198 B.A. L.896 J.D. [Ⓐ Poyner&S.]
Young, James B., Jr. '74 '01 C&L.260 B.S., J.D. [Ⓐ Womble C.S.&R.]
Young, Jay A. '69 '86 C.802 B.A. L.623 J.D. VP & Asst. Gen. Coun., Wachovia Corporation (Legal Department)
Young, Joe C., (BV) '40 '66 C&L.145 B.S., J.D. [J.C.Young]
Young, Terri Lynn '61 '88 C.228 A.B. L.896 J.D. 423 S. Sharon Amity Rd.
Young, Anthony G., P.A. 101 North McDowell Street, Suite 106
Young, Joe C., P.A., (BV) 1515 Mockingbird Lane, Ste. 520
Younger, Phillip E. '45 '77 C.277 B.S.I.M. L.969 J.D. (adm. in GA; not adm. in NC) 8525 Fairview Rd.
Youngs, Jennifer A., (BV) '70 '97 C&L.575 B.A., B.A. Asst. U.S. Atty.
Yount, Jacqueline M. '74 '01 C.228 B.A. L.893 J.D. [Ⓐ Hunton&W.]
Yurko, Lyle J., (AV) '48 '76 C.575 B.A. L.425 J.D. [Yurko&Assoc.]
Yurko & Associates, P.A., (AV) 402 West Trade Street, Suite 101

Zaman, Karen, & Associates, (BV) '51 '79 C.228 B.A. L.575 J.D.
P.O. Box 16577, 28209
Telephone: Toll Free: 866-960-8662 Fax: Toll Free: 866-960-8664
URL: http://www.karenzamanandassoc.com
Medical Malpractice, Personal Injury, Auto Accidents, Traumatic Brain Injuries, Birth Injuries, Head Injuries, Nursing Home Negligence, Wrongful Death.

See Professional Biographies, CHARLOTTE, NORTH CAROLINA

Zanoni, Melinda Morris '69 '94 C&L.339 B.S., J.D. RCG Companies Inc.
Zarsadias, Isidore T. '68 '94 C.645 B.S. L.7 J.D. [Dean&G.]
Zeller, Michael E. '67 '93 C.867 B.A. L.831 J.D. [Moore&V.P.]
Zhao, Laura Kay '67 '01 C.608 B.A. L.989 J.D. 6600 Summer Darby Lane
Ziemba, Heather Manry '71 '96 C.228 A.B. L.880 J.D. Legal Servs. of Southern Piedmont, Inc.
Zimmermann, Cynthia Ann Brewer '53 '86 C.1128 B.A. L.790 J.D. (adm. in SC; not adm. in NC) 2800 Edsel Pl.‡
Zion, Eric M.D. '75 '01 C.576 B.A. L.1119 J.D. [Ⓐ Womble C.S.&R.]
Zolfaghari, Alexander '66 '93 C.1036 B.A. L.659 J.D. (adm. in PA; not adm. in NC) [Ⓒ Cadwalader,W.&T.]
Zolot, Miranda M. '75 '98 C.94 B.A. L.228 J.D. (adm. in NJ; not adm. in NC) [Ⓐ McGuireWoods]
Zurosky, Kirk Steven, (CV) '69 '96 C.1134 B.S. L.818 J.D. [Tippens&Z.]

CHEROKEE, —, *Swain Co.*

Kilbourne, James W., Jr. '71 '97 C.968 B.A. L.575 J.D. Tribal Prosecutor, Eastern Band of Cherokee Indians
Lambert, Patrick Henry '63 '94 C.834 B.S. L.575 J.D. Exec. Dir., Cherokee Tribal Gaming Comm.
Vespereny, Linda E. '56 '81 C.502 B.S. L.273 J.D. Off. of Atty. Gen.

CHERRYVILLE, 5,361, *Gaston Co.*

Allran, William J., III, (BV) '46 '72 C&L.575 A.B., J.D. Off. of Dist. Atty.
Black, Mel '64 '98 L.574 J.D. [A.M.Black,Jr.]

Black, A. Melton, Jr., Attorney at Law, PA
201 North Cherry Street, P.O. Box 459, 28021
Telephone: 704-435-0753 Fax: 704-435-8181
Email: mel@melblack.us URL: http://www.melblack.us
Mel Black.
Administrative Law, Licensing Law, Real Estate.
See Professional Biographies, CHERRYVILLE, NORTH CAROLINA

Grigg, Eugene D., (AV) .... '43 '73 C.1228 B.A. L.575 J.D. P.O. Box 206
Huffstetler, Palmer E., (BV) .... '37 '61 C&L.896 B.A., LL.B. Hwy 150
Huffstetler, Palmer E., Jr., (BV) .... '62 '87 C&L.896 B.A., J.D. [Huffstetler]

Huffstetler Law Offices, (BV)
106 North Cherry Street, 28021-2903
Telephone: 704-435-4907; 800-259-9552 Fax: 704-435-1275
Email: huffstetler@lawyers.com URL: http://www.lawyers.com/huffstetler
Palmer E. Huffstetler, Jr.
General Practice, Real Estate, Loan Closings, Estates, Wills, Criminal Law, Traffic, Uncontested Divorce, Separation Agreements, Business Law.
See Professional Biographies, CHERRYVILLE, NORTH CAROLINA

Kirby, Robert W. .... '28 '52 C.316 A.B. L.575 LL.B. Ret. Supr. Ct. J.

CHINA GROVE, 3,616, *Rowan Co.*

Brooke, Carole Carlton, (BV) .... '55 '82 C.575 B.S. L.1228 J.D. [Brooke&B.]
Brooke, Thomas M., (BV) .... '52 '80 C.232 B.A. L.1228 J.D. [Brooke&B.]
Brooke & Brooke, (BV) .... 101 South Main Street

CLAREMONT, 980, *Catawba Co.*

Priestley, Meredith O. '78 '04
C.404 B.A. L.644 J.D. Corp. Coun., Catawba Rental Company, Inc.

CLARKTON, 739, *Bladen Co.*

McDougald, John G. .... '46 '73 C.575 A.B. L.896 J.D. P.O. Box 386‡

CLAYTON, 6,973, *Johnston Co.*

Conaway, Amy .... '— '04 C.201 B.A. L.1228 J.D. [Hales&C.P.]
De Laine, Allan C., (CV) .... '55 '81 C&L.228 A.B., J.D. P.O. Box 846
Goodman, Cynthia Stephens '54 '79 C.1059 B.B.A. L.245 J.D.
(adm. in GA; not adm. in NC) 2199 Government Rd.
Hales, Melissa Iversen .... '— '04 C.228 B.A. L.1228 J.D. [Hales&C.P.]

Hales & Conaway, PLLC, The Law Offices of
490 Highway 42 West, P.O. Box 1025, 27528
Telephone: 919-359-3093 Toll Free: 1-877-359-3093 Fax: 919-359-3095
URL: http://www.halesandconawaylaw.com
Melissa Iversen Hales; Amy Conaway.
Family Law, Divorce, Adoption, Custody, Child Support, Premarital Agreements, Separation Agreements, Criminal Defense, Social Security Disability, Collections, Debtor, Creditor, Juvenile Law, Estate Administration and Estate Planning, Civil Litigation, Workers Compensation, Personal Injury, Traffic, DWI.
Clinton, North Carolina Office: 100 Fayetteville Street, Suite 103, 28328. Telephone: 919-359-3093. Toll Free: 877-359-3093.
See Professional Biographies, CLAYTON, NORTH CAROLINA

Kristoff, Lawrence E., II, (BV) .... '69 '94 C.692 L.1345 J.D. [Kristoff]
Kristoff Law Offices, (BV) .... P.O. Box 495
Neighbors, Patrick Edward .... '68 '94 C&L.893 B.S., J.D. [Neighbors&Assoc.]★
Neighbors & Associates .... 106 Holly Point Place

Pleasant, Robert S., Law Office of, (BV) '69 '94 C&L.575 B.A., J.D.
224 West Main Street, 27520
Mailing Address: P.O. Box 1191, Clayton, NC 27528
Telephone: 919-550-5677 Fax: 919-550-7677
Email: robert.pleasant@earthlink.net URL: http://www.rpleasantlaw.com
Personal Injury, Wrongful Death, Auto Accidents, Workers Compensation, Criminal, DWI, Traffic Offenses, Family Law, Divorce, Child Custody.
See Professional Biographies, CLAYTON, NORTH CAROLINA

Price, Richard M., (BV) .... '56 '81 C.232 B.S. L.45 J.D. 11181 Hwy. 70 West
Ragland, Gary W., (BV) .... '47 '79 C.316 B.A. L.1228 J.D. 446 E. Main St.
Romary, Peter John Michael, (BV) .... '71 '94 L.575 J.D. [Tanner&R.] ⊙

Stewart Law Office, PLLC
(See Cary)

Tanner, Jeremy K., (CV) .... '69 '95 C.1130 B.A. L.1338 J.D. [Tanner&R.]
Tanner & Romary, P.A., (BV) .... Highway 70 West (⊙Greenville)
Tew, Allen R., (AV) .... '44 '71 C.575 A.B. L.790 J.D. [A.R.Tew]

Tew, Allen R., P.A., (AV) [BR]
202 South Lombard Street, P.O. Box 145, 27528
Telephone: 919-553-6142; 553-2143 Fax: 919-553-8742
Email: allen@atewlawfirm.com URL: http://www.lawyers.com/allentewpa
Allen R. Tew.
General and Trial Practice in all State and Federal Courts, Civil Litigation, Personal Injury Law, Automobile Accidents, Wrongful Death, Domestic Relations and Real Estate, Construction Litigation, Mediation.
See Professional Biographies, CLAYTON, NORTH CAROLINA

Underwood, R. Dannette, (BV) .... '63 '88 C&L.1228 B.A., J.D. [Underwood]
Underwood Law Office, (BV) .... P.O. Box 141

CLEMMONS, 13,827, *Forsyth Co.*

Brewer, Edward Y., (BV) .... '41 '72 C.838 A.B. L.575 J.D. [Davis&B.]
Crotts, Milton B. .... '42 '67 C.296 B.A. L.896 J.D. 1221 Brook Acres Trail‡
Davis, Gilbert T., Jr., (BV) .... '42 '71 C&L.575 A.B., J.D. [Davis&B.]
Davis and Brewer, (BV) .... P.O. Box 786
Frankel, Jill K. .... '65 '90 C.788 A.B.A. L.1365 J.D. [Ⓐ W.E.Kasper]
Goldsmith, Earl J., Jr., (AVⓉ) '24 '50 C&L.150 B.B.A., LL.B.
(adm. in OH; not adm. in NC) [Goldsmith&T.]
Goldsmith & Tuch, (AVⓉ) .... P.O. Box 1006
Kasper, Warren E., (BV) .... '51 '78 C.576 B.A. L.896 J.D. [W.E.Kasper]
Kasper, Warren E., P.A., (BV) .... 3626 Clemmons Rd.
Scales, Archibald H., III, (BV) .... '41 '66 C.198 A.B. L.575 LL.B. 2601 Burke Farm Rd.
Sipprell, Kyla J. .... '71 '96 C&L.575 B.A., J.D. [Ⓐ W.E.Kasper]

Sloan, Norman L., (BV) '47 '72 C.575 A.B. L.896 J.D.
3550 Clemmons Road, Suite 110, 27012
Telephone: 336-748-0008 Fax: 336-766-0903
Email: nlsloanlaw@aol.com URL: http://www.nsloan.com
General and Complex Litigation, Franchise Law and Franchising, Corporate Law, Business Law, Commercial Law, Personal Injury, Trademarks, Copyrights, Intellectual Property Law, Entertainment Law, Unfair Trade Practice Law, and Bankruptcy.
Representative Clients: Leonard Aluminum Utility Building, Inc.; Doctor's Associates Inc.; Subway Restaurants, Inc.; Meridian Aerospace Group, Ltd.; Longhorn Finance, LLC; Slick Enterprises; Bagel Station, Inc.; MRV International, LLC; Lydall, Inc.; Welch-Fulk Enterprises, Inc. References: Branch Bank & Trust; Wachovia Bank & Trust.
See Professional Biographies, CLEMMONS, NORTH CAROLINA

Womble, T. Dan, (BV) .... '61 '86 C&L.896 B.A., J.D. 3802-A Clemmons Road

CLINTON, * 8,600, *Sampson Co.*

Bacon, William M., III, Attorney at Law, (CV) '46 '72
C.198 A.B. L.575 J.D. 101 W. Main St.
Britt, Walter T. .... '13 '37 C&L.575 A.B., LL.B. P.O. Box 137‡
Butler, Gregory C., (BV) .... '59 '85 C&L.575 A.B., J.D. Asst. Dist. Atty.
Butler, Jesse L. .... '29 '58 C&L.575 LL.B. 404 W. Main St.‡

Clark, William E.
(See Fayetteville)

David, G. Phillip .... '59 '88 C.232 B.S.B.A. L.574 J.D. [David&Assoc.] ⊙

David and Associates, pllc
610 Beaman Street, 28328 ⊙
Telephone: 910-592-8400 Toll Free: 1-800-856-9927
Email: aeverhart@davidandassociates.com URL: http://www.wilmingtonpiattorneys.com
G. Phillip David.
Personal Injury, Medical Malpractice, Wrongful Death, Products Liability, Workers Compensation, Aviation, Airplane Crashes, Negligence, Class Actions, Maritime Accidents, Boating Accidents, Bicycle Accidents, Motorcycle Accidents, Truck Accidents, School Bus Accidents, Railroad Accidents, Dog Bites, Slip and Fall, Birth Trauma, Brain Injury, Spinal Injury, Head Injury, Catastrophic Injury, Vehicular Homicide, Personal Injury Mediation, Products Liability, Drug and Medical Device Litigation, Product Defects, Automobile Liability, Motorcycle Products Liability, Amusement Park Liability, Hotel Liability, Marina Liability, Sports Injury.
Jacksonville, North Carolina Office: 405-B Western Boulevard. 28546. Telephone: 910-219-4878.
Supply, North Carolina Office: Highway 17. 28462. Telephone: 910-754-8465.
Wallace, North Carolina Office: 107 North Norwood Street. 28466. Telephone: 910-285-8777.
Wilmington, North Carolina Office: 1516 Dawson Street. 28401. Telephone: 910-251-8088.
Winston-Salem, North Carolina Office: 1100-A South Stratford Road. 27103. Telephone: 336-354-1040.
Greensboro, North Carolina Office: 529 College Road. Suite G. 27410. Telephone: 336-354-1040.
See Professional Biographies, CLINTON, NORTH CAROLINA

Faircloth, Croom M., (AV) .... '10 '34 C.16 B.S. L.896 [Faircloth&F.]
Faircloth, Cyrus J., (AV) .... '36 '60 C&L.896 B.S., LL.B. 114 Lisbon St.
Faircloth, Wilbert M., (AV) .... '42 '67 C&L.896 B.A., J.D. [Faircloth&F.]
Faircloth & Faircloth, (AV) .... 108 W. Elizabeth St.
Fowler, Miles B., (AV) .... '30 '56 C.198 B.S. L.575 LL.B. 126 Elizabeth Street
Griffin, Gregory T., Attorney at Law .... '53 '79 C.34 B.A. L.1228 J.D. 211 E. Main St.

Hales & Conaway, PLLC, The Law Offices of
(See Clinton)

Hobson, David H., (BV) .... '70 '95 C.576 B.A. L.1228 J.D. [Johnson,P.&H.]
Holland, Roscoe "Ross" M., Jr., (BV) '55 '81 C.575 B.A. L.1228 J.D.
[Holland,P.H.&S.]

Holland, Poole, Holland & Sanderson, P.A., (AV)
212 West Main Street, P.O. Box 1046, 28328
Telephone: 910-592-5751 Fax: 910-592-7127
Email: rmholland@intrstar.net URL: http://www.attorneyshphs.com
R. Maurice Holland (1922-1996); Billie L. Poole; Roscoe "Ross" M. Holland, Jr.; Hebern "Sandy" W. Sanderson, Jr.
General Civil and Criminal Practice. Trials in all State Courts. Negligence, Probate, Real Estate, Contract and Insurance Law, Domestic Relations, Traffic Violations, DWI, Personal Injury, Workers Compensation, Social Security Disability.
Representative Clients: First-Citizens Bank & Trust Co.; Boren Clay Products Co.; Plastic Tubing, Inc.; Southern National Bank; Star Telephone Membership Corp.
Approved Attorneys for: Lawyers Title Insurance Corp.; Cape Fear Farm Service; First Title Insurance Co.
See Professional Biographies, CLINTON, NORTH CAROLINA

Howard, Timothy W., (BV) .... '49 '74 C.886 B.A. L.838 J.D. 312 College Street
Johnson, Dale P., (AV) .... '43 '68 C&L.575 A.B., J.D. [Johnson,P.&H.]

Johnson, Parsons & Hobson, P.L.L.C., (AV)
500 College Street, P.O. Drawer 1049, 28329-4012
Telephone: 910-592-7066 Fax: 910-592-9144 URL: http://www.johnsonandparsons.com
URL: http://www.lawyers.com/johnson&parsons
Dale P. Johnson; W. Douglas Parsons (Board Certified Specialist in State Criminal Law and Federal Criminal Law, North Carolina State Board of Legal Specialization); David H. Hobson.
General Civil and Criminal Practice. Trials in all State and Federal Courts. Negligence, Workers Compensation, Insurance and Personal Injury Law.
Reference: United Carolina Bank.
See Professional Biographies, CLINTON, NORTH CAROLINA

Jones, D. Stephen .... '24 '53 C&L.575 B.S., J.D. 312 College St.
Kirby, Albert D., Jr., (BV) .... '58 '87 C.896 B.A. L.1228 J.D. [Kirby]

Kirby Law Firm, The, (BV)
118 Lisbon Street, P.O. Box 1250, 28329-1250
Telephone: 910-592-4481 Facsimile: 910-596-0159
Email: kirbylaw@earthlink.net URL: http://www.kirbylawfirm.com
Member: Albert D. Kirby, Jr.
Personal Injury, Workers Compensation, Criminal Defense, Domestic Relations.
See Professional Biographies, CLINTON, NORTH CAROLINA

Lee, Harry M., (AV) .... '24 '51 C&L.896 B.S., LL.B. 306 Herring St.
Lockerman, Ted B., (AV) .... '36 '61 C&L.896 B.A., LL.B. P.O. Box 27
McCullen Weddle, Shurley R. '74 '99
C.471 B.A. L.1228 J.D. Asst. Clerk of Ct., Sampson Co.
Paderick, Clifton W., (BV) '38 '62
C&L.575 B.S., J.D. Pres., Sampson Community College
Parker, John R., Jr., (BV) .... '31 '61 C&L.575 A.B. 200 W. Main St.
Parsons, W. Douglas, (AV) .... '50 '75 C.575 A.B. L.896 J.D. [Johnson,P.&H.]
Poole, Billie L., (AV) .... '36 '65 C&L.896 B.S., J.D. [Holland,P.H.&S.]
Railey, Corinne A. .... '69 '98 C&L.352 B.A., J.D. [Ⓐ B.R.Warrick]

Rivenbark, Christina, & Associates, (CV) '62 '87 C&L.575 B.A., J.D.
603A Northeast Boulevard, 28328 ⊙
Telephone: 1-800-777-5159
Personal Injury, Automobile Accidents, Workers Compensation, Wrongful Death, Medical Malpractice, Slip and Fall, Criminal Law, Driving While Intoxicated, Traffic Violations, Drug Offenses, Misdemeanors, Felonies, Sexual Assaults, Assaults, Burglary, Motorcycle Accidents, Head Injuries.
Wilmington, North Carolina Office: 4009 Oleander Drive, 28403. Telephone: 1-800-806-8896.
Garner, North Carolina Office: 5533 NC Highway 42 West, 27529. Telephone: 1-800-561-9221.
See Professional Biographies, CLINTON, NORTH CAROLINA

Roberson, Keisha Nicole .... '75 '00 C&L.574 B.A., J.D. P.O. Box 1250
Sanderson, Hebern "Sandy" W., Jr., (BV) '66 '92
C.576 B.A. L.1228 J.D. [Holland,P.H.&S.]
Sutton, William B., Jr., (BV) .... '55 '81 C.228 B.S.E. L.1228 J.D. 600 College St.
Thagard, Leonard W. .... '44 '75 C.1309 B.A. L.575 J.D. Dist. J.

Warrick, Benjamin R., (AV) '36 '67 C&L.575 A.B., J.D.
609 College Street, P.O. Box 1216, 28328
Telephone: 910-590-2900 Fax: 910-590-2555
Email: bwarrick.01*@earthlink.net
Associate: Corinne A. Railey.

(This Listing Continued)

Warrick, Benjamin R. (Continued)

General Civil Practice. Trials in all State Courts. Family, Juvenile Law, Probate, Real Estate and Corporation Law.

See Professional Biographies, CLINTON, NORTH CAROLINA

White, Mario M. .... '66 '92 C&L.574 B.S., J.D. P.O. Box 957
Wright, Benjamin L., (BV) .... '55 '80 C&L.1228 B.S., J.D. [B.Wright]
Wright, Benjamin, (BV) .... 600 College St.

CLYDE, 1,324, *Haywood Co.*

Brown, Bruce B. .... '21 '48 C&L.896 LL.B. 548 Mulberry St.‡
Patton, Roy H., Jr., (BV) .... '43 '69 C.1318 B.S. L.575 J.D. [R.H.Patton,Jr.]
Patton, Roy H., Jr., Law Firm, (BV) .... 5593 Old Clyde Road

COATS, 1,845, *Harnett Co.*

Jones, Norwood E., Jr., (BV) ....'53 '79 C.575 B.S. L.1228 J.D. 302 Cottle Lake Dr.

COLUMBIA, * 836, *Tyrrell Co.*

Ogletree, Charles W., (AV) ....'39 '65 C&L.575 A.B., J.D. 211 W. Main St.
Wheless, Dwight H., (BV) ....'40 '67 C&L.575 A.B., J.D. [Wheless&W.] ⊙

Wheless & Wheless, PLLC, (BV)
402 Main Street, 27925 ⊙
Telephone: 252-796-5500 Fax: 252-796-1154
URL: http://www.whelesslawfirm.com
Dwight H. Wheless.
Traffic Violations, General Practice. Real Estate, Driving While Intoxicated, Civil Litigation, County Government Law, Insurance Defense, Real Estate Development, Residential Real Estate Development, Waterfront Development, Zoning Law, Ship Documentation and Ship Finance and Family Law.
References: East Carolina Bank; Bank of America; RBC Centura; Wachovia Bank; Cooperative Savings & Loan Assn.
Manteo, North Carolina Office: 101 South Virginia Dare Road, P.O. Box 500, 27954. Telephone: 252-473-5500. Fax: 252-473-1154.

See Professional Biographies, COLUMBIA, NORTH CAROLINA

COLUMBUS, * 992, *Polk Co.*

Blanchard, Newman & Hayes
(See Hendersonville)

Gilliam, Thomas A. .... '40 '65 C&L.575 A.B., LL.B. P.O. Box 582★

Haynes, R. Anderson
(See Tryon)

Schappert, Joseph M. '23 '52 C.994 B.A. L.273 J.D.
(adm. in NY; not adm. in NC) 71 Mountain Laurel Dr.

CONCORD, * 55,977, *Cabarrus Co.*

Adams, Scott M., (CV) .... '71 '97 C.945 B.A. L.896 J.D. [Patterson&A.P.] ⊙
Aiken, Victoria S. .... '68 '92 C&L.790 B.A., J.D. 555 Concord Parkway, South
Alcorn, Susan Leigh Boylan .... '53 '01 C.494 B.S. L.896 J.D. [S.B.Alcorn]
Alcorn, Susan B. .... 908 Tartan Lane N.W.
Armistead, David H. .... '71 '97 C.880 B.A. L.280 J.D. CT Communications, Inc.
Arrowood, William D. .... '36 '60 C&L.896 B.A., J.D. 20 Cabarrus Ave. E.
Barnes, Lani Michelle '68 '93 C.679 B.A. L.345 J.D.
(adm. in GA; not adm. in NC) 78 Buffalo Ave., Ste. 200
Barnhardt, John M. .... '36 '61 C&L.575 A.B., LL.B. P.O. Box 163

Basinger, John A., Attorney at Law
(See Salisbury)

Belo, Gordon L., (BV) .... '46 '74 C.575 B.S. L.896 J.D. [Plummer,B.&R.]
Birmingham, Suzanne Hornaday, (BV) .... '52 '81 C.1128 B.A. L.228 J.D. [R.M.Critz]
Black, David H., (BV) .... '55 '81 C&L.575 B.S., J.D. [Black,R.R.&G.]

Black, Rogers, Ruth, & Grossman, P.L.L.C., (BV)
47 Union Street North, P.O. Box 770, 28026-0770
Telephone: 704-788-3900 Fax: 704-782-6288
Members of Firm: David H. Black; William F. Rogers, Jr.; Hilton L. Ruth, III; Steven A. Grossman; Aimee E. Cain.
Personal Injury, Automobile Accidents, Dog Bites, Slip and Fall, Wrongful Death, Social Security Disability, Criminal Law, Driving While Intoxicated (DWI), Drug Crimes, Traffic Violations, Family Law, Adoptions, Child Support, Child Custody, Divorce, Real Estate, Eminent Domain, Landlord Tenant, Business, Corporate, Limited Liability, Trust and Estates, Estate Planning, Wills and Probate.

See Professional Biographies, CONCORD, NORTH CAROLINA

Blanton Law Firm, P.A.
(See Salisbury)

Boger, John R., Jr., (AV) .... '29 '52 C&L.228 B.A., LL.B. [⊡ Hartsell&W.]

Bolduc Law Firm, The, PLLC
(See Charlotte)

Borras, Christopher W. '70 '96
C.160 B.S. L.575 J.D. Investment Rep., Edward Jones Investments‡
Cain, Aimee E. .... '64 '97 C.1494 B.A. L.1522 J.D. [Black,R.R.&G.]
Cansler, Robert E. .... '51 '78 C.48 B.A. L.201 J.D. Chief of Police
Carroll, Phillip G., (BV) ....'40 '69 C&L.575 B.S., J.D. 147 Church St. N.E.
Carter, Wanda L. ....'63 '89 C.839 B.A. L.802 J.D. Legal Servs. of Southern Piedmont

Cloninger Law Office
(See Mount Pleasant)

Combs, Randall R. .... '59 '86 C.896 B.A. L.1228 J.D. Dist. J.
Conner, Taylor Laumann .... '77 '02 C.575 B.A. L.1228 J.D. [T.L.Conner]
Conner, Taylor Laumann, P.A. .... 125 Union St. S., Ste. 30

Conrad Trosch & Kemmy, P.A.
(See Charlotte)

Conroy, Carl S. .... '58 '91 C&L.823 B.A., J.D. 154 Cabarrus Ave. E.
Cook, Brandy Lea .... '— '01 C.125 B.A. L.607 J.D. Pros.
Cooper, Cynthia Penney '51 '87 C.1331 B.A. L.1051 J.D.
(adm. in KS; not adm. in NC) P.O. Box 3131‡
Critz, Robert M., (BV) .... '48 '73 C.575 A.B. L.500 J.D. [R.M.Critz]
Critz, Robert M., P.A., Law Offices of, (BV) .... 33 Church St. S.E.
Cruse, Kenneth B. .... '29 '51 C&L.75 A.B., LL.B. P.O. Box 67

Davis, Amy S. '68 '96 C.1288 B.S. L.1339 J.D.
235 Cabarras Avenue East, 28025
Mailing Address: P.O. Box 1394, Concord, NC 28026
Telephone: 704-784-9440 Fax: 704-721-5175
URL: http://www.amysdavislaw.com
Personal Bankruptcy, Business Bankruptcy, Foreclosures, Adoptions, Child Custody, Child Support.

See Professional Biographies, CONCORD, NORTH CAROLINA

Davis, James C. .... '29 '60 C.125 B.A. L.896 J.D. Sr. Resident Supr. Ct. J.
Davis, Samuel F., Jr., (AV) ....'47 '72 C.198 A.B. L.575 J.D. [Hartsell&W.]
Denny, Mark S., (CV) ....'71 '97 C.925 B.S.B.A. L.615 J.D. 4400 Republic Ct. N.W.
Eaves, Karla G. .... '72 '03 C.198 B.A. L.692 J.D. [Ⓐ Hartsell&W.]
Elliott, J. Maxton .... '28 '60 C&L.575 B.S., J.D. [Hartsell&W.] ‡

Elliott Law Firm, P.C.
(See Huntersville)

Ferguson, Edwin H., Jr., (BV) .... '46 '74 C&L.896 B.B.A., J.D. [Ferguson&S.]
Ferguson & Scarbrough, P.A., (BV) .... 65 McCachern Boulevard, S.E.

Gach Law Firm, PLLC
(See Charlotte)

Goldsmith, Esten H., (BV) .... '45 '91 C.896 B.A. L.904 J.D. [Goldsmith]
Goldsmith Law Office, (BV) .... 81 McCachern Boulevard
Goode, David L. .... '63 '90 C.575 A.B. L.902 J.D. 8385 Bampton Drive
Grant, Adam C., Jr. .... '47 '71 C&L.896 B.A., J.D. Dist. J.
Grant, Wesley B., (AV) .... '43 '69 C.228 A.B. L.896 J.D. [W.B.Grant]
Grant, Wesley B., P.A., (AV) .... 49 Means Avenue, S.E.
Grossman, Steven A., (BV) .... '52 '77 C&L.896 B.A., J.D. [Black,R.R.&G.]
Hamby, William G., Jr., (BV) .... '56 '83 C.575 B.A. L.896 J.D. 45 Church St., S.E.
Harris, Larry E., (BV) .... '39 '65 C.575 A.B. L.896 LL.B. 92 Union St. S.
Hartsell, Fletcher L., Jr., (AV) .... '47 '72 C.198 A.B. L.575 J.D. [Hartsell&W.]

Hartsell & Williams, P.A., (AV)
71 McCachern Boulevard, S.E., P.O. Box 368, 28025 ⊙
Telephone: 704-786-5161 Facsimile: 704-788-8058
Email: hwpalaw@hwpalaw.com URL: http://www.hwpalaw.com
Luther T. Hartsell (1870-1961); Luther T. Hartsell, Jr. (1902-1961); John Hugh Williams (1913-1995); John Sharpe Hartsell (1907-2004); Fletcher L. Hartsell, Jr.; Samuel F. Davis, Jr.; Herbert J. White, Sr.; David C. Williams; K. Todd Phillips. Associate: Karla G. Eaves. Of Counsel: John R. Boger, Jr. Retired: J. Maxton Elliott (Retired).
Languages: English and Spanish.
General Civil and Criminal Practice in all Courts. Workers Compensation, Corporation, Insurance, Real Estate, Taxation, Probate Law, Estate Planning, Family Law and Motor Sports (Racing).
Representative Clients: First Charter National Bank; Southern Railway Co.; Nationwide Insurance Co.; Travelers Indemnity Co.; The Shoe Show, Inc.; S & D Coffee, Inc.; Cabarrus County Board of Education; North East Medical Center; Lawyers Title Insurance Corp.; Cabarrus County.
Kannapolis, North Carolina Office: 708 McLain Road, P.O. Box 2, 28082. Telephone: 704-932-3157. Facsimile: 704-932-9597.

See Professional Biographies, CONCORD, NORTH CAROLINA

Hastings, Randell F., The Law Office of, (BV) '53 '78 C.198 B.A. L.575 J.D.
77 McCachern Boulevard S.E., 28025
Mailing Address: P.O. Box 666, Concord, NC 28026-0666
Telephone: 704-786-4567 Fax: 704-786-2664
Email: rfhastings@aol.com URL: http://www.rhastingslaw.com
Family Law, Divorce, Child Custody, Child Support, Visitation Rights, Domestic Violence, Personal injury, Automobile Accidents, Wrongful Death, Civil Litigation.

See Professional Biographies, CONCORD, NORTH CAROLINA

Hawkins, Timothy M., (AV) .... '48 '73 C&L.575 B.A., J.D. [Koontz,H.N.&M.]
Hazzard, John P., IV '34 '64 C.575 B.A. L.790 LL.B.
(adm. in SC; not adm. in NC) 134 Wilkinson Ct., S.E.‡

Helms, Henderson & Associates, P.A.
(See Charlotte)

Irvin, Howard S., (BV) .... '41 '65 C&L.575 A.B., LL.B. 43 Church St.

Johnson, James C., Jr., Attorney at Law, (AV) '35 '62 C.835 B.S. L.896 LL.B.
400 Church Street, North, 28025
Telephone: 704-784-8404 Fax: 704-784-8714
Email: jjohnson01@vnet.net URL: http://www.lawyers.com/jamescjohnson
Criminal Law, DWI, Drug Crimes, Felonies, Homicide, Misdemeanors, Parole, Traffic Violations.

See Professional Biographies, CONCORD, NORTH CAROLINA

Johnson, Michael A., Jr., (CV) '58 '84 C.1128 B.A. L.1345 J.D.
153 Church Street, N.E.
Jones, Jeffrey D., (BV) .... '65 '90 C.1318 B.A. L.1228 J.D. P.O. Box 382

King Law Firm, The, PLLC
(See Huntersville)

Kluttz, Reamer, Hayes, Randolph & Adkins, L.L.P.
(See Salisbury)

Koontz, K. Michael, (AV) .... '36 '65 C.404 L.896 LL.B. [Koontz,H.N.&M.]

Koontz, Hawkins, Nixon & Miller, (AV)
2 Church Street, S.E., P.O. Box 744, 28026-0744
Telephone: 704-786-3145 Fax: 704-782-4314
Email: khnlaw@vnet.net URL: http://www.concordnclaw.com
Members of Firm: K. Michael Koontz; Timothy M. Hawkins; M. Wayne Nixon, Jr.; Duane S. Miller.
Civil Trial Practice, Criminal Trial Practice, Driving While Intoxicated, Drug Crimes, Juvenile Crimes, Parole and Probation, Traffic Violations, White Collar Crimes, Personal Injury, Automobile Accidents, Wrongful Death, Social Security Disability, Workers Compensation, Family Law, Divorce, Domestic Violence, Child Support, Child Custody.

See Professional Biographies, CONCORD, NORTH CAROLINA

Lauro, Linda M. Boswell '63 '89 C.573 B.A. L.1187 J.D.
(adm. in NY; not adm. in NC) 1507 Chadmore Lane‡
Lueders, G. Spencer, Jr. .... '— '99 C&L.790 B.S., J.D. NASCAR, Inc. (Pat.)
Marshall, Huey B., (BV) .... '52 '84 C.896 B.A. L.574 J.D. Asst. Dist. Atty.
Martin, G. Lee, (BV) .... '65 '90 C.896 B.A. L.575 J.D. 908 Copperfield Boulevard
McGee, Martin B., (BV) .... '67 '95 C.575 B.A. L.896 J.D. Dist. Ct. J.
Medlin, Steven L., (BV) .... '52 '77 C.1128 B.A. L.575 J.D. [Medlin&M.]
Medlin & Medlin, PA, (BV) .... 43 Union St. S.
Miller, Duane S., (BV) .... '66 '91 C.1128 B.S. L.575 J.D. [Koontz,H.N.&M.]
Mills, William L., III, (BV) .... '54 '80 C.575 B.A. L.896 J.D. [Mills L.]

Mills Law, P.A., (BV)
45 Church Street, S.E., 28026-0528
Mailing Address: P.O. Box 528, Concord, NC 28026-0528
Telephone: 704-782-3315 Fax: 704-782-0436
URL: http://www.millslawfirmpa.com
William L. Mills, III (Board Certified Specialist in Estate Planning and Probate Law, North Carolina State Board of Legal Specialization).
Trusts and Estates, Asset Protection, Estate Planning, Probate, Taxation, Corporate Law, Real Estate.

See Professional Biographies, CONCORD, NORTH CAROLINA

Morrison, Anne W. .... '72 '99 C.198 B.A. L.575 J.D. 282 Corban Avenue
Morrison, H. Holt, Jr. .... '73 '02 C.198 A.B. L.896 J.D. 282 Corban Ave.
Nance, John R. .... '55 '92 C.612 B.S. L.1339 J.D. [J.R.Nance]

Nance, John R., P.A., The Law Office of
5 Cabarrus Avenue West, P.O. Box 1149, 28025
Telephone: 704-782-9138 Fax: 704-782-4767
Email: lawyernance@vnet.net URL: http://www.jnancelaw.com
John R. Nance.
Criminal Defense, Driving While Impaired, Traffic Violations, Juvenile Law, Custody Agreements and Child Support, Guardianship, Incompetency Proceedings, Wills, Powers of Attorney, Adoptions, Family Law.

See Professional Biographies, CONCORD, NORTH CAROLINA

Nickerson Law Firm, The
(See Charlotte)
Nixon, M. Wayne, Jr., (AV) .... '51 '77 C.575 B.A. L.896 J.D. [Koontz,H.N.&M.]
Nofal, Philip A., Jr. '53 '82 C.1126 B.A. L.790 J.D.
(adm. in SC; not adm. in NC) 188 Union St. S.
Patterson, Brent A., (BV) ....'67 '92 [Patterson&A.P.] ⊙

Patterson and Adams PLLC, (BV)
433 Church Street North, 28025 ⊙
Telephone: 704-795-4317 Fax: 704-795-5738 URL: http://www.patterson-adams.com
URL: http://www.pattersonadamslawoffice.com
Scott M. Adams; Brent A. Patterson.
Personal Injury, Automobile Accidents, Wrongful Deaths, Workers Compensation, Medical Malpractice.
Gastonia, North Carolina Office: 1305 East Garrison Boulevard, 28054. Telephone: 704-867-1955. Fax: 704-853-1875.
Salisbury, North Carolina Office: 710 North Main Street, 28144. Telephone: 704-795-4317.
See Professional Biographies, CONCORD, NORTH CAROLINA

Phillips, K. Todd, (BV) ....'62 '86 C.999 B.A. L.575 J.D. [Hartsell&W.]

Pickett, R. Wayne, (BV) '46 '74 C&L.575 A.B., J.D.
20 Cabarrus Avenue East, 28025
Telephone: 704-786-5115 Fax: 704-786-5116
Email: rwaynepickett@ctc.net URL: http://www.rwaynepickett.com
Criminal Law, Driving While Intoxicated, Drug Crimes, Felonies, Homicide, Misdemeanors, Parole, Assault, Traffic Violations.
See Professional Biographies, CONCORD, NORTH CAROLINA

Plummer, Franklin R., (BV) .... '48 '73 C.896 B.A. L.192 J.D. [Plummer,B.&R.]
Plummer, Joseph Holland ....'76 '01 C.34 B.S. L.1228 J.D. [⊠ Plummer,B.&R.]
Plummer, Belo & Russell, P.A., (BV) ....29 Church St., S.E.
Porter, Marilyn D. .... '52 '79 C.280 B.S. L.896 J.D. P.O. Box 707
Robertson, Scott C. .... '69 '94 C&L.575 B.A., J.D. 113 Cabarrus Ave. E.
Rogers, William F., Jr., (BV) .... '54 '79 C&L.838 B.S., J.D. [Black,R.R.&G.]
Russell, Vernon A., (BV) .... '56 '81 C.574 B.A. L.575 J.D. [Plummer,B.&R.]
Ruth, Hilton L., III, (BV) .... '57 '83 C.198 B.A. L.1228 J.D. [Black,R.R.&G.]
Scarbrough, James E., (BV) .... '48 '74 C&L.575 B.A., J.D. [Ferguson&S.]
Schneider, Susan E. ....'56 '93 C.472 B.M. L.1340 J.D. 247 Church Street
Shanley, Ashlie P. .... '70 '96 C.576 B.A. L.1228 J.D. Dist. Atty.

Shelley, Mark E., (AV) '56 '83 C.198 A.B. L.896 J.D.
115 Church Street North, P.O. Box 683, 28026
Telephone: 704-782-8282 Facsimile: 704-782-8285
Email: MarkShelley@ctc.net URL: http://www.shelleylaw.com
Tax, IRS Audits, Property Tax, Tax Planning, Trust and Estates, Asset Protection, Estate Planning, Wills and Probate.
See Professional Biographies, CONCORD, NORTH CAROLINA

Smith, Harold H., (AV) .... '18 '50 C.923 B.S. L.309 LL.B. 142 Union St., S.
Smith, Douglas A.
(See Salisbury)
Smith, Timothy D., Law Office of
(See Charlotte)
Spainhour, William Erwin ....'42 '70 C.198 A.B. L.575 J.D. Sr. Resident Supr. Ct. J.
Spence, Thomas K., (CV) .... '31 '60 C.387 A.B. L.575 J.D. 81 McCalhern Blvd.
Stewart, Mary Elizabeth ....'64 '94 C.896 B.A. L.1228 J.D. [R.M.Critz]
Thomas, Linda M. '71 '97 C.811 B.A. L.575 J.D.
Legal Servs. of Southern Piedmont, Inc.
Turnbull, Jeffrey B. ....'57 '86 C.473 B.S. L.851 J.D. 4971 Stough Rd.
White, Herbert J., Sr., (BV) ....'64 '91 C.296 B.S. L.1345 J.D. [Hartsell&W.]
Wilks, Marylaurel E. .... '68 '93 C.129 B.A. L.896 J.D. Speedway Motorsports, Inc.
Williams, David C., (BV) .... '68 '95 C.228 A.B. L.1228 J.D. [Hartsell&W.]
Wiseman, George W. ......'67 '94 C.575 B.A. L.1228 J.D. 42 Union Street South, Suite G
Woodson, Sayers, Lawther, Short, Parrott & Walker, LLP
(See Salisbury)
Zacharias, Amy F. Hahn, (BV) .... '59 '86 C.607 B.A. L.896 J.D. 82-C Union St. S.

CONETOE, 292, *Edgecombe Co.*

Naylor, Wanda M., (CV) ....'53 '83 C.575 B.S. L.574 J.D. P.O. Box 99

CONOVER, 6,604, *Catawba Co.*

Buchanan, James W., (BV) ....'45 '80 C.999 B.A. L.1228 J.D. Asst. Dist. Atty.
Crowe, Harding K. .... '61 '87 C.575 B.A. L.1228 J.D. P.O. Box 1509
Crowe & Davis, P.A., (CV) ....121 1st Avenue South
Davis, Crystal A., (CV) ....'68 '93 C&L.575 B.A., J.D. [Crowe&D.]
Pannell, Martin C., (BV) ....'33 '60 C&L.575 B.A., LL.B. [Pannell&P.]
Pannell, Martin Monroe, (BV) ....'55 '84 C.896 B.A. L.221 J.D. [Pannell&P.]
Pannell & Pannell, (BV) ....233 E. 1st St.

CORNELIUS, 11,969, *Mecklenburg Co.*

Ashley, Joanne E. ...... '64 '00 C.1128 B.A. L.575 J.D. 19109 W. Catawba Ave., Ste. 120
Austin, William O., (BV) ....'44 '69 C.319 B.A. L.575 J.D. [Austin]
Austin Law Firm, The, (BV) ....19453-E N.C. Hwy. 73
Barone, Charles F. .... '59 '87 C.107 B.A. 1983 L.1187 J.D. [Barone]

Barone Law Firm, The, P.A.
9735 Caldwell Commons Circle Suite 100, 28031
Telephone: 704-895-2792 Fax: 704-895-2793
Email: cbarone@baronelawfirm.com URL: http://www.baronefirm.com
Charles F. Barone.
Real Estate, Buying and Selling a Home, Construction, Landlord and Tenant, Zoning Planning and Land Use, Business Law, Corporate, Limited Liability Companies, Partnerships, Trusts and Estates, Asset Protection, Estate Planning, Bankruptcy, Foreclosures, Personal Injury, Automobile Accidents, Dog Bites, Wrongful Death, Criminal Law, Traffic Violations, Driving While Intoxicated, Parole and Probation, Federal Criminal Law, Collections, Contracts, Intellectual Property.
See Professional Biographies, CORNELIUS, NORTH CAROLINA

Bentz, Catherine Marker ....'58 '86 C.610 B.S.S.E. L.831 J.D. [Bentz&Assoc.]
Bentz & Associates, PA ....19453-E West Catawba Avenue
Bolduc Law Firm, The, PLLC
(See Charlotte)
Brennan, Martin M., Jr., (BV) ....'60 '87 C.645 B.S. L.229 J.D. [Brennan]

Brennan Law Firm, PLLC, (BV)
17115 Kenton Drive, Suite 204A, 28031
Telephone: 704-876-6441 Fax: 704-896-6449
Martin M. Brennan, Jr.
Employee Benefits, ERISA, Pension and Profit Sharing Plans, Taxation, Tax Planning, Estate and Gift Taxation, Estate Planning, Business Law, Joint Ventures, Limited Liability Law, Partnership Insurance, Nonprofit and Charitable Organizations.
See Professional Biographies, CORNELIUS, NORTH CAROLINA

Bryan, Callan H. .... '72 '99 C.34 B.A. L.1228 J.D. [Firm of Estate&E.V.&B.]
Bryan, Nicole Vandiver ...... '74 '99 C.575 B.A. L.1228 J.D. [Firm of Estate&E.V.&B.]
DeArmon, Edd W., Jr., (AV) ....'30 '60 C&L.896 B.S., J.D. [Merryman&D.] ‡
Delp, Dorthea Jane '62 '95 C.937 B.A. L.8 J.D.
(adm. in PA; not adm. in NC) 17215 Chabliss Court
Druar, Jacqueline M. .... '74 '03 C.1373 B.A. L.107 J.D. 9735 Caldwell Common
Fox, Kimberly Elise, (CV) ....'58 '84 C&L.575 B.S., J.D. [Kimberly E.F.]
Friguglietti, John M., Jr. .... '71 '96 C.198 B.A. L.923 J.D. [J.M.Friguglietti,Jr.]
Friguglietti, John M., Jr. PA ....19109 West Catawba, Suite 120
Hanzel, John F. ....'49 '74 C.160 B.A. L.902 J.D. [Hanzel&N.]
Hanzel & Newkirk, LLP, (BV) .... 19425 Liverpool Parkway
Hayes, Ray .... '77 '04 C.575 B.A. L.564 J.D. [R.A.Hayes,II]

Hayes, Ray A., II, P.A.
19425-E Liverpool Parkway, 28031
Telephone: 704-987-3807 Fax: 704-987-3808 http://www.ncattorneyatlawfirm.com
Email: rayhayes2@aol.com URL: http://www.ncattorneyatlaw.com
Ray Hayes.
Business Transactions, Business Litigation, Corporate Law, Business Planning, Buying or Selling a Business, Securities, Contracts, Trusts and Estates, Wills and Probate, Bankruptcy, Consumer Bankruptcy, Traffic Violations.
See Professional Biographies, CORNELIUS, NORTH CAROLINA

Hess, Jerry E. ....'42 '72 C&L.494 B.A., J.D. 501 Harborgate Court
Junker, R. Norman .... '44 '69 C.198 A.B. L.228 J.D. 18919 W. Catawba Ave.
Kimberly E. Fox, PLLC ....19826 North Cove Road, Suite E
King, Arris N. ....'70 '98 C.930 B.A. L.8 J.D. [Lakeside]
Knox, Sandra L., (BV) .... '67 '97 C.198 A.B. L.1209 J.D. [S.L.Knox]

Knox, Sandra L., P.C., (BV)
Lakeside Professional Building, 19453 West Catawba Avenue, Suite E, P.O. Box 756, 28031
Telephone: 704-892-1636 Fax: 704-892-6910
Email: sknoxlaw@aol.com URL: http://www.lawyers.com/sknoxlaw
Sandra L. Knox.
Commercial and Residential Real Estate, Condominium Law, Wills, Probate, Estate Planning, Trust, Small Business, Partnership.
See Professional Biographies, CORNELIUS, NORTH CAROLINA

Lakeside Law Offices .... 19901 West Catawba Avenue, Suite 105
Markey, Margaret B. ....'35 '88 C&L.174 B.A., J.D. 18716 W. Catawba Ave., Ste. 300
Matthews, Michael V., (AV) ....'58 '86 C.575 B.S. L.896 J.D. [M.V.Matthews]

Matthews, Michael V., P.C., The Law Offices of, (AV)
19300 Statesville Road, Suite 300, 28031
Telephone: 704-655-8786 Fax: 704-655-8796
Email: mvmlaw@mindspring.com URL: http://www.mvmlaw.com
Michael V. Matthews.
Labor and Employment, Employment Litigation, Employment Rights, Employment Contracts, Employment Discrimination, Family and Medical Leave Act, Sexual Harassment, Wage and Hour Law, Non-Competition/Non-Solicitation Agreements.
See Professional Biographies, CORNELIUS, NORTH CAROLINA

Mauriello, Christopher D. ....'59 '86 C.1044 B.S. L.1206 J.D. [Mauriello]
Mauriello Law Offices ....19810 West Catawba Avenue, Suite E
McGirt, Joe ....'45 '78 C&L.575 B.S., J.D. [J.McGirt]
McGirt, Joe, PLLC .... 19109 W. Catawba Avenue, Suite 200-1
Merryman, Charles B., Jr., (BV) .... '38 '62 C&L.896 A.B., LL.B. [Merryman&D.]
Merryman and DeArmon, (AV) ....19430 NC Highway 73, Suite 200
Newkirk, Robert B., III, (BV) ....'58 '88 C.1128 B.A. L.575 J.D. [Hanzel&N.]
Pross, Kimberly L. .... '69 '97 C.913 B.A. L.1187 J.D. [Surane&P.P.]
Seymour, John R. ....'76 '03 C.576 B.S. L.1228 J.D. [Hanzel&N.]
Singletary, Jocelyn Davis ....'50 '00 C.1016 B.A. L.836 J.D. [Singletary]

Singletary Law Firm, PLLC
19109 West Catawba Avenue, Suite 200, 28031
Telephone: 704-895-4449 Toll Free: 866-895-LAW1 Fax: 704-895-1170
Email: jdsingletary@singletarylawfirm.com URL: http://www.singletarylawfirm.com
Member of Firm: Jocelyn Davis Singletary.
Immigration, Sports and Entertainment, Business Law, Business Formation, Buying and Selling a Business.
See Professional Biographies, CORNELIUS, NORTH CAROLINA

Surane, James W. .... '62 '92 C.1237 B.A. L.940 J.D. [Surane&P.P.]
Surane & Pross PLLC ....19410 Jetton Road, Suite 110

Thomas, Susan V. '61 '86 C.575 B.A. L.30 J.D.
19453 West Catawba Avenue, Suite E, 28031
Telephone: 704-896-7570 Facsimile: 704-892-6910
Email: susanvthomas1@aol.com URL: http://www.susanvthomas.com
Family Law, Domestic Relations, Premarital Agreements, Child Custody, Child Support, Visitation Rights, Alimony, Divorce, Settlements, Paternity, Name Changes.
See Professional Biographies, CORNELIUS, NORTH CAROLINA

Vandiver & Bryan, Estate & Elder Law Firm of
18809 West Catawba Avenue, Suite 102, 28031
Telephone: 704-892-9355 Facsimile: 704-892-9309
Email: chbryan@vbfirm.com URL: http://www.nclaw1.com
Nicole Vandiver Bryan; Callan H. Bryan.
Elder Law, Estate Planning, Estate and Trust Administration, Medicaid Planning and Application, Wills, Trusts and Estates, Advance Directives, Taxation, Probate, Guardianship, Incompetency Proceedings, Medicare, Special Needs Trusts, Disability Law, Social Security, Veteran's Benefits, Long Term Care Planning, Estate Planning for the Disabled, Estate Planning for the Elderly, Business Law, Corporate Law, Business Succession Planning, Family Limited Partnerships, Limited Liability Company Law, Commercial and Contracts.
See Professional Biographies, CORNELIUS, NORTH CAROLINA

Williams, Patteson (Pat), (BV) ....'57 '86 C.575 B.A. L.896 J.D. [G.P.Williams]

Williams, G. Patteson, (BV)
19700-J West Catawba Avenue, P.O. Box 2009, 28031
Telephone: 704-892-0474 Fax: 704-892-0494
Email: attygpw@adelphia.net
Patteson (Pat) Williams.
Real Estate, Residential Real Estate, Commercial Real Estate, Wills, Estates, Estate Administration, Business, Corporate, Automobile Accidents, Personal Injury.
See Professional Biographies, CORNELIUS, NORTH CAROLINA

COROLLA, 1,000, *Currituck Co.*

Malarney, Jeffery, (BV) ....'66 '91 C.20 B.A. L.896 J.D. P.O. Box 369

CREEDMOOR, 2,232, Granville Co.

Armstrong, Charlene Y. '69 '97
C.955 B.S. L.574 J.D. [⊠ Browne,F.W.&W.] (⊙Greensboro)
Browne, T. Marcus, III, (BV) '51 '80
C.232 B.A. L.574 J.D. [Browne,F.W.&W.] (⊙Durham, Greensboro)
Browne, Flebotte, Wilson & Webb, PLLC, (BV)
506 N. Main St. (⊙Charlotte, Durham, Fayetteville, Greensboro)

Flebotte, Daniel R., (BV) '52 '81
C.228 B.A. L.910 J.D. [Browne,F.W.&W.] (ⓞDurham, Greensboro)
Foley, William Andrew, III, (BV) ..... '63 '89 C.575 B.A. L.574 J.D. 2579 Brassfield Rd.
Webb, Joy Rhyne, (BV) '69 '95
C&L.575 B.A., J.D. [Browne,F.W.&W.] (ⓞDurham, Greensboro)
Whitfield, Robert E., (BV) '47 '78
C.232 B.A. L.574 J.D. [Browne,F.W.&W.] (ⓞDurham, Greensboro)
Wilson, Joseph M., Jr., (BV) '61 '91
C.790 B.A. L.574 J.D. [Browne,F.W.&W.] (ⓞDurham, Greensboro)

CULLOWHEE, 3,579, *Jackson Co.*

Hyatt, William D. '39 '65 C.929 A.B. L.150 J.D.
(adm. in OH; not adm. in NC) Western Carolina Univ.
Kucharski, Richard L. '48 '74 C.98 B.S. L.188 J.D.
Gen. Coun., Western Carolina Univ.
Scott, William E. .... '17 '46 C.280 B.B.A. L.51 LL.B. P.O. Box 1149‡
Wilson, Le Von E. ......'54 '81 C.925 B.S. L.574 J.D. Asst. Prof., Western Carolina Univ.

CURRITUCK, * —, *Currituck Co.*

Brumsey, William, III ....'41 '69 C&L.896 B.A., J.D. U.S. Highway 168
Brumsey, William, IV, (BV) .... '70 '99 C&L.896 B.A., J.D. P.O. Box 100
DeVeau, Ronald E., P.C.
(See Nags Head)
Romm, William H., Jr., (BV) .... '48 '77 C.575 B.A. L.796 J.D. Court House Square
Vincent Law Firm, The, PC
(See Southern Shores)

DALLAS, 3,402, *Gaston Co.*

Cloninger, Alan G., (BV) .... '58 '88 C.1128 B.S. L.1228 J.D. 140 W. Trade St.
Hayes, Anne Marie H. ....'65 '91 C.296 B.S. L.124 J.D. Law Prof.
Thrower, Pennie M., (CV) '63 '96 C.577 B.A. L.1228 J.D.
140 West Trade Street, P.O. Box 459, 28034
Telephone: 704-922-6739 Fax: 704-922-0650
Email: Pennie@penniethrowerlaw.com URL: http://www.penniethrowerlaw.com
Residence Real Estate, Traffic Offenses, Wills, Powers of Attorney, Living Wills, Incorporations.
See Professional Biographies, DALLAS, NORTH CAROLINA

DANBURY, * 119, *Stokes Co.*

Badgett, Robyn Jill Lazenby ....'58 '83 C.296 B.A. L.896 J.D. Dist. Ct. Mag.
Bruce, R. Michael, (BV) .... '42 '69 C&L.575 B.S., J.D. 404 N. Main St.
Dellinger, James L., Jr., (BV) ....'46 '72 C.692 B.A. L.896 J.D. Dist. Atty.
Marshall, William F., Jr., (AV) .....'25 '60 C.575 B.S. L.896 LL.B. 113 Courthouse Circle
Massey, A. Moses .... '48 '76 C.101 B.S. L.575 J.D. Dist. J.

DAVIDSON, 7,139, *Mecklenburg Co.*

Ahlers, Jennifer Susan, (CV) .... '68 '96 C.953 B.A. L.1228 J.D. [McIntosh]
Booker, Edward L., (BV) .... '48 '83 C.1128 B.A. L.574 J.D. [E.L.Booker]
Booker, Edward L., PA, (BV) .... P.O. Box 1479
Bruce, Robert A. ....'55 '81 C.349 B.A. L.1292 J.D. 230 S. Main St.
Carnegie, Prosser D., (BV) .... '51 '77 C.198 B.A. L.692 J.D. [McIntosh]
Carter, Beth B. ....'65 '95 C.884 B.S. L.644 J.D. [McIntosh]
Casey, Hugh G., Jr., (AV) ....'27 '56 C&L.145 Ph.B., J.D. P.O. Box 954‡
Chagaris, Christopher G., (CV) .... '69 '94 C.152 B.S. L.425 J.D. [Chagaris]
Chagaris Law Firm, (CV) .... P.O. Box 1408
Cunningham, John R., III, (AV) .... '57 '86 C.198 B.A. L.976 J.D. [J.R.Cunningham,III]
Cunningham, John R., III, P.A., (AV) ....201 South Street
Ellison, William Lewis, Jr. ....'70 '96 C&L.1228 M.A., J.D. [McIntosh]
Fuller, James C., (AV) .... '42 '71 C.198 B.A. L.575 J.D. [ⓒ McIntosh]
Gibert, James M., III ....'57 '84 C.198 A.B. L.245 J.D. Davidson College
Hartsell & Williams, P.A.
(See Concord)
Hayes, Ray A., II, P.A.
(See Cornelius)
Hendrix, Roger B., (AV) .... '23 '53 C.597 B.S. L.575 J.D. 400 Avinger Lane
Horack, Talley, Pharr & Lowndes, A Professional Association
(See Charlotte)
Irvin, Susan K., (AV) '— '84 C.228 B.A. L.846 J.D. BB
P.O. Box 2376, 28036
Telephone: 704-896-0820 Fax: 704-896-0875
Email: susan@skirvinlaw.com URL: http://www.skirvinlaw.com
Commercial Real Estate Development, Zoning, Planning and Land Use Law.
See Professional Biographies, DAVIDSON, NORTH CAROLINA
Kline, Richard J., (AV) '47 '72 C.608 B.S.B.A. L.7 J.D.
230 South Main Street, P.O. Box 1508, 28036
Telephone: 704-892-8823 Fax: 704-892-8683
Email: rjkline@bellsouth.net URL: http://www.lawyers.com/rjkline
Commercial Real Estate, Real Estate Lending, Municipal Law, Zoning and Land Use.
See Professional Biographies, DAVIDSON, NORTH CAROLINA
McIntosh, Robert G., (BV) .... '62 '87 C&L.575 B.S., J.D. [McIntosh]
McIntosh Law Firm, The, P.C., (BV)
The Davidson Cotton Mill, P.O. Box 2270, 28036
Telephone: 704-892-1699 Telecopier: 704-892-8664
Email: bob@mcintoshlawfirm.com URL: http://www.mcintoshlawfirm.com
Robert G. McIntosh; Robert Edward Wick, III; Prosser D. Carnegie; Amanda L. Shue; Jennifer Susan Ahlers; William Lewis Ellison, Jr.; Beth B. Carter. Of Counsel: James C. Fuller.
Adoptions, Appeals, Bankruptcy, Business Law, Civil Litigation, Commercial and Consumer Collections, Commercial and Residential Real Estate, Corporate Law, Foreclosures, Insurance Subrogation, Estate Administration, Family Law, Personal Injury, Wrongful Death, Wills, Workers Compensation, Planning and Land Use.
See Professional Biographies, DAVIDSON, NORTH CAROLINA
Moran, Gerald T., Jr. '63 '89 C.20 B.A. L.880 J.D.
Dep. Gen. Coun.-Commerce & Asst. Secy., Ingersoll-Rand Co.
Roberto, Barbara ....'61 '88 C.105 B.A. L.724 J.D. 17834 River Ford Dr.
Shue, Amanda L. .... '70 '00 C.1128 B.A. L.1228 J.D. [Ⓐ McIntosh]
Todd, Ann C. .... '70 '98 C.198 B.A. L.546 J.D. Integrity Sports Marketing
Trumpower, Michelle D. '72 '99 C.205 B.A. L.1338 J.D.
(adm. in PA; not adm. in NC) Asst. Gen. Coun., Ingersoll-Rand Co.
Wardlow, Richard E., (AV) ....'23 '50 C&L.575 A.B., LL.B. 21205 Senlac Lane‡
Wick, Robert Edward, III .... '72 '99 C.152 B.A. L.192 J.D. [McIntosh]
Williams, G. Patteson
(See Cornelius)

DENTON, 1,450, *Davidson Co.*

Mitchell, Paul Rush ....'53 '78 C.198 B.A. L.896 J.D. Town Atty. (ⓞThomasville)
Whitley, Wesley D. .... '71 '96 C.576 B.S. L.1228 J.D. P.O. Box 1600

DENVER, —, *Lincoln Co.*

Brown, Robert J., (BV) ....'68 '95 C.34 B.S. L.1339 J.D. [R.J.Brown]
Brown, Robert J., P.A., (BV) ....328 Highway 16 North
Capece, Peter C. ....'76 '02 C.125 B.A. L.574 J.D. [Ⓐ Kennedy&W.]
Easterling, Elaine A. '63 '89 C.532 B.A. L.8 J.D.
(adm. in OH; not adm. in NC) 7887 Golf Course Dr. N.
Kennedy, Richard L., (BV) ....'32 '56 C&L.896 B.B.A., J.D. [ⓒ Kennedy&W.]
Kennedy & Wulfhorst, P.A., (BV)
3758 Highway 16 North, 28037
Telephone: 704-483-3415 Telecopier: 704-483-9755 URL: http://www.kennedyandwulfhorst.com
URL: http://www.kandwlaw.com
D. Todd Wulfhorst;—Peter C. Capece. Of Counsel: Richard L. Kennedy.
Residential and Commercial Real Estate, Corporate and Business Law, Wills, Probate, Estate Planning, Domestic and Family Law, Criminal Law, Traffic, Juvenile, Divorce, Collections.
See Professional Biographies, DENVER, NORTH CAROLINA
Wulfhorst, D. Todd, (BV) .... '67 '92 C.645 B.S.M.E. L.575 J.D. [Kennedy&W.]

DOBSON, * 1,457, *Surry Co.*

Adams, Karen J. '70 '97 C.1128 B.S. L.574 J.D.
124 West Kapp Street, P.O. Box 1271, 27017
Telephone: 336-356-4900 Fax: 336-356-2900
Email: kjadams@surry.net URL: http://www.karenadamslaw.com
Criminal Law, Divorce, Speeding Tickets, DUI, DWI.
See Professional Biographies, DOBSON, NORTH CAROLINA
Bowman, C. Ricky, (BV) ....'56 '84 C.896 B.A. L.1228 J.D. Dist. Atty.
Gillespie, Regina Robinson, (CV) .... '58 '93 C.783 B.S. L.896 J.D. P.O. Box 312
Key, Spencer G., Jr., (BV) ....'67 '92 C.896 B.A. L.575 J.D. Dist. Ct. Judge
Langan, Thomas Byron ....'73 '99 C.228 A.B. L.896 J.D. Asst. Dist. Atty.
McNeil, Marion D., (BV) ....'62 '86 C&L.1228 B.A., J.D. P.O. Box 1312
Puckett, Angela Brown, (BV) ....'70 '94 C.577 B.A. L.575 J.D. Asst. Dist. Atty.
Royster and Royster
(See Mount Airy)
White, W. David, (AV) ....'51 '80 C.925 B.S. L.1228 J.D. [W.D.White]
White, W. David, P.A., (AV)
220 West Kapp Street, P.O. Box 1061, 27017
Telephone: 336-386-8225 Fax: 336-386-8227
Email: wileywhite51@hotmail.com URL: http://www.wdavidwhitelaw.com
W. David White.
Civil, Criminal, Family, Alimony, Cohabitation Agreements, Divorce, Divorce Mediation, Domestic Partnerships, Domestic Relations, Domestic Torts, Domestic Violence, Equitable Distribution, Family Arbitration, Family Mediation, Name Changes, Non Traditional Family Law, Paternity, Post Divorce Modification, Postnuptial Agreements, Premarital Agreements, Qualified Domestic Relations Orders, Restraining Orders, Separation Agreements, Spousal Support, Personal Injury, Personal Injury Mediation, Plaintiffs Personal Injury, Accidents, Auto Accidents, Automobile Negligence, School Bus Accidents, Bodily Injury, Brain Injury, Catastrophic Injury, Head Injury, Spinal Injury, Tourist Injuries, Motor Vehicle Accidents and Injuries, Motorcycle Accidents, Wrongful Death, DWI, Speeding Tickets, Traffic Violations.
See Professional Biographies, DOBSON, NORTH CAROLINA

DRAPER, —, *Rockingham Co.*

(See Eden)

DREXEL, 1,938, *Burke Co.*

Cline, Jeffrey L. .... '51 '79 C.575 B.S. L.469 J.D. P.O. Box 2088

DUCK, 200, *Dare Co.*

Hornthal, Riley, Ellis & Maland, L.L.P.
(See Elizabeth City)

DUNN, 9,196, *Harnett Co.*

Adams, Brenton, (BV) .... '46 '72 C&L.896 B.A., J.D. 119 Lucknow Square
Bryan, Robert C., (AV) .... '24 '55 C.871 B.S. L.575 J.D. 302 W. Edgerton St.‡
Cumbie, Lee D. .... '60 '97 C.999 B.S. L.1345 J.D. [Cumbie C.]
Cumbie Consulting .... 111 W. Pearsall St.
Daughtry, Parrish Hayes ....'75 '00 C.575 B.S. L.1228 J.D. [Hayes,W.T.&D.]
Edwards, Charlene, Law Office
(See Lillington)
Fusco, Phillip A., (BV) ....'60 '85 C&L.1228 B.B.A., J.D. [Tart,W.&F.]
Hardison, Kenneth L., (BV) ....'56 '82 C&L.1228 B.S., J.D. [Hardison&L.] ⊙
Hardison & Leone, L.L.P., (AV)
212 S. Wilson Avenue, P.O. Box 759, 28335-0759 ⊙
Telephone: 910-892-1181; Toll-Free 1-888-892-1181 Fax: 910-892-7874
URL: http://www.hardisonandleone.com
Kenneth L. Hardison.
Personal Injury, Auto and Trucking Accidents, Pedestrian Accidents, Catastrophic Injury, Medical Malpractice, Workers' Compensation, Social Security Disability, Nursing Home Negligence, Security Investment Fraud, Inadequate Security Claims, Premises Liability, Mass Torts, Drug Liability Claims, Employment Law, Appellate Practice.
See Professional Biographies, DUNN, NORTH CAROLINA
Harrop, Donald E., Jr., (BV) ....'58 '86 C.228 A.B. L.345 J.D. [McLeod&H.]
Hayes, Gerald W., Jr., (AV) ....'43 '69 C.575 A.B. L.896 J.D. [Hayes,W.T.&D.] ⊙
Hayes, Williams, Turner & Daughtry, P.A., (AV)
804 West Broad Street, 28334 ⊙
Telephone: 910-892-2178 Fax: 910-891-1198 Email: ghayes@harnettlaw.com Email: hwilliams@harnettlaw.com Email: pdaughtry@harnettlaw.com
Email: dturner@harnettlaw.com URL: http://www.harnettlaw.com
Gerald W. Hayes, Jr.; Heather Hayes Williams; Douglas Eugene Turner, Jr.; Parrish Hayes Daughtry.
General Criminal and Civil Practice. Personal Injury, Traffic Court, Real Estate, Probate, Juvenile, Family and Corporation Law. Trials in all Courts.
Reference: United Carolina Bank.
See Professional Biographies, DUNN, NORTH CAROLINA
Johnson, James M., (AV) .... '32 '57 C.198 B.S. L.575 J.D. 302 W. Edgerton St.
Jones, Cecil B., (BV) ....'64 '90 C.896 B.A. L.1228 J.D. [Jones&J.]
Jones, Robert H., (BV) ....'26 '52 C&L.896 B.S., J.D. [Jones&J.]
Jones and Jones, P.L.L.C., (BV) ....302 West Edgerton Street
Lytch, R. Allen, (BV) ....'41 '69 C.1228 B.S. L.575 J.D. 602 W. Broad St.
McCool, Dennis M. '51 '77 C&L.900 B.E., J.D.
(adm. in KS; not adm. in NC) 701 N. Ellis Ave.‡
McLeod, J. Michael, (BV) ....'44 '69 C&L.896 B.A., J.D. [McLeod&H.]
McLeod & Harrop, (BV) .... 209 South Wilson Avenue
Miller, Marshall L., III ....'70 '98 C.1083 B.S. L.1228 J.D. 602 W. Broad St.
Munz, Christopher D. ....'76 '01 C.575 B.A. L.1228 J.D. [Ⓐ Stewart]
Parker, Jerry D., Jr., (CV) ...'60 '87 C.232 B.S.B.A. L.1345 J.D. 1208 W. Cumberland St.
Pope, P. Tilghman ....'72 '99 C.575 B.A. L.1228 J.D. P.O. Box 928

Pope, Patrick H., (AV) . . . '44 '69 C&L.575 B.S., J.D. [Pope,T.&T.]
Pope, Wiley Jackson . . . '76 '01 C.1228 B.B.A. L.1345 J.D. 403 W. Broad St.
Pope, Tilghman & Tart, (AV) . . . 403 W. Broad St.
Slusser, Scott T., (CV) . . . '72 '97 C.1128 B.S. L.1228 J.D. [S.Slusser]
Slusser, Scott, Attorney at Law, (CV) . . . 703 E. Morris Cir.
Snow, Dwight W., (BV) . . . '54 '81 C.896 B.S. L.1228 J.D. 302 West Edgerton
Stewart, Caron H., (BV) . . . '61 '86 C.232 B.S. L.1228 J.D. [Stewart]
Stewart, Vernon K., (BV) . . . '60 '86 C&L.1228 B.B.A., J.D. [Stewart]

Stewart Law Firm, (BV)
111 Commerce Drive, 28334
Telephone: 910-892-4970 Fax: 910-892-4976 URL: http://www.stewartlawfirmnc.com
URL: stewartlaw-firm.com
Email: stewartlaw@dockport.net URL: http://www.stewartlawfirm.com
Members of Firm: Vernon K. Stewart; Caron H. Stewart. Associate: Christopher D. Munz.
Personal Injury, Automobile Accidents, Criminal Law, Traffic Violations, Real Estate, Corporate Law, Family Law, Divorce, Child Custody and Child Support.
See Professional Biographies, DUNN, NORTH CAROLINA

Tart, John P., (BV) . . . '44 '69 C&L.575 B.S., J.D. [Pope,T.&T.]
Tart, Joseph L., (BV) . . . '47 '82 C.232 B.S. L.1228 J.D. [Tart,W.&F.]
Tart, Willis & Fusco, P.A., (BV) . . . 511 N. Ellis Avenue
Taylor, Ann Callison, (CV) . . . '49 '83 C&L.1228 B.A., J.D. 307 Coleridge Dr.
Tilghman, Johnson, (BV) . . . '42 '70 C.1228 B.S. L.575 J.D. [Pope,T.&T.]
Turner, Douglas Eugene, Jr., (CV) . . . '71 '97 C.999 B.A. L.1228 J.D. [Hayes,W.T.&D.]
Williams, Heather Hayes, (BV) . . . '69 '94 C.575 B.S.P.H. L.1228 J.D. [Hayes,W.T.&D.]
Willis, O. Henry, Jr., (BV) . . . '50 '79 C.576 B.A. L.1228 J.D. [Tart,W.&F.]
Yopp, Michael S. . . . '73 '98 C.575 B.S.B.A. L.356 J.D. 611 N. Orange Ave.

DURHAM, * 187,035, *Durham Co.*

Adams, Jennifer Westerhaus . . . '74 '02 C.800 B.A./B.A. L.228 J.D. [Ⓐ Walker&L.]
Adcock, Cynthia F. . . . '61 '91 C.122 B.A. L.228 J.D. Duke Univ. Law Sch.
Adcock, David B. '51 '76 C.575 A.B. L.228 J.D.
(adm. in GA; not adm. in NC) Gen. Coun., Duke Univ.
Adkins, Philip S., (BV) . . . '55 '81 C&L.575 B.A., J.D. [Adkins&F.]
Adkins & Flowers, PA, (BV) . . . 1502 West North Carolina Highway 54, Suite 501
Agusta, Joseph B. . . . '65 '97 C.158 B.S.E.E. L.574 J.D. 5015 Southpark, Ste. 230
Akachukwu, Mildred A. . . . '63 '98 C.1197 B.S. L.574 J.D. P.O. Box 989
Alberti, William T., (BV) '48 '80 C.575 B.A. L.862 J.D.
Sr. Coun., Blue Cross Blue Shield of North Carolina
Aldred, Jo E. '60 '87 C.228 B.A. L.575 J.D.
(adm. in MA; not adm. in NC) Instructor, UNC- Chapel Hill‡
Alexander, David Benjamin . . . '63 '00 C.881 B.A. L.575 J.D. 1415 W. NC Highway 54
Alexander, Helen E. . . . '41 '84 C.352 B.S.N. L.574 J.D. 100 E. Parrish
Allen, Michael S. . . . '70 '95 C&L.575 B.A., J.D. 4104 Cherry Blossom Cir.
Alphin, Alesia R., (BV) . . . '60 '87 C.228 B.S. L.575 J.D. [Moore&A.] (ⒸRaleigh)
Alphin, Oliver W., (AV) . . . '33 '61 C&L.575 B.S., J.D. [Ⓒ Moore&A.] ⊙
Alston, Kären Frasier, (BV) . . . '63 '94 C.302 B.A. L.574 J.D. [Frasier&A.]
Amana, Cheryl E. '— '84 C.705 B.A. L.659 J.D.
(adm. in PA; not adm. in NC) N.C. Central Univ. School of Law‡
Anderson, William Albert, III . . . '72 '00 C&L.575 B.A., J.D. [Kennon,C.B.C.&M.]
Anthony, Joseph E., (BV) . . . '47 '87 C.232 B.A. L.574 J.D. 3101 Petty Rd., 5th Fl.
Ashhurst, Tiffany L. . . . '72 '99 C&L.575 B.A., J.D. [Ashhurst&B.P.]
Ashhurst & Brown PLLC . . . 3622 Lyckan Pkwy
Ashmore, Louise, (BV) . . . '57 '83 C&L.575 B.A., J.D. Employment Law Research, Inc.
Aus, Brian M., (BV) . . . '54 '85 C.705 B.A. L.575 J.D. 124 E. Main St.
Bachman, Glen D., (BV) . . . '67 '95 C.228 B.A. L.910 J.D. 714 9th St.

Bagwell, Holt & Smith, P.A.
(See Chapel Hill)

Baker, Patrick W., (AV) . . . '67 '94 C&L.896 B.A., J.D. 401 N. Mangum St.
Baker, Robert F., (AV) . . . '35 '61 C.198 A.B. L.228 J.D. 3126 Cornwall Road

Baloch, Omar, The Law Offices of
(See Raleigh)

Barco, Susan E., (BV) . . . '46 '74 C.25 B.S. L.228 J.D. 5215 Tahoe Dr.
Barefoot, Robin M., (AV) . . . '58 '85 C.575 B.A. L.574 J.D. [Ⓐ Stubbs,C.B.P.&B.]
Barley, Tracy Hicks . . . '— '93 C.955 B.A. L.574 J.D. [T.H.Barley&Assoc.]

Barley, Tracy Hicks, & Associates, P.A.
413 E. Chapel Hill Street Suite 112, 27702
Telephone: 919-956-9440 Fax: 919-956-9443
Email: thbarley@nc.rr.com URL: http://www.tracybarleylaw.com
Tracy Hicks Barley.
Bankruptcy - Chapters 7 and 13, Family Law, Equitable Distribution, Divorce, Child Custody, Child Support, Estates, Juvenile Law, Incorporations, Personal Injury.
See Professional Biographies, DURHAM, NORTH CAROLINA

Bartlett, Katharine T. '47 '75 C.938 B.A. L.1066 J.D.
Prof. of Law, Duke Univ. Law Sch.
Battaglia, Frederick S., Jr., (BV) . . . '56 '86 C.232 B.S.B.A. L.574 J.D. P.O. Box 2301
Beale, Sara Sun '49 '74 C&L.477 B.A., J.D.
(adm. in MI; not adm. in NC) Duke Univ. Sch. of Law
Beason, Robert A., (AV) . . . '48 '73 C.945 B.A. L.575 J.D. 2741 University Drive
Beckwith, James Payne, Jr. '49 '74
C.575 B.A. L.145 J.D. N.C. Central Univ. School of Law

Becton, Slifkin & Bell, P.A.
(See Raleigh)

Beightol, Kristen L. . . . '75 '01 C.575 B.A. L.1228 J.D. P.O. Box 51729
Beischer, David Dietrich, (AV) . . . '66 '94 C.951 B.A. L.896 J.D. [Beischer,B.&B.]
Beischer, George D., (BV) . . . '42 '66 C.228 B.A. L.575 LL.B. [Beischer,B.&B.]
Beischer, Boles & Beischer, (AV) . . . Suite 101 2726 Croasdaile Drive
Belo, Robert O., (AV) . . . '50 '79 C&L.575 B.S., J.D. [Kennon,C.B.C.&M.]

Bennick, Donna E., P.C.
(See Chapel Hill)

Bentley, Charles A., Jr., (AV) . . . '46 '71 C.10 B.A. L.893 J.D. [Bentley]

Bentley Law Offices, P.A., (AV)
Suite 501 Southbank Building, 400 West Main Street, P.O. Box 52089, 27717-2089
Telephone: 919-682-3700 Fax: 919-419-1847 URL: http://www.lawyers.com/bentleylawoffices
Email: cbentley@bentleylawfirm.com URL: http://www.bentleylawfirm.com
Charles A. Bentley, Jr.
Medical Malpractice Law, Wrongful Death, Personal Injury, Consumer Fraud, Predatory Lending and Unfair and Deceptive Trade Practices, Commercial Litigation, Products Liability, Truck Accidents, Premises Liability and Inadequate Security.
See Professional Biographies, DURHAM, NORTH CAROLINA

Berman, Gary K., (BV) . . . '50 '75 C.659 B.A. L.228 J.D. 315 E. Chapel Hill St., Ste. 400
Bethea-Shields, Karen . . . '49 '74 C.232 B.A. L.228 J.D. 123 Orange St.

Biagiotti Schneider, Tracey '68 '93 C.269 B.A. L.259 J.D.
(adm. in FL; not adm. in NC) 4906 Fortunes Ridge Drive
Biggs, C. Thomas, (BV) . . . '37 '62 C&L.228 B.S.C.E., LL.B. [Stubbs,C.B.P.&B.]
Biggs, Jonathan W., (BV) . . . '64 '91 C.228 A.B. L.896 J.D. [Stubbs,C.B.P.&B.]
Bishop, Keith A. . . . '63 '92 C.1507 B.A. L.574 J.D. [K.A.Bishop]
Bishop, Keith A., PLLC . . . 1802 Martin Luther King Pkwy., Ste. 105
Black, Freda B. . . . '60 '85 C.896 B.A. L.1345 J.D. Off. of Dist. Atty
Blake, Eaddy H. '67 '96
C.576 B.S. L.1228 J.D. Corp. Coun., Bowe Bell & Howell Company
Bland, David H., (AV) '54 '78 C.575 B.A. L.896 J.D.
Div. Atty., Nature Conservancy, The
Blinder, Henry D., (AV) . . . '51 '77 C.696 B.A. L.228 J.D. City Atty.
Bobroff, Harold, (AVⓉ) '20 '52 C.563 B.B.A. L.569 J.D.
(adm. in NY; not adm. in NC) 2701 Pickett Rd., Apt. 3047‡
Boddie, Grace C. . . . '17 '51 C.889 B.S. L.228 J.D. 3636 Hope Valley Road
Boles, Richard J., (AV) . . . '36 '66 C.1308 B.S. L.575 J.D. [Beischer,B.&B.]
Boswell Jones, Keava . . . '73 '01 C.16 B.M. L.1187 J.D. P.O. Box 794
Boulden, Richard S., (BV) . . . '60 '86 C.674 A.B. L.228 J.D. 3208 Denise St.
Boutwell, Rufus C., Jr. . . . '18 '47 C&L.228 B.A., LL.B. 2807 Friendship Cir.‡
Bowens, Florence A. . . . '59 '90 C.404 B.A. L.574 J.D. 3020 Pickett Road, Suite 141
Bowens, Marilyn . . . '55 '92 L.574 J.D. N.C. Central Univ. School of Law
Bowman, John A., (AV) . . . '56 '87 C.885 B.A. L.1228 J.D. [Maxwell,F.&B.]
Boyd, Richard C., Attorney at Law, (BV) '47 '81
C.228 A.B. L.692 J.D. 400 W. Main, Ste. 401
Boyden, Jacquelyn K., (BV) '55 '80 C.477 B.A. L.902 J.D.
(adm. in VA; not adm. in NC)
V.P., Corp. Integrity, Blue Cross Blue Shield of North Carolina
Bracy, Warren D. '42 '75 C.424 B.S. L.188 J.D.
(adm. in MI; not adm. in NC) Prof. of Law, N.C. Central Univ.
Bradley, Kevin P., (BV) . . . '52 '82 C.976 B.A. L.309 J.D. 123 Orange St.

Brady, Nordgren, Klym & Morton, PLLC
(See Raleigh)

Brannon, Anthony M. . . . '37 '62 C&L.575 A.B., LL.B. 3817 Somerset Dr.
Brantley-Lemons, Carena R. . . . '76 '02 C.790 B.A. L.574 J.D. [C.Brantley-Lemons]
Brantley-Lemons, Carena, Attorney at Law . . . 400 W. Main St., Ste. 611
Brawley, Edward T., (BV) . . . '36 '69 C.575 B.A. L.1000 J.D. [Brawley&B.]
Brawley, Sumter C., Jr., (AV) . . . '08 '33 C.228 L.16 [Brawley&B.]
Brawley & Brawley, (AV) . . . 505 S. Duke St.

Brenman, Lisa R.
(See Carrboro)

Briggs, John G., III . . . '72 '00 C.838 B.A. L.574 J.D. P.O. Box 12237
Britt, John G. . . . '46 '78 C&L.575 B.A., J.D. Capital Def. Off.
Brock, Paul B., (BV) . . . '66 '92 C&L.575 B.S.B.A., J.D. [Brock,P.&M.]

Brock, Payne & Meece, P.A., (BV)
3130 Hope Valley Road, 27707
Telephone: 919-401-5913 Fax: 919-419-1018
Email: paul.brock@verizon.net
Paul B. Brock; Barri Hilton Payne; Darin P. Meece.
General Practice, Family Law, Child Custody, Child Support, Divorce, Alimony, Separation Agreements, Spousal Support, Equitable Distribution, Misdemeanors, Traffic, Personal Injury, Contracts, Mediation, Civil Litigation, Wills, Real Estate.
See Professional Biographies, DURHAM, NORTH CAROLINA

Brooks, Gwendolyn C., Ph.D. . . . '64 '99 C.674 B.A. L.228 J.D. [Kennon,C.B.C.&M.]
Brooks, Susan E. '68 '94
C.576 B.A. L.309 J.D. Contracts Admin./Sentencing Servs. Admin.
Broome, Adam H., (AV) '56 '82
C.500 B.S. L.309 J.D. Gen. Coun. & Corp. Sec., Cree, Inc.
Brown, Kelton T. . . . '71 '00 C.1128 B.A. L.607 J.D. [K.Brown&Assoc.]
Brown, Robert, Jr., (BV) . . . '50 '75 C.228 B.A. L.188 J.D. Pub. Def.
Brown, Saprina Elette . . . '72 '99 C&L.574 B.A., J.D. [Ashhurst&B.P.]

Brown & Bunch, PLLC, (AV)
21 West Colony Place, Suite 250, 27705 ⊙
Telephone: 919-490-9700 Fax: 919-419-9736
A. Vann Irvin (Board Certified Specialist in Estate Planning and Probate Law, North Carolina State Board of Legal Specialization) (Resident).
Chapel Hill, North Carolina Office: 101 North Columbia Street, 27514. Telephone: 919-968-1111. Fax: 919-968-1444.
Raleigh, North Carolina Office: 4900 Falls of Neuse Road, Suite 210, Post Office Box 19409. Telephone: 919-878-8060. Fax: 919-878-8062.
See Professional Biographies, DURHAM, NORTH CAROLINA

Brown, K. & Associates, PLLC . . . 4819 Emperor Boulevard, 4th Floor
Browne, T. Marcus, III, (BV) '51 '80 C.232 B.A. L.574 J.D.
[Browne,F.W.&W.] (ⒸCreedmoor, Greensboro)

Browne, Flebotte, Wilson & Webb, PLLC, (BV)
Meridian Business Campus, 2525 Meridian Parkway, Suite 300, P.O. Box 2247, 27702 ⊙
Telephone: 919-688-7393 919-688-1580 Toll Free: 800-556-8404 Facsimile: 919-683-6323
Email: bfwh@browneflebotte.com URL: http://www.browneflebotte.com
T. Marcus Browne, III; Daniel R. Flebotte; Joseph M. Wilson, Jr.; Joy Rhyne Webb; Robert E. Whitfield.
General Civil and Criminal Trial Practice in State and Federal Courts. Personal Injury Litigation, Wrongful Death, Workers Compensation, Bankruptcy, Employment Law, Appellate Practice, Construction Law, Real Estate, Domestic Relations, Traffic Violations, Corporate Law, Labor Law.
Creedmoor, North Carolina Office: 506 North Main Street, P.O. Box 886, 27522. Telephone: 919-528-3061. Fax: 919-528-3505.
Greensboro, North Carolina Office: 503 West McGee Street, 27401. Telephone: 336-273-4480. Fax: 336-273-4362.
Charlotte, North Carolina Office: Cameron Brown Building, 301 South McDowell Street, Suite 1201, 28204. Telephone: 704-370-7771. Fax: 704-370-7798.
Fayetteville, North Carolina Office: Systel Building, 225 Green Street, Suite 204, 28301. Telephone: 910-323-3435. Fax: 910-323-2645.
See Professional Biographies, DURHAM, NORTH CAROLINA

Browning, William W., (BV) . . . '56 '84 C.228 A.B. L.575 J.D. 120 E. Main St.

Brownlee Law Firm
(See Raleigh)

Bryant, Patterson, Covington Idol & Lewis, P.A., (AV) BB
103 West Main Street, Kress Building, Mezzanine Floor, P.O. Box 341, 27702
Telephone: 919-688-6341 Fax: 919-688-6343
URL: http://www.bpcilaw.com
J. Wesley Covington; Robert A. Idol; David O. Lewis;—Jeremy D. Lindsley; P. Lee Craven, III; Andrew L. Peterson.
Trial and Appeals in all State and Federal Courts, Personal Injury, Insurance, Medical and Legal Malpractice, Commercial Litigation, Workers Compensation, Corporation Law, Banking, Estate Planning and Administration, Taxation, Criminal and Traffic.
See Professional Biographies, DURHAM, NORTH CAROLINA

Buchanan, Katharine B. ....'70 '01 C.228 A.B. L.893 J.D. [Ⓒ Walker&L.]
Bugg, John E., (AV) ....'44 '70 C.228 A.B. L.575 J.D. [Bugg&W.]
Bugg, Mary Margaret .... '64 '89 C.575 B.S. L.692 J.D. 3815 Nottaway Rd.

Bugg & Wolf, P.A., (AV)
Suite 170 University Office Park, 411 Andrews Road, 27705
Mailing Address: P.O. Box 2917, Durham, NC 27715
Telephone: 919-383-9431 FAX: 919-383-9771
John E. Bugg; William J. Wolf;—William R. Sparrow; Allen T. Wiggins.
Public and Private Construction Law, including OSHA Proceedings and Litigation. General Civil and Appellate Practice in State, Federal Courts and Administrative Agencies.
See Professional Biographies, DURHAM, NORTH CAROLINA

Bumm, J. Luke .... '76 '03 C.893 B.A. L.575 J.D. Durham District Atty's Office
Burdick, Kimberly L. ....'50 '75 C.787 L.575 J.D. 34 Lure Ct.‡
Burke, Andrew John '59 '93
(adm. in NY; not adm. in NC) Tereck Off. Solutions

Burke, Frederick A., (AV) '39 '64 C&L.107 B.A., J.D.
3622 Lyckan Parkway Suite 5008, 27707
Telephone: 919-489-7788 Fax: 919-489-2699
Email: f.burke.attorney@att.net
Corporations, Commercial Transactions and Real Estate.
See Professional Biographies, DURHAM, NORTH CAROLINA

Burnett, Kandas D. .... '76 '01 C.1128 B.A. L.862 J.D. [Ⓐ Morris,M.&M.]
Burns, Keith D., (BV) ....'68 '93 C.575 B.A. L.896 J.D. [Ⓒ Morris,M.&M.]
Burton, Jill E., (BV) ....'67 '92 C.316 B.S. L.574 J.D. 100 E. Parrish St.
Butterfield, Kevin W., (BV) .... '57 '86 C.373 B.A. L.575 J.D. [Haywood,D.&M.]
Calhoun, Michael D., (AV) ....'53 '78 C.228 A.B. L.575 J.D. [Gulley&C.]
Calore, William J. '57 '82 C.321 B.A. L.902 J.D.
(adm. in VA; not adm. in NC) Asst. Gen. Coun., Reichhold, Inc. (Legal Department)
Campbell, J. Alan, (BV) ....'70 '95 C.896 B.S. L.228 J.D. [Kennon,C.B.C.&M.]
Campbell, Lawrence M., (BV) .... '53 '87 C.228 A.B. L.574 J.D. 2105 Duncan St.
Capron, Cheryl Y., (BV) ....'53 '89 C.428 B.A. L.896 J.D. [C.Capron]
Capron, Cheryl, (BV) ....3819 Cole Mill Road
Carey, James D. '66 '91 C&L.93 B.S., J.D.
(adm. in CT; not adm. in NC) 802 W. Main St.‡
Carman, Danielle M. ....'70 '97 C.1356 B.S. L.575 J.D. Asst. Appl. Def.
Carpenter, Charles F., (AV) ....'57 '82 C&L.575 B.A., J.D. [Pulley,W.K.&L.]
Carr, James L., (BV) ....'36 '65 C&L.575 A.B. Supr. Ct. Clk.
Carrington, Paul D. '31 '55 C.846 B.A. L.309 LL.B.
(adm. in TX; not adm. in NC) Prof. of Law, Duke Univ.
Castle, Leroy R., (CV) ....'36 '84 C.923 B.A. L.1228 J.D. 123 Wicklow Lane
Chaney, Richard G. ....'50 '76 C.228 B.A. L.575 J.D. Dist. J.
Chapin, Denise D. .... '61 '91 C.317 B.A. L.896 J.D. Duke Univ., School of Law

Chapman, Heidi G., P.L.L.C.
(See Chapel Hill)

Charns, D. Tucker, (BV) ....'61 '89 C&L.575 B.A., J.D. [Charns&C.]
Charns, M. Alexander, (BV) ....'56 '82 C.112 B.A. L.575 J.D. [Charns&C.]

Charns & Charns, (BV)
123 Orange Street, P.O. Box 59, 27702
Telephone: 919-956-7564 Fax: 919-956-7409
Email: charnsandcharns@verizon.net URL: http://www.charns-charnslaw.com
Members of Firm: M. Alexander Charns; D. Tucker Charns.
Personal Injury, Automobile Accidents, Wrongful Death, Criminal Law, Driving While Intoxicated, Drug Crimes, Felonies, Misdemeanors, Traffic Violations, Civil Rights, Police Misconduct, Freedom of Information, Public Records, Automobile Negligence, Motor Vehicle Accidents and Injuries, Plaintiff's Personal Injury, Information and Privacy, Civil Appeals, Criminal Appeals, Civil Liberties, Civil Rights Section 1983, Constitutional Law, First Amendment Law, Fourth Amendment Law, Wiretapping, Electronic Surveillance, Malicious Prosecution, Search and Seizure, Criminal Defense, Capital Offenses, Death Penalty, False Arrest, Excessive Use of Force, False Imprisonment, Police Brutality.
See Professional Biographies, DURHAM, NORTH CAROLINA

Cheek, Lewis A., (AV) ....'51 '76 C&L.896 B.A., J.D. [Hedrick M.&C.P.]
Childers, Jeffrey W., Ph.D. ....'58 '03 C.923 B.S. L.575 J.D. [Ⓐ Jenkins,W.&T.]
Childers, Leonor Ortiz, (BV) ....'63 '00 C.469 B.S. L.575 J.D. P.O. Box 2287
Chmura, Donna Ray, (BV) ....'67 '95 C.597 B.S.J. L.273 J.D. [Ⓐ Walker&L.]
Christie, George C. '34 '57 C&L.178 A.B., J.D.
(adm. in NY; not adm. in NC) Prof., Duke Univ. Sch. of Law
Christie, Kathryn McLean ....'49 '80 C.228 B.A. L.339 J.D. W. Durham Station
Chua, Amy L. '62 '90 C&L.309 A.B., J.D.
(adm. in NY; not adm. in NC) Assoc. Prof., Duke Univ. Sch. of Law
Ciompi, N. A., (AV) ....'44 '73 C&L.228 A.B., J.D. Assoc. Univ. Coun., Duke Univ.
Clark, James A. ....'67 '99 C.1301 B.S. L.45 J.D. [Ⓒ Pulley,W.K.&L.]
Clarke, Margaret Madison .... '60 '89 C.228 B.A./B.S. L.575 J.D. 4101 Grove Ridge‡
Clayton, Jerry B., (BV) ....'45 '70 C.575 B.A. L.37 J.D. [Clayton,M.M.&C.]
Clayton, Myrick, McClanahan & Coulter, PLLC, (AV) ....121 E. Parrish St.
Clement, Arthur J., III '34 '60 C&L.329 B.A., LL.B.
(adm. in SC; not adm. in NC) Dir., Advertising & Pub. Rel., N.C. Mut. Life Ins. Co.
Cofield, Erica D. ....'70 '96 C.228 A.B. L.575 J.D. Off. of Dist. Atty.
Cole, James A., Jr., (AV) ....'35 '61 C&L.575 A.B., LL.B. [Stubbs,C.B.P.&B.]
Cole, Kathryn B. ....'51 '90 C.575 B.A. L.574 J.D. 128 E. Parrish St.
Coleman, James E., Jr., (AVⓉ) '46 '75 C.309 A.B. L.178 J.D.
(adm. in NY; not adm. in NC) Prof., Duke Univ. Sch. of Law

Coleman, Gledhill, Hargrave & Peek, P.C.
(See Hillsborough)

Constantinou, Catherine L., (BV) ....'— '93 C.577 B.A. L.574 J.D. [Constantinou]
Constantinou Law Group, (BV) ....120 E. Parrish St. Ste. 300
Costley, Mark O., (AV) ....'60 '85 C&L.228 A.B., J.D. [Walker&L.]
Cotter, William J., (AV) ....'47 '79 C.232 B.S. L.228 J.D. [W.J.Cotter]

Cotter, William J., P.A., (AV)
2003 Chapel Hill Road, P.O. Box 3507, 27702
Telephone: 919-489-0339 Fax: 919-683-3290
URL: http://www.williamjcotterlaw.com
William J. Cotter.
Criminal Law, Family Law, Traffic Violations in State and Federal Courts. Personal Injury.
See Professional Biographies, DURHAM, NORTH CAROLINA

Coulter, Ronald G., (BV) ....'54 '80 C&L.575 B.A., J.D. [Clayton,M.M.&C.]
Covington, J. Wesley ....'50 '81 C.228 B.A. L.574 J.D. [Bryant,P.C.I.&L.]
Cox, James D. '43 '70 L.1065 J.D.
(adm. in CA; not adm. in NC) Prof., Duke Univ. Sch. of Law
Crabtree, Guy W., (AV) ....'48 '78 C.575 B.A. L.574 J.D. [Pulley,W.K.&L.]
Craig, Joel M., (AV) ....'54 '80 C&L.575 A.B., J.D. [Kennon,C.B.C.&M.]

Craven, James B., III, (AV) '42 '67 C.575 A.B. L.228 J.D.
349 West Main Street, P.O. Box 1366, 27702
Telephone: 919-688-8295 Fax: 919-688-7832
Email: jbc64@mindspring.com

(This Listing Continued)

Craven, James B., III (Continued)

Federal and General Practice. International Law, Bankruptcy, Collections, Real Estate, Federal Criminal Law and Federal Appellate Practice, Federal Executive Clemency.
Reference: First Union National Bank.
See Professional Biographies, DURHAM, NORTH CAROLINA

Craven, P. Lee, III ....'75 '02 C&L.575 B.A., J.D. [Ⓐ Bryant,P.C.I.&L.]
Craver, G. Rhodes, (AV) .... '56 '82 C.575 B.S. L.896 J.D. [Kennon,C.B.C.&M.]
Crawford-Turner, Audrey L. ....'55 '94 C&L.574 B.A., J.D. [Ⓒ Frasier&A.]
Credle, Ann M., (BV) ....'67 '93 C.953 B.A. L.1345 J.D. [A.M.Credle]
Credle, Ann M., P.A., (BV) ....212 W. Main. St., Ste. 100
Creekmore, Joseph P. ....'38 '62 C&L.575 A.B., LL.B. Clk., U.S. Dist. Ct.
Crook, C. Connor ....'— '99 C.999 B.A. L.893 J.D. [Ⓒ H.Hofler]
Crossman, Colin R., Esq. ..... '78 '03 C.119 B.S. L.228 J.D. 762 Ninth St., Ste. 591 (Pat.)
Curran, Kathryn T. ....'59 '85 C&L.575 B.S., J.D. [Ⓐ McPherson&R.]
Daly, James, IV, Ph.D. '68 '01 C.1150 B.A. L.421 J.D.
(adm. in KY; not adm. in NC; See Pat. Sect.) [Ⓐ Jenkins,W.&T.]

Daniels Daniels & Verdonik, P.A.
(See Research Triangle Park)

Daniel-Weeks, Bernell .... '68 '97 C.73 B.S. L.574 J.D. P.O. Box 52405
Danner, Richard A. '47 '79 C&L.966 B.A., J.D.
(adm. in WI; not adm. in NC) Assoc. Dean, Duke Univ. Sch. of Law
Darden, P. Ashley ....'74 '03 C.576 B.A. L.1228 J.D. [Ⓐ Jenkins,W.&T.]
Darsie, Charles, (AV) ....'40 '69 C.318 B.A. L.575 J.D. [Darsie,S.M.&D.]
Darsie, Sharpe, Mackritis & Dukelow, P.L.L.C., (AV) .... 128 East Parrish Street
Dayan, Marshall '58 '86 C.280 A.B. L.469 J.D.
North Carolina Central Univ., Sch. of Law
DeBank, Douglas F., (AV) ....'37 '62 C.575 B.S. L.228 J.D. 3622 Lyckan Pkwy.
DeBruyn, F. Robert, (BVⓉ) '34 '62 C.197 A.B. L.911 J.D.
(adm. in WA; not adm. in NC) 4710 Regency Drive
DeMott, Deborah A. '48 '74 C.821 B.A. L.569 J.D.
(adm. in NY; not adm. in NC) Prof., Duke Univ., Sch. of Law
Dempson, Zabrina White, (CV) ....'69 '95 C&L.574 B.A., J.D. [Z.W.Dempson]
Dempson, Zabrina White, P.C., Law Office of, (CV) ....122 E. Main Street
Derr, Dailey J., (AV) ....'41 '72 C&L.575 B.A., J.D. [Ⓒ Sands A.M.&M.]
Dimond, Diane '51 '78 C.352 B.A. L.309 J.D.
Clinical Professor of Law, Duke Univ. School of Law
DiStefano, Pamela R., (BV) ....'57 '84 C.205 B.A. L.1338 J.D. 1316 Broad Street
Dixon, Wallace W. ....'43 '72 C.575 B.S. L.896 J.D. U.S. Mag.
Drake, Wilfred F., (BV) ....'49 '78 C.24 B.A. L.945 J.D. [W.F.Drake]

Drake, Wilfred F., P.C., (BV)
1007 Vickers Avenue, 27707
Telephone: 919-683-8441
Email: wfd17@netzero.com URL: http://www.lawyers.com/wdrakelaw
Wilfred F. Drake.
General Civil Practice. Estate Planning and Estate Administration.
See Professional Biographies, DURHAM, NORTH CAROLINA

Driansky, Richard ....'50 '75 C.994 B.A. L.94 J.D. 4611 University Dr.

Duke, Kenneth J., (BV) '57 '84 C.896 B.A. L.469 J.D.
100 East Parrish Street, Suite 300 West, 27702
Telephone: 919-683-2175 Fax: 919-680-3500
Email: kennethduke.attorney@verizon.net URL: http://www.lawyers.com/kennethduke
Languages: Spanish and English.
Workers Compensation, Traffic Violations, Driving While Intoxicated, Drivers License Suspension, Personal Injury.
Reference: Bank of America.
See Professional Biographies, DURHAM, NORTH CAROLINA

Dukelow, Lisa M., (BV) .... '68 '95 C.575 B.A. L.574 J.D. [Darsie,S.M.&D.]
Dyer, Frances L. ....'45 '76 C.811 B.A. L.574 J.D. 915 Lamond Ave.
Eaddy, H. Blake '67 '96 C.576 B.S. L.1345 J.D.
Corporate Counsel, Bell & Howell Mail & Messaging Tech.
Eagen, Elizabeth S., (BV) ....'43 '78 C.577 B.A. L.61 J.D. [Eagen&E.]
Eagen, Thomas H., (BV) ....'43 '77 C.529 A.B. L.61 J.D. [Eagen&E.]
Eagen & Eagen, (BV) ....4 Consultant Place
Eakes, Martin D., (AV) ....'54 '80 C.198 B.A. L.976 J.D. P.O. Box 3619
Earnhardt, Thomas Wright '45 '71
C.198 A.B. L.575 J.D. N.C. Central Univ. School of Law‡
Easley, Mary Pipines, (AV) '50 '75 C&L.896 B.A., J.D.
N.C. Central Univ. School of Law
Easthom, James R., (CV) ....'63 '91 C.228 A.B. L.893 J.D. [Kennon,C.B.C.&M.]
Edwards, Mark E., (AV) ....'59 '85 C&L.575 B.A., J.D. [Edwards&T.] ⊙
Edwards, Rudolph L., (BV) ....'38 '64 C&L.575 A.B., LL.B. 128 E. Parrish St.
Edwards, S. Matthew ....'80 '05 C&L.1228 B.S., J.D. [Ⓐ Olive&O.]

Edwards & Trenkle, PLLC, (AV)
331 West Main Street, Suite 508, P.O. Box 77, 27701-3232 ⊙
Telephone: 919-688-9555 Fax: 919-683-5650
URL: http://www.edwardstrenkle.com
Mark E. Edwards (Board Certified Specialist in Federal Criminal Law and State Criminal Law, North Carolina State Board of Legal Specialization); Robert C. Trenkle;—Dionne R. Gonder.
Criminal Law, Driving While Intoxicated (DWI), Drug Crimes, Felonies, Parole and Probation, Traffic Violations, Personal Injury, Auto Accidents, Dog Bites, Sexual Abuse, Wrongful Death.
Pittsboro, North Carolina Office: 72 Hillsborough Street, PO Box 541, 27312. Telephone: 919-545-5626. Fax: 919-545-0991.
See Professional Biographies, DURHAM, NORTH CAROLINA

Ekstrand, Robert C. .... '— '98 C.446 B.A. L.228 J.D. [Ekstrand&E.]
Ekstrand, Samantha Sparks .... '74 '01 C.197 A.B. L.228 J.D. [Ekstrand&E.]

Ekstrand & Ekstrand, LLP
811 Ninth Street, Suite 260, 27705
Telephone: 919-416-4590 Fax: 919-416-4591 URL: http://www.ninthstreetlaw.com
Email: sje@ninthstreetlaw.com URL: http://www.ekstrand-law.com
Robert C. Ekstrand; Samantha Sparks Ekstrand.
Criminal Law, Driving While Intoxicated (DWI), Drug Crimes, Felonies, Misdemeanors, Traffic Violations, Personal Injury, Automobile Accidents, Wrongful Death, Medical Malpractice, Wills, Probate, Commercial Bankruptcy, Contracts, Legal Malpractice, Education.
See Professional Biographies, DURHAM, NORTH CAROLINA

Ellison, Daniel Martin '55 '84 C.228 A.B. L.575 J.D.
Legal Editor/Writer, Employment Law Research, Inc.
Elvin, Bruce A. '68 '94 C.813 B.A. L.228 J.D.
(adm. in NY; not adm. in NC) P.O. Box 90362
Erca, Alison A. ....'52 '83 C.610 B.S. L.284 J.D. 1316 Broad Street
Erickson, Ian Andrew ....'— '01 C&L.575 B.A., J.D. U.S. District Court
Ernst, Janis C. ....'61 '87 C.477 B.A. L.329 J.D. 1707 Haddington Dr.
Everett, Robinson O. ....'28 '50 C&L.309 A.B., J.D. [Everett&E.] (⊙Raleigh)
Everett & Everett ....103 W. Main St., Ste. 200

Everett-Perry, Kathy R., (BV) '62 '94 C.1378 B.S. L.574 J.D.
100 E. Parrish St., Ste. 200
Ewing, Carey L. . . . . . . '58 '83 C.602 B.A. L.796 J.D. [Ewing]
Ewing Law Center, P.C. . . . . . . 2304 S. Miami Blvd., Ste. 221
Eyster, Donna Turner . . . . . . '48 '01 C.471 B.A. L.575 J.D. [Mitchell,E.&W.]
Falcone, Edward J., (BV) . . . . . '52 '79 C.228 B.A. L.790 J.D. [H.W.a.E.J.F.Vann]
Farrin, James Scott, Law Offices of '62 '90
C.855 B.A. L.228 J.D. 4819 Emperor Blvd., Suite 200
Fenhagen, Melinda Caitlin '69 '94
C&L.575 B.A., J.D. The Center for Death Penalty Litigation, Inc.
Ferguson, Jay H., (AV) . . . . . . '63 '89 C.34 B.S. L.574 J.D. [Thomas,F.&M.]
Fisher, Stewart W., (AV) . . . . . . '50 '82 C.228 B.A. L.575 J.D. [Glenn,M.&F.]
Fitzpatrick, John C., II . . . . . . '71 '96 C&L.575 B.A., J.D. [J.C.Fitzpatrick]

Fitzpatrick, John C., P.C., Law Office of
116 W. Main Street, 27701
Telephone: 919-683-9500 Fax: 919-683-8400
URL: http://www.johncfitzpatrick.com
John C. Fitzpatrick, II.
DWI, Traffic, Criminal, Personal Injury.
See Professional Biographies, DURHAM, NORTH CAROLINA

Flebotte, Daniel R., (BV) '52 '81 C.228 B.A. L.910 J.D.
[Browne,F.W.&W.] (⊙Creedmoor, Greensboro)
Fleishman, Joel L. . . . . . . '34 '59 C&L.575 A.B., J.D. Prof., Duke Univ. Sch. of Law
Fleshner, Mark L. . . . . . . '60 '94 C.350 B.S. L.273 J.D. [Fleshner&K.] (Pat.) ⊙
Fleshner & Kim, LLP . . . . . . 2304 S. Miami Blvd. (Pat.) (⊙Herndon, VA)
Flowers, Charles E., III . . . . . . '59 '96 C.17 B.A. L.575 J.D. [Adkins&F.]
Fogel, Mark E., (AV) . . . . '42 '74 C.186 B.E. L.575 J.D. [Ⓖ Pulley,W.K.&L.] (⊙Raleigh)
Foil, N. Joanne, (AV) . . . . . . '52 '76 C.1130 B.A. L.575 J.D. [Foil]
Foil Law Offices, (AV) . . . . . . 112 E. Main St.

Fontana, Lynn, (BV) '59 '88 C.48 B.A. L.575 J.D.
1316 Broad Street, 27705
Telephone: 919-286-2500 Facsimile: 919-286-2544
Email: lyfontana@aol.com URL: http://www.lawyers.com/lynnfontana
Plaintiff's Employment Law and Litigation including Discrimination, Wrongful Discharge, Employment Contracts and Separation Agreements.
See Professional Biographies, DURHAM, NORTH CAROLINA

Fox, Adrienne M. '48 '74 C.289 A.B. L.128 J.D.
Prof. of Law, N.C. Central Univ. School of Law
Foye, Anita . . . . . . '72 '97 C&L.575 B.A., J.D. 2515 Apex Hwy.
Frasier, Ralph K., Jr., (BV) . . . . . . '69 '94 C.302 B.S. L.574 J.D. [Frasier&A.]
Frasier & Alston, P.A., (BV) . . . . . . 100 East Parrish Street, Suite 350
Freeman, Homa J., Jr., (AV) . . . . . . '49 '74 C&L.575 A.B., J.D. [Maxwell,F.&B.]
French, Jan H. '53 '83 C.831 B.A. L.184 J.D.
(adm. in CT; not adm. in NC) 3106 Ithaca St.
Fulghum, Caitlyn T., (BV) . . . . . . '72 '98 C.37 B.A. L.228 J.D. 100 E. Parrish St., Ste. 300
Galifianakis, Nick, & Associates, (AV) '28 '56
C&L.228 A.B., LL.B. Suite 200, 301 West Main Street
Gann, Pamela Brooks . . . . . . '48 '73 C.575 B.A. L.228 J.D. Dean, Duke Univ. Sch. of Law
Garrett, Nathan T. . . . . . . '31 '86 C.976 A.B. L.574 J.D. 3923 Northhampton Rd.
Gebeaux, Steven Matthew . . . . . . '69 '99 C.34 B.S. L.575 J.D. [Eagen&E.]
Glean, Pamela Stanback '56 '80 C.228 B.A. L.574 J.D.
N.C. Central Univ. School of Law
Glenn, Robert B., Jr., (AV) . . . . . . '49 '74 C.682 B.A. L.575 J.D. [Glenn,M.&F.]

Glenn, Mills & Fisher, P.A., (AV) BB
Suite 709, South Bank Building, 400 West Main Street, P.O. Drawer 3865, 27702-3865
Telephone: 919-683-2135 Fax: 919-688-9339
Email: GMF-Law.com URL: http://www.gmf-law.com
Robert B. Glenn, Jr.; William S. Mills; Stewart W. Fisher; Carlos E. Mahoney.
General Civil Trial Practice in State and Federal Courts, Personal Injury, Wrongful Death, Professional Negligence, Commercial and Civil Rights Law and Employment Law.
See Professional Biographies, DURHAM, NORTH CAROLINA

Goff, Milton Tremayne, The Law Office of '74 '01
C.884 B.S.B.A. L.574 J.D. 3020 Pickett Road, Suite 424
Goldston, William G., (AV) . . . . . . '52 '81 C.577 B.S. L.574 J.D. 123 Orange Street
Gomez, Anne M. . . . . . . '66 '97 C.597 A.B. L.575 J.D. Asst. Appl. Def.
Gonder, Dionne R. . . . . . . '73 '97 C.228 B.A. L.569 J.D. [Ⓐ Edwards&T.]
Goodson, Paul M. '68 '95 C.575 B.S. L.896 J.D.
3101 Guess Road, F-106 (⊙Charlotte, Raleigh)
Gordon, Elaine M. . . . . . . '52 '82 C.280 B.A. L.1162 J.D. Ctr. for Death Penalty Litig.
Gordon, Nancy E., (AV) . . . . . . '54 '79 C.477 B.A. L.930 J.D. [N.E.Gordon]
Gordon, Nancy E., P.C., Law Offices of, (AV) . . . . . . 3717 A University Drive
Grace, Joan M. . . . . . . '50 Reichhold, Inc. (Legal Department)
Grantham, Kimberly M. . . . . . . '69 '94 C.575 A.B. L.228 J.D. 203 Brandermill Drive
Green, Paul M., Attorney at Law, (AV) . . . '57 '85 C&L.228 B.S., J.D. 1304 Carolina Ave.
Griffin, John R., III . . . . . . '70 '98 C.575 B.S. L.574 J.D. [J.D.Williams,Jr.]
Gudaitis, Christy Myers, (AV) '59 '86 C&L.228 A.B., J.D.
Asst. Univ. Coun., Duke Univ.
Gulley, Wilbur P., (AV) . . . . . . '48 '81 C.228 B.A. L.588 J.D. Sen. [Gulley&C.]
Gulley & Calhoun, (AV) . . . . . . 400 W. Main Street, Suite 501
Gump, Elli Royak '49 '75 C&L.767 B.S., J.D.
(adm. in CA; not adm. in NC) 911 Broad‡
Gustafson, Mark D., (AV) '61 '86 C.112 B.A. L.228 J.D.
Asst. Univ. Coun., Duke Univ.
Guze, Jonathan David . . . . . . '50 '94 C.309 A.B. L.228 J.D. [J.D.Guze]
Guze, Jonathan D. . . . . . . 2507 Wrightwood Ave.
Haagen, Paul H. '50 '83 C.311 B.A. L.976 J.D.
(adm. in PA; not adm. in NC) Prof., Duke Univ. Sch. of Law
Hailey, Gwendolyn S., Law Offices of '61 '89 C.575 A.B. L.574 J.D.
(adm. in PA; not adm. in NC) 315 E. Chapel Hill St., Ste. 405

Hairston, Dorothy, Law Office of '77 '03 C&L.574 B.A., J.D.
400 West Main Street, Suite 611, 27701
Telephone: 919-682-3200 Fax: 919-682-3422
Email: dhairston21@msn.com URL: http://www.dorothyhairstonlaw.com
Family Law, Criminal Law, Traffic Violations, Personal Injury, Medical Malpractice, Workers Compensation, Real Estate, Business, Military Law, Bankruptcy.
See Professional Biographies, DURHAM, NORTH CAROLINA

Hairston, James E., Jr., (BV) '64 '90 C.1369 B.S. L.574 J.D.
100 E. Parrish St., Ste. 350
Hall, David Charles '66 '93 C.576 B.S. L.575 J.D.
Assoc. Gen. Coun., Intell. Prop., Cree, Inc. (Pat.)
Hammer, Ruth Cohen, (BV) . . . . . . '57 '84 C.674 A.B. L.228 J.D. [Roberti,W.L.&W.]
Harbour, Clifford P. '56 '81 C.689 B.A. L.607 J.D.
(adm. in CO; not adm. in NC) P.O. Box 61054‡

Harkins, Harry H., Jr., (AVⓉ) '51 '76
C.228 A.B. L.880 J.D. 1822 N.C. Highway 54 East (⊙Atlanta, GA)

Harper, Theodore R., (AV) '51 '79 C.174 B.A. L.1066 J.D.
PMB 336 6409 Fayetteville Road, Suite 120, 27713
Telephone: 919-544-1137 Fax: 919-544-1139
Email: ted@trianglelegalsolutions.com URL: http://www.trianglelegalsolutions.com
Technology Contracts, Software Licensing, Mergers and Acquisitions, Business Start-Ups, Incorporation, Venture Capital, Strategic Alliances, E-commerce, Internet Licensing, Intellectual Property, Copyrights, Joint Ventures, Distribution Agreements.
See Professional Biographies, DURHAM, NORTH CAROLINA

Harris, Robert J., (CV) '71 '97 C&L.574 B.A., J.D.
315 East Chapel Hill Street, Suite 208
Harriss, William G., (AV) . . . . . . '40 '66 C.575 B.A. L.228 LL.B. [Harriss&M.]
Harriss & Marion, P.L.L.C., (AV) . . . . . . 3326 Chapel Hill Blvd.
Hart, Jane R. . . . . . . '33 '91 C.914 B.A. L.575 J.D. 3915 Regent Rd.
Hartsell, Laura E. . . . . . . '70 '96 C&L.575 B.A., J.D. P.O. Box 2247
Hatch, William A. . . . . . . '61 '94 C.649 B.S. L.574 J.D. [Ⓐ Hutson H.&P.]
Hatfield, Patricia M. '51 '87 C.477 A.B. L.575 J.D.
Dep. Gen. Coun., Health Plans & Litig., Blue Cross Blue Shield of N.C.
Hauser, Susan E. . . . . . . '58 '84 C.896 B.A. L.575 J.D. Staff Atty., Admin. Off. of the Cts.
Havighurst, Clark C. '33 '58 C.674 A.B. L.597 J.D.
(adm. in IL; not adm. in NC) Prof., Duke Univ., Sch. of Law
Haywood, John D. . . . . . . '45 '70 C&L.575 B.A., J.D. 3106 Cornwall Rd.‡

Haywood, Denny & Miller, L.L.P., (AV)
3511 Shannon Road Suite 140, 27707
Mailing Address: P.O. Box 51429, Durham, NC 27717
Telephone: 919-403-0000 Fax: 919-403-0001
Email: hdmllp@hdmllp.com
Members of Firm: Egbert L. Haywood (1911-1985); Emery B. Denny, Jr. (1924-1982); George W. Miller, Jr.; Kevin W. Butterfield; Robert E. Levin; John R. Kincaid; George W. Miller, III.
General Civil, Trial and Appellate Practice in State and Federal Courts. Insurance, Corporations, Bankruptcy, Government Relations and Probate Law.
Representative Clients: State Farm Mutual Insurance Cos.; Herald-Sun Papers; Allstate Insurance Co.; Pepsi-Cola Bottling Co. of Roxboro, North Carolina, Inc.; Carolina Canners, Inc.; North Carolina Farm Bureau Mutual Insurance Co.; Wausau Insurance Co.
See Professional Biographies, DURHAM, NORTH CAROLINA

Hearn, Tarrow Leigh '70 '96 C.10 B.A. L.192 J.D.
(adm. in AL; not adm. in NC) Harcourt Brace
Hedrick, James T., (AV) . . . . . . '28 '53 C.902 B.A. L.575 J.D [Hedrick M.&C.P.]

Hedrick Murray & Cheek PLLC, (AV)
3511 Shannon Road, Suite 200, 27707
Mailing Address: P.O. Box 52394, Durham, NC 27717-2394
Telephone: 919-419-3300 Telecopier: 919-419-1600
Email: name@hmclegal.com URL: http://www.hmclegal.com
James T. Hedrick; Josiah S. Murray, III; Lewis A. Cheek; David S. Kennett; John C. Rogers, III;—Martha E. Soule.
General Practice in all State and Federal Courts. Litigation, Real Estate, Land Use and Development Law, Insurance, Labor and Employment, Commercial Transactions, Probate.
Representative Clients: Wachovia Bank & Trust Co.; Duke Power Co.; Liggett Group Inc.; General Telephone Company of the South; Exxon Corp.
See Professional Biographies, DURHAM, NORTH CAROLINA

Hendricks, Kate Sigman, (BV) . . . . '57 '83 C.273 B.A. L.228 J.D. Asst. Coun., Duke Univ.
Herndon, M. Faith, Law Offices of, (AV) '58 '90 C.976 B.A. L.569 J.D.
P.O. Box 51908
Herrin, Mickey A., Jr. '68 '94 C.575 B.S. L.896 J.D.
Dir. of Legal Affs., SportsMEDIA Technology Corp.
Herring, Sandra G. . . . . . . '51 '95 C.822 A.B. L.228 J.D. [Ⓐ Everett&E.]
Hershner, Mildred Ernau . . . . . . '45 '01 C.518 B.A. L.574 J.D. 301 W. Main St., Ste. 200

Higgins, Frankstone, Graves & Morris, P.A.
(See Chapel Hill)

Hill, Daniel B., (BV) . . . . . . '41 '92 C.610 B.A. L.1128 J.D. [Ⓖ H.Hofler]
Hill, James R. . . . . . . '51 '75 C.1378 L.574 J.D. 521 Burlington Ave.★
Hill, James T., (BV) . . . . . . '50 '77 C.575 A.B. L.192 J.D. [Randall&H.]
Hill, Marcus E., (BV) . . . . . . '55 '84 C&L.575 B.A., J.D. 311 East Main Street
Hill, Renée F. . . . . . . '57 '82 C.103 B.S. L.309 J.D. N.C. Central Univ. School of Law
Hilliard, Antoinette D. Rosetta . . . . . . '70 '99 C.575 B.A. L.574 J.D. Pub. Def. Off.
Hirsh, Kenneth J. '53 '77 C.472 A.B. L.260 J.D.
(adm. in FL; not adm. in NC) Duke University
Hobin, Raymond M. . . . . . . '35 '86 C.749 B.S. L.574 J.D. 3609 Britt St.‡
Hofler, R. Hayes, (AV) . . . . . . '46 '74 C.896 B.A. L.893 J.D. [H.Hofler]

Hofler, Hayes, P.A., (AV) BB
1007 Vickers Avenue, 27707-1355
Telephone: 919-682-9663 Fax: 919-682-2016
URL: http://www.lawyers.com/hha
R. Hayes Hofler. Of Counsel: Daniel B. Hill; C. Connor Crook.
Business and Commercial, Construction, Divorce, Family, Legal Malpractice, Litigation and Appeals, Medical Malpractice, Insurance, Personal Injury, Products Liability, Professional Malpractice.
See Professional Biographies, DURHAM, NORTH CAROLINA

Holder, Angela Roddey . . . . . . '38 '60 C.298 B.A. L.861 J.D. Duke Univ. Med. Ctr.
Holleman, Robert D. . . . . . . '14 '35 C&L.896 B.A., J.D. [Ⓖ Everett&E.] ‡

Hollowell Law Offices, P.A.
(See Cary)

Holmes, C. Scott . . . . . . '72 '98 C&L.575 B.A, J.D. [Ⓐ Stubbs,C.B.P.&B.]
Hoof, J. Bruce, (AV) . . . . . . '48 '73 C.575 A.B. L.880 J.D. [Poe&H.P.]
Hopkins, Harriet S., Attorney at Law, (BV) '53 '82
C.228 B.S. L.575 J.D. 2960 Friendship Road
Horowitz, Donald L. '39 '62 C&L.823 A.B., LL.B.
(adm. in NY; not adm. in NC) Prof. of Law, Duke Univ.

Howard, Stallings, From & Hutson, P.A.
(See Raleigh)

Huber, Jay Patrick '66 '94 C.209 B.A. L.575 J.D.
Writer/Editor, Employment Law Research, Inc.
Hudson, Michael C., (BV) '56 '81 C.240 B.A. L.1228 J.D.
1058 W. Club Blvd., Ste. 6603
Huggins, Shelia A. . . . . . . '67 '02 C.576 B.S. L.575 J.D. 2726 Croasdaile Drive, Suite 202
Hughes, James H., (AV) . . . . . . '50 '78 C.232 B.A. L.574 J.D. [Hutson H.&P.]
Hughes, Staples . . . . . . '51 '80 C.259 B.A. L.575 J.D. Asst. Appl. Def.
Hunt, Anita B. . . . . . . '65 '98 C&L.574 B.A., J.D. [Hunt,P.]
Hunt, Gregory A. '69 '96 C.576 B.S.E.E. L.575 J.D.
[Jenkins,W.&T.] (See Pat. Sect.) ⊙
Hunt Law Firm, The, PLLC . . . . . . P.O. Box 130
Hutchins, William T., Jr., (AV) . . . . . . '70 '95 C&L.575 B.A., J.D. [Kennon,C.B.C.&M.]
Hutson, Richard M., II, (AV) . . . . . . '40 '64 C.575 A.B. L.896 LL.B. [Hutson H.&P.]

Hutson Hughes & Powell, P.A., (AV)
Suite 1500 Durham Centre, 300 West Morgan Street, P.O. Drawer 2252-A, 27702
Telephone: 919-683-1561 FAX: 919-683-1276
Richard M. Hutson, II (Board Certified Specialist in Bankruptcy Law, North Carolina State Board of Legal Specialization); James H. Hughes; Stephanie C. Powell;—William A. Hatch.
General Civil Practice, Bankruptcy, Reorganization, Corporate, Commercial Real Estate, Commercial Litigation, Estate Planning and Probate. Trials in all State and Federal Courts.
Representative Clients: Durham County Hospital Corp.; Peoples Security Life Insurance Co.
Approved Attorneys for: Lawyers Title Insurance Corp.; Investors Title Insurance Corp.; Chicago Title Insurance Co.
See Professional Biographies, DURHAM, NORTH CAROLINA

Hyland, D. Christopher, (BV) .... '68 '95 C.970 B.A. L.1345 J.D. P.O. Box 52149

Hyman, Phelps & McNamara, P.C., (BVⓉ)
4819 Emperor Boulevard, Suite 400, 27703 ⊙
Telephone: 919-313-4750 Fax: 919-313-4751
URL: http://www.hpm.com
Marc H. Shapiro (Resident).
Practice before all Courts, Government Agencies and International Regulatory Authorities involving Foods, Drugs, Cosmetics, Medical Devices, Biologics, Pesticides, Controlled Substances and Consumer Products.
Irvine, California Office: Hyman, Phelps & McNamara. 2603 Main Street, Suite 760. Telephone: 949-553-7400. Fax: 949-553-7433.
Washington, D.C. Office: Hyman, Phelps & McNamara, P.C. 700 Thirteenth Street, N.W., Suite 1200. Telephone: 202-737-5600. Fax: 202-737-9329.
See Professional Biographies, DURHAM, NORTH CAROLINA

Idol, Robert A., (BV) .... '56 '81 C&L.575 B.S., J.D. [Bryant,P.C.I.&L.]
Irvin, A. Vann, (BV) .... '51 '82 C&L.575 B.A., J.D. [Brown&B.]
Jacobson, Paul C. .... '56 '81 C.668 B.A. L.36 J.D. [Sands A.M.&M.]
Jacobson, Sandra W., (AVⓉ) '30 '55 C.881 B.A. L.976 J.D.
(adm. in NY; not adm. in NC) 910 Constitution Dr., Apt. 820
Jefferies, Deborah Mayo '52 '79 C.575 B.A. L.574 J.D.
Law Libr. & Assoc. Prof., N.C. Central Univ. School of Law
Jenkins, Richard E., (AV) '46 '75
C.576 B.S. L.575 J.D. [Jenkins,W.&T.] (See Pat. Sect.) ⊙

Jenkins, Wilson & Taylor, P.A., (AV) BB
University Tower, Suite 1400, 3100 Tower Boulevard, 27707 ⊙
Telephone: 919-493-8000 Fax: 919-419-0383
URL: http://www.jenkinswilsontaylor.com
Richard E. Jenkins; Jeffrey L. Wilson; Arles A. Taylor, Jr.; Gregory A. Hunt;—Bentley J. Olive; E. Eric Mills; Christopher P. Perkins, Ph.D. (Not admitted in NC); James Daly IV, Ph.D. (Not admitted in NC); Jeffrey W. Childers, Ph.D.; P. Ashley Darden.
Patent, Trademark and Copyright Law.
Representative Clients: Böwe Bell and Howell Mail Co.; Duke University; Freudenberg Spunweb Co.; GlaxoSmithKline, Inc.; Huesker, Inc.; North Carolina State University; Sumitomo Electric Lightwave Corp.; The University of North Carolina at Chapel Hill; Vanderbilt University.
Raleigh, North Carolina Office: NCSU Centennial Campus, Suite 101, Venture II, 920 Main Campus Drive, 27606. Telephone: 919-424-3710. Fax: 919-424-3711.
See Professional Biographies, DURHAM, NORTH CAROLINA

Jervis, Robert B., (AV) .... '47 '72 C.1309 A.B. L.575 J.D. [R.B.Jervis]
Jervis, Robert B., P.C., Law Office of, (AV) ..... 3326 Chapel Hill Boulevard, Suite B-110
Johnson, Monte E. '52 '79 C&L.623 B.A., J.D.
(adm. in OK; not adm. in NC) 4525 Murphy School Rd.‡
Johnson, Reginald James '67 '98 C.803 B.S. L.575 J.D.
Legis. & Policy Coun., Ctr. for Responsible Lending

Johnson, Hearn, Vinegar, Gee & Glass, PLLC, (AV)
Generation Plaza Suite 200, 1822 N.C. Highway 54 East, 27713 ⊙
Telephone: 919-544-3302 Fax: 919-544-5920
Email: jhvgg@jhvgglaw.com
Richard J. Vinegar.
Civil trial and appellate practice before all state and federal courts and administrative agencies, administrative law, including occupational licensing, alternative dispute resolution, automobile dealer law, business and corporate law, franchise law, government relations, including representation before the General Assembly and regulatory agencies, insurance insolvency, state and local taxation, trade association law, wills, trusts and estates and unfair competition.
Raleigh, North Carolina Office: Two Hannover Square, 434 Fayetteville Street Mall, Suite 2200, P.O. Box 1776, 27602. Telephone: 919-743-2200. Fax: 919-743-2201. Email: jhvgm@jhvgmlaw.com
See Professional Biographies, DURHAM, NORTH CAROLINA

Johnston, Douglas A. .... '46 '71 C&L.575 B.A., J.D. Asst. City Atty.
Johnston, James J., (BV) .... '47 '75 C.205 B.A. L.574 J.D. 3721 University Dr.

Jones, Dana G. '— '98 C.966 B.S. L.574 J.D.
14 Grove Park, 27705
Telephone: 919-309-2411 Fax: 919-383-2078
Email: loodgj@aol.com URL: http://www.keepthefaithlawfirm.com
Divorce, Child Custody and Child Support, Bankruptcy, Adoption.
See Professional Biographies, DURHAM, NORTH CAROLINA

Jones, Michael A. .... '— '92 C.198 B.A. L.574 J.D. [M.A.Jones&Assoc.]
Jones, Trina .... '66 '92 C.188 B.A. L.477 J.D. Asst. Prof., Duke Univ. Sch. of Law
Jones, Michael A., & Associates, PLLC .... 100 East Parrish Street
Jones-Peretto, Lenore A. .... '69 '97 C.681 A.B. L.569 J.D. 4819 Emperor Blvd.
Jones-Richardson, Vedia, (BV) '56 '83
C.329 B.F.A. L.276 J.D. [A Olive&O.] (See Pat. Sect.)
Jones-Smith, Kimberly Jonita .... '66 '92 C.369 B.S. L.574 J.D. 301 W. Main Street
Jordan, Jennifer '55 '84 C.1222 B.B.A. L.472 J.D.
(adm. in FL; not adm. in NC) 15 Briarfield Ct.‡
Jordan, Michael A., (BV) .... '66 '93 C.575 B.A. L.574 J.D. [A J.S.Farrin]
Jordan, Thomas W., Jr., (BV) .....'49 '74 C.797 B.A. L.575 J.D. Off. of Durham Co. Atty
Joyce, Diane Scobie ...... '66 '94 C&L.575 B.S.B.A., J.D. Triangle Pharmaceuticals, Inc.
Joyner, Irving L. ....'— '77 C.415 B.S. L.1292 J.D. N.C. Central Univ. School of Law
Kalfas, Nahale Freeland, (BV) '70 '99 C.576 B.A. L.228 J.D.
[A N.Galifianakis&Assoc.]
Kalo, Monica Kivel ..... '47 '75 C.577 B.A. L.575 J.D. N.C. Central Univ. School of Law
Kaluzny, Melissa K. '69 '97 C.385 B.A. L.300 J.D.
Asst. Coun., Blue Cross Blue Shield of North Carolina
Kaminetzky, Eric C., (BV) .... '63 '92 C&L.174 B.A., J.D. [Triangle T.T.]
Kaminski, Cheryl L. .... '59 '92 C.509 B.S. L.229 J.D. P.O. Box 71975
Kellogg, Leigh R. .... '64 '90 C.896 B.A. L.228 J.D. 814 Onslow St.
Kennett, David S., (BV) .... '57 '83 C&L.575 B.S., J.D. [Hedrick M.&C.P.]
Kennon, A. William, (AV) .... '40 '67 C.228 B.A. L.575 J.D. [Kennon,C.B.C.&M.]

Kennon, Craver, Belo, Craig & McKee, PLLC, (AV)
4011 University Drive, Suite 300, P.O. Box 51579, 27717-1579
Telephone: 919-490-0500 Telecopier: 919-490-0873
Email: name@kennoncraver.com URL: http://www.kennoncraver.com
A. William Kennon; Katherine L. McKee; Robert O. Belo; Joel M. Craig; G. Rhodes Craver; J. Alan Campbell; James R. Easthom; William T. Hutchins, Jr. (Board Certified Specialist in Real Property, Business, Commercial and Industrial Transactions, North Carolina State Board of Legal Specialization); Gwendolyn C. Brooks, Ph.D.; William Albert Anderson, III;—Erin M. Locklear.

(This Listing Continued)

Kennon, Craver, Belo, Craig & McKee, PLLC (Continued)
General Practice in all State and Federal Courts. Corporation, Health Care, Insurance, Labor and Employment, Land Use and Development Law, Litigation, Probate, Real Estate, Taxation, Banking Law.
See Professional Biographies, DURHAM, NORTH CAROLINA

Kerin, Theodore F. '53 '80 C.602 B.A. L.94 J.D.
(adm. in NY; not adm. in NC) 5211 Oakbrook Drive
Kestenbaum, Jane, (AV) .... '55 '83 C.66 A.B. L.930 J.D. [Kestenbaum]

Kestenbaum Law Firm, P.C., (AV) BB
P.O. Box 51939, 27717
Telephone: 919-459-2360 Fax: 919-459-2365
Jane Kestenbaum;—John W. Strange.
Workers' Compensation, Employment Law, Appellate Practice.
Representative Clients: American Red Cross; Broyhill Furniture Industries; Eaton Corporation; Gates McDonald; Comp Management; Key Risk Management; Gallagher Bassett Services; Express Personnel.
See Professional Biographies, DURHAM, NORTH CAROLINA

Kilzer, Susan B., (BV) .... '54 '89 C.838 B.S. L.575 J.D. 3708 Lyckan Pkwy., Ste. 102
Kim, Moses .... '79 '04 C.1365 B.A. L.575 J.D. 5517 Chapel Hill Blvd., Ste. 2000
Kincaid, John R., (BV) ....'65 '91 C&L.575 B.A., J.D. [Haywood,D.&M.]
King, Malvern F., Jr., (AV) ....'43 '68 C&L.575 A.B., J.D. [Pulley,W.K.&L.]
Kirby, Freeman E., Jr. .... '70 '96 C&L.575 B.A., J.D. Nursing Home Abuse Law Ctr.
Kleinschmidt, Mark James ....'70 '00 C&L.575 B.A., J.D. 123 W. Main Street

Knott, Clark & Berger, L.L.P.
(See Raleigh)

Knudsen, Karl E., Law Offices of
(See Raleigh)

Kornberg, Mindy R., (BVⓉ) '60 '85 C.861 B.A. L.575 J.D.
(adm. in AK; not adm. in NC) Duke Univ.
Kornbluth, Michael A. ....'73 '01 C.696 B.A. L.273 J.D. [Kornbluth]

Kornbluth Law Firm, The, P.A.
120 East Parrish Street, Suite 210, 27702
Telephone: 919-680-8575 Fax: 919-688-4335
Email: mak@kornbluthlaw.com URL: http://www.lawyers.com/kornbluthlaw
Michael A. Kornbluth.
Personal Injury, Automobile Accidents, Wrongful Death, Workers Compensation, Employment Law, Discrimination, Sexual Harassment, Employee Benefits, Civil Litigation, Criminal, Satellite Litigation, Traffic.
See Professional Biographies, DURHAM, NORTH CAROLINA

Kreivenas, Algirdas J. .... '65 '92 C.260 L.575 J.D. 2108 Sprunt Ave.
Kurtz, Spencer C. '30 '54 C&L.831 B.S., LL.B.
(adm. in PA; not adm. in NC) Alumacraft Mfg. Co.
LaBarre, David Q. .... '46 '72 C&L.575 B.S., J.D. Superior Ct. J.
Lambe, William H., Jr., (AV) .... '46 '73 C&L.896 B.A., J.D. [Walker&L.]
Langstaff, Frances Lycan .... '37 '84 C.1044 B.P.S. L.1019 J.D. 4 Bobby Parker Place‡
Lanier, Lisa, (BV) .... '67 '92 C&L.575 B.A., J.D. [Lanier]
Lanier Law Group, (BV) ....600 S. Duke St.
Larson, Lex K. ... '39 '66 C.311 B.A. L.309 LL.B. Pres., Employment Law Research, Inc.
Lauffer, Daniel R., (BV) .... '55 '80 C.575 B.A. L.469 J.D. [Roberti,W.L.&W.]
Levin, Robert E., (BV) .... '61 '86 C.576 B.A. L.575 J.D. [Haywood,D.&M.]
Lewis, David O., (AV) .... '56 '81 C.953 B.S. L.575 J.D. [Bryant,P.C.I.&L.]
Lewis, Kenneth W., (AV) ....'61 '86 C.228 B.A. L.309 J.D. 411 W. Chapel Hill St.

Lewis, Anderson, Phillips, Greene & Hinkle, PLLC
(See Chapel Hill)

Lindsley, Jeremy D., (BV) ....'71 '99 C.94 B.A. L.1292 J.D. [A Bryant,P.C.I.&L.]
Linnartz, Hans Christian .... '54 '80 C.893 B.A. L.228 J.D. P.O. Box 1847
Lippincott, Elizabeth Barrett '72 '97
C.112 B.A. L.880 J.D. Assoc. Coun., Blue Cross Blue Shield of NC
Lischer, Tracy Kenyon, (BV) .... '44 '84 C.502 B.A. L.575 J.D. [Pulley,W.K.&L.]
Lischwe, Joseph Michael, (AV) '56 '86 C.602 A.B. L.734 J.D.
Asst. Gen. Coun., Reichhold, Inc. (Legal Department)
Locklear, Erin M. .... '75 '02 C.674 A.B. L.575 J.D. [A Kennon,C.B.C.&M.]
Loflin, Thomas F., III, (AV) .... '42 '70 C.198 A.B. L.575 J.D. 123 Orange St.
Logan, Lisa M., Law Office of, (BV) '65 '91
C.575 B.A. L.574 J.D. 400 West Main Street, Suite 501
Long, Austine M. ....'62 '00 C.445 B.S. L.64 J.D. 1105 W. Chapel Hill Street, Suite 3
Love, Robert M. .... '62 '90 C&L.228 B.S., J.D. [Love L.]
Love Law .... 1415 W. NC Hwy. 54, Ste. 124
Lovell, Benjamin E. .... '71 '96 C.576 B.A. L.575 J.D. Chapter 13 Off.
Luney, Percy Robert, Jr. '49 '75 C.299 B.A. L.309 J.D.
(adm. in DC; not adm. in NC)
Dean and Prof. of Law, N.C. Central Univ. School of Law
Mackritis, Rosemary D., (BV) ....'59 '90 C.577 B.S. L.575 J.D. [Darsie,S.M.&D.]
Mahoney, Carlos E., (BV) .... '74 '99 C&L.575 B.A., J.D. [Glenn,M.&F.]

Maitland & Maitland, PLLC
(See Chapel Hill)

Marion, Joseph W., (AV) ....'49 '78 C&L.228 B.A., J.D. [Harriss&M.]
Markert, Bobbi Jo .... '72 '98 C.925 B.S. L.575 J.D. Asst. Appl. Def.
Markham, Charles B. .... '26 '51 C.228 A.B. L.273 LL.B. 204 N. Dillard St.‡
Marsh, William A., Jr., (BV) ....'27 '53 C&L.574 B.S., LL.B [Marsh&M.]
Marsh, William Andrew, III, (BV) .... '58 '83 C.302 B.A. L.575 J.D. [Marsh&M.]
Marsh and Marsh, (BV) .... 120 E. Parrish St., Suite 310

Martin & Jones, (AV)
University Towers, Suite 526, 3100 Tower Boulevard, 27707 ⊙
Telephone: 919-544-3000
URL: http://www.MartinandJones.com
Hoyt G. Tessener.
Asbestos Litigation, Bad Faith and Unfair Competition, Business Litigation, Construction Site Injuries, Inadequate Security, Medical Malpractice, Nursing/Rest Home Negligence, Personal Injury, Pharmaceutical and Medical Device Litigation, Product Liability, Social Security Disability, Toxic Torts, Trucking Accidents, Workers' Compensation and Wrongful Death, Land Condemnation, FELA (Federal Employers' Liability Act), Securities Fraud.
Raleigh, North Carolina Office: 410 Glenwood Avenue, 27603. Telephone: 919-821-0005.
Wilmington, North Carolina Office: 1213 Culbreth Drive, Suite 121, 28405. Telephone: 910-256-4005.
Atlanta, Georgia Office: 3353 Peachtree Road, NE, Suite 510, 30326. Telephone: 404-257-1117.
See Professional Biographies, DURHAM, NORTH CAROLINA

Matthews, Gabriela J., (BV) ....'63 '89 C.575 B.A. L.276 J.D. [G.J.Matthews&Assoc.]

Matthews, Gabriela J., & Associates, P.A., (BV)
100 East Parrish Street Suite 400, 27701
Telephone: 919-956-7888 Fax: 919-956-7833
Email: attorney.gmatthews@verizon.net URL: http://www.ncdivorcelawfirm.com
Gabriela J. Matthews.

(This Listing Continued)

Matthews, Gabriela J., & Associates, P.A. (Continued)

Family Law, Child Custody, Child Support, Divorce, Personal Injury, Adoption Law, Domestic Violence, Visitation Rights.

See Professional Biographies, DURHAM, NORTH CAROLINA

Mattunoe, Lisa C. ..... '67 '92 C.93 B.A. L.723 J.D. Div. Atty., Nature Conservancy, The
Mauch, Dieter, (BV) ....'59 '89 C&L.575 B.A., J.D. [Pulley,W.K.&L.]

Maupin Taylor, P.A.
(See Research Triangle Park)

Maxwell, James B., (AV) .... '41 '66 C.682 B.A. L.228 LL.B. [Maxwell,F.&B.]

Maxwell, Freeman & Bowman, P.A., (AV)
2741 University Drive, P.O. Box 52396, 27717-2396
Telephone: 919-493-6464 Telecopier: 919-493-1218
James B. Maxwell; Homa J. Freeman, Jr.; John A. Bowman.
Medical and Legal Negligence, Professional Responsibility, Wrongful Death and Serious Personal Injury, Business and Corporate Law, Residential and Commercial Real Estate, Estate Planning and Estate and Trust Administration, Domestic Relations, Family and Divorce Mediation and Collaborative Family Law, Civil Litigation and Traffic Violations.

See Professional Biographies, DURHAM, NORTH CAROLINA

McCaughan, Ralph Lee '39 '66
C&L.228 A.B., LL.B. Off. of Coun., Duke Univ. (⊙Durham)
McCaughan, Ralph Lee ....'39 '66 C&L.228 A.B., LL.B. [⊡ Walker&L.] (⊙Durham)
McClanahan, Robert D., (AV) ....'52 '78 C&L.575 B.A., J.D. [Clayton,M.M.&C.]
McConchie, Marty S. ....'75 '00 C.896 B.A. L.1209 J.D. [Ⓐ Solomon&M.]
McCreary, Margaret Jane, (BV) ....'48 '75 C.183 B.A. L.1067 J.D. [M.J.McCreary]
McCreary, Margaret J., (BV) .... 112 Swift Ave.
McDonald, Arthur A., Jr. ....'19 '53 C.575 A.B. L.692 LL.B. P.O. Box 25344
McDonald, Eugene J. ....'32 '58 C&L.767 B.S., J.D. Pres., Duke Mgmt. Co.
McDougall, Kevin L. '58 '83 C&L.896 B.A., J.D.
Vice President & General Counsel- Worldwide, Bell & Howell Mail & Messaging Tech.
McGill, Christa A., (BV) ....'63 '88 C.276 A.B. L.228 J.D. [McGill&N.]
McGill & Noble, (BV) ....3325 Chapel Hill Blvd.
McGirt, Emanuel D., (BV) ....'66 '94 C.511 B.A. L.575 J.D. Durham City Atty. Off.
McGrady, David J. ....'56 '81 C.387 B.A. L.309 J.D. Center for Community Self-Help
McKee, Katherine L., (AV) .... '51 '76 C&L.575 B.A., J.D. [Kennon,C.B.C.&M.]
McKee, Martha, (BV) ....'60 '88 C.970 B.A. L.228 J.D. 311 East Main Street
McKinney, Natalie J. ......'68 '93 C.811 B.A. L.1066 J.D. N.C. Central Univ. Sch. of Law
McKissick, Floyd B., Jr., (BV) ....'52 '84 C.156 A.B. L.228 J.D. [McKissick&M.]

McKissick & McKissick, (BV)
The BB&T Building, 4011 University Drive, Suite 203, 27707
Telephone: 919-490-5373 Fax: 919-493-0488 URL: http://www.FloydMcKissick.com
URL: http://www.lawyers.com/mckissicklaw
Floyd B. McKissick, Jr.
Family Law, Premarital Agreements, Equitable Distribution, Divorce, Child Custody, Child Support, Separation and Property Settlement Agreements, Contracts Disputes, Criminal Law, Civil Litigation, Business Law, Commercial Litigation, Zoning, Planning and Land Use, Governmental Relations, Construction Litigation.

See Professional Biographies, DURHAM, NORTH CAROLINA

McKown, Ann E. ....'49 '77 C.575 B.A. L.896 J.D. Dist. Ct. J.
McLaughlin, Christopher B. '69 '96 C.659 B.A. L.228 J.D.
(adm. in MA; not adm. in NC) Towerview Road
McMahon, J. Alexander ....'21 '50 C.228 A.B. L.309 J.D. Duke Univ.
McPherson, William V., Jr., (AV) ......'42 '69 C.228 A.B. L.575 J.D. [McPherson&R.]

McPherson & Rocamora, PLLC, (AV) BB
3211 Shannon Road Suite 620, 27707
Telephone: 919-493-0584 Facsimile: 919-493-0856
William V. McPherson, Jr.; Larry H. Rocamora (Board Certified Specialist in Estate Planning and Probate Law, North Carolina State Board of Legal Specialization);—Kathryn T. Curran.
Estate Planning, Probate Administration Law, Taxation.

See Professional Biographies, DURHAM, NORTH CAROLINA

McReynolds, Roland G. .....'72 '97 C.502 B.A. L.575 J.D. Mng. Editor, Eli Research Inc.
Meddock, Adrienne Lea '62 '91 C.575 A.B. L.574 J.D.
Asst. Dean, Evening Prog., NC Central Univ. Sch. of Law‡
Meece, Darin P., (BV) ....'70 '95 C.1128 B.A. L.575 J.D. [Brock,P.&M.]
Mendini, Mary Guy, (CV) ....'57 '92 C.790 B.A. L.574 J.D. P.O. Box 15025
Metzloff, Thomas B. '54 '82 C.976 B.A. L.309 J.D.
(adm. in GA; not adm. in NC) Prof., Duke Univ. Sch. of Law
Meurer, Michael James '58 '92 C.453 S.B. L.494 J.D.
(adm. in NY; not adm. in NC) Duke University
Michaux, Eric C., (BV) ....'41 '66 C.94 B.S. L.228 LL.B. [Michaux&M.]
Michaux, H. M., Jr., (BV) ....'30 '66 C&L.574 B.S., LL.B. [Michaux&M.]
Michaux & Michaux, P.A., (BV) .... P.O. Box 2152
Mikhail, Sheila A. ....'66 '98 C.339 B.S. L.597 J.D. Life Sciences Law, PLLC
Miles, Lisa M. ....'64 '91 C.577 B.A. L.1345 J.D. 212 W. Main St., Ste. 317
Miller, George W., III, (BV) ....'65 '96 C.575 B.A. L.1228 J.D. [Haywood,D.&M.]
Miller, George W., Jr., (AV) ....'30 '57 C&L.575 B.S., LL.B. [Haywood,D.&M.]
Mills, E. Eric ....'70 '01 C.576 B.S. L.575 J.D. [Ⓐ Jenkins,W.&T.] (See Pat. Sect.)
Mills, Gary S., (BV) '51 '78 C.925 B.S. L.575 J.D.
Assistant General Counsel, AKZO NOBEL, INC.
Mills, Janice L. '53 '77 C.575 B.A. L.228 J.D.
Dean & Prof. of Law, N.C. Central Univ. Sch. of Law
Mills, William S., (AV) ....'52 '79 C&L.575 B.A., J.D. [Glenn,M.&F.]
Miranda-Watkins, Frances, (BV) ....'51 '94 C.959 B.A. L.588 J.D. 201 N. Church St.
Mitchell, Henry A., III, (BV) ....'62 '91 C.198 B.A. L.896 J.D. [Solomon&M.]
Mitchell, Joan M., (BV) ....'43 '91 C&L.575 B.A., J.D. [Mitchell,E.&W.]

Mitchell, Eyster & Warner, P.A., (BV)
2004 S. Miami Boulevard, 27703
Telephone: 919-598-9000 Facsimile: 919-598-9090
Email: attorney@nchealthlaw.com URL: http://www.nchealthlaw.com
Joan M. Mitchell; Donna Turner Eyster; H. Lawrence Warner, Jr.
Comprehensive Health Care Law including Administrative Law, Corporate Law, Business Law, Tax Law, Employment, Estate Planning, Trusts and Estates, Collections.

See Professional Biographies, DURHAM, NORTH CAROLINA

Monks, R. S. (Steve), (BVⓉ) ....'62 '87 C.326 B.B.A. L.796 J.D. [Monks]
Monks Law Firm, The, (BVⓉ) .... P.O. Box 51666
Montgomery, Mark ....'49 '86 C&L.896 B.A., J.D. P.O. Box 161
Moore, *Cathy Lynn* ....'51 '77 C.102 B.A. L.809 J.D. Asst. Co. Atty., Co. Atty. Off.
Moore & Alphin, PLLC, (BV) .... 1000 Park Forty Plaza Suite 100 (⊙Raleigh)

Moore & Van Allen PLLC
(See Research Triangle Park)

Morey, Marcia H., (BV) ....'55 '82 C.357 B.A. L.1051 J.D. Dist. Ct. J.
Morgan, Lisa G. ....'61 '87 C.575 B.S. L.329 J.D. Dir., Career Srvs.
Morris, Mark W. ....'51 '82 C.575 B.A. L.574 J.D. N.C. Central Univ., School of Law

Morris, Manning & Martin, LLP
A Limited Liability Partnership
1000 Park 40 Plaza, Suite 300, 28262 ⊙
Telephone: 704-369-7012 Fax: 704-369-7071
Email: kburns@mmmlaw.com URL: http://www.mmmlaw.com
Of Counsel: Keith D. Burns. Associate: Kandas D. Burnett.
Benefits and Compensation, Commercial Lending, Construction, Corporate, Corporate Technology, Creditor's Rights and Bankruptcy, Emerging Companies, Employment, Environmental, Healthcare, Hospitality, Insurance and Reinsurance, Insurance and Reinsurance Dispute Resolution, Intellectual Property, International, Life Sciences, Litigation, Medical Device, Mergers and Acquisitions, Privacy and Security, Products Liability and Toxic Torts, Real Estate Capital Markets, Real Estate Development and Finance, Residential Real Estate, Securities, Taxation, Technology, Technology Litigation, Telecommunications, Wealth Planning.
Charlotte, NC Office: 201 South College Street, Suite 2300, 28244. Telephone: 704-554-7070. Fax: 704-556-5050.
Charlotte, NC Office: 10150 Mallard Creek Drive, Suite 105, 28262. Telephone: 704-369-7012. Fax: 704-369-7071.
Washington, D.C. Office: City Center Building, 1401 H Street, N.W., Suite 760, 20005. Telephone: 202-408-5153. Fax: 202-408-5146.
Princeton, NJ Office: 601 Ewing Street, Suite C-8, 08540. Telephone: 609-430-1414. Fax: 609-430-1411.
Georgia Office Addresses:
Atlanta (Buckhead) Office: 1600 Atlanta Financial Center, 3343 Peachtree Road, N.E., Atlanta, GA 30326. Telephone: 404-233-7000.
Peachtree Dunwoody Office: 5775-C Peachtree Dunwoody Road, Suite 150, Atlanta, GA 30342. Telephone: 404-255-6900. Fax: 404-843-2317.
Duluth Office: 2180 Satellite Boulevard, Suite 180, Duluth, GA 30097. Telephone: 678-987-2800. Fax: 678-417-0056.
Cumming Office: 307 Atlanta Highway, Cumming, GA 30040. Telephone: 770-781-3000. Fax: 770-781-3007.
Alpharetta Office: 5780 Windward Parkway, Suite 225, Alpharetta, GA 30005. Telephone: 770-781-3000. Fax: 770-781-3007.

See Professional Biographies, DURHAM, NORTH CAROLINA

Mosteller, Robert P. ....'48 '75 C.575 B.A. L.976 J.D. Prof., Duke Law School
Mpare, Nelwyn McDuffie '55 '81
C.811 B.A. L.574 J.D. N. Carolina Central Univ. Sch. of Law
Mullens, Julie Ann ....'66 '92 C.476 B.S. L.215 J.D. 2603 Glendale Ave.
Mullins, Philip A., IV, (BV) ....'65 '93 C.938 B.A. L.1228 J.D. [Thomas,F.&M.]
Mumma, Christine Cecchetti ....'62 '99 C&L.575 B.S. 3124 Surrey Road
Murray, Josiah S., III, (AV) ....'35 '62 C.575 B.S. L.309 LL.B. [Hedrick M.&C.P.]
Myrick, Robert W., (BV) ....'45 '71 C&L.575 B.A., J.D. [Clayton,M.M.&C.]
Nauseef, Robert J., II, (BV) .... '65 '90 C.1236 B.A. L.982 J.D. [Ⓐ Clayton,M.M.&C.]
Newsom, James L., (AV) ....'14 '38 C&L.228 A.B., LL.B. 3100 Tower Boulevard
Nichols, Tara L. ....'70 '03 C.575 B.S. L.574 J.D. [Nichols&S.]
Nichols & Satterfield, PLLC ....3708 Lyckan Parkway, Suite 205
Nifong, Michael B., (AV) ....'50 '78 C&L.575 A.B., J.D. Asst. Dist. Atty.
Nifong, Timothy D., (BV) ....'— '86 L.575 J.D. 5217 George King Rd.
Noble, Virginia A. ....'63 '88 C.575 B.A. L.228 J.D. [McGill&N.]
Noga, Daniel J. ....'68 '96 C.575 B.S. L.896 J.D. Bowe Bell & Howell Company
Nunnallee, Walter H. ......'53 '81 C.259 B.S. L.575 J.D. N.C. Central Univ. School of Law
O'Connor, Maureen Kelley '54 '83 C.321 A.B. L.818 J.D.
Sr. V.P. & Gen. Coun., Blue Cross Blue Shield of North Carolina
O'Foghludha, Michael J., (AV) .... '56 '82 C.228 A.B. L.575 J.D. [Pulley,W.K.&L.]
Olive, B. B., (AV) ....'21 '53 C.228 B.S.E.E. L.724 J.D. [Olive&O.] (See Pat. Sect.)
Olive, Bentley J. ....'75 '01 C.576 B.S. L.577 J.D. [Ⓐ Jenkins,W.&T.] (See Pat. Sect.)
Olive, Susan Freya, (AV) ....'52 '76 C.103 A.B. L.228 J.D. [Olive&O.] (See Pat. Sect.)

Olive and Olive, P.A., (AV) BB
500 Memorial Street, P.O. Box 2049, 27702-2049
Telephone: 919-683-5514 Fax: 919-688-3781 URL: http://www.lawyers.com/oliveandolive
Email: iplaw@oliveandolive.com URL: http://www.oliveandolive.com
B. B. Olive; Susan Freya Olive;—Vedia Jones-Richardson; Joshua L. Price; Andrew T. Prokopetz; Devon E. White; S. Matthew Edwards.
Intellectual Property, Patent, Trademark, Copyright, Computer and Biotechnology Law and Related Litigation.
Reference: North Carolina Bar Assn.

See Professional Biographies, DURHAM, NORTH CAROLINA

O'Neal, Elaine M. .... '62 '91 C&L.574 B.S., J.D. Dist. Ct. J.

Osborn, J. Kirk
(See Chapel Hill)

O'Toole, Neil, (BV) ....'54 '80 C.228 B.A. L.260 J.D. 3100 Tower Boulevard
Ovsenik, Edward C. '56 '84 C.1192 B.A. L.107 J.D.
Ast. Gen. Coun., Reichhold, Inc. (Legal Department)
Padilla, John J., (BV) ....'65 '90 C.1365 B.A. L.575 J.D. P.O. Box 52149
Page, Troy R. '70 '95 C&L.575 B.S.B.A., J.D.
Assoc. Coun., Blue Cross Blue Shield of North Carolina
Parham, Eric J., Law Offices of, (BV) .....'60 '88 C.228 A.B. L.276 J.D. P.O. Box 61582
Parks, William Land ....'36 '72 C.575 B.S. L.574 J.D. 400 W. Main St.
Parris, James W., Jr. ....'54 '98 C&L.574 B.A., J.D. 508 Fulton St.
Patalano, Louis, IV '73 '00
C.575 B.A. L.446 J.D. Blue Cross Blue Shield of North Carolina
Pate, William H. ....'78 '04 C.575 B.S. L.1228 J.D. [Ⓐ Stubbs,C.B.P.&B.]
Patrick, Cheri C., (BV) .....'62 '99 C.225 B.A. L.228 J.D. 100 E. Parrish Street, Suite 400
Patterson, Henry Newton, V ....'66 '94 C.576 B.S.E.E. L.575 J.D. Northern Telecom, Inc.
Payne, Barri Hilton, (BV) ....'70 '99 C.1128 B.A. L.575 J.D. [Brock,P.&M.]
Payne, Silas Mark '57 '83 C.1195 B.A. L.192 J.D.
V.P. & Chf. Compl. Offr., Blue Cross and Blue Shield of North Carolina
Perkins, Christopher P., Ph.D. '63 '01 C.821 B.A. L.800 J.D.
(adm. in CA; not adm. in NC; See Pat. Sect.) [Ⓐ Jenkins,W.&T.]
Perry, Nichelle Jones .... '67 '93 C.999 B.A. L.574 J.D. N.C. Central Univ. School of Law
Perry, W. Wayne ....'31 '59 C&L.574 A.B., LL.B. N.C. Mut. Life Ins. Co.
Perry, Willie R., Jr., Law Office of .....'50 '79 C.1378 B.S. L.575 J.D. 201 N. Church St.
Peterson, Andrew L. ....'74 '03 C.160 B.A. L.574 J.D. [Ⓐ Bryant,P.C.I.&L.]
Phelps, Lou Ann ....'51 '81 C.118 B.A. L.1065 J.D. 27 Bermouth Ct.
Phillips Hayes, Deria, (BV) ....'— '98 C&L.574 B.B.A., J.D. [J.D.Williams,Jr.]
Pita, Frank J. '57 '98 C.472 B.S.E.E. L.574 J.D.
Gen. Coun., Semiconductor Research Corp. (Pat.)
Poe, G. Jona, Jr., (AV) .... '45 '70 C.228 B.S. L.178 J.D. [Poe&H.P.]

Poe & Hoof PLLC, (AV)
3612 Shannon Road, Suite 101, P.O. Box 51909, 27717
Telephone: 919-489-9100 Fax: 919-489-9090
Email: postmaster@phalaw.com URL: http://www.phalaw.com
Members of Firm: G. Jona Poe, Jr.; J. Bruce Hoof.
General Civil Trial and Appellate Practice, Commercial Litigation, Insurance Defense, Personal Injury, Plaintiff's and Workers Compensation.
Representative Clients: Aetna Casualty & Surety Co.; Alliance Mutual Insurance Co.; Bankers and Shippers Insurance Co.; Central Carolina Bank & Trust Co.; Church Mutual Insurance Co.; Crown American Corp.; Crum & Forster Personal Insurance Co.

See Professional Biographies, DURHAM, NORTH CAROLINA

Pokrass, Tyler Seth, (BV) ....'70 '97 C.575 B.A. L.574 J.D. [Ⓐ H.W.a.E.J.F.Vann]

Polin, Sandra Jyll '58 '84 C.951 B.A. L.851 J.D.
(adm. in NY; not adm. in NC) N. C. Central Univ. School of Law
Poole, Robert S. '52 '95 C.228 B.A. L.477 J.D. P.O. Box 371
Post, Garrod S. '54 '81 C.477 B.G.S. L.213 J.D. 1022 Westwood Dr.
Postlethwait, Raymond W., Jr., (BV) '44 '71 C.228 A.B. L.575 J.D. Northgate Mall
Potter, Jeffrey H. '54 '80 C&L.228 A.B., J.D. Dir., Real Estate Admn., Duke University
Powell, H. J. '54 '82 C.999 B.A. L.976 J.D. Duke Law Sch.
Powell, Lisa Holland, (BV) '51 '77 C.228 B.A. L.896 J.D. [Ⓒ Walker&L.]
Powell, Stephanie C., (AV) '48 '84 C.923 B.S. L.575 J.D. [Hutson H.&P.]
Prather, N. King '58 '97 C.893 B.A. L.574 J.D.
Dep. Gen. Coun., Corp. Law & Contract Mgmt., Blue Cross Blue Shield of North Carolina
Prentis, Richard F., Jr., (AV) '46 '73 C.228 A.B. L.575 J.D. [Stubbs,C.B.P.&B.]
Price, Joshua L. '75 '02 C.628 B.S. L.629 J.D. [Ⓐ Olive&O.] (See Pat. Sect.)
Prokopetz, Andrew T. '55 '88 C.693 B.S. L.574 J.D. [Ⓐ Olive&O.] (See Pat. Sect.)
Pulley, W. Paul, Jr., (AV) '36 '61 C&L.575 A.B., LL.B. [Ⓒ Pulley,W.K.&L.]

Pulley, Watson, King & Lischer, P.A., (AV)
21-F Brightleaf Square, 905 West Main Street, P.O. Box 3600, 27702
Telephone: 919-682-9691 Telecopier: 919-688-9107
URL: http://www.pwkl.com
Malvern F. King, Jr.; Richard N. Watson; Tracy Kenyon Lischer; Michael J. O'Foghludha; Charles F. Carpenter; Guy W. Crabtree; Dieter Mauch. Of Counsel: W. Paul Pulley, Jr.; Mark E. Fogel; William L. Stanford, Jr.; James A. Clark.
General Civil and Criminal Trial and Appellate Practice, Personal Injury, Commercial Litigation, Commercial Real Estate, Corporate, Bankruptcy, Environmental Law, Government Contracts Law, Professional Negligence.
References: Wachovia Bank and Trust Co., N.A.; Central Carolina Bank and Trust Co.; NationsBank of North Carolina; Cardinal State Bank.
See Professional Biographies, DURHAM, NORTH CAROLINA

Rallis, Chris A. '53 '78 C.309 A.B. L.228 J.D.
VP, Business Development & General Counsel, Triangle Pharmaceuticals, Inc.
Randall, John C., (BV) '39 '66 C&L.575 A.B., LL.B. [Randall&H.]
Randall & Hill, (BV) 3100 Tower Boulevard, 5th fl.
Ratliff, Alice A. '49 '76 C.228 A.B. L.575 J.D. N. Central Legal Assist. Program
Read, Daniel F., Attorney at Law, (BV) '53 '83
C&L.575 B.A., J.D. 112 Swift Ave., 2nd Fl.
Read, J. Milton, Jr. '37 '63 C&L.575 A.B., LL.B. Ret. Supr. Ct. J.
Reinhardt, Charles A., Jr., (AV) '53 '76 C.247 B.A. L.260 J.D. P.O. Box 1452
Reppy, William A., Jr. '41 '66 C&L.813 A.B., J.D. Prof. of Law, Duke Univ.
Reyman, Gina L. '62 '87 C.546 B.A.B.A. L.575 J.D. Legal Aid
Rhudy, Stephen C., (BV) '51 '77 C.1044 B.A. L.228 J.D. [Walker&L.]
Rice, G. Johnson, Jr., (CVⓉ) '61 '86 C.497 B.B.A. L.500 J.D.
(adm. in AL; not adm. in NC) General Counsel, Kerr Drug, Inc.
Richardson, Celie B. '51 '98 C.575 A.B. L.577 J.D. [Ⓐ Sands A.M.&M.]
Richardson, Kathy Williams, (CV) '65 '92 C.232 B.S. L.896 J.D. [Richardson,P.]

Richardson Law Firm, The, PLLC, (CV)
125 East Parrish Street, 27701
Telephone: 919-680-2300 Fax: 919-680-2500 URL: http://www.kwrlaw.net
Email: info@kwrlaw.net URL: http://www.lawyers.com/katwilliamslaw
Kathy Williams Richardson.
Personal Injury, Family Law, Traffic Violations, Civil Practice, Criminal Law, Collection.
See Professional Biographies, DURHAM, NORTH CAROLINA

Richey, Merle U., P.A. '42 '77 C.228 A.B. L.705 J.D. [M.U.Richey]
Richey, Merle U., P.A. P.O. Box 51382
Richmond, James B. '31 '58 C.228 B.S. L.575 LL.B. 140 Pinecrest Rd.‡
Ringer, Thomas Mdodana '45 '70
C.511 B.A. L.309 J.D. N.C. Central Univ. School of Law
Roberti, Samuel, (BV) '51 '75 C.25 B.A. L.362 J.D. [Roberti,W.L.&W.]
Roberti, Wittenberg, Lauffer & Wicker, P.A., (BV) 100 East Parrish Street
Robertson, Horace B. '23 '53 C.871 B.S. L.276 J.D.
(adm. in DC; not adm. in NC) Prof. of Law, Emeritus, Duke Univ.
Rocamora, Larry H., (AV) '58 '88 C.575 B.S. L.1065 J.D. [McPherson&R.]
Rogers, James E. '57 '87 C&L.574 B.A., J.D. [Rogers,J.E.]
Rogers, John C., III '72 '98 C.198 B.A. L.902 J.D. [Hedrick M.&C.P.]
Rogers, Lee C., (BV) '55 '82 C.228 B.A. L.574 J.D. [Sessoms&R.]
Rogers, James E., P.C. P.O. Box 25198
Rose, Kenneth J. '56 '90 C.910 B.S. L.94 J.D. Center for Death Penalty Litigation
Rosenberg, Paul M. '50 '79 C.103 A.B. L.150 J.D.
(adm. in OH; not adm. in NC) Duke Univ. Med. Ctr.
Rosenthal, David M., (BV) '47 '73 C.424 B.B.A. L.597 J.D. [Rosenthal&Assoc.]
Rosenthal & Associates, (BV) P.O. Box 11506
Ross, Howard K., (BV) '58 '88 C.1128 B.A. L.574 J.D. 3100 Tower Blvd., 5th Fl.
Rothschild, Sandra '49 '97 C.575 B.A. L.574 J.D. N.C. Sch. of Sci. & Mathematics
Rowe, Beth L. '67 '96 C.280 B.A. L.1059 J.D.
(adm. in GA; not adm. in NC) 5017 Wineberry Dr.‡
Rowe, Thomas D., Jr. '42 '71 C.976 B.A. L.309 J.D. Sch. of Law, Duke Univ.
Rupp, Lynne Ann, (CV) '63 '97 C.232 B.A. L.574 J.D. 520 Valley Dr.
Russell, John S., (AV) '54 '85 C.575 B.A. L.309 J.D. Quintiles Transnational Corp.
Sanders, Sheila Mathis '57 '91 C.575 B.A. L.574 J.D. 2424 Erwin Rd., Ste. 501

Sands Anderson Marks & Miller, A Professional Corporation
3622 Lyckan Parkway, Suite 4005, P.O. Box 51266 (27717), 27707 ☉
Telephone: 919-401-6818 Facsimile: 919-401-8114
URL: http://www.SandsAnderson.com
Principal: Paul C. Jacobson. Counsel: Dailey J. Derr. Associate: Celie B. Richardson.
Government, Municipal Law, Securities, Environmental Law, Civil Litigation, Construction Law.
Radford, Virginia Office: 101 W. Main Street, P.O. Box 1052, 24143-1052. Telephone: 540-639-1601. Facsimile: 540-639-6802.
Richmond, Virginia Office: 801 East Main Street, Suite 1800, P.O. Box 1998, 23218-1998. Telephone: 804-648-1636. Facsimile: 804-783-7291.
Fredericksburg, Virginia Office: 904 Princess Anne Street, Suite 407, P.O. Box 907, 22404-0907. Telephone: 540-373-2504. Fax: 540-371-8158.
McLean, Virginia Office: 1481 Chain Bridge Road, Suite 200, 22101. Telephone: 703-893-3600. Facsimile: 703-893-8484.
See Professional Biographies, DURHAM, NORTH CAROLINA

Satterfield, Daron D. '76 '02 C&L.574 B.S., J.D. [Nichols&S.]
Schmalbeck, Richard L. '47 '75 C&L.145 A.B., J.D.
(adm. in OH; not adm. in NC) Prof. of Law, Duke University
Schneider, Brian C. '68 '94 C&L.260 B.S.B.A., J.D. 4906 Fortunes Ridge Drive
Schrader, Phyllis G., (AVⓉ) '45 '86 C.228 B.A. L.326 J.D. Attorney, Self-Help
Schroeder, Christopher H. '48 '74 C.674 A.B. L.1066 J.D.
(adm. in CA; not adm. in NC) Prof., Duke Univ. Sch. of Law
Semonche, John E. '33 '67 C.103 A.B. L.228 LL.B. Prof., Univ. of N. C.
Sendor, Benjamin B. '53 '77 C&L.309 B.A., J.D. Asst. Appl. Def.
Sessoms, Stuart M., Jr., (BV) '47 '74 C.575 A.B. L.228 J.D. [Sessoms&R.]

Sessoms & Rogers, P.A., (BV)
3326 Chapel Hill Blvd., Suite A-200, 27707
Mailing Address: P.O. Box 52508, Durham, NC 27717
Telephone: 919-688-1000 Fax: 919-688-9000
Email: mail@sessomslaw.com URL: http://www.sessomslaw.com
Stuart M. Sessoms, Jr.; Lee C. Rogers.
Collections, Civil Litigation, Commercial Litigation, Banking Law, Consumer Bankruptcy, Traffic Violations.
Representative Clients: Providian National Bank; Branch Banking & Trust Co.; First Select, Inc.
See Professional Biographies, DURHAM, NORTH CAROLINA

Shapiro, Marc H., (BVⓉ) '50 '75 C.575 A.B. L.893 J.D.
[Hyman,P.&M.] (☉Wash., DC)
Sharpe, Jimmy D., (BV) '54 '81 C.577 B.A. L.574 J.D. [Darsie,S.M.&D.]
Shimm, Melvin G. '26 '50 C.178 A.B. L.976 LL.B.
(adm. in NY; not adm. in NC) 2429 Wrightwood Ave.‡
Siegel, Judith V., (CV) '40 '86 C.289 B.A. L.575 J.D.
Mng. Atty., N. Central Legal Assistance Prog., Inc.
Silverstein, Norman P. '15 '40 C.912 L.213 LL.B.
(adm. in MI; not adm. in NC) 4900 Vistawood Way
Simmons, Pamela Robinson '50 '76 C&L.280 B.A., J.D.
(adm. in GA; not adm. in NC) 5306 Oakbrook Dr.‡
Singleton, David G., Jr., (BV) '— '77
C.577 B.S. L.896 J.D. Asst. Univ. Coun., Duke Univ.
Sinor, Morris L. '40 '64 C&L.546 B.S., J.D.
(adm. in NE; not adm. in NC) GTE - NC999191
Skinner, Laura L., (BV) '70 '95 C.1128 B.S. L.575 J.D. 109 Church St.
Skumanich, Nonna '— '91 C.174 L.911 J.D.
Legal Writer & Editor, Employment Law Research, Inc.

Slade, Nicole D., Law Office of '71 '01 C.575 B.A. L.574 J.D.
315 East Chapel Hill Street, Suite 204, 27702
Telephone: 919-680-6521 Fax: 919-680-6704
Email: attyndslade@verizon.net URL: http://www.sladelawofc.com
Family Law, Civil Litigation, Bankruptcy, Personal Injury, Traffic.
See Professional Biographies, DURHAM, NORTH CAROLINA

Slawson, Donna B. '55 '82 C.604 B.A. L.575 J.D. U.S. Ct. of App., Cir. Med.
Sloan, Maceo K., (BV) '49 '79
C.511 B.A. L.574 J.D. 2634 Durham Chapel Hill Blvd., Ste. 206‡
Sloane, Margaret A. '50 '76 C.668 B.A. L.851 J.D. Sloane Mediation Services
Slotkin, Matthew B., (CV) '65 '95 C&L.575 B.A., J.D. [M.B.Slotkin]
Slotkin, Matthew B., P.A., Law Offices of, (CV) 100 East Parrish Street, Suite 400
Smith, Anita L. '— '91 C&L.574 B.A., J.D. 315 E. Chapel Hill St., Ste. 405
Smith, Archie L., III '50 '76 C.575 B.A. L.574 J.D. Durham Co. Clk. of Supr. Ct.
Smith, Cynthia Gail '63 '90
C.945 B.B.A. L.575 J.D. Assoc. Gen. Coun., Corp. Coml., Cree, Inc.
Smith, D. Joe, (AVⓉ) '48 '74 C.992 B.A. L.976 J.D.
(adm. in CT; not adm. in NC) Pres. & Gen. Coun., Novalon Pharmaceutical Corp.
Smith, David C., & Associates '68 '99 2530 Meridian Pkwy., Suite 200
Solari, Frances C., (BV) '52 '82 C.575 B.S. L.574 J.D.
1512 S Alston Ave, NC Central Univ Law Sch
Solomon, Laurel E., (BV) '62 '88 C.1044 B.A. L.228 J.D. [Solomon&M.]

Solomon & Mitchell, PLLC, (BV)
5850 Fayetteville Road - Suite 210, 27713
Telephone: 919-687-4577 Fax: 919-687-4578
URL: http://www.solomonmitchell.com
Laurel E. Solomon; Henry A. Mitchell, III. Associate: Marty S. McConchie.
General Civil Practice. Business Transactions, Family Law, Real Property, Personal Injury, Estate Planning, Creditors' Rights, Health Care, Litigation and Appeals.
See Professional Biographies, DURHAM, NORTH CAROLINA

Sotolongo, Wendy C., (BV) '60 '87 C.228 B.A. L.575 J.D. P.O. Box 51486
Soule, Martha E. '76 '03 C.896 B.S. L.94 J.D. [Ⓐ Hedrick M.&C.P.]
Sparks, Bertel M. '18 '48 C.235 B.S. L.383 LL.B.
(adm. in KY; not adm. in NC) 1707 Woodburn Rd.‡
Sparrow, William R. '80 '05 C.577 B.A. L.896 J.D. [Ⓐ Bugg&W.]
Spaulding, Kenneth B., (AV) '44 '70 C.329 B.A. L.575 J.D.
3100 Tower Blvd., Ste. 300
Spearman, Patricia H. '33 '55
C&L.846 B.A., J.D. Law Prof., N. C. Central Univ. Law Sch.
Speight, Jonathan '74 '01 C.575 B.A. L.574 J.D. [Roberti,W.L.&W.]
Spillman, Ray A. '46 '72 C.575 A.B. L.178 J.D. Coastal Physician Group Inc.
Spritzer, Marlene Alpern '55 '81 C.119 B.S. L.229 J.D. 5225 Pine Cone Lane
Spruill, E. Carol '49 '75 C&L.575 B.A., J.D.
Sr. Lecturing Fellow & Assoc. Dean, Duke Univ. Sch. of Law
Stanback, A. Leon, Jr. '42 '68 C&L.574 B.S., J.D. Supr. Ct. J.
Stanford, William L., Jr. '41 '71 C.260 B.A. L.629 J.D. [Ⓒ Pulley,W.K.&L.]

Stark Law Group, PLLC
(See Chapel Hill)

Steinberg, Kenneth J., (BV) '67 '93 C.205 B.A. L.1003 J.D. [K.J.Steinberg]
Steinberg, Kenneth J., P.A., Law Offices of, (BV) 3600 N. Duke St., Ste. 005
Stephens, Ronald L. '45 '74 C&L.575 B.S., J.D. Supr. Ct. J.
Stern, Thomas M., (AV) '56 '83 C.860 B.A. L.309 J.D.
400 West main Street, Suite 501
Stevens, Thomas J., (AV) '41 '67 C.228 B.A. L.575 J.D. [T.J.Stevens]
Stevens, Thomas J., P.A., (AV) 1911 Hillandale Road
Stocking, Kathryn A. '62 '87 C&L.477 B.A., J.D.
(adm. in IL; not adm. in NC) Custom Molders, Inc.‡
Strange, John W. '74 '01 C.210 B.A. L.192 J.D. [Ⓐ Kestenbaum]

Stubbs, Cole, Breedlove, Prentis & Biggs, P.L.L.C., (AV)
122 East Parrish Street, P.O. Box 376, 27702
Telephone: 919-682-9331 Fax: 919-682-5590 Real Estate Fax: 919-688-0277
Email: stubbscole@aol.com URL: http://www.stubbscole.com
Allston J. Stubbs (1909-2003); Irvin P. Breedlove, Jr. (1946-2003). Members of Firm: James A. Cole, Jr.; Richard F. Prentis, Jr.; C. Thomas Biggs; Jonathan W. Biggs. Associates: C. Scott Holmes; William H. Pate; Robin M. Barefoot.
General Civil and Criminal Trial Practice. Banking, Corporate, Real Estate, Wills and Estates, Estate Planning, Construction and Personal Injury Law.
See Professional Biographies, DURHAM, NORTH CAROLINA

Sutton, Kerstin Walker, Law Office of '61 '01 C.575 B.A. L.574 J.D. P.O. Box 52551
Taflan, Deborah L. '50 '83 C.381 B.A. L.7 J.D.
(adm. in OH; not adm. in NC) Peter Taflan Mktg. Comm., Inc.
Tatum, H. Eugene, III, (BV) '60 '87 C.329 B.A. L.575 J.D. 116 E. Main St.
Taylor, Arles A., Jr. '68 '94
C.576 B.S.B.A. L.575 J.D. [Jenkins,W.&T.] (See Pat. Sect.) ☉
Taylor, Chandra T. '75 '01 C&L.575 B.A., J.D. P.O. Box 3416
Taylor, Samuel B., (BV) '58 '86 C.228 A.B. L.464 J.D. 100 E. Parrish St., Ste. 451

Teague, G. Mark, (BV) '67 '93 C.575 B.A. L.896 J.D. [Moore&A.] ⊙
Tessener, Hoyt G., (AV) '— '88 C.575 B.S. L.228 J.D. [Martin&J.] (⊙Raleigh)

Tharrington Smith
(See Raleigh)

Thomas, William J., II, (AV) '53 '79 C.53 B.S. L.574 J.D. [Thomas,F.&M.]
Thomas, Ferguson & Mullins, LLP, (AV) 119 E. Main Street
Thompson, Sharon A., (BV) '48 '76 C.475 B.S. L.1162 J.D. [S.Thompson]
Thompson, Sharon, Law Group, (BV) 400 W. Main St.
Thornton, William I., Jr., (AV) '40 '66 C.910 B.A. L.575 LL.B. City Atty.
Thuotte, Laura M. '79 '03 C.1128 B.S. L.48 J.D. [🄰 Foil]
Titus, Kenneth C. '51 '76 C&L.575 A.B., J.D. Chf. Dist. J.
Trenkle, Robert C. '60 '86 C.446 B.S. L.575 J.D. [Edwards&T.] ⊙
Triangle Traffic Ticket Clinic, (BV) 620 Executive Pk.
Trottier, Richard O. '51 '95
C.689 B.A. L.588 J.D. State Occupational Health & Safety Proj.
Trustin, Mark S., (BV) '52 '78 C.208 B.A. L.190 J.D. 4312 W. Cornwallis Rd.
Tseng, Judy Y. '74 '00 C.1375 B.A. L.276 J.D. [🄰 M.F.Herndon]
Tucker, Shannon A., (BV) '65 '92 C&L.575 B.A., J.D. Off. of Pub. Def.
Turner, Brendan W. '— '99 C&L.574 B.S., J.D. P.O. Box 1452

Twiggs, Beskind, Strickland & Rabenau, P.A.
(See Raleigh)

Underkuffler, Laura S. '51 '78 C.118 B.A. L.1035 J.D.
(adm. in MN; not adm. in NC) Prof., Duke Univ. Sch of Law
Upchurch, Roger S., (AV) '25 '52 C&L.228 A.B., LL.B. 301 W. Main St.
Uyesato, Daniel E. '54 '80 C.378 B.A. L.813 J.D.
Gen. Coun. & Secy., Reichhold, Inc. (Legal Department)
VanAlstyne, William W. '34 '58 C.800 B.A. L.813 J.D.
(adm. in CA; not adm. in NC) Prof. of Law, Duke Univ.
Vann, Arthur '22 '51 C&L.228 A.B., LL.B. 120 E. Parrish St.‡
Vann, H. Wood, (BV) '57 '82 C.896 B.A. L.575 J.D. [H.W.a.E.J.F.Vann]

Vann, H. Wood and Edward J. Falcone, The Law Offices of, (BV)
Suite 200, 120 East Parrish Street, 27701
Telephone: 919-682-9273; 919-682-4638 Facsimile: 919-683-5533
URL: http://www.lawyers.com/vannandfalcone
H. Wood Vann; Edward J. Falcone. Associate: Tyler Seth Pokrass.
Criminal Law, Personal Injury, Auto Accidents, Family Law, Divorce, Traffic Violations, Driving While Intoxicated..
See Professional Biographies, DURHAM, NORTH CAROLINA

VanSant, Susan B. '55 '84 C.228 A.B. L.575 J.D. 2419 Alpine Rd.‡
Vinegar, Richard J., (AV) '54 '79 C.228 A.B. L.188 J.D. [Johnson,H.V.G.&G.]
Vira, Lisa Khim '70 '00 C.10 B.S. L.574 J.D. [Vira] ⊙

Vira Law Firm, The, PA
133 Celeste Circle, 27517 ⊙
Telephone: 919-918-8000 Fax: 919-918-7887
Email: lisa_vira@nc.rr.com URL: http://www.lisakvira.com
Lisa Khim Vira.
Trusts and Estates, Probate, Wills, Real Estate, Taxation, Business Law.
Carrboro Office: 205 W. Main Street, Suite 207, 27510. Telephone: 919-918-8000. Fax: 919-918-7887.
See Professional Biographies, DURHAM, NORTH CAROLINA

Von Hagen, Beth Poinsett, (BV) '68 '93 C&L.575 B.A., J.D. [Foil]
Walker, Doretta L., (BV) '67 '93 C&L.575 B.A., J.D. Dist. Atty. Off.
Walker, Edwin J., Jr., (AV) '44 '69 C.198 B.A. L.575 J.D. [Walker&L.]

Walker & Lambe, P.L.L.C., (AV)
South Square Corporate Centre II, 3708 Mayfair Street, Suite 100, P.O. Box 51549, 27717-1549
Telephone: 919-493-8411 Fax: 919-493-2047
URL: http://www.WalkerLambe.com
Members of Firm: William H. Lambe, Jr.; Edwin J. Walker, Jr. (Board Certified Specialist in Estate Planning and Probate Law, North Carolinas State Board of Legal Specialization); Stephen C. Rhudy; Mark O. Costley. Of Counsel: Ralph Lee McCaughan; Katharine B. Buchanan; Charles W. White (Retired); Lisa Holland Powell (Retired). Associates: Donna Ray Chmura; Jennifer Westerhaus Adams.
Business Law, Corporate Law, Corporation, Taxation, Real Estate, Estate Planning and Probate Law, Trusts Administration.
Approved Attorneys for: Lawyers Title of North Carolina; Investors Title Insurance Co.; Chicago Title Insurance Co.; Security Union Title Insurance Co.; The Title Company of North Carolina; United Title Insurance Co.; First American Title Insurance Co.; Commonwealth Land Title Insurance Co.; Fidelity National Title Insurance Co.
See Professional Biographies, DURHAM, NORTH CAROLINA

Warner, H. Lawrence, Jr. '61 '92 C.575 B.S. L.128 J.D. [Mitchell,E.&W.]
Warren, David G. '36 '64 C.473 A.B. L.228 J.D. Prof. of Law, Duke Univ.
Warren, Loretta Keimes '59 '89 C.994 B.A. L.724 J.D.
(adm. in NY; not adm. in NC) 2800 Bainbridge Dr.‡
Washington, Judith E. '41 '77 C.369 B.S. L.574 J.D. P.O. Box 52615
Watson, Anne Page, (AV) '49 '75 C.575 A.B. L.896 J.D. [A.P.Watson]
Watson, Richard N., (AV) '46 '74 C&L.575 B.A., J.D. [Pulley,W.K.&L.]

Watson, Anne Page, PLLC, Law Office of, (AV)
3500 Westgate Drive, Suite 604, 27707
Telephone: 919-489-9058 Fax: 919-489-9309 URL: http://www.apwatson.com
Email: annepagewatson@apwatson.com URL: http://www.lawyers.com/annepagewatson
Anne Page Watson.
Estate Planning, Estate Administration, Estate and Gift Taxation, Asset Protection, Small Business Law, Commercial Real Estate, Residential Real Estate, Condominium Law, Charitable Giving, Wills and Probate.
See Professional Biographies, DURHAM, NORTH CAROLINA

Watts, Charles D., Jr. '55 '86 C.575 B.A. L.329 J.D.
Gen. Coun. & Corp. Secy., N.C. Mutual Life Ins. Co.
Webb, Joy Rhyne, (BV) '69 '95 C&L.575 B.A., J.D.
[Browne,F.W.&W.] (⊙Creedmoor, Greensboro)
Webb, Kaye R. '52 '77 C.329 B.A. L.950 J.D. NC Central Univ.
Weeden, Joseph A. '76 '02 C&L.575 B.A., J.D.
(adm. in VA; not adm. in NC) Pres. & Chief Coun., Team HC, LLC
Weintraub, Richard N. '— '76 C.1036 B.A. L.228 J.D. City Atty. Off.
Weistart, John C. '43 '68 C.340 B.A. L.228 J.D. Prof., Duke Univ.

Wellons Law Firm, The
(See Raleigh)

Whisnant, Judy, (BV) '56 '85 C.296 A.B. L.588 J.D. 301 W. Main St., Ste. 400
White, Charles W., (AV) '19 '48 C.896 B.S. L.228 J.D. [🄲 Walker&L.] ‡
White, Devon E. '— '02 C.953 B.A. L.574 J.D. [🄰 Olive&O.] (See Pat. Sect.)
Whitfield, Nathaniel '42 '86 C&L.574 B.A., J.D. Spec. Coun., Duke Univ.
Whitfield, Robert E., (BV) '47 '78 C.232 B.A. L.574 J.D.
[Browne,F.W.&W.] (⊙Creedmoor, Greensboro)
Whitling, Dennis A. '55 '83 C.648 B.S. L.575 J.D. [T.J.Stevens]

Wicker, R. David, Jr., (BV) '60 '85 C.577 B.A. L.574 J.D. [Roberti,W.L.&W.]
Wickham, Leslie Oliver, Jr., (AV) '52 '84 C.575 B.A. L.574 J.D. 3200 Croasdaile Dr.
Widenhouse, Constance E. '54 '86 C.896 B.A. L.575 J.D. Off. of Appl. Def.
Wiggins, Allen T. '69 '02 C.183 B.A. L.575 J.D. [🄰 Bugg&W.]
Wilks, Brian C. '71 '96 C.790 B.S. L.574 J.D. 9 N. Indiancreek Pl.
Williams, Fred J. '51 '76 C.228 B.A. L.575 J.D. N.C. Central Univ. School of Law
Williams, James D., Jr., (AV) '54 '79 C&L.574 B.A., J.D. [J.D.Williams,Jr.]
Williams, Norman Cole, (BV) '66 '94 C.576 B.A. L.724 J.D. [N.Williams]
Williams, Norman E., (BV) '37 '65 C&L.575 A.B., LL.B. 205 N. Church St.
Williams, James D., Jr., P.A., The Law Offices of, (AV)
3400 Croasdaile Drive, Suite 205
Williams, Norman, (BV) 205 N. Church St.
Willis, Albert L. '37 '77 C&L.574 B.A., J.D. 411 W. Chapel Hill St.‡

Wilson, James A., (AV) '61 '89 C&L.575 B.S., J.D.
5322 Highgate Drive, Suite 243, 27713
Telephone: 919-361-4300 Fax: 919-361-4305
Email: jim@jamesawilson.com URL: http://www.jamesawilson.com
Physicians Licensing, Medical Disciplinary Proceedings, Controlled Substances Law, Professional Conduct, Professional Discipline, Professional Sexual Misconduct, Hospital Peer Review, Hospital Privilege, Medical Staff Credentialing, Health Law, Medical Ethics, Medical-Legal Law, Physicians Rights, Professional Licensing, Professional Licensing Regulation, Health Care Licensing, Nurses Licensing.
See Professional Biographies, DURHAM, NORTH CAROLINA

Wilson, James Bradley, (BV) '53 '78 C.34 B.A. L.896 J.D.
Exec. V.P., Chf. Adm. Offr. & Corp. Secy., Blue Cross Blue Shield of N.C.
Wilson, Jeffrey L., (AV) '65 '90
C.575 B.A. L.1228 J.D. [Jenkins,W.&T.] (See Pat. Sect.) ⊙
Wilson, Joseph M., Jr., (BV) '61 '91 C.790 B.A. L.574 J.D.
[Browne,F.W.&W.] (⊙Creedmoor, Greensboro)
Wilson, Mary Jean '46 '74 C.104 B.A. L.228 J.D. 400 W. Main St.

Winston & Maher
(See Chapel Hill)

Wittenberg, Lawrence, (BV) '58 '85 C.1019 B.B.A. L.574 J.D. [Roberti,W.L.&W.]
Wolf, William J., (BV) '63 '87 C.27 B.A. L.896 J.D. [Bugg&W.]
Woodmansee, Julianna Cheek, (BV) '62 '90 C.198 B.A. L.575 J.D. 301 W. Main Street
Wootton, Clyde A., III '41 '65 C&L.896 B.A., J.D. [Wootton&W.]
Wootton, Lance A., (CV) '70 '95 C.896 LL.B. L.1228 J.D. [Wootton&W.]
Wootton and Wootton PC, (CV) 3200 Croasdaile Dr.
Wright, Andrew W.B. '69 '94
C.893 B.A. L.228 J.D. Staff Counsel, IBM Corp. Pers. Sys. Grp.
Wright, Mary E. '52 '76 C.577 B.A. L.273 J.D. N.C. Central Univ. School of Law

Yaeger, William L., (AV) '47 '72 C.228 A.B. L.245 J.D.
400 West Main Street, Suite 501, P.O. Box 100, 27702-0100
Telephone: 919-683-5858 Fax: 919-683-1395
Email: wyaeger431@aol.com
Bankruptcy and Insolvency, Consumer Bankruptcy, Personal Bankruptcy, Bankruptcy Chapter 7, Bankruptcy Chapter 13.

Yager, Clara T. '25 '49 C&L.188 A.B., LL.B.
(adm. in NY; not adm. in NC) 5405 Beaumont Dr.‡
Yova, Steven P., (BV) '52 '84 C.381 B.A. L.896 J.D. Sr. Coun., bioMerieux, Inc.
Zells, Evette J. '39 '83 C.228 M.Ed. L.146 J.D.
(adm. in IL; not adm. in NC) 8 Siena St.

EDEN, 15,908, *Rockingham Co.*

Berger, Philip E., (AV) '52 '83 C.999 B.S. L.896 J.D. [Berger]
Berger, Philip E., Jr. '72 '99 C.953 B.A. L.896 J.D. [🄰 Berger]
Berger Law Firm, The, (AV) 608 Linden Drive (⊙Madison)
Cresenzo, J. Randolph, (BV) '51 '76 C.575 B.A. L.896 J.D. 612-A Business Park Dr.

Deuterman Law Group, The, P.A.
(See Greensboro)

Dilley, David D., & Associates '47 '77 C.608 B.S. L.851 J.D.
(adm. in OH; not adm. in NC) 168 Beaver Run
Etringer, Walter J. '47 '76 C.576 B.A. L.896 J.D. [Maddrey E.&S.]
Harrington, Thomas S., (AV) '26 '56
C.228 L.575 LL.B. 708 West Washington Street (⊙Wentworth)

Holt & Watt
(See Reidsville)

Hux, Douglas R. '50 '75 C&L.896 B.A., J.D. 703 Washington St.‡

Light, C. Orville '— '60 C.240 L.896 J.D.
407 S. Van Buren Road, Suite C-D, 27288
Telephone: 336-627-4566
Email: orvillelight@earthlink.net URL: http://www.corvillelightlaw.com
General Practice. Workers Compensation, Real Estate, Corporation, Business Law, Family, Divorce, Adoptions, Child Custody and Support, Automobile Accidents, Wrongful Death, Trusts and Estates, Wills and Probate, Estate Planning and Personal Injury Law.
See Professional Biographies, EDEN, NORTH CAROLINA

Maddrey, Joseph G., (AV) '41 '67 C&L.896 B.A., J.D. [Maddrey E.&S.]

Maddrey Etringer & Smith, L.L.P., (AV)
610 Henry Street, P.O. Box 507, 27288
Telephone: 336-623-4491 Fax: 336-623-7308
Email: edenlawfirm@earthlink.net
Members of Firm: Joseph G. Maddrey (Board Certified Specialist in Real Property Law, North Carolina State Board of Legal Specialization); Walter J. Etringer; Matthew W. Smith.
General Trial Practice in all State and Federal Courts. Personal Injury, Automobile Accidents, Wrongful Death, Real Estate, Banking, Business and Corporate Law, Probate Law, Family Law, Divorce, Child Custody, Bankruptcy, Collections, Criminal, DWI, Traffic, Zoning, Planning and Land Use Law, Construction Law, Foreclosures.
Reference: Southern National Bank.
See Professional Biographies, EDEN, NORTH CAROLINA

Medlin, Thomas E., Jr., (AV) '60 '85 C.575 B.S. L.896 J.D. [Medlin]
Medlin Law Office, (AV) 230A W, Jubgs Hwy.
Melvin, R. Martin, (AV) '48 '73 C&L.575 B.S., J.D. [Walker&M.]
Nooe, Charles J., (AV) '30 '58 C&L.575 B.S., J.D. 607 Washington Street
Nooe, John W., (BV) '64 '95 C.575 B.S.B.A. L.1345 J.D. [🄰 C.J.Nooe]
Rush, John H. '28 '55 C.316 B.S. L.896 LL.B. 620 Washington St.
Smith, Matthew W., (BV) '73 '98 C&L.1228 B.A., J.D. [Maddrey E.&S.]
Walker, James R., (AV) '40 '65 C&L.896 A.B., LL.B. [Walker&M.]

Walker & Melvin, LLP, (AV)
640 Fagg Drive, P.O. Box 528, 27289
Telephone: 336-623-3138 Fax: 336-623-2023
Email: walkermelvin@earthlink.net URL: http://www.walkermelvin.com
Members of Firm: James R. Walker; R. Martin Melvin.
Civil Practice, Criminal Law, Driving While Intoxicated, Traffic Violations, Wrongful Death, Probate, Real Estate, Personal Injury, Automobile Accidents, Corporate Law, Family Law, Divorce, Child Custody, Adoptions.

(This Listing Continued)

Walker & Melvin, LLP (Continued)

Local Counsel for: Wachovia Bank & Trust Co., N.A.; Safeway Finance Co.
Representative Clients: Morehead Memorial Hospital; NCNB National Bank; Home Savings Bank.
References: Wachovia Bank and Trust Co.; NCNB National Bank of North Carolina.

See Professional Biographies, EDEN, NORTH CAROLINA

EDENTON, * 5,394, *Chowan Co.*

Badger, Jimmy L. '40 '88 C.502 B.A. L.1045 J.D.
(adm. in TN; not adm. in NC) 910 W. Queen St.‡
Bean, C. Christopher .... '48 '75 C.575 B.A. L.896 J.D. Dist. J.
Busby, Charles T., (BV) .... '53 '78 C.575 A.B. L.896 J.D. [C.T.Busby]
Busby, Max S. .... '45 '72 C.576 B.S. L.896 J.D. [M.S.Busby]
Busby, Charles T., P.A., (BV) .... 102 S. Broad St.
Busby, Max S., P.A. .... 110 E. Queen St.
Culpepper, William T., III, (BV) .....'47 '73 C.301 B.S. L.896 J.D. 106 East Queen Street

Dixon, Samuel Bobbitt, (BV) '61 '88 C.575 B.A. L.896 J.D.
117 West Eden Street, 27932
Telephone: 252-482-8696 Fax: 252-482-1493
Email: dixonlaw@thedixonlawfirm.com
Real Estate, Buying and Selling a Home, Criminal Law, Traffic and DWI Offenses, Drug Crimes, Capital Offenses, Murder, Historic Preservation, Juvenile Law, Personal Injury, Automobile Accidents, and Wrongful Death.

See Professional Biographies, EDENTON, NORTH CAROLINA

Ellis, A. Travis .... '66 '99 C.575 B.S. L.1338 J.D. P.O. Box 275
Halloran, Dennis E. .... '52 '81 C.608 B.A. L.365 J.D. 111 Pelican Court
High, W. Hackney, Jr., (BV) .... '65 '90 C.575 B.S. L.1228 J.D. [Holt Y.M.&H.] ⊙
Holt York McDarris & High, LLP, (AV) .... 102 East Queen Street (⊙Raleigh)
Morehead, John C., (BV) .... '50 '76 C.575 B.S. L.945 J.D. 112 E. Queen St.
Rascoe, J. Peter, III .... '57 '82 C.576 B.A. L.790 J.D. Staff Atty.

Vincent Law Firm, The, PC
(See Southern Shores)

Weinrich, Phyllis Page, Mrs. '27 '51 C.882 A.B. L.94 LL.B.
(adm. in VT; not adm. in NC) 804 Surfside Dr.‡

EFLAND, —, *Orange Co.*

Hartsell, Marsha L. .... '48 '84 C.34 B.S. L.574 J.D. 7329 Apple Mill Rd.
Henkels, Maurice M., Jr. .... '33 '62 C&L.309 A.B., J.D. Thunder Mountain
Laughter, Mabel Y. .... '41 '98 C.925 B.S. L.574 J.D. P.O. Box 357

ELIZABETH CITY, * 17,188, *Pasquotank Co.*

Alexy, Fletcher, Wills & Wills, P.C.
(See Point Harbor)

Austin, C. Glenn, (BV) .... '29 '73 C.896 B.S. L.836 J.D. 1408 Horner St.
Beaman, Grafton G. .... '40 '66 C&L.575 B.S., LL.B. Chf. Dist. J.
Boyle, Terrence William .... '45 '70 C.103 B.A. L.904 J.D. U.S. Dist. J.
Cheek, Clayton W. ....'73 '03 C&L.896 B.A., J.D. [A Hornthal,R.E.&M.]
Culpepper, Michael L., (CV) .... '46 '74 C&L.575 A.B., J.D. P.O. Box 772
Eisenbeis, Mary Jane, Attorney at Law, (CV) '52 '98
C.516 B.S. L.923 J.D. 101 E. Elizabeth St.
Ellis, M. H. Hood, (AV) ....'49 '75 C.576 B.S. L.896 J.D. [Hornthal,R.E.&M.]
Etheridge, E. Ray, (BV) .... '29 '53 C&L.896 B.S., J.D. 201 Kramer Bldg.
Forbes, Joseph H., Jr., (BV) .... '59 '84 C.575 B.S. L.1228 J.D. 307 E. Church St.
Glover, Danny R., Jr., (BV) .... '70 '95 C.1302 B.S. L.575 J.D. [D.K.Teague]
Halen, John T. '22 '49 C.102 A.B. L.724 LL.B.
(adm. in NY; not adm. in NC) 139 Spindrift Trail, Glen Cove‡
Halstead, John W., Jr., Attorney at Law '49 '79 C.790 B.S. L.1228 J.D.
508 Kramer Bldg.
Harman, Lisa, (BV) .... '59 '93 C.296 B.A. L.896 J.D. [Trimpi,N.&H.]
Hawkins, Christy Leigh .... '75 '00 C.576 B.A. L.1228 J.D. Dist. Atty.'s Off.
Hiner, Frank P., IV, (BV) .... '63 '97 C.769 B.A. L.192 J.D. P.O. Box 97
Hobbs, Robert B., Jr., (BV) .... '60 '86 [Hornthal,R.E.&M.]
Hornthal, L. P., Jr., (AV) .... '36 '63 C&L.575 A.B., LL.B. [Hornthal,R.E.&M.]
Hornthal, L. Phillip, III, (BV) .... '67 '93 C.575 B.A. L.1345 J.D. [Hornthal,R.E.&M.]

Hornthal, Riley, Ellis & Maland, L.L.P., (AV)
301 East Main Street, P.O. Box 220, 27907-0220 ⊙
Telephone: 252-335-0871 Fax: 252-335-4223
URL: http://www.hrem.com
L. P. Hornthal, Jr.; M. H. Hood Ellis; Mark M. Maland; Donald C. Prentiss; Robert B. Hobbs, Jr. (Also at Nags Head Office) (Board Certified Specialist in Real Property Law-Residential, Business, Commercial and Industrial Transactions, North Carolina State Bar Board of Legal Specialization); Donald I. McRee, Jr.; John D. Leidy; Michael P. Sanders; L. Phillip Hornthal III;—William Brock Mitchell; Clayton W. Cheek. Of Counsel: J. Fred Riley; Thomas L. White, Jr. (Resident, Nags Head Office).
General Trial and Appellate Practice in all Courts. Personal Injury, Products Liability, Professional Malpractice, Corporate, Tax, Bankruptcy, Employment, Education, Criminal, Insurance, Construction, Real Estate, Environmental, Elder, Local Government, Wills and Trusts, Probate and Admiralty Law.
Representative Clients: CIGNA Group; Elizabeth City-Pasquotank County Board of Education; Camden County Board of Education; Kemper Insurance Group; State Farm Mutual; Travelers Insurance Co.; Wachovia Bank of North Carolina, N.A.; Branch Banking & Trust Co.; College of the Albemarle; USF&G.
Nags Head, North Carolina Office: 2502 South Croatan Highway, P.O. Box 310, 27959-0310. Telephone: 252-441-0871. Telefax: 252-441-8822.

See Professional Biographies, ELIZABETH CITY, NORTH CAROLINA

Hughes, Lennie L., (BV) ....'41 '74 C.232 A.B. L.836 J.D. 412 East Colonial Avenue
Johnson, Van H. .... '42 '75 C.575 A.B. L.744 J.D. 108 E. Main St.
Lamb, Nancy B., (BV) .... '55 '82 C.34 B.S. L.896 J.D. Asst. Dist. Atty.
Leidy, John D., (BV) .... '62 '87 C.207 B.A. L.575 J.D. [Hornthal,R.E.&M.]
Maland, Mark M., (AV) .... '48 '77 C.575 A.B. L.896 J.D. [Hornthal,R.E.&M.]
McRee, Donald I., Jr., (BV) .....'61 '87 C.1130 B.A. L.1228 J.D. [Hornthal,R.E.&M.] ⊙
Mitchell, William Brock .... '73 '02 C.140 B.A. L.356 J.D. [A Hornthal,R.E.&M.]
Morgan, William H., Jr., (BV) .... '59 '85 C.301 B.A. L.692 J.D. 410 E. Main St.
Mullen, Herbert T., Jr., (BV) ....'42 '67 C.1228 B.S. L.896 J.D. 101 E. Elizabeth St.
Nash, Thomas P., IV, (BV) .... '49 '79 C.575 A.B. L.861 J.D. [Trimpi,N.&H.]
Parrish, Frank R., (BV) .... '49 '79 C.575 A.B. L.1345 J.D. Dist. Atty.
Prentiss, Donald C., (BV) ....'55 '81 C&L.896 B.A., J.D. [Hornthal,R.E.&M.]
Pureza, David R. .... '69 '96 C.232 B.A. L.500 J.D. [A Twiford]
Riley, J. Fred, (AV) ....'38 '67 C.896 A.B. L.575 J.D. [C Hornthal,R.E.&M.]
Sanders, Michael P., (BV) ....'64 '90 C.575 B.A. L.1345 J.D. [Hornthal,R.E.&M.]
Small, G. Elvin, III, (BV) .... '51 '77 C.228 B.A. L.896 J.D. P.O. Box 69
Small, J. H. W. ....'25 '49 C.893 B.S. L.575 LL.B. Emer. Supr. Ct. J.
Spivey, Gorden W., (BV) .... '42 '77 C.232 B.S. L.574 J.D. [G.W.Spivey]
Spivey, G. Wendell, (BV) .... 303 E. Main St.
Stanley, Nita K., (BV) ....'51 '87 C.999 B.B.A. L.692 J.D. 2035 North Road Street
Teague, D. Keith, (BV) .... '48 '73 C.240 A.B. L.896 J.D. [D.K.Teague]
Teague, D. Keith, P.A., (BV) .... 408 East Colonial Avenue
Thompson, C. Everett, II, (BV) .... '46 '73 C.575 A.B. L.896 J.D. [C.E.Thompson,II]
Thompson, C. Everett, II, P.A., (BV) .... 101 W. Main St.
Trimpi, John G., (BV) .... '46 '72 C.296 B.A. L.896 J.D. [Trimpi,N.&H.]
Trimpi, Nash & Harman, L.L.P., (BV) .... 200 North Water Street, Suite 2A
Twiford Law Firm, The, L.L.P., (BV) .... P.O. Box 99 (⊙Southern Shores)
Underhill, Gary M., Jr., (CV) ....'41 '81 C.575 B.A. L.1228 J.D. 105 A E. Main St.

Vincent Law Firm, The, PC
(See Southern Shores)

Warren, Ronald M. .... '63 '92 C.232 B.S. L.1228 J.D. Dist. Atty. Off.
White, Gerald F., (AV) .... '26 '52 C&L.896 B.S., LL.B. 410 E. Main St.

ELIZABETHTOWN, * 3,704, *Bladen Co.*

Baker, H. Mitchell, III, (AV) .... '51 '76 C&L.896 B.S., J.D. [Baker&S.] ⊙
Baker & Slaughter, P.A., (AV) .... 608 West Broad (⊙Wilmington)

Britt, William S., Law Offices of
(See Lumberton)

Brumbaugh, Mu & King, P.A., (BV)
102 West Broad Street, 28337-0995 ⊙
Telephone: 910-862-2211
URL: http://www.bmklaw.net
Kenneth W. King, Jr.
Practice Limited to Injury Cases. Automobile, Wrongful Death, Medical Malpractice, Workers' Compensation, Products Liability and Social Security Claims.

See Professional Biographies, ELIZABETHTOWN, NORTH CAROLINA

Campbell, William Seth .... '72 '00 C.301 B.A. L.192 J.D. 608 W Broadstreet
Clark, Edward B., (AV) .... '16 '39 C&L.575 B.S., LL.B. P.O. Box 727‡
Clark, Giles R. .... '29 '58 C.232 B.S. L.575 LL.B. Emer. Supr. Ct. J.
Dixon, Matthew J. .... '70 '96 C.575 B.A. L.615 J.D. [A Maynard]
Freedman, Lisa Snyder, (CV) .... '68 '93 C.163 B.A. L.790 J.D. Asst. Dist. Atty.
Grady, Frank T., (AV) .... '19 '49 C&L.575 A.B., J.D. [C Hester,G.&H.]
Grady, Gary A., (BV) .... '54 '79 C.34 B.A. L.574 J.D. [Hester,G.&H.]
Hester, H. Clifton, (AV) .... '56 '81 C.198 A.B. L.575 J.D. [Hester,G.&H.]
Hester, Worth H., (AV) .... '23 '50 C&L.896 B.S., J.D. [C Hester,G.&H.]

Hester, Grady & Hester, P.L.L.C., (AV) BB
115 Courthouse Drive, P.O. Drawer 130, 28337
Telephone: 910-862-3191 FAX: 910-862-4802
URL: http://www.lawyers.com/hestergradyhester
Members of Firm: Gary A. Grady; H. Clifton Hester. Of Counsel: Worth H. Hester; Frank T. Grady; Myra Gooden Pate;—Scoti L. Ussery.
General Practice. Domestic, Real Estate, Personal Injury, Negligence, Workers Compensation, Corporate Law, Criminal Law, Municipal Law, School Law, Divorce, Driving While Intoxicated, Child Support, Contracts, Business Law, Automobile Accidents and Injuries, Wills, Probate, Insurance.

See Professional Biographies, ELIZABETHTOWN, NORTH CAROLINA

Jones, Greg, & Associates, P.A.
(See Wilmington)

King, Kenneth W., Jr., (BV) ...... '61 '86 C.575 B.S. L.469 J.D. [Brumbaugh,M.&K.] ⊙
Maynard, Alan I., (BV) .... '57 '83 C&L.575 B.A., J.D. [Maynard]

Maynard Law Firm, The, (BV)
101 Courthouse Drive, P.O. Box 875, 28337
Telephone: 910-862-8461 FAX: 910-862-6171
Email: maynard_alan@hotmail.com
Member of Firm: Alan I. Maynard. Associates: Matthew J. Dixon; Irene G. Riel. Of Counsel: Reuben L. Moore, Jr.
General Practice. Civil and Criminal Litigation. Family, Probate, Real Estate, Corporate Law, Workman's Compensation, Social Security Law and Personal Injury Law .
Representative Clients: Clarkton Housing Authority; Bladenboro Housing Authority; TranSouth Financial Corp.; Farmers Home Administration; Town of East Arcadia; American General Finance Corp.; United Carolina Bank.
References: United Carolina Bank; Wachovia Bank and Trust Co.; Nations Bank.

See Professional Biographies, ELIZABETHTOWN, NORTH CAROLINA

McGuinness, J. Michael, (AV) '57 '84 C.953 B.A. L.574 J.D.
2034 Highway, 701 North Lakewood Plaza, P.O. Box 952, 28337-0952 ⊙
Telephone: 910-862-7087 Fax: 910-862-8865
Email: jmichael@mcguinnesslaw.com URL: http://www.mcguinnesslaw.com
Personal Injury Law, Products Liability, Wrongful Death, Automobile Accidents, Labor and Employment, Civil Rights, Law Enforcement Liability, Criminal Law, Constitutional Law.
Washington, D.C. Office: 1300 Pennsylvania Avenue, N.W., Suite 700. 20004.
Boston, Massachusetts Office: 28 State Street, Suite 1100, 02109.

See Professional Biographies, ELIZABETHTOWN, NORTH CAROLINA

Melvin, James R., (AV) .... '42 '66 C&L.896 B.A., J.D. 1900 W. Broad St.‡
Moore, Reuben L., Jr., (AV) .... '41 '65 C&L.575 B .A., LL.B. [C Maynard]
Pate, Myra Gooden .... '— '02 C.759 B.A. L.1228 J.D. [C Hester,G.&H.]
Riel, Irene G., (CV) .... '57 '92 C.1309 B.A. L.1345 J.D. [A Maynard]
Singletary, Cynthia A., (BV) .... '60 '87 190 S. Poplar St.
Slaughter, Martin T. .... '65 '93 C.575 B.A. L.838 J.D. [Baker&S.]
Strickland, Kevin Joseph .... '71 '01 C&L.1228 B.A., J.D. P.O. Box 936
Ussery, Scoti L. .... '71 '03 C.953 B.A. L.574 J.D. [A Hester,G.&H.]
Wall, David Garrett, (AV) .... '52 '77 C.198 B.A. L.575 J.D. [D.G.Wall]
Wall, David G., Attorney At Law, (AV) .... 1117-B W. Broad St.
Womble, Harry G., Jr. .... '50 '75 C.575 B.S.B.A. L.192 J.D. P.O. Box 1389

ELKIN, 4,109, *Surry & Wilkes Cos.*

Alexander, R. Lewis, (AV) .... '19 '42 C&L.896 LL.B. Town Atty.
Davis, Vance T. .... '68 '00 C.443 B.S. L.896 J.D. [A J.W.Partin]
Everett, James A., (BV) .... '48 '74 C.575 B.A. L.896 J.D. [Everett&E.]
Everett, William Harrell, (AV) '34 '62 C&L.575 B.A., J.D.
[Everett&E.] (⊙Goldsboro)

Everett & Everett, PLLC, (AV)
1106 N. Bridge Street, Post Office Drawer 189, 28621
Telephone: 336-835-1210 Facsimile: 336-835-7177
Email: jeverett@rivercto.net URL: http://www.everettlawoffice.com
James A. Everett; William Harrell Everett.
Specializing in injury related cases.

See Professional Biographies, ELKIN, NORTH CAROLINA

Flippin, Thomas Clay .... '75 '00 C.34 B.S. L.1228 J.D. [T.C.Flippin]

Flippin, Thomas C., PC, Law Offices of
1435 N. Bridge Street, 28621-2334
Telephone: 336-526-2280 Fax: 336-526-5612
Email: tom@flippinlaw.com URL: http://www.flippinlawfirm.com
Thomas Clay Flippin.
Bankruptcy, Real Estate.

See Professional Biographies, ELKIN, NORTH CAROLINA

Freeman, James N., Jr. .... '66 '91 C&L.575 B.A., J.D. [J.N.Freeman,Jr.]

Freeman, James N., Jr., P.C.
117 Church Street, P.O. Box 347, 28621
Telephone: 336-835-4407 Fax: 336-526-3908
Email: jnfheel@hotmail.com
James N. Freeman, Jr.
Civil Litigation, Appellate Practice, General Practice, Trusts & Estates, Wills & Probate, Real Estate, Traffic Offenses, Business, Corporate, Personal Injury, Wrongful Death, Automobile Accidents.
See Professional Biographies, ELKIN, NORTH CAROLINA

Gillespie, James D., (BV) .... '55 '80 C.575 B.A. L.192 J.D. P.O. Box 771
Park, Daniel J., (AV) ......'34 '59 C&L.228 A.B., LL.B. 121 West Market Street at Church
Partin, James W. (Jack), (BV) .... '53 '79 C.576 B.A. L.1228 J.D. [J.W.Partin]
Partin, James W., (BV) .... 210 W. Main Street
Smith, Franklin D., (BV) .... '32 '64 C.125 B.A. L.896 LL.B. P.O. Box 307
Stewart, Susan R. ....'59 '84 C&L.846 B.A., J.D. Admr., Parkwood Eye Ctr.

ELM CITY, 1,165, *Wilson Co.*

Miles, James E. M. ....'17 '49 C.55 A.B. L.896 LL.B. Rt. 2, Box 373-M‡

ELON COLLEGE, 6,738, *Alamance Co.*

Martin, Robert H. .... '50 '77 C.672 B.S. L.1206 J.D. 1211 Jamestowne Dr.

EMERALD ISLE, 3,488, *Carteret Co.*

Collins and Moore, PLLC
(See Jacksonville)

Edington, Mark M. '65 '91 C.587 B.S. L.502 J.D.
(adm. in MO; not adm. in NC) P.O. Box 4178★
Hart, John M. ....'31 '61 C.262 B.S. L.724 J.D. 604 Cedar Point Blvd.
Lincoln, Michael P., (CV) ....'53 '81 C.1102 B.A. L.1029 J.D. P.O. Box 4130
Lumsden, Treve B., (BV) ....'54 '79 C.1104 B.S. L.990 J.D. [Stone&L.]
Stone, Arnold M., (AVⓉ) ......'30 '59 C.472 B.A. L.896 LL.B. 8752 Reed Drive, Suite 3
Stone & Lumsden, A Professional Corporation, (BV) ....8752 Reed Dr.
Tantum, John E., (AV) ...... '48 '73 C&L.896 B.S., J.D. 8101 Emerald Drive (⊙Wendell)
Toomes, Elizabeth M., (CV) ....'65 '91 C.575 B.S. L.896 J.D. [Ⓐ A.M.Stone]

ENFIELD, 2,347, *Halifax Co.*

Armstrong, H. Lawrence, Jr., (AV) ....'50 '75 C&L.575 A.B., J.D. [Hux,L.&A.]
Hux, George A., (AV) ....'— '37 C&L.575 B.A., J.D. 114 Whitfield St.

Hux, Livermon & Armstrong, L.L.P., (AV)
114 Whitfield Street, P.O. Box 217, 27823
Telephone: 252-445-5188 Fax: 252-445-3285
Email: hla@hlalaw.net
Members of Firm: James S. Livermon, Jr.; H. Lawrence Armstrong, Jr.
General Practice. Criminal including DWI, Traffic Offenses, and Civil Trials in all Courts. Wills and Probate, Trusts and Estates, Corporation, Insurance and Real Property Law, Personal Injury, Automobile Accidents, Family Law.
Local Counsel for: Enfield Building & Loan Assn.; Halifax Electric Membership Corp.; Halifax County Mutual Fire Insurance Co.; Enfield Grain and Fertilizer Co.; Farmers Home Administration; Halifax County Board of Education.
See Professional Biographies, ENFIELD, NORTH CAROLINA

Livermon, James S., Jr., (AV) ....'43 '67 C&L.896 B.A., J.D. [Hux,L.&A.]
Parker, Rom B., Jr. ....'46 '72 C.125 A.B. L.896 J.D. 105 Whitfield St.‡

ENGELHARD, 500, *Hyde Co.*

Midyette, James Emery, Jr. .... '60 '01 C.576 B.S. L.1339 J.D. 1441 Nebraska Rd.

ENKA, —, *Buncombe Co.*

Howard, William P. '13 '42 C.48 L.180 LL.B.
(adm. in DC; not adm. in NC) P.O. Box 1304‡
Miller, James H. '40 '64 C.575 A.B. L.802 LL.B.
(adm. in TX; not adm. in NC) Amer. Enka Corp.
Winger, Maurice, Jr. ....'17 '43 C.947 A.B. L.228 LL.B. Pres., Amer. Enka Corp.

ERWIN, 4,537, *Harnett Co.*

Faircloth, Resson Oliver, II ....'62 '94 C&L.1228 B.B.A., J.D. P.O. Box 8
Hoyle, Barry L. ....'59 '86 C&L.1228 B.S., J.D. 102 E. H St.‡
Hunter, C. Mac, (BV) ....'42 '67 C.125 B.A. L.896 J.D. [C.Mac Hunter]
Hunter, C. Mac, P.A., (BV) ....102 East H Street

FAIRMONT, 2,604, *Robeson Co.*

Floyd, Charles E., (BV) ....'56 '81 C&L.1228 B.S., J.D. 200 S. Main St.

FAIRVIEW, 2,495, *Buncombe Co.*

Rhynedance, Harold D., Jr., (AVⓉ) '22 '49 C&L.188 B.A., J.D.
(adm. in NY; not adm. in NC) 286 Sugar Hollow Rd.

FARMVILLE, 4,392, *Pitt Co.*

Burti, Christopher L., (AV) ....'50 '79 C.232 B.S.B.A. L.575 J.D. 404 W. Church St.
Edwards, Christopher P., (BV) .... '64 '89 C&L.575 B.A., J.D. 131 N. Main St.
Hines, John M., (AV) ....'39 '65 C&L.228 B.A., LL.B. Exec. V.P., Dimon Inc.
Lewis, John B., Jr. ....'36 '61 C&L.575 A.B., LL.B. P.O. Box 4‡

Owens & Nelson, P.L.L.C.
(See Greenville)

FAYETTEVILLE, * 121,015, *Cumberland Co.*

Adams, Gale M., (BV) ....'59 '84 C.575 B.A. L.574 J.D. Fed. Pub. Def. Off.
Allen, Bruce K., Attorney at Law, (CV) '56 '81
C.328 B.A. L.405 J.D. 1000 Wildwood Dr.
Ammons, James Floyd, Jr. ....'55 '81 C&L.575 B.A., J.D. Supr. Ct. J.
Anderson, J. William, (BV) .... '27 '53 C&L.575 B.A., LL.B. [Anderson&S.]
Anderson, James R. .... '70 '97 C.953 B.A. L.1345 J.D. [Ⓐ Browne,F.W.&W.]
Anderson, John Huske, II, (AV) ....'46 '75 C.576 B.S. L.896 J.D. [Anderson,J.L.B.&B.]

Anderson, Johnson, Lawrence, Butler & Bock, L.L.P., (AV) BR
Suite 204 First-Citizens Bank Building, P.O. Drawer 2737, 28302-2737
Telephone: 910-483-1171 FAX: 910-483-5005
Email: ajlbb@andersonjohnson.com URL: http://www.andersonjohnson.com
Members of Firm: Henry L. Anderson (1911-1986); Hal W. Broadfoot (1929-1994); Lee Best Johnson; John Huske Anderson, II; Steven C. Lawrence; J. Stewart Butler, III; A. David Bock. Associate: Robert A. Hasty, Jr.
Civil Trials in all Courts, State and Federal. General Insurance Defense, Medical Malpractice and Professional Malpractice Claims, Product Liability Claims, Drug and Medical Device Claims, Construction Claims, Fire, Arson and Fraud Claims, Fidelity and Surety Claims, Life, Accident and Health Insurance Coverage Claims, Personal Injury and Worker's Compensation, Business and Insurance Litigation, Excess and Reinsurance, Health and Hospital Law.
Representative Clients: North Carolina Farm Bureau Mutual Insurance Co.; Integon; Nationwide Insurance Company; GEICO; Allstate Insurance Company; Shelter Insurance Company; Canal Insurance Company; Providian Insurance Company; Professional Risk Management Services, Inc.; TIG.
See Professional Biographies, FAYETTEVILLE, NORTH CAROLINA

Anderson, Jones & Gengo, PLLC
(See Raleigh)

Anderson & Strickland, (BV) ....210 E. Russell St.
Armstrong, Charles B., (BV) ....'48 '73 C&L.575 B.A., J.D. [Armstrong&B.]
Armstrong & Baggett, (BV) .... 127 South Cool Spring Street
Aycock, Gretchen D. .... '62 '96 C.575 B.A. L.574 J.D. 157 Gillespie St.
Aycock, William W., Jr., (AV) .... '37 '61 C.673 B.S. L.896 LL.B. [McLeod]
Baer, Bruce F., (BV) .... '57 '84 C&L.575 B.S.B.A., J.D. [Baer&B.]

Baer & Baer, Attorneys At Law, P.A., (BV)
Suite 211, McNairy Building, Eutaw Village North 823 Elm Street, P.O. Box 35110, 28303
Telephone: 910-483-8066 Fax: 910-483-7261
Email: baer.baer@earthlink.net URL: http://www.lawyers.com/baerattorneyatlaw
Ervin I. Baer (1928-2004); Bruce F. Baer;—Jennifer R. Cooney.
General Civil Practice. Trials in all Courts. Personal Injury Litigation, Probate, Estate Planning, Corporate, Business and Tax Law, Real Estate, Bankruptcy.
Representative Clients: Branch Banking and Trust Co.; Powers-Swain Chevrolet, Inc.; Stout Properties, Inc.; Paris and Potter Management Corp.; Cape Fear Cardiology Associates, P.A.; McDonald Lumber Co., Inc.; Park N' Shop Food Mart, Inc.
Approved Attorneys for: Chicago Title Insurance Corp.; First American Title Co.
Reference: Branch Banking and Trust Co.
See Professional Biographies, FAYETTEVILLE, NORTH CAROLINA

Baggett, Talmage S., Jr., (BV) ....'50 '85 C.34 B.T. L.1228 J.D. [Armstrong&B.]
Bailey, Stephen '75 '03 C.34 B.S. L.469 J.D.
[Ⓐ Firm of Hutchens,S.&B.] (⊙Wilmington)
Banks, Kenneth E., (BV) .... '43 '73 C.34 B.S. L.575 J.D. [Banks&Assoc.]
Banks and Associates, (BV) .... 125 Reilly Road, Suite 105
Barrett, Grainger R., (BV) .... '49 '74 C&L.575 A.B., J.D. Co. Atty.
Barrington and Jones Law Firm, The, P.A., (AV) .... Heritage Square at 213 Dick Street
Battle, Carmen J. .... '58 '88 C.575 B.A. L.602 J.D. 122 Lamon St.
Beaver, H. Gerald, (AV) .... '47 '73 C.232 B.A. L.575 J.D. [Beaver H.S.&C.]

Beaver Holt Sternlicht & Courie, P.A., (AV) BR
230 Green Street, 28301 ⊙
Telephone: 910-323-4600 FAX: 910-323-3403
Email: info@beaverholt.com URL: http://www.beaverholt.com
H. Gerald Beaver; F. Thomas III Holt; Mark A. Sternlicht; David T. Courie;—Hal Broadfoot Jr.; Mark Hearp. Of Counsel: Janet Holland Downing.
Civil and Criminal Litigation in all State and Federal Courts. Personal Injury, Medical Negligence, Wrongful Death, Workers Compensation, Criminal Defense, Corporate Litigation, Commercial Litigation, Employment and Labor Law, DWI, Traffic Violations.
References: Available Upon Request.
Raeford, North Carolina Office: 127 West Edinborough Avenue. Telephone: 910-875-3379. FAX: 910-875-4030.
See Professional Biographies, FAYETTEVILLE, NORTH CAROLINA

Bennington, Erik T. '78 '03
C.1228 B.B.A. L.896 J.D. [Ⓐ Firm of Hutchens,S.&B.] (⊙Wilmington)
Berg, Stephen J. '63 '88 C.723 B.S. L.300 J.D.
(adm. in MN; not adm. in NC) 7521 McFrench Dr.
Berry, Doran J., (BV) ..... '29 '53 C&L.575 A.B., LL.B. 5085 Morganton Rd., Ste. 102-D
Berry, H. Dolph, (AV) .... '34 '62 C&L.575 A.B., LL.B. 214 Fairway Drive
Blackwell, John V., Jr., (AV) .... '32 '55 C&L.896 B.A., LL.B. [Blackwell&E.] ‡

Blackwell & Edwards, P.A., (AV)
300 Dick Street, Heritage Square, P.O. Box 469, 28302
Telephone: 910-483-5176 Fax: 910-483-9653
Email: TDEdwards@nc.rr.com URL: http://www.blackwellandedwards.com
John V. Blackwell, Jr. (Retired); Timothy D. Edwards.
Family Law, Probate.
See Professional Biographies, FAYETTEVILLE, NORTH CAROLINA

Bock, A. David, (BV) .... '58 '87 C.575 B.A. L.1228 J.D. [Anderson,J.L.B.&B.]
Boliek, David Luther, Jr. .... '67 '97 C.575 B.A. L.1228 J.D. [Williford,H.C.&B.]

Boose, Michael C., (BV) '55 '81 C.232 B.S. L.1228 J.D.
214 Dick Street, 28302
Telephone: 910-486-9292 Fax: 910-221-0750
URL: http://www.boose-law.com
Criminal Law, Personal Injury, Family Law.
See Professional Biographies, FAYETTEVILLE, NORTH CAROLINA

Brady, B. Dianne, (BV) .... '47 '85 C.398 B.A. L.1228 J.D. [Brady]
Brady Law Firm, The, (BV) .... 325 Green St.
Braswell, E. Maurice ....'22 '50 C&L.575 LL.B. 333 DeVane St.‡
Brewer, Coy E., Jr. ....'47 '72 C.896 B.A. L.575 J.D. [Mitchell B.R.]
Brisson, L. Clifford, Jr., (BV) ....'53 '78 C.575 B.S. L.574 J.D. [Craig B.&C.]
Britt, Carl L., Jr. (Woody), (BV) ....'55 '80 C.575 B.A. L.1228 J.D. [C.L.Britt,Jr.]

Britt, Carl L., Jr., Attorney at Law, (BV)
224 Dick Street, 28302
Telephone: 910-483-1176 Fax: 910-483-5201
Email: carl@carlbritt.com URL: http://www.carlbrittjr.com
Carl L. Britt, Jr. (Woody).
Personal Injury, Wrongful Death, Traffic Violations, Driving While Intoxicated, Driving Under the Influence, Criminal Law.
See Professional Biographies, FAYETTEVILLE, NORTH CAROLINA

Brittain, Charles M., (CV) ....'69 '96 C.575 B.A. L.1345 J.D. [Ⓐ Mitchell B.R.]
Britton, John H., (BV) .... '62 '95 C.431 B.S. L.1345 J.D. [Firm of Hutchens,S.&B.]
Britton, Rebecca J., (BV) ...... '63 '92 C.431 B.A L.1228 J.D. [Firm of Hutchens,S.&B.]
Broadfoot, Hal, Jr. .... '62 '02 C.575 B.S.B.A. L.1228 J.D. [Ⓐ Beaver H.S.&C.]
Brown, Raymond F. .... '45 '75 C.138 B.A. L.228 J.D. 205 Bedell Place
Brown, William E., Law Office of ....'55 '93 C.1309 B.S. L.896 J.D. 1305 Hope Mills Rd.
Brown, Willis D. ....'29 '53 C&L.575 A.B., LL.B. 109 Green St., Ste. 302‡

Brown & Moss, P.A., (BV)
Suite 302, New First Citizens Bank Building, 109 Green Street, 28301-5044
Telephone: 910-433-2800 Fax: 910-433-4427
Email: mosspr@aol.com URL: http://www.lawyers.com/mosspr
Patricia R. Moss.
Traffic Offenses, Criminal, DWI, Bond Reductions, Misdemeanors, Felonies, Criminal Practice in State and Federal Courts.
See Professional Biographies, FAYETTEVILLE, NORTH CAROLINA

Brownback, Peter Evans '47 '77 C.367 B.A. L.692 J.D.
(adm. in VA; not adm. in NC) 305 Pinkney Ct.‡
Browne, Flebotte, Wilson & Webb, PLLC, (BV)
225 Green Street, Suite 204 (⊙Charlotte, Creedmoor, Durham, Greensboro)

Brumbaugh, Mu & King, P.A., (BV)
609 Executive Place, 28305 ⊙
Telephone: 910-630-2099
URL: http://www.bmklaw.net
Kenneth W. King, Jr.

(This Listing Continued)

Brumbaugh, Mu & King, P.A. (Continued)
Practice Limited to Injury Cases. Automobile, Wrongful Death, Medical Malpractice, Workers' Compensation, Products Liability and Social Security Claims.
See Professional Biographies, FAYETTEVILLE, NORTH CAROLINA

Bryan, Norwood E., Jr. ....'35 '63 C.575 A.B. L.976 LL.B. P.O. Box 24
Bullard, Ruby Warren, (BV) ....'57 '81 C&L.896 B.A., J.D. [Ⓑ Parish&C.]
Bunce, Steve, (BV) ....'51 '76 C.575 BS L.420 JD 1003 Hay St.
Burge, Vickie L., (BV) ....'60 '85 C.896 B.A. L.1228 J.D. P.O. Box 1901
Burke, Mona E. ....'72 '98 C.575 B.A. L.1345 J.D. [Firm of Dache&B.]
Burns, Kenneth D., (BV) ....'64 '90 C.576 B.A. L.1228 J.D. 3405 Arboretum Pl.
Butler, J. Stewart, III, (BV) ....'57 '85 C.575 B.A. L.574 J.D. [Anderson,J.L.B.&B.]
Butler, Robert H. ....'19 '48 C.896 L.575 LL.B. 511 Forest Lake Rd.‡

Byrd, Gregory M., (CV) '63 '95 C.576 B.S. L.1228 J.D.
214 Dick Street, Suite B, P.O. Box 332, 28302-0332
Telephone: 910-678-0966 1-800-793-1962 Fax: 910-678-0677 URL: http://www.ncdrunkdriving.com
Email: gbyrdlaw@aol.com URL: http://www.lawyers.com/gregorymbyrd-com
Criminal Law, Criminal Defense, Drugs and Narcotics, Traffic Violations/Speeding, DWI, Personal Injury, Automobile Accidents and Injuries, Employment Law, Unemployment Compensation, Wrongful Termination.
See Professional Biographies, FAYETTEVILLE, NORTH CAROLINA

Byrd, Wade E., (AV) ....'48 '73 C.1309 B.A. L.896 J.D. [W.E.Byrd]
Byrd, Wade E., PA, Law Offices of, (AV) .... Drawer 2797
Canady, Donald R., (AV) ....'34 '60 C&L.896 B.B.A., LL.B. 224 Dick St.‡
Canders, Douglas E., (CV) ....'44 '72 C.921 B.S. L.744 J.D. Asst. Co. Atty.
Carlin, Haral E., (BV) ....'47 '90 C.1011 B.A. L.574 J.D. [H.E.Carlin]
Carlin, Haral E., PLLC, (BV) ....214 Dick Street
Carpenter, Jodi V., (CV) '73 '98
C.1228 B.A. L.1345 J.D. [Ⓐ Smith,D.S.H.&D.] (⊙Fayetteville)
Carter, Deborah Powers, (CV) ....'44 '81 C.1317 B.A. L.1228 J.D. [D.P.Carter]
Carter, Lester G., Jr., (BV) ....'25 '49 C.673 B.A. L.575 210 E. Russell St.
Carter, Deborah P., (CV) .... 5746 Dobson Dr.
Chandler, Carl P., II ....'46 '83 C.1309 B.A. L.1228 J.D. P.O. Box 87115
Cheatwood, Philip H., (AV) ....'46 '71 C&L.896 B.A., J.D. [Russ,W.C.&H.]
Cherry, Sol G. ....'32 '56 C&L.575 A.B., LL.B. Ret. Chf. Dist. J.
Ciccone, J. Gary, (BV) ....'46 '74 C&L.575 B.S., J.D. P.O. Box 53668
Clark, Dougald N., Jr. ....'38 '66 C.673 B.A. L.896 LL.B. Dist. J.
Clark, Martha H., (CV) ....'53 '79 C.575 B.A. L.896 LL.B. Asst. Dist. Atty.

Clark, William E., (BV) '43 '68 C.198 B.A. L.575 J.D.
2850 Village Drive, Suite 204, 28304
Telephone: 910-323-2020 FAX: 910-485-8320
Email: weclark@earthlink.net
General Civil Practice. Wills, Estate Planning and Probate. Corporate and Business Law. Real Estate Closings and Development.
Representative Clients: South River R.E.A. Cooperative; Cumberland County Hospital System, Inc.
Approved Attorneys for: Lawyers Title Insurance Corp.
See Professional Biographies, FAYETTEVILLE, NORTH CAROLINA

Clarke, F. Stuart, (AV) ....'42 '71 C&L.575 A.B., J.D. [Thorp,C.&N.]
Clements, Thomas H. ....'52 '83 C.1011 B.S. L.1228 J.D. [Craig B.&C.]
Cleveland, Alfred E., (AV) ....'35 '59 C.276 B.S. L.575 LL.B. [McCoy W.W.C.R.R.P.]
Coffey, Joseph H., Jr., (CV) ....'53 '81 C.1126 B.A. L.1228 J.D. Pub. Def. Off.

Compton, Roger R., (BV) '46 '79 C&L.1228 B.S., J.D.
5311 Raeford Road, P.O. Box 42836, 28309-2836
Telephone: 910-424-6393 Fax: 910-424-2212
Email: adminoffice@nc.rr.com URL: http://www.rogercompton.com
Associate: Melinda C. Flinn.
Family Law, including Divorce, Child Custody, Child Support, Spousal Support; Consumer Bankruptcy Chapter 7,11 and 13; Criminal Defense, Traffic Violations.
See Professional Biographies, FAYETTEVILLE, NORTH CAROLINA

Condlin, Bernard P., (CV) ....'66 '99 C.1031 B.S. L.823 J.D. [Ⓐ Smith,D.S.H.&D.]
Conormon, Todd Clark, (BV) ....'56 '81 C.712 B.A. L.564 J.D. 603 Argyll Rd.
Cook, Owen W., (BV) ....'34 '65 C&L.575 A.B., LL.B. [Cook,I.&S.]
Cook, Ivarsson & Shober, (BV) ....225 Person Street
Cooke, James H., Jr., (BV) ....'51 '77 C.575 B.S. L.896 J.D. [Parish&C.]
Cooney, Jennifer R. ....'— '03 C.575 B.S.B.A. L.1228 J.D. [Ⓐ Baer&B.]
Courie, David T., (BV) ....'70 '97 C&L.1228 B.B.A., J.D. [Beaver H.S.&C.] ⊙
Cowling, Catherine Beckett ....'70 '99 C&L.1228 B.S., J.D. 157 Gillespie St.
Craig, David B. ....'39 '72 C.627 B.S. L.846 J.D. [Craig B.&C.] ‡
Craig Brisson & Clements, P.A., (BV) ....806 Hay Street
Craven, Richard T., (AV) ....'53 '79 C.575 B.A. L.192 J.D. [Murray,C.&I.]
Crenshaw, Paul M. ....'71 '98 C.1309 B.S. L.1228 J.D. [Williford,H.C.&B.]
Crosby, Ronald C., Jr. ....'71 '97 C.575 B.A. L.896 J.D. [Crosby]

Crosby Law Firm, The
210 East Russell Street, Suite 105, 28302
Telephone: 910-483-0458 Fax: 910-483-8689
Email: rcrosby@crosbylawoffices.com URL: http://www.crosbylawfirms.com
Ronald C. Crosby, Jr.
Traffic Violations, Criminal Law, Driving While Intoxicated, Military Law, Personal Injury.
See Professional Biographies, FAYETTEVILLE, NORTH CAROLINA

Dache, Juanita U. ....'66 '98 C.575 B.A. L.1345 J.D. [Firm of Dache&B.]
Dache & Burke, The Law Firm of ....111 Lamon St., Ste. 204
Dardess, Theodore O. ....'72 '99 C.604 B.A. L.575 J.D. Pub. Def. Off.
David, Edward J., (BV) ....'33 '58 C.602 B.S. L.896 J.D. [Downing,D.D.&P.]
Deese, Renny W., (AV) ....'46 '71 C.152 B.A. L.896 J.D. [Reid,L.D.N.&P.]
Dempster, Andrew R., (BV) ....'60 '86 C.953 B.A. L.1228 J.D. [Smith,D.S.H.&D.]
Devan, Laura A., (BV) ....'67 '94 C.390 B.A. L.575 J.D. [Rand&G.]
Devore, Linda S. '50 '76 C.937 B.S. L.879 J.D.
(adm. in IL; not adm. in NC) 2616 Dartmouth Dr.‡
Dickey, Carol D. '49 '74 C&L.575 B.A., J.D.
Chmn., Paralegal Dept., Fayetteville Tech. Comm. College
Dickey, D. Pittman, (BV) ....'50 '74 C&L.575 B.A., J.D. [Smith,D.S.H.&D.]
Downing, Harold D., (BV) ....'33 '58 C&L.575 A.B., J.D. [Downing,D.D.&P.]
Downing, Janet Holland ....'— '77 C.1318 B.A. L.575 J.D. [Ⓑ Beaver H.S.&C.]
Downing, Thaddeus P., (BV) ....'66 '94 C.576 B.A. L.1228 J.D. [Downing,D.D.&P.]
Downing, David, Downing & Pechmann, (BV) ....219 Dick Street, Heritage Square
Dunham, Catherine Ross ....'63 '96 C.575 B.A. L.1228 J.D. 117 Magnolia Ave.
Dunham, Jeff, (BV) ....'60 '85 C.896 B.A. L.575 J.D. [McCoy W.W.C.R.R.P.]
Dunn, Timothy M., (BV) ....'60 '87 C.575 B.S. L.1345 J.D. [T.M.Dunn]
Dunn, Timothy M., P.A., Law Offices of, (BV) ....331 Glenbarney Dr.

Edwards, R. Gregg, (CV) '57 '83 C.576 B.S. L.896 J.D.
1003 Hay Street, Suite 3, P.O. Box 53885, 28305
Telephone: 910-483-3399 Fax: 910-483-9585
Email: rgrdedwards@hotmail.com URL: http://www.lawyers.com/rgedwards
Bankruptcy (including Small Business), Personal Injury, Automobile Accidents and Injuries, Workers Compensation, Back Injuries, Medical Malpractice, Civil Litigation.
See Professional Biographies, FAYETTEVILLE, NORTH CAROLINA

Edwards, Timothy D., (BV) ....'69 '95 C.999 B.S. L.1345 J.D. [Blackwell&E.]
Eller, Sanya T. ....'61 '94 C.1378 B.A. L.574 J.D. P.O. Box 148
Evans, Anne Mayo, (BV) ....'56 '87 C.575 B.A. L.1228 J.D. [McCoy W.W.C.R.R.P.]
Feldbusch, Risa Quinn, (BV) ....'56 '81 C.232 B.S. L.1228 J.D. [Noble&Q.]

Ferguson, Patricia A. Wilson '51 '01 C.576 B.A. L.575 J.D.
201 South McPherson Church Road Suite 209, 28303
Mailing Address: P.O. Box 816, Fayetteville, NC 28302
Telephone: 910-860-2889 Fax: 910-860-2880
Email: tfergie@earthlink.net URL: http://www.fergusonhyattlaw.com
Workers Compensation, Family Law, Domestic Law, Civil Litigation, Corporate Law, Business Law, Criminal, Real Estate, Zoning.
See Professional Biographies, FAYETTEVILLE, NORTH CAROLINA

Flinn, Melinda C. ....'— '02 C&L.1228 B.S., J.D. [Ⓐ R.R.Compton]
Flowers, J. Scott ....'77 '03 C.232 B.A. L.1228 J.D. [Ⓐ Firm of Hutchens,S.&B.]
Franks, George J., (BV) ....'48 '83 C.260 B.S. L.1228 J.D. [G.J.Franks]

Franks, George J., P.A., (BV)
115 South Cool Spring Street, 28301
Telephone: 910-323-2834 Fax: 910-323-4923
Email: frankstrafficlaw@nc.rr.com URL: http://.georgejfranks.com
George J. Franks.
Criminal Law, Traffic Law, Personal Injury, Representation of Professionals before Boards, Representation of Law Enforcement Officers.
See Professional Biographies, FAYETTEVILLE, NORTH CAROLINA

Freedman, Stephen C., (BV) ....'52 '77 C.575 B.A. L.117 J.D. Pub. Defender's Office
Gadsden, M. E. ....'25 '52 C.26 A.B. L.574 LL.B. 1332 Ramsey St.
Galt, Richard Andrew ....'64 '95 C.1044 B.S. L.982 J.D. 2517 Raeford Rd.
George, Marion C., Jr., (CV) ....'22 '58 C.1378 B.S. L.276 J.D. 125 Person St.
Gilliam, J. Duane, (AV) ....'30 '57 C&L.575 B.S., J.D. 3340 Quarry Rd.
Gilliam, Joseph Duane, Jr., (CV) ....'69 '00 C.576 B.S. L.1228 J.D. [Gilliam]
Gilliam, J.D., (CV) ....307 Person St.
Godwin, Christopher B., (BV) '54 '79 C.575 B.A. L.896 J.D.
2513 Raeford Road, Suite A
Goodman, Jim Wade, (BV) ....'63 '88 C&L.575 B.S., J.D. [McCoy W.W.C.R.R.P.]
Grannis, Edward W., Jr., (AV) ....'43 '68 C&L.896 B.A., J.D. Dist. Atty.
Green, Deon Machell '72 '97 C.435 B.S.B.A. L.436 J.D.
(adm. in WI; not adm. in NC) Enkee Mgmt.
Gregory, Randy S., (BV) ....'47 '73 C.1228 B.A. L.896 J.D. [Rand&G.]
Hair, Lacy S. ....'25 '52 C&L.896 B.S., LL.B. 2103 Fordham Dr.
Hall, Beth A. ....'67 '93 C.329 B.A. L.150 J.D. P.O. Box 53592
Hall, Susan Joyce, (CV) ....'59 '95 C.1011 B.S. L.574 J.D. 111 Lamon St.
Hancox, Bradford Scott, (BV) ....'54 '87 C.838 B.A. L.1228 J.D. [Russ,W.C.&H.]
Hancox, Ellen B., (BV) '54 '85
C.890 B.A. L.1228 J.D. Trial Ct. Admr., Cumberland Co. Courthouse
Hardison, Kenneth L., (BV) ....'56 '82 C&L.1228 B.S., J.D. [Hardison&L.] ⊙

Hardison & Leone, L.L.P., (AV)
1014 Hay Street, Drawer 53037, 28305-5316 ⊙
Telephone: 910-223-3022 Toll Free: 800-782-3145 Fax: 910-223-9006
URL: http://www.hardisonandleone.com
Kenneth L. Hardison.
Personal Injury, Auto and Trucking Accidents, Pedestrian Accidents, Catastrophic Injury, Medical Malpractice, Workers' Compensation, Social Security Disability, Nursing Home Negligence, Security Investment Fraud, Inadequate Security Claims, Premises Liability, Mass Torts, Drug Liability Claims, Employment Law, Appellate Practice.
See Professional Biographies, FAYETTEVILLE, NORTH CAROLINA

Harris, Mark ....'73 '03 C.575 B.A. L.1339 J.D. [Ⓐ Smith,D.S.H.&D.]
Hasty, David H., (BV) ....'61 '87 C.575 B.A. L.574 J.D. [Smith,D.S.H.&D.]
Hasty, Robert A., Jr. ....'66 '98 C.232 B.S. L.192 J.D. [Ⓐ Anderson,J.L.B.&B.]
Hatley, Angela M. ....'— '93 C.575 B.S.N. L.1228 J.D. [Hatley&S.]
Hatley & Stone, P.A. ....709 Hay Street
Hearp, Mark ....'75 '01 C.575 B.A. L.1228 J.D. [Ⓐ Beaver H.S.&C.]
Hedahl, Joan E., (BV) ....'53 '76 [Hedahl&R.]
Hedahl & Radtke, (BV) ....1015 Arsenal Ave.
Herring, Darius B., Jr. ....'29 '58 C&L.575 B.A., LL.B. Emer. Supr. Ct. J.‡

Herzog, Paul F., (BV) '53 '78 C.228 B.A. L.575 J.D.
210 East Russell Street, Suite 101-103, P.O. Box 3097, 28302-3097
Telephone: 910-483-9500 Fax: 910-483-9524 URL: http://www.lawyers.com/theherzogfirm
Email: paulfherzog@hotmail.com URL: http://www.theherzogfirm.com
Criminal Defense, Traffic Violations, Drug Crimes, Narcotics, DWI, Homicide, Assault, Sexual Assault, Personal Injury.
See Professional Biographies, FAYETTEVILLE, NORTH CAROLINA

Hicks, George R., III, (BV) ....'64 '90 C.549 B.A. L.1228 J.D. Asst. Dist. Atty.
Hicks, Margit Monaco, (BV) ....'63 '91 C.575 B.A. L.1345 J.D. 1013 Arsenal Avenue
High, L. Sneed, (AV) ....'15 '41 C.870 L.575 LL.B. P.O. Box 409
Hill, Claire V., (BV) ....'65 '90 C.575 B.A. L.1345 J.D. Asst. Dist. Atty.
Hockman, Mark D. ....'54 '79 C.339 B.A. L.910 J.D. [M.D.Hockman]
Hockman, Mark D., P.A., The Law Offices of ....1310 Raeford Rd.
Hollers, Jeffrey C., Jr, (CV) ....'63 '90 C.575 A.B. L.1228 J.D. [Williford,H.C.&B.]
Holt, F. Thomas III, (BV) ....'52 '80 C.575 A.B. L.1228 J.D. [Beaver H.S.&C.] ⊙
Howard, Charles F. ....'27 '80 C.640 B.A. L.1228 J.D. 417 Hallmark Rd.‡
Hudson, Donald, (BV) ....'55 '80 C&L.575 B.S., J.D. [McGeachy,H.&Z.]
Huff, James C. ....'69 '99 C&L.1228 B.B.A., J.D. [Ⓐ Firm of Hutchens,S.&B.]
Hughes, Wendy H. ....'69 '99 C.575 B.S. L.1228 J.D. [Ⓐ Firm of Hutchens,S.&B.]
Hurmence, Roberta (Robin) Weaver, (BV) '56 '83
C.446 B.A. L.574 J.D. 1017 Arsenal Ave.
Hutchens, H. Terry, (AV) ....'50 '77 C.576 B.A. L.896 J.D. [Firm of Hutchens,S.&B.]

Hutchens, Senter & Britton, P.A., The Law Firm of, (AV)
4317 Ramsey Street, 28311 ⊙
Mailing Address: P.O. Box 2505, Fayetteville, NC 28302
Telephone: 910-864-6888 Facsimile: 910-864-6848
Email: lawfirm@hutchensandsenter.com URL: http://www.hutchensandsenter.com
H. Terry Hutchens; William L. Senter; John H. Britton; Joseph J. Vonnegut; Rebecca J. Britton; Shawna Y. Staton (Resident, Raleigh, North Carolina Office). Associates: Wendy H. Hughes; Lonnie M. Player, Jr.; James C. Huff; John A. Mandulak; Sarah Miranda; J. Scott Flowers; Erik T. Bennington (Also at Wilmington, North Carolina Office); Stephen Bailey (Also at Wilmington, North Carolina Office). Of Counsel: Rudolph G. Singleton, Jr.
General Civil Practice, Trials in all State and Federal Courts, Creditor Bankruptcy, Foreclosures and Collection, Personal Injury, Wrongful Death, Worker's Compensation, Insurance Law, Corporation, Business and Real Estate.
Wilmington, North Carolina Office: Suite 210, 1437 Military Cutoff Road, P.O. Box 12969. Telephone: 910-509-7480. Fax: 910-509-7448.
Raleigh, North Carolina Office: Suite 1540, Two Hanover Square. Telephone: 919-834-2688. Fax: 919-834-3373.
See Professional Biographies, FAYETTEVILLE, NORTH CAROLINA

Hyatt, Susan E., (CV) ....'65 '92 C.1309 B.A. L.1228 J.D. [S.E.Hyatt]
Hyatt, Susan E., P.A., (CV) ....213 Dick Street, Suite 204

Inman, Stephen G., (BV) ....'47 '88 C.575 A.B. L.1228 J.D. [Murray,C.&I.]
Ivarsson, Carl G., Jr., (BV) ....'60 '86 C&L.1228 B.A., J.D. [Cook,I.&S.]
Jackson, John Hamilton ....'39 '71 C.314 B.S.E. L.45 J.D. [[A] Yarborough]
Jenkins, Wanda L. .... '58 '91 C&L.329 B.B.A., J.D. Fayetteville State Univ.
Johnson, Edwin Lynn ....'41 '66 C&L.575 B.S., LL.B. Supr. Ct. J.
Johnson, G. B. ....'36 '77 C.257 B.S. L.831 J.D. Co. Atty.
Johnson, Laura G. .... '52 '78 C.994 B.A. L.705 J.D. P.O. Box 1829
Johnson, Lee Best, (AV) ....'46 '74 C.575 B.S. L.192 J.D. [Anderson,J.L.B.&B.]
Jones, Benner, III ....'39 '65 C&L.575 A.B., LL.B. [Barrington&J.]
Keever, A. Elizabeth ....'50 '75 C.577 B.A. L.575 J.D. Chf. Dist. J.
Kelley, Elaine Strickland, (BV) ....'59 '86 C&L.1228 B.S., J.D. Asst. Dist. Atty.

Kelly, Colleen J. '66 '01 C.1011 B.S. L.1228 J.D.
350 Dick Street, 28302
Telephone: 910-424-6699 Fax: 910-426-8463
Email: ckellylaw@earthlink.net
Family Law, Domestic Relations, Juvenile Law, Traffic Violations.
See Professional Biographies, FAYETTEVILLE, NORTH CAROLINA

Kelly, Elaine S. .... '59 '86 C&L.1228 B.A., J.D. [[A] Smith,D.S.H.&D.]
Kennedy-Gurnee, Elizabeth, (CV) ....'67 '92 C&L.1228 B.A., J.D. P.O. Box 53965
King, Kenneth W., Jr., (BV) ...... '61 '86 C.575 B.S. L.469 J.D. [Brumbaugh,M.&K.] ⊙
King, Toni S., (CV) ....'73 '00 C&L.574 B.A., J.D. [[A] Rogers&M.]
Koenig, Deborah Bland, (CV) '59 '84
C.198 B.A. L.575 J.D. Legal Advsr., Co. Sheriff's Off.
Kulich, Ann ....'78 '03 C.575 B.A. L.1228 J.D. [[A] Smith,D.S.H.&D.]
Lawrence, Steven C., (BV) .... '59 '84 C.575 B.A. L.1228 J.D. [Anderson,J.L.B.&B.]
Leary, Sarilyn Hardee .... '78 '03 C&L.1228 B.A., J.D. [[A] Raper,P.]

Ledbetter & Titsworth, P.A.
(See Cary)

Lesica, Catherine H., (BV) ....'56 '81 C.645 B.S. L.904 J.D. [McLeod]
Lewis, Richard M., Jr., (AV) ....'35 '63 C.602 A.B. L.575 LL.B. [Reid,L.D.N.&P.]
Lingle, Dena S., (BV) .... '52 '79 C.577 B.S. L.575 J.D. 997 S. McPherson Chruch Rd.
Little, Amanda P. ....'73 '98 C.886 B.A. L.1228 J.D. P.O. Box 1513
MacRae, James C., (AV) ....'33 '61 C&L.575 A.B., LL.B. [MacRae P.&M.]
MacRae, James C., Jr., (BV) .... '60 '88 C.925 B.S. L.574 J.D. [MacRae P.&M.]
MacRae Perry & MacRae, (AV) .... 131 South Cool Spring Street
Malcolm, Joshua D. '70 '04 C.999 B.A. L.574 J.D.
Asst. Univ. Legal Coun., Fayetteville State Univ.
Mallonee, Paul G. ....'25 '52 C.813 A.B. L.878 J.D. P.O. Box 35712‡
Mandulak, John A. ....'76 '02 C.575 B.A. L.200 J.D. [[A] Firm of Hutchens,S.&B.]
Martin, Kathy J. .... '63 '98 C.1317 B.A. L.1325 J.D. 6419 Rannock Dr.★
Maxwell, C. Douglas, Jr., (BV) .... '40 '70 C.1130 B.S. L.575 J.D. [Maxwell&M.]

Maxwell & Melvin, (BV)
116 North Cool Spring Street, 28301
Telephone: 910-483-1414 FAX: 910-483-7443
Members of Firm: C. Douglas Maxwell, Jr.; Stephen R. Melvin.
General Practice, Personal Injury, Wrongful Death, Medical Malpractice, Real Estate, Workers Compensation, Collections, Bankruptcy, Criminal, Traffic, Corporations, Elder Law, Wills and Estates.
See Professional Biographies, FAYETTEVILLE, NORTH CAROLINA

McCauley, R. Williford, (BV) ... '65 '91 C.198 B.A. L.896 J.D. [McCoy W.W.C.R.R.P.]

McCoy Weaver Wiggins Cleveland Rose Ray PLLC, (AV) [BR]
202 Fairway Drive, P.O. Box 87009, 28304
Telephone: 910-483-8104 FAX: 910-483-0094
Email: office@mccoyrose.com
Members of Firm: Donald W. McCoy (1919-1995); Charles G. Rose, Jr. (1912-1996); Richard M. Wiggins; Alfred E. Cleveland; Robert G. Ray (Board Certified Specialist in Estate Planning and Probate Law, North Carolina State Board of Legal Specialization); Steven J. O'Connor; Anne Mayo Evans; Jeff Dunham (Board Certified Specialist in Real Property Law; Business, Commercial and Industrial Transactions; and Residential Transactions, North Carolina State Board of Legal Specialization); Jim Wade Goodman; R. Williford McCauley; James Albert McLean, III. Of Counsel: L. Stacy Weaver, Jr.
Civil Litigation, Corporate, Wills and Estates, Taxation, Municipal and Institutional Bonds, Real Estate and Immigration.
Representative Clients: Fayetteville Technical Community College; Methodist College, Inc.; St. Paul Companies; Ellis-Walker Builders, Inc.; Time-Warner, Inc.; The McLean Foundation.
See Professional Biographies, FAYETTEVILLE, NORTH CAROLINA

McFarland, Leighton W., III ....'46 '74 C&L.575 B.S., J.D. 3405 Arboretum Place‡
McGeachy, N. Hector, Jr., (AV) .... '17 '41 C.198 B.S. L.575 J.D. [McGeachy,H.&Z.]
McGeachy, Hudson & Zuravel, (AV) ....138 Dick Street
McGlothlin, Larry J. ....'45 '69 C&L.7 B.A., J.D. 210 E. Russell St.
McLean, James Albert, III ...... '76 '01 C.228 A.B. L.575 J.D. [McCoy W.W.C.R.R.P.]
McLeod, Joe, (AV) ....'37 '63 C&L.575 A.B., J.D. [McLeod]

McLeod Law Firm, The, P.A., (AV)
First Citizens Bank Building Suite One, 109 Green Street, P.O. Box 1539, 28302
Telephone: 910-323-1425 800-446-8259 Fax: 910-323-4582
Email: theMcLeodlawfirm@aol.com
Joe McLeod; Catherine H. Lesica; William W. Aycock, Jr.
Practice limited to Civil Litigation in State and Federal Courts.
Reference: First Citizens Bank & Trust Co.
See Professional Biographies, FAYETTEVILLE, NORTH CAROLINA

McSwain, Ronald D., (BV) ....'55 '81 C.896 B.A. L.1228 J.D. 708 Packard Pl
Melvin, Stephen R., (BV) ....'52 '81 C.896 B.A. L.1228 J.D. [Maxwell&M.]
Milazzo, Carl J. ....'63 '87 C.927 B.S. L.146 J.D. City Police Dept.
Miller, Sherry E., (BV) .... '65 '95 C.575 B.A. L.574 J.D. [Rogers&M.]
Miranda, Sarah ....'72 '99 C.575 B.A. L.1339 J.D. [[A] Firm of Hutchens,S.&B.]
Mitchell, Ronnie Monroe, (AV) ....'52 '78 C&L.896 B.A., J.D. [Mitchell B.R.]

Mitchell Brewer Richardson, PLLC, (AV)
2950 Village Drive, 28304
Telephone: 910-678-7100 Fax: 910-678-9099
Members of Firm: Ronnie Monroe Mitchell; Coy E. Brewer, Jr.; William O. Richardson. Associate: Charles M. Brittain.
Personal Injury, Medical Malpractice, Traffic, Criminal, Workers Compensation, Appellate Law, General Civil and Criminal Practice, Trials in all State and Federal Courts.
Other Fayetteville Office: 2950 Village Drive, 28304. Telephone: 910-678-7100. Fax: 910-678-9099.
See Professional Biographies, FAYETTEVILLE, NORTH CAROLINA

Morris, Joe H., (BV) .... '28 '59 C&L.896 B.S., LL.B. 2608 Elmhurst Dr.‡
Moss, Patricia R., (BV) ....'47 '82 C&L.1228 B.A., J.D. [Brown&M.]
Muncaster, James R. ....'46 '71 C&L.260 B.A., J.D. P.O. Box 25657‡
Murray, Ocie F., Jr., (AV) ....'41 '67 C.240 A.B. L.945 J.D. [Murray,C.&I.]

Murray, Craven & Inman, L.L.P., (AV)
Highland Place, 2517 Raeford Road, P.O. Drawer 53007, 28305-3007
Telephone: 910-483-4990 FAX: 910-483-6822
Members of Firm: Ocie F. Murray, Jr.; Richard T. Craven; Stephen G. Inman;—Thomas Waitt Pleasant.

(This Listing Continued)

Murray, Craven & Inman, L.L.P. (Continued)
General Civil and Criminal Trial Practice before all State and Federal Courts. Corporation, Insurance, Bankruptcy, Personal Injury, Probate, Taxation, Estate Planning, Construction Law.
Representative Clients: E. I. duPont de Nemours & Co.; State Farm Insurance Cos.; Ford Motor Co.; Metropolitan Life Insurance Co.; Westinghouse Corp.; Amerisure Cos.; Southeastern Hospital Supply Co.; Lawyers Mutual Liability Insurance Company of North Carolina.
See Professional Biographies, FAYETTEVILLE, NORTH CAROLINA

Nance, James Kirkman .... '70 '01 C.953 B.A. L.1339 J.D. [[A] Reid,L.D.N.&P.]
Nance, James R., Jr., (AV) ....'40 '65 C&L.896 B.A., J.D. [Reid,L.D.N.&P.]
Neier, Bryce Denman .... '61 '92 C.362 B.B.A. L.1228 J.D. 2581 Ravenhill Road
Neville, J. Thomas ....'66 '04 C.576 B.A. L.1228 J.D. [Thorp,C.&N.]

Nichols, Heather D. Miller '72 '03 C.1309 B.A. L.1228 J.D.
213 Dick Street, Suite 204, P.O. Box 2302, 28302
Mailing Address: P.O. Box 2302, Fayetteville, NC 28302
Telephone: 910-484-4876 Fax: 910-484-7352
Email: heather@heathernicholslaw.com URL: http://www.heathernicholslaw.com
Family Law, Civil Litigation, Real Estate Litigation, Wills, Estates.
See Professional Biographies, FAYETTEVILLE, NORTH CAROLINA

Noble, Reed N., (CV) ....'55 '81 C.692 B.S.B.A. L.1228 J.D. [Noble&Q.]
Noble & Quinn, (BV) ....5114 Yadkin Road, Suite 100
Noe, Timothy A., (CV) ....'51 '82 C.228 A.B. L.1228 J.D. [T.A.Noe]

Noe, Timothy A., P.A., (CV)
507 Owen Drive, 28304
Telephone: 910-485-8805 Fax: 910-485-8807
Email: timothynoe@aol.com URL: http://www.lawyers.com/noelaw
Timothy A. Noe.
Personal Injury, Criminal Law, Traffic Violations, Driving While Intoxicated, Medical Malpractice, Wrongful Death.
See Professional Biographies, FAYETTEVILLE, NORTH CAROLINA

Null, Jeffrey D., (CV) ....'68 '94 C&L.575 B.S.B.A., J.D. [Rand&G.]
O'Connor, Steven J., (BV) ....'58 '83 C&L.575 B.A., J.D. [McCoy W.W.C.R.R.P.]
Olivera, Luis John, (CV) ....'70 '00 C.1317 B.A. L.1228 J.D. Pros.
Page, Richmond H. "Dick", (BV) '47 '73
C.115 B.S. L.896 J.D. Title Underwriting, Consumers Title Co.
Parish, James R., (AV) ....'50 '76 C.198 B.A. L.896 J.D. [Parish&C.]
Parish & Cooke, (AV) ....343 Person Street
Patten, John P. ....'18 '77 C&L.262 J.D. 4310 Coventry Rd.
Pearce, Richard W. '24 '50 C.575 L.362 LL.B.
(adm. in FL; not adm. in NC) Pres., Methodist College
Pechmann, John E., (BV) .... '48 '73 C.925 A.B. L.575 J.D. [Downing,D.D.&P.]
Perry, Daniel Thaddeus, III, (AV) ....'44 '69 C.575 A.B. L.790 J.D. [MacRae P.&M.]
Person, Rebecca F., (BV) ....'58 '83 C.575 B.S.B.A. L.896 J.D. [Reid,L.D.N.&P.]
Pittman, Alan, (BV) .... '46 '79 C.1309 B.A. L.1228 J.D. 2413 Robeson Street Suite 7
Pitts, Marshall B., Jr., (CV) ....'64 '90 C.34 B.S. L.574 J.D. P.O. Box 207
Player, Lonnie M., Jr., (CV) '70 '98 C.228 A.B. L.575 J.D.
[[A] Firm of Hutchens,S.&B.]
Pleasant, Thomas Waitt, (CV) ....'70 '96 C&L.896 B.A., J.D. [[A] Murray,C.&I.]
Plyler, Matthew R., (CV) ....'66 '93 C&L.575 B.A., J.D. [Plyler]
Plyler Law Firm, P.A., (CV) .... 4140 Ferncreek Drive, Suite 104
Praschan, Kenneth C., (BV) ....'58 '84 C.999 B.S. L.1228 J.D. 2547 Ravenhill Rd.
Price, Gary A., (CV) ....'67 '94 C.296 B.A. L.1302 J.D. [[A] Smith,D.S.H.&D.]
Privette, Jodi V., (CV) '73 '98 C.1228 B.A. L.1345 J.D.
309 Person Street (⊙Fayetteville)
Proctor, James Crowell .... '58 '86 C.55 B.S. L.1228 J.D. Employ. Sec. Comm. of N.C.
Radtke, Debra J., (BV) ....'54 '79 C&L.494 B.A., J.D. [Hedahl&R.]
Rand, Anthony E., (BV) ....'39 '64 C&L.575 A.B., LL.B. [Rand&G.]
Rand & Gregory PA, (BV) .... 405 Barrington Cross
Raper, John E., Jr., (AV) .... '35 '61 C.575 A.B. L.569 J.D. [Raper,P.]

Raper Law Firm PLLC, The, (AV)
2543 Ravenhill Drive, Suite C, 28303
Mailing Address: P.O. Box 87409, Fayetteville, NC 28304
Telephone: 910-764-9200 Fax: 910-486-5358
Member of Firm: John E. Raper, Jr. Associate: Sarilyn Hardee Leary.
Corporate Law, Tax Law, Trusts and Estates, Commercial Real Estate, Finance, Business and Construction Litigation.
See Professional Biographies, FAYETTEVILLE, NORTH CAROLINA

Ray, Robert G., (AV) ....'43 '68 C&L.575 B.S., J.D. [McCoy W.W.C.R.R.P.]
Reaves, John C., (BV) ....'67 '92 C.228 A.B. L.575 J.D. P.O. Box 53555
Redding, Bobbie N., (BV) ....'35 '86 C.575 A.B. L.1228 J.D. Dept. of Soc. Serv.
Regan, A M. ....'43 '81 C.471 A.B. L.1228 J.D. P.O. Box 2357

Reid, Lewis, Deese, Nance & Person, L.L.P., (AV)
330 Dick Street, Heritage Square, 28301
Mailing Address: P.O. Drawer 1358, Fayetteville, NC 28302
Telephone: 910-323-3500 Fax: 910-323-0066
URL: http://www.rldnp.com
Members of Firm: Marland C. Reid (1934-1998); Richard M. Lewis, Jr.; Renny W. Deese (Board Certified Specialist in Family Law, North Carolina State Board of Legal Specialization); James R. Nance, Jr.; Rebecca F. Person. Associate: James Kirkman Nance.
General Civil and Criminal Trial Practice in State and Federal Courts. Personal Injury, Negligence, Family Law, Construction Insurance, Corporation, Probate and Real Estate Law.
See Professional Biographies, FAYETTEVILLE, NORTH CAROLINA

Richardson, William O., (BV) ....'55 '80 C.575 B.A. L.1228 J.D. [Mitchell B.R.]
Rigby-Conyers, Kimberly A. '64 '94 C.269 B.A. L.1345 J.D.
Claim Rep., State Farm Mutual Insurance Co.
Rogers, Allen W. .... '60 '86 C.329 B.A. L.575 J.D. [Rogers&M.]
Rogers & Miller Firm, The, P.A., (BV) .... P.O. Box 1361
Rose, Charles G., III ....'39 '64 C.198 A.B. L.575 LL.B. (M.C.)
Roupas, Thomas F., Jr. ....'62 '97 C.232 B.S. L.260 J.D. P.O. Box 35087
Rouse, J. B. (Mickey), (CV) ......'46 '83 C&L.1228 B.B.A., J.D. [J.B.Rouse,III&Assoc.]

Rouse, J.B., III & Associates, (CV)
1300 A Pamalee Drive, 28303
Telephone: 910-488-2100 Fax: 910-488-5515
URL: http://www.jbrouselaw.com
J. B. (Mickey) Rouse.
Personal Injury, Automobile Accidents, Serious Accidents, Lemon Law, Traffic Violations, DWI, Wills, Probate, Trusts and Estates, Business Litigation.
See Professional Biographies, FAYETTEVILLE, NORTH CAROLINA

Rudisill, Clinton L. .... '57 '99 C.925 B.S. L.1228 J.D. [Rudisill&Assoc.]
Rudisill & Associates, P.A. .... 439 Westwood S/C
Ruppe, A. Maxwell .... '28 '52 C&L.575 A.B., J.D. 336 Summertime Rd.‡
Russ, D. P., Jr., (AV) ....'18 '40 C&L.575 B.S., LL.B. [Russ,W.C.&H.] ‡
Russ, Margaret Riddle, (BV) ....'43 '85 C.1317 B.A. L.575 J.D. Asst. Dist. Atty.
Russ, Worth, Cheatwood & Hancox, (AV) .... 717 Hay Street

Senter, William L., (AV) .... '50 '75 C.575 B.S. L.896 J.D. [Firm of Hutchens,S.&B.]
Sexton, Cristie A. .... '65 '92 C.160 B.S. L.1228 J.D. 1300-A Pamalee Dr.
Shober, Joanna M., (CV) .... '63 '96 C.999 B.S. L.1228 J.D. [Cook,I.&S.]
Siler, Cheri L., (CV) .... '65 '91 C&L.574 B.A., J.D. Off. of Dist. Atty.
Singleton, Rudolph G., Jr., (AV) '30 '54
C&L.896 A.B., J.D. [Firm of Hutchens,S.&B.]
Sisk, Nicholas C. P. .....'— '00 C.152 B.A. L.1228 J.D. Legal Aid of North Carolina, Inc.
Smith, Allen D., (BV) .... '61 '87 C&L.575 B.A., J.D. [Smith,D.S.H.&D.]
Smith, Sharon R., (CV) .... '59 '85 C.575 B.A. L.1228 J.D. Asst. Dist. Atty.
Smith, W. David, Jr., (BV) .... '55 '89 C.575 B.A. L.1228 J.D. Pub. Def. Off.
Smith, W. Ritchie, Jr., (BV) .... '34 '58 C&L.575 A.B., J.D. [Smith,D.S.H.&D.]
Smith, Dickey, Smith, Hasty & Dempster, P.A., (BV) ....309 - 315 Person Street
Stanton, Robert R. .... '27 '51 C.968 A.B. L.790 LL.B. 3417 Florida Dr.‡
Sternlicht, Mark A., (BV) ....'54 '78 C&L.575 A.B., J.D. [Beaver H.S.&C.]
Stokes, Stephen Craig, (CV) .... '55 '92 C&L.259 B.S., J.D. 117 Person St.
Stone, Michael A. .... '— '95 C.1309 B.A. L.1228 J.D. [Hatley&S.]
Strickland, Michael W., (BV) ....'60 '85 C.1309 B.A. L.1228 J.D. [Anderson&S.]
Stuhl, George Z. ....'08 '32 C.228 L.896 305 Murray Hill Rd.‡
Sutton, Jason B. .... '74 '01 C.576 B.S. L.192 J.D. [Sutton P.]
Sutton Law Firm PLLC ....2529 Raeford Rd.
Sweeny, Chuck, (BV) .... '43 '72 C.165 B.A. L.896 J.D. [Yarborough]
Tally, John C., (BV) ....'49 '74 C.575 A.B. L.228 J.D. [Tally&T.]
Tally, Mary Ann, (AV) ....'49 '74 C.838 A.B. L.228 J.D. [Tally&T.]
Tally & Tally, (AV) .... 235 Tallywood Shopping Center
Thompson, Jack A. ....'41 '65 C&L.896 B.A., J.D. Supr. Ct. J.

Thorp, Clarke & Neville, P.A., (AV)
150 N. McPherson Church Road, Suite B, 28303
Telephone: 910-323-4111 Fax: 910-483-1247
Email: thorpclark@aol.com URL: http://www.lawyers.com/thorpclarke
Members of Firm: Herbert H. Thorp (1932-1996); F. Stuart Clarke; J. Thomas Neville.
General and Trial Practice. Personal Injury, Medical Negligence, Real Estate, Probate, Criminal, Corporate and Bankruptcy Law.
Counsel for: W. R. Co.; W.S. Wellons Realty, Inc.; Cape Fear Broadcasting Co.; Cross Creek Mall; Cross Creek Plaza, Inc.; Centura Bank, Inc.; Bass Construction; Dickens Construction.
Reference: Branch Banking & Trust.
See Professional Biographies, FAYETTEVILLE, NORTH CAROLINA

Tinney, Larry L. '45 '70 C&L.846 B.B.A., J.D.
(adm. in TX; not adm. in NC) Pres. & CEO, Royal Crown Leasing, Inc.
Townley, Robert C. '64 '00 C.870 B.S. L.1059 J.D.
Chf. Legal Offr., Advanced Internet Technologies, Inc.
Tucker, Kimbrell K. .... '65 '89 C.673 B.S. L.1228 J.D. State Dist. Ct. J.

Tyson, H. Mac, II
(See Shallotte)

Umerah, Chukwudi E. ....'63 '97 C.1309 B.S. L.1178 J.D. Pub. Def.
Vallery, Ray Colton, (BV) .... '42 '66 C&L.575 A.B., LL.B. 596 Executive Pl.

Vaughan, Christopher V., The Law Offices of
(See Raeford)

Vonnegut, Joseph J. ....'63 '89 C.152 B.A. L.469 J.D. [Firm of Hutchens,S.&B.]
Waple, Mark L., (BV) .... '45 '74 C.870 B.S. L.575 J.D. [Waple&Assoc.]

Waple & Associates, (BV)
No. 6, Georgetown Square, 120 Westlake Road, 28314
Telephone: 910-864-3737 Fax: 910-864-3284
Email: waplelaw@earthlink.net URL: http://www.waplelaw.com
Mark L. Waple.
Medical Negligence, including Obstetric Malpractice, Birth Trauma, Surgical Malpractice, Oncological Malpractice, Failure to Diagnose Disease, Medication Errors, Military Medical Negligence; Armed Forces Law, including practice in all Military Trials and Appellate Courts, all Service Boards for Correction of Military Records, Military Personnel Law, Personal Injury.
See Professional Biographies, FAYETTEVILLE, NORTH CAROLINA

Washington, Lila E. .... '57 '83 C.1378 B.A. L.329 J.D. P.O. Box 207
Weaver, L. Stacy, Jr., (AV) ......'29 '53 C&L.228 A.B., J.D. [McCoy W.W.C.R.R.P.]
Weeks, Gregory A. ....'46 '77 C.1378 B.S. L.575 J.D. Supr. Ct. J.
West, Clifton C., (CV) ....'56 '89 C.575 B.S. L.1228 J.D. 2018 Ft. Bragg Road, Suite 118
Wiggins, Richard M., (AV) ....'33 '58 C&L.575 A.B., J.D. [McCoy W.W.C.R.R.P.]
Williams, Thomas H., (BV) ....'16 '41 C.240 B.A. L.896 LL.B. 1037 Bragg Blvd.
Williford, Michael Leighton, (BV) .... '57 '83 C.575 B.A. L.574 J.D. [Williford,H.C.&B.]
Williford, Hollers, Crenshaw & Boliek, L.L.P., (BV) .... 138 Dick Street Suite 200
Wilson, Paul S. '64 '89 C.1369 B.S. L.893 J.D.
(adm. in GA; not adm. in NC) 6450 Kelmscot Ct.‡

Winesette, John Michael, (BV) '52 '78 C.575 B.A. L.574 J.D.
202 Fairway Drive, Suite A, 28305
Telephone: 910-433-2400 Fax: 910-433-2618
Email: MikeWnst@prodigy.net
Personal Injury, Automobile Accidents, Aviation, Products Liability, Medical Negligence including Obstetric, Emergency Room and Surgical Negligence, Wrongful Death Litigation.
See Professional Biographies, FAYETTEVILLE, NORTH CAROLINA

Winfrey, Ronald E., (BV) .... '45 '76 C&L.575 A.B., J.D. P.O. Box 1658
Winters, Hugh Addison, III, (BV) .... '57 '85 C.276 B.A. L.575 J.D. [Yarborough]
Witcover, Henry W. ....'17 '51 C.228 A.B. L.813 J.D. 716 Fairfield Rd.‡
Worth, Walker Y., Jr., (AV) .... '28 '53 C&L.575 B.S., J.D. [Russ,W.C.&H.]
Yarborough, Garris Neil, (BV) ....'51 '77 C&L.575 B.A., J.D. [Yarborough]

Yarborough Law Firm, The, (BV)
115 East Russell Street, 28301
Telephone: 910-433-4433 Fax: 910-433-2233
Email: gnyesq@yarboroughlawfirm.com URL: http://www.yarboroughlawfirm.com
Garris Neil Yarborough. Associates: Hugh Addison Winters, III; John Hamilton Jackson; Chuck Sweeny.
General Civil Trial Practice in all State and Federal Courts. Construction, Municipal, Real Estate, Land Condemnation, Corporation, Collections, Personal Injury, Administrative and Probate Law.
See Professional Biographies, FAYETTEVILLE, NORTH CAROLINA

Zuravel, David Lee, (BV) ....'60 '94 C.953 B.S. L.1228 J.D. [McGeachy,H.&Z.]

FLAT ROCK, 2,565, *Henderson Co.*

Dill, David G. ....'40 '68 C.610 B.B.A. L.608 J.D. 104 Scenic Drive‡
Koopmann, Ann S. '42 '88 C.966 B.S. L.1040 J.D.
(adm. in XX; not adm. in NC) 105 Aldseyshire Way
Monti, Donald P. '41 '66 C.119 B.S. L.229 J.D.
(adm. in PA; not adm. in NC) Pres., Performance Evaluation Consultants, Inc.
Robbinson, William H. '27 '57 C&L.260 LL.B.
(adm. in FL; not adm. in NC) P.O. Box 786‡
Webster, Ben H. '33 '74 C.198 B.S. L.1137 J.D.
(adm. in CA; not adm. in NC) P.O. Box 608‡

FLETCHER, 4,185, *Henderson Co.*

Blanchard, Newman & Hayes
(See Hendersonville)

Lenell, Meredith, (BV(T)) ....'47 '79 C.597 B.A. L.284 J.D. 99 Shadow Ridge Dr.
Seagle, J. Harold, (AV) ....'47 '77 C&L.575 A.B., J.D. 311 Bradenton Knoll
Seagle, J. Mark .... '70 '98 C.953 B.A. L.1228 J.D. 311 Bradenton Knoll

FOREST CITY, 7,475, *Rutherford Co.*

Baldwin, T. Kent, (CV) ....'69 '94 C.999 B.S. L.574 J.D. [Baldwin]
Baldwin Law Firm, (CV) ....280 E. Main Street
Benoy, Jean A., (Mr.), (AV) .... '29 '63 C.1032 L.575 LL.B. 509 W. Main St.‡
Davis, J. Thomas, (AV) .... '56 '84 C.999 B.S. L.1228 J.D. 142 E. Main St.

Hamrick, Bowen, Mebane, Greenway & Lloyd, L.L.P.
(See Rutherfordton)

King, Brian Wayne, (CV) .... '73 '98 C.1128 B.A. L.1228 J.D. 138 South Broadway
Morrow, George R. .... '25 '51 C.561 B.A. L.228 LL.B. 104 Yarboro St.
Petho, Douglas A., (BV) .... '66 '91 C&L.575 B.S., J.D. [Price,S.H.P.&A.] ⊙

Price, Smith, Hargett, Petho & Anderson, (AV)
552 Oak Street, 28043 ⊙
Telephone: 828-248-1448 Fax: 828-248-4405
Email: priceatty@aol.com URL: http://www.lawyers.com/pshp&a
Douglas A. Petho.
Plaintiffs Catastrophic Personal Injury, Medical Malpractice, Wrongful Death, Workers Compensation, Insurance Litigation for Plaintiff, Motor Vehicle Accidents, Criminal Defense.
See Professional Biographies, FOREST CITY, NORTH CAROLINA

Summey, Robert G. .... '27 '53 C&L.896 B.S., LL.B. 358 Walter Horn Rd.
Wolf, Robert W., (AV) .... '44 '70 C.152 B.A. L.896 J.D. 138 S. Bway.

FORT BRAGG, 29,183, *Cumberland Co.*

Govern, Kevin Hugh '62 '87 C&L.436 B.A., J.D.
(adm. in WI; not adm. in NC) USASOC★
Kiel, John Loran, Jr. .... '70 '99 C.101 B.A. L.259 J.D. U.S. Army JAG Corp.
Schwenk, Alyssa M. '73 '98 C.164 B.A. L.1194 J.D.
(adm. in NY; not adm. in NC) JAG Atty.★
Thoman, Jay L. '74 '00 C.285 B.A. L.950 J.D.
(adm. in OR; not adm. in NC) Chief of Jus.★
Topping, Richard F. ....'76 '01 C.321 B.A. L.184 J.D. Asst. Ctr. JAG
Verma, Ravender K. '71 '98 C.446 B.A. L.64 J.D.
(adm. in MD; not adm. in NC) JAG Officer★
Vinton, Matthew '75 '03 C.870 B.S. L.260 J.D.
(adm. in FL; not adm. in NC) Trial Coun., Off. of the Staff J. Adv.

Yarborough Law Firm, The
(See Fayetteville)

FOUR OAKS, 1,424, *Johnston Co.*

Lee, Jacquelyn L., (BV) ....'49 '91 C.1228 B.A. L.1345 J.D. P.O. Box 1417
Shaw, Philip C., (BV) ....'42 '69 C.575 A.B. L.896 J.D. 102 Wellons St.

FRANKLIN, * 3,490, *Macon Co.*

Beck, Monty C., (BV) ....'58 '84 C.575 B.S. L.1228 J.D. [Coward,H.&S.]
Beran, Milo Richard ....'33 '68 C.871 B.S. L.1161 J.D. 595 Bailey Road
Berger Brown, Jennifer ....'75 '05 C.228 B.S. L.280 J.D. 61 E. Main St.

Bowling, Russell R., (BV) '54 '79 C&L.896 B.A., J.D.
77 West Main Street, 28734
Telephone: 828-524-5070 Fax: 828-524-5380
Email: rbowling@russellbowling.com URL: http://www.russellbowling.com
General Civil and Criminal Practice. Real Estate, Wills, Estates and Estate Administration, Criminal and Traffic and Motor Vehicle Law, Social Security Disability.
Representative Clients: Furnished Upon Request.
See Professional Biographies, FRANKLIN, NORTH CAROLINA

Boyer, Gregory F. ....'49 '86 C.259 B.S. L.1288 J.D. [Jones,K.M.&P.]
Collins, Joseph M., (BV) ....'55 '87 C.575 B.A. L.1345 J.D. [Collins&H.]

Collins & Hensley, P.A., (BV)
217 Iotla Street, 28734
Telephone: 828-524-0017 Telecopier: 828-524-0024
Email: colhen@dnet.net URL: http://www.lawyers.com/colhen
Joseph M. Collins; Robert E. Hensley (Board Certified Specialist in Criminal Law, North Carolina State Board of Legal Specialization).
Civil Litigation, Criminal, Real Property, Personal Injury, Automobile Accidents and Injuries, Wrongful Death, Domestic Relations Family Law, Divorce, Child Custody, Equitable Distribution, Adoption Law, Social Security Disability Law, Workers Compensation.
See Professional Biographies, FRANKLIN, NORTH CAROLINA

Coward, Orville D., Jr., (AV) ....'53 '79 C.976 B.A. L.575 J.D. [Coward,H.&S.]

Coward, Hicks & Siler, P.A., (AV)
43 West Main Street, 28734 ⊙
Telephone: 828-524-6475 Fax: 828-524-9833
Orville D. Coward, Jr.; Robert F. Siler; Monty C. Beck; Richard K. Walker (Resident).
General Practice in all Courts. Trials, Eminent Domain, Personal Injury and Workers Compensation, Probate, Estate Planning, Real Estate, Corporations, Family Law.
Sylva, North Carolina Office: 705 West Main Street, 28779. Telephone: 828-586-2147. Fax: 828-586-2605.
Cashiers, North Carolina Office: 211 Cashiers School Road, P.O. Box 1918, 28717. Telephone: 828-743-2401. Fax: 828-743-2403.
See Professional Biographies, FRANKLIN, NORTH CAROLINA

Davis, Bruce G. '25 '50 C.228 A.B. L.260 J.D.
(adm. in FL; not adm. in NC) 396 Cat Creek Rd.‡
Downs, James U. ....'41 '66 C.885 B.A. L.425 LL.B. Supr. Ct. J.
Fromknecht, Kenneth W., II, (BV) '58 '89 C.1111 B.A. L.362 J.D.
[K.W.Fromknecht,II]

Fromknecht, Kenneth W., II, P.A., Law Offices of, (BV)
29 Iotla Street P.O. Drawer 1146, 28744-1146
Telephone: 888-349-9911 Telecopier: 828-349-9944
Email: kwflaw@dnet.net URL: http://www.lawyers.com/fromknechtlaw
Kenneth W. Fromknecht, II.
Real Estate, Land Use, Inheritance, Business Formation, Construction Litigation, Complex Commercial Litigation, Catastrophic Injury, Insurance Litigation.
See Professional Biographies, FRANKLIN, NORTH CAROLINA

Henning, John F., (BV) ....'48 '74 C.925 B.S. L.575 J.D. 139 Lotla St.
Hensley, Robert E., (BV) ....'63 '88 C.953 B.A. L.1228 J.D. [Collins&H.]
Jones, Chester M., (BV) .... '59 '83 C.1365 B.B.A. L.896 J.D. [Jones,K.M.&P.]
Jones, Fred Howell, (BV) ....'65 '90 C&L.575 B.A., J.D. [Jones,K.M.&P.]
Jones, Richard S., Jr., (AV) ....'34 '61 C.198 B.S. L.575 J.D. [Jones,K.M.&P.]

Jones, Key, Melvin & Patton, P.A., (AV)
61 East Main Street, 28734 ⊙
Telephone: 828-524-4444 Fax: 828-369-7343
Email: jkmp@smnet.net URL: http://www.joneskey.com

(This Listing Continued)

Jones, Key, Melvin & Patton, P.A. (Continued)

Richard S. Jones, Jr.; Bobby Joe Key; Richard F. Melvin; Lawrence M. Patton, Jr.; Fred Howell Jones; Chester M. Jones; Camila J. Wright; Gregory F. Boyer.
Civil Trial Practice in all Courts. Real Estate, Insurance, Corporate Law, Probate, Family Law, Divorce, Adoptions, Equitable Distribution, Pre-Nuptial Agreements, Child Custody, Child Support, Domestic Violence, Alimony, Personal Injury, Auto Accidents, Wrongful Death, Estate and Gift Taxation, Taxation, Government, Mediation; Business Law, Litigation, Trusts and Estates, Wills, Criminal Law, DWI, Traffic Offenses.
Representative Clients: John C. Campbell Folk School; Macon Savings Bank; Wildcat Cliffs Country Club; County of Macon; Wachovia Bank of Trust Co., NA; Town of Franklin; Regions Bank of Clayton.
Highlands, North Carolina Office: Professional Building, Suite 3, South Street, 28741. Telephone: 828-526-3762.

See Professional Biographies, FRANKLIN, NORTH CAROLINA

Key, Bobby Joe, (BV) ... '33 '64 C.198 B.S. L.575 J.D. [Jones,K.M.&P.]
Patton, Lawrence M., Jr., (BV) ... '46 '73 C.198 A.B. L.575 J.D. [Jones,K.M.&P.]
Phillips, Leo J. ... '64 '89 C.1126 B.A. L.192 J.D. 3 1/2 E. Main St.
Philo, Steven E., (BV) ... '42 '74 C.870 B.S. L.896 J.D. [Philo&S.]

Philo & Spivey, P.A., (BV)
587 West Main Street, 28734
Telephone: 828-524-6377 Fax: 828-369-8054 Email: sphilo@mchsi.com
Email: s.philo@mchsi.com URL: http://www.lawyers.com/philo&spiveypa
Steven E. Philo; David C. Spivey.
Criminal Law, DWI, Traffic Violations, Civil Trial and Appellate Practice in all Courts. Real Property, Probate, Corporate Law, Domestic Relations and Family Law, Divorce.
References: Wachovia Bank & Trust Co., N.A.; Macon Savings and Loan Assn.

See Professional Biographies, FRANKLIN, NORTH CAROLINA

Siler, Robert F., (AV) ... '37 '75 C.228 A.B. L.896 J.D. [Coward,H.&S.]
Spivey, David C., (BV) ... '57 '82 C&L.896 B.S., J.D. [Philo&S.]
Steadham, John M., (AV Ⓣ) '41 '72
C.259 B.S. L.260 J.D. 5318 Lower Burningtown Road‡
Tisdale, Bradley Shannon ... '55 '87 C&L.836 B.A., J.D. 90 Wild Cove Road
Wall, Eileen J. '16 '48 C.150 L.1340 LL.B.
(adm. in OH; not adm. in NC) 1162 Trimont Mt. Rd.‡
Wright, Camila J. ... '78 '03 C.838 B.A. L.575 J.D. [Jones,K.M.&P.]

FRANKLINTON, 1,745, *Franklin Co.*

Draughn, Charles M., III, (BV) ... '55 '86 C.576 B.A. L.574 J.D. 105 S. Main St.
Shapiro, Charles D. '65 '91 C.94 B.A. L.276 J.D.
(adm. in NY; not adm. in NC) U.S. Gen Coun, Novozymes North America, Inc.

FREMONT, 1,463, *Wayne Co.*

Hollowell, David E., (BV) ... '54 '81 C.576 B.A. L.896 J.D. 1730 Memorial Church Road

FUQUAY-VARINA, 7,898, *Wake Co.*

Aguirre, Bridgett B., (BV) ... '59 '90 C.1317 B.A. L.1345 J.D. 202 E. Academy
Akins, John Waverly, (BV) ... '71 '00 C.576 B.A. L.1202 J.D. [J.W.Akins]
Akins, Waverly F., Law Offices of, (BV) '32 '61
C.232 A.B. L.575 J.D. 205 S. Fuquay Ave.
Akins, John W., Law Office of, (BV) ... 205 S. Fuquay Ave.
Cumalander, Tonya C., (BV) ... '61 '88 C.953 B.A. L.1228 J.D. P.O. Box 1055
Evans, Steven L., (AV) ... '51 '76 C&L.575 B.S., J.D. [S.L.Evans]
Evans, Steven L., P.C., Law Offices of, (AV) ... P.O. Box 146
Griffin, Robert E. ... '40 '77 C&L.574 B.A., J.D. 142 South Spring Street
Johnson, Linda Funke, (CV) ... '60 '85 C.1030 B.S. L.1252 J.D. P.O. Box 446
Mercogliano, Kathy Anderson ... '— '01 C.577 B.S.N. L.1228 J.D. [K.A.Mercogliano]
Mercogliano, Kathy Anderson, PA, The Law Office of ... 1000 N. Main St., Ste. 200
Mills, Amos T., III ... '47 '72 C.329 B.A. L.228 J.D. 4820 Cypress Ford Rd.‡
Rogel, Todd S. ... '52 '78 C.575 B.A. L.276 J.D. [Tanner&R.]
Senter, Jack, (BV) ... '23 '53 C.125 A.B. L.469 LL.B. [Senter&S.]
Senter & Stephenson, (AV) ... 114 Raleigh St.
Stephenson, Larry A., (AV) ... '37 '62 C&L.575 B.S., LL.B. [Senter&S.]
Tanner, LeAnn M., (BV) ... '57 '86 C.34 B.S. L.1228 J.D. [Tanner&R.]
Tanner & Rogel, P.A., (BV) ... 5048 Allanbrooke Lane
Treece, Annette C. ... '44 '01 C.576 B.A. L.574 J.D. P.O. Box 1148
Vavonese, Jamie ... '78 '05 C.576 B.A. L.1228 J.D. 134 N. Main St., Ste. 204

GARNER, 17,757, *Wake Co.*

Atchinson, M. Michele ... '72 '98 C.1128 B.S. L.836 J.D. Asst. Gen. Cnsl, Hillco, Ltd.
Aughenbaugh, Leigh A. '70 '95
C.471 B.A. L.1345 J.D. 5533 N.C. Hwy. 42 W., Ste. A6B‡
Bingham, William H., Jr., (BV) ... '47 '80 C&L.575 A.B., J.D. P.O. Box 1333
Bowling, J. Carleton '44 '85 C.235 B.A.B.S. L.383 J.D.
(adm. in KY; not adm. in NC) 1530 Gleneagle Drive

Breeden, Jonathan D. '75 '00 C.576 B.A. L.1228 J.D.
Int. 1-40, Highway 42, Exit 312, 100 Professional Court, Suite 2, 27529
Mailing Address: P.O. Box 967, Clayton, NC 27528
Telephone: 919-661-4970 Fax: 919-661-4971 URL: http://www.jbreedenlaw.com
Email: jonathan@breedenlaw.com URL: http://www.breedenlaw.com
Criminal Law, Driving While Intoxicated (DWI), Drug Crimes, Traffic Violations, Family Law, Child Custody, Child Support, Divorce, Education Law, Contracts, Wills.

See Professional Biographies, GARNER, NORTH CAROLINA

Calder, Joseph A., (BV) ... '47 '72 C.576 B.A. L.575 J.D. [Calder,W.M.&B.]
Calder, Watkins, McWilliam & Beaver, P.L.L.C., (BV) ... 126 U.S. Hwy. 70 W.
Covington, L. Philip ... '37 '64 C&L.575 LL.B. 139 W. Main St.
Crawford, Troy G. ... '75 '00 C.576 B.S. L.1228 J.D. 1027 Highway 70 West, Suite 202
Eatmon, Joseph Michael, Law Offices of '70 '01
C.576 B.A. L.1228 J.D. 100 Professional Court
Fowler, Timothy Gerald ... '64 '99 C.575 B.A. L.221 J.D. [T.G.Fowler]
Fowler, Tim G., Law Office of ... 1027 U.S. Hwy. 70 E., Ste. 208-210
Hagler-Gray, Terrie V. ... '68 '93 C.269 B.A. L.228 J.D. Assoc. Gen. Coun., Hillco, Ltd.

Hilbert Law Firm, The, PLLC
(See Raleigh)

Johnson, Scott N., (BV) ... '64 '89 C.575 B.A. L.896 J.D. [Mast,S.M.M.S.&J.]
Mason, Nancy O., (BV) ... '47 '85 C.119 B.A. L.575 J.D. Gen. Coun., Hillco, Ltd.
Mast, Schulz, Mast, Mills, Stem & Johnson, P.A., (AV)
5842 Highway 42 West (⊙Smithfield)
Prather, J. D., (AV) ... '62 '88 C&L.228 A.B., J.D. [Prather]

Prather Law Firm, P.C., (AV)
402 St. Mary's Street, 27529
Telephone: 919-772-0699 Fax: 919-772-0682
Email: jdp@pratherlaw.com
J. D. Prather.
Workers Compensation, Social Security Disability, Disability Claims, Personal Injury, Automobile Accidents, Slip and Fall, Wrongful Death, Toxic Tort, Mold Exposure.

See Professional Biographies, GARNER, NORTH CAROLINA

Richardson, Jonathan, The Law Office of
(See Cary)

Rivenbark, Christina, & Associates, (CV) '62 '87 C&L.575 B.A., J.D.
5533 NC Highway 42 West, 27529 ⊙
Telephone: 1-800-561-9221
Personal Injury, Automobile Accidents, Workers Compensation, Wrongful Death, Medical Malpractice, Slip and Fall, Criminal Law, Driving While Intoxicated, Traffic Violations, Drug Offenses, Misdemeanors, Felonies, Sexual Assaults, Assaults, Burglary, Motorcycle Accidents, Head Injuries.
Wilmington, North Carolina Office: 4009 Oleander Drive, 28403. Telephone: 1-800-806-8896.
Clinton, North Carolina Office: 603A Northeast Boulevard, 28328. Telephone: 1-800-777-5159.

See Professional Biographies, GARNER, NORTH CAROLINA

Tope, Jacqueline A. ... '54 '97 C.471 B.S. L.1228 J.D. [Tope]
Tope Law Offices, PLLC ... 2704 Falkirk Pl.
Turner, Phyllis A. ... '62 '92 C.575 B.S. L.1526 J.D. [P.A.Turner]
Turner, Phyllis A., P.C. ... P.O. Box 1385
Valsame, George T., Attorney at Law '63 '88
C.575 B.S.B.A. L.1228 J.D. 302 Tiffany Circle
Watkins, Stephen P. ... '65 '93 C.122 B.A. L.1228 J.D. [Calder,W.M.&B.]
Wells, Don R. ... '69 '00 C.576 B.S. L.1228 J.D. [Mast,S.M.M.S.&J.]

GASTONIA, * 66,277, *Gaston Co.*

Abernethy, Richard B., (BV) ... '53 '80 C.968 B.A. L.1228 J.D. 212-C W. Second Ave.
Adams, Scott M., (CV) ... '71 '97 C.945 B.A. L.896 J.D. [Patterson&A.P.] ⊙
Albright, S. Alan, (AV) ... '48 '73 C.575 B.S.B.A. L.228 J.D. [Albright&S.]
Albright & Sumner, (AV) ... 209 West Second Avenue
Albright-Jurs, Lisa, (CV) ... '67 '94 C.575 B.A. L.245 J.D. 2405 Rosemond Cir.
Anthony, William A., III, (CV) ... '64 '96 C.1128 B.A. L.192 J.D. [Bogle,A.&L.]
Arthurs, Douglas P., (AV) ... '54 '82 C.575 B.A. L.896 J.D. [Arthurs&F.]

Arthurs & Foltz, (AV)
420 East Long Avenue, P.O. Box 2206, 28053-2206
Telephone: 704-865-1900 Fax: 704-854-9323
Email: dpa@arthursfoltz.com
Members of Firm: Douglas P. Arthurs; Nancy Ewinger Foltz; Ann Brittian Green. Associate: Tara Reavis Sain.
General Civil and Trial Practice before all State Courts. Real Estate, Eminent Domain, Buying or Selling, Commercial Leasing, Construction, Landlord and Tenant, Zoning and Land Use, Insurance Defense, Personal Injury, Automobile Accidents, Dog Bites, Slip and Fall, Wrongful Death, Insurance, Property Damage, Domestic/Family Law, Adoptions, Child Support, Child Custody, Divorce, Domestic Violence, Visitation Rights, Wills and Estates, Zoning, Planning and Land Use, Debt and Credit, Collections, Creditors Rights.

See Professional Biographies, GASTONIA, NORTH CAROLINA

Atkins, James H., (BV) ... '31 '56 C&L.228 A.B., J.D. 625 E. Second Ave.
Aycock, David W. ... '76 '05 C.198 A.B. L.896 J.D. [Ⓐ Stott,H.P.&W.]
Bell, R. Locke, (BV) ... '50 '83 C.575 A.B. L.896 J.D. [L.Bell]
Bell, Locke, (BV) ... 125 E. Main Ave.
Bogle, Edgar F., (BV) ... '68 '95 C.575 B.A. L.896 J.D. [Bogle,A.&L.]

Bogle, Anthony & Leach, P.A., (BV)
223 West Main Avenue, Suite A, P.O. Box 981, 28053-0981
Telephone: 704-867-3688 800-422-4988 Fax: 704-867-1938
Email: WilliamAAnthony@aol.com URL: http://www.bogleanthonylaw.com
Edgar F. Bogle; William A. Anthony, III; Timothy T. Leach.
Workers Compensation, Personal Injury, Wrongful Death, Criminal Defense, Traffic Violations, Driving While Intoxicated, Corporate Law, Wills, Trust Law, Family Law/Domestic, Divorce, Child Custody, Child Support.

See Professional Biographies, GASTONIA, NORTH CAROLINA

Bollinger & Piemonte, PC
(See Charlotte)

Bone, Jesse V., Jr., (BV) ... '60 '91 C.575 B.A. L.896 J.D. [Mullen H.&C.]
Bowman, James L., (CV) ... '50 '91 C.575 B.A. L.790 J.D. P.O. Box 872

Bradshaw, Aaron E., Law Office of, (BV) '56 '85 C.34 B.A. L.192 J.D.
313 S. South Street, P.O. Box 1072, 28053
Telephone: 704-866-8289 Fax: 704-866-9429
Email: info@gastonlaw.com URL: http://www.gastonlaw.com
Civil Litigation, Insurance Defense, General Liability, Automobile Liability, Product Liability, Construction Litigation, Commercial Litigation, Insurance Law.

See Professional Biographies, GASTONIA, NORTH CAROLINA

Broome, Dennis L., (BV) ... '50 '84 C.575 A.B. L.469 J.D. 330 N. Marietta St.
Broussard, Lester H. ... '34 '63 C.420 B.A. L.365 LL.B. 3019 Gaston Day School Rd.
Brown, Joyce A. ... '32 '56 C.435 A.B. L.575 J.D. Dist. J.
Buerkert, John E., Jr. '66 '93
C.918 B.A. L.734 J.D. V.P. & Gen. Coun., Gaston Health Care, Inc.

Bumgardner, Don H., (AV) '45 '70 C&L.575 A.B., J.D.
219 West Main Avenue, 28052
Telephone: 704-868-9293 Fax: 704-868-9296
Email: bumgardd@bellsouth.net URL: http://www.bumgardner.lawoffice.com
General Civil and Appellate Practice in all State and Federal Courts. Personal Injury, Products Liability, Workers Compensation and Medical Malpractice.

See Professional Biographies, GASTONIA, NORTH CAROLINA

Caldwell, Jesse B., III ... '49 '73 C&L.575 A.B., J.D. Supr. Ct. J.
Campbell, Clair G., (BV) ... '61 '85 C.16 B.A. L.192 J.D. [Campbell&Assoc.]
Campbell & Associates, PLC, (BV)
359 W. Main Avenue, Suite F (⊙Charlotte, Hickory)
Carpenter, Berlin H., Jr. ... '27 '52 C.404 A.B. L.575 LL.B. Ret. Dist. Ct. J.‡
Carpenter, James R., (AV) ... '45 '69 C&L.575 A.B., J.D. 311 S. South St.
Carpenter, Robert Wade ... '74 '01 C&L.575 B.A., J.D. P.O. Box 1058
Collins, Craig R. ... '71 '97 C.665 B.A. L.884 J.D. Dist. Atty. Off.
Collins, D. Brad ... '78 '04 C.577 B.A. L.838 J.D. [Mullen H.&C.]
Cooper, Langdon M., (AV) ... '41 '69 C.228 A.B. L.575 J.D. [Mullen H.&C.]
Crawford, Laura Leipold ... '71 '00 C.858 B.A. L.107 J.D. 104 E. Main Ave.
Dorsett, Charles H., (AV) ... '13 '40 C&L.896 LL.B. 1604 Nottingham Dr.
Douglas, J. Paul, (AV Ⓣ) '47 '75 C.45 B.S.Ch.E. L.276 J.D.
(adm. in DC; not adm. in NC)
V.P., Corp. Coun. & Secy., Public Service Company of North Carolina, Inc.
Drum, Jack D., (AV) ... '48 '74 C&L.575 B.S.B.A., J.D. [Stott,H.P.&W.]
Eckerman, Thomas Patrick ... '64 '99 C.575 B.A. L.861 J.D. [Ⓐ N.Street]
Efird, Tom D. ... '39 '64 C&L.575 A.B., LL.B. Pres., Standard Distributors, Inc.
Ferguson, Robert Warner, (BV) ... '58 '83 C.1128 B.A. L.896 J.D. [Ferguson&M.]
Ferguson & McGraw, (BV) ... 211 West Third Avenue
Foltz, Nancy Ewinger, (AV) ... '54 '80 C.352 B.S. L.896 J.D. [Arthurs&F.]
Forbes, Robert H., (BV) ... '30 '60 C.1126 B.S. L.896 J.D. P.O. Box 2377
Funderburk, Jim R., (AV) ... '45 '72 C&L.896 B.A., J.D. [J.Funderburk]
Funderburk, Jim, PLLC, (AV) ... 407 S. York St.
Furr, David M., (AV) ... '57 '82 C&L.896 B.A., J.D. [Gray,L.K.S.S.F.&S.]
Gadd, Kathleen M. ... '72 '98 C&L.851 B.B.A., J.D. Gaston Co.

Gallagher, Cherlyn Rae '60 '85 C.607 B.A. L.7 J.D. (adm. in OH; not adm. in NC) State Farm Ins.
Gallagher, Robert M., (BV) '50 '75 C.1126 B.A. L.192 J.D. Pres. & CEO, Good Will, Inc.
Garland, J. Boyce, Jr., (BV) '59 '87 C.575 B.A. L.1228 J.D. [J.B.Garland,Jr.]

Garland, J. Boyce, Jr., (BV)
223 West Main Avenue, Suite M, P.O. Box 1657, 28053
Telephone: 704-867-1113 Fax: 704-867-4792
Email: jboycejr@bellsouth.net URL: http://www.jboycegarland.com
James B. Garland (1920-2002); J. Boyce Garland, Jr.
Language: German.
General Civil and Criminal Practice in all Courts. Corporations, Business, Estate Planning and Administration, Probate, Real Estate, Personal Injury, Automobile Accidents, and Criminal.
Representative Clients: Oakwood Mobile Homes, Inc.; SET Enterprises, Inc.; Wachovia Bank; NA and Branch Banking and Trust Company.
See Professional Biographies, GASTONIA, NORTH CAROLINA

Gaston, Harley B., Jr. '29 '56 C&L.228 A.B., J.D. Dist. J.
Gingles, Ralph C., Jr. '46 '71 C.575 B.S. L.893 J.D. Dist. Ct. J.
Graham, Charles L., Jr., (BV) '61 '86 C.1126 B.A. L.1228 J.D. [Stott,H.P.&W.]
Gray, Charles D., III, (AV) '38 '63 C.575 A.B. L.569 LL.B. [Gray,L.K.S.S.F.&S.]
Gray, James C., (AV) '43 '68 C&L.575 A.B., J.D. [J.C.Gray]
Gray and Hunn, P.A., (BV) 233 W. Main Ave.
Gray, James C., P.A., (AV) 233 W. Main Avenue

Gray, Layton, Kersh, Solomon, Sigmon, Furr & Smith, P.A., (AV)
516 South New Hope Road, P.O. Box 2636, 28053-2636
Telephone: 704-865-4400 FAX: 704-866-8010
URL: http://www.gastonlegal.com
David A. Layton; John D. Kersh, Jr. (Board Certified Specialist in Estate Planning and Probate Law, North Carolina State Board of Legal Specialization); T. J. Solomon, II; P. Wayne Sigmon (Board Certified Specialist in Bankruptcy Law, North Carolina State Board of Legal Specialization); David M. Furr; David W. Smith, III; William E. Moore, Jr.; John H. Griffing (Board Certified Specialist in Estate Planning and Probate Law, North Carolina State Board of Legal Specialization);—Emily H. Leazer; Ted F. Mitchell. Of Counsel: Charles D. Gray, III.
General Civil Trial Practice, Arbitration, Corporation Law, Construction Law, Real Estate Law, Mediation, Municipal and Zoning Law, Mergers and Acquisitions, Bankruptcy, Family, Tax, Estate Planning and Probate Law, Personal Injury Law, Traffic, Professional Sports Representation, Community Association Law.
References: RBC Centura; Wachovia Bank & Trust Company, N.A.
See Professional Biographies, GASTONIA, NORTH CAROLINA

Green, Ann Brittian, (BV) '71 '96 C.575 B.A. L.896 J.D. [Arthurs&F.]
Griffing, John H., (BV) '62 '88 C.575 B.S. L.896 J.D. [Gray,L.K.S.S.F.&S.]
Hance, Julie Moser, (CV) '70 '95 C.8 B.S. L.7 J.D. [Hance&H.]
Hance, L. Keith, (CV) '67 '95 C.1126 B.A. L.8 J.D. [Hance&H.]
Hance & Hance, P.A., (CV) 317 South Street
Hassan, Blake W., (BV) '63 '93 C.420 B.S. L.575 J.D. 301 S. York St.
Heavner, J. Mark, (BV) '59 '84 C.198 A.B. L.896 J.D. [Mullen H.&C.]

Helms, Henderson & Associates, P.A.
(See Charlotte)

Hodnett, Michael K., (AV) '45 '73 C.945 A.B. L.896 J.D, [Hodnett]
Hodnett Law, P.A., (AV) 233 West Main Avenue
Holland, Lucretia Nashon '75 '01 C.956 B.A. L.608 J.D. Pub. Def. Off.
Holland, William G., (BV) '30 '62 C.871 B.S. L.575 LL.B. 155 S. York St.
Hollowell, Linwood Branton, Jr., (AV) '37 '63 C&L.228 A.B., LL.B. [Stott,H.P.&W.]
Hoyle, Angela G. '68 '93 C.576 B.A. L.575 J.D. Co. J.
Hoyle, Larry Glenn, (BV) '59 '90 C.1128 B.A. L.1345 J.D. 311 S. South St.
Hunn, J. Thomas, (BV) '61 '89 C.1290 L.1187 J.D. [Gray&H.]
James, Reid C., Law Office of, (BV) '51 '77 C.575 B.A. L.421 J.D. 407 S. Maritta St.
Joyce, D. Kevin '73 '98 C.575 B.S. L.574 J.D. [Stott,H.P.&W.]
Kakassy, Thomas B., (BV) '55 '80 C.575 B.A. L.896 J.D. [T.B.Kakassy]

Kakassy, Thomas B., P.A., (BV)
414 South Street, P.O. Box 2436, 28053
Telephone: 704-867-1795 Fax: 704-867-1820
Email: ThomasKakassy@Carolina.rr.com URL: http://www.kakassy.com
Thomas B. Kakassy.
Civil Litigation, Personal Injury, Workers Compensation, Social Security Disability, Bankruptcy, Business, Domestic Relations, Family Law, Criminal, Traffic, Real Estate, Estates and Guardianships.
See Professional Biographies, GASTONIA, NORTH CAROLINA

Katzenstein, Charles J., Jr., (BV) '34 '64 C&L.575 A.B., LL.B. [Katzenstein&L.]
Katzenstein & Lorance, (BV) 223 West Main Avenue, Suite C

Keeter, Morris W., (AV) '50 '75 C.404 A.B. L.896 J.D.
309 South Street, P.O. Box 1575, 28053-1575
Telephone: 704-864-5425 Telecopier: 704-864-5426
Email: mwkeeter@bellsouth.net URL: http://www.lawyers.com/morriswkeeter
See Professional Biographies, GASTONIA, NORTH CAROLINA

Kelso, Lloyd T., & Associates, (BV) '50 '76 C.247 B.A. L.790 J.D. 413 South York Street
Kenny, Terry Albright, (BV) '— '87 C.577 B.A. L.896 J.D. [Whitesides&K.]
Kersh, John D., Jr., (AV) '50 '78 C.1128 B.A. L.896 J.D. [Gray,L.K.S.S.F.&S.]

King Law Firm, The, PLLC
(See Huntersville)

LaFar, W. Marshall, (BV) '39 '66 C.198 A.B. L.896 LL.B. 1331 E. Garrison Blvd.
Lawing, Bob W., (BV) '30 '60 C&L.896 B.A., LL.B. 117 W. 3rd Ave.
Laws, Richard D., (AV) '54 '79 C&L.896 B.S., J.D. [R.D.Laws]

Laws, Richard D., P.A., (AV)
418 South Street, 28052
Mailing Address: P.O. Box 1985, Gastonia, NC 28053
Telephone: 704-861-0575 Facsimile: 704-868-9132
Email: rlaws92022@aol.com URL: http://www.lawyers.com/rlaws
Richard D. Laws.
Residential Real Estate, Commercial Real Estate, Estate Planning, Estate Administration, Wills, Probate, Trusts.
See Professional Biographies, GASTONIA, NORTH CAROLINA

Layton, David A., (AV) '43 '68 C&L.575 A.B., J.D. [Gray,L.K.S.S.F.&S.]
Leach, Timothy T., (BV) '66 '91 C.1128 B.A. L.228 J.D. [Bogle,A.&L.]
Leazer, Emily H., (CV) '69 '94 C.575 B.S.B.A. L.1228 J.D. [Gray,L.K.S.S.F.&S.]
Leissner, Richard P., Jr. '77 '02 C&L.575 B.A., J.D. [J.B.Morrow]
Lorance, R. Dennis, (BV) '53 '78 C&L.575 A.B., J.D. [Katzenstein&L.]
Martin, James R. '71 '97 C.188 B.A. L.896 J.D. [Mullen H.&C.]
Mazzariello, Arcangela M., Law Office of, (CV) '54 '95 C.731 B.S. L.1178 J.D. P.O. Box 1574
McGraw, J. Reid, Jr., (AV) '62 '89 C.1128 B.A. L.896 J.D. [Mullen H.&C.]
McGraw, Sonya Campbell, (BV) '66 '91 C.232 B.S. L.896 J.D. [Ferguson&M.]
McSpadden, Malcolm B., (CV) '55 '81 C.576 B.S.M.E. L.896 J.D. P.O. Box 2336
Mitchell, Ted F., (CV) '67 '96 C.160 B.A. L.1228 J.D. [Gray,L.K.S.S.F.&S.]
Mitchem, Wade W., (BV) '23 '54 C&L.575 A.B., LL.B. 105 S. Marietta St.
Moore, Charles L., (BV) '53 '79 C.575 B.A. L.1228 J.D. Co. Atty.
Moore, William E., Jr., (BV) '58 '81 C.260 B.A. L.228 J.D. [Gray,L.K.S.S.F.&S.]
Morris, Kellum, (AV) '50 '77 C.228 A.B. L.896 J.D. Pub. Def.
Morrow, J. Ben, (AV) '36 '65 C.790 B.S. L.896 J.D. [J.B.Morrow]
Morrow, J. Ben, P.A., (AV) 312 South Chester Street

Mullen Holland & Cooper P.A., (AV)
301 South York Street, P.O. Box 488, 28053
Telephone: 704-864-6751 Facsimile: 704-861-8394
URL: http://www.mhc-law.com
Langdon M. Cooper (Board Certified Specialist in Bankruptcy Law by North Carolina State Board of Legal Specialization); H. Randolph Sumner; Nancy Borders Paschall; J. Mark Heavner; J. Reid McGraw, Jr.; Jesse V. Bone, Jr.; Elizabeth Neisler Sumner (Board Certified Specialist in Estate Planning and Probate Law, North Carolina State Board of Legal Specialization); James R. Martin; Jane Foy Painter; John H. Russell, Jr.; Lee A. Peindl; Jason R. Shoemaker; D. Brad Collins.
General Civil Trial and Appellate Practice, all Federal and State Courts. Banking, Bankruptcy and Reorganization, Construction, Corporate and Commercial, Employment Discrimination, Estate Planning and Administration, Health Care, Insurance, Mergers and Acquisitions, Negligence, Personal Injury, Professional Malpractice, Real Estate, Workers' Compensation.
Representative Client: Bankers Trust Company of New York; Duke Power Company; First of Georgia Insurance; Gaston Memorial Hospital; Liberty Mutual Insurance Co.; Spectrum Dyed Yarns; Eastridge Mall, L.L.P.; FMC Corporation-Lithium Division; Freightliner; Gastonia Housing Authority.
See Professional Biographies, GASTONIA, NORTH CAROLINA

Murthy, Anu '65 '95 C.608 B.A. L.94 J.D. P.O. Box 2636
Ness, Aimee McHale '64 '88 C.321 B.A. L.734 J.D. 2885 Old Well Ln.‡
Nichols, Nicole L., (CV) '73 '98 C.1128 B.A. L.1228 J.D. [Nichols&A.]

Nichols and Austell L.L.P., (CV)
600 East Franklin Boulevard, 28054
Telephone: 704-868-4340 Fax: 704-868-4342
URL: http://www.nicholsaustell.com
Members of Firm: Nicole L. Nichols; Stacey Parker Austell.
Wills, Probate, Real Estate, Residential Real Estate.
See Professional Biographies, GASTONIA, NORTH CAROLINA

Painter, Jane Foy, (BV) '60 '86 C&L.575 B.A., J.D. [Mullen H.&C.]
Palmer, H. William, (AV) '30 '54 C&L.575 A.B., LL.B. [Stott,H.P.&W.]
Parker, James T., (CV) '63 '91 C.1128 B.A. L.574 J.D. 3243 Deerwood Dr.
Parker Austell, Stacey '77 '02 C.228 A.B. L.575 J.D. [Nichols&A.]

Parker, Poe, Adams & Bernstein L.L.P.
(See Charlotte)

Paschall, Nancy Borders, (AV) '60 '85 C&L.896 B.A., J.D. [Mullen H.&C.]
Patterson, Brent A., (BV) '67 '92 [Patterson&A.P.] ⊙

Patterson and Adams PLLC, (BV)
1305 East Garrison Boulevard, 28054 ⊙
Telephone: 704-867-1955 Fax: 704-853-1875 URL: http://www.patterson-adams.com
URL: http://www.pattersonadamslawoffice.com
Scott M. Adams; Brent A. Patterson.
Personal Injury, Automobile Accidents, Wrongful Deaths, Workers Compensation, Medical Malpractice.
Concord, North Carolina Office: 433 Church Street North, 28025. Telephone: 704-795-4317. Fax: 704-795-5738.
Salisbury, North Carolina Office: 710 North Main Street, 28144. Telephone: 704-795-4317.
See Professional Biographies, GASTONIA, NORTH CAROLINA

Patti, Timothy Lee '54 '80 C.1126 B.A. L.1228 J.D. Supr. Ct. J.
Peindl, Lee A. '76 '03 C.935 B.A. L.124 J.D. [Mullen H.&C.]
Pfingstl, Stefanie '48 '93 C.831 B.A. L.284 J.D. Asst. Staff Atty., Co. Dept. of Soc. Servs.
Phillips, David A., (BV) '59 '90 C.34 B.S. L.469 J.D. [Phillips]
Phillips Law Firm, The, (BV) 102 E. Main Ave.
Pickard, Rachel, (AV) '55 '80 C.37 B.A. L.575 J.D. 333 S. York Street
Planer, Geoffrey A., (BV) '49 '74 C.198 B.A. L.575 J.D. 216 South Marietta Street
Ragan, James W. '51 '77 C.893 B.A. L.790 J.D. [Ragan&R.P.]
Ragan, Jerry Neil, (AV) '55 '80 [Ragan&R.P.]

Ragan & Ragan PLLC, (AV) BB
616 Cox Road, P.O. Box 249, 28053-0249
Telephone: 704-864-3409 Fax: 704-853-1040
Email: info@ragan-ragan.com URL: http://www.ragan-ragan.com
Members of Firm: Jerry Neil Ragan; James W. Ragan.
Personal Injury, Workers Compensation, Medical Malpractice, Wrongful Death, Automobile Accidents, Products Liability.
See Professional Biographies, GASTONIA, NORTH CAROLINA

Ratchford, Brent D., (CV) '70 '96 C.1128 B.S. L.1345 J.D.
223 W. Main Avenue, Suite B, P.O. Box 726, 28053-0726
Telephone: 704-868-3434 Fax: 704-868-3225
Email: bdrattorneyatlaw@aol.com URL: http://www.brentratchford.com
Criminal Law, Juvenile Law, Traffic Law, Federal Law.
See Professional Biographies, GASTONIA, NORTH CAROLINA

Redwing, Dennis J. '48 '76 C.493 B.S. L.494 J.D. Cir.J.
Roberts, Joseph B., III, (AV) '40 '64 C&L.575 A.B., LL.B. [Roberts]
Roberts, Scott W., (BV) '68 '94 C.575 B.A. L.790 J.D. [Roberts]

Roberts Law Firm, The, P.A., (AV)
302 South York Street, P.O. Box 2335, 28053-2335
Telephone: 704-865-1271 Fax: 704-865-1488
Joseph B. Roberts, III; Scott W. Roberts.
Trial Practice. Personal Injury, Workers Compensation, Social Security Disability, Medical Malpractice, Nursing home Litigation, Products Liability and Wrongful Death.
See Professional Biographies, GASTONIA, NORTH CAROLINA

Robinson, A. Douglas, Jr., (BV) '70 '95 C.311 B.A. L.575 J.D. [Robinson&W.]
Robinson, Theodore Lamar, Jr., (AV) '43 '68 C.1126 A.B. L.896 J.D. [Robinson&W.]
Robinson & Wilson, L.L.P., (AV) 246 West Main Avenue (⊙Belmont)

Rodgers, J. Neal, PLLC, Law Offices of
(See Charlotte)

Rosenberg, Scott R. '70 '97 C.16 B.A. L.1187 J.D.
201 West Second Avenue, Suite B, 28052
Mailing Address: P.O. Box 278, Gastonia, NC 28053-0278
Telephone: 704-865-3600 Fax: 704-865-3792
Email: rosenbergscottra@bellsouth.net
Criminal Law, Traffic, Driving While Intoxicated, Juvenile Crimes, Parole and Probation.
See Professional Biographies, GASTONIA, NORTH CAROLINA

Russell, John H., Jr., (BV) '67 '93 C.674 B.A. L.575 J.D. [Mullen H.&C.]
Rutledge, Ralph M., (BV) '57 '82 C&L.575 B.S., J.D. Pub. Def.
Sain, Tara Reavis, (CV) '72 '98 C.575 B.A. L.1345 J.D. [Arthurs&F.]
Sanchez, Jill Yvonne '74 '01 C.150 B.A. L.575 J.D. Gaston Co. Dept. of Soc. Servs.

Schultz, Richard B., (BV) .... '50 '75 C.576 B.A. L.862 J.D. 212-C W. Second Ave.
Shaw, Robert H. '52 '78
C.228 B.A. L.896 J.D. Gen. Coun., Curtiss-Wright Flight Systems
Shoemaker, Jason R. .... '78 '03 C&L.896 B.A., J.D. [Mullen H.&C.]
Short, M. Roy, Jr. .... '35 '60 C.404 A.B. L.575 LL.B. 1006 S. Union Rd.‡
Shovelin, Julia Manning .... '49 '81 C&L.896 B.A., J.D. Co. Bd. of Educ.
Sigmon, P. Wayne, (AV) .... '49 '76 C.576 B.S.I.E. L.362 J.D. [Gray,L.K.S.S.F.&S.]
Smith, David W., III, (AV) .... '54 '80 C.269 B.A. L.896 J.D. [Gray,L.K.S.S.F.&S.]
Smith, Lloyd Ashley .... '67 '92 C.576 B.S. L.575 J.D. City Atty.
Solomon, T. J., II, (AV) .... '49 '74 C.162 B.A. L.790 J.D. [Gray,L.K.S.S.F.&S.]
Stann, Frederick R., (BV) .... '48 '75 C.1126 B.A. L.575 J.D. 502 E. Garrison Blvd.
Stevens, Catherine A. .... '51 '77 C&L.575 B.A., J.D. Dist. Ct. J.
Stewart, Carl J., Jr., (BV) .... '36 '61 C&L.228 A.B., J.D. 283 W. Main Ave.
Stott, Grady B., (AV) .... '21 '52 C&L.228 A.B., LL.B. [Stott,H.P.&W.]

Stott, Hollowell, Palmer & Windham, L.L.P., (AV)
401 East Franklin Boulevard, P.O. Box 995, 28053-0995
Telephone: 704-864-3425 Fax: 704-864-0478
Members of Firm: L. B. Hollowell (1904-1981); Grady B. Stott; James C. Windham, Jr.; H. William Palmer; Martha R. Thompson; Charlton K. Torrence, III; Jack D. Drum; D. Kevin Joyce. Associate: David W. Aycock. Of Counsel: Linwood Branton Hollowell, Jr.; Charles L. Graham, Jr.
General Civil and Trial Practice in all Courts. Corporation, Real Estate, Estate Planning and Probate, Insurance, Commercial Law, Municipal Law, Worker Compensation, Bankruptcy, Labor and Employment Law.
Representative Clients: Parkdale Mills Inc.; Wix Corp.; Gaston County; Citizens South Bank; Gastonia ABC Board.
See Professional Biographies, GASTONIA, NORTH CAROLINA

Street, Nicholas, (BV) .... '42 '72 C&L.575 A.B., J.D. 269 West Main Avenue
Sumner, Elizabeth Neisler, (AV) .... '58 '82 C.198 A.B. L.896 J.D. [Mullen H.&C.]
Sumner, H. Randolph, (AV) .... '57 '82 C.575 B.A. L.896 J.D. [Mullen H.&C.]
Sumner, Robert T., (AV) .... '53 '79 C&L.575 B.A., J.D. [Albright&S.]

Taylor, Regina Mitchell '65 '91 C.1378 B.S. L.574 J.D.
1568-E Union Road, 28054
Telephone: 704-861-0700 Fax: 704-861-0488
Email: rmtatty@bellsouth.net URL: http://www.regina-taylorlaw.com
Business Law, Corporate Law, Family Business Law, Small Business Law, Bankruptcy, Fair Debt Collections Act, Creditors Rights, Landlord and Tenant Law, Criminal, DWI, Traffic Violations, Domestic Relations, Family Law, Divorce, Child Custody, Adoptions, Child Support, Religious Institutions, Non Profit Organizations, Real Estate Title Examinations, Land Acquisitions, Wills, Decedents Estates.
See Professional Biographies, GASTONIA, NORTH CAROLINA

Thompson, Martha R., (AV) .... '63 '88 C.269 B.A. L.790 J.D. [Stott,H.P.&W.]

Thrower, Pennie M.
(See Dallas)

Torrence, Charlton K., III, (BV) .... '62 '89 C&L.575 B.A., J.D. [Stott,H.P.&W.]
Trakas, Andrew G., (CV) .... '53 '84 C.968 B.A. L.896 J.D. 931 Scotch Dr.
Warshawsky, Mark, (BV) .... '48 '74 C&L.575 A.B., J.D. 359 West Main Avenue
Wertz, Carol B., (CV) .... '72 '98 C.198 B.A. L.1345 J.D. [🄰 J.B.Morrow]
Whitesides, Henry M., (AV) .... '28 '57 C&L.575 B.S., J.D. [Whitesides&K.]
Whitesides & Kenny, L.L.P., (AV) .... 117 East Main Avenue
Wilson, Parks H., Jr., (AV) .... '53 '79 C.198 B.A. L.192 J.D. [Robinson&W.]
Windham, James C., Jr., (AV) .... '47 '72 C.269 B.A. L.575 J.D. [Stott,H.P.&W.]
Wise, Amy F. .... '72 '98 C.280 B.A. L.469 J.D. 325 N. Marietta Street

Yelton, Farfour, McCartney, Lutz & Craig, P.A.
(See Shelby)

GATESVILLE, * 308, *Gates Co.*

Godwin, Philip P. .... '24 '56 C&L.896 B.S., LL.B. [Godwin&G.] ‡
Godwin, Philip P., Jr., (BV) .... '52 '80 C.896 B.A. L.574 J.D. [Godwin&G.]
Godwin & Godwin, (BV) .... 110 Court St.

GIBSONVILLE, 4,372, *Alamance & Guilford Cos.*

Bullard, Daniel S., (BV) .... '68 '93 C&L.896 B.A., J.D. [Walker&B.]
Bullard, Lisa Wallace, (BV) .... '68 '94 C.896 B.A. L.383 [Walker&B.]
Walker, James F. .... '46 '79 C.576 B.A. L.896 J.D. [Walker&B.]
Walker & Bullard, P.A., (BV) .... 229 E. Main St.

GLADE VALLEY, 1,115, *Alleghany Co.*

Cruciani, Joseph R., (BV) .... '28 '57 C&L.575 LL.B. [Cruciani]
Cruciani Professional Association, (BV) .... 548 Scenic Valley Rd.

GOLDSBORO, * 39,043, *Wayne Co.*

Agner, John M., (CV) .... '66 '98 C.404 B.A. L.574 J.D. [J.M.Agner]
Agner, John Michael, Attorney at Law, (CV) .... 214 S. William St., Ste. 3
Allen, Jerry A., Jr., (BV) .... '62 '89 C.575 B.A. L.1228 J.D. [Walker,C.A.G.&A.]
Ammons, Jeffrey T., (BV) .... '70 '96 C.790 B.A. L.1345 J.D. [Walker,C.A.G.&A.]
Baddour, Philip A., Jr., (AV) .... '42 '67 C&L.575 A.B., J.D. [Baddour,P.&H.]

Baddour, Parker & Hine, P.C., (AV) 🄱🄱
208 South William Street, P.O. Drawer 916, 27530
Telephone: 919-735-7275 Fax: 919-736-3297
Email: info@goldsborolawyers.com URL: http://www.lawyers.com/baddourparkerhine&orander
Philip A. Baddour, Jr.; E. B. Borden Parker; John C. Hine (Board Certified Specialist in Estate Planning and Probate Law, North Carolina State Board of Legal Specialization).
Automobile Accidents and Injuries, Personal Injury, Wrongful Death, Workers Compensation, Real Estate, Social Security Disability, Wills, Trusts and States, Taxation, Family Law, Divorce, Business Law, Civil Litigation, Products Liability.
Representative Clients: Wayne County; Wayne County Department of Social Services; Southern Medical Oncology Center, P.A.; Goldsboro Neurological Surgery, P.A.; Shepherd Electric Supply Co., Inc.; Quality Forest Products, Inc.; Seegars Fence Co.
See Professional Biographies, GOLDSBORO, NORTH CAROLINA

Barfield, Glenn A., (BV) .... '60 '86 C&L.575 B.A., J.D. [Barnes,B.&H.]
Barnes, Henson P., (AV) .... '34 '61 C&L.575 A.B., LL.B. [Barnes,B.&H.] ‡
Barnes, Braswell & Haithcock, P.A., (AV) .... 231 East Walnut Street
Benton, Shelby D., (AV) .... '61 '85 C.576 B.A. L.1345 J.D. [Hollowell&B.]
Bland, William W., (BV) .... '60 '92 C.228 A.B. L.575 J.D. Asst. Dist. Atty.
Brantley, J. Christopher, (BV) '66 '93 C.232 B.A. L.1345 J.D.
[Brantley,J.R.H.&H.] ⊙
Brantley, Jesse C. .... '66 '93 C.232 B.A. L.1228 J.D. 601 N. Spence Ave.

Brantley, Jenkins, Riddle, Hardee & Hardee, (BV)
601 North Spence Avenue, 27534 ⊙
Telephone: 919-778-9700 Fax: 919-778-1938 URL: http://www.bjrhhlawyers.com
URL: http://www.bjrhhatty.com
J. Christopher Brantley; Eugene G. Jenkins (1961-2003); Gene A. Riddle; Charles R. Hardee; G. Wayne Hardee. Associates: Brian Christopher (Chris) Daniels; Thomas Moore.
Personal Injury, Wrongful Death, Automobile Accidents, Head and Spinal Injury, Nursing Home Abuse and Neglect, Workers Compensation, Insurance, Products Liability, Social Security Disability, Medical Malpractice.

(This Listing Continued)

Brantley, Jenkins, Riddle, Hardee & Hardee (Continued)
Greenville, North Carolina Office: 202 East Arlington Boulevard, P.O. Box 924, 27858. Telephone: 252-355-1998. Fax: 252-321-2948.
Jacksonville, North Carolina Office: 901 Hargett Street, P.O. Box 7070, 28540. Telephone: 910-455-5599. Fax: 910-455-7191.
Kinston, North Carolina Office: 2506 Heritage Street, Suite A, 28501. Telephone: 252-522-1500.
See Professional Biographies, GOLDSBORO, NORTH CAROLINA

Braswell, R. Gene, (AV) .... '42 '70 C.55 A.B. L.869 J.D. [Barnes,B.&H.]
Brown, Darrell Keith .... '74 '00 C.1228 B.A. L.575 J.D. [Everett,W.F.L.&B.]
Brown, J. Thomas, Jr., (BV) .... '39 '63 C&L.575 LL.B. [Duke&B.]
Bryant, Craig I., (BV) .... '53 '78 C.1103 B.A. L.245 J.D. [C.I.Bryant]
Bryant, Craig I., P.A., (BV) .... 202 S. William St.
Clark, Donald E., Jr., (BV) .... '64 '89 C&L.1228 B.A., J.D. [Walker,C.A.G.&A.]
Copeland, James W., Jr., (BV) .... '52 '77 C&L.575 A.B., J.D. Asst. Dist. Atty.
Corbett, Lisa Granberry, (BV) .... '63 '88 C.575 B.S. L.1228 J.D. Asst. Atty. Gen.
Daniels, Brian Christopher (Chris) '72 '00
C.999 B.A. L.1187 J.D. [🄰 Brantley,J.R.H.&H.]
Davis, Joseph H., (BV) .... '27 '55 C.575 A.B. L.846 J.D. Edgerton Bldg.
Dees, John W., (AV) .... '47 '72 C&L.575 A.B., J.D. [Dees,S.P.J.D.&J.]
Dees, William A., Jr., (AV) .... '20 '48 C&L.575 A.B., J.D. [Dees,S.P.J.D.&J.]

Dees, Smith, Powell, Jarrett, Dees & Jones, (AV)
100 North William Street Post Office Drawer 8, 27533-0008
Telephone: 919-735-8311 Fax: 919-735-0234
Email: emilyp@deeslaw.com URL: http://www.deeslaw.com
Members of Firm: W. Archie Dees (1887-1979); William A. Dees, Jr.; William W. Smith (Retired); William L. Powell, Jr. (Retired); Tommy W. Jarrett; John W. Dees; Michael M. Jones. Associates: Joyce Ann Keller; Billy J. Strickland II.
General Trial and Appellate Practice in all State and Federal Courts, Personal Injury, Medical Malpractice, Workers Compensation, Dispute Resolution, Corporate Law and Business Law, Contracts, Traffic Offenses, DWI, Commercial, Environmental, Banking, Real Property, Timber Transactions, Estate Administration, Trusts and Estates, Wills and Probate, Negligence and Traffic Law.
Representative Clients: Branch Banking & Trust Co.; Georgia Pacific Corporation; Crawford-Norwood Co. (Real Estate).
Approved Attorneys for: Lawyers Title Insurance Corp.; Chicago Title Insurance Co.; Investors Title Insurance Co.; First American Title Insurance Co.; Fidelity National Title.
See Professional Biographies, GOLDSBORO, NORTH CAROLINA

Dobbs, Thomas H. '66 '95 C.309 B.A. L.896 J.D.
(adm. in GA; not adm. in NC) 308 Carswell Ln.
Duke, John E., (AV) .... '29 '57 C&L.575 B.S., LL.B. [Duke&B.]
Duke and Brown, (AV) .... 213 E. Walnut St.
Duncan, Farris A., (BV) .... '44 '70 C.576 B.A. L.575 J.D. [F.A.Duncan]
Duncan, Farris A., P.A., (BV) .... 1401 No. Berkeley Blvd. Ste. A
Edmundson, Paul B., Jr., (BV) .... '29 '55 C&L.575 LL.B. 200 W. Ash St., Suite 203
Edwards, H. Jack, (AV) .... '42 '67 C&L.575 A.B., J.D. 660 N. Spence Ave.
Ellis, Kenneth R. .... '45 '71 C&L.896 B.A., J.D. Dist. J.
Everett, William Harrell, (AV) '34 '62
C.575 B.A. L.896 J.D. [Everett,W.F.L.&B.] (⊙Elkin)
Everett, Womble, Finan, Lawrence & Brown, L.L.P., (AV) .... 507 B Spence Avenue
Ferguson, Claud F., Jr., (BV) .... '53 '78 C.577 B.A. L.575 J.D. Asst. Dist. Atty.
Finan, Timothy I., (AV) .... '52 '77 C.576 B.A. L.575 J.D. [Everett,W.F.L.&B.]
Foy, Louis F., III .... '74 '00 C.240 B.S. L.1228 J.D. [🄰 Walker,C.A.G.&A.]
Franklin, E. Thomas, Jr. .... '44 '69 C&L.575 B.S., J.D. Franklin Bkg. Co., Inc.
Franklin, Eugene T., Jr. .... '44 '69 C&L.575 B.S. in B.A., J.D. 706 E. Beach St.
Fuller, Robert E., Jr., (BV) .... '49 '74 C&L.896 B.A., J.D. 109 N. William St.
Gaylor, Charles P., III, (BV) .... '49 '77 C.575 A.B. L.1338 J.D. [C.P.Gaylor,III]
Gaylor, Charles P., III, PA, (BV) .... 109 N. William St.
Gomulka, John Kevin, (BV) .... '61 '89 C.928 B.A. L.1358 J.D. 109 N. William St.
Grice, O. Drew, Jr. .... '69 '95 C.301 B.A. L.192 J.D. [Walker,C.A.G.&A.]
Gurley, Charles R., (CV) .... '63 '91 C.232 B.A. L.574 J.D. 112 N. William St.
Haithcock, W. Timothy, (AV) .... '44 '69 C&L.575 A.B., J.D. [Barnes,B.&H.]
Hardee, Charles R., (BV) .... '56 '81 C.575 B.S. L.1228 J.D. [Brantley,J.R.H.&H.]
Hardee, G. Wayne, (BV) .... '57 '82 C.575 B.S. L.1228 J.D. [Brantley,J.R.H.&H.]
Hedrick, Bryan Harlan .... '73 '00 C.999 B.S. L.575 J.D. Law Clk.
Heekin, Sarah L. .... '71 '00 C.577 B.A. L.1228 J.D. [🄰 Barnes,B.&H.]
Helmer, Christopher A. .... '71 '01 C.608 B.A. L.117 J.D. P.O. Box 175
Hine, John C., (AV) .... '48 '74 C.575 B.S. L.838 J.D. [Baddour,P.&H.]
Hollowell, Jean P., (BV) .... '53 '82 C.645 B.A. L.1345 J.D. [Hollowell&B.]
Hollowell & Benton, P.A., (AV) .... 130 S. John Street
Hulse, B. Geoffrey, (BV) .... '55 '85 C.575 B.A. L.1228 J.D. [Barnes,B.&H.]
Hulse, H. Bruce, Jr., (BV) .... '48 '75 C.1228 B.A. L.574 J.D. 219 E. Walnut St.
Jacobs, Donald M. .... '37 '64 C&L.575 A.B., LL.B. Emer. Supr. Ct. J.
Jarrett, Tommy W., (AV) .... '43 '67 C&L.575 A.B., J.D. [Dees,S.P.J.D.&J.]
Jones, Arnold O., II, (BV) .... '65 '90 C.575 B.S. L.896 J.D. 112 S. John St.
Jones, Michael M., (AV) .... '53 '79 C&L.575 A.B., J.D. [Dees,S.P.J.D.&J.]
Jordan, Louis, Law Offices, (BV) .... '45 '71 C.709 B.A. L.574 J.D. 112 E. Walnut St.
Keller, Joyce Ann, (BV) .... '50 '78 C.280 B.A. L.245 J.D. [🄰 Dees,S.P.J.D.&J.]
Kellum, Norman B., Jr., (AV) .... '37 '65 C&L.896 B.S., J.D. [Kellum] ⊙

Kellum Law Firm, (AV)
2005 East Ash Street, P.O. Box 1085, 27533 ⊙
Telephone: 919-722-6955 Fax: 919-722-6922
Email: ckeenhold@kellumlawfirm.com URL: http://www.lawyers.com/kellumlawfirm
Norman B. Kellum, Jr.
State and Federal Civil Trial Practice, Personal Injury Law, Wrongful Death, Workers' Compensation, Social Security, Defective Products, Mass Torts and Insurance Law.
See Professional Biographies, GOLDSBORO, NORTH CAROLINA

Kerr, John H., III, (AV) .... '36 '61 C&L.575 A.B., LL.B. [Warren,K.W.T.&S.]
Kinsey, Rebecca B., (BV) .... '63 '92 C.575 A.B. L.574 J.D. [Barnes,B.&H.]
Kroboth, Jan T., (BV) .... '45 '88 C.1044 B.S. L.1228 J.D. Asst. Dist. Atty.
Langston, W. Dortch, Jr., (AV) ... '37 '64 C.228 B.A. L.896 J.D. 206 East Chestnut Street
Lapas, Adrian M., (BV) .... '64 '93 C.575 B.A. L.896 J.D. [A.M.Lapas]
Lapas, Adrian M., P.A., (BV) .... 206 E. Chestnut St.
Lawrence, Ronald T., II, (BV) .... '65 '95 C.953 B.A. L.1228 J.D. [Everett,W.F.L.&B.]
Moore, Thomas .... '— '03 C.576 B.A. L.425 J.D. [🄰 Brantley,J.R.H.&H.]
Nowachek, Deborah L. .... '62 '89 C.424 A.B. L.365 J.D. [D.L.Nowachek]
Nowachek, Deborah L., P.A. .... 145 Meadowlark Road
Parker, E. B. Borden, (AV) .... '44 '69 C&L.575 A.B., J.D. [Baddour,P.&H.]
Parker, Wylie F. .... '14 '39 C&L.575 B.A., LL.B. P.O. Box 6‡
Powell, William L., Jr., (AV) .... '36 '61 C&L.896 B.A., LL.B. [Dees,S.P.J.D.&J.] ⊙
Riddle, Gene A., (BV) .... '59 '85 C.575 B.A. L.896 J.D. [Brantley,J.R.H.&H.]

Rose Rand Attorneys, P.A.
(See Wilson)

Rouse, David M., (AV) .... '42 '66 C&L.575 A.B., J.D. 312 East Walnut Street
Samelson, Samuel L. '40 '65 C&L.472 B.B.A., LL.B.
(adm. in FL; not adm. in NC) Pres., Linde Products Mfg. Co.

Sauls, Randall M., (BV) '57 '84 C.575 B.A. L.1228 J.D.
Atty. & Branch Mgr., First American Title Ins. Co.
Setzer, Joseph E., Jr. ....'48 '73 C&L.575 B.S., J.D. Dist. J.
Smith, Henry C., (BV) ....'56 '81 C&L.575 B.S., J.D. [Warren,K.W.T.&S.]
Smith, Norborne G., Jr. ....'20 '47 C.96 B.S. L.893 LL.B. 1500 E. Ash St.
Smith, Robert Morgan ....'69 '03 C.999 B.S. L.1187 J.D. [Smith&S.]
Smith, William W., (AV) ....'28 '53 C.198 A.B. L.575 LL.B. [Dees,S.P.J.D.&J.] ‡

Smith and Strickland, PLLC
104 S. William Street, Suite A, P.O. Box 1657, 27533
Telephone: 919-735-5252 Fax: 919-735-5696
URL: http://www.smithandstrickland.com
Robert Morgan Smith; Donald B. Strickland.
Criminal Defense, Driving While Impaired, DUI, DWI, Traffic Violations, Parole and Probation, Drug Crimes, White Collar Crimes, Juvenile Crimes, Personal Injury, Military Law.
See Professional Biographies, GOLDSBORO, NORTH CAROLINA

Strickland, Billy J., II ....'73 '05 C.1228 B.S. L.1339 J.D. [Ⓐ Dees,S.P.J.D.&J.]
Strickland, Donald B. ....'31 '56 C&L.228 B.A., J.D. [Smith&S.]
Taylor, L. E. (Trey), III, (BV) ....'62 '87 C&L.575 B.S., J.D. [Warren,K.W.T.&S.]
Vickory, Charles B., III, (AV) ....'56 '81 C.575 B.S. L.896 J.D. Dist. Atty.
Vinson, James A., III, (BV) ....'45 '71 C&L.575 A.B., J.D. 235 E. Walnut
Walker, Robert D., Jr., (AV) ....'49 '74 C.576 B.A. L.896 J.D. [Walker,C.A.G.&A.]
Walker, Clark, Allen, Grice & Ammons, LLP, (AV) .... 1407 W. Grantham St.

Wallace, Morris, Barwick, Landis & Stroud, P.A.
(See Kinston)

Walston, John T., (BV) ....'52 '77 C&L.575 A.B., J.D. [Warren,K.W.T.&S.]
Warren, Lindsay C., Jr., (AV) ....'24 '51 C&L.575 B.S., J.D. [Ⓒ Warren,K.W.T.&S.]
Warren, S. Reed, (AV) ....'57 '82 C.232 B.A. L.896 J.D. [S.R.Warren]

Warren, Kerr, Walston, Taylor & Smith, L.L.P., (AV)
117 Ormond Avenue, P.O. Box 1616, 27533-1616
Telephone: 919-734-1841 Fax: 919-734-4215
William R. Allen (1896-1972); Walter Frank Taylor (1889-1977). Of Counsel: Lindsay C. Warren, Jr. Members of Firm: John H. Kerr, III; John T. Walston; L. E. (Trey) Taylor, III; Henry C. Smith.
General Civil Practice. Corporate and Business Law, Wills and Probate, Trusts and Estates, Banking, Tax, Labor, Insurance, Collections, Real Estate, and Traffic Violations.
Counsel for: Southern Railway Co.; Carolina Power & Light Co.; Travelers Group; Fireman's Fund Insurance Co.; Mount Olive Pickle Co., Inc.; Goldsboro Milling Co. and Affiliates; Southern Bell Telephone Co.; T.A. Loving Co.
See Professional Biographies, GOLDSBORO, NORTH CAROLINA

Warren, S. Reed, PA, (AV) ....642 N. Spence Ave.
Williams, Jonathan S., (BV) ....'63 '90 C&L.575 B.A., J.D. [J.S.Williams]
Williams, Jonathan S., P.C., (BV) .... 106 Cassedale Dr.
Womble, James D., Jr., (BV) ....'45 '72 C&L.575 A.B., J.D. [Everett,W.F.L.&B.]
Wood, J. Darby, (AV) ....'40 '65 C&L.575 A.B., LL.B. 664 N. Spence Ave.
Wright, Paul M. ....'48 '75 C.937 B.A. L.228 J.D. Supr. Ct. J.

GRAHAM, * 12,833, *Alamance Co.*

Abernathy, G. Wayne, (BV) '47 '75 C&L.575 A.B., J.D.
Suite A 108 South Maple Street
Allen, Bradley R. ....'62 '88 C.575 B.S. L.1345 J.D. Alamance Co. Dist. Atty.'s Off.
Balog, Steve A., (AV) ....'50 '75 C&L.575 B.S., J.D. Supr. Ct. J.
Bass, James A., III ....'56 '92 C.198 B.A. L.896 J.D. Off. of Co. Dist. Atty.
Bass, Misti Carden ....'69 '95 C.1128 B.A. L.575 J.D. Alamance Co. Atty. Off.
Boone, Haley S. ....'68 '97 C.576 B.A. L.575 J.D. Off. of Dist. Atty.
Camp, Patricia '53 '93 C.691 B.A. L.145 J.D.
(adm. in OH; not adm. in NC) P.O. Box 922
Collins, Robert E., (P.A.), (BV) ....'51 '76 C.290 B.A. L.575 J.D. P.O. Box 822

Daniel, George B., P.A.
(See Yanceyville)

Daniel, William H., P.A.
(See Yanceyville)

Dawson, Alexander, (BV) ....'43 '86 C.1378 B.S. L.574 J.D. [Dawson,D.&D.]
Dawson, Alexander, III ....'64 '95 C.1378 B.S. L.329 J.D. [Dawson,D.&D.]
Dawson, April Gordon ....'66 '95 C.1298 B.S. L.329 J.D. [Dawson,D.&D.]
Dawson, Dawson, and Dawson, P. A., (BV) ....20 Court Square, Southwest
DiLello, Anthony C., (CV) ....'70 '95 C.576 B.A. L.574 J.D. [McEntire&D.]
Doby, Julian M., (BV) ....'72 '98 C.1228 B.A. L.1345 J.D. [J.M.Doby]
Doby, Julian M., PA, (BV) ....P.O. Box 722
Dorrestein, Ronald, (CV) ....'62 '94 C.240 B.A. L.574 J.D. [Latham,W.&D.]

Hairston, Dorothy, Law Office of
(See Durham)

Hall, Forrest C., (BV) ....'22 '48 C.240 A.B. L.228 LL.B. 205 N. Main St.
Hardy, Mildred T., (BV) ....'43 '87 C&L.574 B.A., J.D. 106 S. Maple St., Ste. B
Harris, David L., (BV) ....'49 '80 C.240 B.S.B.A. L.1228 J.D. 122 S. Main St.
Harris, Rebecca Burns ....'72 '99 C.454 B.A. L.575 J.D. 154 S. Main St.
Harviel, Ernest J. ....'50 '75 C.34 B.S. L.575 J.D. Dist. J.
Hassell, Robert A., (CV) ....'46 '73 C.853 A.B. L.228 J.D. [R.A.Hassell]
Hassell, Robert A., PLLC, Law Office of, (CV) ....108 W. Elm St.
Hayes, Robert R. ....'30 '60 C.240 A.B. L.575 LL.B. 207 N. Main St., Suite 1
Holley, David Kent, (BV) ....'62 '87 C.34 B.A. L.896 J.D. [Ridge&H.]
Horn, Michelle Delgado ....'48 '79 C.838 B.A. L.575 J.D. 112 South Maple Street
Huffman, David R., (BV) ....'55 '86 C.896 B.S. L.469 J.D. 103 W. Elm St.
Hunt, George E., (AV) ....'44 '75 C.925 B.A. L.575 J.D. [Hunt&W.]
Hunt & White, (AV) ....106 South Maple St.
Jacobs, Robert J., (BV) ....'53 '79 C&L.575 A.B., J.D. 140 E. Elm Street
Kitchen, S.C., (BV) ....'54 '80 C.1128 B.A. L.575 J.D. Co. Atty.
Laskody, Lee, (CV) ....'68 '98 C&L.575 B.A., J.D. P.O. Box 1240
Latham, James F., (AV) ....'20 '42 C&L.228 A.B., J.D. [Latham,W.&D.] ⊙
Latham, Wood & Dorrestein, L.L.P., (AV) .... 10 N.W. Court Sq. (⊙Burlington)
Manning, P. Bryden, (CV) ....'43 '79 C.575 B.A. L.184 J.D. P.O. Box 28
McEntire, Mitchell M., (BV) ....'45 '70 C&L.575 B.A., J.D. [McEntire&D.]

McEntire & DiLello, (BV)
103 West Elm Street, P.O. Drawer 471, 27253
Telephone: 336-228-1341 Fax: 336-229-7465
Email: mmmfirm@aol.com
Mitchell M. McEntire; Anthony C. DiLello.
Criminal and Traffic, DWI, Municipal, Personal Injury and Estates.
See Professional Biographies, GRAHAM, NORTH CAROLINA

Monroe, Daniel H., Jr., (AV) ....'48 '74 C.269 B.A. L.575 J.D. 111 S. Main St.
Moorefield, Rickey L., (CV) ....'54 '79 C&L.575 B.A., J.D. 103 W. Elm St.
Morris, Eugene T., Jr., (AV) ....'53 '80 C.790 B.A. L.245 J.D. Dist. Atty. Off.
Paisley, John P., Jr., (BV) ....'48 '73 C.240 B.A. L.896 J.D. 10 N.W. Court Sq.
Plunkett, Richard Clay ....'73 '00 C.575 B.A. L.574 J.D. P.O. Box 994
Ramaswamy, Anand P., (CV) '64 '98
C.577 B.A. L.575 J.D. Off. of the Dist. Atty., Pros. Dist. 15A
Richardson, R. Nelson, (BV) ....'49 '75 C.575 B.A. L.896 J.D. [Roberson&R.]
Ridge, Paul H., (P.A.), (AV) ....'23 '49 C.240 A.B. L.575 LL.B. [Ridge&H.]
Ridge & Holley, (AV) ....114 S. Maple St.
Roberson, James K., (AV) ....'50 '75 C.232 B.S. L.896 J.D. [Roberson&R.]
Roberson & Richardson, (AV) ....P.O. Box 394
Spencer, James C., Jr. ....'40 '67 C&L.575 A.B., J.D. Supr. Ct. J.

Stedman Law Firm
(See Burlington)

Sternberg, Frederick J., (BV) ....'41 '66 C.105 A.B. L.896 LL.B. [F.J.Sternberg]
Sternberg, Frederick J., P.A., (BV) .... 38 Court Square, S.W.
Swiggett, R. Horace, Jr. ....'32 '57 C.296 B.A. L.228 J.D. 134 S. Main St.
Thompson, Charles C., III, (CV) ....'39 '74 C.575 A.B. L.838 LL.B. 11 N.W. Court Sq.
Wagoner, Mary M. ....'66 '91 C.576 B.A. L.575 J.D. Off. of Co. Atty.
Watkins, Christopher T., (CV) ....'50 '84 C&L.574 B.A., J.D. [C.Watkins]
Watkins, Christopher, (CV) ....112 W. Elm St.
Wheeler, Grady Joseph, Jr., (BV) ....'50 '77 C.575 B.A. L.192 J.D. 207 N. Main St.
White, Octavis, (BV) ....'55 '84 C.576 B.A. L.1119 J.D. [Hunt&W.]
Whited, G. Keith, (CV) ....'55 '81 C.575 B.A. L.574 J.D. 110 S. Maple St., Ste. B
Wood, B. F., (AV) ....'25 '53 C&L.575 B.A., J.D. [Latham,W.&D.]

GRANITE FALLS, 4,612, *Caldwell Co.*

Hamby, Penelope E. Joyner, (BV) ....'65 '92 C.1228 L.1345 J.D. 115 N. Main St.

GRANITE QUARRY, 2,175, *Rowan Co.*

Fisher, J. Steven '66 '92 C.575 B.A. L.896 J.D.
(adm. in GA; not adm. in NC) S&M Bank

GREENSBORO, * 223,891, *Guilford Co.*

Abel, Michael R., (AV) ....'45 '70 C.198 A.B. L.575 J.D. [Schell B.A.A.&L.]
Aberman, Debbi L. ....'56 '81 C&L.260 B.A., J.D. [Ⓐ Isaacson I.&S.]
Ackerman, Nicholas S., (BV) '68 '98
C.575 A.B L.1338 J.D. 416 Gallimore Dairy Road, Suite D
Adams, J. Patrick, (AV) ....'36 '61 C&L.575 A.B., LL.B. [Adams&O.]
Adams, James C., II, (BV) ....'66 '91 C.575 B.A. L.276 J.D. [Brooks,P.M.H.&L.]
Adams, Jennifer F. ....'76 '01 C.198 B.A. L.896 J.D. [Ⓐ Hunter,H.M.E.&B.]
Adams, Rayford K., III, (AV) ....'— '79 C.198 B.S. L.896 J.D. [Hunter,H.M.E.&B.]

Adams Kleemeier Hagan Hannah & Fouts PLLC
(See Nexsen Pruet Adams Kleemeier, PLLC)

Adams & Osteen, (AV)
BB&T Building-Suite 410, 201 West Market Street, 27401-2527
Telephone: 336-274-2947 Fax: 336-274-2940
Email: osteena@bellsouth.net
J. Patrick Adams; William L. Osteen, Jr.
Civil and Criminal Trial and Appeals in all State and Federal Courts. Real Estate, Corporation and Wills and Probate, Commercial Law, Business and Construction Law.
See Professional Biographies, GREENSBORO, NORTH CAROLINA

Adamson, Eric Andrew '70 '97
C.347 B.S. L.1209 J.D. Asst. Gen. Coun, The Fresh Market Inc.
Agapion, Bill ....'26 '52 C&L.575 A.B., LL.B. 625 S. Elm St.
Albright, D. Erik, (AV) ....'65 '90 C.228 A.B. L.880 J.D. [Smith M.]
Albright, Lonnie G., III, (BV) ....'56 '86 C.577 B.A. L.574 J.D. 322 S. Eugene St.
Albright, W. Douglas ....'39 '64 C.228 A.B. L.30 LL.B. Supr. Ct. J.
Alderman, Holly H. ....'64 '89 C&L.575 B.S., J.D. [Schell B.A.A.&L.]
Alexander, E. Raymond, Jr., (BV) ....'37 '65 C&L.896 B.A., LL.B. #2 Government Plz.

Alexander Ralston, Speckhard & Speckhard, L.L.P., (AV)
221 Commerce Place, Suite D, 27401
Telephone: 336-379-9302 Fax: 336-370-1232
URL: http://www.speckhardandspeckhard.com
Donald K. Speckhard; Stanley E. Speckhard.
General Practice in all Courts. Corporate, Bankruptcy, Commercial, Personal Injury, Medical Malpractice, Product Liability, Wrongful Death, Brain Injury, Real Estate, Wills, Probate and Estate Planning, Civil Litigation, Workers Compensation and Appellate Law.
See Professional Biographies, GREENSBORO, NORTH CAROLINA

Allen, Derek J., (BV) ....'71 '97 C&L.48 B.A., J.D. [Brooks,P.M.H.&L.]
Allen, Michael J., (AV) ....'60 '85 C.934 B.A. L.602 J.D. [Carruthers&R.]
Allen, Rose M. ....'48 '88 C.1298 B.S. L.574 J.D. 410 Swing Road (Pat.)
Allen, Sharon K., (BV) ... '56 '82 C.575 A.B. L.1228 J.D. 333 N. Greene Street, Suite 500
Alligood, Brian H., (BV) ....'67 '92 C.575 B.A. L.228 J.D. [Sharpless&S.]
Alloway, Sherry Fowler ....'55 '80 C.999 B.A. L.1228 J.D. Dist. J.
Alspaugh, James A., (BV) ....'30 '57 C&L.575 B.S., J.D. 903 W. Market St.
Anderson, Francis I. ....'11 '35 C&L.575 A.B., LL.B. 712 Kemp Rd., W.‡
Anderson, Stephanie W. ....'71 '01 C.240 B.A. L.1228 J.D. [Ⓐ Burton&S.]
Anderson, Thomas L. '50 '78 C.494 B.S. L.477 J.D.
(adm. in DC; not adm. in NC) Lorillard Tobacco Company (Legal Department)

Anderson Korzen & Associates, P.C.
(See Kernersville)

Andia, Gilbert J., Jr., (BV) ....'60 '89 C.886 B.S. L.896 J.D. [Hunter,H.M.E.&B.] (Pat.)
Andrews, Lee D. ....'— '70 C.1378 B.A.B.A. L.329 J.D. P.O. Box 21472
Antolin, Stanislav ....'— '94 C.223 B.S. L.1338 J.D. [Ⓒ Smith M.] (Pat.)
Armstrong, Charlene Y. '69 '97
C.955 B.S. L.574 J.D. [Ⓐ Browne,F.W.&W.] (⊙Creedmoor)
Asby, Phillip G., (CV) ....'67 '95 C.575 B.A. L.896 J.D. 228 W. Market St.
Ashley, Bruce P., (AV) ....'61 '86 C.575 A.B. L.477 J.D. [Smith M.]
Ashley, Elaine Hedrick, (BV) ....'54 '98 C.575 B.M. L.574 J.D. [Hill,E.D.J.&B.]
Atwell, J. Stanley, (AV) ....'56 '84 C.575 B.S. L.896 J.D. [Carruthers&R.]
Auberry, Evan Kent, (AV) ....'56 '82 C&L.575 A.B., J.D. [Smith M.]
Audilet, W. Alexander, (BV) ....'61 '88 C.893 B.A. L.896 J.D. [Smith M.]
Avery, Margaret DuBose, (AV) '48 '75 C.575 A.B. L.145 J.D.
V.P. & Assoc. Gen. Coun., United Guaranty Corp.
Aycock, George W. (Trey), III, (BV) ....'67 '94 C.575 B.A. L.879 J.D. [Coltrane A.&O.]
Aycock, William P., II, (AV) ....'43 '70 C&L.575 A.B., J.D. [Schell B.A.A.&L.]
Baier, Richard C. '50 '77 C.101 B.A. L.345 J.D.
(adm. in IN; not adm. in NC) Jefferson-Pilot Communications Co.
Bailey, Sabrina M., (BV) ....'72 '97 C.316 B.A. L.923 J.D. P.O. Box 2368

Bailey & Thomas, P.A.
(See Winston-Salem)

Baker, Marcia E. ....'— '84 C.477 A.B. L.575 J.D. 605 Foxbriar Dr.
Baker, Wendy J. ....'68 '95 C.313 B.S. L.930 J.D. 3300 Battleground Ave.
Ballinger, Max D. ....'32 '60 C&L.575 B.S.B.A., J.D. 6200 Ballinger Rd.
Barbee, Ronald, (BV) ....'38 '70 C&L.574 B.S., J.D. 101 S. Elm Street, Suite 130
Barbour, William G., (BV) ....'51 '81 C.925 B.S.B.A. L.192 J.D. 314 S. Eugene St.
Barker, Dan T., Jr., (BV) ....'60 '87 C.198 B.A. L.575 J.D. 3525 Primrose Avenue

Barlow, Jodi S., (BV) .... '63 '94 C.935 B.A. L.574 J.D. Off. of Dist. Atty.
Barlow, John R., II, (AV) .... '41 '70 C.575 A.B. L.896 J.D. [Tuggle D.&M.]
Barnes, Robert J. .... '43 '75 C&L.790 B.S., J.D. 12 Knoll Brook Ct.
Barrett, Clifton T., (AV) .... '59 '85 C&L.896 B.A., J.D. Asst. U.S. Atty.
Barrett, J. Alexander S., (AV) .... '— '85 C.1365 B.A. L.880 J.D. [Nexsen P.A.K.]
Barron, Vance, Jr., (AV) .... '43 '73 C&L.575 B.A., J.D. [Barron&B.]

Barron & Berry, L.L.P., (AV) [BB]
301 South Greene Street, Suite 310, 27401
Mailing Address: P.O. Box 2370, Greensboro, NC 27402-2370
Telephone: 336-274-4782 Fax: 336-379-8592 URL: http://www.barronberry.com
Email: barronberry@bellsouth.net URL: http://www.lawyers.com/barronberrylaw
Vance Barron, Jr.; Frederick L. Berry. Associate: Jamie Lisa Forbes.
Personal Injury, Medical Malpractice, Automobile Accidents, Wrongful Death, Products Liability and Brain Injury.
See Professional Biographies, GREENSBORO, NORTH CAROLINA

Bartenfield, John David .... '62 '97 C.240 B.A. L.1228 J.D. 903 W., Market St.
Basden, June L., (AV) .... '53 '86 C.577 B.S. L.575 J.D. [Carruthers&R.]
Bates, Mathew E., (BV) .... '48 '74 C.1318 A.B. L.896 J.D. [M.E.Bates]

Bates, Mathew E., P.A., (BV)
5501 Adams Farm Lane, Suite D, P.O. Box 7219, 27417
Telephone: 336-854-9500 Fax: 336-854-9566
URL: http://www.lawyers.com/mathewbates
Mathew E. Bates.
Taxation, Securities Arbitration, Commodities Arbitration, Bankruptcy, Business, Corporate and Wills, Chapter 7 Bankruptcy, Chapter 13 Bankruptcy.
See Professional Biographies, GREENSBORO, NORTH CAROLINA

Bayliss, Jack B., Jr., (AV) .... '54 '79 C&L.575 A.B., J.D. [Carruthers&R.]
Baynes, Robert G., (AV) .... '— '64 C&L.575 B.A., J.D. [Nexsen P.A.K.]
Beatty, Joseph R., (AV) .... '44 '69 C.575 A.B. L.228 J.D. [Hill,E.D.J.&B.]
Beaver, Gary L., (AV) .... '55 '82 C.871 B.S. L.228 J.D. [Nexsen P.A.K.]
Beavers, Harold W., (BV) .... '55 '81 C&L.896 B.A., J.D. [Beavers&B.]

Beavers, Walter L., (AV) '38 '72 C.296 B.S. L.836 J.D.
326 South Eugene Street, 27401
Telephone: 336-275-7601 Facsimile: 336-275-2009
Email: wbeavers@bellsouth.net
Practice Limited to Intellectual Property Law including Patent, Trademark, Copyright and Unfair Competition.
See Professional Biographies, GREENSBORO, NORTH CAROLINA

Beavers & Boydoh, LLP, (BV) .... 400 West Market Street, Suite 201
Bell, Haney H., III, (AV) '44 '74 C.893 B.A. L.966 J.D.
(adm. in VA; not adm. in NC) Assoc. Gen. Coun., Lorillard Tobacco Co.
Benjamin, William P., (BV) .... '53 '79 C.575 B.S, L.861 J.D. [Hunter,H.M.E.&B.]
Benson, Robert A., (BV) .... '50 '75 C&L.896 B.A., J.D. [Benson&M.]

Benson & Marshall, L.L.P., (BV)
221 Commerce Place, 27401
Telephone: 336-691-1044 Fax: 336-691-1428
URL: http://www.bensonandmarshall.com
Robert A. Benson; Michael T. Marshall.
General Civil Practice, Corporation, Commercial, Personal Injury and Insurance, Real Estate, Business Acquisitions, Probate, Wills and Estate Planning, Elder Law, Business, Contracts, Collections, Civil Litigation, Domestic Relations, Family Law, Divorce, Adoptions, Foreclosures, General Practice.
See Professional Biographies, GREENSBORO, NORTH CAROLINA

Bergman, Joan M. .... '72 '98 C.423 B.A. L.1338 J.D. [[A] Isaacson I.&S.]
Berkelhammer, Jonathan A., (AV) .... '55 '82 C.577 B.S. L.575 J.D. [Smith M.]

Berman, Jeffrey S., (BV) '51 '88 C.24 B.A. L.851 J.D.
216 Commerce Place, 27401
Telephone: 336-691-0054 Fax: 336-691-0530
Email: jberman@triad.rr.com URL: http://www.jeffreybermanlawfirm.com
Family Law, Divorce, Child Custody, Alimony, Criminal Law, Traffic Violations, Driving While Intoxicated, Civil Litigation, Personal Injury, Wills and Estates.
See Professional Biographies, GREENSBORO, NORTH CAROLINA

Bernhardt, Richmond G., Jr., (AV) .... '30 '57 C&L.575 A.B., J.D. 810 Dover Road
Berry, Frederick L., (AV) .... '56 '81 C&L.896 B.A., J.D. [Barron&B.]
Berry, M. Douglas, (AV) .... '48 '75 C&L.575 B.A., J.D. [Gabriel B.&W.]
Biesecker, Eric H., (BV) .... '— '96 C.896 B.A. L.575 J.D. [[A] Nexsen P.A.K.]
Biggers, Carole L. .... '59 '85 C.659 B.A. L.569 J.D. Novartis Crop Protection, Inc.
Binkley, Joan B. .... '65 '91 C&L.896 B.A., J.D. Off. of U.S. Atty.‡
Bishop, Diane P. .... '59 '85 C.880 B.A. L.575 J.D. 4000 Westmount Dr.‡
Bishop, Marc D., (AV) .... '59 '84 C&L.575 B.A., J.D. [Brooks,P.M.H.&L.] ⊙
Black, Janet Ward, (AV) .... '59 '85 C.198 B.A. L.228 J.D. [Donaldson&B.]
Black, Steven E., (BV) .... '71 '99 C.577 B.S. L.1187 J.D. [Forman R.B.]
Black, T. Keith, (BV) .... '59 '84 C&L.575 B.S., J.D. [Forman R.B.]
Blackwood, L. James, II, (AV) .... '49 '74 C.576 B.S. L.575 J.D. [Coggin,B.&B.]
Bloss, John F., (BV) .... '65 '93 C.945 B.S. L.1209 J.D. [Clark B.&W.]
Blust, John M., (BV) .... '54 '82 C&L.575 B.S., J.D. [[A] Ivey,M.G.&T.]
Boddie, John H., (BV) .... '52 '77 C.228 A.B. L.575 J.D. 403 E. Parkway
Bolick, H. Arthur, II, (BV) .... '69 '94 C&L.575 B.A., J.D. [Brooks,P.M.H.&L.]
Bolton, Phillip E., (AV) .... '59 '84 C&L.575 B.S., J.D. [Bolton]
Bolton Law Offices, P.A., (AV) .... 604 Green Valley Rd., Suite 406
Bonuomo, Kim R., (AV) .... '61 '88 C.692 B.A. L.893 J.D. [Morgenstern&B.]
Booker, Virginia G. .... '45 '75 C.577 B.A. L.575 J.D. Piedmont Triad Coun. of Gov.
Boone, Edwin E., Jr., (AV) .... '21 '49 C.575 B.S. L.228 LL.B. [[C] Turner&L.]
Booth, Joseph P., III, (BV) .... '69 '97 C.953 B.S. L.823 J.D. [Sharpless&S.]

Booth Harrington & Johns, LLP, (AV) [BB]
239 N. Edgeworth Street, P.O. Box 3585, 27402
Telephone: 336-275-9567 Fax: 336-373-8747
Email: kdm@nc-law.com URL: http://www.nc-law.com
Members of Firm: Roy M. Booth (1911-1995); E. Jackson Harrington, Jr.; A. Frank Johns; R. Harbour Partesotti.
State and Federal Civil Litigation, Personal Injury, Elder Law, Estate Planning, Trusts and Probate, Special Needs Trusts, Guardianships, Education and Disability Law.
See Professional Biographies, GREENSBORO, NORTH CAROLINA

Boring, Dennis Edgar, (BV) .... '46 '72 C&L.575 B.A., J.D. [D.E.Boring]
Boring, Dennis E., (BV) .... 318 S. Eugene St., Ste. 101
Boroughs, Lewis E. .... '20 '48 L.273 LL.B. 3518 Old Onslow Rd.‡
Borum, Howard L., (AV) .... '55 '80 C.576 B.S. L.896 J.D. [Carruthers&R.]
Bossong, Brooks F., (BV) .... '— '93 C.575 B.A. L.420 J.D. [[A] Nexsen P.A.K.]
Bost, Deborah J., (AV) .... '50 '79 C.576 B.A.E. L.896 J.D. [D.Bost]
Bost, Deborah, (AV) .... 3935 Starmount Dr.
Botwright, Richard M. .... '70 '04 C.652 B.S. L.575 J.D. [[A] Carruthers&R.]
Bowden, R. Steve, & Associates ..... '49 '79 C.896 B.A. L.1345 J.D. 806 Summit Avenue
Bowers, Deborah J., (BV) .... '52 '80 C.846 B.A. L.326 J.D. [Pinto C.K.&B.]
Bowman, Marianne L. .... '65 '93 C.577 B.S. L.1206 J.D. 3901 Gaston Rd.

Boyd, Martha P. '61 '86 C.16 B.A. L.902 J.D.
(adm. in AL; not adm. in NC) Assoc. Gen. Coun., Volvo GM Heavy Truck Corp.
Boyd, Walter Y., Jr., (AVⓉ) .... '56 '84 C.240 B.A. L.574 J.D. [[C] Smith M.] (Pat.)
Boydoh, Robert E., Jr., (BV) .... '65 '91 C.301 B.A. L.896 J.D. [Beavers&B.]
Brackett, Kevin R., Attorney at Law '62 '90 C.575 B.S. L.1228 J.D.
1101 W. Market St.
Brady, Stacey A. .... '72 '98 C.160 B.A. L.575 J.D. [[A] Schell B.A.A.&L.]
Brandon, H. Bruce .... '50 '85 C.1070 B.S. L.896 J.D. [[C] Younce,M.&M.]
Brannan, W. Scott, (BV) .... '53 '80 C&L.575 B.A., J.D. [Coggin,B.&B.]

Brannon Strickland, PLLC
(See Raleigh)

Brantley, F. Cooper, (AV) .... '— '73 C.198 B.A. L.575 J.D. [[C] Nexsen P.A.K.]
Bray, Doris R., (AV) .... '38 '66 C.392 A.B. L.575 LL.B. [Schell B.A.A.&L.]
Bray, Susan Elizabeth .... '61 '87 C.896 B.A. L.802 J.D. Dist. J.

Brevorka, Peter J., (AVⓉ) '43 '68 C.999 L.107 J.D.
1515 West Cornwallis Drive, Suite 101, 27408 ⊙
Telephone: 336-271-4016 Fax: 336-271-8448
Email: brevorka@bellsouth.net
(Board Certified Specialist in Estate Planning and Probate Law, North Carolina State Board of Legal Specialization).
Probate, Estate Planning, Trusts and Estates.
See Professional Biographies, GREENSBORO, NORTH CAROLINA

Brewington, Elizabeth S., (AV) ...... '65 '92 C.198 B.A. L.575 J.D. [Brooks,P.M.H.&L.]
Brinkey, Kathleen Murphy .... '63 '89 C.751 B.S. L.838 J.D. [[A] Stern,K.&W.]
Britt, C. Robin, Jr. .... '72 '01 C&L.577 B.A., J.D. [Brooks,P.M.H.&L.]
Brock, Florence C. .... '48 '91 C.823 B.A. L.896 J.D. [Bolton]
Brooks, Jean C., (AV) .... '47 '91 C.577 B.A. L.896 J.D. [Brooks,P.M.H.&L.]

Brooks, Pierce, McLendon, Humphrey & Leonard, L.L.P., (AV) [BB]
2000 Renaissance Plaza, 230 North Elm Street (27401), P.O. Box 26000, 27420-6000 ⊙
Telephone: 336-373-8850 Facsimile: 336-378-1001
URL: http://www.brookspierce.com
Aubrey L. Brooks (1872-1958); William H. Holderness (1904-1965); Lennox P. McLendon (1890-1968); Kenneth M. Brim (1898-1974); C. Theodore Leonard, Jr. (1929-1983); Claude C. Pierce (1913-1988); Thornton H. Brooks (1912-1988); G. Neil Daniels (1911-1997); Hubert Humphrey (1928-2003). Of Counsel: Henry E. Frye. Special Counsel: J. Lee Lloyd. Members of Firm: Lennox P. McLendon, Jr.; Edgar B. Fisher, Jr.; W. Erwin Fuller, Jr.; James T. Williams, Jr.; Wade H. Hargrove; M. Daniel McGinn; Michael D. Meeker; William G. McNairy; Edward C. Winslow, III; Howard L. Williams; George W. House; William P. H. Cary; Reid L. Phillips; Robert A. Singer; John H. Small (Board Certified Specialist in Business and Consumer Bankruptcy Law, North Carolina State Board of Legal Specialization); Randall A. Underwood; S. Leigh Rodenbough, IV; Mark J. Prak; Jill R. Wilson; Marc D. Bishop; Jim W. Phillips, Jr.; Mack Sperling; Jeffrey E. Oleynik; Mark Davidson; John W. Ormand, III; Robert J. King, III; V. Randall Tinsley; S. Kyle Woosley; Forrest W. Campbell, Jr.; Marcus W. Trathen; Jean C. Brooks; James C. Adams, II; Allison M. Grimm; Elizabeth S. Brewington; H. Arthur Bolick, II; J. Edwin Turlington; John M. Cross, Jr.; Jennifer K. Van Zant; David W. Sar; Brian J. McMillan; Natalie Kay Sanders; David Kushner; Derek J. Allen; Clinton R. Pinyan; Teresa DeLoatch Bryant; Coe W. Ramsey; Robert W. Saunders; Elizabeth V. LaFollette; Ginger S. Shields; Jennifer T. Harrod; Charles E. Coble; Charles F. Marshall, III; Patrick J. Johnson; John M. DeAngelis; Stephen G. Hartzell; Jessica M. Marlies; Andrew J. Haile; J. Benjamin Davis; Caroline Elizabeth Ritchie; Katherine A. Murphy; Sara R. Vizithum; C. Scott Meyers; John S. Buford; Nicole A. Crawford; Alexander Elkan; C. Robin Britt, Jr.; Katherine J. Clayton; Jennifer Ann Galassi; Kathleen A. Gleason; Janice L. Kopec; Susan M. Young; Darrell A. Fruth; Iain MacSween; Benjamin R. Norman; Elizabeth E. Spainhour.
General Practice in State and Federal Courts. Administrative, Antitrust, Banking, Bankruptcy, Bonds, Business Litigation, Communications and Media, Corporate, Corporate Finance, Energy, Environmental, Foundations, Insurance, Intellectual Property, Internet, Labor, Legislative, Mergers and Acquisitions, Probate, Public Utilities, Real Estate, Securities, Taxation, Telecommunications and Trade Associations Law.
Raleigh, North Carolina Office: 1600 Wachovia Capitol Center, 150 Fayetteville Street Mall, 27601, P.O. Box 1800, 27602-1800. Telephone: 919-839-0300. Facsimile: 919-839-0304.
See Professional Biographies, GREENSBORO, NORTH CAROLINA

Brotherton, Joseph F., (AV) .... '54 '79 C&L.575 A.B., J.D. [Brotherton F.Y.&W.]

Brotherton Ford Yeoman & Worley, PLLC, (AV) [BB]
127 North Greene Street, Fourth Floor, P.O. Box 21327, 27401
Telephone: 336-346-1116 Fax: 336-346-1117
URL: http://www.bfyandw.com
Joseph F. Brotherton; Robert A. Ford; Richard D. Yeoman; Demetrius L. Worley;—Steven P. Weaver; Marian Smith Kshetrapal.
Employment Litigation, Medical Malpractice, Commercial Claims, Business Torts, General Liability Claims, Insurance Defense, Workers Compensation, Insurance Coverage, Business Litigation, Commercial Litigation, Professional Malpractice.
See Professional Biographies, GREENSBORO, NORTH CAROLINA

Brown, Allen W. .... '12 '49 C&L.896 LL.B. 1101 N. Elm St.‡
Brown, Charles D. ... '25 '57 C.901 B.A. L.912 LL.B. Sr. Admn. Law J., Soc. Sec. Admn.
Brown, David L., (AV) .... '66 '92 C.577 B.A. L.575 J.D. [Pinto C.K.&B.]
Brown, Drew .... '76 '02 C.896 B.A. L.228 J.D. [[A] Smith M.]
Brown, Martha P., (BV) .... '68 '93 C.1030 B.A. L.575 J.D. [Pinto C.K.&B.]
Brown, T. W. .... '51 '89 C.318 B.A. L.575 J.D. 1003 Kemp Rd. W.
Browne, T. Marcus, III, (BV) '51 '80
C.232 B.A. L.574 J.D. [Browne,F.W.&W.] (⊙Creedmoor, Durham)
Browne, Flebotte, Wilson & Webb, PLLC, (BV)
503 West McGee Street (⊙Charlotte, Creedmoor, Durham, Fayetteville)
Bruce, Carole Watkins, (AV) .... '45 '80 C.10 B.S. L.896 J.D. [Smith M.]
Bryan, James W., (AV) .... '58 '89 C.575 B.A. L.896 J.D. [Nexsen P.A.K.]
Bryan, Tomi White .... '64 '89 C.576 B.A. L.896 J.D. 4230 Beechwood Drive
Bryant, Teresa DeLoatch, (BV) ...... '68 '93 C.576 B.A. L.228 J.D. [Brooks,P.M.H.&L.]
Buford, John S. .... '77 '02 C.893 B.A. L.902 J.D. [Brooks,P.M.H.&L.]
Bullock, Frank W., Jr. .... '38 '63 C&L.575 B.S., LL.B. U.S. Dist. J.
Bunton, Albert .... '21 '55 C.296 L.896 LL.B. 909 Meade Dr.‡
Burgin, William G., III, (BV) .... '52 '88 C.500 B.A. L.893 J.D. [Tuggle D.&M.]
Burnham, Margaret Shea, (AV) .... '— '83 C.886 B.A. L.896 J.D. [Nexsen P.A.K.]
Burns, Nancy K. .... '78 '05 C&L.896 B.A, J.D. [[A] MacCord M.P.]
Burton, Laura Deddish, (AV) .... '70 '97 C.228 B.A. L.893 J.D. [[A] Smith M.]
Burton, Walter K., (AV) .... '59 '84 C.437 B.A. L.365 J.D. [Burton&S.]
Burton, William E., III .... '68 '93 C.576 B.S.B.A. L.896 J.D. [Smith M.]

Burton & Sue, L.L.P., (AV) [BB]
419 North Elm Street, P.O. Box 20083, 27420
Telephone: 336-275-0512 Facsimile: 336-378-1390
Email: burtnsue@bellsouth.net
Members of Firm: Gary K. Sue; Walter K. Burton. Associates: Stephanie W. Anderson; Julie A. Connolly; Desiré E. Carter; C. Michael Day.
General Practice. Trials in all State and Federal Courts. Negligence, Automobile, Workers' Compensation, Medical, Legal and Professional Malpractice, Products Liability, Fire, Casualty, Surety and General Insurance Defense Practice.
See Professional Biographies, GREENSBORO, NORTH CAROLINA

Bynum, Harold N., (AV) .... '39 '69 C.198 B.S. L.575 J.D. [Smith M.]
Byrd, Brian W., (AV) .... '72 '97 C&L.893 B.A., J.D. [[A] Smith M.]

Cabbell, Diane Benedict '66 '93 C.813 B.A. L.477 J.D.
(adm. in MI; not adm. in NC) 1209 Lakewood Dr.
Cahoon, Marilyn, (BV) .... '46 '83 C.577 B.A. L.896 J.D. 100 S. Elm St., Ste. 300
Cahoon, Robert S., (AV) .... '15 '42 C&L.896 B.S., J.D. [C Cahoon&S.N.C.&L.]
Cahoon & Swisher, North, Cooke & Landreth, (AV) ......100 South Elm Street, Suite 300
Cain, Mark T. .... '61 '87 C.477 B.A. L.575 J.D. [Schell B.A.A.&L.]
Callahan, Megan E. .... '78 '04 C.576 B.A. L.1228 J.D. [A Moss,M.&H.]
Camp, Jacqueline E., (BV) .... '63 '88 C.893 B.A. L.1565 J.D. [C Womble C.S.&R.]
Camp, Robert H. .... '33 '65 C.524 B.S. L.446 J.D. Sr. Atty., Lucent Technologies, Inc.
Campbell, Forrest E., (BV) .... '29 '55 C.670 A.B. L.228 J.D. [Fisher P.]
Campbell, Forrest W., Jr., (AV) .... '55 '90 C.999 B.M. L.896 J.D. [Brooks,P.M.H.&L.]
Campbell, Frank A., (AV) .... '41 '68 C&L.228 B.A., J.D. 338 N. Elm St., Ste. 301
Cannon, Douglas, (AV) .... '46 '72 C.589 B.S. L.94 J.D. Asst. U.S. Atty.
Capone, Lucien, III '51 '77
C.576 B.A. L.896 J.D. Univ. Coun., Univ. of N.C. at Greensboro
Carbia, James E. '58 '83 C.258 B.S. L.362 J.D.
(adm. in FL; not adm. in NC) 321 S. Elm St.‡
Carlson, Charles E., Jr. '43 '67 C.222 B.A. L.705 J.D.
(adm. in NJ; not adm. in NC)
Vice President, General Counsel & Secretary, Marconi Commerce Systems Inc.
Carruthers, Thomas D., (BV) .... '60 '86 C.228 B.A. L.1228 J.D. [Henson&H.]

Carruthers & Roth, P.A., (AV) BB
235 North Edgeworth Street (27401), P.O. Box 540, 27402
Telephone: 336-379-8651 Fax: 336-273-7885
Email: rrk@crlaw.com URL: http://www.crlaw.com
Joseph T. Carruthers, Jr. (1906-1992); Charles E. Roth (1917-1992); Kenneth M. Greene; Richard L. Vanore; Kenneth R. Keller; L. Worth Holleman, Jr.; Jack B. Bayliss, Jr.; Howard L. Borum (Board Certified Specialist in Real Property Law-Business, Commercial and Industrial Transactions, North Carolina State Board of Legal Specialization); J. Scott Dillon; J. Stanley Atwell (Board Certified Specialist in Estate Planning and Probate Law, North Carolina State Board of Legal Specialization); Kenneth L. Jones; June L. Basden; Michael J. Allen; Gregory S. Williams (Board Certified Specialist in Estate Planning and Probate Law, North Carolina State Board of Legal Specialization); John M. Flynn; Keith A. Wood; Christopher J. Vaughn; Norman F. Klick, Jr.;—Carey A. McAlister; J. Patrick Haywood; Craig A. Taylor; C. Mark Stevenson; Elizabeth S. Jester; Richard M. Botwright. Of Counsel: William L. Tankersley, III.
Business and Civil Trial Practice. Trials in all State and Federal Courts. Administrative, Hearings, Arbitration, Business, Corporation, Partnership, Limited Liability Company, Secured Transactions, Banking, Pension, Profit-Sharing and Employee Benefits, Employment, International, Intellectual Property, Corporate Reorganization, Bankruptcy, Debtors' and Creditors' Rights, Estate Planning, Probate and Trust, Elder Law, Medicaid Planning, Real Estate, Administrative, Environmental, Taxation, Construction, Product Liability, Professional Liability, Negligence, Insurance, Personal Injury and Workers Compensation Law.
Representative Clients: AC Corp.; American South Construction Company; Branch Banking and Trust Company; Fleet Capital Corporation; FNB Southeast; GE Capital Commercial Services, Inc.; Glenwood Development Company; Medical Mutual Insurance Company; General Electric Capital Corporation; Penn-America Group, Inc.; Rentenbach Construction Co.
See Professional Biographies, GREENSBORO, NORTH CAROLINA

Carter, Desiré E. .... '77 '04 C.759 B.A. L.575 J.D. [A Burton&S.]
Carter, Robert Bryson .... '66 '94 C.797 B.A. L.575 J.D. 300 N. Greene St., Ste. 1900

Carter, Ewing, III, P.A.
(See High Point)

Cary, William P. H., (AV) .... '49 '76 C&L.893 B.A., J.D. [Brooks,P.M.H.&L.]
Cawn, Maurice A. .... '42 '73 C.1126 B.A. L.575 J.D. City Police Atty.
Chabon, Gregory M., (BV) .... '59 '96 C.160 B.S.M.E. L.259 J.D. [Womble C.S.&R.]

Chamberlin, Ames C., (AV) '67 '95 C.78 B.A. L.1228 J.D.
First Citizens Building Suite 430, 100 South Elm Street, 27401
Telephone: 336-272-6867 Fax: 336-272-7778
Email: ameschamberlin@msn.com URL: http://www.chamberlinlaw.com
(Board Certified Specialist in State Criminal Law and Federal Criminal Law, North Carolina State Board of Legal Specialization).
Drug Cases, Drunk Driving Cases, Homicide/Capital Cases, Traffic Cases, Federal Cases; Assault Cases, Expunctions, Probation Violation Cases, Fraud Cases; White Collar Crime, and Domestic Violence Cases.
See Professional Biographies, GREENSBORO, NORTH CAROLINA

Chamberlin, Andrew S., (AV) .... '64 '90 C&L.280 B.A., J.D. [Ellis&W.] (⊙Cary)
Chandler, Michael R., (CV) .... '59 '87 C&L.575 B.A., J.D. [Chandler,S.&Assoc.]
Chandler, Schiffman, & Associates, (BV) ....127 N. Greene St.
Chapman, Deborah C. ...... '68 '93 C.575 B.A. L.1228 J.D. 2311 W. Cone Blvd., Ste. 234
Chapman, Gerard M., (AV) .... '51 '78 C.575 B.A. L.280 J.D. [Chapman]
Chapman Law Firm, (AV) .... 403 N. Elm Street, Suite A
Chase, Margaret M. .... '76 '04 C.269 B.A. L.896 J.D. 125 S. Elm St., Ste. 400
Chastain, Peter F., (AV) .... '45 '74 C.790 A.B. L.575 J.D. [P.Chastain&Assoc.]

Chastain, Peter, & Associates, P.A., (AV) BB
3705 West Market Street, Suite C, 27403
Telephone: 336-297-0711 Fax: 336-297-4099
Email: pchastain@chastain-law.com URL: http://www.hudclosingagentnc.com
Peter F. Chastain;—Moshera Mohamed. Of Counsel: Charles B. Hahn (Board Certified Specialist in Estate Planning and Probate Law, North Carolina State Bar Board of Legal Specialization).
Real Estate, Commercial Law.
See Professional Biographies, GREENSBORO, NORTH CAROLINA

Chatlain, Dean F. '50 '75 C.611 B.A. L.880 J.D.
V.P. & Tax Coun., Jefferson-Pilot Corporation & Subsidiaries
Chilson, John A. .... '69 '99 C.871 B.S. L.477 J.D. [A Ellis&W.] ⊙
Christy, Barbara R., (AV) .... '58 '83 C.34 B.S. L.575 J.D. [Schell B.A.A.&L.]
Churchill, David L., (BV) .... '55 '80 C.970 B.A. L.896 J.D. Superior Ct. Probate J.

Chut, Mercedes Oglukian, (BV) '63 '90 C.198 B.A. L.228 J.D.
201 West Market Street, Suite 409, 27401
Telephone: 336-274-0352 Fax: 336-373-0947
Email: MercedesChut@aol.com
Civil Litigation in State and Federal Courts, Appellate Law, Bankruptcy, Business, Local Government, Employment (Employer), Divorce.
See Professional Biographies, GREENSBORO, NORTH CAROLINA

Clark, David M., (AV) .... '29 '58 C.896 A.B. L.569 LL.B. [Clark B.&W.]

Clark Bloss & Wall, PLLC, (AV) BB
600 Dixie Building, 125 South Elm Street, P.O. Box 1349, 27402
Telephone: 336-275-7275 Fax: 336-275-7276
Email: cbw@cbw-law.com
David M. Clark; John F. Bloss; Jonathan Wall.
General Practice. Trials in all State and Federal Courts. Commercial, Securities, Corporations, Personal Injury, Medical Malpractice, Professional Liability, Insurance, Contracts, Class Actions, and Probate Law.
Representative Clients: The Prudential Insurance Company of America (litigation); Johnson Controls, Inc.
Approved Attorneys for: Jefferson-Pilot Insurance Co.
See Professional Biographies, GREENSBORO, NORTH CAROLINA

Clarke, Brian S., (BV) .... '— '99 C.575 B.A. L.902 J.D. [A Nexsen P.A.K.]

Clawson, Thomas G. '50 '79 C.152 B.A. L.790 J.D.
(adm. in MD; not adm. in NC) 3100 N. Elm St.‡
Clayton, Katherine J. .... '49 '04 C.880 B.E. L.577 J.D. [Brooks,P.M.H.&L.] ⊙
Clendenin, Harry H., III, (AV) .... '45 '70 C.576 B.A. L.896 J.D. [Clifford C.O.&J.]
Clifford, Locke T., (AV) .... '42 '67 C&L.575 A.B., J.D. [Clifford C.O.&J.]

Clifford Clendenin O'Hale & Jones, LLP, (AV)
415 West Friendly Avenue, 27401
Telephone: 336-378-1212 Fax: 336-333-9820 Email: frontdesk@ccojcd.com URL: http://www.ccojcd.com
Email: coachclendenin@aol.com URL: http://www.greensborocriminallawyers.com
Members of Firm: Locke T. Clifford (Board Certified Specialist in Criminal Law, North Carolina State Board of Legal Specialization); Harry H. Clendenin, III; Robert O'Hale (Board Certified Specialist in Criminal Law, North Carolina State Board of Legal Specialization); Walter L. Jones.
General Civil and Criminal Practice. Trials in all State and Federal Courts. Personal Injury, Wrongful Death, Products Liability, Workers Compensation, Criminal Trials and Appeals, Federal Forfeitures, Grand Jury Practice, Criminal Law, Drugs and Narcotics, Fraud and Deceit, Money Laundering, white Collar Crime, Occupational Safety and Health, Workers Compensation, Premises Liability, Personal Injury, Criminal Appeals, Capital Offenses.
See Professional Biographies, GREENSBORO, NORTH CAROLINA

Coalter, J. Scott, (BV) .... '65 '96 C.846 B.A. L.1345 J.D. Asst. Pub. Def.
Coates, Paul D., (AV) .... '56 '81 C.577 B.S. L.575 J.D. [Pinto C.K.&B.]
Coble, Charles E. .... '72 '98 C.976 B.A. L.309 J.D. [Brooks,P.M.H.&L.] ⊙
Coble, J. Howard .... '31 '66 C.296 B.A. L.575 J.D. (MC)
Coggin, George W., (AV) .... '31 '59 C&L.575 A.B., LL.B. [C Coggin,B.&B.]
Coggin, Blackwood & Brannan, (AV) .... 108 Commerce Place
Cohen, Seth R., (AV) .... '57 '91 C.280 B.A. L.575 J.D. [Smith,J.R.&C.]
Coltrane, Charles W., (AV) .... '63 '91 C.575 B.S.B.A. L.896 J.D. [Coltrane A.&O.]
Coltrane, James E. .... '06 '29 C&L.228 B.A., M.A. 401 Mimosa Dr.‡

Coltrane Aycock & Overfield, PLLC, (AV)
106 North Elm Street, Suite 300, 27401
Telephone: 336-279-8707 Fax: 336-279-8849
Charles W. Coltrane (Board Certified Specialist in Family Law, North Carolina State Board of Legal Specialization); George W. (Trey) Aycock, III; John Covington Overfield.
Family Law, Civil Litigation, Equitable Distribution, Domestic Relations, Real Property, Creditors Rights, Collections, Corporate Law, Business Law, Trusts and Estates.
See Professional Biographies, GREENSBORO, NORTH CAROLINA

Comer, John F., (BV) .... '34 '58 C&L.575 A.B., LL.B. 119 N. Greene St.
Cone, Robert C., (AV) .... '52 '78 C&L.575 B.A., J.D. [Tuggle D.&M.]
Cone, Sally B. .... '54 '78 C&L.575 B.A., J.D. [A Stern,K.&W.]
Cone, Thomas E., (AV) .... '54 '81 C.31 B.A. L.228 J.D. [Ott C.&R.]
Conner, Richard D., (AV) .... '45 '73 C.296 A.B. L.577 J.D. [Conner G.S.]

Conner Gwyn Schenck PLLC, (AV)
306 E. Market Street, Suite One, 27401 ⊙
Mailing Address: P.O. Box 20744, Greensboro, NC 27420
Telephone: 336-691-9222 Fax: 336-691-9259
URL: http://www.cgspllc.com
Richard D. Conner (Resident); Allen Holt Gwyn (Resident); James S. Schenck, IV (Resident, Raleigh Office); C. Hamilton Jarrett, III (Resident, Raleigh Office); Paul E. Davis (Resident, Raleigh Office); Jay M. Wilkerson (Resident);—Edward N. Pollard (Resident). Of Counsel: Jeffrey B. Parsons (Resident, Raleigh Office).
Construction Law, Trials, Contract Law, Mediation, Arbitration.
Raleigh, North Carolina Office: 2626 Glenwood Avenue, Suite 180, 27608. Telephone: 919-789-9242. Fax: 919-789-9210.
See Professional Biographies, GREENSBORO, NORTH CAROLINA

Connolly, Julie A. .... '77 '04 C.575 B.A. L.259 J.D. [A Burton&S.]
Connor, William C., (AV) .... '54 '79 C.428 B.A. L.902 J.D. [Tuggle D.&M.]
Connors, Manning A., III, (BV) .... '70 '95 C.269 B.A. L.896 J.D. [Smith M.]

Constangy, Brooks & Smith, LLC
(See Winston-Salem, North Carolina)

Cooke, A. Wayland, (AV) .... '49 '76 C.575 A.B. L.574 J.D. [Cahoon&S.N.C.&L.]
Cooke, Barden W., (AV) .... '49 '76 C.198 B.A. L.896 J.D. [Cooke&C.]
Cooke, R. Cameron, (AV) .... '37 '64 C&L.575 B.S.B.A., LL.B. 100 Wedgedale Ave.
Cooke, William O., Jr., (AV) .... '52 '78 C.31 B.A. L.228 J.D. [Cooke&C.]
Cooke, William Owen, (AV) .... '17 '41 C.198 A.B. L.575 J.D. [Cooke&C.]

Cooke & Cooke, LLP, (AV)
Suite 301 First Citizens Bank Building, 100 South Elm Street, P.O. Box 187, 27402
Telephone: 336-272-4514 Facsimile: 336-272-4516
Members of Firm: Arthur O. Cooke (1916-1983); William Owen Cooke; Barden W. Cooke; William O. Cooke, Jr.
General Civil Practice, Trials in all State Courts, Business, Corporate, Limited Liability, Partnership Trust and Estates, Estate Planning and Administration, Wills and Probate, Real Estate, Eminent Domain, Landlord Tenant, Foreclosures.
Representative Clients: N. C. Grange Mutual Insurance Co.; Piedmont Triad Airport Authority; Brown-Gardiner Drug Co.; Engineered Plastics, Inc.; Strandberg Engineering Laboratories; ICBT, Inc.
See Professional Biographies, GREENSBORO, NORTH CAROLINA

Coughenour, Leigh .... '77 '04 C.577 B.S. L.896 J.D. [A Nexsen P.A.K.]
Coughlin, Richard A., (AV) .... '68 '93 C.269 B.A. L.280 J.D. [Smith M.]
Cowan, J. Donald, Jr., (AV) .... '43 '68 C&L.896 B.A., J.D. [Smith M.] (⊙Raleigh)
Crawford, Nicole A. .... '69 '03 C.1494 B.A. L.228 J.D. [Brooks,P.M.H.&L.]
Crews, Crystal Bowman .... '— '03 C.576 B.A. L.896 J.D. [A Smith M.]
Crihfield, Glenn Stevenson, (AV) '36 '63 C.228 A.B. L.575 LL.B.
[Douglas,R.H.C.&H.]
Cross, John M., Jr., (AV) .... '70 '95 C&L.575 B.S., J.D. [Brooks,P.M.H.&L.]
Crumley, Bobby J., (BV) .... '56 '80 C.34 B.A. L.896 J.D. [Crumley&Assoc.]

Crumley & Associates, (BV)
2400 Freeman Mill Road, Suite 200, 27406
Telephone: Toll Free: 800-288-1529 Fax: 336-333-9894
URL: http://www.crumleyandassociates.com
Bobby J. Crumley.
Workers' Compensation, Automobile Accidents, Nursing Home Abuse, Social Security Disability, Traumatic Brain Injury, Wrongful Death, Slip and Fall Injury, Drug Injury, Product Liability and Consumer Fraud.
See Professional Biographies, GREENSBORO, NORTH CAROLINA

Cummings, Candace S., (AV⊤) '47 '72
C.478 B.A. L.893 J.D. V.P. Admin. & Gen. Coun., VF Corp.
Curley, Sean B. .... '46 '81 C.914 B.A. L.575 J.D. Soc. Sec. Admn.

Dail & Linton
(See High Point)

Daisy, William L. .... '43 '68 C.198 B.A. L.575 J.D. Dist. J.
D'Amelio, Lawrence J., III, (BV) .... '61 '88 C.1228 B.A. L.851 J.D. [D'Amelio]
D'Amelio Law Firm, (BV) .... 203 Pomona Dr.
Daniel, Sharon C., (AV) '53 '78
C&L.575 A.B., J.D. Sr. V.P., North Carolina Trust Company

Daniels, Paul A., (CV) '64 '97 C.1309 B.S. L.1209 J.D.
101 South Elm Street, Suite 350
Dansby, David M., Jr., (CV) '39 '64
C&L.575 A.B., LL.B. Cor. Friendly Ave. & Morrow Blvd.

David, Cheryl K., (BV) '62 '87 C.575 B.S. L.1002 J.D.
5606 West Friendly Avenue, 27410
Telephone: 336-275-0804 Fax: 336-272-2441 URL: http://www.cherylldavid.com
Email: cheryl@cheryldavid.com URL: http://www.greensboroestateplanning.com
Estate Planning, Elder Law, Asset Protection, Trusts and Estates, Wills and Probate, Guardianship.
See Professional Biographies, GREENSBORO, NORTH CAROLINA

David, G. Phillip .... '59 '88 C.232 B.S.B.A. L.574 J.D. [David&Assoc.] ⊙

David and Associates, pllc
529 College Road, Suite G, 27410 ⊙
Telephone: 336-354-1040 Toll Free: 1-800-856-9927
Email: aeverhart@davidandassociates.com URL: http://www.wilmingtonpiattorneys.com
G. Phillip David.
Personal Injury, Medical Malpractice, Wrongful Death, Products Liability, Workers Compensation, Aviation, Airplane Crashes, Negligence, Class Actions, Maritime Accidents, Boating Accidents, Bicycle Accidents, Motorcycle Accidents, Truck Accidents, School Bus Accidents, Railroad Accidents, Dog Bites, Slip and Fall, Birth Trauma, Brain Injury, Spinal Injury, Head Injury, Catastrophic Injury, Vehicular Homicide, Personal Injury Mediation, Products Liability, Drug and Medical Device Litigation, Product Defects, Automobile Liability, Motorcycle Products Liability, Amusement Park Liability, Hotel Liability, Marina Liability, Sports Injury.
Jacksonville, North Carolina Office: 405-B Western Boulevard. 28546. Telephone: 910-219-4878.
Supply, North Carolina Office: Highway 17. 28462. Telephone: 910-754-8465.
Wallace, North Carolina Office: 107 North Norwood Street. 28466. Telephone: 910-285-8777.
Clinton, North Carolina Office: 610 Beaman Street. 28328. Telephone: 910-592-8400.
Winston-Salem, North Carolina Office: 1100-A South Stratford Road. 27103. Telephone: 336-354-1040.
Wilmington, North Carolina Office: 1516 Dawson Street. 28401. Telephone: 910-251-8088.
See Professional Biographies, GREENSBORO, NORTH CAROLINA

Davidson, Barney M. .... '57 '83 C.575 B.A. L.893 J.D. P.O. Box 26000
Davidson, Gerard H., Jr., (AV) .... '43 '68 C&L.896 B.A., J.D. [Smith M.]
Davidson, Mark, (AV) .... '57 '83 C.575 B.A. L.893 J.D. [Brooks,P.M.H.&L.]
Davidson, Teresa D., (BVⓉ) '59 '84 C.893 B.A. L.838 J.D.
(adm. in AZ; not adm. in NC)
Legal V.P. & Gen. Coun., Volvo Coml. Fin. LLC, The Americas
Davis, Herbert O., (AV) .... '35 '60 C.575 A.B. L.228 J.D. [Smith M.]
Davis, J. Benjamin, (BV) .... '71 '98 C.896 B.A. L.976 J.D. [Brooks,P.M.H.&L.] ⊙
Davis, Jeffery M. .... '— '03 C.160 B.A. L.575 J.D. [Ⓐ Evans]
Davis, Jeffrey M. .... '78 '03 C.160 B.A. L.575 J.D. [Hunter,H.M.E.&B.]
Davis, Joel W. .... '74 '00 C.1063 B.B.A. L.861 J.D. [Ⓐ Deuterman]
Davis, Kearns .... '69 '95 C.198 B.A. L.577 J.D. U.S. Dept. of Justice
Davis, Lindsay Reeves, Jr. .... '46 '71 C.198 A.B. L.575 J.D. Supr. Ct. J.
Davis, Ronald R., (AVⓉ) '58 '87
C.198 B.A. L.575 J.D. [Womble C.S.&R.] (⊙Winston-Salem)
Davis, W. B. Rodman, (AV) .... '— '78 C.575 B.A. L.1365 J.D. [Nexsen P.A.K.]
Day, C. Michael, (BV) .... '61 '91 C.575 B.A. L.896 J.D. [Ⓐ Burton&S.]
DeAngelis, John M., (BV) .... '68 '98 C.309 A.B. L.575 J.D. [Brooks,P.M.H.&L.]
Decker, Rachel Scott, (BV) .... '71 '95 C.575 B.A. L.790 J.D. [Ⓐ Donaldson&B.]
DeNicola, George Randall .... '48 '76 C.838 B.A. L.608 J.D. [G.R.DeNicola]
DeNicola, G. Randall .... 1400 Battleground Ave., Ste. 209
Dennis, Paul M., Jr., (AV) .... '50 '75 C.228 B.A. L.575 J.D. [Tuggle D.&M.]
Dettor, Douglas P., (BV) .... '26 '50 C.296 L.692 J.D. 316 S. Eugene St.
Deuterman, Daniel L., (AV) .... '65 '91 C&L.575 B.A., J.D. [Deuterman]

Deuterman Law Group, The, P.A., (AV)
101 South Elm Street, Suite 170, 27401
Telephone: Toll Free: 866-373-1130 Fax: 336-373-1466 URL: http://www.lawyers.com/deutermanlaw
Email: info@deutermanlaw.com URL: http://www.deutermanlaw.com
Daniel L. Deuterman (Board Certified Specialist in Workers' Compensation, North Carolina State Board of Legal Specialization);—Joel W. Davis.
Languages: Spanish and Russian.
Workers Compensation, Auto Accidents, Social Security Disability, Wrongful Death, Nursing Home Neglect, Slip and Fall, Products Liability.
See Professional Biographies, GREENSBORO, NORTH CAROLINA

DeVaney, M. Jay, (AV) .... '— '71 C&L.896 B.A., J.D. [Nexsen P.A.K.]
Dewey, James M. .... '— '02 C.896 B.A. L.577 J.D. [Ⓐ Smith M.]
Diamond, Patrick L. .... '66 '02 C.820 B.A. L.896 J.D. [Ⓐ R.I.Shope]
Dillon, J. Scott, (AV) .... '56 '83 C.576 B.S. L.575 J.D. [Carruthers&R.]
D'Lugin, Jeri Kay .... '55 '80 C.861 B.A. L.823 J.D. 201 Stauton Dr.
Donaldson, Arthur J., (AV) .... '38 '65 C&L.128 B.A., J.D. [Donaldson&B.]

Donaldson & Black, P.A., (AV) ⊞
208 West Wendover Avenue, 27401-1307
Telephone: 336-273-3812 N.C. Toll Free: 800-531-9191 Fax: 336-379-9415
Email: postmaster@donaldsonandblack.com URL: http://www.donaldsonandblack.com
Arthur J. Donaldson; Janet Ward Black;—Rachel Scott Decker; Phyllis J. Lile-King; S. Camille Payton; John T. O'Neal.
Personal Injury, Wrongful Death, Products Liability, Worker's Compensation, Professional Malpractice, Nursing Home Neglect and Abuse, Inadequate Security, Eminent Domain, Qui Tam Fraud, Lead Poisoning and Domestic.
See Professional Biographies, GREENSBORO, NORTH CAROLINA

Donato, Anthony P. .... '69 '95 C.62 B.A. L.117 J.D. 2016 New Garden Rd., Ste. A
Donnell, Jack L., (AV) .... '22 '47 C&L.896 B.S., LL.B. 300 N. Greene St.
Dotson, Marshall Fulton, III, (BV) .... '62 '89 C.576 B.A. L.896 J.D. [M.F.Dotson,III]
Dotson, Marshall F., III, (BV) .... 127 N. Greene St., Ste. 500
Douglas, R. D., Jr., (AV) .... '12 '36 C&L.276 Ph.B., J.D. [Ⓒ Douglas,R.H.C.&H.]
Douglas, Robert D., III, (AV) .... '43 '68 C&L.575 A.B., J.D. [Douglas,R.H.C.&H.]

Douglas, Ravenel, Hardy, Crihfield & Hoyle, L.L.P., (AV)
110 Commerce Place, P.O. Box 419, 27402-0419
Telephone: 336-378-0580 Fax: 336-378-0886
URL: http://www.drhch.com
Members of Firm: R. D. Douglas, Sr. (1875-1960); Thomas P. Ravenel (1916-1992); Glenn Stevenson Crihfield; Robert D. Douglas, III; William R. Hoyle; Amanda L. Fields. Of Counsel: R. D. Douglas, Jr.; John W. Hardy; Robert P. Worth.
General Civil Practice. Trials in all State Courts. Corporation, Real Estate, Estate Planning, Probate, Family, Child Support, Child Custody, Divorce, Arbitrations, Personal Injury, and Mediation Law.
See Professional Biographies, GREENSBORO, NORTH CAROLINA

Dowda, D. Lamar, (AV) .... '29 '60 C&L.896 B.A., LL.B. 48 Buckboard Lane‡
Downs, Patrick, (BV) .... '55 '95 C.907 B.S. L.988 J.D. [Ⓐ R.I.Shope]
Doyle, Connie P. .... '63 '90 C.232 B.A. L.790 J.D. Estate Tax Atty., IRS
Driver, Michael B. .... '66 '94 C.228 A.B. L.896 J.D. Off. of Pub. Def.
Duggins, J. Nathan, III, (BV) .... '69 '95 C.575 B.A. L.896 J.D. [Tuggle D.&M.]
Duggins, James N., Jr., (AV) .... '43 '68 C&L.575 B.S., J.D. [Tuggle D.&M.]
Duncan, Alan W., (AV) .... '54 '79 C.198 A.B. L.880 J.D. [Smith M.]
Duncan, Thomas C., (AV) .... '45 '69 C&L.575 A.B., J.D. [Hill,E.D.J.&B.]

Duquette, Dennis W. '47 '74 C.475 B.A. L.276 J.D.
Tax Coun., Burlington Industries, Inc.
Eagles, Catherine C. .... '58 '82 C.806 B.A. L.273 J.D. Supr. Ct. J.
Eagles, William A., (AV) .... '48 '79 C.576 B.S. L.896 J.D. [Hunter,H.M.E.&B.]
Earp, Stephen W., (AV) .... '52 '77 C.198 B.A. L.893 J.D. [Smith M.]
Edmisten, Veronica .... '76 '03 C.575 B.A. L.574 J.D. Judicial Center
Edwards, Mona Gillis '56 '84 C.893 B.A. L.902 J.D.
(adm. in VA; not adm. in NC) Dep. City Mgr.
Egerton, Lawrence, Jr., (BV) .... '31 '56 C&L.575 B.S., J.D. [Egerton&Assoc.]
Egerton & Associates, P.A., (BV) .... 222 Commerce Place
Eggleston, Donald P., (BV) .... '49 '74 C&L.575 A.B., J.D. [D.P.Eggleston]
Eggleston, Donald P., P.A., (BV) .... 305 Blandwood Ave., 2nd Fl.
Elam, John C., (BV) .... '53 '81 C.575 B.A. L.896 J.D. [Hunter,H.M.E.&B.]
Elkan, Alexander .... '69 '03 C.865 B.S. L.577 J.D. [Brooks,P.M.H.&L.]

Ellis & Winters LLP, (AV)
100 N. Greene Street, Suite 102, 27401 ⊙
Telephone: 336-217-4193 Facsimile: 336-217-4198
URL: http://www.elliswinters.com
Andrew S. Chamberlin; Curtis J. Shipley. Associate: John A. Chilson.
Trial and Appellate Practice in all State and Federal Courts. Commercial Litigation, Administrative Litigation, Medical Malpractice, Products Liability, Antitrust, Corporate, Real Estate and Finance.
Cary, North Carolina Office: 1100 Crescent Green, Suite 200, 27511-8105. Telephone: 919-865-7000. Facsimile: 919-865-7010.
Raleigh, North Carolina Office: P.O. Box 33550, 27636. Telephone: 919-865-7000. Facsimile: 919-865-7010.
See Professional Biographies, GREENSBORO, NORTH CAROLINA

Ellison Law Firm, The
(See Winston-Salem)

Elrod Lawing & Sharpless, P.A.
(See Sharpless & Stavola, P.A.)

Emken, Robert A., Jr., (BV) '63 '88
C.896 B.A. L.575 J.D. Gen. Coun. & Secy., Guilford Mills, Inc.
Englar, John D., (AV) '47 '73 C&L.228 B.A., J.D.
(adm. in NY; not adm. in NC)
Sr. V.P., Corp. Develop. & Law & Dir., Burlington Industries, Inc.
Ennis, Stephanie Renee .... '— '04 C&L.577 B.A., J.D. [Ⓐ Nexsen P.A.K.]
Ennis, Trudy A., (AV) .... '— '87 C.925 B.A. L.575 J.D. [Nexsen P.A.K.]
Enochs, Herman G., Jr., (AV) .... '29 '56 C.296 A.B. L.575 LL.B. [Ⓒ Ott C.&R.]
Enochs, Wendy M. .... '66 '91 C.577 L.1345 J.D. Dist. J.

Ernest, Jodi A., Law Office of, (CV) '70 '96 C.164 B.A. L.61 J.D.
3703-D W. Market Street, 27403
Mailing Address: P.O. Box 1738, Greensboro, NC 27402-1738
Telephone: 336-315-2266 Fax: 336-315-2257
Email: earnestlaw@hotmail.com URL: http://www.ernestlaw.com
Real Estate, Residential, Buying or Selling Home, Commercial Real Estate, Conveyancing, Living Wills, Wills.
See Professional Biographies, GREENSBORO, NORTH CAROLINA

Erwin, Martin N., (AV) .... '38 '67 C.896 B.A. L.575 J.D. [Smith M.]
Eudy, Clinton, Jr., (AV) .... '43 '71 C&L.575 B.A., J.D. 400 W. Market St., Suite 312‡
Euliss, Wade C. .... '26 '54 C.240 A.B. L.607 LL.B. 829 Southeastern Bldg.
Evans, G. Marlin, (AV) .... '36 '62 C&L.575 B.S.B.A., J.D. [Hill,E.D.J.&B.] ‡
Evans, Robert C., (BVⓉ) '54 '80 C.176 B.A. L.446 J.D.
(adm. in LA; not adm. in NC) [Evans] ⊙

Evans & Co., (BVⓉ)
101 West Friendly Avenue, Suite 500, 27401 ⊙
Telephone: 336-275-1400 Fax: 336-275-1401
URL: http://www.evanslawfirm.com
Member of Firm: Robert C. Evans (Not admitted in NC). Associate: Jeffery M. Davis.
General Insurance Defense, Admiralty, Aviation, Comprehensive General Liability, Cargo, Construction, Energy, Environmental, Toxic Torts, Errors and Omissions, Excess and Umbrella, Motor Carriers, Railroad, Insurance Coverage, Oil and Gas, Products Liability, Professional Liability, Directors and Officers Liability, Property and Casualty.
New Orleans, Louisiana Office: 629 Cherokee Street, 70118. Telephone: 504-522-1400. Fax: 504-522-1401.
Durango, Colorado Office: 823 East 4th Avenue, 81301. Telephone: 970-375-9300. Fax: 970-375-9301.
Houston, Texas Office: 13700 Veterans Memorial Drive, Suite 250, 77014. Telephone: 713+522-1400. Fax: 713-522-1401.
See Professional Biographies, GREENSBORO, NORTH CAROLINA

Evenson, Peter O., Sr., (AV) .... '50 '77 C.945 A.B. L.896 J.D. [Tuggle D.&M.]
Everhardt, Jerry R., (AV) .... '48 '74 C.575 A.B. L.145 J.D. P.O. Box 4065
Ewalt, Robert M., Jr. .... '39 '65 C&L.665 B.S., LL.B. 2411 Veranda Lane
Exum, James G., Jr., (AV) .... '35 '60 C.575 A.B. L.569 LL.B. [Ⓒ Smith M.]
Falk, Harry S. '61 '87 C.910 B.S.B.A. L.1009 J.D.
(adm. in NY; not adm. in NC) Pres., SSA Southeast
Falk, Herbert S., Jr., (AV) .... '31 '56 C.902 A.B. L.575 J.D. [Turner&L.]
Falk, Orren B., (BV) .... '58 '87 C.75 B.A. L.1009 J.D. 111 Arden Place
Farabow, Stephanie T., (BV) '65 '91 C.198 B.A. L.896 J.D.
Asst. V.P. & Assoc. Coun., Jefferson-Pilot Corp.& Subsidiaries (Legal Department)
Farland, Joy Parks, (BV) .... '54 '78 C&L.575 B.A., J.D. [J.P.Farland]
Farland, Joy P., Attorney at Law, (BV) .... 419 N. Edgeworth St., Ste. 200
Farran, Jeffrey P., (BV) .... '45 '73 C.880 B.A. L.575 J.D. [Ling&F.]
Farrior, James R., Jr. .... '56 '81 C.1378 B.A. L.575 J.D. [J.R.Farrior]
Farrior, J. Rufus, P.A. .... 400 W. Fisher Ave.
Faucher, Emily C. .... '78 '03 C.500 B.A. L.902 J.D. Asst. Dist. Atty.
Faucher, James R. .... '— '03 C.896 B.A. L.902 J.D. [Ⓐ Smith M.]
Felt, James S. .... '67 '93 C.1365 B.A. L.276 J.D. [Purrington M.]
Ferguson, Alan E., (AV) .... '55 '83 C&L.575 B.A., J.D. [Fisher P.]
Ferguson, Blake Walter '52 '83 C.907 B.A.Ed. L.494 J.D.
(adm. in WA; not adm. in NC) 320 Federal Place
Ferguson, Nancy Short, (AV) ..... '56 '83 C&L.575 B.S., J.D. V.P., Chicago Title Ins. Co.
Feuchs-Marker, Marilyn, (AV) .... '53 '88 C.446 B.A. L.426 J.D. [Smith M.]
Fields, Amanda L., (BV) .... '65 '98 C.577 B.A. L.575 J.D. [Douglas,R.H.C.&H.]
The Firm At Fisher Park, (AV) .... 314 North Church Street
Fish, Konrad K., (BV) .... '35 '59 C&L.228 A.B., LL.B. [Ⓐ Fisher P.]
Fisher, Edgar B., Jr., (AV) .... '35 '61 C&L.228 A.B., LL.B. [Brooks,P.M.H.&L.]
Flebotte, Daniel R., (BV) '52 '81
C.228 B.A. L.910 J.D. [Browne,F.W.&W.] (⊙Creedmoor, Durham)
Floyd, Jack W., (AV) .... '34 '61 C&L.575 B.S., J.D. 125 S. Elm St., Ste. 300
Flynn, John M., (AV) .... '64 '90 C&L.896 B.A., J.D. [Carruthers&R.]
Folmar, David P., Jr. .... '63 '88 C.125 B.A. L.472 J.D. Asst. U.S. Atty.
Forbes, Jamie Lisa .... '55 '01 C.174 B.A. L.575 J.D. [Ⓐ Barron&B.]
Ford, Robert A., (AV) .... '55 '84 C.902 B.A. L.896 J.D. [Brotherton F.Y.&W.]
Forman, Jacqueline .... '48 '77 C.107 B.A. L.1009 J.D. 7 Gwyn Lane‡
Forman, Richard C., (AV) .... '29 '53 C.280 A.B. L.245 J.D. [Ⓒ Forman R.B.]

Forman, Scott .... '46 '71 C.107 B.A. L.94 J.D. 7 Gwyn Lane

Forman Rossabi Black, P.A., (AV)
3623 North Elm Street, Suite 200, P.O. Box 41027, 27455-2586
Telephone: 336-378-1899; 1-800-805-0425 Fax: 336-378-1850
Email: firm@frb-law.com URL: http://www.frb-law.com
Amiel J. Rossabi; T. Keith Black; James H. Slaughter; Steven E. Black; William F. Patterson, Jr.;—Emily Jeffords Meister; Barbara Lynn Stewart; Theodora A. Vaporis; Jason M. Goins; Erinn McKee Hannigan. Of Counsel: Richard C. Forman; Paul E. Marth.
Appellate Practice, Business Law, Commercial Law, Community Association Law, Construction Law, Contracts, Corporate Law, Debtor and Creditor, Family Law, Insurance, Labor and Employment, Litigation, Parliamentary Law, Personal Injury, Real Estate, Taxation, Trusts and Estates, Trial Practice in all State and Federal Courts.
References: Wachovia Bank & Trust Co., N.A.; Triad Bank.
See Professional Biographies, GREENSBORO, NORTH CAROLINA

Foskett, Steven E., (BV) .... '57 '87 C.575 B.A. L.574 J.D. 1111 West Friendly Avenue
Foster, Thomas G., Jr. .... '46 '74 C.893 B.A. L.421 J.D. Dist. J.
Fountain, Jennifer N., (BV) .... '72 '99 C.280 B.A. L.692 J.D. [Isaacson I.&S.]
Foust, Richard Russell .... '70 '00 C&L.896 B.A., J.D. [Stamey,F.&D.]
Fox, Andrea Harris, (BV) '65 '90 C.790 B.S. L.575 J.D.
Asst. V.P. & Assoc. Coun., Jefferson-Pilot Corporation & Subsidiaries
Fox, Michael S., (BV) .... '63 '89 C.34 B.A. L.575 J.D. [Tuggle D.&M.]
Fox, Pamela Sarsfield, (AV) .... '62 '88 C.893 B.A. L.902 J.D. VP, Wachovia Bank, N.A.
Fox, Steven B., (BV) .... '62 '87 C.20 B.A. L.896 J.D. 101 South Elm Street, Suite 350
Fradenburg, Susan McNear, (BV) .... '68 '93 C.378 B.A. L.896 J.D. [Smith M.]
Franklin, Robert A., (AV) .... '42 '72 C.575 A.B. L.896 J.D. [Frazier&F.]

Frassineti and Glover, (AV)
Suite 403, 201 West Market Street, P.O. Drawer 1799, 27402
Telephone: 336-273-9794 Fax: 336-273-1570
Email: dmglover@bellsouth.net
Jordan J. Frassineti (1929-1996); Durant M. Glover.
Business Litigation, Bankruptcy, Collections, Incorporation, Probate and Real Estate.
See Professional Biographies, GREENSBORO, NORTH CAROLINA

Frazier, Cyrus Clifford, Jr., (AV) .... '23 '51 C&L.575 A.B., LL.B. [Frazier&F.]

Frazier & Frazier, LLP, (AV)
Suite 206 Southeastern Building, 102 North Elm Street, P.O. Drawer 1559, 27402
Telephone: 336-378-9411 Telecopier: 336-274-7358
URL: http://www.frazier-lawnc.com
Members of Firm: C. Clifford Frazier (1884-1967); Robert H. Frazier (1899-1978); Cyrus Clifford Frazier, Jr.; Robert A. Franklin; Torin Lane Fury; G. Clark Hering, IV.
General Practice. Trials in all State and Federal Courts, Corporate and Commercial Transactions, Estate Planning and Administration, Civil Litigation, Personal Injury and Insurance Litigation, Taxation and Real Estate Development, Commercial and Residential Transactions.
Representative Clients: Montgomery Ward Co.; NCNB National Bank of North Carolina (Trust Dept.); Wachovia Bank & Trust Co., N.A. (Trust Dept.); State Farm Mutual Automobile Insurance Co.; Integon Corp.; Foremost Insurance Co.; Neese Country Sausage, Inc.; Unifi, Inc.
See Professional Biographies, GREENSBORO, NORTH CAROLINA

Freedman, Brian M., (AV) .... '64 '89 C.228 B.A. L.896 J.D. [Ogletree,D.N.S.&S.]
Freeman, Christina N. .... '— '98 C.577 B.S.W. L.574 J.D. [A Schell B.A.A.&L.]
Friend, Robert H., (BV) .... '47 '78 C.233 B.S. L.896 J.D. 301 N. Elm St.
Fruth, Darrell A. .... '72 '01 C.453 S.B. L.976 J.D. [Brooks,P.M.H.&L.] (Pat.)
Frye, Henry E. .... '32 '59 C.1378 B.S. L.575 J.D. [G Brooks,P.M.H.&L.] ⊙
Fuller, W. Erwin, Jr., (AV) .... '38 '64 C.575 B.S. L.228 LL.B. [Brooks,P.M.H.&L.]
Fury, Torin Lane, (BV) .... '64 '91 C.1228 J.D. L.576 B.A. [Frazier&F.]
Gabriel, Richard W., (AV) .... '49 '75 C.228 A.B. L.896 J.D. [Gabriel B.&W.]

Gabriel Berry & Weston, L.L.P., (AV)
214 Commerce Place, 27401
Telephone: 336-275-9381 Fax: 336-275-7864 URL: http://www.gabrielberrywestonlaw.com
URL: http://www.lawyers.com/gbwlaw
Members of Firm: Richard W. Gabriel; M. Douglas Berry (Board Certified Specialist in Family Law, North Carolina State Board of Legal Specialization); Robert A. Wells.
General Civil Practice in all Courts. Insurance, Real Estate, Civil Litigation, Personal Injury, Family, Divorce, Custody, Taxation, Probate, Estate Planning Corporation Law.
See Professional Biographies, GREENSBORO, NORTH CAROLINA

Galassi, Jennifer Ann .... '79 '04 C&L.577 B.A., J.D. [Brooks,P.M.H.&L.]
Galiger, Scott G., (CV) .... '69 '94 C.874 B.A. L.245 J.D. [A Schlosser&P.]
Galloway, Edward H., (BV) ....'51 '76 C.31 B.A. L.575 J.D. 201 W. Market St., Rm. 409
Galloway, Hunter H., III, (AV) .... '45 '72 C&L.575 B.S., J.D. 201 W. Market St.
Gardner, T. Alfred ..... '38 '66 C.404 B.A. L.896 J.D. Spec. Coun., Chicago Title Ins. Co.
Garrison, Lisa Frye, (BV) .... '69 '94 C&L.575 B.A., J.D. [Smith M.]
Gasparovic, Ladd S. .... '76 '01 C.953 B.A. L.1228 J.D. Dist. Atty.'s Off.
Gatling, Kimberly Bullock .... '74 '00 C.1378 B.S. L.273 J.D. [A Smith M.] (Pat.)
Gatton, Edwin R., (AV) .... '47 '73 C.34 B.S. L.896 J.D. [Ivey,M.G.&T.]
Gauffreau, Stuart C., (BV) .... '— '96 C.228 B.A. L.575 J.D. [A Nexsen P.A.K.]
Gayle, Scott C., (AV) .... '51 '77 C.575 A.B. L.228 J.D. [Tuggle D.&M.]
Gaylord, T.M. (Mark), Jr., (AV) .... '54 '79 C&L.575 B.S., J.D. [Tate,G.L.P.&W.]
Gerhardt, Maureen Breen, (AV) .... '56 '84 C.893 B.S.N. L.880 J.D. [A Stern,K.&W.]
Gertz, Gregory M. .... '56 '85 C.494 B.A. L.300 J.D. UnitedHealthcare
Gervasi, Jay A., Jr., (BV) .... '58 '86 C.228 B.S. L.880 J.D. [J.Gervasi]

Gervasi, Jay, P.A., (BV)
910 North Elm Street, 27401
Telephone: 336-574-0174 Fax: 336-574-2541
Email: jay@gervasilaw.com URL: http://www.jgervasilaw.com
Jay A. Gervasi, Jr. (Board Certified, Specialist in Worker's Compensation Law, North Carolina State Bar, Board of Legal Specialization).
Workers Compensation, Personal Injury.
See Professional Biographies, GREENSBORO, NORTH CAROLINA

Gifford, William H., Jr. .... '55 '80 C.659 B.A. L.575 J.D. Oakwood Homes Corp.
Giles, H. M., Jr., (AV) .... '36 '61 C&L.575 B.S., LL.B. [Tate,G.L.P.&W.] ‡
Gill, Mary E. .... '58 '85 C.801 B.A. L.424 J.D. Coun., Lucent Technologies, Inc.
Gillis, Eileen King .... '69 '94 C.770 B.S. L.228 J.D. [A Smith M.]
Glasgow, JiNan '68 '99 C.576 B.S. L.575 J.D.
[G MacCord M.P.] (See Pat. Sect.) (⊙Raleigh)
Gleason, Kathleen A. .... '64 '03 C.957 B.S. L.574 J.D. [Brooks,P.M.H.&L.]
Glover, Durant M., (AV) .... '51 '76 C.228 A.B. L.575 J.D. [Frassineti&G.]
Godwin, Michael H., (AV) .... '49 '74 C&L.575 B.A., J.D. [Schell B.A.A.&L.]
Goins, Jason M. .... '78 '03 C&L.896 B.S., J.D. [A Forman R.B.]
Goodman, Gary B. .... '46 '71 C.608 B.A. L.930 J.D. Asst. Dist. Atty.
Gordon, Geo. W., (CV) .... '24 '54 C&L.575 A.B., LL.B. 201 W. Market St.
Gordon, Harry G. .... '45 '72 C&L.893 B.A., J.D. [Gordon]
Gordon Law Offices .... 400 W. Market St.
Gorham, F. Kevin, (BV) .... '58 '84 C.34 B.S. L.365 J.D. [Maddox&G.]
Gorham, Gregory L., (BV) .... '56 '82 C.228 A.B. L.200 J.D. 119 North Greene Street
Gorrell, Ralph W., (BV) .... '51 '88 C.198 B.A. L.575 J.D. [A Pell&P.]
Goulder, Gerald P. .... '53 '79 C.608 B.A. L.910 J.D. [Goulder I.]

Goulder Immigration Law Firm
3200 Northline Avenue, Suite 130, 27408
Telephone: 336-808-1119 Fax: 336-294-3063 Toll Free Voice/Fax: 1-866-878-4727
Email: Goulder@gouldervisa.com URL: http://www.gouldervisa.com
Gerald P. Goulder.
Immigration and Naturalization, Visas, U.S. Citizenship, Student Visa, HI-B, L Visas, E Visas, Employment Visa, J-Visa, Fiancée Visas, all Family-Based Immigration Visas and Adjustments of Status.
See Professional Biographies, GREENSBORO, NORTH CAROLINA

Grace Holton Tisdale & Clifton P.A.
(See Winston-Salem)

Graham, Edward N. .... '40 '70 C.575 A.B. L.309 J.D. Off. of Hearings & Appeals
Graham, Garland G., (BV) .... '75 '99 C&L.260 B.A., J.D. [A Schell B.A.A.&L.]
Gram, Joseph P., (BV) .... '70 '95 C&L.575 B.A., J.D. [Hill,E.D.J.&B.]
Granowsky, Richard T. .... '64 '99 C.34 B.A. L.575 J.D. [Hill,E.D.J.&B.]
Gray, Angela Newell, (BV) .... '63 '94 C.575 B.A. L.574 J.D. 108 N. Elm St.
Gray, Jeanette F. .... '74 '99 C.575 B.A. L.1228 J.D. [K.G.Sumner]
Gray, Mark V.L. .... '56 '82 C.232 B.A. L.575 J.D. [Gray]
Gray, Richard L., (AV) '47 '73 C.576 B.S. L.575 J.D.
Gen. Coun. & Sen. V.P., United Guaranty Corp.
Gray, Robert E., III .... '61 '04 C.316 B.A. L.577 J.D. [A Hill,E.D.J.&B.]

Gray Legal Group
108 N. Elm Street, 27401
Telephone: 336-691-9200 Fax: 336-691-0888
Email: markvlgray@gnjblaw.com URL: http://www.graylegalgroup.com
Mark V.L. Gray.
Workers Compensation, Injuries, Wrongful Death, Life and Disability Insurance Claims, Auto Accidents.
See Professional Biographies, GREENSBORO, NORTH CAROLINA

Greene, Kenneth M., (AV) .... '45 '70 C.902 B.S. L.893 J.D. [Carruthers&R.]
Greene, Richard M., (BV) .... '48 '75 C&L.575 B.S., J.D. 230 N. Spring St.
Greeson, Harold F., (AV) .... '41 '66 C&L.896 B.A., LL.B [Greeson]
Greeson Law Offices, (AV) .... 1515 West Cornwallas Suite 203
Grewal, Dalmir S. .... '66 '98 C.575 B.A. L.496 J.D. [A J.B.Weeks]
Griffin, Mark F., (BV) .....'61 '86 C.1128 B.A. L.896 J.D. Gen.Coun., USA Staffing, Inc.
Griffin, Robert G., (BV) .... '62 '89 C&L.575 B.A., J.D. Coun., Koury Corp.
Grimes, Elizabeth G., (AV) .... '64 '89 C.575 B.A. L.896 J.D. [Grimes&G.N.C.]
Grimes, L. Charles, (BV) .... '62 '89 C&L.575 B.S., J.D. [Grimes&G.N.C.]

Grimes & Grimes of North Carolina, P.A., (AV) BB
307 South Swing Road, 27409
Mailing Address: P.O. Box 8009, Greensboro, NC 27419
Telephone: 336-232-5921 Fax: 336-217-4357
L. Charles Grimes; Elizabeth G. Grimes.
Entertainment Law, Entertainment Litigation, Business and Commercial Litigation, Administrative Agency Practice, Construction Law and Collections and Business Law.
See Professional Biographies, GREENSBORO, NORTH CAROLINA

Grimm, Allison M., (AV) .... '63 '90 C.575 B.S. L.896 J.D. [Brooks,P.M.H.&L.]
Grossi, Charles '26 '53 C&L.280 LL.B.
(adm. in GA; not adm. in NC) 2700 Cottage Pl.‡
Gullick, Lynn G., (AV) .... '53 '86 C.10 B.S. L.245 J.D. P.O. Box 386
Gumbiner, Kenneth J., (AV) .... '46 '71 C.679 B.S.I.E. L.339 J.D. [Tuggle D.&M.]
Guynn, Elizabeth C. '61 '89 C.896 B.A. L.945 J.D.
(adm. in VA; not adm. in NC) 3520 Drawbridge Pky‡
Gwyn, Allen Holt, (AV) .... '49 '76 C.575 A.B. L.896 J.D. [Conner G.S.]
Hackworth, Roydera Dolores .... '59 '97 C.94 B.A. L.574 J.D. P.O. Box 18300
Hagan, Charles T., III, (AV) .... '— '77 C.575 B.A. L.896 J.D. [Nexsen P.A.K.]
Hagan, Charles T., Jr., (AV) .... '— '36 C.575 L.893 J.D. [G Nexsen P.A.K.] ‡
Hagan, Kay Ruthven ...... '53 '78 C.259 B.S. L.896 J.D. V.P., NationsBank of N.C., N.A.
Hahn, Charles B., (AV) '47 '71
C.247 B.A. L.861 J.D. [G P.Chastain&Assoc.] (⊙Greensboro)
Hahn, Charles B., (AV) .... '47 '71 C.247 B.A. L.861 J.D. [Hahn&C.] (⊙Greensboro)

Hahn & Chastain, P.A., (AV) BB
3705 West Market Street, Suite C, 27403
Telephone: 336-297-0530
URL: http://www.hahnchastainlaw.com
Charles B. Hahn (Board Certified Specialist in Estate Planning and Probate Law, North Carolina State Bar Board of Legal Specialization); Peter F. Chastain (Also Member, Peter F. Chastain & Associates, P.A.).
Corporate Law, Taxation, Estate Planning, Wills, Probate, Elder Law, Real Estate, Trusts and Estates, Business Law, Commercial Law.
See Professional Biographies, GREENSBORO, NORTH CAROLINA

Haile, Andrew J. .... '72 '00 C.198 B.S. L.813 J.D. [Brooks,P.M.H.&L.]
Hairston, Sandra J., (AV) .... '58 '87 C.1128 B.A. L.574 J.D. Off. of U.S. Atty.
Hale, J. Scott, (BV) .... '— '96 C.575 B.A. L.469 J.D. [Nexsen P.A.K.]
Haley, Daniel W. .... '35 '61 C&L.575 B.S., J.D. Pres., Daniel Haley & Co.
Halkiotis, Christon S. ...... '78 '04 C.705 B.A. L.574 J.D. Asst. Dist. Atty., Dist. Atty. Off.
Hall, Elizabeth Davis .... '— '02 C.198 B.A. L.893 J.D. [A Nexsen P.A.K.]
Hall, Harrison M. .... '— '02 C.198 A.B. L.896 J.D. [A Purrington M.]
Hall, Richard D., Jr. .... '41 '69 C.10 B.S. L.469 LL.B. [R.D.Hall,Jr.]
Hall, William F., (AV) '62 '87 C.198 B.A. L.575 J.D.
V.P. & Assoc. Gen. Coun., United Guaranty Corp.
Hall, Richard D., Jr., P.A., (AV) .... 221 Commerce Pl., Ste. A
Halpern, Ronald Barry ......'49 '74 C.1046 B.A. L.117 J.D. Central Carolina Legal Servs.
Halsey, Hardin G., (AV) '55 '83
C.886 B.S. L.383 J.D. [Womble C.S.&R.] (⊙Winston-Salem)
Hamilton, D. Ross, Jr., (BV) .... '69 '94 C.228 A.B. L.896 J.D. [G Womble C.S.&R.]
Hamilton, Melanie Martin, (BV) .... '68 '93 C.27 B.A. L.896 J.D. [Ott C.&R.]
Hamlet, Fred T., (AV) '47 '73 C.575 A.B. L.309 J.D.
300 North Greene Street, Suite 2175 (⊙Wilmington)

Handler & Brown, P.L.L.C.
(See Winston-Salem)

Hanks, Ann E.
(See High Point)

Hannah, Walter L., (AV) .... '— '53 C.886 L.902 J.D. [G Nexsen P.A.K.]
Hannigan, Erinn McKee .... '74 '02 C.63 B.A. L.424 J.D. [A Forman R.B.]
Hansen, Gregg A., (BV) '46 '71 C.945 A.B. L.575 J.D.
V.P. & Assoc. Gen. Coun., Jefferson-Pilot Corporation & Subsidiaries
Hanson, Randall A., (BV) .... '60 '85 C&L.575 A.B., J.D. [Womble C.S.&R.]
Hardin, Eric W., (BV) .... '69 '96 C.951 B.A. L.575 J.D. [Tuggle D.&M.]
Hardison, Kenneth L., (BV) .... '56 '82 C&L.1228 B.S., J.D. [Hardison&L.] ⊙
Hardison & Leone, L.L.P., (AV)
7B Corporate Center Court (⊙Charlotte, Dunn, Fayetteville, Raleigh, Southern Pines, NC; Myrtle Beach, SC)

Hardy, John W., (AV) ....'25 '52 C&L.896 B.S., LL.B. [Ⓒ Douglas,R.H.C.&H.]
Hargrove, Wade H., (AV) ....'40 '65 C&L.575 A.B., J.D. [Brooks,P.M.H.&L.] ⊙
Harkavy, Jonathan R., (AV) ....'43 '69 C.378 A.B. L.178 LL.B. [Patterson H.]
Harkavy, Nahomi, (AV) ....'45 '72 C.66 B.A. L.178 J.D. [Ⓒ Patterson H.]
Harrell, L. Cooper ....'76 '01 C&L.577 B.A., J.D. [Ⓐ Smith M.]
Harrelson, Wallace C., (AV) ......'36 '63 C&L.228 A.B., LL.B. Pub. Def., 18th Jud. Dist.
Harrington, E. Jackson, Jr., (AV) ....'44 '69 C&L.575 A.B., J.D. [Booth H.&J.]
Harrington, Lucy '64 '94 C.162 B.A. L.352 J.D.
(adm. in IA; not adm. in NC) [Ⓐ Woodruff]
Harris, Margaret A. ....'16 '40 C&L.228 A.B., LL.B. 305 Victoria St.‡
Harris, Terrill Johnson, (AV) ....'65 '90 C.896 B.A. L.228 J.D. [Smith M.]

Harrison, A. Wayne, (AV) '42 '69 C&L.575 LL.B.
101 S. Elm Street, Suite 230, 27401
Telephone: 336-378-0616 Fax: 336-378-1172
Email: wayno@triad.rr.com URL: http://www.lawyers.com/harrisenlaw
Criminal Law, Constitutional Law, Civil Forfeiture, Criminal Forfeiture, Criminal Appeals, White Collar Crimes.
See Professional Biographies, GREENSBORO, NORTH CAROLINA

Harrod, Jennifer T. ....'68 '97 C.575 B.A. L.228 J.D. [Brooks,P.M.H.&L.]
Harshman, Beth B. ....'63 '91 C.886 B.S. L.896 J.D. 3825 Pinetop Rd.
Hartwell, Linda J., Attorney at Law .....'59 '89 C.1086 B.S. L.1228 J.D. 9C Terrace Way
Hartzell, Stephen G. ....'69 '00 C.326 B.A. L.577 J.D. [Brooks,P.M.H.&L.] ⊙
Haskins, Donald B. ....'34 '59 C.296 A.B. L.896 LL.B. 3000 W. Market St.
Hassell, A. Robinson ....'61 '86 C&L.575 B.A., J.D. Dist. J.
Hassell, Mary E. ....'58 '84 C.575 B.A. L.896 J.D. Univ. of NC-Greensboro
Hassenfelt, Stephen C., (AV) '50 '76 C.575 B.S. L.896 J.D.
Chmn. & CEO, North Carolina Trust Company
Hatfield, Cynthia A., (BV) ....'63 '88 C.197 B.A. L.575 J.D. 219 N.Washington St.
Hayes, Deborah K. '61 '86 C&L.838 B.S., J.D.
Assoc. Gen. Coun., Volvo Commercial Finance

Hayes, Mark E. '58 '86 C.240 B.A. L.469 J.D.
101 South Elm Street, Suite 142, 27401
Telephone: 336-333-2900 Fax: 336-333-2995
URL: http://www.markhayeslaw.com
Criminal Law. Trials and Appeals in all State Courts. DUI/DWI, Traffic Violations, Drug Crimes, Felonies, Misdemeanors, Sexual Assault, White Collar Crime.
See Professional Biographies, GREENSBORO, NORTH CAROLINA

Haynsworth Baldwin Johnson & Greaves LLC
(See Ogletree, Deakins, Nash, Smoak & Stewart, P.C.)

Haywood, J. Patrick ....'72 '01 C.576 B.A. L.575 J.D. [Ⓐ Carruthers&R.]
Head, Dora L. ....'42 '68 C.851 B.S. L.734 J.D. 1700 Natchez Trace
Heberle, Douglas M., (BV) ....'70 '97 C.602 B.A. L.575 J.D. 5503 Copper Hill Court
Heckman, R. Harper, (AV) ....'— '91 C&L.575 B.A., J.D. [Nexsen P.A.K.]
Hedges, Steven D., (AV) ....'— '82 C.886 B.Arch. L.896 J.D. [Nexsen P.A.K.]
Henderson, Fredk. G., Jr. ....'13 '38 C&L.575 A.B., LL.B. 1501 Garland Dr.‡
Henson, Perry C., Jr., (AV) ....'52 '77 C&L.575 A.B., J.D. [Henson&H.]

Henson & Henson, L.L.P., (AV) BB
Suite 600, The Piedmont Building, 114 North Elm Street, 27401
Mailing Address: P.O. Box 3525, Greensboro, NC 27402-3525
Telephone: 336-275-0587 Facsimile: 336-273-2585
Email: phenson@hensonlawyers.com URL: http://www.lawyers.com/hensonandhenson
Perry C. Henson (1922-2003); Perry C. Henson, Jr.; Thomas D. Carruthers; Karen Strom Talley.
General Civil Practice, Trials and Appeals in all State and Federal Courts, Personal Injury, Automobile, Workers' Compensation, Wrongful Death, Medical Malpractice, Legal Malpractice, Insurance, Professional Malpractice, Products Liability, Fire, ERISA and Insurance Defense.
Representative Clients: Allgood Construction Co., Inc.; Atlantic Mutual Ins. Company; Canal Ins. Company; Carolina Bank Holdings, Inc.; Discovery Ins. Co.; Epes Transport System, Inc.; GEICO Direct Insurance Company; Kmart Corporation Old Dominion Freight Line, Inc.; Lawyers Mutual Liability Ins. Co.; N.C. Farm Bureau Mutual Ins. Co.
See Professional Biographies, GREENSBORO, NORTH CAROLINA

Hering, G. Clark, IV, (BV) ....'62 '92 C.896 B.A. L.1017 J.D. [Frazier&F.]
Herman, Victoria M. ....'54 '79 C&L.575 B.A., J.D. 611 Wicker St.★
Heyl, Jonathan ....'65 '98 C.232 B.A. L.575 J.D. [Ⓐ Smith M.]
Hicks, Daniel K., (AV) ....'— '97 C.92 B.A. L.575 J.D. [Ⓒ Nexsen P.A.K.]
Hicks, Jack B., (AV) ....'57 '87 C.893 B.S.M.E. L.846 J.D. [Womble C.S.&R.] (Pat.)
Hicks, Richard H., Jr., (AV) ....'45 '69 C.198 A.B. L.575 J.D. [Hicks M.N.]
Hicks McDonald Noecker, LLP, (AV) ....100 S. Elm St., Ste. 510
Higgins, Gregory T., (BV) ....'— '00 C.260 B.A. L.896 J.D. [Ⓐ Nexsen P.A.K.]
Higgins, John T., Jr., (AV) ....'47 '72 C.659 B.A. L.575 J.D. [Hunter,H.M.E.&B.]
Hill, Karl N., Jr., (AV) ....'30 '58 C&L.575 B.S., J.D. [Hill,E.D.J.&B.]
Hill, William L., (BV) ....'65 '94 C.1128 B.S. L.421 J.D. [Ⓐ Moss,M.&H.]

Hill, Evans, Duncan, Jordan & Beatty, (AV) BB
A Professional Limited Liability Company
1400 Renaissance Plaza, 230 North Elm Street, P.O. Box 989, 27402
Telephone: 336-379-1390 Fax: 336-379-1198
Email: generalmail@hillevans.com URL: http://www.hillevans.com
Members of Firm: Welch Jordan (1912-1976); William D. Caffrey (1928-1991); Karl N. Hill, Jr.; Thomas C. Duncan; William Welch Jordan (Board Certified Specialist in Family Law, North Carolina State Board of Legal Specialization); Joseph R. Beatty; R. Thompson Wright; Everett B. Saslow, Jr.; Polly D. Sizemore; Michele G. Smith; Joseph P. Gram; Elaine Hedrick Ashley; Richard T. Granowsky; G. Marlin Evans (Retired). Associates: Martha R. Sacrinty; Robert E. Gray, III; Shawn C. Troxler.
General Civil Practice. Banking, Bankruptcy, Construction, Corporation, Mediation, Employment, Environmental, Estate Planning, Family, Insurance, Labor, Personal Injury, Product Liability, Real Estate, Surety, Taxation, Trade Regulation, Wills and Trusts, Workers Compensation Law, Municipal and Police Liability, Criminal and Traffic.
Representative Clients: City of Greensboro; Ford Motor Credit Co.; Gilbarco Inc.; Jefferson-Pilot Corp.; Rheem Manufacturing Co.; Overnight Transportation Co.
See Professional Biographies, GREENSBORO, NORTH CAROLINA

Hinds, Elizabeth A., (CV) ....'65 '93 C.320 B.A. L.192 J.D. [Ⓐ Egerton&Assoc.]
Hinnant, Patrice A. ....'53 '78 C.811 B.A. L.574 J.D. Dist. Ct.
Hobgood, Harry L. '46 '72 C.976 B.A. L.228 J.D.
U.S. Atty. Off., U.S. Dep. of U.S. Dept. of Jus.
Hodgman, Heather Paige ....'79 '04 C.228 A.B. L.945 J.D. [Hodgman]
Hodgman, Robert S., (AV) ....'47 '72 C.228 A.B. L.575 J.D. [Hodgman]

Hodgman Law Firm, The, (AV)
First Citizens Bank Building, 100 South Elm Street, Suite 514, P.O. Box 3245, 27402
Telephone: 336-373-0934 Fax: 336-373-0160 URL: http://www.hodgmanlaw.com
Email: rshodgman@aol.com URL: http://www.lawyers.com/hodgmanlawfirm
Robert S. Hodgman (Board Certified Specialist in Workers Compensation Law, North Carolina State Board of Legal Specialization); Heather Paige Hodgman.
Language: Spanish.
Workers Compensation, Personal Injury, Automobile Accidents and Injuries, Products Liability, Social Security.
See Professional Biographies, GREENSBORO, NORTH CAROLINA

Hoffman, James Allen, (BVⓉ) '56 '86 C.870 B.S. L.945 J.D.
(adm. in VA; not adm. in NC) V.P. & Assoc. Gen. Coun., Litig., Jefferson-Pilot Corporation and Subsidiaries (Legal Department)
Holland, Gregory G., (AV) ....'67 '92 C.1365 B.A. L.280 J.D. [Smith M.]
Holleman, L. Worth, Jr., (AV) ....'48 '74 C&L.575 B.S., J.D. [Carruthers&R.]
Holloway, James C. '53 '78
C.960 B.S. L.801 J.D. Admin. Law J., N.C. Employ. Sec. Comm.
Holt, Michael D., (AV) ....'52 '86 C.576 B.A. L.575 J.D. 101 South Elm Street, Suite 350
Horne, Maurice Westbrook ....'38 '66 C&L.896 B.A., J.D. Admn. Law J.
Horsley, William F., (AV) ....'47 '72 C.272 B.A. L.896 J.D. [W.F.Horsley]

Horsley, William F., P.A., (AV) BB
500-D State Street, 27405
Telephone: 336-691-0077; 1-800-953-2542 Fax: 336-691-8083 URL: http://www.lawyers.com/horsleylawfirm
Email: wfh@horsleylawfirm.com URL: http://www.horsleylawfirm.com
William F. Horsley.
Personal Injury, Product Liability, Auto Accidents, Wrongful Death, Nursing Home Negligence, Medical Malpractice, Premises Liability, Inadequate Security, Land Condemnation.
See Professional Biographies, GREENSBORO, NORTH CAROLINA

House, George W., (AV) ....'46 '73 C.198 B.A. L.893 J.D. [Brooks,P.M.H.&L.] ⊙
House, Sara S. '48 '74 C.276 B.S.F.S. L.893 J.D.
Gen. Coun., T.H.E.M. International, Inc.
Howard, D. Christopher '71 '97 C.1369 B.B.A. L.1509 J.D.
In-house Coun., Syngenta Crop Protection, Inc.
Howell, Sue ....'50 '97 C.575 B.A. L.574 J.D. P.O. Box 13770
Hoyle, William R., (AV) ....'41 '66 C&L.575 A.B. [Douglas,R.H.C.&H.]
Hubbard, Gerald J. '49 '80 C.1044 B.S. L.1202 J.D.
(adm. in MA; not adm. in NC) 111F Shorelake Dr.‡
Hubbard, Maury A., III ....'62 '87 C&L.575 B.A., J.D. P.O. Box 10769
Hunt, Susan L., (BV) ....'64 '94 C.577 B.A. L.896 J.D. [S.L.Hunt]
Hunt, Susan L., PC, (BV) ....501 Simpson Street
Hunter, Bynum M., (AV) ....'25 '49 C&L.575 A.B., LL.B. [Ⓒ Smith M.]
Hunter, Robert N., Jr., (AV) ....'47 '73 C&L.575 B.A., J.D. [Hunter,H.M.E.&B.]

Hunter, Higgins, Miles, Elam & Benjamin, PLLC, (AV)
101 West Friendly Avenue, Suite 500, 27401
Mailing Address: P.O. Box 20570, Greensboro, NC 27420
Telephone: 336-273-1600 Fax: 336-274-4650 URL: http://www.greensborolaw.com
Email: hjeb@greensborolaw.com URL: http://www.lawyers.com/hunterhiggins
John T. Higgins, Jr.; Robert N. Hunter, Jr.; James W. Miles, Jr.; Rayford K. Adams III (Board Certified Specialist in Business and Consumer Bankruptcy Law, North Carolina State Bar Board of Legal Specialization); William P. Benjamin; William A. Eagles; John C. Elam; Robert G. McIver; Gilbert J. Andia, Jr.; Ronda L. Lowe; Brian Tomlin; Jeffrey M. Davis. Associates: Jennifer F. Adams; Lisa Johnson-Tonkins; Amanda M. Patty. Of Counsel: James N. Rogers (Not admitted in NC).
General Business, Commercial, Real Estate, Arbitration and Mediation, Securities, Election Law, Business Bankruptcy and Workouts, Business and Civil Litigation, Appeals, Personal Injury, Wrongful Death, Medical Malpractice, Criminal Defense, Family Law, Insurance, Construction, Employment, Education, Environmental Law, Tax, Estate Planning, Estate Administration, Intellectual Property Law.
See Professional Biographies, GREENSBORO, NORTH CAROLINA

Hurley, Marshall R., (BV) ....'55 '81 C.575 B.A. L.896 J.D. [M.Hurley]
Hurley, Marshall, PLLC, (BV) ....2400 Freeman Mill Road
Hurst, Margaret A., (AVⓉ) '57 '83 C.290 L.896 J.D.
(adm. in FL; not adm. in NC) 7300 W. Friendly Ave.
Iddings, Jeffrey S., Attorney at Law, (BV) '66 '91
C.575 B.A. L.280 J.D. 338 N. Elm St, Ste. 201
Iorio, John S., (BV) ....'60 '85 C.446 B.A. L.896 J.D. [J.Iorio]
Iorio, John, (BV) ....102 N. Elm St., Ste. 304
Isaac, Anne A., (BV) ....'— '83 C.555 M.A. L.896 J.D. 437 W. Friendly Ave.
Isaacson, Henry H., (AV) ....'33 '58 C&L.575 A.B., J.D. [Isaacson I.&S.]
Isaacson, Marc L., (AV) ....'56 '83 C.575 B.A. L.896 J.D. [Isaacson I.&S.]

Isaacson Isaacson & Sheridan, LLP, (AV) BB
Suite 400 Bank of America Building, 101 West Friendly Avenue, P.O. Box 1888, 27402
Telephone: 336-275-7626 Fax: 336-273-7293
URL: http://www.lawyers.com/iislaw
Members of Firm: Henry H. Isaacson; Marc L. Isaacson; Desmond G. Sheridan; Jennifer N. Fountain. Associates: Debbi L. Aberman; Joan M. Bergman.
General Practice in State and Federal Courts. Business & Corporate, Real Estate (Residential and Commercial), Municipal/Zoning, Commercial, Tax, Probate and International Law.
See Professional Biographies, GREENSBORO, NORTH CAROLINA

Ivey, Charles M., III, (AV) ....'53 '78 C.575 A.B. L.896 J.D. [Ivey,M.G.&T.]

Ivey, McClellan, Gatton & Talcott, L.L.P., (AV) BB
121 South Elm Street, P.O. Box 3324, 27402
Telephone: 336-274-4658 Telefax: 336-274-4540
Members of Firm: Charles M. Ivey, Jr. (1914-1993); Charles M. Ivey, III (Board Certified Specialist in Business and Consumer Bankruptcy Law, North Carolina State Bar Board of Legal Specialization); Robert L. McClellan; Edwin R. Gatton; James K. Talcott (Board Certified Specialist in Business and Consumer Bankruptcy Law, North Carolina State Bar Board of Legal Specialization); Dirk W. Siegmund (Board Certified Specialist in Business and Consumer Bankruptcy Law, North Carolina State Board of Legal Specialization); Eric A. Richardson. Associates: John M. Blust; Mary Beth B. Swecker; J. Marshall Shelton.
General Practice in all State and Federal Courts. Litigation, Insurance, Tax, Bankruptcy, Commercial, Corporation, Real Estate, Domestic, Criminal and Probate Law.
Representative Clients: Laurel Hill Paper Company; Alexander Community Hospital, Inc.; Rite Industries, Inc.; Mercedes-Benz Credit Corporation; Sedgewick Industries, Inc.; Greensboro Academy; Oak Ridge Military Academy; Computer Net Inc.
Approved Attorneys For: Jefferson-Pilot Title Insurance Co.; Lawyers Title Insurance Corp.
See Professional Biographies, GREENSBORO, NORTH CAROLINA

Jackson, A. Scott, (AV) ....'— '88 C.437 B.B.A. L.575 J.D. [Nexsen P.A.K.]
Jacobs, Bradley L., (AV) ....'61 '86 C.346 B.S. L.383 J.D. [Tuggle D.&M.]
Jacobson, Denis E., (AV) ....'57 '86 C.475 B.A. L.896 J.D. [Tuggle D.&M.]
James, J. David, (AV) ....'44 '71 C.198 A.B. L.575 J.D. [Smith,J.R.&C.]
Jeffries, James H., III ....'34 '62 C&L.383 A.B., J.D. 3019 Lake Forest Dr.
Jennings, Neill A., Jr. ....'41 '67 C.301 A.B. L.575 J.D. [N.A.Jennings,Jr.]
Jennings, Neill A., Jr., P.A. ....102 N. Elm Street
Jester, Elizabeth S. ....'73 '03 C.575 B.A. L.896 J.D. [Ⓐ Carruthers&R.]
Jimison, Holly Hendrix ....'53 '79 C.362 B.A. L.260 J.D. 1105 Hammel Rd.
Johns, A. Frank, (AV) ....'45 '77 C&L.259 B.S., J.D. [Booth H.&J.]
Johnson, Kenneth M., (AV) ....'59 '84 C.577 B.A. L.273 J.D. [Tuggle D.&M.]
Johnson, Neale T., (BV) ....'66 '98 C.790 B.A. L.893 J.D. [Ⓐ Smith M.]
Johnson, Patrick J. ....'69 '94 C&L.893 B.A., J.D. [Brooks,P.M.H.&L.] ⊙
Johnson, Ronald P., (AV) ....'49 '74 C&L.790 B.A., J.D. [Johnson,P.K.&M.]

Johnson, Peddrick, Kantlehner & McDonald, P.L.L.C., (AV)
440 West Market Street, Suite 300, 27401
Telephone: 336-574-9720 Telefax: 336-574-9734
URL: http://www.lawyers.com/jpmck

(This Listing Continued)

Johnson, Peddrick, Kantlehner & McDonald, P.L.L.C. (Continued)

Ronald P. Johnson (Board Certified Specialist in Estate Planning and Probate Law, North Carolina Board of Legal Specialization).; Martha Taylor Peddrick (Board Certified Specialist in Estate Planning and Probate Law, North Carolina Board of Legal Specialization); Margaret Robison Kantlehner; Davis McDonald; David B. McLean.
Estate Planning, Estate and Trust Administration, Probate, Corporate and Business Law, Tax Services, Elder Law, Guardianship.
See Professional Biographies, GREENSBORO, NORTH CAROLINA

Johnson-Tonkins, Lisa ....'72 '03 C.1378 B.A. L.574 J.D. [Ⓐ Hunter,H.M.E.&B.]
Johnston, David G. '54 '79 C.1365 B.S. L.245 J.D.
(adm. in GA; not adm. in NC) BDO Seidman
Johnston, Eugene ....'36 '61 C&L.896 B.A., J.D. 338 N. Greene St.
Johnston, J. Phillips L. ....'— '63 C.228 A.B. L.575 LL.B. [Ⓒ Nexsen P.A.K.]
Johnston, J. Reed, Jr., (AV) ....'44 '68 C&L.575 A.B., J.D. [Tuggle D.&M.]
Johnston, Sharon A., (BV) ....'63 '89 C.575 B.A. L.1228 J.D. Employ. Sec. Comm.
Johnston, Sharon M. ....'44 '70 C&L.575 B.A., J.D. 3014 Redford Dr.
Jones, Jeffrey A. ....'64 '92 C.859 B.S. L.276 J.D. [Purrington M.]
Jones, Kenneth L., (AV) ....'60 '85 C&L.575 B.S., J.D. [Carruthers&R.]
Jones, R. Kody ....'77 '05 C.575 B.S. L.1218 J.D. [Ⓐ MacCord M.P.] (See Pat. Sect.)
Jones, R. Turner '10 '33 C.682 L.893 LL.B.
(adm. in VA; not adm. in NC) 6100 W. Friendly Ave.‡
Jones, Walter L., (AV) ....'64 '89 C.576 B.A. L.1228 J.D. [Clifford C.O.&J.]
Jordan, William Welch, (AV) ....'45 '70 C&L.575 A.B., J.D. [Hill,E.D.J.&B.]
Joseph, Michael F., (BV) .....'50 '75 C&L.896 B.A., J.D. Asst. U.S. Atty, U.S. Atty. Off.
Joseph, R. David ....'62 '88 C&L.896 B.A., J.D. 104 W. Northwood St.
Joyce, Melissa J. ....'55 '83 C.1154 B.A. L.838 J.D. 3 Lake Forest Ct.
Kahn, Benjamin A., (AV) ....'— '93 C&L.575 B.A., J.D. [Nexsen P.A.K.]
Kahn, Joseph M. ....'— '00 C.910 B.A. L.790 J.D. [Ⓐ Nexsen P.A.K.]
Kantlehner, Margaret Robison, (AV) '59 '84
C.197 A.B. L.1228 J.D. [Johnson,P.K.&M.]
Kapanka, Richard A., (AV) '46 '73 C.475 B.S. L.477 J.D.
(adm. in CT; not adm. in NC)
V.P. & Assoc. Gen. Coun., Jefferson-Pilot Corporation & Subsidiaries
Kaplan, Barbara J. '65 '92 C.309 A.B. L.569 J.D.
(adm. in NY; not adm. in NC) Sr. Coun., VF Corp.
Kaye, Lori-Nan '56 '79 C.787 B.A. L.276 J.D.
(adm. in DC; not adm. in NC) P.O. Box 10391
Keever, J. Thomas, Jr., (BV) ....'48 '73 C.576 B.A. L.575 J.D. [Ⓐ Fisher P.]
Keller, Kenneth R., (AV) ....'46 '74 C.576 B.A. L.575 J.D. [Carruthers&R.]
Kelly, Michael E., (AV) ....'49 '74 C&L.575 A.B., J.D. [Smith M.]
Kidwell, Robert D. ....'73 '98 C.835 B.B.A. L.896 J.D. [Ⓐ Smith M.]

Kimel, Horace M., Jr., (AV) '48 '73 C&L.575 B.A., J.D.
BB&T Building, 201 W. Market Street, Suite 409, 27401
Telephone: 336-389-0830 Fax: 336-373-0947
Criminal, Traffic Offenses, Traffic Violations, Drug Offense, Homicide and Serious Offenses Against Persons. Personal Injury, Felonies, Misdemeanors, DWI, DMV Hearings, Driving While License Revoked.
See Professional Biographies, GREENSBORO, NORTH CAROLINA

Kincaid, Amy H. ....'70 '98 C.160 B.S. L.575 J.D. [Ⓐ Smith M.]
King, Bailey ....'80 '05 C.968 B.A. L.575 J.D. [Ⓐ Smith M.]
King, Robert J., III, (AV) ....'62 '88 C.1128 B.A. L.896 J.D. [Brooks,P.M.H.&L.]
King, W. Winburne, III, (AV) ....'— '75 C&L.575 B.A., J.D. [Ⓒ Nexsen P.A.K.]
Kirkman, John W., Jr., (BV) ....'50 '77 C.316 B.A. L.574 J.D. 127 N. Greene St.
Kiser, John Craig ....'76 '02 C.575 B.A. L.896 J.D. [Ⓐ Schell B.A.A.&L.]

Kiser, Aleta B.
(See High Point)

Klass, Amy Smith, (AV) ....'62 '87 C&L.575 B.S., J.D. [Ⓒ Smith M.]
Klauer, Lynne P. ....'58 '85 C.201 B.S. L.1017 J.D. U.S. Atty Off.
Klee, Stephen E., (AV) ....'68 '93 C.1365 B.A. L.896 J.D. [Smith M.]
Klepfer, Robert O., Jr., (AV) ....'42 '66 C&L.575 A.B., LL.B. [Stern,K.&W.]
Klick, Norman F., Jr., (AV) ....'71 '97 C.576 B.A. L.896 J.D. [Carruthers&R.]
Kluttz, Lucy K., (BV) ....'60 '85 C&L.575 B.A., J.D. [Bolton]
Koenig, Daniel W., (BV) ....'— '97 C.228 A.B. L.802 J.D. [Ⓐ Nexsen P.A.K.]
Koenig, Jennifer L.J., (AV) ....'72 '97 C&L.575 A.B., J.D. [Schell B.A.A.&L.]
Koonce, Neil W., (AV) '47 '73
C.575 A.B. L.896 J.D. V.P., Gen. Coun. & Secy., Cone Mills Corp.
Koonts, Robert H., (AV) ....'27 '52 C&L.575 B.S., LL.B. 100 N. Greene St.
Kopec, Janice L. ....'77 '04 C.321 B.A. L.902 J.D. [Brooks,P.M.H.&L.]
Kornegay, John H. ....'54 '80 C.790 B. A. L.896 J.D. [Ⓐ Fisher P.]
Kramer, Douglas B. ....'47 '73 C&L.150 B.S., J.D. 5303 Coveview Court

Krohn, Clayton B., (CV) '63 '98 C.475 B.A. L.902 J.D.
100 South Elm Street, Suite 430, 27401
Telephone: 336-379-7159 Fax: 336-272-7778
Email: claytonkrohn@yahoo.com URL: http://www.claytonkrohnlaw.com
Civil Litigation, Juvenile Delinquency, Insurance, Copyrights, Trademarks, Collections, Traffic Violations, Personal Injury.
See Professional Biographies, GREENSBORO, NORTH CAROLINA

Kshetrapal, Marian Smith ......'78 '04 C.575 B.A. L.896 J.D. [Ⓐ Brotherton F.Y.&W.]
Kuoni, Elizabeth B. '58 '84 C.966 B.A. L.273 J.D.
(adm. in IL; not adm. in NC) P.O. Box 540‡
Kushner, David, (AV) ....'63 '96 C.575 A.B. L.228 J.D. [Brooks,P.M.H.&L.] ⊙
Kyger, David L. ....'55 '79 C.880 A.B. L.893 J.D. [Smith M.]
Kyre, Kenneth, Jr., (AV) ....'51 '77 C.1130 B.A. L.896 J.D. [Pinto C.K.&B.]
Lackey, L. C. ....'45 '74 C.575 B.S. L.896 J.D. Secy. & Treas., Wysong & Miles Co.
LaFollette, Elizabeth V., (BV) ....'72 '97 C.37 B.A. L.575 J.D. [Brooks,P.M.H.&L.]
Lampe, Donald C., (AV) '57 '82 C.453 B.S. L.228 J.D.
[Womble C.S.&R.] (⊙Charlotte)
Landreth, Michael C., (BV) ....'53 '81 C&L.577 B.A., J.D. [Cahoon&S.N.C.&L.]
Langley, D. Beth, (AV) ....'— '92 C&L.896 B.A., J.D. [Nexsen P.A.K.]
Lauver, Linda B. ....'54 '86 C&L.896 B.A., J.D. Compliance Mgr., Wrangler, Inc.
Lavigne, John J. '58 '87 C.025 B.Com. L.028 LL.B.
(adm. in ON; not adm. in NC)
Assoc. Coun., Canada, Volvo Coml. Fin. LLC, The Americas
Lawing, Sally A., (AV) ....'54 '82 C.1128 B.A. L.575 J.D. [Lawing]

Lawing Firm, The, P.A., (AV)
3859 Battleground Avenue, Suite 210, 27410
Telephone: 336-288-0808 Fax: 336-288-0858
Email: sally@lawingfirm.com
Sally A. Lawing.
Medical Malpractice.
See Professional Biographies, GREENSBORO, NORTH CAROLINA

Lawing Sharpless & Stavola, P.A.
(See Sharpless & Stavola, P.A.)

Lazala, Virginia A. '61 '86 C.914 B.A. L.276 J.D.
V.P. & Gen. Coun., Novartis Animal Health US, Inc.
Lee, Bruce A., (BV) ....'58 '89 C&L.574 B.A., J.D. [B.A.Lee]
Lee, John K. ....'23 '52 C.1378 B.S.E.E. L.575 J.D. P.O. Box 20027
Lee, Bruce A., P.A., (BV) ....701 E. Market

Leigh, Rebecca A., Law Offices of, (AVⓉ) '51 '84 C.239 B.A. L.796 J.D. BB
301 South Greene Street, Suite 201, 27401
Telephone: 336-389-1800 Fax: 336-389-0060; URL: http://www.leighlawnc.com
Email: rebecca@leighlaw.com URL: http://www.leighlaw.com
Business Litigation, Creditors Rights, Creditor Bankruptcy, Corporate Law, Banking Law, Civil Litigation, Equipment Financing and Leasing.
See Professional Biographies, GREENSBORO, NORTH CAROLINA

Lester, Eugene E., III, (BV) ....'71 '96 C.999 B.S. L.896 J.D. [Sharpless&S.]
Lester, James L., (AV) ...'57 '82 C.453 S.B. L.228 J.D. [MacCord M.P.] (See Pat. Sect.)
Levin, Steven H. ....'66 '92 C.575 B.A. L.896 J.D. U.S. Atty.'s Off.
Levitt, Robert A. ....'16 '39 C.563 B.A. L.1009 LL.B. 2802 St. Regis Rd.‡
Lewis, Christina L. ....'— '02 C.846 B.A. L.228 J.D. [Ⓐ Sharpless&S.]
Lile-King, Phyllis J., (BV) ....'64 '92 C.275 B.A. L.893 J.D. [Ⓐ Donaldson&B.]
Lind, Frederick G., (AV) ....'47 '74 C.228 B.A. L.209 J.D. Asst. Pub. Def.

Lindley, Kathryn S., (BV) '— '97 C.577 B.S. L.896 J.D.
314 S. Eugene Street, 27402
Mailing Address: P.O. Box 3272, Greensboro, NC 27402
Telephone: 336-333-9600 Fax: 336-274-6956
Email: lindleylaw@mindspring.com URL: http://www.lindleylawfirm.com
Family Law, Divorce, Visitation Rights, Domestic Violence, Child Support, Child Custody, Adoptions, Criminal Law, Driving While Intoxicated, Traffic Violations, Trusts and Estates, Estate Planning, Wills and Probate, Corporate, Business, Real Estate, Collections.
See Professional Biographies, GREENSBORO, NORTH CAROLINA

Lindsey, Christopher E. ....'66 '93 C.893 B.A. L.846 J.D. [Purrington M.]
Ling, Stephen D., (BV) ....'48 '73 C.45 B.S.B.A. L.575 J.D. [Ling&F.]
Ling & Farran, (BV) ....706 Green Valley Road, Suite 505
Lingle, Robert J., (BV) ....'65 '91 C.1128 B.A. L.575 J.D. [Puryear&L.]
Little, Angela L. ....'70 '00 C.945 B.A. L.893 J.D. [Ⓐ Smith M.]
Lively, Kent, (CV) ....'35 '63 C&L.575 A.B., J.D. 423 South Eugene Court
Livingston, Paul H., Jr., (AV) ....'46 '71 C.575 B.S. L.896 J.D. [Schell B.A.A.&L.]

Lloyd, Charles A., (AV) '44 '69 C.198 B.A. L.575 J.D.
301 South Greene Street Suite 100, 27401
Telephone: 336-275-9358 Fax: 336-273-0502
URL: http://www.lawyers.com/charleslloyd
Criminal, Traffic, Driving While Impaired, Conspiracy, Felony, Drug Cases. Trials and Appeals in State and Federal Courts.
See Professional Biographies, GREENSBORO, NORTH CAROLINA

Lloyd, Harold A., (AV) '59 '85
C.198 A.B. L.228 J.D. General Counsel, The Fresh Market Inc.
Lloyd, J. Lee ....'59 '86 C&L.575 B.S.B.A., J.D. [Ⓒ Brooks,P.M.H.&L.]
Lloyd, Robert B., Jr., (AV) ....'26 '50 C.309 A.B. L.228 J.D. [Lloyd M.&Assoc.]
Lloyd, W. David, (AV) ....'48 '87 C.806 B.A. L.574 J.D. 3505 Smoketree Drive

Lloyd Miller & Associates, P.A., (AV) BB
Piedmont Natural Gas Building, 806 Green Valley Road, Suite 203, 27408-7076
Mailing Address: P.O. Box 29247, Greensboro, NC 27429-9247
Telephone: 336-373-5991 Fax: 336-272-2180 URL: http://www.lloydmiller.com
URL: http://www.lloydmillerlaw.com
Robert B. Lloyd, Jr. (Board Certified Specialist in Estate Planning and Probate Law, North Carolina State Board of Legal Specialization); Peter J. Miller (Board Certified Specialist in Estate Planning and Probate Law, North Carolina State Board of Legal Specialization).
Trust Administration, Estate Administration, Estate Planning, Probate Administration, Taxation, Corporate Law, Limited Liability Company Law, Employee Benefits, Business Start Up, Partnership Law, Mergers and Acquisitions, Wills and Probate.
See Professional Biographies, GREENSBORO, NORTH CAROLINA

Lock, Caroline Hudson, (AV) ....'56 '81 C.228 A.B. L.880 J.D. [Smith M.]
Loftin, Robert M. '56 '82 C&L.575 B.A., J.D.
(adm. in MD; not adm. in NC) 1900 Falmouth Dr.
Loftin, Valerie W. ....'56 '81 C&L.575 B.A., J.D. 100 N. Greene St.
Long, Janie L. ....'60 '99 C.316 B.S. L.1228 J.D. [Tuggle D.&M.]
Lowe, Ronda L., (BV) ....'57 '90 C.577 B.A. L.1228 J.D. [Hunter,H.M.E.&B.]
Lucas, Kenneth S., Jr., (BV) ....'60 '85 C.902 B.A. L.896 J.D. [Tate,G.L.P.&W.]
Lucas, Lacy L., Jr., (AV) ....'30 '55 C&L.575 B.S., LL.B. 301 N. Elm St.
Lunsford, John W., (BV) '47 '73
C.575 A.B. L.893 J.D. 3825 West Market Street, Suite 101
Lupton, Anne B., (AV) ....'42 '75 C.575 A.B. L.896 J.D. Asst. Pub. Def.
Lupton, Stevenson, Jr. ....'44 '73 C&L.896 B.A., J.D. 2900 Turner Grove Dr. N.
MacCord, Howard A., Jr., (AV) '50 '78
C.893 B.A. L.273 J.D. [MacCord M.P.] (See Pat. Sect.)

MacCord Mason PLLC, (AV)
300 North Greene Street, Suite 1600, P.O. Box 2974, 27402 ⊙
Telephone: 336-273-4422 Fax: 336-271-2830
URL: http://www.maccordmason.com
Members of Firm: Edward W. Rilee; Howard A. MacCord, Jr.; William J. Mason (Resident, Wilmington Office); James L. Lester. Associates: Dean Turman; Nancy K. Burns; R. Kody Jones. Of Counsel: JiNan Glasgow.
Patent, Trademark, Copyright and Unfair Competition. Trade Secret Practice before all Courts. Intellectual Property Law, Litigation.
Wilmington, North Carolina Office: 1209 Culbreth Drive, Suite 103, 28405. Telephone: 910-256-3557. Fax: 910-256-0523.
Raleigh, North Carolina Office: 510 Glenwood Avenue, Suite 321, 27611. Telephone: 919-664-8624. Fax: 919-664-8625.
See Professional Biographies, GREENSBORO, NORTH CAROLINA

Mack, Ronald W., (AV) '54 '82 C.575 B.S. L.896 J.D.
Exec. V.P. Retail & Gen. Coun., Koury Corporation
MacSween, Iain ....'72 '96 L.1515 LL.B. [Brooks,P.M.H.&L.]
Maddox, E. Thomas, Jr., (BV) ....'41 '72 C.232 A.B. L.575 J.D. [Maddox&G.]
Maddox and Gorham, P.A., (BV) ....220 North Eugene Street
Mahler, Harold C., (AV) ....'31 '62 C&L.575 LL.B. 102 N. Elm Street, Suite 206
Maier, John B., (AV) '35 '65 C.696 B.S. L.64 J.D.
Intell. Prop. Coun., Burlington Industries, Inc. (Pat.)
Malone, Charles F. '51 '77 L.94 J.D.
(adm. in MA; not adm. in NC) Assoc. Prof., North Carolina A&T State University
Malone, John I., Jr., (BV) ....'68 '95 C&L.896 B.A., J.D. [Pinto C.K.&B.]
Mangum, Henry B., Jr., (AV) ....'55 '81 C&L.896 B.S., J.D. [Nexsen P.A.K.]
Marcus, Robert R., (AV) ....'68 '93 C.299 B.A. L.228 J.D. [Smith M.]
Marks, Benjamin S., Jr. ....'34 '58 C&L.575 B.S., J.D. 437 West Friendly Ave.
Marley, A. Ray, Jr. ....'38 '68 C.575 A.B. L.896 J.D. 201 W. Market St.‡
Marlies, Jessica M., (BV) ....'69 '00 C.178 B.A. L.577 J.D. [Brooks,P.M.H.&L.]

Marshall, Charles F., III ... '70 '96 C&L.575 B.A., J.D. [Brooks,P.M.H.&L.] ⊙
Marshall, Michael T., (BV) ... '49 '74 C.575 A.B. L.836 J.D. [Benson&M.]
Marth, Paul E., (AV) ... '50 '75 C&L.896 B.A., J.D. [Ⓒ Forman R.B.]
Martin, B. Douglas, (BV) ... '57 '83 C&L.896 B.A., J.D. [Ⓐ Fisher P.]
Martin, Travis W. ... '— '02 C.34 B.S. L.896 J.D. [Ⓐ Smith M.]
Martinek, Robin K. ... '71 '02 C&L.575 B.A., J.D. 806 Summit Ave.
Mason, Matthew L., (AV) ... '65 '90 C.296 B.S. L.893 J.D. [Moss,M.&H.]
Maultsby, Alexander L., (AV) ... '65 '91 C.198 B.A. L.575 J.D. [Smith M.]
Maury, Deborah F. ... '50 '76 C.205 B.A. L.446 J.D. 628 N. Elm Street
Maxwell, Jonathan V. ... '49 '74 C.968 B.A. L.575 J.D. Co. Atty.
Mayes, James P. '52 '92 C.674 B.A. L.64 J.D.
(adm. in MD; not adm. in NC) Exec. Dir., International Civil Rights Center
Mazzoli, Henri R., (BV) ... '36 '65 C.316 A.B. L.896 LL.B. 403 Blandwood Ave.
McAlister, Carey A. ... '74 '00 C.198 A.B. L.1228 J.D. [Ⓐ Carruthers&R.]
McAlister, Daniel K. ... '38 '63 C.198 A.B. L.228 LL.B. 100 N. Greene St.‡
McCann, Philip P. ... '49 '84 C.999 B.S. L.8 J.D. [Smith M.] (Pat.)
McCarty, Thomas Chester, (BVⓉ) '57 '83 C.575 B.A. L.260 J.D.
(adm. in FL; not adm. in NC) P.O. Box 9904
McClanahan, Frank C., III '46 '75 C.546 B.A. L.569 J.D.
(adm. in NY; not adm. in NC) Chf. Coun. LMSB, I.R.S.
McClearn, Brenda S., (BV) ... '— '94 C.174 B.S. L.273 J.D. [Sharpless&S.]
McClellan, Robert L., (AV) ... '52 '78 C.575 B.A. L.896 J.D. [Ivey,M.G.&T.]
McDiarmid, Katherine Bonan, (AV) ... '59 '84 C.893 B.A. L.896 J.D. 500 Rockford Road
McDonald, David W., (BV) ... '54 '81 C&L.575 B.A., J.D. [Hicks M.N.]
McDonald, Davis, (BV) ... '57 '86 C.311 A.B. L.575 J.D. [Johnson,P.K.&M.]
McGee, Catherine T., (BV) ... '61 '87 C.309 A.B. L.893 J.D. [McGee&Assoc.]
McGee & Associates, (BV) ... 3 Chowan Road
McGinn, Brian J., (BV) ... '68 '94 C&L.896 B.A., J.D. Laura Lard Tobacco Co.
McGinn, M. Daniel, (AV) ... '42 '67 C&L.896 A.B., J.D. [Brooks,P.M.H.&L.] ⊙
McIver, Robert G., (BV) ... '52 '81 C.309 B.A. L.893 J.D. [Hunter,H.M.E.&B.]
McKinney, James H., (BV) ... '50 '77 C.576 B.S. L.575 J.D. 210 W. Friendly Ave.
McKinney, Jeremy L., (BV) ... '71 '96 C.1090 B.A. L.1345 J.D. 436 Spring Garden Road

McLaughlin, Anthony C., (BV) '55 '80 C.1292 B.A. L.724 J.D.
125 South Elm Street, Suite 604, P.O. Box 217, 27402
Telephone: 336-274-8441 Fax: 336-274-8422 URL: http://www.lawyers.com/ncdirtlawyer
Email: dirt_law@bellsouth.net URL: http://www.ncdirtlawyer.com
General Practice, Residential Real Estate, Commercial Real Estate, Wills and Probate.
See Professional Biographies, GREENSBORO, NORTH CAROLINA

McLean, David B. ... '66 '99 C.269 B.A. L.896 J.D. [Johnson,P.K.&M.]
McLendon, John A., Jr., (AV) ... '58 '87 C.478 B.A. L.575 J.D. [Schell B.A.A.&L.]
McLendon, Lennox P., Jr., (AV) ... '21 '48 C&L.575 A.B., J.D. [Brooks,P.M.H.&L.]
McMillan, Brian J., (BV) ... '57 '97 C.208 B.S.B.A. L.1068 J.D. [Brooks,P.M.H.&L.]
McMillion, Donald C. ... '38 '63 C&L.575 B.S., LL.B. P.O. Box 21447
McNairy, William G., (AV) ... '43 '73 C.575 B.S. L.945 J.D. [Brooks,P.M.H.&L.] ⊙
McNulty, Joseph F., Jr., (AV) '46 '79
C.316 B.A. L.896 J.D. Tax, Estate & Elder Planning Ctr.
McVey, Edward L., III, (BV) ... '47 '72 C&L.69 B.A., J.D. 330 S. Greene St.
Meagher, Laura C. '60 '89 C.910 B.A. L.930 J.D.
(adm. in OH; not adm. in NC) Asst. Gen. Coun., VF Corp.
Medford, James A., (AV) ... '45 '71 C.575 A.B. L.309 J.D. [Smith M.]
Medina, Edward S. ... '67 '95 C&L.893 B.A., J.D. Gen. Coun., Market America, Inc.
Meeker, Michael D., (AV) ... '47 '72 C&L.575 B.S., J.D. [Brooks,P.M.H.&L.]
MeHaffey, Elizabeth T. '66 '01 C.577 B.A. L.575 J.D.
V.P., Legal Affairs, Timco Aviation Services, Inc.
Meister, Emily Jeffords ... '77 '02 C.160 B.S. L.896 J.D. [Ⓐ Forman R.B.]
Melvin, Charles E., Jr., (AV) ... '29 '56 C&L.575 B.S., J.D. [Ⓒ Smith M.]
Meschan, David F., (AV) ... '44 '69 C.198 A.B. L.575 J.D. [Tuggle D.&M.]
Meyers, C. Scott ... '72 '01 C.886 B.A. L.1209 J.D. [Brooks,P.M.H.&L.]
Meyers, Nancy R., (BV) ... '69 '95 C.575 B.S. L.421 J.D. [Pinto C.K.&B.]
Meyland, A. L., (AV) ... '19 '48 C&L.575 LL.B. [Ⓒ Ott C.&R.]
Miles, J. Benjamin, (BV) ... '30 '55 C.296 A.B. L.896 LL.B. 102 N. ELM St.
Miles, James W., Jr., (AV) ... '48 '73 C&L.575 B.A., J.D. [Hunter,H.M.E.&B.]
Miles, Linda A., (AV) ... '48 '72 C&L.575 B.A., J.D. Chief Dep. City Atty.
Miller, Angela Hewlett ... '65 '96 C.1228 B.A. L.574 J.D. United States Attorney's Office
Miller, Peter J., (AV) ... '56 '83 C.896 B.A. L.1228 J.D. [Lloyd M.&Assoc.]
Millikin, Stephen Perry, (AV) ... '26 '52 C&L.575 B.S., J.D. [Ⓒ Smith M.]
Milstein, Ronald S. ... '56 '82 C.1350 B.A. L.1019 J.D. Gen. Coun., Lorillard Tobacco Co.
Mohamed, Moshera ... '75 '02 C.577 B.S. L.574 J.D. [Ⓐ P.Chastain&Assoc.]
Moody, David K. ... '61 '92 C.821 B.A. L.188 J.D. [Purrington M.]
Moore, David M., II, (AV) ... '44 '69 C&L.575 A.B., J.D. [Ⓒ Smith M.]
Moore, Karen Keiger ... '51 '89 C&L.896 B.A., J.D. Central Carolina Legal Servs., Inc.
Moore, Larry I., III, (AV) ... '48 '79 C.871 B.S. L.326 J.D. [Younce,M.&M.]
Moore, Samuel M., (BV) ... '36 '70 C.469 A.B. L.575 J.D. [Ⓒ Smith M.]
Moore, Susan D. ... '52 '77 C.232 B.A. L.896 J.D. Guilford Co. Atty.'s Off.

Morgan, Herring, Morgan, Green, Rosenblutt & Gill, LLP
(See High Point)

Morgenstern, Barbara R., (AV) ... '54 '86 C.347 A.B. L.575 J.D. [Morgenstern&B.]

Morgenstern & Bonuomo, PLLC, (AV)
419 North Edgeworth Street, 27401
Telephone: 336-379-5006 Telefax: 336-275-3901
Barbara R. Morgenstern (Board Certified Specialist in Family Law, North Carolina State Board of Legal Specialization); Kim R. Bonuomo (Board Certified Specialist in Family Law, North Carolina State Board of Legal Specialization).
Practice Limited to Family and Domestic Relations Law.
See Professional Biographies, GREENSBORO, NORTH CAROLINA

Morris, Kevin J. '63 '94 C.706 B.A. L.472 J.D.
V.P. of Admn. & Gen. Coun., Sunstates Maintenance Corporation

Morris York Williams Surles & Barringer, L.L.P.
(See Charlotte)

Morse, Kevin B. ... '62 '93 C.576 B.S. L.574 J.D. 445 Dolly Madison Road
Morton, J. Bruce ... '30 '55 C.296 A.B. L.575 J.D. Dist. J.
Moseley, William O., Jr., (AV) ... '35 '81 C.577 B.S. L.896 J.D. [Younce,M.&M.]
Moses, Margaret D. ... '49 '76 C&L.329 B.A., J.D. P.O. Box 2547
Moss, Joseph W., (AV) ... '41 '66 C.228 B.A. L.896 LL.B. [Ⓒ Moss,M.&H.]

Moss, Mason & Hill, (AV)
Bank of America Building, 101 West Friendly Avenue, Suite 602, 27429
Telephone: 336-370-1282 Fax: 336-271-6838
Matthew L. Mason; William L. Hill. Of Counsel: Joseph W. Moss. Associate: Megan E. Callahan.
Civil Litigation, Construction Litigation, Criminal Defense, Insurance Litigation, Workers Compensation, Personal Injury, Products Liability, Civil Rights, Law Enforcement Liability.
See Professional Biographies, GREENSBORO, NORTH CAROLINA

Murphy, Donald L., (BV) ... '51 '78 C&L.574 B.A., J.D. [D.L.Murphy]
Murphy, Katherine A. ... '58 '99 C.1349 B.A. L.575 J.D. [Brooks,P.M.H.&L.]
Murphy, Romallus O. ... '28 '56 C.329 B.A. L.575 J.D. 1106 E. Market St.
Murphy, Donald L., P.A., (BV) ... 301 South Greene Street Suite 110
Murray, Maureen Demarest, (AV) ... '55 '80 C.228 A.B. L.880 J.D. [Smith M.]
Myatt, Christine L., (AV) ... '— '82 C&L.896 B.A., J.D. [Nexsen P.A.K.]
Nance, Jordan ... '80 '05 C.576 B.A. L.880 J.D. [Ⓐ Smith M.]
Nash, Michael R., (BV) ... '53 '81 C.577 B.A. L.896 J.D. 216 West Smith Street
Neumann, Howard P., (AV) ... '52 '77 C.575 B.A. L.692 J.D. Asst. Dist. Atty.
Newell, Dottie A. ... '42 '88 C.1378 B.A. L.574 J.D. P.O. Box 21863

Nexsen Pruet Adams Kleemeier, PLLC, (AV) BR
701 Green Valley Road, Suite 100, P.O. Box 3463 (27402), 27408 ⊙
Telephone: 336-373-1600 Facsimile: 336-273-5357
URL: http://www.npaklaw.com
Wilburn Brewer, Jr. (1939-2003); C. Alvin Brown (1940-1978); Paul A. Cooper (1889-1956); Frank B. Gary (1900-1971); John A. Kleemeier, Jr. (1911-1973); William J. Adams, Jr. (1908-1993); Elizabeth Dunn White (1954-1995); Daniel W. Fouts (1932-2003). Members of Firm: J. Alexander S. Barrett; Robert G. Baynes; Gary L. Beaver; James W. Bryan; Margaret Shea Burnham (Board Certified Specialist in Real Property Law, Business, Commercial and Industrial Transactions, North Carolina State Board of Legal Specialization); W. B. Rodman Davis; M. Jay DeVaney (Board Certified Specialist in Real Property Law, Business, Commercial and Industrial Transactions, North Carolina State Board of Legal Specialization); Trudy A. Ennis (Board Certified Specialist in Family Law, North Carolina State Board of Legal Specialization); Charles T. Hagan III; J. Scott Hale; R. Harper Heckman; Steven D. Hedges; A. Scott Jackson; Benjamin A. Kahn (Board Certified Specialist in Business and Consumer Bankruptcy, North Carolina State Board of Legal Specialization); D. Beth Langley; Henry B. Mangum, Jr.; Christine L. Myatt (Board Certified Specialist in Business Bankruptcy Law, North Carolina State Board of Legal Specialization); Peter G. Pappas; David S. Pokela; Tonya Bunn Powell (Board Certified Specialist in Real Property Law: Business, Commercial and Industrial Transactions, North Carolina State Board of Legal Specialization); Randall W. Reavis; David A. Senter; Thomas S. Thornton, Jr.; William M. Wilcox IV. Of Counsel: F. Cooper Brantley; Charles T. Hagan, Jr.; Walter L. Hannah; Daniel K. Hicks; W. Winburne King III; John N. Ogburn, Jr. Special Counsel: J. Phillips L. Johnston; R. Scott Tobin. Associates: Eric H. Biesecker; Brooks F. Bossong; Brian S. Clarke; Leigh Coughenour; Stephanie Renee Ennis; Stuart C. Gauffreau; Elizabeth Davis Hall; Gregory T. Higgins; Joseph M. Kahn; Daniel W. Koenig; Brian T. Pearce; James David Yarbrough, Jr.
Acquisitions, Administrative Law, Alternative Dispute Resolution, Antitrust Law, Appellate Practice, Arbitration, Bankruptcy Law, Business Law, Collections Law, Construction Law, Commercial Law, Commercial Real Estate, Computers, Contracts, Copyrights, Corporate Law, Creditor-Debtor Rights, Disabilities, Domestic Relations Law, Economic Development Law, Education Law, Election, Eminent Domain Employee Benefits Law, Employment Law, Environmental Law, Estate Planning, Family Law, Fidelity Law, Finance Law, Governmental Representation, Health Care Law, Hospital Law, Immigration Law, Insurance Law, Insurance Defense, Intellectual Property Law, International Law, Internet Law, Investments, Labor Law, Land Use, Leasing Law, Litigation, Maritime Law, Mediation, Mergers, Naturalization Law, Partnership Law, Patents, Personal Injury, Probate, Products Liability Law, Professional Liability, Public Contracts, Public Finance, Real Estate Law, Real Estate Planning, Regulatory Law, Securities, Surety Law, Taxation Law, Technology Law, Torts, Trade Regulation, Trade Secrets, Trademarks, Transportation, Trusts, Utility Law, Wills, Workers' Compensation and Zoning Law.
See Professional Biographies, GREENSBORO, NORTH CAROLINA

Niburg, Rebecca A. ... '78 '03 C.575 B.A. L.910 J.D. [Ⓐ Tuggle D.&M.]
Nicholson, Mary K., (BV) ... '51 '76 C.575 A.B. L.896 J.D. 1908 Madison Ave.
Nieman, John F., Jr., (BV) ... '52 '92 C.577 B.A. L.574 J.D. Pub. Def.

Nixon & Associates
(See High Point)

Noble, Thomas E. ... '71 '01 C.769 B.A. L.597 J.D. [Ⓐ Tuggle D.&M.]
Noecker, John W., (BVⓉ) ... '41 '66 C&L.608 B.S., J.D. [Hicks M.N.]
Norman, Benjamin R. ... '78 '05 C.575 B.A. L.896 J.D. [Brooks,P.M.H.&L.]
North, H. Davis, III, (AV) ... '48 '80 C.575 A.B. L.896 J.D. [Cahoon&S.N.C.&L.]
Oakley, Daniel C. ... '50 '74 C&L.575 B.S., J.D. 228 W. Market St.
Oakley, Joel N., (AV) ... '60 '86 C.34 B.A. L.574 J.D. 322 S. Eugene St.
O'Bryant, Ramona Cunningham, (AV) ... '58 '85 C.23 B.A. L.575 J.D. [Smith M.]
O'Connor, Harry J., Jr., (BV) ... '31 '59 C.576 B.S. L.228 J.D. P.O. Box 39234
Oden, Wm. K., Jr. ... '29 '58 C.296 A.B. L.228 LL.B. Claims Atty., Allstate Ins. Co.
Ogburn, John N., Jr., (AV) ... '— '57 C&L.575 B.S., J.D. [Ⓒ Nexsen P.A.K.]

Ogletree, Deakins, Nash, Smoak & Stewart, P.C., (AV) BR
2725 Horse Pen Creek Road Suite 101, 27410-8392 ⊙
Mailing Address: P.O. Box 13310, Greensboro, NC
Telephone: 336-375-9737 Facsimile: 336-375-4430
Email: clientservices@ogletreedeakins.com URL: http://www.ogletreedeakins.com
Brian M. Freedman.
Labor Relations, Employment Litigation, Workers' Compensation. Civil Litigation in all State and Federal Courts and Administrative Agencies.
Atlanta, Georgia Office: 600 Peachtree Street, N.E., Suite 2100. Telephone: 404-881-1300.
Austin, Texas Office: 301 Congress Avenue, Suite 1250. Telephone: 512-344-4700.
Birmingham, Alabama Office: One Federal Place, Suite 1000, 1819 Fifth Avenue North. Telephone: 205-328-1900.
Charleston, South Carolina Office: 134 Meeting Street, Suite 160, P.O. Box 1808. Telephone: 843-853-1300.
Charlotte, North Carolina Office: 400 West Trade Street. Telephone: 704-342-2588.
Chicago, Illinois Office: Twenty-Fifth Floor, Two First National Plaza, 20 South Clark Street. Telephone: 312-558-1220.
Columbia, South Carolina Office: 1320 Main Street, Suite 600. Telephone: 803-252-1300.
Dallas, Texas Office: 700 Preston Commons, 8117 Preston Road. Telephone: 214-987-3800.
Greenville, South Carolina Office: The Ogletree Building, 300 North Main Street, P.O. Box 2757. Telephone: 864-271-1300.
Houston, Texas Office: One Allen Center, 500 Dallas Street, Suite 3000. Telephone: 713-655-0855.
Kansas City, Missouri Office: 4717 Grand Avenue, Suite 300. Telephone: 816-471-1301.
Los Angeles, California Office: 633 West Fifth Street, Suite 5300. Telephone: 213-239-9800.
Indianapolis, Indiana Office: Suite 4600, 111 Monument Circle. Telephone: 317-916-1300.
Miami, Florida Office: 80 S.W. 8th Street, Suite 1830. Telephone: 305-374-0506.
Morristown, New Jersey Office: 10 Madison Avenue, Suite 402. Telephone: 973-656-1600.
Nashville, Tennessee Office: SunTrust Center, Suite 800, 424 Church Street. Telephone: 615-254-1900.
Phoenix, Arizona Office: 2415 East Camelback Road, Suite 800. Telephone: 602-778-3700.
Raleigh, North Carolina Office: 2301 Sugar Bush Road, Suite 600, P.O. Box 31608. Telephone: 919-787-9700.
San Antonio, Texas Office: 2600 Weston Centre, 112 East Pecan Street. Telephone: 210-354-1300.
St. Thomas, U.S. Virgin Islands Office: The Tunick Building, 1336 Beltjen Road, Suite 202. Telephone: 340-714-1235.
Tampa, Florida Office: 100 North Tampa Street, Suite 3600. Telephone: 813-289-1247.
Washington, D.C. Office: Fifth Floor, 2400 N Street, N.W. Telephone: 202-887-0855.
See Professional Biographies, GREENSBORO, NORTH CAROLINA

O'Hale, Robert, (AV) ... '54 '81 C.575 B.A. L.1228 J.D. [Clifford C.O.&J.]
Oleynik, Jeffrey E., (AV) ... '58 '83 C.945 B.A. L.893 J.D. [Brooks,P.M.H.&L.] ⊙
O'Neal, Bonnie Lee C. ... '71 '98 C.577 B.A. L.575 J.D. 102 N. Elm St., Ste. 623
O'Neal, John T., (CV) ... '71 '96 C.577 B.A. L.575 J.D. [Ⓐ Donaldson&B.]
Ormand, John W., III, (AV) ... '62 '87 C.896 B.A. L.575 J.D. [Brooks,P.M.H.&L.] ⊙
Osteen, William L., Jr., (AV) ... '60 '87 C&L.575 B.S., J.D. [Adams&O.]
Osteen, William L., Sr. ... '30 '56 C.296 A.B. L.575 LL.B. U.S. Dist. J.
Ott, Wendell H., (AV) ... '40 '76 C.499 B.S. L.575 J.D. [Ott C.&R.]

Ott Cone & Redpath, P.A., (AV)
1501 Highwoods Boulevard, Suite 101, 27410
Telephone: 336-373-1300 Fax: 336-273-9353
URL: http://www.ottconeredpath.com

(This Listing Continued)

Ott Cone & Redpath, P.A. (Continued)

Thomas E. Cone; Melanie Martin Hamilton; Wendell H. Ott; Randolph A. Redpath; Laurie S. Truesdell; Richard L. Wells. Of Counsel: Herman G. Enochs, Jr.; A. L. Meyland.
Trial and Appellate Practice in all State and Federal Courts. Administrative, Regulatory, Health Care, Hospital, Labor and Employment Law.

See Professional Biographies, GREENSBORO, NORTH CAROLINA

Overfield, John Covington, (BV) ....'70 '95 C.880 B.A. L.896 J.D. [Coltrane A.&O.]
Oxner, Todd P., (AV) .... '62 '93 C.768 B.A. L.352 J.D. [Oxner T.&P.]
Oxner Thomas & Permar, PLLC, (AV) ....800 Green Valley Road, Suite 304
Palancia, Jennifer A. '71 '01 C.184 B.A. L.1228 J.D.
Asst. Univ. Atty., Univ. of NC at Greensboro - Univ. Coun.
Palecek, Diana R. '66 '92 C.247 A.B. L.896 J.D.
Asst. V.P. & Assoc. Coun., Jefferson-Pilot Corp. & Subsidiaries (Legal Department)
Palenske, Robin R. ....'59 '86 C.339 B.S. L.575 J.D. Admin. Law J., Soc. Sec. Admn.
Pappas, Peter G., (AV) ....'— '82 C&L.575 B.A., J.D. [Nexsen P.A.K.]
Park, Laurie Pearlman .... '62 '89 C.103 B.A. L.273 J.D. 1515 Worthington Place‡
Parker, Gerald C. ....'33 '58 C&L.575 A.B., J.D. 212 W. Friendly Ave.
Parrish, Michael R., (BV) ....'53 '86 C.896 B.A. L.902 J.D. 701 North Eugene Street
Partesotti, R. Harbour ....'77 '03 C.16 B.S. L.575 J.D. [Booth H.&J.]
Patterson, William F., Jr., (AV) ....'54 '82 C&L.575 B.A., J.D. [Forman R.B.]

Patterson Harkavy LLP, (AV)
101 South Elm Street, P.O. Box 29269, 27429-9269
Telephone: 336-370-4200 Facsimile: 336-274-8490
URL: http://www.pathlaw.com
Jonathan R. Harkavy (Resident). Of Counsel: Nahomi Harkavy (Resident).
Dispute Resolution Practice in all State and Federal Courts.
Raleigh, North Carolina Office: 414 West Jones Street, P.O. Box 27927, 27611. Telephone: 919-755-1812. Facsimile: 919-755-0124.
Chapel Hill, North Carolina Office: 100 Europa Drive, Suite 250, 27517. Telephone: 919-942-5200. Toll Free: 800-458-2541. Fax: 919-942-5256.

See Professional Biographies, GREENSBORO, NORTH CAROLINA

Patty, Amanda M. ....'78 '04 C.577 B.A. L.665 J.D. [Hunter,H.M.E.&B.]
Patty, Seldon E., (AV) .... '43 '68 C&L.575 B.S., J.D. Ste 100, 109 Muirs Chapel Rd
Payne, Robert S., Law Office of ....'45 '74 C&L.575 B.A., J.D. 226 E. Avondale Dr.
Payton, Mildred B. ....'18 '63 C.1378 B.S. L.576 LL.B. 1008 S. Benbow Rd.‡
Payton, S. Camille, (BV) ....'62 '93 C.575 B.A. L.846 J.D. [Donaldson&B.]
Pearce, Betty J., (AV) ....'46 '75 C.914 B.A. L.569 J.D. P.O. Box 4483
Pearce, Brian T. ....'— '03 C.160 B.S. L.896 J.D. [Nexsen P.A.K.]
Pearman, Larry W., (BV) .....'49 '80 C.575 B.S. L.1228 J.D. 5405 West Friendly Avenue
Pearman, Richard M., Jr. ....'43 '70 C&L.896 B.A., J.D. 201 I Pomona Dr.
Peck, Timothy, (AV) ....'55 '81 C.198 B.A. L.896 J.D. [Smith M.]
Peddrick, Martha Taylor, (AV) ....'50 '84 C.205 B.A. L.896 J.D. [Johnson,P.K.&M.]
Pell, Gerald A., (AV) ....'39 '65 C.930 B.B.A. L.575 J.D. [Pell&P.]
Pell, James E., (BV) ....'42 '65 C&L.575 B.S., J.D. [Pell&P.]
Pell and Pell, L.L.P., (AV) ....220 Commerce Pl.
Pendergraft, Michael R., (AV) ....'50 '76 C&L.575 B.A., J.D. [Turner&L.]
Peraldo, Jeffrey K., (AV) ....'58 '90 C&L.896 B.A., J.D. [J.K.Peraldo]

Peraldo, Jeffrey K., P.A., The Law Offices of, (AV)
500-D State Street, 27405
Telephone: 336-458-0058 Fax: 336-691-8083 URL: http://www.greensborolawyer.com
Email: jkp@greensborolawyer.com URL: http://www.jkperaldolaw.com
Jeffrey K. Peraldo.
Serious Personal Injury, Wrongful Death, Automobile Accidents, Trucking Accidents, Medical Malpractice, Hospital Malpractice, Nursing Home Neglect and Abuse, Product Liability, Construction Accidents, Consumer Fraud, Land Condemnation, Negligent Security.

See Professional Biographies, GREENSBORO, NORTH CAROLINA

Perkins, Patricia Carole ....'76 '01 C.198 B.A. L.880 J.D. [Smith M.]
Permar, Rufus Howard "Chip", III ....'75 '01 C.576 B.A. L.192 J.D. [Oxner T.&P.]
Perry, Rebecca, (BV) ....'63 '95 C.623 B.A. L.896 J.D. [R.Perry]
Perry, Rebecca, PLLC, (BV) ....436 Spring Garden Street
Peters, Robert Y. ....'34 '61 C.215 B.E.E. L.276 J.D. Lucent Technologies, Inc. (Pat.)‡
Peterson-Buie, Becky Jo, (BV) ....'56 '84 C.811 B.A. L.574 J.D. Dep. City Atty.
Pfaff, J.S. ....'44 '70 C.575 A.B. L.896 J.D. 201 W. Market St., Ste. 409
Phillips, Jim W., Jr., (AV) ....'57 '84 C.575 A.B. L.896 J.D. [Brooks,P.M.H.&L.]
Phillips, Paige Michaux .....'68 '96 C.575 B.S.B.A. L.861 J.D. Asst. Mgr., Jefferson-Pilot
Phillips, Reid L., (AV) ....'52 '77 C.575 B.A. L.846 J.D. [Brooks,P.M.H.&L.]
Phillips, Susan J., (CV) ....'59 '85 C.575 B.A. L.896 J.D. 2601 W. Market Street
Pickett, Therence O. '66 '91 C.576 B.A. L.228 J.D.
(adm. in VA; not adm. in NC)
VP, Gen. Coun. & Sec., Mack Trucks, Inc., Volvo Trucks North America, Inc.
Pickup, Caroline Collins ....'75 '00 C.575 B.A. L.880 J.D. [Smith M.]
Pinsker, Jerrold B. ....'49 '75 C.228 B.A. L.575 J.D. 2000 Burntleaf Pl.‡
Pinto, Lillian H., (BV) ....'58 '83 C&L.896 B.A., J.D. [Womble C.S.&R.]
Pinto, Michelle '76 '01 C.48 B.A. L.469 J.D.
(adm. in GA; not adm. in NC) 1302 Pleasant Ridge Road
Pinto, Richard L., (AV) ....'55 '80 C&L.896 B.A., J.D. [Pinto C.K.&B.]

Pinto Coates Kyre & Brown, PLLC, (AV)
3203 Brassfield Road, 27410
Mailing Address: P.O. Box 4848, Greensboro, NC 27404
Telephone: 336-282-8848 Facsimile: 336-282-8409
URL: http://www.pckb-law.com
Members of Firm: Richard L. Pinto; Paul D. Coates; Kenneth Kyre, Jr.; David L. Brown; Martha P. Brown; Nancy R. Meyers; John I. Malone, Jr.; Deborah J. Bowers; Brady A. Yntema. Associates: Bryan G. Scott; Kimberly A. Schell.
Civil Litigation, Insurance Defense, Insurance Coverage, Commercial Litigation, Personal Injury, Products Liability, Wrongful Death, Medical Malpractice, Workers Compensation, Labor and Employment, Appellate Practice.
Representative Clients: Penn National Insurance Co.; St. Paul Travelers; Grain Dealers Mutual Insurance Co.; N.C. Farm Bureau Insurance Co.; Virginia Mutual Insurance Co.; Harleysville Mutual Insurance Co.; Selective Insurance; Auto-Owners Insurance Co.; General Casualty Insurance Co.

See Professional Biographies, GREENSBORO, NORTH CAROLINA

Pinyan, Clinton R., (AV) ....'68 '95 C.896 B.A. L.145 J.D. [Brooks,P.M.H.&L.]
Placke, Eric D., (BV) ....'61 '86 C&L.45 B.A., J.D. Asst. Fed. Pub. Def.
Pokela, David S., (AV) ....'— '92 C.575 B.S. L.896 J.D. [Nexsen P.A.K.]
Polinsky, David B. ....'46 '76 C.679 B.S.E.E. L.705 J.D. [Polinsky]
Polinsky Law Offices ....P.O. Box 4452
Pollard, Edward N., (BV) ....'— '93 C.576 B.S.C.E. L.896 J.D. [Conner G.S.]
Pomerantz, Eric P. '57 '83 C.1349 B.A. L.30 J.D.
(adm. in NY; not adm. in NC) Novartis
Pons, J. Edwin, (BV) ....'51 '78 C.871 B.S. L.575 J.D. Dep. Co. Atty.
Poole, J. Gregory '64 '89 C.575 A.B. L.896 J.D.
Assoc. Coun., Construction, Volvo Coml. Fin. LLC, The Americas

Poortvliet, Kenneth L. '61 '99 C.774 B.A. L.1339 J.D.
318 S. Eugene Street, Suite 103, 27405
Telephone: 336-370-1614 Fax: 336-370-1732
Email: ken@poortvlietlaw.com URL: http://www.kpoortvlietlaw.com

(This Listing Continued)

Poortvliet, Kenneth L. (Continued)

Family Law, Divorce, Child Custody, Child Support, Adoptions, Domestic Violence, Visitation Rights, Criminal Law, Traffic Violations and Driving While Intoxicated.

See Professional Biographies, GREENSBORO, NORTH CAROLINA

Popalis, Craig H. ....'55 '00 C&L.260 B.S.M.E., J.D. [Womble C.S.&R.]
Pope, A. Harrell ....'18 '40 C&L.228 A.B., LL.B. 300 N. Greene St.
Porter, Leon E., Jr., (AV) '— '78 C.575 A.B. L.896 J.D.
V.P., Gen. Coun. & Secy., Jefferson-Pilot Communications Co.
Powell, James M., (AV) ....'— '77 C.10 B.A. L.16 J.D. [Womble C.S.&R.]
Powell, Tonya Bunn, (AV) ....'— '96 C.896 B.A. L.575 J.D. [Nexsen P.A.K.]
Prak, Mark J., (AV) ....'55 '80 C&L.228 A.B., J.D. [Brooks,P.M.H.&L.]
Prause, D. Marsh, (BV) ....'68 '93 C.674 B.S.E. L.896 J.D. [Smith M.]
Pritchett, Jan Elliott, (BV) ....'68 '95 C.955 B.A. L.803 J.D. [Schlosser&P.]
Purdom, Eugene W., (AV) ....'41 '68 C&L.575 A.B., J.D. [Tate,G.L.P.&W.]
Purrington, Alfred L., III, (AV) ....'33 '61 C.575 A.B. L.309 LL.B. [Purrington M.]
Purrington, Alfred Nicholas, (AV) ....'66 '94 C.674 A.B. L.276 J.D. [Purrington M.]

Purrington Moody LLP, (AV)
301 North Elm Street, Suite 115, 27401
Telephone: 336-510-5880 Fax: 336-510-5888
URL: http://www.purringtonmoody.com
Members of Firm: Alfred Nicholas Purrington; David K. Moody (Resident, New York, New York Office); James S. Felt; Neil M. Freeman (Not admitted in NC; Resident, New York, New York Office); Jeffrey A. Jones; Stephen L. Pampush (Resident, New York, New York Office); Christopher E. Lindsey. Associate: Harrison M. Hall. Senior Counsel: Alfred L. Purrington, III.
Investments, Investment Funds, Private Equity, Corporate Law, Partnership Law, Limited Liability Companies, Securities, Business Law, Finance, Mergers and Acquisitions.
New York, New York Office: 105 Hudson Street, Suite 304, 10013. Telephone: 212-431-7129. Fax: 212-431-7124.

See Professional Biographies, GREENSBORO, NORTH CAROLINA

Puryear, David B., Jr., (BV) ....'53 '83 C.1378 B.A. L.575 J.D. [Puryear&L.]

Puryear and Lingle, P.L.L.C., (BV)
5501-E Adams Farm Lane, 27407-6396
Telephone: 336-218-0227 Telecopier: 336-218-0240
Email: admin@puryearandlingle.com URL: http://www.puryearandlingle.com
David B. Puryear, Jr.; Robert J. Lingle.
Commercial Litigation, Personal Injury, Employment Law, Business Law, Libel/Slander, Antitrust, Unfair Trade Practices, Fraud, Copyright/Trademark Infringement, Contracts, Elder Law, Wills, Trusts, Estate Planning, Disability Claims, ERISA, Pension and Profit Sharing Plan Claims, Mediation.
Jefferson Pilot Financial Services; ABI-Accessory Brands, Inc.; ALEM Airways, Inc.; Intensa, Inc.; Yates Food Products, Inc.; Coating Concepts International; Impak Industries, LLC; NICCE Welding Technology, Inc.; Salem Medical Electronics, Inc.; KC Enterprises, Inc.

Quinn, Nancy P., (CV) ....'56 '89 C.1287 B.A. L.896 J.D. [Quinn]

Quinn Law Firm, The, (CV)
315 Spring Garden Street, Suite 1D, 27401
Telephone: 336-272-9072 Fax: 336-272-2289
Email: quinnlaw@triadbiz.rr.com URL: http://www.quinnlawnc.com
Nancy P. Quinn.
Workers Compensation, Personal Injury, Automobile Accidents and Injuries, Employment Discrimination, Immigration.

See Professional Biographies, GREENSBORO, NORTH CAROLINA

Ramseur, Patti West ....'— '99 C.576 B.S. L.896 J.D. [Smith M.]
Ramsey, Coe W. ....'72 '98 C.575 B.A. L.896 J.D. [Brooks,P.M.H.&L.]
Ramsey, H. Vaughn, (AV) ....'56 '83 C&L.575 B.A., J.D. [Tuggle D.&M.]
Raspet, Jill L. ....'78 '02 C.953 B.S. L.896 J.D. [Schell B.A.A.&L.]
Ray, William C. ....'46 '73 C.575 A.B. L.472 J.D. 80 Mansfield Cir., Ste. B
Reavis, Randall W., (AV) ....'— '89 C.125 B.A. L.575 J.D. [Nexsen P.A.K.]
Redman, Barbara J. '54 '86 C.383 B.A. L.280 J.D.
(adm. in GA; not adm. in NC) Assoc. Prof. of Bus. Admin., N.C. A&T State Univ.
Redpath, Randolph A., (AV) ....'52 '83 C.378 B.A. L.896 J.D. [Ott C.&R.]
Reed, Robert A. '42 '68 C.679 B.S. L.665 LL.B.
(adm. in PA; not adm. in NC)
V.P., Secy. & Assoc. Gen. Coun., Jefferson-Pilot Corporation & Subsidiaries
Reeve, Brian C. '62 '87 C.276 B.S. L.575 J.D.
Corporate & Commercial Counsel, Novartis Crop Protection, Inc.
Reilly, John P. '62 '88 C&L.188 B.A., J.D.
Assoc. Gen. Coun., Litig., Lorillard Tobacco Co.
Reynolds, Rufus W. ....'07 '32 C&L.228 B.A., LL.B. Ret. U.S. Bkrptcy. J.
Rhodes, C. Robert, (AV) ....'36 '67 C.576 B.S. L.273 LL.B. [Womble C.S.&R.] (Pat.)
Rich, James R. ......'52 '77 C.575 B.A. L.574 J.D. Area Coun., I.R.S., Off. of Chf. Coun.
Richardson, Eric A., (BV) ....'68 '96 C.945 B.A. L.896 J.D. [Ivey,M.G.&T.]
Ridenhour, Patricia P., (BV) ....'42 '91 C.575 A.B. L.896 J.D. 301 S. Greene Street
Rierson, Jennifer L. ....'67 '94 C.896 B.A. L.574 J.D. Pub. Def. Off.
Rightsell, William T., Jr., (BV) '36 '61
C&L.575 A.B., J.D. Rightsell Eggleston Forrester & Donato LLP
Rilee, Edward W., (AV) .....'49 '82 C.886 B.S. L.7 J.D. [MacCord M.P.] (See Pat. Sect.)
Riotte, Christina L. '62 '87 C.259 B.S. L.260 J.D.
(adm. in FL; not adm. in NC) 1802 Saint Andrews Rd.‡
Ritchie, Caroline Elizabeth ....'74 '01 C.198 B.A. L.790 J.D. [Brooks,P.M.H.&L.]
Ritter, Joseph M., (AV) '50 '77 C.575 A.B. L.192 J.D.
State Coun., Fidelity Natl. Title Ins. Co. of N.Y.

Roberson, Haworth & Reese, P.L.L.C.
(See High Point)

Robertson, Pamela A., (AV) ....'55 '82 C.471 B.A. L.446 J.D. [Sharpless&S.]
Robinson, Russell M., III, (BV) '58 '91
C.228 B.A. L.896 J.D. Asst. Gen. Coun., Burlington Industries, Inc.

Robinson & Lawing, L.L.P.
(See Winston-Salem)

Rodenbough, S. Leigh, IV, (AV) ....'55 '81 C&L.575 B.A., J.D. [Brooks,P.M.H.&L.]
Roessler, Todd S. ....'70 '01 C&L.575 B.S., J.D. Law Clk., Dist. Ct.
Rogers, James N. '41 '66 C.588 B.S. L.107 J.D.
(adm. in NY; not adm. in NC; Pat.) [Hunter,H.M.E.&B.]
Rollins, Elizabeth O., (BV) ....'25 '49 C.6 A.B. L.575 J.D. 1809 Madison Avenue
Rossabi, Amiel J., (AV) ....'63 '88 C.575 B.A. L.724 J.D. [Forman R.B.]
Rossi, Bonnie E., (CV) ....'48 '99 C.296 B.S. L.1360 J.D. [Woodruff]
Rotenstreich, Kenneth B., (AV) '62 '87
C.88 B.A. L.896 J.D. 101 South Elm Street, Suite 350
Rothenberg, Jerome S. ......'44 '79 C.264 A.B. L.574 J.D. Pres., Jerome Rothenberg, PC
Rowell, Lewis S. ....'55 '98 C.870 B.S. L.574 J.D. [Womble C.S.&R.] (Pat.)
Rowlett, Margaret F., (BV) ....'64 '90 C.244 B.A. L.228 J.D. [Smith,J.R.&C.]
Ruby, Barbara C., (AV) ....'49 '76 C.228 B.A. L.575 J.D. [Smith M.]
Sacrinty, Martha R. ....'79 '04 C.577 B.A. L.575 J.D. [Hill,E.D.J.&B.]
Saintsing, James R., (AV) ....'57 '85 C.896 B.A. L.575 J.D. [Saintsing P.]
Saintsing PLLC, (AV) ....403 A North Elm Street

Sampson, J. Mark ....'72 '99 C.228 A.B. L.896 J.D. [[A] Womble C.S.&R.]
Sánchez Valencia, Carlos F. '70 '95 C&L.999
Legal Dir. & Corp. Secy., Volvo Coml. Fin. LLC, The Americas
Sanders, Craig E. ....'70 '95 C.575 B.S. L.228 J.D. 4206 Bitternut Trl
Sanders, Natalie Kay, (BV) ....'70 '95 C.106 B.A. L.228 J.D. [Brooks,P.M.H.&L.]
Sansone, Jos. A. ....'23 '54 C&L.602 B.S., LL.B. 1808 Spring Garden St.
Sar, David W., (BV) ....'71 '96 C.228 B.A. L.976 J.D. [Brooks,P.M.H.&L.] ⊙
Saslow, Everett B., Jr., (AV) ....'51 '76 C&L.575 B.A., J.D. [Hill,E.D.J.&B.]
Saunders, Charles W., Jr. '42 '70 C.968 A.B. L.575 J.D.
V.P. & Reg. Tr. Offr., First Union National Bank
Saunders, Robert W., (AV) .... '59 '87 C.575 B.A. L.893 J.D. [Brooks,P.M.H.&L.] ⊙
Sawyer, Wendell H., (BV) ....'51 '80 C.316 B.A. L.45 J.D. P.O. Box 4203
Schaaf, Scott A. ....'77 '02 C&L.575 B.A., J.D. [Tuggle D.&M.]

Schafer, Gerald S., (AV) '44 '70 C&L.575 A.B., J.D. [BB]
220 Commerce Place, 27401
Telephone: 336-273-9309 Fax: 336-273-2700
General Civil Practice. Bankruptcy, Debtor/Creditors Rights Law, Collection and Criminal Law.
See Professional Biographies, GREENSBORO, NORTH CAROLINA

Scharf, Heino W. '45 '74 C.234 B.S. L.1095 J.D.
(adm. in CA; not adm. in NC) Mgr., Product Assurance, Volvo GM Heavy Truck Corp.
Schell, Braxton, (AV) ....'24 '51 C&L.575 B.S., J.D. [Schell B.A.A.&L.]
Schell, Kimberly A. ....'79 '05 C.692 B.A. L.896 J.D. [[A] Pinto C.K.&B.]

Schell Bray Aycock Abel & Livingston P.L.L.C., (AV) [BB]
1500 Renaissance Plaza, 230 North Elm Street, P.O. Box 21847, 27420
Telephone: 336-370-8800 Fax: 336-370-8830
Email: Info@sbaal.com URL: http://www.sbaal.com
Members of Firm: Braxton Schell; Doris R. Bray; William P. Aycock, II (Board Certified Specialist in Real Property Law - Business, Commercial and Industrial Transactions, North Carolina State Board of Legal Specialization); Michael R. Abel; Paul H. Livingston, Jr. (Board Certified Specialist in Estate Planning and Probate Law, North Carolina State Board of Legal Specialization); Thomas C. Watkins; Michael H. Godwin; Barbara R. Christy; John A. McLendon, Jr.; Melanie Samson Tuttle; Jennifer L.J. Koenig (Board Certified Specialist in Estate Planning and Probate Law, North Carolina State Board of Legal Specialization); Holly H. Alderman (Resident, Chapel Hill, North Carolina Office) (Board Certified Specialist in Real Property Law: Business, Commercial and Industrial Transactions, North Carolina State Board of Legal Specialization); Mark T. Cain. Associates: Garland G. Graham; Stacey A. Brady; Jill L. Raspet; John Craig Kiser; Christina N. Freeman; Samantha G. Steffen.
Corporate, Taxation, Securities Regulation, Venture Capital, Real Estate and Real Estate Finance, Mergers and Acquisitions, Health Care, Antitrust and Trade Regulation, Banking, Commercial, Employee Benefits, Estate Planning and Administration.
See Professional Biographies, GREENSBORO, NORTH CAROLINA

Schiffman, Adelia T., (BV) ....'65 '90 C.577 B.A. L.896 J.D. [Chandler,S.&Assoc.]
Schiftan, Lynne G., (AV) ....'52 '79 C.575 B.A. L.574 J.D. Dept. Co. Atty.
Schlosser, E. S., Jr., (BV) ....'39 '65 C&L.575 A.B., LL.B. 101 S. Elm St.
Schlosser, Michael A., (BV) ....'45 '73 C.885 B.A. L.896 J.D. [Schlosser&P.]

Schlosser & Pritchett, (BV)
5709 W. Friendly Avenue, 27410
Telephone: 336-292-4076 Fax: 336-292-8003
URL: http://www.schlosserpritchett.com
Michael A. Schlosser; Jan Elliott Pritchett. Associates: L. Steven Wayne; Scott G. Galiger.
Criminal Law, Wrongful Death, Automobile Accidents, Felonies, Misdemeanors, Traffic, Personal Injury, Litigation in State and Federal Courts.
See Professional Biographies, GREENSBORO, NORTH CAROLINA

Schultz, Lawrence H., Jr., (BVⓣ) '26 '53 C.976 A.B. L.188 J.D.
3017 W. Cornwallis Dr.
Schwartz, Eugenia S. '42 '80 C.577 B.A. L.602 J.D.
(adm. in IN; not adm. in NC) 422A Fisher Park Circle‡
Schwenn, William L. .... '48 '73 C&L.575 A.B., J.D. Court Clk., U.S. Bkrptcy. Ct.
Scott, Bryan G. ....'79 '04 C.34 B.A. L.896 J.D. [[A] Pinto C.K.&B.]
Scott, Robert L. '43 '75 C.1016 B.A. L.1119 J.D.
(adm. in IL; not adm. in NC) 305 E. Montcastle Dr., Apt. A‡
Seals, Amy Dyar '63 '88 C.572 B.S. L.1059 J.D.
(adm. in GA; not adm. in NC) 320 Federal Place
Semmler, Carl D., (BV) '58 '87 C.575 B.A. L.896 J.D.
Assist. V.P. and Assoc. Coun., Jefferson-Pilot Corporation & Subsidiaries
Senter, David A., (AV) ....'— '84 C&L.896 B.S., J.D. [Nexsen P.A.K.]
Seymour, Hubert E., Jr. ....'24 '51 C.309 A.B. L.477 J.D. 1105 Pender Lane‡
Shannon, Michael J. '65 '95 C.602 B.B.A. L.429 J.D
(adm. in KY; not adm. in NC) Assoc. G.C., Dir. Gov't Rel., Lorillard Tobacco Co.
Sharp, Edward R. ....'— '02 C.858 B.A. L.896 J.D. [[A] Smith M.]
Sharp, P. Trevor ....'47 '74 C.970 B.A. L.477 J.D. U.S. Mag.
Sharpless, Frederick K., (AV) ....'— '84 C.197 A.B. L.575 J.D. [Sharpless&S.]

Sharpless & Stavola, P.A., (AV) [BB]
826 North Elm Street, P.O. Box 22106, 27420
Telephone: 336-333-6400 Facsimile: 336-333-6399
URL: http://www.sharpless-stavola.com
Frederick K. Sharpless; Pamela A. Robertson; Joseph M. Stavola; Brenda S. McClearn; Joseph P. Booth, III; Brian H. Alligood; Eugene E. Lester, III;—Christina L. Lewis.
General Civil Litigation, Trials and Appeals in all State and Federal Courts, Professional and Medical Malpractice, Construction and Commercial Litigation, Business Torts, Hospitals and Health Care, Employment and Administrative Law, Insurance Coverage, Wrongful Death, Product Liability Defense, Toxic Torts, Environmental Litigation.
Representative Clients: Jefferson Pilot Corporation; Church Mutual Insurance Co.; CNA Insurance Group; Senergy, Inc.; The Medical Protective Company; AIG Companies; Beverly Enterprises; Dixon Hughes, P.L.L.C.; Davenport, Marvin, Joyce & Co., L.L.P.
See Professional Biographies, GREENSBORO, NORTH CAROLINA

Shaw, John E. '42 '83 C.832 B.S. L.370 J.D.
(adm. in AL; not adm. in NC) Exec. Dir., City Human Rel. Dept.
Shelton, J. Marshall ....'75 '03 C.575 B.S. L.607 J.D. [[A] Ivey,M.G.&T.]
Sheridan, Desmond G., (AV) ....'57 '86 C.260 B.S. L.575 J.D. [Isaacson I.&S.]
Sherrill, David E., Law Office of .....'67 '02 C.955 B.S.N. L.574 J.D. 1101 W. Market St.
Shields, Ginger S., (BV) ....'71 '97 C.198 B.A. L.228 J.D. [Brooks,P.M.H.&L.]
Shipley, Curtis J. ....'63 '90 C.597 B.S. L.352 J.D. [Ellis&W.] ⊙
Sholtz, Michael C. ....'55 '88 C.976 B.A. L.884 LL.M U.S. Trust Co. of North Carolina
Shope, Richard I., (BV) ....'44 '73 C&L.575 A.B., J.D. [R.I.Shope]
Shope, Richard I., Attorneys At Law, P.A., (BV) .... 426 W. Friendly Avenue
Shortt, Lisa Kaminski ....'66 '00 C.296 B.S. L.896 J.D. [[A] Smith M.]
Siegmund, Dirk W., (BV) ....'59 '94 C.205 B.S.B.A. L.896 J.D. [Ivey,M.G.&T.]
Singer, Larry A. '48 '74 C.831 B.B.A. L.472 J.D.
(adm. in FL; not adm. in NC) 3615 Friendly Acres Dr.
Singer, Robert A., (AV) ....'52 '79 C.575 B.A. L.896 J.D. [Brooks,P.M.H.&L.]
Sinks, Thomas W., (AV) ....'50 '76 C.198 A.B. L.575 J.D. 5305 Century Oaks Dr.‡
Sitton, Larry B., (AV) ....'40 '64 C&L.896 B.A., LL.B. [Smith M.]
Sizemore, Polly D., (AV) ....'52 '88 C.34 B.A. L.896 J.D. [Hill,E.D.J.&B.]
Slaughter, James H., (AV) ....'64 '89 C&L.575 B.A., J.D. [Forman R.B.]
Small, John H., (AV) ....'54 '79 C.575 B.A. L.976 J.D. [Brooks,P.M.H.&L.]

Smalls, Harriett T. ....'55 '99 C.577 B.S.N. L.575 J.D. [[A] Smith M.]
Smith, Daniel E. ....'57 '82 C.232 B.S.B.A. L.1228 J.D. 404 W. Bessemer Ave.

Smith, David B., (AV) '48 '73 C.1378 B.S. L.575 J.D. [BB]
First Citizens Bank Building, 100 South Elm Street, Suite 520, 27402
Mailing Address: P.O. Box 2097, Greensboro, NC 27402-2097
Telephone: 336-574-2533 Fax: 336-574-3378
Email: dbsmithattorney@msn.com URL: http://www.dbsmithattorney.net
Criminal Practice in all State and Federal Courts, Criminal Law, Driving While Intoxicated (DWI), Drug Crimes, Juvenile Crimes, Parole and Probation, Traffic Violations, White Collar Crimes, Federal Appellate, Federal Forfeitures, Fraud.
See Professional Biographies, GREENSBORO, NORTH CAROLINA

Smith, Jeffrey L. '66 '91 C&L.575 A.B., J.D.
Asst. V.P. & Assoc. Coun., Jefferson-Pilot Corporation & Subsidiaries
Smith, Julius C., III, (AV) ....'22 '49 C&L.575 A.B., LL.B. 300 North Greene Street‡
Smith, McNeill, (AV) ....'18 '41 C.575 A.B. L.178 LL.B. 300 North Greene Street
Smith, Michele G., (AV) ....'51 '93 C.34 B.S. L.896 J.D. [Hill,E.D.J.&B.]
Smith, Norman B., (AV) ....'38 '65 C.575 A.B. L.309 LL.B. [[S] Smith,J.R.&C.]
Smith Daniel, Paula ....'64 '93 C.188 B.S. L.659 J.D. 3607 Shenango Rd.

Smith, James, Rowlett & Cohen, L.L.P., (AV)
101 South Elm Street, Suite 310, P.O. Box 990, 27402
Telephone: 336-274-2992 FAX: 336-274-8490
Email: sjrclaw@earthlink.net URL: http://www.sjrclaw.com
Members of Firm: J. David James; Margaret F. Rowlett; Seth R. Cohen. Of Counsel: Norman B. Smith.
General Practice in all State and Federal Courts. Antitrust, Employment, Labor, Constitutional, Divorce, Environmental, Probate, Workers Compensation, Negligence, Personal Injury, Product Liability; Shareholder and Investor Rights; Civil and Criminal Trial and Appellate Practice, Wills.
See Professional Biographies, GREENSBORO, NORTH CAROLINA

Smith Moore LLP, (AV) [BB]
Wachovia Tower, 300 North Greene Street, Suite 1400, P.O. Box 21927, 27420 ⊙
Telephone: 336-378-5200 Fax: 336-378-5400
Email: smith.moore@smithmoorelaw.com URL: http://www.smithmoorelaw.com
Partners: D. Erik Albright; Bruce P. Ashley; Evan Kent Auberry; W. Alexander Audilet; Jonathan A. Berkelhammer; Carole Watkins Bruce; William E. Burton III; Harold N. Bynum; Manning A. Connors, III; Richard A. Coughlin; J. Donald Cowan, Jr.; Gerard H. Davidson, Jr.; Herbert O. Davis; Alan W. Duncan; Stephen W. Earp; Martin N. Erwin; Marilyn Feuchs-Marker; Susan McNear Fradenburg; Lisa Frye Garrison; Terrill Johnson Harris; Gregory G. Holland; Michael E. Kelly; Stephen E. Klee; David L. Kyger; Michael V. Lee (Resident, Wilmington Office); Caroline Hudson Lock; Robert R. Marcus; Alexander L. Maultsby; Philip P. McCann; James A. Medford; Maureen Demarest Murray; Ramona Cunningham O'Bryant; Timothy Peck; Barbara C. Ruby (Board Certified Specialist in Estate Planning and Probate Law, North Carolina State Board of Legal Specialization); Larry B. Sitton; Thomas E. Terrell, Jr.; Julianna C. Theall; Allison Overbay Van Laningham; E. Garrett Walker; Jeri L. Whitfield (Board Certified Specialist in Worker's Compensation Law, North Carolina State Board of Legal Specialization). Associates: Drew Brown; Laura Deddish Burton; Brian W. Byrd; Crystal Bowman Crews; James M. Dewey; James R. Faucher; Kimberly Bullock Gatling; Eileen King Gillis; L. Cooper Harrell; Jonathan Heyl; Neale T. Johnson; Robert D. Kidwell; Amy H. Kincaid; Bailey King; Angela L. Little; Travis W. Martin; Jordan Nance; Patricia Carole Perkins; Caroline Collins Pickup; Patti West Ramseur (Resident); Edward R. Sharp; Lisa Kaminski Shortt; Harriett T. Smalls; Heather Howell Wright. Counsel: Stanislav Antolin; Walter Y. Boyd Jr.; James G. Exum, Jr.; Bynum M. Hunter; Amy Smith Klass; Charles E. Melvin, Jr.; Stephen Perry Millikin; David M. Moore II; Samuel M. Moore; D. Marsh Prause.
General, Trial and Appellate Practice in All State and Federal Courts, Dispute Resolution, Corporate, Taxation, Securities Regulation, Real Property and Finance, Labor and Employment (Management) Law, Employee Benefits, International and Immigration, Antitrust and Trade Regulation, Negligence, Products Liability, Insurance Coverage, Media, Banking, Commercial, Bankruptcy, Administrative, Environmental, Hospital and Health Care, Public Authority and Public Finance, Estate Planning and Administration, Probate, Legislative, Intellectual Property, Education, and Sports Law.
Raleigh, North Carolina Office: 2800 Two Hannover Square, P.O. Box 27525. Telephone: 919-755-8700. Fax: 919-755-8800.
Atlanta, Georgia Office: One Atlantic Center, Suite 3700, 1201 West Peachtree Street. Telephone: 404-962-1000. Fax: 404-962-1200.
Wilmington, North Carolina Office: 300 North Third Street, Suite 301. Telephone: 910-251-7001. Fax: 910-251-7007.
See Professional Biographies, GREENSBORO, NORTH CAROLINA

Snyder, Barry C., (BV) ....'50 '78 C.577 B.A. L.575 J.D. 210 W. Friendly Ave.
Spagnola, Samuel S., (BV) '70 '98 C.296 B.A. L.802 J.D.
100 South Elm Street, Suite 430
Spainhour, Elizabeth E. .... '73 '05 C.197 B.A. L.575 J.D. [Brooks,P.M.H.&L.] ⊙
Spainhour, R. Andrew, (BV) '71 '98
C.198 B.A. L.575 J.D. Gen. Coun., Replacements, Ltd.
Spangler, David B., (BV) ....'50 '77 C.575 B.A. L.362 J.D. [D.B.Spangler]
Spangler, David B., P.A., (BV) ....337 S. Greene St.
Sparrow, Donald G., (AV) ....'45 '70 C&L.575 A.B., J.D. [Sparrow W.&S.]
Sparrow, Jason B., (BV) ....'71 '98 C&L.575 B.A., J.D. [Sparrow W.&S.]
Sparrow, Sarah F., (AV) ....'45 '85 C.228 B.S.N. L.575 J.D. [Tuggle D.&M.]

Sparrow Wolf & Sparrow, P.A., (AV) [BB]
812 North Elm Street, P.O. Box 308, 27401
Telephone: 336-544-5080 Fax: 336-544-5085
URL: http://www.sparrowwolflaw.com
Donald G. Sparrow; Gary R. Wolf; Jason B. Sparrow.
General Trial Practice in all State and Federal Courts. Business Law, Corporate Law, Commercial Finance, Real Estate, Construction Law, Personal Injury, Motor Vehicle Law.
See Professional Biographies, GREENSBORO, NORTH CAROLINA

Speckhard, Donald K., (BV) ....'41 '70 C.404 B.A. L.575 J.D. [Alexander,R.S.&S.]
Speckhard, Stanley E., (AV) ....'49 '75 C&L.575 B.A., J.D. [Alexander,R.S.&S.]
Sperling, Mack, (AV) ....'58 '83 C.867 B.A. L.575 J.D. [Brooks,P.M.H.&L.]
Spiker, Randa H., (BV) ....'71 '97 C.575 B.A. L.1228 J.D. P.O. Box 10769
Sroka, Daniel M., (AV) .... '62 '89 C.966 B.B.A. L.896 J.D. [D.Sroka,Sr.]

Sroka, Daniel, P.C., (AV)
3625 North Elm Street, Suite 107A, P.O. Box 1658, 27402
Telephone: 336-282-5584 Facsimile: 336-282-5796
Email: Dan@Srokaweb.com URL: http://www.Srokaweb.com
Daniel M. Sroka.
Corporate Law, Mergers and Acquisitions, Commercial Transactions, Franchise Law, Intellectual Property Licensing, Business Law, Commercial Real Estate.
See Professional Biographies, GREENSBORO, NORTH CAROLINA

Stamey, Foust & Dwyer, LLP, (BV) ......204 Muirs Chapel Road, Ste. 300 (⊙Jamestown)
Stanaland, Elizabeth M., (AV) '58 '85
C&L.260 B.A., J.D. 101 South Elm Street, Suite 350
Stanaland, Terence B., (AV) '56 '84
C.232 B.S.B.A. L.260 J.D. 101 South Elm Street, Suite 350
Standish, Myles E., (BV) ....'54 '82 C.309 B.A. L.575 J.D. Oakwood Homes Corp.
Stange, Richard T., (AV) '47 '72 C&L.896 B.A., J.D.
V.P. & Dep. Gen. Coun., Jefferson-Pilot Corporation & Subsidiaries
Stavola, Joseph M., (AVⓣ) ....'— '79 C.1044 B.A. L.564 J.D. [Sharpless&S.]
Steffen, Samantha G. ....'73 '98 C.1175 B.S.B.A. L.260 J.D. [[A] Schell B.A.A.&L.]
Stegall, Laurie R., (BV) ....'68 '93 C.296 B.A. L.575 J.D. [L.R.Stegall]

Stegall, Laurie R., P.A., Law Office of, (BV)
529 College Road, Suite C, 27410
Telephone: 336-299-0170 Facsimile: 336-299-0740
Email: stegalllaw@aol.com URL: http://www.lauriestegalllaw.com
Laurie R. Stegall.
Residential Real Estate, Real Estate Closings, Estate Planning, Wills.

See Professional Biographies, GREENSBORO, NORTH CAROLINA

Stein, Daniel J. .... '47 '75 C.446 B.A. L.128 J.D. U.S. Admin. Law J.
Stelts, Anne E. .... '74 '99 C&L.896 B.A., J.D. Pro Se Law Clk.

Stern, Klepfer & Wright, PLLC, (AV)
101 West Friendly Avenue, Suite 600, 27401
Telephone: 336-373-1500 Fax: 336-272-8258
Sidney J. Stern, Jr. (1914-1991); John L. Rendleman (1932-1983). Members of Firm: Robert O. Klepfer, Jr.; Brinton D. Wright. Associates: Sally B. Cone; Maureen Breen Gerhardt; Kathleen Murphy Brinkey.
General Practice in State and Federal Courts, before Administrative Tribunals. Adoptions, Business, Closely Held Business, Limited Liability Companies, Contracts, Real Property, Real Estate, Commercial Leasing, Trusts and Estates, Estate Planning, Wills, Probate, Elder Law.
Representative Clients: SouthTrust Bank; Bank of America, N.A.; Tannenbaum-Sternberger Foundation; Bennett College; Robins & Weill, Inc.; Carlyle & Co. Jewelers.

See Professional Biographies, GREENSBORO, NORTH CAROLINA

Stevenson, C. Mark .... '73 '02 C.1175 B.S. L.472 J.D. [A Carruthers&R.]
Stewart, Barbara Lynn .... '57 '90 C.805 B.A. L.846 J.D. [A Forman R.B.]
Stockdale, Matthew Alan .... '75 '00 C.20 B.A. L.896 J.D. [M.A.Stockdale]

Stockdale, Matt A., PLLC, Law Office of
313 South Greene Street, Suite 303, 27401
Telephone: 336-510-0941 Fax: 336-510-0967 URL: http://www.mattstockdalelaw.com
Email: matt@mattstockdalelaw.com URL: http://www.mstockdalelaw.com
Member of Firm: Matthew Alan Stockdale.
Criminal Law, Traffic Violations, Driving While Intoxicated, Drug Crimes, Parole and Probate, White Collar Crime, Trust and Estates, Estate Planning, Business Law, Child Support.

See Professional Biographies, GREENSBORO, NORTH CAROLINA

Stocks, William L. .... '42 '66 C.232 L.575 J.D. U.S. Bkrptcy. J.
Stokes, Theophilus O., III .. '56 '84 C.296 B.A. L.896 J.D. 106 S. Murrow Blvd., Ste. 200
Stone, Kenneth W., (AV) '60 '85 C.953 B.S. L.575 J.D.
Mgr. & Underwriting Coun., Fidelity Natl. Title Ins. Co.
Strange, Ross E. .... '28 '61 C&L.472 B.S.Ed., LL.B. Southeastern Bldg.
Street, Marquis D., (P.A.) .... '46 '71 C.1378 B.S. L.352 J.D. [M.D.Street]
Street, Marquis D., P.A. .... 125 South Elm Street, Suite 400
Stuart, Carmon J. .... '14 '38 C.34 B.S. L.228 LL.B. 101 W. Friendly Ave.
Stukes, Thomas S., (AV) '47 '74 C&L.575 A.B., J.D.
300 North Greene Street, Suite 1900
Sudermann, Emily E. '67 '97 C.198 B.A. L.180 J.D.
Assoc. Coun., Jefferson-Pilot Corporation & Subsidiaries
Sue, Gary K., (AV) .... '58 '85 C.896 B.A. L.356 J.D. [Burton&S.]
Suher, Thomas R. '50 '74 C.31 B.A. L.575 J.D.
Corp. Coun., Lucent Technologies Inc.
Sumner, Kathleen G., (BV) .... '50 '90 C.763 B.A. L.1228 J.D. [K.G.Sumner]

Sumner, Kathleen G., Law Offices of, (BV)
9 Terrace Way, Suite B, 27403
Mailing Address: P.O. Box 7915, Greensboro, NC 27417-0915
Telephone: 336-294-9388 Toll Free: 800-376-9718 Fax: 336-294-9144
Email: KSumner@sumnerlaw.net URL: http://www.sumnerlaw.net
Attorneys: Kathleen G. Sumner; Jeanette F. Gray.
Worker Compensation, Appellate Practice.

See Professional Biographies, GREENSBORO, NORTH CAROLINA

Sutherland, Francis A., Jr. '40 '65 C.478 A.B. L.902 LL.B.
V.P. & Ins. Coun., Jefferson-Pilot Corporation & Subsidiaries
Sutton, Roger B., (AV) '47 '76 C&L.575 B.S., J.D.
Sr. V.P. & Gen. Coun., The Todd Organization of the Carolinas, L.L.C.
Swecker, Mary Beth B., (BV) .... '61 '88 C.893 B.S. L.896 J.D. [Ivey,M.G.&T.] ‡
Swindlehurst, Cynthia Munk .... '— '03 C.101 B.A. L.228 J.D. [A Tuggle D.&M.]
Swisher, James L. .... '38 '62 C&L.896 B.A., J.D. [Cahoon&S.N.C.&L.]
Talcott, James K., (AV) .... '46 '85 C.260 B.S.B.A. L.896 J.D. [Ivey,M.G.&T.]
Talley, Karen Strom .... '77 '02 C.577 B.A. L.575 J.D. [Henson&H.]
Tankersley, Tracey G., (BV) .... '68 '94 C.575 B.A. L.896 J.D. [T.Tankersley]
Tankersley, William L., III, (AV) .... '48 '74 C.269 B.A. L.575 J.D. [C Carruthers&R.]
Tankersley, Tracey, (BV) .... 314 S. Eugene St.
Tate, Charles M., (AV) .... '43 '68 C&L.575 A.B., J.D. [Tate,G.L.P.&W.]

Tate, Gaylord, Lucas, Purdom & Workman, L.L.P., (AV)
Suite 101, Friendly Holden Building, 3608 West Friendly Avenue, 27410
Mailing Address: P.O. Box 4544, Greensboro, NC 27404
Telephone: 336-218-0602 Fax: 336-218-0025
Members of Firm: Charles M. Tate; T.M. (Mark) Gaylord, Jr.; Kenneth S. Lucas, Jr.; Eugene W. Purdom; Jeffrey T. Workman. Retired: Julius Dees, Jr. (1925-2001); H. M. Giles, Jr. (Retired); Charles R. Tedder (Retired).
General Practice. Trials in all State and Federal Courts. Business, Corporate, Commercial, Real Estate, Foreclosure, Construction, Probate, Bankruptcy, Personal Injury, Wrongful Death, Estate Planning and Administration, Mediation, Collections.
Counsel for: Pegram-West, Inc.; Coyne Beahm Shouse, Inc.; Offutt Systems, Inc.; Jarrett Construction Co., Inc.
Representative Client: Nations Bank.
Approved Attorneys for: Lawyers Title Insurance Corp.

See Professional Biographies, GREENSBORO, NORTH CAROLINA

Taylor, Craig A. .... '76 '01 C&L.896 B.A., J.D. [A Carruthers&R.]
Teague, Stephen G., (AV) '58 '83 C.575 B.A. L.896 J.D.
101 South Elm Street, Suite 350
Tedder, Charles R., (AV) .... '34 '62 C.258 B.S. L.896 LL.B. [Tate,G.L.P.&W.] ‡

Temple Law Firm, PLLC
(See Raleigh)

Tennille, Ben F. '45 '71 C&L.575 B.A., J.D.
Spec. Supr. Ct. J., Complex. Bus., NC Bus. Ct.
Terrell, Thomas E., Jr., (AV) .... '57 '85 C&L.575 B.A., J.D. [Smith M.]
Tewkesbury, Edward P., (AV) .... '52 '78 C.968 B.A. L.228 J.D. [Tewkesbury]
Tewkesbury Law Offices, (AV) .... 1604 B Battleground Avenue
Theall, Julianna C., (AV) .... '61 '86 C&L.280 B.B.A., J.D. [Smith M.]
Thomas, Devin Ferree .... '69 '97 C.575 B.A. L.896 J.D. [Oxner T.&P.]

Thomas, J. Michael, (AV) '57 '84 C.896 B.A. L.575 J.D.
318 S. Eugene Street, Suite 107, 27401
Telephone: 336-691-8150 Fax: 336-691-8151
Email: thomasjmtlawyer@aol.com
Construction Law, Municipal Law, Civil Litigation, Alimony, Divorce, Equitable Distribution, Separation Agreements, Zoning and Land Use.
Representative Clients: Bank of America; City of Reidsville; Town of Oak Ridge.
Approved Attorney for: First American Title Insurance Co.; Chicago Title Insurance Co.; Investors Title Insurance Co.; Lawyers Title Insurance Co.

See Professional Biographies, GREENSBORO, NORTH CAROLINA

Thomas, Nancy Payne .... '61 '00 C.577 B.S. L.574 J.D. 14 Moss Cove Court
Thornton, Thomas S., Jr., (AV) .... '— '69 C.228 B.A. L.896 J.D. [Nexsen P.A.K.]
Tilley, N. Carlton, Jr. .... '43 '69 C&L.896 B.S., J.D. Chf. U.S. Dist. J.
Tinsley, V. Randall, (AV) .... '58 '87 C.608 B.S. L.893 J.D. [Brooks,P.M.H.&L.]
Tobin, R. Scott, (AV(T)) .... '— '81 C&L.575 B.A., J.D. [G Nexsen P.A.K.]
Toman, Dennis J., (AV) .... '59 '84 C.966 B.B.A. L.575 J.D. [D.J.Toman]
Toman, Dennis J., PC, Law Offices of, (AV) .... P.O. Box 18322
Tomlin, Brian, (BV) .... '60 '96 C.893 B.A. L.574 J.D. [Hunter,H.M.E.&B.]
Townsend, Mark R. .... '60 '85 C&L.896 B.A., J.D. Asst. Gen. Coun., VF Corp.
Trathen, Marcus W., (AV) .... '65 '90 C&L.575 B.A., J.D. [Brooks,P.M.H.&L.] ⊙
Trevorrow, William B., (AV) .... '34 '66 C.316 A.B. L.896 LL.B. [R.D.Hall,Jr.]
Trivette, William S. .... '48 '78 C.870 B.S. L.744 J.D. Asst. Fed. Pub. Def.
Troutman, Michael K. .... '— '94 C.1378 L.574 J.D. [M.K.Troutman]
Troutman, Michael K., P.A., Law Offices of .... 400 W. Market Street, Suite 501
Troxler, Shawn C. .... '78 '05 C.576 B.S. L.577 J.D. [A Hill,E.D.J.&B.]
Truesdell, Laurie S., (BV) .... '58 '87 C&L.575 B.S., J.D. [Ott C.&R.]
Tucker, Catherine I. '67 '93 C.420 B.A. L.1017 J.D.
Assoc. Coun., Specialty Fin., Volvo Coml. Fin. LLC, The Americas
Tucker, R. Rand, (AV) .... '60 '85 C.575 B.A. L.477 J.D. Corp. Coun., La-Z-Boy Inc.
Tuggle, Richard J., (AV) .... '30 '59 C&L.575 B.S., J.D. [Tuggle D.&M.]

Tuggle Duggins & Meschan, P.A., (AV) BR
228 West Market Street, P.O. Box 2888, 27402-2888
Telephone: 336-378-1431 Telecopier: 336-274-6590
URL: http://www.tuggleduggins.com
Richard J. Tuggle; James N. Duggins, Jr.; David F. Meschan; J. Reed Johnston, Jr.; Paul M. Dennis, Jr.; Robert C. Cone; John R. Barlow, II (Board Certified Specialist in Real Property Law-Residential, Business, Commercial and Industrial Transactions, North Carolina State Board of Legal Specialization); H. Vaughn Ramsey; William C. Connor; Bradley L. Jacobs (Board Certified Specialist in Estate Planning and Probate Law, North Carolina State Board of Legal Specialization); Michael J. Wenig; Denis E. Jacobson; William G. Burgin, III (Board Certified Specialist in Real Property Law, Residential, Business, Commercial and Industrial Transactions, North Carolina State Board of Legal Specialization); Scott C. Gayle; Kenneth J. Gumbiner; Sarah F. Sparrow (Board Certified Specialist in Business and Consumer Bankruptcy Law, North Carolina State Board of Legal Specialization); Kenneth M. Johnson; Peter O. Evenson, Sr.; Michael S. Fox; Eric W. Hardin; J. Nathan Duggins III; Janie L. Long; Scott A. Schaaf; Cynthia Munk Swindlehurst; Thomas E. Noble; Rebecca A. Niburg.
General Civil Practice. Corporation, Tax, Insurance, Banking, Pension and Profit Sharing, Bankruptcy and Creditors' Rights, Trust and Estate, Construction and Real Estate Law. Trials and Appeals in all State and Federal Courts.
Representative Clients: Allen Industries, Inc.; Beacon Technologies, Inc.; The Fresh Market, Inc.; Highland Industries, Inc.; Kingsdown, Inc.; Shamrock Environmental Corporation; Southern Foods Group, Inc.; Takata Restraint Systems, Inc.
References: Wachovia Bank, N.A.

See Professional Biographies, GREENSBORO, NORTH CAROLINA

Turlington, J. Edwin, (AV) .... '57 '82 C.228 B.A. L.575 J.D. [Brooks,P.M.H.&L.] ⊙
Turman, Dean .... '69 '01 C.576 B.S. L.312 J.D. [A MacCord M.P.] (See Pat. Sect.)
Turner, James R., (AV) .... '34 '63 C.575 A.B. L.976 LL.B. 505 Willoughby Boulevard
Turner, Joseph E. .... '50 '76 C.198 B.A. L.575 J.D. Dist. J.
Turner & Lloyd, P.A., (AV) .... 806 Green Valley Road, Suite 203
Tuttle, Melanie Samson .... '54 '83 C.477 B.S.E. L.150 J.D. [Schell B.A.A.&L.]

Twiggs, Beskind, Strickland & Rabenau, P.A.
(See Raleigh)

Tyser, Wallace C., Jr. '44 '68 C&L.575 B.A., J.D.
Gen. Coun., Oakwood Acceptance Corp., LLC
Underwood, Randall A., (AV) .... '52 '79 C.575 B.S. L.893 J.D. [Brooks,P.M.H.&L.]
Upchurch, Fred M., (AV) .... '31 '58 C&L.896 B.S., LL.B. P.O. Box 29202‡
Van Laningham, Allison Overbay, (AV) .... '71 '96 C&L.896 B.A., J.D. [Smith M.]
Van Noppen, Leonard H. .... '15 '37 C&L.896 LL.B. Ret. Dist. J.
Vanore, Richard L., (AV) .... '47 '73 C&L.575 A.B., J.D. [Carruthers&R.]
Van Zant, Jennifer K., (AV) .... '69 '94 C.228 B.S. L.896 J.D. [Brooks,P.M.H.&L.]
Vaporis, Theodora A. .... '64 '88 C.999 B.A. L.128 J.D. [A Forman R.B.]
Vaughan, Donald (Don) R. .... '52 '82 C.575 B.A. L.896 J.D. [D.R.Vaughan&Assoc.]

Vaughan, Donald R., and Associates
Attorneys and Counselors at Law
612 W. Friendly Avenue, 27401
Telephone: 336-273-1415 Fax: 336-273-1445
Email: vaughanlaw@aol.com
Donald (Don) R. Vaughan.
Traffic Violations and Criminal Law.

See Professional Biographies, GREENSBORO, NORTH CAROLINA

Vaughn, Christopher J., (BV) .... '68 '94 C.577 B.S. L.228 J.D. [Carruthers&R.]
Vizithum, Sara R. .... '75 '02 C.323 B.A. L.575 J.D. [Brooks,P.M.H.&L.]
Vreeland, Arthur A., (AV) .... '44 '75 C.228 A.B. L.188 J.D. 4 Parkmont Court
Wagoner, Anna Mills S. '49 '85 C.6 B.A. L.896 J.D.
U.S. Atty., U.S. Dist. Ct., Middle Dist. of North Carolina
Waldrep, Thomas W., Jr. .... '57 '83 C.679 B.A. L.1119 J.D. U.S. Bkrptcy. J.
Walker, E. Garrett, (AV) .... '50 '75 C&L.575 A.B., J.D. [Smith M.]
Walker, Perry N., (AV) .... '25 '55 C.296 A.B. L.896 LL.B. 400 W. Market St.‡

Walker, R. Shane '74 '01 C.575 B.A. L.1228 J.D.
520 South Elm Street, Suite 204, 27420
Mailing Address: P.O. Box 20448, Greensboro, NC 27420
Telephone: 336-373-9902 Fax: 336-373-9903
Email: rshanewalkerlaw@yahoo.com URL: http://www.rshanewalkerlaw.com
Automobile Accidents and Injuries, Traffic Violations, Wills, Civil Litigation, General Practice.

See Professional Biographies, GREENSBORO, NORTH CAROLINA

Wall, John W., Jr., (AV) ... '48 '74 C.316 B.A. L.896 J.D. 604 Green Valley Rd., Ste. 210
Wall, Jonathan, (BV) .... '64 '94 C.228 B.A. L.902 J.D. [Clark B.&W.]
Wall, Percy L., (AV) .... '25 '51 C&L.575 A.B., LL.B. [P.L.Wall]
Wall, Philip T. .... '30 '56 C.316 B.S. L.896 LL.B. 536 Woodvale Dr.‡

Wall Law Firm, P.C.
(See Winston-Salem)

Wall, Percy L., P.A., (AV) .... 314 S. Eugene Street

Wallace Law Firm, The
(See High Point)

Wannamaker, Charles W., III .... '45 '72 C&L.575 B.A., J.D. 612 W. Cornwallis Dr.
Warner, Joseph E., III '56 '81
C.228 A.B. L.896 J.D. Breslow, Starling, Frost, Warner & Boger
Warner, Timothy G., (BV) .... '26 '48 C&L.228 A.B., LL.B. 10 Provincetown Ct.
Warren, Jesse L., (AV) .... '33 '57 C&L.575 B.S., LL.B. City Atty.
Washington, Barbara Gore .... '— '74 C.1378 B.S. L.1292 J.D. P.O. Box 21242
Watkins, Thomas C., (AV) .... '51 '78 C&L.575 B.S., J.D. [Schell B.A.A.&L.]
Wattleworth, C. Andrew, (BV) .... '66 '96 C.896 B.A. L.192 J.D. Market America, Inc.
Watts, W. Graham .... '50 '89 C.1378 B.S. L.574 J.D. 2506 Four Seasons Blvd.
Wayne, L. Steven .... '72 '98 C.575 B.A. L.1228 J.D. [A Schlosser&P.]
Weatherford, Terry L. .... '42 '71 C.531 B.S. L.838 J.D. 804 Green Valley Road

Weaver, Steven P. ....'76 '02 C&L.575 B.A., J.D. [Brotherton F.Y.&W.]
Webb, Joy Rhyne, (BV) '69 '95
C&L.575 B.A., J.D. [Browne,F.W.&W.] (⊙Creedmoor, Durham)
Weckworth, Robert N. ....'62 '89 C.316 B.A. L.724 J.D. [R.Weckworth]
Weckworth, Robert ....101 South Elm Street, Suite 228

Weeks, James B., (BV) '41 '76 C&L.575 B.A., J.D.
119 North Greene Street, Suite 100, 27401
Telephone: 336-272-7272 Fax: 336-275-0999
Email: weekslaw@xspedius.net URL: http://www.lawyers.com/jamesbweeks
Associate: Dalmir S. Grewal.
General Civil Practice in all State and Federal Courts. Buying and Selling Homes, Commercial Real Estate, Residential Real Estate, Civil Litigation, Personal Injury, Probate, Estate Planning, Corporate Law, Social Security Disability, Criminal Law, Traffic Violations, Driving While Intoxicated.
See Professional Biographies, GREENSBORO, NORTH CAROLINA

Weinstein, Robert M., (BV) ....'36 '61 C.575 A.B. L.896 J.D. [Weinstein]
Weinstein Law Offices, (BV) .... 437 W. Friendly Ave., Suite 111
Weiss, Paul J., Jr. '22 '51 C.260 A.B. L.477 LL.B.
(adm. in FL; not adm. in NC) 2406 Hawthorne St.‡
Wells, Richard L. ....'47 '74 C.475 B.S. L.477 J.D. [Ott C.&R.]
Wells, Robert A., (BV) ....'70 '96 C.886 B.A. L.896 J.D. [Gabriel B.&W.]
Wendling, Gregory A., (BV) '60 '85 C.323 A.B. L.896 J.D.
426 W. Friendly Ave., Ste. A
Wenig, Michael J., (AV) ....'58 '86 C.588 B.S.B.A. L.1119 J.D. [Tuggle D.&M.]
West, Michael D. '50 '75 C&L.575 A.B., J.D.
U.S. Bkrptcy. Admr. for Middle Dist. of N.C.
West, Samuel E., (AV) '47 '77 C.610 A.B. L.575 J.D.
Asst. V.P. & State Coun., First American Title Ins. Co.
Weston, Jerry S. ....'41 '66 C&L.575 A.B., LL.B. 214 Commerce Place‡
Westwater, D. Brooks, Jr. ....'41 '69 C&L.608 B.A., J.D. 104 Erskine Dr.
White, Benjamin Harvey, Jr. ....'42 '68 C&L.896 B.S., J.D. Chf. Asst. U.S. Atty.

White, Charles L., II, (AV) '54 '80 C.228 B.S. L.896 J.D.
330 South Greene Street, 27401
Mailing Address: P.O. Box 9518, Greensboro, NC 27429
Telephone: 336-378-2746 Fax: 336-378-2749
Email: cleroy@mindspring.com URL: http://www.chuckwhitelaw.com
Languages: Spanish.
Criminal Law, Felonies, Misdemeanors, Drug Crimes, State and Federal Court, Drug Forfeiture, Driving While Intoxicated, Traffic Violations, Mediation, Arbitration, Alternative Dispute Resolution, Juvenile Delinquency Law, Child Abuse Neglect and Dependency.
See Professional Biographies, GREENSBORO, NORTH CAROLINA

Whited, Debra L. '58 '83 C&L.575 B.A., J.D.
Asst. Gen. Coun., General Dynamics Advanced Info. Systems
Whiteheart, Kevin W., (BV) '60 '88 C.577 B.A. L.1228 J.D.
Bkrptcy Coun., U.S. Transporation, Volvo Coml. Fin. LLC, The Americas
Whitfield, Jeri L., (AV) ....'50 '77 C.188 B.S. L.273 J.D. [Smith M.]
Whitfield, Robert E., (BV) '47 '78
C.232 B.A. L.574 J.D. [Browne,F.W.&W.] (⊙Creedmoor, Durham)
Whitman, Robyn R. Compton, (AV) '61 '89
C.471 B.A. L.1345 J.D. U.S. Bkrptcy. Admr. Off.
Wiener, Arthur W. ....'17 '46 C.477 B.S.Ed. L.262 J.D. 5005 Tower Rd.‡
Wilcox, William M., IV, (AV) ....'— '83 C.473 B.S. L.896 J.D. [Nexsen P.A.K.]
Wilkerson, Jay M., (BV) .... '— '92 C&L.575 B.S., J.D. [Conner G.S.]
Williams, Gregory S., (AV) ....'65 '90 C.893 B.A. L.945 J.D. [Carruthers&R.]
Williams, Howard L., (AV) ....'45 '72 C.576 B.S. L.896 J.D. [Brooks,P.M.H.&L.]
Williams, James T., Jr., (AV) ......'40 '66 C&L.896 B.A., LL.B. [Brooks,P.M.H.&L.] ⊙
Williams, Miriam '17 '53 C&L.569 LL.B.
(adm. in NY; not adm. in NC) 1800 Dunleith Way‡
Williams, Paul T. ....'45 '77 C.575 B.A. L.896 J.D. Admin. Law J., OHA, SSA
Williams, W. Fred ....'15 '40 C&L.896 B.S., LL.B. 1813 Pembroke Rd.‡

Willis, Amanda M. '68 '93 C.188 B.A. L.588 J.D.
Plaza Station, Banking Street, P.O. Box 9593, 27429
Telephone: 336-688-4638
URL: http://www.amandawillislaw.com
Business and Commercial Litigation, Bankruptcy, Debt and Credit, Real Estate, Construction, Eminent Domain, Land Lord/Tenant, Animal Law and Animal Cruelty Law.
See Professional Biographies, GREENSBORO, NORTH CAROLINA

Wilson, Jill R., (AV) ....'57 '82 C.317 B.A. L.896 J.D. [Brooks,P.M.H.&L.]
Wilson, Joseph M., Jr., (BV) '61 '91
C.790 B.A. L.574 J.D. [Browne,F.W.&W.] (⊙Creedmoor, Durham)
Wilson, Mark T. '52 '79 C.228 B.A. L.575 J.D.
Credit Servs. Atty., NationsBank of North Carolina, N.A.

Wilson & Iseman, L.L.P.
(See Winston-Salem)

Winfree, Charles H., (BV) ....'59 '89 C.576 B.S. L.575 J.D. [Winfree&W.]

Winfree & Winfree, (BV)
201 West Market Street Suite 408, 27401
Telephone: 336-273-8998 Fax: 336-272-3065
URL: http://www.winfreelawoffice.com
Charles H. Winfree.
Consumer Law, Lemon Law, Consumer Rights, Collections, Family Law, Divorce, Alimony, Civil Litigation, Business Litigation, Business Property, Traffic Violations.
See Professional Biographies, GREENSBORO, NORTH CAROLINA

Winkelstein, Harris J. ....'18 '51 C&L.446 A.B., LL.B. 4907-E Tower Rd.‡
Winslow, Edward C., III, (AV) ... '46 '74 C.198 B.A. L.575 J.D. [Brooks,P.M.H.&L.] ⊙
Wolf, Gary R., (AV) ....'54 '84 C.576 B.E.D. L.896 J.D. [Sparrow W.&S.]
Wolfe, James B., Jr. ....'21 '51 C&L.228 A.B., LL.B. Chf. U.S. Bkrptcy. J.

Womble Carlyle Sandridge & Rice, (AV)
A Professional Limited Liability Company
300 North Greene Street, 27402 ⊙
Telephone: 336-574-8030 Fax: 336-574-4520
Email: lawyers@wcsr.com URL: http://www.wcsr.com
Members of Firm: Gregory M. Chabon; Ronald R. Davis (Also at Winston-Salem Office); Hardin G. Halsey (Also at Winston-Salem Office); Randall A. Hanson; Jack B. Hicks; Donald C. Lampe (Also at Charlotte, North Carolina Office); James M. Powell; C. Robert Rhodes. Associates: Craig H. Popalis; Lewis S. Rowell; J. Mark Sampson. Of Counsel: Jacqueline E. Camp; D. Ross Hamilton, Jr.; Lillian H. Pinto.
General Civil Practice, Trial and Appellate Litigation. Administrative, Antitrust, Aviation, Banking, Bankruptcy and Creditor's Rights, Bond Financing, Civil Rights, Commercial, Construction, Consumer Lending, Corporate, E-Commerce, Employee Benefits, Environmental, Estate Planning, Family, Government Relations, Health Care, Insurance, Intellectual Property, International, Labor and Employment, Municipal, Negligence, Probate, Product Liability, Real Estate, Retirement Plans, Securities, Taxation, Toxic Tort, Wills and Trusts Law.
Representative Clients: Brad Ragan, Inc.; Brenner Companies; Food Lion, Inc.; Hanes Companies, Inc.; North Carolina Baptist Hospitals, Inc.; R.J. Reynolds Tobacco Co.; Wachovia Corp.; Wake Forest University.
Charlotte, North Carolina Office: 3500 One Wachovia Center, 301 South College Street. Telephone: 704-331-4900. Fax: 704-331-4955.

(This Listing Continued)

Womble Carlyle Sandridge & Rice (Continued)
Winston-Salem, North Carolina Office: One West Fourth Street, 27101. Telephone: 336-721-3600. Fax: 336-721-3660.
Raleigh, North Carolina Office: 2100 First Union Capitol Center, 150 Fayetteville Street Mall, P.O. Box 831. Telephone: 919-755-2100. Fax: 919-755-2150.
Research Triangle Park, North Carolina Office: 2530 Meridian Parkway, Suite 400 (Durham), 27713, P.O. Box 13069, Research Triangle Park, 27709. Telephone: 919-484-2300. Fax: 919-484-2340.
Atlanta, Georgia Office: One Atlantic Center, 1201 West Peachtree Street, Suite 3500. Telephone: 404-872-7000. Fax: 404-888-7490.
Other Atlanta, Georgia Office: Suite 404, 2296 Henderson Mill Road, N.E. Telephone: 770-492-9030. Fax: 770-492-9609.
Washington, D.C. Office: Suite 700, 1401 Eye Street. Telephone: 202-857-4400. Fax: 202-467-6910.
Greenville, South Carolina Office: 700 Poinsett Plaza, 104 South Main Street, P.O. Box 10208. Telephone: 864-255-5400. Fax: 864-255-5440.
Tysons Corner, Virginia Office: 8065 Leesburg Pike, Fourth Floor. Telephone: 703-790-3310. Fax: 703-790-2623.
Reviser of the North Carolina Law Digest for this Directory.
See Professional Biographies, GREENSBORO, NORTH CAROLINA

Wood, A. Terry, (AV) ....'36 '64 C&L.575 B.S., LL.B. Chf. Dep. City Atty.
Wood, Jody Burig, (BV) ....'68 '93 C.119 B.S. L.575 J.D. Off. of Dist. Atty.
Wood, Keith A., (AV) ....'65 '91 C&L.575 B.S., J.D. [Carruthers&R.]
Woodruff, Carolyn J., (AV) ....'— '83 L.228 J.D. [Woodruff]

Woodruff Law Firm, P.A., (AV)
420 W. Market Street, 27401
Telephone: 336-272-9122 Telecopier: 336-272-7991 URL: http://www.lawyers.com/woodruff
Email: cwoodruff@woodrufflawfirm.com URL: http://www.woodrufflawfirm.com
Carolyn J. Woodruff;—Bonnie E. Rossi; Lucy Harrington (Not admitted in NC).
Family Law, Taxation, Divorce, Mediation and Arbitration Child Custody and Child Support.
See Professional Biographies, GREENSBORO, NORTH CAROLINA

Woosley, S. Kyle, (AV) ....'54 '80 C.575 B.A. L.813 J.D. [Brooks,P.M.H.&L.]
Workman, Jeffrey T., (BV) ....'69 '95 C.575 B.A. L.896 J.D. [Tate,G.L.P.&W.]
Worley, Demetrius L. ....'72 '97 C.1228 B.A. L.575 J.D. [Brotherton F.Y.&W.]
Worsham, Jack W. ....'26 '52 C&L.575 B.S., LL.B. Pres., Intertech Corp.
Worth, Robert P., (BV) ....'50 '75 C&L.575 B.A., J.D. [Douglas,R.H.C.&H.]
Worth, Thomas A., (AV) ....'55 '82 C.575 B.A. L.896 J.D. [Worth]
Worth Law Firm, The, (AV) .... 301 S. Greene St., Ste. 300
Wright, Brinton D., (AV) ....'49 '76 C.367 B.A. L.896 J.D. [Stern,K.&W.]
Wright, Donna Michelle ....'59 '00 C.411 B.S. L.802 J.D. P.O. Box 3008
Wright, Douglas E., (AV) ....'57 '82 C.893 B.A. L.945 J.D. 114 N. Elm Street
Wright, Heather Howell ....'— '02 C.797 B.A. L.896 J.D. [Smith M.]
Wright, R. Thompson, (AV) ....'49 '75 C.311 A.B. L.575 J.D. [Hill,E.D.J.&B.]

Wyatt Early Harris Wheeler L.L.P.
(See High Point)

Yarbrough, James David, Jr. ....'— '02 C.575 B.A. L.861 J.D. [Nexsen P.A.K.]
Yeoman, Richard D. ....'70 '97 C&L.101 B.A., J.D. [Brotherton F.Y.&W.]
Yntema, Brady A., (BV) ....'73 '98 C.240 B.S. L.201 J.D. [Pinto C.K.&B.]
York, Frank W. ....'34 '60 C&L.575 B.S., LL.B. Pres. & CEO, Newman Mach. Co.
Younce, Charles P., (AV) ....'37 '66 C&L.575 A.B. [Younce,M.&M.]

Younce, Moore & Moseley, L.L.P., (AV)
333 North Greene Street, Suite 404, P.O. Box 3486, 27402
Telephone: 336-379-0123 Fax: 336-379-9894
URL: http://www.ymmlaw.com
Members of Firm: Charles P. Younce; Larry I. Moore III; William O. Moseley, Jr. Of Counsel: H. Bruce Brandon.
General Practice in All State and Federal Courts, Civil Litigation, Products Liability, Aviation Litigation, Personal Injury, Bankruptcy. Commercial Law, Collections, Homeowners Association Law, Mediation, Arbitration, Wills, Estates, General Practice in all State and Federal Courts, Litigation, Bankruptcy, Employment, Real Estate, Domestic Relations, Criminal.
See Professional Biographies, GREENSBORO, NORTH CAROLINA

Young, Susan M. ....'77 '04 C.966 B.A. L.896 J.D. [Brooks,P.M.H.&L.]
Zellinger, James A. ....'52 '77 C.228 B.A. L.262 J.D. 3704 Moss Creek Drive
Zigler, Albert M. ....'24 '52 C.105 A.B. L.659 LL.B. 3100 N. Elm St.‡

GREENVILLE, * 60,476, *Pitt Co.*

Akins, Darth D. .... '61 '97 C.932 B.S. L.213 J.D. Pitt Co. Dist. Atty. Off.
Albritton, Harry Humphrey, Jr. ....'76 '02 C.232 B.A. L.607 J.D. [Blount]
Allen, W. L., III, (BV) ....'— '92 C.232 B.S. L.896 J.D. [Ward&S.] (⊙New Bern)
Andrews, Deborah B. .... '— '97 C.576 B.A. L.575 J.D. [Ward&S.] (⊙New Bern)
Antinore, James K., Law Offices of '64 '92 C.732 B.A. L.896 J.D.
110 Kimberley Drive
Avery, E. Cordell, (AV) ....'— '76 C&L.575 A.B., J.D. [Everett&H.]
Aycock, E. Burt, Jr. ....'42 '68 C&L.575 B.A., J.D. Chf. Dist. J.‡

Baker, Jones, Daly, Murray, Carter & Daughtry, P.A.
(See Ahoskie)

Ball, Micah D., (BV) ....'56 '82 C.232 B.S.B.A. L.896 J.D. [Colombo,K.D.&B.]
Barber, Timothy C., (AV) ....'56 '82 C.228 B.A. L.575 J.D. [Barber&W.]
Barber & Wilson, P.A., (AV) ....1708 East Arlington Boulevard
Barnhill, Ann H., (BV) ....'54 '79 C&L.896 B.A., J.D. [Mattox,D.&B.]
Bennett, John H., (BV) ....'60 '85 C&L.896 B.A., J.D. Asst. U.S. Atty.
Bivins, William P., Jr., (BV⊙) '45 '74 C.228 A.B. L.802 J.D.
V.P., Corp. Legal Affs., DSM Pharmaceuticals, Inc.
Blick, Joseph A., Jr., (BV) ....'54 '81 C.575 B.A. L.896 J.D. Asst. Dist. Atty.

Block, Victoria L.
(See New Bern)

Blount, Judson H., III, (CV) ....'59 '86 C&L.575 B.A., J.D. 119 West Fourth Street
Blount, Marvin K., III ....'64 '96 C.232 B.S.B.A. L.896 J.D. [Blount]
Blount, Marvin K., Jr., (AV) ....'39 '66 C.280 A.B. L.896 J.D. [Blount]
Blount, Rebecca C. ....'71 '01 C.893 L.896 J.D. [Blount]
Blount & Crisp Law Offices, (AV) ....119 West Third Street

Blount Law Firm, The, P.A., (AV)
400 West First Street, P.O. Drawer 58, 27835-0058
Telephone: 252-752-6000; 800-851-1818 Fax: 252-752-2174 URL: http://www.theblountlawfirmnc.com
Email: louise@theblountlawfirm.com URL: http://www.theblountlawfirm.com
Marvin K. Blount, Jr.;—Darren M. Dawson; Marvin K. Blount, III; Rebecca C. Blount; Harry Humphrey Albritton, Jr.
General Civil Practice in all State and Federal Courts. Personal Injury, Wrongful Death, Medical Malpractice, Legal Malpractice, Mass Torts, Complex and Multi-District Litigation, Class Actions, Antitrust, Products Liability, Nursing Home Negligence, Logging Truck Accidents, Spectator Injuries, Safety.
Reference: First Citizens Bank, Greenville, N.C.
See Professional Biographies, GREENVILLE, NORTH CAROLINA

Braddy, G. Galen, (BV) ....'66 '92 C.575 B.A. L.574 J.D. [Harrington&B.]
Brantley, J. Christopher, (BV) '66 '93 C.232 B.A. L.1345 J.D.
[Brantley,J.R.H.&H.] ⊙

Brantley, Jenkins, Riddle, Hardee & Hardee, (BV)
202 East Arlington Boulevard, P.O. Box 924, 27858 ⊙
Telephone: 252-355-1998 Fax: 252-321-2948 URL: http://www.bjrhhlawyers.com
URL: http://www.bjrhhatty.com
J. Christopher Brantley.
Personal Injury, Wrongful Death, Automobile Accidents, Head and Spinal Injury, Nursing Home Abuse and Neglect, Workers Compensation, Insurance, Products Liability, Social Security Disability, Medical Malpractice.
Goldsboro, North Carolina Office: 601 North Spence Avenue, 27534. Telephone: 919-778-9700. Fax: 919-778-1938.
Jacksonville, North Carolina Office: 901 Hargett Street, P.O. Box 7070, 28540. Telephone: 910-455-5599. Fax: 910-455-7191.
Kinston, North Carolina Office: 2506 Heritage Street, Suite A, 28501. Telephone: 252-522-1500.
See Professional Biographies, GREENVILLE, NORTH CAROLINA

Brewer, William Clarence, Jr., (AV) .... '31 '56 C&L.575 B.A., J.D. [Speight,W.&B.]
Brown, Allen C., (CV) .... '50 '83 C.575 B.A. L.1228 J.D. 3493-C South Evans Street
Brown, Angela H. .... '66 '95 C.339 B.S. L.1187 J.D. [R.M. .&A.H.B.Brown,III]
Brown, Earl T., (BV) .... '51 '91 C.1378 B.S. L.1228 J.D. 410 W. 14 St.
Brown, Larry W., Jr. .... '67 '97 C.232 B.S. L.575 J.D. 321 S. Evans Street
Brown, Roddey Middleton, III '62 '94
C.1069 B.A. L.1187 J.D. [R.M. .&A.H.B.Brown,III]

Brown, Roddey M. III, & Angela H. Brown, P.A.
123 West Third Street, 27858
Telephone: 252-317-4000 Fax: 252-317-4444
URL: http://www.roddeyandangelabrownattorneys.com
Roddey Middleton Brown, III; Angela H. Brown.
Criminal Law, DWI, Drug Crimes, Juvenile Crimes, Parole and Probation, Traffic Violations, White Collar Crime, Education, Elder Law, Nursing Home Abuse, Workers Compensation, Medical Malpractice, Personal Injury, Automobile Accidents, Sexual Abuse, Slip and Fall, Wrongfull Death and Appellate Practice.
See Professional Biographies, GREENVILLE, NORTH CAROLINA

Browning, Robert R., (AV) .... '36 '66 C.228 B.A. L.575 J.D. [Browning&H.]
Browning, William Scott .... '70 '97 C.232 B.S./B.A. L.574 J.D. [A Browning&H.]
Browning & Hill, L.L.P., (AV) .... 200 East Fourth Street
Bruner, James R. .... '32 '54 C.421 L.383 J.D. Assoc. Prof., East Carolina Univ.★
Burch, Timothy E., (BV) .... '68 '96 C.906 B.A. L.36 J.D. [Burch]

Burch Law Office, (BV)
311 South Evans Street, 27858
Telephone: 252-830-5291 Fax: 252-830-9234
Email: tim@burchlawoffice.com URL: http://www.burchlaw-office.com
Timothy E. Burch.
Personal Injury, Automobile Accidents, Wrongful Death, Medical Malpractice, Criminal Law, Driving While Intoxicated, Drug Crimes, Traffic Violations, White Collar Crime, Worker Compensation, Adoptions, Child Custody, Child Support, Divorce, Visitation Rights, Wills and Probate, Trust and Estates, Estate Planning, Social Security Disability, Eminent Domain, Zoning and Planning, Traumatic Brain Injury, Corporate-Business Formation.
See Professional Biographies, GREENVILLE, NORTH CAROLINA

Burgdorff, Joanne K. .... '40 '81 C.326 B.S. L.796 J.D. Co. Atty.
Campbell, Steven V. '57 '83 C&L.339 B.S., J.D.
(adm. in ID; not adm. in NC) 2078 Hyde Dr.‡
Cannon, Richard L., III, (BV) .... '55 '83 C.575 B.S. L.1228 J.D. [Cannon&T.]
Cannon & Taylor, LLP, (BV) .... 300 E. Arlington Boulevard, Suite 5
Carr, Mary Blair '61 '87 C.232 B.A. L.896 J.D.
(adm. in FL; not adm. in NC) P.O. Box 7201‡
Carroll, Kathryn Slocumb .... '69 '96 Pitt Co. Legal Dept.
Cassiano, Frank A., Jr., Law Offices of, (BV) '57 '88
C.871 B.S. L.1194 J.D. 310 South Pitt Street
Cavanagh, Mary V. .... '— '89 C.896 B.A. L.893 J.D. [Ward&S.] (⊙New Bern)
Clark, Dallas, Jr., (AV) .... '43 '68 C&L.896 B.A., J.D. [D.Clark,Jr.]
Clark, Melanie Hite, (BV) .... '57 '87 C.232 B.S. L.1228 J.D. 301 Crown Point Rd.
Clark, Dallas, Jr., P.A., (AV) .... 321 South Evans Street
Cole, Alden Brewer .... '69 '98 C.953 B.A. L.420 J.D. [Wells&C.]
Coleman, Curtis C., III, (BV) .... '58 '84 C.896 B.A. L.575 J.D. [C.C.Coleman,III]
Coleman, Curtis C., III, P.A., (BV) .... 916 S. Evans St.
Colombo, Michael A., (AV) .... '48 '79 C.576 B.S. L.790 J.D. [Colombo,K.D.&B.]
Colombo, Kitchin, Dunn & Ball, L.L.P., (AV) .... 1698 East Arlington Boulevard
Conner, Ernest L., Jr., (BV) .... '55 '87 C.232 B.A. L.575 J.D. [E.L.Conner,Jr.]
Conner, Ernest L., Jr., P.A., (BV) .... 115 Fort Sumter Drive
Cordes, Chris, (CV) .... '58 '93 C.1365 B.A. L.245 J.D. Asst. Fed. Def.
Cox, Hugh D., (BV) .... '42 '75 C.576 B.A. L.574 J.D. 321 Evans Street, Suite 102
Crisp, Nelson B., (AV) .... '38 '68 C.228 B.A. L.575 J.D. [Blount&C.]
Daniel, David W. .... '60 '85 C&L.896 B.A., J.D. U.S. Mag.
Davenport, Matthew James '74 '00 C&L.1228 B.B.A., J.D.
Asst. Dist. Atty., Pitt Co. Off. of the Dist. Atty.
Davis, Gary B., (BV) .... '50 '75 C&L.575 B.S., J.D. [Mattox,D.&B.]
Dawson, Darren M., (BV) .... '67 '92 C&L.1228 B.A., J.D. [A Blount]
Dixon, Phillip R., Sr., (AV) .... '49 '74 C.232 B.S.B.A. L.575 J.D. [P.R.Dixon]

Dixon, Phillip R., P.A., (AV) BB
110 East Arlington Boulevard, P.O. Drawer 8668, 27835-8668
Telephone: 252-355-8100 Telecopier: 252-355-0271
Email: phildixon@coastalnet.com URL: http://www.downeast-law.com
Phillip R. Dixon, Sr.
Administrative Law, Business Law, Construction Law, Corporate Law, Education Law, Elder Law, Eminent Domain, Franchise Law, General Practice, Land Use Law, Municipal and Zoning Law, Partnership Law, Public Utilities Law, Real Estate Law, Trusts and Estates, Wills and Probate.
See Professional Biographies, GREENVILLE, NORTH CAROLINA

Doub, Randy D., (BV) .... '55 '80 C.232 B.A. L.575 J.D. P.O. Box 8668

Duke, W. Gregory, (BV) '65 '90 C&L.575 B.A., J.D.
119 West Fourth Street, 27835
Telephone: 252-758-4444 Fax: 252-758-4080
Email: wgd1070@aol.com URL: http://www.wgdukelaw.com
General Trial and Appellate in all State and Federal Courts. Criminal Law, Drug Crimes, Felonies, Homicide, Misdemeanors, Driving While Intoxicated, Traffic Violations, Domestic Relations, Divorce, Child Custody, Child Support, Alimony, Equitable Distribution.
See Professional Biographies, GREENVILLE, NORTH CAROLINA

Duke, W. Russell, Jr. .... '47 '74 C&L.896 B.A., J.D. Supr. Ct. J.
Dunn, John B., Jr., (BV) .... '63 '89 C.232 B.A. L.1228 J.D. [Colombo,K.D.&B.]
Dupree, Joseph B., II, (CV) .... '68 '93 C.575 A.B. L.1228 J.D. [Owens&N.]
Edwards, Amy Ann .... '69 '00 C.232 B.A. L.575 J.D. P.O. Box 686
Edwards, Charles C., Jr. .... '78 '04 C.576 B.S. L.1228 J.D. [A Hopf&H.]
Edwards, Joseph T., (BV) .... '60 '85 C&L.575 B.S., J.D. [Edwards&E.]
Edwards, Sharron R., (BV) .... '62 '87 C&L.575 B.A., J.D. [Edwards&E.]

Edwards & Edwards, L.L.P., (BV)
2192 South Evans Street, P.O. Drawer 1425, 27835-1425
Telephone: 252-353-1200 Fax: 252-353-1301
Email: Edwards.attys@earthlink.net URL: http://www.edwardsattorneys.com

(This Listing Continued)

Edwards & Edwards, L.L.P. (Continued)
Members of Firm: Joseph T. Edwards; Sharron R. Edwards.
General Civil Practice in all State and Federal Courts. Personal Injury and Wrongful Death, Automobile Accidents, Professional Malpractice and Products Liability.
See Professional Biographies, GREENVILLE, NORTH CAROLINA

Eglinton, Donalt J., (AV) '— '82
C.136 M.A. L.896 J.D. [Ward&S.] (⊙New Bern, Raleigh)
Ellis, A. Charles, (AV) '— '83 C.575 A.B. L.1228 J.D.
[Ward&S.] (⊙New Bern, Raleigh)
Evans, E. Bradley .... '— '02 C&L.896 B.A., J.D. [Ward&S.] (⊙New Bern)
Evans, Lynwood P., (BV) '— '99 C.575 B.S.B.A. L.1228 J.D.
[Ward&S.] (⊙New Bern)
Everett, Clifton W., Jr. .... '42 '67 C&L.896 B.A., J.D. Supr. Ct. J.
Everett & Hite, L.L.P., (AV) .... 200 South Washington Street
Fanning, Paul A., (BV) .... '— '98 C.48 B.A. L.896 J.D. [Ward&S.] (⊙New Bern)
Fields, J. Michael, (BV) .... '— '91 C&L.575 B.S., J.D. [Ward&S.] (⊙New Bern)
Fisher, Steven M. .... '59 '91 C.232 B.A. L.896 J.D. 315 S. Evans St., Ste. A
Flanagan, Michael P., (AV) .... '— '71 C&L.575 A.B., J.D. [Ward&S.] (⊙New Bern)
Fox, Michael A. .... '54 '89 C.232 B.S. L.574 J.D. [M.Fox&Assoc.]
Fox, Michael, & Associates .... 123 W. Fourth St.
Funderburk, Amy L. .... '72 '03 C.232 B.S. L.575 J.D. [A Barber&W.]
Gallagher, Janis E. .... '68 '96 C.216 B.A. L.896 J.D. Asst. Co. Atty.
Gaylord, Louis W., Jr., (AV) .... '18 '47 C&L.575 A.B., LL.B. [Gaylord,M.S.S.&H.] ‡

Gaylord, McNally, Strickland, Snyder & Holscher, L.L.P., (AV) BB
498 Red Banks Road, P.O. Drawer 545, 27835-0545
Telephone: 252-321-7111 Fax: 252-321-7112
URL: http://www.lawyers.com/gmsslaw
Members of Firm: Louis W. Gaylord, Jr. (Retired); Danny D. McNally; D. Michael Strickland; Vernon G. Snyder, III; Emma Stallings Holscher.
General Practice, Civil Practice, Real Estate, Real Property, Residential Real Estate, Commercial Real Estate, Commercial Law, Business Law, Business Transactions, Construction Law, Corporate Law, Contracts, Debtor and Creditor, Collections, Insurance, Litigation, Trial Practice, Personal Injury, Automobile Accidents and Injuries, Wrongful Death, Probate, Trusts and Estates, Estate Administration, Estate Planning, Wills, Contested Wills.
Representative Clients: Wachovia Bank, N.A.; Bank of America; Garris Evans Lumber Co., Inc.; United States Fidelity and Guaranty Co.; The Daily Reflector, Inc.; Nationwide Mutual Insurance Co.; Ironwood Development, Inc.; Lawyers Title Insurance Corp.
See Professional Biographies, GREENVILLE, NORTH CAROLINA

Gilliland, Gary '42 '75 C.845
(adm. in TX; not adm. in NC) 216 Pineview Dr.‡
Gowen, Richard T. .... '73 '02 L.575 J.D. [A Barber&W.]
Griffin, Richard L., (BV) '58 '87
C.232 B.S.B.A. L.1228 J.D. 202 E. Arlington Blvd., Ste. B
Groh, Ellen G. .... '61 '91 C.1044 B.S. L.575 J.D. Panlico Sound Legal Servs.
Haddock, Larry Christopher .... '73 '00 C.232 B.S. L.383 J.D. 202 E. Arlington Blvd.
Hagen, Stephan M. .... '65 '93 C.966 B.S. L.896 J.D. Off. of Pub. Def.
Hahn, L. Allen, (AV) .... '48 '73 C.575 A.B. L.838 J.D. [L.A.Hahn]

Hahn, L. Allen, P.A., (AV)
504-A Red Banks Road, Drawer 665, 27835-0665
Telephone: 252-756-6970 Fax: 252-756-2837
Email: packages@earthlink.net URL: http://www.lallenhahn.com
L. Allen Hahn.
Real Property, Real Estate, Corporations, Collections, Wills and Estates Law, Loan Closings.
See Professional Biographies, GREENVILLE, NORTH CAROLINA

Haigwood, Thomas D., (AV) ... '45 '70 C&L.575 LL.B. Spec. Supr. Ct. J., Spec. Supr. Ct.
Hamilton, Clovia A. '66 '97 C.339 B.S. L.1000 J.D.
(adm. in GA; not adm. in NC) Asst. Prof. Planning Law, East Carolina Univ.
Harper, Edward J., II, (AV) .... '46 '74 C.232 B.A. L.896 J.D. 1607 East Fifth Street
Harrington, Danny A., (BV) .... '57 '82 C.232 B.S.B.A. L.575 J.D. [Harrington&B.]
Harrington & Braddy, (BV) .... 211 W. 14th St. Ste. B
Harris, Thomas E., (AV) .... '40 '65 C&L.383 B.S., J.D. [Harris,C.W.&B.] ⊙
Harris, Creech, Ward and Blackerby, P.A., (AV)
219 Commerce Street Suite C (⊙New Bern)
Hassler, Gregory L., (BV) '52 '87
C.34 B.A. L.245 J.D. Asst. Univ. Atty., East Carolina University
Herrin, Mickey A., (AV) .... '41 '69 C.296 B.S. L.575 J.D. [Herrin&M.]
Herrin & Morano, (AV) .... 210 South Washington Street
Higley, Donald S., II, (BV) .... '63 '94 C.575 B.A. L.1228 J.D. [Hopf&H.]
Hilburn, Patricia Gwynett .... '47 '81 C.1111 B.A. L.861 J.D. Dist. J.
Hill, Kathryn (Kitty) Hart .... '74 '99 C.232 B.A. L.575 J.D. 210 Spilman Building
Hill, Myron T., Jr., (AV) .... '58 '84 C.228 B.A. L.896 J.D. [Browning&H.]
Hill, William F., (BV) .... '58 '84 C.902 B.A. L.893 J.D. [W.F.Hill]

Hill, William F., P.A., (BV)
2470 Emerald Place Drive Suite D, 27834
Telephone: 252-355-4277 Fax: 252-355-2797
Email: billhill@williamfhillpa.com URL: http://www.williamfhillpalaw.com
William F. Hill.
Creditor's Rights, Collections, Small Business, Buying or Selling a Business, Employment Contracts, General Business, Contracts, Starting a Business, Corporate Law, Family Law, Divorce.
See Professional Biographies, GREENVILLE, NORTH CAROLINA

Holloway, James E. '49 '91 C.232 M.B.A. L.575 J.D.
(adm. in NJ; not adm. in NC) Assoc. Prof. of Bus. Law, East Carolina University
Holscher, Emma Stallings, (BV) ... '69 '97 C.575 B.A. L.1345 J.D. [Gaylord,M.S.S.&H.]
Hopf, James F., (BV) .... '61 '86 C.1228 B.A. L.575 J.D. [Hopf&H.]

Hopf & Higley, P.A., (BV)
1694 East Arlington Boulevard, Suite E, 27858
Telephone: 252-756-1883 Fax: 252-756-1797
URL: http://www.hopfhigley.com
James F. Hopf; Donald S. Higley, II;—Charles C. Edwards, Jr.
Environmental, Toxic Tort, Plaintiffs' Personal Injury and other Complex Litigation in all State and Federal Courts.
See Professional Biographies, GREENVILLE, NORTH CAROLINA

Horne, Stephen F., II, (BV) .... '48 '76 C.232 B.A. L.790 J.D. 300 Cotanche Street
Howard, Malcolm J. .... '39 '70 C.870 B.S. L.896 J.D. U.S. Dist. J.
Irons, Ben G., II, (BV) '49 '74 C&L.575 B.A., J.D.
Univ. Atty., East Carolina University
James, Gregory K., (BV) .... '58 '86 C.575 A.B. L.1228 J.D. [James&S.]
James & Sutton, P.A., (BV) .... 315 S. Evans St.
Jenkins, Kimberly Smith, (BV) .... '63 '88 C.802 B.A. L.846 J.D. Asst. Dist. Atty.
Jones, David A. .... '75 '01 C.577 B.A. L.1228 J.D. 105 Lamont Rd.
Jones, Merrill G., II .... '— '97 C&L.896 B.S., J.D. [Ward&S.] (⊙New Bern)
Jones, Steven R. .... '71 '99 C.232 B.S. L.1345 J.D. [Jones&S.]
Jones & Saunders .... P.O. Box 1726
Keegan, Mark S. .... '51 '77 C.1229 B.I.A. L.477 J.D. [Keegan]

Keegan Law Firm, LLC .... 233 N. Main Street, Suite 7
Kellum, Norman B., Jr., (AV) .... '37 '65 C&L.896 B.S., J.D. [Kellum] ⊙

Kellum Law Firm, (AV)
205 S.W. Greenville Boulevard, P.O. Box 20727, 27858 ⊙
Telephone: 252-353-4100 Fax: 252-353-8754
Email: ckeenhold@kellumlawfirm.com URL: http://www.lawyers.com/kellumlawfirm
Norman B. Kellum, Jr.;—Russell L. Needell.
State and Federal Civil Trial Practice, Personal Injury Law, Wrongful Death, Workers' Compensation, Social Security, Defective Products, Mass Torts and Insurance Law.
See Professional Biographies, GREENVILLE, NORTH CAROLINA

Kemp, Robert C., III .... '71 '96 C.575 B.A. L.896 J.D. P.O. Box 8047
Kiess, Stephen D., (BV) .... '— '91 C.477 B.B.A. L.896 J.D. [Everett&H.]
King, Jeremy C. .... '— '02 C&L.790 B.A., J.D. [J.C.King]
King, Jeremy Clayton, Law Offices of .... P.O. Box 20400
Kitchin, W. Walton, (BV) .... '46 '77 C&L.896 B.A., J.D. [Colombo,K.D.&B.]
Lanier, James C., Jr., (BV) .... '27 '52 C&L.575 B.A., LL.B. 219 Cotanche St., Suite 11
Lederer, William M. .... '43 '70 C.1457 B.A. L.260 J.D. [Lederer&Assoc.]
Lederer & Associates, P.A. .... 708 Cromwell Drive
Leech, David A. .... '51 '78 C.228 B.S. L.575 J.D. Dist. J.
Leon, Mary-Ann .... '— '99 C.1109 B.A. L.575 J.D. [L.]

LeonLaw Firm, The
P.O. Box 20338, 27858
Telephone: 252-830-5366
Email: maleon@leonlaw.org URL: http://www.leonlaw.org
Member of Firm: Mary-Ann Leon.
Employment Law, Personal Injury, Workers Compensation, Contracts.
See Professional Biographies, GREENVILLE, NORTH CAROLINA

Lewis, Katherine Evans .... '— '93 C.43 B.S. L.500 J.D. [Ward&S.] (⊙New Bern)
Mackall, Theodore E., Jr. .... '50 '85 C&L.45 B.S.P.A., J.D. P.O. Box 58
Martin, John M., (AV) .... '— '75 C.576 B.A. L.896 J.D. [Ward&S.] (⊙New Bern)
Martin, Lance P., (BV) .... '— '95 C.812 B.S. L.861 J.D. [Ward&S.] (⊙New Bern)
Mattox, Fred T., (AV) .... '31 '56 C&L.575 A.B., J.D. [Mattox,D.&B.]
Mattox, Davis & Barnhill, P.A., (AV) .... 315 W. 2nd St.
McLawhorn, Charles L., Jr., (BV) .... '47 '76 C.232 A.B. L.616 J.D. [McLawhorn&Assoc.]
McLawhorn & Associates, (BV) .... 501 Greenville Blvd.
McNally, Danny D., (AV) .... '46 '73 C&L.575 B.S., J.D. [Gaylord,M.S.S.&H.]
Melvin, R. Bailey, (BV) .... '66 '92 C&L.575 B.A., J.D. [Melvin]
Melvin Law Firm, The, P.A., (BV) .... 610-A Lynndale Court
Miller, Jeffrey L., (AV) .... '50 '75 C.232 B.A. L.472 J.D. 2510 E. 10th St.
Morano, Mark R., (BV) .... '53 '78 C.724 B.A. L.228 J.D. [Herrin&M.]
Needell, Russell L., (BV) .... '56 '81 C.1170 B.A. L.117 J.D. [Kellum] (⊙Rocky Mount)
Nelson, James A., Jr., (BV) .... '54 '80 C.575 B.A. L.1225 J.D. [Owens&N.]
Oliver, Tonya Y. .... '71 '96 C.575 B.A. L.896 J.D. Asst. Dist. Atty.
Owens, Mark W., III, (BV) .... '61 '86 C.575 B.A. L.896 J.D. [Owens&N.]
Owens, Mark W., Jr., (AV) .... '37 '63 C.575 A.B. L.896 LL.B. [Owens&N.]

Owens & Nelson, P.L.L.C., (AV) BR
201 West Third Street, P.O. Box 36, 27834
Telephone: 252-757-3300 Fax: 252-758-9777
URL: http://www.owensrouseandnelson.com
Members of Firm: Mark W. Owens, Jr.; James A. Nelson, Jr.; Mark W. Owens, III; Joseph B. Dupree, II.
General Civil and Criminal Trial Practice before all State and Federal Courts. Alternative Dispute Resolution, Civil Practice, Commercial Real Estate, Criminal Law, Domestic Relations, DUI and DWI Law, Eminent Domain, Estates, Family Law, Fraud and Deceit, General Practice, Guardianship Law, Insurance, Litigation, Medical Malpractice, Mortgages, Negligence, Personal Injury, Premises Liability, Probate, Professional Liability, Property Law, Real Estate, Torts, Traffic, Trusts and Estates, Unfair Competition, White Collar Crime, Wills and Workers Compensation Law.
See Professional Biographies, GREENVILLE, NORTH CAROLINA

Paramore, Kenneth D. .... '60 '86 C.232 B.S. L.575 J.D. 102 Eagle Ct.
Parker, Darnell .... '70 '97 C.575 B.A. L.574 J.D. 408 West First Street, Suite 1-B
Paysour, Conrad E., III, (BV) .... '61 '88 C.1128 B.A. L.838 J.D. 315 W. 2nd St.
Peacock, Gregory T., (AV) '— '96 C.575 B.S.B.A. L.896 J.D. [Ward&S.] (⊙New Bern)
Perez, Mario E., (BV) .... '59 '84 C.744 B.A. L.276 J.D. 310 South Evans Street
Poole, Richard C., (BV) .... '54 '80 C.228 B.A. L.896 J.D. 1510 E. Arlington Blvd.
Porter, Christian E. .... '74 '99 C.228 B.A. L.1128 J.D. [Colombo,K.D.&B.]
Ramey, Jerome, (CV) .... '58 '83 C.454 B.A. L.588 J.D. 112 S. Pitt St.
Ricci, Brian M. .... '72 '97 C.232 B.A. L.1228 J.D. 321 S. Evans Street
Rickner, Gary J., (AV⊤) '— '74 C.827 B.A. L.192 J.D. [Ward&S.] (⊙New Bern, Raleigh)
Riggsbee, Leslie Shea .... '72 '98 C&L.575 B.A., J.D. Law Clk., U.S. Dist. Ct.
Roberts, James M., (BV) .... '42 '70 C.232 A.B. L.575 J.D. 321 Evans St.
Robinson, Leslie S., (BV) .... '61 '86 C.232 B.S. L.1228 J.D. [Robinson]

Robinson Law Firm, The, P.A., (BV)
1510 East Arlington Boulevard, 27858
Telephone: 252-758-4100 Fax: 252-758-0876
Email: contactus@therobinsonlawfirm.com URL: http://www.therobinsonlawfirm.com
Leslie S. Robinson.
Criminal Law, Driving While Intoxicated, Alcohol Violations, Controlled Substance Violations.
See Professional Biographies, GREENVILLE, NORTH CAROLINA

Romary, Peter John Michael, (BV) .... '71 '94 L.575 J.D. [Tanner&R.] ⊙
Rouse, Robert D., III, (BV) .... '— '73 C&L.575 A.B., J.D. [R.D.Rouse,III]

Rouse, Robert D., III, PLLC., Law Offices of, (BV)
610 Lynndale Court, Suite D., 27858
Telephone: 252-752-4200 Fax: 252-752-9200
URL: http://www.rrouselaw.com
Robert D. Rouse, III.
Personal Injury, Property Damage, Premises Liability, Auto Accidents, Bus Accidents, Motorcycle Accidents, Truck and Tractor-Trailer Collisions, Wrongful Death Claims, Dog Bites, Head and Spinal Injuries, Civil Litigation, Medical Malpractice, Nursing Home Abuse/Negligence, Bad Faith, Unfair Competition.
See Professional Biographies, GREENVILLE, NORTH CAROLINA

Sams, Stanley M., (AV) .... '— '79 C.232 B.S.B.A. L.575 J.D. [Ward&S.] (⊙New Bern)
Saunders, James R. .... '73 '99 C.1128 B.A. L.1228 J.D. [Jones&S.]
Savage, John M., (BV) .... '40 '66 C.93 A.B. L.262 LL.B. 313 S. Evans St.
Shoffner, Robert L., Jr., (BV) .... '42 '67 C&L.575 B.S.B.A., J.D. Pub. Def.
Silver, David .... '69 '97 C.645 B.S. L.575 J.D. P.O. Box 7384
Singleton, A. Louis, (AV) .... '30 '61 C.232 B.S. L.575 LL.B. 498 Red Banks Rd.‡
Smith, J. Troy, Jr., (AV) .... '— '67 C&L.575 A.B., J.D. [Ward&S.] (⊙New Bern)
Smith, Peggy T. .... '77 '03 C&L.1019 B.A., J.D. [Colombo,K.D.&B.]
Snyder, Vernon G., III, (BV) .... '52 '80 C.575 A.B. L.1228 J.D. [Gaylord,M.S.S.&H.]
Speight, Watson and Brewer, (AV) .... 109 South Evans Street
Stephenson, H. L., III, (AV) .... '— '82 C&L.575 A.B., J.D. [Ward&S.] (⊙New Bern)
Stillerman, Shelli S. '68 '94 C.471 B.A. L.1228 J.D. University Health Systems of Eastern California
Stokes, R. Cherry .... '46 '72 C.232 B.S.B.A. L.575 J.D. 107 W. 3rd St.
Stone, Meredith B., (AV⊤) '59 '85 C.882 B.A. L.724 J.D. V.P. Gen. Coun., NACCO Materials Handling Group, Inc., Americas
Strickland, D. Michael, (BV) .... '53 '78 C.576 B.S. L.896 J.D. [Gaylord,M.S.S.&H.]
Stroud, Donald R., Jr., (CV) .... '65 '90 C.232 B.S.B.A. L.1228 J.D. [D.Stroud,Jr.]
Stroud, Donald, Jr., Attorney at Law, (CV) .... 311 S. Evans St. Mall

Sumrell, Sugg, Carmichael, Hicks & Hart, P.A.
(See New Bern)

Sutton, David C., (BV⊤) .... '62 '90 C.1175 B.S.B.A. L.259 J.D. [James&S.]
Swank, Kimberly A., (BV) .... '— '91 C.232 B.A. L.1228 J.D. [Everett&H.]
Taggart, J. Scott .... '64 '96 C.953 B.S. L.1339 J.D. P.O. Box 1505
Tanner & Romary P.A., (BV) .... 600 Lynndale Court, Suite C (⊙Clayton)
Taylor, Terence Lee, (BV) .... '68 '93 C&L.1345 B.A., J.D. [Cannon&T.]
Waddell, Robert W. .... '66 '02 C.890 B.A. L.1228 J.D. P.O. Box 7283

Wallace, Morris, Barwick, Landis & Stroud, P.A.
(See Kinston)

Waller, Benjamin E. F. B. .... '— '98 C.289 B.A. L.228 J.D. [Ward&S.]

Ward and Smith, P.A., (AV)
120 West Fire Tower Road, P.O. Box 8088, 27835-8088 ⊙
Telephone: 252-215-4000 Facsimile: 252-215-4077
Email: wardsmith@wardandsmith.com URL: http://www.wardandsmith.com
W. L. Allen, III; Deborah B. Andrews; Mary V. Cavanagh; Donalt J. Eglinton; A. Charles Ellis; E. Bradley Evans; Lynwood P. Evans; Paul A. Fanning; J. Michael Fields; Michael P. Flanagan; Merrill G. Jones II; Katherine Evans Lewis; John M. Martin; Lance P. Martin; Gregory T. Peacock (Board Certified Specialist in Estate Planning and Probate Law, North Carolina State Board of Legal Specialization); Gary J. Rickner; Stanley M. Sams; J. Troy Smith, Jr.; H. L. Stephenson, III; Benjamin E. F. B. Waller; Kenneth R. Wooten.
General and Trial Practice. Admiralty Law; Bankruptcy; Banks and Banking; Business Law; Civil Rights; Commercial Law; Construction Law; Contracts; Copyrights; Corporate Law; Debtor and Creditor; Elder Law; Eminent Domain; Employee Benefits; Environmental Law; Family Law including Divorce; Finance; Franchise Law; Government; Government Contracts; Health Care Law; Immigration and Naturalization; Insurance; International Law; International Trade; Investments; Labor and Employment including Discrimination, Sexual Harassment, and Workers' Compensation; Landlord and Tenant; Litigation; Personal Injury including Automobile Accidents, Legal Malpractice and Medical Malpractice; Products Liability; Real Estate; Securities; Taxation; Technology and Science including Internet Law, Trademarks, and Patents; Trusts and Estates including Estate Planning and Wills and Probate; Zoning and Land Use.
Barnhill Contracting Company; Chubb Insurance; Daedong-USA, Inc.; First-Citizens Bank & Trust Company; First Flight Federal Credit Union; Fountain Powerboats, Inc.; NC State Firemen's Association; Potash Corp.; State of North Carolina; Weyerhaeuser Co.
New Bern, North Carolina Office: 1001 College Court, P.O. Box 867. Telephone: 252-672-5400. Facsimile: 252-672-5477.
Raleigh, North Carolina Office: Suite 2400, Two Hannover Square, Fayetteville Street Mall, P.O. Box 2091. Telephone: 919-836-4260. Facsimile: 919-836-4277.
Wilmington, North Carolina Office: University Corporate Center, 127 Racine Drive, P.O. Box 7068. Telephone: 910-794-4800. Facsimile: 910-794-4877.
See Professional Biographies, GREENVILLE, NORTH CAROLINA

Warren, Tyler B., (AV) .... '— '74 C.576 B.S. L.896 J.D. [Everett&H.]
Watson, William H., (AV) .... '23 '50 C&L.575 B.S., J.D. [Speight,W.&B.]
Wells, J. Warner, II, (CV) .... '69 '96 C.198 B.A. L.790 J.D. [Wells&C.]
Wells & Cole, PLLC, (CV) .... 414 South Evans Street
Whitley, Robert E., (AV) '49 '74 C.232 B.S.B.A. L.896 J.D. [Whitley,R.&W.] (⊙Jacksonville, Kinston, Raleigh)
Whitley, Rodgman & Whitley, (AV) 1702-A E. Arlington Boulevard, Suite 100 (⊙Jacksonville, Kinston, New Bern, Raleigh)

Willey, Ralph G., P.A.
(See Rocky Mount)

Williams, Keith Alan, (BV) .... '67 '92 C.1053 B.A. L.575 J.D. [K.A.Williams]

Williams, Keith A., P.A., Law Offices of, (BV)
321 South Evans Street, Suite 103, P.O. Box 1965, 27835-1965
Telephone: 252-931-9362 Fax: 252-830-5155
Email: kwlaw@earthlink.net URL: http://www.lawyers.com/keithwilliams
Keith Alan Williams (Board Certified Specialist in Federal and State Criminal Law, North Carolina State Board of Legal Specialization).
Criminal and Civil Litigation in Federal and State Courts.
See Professional Biographies, GREENVILLE, NORTH CAROLINA

Wilson, Andrew H.D., (BV) .... '64 '92 C.152 B.A. L.692 J.D. [Barber&W.]
Wooten, Kenneth R., (AV) '— '79 C.596 B.A. L.595 J.D. [Ward&S.] (⊙New Bern, Raleigh)
Wooten, William I., Jr., (BV) .... '34 '63 C.228 A.B. L.575 J.D. 111 West Third St.
Wright, Ernest B. '24 '49 C.418 B.A. L.45 LL.B. (adm. in AR; not adm. in NC) 305 Francis Asbury Lane‡

GRIFTON, 2,073, *Lenoir & Pitt Cos.*

Houston, Russell, III, (BV) .... '40 '74 C.383 B.A. L.421 J.D. 406 W. McCrae St.

HALIFAX, * 327, *Halifax Co.*

Cranford, Dwight L. .... '32 '60 C&L.575 A.B., J.D. Dist. J.

Hux, Livermon & Armstrong, L.L.P.
(See Enfield)

Jones, Franklin L., Jr., Law Office of, (BV) '66 '95 C.575 B.S. L.1345 J.D.
462 Highway 301 South, P.O. Box 556, 27839
Telephone: 252-583-1515 Fax: 252-583-1818
Email: fjoneslaw@coastalnet.com URL: http://www.franklinljones.com
Criminal Defense, Personal Injury, Workers Compensation.
See Professional Biographies, HALIFAX, NORTH CAROLINA

McCoy, H. Paul, Jr. .... '48 '73 C&L.896 B.A., J.D. Chf. Dist. Ct. J.

Moseley, Elliott & Dickens, L.L.P.
(See Roanoke Rapids)

Robinson, Teresa Raquel .... '76 '01 C.1378 B.S. L.574 J.D. Asst. U.S. Dist. Atty.

HAMLET, 6,018, *Richmond Co.*

Crawford, Derek G., (CV) .... '65 '92 C.575 B.S. L.574 J.D. [Crawford]
Crawford Law Office PC, (CV) .... 203 Willow Ln., Hwy. 74 & 15 Williams St.
Futrell, Stephan R., (BV) .... '56 '81 C.896 B.A. L.276 J.D. [Kitchin,N.W.W.&F.] ⊙
Goodwin, George Wayne, (BV) .... '67 '92 C&L.575 B.A., J.D. [Goodwin]
Goodwin, Melanie Wade .... '70 '00 C.575 B.A. L.1228 J.D. [Goodwin]
Goodwin Law Offices, P.A., (BV) .... P.O. Box 1166
Kitchin, Henry L., (AV) .... '39 '63 C&L.896 B.A., LL.B. [Kitchin,N.W.W.&F.] ⊙
Kitchin, Neal, Webb, Webb & Futrell, P.A., (AV) .... 54 Main Street (⊙Rockingham)
Neal, F. Brent, (AV) .... '44 '72 C&L.575 A.B., J.D. [Kitchin,N.W.W.&F.] ⊙
Webb, William R., Jr., (BV) .... '53 '79 C&L.896 B.A., J.D. [Kitchin,N.W.W.&F.] ⊙

HAMPSTEAD, —, *Pender Co.*

Biberstein & Nunalee, L.L.P., (AV) .... 16191 U.S. Highway 17 (⊙Burgaw)

Brandon, Walter J., (BV) .... '48 '81 C.894 B.A. L.607 J.D. P.O. Box 40
Ciardella, Margaret C. .... '42 '87 C.953 B.S. L.575 J.D. 107 Topsail Watch Ln.
Jones, G. A., Jr. .... '20 '49 C.362 L.575 LL.B. 115 Bellowing Doe Rd.
Kilroy, Robert W., (BV) .... '38 '73 C.93 A.B. L.347 J.D. 14889 U.S. Hwy. 17
Nunalee, Mark I., (BV) .... '55 '81 C&L.575 B.S., J.D. [Biberstein&N.] ⊙

HARBINGER, 400, *Currituck Co.*

Edsall, James T., (BV) .... '61 '96 C.575 B.A. L.1339 J.D. 8562 Caratoke Hwy.
Epp, James Douglas, (CV) .... '69 '96 C.999 B.A. L.1339 J.D. 8562 Caratoke Hwy.

HARRELLSVILLE, 106, *Hertford Co.*

Moore, Darlene .... '60 '86 C.575 B.A. L.574 J.D. Rte. 1, Box 158★

HARRISBURG, 4,493, *Cabarrus Co.*

Angel, Kirk J. .... '70 '97 C.48 B.A. L.838 J.D. [Angel]
Angel Law Firm, The .... P.O. Box 692
Cook, Brian P., (AV Ⓣ) .... '56 '89 C.116 B.A. L.607 J.D. P.O. Box 1448
Cox, Ben Allen .... '59 '01 C.999 B.B.A. L.1228 J.D. [B.A.Cox]
Cox, Ben A., PLLC, Law Offices of .... P.O. Box 1420
Hollingsworth, Barbara D. .... '45 '83 C.418 B.S. L.1345 J.D. P.O. Box 1224

HAVELOCK, 22,442, *Craven Co.*

Brown, Jennifer J. '69 '95 C&L.629 B.A, J.D
(adm. in OR; not adm. in NC) Dept. of Navy, NAVAIRDEPOT

Brumbaugh, Mu & King, P.A., (BV)
404 East Main Street, 28532 ⊙
Telephone: 252-447-4445
URL: http://www.bmklaw.net
Kenneth W. King, Jr.
Practice Limited to Injury Cases. Automobile, Wrongful Death, Medical Malpractice, Workers' Compensation, Products Liability and Social Security Claims.
See Professional Biographies, HAVELOCK, NORTH CAROLINA

Glenn, Julie Bailey .... '59 '84 C&L.260 B.A., J.D. 803-A E. Main St.‡
Haner, Annemarie Spadaro .... '44 '80 C&L.588 B.A., J.D. 803 E. Main St.‡
King, Kenneth W., Jr., (BV) ...... '61 '86 C.575 B.S. L.469 J.D. [Brumbaugh,M.&K.] ⊙

Mills & Willey
(See New Bern)

Palmer, Robert G. '68 '02 C.1287 B.A. L.356 J.D.
(adm. in FL; not adm. in NC) J. Advocate
Rice, W. Mack .... '67 '93 C.232 B.S.B.A. L.574 J.D. [W.M.Rice]
Rice, W. Mack, P.A. .... 308 W. Main St., Ste. 102
Stricklin, Bobby J., (CV) .... '51 '87 L.1228 J.D. 448 Westbrooke Shopping Ctr.

Stubbs & Perdue, P.A.
(See New Bern)

Sumrell, Sugg, Carmichael, Hicks & Hart, P.A.
(See New Bern)

Wall, Bevin W.
(See Newport)

HAYESVILLE, * 279, *Clay Co.*

Bius, Dana L. .... '71 '97 C.48 B.A. L.1228 J.D. [Ⓐ McKeever,E.D.&H.] (⊙Murphy)
Carter, William E., (BV) .... '30 '55 C.77 B.S. L.575 LL.B. P.O. Box 525

Ford, Larry J., Attorney at Law, (BV) '— '76 C.925 B.A. L.575 J.D.
46 Church Street, Suite 22, P.O. Box 750, 28904-0750
Telephone: 828-389-3726 Fax: 828-389-3816
Email: fordlaw@usa.net URL: http://www.lfordlaw.com
Real Estate, Trusts and Estates, Elder Law, Business Law, Corporate Law, Wills & Probate.
See Professional Biographies, HAYESVILLE, NORTH CAROLINA

Hendrix, Dina M., (CV) .... '68 '94 C.198 B.A. L.896 J.D. P.O. Box 1068
Hendrix, Michael E., (CV) .... '66 '92 C.925 B.A. L.469 J.D. P.O. Box 1068
McKeever, Edwards, Davis & Hays, P.A., (AV)
Court House Square (⊙Bryson City, Murphy)
Nichols, Deborah L., (BV) .... '53 '77 C&L.469 A.B., J.D. [Nichols&N.]
Nichols, Gary W., (BV) .... '49 '74 C.280 B.A. L.469 J.D. [Nichols&N.]
Nichols & Nichols, (BV) .... 40 Church St.
Patterson, Ronald S., (CV) .... '51 '80 C.925 B.S. L.574 J.D. P.O. Box 660
Woody, Merinda Swanson, (BV) .... '52 '83 C.577 B.A. L.1228 J.D. [M.S.Woody]

Woody, Merinda Swanson, P.A., Law Offices of, (BV)
137 Tusquittee Street, P.O. Box 1519, 28904
Telephone: 828-389-0202
URL: http://www.lawyers.com/woody
Merinda Swanson Woody.
Residential and Commercial Real Estate, Buying or Selling a Home or Business, Business Law, Construction Law, Contract Law, Estate Planning, Wills and Probate, Trusts and Estates, Asset Protection.
See Professional Biographies, HAYESVILLE, NORTH CAROLINA

HENDERSON, * 16,095, *Vance Co.*

Allen, Ben U. .... '30 '63 C.232 B.S. L.575 LL.B. Ret. Dist. J.
Alston, D. Bermard .... '— '85 C&L.575 B.S., J.D. [Alston,G.&D.]
Alston, Green & Durrante .... 626 S. Garnett Street
Blackburn, Charles F., (AV) .... '25 '49 C.198 L.902 LL.B. 109 Young Street
Blackburn, George T., (AV) .... '21 '49 C&L.902 B.A., J.D. 109 Young Street
Blackburn, George T., II, (AV) '50 '76 C&L.575 A.B., J.D.
Sr. V.P. & Gen. Coun., Rose's Stores, Inc. (⊙Raleigh)
Burnette, Caroline Slater .... '— '04 C.853 B.A. L.1345 J.D. [Ⓐ Stainback&S.]
Care, Jonathan S., (CV) .... '73 '99 C&L.1228 B.A., J.D. [Ⓐ Hight&F.]
Carraway, Melissa J., (BV) .... '56 '85 C.471 B.A. L.1228 J.D. 203 N. Chestnut St.
Cloninger, D. Randall, Attorney at Law, (BV) '53 '88
C.575 B.S.M.T. L.574 J.D. 115 Young St., Ste. 3

Davis, Sturges & Tomlinson
(See Louisburg)

DeCillis, Steven B., (BV) .... '68 '94 C.705 B.S. L.575 J.D. 804 S. Garnett St.
Faulkner, Arthur D., (CV) .... '47 '78 C.1228 B.S. L.574 J.D. [A.D.Faulkner]
Faulkner, Lee A., (AV) .... '46 '74 C.575 A.B. L.896 J.D. [Hight&F.]
Faulkner, A. D., (CV) .... 115 Young, Ste. 2
Fleming, Robert F., (AV) .... '44 '69 C.228 A.B. L.896 J.D. 128 Cedarwood Dr.‡
Green, James P., Jr. .... '58 '86 C&L.574 B.A., J.D. [Alston,G.&D.]
Hight, Henry W., Jr. .... '49 '74 C&L.575 A.B., J.D. Supr. Ct. J.
Hight, Robert S., (AV) .... '28 '54 C&L.575 A.B., LL.B. [Hight&F.]
Hight & Faulkner, (AV) .... 109 Church Street

Jackson, Harvey D., Attorney at Law '47 '78 C.198 B.A. L.575 J.D.
125 N. Garnett Street, 27536
Telephone: 252-492-7929 Fax: 252-492-4799
Email: hjackson@inet4u.com URL: http://www.harveyjacksonlaw.com

(This Listing Continued)

Jackson, Harvey D., Attorney at Law (Continued)
Worker's Compensation, Personal Injury, Auto Accident and Insurance Claims, Wrongful Death, Traffic Violations.
See Professional Biographies, HENDERSON, NORTH CAROLINA

Kittrell, Robert G., Jr., (AV) .... '21 '48 C&L.575 B.S., J.D. 109 Young Street
Lemmond, Melissa C. .... '56 '85 C.471 B.A. L.1228 J.D. Melissa Carraway Lemmond
McGill, Rosha Ward '51 '84
C.588 B.S. L.276 J.D. Mgn. Atty., N. Central Legal Assist. Prog.
Noel, William W., III, (CV) .... '58 '91 C.296 B.S. L.574 J.D. P.O. Box 4
Pergerson, Donald D., (BV) .... '48 '85 C&L.575 B.A., J.D. 140 W. Andrews Ave.
Perry, Bennett H., Jr., (AV) .... '29 '55 C&L.575 A.B., LL.B. 109 Young Street

Pike, John H.
(See Oxford)

Rogers, Bobby W., (AV) .... '34 '63 C.576 B.S.C.E. L.273 LL.B. 229 Young St.
Rogers, Michael F., (BV) .... '66 '91 C.232 B.A. L.1228 J.D. 229 Young St.
Ross, Paul R., (BV) .... '61 '88 C.576 B.S. L.1228 J.D. P.O. Box 45
Satterwhite, Michael E., (AV) .... '52 '77 C.575 B.A. L.469 J.D. [Stainback&S.]
Stainback, Paul J., (BV) .... '49 '76 C&L.896 B.A., J.D. [Stainback&S.]

Stainback & Satterwhite, (AV)
115 N. Garnett Street, P.O. Box 1820, 27536-4637
Telephone: 252-438-4136 FAX: 252-438-6044
Members of Firm: Paul J. Stainback; Michael E. Satterwhite. Associate: Caroline Slater Burnette.
General Civil and Criminal Practice. Trials in all Courts. Probate, Real Estate, Corporation, Commercial and School District Law.
References: First-Citizens Bank & Trust Co.; Southern National Bank.
See Professional Biographies, HENDERSON, NORTH CAROLINA

Stevenson, Amanda E., (BV) .... '62 '88 C&L.575 B.A., J.D. 203 N. Chestnut St.
Yancey, Carolyn J., Attorney at Law, (CV) '68 '96
C.302 B.A. L.574 J.D. 246 Dabney Drive
Zollicoffer, John H., Jr., (AV) .... '36 '61 C.575 A.B. L.228 J.D. [Zollicoffer]

Zollicoffer Law Office, (AV)
215 North Garnett Street, P.O. Drawer 19, 27536
Telephone: 252-438-4134 Fax: 252-438-2700
Members of Firm: Allison C. Zollicoffer (1854-1922); Jere P. Zollicoffer (1890-1944); John H. Zollicoffer (1902-1975); A. Augustus Zollicoffer, Jr. (1924-1991); John H. Zollicoffer, Jr.
General Practice, Litigation Torts, Trials, Personal Injury, Corporation, Insurance Law, Trusts and Estates, Wills, Traffic Citations; Real Estate, Mediation.
See Professional Biographies, HENDERSON, NORTH CAROLINA

HENDERSONVILLE, * 10,420, *Henderson Co.*

Adams, Hoyle B. .... '21 '53 C.576 B.S. L.575 LL.B. P.O. Box 1861
Alexander, Sharon B., (AV) .... '56 '81 C.122 B.A. L.838 J.D. [Prince,Y.&M.]
Bazzle, Ervin W., (BV) .... '48 '76 C.870 B.S. L.790 J.D. [Bazzle&C.]
Bazzle & Carr, P.A., (BV) .... 206 Third Avenue West
Beeker, Angela Skerrett .... '— '91 C.228 B.S.E. L.1228 J.D. [Whitmire B.&T.]
Binkowski, Don '29 '57 C.477 A.B. L.912 LL.B.
(adm. in MI; not adm. in NC) 2110 Cumming Woods Court‡
Blanchard, Ronald G., (BV) .... '48 '77 C.896 B.A. L.574 J.D. [Blanchard,N.&H.]

Blanchard, Newman & Hayes, (BV)
112 South Washington Street, P.O. Box 868, 28793
Telephone: 828-693-0222 Fax: 828-693-0454
Email: bcbattys@brinet.com URL: http://www.lawyers.com/bbn&j
Members of Firm: Ronald G. Blanchard; Gregory A. Newman; Jason Randolph Hayes.
General Civil Litigation, Family Law, Divorce, Criminal in all State and Federal Courts, Traffic, DWI.
See Professional Biographies, HENDERSONVILLE, NORTH CAROLINA

Brewer, Mitchell K. .... '77 '05 C.999 B.S. L.1228 J.D. 206 3rd Ave. W.
Brinkley, Robert G. '41 '77 C.679 B.S.Ch.E. L.818 J.D.
(adm. in MA; not adm. in NC) Chem Design Corp.
Brittain, Thomas M., Jr., (BV) .... '62 '87 C.160 B.A. L.1228 J.D. Asst. Dist. Atty.
Brooks, Athena Fox, (BV) .... '66 '91 C.48 B.A. L.575 J.D. 200 N. Grove St.
Bruton, Jefferson H., (BV) .... '39 '65 C.198 B.A. L.896 LL.B. [Ⓐ Stepp,G.&Assoc.]
Bryant, John D., (AV Ⓣ) .... '26 '61 C.597 B.S. L.188 J.D. 227 Raintree Dr.
Burrell, Charles Russell, (BV) .... '60 '85 C.228 A.B. L.575 J.D. 501 N. Justice St.

Carpenter, Walter C., (BV) '58 '85 C.575 B.A. L.469 J.D.
132 South Main Street, 28792
Telephone: 628-692-1919 Fax: 628-692-2647
Civil and Criminal Litigation, Traffic Violations, Driving While Intoxicated, Real Estate, Buying and Selling a Home, Commercial Real Estate, Wills, Probate, Estate Planning, Trusts and Estates.
See Professional Biographies, HENDERSONVILLE, NORTH CAROLINA

Carr, Eugene M., III, (BV) .... '56 '85 C.976 B.A. L.575 J.D. [Bazzle&C.]
Cathey, William J., III, (BV) .... '54 '79 C.48 B.A. L.245 J.D. 131 4th Avenue W.
Cheaney, Philip N., (AV) '20 '48 C&L.260 J.D.
(adm. in FL; not adm. in NC) 285 Sabine Dr.‡
Collie, C. Page .... '69 '95 C.34 B.S. L.575 J.D. 2110 North Stoney View Drive
Collins, Patrick H. .... '40 '67 C.165 B.A. L.228 LL.B. 318 N. Main St.

Cosgrove, Timithy R., (BV) '48 '75 C.103 A.B. L.896 J.D.
100-A Chadwick Square Court, 28739
Telephone: 828-696-7993 Facsimile: 828-696-7928
Email: doryyoung@aol.com
Civil and Criminal Litigation in all State and Federal Courts. Real Estate, Probate, Estate Planning, Traffic Matters, DWI, Family Law, Divorce, Equitable Distribution, Adoption, Personal Injury Litigation.
See Professional Biographies, HENDERSONVILLE, NORTH CAROLINA

Costello, James A. .... '37 '66 C.1031 B.S. L.982 LL.B. 2 Whirlaway Ct.

Deutsch, Robert J., P.A.
(See Asheville)

Dierauf, Elizabeth M. Fay, (BV) '67 '94
C.1369 B.A. L.896 J.D. Asst. Dist. Atty., Dist. Atty. Off.
Edney, J. Michael, Law Office of '60 '85 C.48 B.A. L.790 J.D.
1509 Haywood Rd., Ste. C
Egan, Michael E., (BV Ⓣ) .... '46 '75 C.362 B.A. L.259 J.D. 318 N. Whitted St.

Ehrmann, Jacob C.
(See Asheville)

Elkins, Don H., (BV) .... '39 '69 C.125 A.B. L.896 J.D. [Elkins&E.]
Elkins, H. Trade .... '74 '00 C.925 B.S.B.A. L.1338 J.D. [Elkins&E.]

Elkins & Elkins, (BV)
228 6th Avenue East, Suite 1B, 28792
Telephone: 828-692-2205 Fax: 828-692-8469
Email: htelkins@prodigy.net
Members of Firm: Don H. Elkins; H. Trade Elkins.
Bankruptcy, Real Estate, Residential Real Estate, Buying and Selling a Home, Probate, Corporation, Civil Trial Practice, Out of Court Debt Restructuring.
See Professional Biographies, HENDERSONVILLE, NORTH CAROLINA

Eubanks, Michael C.
(See Brevard)

Ferikes & Bleynat, PLLC
(See Asheville)

Fosmire, Susan L., (BV) .... '60 '91 C.258 B.A. L.574 J.D. P.O. Box 948
Fox, David K., (AV) '54 '82 C&L.575 B.A., J.D.
210 3rd Ave. W. (⊙New Orleans, LA)
Fritschner, Samuel H., (BV) .... '52 '81 C.896 B.A. L.421 J.D. [Whitmire&F.]

Frue Law Firm, The, PLLC
(See Asheville)

Gantt, David, Law Office
(See Asheville)

Gardo, William L., II, (BV) '62 '87 C.34 B.A. L.575 J.D.
921 Oakland Street, 28791
Telephone: 828-697-9964 Fax: 828-697-9495
URL: http://www.lawyers.com/gardolaw
General Civil Trial Practice, Personal Injury, Automobile Accidents, Wrongful Death, Family Law, Divorce, Child Custody, Child Support, Adoptions, Workers Compensation, Criminal Law, Driving While Intoxicated, Traffic Violations, Drug Offenses.
See Professional Biographies, HENDERSONVILLE, NORTH CAROLINA

Garren, Don H., (BV) .... '33 '63 C.575 A.B. L.896 J.D. 422 N. Church St.
Gasperson-Justice, Kimberly, (BV) '64 '89
C.1129 B.A. L.1228 J.D. 501 North Justice Street
Gilliam, Sue Ballard, (BV) ......'34 '85 C.1111 B.A. L.469 J.D. 303 S. Church St., Ste. 2
Goldsmith, James L., Jr., (BV) .... '53 '82 P.O. Box 752

Grimes & Teich
(See Asheville)

Groce, Edwin R., (BV) .... '37 '63 C.896 B.B.A. L.575 J.D. [Stepp,G.&Assoc.]
Gudger, Lamar, (AV) ....'19 '42 C&L.575 A.B., LL.B. 201 N. Main St. (⊙Asheville)
Haggard, Robert H., (AV) ....'49 '74 C.198 B.A. L.259 J.D. [VanWinkle,B.W.S.&D.]
Hall, Stephen K. '49 '76 C&L.966 B.A., J.D.
(adm. in WI; not adm. in NC) 203 White Oak Dr.‡
Harrelson, Edward L. ....'68 '93 C&L.575 B.A., J.D. 210 3rd Ave. W.
Hayes, Jason Randolph .... '72 '01 C.232 B.A. L.896 J.D. [Blanchard,N.&H.]

Hix, Thomas N., (AV) '50 '76 C.692 B.A. L.192 J.D.
422 N. Church Street, 28792
Telephone: 828-697-5410 Fax: 828-692-5373
URL: http://www.thomashix.com
Family Law, Divorce, Equitable Distribution, Child Custody, Child Support, Adoption, Prenuptial Agreements, Domestic Violence, Criminal Law, DWI, Traffic Violations, Drug Offenses, Civil Litigation, Wills.
See Professional Biographies, HENDERSONVILLE, NORTH CAROLINA

Hoffman, Stephen P., (AVⓉ) ...... '46 '75 C.994 B.A. L.1009 J.D. 220 Bent Pine Terrace
Hogan, Lawrence A., (BV) .... '43 '71 C.375 B.S. L.378 J.D. 229 N. Main
Hogan, Robert L., (BV) .... '48 '85 C.375 B.S.B.A. L.190 J.D. P.O. Box 1688

Howe, Waters & Moxley, P.A., (AV) BB
P.O. Box 586, 28793
Telephone: 828-692-9636
Email: HWCM@bellsouth.net
William B. W. Howe (1928-2003); R. Charles Waters; Linda A. Moxley.
General Civil Practice. Civil and Criminal Litigation, Real Estate, Residential and Commercial Real Estate, Guardianships, Wills and Probate, Trusts and Estates, Business Law, Contracts.
See Professional Biographies, HENDERSONVILLE, NORTH CAROLINA

Jackson, Frank B., Law Offices of, (AV) '47 '72 C&L.575 A.B., J.D. BB
422 North Church Street, P.O. Box 1666, 28792
Mailing Address: P.O. Box 1666, Hendersonville, NC
Telephone: 828-697-5410 Fax: 828-692-5373
URL: http://www.frankbjacksonlaw.com
Associate: James Lamar Palmer.
Civil Litigation in all State and Federal Courts. Domestic Litigation, Divorce, Child Custody, Child Support, Equitable Distribution, Spousal Support, General Civil Practice, Appeals, Probate and Estate Planning.
See Professional Biographies, HENDERSONVILLE, NORTH CAROLINA

Johnston, Diana Armatage, (BV) '39 '73
C.024 B.A. L.569 J.D. 1612 Asheville Hwy, Ste.3
Knox, Caroline T. ....'70 '00 C.945 B.A. L.896 J.D. [VanWinkle,B.W.S.&D.]
Kropp, Richard V. '28 '53 C.604 A.B. L.309 LL.B.
(adm. in OH; not adm. in NC) 1103 Red Oak Dr.‡
Layburn, Donald W., Jr. '48 '84 C.1099 B.A. L.425 J.D.
(adm. in LA; not adm. in NC) 1954 Cambridge Dr., Ste. B
Lebensburger, Scott E., (BV) ....'50 '77 C.902 B.A. L.862 J.D. 211 N. Main St.
Lemke, William A. '12 '43 C.910 A.B. L.999 LL.B.
(adm. in MO; not adm. in NC) 1017 Saddlebrook Dr.‡
Linkous, Eugene T., Jr., (BV) .... '54 '83 C&L.575 B.A., J.D. [Linkous&Assoc.]
Linkous and Associates, (BV) .... P.O. Box 2807
Lowry, Wm. J. ....'22 '49 C&L.228 A.B., LL.B. 320 Colony Ln.‡
Madden, Frank H. '05 '27 L.146 LL.B.
(adm. in IL; not adm. in NC) 333 Thompson St., Rm. 217‡
Marquis, Stephen B. '32 '67 C.999 B.A. L.213 J.D.
(adm. in MI; not adm. in NC) 323 Cummings Pkwy.
Massagee, B. B., III, (AV) ....'54 '79 C&L.896 B.A., J.D. [Prince,Y.&M.]
Massagee, Boyd B., Jr., (AV) ....'32 '59 C.198 B.S. L.575 LL.B. [Prince,Y.&M.]
McAllister, Bowdre Mays ....'62 '87 C.280 A.B. L.1059 J.D. P.O. Box 178
Moore, Deborah S. ....'53 '83 C.575 B.A. L.838 J.D. P.O. Box 1477
Morley, E.K., (BV) .... '31 '82 C.645 B.A. L.896 J.D. [E.K.Morley]

Morley, E.K., PLLC, Law Offices of, (BV)
104 First Avenue East, 28792
Telephone: 828-697-6285 Fax: 828-697-6287
Email: ekmorley@ioa.com URL: http://www.lawyers.com/ekmorley
E.K. Morley (Board Certified Specialist in Estate Planning and Probate Law, North Carolina State Board of Legal Specialization).
Contested Wills, Will Contests, Estate Litigation, Decedents Estates, Inheritance, Successions, Trusts and Estates, Surrogates Court Practice, Contested Trusts and Estates, Estate Administration, Estate Settlements, Fiduciary Law, Fiduciary Liability, Fiduciary Litigation, Trust Law, Trust Litigation, Ancillary Probate, Probate Litigation.
See Professional Biographies, HENDERSONVILLE, NORTH CAROLINA

Morris, Waymon L. ....'36 '65 L.770 J.D. 308 6th Ave. E.
Moxley, Linda A., (CV) .... '52 '94 C.160 B.A. L.469 J.D. [Howe,W.&M.]
Mulligan, Thomas .... '49 '77 C.693 B.A. L.564 J.D. 190 Ridgeview Dr.
Mundy, John D., (CV) ....'67 '97 C.575 B.A. L.574 J.D. Asst. Dist. Atty.

Neill, D. Samuel, (BV) '49 '75 C&L.896 B.A., J.D.
222 Third Avenue West, 28739
Telephone: 828-693-1739 Faxline: 828-696-9163
Email: samneill@bellsouth.net URL: http://www.samneillaw.com
(This Listing Continued)

Neill, D. Samuel (Continued)
Estate Planning, Wills and Probate, Trusts and Estates, Real Estate, Residential Real Estate, Commercial Real Estate, Personal Injury, Business Law and Elder Law.
Representative Client: Town of Laurel Park.
See Professional Biographies, HENDERSONVILLE, NORTH CAROLINA

Neill, Roy D., (BV) ....'57 '85 C.34 B.S. L.896 J.D. 144 Third Avenue East

Neumann, Scott D.
(See Brevard)

Newman, Gregory A., (BV) ....'61 '89 C.1178 B.A. L.201 J.D. [Blanchard,N.&H.]
O'Dowd, John H., Jr., (BVⓉ) '49 '77 C.152 B.A. L.790 J.D.
(adm. in SC; not adm. in NC) P.O. Box 687
Oxley, Merrimon Burwell ....'62 '87 C.575 B.A. L.692 J.D. Dist. Atty. Off.
Palmer, James Lamar .... '76 '02 C.575 B.A. L.574 J.D. [Ⓐ F.B.Jackson]
Patty, Clarence R., Jr. '17 '51 C.838 B.S. L.273 J.D.
(adm. in DC; not adm. in NC) 9 Curlew Ct.‡
Powell, Mark E. ....'58 '83 C&L.575 B.S., J.D. Dist. J.

Prince, Youngblood & Massagee, (AV) BB
240 Third Avenue, West, 28739
Telephone: 828-692-2595 FAX: 828-693-0177
Members of Firm: L. B. Prince (1898-1982); Kenneth R. Youngblood; Boyd B. Massagee, Jr.; B. B. Massagee, III; Sharon B. Alexander.
General Practice. Probate, Civil Litigation, Commercial, Residential Real Estate, Corporate, Arbitration, Mediation, Healthcare, Employment Law, Family Law, Equitable Distribution, Child Custody, Adoptions.
Representative Clients: Margaret R. Pardee Memorial Hospital; Nations Bank; First Citizens Bank and Trust Co.; Duke Power Co.; Blue Cross & Blue Shield of North Carolina; Blue Ridge Community College; Fletcher Motor Co., Inc.; Hunter Chevrolet-Volvo-Subaru Co., Inc.; Village of Flat Rock.
See Professional Biographies, HENDERSONVILLE, NORTH CAROLINA

Redden, Arthur J., Jr., (BV) .... '35 '64 C.925 B.A. L.896 LL.B. 326-A 1st Ave. E.
Romeo, Randolph C., (BV) .... '48 '76 C.602 B.B.A. L.192 J.D. 136 S. King St.
Shealy, Adam L. ....'68 '96 C.140 B.S. L.280 J.D. [VanWinkle,B.W.S.&D.]
Sheffron, Scott H. ....'67 '98 C&L.1206 B.S., J.D. [Sheffron]
Sheffron Law Firm .... 329 N. Washington Street
Shelton, Scott H., (CV) ....'67 '93 C&L.575 B.A., J.D. 206 3rd Ave. W.
Shobe, William M., II '54 '84 C.880 B.A. L.1051 J.D.
(adm. in MN; not adm. in NC) 2012 Laurel Pk. Hwy.‡

Sluder, Curtis Alan
(See Asheville)

Smith, Stephen R. '24 '51 C.893 B.A. L.976 LL.B.
(adm. in NY; not adm. in NC) Dampp-Chaser Electronics Corp.
Stein, William J. '28 '73 C.966 M.S. L.128 J.D.
(adm. in OH; not adm. in NC) 106 Kenwood Dr.‡
Stepp, Christopher Samuel, (BV) ...... '65 '91 C.575 B.A. L.1228 J.D. [Stepp,G.&Assoc.]
Stepp, W. Harley, Jr., (AV) .... '34 '64 C&L.575 B.S., J.D. [Stepp,G.&Assoc.]
Stepp, Groce & Associates, (AV) .... 112 South Main Street
Thompson, Michael M., (BV) .... '57 '85 C.48 B.S. L.1228 J.D. [VanWinkle,B.W.S.&D.]
Todd, Frank L., Sr. ....'22 '48 C&L.896 B.S., LL.B. P.O. Box 2150‡
Toms, Fred '25 '56 C.228 L.245 J.D.
(adm. in MS; not adm. in NC) 1809 Country Club Rd.‡
Townsend, Teresa L. .... '50 '86 C.235 B.S. L.896 J.D. [Whitmire B.&T.]
Tylander, Robert D., (AVⓉ) '18 '43 C&L.260 B.S., J.D.
(adm. in FL; not adm. in NC) 40 High Rocks Trail‡

Van Winkle, Buck, Wall, Starnes and Davis, P.A., (AV)
422 South Main Street, 28792 ⊙
Telephone: 828-697-6196 FAX: 828-693-3999
Email: vw@vwlawfirm.com URL: http://www.vwlawfirm.com
Robert H. Haggard (Board Certified Specialist in Estate Planning and Probate Law, North Carolina State Board of Legal Specialization); Michael M. Thompson; Adam L. Shealy (Board Certified Specialist in Estate Planning and Probate Law, North Carolina State Board of Legal Specialization); Caroline T. Knox.
Administrative, Banking, Bankruptcy, Business Law, Creditor's Rights, Estates and Trusts, Litigation, Real Estate, Taxation.
Western Region General Counsel for: Wachovia Bank & Trust Co.
Attorneys for: Carolina Power & Light Co.; Charles D. Owen Manufacturing Co.; Clyde Savings and Loan Assn.; Continental Telephone Company of N.C.; Gerber Products Co.; Liberty Mutual Insurance Co.; Reliance Insurance Co.; State Farm Mutual Automobile Insurance Co.; United States Fidelity & Guaranty Co.
Asheville, North Carolina Office: 11 North Market Street, P.O. Box 7376. Telephone: 828-258-2991. FAX: 828-255-0255; 257-2767.
See Professional Biographies, HENDERSONVILLE, NORTH CAROLINA

Veazey, Alexander (Lex) H., III, (CV) .....'53 '78 C.198 B.A. L.896 J.D. 210 N. Main St.
Walicki, Nicole J. ....'71 '96 C.577 L.575 J.D. [Ⓐ Linkous&Assoc.]
Walker, Charlie C., Jr, (BV) ....'49 '75 C.244 B.A. L.896 J.D. Dist. Atty.
Waters, R. Charles, (AV) ....'38 '68 C.228 A.B. L.575 J.D. [Howe,W.&M.]
Welch, Brian S., (BV) ....'62 '91 C.48 J.D. L.574 B.S. P.O. Box 887

Whitmire Beeker & Townsend
120 West Allen Street, 28792
Telephone: 828-692-8201 Fax: 828-692-7032
URL: http://www.wbtlawfirm.com
Angela Skerrett Beeker; Teresa L. Townsend.
Real Estate - Residential and Commercial, Local Government Law, Land Development, Business and Corporations, Wills and Estates, Bankruptcy, Family Law, Environmental Law, Litigation.
See Professional Biographies, HENDERSONVILLE, NORTH CAROLINA

Whitmire & Fritschner, (BV) ....120 W. Allen St.
Winson, Lawrence D. ....'51 '75 C&L.260 B.S., J.D. 140 4th Avenue West, Suite 102
Yelverton, Richard Lee, III .... '70 '00 C.999 B.S. L.574 J.D. 210 N. Main St.
Youngblood, Kenneth R., (AV) ....'31 '55 C&L.575 A.B., LL.B. [Prince,Y.&M.]

HERTFORD, * 2,105, *Perquimans Co.*

Cole, J. Carlton ....'49 '87 C.414 B.S. L.574 J.D. Dist. J.
Edwards, Walter G., Jr., (CV) ....'50 '77 C.575 B.A. L.574 J.D. P.O. Box 245
James, Melanie M. ....'61 '86 C.575 B.A. L.1345 J.D. 200 W. Punch Alley
Matthews, John V., Jr., (BV) ....'41 '71 C.232 A.B. L.800 J.D. 129 N. Church St.
Pinsak, William F. '30 '58 C.679 B.S. L.347 J.D.
(adm. in IN; not adm. in NC) 11 Cashie Dr.
Vayda, George T. '— '54 C.1025 L.446 LL.B.
(adm. in NY; not adm. in NC) 405 Church St.‡

Vincent Law Firm, The, PC
(See Southern Shores)

HICKORY, 37,222, *Burke, Caldwell & Catawba Cos.*

Aberle, Timothy J. '59 '96
C.223 B.S.M.E. L.1338 J.D. Patent Coun., Corning Cable Systems

Abernethy, J. Carroll, Jr., (AV) .... '24 '49 C.404 A.B. L.896 J.D. 328 4th St., S.W.
Abernethy, Jesse David, (BV) '54 '79
C.896 B.S. L.575 J.D. Pat. Coun., Siecor Corporation
Adams, Valeree R. .... '75 '00 C.125 B.A. L.1228 J.D. [Young,M.B.&T.]
Allport, Ptolemy Taylor, (CV) .... '63 '93 C.839 B.S. L.861 J.D. [Patrick,H.&D.]
Allran, Austin M. .... '51 '79 C.228 B.A. L.802 J.D. NC State Sen.
Amos, T. Dean, (BV) .... '60 '87 C.575 B.S. L.896 J.D. [Young,M.B.&T.]
Anthony, Shirley Herman, (BV) .... '46 '88 C.404 B.A. L.896 J.D. 208 Union Sq.
Bach, Wayne M., (AV) .... '46 '73 C.232 A.B. L.421 J.D. [Young,M.B.&T.]
Barnett, Michael J. .... '77 '02 C.1044 B.A. L.575 J.D. [Patrick,H.&D.]
Brackett, J. Steven, (BV) .... '47 '73 C.152 B.A. L.896 J.D. [J.S.Brackett]
Brackett, J. Steven, Law Office, (BV) .... 1985 Tate Blvd. SE
Bradshaw, Eloise DeLaney, (BV) .... '55 '80 C&L.575 A.B., J.D. [Patrick,H.&D.]

Bumgardner, Don H.
(See Gastonia)

Cagle, Joe N., (BV) .... '39 '64 C.625 B.S. L.896 J.D. 109 First Ave., N.E.
Campbell, Clair G., (BV) .... '61 '85 C.16 B.A. L.192 J.D. [Campbell&Assoc.]
Campbell & Associates, PLC, (BV) .... 104 3rd St. (⊙Charlotte, Gastonia)
Carter, Sherwood J., (BV) .... '42 '72 C&L.575 A.B., J.D. 620 Fourth St., S.W.
Chamblee, Wm. H., (CV) .... '20 '48 C.896 B.S. L.575 LL.B. 327 Third Ave., N.W.
Cherry, Burford A., (BV) ...... '57 '82 C.576 B.A. L.1228 J.D. Dist. Ct. J., 25th Jud. Dist.
Christian, Daniel G., (BV) .... '54 '79 C.1129 B.S. L.1228 J.D. 18 3rd Ave., N.E.
Clark, D. Shawn, (CV) .... '72 '97 C.1128 B.S. L.1345 J.D. [D.S.Clark]
Clark, David Shawn, (CV) .... 316 4th St. N.W., Ste. B
Cody, Blair E., III .... '74 '00 C.404 B.A. L.574 J.D. [Gorham,C.M.G.&C.]
Connor, Bradley Ellis '73 '01 C.610 B.A. L.823 J.D.
(adm. in GA; not adm. in NC) Corp. Atty., CommScope, Inc.

Conrad, Scott D.
(See Newton)

Corne, Corne & Grant, P.A.
(See Newton)

Crone, John W., III, (BV) .... '54 '80 C.575 B.A. L.896 J.D. [Gorham,C.M.G.&C.]
Crouch, Carolyn, (CV) .... '53 '84 C.736 B.A. L.796 J.D. 110 N. Center St.
Culpepper, Paul E., (BV) .... '67 '93 C.896 B.A. L.1345 J.D. [Young,M.B.&T.]
Cummings, Theodore F., III, (BV) '41 '78
C.404 B.A. L.896 J.D. 116 2nd St. N.W., Ste. 201

Dark, L. Talton, III
(See Morganton)

DeMayo, Michael A., (BV) .... '65 '91 C.896 B.A. L.575 J.D. [M.A.DeMayo] ⊙
DeMayo, Michael A., L.L.P., Law Offices of, (BV)
321 Third Avenue, N.W. (⊙Charlotte, Monroe)
Dixon, Charles D., (AV) .... '26 '52 C.575 A.B. L.309 LL.B. [Patrick,H.&D.]
Eaker, Jennifer .... '74 '03 C.575 B.A. L.192 J.D. [Eaker&F.]

Eaker & Fulkerson, PC
110 N. Center Street, Suite 203, 28603-9249
Telephone: 828-267-2923 Fax: 828-267-2924
Jennifer Eaker; Daniel R. Fulkerson.
Criminal Law, Driving Under the Influence, Real Estate, Domestic.
See Professional Biographies, HICKORY, NORTH CAROLINA

Elliott, J. Bryan, (BV) '49 '75 C&L.575 A.B., J.D.
21 First Street NW, Suite 400, P.O. Box 2047, 28603-2047
Telephone: 828-324-5200 Fax: 828-324-0498
Email: elliottbk@earthlink.net URL: http://www.jbryanelliottlawfirm.com
Bankruptcy, Social Security Disability.
See Professional Biographies, HICKORY, NORTH CAROLINA

Eustice, Benjamin R. '68 '94 C.1027 B.S. L.425 J.D.
(adm. in LA; not adm. in NC) [B.R.Eustice]
Eustice, Benjamin R., PLLC .... 101 Government Ave. S.W.
Evans, Joe H. .... '28 '52 C.404 A.B. L.896 LL.B. 433 4th St., S.W.‡
Ferrell, Forrest A., (AV) .... '38 '63 C.316 A.B. L.575 LL.B. [Sigmon,C.M.H.H.&F.]
Fisher, Evans W. .... '52 '78 C.198 B.A. L.228 J.D. [Patrick,H.&D.]
Fulkerson, Daniel R. .... '— '01 C.577 B.A. L.966 J.D. [Eaker&F.]
Fuller, Donald R., Jr., (BV) .... '48 '73 C.575 B.S. L.893 J.D. [Patrick,H.&D.]
Gaither, James M., Jr., (AV) .... '42 '67 C&L.896 B.A., J.D. 110 N. Center St.
George, Boyd L. .... '42 '66 C.602 B.B.A. L.893 LL.B. 835 18th Ave. Dr., N.W.‡
Goodman, Ann R., Attorney at Law ..... '— '80 C.228 A.B. L.896 J.D. 126 1st Ave. N.E.
Gorham, B. Gregory .... '74 '99 C.893 B.S. L.1128 J.D. [Gorham,C.M.G.&C.]
Gorham, J. Samuel, III, (AV) '42 '71 C.575 B.S.B.A. L.896 J.D.
[Gorham,C.M.G.&C.]

Gorham, Crone, Mace, Green & Cody, LLP, (AV)
Fidelity Professional Building, 27 First Avenue, N.E., Suite 203, P.O. Box 2507, 28603-2507
Telephone: 828-322-5505 Telefax: 828-328-1882
Members of Firm: J. Samuel Gorham, III; John W. Crone, III; Derek L. Mace; Daniel R. Green, Jr.; Blair E. Cody, III. Associate: B. Gregory Gorham.
General Practice, Bankruptcy, Criminal, Driving While Intoxicated, Drug Crimes, Parole and Probation, Traffic Violations, White Collar Crime, Family Law, Adoption Law, Child Custody, Child Support, Divorce, Domestic Violence, Visitation Rights, Municipal Law, Personal Injury, Automobile Accidents, Wrongful Death, Real Estate, Buying or Selling a Home, Construction, Eminent Domain, Zoning and Land Use, Trust and Estates, Asset Protection, Estate Planning, Wills and Probate. Litigation in all State and Federal Courts.
Representative Client: NationsBank of North Carolina, N.A.
Approved Attorneys for: Lawyers Title Insurance Corp.; Chicago Title Insurance Co.
References: NationsBank of North Carolina, N.A.; First Union National Bank; Bank of Granite.
See Professional Biographies, HICKORY, NORTH CAROLINA

Gray, Layton, Kersh, Solomon, Sigmon, Furr & Smith, P.A.
(See Gastonia)

Green, Daniel R., Jr., (BV) .... '54 '79 C.404 B.A. L.575 J.D. [Gorham,C.M.G.&C.]
Hannah, Thomas N., (BV) .... '48 '79 C.1317 B.A. L.896 J.D. 785 U.S. Hwy. 70, S.W.
Hanvey, J. Scott, (BV) .... '67 '92 C.575 B.A. L.1228 J.D. [Sigmon,C.M.H.H.&F.]
Hawkins, Vanessa Barlow, (BV) .... '60 '85 C&L.575 B.S., J.D. 423 4th Street S.W.
Hayes, Gregory R. .... '57 '83 C&L.896 B.A., J.D. Dist. J.
Helton, Lyndon R., (BV) .... '65 '93 C.404 B.A. L.896 J.D. [L.R.Helton]

Helton, Lyndon R., PLLC, (BV)
827 Highland Avenue NE, P.O. Box 909, 28601
Telephone: 828-328-9966 Fax: 828-328-9996
URL: http://www.lyndonheltonlaw.com
Lyndon R. Helton.
Workers Compensation, Personal Injury.
See Professional Biographies, HICKORY, NORTH CAROLINA

Hester, Oma H., Jr., (BV) .... '25 '50 C.575 L.477 J.D. P.O. Box 2882
Hood, David Wallace, (BV) .... '66 '91 C&L.575 B.A., J.D. [Patrick,H.&D.]
Hovey, George D., (AV) .... '13 '40 C.390 B.S. L.228 LL.B. 328 1st Ave. N.W.‡
Huegerich, Nancy L. .... '76 '03 C.576 B.A. L.575 J.D. [Sigmon,C.M.H.H.&F.]
Huffman, W. George, (AV) .... '36 '64 C.797 A.B. L.575 J.D. 127 1st Ave., N.E.
Hutton, Warren A., (BV) .... '57 '83 C.861 B.A. L.896 J.D. [Sigmon,C.M.H.H.&F.]
Inglefield, Rebecca A. .... '56 '87 C.575 B.A. L.744 J.D. 220 18th St. Cir. SE
Jayne, M. Victoria, Law Offices of '— '86
C.471 B.A. L.575 J.D. 201 Government Avenue, S.W.
Jennings, William Andrew, (BV) .... '62 '87 C.280 B.B.A. L.896 J.D. P.O. Box 2284
Jones, Jonathan L. .... '53 '79 C.886 B.S. L.896 J.D. Dist. J.
Keener, Hurshell H., (AV) '29 '53 C&L.575 B.S., J.D.
Chmn. of the Bd., Leathercraft, Inc.
Kepford, Kirby, (BV) .... '50 '76 C&L.339 B.S., J.D. 260 1st Ave., N.W.
Killian, Mark L., (BV) .... '61 '88 C&L.575 B.A., J.D. P.O. Box 11139
Leak, Frank W. .... '68 '01 C&L.575 B.A., J.D. [Young,M.B.&T.] (Pat.)
Lewis, John Malachi .... '72 '98 C.152 B.A. L.575 J.D. [J.R.Rudisill,Jr.]
Lovekin, Stephen L., (BV) .... '40 '68 C.125 B.A. L.896 J.D. [Lovekin,Y.&O.]

Lovekin, Young & Orndoff, PC, (BV)
27 First Avenue, N.E., 28601
Mailing Address: P.O. Box 2087, Hickory, NC 28603
Telephone: 828-322-5435 Toll Free: 1-800-241-2001 Fax: 828-322-3973
Email: lovekin@charter.net URL: http://www.stephenlovekinlaw.com
Members of Firm: Stephen L. Lovekin; Gary F. Young; Jason Alexander Orndoff.
Personal Injury, Automobile Accidents, Bodily Injury, Wrongful Death, Workers Compensation, Products Liability, Family Law, Divorce, Child Custody, Child Support, Step-Parent Adoptions, Employment Insurance, Traffic Violations, Wills.
See Professional Biographies, HICKORY, NORTH CAROLINA

Mace, Derek L. .... '72 '97 C.404 B.A. L.575 J.D. [Gorham,C.M.G.&C.]
Mackie, Jeffrey T., (AV) .... '47 '73 C.896 B.A. L.575 J.D. [Sigmon,C.M.H.H.&F.]
Matthews, Scott A., (CV) .... '66 '92 C.575 B.S. L.940 J.D. [S.Matthews]
Matthews, Scott, (CV) .... 200 First Ave. N.W., Ste 501
McGee, Victoria J. .... '56 '86 C.471 B.A. L.575 J.D. City Atty's. Off.
McIntosh, Kevin C., (CV) .... '67 '93 C.575 B.S. L.1228 J.D. [Young,M.B.&T.]
Mitchell, Chrisanne Worthington '56 '83 C&L.280 B.S., J.D.
(adm. in GA; not adm. in NC) The Trust for Public Land
Morphis, Thomas C., Sr., (AV) .... '47 '72 C.296 B.A. L.575 J.D. [Young,M.B.&T.]

Mullen Holland & Cooper P.A.
(See Gastonia)

Noble, L. Oliver, Jr. .... '46 '70 C.576 B.S. L.575 J.D. [Patrick,H.&D.]
Orgain, John B., IV, (BV) '59 '86
C.228 A.B. L.309 J.D. General Counsel, Alex Lee, Inc.
Orndoff, Jason Alexander .... '75 '01 C&L.575 B.A., J.D. [Lovekin,Y.&O.]
Owsley, Lisa Suzanne .... '55 '82 C.1365 B.A. L.896 J.D. Dist. J.
Palmer, Stephen L., (BV) .... '70 '97 C.160 B.S. L.1228 J.D. [Sigmon,C.M.H.H.&F.]

Patrick, Harper & Dixon L.L.P., (AV)
Centura Bank Building, 34 Second Street, N.W., P.O. Box 218, 28603
Telephone: 828-322-7741 Fax: 828-322-9340
Members of Firm: Bailey Patrick (1898-1989); James T. Patrick (1936-1990); F. Gwyn Harper, Jr. (1911-1994); Stephen Mason Thomas; Donald R. Fuller, Jr.; Eloise DeLaney Bradshaw; David Wallace Hood; Kimberly H. Whitley; Evans W. Fisher; L. Oliver Noble, Jr. Associates: Ptolemy Taylor Allport; Michael J. Barnett; Michael P. Thomas; Sarah M. White. Of Counsel: Charles D. Dixon (Board Certified Specialist in Estate Planning and Probate Law, North Carolina State Board of Legal Specialization).
General Practice, State and Federal Courts. Insurance, Tax, Probate, Estate Planning and Corporation Law. Real Property and Litigation.
General Counsel for: Century Furniture Co.; Shuford Mills, Inc.; Hickory Springs Manufacturing Co.; Southern Furniture Co. of Conover, Inc.; Hickory Construction Co.
Special Counsel for: Norfolk-Southern Railway Co.
Local Counsel for: Duke Power Co.; Martin Marietta Corp.; The Lane Co.; Nationwide Insurance Co.
See Professional Biographies, HICKORY, NORTH CAROLINA

Paulette, Janet S. .... '47 '77 C.692 B.A. L.421 J.D. 543 7th St. N.W.‡
Pitofsky, Alexander H. .... '63 '89 C.178 B.A. L.276 J.D. 3621 9th Street Dr. N.E.
Pleasant, William R., Jr. '69 '94 C&L.896 B.A., J.D.
Sr. Corp. Atty., CommScope, Inc.
Posey, Donald R., (CV) .... '38 '95 C.398 B.A. L.809 J.D. P.O. Box 9348
Poteet, Matthew S., (CV) .... '62 '95 C.575 B.A. L.861 J.D. 327 3rd Ave. N.W.

Rigsbee, Keith W., PLLC, Law Office of
(See Morganton)

Robbins, D. Steve .... '46 '74 C.232 B.S.B.A. L.575 J.D. 282 1st Ave. S.E.
Rudisill, J. Richardson, Jr. .... '47 '73 C&L.575 B.S., J.D. [J.R.Rudisill,Jr.]
Rudisill, Jesse R., Jr. .... '47 '73 C&L.577 B.S., J.D. [Firm of J.R.Rudisill,Jr.]
Rudisill, J. Richardson, Jr., Law Firm of .... 100 Main Avenue, N.W., 3rd Floor
Rudisill, J. Richardson, Jr., Law Firm of .... P.O. Box 516
Sharpe, Curtis Randolph, Jr., (CV) ..... '60 '85 C.575 B.A. L.896 J.D. 18 Third Ave., N.E.
Shores, Thomas Haynes, Jr. .... '66 '94 C.880 B.S. L.910 J.D. Pres., Classic Leather, Inc.
Sigmon, William R., (AV) .... '35 '63 C.404 B.S. L.896 LL.B. [Sigmon,C.M.H.H.&F.]

Sigmon, Clark, Mackie, Hutton, Hanvey & Ferrell, P.A., (AV)
420 Third Avenue, N.W., P.O. Drawer 1470, 28603
Telephone: 828-328-2596 FAX: 828-328-6876
URL: http://www.sigmonclark.com
William R. Sigmon; Jeffrey T. Mackie; Warren A. Hutton; J. Scott Hanvey; Forrest A. Ferrell; Stephen L. Palmer;—R. Jason White; Nancy L. Huegerich. Of Counsel: Marshall V. Yount.
General Practice. Probate, Corporate, Trials concerning all phases of the law and Real Estate Law.
Representative Clients: Cox Manufacturing Co.; Alba-Waldensian, Inc.; Hancock & Moore, Inc.; Disque Furniture, LLC; Taylor-King Furniture, Inc.; Hickory Board of Education.
Local Counsel for: Erie Insurance Co.
See Professional Biographies, HICKORY, NORTH CAROLINA

Smith, Young M., Jr., (BV) .... '44 '69 C.575 A.B. L.228 J.D. Drawer 1948
Steele, Martin Edward .... '55 '81 C.339 B.A. L.1049 J.D. [M.E.Steele]
Steele, Martin E., PLLC, Law Offices of .... 2050 Catawba Valley Blvd., S.E.

Stott, Hollowell, Palmer & Windham, L.L.P.
(See Gastonia)

Stroupe, John C., Jr. .... '25 '58 C.404 A.B. L.896 LL.B. 1350 10th Street Pl., N. W.‡
Summerlin, Jimmy R., Jr. .... '73 '03 C.576 B.S. L.838 J.D. [Young,M.B.&T.]

Taylor, Jason E., Law Offices of, (BV) '67 '93 C.319 B.A. L.904 J.D.
120 Third Street, NE, 28601 ⊙
Mailing Address: P.O. Box 2688 28603-2688
Telephone: 828-327-9004; Toll Free: 800-351-3008 Fax: 828-327-9008 URL: http://www.jasonetaylor.com
Email: Jason@JasonETaylor.com
Personal Injury, Automobile Accidents, Motorcycle Accidents, Wrongful Death, Slip and Fall, Medical Malpractice, Workers Compensation, Criminal.
Charlotte, North Carolina Office: 200 North McDowell, 28204. Telephone: 704-350-1646. Fax: 704-350-1648. Toll Free: 1-877-350-1646.
See Professional Biographies, HICKORY, NORTH CAROLINA

Taylor, K. McNeill, Jr. '54 '80 C.228 A.B. L.145 J.D.
V.P. & Gen. Coun., Siecor Corporation (Pat.)
Taylor, Terry M., (BV) ....'55 '84 C.927 B.S. L.896 J.D. [Young,M.B.&T.]
Teague, Beverly D., (CV) ....'53 '89 C.404 A.B. L.1228 J.D. [B.D.Teague]
Teague, Beverly D., P.C., (CV) ....7625 No. Hwy. 127
Thomas, Bryce O., Jr., (BV) ....'47 '74 C&L.575 A.B., J.D. 21 1st St. N.W.
Thomas, Laura Johnson ... '— '01 C.160 B.A. L.790 J.D. Corp. Atty., CommScope Inc.
Thomas, Michael P. ....'76 '01 C.674 A.B. L.902 J.D. [A Patrick,H.&D.]
Thomas, Stephen Mason, (AV) ....'45 '70 C&L.575 B.A., J.D. [Patrick,H.&D.]
Thomas, Tara Elizabeth Cannon '— '99 C.482 B.S. L.838 J.D.
1282 12th Street Dr. NW

Trimble, Blake W. '48 '73 C.282 B.A. L.896 J.D.
Gen. Coun., Hickory Springs Manufacturing Co.
Vaught, Curt J., (BV) ....'46 '76 C.576 B.S. L.896 J.D. 112 Fifth St., S.W.
Vujovic, Radoje "Rod" A. ....'66 '96 C.34 B.S. L.209 J.D. [R.A.Vujovic]
Vujovic, Rod A., Attorney at Law, P.A. ....118 Highway 321 SW

Walker, Rufus F., Jr., (BV) '46 '75 C.94 A.B. L.818 J.D.
110 Third Street, North East, 28601
Telephone: 828-328-8101 Fax: 828-328-8103
Email: rfw@charter.net URL: http://www.lawyers.com/rufuswalkerlaw
General Civil Practice. Trials. Real Estate, Corporation, Estate Planning, Probate, Elder Law and Personal Injury.
See Professional Biographies, HICKORY, NORTH CAROLINA

Weathers, Carroll W., Jr. ....'31 '56 C&L.896 A.B., LL.B. 24 2nd Ave., N.E.
White, R. Jason ....'77 '03 C.577 B.A. L.1228 J.D. [A Sigmon,C.M.H.H.&F.]
White, Sarah M. ....'78 '03 C&L.575 B.A., J.D. [A Patrick,H.&D.]
Whitener, Joe P., (BV) ....'25 '49 C.569 E.E. L.228 LL.B. 110 3rd St., N.W.
Whitley, Kimberly H., (BV) ....'67 '93 C&L.575 B.A., J.D. [Patrick,H.&D.]
Williams, M. Elizabeth ....'75 '03 C.576 B.S. L.1228 J.D. [Williams]
Williams, R. Kelsey ....'75 '02 C.404 B.A. L.1228 J.D. [Williams]
Williams Law Firm, The ....415 First Avenue, N.W.
Wyatt, Frank Burkhead, II '62 '88 C.576 B.S.E.E. L.896 J.D.
Sr. V.P., Gen. Coun. & Secy., CommScope, Inc. (Pat.)
Young, Charles R., (AV) ....'42 '68 C.968 B.A. L.896 J.D. [Young,M.B.&T.]
Young, Gary F., (BV) ....'54 '79 C.597 B.A. L.575 J.D. [Lovekin,Y.&O.]

Young, Morphis, Bach and Taylor, L.L.P., (AV) BB
First Lawyers Building, 400 Second Avenue, N.W., P.O. Drawer 2428, 28603
Telephone: 828-322-4663 FAX: 828-322-2023
Email: lawyers@hickorylaw.com URL: http://www.hickorylaw.com
Members of Firm: Charles R. Young; Thomas C. Morphis, Sr.; Wayne M. Bach; Terry M. Taylor (Certified Specialist, Real Property Law, North Carolina State Board of Legal Specialization); T. Dean Amos; Paul E. Culpepper; Kevin C. McIntosh. Associates: Valeree R. Adams; Jimmy R. Summerlin, Jr.; Frank W. Leak.
General, Civil and Criminal Practice. Trials in all State and Federal Courts and the U.S. Supreme Court. Corporations, Taxation, Probate, Trusts, Real Estate, Commercial, Complex Business and Commercial, Municipal, Family Law, Complex Matrimonial Law, Negligence, Products Liability, Personal Injury, Workers Compensation, Insurance Law, Bankruptcy, Patent Law.
Representative Clients: First Citizens Bank & Trust Co.; Shuford Mills, Inc.; United States Hosiery Corp.; Graystone Ophthalmology Associates, P.A.; Living Centers of America, Inc.
Approved Attorneys for: Lawyers Title Insurance Corp.; Chicago Title Insurance Corp.; NationsBank of North Carolina; Branch Banking & Trust Co.; First Union National Bank.
See Professional Biographies, HICKORY, NORTH CAROLINA

Yount, Leslie M., (BV) ....'63 '90 C.575 B.S. L.469 J.D. 248 Ninth Ave. Dr. N.E.
Yount, Marshall V., (AV) ......'17 '40 C&L.575 B.S., LL.B. 110 Third Street, North East
Yount, Ralph D., (BV) ....'52 '77 C&L.575 B.A., J.D. 1930 1st Ave. S.W.

HIGHLANDS, 948, *Macon Co.*

Ashburn, William W., III '47 '74 C.572 B.A. L.469 J.D.
(adm. in GA; not adm. in NC) Coldwell Banker Ashburn Real Estate
Baer, Leonard F., (AVⓉ) ....'— '77 C.354 B.S. L.669 J.D. [L.F.Baer]

Baer, Leonard F., PLLC, Law Offices of, (AVⓉ) BB
511 Smallwood Avenue, P.O. Box 2619, 28741
Telephone: 828-526-8411 Fax: 826-526-9834
Email: LegalBaer@aol.com URL: http://www.LegalBaer.com
Leonard F. Baer.
Construction Law, Employment Law, Elder Law, Immigration Law.
See Professional Biographies, HIGHLANDS, NORTH CAROLINA

Berkens, Michael H. ....'58 '83 C.102 B.A. L.362 J.D. P.O. Box 129‡
Bowen, Louis R., Jr., (BVⓉ) ....'37 '66 C.1365 L.902 LL.B. 494 N. Cobb Rd.
Burns, Douglas J. '56 '84 C.259 B.S. L.192 J.D.
(adm. in FL; not adm. in NC) R.R. 1, Box 350‡
Cabler, James A., Jr ....'33 '59 C.695 B.A. L.893 LL.B. 125 Pine St.
Dunwody, W. E., III, (AVⓉ) '43 '70 C.362 B.S. L.260 J.D.
(adm. in FL; not adm. in NC) [W.E.Dunwody,III]
Dunwody, W. E., III, P.A., (AVⓉ) ....129 Cullasaja Club Dr.

Jones, Key, Melvin & Patton, P.A., (AV)
Professional Building, Suite 3, South Street, 28741 ⊙
Telephone: 828-526-3762
Richard F. Melvin (Resident Partner).
Civil and Criminal Trial Practice in all Courts. Real Estate, Insurance, Taxation, Probate Law, Domestic Relations, Personal Injury, Social Security Disability Law and Local Government Law, Mediation.
Representative Clients: Macon Savings Bank; Wildcat Cliffs Country Club; County of Graham; County of Macon; First Union National Bank; Town of Franklin.
Approved Attorneys for: Fidelity National Title Insurance Co.; Lawyers Title Insurance Corp.; Investors Title Insurance Company.
Franklin, North Carolina Office: 61 East Main Street, 28734. Telephone: 828-524-4444. Fax: 828-369-7343.
See Professional Biographies, FRANKLIN, NORTH CAROLINA

Mariani, George E. '25 '50 C.473 B.S. L.150 LL.B.
(adm. in OH; not adm. in NC) 120 Brushy Face Rd. N.‡
Mavar, Gerald M. '46 '72 C&L.500 B.A., J.D.
(adm. in MS; not adm. in NC) R.R. 2, Box 472‡
Mavar, Nick A., Jr. '41 '66 C&L.500 B.B.A., J.D.
(adm. in MS; not adm. in NC) R.R. 2, Box 472‡
Mayer, John R., (AV) ....'39 '70 C&L.421 B.A., J.D. [J.R.Mayer]

Mayer, John R., Attorney At Law, PLLC, (AV) BB
511 Smallwood Avenue, P.O. Box 750, 28741
Telephone: 828-526-3731 Fax: 828-526-3734
Email: jack@jackmayerlaw.com
John R. Mayer.
General Practice including Civil Rights, Class Actions, Employment Law, Personal Injury, Products Liability, Professional Liability, Toxic Torts, Wrongful Death.
See Professional Biographies, HIGHLANDS, NORTH CAROLINA

Melvin, Richard F., (BV) ....'41 '66 C.228 A.B. L.260 J.D. [Jones,K.M.&P.]
Oxford, Charles Oliver, (AVⓉ) ....'41 '65 C&L.280 B.B.A., LL.B. P.O. Box 1204‡
Patten, Woolvin, (AVⓉ) '14 '36 C&L.469 A.B., LL.B.
(adm. in GA; not adm. in NC) 84 Clubhouse TR#104‡
Riser, Christopher M. ....'66 '97 C&L.575 B.A., J.D. [Riser,P.]
Riser, Elizabeth Mayer ....'73 '97 C.296 B.S. L.575 J.D. [Riser,P.]
Riser Law Firm, The, PLLC ....3356 Clear Creek Road
Rodenbough, Leigh, (AV) ....'24 '50 C&L.575 A.B., LL.B. P.O. Box 2744
Schaub, Frank '21 '49 C.336 B.A. L.362 LL.B.
(adm. in FL; not adm. in NC) RR 2 Box 4C‡

Sossomon, Creighton W., (BV) '44 '69 C&L.575 A.B., J.D.
125 Pine Street, P.O. Box 9, 28741
Telephone: 828-526-2101 Fax: 828-526-3654
General Civil Trial Practice. Civil Litigation, Real Estate, Estate Planning and Probate Law.
A List of Representative Clients will be furnished upon request.
See Professional Biographies, HIGHLANDS, NORTH CAROLINA

Thompson, Lawrence E., II '15 '41 C.250 A.B. L.923 J.D.
(adm. in WV; not adm. in NC) Rte. 1, Box 360‡
Whittle, Chester E. '16 '41 C&L.260 B.S., J.D.
(adm. in FL; not adm. in NC) P.O. Box 1222

HIGH POINT, 85,839, *Davidson, Forsyth, Guilford & Randolph Cos.*

Aldridge, Bryant T., Jr., (BV) ....'57 '83 C.228 A.B. L.896 J.D. [Bretzmann&A.]
Almond, Grant W. ....'76 '00 C.575 B.A. L.1228 J.D. [A Keziah,G.&S.]
Alt, Charles A., (AV) ....'55 '80 C.902 B.S. L.945 J.D. [Wyatt E.H.W.]
Ashcraft, David B., (BV) ....'47 '74 C&L.896 B.S., J.D. [Wyatt E.H.W.]
Baggett, Fred P., (BV) ....'47 '71 C&L.575 B.A.B.L., J.D. City Atty.
Baker, Walter W., Jr., (AV) ....'42 '66 C&L.575 A.B., J.D. [Baker]
Baker, Walter W. (Trip), III ....'77 '04 C.577 B.A. L.896 J.D. [A Baker]

Baker Law Offices, PLLC, (AV)
820 North Elm Street, 27262
Telephone: 336-885-0111 Fax: 336-885-1460 URL: http://www.baker-lawoffices.com
URL: http://www.lawyers.com/bakerlawofficepllc
Walter W. Baker, Jr.; Jeffrey L. Mabe. Associate: Walter W. (Trip) Baker III.
General Civil and Criminal Trial Practice. Personal Injury, Criminal, Traffic, Worker's Compensation, Social Security, Estate and Probate.
See Professional Biographies, HIGH POINT, NORTH CAROLINA

Barron & Berry, L.L.P.
(See Greensboro)

Bauman, Kim R., (AV) ....'55 '80 C.228 B.A. L.896 J.D. [Wyatt E.H.W.]
Bennett, Hugh C., Jr., (BV) ....'37 '69 C.576 B.S. L.575 J.D. 1506 Johnson St.
Berger, Lori Watson, (BV) ....'66 '93 C.471 B.S. L.896 J.D. 1422 S. Main St.

Berman, Jeffrey S.
(See Greensboro)

Bernadett Clark, Leah-Flora ....'63 '94 C.846 B.A. L.326 J.D. 1009 Leonard Ave.
Blocker, Adrienne S. ....'63 '98 C.584 B.A. L.1345 J.D. 1810 Westchester Dr.
Boone, Donald L. ....'34 '61 C&L.575 A.B., LL.B. Dist. J.

Booth Harrington & Johns, LLP
(See Greensboro)

Bouldin, Steven H., (BV) ....'62 '88 C.228 A.B. L.896 J.D. [Keziah,G.&S.]
Boyan, Robert S., (BV) ....'54 '81 C.575 B.A. L.896 J.D. P.O. Box 909
Bradley, William Ray "Pete", (BV) ....'57 '89 C.575 B.A. L.1228 J.D. [Bradley&S.]
Bradley & Smothers, P.L.L.C., (BV) ....210 East Lexington
Bretzmann, Raymond A., (BV) ....'49 '74 C&L.896 B.A., J.D. [Bretzmann&A.]
Bretzmann & Aldridge, L.L.P., (BV) ....500 East Green Drive, Suite 201
Brinson, Robert A., (AV) ....'50 '76 C.968 A.B. L.896 J.D. [Roberson,H.&R.]

Bruner, Joseph E., Law Offices of, (BV) '48 '74 C.280 B.B.A. L.575 J.D.
510 Ferndale Boulevard, Suite 101, 27262
Telephone: 336-889-7277 Fax: 336-889-5155 URL: http://wwwbrunerlawfirm.com
Email: joebruner@brunerlaw.com URL: http://www.brunerlaw.com
Associate: Juan F. Zuluaga.
Languages: Spanish.
Criminal Defense, Felonies, Drug Crimes, White Collar Crimes, Driving While Impaired, Traffic Violations, Automobile Accidents, Personal Injury, Medical Malpractice, Workers Compensation, Business Law, Tax Law.
See Professional Biographies, HIGH POINT, NORTH CAROLINA

Bryant, Calvin B., (BV) ....'28 '55 C&L.575 A.B., J.D. [C Wyatt E.H.W.]
Bryson, John D., (AV) ....'58 '85 C&L.896 B.A., J.D. [Wyatt E.H.W.]
Burch, Susan R. ....'67 '95 C&L.896 B.A., J.D. Dist. Ct. Judge
Butler, Ronald P., (BV) ....'52 '82 C.240 B.A. L.574 J.D. [R.Butler]

Butler, Ron, (BV)
322 South Wrenn Street, P.O. Box 2594, 27261
Telephone: 336-841-7915 Fax: 336-885-5152
Email: hplaw@prodigy.net URL: http://www.ronbutlerlawfirm.com
Ronald P. Butler.
Traffic Violations, Criminal Law, Driving While Intoxicated, Family Law, Divorce and Juvenile Law. Wills.
See Professional Biographies, HIGH POINT, NORTH CAROLINA

Byerly, Steven E., (BV) ....'48 '73 C&L.896 B.A., J.D. [Byerly]
Byerly, W. B. Jack, Jr., (AV) ....'27 '50 C.316 L.896 LL.B. [Byerly]
Byerly Law Offices, (AV) ....505 E. Commerce Ave.
Cain, Charles L. '55 '81 C.896 B.A. L.575 J.D.
Sr. Vice Pres., Legal Affair, Banner Pharmacaps Inc.
Carpenter, Harvey A., IV ....'69 '96 C.575 B.A. L.285 J.D. 1422 S. Main St.
Carroll, E. Randolph, (AV) ....'52 '78 C.575 A.B. L.896 J.D. P.O. Box 2434

Carruthers & Roth, P.A.
(See Greensboro)

Carter, Ewing, III ....'59 '91 C.952 B.A. L.150 J.D. [E.Carter,III]

Carter, Ewing, III, P.A.
1004 N. Main Street, Suite 102, 27262
Telephone: 336-883-2247 Fax: 336-883-2696
Email: lawoffice@ecarterlaw.com
Ewing Carter III.
Personal Injury, Workers Compensation, Driving While Intoxicated, Driving While License Revoked, Speeding Tickets, Auto Accidents, Wrongful Death, Traffic Violations, Slip and Fall.
See Professional Biographies, HIGH POINT, NORTH CAROLINA

Cecil, David Lohr, (BV) ....'65 '92 C.896 B.S. L.1228 J.D. [Cecil&C.]
Cecil, Lee M., (BV) ....'62 '87 C.576 B.A. L.896 J.D. P.O. Box 2632
Cecil, Robert L. ....'36 '62 C&L.896 B.A., LL.B. [Cecil&C.]
Cecil & Cecil, P.A., (BV) ....P.O. Box 5666

Chamberlin, Ames C.
(See Greensboro)

Chess, Sammie, Jr., (BV) '34 '58 C&L.574 A.B., LL.B. Admin. Law J., State Off. of Admin. Hearings

Chut, Mercedes Oglukian
(See Greensboro)

Clifford Clendenin O'Hale & Jones, LLP
(See Greensboro)

Clinard, Aaron Neal, (AV) ... '47 '77 C.575 A.B. L.896 J.D. [Fisher,C.&C.]
Clontz, J. W., (AV) ... '18 '46 C&L.896 A.B., LL.B. 164 S. Main St.‡
Coalter, John S. ... '65 '96 C.846 B.A. L.1228 J.D. [[A] Morgan,H.M.G.R.&G.]
Combs, Todd J. ... '68 '96 C.140 B.S. L.615 J.D. [[A] Morgan,H.M.G.R.&G.]
Cornwell, Rick, (BV) ... '49 '74 C.612 B.A. L.623 J.D. [Fisher,C.&C.]
Coughlin, Barbara B. ... '52 '78 C&L.575 A.B., J.D. 908 Forest Hill Dr.‡
Craig, John O., III ... '55 '82 C.198 A.B. L.575 J.D. Supr. Ct. Judge
Crawford, Bonnie Brade, (BV) ... '52 '89 C.1378 B.S. L.575 J.D. 1109 W. Green Dr.
Dail, Richard T., (BV) ... '63 '98 C.1333 B.S. L.1228 J.D. [Dail&L.]

Dail & Linton, (BV)
407 Ferndale Boulevard, 27262
Telephone: 336-889-0138 Fax: 336-889-0341
Email: dail-linton@northstate.net URL: http://www.dailandlinton.com
Members of Firm: Richard T. Dail; Wilbur L. Linton, Jr.
Personal Injury, Automobile Accidents, Slip and Fall, Wrongful Death, Family Law, Adoption Law, Child Custody, Child Support, Divorce, Domestic Violence, Criminal Law, Driving While Intoxicated, Drug Crimes, Traffic Violations, Business Litigation, Trial Practice, General Practice, Workers Compensation.
See Professional Biographies, HIGH POINT, NORTH CAROLINA

Daniel, Judy J. ... '54 '92 C.215 B.B.A. L.36 J.D. 2506 Westchester Dr.

David, Cheryl K.
(See Greensboro)

Davidson, Bob, Jr. ... '— '85 C.577 B.S. L.192 J.D. [B.Davidson,Jr.]
Davidson, Bob, Jr. ... 804 North Hamilton Street

Deuterman Law Group, The, P.A.
(See Greensboro)

Douglas, Ravenel, Hardy, Crihfield & Hoyle, L.L.P.
(See Greensboro)

Dula, Arnita Maria ... '62 '01 C.577 B.A. L.575 J.D. Guilford Co. Schools
Early, A. Doyle, Jr., (AV) ... '43 '67 C&L.896 B.A., J.D. [Wyatt E.H.W.]

Ernest, Jodi A., Law Office of
(See Greensboro)

Finan, Christopher C. ... '75 '01 C.645 B.S. L.896 J.D. [Roberson,H.&R.]

Fisher, Clinard & Cornwell, PLLC, (AV) [BB]
Suite 800 GE Capital Building, 101 S. Main Street, P.O. Box 1150, 27261
Telephone: 336-883-9156 Fax: 336-886-8593
URL: http://www.highpointlaw.com
Louis J. Fisher, Sr. (1901-1981); Louis J. Fisher, Jr. (1935-2004); Aaron Neal Clinard; Rick Cornwell; Shane T. Stutts;—Robert A. Lefkowitz; Jay W. Wagner.
Corporation and Business, General Trial and Appellate Practice, Estate Planning and Administration, Taxation, Bankruptcy, Inter-creditor workouts, Commercial Real Estate, Banking, Commercial and Construction Litigation, Municipal Law, Zoning, Mediation and Dispute Resolution, Criminal, Traffic, Personal Injury and Wrongful Death.
See Professional Biographies, HIGH POINT, NORTH CAROLINA

Floyd, Joe D., (AV) ... '30 '65 C.296 B.A. L.896 J.D. [J.D.Floyd]
Floyd, Joseph Donald, II, (BV) ... '67 '94 C.896 B.A. L.1228 J.D. [J.D.Floyd]
Floyd, Kimberly Hayes, (BV) ... '58 '85 C&L.1228 B.S., J.D. [J.D.Floyd]
Floyd, Joe D., P.A., Law Firm, (AV) ... 401 South Main Street
Forrester, Richard W., (BV) ... '48 '77 C.577 B.A. L.896 J.D. 3609 Blairwood St.
Foster, Thomas F. ... '48 '77 C&L.575 B.A., J.D. [[A] Roberson,H.&R.]

Frazier & Frazier, LLP
(See Greensboro)

Gabell, Margaret M., (BV) ... '68 '97 C.223 B.S. L.1338 J.D. 1810 Westchester Dr.

Gabriel Berry & Weston, L.L.P.
(See Greensboro)

Gallimore, Kim W., (AV) ... '55 '80 C.228 A.B. L.896 J.D. [Wyatt E.H.W.]
Gardner, Rossie G., (BV) ... '31 '59 C.316 L.896 LL.B. 518 N. Hamilton St., Suite 202
Gates, Gilbert L., (AV) ... '42 '68 C&L.228 A.B., J.D. [Keziah,G.&S.]
Gerber, Ellen W., (BV) '36 '77 C.94 B.S. L.575 J.D. Legal Aid Soc. of Northwest N.C., Inc.
Gill, James E., Jr., (BV) ... '44 '71 C.296 B.A. L.192 J.D. [Morgan,H.M.G.R.&G.]

Goulder Immigration Law Firm
(See Greensboro)

Green, James M., Jr., (BV) ... '46 '72 C.296 B.A. L.192 J.D. [Morgan,H.M.G.R.&G.]
Greeson, Howard R., Jr. ... '43 '71 C.575 A.B. L.896 J.D. Supr. Ct. J.
Hammer, Stanley F., (AV) ... '53 '84 C.790 B.A. L.1228 J.D. [Wyatt E.H.W.]
Hamrick, Diane Q., (BV) ... '45 '81 C.1377 B.A. L.245 J.D. [Hamrick&Assoc.]
Hamrick & Associates, (BV) ... 510 Ferndale Boulevard, Suite 101

Handler & Brown, P.L.L.C.
(See Winston-Salem)

Hanks, Ann E., (AV) '54 '79 C&L.575 A.B., J.D.
202 W. Lexington Avenue, 27262
Mailing Address: P.O. Box 5064, High Point, NC 27262
Telephone: 336-812-3073 Fax: 1-866-521-5296
Email: ahanks@triad.rr.com URL: http://www.annhankslaw.com
(Board Certified Specialist in Estate Planning and Probate Law, North Carolina State Board of Legal Specialization).
Trusts and Estates, Asset Protection, Estate Planning, Guardianship, Wills and Probate, Tax Planning, Elder Law.
See Professional Biographies, HIGH POINT, NORTH CAROLINA

Harris, William P., (AV) ... '42 '68 C.316 A.B. L.896 J.D. [Wyatt E.H.W.]
Hauser, Robert E., (AV) ... '28 '77 C.228 B.A. L.896 J.D. 1111 Gatehouse Rd.‡
Haworth, John, (AV) ... '27 '50 C.296 A.B. L.575 LL.B. [[C] Morgan,H.M.G.R.&G.]
Hayes, Marcus Edward, Sr. ... '61 '88 C.575 B.A. L.1228 J.D. 1810 Westchester Drive
Haynes, Christie D. ... '— '04 C.296 B.S. L.896 J.D. [[A] Cecil&C.]
Hayworth, Joseph A., Jr., (CV) ... '53 '89 C.296 B.S. L.896 J.D. 1231 Wales Court

Henson & Henson, L.L.P.
(See Greensboro)

Herring, W. Dan, (BV) ... '33 '63 C&L.896 B.S., J.D. [Morgan,H.M.G.R.&G.]
Hill, Raymond T. ... '48 '74 C.290 A.B. L.790 J.D. 500 E. Green Dr.

Hill, Evans, Duncan, Jordan & Beatty
(See Greensboro)

Horner, Shaida Jarrahi ... '71 '99 C.575 B.A. L.896 J.D. V.P., Wachovia Bank, N.A.
Howard, D. Darren ... '68 '97 C.228 B.A. L.896 J.D. [Howard]
Howard, Molly Nall, (BV) ... '69 '94 C.228 B.A. L.896 J.D. [Howard]

Howard Law Firm, The, P.C., (BV)
Spring Tree Office Park, 2115 Eastchester Drive, 27265
Telephone: 336-885-3124 Fax: 336-889-3116
Molly Nall Howard; D. Darren Howard.
Family Law, Adoptions, Child Custody, Divorce, Child Support, Domestic Violence, Alimony, Contempt, Interstate Child Custody Matters, Termination of Parental Rights.
See Professional Biographies, HIGH POINT, NORTH CAROLINA

Hull, Maurice S. S., (AV) ... '53 '79 C.968 B.A. L.896 J.D. [[C] Keziah,G.&S.]
Hundley, James R., (AV) ... '56 '85 C.577 B.A. L.896 J.D. [Wyatt E.H.W.]

Idol, David H., (BV) '46 '73 C&L.575 A.B., J.D.
704 North Main Street, P.O. Box 1776, 27261-1776
Telephone: 336-889-8111 Fax: 336-889-7764
Personal Injury, General Civil and Criminal Practice, Bankruptcy, Real Estate, Commercial, Wills and Estates, Corporations and Partnerships, Traffic Violations, Driving While Intoxicated, Social Security Disability.
See Professional Biographies, HIGH POINT, NORTH CAROLINA

Jarrell, Chas. R., (CV) ... '18 '42 C.316 A.B. L.896 LL.B. 401 Park St.
Jarrell, Cynthia Roberson, (BV) ... '62 '88 C.575 B.S. L.1228 J.D. 217 Edgedale Drive‡
Jarrell, Elsie, (CV) ... '42 '93 C.296 B.A. L.574 J.D. 802 Miriam Ave.
Jobe, Matthew C. ... '71 '01 C.575 B.S.B.A. L.896 J.D. [[A] Wyatt E.H.W.]
Keziah, S. Perry, (AV) ... '30 '54 C&L.228 A.B., J.D. [Keziah,G.&S.]

Keziah, Gates & Samet, L.L.P., (AV) [BB]
Suite 400 High Point Bank & Trust Building, 300 North Main Street, P.O. Box 2608, 27261-2608
Telephone: 336-889-6900 336-889-7055
Email: info@keziahgates.com URL: http://www.keziahgates.com
Partners: S. Perry Keziah; Gilbert L. Gates; Jan H. Samet; Charles E. Lynch, Jr.; Andrew S. Lasine; Steven H. Bouldin; Alan N. Post. Of Counsel: Maurice S. S. Hull. Associate: Grant W. Almond.
General Civil Practice in State and Federal Courts. Trials and Appeals, Real Estate, Banking, Corporate Law, Estate Planning and Probate, Construction Law, Taxation, Commercial Law and Collections.
Counsel for: Bank of America, N.A.; Furniture Manufacturers Credit Assn., Inc.; High Point Bank & Trust Co.; IHFC, Properties, LLC; Harris Teeter, Inc.; Mickey Truck Bodies, Inc.; North Pointe Partners, LLC.
See Professional Biographies, HIGH POINT, NORTH CAROLINA

Kimel, Horace M., Jr.
(See Greensboro)

Kiser, Aleta B. '61 '95 C.886 B.A. L.896 J.D.
2201 Eastchester Drive, Suite 105, 27265
Telephone: 336-885-5580 Fax: 336-885-8592
Email: aletakiser@northstate.net
Bankruptcy, Traffic Violations, Criminal, Real Estate, Buying or Selling a Home, Personal Injury, Estate Planning, Social Security, Wills and Probate, Trusts and Estates, Probate, Estate Planning and General Practice.
See Professional Biographies, HIGH POINT, NORTH CAROLINA

Koonce, Elizabeth MacLean, (AV) ... '54 '80 C&L.575 B.A., J.D. [Roberson,H.&R.]
Kreager, Alex C., Law Offices of, (BV) '66 '95 C.968 B.A. L.192 J.D. 1207 Brentwood St.
Kroger, Christopher M., (BV) ... '63 '94 C.437 B.B.A. L.923 J.D. [[A] Wyatt E.H.W.]

Krohn, Clayton B.
(See Greensboro)

Laney, R. Bruce, (BV) ... '49 '73 C&L.575 A.B., J.D. [Wyatt E.H.W.]
Langford, John W., (CV) ... '14 '47 C.155 A.B. L.574 LL.B. 414 Cedar St.
Lanik, James C., (BV) ... '69 '95 C.399 B.A. L.208 J.D. [[A] Roberson,H.&R.]
Lansberg Sams, Melissa E. ... '75 '01 C.316 B.A. L.1228 J.D. 210 E. Lexington Ave.
Lasine, Andrew S., (AV) ... '57 '83 C.228 A.B. L.902 J.D. [Keziah,G.&S.]
Lawing, Stephen E., (AV) '41 '66 C&L.896 B.A., J.D. 101 South Main Street, Suite 416
Lefkowitz, Robert A., (BV) ... '58 '84 C.692 B.A. L.945 J.D. [[A] Fisher,C.&C.]
Levy, Edgar S., III ... '55 '80 C.893 B.S. L.945 J.D. [Wyatt E.H.W.]
Linton, Wilbur L., Jr., (BV) ... '67 '98 C.290 B.A. L.1228 J.D. [Dail&L.]

Lloyd, Charles A.
(See Greensboro)

Lyle, Richard R., (BV) ... '46 '70 C&L.896 B.A., J.D. Asst. Dist. Atty.
Lynch, Charles E., Jr., (AV) ... '47 '71 C.575 A.B. L.790 J.D. [Keziah,G.&S.]
Maas, David E. '14 '40 C.451 L.1340 LL.B. (adm. in OH; not adm. in NC) 800 W. Parkway Ave.
Mabe, Jeffrey L., (BV) ... '56 '82 C.577 B.A. L.896 J.D. [Baker]
Manger, Richard A., (AV) ... '52 '77 C&L.896 B.A., J.D. [Manger]

Manger Law Firm, (AV)
The Arboretum, Suite 230, 1208 Eastchester Drive, 27265
Telephone: 336-889-4334 Fax: 336-889-3977
Email: ram@mangerlaw.com URL: http://www.mangerlawfirm.com
Richard A. Manger.
Personal Injury, Workers Compensation, Wrongful Death, Automobile Accidents, Trucking Accidents.
See Professional Biographies, HIGH POINT, NORTH CAROLINA

Massie, Martha C. ... '60 '03 C.296 B.S. L.575 J.D. [[A] Wyatt E.H.W.]
Mattocks, Clarence V., (BV) ... '47 '74 C.296 B.A. L.575 J.D. [Mattocks&M.]
Mattocks, James, (AV) ... '19 '41 C.316 B.A. L.228 J.D. [Mattocks&M.] ‡
Mattocks & Mattocks, (BV) ... 1638 Westchester Drive, Suite 101
May, J. Randall, (BV) ... '46 '74 C.925 B.A. L.192 J.D. Asst. Pub. Def.
Mayberry, Bryce B., Law Office of, (BV) '64 '94 C.502 B.S. L.1439 J.D. 1403 Eastchester Dr.
Maynard, David L., (AV) ... '37 '63 C&L.228 A.B., LL.B. [Roberson,H.&R.]
McAllister, Kenneth W., (AV) ... '49 '74 C.575 A.B. L.228 J.D. [McAllister,P.]

McAllister Firm, The, PLLC, (AV) [BB]
201 Neal Place, P.O. Box 5006, 27262
Telephone: 336-882-4300 Fax: 336-882-4306
Email: kmcallister@mcallisterlawfirm.com URL: http://www.mcallisterlawfirm.com
Kenneth W. McAllister. Attorney: Marc R. Tyrey.
General Civil and Criminal Trial Practice in State and Federal Court. Traffic Violations, White Collar Crime, Corporation and Business, Trusts and Estates, Wills and Probate, Estate Planning and Administration, Banking, Family Law, Personal Injury.
See Professional Biographies, HIGH POINT, NORTH CAROLINA

Merritt, Colin D., (BV) ... '72 '98 C&L.896 B.S., J.D. [Roberson,H.&R.]
Miller, William P., (AV) ... '55 '80 C.228 A.B. L.575 J.D. [Roberson,H.&R.]

Moreno, Barbara Kumm .... '56 '85 C.529 B.S. L.724 J.D. 304 Lindsay St
Morgan, James F., (BV) .... '43 '69 C.296 B.A. L.192 J.D. [Morgan,H.M.G.R.&G.]

Morgan, Herring, Morgan, Green, Rosenblutt & Gill, LLP, (BV)
1801 Westchester Drive, Suite 200, P.O. Box 2756, 27262
Telephone: 336-883-6177 FAX: 336-883-6647
Members of Firm: J.V. Morgan (1918-1982); W. Dan Herring; James F. Morgan; James M. Green, Jr.; David K. Rosenblutt; James E. Gill, Jr. Associates: Todd J. Combs; John S. Coalter. Of Counsel: John Haworth; John C. Riggs.
General Civil and Criminal Trial Practice in all State and Federal Courts. Interstate Commerce, Probate, Real Estate, Corporation and Tax Law. Torts. Traffic Violations and Driving Under the Influence, Personal Injury, Auto Accidents, Wills and Estates, Family Law, Divorce, Custody, Support, Adoption, Workers Compensation, Bankruptcy, Social Security, Employment Discrimination.
Representative Clients: High Point Merchants Assn.; North State Telephone Co.; NCNB National Bank of North Carolina; Arthur A. Oliver & Son, Inc.; Royals, Inc.
See Professional Biographies, HIGH POINT, NORTH CAROLINA

Moss, Jason E., (BV) .... '74 '99 C&L.896 B.A., J.D. [Wyatt E.H.W.]
Nix, Kathleen E., (AV) .... '51 '78 C.790 B.A. L.896 J.D. 601-B Eastchester Dr.
Nixon, Georgia S., (BV) '65 '91 C.576 B.A. L.1345 J.D.
[Nixon&Assoc.] (Lexington)

Nixon & Associates, (BV)
210 East Lexington Avenue, 27262
Telephone: 336-885-5959 Fax: 336-885-7400
Email: gnixon@northstate.net URL: http://www.nixonlawoffices.com
Georgia S. Nixon (Board Certified Specialist in Criminal Law, North Carolina State Board of Legal Specialization).
Traffic Violations, Criminal Defense, DWI, Drug Charges, License Restoration, Personal Injury, Auto Accidents, Domestic Law.
See Professional Biographies, HIGH POINT, NORTH CAROLINA

Peraldo, Jeffrey K., P.A., The Law Offices of
(See Greensboro)

Peterson, Michael J., (CV) .... '52 '78 C&L.420 B.S., J.D. 210 E. Lexington Ave.

Poortvliet, Kenneth L.
(See Greensboro)

Post, Alan N., (BV) .... '58 '86 C.103 A.B. L.192 J.D. [Keziah,G.&S.]
Powell, Alan B., (BV) .... '65 '90 C.880 B.A. L.896 J.D. [Roberson,H.&R.]
Powell, Lisa W. .... '65 '91 C.174 B.A. L.896 J.D. [Roberson,H.&R.]

Puryear and Lingle, P.L.L.C.
(See Greensboro)

Quick, Valerie G., (BV) .... '56 '91 C.575 B.A. L.896 J.D. 2506 Westchester Dr.
Rayborn, Cory A. .... '75 '03 C.228 B.S. L.575 J.D. [Wyatt E.H.W.]
Reardon, Arlene W. .... '75 '01 C.415 B.A.M.A. L.896 J.D. [Wyatt E.H.W.]

Reitzel, J. Brooks, Jr. '45 '71 C&L.575 B.A., J.D.
SunTrust Bank Building, 1301 Eastchester Drive, Suite 201, P.O. Box 5544, 27265
Telephone: 336-885-7900 Fax: 336-885-7925
URL: http://www.reitzellaw.com
Bankruptcy, Debtor/Creditor Relations, Banking Law, Commercial Law, Corporate Law, Wills, Probate, Trust and Estate, Estate Planning, Real Estate, Trial Practice in State and Federal Courts. Representing Furniture Designers, Importers, Manufacturers, Retailers throughout the United States.
See Professional Biographies, HIGH POINT, NORTH CAROLINA

Riedlinger, Cheryl S., Law Offices of, (BV) '60 '85
C.033 B.A. L.896 J.D. 107 W. Lexington Ave.
Riggs, John C., (AV) .... '27 '56 C&L.896 B.S., LL.B. [Morgan,H.M.G.R.&G.]

Roberson, Haworth & Reese, P.L.L.C., (AV)
High Point Bank & Trust Company Building, Suite 300, 300 North Main Street, P.O. Box 1550, 27261
Telephone: 336-889-8733 FAX: 336-885-1280
Email: mail@rhrlaw.com URL: http://www.rhrlaw.com
Members of Firm: Wescott Roberson (1875-1938); Horace S. Haworth (1892-1978); Owen Reese (1896-1970); Arthur M. Utley, Jr. (1923-1987); Robert A. Brinson; Elizabeth MacLean Koonce; David L. Maynard; William P. Miller; Alan B. Powell; Colin D. Merritt; Christopher C. Finan. Associates: Lisa W. Powell; Thomas F. Foster; James C. Lanik.
General and Trial Practice in State and Federal Courts. Banking, Corporation, Probate, Real Estate, Bankruptcy, Commercial, Municipal Corporations, Personal Injury, Products Liability, Zoning and Land Use, Condemnation.
See Professional Biographies, HIGH POINT, NORTH CAROLINA

Robinson & Lawing, L.L.P.
(See Winston-Salem)

Rosenblutt, David K., (BV) .... '52 '77 C.951 B.A. L.94 J.D. [Morgan,H.M.G.R.&G.]
Samet, Jan H., (AV) .... '45 '73 C.577 B.A. L.575 J.D. [Keziah,G.&S.]
Sawyer, Frederick G., (BV) .... '59 '84 C&L.575 B.S., J.D. [Wyatt E.H.W.]

Schell Bray Aycock Abel & Livingston P.L.L.C.
(See Greensboro)

Schlosser & Pritchett
(See Greensboro)

Schoch, Arch K., IV, (AV) .... '40 '64 C&L.575 B.A., LL.B. [Schoch&S.]
Schoch, Arch K., V, (AV) .... '67 '97 C.893 B.A. L.192 J.D. [Schoch&S.]

Schoch & Schoch, (AV)
500 East Green Drive, P.O. Box 1893, 27261
Telephone: 336-884-4151 Telecopier: 336-883-7151
Members of Firm: Arch K. Schoch (1909-1980); Louise Rodes Schoch (1909-1995).
Arch K. Schoch IV; Arch K. Schoch V.
General Civil Trial Practice. Personal Injury, Automobile Accidents, Wrongful Death, Civil Litigation, Criminal Defense, Traffic Violations, Condemnation.
Representative Clients: Archdale Oil Co.; Classic Gallery, Inc.; Cramer Wood Products, Inc.; Jones & Peacock Insurance, Inc.; Phillips Industries, Inc.; Piedmont Chemical Industries, Inc.
See Professional Biographies, HIGH POINT, NORTH CAROLINA

Scott, Robert J., (BV) ...... '42 '69 C.397 B.S. L.896 J.D. 132 Church St. (Kernersville)
Sheahan, Robert E., & Associates, (AV) '42 '67
C.340 B.A. L.228 LL.B. 603-B Eastchester Drive
Skager, Philip R. .... '49 '74 C.347 A.B. L.1119 J.D. [P.Skager]
Skager, Philip .... 206 Church Ave.
Smothers, Thomas W., (BV) .... '66 '94 C.575 B.S.B.A. L.1228 J.D. [Bradley&S.]
Snow, James M., (BV) .... '51 '76 C&L.575 A.B., J.D. 150 Church Ave.
Snow, Richard A., (AV) '54 '90 C&L.880 B.A., J.D.
(adm. in GA; not adm. in NC) P.O. Box 6633

Stegall, Laurie R., P.A., Law Office of
(See Greensboro)

Stockdale, Matt A., PLLC, Law Office of
(See Greensboro)

Stutts, Shane T., (BV) .... '72 '97 C.575 B.A. L.692 J.D. [Fisher,C.&C.]

Sullivan, Jack D. '20 '56 C.846 B.B.A. L.796 LL.B.
(adm. in TX; not adm. in NC) 304 E. Springfield Rd.‡
Tate, C. Richard, Jr., (BV) .... '34 '63 C&L.896 B.A., LL.B. 115 W. High Ave.
Terres, Joyce L., Attorney at Law, (BV) '56 '91
C.999 B.S. L.896 J.D. 202 W. Lexington Ave.
Tobin, Victoria H., (AV) '46 '81 C.437 B.A. L.575 J.D.
V.P. & Gen. Coun., Wellington Hall Designs, LLC
Towers, Richard S., (BV) .... '43 '68 C.1108 B.A. L.896 J.D. 322 S. Wrenn St.

Tuggle Duggins & Meschan, P.A.
(See Greensboro)

Tyrey, Marc R., (BV) .... '71 '97 C.296 B.A. L.1228 J.D. [McAllister,P.]
Valitutto, Richard E.F. '59 '84 C.575 B.A. L.201 J.D.
Gen. Coun. & Sec., New Breed Transfer Corp.
Wagner, Jay W. .... '68 '98 C.575 B.A. L.574 J.D. [Fisher,C.&C.]
Wallace, Stephen F. .... '69 '03 C.576 B.A. L.1339 J.D. [Wallace]

Wallace Law Firm, The
300 N. Lindsay Street, Suite 101, 27262
Telephone: 336-882-4940 Fax: 336-882-4945
Email: Mercy@wlfnc.com URL: http://www.WLFCarolinas.com
Stephen F. Wallace.
Languages: English and Spanish.
Real Property, Business Law, Corporate Law, Intellectual Property, Traffic.
See Professional Biographies, HIGH POINT, NORTH CAROLINA

Wheeler, William E., (AV) .... '45 '75 C.575 A.B. L.896 J.D. [Wyatt E.H.W.]

White, Charles L., II
(See Greensboro)

Whitley, D. P., Jr., (AV) .... '18 '41 C&L.575 A.B., J.D. 164 S. Main St.

Winfree & Winfree
(See Greensboro)

Woodruff Law Firm, P.A.
(See Greensboro)

Woods, David Neal .... '75 '00 C.404 B.A. L.575 J.D. [Wyatt E.H.W.]
Wright, Carl R., (BV) .... '53 '81 C.296 B.A. L.896 J.D. 1312 Long St., Ste. 102
Wyatt, Frank Burkhead, (AV) .... '34 '59 C&L.896 B.S., J.D. [Wyatt E.H.W.]
Wyatt, Scott Fitzgerald, (BV) .... '66 '92 C&L.896 B.A., J.D. [Wyatt E.H.W.]

Wyatt Early Harris Wheeler L.L.P., (AV)
1912 Eastchester Drive, Suite 400, P.O. Drawer 2086, 27261
Telephone: 336-884-4444 Fax: 336-889-5232
URL: http://www.wehwlaw.com
Members of Firm: Frank Burkhead Wyatt; William P. Harris; A. Doyle Early, Jr. (Board Certified Specialist in Family Law, North Carolina State Board of Legal Specialization); William E. Wheeler; David B. Ashcraft; Kim W. Gallimore (Board Certified Specialist in Real Property Law: Business, Commercial, Industrial and Residential Transactions, North Carolina State Board of Legal Specialization); Kim R. Bauman; R. Bruce Laney; Charles A. Alt; Frederick G. Sawyer; James R. Hundley; Edgar S. Levy, III (Board Certified Specialist in Estate Planning and Probate Law, North Carolina State Board of Legal Specialization); John D. Bryson (Board Certified Specialist in Criminal Law including Appellate Practice, North Carolina State Board of Legal Specialization); Stanley F. Hammer (Board Certified Specialist in Criminal Law including Appellate Practice, North Carolina State Board of Legal Specialization); Scott Fitzgerald Wyatt; David Neal Woods; Christopher M. Kroger; Matthew C. Jobe; Arlene W. Reardon; Jason E. Moss; Cory A. Rayborn; Martha C. Massie. Of Counsel: Calvin B. Bryant (Board Certified Specialist in Estate Planning and Probate Law, North Carolina State Board of Legal Specialization).
Litigation, Legal and Regulatory matters in Furniture/Home Furnishings Industries, General Civil, Insurance, Business, Securities, Taxation and Criminal Practice. Trials and Appeals in all State and Federal Courts. Probate and Estate Planning, Real Estate, Bankruptcy, Corporation, Banking, Negligence, Workers Compensation and Family Law.
Representative Clients: Allstate Insurance Co.; Banner Pharmacaps, Inc.; BB&T Factors Corp.; Davis Furniture Industries; Dar-Ran Furniture Industries; Mid-State Petroleum; British Vita; J & S Cafeterias; The Presbyterian Homes, Inc.; Palliser Furniture Corp.
See Professional Biographies, HIGH POINT, NORTH CAROLINA

Zuluaga, Juan F. .... '72 '03 C.577 B.S. L.575 J.D. [J.E.Bruner]

HILLSBOROUGH, * 5,446, *Orange Co.*

Anderson, Charles T. L., (BV) ...... '50 '76 C&L.575 A.B., J.D. 15B District Court Judge
Barber, Wade .... '44 '70 C.198 B.A. L.575 J.D. Sr. Resident, Supr. Ct. J.
Borhanian, S. Sean .... '58 '91 C.705 B.A. L.790 J.D. [Coleman,G.H.&P.]
Buckner, Joe Ed .... '60 '87 C&L.575 B.A., J.D. Trial J.
Butler, Rick, (BV) .... '53 '87 C.125 B.A. L.1345 J.D. 100 N. Churton St.
Cheasty, John C. '07 '33 C.433 A.B. L.262 LL.B.
(adm. in NY; not adm. in NC) 513 Hardscrabble Dr.‡
Cheshire, Lucius M., (AV) .... '25 '65 L.575 [Cheshire&P.] ‡
Cheshire & Parker, (AV) .... P.O. Box 100
Coleman, Alonzo B., Jr. .... '37 '65 C.249 B.S. L.575 LL.B. Dist. J.
Coleman, Samuel E., (CV) .... '63 '94 C&L.575 B.A., J.D. [Coleman,G.H.&P.]

Coleman, Gledhill, Hargrave & Peek, P.C., (AV)
129 East Tryon Street, P.O. Drawer 1529, 27278
Telephone: 919-732-2196 FAX: 919-732-7997
URL: http://www.cgandh.com
Geoffrey E. Gledhill; Douglas Hargrave; Samuel E. Coleman; Leigh Ann Peek;—S. Sean Borhanian; Markee L. Squire.
General Civil and Criminal Trial Practice in all State and Federal Courts. Litigation, Negligence, Domestic, Real Estate, Corporate, Municipal and Probate Law, Commercial Transactions and Litigation.
See Professional Biographies, HILLSBOROUGH, NORTH CAROLINA

Cooley, Ronald Edwin .... '57 '00 C.1213 B.E. L.577 J.D. [Cooley]
Cooley Law Offices .... 2203 Rhonda Road
DeFranco, Michael A., (BV) .... '67 '96 C.896 B.A. L.861 J.D. 1414 Ainsworth Blvd.
Delamar, Paul Johnson, III ..... '76 '01 C&L.575 B.A., J.D. 400 Millstone Drive, Suite 200
Dickerson, Donald R., (BV) .... '48 '73 C&L.575 B.A., J.D. [D.R.Dickerson]
Dickerson, Lauren O. .... '75 '01 C.575 B.A. L.1228 J.D. [D.R.Dickerson]

Dickerson, Donald R., P.A., (BV)
106 North Churton Street, 27278
Telephone: 919-644-0021 Toll Free: 888-920-0021 Facsimile: 919-732-1002 Email: lodickerson@mindspring.com
Email: drdpa@earthlink.net URL: http://www.dickerson-law-firm.com
Donald R. Dickerson;—Lauren O. Dickerson.
General Civil and Criminal Trial Practice. Criminal, Civil, Domestic Relations, Family, Personal Injury, Traffic Violations.
See Professional Biographies, HILLSBOROUGH, NORTH CAROLINA

Drummond, Josune .... '48 '97 C.1222 B.S. L.229 J.D. 106 E. Margaret Ln.
Earnhardt Breen, Melany ...... '62 '92 C.1090 B.G.S. L.575 J.D. North State Legal Servs.

Epting & Hackney
(See Chapel Hill)

Fitzpatrick, John C., P.C., Law Office of
(See Durham)

Franklin Law Center, PLLC
(See Chapel Hill)

Gay, James Michael, (BV) ....'49 '92 C.999 B.S. L.1228 J.D. [J.M.Gay]
Gay, James Michael, P.A., (BV) .... 100 North Churton Street, Suite 209
Gidcumb, Lance E., Attorney at Law, (BVⓣ) '50 '75
C.338 B.S. L.69 J.D. 1826 Patrick Henry Lane
Gledhill, Geoffrey E., (AV) ....'44 '75 C.1338 B.S. L.574 J.D. [Coleman,G.H.&P.]
Gooding-Ray, Theresa N. .... '72 '99 C&L.575 B.A., J.D. Legal Aid of NC
Guibert, Judith K. .....'46 '92 C.446 B.A. L.575 J.D. 100 North Churton Street, Suite 204

Hairston, Dorothy, Law Office of
(See Durham)

Hargrave, Douglas, (AV) ....'50 '76 C.896 B.A. L.575 J.D. [Coleman,G.H.&P.]

Hauser, Judith M., (BV) '— '85 C&L.575 B.A., J.D.
127 West King Street, 27278-2543
Telephone: 919-732-6131 Fax: 919-732-6229
Email: closings@mindspring.com
General Practice. Real Estate, Wills and Estates.
See Professional Biographies, HILLSBOROUGH, NORTH CAROLINA

Hogue, Cyrus D., III, (BV) ....'49 '75 C.976 B.A. L.575 J.D. [C.D.Hogue III]
Hogue, Cyrus D. III, P.A., (BV) .... 110 W. Margaret Lane
Koelling, Gerald R., (BVⓣ) '40 '71 C.766 B.S. L.1066 J.D.
(adm. in CA; not adm. in NC) Mag.‡
Ledbetter, Janet Knight, Law Office ....'45 '77 C.302 B.A. L.574 J.D. P.O. Box 1108
Littman, James F. '23 '64 C.260 B.S. L.362 J.D.
(adm. in FL; not adm. in NC) 1651 St. Mary's Road‡
Loftin, Dalton Hartwell, (AV) .... '31 '59 C&L.575 B.S., J.D. [🄲 Loftin&L.]
Loftin, John D., (BV) .... '55 '89 C&L.575 A.B., J.D. [Loftin&L.]

Loftin and Loftin, P.A., (BV)
117 North Churton Street, P.O. Box 733, 27278
Telephone: 919-732-9748 Fax: 919-732-4241
Email: jdloftin@mindspring.com URL: http://www.jdloftinlaw.com
John D. Loftin. Of Counsel: Dalton Hartwell Loftin.
General Practice, General Civil and Criminal Trial and Appellate Practice. Personal Injury, Real Estate, Contracts, Constitutional, American Indian Law, Condemnation, Subdivision, Zoning, Family, Probate and Corporation Law.
Representative Clients: Hillsborough Savings Bank; Orange County Medical Foundation, Inc.
References: Hillsborough Savings Bank; Central Carolina Bank; NationsBank; Federal Land Bank; Farmers Home Administration.
See Professional Biographies, HILLSBOROUGH, NORTH CAROLINA

Love, Patricia Stanford ....'28 '78 C&L.575 B.A., LL.D. Ret. Chf. Dist. J.
Martin, Harry C., (AV) .... '20 '48 C.575 A.B. L.309 LL.B. [Martin&M.] ⊙
Martin, John A. ....'50 '92 C.48 B.A. L.790 J.D. [Martin&M.]
Martin & Martin, P.A., A Professional Association, (AV)
133 East King Street (⊙Asheville)
Mead, Dale C. ....'55 '79 C.1239 B.A. L.284 J.D. 1702 McRae Pl.
Meggett, Paul A. ....'69 '98 C.576 B.S. L.575 J.D. 2205 Beckette Rdg.
Parker, D. Michael, (AV) ....'51 '78 C.575 B.A. L.896 J.D. [Cheshire&P.]
Peek, Leigh Ann, (BV) ....'60 '95 C.232 B.A. L.575 J.D. [Coleman,G.H.&P.]
Powell, Susie R. ....'42 '73 C.1298 B.A. L.930 J.D. Orange Chatham Legal Servs.
Rothrock, Kenneth Price ....'50 '81 C.34 B.A. L.574 J.D. P.O. Box 1347
Sandling, Kelly Leann '76 '01 C.576 B.A. L.1228 J.D.
Legal Aid of North Carolina, Inc.
Skvarla, John E., III, (AV) '48 '73
C.433 B.A. L.575 J.D. Pres. & Gen. Coun., Isotechnologies, Inc.
Squire, Markee L. ....'77 '02 C.1378 B.S. L.575 J.D. [🄰 Coleman,G.H.&P.]
Steffan, Kim K., (BV) ....'62 '86 C.228 B.A. L.575 J.D. 400 Millstone Dr., Ste. 200
Strange, LaShawn Lanea .... '73 '99 C.160 B.A. L.574 J.D. Legal Servs.
Troy, Michael C. .... '38 '62 C&L.228 A.B., LL.B. 807 Benton St.
Veit, Glenn C., (BV) ....'54 '87 C.228 A.B. L.574 J.D. 110 W. Margaret Lane
Woodall, Jack C. ....'24 '47 C&L.228 LL.B. P.O. Box 483
Zwilling, Andre W. .... '67 '93 C.575 B.A. L.838 J.D. 1615 Ainsworth Blvd.

HOLDEN BEACH, 787, *Brunswick Co.*

Del Ré, Benedict J., Jr. '59 '86 C.273 B.B.A. L.1148 J.D.
1111 Sabbath Home Rd. S.W.
Lizak, Laura Lee ....'67 '96 C.472 B.S.C. L.1228 J.D. Corp. Coun.

HOLLY RIDGE, 831, *Onslow Co.*

Eckert, Lorraine D. '51 '79 C.222 B.A. L.1048 J.D.
(adm. in CT; not adm. in NC) 318A N. Shore Dr.

HOLLY SPRINGS, 9,192, *Wake Co.*

Bryan, David Newman ....'70 '99 C.575 B.A. L.1228 J.D. P.O. Box 1238
Bryan, Donald R., Jr. ....'54 '85 C.232 B.S. L.896 J.D. Bryan Properties, Inc.
Miller, John J., III ....'64 '90 C.896 B.A. L.1228 J.D. The Holland Company Inc.

Richardson, Jonathan, The Law Office of
(See Cary)

HOPE MILLS, 11,237, *Cumberland Co.*

Clark, William E.
(See Fayetteville)

HORSE SHOE, —, *Henderson Co.*

Robinson, Allen J. B. .... '46 '72 C&L.790 A.B., J.D. 259 Adventure Trail‡

HOT SPRINGS, 645, *Madison Co.*

Clary, Bruce E. '30 '55
(adm. in FL; not adm. in NC) Rte. 1
Cury, Alexandra '57 '81 C.659 B.A. L.893 J.D.
(adm. in FL; not adm. in NC) 1717 Howard Moore Rd.

HUBERT, —, *Onslow Co.*

Jennings, Robert L. ....'— '96 204 Blueberry Court

HUNTERSVILLE, 24,960, *Mecklenburg Co.*

Baker, David J. ....'70 '95 C.896 B.A. L.1228 J.D. [Baker&B.P.]
Baker, Laura S. ....'68 '95 C.896 B.A. L.1228 J.D. [Baker&B.P.]
Baker & Baker, PLLC ....9620 Holly Point Drive, Ste. 102

Bolduc Law Firm, The, PLLC
(See Charlotte)

Clark, Xonna M. '61 '86 C.309 A.B. L.659 J.D.
(adm. in MD; not adm. in NC)
Sr. Bus. Coun., Commercial Transactions, GE Advanced Materials
Constitution Law Associates, LLC
7930 W. Kenton Circle (⊙Charlotte, Monroe, NC; Fort Mill, Lake Wylie, Rock Hill, SC)
Elliott, Michael K. ....'67 '03 C.576 B.S. L.1339 J.D. [Elliott]

Elliott Law Firm, P.C.
P.O. Box 1821, 28078
Telephone: 704-491-0365 URL: http://www.mkelliott-law.com
Email: mikeelliott@legalemail.com URL: http://www.elliottlawfirm.net
Michael K. Elliott.
Business Law, Limited Liability Company Law, Incorporations, Corporate Law, Mergers and Acquisitions, Tax Law, Real Estate, Construction Law, Trusts and Estates, Asset Protection, Estate Planning, Guardianship, Bankruptcy, Traffic Violations.
See Professional Biographies, HUNTERSVILLE, NORTH CAROLINA

Hayes, Ray A., II, P.A.
(See Cornelius)

Hesse, Karl O. .... '38 '72 C.494 B.E.E. L.276 J.D. 13324 Mayes Rd. (Pat.)‡
Hochman, Brian R. ....'66 '92 C.896 B.A. L.884 J.D. 11928 Cupworth Court

James, Bruce L. '61 '86 C.1128 B.S. L.1228 J.D.
Rosedale Commons Executive Suites, 10105 Hickorywood Hill Avenue Suite B-3, 28078
Mailing Address: P.O. Box 657, Huntersville, NC 28070
Telephone: 704-992-6556 Facsimile: 704-992-6559 Charlotte: 704-372-1202
Email: brucejames1@aol.com URL: http://www.brucejameslaw.com
Estate Planning, Asset Protection, Estate Litigation, Tax, Wills and Probate, Non Profit and Charitable Organizations, Business Law, Corporate Law, Collections, Eminent Domain, Employee Benefits, Civil Litigation, Taxation.
See Professional Biographies, HUNTERSVILLE, NORTH CAROLINA

Johnson, Robin M. .... '63 '93 C.152 B.S. L.790 J.D. Coun.
King, Brent F., (CV) .... '70 '96 C.575 B.A. L.896 J.D. [King,P.]

King Law Firm, The, PLLC, (CV)
7930 W. Kenton Circle, Suite 100, 28078
Telephone: 704-892-5533 Fax: 704-892-9191
Email: bking@brentkinglaw.com URL: http://www.brent-kinglawfirm.com
Brent F. King.
Bankruptcy, Domestic, Family, Wills, Trusts, Criminal.
See Professional Biographies, HUNTERSVILLE, NORTH CAROLINA

Knox, Charles E., (AV) ...'26 '51 C&L.575 B.S., J.D. 16740 Birkdale Commons Parkway
Legg, Basil R., Jr. '56 '84 C.575 A.B. L.923 J.D.
(adm. in WV; not adm. in NC) 14537 Maclauren Ln.
Nason, Allen M. '72 '99 C.956 B.S. L.1358 J.D.
[Constitution&Assoc.] (⊙Charlotte, Monroe, NC; Rock Hill, SC)
Peterffy, Jan L.A. von ....'61 '88 C.1236 B.A. L.464 J.D. P.O. Box 1346
Thebeau, Cheri A., (CVⓣ) ....'61 '89 C.900 B.A. L.616 J.D. [Thebeau&Assoc.]
Thebeau & Associates, P.A., (CVⓣ) ....7930 W. Kenton Circle, Suite 230
Tokunboh, Olufemi ....'— '93 L.999 J.D. 15834 Waldrop Hill Court
Von Peterffy, Jan L. ....'61 '88 C.1236 B.A. L.464 J.D. P.O. Box 1346

Williams, G. Patteson
(See Cornelius)

INDIAN TRAIL, 11,905, *Union Co.*

Goodwin, S. Stephen, (CV) ....'66 '92 C.575 B.A. L.192 J.D. [Goodwin&H.]
Goodwin & Hinson, P.A., (CV) ....309 Post Office Drive
Hinson, Wesley S. ....'73 '99 C.575 B.A. L.1228 J.D. [Goodwin&H.]
Levine, Shelley K. .... '78 '04 C&L.575 B.S.B.A., J.D. [🄰 Goodwin&H.]
Pamperin, Claudia J. ....'71 '02 C.362 B.A. L.259 J.D. [Pamperin]
Pamperin Law Firm ....1012 Onotoa Drive
Smith, Matthew Brian ....'— '02 C.575 B.A. L.1228 J.D. [🄰 Goodwin&H.]

JACKSON, * 695, *Northampton Co.*

Bridgers, David C., Jr. ....'40 '72 C.232 A.B. L.574 J.D. Co. Clk. of Supr. Ct.
McKellar, John F., (BV) .... '49 '75 C.575 A.B. L.896 J.D. 109 Thomas Bragg Drive

Moseley, Elliott & Dickens, L.L.P.
(See Roanoke Rapids)

Turner, Felton, Jr., (AV) .... '28 '56 C.576 B.S. L.575 LL.B. 110 E. Jefferson St.

JACKSON SPRINGS, —, *Moore Co.*

Lacher, Richd. W. '16 '50 C.966 B.S. L.209 J.D.
(adm. in IL; not adm. in NC) Rte. 1‡

JACKSONVILLE, * 66,715, *Onslow Co.*

Adams, Mark R. ....'68 '00 C.953 B.A. L.1187 J.D. [Morton&A.]
Andrews, William H., (AV) ....'46 '72 C&L.896 B.A., J.D. 2229 Perry Dr.‡
Bailey, Edward G., (AV) ....'40 '65 C&L.896 B.A., LL.B. 314 New Bridge Street
Baldwin, C. Mark .... '51 '80 C.575 A.B. L.228 J.D. [🄰 Brumbaugh,M.&K.]
Basham, Owen D. '42 '67 C.531 B.A. L.383 J.D.
(adm. in KY; not adm. in NC) [Taylor&B.]
Bell, Hiram C., Jr., (BV) ....'47 '77 C.576 B.S. L.192 J.D. [Bell]
Bell Law Firm, (BV) ....410 New Bridge Street, Suite 8A
Best, David L., (CV) .... '49 '75 C.232 B.A. L.574 J.D. 410 New Bridge St.
Blackwell, Edwin H., III, (BV) ....'54 '79 C.575 B.A. L.790 J.D. P.O. Box 1379

Block, Victoria L.
(See New Bern)

Blum, Andrew Franklin ......'58 '86 100 Brewster Blvd., PSC Box 125 (Camp Lejeune)★
Brantley, J. Christopher, (BV) '66 '93 C.232 B.A. L.1345 J.D.
[Brantley,J.R.H.&H.] ⊙

Brantley, Jenkins, Riddle, Hardee & Hardee, (BV)
901 Hargett Street, P.O. Box 7070, 28540 ⊙
Telephone: 910-455-5599 Fax: 910-455-7191 URL: http://www.bjrhhlawyers.com
URL: http://www.bjrhhatty.com
J. Christopher Brantley.
Personal Injury, Wrongful Death, Automobile Accidents, Head and Spinal Injury, Nursing Home Abuse and Neglect, Workers Compensation, Insurance, Products Liability, Social Security Disability, Medical Malpractice.
Goldsboro, North Carolina Office: 601 North Spence Avenue, 27534. Telephone: 919-778-9700. Fax: 919-778-1938.
Greenville, North Carolina Office: 202 East Arlington Boulevard, P.O. Box 924, 27858. Telephone: 252-355-1998. Fax: 252-321-2948.
Kinston, North Carolina Office: 2506 Heritage Street, Suite A, 28501. Telephone: 252-522-1500.
See Professional Biographies, JACKSONVILLE, NORTH CAROLINA

Brumbaugh, Clay A., (BV) .... '40 '72 C.174 B.A. L.1065 J.D. [Brumbaugh,M.&K.]

Brumbaugh, Mu & King, P.A., (BV)
112 Old Bridge Street, P.O. Box 1088, 28541-1088 ⊙
Telephone: 910-455-4065; 800-635-1683 Fax: 910-455-5539 URL: http://www.lawyers.com/brumbaughmuandking
URL: http://www.bmklaw.net

(This Listing Continued)

Brumbaugh, Mu & King, P.A. (Continued)
Richard A. Mu; Clay A. Brumbaugh; Kenneth W. King, Jr.; Leah L. King. Associates: Nicole D. Wray; Angela D. Vandivier-Stanley; C. Mark Baldwin.
Practice Limited to Injury Cases. Automobile, Wrongful Death, Medical Malpractice, Workers' Compensation, Products Liability and Social Security Claims.
Reference: First Citizens Bank, Jacksonville, NC.
Wilmington, North Carolina Office: 2018 South 16th Street. Telephone: 910-763-2111.
Elizabethtown, North Carolina Office: 102 West Broad Street. Telephone: 910-862-2211.
Fayetteville, North Carolina Office: 609 Executive Place. Telephone: 910-630-2099.
New Bern, North Carolina, Office: McCarthy Square Office Suites, 790 Cardinal Road, Suite 6. Telephone: 252-636-2099.
Shallotte, North Carolina Office: 143 Holden Beach Rd., Suite #6-A. Telephone: 910-754-3660.
Washington, North Carolina Office: 110 West Third Street, P.O. Box 338. Telephone: 252-946-0793.
Havelock, North Carolina Office: 404 East Main Street, 28532. Telephone: 252-447-4445.
Kinston, North Carolina Office: 414 South Queen Street, 28501. Telephone: 252-939-1800.
Rocky Mt., North Carolina Office: 876 Country Club Rd., 27804. Telephone: 252-451-4090.
See Professional Biographies, JACKSONVILLE, NORTH CAROLINA

Carter, John T., Jr., (AV) ....'50 '76 C.1128 B.A. L.575 J.D. [Warlick M.D.&C.]
Ceruzzi, John W., (BV) ....'70 '97 C.896 B.A. L.1228 J.D. 114 Old Bridge St.
Cloutier, Margaret, (BV) ....'56 '93 C.232 B.A. L.1228 J.D. 634 Court St.
Coleman, R. Lynn, (BV) ....'54 '80 C.575 B.S. L.1228 J.D. [Coleman]
Coleman Law Firm, (BV) ....410 New Bridge St.
Collins, George L., (BV) ....'44 '83 C.575 B.S. L.1228 J.D. [Collins&M.]

Collins and Moore, PLLC, (BV)
634 Court St., 28540
Telephone: 910-347-7100 Fax: 910-455-1496 URL: http://www.collinsandmoore.com
Email: glcatty@earthlink.net URL: http://www.lawyers.com/collinsandmoore
Members of Firm: George L. Collins; James L. Moore, Jr.;—Ann D. Maready.
Personal Injury including Wrongful Death, Automobile Accidents and Injuries, Medical Malpractice, Premises Liability; Corporate and Business Law including Contracts, Disputes, Commercial Litigation, Taxation; Estate Planning including Wills, Trusts, Retirement Planning, Wealth Preservation; Criminal Defense including Felonies, Misdemeanors, Drugs, Traffic Violations, Speeding, Parole and Probation, DWI; Family Law including Divorce, Child Custody, Alimony, Separation Agreements; Workers Compensation.
References: NationsBank; Wachovia Bank and Trust Co.
See Professional Biographies, JACKSONVILLE, NORTH CAROLINA

Coxe, L. Robert, III, (BV) ....'50 '78 C.576 B.A. L.1048 J.D. [Coxe]
Coxe Legal Clinic, The, (BV) ....3884 Henderson Dr.
David, G. Phillip ....'59 '88 C.232 B.S.B.A. L.574 J.D. [David&Assoc.] ⊙

David and Associates, pllc
405-B Western Boulevard, 28546 ⊙
Telephone: 910-219-4878 Toll Free: 1-800-856-9927
Email: aeverhart@davidandassociates.com URL: http://www.wilmingtonpiattorneys.com
G. Phillip David.
Personal Injury, Medical Malpractice, Wrongful Death, Products Liability, Workers Compensation, Aviation, Airplane Crashes, Negligence, Class Actions, Maritime Accidents, Boating Accidents, Bicycle Accidents, Motorcycle Accidents, Truck Accidents, School Bus Accidents, Railroad Accidents, Dog Bites, Slip and Fall, Birth Trauma, Brain Injury, Spinal Injury, Head Injury, Catastrophic Injury, Vehicular Homicide, Personal Injury Mediation, Products Liability, Drug and Medical Device Litigation, Product Defects, Automobile Liability, Motorcycle Products Liability, Amusement Park Liability, Hotel Liability, Marina Liability, Sports Injury.
Wilmington, North Carolina Office: 1516 Dawson Street. 28401. Telephone: 910-251-8088.
Supply, North Carolina Office: Highway 17. 28462. Telephone: 910-754-8465.
Wallace, North Carolina Office: 107 North Norwood Street. 28466. Telephone: 910-285-8777.
Clinton, North Carolina Office: 610 Beaman Street. 28328. Telephone: 910-592-8400.
Winston-Salem, North Carolina Office: 1100-A South Stratford Road. 27103. Telephone: 336-354-1040.
Greensboro, North Carolina Office: 529 College Road. Suite G. 27410. Telephone: 336-354-1040.
See Professional Biographies, JACKSONVILLE, NORTH CAROLINA

Detwiler, Robert W., (BV) ....'50 '76 C&L.608 B.A., J.D. 327 New Bridge Street
Dotson, Marshall F., Jr., (AV) ....'30 '60 C.296 B.A. L.896 J.D. [Warlick M.D.&C.]
Edwards, J. Dewey, Jr., (BV) ....'51 '76 C&L.896 B.A., J.D. [Gaylor,E.&V.]
Erwin, E. Alex, III, (BV) ....'46 '72 C.673 B.A. L.896 J.D. 1003 Greenway Dr
Erwin, Frank W., (BV) ....'52 '77 C.198 A.B. L.228 J.D. [Erwin,S.&S.] ⊙

Erwin, Simpson & Stroud, P.L.L.C., (BV)
825 Gum Branch Road, Suite 115, 28540 ⊙
Telephone: 910-455-1800 Facsimile: 910-346-5883
URL: http://www.essnc.com
Frank W. Erwin (Board Certified Specialist in Real Property Law, Residential Transactions, North Carolina State Board of Legal Specialization); John P. Simpson; Joseph E. Stroud, Jr. (Board Certified Specialist in State Criminal Law, North Carolina State Board of Legal Specialization).
Appellate Practice, Bankruptcy, Civil Practice, Commercial Real Estate, Condominium Law, Construction Law, Contracts, Corporate Law, Criminal Law, Debtor and Creditor, Family Law, Real Estate Foreclosure, Homeowners Association Law, Civil Litigation, Municipal Law, Personal Injury, Real Estate, Trusts and Estates, Wills.
Cedar Point, North Carolina Office: 708 Cedar Point Boulevard, 28584. Telephone: 910-326-4008.
See Professional Biographies, JACKSONVILLE, NORTH CAROLINA

Faison, Dolores Jones, (CV) ....'52 '81 C.575 B.A. L.574 J.D. 410 New Bridge St., Ste. 3

Fisher, Glenn O'Keith, Attorney at Law, (BV) '57 '82 C.575 B.A. L.896 J.D.
2505 Henderson Drive, 28546-5253
Telephone: 910-347-8800 Fax: 910-455-4440
Email: fmlaw@coastalnet.com
Real Estate, Criminal Law, Civil Litigation, Probate, Corporation, Personal Injury, Municipal Law.
See Professional Biographies, JACKSONVILLE, NORTH CAROLINA

Fountain, Keith E., (BV) ....'54 '80 C.953 B.A. L.192 J.D. [Lanier&F.]
Gatewood, Sheryl G. '63 '89 C.187 B.A. L.910 J.D.
(adm. in MO; not adm. in NC) 123 Plantation Blvd.
Gaylor, Jimmy F., (AV) ....'49 '74 C.232 B.A. L.896 J.D. [Gaylor,E.&V.]

Gaylor, Edwards and Vatcher, (AV)
219 New Bridge Street, P.O. Box 1057, 28541-1057
Telephone: 910-455-9494 FAX: 910-455-0117
Jimmy F. Gaylor; J. Dewey Edwards, Jr.; Walter W. Vatcher.
General Civil and Criminal Practice. Real Estate, Personal Injury, Traffic Violation, DWI, Felonies, Misdemeanor, Driver License Restoration, Medical Malpractice, Auto Accidents, Wrongful Death, Trust & Estate.
Approved Attorneys for: Fidelity Title Insurance Co.; Investors Title Insurance Co.
Reference: First Citizens Bank & Trust Co.
See Professional Biographies, JACKSONVILLE, NORTH CAROLINA

Geracos, Georgann, (BV) ....'47 '83 C&L.1044 B.A., J.D. 323 New Bridge Street
Gleason, Robert J., (CV) ....'61 '88 C.602 B.A. L.228 J.D. Asst. Dist. Atty.
Hamilton, F. Cooper, (AV) ....'28 '55 C.575 A.B. L.896 LL.B. 222 New Bridge St.
Hardison, Paul A. ....'52 '84 C.953 B.A. L.574 J.D. Dist. J.
Harris, Rodger Craig '49 '87 C.1111 B.A. L.537 J.D.
(adm. in CA; not adm. in NC) P.O. Box 1516★
Hart, Leon T. ....'16 '56 C.563 B.B.A. L.1009 J.D. 327 New Bridge St.‡
Healey, Ellen B. '51 '78 C.960 B.S. L.1018 J.D.
(adm. in MN; not adm. in NC) 1016 Beech Tree Road
Henry, Charles H., Jr., (AV) ....'50 '75 C.575 A.B. L.896 J.D. 313 New Bridge St.

Jones, Carol Ann, (CV) ....'66 '94 C.575 B.A. L.574 J.D. Asst. Dist. Atty.
Jungreis, Jeremy Nathan '71 '96 C.1175 B.S. L.259 J.D.
U.S. Marine Corps, Eastern Area Counsel Off.★
Kellum, Norman B., Jr., (AV) ....'37 '65 C&L.896 B.S., J.D. [Kellum] ⊙

Kellum Law Firm, (AV)
445-A Western Boulevard, P.O. Box 12155, 28546 ⊙
Telephone: 910-455-4546 Fax: 910-455-2422
Email: ckeenhold@kellumlawfirm.com URL: http://www.lawyers.com/kellumlawfirm
Norman B. Kellum, Jr.
State and Federal Civil Trial Practice, Personal Injury Law, Wrongful Death, Workers' Compensation, Social Security, Defective Products, Mass Torts and Insurance Law.
See Professional Biographies, JACKSONVILLE, NORTH CAROLINA

King, Kenneth W., Jr., (BV) ......'61 '86 C.575 B.S. L.469 J.D. [Brumbaugh,M.&K.] ⊙
King, Leah L., (CV) ....'67 '92 C.232 B.S. L.1228 J.D. [Brumbaugh,M.&K.]
Lanier, Charles S., (BV) ....'47 '72 C.232 A.B. L.896 J.D. [Lanier&F.]
Lanier & Fountain, (BV) ....114 Old Bridge Street
Leas, R. W. '49 '79 C&L.744 B.A., J.D.
(adm. in TX; not adm. in NC) 1302 Decatur★
Lee, Ernest R., (BV) ....'60 '86 C.55 B.S. L.1228 J.D. Asst. Dist. Atty.
Lock, Robert E., (AV) ....'25 '53 C&L.575 B.S., LL.B 400 New Bridge St.

Mako & Associates, P.A.
(See Wilmington)

Maready, Ann D. ....'68 '93 C.896 B.A. L.1228 J.D. [Ⓐ Collins&M.]
Maultsby, Michael D., (BV) ....'67 '92 C.953 B.A. L.574 J.D. Asst. Dist. Atty.
McConnell, Kevin, (BV) ....'58 '87 C.160 B.S. L.201 J.D. [Ⓐ N.B.Tisdale]
McNamara, Thomas D., (BV) ....'54 '93 C.871 B.S. L.1228 J.D. [McNamara&S.]

McNamara & Smith, P.C., (BV)
309 New Bridge Street, 28540-4757
Telephone: 910-938-7191 Fax: 910-938-7833
Email: thomasmcnamara1@earthlink.net URL: http://www.lawyers.com/mcnamaraandsmith
Thomas D. McNamara (Board Certified Specialist in Family Law, North Carolina State Board of Legal Specialization); M. Lynn Smith (Board Certified Specialist in Family Law, North Carolina State Board of Legal Specialization).
Family Law, including Divorce, Separation Agreements, Child Custody, Child Support, Alimony, Property Distribution.
See Professional Biographies, JACKSONVILLE, NORTH CAROLINA

Mercer, Grady, Jr., (BV) ....'41 '68 C.232 L.838 J.D. P.O. Box 386
Mewborn, Christopher L., (BV) ....'66 '91 C&L.1228 B.S., J.D. [C.L.Mewborn]
Mewborn, Christopher L., Attorney P.A., (BV) ....825 Gum Branch Rd., Ste. 130
Milsted, Carl S., (AV) ....'34 '59 C&L.575 B.S., J.D. [Warlick M.D.&C.]
Moore, James L., Jr., (BV) ....'59 '85 C.575 B.A. L.1228 J.D. [Collins&M.]

Moore, Roger A., (AV) '46 '73 C&L.575 A.B., J.D.
100 Old Bridge Street, P.O. Drawer 886, 28540
Telephone: 910-455-0448; 455-0449 Fax: 910-347-6343
Email: rogermooreatty4u@earthlink.net URL: http://www.ncbankruptcylaw.com
(Board Certified Specialist in Bankruptcy Law, North Carolina State Board of Legal Specialization).
Bankruptcy, Municipal Law.
See Professional Biographies, JACKSONVILLE, NORTH CAROLINA

Moore, Thomasine E., and Associates, (CV) '49 '75
C&L.574 B.S., J.D. 410 New Bridge St.

Morgan, Victor H.E., Jr., Attorney at Law, (BV) '57 '83 C.953 B.A. L.896 J.D.
732 Court Street, P.O. Box 746, 28541
Telephone: 910-455-6555 Facsimile: 910-455-5149
Personal Injury, Auto Accidents, Workers' Compensation, Social Security Disability, Domestic Relations, Divorce, Criminal, Traffic Violations, DWI.
See Professional Biographies, JACKSONVILLE, NORTH CAROLINA

Morgan, William J., (AV) ....'41 '67 C.198 A.B. L.575 J.D. [W.J.Morgan]

Morgan, William J., P.A., (AV)
127 Chaney Avenue, P.O. Drawer 700, 28541-0700
Telephone: 910-989-1234 Fax: 910-455-8988 URL: http://www.morganlaw-nc.com
Email: wjm@morganlaw-nc.com URL: http://morganlawfirm-nc.com
William J. Morgan.
Personal Injury Law, General Civil Litigation, Medical Negligence Law, Major Criminal Defense.
See Professional Biographies, JACKSONVILLE, NORTH CAROLINA

Morton, Joseph W. ....'67 '97 C.953 B.A. L.1187 J.D. [Morton&A.]
Morton & Adams, P.C. ....1007 Hargett Street, Suite 2
Motelewski, Joseph R. ....'18 '42 L.209 LL.B. 224 Country Club Dr.‡
Mu, Richard A., (BV) ....'50 '80 C.871 B.S. L.896 J.D. [Brumbaugh,M.&K.]
Neal, Kelly B., (CV) ....'70 '98 C.953 B.A. L.1187 J.D. Off. of Dist. Atty.
Nodine, Matthew P. '71 '01 C.956 B.S. in B.A. L.790 J.D.
(adm. in SC; not adm. in NC) Pros. Atty., Camp Lejeune, U.S. Marine Corps.
Oswalt, Timothy R., (CV) ....'62 '97 C.1317 B.A. L.1228 J.D. [Ⓐ Lanier&F.]
Owens, Deke Slayton, (CV) ....'71 '96 C.232 B.S. L.327 J.D. [Ⓐ J.D.Warlick]
Paramore, W.H., III, (BV) '51 '76 C&L.575 B.A., J.D.
410 New Bridge Street, Suite Four
Patterson, Robert E., (BV) ....'23 '49 C.611 A.B. L.608 J.D. [R.E.Patterson]
Patterson, Robert E., P.A., (BV) ....221 New Bridge St.
Pope, Franklin D. ....'— '88 C.953 B.A. L.575 J.D. [Pope] (⊙Wilmington)
Pope Firm, The ....825 Gum Branch Road, Suite 107

Popkin, Samuel Stuart '52 '78 C.228 B.A. L.574 J.D.
1007 Hargett Street, Suite 1, 28540
Telephone: 910-347-0100 Fax: 910-989-1202
Email: spopkinattrny@ec.rr.com URL: http://www.popkinlaw.com
Criminal Law, Traffic Violations, Juvenile Delinquency, Divorce, Negligence, Abuse.
See Professional Biographies, JACKSONVILLE, NORTH CAROLINA

Quinn, Steve A., (CV) ....'65 '91 C.953 B.A. L.1345 J.D. [Ⓐ Lanier&F.]
Reed, Janet Pittman, The Law Office of '61 '88
C.260 B.A. L.339 J.D. 410 New Bridge Street
Robinson, Gordon E., Jr., (BV) .....'58 '84 C.228 B.A. L.575 J.D. 410 New Bridge Street

Robinson, Bruce H., Jr.
(See Wilmington)

Sandlin, Billy G., (BV) ....'41 '74 C&L.575 B.A., J.D. 220A New Bridge St.
Seaton, Sarah C. Cowen ....'60 '86 C.576 B.A. L.1228 J.D. Dist. Ct. J.
Simpson, John P., (BV) ....'45 '72 C&L.896 B.A., J.D. [Erwin,S.&S.] ⊙
Sims, Hurman R. ....'44 '68 C&L.846 B.A., J.D. 825 Gum Branch Rd., Ste. 103
Smith, M. Lynn, (BV) ....'69 '95 C&L.575 B.S., J.D. [McNamara&S.]
Strickland, James R. ....'28 '55 C&L.575 B.S., LL.B. Supr. Ct. J.
Stroud, Joseph E., Jr., (BV) ....'51 '77 C.232 B.A. L.896 J.D. [Erwin,S.&S.] ⊙
Taylor, Vaughan E., (AV) ....'47 '72 C.197 B.A. L.893 J.D. [Taylor&B.]

Taylor and Basham, (AV)
Suite 117, 825 Gum Branch Road, 28540
Telephone: 910-455-6300 Fax: 910-455-3012
Email: vaughantaylor@att.net URL: http://www.lawyers.com/militarylaw

(This Listing Continued)

Taylor and Basham (Continued)
Vaughan E. Taylor; Owen D. Basham (Not admitted in NC).
Military Law, Military Courts Martial, Military Criminal Law, Military Justice and Military Administrative Law.
See Professional Biographies, JACKSONVILLE, NORTH CAROLINA

Tisdale, Norwood Boyd, (BV) ....'45 '75 C&L.228 A.B., J.D. 400 New Bridge Street
Vandivier-Stanley, Angela D. ....'70 '00 C.63 B.S. L.1187 J.D. [Brumbaugh,M.&K.]
Vatcher, Walter W., (AV) ....'52 '79 C.575 B.S. L.1228 J.D. [Gaylor,E.&V.]

Wallace, Morris, Barwick, Landis & Stroud, P.A.
(See Kinston)

Walton, Donald G., Jr., (BV) ....'61 '89 C.953 B.A. L.383 J.D. 722 New Bridge St.

Ward and Smith, P.A.
(See New Bern)

Warlick, Alex, Jr., (AV) ....'30 '55 C.404 A.B. L.575 J.D. [Warlick M.D.&C.]
Warlick, John D., Jr., (AV) ....'34 '62 C&L.575 A.B., J.D. [J.D.Warlick]

Warlick, Lana S., (AV) '51 '76 C&L.575 A.B., J.D.
410 New Bridge Street Suite 1A, P.O. Box 1393, 28540
Telephone: 910-347-4400 Fax: 910-347-3736
(Board Certified Specialist in Family Law, North Carolina State Board of Legal Specialization).
Family Law, Divorce Law, Separation Agreements, Custody, Child Support, Alimony, Property Distribution, Adoption and Appellate Practice.
References: First Citizens Bank and Trust Co.; BB & T; RBC Centura.
See Professional Biographies, JACKSONVILLE, NORTH CAROLINA

Warlick, Robert A., (CV) ....'71 '97 C.953 B.A. L.1228 J.D. [J.D.Warlick]

Warlick, John Drew, P.A., The Law Offices of, (AV)
313 New Bridge Street, 28540
Telephone: 910-455-7700 Fax: 910-455-4068
Email: jdw@warlicklaw.com URL: http://www.warlicklawoffice.com
John D. Warlick, Jr.; Robert A. Warlick;—Deke Slayton Owens.
Personal Injury Law, Medical Negligence Law, General Civil Litigation, Automobile Accidents and Injuries, Wrongful Death, DWI, Traffic and Family Law.
See Professional Biographies, JACKSONVILLE, NORTH CAROLINA

Warlick Milsted Dotson & Carter, (AV) ....320 New Bridge Street
Waters, Harold L., (AV) ....'35 '60 C&L.575 A.B., J.D. 307 Freeman
Welch, Christopher J. ....'75 '00 C.855 B.A. L.896 J.D. [Welch]

Welch Law Firm, The, P.C.
220 Old Bridge Street, 28540
Telephone: 910-347-0161 Fax: 910-347-0164
Christopher J. Welch.
Criminal Law, General Practice.
See Professional Biographies, JACKSONVILLE, NORTH CAROLINA

Whitley, Robert E., (AV) '49 '74 C.232 B.S.B.A. L.896 J.D. [Whitley,R.&W.] (⊙Greenville, Kinston, Raleigh)
Whitley, Rodgman & Whitley, (AV) 200 Valencia Drive, Suite 101 (⊙Greenville, Kinston, New Bern, Raleigh)
Wigmore, Andrew Kent, Attorney at Law, (CV) '61 '93 C.999 B.S. L.1345 J.D. P.O. Box 208
Williams, Alan F. '64 '98 C.886 B.A. L.276 J.D. (adm. in VA; not adm. in NC) Milit. J.
Wray, Nicole D., (CV) ....'70 '95 C.232 B.A. L.1228 J.D. [Brumbaugh,M.&K.]
Wright, Ernest J., (BV) ....'53 '78 C.329 B.A. L.930 J.D. [E.J.Wright]
Wright, Ernest J., P.A., (BV) ....410 New Bridge Street
Wunder, David M. ....'56 '86 C.696 B.A. L.208 J.D. Psc Box 20080★

JAMESTOWN, 3,088, *Guilford Co.*

Chang, Ae Kyung ....'71 '98 C.575 B.A. L.896 J.D. 4915 Piedmont Pkwy., Ste. 103
Dwyer, David C. ....'74 '01 C.198 B.A L.896 J.D. [Stamey,F.&D.]
Edwards, Billy G. ....'42 '78 C.296 B.S. L.896 J.D. 200A Hillstone Dr.
Farmer, Ben, (BV) ....'45 '70 C.575 A.B. L.896 J.D. 720 W. Main St.
Paul, Daniel ....'54 '83 C.92 B.A. L.1218 J.D. Gen. Coun., Furnitureland South, Inc.‡
Schmitt, Allen ....'09 '36 P.O. Box 997
Stamey, Michael C., (BV) ....'57 '83 C.575 B.A. L.1228 J.D. [Stamey,F.&D.]
Stamey, Foust & Dwyer, LLP, (BV) .......P.O. Box 578 (⊙Greensboro)
Washington, Edw. K. ....'23 '55 C&L.575 A.B., LL.B. P.O. Box 1146‡

JEFFERSON, * 1,422, *Ashe Co.*

Hodges, Sherrie R., (BV) '57 '82 C.576 B.A. L.896 J.D.
401 East Main Street, Suite 3, P.O. Box 908, 28640
Telephone: 336-846-2511 Fax: 336-846-2514
Real Estate, Family Law, Social Security.

Hurley, Grier, (BV) ....'61 '89 C.953 B.A. L.1228 J.D. Staff Atty.
Johnston, John C., (BV) ....'58 '86 C.34 B.S.C.J. L.574 J.D. [Johnston&J.]
Johnston, Thomas S., (AV) ....'25 '49 C&L.896 B.S., LL.B. [Johnston&J.]

Johnston and Johnston, (BV)
306 East Main Street, P.O. Box 398, 28640
Telephone: 336-246-3311 Fax: 336-246-7194
Members of Firm: Ira T. Johnston (1892-1971); John C. Johnston. Of Counsel: Thomas S. Johnston.
General Practice. Domestic, Traffic and DWI, Probate, Real Estate, Personal Injury and Corporation Law. Trials in all Courts.
Representative Client: Town of Jefferson, North Carolina.
Approved Attorneys for: Investors Title Insurance Company; The Federal LandBank of Columbia; Statewide Title; Lawyers Title; Fidelity National Title.
References: First Charter; AF Bank.

Kilby & Hurley
(See West Jefferson)

Lonon, Grady, (CV) ....'49 '81 C.575 B.A. L.940 J.D. P.O. Box 422
Shepherd, Michelle T. ....'71 '96 C.34 B.S. L.1345 J.D. 401 East Main Street

Vannoy & Reeves, PLLC
(See West Jefferson)

Worth, Allen, (AV) ....'22 '52 C&L.575 A.B., LL.B. P.O. Box 26

JONESVILLE, 1,549, *Yadkin Co.*

Brown, Andrew G. ....'77 '02 C.1126 B.A. L.1228 J.D. [Finger,P.A.&R.]
Finger, M. Neil, (AV) ....'30 '55 C.34 B.S. L.575 LL.B. [Finger,P.A.&R.]
Finger, Parker, Avram, & Roemer, L.L.P., (AV) ..... 105 S. Bridge St. (⊙Winston-Salem)
Martin, Dennis G., (BV) ....'49 '93 C.575 B.A. L.574 J.D. [Martin,D.G.]
Martin, Dennis G., P.C., (BV) ....105 S. Bridge St.
Parker, Raymond A., (AV) ....'44 '74 C.576 B.A. L.896 J.D. [Finger,P.A.&R.]

KANNAPOLIS, 36,910, *Cabarrus & Rowan Cos.*

Blough, Eric J. .....'66 '96 C.25 B.S. L.896 J.D. Assoc. Gen. Coun., Pillowtex Corporation
Brown, Bachman S., Jr., (AV) ....'26 '50 C&L.228 A.B., LL.B. 121 S. Main St.
Burgner, Michael R. ....'72 '99 C.228 A.B. L.276 J.D. [Hartsell&W.]
Clement, Andrew P. ....'68 '94 C.232 B.A. L.575 J.D. 411 Jackson Park Road
Forbis, Clinton S., Jr., (BV) ....'44 '72 C.316 A.B. L.896 J.D. 1112 Centergrove Rd.
Grady, Thomas Myers, (AV) ....'41 '66 C.1318 B.S. L.896 J.D. [Hartsell&W.]
Griggs, Farrar O., Jr., (BV) ....'48 '77 C.575 A.B. L.365 J.D. 601 Coach St.

Hartsell & Williams, P.A., (AV)
708 McLain Road, P.O. Box 2, 28082 ⊙
Telephone: 704-932-3157 Facsimile: 704-932-9597
Luther T. Hartsell (1870-1961); Luther T. Hartsell, Jr. (1902-1961); John Hugh Williams (1913-1995); Thomas Myers Grady; J. Merritt White, III; Michael R. Burgner. Associate: Christy E. Wilhelm.
General Civil and Criminal Practice in all Courts. Workers Compensation, Corporation, Insurance, Real Estate, Taxation, Probate Law, Estate Planning, Family Law and Motor Sports (Racing).
Representative Clients: First Charter National Bank; Southern Railway Co.; Nationwide Insurance Co.; Travelers Indemnity Co.; The Shoe Show, Inc.; S & D Coffee, Inc.; Cabarrus County Board of Education; North East Medical Center; Lawyers Title Insurance Corp.; Cabarrus County.
Concord, North Carolina Office: 71 McCachern Boulevard, S.E., P.O. Box 368, 28025. Telephone: 704-786-5161. Facsimile: 704-788-8058.
See Professional Biographies, KANNAPOLIS, NORTH CAROLINA

Hastings, Randell F., The Law Office of
(See Concord)

Koontz, Hawkins, Nixon & Miller
(See Concord)

Mills Law, P.A.
(See Concord)

Rutledge, J. Carlyle, (AV) ....'09 '36 C&L.575 B.A., LL.B. [Rutledge,F.S.&S.] ‡
Rutledge, Friday, Safrit & Smith, (AV) ....1910 Dale Earnhardt Blvd.
Safrit, Walter M., II, (AV) ....'49 '74 C.247 B.A. L.790 J.D. [Rutledge,F.S.&S.]

Shelley, Mark E.
(See Concord)

Smith, Reginald K., (BV) ....'49 '73 C.575 B.S. L.500 J.D. [Rutledge,F.S.&S.]
White, J. Merritt, III, (BV) ....'59 '87 C&L.1228 B.B.A., J.D. [Hartsell&W.]
Widelski, Kathleen A. '57 '87 C.575 B.A. L.1228 J.D. Cabarrus Cty. Dept. of Social Svcs.
Wilhelm, Christy E. ....'— '02 C.228 B.A. L.1228 J.D. [Hartsell&W.]
Williford, C. Todd, (BV) ....'58 '83 C.575 B.A. L.469 J.D. 807 Centergrove Road

KENANSVILLE, * 856, *Duplin Co.*

Blizzard, Melissa K. ....'— '94 C.232 B.A. L.1228 J.D. 100 Front Street
Craft, Wm. E., (BV) ....'24 '50 L.896 J.D. 115 Front St.

Hale & Harrell
(See Burgaw)

Ingram, Carolyn Burnette, (BV) ....'46 '72 C.577 B.A. L.896 J.D. [Ingram&I.]
Ingram, Charles M., (BV) ....'48 '78 C.575 A.B. L.192 J.D. [Ingram&I.]
Ingram & Ingram, (BV) ....210 Seminary Street
Lanier, Russell J., Jr. ....'44 '68 C.1228 A.B. L.575 J.D. Sr. Res. Supr. Ct. J.

Ludlum Law Firm
(See Warsaw)

Phillips, David T., (BV) ....'52 '81 C.1228 B.S. L.896 J.D. [Phillips&P.]

Phillips & Phillips, (BV)
112 Front Street, P.O. Box 720, 28349
Telephone: 910-296-0215 Fax: 910-296-0923
Email: phillipsattn@earthlink.net
Member of Firm: David T. Phillips.
Traffic Violations, Driving While Intoxicated, Personal Injury, Probate, Estate Planning, Real Estate, General Practice.
See Professional Biographies, KENANSVILLE, NORTH CAROLINA

Poirier, Dean R. ....'57 '93 C.455 B.S. L.575 J.D. State Employ. Sec. Comm.
Rhodes, Robin Neil ....'63 '98 C.575 B.A. L.1243 J.D. [R.N.Rhodes]

Rhodes, Robin Neil, PLLC
310 N. Main Street, P.O. Box 717, 28349
Telephone: 910-296-6090 Fax: 910-296-6091
Email: rhodeslawfirm@earthlink.net
Member of Firm: Robin Neil Rhodes.
Criminal Law, Traffic Violations, Driving While Intoxicated, Felonies, Misdemeanors. Real Estate, Personal Injury, Divorce.
See Professional Biographies, KENANSVILLE, NORTH CAROLINA

Smith, Timothy Wayne, (BV) ....'59 '86 C.232 B.S. L.1228 J.D. [T.W.Smith]
Smith, Timothy W., P.A., (BV) ....100 Front St.
Stevens, Henry L., III ....'23 '51 C.575 A.B. L.896 J.D. Supr. Ct. J.

Thompson & Thompson, P.C.
(See Warsaw)

Wallace, Morris, Barwick, Landis & Stroud, P.A.
(See Kinston)

Welch Law Firm, The, P.C.
(See Jacksonville)

KENLY, 1,569, *Johnston & Wilson Cos.*

Lucas, Leon A., Attorney at Law, (BV) .....'53 '79 C.896 B.A. L.1228 J.D. P.O. Box 910

KERNERSVILLE, 17,126, *Forsyth Co.*

Aktug, Kurt B. ....'70 '97 C.160 B.A. L.8 J.D. 7755 Fording Bridge Rd.
Anderson, Joseph L., (BV) ....'62 '89 C.112 B.A. L.309 J.D. [Anderson K.&Assoc.]

Anderson Korzen & Associates, P.C., (BV)
233 West Mountain Street, 27284
Telephone: 336-993-7958 Fax: 336-993-7964 URL: http://www.lawyers.com/anderson
Email: janderson@andersonkorzen.com URL: http://www.andersonkorzen.com
Joseph L. Anderson;—Jeffrey G. Weber; Katherine Flynn Henry. Of Counsel: John J. Korzen; Law Offices of Michael J. Pangia (Not admitted in NC).
Complex Litigation and Trials, Long Term Care and Nursing Home Abuse and Neglect, Serious Personal Injuries, Wrongful Death, Medical Malpractice, Aviation Torts and Air Crash Disasters, Serious Professional Negligence, Tractor Trailer Collisions, Product Liability.
See Professional Biographies, KERNERSVILLE, NORTH CAROLINA

Apple, Willis W., (BV) ....'51 '80 C&L.575 B.S., J.D. 101 S. Main St.
Bain, John H., (BV) ....'53 '91 C.577 B.A. L.896 J.D. 101 S. Main St.
Barrow, John J., (BV) ....'54 '91 C.577 B.S. L.1228 J.D. [J.Barrow]
Barrow, John, P.A., Law Offices of, (BV) ....130 West Mountain Street
Bennett, N. Alan, (BV) ....'56 '81 C.232 B.S. L.1228 J.D. [Thomas&B.]
Boles, Harry A., (BV) ....'47 '79 C&L.896 B.S., J.D. 115 South Main Street
Collins, Arvil Lee, (BV) ....'57 '82 C.576 B.A. L.1228 J.D. P.O. Box 829
Coltrane, Joseph M., Jr., Law Office of, (BV) '46 '77 C&L.575 B.A., J.D. 225 W. Mountain St.
Craddock, Jean M., (BV) ....'53 '81 C&L.896 B.A., J.D. 566 Linville Rd.
Davis, Chester C. ....'42 '72 C.198 A.B. L.575 J.D. Dist. Ct. J.

Dean, Stanley P., (BV) .... '65 '93 C.228 A.B. L.045 J.D. Pres., SPD Invest., Inc.
Grubbs, Jason T. .... '76 '03 C.886 B.A. L.896 J.D. 430 W. Mountain St.
Henry, Katherine Flynn, (CV) ...... '73 '98 C.473 B.A. L.896 J.D. [Anderson K.&Assoc.]
James, Wendy Hobson .... '77 '04 C.471 B.A. L.574 J.D. 225 W. Mountain St.

Jordan, Jerry D.
(See Winston-Salem)

Korzen, John J., (AV) .... '60 '91 C&L.896 B.A., J.D. [⊡ Anderson K.&Assoc.]
Lauver, Robert A., (BV) .... '58 '86 C.1326 B.A. L.896 J.D. [R.A.Lauver]
Lauver, Robert A., P.A., (BV) .... 113 W. Mountain St.
Moore, Thomas O., Jr. '34 '61
C.575 B.S. L.893 LL.B. Pres. & CEO, Blue Ox Industries, Inc.
Morgan, Eric C., (BV) .... '65 '91 C.893 B.A. L.846 J.D. [E.C.Morgan]
Morgan, Eric C., PA, (BV) .... P.O. Box 2424
Mundorf, Nancy Sellars, (BV) .... '51 '75 C&L.896 B.A., J.D. 118 W. Mountain St.
Oglesby, Ursula D. .... '66 '91 C&L.309 B.A., J.D. Dudley Prods., Inc.
Pangia, Michael J., Law Offices of, (AV Ⓣ) '42 '67 C.1027 B.S. L.724 J.D.
(adm. in NY; not adm. in NC) [⊡ Anderson K.&Assoc.] (⊙Wash., DC)
Parks, William Raymond, II '48 '88 C.1377 B.S.C.J. L.790 J.D.
(adm. in SC; not adm. in NC) 813 Branchwood Dr.‡
Prince, Thomas W. .... '46 '73 C.999 B.S. L.896 J.D. P.O. Box 1054

Rutledge, Dean B.
(See Winston-Salem)

Scott, Robert G., (BV) .... '70 '99 C.999 B.A. L.1187 J.D. [Scott]
Scott, Robert J., (BV) '42 '69
C.397 B.S. L.896 J.D. 109 East Mountain Street (⊙High Point)
Scott Law Offices, (BV) .... 109 E. Mountain St.

Surratt & Thompson, PLLC
(See Winston-Salem)

Thomas, Raymond D., (AV) .... '39 '64 C.198 A.B. L.896 J.D. [Thomas&B.]
Thomas & Bennett, (AV) .... 116 S. Cherry St.
Walters, Bambi Faivre .... '70 '97 C.893 B.S. L.861 J.D. P.O. Box 622 (Pat.)
Weber, Jeffrey G. .... '58 '91 C.999 B.A. L.790 J.D. [Anderson K.&Assoc.]

Winfree & Winfree
(See Greensboro)

Wolfe, John G., III, (AV) .... '45 '70 C.451 B.A. L.896 J.D. Town Atty.

KILL DEVIL HILLS, 5,897, *Dare Co.*

Archbell, Roy A., Jr.
(See Kitty Hawk)

Coppage, Charles D., (CV) .... '48 '74 C.1365 B.A. L.896 J.D. [Coppage]
Coppage Law Firm, P.A., The, (CV) .... 208 W. Walker St.

DeVeau, Ronald E., P.C.
(See Nags Head)

Forbes, James D. '10 '33 C.276 L.799 LL.B.
(adm. in MD; not adm. in NC) P.O. Box 3570‡
Gray, E. Crouse, Jr., (BV) .... '50 '77 C&L.575 B.A., J.D. [Gray&L.]
Gray & Lloyd, LLP, (BV) .... 3120 N. Croatan Highway
Hardman, Joseph M. '29 '74 C.685 B.A. L.950 J.D.
(adm. in MD; not adm. in NC) P.O. Box 95‡
Hess, Harvey K., Jr. '50 '78 C.658 B.S. L.969 J.D.
(adm. in GA; not adm. in NC) P.O. Box 7‡

Hornthal, Riley, Ellis & Maland, L.L.P.
(See Elizabeth City)

Jessup, Sidney P., (CV) ... '56 '86 C.890 B.A. L.1228 J.D. 3116 N. Costan Hwy., Ste. 101

Kellogg and Evans, P.A.
(See Manteo)

Lloyd, Benita A., (BV) .... '63 '87 C.838 B.A. L.1228 J.D. [Gray&L.]

Vincent Law Firm, The, PC
(See Southern Shores)

KING, 5,952, *Forsyth & Stokes Cos.*

Bennett, Michael R., (BV) .... '61 '89 C.577 B.S. L.896 J.D. [Stover&B.]
Browder, J. Tyrone, (BV) .... '45 '74 C&L.575 B.S., J.D. [J.T.Browder]
Browder, J. Tyrone, P.A., (BV) .... 153-A Jefferson Church Rd.
Carter, Clarence W., Jr. .... '32 '64 C&L.575 A.B., LL.B. Sr. Res. Supr. Ct. J.
Cromer, Anderson D. .... '53 '82 C&L.896 B.A., J.D. Supr. Ct. J.
McGrath, John L., (BV) .... '65 '92 C.423 B.A. L.904 J.D. 153 Jefferson Church Rd.
O'Neal, Elizabeth M., (BV) .... '54 '79 C&L.575 B.A., J.D. 201 E. King St.
Stover, Richard E., (AV) .... '39 '64 C.125 A.B. L.896 J.D. [⊡ Stover&B.]
Stover & Bennett, (BV) .... 607-D South Main Street
West, R. Brandon .... '77 '02 C.575 B.A. L.896 J.D. [⊡ Stover&B.]

KINGS MOUNTAIN, 9,693, *Cleveland & Gaston Cos.*

Cloninger, E. Scott, (BV) .... '48 '74 C&L.575 A.B., J.D. [Cloninger&N.]
Cloninger & Neisler, (BV) .... P.O. Box 515
Corry, Clayward C., Jr., (BV) .... '50 '76 C&L.574 B.A., J.D. 117 S. Battleground Ave.
Hoyle, J. Charles '52 '94 C.1070 B.S. L.408 J.D.
(adm. in CA; not adm. in NC) 207 Hoyle's Rd.

Hullender, David Mark, (BV) '62 '89 C.575 B.A. L.574 J.D.
235 S. Battleground Avenue, 28086
Telephone: 704-739-2965 Fax: 704-739-2966
Email: Hullylaw@bellsouth.net URL: http://www.hullenderlaw.com
General Practice, Traffic Violations, Driving While Intoxicated, Real Estate, Family Law, Divorce, Wills, Probate.
See Professional Biographies, KINGS MOUNTAIN, NORTH CAROLINA

Luptak, Richard J., (BV) .... '60 '88 C.848 B.A. L.1187 J.D. 117 S. Battleground Ave.
Neisler, C. Andrew, Jr., (BV) .... '52 '77 C.198 A.B. L.790 J.D. [Cloninger&N.]
Thomasson, George B., (BV) .... '24 '52 C.198 B.S. L.228 J.D. 110 W. Mountain St.

KINSTON, * 23,688, *Lenoir Co.*

Amodeo, Nancy F. .... '67 '95 C.1350 B.A. L.107 J.D. 2170 Autumn Dr.
Archie, John C., (AV) .... '51 '78 C.575 B.A. L.192 J.D. [White&A.]
Archie, Richard J., (BV) .... '67 '91 C&L.575 B.A., J.D. [White&A.]
Barwick, P. C., Jr., (AV) .... '37 '61 C&L.896 B.A., LL.B. [Wallace,M.B.L.&S.]
Beam, Martha B., (CV) .... '49 '88 C.575 B.A. L.1228 J.D. 131 S. Queen St.
Beech, Harvey E., (BV) .... '24 '52 C.511 A.B. L.575 LL.B. 308 S. Queen St.
Bower, Joseph Sidney, (BV) .... '51 '79 C.575 B.A. L.192 J.D. [White&A.]
Boyd, Delaina Davis .... '74 '99 C.576 B.S. L.1228 J.D. [White&A.] ⊙

Brantley, J. Christopher, (BV) '66 '93 C.232 B.A. L.1345 J.D.
[Brantley,J.R.H.&H.] ⊙

Brantley, Jenkins, Riddle, Hardee & Hardee, (BV)
2506 Herritage Street, Suite A, 28501 ⊙
Telephone: 252-522-1500 Fax: 252-522-0556 URL: http://www.bjrhhlawyers.com
URL: http://www.bjrhhatty.com
J. Christopher Brantley.
Personal Injury, Wrongful Death, Motor Vehicle Automobile Accidents, Head and Spinal Injury, Nursing Home Abuse and Neglect, Workers Compensation, Insurance, Products Liability, Social Security Disability, Medical Malpractice.
Goldsboro, North Carolina Office: 601 North Spence Avenue, 27534. Telephone: 919-778-9700. Fax: 919-778-1938.
Greenville, North Carolina Office: 202 East Arlington Boulevard, P.O. Box 924, 27858. Telephone: 252-355-1998. Fax: 252-321-2948.
Jacksonville, North Carolina Office: 901 Hargett Street, P.O. Box 7070, 28540. Telephone: 910-455-5599. Fax: 910-455-7191.
See Professional Biographies, KINSTON, NORTH CAROLINA

Brumbaugh, Mu & King, P.A., (BV)
414 South Queen Street, 28501 ⊙
Telephone: 252-939-1800
URL: http://www.bmklaw.net
Kenneth W. King, Jr.
Practice Limited to Injury Cases. Automobile, Wrongful Death, Medical Malpractice, Workers' Compensation, Products Liability and Social Security Claims.
See Professional Biographies, KINSTON, NORTH CAROLINA

Burch Law Office
(See Greenville)

Cleavenger, Paul T., (CV) .... '45 '89 C.174 B.S. L.900 J.D. [Cleavenger]
Cleavenger Law Firm, The, P.C., (CV) .... 127 S. Queen Street
Coley, William C., III .... '52 '81 C.575 B.A. L.1228 J.D. [Wooten&C.]
Connor, Kimberly A. .... '77 '02 C.210 B.A. L.879 J.D. [⊡ Wallace,M.B.L.&S.]
Cowper, Albert W. .... '11 '34 C&L.575 LL.B. Ret. Supr. Ct. J.
Duke, David R., (BV) .... '51 '77 C&L.896 B.A., J.D. [R.Duke]
Duke, Rod, Attorney at Law, (BV) .... 110 S. Queen St., Ste. 108-109
Durant, Joretta, (BV) .... '55 '80 C.575 L.245 J.D. 207 S. Queen St.
Fillippeli, David J., Jr., (BV) .... '60 '85 C.576 B.A. L.575 J.D. [White&A.] ⊙
Floyd, Gregory E. .... '76 '02 C.685 B.A. L.1228 J.D. [White&A.]
Foster, Allen C., II .... '62 '91 C.576 B.A. L.1339 J.D. [Gerrans,F.&S.]
Gerrans, William W. .... '56 '82 C&L.575 B.S.B.A., J.D. [Gerrans,F.&S.]
Gerrans, Foster & Sargeant, P.A., (BV) .... 109 E. Gordon Street
Griffin, Robert W., (BV) .... '52 '77 C&L.575 A.B., J.D. [Griffin&G.]
Griffin & Griffin, (BV) .... 213 E. Gordon St.
Harrison, Fred W., (BV) .... '30 '56 C.232 B.S. L.575 J.D. [Harrison&S.] ‡
Harrison and Simpson, P.A., (BV) .... 1331 Rusty Lee Rd.
Henderson, Sherwood C. .... '70 '96 C.198 B.A. L.1228 J.D. [White&A.]
Herring, J. Mark .... '74 '00 C.576 B.A. L.192 J.D. [White&A.]
Hooten, John R., (AV) .... '35 '63 C.575 B.S. L.896 J.D. [White&A.]
Hoover, Payton D. .... '71 '03 C.575 B.A. L.1228 J.D. [⊡ Wallace,M.B.L.&S.]

Jenkins, George L., Jr., (BV) '52 '82 C.575 B.A. L.1228 J.D.
111 East Gordon Street, P.O. Box 303, 28502-0303
Telephone: 252-523-4000 Fax: 252-523-0980
Email: kinstonlawyer@mac.com URL: http://www.lawyers.com/georgejenkins
Real Estate, Traffic Tickets, Divorce, Adoption, Real Estate Acquisition and Real Estate Foreclosure.
See Professional Biographies, KINSTON, NORTH CAROLINA

Johnsey, C. Gray, (AV) .... '49 '78 C.575 B.A. L.192 J.D. [White&A.]
Johnson, E. Wyles, Jr. .... '56 '02 C.1083 B.S. L.1228 J.D. [White&A.]
King, Kenneth W., Jr., (BV) ...... '61 '86 C.575 B.S. L.469 J.D. [Brumbaugh,M.&K.] ⊙
Landis, Richard F., II, (BV) .... '48 '73 C.125 A.B. L.896 J.D. [Wallace,M.B.L.&S.]
Llewellyn, James D. (Lew) .... '40 '69 C&L.575 B.S., J.D. Courthouse‡
Manning, William E., Jr., (BV) .... '66 '91 C&L.575 B.S.B.A., J.D. [White&A.] ⊙
Marshall, John P., (BV) .... '62 '89 C&L.1228 B.A., J.D. Tands, Inc.
McNairy, John O. '48 '74 C&L.575 B.S., J.D.
(adm. in GA; not adm. in NC) V.P., L. Harvey & Son Co.
McRae, John A., Jr., (BV) .... '17 '40 C&L.575 B.A., LL.B. P.O. Box 704
Morris, Thomas H., (AV) .... '36 '63 C&L.896 B.A., LL.B. [Wallace,M.B.L.&S.]
Parrott, Marion A., (BV) .... '18 '47 C.152 B.A. L.575 LL.B. P.O. Box 3547
Pate, Imelda J., (BV) .... '59 '83 C.576 B.A. L.1228 J.D. Asst. Dist. Atty.
Perry, Barbara S. .... '26 '50 C.99 A.B. L.575 LL.B. [⊡ Perry,P.&P.] ‡
Perry, Dan E., (BV) .... '31 '59 C&L.575 B.S., LL.B. [Perry,P.&P.]
Perry, James Stockton, (BV) .... '55 '80 C&L.575 B.S., J.D. [Perry,P.&P.]
Perry, Warren S., (BV) .... '24 '50 C&L.575 A.B., LL.B. [Perry,P.&P.]
Perry, Perry & Perry, (BV) .... 518 Plaza Blvd.
Rochelle, Vernon H., (AV) .... '38 '65 C.228 A.B. L.575 LL.B. City Atty.
Rodgman, Paul A., (AV) .... '50 '76 C.228 B.A. L.575 J.D. [Whitley,R.&W.]
Rogerson, Christopher Alan, (CV) .... '71 '97 C&L.1228 B.A., J.D. 518 Plaza Blvd.

Rose Rand Attorneys, P.A.
(See Wilson)

Sargeant, Jonathon L., (BV) .... '67 '92 C&L.575 B.S.B.A., J.D. [Gerrans,F.&S.]
Simpson, William F., Jr., (BV) .... '45 '75 C.575 A.B. L.616 J.D. [Harrison&S.]

Smith and Strickland, PLLC
(See Goldsboro)

Stearns, Richard M., (AV) .... '48 '81 C.871 B.S. L.64 J.D. P.O. Box 2218
Stroud, Stuart L., (BV) .... '67 '92 C.575 B.A. L.1228 J.D. [Wallace,M.B.L.&S.]
Sullivan, Matthew S., (BV) .... '68 '95 C.1090 B.S. L.1228 J.D. [White&A.]

Sumrell, Sugg, Carmichael, Hicks & Hart, P.A.
(See New Bern)

Vincent, Charles R. .... '34 '63 C&L.575 A.B., LL.B. 1903 Pawnee Dr.‡
Wallace, Fitzhugh E., Jr., (AV) ...... '17 '49 C.575 L.896 LL.B. [Wallace,M.B.L.&S.] ‡

Wallace, Morris, Barwick, Landis & Stroud, P.A., (AV) ⊞
131 South Queen Street, P.O. Box 3557, 28502-3557
Telephone: 252-523-2000 Fax: 252-523-0408
URL: http://www.wmbattorneys.com
Fitzhugh E. Wallace, Jr. (Retired); Thomas H. Morris; P. C. Barwick, Jr.; Richard F. Landis, II; Stuart L. Stroud;—Kimberly A. Connor; Payton D. Hoover.
General Civil and Trial Practice in all State and Federal Courts. Aviation, Banking, Corporate Law, Insurance, Personal Injury, Probate, Product Liability, Real Estate and Taxation.
Representative Clients: Branch Banking & Trust Co.; E.I. du Pont De Nemours & Co., Inc.; First Citizens Bank & Trust Co.; City of Kinston; Kinston Daily Free Press Co.
Insurance Clients: Nationwide Mutual Insurance Co.; State Farm Insurance Cos.; USAA Insurance Co.
See Professional Biographies, KINSTON, NORTH CAROLINA

Ward and Smith, P.A.
(See New Bern)

White, Thomas J., III, (AV) .... '41 '66 C&L.575 B.A., LL.B. [White&A.]

White & Allen, P.A., (AV)
106 South McLewean Street, P.O. Box 3169, 28501 ⊙
Telephone: 252-527-8000 Telecopier: 252-527-8128
Email: law@whiteandallen.com URL: http://www.whiteandallen.com
Thomas J. White (1903-1991); William A. Allen, Jr. (1920-2001); John R. Hooten; John C. Archie; C. Gray Johnsey (Board Certified Specialist in Estate Planning and Probate Law, North Carolina State Board of Legal Specialization); Joseph Sidney Bower; David J. Fillippeli, Jr.; Matthew S. Sullivan; Sherwood C. Henderson; Richard J. Archie; William E. Manning, Jr. (Board Certified Specialist in Real Property Law-Residential Transactions, North Carolina State Board of Legal Specialization); Delaina Davis Boyd; Thomas J. White, III; J. Mark Herring; E. Wyles Johnson, Jr.; Gregory E. Floyd.
General Civil Practice in all State and Federal Courts. Personal Injury, Automobile Accidents, Wrongful Death, Insurance, Real Estate, Corporation, Taxation, Commercial, Trusts and Estates, Wills and Probate.
Special Counsel for: Southern Railway Co.
Representative Clients: Carolina Power & Light Co.; First American Savings Bank; Kinston Housing Authority; First Citizens Bank & Trust Co.; Wachovia Bank of North Carolina, N.A.; NationsBank, N.A.; Kemper National Group; Hampton Industries, Inc.
Snow Hill, North Carolina Office: 109 S.E. Second Street. 28580. Telephone: 252-747-5152. Telecopier: 252-747-4657. Email: law@whiteandallen.com.
See Professional Biographies, KINSTON, NORTH CAROLINA

Whitley, Robert E., (AV) '49 '74 C.232 B.S.B.A. L.896 J.D. [Whitley,R.&W.] (⊙Greenville, Jacksonville, Raleigh)
Whitley, Robert E., Jr., (BV) '69 '95 C.34 B.A. L.1228 J.D. [Whitley,R.&W.] (⊙New Bern)

Whitley, Rodgman & Whitley, (AV)
2902-B North Herritage Street, P.O. Box 5309, 28503-5309 ⊙
Telephone: 252-523-3000 Fax: 252-523-3433 URL: http://www.wrwlaw.com
Email: rew@wrwlaw.com URL: http://www.whitleyrodgmanwhitley.com
Partners: Robert E. Whitley; Paul A. Rodgman; Robert E. Whitley, Jr.;—Benjamin H. Whitley (Resident, Raleigh Office); Brian E. Clemmons (Resident, Raleigh Office); Juan A. Flores (Resident, Raleigh Office).
Personal Injury, Wrongful Death, Workers' Compensation, Social Security Disability, Nursing Home Negligence.
New Bern, North Carolina Office: 701 McCarthy Boulevard, P.O. Box 12550. Telephone: 252-633-6601. Fax: 252-635-6621.
Raleigh, North Carolina Office: 3605 Glenwood Avenue, Suite 350. Telephone: 919-785-5000. Fax: 919-785-3729.
Jacksonville, North Carolina Office: 200 Valencia Drive, Suite 101. Telephone: 910-219-1000. Fax: 910-219-1111.
Greenville, North Carolina Office: 1702-A E. Arlington Boulevard, Suite 100. Telephone: 252-353-5500. Fax: 252-352-0405.
See Professional Biographies, KINSTON, NORTH CAROLINA

Willey, Ralph G., P.A.
(See Rocky Mount)

Williams, Rose Vaughn .... '64 '90 C&L.575 B.S., J.D. Dist. Ct. J.
Wooten, Dal F., III, Law Office of, (BV) '57 '82 C.575 B.S.B.A. L.1228 J.D. P.O. Box 2163
Wooten, Everette L., Jr., (BV) .... '43 '67 C&L.575 B.S., J.D. [Wooten&C.]
Wooten & Coley, (BV) .... 600 Plaza Blvd.
Worthington, Elizabeth P., (CV) .... '53 '78 C&L.575 B.S., J.D. [Perry,P.&P.]

KITTY HAWK, 2,991, *Dare Co.*

Alexy, James A. .... '38 '64 C.645 B.S. L.884 LL.B. 4713 N. Croatan Hwy.

Alexy, Fletcher, Wills & Wills, P.C.
(See Point Harbor)

Archbell, Roy A., Jr., (AV) '49 '74 C&L.896 B.A., J.D.
12 Juniper Trail Center, P.O. Box 57, 27949
Telephone: 252-261-7555 Fax: 252-261-6444
Email: archbell.roy@earthlink.net URL: http://www.lawyers.com/archbell
General Civil Trial Practice in State and Federal Courts. Family, Personal Injury, Collection, Corporate, Construction, Insurance, Real Estate, Domestic Relations, Divorce.
See Professional Biographies, KITTY HAWK, NORTH CAROLINA

Birkhead, G. William, (AVⓉ) '41 '66 C.999 B.S. L.893 LL.B. [Vandeventer B.] (⊙Raleigh, NC; Norfolk, VA)
Booth, Wyatt M. .... '— '01 C.576 B.S.C.E. L.902 J.D. [🄰 Vandeventer B.] (⊙Raleigh)
Buckius, Dean T., (AVⓉ) .... '59 '84 C.945 B.A. L.896 J.D. [Vandeventer B.] ⊙

DeVeau, Ronald E., P.C.
(See Nags Head)

Evans, Jeanine C., (BV) .... '70 '95 C.575 B.A. L.1345 J.D. [Sharp,M.O.&G.]
Fenstermaker, Norman K. '21 '50 C&L.608 B.S., LL.D. (adm. in OH; not adm. in NC) 51 Deer Path Lane‡
Ferrell, David P. '71 '96 C.575 B.A. L.1228 J.D. [🄰 Vandeventer B.] (⊙Raleigh, NC; Norfolk, VA)
Frank, Terry C. '73 '03 C.890 B.A. L.692 J.D. [🄰 Vandeventer B.] (⊙Raleigh, NC; Norfolk, VA)
Gaw, John G., Jr., (BV) ...... '45 '71 C.673 B.S. L.790 J.D. 5121 North Croatan Highway
Genzler, Patrick A. '49 '78 C.886 B.S. L.945 J.D. [Vandeventer B.] (⊙Raleigh, NC; Norfolk, VA)
Graf, Richard J. '23 '50 C.299 A.B. L.309 LL.B. (adm. in NY; not adm. in NC) 4024 Martins Point Rd.‡
Graham, John C., III, (BV) .... '60 '85 C.576 B.A. L.469 J.D. [Sharp,M.O.&G.]
Guy, Richard S., (BVⓉ) '51 '82 C.197 A.B. L.893 J.D. [Vandeventer B.] (⊙Raleigh, NC; Norfolk, VA)
Herman, Patrick W., (AVⓉ) '52 '82 C.886 B.A. L.945 J.D. [Vandeventer B.] (⊙Raleigh, NC; Norfolk, VA)

Hornthal, Riley, Ellis & Maland, L.L.P.
(See Elizabeth City)

Khoury, Daniel D., (AV) .... '50 '77 C.608 B.S.Ed. L.896 J.D. [Vandeventer B.]
Lenard, Lynette B. .... '49 '82 C.575 B.S. L.30 J.D. 4021 Creek Road
Logan, Leonard G., Jr., (CV) .... '37 '62 C&L.228 A.B., LL.B. P.O. Box 470
Lowenstein, Neil S., (BVⓉ) '63 '89 C.885 B.A. L.692 J.D. [Vandeventer B.] (⊙Raleigh, NC; Norfolk, VA)
MacIver, Byrnn L. '52 '79 C.860 B.A. L.1292 J.D. (adm. in PA; not adm. in NC) P.O. Box 8308
Michael, Steven D., (BV) .... '49 '75 C.232 B.S. L.575 J.D. [Sharp,M.O.&G.]

Moore Law Firm, The, P.C.
(See Manns Harbor)

Norcross, Angelea C., (BV) '59 '90 C.893 B.A. L.1209 J.D. 4425 North Croatan Highway
O'Donnell, Robert L., (AVⓉ) '46 '75 C.812 B.S. L.893 J.D. [Vandeventer B.] (⊙Raleigh, NC; Norfolk, VA)
Outten, Robert L., (BV) .... '56 '82 C.575 B.S.B.A. L.896 J.D. [Sharp,M.O.&G.]
Powers, Edward J., (BVⓉ) '65 '90 C.886 B.A. L.692 J.D. [Vandeventer B.] (⊙Raleigh, NC; Norfolk, VA)
Reeves, Michael C. .... '47 '73 C.673 B.A. L.896 J.D. [Sharp,M.O.&G.]
Russotto, David S. .... '62 '87 C.1365 B.A. L.896 J.D. 3512 North Croatan Highway
Sharp, Starkey, (BV) .... '52 '77 C.809 B.B.A. L.228 J.D. [Sharp,M.O.&G.]

Sharp, Michael, Outten and Graham, (BV)
4417 North Croatan Highway, P.O. Drawer 1027, 27949
Telephone: 252-261-2126 Fax: 252-261-1188
URL: http://www.lawyers.com/smo&glaw
Members of Firm: Starkey Sharp; Steven D. Michael; Robert L. Outten; John C. Graham, III; Jeanine C. Evans; Michael C. Reeves.
General Civil and Criminal Practice, Commercial and Residential Real Estate, Municipal and Administrative, Family and Domestic Relations, Personal Injury, Probate, Banking, Corporations, Traffic, Driving While Intoxicated, Mediation, Arbitration, Ship Documentation, Estate Planning, Elder Law.
Approved Attorneys for: Lawyers Title Insurance Corp.; Chicago Title Insurance Co.; The Title Guarantee Co.; American Title Insurance Co.; First Title Insurance Co.; United Title Insurance Co.
See Professional Biographies, KITTY HAWK, NORTH CAROLINA

Shearin, Norman W., Jr., (AV) .... '45 '71 [Vandeventer B.]

Shearin, Norman W., Jr.
(See Vandeventer Black LLP, Norfolk, Virginia)

Smallwood, Gerald E. '29 '61 C.885 B.S. L.902 J.D. (adm. in VA; not adm. in NC) P.O. Box 1131‡
Trivette, Robert P., (BV) '56 '89 C.999 B.A. L.575 J.D. [🄰 Vandeventer B.] (⊙Raleigh, NC; Norfolk, VA)

Vandeventer Black LLP, (AV)
Southern Shores Law Building, 6 Juniper Trail, P.O. Box 1042, 27949 ⊙
Telephone: 252-261-5055 Facsimile: 252-261-8444
Email: nshearin@vanblk.com URL: http://www.vanblk.com
Partners: G. William Birkhead; Dean T. Buckius; Patrick A. Genzler; Richard S. Guy; Patrick W. Herman; Daniel D. Khoury (Board Certified Specialists in Real Property Law-Business, Commercial and Industrial Transactions); Neil S. Lowenstein; Robert L. O'Donnell; Edward J. Powers; Norman W. Shearin, Jr. (Board Certified Specialist in Real Property Law- Business, Commercial and Industrial Transactions, North Carolina State Board of Legal Specialization). Associates: Wyatt M. Booth; David P. Ferrell; Terry C. Frank (Resident, Kitty Hawk, North Carolina Office); Robert P. Trivette.
Admiralty, Arbitration and Mediation, Aviation, Banking, Bankruptcy and Creditors' Rights, Commercial Transactions, Community Associations, Construction Law, Environmental Law, Estate Planning, General Litigation in State and Federal Courts, Government/Public Contracts, Health Care Law, Immigration Law, International, Intellectual Property, Insurance Defense, Labor and Employment Law, Land Use, Local Government/Municipal Law, Malpractice, Maritime, Mergers and Acquisitions, Products Liability, Public Utilities, Real Estate, Taxation, Technology, Workers' Compensation.
Norfolk, Virginia Office: 500 World Trade Center, 23510-1699. Telephone: 757-446-8600. Telecopier: 757-446-8670.
Richmond, Virginia Office: Eighth & Main Building, 707 East Main Street, P.O. Box 1558, 23218-1558. Telephone: 804-237-8800. Fax: 804-237-8801.
Roanoke Island, North Carolina Office: 305 Essex Square, Sir Walter Raleigh Street. Telephone: 252-473-1888. Fax: 252-261-5374.
London, England Office: Blackwell House, 23 Guildhall Yard, EC2V 5AE. Telephone: 011 44 020 7917 6053. Facsimile: 011 44 020 7917 6054.
Raleigh, North Carolina Office: Two Hannover Square, Suite 1530, 434 Fayetteville Street Mall, P.O. Box 2599. Telephone: 919-754-1171. Fax: 919-754-1317.
See Professional Biographies, KITTY HAWK, NORTH CAROLINA

Vincent Law Firm, The, PC
(See Southern Shores)

Wills, J. Robert .... '31 '58 4425 N. Croatan Hwy.

KNIGHTDALE, 5,958, *Wake Co.*

Davis & McCabe, P.A.
(See Raleigh)

Doyle, Glenn S., (CV) .... '71 '98 C.232 B.S. L.1228 J.D. [Doyle&D.]
Doyle, Henry M., (BV) .... '69 '95 C.575 B.A. L.574 J.D. [Doyle&D.]
Doyle & Doyle, LLP, (BV) .... 100 S. Smithfield Road
Young, Lavette H. .... '65 '92 C&L.101 B.A., J.D. 1132 Amber Acres Lane

KURE BEACH, 1,573, *New Hanover Co.*

Bell, W. Dan .... '42 '76 C.174 B.A. L.966 J.D. 206 K Ave., Ste. 205‡

LA GRANGE, 2,805, *Lenoir Co.*

Mooring, Thomas D., Jr., (BV) .... '41 '71 C&L.575 B.A., J.D. P.O. Box 158

LAKE LURE, 1,027, *Rutherford Co.*

Doti, Joseph E. '15 '37 C.563 L.262 LL.B. (adm. in NY; not adm. in NC) P.O. Box 195
Fuleihan, Neville S., (BV) '31 '89 C.165 B.A. L.1338 J.D. 115 Bent Creek Blvd., Ste. 18
Kaufman, Robert E. '30 '58 C.575 B.S. L.569 LL.B. (adm. in NY; not adm. in NC) Route 1‡
Weisgerber, Robert G. '45 '69 C.913 B.A. L.259 J.D. (adm. in PA; not adm. in NC) RR 1‡

LAKE TOXAWAY, —, *Transylvania Co.*

Battista, Peter L., Jr. '35 '59 C.976 B.A. L.178 LL.B. (adm. in NY; not adm. in NC) Lake Toxaway Country Club‡

LANDIS, 2,996, *Rowan Co.*

Corriher, James A., (BV) .... '45 '80 C.1128 B.S. L.1228 J.D. [Corriher&K.] ⊙
Corriher & Koontz, (BV) .... 101 S. Central Ave. (⊙Salisbury)

LAUREL PARK, 1,835, *Henderson Co.*

Coira, Charles F., Jr., (AV) .... '23 '46 C&L.575 A.B., LL.B. 300 Roberts Dr.‡

LAURINBURG, * 15,874, *Scotland Co.*

Baker, Debbie Goronet
(See Raeford)

Berwick, Roy William '48 '80 C.627 B.G.S. L.190 J.D. (adm. in NE; not adm. in NC) 408 Avery St.‡

Britt, William S., Law Offices of
(See Lumberton)

Bruner, Jerry L., (BV) .... '61 '86 C.232 B.S. L.1228 J.D. [Moser,G.B.&W.]
Bruner, Leslie M. .... '61 '86 C.198 B.A. L.1228 J.D. 12361 Olde Farm Circle

Daniel, John R., Law Office of
(See Rockingham)

Dean, Daniel B., (AV) .... '47 '75 C.198 B.S. L.575 J.D. [Williamson,D.W.&S.]
Ellis, B. Craig .... '41 '70 C.893 B.S.Ed. L.575 J.D. Supr. Ct. J.
Etheridge, Kennieth S., (AV) '36 '60 C&L.896 B.S., LL.B. 600 E. South Main Street, Suite E‡
Floyd, William P., Jr., (BV) .... '64 '94 C.575 B.A. L.896 J.D. [Gordon,H.H.&F.]

Garner, Terry R., (AV) .... '47 '72 C&L.575 A.B., J.D. [Moser,G.B.&W.]
Gordon, J. Robert, (AV) .... '39 '64 C.198 B.A. L.575 J.D. [Gordon,H.H.&F.]

Gordon, Horne, Hicks and Floyd, P.A., (AV)
609 South Atkinson Street, P.O. Box 587, 28352
Telephone: 910-276-7825 Fax: 910-277-8430
URL: http://www.lawyers.com/ghandhlaw
J. Robert Gordon; John H. Horne, Jr.; Charles L. Hicks, Jr.; William P. Floyd, Jr.
General, Civil and Criminal Trial Practice, Probate, Corporation, Real Estate, Personal Injury, Estate Planning, Social Security Disability, Workers' Compensation and Family Law.
Representative Clients: Southern National Bank; First Southern Savings and Loan Assn.; City of Laurinburg; Travelers Insurance Co.; Carolina Power and Light Co.
Approved Attorneys for: Lawyers Title Insurance Corp.; First Title Insurance Co.; United Title Insurance Co.
References: Southern National Bank of North Carolina; First Southern Savings & Loan Assn.
See Professional Biographies, LAURINBURG, NORTH CAROLINA

Griffin Law Office
(See Red Springs)

Griswold, Lisa D., (BV) .... '66 '92 C&L.575 B.A., J.D. [Purcell&G.]
Hicks, Charles L., Jr., (BV) .... '56 '81 C&L.575 A.B., J.D. [Gordon,H.H.&F.]
Horne, John H., Jr., (AV) .... '46 '72 C&L.575 A.B., J.D. [Gordon,H.H.&F.]
Johnston, Edward H., Jr., (BV) .... '51 '76 C.198 B.A. L.896 J.D. Co. Atty.

Jones, Greg, & Associates, P.A.
(See Wilmington)

Mason, James W., (AV) .... '16 '38 C&L.896 LL.B. 213-E East Cronly Street
McIlwain, William C., III .... '51 '77 C.198 B.A. L.896 J.D. Dist. J.
McInnis, Jonathan L., (CV) .... '71 '98 C.896 B.A. L.1345 J.D. 303B Atkinson St.
McRae, W. Philip, (BV) .... '54 '81 C.1317 B.A. L.574 J.D. 138 S. Main St.
Moser, William F., (AV) .... '42 '67 C&L.896 B.A., J.D. [Moser,G.B.&W.]

Moser, Garner, Bruner & Wansker, P.A., (AV)
600 E. South Main Street, Suite E, P.O. Box 1827, 28353-1827
Telephone: 910-276-2631 Fax: 910-276-0326
Email: emgbw@carolina.net URL: http://www.lawyers.com/emgblaw
William F. Moser; Terry R. Garner; Jerry L. Bruner. Of Counsel: Henry B. Wansker.
General Civil and Criminal Trial Practice, Insurance, Social Security, Disability Law, Workers Compensation, Administrative, Corporate Law, Commercial and Residential Real Estate, Probate Law, Personal Injury and Negligence Litigation, Family Law, Motor Vehicle Law.
Representative Clients: First Union National Bank of North Carolina; Jasper Textiles, Inc.; Laurinburg-Maxton Airport Commission; Scotland Container, Inc.; Wachovia Bank, N.A.
See Professional Biographies, LAURINBURG, NORTH CAROLINA

Purcell, William R., II, (AV) .... '60 '85 C.198 B.A. L.575 J.D. [Purcell&G.]

Purcell & Griswold, LLP, (AV) BB
210 West Cronly Street, P.O. Box 1567, 28353
Telephone: 910-277-1980 Fax: 910-277-1480
URL: http://www.purcellandgriswold.com
William R. Purcell, II; Lisa D. Griswold.
General Civil and Criminal Litigation, Health Care, Criminal Law, Traffic Violations, Personal Injury, Real Estate, Business Law, Wills and Estates.
See Professional Biographies, LAURINBURG, NORTH CAROLINA

Rhue, Christopher Windly, (CV) .... '71 '96 C.953 B.A. L.192 J.D. Dist. Atty. Off.
Sojka, Nickolas J., Jr., (BV) .... '62 '87 C.945 B.A. L.893 J.D. [Williamson,D.W.&S.]

Vaughan, Christopher V., The Law Offices of
(See Raeford)

Wansker, Henry B., (AV) '52 '78
C.575 B.A. L.896 J.D. [⊡ Moser,G.B.&W.] (©Salt Lake City, UT)
Williamson, Andrew G., (AV) .... '25 '50 C&L.575 LL.B. [⊡ Williamson,D.W.&S.] ‡
Williamson, Andrew G., Jr., (BV) '58 '84 C.575 B.A. L.896 J.D.
[Williamson,D.W.&S.]

Williamson, Dean, Williamson & Sojka, L.L.P., (AV) BB
213C East Cronly Street, P.O. Box 1627, 28353
Telephone: 910-276-8082 Fax: 910-276-1011
URL: http://www.williamsondean.com
Andrew G. Williamson (Retired). Members of Firm: Daniel B. Dean; Andrew G. Williamson, Jr.; Nickolas J. Sojka, Jr.
General Civil and Criminal Practice. Real Estate, Business Law, Probate, Workers Compensation, Personal Injury, Traffic, Education, Labor and Employment, Construction and Family Law. Trials in all Courts.
Counsel for: Scotland County Board of Education; Hoke County Board of Education; Laurinburg Housing Authority; Kordsa USA, Inc.; InterKordsa, Inc.
Representative Clients: St. Andrews Presbyterian College; The Morgan Co.; McCarter Electrical Co.; Cooper Petroleum, Inc.; McArthur Construction Company; GMAC/Integon Insurance Co.
See Professional Biographies, LAURINBURG, NORTH CAROLINA

Wood, Christopher M., Law Office of, (CV) '57 '94
C.956 B.A. L.1339 J.D. 124 East Cronly Street

LEAKSVILLE, —, *Rockingham Co.*

(See Eden)

LELAND, 1,938, *Brunswick Co.*

Barnhardt, Zeb E., Jr., (AV) ...... '41 '69 C.228 A.B. L.880 J.D. 1158 Willow Pond Lane

Mako & Associates, P.A.
(See Wilmington)

Peterson, Robert G., (CV) '54 '82 C&L.575 B.A., J.D.
10089 N. Olde Towne Wynd S.E.

LENOIR, * 14,192, *Caldwell Co.*

Baumberger, Michael P., (BV) .... '46 '73 C.925 B.A. L.362 J.D. 108 Mulberry St. NW
Beach, Benjamin .... '— '49 511 Mountain View St.‡
Beach, N. Douglas, Jr., (BV) .... '61 '88 C.575 B.A. L.896 J.D. [Beach]
Beach, Neil D., (BV) .... '42 '67 C&L.575 A.B., J.D. [Beach]
Beach Law Offices, (BV) .... 226 Mulberry St., N.W.
Beal, Beverly T. .... '47 '74 C&L.896 B.A., J.D. Supr. Ct. J.
Blair, Edward H., Jr., (BV) .... '— '78 C.575 A.B. L.790 J.D. [Groome,T.P.&B.]
Brady, Charles A., III, (BV) .... '55 '81 C.575 B.A. L.896 J.D. [Todd,V.&B.]
Brady, Robert M. .... '49 '74 C&L.896 B.A., J.D. Dist. Ct. J.
Cannon, Bruce L., (BV) .... '50 '76 C&L.575 B.S., J.D. [Cannon&C.]
Cannon & Correll, P.A., (BV) .... 132 Main Street, NW
Carpenter, Walter T., Jr., (AV) .... '21 '49 C.896 B.A. L.309 J.D. 101 Willow St.‡
Clark, Macon A., P.A. .... '52 '93 C.999 B.A. L.362 J.D. Asst. State Atty.
Correll, J. Michael, (BV) .... '47 '73 C&L.575 A.B., J.D. [Cannon&C.]
Correll, Michael David .... '77 '03 C.34 B.S. L.1339 J.D. [Cannon&C.]

Dark, L. Talton, III
(See Morganton)

Delk, Joseph C., III, (BV) .... '50 '76 C.198 B.A. L.575 J.D. 1002 West Ave.
Dobbin, Charles E. .... '27 '82 C.575 B.S. L.896 J.D. Pres., Caldwell Savings Bk.
Douglas, Ted S., (CV) .... '32 '66 C.404 A.B. L.128 LL.B. 215 Main St., N.W.

Eaker & Fulkerson, PC
(See Hickory)

Elliott, J. Bryan
(See Hickory)

Groome, H. Houston, Jr., (AV) .... '— '65 C.228 A.B. L.575 LL.B. [Groome,T.P.&B.]

Groome, Tuttle, Pike & Blair, (AV)
210 Ridge Street, N.W., P.O. Box 776, 28645
Telephone: 828-758-0141 Fax: 828-758-5326
Members of Firm: H. Houston Groome, Jr.; Carroll D. Tuttle; Fred D. Pike; Edward H. Blair, Jr.
Representative Client: CCB Savings Bank.
See Professional Biographies, LENOIR, NORTH CAROLINA

Hebel, Linda G., (CV) .... '43 '74 C.188 A.B. L.30 J.D. 215 Main St., N.W.

Helton, Lyndon R., PLLC
(See Hickory)

Holloway, Richard S. .... '70 '95 C.577 L.1228 J.D. Asst. Dist. Atty.
Jud, Austen D. .... '72 '97 C.576 B.A. L.1228 J.D. P.O. Box 1050
Keller, Dewey L., (BV) .... '47 '82 C.1222 B.S. L.1206 J.D. P.O. Box 2437
Lackey, David S., (BV) .... '54 '81 C.228 B.A. L.575 J.D. [Wilson,L.&R.]
McCarl, Lucy R., (BV) .... '58 '89 C.140 B.A. L.896 J.D. 223-A Main Street, NW
Pearce, Herbert H., (BV) .... '49 '78 C.925 B.A. L.575 J.D. 814 Harper Ave., S.W.
Pearce, Shelley Ryan .... '72 '01 C.925 B.A. L.1228 J.D. 814 Harper Ave.
Pike, Fred D., (BV) .... '— '79 C.152 B.A. L.790 J.D. [Groome,T.P.&B.]
Pope, W. Darrell, (BV) .... '53 '86 C.48 B.A. L.574 J.D. State Dept. of Soc. Servs.
Potter, Steve B., (BV) .... '62 '88 C.575 B.A. L.1345 J.D. 622 West Ave. N.W.
Robbins, Robert J., Jr., (BV) .... '50 '76 C.575 A.B. L.574 J.D. P.O. Box 718
Rohr, Timothy J., (BV) .... '69 '94 C&L.575 B.A., J.D. [Wilson,L.&R.]
Todd, James R., Jr., (AV) .... '20 '51 C&L.575 B.A. [Todd,V.&B.]

Todd, Vanderbloemen and Brady, P.A., (AV) BB
214 Ridge Street, Northwest, P.O. Drawer 1320, 28645-5227
Telephone: 828-758-0044 Fax: 828-758-8467
Folger L. Townsend (1899-1973); James R. Todd, Jr.; Bruce W. Vanderbloemen; Charles A. Brady, III.
General Civil and Criminal Practice. Trials in all Courts. Real Estate, Probate, Corporation, Administrative, Family and Personal Injury Law.
Representative Clients: NationsBank; Beall Oil Company; Duke Power Company; Southern Bell Telephone & Telegraph Company; Bush Oldsmobile, Inc.; Integon Indemnity Corp.; Nationwide Mutual Insurance Company; Anderson Truck Lines, Inc.; Stevens Furniture Company, Inc.; First Union National Bank.
See Professional Biographies, LENOIR, NORTH CAROLINA

Topkins, Elyse Michelle .... '51 '80 C.577 A.B. L.575 J.D. 1002 West Ave.
Tuttle, Carroll D., (BV) .... '— '74 C.34 B.S. L.575 J.D. [Groome,T.P.&B.]
Vanderbloemen, Bruce W., (AV) .... '47 '71 C.198 B.A. L.575 J.D. [Todd,V.&B.]
Whisnant, Thomas W., P.A., Law Offices of, (BV) '49 '91
C&L.575 B.A., J.D. 808 Harper Avenue, NW
Wilson, Hugh M., (AV) .... '30 '56 C&L.896 B.B.A., LL.B. [Wilson,L.&R.]
Wilson, Lackey & Rohr, P.C., (AV) .... 606 College Avenue SW

LEWISVILLE, 8,826, *Forsyth Co.*

Billings, Donald R., (AV) .... '34 '63 C&L.228 A.B., J.D. 5525 Williams Rd.‡
Davis, V. Tate .... '68 '00 C.443 B.S. L.896 J.D. [Davis E.&D.L.]

Davis Elder & Disability Law
6620 Shallowford Road, P.O. Box 754, 27023
Telephone: 336-946-0266 Fax: 336-946-0499 URL: http://www.tatedavis.com
Email: tate@daviselderlaw.com URL: http://www.daviselderlawoffice.com
V. Tate Davis.
Elder Law.
See Professional Biographies, LEWISVILLE, NORTH CAROLINA

Feder, Joan L. '60 '84 C.589 B.A. L.424 J.D.
(adm. in IL; not adm. in NC) 8341 Tuscany Dr.
Gelbin, Ellen R., (AV) .... '— '85 C&L.575 B.S., J.D. 743 Big Tree Drive
Huffines, James P., Jr. .... '57 '83 C.575 B.S. L.1228 J.D. P.O. Box 302
Johe, Sharon D. '39 '73 L.569 J.D.
(adm. in NY; not adm. in NC) 278 Riverwood Dr.‡
Kegler, Kimbrelly N. .... '73 '98 C&L.575 B.S.B.A, J.D. [Kegler]
Kegler Group, The .... 875 Crafton Creek Dr., Ste. B
Mattocks, N. Randolph, Jr. .... '44 '69 C&L.896 B.B.A., J.D. 5180 Riverwest Rd.
Motsinger, John K., Sr., Law Offices of, (BV) '47 '83
C.902 B.A. L.896 J.D. P.O. Box 445

LEXINGTON, * 19,953, *Davidson Co.*

Anthony, Daniel B., PC, The Law Practice of
(See Winston-Salem)

Ayers, Dennis R. .... '50 '76 C.575 A.B. L.896 J.D. Lexington Memorial Hosp., Inc.
Baker, Rosalind, Law Offices of, (BV) ... '58 '84 C.1378 B.A. L.574 J.D. 136 W. 1st Ave.

Barnes, Grimes, Bunce & Fraley, PLLC, (BV)
20 South Main Street, P.O. Box 476, 27292-0476
Telephone: 336-249-9128 Fax: 336-249-9129
Email: linwoodbunce@bgblawoffice.com URL: http://www.lawyers.com/bgblawoffice
Beamer H. Barnes (1915-2002); Jerry B. Grimes; D. Linwood Bunce, II; Shawn L. Fraley.
Personal Injury, Auto Accidents, Wrongful Death, Workers Compensation, Criminal Law, DWI, Drug Crimes, Traffic Violations, Real Estate, Mortgages, Landlord and Tenant Law, Wills and Probate, Family Law, Child Custody, Child Support, Divorce, Elder Law.
See Professional Biographies, LEXINGTON, NORTH CAROLINA

Barnhill, Stephen D., (BV) .... '58 '90 C.316 B.S. L.896 J.D. [Brinkley W.]
Beeker, Ned Arthur, (AV) .... '32 '60 C&L.575 LL.B. 416 Country Club Blvd.

Berg, Jeffrey J., (BV) '61 '89 C.622 B.S. L.623 J.D.
401 West Center Street, 27292
Telephone: 336-249-3870 Fax: 336-243-3059
Email: lawyer@jberglaw.com URL: http://www.jberglaw.com
Criminal Defense, Driving While Intoxicated (DWI), Misdemeanors, Traffic Violations, Speeding Tickets, Residential Real Estate, Commercial Real Estate, Mortgages, Deeds, Land Sales, Trusts and Estates, Corporations, Wills and Probate.
See Professional Biographies, LEXINGTON, NORTH CAROLINA

Biesecker, Joe E., (AV) .... '37 '68 C.125 A.B. L.896 J.D. [Wilson,B.T.&S.]
Bodenheimer, Laura G., (CV) .... '65 '91 C.34 B.A. L.469 J.D. P.O. Box 766
Bowers, Bob W., (AV) .... '40 '64 C&L.896 A.B., LL.B. [Stoner,B.&G.]
Brinkley, Walter F., (AV) .... '26 '49 C&L.575 LL.B. [Brinkley W.]

Brinkley Walser, PLLC, (AV)
10 LSB Plaza, P.O. Box 1657, 27292
Telephone: 336-249-2101 Fax: 336-249-4572

(This Listing Continued)

Brinkley Walser, PLLC (Continued)

Zeb Vance Walser (1863-1940); Don A. Walser (1899-1977); Gaither S. Walser (1934-2001); Walter F. Brinkley; Charles H. McGirt; G. Thompson Miller; D. Clark Smith, Jr.; Stephen W. Coles; David E. Inabinett; Stephen D. Barnhill. Associates: April D. Craft; Bradley S. Hunt.
General Practice in State and Federal Courts. Insurance, Corporation, Probate, Real Estate Law, Medical Malpractice Defense, Personal Injury Litigation, Workers' Compensation, Elder Law, Social Security, Criminal Law, Domestic Relations, Banking Law.

See Professional Biographies, LEXINGTON, NORTH CAROLINA

Buggs, Corey D., (BV) .... '69 '97 C.576 B.S.E.E. L.896 J.D. Asst. Dist. Atty.
Bunce, D. Linwood, II, (BV) .... '53 '79 C&L.1228 B.S., J.D. [Barnes,G.B.&F.]
Coles, Stephen W., (AV) .... '56 '80 C&L.896 B.A., J.D. [Brinkley W.]
Craft, April D. .... '71 '01 C.240 B.A. L.896 J.D. [A Brinkley W.]
Crump, R. Flint, (CV) .... '72 '98 C.839 B.S. L.896 J.D. [Cunningham&C.]
Cunningham, J. Calvin, (BV) .... '47 '74 C.404 B.A. L.896 J.D. [Cunningham&C.]
Cunningham & Crump, PLLC, (BV) .... 18 South Main Street
Curry, Holly B., (BV) .... '61 '88 C.577 B.A. L.574 J.D. 113 W. Center St.
Curry, Scott Y., (BV) .... '56 '82 C.404 B.A. L.1228 J.D. 111 W. Center St.

Davidson, Daryl G., Sr., PC, Law Office of
(See Statesville)

Elkins, Thomas James '50 '75 C.1130 B.A. L.862 J.D.
(adm. in OK; not adm. in NC) 110 Ridgewood Dr.‡
Fraley, Shawn L. .... '75 '01 C&L.575 B.A., J.D. [Barnes,G.B.&F.]
Frank, Garry W., (AV) .... '53 '78 C.198 B.A. L.896 J.D. P.O. Box 1067
Fritts, William F., (BV) .... '57 '85 C&L.575 B.A., J.D. [Wilson,B.T.&S.]
Frye, Charles E., III, (BV) .... '57 '82 C&L.896 B.A., J.D. P.O. Box 788
Gamblin, Doris C., (BV) .... '57 '86 C&L.896 B.A., J.D. [Smith&G.]
Gray, Carl W., (BV) .... '45 '75 C.125 B.A. L.896 J.D. [Stoner,B.&G.]
Grimes, Jerry B., (BV) .... '38 '63 C&L.896 LL.B. [Barnes,G.B.&F.]

Handler & Brown, P.L.L.C.
(See Winston-Salem)

Harp, Charles H., II, (BV) .... '44 '72 C.1128 B.A. L.896 J.D. 28 Vance Circle
Hedrick, Laura Lucile, (CV) .... '61 '86 C&L.896 B.A., J.D. 113 W. Center St.
Holton, Stephen C., (BV) .... '55 '81 C.577 B.S. L.896 J.D. [Holton&H.]
Holton & Holton, (BV) ....115 W. Center St.
Honeycutt, James M. .... '48 '74 C&L.575 B.S., J.D. Dist. J.
Hunt, Bradley S. .... '75 '02 C.575 B.A. L.923 J.D. [A Brinkley W.]
Inabinett, David E., (BV) .... '70 '96 C&L.896 B.A., J.D. [Brinkley W.]
Jane', Carlos E., (BV) .... '69 '97 C.577 B.A. L.896 J.D. 2 Williams St.

Ketner & Dees, P.A.
(See Salisbury)

Klass, Jack E. .... '29 '56 C.316 A.B. L.896 J.D. Dist. Ct. J.
Klass, Mark E. .... '56 '84 C.575 B.A. L.1228 J.D. Supr. Ct. J.
Krueger, Charles R., (BV) .... '46 '73 C.575 B.S. L.896 J.D. [C.R.Krueger]
Krueger, C. Roland, Attorney at Law, (BV) .... 4 Williams St.
Labosky, Jennifer A. .... '61 '86 C&L.896 B.A., J.D. Davidson Co. Community Coll.
Leonard, Joe H., (AV) .... '19 '47 C.896 A.B. L.575 J.D. 113 W. Center St.‡
Lohr, Philip B., (BV) .... '49 '74 C.404 A.B. L.836 J.D. 111 W. Center St.
Martin, Alan Braddy, (BV) .... '69 '94 C&L.575 A.B., J.D. Asst. Dist. Atty.
McCain, Richard J. .... '66 '93 C.1058 B.A. L.425 J.D. 16 Court Square
McGirt, Charles H., (AV) .... '36 '61 C.404 A.B. L.575 J.D. [Brinkley W.]
Meinecke, Terry Michael '68 '01 C.577 B. S. L.546 J.D.
Asst. Dist. Atty., Dist. Attys. Off.
Michael, Jon C., (CV) .... '68 '98 C.1128 B.A. L.1187 J.D. 23 W. 2nd St.
Michael, Wayne L., (BV) .... '51 '77 C&L.575 B.A., J.D. Dist. Ct. Judge
Miller, G. Thompson, (AV) .... '46 '72 C&L.896 B.A., J.D. [Brinkley W.]
Mock, James F., (BV) .... '42 '71 C&L.823 A.B., J.D. Asst. Dist Atty.

Morgan, Herring, Morgan, Green, Rosenblutt & Gill, LLP
(See High Point)

Myers, Jon W. .... '66 '92 C&L.896 B.A., J.D. P.O. Box 146
Nixon, Georgia S., (BV) '65 '91 C.576 B.A. L.1345 J.D.
101 West Center St. Extension (⊙High Point)
Penry, J. Rodwell, Jr., (BV) .... '45 '71 C&L.896 B.A., J.D. 17 E. Center St.
Penry, Phyllis S., (AV) .... '46 '75 C.316 A.B. L.896 J.D. 17 E. Center St.
Priest, Gwenda, (BV) .... '52 '81 C.575 B.A. L.117 J.D. Asst. Dist. Atty.
Raines, Christopher A., (CV) .... '70 '96 C&L.575 B.A., J.D. [Wilson,B.T.&S.]
Rodden, Max R., (BV) .... '63 '91 C&L.896 B.S., J.D. [Wilson,B.T.&S.]
Rosin, Marla Jo .... '64 '89 C.298 B.A. L.362 J.D. [Rosin]
Rosin Law Offices .... 670 Jes Wes Lane
Royster, Theodore S., Jr., (BV) .... '45 '73 C.896 B.A. L.192 J.D. 8 Vance St.
Sink, Irvin R., (BV) .... '50 '76 C.576 B.A. L.896 J.D. [Wilson,B.T.&S.]
Smith, D. Clark, Jr., (AV) .... '50 '75 C&L.896 B.S., J.D. [Brinkley W.]
Smith, Robert B., Jr., (AV) .... '38 '64 C&L.575 B.S.B.A., LL.B. [Smith&G.]
Smith, Timothy Dean .... '60 '89 C&L.575 B.A., J.D. P.O. Box 1702
Smith & Gamblin, (AV) .... 1 W. Center St.

Snyder, James Eugene, Jr., (AV) '45 '70 C&L.896 B.A., J.D.
16 West 1st Avenue, P.O. Box 482, 27293
Telephone: 336-249-3399 Fax: 336-243-7800
Email: JamesSnyder@jamesesnyderjr.com URL: http://www.jamesesnyderjr.com
General Civil and Criminal Trial Practice in State and Federal Courts. Corporations, Real Property, Family and Probate Law with Personal Injury and Medical Malpractice concentration.

See Professional Biographies, LEXINGTON, NORTH CAROLINA

Stoner, Bowers & Gray, P.A., (AV) .... 38 Vance Circle
Swann, Michael A., (AV) .... '47 '77 C&L.575 A.B., J.D. [M.A.Swann]

Swann, Michael A., P.A., (AV)
21 Vance Circle, P.O. Box 1503, 27293
Telephone: 336-249-7777 Facsimile: 336-249-9988
Email: michaelswann@lexcominc.net
Michael A. Swann.
Practice Limited to: Workers' Compensation, Personal Injury, Civil Litigation, Mediation.

See Professional Biographies, LEXINGTON, NORTH CAROLINA

Taylor, Robert Samuel, III, (BV) .... '68 '94 C&L.575 B.A., J.D. Asst. Dist. Atty.
Tripp, Roger S., (BV) .... '49 '74 C.232 B.A. L.896 J.D. [Wilson,B.T.&S.]
Wall, Carroll C., III .... '48 '72 C&L.896 B.A., J.D. 129 W. Center St.
Wilson, Biesecker, Tripp & Sink, (AV) .... 118 West First Avenue
Wood, April C. .... '73 '97 C.999 B.A. L.1339 J.D. Dist. J.

Wyatt Early Harris Wheeler L.L.P.
(See High Point)

Zimmerman, Herman W., Jr., (AV) .... '39 '67 C.198 A.B. L.896 J.D. 114 W. 2nd Ave.

LIBERTY, 2,661, *Randolph Co.*

Flowe, William H., Jr., Law Offices of '51 '76 C&L.896 B.A., J.D.
124 S. Fayetteville Street, 27298-1315
Telephone: 336-622-2278 Fax: 336-622-5944
Email: flowe51@rtelco.net URL: http://www.williamflowelaw.com
Real Estate, Closings, Buying and Selling, Wills, Trust and Estates, Estates Planning, Small Business, Limited Liability Companies, Business Enterprises, Family Law, Divorce.

See Professional Biographies, LIBERTY, NORTH CAROLINA

Wilson, James L., (BV) .... '41 '70 C.240 A.B. L.896 J.D. P.O. Box 70

LILLINGTON, * 2,915, *Harnett Co.*

Bain, Alton D., (BV) .... '60 '85 C.228 A.B. L.575 J.D. [Bain,B.&M.]
Bain, Edgar R., (AV) .... '33 '57 C&L.896 B.S., LL.B. [Bain,B.&M.]

Bain, Buzzard & McRae, LLP, (AV)
65 Bain Street, 27546
Telephone: 910-893-5111 Fax: 910-893-6956 URL: http://www.bainlawyers.com
URL: http://www.bainandmcrae.com
Members of Firm: Edgar R. Bain; Alton D. Bain; Robert A. Buzzard; David F. McRae;—L. Stacy Weaver, III.
General Civil and Criminal Practice. Trials in all State and Federal Courts. Real Estate, Trusts and Estates, Wills and Probate, Medicaid Planning, Elder Law, Business and Corporate Law, Taxation, Tax Planning, Personal Injury, Automobile Accidents, Wrongful Death, Medical Malpractice, Criminal Law, DWI, Traffic Offenses.

See Professional Biographies, LILLINGTON, NORTH CAROLINA

Breeden, Jonathan D.
(See Garner)

Buzzard, Robert A., (BV) .... '65 '91 C.338 B.S. L.1228 J.D. [Bain,B.&M.]
Carr, Christopher L., (CV) .... '63 '91 C&L.1228 B.A., J.D. P.O. Box 10
Chriscoe, Johnny C., Jr. ... '57 '90 C.1317 B.A. L.1345 J.D. Assoc. Dean, Campbell Univ.
Davidson, James P. .... '52 '89 C.575 B.A. L.1345 J.D. 101 E. Front St.
Davidson, Rebecca J., (BV) .... '53 '84 C&L.575 B.A., J.D. [Johnson&J.]

Edwards, Charlene, Law Office, (CV) '68 '93 C&L.1228 B.A., J.D.
Cape Fear Plaza, 133C West Cornelius Harnett Boulevard, 27546
Mailing Address: P.O. Box 2446, Lillington, NC 27546
Telephone: 910-893-1128 Fax: 910-893-1138
Email: edwardslaw1@earthlink.net URL: http://www.lillingtonlawyers.com
Associate: Ben L. Roberts.
Family Law, Divorce, Domestic Relations, Personal Injury, Automobile Accidents, Wrongful Death, Construction Accidents, Criminal Law, Workers Compensation, Social Security Disability, Traffic Law.

See Professional Biographies, LILLINGTON, NORTH CAROLINA

Ennis, Rhonda H., (BV) .... '42 '81 C&L.1228 B.A., J.D. 602 W. Front St.
Felmet, L. Holt, (BV) .... '46 '74 C&L.896 B.A., J.D. [L.H.Felmet]

Felmet, L. Holt, P.A., (BV)
32 East Front Street, P.O. Box 1689, 27546
Telephone: 910-893-2999 Fax: 910-893-3255
Email: hfelmet@aol.com URL: http://www.felmetlaw.com
L. Holt Felmet.
General Civil and Criminal Trial Practice in all Courts. Personal Injury Litigation, Domestic Relations and Family Law, Real Estate, Criminal Defense (including traffic) and Estate Administration.
Approved Attorney for: Commonwealth Land Title Insurance Co.; Lawyers Title Insurance Co.; Jefferson-Pilot Insurance Co.; Chicago Title Insurance Co.; Investors Title Insurance Co.; Old Republic Title Insurance Co.

See Professional Biographies, LILLINGTON, NORTH CAROLINA

Frost, Elisabeth Garner .... '71 '00 C.228 B.A. L.575 J.D. Dist. Atty.'s Off., 11th Dist.
Gilchrist, C. Winston, (BV) .... '63 '88 C&L.575 B.A., J.D. [Morgan,R.&G.]

Hales & Conaway, PLLC, The Law Offices of
(See Clinton)

Hartley, David V., Law Office of, (CV) '44 '91
C.259 B.S. L.1345 LL.D. 829 S. Eighth St.
Hayes, Gerald W., Jr., (AV) .... '43 '69 C.575 A.B. L.896 J.D. [Hayes,W.T.&D.] ⊙

Hayes, Williams, Turner & Daughtry, P.A., (AV)
950 Main Street, 27546 ⊙
Mailing Address: 804 West Broad Street, Dunn, NC 28334
Telephone: 910-814-1111 Fax: 910-891-1198
Gerald W. Hayes, Jr.
General Criminal and Civil Practice. Traffic Court, Personal Injury, Real Estate, Probate, Family and Corporation Law. Trials in all Courts.
Reference: United Carolina Bank.

See Professional Biographies, LILLINGTON, NORTH CAROLINA

Johnson, Sandra L., (BV) .... '45 '75 C.228 B.A. L.575 J.D. [Johnson&J.]
Johnson, W. A., (AV) .... '20 '44 C&L.575 A.B., J.D. [Johnson&J.]
Johnson, W. Glenn, (BV) .... '46 '73 C&L.575 B.A., J.D. [Johnson&J.]
Johnson and Johnson, P.A., (AV) .... 31 East Harnett Street

Jones, Jesse W. '64 '94 C.576 B.S. L.1228 J.D.
700 South 8th Street, 27546
Telephone: 910-814-2661 Fax: 910-814-3709
Email: jessejoneslaw@yahoo.com URL: http://www.jessejoneslaw.com
Criminal Law, Felonies, Misdemeanors, Murder, Manslaughter, Parole and Probation, Sex Crimes, Capital Offenses, Personal Injury, Automobile Accidents and Injuries, Wrongful Death, Family Law, Child Custody, Divorce, Alimony, Spousal Support, Traffic Violations, Driving While Intoxicated.

See Professional Biographies, LILLINGTON, NORTH CAROLINA

Kelly, Reginald B., (BV) .... '50 '81 C.576 B.S. L.1228 J.D. [Kelly&W.]

Kelly & West, P.A., (BV)
900 S. Main Street, P.O. Box 1118, 27546
Telephone: 910-893-8183 Toll Free: 1-800-936-3133 Fax: 910-893-5814
Email: info@kelly-west.com URL: http://www.kelly-westlaw.com
Reginald B. Kelly; J. Thomas West. Associate: J. David Lewis.
Personal Injury and Wrongful Death Litigation, Automobile Negligence, Medical Negligence, Workers Compensation, Trials and Appeals, Real Estate, Wills, Traffic and DWI Law.

See Professional Biographies, LILLINGTON, NORTH CAROLINA

Lewis, J. David, (BV) .... '61 '88 C.575 B.A. L.896 J.D. [A Kelly&W.]
McCormick, Duncan B. .... '67 '95 C.575 B.A. L.1228 J.D. P.O. Box 1629
McCormick, Edward H. .... '35 '64 C&L.575 A.B., LL.B. Dist. J.
McRae, David F., (BV) .... '57 '89 C.232 B.A. L.1345 J.D. [Bain,B.&M.]
Morgan, Robert B. .... '15 '45 C.896 L.192 J.D. Rte. 1
Morgan, Robert B., (AV) .... '25 '50 C.232 B.S. L.896 LL.B. [Morgan,R.&G.] ⊙
Morgan, Reeves & Gilchrist, (AV) .... 101 East Front St. (⊙Raleigh)
Penny, Mark L. .... '— '03 C&L.1228 B.A., J.D. 809 South 8th Street
Reeves, Mary Morgan, (BV) .... '62 '88 C.228 A.B. L.896 J.D. [Morgan,R.&G.]
Roberts, Ben L. .... '79 '04 C&L.1228 B.A., J.D. [A C.Edwards]
Smith, Reba Sloan, (CV) .... '51 '91 C.778 B.A. L.1228 J.D. P.O. Box 754

Stewart Law Firm
(See Dunn)

Strickland, Peter B. .... '62 '93 C.575 A.B. L.896 J.D. P.O. Box 2259

Weaver, L. Stacy, III ......'56 '04 C.228 B.A. L.1228 J.D. [Ⓐ Bain,B.&M.]
West, J. Thomas, (BV) ......'51 '81 C&L.1228 B.B.A., J.D. [Kelly&W.]
Woodall, E. Marshall, (BV) ......'38 '63 C&L.575 B.S., LL.B. [Woodall]
Woodall Law Firm, The, P.A., (BV) ...... 609 1st St.

LINCOLNTON, * 9,965, *Lincoln Co.*

Barefoot, Daniel W., (BV) ......'51 '76 C&L.575 A.B., J.D. 119 1/2 E. Main
Black, David M., (BV) ......'57 '83 C.34 B.S. L.575 J.D. [D.M.Black]

Black, David M., P.A., (BV)
333 East Main Street, Suite 105, P.O. Box 2000, 28093
Telephone: 704-732-1778 Fax: 704-732-9927
Email: dblack@davidmblack.com URL: http://www.dblacklaw.com
David M. Black.
See Professional Biographies, LINCOLNTON, NORTH CAROLINA

Childs, W. H., Jr., (AV) ......'23 '48 C.152 L.896 LL.B. P.O. Box 103‡
Deaton, Wesley L., (CV) ......'72 '98 C.575 A.B.J.M. L.280 J.D. [Pendleton&P.]

Elliott, J. Bryan
(See Hickory)

Garland, J. Boyce, Jr.
(See Gastonia)

Gray, Layton, Kersh, Solomon, Sigmon, Furr & Smith, P.A.
(See Gastonia)

Huffstetler Law Offices
(See Cherryville)

Jonas, Harvey A., Jr., (AV) ......'19 '42 C&L.575 B.A., J.D. [Ⓒ Jonas]
Jonas, Richard E., (AV) ......'43 '68 C.575 B.A. L.228 J.D. [Jonas]

Jonas Law Firm, The, P.L.L.C., (AV)
210 East Main Street, P.O. Box 38, 28092
Telephone: 704-735-1423 Fax: 704-735-1490
URL: http://www.jonaslawfirm.com
Members of Firm: Charles A. Jonas (1876-1955); Charles R. Jonas (1904-1988); Richard E. Jonas; Johnathan L. Rhyne, Jr. (Board Certified Specialist in Family Law, North Carolina State Board of Legal Specialization); W. Todd Pomeroy; Rebecca J. Pomeroy. Of Counsel: Harvey A. Jonas, Jr. Associate: Jeremy S. Wilson.
General Civil and Criminal Litigation Practice. Corporation, Banking, Real Estate, Probate Estate Planning, Elder and Family Law.
Counsel for: NationsBank; First Federal Savings & Loan Assn.; Lineberger Brothers, Inc.; Abernethy Chevrolet-Oldsmobile, Inc.; Rhyne Mills, Inc.; Lincoln Bank of North Carolina.
Local Counsel for: Southern Railway; Seaboard Coastline Railway; Nationwide Mutual Insurance Co.
See Professional Biographies, LINCOLNTON, NORTH CAROLINA

Kennedy & Wulfhorst, P.A.
(See Denver)

Lewis, Robert C., (BV) ......'44 '71 C&L.575 A.B., J.D. [Lewis&S.]
Lewis & Shuford, P.A., (BV) ......101 W. Court Sq.
Nachamie, Deirdre H. ......'69 '96 C.576 B.A. L.1228 J.D. P.O. Box 853

Patterson and Adams PLLC
(See Concord)

Pendleton, Clay, (BV) ......'62 '87 C.575 B.S. L.896 J.D. [Pendleton&P.]
Pendleton, Don M., (AV) ......'35 '58 C.34 L.896 LL.B. [Pendleton&P.]
Pendleton & Pendleton, P.A., (AV) ......211 North Academy Street
Pomeroy, Rebecca J., (BV) ......'71 '96 C.575 B.A. L.192 J.D. [Jonas]
Pomeroy, W. Todd ......'70 '96 C.880 B.S. L.192 J.D. [Jonas]
Powell, Robert C. ......'39 '63 C.228 L.575 J.D. P.O. Box 1587
Rhyne, Johnathan L., Jr., (AV) ......'55 '81 C.198 B.A. L.1228 J.D. [Jonas]
Shaffer, Richard L., Jr., (BV) ......'60 '85 C&L.575 B.S., J.D. Off. of Dist. Atty.
Shuford, Meredith A. ......'69 '97 C.576 B.A. L.574 J.D. [Lewis&S.]
Shuford, Thomas M., Jr., (BV) ......'44 '73 C.34 B.S. L.574 J.D. [Lewis&S.]

Singletary Law Firm, PLLC
(See Cornelius)

Taylor, Jeffrey A., (BV) ......'62 '87 C&L.896 B.A., J.D. [Pendleton&P.]
Wilkie, Lynn Broadway ......'65 '93 C.34 B.S. L.896 J.D. [L.B.Wilkie]

Wilkie, Lynn Broadway, Law Office of
214 East Main Street, 28054
Telephone: 704-732-7417 Fax: 704-732-7418 URL: http://www.wilkielawfirm.com
Email: lynn@wilkie.net URL: http://www.wilkielaw.com
Lynn Broadway Wilkie.
See Professional Biographies, LINCOLNTON, NORTH CAROLINA

Wilson, Jeremy S. ......'78 '03 C.1309 B.S. L.1228 J.D. [Ⓐ Jonas]
Wilson, Thomas J., (BV) ......'14 '49 C.198 L.575 LL.B. [T.J.Wilson]
Wilson, Thomas J., Jr., (BV) ......'57 '84 C.1128 B.A. L.1228 J.D. [T.J.Wilson]
Wilson, Thomas J., P.A., (BV) ......228 E. Main St.

Yelton, Farfour, McCartney, Lutz & Craig, P.A.
(See Shelby)

LINVILLE, 244, *Avery Co.*

Burbacher, Charles R., II '38 '65 C.880 B.A. L.260 LL.B.
(adm. in FL; not adm. in NC) P.O. Box 184‡
Feinberg, Louis E. ......'41 '65 C.575 A.B. L.260 J.D. P.O. Box 705

LITTLE SWITZELAND, —, *McDowell Co.*

Furnell, Terry B. '37 '64 C.663 B.A. L.362 LL.B.
(adm. in FL; not adm. in NC) 355 Firetower Rd.‡

LITTLETON, 692, *Halifax Co.*

Pelfrey, Melissa D., (BV) ......'69 '94 C.575 B.A. L.1345 J.D. [Pelfrey&P.]
Pelfrey, Stephen Walter, (BV) ......'68 '94 C.890 B.S. L.1209 J.D. [Pelfrey&P.]
Pelfrey & Pelfrey, (BV) ......P.O. Box 369
Skinner, William T., IV, (CV) ......'60 '87 C.576 B.S. L.1345 J.D. 115 N. Mosby Ave.

LONG BEACH, —, *Brunswick Co.*

(See Oak Island)

LOUISBURG, * 3,037, *Franklin Co.*

Batton, Darnell A., (BV) ......'56 '84 C.232 B.S. L.1228 J.D. [Batton&G.]
Batton & Guin, (BV) ......107 S. Main Street
Davis, Charles M., (AV) ......'36 '61 C.575 A.B. L.896 LL.B. [Davis,S.&T.]

Davis, Sturges & Tomlinson, (AV) BB
DSS Building, 101 North Church Street, P.O. Drawer 708, 27549
Telephone: 919-496-2137 Telecopier: 919-496-6291
Email: name@dstattys.com URL: http://www.louisburglawyers.com
Members of Firm: Charles M. Davis; Aubrey S. Tomlinson, Jr.; C. Boyd Sturges, III.

(This Listing Continued)

Davis, Sturges & Tomlinson (Continued)
General Civil and Criminal Trial Practice in State and Federal Courts. Estate and Probate, Real Estate and Corporation Law. Personal Injury, Automobile Accidents, Truck Accidents, Wrongful Death, Traffic Violations, DWI, Litigation, Land Condemnation.
Approved Attorneys for: Lawyers Title Insurance Corp.; Fidelity National Insurance Co.; Investigators Title Ins.; Statewide Title Ins.
References: First Citizens Bank & Trust Co.; Branch bank & Trust Co.
See Professional Biographies, LOUISBURG, NORTH CAROLINA

Guin, David R., (BV) ......'58 '89 C.871 B.S. L.1228 J.D. [Batton&G.]
Hobgood, Robert H. ......'46 '74 C&L.575 A.B., J.D. Supr. Ct. J.

Jolly, Williamson & Williamson, (AV)
106 East Nash Street, 27549
Telephone: 919-496-4152 Fax: 919-496-5270
Email: jollywilliamson@aol.com
John P. Williamson, Jr.; Benjamin N. Williamson, III.
General Practice in State and Federal Courts. Trials. Wills, Trusts, Probate, Civil, Criminal, DWI, Real Estate, Personal Injury Law, Automobile Accidents and Wrongful Death.
See Professional Biographies, LOUISBURG, NORTH CAROLINA

McFarlane, Steven H., (BV) ......'63 '90 C.532 B.A. L.575 J.D. [McFarlane]
McFarlane, Susan S. ......'62 '89 C&L.575 B.A., J.D. [Ⓒ McFarlane]
McFarlane Law Office, P.A., (BV) ......102 E. Nash St.
Norman, Larry E., (BV) ......'52 '79 C.576 B.A. L.1228 J.D. 101 S. Main St.
Senter, James Larry ......'43 '69 C.115 B.S. L.500 J.D. Dist. J.
Sturges, C. Boyd, III, (BV) ......'69 '95 C&L.896 B.A., J.D. [Davis,S.&T.]
Tomlinson, Aubrey S., Jr., (AV) ......'43 '68 C.896 B.A. L.575 J.D. [Davis,S.&T.]
Toppen, Jon P. '61 '88 C.323 B.A. L.912 J.D.
(adm. in MI; not adm. in NC) Louisburg College
Williamson, Benjamin N., III, (AV) ......'43 '69 C.575 B.S. L.838 J.D. [Jolly,W.&W.]
Williamson, John P., Jr., (AV) ......'43 '69 C.575 A.B. L.838 J.D. [Jolly,W.&W.]

LOWELL, 2,704, *Gaston Co.*

Isbill, Charlotte Shuford ......'41 '72 C.228 B.A. L.575 J.D. 205 Mill St.

LUMBERTON, * 20,795, *Robeson Co.*

Berry, Sue A., (BV) ......'50 '79 C&L.846 B.A., J.D. Asst. Pub. Def. [Bowen&B.]
Biggs, Gayla G., (BV) ......'64 '90 C.1228 B.A. L.1345 J.D. Pub. Def. Off.
Biggs, I. Murchison, (AV) ......'24 '45 C&L.896 B.S., LL.B. 3550 E. Elizabethtown Rd.
Bowen, Woodberry L., (BV) '47 '74
C&L.575 B.A., J.D. 910 Walnut Street (⊙Lumberton)
Bowen, Woodberry L., (BV) ......'47 '74 C&L.575 A.B., J.D. [Bowen&B.] (⊙Lumberton)
Bowen & Berry, PLLC, (BV) ......910 North Walnut Street
Branch, David F., Jr., (BV) ......'55 '81 C.896 B.A. L.192 J.D. [Musselwhite,M.M.&B.]
Britt, Evander M., III, (BV) ......'54 '81 C&L.896 B.A., J.D. [Britt&B.]
Britt, Joe Freeman, (AV) ......'35 '63 C.896 A.B. L.362 J.D. P.O. Box 99‡
Britt, L. Johnson, III, (BV) '60 '87
C.896 B.A. L.1228 J.D. Robertson Co. Courthouse Atty.'s Off.

Britt, William S., Law Offices of, (BV) '54 '81 C&L.896 B.A., J.D.
106 W. Fifth Street, 28358
Telephone: 910-739-7141 Fax: 910-739-7906
URL: http://www.wsbritt.com
Medical Malpractice, Wrongful Death, Automobile Accidents and Injuries, Truck Accidents, Motorcycle Accidents, Construction Accidents, Dog Bites and Personal Injury Law.
See Professional Biographies, LUMBERTON, NORTH CAROLINA

Britt & Britt, P.A., (BV) ......411 North Elm Street
Brooks, Dexter ......'43 '76 C.576 B.S.E.E. L.575 J.D. Supr. Ct. J.
Bullard, Edward J., Attorney at Law ......'62 '93 C.577 B.A. L.574 J.D. 424 N. Chestnut St.
Caldwell, S. F. ......'17 '40 C&L.896 B.A., LL.B. 202 E. 19th St.‡
Campbell, John Wishart, (AV) ......'23 '49 C&L.575 LL.B. [Ⓒ Teague,C.D.&G.]
Carmical, J. Stanley ......'54 '80 C.896 B.A. L.575 J.D. Dist. J.
Carter, John B., Jr. ......'51 '79 C.1011 B.A. L.574 J.D. Dist. J.
Chavis, Ertle Knox, (CV) ......'42 '75 C.1317 B.A. L.574 J.D. P.O. Box 877
Daniels, Judith Milsap, (BV) ......'59 '84 C.896 B.A. L.575 J.D. 347 Forest Rd.
Davis, Katherine H., (BV) ......'69 '94 C&L.575 A.B., J.D. [Huggins,P.&D.]
Davis, William L., III, (CV) ......'45 '77 101 N. Court Sq.
Duvall, Martha J., (BV) ......'58 '83 C.30 B.S. L.665 J.D. 243 Oakwood Heights Dr.

Edwards, R. Gregg
(See Fayetteville)

Floyd, Robert F., Jr. ......'54 '79 C&L.115 B.S., J.D. Judge of the Supr. Crt.

Gordon, Horne, Hicks and Floyd, P.A.
(See Laurinburg)

Grantham, Norris Musselwhite, (BV) '65 '90
C.575 B.A. L.1345 J.D. [Musselwhite,M.M.&B.]

Griffin Law Office
(See Red Springs)

Hedgpeth, James F., Jr. ......'68 '01 C.576 B.A./M.A. L.1228 J.D. [Huggins,P.&D.]
Holec, David A., (BV) ......'55 '80 C.339 B.S. L.896 J.D. City Atty.
Huggins, Bruce W., (BV) ......'41 '70 C&L.575 A.B., J.D. [Huggins,P.&D.]
Huggins, Pounds & Davis, L.L.P., (BV) ......503 North Elm Street
Jacobson, Robert D., (BV) ......'42 '67 C&L.352 B.A., J.D. 305 E. 5th St.
Jobe, Bruce F., (BV) ......'52 '80 C.896 B.A. L.1228 J.D. [B.F.Jobe]
Jobe, Bruce F., P.A., Law Offices of, (BV) ......4312 Ludgate Street

Jones, Greg, & Associates, P.A.
(See Wilmington)

Kinlaw, J. Hal, Jr., (BV) ......'52 '78 C.576 B.A. L.896 J.D. Co. Atty.
Locklear, Gary L. ......'49 '79 C&L.575 B.A., J.D. Supr. Ct. J.
MacLean, Hector ......'20 '48 C.198 B.S. L.575 LL.B. 316 Elm St.‡
McIntyre, D. Carmichael (Mike), II, (BV) ......'56 '81 C&L.575 A.B., J.D. [McIntyre]
McIntyre Law Firm, Professional Association, (BV) ......701 N. Elm St.
McKinnon, Henry A., Jr. ......'22 '47 C&L.228 A.B., LL.B. Supr. Ct. J.
McLean, Charles G. ......'23 '52 C&L.273 A.B., LL.B. Chief Dist. Ct. J.‡
McLean, Dickson, Jr., (AV) ......'27 '52 C&L.575 A.B., J.D. [Ⓒ Ramsaur&M.]
McLean, William S., (AV) '35 '60
C.575 A.B. L.228 LL.B. Suite 302, 500 North Chestnut Street‡
Moody, Jack H., Jr., (BV) ......'65 '91 C.575 B.S. L.1228 J.D. Asst. Pub. Def.
Musselwhite, Fred L., (AV) ......'39 '63 C&L.896 B.S., LL.B. [Musselwhite,M.M.&B.]
Musselwhite, James W., (BV) ......'57 '81 C.576 B.S. L.1228 J.D. [Musselwhite,M.M.&B.]
Musselwhite, W. Edward, Jr., (BV) '55 '81
C.896 B.S. L.1228 J.D. [Musselwhite,M.M.&B.]
Musselwhite, Musselwhite, Musselwhite & Branch, (AV) ......606 North Elm Street
Oxendine, Rodney, (BV) ......'— '98 C.1317 B.S. L.574 J.D. Robeson Count Courthouse
Pounds, Dallas M., (BV) ......'60 '88 C.12 B.S. L.1228 J.D. [Huggins,P.&D.]

Ramsaur, David J., (BV) ....'62 '87 C.896 B.A. L.1228 J.D. [Ramsaur&M.]
Ramsaur & McLean, Professional Association, (AV)
Suite 302, 500 North Chestnut Street
Regan, John Breckenridge, III, (AV) ....'40 '68 C.575 A.B. L.896 J.D. 408 N. Chestnut St.
Richardson, Herbert L. ....'52 '76 C&L.574 B.A., J.D. Dist. J.
Rogers, D. Jeffrey, (BV) ....'55 '82 C.1317 B.A. L.574 J.D. 114 W. 5th St.
Rogers, Hubert N., III, (BV) ....'54 '80 C&L.1228 B.S., J.D. 101 N. Court Sq.

Rouse, J.B., III & Associates
(See Fayetteville)

Smith, C. Christopher, (BV) ....'46 '72 C.575 A.B. L.790 J.D. [C.C.Smith]
Smith, Troy A., (CV) ....'67 '94 C.838 B.A. L.574 J.D. [T.A.Smith]

Smith, C. Christopher, P.A., (BV)
4850 Fayetteville Road, Suite C, 28358
Telephone: 910-738-8131 Fax: 910-738-6078
Email: smithlaw@carolina.net URL: http://www.cchristophersmith.com
C. Christopher Smith.
Real Estate, Bankruptcy, Wills, Estate Administration, Business Law, Corporation Law, Limited Liability Company Law, Partnership Law, General Practice.
Approved Attorney for: Chicago Title Insurance Co.; Lawyerstitle; Investors Title; Statewide Title; Network Title.

See Professional Biographies, LUMBERTON, NORTH CAROLINA

Smith, Troy A., PC, (CV) ....P.O. Box 735
Stacy, Horace E., Jr., (AV) ....'29 '56 C&L.575 A.B., LL.B. P.O. Box 7405
Teague, Campbell, Dennis & Gorham, L.L.P., (AV)
408 North Chestnut Street (⊙Raleigh)
Todd, Stanley M., (BV) ....'47 '88 C.176 B.A. L.1228 J.D. Asst. Dist. Atty.

Townsend, J. Richard, (BV) '52 '78 C.232 B.A. L.896 J.D.
Salem Square Professional Park, 4904 Fayetteville Road, 28358
Telephone: 910-739-7518 1-800-542-2664 Fax: 910-671-8433
URL: http://www.lawyers.com/richardtownsend
Personal Injury, Automobile Accidents, Truck Accidents, Motorcycle Accidents, Bicycle Accidents, Dog Bites, Hospital Negligence, Nursing Home Negligence, Criminal Law, Misdemeanors, Assaults, Traffic Violations, Driving While Intoxicated, Estate Planning, Wills, Trusts and Estates.

See Professional Biographies, LUMBERTON, NORTH CAROLINA

Ward, Joseph C., Jr. ....'24 '52 C&L.575 B.S.B.A., J.D. 707 N. Chestnut St.‡
West, Heath E. ....'73 '02 C.34 B.S. L.327 J.D. [E.West]
West, Eric, Office ....318-B E. Fifth St.
Williams, Marcus W., (BV) ....'53 '79 C.575 B.A. L.494 J.D. Asst. Pub. Def.

MADISON, 2,262, *Rockingham Co.*

Berger, P. Kevin ....'74 '00 C.577 B.S. L.896 J.D. [Berger]
Berger Law Firm, The, (AV) ....114 West Murphy Street (⊙Eden)
Cardwell, Vernon E., (AV) ....'41 '69 C.316 A.B. L.896 J.D. 109 Midtown Arcade
Cassidy, Michael J., (BV) ....'67 '92 C.896 B.A. L.575 J.D. [Webster&C.]

Folger & Tucker, P.A., (AV)
117 East Murphy Street, 27025
Telephone: 336-548-2309 Fax: 336-548-1751
Email: fthlaw@earthlink.net
Members of Firm: Alonzo D. Folger, Jr. (1922-2000); Benjamin F. Tucker.
General Civil and Criminal Practice in State Courts. Personal Injury, Automobile Accidents, Wrongful Death, Workers Compensation, Real Estate, Family Law, Divorce, Child Custody, Traffic Violations, Corporations and Probate Law.
Representative Clients: Guaranteed Systems, Inc.; BB&T, Madison, N.C.; McMichael Mills, Inc.
Approved Attorneys for: Investors Title Insurance Co.; Fidelity National Title Insurance Co.
References: Branch Banking and Trust Company, Madison, N.C.; FNB Southeast, Madison, N.C.

See Professional Biographies, MADISON, NORTH CAROLINA

Fulp, George T., (BV) ....'46 '73 C&L.575 A.B., J.D. 138 E. Murphy St.
Hundley, Wayland E., (CVⓉ) '62 '88 C.886 B.S. L.692 J.D.
(adm. in VA; not adm. in NC) 870 Remington Dr.‡
Knight, Kenneth D., (AV) ....'49 '74 C.575 B.S. L.896 J.D. 405 West Decatur Street
Rodenbough, S L., III ....'24 '50 C&L.575 B.A., LL.B. 129 East Murphy Street‡
Tucker, Benjamin F., (AV) ....'51 '76 C.575 A.B. L.692 J.D. [Folger&T.]
Webster, S. J., Jr., (AV) ....'34 '59 C.316 B.A. L.896 LL.B. [Webster&C.]
Webster & Cassidy, (AV) ....114 W. Murphy St.

MAGGIE VALLEY, 607, *Haywood Co.*

Haddock, R. Philip '19 '47 C.945 A.B. L.362 J.D.
(adm. in FL; not adm. in NC) P.O. Box 606‡
Schild, Marvin '29 '53 C&L.472 B.B.A., LL.B.
(adm. in FL; not adm. in NC) 211 Cedar Dr.‡

MANNS HARBOR, 1,167, *Dare Co.*

Moore, Ronda G., (CV) ....'68 '94 C.902 B.S. L.607 J.D. [Moore]

Moore Law Firm, The, P.C., (CV)
6983 Old Manns Harbor Road, P.O. Box 150, 27953
Telephone: 252-473-9777 Fax: 252-473-9801
Email: rondamoore@charter.net URL: http://www.mooreouterbankslaw.com
Ronda G. Moore.
Real Estate, Corporate Law.

See Professional Biographies, MANNS HARBOR, NORTH CAROLINA

MANTEO, * 991, *Dare Co.*

Aldridge, George Irvin ....'34 '72 C.240 A.B. L.575 J.D. [Aldridge,S.S.&F.] ‡

Aldridge, Seawell, Spence & Felthousen, L.L.P., (AV)
805 North Main Highway, P.O. Box 339, 27954
Telephone: 252-473-3484 Facsimile: 252-473-2046
URL: http://www.lawyers.com/aldridgeseawellfelthousen
Members of Firm: George Irvin Aldridge (Retired); Christopher L. Seawell; W. Mark Spence; Kris J. Felthousen. Associates: Paddison P. Hudspeth; Thomas P. Routten.
General Civil and Criminal Trial Practice. Real Estate, Wills and Probate, Corporate, Domestic Relations Law, Family, Divorce, Child Custody, Personal Injury, Automobile Accidents and Wrongful Death.
References: East Carolina Bank; Centura Bank.

See Professional Biographies, MANTEO, NORTH CAROLINA

Archbell, Roy A., Jr.
(See Kitty Hawk)

Barnes, Edgar L. ....'59 '86 C.953 B.A. L.574 J.D. Dist. Ct. J.
Cannon, William H., (AV) ....'39 '66 C.198 B.A. L.575 LL.B. [W.H.Cannon] ⊙
Cannon, William H., P.A., (AV) ...... 207 Queen Elizabeth Avenue, Suite 1 (⊙Charlotte)
Cole, Herman A., Jr., (CV) ....'38 '64 C&L.575 B.A., LL.B. Co. Atty.

DeVeau, Ronald E., P.C.
(See Nags Head)

Evans, Charles D., (BV) .... '44 '73 C&L.575 A.B., J.D. [Kellogg&E.]
Felthousen, Kris J., (BV) .... '66 '92 C.893 B.A. L.1209 J.D. [Aldridge,S.S.&F.]

Grimsley, Allan R. ....'69 '99 C.1369 B.S. L.896 J.D. Asst. Dist. Atty.
Harden, Matthew J. ....'76 '02 C.1083 B.S. L.1339 J.D. [A Wheless&W.]
Harman-Scott, Susan, (CV) ....'54 '86 C.577 B.A. L.896 J.D. [A Kellogg&E.]

Hornthal, Riley, Ellis & Maland, L.L.P.
(See Elizabeth City)

Hudspeth, Paddison P. ....'79 '04 C&L.576 B.A., J.D. [A Aldridge,S.S.&F.]

Kellogg and Evans, P.A., (BV)
201 Ananias Dare Street, P.O. Box 189, 27954
Telephone: 252-473-5500 Fax: 252-473-1214, 2157
Email: kandelaw@kelloggandevans.com URL: http://www.lawyers.com/kelloggandevans
Members of Firm: Martin Kellogg, Jr. (1908-2001); Charles D. Evans. Associate: Susan Harman-Scott.
General Civil Practice in State Courts, Family Law, Probate, Real Estate, Business Law, Vessel Documentation and Financing, and Estate Planning and Administration.
Representative Clients: Centura Bank; Wachovia Bank; East Carolina Bank; First Union National Bank; NationsBank; Cooperative Savings Bank, FSB; Wanchesc Fish Co.; Outer Banks Ventures, Inc.; Norwest Mortgage, Inc.; Chase Manhattan Mortgage Corp.

See Professional Biographies, MANTEO, NORTH CAROLINA

McCown, Linda H., (BV) ....'57 '89 C&L.228 B.S., J.D. [McCown&M.]
McCown & McCown, P.A., (BV) ....300 Sir Walter Raleigh Street
Parker, John R. ....'48 '74 C.575 A.B. L.896 J.D. Supr. Ct. J.
Routten, Thomas P. ....'78 '04 C.893 B.A. L.692 J.D. [A Aldridge,S.S.&F.]
Seawell, Christopher L., (AV) ....'46 '71 C&L.575 B.S., J.D. [Aldridge,S.S.&F.]

Sharp, Michael, Outten and Graham
(See Kitty Hawk)

Spence, W. Mark, (BV) ....'51 '79 C.55 B.S. L.1228 J.D. [Aldridge,S.S.&F.]

Vandeventer Black LLP
(See Kitty Hawk)

Vincent Law Firm, The, PC
(See Southern Shores)

Wheless, Dwight H., (BV) ....'40 '67 C&L.575 A.B., J.D. [Wheless&W.] ⊙
Wheless, W. Jay, (BV) ....'64 '89 C.575 A.B. L.1228 J.D. [Wheless&W.]

Wheless & Wheless, PLLC, (BV)
101 South Virginia Dare Road, P.O. Box 500, 27954 ⊙
Telephone: 252-473-5500 Fax: 252-473-1154 Real Estate Processing Email: whelesslawfirm@earthlink.net
Email: whelesslawfirm@earthlink.net URL: http://www.whelesslawfirm.com
Members of Firm: Dwight H. Wheless; W. Jay Wheless;—Matthew J. Harden.
Traffic Violations, General Practice. Real Estate, Driving While Intoxicated, Civil Litigation, County Government Law, Insurance Defense, Real Estate Development, Residential Real Estate Development, Waterfront Development, Zoning Law, Ship Documentation and Ship Finance and Family Law.
References: East Carolina Bank; Bank of America; RBC Centura; Wachovia Bank; Cooperative Savings & Loan Assn.
Columbia, North Carolina Office: 402 Main Street, 27925. Telephone: 252-796-5500. Fax: 252-796-1154.

See Professional Biographies, MANTEO, NORTH CAROLINA

MARBLE, —, *Cherokee Co.*

Harris, Glenn E. ....'28 '57 C.77 B.A. L.893 J.D. P.O. Box 190‡

MARION, * 4,943, *McDowell Co.*

Bibb, Eleanor B., (BVⓉ) '61 '92 C.822 B.A. L.744 J.D.
(adm. in TX; not adm. in NC) P.O. Box 669
Burgin, Charles E., (AV) ....'38 '65 C.575 A.B. L.228 LL.B. [Dameron,B.&P.]
Carnes, Everette C., (AV) ....'21 '48 C&L.896 J.D. [C Carnes&F.]
Carnes & Franklin, P.A., (BV) ....97 South Main Street
Caviness, Loto Greenlee ....'51 '77 C.404 B.A. L.896 J.D. Supr. Ct. J.
Clark, Bay '27 '55 C&L.94 LL.B.
(adm. in TX; not adm. in NC) Rte 2 Box 767‡
Coats, Donald F., (BV) ....'47 '74 C.10 B.S. L.192 J.D. 25 W Henderson St.
Dameron, E. Penn, Jr. ....'50 '75 C&L.575 B.A., J.D. Supr. Ct. J.

Dameron, Burgin & Parker, P.A., (AV)
26 West Court Street, P.O. Drawer 1049, 28752
Telephone: 828-652-2441 Telecopier: 828-652-9579
Email: dameronburgin@dameronburginlaw.com URL: http://www.dameronburginlaw.com
Emerson P. Dameron (1909-2000); Charles E. Burgin; Sharon L. Parker; Margaret A. Lorenz; Phillip T. Jackson;—Jennifer O. Jackson; Aaron G. Walker.
General Practice and Litigation in all State and Federal Courts, Medical Malpractice, Municipal Law; Education Law, Health Care, Corporate Law, Insurance, Real Estate, Probate Law, and Professional Liability.
Counsel for: Norfolk Southern Railway Co.; Jefferson-Pilot Insurance Cos.; Security Life & Trust Co.; American Thread Co.; United Merchants & Manufacturers Corp.

See Professional Biographies, MARION, NORTH CAROLINA

Dews, Julie, (AV) ....'51 '90 C.1178 B.A. L.588 J.D. [Goldsmith,G.&D.]
Edwards, A. Michael, (BV) ....'59 '85 C&L.575 B.S., J.D. 137 Logan St.
Evans, Hill, (AV) ....'55 '80 C&L.896 B.A., J.D. [W.H.Evans]
Evans, W. Hill, P.A., (AV) ....69 South Main Street
Franklin, Hugh J., (BV) .... '53 '81 C.34 B.A. L.1228 J.D. [Carnes&F.]
Goldsmith, C. Frank, Jr., (AV) ....'45 '70 C.198 A.B. L.575 J.D. [Goldsmith,G.&D.]
Goldsmith, James W., (AV) ....'48 '75 C.576 B.S. L.575 J.D. [Goldsmith,G.&D.]

Goldsmith, Goldsmith & Dews, P.A., (AV)
57 South Main Street, P.O. Box 1107, 28752
Telephone: 828-652-3000 Fax: 828-652-9196
Email: lawfirm@GoldsmithDews.com URL: http://www.GoldsmithDews.com
C. Frank Goldsmith, Jr.; James W. Goldsmith; Julie Dews.
General Trial and Appellate Practice, Civil and Criminal, before all State and Federal Courts. Personal Injury, Workers Compensation, Family, Employment, Real Estate, Probate, Commercial and Constitutional Law.

See Professional Biographies, MARION, NORTH CAROLINA

Golsan, Roy W. ....'72 '00 C.840 B.B.A. L.896 J.D. [Little,S.&G.]
Jackson, Jennifer O., (BV) ....'68 '93 C.160 B.S. L.575 J.D. [A Dameron,B.&P.]
Jackson, Phillip T., (BV) ....'68 '94 C.576 B.A. L.575 J.D. [Dameron,B.&P.]
Little, Stephen R., (AV) ....'51 '77 C&L.896 B.A., J.D. [Little,S.&G.]
Little, Sheffer and Golsan, P.A., (AV) ....20 North Main Street
Lorenz, Margaret A., (BV) ....'67 '93 C.945 B.A. L.896 J.D. [Dameron,B.&P.]
Lynch & Taylor, P.A., (BV) ....94 West Fort St.
Parker, Sharon L., (AV) ....'59 '87 C&L.575 B.A., J.D. [Dameron,B.&P.]
Rivera-Carretero, Armando A., (CV) ....'42 '74 C&L.677 B.B.A., J.D. P.O. Box 2956
Sheffer, Andrew R., (CV) ....'72 '97 C.893 B.A. L.896 J.D. [Little,S.&G.]
Taylor, Lee F., (BV) ....'68 '96 C.576 B.S. L.362 J.D. [Lynch&T.]
Walker, Aaron G. ....'79 '04 C.34 B.S. L.575 J.D. [A Dameron,B.&P.]
Yancey, Robert Anthony, (BV) ....'51 '76 C.575 B.S. L.790 J.D. [Yancey,R.A.]
Yancey, Robert A., P.A., (BV) ....81 W. Fort St.

MARSHALL, * 809, *Madison Co.*

Baker, James L., Jr. ....'54 '82 C.1129 B.A. L.469 J.D. Sr. Res. Supr. Ct. J.
Hager, Judy S. ....'46 '96 C.34 B.A. L.574 J.D. [J.S.Hager]

Hager, Judy Shelton, Attorney at Law .................................P.O. Box 669
Huff, Joseph B., (AV) .... '19 '42 C.1129 L.896 LL.B. 108 E. Main Street

Huff, Stephen E., (AV) '50 '78 C.575 B.A. L.896 J.D.
30 South Main Street, P.O. Box 758, 28753
Telephone: 828-649-2851 Fax: 828-649-9135
General Civil and Criminal Practice. Trials in all Courts. Administrative, Personal Injury, Probate, Corporation and Real Estate Law.
Representative Clients: Southern Railway System; Wachovja Bank of North Carolina; Asheville Federal Savings and Loan Assn.; Continental Trailways; Dickerson, Inc.; United States Fidelity and Guaranty Co.; Aetna Casualty and Surety Co.; Insurance Companies of North America; Clyde Savings and Loan Assn.

Leake, Larry B., (AV) ....'50 '74 C&L.575 B.A., J.D. [Leake&S.] ⊙

Leake & Scott, (AV)
Mashburn Building, P.O. Box 451, 28753 ⊙
Telephone: 828-649-3883
Email: harrell_leake@law.com
Larry B. Leake.
General Practice and Trial in all Courts. Interstate Commerce, Insurance, Corporation, Real Estate, Governmental, Medical Malpractice, Personal Injury, Taxation Law.
Asheville, North Carolina Office: 501 BB&T Building, 28801. Telephone: 828-253-3661.
See Professional Biographies, MARSHALL, NORTH CAROLINA

Mashburn, Charles E., (AV) ....'19 '47 C&L.575 A.B., LL.B. P.O. Box 98‡
Plaut, Tanya M., (AVⓉ) '36 '69 C.94 B.S.B.A. L.818 J.D.
(adm. in FL; not adm. in NC) [T.M.Plaut]
Plaut, Tanya M., P.A., (AVⓉ) ....P.O. Box 218
Rockey, Arlaine ....'62 '89 C.575 B.A. L.472 J.D. P.O. Box 656

Sluder, Curtis Alan
(See Asheville)

MARS HILL, 1,764, *Madison Co.*

Blackwell, Steven, (BV) ....'36 '65 C.896 A.B. L.575 J.D. P.O. Box 1418
Blume, George B. '31 '61 C.608 B.S. L.362 J.D.
(adm. in FL; not adm. in NC) 71 English Ridge‡
Briggs, Bruce B., (AV) ....'37 '62 C.1129 L.896 LL.B. Dist. J.
Van Helden, Diane C., (AVⓉ) ....'43 '73 C.705 A.B. L.326 J.D. P.O. Box 1441

MATTHEWS, 22,127, *Mecklenburg Co.*

Adams, Andrew M., (CVⓉ) ...... '63 '89 C.1083 B.S. L.1209 J.D. 8534 Castle Cliff Drive
Adams, Heather Brantley '71 '97 C.893 B.A. L.1356 J.D.
Sr. Real Estate Atty., Family Dollar Stores, Inc.
Allen, William J. ..... '— '98 C.829 B.A. L.1252 J.D. 2435 Plantation Center Dr., Ste. 205
Athans, Athanasios G. ....'62 '86 C&L.228 B.A., J.D. 300 Auckland Lane
Bennett, Charles W., (BV) ....'46 '77 C.48 B.A. L.575 J.D. 196 N. Trade St.
Bentsi-Enchill, Jatrine '64 '91 C.951 B.A. L.1068 J.D.
(adm. in CA; not adm. in NC) 2930 Providence Hills Dr.
Bland, Michael D., (BV) ....'52 '78 C&L.896 B.A., J.D. 196 N. Trade St.
Brogan, Byron J. .... '47 '73 C&L.546 B.S., J.D. Insurance Counsel, Family Dollar Stores

Carter, James H., (BV) '46 '79 C.1128 B.A. L.1228 J.D.
131 Matthews Station Street, Suite 2C, 28105
Mailing Address: P.O. Box 2638, Matthews, NC 28206
Telephone: 704-844-8926 Fax: 704-844-8936
Email: jamescarterlaw@alltel.net
Construction Law, Personal Injury.
See Professional Biographies, MATTHEWS, NORTH CAROLINA

Clifford, John G. '55 '81
C.893 B.A. L.896 J.D. Asst. Gen. Coun., Family Dollar Stores, Inc.
Coffman, E. Ronald .... '36 '54 C.477 B.S.M.E. L.273 J.D. 3617 Bounty Ct.
Dalrymple, Jeffrey G. ....'64 '89 C.1044 B.S. L.201 J.D. [Lynch&D.]
Farris, Richard S., (BV) ....'61 '92 C.999 B.S. L.1228 J.D. 250 N. Trade St., Ste. 300

Garis Law Firm
(See Charlotte)

Gessner, L. Michelle '72 '99
C.999 B.S. L.923 J.D. Atty., Legal Dept., Family Dollar Stores, Inc.
Gessner, Michelle '72 '99 C.999 B.S. L.923 J.D.
Sr. Litig. Atty., Family Dollar Stores, Inc.
Hamilton, Jack T. ....'27 '57 C&L.575 B.S., J.D. 601 Evams Manor Dr.
Harwell, Helen Ruth ....'72 '97 C.10 B.S.B.A. L.192 J.D. 196 N. Trade St.

Heasley, C. Wayne
(See Charlotte)

Howell, James D. .... '33 '70 C&L.575 B.S., J.D. [J.D.Howell]
Howell, James D., P.A., Law Office of .... 9930 Monroe Rd., Ste. 103
Hughes, Rebekah Tinsley '72 '97 C&L.790 B.A., J.D.
(adm. in SC; not adm. in NC) Corp. Coun., Family Dollar
Hutchens, John G., Jr. ....'52 '79 C.198 A.B. L.896 J.D. V.P., Harris Teeter, Inc.
Kaplan, Alan M. ....'57 '82 C.577 B.A. L.575 J.D. 629 Elizabeth Ln.‡
Karres, Matthew S. '58 '84
C&L.575 A.B., J.D. Atty., Legal Dept., Family Dollar Stores, Inc.
Kelley, Janet G., (BVⓉ) '53 '78 C.510 B.A. L.383 J.D.
(adm. in KY; not adm. in NC) Family Dollar Stores, Inc.
Labiner, Howard Mark ....'58 '83 C.1349 B.A. L.575 J.D. P.O. Box 3425
Leder, Joseph, (AVⓉ) ....'27 '52 C.331 B.A. L.569 LL.B. 3009 Michelle Dr.‡
Leger, Lindy Thomas .... '63 '89 C.575 A.B. L.1345 J.D. 234 Benton Woods Dr.
Lynch, John R., Jr., (BVⓉ) ....'54 '80 C.354 B.A. L.94 J.D. [Lynch&D.]
Lynch & Dalrymple, P.A., (BVⓉ) .... 9912 Monroe Rd., Ste. 201
Mahoney, George R., Jr. '42 '67 C.611 A.B. L.228 LL.B.
Exec. V.P., Gen. Coun., Secy. & Dir., Family Dollar Stores, Inc.
Marino, Matthew A. ....'63 '88 C&L.569 B.A., J.D. 105 Pineville-Matthews Road
Matre, Abigail P. .... '68 '00 C.886 B.S. L.790 J.D. Family Dollar Stores, Inc.
McLean, Amy Clayborne '71 '97 C.232 B.A. L.575 J.D.
Atty., Family Dollar Stores, Inc.
Miller, Nick J., (AV) ....'30 '59 C&L.575 B.A., J.D. 1216 Reverdy (⊙Charlotte)
Mullican, Michael P. ....'75 '04 C.576 B.A. L.145 J.D. Family Dollar Stores, Inc.
Nantz, Richard Edward ....'54 '01 C.1128 B.S. L.862 J.D. P.O. Box 2570
Newkirk, Krista Lyn ...... '72 '98 C.546 B.A. L.945 J.D. Atty., Family Dollar Stores, Inc.
Pope, Tina Blalock ....'74 '00 C.999 B.S. L.1526 J.D. Asst. Dist. Atty.
Reed, Jill E. ....'67 '96 C.473 B.A. L.117 J.D. 7031 Kidwelly Lane
Schoenheit, Thomas E. '53 '78 C.575 B.A. L.880 J.D.
Asst. Gen. Coun., Real Estate, Family Dollar Stores, Inc.
Simms, Stephen G. '40 '65 C.705 B.A. L.923 J.D.
(adm. in WV; not adm. in NC) Family Dollar Stores, Inc.
Smalley, Ryan James ....'74 '99 C.902 B.A. L.896 J.D. Family Dollar Stores, Inc.
Sperry, George H., Jr. ....'66 '99 C.953 B.S. L.575 J.D. [Sperry&T.]

Sperry & Tyson, PLLC
100-E West John Street, 28105
Mailing Address: P.O. Box 2475, Matthews, NC 28106
Telephone: 704-845-2600 Fax: 704-845-1339
George H. Sperry, Jr.; Adam M. Tyson.
Real Estate, Residential Real Estate, Commercial Real Estate, Mortgages, Trusts and Estates, Estate Planning, Business Law, Partnerships, Contracts, Collections, Corporate, Taxation, Bankruptcy.
See Professional Biographies, MATTHEWS, NORTH CAROLINA

Stoner, Sean A. '72 '99 C.97 B.A. L.608 J.D.
Corp. Real Estate Atty., Family Dollar Stores, Inc.
Tillotson, Suzanne C. '70 '96
C&L.575 B.A., J.D. Real Estate Atty., Family Dollar Stores, Inc.
Tyson, Adam M. ....'66 '02 C.1102 B.S. L.574 J.D. [Sperry&T.]
Unger, Rebekah Hughes '72 '97 C&L.790 B.A., J.D.
(adm. in SC; not adm. in NC) Real Estate Atty., Family Dollar Stores, Inc.
Usher, Jeffrey R. .... '54 '82 C.679 B.S. L.896 J.D. P.O. Box 1792
Vann, Christopher M., (CV) .... '68 '93 C.228 B.A. L.575 J.D. [Vann]

Vann Law Firm, P.A., (CV)
9930 Monroe Road, Suite 103, 28105
Telephone: 704-846-6050 Fax: 704-845-1662
URL: http://www.vannlawfirm.com
Member of Firm: Christopher M. Vann.
Business Law, Corporate, Limited Liability Companies, Small Business, Contracts, Collections, Creditor Rights, Employment, Discrimination, Driving While Intoxicated, Traffic Violations and Wrongful Termination Law.
See Professional Biographies, MATTHEWS, NORTH CAROLINA

Varriale, Corinne D. '63 '87 C.1505 B.A. L.564 J.D.
(adm. in NY; not adm. in NC) Family Dollar Stores, Inc.
Weaver, Eran Lee ....'70 '97 C.896 B.A. L.692 J.D. P.O. Box 2570
Whittaker, William G. ....'57 '82 C.1128 B.A. L.838 J.D. 196 N. Trade St.
Wieboldt, Stephanie Carol '68 '93
C.210 B.S. L.896 J.D. Real Estate Atty., Family Dollar Stores, Inc.
Wood, Sylvia Stanley ......'66 '91 C.838 B.S. L.896 J.D. Atty., Family Dollar Stores, Inc.
Wren, J. Robert, Jr., (BV) '47 '72
C.896 B.B.A. L.273 J.D. Exec. V.P. & Gen. Coun., PCA Intl., Inc.

MAXTON, 2,551, *Robeson & Scotland Cos.*

Hammonds, Chad Wyatt, (CV) ....'69 '94 C.602 B.S. L.896 J.D. P.O. Box 7

MEBANE, 7,284, *Alamance & Orange Cos.*

Davis, Charles E., (BV) ....'51 '76 C.198 B.A. L.575 J.D. [Davis&H.]
Davis & Humbert, P.A., (BV) ....200 W. Center St.
Hollowood, Edward F., (BVⓉ) '49 '81 C&L.262 B.A., J.D.
(adm. in TX; not adm. in NC) 101 W. Roosevelt St.
Humbert, William H., (BV) ....'50 '76 C.198 B.A. L.575 J.D. [Davis&H.]
Long, John R., (AV) '51 '79
C.228 B.A. L.245 J.D. V.P. & Gen. Coun., Liggett Group Inc.
Settle, Lee W., (BV) .... '19 '48 C.896 B.A. L.575 LL.B. 105 S. 4th
Springer, Matt Lawrence '64 '90 C.94 B.S. L.904 J.D.
(adm. in NY; not adm. in NC) V.P. & Gen. Coun., Madison River Communication

Vira Law Firm, The, PA
(See Carrboro)

MIDLAND, 950, *Cabarrus Co.*

Witt, Deborah Williamson, (AVⓉ) '55 '86
C.806 B.A. L.790 J.D. 14525 Cabarrus Station Rd.

MOCKSVILLE, * 4,178, *Davie Co.*

Culler, Mark S., (BV) ....'59 '86 C.806 B.A. L.896 J.D. P.O. Box 654
Fleming, Tamara Allen, (BV) ....'61 '86 C.575 B.A. L.1228 J.D. [Martin&V.]
Hall, William E., (AV) ....'25 '60 C.576 B.S. L.896 J.D. 181 South Main Street‡

Leonard, Wade H., Jr., (BV) '42 '72 C.34 B.S. L.575 J.D.
34 Town Square, 27028
Telephone: 336-751-5020 Fax: 336-751-9640
General Civil and Criminal Practice. Probate, Real Estate, Family, Corporation and Personal Injury Law. Trials.
Approved Attorney for: Lawyers Title Insurance Corp.; Farmers Home Administration, V.A. Approved; AMI Title Insurance Co.; Jefferson Pilot Title Insurance Co.; Investors Title; Stewart Title Insurance Co.; Chicago Title Insurance, The Title Company of North Carolina; First American Title; Statewide Title Company.

Martin, George W., (AV) .... '27 '52 C&L.228 A.B., J.D. [Martin&V.]
Martin, Lester P., Jr. ....'24 '55 C.575 A.B. L.896 LL.B. Ret. Supr. Ct. J.

Martin & Van Hoy LLP, (AV)
10 Court Square, 27028-2415
Telephone: 336-751-2171 Fax: 336-751-1773
Members of Firm: George W. Martin; Henry P. Van Hoy, II; Sally Womack Smith; Robert H. Raisbeck, Jr.; Tamara Allen Fleming; Brian F. Williams.
General Civil Practice. Trials. Probate, Real Estate, Corporation, Insurance and Personal Injury Law, Criminal Defense, Family Law, Estate Planning, Business Law, Mediation.
Representative Clients: Central Carolina Bank and Trust Co.; Funder America, Inc.; Town of Mocksville.
Approved Attorneys for: Lawyers Title Insurance; Commonwealth Title Insurance; Jefferson Pilot Title Insurance; Investors Title Insurance.
See Professional Biographies, MOCKSVILLE, NORTH CAROLINA

McClamrock, Grady L., Jr., (BV) ....'52 '77 C.576 B.S. L.896 J.D. 161 S. Main St.
Nesbit, Thomas L., (BV) ....'59 '84 C&L.575 B.A., J.D. [T.L.Nesbit]
Nesbit, Thomas L., P.C., (BV) .... 65 Court Sq.
Parker, Julie A., (BV) .... '61 '87 C&L.896 B.A., J.D. 854 Valley Rd., Ste. 200
Parker, Michael J., (BV) ....'62 '87 C.1083 B.A. L.896 J.D. 854 Valley Rd.
Raisbeck, Robert H., Jr., (AV) ....'63 '89 C&L.896 B.A., J.D. [Martin&V.]
Smith, Sally Womack, (AV) ....'57 '82 C.260 B.A. L.896 J.D. [Martin&V.]
Springer, Frank David '12 '38 C.813 A.B. L.309 J.D.
(adm. in CA; not adm. in NC) 1372 Point Rd.‡

Teeter Law Firm
(See Winston-Salem)

Van Hoy, Henry P., II, (AV) ....'49 '74 C&L.575 A.B., J.D. [Martin&V.]
Vogler, E. Edward, Jr., (P.A.), (AV) .... '51 '77 C.575 B.A. L.896 J.D. [E.E.Vogler,Jr.]
Vogler, E. Edward, Jr., P.A., (AV) .... 181 South Main Street
White, Andrew ....'57 '83 C.296 B.S. L.930 J.D. 132 W. Lexington Rd.
Williams, Brian F. ....'71 '99 C.575 B.A. L.896 J.D. [Martin&V.]
Womack, Joseph W., (AVⓉ) '26 '56 C.260 B.A. L.472 J.D.
(adm. in FL; not adm. in NC) 1317 Jericho Church Rd.‡

MONROE, * 26,228, *Union Co.*

Adams, Robert C.
(See Charlotte)

Asti, Russell Z., (BV) .... '49 '75 C.896 B.A. L.836 J.D. 121 E. Phifer St.

Berger, Hal, P.A., A Professional Law Corporation
(See Charlotte)

Brooks, Charles B., II, (BV) '60 '85 C.296 A.B. L.575 J.D.
313 North Main Street, 28112
Telephone: 704-283-9363 Fax: 704-289-8327
Criminal Defense, Driving While Intoxicated (DWI Defense), Drug Crimes, Assault, Traffic Violations, Child Custody, Child Support, Divorce, Products Liability, Medical Malpractice, Automobile Accidents, Wrongful Death, Products Liability and Medical Malpractice. Litigation.
See Professional Biographies, MONROE, NORTH CAROLINA

Brooks Law Office
(See Charlotte)

Brown, Richard L., Jr. '69 '96 C.511 B.A. L.575 J.D.
310 N. Church Street, P.O. Box 3326, 28112
Telephone: 704-283-6800 Fax: 704-291-7725
Email: arichardbrownl@carolina.rr.com URL: http://www.richardbrownlaw.com
Real Estate-Buying and Selling, Landlord and Tenant, Personal Injury, Automobile Accidents, Dog Bites, Criminal Law, White Collar Crime, Traffic Violations, Driving While Intoxicated, Employment Law, Wrongful Terminations, Bankruptcy, Civil Rights, Health Care, Nursing Home Issues.
See Professional Biographies, MONROE, NORTH CAROLINA

Bundy, H. Ligon, (AV) .... '49 '76 C&L.575 B.A., J.D. [Perry,B.P.&L.]
Caldwell, Thomas J., (AV) .... '46 '71 C.198 A.B. L.575 J.D. [Griffin,S.C.H.&H.]
Clark, Griffin & McCollum, L.L.P., (BV) .... 238 East Franklin Street

Clodfelter Law Office
(See Wadesboro)

Cohen, Zachary A. '78 '05 C.999 B.A. L.1363 J.D.
201 N. Main Street, Suite 101, 28112
Telephone: 704-283-9090
Email: zcohen@lawyer.com URL: http://www.zachcohenlaw.com
Criminal Law, Traffic Violations, Drug Crimes, Driving While Intoxicated, Sex Crimes.
See Professional Biographies, MONROE, NORTH CAROLINA

Collins, Shawna Davis '70 '95 C.140 B.A. L.260 J.D.
315-A N. Main Street Suite 201, 28112
Telephone: 704-289-3250 Facsimile: 704-283-9539
Email: info@shawnacollins.com URL: http://www.lawyers.com/sdcollins
Family Law, Adoption Law, Child Custody, Child Support, Divorce, Criminal Law, Driving While Intoxicated, Drug Crimes, Felonies, Traffic Violations, Trusts and Estates, Wills, Probate.
See Professional Biographies, MONROE, NORTH CAROLINA

Constitution Law Associates, LLC
2649 Breckenridge Centre Drive (⊙Charlotte, Huntersville, NC; Fort Mill, Lake Wylie, Rock Hill, SC)
Cox, Christopher L. .... '74 '99 C&L.1228 Asst. Dist. Atty.
Cox, Ronald H., (BV) .... '52 '80 C.575 B.A. L.896 J.D. 100 W. Jefferson
Crook, Jeffrey L. .... '61 '88 C&L.896 B.A., J.D. 500 N. Main St., Ste. 826
Crow, Harry B., Jr. .... '44 '69 C&L.575 B.A., J.D. 315-B N. Main St.
Crow, Marcus D. .... '72 '01 C.575 B.S. L.692 J.D. [Crow]
Crow, Matthew Hung .... '70 '99 C.575 B.A. L.692 J.D. [Ⓐ Crow]
Crow Law Firm, The .... 315-B N. Main St.
Dawkins, Koy E., (AV) .... '34 '59 C.316 B.S. L.896 LL.B. [K.E.Dawkins]

Dawkins, Koy E., P.A., (AV)
212 East Jefferson Street, P.O. Drawer 399, 28111-0399
Telephone: 704-283-8501 Fax: 704-283-1371
Email: kdawkins@koydawkins.com URL: http://www.koydawkins.com
Koy E. Dawkins.
General Practice in all State and Federal Courts. Real Estate, Commercial and Business Law. Construction Law, Education Law, Personal Injury, Trusts and Estates, Civil Litigation, Wills and Probate.
See Professional Biographies, MONROE, NORTH CAROLINA

DeMayo, Michael A., (BV) .... '65 '91 C.896 B.A. L.575 J.D. [M.A.DeMayo] ⊙
DeMayo, Michael A., L.L.P., Law Offices of, (BV)
406 S. Sutherland Ave. (⊙Charlotte, Hickory)
Doule, Melanie Elizabeth .... '76 '01 C.128 B.A. L.575 J.D. Dist. Atty.'s Off.

Everett, Kerry B.
(See Charlotte)

Fisher, Lewis R., (BV) .... '50 '74 C.273 B.A. L.575 J.D. 105 S. Hayne St.

Garis Law Firm
(See Charlotte)

Glass, J. Bennett, P.A., (AV) ..... '40 '66 C.269 A.B. L.575 LL.B. 108-A W. Jefferson St.

Goldfarb, William K., Law Offices of, (BV) '64 '91 C.576 B.A. L.1228 J.D.
301 South Charlotte Avenue, P.O. Box 3200, 28111
Telephone: 704-296-0055 Fax: 704-296-0053
Email: goldfarb_law@hotmail.com
Personal Injury, Professional Negligence, Medical Malpractice, Workers' Compensation, Traffic Violations.
See Professional Biographies, MONROE, NORTH CAROLINA

Griffin, Bobby H., (BV) .... '38 '67 C.1318 B.A. L.896 J.D. [Clark,G.&M.]
Griffin, C. Frank, (AV) .... '26 '50 C.575 B.S. L.228 LL.B. [Ⓒ Griffin,S.C.H.&H.]

Griffin, Smith, Caldwell, Helder & Helms, P.A., (AV)
314 North Hayne Street, P.O. Drawer 99, 28111-0099
Telephone: 704-289-4577 Toll Free from Charlotte: 704-372-4808 Fax: 704-289-4218 (Real Estate); 704-283-1122 (General)
URL: http://www.griffinsmithcaldwell.com
Thomas J. Caldwell (Certified Mediator); Jake C. Helder; R. Kenneth Helms, Jr.;—Trey Robison; Rebecca L. Robison; Kimberly B. Loia; James A. Lee, III. Of Counsel: C. Frank Griffin; Henry B. Smith, Jr.
Personal Injury, Worker's Compensation, General Civil Litigation, Residential and Commercial Real Estate Finance and Development, Land Use Planning and Zoning, Wills, Trusts, Estate Planning and Administration, Business and Corporate Law, General Practice, Family Law, Traffic.
See Professional Biographies, MONROE, NORTH CAROLINA

Hancock, Franklin S., (CV) .... '54 '79 C.198 B.A. L.896 J.D. 1201 Concord Ave.
Harrington, James J. .... '73 '02 C.968 B.A. L.192 J.D. [Harrington]
Harrington, Larry E., (AV) .... '40 '64 C.404 L.896 LL.B. [Harrington]

Harrington Law Firm, (AV)
315 A North Main Street, P.O. Box 1003, 28112
Telephone: 704-289-2548 Fax: 704-283-9539
URL: http://www.lawyers.com/larryeharrington
Larry E. Harrington; James J. Harrington.
Civil and Criminal Trials in all Courts. Corporation, Wills, Probate and Estates, Insurance Law, Personal Injury, Traffic Violations.
See Professional Biographies, MONROE, NORTH CAROLINA

Helder, Jake C., (BV) .... '45 '70 C.575 B.S. L.896 J.D. [Griffin,S.C.H.&H.]
Helms, R. Kenneth, Jr., (BV) .... '62 '88 C.575 B.A. L.896 J.D. [Griffin,S.C.H.&H.]
Helms, William Franklin, III .... '68 '97 C.198 B.A. L.575 J.D. P.O. Box 850
Helms, William H. .... '46 '72 C&L.575 B.S., J.D. Supr. Ct. J.‡

Helms, Henderson & Associates, P.A.
(See Charlotte)

Higdon, Stephen V., (BV) .... '71 '97 C.575 B.A. L.896 J.D. Off. of Dist. Atty.
Hipps, Jonathan L., (CV) .... '70 '97 C.34 B.S. L.574 J.D. Asst. Dist. Atty.
Honeycutt, Kenneth W., (AV) .... '47 '72 C.115 B.S. L.896 J.D. Asst. Dist. Atty.

Honnold Law Firm, The, P.A.
(See Charlotte)

Huffman, Carol L., (BV) .... '68 '96 C.575 B.A. L.896 J.D. P.O. Box 1008
Huffman, Robert L., (BV) .... '32 '61 C.34 B.S. L.575 LL.B. 340 W. Morgan St.
Hutaff, Richard R., (BV) .... '54 '80 C.576 B.A. L.192 J.D. 108 E. Jefferson St.
Hutcherson, Joseph L., II, Attorney at Law, (BV) '44 '76
C&L.575 B.A., J.D. 315 N. Main St.
Jones, Daniell .... '79 '04 C.1378 B.A. L.896 J.D. [Wilson&J.]
Larocque, Jeremy P., (CV) .... '72 '98 C.576 B.S.M.E. L.575 J.D. [Lehnhardt&L.]
Lee, James A., III .... '75 '05 C.576 B.S. L.1228 [Ⓐ Griffin,S.C.H.&H.]
Lee, W. David .... '50 '75 C.925 B.A. L.896 J.D. Supr. Ct. J.
Lehnhardt, Dana Belk, (CV) .... '73 '98 C.1128 B.A. L.575 J.D. [Lehnhardt&L.]
Lehnhardt & Larocque, LLP, (CV) .... 107-A E. Jefferson Street

Lezman, Jack G., P.A.
(See Charlotte)

Loia, Kimberly B. .... '75 '01 C.140 B.S. L.1370 J.D. [Ⓐ Griffin,S.C.H.&H.]
Long, Richard G., Jr., (BV) .... '57 '82 C.575 B.A. L.896 J.D. [Perry,B.P.&L.]
Love, Walter B., Jr., (AV) .... '21 '49 C&L.575 B.S., J.D. 108 E. Jefferson St.
MacConnachie, Ian M., Jr. '46 '73 C.184 B.A. L.851 J.D.
(adm. in NJ; not adm. in NC) 1220 Irongate Dr.‡
Maness, Jayrene R., (BV) .... '56 '81 C.575 B.A. L.896 J.D. Asst. Dist. Atty.
McCollum, Joe P., Jr., (BV) .... '42 '67 C&L.896 B.A., J.D. [Clark,G.&M.]
McGuirt, William L., (BV) .... '55 '84 C.34 B.S. L.1228 J.D. [W.L.McGuirt]
McGuirt, William L., P.C., (BV) .... P.O. Box 3154
Milliken, John R., (AV) .... '31 '58 C.575 A.B. L.273 LL.B. City Atty.
Murray, Kimlani S. .... '72 '98 C.645 B.A. L.896 J.D. Dist. Atty. Off.
Nanney, Kenneth M. '67 '92
C.1128 B.A. L.790 J.D. In-House Coun., Union Reg. Med. Ctr.
Nason, Allen M. '72 '99 C.956 B.S. L.1358 J.D.
[Constitution&Assoc.] (⊙Charlotte, Huntersville, NC; Rock Hill, SC)
Painter, John H., (BV) .... '56 '81 C.34 B.S. L.1228 J.D. 108 W. Jefferson St.
Parker, Michael Dean, (BV) .... '64 '89 C.576 B.S. L.575 J.D. Asst. Dist. Atty.
Peniston, Richard A., (BV) ..... '49 '77 C.1128 B.A. L.575 J.D. [R.A.Peniston&Assoc.] ⊙
Peniston, Richard A., & Associates, P.A., (BV)
211 Lancaster Avenue (⊙Charlotte, Raleigh)
Perry, Donald C., (BV) .... '40 '64 C&L.896 B.A., LL.B. [Perry,B.P.&L.]

Perry, Bundy, Plyler & Long, L.L.P., (AV)
316 North Hayne Street, P.O. Box 7, 28111-0007
Telephone: 704-289-2519 Fax: 704-282-0105
Members of Firm: Donald C. Perry; H. Ligon Bundy; Dale Ann Wilkinson Plyler; Richard G. Long, Jr.
General Practice. Trials in all State and Federal Courts. Real Estate and Probate, Corporation, Worker's Compensation, Personal Injury, Family Law, Local Government Law, Traffic Violations, Social Security Disability.
Representative Clients: Town of Wingate; Wildred, Inc.; Smith York & Co.; Taylor's Motor Co.; Computing Solutions, Inc.; Union County Department of Social Services.
References: United Carolina Bank; NCNB National Bank of North Carolina; First Citizens Bank.
See Professional Biographies, MONROE, NORTH CAROLINA

Plyler, Dale Ann Wilkinson, (BV) .... '64 '90 C.925 B.S. L.1228 J.D. [Perry,B.P.&L.]
Prevost, Robert .... '55 '91 C.69 B.A. L.846 J.D. 1000 E. Franklin St.
Robison, Pat S., III .... '67 '96 C.623 B.A. L.896 J.D. P.O. Drawer 99
Robison, Rebecca L., (BV) .... '70 '98 C.608 B.A. L.117 J.D. [Ⓐ Griffin,S.C.H.&H.]
Robison, Trey .... '67 '96 C.623 B.A. L.896 J.D. [Ⓐ Griffin,S.C.H.&H.]
Rodgers, Timothy R., (CV) .... '72 '98 C.838 B.A. L.575 J.D. Asst. Dist. Atty.

Schattenfield Law Firm, The, PLLC
(See Charlotte)

Smith, Henry B., Jr., (BV) .... '36 '61 C&L.575 B.A., LL.B. [Ⓒ Griffin,S.C.H.&H.]

Sperry & Tyson, PLLC
(See Matthews)

Starnes, Steven D., (BV) .... '65 '90 C.999 B.S. L.192 J.D. [S.D.Starnes]
Starnes, Steven D., P.A., (BV) .... 107 N. Main St.
Stepp, Donna B., (BV) .... '69 '93 C.1356 B.A. L.1228 J.D. [D.B.Stepp]

Stepp, Donna B., P.C., Law Office of, (BV)
105 C East Jefferson Street, P.O. Box 2526, 28111
Telephone: 704-283-5353 Fax: 704-289-2528
Email: dbstepp@gte.net
Donna B. Stepp.
Family Law, Divorce, Separation, Child Custody, Traffic Violations, DWI, Criminal Defense.
See Professional Biographies, MONROE, NORTH CAROLINA

Westmoreland, Anna N., Law Office of
(See Charlotte)

Williams, Joseph J. .... '64 '88 C.575 B.A. L.574 J.D. Dist. J.
Wilson, Tiffany N. .... '77 '03 C.329 B.A. L.574 J.D. [Wilson&J.]

Wilson & Jones
111 Winchester Avenue, 28110
Telephone: 704-283-1500
URL: http://www.wilsonjoneslaw.com
Members of Firm: Tiffany N. Wilson; Daniell Jones.
Criminal Law, Bankruptcy, Workers Compensation, Personal Injury, Family Law, Traffic Violations, Social Security, Automobile Accidents, Elder Law.
See Professional Biographies, MONROE, NORTH CAROLINA

MOORESVILLE, 18,823, *Iredell Co.*

Anderson, Christopher C. "Kit" .... '77 '04 C.896 B.A. L.280 J.D. [Ⓐ Homesley G.&W.]
Bain, Brian T. .... '76 '01 C.925 B.S.B.A. L.1228 J.D. [Ⓐ Lutzel,G.&B.]

Barone Law Firm, The, P.A.
(See Cornelius)

Bolduc Law Firm, The, PLLC
(See Charlotte)

Brawley, P.B., Jr., (AV) .... '30 '60 C.576 B.S. L.896 J.D. [P.B.Brawley]
Brawley, P.B., P.A., (AV) .... 283 N. Main St.
Carson, Evalyn B. .... '11 '65 C.577 L.981 LL.B. 125 N. Sycamore St.‡
Childers, Mark L., (BV) .... '64 '90 C.1128 B.A. L.896 J.D. [Thomas,G.&C.]

Corbett, William T., Jr., Law Office of, (BV) '64 '89 C&L.1228 B.A., J.D.
755 North Main Street, Suite A, P.O. Box 1227, 28115
Telephone: 704-799-7076 Fax: 704-663-5455
Email: billcorbettlaw@msn.com URL: http://www.billcorbettlaw.com

(This Listing Continued)

Corbett, William T., Jr., Law Office of (Continued)
Insurance Defense, Wills and Probate, Estates, Criminal Law, Traffic Violations, General Civil Litigation.
See Professional Biographies, MOORESVILLE, NORTH CAROLINA

Cornelius, Preston .... '41 '67 C.576 B.S. L.575 J.D. Supr. J.‡
Crisco, Ronnie D., Jr. .... '80 '05 C.228 B.A. L.575 J.D. [A Homesley G.&W.]

Dalton, Judy
(See Troutman)

Davidson, Daryl G., Sr., PC, Law Office of
(See Statesville)

Donaldson, Kevin C. .... '73 '99 C.247 B.A. L.1345 J.D. [Homesley,J.G.D.M.&D.]
Fields, T. Eric, (BV) .... '48 '73 C.404 B.A. L.896 J.D. P.O. Box 1573
Gambill, Stephen P. .... '58 '85 C.34 B.S. L.574 J.D. Town Atty.
Godley, T. Michael, (BV) .... '60 '86 C.575 B.S. L.1228 J.D. [Thomas,G.&C.]
Goodman, Nancy Barlow .... '66 '94 C.1365 B.A. L.790 J.D. [Homesley G.&W.]

Hartsell & Williams, P.A.
(See Concord)

Hayes, Ray A., II, P.A.
(See Cornelius)

Holden, Matthew J. '64 '90
C.884 B.A. L.1017 J.D. Sr. Corp. Coun., Lowe's Companies Inc.
Homesley, Clifton W., (BV) .... '60 '86 C.575 B.S. L.1228 J.D. [Homesley G.&W.]
Homesley, Troy C., Jr., (AV) ... '34 '58 C&L.575 A.B., J.D. [Homesley,J.G.D.M.&D.] ⊙

Homesley Goodman & Wingo, PLLC, (BV)
330 South Main Street, 28115
Telephone: 704-664-2162 Fax: 704-664-0267
Email: HGWinfo@lakenormanlaw.com URL: http://www.lakenormanlaw.com
Members of the Firm: Clifton W. Homesley; Andrew J. Wingo; Nancy Barlow Goodman. Associates: Christopher C. "Kit" Anderson; Ronnie D. Crisco, Jr.
Languages: Spanish.
Contract Law, Commercial and Business Law, Trademark Law, Civil Litigation, Corporate Law, Residential and Commercial Real Estate, Domestic and Family Law, Elder Law, Estate Planning and Administration, Wills and Trusts, Personal Injury, Worker's Compensation, Traffic and Criminal Law.
See Professional Biographies, MOORESVILLE, NORTH CAROLINA

Homesley, Jones, Gaines, Dudley, McLurkin & Donaldson, PLLC, (AV)
236 Raceway Drive, Suite 7, Lakeside Business Park, 28117 ⊙
Mailing Address: P.O. Box 3010, Mooresville, NC 28117
Telephone: 704-664-1127 Real Estate Telephone: 704-664-2145 Fax: 704-663-0939 Real Estate Fax: 704-664-6596 Real Estate Email: lakenormanrealestate@alltel.net
URL: http://www.mooresvillelakelaw.com
Troy C. Homesley, Jr.; Walter H. Jones, Jr.; Elise B. McLurkin; Kevin C. Donaldson;—John P. Stutts.
General Civil and Criminal Trial Practice in all State and Federal Courts. Probate, Real Estate, Personal Injury, Family, Corporation, Insurance, Negligence.
References: Branch Bank and Trust Co., Statesville, North Carolina; First Union National Bank, Mooresville, North Carolina.
Statesville, North Carolina Office: 316 East Broad Street, P.O. Box 149. Telephone: 704-873-2172. Fax: 704-924-2103; 704-873-5908. Email: hjgd@statesville.net. Real Estate Email: realestate@statesville.net.
See Professional Biographies, MOORESVILLE, NORTH CAROLINA

Howard, William G., (BVⓉ) .... '58 '83 C&L.378 B.A., J.D. Asst. Co. Atty.
Johnson, Leslie Gandy .... '74 '98 C.240 B.A. L.1228 J.D. [Lutzel,G.&B.] ⊙
Jones, Harley H., (BV) '60 '85 C&L.575 B.A., J.D.
Asst. Gen. Coun., Lowe's Cos. Inc.
Jones, Walter H., Jr., (AV) ..... '41 '66 C.575 B.A. L.896 J.D. [Homesley,J.G.D.M.&D.]
Keener, Gaither M., Jr., (AV) '49 '76 C.925 B.A. L.896 J.D.
V.P., Deputy Gen. Coun. & Asst. Secy., Lowe's Companies Inc.

Kluttz, Reamer, Hayes, Randolph & Adkins, L.L.P.
(See Salisbury)

Levine, Michael J. .... '68 '97 C.575 B.A. L.356 J.D. 109 Professional Park Dr.
Lutzel, Richard J., (BV) .... '66 '92 C.567 B.A. L.823 J.D. [Lutzel,G.&B.] ⊙
Lutzel, Gandy & Broadway, (BV) .... 542 Williamson Rd., Ste. A (⊙Charlotte)
Mathews, Jennifer .... '73 '00 C.575 B.A. L.880 J.D. Corp. Coun., Lowe's Cos. Inc.
McCanless, R. William '57 '82 C.1128 B.S. L.896 J.D.
Sr. V.P., Gen. Coun. & Secy., Lowe's Companies, Inc.

McIntosh Law Firm, The, P.C.
(See Davidson)

McLurkin, Elise B., (BV) ...... '70 '97 C.247 B.S. L.1228 J.D. [Homesley,J.G.D.M.&D.]
Mills, Paul Grey, Jr., (CV) '66 '95
C.34 B.S. L.1339 J.D. 109 Professional Park Dr., Ste. 200
Mock, Franklin .... '74 '99 C.575 B.A. L.896 J.D. [Whitfield&M.]
Morris, Bradley C., (BVⓉ) .... '54 '89 C.679 B.A. L.347 J.D. [B.C.Morris]

Morris, Bradley C., PLLC, (BVⓉ)
174 North Main Street, 28115
Telephone: 704-799-6662 Fax: 704-799-6554
Email: brad@bradmorrislaw.com URL: http://www.bradmorrislaw.com
Bradley C. Morris.
Civil Litigation, Complex Business Litigation, Construction Law, Employment Contract Disputes, Business Law.
See Professional Biographies, MOORESVILLE, NORTH CAROLINA

Nall, Thomas G. .... '30 '55 C.198 B.S. L.575 J.D. 522 Canvasback Rd.‡
Neel and Randall, (AV) .... 149 East Iredell Avenue
O'Neale, R. S. "Trey" '67 '98
C.1128 B.A. L.790 J.D. Corp. Coun., Lowe's Companies, Inc.
Painter, Natalie J., Law Office of '76 '04
C.800 B.S. L.896 J.D. 201 N. Church St., Ste. 200
Parker, Viki West, (BV) '64 '93
C.575 B.A. L.790 J.D. 427 East Statesville Avenue, Suite 203
Perkins, Kathryn Haggerson ..... '70 '99 C.575 B.A. L.896 J.D. Lowe's Companies Inc.
Pope, Elaine R. .... '53 '77 C&L.896 B.A., J.D. Corp. Coun., Lowe's Companies, Inc.
Pope, William R., (AV) .... '18 '48 C.198 B.S. L.575 LL.B. 283 North Main St.‡
Pratt, Richard G., (BV) '51 '78 C.575 B.A. L.896 J.D.
Sr. Coun., Lowe's Companies, Inc.
Randall, Robert N., (AV) .... '32 '60 C&L.575 A.B., LL.B. [Neel&R.]
Reeves, M. Lee '67 '97 C&L.800 B.B.A., J.D.
(adm. in NY; not adm. in NC) Asst. Gen. Coun. & Asst. Sec., Lowes Companies, Inc.
Reische, Christin J. '55 '89
C.198 B.A. L.896 J.D. Asst. Gen. Coun., Lowes Companies, Inc.
Riddick, Patricia L., (CV) .... '69 '96 C.886 B.A. L.1187 J.D. [P.L.Riddick]
Riddick, Patricia L., PLLC, (CV) .... 182 East Plaza Drive, Suite B
Sandler, Neil F., (AVⓉ) .... '36 '62 C.347 B.S. L.912 J.D. 406 Catalina Dr.
Saul, Jeffrey A., (BVⓉ) ...... '60 '86 C.475 B.S. L.1187 J.D. Glenwood Development Co.

Singletary Law Firm, PLLC
(See Cornelius)

Smith, Douglas A.
(See Salisbury)

Stutts, John P. .... '77 '03 C.885 B.A. L.1228 J.D. [A Homesley,J.G.D.M.&D.]
Thomas, Ben S., (BV) .... '57 '89 C&L.420 B.S., J.D. [Thomas,G.&C.]
Thomas, Godley & Childers, P.A., (BV) .... 514 Williamson Road, Suite 421
Turner, D. Scott .... '72 '00 C.198 B.A. L.1119 J.D. [D.S.Turner]
Turner, D. Scott, Attorney At Law, PLLC .... 174 North Main Street
Tyndall, Richard, (AV) .... '36 '65 C.404 A.B. L.896 LL.B. 116 Laurel Hedge LN
West, Viki Melissa, (BV) .... '64 '93 C.575 B.A. L.790 J.D. [West]
West Law Firm, P.L.L.C., (BV) .... 548 C N. Main St.
White, Jay K., (BV) .... '60 '86 C.575 B.S. L.1228 J.D. [J.K.White]
White, Jay Kevin, Attorney at Law, (BV) .... 207 S. Broad St.
Whitfield, M. Gregory, (BV) .... '65 '91 C&L.575 B.S.B.A., J.D. [Whitfield&M.]

Whitfield & Mock, P.A., (BV)
609 East Center Avenue, P.O. Box 1616, 28115
Telephone: 704-663-5350 Fax: 704-663-4001
URL: http://www.whitfieldandmocklaw.com
M. Gregory Whitfield; Franklin Mock.
Personal Injury, Workers Compensation, Traffic Violations, Driving While Intoxicated, Criminal Law, Civil Litigation, Family Law, Social Security Disability, Wills and Probate.
See Professional Biographies, MOORESVILLE, NORTH CAROLINA

Williams, Robert G. .... '38 '67 C.611 B.A. L.347 J.D. 185 Ruby Rd.

Williams, G. Patteson
(See Cornelius)

Willis, William M., IV, Attorney at Law, (CV) '70 '95 C.160 B.S. L.280 J.D.
201 N. Church Street, Suite 501, P.O. Box 707, 28115
Telephone: 704-660-8019 Fax: 704-663-5914 URL: http://www.willislaw-office.com URL: http://www.willislawyer.com
Email: william@willislawyer.com URL: http://www.willislawoffice.com
Criminal Law, Traffic Violations, Drug Crimes, Personal Injury, Automobile Accidents, Family Law, Workers Compensation.
See Professional Biographies, MOORESVILLE, NORTH CAROLINA

Wingo, Andrew J., (CV) .... '72 '98 C.125 B.A. L.1228 J.D. [Homesley G.&W.]
Woods, Todd I., (BVⓉ) '68 '94
C.500 B.B.A. L.356 J.D. Asst. Gen. Coun., Lowe's Cos. Inc.

MOREHEAD CITY, 7,691, *Carteret Co.*

Bailey, Glenn B., (BV) .... '29 '63 C&L.575 B.A., LL.B. 821 Arendell St.
Barkman, Francis E. '16 '41 C.722 B.A. L.228 J.D.
(adm. in MD; not adm. in NC) 3504 Sunny Dr.‡
Bennett, Thomas S., (AV) .... '34 '58 C&L.575 A.B., LL.B. P.O. Box 189
Berryman, Melissa .... '73 '98 C.320 B.A. L.1228 J.D. [Kirkman,W.B.&B.]
Beswick, George W., (BV) .... '41 '75 C&L.575 A.B., J.D. [Beswick,G.&S.]

Beswick, Goines & Stephenson, P.A., (BV)
911 Arendell Street, 28557
Telephone: 252-726-2134 Facsimile: 252-726-7438
Email: bmg@coastalaw.com URL: http://www.coastalaw.com
George W. Beswick; M. Douglas Goines; Sundee G. Stephenson.
General Civil and Trial Practice, Personal Injury, Wrongful Death, Medical Malpractice, Workers Compensation, Civil Litigation, Business and Commercial Litigation, Construction, Real Estate (Commercial and Residential), Wills, Trust, Estates, Traffic Matters, Criminal Law, Juvenile Matters, Domestic (Divorce, Alimony, Child Custody, Child Support), Social Security Disability.
See Professional Biographies, MOREHEAD CITY, NORTH CAROLINA

Boshamer, H. C., (BV) .... '32 '64 C.228 A.B. L.575 LL.B. 3512 Country Club Road
Brady, Carolyn Barnett, (CV) .... '59 '85 C.198 B.A. L.896 J.D. [Kirkman,W.B.&B.]
Briggs, John T., (BV) .... '65 '91 C.232 B.S. L.1228 J.D. [A Kellum] (⊙New Bern)
Brothers, Catherine E., (BV) .... '60 '87 C.185 B.A. L.1228 J.D. 821 Arendell St.
Bryant, Alfred S., (AV) .... '33 '60 C.575 A.B. L.976 LL.B. 103 S. 11th St., #B
Burke, Jane F. ....'61 '92 C.577 B.S. L.574 J.D. 2105 Emeline Place
Couch, V. Stuart .... '65 '96 C.228 A.B. L.1228 J.D. J. Advocate
Cummings, Robert L., (CV) .... '46 '75 C.790 B.A. L.896 J.D. 1210 Arendell St.
Cummings, Sydney L. .... '76 '01 C.575 B.A. L.1345 J.D. 1210 Arendell Street
Darden, Robert D., Jr., (BV) .... '27 '72 C.453 B.S. L.575 J.D. 304 North 35th Street
Davis, Gus L., Jr., (BV) .... '35 '61 C.575 A.B. L.896 J.D. 105 N. 10th St.
Davis, Louis James .... '43 '68 C&L.575 A.B., J.D. 105 N. 10th St.
Dubois, Alan F., (CV) .... '66 '93 C&L.896 B.A., J.D. 1007 Shepard St.

Garner, Margaret Ann '54 '82 C&L.37 B.A., J.D.
3332 Bridges Street, Suite # 2B, 28557
Telephone: 252-726-1810 Fax: 252-726-0980
Email: mgarner@coastalnet.com URL: http://www.lawyers.com/margaretanngarner
Estate Planning, Probate and Estate Administration, Commercial and Residential Real Estate, Corporations, Partnerships and LLCs, Bankruptcy.
See Professional Biographies, MOREHEAD CITY, NORTH CAROLINA

Goines, M. Douglas, (BV) .... '47 '75 C.575 B.S.B.A. L.896 J.D. [Beswick,G.&S.]
Graham, C. Barrett, (CV) .... '44 '76 C.885 B.A. L.575 J.D. 610 Arendell Street
Harris, John M., (BV) .... '55 '81 C.576 B.A. L.1228 J.D. [Harris]
Harris, R. Andrew .... '69 '94 C.576 B.A. L.896 J.D. [Harris]
Harris Law Firm, PLLC, (BV) .... 304 N. 35th St.
Harvell, Cecil S., (BV) .... '58 '83 C.1365 B.A. L.1228 J.D. [C.S.Harvell]
Harvell, Cecil S., P.A., (BV) .... 1107 Bridges Street
Hurst, George K. .... '45 '91 C.598 B.A. L.1292 J.D. P.O. Box 769

Kellum Law Firm, (AV)
5178 Highway 70 West, 28557 ⊙
Telephone: 252-726-7000 Fax: 252-726-8888
Email: ckeenhold@kellumlawfirm.com URL: http://www.lawyers.com/kellumlawfirm
Associate: John T. Briggs.
State and Federal Civil Trial Practice, Personal Injury Law, Wrongful Death, Workers' Compensation, Social Security, Defective Products, Mass Torts and Insurance Law.
See Professional Biographies, MOREHEAD CITY, NORTH CAROLINA

Kinnaman, Bruce E., (CV) .... '49 '80 C.37 B.S. L.1228 J.D. 700 Arendell St., Ste. 9

Kirkman, Whitford, Brady & Berryman, P.A., (BV)
710 Arendell Street - Suite 105, P.O. Drawer 1347, 28557-4240
Telephone: 252-726-8411 Fax: 252-726-6974
Email: kirkwhit@mail.clis.com URL: http://www.kirkmanwhitford.com
Neil B. Whitford; Carolyn Barnett Brady; Melissa Berryman.
General Civil Practice. Real Estate, Development and Land Use, Condominium, Corporate, Probate, Municipal, Business, Education, Civil Litigation, Environmental Law.
Representative Client: Roosevelt Partnership, Inc.
References: Wachovia Bank and Trust Co.; Branch Bank and Trust Co.
See Professional Biographies, MOREHEAD CITY, NORTH CAROLINA

Lassiter, Andrew A., (CV) .... '58 '86 C.902 B.A. L.1228 J.D. P.O. Box 1645

Marquardt, Dennis M., (BV) ....'41 '70 C.117 B.A. L.575 J.D. [D.M.Marquardt]

Marquardt, Dennis M., PA, (BV)
1210 Arendell Street, 28557
Telephone: 252-726-4114 Fax: 252-726-4720
Email: dmmlaw@ec.rr.com
Dennis M. Marquardt.
Real Estate, Real Estate Foreclosure, Condominiums, Probate, Wills & Estates, Corporate Law.
See Professional Biographies, MOREHEAD CITY, NORTH CAROLINA

Mason, Edith W., (BV) ....'50 '80 C.471 B.A. L.896 J.D. [Mason&M.]
Mason, L. Patten, (AV) ....'41 '67 C&L.575 B.S., J.D. [Mason&M.]

Mason & Mason, P.A., (AV)
225 Professional Circle P.O. Drawer 99, 28557
Telephone: 252-247-5303 Fax: 252-240-4848
Email: pat@masonattorneys.com
L. Patten Mason; Edith W. Mason.
General Civil Trial Practice. Real Estate Law, Admiralty, Probate, Corporate.
See Professional Biographies, MOREHEAD CITY, NORTH CAROLINA

McNeill, Robert H., II ....'40 '69 C.870 B.S. L.896 J.D. P.O. Box 843
Nobles, John E., Jr., (AV) ....'48 '77 C.575 B.A. L.896 J.D. P.O. Box 1805
Phillips, Herbert O., III ....'28 '51 C&L.575 B.S., LL.B. Supr. J.
Phillips, John H., (AV) ....'42 '68 C&L.575 B.A., J.D. [J.H.Phillips]
Phillips, John H., P.A., (AV) ....4913 Holly Ln.
Ross, John Bowen, Jr. ....'38 '63 C&L.228 B.S.M.E., LL.B. 1107 Bridges St.
Stephenson, Sundee G. ....'70 '01 C.576 B.S.W. L.1228 J.D. [Beswick,G.&S.]

Sumrell, Sugg, Carmichael, Hicks & Hart, P.A.
(See New Bern)

Taylor, Derek, (CV) ....'53 '96 C&L.575 B.S., J.D. [Taylor&T.]
Taylor, Nelson W., III, (AV) ....'28 '55 C&L.575 A.B., J.D. [Taylor&T.]
Taylor & Taylor, (AV) ....610 Arendell Street
Thompson, James W., III, Law Office of '44 '73 C&L.575 B.A., J.D.
1207-A Arendell St.

Wall, Bevin W.
(See Newport)

Wallace, James Q., III, (CV) ....'53 '81 C.576 B.A. L.1228 J.D. 3409 Pine St.

Wallace, Morris, Barwick, Landis & Stroud, P.A.
(See Kinston)

Ward and Smith, P.A.
(See New Bern)

Way, John E., Jr., (BV) ....'47 '81 C.575 B.A. L.1228 J.D. 821 Arendell St.
Whaley, Debra, Attorney At Law ....'77 '02 209 N. 35th St.
Whitford, Neil B., (BV) ....'51 '76 C.576 B.A. L.575 J.D. [Kirkman,W.B.&B.]

MORGANTON, * 17,310, *Burke Co.*

Avery, Richard C., (BV) ....'64 '93 C.198 B.A. L.896 J.D. 203 E. Union St.
Aycock, Ellis L., (BV) ....'39 '65 C&L.896 B.B.A., J.D. 1180 Sundance Lane
Aycock, Samuel E., (AV) ....'46 '72 C.198 A.B. L.575 J.D. [Starnes,A.H.&E.]
Becker, Russell R., (BV) ....'47 '89 C.585 B.S. L.896 J.D. [Becker]
Becker Law Firm, (BV) ....204 E. McDowell St., Ste. A.
Beyer, Richard W., (BV) ....'52 '76 C&L.896 B.S., J.D. P.O. Box 2100
Blanton, Thomas R., III, (AV) ....'42 '69 C.896 B.A. L.575 J.D. [T.R.Blanton,III]
Blanton, Thomas R., III, P.A., (AV) ....220 West Union Street
Bostian, Charles Marcus ....'68 '95 C.925 B.S. L.1228 J.D. [[A] V.N.Yamouti]
Byrd, Joe K., (AV) ....'23 '50 C&L.575 A.B., J.D. [Byrd,B.E.W.&M.] ‡

Byrd, Byrd, Ervin, Whisnant & McMahon, P.A., (AV) [BB]
One Northsquare, 301 East Meeting Street, 28655
Telephone: 828-437-4220 Fax: 828-438-4517
Email: skp@byrdlaw.com URL: http://www.lawyers.com/byrdbyrdervin
Joe K. Byrd (Retired); Robert B. Byrd (1930-2002); John W. Ervin, Jr.; C. Scott Whisnant; Lawrence D. McMahon, Jr.;—Michelle C. Pritchard; Robert K. Denton.
Business Law, Business Dissolutions, Business Estate Planning, Business Formation, Buy-Sell Agreements, Closely Held Business Estate Planning, Civil Litigation, Commercial Litigation, Common Carrier Liability Law, Contested Wills, Corporate Law, Closely Held Corporations, Corporate Dissolutions, Corporate Formation, Criminal, Drivers' License Suspension, Driving While Intoxicated, Motor Carrier Liability, Partnership Law, Limited Liability Partnerships, Partnership Dissolution, Partnership Formation, Personal Injury, Accidents, Auto Accidents, Auto Negligence, Bodily Injury, Brain Injury, Carpal Tunnel Syndrome, Catastrophic Injury, Commercial Vehicle Liability, Head Injury, Motor Vehicle Accidents & Injuries, Motorcycle Accidents, Pedestrian Injuries, School Bus Accident, Severe Burns, Slip and Fall, Spinal Injury, Third Party Wrongful Death, TMS Dysfunction, Wrongful Death, Social Security, Social Security Disability, Truck Accidents, Trusts & Estates, Decedent's Estate, Estate Administration, Estate Planning, Workers' Compensation, Industrial Insurance, Workers' Compensation Appeals.
See Professional Biographies, MORGANTON, NORTH CAROLINA

Carswell-Pritchard, Michelle L. ....'70 '96 C.198 B.A. L.990 J.D. P.O. Box 1269
Cheuvront, Steven M. ....'70 '98 C.250 B.S. L.923 J.D. 211 E. Union St.
Clontz, Wayne O., (CV) ....'52 '79 C.228 B.A. L.574 J.D. 400 E. Meeting St.
Collett, Mary Ruffin ....'52 '81 C.604 B.A. L.896 J.D. 111 Riverside Ct.‡
Cox, Amy L., (BV) ....'50 '76 C&L.575 B.A., J.D. 207 Avery Avenue
Dale, Wheeler ....'15 '42 C&L.896 B.S., LL.B. 103 N. Sterling St.‡
Daniel, Stephen T. ....'44 '69 C&L.896 B.A., J.D. P.O. Box 1825
Daniel, Warren Todd ....'68 '00 C.870 B.S. L.575 J.D. P.O. Box 1825

Dark, L. Talton, III, (BV) '53 '79 C.34 B.S.B.A. L.896 J.D.
211 East Union Street, 28655-3449
Telephone: 828-433-0103 Fax: 828-437-9397 Toll Free #: 1-888-433-0103
Email: darklaw@bellsouth.net URL: http://www.taltondark.com
Criminal Law, Driving While Intoxicated, Traffic Violations.
See Professional Biographies, MORGANTON, NORTH CAROLINA

Denton, Robert K. ....'74 '03 C.575 B.A. L.1228 J.D. [[A] Byrd,B.E.W.&M.]
Dyer, William, (BV(T)) ....'19 '69 C.192 A.B. L.1045 LL.B. 500 Lenoir Road

Eaker & Fulkerson, PC
(See Hickory)

Edwards, C. Thomas, (BV) ....'48 '77 C.228 B.A. L.790 J.D. [Ledford&E.]
Einstein, Nancy L. ....'55 '84 C.475 B.A. L.64 J.D. [Starnes,A.H.&E.]

Elliott, J. Bryan
(See Hickory)

Ervin, John W., Jr., (AV) ....'37 '62 C&L.575 A.B., LL.B. [Byrd,B.E.W.&M.]
Ervin, Robert C. ....'60 '85 C.198 B.A. L.309 J.D. Co. J.
Ervin, Sam J., IV, (AV) ....'55 '81 C.198 A.B. L.309 J.D. State Util. Comm.‡
Gage, Robert H., (BV) ....'48 '76 C.309 B.A. L.575 J.D. 207 Avery Avenue
Haire, Susan L. ....'70 '96 C.575 B.S. L.574 J.D. [Starnes,A.H.&E.]
Hall, Douglas L. ....'— '95 C.296 B.A. L.1228 J.D. [Hall&H.] ⊙
Hall, Susan P., (CV) ....'— '95 C.269 B.A. L.1228 J.D. [Hall&H.]

Hall & Hall, Attorneys At Law, P.C., (CV)
Suite 200 305 S. Green Street, 28655 ⊙
Telephone: 828-433-9100 Fax: 828-433-9339
Email: hallandhall@bellsouth.net
Douglas L. Hall; Susan P. Hall.
Estates, Real Estate, Workers Compensation, Family Law, Divorce, Equitable Distribution, Personal Injury, Traffic Violations, Driving While Intoxicated, Criminal Law, Collections, Child Custody, Corporate Law, Employment Discrimination.
Newland, North Carolina Office: 118 Elk Street, 28657. Telephone: 828-733-9222.
See Professional Biographies, MORGANTON, NORTH CAROLINA

Helton, Lyndon R., PLLC
(See Hickory)

Hennessee, Heather M. ....'74 '99 C&L.1228 B.A., J.D. Staff Atty.
Kuehnert, Daniel A., (BV) ....'54 '83 C.1044 B.A. L.896 J.D. 216 N. Sterling St.
Lail, Warren K. ....'50 '89 C.575 A.B. L.896 J.D. 215 Brentwood RD.
LeCroy, M. Alan, (BV) ....'65 '91 C.896 B.A. L.575 J.D. [LeCroy A.&W.]
LeCroy Ayers & Willcox, (BV) ........................P.O. Box 1785
Ledford, Bob A., (BV) ....'43 '80 C.34 B.S. L.575 J.D. [Ledford&E.]
Ledford & Edwards, (BV) ....205 S. King St.
Martin, Wayne W., (BV) ....'34 '67 C.240 A.B. L.192 J.D. 111 West McDowell Street
McGee, David Howell '57 '81
C.1128 B.A. L.575 J.D. Coordinator of Paralegal Tech. Program
McKay, Mary R., (CV) ....'53 '78 C&L.16 A.B., J.D. 216 N. Sterling St.
McMahon, Lawrence D., Jr., (AV) ......'53 '78 C&L.575 B.A., J.D. [Byrd,B.E.W.&M.]
McMurray Law Office, (BV) ....202 S. Green St.
McMurray-Russ, Martha L., (BV) ....'53 '79 C&L.575 B.S., J.D. [McMurray]
Mull, John R., (BV) ....'49 '77 C&L.896 B.A., J.D. 204 S. Green St.
Palmieri, Phyllis ....'48 '85 C&L.923 B.A., J.D. Catawba Valley Legal Servs.
Peters, Troy A., (CV) ....'66 '91 C&L.896 B.A., J.D. Asst. Dist. Atty.
Phifer, Rebecca R., (BV) ....'50 '79 C.608 B.S. L.575 J.D. Asst. Atty. Gen.
Pritchard, Michelle C., (CV) ....'70 '96 C.198 B.A. L.990 J.D. [[A] Byrd,B.E.W.&M.]
Rigsbee, Keith W., (BV) ....'65 '90 C&L.896 B.A., J.D. [K.W.Rigsbee]

Rigsbee, Keith W., PLLC, Law Office of, (BV)
204 South Green Street, 28655
Telephone: 828-430-7540 Fax: 828-430-7540
Email: rigsbeek@bellsouth.net URL: http://www.rigsbeelawoffice.com
Keith W. Rigsbee.
Family Law, Criminal Law, Personal Injury, Small Business Corporations, Real Estate.
See Professional Biographies, MORGANTON, NORTH CAROLINA

Rooks, Timothy J., Law Offices of, (BV(T)) '68 '93
C.222 B.A. L.896 J.D. 122 W. Union St.

Saunders, Peggy M., (AV) '52 '89 C.77 B.A. L.575 J.D.
500 South Green Street, P.O. Box 790, 28680-0790
Telephone: 828-437-8333 Facsimile: 828-430-9333
Email: psaunders@hci.net
Real Property, Real Estate, Probate, Trusts, Wills and Estates.
See Professional Biographies, MORGANTON, NORTH CAROLINA

Schoeberle, Stephen M., (BV) ....'57 '82 C.576 B.A. L.575 J.D. Co. Dept. of Soc. Servs.
Settlemyer, Steve B., (BV) ....'44 '69 C.125 B.A. L.575 J.D. 201 W. Meeting
Simpson, Dan R., (AV) ....'27 '51 C&L.896 B.S., LL.B. [Simpson,S.&V.]
Simpson, James A., (BV) ....'26 '53 C&L.896 B.S., LL.B. Professional Bldg.
Simpson, James Reid, II, (BV) ....'54 '79 C.813 B.A. L.228 J.D. [Simpson,S.&V.]
Simpson, Simpson & Vinay, P.A., (AV) ....204 East McDowell Street
Sitton, Claude S. ....'37 '63 C.575 A.B. L.896 LL.B. Supr. Ct. J.
Sitton, Jaye ....'65 '94 C&L.575 B.A., J.D. Jud. Clk., U.S. Ct. of App.
Starnes, Thomas M., (AV) ....'36 '63 C&L.575 B.S., LL.B. [Starnes,A.H.&E.]

Starnes, Aycock, Haire & Einstein, P.A., (AV)
118 North Sterling Street, 28655
Telephone: 828-437-3335 Fax: 828-438-4929; 828-437-9832
Thomas M. Starnes; Samuel E. Aycock; Susan L. Haire; Nancy L. Einstein.
General Civil Trial Practice in all Courts, Business Law, Real Estate, Probate, Trusts and Estates Wills.
Representative Clients: Duke Power Co.; Wachovia Bank of N.C.; Grace Hospital, Inc.; The Aetna Insurance Group; Kemper Insurance Group; North Carolina Farm Bureau Insurance Co.
Approved Attorneys for: Lawyers Title Insurance Corp.
Reference: Wachovia Bank of N.C.
See Professional Biographies, MORGANTON, NORTH CAROLINA

Tate, Samuel McDowell ....'23 '53 C.198 A.B. L.575 J.D. Ret. Dist. J.
Teele, H. Dockery, Jr., (AV) ....'43 '68 C&L.575 B.S., J.D. 122 W. Union St.
Triggs, Clyde G. ....'47 '73 C.34 B.A. L.896 J.D. P.O. Box 579
Vernon, Livingston ....'22 '49 C&L.575 A.B., J.D. Emer. Dist. J.
Vinay, Louis E., Jr., (BV) ....'55 '79 C.575 B.A. L.228 J.D. [Simpson,S.&V.]
Whisnant, C. Scott, (BV) ....'50 '75 C.575 B.A. L.192 J.D. [Byrd,B.E.W.&M.]
Willcox, Roderick H., Jr., (BV) ....'63 '89 C.207 B.A. L.896 J.D. [LeCroy A.&W.]
Wojcik, Donna B. ....'60 '91 C.1176 B.A. L.1228 J.D. Atty. Gen. Off.
Yamouti, Victor N., Law Office of, (CV) '66 '93
C.953 B.S. L.896 J.D. 216 East Concord Street

Young, Morphis, Bach and Taylor, L.L.P.
(See Hickory)

MORRISVILLE, 5,208, *Durham & Wake Cos.*

Alrutz, Michael A. '69 '03 C.659 B.A. L.228 J.D.
(adm. in NY; not adm. in NC) Legal Coun., Trimers, Inc.
Andrew L. Liput, LLP ....105 Gambardelli Ct.
Bonczek, Robert R. '45 '70 C&L.575 B.S., J.D.
(adm. in FL; not adm. in NC; Pat.) Trimeris, Inc.
Carrow, H. Hill, Jr. ....'55 '80 C.575 A.B. L.178 J.D. 205 Keybridge Dr.
Gillan, John A., (BV(T)) '65 '90 C.222 B.A. L.276 J.D.
(adm. in NJ; not adm. in NC) Division Counsel, Hanson Building Materials America
Hallajian, Andrew H. ....'66 '92 [[C] Andrew,L.L.]
Jefferson, Jeffrey L. '61 '95 C.838 B.S. L.309 J.D.
(adm. in GA; not adm. in NC) 105 Grahamwood Ct.
Lapine, Bernard J. ....'69 '96 C.282 B.A. L.1187 J.D. Mid Atlantic Medical Services, Inc.
Liput, Andrew L. '62 '87 C.222 B.A. L.262 J.D.
(adm. in NJ; not adm. in NC) [Andrew,L.L.]
Nelson, M. Bud ....'56 '94 C.1372 B.S. L.107 J.D. Trimeris, Inc. (Pat.)
Nye, C. Howard, (AV) .....'62 '87 C.228 A.B. L.896 J.D. Pres., Hanson Aggregates East
Oechsle, Jonathan D. '64 '91 C.893 B.A. L.945 J.D.
Sr. Coun./Gen. Coun., Diosynth. RTP Inc., Azko Nobel Inc.
Pandite, Prasan A. '— '93 C.112 A.B. L.597 J.D.
(adm. in MA; not adm. in NC) President, Advanced Medical Institute
Powell, William P., Jr., (BV) '59 '82 C.1129 B.A. L.896 J.D.
Gen. Coun., Empire Distributors of N.C., Inc.

Richardson, Jonathan, The Law Office of
(See Cary)

Wade, Elizabeth . . . . '78 '04 C.623 B.A. L.228 J.D. Carolina Dispute Resolution

MOUNTAIN HOME, 2,169, *Henderson Co.*

Ahrens, Robert W. '35 '63 C&L.893 B.S., LL.B.
(adm. in VA; not adm. in NC) P.O. Box 697‡

MOUNT AIRY, 8,484, *Surry Co.*

Adams, Karen J.
(See Dobson)

Beal, Michael D., (BV) . . . . '66 '91 C.576 B.A. L.896 J.D. [Ⓐ Royster&R.]
Bell, Carl E., (AV) . . . . '40 '70 C.1318 B.S. L.896 J.D. 140 Franklin Street
Campbell, Hugh B., III, (BV) . . . . '67 '92 C.198 B.A. L.896 J.D. [Gardner,G.&C.P.]

Davis Elder & Disability Law
(See Lewisville)

Donnelly, Gus L., (BV) . . . . '40 '78 C.575 B.A. L.896 J.D. 134 Moore Ave.
Faw, Thomas M., (AV) . . . . '24 '54 C.198 A.B. L.896 LL.B. [Ⓒ Faw,F.&J.]

Faw, Folger & Johnson, P.C., (AV) BR
Branch Banking and Trust Building, 541 North Main Street, P.O. Drawer 512, 27030
Telephone: 336-786-2401 Fax: 336-786-2620
Email: fawfolger1@earthlink.net URL: http://www.fgjohnson.com
Charles L. Folger (1911-1998); Fredrick G. Johnson. Of Counsel: Thomas M. Faw.
General and Trial Practice. Business and Corporate, Commercial, Education, Municipal, Trusts and Estates, Wills, Probate, Real Estate Law.
Approved Attorneys for: Lawyers Title Insurance Co.
See Professional Biographies, MOUNT AIRY, NORTH CAROLINA

Fawcett, Richard M., (AV) . . . . '49 '74 C&L.575 B.S., J.D. 603 N. Main St.
Folger, Fred, Jr., (AV) . . . . '26 '52 C&L.228 A.B., LL.B. [Folger&F.]
Folger and Folger, (AV) . . . . 129 Moore Ave.
Gardner, John C. W., (AV) . . . . '29 '56 C.404 A.B. L.896 J.D. [Ⓒ Gardner,G.&C.P.]
Gardner, John C. W., Jr., (BV) . . . . '58 '85 C&L.896 B.A., J.D. [Gardner,G.&C.P.]

Gardner, Gardner and Campbell PLLC, (BV)
304 Franklin Street, P.O. Box 866, 27030
Telephone: 336-789-5502 Fax: 336-789-5506
URL: http://www.lawyers.com/ggs&m
Members of Firm: Carroll F. Gardner (1934-2004); John C. W. Gardner, Jr.; Hugh B. Campbell, III. Of Counsel: John C. W. Gardner; Matthew J. Middleton.
General Civil and Criminal Practice in all State and Federal Courts, including Corporate and Real Property Practice.
Local Counsel for: Housing Authority of the Town of Mt. Airy; Cooke Trucking Co.; Wachovia Bank; N. C. Granite Corp.; Federal Land Bank of Columbia.
Approved Attorneys for: Lawyers Title Insurance Corp.; Jefferson-Pilot Title Insurance Co.; Commercial Standard Title Insurance Co.; Workmen's Federal Savings Bank.
See Professional Biographies, MOUNT AIRY, NORTH CAROLINA

Hansen, Gerald H. '57 '84 C.259 B.S. L.845 J.D.
(adm. in FL; not adm. in NC) 330D Cross Creek Dr.
Haxton, Manford R. . . . . '28 '62 C.623 B.S. L.326 LL.B. 2893 W. Pine St.‡
Hiatt, V. Talmage . . . . '24 '51 C&L.575 A.B., LL.B. 1010 S. Main St.‡

Jessup, Ron L., The Law Offices of, (CV) '53 '91 C.576 B.A. L.574 J.D.
132 Moore Avenue, 27030
Telephone: 336-786-5200 Fax: 336-786-1504
Email: jessuplaw@hotmail.com
Consumer Protection Law, Unfair and Deceptive Trade Practices, Employment and Labor Law, Sexual Harassment and Discrimination, U.S. Title VII Discrimination, Criminal Law, Civil and Criminal Trial Litigation, State and Federal Courts.
See Professional Biographies, MOUNT AIRY, NORTH CAROLINA

Johnson, Fredrick G., (AV) . . . . '48 '73 C.896 B.A. L.575 J.D. [Faw,F.&J.]
LaPrade, F. Grey, Jr., (BV) . . . . '43 '71 C&L.896 B.A., J.D. [Woltz,L.&L.]
Lewis, Fred E., III, (BV) . . . . '43 '71 C.198 A.B. L.896 J.D. [Woltz,L.&L.]
Lowe, Sharon Hice, (BV) . . . . . . '58 '84 C.575 B.A. L.896 J.D. 708 S. Main St., Ste. 1463
Massey, Aaron M. . . . . '48 '76 C.101 B.S. L.575 J.D. Supr. Ct. J.
Merritt, Cama C. . . . . '28 '75 C.6 A.B. L.896 J.D. 832 Country Club Rd‡
Merritt, H. Lee, Jr., (BV) . . . . '50 '77 C.575 B.A. L.469 J.D. 129 Moore Ave.
Middleton, Matthew J. . . . . '74 '04 C.34 B.A. L.862 J.D. [Ⓒ Gardner,G.&C.P.]
Oliver, Otis M. . . . . '38 '63 C&L.575 LL.B. Dist. J.
Pardue, T. Richard, Jr. '53 '78 C&L.575 B.A., J.D. P.O. Box 1466
Peoples, Hugh H. . . . . '43 '74 C.198 B.A. L.575 J.D. 302 Grace St.‡
Pfitzner, Helen S. . . . . '62 '88 C.569 B.A. L.813 J.D. 442 Montclair Drive
Royster, Michael F., (AV) . . . . '46 '75 C.896 B.A. L.192 J.D. [Royster&R.] ⊙
Royster, Stephen G., (AV) . . . . '46 '74 C.896 B.A. L.192 J.D. [Royster&R.]

Royster and Royster, (AV)
851 Marshall Street, P.O. Box 1005, 27030 ⊙
Telephone: 336-789-5127 Fax: 336-789-6650
Email: sgr@roysterandroyster.com URL: http://www.lawyers.com/roysterandroyster
Members of Firm: Stephen G. Royster; Michael F. Royster. Associate: Michael D. Beal.
General Civil and Criminal Trial Practice. DWI, Traffic Offenses, Felonies. Personal Injury, Automobile Accidents, Wrongful Death, Real Estate Law, Trusts and Estates, Wills and Probate, Probate Law and Workers Compensation.
Pilot Mountain, North Carolina Office: 110 South Davis Street, P.O. Box 1396. Telephone: 919-368-4455. Fax: 919-368-1279. Email: mroyster@surry.net.
See Professional Biographies, MOUNT AIRY, NORTH CAROLINA

Sharpe, Patrick M., (BV) . . . . '34 '59 C&L.896 B.A., LL.B. [P.M.Sharpe]
Sharpe, P.M., Law Offices of, PLLC, (BV) . . . . 902 S. Renfro Street
Stevens, Sarah S., (BV) . . . . '60 '86 C.577 B.S. L.1228 J.D. 1835 Westfield Rd.
Williams, Joseph Howard, (CV) . . . . '68 '94 C.896 B.A. L.192 J.D. 708 S Main St
Woltz, Edwin Moore, (BV) . . . . '58 '83 C.575 B.S. L.896 J.D. P.O. Box 4600
Woltz, Lewis & LaPrade, (BV) . . . . 145 W. Independence Bld.

MOUNT GILEAD, 1,336, *Montgomery Co.*

Lehrer, Robert W. . . . . '49 '78 C.475 B.A. L.896 J.D. 1779 Yank Rd.

MOUNT HOLLY, 9,618, *Gaston Co.*

Childers, David C., (BV) . . . . '51 '81 C.575 B.A. L.1228 J.D. [Childers,F.&C.]
Childers, Fowler & Childers, P.A., (BV) . . . . 135 S. Main St.
Michael, Kemp A., Attorney at Law, (BV) '47 '72
C.1318 B.A. L.896 J.D. 124 W. Catawba Ave.
Miller, Andrea L., (BV) . . . . '72 '97 C&L.1345 B.A., J.D. 129 W. Catawba Ave.
Stancil, James W. . . . . '15 '41 L.799 LL.B. 129 W. Catawba Ave.‡
Stancil, James W., (AV) . . . . '52 '78 C&L.896 J.D. 129 W. Catawba Ave.
Whitt, Robert C., (AV) . . . . '49 '75 C.198 B.A. L.575 J.D. 601 S. Main St.

MOUNT OLIVE, 4,582, *Wayne Co.*

Connor, Douglas P. '34 '64 C.296 A.B. L.896 J.D. 209 N. Center St.‡
Edwards, John P., Jr., (BV) . . . . '51 '77 C.228 A.B. L.575 J.D. P.O. Box 120
Macartney, Richard K. '42 '81 C.393 B.A. L.1048 J.D.
(adm. in MA; not adm. in NC) Carolina Turkey
Rice, Robert T., (BV) . . . . '42 '73 C.576 B.S. L.575 J.D. P.O. Box 120
Turner, W. Carroll, (BV) . . . . '49 '74 C&L.896 B.A., J.D. [Turner]
Turner Law Offices, L.L.P., (BV) . . . . 117 S. Center St.

MOUNT PLEASANT, 1,259, *Cabarrus Co.*

Cloninger, Brent . . . . '63 '93 C.575 B.A. L.1228 J.D. [Cloninger]

Cloninger Law Office
1453 N. Main Street, 28124
Mailing Address: P.O. Box 1518, Mount Pleasant, NC 28124
Telephone: 704-436-2233 Fax: 704-436-2244
Email: bcloninger@ctc.net URL: http://www.cloningerlawfirm.com
Brent Cloninger.
Criminal, Traffic, Driving While Intoxicated, Family Law, Custody, Divorce, Child Support, Visitation Rights, Wills and Probate.
See Professional Biographies, MOUNT PLEASANT, NORTH CAROLINA

MOUNT ULLA, —, *Rowan Co.*

Sherrill, John C., III, (BV) . . . . '53 '81 C.198 B.A. L.64 J.D. P.O. Box 599

MOYOCK, 700, *Currituck Co.*

Innes, Amy J. . . . . '71 '99 C.1356 B.A. L.1206 J.D. 257 Caratoke Hwy., Ste. B
Innes, James Brian . . . . '71 '97 C.1356 B.A. L.1206 J.D. 257 Caratoke Hwy., Ste. B

MURFREESBORO, 2,045, *Hertford Co.*

Howard, Vernice Britt, (CV) . . . . '53 '85 C.709 B.A. L.273 J.D. 1131 Va. Blvd.
Jones, Thomas L., Jr., (BV) . . . . '53 '81 C.575 B.A. L.574 J.D. 207 East Main Street
Lee, Robert Edward, Jr., (AV) . . . . '45 '72 C&L.896 B.A., J.D. [Revelle&L.]

LeonLaw Firm, The
(See Greenville)

Revelle, Charles L., III, (AV) . . . . '52 '77 C.575 A.B. L.228 J.D. [Revelle&L.]
Revelle, J. Guy, Jr., (AV) . . . . '32 '57 C&L.896 B.A., LL.B. [Ⓒ Revelle&L.]

Revelle & Lee, LLP, (AV)
201 East Main Street, P.O. Box 448, 27855
Telephone: 252-398-4171 Fax: 252-398-4051
Email: revellelawfirm@coastalnet.com
Members of Firm: Robert Edward Lee, Jr.; Charles L. Revelle, III. Associate: J. Jerry Vick, Jr. Of Counsel: J. Guy Revelle, Jr.
Probate, Real Estate, Corporation, Taxation and Municipal Corporations Law.
General Counsel for: Hertford County; Chowan College; Town of Murfreesboro; Roanoke Chowan Human Services; Hertford County Department of Social Service.
Representative Clients: Severn Peanut Company; United Turf, Inc.
Approved Attorneys for: Rural Economic Development Services; Lawyers Title Insurance Corp.; United Title Insurance Co.
See Professional Biographies, MURFREESBORO, NORTH CAROLINA

Spruill, Gerald W., Law Offices of, (CV) . . . . '67 '97 C.953 B.A. L.574 J.D. P.O. Box 741
Vick, J. Jerry, Jr., (BV) . . . . '56 '81 C&L.575 A.B., J.D. [Ⓐ Revelle&L.]

MURPHY, * 1,575, *Cherokee Co.*

Bata, Rudolph A., Jr., (BV) . . . . '47 '73 C.999 B.S. L.245 J.D. [R.A.Bata,Jr.]

Bata, Rudolph A., Jr., P.A., (BV)
225 Valley River Avenue Suite A, 28906
Telephone: 828-837-8684 Fax: 828-837-2174
Email: batalaw@yahoo.com URL: http://www.lawyers.com/batalaw
Rudolph A. Bata, Jr.
General Civil Practice, Civil Litigation in State and Federal Courts, Personal Injury, Negligence, Real Estate Litigation, Residential and Commercial Transactions, Probate Law.
References: First Citizens Bank; First Union National Bank.
See Professional Biographies, MURPHY, NORTH CAROLINA

Bius, Dana L. . . . . . . '71 '97 C.48 B.A. L.1228 J.D. [Ⓐ McKeever,E.D.&H.] (⊙Hayesville)
Blomeley, James L., Jr., (BV) '56 '81 C.280 B.S. L.896 J.D.
53 Peachtree Street, Suite 201
Brown, Darryl R. . . . . '67 '92 C.48 B.A. L.575 J.D. [D.R.Brown]
Brown, Darryl R., Attorney at Law, P.A. . . . . 157 Hiwassee St.
Collins, Gerald R., Jr., (BV) . . . . '53 '80 C.896 B.A. L.1228 J.D. [Collins,P.]
Collins Law Firm, The, PLLC, (BV) . . . . 53 Peachtree Street, Suite 202
Cook, Beverly B. . . . . '72 '99 C.925 B.S. L.574 J.D. [B.B.Cook]
Cook, Beverly B., P.A. . . . . 800 Andrews Rd., Ste. B
Cowan, David E. . . . . '76 '02 C.925 B.S. L.1228 J.D. [Cowan&C.]
Cowan, Ronald M., (AV) . . . . '50 '75 C.575 B.S. L.896 J.D. [Cowan&C.]

Cowan & Cowan, P.A., (AV)
26 Tennessee Street, P.O. Box 579, 28906-0579
Telephone: 828-873-2332 Fax: 828-837-2336
Email: cowanlawyers@brmemc.net
Ronald M. Cowan; David E. Cowan.
Civil Litigation, Criminal Defense, Traffic Violations, Real Estate, Residential Transactions, Commercial Transactions.
See Professional Biographies, MURPHY, NORTH CAROLINA

Davis, Todd W., (CV) . . . . '70 '95 C.575 B.A. L.838 J.D. P.O. Box 920

Ford, Larry J., Attorney at Law
(See Hayesville)

Hays, W. Arthur, Jr., (AV) . . . . '42 '68 C&L.575 A.B., J.D. [McKeever,E.D.&H.]
Lindsay, R. Scott, (BV) . . . . '51 '77 C.925 B.A. L.896 J.D. P.O. Box 580
McKeever, William H., (BV) . . . . '53 '81 C.575 B.A. L.574 J.D. [McKeever,E.D.&H.]
McKeever, Edwards, Davis & Hays, P.A., (AV)
139 Peachtree Street (⊙Bryson City, Hayesville)
Sanders, Deborah Kay . . . . '72 '98 C.576 B.A. L.896 J.D. P.O. Box 596
Smith, Noland W., (BV) . . . . '57 '82 C.575 B.S. L.896 J.D. [McKeever,E.D.&H.]
Snow, John J., Jr. . . . . '45 '71 C&L.896 B.A., J.D. Chf. Dist. J.
Steinbronn, Richard E., (AVⓉ) . . . . '— '66 C.723 B.A. L.602 LL.B. [Steinbronn,R.E.]
Steinbronn, Richard E., PC, (AVⓉ) . . . . 26 Tennessee Street
Sumpter, W. David, III, (BV) . . . . '45 '75 C.797 B.A. L.838 J.D. 115 Hiwassee St.

NAGS HEAD, 2,700, *Dare Co.*

Alexy, Fletcher, Wills & Wills, P.C.
(See Point Harbor)

Archbell, Roy A., Jr.
(See Kitty Hawk)

DeVeau, Ronald E., (BV) . . . . '44 '70 C.401 B.S. L.228 J.D. [R.E.DeVeau]

DeVeau, Ronald E., P.C., (BV)
2224 S. Croatan Highway, #14, 27959
Telephone: 252-480-2828 Fax: 252-480-2929
Email: ron@deveaulaw.com URL: http://www.lawyers.com/deveaulaw
Ronald E. DeVeau.
General Civil and Trial Practice in State and Federal Courts, Personal Injury and Negligence, Workers Compensation, Family Law, Business Torts, Estates.
See Professional Biographies, NAGS HEAD, NORTH CAROLINA

Gilreath, James R., Jr., (BV) .... '71 '97 C.902 B.A. L.790 J.D. P.O. Box 1087
Harrison, M. Peebles .... '67 '92 C.301 B.A. L.902 J.D. [Rose&H.]
Hobbs, Robert B., Jr., (BV) .... '60 '86 [Hornthal,R.E.&M.]

Hornthal, Riley, Ellis & Maland, L.L.P., (AV)
2502 South Croatan Highway, P.O. Box 310, 27959-0310 ⊙
Telephone: 252-441-0871 Telefax: 252-441-8822
Email: hrem@hrem.com URL: http://www.hrem.com
Robert B. Hobbs, Jr. (Also at Elizabeth City Office) (Board Certified Specialist in Real Property Law-Residential, Business, Commercial and Industrial Transactions, North Carolina State Bar Board of Legal Specialization); Donald I. McRee, Jr. Of Counsel: Thomas L. White, Jr. (Resident).
General Trial and Appellate Practice in all Courts. Personal Injury, Products Liability, Professional Malpractice, Corporate, Tax, Bankruptcy, Employment, Education, Family, Construction, Real Estate, Environment, Elder, Local Government, Wills and Trusts, Probate and Admiralty Law.
Representative Clients: CIGNA Group; Elizabeth City-Pasquotank County Board of Education; Camden County Board of Education; Kemper Insurance Group; State Farm Mutual; Travelers Insurance Co.; Wachovia Bank of North Carolina, N.A.; Branch Banking & Trust Co.; College of the Albemarle; USF&G.
Elizabeth City, North Carolina Office: 301 East Main Street, P.O. Box 220. Telephone: 252-335-0871. Fax: 252-335-4223.
See Professional Biographies, NAGS HEAD, NORTH CAROLINA

Kellogg and Evans, P.A.
(See Manteo)

Mauney, John A. .... '50 '79 C&L.574 LL.B. 2224 S. CroatanHwy. 9
McRee, Donald I., Jr., (BV) .....'61 '87 C.1130 B.A. L.1228 J.D. [Hornthal,R.E.&M.] ⊙

Moore Law Firm, The, P.C.
(See Manns Harbor)

Rose, Dennis C., (BV) .... '53 '92 C.1369 B.S. L.500 J.D. [Rose&H.]
Rose & Harrison, P.C., (BV) .... 119 Woodhill Drive, Suite 3

Sharp, Michael, Outten and Graham
(See Kitty Hawk)

Vandeventer Black LLP
(See Kitty Hawk)

Vincent Law Firm, The, PC
(See Southern Shores)

White, Thomas L., Jr., (AV) ....'38 '70 C&L.575 A.B., J.D. [Ⓒ Hornthal,R.E.&M.]

NASHVILLE, * 4,309, *Nash Co.*

Adams, Franklin L., Jr., (AV) .... '39 '63 C&L.575 B.A., LL.B. [Valentine,A.&L.]
Beckham, Sonja S. '49 '82
C.925 B.S.Ed. L.574 J.D. Staff Atty., Co. Dept. of Social Servs.
Cooper, Pell C. .... '59 '88 C&L.575 B.A., J.D. Dist. Ct. J.
Cooper, Roy A., Jr., (AV) .... '27 '56 C.896 B.S. L.575 J.D. [Fields&C.] ‡
Davenport, John E., (AV) .... '28 '52 C&L.575 A.B., J.D. [J.E.Davenport]

Davenport, John E., P.A., (AV)
207 West Washington Street, P.O. Box 938, 27856
Telephone: 252-459-2124 Fax: 252-459-7691
John E. Davenport.
General Civil and Criminal Practice. Probate, Real Estate, and Taxation.
Reference: Centura Bank.
See Professional Biographies, NASHVILLE, NORTH CAROLINA

Edmondson, Stephanie James ......'72 '97 C.232 B.A. L.575 J.D. 1595 Sarah Ruppert Rd.
Edwards, Mark E., (BV) .... '71 '97 C&L.896 B.A., J.D. [Fields&C.]
Etheridge, William D., (AV) ....'37 '62 C&L.575 A.B., LL.B. [Etheridge,S.&H.]
Etheridge, Sykes & Hamlett, L.L.P., (AV) .... 212 West Church Street

Fields & Cooper, PLLC, (AV)
113 Court Street, P.O. Box 757, 27856 ⊙
Telephone: 252-459-2121 Fax: 252-459-2123
Roy A. Cooper, Jr. (Retired); Mark E. Edwards (Resident);—Michael D. Gaynor (Resident, Nashville Office).
General Civil and Trial Practice in State and Federal Courts. Personal Injury, Creditor Bankruptcy and Collections, Construction, Corporation, Probate, Real Estate, Traffic, and Elder Law.
Rocky Mount, North Carolina Office: 422 Sunset Avenue, P.O. Box 4538. Telephone: 252-442-3115. Fax: 252-442-4170. Email: nashville.fclaw@earthlink.net.
See Professional Biographies, NASHVILLE, NORTH CAROLINA

Fisher, Henry M., (BV) ....'41 '69 C&L.575 A.B., J.D. 210 W. Church St.
Gaynor, Michael D. .... '76 '02 C&L.1228 B.B.A., J.D. [Ⓐ Fields&C.] ⊙
Graham, Steven A., (BV) ....'54 '79 C.576 B.S. L.1228 J.D. Asst. Dist. Atty.
Hamlett, J. Richard, II, (BV) ....'68 '94 C.232 B.S. L.1228 J.D. [Etheridge,S.&H.]
Lamar, L. Wardlaw, (AV) ....'36 '68 C.10 B.A. L.575 J.D. [Valentine,A.&L.]
Lamar, Lewis W., Jr., (BV) ....'68 '95 C.575 B.A. L.1228 J.D. [Valentine,A.&L.]

Murphy, Michael P., P.A.
(See Rocky Mount)

Sykes, Raymond M., Jr., (BV) .... '53 '78 C&L.575 B.A., J.D. [Etheridge,S.&H.]
Valentine, I.T. "Tim", (AV) .... '26 '52 C.152 A.B. L.575 LL.B. [Valentine,A.&L.]

Valentine, Adams & Lamar, L.L.P., (AV)
203 South Barnes Street, P.O. Box 847, 27856
Telephone: 252-459-1111
Email: 2lewis@nashvillenc.com
Members of Firm: I.T. "Tim" Valentine (Retired) (U.S. Congressman); Franklin L. Adams, Jr.; L. Wardlaw Lamar; Lewis W. Lamar, Jr.
Personal Injury, Automobile Accidents, Wrongful Death, Criminal, DWI, Traffic, Real Estate, Business, Wills, Trusts, Estate, Elder Law, Education Law.
See Professional Biographies, NASHVILLE, NORTH CAROLINA

Werner, Keith E., (BV) .... '54 '86 C.645 B.S. L.1228 J.D. Asst. Dist. Atty.

NEBO, —, *McDowell Co.*

Lian, Steven C., (BVⓉ) ....'47 '72 C&L.585 B.S., J.D. [Lian]
Lian Law Firm, (BVⓉ) ....2680 Laurel Pointe Drive

NEW BERN, * 23,128, *Craven Co.*

Adair, Geoffrey G. .... '55 '93 C.575 B.S. L.574 J.D. Dist. Atty. Off.
Alford, Benjamin G. .... '50 '78 C.575 A.B. L.574 J.D. Supr. Ct. J.
Allen, W. L., III, (BV) .... '— '92 C.232 B.S. L.896 J.D. [Ward&S.] (⊙Greenville)
Andrews, Deborah B. .... '— '97 C.576 B.A. L.575 J.D. [Ward&S.] (⊙Greenville)
Arno-Wood, Jennifer M. .... '— '04 C.1031 B.A. L.107 J.D. [Ⓐ Harris,C.W.&B.]
Ashton, Rudolph Alexander, III, (BV) '46 '71 C.896 B.S. L.893 J.D.
[McCotter,A.&S.]
Atkins, Beth Ferebee, (BV) ....'60 '85 C.575 B.S. L.893 J.D. [Howard,S.F.&H.] ⊙
Austin, William Joseph, Jr., (AV) .... '— '78 C&L.575 A.B., J.D. [Ward&S.] (⊙Raleigh)
Ayers, James M., II, (BV) ....'62 '91 C.790 B.S. L.1345 J.D. 307 Metcalf St.
Beaudoin, Adam M. ....'— '01 C.1369 B.A. L.692 J.D. [Ward&S.] (⊙Wilmington)
Bell, Albert R., Jr., (AV) ....'— '75 C.1228 B.S. L.896 J.D. [Ward&S.] (⊙Raleigh)
Bell, Laura Jean A. .... '65 '94 C.999 B.S. L.1345 J.D. Asst. Dist. Atty.
Bell, Steven K., (CV) .... '69 '94 C.232 B.S. L.1345 J.D. P.O. Box 1355
Bettis, Lee W., Jr. .... '64 '01 C.657 B.A. L.1009 J.D. [Emanuel&D.]
Bircher, John C., III, (BV) .... '70 '97 C.575 B.S.C.J. L.1228 J.D. [Hunter B.]
Blackerby, Melissa G. .... '66 '92 C.575 B.A. L.1345 J.D. 108 Virginia Ln.
Blackerby, R. Brittain, (AV) .... '65 '92 C.953 B.A. L.1228 J.D. [Harris,C.W.&B.]

Block, Victoria L. '48 '77 C.813 A.B. L.1068 J.D.
315 Metcalf Street, 28562
Telephone: 252-636-0600 Fax: 252-636-0527
Email: vblock@mindspring.com URL: http://www.victoriablocklaw.com
Immigration Law, Social Security Law, Wills.
See Professional Biographies, NEW BERN, NORTH CAROLINA

Booker, Nichole G. .... '74 '04 C.577 B.A. L.1228 J.D. [Ⓐ Harris,C.W.&B.]
Bowers, Robert G., (CV) .... '27 '52 C.404 A.B. L.896 J.D. 2807 Neuse Blvd., Ste. 1
Bowman, Jennifer Lynn, (BV) .... '— '93 C&L.575 A.B., J.D. [Ward&S.]
Braswell, Edwin M., Jr., (BV) ....'52 '78 C.575 B.S. L.574 J.D. [Ⓐ Kellum]
Briggs, John T., (BV) ..... '65 '91 C.232 B.S. L.1228 J.D. [Ⓐ Kellum] (⊙Morehead City)
Bruce, Patricia G., (CV) .... '53 '81 C.89 B.A. L.705 J.D. Asst. Dist. Atty.

Brumbaugh, Mu & King, P.A., (BV)
McCarthy Square Office Suites, 790 Cardinal Road, Suite 6, 28562 ⊙
Telephone: 252-636-2099
URL: http://www.bmklaw.net
Kenneth W. King, Jr.
Practice Limited to Injury Cases. Automobile, Wrongful Death, Medical Malpractice, Workers' Compensation, Products Liability and Social Security Claims.
See Professional Biographies, NEW BERN, NORTH CAROLINA

Bryant, Brenda J. ....'50 '83 C.1111 B.A. L.362 J.D. [King&B.]
Butler, Jenna Fruechtenicht, (BV) '— '96
C&L.896 B.A., J.D. [Ward&S.] (⊙Wilmington)
Byrum, Jill Quattlebaum .... '68 '92 C&L.790 B.S., J.D. [Sumrell,S.C.H.&H.]
Carmichael, Fred M., (BV) .... '37 '65 C.896 B.A. L.575 J.D. [Sumrell,S.C.H.&H.]
Carroll, Cynthia Y., (BV) .... '52 '92 C.1128 B.A. L.574 J.D. [Carroll&P.]
Carroll & Potter, P.A, (BV) .... 3601 Trent Road, Suite 7
Cavanagh, Mary V. .... '— '89 C.896 B.A. L.893 J.D. [Ward&S.] (⊙Greenville)
Chesnutt, Marcus W., (AV) .... '53 '78 C.575 B.A. L.192 J.D. [Chesnutt,C.T.&P.]

Chesnutt, Clemmons, Thomas & Peacock, P.A., (AV) BB
225-C Broad Street, P.O. Box 12530, 28561
Telephone: 252-633-6868 Fax: 252-637-2450
Email: gary@nclegalnet.com
Marcus W. Chesnutt; Gary H. Clemmons; Scott E. Thomas; Carolyn Taylor Peacock.
General Practice in all State and Federal Courts. Personal Injury, Wrongful Death, Civil Litigation, DWI, Traffic Offenses, Family and Domestic Law. Social Security, Workers' Compensation, Homeowners Associations, Criminal Defense, DMV Hearings.
See Professional Biographies, NEW BERN, NORTH CAROLINA

Clarke, Ernest H. '30 '58 C&L.902 A.B., LL.B.
(adm. in KY; not adm. in NC) 505 E. Front St.‡
Clemmons, Gary H., (AV) ....'55 '81 C.575 B.A. L.1228 J.D. [Chesnutt,C.T.&P.]
Creech, C. David, (AV) ....'59 '88 C.232 B.S. L.575 J.D. [Harris,C.W.&B.]
Crow, Kenneth F. '62 '91 C.575 B.A. L.1345 J.D.
Supr. Ct. J., The Perrier Ct. Judges Chambers
Crow, Richard J. ....'— '04 C.577 B.A. L.574 J.D. [Ⓐ Ward&S.]
Currin, Rodney A., (AV) ....'— '76 C&L.575 B.S., J.D. [Ⓐ Stubbs&P.]
Dale, Alexander C. ....'— '01 C.577 B.A. L.228 J.D. [Ward&S.] (⊙Wilmington)
Daniels, Edwin H., Sr. ....'29 '63 C.869 B.S. L.273 LL.B. 206 W. Palmer Dr.‡
Davis, James Lee, (AV) ....'— '71 C.296 A.B. L.575 J.D. [Ward&S.]
Davis, Michael Scott, (BV) .... '66 '94 C.575 B.A. L.896 J.D. [Ward&D.]
De Young, Richard C., III, (BV) ....'46 '73 C.420 B.A. L.945 J.D. 4502 Stratton Dr.
Dickerson, B. Kyle .... '74 '00 C.575 B.A. L.836 J.D. [Ⓐ Sumrell,S.C.H.&H.]
Dorsett, Stuart B., (AV) ....'— '85 C.198 A.B. L.575 J.D. [Ward&S.] (⊙Raleigh)
Dunn, Donald J., (BV) .... '54 '79 C.575 B.A. L.192 J.D. [D.J.Dunn]
Dunn, Raymond E., Jr., (AV) ....'51 '79 C.575 B.A. L.896 J.D. [Emanuel&D.] ⊙
Dunn, Donald J., P.A., (BV) .... 245 Craven St.
Durr, William S., (BVⓉ) ....'— '91 C.696 B.A. L.910 J.D. [Ward&S.]
Edwards, Anne Duncan, (BV) ....'55 '91 C.886 B.S. L.945 J.D. [Emanuel&D.]
Eglinton, Donalt J., (AV) '— '82
C.136 M.A. L.896 J.D. [Ward&S.] (⊙Greenville, Raleigh)
Ellis, A. Charles, (AV) '— '83
C.575 A.B. L.1228 J.D. [Ward&S.] (⊙Greenville, Raleigh)

Emanuel & Dunn, PLLC, (AV)
3230 Country Club Road, P.O. Box 1389, 28563 ⊙
Telephone: 252-633-3800 Fax: 252-633-6669
Members of Firm: J. L. Emanuel (1894-1968); Raymond E. Dunn (1922-2001); Robert L. Emanuel (Resident, Raleigh Office); Stephen A. Dunn (Resident, Raleigh Office); James M. Mason; Raymond E. Dunn, Jr.; Pat Leigh Pittman; Anne Duncan Edwards; Joanne K. Partin (Board Certified Specialist in Estate Planning and Probate Law, North Carolina State Board of Legal Specialization); Lee W. Bettis, Jr.; Mary Thompson Skinner.
Civil Trials in all State and Federal Courts. Business Litigation, Employment Litigation, Personal Injury Litigation, ERISA Litigation, Business Law, Contracts, Real Estate, Estate Planning and Probate, Employment Law.
Representative Clients: Metropolitan Life Insurance Co.; BellSouth Telecommunications, Inc.; Prudential Insurance Company of America; Cargill, Incorporated.
Raleigh, North Carolina Office) 130 South Salisbury Street, P.O. Box 426, 27602. Telephone: 919-832-0329; 919-832-0320.
See Professional Biographies, NEW BERN, NORTH CAROLINA

Evans, E. Bradley .... '— '02 C&L.896 B.A., J.D. [Ward&S.] (⊙Greenville)
Evans, Lynwood P., (BV) '— '99 C.575 B.S.B.A. L.1228 J.D.
[Ward&S.] (⊙Greenville)
Fanning, Paul A., (BV) .... '— '98 C.48 B.A. L.896 J.D. [Ward&S.] (⊙Greenville)
Fields, J. Michael, (BV) ....'— '91 C&L.575 B.S., J.D. [Ward&S.] (⊙Greenville)
Finney, Irene Constance, (BV) ....'63 '94 C.575 B.A. L.574 J.D. Asst. Dist. Atty.
Flanagan, Louise W. ....'62 '88 C.896 B.A. L.893 J.D. Chf. U.S. Dist. J.
Flanagan, Michael P., (AV) ...... '— '71 C&L.575 A.B., J.D. [Ward&S.] (⊙Greenville)
Flanders, Dale C. '23 '51 C.560 B.A. L.597 J.D.
(adm. in IL; not adm. in NC) 901 Plantation Dr.‡
Flowers, Kent G., Jr., (CV) .... '55 '82 C.953 B.A. L.42 J.D. 2818 Neuse Blvd.
Freeman, George K., Jr., (AV) '— '55
C.575 B.S.B.A. L.309 LL.B. [Ward&S.] (⊙Wilmington)
Friday, Grady L. ....'26 '78 C&L.896 B.S., J.D. 1001 College Ct.‡

Fulk, Jeffrey S., (CV) ....'56 '83 C.1128 B.S. L.896 J.D. 320 Craven St.
Garland, Michael E., (CV) ....'64 '91 C.575 B.A. L.1228 J.D. [Jones G.&P.P.]
Gatchel, Brian J., (BV) ....'68 '95 C.198 B.A. L.383 J.D. [Henderson,B.T.&G.]
Gillespie, Kenneth R., (BV) ....'48 '81 C.577 B.S. L.896 J.D. [Gillespie&M.]
Gillespie & Murphy, P.A., (BV) ....320 Middle St.
Godette, Franklin D. ....'32 '58 C&L.329 B.A., J.D. 821 Queen St.
Godwin, Jenny Phillips '51 '77 C.976 B.A. L.245 J.D.
(adm. in GA; not adm. in NC) 2439 W. Rock Creek Rd.‡
Grady, Arey W., III ....'72 '98 C&L.575 B.A., J.D. [Sumrell,S.C.H.&H.]
Gray, S. McKinley, III, (AV) ....'— '93 C.575 B.S. L.1228 J.D. [Ward&S.]
Greene, Kelly L., (CV) ....'73 '99 C.896 B.A. L.1228 J.D. [Stubbs&P.]
Gurganus, David E. ....'— '99 C.232 B.A. L.475 J.D. P.O. Box 12485
Haidt, David James, (CV) ....'69 '95 C.575 B.A. L.1294 J.D. 310 Craven St.
Handy, Mary Z. ....'— '99 C.575 B.A. L.1365 J.D. [Ⓐ Howard,S.F.&H.] ⊙
Harris, Barry P., IV ....'— '79 C&L.280 B.A., J.D. [Ward&S.]
Harris, Thomas E., (AV) ....'40 '65 C&L.383 B.S., J.D. [Harris,C.W.&B.] ⊙

Harris, Creech, Ward & Blackerby, P.A., (AV)
325 Pollock Street P.O. Drawer 1168, 28563-1168 ⊙
Telephone: 252-638-6666 Facsimile: 252-638-3542
Email: info@hcwb.net
Thomas E. Harris; C. David Creech; Thomas M. Ward; R. Brittain Blackerby; Charles Everett Simpson, Jr.; Bonnie J. Refinski-Knight; Walter Gregory Merritt;—Marie C. Moseley; Nichole G. Booker; Jennifer M. Arno-Wood.
General Practice.
Greenville, North Carolina Office: 219 Commerce Street, Suite C. 27858.
See Professional Biographies, NEW BERN, NORTH CAROLINA

Hart, Scott C., (BV) ....'68 '92 C&L.575 B.A., J.D. [Sumrell,S.C.H.&H.]
Henderson, David S., (BV) ....'33 '59 C.902 B.A. L.896 LL.B. [Henderson,B.T.&G.]

Henderson, Baxter, Taylor & Gatchel, P.A., (BV)
1319 Commerce Drive, 28562
Mailing Address: Post Office Drawer U, New Bern, NC 28653
Telephone: 252-638-5792 Fax: 252-637-7548
URL: http://www.ncfirm.com
David S. Henderson; Brian Zachary Taylor; Brian J. Gatchel.
General Civil and Criminal Practice in all State and Federal Courts. Estate Planning, Estate Administration, Real Estate Law, Corporations, Collections, Social Security Law, Foreclosure, Business Law, Family Law and Administrative Law.
Representative Client: Craven County Board of Education.
See Professional Biographies, NEW BERN, NORTH CAROLINA

Hicks, Donald C., (CV) ....'48 '74 C&L.575 A.B., J.D. Asst. Dist. Atty.
Hicks, Jimmie B., Jr., (BV) ....'65 '91 C.576 C.S.C. L.575 J.D. [Sumrell,S.C.H.&H.]
Hiner, J. Randall, (BV) ....'— '67 C.682 B.A. L.575 J.D. [J.R.Hiner]
Hiner, J. Randall, PLLC, (BV) ....409 Pollock Street
Hingson, Constantine C. .....'— '04 C.575 B.A. L.1228 J.D. [Ward&S.] (⊙Wilmington)
Hobbs, Karen C., (BV) ....'63 '90 C.575 B.A. L.1228 J.D. Dist. Atty.'s Off.
Hollows, William H., (BV) ....'47 '78 C.575 B.A. L.838 J.D. 223 Broad St.

Howard, Stallings, From & Hutson, P.A., (AV)
2407 Grace Avenue, P.O. Box 975, 28563 ⊙
Telephone: 252-633-3006 Fax: 252-633-3097
URL: http://www.howardstallings.com
Joseph H. Stallings; Beth Ferebee Atkins; Mary Z. Handy.
General, Civil and Commercial Litigation, Business Law, Construction Law, Family and Domestic Relations Law, Commercial Real Estate, Taxation, Employment Law, Computer Law, Estate Planning and Administration, Employment Law, Computer Law, Representation of Creditors, Debtors and Trustees in Bankruptcy Cases, Out-of-Court Debt Restructuring, Foreclosure Proceedings, Project Finance, Landlord-Tenant Law, Intellectual Property; Contract Litigation; Contracts.
Representative Clients: Marmon Industrial Corp; Eckerd Corp; VR Business Brokers; Microspace Communications Corp.; Extend Stay America, Inc.; Tricor Development Corp.; L&M Brokerage, Inc.; CRTS, Inc.; Executive Staffing Services; Branch Banking & Trust Co.
Raleigh, North Carolina Office: Suite 400, 4000 Westchase Boulevard, 27607, P.O. Box 12347. Telephone: 919-821-7700. Fax: 919-821-7703.
See Professional Biographies, NEW BERN, NORTH CAROLINA

Hunter, J. Randal, (BV) ....'54 '79 C.198 B.A. L.896 J.D. [Hunter B.]

Hunter Bircher, LLP, (BV)
220 East Front Street, P.O. Box 567, 28563
Telephone: 252-638-3222 Facsimile: 252-638-1113
Email: jcb@hunterbircher.com
J. Randal Hunter (Board Certified Specialist in Family Law, North Carolina State Board of Legal Specialization); John C. Bircher III; Aisha Pridgen.
Debtor Creditor Law, Family Law, Bankruptcy, Federal Law, Administrative, Civil Litigation, Corporate Law, Small Business, Divorce, Child Custody, Commercial Law, Collections.
See Professional Biographies, NEW BERN, NORTH CAROLINA

Johnson, Douglas B., Jr. ....'66 '97 C.232 B.A. L.1228 J.D. [Ⓐ Kellum]
Johnson, Thomas H., Jr., (BV) '— '85 C&L.575 B.S., J.D.
[Ward&S.] (⊙Wilmington)
Jones, Cathy F. ....'60 '92 C.576 B.A. L.1228 J.D. Law Clk., U.S. Mag. J.
Jones, Douglas M., (BV) ....'56 '84 C.232 B.A. L.896 J.D. [Jones G.&P.P.]
Jones, J. Kevin, (BV) ....'67 '92 C.575 B.S. L.1345 J.D. [Ⓐ Kellum]
Jones, Merrill G., II ....'— '97 C&L.896 B.S., J.D. [Ward&S.] (⊙Greenville)
Jones Garland & Peterman PLLC, (BV) ....1721 South Glenburnie Road
Kafer, Charles William, (AV) ....'44 '69 C&L.896 B.A., J.D. 209 Pollock Street
Kellum, Norman B., Jr., (AV) ....'37 '65 C&L.896 B.S., J.D. [Kellum] ⊙

Kellum Law Firm, (AV)
219 Broad Street, P.O. Box 866, 28563 ⊙
Telephone: 252-633-2550 Fax: 252-672-0536
Email: ckeenhold@kellumlawfirm.com URL: http://www.lawyers.com/kellumlawfirm
John W. Beaman (1911-1984); Norman B. Kellum, Jr.;—John T. Briggs; Russell L. Needell; J. Kevin Jones (Board Certified Specialist in Workers' Compensation Law, North Carolina State Board of Legal Specialization); Douglas B. Johnson, Jr.; Jeffrey W. Phillips; Edwin M. Braswell, Jr.
State and Federal Civil Trial Practice, Personal Injury Law, Wrongful Death, Workers' Compensation, Social Security, Defective Products, Mass Torts and Insurance Law.
Jacksonville, North Carolina Office: 445-A Western Boulevard, P.O. Box 12155, 28546. Telephone: 910-455-4546. Fax: 910-455-2422.
Greenville, North Carolina Office: 205 S.W. Greenville Boulevard, P.O. Box 20727, 27858. Telephone: 252-353-4100. Fax: 252-353-8754.
Goldsboro, North Carolina Office: 2005 East Ash Street, P.O. Box 1085, 27533. Telephone: 919-722-6955. Fax: 919-722-6922.
Rocky Mount, North Carolina Office: 3250 Zebulon Road, 27804. Telephone: 252-442-3975. Fax: 252-442-7309.
Morehead City, North Carolina Office: 5178 Highway 70 West, 28557. Telephone: 252-726-7000. Fax: 252-726-8888.
See Professional Biographies, NEW BERN, NORTH CAROLINA

King, Calvin R., (AVⓉ) ....'23 '48 C&L.500 LL.B. P.O. Box 1124
King, D. Mitchell, (BVⓉ) ....'48 '73 C.232 A.B. L.575 J.D. [King&B.]
King, John W., Jr., (BV) ....'54 '80 C.896 B.A. L.1228 J.D. [Stubbs&P.]
King, Kenneth W., Jr., (BV) ......'61 '86 C.575 B.S. L.469 J.D. [Brumbaugh,M.&K.] ⊙
King & Bryant, P.A., (BVⓉ) ....410 Tar Landing

Lacy, Steven E., (BV) ....'51 '80 C.576 B.A. L.472 J.D. 225 Broad St.
Lasitter, Moses Dow, (BV) ....'42 '73 C.575 A.B. L.896 J.D. [Lee,H.&L.]
Lathan, William R., Jr., (AV) ....'— '75 C&L.575 A.B., J.D. [Ward&S.] (⊙Raleigh)
Lee, Edward Y. '68 '94 C.276 B.S.F.S. L.802 J.D.
(adm. in PA; not adm. in NC) 1563 College Way★
Lee, Hancock & Lasitter, P.A., (BV) ....507 Pollock Street, Suite 5

LeonLaw Firm, The
(See Greenville)

Lewis, Katherine Evans ....'— '93 C.43 B.S. L.500 J.D. [Ward&S.] (⊙Greenville)
Loest, Craig J. '— '00 C.436 B.S.M.E. L.94 J.D.
(adm. in WI; not adm. in NC) I.P. Coun., BSH Home Appliances Corp.
Long, Steven N. ....'72 '03 C.1128 B.S. L.1228 J.D. [Long&M.]
Long & Mezzullo, PLLC ....243 Craven St.
Markovich, Mary M. ....'— '94 C.999 B.S. L.574 J.D. 327 Pollock St.
Marteney, Cheryl A., (BV) ....'— '89 C.924 B.A. L.945 J.D. [Ward&S.]
Martin, John M., (AV) ....'— '75 C.576 B.A. L.896 J.D. [Ward&S.] (⊙Greenville)
Martin, Lance P., (BV) ....'— '95 C.812 B.S. L.861 J.D. [Ward&S.] (⊙Greenville)
Martin, W. Daniel, III, (AV) '— '73 C.576 B.A. L.575 J.D.
[Ward&S.] (⊙Wilmington)
Martin, William E., (AV) ....'— '75 C&L.896 B.A., J.D. [Ward&S.]
Mayo, Hiram J., Jr., (CV) ....'47 '74 C.575 A.B. L.896 J.D. P.O. Box 1734
McClees, Susan H., (CV) ....'49 '77 C&L.575 B.A., J.D. 507 Pollock St.
McCotter, Charles K., Jr., (BV) ....'46 '71 C&L.575 B.S., J.D. [McCotter,A.&S.]

McCotter, Ashton & Smith, P.A., (BV)
3515 Trent Road, Suite 10, P.O. Box 12800, 28561
Telephone: 252-635-1005 Fax: 252-635-5050
Email: maslaw@justice.com URL: http://www.lawyers.com/mmalaw
Members: Charles K. McCotter, Jr.; Rudolph Alexander Ashton, III; Kirby H. Smith, III. Associate: Terri Woodard Sharp.
General Civil and Criminal Practice and Appeals in all State and Federal Courts. Probate, Real Property, Corporation, Business, Construction, Administrative, Negligence, Workers' Compensation, Admiralty and Maritime, Federal and State Criminal Defense, Mediation and Arbitration.
See Professional Biographies, NEW BERN, NORTH CAROLINA

McFadyen, W. David, Jr., (AV) ....'53 '79 C.232 B.S. L.574 J.D. Dist. Atty.
Merritt, Walter Gregory, (BV) ... '68 '96 C.575 B.S.B.A. L.1228 J.D. [Harris,C.W.&B.]
Mezzullo, Crystal B. ....'66 '02 C.232 B.S.N. L.1228 [Long&M.]
Mills, J. Michael, (BV) ....'64 '90 C.575 B.A. L.896 J.D. [Mills&W.]

Mills & Willey, (BV)
201 Broad Street, Drawer 1638, 28563
Telephone: 252-638-1111 Telecopier: 252-638-8499
Email: mills@cconnect.net
J. Michael Mills; Joshua W. Willey, Jr.
Accident, Personal Injury Law, Workers Compensation, Criminal Law, General Civil and Criminal Litigation in State and Federal Courts.
See Professional Biographies, NEW BERN, NORTH CAROLINA

Moseley, Marie C. ....'54 '00 C.1128 B.S.N. L.575 J.D. [Ⓐ Harris,C.W.&B.]
Murphy, J. Allen, (BV) ....'53 '85 C.232 B.A. L.574 J.D. [Gillespie&M.]
Navin, Kathryn M. ..... '73 '99 C.965 B.A. L.665 J.D. Marine Corps Air Station Cherry Pt.
Norment, James W. ....'— '01 C&L.577 B.A., J.D. [Ward&S.]
Norris, Grady J. '37 '66 C.88 A.B. L.145 J.D.
(adm. in DC; not adm. in NC) 301 Juanita Lane‡
Oden, William A., III ....'— '04 C.575 B.A. L.1228 J.D. [Ward&S.]
Oliver, George Mason ....'74 '99 C&L.575 B.A., J.D. [Stubbs&P.]
Osterhout, Anna B. ....'65 '93 C.575 B.A. L.1228 J.D. 1001 College Ct.
Overholt, Hugh R., (AV) ....'— '57 C&L.45 A.B., J.D. [Ward&S.]
Parrott, Jeannette A., (CV) ....'— '90 C.228 B.A. L.893 J.D. [Ward&S.]
Parson, Clifford P. ....'— '92 C.301 B.A. L.896 J.D. [Ward&S.]
Partin, Joanne K., (BV) ....'46 '81 C.896 B.A. L.575 J.D. [Emanuel&D.]
Peacock, Carolyn Taylor, (BV) .... '72 '96 C.259 B.S. L.896 J.D. [Chesnutt,C.T.&P.]
Peacock, Gregory T., (AV) '— '96 C.575 B.S.B.A. L.896 J.D.
[Ward&S.] (⊙Greenville)
Pearson, David S., (CVⓉ) '66 '91 C.549 B.S. L.1065 J.D.
(adm. in CA; not adm. in NC) 105 Pinehurst Dr.
Peiffer, William A. '20 '49 C.650 B.S. L.1017 LL.B.
(adm. in PA; not adm. in NC) 50 Shoreline Dr.‡
Peterman, T. Russell, Jr. ....'62 '88 C.160 B.A. L.16 J.D. [Jones G.&P.P.]
Phillips, Jeffrey W. ....'77 '03 C.575 B.A. L.896 J.D. [Ⓐ Kellum]
Pittman, Pat Leigh ....'63 '88 C.896 B.A. L.575 J.D. [Emanuel&D.]
Piwowarski, Catherine Ricks, (CV) '65 '96 C.575 B.A. L.228 J.D.
205 W. Rock Creek Rd.
Poole, Samuel H. ....'— '62 C&L.575 A.B., LL.B. [Ward&S.] (⊙Raleigh)
Pope, C. H., Jr., (AV) ....'— '72 C&L.575 B.S., J.D. [Ward&S.]
Potter, Daniel E. ....'66 '92 C.228 A.B. L.469 J.D. [Carroll&P.]
Pridgen, Aisha ....'76 '02 C.577 B.A. L.575 J.D. [Hunter B.]
Proctor, E. Knox, V ....'— '87 C&L.575 A.B., J.D. [Ward&S.] (⊙Raleigh)
Quay, Cindi M. ....'— '00 C.999 B.A. L.574 J.D. [Ward&S.]
Raynor, Robert G., Jr., (BV) ....'54 '84 C&L.574 B.A., J.D. 417-B Broad St.
Refinski-Knight, Bonnie J., (AV) ....'60 '90 C&L.966 B.A., J.D. [Harris,C.W.&B.]
Remington, Eric J., (BV) ....'— '93 C.350 B.S. L.190 J.D. [Ward&S.]
Richards, Juliana Cleland ....'— '05 C.871 B.S. L.228 J.D. [Ward&S.]
Richardson, Ernest C., III, (BV) ....'47 '72 C&L.575 B.S., J.D. 503 Pollock Street
Rickner, Gary J., (AVⓉ) '— '74
C.827 B.A. L.192 J.D. [Ward&S.] (⊙Greenville, Raleigh)
Routson, Clint D., (AV) ....'— '83 C.138 B.S. L.945 J.D. [Ward&S.]
Sams, Stanley M., (AV) .... '— '79 C.232 B.S.B.A. L.575 J.D. [Ward&S.] (⊙Greenville)
Sayre, Jeremy R. ....'— '98 C.363 B.S. L.608 J.D. [Ward&S.] (⊙Raleigh)
Sharp, Terri Woodard ....'62 '00 C.999 B.S. L.574 J.D [Ⓐ McCotter,A.&S.]
Sheffield, Frank H., Jr., (AV) ....'— '75 C&L.846 B.A., J.D. [Ward&S.]
Shields, Buren R., III ....'46 '75 C.870 B.S. L.878 J.D. Atty. Gen Off.
Shields, Robert S., Jr., (AV) ....'56 '81 C&L.575 B.A., J.D. [R.S.Shields,Jr.]
Shields, Robert S., Jr., PLLC, (AV) ....218C S. Front St.
Simpson, Charles Everett, Jr., (BV) ... '68 '93 C.575 B.A. L.1228 J.D. [Harris,C.W.&B.]
Skinner, Mary Thompson, (BV) ....'54 '81 C&L.575 B.S., J.D. [Emanuel&D.]
Skipper, Nathan R., Jr., (AV) ....'34 '63 C&L.228 B.A., J.D. 1108 Country Club Dr.
Sloan, John Reeves, (BV) ....'— '90 C&L.575 A.B., J.D. [Ward&S.] (⊙Wilmington)
Smith, J. Troy, Jr., (AV) ....'— '67 C&L.575 A.B., J.D. [Ward&S.] (⊙Greenville)
Smith, Kirby H., III ....'65 '92 C.575 B.S. L.896 J.D. [McCotter,A.&S.]
Snyder, D. Joseph '28 '58 C.802 B.B.A. L.472 LL.B.
(adm. in FL; not adm. in NC) 5700 Sloop Ct.‡
Stallings, Joseph H., (AV) ....'50 '76 C&L.575 A.B., J.D. [Howard,S.F.&H.] ⊙
Stephenson, H. L., III, (AV) ...... '— '82 C&L.575 A.B., J.D. [Ward&S.] (⊙Greenville)
Stith, Francis B., (BV) ....'39 '69 C.232 A.B. L.469 LL.B. [Stith&S.]
Stith & Stith, P.A., (BV) ....213 Broad Street
Stubbs, Trawick H., Jr., (AV) ....'42 '67 C.575 A.B. L.228 J.D. [Stubbs&P.] ⊙

Stubbs & Perdue, P.A., (AV) BR
310 Craven Street, P.O. Box 1654, 28563-1654 ⊙
Telephone: 252-633-2700 Fax: 252-633-9600 URL: http://www.stubbsperdue.com
Email: law@stubbsperdue.com URL: http://www.lawyers.com/stubbsperdue
Gary R. Perdue, Sr. (1947-1997); Trawick H. Stubbs, Jr.; John W. King, Jr.; Kelly L. Greene; George Mason Oliver;—Rodney A. Currin; Thomas R. Wilson.
General Practice in all Courts. Probate, Real Estate, Personal Injury, Bankruptcy Reorganization, Domestic Relations, Corporation and Criminal Law, Environmental Law, Toxic Torts.
Approved Attorneys For : Lawyers Title Insurance Corp.
References: First Citizens Bank; Branch Banking & Trust Co.
Raleigh, North Carolina Office: Two Hannover Square, 434 Fayetteville Street Mall, Suite 1630, P.O. Box 1630, 27602-1630. Telephone: 919-856-9400. Fax: 919-856-9300. Email: law@stubbsperdue.com
See Professional Biographies, NEW BERN, NORTH CAROLINA

Sugg, James R., (AV) .... '31 '59 C.316 A.B. L.896 J.D. [Sumrell,S.C.H.&H.]

Sumrell, Sugg, Carmichael, Hicks & Hart, P.A., (AV)
416 Pollock Street, P.O. Drawer 889, 28563
Telephone: 252-633-3131 Fax: 252-633-3507
Email: email@nclawyers.com URL: http://www.nclawyers.com
Raymond E. Sumrell (1924-2004);—James R. Sugg; Fred M. Carmichael; Jimmie B. Hicks, Jr.; Scott C. Hart; Jill Quattlebaum Byrum; Arey W. Grady, III;—B. Kyle Dickerson.
General Civil. Trials and Appeals in all Civil Courts. Wills and Estates, Real Estate, Corporate Law, Financial Transactions, Insurance and Negligence, Employment Law, Municipal Law, Law Enforcement Liability Defense, Health Care Law and Intellectual Property.
References: Branch Bank & Trust Company of New Bern; Bank of America; First Citizens Bank, New Bern.
See Professional Biographies, NEW BERN, NORTH CAROLINA

Swart, John P., (BV) ....'— '81 C.835 B.S. L.838 J.D. [Ward&S.] (⊙Wilmington)
Tayloe, Ryal W., (AV) ....'— '82 C.575 A.B. L.896 J.D. [Ward&S.] (⊙Wilmington)
Taylor, Brian Zachary, (CV) ...... '64 '91 C.575 B.S. L.1228 J.D. [Henderson,B.T.&G.]
Thomas, Scott E., (CV) .... '66 '92 C.232 B.S. L.574 J.D. [Chesnutt,C.T.&P.]
Thompson, Matthew W. ......'— '04 C.205 B.A. L.945 J.D. [Ward&S.] (⊙Wilmington)
Tierney-White, Barbara '— '93 C&L.1241 B.A., J.D.
(adm. in CA; not adm. in NC) 2006 Caracara Dr.
Turco, Cynthia L. ....'48 '75 C.651 B.S. L.923 J.D. Vice Pres., Craven Reg. Med. Ctr.
Voerman, David P. ....'47 '72 C.321 A.B. L.228 J.D. P.O. Box 12485
Waddell, Jerry F. .... '48 '73 C.937 B.A. L.896 J.D. Dist. J.

Wallace, Morris, Barwick, Landis & Stroud, P.A.
(See Kinston)

Wang, Amy P., (BV) ....'— '96 C.893 B.A. L.896 J.D. [Ward&S.]
Ward, Alfred Decatur, Jr., (BV) ....'49 '74 C.232 B.S. L.896 J.D. [Ward&D.]
Ward, David L., Jr., (AV) ....'— '62 C.575 B.S. L.228 J.D. [Ward&S.] (⊙Raleigh)
Ward, John A. J., (AV) .... '44 '73 C&L.575 A.B., J.D. [Ward&D.]
Ward, Kennedy W., (BV) .... '30 '54 C&L.896 B.S., J.D. [K.W.Ward]
Ward, Thomas M., (AV) .... '52 '78 C&L.575 B.S., J.D. [Harris,C.W.&B.]
Ward and Davis, LLP, (AV) .... P.O. Box 1428
Ward, Kennedy W., P.A., (BV) .... 409 Pollock St.

Ward and Smith, P.A., (AV)
1001 College Court, P.O. Box 867, 28563-0867 ⊙
Telephone: 252-672-5400 Facsimile: 252-672-5477
Email: wardsmith@wardandsmith.com URL: http://www.wardandsmith.com
D. L. Ward (1903-1971); W. L. Allen, III; Deborah B. Andrews; William Joseph Austin, Jr.; Adam M. Beaudoin; Albert R. Bell, Jr.; Jennifer Lynn Bowman; Jenna Fruechtenicht Butler; Mary V. Cavanagh; Alexander C. Dale; James Lee Davis; Stuart B. Dorsett (Board Certified Specialist in Estate Planning and Probate Law, North Carolina State Board of Legal Specialization); Richard J. Crow; William S. Durr; Donalt J. Eglinton; A. Charles Ellis; E. Bradley Evans; Lynwood P. Evans; Paul A. Fanning; J. Michael Fields; Michael P. Flanagan; George K. Freeman, Jr.; S. McKinley Gray, III; Barry P. Harris, IV; Constantine C. Hingson; Thomas H. Johnson, Jr.; Merrill G. Jones II; William R. Lathan, Jr.; Katherine Evans Lewis; Cheryl A. Marteney; John M. Martin; Lance P. Martin; W. Daniel Martin, III; William E. Martin; James W. Norment; William A. Oden, III; Hugh R. Overholt; Jeannette A. Parrott; Clifford P. Parson; Gregory T. Peacock (Board Certified Specialist in Estate Planning and Probate Law, North Carolina State Board of Legal Specialization); Samuel H. Poole; C. H. Pope, Jr.; E. Knox Proctor V; Cindi M. Quay; Eric J. Remington; Juliana Cleland Richards; Gary J. Rickner; Clint D. Routson; Stanley M. Sams; Jeremy R. Sayre; Frank H. Sheffield, Jr.; John Reeves Sloan (Board Certified Specialist in Estate Planning and Probate Law, North Carolina State Board of Legal Specialization); J. Troy Smith, Jr.; H. L. Stephenson, III; John P. Swart; Ryal W. Tayloe; Matthew W. Thompson; Benjamin E. F. B. Waller; Amy P. Wang; David L. Ward, Jr.; Leigh Allred Wilkinson; A. Rexford Willis, III; Kenneth R. Wooten.
General and Trial Practice. Admiralty Law; Bankruptcy; Banks and Banking; Business Law; Civil Rights; Commercial Law; Construction Law; Contracts; Copyrights; Corporate Law; Debtor and Creditor; Elder Law; Eminent Domain; Employee Benefits; Environmental Law; Family Law including Divorce; Finance; Franchise Law; Government; Government Contracts; Health Care Law; Immigration and Naturalization; Insurance; International Law; International Trade; Investments; Labor and Employment including Discrimination, Sexual Harassment, and Workers' Compensation; Landlord and Tenant; Litigation; Personal Injury including Automobile Accidents, Legal Malpractice and Medical Malpractice; Products Liability; Real Estate; Securities; Taxation; Technology and Science including Internet Law, Trademarks, and Patents; Trusts and Estates including Estate Planning and Wills and Probate; Zoning and Land Use.
Barnhill Contracting Company; Chubb Insurance; Daedong-USA, Inc.; First-Citizens Bank & Trust Company; First Flight Federal Credit Union; Fountain Powerboats, Inc.; NC State Firemen's Association; Potash Corp.; State of North Carolina; Weyerhaeuser Co.
Greenville, North Carolina Office: 120 West Fire Tower Road, P.O. Box 8088. Telephone: 252-215-4000. Facsimile: 252-215-4077.
Raleigh, North Carolina Office: Suite 2400, Two Hannover Square, Fayetteville Street Mall, P.O. Box 2091. Telephone: 919-836-4260. Facsimile: 919-836-4277.
Wilmington, North Carolina Office: University Corporate Center, 127 Racine Drive, P.O. Box 7068. Telephone: 910-794-4800. Facsimile: 910-794-4877.
See Professional Biographies, NEW BERN, NORTH CAROLINA

Warnock, Russell William '56 '86 C.971 B.S.M.E. L.276 J.D.
(adm. in CO; not adm. in NC; Pat.) Sr. I.P. Coun., BSH Home Appliances Corp.
Whitley, Laura M. W. ....'69 '96 C.471 B.A. L.1345 J.D. 701 McCarthy Blvd.
Whitley, Robert E., Jr., (BV) '69 '95 C.34 B.A. L.1228 J.D.
[Whitley,R.&W.] (⊙Kinston)
Whitley, Rodgman & Whitley, (AV)
701 McCarthy Boulevard (⊙Greenville, Jacksonville, Kinston, Raleigh)
Wilkinson, Leigh Allred, (BV) ....'— '85 C.576 B.S. L.575 J.D. [Ward&S.]
Willey, Joshua W., Jr., (BV) .... '52 '77 C&L.896 B.A., J.D. [Mills&W.]
Williams, Michael J. ....'72 '97 C.232 B.S.B.A. L.260 J.D. P.O. Box 1167
Willis, A. Rexford, III, (AV) ..... '— '80 C&L.575 B.S., J.D. [Ward&S.] (⊙Wilmington)
Wilson, Thomas R. ....'76 '03 C.473 B.A. L.734 J.D. [Ⓐ Stubbs&P.]
Winburn, John Temple, (AVⓉ) '42 '74 C.339 B.S.E.E. L.128 J.D.
(adm. in IL; not adm. in NC; Pat.) Corp. I.P. Coun., BSH Home Appliance Corp.
Wooten, Kenneth R., (AV) '— '79
C.596 B.A. L.595 J.D. [Ward&S.] (⊙Greenville, Raleigh)
Wright, I. Clark, Jr., (AV) .... '57 '83 C&L.575 A.B., J.D. [Ward&D.]
Wright, Patricia Easton ....'48 '89 C.947 B.A. L.1228 J.d. 310 Craven St.
Zemek, Elliot ....'30 '55 C.569 L.1009 J.D. 310 Broad St.

NEWLAND, * 645, *Avery Co.*

Capua, Andrea N., (BV) .... '62 '88 C.1222 B.S. L.796 J.D. [DiSanti W.C.&W.] ⊙
Carpenter, Randy A. .... '57 '97 C.999 B.A. L.1194 J.D. 1751-B Three Mile Hwy.
Castengera, Cynthia B. ....'65 '96 C.269 B.A. L.790 J.D. 616 Cranberry Street
Cocke, William B., Jr., (BV) .... '47 '72 C&L.575 B.A., J.D. P.O. Box 606
Di Santi, Anthony S., (AV) .... '47 '75 C.575 B.S. L.896 J.D. [DiSanti W.C.&W.] ⊙

Di Santi Watson Capua & Wilson, (AV)
102 Elk Street, 28657 ⊙
Telephone: 828-733-9273
URL: http://www.lawyers.com/disantiwatson&capua
Members of Firm: Anthony S. Di Santi; Donald M. Watson, Jr.; Andrea N. Capua; Frank C. Wilson, III. Of Counsel: W. Kelly Johnson (Not admitted in NC).
General Civil Practice and in all State and Federal Courts. Corporation, Real Property, Insurance, Family, Municipal, Personal Injury, Automobile Accidents and Injuries, Estate Planning, Probate, Real Estate Development and Interstate Land Sales.
Reference: NCNB National Bank of North Carolina, Boone, North Carolina.
Boone, North Carolina Office: 642 West King Street, P.O. Box 193, 28607-4040. Telephone: 828-264-6126.
See Professional Biographies, NEWLAND, NORTH CAROLINA

Hall, Douglas L. ....'— '95 C.296 B.A. L.1228 J.D. [Hall&H.] ⊙

Hall & Hall, Attorneys At Law, P.C., (CV)
118 Elk Street, P.O. Box 898, 28657 ⊙
Telephone: 828-733-9222 Fax: 828-737-9009
Email: hallandhall@bellsouth.net
Douglas L. Hall.
Estates, Real Estate, Workers Compensation, Family Law, Divorce, Equitable Distribution, Personal Injury, Traffic Violations, Driving While Intoxicated, Criminal Law, Collections, Child Custody, Corporate Law, Employment Discrimination.
Morganton, North Carolina Office: 305 S. Green Street, 28655. Telephone: 828-433-9100. Fax: 828-433-9339
See Professional Biographies, NEWLAND, NORTH CAROLINA

Hemphill, Kathryn G., (BV) '46 '81 C.822 B.A. L.896 J.D.
299 Sokossa Road, P.O. Drawer 849, 28657
Telephone: 828-733-6004 Fax: 828-733-2091
Email: khemphill@goboone.net
General Trial Practice. Civil Practice in State Courts. Domestic Relations and Real Estate Law. Estates and Wills.
See Professional Biographies, NEWLAND, NORTH CAROLINA

Johnson, Kelly, (AV) .... '40 '68 C.34 B.S. L.896 J.D. [K.Johnson]
Johnson, W. Kelly, (AVⓉ) '61 '86 C.347 B.A. L.150 J.D.
(adm. in OH; not adm. in NC) [Ⓞ DiSanti W.C.&W.] ⊙
Johnson, William K. .... '40 '68 C.34 B.A. L.896 J.D. 1 Avery Square
Johnson, Kelly, P.A., (AV) .... Avery Square
Lacey, R. Bruce, (BV) ....'55 '81 C.575 B.S. L.1228 J.D. Main St.
Lacey, Robert H. ....'27 '49 C.34 B.S. L.896 LL.B. Ret. Dist. Ct. J.
Lyerly, Alexander .... '44 '75 C.34 B.S. L.796 J.D. Chief J.
McKinney, Gerald R., (BV) .... '55 '80 C&L.575 B.S., J.D. [G.R.McKinney]

McKinney, Gerald R., P.A., (BV)
390 Sokassa Road, P.O. Box 9, 28657
Telephone: 828-733-5199; 733-5299 Fax: 828-733-1582
Email: geraldlaw1@bellsouth.net
Gerald R. McKinney.
General Civil and Criminal Trial Practice. Workers Compensation, and Personal Injury Law. Mediation; Real Estate.
See Professional Biographies, NEWLAND, NORTH CAROLINA

Poore, Lisa M. .... '66 '91 C.198 A.B. L.577 J.D. 118 Elk St.

Seegers, Joseph W., (BV) '47 '72 C.301 B.S. L.790 J.D.
125 Pineola, P.O. Box 490, 28657
Telephone: 828-733-9206 Fax: 828-733-3291
General Civil and Criminal Trial Practice before all Courts. Criminal Law, Capital Offenses, D.U.I., Traffic Violations, Probate, Estates, Estate Planning, Business and Commercial Law, Negligence Law, Workers Compensation, Municipal Law, Juvenile Law, Family Law, Divorce, Child Custody.
See Professional Biographies, NEWLAND, NORTH CAROLINA

Teasley, Thomas H., (AVⓉ) '11 '36 C.1365 L.362 LL.B.
(adm. in FL; not adm. in NC) R.R. 2, Box 467A‡
Watson, Donald M., Jr., (BV) ....'49 '74 C&L.575 B.S., J.D. [DiSanti W.C.&W.] ⊙
Wilson, Frank C., III, (BV) ....'54 '83 C.16 B.A. L.192 J.D. [DiSanti W.C.&W.] ⊙

NEWPORT, 3,349, *Carteret Co.*

Davis, Rosalee H., (CVⓉ) ....'63 '93 C&L.790 B.A., J.D. 905 Sunset Boulevard
Herring, Stephen J., (BV) ....'51 '76 C&L.575 B.A., J.D. 267 Howard Blvd.
von Staudach, Matthew L. '39 '70 C.665 A.B. L.229 J.D.
(adm. in PA; not adm. in NC) 305 Carrie Ct.

Wall, Bevin W., (CV) '63 '88 C.1130 B.A. L.575 J.D.
Ocean Way Plaza, Suite F, 7025 Highway 70, 28570
Telephone: 252-223-4411 Fax: 252-223-5104
Bankruptcy, Real Estate, Traffic, DWI, Juvenile.
See Professional Biographies, NEWPORT, NORTH CAROLINA

NEWTON, * 12,560, *Catawba Co.*

Barkley, Wesley W. ....'78 '03 C.999 B.A. L.1228 J.D. [Ⓐ Sigmon,S.&I.]
Bechtel, Debra ....'64 '92 C&L.260 B.A., J.D. Catawba Co. Atty. Off.
Childs, Charles W., Jr., (BV) .... '52 '77 C.576 B.A. L.575 J.D. P.O. Box 1207
Cilley, John H., IV, (BV) .... '59 '85 C.276 B.S.F.S. L.896 J.D. [Isenhower,W.&C.]

Conrad, Scott D., (BV) '68 '96 C.34 B.S. L.1345 J.D.
11 East "A" Street, P.O. Box 42, 28658
Telephone: 828-466-3858 Fax: 828-466-3808
Email: Killian&Reilley@w3link.com URL: http://www.lawyers.com/scottdconrad
Criminal, Domestic/Family, Child Custody, Juvenile, Traffic, Divorce, Real Estate, Wills.
See Professional Biographies, NEWTON, NORTH CAROLINA

Corne, Ray Garrison, (BV) .... '52 '77 C.198 B.A. L.896 J.D. [Corne,C.&G.]

Corne, Corne & Grant, P.A., (AV)
217 North Main Avenue, P.O. Drawer 166, 28658
Telephone: 828-464-2371 Fax: 828-465-5422
Email: ccg@newtonslaw.com URL: http://www.newtonslaw.com
Stanley J. Corne (1924-2003); Ray Garrison Corne; Robert M. Grant, Jr.; Chrystal N. Dehart.
Personal Injury, Automobile Accidents, Slip and Fall, Wrongful Death, Medical Malpractice, Family Law, Child Custody, Child Support, Divorce, Visitation Rights, Real Estate, Residential Real Estate, Criminal Law, Business Law, Joint Ventures, Limited Liability Company Law, Partnership, Corporate Law, Trusts and Estates.
Representative Clients: Carolina Glove Co.; City of Claremont; Conover Lumber Co.; Hendrick Motors.
References: Bank of Granite; Peoples Bank; Branch Banking & Trust.
See Professional Biographies, NEWTON, NORTH CAROLINA

Cutchin, John F., (BV) ....'49 '75 C.198 A.B. L.575 J.D. [J.F.Cutchin]
Cutchin, John F., P.A., (BV) .... 16 S. College Ave.
Dehart, Chrystal N. ....'76 '02 C.575 B.A. L.245 J.D. [Corne,C.&G.]
de Torres, Eduardo X., (CV) ....'51 '76 C.1126 B.A. L.602 J.D. [E.X.deTorres]

de Torres, E. X., (CV) .... 30 W. A St.

Eaker & Fulkerson, PC
(See Hickory)

Fox, Martha Erwin, (BV) .... '41 '83 C.34 B.S. L.896 J.D. P.O. Box 1299

Gorham, Crone, Mace, Green & Cody, LLP
(See Hickory)

Grant, Robert M., Jr., (AV) .... '49 '74 C&L.896 B.A., J.D. [Corne,C.&G.]
Haddock, Rebecca H. .... '54 '89 C.1228 B.S. L.229 J.D. P.O. Box 669
Hatcher, Linda J., (CV) .... '61 '87 C&L.838 B.A., J.D. 217 N. Main Ave.
Huffman, Gregory D., (CV) .... '71 '96 C.576 B.A. L.1345 J.D. P.O. Box 148
Isenhower, C. Randall, (BV) .... '53 '79 C.576 B.S.C.E. L.575 J.D. [Sigmon,S.&I.]
Isenhower, David L., (BV) .... '48 '74 C.404 A.B. L.575 J.D. [Isenhower,W.&C.]

Isenhower, Wood & Cilley, P.A., (BV)
7 East Second Street, P.O. Box 145, 28658
Telephone: 828-465-2100 Fax: 828-465-3707
Email: iwc@iwc-law.com
David L. Isenhower; Allen W. Wood, III; John H. Cilley, IV.
Aged and Aging, Bankruptcy, Commercial, Corporate, Foreclosures, Probate, Real Estate, Trusts and Estates and Wills.
See Professional Biographies, NEWTON, NORTH CAROLINA

Kincaid, Timothy S. .... '52 '79 C.925 B.S. L.1228 J.D. Dist. J.
Moose, David R., (BV) .... '52 '80 C.925 B.S.Fin. L.285 J.D. P.O. Box 168
Mullinax, Robert A., (BV) .... '52 '77 C.575 A.B. L.896 J.D. 22 S Main Ave Fl 3

Patrick, Harper & Dixon L.L.P.
(See Hickory)

Pitts, Larry W., (AV) .... '37 '67 C.870 B.S. L.896 J.D. 310 N. College Ave.
Poovey, Nathaniel J., (BV) '71 '96 C.152 B.A. L.1228 J.D.
Catawba Co. Jus. & Govt. Ctr.
Powell, William D., (CV) .... '55 '83 C.575 B.S. L.896 J.D. 232 W. A St.
Reilly, D. Scott, (BV) .... '62 '89 C.404 B.S. L.1187 J.D. 11 East "A" Street
Sigmon, Gene, (AV) .... '41 '67 C&L.575 B.A., J.D. [Sigmon,S.&I.]
Sigmon, Lance B., Attorney at Law '58 '88
C.925 B.S.B.A. L.896 J.D. 1425 Brentwood Dr.

Sigmon, Clark, Mackie, Hutton, Hanvey & Ferrell, P.A.
(See Hickory)

Sigmon, Sigmon & Isenhower, (AV)
P.O. Box 88, 28658
Telephone: 828-464-0101 Fax: 828-464-9062
Members of Firm: Jesse C. Sigmon (1885-1967); Jesse C. Sigmon, Jr. (1922-1997); Gene Sigmon; C. Randall Isenhower. Associate: Wesley W. Barkley.
General Civil and Criminal Practice, Driving While Intoxicated, Felonies, Traffic Violations, Probate, Real Estate, Corporation, Business Law, Family Law, Adoptions, Child Custody, Child Support, Divorce, Personal Injury, Tort Law.
Representative Clients: Furnished Upon Request.
See Professional Biographies, NEWTON, NORTH CAROLINA

Thomas, Robert E. .... '29 '57 C&L.575 B.A., J.D. Dist. Atty.
Waddell, Lewis E., Jr., (BV) .... '42 '66 C&L.575 B.A., J.D. 22 South Main Avenue
Warlick, Thomas W., (BV) .... '34 '59 C.198 B.S. L.575 J.D. 11 South College Avenue
Weathers, Jeffrey S., (CV) .... '69 '98 C.790 B.S. L.1339 J.D. P.O. Box 148
Williams, Richard A., (AV) .... '23 '49 C&L.896 B.A., LL.B. Citizens Svgs. Bk. Bldg.
Wood, Allen W., III, (BV) .... '51 '77 C.896 B.A. L.575 J.D. [Isenhower,W.&C.]

Young, Morphis, Bach and Taylor, L.L.P.
(See Hickory)

NEWTON GROVE, 511, *Sampson Co.*

Geimer, William S., (BV) '40 '69
C.835 B.S. L.575 J.D. Farmworkers Legal Servs. of N. C.

NORTH WILKESBORO, 4,116, *Wilkes Co.*

Bennett, Kevin D. '54 '80 C.101 B.A. L.846 J.D.
(adm. in TX; not adm. in NC) Highway 268 East
Bentley, Lee C., (BV) .... '66 '92 C.34 B.A. L.1228 J.D. Corp. Coun., Lowe's Cos., Inc.
Colvard, Howard C., Jr., (AV) .... '46 '71 C&L.896 B.A., J.D. [Vannoy,C.T.&V.]
Davis, Eric .... '42 '69 C&L.575 B.A., J.D. P.O. Box 426‡
Ferrell, R. Tyson, (BV) .... '65 '91 C.232 B.A. L.1128 J.D. [Ⓐ McElwee]
Gray, Jeffrey E., (BV) .... '60 '86 C&L.575 B.A., J.D. Sr. Corp. Coun., Lowe's Cos., Inc.
Harris, Wayne W. '61 '86 C.837 B.S. L.880 J.D.
(adm. in TN; not adm. in NC) Asst. Gen. Coun., Lowe's Cos., Inc.
Hayes, J. Allie .... '10 '35 C&L.896 LL.B. Hayes Bros. Bldg.‡
James, Carmen Elizabeth .... '58 '01 C.896 B.A. L.574 J.D. [Ⓐ Vannoy,C.T.&V.]
Johnson, Daniel Stuart .... '75 '00 C.575 B.S./B.A. L.896 J.D. [Ⓐ Vannoy,C.T.&V.]
Lane, Christopher Decker, (BV) .... '64 '93 C.20 B.A. L.896 J.D. [Ⓐ McElwee]
Laney, Robert P., (BV) .... '52 '77 C.896 B.A. L.575 J.D. [Ⓐ McElwee]
Logsdon, John Michael, (BV) .... '52 '95 C.228 B.S. L.574 J.D. [Ⓐ McElwee]
Mahan, Elizabeth K. .... '68 '93 C.228 B.A. L.896 J.D. [Ⓐ McElwee]
Maloney, James, (CV) .... '70 '97 C.34 B.S. L.574 J.D. [Ⓐ McElwee]
McElwee, Karen Inscore, (BV) .... '55 '93 C.999 B.S. L.896 J.D. [Ⓐ McElwee]
McElwee, W. H., III, (AV) .... '45 '71 C&L.896 B.A., J.D. [McElwee]
McElwee Firm, PLLC, (AV) .... 906 Main Street
Miller, Michael T. '59 '84 C.927 B.S. L.365 J.D.
(adm. in IL; not adm. in NC) P.O. Box 1111‡
Moore, E. James, (AV) .... '26 '51 C&L.896 B.S., J.D. 207 Tenth Street
Moore, Jerry D., (AV) .... '40 '67 C&L.896 B.A., J.D. 214 9th St.
Porter, Cecil Lee, (AV) .... '27 '51 C.880 L.896 J.D. 312 9th St.
Potter, James W. '60 '85 C.477 B.A. L.665 J.D.
(adm. in PA; not adm. in NC) Asst. Gen. Coun., Lowe's Cos., Inc.
Rowley, Lisa J., (BVⓉ) .... '56 '91 C.438 A.B. L.629 J.D. [L.J.Rowley]
Rowley, Lisa J., PLLC, (BVⓉ) .... 809 Main St., Ste. 33
Stevens, Kimberly C., (BV) .... '67 '92 C.906 B.A. L.893 J.D. [Ⓐ McElwee]
Triplett, Anthony R., (AV) .... '55 '81 C&L.575 B.S., J.D. [Vannoy,C.T.&V.]
Vannoy, J. Gary, (AV) .... '40 '64 C&L.896 B.A., LL.B. [Vannoy,C.T.&V.]
Vannoy, John G. (Jay), Jr., (AV) .... '67 '92 C.296 B.S. L.1228 J.D. [Vannoy,C.T.&V.]

Vannoy, Colvard, Triplett & Vannoy, P.L.L.C., (AV) BR
922 "C" Street, P.O. Box 1388, 28659
Telephone: 336-667-7201 Fax: 336-838-7250
URL: http://www.vannoylaw.com
Members of Firm: J. Gary Vannoy; Howard C. Colvard, Jr.; Anthony R. Triplett; John G. (Jay) Vannoy, Jr.;—Daniel Stuart Johnson; Carmen Elizabeth James.
Civil and Criminal Litigation, Corporations, Personal Injury, Automobile Accidents, Traffic, Driving While Intoxicated, DWI, Real Estate, Wills, Trusts and Estates, Workers' Compensation, Social Security Disability.
Representative Clients: Branch Bank & Trust Co.; Wilkes County, ECMD, Inc.
References: Branch Bank & Trust Co.; 1st Citizens Bank & Trust Co.
See Professional Biographies, NORTH WILKESBORO, NORTH CAROLINA

Wiebel, George C. .... '44 '70 C.575 A.B. L.469 J.D. 205 10th St.‡

NORWOOD, 2,216, *Stanly Co.*

Harris, William H. .... '19 '48 C&L.896 B.S., J.D. 16426 Chicora Ct.‡

OAK ISLAND, 6,571, *Brunswick Co.*

Banks, Lawrence K., (AVⓉ) '43 '67
C&L.228 A.B., LL.B. 1000 Caswell Beach Road, Suite 1201
Edwards, Roger Lee, (BV) .... '53 '79 C.34 B.A. L.115 J.D. [R.L.Edwards]

Edwards, Roger Lee, P.A., (BV)
7201 East Oak Island Drive, 28465
Telephone: 910-278-3100 Fax: 910-278-3320
Email: rledwardsesq@bellsouth.net
Roger Lee Edwards.
General Civil State and Federal Courts. Municipal and Local Government Law, Real Estate, Corporate, Commercial, Probate, Family, Personal Injury.
See Professional Biographies, OAK ISLAND, NORTH CAROLINA

Serra, Robert K., (BV) .... '54 '84 C.477 B.S. L.575 J.D. [Serra P.]
Serra Law Firm, PLLC, (BV) .... 104 Price St.
Sullivan, Richard Patrick, Jr. '49 '87 C.1290 B.A. L.950 J.D.
(adm. in AZ; not adm. in NC) Asst. Atty. Gen.

OAK RIDGE, 3,988, *Guilford Co.*

Goslen, Frank O. .... '27 '52 C.1129 L.896 J.D. Pres., Southeastern Adjustment Co., Inc.
Wiener, Alan D. '50 '74 C&L.273 B.B.A., J.D.
(adm. in FL; not adm. in NC) 8326 W. Harrell Rd.‡

OCEAN ISLE BEACH, 523, *Brunswick Co.*

Atkins, Amy Renee .... '75 '01 C.228 B.A. L.1228 J.D. 6406 Beach Drive, S.W.
Lominac, Karen T. .... '70 '97 C.1228 B.B.A. L.1345 J.D. 6406 Beach Dr.
Smith, Cynthia D., (CV) .... '66 '97 C.576 B.A. L.1228 J.D. [C.D.Smith]
Smith, Cynthia D., PC, (CV) .... 7199 Beach Dr. S.W., Ste. 5
Stanley, Davey L., (CV) .... '30 '79 C.627 B.G.E. L.1228 J.D. [Stanley&S.]
Stanley, Karin L., (BV) .... '58 '87 C.953 B.A. L.1228 J.D. [Stanley&S.]
Stanley & Stanley, (BV) .... 6655A Beach Dr. S.W.

OCRACOKE, 769, *Hyde Co.*

Parker-Lowe, Katherine .... '59 '86 C.577 B.A. L.1228 J.D. [K.S.Parker-Lowe]

Parker-Lowe, Katherine S.
35 Miss Elecia Lane, Suite 101, P.O. Box 730, 27960-0730
Telephone: 252-928-1000 Fax: 252-928-3037
Email: katherine@parker-lowe.net
Katherine Parker-Lowe.
Real Estate, Civil Practice, Consumer Law, Traffic, Bankruptcy, Business.
See Professional Biographies, OCRACOKE, NORTH CAROLINA

ORIENTAL, 786, *Pamlico Co.*

Moore, Elliott '27 '56 C.228 A.B. L.260 LL.B.
(adm. in GA; not adm. in NC) P.O. Box 779‡
Sage, William R., (AV) .... '48 '75 C.232 A.B. L.575 J.D. 403 Neuse St.

OTTO, —, *Macon Co.*

Dunn, Edgar H., Jr. '19 '47 C.383 L.260 J.D.
(adm. in FL; not adm. in NC) 388 Southgate Rd.‡

OXFORD, * 8,338, *Granville Co.*

Allen, Claude W., Jr. .... '28 '62 C.576 B.S. L.575 LL.B. Ret. Chief Dist. Ct. J.
Bostic, Cindy K. Pulley, (BV) .... '70 '95 C.888 B.A. L.1345 J.D. Off. of Dist. Atty.
Bradsher, Ronald S., Jr., (BV) .... '58 '83 C.925 B.S.B.A. L.896 J.D. 135 1/2 Main Street
Burnette, J. Thomas, (AV) .... '59 '85 C.1228 B.S. L.896 J.D. [Edmundson&B.]
Burnette, Michael P. .... '70 '95 C&L.575 B.A., J.D. P.O. Box 1285
Catherwood, Robert K., (BV) .... '44 '73 C.645 B.S. L.896 J.D. 104 Court St.
Cross, James E., Jr., (AV) .... '47 '73 C&L.896 B.A., J.D. [Royster,C.&C.]
Currin, Hugh M., Jr., (AV) .... '51 '80 C.576 B.A. L.1228 J.D. [Royster,C.&C.]
Currin, Sam B., III, (AV) .... '46 '71 C&L.896 B.A., J.D. Dist. Atty.
Currin, Thomas L., (AV) .... '51 '76 C&L.575 B.A., J.D. [Currin&D.]

Currin & Dutra, LLP, (AV)
118 Main Street, P.O. Box 1226, 27565
Telephone: 919-693-8011 Fax: 919-690-1415
Email: oxfordlaw@earthlink.net
Members of Firm: Thomas L. Currin; Lori A. Dutra. Associate: Amy R. Edge.
General Practice, Civil Litigation in all Courts, Criminal Litigation in all Courts, Traffic Offenses, Personal Injury, Small Business Law, Corporate Law, Residential Real Estate, Commercial Real Estate, Land Use Planning, Estate Planning, Probate, Workers Compensation and Social Security Disability.
See Professional Biographies, OXFORD, NORTH CAROLINA

Davis, Drew H. .... '74 '00 C&L.896 B.A., J.D. 135 College St.
Duckworth, James T., III, (BV) .... '66 '92 C.228 A.B. L.575 J.D. [Edmundson&B.]
Dunlow, John M., (BV) .... '68 '94 C.34 B.S. L.1228 J.D. [Ⓐ J.W.Watson,Jr.]
DuRant, Barbara Bolton .... '60 '01 C.577 B.A. L.574 J.D. P.O. Box 2115
Dutra, Lori A., (BV) .... '60 '87 C.1128 B.A. L.575 J.D. [Currin&D.]
Edge, Amy R., (BV) .... '69 '95 C.228 A.B. L.575 J.D. [Ⓐ Currin&D.]
Edmundson, R. Gene, (AV) .... '36 '63 C.228 A.B. L.896 LL.B. [Edmundson&B.]

Edmundson & Burnette, L.L.P., (AV)
106 Main Street, P.O. Box 428, 27565
Telephone: 919-693-7087 FAX: 919-693-7979
Email: tburnette@enblaw.com
R. Gene Edmundson; J. Thomas Burnette; James T. Duckworth, III.
General Civil and Trial Practice in State and Federal Courts. Criminal, Probate, Real Estate, Corporate, Family and Personal Injury Law.
References: Capital Bank; Branch Banking and Trust Company; Centura Bank; United Title Company; Central Carolina Bank.

Finch, Daniel F., (AV) .... '44 '73 C.575 A.B. L.469 J.D. Dist. Co. J.
Gibson, Teresa M., (BV) .... '60 '94 C.260 B.A. L.575 J.D. [T.Gibson]
Gibson, Teresa, PA, (BV) .... 121 E. McClanahan St.
Gregory, Mark L. .... '74 '01 C.896 B.A. L.362 J.D. Asst. Dist. Atty.
Hensley, Dale W., (BV) .... '69 '98 C.48 B.A. L.575 J.D. [Royster,C.&C.]
Hicks, N. Kyle, (BV) .... '58 '84 C.575 B.S. L.896 J.D. [Hopper&H.]
Hopper, William L., (AV) .... '41 '66 C.168 B.S. L.45 LL.B. [Hopper&H.]

Hopper & Hicks, L.L.P., (AV)
111 Gilliam Street, P.O. Box 247, 27565
Telephone: 919-693-8161 Fax: 919-693-9938
URL: http://www.hopperhicks.com
Members of Firm: William L. Hopper; N. Kyle Hicks;—James C. Wrenn, Jr.
General Civil and Criminal Practice. Trials in all Courts. Probate, Wills and Probate, Real Estate, Automobile Accidents, Wrongful Death, Personal Injury, Family Law, Divorce, Child Custody, Adoptions, Business and Corporate Law, Administrative Law, Immigration Law, Taxation.

(This Listing Continued)

Hopper & Hicks, L.L.P. (Continued)
Counsel for: Granville United Bank.
Representative Clients: Centura Bank; Southern National Bank; Premier Quilting Corp.
See Professional Biographies, OXFORD, NORTH CAROLINA

Jackson, Harvey D., Attorney at Law
(See Henderson)

Nichol, Charm M. ....'— '97 C.446 B.A. L.574 J.D. 229 Hillsboro St.

Pike, John H., (BV) '47 '76 C&L.575 B.S., J.D.
129 Williamsboro Street Suite 1, P.O. Box 1165, 27565
Telephone: 919-693-2412 Fax: 919-693-1652
Email: JPIKE@GLORYROAD.net URL: http://www.lawyers.com/johnhpike
Traffic Violations, DWI, Criminal Law (all except capital), Family Law, Child Custody, Divorce, Adoptions, Personal Injury, Automobile Accidents, Truck and Motorcycle Accidents, Civil Litigation, Wrongful Death.
See Professional Biographies, OXFORD, NORTH CAROLINA

Royster, Thomas S., Jr., (AV) ....'37 '61 C&L.896 B.S., LL.B. [Royster,C.&C.]

Royster, Cross & Currin, LLP, (AV)
135 College Street, P.O. Drawer 1168, 27565
Telephone: 919-693-3131 Fax: 919-693-2919
Members of Firm: Thomas S. Royster, Jr. (Board Certified Specialist in Estate Planning and Probate Law, North Carolina State Board of Legal Specialization); James E. Cross, Jr. (Board Certified Specialist in Real Property Law-Residential Transactions, North Carolina State Board of Legal Specialization); Hugh M. Currin, Jr.; Dale W. Hensley.
Business Law, Corporate Law, Wills and Probate, Trusts and Estates, Commercial and Residential Real Estate, Personal Injury, Traffic, Family Law, Divorce, Child Custody, Adoptions.
See Professional Biographies, OXFORD, NORTH CAROLINA

Thorp, H. Norman, III, (BV) '63 '88 C.34 B.S. L.1228 J.D.
133 Williamsboro Street, P.O. Box 1027, 27565
Telephone: 919-693-3232 Telecopier: 919-693-2322
Email: hnthorp@gloryroad.net URL: http://www.lawyers.com/hnthorp
Criminal Law, Traffic Violations, DWI, Drug Violations, Theft, Personal Injury, Automobile Accidents, Residential Real Estate, Creditor Bankruptcy, Small Business Law, Business Startup, Wills and Probate.
See Professional Biographies, OXFORD, NORTH CAROLINA

Watson, John W., Jr., (BV) '54 '82 C.575 B.A. L.1228 J.D.
204 Williamsboro Street, P.O. Box 100, 27565-0100
Telephone: 919-693-5697 Facsimile: 919-693-1192
Email: jwwatsonjr@earthlink.net URL: http://www.jwatsonlaw.com
Associate: John M. Dunlow.
Workers Compensation Law, Criminal Law, Estates, Personal Injury, Automobile Accidents, Wrongful Death, Traffic Violations, DWI, Family Law, Divorce, Child Custody.
See Professional Biographies, OXFORD, NORTH CAROLINA

Wilkinson, Aaron C. ....'70 '95 C.575 B.A. L.896 J.D. P.O. Box 1285
Wilkinson, Charles W., Jr. ....'41 '67 C.232 B.S. L.575 J.D. Chf. Dist. Ct. J.
Wrenn, James C., Jr. ....'75 '00 C.885 B.A. L.309 J.D. [A Hopper&H.]

PAW CREEK, —, *Mecklenburg Co.*

Shabica, Carl S. ....'48 '75 C.303 B.A. L.574 J.D. [C.Shabica]
Shabica, Carl ....P.O. Box 804

PEMBROKE, 2,399, *Robeson Co.*

Baker, Ida T. ....'63 '91 C.1317 B.A. L.1378 J.D. Legal Aid of North Carolina, Inc.
Brooks, Brian Keith, (BV) ....'68 '94 C&L.575 B.A., J.D. 203 S. Vance St.
Hunt, Grady L., (BV) .... '61 '89 C.1317 B.A. L.575 J.D. [Locklear,J.S.&H.]
Jacobs, Arlie ....'47 '77 C.103 B.S. L.575 J.D. [Locklear,J.S.&H.]
Kimmel, Angela M. ....'57 '88 C.300 B.A. L.139 J.D. Lumbee River Legal Servs.
Locklear, Arnold .... '44 '73 C.1317 B.A. L.574 J.D. [Locklear,J.S.&H.]
Locklear, Jacobs, Sutton & Hunt, (BV) ....203 S. Vance St.
Oxendine, Henry W., (CV) .... '40 '73 C.1317 B.S. L.574 J.D. 208 Union Chapel Rd.
Payne, Donna Gooden, (CV) .... '65 '92 C.575 B.A. L.846 J.D. Univ. of N.C.
Roach, Janet H. ....'40 '84 C.309 B.A. L.1228 J.D. Lumbee River Legal Servs.
Sutton, Ronnie N., (CV) ....'41 '85 C.1176 B.A. L.575 J.D. [Locklear,J.S.&H.]

PFAFFTOWN, 900, *Forsyth Co.*

Crowell, Steven J., (CV) ....'56 '95 C.575 B.S. L.896 J.D. 7250 Pellinore Dr.
Hall, Roy G., Jr., (AV) ....'26 '55 C&L.575 A.B., J.D. 3960 Lakeview Drive
Northcraft, Julian O. '23 '50 C&L.608 B.S., J.D.
(adm. in OH; not adm. in NC) 3513 Waterway Dr.‡

PILOT MOUNTAIN, 1,181, *Surry Co.*

Anderson, M. Ann, (AV) ....'55 '81 C&L.575 B.A., J.D. [A T.W.Anderson]

Anderson, Thomas W., (BV) '54 '79 C&L.575 B.A., J.D.
214 E. Marion Street, P.O. Box 1273, 27041
Telephone: 336-368-9621 Fax: 336-368-9168
Email: thanderson54@hotmail.com URL: http://www.lawyers.com/thomaswandersonlaw
—M. Ann Anderson.
Bankruptcy, Mediation, Employment Law and Criminal.
See Professional Biographies, PILOT MOUNTAIN, NORTH CAROLINA

Long, James M. ....'37 '63 C&L.575 A.B., LL.B. Ret. Supr. Ct. J.
Martin, Watt N. ....'23 '50 C&L.273 A.B., LL.B. 211 E. Main St.
Reid, William G. ....'28 '55 C.925 B.S. L.575 LL.B. 101 E. Main St.‡
Royster, Michael F., (AV) ....'46 '75 C.896 B.A. L.192 J.D. [Royster&R.] ⊙
Royster and Royster, P.A., (AV) .... 110 S. Davis St. (⊙Mount Airy)
Sherrill, Everett C. ....'42 '67 C.198 B.A. L.896 J.D. Pres., Armtex, Inc.
Smith, Kenneth A. ....'43 '68 C&L.896 B.B.A., J.D. P.O. Box 850
Swanson, Edward N., (AV) ....'30 '55 C&L.228 A.B., LL.B. 115 West Main Street

PINEHURST, 9,706, *Moore Co.*

Bost, William Clarence "Bill" ....'52 '80 C.228 B.A. L.1228 J.D. P.O. Box 156
Brenner, Victoria P., (BV) ....'— '81 C.1365 B.A. L.472 J.D. [Robbins M.&R.]
Bynum, Fred W., Jr., (AV) ....'21 '48 C.228 A.B. L.309 LL.B. 1600 Morganton Rd.‡
Carlisle, Sam Q., II, (AV) ....'47 '74 C.575 B.A. L.896 J.D. P.O. Box 1209
Clarke, Mynell James, II, (BV) .... '55 '81 C.1130 B.A. L.896 J.D. [Clarke&P.]
Clarke & Phifer, LLP, (BV) .... 135 Applecross Road
Creed, Laura S. .... '73 '98 C.10 B.S. L.356 J.D. [A VanCamp,M.&N.]
Ecker, Karl L., (AVⓉ) '39 '64 C.477 A.B. L.912 J.D.
(adm. in MI; not adm. in NC) 40 Oxton Circle‡
Force, Frank J. '20 '49 C.136 B.A. L.477 J.D.
(adm. in MI; not adm. in NC) 430 Midland Dr.‡
Friesen, Robert M., (BV) ....'— '90 C&L.378 B.A., J.D. [Robbins M.&R.]
Garner, Jennifer B., (CV) ....'69 '94 C.577 B.A. L.896 J.D. [Garner&H.]
Garner & Hayes, PLLC, (BV) .... 125 Applecross Road
Gentry, Louis F. '42 '66 C.835 B.S. L.838 LL.B.
(adm. in TN; not adm. in NC) V.P. & Reg. Tr. Mgr., Branch Banking & Tr. Co.

Gorman, F. David '26 '53 C.976 B.A. L.309 LL.B.
(adm. in CT; not adm. in NC) 80 McCaskill Road West
Hayes, Lu Pendleton, (BV) .... '52 '84 C.680 B.S. L.1228 J.D. [Garner&H.]
Holshouser, James E., Jr., (AV) ....'34 '60 C.198 B.A. L.575 LL.B. [Sanford H.] ⊙
Jacobson, Ralph .... '28 '53 C.563 B.B.A. L.569 LL.B. 305 Donald Ross Dr.‡
Later, Stephen F., (BV) ....'— '94 C.178 B.A. L.575 J.D. [Robbins M.&R.]
May, John M., (AV) ....'— '72 C&L.896 B.A., J.D. [Robbins M.&R.]
McInerney, James L. '31 '78 C.477 B.B.A. L.213 J.D.
(adm. in MI; not adm. in NC) 200 Fairway Dr.‡
McNeill, James E. ....'75 '01 C.575 B.S. L.192 J.D. [A Clarke&P.]
Meacham, Eddie H., (BV) ....'58 '83 C.240 B.A. L.896 J.D. [VanCamp,M.&N.]

Morris Law Office
(See Whispering Pines)

Neville, Warwick Fay, (BV) ....'30 '55 C.674 A.B. L.659 LL.B. 16 Parker Ln.
Newman, Michael J., (BV) .... '62 '88 C.925 B.S. L.896 J.D. [VanCamp,M.&N.]
Oxendine, Ryan D. ....'75 '01 C.575 B.A. L.574 J.D. [A VanCamp,M.&N.]
Page, Robert N., III, (BV) ....'22 '48 C&L.575 A.B., LL.B. P.O. Box 4152‡
Parks, Owen Tracy, III, (AV) ....'43 '68 C&L.575 B.S., J.D. P.O. Box 4077
Pate, W. Daniel, (BV) ....'48 '74 C.575 B.S. L.896 J.D. [Pate&S.]

Pate & Scarborough, L.L.P., (AV)
15 Chinquapin Road, P.O. Box 1669, 28370
Telephone: 910-295-2161 Fax: 910-295-3247
W. Daniel Pate; Dewitt Talmadge Scarborough, III (Board Certified Specialist in Real Property Law-Residential, North Carolina State Board of Legal Specialization).
Real Property, Trust and Estate Planning and Administration, Business Formation.
See Professional Biographies, PINEHURST, NORTH CAROLINA

Phifer, H. Craig, III, (BV) ....'56 '82 C.575 B.A. L.896 J.D. [Clarke&P.]
Rich, Dean A., (AV) ....'28 '57 C.388 B.A. L.575 J.D. [Robbins M.&R.] ‡
Richardson, Arthur L. B. '12 '38 C.309 B.S. L.273
(adm. in DC; not adm. in NC) P.O. Box 1986‡
Robbins, Phillip Wayne, (BV) ....'— '66 C.178 A.B. L.575 J.D. [Robbins M.&R.]

Robbins May & Rich LLP, (AV)
120 Applecross Road, 28374
Telephone: 910-692-4900 Fax: 910-692-4286 (Real Estate and Corporate) Fax: 910-692-1768 (Trusts and Estates and Litigation)
URL: http://www.rmrattorneys.com
Partners: Phillip Wayne Robbins; John M. May; Carol M. White; Mark D. Vaughn; Victoria P. Brenner; Robert M. Friesen; Stephen F. Later. Retired Partner: Dean A. Rich. Associate: Janet C. Smith.
General Civil and Criminal Litigation in all Courts. Traffic Violations, Real Property, Trust and Estate Planning and Administration, Commercial and Residential Real Estate Transactions, Banking, Taxation, Personal Injury, Family Law, Divorce, Worker's Compensation, Business Formations and Transactions and Social Security Disability.
See Professional Biographies, PINEHURST, NORTH CAROLINA

Ryan, Raymond J. ....'29 '56 C.433 B.S. L.262 LL.B. P.O. Box 756
St. John, Donald J. ....'34 '63 C.1030 B.S.S. L.306 LL.B. P.O. Box 3313
Sanford Holshouser LLP, (AV) ....100 Market Square (⊙Raleigh)
Scarborough, Dewitt Talmadge, III, (AV) ....'50 '75 C&L.575 A.B., J.D. [Pate&S.]
Shelton, Randolph E., Jr., (BV) '50 '75
C.893 B.A. L.896 J.D. 1600 Morganton Rd., Lot P-2
Shields, Mary C. '57 '86 C.205 B.S.
(adm. in LA; not adm. in NC) P.O. Box 3819‡
Sizoo, Joseph A. '10 '38 C&L.273 LL.B.
(adm. in DC; not adm. in NC) 2092 Airport Rd.‡
Skillman, Tiffany J. ....'77 '02 C.575 B.A. L.1228 J.D. [A VanCamp,M.&N.]
Skipton, John A. '19 '48 C&L.608 B.S., LL.B.
(adm. in OH; not adm. in NC) 145 St. Andrews Dr.‡
Slagle, Craig A. ....'76 '05 C.34 B.S. L.1228 J.D. [A VanCamp,M.&N.]
Smith, Janet C., (CV) ....'59 '95 C.228 A.B. L.128 J.D. [A Robbins M.&R.]
Street, Thomas Barrett '74 '00 C.896 B.A. L.128 J.D. 210 Woodland Drive
Suggs, Robert V. ....'34 '64 C&L.896 B.S., LL.B. [P.B.Trevarrow] (⊙Southern Pines)‡

Thompson, Hurley E., Jr.
(See Carthage)

Thompson, Robert S., P.A.
(See Southern Pines)

Trevarrow, Paul B., (CV) ....'70 '96 C.477 A.B. L.912 J.D. [P.B.Trevarrow]
Trevarrow, Paul B., PLLC, (CV) ....285 Olmsted Boulevard, Suite 3
Van Camp, James R., (AV) ....'40 '65 C.55 A.B. L.896 LL.B. [VanCamp,M.&N.]
Van Camp, Thomas M., (BV) ....'63 '89 C.264 B.A. L.896 J.D. [VanCamp,M.&N.]

Van Camp, Meacham & Newman, PLLC, (AV) BB
Two Regional Circle, 28374
Telephone: 910-295-2525 Fax: 910-295-2001; 910-295-1520 (Litigation)
URL: http://www.lawyers.com/vancampmeacham&newman
James R. Van Camp; Eddie H. Meacham; Michael J. Newman; Thomas M. Van Camp;—Laura S. Creed; Ryan D. Oxendine; Tiffany J. Skillman; Craig A. Slagle.
General Civil and Criminal Litigation and Appellate Practice in State and Federal Courts. Personal Injury, Commercial, Medical Malpractice, Wrongful Death, Worker's Compensation, Insurance, Land Condemnation, Constitutional and Civil Rights, Family, Corporate, Real Estate, Administrative, Social Security Disability, Construction Law, Labor and Employment, Wills, Estate Planning and Probate Law.
See Professional Biographies, PINEHURST, NORTH CAROLINA

Vaughn, Mark D., (AV) ....'— '88 C.937 B.A. L.896 J.D. [Robbins M.&R.]
Wagnitz, John H. '09 '33 C&L.608 J.D.
(adm. in OH; not adm. in NC) 200 Blake Blvd.‡

West & Smith, L.L.P.
(See Southern Pines)

White, Carol M., (BV) ....'— '88 C.575 B.S. L.1345 J.D. [Robbins M.&R.]

PINE KNOLL SHORES, 1,524, *Carteret Co.*

Halada, John R., Law Office of '43 '00 C.667 B.S.E.E. L.575 J.D.
153 Mimosa Boulevard

PINETOPS, 1,514, *Edgecombe Co.*

Carlton, J. Phil, (AV) ....'38 '63 C.576 B.S. L.575 J.D. 108 N. Third Street
Pitt, Robert D., (BV) ....'57 '82 C.232 B.S. L.575 J.D. 121 W. Hamlet St.

PINEVILLE, 3,449, *Mecklenburg Co.*

Downs, Kenneth R. ....'21 '53 C.472 L.575 LL.B. 810 Main St.‡

PINNACLE, —, *Stokes Co.*

McNaught, Mary C. ....'46 '76 C.896 B.A. L.818 J.D. 1689 Brim's Grove Rd.

PISGAH FOREST, —, *Transylvania Co.*

Blyler, William E., (AVⓉ) '36 '65 C.259 B.A. L.260 J.D.
(adm. in FL; not adm. in NC) 112 Gordon Rd.
Cilley, Robert S. ....'48 '74 C&L.575 A.B., J.D. Chf. Dist. J.
Hooper, Alvin D. .... '39 '72 C.576 B.S. L.776 J.D. 55 Sweetwater Lane
Jordan, Elizabeth K. ....'55 '80 C.880 B.A. L.174 J.D. 16 Timberlane Dr.

PITTSBORO, * 2,226, *Chatham Co.*

Baroff, Roy J., Office of, (BV) .... '56 '87 C&L.575 B.A., J.D. 240 Buteo Rdg.
Betts, Lowry M. ....'30 '56 C.790 A.B. L.575 J.D. Ret. Chf. Dist. J.‡
Bland, Cynthia Sax, (CV) ....'47 '89 C.296 A.B. L.1345 J.D. 179 Hillsboro St.
Bowen, Courtney A. ....'77 '03 C&L.575 B.A., J.D. [[A] Bradshaw&R.]
Bradshaw, Patrick E., (BV) ....'64 '89 C&L.575 B.A., J.D. [Bradshaw&R.]

Bradshaw & Robinson, L.L.P., (BV)
Hall-London House, 128 Hillsboro Street, P.O. Box 607, 27312
Telephone: 919-542-2400 Fax: 919-542-1319
Email: law@bradshawrobinson.com
Patrick E. Bradshaw; Nicolas P. Robinson. Associate: Courtney A. Bowen.
Civil and Criminal Practice. Development and Zoning, Business, Corporation, Bankruptcy, Wills, Probate, Estate Administration, Real Estate and Traffic Law.
See Professional Biographies, PITTSBORO, NORTH CAROLINA

Chut, Frank J., Jr. ....'65 '90 C&L.228 B.A., J.D. 1355 Fearrington Post
Collins, Virginia B. ....'45 '93 C.576 B.A. L.574 J.D. 240 Havis Creek Dr.
Collins, William F. '19 '45 C&L.966 A.B., LL.B.
(adm. in NY; not adm. in NC) 656 Fearrington Post‡
Collura, Vincent Paul ....'37 '62 C&L.575 B.A., J.D. 45 Fearrington Post
Cooper, David Samuel, (BV) ....'55 '86 C.575 B.A. L.1228 J.D. Asst. Dist. Atty.
Edwards, Mark E., (AV) ....'59 '85 C&L.575 B.A., J.D. [Edwards&T.] ⊙
Edwards & Trenkle, (AV) .... 72 Hillsborough Street (⊙Durham)
Franklin, Susan R. ....'49 '79 C.999 B.A. L.146 J.D. [Franklin] ⊙

Franklin Law Center, PLLC
60 West Street, P.O. Box 685, 27312 ⊙
Telephone: 919-942-0800 Fax: 919-942-0607
Email: sfranklin@franklinlawcenter.com URL: http://www.franklinlawcenter.com
Susan R. Franklin.
Divorce, Alimony, Spousal Support, Separation Agreements, Marital Property Settlements, Equitable Distribution of Assets, Cohabitation Agreements, Community Property Law, Non-Traditional Family Law, Divorce Mediation, Divorce Arbitration, Collaborative Family Law, Adoption, International Family Law, Child Custody, Military Divorce, Military Family Law, Trial Practice in all Courts.
Chapel Hill Office: Exchange West at Meadowmont, 1414 Raleigh Road, Suite 290. 27517-8834. Telephone: 919-942-0800. Fax: 919-942-0607.
See Professional Biographies, PITTSBORO, NORTH CAROLINA

Gunn, Robert L., (AV) ....'31 '63 C&L.575 B.S., LL.B. [Gunn&M.]

Gunn & Messick, LLP, (AV)
90 West Salisbury Street, P.O. Box 880, 27312-0880
Telephone: 919-542-3253 Fax: 919-542-0257
Members of Firm: Robert L. Gunn; Paul S. Messick, Jr.
General Civil and Criminal Practice. Trials in all State Courts. Estate Planning, Corporation, Personal Injury, Real Estate and Administrative Law.
Representative Client: Chatham Mills, Inc.
Reference: First Citizens Bank & Trust Company, Pittsboro.
See Professional Biographies, PITTSBORO, NORTH CAROLINA

Henke, Robert J. .... '34 '80 C.339 B.S. L.589 J.D. 1024 Fearington Post‡
Holmes, Edward S., (AV) .... '— '58 C&L.575 B.A., LL.B. [Holmes&M.]
Holmes & McLaurin, (AV) ....27 Hillsboro Street
Hubbard, Thomas E. '— '73 C.228 L.577 J.D.
Consultant, Tim Hubbard Med. Consultant, Regulatory
Hunt, John E. '23 '48 C.299 L.982 LL.B.
(adm. in NY; not adm. in NC) 190 Weatherbend, Fearrington Post
Ising, Judith G., (BVⓉ) .... '43 '86 C.1118 B.A. L.284 J.D. 808 Fearrington Post

Jones, Dana G.
(See Durham)

Lamb, Bradley Robert ....'56 '89 C.575 B.A. L.574 J.D. P.O. Box 453
Lewis, Henry W. .... '16 '40 C.575 A.B. L.309 J.D. 386 Fearrington Post‡

Maitland & Maitland, PLLC
(See Chapel Hill)

Mathias, F. Gregory, (BVⓉ) '41 '76 C.11 A.B. L.900 J.D.
(adm. in KS; not adm. in NC) 823 Fearrington Post
McKinney, Ruth A., (BV) .... '51 '89 C.228 B.A. L.575 J.D. 169 Wintersage
McLaurin, R. Edward, Jr., (BV) .... '49 '75 C&L.575 B.S., J.D. [Holmes&M.]
Messick, Paul S., Jr., (BV) ....'46 '71 C.228 A.B. L.575 J.D. [Gunn&M.]

Miller, Charles W. '58 '81 C.932 B.B.A. L.912 J.D.
288 East Street, Suite 2004, P.O. Box 1549, 27312
Telephone: 919-542-9820 Fax: 919-542-5624 URL: http://www.pittsborolaw.com
Email: charlesmiller@pittsborolaw.com URL: http://www.lawyers.com/pittsborolaw
Collections, Bankruptcy, Commercial Litigation, Business Contracts, Credit Law, Administrative Law, Real Estate, Mediation, Securities Arbitration, Investment Fund.
See Professional Biographies, PITTSBORO, NORTH CAROLINA

Perry, James F. ....'26 '51 C.475 B.A. L.228 LL.B. 1012 Fearrington Post‡
Robinson, Nicolas P., (BV) ....'64 '89 C&L.575 B.A., J.D. [Bradshaw&R.]
Spritzer, Martin A. '27 '52 C.705 A.B. L.309 LL.B.
(adm. in NJ; not adm. in NC) 595 E. Fearrington Post‡
Starkweather, Jeffrey L. ....'47 '89 C.684 B.A. L.574 J.D. P.O. Box 217
Trenkle, Robert C. ....'60 '86 C.446 B.S. L.575 J.D. [Edwards&T.] ⊙

Vira Law Firm, The, PA
(See Carrboro)

Webster, Joe L., (BV) ....'54 '79 C&L.329 B.A., J.D. 200 Sanford Rd.
Wiles, James E. .... '46 '86 C.575 B.A. L.574 J.D. 241 Nicks Bend E.

Willis, Robert J., Law Offices of
(See Raleigh)

Winston & Maher
(See Chapel Hill)

PLYMOUTH, * 4,107, *Washington Co.*

Cockrell, Arthur E., (BV) ....'39 '69 C&L.575 B.S., J.D. 119 E. Water St.
Harrell, Maynard A., Jr., (BV) ....'44 '72 C.206 B.S. L.500 J.D. P.O. Box 369
Hutchins, Robert Wendel, (BV) ....'45 '72 C&L.575 B.A., J.D. [Hutchins]
Hutchins Law Firm, P.A., (BV) .... 115 W. Water St.

Willey, Ralph G., P.A.
(See Rocky Mount)

Womble, R. Andrew, (CV) ....'71 '96 C&L.575 B.S., J.D. 114 Main Street

POINT HARBOR, —, *Currituck Co.*

Alexy, Fletcher, Wills & Wills, P.C., (BV)
8845 Caratoke Highway, 27964
Telephone: 252-491-8497 Fax: 252-491-8723
URL: http://www.obxlawfirm.com
Grant E. Fletcher; Gregory E. Wills; James R. Wills, III;—Bernard "B.J." B. McAvoy, Jr.
Business Law, Child Custody, Civil Litigation, Criminal Law, Domestic Relations, Divorce Law, Family Law, Medical Malpractice, Personal Injury, Real Estate Law and Workers Compensation Law, Traffic Violations, Driving While Intoxicated, Buying or Selling a Home, Buying or Selling a Business, Corporate, Small Business.
See Professional Biographies, POINT HARBOR, NORTH CAROLINA

Fletcher, Grant E. ....'65 '95 C.215 B.A. L.475 J.D. [Alexy,F.W.&W.]
McAvoy, Bernard "B.J." B., Jr. .... '76 '04 C.576 B.S. L.1228 J.D. [[A] Alexy,F.W.&W.]
Stott, William C., Jr. '32 '59 C&L.893 B.A., LL.B.
(adm. in VA; not adm. in NC) P.O. Box 259‡
Wills, Gregory E., (BV) ....'64 '93 C.1356 B.A. L.1228 J.D. [Alexy,F.W.&W.]
Wills, James R., III, (CV) .... '61 '93 C.1356 B.S. L.616 J.D. [Alexy,F.W.&W.]

RAEFORD, * 3,469, *Hoke Co.*

Adair, Meredith Page ....'69 '94 C&L.575 B.A., J.D. Pros. Atty.

Baker, Debbie Goronet '68 '94 C.575 B.A. L.574 J.D.
112 E. Elwood Avenue, 28376
Mailing Address: P.O. Box 726, Raeford, NC 28376
Telephone: 910-904-5585; Toll Free: 866-423-6084 Fax: 910-904-5589 URL: http://www.debbiebaker.com
Email: DBakerattorney@aol.com URL: http://www.hoke-raeford.com/debbiebaker
General Practice, Personal Injury, Automobile Accidents and Injuries, Wrongful Death, Criminal Defense, Misdemeanors, Felonies, DWI, Traffic Violations, Revoked Licenses/DMV Hearings, Uncontested Divorces, Workers Compensation, Child Support, Child Custody.
See Professional Biographies, RAEFORD, NORTH CAROLINA

Banks, Brian S. '55 '87 C.174 B.A. L.900 J.D.
(adm. in KS; not adm. in NC) 301 Harris Street★
Beaver Holt Sternlicht Glazier Carlin Britton & Courie, P.A., (AV)
127 W. Edinborough Ave. (⊙Fayetteville)

Britt, William S., Law Offices of
(See Lumberton)

Byrd, Gregory M.
(See Fayetteville)

Courie, David T., (BV) ....'70 '97 C&L.1228 B.B.A., J.D. [Beaver H.S.G.C.B.&C.] ⊙
Diehl, Philip A., (AV) ....'37 '61 C&L.896 B.A., J.D. [Diehl&G.]
Diehl & Gibson, (AV) .... 127 West Edinborough Avenue
Fields, William Corbett, Jr., (BV) .... '66 '92 C.34 B.A. L.1228 J.D. [Willcox,M.F.&S.]
Gibson Diehl, Millicent ....'48 '74 C.1130 B.A. L.575 J.D. [Diehl&G.] ‡

Gordon, Horne, Hicks and Floyd, P.A.
(See Laurinburg)

Griffin Law Office
(See Red Springs)

Holt, F. Thomas III, (BV) .... '52 '80 C.575 A.B. L.1228 J.D. [Beaver H.S.G.C.B.&C.] ⊙
Hostetler, Charles A., (AV) ....'24 '49 C&L.896 LL.B. [Hostetler&M.] ‡
Hostetler & McNeill, (AV) ....109 Campus Avenue
McFadyen, Duncan B., III, (AV) ...... '48 '73 C.673 B.A. L.575 J.D. [Willcox,M.F.&S.]
McNeill, Bobby Burns, (AV) .... '31 '58 C&L.575 B.S., J.D. [Hostetler&M.]
Moses, William L. ....'30 '55 C&L.896 B.S., LL.B. 705 Harris Ave.‡
Powell, Jean E., (BV) ....'50 '75 C&L.575 A.B., J.D. Dist. Atty.
Sutherland, Regina Roberts, (BV) '71 '00 C.232 B.S.C.J. L.1228 J.D.
[Willcox,M.F.&S.]
Teal, Linda Kaye, (BV) .... '55 '84 C.471 B.S. L.575 J.D. P.O. Box 143

Vaughan, Christopher V., The Law Offices of '69 '01 C.1317 B.S. L.1345 J.D.
131 West Edinborough Avenue, 28376
Mailing Address: P.O. Box 35590, Fayetteville, NC 28303
Telephone: 910-875-0955 Fax: 910-875-0233
Email: izzydaddy@hotmail.com URL: http://www.vaughanlawoffice.com
Criminal Law, Traffic, DWI, Family Law, Divorce, Child Support and Child Custody.
See Professional Biographies, RAEFORD, NORTH CAROLINA

Willcox, R. Palmer, (AV) ....'35 '61 C&L.790 B.S., LL.B. [Willcox,M.F.&S.] ‡

Willcox, McFadyen, Fields & Sutherland, (AV)
112 E. Edinborough Avenue, 28376
Telephone: 910-875-4065 Fax: 910-875-6710
Email: wmfs@nc.rr.com URL: http://www.racefordlawyers.com
Members of Firm: R. Palmer Willcox (Retired); Duncan B. McFadyen, III; William Corbett Fields, Jr.; Regina Roberts Sutherland.
General Civil and Criminal Trial Practice. Personal Injury, Probate and Real Estate Law.
Representative Clients: County of Hoke.
Approved Attorneys for: Lawyers Title Insurance Corp.
References: United Carolina Bank of Raeford, North Carolina; Southern National Bank.
See Professional Biographies, RAEFORD, NORTH CAROLINA

RALEIGH, * 276,093, *Wake Co.*

Abrams, Douglas B., (AV) .... '54 '79 C&L.896 B.A., J.D. [Abrams&A.]
Abrams, Margaret Smith, (AV) .... '54 '80 C&L.896 B.A., J.D. [Abrams&A.]

Abrams & Abrams, P.A., (AV)
414 West Jones Street, 27603
Mailing Address: P.O. Box 26025, Raleigh, NC 27611
Telephone: 919-755-9166 Fax: 919-755-9396 URL: http://www.abramslawfirm.com
Email: dabrams@abramslawfirm.com URL: http://www.lawyers.com/abramslawfirm
Douglas B. Abrams; Margaret Smith Abrams.
Catastrophic Personal Injury, Tractor Trailer Wrecks, Traumatic Brain Injury, Products Liability, Wrongful Death, Electrocutions, Toxic Torts, Insurance Litigation, Industrial/Construction Explosions, Railroad Litigation, Professional Negligence, Maritime Litigation.
See Professional Biographies, RALEIGH, NORTH CAROLINA

Abramson, Jarett K. '71 '97 C.659 B.A. L.878 J.D.
[[A] Myers B.S.&S.] (See Pat. Sect.)
Acree, Kara Grice ....'70 '00 C.228 B.A. L.575 J.D. [[A] Tharrington S.]
Acree, Sharon S. ....'62 '89 C.893 B.A. L.796 J.D. [Acree]
Acree Law Offices, PLLC .... 6101 Grove Crest Ct., Apt. 221
Adams, Christopher A. '70 '99
C.575 B.A. L.1345 J.D. NC Employ. Sec. Comm., App. Dept.
Adams, Geoffrey William .... '72 '98 C.878 B.S. L.228 J.D. [[A] Smith,A.B.D.M.&J.]
Adams, J. Allen, (AV) .... '32 '54 C&L.575 A.B., J.D. [[C] Parker,P.A.&B.]
Adams, Jeff H., Attorney at Law .... '56 '84 C&L.575 B.A., J.D. P.O. Box 10651
Adams, R. L., (AV) ....'57 '83 C&L.575 B.A., J.D. [R.L.Adams]
Adams, Ryan J., (BV) ....'75 '01 C.228 B.A. L.575 J.D. [Shirley&A.]
Adams, Thomas F., Jr., (AV) ....'21 '49 C&L.575 A.B., LL.B. [Adams,P.&B.]

Adams, Virginia Green ....'66 '92 C&L.575 B.A., J.D. 2326 Hathaway Rd.

Adams, McCullough & Beard
(See Parker, Poe, Adams & Bernstein L.L.P.)

Adams, Portnoy & Berggren, P.A., (AV) ....4000 Blue Ridge Rd.

Adams, R. L., PLLC, (AV)
3737 Glenwood Avenue, Suite 100, 27612
Mailing Address: P.O. Box 31703, Raleigh, NC, 27622-1703
Telephone: 919-573-1868 Telefax: 919-239-2687
Email: rl@rladams.com URL: http://www.rladams.com
R. L. Adams.
Equine Law, Civil Litigation, Real Estate Litigation, Business Torts, Products Liability.

See Professional Biographies, RALEIGH, NORTH CAROLINA

Addleton, Jennifer A. ....'— '03 C.953 B.A. L.1228 J.D. [Cranfill,S.&H.]
Agraz, Rodolfo R., (AV) ....'62 '88 C.228 B.S. L.280 J.D. [Ogletree,D.N.S.&S.]
Ailsworth, Timothy S. ....'55 '84 C.301 B.A. L.1209 J.D. NC Leaque of Municipalities
Albright, Karen M. '59 '84 C.446 B.A. L.228 J.D.
(adm. in MD; not adm. in NC) Assoc. General Counsel, Martin Marietta Materials, Inc.
Alcoke, Meredith Jo '71 '97 C&L.575 B.A., J.D.
Asst. Atty. Gen., Atty. Gen. Off., Div of Customs Mgmt.
Aldridge, W. Sidney, (AV) ....'52 '77 C&L.575 A.B., J.D. [Nicholls&C.]
Alexander, Barry D. ....'— '94 C&L.1356 B.S., J.D. [Nelson M.R.&S.]
Alexander, DeLisa K. ....'65 '95 C.1369 B.B.A. L.1209 J.D. Corp. Coun., Red Hat, Inc.
Alexander, Thomas Willis Haywood, (AV) '40 '68 C.575 A.B. L.896 J.D.
[Maupin T.]
Alexander, William G., (AV) ....'51 '76 C.198 A.B. L.896 J.D. [Legacy]

Alexander & Doyle, P.A.
(See Cary)

Allen, Arch T., III, (AV) ....'40 '65 C&L.575 B.S., J.D. [Allen&M.]
Allen, Dwight W. ....'46 '73 C.575 B.A. L.896 J.D. [🄲 Smith,A.B.D.M.&J.]
Allen, F. Hill, (AV) ....'67 '92 C.575 B.A. L.893 J.D. [Tharrington S.]
Allen, James P. ....'52 '86 C.575 B.A. L.309 J.D. Asst. Atty. Gen., Dept. of Jus.
Allen, Michael C. ....'57 '99 C.575 B.S. L.1345 J.D. [Cranfill,S.&H.]
Allen, Noel L., (AV) ....'47 '74 C.240 B.A. L.575 J.D. [Allen&P.]
Allen, Sonya Maria ....'— '00 C.16 B.A. L.574 J.D. NC Dept. of Jus.

Allen & Moore, L.L.P., (AV)
3700 Computer Drive, Suite 320, 27609-8627
Telephone: 919-783-8023 Fax: 919-783-8282
Email: ALLNMOORE@AOL.COM
Arch T. Allen, III; Joseph C. Moore, III; Ann Strader Hanley.
General Civil Practice. Administrative, Business and Corporate Law, Insurance Law, Construction Law and Litigation in all State and Federal Courts.

See Professional Biographies, RALEIGH, NORTH CAROLINA

Allen and Pinnix, P.A., (AV) BR
333 Fayetteville Street Mall Suite 1200, 27601
Telephone: 919-755-0505 Facsimile: 919-829-8098
Email: tmr@allen-pinnix.com URL: http://www.allen-pinnix.com
Noel L. Allen; John L. Pinnix (Board Certified Specialist in Immigration Law, North Carolina State Board of Legal Specialization); C. Lynn Calder (Board Certified Specialist in Immigration Law, North Carolina State Board of Legal Specialization); M. Jackson Nichols; J. Heydt Philbeck; D. James Jones, Jr.; Alice S. Glover; Kenneth C. Day; Angela Long Carter.
Antitrust, Immigration, Administrative, International Trade, Corporate, Construction, Insurance, Employment, Arbitration, Mediation, Franchise, Unfair Trade Practices, Unfair Competition, Mergers and Acquisitions, Business Litigation and Appellate Practice in all State and Federal Courts.

See Professional Biographies, RALEIGH, NORTH CAROLINA

Allen-Steele, Nicholle .... '70 '00 C.223 B.S. L.180 J.D. [🄰 Parker,P.A.&B.]
Alley, Zebulon D., (AV) ....'28 '55 C&L.575 A.B., LL.B. [Z.D.Alley]
Alley, Zebulon D., P.A., (AV) .... 863 Washington Street
Alphin, Alesia R., (BV) ...'60 '87 C.228 B.S. L.575 J.D. 3716 National Drive (⊙Durham)
Alphin, Fred, Jr., (BV) '36 '87 C.575 B.S. L.574 J.D.
Assoc. Gen. Coun., N.C. Farm Bureau Federation, Inc.
Alphin, Oliver W., (AV) .... '33 '61 C&L.575 B.S., J.D. [🄲 Moore&A.] ⊙

Alston & Bird LLP, (AV) BR
3201 Beechleaf Court, Suite 600, 27604-1062 ⊙
Telephone: 919-862-2200 Telecopier: 919-862-2260 Cable Address: AMGRAM GA Telex: 54-2 996
Easylink: 62985848
Email: info@alston.com URL: http://www.alston.com
Members of Firm: W. Murray Spruill; Christopher M. Humphrey. Of Counsel: Jasper L. Cummings, Jr. Associates: Ryan W. Cagle; Michelle L. Cunningham; Edward R. Ergenzinger, Jr.; Kevin R. Lyn; Jason O. Piche; David M. Saravitz; Leigh W. Thorne.
Languages: Bangla, Bulgarian, Croatian, French, German, Gujarati, Hindi, Italian, Japanese, Korean, Portuguese, Russian, Spanish, Tamil, Thai, Turkish, Urdu.
Administrative Law, Alternative Dispute Resolution, Antitrust and Trade Regulation, Appellate Practice, Bankruptcy, Banks and Banking, Biotechnology, Business Law, Class Actions, Commercial Real Estate, FCC Licensing, FCC Regulation, Wireless Communications, Complex and Multi-District Litigation, Computers and Software, Constitutional Law, Construction Law, Copyrights, Corporate Ethics, Corporate Governance, Corporate Law, Criminal Law, Debtor and Creditor, Electronic Commerce, Emerging Growth Companies, Employee Benefits, Employment Law, Entertainment Law, ERISA, ERISA Litigation, Energy, Environmental Law, Environmental Litigation, Executive Compensation; Finance, Franchises and Franchising, Government Investigations; Health Care Corporate Law, Health Care Regulation, Immigration Law, Insurance Defense, Intellectual Property, International Finance, International Law, International Taxation, International Trade, Internet Law, Labor Law, Labor and Employment, Land Use, Legislative Practice, Life Sciences, Litigation, Local Taxation, Medical Malpractice, Mergers, Acquisitions and Divestitures, Multimedia Law, Municipal Law, Nonprofit and Charitable Organizations, Occupational Safety and Health, Partnership Law, Patents, Privacy Law, Products Liability, Professional Liability, Public Finance, Public Policy, Real Estate Finance, Regulatory Law, RICO, Securities, Securities Litigation, State Taxation, Taxation, Tax Litigation, Technology and Science, Telecommunications Law, Trademarks, Trusts and Estates, Utility Law, Venture Capital, White Collar Crime, Zoning.
Atlanta, Georgia Office: One Atlantic Center, 1201 West Peachtree Street, 30309-3424. Telephone: 404-881-7000. Telecopier: 404-881-7777.
Washington, D.C. Office: 601 Pennsylvania Avenue, N.W., North Building, 10th Floor, 20004-2601. Telephone: 202-756-3300. Telecopier: 202-756-3333.
Charlotte, North Carolina Office: Bank of America Plaza, 101 South Tryon Street, Suite 4000, 28280-4000. Telephone: 704-444-1000. Fax: 704-444-1111.
New York, New York Office: 90 Park Avenue, 10016-1387. Telephone: 212-210-9400. Fax: 212-210-9444.
(Liaison) Munich, Germany Office: Brienner Strasse 11/V, 80333 Munich. Telephone: (49) (89) 238-0-70. Telecopier: (49) (89) 238-0-7110.

See Professional Biographies, RALEIGH, NORTH CAROLINA

Ambrose, Bruce S. ....'53 '77 C.228 B.A. L.923 J.D. Asst. Atty. Gen.
Anders, Jonathan C., (BV) ....'70 '96 C.575 B.A. L.1228 J.D. [Cranfill,S.&H.]
Anderson, Albeon G., Jr. ....'41 '68 C.611 B.A. L.597 J.D. [Anderson&A.] ⊙
Anderson, Ann M. ....'— '01 C&L.575 B.A., J.D. [🄰 Kennedy C.L.&H.]
Anderson, Charles N., Jr., (BV) ..... '56 '86 C.576 B.A. L.575 J.D. [Ellis&W.] (⊙Cary)
Anderson, Deanna Davis ....'69 '95 C.1077 B.A. L.896 J.D. [Smith,A.B.D.M.&J.]
Anderson, George M., (BV) ....'21 '51 C&L.896 B.S., J.D. [Anderson&R.]
Anderson, Mark E., (AV) ....'63 '88 C.228 A.B. L.575 J.D. [Patterson,D.C.B.&A.]
Anderson, Michael J., (AV) ....'43 '69 C.611 B.A. L.607 J.D. [Anderson&A.] ⊙

Anderson, Robin Adams, (AV) ....'58 '90 C.454 B.A. L.575 J.D. [Nicholls&C.]
Anderson, Thomas B., Jr., (AVⓉ) .... '42 '70 C.198 B.A. L.575 J.D. [Womble C.S.&R.]
Anderson, Victor A., Jr. ....'52 '88 C&L.1228 B.A., J.D. [Anderson,J.&G.]
Anderson, William Eugene, (AV) ....'44 '69 C.228 B.A. L.575 J.D. [McDaniel&A.]
Anderson, Zebulon D., (AV) ....'69 '94 C.228 B.A. L.893 J.D. [Smith,A.B.D.M.&J.]
Anderson and Anderson, (AV) ....19 West Hargett Street (⊙Rocky Mount)

Anderson, Jones & Gengo, PLLC
1305 Navaho Drive, Suite 103, 27609
Telephone: 919-277-2541 Fax: 919-277-2544
Email: lgengo@ajgpllc.com URL: http://www.ajgpllc.com
Members of the Firm: Victor A. Anderson, Jr.; Todd Allen Jones; Laurie B. Gengo.
Construction Law, Construction Litigation, Collections, OSHA Defense, Contracts, Administrative Law, Administrative Litigation, Real Estate, Environmental Law, Environmental Litigation, Toxic Mold Litigation.

See Professional Biographies, RALEIGH, NORTH CAROLINA

Anderson & Rutherford, L.L.P., (BV) ....150 Fayetteville Mall, Ste. 2200
Andrews, Thomas J., (BV) '38 '66 C.197 A.B. L.228 LL.B.
Coun., Admin. Off. of the Cts.
Andrews, William P., Jr., (AV) .... '49 '75 C&L.575 B.A., J.D. [🄲 Hunton&W.]
Andrussier, Sean E. ....'67 '92 C.1365 B.A. L.228 J.D. [Womble C.S.&R.]
Ange, Robert L. .... '78 '03 C.575 B.A. L.1228 J.D. [🄰 Jordan P.W.G.J.&C.]
Angel, Lisa M., (BV) ....'68 '93 C.575 B.A. L.896 J.D. 4101 Lake Boone Trail, Suite 500
Angell, James B., (BV) .... '56 '85 C&L.575 B.A., J.D. [Howard,S.F.&H.]
Ansley, James R., Law Offices of, (BV) '61 '91
C.576 B.S. L.356 J.D. 19 W. Hargett St., Ste. 406
Anthony, Keith P. ....'— '02 C.893 B.A. L.575 J.D. [🄰 Helms M.&W.]
Anthony, Len S., (AV) '58 '83 C&L.896 B.S., J.D.
Dep. Gen. Coun., Regulatory Affs., Progress Energy
Anthony, Phillip J., (AV) .... '58 '92 C.8 B.A. L.1228 J.D. [Patterson,D.C.B.&A.]
Araneda, Jorgelina Elcira .... '— '90 C&L.575 B.A., J.D. [Araneda] ⊙

Araneda Law Firm, P.C.
4600 Marriott Drive, Suite 350, 27612 ⊙
Mailing Address: P.O. Box 31383, Raleigh, NC 27622-1383
Telephone: 919-788-9225 Fax: 919-788-9151
Email: alf-law@att.net URL: http://www.aranedalaw.com
Jorgelina Elcira Araneda (Board Certified Specialist in Immigration Law, North Carolina State Board of Legal Specialization),.
Languages: English and Spanish.
Immigration Law, Business Immigration, Citizenship, Consular Law, Employment Authorizations, Employment Immigration, Employment Visas, Family Immigration Law, Labor Certifications, Permanent Visas, Religious Visas, Visas, Federal Criminal Law, Immigration Defense.
New York, New York Office: 48 Wall Street, Suite 1100. 10005. Telephone: 212-918-4625. Fax: 212-918-4801.

See Professional Biographies, RALEIGH, NORTH CAROLINA

Arbogast, Steven M. ....'56 '85 C.473 B.A. L.851 J.D. Atty. Gen. Off.
Archer, Amy Alana .... '68 '94 C.575 B.A. L.1228 J.D. State Farm Insurance Co.
Arena, Paul A. .... '70 '96 C&L.575 B.A., J.D. [🄰 Poyner&S.]
Armbruster, J. Mitchell .... '71 '99 C.188 B.S. L.577 J.D. [🄰 Smith,A.B.D.M.&J.]
Armstrong, Carol A. .... '— '91 C.575 A.B. L.574 J.D. [Armstrong]
Armstrong, Laurie G. ....'— '04 C&L.575 B.S., J.D. [🄰 Kirby&H.]
Armstrong Law Offices, PLLC ....316 West Millbrook Road Suite 117
Arnold, Gerald ....'40 '66 C.232 A.B. L.575 LL.B. Chf. Appl. Ct. J.
Arnold, Robert Marks, (AV) .... '51 '78 C.674 B.A. L.896 J.D. [Smith,A.B.D.M.&J.]
Arrowood, Catharine Biggs, (AV) .... '51 '76 C&L.896 B.A., J.D. [Parker,P.A.&B.]
Ash, Mark A., (AV) .... '53 '79 C.309 A.B. L.893 J.D. [Smith,A.B.D.M.&J.]
Askew, Garland L., (BV) ....'43 '69 C.232 A.B. L.575 J.D. [DeMent,A.G.&D.]
Askew, Roger Allan, (BV) ....'64 '91 C.1228 B.A. L.1345 J.D. [Larcade,H.&A.P.]
Atchison, Alexander R. ....'72 '98 C.1128 B.A. L.192 J.D. [🄰 Young M.&H.]
Atkins, Beth Ferebee .... '60 '85 [Howard,S.F.&H.] ⊙
Atkinson, Season D. ....'73 '01 C.437 B.A. L.1017 J.D. [🄰 Teague,C.D.&G.]
Attanasio, John R. '49 '75 C.309 A.B. L.273 J.D.
(adm. in DC; not adm. in NC) Of Coun., ABB Inc.
Austin, Joe E., Jr., (AV) ....'65 '89 C.198 A.B. L.896 J.D. [Young M.&H.]
Austin, John Scott, (BV) .... '64 '94 C.576 B.A. L.1228 J.D. [Francis&A.]
Austin, Thomas K. '44 '77 C&L.575 B.A., J.D.
Assoc. Gen. Coun., North Carolina Elec. Membership Corp.
Austin, William Joseph, Jr., (AV) '— '78 C&L.575 A.B., J.D.
[Ward&S.] (⊙New Bern)
Autry, George B., Jr. ....'63 '91 C.846 B.A. L.575 J.D. [Cranfill,S.&H.]
Autry, Stephanie Hutchins, (BV) ....'62 '87 C.577 B.A. L.575 J.D. [Cranfill,S.&H.]
Avery, Isaac T., III, (AV) .... '49 '74 C&L.575 B.S., J.D. Spec. Dep. Atty. Gen.
Avram, Randall David, (AV) .... '— '86 C.575 B.A. L.896 J.D. [Kilpatrick S.]
Aycock, C. Ronald .....'40 '66 C&L.575 B.S., J.D. Exec. Dir., State Assn. of Co. Comrs.
Ayers, Christopher J. ....'77 '02 C.228 B.A. L.575 J.D. [🄰 Hunton&W.]
Ayers, D. Randal ....'63 '94 C&L.893 B.S.E.E., J.D. [Myers B.S.&S.] (See Pat. Sect.)
Babb, Amy Barnes ....'66 '91 C&L.575 A.B., J.D. Staff Atty., NC Util. Comm., Pub. Staff
Babb, Jonathan Porter ....'63 '94 C.576 B.A. L.574 J.D. State Dept. of Jus.
Babb, Russell David .... '73 '99 C&L.575 B.A., J.D. [🄰 Temple]
Bachl, Carolyn A. ....'— '04 C&L.575 B.S., J.D. [🄰 Kilpatrick S.]
Baddour, Philip A., III, (BV) ... '70 '96 C.575 B.A. L.1228 J.D. 4338 Mail Service Center
Badham, R. Paxton, Jr. ......'50 '75 C.575 B.S. L.896 J.D. Martin Marietta Materials, Inc.
Baer, Miriam J. .... '59 '84 C.378 B.A. L.575 J.D. Coun., State Real Estate Comm.
Bagbey, Francis C., (AV) ....'49 '80 C.674 A.B. L.945 J.D. [Smith,A.B.D.M.&J.]
Bagchi, Neil S. ....'77 '04 C&L.575 B.A., J.D. [🄰 Hutchison&M.]

Bagwell, Holt & Smith, P.A.
(See Chapel Hill)

Bailey, Aaron N. ....'73 '99 C.576 B.A. L.1228 J.D. [🄰 Smith D.N.W.S.&M.]
Bailey, Kris D. .... '56 '95 C.1420 B.S. L.280 J.D. Co. Cthse.
Bailey, Yvonne C., (AV) '52 '81 C.1262 B.A. L.208 J.D.
Asst. Genenral Counsel, Martin Marietta Materials, Inc.

Bailey & Dixon, L.L.P., (AV) BR
2500 Two Hannover Square, 434 Fayetteville Street Mall, P.O. Box 1351, 27602
Telephone: 919-828-0731 Facsimile: 919-828-6592
Email: info@bdixon.com URL: http://www.bdixon.com
Members of Firm: Ralph McDonald; Gary S. Parsons; Carson Carmichael, III; Robert H. Merritt, Jr.; Patricia P. Kerner; Cathleen M. Plaut; David S. Coats; M. Denise Stanford; David S. Wisz; Warren Tobin Savage, IV; Dayatra T. King. Associates: Anna Baird Choi; Donald T. O'Toole; Gavin B. Parsons; Hannah G. Styron.
General Civil Trial, Appellate and Administrative Practice. Litigation: Insurance Regulation, Defense of Personal Injury and Professional Malpractice Claims, Commercial Litigation, Including Environmental Law, Employment Law, Insurance Coverage Disputes, Construction, Land Use, Municipal and Police Liability, Products Liability, Drug and Medical Device Liability, Business Torts, and Workers' Compensation. Administrative Law: Public Utilities, Including Electric, Telecommunications, Gas, Transportation, Water and Sewer. Professional and Occupational Licensing, Healthcare, Labor and Employment Law, Business and Corporate Law, Commercial Real Estate, Estate Administration and Taxation.

(This Listing Continued)

Bailey & Dixon, L.L.P. (Continued)

Representative Clients: Nationwide Insurance Co.; Lawyers Mutual Liability Insurance Co. of North Carolina; Aetna Life and Casualty Insurance Co.; Santee Carriers; Commonwealth Land Title Co.; First Title Insurance Co.; Investors Title Insurance Co.; Chicago Title Insurance Co.; Security Union Title Insurance Co.
Approved Attorneys For: Lawyers Title Insurance Corp.

See Professional Biographies, RALEIGH, NORTH CAROLINA

Baird, Stanford D., (BV) .... '— '95 C.228 A.B. L.896 J.D. [Kennedy C.L.&H.]
Bakewell, Carolin D. .... '54 '83 C&L.575 B.A., J.D. North Carolina Bar
Baldwin, Kathleen Uebele ....'64 '90 C&L.575 B.A., J.D. Asst. Atty. Gen.
Balentine, Grady L., Jr. .... '58 '93 C.48 B.A. L.575 J.D. Assoc. Atty. Gen.
Balestrieri, Patrick F. ....'68 '94 C.575 B.A. L.469 J.D. [Ⓐ Kuniholm]
Ballance, Michael W. ....'69 '96 C.576 B.A. L.575 J.D. [Ⓐ Young M.&H.]
Ballard, Melinda Meador .... '60 '86 C.575 B.A. L.896 J.D. N.C. State Univ.

Baloch, Omar, The Law Offices of '— '04 C.575 B.A. L.608 J.D.
5104 Western Boulevard, Suite C, 27606
Telephone: 919-233-4999 Fax: 919-859-5321
Email: mobaloch@balochlaw.com URL: http://www.balochlaw.com
Languages: Hindi and Urdo.
Immigration, Traffic Violations, Personal Injury, Small Business and Business Enterprises.

See Professional Biographies, RALEIGH, NORTH CAROLINA

Banat, Amanda B. .... '78 '03 C.802 B.A. L.37 J.D. [Ⓐ Smith D.N.W.S.&M.]
Bandini, Jeffrey A. ....'71 '98 C&L.575 B.A., J.D. [Ⓐ Parker,P.A.&B.]
Banks, Myron C., (AV) ..... '31 '55 C&L.575 A.B., J.D. Dep. Secy., N.C. Dept. of Rev.‡
Bannon, Bradley J. ....'70 '97 C.790 B.A. L.1228 J.D. [Cheshire,P.S.B.&V.]
Banzet, Ann Howard ....'70 '95 C.576 B.A. L.575 J.D. Box 7316
Bar, Roselyn R. '58 '84 C.696 B.A. L.1009 J.D.
(adm. in NY; not adm. in NC)
Vice Pres., Gen. Coun./Corp. Sec., Martin Marietta Materials, Inc.
Barefoot, D. Caldwell, Jr. ....'67 '94 C.896 B.A. L.1228 J.D. [Wyrick R.Y.&P.]
Barefoot, Thomas N., (AV) .... '51 '77 C&L.896 B.A., J.D. [T.N.Barefoot]
Barefoot, Thomas N., P.A., Law Offices of, (AV) .... 8273 Hillside Dr.
Barham, Charles D., Jr., (AV) '30 '54 C&L.896 B.S., J.D.
Exec. V.P., Fin., Carolina Power & Light Co.
Barkley, John P. ....'59 '84 C.575 B.A. L.1228 J.D. Asst. Atty. Gen.
Barkley, W. Travis ....'68 '94 C.575 B.S. L.7 J.D. [Barkley]
Barkley Law Offices, P.C. ....5561 McNeely Drive, Suite 203
Barnes, David M., (AV) .... '59 '85 C&L.896 B.A., J.D. [Poyner&S.]
Barnes, W. Joey, (AV) ...... '61 '86 C&L.575 B.A., J.D. Dep. Comr., State Indus. Comm.
Barnett, William T., Jr., (AV) ...... '57 '85 C.198 B.A. L.575 J.D. [Smith,A.B.D.M.&J.]
Barnette, H. Vance, III, (BV) ....'69 '97 C.896 B.A. L.1338 J.D. [Cranfill,S.&H.]
Barnette, Henry V., Jr. .... '39 '64 C.228 A.B. L.896 J.D. Supr. Ct. J.
Barnwell, John G. ..... '47 '89 C.1365 B.A. L.575 J.D. Asst. Atty. Gen., NC Dept. of Jus.
Baron, Sidney S. .... '20 '74 C&L.912 B.S., J.D. 7931 Footman Way‡
Barrett, George R., (BV) .... '44 '73 C.576 B.S.E.E. L.575 J.D. 420 S. McDowell St.
Barrett, William P., (AV) ....'63 '88 C&L.502 B.J., J.D. [Maupin T.]
Barron, Jason L. .... '— '02 C.576 B.A. L.896 J.D. [Ⓐ Kennedy C.L.&H.]
Barrow, H. Spencer, (AV) ....'45 '70 C.575 B.S.B.A. L.896 J.D. [H.S.Barrow]

Barrow, Nigle B., Jr., (AV) '49 '77 C.115 B.A. L.575 J.D.
1635 Two Hanover Square, P.O. Box 2714, 27602-2714
Mailing Address: P.O. Box 2714, Raleigh, NC 27602-2714
Telephone: 919-834-2116 Fax: 919-831-4789
Email: texbarrow@att.net URL: http://www.lawyers.com/niglebbarrowjr
Complex Commercial Litigation, Civil Litigation, Trial Practice, Construction Litigation, Class Actions Litigation, Personal Injury Litigation.

See Professional Biographies, RALEIGH, NORTH CAROLINA

Barrow, H. Spencer, P.A., (AV) ....16 W. Martin St., Ste. 700
Barry, Elizabeth A. ....'69 '94 C.339 B.S. L.228 J.D. N.C. Prisoner Legal Servs.
Bartis, Patricia T., (AV) ....'65 '94 C.105 B.A. L.575 J.D. [Parker,P.A.&B.]
Barwick, P. Collins, III, (AV) ....'61 '88 C&L.896 B.A., J.D. [Cranfill,S.&H.]
Barwick, Thomas E., (AV) ....'54 '80 C.232 B.A. L.692 J.D. [Martin&J.]
Bashyam, Murali .... '70 '95 C&L.896 B.A., J.D. [Bashyam&S.]

Bashyam & Spiro, LLP
4101 Lake Boone Trail, Suite 200, 27607
Telephone: 919-833-0840 Fax: 919-833-4722
URL: http://www.lawyers.com/immigrationcounsel
Members of Firm: Murali Bashyam; Robert B. Spiro. Associate: Carrie Amelia (Ame) Coats.
U.S. and Foreign Immigration and Nationality Law.

See Professional Biographies, RALEIGH, NORTH CAROLINA

Bason, Amy Y. .... '71 '96 C.705 B.A. L.575 J.D. [Ⓐ Kirschbaum,N.K.&G.]
Bason, George F. ....'26 '51 C&L.575 A.B., LL.B. Ret. Chf. Dist. J.
Bason, Wm. A., (BV) ....'24 '51 C&L.575 LL.B. 505 Oberlin Rd.
Bass, Gerald L., (AV) ....'33 '62 C&L.575 B.S., LL.B. [Ⓒ Bass,B.&F.]

Bass, Bryant & Fanney, P.L.L.C., (AV)
16 West Martin Street, Suite 900, Drawer 909, 27602
Telephone: 919-832-9661 Fax: 919-831-9211
URL: http://www.lawyers.com/bassbryant&fanney
John Walter Bryant; John K. Fanney (Board Certified Specialist in Federal Criminal Law and State Criminal Law, North Carolina State Board of Legal Specialization). Associates: James K. Jackson; Eva C. Currin. Of Counsel: Gerald L. Bass.
General Trial Practice in all Courts, Criminal Law, Driving While Impaired, (DWI), Federal Criminal Offenses, Felonies, Misdemeanors, Traffic Violations, Personal Injury, Wrongful Death, Professional Malpractice, Construction Law, Corporate, Business Litigation, Collections, Landlord/Tenant, Appellate, Administrative, Contract, Fiduciary, Estates and Wills.

See Professional Biographies, RALEIGH, NORTH CAROLINA

Bateman, Valerie L. ....'61 '86 C&L.575 B.A., J.D. Asst. Atty. Gen.
Batten, Amy Meyers, (AV) .... '67 '92 C.659 B.S. L.228 J.D. [Smith,A.B.D.M.&J.]
Batten, David H., (AV) ....'57 '83 C.575 B.A. L.896 J.D. [Cranfill,S.&H.]

Battle, Winslow, Scott & Wiley, P.A., (AV)
3737 Glenwood Avenue, Suite 100, 27612 ⊙
Telephone: 919-573-1877 Facsimile: 919-573-1878
J. Brian Scott;—Eileen M. Bornstein.
Administrative, Alternative Dispute Resolution, Banking, Bankruptcy, Construction, Commercial, Corporate, Environmental, Estate Planning, General Trial and Appellate Practice in all State and Federal Courts. Health Care, Insurance, Insurance Defense, Labor and Employment, Local Government Law, Personal Injury, Probate and Estate Planning, Real Estate, Tax, Workers' Compensation.
General Counsel for: Nash County; Nash Health Care Systems; Rocky Mount Redevelopment Commission.
Rocky Mount, North Carolina Office: 2343 Professional Drive, PO Box 7100, 27804. Telephone: 252-937-2200. Facsimile: 252-937-8100.

See Professional Biographies, RALEIGH, NORTH CAROLINA

Baum, Allen R. .... '67 '92 C.529 B.S. L.1338 J.D. [Hutchison&M.] (Pat.)
Baumer, David L. .... '49 '80 C.610 B.A. L.472 J.D. Assoc. Prof., N.C. State Univ.
Bayzle, Scott E. ....'77 '05 C&L.896 B.S., J.D. [Ⓐ Parker,P.A.&B.]

Beall, Elizabeth Todd ....'68 '96 C.577 B.A. L.896 J.D. [Martin&J.]
Beard, John Q., (AV) '33 '60 C&L.228 A.B., LL.B.
Pres., CEO & Gen. Coun., Builders Mutual Ins. Co.
Beatty, Bryan Elliot, (AV) ....'58 '87 C.1350 B.A. L.575 J.D. Asst. Atty. Gen.
Beatty, David D., (AV) ... '68 '93 C.576 B.S. L.575 J.D. [Myers B.S.&S.] (See Pat. Sect.)
Beci, Donald L. ....'54 '84 C&L.339 B.S.W., J.D. [Ⓐ Wyrick R.Y.&P.]
Becker, Britne Nicole .... '75 '01 C.473 B.S. L.124 J.D. Dept. of Jus., Crime Control Sect.
Becker, Diane R. ....'67 '93 C.381 B.A. L.574 J.D. [Becker P.]
Becker, Gloria Taft ....'74 '00 C.575 B.A. L.1228 J.D. [Cranfill,S.&H.]
Becker Law Offices PLLC .... 6030 Creedmoor Rd., Ste. 200
Becton, Charles L., (AV) ....'44 '69 C.329 B.A. L.228 J.D. [Becton,S.&B.]

Becton, Slifkin & Bell, P.A., (AV)
4000 Westchase Boulevard Suite 500, 27607
Telephone: 919-755-1068 Fax: 919-828-7543
Email: bsb@bsblawfirm.com URL: http://www.lawyers.com/bsblawfirm
Members of Firm: Charles L. Becton; Anne R. Slifkin; Asa L. Bell, Jr. Associate: Judith M. Pope.
Personal Injury and Wrongful Death, Vehicle Collisions, Medical Malpractice and Product Liability.

See Professional Biographies, RALEIGH, NORTH CAROLINA

Beddingfield, Julie .... '68 '00 C.424 B.A. L.260 J.D. [Ⓐ Hunton&W.]
Beeton, Sarah E. '60 '87 C.478 B.A. L.893 J.D.
(adm. in NY; not adm. in NC) 2106 Cowper Dr.

Belk, Sherri D. '73 '03 C.577 B.A. L.796 J.D.
The Capital Club Building, 16 West Martin Street, Suite 604, 27601
Telephone: 919-834-3533 Fax: 919-829-1600
Email: sherribelklaw@aol.com
Family Law, Divorce, Child Custody, Child Support, Visitation Rights, Criminal Law, Traffic Violations, Driving While Intoxicated, Misdemeanors, Wills, Probate, Personal Injury, Automobile Accidents.

See Professional Biographies, RALEIGH, NORTH CAROLINA

Bell, Albert R., Jr., (AV) ....'— '75 C.1228 B.S. L.896 J.D. [Ward&S.] (⊙New Bern)
Bell, Asa L., Jr., (AV) .... '65 '91 C&L.575 B.A., J.D. [Becton,S.&B.]
Bell, F. Daniel, III, (AV) ....'— '80 C.575 B.S. L.425 J.D. [Kennedy C.L.&H.]
Bell, Julie L., (BV) ....'67 '92 C.577 B.A. L.575 J.D. [Patterson,D.C.B.&A.]
Bellamy, Kristi Michelle ....'75 '01 C.575 B.A. L.352 J.D. NC Indus. Comm.
Bender, Victoria, (BV) .... '50 '78 C.1350 B.A. L.1065 J.D. [Bender]

Bender Law Offices, (BV)
6608-204 Six Forks Road, 27615
Telephone: 919-870-9600 Fax: 919-847-2473
Email: info@benderlaw.com URL: http://www.benderlaw.com
Victoria Bender.
Family Law, Divorce, Child Custody, Child Support, Spousal Support, Alimony, Equitable Distribution, Domestic Violence.

See Professional Biographies, RALEIGH, NORTH CAROLINA

Bendiks-Perna, Sohni Y. '62 '87 C&L.846 B.A., J.D.
(adm. in TX; not adm. in NC) Off. of Hearings & App.
Benedict, Kevin W., (BV) .... '69 '95 C.576 B.S. L.838 J.D. [Maupin T.]
Benge, Alison J. .... '76 '05 C.303 B.A. L.228 J.D. [Ⓐ Hunton&W.]

Benjamin, John T., Jr., Law Offices of, (AV) '66 '92 C.105 B.A. L.94 J.D.
227 West Martin Street, 27601
Telephone: 919-755-0060 Fax: 919-755-0069
Email: benjamin@lawjtb.com
Associates: William E. Hubbard; Mitchell A. Meyers.
Civil Litigation, Commercial Litigation, Construction Litigation, Banking Litigation, Commercial Leasing Litigation, Commercial Debt, Creditors Rights, Negligence Defense, Business Law, Contracts, Appellate Practice.
Representative Clients: Food Lion, LLC; Kash n' Karry; Kimco, Inc.; EMC Mortgage Corp.; LaSalle Bank, N.A.; Fairbanks Capital Corp.; Wells Fargo; Ohio Savings Bank; Western Union Financial Services; Kline Iron & Steel, Co., Inc.

See Professional Biographies, RALEIGH, NORTH CAROLINA

Bennett, Calvin B., III, (AV) '62 '91 C.10 B.A. L.228 J.D.
P.O. Box 90574, 27675
Telephone: 919-844-3989 Fax: 919-848-6261
Email: cal@bennett-law.com URL: http://www.bennett-law.com
Mediation, Real Estate Investment and Executive Compensation.

See Professional Biographies, RALEIGH, NORTH CAROLINA

Bennett, Danielle .... '73 '99 C.228 A.B. L.574 J.D. [Ⓐ Hunton&W.]
Bennett, Lesley W. .... '70 '97 C.577 B.S. L.575 J.D. [Wilson&R.]
Bennink, Robert H., Jr., (AV) '45 '75
C.384 B.A. L.575 J.D. Gen. Coun., State Utilities Comm.
Benson, Jeffrey A., (AV) .... '— '93 C.475 B.A. L.228 J.D. [Kilpatrick S.]
Bergdolt, Marian Hill ....'61 '86 C.198 B.A. L.923 J.D. 8605 Wheeling Dr.‡
Bergdolt, Robert H. ....'—, '91 C.228 A.B. L.976 J.D. [DLPiper R.G.C.U.]
Berger, Bruce W., (AV) ....'55 '80 C.880 B.A. L.802 J.D. [Knott,C.&B.]
Berggren, William G. ....'63 '89 C.705 B.A. L.809 J.D. [Adams,P.&B.]
Bernstein, Marc D. .... '67 '95 C.228 B.S. L.945 J.D. Asst. Atty. Gen., Atty. Gen. Off.
Berry, David W. ....'63 '92 C.575 B.A. L.861 J.D. [Smith,A.B.D.M.&J.]
Berry, Harold W., Jr., (AV) ....'45 '71 C&L.575 A.B., J.D. [Hatch,L.&B.]
Berry, Lynne E. .... '52 '87 C&L.588 B.S., J.D. Div. of Aging
Beskind, Donald H., (AV) ....'48 '73 C.273 A.B. L.184 J.D. [Twiggs,B.S.&R.]
Best, Pamela Weaver, (BV) ....'55 '84 C.232 B.S. L.1228 J.D. Assoc. Atty., AOC
Betts, Rachel S. ....'75 '00 C&L.575 B.A., J.D. [Ⓐ Smith,A.B.D.M.&J.]
Beverly, Brian O., (BV) ....'68 '95 C.575 B.A. L.574 J.D. [Young M.&H.]
Bibbs, Mark L. ....'70 '96 C&L.575 B.A., J.D. 512 Brickhaven Drive, Suite 220
Bigel, Mitchell S., (AV) '53 '82 C.563 B.E.E. L.273 J.D.
[Myers B.S.&S.] (See Pat. Sect.)
Biggs, Laurie B. .... '77 '03 C.477 B.A. L.383 J.D. [Stubbs&P.]
Billings, James G., (AV) '42 '69 C.576 B.S. L.575 J.D.
3737 Glenwood Avenue, Suite 100
Billingsley, Carlton C., Jr. .....'46 '71 C.1038 B.A. L.896 J.D. State Employ. Sec. Comm.
Billow, Paul H. .... '64 '89 C.575 B.S. L.896 J.D. [Womble C.S.&R.]
Bingham, Jaye Elizabeth, (AV) ....'72 '97 C.228 A.B. L.575 J.D. [Cranfill,S.&H.]
Birkhead, G. William, (AVⓣ) '41 '66 C.999 B.S. L.893 LL.B.
[Vandeventer B.] (⊙Kitty Hawk, NC; Norfolk, VA)
Bishop, Marc D., (AV) ....'59 '84 C&L.575 B.A., J.D. [Brooks,P.M.H.&L.] ⊙
Bishop, Zachary R. .... '75 '01 C.228 A.B. L.861 J.D. [Ⓐ Hunton&W.]
Bissette, Hannah C. ....'— '04 C.575 B.A. L.896 J.D. [Ⓐ Ragsdale L.]
Black, James Bell, IV ....'74 '99 C.575 B.S.B.A. L.896 J.D. [Cranfill,S.&H.]
Black, Matthew S. .... '73 '98 C.575 B.S. L.896 J.D. [Pinna J.&B.]
Black, Meredith T. ....'— '98 C.471 B.A. L.896 J.D. [Cranfill,S.&H.]
Black, Nancy Fountain, (BV) ..... '58 '83 C.575 B.A. L.896 J.D. 209 Fayetteville St. Mall
Black, William M., Jr., (BV) ...... '53 '84 C&L.575 B.A., J.D. 2209 Century Dr., Ste. 302
Blackburn, George T., II, (AV) '50 '76 C&L.575 A.B., J.D.
Sr. V.P. & Gen. Coun., Variety Wholesalers, Inc. (⊙Henderson)
Blake, Christopher J., (AV) ....'61 '86 C.1040 B.A. L.128 J.D. [Nelson M.R.&S.]

Blanchard, Charles F., (AV) ..... '23 '50 C&L.228 A.B., LL.B. [⊡ Blanchard,J.M.L.&S.]

Blanchard, Jenkins, Miller, Lewis & Styers, P.A., (AV)
1117 Hillsborough Street, 27603-1505
Telephone: 919-755-3993 Fax: 919-755-3994
URL: http://www.bjmls-law.com
Robert O. Jenkins; Philip R. Miller, III; E. Hardy Lewis; M. Gray Styers, Jr. Of Counsel: Charles F. Blanchard; Eric Miller Reeves. Associate: Karen Kemerait Prather.
Civil and Business Litigation, Administrative Law, Serious Personal Injury and Wrongful Death in following areas: Nursing Home Negligence, Medical and Professional Negligence, Automobile and Trucking Accidents, and Premises Liability, Commercial Torts, Utilities Law, Land Use and Zoning; Alcoholic Beverage Control Law, Federal and State Criminal Defense, Federal Grand jury Practice, Appellate Practice.
See Professional Biographies, RALEIGH, NORTH CAROLINA

Bledsoe, Joseph A., III ....'67 '93 C.576 B.A. L.575 J.D. 6616-203 Six Forks Rd.
Bloch, Barry H. .... '60 '85 C.1036 B.A. L.665 J.D. N C Board of Mortuary Science
Block, Kyla K. .... '— '05 C.165 B.A. L.896 J.D. [⊡ Hedrick E.G.&K.]
Bloom, Heidi C., (BV) .... '69 '96 C.575 B.A. L.896 J.D. [⊡ Wyrick R.Y.&P.]
Blount, James D., Jr., (AV) .... '27 '52 C&L.575 A.B., J.D. [Smith,A.B.D.M.&J.]
Blow, Beverly G. .... '— '84 C.576 B.A. L.1206 J.D. North Carolina State Univ.
Blue, Daniel T., Jr., (AV) .... '49 '73 C.574 B.S. L.228 J.D. [Thigpen,B.S.&F.]
Blue, Thomas D., Jr. .... '60 '97 C.48 B.A. L.575 J.D. [Ellis&W.] (⊙Cary)
Blum, Robert J. .... '34 '59 C.880 B.A. L.575 J.D. P.O. Box 629
Blum, Seth A., (BV) .... '68 '93 C.860 B.S. L.228 J.D. [Kurtz&B.]
Blumberg, Donna K., (BV) .... '59 '85 C&L.575 B.A., J.D. [⊡ Ellis&W.] (⊙Cary)
Blumberg, Jonathan A. .... '60 '86 C&L.575 B.A., J.D. [Tharrington S.]
Bobbitt, Julian D., Jr., (AV) .... '51 '77 C.575 B.A. L.893 J.D. [Smith,A.B.D.M.&J.]
Boddie, Needham J., II '56 '94
C.228 B.S.M.E. L.896 J.D. [Myers B.S.&S.] (See Pat. Sect.)
Bode, John T., (AV) .... '41 '70 C.870 B.S. L.575 J.D. [Bode,C.&S.]
Bode, Robert V., (AV) .... '48 '74 C&L.575 B.A., J.D. [Bode,C.&S.]

Bode, Call & Stroupe, L.L.P., (AV)
3105 Glenwood Avenue, Suite 300, P.O. Box 6338, 27628-6338
Telephone: 919-881-0338 Telecopier: 919-881-9548
Members of Firm: David P. Green (1945-1985); John V. Hunter III (Retired); John T. Bode; W. Davidson Call; Robert V. Bode; Odes L. Stroupe, Jr.; V. Lane Wharton, Jr.; S. Todd Hemphill; Diana Evans Ricketts. Associates: John S. Byrd, II; Matthew A. Fisher.
General Civil and Trial Practice. Utility Regulation, Energy, Corporation, Contract, Commercial Law, Real Estate, Hospital, Health Care and Administrative Law, Legislative Representation, Securities and Municipal Finance, Trials and Appeals in all State and Federal Courts, Land Use and Insurance Regulation.
Reference: Bank of America.
See Professional Biographies, RALEIGH, NORTH CAROLINA

Bolch, Thomas J., (AV) .... '39 '66 C&L.575 B.S., J.D. Comr.
Bolen, Zachary C. .... '73 '00 C.575 B.A. L.1228 J.D. [⊡ Young M.&H.]
Bolton, Everett M. .... '73 '05 C.896 B.A. L.1228 J.D. [⊡ Boxley,B.G.&H.]
Bolton, Lawrence E., (AV) .... '43 '68 C&L.945 B.A., J.D. [Boxley,B.G.&H.]
Bolton, Richard O. .... '72 '98 C&L.896 B.A., J.D. [⊡ Ragsdale L.]
Bonnen, Alice M. .... '56 '04 C.475 B.S. L.896 J.D. [⊡ Myers B.S.&S.]
Bookhout, David A., (AV) .... '48 '74 C.31 B.A. L.309 J.D. [Maupin T.]
Boone, David W., (AV) .... '53 '79 C.232 B.A. L.896 J.D. [Burns,D.&P.]
Boone, Victor J. .... '50 '75 C.575 B.A. L.574 J.D. Legal Aid of North Carolina
Booth, Wyatt M. '— '01 C.576 B.S.C.E. L.902 J.D.
[⊡ Vandeventer B.] (⊙Kitty Hawk)
Borchers, Lynne A. .... '64 '91 C.1044 B.S.E.E. L.776 J.D. [Myers B.S.&S.]
Bordeaux, Brandon G. .... '70 '95 C.823 B.S. L.896 J.D. [Parker,P.A.&B.]
Borden, William H. .... '54 '80 C&L.575 B.A., J.D. Asst. Atty. Gen.
Bornstein, Eileen M. .... '74 '02 C.576 B.A. L.1228 J.D. [⊡ Battle,W.S.&W.]
Bost, William S., III, (BV) .... '63 '89 C&L.575 B.A., J.D. [Ragsdale L.]
Botvinick, Ira J. .... '50 '76 C.102 B.A. L.575 J.D. 222 W. Hargett St.
Bowen, Wiley F. .... '31 '61 C&L.896 B.S., LL.B. [⊡ Wyrick R.Y.&P.]
Bowler, John S., (BV) .... '51 '76 C.1031 B.A. L.823 J.D. U.S. Atty. Off.
Bowman, Kendal Crowder '71 '97
C.893 B.A. L.362 J.D. Assoc. Gen. Coun., Progress Energy
Boxley, John Maclachlan, (AV) .... '42 '67 C&L.575 B.A., J.D. [Boxley,B.G.&H.]

Boxley, Bolton, Garber & Haywood, L.L.P., (AV)
The Nash Square Building, 227 West Martin Street P.O. Drawer 1429, 27602
Telephone: 919-832-3915 Fax: 919-832-3918
John Maclachlan Boxley; Lawrence E. Bolton (Board Certified Specialist in Estate Planning and Probate Law, North Carolina State Board of Legal Specialization); Ronald Hill Garber; Kenneth C. Haywood. Associates: Brian C. Setliff; Everett M. Bolton.
General Civil Trial Practice in State and Federal Courts. Probate, Family, Personal Injury, Administrative, Corporation, Taxation, Real Estate, Eminent Domain, Business, Legislative and Construction.
Representative Clients: N.C. Aggregates Assn.; Carolina Ready Mix Concrete Assn.; Sirchie Fingerprint Laboratories, Inc.; Carolina Cardiovascular Surgical Associates, P.A.; First Title Insurance Co.; Fidelity National Title Insurance Company of Pennsylvania; Home Builders Association of Raleigh and Wake County; N.C. Podiatric Medical Society.
See Professional Biographies, RALEIGH, NORTH CAROLINA

Boyce, G. Eugene, (AV) .... '32 '56 C&L.896 B.S., LL.B. [Boyce&I.]
Boyce, R. Daniel, (AV) .... '58 '84 C.896 B.A. L.575 J.D. [Boyce&I.]

Boyce & Isley, PLLC, (AV)
Lawyers Weekly Building, Suite 100, 107 Fayetteville Street Mall, P.O. Box 1990, 27602-1990
Telephone: 919-833-7373 Fax: 919-833-7536
Email: pisley@boyceisley.com URL: http://www.boyce-isleylaw.com
G. Eugene Boyce; R. Daniel Boyce (Board Certified Specialist in State and Federal, Criminal Law, North Carolina State Board of Legal Specialization); Philip R. Isley; Laura Boyce Isley.
Civil Litigation, Class Actions, Taxation, Complex Litigation, Commercial Litigation, Criminal Law, Insurance Defense, Appellate Practice, Employment Law.
See Professional Biographies, RALEIGH, NORTH CAROLINA

Boyd, J. Bryan .... '75 '01 C.1129 B.A. L.1228 J.D. Jud. Law Clk.
Boyd, Kathleen C. .... '54 '95 C.923 B.S. L.575 J.D. Prog. Dir., Durham Pub. Schs.
Boyette, Richard T., (AV) .... '52 '77 C&L.575 B.A., J.D. [Cranfill,S.&H.]
Boylan, George W., (AV) .... '46 '71 C.301 B.A. L.575 J.D. Spec. Dep. Atty. Gen.
Boyles, Jean Winborne, (AV) .... '45 '73 C&L.577 B.A., J.D. [⊡ Johnson,H.V.G.&G.]
Boyles, W. Winborne .... '77 '03 C&L.575 B.A., J.D. [⊡ Maupin T.]
Brachman, Lisa .... '57 '83 C.976 B.A. L.1066 J.D. Exec. Dir., NC Leaf
Brackett-Jones, Kimberly .... '74 '99 C.623 B.A. L.280 J.D. [⊡ Womble C.S.&R.]
Bradley, Jennifer M., (BV) .... '73 '98 C.244 B.S. L.575 J.D. [Sokol M.S.O.L.P.]
Bradshaw, Susan Hatcher, (BV) .... '37 '80 C.228 B.A. L.1228 J.D. 4002 Barrett Dr.
Brady, George T., III .... '72 '98 C&L.575 B.S., J.D. [⊡ Parker,P.A.&B.]
Brady, R. Daniel, (AV) .... '53 '82 C.575 B.S. L.896 J.D. [Brady,N.K.&M.]

Brady, Nordgren, Klym & Morton, PLLC, (AV)
2301 Sugar Bush Road, Suite 450, 27612
Telephone: 919-782-3500 Fax: 919-573-1430
Email: lawyers@bradynordgren.com URL: http://www.bradynordgren.com

(This Listing Continued)

Brady, Nordgren, Klym & Morton, PLLC (Continued)
Members of Firm: R. Daniel Brady (Board Certified Specialist in Estate Planning and Probate Law, North Carolina State Board of Legal Specialization); Mark R. Klym (Board Certified Specialist in Estate Planning and Probate Law, North Carolina State Board of Legal Specialization); Travis K. Morton; Timothy A. Nordgren; J. Michael Malone.
Trusts and Estates, Estate Planning, Estate Litigation, Personal Injury, Civil Litigation, Commercial Litigation, Wills, Probate, Corporate Law, Business Law, Taxation, Elder Law.
See Professional Biographies, RALEIGH, NORTH CAROLINA

Branch, John E. .... '— '04 C&L.575 B.A., J.D. [⊡ Ogletree,D.N.S.&S.]
Brannon, Anthony M. .... '65 '01 C.576 B.S. L.1228 J.D. [Wake T.]
Brannon, David S., (BV) .... '52 '90 C.645 B.S. L.574 J.D. P.O. Box 1027

Brannon Strickland, PLLC
107 Fayetteville Street Mall, Suite 201, 27601
Telephone: 919-838-5295 Fax: 919-838-5299
URL: http://www.brannonstrickland.com
Anthony M. Brannon; Robin Eason Strickland. Associate: Marlet Massey Edwards.
Appellate Advocacy, Civil Litigation. Constitutional Law, Criminal Defense, District Court/Traffic Violations, Divorce, Family Law, Juvenile/DSS, Real Estate.
See Professional Biographies, RALEIGH, NORTH CAROLINA

Brathwaite, Ashley Kamphaus .... '— '05 C.269 B.A. L.1228 J.D. [Cranfill,S.&H.]
Braun, Eric M., (BV) '— '93 C.1369 B.S. L.896 J.D.
[⊡ Kennedy C.L.&H.] (⊙Research Triangle Park)
Brawley, Daniel Lee, (AV) ... '42 '67 C&L.575 A.B., J.D. [⊡ Maupin T.] (⊙Wilmington)
Brennan, Daniel T. '61 '88 C.1296 B.A. L.1338 J.D.
Corp. Coun., Identity Software Inc.
Brewer, Christopher P. .... '49 '74 C.1228 B.B.A. L.192 J.D. Spec. Dep. Atty. Gen.
Brewer, Curtis C., IV, (AV) .... '— '95 C.575 B.A. L.896 J.D. [Kennedy C.L.&H.]
Brewer, J. Clark, (AV) .... '42 '67 C&L.575 B.S., J.D. [Young M.&H.]
Brewer, Lucy T. .... '75 '03 C.575 B.A. L.1228 J.D. [⊡ Clifton&S.]
Brewer, William E., (AV) .... '51 '76 C&L.575 A.B., J.D. [Brewer]

Brewer Law Firm, The, (AV)
619 North Person Street, 27604
Telephone: 919-832-2288; 1-800-899-3328 Fax: 919-834-2011 URL: http://www.brewerlawyers.com
Email: info@brewerwright.com URL: http://www.debtrelief.com
William E. Brewer (Board Certified Specialist in Consumer Bankruptcy Law, North Carolina Board of Legal Specialization); Victoria S. Wright (Board Certified Specialist in Consumer Bankruptcy, North Carolina State Board of Legal Specialization).
Bankruptcy (Debtors and Noninstitutional Creditors), Consumer and Business Bankruptcy.
See Professional Biographies, RALEIGH, NORTH CAROLINA

Brian, William J., (AV) '— '89 C.910 A.B. L.228 J.D.
[Kennedy C.L.&H.] (⊙Research Triangle Park)

Brice, F. Bryan, Jr. '62 '91 C&L.575 B.A., J.D.
19 West Hargett Street, Suite 600, 27601
Telephone: 919-754-1600 Fax: 919-832-0301 URL: http://www.attybryanbrice.com
Email: bryan_brice@yahoo.com URL: http://www.lawyers.com/bryanbrice
Associate: Heather L. Spurlock.
Environmental Law, Brownfields Redevelopment, Underground Storage Tanks, Wetlands, Toxic Torts, Administrative Law, Criminal Law, Driving While Intoxicated (DWI), Traffic Violations, Personal Injury, Condemnation, Eminent Domain.
See Professional Biographies, RALEIGH, NORTH CAROLINA

Bricio, Katherine N. .... '71 '99 C&L.575 B.A., J.D. [Martin&J.]
Bridgers, Heather E. .... '70 '00 C.260 B.A. L.802 J.D. [⊡ Maupin T.]
Briley, Wm. F. .... '30 '58 C&L.575 B.S., LL.B. Asst. Atty. Gen.

Brinkley, Dewey P. '72 '02 C.575 B.A. L.861 J.D.
5 West Hargett Street, Suite 904, 27601
Telephone: 919-616-1269 Fax: 919-833-6106
Email: brinkleylawfirm@bellsouth.net URL: http://www.brinkleylawfirm.com
Criminal Law, Driving While Intoxicated, DWI, Traffic Violations, Drug Crimes, Parole and Probation, Juvenile Crimes, White Collar Crimes.
See Professional Biographies, RALEIGH, NORTH CAROLINA

Brinkley, Martin H., (AV) .... '66 '92 C.309 A.B. L.575 J.D. [Smith,A.B.D.M.&J.]
Brissette, Stephen C., (AV) .... '57 '82 C&L.575 B.A., J.D. [Wyrick R.Y.&P.]
Bristow, John D. .... '— '00 C&L.575 B.S., J.D. [⊡ Troutman S.]
Britt, Courtney C. .... '77 '04 C&L.896 B.S., J.D. [⊡ Teague,C.D.&G.]
Britt, William Earl .... '32 '58 C&L.896 B.S., LL.B. Sr. U.S. Dist. J.
Broadus, Georgia Winstead, (BV) .... '46 '75 C.576 B.A. L.575 J.D. 409 Wake Forest Rd.
Brock, Walter E., Jr., (AV) .... '52 '78 C&L.575 B.A., J.D. [Young M.&H.]
Brocker, Douglas J., (AV) .... '67 '92 C.696 B.A. L.575 J.D. [Millberg,G.&S.]
Brogden, Blackwell M., Jr., (AV) '50 '77 C.34 B.S. L.575 J.D.
Chf. Dep. Legal Coun., State Real Estate Comm.
Bromby, Craig A., (AV) .... '49 '75 C.576 B.S. L.575 J.D. [Hunton&W.]
Brook, Christopher A. .... '— '05 C&L.575 B.A., J.D. [Cranfill,S.&H.]
Brooke, Carol L. '65 '00 C.118 B.A. L.575 J.D.
NC Justice and Community Development Center
Brooks, Christopher W. '72 '98
C.575 B.A. L.1345 J.D. Asst. Atty. Gen., N.C. Department of Justice
Brooks, Edward K. .... '74 '04 C.575 B.A. L.574 J.D. [⊡ Patterson,D.C.B.&A.]
Brooks, John C. .... '37 '64 C.575 A.B. L.145 J.D. 516 N. Blount St.‡
Brooks, M. Guy, III, (AV) '56 '81 C&L.575 B.S., J.D.
Assoc. General Counsel, Martin Marietta Materials, Inc.
Brooks, Sherri L. '68 '96 C.228 A.B. L.574 J.D.
Interim Exec. Dir., Agency Legal Coun., NC Human Relations Commission

Brooks, Pierce, McLendon, Humphrey & Leonard, L.L.P., (AV)
1600 Wachovia Capitol Center, 150 Fayetteville Street Mall (27601), P.O. Box 1800, 27602-1800 ⊙
Telephone: 919-839-0300 Facsimile: 919-839-0304
URL: http://www.brookspierce.com
Of Counsel: Henry E. Frye. Members of Firm: Wade H. Hargrove; Mark J. Prak; John W. Ormand, III; Marcus W. Trathen; J. Edwin Turlington; David Kushner; Coe W. Ramsey; Robert W. Saunders; Charles E. Coble; Charles F. Marshall, III; Patrick J. Johnson; Stephen G. Hartzell; J. Benjamin Davis; Katherine J. Clayton; Elizabeth E. Spainhour; James T. Williams, Jr. (Also at Greensboro Office); M. Daniel McGinn (Also at Greensboro Office); William G. McNairy (Also at Greensboro Office); Edward C. Winslow, III (Also at Greensboro Office); George W. House (Also at Greensboro Office); Marc D. Bishop (Also at Greensboro Office); Jim W. Phillips, Jr. (Also at Greensboro Office); Jeffrey E. Oleynik (Also at Greensboro Office); David W. Sar (Also at Greensboro Office).
General Practice in State and Federal Courts. Administrative, Antitrust, Banking, Bankruptcy, Bonds, Business Litigation, Communications and Media, Corporate, Corporate Finance, Energy, Environmental, Foundations, Insurance, Intellectual Property, Internet, Labor, Legislative, Mergers and Acquisitions, Probate, Public Utilities, Real Estate, Securities, Taxation, Telecommunications and Trade Associations Law.
Greensboro, North Carolina Office: 2000 Renaissance Plaza, 230 North Elm Street, 27401, P.O. Box 26000, 27420-6000. Telephone: 336-373-8850. Facsimile: 336-378-1001.
See Professional Biographies, RALEIGH, NORTH CAROLINA

Brooks, Stevens & Pope, P.A.
(See Cary)
Broome, David E., Jr. .... '50 '76 C&L.575 A.B., J.D. Off. Legal Affairs

Brosius, D. Todd .... '70 '99 C.860 B.A. L.228 J.D. [A Smith M.]
Broughton, Allen L., (AVⓉ) '68 '93 C&L.575 B.S.B.A., J.D.
(adm. in GA; not adm. in NC) [Broughton&F.] (⊙Roswell, GA)
Broughton, Robert B., (AV) .... '24 '51 C.575 A.B. L.896 J.D. [C Maupin T.]

Broughton & Fernandez, (AVⓉ)
4030 Wake Forest Road, Suite 300, 27609
Telephone: 919-719-2722 Fax: 919-719-2799
Email: johnfernandez@raleightriallawyers.com URL: http://www.raleightriallawyers.com
Allen L. Broughton (Not admitted in NC; Resident, Roswell, Georgia Office); John P. Fernandez.
Civil Litigation, Personal Injury, Automobile Accidents, Truck Accidents, Wrongful Death.
See Professional Biographies, RALEIGH, NORTH CAROLINA

Broughton Wilkins Sugg & Thompson, PLLC, (AV)
150 Fayetteville Street Mall (27601)
Brown, Alison M., (BV) .... '68 '95 C.577 B.A. L.575 J.D. 224 S. Dawson St.
Brown, Brian R. .... '52 '79 C.886 B.A. L.245 J.D. [Parker,P.A.&B.]
Brown, Douglas R. .... '59 '88 C.1044 B.S. L.575 J.D. Pros., Asst. Dist. Atty.
Brown, Gregory W. .... '67 '99 C.893 B.A. L.228 J.D. [Ragsdale L.]
Brown, June Hobby '62 '91 C.575 B.S.N. L.1345 J.D.
(adm. in CA; not adm. in NC) 340 Buncombe St.
Brown, R. Scott, (BV) .... '61 '86 C&L.575 B.A., J.D. P.O. Box 1729

Brown, Stephanie J. '66 '92 C.576 B.A. L.896 J.D.
916 Rock Quarry Road, Suite 116, 27610
Telephone: 919-836-9444 Fax: 919-836-9409
Email: sjbrown_law@hotmail.com URL: http://www.sjbrown-law.com
Criminal Law, Driving While Intoxicated, Drug Crimes, Felonies, Misdemeanors, Parole and Probation, Traffic Violations, Family Law, Child Custody, Child Support, Divorce, Visitation Rights, Automobile Accidents, Social Security Disability.
See Professional Biographies, RALEIGH, NORTH CAROLINA

Brown & Bunch, PLLC, (AV)
4900 Falls of Neuse Road, Suite 210 Post Office Box 19409, 27619-9409 ⊙
Telephone: 919-878-8060 FAX: 919-878-8062
Email: brownandbunch@mindspring.com
Members of Firm: Charles Gordon Brown (Resident, Chapel Hill Office); William W. Bunch, III (Resident); William D. Bernard (Resident, Chapel Hill Office); A. Vann Irvin (Board Certified Specialist in Estate Planning and Probate Law, North Carolina State Board of Legal Specialization) (Resident, Durham Office); LeAnn Nease Brown (Resident, Chapel Hill Office); Scott D. Zimmerman (Resident, Chapel Hill Office).
General Practice in all State and Federal Courts, Administrative Law, Antitrust Litigation, Appeals, Collections, Commercial Litigation, Commercial Transactions, Construction, Corporate Practice, Creditors' Rights, Employment Law, Estates and Trusts, Health Law, Lender Liability Defense, Mediation, Municipal and Land Use Law, Real Estate, State and Federal Taxation, Trade Regulation and Trials.
Counsel for: NationsBank; First Union National Bank; Centura Bank; The Chase Manhattan Bank; Mellon Bank, N.A.; Branch Banking and Trust Co.; Central Carolina Bank and Trust Co., N.A.; Triangle East Bank; Ameribanc Savings Bank.
Chapel Hill, North Carolina Office: 101 North Columbia Street, 27514. Telephone: 919-968-1111. Fax: 919-968-1444.
Durham, North Carolina Office: 21 West Colony Place, Suite 250, 27705. Telephone: 919-490-9700. Fax: 919-419-9736.
See Professional Biographies, RALEIGH, NORTH CAROLINA

Browne, Noëlle Stevens, (BV) '59 '85
C&L.575 B.A., J.D. Coun., N.C. Lic. Bd. for Gen. Contractors
Browning, Christopher G., Jr., (AV) '62 '86 C&L.575 B.A., J.D.
Sol. Gen. State of N.C.
Brownlee, William K. .... '71 '99 C.152 B.A. L.574 J.D. [Brownlee]

Brownlee Law Firm
2501 Blue Ridge Road, Suite 150, 27607
Telephone: 919-863-4305 Fax: 919-863-4315
Email: will@wkblawfirm.com URL: http://www.wkblaw-firm.com
William K. Brownlee.
Residential and Commercial Real Estate, Landlord-Tenant Law, Business Law, Contracts, Debtor and Creditor, Commercial Leasing, Mechanics Liens.
See Professional Biographies, RALEIGH, NORTH CAROLINA

Brumback, Melissa Dewey .... '72 '98 C&L.575 B.A., J.D. [A Ragsdale L.]
Bryan, Kimberly W. .... '— '92 C.576 B.A. L.1228 J.D. [Cheshire,P.S.B.&V.]
Bryan, Robert A., Jr. .... '55 '82 C.576 B.A. L.896 J.D. Rules Review Comm.
Bryant, Dawn S., (BV) .... '55 '81 C.575 B.A. L.574 J.D. Raleigh Police Dept.
Bryant, John Walter, (AV) .... '53 '86 C&L.896 B.A., J.D. [Bass,B.&F.]
Bryant, Wanda .... '56 '82 C.228 B.A. L.574 J.D. Sr. Dep. Atty. Gen.
Bryson, Daniel K., (AV) .... '60 '88 C.575 B.A. L.896 J.D. [Lewis&R.]
Bryson, E. C., Jr., (AV) .... '36 '64 C.228 B.A. L.575 LL.B. [Patterson,D.C.B.&A.]
Buckingham, David Todd, (AV) .... '57 '84 C&L.228 B.A., J.D. [Smith,A.B.D.M.&J.]
Buckius, Dean T., (AVⓉ) .... '59 '84 C.945 B.A. L.896 J.D. [Vandeventer B.] ⊙
Buckley, Thomas M. .... '64 '90 C.93 B.A. L.1065 J.D. [Patterson,D.C.B.&A.]
Buckman, Richard C. '43 '68 C&L.861 B.A., J.D.
(adm. in LA; not adm. in NC) 4112 Blue Ridge Rd.‡
Bulfer, William A. .... '78 '03 C.679 B.A. L.896 J.D. [A Teague,C.D.&G.]
Bullard, Madison E., Jr., (AV) .... '56 '81 C.896 B.A. L.575 J.D. [Wyrick R.Y.&P.]
Bullock, Bruce R. '66 '92 C.611 B.A. L.575 J.D.
V.P./Sr. Coun., Business Telecom, Inc.
Bullock, Stafford G. .... '42 '70 C.778 B.A. L.329 J.D. Dist. J.
Bumgardner, Kathryn V., (BV) .... '51 '88 C.576 B.A. L.574 J.D. [Bumgardner&R.]

Bumgardner & Rose, P.A., (BV)
3948 Browning Place, Suite 100, 27609
Telephone: 919-571-1866 Fax: 919-571-0096
Email: bumrose@bumgardner-rose.com URL: http://www.bumgardner-rose.com
Kathryn V. Bumgardner; Margie E. Rose.
Family Law, Domestic Relations, Divorce, Premarital Agreement, Separation Agreement, Child Custody, Child Support, Visitation Rights, Mediation, Collaborative Law.
See Professional Biographies, RALEIGH, NORTH CAROLINA

Bumgarner, Jonathan R. .... '78 '03 C&L.1228 B.A., J.D. [A Maupin T.]
Bunch, William W., III, (BV) .... '54 '80 C&L.575 B.S., J.D. [Brown&B.]
Bunn, J. Howard, Jr. .... '37 '63 C&L.896 B.A., LL.B. Chmn., Comr.
Bunn, Thomas D., (AV) .... '25 '50 C&L.896 LL.B. [Hatch,L.&B.]
Bunting, Elisha H., Jr. .... '45 '74 C&L.575 B.S., J.D. 700 Sampson Street
Burch, Dorothy Bass, (BV) .... '65 '91 C.471 B.A. L.575 J.D. [Ragsdale L.]
Burch, Laurie J. .... '64 '90 C.896 B.A. L.1228 J.D. [Burch,J.&R.]
Burch, Joneth & Rodgers, P.C. .... 2600 Fairview Rd.
Burgess, Cale K., Jr. .... '23 '49 C&L.575 A.B., LL.B. 2803 Oberlin Rd.
Burgin, John S. .... '51 '77 C.853 B.A. L.383 J.D. [Ogletree,D.N.S.&S.]
Burgwyn, Henry H. .... '44 '75 C.575 A.B. L.327 J.D. Assoc. Atty. Gen.
Burke, Judy Jo Ulmer '42 '84 C.508 B.A. L.575 J.D.
Gov. Adv. Council for Persons with Disabilities
Burkhart, Susan K., (AV) .... '55 '82 C.477 B.A. L.1228 J.D. [Cranfill,S.&H.]
Burleson, Lynn P., (AV) .... '48 '80 C.575 A.B. L.896 J.D. [Tharrington S.]
Burns, F. Kent, (AV) .... '29 '55 C.228 A.B. L.575 J.D. [C Burns,D.&P.] ‡
Burns, George V. .... '67 '94 C.1200 B.A. L.1202 J.D. [A Lewis&R.]
Burns, John D. .... '70 '97 C.198 A.B. L.896 J.D. [A Hunton&W.]

Burns, Day & Presnell, P.A., (AV)
Suite 560, 2626 Glenwood Avenue, P.O. Box 10867, 27605
Telephone: 919-782-1441 Fax: 919-782-2311
URL: http://www.burnsdaylaw.com
David W. Boone; James M. Day; Daniel C. Higgins; Greg L. Hinshaw; Lacy M. Presnell III;—Julia M. Young. Retired: F. Kent Burns (Retired).
General Practice in State and Federal Courts and Administrative Agencies. Commercial, Construction and Insurance Litigation, Arbitration and Mediation, Public Utilities, Telecommunication, Real Property, Corporate and Probate Law, Bankruptcy and Business Reorganizations.
See Professional Biographies, RALEIGH, NORTH CAROLINA

Burrows, Melinda '60 '90 C.880 B.A. L.575 J.D.
Dep. Gen. Coun., Compl. & Litig., Progress Energy
Burwell, Walter Brodie, Jr., (BV) .... '53 '83 C.575 B.A. L.1228 J.D. [Pinna J.&B.]
Bussian, John A., III, (AV) .... '— '80 C.228 B.A. L.276 J.D. [Bussian,P.]

Bussian Law Firm, The, (PLLC, (AV)
Wachovia Capitol Center 16th Floor, 150 Fayetteville Street Mall, 27601
Telephone: 919-829-4900 Fax: 919-829-2165
John A. Bussian III.
Constitutional, Intellectual Property, Corporate and Securities Law in all Courts.
See Professional Biographies, RALEIGH, NORTH CAROLINA

Butler, John J., (AV) .... '57 '83 C.577 B.A. L.309 J.D. [Parker,P.A.&B.]
Byassee, William Sam, (AV) '50 '82
C.838 B.A. L.880 J.D. [Maupin T.] (⊙Research Triangle Park)
Byker, Patrick L., (BV) '— '92 C.114 B.A. L.575 J.D.
[C Kennedy C.L.&H.] (⊙Research Triangle Park)
Bynum, Stephanie Fountain, (BV) '52 '80
C.575 B.A. L.1345 J.D. [A Smith D.N.W.S.&M.]
Byrd, John S., II .... '65 '01 C.576 B.A. L.472 J.D. [A Bode,C.&S.]
Byrd, Sandra S. .... '58 '84 C.471 B.S. L.575 J.D. V.P., Wachovia Bk. of N.C., N.A.
Byrd, Stephen T., (AV) .... '57 '84 C&L.575 B.S., J.D. [Manning,F.&S.]
Bystrynski, William B., (AV) .... '57 '94 C.1019 B.A. L.575 J.D. [Kirby&H.]
Cagle, Ryan W. .... '72 '02 C.619 B.S. L.862 J.D. [A Alston&B.] (See Pat. Sect.)
Cahill, Daniel G., (AV) .... '67 '94 C.575 B.A. L.896 J.D. [Poyner&S.]
Calabria, Ann Marie .... '47 '86 C.1046 B.A. L.1228 J.D. Gen. Ct. Jus.
Calder, C. Lynn, (AV) .... '59 '84 C.232 B.A. L.1228 J.D. [Allen&P.]
Caldwell, Charles F., (BV) .... '52 '84 C.1130 B.A. L.1228 J.D. P.O. Box 390
Caldwell, Derek R. .... '59 '95 C.174 B.A. L.146 J.D. [D.R.Caldwell]
Caldwell, Edmond W., Jr., (AV) .... '55 '82 C.575 B.S. L.1228 J.D. [C Holt Y.M.&H.]

Caldwell, Derek R., P.A., Law Office of
211 East Six Forks Road, Suite 210-A, P.O. Box 19242, 27619
Telephone: 919-838-9400 Fax: 919-834-1031 Email: derekcaldwell_attorney@yahoo.com
Email: derek@derekcaldwelllaw.com URL: http://www.derekcaldwelllaw.com
Derek R. Caldwell.
Bankruptcy, Personal Bankruptcy, Chapter 7, Chapter 13, Consumer and Business Bankruptcy, Personal Injury, Automobile Accidents, Wrongful Death, Mediation, Business Law, Consumer Law, Lemon Law, Fair Debt Collection Practices.
See Professional Biographies, RALEIGH, NORTH CAROLINA

Call, W. Davidson, (BV) .... '42 '68 C.893 B.A. L.692 LL.B. [Bode,C.&S.]
Camden, Kerry E. .... '— '05 C.659 B.A. L.896 J.D. [A DLPiper R.G.C.U.]
Cameron, Christie Speir .... '54 '81 C&L.575 B.S., J.D. Clk., Supm. Ct.
Cameron, Dallas A., Jr. .... '39 '73 C&L.575 B.A., J.D. Adm. Off. of the Cts.
Cammarano, Gina E. .... '68 '95 C.602 B.B.A. L.575 J.D. [A Jernigan]
Campbell, Dexter M., III .... '— '03 C.575 B.A. L.1228 J.D. [Cranfill,S.&H.]
Campen, Henry C., Jr., (AV) .... '49 '86 C.896 B.A. L.574 J.D. [Parker,P.A.&B.]

Campion, John E., (AV) '47 '76 C.608 B.A. L.930 J.D.
5 West Hargett Street Suite 810, P.O. Box 2656, 27602
Telephone: 919-239-0260 Fax: 919-239-0261
Email: john@johncampionlaw.com URL: http://www.johncampionlaw.com
Employment Law, Discrimination, Sexual Harassment, Non-Compete Agreements, Wage and Hour Law, Employment Severance Agreements.
See Professional Biographies, RALEIGH, NORTH CAROLINA

Canaday, Marjorie Sibley .... '50 '88 C.259 B.M. L.574 J.D. Law Clk. to Ct. of App.
Canfield, Lisa K. .... '72 '97 C.886 B.A. L.893 J.D. [A Wyrick R.Y.&P.]
Cannon, James R. .... '60 '91 C.840 B.S. L.228 J.D. [Myers B.S.&S.] (See Pat. Sect.)
Capel, Christopher B., (AV) .... '57 '85 C&L.575 A.B., J.D. [Smith,A.B.D.M.&J.]

Capitol District Law Offices, (AV) BR
11 South Blount Street, P.O. Box 25096, 27611-5096
Telephone: 919-828-0363 Fax: 919-832-5205
Email: rweaver@capitolaw.com URL: http://www.capitolaw.com
Member of Firm: Reagan Hale Weaver.
Civil Practice in State and Federal Courts. Trials and Appeals. Employment Law, including Discrimination, Retaliatory Discharge, Whistleblower Litigation, Sexual Harassment, Contracts, Covenants Not To Compete, Executive Severance Contracts, Professional Licensing. False Claims Act, Qui Tam Litigation, Wrongful Death, Personal Injury, Arbitration and Mediation, Wrongful Termination, Title VII Discrimination, Equal Employment Opportunity Law.
See Professional Biographies, RALEIGH, NORTH CAROLINA

Carlton, Alfred P., Jr., (AV) .... '— '75 C&L.575 B.S., J.D. [Kilpatrick S.]
Carlton, Karen Kelly .... '61 '86 C.1083 B.A. L.896 J.D. [C Jordan P.W.G.J.&C.]
Carlton, Richard H., (BV) .... '52 '79 C.575 B.S.B.A. L.1228 J.D. 3717 Benson Dr.
Carlton, Terry J., (BV) .... '61 '86 C.475 B.A. L.896 J.D. [Jordan P.W.G.J.&C.]
Carmack, Amie Flowers, (BV) .... '— '95 C&L.896 B.A., J.D. [Kennedy C.L.&H.]
Carmichael, Carson, III, (AV) .... '54 '81 C.576 B.S. L.896 J.D. [Bailey&D.]
Carmichael, Hope Derby, (BV) .... '66 '91 C.758 B.A. L.575 J.D. [Jordan P.W.G.J.&C.]
Carpenter, J. Michael, (AV) '51 '75 C.576 B.A. L.273 J.D.
Exec. V.P. & Gen. Coun., N.C. Home Builders Assn.
Carr, Anna .... '75 '03 C.945 B.S. L.896 J.D. [A Myers B.S.&S.]
Carr, Jonathan P. .... '66 '92 C.575 B.S. L.1228 J.D. [Jordan P.W.G.J.&C.]
Carr, Steven, (AV) .... '54 '79 C&L.900 B.A., J.D. [Nelson M.R.&S.]
Carrigan, Connie E., (BV) .... '61 '89 C.576 B.A. L.1345 J.D. [Smith D.N.W.S.&M.]
Carrington, Deborah R. '49 '75
C.576 B.A. L.575 J.D. Exec. Secy., N.C. Jud. Standards Comm.

Carruth, Paul, (AV) '48 '74 C.228 B.A. L.575 J.D.
5834 Faringdon Place, Suite 1, 27609
Telephone: 919-872-8225 Fax: 919-872-8335
Email: carruthlaw@aol.com URL: http://www.lawyers.com/carruthlaw
Real Estate, Wills, Trusts and Estates, Probate, Family Law, Mediation and Arbitration, General Practice.
See Professional Biographies, RALEIGH, NORTH CAROLINA

Carter, Angela Long, (BV) .... '75 '00 C.240 B.A. L.575 J.D. [Allen&P.]
Carter, Charles S. .... '— '74 C.228 B.S. L.575 J.D. [McNair]
Carter, Jean Gordon, (AV) .... '55 '83 C.896 B.S. L.228 J.D. [Hunton&W.]

Carter, Laura L. .... '— '01 NC Indus. Commission
Carter, Patrice P. ....'62 '88 C.811 B.A. L.574 J.D. Law Clk. to Ct. of App.
Case, Charles D., (AV) ....'52 '77 C.576 B.S. L.309 J.D. [Hunton&W.]
Case, Margie Toy, (AV) ....'52 '78 C.216 B.A. L.665 J.D. [Maupin T.]
Casey, Warren C. ....'21 '49 C&L.896 B.A., J.D. 1801 Pony Run Rd.‡
Cashwell, Narley L. ....'45 '75 C&L.575 A.B., J.D. Supr. Ct. J.
Castaner, Sarah E. ....'69 '02 C.1380 B.A. L.1292 J.D. 2 Hannover Sq., Ste. 1540
Castelloe, Paul E., The Law Office of, (AV) '44 '68
C&L.575 A.B., J.D. 3950 Blue Ridge Road
Cato, Emily Copeland ....'45 '76 C.914 A.B. L.1119 J.D. 3040 Granville Dr.‡
Cauthen, Robert B. ....'47 '79 C.576 B.S. L.575 J.D. 6111 Lynnridge Ln., Rm. 309‡
Cayton, Alison R., (BV) ....'64 '91 C.797 B.A. L.575 J.D. [Manning,F.&S.]
Celestini, Stephen D. '63 '89
C.886 B.A. L.896 J.D. Gen. Coun., Salix Pharmaceuticals, Inc
Cella, Ansley Chapman ....'73 '98 C.160 B.A. L.790 J.D. [Manning,F.&S.]
Cella, Eugene J. ....'48 '74 C.575 A.B. L.362 J.D. State Secs. Admr.
Cella, John R., Jr. ....'— '00 C.575 B.A. L.790 J.D. [🄰 Manning,F.&S.]

Chambers, David R., (BV) '53 '81 C.575 B.A. L.574 J.D.
3110 Edwards Mill Road, Suite 340, 27612
Telephone: 919-277-2200 Fax: 919-277-2525
Email: drcestate@aol.com URL: http://www.davidrchambers.com
Estate Planning, Wealth Transfer, Asset Protection, Tax Planning, Charitable Giving.
See Professional Biographies, RALEIGH, NORTH CAROLINA

Chambliss, Joseph B., Jr., (AV) ....'54 '85 C.575 B.A. L.1228 J.D. [Cranfill,S.&H.]
Chandler, Paige ....'71 '99 C.575 B.A. L.1228 J.D. [🄰 Vann&S.]
Chapman, Morgan S. ....'54 '78 C&L.896 B.A., J.D. Dep. Comr., State Indus. Comm.
Chasse, Eric Craig ....'68 '93 C.575 B.A. L.945 J.D. 5 West Hargett Street Suite 709

Chastain, Peter, & Associates, P.A.
(See Greensboro)

Cheek, Clyde Alexander, III ....'72 '00 C.953 B.A. L.575 J.D. Law Clk.
Chen, Alyssa M. ....'75 '03 C.174 B.A. L.575 J.D. [🄰 Wyrick R.Y.&P.]
Cherney, Colburn G. '16 '42 C.477 A.B. L.309 J.D.
(adm. in IL; not adm. in NC) 730 Red Forest Trail‡
Cherry, William S., Jr., (AV) ....'50 '75 C.576 B.A. L.896 J.D. [Poyner&S.]
Cheshire, Joseph B., V, (AV) ....'47 '73 C.575 B.A. L.896 J.D. [Cheshire,P.S.B.&V.]

Cheshire, Parker, Schneider, Bryan & Vitale, (AV)
133 Fayetteville Street Mall, Suite 500, P.O. Box 1029, 27602-1029
Telephone: 919-833-3114 Fax: 919-832-0739
Members of Firm: Joseph B. Cheshire, V; John H. Parker; Alan Marc Schneider; Kimberly W. Bryan (Board Certified Specialist in Family Law, North Carolina State Board of Legal Specialization); Jonathan Gordon McGirt (Board Certified Specialist in Family Law, North Carolina Board of Legal Specialization); Lorion Maerae Vitale; John Keating Wiles; Bradley J. Bannon. Associate: Doris K. Jordan.
Federal and State Criminal Trials and Appeals. Professional Discipline and Regulatory Law, Ethics. Family Law, Divorce, Alimony, Child Custody, Equitable Distribution, Civil Trial Defense.
See Professional Biographies, RALEIGH, NORTH CAROLINA

Chester, Suzanne M. ...'61 '95 C.999 B.A. L.575 J.D. E. Central Community Legal Servs.
Chestnut, L. McNeil ....'48 '81 C&L.1228 B.S., J.D. The State Atty. Gen. Off.
Chignell, Kevin L., (BV) ....'70 '95 C&L.575 B.S., J.D. [Parker,P.A.&B.]
Chilson, John A. ....'69 '99 C.871 B.S. L.477 J.D. [🄰 Ellis&W.] ⊙

Chocklett, Gregory P., Law Offices of, (BV) '56 '84 C&L.575 A.B., J.D.
711 Harvey Street, 27608-2403
Telephone: 919-856-0100 Fax: 919-856-0799
Email: chocklett@bellsouth.net URL: http://www.chocklettlaw.com
Commercial Litigation, Bankruptcy/Creditor, Collections, Contracts, Civil Trials and Appeals, Personal Injury. Medical Malpractice, ERISA, Repossessions, Foreclosures.
The CIT Group; General Electric Capital Corp.; Lockheed Martin Lender Services,Inc.; Wells Fargo Bank, N.A.; WFS Financial, Inc.; Triad Financial Corp.; Onyx Acceptance Corp.; Origen Financial LLC; Consumer Portfolio Services, Inc.; Invacare Corp.
See Professional Biographies, RALEIGH, NORTH CAROLINA

Choi, Anna Baird, (BV) ....'68 '94 C.575 B.A. L.1228 J.D. [🄰 Bailey&D.]
Christian, E. Ann, (BV) ....'50 '77 C.575 A.B. L.192 J.D. 122 St. Mary's St.
Christison, Kent F., (AV) ....'— '71 C.967 A.B. L.893 J.D. [Kennedy C.L.&H.]
Chun, Jennifer Miseong ....'67 '95 C.999 B.S. L.900 J.D. [J.Chun]
Chun, Jennifer, Law Office of ....8362-204 Six Forks Road
Church, Kim, (AV) ....'56 '82 C.577 B.A. L.575 J.D. [🄲 Kuniholm]
Cioffi, Andrew P., (AV) ....'59 '85 C.550 B.A. L.904 J.D. [Smyth&C.]
Clanton, Charles W. ....'56 '91 C&L.575 B.A., J.D. [Wyrick R.Y.&P.]
Clare, Jacqueline Riley, (AV) ....'56 '82 C.232 B.A. L.575 J.D. [Clare,J.R.]
Clare, Thomas M., (AV) ....'53 '83 C.232 B.A. L.575 J.D. [Teague,C.D.&G.]
Clare, Jacqueline R., (AV) ....1011 Vance St.
Clark, Daniel W., (BV) ....'63 '88 C&L.575 B.A., J.D. [Tharrington S.]
Clark, Heman R., (AV) '15 '40
C.198 A.B. L.575 LL.B. 150 Fayetteville St. Mall, Suite 1520
Clark, Michael Wood ....'59 '90 C.577 B.S.N. L.1345 J.D. [Knott,C.&B.]
Clark, Reuben G., III, (AV) ....'52 '80 C.813 B.A. L.659 J.D. [Maupin T.]
Clark, Sandra M., (BV) ....'63 '94 C&L.1228 B.B.A., J.D. [Manning,F.&S.]
Clarke, A. Bruce, (AV) '58 '83
C&L.575 B.S., B.A., J.D. Pres. & CEO, Capital Assoc. Industries Inc.
Clauson, Vaughn S. ....'50 '96 C.1070 B.S. L.575 J.D. P.O. Box 10629
Clay, Robert M., (AV) ....'35 '61 C&L.575 A.B., J.D. [Patterson,D.C.B.&A.]
Clayton, Katherine J. ....'49 '04 C.880 B.E. L.577 J.D. [Brooks,P.M.H.&L.] ⊙
Cleary, Melissa R. ....'70 '95 C.741 B.A. L.575 J.D. [Teague,C.D.&G.]
Clegg, David L., (BV) ....'55 '81 C.301 B.A. L.790 J.D. Dep. Comr.
Cleland, Jennifer J. ....'65 '92 C&L.575 B.A., J.D. Jud. Clk., Ct. App. J.
Clement, David B. ....'59 '86 C.871 B.S. L.884 J.D. [🄰 Smith,A.B.D.M.&J.]
Clemmons, Brian E., (BV) ....'61 '87 C&L.575 B.A., J.D. [🄰 Whitley,R.&W.]
Clemmons, Lauren Murphy, (BV) ....'64 '88 C.575 A.B. L.896 J.D. Asst. Atty. Gen.
Clifton, Benjamin F., Jr., (AV) ....'43 '70 C&L.575 B.A., J.D. [Clifton&S.]

Clifton & Singer, L.L.P., (AV)
4900 Falls of Neuse Road, Suite 160, 27609
Telephone: 919-790-7000
URL: http://www.cliftonsingerlaw.com
Members of Firm: Benjamin F. Clifton, Jr.; Richard G. Singer. Associates: Lance R. Fife; Lucy T. Brewer.
Personal Injury, Medical Malpractice, Wrongful Death, Catastrophic Injury, Residential Real Estate, Commercial Real Estate, Family Law, Divorce, Child Custody, Criminal Law, DWI, Traffic Violations.
References: United Carolina Bank; First Citizens Bank & Trust Co.; First Union National Bank; Branch Banking & Trust Co.
See Professional Biographies, RALEIGH, NORTH CAROLINA

Cline, Denise S., (AV) ....'— '83 C.198 A.B. L.575 J.D. [Smith M.]
Cline, James E., (BV) ....'39 '70 C.576 B.A. L.575 J.D. 333 Fayetteville St. Mall
Close, Cary Elizabeth, (BV) ....'59 '91 C.575 B.A. L.1228 J.D. [Manning,F.&S.]

Coates, J. Keith, Jr. '72 '98 C.797 B.A. L.838 J.D.
(adm. in GA; not adm. in NC) [🄰 Hunton&W.]
Coats, Carrie Amelia (Ame) ....'70 '02 C.575 B.A. L.1228 J.D. [🄰 Bashyam&S.]
Coats, David S., (AV) ....'62 '88 C.296 B.S. L.896 J.D. [Bailey&D.]

Coats & Bennett, PLLC
(See Cary)

Cobb, Barry S., (AV) ....'68 '92 C&L.575 B.S., J.D. [Yates,M.&W.]
Cobb, Carla M. ....'74 '01 C.575 B.A. L.1228 J.D. [🄰 Teague,C.D.&G.]
Cobb, James L.S. ....'52 '89 C.228 B.A. L.1065 J.D. [Wyrick R.Y.&P.]
Cobb, Laurence A. ....'33 '58 C&L.575 B.S.B.A., J.D. [🄲 Sanford H.]
Coble, Charles E. ....'72 '98 C.976 B.A. L.309 J.D. [Brooks,P.M.H.&L.] ⊙
Coble, George R. (Ran), Jr. ....'49 '77 C.198 B.A. L.575 J.D. Exec. Dir.
Cochran, Benjamin T. ....'76 '02 C.575 B.A. L.1345 J.D. [🄰 Hardison&L.]
Cockburn, Joscelyn G. '41 '75 C.854 B.S. L.273 J.D.
(adm. in PA; not adm. in NC; Pat.) IBM Corp.
Cockman, David R., (AV) ....'28 '57 C&L.575 A.B., J.D. [🄲 Vann&S.]
Cohen, Donna R. ....'59 '87 C.1044 B.A. L.564 J.D. 2840 Plaza Pl.
Cohen, Gerry ....'50 '75 C&L.575 B.A., J.D. Legislative Off.
Cohen, Keirth '69 '95 C.228 A.B. L.945 J.D.
(adm. in VA; not adm. in NC) Equal Employ. Opportunity Comm.
Colbert, Lois W., (BV) ....'— '88 C.339 B.S. L.477 J.D. [Kilpatrick S.]
Coldiron, Holly Ann ....'63 '97 C&L.575 B.A., J.D. [🄰 Hutchison&M.]
Cole, Janice McKenzie, (BV) ....'47 '80 C.1139 B.A. L.262 J.D. U.S. Atty.
Cole, Sean A.B. ....'71 '97 C.387 B.A. L.896 J.D. [Martin&J.]
Coleman, Daniel T., (CV) ....'57 '88 C.575 B.S. L.574 J.D. Ste 202, 4080 Barrett Dr
Coleman, Peter S. ....'71 '97 C.1228 B.A. L.1345 J.D. [Roper&C.]

Coleman, Gledhill, Hargrave & Peek, P.C.
(See Hillsborough)

Coleman Gray, Elizabeth G. ....'56 '78 C&L.608 B.A., J.D. N.C. Prisoner Legal Serv.
Colgan, Richard J., (BVⓉ) '53 '80 C.107 B.A. L.838 J.D.
16 West Martin Street, Suite 409 (⊙Virginia Beach, VA)
Colgan, Timothy J. ....'58 '91 C.232 B.S. L.574 J.D. 111 Brooks Ave.
Collins, G. Bryan, Jr., (AV) '60 '85
C.198 B.A. L.575 J.D. 16 West Martin Street, Suite 501
Collins, Jennifer Long ....'68 '95 C.160 B.A. L.421 J.D. [🄰 Womble C.S.&R.]
Colston, L. Aylett ....'72 '99 C.198 A.B. L.902 J.D. [🄰 Hutchison&M.]
Coltrain, Keith E. ....'64 '95 C.576 B.S. L.575 J.D. [Elmore&W.]
Coman, James J., (AV) .....'42 '72 C.708 A.B. L.896 J.D. Dir., State Bur. of Investigation
Compton, R. Sarah ....'46 '73 C.446 B.S. L.276 J.D. 1044 Washington Street‡
Condon, Kevin R. '57 '86 C.676 B.A. L.896 J.D.
(adm. in CT; not adm. in NC)
V.P. & Chf. Legal Offr., Invensys Energy Management Division
Cone, Sarah E. ....'78 '05 C.576 B.A. L.1228 J.D. [🄰 Lewis&R.]
Conger-Lane, Dawn ....'69 '96 C.1228 B.B.A. L.574 J.D. [Cranfill,S.&H.]
Conley, David T. ......'54 '79 C.575 B.S. L.896 J.D. Assoc. Gen. Coun., Progress Energy
Connell, John H. ....'59 '85 C&L.575 B.A., J.D. Clk., Ct. of Appeals
Connell, Michael C. ....'— '86 C&L.575 B.A., J.D. [Cranfill,S.&H.]
Conner, James L., II ....'56 '84 C.228 B.A. L.575 J.D. Office of Adm Hearings

Conner Gwyn Schenck PLLC, (AV)
2626 Glenwood Avenue, Suite 180, 27608 ⊙
Mailing Address: P.O. Box 30933, Raleigh, NC 27622
Telephone: 919-789-9242 Facsimile: 919-789-9210
URL: http://www.cgspllc.com
Richard D. Conner (Resident, Greensboro Office); Allen Holt Gwyn (Resident, Greensboro Office); James S. Schenck, IV (Resident); C. Hamilton Jarrett, III (Resident); Paul E. Davis (Resident); Jay M. Wilkerson (Resident, Greensboro Office);—Edward N. Pollard (Resident, Greensboro Office). Of Counsel: Jeffrey B. Parsons.
Construction Law, Trials, Contract Law, Mediation, Arbitration.
Greensboro, North Carolina Office: 306 E. Market Street, Suite One, 27401. Telephone: 336-691-9222. Fax: 336-691-9259.
See Professional Biographies, RALEIGH, NORTH CAROLINA

Cook, Charles Ryan '— '97 C.112 B.A. L.37 J.D.
(adm. in WA; not adm. in NC) [🄰 Ogletree,D.N.S.&S.] (⊙Raleigh)
Cook, Jeffrey M. ....'66 '98 C.689 B.A. L.574 J.D. U.S. Bkrptcy. Admr. Off.
Cook, Terri L., (AV) ....'56 '86 C.383 B.B.A. L.575 J.D. [Silverstein&C.]
Cook, Thomas H., Jr., (AV) ....'58 '87 C.893 B.S. L.945 J.D. [Wyrick R.Y.&P.]
Cook, William Christian ....'67 '99 C.925 B.S. in B.A. L.200 J.D. P.O. Box 2475
Cooke, Betsy ....'— '98 C&L.575 B.A., J.D. [🄰 Kilpatrick S.]
Cooke, John C., (AV) ....'52 '78 C&L.896 B.A., J.D. [Womble C.S.&R.]
Cookson, Andrew ....'68 '03 C.1083 B.A. L.574 J.D. [Gurley&C.]
Cooley, Jessica E. ....'79 '05 C.999 B.A. L.1228 J.D. [🄰 Jordan P.W.G.J.&C.]
Cooper, Kathryn Jones ....'59 '84 C.788 A.B. L.575 J.D. Spec. Dep. Atty. Gen.
Cooper, Ricky William (Rick) '55 '80 C.1204 B.S. L.836 J.D.
V.P., Prob. Mgr., First-Citizens Bank & Trust Company
Cooper, Roy A., III, (AV) ....'57 '82 C&L.575 B.A., J.D. Atty. Gen.
Copeland, Buxton S., (AV) ....'59 '85 C.575 B.A. L.1228 J.D. [Cranfill,S.&H.]
Copeland, Melissa J. '69 '94 C.140 B.A. L.790 J.D.
(adm. in SC; not adm. in NC) [Nelson M.R.&S.]
Copeley, Leto, (AV) ....'54 '84 C.331 B.A. L.309 J.D. [Patterson H.] (⊙Chapel Hill)
Corbett, Brian F. ....'75 '00 C.423 B.A. L.896 J.D. [🄲 Poyner&S.]
Cordell, Sherie Y. '— '85 C.645 B.A. L.564 J.D.
V.P. & Sr. Coun., GE Capital Mortgage Insurance
Corne, John R. ....'46 '75 C&L.575 A.B., J.D. Spec. Dep. Atty. Gen., Dept. of Jus.
Cornelius, Andrew T. ....'79 '04 C.575 B.A. L.1228 J.D. [🄰 J.P.Laurie,III]
Cortes, David J. '50 '78 C.420 B.S. L.425 J.D.
(adm. in LA; not adm. in NC) Asst. U.S. Atty.
Corum, Allison Smith ....'62 '94 C.269 B.A. L.575 J.D. Assoc. Atty. Gen.
Corvette, Theodore E., (BV) ....'45 '73 C.205 B.A. L.228 J.D. [Nelson M.R.&S.]
Costa, Santo J. ....'45 '72 C&L.724 B.S., J.D. [🄲 Maupin T.]
Costanza, Nicholas J. '55 '80 C.705 B.A. L.884 J.D.
(adm. in PA; not adm. in NC)
V.P., Chf. Legal Coun. & Secy., Exide Electronics Grp., Inc.

Cotter, William J., P.A.
(See Durham)

Cowan, J. Donald, Jr., (AV) .....'43 '68 C&L.896 B.A., J.D. [Smith M.] (⊙Greensboro)
Coward, David Scott, (AV) ....'— '89 C.575 B.S. L.178 J.D. [Kennedy C.L.&H.]
Cox, E. Christopher ....'62 '87 C&L.575 B.A., J.D. Assoc. Gen. Coun., Progress Energy
Cox, Joseph B., Jr. ....'48 '76 C.228 A.B. L.575 J.D. [Cox&C.]
Cox, R. James, Jr. ....'69 '01 C.576 B.E.D. L.575 J.D. [🄰 Smith M.]
Cox, W. Robbins, (BV) ....'53 '80 C.228 A.B. L.575 J.D. [Cox&C.]
Cox and Cox, L.L.P., (BV) ....3105 Glenwood Avenue, Suite 302
Cozort, Jack L., (AV) ....'50 '75 C.576 B.A. L.896 J.D. [Parker,P.A.&B.]
Crabill, Robert A. ....'66 '93 C.893 B.A. L.575 J.D. N.C. Dept. of Justice

Craige, Burton, (AV) ...... '49 '80 C.309 B.A. L.575 J.D. [Patterson H.] (⊙Chapel Hill)
Crampton, Gregory B., (AV) ....'47 '72 C.902 B.A. L.575 J.D. [Nicholls&C.]
Cranfill, Paul L., (AV) .... '42 '69 C&L.575 B.S., J.D. [Cranfill,S.&H.]

Cranfill, Sumner & Hartzog, L.L.P., (AV) BR
Hillsborough Place, 225 Hillsborough Street, Suite 300, P.O. Box 27808, 27611-7808 ⊙
Telephone: 919-828-5100 Fax: 919-828-2277
URL: http://www.cshlaw.com
Members Of The Firm: Paul L. Cranfill; Robert W. Sumner; Dan M. Hartzog (Managing Partner); Alene M. Mercer; Richard T. Boyette; David D. Ward; Patricia L. Holland; David H. Batten; H. Lee Evans, Jr.; C. D. Taylor Pace; Susan K. Burkhart; Buxton S. Copeland; P. Collins Barwick, III; Robert H. Griffin; Kari Russwurm Johnson; David A. Rhoades; Brady W. Wells; Joseph B. Chambliss, Jr.; W. Scott Fuller; Robin H. Terry; William W. Pollock; Stephanie Hutchins Autry; Leigh Ann G. Smith; Jonathan C. Anders; Maranda J. Freeman; H. Vance Barnette, III; Kirk D. Kuhns; Jaye Elizabeth Bingham; Beth R. Fleishman; Ann Smith Estridge; J. Gregory Newton; Donna R. Rascoe; C. Houston Foppiano; James Bell Black, IV; Erin Fleming Taylor; F. Marshall Wall; Jesse M. Tillman, III; Michael C. Allen; Melissa Robin Davis; Daniel G. Katzenbach; Gloria Taft Becker; George L. Simpson, IV; Randolph L. Lee; George B. Autry, Jr.; Katherine Hilkey-Boyatt; Jennifer C. Polley-Abramson; J. Greer Vanderberry, Jr.; Tracy C. Myatt; Kathleen Manning Miles; Roy G. Pettigrew; Rachel K. Esposito; Dawn Conger-Lane; Leanne L. Mullis; Amy Harrison Nuttall; John Michael Ricci; Alycia S. Levy; Meredith T. Black; Dexter M. Campbell, III; Ginger Bagley Hunsucker; Jennifer A. Addleton; Stephanie A. Gaston; Michael C. Connell; Amy L. Pfeiffer; Erica Jona Thomas; Katie J. Weaver; Ashley Kamphaus Brathwaite; Christopher A. Brook; Paul Holscher.
General Trial and Appellate Practice before all State and Federal Courts. Litigation of Insurance Law, Personal Injury, Medical Malpractice, Nursing Home Negligence, Professional Malpractice, Products Liability, Premises Liability, Municipal and Police Liability, Intentional Torts, Commercial Litigation, Workers' Compensation, Employment, Education, Construction and Land Condemnation Law.
Representative Clients: NC Association of County Commissioners; Tyson Foods, Inc.
Charlotte, North Carolina Office: 227 West Trade Street, Suite 600. Telephone: 704-332-8300. Fax: 704-332-9994.
Wilmington, North Carolina Office: 1209 Culbreth Drive, Suite 200, 28405. Telephone: 910-509-9778. Fax: 910-509-9676.

See Professional Biographies, RALEIGH, NORTH CAROLINA

Crawford, Renee Billings .... '60 '96 C.831 B.A. L.228 J.D. [Crawford]
Crawford, Robert O., III, (AV) ....'58 '84 C&L.896 B.A., J.D. [Crawford]

Crawford Law Office, (AV)
Landmark Center, 4601 Six Forks Road, Suite 500, 27609
Telephone: 919-510-8140 Facsimile: 919-785-4152
URL: http://www.lawyers.com/crawfordlawoffice
Renee Billings Crawford; Robert O. Crawford, III.
Medical Malpractice Defense, Professional and Occupational Licensing and Discipline Defense, Administrative Law, Employment Law, Insurance Defense, Business Litigation, Civil Appeals.

See Professional Biographies, RALEIGH, NORTH CAROLINA

Crawley, Francis W., (BV) ....'48 '73 C&L.575 A.B., J.D. Spec. Dep. Atty. Gen.
Creech, Paul P., (AV) .... '51 '77 C.575 A.B. L.790 J.D. [P.P.Creech]
Creech, William A. ....'25 '58 C.575 A.B. L.276 J.D. Emerg. Dist. Ct. J.

Creech, Paul P., Attorney at Law, PLLC, (AV)
3605 Glenwood Avenue Suite 220, 27612
Telephone: 919-787-7766 Fax: 919-787-7793
Email: paul@creechlaw.com URL: http://www.creechlawfirm.com
Paul P. Creech.
Business, Corporate, Tax, Estate Planning, Real Estate, Wills Buying and Selling of Businesses.

See Professional Biographies, RALEIGH, NORTH CAROLINA

Creekman, James E., (AV) '47 '74 C&L.893 B.A., J.D.
Grp. V.P., Legal Servs., First-Citizens Bank & Trust Company
Crill, John L., (AV) .... '43 '67 C.25 A.B. L.228 LL.B. [Ⓒ Wyrick R.Y.&P.]

Crisp Page & Currin, LLP, (AV)
1305 Navaho Drive, Suite 302, 27609-7444
Telephone: 919-876-8282 Fax: 919-876-8285 URL: http://www.cpclaw.com
URL: http://crisppageandcurrin.com
William T. Crisp (1924-1992). Members of the Firm: Robert F. Page; Cynthia M. Currin.
General Civil Practice in State and Federal Courts, Trial Practice, Appellate Practice, Civil Litigation, Business Litigation, Utilities, Cellular Telephone, Communications, Corporate Law, Cooperative, Non-Profit Organizations, Employment, Mediation, Administrative Law, Social Security Disability.

See Professional Biographies, RALEIGH, NORTH CAROLINA

Crooks, Susan Davis, (AV) ....'50 '87 C.576 L.1228 J.D. [Womble C.S.&R.]
Croom, Claudia C. .... '67 '97 C.228 A.B. L.574 J.D. 19 W. Hargett, Ste. 420
Croom, Craig ....'67 '94 C.575 B.S. L.574 J.D. Asst. Dist Atty.
Croteau, Anne Elizabeth ....'71 '98 C.228 B.A. L.309 J.D. [Ⓐ Young M.&H.]
Crouch, James A., (BV) .... '66 '92 C.232 B.A. L.1345 J.D. [Manning&C.]
Crouch, Rachelle J. .... '72 '99 C.845 B.B.A. L.802 J.D. [Ⓐ Kirschbaum,N.K.&G.]
Crouse, James T. ....'49 '81 C.198 B.A. L.228 J.D. [Crouse]
Crouse, Robert N. ... '60 '97 C.588 B.S.E.E. L.896 J.D. [Myers B.S.&S.] (See Pat. Sect.)

Crouse Law Offices
Two Hanover Square, Suite 2350, 434 Fayetteville Street Mall, 27601
Telephone: 919-861-0500 Fax: 919-861-0504
Email: JTC@CrouseLaw.com URL: http://www.crouselaw.com
James T. Crouse.
National and International Aviation Litigation, Mass Disaster, Products Liability, Personal Injury Litigation, Appeals in all Courts.

See Professional Biographies, RALEIGH, NORTH CAROLINA

Croutharmel, Richard ....'62 '00 C.1253 B.S. L.574 J.D. 5 West Hargett St.
Crowder, Sarah A. .... '52 '81 C.896 B.A. L.575 J.D. East Central Comm. Legal Servs.
Crowe, William M. ....'66 '02 C.575 B.A. L.574 J.D. [Ⓐ Holt Y.M.&H.]
Crowell, Michael ....'45 '71 C.575 B.A. L.309 J.D. [Tharrington S.]
Crump, David S., (BV) ....'49 '74 C&L.575 A.B., J.D. 4109 Wake Forest Rd., Ste. 307
Crump, Derek M., (BV) '63 '88 C.576 B.A. L.896 J.D.
421 Fayetteville St. Mall, Ste. 1203
Crumpler, Laura E., (AV) ....'50 '79 C.758 B.A. L.896 J.D. P.O. Box 629
Crumpler, William B. (Bud), (AV) ....'41 '71 C.870 B.S. L.575 J.D. State Dept. of Jus.
Cummer, Catharine W. ....'72 '96 C.813 A.B. L.1066 J.D. [Ⓒ Nelson M.R.&S.]
Cummings, Howard J., (AV) ....'53 '80 C.576 B.S. L.1228 J.D. Asst. Dist. Atty.
Cummings, Jasper L., Jr., (AVⓉ) .... '46 '72 C.228 A.B. L.976 J.D. [Ⓒ Alston&B.]
Cunningham, Joan Maria, (BV) ....'44 '84 C.272 B.A. L.575 J.D. State Dept. of Jus.
Cunningham, Matthew S. ....'73 '00 C.576 B.A. L.896 J.D. [Ⓐ Smith M.]
Cunningham, Michelle L. '— '03 C.201 B.S. L.577 J.D.
[Ⓐ Alston&B.] (See Pat. Sect.)
Currie, Nathaniel, (BV) ....'43 '73 C&L.574 B.S.C., J.D. 805 New Bern Ave.
Currin, Cynthia M., (AV) .... '54 '80 C&L.575 A.B., J.D. [Crisp P.&C.]
Currin, Eva C. ....'78 '03 C.576 B.A. L.575 J.D. [Ⓐ Bass,B.&F.]
Currin, George B. .... '61 '87 C.576 B.A. L.1228 J.D. 16 W. Martin St., Suite 700
Currin, Samuel T., (AV) ....'48 '74 C.896 B.A. L.575 J.D. [Currin] ⊙

Currin Law Firm, PLLC, (AV)
Currin Law Building, 20 Market Plaza, P.O. Box 269, 27602-0269 ⊙
Mailing Address: P.O. Box 269, Raleigh, NC
Telephone: 919-833-0888 Facsimile: 919-833-8171 URL: http://www.currinlaw.com
URL: http://www.lawyers.com/currinlaw

(This Listing Continued)

Currin Law Firm, PLLC (Continued)
Samuel T. Currin; Thomas C. Goolsby.
Federal and State Criminal Defense, Civil and Criminal Forfeitures, Serious Personal Injury/Wrongful Death, Medical Malpractice, Government Relations.
Wilmington, North Carolina Office: Goolsby Law Building, 620 Market Street, 28401. Telephone: 910-763-3339. Fax: 910-763-1720.

See Professional Biographies, RALEIGH, NORTH CAROLINA

Dahl, David D., (AV) .... '52 '80 C.902 B.A. L.575 J.D. [Manning,F.&S.]
Daigneault, Melissa S. .... '78 '03 C.839 B.S. L.896 J.D. [Ⓐ Parker,P.A.&B.]
Dail, Francis E. .... '40 '73 C.316 A.B. L.896 J.D. Admin. Coun., Ct. of App.
Dail, Sean B. .... '60 '86 C.576 B.A. L.896 J.D. NC Gen. Assembly, Drafting Div.
Dalonzo-Baker, Sarah '70 '97
C.759 B.A. L.896 J.D. V.P., Total Motion Physical Therapy Inc.
Dalton, Craig G., Jr., (AV) .... '50 '77 C&L.575 A.B., J.D. [Poyner&S.]
Dalton, Mary Ann ....'71 '99 C.575 B.A. L.1228 J.D. [Dalton]

Dalton Law Firm, The, P.A.
2501 Blue Ridge Road Suite 390, 26707
Telephone: 919-755-0255 Fax: 919-785-3422
Email: maryann@daltonlawyer.com URL: http://www.daltonelderlawfirm.com
Mary Ann Dalton.
Elder Law, Medicaid Planning, Estate Planning, Asset Protection, Wills, Probate, Trusts, Collaborative Law, Elder Law Mediation.

See Professional Biographies, RALEIGH, NORTH CAROLINA

Daniel, Royal T., III ....'56 '91 C.576 B.S. L.818 J.D. [R.T.Daniel,III]
Daniel, Royal T., III, P.A., The Law Office of ....1004 Deerfield Dr.
Daniell, William P., (AV) ....'51 '77 C&L.575 A.B., J.D. [Young M.&H.]

Daniels Daniels & Verdonik, P.A.
(See Research Triangle Park)

Dannelly, William D., (AV) .... '51 '77 C.453 S.B. L.575 J.D. [Hunton&W.]
Darden, Josephine R., (AV) ....'52 '85 C.575 B.A. L.93 J.D. [Ⓐ Young M.&H.]
Darden, Thomas F., II '55 '81
C.575 B.A. L.976 J.D. Chmn. of the Bd., Cherokee Sanford Grp.‡
Darer, Brian D. .... '73 '98 C&L.893 B.A., J.D. [Ⓐ Parker,P.A.&B.]
Darrow, Mary Jude, (AVⓉ) '57 '85 C.158 B.S. L.425 J.D.
(adm. in LA; not adm. in NC) 310 New Bern Avenue, Eighth Floor
Daugherty, Hilary D. ....'26 '60 C.576 B.S. L.575 LL.B. 3407 Ocotea St.
Daum, Shiloh A. ....'75 '04 C&L.575 B.A., J.D. [Ⓐ Zaytoun&M.P.]
Daumen, Michael J. ....'67 '94 C.880 B.A. L.966 J.D. 9017 Miranda Drive
Davenport, Katherine Elizabeth '69 '94 C.311 B.A. L.383 J.D.
(adm. in KY; not adm. in NC) Soc. Sec. Admin., Off. Hearings & Appeals
Daves, Bradley J. .... '73 '98 C.576 B.S. L.575 J.D. [Ⓐ Smith,A.B.D.M.&J.]
Davidian, V.A. "Woofer", III .... '— '99 C.575 B.A. L.1339 J.D. [Sandlin&D.]
Davidoff, Janice L. .... '51 '86 C.1374 B.A. L.107 J.D. 1608 Beechwood Dr.
Davis, Adrian Jaye .... '73 '00 C&L.575 B.A., J.D. [A.J.Davis]
Davis, B. Joan, (AV) ....'65 '90 C&L.575 B.A., J.D. [Howard,S.F.&H.]
Davis, Brian F., (AV) ....'65 '91 C.575 B.A. L.896 J.D. [Davis&M.]
Davis, Dana H., (AV) ....'65 '90 C.575 B.A. L.896 J.D. [Young M.&H.]
Davis, Donald A. ....'44 '70 C.576 B.A. L.575 J.D. 5400 Atlantic Springs Rd.
Davis, E. Lawrence, III, (AV) .... '37 '63 C.674 A.B. L.228 LL.B. [Ⓒ Womble C.S.&R.]
Davis, Egbert L., III .... '37 '63 C.674 A.B. L.228 LL.B. Drawer 831
Davis, Frederick M. ....'67 '96 C&L.665 B.S., J.D. Univ. Student Legal. Svcs.
Davis, Hugh W., II, (AV) .... '62 '88 C.228 B.A. L.893 J.D. [Poyner&S.]
Davis, J. Benjamin, (BV) .... '71 '98 C.896 B.A. L.976 J.D. [Brooks,P.M.H.&L.] ⊙
Davis, Jaime Humphries .... '76 '01 C&L.575 B.A., J.D. [Ⓐ Gailor,W.&H.]
Davis, John M., (BV) ...... '44 '72 C&L.575 B.S., J.D. 5901 Falls of Neuse Rd., Ste. 200

Davis, Joyce L., & Associates, (AV) '48 '74 C&L.575 B.S., J.D.
Two Hannover Square Suite 1730, P.O. Box 709, 27602
Telephone: 919-834-6534 Facsimile: 919-834-6536
Email: jldAssoc@jldavis.com URL: http://www.jldavis.com
Associates: Everette P. Winslow; C. Andrew McGuffin. Of Counsel: Laura J. Wetsch.
Employment Law, Civil Litigation, Cooperative Law, Non-Profit Law, and Business Law, including Board of Directors Legal Liability.

See Professional Biographies, RALEIGH, NORTH CAROLINA

Davis, Leslie Hollowell .... '56 '82 C&L.575 B.A., J.D. State Ct. of App.
Davis, Mark A., (AV) .... '66 '91 C&L.575 B.A., J.D. [Womble C.S.&R.]
Davis, Matthew B. .... '78 '04 C&L.575 B.A., J.D. [Ⓐ Young M.&H.]
Davis, Melissa Robin ....'65 '91 C.421 B.A. L.276 J.D. [Cranfill,S.&H.]
Davis, Paul E. .... '— '84 C&L.1128 B.A., J.D. [Conner G.S.]
Davis, Thomas H., Jr., (AV) .... '51 '76 C.576 B.A. L.896 J.D. [Poyner&S.]
Davis, Tonya D. .... '— '01 C&L.575 B.A., J.D. [Ⓐ Hedrick E.G.&K.]
Davis, William A., II, (AV) .... '42 '67 C.575 A.B. L.228 LL.B. [Womble C.S.&R.]

Davis, Adrian J., Attorney at Law
234 Fayetteville Street Mall Suite 200, 27601
Telephone: 919-755-2274 Fax: 919-755-2274
Email: adavis.cclg@notrials.com URL: http://www.wakefamilylawfirm.com
Adrian Jaye Davis.
Family Law, Divorce, Child Custody, Child Support, Collaborative Law.

See Professional Biographies, RALEIGH, NORTH CAROLINA

Davis & McCabe, P.A., (AV)
1115 Hillsborough Street, 27603
Telephone: 919-833-3370 Fax: 919-833-3371
URL: http://www.davismccabe.com
Brian F. Davis; John Matthew McCabe.
Personal Injury, Automobile Accidents and Injuries, Trucking Accidents, Medical Malpractice, Products Liability, Workers Compensation.

See Professional Biographies, RALEIGH, NORTH CAROLINA

Dawson, Amos C., III, (AV) ....'48 '75 C&L.575 B.A., J.D. [Maupin T.]
Day, James M., (AV) ....'50 '75 C.679 B.S.A.E. L.896 J.D. [Burns,D.&P.]
Day, Kenneth C., (AV) ....'47 '73 C&L.575 A.B., J.D. [Allen&P.]
Dean, Christine Witcover, (AV) .... '47 '71 C.822 A.B. L.228 J.D. Asst. U.S. Atty.
Dean, Joseph W. .... '44 '69 C.152 B.A. L.896 J.D. Secy., Crime Control & Pub. Safety
Deans, Marcia M. '58 '85 C.312 B.A. L.502 J.D.
(adm. in CA; not adm. in NC) 5109 Castlebrook Dr.‡
Debnam, Tracy T. .... '69 '97 C.802 B.A. L.616 J.D. [Ⓒ Smith D.N.W.S.&M.]
Debnam, W. Thurston, Jr., (AV) .... '47 '72 C&L.896 B.A., J.D. [Smith D.N.W.S.&M.]
Deerson, Bruce A. '51 '75 C.367 B.A. L.273 J.D.
(adm. in VA; not adm. in NC) General Counsel, Martin Marietta Materials, Inc.
DeFrank, Michael D. ....'74 '00 C.896 B.A. L.245 J.D. [Ⓐ Wyrick R.Y.&P.]
Deiter-Maradei, Kathryn ....'78 '04 C.645 B.A. L.577 J.D. [Ⓐ Teague,C.D.&G.]
Delafield, Michael R. ....'70 '99 C.674 B.A. L.1294 J.D. [Ⓐ Schwartz&S.]
DelForge, Clarence Joe, III, (AV) ....'59 '85 C.198 A.B. L.575 J.D. Asst. Atty. Gen.
Dellinger, Hampton Y., (AV) ....'67 '93 C.477 B.A. L.976 J.D. [Womble C.S.&R.]
DeLuca, John B. ....'56 '81 C.228 B.A. L.813 J.D. State Employ. Sec. Comm.

DeMent, Angela L., (BV) ... '63 '88 C&L.896 B.A., J.D. [DeMent,A.G.&D.]
DeMent, Russell W., III ... '71 '97 C&L.896 B.A., J.D. [DeMent,A.G.&D.]
DeMent, Russell W., Jr., (AV) ... '40 '65 C&L.896 B.A., LL.B. [DeMent,A.G.&D.]

DeMent, Askew, Gammon & DeMent, (AV)
Suite 1513 Branch Bank Building, 333 Fayetteville Street Mall, P.O. Box 711, 27602
Telephone: 919-833-5555 Fax: 919-832-8287
Email: lawdagdo@aol.com
Members of Firm: Russell W. DeMent, Jr.; Garland L. Askew; Richard T. Gammon; Angela L. DeMent; Russell W. DeMent, III; Berryman J. Fitzhugh, III.
Criminal and General Civil Practice in State and Federal Courts and before State Departments and Commissions. Corporation, Real Estate Law, Trusts and Estates.
See Professional Biographies, RALEIGH, NORTH CAROLINA

Demidovich, Brian ... '68 '04 C.980 B.S. L.989 J.D. [Russell,P.&D.]
Dempster, Joseph B., Jr., (AV) ... '65 '90 C.575 B.A. L.896 J.D. [Poyner&S.]
Dennis, George W., III, (AV) ... '50 '75 C.401 B.A. L.228 J.D. [Teague,C.D.&G.]
Dennis, Walter M. ... '51 '82 C.575 B.A. L.838 J.D. 6904-22 River Run
de Rosset, Robert C. ... '69 '96 C.575 B.A. L.790 J.D. [Ⓐ Young M.&H.]
Derrenbacher, Christopher J. ... '72 '98 C.232 B.A. L.1345 J.D. [Patterson,D.C.B.&A.]
Devay, Daniel Alan ... '51 '85 C.30 B.A. L.896 J.D. P.O. Box 19841
Dever, James C., III ... '62 '87 C.602 B.B.A. L.228 J.D. Dist. J.
Dew, Theresa S. ... '75 '00 C.1228 B.A. L.575 J.D. [Ⓐ Stuart]
Dewar, Debra L. ... '— '95 C&L.575 B.S., J.D. [Ⓒ Ogletree,D.N.S.&S.]
Diab, F. Joseph, (BV) ... '65 '93 C.31 B.A. L.228 J.D. [Ⓒ Sanford H.]
Diehl, Charles Frederick ... '63 '92 C.240 B.A. L.896 J.D. P.O. Box 27766
DiLeone, Ralph J., (AVⓉ) ... '55 '84 C.930 B.S. L.851 J.D. [DiLeone&Assoc.]
DiLeone & Associates, P.C., (AVⓉ) ... 900 Ridgefield Drive, Suite 350
Dill, James David ... '76 '02 C.790 B.S. L.446 J.D. [Ⓐ Smith D.N.W.S.&M.]
Dillon, Robert C. ... '65 '90 C&L.575 B.S., J.D. P.O. Box 20255
Dilthey, Ronald C., (AV) ... '35 '60 C&L.896 B.S., LL.B. [Patterson,D.C.B.&A.]
Dimmock, Thomas J., (AV) ... '49 '75 C.576 B.S. L.575 J.D. [Dimmock&D.]
Dimmock & Dodd, (AV) ... 4700 Six Forks Road, Suite 150
Diosegy, Arlene J., (AV) '49 '74
C.25 B.A. L.831 J.D. [Maupin T.] (⊙Research Triangle Park)
Di Pasquantonio, Francis J. ... '42 '71 C.205 B.A. L.575 J.D. N.C. Dept. of Ins.
Dipierro, Joseph V., (CV) ... '48 '90 L.575 J.D. 5 W. Hargett Street, Suite 407
Dixon, Amanda R., Law Office of '70 '96 C.329 B.A. L.575 J.D.
2949 New Bern Avenue
Dixon, Daniel R. ... '11 '41 C.945 A.B. L.228 LL.B. 7 N. Bloodworth St.‡
Dixon, Julia Ellen ... '69 '01 C.471 B.A. L.575 J.D. [Ⓐ Martin&J.]
Dixon, Lisa J., (AV) ... '— '87 C.576 B.A. L.575 J.D. [Kilpatrick S.]
Dixon, Wright T., Jr., (AV) ... '21 '51 C.228 A.B. L.896 J.D. 434 Fayetteville Street Mall‡

DLA Piper Rudnick Gray Cary US LLP, (AV)
Six Forks Center I, 4700 Six Forks Road, Suite 200, 27609 ⊙
Telephone: 919-786-2000 FAX: 919-786-2200
Email: info@dlapiper.com URL: http://www.dlapiper.com
Partners: Robert H. Bergdolt; William R. Klapp, Jr.; Brad S. Markoff; Jeffrey D. Miller; Jeffrey M. Sullivan. Of Counsel: Christine C. Lehr; Bradford R. Lenox. Associates: Kerry E. Camden; Carrie Joan Hartley; Damon M. McLean; Michael S. O'Sullivan.
Advertising, Promotion and Trade Practices; Aerospace and Defense; Antitrust and Trade Regulation; Aviation; Bankruptcy and Business Reorganization; Biosciences; Business and Technology; Class Action Litigation; Communications; Construction; Copyrights; Corporate Governance and Protective Practices; Corporate and Securities; Domain Name Practice; Drug and Medical Device; Electronic Commerce and Privacy; Employee Benefits and Executive Compensation; Energy; Environmental; Federal Affairs and Legislative; Finance; Finance, Financial Services and Bankruptcy; Franchise and Distribution; Franchise and Distribution-International; Franchise and Distribution-Litigation; Franchise and Distribution-Technology; Government Contracts; Government Controversies; Governmental Affairs, Land Use and Development; HIPAA Privacy and Security; Health Care; Homeland Security; Information Technology; Insurance and Reinsurance; Insurance and Surety Litigation; Intellectual Property; International Commerce and Litigation; Iraq Reconstruction; Labor and Employment Law; Leasing; Legislative Financial Services; Litigation; Lodging and Timeshare; Medical Malpractice Defense; Mergers and Acquisitions; Multifamily Housing and Community Development Law; Nonprofit Organizations; Outsourcing; Patent Litigation; Patent Prosecution; Pesticide; Private Client Services; Product Liability and Toxic Torts; Professional Liability; Project Finance; Public Finance; REITs and Real Estate Securitization; Real Estate; Real Estate Finance; Securities Litigation; Sports Facilities Development; State Legislation and Public Policy; Tax; Tax Policy and Legislation; Technology Transfer; Trademark Litigation; Trademarks; Transportation; Venture Capital and Emerging Companies; White Collar; Workout Experience.
Annapolis, Maryland Office: 60 West Street, Suite 401, 21401-2434. Telephone: 443-482-3830. FAX: 443-482-3848.
Baltimore, Maryland Office (Downtown): 111 South Calvert Street, Suite 1950, 21202-6174. Telephone: 410-580-3000. FAX: 410-580-3665.
Baltimore, Maryland Office (Mt. Washington): 6225 Smith Avenue, 21209-3600. Telephone: 410-580-3000. FAX: 410-580-3001.
Boston, Massachusetts Office: One International Place, 21st Floor, 02110-2613. Telephone: 617-406-6000. FAX: 617-406-6100.
Chicago, Illinois Office: 203 North La Salle Street, Suite 1900, 60601-1293. Telephone: 312-368-4000. FAX: 312-236-7516.
Dallas, Texas Office: 1717 Main Street, Suite 4600, 75201-4605. Telephone: 214-743-4500. FAX: 214-743-4545.
Easton, Maryland Office: 117 Bay Street, 21601-2703. Telephone: 410-820-4460. FAX: 410-820- 4463.
Edison, New Jersey Office: Piper Rudnick LLP, A New Jersey Limited Liability Partnership, Robert A. Assuncao, Managing Partner, 379 Thornall Street, Eighth Floor, 08837-2226. Telephone: 732-590-1850. FAX: 732-590-1860.
La Jolla, California Office: 1200 Prospect Street, Suite 575, 92037. Telephone: 858-638-6806. Fax: 858-456-3075.
Las Vegas, Nevada Office: Hughes Center, 3960 Howard Hughes Parkway, Suite 400, 89109. Telephone: 702-737-3433. FAX: 702-737-1612.
Los Angeles, California Office (Century City): 1999 Avenue of the Stars, Fourth Floor, 90067-6022. Telephone: 310-595-3000. FAX: 310-595-3300.
Los Angeles, California Office (Downtown): 550 South Hope Street, Suite 2300, 90071-2631. Telephone: 213-330-7700. FAX: 213-330-7701.
New York, New York Office: 1251 Avenue of the Americas, 10020-1104. Telephone: 212-835-6000. FAX: 212-835-6001.
Paris, France Office: Cariddi, Mee, Rue, Association d'Avocats au Barreau de Paris, Correspondants de Piper Rudnick LLP, 12 rue de la Paix, 75002 Paris, France. Telephone: +33-1 42.61.57.71. FAX: +33-1 42.61.79.21.
Philadelphia, Pennsylvania Office: One Liberty Place, 1650 Market Street, Suite 4900, 19103. Telephone: 215-656-3300. FAX: 215-656-3301.
Reston, Virginia Office: 1775 Wiehle Avenue, Suite 400, 20190-5159. Telephone: 703-773-4000. FAX: 703-773-5000.
San Francisco, California Office: 333 Market Street, Suite 3200, 94105-2150. Telephone: 415-659-7000. FAX: 415-659-7300.
Tampa, Florida Office: 101 East Kennedy Boulevard, Suite 2000, 33602-5149. Telephone: 813-229-2111. FAX: 813-229-1447.
Washington, District of Columbia Office: 1200 Nineteenth Street, NW, Main Reception on 7th Floor, 20036-2412. Telephone: 202-861-3900. FAX: 202-223-2085.
See Professional Biographies, RALEIGH, NORTH CAROLINA

Dodd, Everett E., Jr., (BV) ... '48 '74 C&L.575 A.B., J.D. P.O. Box 21012
Dodd, L. Michael, (AV) ... '50 '77 C.576 B.A. L.896 J.D. [Dimmock&D.]
Doherty, Pearl B. ... '55 '81 C.367 B.A. L.107 J.D. [Ⓐ Poyner&S.]
Dolan, Stephen R., (AV) ... '49 '74 C.385 A.B. L.309 J.D. [Ⓐ Jordan P.W.G.J.&C.]
Dollar, Lorrie L. ... '— '84 C.575 B.A. L.574 J.D. Dep. Comm.
Dombalis, Nicholas J., II, (AV) ... '50 '75 C.301 B.A. L.896 J.D. [Nicholls&C.]
Dominick, L. Allison ... '70 '96 C.575 B.A. L.494 J.D. 6636 Portsmouth Ln.‡
Donadio, Donald A., (AV) ... '43 '67 C&L.896 B.A., J.D. [Womble C.S.&R.]
Donahue, Melissa Dix ... '74 '01 C&L.383 B.A., J.D. [Ⓑ Womble C.S.&R.]
Donaldson, Alexander M., (AV) ... '53 '84 C.575 B.A. L.945 J.D. [Wyrick R.Y.&P.]
Dorsett, James K., III, (AV) ... '51 '77 C.198 B.A. L.896 J.D. [Smith,A.B.D.M.&J.]
Dorsett, Stuart B., (AV) ... '— '85 C.198 A.B. L.575 J.D. [Ward&S.] (⊙New Bern)
Dorsey, John C., (AV) ... '46 '72 C.967 B.A. L.273 J.D. [Manning,F.&S.]
Dorton, David R., (AV) ... '53 '79 C.896 B.A. L.575 J.D. [Maupin T.]
Douglass, Thomas G., (BV) ... '56 '83 C.301 B.A. L.1228 J.D. [Douglass&D.]

Douglass & Douglass, (BV)
Two Hannover Square, Suite 2050, P.O. Box 362, 27602-0362
Telephone: 919-832-1620 FAX: 919-833-8182
Email: douglassatty@earthlink.com URL: http://www.lawyers.com/douglass&douglass
Clyde A. Douglass (1889-1973); Clyde A. Douglass, II (1923-1994); Thomas G. Douglass.
General Civil Litigation, Personal Injury, Automobile Accidents and Injuries, Traffic Violations, Wills, Trusts and Estates, Estate Administration, Real Estate.
Approved Attorneys: First Title Insurance Co.; Lawyers Title Insurance Corp.
References: First Citizens Bank & Trust Co.; NationsBank; Centura Bank; Branch Banking & Trust Co.; Raleigh Federal Savings & Loan Assn.
See Professional Biographies, RALEIGH, NORTH CAROLINA

Dow, Sharon K. ... '73 '97 C.999 B.A. L.1345 J.D. [Ⓐ Hardison&L.]
Downing, Kathrine E. ... '68 '01 C.608 B.S.L.A. L.1228 J.D. [Ⓐ Patterson,D.C.B.&A.]
Doyle, Jeffrey A., (BV) ... '— '93 C&L.575 B.A., J.D. [Hedrick E.G.&K.]
Drake, Franklin, (AVⓉ) ... '53 '78 C&L.575 B.A., J.D. [Smith D.N.W.S.&M.]
Dreifus, David, (AV) ... '52 '82 C.860 B.A. L.228 J.D. [Poyner&S.]
Drennan, James C. ... '49 '74 C.269 B.A. L.228 J.D. Admin. Off. of the Cts.
Driggers, Stephen G. ... '50 '93 C.846 B.A. L.813 J.D. [Ⓐ Smith,A.B.D.M.&J.]
Drooz, David T., (BV) '57 '82 C.311 B.A. L.575 J.D.
Asst. Univ. Coun., North Carolina State Univ.
Dubis, Melanie Black ... '70 '95 C.575 B.A. L.880 J.D. [Parker,P.A.&B.]
Dubois, George A. ... '62 '87 C.228 A.B. L.893 J.D. Fed. Pub. Def.
DuBree, Sonya Elizabeth ... '69 '94 C.577 B.S. L.1228 J.D. 2 Hannover Sq., Ste. 2404
Dudley, William A. '50 '79 C.1378 B.S. L.574 J.D.
Dep. Secy., NC Dept of Crime Control & Pub Safety
Dudzik, Carolyn M. ... '58 '86 C.347 B.A. L.575 J.D. [Wyrick R.Y.&P.]
Duffley, Kimberly Weaver, (BV) ... '68 '94 C.575 B.A. L.469 J.D. State Atty. Gen. Off.
Duffley, Peter J., (BV) ... '67 '94 C.679 B.S. L.896 J.D. [Ⓒ Womble C.S.&R.]
Duggins, Robert E. ... '65 '90 C.576 B.S. L.575 J.D. [Smith,A.B.D.M.&J.]
Duke, David M., (AV) ... '58 '84 C.945 B.A. L.896 J.D. [Young M.&H.]
Dula, Rosa D., (CV) ... '61 '97 C.575 B.S., B.A. L.574 J.D. Dist. Atty. Off.
Dunathan, Susan L. ... '59 '01 C.1365 B.A. L.574 J.D. [Ⓐ Parker,P.A.&B.]
Dunbar, Henry O., Jr. ... '59 '92 C&L.1228 B.S., J.D. 3605 Glenwood Ave.
Duncan, Allyson Kay ... '— '75 C.302 B.S. L.228 J.D. U.S. Ct. App. J.
Duncan, J. Michael ... '50 '92 C.232 B.S. L.574 J.D. P.O. Box 6548
Dunn, H. Glenn, (AV) ... '44 '77 C.260 B.D. L.575 J.D. [Poyner&S.]
Dunn, Raymond E., Jr., (AV) ... '51 '79 C.575 B.A. L.896 J.D. [Emanuel&D.] ⊙
Dunn, Stephen A., (BV) ... '56 '84 C.576 B.A. L.192 J.D. [Emanuel&D.]
Dutton, Janet B., (CV) '63 '88 C.1317 B.S. L.575 J.D.
Assoc. Legal Coun., N.C. Real Estate Comm.
Dyson, Michael Ryan, (BV) ... '50 '75 C.575 B.A. L.802 J.D. [R.Dyson]
Dyson, Ryan, PLLC, (BV) ... 8520 Six Forks Road, Suite 101
Eads, Wayne B., (BV) ... '50 '75 C.232 B.A. L.575 J.D. [W.B.Eads]

Eads, Wayne Buchanan, (BV)
715 West Johnson Street, 27603
Mailing Address: P.O. Box 25789, Raleigh, NC 27611-25789
Telephone: 919-833-3703 Fax: 919-833-0337
Email: waynebuchananeads@yahoo.com
Member of Firm: Wayne B. Eads.
Criminal Defense in State and Federal Courts. All Major Crimes, White Collar Crimes, Drug Offenses, Firearms Offenses, Trials and Appeals.
See Professional Biographies, RALEIGH, NORTH CAROLINA

Eagles, Margaret P. ... '73 '00 C.896 B.A. L.1228 J.D. [Ⓐ Larcade,H.&A.P.]
Eagles, Sidney S., Jr. ... '39 '64 C&L.896 B.A., J.D. [Ⓒ Smith M.]
Earwood, John T. ... '69 '97 C&L.896 B.A., J.D. [Ⓐ Hunton&W.]
Eason, Joseph W., (AV) ... '53 '77 C&L.575 B.A., J.D. [Nelson M.R.&S.]
Eason, Shelley T. ... '49 '78 C&L.575 B.A., J.D. Dep. Co. Atty., Co. Atty. Off.
Eatman, Jerome R., Jr., (AV) ... '56 '82 C&L.575 A.B., J.D. [Lynch&E.]
Eatmon, Christine S. ... '68 '05 C&L.1228 B.A., J.D. [Ⓐ Wyrick R.Y.&P.]
Edgerton, Laura A., (BV) ... '68 '93 C.576 B.A. L.280 J.D. [Maupin T.]
Edlin, Brian S. ... '74 '00 C.925 B.S. L.884 J.D. [Ⓐ Jordan P.W.G.J.&C.]
Edmisten, Rufus L. ... '41 '67 C.575 B.A. L.273 J.D. [Edmisten&W.]

Edmisten & Webb Law Firm, The, (AV)
133 Fayetteville Street Mall, Suite 300, P.O. Box 1509, 27602
Telephone: 919-831-8700 Fax: 919-831-8749 Email: rufus@rufusedmisten.com
Email: woodywebb@ew-law.com URL: http://www.edmisten-webblaw.com
Rufus L. Edmisten; William Woodward Webb; William Woodward Webb, Jr. Associates: Gardner Marshall Payne; Virginia Dockery Webb.
Civil and Criminal Litigation, Business and Corporate Law, Government Relations and Legislative Law, Administrative Law, Sports Law, Real Estate.
Other Raleigh Office: 132 South Salisbury Street, Suite 300. 27601. Telephone: 919-829-1988. Fax: 919-829-1983.
See Professional Biographies, RALEIGH, NORTH CAROLINA

Edmondson, Lucy E. ... '63 '89 C.198 B.A. L.896 J.D. State Util. Comm.
Edmonson, A. Root, (AV) ... '47 '76 C.575 A.B. L.574 J.D. Dep. Coun., N.C. State Bar
Edmunds, Robert H., Jr. ... '49 '75 C.881 A.B. L.575 J.D. Supm Ct. J.
Edwards, Charles A., (AV) ... '45 '70 C.198 A.B. L.575 J.D. [Womble C.S.&R.]
Edwards, Debby B., (BV) ... '60 '90 C.232 B.S. L.1345 J.D. 617 W. Jones St.
Edwards, J. Kenneth, (BV) ... '65 '90 C&L.575 B.A., J.D. [Gwynn&E.]
Edwards, Jeffrey R. '62 '94 C.1128 B.A. L.1228 J.D.
Atty. Gen. Off., Crime Contl. & Motor Vehicle Sec.
Edwards, Kathleen S. '58 '83 C.1111 B.A. L.309 J.D.
(adm. in FL; not adm. in NC) Liberty Mutual Group
Edwards, Marlet Massey ... '75 '02 C.576 B.A. L.1228 J.D. [Ⓐ Brannon S.]
Edwards, Theodore C., II, (AV) ... '— '94 C&L.228 A.B., J.D. [Kilpatrick S.]

Edwards & Edwards, L.L.P.
(See Greenville)

Efird, David B. ... '78 '04 C&L.575 B.S.B.A., J.D. [Ⓐ Manning,F.&S.]
Eglinton, Donalt J., (AV) '— '82
C.136 M.A. L.896 J.D. [Ward&S.] (⊙Greenville, New Bern)
Eheman, Kenneth E., Jr. ... '65 '95 C.575 B.S.B.A. L.659 J.D. [Wyrick R.Y.&P.]
Eichler, John W. ... '68 '96 C.918 B.A. L.823 J.D. Assoc., PricewaterhouseCoopers LLP
Eiden, Thomas W. ... '51 '75 C.228 B.A. L.575 J.D. E.D.S. Fed. Corp.
Elkins, Augustus B., II ... '53 '78 C.575 A.B. L.896 J.D. Admin. Law J.★
Ellen, Phillip A. ... '70 '97 C.240 B.A. L.1345 J.D. Gen. Couns., N.C. Retail Mchts. Assn.
Ellinger, Jeffrey R., (BV) ... '54 '86 C.645 B.A. L.574 J.D. [Jordan P.W.G.J.&C.]

Ellinger, Susan Y., (AV) .... '53 '92 C.790 B.A. L.574 J.D. [Nelson M.R.&S.]
Elliott, Jessica L. '75 '00
C.473 B.A. L.201 J.D. Assoc. Coun., The Jack Parker Corporation
Elliott, Joshua T. .... '73 '99 C.575 B.S. L.201 J.D. [🄰 Hutchison&M.] (Pat.)
Ellis, A. Charles, (AV) '— '83
C.575 A.B. L.1228 J.D. [Ward&S.] (⊙Greenville, New Bern)
Ellis, L. Neal, Jr., (AV) .... '48 '75 C.870 B.S. L.893 J.D. [Hunton&W.]
Ellis, Richard W., (AV) .... '42 '69 C&L.575 A.B., J.D. [Ellis&W.] (⊙Cary)
Ellis, Thomas F., (AV) .... '20 '47 C.575 B.S. L.893 LL.B. [🄲 Ogletree,D.N.S.&S.]

Ellis & Winters LLP, (AV)
P.O. Box 33550, 27636 ⊙
Telephone: 919-865-7000 Fax: 919-865-7010
URL: http://www.elliswinters.com
Richard W. Ellis; Michael G. Winters; Jonathan D. Sasser; Leslie C. O'Toole; Charles N. Anderson, Jr.; Paul K. Sun, Jr.; Matthew W. Sawchak; Alex J. Hagan; Julia F. Youngman; Thomas D. Blue, Jr.; Curtis J. Shipley. Associates: Suzanne Collins Lagerholm; Wendy I. Sexton; George F. Sanderson, III; Danielle Eng Rose; Thomas H. Segars; Brian C. Vick; Stephen C. Keadey; John A. Chilson. Of Counsel: Donna K. Blumberg.
Trial and Appellate Practice in all State and Federal Courts. Commercial Litigation, Administrative Litigation, Medical Malpractice, Products Liability, Antitrust, Corporate, Real Estate and Finance.
Cary, North Carolina Office: 1100 Crescent Green, Suite 200, 27511-8105. Telephone: 919-865-7000. Facsimile: 919-865-7010.
Greensboro, North Carolina Office: 100 N. Greene Street, Suite 102, 27401. Telephone: 336-217-4193. Facsimile: 336-217-4198.
See Professional Biographies, RALEIGH, NORTH CAROLINA

Elmore, Richard A. .... '50 '82 C.296 B.S. L.574 J.D. NC Ct. of App.

Elmore & Wall, P.A.
3737 Glenwood Avenue, Suite 100, 27612 ⊙
Mailing Address: P.O. Box 10937, Raleigh, NC 27605
Telephone: 919-865-9500 Fax: 919-865-9501
Email: keith.coltrain@elmorewall.com URL: http://www.elmorewall.com
Keith E. Coltrain.
Construction, Surety, Complex Litigation, Medical Malpractice, Products Liability, Toxic Torts, Class Actions, Insurance Defense, Arbitration, Mediation.
Charleston, South Carolina Office: 145 King Street, Suite 302. 29401. Telephone: 843-329-9500. Fax: 843-329-9501.
Greenville, South Carolina Office: 301 North Main Street, Suite 2000, 29601. Telephone: 864-255-9500. Fax: 864-255-9505.
See Professional Biographies, RALEIGH, NORTH CAROLINA

Elvers, John D., (AV) .... '63 '89 C&L.575 A.B., J.D. [Lewis&R.]
Emanuel, Robert L., (AV) .... '26 '51 C&L.575 A.B., LL.B. [Emanuel&D.]

Emanuel & Dunn, PLLC, (AV)
130 South Salisbury Street, 27602 ⊙
Telephone: 919-832-0329; 919-832-0320 Fax: 919-832-6731
Members of Firm: Robert L. Emanuel; Stephen A. Dunn (Resident, Raleigh Office); Raymond E. Dunn, Jr.; James M. Mason.
Civil Trials in all State and Federal Courts. Business Litigation, Employment Litigation, Personal Injury Litigation, ERISA Litigation, Business Law, Contracts, Real Estate, Estate Planning and Probate, Employment Law.
Representative Clients: Metropolitan Life Insurance Co.; BellSouth Telecommunications, Inc.; Prudential Insurance Company of America; Cargill, Incorporated.
New Bern, North Carolina Office: 3230 Country Club Road, P.O. Drawer 1389, 28563. Telephone: 252-633-3800. Fax: 252-633-6669.
See Professional Biographies, RALEIGH, NORTH CAROLINA

Empson, Nicholas C.R. .... '57 '84 C.99 B.A. L.228 J.D. 4401 Creedmoor Rd.
Enloe, Caren Davis, (BV) .... '64 '90 C.34 B.A. L.1345 J.D. [Smith D.N.W.S.&M.]
Ennis, Suzanne, (AVⓉ) '61 '88 C.260 B.A. L.362 J.D.
(adm. in FL; not adm. in NC) Assoc. Gen. Coun., Florida Power Corp.
Epstein, Steven B., (AV) .... '65 '90 C&L.575 B.A., J.D. [🄲 Hunton&W.]
Ergenzinger, Edward R., Jr. '72 '02 C&L.896 B.A., J.D.
[🄰 Alston&B.] (See Pat. Sect.)
Erwin, John R. .... '57 '83 C.198 B.A. L.575 J.D. [Parker,P.A.&B.]
Esposito, Donald R., Jr. .... '69 '95 C.575 B.A. L.309 J.D. [🄲 Womble C.S.&R.]
Esposito, Rachel K. .... '71 '00 C.240 B.A. L.575 J.D. [Cranfill,S.&H.]
Estridge, Ann Smith, (BV) .... '69 '96 C.576 B.A. L.575 J.D. [Cranfill,S.&H.]
Etheridge, Tawanda .... '74 '99 C.1378 B.S. L.575 J.D. Research & Policy Assoc.
Evans, Christine A. .... '66 '96 C.207 B.A. L.575 J.D. NC General Assembly
Evans, H. Lee, Jr., (AV) .... '59 '84 C&L.575 B.S., J.D. [Cranfill,S.&H.]
Evans-Stanton, Sherri L. '56 '88 C.846 B.S. L.770 J.D.
Staff Atty. to N. C. Gen. Assembly
Everett, Robinson O. .... '28 '50 C&L.309 A.B., J.D. [🄲 Everett,G.H.&S.] (⊙Durham)

Everett, Gaskins, Hancock & Stevens, LLP, (AV)
The Professional Building, Suite 600, 127 West Hargett Street, P.O. Box 911, 27602-0911
Telephone: 919-755-0025 Fax: 919-755-0009
URL: http://www.eghs.com
Partners: R.O. Everett (1878-1971); Kathrine R. Everett (1893-1992); Hugh Cannon (1931-2005); Ed Gaskins, Jr.; William Gerry Hancock, Jr.; Hugh Stevens; Paul C. Ridgeway; C. Amanda Martin; Louis E. Wooten, III; William P. Janvier (Board Certified Specialist in Business and Consumer Bankruptcy Law, North Carolina State Board of Legal Specialization); K. Matthew Vaughn; Michael J. Tadych. Associate: Ashley Matlock. Of Counsel: Robinson O. Everett.
Administrative Law, Appellate Practice, Bankruptcy, Business Law, Biotechnology, Commercial Law, Commercial Litigation, Communications and Media Law, Construction Law, Corporate Law, Debtor and Creditor Law, Education Law, First Amendment Law, Franchise Law, Intellectual Property, Insurance Law, International Trade Law, Internet Law, Litigation, Lobbying, Non-Profit Corporations and Charitable Organizations, Parliamentary Law, Tax and Estate Planning, Tax Controversies, Taxation, Toxic Torts, Trade Association Law.
See Professional Biographies, RALEIGH, NORTH CAROLINA

Eveson, Erin Dancy .... '— '00 C.125 B.A. L.575 J.D. [🄰 Hedrick E.G.&K.]
Eveson, Todd H. .... '76 '00 C.228 A.B. L.575 J.D. 8305 Falls of Neuse Rd., Ste. 203
Ewalt, Gretchen W., (AV) .... '62 '88 C.1090 B.A. L.893 J.D. [Ogletree,D.N.S.&S.]
Eyster, Kathryn M. .... '74 '03 C.228 B.S. L.896 J.D. [🄰 Womble C.S.&R.]
Faires, Sabra J. .... '55 '80 C.198 A.B. L.575 J.D. N.C. Gen. Assembly
Fanney, John K., (BV) .... '65 '91 C.575 B.A. L.1228 J.D. [Bass,B.&F.]
Farag, Angela N. .... '78 '04 C&L.575 B.A., J.D. [🄰 Young M.&H.]
Farah, N. Victor, (AV) .... '54 '81 C.477 B.A. L.912 J.D. [Jernigan]
Farmer, Robert L. .... '33 '60 C&L.575 B.S., LL.B. Sr. Resident Supr. Ct. J.
Farr, Thomas A., (AV) .... '54 '79 C.317 B.L.S. L.1365 J.D. [Ogletree,D.N.S.&S.]
Farrell, Richard W., (AV) .... '46 '72 C.588 B.A. L.262 J.D. [Farrell&L.]
Farrell, William N., Jr., (AV) '48 '73
C&L.575 A.B., J.D. Sr. Dep. Atty. Gen., State Dept. of Jus.
Farrell & La Mantia, (AV) .... 4900 Falls of Neuse Road, Suite 212
Faucette, Douglas L. .... '70 '95 C&L.575 B.S., J.D. Wake Co. Dist. Atty. Off.
Faucette, Matthew .... '72 '02 C.575 B.A. L.1228 J.D. [Faucette]
Faucette Law Firm, PLLC .... 8601 Six Forks Rd., Suite 400

Faust, Richard S., (AV) '49 '74
C.576 B.S.M.E. L.575 J.D. 8384 Six Forks Road, Suite 204 (Pat.)
Feitshans, Theodore A. '56 '86 C.188 B.S. L.276 J.D.
Lecturer, Extension Specialist, N.C. State University
Fellers, Carlton E., (BV) .... '37 '70 C&L.574 B.S.C., J.D. [Thigpen,B.S.&F.]

Ferguson, Stein, Chambers, Gresham & Sumter, P.A.
(See Charlotte)

Fernandez, John P., (CV) .... '63 '93 C.574 B.A. L.575 J.D. [Broughton&F.]
Ferrell, David P. '71 '96 C.575 B.A. L.1228 J.D.
[🄰 Vandeventer B.] (⊙Kitty Hawk, NC; Norfolk, VA)
Ferrell, June S. .... '56 '85 C.576 B.A. L.1345 J.D. Dept. of Jus.
Ferrell, Michael R., (AV) '48 '76 C.1130 B.A. L.575 J.D.
Co. Atty., Wake Co. Atty. Off.
Ferreri, Eugene A., Jr. '51 '76
C.228 A.B. L.945 J.D. V.P., First-Citizens Bank & Trust Company
Ferris, David J., Jr. .... '67 '00 C.576 B.A. L.1187 J.D. [Ferris&Assoc.]
Ferris & Associates .... 5540 Centerview Dr., Ste. 310
Few, William P., (AV) .... '43 '68 C.228 A.B. L.575 J.D. 4200 Six Forks Road Suite 120
Fields, Robert E., III, (AV) .... '58 '84 C.198 B.A. L.896 J.D. [Womble C.S.&R.]
Fife, Lance R. .... '70 '99 C.877 B.S. L.615 J.D. [🄰 Clifton&S.]
File, Gilbert W., IV, (BV) .... '71 '99 C.152 L.1228 J.D. [🄰 Vann&S.]
Finarelli, Joseph .... '73 '99 C.228 B.A. L.896 J.D. Asst. Atty. Gen.
Finch, Daniel B. .... '75 '01 C.576 B.A. L.1228 J.D. [🄰 Pinna J.&B.]
Finch, Jane Flowers, (AV) .... '53 '78 C.577 B.A. L.574 J.D. 1810 Craig Street
Fine, J. Andrew '71 '97 C&L.260 B.A., J.D.
(adm. in FL; not adm. in NC) [Lewis&R.]
Finkelstein, Lisa Bland, (BV) .... '63 '88 C.575 B.A. L.896 J.D. Asst. Atty. Gen.
Finkelstein, Mark A., (AV) .... '59 '85 C.293 B.A. L.575 J.D. [Herring M.M.&F.]
Finlator, W. Wallace, Jr. .... '45 '87 C.896 B.A. L.574 J.D. Asst. Atty. Gen., Dept. of Jus.
Finley, Edward S., Jr., (AV) .... '49 '74 C&L.575 A.B., J.D. [Hunton&W.]
Finn, William, (BV) .... '— '99 C.576 B.A. L.1228 J.D. [🄰 A.K.Sandman]
Fishburne, Anne M. .... '54 '83 C.577 B.A. L.575 J.D. 1305 Navaho Dr.
Fisher, Benjamin P. .... '76 '01 C.575 B.A. L.896 J.D. [🄰 Troutman S.]
Fisher, Matthew A. .... '76 '01 C.838 B.A. L.575 J.D. [🄰 Bode,C.&S.]
Fisher, Shana G. R. .... '73 '98 C&L.477 B.A., J.D. [🄰 Maupin T.]
Fitzhugh, Berryman J., III .... '72 '98 C.575 B.A. L.1345 J.D. [DeMent,A.G.&D.]
Fitzmorris, Carolyn L. .... '60 '91 C.1494 B.A. L.577 J.D. [🄰 Wyrick R.Y.&P.]

Fitzpatrick, John C., P.C., Law Office of
(See Durham)

Flammia, Dayle A., (AV) .... '53 '81 C.576 B.A. L.574 J.D. [Teague,C.D.&G.]
Flanagan, Anthony Emerson .... '63 '89 C&L.575 B.A., J.D. [Harris F.]
Flatley, Brian K. .... '66 '91 C.93 A.B. L.896 J.D. U.S. Mag.
Fleishman, Beth R., (AV) .... '50 '77 C&L.575 A.B., J.D. [Cranfill,S.&H.]
Fleming, Frederick W. .... '70 '01 C.373 B.A. L.574 J.D. P.O. Box 10629
Flexner, Richard M., (BV) .... '53 '77 C.645 B.A. L.884 J.D. [Flexner]

Flexner Law Firm, The, P.A., (BV)
300 W. Millbrook Road, Suite 101, 27609
Telephone: 919-787-1661; 1-800-FLEXNER Fax: 919-787-1771
Email: flexlaw@flexlaw.com URL: http://www.flexlaw.com
Richard M. Flexner.
Personal Injury, Products Liability, Medical Malpractice, Automobile Accidents and Injuries, Truck Accidents, Motorcycle Accidents, Workers Compensation, Social Security Disability, Wrongful Death, Civil Litigation, Insurance Litigation, Hospital Negligence, Nursing Home Negligence, Catastrophic Injury.
See Professional Biographies, RALEIGH, NORTH CAROLINA

Flick, Paul T., (AV) .... '61 '86 C&L.896 B.A., J.D. [Jordan P.W.G.J.&C.]
Flores, Juan A. .... '— '88 C.143 B.S. L.575 J.D. [🄰 Whitley,R.&W.]
Flynn, Samantha Francis '47 '74 C.665 B.A. L.229 J.D.
Assoc. Gen. Coun., Carolina Power & Light Co.
Flynn, William M., (AV) .... '49 '77 C.276 B.S.F.S. L.945 J.D. [Hunton&W.]
Fodor, Janine .... '62 '90 C.477 B.A. L.976 J.D. [🄲 Unti&L.]
Fogel, Mark E., (AV) '42 '74
C.186 B.E. L.575 J.D. 5 West Hargett Street, Suite 510 (⊙Durham)
Fogel, Sheldon L. .... '42 '65 C&L.575 A.B., J.D. 1708 Falls Church Rd.
Fogg, John M. '68 '94 C.976 B.A. L.178 J.D.
(adm. in CA; not adm. in NC) [Hutchison&M.]
Folger, Frank Wilkinson .... '65 '96 C.198 B.A. L.1345 J.D. 300 N. Salisbury St.
Folger, Lee A., III '36 '77 C.575 B.S. L.896 J.D.
V.P. & Res. Mgr., Robinson Humphrey Amer. Express
Foppiano, C. Houston, (BV) .... '69 '99 C.846 B.S. L.838 J.D. [Cranfill,S.&H.]
Forbes, Marilyn R., (AV) .... '55 '81 C.645 B.A. L.896 J.D. [Womble C.S.&R.]
Ford, Donald B., (BV) .... '45 '91 C.296 B.S. L.1228 J.D. 5720 Six Forks Road
Ford, Sarah L. .... '73 '03 C.473 B.A. L.569 J.D. [🄰 Parker,P.A.&B.]

Ford, Tonya Lynette '74 '99 C.302 B.A. L.574 J.D.
16 West Martin Street, Suite 604, 27601
Telephone: 919-829-1500 Fax: 919-829-1600
Email: tlford@tlfordlaw.com URL: http://www.tlfordlaw.com
Employment Law, Discrimination, Employee Benefits, Sexual Harassment, Wrongful Termination, Criminal Law, Driving While Intoxicated, Juvenile Crimes, Traffic Violations, Business Law, Personal Injury.
See Professional Biographies, RALEIGH, NORTH CAROLINA

Fork, Brian .... '— '05 C.198 B.A. L.575 J.D. [🄰 Kennedy C.L.&H.]
Forro, Lila T. .... '53 '95 C.695 B.A. L.574 J.D. E. Central Community Legal Servs.
Foster, Marion J., (Mr.) .... '25 '51 C.893 B.S. L.273 LL.B. 2723 Anderson Dr.‡
Fountain, David B., (AV) '67 '94 C&L.575 B.A., J.D.
Dep. Gen. Coun., Coml. Trans., Progress Energy
Fountain, John N., (AV) .... '44 '68 C.228 B.A. L.896 J.D. [Young M.&H.]
Fountain, Reed N., (BV) .... '70 '96 C.228 B.A. L.575 J.D. [Young M.&H.]
Fountain, Richard T., III, (AV) '59 '85
C.575 B.A. L.896 J.D. Suite 240, 3605 Glenwood Avenue
Fountain, Susan T. .... '72 '97 C&L.575 B.A., J.D. [🄲 Yates,M.&W.]
Fowler, Thomas L. .... '55 '80 C&L.575 B.A., J.D. Adm. Off. of the Cts.
Fox, Sarah Wesley, (AV) .... '— '83 C.861 B.A. L.896 J.D. [Kilpatrick S.]
Francis, Charles T., (AV) .... '63 '89 C.674 A.B. L.228 J.D. [Francis&A.]

Francis & Austin, PLLC, (AV)
Two Hannover Square, 434 Fayetteville Street Mall Suite 2300, P.O. Box 164, 27602-0164
Telephone: 919-828-0801 Fax: 919-828-0804
URL: http://www.lawyers.com/francis&austin
Charles T. Francis; John Scott Austin. Of Counsel: Alan D. Woodlief, Jr.; Stacie S. Watson.
Appellate Advocacy, Automobile Accidents and Personal Injuries, Business Organization, Complex Business Litigation, Federal Civil Practice, Unfair and Deceptive Trade Practices, Debtor and Creditor Collections, Commercial Litigation, Construction Litigation, Insurance Law, Public Housing,

(This Listing Continued)

Francis & Austin, PLLC (Continued)
Trial Practice, Medical Negligence, Birth Injury, Civil Litigation, Personal Injury, Wrongful Death, Public Finance, Private Finance, Toxic and Environmental Torts, Defamation and Media Torts.
See Professional Biographies, RALEIGH, NORTH CAROLINA

Frank, Terry C. '73 '03 C.890 B.A. L.692 J.D. [Ⓐ Vandeventer B.] (☉Kitty Hawk, NC; Norfolk, VA)
Frankel, Shannon S. '78 '05 C.228 B.A. L.945 J.D. [Ⓐ Young M.&H.]
Frazier, Michael Lee '52 '80 C.575 B.A. L.577 J.D. 2510 Countrywood Rd.
Freeman, Franklin E., Jr. '45 '70 C&L.575 A.B., J.D. Assoc. Jus., Supm. Ct.
Freeman, Maranda J. '60 '96 C.1128 B.S. L.896 J.D. [Cranfill,S.&H.]
Fricke, David R., (AV) '61 '86 C.882 B.A. L.896 J.D. [Hunton&W.]
Friedberg, Edwin P., (AV) '20 '48 C&L.228 B.A., J.D. [© Howard,S.F.&H.]
Friedensen, Jane T., (BV) '61 '86 C&L.575 B.A., J.D. Asst. Atty. Gen.
Friedlander, William A. '20 '51 C.966 B.A. L.276 J.D. (adm. in MD; not adm. in NC) 6016 Bramblewood Dr.‡
Friedman, Terence D. '69 '98 C.502 B.A./B.J. L.69 J.D. [Maupin T.]
Friedrich, Alfred A. '41 '94 C.569 B.E.E. L.575 J.D. 1109 Kimberley Dr.
Fritscher, Leslie Gibbs '74 '01 C.576 B.S.W. L.1228 J.D. 7901 Strickland Rd., Ste 110
From, I. Allan, (AV) '50 '75 C.273 B.B.A. L.790 J.D. [Howard,S.F.&H.]
Frost, Susan Hupman '48 '76 C.228 A.B. L.776 J.D. Staff Dir., Rules Review Comm.
Frye, Henry E. '32 '59 C.1378 B.S. L.575 J.D. [© Brooks,P.M.H.&L.] ☉
Frye, Katherine Ann '75 '01 C.575 B.A. L.1228 J.D. 7901 Strickland Rd.
Fuerst, Robert L., (AV) '48 '73 C&L.575 B.A., J.D. [Henson&F.] ☉
Fuller, V. Lori, (BV) '60 '85 C&L.575 B.A., J.D. Asst. Atty. Gen.
Fuller, W. Scott, (AV) '66 '92 C&L.575 B.A., J.D. [Cranfill,S.&H.]
Fullwood, James R. '42 '68 C&L.575 A.B., J.D. Sr. Resident Dist. Ct. J.
Fulton, Ann Scott, (AV) '50 '75 C&L.896 B.A., J.D. Gen. Coun., NC Alcoh. Beverage Control Comm.
Fulton, Charles L., (AV) '27 '50 C&L.575 A.B., J.D. [Manning,F.&S.]
Furr, James E., IV '74 '01 C.198 B.A. L.575 J.D. [Ⓐ Wyrick R.Y.&P.]
Furr, Kelly D. '73 '01 C.198 B.A. L.577 J.D. [Ⓐ Wyrick R.Y.&P.]
Fuscoe, John M. '58 '96 C.893 B.S. L.228 J.D. [Wyrick R.Y.&P.] (Pat.)
Fussa, Matthew F. '68 '93 C.529 B.A. L.644 J.D. [Ⓐ Maupin T.]
Futrell, Robert E., Jr. '69 '94 C.575 B.S. L.823 J.D. [Wyrick R.Y.&P.]
Gaeta, Anthony, Jr., (AV) '45 '70 C.918 B.A. L.945 J.D. 808 Salem Woods Dr., Ste. 201
Gailor, Carole S., (AV) '45 '77 C.30 B.A. L.904 J.D. [Gailor,W.&H.]
Gailor, Frank R., (AV) '40 '70 C.791 B.S. L.273 J.D. P.O. Box 12929‡

Gailor, Wallis & Hunt, PLLC, (AV) BR
The 1903 Building, 1101 Haynes Street, Suite 201, 27604
Telephone: 919-832-8488 Fax: 919-832-8283
URL: http://www.gailorwallis.com
Carole S. Gailor (Board Certified Specialist in Family Law, North Carolina State Board of Legal Specialization); Kimberly Ann Wallis; Cathy Cubbon Hunt;—Jaime Humphries Davis; Stephanie Thomas Jenkins; Stephanie J. Gibbs.
Equitable Distribution, Divorce Litigation, Child Custody, Child Support, Hague Convention Proceedings, Domestic Relations Appeals, Divorce Mediation, Arbitration and Adoption, Family Law.
See Professional Biographies, RALEIGH, NORTH CAROLINA

Gale, James L., (AV) '47 '74 C.1236 B.A. L.280 J.D. [Smith M.]
Gamble, Richard O., (AV) '32 '55 C&L.575 A.B., J.D. 300 S. Salisbury St.
Gamin, Fred R. '47 '73 C.659 B.A. L.597 J.D. N.C. Employ. Sec. Comm.
Gammon, Richard T. '54 '81 C&L.1228 B.S., J.D. [DeMent,A.G.&D.]
Gammon, William H., (AV) '48 '73 C.198 A.B. L.575 J.D. [Nelson M.R.&S.]
Garber, Ronald Hill, (AV) '51 '77 C&L.575 B.A., J.D. [Boxley,B.G.&H.]
Gardner, Kristopher B. '76 '02 C.575 B.A. L.574 J.D. [Ⓐ Tharrington S.]
Gardner, Robert R. '25 '50 C&L.228 A.B., LL.B. 16 W. Martin St.‡
Gardner, Terri L., (AV) '56 '81 C&L.896 B.A., J.D. [Poyner&S.]
Garlock, Barbara B., (AV) '60 '88 C&L.893 B.A., J.D. [© Wyrick R.Y.&P.]
Garner, Edward, Jr. '42 '75 C.1378 B.S. L.575 J.D. Dep. Comr., State Indus. Comm.
Garrett, Aaron D., Attorney at Law, (BV) '47 '78 C.575 A.B. L.61 J.D. 276 W. Millbrook Rd.
Garrett, David J. '70 '02 C&L.851 B.Ed., J.D. [Ⓐ Sanford H.]
Garriss, James A. '48 '73 C.575 A.B. L.178 J.D. (adm. in NY; not adm. in NC) P.O. Box 20547‡
Gaskins, Ed, Jr., (AV) '41 '66 C.896 B.A. L.228 J.D. [Everett,G.H.&S.]
Gaskins, Gregory C. '47 '78 C&L.896 B.B.A., J.D. Dept. of State Treas.
Gaskins, Johnny S., (AV) '49 '79 C.576 B.A. L.1228 J.D. 2 Hannover Square, Suite 2350
Gaston, Stephanie A. '— '03 C.269 B.A. L.1228 J.D. [Cranfill,S.&H.]
Gates, James E., (AV) '54 '81 C.874 B.A. L.276 J.D. [Maupin T.]
Gee, M. Blen, Jr., (AV) '50 '81 C&L.575 A.B., J.D. [Johnson,H.V.G.&G.]
Geer, Martha A. '58 '84 C.104 A.B. L.575 J.D. N.C. Ct. of Appeals J.
Gehrke, Edward J., II '58 '88 C&L.896 B.S., J.D. 4401 Creedmoor Rd.
Gelblum, Robert R. '50 '85 C.918 B.A. L.575 J.D. Asst. Atty. Gen., Atty. Gen. Off.
Gendy, Laura Jo '75 '01 C.575 B.A. L.896 J.D. Ct. of Appeals
Gengo, Laurie B. '58 '86 C.1372 B.A. L.107 J.D. [Anderson,J.&G.]
Genzler, Patrick A. '49 '78 C.886 B.S. L.945 J.D. [Vandeventer B.] (☉Kitty Hawk, NC; Norfolk, VA)
George, Charles '66 '94 C.477 B.A. L.472 J.D. [Patterson,D.C.B.&A.]
Gerard, Daniele '58 '90 C.367 B.A. L.178 J.D. NC Prisoner Legal Servs.
Gheen, Stephen T., (BV) '50 '84 C.925 M.A. L.574 J.D. J. & Chf. Dep. Commissioner, N.C. Industrial Comm.
Gibbons, Lemuel H., III, (AV) '52 '77 C&L.575 B.A., J.D. [Poyner&S.]
Gibbons, Susanna K., (AV) '63 '89 C&L.896 B.A., J.D. [Poyner&S.]
Gibbs, Stephanie J. '58 '03 C.1381 B.A. L.575 B.A. [Ⓐ Gailor,W.&H.]
Gilbert, James H., Jr., (AVⓉ) '35 '63 C.228 B.A. L.260 J.D. (adm. in FL; not adm. in NC) 187 Howell RD.‡
Gilbert, Seagrumn L. '79 '04 C.577 B.A. L.228 J.D. [Ⓐ Nelson M.R.&S.]
Gilchrist, Jane Ammons, (BV) '66 '91 C&L.575 B.A., J.D. Asst. Atty. Gen., NC Dept. of Jus.
Giles, Roy A., Jr., (BV) '41 '66 C&L.575 A.B., LL.B. Spec. Dep. Atty. Gen.
Gill, Teresa M. '56 '87 C.575 B.A. L.228 J.D. 2601 Oberlin Road, Suite 100
Gilly, Kennedy J., Jr., (AVⓉ) '50 '75 C&L.861 B.A., J.D. Div. Coun., Nationwide Mutual Insurance Company(Legal Department)
Gingerella, Donna M. '59 '84 C.1107 B.A. L.1294 J.D. (adm. in ME; not adm. in NC) IRS - Dept. of Treas.
Giroux, Richard E. '46 '77 C.93 B.A. L.575 J.D. NC Prisoner Legal Servs.
Givens, George Franklin '46 '83 C.1090 B.A. L.574 J.D. Leg. Analyst
Glasgow, JiNan '68 '99 C.576 B.S. L.575 J.D. [© MacCord M.P.] (☉Greensboro)
Glass, F. Stephen, (AV) '40 '66 C&L.896 B.A., J.D. [Johnson,H.V.G.&G.]
Glass, Margaret S. '46 '75 C.518 B.A. L.1065 J.D. V.P. & Treas., Carolina Power & Light Co.
Glass, Philip A., (BV) '59 '84 C.473 B.A. L.575 J.D. [Nodell,G.&H.]
Glatz, Robert W., (AV) '58 '91 C.453 S.B.M.E. L.575 J.D. [Myers B.S.&S.] (See Pat. Sect.)
Glazier, Richard B. '55 '81 C.645 B.A. L.896 J.D. [© Hardison&L.]
Glenn, George T., II, (BV) '53 '82 C.1378 B.S. L.574 J.D. Dep. Comm.
Glenn, R. Alexander '65 '90 C&L.184 B.A., J.D. (adm. in CT; not adm. in NC) Dep. Gen. Coun.-Florida, Florida Power Corp.
Glover, Alice S. '60 '94 C.575 B.A. L.574 J.D. [Allen&P.]
Glover, Lisa C. '74 '99 C.575 B.S. L.228 J.D. Asst. Atty Gen.
Godfrey, Elizabeth B., (BV) '56 '86 C.317 B.A. L.1228 J.D. [© Smith D.N.W.S.&M.]
Godwin, A. Pilston, Jr. '12 '37 C&L.896 LL.B. Ret. Supr. Ct. J.

Godwin, Rosemary, (BV) '58 '91 C.575 B.S.B.A. L.1228 J.D.
434 Fayetteville Street Mall, 27601
Telephone: 919-834-6161 Fax: 919-834-6269
Email: rosemarygodwin@bellsouth.net URL: http://www.rosemarygodwinlaw.com
Criminal Law in all State and Federal Courts. Federal Criminal Law, White Collar Crime, Driving While Intoxicated, Drug Crimes, Felonies, Homicide, Misdemeanors, Sexual Assault, Traffic
See Professional Biographies, RALEIGH, NORTH CAROLINA

Goebel, Jeffrey John '69 '00 C.436 B.A. L.45 J.D. [Ⓐ Jordan P.W.G.J.&C.]
Goettel, Timothy S. '61 '87 C.228 B.A. L.893 J.D. [Hunton&W.]
Golaski, Lorien '— '05 C.597 B.S. L.861 J.D. [Ⓐ Kilpatrick S.]
Goldston, Forrest W., (BV) '49 '77 C.576 B.A. L.896 J.D. 5027 Dunwoody Tr.
Golub, Aaron P. '74 '02 C&L.273 B.A., J.D. [Ⓐ Hutchison&M.]
Goodman, James R., Law Office of '60 '89 C.576 B.A. L.1228 J.D. 8378 Six Forks Rd., Ste. 203
Goodmon, Raymond H., III, (AV) '52 '77 C.575 B.A. L.228 J.D. P.O. Box 12031
Goodson, Patricia W. '— '96 C&L.896 B.A., J.D. [Kilpatrick S.]
Goodson, Paul M. '68 '95 C.575 B.S. L.896 J.D. 422 St. Mary's Street, Suite 1 (☉Charlotte, Durham)
Goodson, Scott Bartley '67 '96 C.575 B.S.B.A. L.896 J.D. [Martin&J.]
Goolsby, Thomas C. '61 '92 C.152 B.S. L.575 J.D. [Currin] ☉
Goray, Caroline Seibert '59 '86 C.813 B.A. L.477 J.D. 7307 Wilderness Rd.‡
Gordon, Frank J., (AV) '62 '88 C.576 B.S.Ch.E. L.896 J.D. [Millberg,G.&S.]
Gordon, Lisa R. '— '99 C.112 A.B. L.494 J.D. [Ⓐ Nelson M.R.&S.]
Gordon, Michael D. '46 '76 C.232 B.S.B.A. L.896 J.D. Atty. Gen's. Off.
Gordon, Michael R. '70 '95 C.861 B.A. L.1009 J.D. [Ⓐ Smith,A.B.D.M.&J.]
Gorham, Henry W., (AV) '48 '74 C.232 B.S.B.A. L.896 J.D. [Teague,C.D.&G.]
Gottsegen, Adam M. '75 '02 C.880 B.A. L.896 J.D. [Ⓐ Smith D.N.W.S.&M.]
Gottsegen, Jennifer Terry '77 '02 C.575 B.A. L.896 J.D. [Ⓐ Young M.&H.]
Gould, Lawrence J. '— '94 C.918 B.A. L.228 J.D. [Ⓐ Kilpatrick S.]
Govert, Gary R., (BV) '52 '86 C.665 B.A. L.575 J.D. N C Department of Justice
Grace, Nancy L., (AV) '— '96 C&L.576 B.A., J.D. [Sullivan&G.]
Graebe, Christopher T., (AV) '61 '90 C.894 B.A. L.575 J.D. [Womble C.S.&R.]
Graf, Wendy L. '71 '97 C.1369 B.S. L.838 J.D. Atty., Research Div., N.C. Gen. Assembly
Grafstein, Lisa, (AV) '66 '95 C.597 B.A. L.575 J.D. [Grafstein&W.]
Grafstein & Walczyk, P.L.L.C., (AV) 617 W. Jones Street
Graham, William E., Jr., (AV) '29 '56 C&L.575 A.B., J.D. [© Hunton&W.]
Graham, William T. '33 '62 C.228 A.B. L.893 J.D. 3421 Williamsborough Court
Granberry, William A. '26 '54 C.277 B.S. L.273 J.D. (adm. in DC; not adm. in NC) Pres., Amer. Mtge. Ins. Co.
Grant, Mary B. '61 '89 C.679 B.S. L.273 J.D. [© Hutchison&M.] (Pat.)
Graves, Debra C. '57 '86 C.577 B.A. L.575 K/D/ U.S. Pub. Def.
Gray, Beecher R. '47 '83 C.575 M.P.H. L.896 J.D. Admin. Law J., Off. of Admin. Hearings
Gray, Jane Powell '49 '79 C.260 B.A. L.1228 J.D. Resident Dist. Ct. J.
Gray, Jeffrey P., (BV) '59 '86 C.925 B.S. L.1228 J.D. [Holt Y.M.&H.]
Gray, Matthew J. '76 '03 C.1378 B.S. L.896 J.D. [Ⓐ Young M.&H.]
Gray, R. Frank, (AV) '48 '73 C.198 B.A. L.260 J.D. [Jordan P.W.G.J.&C.]
Gray, Thomas A. '68 '97 C.665 B.A. L.45 J.D. (adm. in MA; not adm. in NC) [Ⓐ Smith D.N.W.S.&M.]
Graybeal, John F., (AV) '37 '62 C.604 B.A. L.1565 LL.B. [© Parker,P.A.&B.]
Green, Betsy Glenn '72 '98 C.680 B.A. L.1228 J.D. 2000 Nakoma Pl.
Green, Charles P., Jr., (AV) '41 '65 C&L.575 A.B., LL.B. [© Howard,G.&M.]
Green, Jennifer Miller, (BV) '61 '88 C.577 B.S. L.575 J.D. J.
Green, John R., Jr., (BV) '64 '92 C.576 B.A. L.896 J.D. [Ⓐ Wyrick R.Y.&P.]
Green, Leonard G., (BV) '50 '75 C.232 B.S. L.575 J.D. Asst. Atty. Gen., NC Dept. of Jus., Consumer Protec. Div.
Greenblatt, Deborah '46 '72 C.705 A.B. L.228 LL.M. Exec. Dir., Carolina Legal Assistance
Greene, George R. '30 '57 C.778 A.B. L.575 LL.B. Supr. Ct. J.
Greene, K. Edward '44 '69 C.232 A.B. L.575 J.D. [© Wyrick R.Y.&P.]
Greene, Wendy Leigh '63 '00 C.951 B.A. L.575 J.D. P.O. Box 25397

Gregory, Keith O. '66 '95 C.893 B.A. L.574 J.D.
Two Hannover Square, 434 Fayetteville Street Mall, Suite 2310, 27601
Telephone: 919-832-3148
Email: attykeithgregory@aol.com URL: http://www.kogregorylaw.com
Criminal Law, Driving While Intoxicated, Drug Crimes, Felonies, Homicide, Sexual Assault, Traffic Violations, Personal Injury, Automobile Accidents, Wrongful Death, Uncontested Divorces, Entertainment Law, Music Contracts, Athletic Contracts.
See Professional Biographies, RALEIGH, NORTH CAROLINA

Gregory, Nancy Warren '69 '94 C&L.575 B.A., J.D. State Indus. Comm.
Griffin, Charles N., III '68 '97 C.880 B.A. L.896 J.D. [Ⓐ Kirschbaum,N.K.&G.]
Griffin, Diane S., (BV) '49 '86 C&L.575 B.A., J.D. [D.S.Griffin]
Griffin, James P., Jr. '47 '87 C.231 A.B. L.421 J.D. N.C. Prisoner Legal Servs.
Griffin, Robert H., (AV) '61 '86 C&L.896 B.A., J.D. [Cranfill,S.&H.]
Griffin, Suzanne R., (AV) '64 '89 C.339 B.S. L.597 J.D. [Poyner&S.]
Griffin, Diane S., P.C., Law Office of, (BV) P.O. Box 10629
Grigg, Mary Lynne '66 '92 C.1128 B.A. L.228 J.D. [© Womble C.S.&R.]
Grissett, Finley David '50 '76 C.198 B.S. L.969 J.D. V.P. & Tr. Offr., First Union Natl. Bk. of N.C.
Groninger, Ann Elizabeth, (AV) '69 '95 C.475 B.S. L.861 J.D. [Patterson H.] (☉Chapel Hill)
Groon, Gerald H., Jr., (BV) '60 '90 C.575 B.S. L.1345 J.D. [Smith D.N.W.S.&M.]
Groves, James D. '31 '58 C.225 A.B. L.862 LL.B. (adm. in OK; not adm. in NC) 300 Dartmouth Rd.‡
Gruber, Alexandra Sarah '— '00 C.124 B.Mus. L.836 J.D. (adm. in TN; not adm. in NC) Appl. Coord.
Gruber, Robert P. '43 '68 C&L.575 A.B., J.D. Exec. Dir., Pub. Staff-N.C. Util. Comm.
Gulick, James C. '50 '74 C&L.575 B.A., J.D. Spec. Dep. Atty. Gen., State Dept. of Justice
Gunn, Fern E., (BV) '56 '83 C&L.228 A.B., J.D. Dep. Coun., State Bar
Gunter, K. Gregory '73 '01 C.925 B.S. L.575 J.D. [Ⓐ Hardison&L.]
Gunter, Markham B. '65 '94 C.575 A.B. L.1228 J.D. [Gunter P.]
Gunter Law Firm PLLC 123 Glenwood Ave.

Gunther, Timothy A., (BV) .... '58 '92 C.188 B.S. L.1228 J.D. P.O. Box 185
Gupton, John B. ....'66 '92 C&L.575 B.A., J.D. Gen. Coun., Capital Assoc. Industries Inc.
Gurley, Tony .... '54 '03 [Gurley&C.]
Gurley & Cookson, PLLC .... 5986 Six Forks Road
Gusler, Richard Noel, The Law Offices of, (AV) '48 '84
C&L.576 B.A., J.D. 107 Glenwood Ave.
Gutshall, Morgan Carridy .... '80 '05 C.838 B.A. L.1228 J.D. [Hardison&L.]
Guy, Richard S., (BVⓉ) '51 '82 C.197 A.B. L.893 J.D.
[Vandeventer B.] (©Kitty Hawk, NC; Norfolk, VA)
Guy, William H. ...... '55 '84 C.892 B.A. L.1065 J.D. NC Dept. of Health & Human Svcs.
Gwyn, William B., Jr., (AV) .... '50 '81 C&L.896 B.S., J.D. [Maupin T.]
Gwynn, Kenneth B., (AV) .... '59 '84 C&L.896 B.A., J.D. [Gwynn&E.]
Gwynn and Edwards, (AV) .... 5909 Falls of Neuse Road
Haas, Angela L. .... '— '02 C.34 B.S. L.1228 J.D. [Haas M.&Assoc.]

Haas McNeil & Associates, P.A.
801 Oberlin Road Suite 250, 27605
Telephone: 919-783-9669 Fax: 919-783-7235 URL: http://www.carolinafamilylaw.com
Email: inquiry@carolinfamilylaw.com URL: http://www.haasmcneil.com
Angela L. Haas; John P. McNeil.
Family Law, Divorce, Separation Agreements, Child Support, Child Custody, Alimony, Domestic Violence, Visitation Rights, Spousal Support, Property Distribution, Prenuptial Agreements, Alimony, Domestic Law, Adoption, Litigation, Mediation, Collaborative Law, Alternative Dispute Resolution, LGBT Law, and Non-Traditional Family Law.
See Professional Biographies, RALEIGH, NORTH CAROLINA

Hafer, F. Eugene, (AV) .... '34 '66 C&L.575 B.S., J.D. [Holt Y.M.&H.]
Hagan, Alex J., (AV) .... '65 '92 C&L.575 B.A., J.D. [Ellis&W.] (©Cary)
Hahn, Jeffrey M. .... '62 '86 C.893 B.A. L.309 J.D. [Womble C.S.&R.]

Hahn, L. Allen, P.A.
(See Greenville)

Haigh, William L. ......'44 '73 C&L.575 B.A., J.D. Chf. Dep. Comr., N.C. Indus. Comm.
Haislip, Zesely Bryan, Jr., (BV) ....'54 '83 C.575 B.A. L.245 J.D. P.O. Box 20888
Hale, Grayson S. ....'— '98 C.1125 B.S. L.45 J.D. [Kennedy C.L.&H.]
Hale, Robert H., Jr. .... '68 '94 C&L.575 B.A., J.D. [R.H.Hale,Jr.]
Hale, William K. ....'47 '74 C.576 B.A. L.575 J.D. [Jordan P.W.G.J.&C.]
Hale, Robert H., Jr., Attorney at Law, PC .... P.O. Box 1349
Hall, Bly ....'52 '85 C.104 A.B. L.575 J.D. Asst. Atty. Gen.
Hall, Colby L. ....'73 '00 C.576 B.A. L.1228 J.D. P.O. Box 97307
Hall, George R., III ....'61 '96 C.575 B.A. L.1187 J.D. 207 W. Drewry Lane
Hall, Harold G., (AV) ....'35 '61 C.575 A.B. L.896 LL.B. [Hall&O.]
Hall, John T., III, (AV) ....'38 '72 C.216 A.B. L.575 J.D. 420 S. McDowell

Hall, Kyle S., (AV) '44 '70 C&L.575 A.B., J.D.
5 West Hargett Street Suite 810, P.O. Box 2211, 27602
Telephone: 919-831-8901 Fax: 919-831-8719
Email: khall@mindspring.com URL: http://www.lawyers.com/ks-hall
Criminal Law, Homicide, Sexual Assault, Drug Crimes, Felonies, Misdemeanors, Driving While Intoxicated, Traffic Violations, Parole and Probation, Personal Injury, Products Liability, Automobile Accidents and Injuries, Wrongful Death, Railroad Accidents.
See Professional Biographies, RALEIGH, NORTH CAROLINA

Hall, Michael J., J.D., M.S.E.L. '72 '00 C.1203 B.S. L.1194 J.D./M.S.E.L.
(adm. in MA; not adm. in NC) Progress Energy Service Co. LLC
Hall, Patricia B. ....'52 '85 C.104 A.B. L.575 J.D. Dept. of Jus.
Hall & O'Donnell, L.L.P., (AV) .... 4080 Barrett Drive (Cornwallis Square)
Halliday, Chad L. ....'76 '02 C.1044 B.A. L.896 J.D. [Smith D.N.W.S.&M.]
Hamden, Michael S. ....'54 '85 C.1293 B.A. L.838 J.D. [NC P.]
Hamilton, Bruce A., (AV) ....'61 '86 C.861 B.S. L.893 J.D. [Teague,C.D.&G.]
Hamilton, Joyce A. ....'49 '75 C.577 B.S. L.575 J.D. Dist. Ct. J.
Hammond, Robin M., (BV) ....'56 '85 C.232 B.A. L.575 J.D. Real Prop. Coun.
Hampson, Tobias S. ....'75 '02 C.30 B.A. L.1228 J.D. [Patterson,D.C.B.&A.]
Hampton, Julie W. ....'77 '02 C.577 B.A. L.1228 J.D. [Poyner&S.]
Hancock, William Gerry, Jr., (AV) ....'43 '71 C.575 A.B. L.228 J.D. [Everett,G.H.&S.]
Handy, Mary Z. ....'— '99 C.575 B.A. L.1365 J.D. [Howard,S.F.&H.] ⊙
Hankins, S. Ellis, (AV) '54 '80
C&L.575 B.A., J.D. Exec. Dir., NC League of Municipalities
Hanley, Ann Strader, (BV) ....'59 '85 C&L.896 B.A., J.D. [Allen&M.]
Hanna, Brett T. ....'— '97 C.1070 B.S. L.896 J.D. [Kennedy C.L.&H.]
Hanna, Douglas W. ....'66 '91 C.477 B.G.S. L.896 J.D. [Womble C.S.&R.]
Hannah, Nancy Edmunds, (BV) ....'59 '93 C.269 B.A. L.902 J.D. [Vann&S.]
Hanshumaker, Rita Lane .....'69 '97 C.1350 B.A. L.575 J.D. 434 Fayetteville Street Mall
Hanson, James S. ....'71 '01 C.896 B.A. L.577 J.D. [Smith,A.B.D.M.&J.]
Happer, M. Marshall, III, (AV) ....'38 '63 C&L.575 A.B., J.D. [Manning,F.&S.]
Harazin, William D., (AV) '53 '78
C.338 B.S. L.801 J.D. 434 Fayetteville St. Mall, Ste. 2404
Harden, Holmes P., (AV) ....'56 '81 C.198 B.A. L.575 J.D. [Maupin T.]
Hardison, Kenneth L., (BV) ....'56 '82 C&L.1228 B.S., J.D. [Hardison&L.] ⊙

Hardison & Leone, L.L.P., (AV)
225 Hillsborough Place, Suite 400, P.O. Box 27843, 27603-7843 ⊙
Telephone: 919-829-0449 Toll Free: 1-800-738-0449 Fax: 919-835-1379
Email: ken@hardisonandleone.com URL: http://www.hardisonandleone.com
Kenneth L. Hardison; Elizabeth A. Leone;—Benjamin T. Cochran; Jennifer H. Seate; Joseph W. Osman; C. Michael Millard; K. Gregory Gunter; Christopher R. Nichols; Sharon K. Dow; Morgan Carridy Gutshall. Of Counsel: Richard B. Glazier; James T. Irvin, Jr.
Languages: English and Spanish.
Personal Injury, Auto and Trucking Accidents, Pedestrian Accidents, Catastrophic Injury, Medical Malpractice, Workers' Compensation, Social Security Disability, Nursing Home Negligence, Security Investment Fraud, Inadequate Security Claims, Premises Liability, Mass Torts, Drug Liability Claims, Employment Law, Appellate Practice, Immigration.
Dunn, North Carolina Office: 212 S. Wilson Avenue, P.O. Box 759, 28335. Telephone: 910-892-1181. Toll Free: 1-888-892-1181. Fax: 910-892-7874.
Fayetteville, North Carolina Office: 1014 Hay Street, Post Office Drawer 53037, 28305-5316. Telephone: 910-223-3022. Toll Free: 800-782-3145. Fax: 910-223-9006.
Southern Pines, North Carolina Office: 235 E. Pennsylvania Avenue, Sandhills Executive Center, 28387. Telephone: 910-695-1183. Toll Free: 800-600-7969. Fax: 919-835-1379.
Greensboro, North Carolina Office: 7B Corporate Center Court, 27408. Telephone: 336-370-1299. Toll Free: 800-600-7969. Fax: 919-835-1379.
Charlotte, North Carolina Office: 6047 Tyvola Glen Circle, 28217. Telephone: 704-377-3190. Toll Free: 800-600-7969. Fax: 919-835-1379.
Myrtle Beach, South Carolina Office: 115 48th Avenue, Suite 122, 29577. Telephone: 843-467-2100. Toll Free: 800-600-7969. Fax: 919-835-1379.
Durham, North Carolina Office: 2530 Meridian Parkway, Suit 3.
See Professional Biographies, RALEIGH, NORTH CAROLINA

Hargett, Robert T., (BV) ....'57 '82 C.100 B.A. L.607 J.D. NC Dept. of Just.
Hargrove, Susan Haney, (AV) ......'56 '92 C.228 B.A. L.575 J.D. [Smith,A.B.D.M.&J.]
Hargrove, Wade H., (AV) ....'40 '65 C&L.575 A.B., J.D. [Brooks,P.M.H.&L.] ⊙
Harlow, David A., (AV) ....'43 '68 C.401 B.A. L.228 J.D. [Nelson M.R.&S.] (Pat.)
Harrell, Michael S., (AV) ....'62 '90 C.1083 B.A. L.893 J.D. [Manning,F.&S.]
Harriott, Ormond ....'51 '93 C.1036 B.A. L.201 J.D. 805 New Bern Avenue, Suite 200
Harris, Addie M. ....'64 '89 C.896 B.A. L.574 J.D. Law Clk., Ct. of App. J.
Harris, Claude W., (BV) ....'23 '51 C.232 A.B. L.575 LL.B. Atty. Gen. Off.
Harris, Donald J. ....'62 '88 C.1044 B.S. L.107 J.D. [Harris&W.]
Harris, Margaret Winfield ....'69 '94 C&L.893 B.A., J.D. [Harris&W.]
Harris, Nelson G. ....'62 '89 C&L.575 B.S., J.D. [Harris F.]
Harris, Steven Troy ....'72 '00 C.575 B.A. L.574 J.D. [Stratas&W.]
Harris, W. C., Jr., (AV) ....'13 '37 C&L.575 A.B. 3600 Glenwood Ave.‡
Harris, W. Tom, Jr., (BV) '40 '65 C.198 B.A. L.575 LL.B.
Coun., Chicago Title Ins. Co.
Harris Flanagan, LLC .... 7200 Stonehenge Drive, Suite 311

Harris, Malcolm E., P.A.
(See Wake Forest)

Harris & Winfield, llp
1044 Washington Street, 27605
Telephone: 919-546-8788 Fax: 919-546-8789 URL: http://www.harriswinfield.com
Email: email@harriswinfield.com URL: http://www.harris-winfield.com
Donald J. Harris; Margaret Winfield Harris; Clay Hodges.
Language: Spanish, Portuguese.
Business Litigation, Breach of Contract, Trademark and Copyright Litigation, Technology Litigation, Medical Malpractice, Wrongful Death, Unfair Trade Practices Litigation, Catastrophic Injury.
See Professional Biographies, RALEIGH, NORTH CAROLINA

Harrison, Cecil W., Jr., (AV) ....'47 '73 C&L.575 A.B., J.D. [Poyner&S.]
Harrison, Elizabeth R. ....'69 '95 C.575 B.A. L.1228 J.D. P.O. Box 6087
Harrison, Janet DeLaura '54 '78 C.1086 B.A. L.1206 J.D.
(adm. in FL; not adm. in NC) 3536 Durham Rd.‡
Harrold, M. Bradley ....'61 '86 C.198 B.A. L.575 J.D. [Harold P.]
Harrold Law Firm, PLLC ....3323 Alamance Drive
Harshbarger, Marcella A. ....'— '03 C.1208 B.A. L.228 J.D. [Kilpatrick S.]
Hart, William P. ....'52 '78 C.602 B.A. L.228 J.D. N.C. Dept. of Justice
Hartley, Carrie Joan ....'— '01 C.575 B.A. L.1565 J.D. [DLPiper R.G.C.U.]
Hartzell, Adam G. ....'69 '99 C.30 B.A. L.1228 J.D. [Farrell&L.]
Hartzell, J. Jerome, (AV) ....'50 '77 C&L.575 B.A., J.D. [Hartzell&W.]
Hartzell, Stephen G. ....'69 '00 C.326 B.A. L.577 J.D. [Brooks,P.M.H.&L.] ⊙

Hartzell & Whiteman, L.L.P., (AV)
2626 Glenwood Avenue, Suite 500, 27608
Telephone: 919-571-8300 Fax: 919-571-1004
URL: http://www.hwlawyers.com
Members of Firm: J. Jerome Hartzell; Andrew O. Whiteman; John R. Rittelmeyer.
Business Litigation, Securities Claims and Arbitration, Business Ownership Disputes, Consumer Class Actions, Disability/Insurance Claims, Employee Benefits and Workplace Injuries, Wage and Hour/Overtime Disputes, Intellectual Property Claims, Consumer and Employment Disputes, Professional Malpractice.
See Professional Biographies, RALEIGH, NORTH CAROLINA

Hartzog, Dan M., (AV) ....'47 '73 C&L.575 A.B., J.D. [Cranfill,S.&H.]
Haskell, Craig S., (AV) ....'66 '90 C.659 B.A. L.575 J.D. [Nodell,G.&H.]
Hassell, Charles R., Jr., (AV) ....'43 '68 C&L.575 A.B., J.D. 115 S. St. Mary's St.

Hatch, Little & Bunn, L.L.P., (AV)
327 Hillsborough Street, P.O. Box 527, 27602
Telephone: 919-856-3940 Fax: 919-856-3950
URL: http://www.hatchlittlebunn.com
Members of Firm: J. Wilbur Bunn (1883-1969); William T. Hatch (1905-1979); James C. Little (1917-1977); Harold W. Berry, Jr.; Thomas D. Bunn; John N. McClain, Jr.; Tina Frazier Pace; David H. Permar; A. Bartlett White; Douglas Q. Wickham (Board Certified in Business Bankruptcy Law and Consumer Bankruptcy Law, North Carolina State Board of Legal Specialization); William D. Young, IV. Associates: Elizabeth T. Martin; John E. McKnight.
General Practice in all Courts. Bankruptcy, Civil, Commercial, Corporate, Criminal, Driving While Intoxicated, Traffic Violations, Family, Divorce, Child Custody, Child Support, Insurance, Interstate Commerce, Municipal, Zoning, Personal Injury, Probate, Real Property, Utility Law, Home Owners Associations, Foreclosure.
See Professional Biographies, RALEIGH, NORTH CAROLINA

Hatfield, Scott C. ....'65 '93 C&L.880 B.E., J.D. [Myers B.S.&S.] (See Pat. Sect.)
Hawley, David B. ....'58 '99 C.923 B.A. L.575 J.D. [Ogletree,D.N.S.&S.]
Hawn, Heather L. ....'70 '97 C.575 A.B. L.1228 J.D. [Wilson&R.]
Hayes, Amanda A. ....'— '02 C.205 B.A. L.575 J.D. [Parker,P.A.&B.]
Hayes, Anne M. ....'59 '87 C.136 B.S. L.472 J.D. Asst. U.S. Atty.
Hayes, Susanne F., (BV) ....'39 '84 C.8 B.A. L.1228 J.D. 3600 Glenwood Ave.
Haygood, Richard David ....'— '97 C.577 B.A. L.575 J.D. [Kilpatrick S.]
Hayman, Wilson, (AV) ....'54 '79 C.674 A.B. L.575 J.D. [Poyner&S.]
Haynes, Helen R., (BVⓉ) '60 '84 C.597 B.A. L.477 J.D.
(adm. in MI; not adm. in NC)
Associate General Counsel, Martin Marietta Materials, Inc.
Haywood, E. Burke, (BV) '53 '80 C&L.575 B.A., J.D.
Asst. Atty. Gen., State Dept. of Jus.

Haywood, Emmett Boney, (AV) '55 '82 C.575 A.B. L.585 J.D.
3700 National Drive, Suite 112, 27612
Telephone: 919-781-1371 Fax: 919-781-1373
Email: ehaywood@landlaw-nc.com URL: http://www.landlaw-nc.com
Eminent Domain, Land Condemnation, Land Use, Contracts, Civil Litigation and Dispute Resolution.
See Professional Biographies, RALEIGH, NORTH CAROLINA

Haywood, Kenneth C., (BV) ....'66 '92 C.575 B.A. L.896 J.D. [Boxley,B.G.&H.]
Healey, Matthew S. ....'73 '02 C.602 B.A. L.280 J.D. [Womble C.S.&R.]
Hearn, George G., (AV) ....'49 '74 C&L.575 A.B., J.D. [Johnson,H.V.G.&G.]
Heck, Barbara A., (BV) ....'59 '85 C&L.575 B.A., J.D. 2900 ES Kings Vlg.
Hedrick, John A. ....'65 '91 C.575 B.A. L.1228 J.D. [Scudder&H.]
Hedrick, Kristie L. ....'74 '03 C&L.575 B.A., J.D. [Patterson,D.C.B.&A.]
Hedrick, R. A. (Fred) ....'23 '49 C&L.575 B.A., LL.B. Ret. Chf. J., Ct. of App.
Hedrick, Robert T., (BV) ....'34 '61 C&L.896 B.S., J.D. P.O. Box 58004

Hedrick Eatman Gardner & Kincheloe, L.L.P., (AV)
4011 Westchase Boulevard, Suite 300, 27607 ⊙
Telephone: 919-832-9424 Fax: 919-832-9425
URL: http://www.hedrickeatman.com
Partners: Jeffrey A. Doyle (Resident); Thomas M. Morrow (Resident). Associates: Jessica C. Smythe; Erin Dancy Eveson; Jennifer S. Jerzak; Tonya D. Davis; Jennifer Vega Ruiz; Barry C. Jennings; Bettina Mumme; Erika D. Taylor; Stacy M. Race; Dana C. Moody; Susan J. VanDerweert; Kyla K. Block.
General Civil Litigation and Insurance Defense, Legal and Professional Malpractice, Motor Vehicle Negligence, Premises Liability, Product Liability, Construction, Insurance Coverage Disputes, Arson and Fraud, Employment Law, Trucking and Transportation and Worker's Compensation.
Representative Clients: Ace-USA; Carolinas Healthcare Systems; Chubb Group; Continental Tire; Liberty Mutual; Medical Mutual Insurance; PMA Group; St. Paul Travelers Insurance Co.; United Parcel Service; USAA; Wal-Mart Corp.
Charlotte, North Carolina Office: 6000 Fairview Road, Suite 1000, 28210. Mailing Address: P.O. Box 30397, 28230. Telephone: 704-366-1101. Fax: 704-366-6181.
Wilmington, North Carolina Office: 1508 Military Cutoff Road, Suite 202, 28403. Telephone: 910-509-9664. Fax: 910-509-9630.
Columbia, South Carolina Office: 1201 Main Street, Suite 1200, 29201. Mailing Address: P.O. Box 11267, 29211. Telephone: 803-727-1200. Fax: 803-727-1259.
See Professional Biographies, RALEIGH, NORTH CAROLINA

Hedrick Murray & Cheek PLLC
(See Durham)
Hedspeth, Misty Coble ....'78 '03 C.576 B.S. L.1228 J.D. [Hedspeth]
Hedspeth Law Firm, PLLC
410 N. Boylan Avenue, Suite 145, 27603
Telephone: 919-256-3645 Fax: 919-256-3745 URL: http://www.trianglefamilylaw.com
Email: mhedspeth@hedspethlaw.com URL: http://www.hedspethlaw.com
Misty Coble Hedspeth.
Family Law, Traffic Violations, Criminal Law, Misdemeanors.
See Professional Biographies, RALEIGH, NORTH CAROLINA
Heidgerd, C. D., (AV) '47 '72 C&L.896 B.A., J.D.
3737 Glenwood Avenue, Suite 100, 27612
Telephone: 919-861-2484 Fax: 919-861-2486 URL: http://cdheidgerdlaw.com/
Email: cdh@heidgerdlaw.com URL: http://www.heidgerdlaw.com
Civil Trials and Appeals, Personal Injury, Wrongful Death, Eminent Domain, Administrative Law, Professional and Occupational Licensing, Family Law.
See Professional Biographies, RALEIGH, NORTH CAROLINA
Heinberg, Christine O'Connor ....'51 '78 C.823 B.A. L.1019 J.D. N.C. Legal Servs.
Heiskell, Christopher Neil, (AV) ......'68 '93 C.296 B.S. L.1228 J.D. [Larcade,H.&A.P.]
Heitman, Jane Hilary '52 '77 C.103 A.B. L.245 J.D.
(adm. in GA; not adm. in NC) 11008 Brass Kettle Rd.‡
Helms Mulliss & Wicker, PLLC, (AV) BB
2600 Two Hannover Square, 27601 ⊙
Mailing Address: P.O. Box 27507, Raleigh, NC 27611
Telephone: 919-755-6600 Fax: 919-755-6699. Telex: 572460
URL: http://www.hmw.com
Members of Firm: David V. Otterson; Mack A. Paul, IV; David F. Paulson, Jr.; Robert H. Tiller; Dennis A. Wicker; Robert A. Wicker. Associates: Keith P. Anthony; Mathias H. "Matt" Hunoval; Andrew E. Kristianson; Jason R. Schneider; Aaron G. Spencer; Guilford Mattern York.
Banking, Finance, Corporate, Government Relations, Business Litigation, Tax, Securities, Real Property and Finance, Labor and Employment (Management) Law, Employee Benefits, International, Technology, Insurance Coverage, Media, Commercial Bankruptcy, Environmental, Public Finance, ERISA, Estate Planning and Administration, Education, Venture Capital, Intellectual Property.
Charlotte, North Carolina Office: 201 North Tryon Street, P.O. Box 31247 (28231). Telephone: 704-343-2000. Fax: 704-343-2300. Telex: 572460.
Wilmington, North Carolina Office: 127 Grace Street, P.O. Box 599 (28402). Telephone: 910-254-3800. Fax: 910-254-3900.
See Professional Biographies, RALEIGH, NORTH CAROLINA
Hemphill, S. Todd, (AV) ....'56 '82 C.197 A.B. L.575 J.D. [Bode,C.&S.]
Henderson, Charles H. ....'40 '76 C.232 A.B. L.574 J.D. [Ⓟ Poyner&S.]
Henderson, R. David, (AV) ....'58 '86 C.1128 B.A. L.896 J.D. Dep. Coun., N.C. State Bar
Hendren, Jason L. ....'73 '99 C.999 B.A. L.838 J.D. 2418 Blue Ridge Road, Suite 200
Hendricks, David P., The Law Office of ... '60 '01 C.576 B.S. L.574 J.D. P.O. Box 37127
Hendrickson, C. T. ....'57 '84 C.576 B.S. L.896 J.D. P.O. Box 41228
Hensey, Charles McK. ....'34 '62 C.228 A.B. L.575 LL.B. Spec. Dep. Atty. Gen.
Hensley, Robert G., Jr. .... '— '03 C.999 B.A. L.575 J.D. [Ⓐ Kilpatrick S.]
Hensley, S. Scott ....'70 '96 C.576 B.A. L.365 J.D. PricewaterhouseCoopers, LLP
Henson, Carmaletta L. ....'74 '99 C&L.575 B.A., J.D. [Ⓐ Henson&F.] ⊙
Henson, David S., (CV) ....'73 '98 C&L.575 B.A., J.D. [Ⓐ Henson&F.] ⊙
Henson, Thomas W., (AV) ....'42 '67 C&L.575 B.S.B.A., J.D. [Henson&F.]
Henson, Thomas W., Jr., (BV) '65 '89
C&L.575 B.S.B.A., J.D. [Henson&F.] (⊙Asheville, Rocky Mount)
Henson & Fuerst, P.A., (AV)
2501 Blue Ridge Road, Suite 390, 27607 ⊙
Telephone: 919-781-1107 Fax: 919-781-8048
Email: henson-fuerst@lawmed.com URL: http://www.lawmed.com
Thomas W. Henson (Resident); Robert L. Fuerst (Board Certified Specialist in Family Law, North Carolina State Board of Legal Specialization); Thomas W. Henson, Jr.;—David S. Henson; Carmaletta L. Henson; Joseph S. Hodgin.
Civil Trial Practice, Medical Malpractice, Nursing Home Liability, Nursing Home Abuse and Neglect, Personal Injury, Automobile Accidents, Wrongful Death.
Rocky Mount Office: 2317 Sunset Avenue, P.O. Box 7008, 27804-2529. Telephone: 252-443-2111. Fax: 252-443-9429.
See Professional Biographies, RALEIGH, NORTH CAROLINA
Herbert, Gordon B., (BV) '46 '75
C.1309 B.A. L.575 J.D. Pres. & Gen. Coun., United Title Co.
Herman, Patrick W., (AVⓉ) '52 '82 C.886 B.A. L.945 J.D.
[Vandeventer B.] (⊙Kitty Hawk, NC; Norfolk, VA)
Herrin, Joseph E., (BV) ....'63 '90 C.575 B.A. L.1228 J.D. Asst. Atty. Gen.
Herring, E. Parker, (BV) ....'53 '86 C.575 B.A. L.896 J.D. [Herring M.M.&F.]
Herring McBennett Mills & Finkelstein, PLLC, (AV)
Two Hannover Square, 27601
Mailing Address: P.O. Box 1677, Raleigh, NC 27602
Telephone: 919-821-1860 Fax: 919-821-1816
Email: hermcb@hermcb.com URL: http://www.hermcb.com
E. Parker Herring (Board Certified Specialist, Family Law, North Carolina State Board of Legal Specialization); Larry D. McBennett; Bobby D. Mills (Board Certified Specialist in Family Law, North Carolina State Board of Legal Specialization); Mark A. Finkelstein; Stephen W. Petersen. Associate: Anna E. Worley.
Comprehensive Business, Litigation, Real Estate, Domestic and Adoption Practice including, Trial and Appellate Litigation, Administrative, Antitrust, Business Law, Business Crimes, Civil Rights, Commercial, Construction, Corporate, Business Formation, E-Commerce, Employment, Environmental, Estate Planning, Family, Adoption, Equitable Distribution, Divorce, Health Care, Intellectual Property, Negligence, Probate, Products Liability, Real Estate, Toxic Tort, Wills and Trusts Law, Business Ownership Disputes, Disability, Insurance Claims, Wage and Hour, Overtime Disputes, Franchise Disputes, Contracts Disputes, Unfair Trade Practices, Breach of Fiduciary Duty, Partnership Disputes, Non-Compete Covenants, Tortious Interference with Contract, Mergers and Acquisitions, White Collar Criminal Defense, Regulatory Law, Professional Licensing, Eminent Domain and Land Condemnation.
See Professional Biographies, RALEIGH, NORTH CAROLINA
Hewitt, Marcus C. ....'71 '96 C&L.575 B.A., J.D. [Ⓐ Maupin T.]
Heyward, Robert B. '51 '75 C&L.260 B.S.B.A., J.D.
(adm. in FL; not adm. in NC) V.P., Gen. Coun. & Secy., Golden Corral Corporation
Hibbert, Carl W., (AV) ....'— '72 C&L.896 B.A., J.D. [Kilpatrick S.]
Higgins, Daniel C., (AV) ....'54 '81 C.1369 B.A. L.945 J.D. [Burns,D.&P.]
High, Curtis R. ....'67 '94 C&L.790 B.A., J.D. [High]
High, W. Hackney, Jr., (BV) .... '65 '90 C.575 B.S. L.1228 J.D. [Holt Y.M.&H.] ⊙
High Law Firm ....5 W. Hargett St.
Hightower, Alexandra M., (BV) ....'57 '82 C.529 A.B. L.896 J.D. P.O. Box 629
Hilbert, Mary Lifson ....'73 '99 C.880 B.A. L.910 J.D. [Hilbert,P.]
Hilbert Law Firm, The, PLLC
410 N. Boylan Avenue, Suite 152, 27603
Telephone: 919-256-3970 Fax: 919-256-3971
Email: maryhilbertlaw@yahoo.com URL: http://www.raleighdivorcelawfirm.com
Mary Lifson Hilbert.
Family Law, Child Custody, Divorce Litigation, Child Support, Domestic Violence, Equitable Distribution, Alimony, Post-Separation Support, Separation Agreements Premarital Agreements, Adoptions, Visition Rights, Divorce.
See Professional Biographies, RALEIGH, NORTH CAROLINA

Hildebran-Bachofen, Deborah L., (AV) '53 '84
C&L.575 B.S.B.A., J.D. [Manning,F.&S.]
Hilkey-Boyatt, Katherine ....'76 '01 C&L.575 B.A., J.D. [Cranfill,S.&H.]
Hill, Evelyn W. ....'48 '79 C.683 B.A. L.575 J.D. Supr. Ct. J.
Hill, Matt ....'78 '03 [Ⓐ Gurley&C.]
Hill, Melissa, (AV) ....'62 '87 C&L.575 B.A., J.D. [Tharrington S.]
Hill, Michael D., (AV) '60 '87
C.976 B.S. L.790 J.D. V.P. & Gen. Coun., Capitol Bdcstg. Co.
Hill, Randolph J., (BV) '62 '87 C.602 B.A. L.896 J.D.
434 Fayetteville Street Suite 2350, 27601
Telephone: 919-861-0507 Fax: 919-861-0504
Email: rjhlaw@earthlink.net URL: http://www.lawyers.com/rjhilllaw
Criminal, Personal Injury, Automobile Accidents, Civil, Appeals, Business Litigation, Traffic, Driving While Intoxicated, Drug Crimes, Felonies, Homicide, Misdemeanors.
See Professional Biographies, RALEIGH, NORTH CAROLINA
Hill, Richard L. '42 '68 C.882 B.A. L.1294 J.D.
(adm. in VT; not adm. in NC) 5219 Lake Wheeler Rd.‡
Hill, Thelma M. ....'53 '78 C.778 B.S. L.575 J.D. Off. of Chmn., Employ. Sec. Comm.
Hillman, Robert L., (BV) '51 '76 C&L.902 B.A., J.D.
Gen. Coun., Dept. of State Auditor
Hinkle, Jamison H. ....'69 '96 C.228 A.B. L.575 J.D. [Ⓐ Smith,A.B.D.M.&J.]
Hinnant, Christopher M., (CV) '72 '97 C.575 B.A. L.1228 J.D.
[Patterson,D.C.B.&A.]
Hinshaw, Greg L., (AV) ....'50 '75 C&L.575 B.S., J.D. [Burns,D.&P.]
Hinton, Charles L., III, (BV) '47 '73 C&L.575 A.B., J.D.
1620 Hillsborough St., Suite 100
Hipp, Edward B., (AV) ....'21 '50 C.198 B.S. L.575 J.D. 3312 Fairhill Dr.‡
Hirsch, Alan Seth, (BV) ....'50 '74 C.575 B.A. L.178 J.D. Gov. Off.
Hirsch, Frank A., Jr., (BV) ....'60 '87 C.575 B.A. L.880 J.D. [Nelson M.R.&S.]
Hitch, Rachel B. ....'74 '02 C.646 B.A. L.1228 J.D. [Ⓐ Schwartz&S.]
Hobart, John D., Jr. ....'60 '89 C&L.575 B.A., J.D. Gen. Coun., NC Dept. of Com.
Hobgood, Charles H., (AV) ....'51 '77 C&L.575 B.A., J.D. Asst. Atty. Gen.
Hobson, L. Robert ....'66 '92 C.575 B.A. L.896 J.D. 3600 Glenwood Ave.‡
Hockaday, J. Travis ....'78 '03 C.1228 B.A. L.575 J.D. [Ⓐ Smith,A.B.D.M.&J.]
Hodgdon, Thaddeus B., (AV) ....'46 '71 C.347 A.B. L.1119 J.D. [Hodgdon&S.]
Hodgdon & Schuette, P.A., Law Offices of, (AV) ....8340 Bandford Way, Suite 105
Hodge, Leanor Bailey ....'71 '97 C.329 B.B.A. L.831 J.D. [Manning,F.&S.]
Hodges, Clay ....'68 '00 C&L.575 B.A., J.D. [Harris&W.]
Hodgin, Joseph S. ....'76 '02 C.1228 B.A. L.607 J.D. [Ⓐ Henson&F.] ⊙
Hogan, Gentry Case Merritts ......'69 '99 C.1044 B.A. L.1338 J.D. 309 W. Millbrook Rd.
Hogewood, A. Lee, III, (AV) .... '— '90 C.309 A.B. L.896 J.D. [Kennedy C.L.&H.]
Hoke, Chris G. ....'54 '79 C&L.575 B.A., J.D. Dep. State Health Dir.
Holbrook, Cyrus A., (AV) '46 '73
C.437 B.A. L.838 J.D. 5000 Falls of Neuse Road, Suite 102
Holland, James R. ....'— '02 L.575 J.D. [Ⓐ Smith M.]
Holland, Patricia L., (AV) ....'54 '79 C.967 B.A. L.896 J.D. [Cranfill,S.&H.]
Hollander, Reed J. ....'72 '96 C.339 B.A. L.228 J.D. [Ⓟ Nelson M.R.&S.]
Holloman, Sharron D. ....'63 '93 C&L.574 B.A., J.D. 500 King Richard Rd.
Holloway, Margaret W. ....'67 '96 C.198 B.A. L.575 J.D. 4101 Heathgate Ln.
Hollowell, Edward E., (AV) ....'33 '61 C&L.575 B.S., J.D. [Hollowell]
Hollowell, Wallace C., III ....'71 '97 C.575 B.A. L.893 J.D. [Nelson M.R.&S.]
Hollowell Law Offices, P.A., (AV)
5511 Capital Center Drive, Suite 104, 27606
Telephone: 919-852-2211 Fax: 919-852-2233
Email: edhollowell@bellsouth.net URL: http://www.hollowell-lawoffices.com
Member: Edward E. Hollowell.
Health Care Law, Administrative Law, Corporate Law, Business Law, Employment, Governmental Estate Planning and Collection.
See Professional Biographies, RALEIGH, NORTH CAROLINA
Holm, David E. ....'70 '00 C.576 B.A. L.472 J.D. [Holm]
Holm Law Firm, PLLC
Two Hannover Square, Suite 2406, 27601
Telephone: 919-833-4000 Fax: 919-833-0731
Email: dave@holmlawoffice.com URL: http://www.holmlawoffice.com
David E. Holm.
Family Law, Child Support, Child Custody, Divorce, Alimony, Visitation Rights, Collaborative Law, Trusts and Estates, Asset Protection, Guardianship and Wills.
See Professional Biographies, RALEIGH, NORTH CAROLINA
Holmes, Jack Spain, (AV) ....'62 '87 C.575 B.S. L.945 J.D. [Lewis&R.]
Holmes, Phillip A., (BV) ....'50 '80 C.575 A.B. L.1228 J.D. N.C. Industrial Comm.
Holmes, Robert P., IV, (BV) ....'59 '84 C&L.575 B.S.B.A., J.D. 2211 Wheeler Rd.
Holscher, Paul ....'— '05 C.575 B.A. L.1228 J.D. [Cranfill,S.&H.]
Holshouser, James E., Jr., (AV) ....'34 '60 C.198 B.A. L.575 LL.B. [Sanford H.] ⊙
Holt, C. Mark, (AV) ....'60 '87 C.896 B.A. L.575 J.D. [Kirby&H.]
Holt, Clyde, III, (AV) ....'47 '72 C.597 B.A. L.575 J.D. [Holt Y.M.&H.]
Holt, Fred F. ....'42 '97 L.923 J.D. 4928 Misty Oak Dr.
Holt York McDarris & High, LLP, (AV) BB
Two Hannover Square, Suite 2010, 434 Fayetteville Street Mall, 27601 ⊙
Mailing Address: P.O. Box 2060, Raleigh, NC 27602
Telephone: 919-420-7826; Toll Free: 888-285-7634 Fax: 919-420-7838
URL: http://www.hymh.com
Partners: Jeffrey P. Gray; W. Hackney High, Jr.; Clyde Holt, III; Charles F. McDarris; Elizabeth Carr Trahos; David L. York;—William M. Crowe; Colleen Kochanek; Benjamin R. Kuhn; Claudia N. McClinton; David J. Neill; Bradford A. Williams. Of Counsel: F. Eugene Hafer; Edmond W. Caldwell, Jr.
Municipal/Administrative Law, Zoning and Land Use, Real Property, Government Regulations, Condemnation Defense, Corporate Law, Trusts and Estates, Wills and Probate, Alcoholic Beverages, General Trial and Appellate Practice before all State and Federal Courts and Agencies. Legislative Representation before the North Carolina General Assembly.
Edenton, North Carolina Office: 102 East Queen Street, P.O. Box 92, 27932. Telephone: 252-482-4422, Toll-free: 888-256-0219. Fax: 252-482-4423.
See Professional Biographies, RALEIGH, NORTH CAROLINA
Homick, Daniel J. '47 '78 C.363 A.B. L.117 J.D.
(adm. in OH; not adm. in NC) 8608 Cold Springs Rd.
Homick, Victoria M. ....'51 '79 C.706 B.A. L.117 J.D. 8608 Cold Springs Rd.‡
Honeycutt, John T. ....'67 '92 C&L.575 B.A., J.D. [Yates,M.&W.]
Hoomani, Ali John ....'71 '97 C.576 B.A. L.1228 J.D. Dep. Gen. Coun.
Hooten, Julia S. ....'72 '03 C.34 B.A. L.1228 J.D. [Ⓐ Teague,C.D.&G.]
Hopper, Kevin P., (BV) ....'67 '94 C.814 B.S. L.845 J.D. [Hopper]
Hopper Law Firm, (BV)
4601 Six Forks Road, Suite 127, 27609
Telephone: 919-829-5600 Fax: 919-510-5152 URL: http://www.HopperLawfirm.com
URL: http://www.hopperlawoffice.com
Member of Firm: Kevin P. Hopper.

(This Listing Continued)

Hopper Law Firm (Continued)

Family Law, Business Litigation, Construction Law, Child Custody, Divorce, Criminal Law, Traffic Violations, DWI, Commercial Litigation, Alimony and Misdemeanors.

See Professional Biographies, RALEIGH, NORTH CAROLINA

Horne, B. Davis, Jr., (AV) ....'56 '84 C.1309 B.A. L.1228 J.D. [Smith,A.B.D.M.&J.]
Horne, Daniel M., Jr. ....'— '90 C.1228 B.S. L.575 J.D. P.O. Box 2779
Horne, H. Forest, Jr., (AV) ....'60 '89 C.383 B.B.A. L.1228 J.D. [Martin&J.]
Horne, Patricia S., (AV) ....'55 '82 C.228 B.S. L.575 J.D. [Seay&H.]
Horsley, Charles Jeffrey ....'— '01 C.610 B.B.A L.1228 J.D. [A Barkley]
Horton, Clarence E., Jr. ....'40 '65 C&L.575 A.B., LL.B. Appl. Ct. J.
Horton, Walter Lee, Jr., (AV) ....'26 '56 C&L.575 A.B., J.D. 615 Oberlin Rd.
Horwitz, Evan B. ....'75 '01 C.347 B.A. L.1228 J.D. [A Manning,F.&S.]
House, George W., (AV) .... '46 '73 C.198 B.A. L.893 J.D. [Brooks,P.M.H.&L.] ⊙
Houser, Bradley W. ....'67 '93 C&L.575 B.A., J.D. State Indus. Comm.
Howard, Edward Cader, (AV) ....'48 '72 C.198 A.B. L.575 J.D. [Howard,S.F.&H.]
Howard, J. Myrick '53 '78 C&L.575 B.A., J.D.
Exec. Dir., Historic Preservation Found. of N.C.
Howard, Justin D. ....'73 '03 C.953 B.S. L.575 J.D. [A Patterson,D.C.B.&A.]
Howard, Kenneth B. '54 '82 C.575 B.S. L.896 J.D.
(adm. in MI; not adm. in NC) V.P., Medic Computer Systems
Howard, Robert E., Jr. ....'76 '03 C.896 B.A. L.790 J.D. [A Howard,G.&M.]

Howard, Green & Moye, L.L.P., (AV) BB
4000 Westchase Boulevard Suite 200, P.O. Box 10305, 27605
Telephone: 919-833-2422 Fax: 919-833-2430
Email: howardandgreen@mindspring.com URL: http://www.lawyers.com/howardandgreen
Robert E. Howard Sr.; Katherine S. Moye. Associate: Robert E. Howard, Jr. Of Counsel: Charles P. Green, Jr.
General Civil Practice. Real Estate, Family and Domestic Relations Law. Custody and Support and Equitable Distribution Law.
References: Bank of America; First Citizens Bank & Trust, Wachovia Bank.

See Professional Biographies, RALEIGH, NORTH CAROLINA

Howard Sr., Robert E., (AV) ....'45 '70 L.575 LL.B. [Howard,G.&M.]

Howard, Stallings, From & Hutson, P.A., (AV) BB
4000 Westchase Boulevard, Suite 400, P.O. Box 12347, 27607 ⊙
Telephone: 919-821-7700; 800-822-4182 Fax: 919-821-7703; 834-8481
URL: http://www.hsfh.com
Edward Cader Howard; I. Allan From; Joseph H. Stallings; John N. Hutson, Jr.; Beth Ferebee Atkins; James B. Angell (Board Certified Specialist in Business Bankruptcy Law, North Carolina State Board of Legal Specialization); Peggy S. Vincent; B. Joan Davis; Brian E. Moore; Philip W. Paine; Mary Z. Handy; Russell W. Johnson. Of Counsel: Edwin P. Friedberg.
General, Civil and Commercial Litigation, Business Law, Commercial Real Estate, Taxation, Employment Law, Computer Law, Estate Planning and Administration, Bankruptcy Law, Loan Structuring and Workouts, Intellectual Property Law, Personal Injury.
Representative Clients: Marmon Industrial Corp; Eckerd Corp; VR Business Brokers; Microspace Communications Corp.; Extend Stay America, Inc.; Tricor Development Corp.; L&M Brokerage, Inc.; CRTS, Inc.; Executive Staffing Services; Branch Banking & Trust Co.
New Bern, North Carolina Office: 2407 Grace Avenue, 28563, P.O. Box 975. Telephone: 252-633-3006. Fax: 252-633-3097.

See Professional Biographies, RALEIGH, NORTH CAROLINA

Howell, Thomas Cooper ....'70 '99 C.575 B.S. in B.A. L.896 J.D. [A W.B.Howell]
Howell, W. Brian, (AV) ....'43 '69 C.576 B.S. L.575 J.D. 1101 A Haynes Street Suite 213
Howison, Robert C., Jr., (AV) ....'15 '39 C&L.575 A.B., J.D. [C Hunton&W.]
Huang, Hans H., (BV) ....'73 '98 C&L.575 B.A., J.D. [A Maupin T.]
Hubbard, Michael W., (AV) .... '59 '84 C.682 B.S. L.893 J.D. [Smith,A.B.D.M.&J.]
Hubbard, William E. ....'— '96 C.34 B.S. L.1228 J.D. [A J.T.Benjamin,Jr.]

Hubbard, Brett A.
(See Cary)

Hudson, Isham B., Jr. ....'29 '56 C.228 A.B. L.575 LL.B. 2305 Byrd St.‡
Huffstetler, Ashley ....'76 '03 C&L.575 B.A., J.D. [A Ragsdale L.]
Huffstetler, Noah H., III, (AV) ....'51 '76 C&L.575 A.B., J.D. [Nelson M.R.&S.]
Huggard, John P., (BV) ....'45 '75 C&L.575 B.A., J.D. 124 St. Mary's St.
Huggins, Molly G. .... '— '03 C.198 B.A. L.575 J.D. [A Smith M.]
Hughes, George W., (AV) '47 '72
C.240 B.A. L.896 J.D. 133 Fayetteville St. Mall, Ste. 200‡
Hugo, Michael P. ....'58 '86 C.1209 B.S. L.61 J.D. 1304 Paddock Dr., Ste. F100‡
Hulett, Mary ....'42 '77 C.813 B.A. L.273 J.D. [Ragsdale L.]
Humphrey, Christopher M. '71 '98 C.576 B.S. L.575 J.D.
[Alston&B.] (See Pat. Sect.)
Humphrey, Maclyn A. '55 '90
C.228 A.B. L.575 J.D. State Dept. of Envir., Health & Nat. Res.
Humrickhouse, Stephani Wilson, (AV) '56 '80
C.188 B.S.I.L.R L.575 J.D. [Nicholls&C.]
Hunoval, Mathias H. "Matt" ....'— '03 C.198 B.A. L.896 J.D. [A Helms M.&W.]
Hunsucker, Ginger Bagley ....'— '03 C&L.575 B.S., J.D. [Cranfill,S.&H.]
Hunt, Cathi J., (BV) '67 '99 C.685 B.A. L.93 J.D.
Assoc. Gen. Coun., Progress Energy
Hunt, Cathy Cubbon .... '61 '96 C.575 B.S. L.1015 J.D. [Gailor,W.&H.]
Hunt, Gregory A. ....'69 '96 C.576 B.S.E.E. L.575 J.D. [A Jenkins,W.&T.] (Pat.) ⊙
Hunt, James B., Jr. ....'37 '66 C.576 B.S. L.575 J.D. [Womble C.S.&R.]
Hunter, John V., III, (AV) ....'30 '55 C.198 B.S. L.575 J.D. [Bode,C.&S.] ‡

Hunter, Richard S., Jr., (AV) '54 '80 C.575 A.B. L.192 J.D. BB
133 Fayetteville Street Mall, Suite 300 P.O. Drawer 470, 27602-0470
Telephone: 919-831-8722 Fax: 919-831-8734
Email: hunteratty@aol.com URL: http://www.rshunteratty.com
Of Counsel: Karen Britt Peeler.
Litigation, Personal Injury, Wrongful Death, Professional Negligence, Product Liability.

See Professional Biographies, RALEIGH, NORTH CAROLINA

Hunter, Robert C. .... '44 '69 C&L.575 A.B., J.D. Ct. of App. J.

Hunton & Williams LLP, (AV)
One Bank of America Plaza, 421 Fayetteville Street Mall, Suite 1400, 27601 ⊙
Telephone: 919-899-3000 FAX: 919-833-6352; 919-899-3096
URL: http://www.hunton.com
Senior Counsel: Robert C. Howison, Jr.; Walton K. Joyner. Partners: Craig A. Bromby; Jean Gordon Carter (Board Certified Specialist in Estate Planning and Probate Law); Charles D. Case; William D. Dannelly; L. Neal Ellis, Jr.; Edward S. Finley, Jr.; William M. Flynn; David R. Fricke; Timothy S. Goettel; Douglas Wayne Kenyon; Thomas J. Manley; William H. McBride; William S. Patterson; Mary Nash Kelly Rusher. Counsel: William P. Andrews, Jr.; Steven B. Epstein; William E. Graham, Jr. Associates: Christopher J. Ayers; Julie Beddingfield; Alison J. Benge; Danielle Bennett; Zachary R. Bishop; John D. Burns; J. Keith Coates, Jr. (Not admitted in NC); John T. Earwood; Kelli Dutrow Jackson (Not admitted in NC); Elizabeth H. Johnson; Timothy D. Johnson; Christopher R. Stambaugh (Not admitted in NC); Ray A. Starling; Jason S. Thomas; Jennifer J. Tung; Robert C. Van Arnam.
General Practice. Administrative/Regulatory Law, Admiralty, Antitrust, Unfair Trade Practices, Bankruptcy, Business, Corporation, Environmental, Insurance, International, Labor, Municipal Bond and Finance Law, Non-Criminal Trials and Appeals, Real Property, Condemnation, Securities Regulation, Taxation, Trademarks, Copyright, Utilities, Probate and Estate Planning.

(This Listing Continued)

Hunton & Williams LLP (Continued)

Washington, D.C. Office: 1900 K Street, N.W., 20006-1109. Telephone: 202-955-1500. Fax: 202-778-2201.
Miami, Florida Office: 1111 Brickell Avenue, Suite 2500, 33131. Telephone: 305-810-2500. Fax: 305-810-2460.
Atlanta, Georgia Office: Bank of America Plaza, 600 Peachtree Street, N.E., Suite 4100, 30308-2216. Telephone: 404-888-4000. Fax: 404-888-4190 and Georgia-Hill Office: Southside Legal Center, 250 Georgia Avenue, S.E., Suite 211, 30312. Telephone: 404-688-5512; 404-688-5513.
New York, New York Office: 200 Park Avenue, 43rd Floor, 10166-0136. Telephone: 212-309-1000. Fax: 212-309-1100.
Charlotte, North Carolina Office: Bank of America Plaza, 101 South Tryon Street, Suite 3500, 28280. Telephone: 704-378-4700. Fax: 704-378-4890.
Knoxville, Tennessee Office: 2000 Riverview Tower, 900 South Gay Street, 37902. Telephone: 865-549-7700. Fax: 865-549-7704.
Dallas, Texas Office: Energy Plaza, 30th Floor, 1601 Bryan Street, 75201-3402. Telephone: 214-979-3000. Fax: 214-880-0011.
Richmond, Virginia Office: Riverfront Plaza, East Tower, 951 East Byrd Street, 23219-4074. Telephone: 804-788-8200. Fax: 804-788-8218; 804-788-8219 and Church Hill Office: 2300 East Marshall Street, 23223. Telephone: 804-775-2248.
McLean, Virginia Office: 1751 Pinnacle Drive, Suite 1700, Tysons Corner, 22102. Telephone: 703-714-7400. Fax: 703-714-7410.
Norfolk, Virginia Office: 500 East Main Street, Suite 1000, 23510-3889. Telephone: 757-640-5300. Fax: 757-625-7720.
Brussels, Belgium Office: Ave Louise 326, B6, 1050 Brussels, Belgium. Telephone: +32 0-2-643-5800. Fax: +32 0-2-643-5822.
Bangkok, Thailand Office: 34/F Abdulrahim Place, 990 Rama IV Road, Bangkok, Thailand, 1050. Telephone: +011 662 636-2366. Fax: +011 662 636-2377.
London, England Office: Fleetway House, 25 Farringdon Street, London EC4A 4AB, England. Telephone: +44 (0)20 7246 5700. Fax: +44 (0)20 7246 5772.
Singapore, Singapore Office: 6 Battery Road, #24-01, Singapore, 049909. Telephone: +65 6534-5608. Fax: +65 6534-5532.
Beijing, China Office: 517-520 South Office Tower, Beijing Kerry Centre, No. 1 Guanghua Road, Chaoyang District, Beijing, PRC 100020, China. Telephone: +86 10 5863 7500. Fax: +86 10 5863 7591.

See Professional Biographies, RALEIGH, NORTH CAROLINA

Huntwork, Vicki Litwin '65 '91 C.472 B.S. L.575 J.D.
(adm. in CA; not adm. in NC; Pat.) 7305 Still Pond Court
Hurley, Julie R. ....'59 '84 C.446 B.S. L.734 J.D. [C Yates,M.&W.]
Hurley, Michael C., (BV) .... '58 '84 C.446 B.A. L.734 J.D. [Yates,M.&W.]
Hurst, Michael D. ....'55 '84 C.1222 B.P.A. L.896 J.D. Transom Development
Huskins, J. Frank ....'11 '32 C&L.575 A.B. 333 Fayetteville St. Mall

Hutchens, Senter & Britton, P.A., The Law Firm of, (BV)
Suite 1540 Two Hanover Square, 27601 ⊙
Mailing Address: P.O. Box 2505, Fayetteville, NC 28302
Telephone: 919-834-2688 Facsimile: 919-834-3373
Email: lawfirm@hutchensandsenter.com URL: http://www.hutchensandsenter.com
Shawna Y. Staton.
General Civil Practice, Trials in all State and Federal Courts, Creditor Bankruptcy, Foreclosures and Collection, Personal Injury, Wrongful Death, Worker's Compensation, Insurance Law, Corporation, Business and Real Estate.
Fayetteville, North Carolina Office: 4317 Ramsey Street, P.O. Box 2505. Telephone: 910-864-6888. Fax: 910-864-6848.
Wilmington, North Carolina Office: Suite 210, 1437 Military Cutoff Road, P.O. Box 12969. Telephone: 910-509-7480. Fax: 910-509-7448.

See Professional Biographies, RALEIGH, NORTH CAROLINA

Hutchison, Fred D., (AV) ....'49 '75 C.575 B.S. L.893 J.D. [Hutchison&M.]
Hutchison, H. Gray, Jr. ....'48 '73 C&L.575 B.S.B.A., J.D. 1300 St. Mary's St.

Hutchison & Mason PLLC, (AV)
3110 Edwards Mill Road, Suite 100, 27612
Telephone: 919-829-9600 Fax: 919-829-9696
Email: info@hutchlaw.com URL: http://www.hutchlaw.com
Fred D. Hutchison; Merrill McCall Mason; Helga Lura Leftwich; J. Robert Tyler, III; Randall M. Whitmeyer; Allen R. Baum; John M. Fogg (Not admitted in NC); William N. Wofford; Kathleen Nowack Worm;—Neil S. Bagchi; Holly Ann Coldiron; L. Aylett Colston; Joshua T. Elliott; Aaron P. Golub; Justyn J. Kasierski (Not admitted in NC); D. Karen Maready; Donald L. Novajosky (Not admitted in NC). Of Counsel: Mary B. Grant.
Business, Corporate, Securities and Commercial Law, including Start-Up and Emerging Growth Companies, Software and Computer Law, Corporate Finance, including Venture Capital Financings and Private Placements, Public Offerings, Corporate Governance, Corporate Mergers, Acquisitions and Dispositions, Joint Ventures, Intellectual Property (Patents, Trademarks, Copyright, Licensing and Trade Secrets), Executive Employment, Compensation and Termination.

See Professional Biographies, RALEIGH, NORTH CAROLINA

Hutson, John N., Jr., (AV) ....'55 '81 C&L.575 B.A., J.D. [Howard,S.F.&H.]
Hwang, Albert Chen-Huei ....'76 '01 C&L.575 B.A., J.D. [A Troutman S.]
Iddings, Susan S. ....'46 '84 C.260 B.A. L.574 J.D. Leg. Drafting Div.
Imperial, Robert K., (BVⓣ) '62 '88 C.1083 B.A. L.469 J.D.
(adm. in GA; not adm. in NC) [C Maupin T.]
Ingersoll, Shaun A. ....'60 '88 C.92 B.S. L.846 J.D. 3733 National Dr., Ste. 215
Ingram, John Randolph, II, (BV) ....'57 '83 C.232 B.A. L.1228 J.D. [Schilawski&I.]
Inlow, Richard Charles ....'62 '98 C.953 B.S. L.1009 J.D. [A Wilson&R.]
Inman, Bradley ....'73 '05 C&L.575 B.S.B.A., J.D. [A Teague,C.D.&G.]
Inman, Lisa D. ....'66 '97 C.691 B.Mus. L.575 J.D. [Wyrick R.Y.&P.]
Inman, Lucy N., (BV) ....'61 '90 C.576 B.A. L.575 J.D. [A Kuniholm]
Isenberg, Michael L. ....'40 '65 C.945 A.B. L.923 LL.B. 4401 Creedmoor Rd.
Ishman, Mark W. ....'70 '01 C.589 B.S. L.1000 J.D. [M.W.Ishman]

Ishman, Mark W., P.C., The Law Office of
9660 Falls of Neuse Road Suite 138-350, 27615
Telephone: 919-468-3266
Email: mishman@ishmanlaw.com URL: http://www.ishmanlawfirm.com
Mark W. Ishman.
Internet Law, E-Commerce, Intellectual Property, Copyrights, Licensing Agreements, Patents, Trade Secrets, Trademarks, Unfair Trade Practice, Corporate, Cyber Law.

See Professional Biographies, RALEIGH, NORTH CAROLINA

Isley, Laura Boyce, (BV) ....'66 '92 C&L.896 B.A., J.D. [Boyce&I.]
Isley, Philip R., (AV) ....'67 '92 C.902 B.A. L.500 J.D. [Boyce&I.]
Ivey, Reef C., II, (AV) ....'43 '68 C.576 B.S. L.575 J.D. [C Shanahan]
Jacks, Maston T. '47 '76 C.893 B.City Plan. L.945 J.D.
(adm. in DC; not adm. in NC) 2401 Landmark Dr.‡
Jackson, Barbara A., (BV) ....'61 '90 C&L.575 B.A., J.D. Gen. Coun.
Jackson, J. Christopher ....'— '99 C&L.575 B.A., J.D. [A Kilpatrick S.]
Jackson, James K. ....'76 '02 C.576 B.A. L.469 J.D. [A Bass,B.&F.]
Jackson, Jeremiah L. ....'78 '04 C.576 B.A. L.575 J.D. 3716 National Drive, Suite 100
Jackson, Jill Schnabel ....'74 '99 C.494 B.A. L.575 J.D. [A Tharrington S.]
Jackson, Kelli Dutrow '65 '02 C.228 B.A. L.1059 J.D.
(adm. in GA; not adm. in NC) [A Hunton&W.]
James, Nathaniel T. ....'55 '92 C.659 B.S. L.893 J.D. 3606 Pritchard Ct.
Janak, Craig M. ....'71 '98 C.107 B.A. L.1292 J.D. [Janak]

Janak Law Firm, P.A.
7404-D Chapel Hill Road, 27607
Telephone: 919-233-0358 Fax: 919-233-0323
Email: cjanak@janaklaw.com

(This Listing Continued)

Janak Law Firm, P.A. (Continued)

Craig M. Janak.
Bankruptcy, Consumer Bankruptcy, Foreclosures, Real Estate, Buying and Selling, Landlord and Tenant, Business Law, Collections, Creditors Rights.
See Professional Biographies, RALEIGH, NORTH CAROLINA

Janvier, William P., (AV) .... '67 '93 C.691 B.A. L.575 J.D. [Everett,G.H.&S.]
Jarrett, C. Hamilton, III, (AV) .... '52 '83 C.160 B.S.C.E. L.469 J.D. [Conner G.S.]
Jean, Katherine E., (AV) .... '60 '85 C&L.575 B.S., J.D. 16 W. Martin St., Ste. 500
Jeffries, Pamela N. ..... '69 '95 C.575 B.A. L.945 J.D. Hearing Offr., Employ. Sec. Comm.
Jenkins, Jack W. .... '56 '84 C.232 B.S.B.A. L.575 J.D. Spec. Supr. Ct. J.
Jenkins, Laura S. .... '68 '97 C.576 B.A. L.790 J.D. 308 W. Millbrook Rd., Ste. C
Jenkins, Richard E., (AV) .... '46 '75 C.576 B.S. L.575 J.D. [Jenkins,W.&T.] (Pat.) ⊙
Jenkins, Robert O., (AV) .... '62 '92 C&L.575 B.A., J.D. [Blanchard,J.M.L.&S.]
Jenkins, Stephanie Thomas .... '66 '92 C.198 B.A. L.575 J.D. [Ⓐ Gailor,W.&H.]

Jenkins, Wilson & Taylor, P.A., (AV)
NCSU Centennial Campus, Suite 101 Venture 11, 920 Main Campus Drive, 27606 ⊙
Telephone: 919-424-3710 Fax: 919-424-3711
URL: http://www.jenkinswilsontaylor.com
Richard E. Jenkins; Jeffrey L. Wilson; Arles A. Taylor, Jr.;—Gregory A. Hunt.
Patent, Trademark and Copyright Law.
Representative Clients: Böwe Bell and Howell Mail Co.; Duke University; Freudenberg Spunweb Co.; GlaxoSmithKline, Inc.; Huesker, Inc.; North Carolina State University; Sumitomo Electric Lightwave Corp.; The University of North Carolina at Chapel Hill; Vanderbilt University.
Durham, North Carolina Office: University Tower, Suite 1400, 3100 Tower Boulevard, 27707-6226. Telephone: 919-493-8000. Fax: 919-419-0383.
See Professional Biographies, RALEIGH, NORTH CAROLINA

Jennings, Barry C. .... '— '03 C.576 B.S. L.575 J.D. [Ⓐ Hedrick E.G.&K.]
Jernigan, Ellen M. .... '— '02 C.576 B.S. L.896 J.D. [Ⓐ Smith,A.B.D.M.&J.]
Jernigan, J. Allen, (AV) '57 '83
C&L.575 A.B., J.D. Spec. Dep. Atty. Gen., NC Dept. of Jus.
Jernigan, John L., (AV) .... '42 '67 C.198 A.B. L.575 J.D. [Smith,A.B.D.M.&J.]
Jernigan, Leonard T., Jr., (AV) .... '50 '76 C.575 B.A. L.574 J.D. [Jernigan]

Jernigan Law Firm, The, A Professional Law Corporation, (AV)
Wachovia Capitol Center Suite 1910, 150 Fayetteville Street Mall, P.O. Box 847, 27602
Telephone: 919-833-1283 Fax: 919-833-1059
Email: ltj@jernlaw.com URL: http://www.jernlaw.com
Leonard T. Jernigan, Jr. (Board Certified Specialist in Workers Compensation, North Carolina State Board of Legal Specialization); N. Victor Farah (Board Certified Specialist in Workers Compensation, North Carolina State Board of Legal Specialization);—Gina E. Cammarano; Lauren R. Trustman.
Trial and Appellate Practice before State and Federal Courts and Agencies, Personal Injury, Workers' Compensation, Toxic Torts (Asbestos), Products Liability.
See Professional Biographies, RALEIGH, NORTH CAROLINA

Jerzak, Jennifer S. .... '— '97 C.893 B.A. L.896 J.D. [Ⓐ Hedrick E.G.&K.]
Jessup, Dianna W., (BV) ...... '60 '90 C&L.575 B.S., J.D. Staff Atty., NC Gen. Assembly
Jessup, Robert M., Jr., (AV) .... '60 '85 C.188 A.B. L.575 J.D. [Sanford H.]
Jeutter, Gerald A. "Jeb", Jr., (AV) .... '— '85 C.945 B.A. L.356 J.D. [Kilpatrick S.]
Jiménez, Gabriel F. .... '73 '98 C.1222 B.B.A. L.259 J.D. [Jiménez]
Jiménez Law Offices, PLLC .... 3737 Glenwood Avenue, Suite 100
John, Joseph R., Sr. .... '39 '71 C&L.575 A.B., J.D. Ct. of App. J.
Johnsey, Elinor .... '80 '05 C.575 B.A. L.896 J.D. [Ⓐ Young M.&H.]
Johnson, David R. .... '53 '78 C.575 A.B. L.896 J.D. North Carolina State Bar
Johnson, Elizabeth H. .... '77 '04 C.162 B.A. L.228 J.D. [Ⓐ Hunton&W.]
Johnson, Emily Perry .... '53 '78 C.471 B.A. L.575 J.D. State Gen. Assembly
Johnson, Erica Renee .... '73 '00 C.1378 B.A. L.574 J.D. Dist. Atty.'s Off.
Johnson, James T., (BV) .... '66 '92 C.228 B.A. L.575 J.D. [J.T.Johnson]
Johnson, Jeffrey J., (BV) .... '53 '91 C.610 B.G.S. L.575 J.D. [Wyrick R.Y.&P.]
Johnson, Joseph E., (BV) .... '41 '66 C&L.896 B.B.A., J.D. [Ⓒ Ragsdale L.]
Johnson, Kari Russwurm, (BV) .... '62 '88 C.232 B.S. L.896 J.D. [Cranfill,S.&H.]
Johnson, Keith H., (AV) .... '62 '91 C.575 B.A. L.893 J.D. [Poyner&S.]
Johnson, Larry D. .... '37 '67 C&L.575 B.S., J.D. Commonwealth Land Title Co.
Johnson, Lundy L. .... '— '89 C&L.574 B.S., J.D. Jud. Clk., Asso. J. Supm. Ct.
Johnson, Patrick J. .... '69 '94 C&L.893 B.A., J.D. [Brooks,P.M.H.&L.] ⊙
Johnson, Robin S. '50 '88 C.338 B.S.Ed. L.575 J.D.
State Gen. Assembly, Research Div.
Johnson, Russell W. .... '77 '04 C.923 B.A. L.575 J.D. [Ⓐ Howard,S.F.&H.]
Johnson, Samuel H., (AV) .... '27 '53 C&L.575 A.B., J.D. [Johnson,H.V.G.&G.]
Johnson, Sarah M. .... '78 '04 C.999 B.A. L.896 J.D. [Ⓐ Wyrick R.Y.&P.]
Johnson, Timothy D. .... '75 '01 C.827 B.A. L.228 J.D. [Ⓐ Hunton&W.]
Johnson, Valerie Alston .... '64 '94 C&L.575 B.A., J.D. [Patterson H.] (⊙Chapel Hill)

Johnson, Hearn, Vinegar, Gee & Glass, PLLC, (AV)
Two Hannover Square, 434 Fayetteville Street Mall, Suite 2200, P.O. Box 1776, 27602 ⊙
Telephone: 919-743-2200 Fax: 919-743-2201
Email: jhvgg@jhvgglaw.com
Samuel H. Johnson; George G. Hearn; Richard J. Vinegar (Resident, Research Triangle Park Office); M. Blen Gee, Jr.; F. Stephen Glass. Of Counsel: Jean Winborne Boyles.
Civil trial and appellate practice before all state and federal courts and administrative agencies, administrative law, including occupational licensing, alternative dispute resolution, automobile dealer law, business and corporate law, franchise law, government relations, including representation before the General Assembly and regulatory agencies, insurance insolvency, state and local taxation, trade association law, wills, trusts and estates and unfair competition, landlord tenant, property tax appeals, e-commerce, business enterprises, closely held businesses, limited liability companies, partnerships, small businesses, buying or selling a business, employment contracts, human resources, business planning, lawsuits, licensing agreements, internet, starting a business, strategic alliances, joint venture.
Durham Office: Generation Plaza, Suite 200, 1822 N.C. Highway 54 East, 27713. Telephone: 919-544-3302. Fax: 919-544-5920. Email: richard@vinegarlaw.com.
See Professional Biographies, RALEIGH, NORTH CAROLINA

Johnson, James T., P.A., (BV)
The Pilot Mill Building, 1101 Haynes Street, Suite 103, 27604
Mailing Address: P.O. Box 886, Raleigh, NC 27602
Telephone: 919-833-8133 Fax: 919-833-8305
Email: jjohnson@jtjlaw.com URL: http://www.jtjlaw.com
James T. Johnson.
Personal Injury, Automobile Accidents, Wrongful Death, Nursing Home Litigation, Medical Malpractice, Insurance Litigation, Commercial Litigation, Construction Litigation.
See Professional Biographies, RALEIGH, NORTH CAROLINA

Johnston, Margaret G., (AV) .... '47 '74 C.1044 B.A. L.575 J.D. [Pinna J.&B.]
Jolly, Jane Helen .... '57 '83 C&L.280 B.A., J.D. U.S. Attys. Off.
Jolly, John R., Jr., (AV) .... '42 '67 C&L.575 A.B., J.D. J.
Jones, Abraham Penn .... '52 '77 C&L.309 A.B., J.D. Supr. Ct. J.
Jones, Benji Taylor .... '69 '99 C.802 B.F.A. L.178 J.D. [Ⓐ Smith,A.B.D.M.&J.]
Jones, Beth Tyner .... '— '88 C&L.1228 B.A., J.D. [Ⓐ Womble C.S.&R.]
Jones, D. James, Jr., (AV) .... '43 '68 C.198 A.B. L.575 J.D. [Allen&P.]
Jones, E. Richard, Jr., (AV) .... '32 '61 C&L.575 A.B., J.D. 16 W. Martin St., Suite 404
Jones, Henry W., Jr., (AV) .... '52 '78 C.576 B.A. L.692 J.D. [Jordan P.W.G.J.&C.]
Jones, John Alan, (AV) .... '56 '82 C&L.575 B.A., J.D. [Martin&J.] (⊙Wilmington)
Jones, Kelly B. .... '71 '97 C.953 B.S. L.1228 J.D. [Ⓐ Womble C.S.&R.]
Jones, Linwood L. .... '59 '84 C&L.575 B.A., J.D. Coun., State Gen. Assembly
Jones, Lori P. .... '73 '04 C.576 B.S. L.575 J.D. [Ⓐ Patterson,D.C.B.&A.]
Jones, R. Michael '46 '71 C&L.575 A.B., J.D.
V.P., Pub. Affs., Carolina Power & Light Co.
Jones, Richard E., (AV) .... '37 '71 C.451 B.A. L.273 J.D. 4000 Edward Pride Wynd‡
Jones, Roland S., Jr. .... '54 '81 C.575 B.A. L.790 J.D. Capital Advisers, Inc.
Jones, Rose M. '51 '86 C.471 B.A. L.273 J.D.
(adm. in VA; not adm. in NC) Pres., Law Makers, Inc.
Jones, Timothy M. .... '66 '91 C.696 B.A. L.94 J.D. Supr. Ct. Clk.
Jones, Todd Allen .... '71 '98 C.575 B.S.P.H. L.1345 J.D. [Anderson,J.&G.]
Jones, Tracey L. .... '72 '97 C.575 B.A. L.896 J.D. [Ⓐ Teague,C.D.&G.]

Jones Martin Parris & Tessner Law Offices, PLLC
(See Martin & Jones)

Joneth, Robert A. .... '46 '78 C&L.966 B.S., J.D. [Burch,J.&R.]
Jonson, David N. .... '— '97 C.902 B.A. L.790 J.D. [Ⓐ Kennedy C.L.&H.]
Jordan, Doris K. .... '— '04 C.34 B.A. L.577 J.D. [Ⓐ Cheshire,P.S.B.&V.]
Jordan, Evia L. .... '61 '87 C.896 B.A. L.574 J.D. 16 West Martin Street, Suite 601
Jordan, James F. .... '42 '68 C.469 B.A. L.280 LL.B. 8015 Creedmoor Rd.
Jordan, John R., Jr., (AV) .... '21 '48 C&L.575 B.A., J.D. [Ⓒ Jordan P.W.G.J.&C.]
Jordan, Jonathan C. ... '68 '97 C.896 B.A. L.575 J.D. Dir. of Research, John Locke Found.

Jordan Price Wall Gray Jones & Carlton, (AV)
A Professional Limited Liability Company
1951 Clark Avenue, P.O. Box 10669, 27605-0669
Telephone: 919-828-2501 Telecopier: 919-834-8447
Email: law@jordanprice.com URL: http://www.jordanprice.com
Members of Firm: Joseph E. Wall; R. Frank Gray; Henry W. Jones, Jr.; Paul T. Flick; Terry J. Carlton; Hope Derby Carmichael; Jonathan P. Carr; William K. Hale; Jeffrey R. Ellinger. Associates: Stephen R. Dolan; Sara C. Moesta; Brian S. Edlin; Jeffrey John Goebel; Joseph E. Propst; Robert L. Ange; Jessica E. Cooley. Of Counsel: John R. Jordan, Jr.; Robert R. Price; Karen Kelly Carlton.
General Practice in all State and Federal Courts. Trials. Banking, Insurance, Health and Hospital Law. Corporate Practice and Administrative Law, Creditors' Rights and Bankruptcy, Insurance Defense. Condominium and Homeowners' Association Law. Estate Planning. Legislative Representation, Commercial Real Estate and Local Government Law.
Representative Clients: NC Association of Alcoholic Beverage Control Boards; Canal Insurance Company; House of Raeford Farms; NC Association of Plumbing-Heating-Cooling Contractors; Jefferson-Pilot Life Insurance Co.; NC Manufactured Housing Institute; Greentree Servicing, LLC; Paragon Commercial Bank; Daimler Chrysler Corp.; UBS.
See Professional Biographies, RALEIGH, NORTH CAROLINA

Joseph, Shannon R., (BV) .... '69 '95 C.968 B.A. L.896 J.D. [Ⓐ Smith M.]
Joslin, William, (AV) .... '20 '48 C.575 A.B. L.178 J.D. [Joslin,S.&L.]
Joslin, Sedberry & Lamkin, L.L.P., (AV) .... 4006 Barrett Dr.
Joyner, Gary K., (AV) .... '— '82 C.575 B.A. L.896 J.D. [Kilpatrick S.]
Joyner, Kevin S. .... '71 '98 C.232 B.S./B.A. L.1345 J.D. [Ⓐ Ogletree,D.N.S.&S.]
Joyner, Rebecca Blackmon .... '74 '04 C.575 B.A. L.262 J.D. [Ⓟ Parker,P.A.&B.]
Joyner, Walton K., (AV) .... '33 '60 C&L.575 A.B., J.D. [Ⓒ Hunton&W.]
Justus, Kimberly S. .... '72 '97 C.277 B.S. L.896 J.D. [Ⓢ Womble C.S.&R.]
Kane, Gary P. .... '43 '66 C.112 A.B. L.1066 J.D. Exec. Dir., N.C. Housing Fin. Agcy.
Kane, George W., III, Attorney at Law, (BV) '49 '81
C.1275 B.A. L.575 J.D. 242 W. Millbrook Rd.
Kaplan, Harrison J., (BV) .... '59 '87 C&L.575 B.A., J.D. 2304 Sweet Birch Court
Kaplan, Martin L. .... '46 '98 C.563 B.A. L.574 J.D. [Kaplan] (⊙Balt., MD)
Kaplan Law Office, The .... 6200 Falls of Neuse Road, Suite 200
Kapp, M. Keith, (AV) .... '53 '79 C&L.575 A.B., J.D. [Maupin T.]

Kash, Gregory M., Law Offices of, (BV) '62 '87 C.198 B.A. L.1228 J.D.
Two Hannover Square, 434 Fayetteville Street, Suite 2350, 27601
Telephone: 919-861-2006 Facsimile: 919-861-0504
Email: gregkash@mindspring.com URL: http://www.gkashlaw.com
Civil Litigation, Personal Injury, Medical Malpractice, Products Liability, Automobile Accidents, Wrongful Death, Premises Liability, Workers Compensation, Animal Law, Consumer Law, Business Law, Labor and Employment, Military Law.
See Professional Biographies, RALEIGH, NORTH CAROLINA

Kasierski, Justyn J. '72 '00 C.690 B.A. L.228 J.D.
(adm. in MA; not adm. in NC) [Ⓐ Hutchison&M.]
Kassor, Eric H. .... '59 '85 C&L.1019 B.A., J.D. [Kassor&P.]
Kassor & Paluch .... 3000 Highwoods Boulevard
Katzenbach, Daniel G., (BV) .... '72 '97 C.902 B.A. L.896 J.D. [Cranfill,S.&H.]
Kaylor, Robert W., (AV) .... '44 '74 C.232 A.B. L.575 J.D. [R.W.Kaylor]

Kaylor, Robert W., P.A., (AV)
225 Hillsborough Street, Suite 480, 27603
Telephone: 919-828-5250 Fax: 919-828-5240
Email: bkaylor@rwkaylorlaw.com
Robert W. Kaylor.
Public Utility Regulation, State Legislative Practice, Administrative Agency Practice, Workers Compensation.
See Professional Biographies, RALEIGH, NORTH CAROLINA

Keadey, Stephen C. .... '69 '03 C&L.575 A.B., J.D. [Ⓐ Ellis&W.] (⊙Cary)
Kearns, Edwin N., (BV) .... '33 '64 C&L.575 A.B., LL.B. P.O. Box 806
Keating, Marylin A. '69 '95 C&L.575 B.A., J.D.
Vice President, Human Res., Legacy Healthcare Services, Inc.
Keefe, Sarah Anne, (AV) .... '67 '92 C&L.472 B.S., J.D. [Womble C.S.&R.] (Pat.)
Keegan, Amy L. .... '77 '02 C.886 B.A. L.228 J.D. [Ⓐ Nelson M.R.&S.]
Keen, C. Matthew, (BV) .... '61 '87 C.576 B.S. L.575 J.D. [Ogletree,D.N.S.&S.]
Keen, Ruth M. .... '58 '86 C.575 B.A. L.896 J.D. 1508 Brooks Ave.
Keenan, Pamela P., (BV) .... '58 '87 C.1142 B.A. L.802 J.D. [Kirschbaum,N.K.&G.]
Kelley, Laura M. .... '74 '00 C.945 B.S. L.228 J.D. [Ⓐ Myers B.S.&S.] (See Pat. Sect.)
Kelly, George E., III, (BV) .... '56 '84 C.228 B.A. L.896 J.D. [Kelly]
Kelly Law Firm, (BV) .... 284 W. Millbrook Rd., Ste. B

Kelly & West, P.A.
(See Lillington)

Kemp, Daniel W. '45 '70 C.610 A.B. L.150 J.D.
(adm. in OH; not adm. in NC) Assoc. Gen. Coun., Progress Energy
Kennedy, Christian Michael, (AV) '63 '97
C.859 B.A. L.1228 J.D. [Patterson,D.C.B.&A.]
Kennedy, Christine W. .... '54 '01 C.103 B.A. L.94 J.D. Legal Aid of North Carolina

Kennedy Covington Lobdell & Hickman, L.L.P., (AV)
434 Fayetteville Street Mall, 19th Floor, P.O. Box 1070, 27602-1070 ⊙
Telephone: 919-743-7300 Fax: 919-743-7358
URL: http://www.kennedycovington.com
Partners: Stanford D. Baird; F. Daniel Bell, III; Curtis C. Brewer, IV; William J. Brian; Amie Flowers Carmack; Kent F. Christison; David Scott Coward; A. Lee Hogewood III; Alan H. Peterson; Lacy H. Reaves; John L. Sarratt; William G. Scoggin; Michael R. Thornton; Robert B. Womble. Special

(This Listing Continued)

Kennedy Covington Lobdell & Hickman, L.L.P. (Continued)

Counsel: Eric M. Braun (Also at Research Triangle Park, North Carolina Office); Patrick L. Byker; Brett T. Hanna; Thomas I. Lyon; John E. (Jack) Markham, Jr.; Neal B. Wolgin. Associates: Ann M. Anderson; Jason L. Barron; Brian Fork; Grayson S. Hale; David N. Jonson; Michael F. King; Katherine Stukes McKenzie; Daniel J. Palmieri; Craigie D. Sanders; David E. Wagner; Margaret Rose Westbrook; C. Allen York.
Administrative Law, Alternative Dispute Resolution, Antitrust and Trade Regulation, Bankruptcy, Banks and Banking, Business Law, Commercial Law, Commercial Real Estate Development, Construction Law, Corporate Law, Debt and Equity Finance, Emerging Growth Companies, Employee Benefits, Employment Law, Entrepreneurial Business Law, Environmental Law, Family Law, Finance, Governmental, Health Care, Immigration and Naturalization, Intellectual Property, International Law, Labor and Employment, Land Sales, Land Use Regulation, Limited Liability Companies and Partnerships, Litigation, Medical Malpractice, Mergers, Acquisitions and Divestitures, Non-Profit and Charitable Organizations, Patents, Private Equity, Products Liability, Professional Liability, Public Utility Law, Real Estate Development, Real Estate Leasing, Real Estate Finance, Securities, Taxation, Technology Law, Trademarks, Trial Practice, Trusts and Estates, Utility Law, Venture Capital, Zoning, Planning and Land Use.
Charlotte, North Carolina Office: Hearst Tower, 214 North Tryon Street, 47th Floor, 28202. Telephone: 704-331-7400. Fax: 704-331-7598.
Research Triangle Park, North Carolina Office: P.O. Box 14210, Research Triangle Park, 27709-4210, 2801 Slater Road, Suite 120, Morrisville, 27560. Telephone: 919-466-1190. Fax: 919-831-7040.
Columbia, South Carolina Office: NBSC Building, Suite 850, 1122 Lady Street, 29201. Telephone: 803-251-2300. Fax: 803-251-2315.
Rock Hill, South Carolina Office: 140 East Main Street, Suite 220, P.O. Box 11429, 29731-1429. Telephone: 803-329-7600. Fax: 803-329-7677.

See Professional Biographies, RALEIGH, NORTH CAROLINA

Kenney, Kirsten E. .... '— '03 C.914 B.A. L.228 J.D. [Ⓐ Kilpatrick S.]

Kennon, Craver, Belo, Craig & McKee, PLLC
(See Durham)

Kenyon, Douglas Wayne, (AV) .... '54 '79 C&L.602 B.A., J.D. [Hunton&W.]
Kenyon, Rosemary Gill, (AV) ...... '54 '79 C.741 B.A. L.602 J.D. [Smith,A.B.D.M.&J.]
Kerner, Patricia P., (AV) .... '60 '85 C.896 B.A. L.575 J.D. [Bailey&D.]
Kerner, Robert C., Jr., (AV) ....'59 '86 C.896 B.A. L.1228 J.D. [Teague,C.D.&G.]
Kesler, William T., Jr. .... '— '01 C.575 B.A. L.1228 J.D. [Ⓐ Yates,M.&W.]

Kestenbaum Law Firm, P.C.
(See Durham)

Kiger, Christopher R. .... '75 '02 C.240 B.A. L.575 J.D. [Ⓐ Smith,A.B.D.M.&J.]
Kilbride, Nina G. .... '69 '97 C.810 B.A. L.896 J.D. [Kilbride,P.]
Kilbride, Terry M., (BV) .... '65 '90 C.999 B.A. L.896 J.D. [Kilbride,P.]
Kilbride Law Firm, The, PLLC, (BV) .... 741 W. Johnson St.
Killen, Russell B., (AV) ....'69 '94 C.575 B.A. L.228 J.D. [Parker,P.A.&B.]
Killian, Leon M., III, (AV) ....'44 '69 C&L.575 B.S., J.D. [Nelson M.R.&S.]
Kilpatrick, Thomas C. ....'71 '96 C&L.575 B.S., J.D. [Manning,F.&S.]

Kilpatrick Stockton LLP, (AV)
Suite 400, 3737 Glenwood Avenue, 27612 ⊙
Telephone: 919-420-1700 Facsimile: 919-420-1800
Email: info@KilpatrickStockton.com URL: http://www.KilpatrickStockton.com
Members of Firm:
Randall David Avram; Jeffrey A. Benson; Alfred P. Carlton, Jr.; Lois W. Colbert; Lisa J. Dixon; Theodore C. Edwards, II; Sarah Wesley Fox (Resident); Patricia W. Goodson; Richard David Haygood; Carl W. Hibbert (Resident); Gerald A. "Jeb" Jeutter, Jr. (Resident); Gary K. Joyner (Resident); David M. Krasnow; William F. Lane; Steven J. Levitas; W. Christopher Matton; Alan H. McConnell (Resident); Gregg E. McDougal (Resident); Alan D. McInnes; Martha L. Sewell; Hayden J. Silver, III; Jeffrey T. Skinner; Craig B. Wheaton (Resident). Counsel: Michael L. Schenk. Resident Associates: Carolyn A. Bachl; Betsy Cooke; Lorien Golaski; Lawrence J. Gould; Marcella A. Harshbarger; Robert G. Hensley, Jr.; J. Christopher Jackson; Kirsten E. Kenney; David C. Lindsay; Stephen S. Logue; Emily A. Moseley; Jennifer S. O'Connor (Not admitted in NC); Ms. Dorinda L. Peacock; Deborah L. Pritchard; B. Ford Robertson; Sabrina Presnell Rockoff; Catherine L. Thomas; Linda B. Tigges; Elizabeth C. Williamson; W. Swain Wood.
Civil Trial and Appellate Practice in all State and Federal Courts, Federal State and Local Taxation, Probate, Trust and Estate Planning, Real Estate, Environmental, Corporate, Corporate Reorganization, Securities, Banking Commercial, Antitrust, Labor, Employment, Administrative, Bankruptcy, Construction, Healthcare, Intellectual Property, Professional Malpractice, Products Liability and Negligence Law, Domestic Law and Equitable Distribution, Employee Benefits and Executive Compensation, Entrepreneurial Development, Franchising, Insurance Defense, Sports and Entertainment, State Agency and Lobbying Practice.
Atlanta, Georgia Office: Suite 2800, 1100 Peachtree Street. Telephone: 404-815-6500. Facsimile: 404-815-6555. Telex: 54-2307.
Augusta, Georgia Office: 699 Broad Street, Suite 1400, 30903-2043. Telephone: 706-724-2622. Facsimile: 706-722-0219.
Charlotte, North Carolina Office: Suite 2500, 214 North Tryon Street, 28202. Telephone: 704-338-5000. Facsimile: 704-338-5125.
London, England Office: 39th Floor, One Canada Square, London E145 NZ. Telephone: 44 (0)20 7154 6000. Facsimile: 44 (0)20 7154 6100.
New York, New York Office: 805 Third Avenue, 20th Floor, 10022. Telephone: 212-912-3527.
Stockholm, Sweden Office: Box 5421, SE-114 84. Telephone: 46-8-505-646-00. Facsimile: 46-8-505-646-99.
Washington, D.C. Office: Suite 900, 607 14th Street, N.W., 20005-2018. Telephone: 202-508-5800. Facsimile: 202-508-5858.
Winston-Salem, North Carolina Office: 1001 West Fourth Street, 27101-2400. Telephone: 336-607-7300. Facsimile: 336-607-7500.

See Professional Biographies, RALEIGH, NORTH CAROLINA

Kimbrell, Tracy Wood ....'80 '05 C.576 B.A. L.575 J.D. [Ⓐ Parker,P.A.&B.]
Kindel, Christopher M. ....'75 '01 C.846 B.A. L.575 J.D. [Ⓐ Nelson M.R.&S.]
King, Dayatra T., (AV) .... '72 '97 C.575 B.A. L.228 J.D. [Bailey&D.]
King, H. Lloyd, Jr. '53 '78 C.314 B.A. L.45 J.D.
(adm. in FL; not adm. in NC) Admin. Law Judge
King, Katie Hardersen ....'— '02 C.471 B.A. L.1228 J.D. [Ⓐ Sullivan&G.]
King, Michael F. .... '— '98 C.674 A.B. L.846 J.D. [Ⓐ Kennedy C.L.&H.]
Kingsbery, Douglas E., (AV) .... '54 '80 C&L.228 A.B., J.D. [Tharrington S.]
Kirby, David F., (AV) .... '51 '77 C&L.575 A.B., J.D. [Kirby&H.]
Kirby, John M., (BV) .... '66 '94 C.576 B.A. L.575 J.D. [Ⓐ McDaniel&A.]
Kirby, Lee M., Jr., (AV) .... '56 '87 C.118 B.A. L.309 J.D. [Smith,A.B.D.M.&J.]
Kirby, Sammy R. .... '47 '73 C&L.575 A.B., J.D. Atty. Gen. Off.

Kirby & Holt, L.L.P., (AV) BB
(Formerly Edwards & Kirby)
Suite 100 3201 Glenwood Avenue, P.O. Box 31665, 27622
Telephone: 919-881-2111 Fax: 919-781-8630
URL: http://www.kirby-holt.com
David F. Kirby; C. Mark Holt; William B. Bystrynski; Isaac L. Thorp;—Laurie G. Armstrong.
Personal injury, including medical malpractice, products liability and catastrophic injury, and business torts.

See Professional Biographies, RALEIGH, NORTH CAROLINA

***Kirkland, Byron B.**, (AV)* .... *'61 '87 C&L.575 B.A., J.D. [Smith,A.B.D.M.&J.]*
Kirkman, A. Larkin, (BV) ... '37 '65 C.575 A.B. L.145 J.D. 16 W. Martin St., Ste. 808-09
Kirkman, David N. .... '53 '79 C.198 B.A. L.575 J.D. P.O. Box 629
Kirschbaum, Frank S., (AV) ....'69 '96 C&L.575 B.A., J.D. [Kirschbaum,N.K.&G.]
Kirschbaum, Ronald I., (AV) ......'42 '67 C.1365 A.B. L.575 J.D. [Kirschbaum,N.K.&G.]
Kirschbaum, Nanney, Keenan & Griffin, P.A., (AV)
2418 Blue Ridge Rd., Ste. 200 (⊙Charlotte)

Kissling, Lawrence J., III .... '62 '88 C.623 B.S.E.D. L.809 J.D. P.O. Box 99551
Klapp, William R., Jr., (AV) .... '— '86 C.886 B.A. L.262 J.D. [DLPiper R.G.C.U.]
Klein, Jamie W. '65 '92 C.674 A.B. L.569 J.D.
(adm. in NY; not adm. in NC) IBM Corp.
Kleissler, Thomas F. '60 '88 C&L.276 B.A., J.D.
(adm. in NJ; not adm. in NC) Gen. Coun., GE Capital Mortgage Servs., Inc.
Kline, Ray Martin .... '74 '01 C.575 B.A. L.94 J.D. [Kline]
Kline Law Office .... 4030 Wake Forest Road, Suite 300
Klopfer, Eric B. '61 '92 C.665 B.A. L.976 J.D.
(adm. in OH; not adm. in NC) V.P. & Sr. Coun., General Electric Capital Mortgage
Klotzberger, Kathy A., (AV) '51 '81 C.575 B.A. L.180 J.D.
Sr. V. P., First-Citizens Bank & Trust Company
Klym, Mark R. .... '70 '95 C.882 B.A. L.607 J.D. [Brady,N.K.&M.]
Knight, Roger Weldon ....'60 '85 C.953 B.A. L.575 J.D. [Wyrick R.Y.&P.]
Kniskern, Joseph Warren, (AVⓉ) '51 '76 C&L.260 B.S.B.A., J.D.
(adm. in FL; not adm. in NC) 1020 Stradshire Dr.
Knott, Joe Thomas, III, (AV) .... '51 '80 C&L.575 B.S., J.D. [Knott,C.&B.]

Knott, Clark & Berger, L.L.P., (AV)
4800 Six Forks Road, Suite 100, 27609
Telephone: 919-783-5900 Telecopier: 919-783-9650 URL: http://www.knottclarkberger.com
URL: http://www.lawyers.com/pncb
Members of Firm: Joe Thomas Knott, III; Michael Wood Clark; Bruce W. Berger;—Kenneth R. Murphy, III.
General Practice in State and Federal Courts. Medical Malpractice, Nursing Malpractice, Hospital Liability, Plaintiffs Personal Injury, Wrongful Death, Automobile Accidents and Injuries, Commercial Vehicle Liability, Nursing Home Negligence, Workers Compensation, Insurance Bad Faith, Insurance Litigation.

See Professional Biographies, RALEIGH, NORTH CAROLINA

Knox, Jennifer Jane .... '74 '00 C.999 B.A. L.577 J.D. Dist. J.

Knudsen, Karl E., Law Offices of, (AV) '52 '78 C.576 B.A. L.575 J.D.
Five West Hargett Street, Suite 1100, P.O. Box 2386, 27601
Telephone: 919-828-5566 Fax: 919-834-3343
Email: kknudsen@karlkudsenlaw.com URL: http://www.knudsen-law.com
(Board Certified Specialist in State Criminal Law, North Carolina State Board of Legal Specialization).
Associate: Eileen A. Mullen.
Criminal Law, Driving While Intoxicated, Drug Crimes, Felonies, Homicide, Misdemeanors, Traffic Violations, Personal Injury, Medical Malpractice, Auto Accidents, Wrongful Death, Products Liability, Workers Compensation.

See Professional Biographies, RALEIGH, NORTH CAROLINA

Kochanek, Colleen, (CV) ....'67 '92 C.347 B.A. L.896 J.D. [Ⓐ Holt Y.M.&H.]
Kohn, Howard S., (BV) ....'55 '81 C.228 A.B. L.910 J.D. [H.Kohn]
Kohn, Howard, Law Offices of, (BV) .... 4515 Falls of Neuse Rd., Ste. 175
Koman, Leigh Emerson ....'49 '74 C.228 A.B. L.575 J.D. Asst. Atty. Gen.
Konides, James A., (CVⓉ) '61 '86 C.836 B.A. L.260 J.D.
(adm. in FL; not adm. in NC) 9650 Strickland Rd.
Korando, Kimberly J., (AV) ....'59 '86 C&L.623 B.S., J.D. [Smith,A.B.D.M.&J.]
Kornegay-Timmons, Patricia A. '62 '88
C.575 B.A. L.228 J.D. Assoc. Gen. Coun., Progress Energy
Kozar, Carol A. .... '65 '97 C.103 B.A. L.575 J.D. IBM

Kramer, Howard A., (BV) '44 '71 C.966 B.S. L.575 J.D.
300 West Millbrook Road, Suite 101, 27609
Telephone: 919-821-4600 Fax: 919-787-1771
Email: hk11772003@yahoo.com URL: http://www.lawyers.com/kramerlaw
Administrative Law, Health Care Law, Government Relations, Lobbying, Representation before State Agencies and Boards, Professional Licensing.

See Professional Biographies, RALEIGH, NORTH CAROLINA

Krasner, Joshua M., (BV) ....'67 '92 C.575 B.S. L.896 J.D. [Maupin T.]
Krasner, Tina A. ....'67 '93 C.893 B.A. L.896 J.D. Asst. Atty. Gen., Dept. of Jus.
Krasnow, David M., (AV) .... '— '88 C.415 B.S. L.1209 J.D. [Kilpatrick S.] (Pat.)
Kratt, Emil William, (BV) .... '62 '87 C&L.896 B.A., J.D. [Wyrick R.Y.&P.]
Kristianson, Andrew E. ....'— '99 C.939 B.A. L.911 J.D. [Ⓐ Helms M.&W.]
Krosner, David R., (AV) ....'63 '89 C.338 B.S. L.436 J.D. [Poyner&S.]
Kuhn, Benjamin R. ....'70 '97 C.1128 B.A. L.831 J.D. [Ⓐ Holt Y.M.&H.]
Kuhns, Kirk D., (AV) .... '68 '94 C.575 B.S. L.1202 J.D. [Cranfill,S.&H.]
Kuniholm, Elizabeth F., (AV) ....'47 '81 C&L.228 A.B., J.D. [Kuniholm] ⊙

Kuniholm Law Firm, (AV)
1500 Sunday Drive, Suite 208, P.O. Box 30303, 27622 ⊙
Telephone: 919-854-4454 Telecopier: 919-854-4450
Email: kuniholmlaw@kuniholmlaw.com URL: http://www.kuniholmlaw.com
Elizabeth F. Kuniholm;—Lucy N. Inman; Ashley Browning Young; Patrick F. Balestrieri. Of Counsel: Kim Church.
Civil Trial and Appellate Practice in all State and Federal Courts, Personal Injury and Wrongful Death, Medical and Professional Negligence, Obstetric and Pediatric Malpractice, Brain Injury. Trucking Accidents, Automobile Accidents. Insurance Litigation. Sexual Abuse.
Asheville, North Carolina Office: 46 Haywood Street, Suite 250. Telephone: 800-350-7574.

See Professional Biographies, RALEIGH, NORTH CAROLINA

Kunstling, Amy C. .... '71 '96 C&L.228 A.B., J.D. State Dept. of Jus.
Kurtz, Howard A., (BV) .... '67 '92 C&L.575 B.A., J.D. [Kurtz&B.]

Kurtz & Blum, PLLC, (BV)
16 West Martin Street, 10th Floor, 27601
Telephone: 919-832-7700; Toll Free: 888-505-7780 Facsimile: 919-832-2740 URL: http://www.lawyers.com/kurtzandblum
Email: info@kurtzandblum.com URL: http://www.KurtzandBlum.com
Howard A. Kurtz; Seth A. Blum. Associates: Meredith S. Nicholson; Paula K. McGrann; Adam P. Soltys.
Criminal Law, DWI, Drug Crimes, Felonies, Homicides, Misdemeanors, Parole and Probation, Sexual Assaults, Traffic Violations, White Collar Crimes, Family Law, Child Custody, Child Support, Divorce, Domestic Violence, Spousal Support, Personal Injury, Auto Accidents, Sexual Abuse, Wrongful Death, Legal Malpractice, Medical Malpractice, Immigration.

See Professional Biographies, RALEIGH, NORTH CAROLINA

Kurz, Mary Elizabeth ....'44 '72 C.452 B.A. L.446 J.D. Campus Box 7008
Kushner, David, (AV) .... '63 '96 C.575 A.B. L.228 J.D. [Brooks,P.M.H.&L.] ⊙
Kuszaj, James M. ....'47 '75 C.734 B.A. L.912 J.D. 9650 Strickland Rd. (Pat.)
Kyles, Charles C. ....'69 '01 C.576 B.A. L.575 J.D. [Ⓐ Stuart]
Ladd, Suzanne R. .... '71 '97 C&L.575 B.A., J.D. [Sokol M.S.O.L.P.]
Lagerholm, Suzanne Collins .... '67 '99 C&L.575 B.A., J.D. [Ⓐ Ellis&W.] (⊙Cary)
Laite, Gilbert C., III, (AV) '57 '84
C.1248 B.S.B.A. L.896 J.D. [Maupin T.] (⊙Wilmington)
Lake, Brian D., (BV) ....'58 '87 C.885 B.A. L.896 J.D. [Lewis&R.]
Lake, I. Beverly, Jr. .... '34 '60 C&L.896 B.S., J.D. Assoc. Supm. Ct. Jus.
Lakin, Jennifer Karleen '70 '96 C.575 B.A. L.260 J.D.
(adm. in SC; not adm. in NC) Adm. Off. of the Cts.
La Mantia, Mark A., (BV) .... '58 '82 C.597 B.A. L.596 J.D. [Farrell&L.]
Lamb, Zee B. .... '58 '86 C.228 A.B. L.575 J.D. 133 Fayetteville St. Mall, Ste. 100‡

Lamkin, Laura Jean . . . . '60 '94 C.575 B.S. L.574 J.D. [Joslin,S.&L.]
Lane, Leslie C. . . . . '78 '04 C.575 B.A. L.280 J.D. [Ⓐ Nelson M.R.&S.]

Lane, Robert J., III, Law Office of '64 '89 C.1228 B.B.A. L.575 J.D.
107 Fayetteville Street Mall, Suite 201, 27601
Telephone: 919-835-9095 Fax: 919-838-5299
Email: rlane@lawyer.com URL: http://www.robertjlanelaw.com
(Also Member, Wake County Traffic & DWI Center, PLLC).
Criminal Law, Driving While Intoxicated (DWI), Drug Crimes, Felonies, Assault, Traffic, Personal Injury, Auto Accidents, Wrongful Death, Employment, Discrimination, Harassment.
See Professional Biographies, RALEIGH, NORTH CAROLINA

Lane, William F. . . . . '— '97 C.602 B.S. L.515 J.D. [Kilpatrick S.] (Pat.)
Lange, David L. . . . . '38 '64 C&L.339 B.S., LL.B. Prof., Duke Univ. Sch. of Law
Lannom, Sarah A. . . . . '66 '91 C.210 B.A. L.896 J.D. 1505 Mail Service Center
Lapinski, Alexander L. . . . . '66 '03 C.178 B.A. L.1009 J.D. [Ⓐ Farrell&L.]
Larcade, Jodee Sparkman, (AV) . . . . . . '54 '79 C.228 B.A. L.802 J.D. [Larcade,H.&A.P.]

Larcade, Heiskell and Askew PLLC, (AV)
3716 National Drive, Suite 118, 27612
Telephone: 919-785-3494 Facsimile: 919-785-3221
Jodee Sparkman Larcade; Christopher Neil Heiskell; Roger Allan Askew (Resident, Rocky Mount Office);—Margaret P. Eagles.
See Professional Biographies, RALEIGH, NORTH CAROLINA

Larger, Pamela Leonard . . . . . '67 '04 C.383 B.A. L.421 J.D. Staff Atty., Progress Energy
Larson, David D., Jr. . . . . '71 '98 C.896 B.A. L.972 J.D. 5 W. Flargett St., Ste. 310
Lassiter, Melissa Owens '65 '90
C.575 B.A. L.1228 J.D. Admin. Law J., Off. of Admin. Hearings
Lasso, Scott J., (BV) . . . . '67 '92 C.500 B.B.A. L.896 J.D. [Ⓐ Lewis&R.]
Lathan, William R., Jr., (AV) . . . . . '— '75 C&L.575 A.B., J.D. [Ward&S.] (⊙New Bern)
Laton, Donald W., (BV) . . . . '59 '86 C.575 B.S. L.469 J.D. Asst. Atty. Gen.
Laufer, Leslie Ann . . . . '53 '91 C.914 B.A. L.575 J.D. Law Clk., Supm. Ct. Jus.
Laughinghouse, Durwood S., (AV) '48 '74
C.576 B.S. L.896 J.D. Resident V.P., Norfolk Southern Corp.
Laurie, James P., III, (BV) . . . . '62 '92 C.902 B.A. L.1228 J.D. [J.P.Laurie,III]

Laurie, James P., III, PLLC, The Law Office of, (BV)
8311 Six Forks Road, Suite 111, 27615
Telephone: 919-256-4455 Fax: 919-256-4466
Email: jameslaurie@laurielaw.com URL: http://www.laurielaw.com
James P. Laurie, III. Associates: Jina B. Propst; Andrew T. Cornelius.
Construction Law, Mechanics Liens and Bond Claims, Construction Litigation, Construction Defects, Arbitration, Commercial Law.
See Professional Biographies, RALEIGH, NORTH CAROLINA

Laws, Gwenda L., (BV) . . . . '66 '91 C.228 B.A. L.575 J.D. [Ⓒ Womble C.S.&R.]
Lawson, Robert Charles . . . . '76 '03 C.893 B.A. L.896 J.D. [Ⓐ Pinna J.&B.]
Lawton, Thomas Oregon, III . . . . '57 '91 C.103 A.B. L.276 J.D. Asst. Atty. Gen.
Lawton, William C. . . . . '46 '72 C.576 B.S. L.276 J.D. Dist. J.
Layton, Thomas E., (AV) . . . . '53 '83 C.446 B.S. L.64 J.D. P.O. Box 97845
Leager, Samuel R., (AV) . . . . '16 '41 C&L.575 B.S., J.D. 3600 Glenwood Ave.‡
League, Richard N. . . . . '38 '66 C&L.575 A.B., LL.B. 6228 Lookout Loop‡
Ledford Cheek, Jill . . . . . . '55 '80 C.1128 B.A. L.575 J.D. Special Dep. Atty., Dept. of Jus.
Lee, Donna M. . . . . '66 '93 C.576 B.A./B.A. L.1228 J.D. [D.M.Lee]
Lee, G. Thomas, (AV) . . . . '57 '85 C.576 A.B. L.896 J.D. [Womble C.S.&R.]
Lee, Michael E. . . . . '45 '75 C.1378 B.S. L.574 J.D. Research Asst., Ct. of App.
Lee, Monica Langdon . . . . '73 '98 C.576 B.A. L.1228 J.D. [Ⓐ Yates,M.&W.]
Lee, Randolph L., (BV) . . . . '56 '99 C.597 B.A. L.574 J.D. [Cranfill,S.&H.]
Lee, Donna M., Law Group, PLLC . . . . 3957 Stags Leap Circle
Leech, Jennifer Yow . . . . '64 '92 C.575 B.A. L.61 J.D. P.O. Box 30503
Leftwich, Helga Lura, (AV) . . . . '52 '93 C.228 B.A. L.575 J.D. [Hutchison&M.]
Legacy Lawyers, PLLC, (AV) . . . . 3717 Benson Dr.
Lehan, Timothy P., (AV) . . . . '51 '82 C.1126 B.A. L.575 J.D. [Smith,A.B.D.M.&J.]
Lehman, Kathryn S. . . . . '— '04 C.576 B.A. L.575 J.D. [Ⓐ Parker,P.A.&B.]
Lehman, Philip A. . . . . . . '46 '75 C.309 B.A. L.128 J.D. Asst. Atty. Gen., NC Dept. of Jus.
Lehr, Christine C., (BV) . . . . '— '96 C.575 B.S. L.228 J.D. [Ⓒ DLPiper R.G.C.U.]
Lemon, Shawna Cannon '68 '01
C.968 B.S. L.575 J.D. [Ⓐ Myers B.S.&S.] (See Pat. Sect.)
Lennon, David D., (BV) . . . . '52 '82 C.575 B.A. L.896 J.D. [Lennon]
Lennon, George W., (AV) . . . . '47 '76 C.575 A.B. L.61 J.D. 425 North Boylan Ave.
Lennon Law Firm, The, P.A., (BV) . . . . 176 Mine Lake Court, Suite 100
Lenox, Bradford R. . . . . '— '96 C.945 B.B.A. L.228 J.D. [Ⓒ DLPiper R.G.C.U.]
Leonard, Jerry W., Law Offices of . . . . . '45 '71 C.301 B.S. L.575 J.D. 5 W. Hargett Street
Leonard, Krista F. Norstog, (BV) '66 '91 C.1058 B.A. L.228 J.D.
[Smith D.N.W.S.&M.]
Leone, Elizabeth A., (AV) . . . . '69 '98 C.1228 B.S. L.1345 J.D. [Hardison&L.]
Levenbook, Kenneth T. . . . . '47 '73 C.696 A.B. L.107 J.D. NC Gen. Assembly
Levinson, Eric L. . . . . '67 '92 C.280 B.B.A. L.525 J.D. J., N.C. State Ct. of Appls.
Levitas, Steven J., (AV) . . . . '— '83 C.575 B.A. L.309 J.D. [Kilpatrick S.]
Levy, Alycia S. . . . . '— '02 C.1365 B.A. L.692 J.D. [Cranfill,S.&H.]
Lewandowski, Dona . . . . '55 '83 C.837 B.S. L.575 J.D. Resch. Asst., State Ct. of App.
Lewis, Christopher G. . . . . '69 '98 C.575 B.A. L.1228 J.D. [Ⓐ Teague,C.D.&G.]
Lewis, E. Hardy, (AV) . . . . '65 '91 C.602 B.A. L.575 J.D. [Blanchard,J.M.L.&S.]
Lewis, Floyd M. . . . . '50 '75 C&L.574 B.S., J.D. Asst. Atty. Gen., Dept. of Jus.
Lewis, James Matthew . . . . '69 '00 C.383 B.A. L.574 J.D. Admin. Law J.
Lewis, Jennifer B. . . . . '66 '93 C.232 B.A. L.1048 J.D. State Land Title Co.
Lewis, Jessica M. . . . . '76 '05 C&L.575 B.S., J.D. [Ⓐ Patterson,D.C.B.&A.]
Lewis, Richard M., (AV) . . . . '50 '75 C&L.896 B.A., J.D. [Lewis&R.]

Lewis & Roberts, P.L.L.C., (AV) BR
1305 Navaho Drive, Suite 400, 27609-7482 ⊙
Mailing Address: P.O. Box 17529, Raleigh, NC 27619-7529
Telephone: 919-981-0191 888-981-0939 Facsimile: 919-981-0199
URL: http://www.lewis-roberts.com
Richard M. Lewis; James A. Roberts, III; Winston L. Page, Jr.; Timothy S. Riordan; Jack Spain Holmes; Daniel K. Bryson; John D. Elvers; Brian D. Lake; John H. Ruocchio; Gary Vance Mauney (Resident, Charlotte Office); Scott J. Lasso; Kimberly R. Wilson; Jeffrey Allen Misenheimer; Paul R. Dickinson, Jr. (Resident, Charlotte Office); George V. Burns; J. Andrew Fine (Not admitted in NC); Bryant D. Paris, III; Geoffrey S. Proud; Sarah E. Cone.
Workers' Compensation Law, Commercial Litigation, Construction Law, Surety Law, Civil Trial Practice.
Charlotte, North Carolina Office: 128 South Tryon Street, Suite 1100, 28202-5012. Telephone: 704-347-8990. Facsimile: 704-347-8929.
See Professional Biographies, RALEIGH, NORTH CAROLINA

Liggett, David K., (BV) . . . . '65 '95 C&L.575 B.A., J.D. [Ragsdale L.]
Liggett, Frank R., III, (AV) . . . . '40 '66 C&L.575 A.B., J.D. [Ragsdale L.]
Ligon, George, Jr . . . . '51 '77 C.577 B.S. L.608 J.D. P.O. Box 1106
Liles, John W., Jr., (BV) . . . . '34 '59 C.198 B.S. L.575 J.D. 1228 Shadowbark Ct.
Lilliston, Andrew W., Jr. '46 '75 C.347 B.S. L.893 J.D.
(adm. in IN; not adm. in NC) Dep. Gen. Coun., Golden Corral Corporation
Linder, Jeffrey T. . . . . '69 '95 C.112 B.A. L.575 J.D. [Young M.&H.]

Lindsay, David C. . . . . '— '97 C.575 B.A. L.228 J.D. [Ⓐ Kilpatrick S.]
Lingo, Kristen Gardner, (BV) . . . . '67 '93 C&L.575 B.A., J.D. [Manning,F.&S.]
Link, Amos E., Jr. '46 '73 C.709 B.A. L.574 J.D. 541 New Bern Ave.
Little, Cathryn M. . . . . '60 '85 C.893 B.A. L.260 J.D. [Little&L.]
Little, J. Matthew, (BV) . . . . '66 '93 C.575 B.A. L.896 J.D. [Teague,C.D.&G.]
Little, James D., (BV) '44 '72
C&L.575 A.B., J.D. Staff Atty., NC Utilities Comm, Pub. Staff
Little, Melissa E. . . . . '59 '00 C&L.575 B.A., J.D. P.O. Box 30036
Little, Sue Yielding, (AV) . . . . '44 '79 C.1365 A.B. L.575 J.D. Asst. Atty. Gen.
Little, William B. L. . . . . '59 '92 C.576 B.A. L.1228 J.D. [Little&L.]
Little & Little, PLLC . . . . 16 N. Boylan Avenue
Litz, Matthew C. . . . . '73 '03 C.1222 B.B.A. L.259 J.D. [Ⓐ Young M.&H.]
Lively, Donald F., (BV) . . . . '55 '80 C.280 B.A. L.69 J.D. [Teague,C.D.&G.]
Lloyd, John C. . . . . '— '97 C.754 B.A. L.1338 J.D. [Ⓐ McDaniel&A.]
Lloyd, Winston P. . . . . '66 '95 C.575 B.A. L.896 J.D. [Wyrick R.Y.&P.]
Locke, Donald T. '58 '87 C.269 B.A. L.790 J.D.
(adm. in TX; not adm. in NC) CFO & Gen. Coun., Summus, Inc.
Loeffler, Nicole Sabourin . . . . '73 '00 C.629 B.I.arc L.575 J.D. [Ⓐ Manning,F.&S.]
Logan, John F., (AV) . . . . '58 '84 C.692 B.A. L.1228 J.D. 4501 Atlantic Ave., Ste. 132
Logue, Stephen S. . . . . '— '05 C.576 B.S. L.577 J.D. [Ⓐ Kilpatrick S.]
Long, David W., (AV) . . . . '42 '67 C.228 A.B. L.575 J.D. [Poyner&S.]
Long, James E., (AV) . . . . '40 '66 C&L.575 A.B., J.D. Comm., State Dept. of Ins.
Long, Steven B., (AV) . . . . '60 '91 C.575 B.S. L.276 J.D. [Maupin T.]
Loper, Johnny M., (AV) . . . . '52 '83 C.497 B.S. L.500 J.D. [Womble C.S.&R.]
Lopp, William F. . . . . '39 '68 C.575 A.B. L.896 Dept. Human Res.
Lord, Michael C., (AV) . . . . '63 '88 C.902 B.A. L.896 J.D. [Maupin T.]
Lore, R. James, (AV) . . . . '50 '76 C.576 B.S. L.574 J.D. 1312 Annapolis Drive
Lovett, James F., Jr., (CV) . . . . '57 '90 C.269 B.A. L.896 J.D. 4048 Barrett Dr.
Lowenstein, Neil S., (BVⓉ) '63 '89 C.885 B.A. L.692 J.D.
[Vandeventer B.] (⊙Kitty Hawk, NC; Norfolk, VA)
Lowrance, Martha W. . . . . '50 '84 C.577 B.A. L.1228 J.D. Exec. Dir., N.C. State Bar
Lowry, Stephen D., (AV) . . . . '55 '80 C.1064 B.A. L.228 J.D. [Lowry&Assoc.]

Lowry & Associates, The Law Offices of, (AV)
8358 Six Forks Road, Suite 104, 27615
Telephone: 919-518-0783 Fax: 919-518-8375
Stephen D. Lowry.
Residential Real Estate, Commercial Real Estate, Trusts and Estates, Estate Planning, Asset Protection, Wills, Probate, Business Law, Limited Liability Company Law, Tax Law, Non-Profit and Charitable Organizations.
See Professional Biographies, RALEIGH, NORTH CAROLINA

Loyek, Laura Murray . . . . '— '02 C.896 B.A. L.309 J.D. [Ⓐ Smith M.]
Lughes, Joseph A. '28 '55 C.838 L.192 LL.B.
(adm. in TN; not adm. in NC) Pres., Great Amer. South Ins. Co., Inc.
Lumsden, Margaret C., (BV) . . . . '62 '88 C.674 A.B. L.228 J.D. [Unti&L.]
Lundberg, Susan R., (BVⓉ) . . . . '56 '88 C.351 B.A. L.174 J.D. NC Dept. of Jus.
Lung, Matthew K. . . . . '71 '00 C.999 B.S. L.896 J.D. [Ⓐ Womble C.S.&R.]
Lunsford, L. Thomas, II . . . . '53 '78 C&L.575 B.A., J.D. Exec. Dir., N.C. State Bar
Lupton, Lynn Wilson . . . . '76 '03 C.575 B.A. L.1228 J.D. [Ⓐ Smith D.N.W.S.&M.]
Luzzi, Joseph M. . . . . '65 '91 C&L.575 B.A., J.D. [J.Luzzi]
Luzzi, Joseph . . . . 5 W. Hargett St., Ste. 407
Lyn, Kevin R. . . . . '66 '98 C.228 B.S.E. L.575 J.D. [Ⓐ Alston&B.] (See Pat. Sect.)
Lynch, Arch E., Jr., (AV) . . . . '30 '57 C&L.896 B.S., J.D. [Ⓒ Poyner&S.]
Lynch, Donna S. McLamb . . . . '65 '91 C.575 B.A. L.896 J.D. State School Board Assn.
Lynch, J. Christopher, (AV) . . . . '62 '88 C.893 B.A. L.309 J.D. [Wyrick R.Y.&P.]
Lynch, Maria M., (AV) . . . . '53 '79 C.838 B.A. L.575 J.D. [Lynch&E.]

Lynch & Eatman, L.L.P., (AV)
Carolina Corporate Center, Suite 201, 5400 Glenwood Avenue, P.O. Box 30515, 27622-0515
Telephone: 919-571-3332 Fax: 919-571-9983
URL: http://www.lyncheatman.com
Members of Firm: Maria M. Lynch; Jerome R. Eatman, Jr.; Katherine B. Wilkerson.
Business and Corporate Law, Mergers and Acquisitions, Zoning and Real Estate, Probate, Wills and Estate Administration and Taxation Law.
Representative Client: The Morgan Co.
See Professional Biographies, RALEIGH, NORTH CAROLINA

Lyon, Thomas I., (BV) . . . . '— '98 C.575 B.S.B.A. L.383 J.D. [Ⓒ Kennedy C.L.&H.]
Mabe, John I., Jr., (AV) . . . . '54 '80 C&L.575 A.B., J.D. [Maupin T.]

MacCord Mason PLLC, (AV)
510 Glenwood Avenue, Suite 321, 27611 ⊙
Telephone: 919-664-8624 Fax: 919-664-8625
URL: http://www.maccordmason.com
Of Counsel: JiNan Glasgow.
Patent, Trademark, Copyright and Unfair Competition. Trade Secret Practice before all Courts. Intellectual Property Law, Litigation.
Wilmington, North Carolina Office: 1209 Culbreth Drive, Suite 103, 28405. Telephone: 910-256-3557. Fax: 910-256-0523.
Greensboro, North Carolina Office: 300 North Greene Street, Suite 1600, 27402. Telephone: 336-273-4422. Fax: 336-271-2830.
See Professional Biographies, RALEIGH, NORTH CAROLINA

MacKethan, John A., (AV) . . . . '42 '68 C&L.575 B.S., J.D. [Ⓒ Poyner&S.]
Madden, John D., (AV) . . . . '57 '83 C.198 B.A. L.896 J.D. [Smith,A.B.D.M.&J.]
Maddrey, John F., (AV) . . . . '54 '79 C.575 A.B. L.893 J.D. Asst. Atty. Gen.
Madison, Caryn . . . . '73 '02 C&L.577 B.A., J.D. [Ⓐ White&S.]
Madison, Charles A., (AV) '62 '87
C&L.575 B.A., J.D. Assoc. Gen. Coun., Progress Energy
Magri, Karen A. . . . . '63 '96 C.188 B.S. L.228 J.D. [Myers B.S.&S.] (See Pat. Sect.)
Mahley, Gordon H., Jr. '31 '57 C.732 B.A. L.982 LL.B.
Admin. Law J., Soc. Sec. Admn.
Mahood, Zoe Gabriele '67 '94 C.228 A.B. L.260 J.D.
U.S. Equal Employment Opportunity
Maiorano, Wayne K. . . . . '66 '98 C.884 B.A. L.575 J.D. [Ⓐ Smith,A.B.D.M.&J.]
Maitin, Lawrence S. . . . . '68 '94 C.1505 B.A. L.607 J.D. [Maitin]

Maitin Law Firm
8396 Six Forks Road, Suite 201, 27615
Telephone: 919-846-1057 Fax: 919-846-1058
Email: Larry@Maitinlaw.com
Lawrence S. Maitin.
Creditors Rights, Real Estate, Foreclosures, Collections, Bankruptcy.
See Professional Biographies, RALEIGH, NORTH CAROLINA

Maitland & Maitland, PLLC
(See Chapel Hill)

Majestic, Ann L., (AV) . . . . '52 '82 C&L.228 B.A., J.D. [Tharrington S.]
Maldonado, Jennifer D. . . . . '72 '98 C.575 B.A. L.1228 J.D. [Ⓐ Yates,M.&W.]
Malik, Tania S. '67 '92 C.575 B.A. L.1059 J.D. Off. of Comr. of Ins.

Mallard, Heather K., (AV) . . . . '63 '88 C.294 B.A. L.902 J.D. [Womble C.S.&R.]
Malone, J. Michael . . . . '68 '99 C.576 B.S.C.E. L.575 J.D. [Brady,N.K.&M.]
Malone, Rod, (BV) . . . . '64 '89 C.576 B.S.E.E. L.575 J.D. [Tharrington S.]
Mangum, Ned Wilson, (BV) . . . . '72 '98 C.576 L.575 J.D. Asst. Dist. Atty.
Manley, Thomas J., (AV) . . . . '46 '72 C.575 A.B. L.309 J.D. [Hunton&W.]
Mann, Barry D., (AV) . . . . '56 '82 C&L.575 B.S., J.D. [Manning,F.&S.]
Mann, John W. . . . . '66 '98 C&L.575 B.A., J.D. [A Smith M.]
Mann, Julian, III '47 '74
C.575 B.S. L.192 J.D. Chf. Adm. J. & Dir. Off. of Adm. Hearings
Mann, William A., (AV) . . . . '44 '68 C&L.575 A.B., J.D. [Ragsdale L.]
Mannheim, W. David, (CV) . . . . '— '97 C&L.280 B.B.A., J.D. [A Wyrick R.Y.&P.]
Manning, Howard E., Jr., (AV) . . . . '43 '68 C&L.575 A.B., J.D. Supr. Ct. J.
Manning, Thomas C., (AV) . . . . '52 '77 C.575 A.B. L.790 J.D. [Manning&C.]

Manning & Crouch, (AV) BR
Capital Club Building, Suite 1104, 16 West Martin Street, P.O. Box 350, 27602
Telephone: 919-828-5778 Fax: 919-828-5045
Email: manninglaw@att.net URL: http://www.lawyers.com/manning&crouch
Thomas C. Manning; James A. Crouch.
Criminal Trials in State and Federal Courts, Criminal Fraud, Criminal Tax Matters, Grand Jury Investigation, Homicide, Federal Grand Jury, Criminal and Regulatory Investigations, Driving While Intoxicated (DWI), Driving While Impaired, Traffic Violations, Homicide, Sex Crimes, Drug Crimes.
See Professional Biographies, RALEIGH, NORTH CAROLINA

Manning, Fulton & Skinner, P.A., (AV) BR
Glenwood Plaza, Suite 500, 3605 Glenwood Avenue, P.O. Box 20389, 27619-0389
Telephone: 919-787-8880 Telecopier: 919-787-8902 (Litigation); 781-0811 (Real Estate); 571-2504 (Business-Tax)
Email: manager@manningfulton.com URL: http://www.manningfulton.com
Howard E. Manning (1914-2002); Charles L. Fulton (Board Certified Specialist in Real Property Law-Business, Commercial and Industrial Transactions, North Carolina State Board of Legal Specialization); William P. Skinner, Jr.; John B. McMillan; W. Gerald Thornton; Charles B. Morris, Jr. (1936-1995); M. Marshall Happer III; Michael T. Medford; Samuel T. Oliver, Jr. (Board Certified Specialist in Real Property Law-Business, Commercial and Industrial Transactions, North Carolina State Board of Legal Specialization); David D. Dahl; Charles E. Nichols, Jr. (Board Certified Specialist in Real Property Law: Business, Commercial and Industrial Transactions, North Carolina State Board of Legal Specialization); Barry D. Mann; John C. Dorsey; William C. Smith, Jr.; Deborah L. Hildebran-Bachofen (Board Certified Specialist in Estate Planning and Probate Law, North Carolina State Board of Legal Specialization); Stephen T. Byrd (Board Certified Specialist in Estate Planning and Probate Law, North Carolina State Board of Legal Specialization); Michael S. Harrell; Alison R. Cayton (Board Certified Specialist in Real Property Law: Business, Commercial and Industrial Transactions, North Carolina State Board of Legal Specialization); Cary Elizabeth Close; Kristen Gardner Lingo; Thomas C. Kilpatrick; S. Nicole Taylor; Judson A. Welborn; Sandra M. Clark (Board Certified Specialist in Estate Planning and Probate Law, North Carolina State Board of Legal Specialization); Leanor Bailey Hodge; Ritchie W. Taylor; Ansley Chapman Cella; David G. Martin; Franklin E. Martin (Board Certified Specialist in Real Property Law - Residential Transactions, North Carolina State Board of Legal Specialization);—Nicole Sabourin Loeffler; Evan B. Horwitz; John R. Cella, Jr.; Jennifer L. Weaver; David B. Efird.
Alternative Dispute Resolution, Appellate; Bankruptcy, Condemnation, Corporate/Business Entities, Corporate Finance, Employee Benefits/ERISA, Employment, Estate/Trust Administration, Estate Planning/Wealth Transfer, Family Law, Franchise, Government Relations, Litigation, Mergers/Acquisitions, Real Property, Sports/Entertainment, Tax Controversies, Tax Planning.
Representative Clients: International Business Machines Corp.; Allstate Insurance Co.; Anheuser-Busch Cos.; Pharmaceutical Research and Manufacturers of America; Employers Reinsurance Corp.; General Electric Capital Corp.; SiemensEnergy & Automation, Inc.; E.J. Victor, Inc.; General Parts, Inc.; Carquest Corporation.
See Professional Biographies, RALEIGH, NORTH CAROLINA

Manthei, Gayl M. '52 '80 C.957 B.A. L.966 J.D. Spec. Dep. Atty. Gen.
Mantle, Holly A. . . . . '76 '05 C.575 B.S. L.1148 J.D. [A Patterson,D.C.B.&A.]

Manus, Roger, (AV) '— '79 C.429 B.A. L.569 J.D.
1312 Annapolis Drive, Suite 103, 27608-2146
Telephone: 919-833-4600 Fax: 919-833-4726
Email: manuslaw@bellsouth.net URL: http://www.manuslaw.com
Nursing Home Negligence, Class Actions, Mental Disability Law, Medicaid Appeals, Wrongful Death, Medical Malpractice, Disability Rights, Americans with Disabilities Act (ADA), Employment Discrimination, False Claims Act, Mental Health Law.
See Professional Biographies, RALEIGH, NORTH CAROLINA

March, Rachel B. . . . . '69 '97 C&L.896 B.A., J.D. [A Ogletree,D.N.S.&S.]
Maready, D. Karen . . . . '74 '03 C.1335 B.A. L.500 J.D. [A Hutchison&M.]
Mariencheck, S. Nikole . . . . '71 '97 C.280 B.A. L.790 J.D. [A Smith,A.B.D.M.&J.]
Marin, John W. (Jack), (AV) . . . . '44 '80 C&L.228 A.B., J.D. [Maupin T.]
Marino, Peter J., (AV) . . . . '65 '90 C.1031 B.A. L.575 J.D. [Smith,A.B.D.M.&J.]
Markham, Jennifer B. . . . . '77 '03 C.575 B.A. L.1509 J.D. [A Smith,A.B.D.M.&J.]
Markham, John E. (Jack), Jr., (AV) '— '73 C&L.575 A.B., J.D.
[C Kennedy C,L.&H.] (⊙Research Triangle Park)
Markoff, Brad S., (AV) . . . . '— '82 C.228 A.B. L.910 J.D. [DLPiper R.G.C.U.]
Markus, Patricia A. . . . . '67 '92 C.311 B.A. L.93 J.D. [Smith M.]
Markworth, Robert Bruce . . . . '67 '98 C.1128 B.A. L.575 J.D. [A Shanahan]
Marquette, Ronald M., (BV) . . . . '45 '73 C.1070 B.S. L.228 J.D. P.O. Box 629
Marquis, A. Danielle, (BV) '68 '92
C.838 B.A. L.192 J.D. Special Dep. Atty. Gen., Atty. Gen. Off.
Marshall, Charles F., III . . . . '70 '96 C&L.575 B.A., J.D. [Brooks,P.M.H.&L.] ⊙
Marshall, Elaine F., (BV) . . . . '45 '81 C.446 B.S. L.1228 J.D. Secy. of State‡
Marshall, Jeffrey E., (BV) . . . . '70 '96 C.107 B.S.B.A. L.117 J.D. 221 Glenwood Ave.
Marshall, William E., Jr., (P.A.), (BV) . . . . . . '42 '70 C.576 B.S. L.896 J.D. 2 Hannover Sq.
Marshbanks, M. Lynn . . . . '61 '87 C&L.575 B.A., J.D. N.C. Gen. Assembly
Marsocci, Jeffrey . . . . '70 '95 C&L.1019 B.B.A., J.D. [J.G.Marsocci]
Marsocci, Jeffrey G., PLLC, The Law Offices of . . . . 8406 Six Forks Rd.

Martin, Andrew S., (AV) '43 '69 C.575 B.S. L.896 J.D.
1026 Washington Street, P.O. Box 10406, 27605-0406
Telephone: 919-828-5620 Telecopier: 919-828-5211
Email: asm@martinlaw.net
Residential and Commercial Real Estate Transactions, Estate Planning, Probate and Trusts, Corporations, Limited Liability Companies.
See Professional Biographies, RALEIGH, NORTH CAROLINA

Martin, Brenda F. . . . . '59 '00 C.232 B.S.B.A. L.574 J.D. [B.F.Martin]
Martin, C. Amanda, (AV) . . . . '67 '92 C.260 B.S. L.575 J.D. [Everett,G.H.&S.]
Martin, David G., (BV) . . . . '65 '96 C.575 B.A. L.1345 J.D. [Manning,F.&S.]
Martin, David Grier, III '68 '95 C.198 B.A. L.575 J.D.
Coun., Preservation North Carolina
Martin, Elizabeth T. . . . . '76 '02 C.222 B.A. L.575 J.D. [A Hatch,L.&B.]
Martin, Franklin E., (AV) . . . . '38 '68 C&L.575 B.A., J.D. [Manning,F.&S.]
Martin, Gregory M., (AV) . . . . '57 '82 C&L.575 B.A., J.D. [Martin&J.]
Martin, Homer D., Jr. . . . . '52 '77 C.575 B.A. L.1048 J.D. P.O. Box 19636
Martin, John C. . . . . '43 '67 C&L.896 B.A., J.D. App. Ct. J.
Martin, Margaret Rand, (AV) . . . . '49 '77 C&L.575 A.B., J.D. P.O. Box 18463
Martin, Mark D. . . . . '63 '88 C.925 B.S.B.A. L.575 J.D. Supm. J.
Martin, Marty, (BV) . . . . '52 '77 C.575 B.A. L.1048 J.D. P.O. Box 19636
Martin, Stephen D. . . . . '75 '02 C.611 B.A. L.597 J.D. [A Nelson M.R.&S.]
Martin, Brenda F., Attorney at Law, P.A. . . . . 124 St. Mary St.

Martin & Jones, (AV) BR
Suite 200, 410 Glenwood Avenue, 27603 ⊙
Telephone: 919-821-0005
URL: http://www.MartinandJones.com
John Alan Jones; Gregory M. Martin; E. Spencer Parris; Hoyt G. Tessener; H. Forest Horne, Jr.; John Michael Riley; Thomas E. Barwick; G. Christopher Olson; Scott Bartley Goodson; Elizabeth Todd Beall; Sean A.B. Cole; Katherine N. Bricio; Julia Ellen Dixon; Martin A. Ramey; Clint W. Sitton (Not admitted in NC); Samuel L. Starks (Not admitted in NC).
Asbestos Litigation, Bad Faith and Unfair Competition, Business Litigation, Construction Site Injuries, Inadequate Security, Medical Malpractice, Nursing/Rest Home Negligence, Personal Injury, Pharmaceutical and Medical Device Litigation, Product Liability, Social Security Disability, Toxic Torts, Trucking Accidents, Workers' Compensation and Wrongful Death, Land Condemnation, FELA (Federal Employers' Liability Act), Securities Fraud.
Durham, North Carolina Office: University Towers, Suite 526. 3100 Tower Boulevard, 27707. Telephone: 919-544-3000.
Wilmington, North Carolina Office: 1213 Culbreth Drive, Suite 121, 28405. Telephone: 910-256-4005.
Atlanta, Georgia Office: 3353 Peachtree Road, NE, Suite 510, 30326. Telephone: 404-257-1117.
See Professional Biographies, RALEIGH, NORTH CAROLINA

Martinez, Jason L., (AV) . . . . '69 '94 C.276 B.S. L.262 J.D. [Smith,A.B.D.M.&J.]
Mason, C. Steven, (AV) . . . . '56 '81 C.575 B.A. L.893 J.D. [Smith,A.B.D.M.&J.]
Mason, James M. . . . . '72 '04 C.228 B.A. L.896 J.D. [Emanuel&D.]
Mason, Merrill McCall, (AV) . . . . '60 '89 C&L.575 B.A., J.D. [Hutchison&M.]
Massey, David Sanders, (AV) . . . . '45 '82 C.53 B.S. L.896 J.D. Dir., Dept. of Secy. of State
Matlock, Ashley . . . . '— '01 C&L.575 B.A., J.D. [A Everett,G.H.&S.]
Matthews, Ann W. '— '88 C.846 B.J. L.902 J.D.
Asst. Atty. Gen., NC Dept. of Justice, Atty General's Office
Matthews, William C., Jr., (AV) . . . . . . '49 '77 C.806 B.A. L.692 J.D. [Womble C.S.&R.]
Matthis, John R. B. . . . . '20 '51 C&L.896 B.S., J.D. Dep. Atty. Gen.
Matton, W. Christopher, (AV) . . . . '— '94 C.659 B.S.E. L.896 J.D. [Kilpatrick S.]
Mattox, Isabel Worthy, (AV) . . . . '58 '86 C&L.575 B.A., J.D. P.O. Box 389
Mau, Jennie W. . . . . '62 '88 C.1130 B.A. L.575 J.D. NC Atty. Gen. Off.

Maupin Taylor, P.A., (AV) BR
Highwoods Tower One, Suite 500, 3200 Beechleaf Court, P.O. Drawer 19764, 27604-1064 ⊙
Telephone: 919-981-4000 Telecopier: 919-981-4300
URL: http://www.maupintaylor.com
Armistead J. Maupin (1914-2005); William W. Taylor, Jr. (Retired); Charles B. Neely, Jr.; Thomas Willis Haywood Alexander; Robert A. Valois; John T. Williamson; Frank P. Ward, Jr.; Nancy S. Rendleman (Board Certified Specialist in Estate Planning and Probate Law, North Carolina State Board of Legal Specialization); Margie Toy Case; M. Keith Kapp; Mark S. Thomas; David R. Dorton (Board Certified Specialist in Real Property Law, Business, Commercial and Industrial Transactions, North Carolina State Board of Legal Specialization); Holmes P. Harden (Certified Specialist, Business and Consumer Bankruptcy Law, North Carolina State Board of Legal Specialization); D. Royce Powell; William B. Gwyn, Jr.; James E. Gates; Amos C. Dawson, III; Gilbert C. Laite, III; Ronald R. Rogers; Elizabeth Davenport Scott; Reuben G. Clark, III; Arlene J. Diosegy; Michael C. Lord; Karon B. Thornton; Theron McK. vanDusen; William P. Barrett; Kurt J. Olson; John W. (Jack) Marin; John I. Mabe, Jr.; David A. Bookhout; Charles L. Steel, IV; Steven B. Long; Laura A. Edgerton; Ronald D. Raxter; Gerald A. Tingen; Roy H. Wyman, Jr.; Kevin W. Benedict; Joshua M. Krasner; Camden R. Webb; Terence D. Friedman; William Sam Byassee;—Mark A. Whitson; Marcus C. Hewitt; Hans H. Huang; Heather E. Bridgers; Shana G. R. Fisher; Matthew F. Fussa; W. Winborne Boyles; Jonathan R. Bumgarner; Brenda J. Thissen (Not admitted in NC); Robert W. Shaw; Jennifer A. Morgan; Nicholas A. Nance. Of Counsel: Daniel Lee Brawley; Robert B. Broughton; Santo J. Costa; Robert K. Imperial (Not admitted in NC); W. Travis Porter; Kevin A. Prakke.
Agribusiness, Administrative, Alcoholic Beverages, Alternative Dispute Resolution, Antitrust and Trade Regulation, Aviation Law, Bankruptcy, Banking Law, Business Litigation, Charitable Organizations, Collective Bargaining, Commercial Leases, Commercial Real Estate, Computers and Software, Construction Law, Copyrights, Corporate Finance, Corporate Law, Creditors' Rights, Employee Benefits, Employer Liability, Employment Discrimination, Employment Law, Employment Litigation, Environmental Law, Franchises and Franchising, Government Contracts, Governmental (State and Local) Law, Health Law, Hospital Law, Immigration and Naturalization, Industrial Accidents, Industrial Relations, Intellectual Property, Labor Arbitration, Labor Law, Labor Legislation, Labor Relations, Management Labor Law, Medical Malpractice Defense, Mergers and Acquisitions, Occupational Health and Safety, Patent Litigation, Products Liability, Real Estate Finance, Secured Lending, Securities Regulation, Sports Law, Taxation, Technology Law, Trademark, Trusts and Estates, Venture Capital, Zoning Law.
Representative Clients: American International Group; Blue Cross/Blue Shield of North Carolina; CSX Transportation, Inc.; Fluor Daniel Midland, Inc.; E & J Gallo Winery; Glaxo Wellcome; Northern Telecom Inc.; Reichhold Chemical Co. Inc.; Sampson Regional Medical Center; Smithfield Foods, Inc.; SouthTrust Bank, N.A.
Research Triangle Park, North Carolina Office: 480 Beta Building, Headquarters Park, Post Office Box 13646, 27709-3646. Telephone: 919-361-4900. Telecopier: 919-361-2262.
Wilmington, North Carolina Office: Landfall Park North, 1985 Eastwood Road, Suite 200, 28403. Telephone: 910-256-5135. Telecopier: 910-256-6451.
See Professional Biographies, RALEIGH, NORTH CAROLINA

Mavretic, Laura K. . . . . '49 '81 C.269 B.A. L.1345 J.D. Comr., State Indus. Comm.
Maxfield, John A., (BV) . . . . '49 '84 C.999 B.S. L.1228 J.D. Wake Cnty Sheriff Dept
Mayhew, Christine F. . . . . '75 '00 C.160 B.A. L.790 J.D. [A Wyrick R.Y.&P.]
Mazer, Lawrence F., (AV) '49 '83
C.30 B.A. L.1228 J.D. Assoc. Gen. Coun., Progress Energy
Mazzone, Erik Louis . . . . '70 '96 C&L.93 B.A., J.D. 4101 Lake Boone Trl., Ste. 200
McAlister, Cynthia V., (BV) . . . . '51 '96 C.576 B.A. L.578 J.D. [Smith D.N.W.S.&M.]
McArthur, John R. '56 '82 C.198 B.A. L.790 J.D.
Sr. V.P., Gen. Coun. & Secy., Progress Energy
McBennett, Larry D., (BV) . . . . '49 '77 C&L.575 B.A., J.D. [Herring M.M.&F.]
McBride, William H., (AV) . . . . '48 '76 C.674 A.B. L.846 J.D. [Hunton&W.]
McCabe, John Matthew, (AV) . . . . '— '94 C.575 A.B. L.1345 J.D. [Davis&M.]
McCallister, Steven K. . . . . '72 '98 C.34 B.A. L.896 J.D. [A Shanahan]
McCants, Jo Ann Bernard . . . . '65 '90 C&L.574 B.A., J.D. Assoc. Coun.
McClain, John N., Jr., (AV) . . . . '49 '74 C.575 A.B. L.838 J.D. [Hatch,L.&B.]
McClanahan, Doug . . . . '71 '95 C.34 B.A L.1228 J.D. [McClanahan]
McClanahan Law Firm, PLLC . . . . 343 E. Six Forks Road Suite 288
McClearen, R. Edwin, (AV) . . . . '46 '76 C.576 B.S. L.596 J.D. 1312 Annapolis Drive‡
McClinton, Claudia N. . . . . '76 '04 C&L.575 B.A., J.D. [A Holt Y.M.&H.]
McColl, Ann W. . . . . '61 '91 C&L.575 B.A., J.D. P.O. Box 17505
McConkey, Brenton W. . . . . '— '04 C.896 B.A. L.575 J.D. [A Parker,P.A.&B.]
McConnell, Alan H. . . . . '— '88 C.280 B.S. L.273 J.D. [Kilpatrick S.]
McConnell, Kathleen C. . . . . '63 '91 C.331 B.A. L.564 J.D. Plaza Assoc. Inc.

McCoppin, Andrew, P.A., The Law Office of
(See Cary)

McCord, Dean M. . . . . '63 '95 C.575 B.A. L.436 J.D. [Wyrick R.Y.&P.]
Mccormick, Thomas A., JR. . . . . '45 '73 C&L.575 BSBA, J.D. City of Raleigh
McCotter, DeWitt C., III, (AV) . . . . '39 '64 C&L.575 B.S., J.D. [C Poyner&S.]
McCoy, David, (AV) . . . . '52 '91 C.280 B.S.Ed. L.575 J.D. Dep. Sec. of Transp.
McCoy, Leigh A. . . . . '67 '91 C.198 B.A. L.575 J.D. Law Clk., Ct. of App. J.
McCrary, Thomas M. '22 '43 C.38 A.A. L.45 LL.B. 3509 Ranlo Dr.‡
McCullough, Elizabeth P. . . . . '74 '99 C.198 B.A. L.896 J.D. [A Young M.&H.]
McCullough, John D. . . . . '45 '70 C.575 A.B. L.790 J.D. Appl. Ct. J.
McCullough, William H., (AV) . . . . '34 '59 C.404 A.B. L.575 J.D. [C Parker,P.A.&B.]
McDaniel, Andrew H., (AV) . . . . '29 '57 C&L.575 B.S., LL.B. 608 Sampson St.‡
McDaniel, L. Bruce, (AV) . . . . '33 '58 C&L.896 B.S., J.D. [McDaniel&A.]

McDaniel, Michael E. '66 '93 C.576 B.A. L.1345 J.D.
421 Fayetteville St. Mall, Ste. 1203

McDaniel & Anderson, L.L.P., (AV)
Lafayette Square, 4942 Windy Hill Drive, P.O. Box 58186, 27658
Telephone: 919-872-3000 Fax: 919-790-9273
Members of Firm: L. Bruce McDaniel; William Eugene Anderson;—John M. Kirby; John C. Lloyd.
Civil Trials and Appeals, Corporations, Securities, Administrative, Personal Injury, Construction Law, Insurance, Negligence, Zoning and Municipal Law.
Representative Clients: Dean Witter Reynolds, Inc.; Peat, Marwick, Mitchell & Co.
See Professional Biographies, RALEIGH, NORTH CAROLINA

McDarris, Charles F., (AV) '63 '91 C.673 B.S. L.896 J.D. [Holt Y.M.&H.]
McDonald, Ralph, (AV) '40 '64 C&L.575 A.B., LL.B. [Bailey&D.]
McDougal, Gregg E., (AVⓉ) '— '87 C.473 B.S. L.896 J.D. [Kilpatrick S.]
McElroy, Richard C., III, (AV) '51 '81 C.575 B.S. L.1228 J.D. 324 Yadkin Dr.
McGann, Bryan A. '61 '01 C.232 B.S. L.577 J.D. [Ⓐ Smith,A.B.D.M.&J.]
McGaughey, Terri Toth, (AV) '55 '80
C.575 B.A. L.1228 J.D. 150 Fayetteville Street Mall, Suite 1400‡
McGinn, M. Daniel, (AV) '42 '67 C&L.896 A.B., J.D. [Brooks,P.M.H.&L.] ⊙
McGirt, Jonathan Gordon, (AV) '63 '93 C&L.575 B.A., J.D. [Cheshire,P.S.B.&V.]
McGrann, Paula K. '— '01 C.1309 B.A. L.575 J.D. [Ⓐ Kurtz&B.]
McGuffin, C. Andrew '69 '03 C.330 B.A. L.1065 J.D. [Ⓐ J.L.Davis&Assoc.]
McGuire, Gregory P. '62 '87 C.188 B.S. L.575 J.D. [Ogletree,D.N.S.&S.]
McGuire, Matthew P., (AV) '66 '93 C.602 B.A. L.575 J.D. [Nelson M.R.&S.]
McInnes, Alan D., (BV) '— '94 C.228 B.A. L.575 J.D. [Kilpatrick S.]
McKay, Elizabeth Leonard '61 '87 C.896 B.A. L.575 J.D. Ct. of App.
McKenzie, Katherine Stukes '— '03 C&L.575 B.A., J.D. [Ⓐ Kennedy C.L.&H.]
McKnight, John E. '73 '04 C.1175 B.A. L.896 J.D. [Ⓐ Hatch,L.&B.]
McLamb, Catherine C., (AV) '49 '75 C&L.575 B.A., J.D. [Sokol M.S.O.L.P.]
McLamb, Dan J., (AV) '49 '74 C&L.575 A.B., J.D. [Yates,M.&W.]
McLawhorn, Daniel F. '48 '74 C.198 A.B. L.575 J.D. Raleigh City Atty.
McLean, Carley B., Jr. '57 '83 C&L.575 B.A., J.D. [C.B.McLean,Jr.]
McLean, Damon M. '— '02 C.674 A.B. L.228 J.D. [Ⓐ DLPiper R.G.C.U.]
McLean, C. B., Jr., Attorney at Law 4000 Wake Forest Rd., Ste. 118
McLeod, David S. '52 '77 C.575 B.A. L.472 J.D. 2 W. Edenton St.
McMahon, Timothy L. '60 '87 C.602 B.B.A. L.734 J.D. 3600 Glenwood Ave.‡
McMillan, Duncan A., (AV) '52 '77 C.896 B.A. L.575 J.D. [McMillan,S.&P.]
McMillan, John B., (AV) '42 '67 C&L.575 A.B., J.D. [Manning,F.&S.]
McMillan, Robert L., (AV) '23 '49 C.896 B.S. L.575 LL.B. [McMillan,S.&P.]
McMillan, Taylor '38 '64 C.575 A.B. L.145 J.D. Chf. Dep. Comr., State Dept of Labor

McMillan, Smith & Plyler, (AV)
205 West Martin Street, 27602
Telephone: 919-821-5124 Fax: 919-821-5129
Email: plyler@mspraleigh.com
Members of Firm: Robert L. McMillan; Stephen T. Smith; Duncan A. McMillan; William Webb Plyler.
Languages: Spanish and English.
Civil and Criminal Trials and Appeals in all State and Federal Courts. Commercial Litigation, False Claims Act Litigation, Business Torts, Antitrust, Personal Injury, Negligence, Criminal Defense and White Collar Criminal Defense, N.C. Election Law.
See Professional Biographies, RALEIGH, NORTH CAROLINA

McNair Law Firm, P.A., (AV)
Landmark Center, Suite 500, 4601 Six Forks Road, 27609 ⊙
Telephone: 919-786-4061 Facsimile: 919-786-4076
Email: cfort@mcnair.net URL: http://www.mcnair.net
Charles S. Carter.
Administrative, Admiralty, Antitrust, Banking, Bankruptcy, Civil and Criminal Practice in all State and Federal Courts of Record, Corporate, Environmental, ERISA, Estate Planning, Health Care, Intellectual Property, Immigration, International, Interstate Land Sales, Labor and Employment Relations, Legislative/Governmental (National and State), Mergers and Acquisitions, Municipal Finance, Probate, Real Estate, Regulatory, Securities, Tax, Telecommunications, and Utility Law.
Representative Clients: Fuji Photo Film, Inc.; Georgia-Pacific Corp.; Milliken & Co.; Bank of America Corp.; Norfolk Southern Corp.; Pirelli Cable Corp.; SCANA Corp.; Westinghouse Electric Corp.
Columbia, South Carolina Office: 1301 Gervais Street, P.O. Box 11390, 29211. Telephone: 803-799-9800. Facsimile: 803-799-9804.
Anderson, South Carolina Office: 500 South McDuffie Street, P.O. Box 4086, 29621. Telephone: 864-226-1688. Facsimile: 864-225-6456.
Bluffton, South Carolina Office: 5 Belfair Village Drive, 29910-2605. Telephone: 843-815-2171. Facsimile: 843-815-5991.
Charleston, South Carolina Office: 100 Calhoun Street, Suite 400, 29401. Telephone: 843-723-7831. Facsimile: 843-722-3227.
Georgetown, South Carolina Office: 121 Screven Street, P.O. Drawer 418, 29442. Telephone: 843-546-6102. Facsimile: 843-546-0096.
Greenville, South Carolina Office: Bank of America Plaza, 7 North Laurens Street-Suite 600, P.O. Box 447. 29602. Telephone: 864-271-4940. Facsimile: 864-233-0423; 864-271-4015.
Hilton Head Island, South Carolina Office: Shelter Cove Executive Park, 23-B Shelter Cove Lane, Suite 400, P.O. Drawer 3, 29938-0003. Telephone: 843-785-2171. Facsimile: 843-686-5991.
Myrtle Beach, South Carolina Office: Founders Centre, 2411 Oak Street, Suite 206, 29577. Telephone: 843-444-1107. Facsimile: 843-444-4729.
Charlotte, North Carolina Office: Two Wachovia Center, 301 South Tryon Street, Suite 1615, 28282. Telephone: 704-347-1170. Facsimile: 704-347-4467.
See Professional Biographies, RALEIGH, NORTH CAROLINA

McNairy, William G., (AV) '43 '73 C.575 B.S. L.945 J.D. [Brooks,P.M.H.&L.] ⊙
McNeil, Erin D. '74 '99 C.577 B.A. L.575 J.D. [Ⓐ Yates,M.&W.]
McNeil, John P. '68 '01 C.953 B.A. L.896 J.D. [Haas M.&Assoc.]
McNeill, Barry S., (AV) '54 '79 C.575 B.S. L.574 J.D. Spec. Dep. Atty. Gen.
McNeill, Caryn Coppedge, (AV) '66 '91 C.198 B.A. L.228 J.D. [Smith,A.B.D.M.&J.]
McNeill, John P. '55 '92 C.640 B.S. L.273 J.D. [Ⓒ Smith D.N.W.S.&M.]
McNish, Susan K., (AVⓉ) '40 '81 C.112 A.B. L.770 J.D. 11010 Louson Place‡
McPherson, Michelle Bagley '56 '85
C.70 B.A. L.276 J.D. Asst. Atty. Gen., Consumer Protec.
Mcquade, Mark A. '69 '96 C&L.190 B.S., J.D. Assoc. Gen. Coun., Progress Energy
Meacham, Brian D. '— '03 C&L.575 B.S., J.D. [Ⓐ Smith,A.B.D.M.&J.]
Meacham, Patrick M. '66 '99 C.378 B.A. L.1228 J.D. [Patterson,D.C.B.&A.]
Meares, Beth Kelly '68 '92 C&L.1228 B.B.A., J.D. State Farm Ins. Co.
Medford, Michael T., (AV) '51 '76 C.575 A.B. L.178 J.D. [Manning,F.&S.]
Mediratta, Paul '— '03 C.446 B.S. L.1187 J.D. [Mediratta]

Mediratta Law Firm
5 West Hargett Street, Suite 700, 27601
Telephone: 919-833-6105 Fax: 919-833-6106 URL: http://www.medirattalawoffice.com
Email: medirattalawfirm@bellsouth.net URL: http://www.medirattalawfirm.com
Paul Mediratta.
Criminal Law, Driving While Intoxicated, Traffic Violations, Personal Injury, Civil Litigation, Immigration, Automobile Accidents, Juvenile Law.
See Professional Biographies, RALEIGH, NORTH CAROLINA

Meeker, Charles C., (AV) '50 '75 C.976 B.A. L.178 J.D. [Parker,P.A.&B.]
Meeks, Kevin G. '70 '99 C.228 A.B. L.280 J.D. [Ⓐ Troutman S.] (⊙Atlanta, GA)
Meeks, Robert M. '59 '95 C.277 B.S.E.E. L.280 J.D. [Myers B.S.&S.] (See Pat. Sect.)
Meelheim, Helen D. '52 '95 C&L.575 B.S.N., J.D. [Ⓐ Patterson,D.C.B.&A.]
Meigs, Carrie E. '74 '98 C&L.575 B.A., J.D. [Patterson,D.C.B.&A.]
Meir, Victor N., (CV) '69 '97 C.575 B.S. L.1048 J.D. P.O. Box 2475
Melott, Robert A. '36 '65
C.870 B.S. L.575 J.D. Chf. Admin. Law J., Off. of Adm. Hearings
Melvin, Wm. W., (AV) '23 '51 C.428 L.896 J.D. 150 Fayetteville St. Mall
Mercer, Alene M., (AV) '48 '77 C.575 B.S. L.569 J.D. [Cranfill,S.&H.]
Mercer, Charles H., Jr., (AV) '47 '75 C.575 A.B. L.472 J.D. [Nelson M.R.&S.]
Mermelstein, Robert J. '61 '96 C.667 B.S.M.E. L.978 J.D.
8212 Creedmoor Rd., Ste. 101
Merrills, Andrew W., (BV) '65 '91 C.228 A.B. L.469 J.D. [Ogletree,D.N.S.&S.]
Merriman, William W., III, (AV) '37 '63 C&L.575 A.B., LL.B. [W.Merriman]
Merriman, William, (AV) 100 St. Albans Dr., Ste. 201
Merritt, D. Donovan, (BV) '53 '78 C&L.575 A.B., J.D. [Wyrick R.Y.&P.]
Merritt, Robert H., Jr., (AV) '48 '74 C.575 B.A. L.802 J.D. [Bailey&D.]
Metz, Bruce N. '34 '66 C.8 B.A. L.7 J.D. 5 W. Hargett St., Ste. 902
Meyer, Deborah N. '50 '92 C.1377 B.S.N. L.1228 J.D. 4030 Wake Forest Rd., Ste. 101
Meyer, Jaye Powell, (AV) '61 '90 C.896 B.A. L.575 J.D. [Tharrington S.] ⊙
Meyer, Louis B. '33 '60 C&L.896 B.A., J.D. Spec. Supr. Ct. J.
Meyer, Louis B., III, (AV) '57 '83 C&L.896 B.A., J.D. [Poyner&S.]
Meyer, Paul A. '70 '97 C.896 B.S. L.1345 J.D. Asst. Gen. Coun., Assn. of Co. Comrs.
Meyers, Mitchell A. '71 '98 C.260 B.A. L.1206 J.D. [Ⓐ J.T.Benjamin,Jr.]
Meynardie, Robert A., (AV) '59 '91 C.659 B.S. L.245 J.D. [Nelson M.R.&S.]
Michaels, John A., (AV) '51 '77 C.576 B.A. L.790 J.D. [Michaels&M.]
Michaels, Paul J., (AV) '47 '73 C.576 B.A. L.575 J.D. [Michaels&M.]
Michaels & Michaels, P.A., (AV) 107 Glenwood Avenue
Midgette, Nonnie F. '43 '71 C&L.329 B.A., J.D. Asst. Atty. Gen.
Milak, Jennifer B. '71 '97 C.526 B.A. L.1228 J.D. [Ⓐ Teague,C.D.&G.]
Miles, J. Hart, Jr. '68 '96 C.575 B.A. L.1228 J.D. [H.Miles]
Miles, Kathleen Manning, (BV) '72 '98 C.576 B.A. L.1228 J.D. [Cranfill,S.&H.]
Miles, Hart, Attorney At Law, P.A. 19 W Hargett Street, Suite 200
Millard, C. Michael '57 '93 C.92 B.S. L.790 J.D. [Ⓐ Hardison&L.]
Millberg, John C., (AV) '56 '80 C.97 B.A. L.896 J.D. [Millberg,G.&S.]

Millberg, Gordon & Stewart, PLLC, (AV)
1101 Haynes Street, Suite 104, 27604-1455
Telephone: 919-836-0090 Fax: 919-836-8027
Email: mgsfirm@mgsattorneys.com URL: http://www.mgsattorneys.com
John C. Millberg; Frank J. Gordon; William W. Stewart, Jr.; Douglas J. Brocker;—Seth C. Turner; Elizabeth H. Poremba.
Civil Trial, Product Liability, Railroad Litigation, Trucking Liability, Construction Litigation, Toxic Torts, Professional Liability and Professional Ethics, Occupational Licensing and Discipline.
See Professional Biographies, RALEIGH, NORTH CAROLINA

Millen, Pressly M., (AV) '60 '86 C.976 A.B. L.228 J.D. [Womble C.S.&R.]
Miller, Diane G. '51 '86 C.645 B.S. L.575 J.D. P.O. Box 629
Miller, Gerhard A. '51 '79 C.165 A.B. L.569 J.D.
Sr. V.P. & Gen. Coun., GE Financial Assurance, GE Capital Mortgage Corp.
Miller, Jeffrey D., (AV) '— '96 C.645 B.A. L.896 J.D. [DLPiper R.G.C.U.]
Miller, Jennifer M. '72 '98 C.347 B.A. L.896 J.D. [Ⓐ Wyrick R.Y.&P.]
Miller, Mary L. '56 '97 C.1111 B.A. L.1059 J.D. [Myers B.S.&S.] (See Pat. Sect.)
Miller, Miranda R. '64 '95 C.112 B.A. L.178 J.D. [Ⓐ Smith,A.B.D.M.&J.]
Miller, Philip R., III, (AV) '66 '92 C.575 B.A. L.1345 J.D. [Blanchard,J.M.L.&S.]
Miller, R. Bradley, (AV) '53 '79 C.575 B.A. L.178 J.D. 2308 Beachridge Road
Miller, Robert A. '51 '77 C.260 B.A. L.575 J.D. 127 W. Hargett Street
Miller, Robert J. '33 '85 C.576 B.S. L.574 J.D. 3404 Lake Boone Trail
Miller, W. Stacy, II, (AV) '65 '94 C.896 B.A. L.1228 J.D. [Zaytoun&M.P.]
Miller, William R. '49 '83 C.576 B.A. L.326 J.D. Atty. Gen. Off.

Miller, Charles W.
(See Pittsboro)

Miller & Shedor, PLLC
(See Cary)

Mills, Bobby D., (BV) '60 '85 C.48 B.A. L.896 J.D. [Herring M.M.&F.]
Mineo, Athena R. '57 '82 C.575 B.A. L.1228 J.D. [Mineo&M.]
Mineo, Robert A., (AV) '48 '81 C.576 B.S. L.1228 J.D. [Mineo&M.]

Mineo & Mineo, (AV)
Two Hanover Square, Suite 2350, 434 Fayetteville Street Mall, 27601
Telephone: 919-861-0501 Fax: 919-861-0504
URL: http://www.airlawus.com
Members of Firm: Robert A. Mineo; Athena R. Mineo.
National and International Aviation Litigation, Aircraft Crash and Regulatory Law, Mass Disaster, Product Liability, and Personal Injury Litigation. Appeals in all Courts.
See Professional Biographies, RALEIGH, NORTH CAROLINA

Minges, David R. '56 '82 C.232 B.S. L.1228 J.D.
4401 Revere Drive, 27609
Telephone: 919-782-4476 Fax: 919-782-4277
Email: dminges@nc.rr.com URL: http://www.lawyers.com/davidminges
Eminent Domain, Condemnation, Real Estate.
See Professional Biographies, RALEIGH, NORTH CAROLINA

Minier, John W., (AV) '62 '89 C.197 B.A. L.228 J.D. [Yates,M.&W.]
Misenheimer, Jeffrey Allen '73 '99 C.301 B.A. L.192 J.D. [Lewis&R.]
Miskimon, Scott A., (AV) '60 '92 C.502 B.J. L.575 J.D. [Smith,A.B.D.M.&J.]
Mitchell, Burley B., Jr., (AV) '40 '69 C.576 B.A. L.575 J.D. [Womble C.S.&R.]
Mitchell, Henry A., Jr., (AV) '35 '61 C.296 A.B. L.896 J.D. [Smith,A.B.D.M.&J.]
Mitchell, John F., (AV) '50 '75 C.896 B.A. L.575 J.D. Bus. & Estate Analysis, Inc.
Mitchell, Memory F. '24 '47 C.471 A.B. L.575 J.D. 2431 Medway Dr.‡
Mitchell, Michael W., (AV) '64 '89 C&L.896 B.A., J.D. [Smith,A.B.D.M.&J.]

Mitchell, Eyster & Warner, P.A.
(See Durham)

Mitchiner, Joseph H., (AV) '51 '77 C.575 B.S. L.574 J.D. [Mitchiner]

Mitchiner Law Firm, PLLC, (AV)
3110 Edwards Mill Road, Suite 340, 27612-5419
Telephone: 919-277-2600 Fax: 919-277-2626
Email: joe.mitchiner@mitchinerlaw.com
Joseph H. Mitchiner.
Wills, Trusts and Estates, including Estate Planning, Family Wealth Transfer, Living Trusts, Trust Planning and Wealth Preservation.
See Professional Biographies, RALEIGH, NORTH CAROLINA

Mitterling, Sandra W. '66 '95 C&L.575 B.A., J.D. [Ⓐ Ragsdale L.]
Mobley, Linda C., (BV) '49 '78 C.778 B.S. L.574 J.D. 3505 Barron Berkeley Way
Modlin, Claire A., (BV) '70 '95 C.575 B.S. L.1228 J.D. [Ⓒ Patterson,D.C.B.&A.]
Moesta, Sara C. '76 '00 C.1369 B.A. L.896 J.D. [Ⓐ Jordan P.W.G.J.&C.]
Moesta, Scott C. '73 '98 C.229 B.A. L.201 J.D. 5640 Six Forks Rd., Ste. 203
Moffitt, Donna Dutty '47 '84 C.576 B.E.D. L.575 J.D.
Asst. Dir., State Div. of Community Assistance
Moffitt, Thomas F., (AV) '47 '75 C.577 B.A. L.575 J.D. Dep. Coun.

Moir, Vickie L., (BV) . . . '52 '78 C.758 B.A. L.575 J.D. 1008 Winona Rd.
Molleur, John T., (BV) . . . '64 '96 C.228 A.B. L.945 J.D. [A Yates,M.&W.]
Monchick, Randolph B. . . . '47 '89 C.259 B.S. L.575 J.D. Asst. Fed. Pub. Def.
Monroe, Robert E., (BV) . . . '49 '74 C.158 B.S. L.607 J.D. [Monroe,W.&W.]
Monroe, Wyne & Wallace, P.A., (AV) . . . 3225 Blue Ridge Road, Suite 117
Montgomery, John Robert . . . '27 '53 C&L.575 B.S., J.D. 1408 Pony Run Rd.‡
Montgomery, Renee J., (AV) . . . '50 '78 C&L.228 B.A., J.D. [Parker,P.A.&B.]
Montgomery, Robert C., (AV) . . . '62 '87 C&L.575 A.B., J.D. P.O. Box 629

Montgomery, Charles H., Law Offices of
(See Cary)

Moody, Dana C. . . . '— '01 C&L.575 B.A., J.D. [A Hedrick E.G.&K.]
Moog, Robert S. '49 '74 C.107 B.A. L.94 J.D.
(adm. in OR; not adm. in NC) Asst. Prof., N.C. State Univ.
Moore, Brian E., (BV) . . . '74 '99 C.575 B.A. L.1228 J.D. [Howard,S.F.&H.]
Moore, D. Scott . . . '63 '96 C.339 B.S.E.E. L.146 J.D. [Myers B.S.&S.] (See Pat. Sect.)
Moore, Jackson W., (BV) . . . '70 '95 C.893 B.A. L.228 J.D. [A Smith,A.B.D.M.&J.]
Moore, Joseph C., III, (AV) . . . '48 '74 C.575 A.B. L.896 J.D. [Allen&M.]
Moore, Michael D. . . . '64 '96 C.585 B.A. L.1228 J.D. [A Teague,C.D.&G.]
Moore, Richard W., (BV) . . . '47 '77 C.10 B.S. L.893 J.D. [Moore&A.]
Moore, Thomas Henry, (CV) . . . '58 '94 C&L.575 B.A., J.D. NC Dept. of Jus.
Moore, W. Richard, (BV) . . . '49 '74 C&L.896 B.A., J.D. P.O. Box 25201

Moore & Alphin, PLLC, (BV)
3716 National Drive, Suite 100, 27612 ⊙
Telephone: 919-787-8812 Facsimile: 919-787-3312
URL: http://www.lawyers.com/moorealphin
Richard W. Moore; G. Mark Teague; S. Amanda Palmer. Of Counsel: Oliver W. Alphin.
Residential and Commercial Real Estate, Zoning, Planning and Land Use, Corporate, Business Law, Small Business, Estate Planning, Wills.
Durham, North Carolina Office: 1000 Park Forty Plaza, Suite 100, 27713. Telephone: 919-544-0092. Facsimile: 919-544-1059.
See Professional Biographies, RALEIGH, NORTH CAROLINA

Moore & Van Allen PLLC
(See Research Triangle Park)

Morelock, Fred M., (AV) . . . '52 '76 C&L.575 B.A., J.D. [Tharrington S.]
Morgan, Clayton D. . . . '65 '91 C.575 B.S. L.896 J.D. Staff Atty., Progress Energy
Morgan, Jennifer A. . . . '79 '05 C.576 B.S. L.1228 J.D. [A Maupin T.]
Morgan, Margaret, (BV) . . . '61 '86 C.228 A.B. L.1228 J.D. [Morgan&R.]
Morgan, Patsy S. . . . '55 '80 C.254 B.A. L.880 J.D. 323 Golf Course Dr.
Morgan, Robert B., (AV) . . . '25 '50 C.232 B.S. L.896 J.D. [Morgan&R.] ⊙
Morgan & Reeves, (AV) . . . 16 W. Martin St. (⊙Lillington)
Moritz, Claire L., (AV) . . . '54 '80 C.94 B.S. L.228 J.D. V.P., Legal Servs., WakeMed
Mormando, Mark A. '62 '89 C.690 B.S. L.61 J.D.
(adm. in CA; not adm. in NC) Tax Mgr., Invensys, plc
Morris, Fenita T. '67 '92 C.575 B.S. L.574 J.D.
(adm. in TX; not adm. in NC) U.S. Atty's Off.
Morris, Robert Joseph . . . '63 '88 C&L.228 A.B., J.D. [Smith,A.B.D.M.&J.]
Morris, Schneider & Prior, L.L.C.
7330 Chapel Hill Road, Suite 104 (⊙Atlanta, GA; Winchester, VA)

Morris York Williams Surles & Barringer, L.L.P.
(See Charlotte)

Morrison, Fred G., Jr. '39 '63 C.451 L.896 J.D.
Sr. Admin. Law J., Off. of Adm. Hearings
Morrison, Marifrances . . . '68 '94 C.454 B.A. L.1202 J.D. [Ogletree,D.N.S.&S.]
Morrison, Steven C., (AVⓣ) '53 '79
C.347 B.S. L.345 J.D. Chief Legal Offr., Togethersoft Corp.
Morrow, Thomas M. . . . '— '97 C.893 B.S. L.896 J.D. [Hedrick E.G.&K.]
Morton, Robert L., (CVⓣ) . . . '34 '66 C&L.376 B.S., J.D. [Wallis&M.]
Morton, Travis K., (BV) . . . '69 '94 C.576 B.A. L.575 J.D. [Brady,N.K.&M.]
Moseley, Alice Neece, (BV) '56 '85
C.576 B.S.W. L.575 J.D. Asst. Exec. Dir., N.C. State Bar
Moseley, Emily A. . . . '— '98 C.668 B.A. L.880 J.D. [A Kilpatrick S.]
Moss, William H., (AV) . . . '56 '84 C&L.575 B.A., J.D. [Smith,A.B.D.M.&J.]
Moye, Katherine S., (BV) . . . '68 '94 C.420 B.A. L.575 J.D. [Howard,G.&M.]
Moylan, Patricia A. '56 '81
C.575 B.A. L.851 J.D. Legal Educ. Offr., NC Real Estate Comm.
Mueller, Bernhard . . . '68 '01 C&L.790 B.A., J.D. [A Ogletree,D.N.S.&S.]
Mullen, Eileen A. . . . '70 '97 C.823 B.A. L.229 J.D. [A K.E.Knudsen]
Muller, Tara D. . . . '75 '00 C.576 B.A. L.1228 J.D. [A Teague,C.D.&G.]
Mullis, Leanne L. . . . '72 '02 C.881 B.A. L.1228 J.D. [Cranfill,S.&H.]
Mumme, Bettina . . . '— '01 C.645 B.S. L.575 J.D. [A Hedrick E.G.&K.]
Mund, Nathaniel B. '71 '96 C.475 B.A. L.575 J.D.
Dir., Gov. Rel., State Conserv. Coun.
Munford, R. Donavon, Jr., (AV) . . . '54 '79 C.198 A.B. L.575 J.D. [Smith,A.B.D.M.&J.]
Munn, Charles H., Jr. . . . '64 '91 C.896 B.S. L.1228 J.D. 4101 Lake Boone Trail, Suite 300
Murphy, Gerald P. . . . '57 '82 C.34 B.A. L.1228 J.D. Spec. Dep. Atty. Gen.
Murphy, Hope D. . . . '74 '99 C&L.575 B.A., J.D. 6608 Six Forks Road
Murphy, Kathleen, (CV) . . . '62 '85 C.576 B.A. L.1228 J.D. 333 Fayetteville St. Mall
Murphy, Kenneth R., III . . . '69 '99 C&L.575 B.A., J.D. [A Knott,C.&B.]
Murphy, Margaret Louise . . . '71 '99 C.1185 B.S.W. L.1228 J.D. [A Sandman&R.]
Murray, Charles J. . . . '43 '68 C&L.575 A.B., J.D. Atty. Gen. Off.
Musselwhite, Marvin D., Jr., (AV) . . . '38 '63 C&L.228 A.B., J.D. [Poyner&S.]
Myatt, Tracy C. . . . '64 '94 C.576 B.A. L.575 J.D. [Cranfill,S.&H.]
Myers, James D. . . . '40 '72 C&L.790 B.S.Ch.E., J.D. [Myers B.S.&S.] (See Pat. Sect.)
Myers, Jerry T., (AV) . . . '58 '84 C&L.896 B.S., J.D. [Smith D.N.W.S.&M.]

Myers Bigel Sibley & Sajovec, P.A., (AV)
4140 Parklake Avenue, Suite 600, 27612
Telephone: 919-854-1400 Fax: 919-854-1401
Email: mbss@myersbigel.com URL: http://www.myersbigel.com
D. Randal Ayers; David D. Beatty; Mitchell S. Bigel; Needham J. Boddie, II; Lynne A. Borchers; James R. Cannon; Robert N. Crouse; Robert W. Glatz; Scott C. Hatfield; Dr. Karen A. Magri; Robert M. Meeks; Dr. Mary L. Miller; D. Scott Moore; James D. Myers; Timothy J. O'Sullivan; David K. Purks; Julie H. Richardson; F. Michael Sajovec; Grant J. Scott; Kenneth D. Sibley; Richard P. Vitek;—Jarett K. Abramson; Dr. Alice M. Bonnen; Anna Carr; Laura M. Kelley; Dr. Shawna Cannon Lemon; Rohan G. Sabapathypillai; Elizabeth A. Stanek.
Intellectual Property Law: Patents, Trademarks, Copyrights and related Litigation.
See Professional Biographies, RALEIGH, NORTH CAROLINA

Nachtrieb, Dennis W. . . . '56 '95 C.1044 B.A. L.574 B.S. [A Gurley&C.]
Nager, Elizabeth Carr . . . '63 '88 C.228 A.B. L.1068 J.D. 1300 Canterbury Rd.‡
Nance, Lars F., (BV) . . . '54 '80 C&L.575 B.A., J.D. Spec. Dep. Atty. Gen.
Nance, Nicholas A. . . . '79 '05 C.34 B.S.B.A. L.1228 J.D. [A Maupin T.]
Nance, Tamara R., (AV) . . . '57 '83 C&L.608 B.A., J.D. P.O. Box 37010
Nanney, David P., Jr., (AV) . . . '58 '85 C.1128 B.S. L.1228 J.D. [Kirschbaum,N.K.&G.]
Nanney, Joseph H., Jr., (AV) . . . '61 '91 C.1129 B.M. L.575 J.D. [Wyrick R.Y.&P.]
Narayan, Rajeev . . . '70 '98 C.575 B.S.B.A. L.260 J.D. N.C. State University

Narron, John W., (AV) . . . '51 '77 C.232 B.A. L.500 J.D. [Smith D.N.W.S.&M.]
Nazareth, Natasha M. . . . '71 '97 C.228 A.B. L.575 J.D. Staff Atty.
NC Prisoner Legal Services . . . 1110 Wake Forest Rd.
Neely, Charles B., Jr., (AV) . . . '43 '70 C.575 A.B. L.228 J.D. [Maupin T.]
Neijna, Adam M., (BV) . . . '66 '91 C.1365 B.A. L.472 J.D. [A.Neijna]

Neijna, Adam, PLLC, The Law Offices of, (BV)
8601 Six Forks Road, Suite 400, 27615
Telephone: 919-844-0900 Fax: 919-882-2110
Email: amn@amnlawfirm.com URL: http://www.amnlawfirm.com
Member: Adam M. Neijna.
Civil Litigation, Construction Law, Commercial Law, Products Liability, Personal Injury.
See Professional Biographies, RALEIGH, NORTH CAROLINA

Neill, David J. . . . '73 '04 C&L.575 A.B., J.D. [A Holt Y.M.&H.]
Nelson, Ilene Berenter . . . '48 '80 C.174 B.S. L.1065 J.D. Admr., Admin. Off. of the Cts.
Nelson, William W., (AV) . . . '60 '86 C&L.575 A.B., J.D. [Smith,A.B.D.M.&J.]

Nelson Mullins Riley & Scarborough LLP, (AV)
GlenLake One, Suite 200, 4140 Parklake Avenue, 27612 ⊙
Telephone: 919-877-3800 Telecopy: 919-877-3799
URL: http://www.nelsonmullins.com
Of Counsel: Catharine W. Cummer; Reed J. Hollander. Partners: Barry D. Alexander; Christopher J. Blake; Steven Carr; Melissa J. Copeland (Not admitted in NC); Theodore E. Corvette; Joseph W. Eason; Susan Y. Ellinger; William H. Gammon; David A. Harlow; Frank A. Hirsch, Jr.; Wallace C. Hollowell, III; Noah H. Huffstetler, III (Managing Partner, Raleigh Office); Leon M. Killian, III (Board Certified Specialist in Real Property Law, Residential, Business, Commercial and Industrial Transactions, North Carolina State Board of Legal Specialization); Matthew P. McGuire; Charles H. Mercer, Jr.; Robert A. Meynardie; Cathy M. Rudisill; George M. Teague. Associates: Seagrumn L. Gilbert; Lisa R. Gordon; Amy L. Keegan; Christopher M. Kindel; Leslie C. Lane; Stephen D. Martin; Ross E. Sallade; Christopher M. Thomas.
Health Care; Intellectual Property; labor and Employment; Low Income Housing Tax Credits.
Atlanta, Georgia Office: 999 Peachtree Street, N.E., Suite 1400, 30309-3964. P.O. Box 77707, 30357-0707. Telephone: 404-817-6000. Telecopy: 404-817-6050.
Charleston, South Carolina Office: Liberty Center, Suite 600, 151 Meeting Street, 29401-2239. P.O. Box 1806, 29402-1806. Telephone: 843-853-5200. Telecopy: 843-722-8700.
Charlotte, North Carolina Office: Bank of America Corporate Center, Suite 2400, 100 North Tryon Street, 28202-4007. Telephone: 704-417-3000. Telecopy: 704-377-4814.
Columbia, South Carolina Office: Meridian, 17th Floor, 1320 Main Street, 29201, P.O. Box 11070, 29211-1070. Telephone: 803-799-2000. Telecopy: 803-256-7500.
Greenville, South Carolina Office: Poinsett Plaza, 104 South Main Street, Suite 900, 29601. P.O. Box 10084, 29603-0084. Telephone: 864-250-2300. Telecopy: 864-232-2925.
Myrtle Beach, South Carolina Office: Founders Centre, Suite 301, 2411 North Oak Street, 29577-3165. P.O. Box 3939, 29578-3939. Telephone: 843-448-3500. Telecopy: 843-448-3437.
Washington, D.C. Office: 101 Constitution Avenue, NW, Suite 900, 20001. Telephone: 202-712-2800. Fax: 202-712-2860.
Winston-Salem, North Carolina Office: The Knollwood, 380 Knollwood Street, Suite 530, 27103. Telephone: 336-774-3300. Fax: 336-774-3299.
See Professional Biographies, RALEIGH, NORTH CAROLINA

Nesnow, Dolores O. '45 '76
C.178 B.S. L.966 J.D. Admin. Law J., Off. of Admin. Hearings
Newby, Paul M. . . . '55 '80 C.228 B.A. L.575 J.D. Assoc. J. Supm. Ct.
Newman, James T., Jr. . . . '— '02 C.576 B.A. L.1228 J.D. [A Yates,M.&W.]
Newman, Jan L. . . . '73 '01 C.471 B.A. L.1128 J.D. [A Smith,A.B.D.M.&J.]
Newman, Lou A., (AV) . . . '55 '80 C.228 B.A. L.575 J.D. Asst. Clk.
Newsome, George H. . . . '22 '48 L.228 LL.B. 717 Yarmouth Rd
Newsome, Joseph A. . . . '71 '98 C.228 A.B. L.896 J.D. [A Wallace,N.&S.]
Newson, Perry Y., (BV) '56 '83
C.682 B.A. L.945 J.D. Exec. Dir. & Coun., State Bd. of Ethics
Newton, Deborrah L. . . . '— '99 C.953 B.A. L.1228 J.D. [Newton L.]
Newton, J. Gregory, (BV) . . . '70 '96 C.575 B.A. L.1228 J.D. [Cranfill,S.&H.]
Newton, Jason D. . . . '72 '99 C.575 B.A. L.896 J.D. [A Yates,M.&W.]
Newton Law . . . 300 Blake Street, Suite 207
Nicholls, F. Timothy, (AV) . . . '43 '67 C&L.575 B.A., J.D. [Nicholls&C.]

Nicholls & Crampton, P.A., (AV)
4300 Six Forks Road Suite 700, P.O. Box 18237, 27609
Telephone: 919-781-1311 Telecopier: 919-782-0465
URL: http://www.nichollscrampton.com
W. Sidney Aldridge; Robin Adams Anderson; Gregory B. Crampton (Board Certified Specialist in Bankruptcy Law, North Carolina State Board of Legal Specialization); Nicholas J. Dombalis, II; Stephani Wilson Humrickhouse (Board Certified Specialist in Bankruptcy Law, North Carolina State Board of Legal Specialization); F. Timothy Nicholls; Kevin L. Sink (Board Certified Specialist in Business Bankruptcy Law, North Carolina State Board of Legal Specialization).
Trust, Estate Planning, Probate, Bankruptcy and Business Law, Civil Trial Practice, Construction Litigation, Commercial Trial Practice, Corporation, Criminal Trial Practice, Employment Law, Family Law, Personal Injury, Products Liability, Real Estate and Wrongful Death.
See Professional Biographies, RALEIGH, NORTH CAROLINA

Nichols, Charles E., Jr., (AV) . . . '56 '82 C.228 B.A. L.575 J.D. [Manning,F.&S.]
Nichols, Christopher R., (BV) . . . '69 '94 C&L.896 B.A., J.D. [A Hardison&L.]
Nichols, M. Jackson, (AV) . . . '51 '77 C.198 B.A. L.896 J.D. [Allen&P.]
Nicholson, Meredith S. . . . '73 '00 C&L.575 B.A., J.D. [A Kurtz&B.]
Nicholson, Tammy D. '72 '99
C.575 B.S. L.574 J.D. Title Coun., Fidelity Natl. Title Ins. Co.
Nipper, J. Russell . . . '20 '47 C&L.896 B.S., LL.B. 2514 St. Mary's St.‡
Nodell, Theodore A., (AV) . . . '47 '72 C&L.896 B.A., J.D. [Nodell,G.&H.]

Nodell, Glass & Haskell, L.L.P., (AV)
5540 Centerview Drive, Suite 416, 27606
Telephone: 919-821-2600 Fax: 919-821-7744
URL: http://www.nodglahaslaw.com
Members of Firm: Theodore A. Nodell; Philip A. Glass; Craig S. Haskell. Associate: James R. White.
Creditor Bankruptcy, Creditor Rights, Secured Transactions, Foreclosure, Collections, Commercial Litigation and Workouts.
Reference: Branch Banking and Trust Company.
See Professional Biographies, RALEIGH, NORTH CAROLINA

Noland, John Everette, Jr., (BV) '41 '68 C.1365 A.B. L.477 LL.B.
5 West Hargett Street
Nordan, Richard P., (AV) . . . '56 '85 C.576 B.A. L.575 J.D. [Wallace,N.&S.]
Nordgren, Timothy A., (AV) . . . '69 '95 C.352 B.B.A. L.575 J.D. [Brady,N.K.&M.]
Norman, Bartley A. . . . '72 '02 C.576 B.A. L.575 J.D. [A Smith,A.B.D.M.&J.]
Norris, Thomas L., Jr., (AV) . . . '33 '60 C&L.575 B.S., J.D. [C Poyner&S.]
Novajosky, Donald L. '71 '00 C.645 B.S. L.564 J.D.
(adm. in NJ; not adm. in NC) [A Hutchison&M.]
Noyes, Craig W. . . . '77 '02 C.259 B.S. L.575 J.D. [A Schwartz&S.]
Nunnally, John M., (BV) . . . '65 '92 C.576 B.A. L.1228 J.D. [Ragsdale L.]
Nuttall, Amy Harrison . . . '58 '02 C.472 B.S. L.1228 J.D. [Cranfill,S.&H.]
Oates, John Frances, Jr., (BV) . . . '61 '87 C.976 A.B. L.896 J.D. Asst. Atty. Gen.
O'Brien, Daniel P. . . . '— '95 C.118 B.A. L.575 J.D. Dept. of Jus., Appl. Sect.
O'Brien, James M., III, (AV) . . . '66 '92 C.953 B.A. L.1066 J.D. [Poyner&S.]
O'Connor, Arthur W., Jr. '59 '84 C.228 A.B. L.880 J.D.
V.P. & Sr. Coun., GE Financial Assurance, GE Mtge. Holdings, LLC

O'Connor, Jennifer S. '— '98 C.228 B.A. L.818 J.D.
(adm. in FL; not adm. in NC) [[A] Kilpatrick S.]
O'Connor, Liam T. .... '54 '81 C.102 B.A. L.1009 J.D. P.O. Box 97425
Odom, T. LaFontine, Sr., (AV) .... '38 '62 C&L.575 A.B., LL.B. [Odom] ⊙
Odom Firm, The, PLLC, (AV) .... 1046 Washington Street (⊙Charlotte)
O'Donnell, John B., Jr., (AV) .... '48 '74 C.575 A.B. L.896 J.D. [Hall&O.]
O'Donnell, Robert L., (AVⓉ) '46 '75 C.812 B.S. L.893 J.D.
[Vandeventer B.] (⊙Kitty Hawk, NC; Norfolk, VA)
O'Donoghue, Roderick W., Jr., (BV) '52 '80
C.1128 B.A. L.1228 J.D. 1100 Navaho Dr., Ste. 106
O'Duffy, Siobhan T. .... '59 '86 C.103 B.A. L.228 J.D. 2708 Kittrell Dr.‡
Oettinger, Kenneth B., (AV) .... '44 '71 C&L.575 A.B., J.D. [Oettinger&P.]

Oettinger & Peebles, LLP, (AV)
3737 Glenwood Avenue, Suite 100, 27612
Telephone: 919-573-1860 Fax: 919-573-1861
Members of the Firm: Kenneth B. Oettinger; Monique M. Peebles.
See Professional Biographies, RALEIGH, NORTH CAROLINA

Ogburn, Rudy L., (AV) .... '56 '82 C&L.896 B.A., J.D. [Young M.&H.]

Ogletree, Deakins, Nash, Smoak & Stewart, P.C., (AV) BB
2301 Sugar Bush Road Suite 600, 27612 ⊙
Mailing Address: P.O. Box 31608, Raleigh, NC 27622
Telephone: 919-787-9700 Facsimile: 919-783-9412 Immigration Telephone: 919-760-3000 Immigration Facsimile: 919-787-2934 URL: http://www.visatrax.com
Email: clientservices@ogletreedeakins.com URL: http://www.ogletreedeakins.com
Guy F. Driver (1940-2001); John S. Burgin; C. Matthew Keen; Andrew W. Merrills; Robert A. Sar; Bruce A. Petesch; Thomas A. Farr; Gregory P. McGuire; Rodolfo R. Agraz; Gretchen W. Ewalt; Stephen H. Smalley; Marifrances Morrison;—Rachel B. March; Phillip J. Strach; Kevin S. Joyner; Bernhard Mueller; David B. Hawley; Kevin J. O'Sullivan (Not admitted in NC); John E. Branch; Charles Ryan Cook (Not admitted in NC). Of Counsel: Debra L. Dewar; Thomas F. Ellis.
Labor Relations, Employment Litigation, Workers' Compensation. Civil Litigation in all State and Federal Courts and Administrative Agencies.
Representative Clients: Duke Energy Corp.; General Electric Co.; W. R. Grace & Co.
Atlanta, Georgia Office: 600 Peachtree Street, N.E., Suite 2100. Telephone: 404-881-1300.
Austin, Texas Office: 301 Congress Avenue, Suite 1250. Telephone: 512-344-4700.
Birmingham, Alabama Office: One Federal Place, Suite 1000, 1819 Fifth Avenue North. Telephone: 205-328-1900.
Charleston, South Carolina Office: 134 Meeting Street, Suite 160, P.O. Box 1808. Telephone: 843-853-1300.
Charlotte, North Carolina Office: 400 West Trade Street. Telephone: 704-342-2588.
Chicago, Illinois Office: Twenty-Fifth Floor, Two First National Plaza, 20 South Clark Street. Telephone: 312-558-1220.
Columbia, South Carolina Office: 1320 Main Street, Suite 600. Telephone: 803-252-1300.
Dallas, Texas Office: 700 Preston Commons, 8117 Preston Road. Telephone: 214-987-3800.
Greensboro, North Carolina Office: 2725 Horse Pen Creek Road, Suite 101. Telephone: 336-375-9737.
Greenville, South Carolina Office: The Ogletree Building, 300 North Main Street, P.O. Box 2757. Telephone: 864-271-1300.
Houston, Texas Office: One Allen Center, 500 Dallas Street, Suite 3000. Telephone: 713-655-0855.
Kansas City, Missouri Office: 4717 Grand Avenue, Suite 300. Telephone: 816-471-1301.
Los Angeles, California Office: 633 West Fifth Street, Suite 5300. Telephone: 213-239-9800.
Indianapolis, Indiana Office: Suite 4600, 111 Monument Circle. Telephone: 317-916-1300.
Miami, Florida Office: 80 S.W. 8th Street, Suite 1830. Telephone: 305-374-0506.
Morristown, New Jersey Office: 10 Madison Avenue, Suite 402. Telephone: 973-656-1600.
Nashville, Tennessee Office: SunTrust Center, Suite 800, 424 Church Street. Telephone: 615-254-1900.
Phoenix, Arizona Office: 2415 East Camelback Road, Suite 800. Telephone: 602-778-3700.
San Antonio, Texas Office: 2600 Weston Centre, 112 East Pecan Street. Telephone: 210-354-1300.
St. Thomas, U.S. Virgin Islands Office: The Tunick Building, 1336 Beltjen Road, Suite 202. Telephone: 340-714-1235.
Tampa, Florida Office: 100 North Tampa Street, Suite 3600. Telephone: 813-289-1247.
Washington, D.C. Office: Fifth Floor, 2400 N Street, N.W. Telephone: 202-887-0855.
See Professional Biographies, RALEIGH, NORTH CAROLINA

Okun, Michael G., (AV) ...... '47 '80 C.33 B.A. L.575 J.D. [Patterson H.] (⊙Chapel Hill)
Oleynik, Jeffrey E., (AV) .... '58 '83 C.945 B.A. L.893 J.D. [Brooks,P.M.H.&L.] ⊙

Olive and Olive, P.A.
(See Durham)

Oliver, Cindy G., (BV) .... '62 '87 C.1365 B.A. L.896 J.D. P.O. Box 10349
Oliver, George J., (AVⓉ) .... '43 '73 C.1228 B.S. L.838 J.D. [Smith M.]
Oliver, Helen M. .... '73 '97 C.216 B.A. L.1338 J.D. [Sokol M.S.O.L.P.]
Oliver, James .... '71 '97 C.216 B.A. L.1338 J.D. 4809 Delta Vision Ct.
Oliver, Samuel T., Jr., (AV) .... '52 '79 C.896 B.A. L.575 J.D. [Manning,F.&S.]
Olivieri, Joseph Patrick '73 '01 C.659 B.A. L.575 J.D.
100 East Six Forks Rd., Suite 304
Olson, G. Christopher, (AV) .... '67 '94 C.575 B.A. L.1228 J.D. [Martin&J.]
Olson, Kurt J., (BV) .... '52 '84 C.454 B.S. L.128 J.D. [Maupin T.]
O'Neal, Cynthia A. .... '74 '99 C&L.228 B.A., J.D. [[A] Taylor,P.R.&R.]
Onuscheck, David '57 '82 C.602 B.A. L.276 J.D.
(adm. in PA; not adm. in NC)
V.P., Gen. Coun., Power Tech. Div., Asst. Secy., ABB Inc.
Ormand, John W., III, (AV) ..... '62 '87 C.896 B.A. L.575 J.D. [Brooks,P.M.H.&L.] ⊙
Orr, Robert F. .... '46 '75 C&L.575 A.B., J.D. Assoc. Jus., Supm. Ct.

Osborn, J. Kirk
(See Chapel Hill)

Osborne, Jay L. .... '64 '90 C&L.575 B.A., J.D. NC Atty. Gen. Off.
Osman, Joseph W. .... '70 '96 C.999 B.A. L.1228 J.D. [[A] Hardison&L.]
O'Sullivan, Kevin J. '— '03 C.390 B.A. L.262 J.D.
(adm. in NY; not adm. in NC) [[A] Ogletree,D.N.S.&S.]
O'Sullivan, Michael S. .... '— '02 C.645 B.A. L.575 J.D. [[A] DLPiper R.G.C.U.]
O'Sullivan, Timothy J. '61 '90
C.502 B.S.E.E. L.228 J.D. [Myers B.S.&S.] (See Pat. Sect.)
O'Toole, Donald T. .... '60 '00 C.103 Sc.B. L.575 J.D. [[A] Bailey&D.]
O'Toole, Leslie C., (AV) .... '61 '86 C.103 A.B. L.575 J.D. [Ellis&W.] (⊙Cary)
Otterson, David V., (AVⓉ) .... '53 '80 C.147 B.A. L.1065 J.D. [Helms M.&W.]
Otto, Catherine E. .... '75 '03 C&L.575 A.B., J.D. [[A] Womble C.S.&R.]
Ouellette, Roberta A. .... '53 '80 C.550 B.A. L.1294 J.D. 3900 Barrett Dr., Ste. 101
Outlaw, Larry A. .... '44 '75 C.198 A.B. L.575 J.D. NC Real Estate Comm.
Owens, Terryn D. .... '58 '83 C&L.575 B.S., J.D. P.O. Box 31627‡
Oxley, Elizabeth Lerch, (AV) '53 '83
C.385 A.B. L.352 J.D. Asst. Atty. Gen., N.C. Dept. of Justice
Pace, C. D. Taylor, (AV) .... '60 '85 C&L.575 B.A., J.D. [Cranfill,S.&H.]
Pace, Tina Frazier, (BV) .... '68 '94 C.228 A.B. L.575 J.D. [Hatch,L.&B.]
Page, Christopher A., (BV) .... '66 '93 C.228 B.A. L.976 J.D. [Young M.&H.]
Page, Edgar Moore .... '75 '00 C&L.575 B.S.B.A., J.D. [[A] Yates,M.&W.]
Page, Robert F., (AV) .... '44 '69 C&L.228 B.A., J.D. [Crisp P.&C.]
Page, Winston L., Jr., (AV) .... '48 '75 C&L.575 B.A., J.D. [Lewis&R.]
Paine, Philip W. .... '77 '03 C.790 B.S. L.575 J.D. [[A] Howard,S.F.&H.]
Palmer, S. Amanda .... '70 '98 C.30 B.S. L.1209 J.D. [Moore&A.]
Palmieri, Daniel J. .... '— '04 C&L.577 B.A., J.D. [[A] Kennedy C.L.&H.]
Paluch, Stephen James .... '69 '99 C.1529 B.A. L.7 J.D. [Kassor&P.]
Panico, Sondra C., (BV) .... '66 '93 C.477 B.A. L.276 J.D. Assoc. Atty. Gen.

Pappas, William G., (AV) .... '52 '77 C&L.575 B.A., J.D. [Parker,P.A.&B.]
Parascandola, Stephen T. .... '62 '89 C.1236 B.A. L.362 J.D. [Smith,A.B.D.M.&J.]
Paris, Bryant D., III .... '75 '02 C.575 A.B. L.500 J.D. [Lewis&R.]
Parker, Fred P., III '39 '64 C&L.575 A.B., LL.B.
Executive Director, NC Board of Law Examiners
Parker, John H., (AV) .... '44 '69 C.575 B.A. L.838 J.D. [Cheshire,P.S.B.&V.]
Parker, Joseph M. '31 '60
C.240 A.B. L.228 LL.B. Pres. & Gen. Coun., Lawyers Title of N.C.
Parker, Sarah Elizabeth .... '42 '69 C&L.575 A.B., J.D. Assoc. Jus., Supm. Ct.
Parker, Susan Milner, (AV) .... '51 '81 C.228 B.A. L.1194 J.D. [Smith,A.B.D.M.&J.]

Parker, Poe, Adams & Bernstein L.L.P., (AV) BB
Wachovia Capitol Center, 150 Fayetteville Street Mall, Suite 1400, P.O. Box 389, 27602-0389 ⊙
Telephone: 919-828-0564 Facsimile: 919-834-4564
Email: info@parkerpoe.com URL: http://www.parkerpoe.com
Partners: Catharine Biggs Arrowood; Patricia T. Bartis; Brandon G. Bordeaux; Brian R. Brown; John J. Butler; Henry C. Campen, Jr.; Kevin L. Chignell; Jack L. Cozort; Melanie Black Dubis; John R. Erwin; Russell B. Killen; Charles C. Meeker; Renee J. Montgomery; William G. Pappas; Frank E. Silber; Robert W. Spearman; James A. Thomas; R. Bruce Thompson, II; James C. Thornton; Cynthia Leigh Wittmer. Special Counsel: Rebecca Blackmon Joyner; Todd M. Rubin. Of Counsel: J. Allen Adams; John F. Graybeal; William H. McCullough (Board Certified Specialist in Real Property Law and Business, Commercial and Industrial Transactions, North Carolina Board of Legal Specialization). Associates: Nicholle Allen-Steele; Jeffrey A. Bandini; Scott E. Bayzle; George T. Brady III; Melissa S. Daigneault; Brian D. Darer; Susan L. Dunathan; Sarah L. Ford; Amanda A. Hayes; Tracy Wood Kimbrell; Kathryn S. Lehman; Brenton W. McConkey; Charles E. Raynal, IV.
Administrative and Regulatory, Antitrust and Trade Regulation, Arbitration, Banking, Bankruptcy, Insolvency and Reorganization, Biotechnology, Capital Markets, Computer, Construction, Copyright, Corporate, Corporate Finance, Education, Employee Benefits and Compensation Plans, Employment, Environmental, Estate Planning and Administration, Governmental Contracts and Procurement, Governmental Relations, Health Care, Immigration, Insurance, Intellectual Property, International Trade and Investment, Joint Ventures, Lending and Finance, Limited Liability Companies and Partnerships, Litigation, Malpractice Defense, Mergers and Acquisitions, Municipal, Products Liability, Project Development, Project Finance, Public Finance, Commercial Real Estate, Securities, Tax Exempt Organizations, Taxation, Technology Management and Licensing, Telecommunications, Trademark, Transportation, Utilities Regulation, Zoning.
Representative Clients: Board of Governors of the University of North Carolina; Charlotte Mecklenburg Hospital Authority; Crescent Resources LLC, Duke Energy; Laboratory Corporation of America Holdings; North Carolina Biotechnology Center; Sonic Automotive; Speedway Motorsports; Sunbelt Rentals, Inc.; Wachovia.
Charlotte, North Carolina Offices: Three Wachovia Center, 401 South Tryon Street, Suite 3000, 28202. Telephone: 704-372-9000. Facsimile: 704-334-4706.
Columbia, South Carolina Office: 1201 Main Street, Suite 1450, 29201. Telephone: 803-255-8000. Facsimile: 803-255-8017.
Spartanburg, South Carolina Office: 101 W. St. John Street, Suite 203, 29306. Telephone: 803-591-2030. Facsimile: 803-591-2050.
Charleston, South Carolina Office: 200 Meeting Street, Suite 301, 29401. Telephone: 843-727-2650. Facsimile: 843-727-2680.
See Professional Biographies, RALEIGH, NORTH CAROLINA

Parkman, Kimberly K. .... '75 '03 C.840 B.S.N. L.575 J.D. [[A] Patterson,D.C.B.&A.]
Parks, Kristin D. .... '68 '95 C.575 B.A. L.896 J.D. P.O. Box 25397
Parris, E. Spencer, (AV) .... '50 '83 C.160 B.S. L.790 J.D. [Martin&J.]
Parrott, Hillary Bailey .... '74 '00 C&L.575 B.A., J.D. [[A] Michaels&M.]
Parry, K. Alan, Jr., (AV) .... '73 '98 C.840 B.S. L.228 J.D. [[A] Smith,A.B.D.M.&J.]
Parsons, Aubrey E. .... '46 '89 C.576 B.A. L.575 J.D. Atty. Gen.
Parsons, Elizabeth F. .... '46 '89 C.576 B.A. L.575 J.D. Asst. Atty. Gen.
Parsons, Gary S., (AV) .... '52 '77 C.576 B.S. L.575 J.D. [Bailey&D.]
Parsons, Gavin B. .... '75 '01 C.576 B.A. L.896 J.D. [[A] Bailey&D.]
Parsons, Jeffrey B., (BV) .... '62 '88 C&L.575 B.A., J.D. [[C] Conner G.S.]
Partin, Wilson B., Jr. '37 '64 C&L.575 A.B., J.D.
Dep. Gen. Coun., N.C. Utilities Comm.
Partrick, Sean T., (BV) .... '63 '97 C.575 B.A. L.1345 J.D. [[A] Yates,M.&W.]
Paschal, Robert C., (AV) .... '51 '78 C.575 B.A. L.228 J.D. [Young M.&H.]
Passé, James G. '51 '79 C.339 B.S. L.146 J.D.
(adm. in MI; not adm. in NC; Pat.) [Passé]

Passé Intellectual Property, LLC
1717 Brassfield Road, 27614-9448
Telephone: 919-256-8196 Fax: 919-878-0101
Email: jpasse@passeip.com
James G. Passé (Not admitted in NC).
Patent Drafting, Patent Prosecution, Patents, Intellectual Property, Trademarks.
See Professional Biographies, RALEIGH, NORTH CAROLINA

Patel, Sandhya G. .... '78 '04 C&L.575 B.A., J.D. [[A] Stuart]

Patrick, Michael W.
(See Chapel Hill)

Patrick-Wilson, Sharon .... '69 '94 C.329 B.A. L.472 J.D. Spec. Dep. Atty. Gen.
Patt, yh '58 '96 L.1364 J.D.
(adm. in MD; not adm. in NC) P.O. Box 25496
Patterson, Carl N., Jr., (AV) .... '51 '76 C.198 B.A. L.575 J.D. [Smith,A.B.D.M.&J.]
Patterson, Grady S., Jr., (AV) ..... '28 '50 C&L.896 B.A., J.D. [Patterson,D.C.B.&A.] ‡
Patterson, Henry N., Jr., (AV) '40 '66
C&L.575 A.B., LL.B. [Patterson H.] (⊙Chapel Hill)
Patterson, Vidalia .... '75 '01 C.198 B.A. L.180 J.D. [[A] Womble C.S.&R.]
Patterson, William S., (AV) .... '47 '73 C.896 B.A. L.575 J.D. [Hunton&W.]

Patterson, Dilthey, Clay, Bryson & Anderson, L.L.P., (AV)
4020 WestChase Boulevard, Suite 550, 27607 ⊙
Telephone: 919-821-4020 Fax: 919-829-0055
URL: http://www.pattersondilthey.com
Members of Firm: Grady S. Patterson, Jr. (Retired); Ronald C. Dilthey; Robert M. Clay; E. C. Bryson, Jr.; Reid Russell; Mark E. Anderson; Donna Renfrow Rutala; Phillip J. Anthony; G. Lawrence Reeves, Jr.; Charles George; Mary McHugh Webb; Christian Michael Kennedy; Christopher J. Derrenbacher; Christopher M. Hinnant; Patrick M. Meacham; Julie L. Bell; Carrie E. Meigs; Thomas M. Buckley. Associates: Heather R. Wilson; Kathrine E. Downing; Helen D. Meelheim; Kimberly K. Parkman; Kristie L. Hedrick; Justin D. Howard; Tobias S. Hampson; Edward K. Brooks; Jennifer M. St. Clair; Mindi L. Schulze; Lori P. Jones; Holly A. Mantle; Jessica M. Lewis. Of Counsel: Claire A. Modlin.
General Trial and Appellate Practice before all State and Federal Courts. Litigation of Insurance Law, Personal Injury, Medical Malpractice, Legal Malpractice, Workers Compensation and Intentional Torts, Construction Law and Litigation, Products Liability and General Civil and Commercial Litigation.
Representative Clients: Amica Mutual Insurance Co.; Great American Insurance Group; Kemper Insurance Group; Medical Protective Insurance Co.
Wilmington, North Carolina Office: 2516 Independence Boulevard, Suite 200. Telephone: 910-452-2797. Toll-Free: 877-731-5007. Fax: 910-452-4151.
See Professional Biographies, RALEIGH, NORTH CAROLINA

Patterson Harkavy LLP, (AV)
414 West Jones Street, 27603 ⊙
Mailing Address: P.O. Box 27927, Raleigh, NC 27611
Telephone: 919-755-1812 Facsimile: 919-755-0124
URL: http://www.pathlaw.com

(This Listing Continued)

Patterson Harkavy LLP (Continued)

Members of Firm: Henry N. Patterson, Jr. (Resident, Chapel Hill, North Carolina Office); Leto Copeley (Resident, Chapel Hill, North Carolina Office); Valerie Alston Johnson (Resident, Chapel Hill, North Carolina Office); Burton Craige; Ann Elizabeth Groninger; Jonathan R. Harkavy (Resident, Greensboro, North Carolina Office); Michael G. Okun. Of Counsel: Nahomi Harkavy (Resident, Greensboro, North Carolina Office).
Trial, Appellate and Dispute Resolution Practice in all State and Federal Courts. Personal Injury, Wrongful Death, Medical Malpractice, Workers' Compensation, Labor, Employment, Civil Rights, and Criminal.
Greensboro, North Carolina Office: 101 South Elm Street, P.O. Box 29269, 27429-9269. Telephone: 336-370-4200. Facsimile: 336-274-8490.
Chapel Hill, North Carolina Office: 100 Europa Drive, Suite 250, 27517. Telephone: 919-942-5200. Toll Free: 800-458-2541. Fax: 919-942-5256.
See Professional Biographies, RALEIGH, NORTH CAROLINA

Paul, Mack A., IV ....'62 '91 C.197 B.A. L.178 J.D. [Helms M.&W.]
Paulson, David F., Jr. ....'64 '91 C.228 B.A. L.896 J.D. [Helms M.&W.]
Pawl, Debra L. '52 '83 C.363 B.S. L.851 J.D.
(adm. in OH; not adm. in NC; Pat.) Closure Medical Corporation
Payne, Gardner Marshall ....'72 '01 C.576 B.A. L.1228 J.D. [Ⓐ Edmisten&W.]
Payne, Harry E., Jr. ....'52 '77 C.575 B.A. L.896 J.D. Comr. of Labor
Payne, M. Travis, (AV) ....'47 '78 C.112 B.A. L.477 J.D. 315 E. Jones St.
Peacock, Dorinda L. ....'— '98 C.198 A.B. L.575 J.D. [Ⓐ Kilpatrick S.]
Pearson, Ernest C., (AV) ....'50 '75 C.576 B.A. L.575 J.D. [Sanford H.]
Peck, Christopher L. ....'64 '94 C.140 B.A. L.1194 J.D. [Peck]

Peck Law Firm, The, P.A.
7511 Mourning Dove Road, Suite 104, 27615-5097
Telephone: 919-376-5411 Telcopier: 919-782-9493
Email: Chris@PeckLawFirm.Net URL: http://www.pecklawfirm.net
Member of the Firm: Christopher L. Peck.
Business Acquisitions and Divestitures, Corporation, Finance and Commercial Law, Real Property, Construction Law, Franchise Law, Entertainment Law and Intellectual Property.
See Professional Biographies, RALEIGH, NORTH CAROLINA

Peebles, Monique M., (BV) ....'68 '94 C.576 B.A. L.574 J.D. [Oettinger&P.]
Peeler, Karen Britt, (AV) ....'54 '80 C.471 B.A. L.896 J.D. [Ⓑ R.S.Hunter,Jr.]
Pelaez, Perry J., (CVⓉ) ....'61 '91 C.446 B.A. L.201 J.D. [Ⓐ Wilson&R.]
Pender, George H., (BV) ....'56 '91 C.34 B.S.B.A. L.1228 J.D. [Teague,C.D.&G.]
Pendergrass, James K., Jr., (BV) ....'60 '87 C.240 B.S. L.896 J.D. [Pendergrass]

Pendergrass Law Firm, PLLC, (BV)
4101 Lake Boone Trail, Suite 202, 27607
Telephone: 919-510-9559 Fax: 919-510-0190
Email: mailbox@pendergrasslawfirm.com URL: http://www.lawyers.com/pendergrasslaw
James K. Pendergrass, Jr. (Board Certified Specialist in Residential, Business, Commercial and Industrial Transactions, North Carolina State Board of Legal Specialization); Bernard Richards, Jr. Commercial Real Estate, Residential Real Estate, Real Estate Litigation, Legal Malpractice Defense, Corporate and Banking Law.
See Professional Biographies, RALEIGH, NORTH CAROLINA

Peniston, Richard A., (BV) ....'49 '77 C.1128 B.A. L.575 J.D. [R.A.Peniston&Assoc.] ⊙
Peniston, Richard A., & Associates, P.A., (BV)
811 W. Morgan St. (⊙Charlotte, Monroe)
Penry, J. Anthony, (AV) ....'54 '79 C.575 B.A. L.896 J.D. [Taylor,P.R.&R.]
Perdue, Garrett R. ....'76 '04 C&L.575 B.A., J.D. [Ⓐ Womble C.S.&R.]
Permar, David H., (AV) ....'43 '72 C.446 B.S. L.273 J.D. [Hatch,L.&B.]
Perry, Cheryl A. ....'62 '89 C.228 B.A. L.575 J.D. State Dept. of Jus.
Perry, Mark A. ....'58 '87 C.576 B.A. L.574 J.D. 715 W. Johnson St.
Persinger, Morgan E. ....'75 '00 C&L.923 B.A., J.D. [Ⓐ Womble C.S.&R.]
Peters, Alexander McC., (BV) ....'61 '86 C.577 B.M. L.575 J.D. Spec. Dep. Atty. Gen.
Petersen, Stephen W., (AV) ....'52 '96 C.296 A.B. L.575 J.D. [Herring M.M.&F.]
Peterson, Alan H., (AV) ....'— '77 C.429 B.A. L.575 J.D. [Kennedy C.L.&H.]
Peterson, Elizabeth C. ....'44 '87 C.577 B.A. L.574 J.D. P.O. Box 629
Petesch, Bruce A., (AV) ....'43 '69 C.694 A.B. L.209 J.D. [Ogletree,D.N.S.&S.]
Pettey, Rodney E., (AV) ....'64 '90 C.92 B.S. L.896 J.D. [Yates,M.&W.]
Pettigrew, Roy G. ....'73 '01 C.575 B.A. L.896 J.D. [Cranfill,S.&H.]
Petty, Amy Campbell ....'66 '94 C.575 B.S.B.A. L.1228 J.D. P.O. Box 27504

Petty, Michael Scott, (BV) '67 '95 C.575 B.A. L.1228 J.D.
133 Fayetteville Street Mall, Suite 300, 27602
Mailing Address: P.O. Box 2298, Raleigh, NC 27602
Telephone: 919-821-5959 Facsimile: 919-821-9303 URL: http://www.michaelpettylaw.com
Email: mpetty@michaelpettylaw.com URL: http://www.michaelscottpetty.com
Criminal Defense in State and Federal Courts, White Collar Crimes, Sexual Offenses, Traffic Offenses, Personal Injury, Auto Accidents, Products Liability, Unfair and Deceptive Trade Practice, Antitrust Litigation, Premises Liability, Intentional Torts, Dental and Medical Malpractice, Unfair and Deceptive Trade Practice Litigation.
See Professional Biographies, RALEIGH, NORTH CAROLINA

Pfeiffer, Amy L. ....'— '91 C.576 B.A. L.180 J.D. [Cranfill,S.&H.]
Phelps, John M., II, (BV) ....'58 '82 C&L.1228 B.A., J.D. Asst. Gen. Coun.
Philbeck, J. Heydt, (BV) ....'67 '92 C.240 B.A. L.879 J.D. [Allen&P.]
Phillips, Donald K. ....'72 '99 C.575 B.A. L.644 J.D. Crim. Div., Atty. Gen. Off.
Phillips, Jim W., Jr., (AV) ....'57 '84 C.575 A.B. L.896 J.D. [Brooks,P.M.H.&L.] ⊙
Philpott, H. Julian, Jr., (AV) '50 '78 C.575 B.S. L.896 J.D.
Secy. & Gen. Coun., N.C. Farm Bureau Federation, Inc.
Phipps, Stacey Alayne ....'68 '01 C.45 B.S. L.574 J.D. Atty. Gen.'s Off.
Piche, Jason O. ....'75 '03 C.228 B.S.E. L.893 J.D. [Ⓐ Alston&B.]
Pickett, Phyllis B., (BV) ....'58 '83 C&L.575 A.B., J.D. Staff Atty., NC Gen. Assembly
Pinna, William P., (BV) ....'43 '68 C.209 B.S.C. L.228 J.D. [Pinna J.&B.]

Pinna Johnston & Burwell, P.A., (AV)
2601 Oberlin Road, Suite 100, P.O. Box 31788, 27622
Telephone: 919-755-1317; 782-0450 Fax: 919-782-0452 URL: http://www.pjb-law.com
URL: http://www.pinnajohnstonburwell.com
William P. Pinna; Margaret G. Johnston; Walter Brodie Burwell, Jr.; Robin E. Pipkin; Matthew S. Black;—Daniel B. Finch; Robert Charles Lawson.
Corporation, Mergers and Acquisitions, Probate, Trusts, Real Estate Law, Taxation and Estate Planning, Wills and Trusts. General Civil Practice in all State and Federal Courts.
Representative Client: Lewis Clarke & McBride, P.A.
See Professional Biographies, RALEIGH, NORTH CAROLINA

Pinnix, John L., (AV) ....'47 '73 C.577 B.A. L.896 J.D. [Allen&P.]
Pinnix, Lorita K. '58 '94 C.576 B.A. L.893 J.D.
Asst. Coun., State Dept of Commerce/ABC Comm.
Pipkin, Robin E., (BV) ....'56 '81 C&L.575 B.S., J.D. [Pinna J.&B.]
Pitman, Thomas J., (BV) ....'46 '81 C.871 B.S. L.896 J.D. Special Dep. Atty. Gen.
Pittman, Jan N. ....'48 '76 C.232 B.S. L.790 J.D. [Teague,C.D.&G.]
Pittman, William B., (AV) ....'34 '61 C&L.575 A.B., LL.B. 2116 White Oak Road
Plaut, Cathleen M., (AV) ....'60 '86 C.473 B.S. L.575 J.D. [Bailey&D.]
Pletzke, Mark J. ....'59 '84 C.27 L.912 J.D. P.O. Box 629
Plyler, William Webb, (AV) ....'55 '82 C&L.575 A.B., J.D. [McMillan,S.&P.]
Podger, Kelly L. ....'74 '02 C&L.575 B.A., J.D. [Ⓐ Smith,A.B.D.M.&J.]

Poley, Jeffrey A. ....'70 '96 C.278 B.A. L.575 J.D. [Womble C.S.&R.]
Polk, William M. '73 '00 C.576 B.S. L.574 J.D.
Dir., Victims & Citizen's Rights Sect., NC Atty. Gen. Off.
Pollard, T. Lawrence ....'48 '74 C.575 A.B. L.896 J.D. Asso. Atty. Gen.
Polley-Abramson, Jennifer C. ....'69 '02 C.383 B.A. L.878 J.D. [Cranfill,S.&H.]
Pollock, William W., (AV) ....'61 '92 C.896 B.A. L.790 J.D. [Cranfill,S.&H.]
Pomper, Diane Martin ....'47 '75 C&L.208 B.A., J.D. 2833 Sterling Park Dr.
Ponton, Robert A., Jr., (AV) ....'54 '79 C&L.575 B.A., J.D. [Wyrick R.Y.&P.]
Poole, C. Ruffin ....'72 '98 C.575 B.A. L.574 J.D. The Gov. Off. State of NC
Poole, Carlyn G., (AV) ....'40 '79 C.845 B.A. L.575 J.D. [Tharrington S.]
Poole, Charles Ruffin ....'72 '98 C.575 B.A. L.574 J.D. Spec. Coun. to Gov.
Poole, Samuel H. ....'— '62 C&L.575 A.B., LL.B. [Ward&S.] (⊙New Bern)
Pope, James Arthur, (BV) '56 '82 C.575 B.A. L.228 J.D.
Exec. V.P. & CFO, Variety Wholesalers, Inc.
Pope, Judith M. ....'64 '00 [Ⓐ Becton,S.&B.]
Pope, Ricky L. ....'62 '00 C.16 B.S. L.1243 J.D. 4905 Waters Edge Drive‡
Poremba, Elizabeth H. ....'77 '03 C.34 B.S.C.J. L.1228 J.D. [Ⓐ Millberg,G.&S.]
Porper, Daniel S. ....'72 '98 C.1111 B.A. L.823 J.D. [Ⓐ Wyrick R.Y.&P.]
Porter, W. Travis, (AV) '31 '60
C&L.575 A.B., J.D. [Ⓑ Maupin T.] (⊙Research Triangle Park)
Portnoy, Douglas E., (BV) ....'66 '91 C.860 B.A. L.575 J.D. [Adams,P.&B.]
Posner, Beth Sheba ....'67 '97 C.104 A.B. L.575 J.D. Legal Servs. of N.C.
Poteat, Earmine L., Jr. ....'31 '59 C&L.575 A.B., LL.B. 8520 Davishire Dr.‡
Potter, William H., Jr., (AV) ....'43 '69 C&L.575 A.B., J.D. [Sink&P.]
Powell, D. Royce, (AV) ....'51 '79 C&L.575 B.S., J.D. [Maupin T.]
Powell, Frank Grey '69 '98 C.296 B.A. L.896 J.D.
NC Gov. Advocacy Council for Persons with Disab.
Powell, Peter E., (AV) ....'48 '73 C&L.575 B.A., J.D. Admin. Off. of the Cts.
Powers, Charles F., III, (AV) ....'43 '66 C.1126 A.B. L.575 LL.B. [Poyner&S.]
Powers, Dorothy ....'56 '86 C.1086 B.A. L.1206 J.D. Jus. Dept.
Powers, Edward J., (BVⓉ) '65 '90 C.886 B.A. L.692 J.D.
[Vandeventer B.] (⊙Kitty Hawk, NC; Norfolk, VA)
Poyner, James M., (AV) ....'14 '40 C.576 B.S. L.228 J.D. 3600 Glenwood Ave.‡

Poyner & Spruill LLP, (AV)
3600 Glenwood Avenue, P.O. Box 10096, 27605-0096 ⊙
Telephone: 919-783-6400 Telecopier: 919-783-1075
URL: http://www.poynerspruill.com
Members of Firm: Marvin D. Musselwhite, Jr.; David W. Long; John L. Shaw; Cecil W. Harrison, Jr.; William S. Cherry, Jr.; Lemuel H. Gibbons, III; H. Glenn Dunn; Susanna K. Gibbons; Louis B. Meyer III; David Dreifus; David M. Barnes; Thomas H. Davis, Jr.; Wilson Hayman; Craig G. Dalton, Jr.; Edwin Marion Speas, Jr.; Timothy P. Sullivan; Hugh W. Davis II; Keith H. Johnson; Joseph B. Dempster, Jr.; Thomas R. West; Eric P. Stevens; Robin L. Tatum; Steven Mansfield Shaber; William R. Shenton; David R. Krosner; James M. O'Brien, III; Joseph E. Zeszotarski, Jr.; Terri L. Gardner; Charles F. Powers, III; Suzanne R. Griffin; David L. Woodard; Daniel G. Cahill; Lisa P. Sumner. Associates: Pearl B. Doherty; Pamela A. Scott; Anuja Guleria Purohit; Kacey S. Ragsdale; Edward Bardin Simmons, Jr.; Anne C. Sherman; Julie W. Hampton; Heather F. Riley; Bryn D. Wilson; Adam B. Snyder (Not admitted in NC); Paul A. Arena. Of Counsel: Arch E. Lynch, Jr.; DeWitt C. McCotter, III; Thomas L. Norris, Jr.; Robert W. Wilson, Jr.; Charles H. Henderson; John A. MacKethan. Associate Counsel: Brian F. Corbett.
Comprehensive business and litigation practice including: Appellate, Arbitration, Banking, Bankruptcy/Creditors' Rights, Complex Business Litigation, Construction, Credit and Financial Services, Eminent Domain/Condemnation, Employment Benefits, Employment Practices, Entertainment Law, Environmental, Estate, Exempt Organizations, General Corporate, Governmental Relations, Health Care, Intellectual Property Law, International, Land Use and Zoning, Limited Liability Companies, Local Government, Mediation, Partnerships, Personal and Financial Planning, Probate, Product Liability, Professional Liability, Railroad, Real Estate, Regulatory and Municipal, Securities, Sports Law, Tax, Technology and Emerging Business, Tort Litigation and Insurance Defense, Transactional including Mergers and Acquisitions, Transportation, Utilities, White Collar Criminal Defense.
Rocky Mount, North Carolina Office: 130 S. Franklin Street, P.O. Box 353, 27802-0353. Telephone: 252-446-2341. Telecopier: 252-972-7045.
Charlotte, North Carolina Office: One Wachovia Center, 301 South College Street, Suite 2300, 28202. Telephone: 704-342-5250. Telecopier: 704-342-5264.
Southern Pines, North Carolina Office: 135 West New Hampshire Avenue, 28388-0371. Telephone: 910-692-6866. Telecopier: 910-695-3036.
See Professional Biographies, RALEIGH, NORTH CAROLINA

Prak, Mark J., (AV) ....'55 '80 C&L.228 A.B., J.D. [Brooks,P.M.H.&L.] ⊙
Prakke, Kevin A., (BV) ....'68 '93 C&L.575 B.S., J.D. [Ⓑ Maupin T.]
Prather, Karen Kemerait, (BV) '66 '91 C.198 B.A. L.896 J.D.
[Ⓐ Blanchard,J.M.L.&S.]

Prather Law Firm, P.C.
(See Garner)

Prati, Kristine L. ....'78 '03 C.107 B.A. L.339 J.D. [Ⓐ Wilson&R.]
Presnell, Gary L., Law Office, (AV) '50 '83
C.575 B.A. L.574 J.D. 400 Oberlin Bldg., Ste. 380
Presnell, Lacy M., III, (AV) ....'51 '76 C.575 A.B. L.896 J.D. [Burns,D.&P.]
Pressley, R. L. "Bit" ....'62 '96 C.1040 B.A. L.575 J.D. [Russell,P.&D.]
Price, Robert R., (AV) ....'49 '74 C.296 B.A. L.597 J.D. [Ⓑ Jordan P.W.G.J.&C.]
Pridgen, Eric E. ....'76 '03 C.577 B.A. L.574 J.D. [Ⓐ Underwood&R.] (⊙Orlando, FL)
Priester, Amos U., IV, (AV) ....'56 '82 C&L.575 B.S., J.D. [Smith,A.B.D.M.&J.]
Prince, John Matthew '63 '94 C.280 B.A. L.383 J.D.
(adm. in GA; not adm. in NC) Soc. Sec. Admin.
Pritchard, Deborah L. ....'— '04 C.205 B.S. L.574 J.D. [Ⓐ Kilpatrick S.]
Pritchett, Newton G., Jr. ....'54 '82 C.228 B.A. L.575 J.D. Asst. Atty. Gen.
Proctor, E. Knox, V ....'— '87 C&L.575 A.B., J.D. [Ward&S.] (⊙New Bern)
Propst, Jina B. ....'70 '98 C.896 B.A. L.1228 J.D. [Ⓐ J.P.Laurie,III]
Propst, Joseph E. ....'69 '99 C.575 B.A. L.192 J.D. [Ⓐ Jordan P.W.G.J.&C.]
Proud, Geoffrey S. ....'77 '03 C.896 B.A. L.93 J.D. [Ⓐ Lewis&R.]
Provenza Benko, Kristen S. ....'74 '99 C.425 B.A. L.575 J.D. [Ⓐ Womble C.S.&R.]
Pruitt, Shirley Maring ....'61 '92 C.999 A.D. L.896 J.D. [Ⓑ Yates,M.&W.]
Pryzwansky, David T., (AV) ....'65 '92 C.893 B.A. L.575 J.D. [Pryzwansky&C.]
Pryzwansky & Cook, PLLC, (AV) .... 5 West Hargett St., Suite 910
Pueschel, Janet I. ....'45 '92 C.232 B.S. L.574 J.D. 8901 Pleasant Meadow Dr.
Pugh, Elizabeth Y. ....'48 '74 C&L.574 B.A., J.D. P.O. Box 28630
Pullen, Lucius W., (AV) ....'27 '54 C.896 B.A. L.575 J.D. P.O. Box 6527
Purks, David K. ....'63 '94 C.886 B.S. L.734 J.D. [Myers B.S.&S.] (See Pat. Sect.)
Purohit, Anuja Guleria ....'67 '93 C.207 B.A. L.228 J.D. [Ⓐ Poyner&S.]
Purrington, J. Ward, (AV) ....'40 '67 C&L.575 A.B., J.D. 2723 Riddick Dr.
Purser, Earle R., (BV) ....'20 '50 C&L.896 B.A., LL.B. P.O. Box 1332
Pursley, Evelyn M. ....'52 '86 C.623 B.A. L.228 J.D. Exec. Dir., NC IOLTA
Putterman, Charles M., (BV) '54 '79
C.569 B.A. L.1019 J.D. 5 W. Hargett Street, Suite 700
Quinn, Kevin A. '41 '68 C&L.262 B.A., J.D.
(adm. in NY; not adm. in NC) V.P., Gen. Coun. & Secy., Adco Global, Inc.
Rabenau, Karen M., (BV) ....'67 '92 C.320 B.A. L.575 J.D. [Twiggs,B.S.&R.]
Rabil, Michael J., (BV) ....'31 '60 C&L.575 B.S., LL.B. 4504 Wilkes St.
Rabon, Susan Warren, (CV) ....'60 '86 C.576 B.A. L.893 J.D. Sr. Asst., Off. of the Gov.
Race, Stacy M. ....'— '03 C.790 B.A. L.93 J.D. [Ⓐ Hedrick E.G.&K.]

Rafferty, John F. '21 '49
C.565 B.S. L.823 J.D. Admin. Law J., Off. of Hearings & Appeals
Raghunanan, Elizabeth . . . . '75 '01 C.1376 B.S. L.574 J.D. 224 S. Dawson St.
Ragsdale, George R., (AV) . . . . '36 '62 C&L.575 A.B., LL.B. [Ragsdale L.]
Ragsdale, Kacey S. . . . . '73 '00 C&L.575 B.A., J.D. [Ⓐ Poyner&S.]
Ragsdale, William L., (AV) . . . . . . '31 '64 C&L.228 B.S.E.E., LL.B. 300 W. Millbrook Rd.

Ragsdale Liggett PLLC, (AV) BR
A Professional Limited Liability Company
Crosspointe Plaza, Suite 400, 2840 Plaza Place, P.O. Box 31507, 27612
Mailing Address: P.O. Box 31507, Raleigh, NC 27622-1507
Telephone: 919-787-5200 Fax: 919-783-8991
URL: http://www.rl-law.com
Members of Firm: Dan K. Moore (1906-1986); George R. Ragsdale; Frank R. Liggett III; William A. Mann; William B. Bost III; Dorothy Bass Burch; Mary Hulett; Walter L. Tippett, Jr.; David K. Liggett; John M. Nunnally; Robert J. Ramseur, Jr.; Gregory W. Brown. Of Counsel: Joseph E. Johnson. Associates: Sarah E. Winslow; Melissa Dewey Brumback; Jessica C. Tyndall; Sandra W. Mitterling; Hannah C. Bissette; Richard O. Bolton; Charles Vaughan, III; Ashley Huffstetler.
General Civil Litigation and Administrative Law in State and Federal Courts and Agencies. Taxation, Estate Planning, Partnership, Landlord and Tenant, Real Estate, Insurance and Reinsurance Law. Corporate, Business, International, Environmental Law. Construction Law, Employment Discrimination and Administrative Hearings and Appeals.
See Professional Biographies, RALEIGH, NORTH CAROLINA

Raines, Julie B. . . . . '67 '97 C.576 B.A. L.128 J.D. P.O. Box 7229
Rak, Walter N., (BV) . . . . '65 '90 C.228 B.A. L.575 J.D. 3950 Blue Ridge Road
Ramage, Gregory J. . . . . '— '93 C.679 B.S. L.575 J.D. 5540 Centerview Dr.
Ramey, Martin A. . . . . '66 '02 C.36 B.A. L.1049 J.D. [Ⓐ Martin&J.]
Ramseur, Robert J., Jr., (BV) . . . . '70 '96 C&L.896 A.B., J.D. [Ragsdale L.]
Ramsey, Coe W. . . . . '72 '98 C.575 B.A. L.896 J.D. [Brooks,P.M.H.&L.] ⊙
Rand, Walter, (AV) . . . . '36 '64 C&L.575 A.B., LL.B. 19 W. Hargett St., Ste. 601
Rand, Walter B. . . . . '62 '95 C.575 B.A. L.736 J.D. 19 W. Hargett, Suite 601
Rankin, Gisele Lunsford . . . . '55 '80 C&L.575 B.A., J.D. State Utilities Comm.
Ranney, John C. . . . . '30 '57 C.321 A.B. L.276 J.D. Ret. Admin. Law J.
Ransdell, Phillip C., (AV) . . . . '31 '58 C&L.575 B.S., LL.B. 333 Fayetteville St. Mall
Rasberry, Francis P., Jr., (AV) . . . . '48 '73 C.902 B.A. L.575 J.D. Dep. City. Atty.
Rascoe, Donna R., (BV) . . . . '58 '93 C.577 B.A. L.575 J.D. [Cranfill,S.&H.]
Ratledge, James E. R., (BV) . . . . '61 '88 C&L.575 B.A., J.D. [Wilson&R.]
Ratledge, Toler Workman '63 '88
C.576 B.A. L.575 J.D. Gen. Coun., The Jack Parker Corp.
Ravert, Kristie Marie . . . . '73 '01 C.820 L.607 [Ⓐ]
Raxter, Ronald D., (BV) . . . . '53 '77 C&L.575 B.A., J.D. [Maupin T.]
Ray, James C., (BV) . . . . '45 '73 C&L.228 A.B., J.D. V.P., Sycamore Virginia Corp.
Raynal, Charles E., IV . . . . '73 '00 C.198 B.A. L.896 J.D. [Ⓐ Parker,P.A.&B.]
Raynor, Dawn Dillon, (BV) . . . . '— '95 C.890 B.A. L.896 J.D. [Young M.&H.]
Raynor, Glenn C., (BV) . . . . '65 '91 C&L.575 B.S., J.D. [Young M.&H.]
Ray-Welborn, Melody C. . . . . '76 '01 C.228 A.B. L.245 J.D. [Ⓐ Womble C.S.&R.]
Reagan, O. Walker, III, (BV) '52 '78 C.228 A.B. L.575 J.D.
Staff Atty., Legis. Res. Div.
Reaves, Lacy H., (AV) . . . . '— '72 C&L.575 A.B., J.D. [Kennedy C.L.&H.]
Redwine, Philip O., (AV) . . . . '38 '65 C.576 B.S. L.896 J.D. [P.O.Redwine]
Redwine, Philip O., P.A., (AV) . . . . 14005 Bingham Drive
Reed, M. Ann, (AV) . . . . '47 '71 C&L.575 A.B., J.D. Sr. Dep. Atty. Gen.
Reed, Mary Z. . . . . '50 '83 C.575 B.A. L.574 J.D. 400 Oberlin Rd.
Reeves, Diane A. . . . . '52 '79 C.228 B.A. L.896 J.D. P.O. Box 629
Reeves, Eric Miller, (BV) . . . . '63 '90 C.228 B.A. L.896 J.D. [© Blanchard,J.M.L.&S.]
Reeves, G. Lawrence, Jr., (AV) . . . . '52 '78 C&L.575 B.S., J.D. [Patterson,D.C.B.&A.]
Reichbind, Joseph . . . . '46 '73 C.976 B.A. L.724 J.D. V.P., Leith Leasing, Inc.
Reilly, Robert R., Jr. '47 '72 C.705 B.A. L.575 J.D.
Admin. Law J., Off. of Adm. Hearings
Rendleman, Nancy S., (AV) . . . . '52 '77 C&L.575 B.S., J.D. [Maupin T.]
Renfer, R. A., Jr. . . . . '40 '66 C.937 B.A. L.846 LL.B. Asst. U.S. Atty.
Renfer, Rudy E., (BV) . . . . '69 '96 C.576 B.A. L.209 J.D. Assoc. Atty. Gen., Divil Div.
Renfer, Susan Oliver '53 '81
C.886 B.A. L.893 J.D. Pres., North Carolina Family Policy Council
Resnick & Abraham, L.L.C.
6200 Falls of Neuse Road, Suite 200 (⊙Wash., DC; Wilmington, DE; Balt., MD; Fairfax, VA)
Reynolds, David Reaves, (BV) . . . . '65 '94 C&L.575 B.A., J.D. [Reynolds&P.]
Reynolds, Donald R., (AV) . . . . '62 '89 C.939 B.A. L.569 J.D. [Wyrick R.Y.&P.]
Reynolds, Ted R., (AV) . . . . '32 '59 C&L.575 A.B., J.D. [Reynolds&P.]
Reynolds & Pendergrass, P.A., (AV) . . . . 316 W. Edenton St.
Rhinehardt, Jamal A. . . . . '70 '03 C.999 B.S. L.575 J.D. [Ⓐ Smith,A.B.D.M.&J.]
Rhoad, Matthew D. . . . . '75 '00 C.896 B.A. L.575 J.D. [Ⓐ Smith,A.B.D.M.&J.]
Rhoades, David A., (AV) . . . . '62 '89 C.575 B.A. L.896 J.D. [Cranfill,S.&H.]
Ricci, John Michael . . . . '77 '02 C.575 B.A. L.1228 J.D. [Cranfill,S.&H.]
Rich, Millard R., Jr., (BV) . . . . '29 '56 C&L.575 A.B., LL.B. Dep. Atty. Gen.
Richards, Bernard, Jr. . . . . '67 '93 C.280 B.A. L.1228 J.D. [Pendergrass]
Richardson, Julie H. '59 '95 C.679 B.S.M.E. L.228 J.D.
[Myers B.S.&S.] (See Pat. Sect.)
Richardson, Mark E. '28 '56 C.931 A.B. L.273 J.D.
(adm. in DC; not adm. in NC) 11105 Woodmont Dr.‡
Ricketts, Diana Evans . . . . '49 '74 C&L.575 B.A., J.D. [Bode,C.&S.]
Rickner, Gary J., (AVⓉ) '— '74
C.827 B.A. L.192 J.D. [Ward&S.] (⊙Greenville, New Bern)
Ridgeway, Paul C., (AV) . . . . '60 '86 C.576 B.S. L.1228 J.D. [Everett,G.H.&S.]
Riemann, Neil A. . . . . '66 '92 C.575 A.B. L.477 J.D. [Taylor,P.R.&R.]
Ries, Addie K.S. . . . . '78 '03 C.280 B.A. L.575 J.D. [Ⓐ Smith,A.B.D.M.&J.]
Riley, Elizabeth LeVan, (AV) . . . . '58 '83 C.880 B.A. L.383 J.D. [© Womble C.S.&R.]
Riley, Heather F. . . . . '— '03 C.575 B.A. L.896 J.D. [Ⓐ Poyner&S.]
Riley, John Michael . . . . '66 '91 C.896 B.S. L.575 J.D. [Martin&J.]
Riordan, Timothy S., (AV) . . . . '60 '87 C.317 B.A. L.602 J.D. [Lewis&R.]
Risinger, Bradley M., (AV) . . . . '64 '90 C.347 B.A. L.276 J.D. [Smith M.]
Rittelmeyer, John R. . . . . '55 '88 C.276 B.S. L.500 J.D. [Hartzell&W.]

Rivenbark, Christina, & Associates
(See Wilmington)

Rivera, Maria '73 '98 C.259 B.A. L.262 J.D.
(adm. in FL; not adm. in NC) Office of Hearings & Appeals, SSA
Roach, Gerald F., (AV) . . . . '58 '82 C&L.896 B.A., J.D. [Smith,A.B.D.M.&J.]
Roach, Suzanne P. . . . . '54 '86 C.232 B.S.B.A. L.575 J.D. 5025 Trail Ridge Dr.
Roach, W. Linville, (AV) . . . . '31 '55 C&L.896 B.S., LL.B. [© Smith,A.B.D.M.&J.]
Robbins, Larry E., (AV) . . . . '51 '80 C&L.575 B.A., J.D. [Wyrick R.Y.&P.]
Roberson, Sheri, (BV) . . . . '71 '96 C.893 B.A. L.802 J.D. [Ⓐ Womble C.S.&R.]
Roberts, James A., III, (AV) . . . . '56 '82 C&L.896 B.A., J.D. [Lewis&R.]
Roberts, Jeffery G. '69 '94 C.896 B.S. L.421 J.D.
[Underwood&R.] (⊙Orlando, FL; Lexington, KY)
Robertson, Ann . . . . '48 '91 C&L.575 B.A., J.D. [Robertson I.]
Robertson, B. Ford . . . . '— '96 C.893 B.A. L.896 J.D. [Ⓐ Kilpatrick S.]

Robertson Immigration Law Firm
The Capital Club Building, 16 West Martin Street, Suite 1101, 27601-2977
Telephone: 919-834-7004 Fax: 919-834-0428
Email: immigrationlaw@nc.rr.com URL: http://www.robertsonimmigrationlaw.com
Ann Robertson (Board Certified Specialist in Immigration Law, North Carolina State Board of Legal Specialization).
Immigration and Naturalization, Business Immigration, Citizenship, Consular Law, Employment Visas, Political Asylum, Non-Immigrant Visas.
See Professional Biographies, RALEIGH, NORTH CAROLINA

Robinson, David S. . . . . '65 '90 C.276 L.273 J.D. [D.S.Robinson]
Robinson, David S., Esq., PC . . . . P.O. Box 99766
Roccesano, Susan Calabrese . . . . '62 '88 12433 Bayleaf Church Rd.
Rockoff, Sabrina Presnell . . . . '— '02 C&L.575 J.D. [Ⓐ Kilpatrick S.]
Roden, Randall M., (AV) . . . . '46 '76 C&L.575 B.A., J.D. [Tharrington S.]
Rodgers, Kevin D. . . . . '61 '87 C.1228 B.S. L.896 J.D. [Burch,J.&R.]
Rogan, Robert '— '92 C.999 D.O. L.1339 J.D.
(adm. in PA; not adm. in NC) 3704-304 Horton St.‡
Rogers, Jeff D., (BV) . . . . '62 '87 C.953 B.A. L.1228 J.D. [Smith D.N.W.S.&M.]
Rogers, Richard A., Jr., (AV) . . . . '53 '78 C.893 B.A. L.902 J.D. [© Wyrick R.Y.&P.]
Rogers, Ronald R., (AV) . . . . '60 '86 C.896 B.A. L.575 J.D. [Maupin T.]
Rogers, Walter R., Jr., (AV) . . . . '52 '77 C.228 B.A. L.813 J.D. [Smith,A.B.D.M.&J.]
Romanet, Andrew L., Jr. '40 '67
C&L.575 A.B., J.D. Gen. Coun., N.C. League of Municipalities
Roney, Gregory P. . . . . '70 '96 C&L.575 B.A., J.D. Asst. Atty. Gen.
Roper, Wayne A., (BV) . . . . '59 '94 C.232 B.S.B.A. L.1345 J.D. [Roper&C.]
Roper & Coleman, P.A., (BV) . . . . 5660 Six Forks Rd., Ste. 104
Rose, Danielle Eng . . . . '72 '00 C.945 B.A. L.228 J.D. [Ⓐ Ellis&W.] (⊙Cary)
Rose, Jeffrey . . . . '66 '99 C.1128 B.A. L.574 J.D. 150 Fayetteville St. Mall, Ste. 2300
Rose, Margie E. . . . . '39 '88 C.228 B.A. L.574 J.D. [Bumgardner&R.]
Rose, Steven J. . . . . '43 '68 C&L.472 B.B.A., J.D. Coun., State Gen. Assembly

Rose Rand Attorneys, P.A., (AV)
Corporate Plaza Building, Suite 1508, 333 Fayetteville Street, 27601 ⊙
Telephone: 919-832-4040 Fax: 919-832-4050
—J. Yancey Washington.
General Practice, all Courts. Corporation, Labor and Insurance Law. Trials, including Personal Injury, Wrongful Death and Workers Compensation, Eminent Domain, Tax, Estate Planning and Administration, Municipal, Environmental, Real Estate, Bankruptcy.
Wilson, North Carolina Office: 2500 West Nash Street, Unit C, P.O. Drawer 2367, 27894-2367. Telephone: 252-291-3848. Telecopier: 252-291-9555.
See Professional Biographies, RALEIGH, NORTH CAROLINA

Rosefielde-Keller, Cindy S. . . . . '62 '90 C.1111 B.A. L.61 J.D. [Sandman&R.]
Rosen, Lee S., (AV) . . . . '61 '87 C.48 B.A. L.896 J.D. [Rosen]
Rosen Law Firm, The, (AV) . . . . 4101 Lake Boone Tr., Ste. 500
Rosenberg, Bryan D., (BV) '61 '93 C.475 B.A. L.1228 J.D.
State Mgr., Fidelity Natl. Title Ins. Co. of New York
Rosenberg, Theresa Joan . . . . '46 '00 C.576 B.A. L.575 J.D. 2742 Rue Sans Famille
Rosenfeld, Margaret N. . . . . '70 '01 C.571 B.A. L.273 J.D. [Ⓐ Smith,A.B.D.M.&J.]
Rosner, Jeffrey E. . . . . '74 '02 C.94 B.S. L.575 J.D. [Rosner]
Rosner Law Firm, P.A. . . . . 5858 Faringdon Place
Ross, Bruce A. '50 '89 C.801 B.A. L.146 J.D.
(adm. in IL; not adm. in NC) General Electric Capital Mortgage
Ross, Deborah K. . . . . '63 '90 C.103 B.A. L.575 J.D. House of Rep.
Ross, William G., Jr., (AV) . . . . '47 '72 C.198 B.A. L.893 J.D. Secy.
Rouse, William E., Jr., (AV) . . . . '29 '56 C&L.575 B.S., LL.B. 1042 Washington St.
Rubin, Todd M., (BV) . . . . '54 '85 C.1168 B.A. L.107 J.D. [© Parker,P.A.&B.]
Rudisill, Cathy M., (AV) . . . . '— '84 C&L.575 B.A., J.D. [Nelson M.R.&S.]
Rudisill, Justus C. . . . . '23 '52 C.404 A.B. L.896 LL.B. Off. of the Atty. Gen.
Ruegger, Robert E., (AV) . . . . '64 '89 C.1228 B.A. L.896 J.D. 5858 Faringdon Place
Ruiz, Jennifer Vega . . . . '— '02 C.999 B.A. L.575 J.D. [Ⓐ Hedrick E.G.&K.]
Ruocchio, John H. . . . . '65 '95 C.575 B.A. L.1228 J.D. [Lewis&R.]
Rush, John Charles . . . . '28 '68 C&L.575 A.B., J.D. 1835 C Hilton St.‡
Rusher, Mary Nash Kelly, (AV) . . . . '58 '85 C.896 B.A. L.893 J.D. [Hunton&W.]
Russell, Corinne Griffin, (AV) . . . . '49 '77 C.575 A.B. L.790 J.D. Asst. Co. Atty.
Russell, F. Alton, (AV) '40 '69 C&L.575 B.S., J.D.
Pres. & Gen. Coun., Title Co. of N.C., Inc., The
Russell, Kathie L. . . . . '63 '94 C.1111 B.A. L.953 J.D. [Russell,P.&D.]
Russell, Reid, (AV) . . . . '52 '80 C.867 B.A. L.575 J.D. [Patterson,D.C.B.&A.]
Russell, Samuel R., III . . . . '— '80 4020 Westchase Blvd., Suite 550
Russell, Pressley & Demidovich, P.C. . . . . 727 W. Hargett St., Ste. 109
Rutala, Donna Renfrow, (AV) . . . '57 '89 C.575 B.S.N. L.574 J.D. [Patterson,D.C.B.&A.]
Ruth, Kristin H. . . . . '56 '91 C.375 B.S. L.1345 J.D. Dist. J.
Rutherford, Marjorie M. . . . . '53 '78 C.788 A.B. L.893 J.D. 12517 Shallowford Dr.
Rutherford, Richard W., (AV) '51 '76 C.309 B.A. L.178 J.D.
701 Corporate Center Drive
Sabapathypillai, Rohan G. . . . . '74 '03 C.886 B.S.E.E. L.1128 J.D. [Ⓐ Myers B.S.&S.]
Saber, Jacquelyn D. '62 '89 C.280 A.B.J. L.245 J.D.
(adm. in PA; not adm. in NC) 3904 City of Oaks Wynd
Saber, Michael P., (AV) . . . . '61 '89 C.178 B.A. L.245 J.D. [Smith,A.B.D.M.&J.]
Safran, Perry R. . . . . '50 '81 C.576 B.S. L.1228 J.D. [Safran]
Safran Law Office . . . . 120 S. Boylan Ave.
St. Clair, Jennifer M. . . . . '79 '04 C.575 B.A. L.1228 J.D. [Ⓐ Patterson,D.C.B.&A.]
Saintsing, Byron L., (AV) . . . . '63 '88 C.896 B.A. L.575 J.D. [Smith D.N.W.S.&M.]
Sajovec, F. Michael, (AV) '59 '86
C.119 B.S. L.1003 J.D. [Myers B.S.&S.] (See Pat. Sect.)
Salisbury, Anne B. . . . . '49 '82 C.758 A.B. L.1228 J.D. Dist. J.
Salisbury, Stephen R. . . . . '42 '67 C.228 A.B. L.659 LL.B. Sr. V.P., Triangle Bk.
Sallade, Ross E. . . . . '69 '00 C.301 B.S. L.893 J.D. [Ⓐ Nelson M.R.&S.]
Salmony, Edith R. . . . . '48 '86 C.575 B.A. L.574 J.D. [Ⓐ Temple]
Sampson, Larry B. '55 '89 C.273 B.A. L.1209 J.D.
(adm. in VA; not adm. in NC) Coun., Electronic Data Systems Corp.
Sanders, Craigie D. '— '03 C.383 B.A. L.574 J.D.
[Ⓐ Kennedy C.L.&H.] (⊙Research Triangle Park)
Sanderson, George F., III . . . . '73 '00 C.276 A.B. L.569 J.D. [Ⓐ Ellis&W.] (⊙Cary)
Sandlin, Deborah . . . . '— '98 C.235 B.A. L.574 J.D. [Sandlin&D.]

Sandlin & Davidian
5617 Departure Drive, 27616
Telephone: 919-850-9199 Fax: 919-850-9699
URL: http://www.sandlin-law.com
Deborah Sandlin (Board Certified Specialist in Family Law, North Carolina State Board of Legal Specialization); V.A. "Woofer" Davidian III.
Family Law, Divorce, Equitable Distribution, Child Custody, Child Support, Alimony, Premarital Agreements, Domestic Partnership Agreements, Domestic Violence, Driving While Intoxicated (DWI), Drug Crimes, Parole and Probation, Traffic Violations, Appellate Practice.
See Professional Biographies, RALEIGH, NORTH CAROLINA

Sandman, Andrew K., (BV) '68 '93 C.576 B.S. L.115 J.D.
7101 Creedmoor Road Suite 122, 27613
Telephone: 919-845-6688 Facsimile: 919-845-6639
Email: asandlaw@bellsouth.net URL: http://www.andrewsandmanlaw.com
Associate: William Finn.
Criminal Law, Drug Crimes, Driving While Intoxicated, Assaults, Traffic Violations, Personal Injury.
See Professional Biographies, RALEIGH, NORTH CAROLINA

Sandman, Michael G., (BV) . . . '61 '85 C.30 B.S. L.575 J.D. [Sandman&R.]
Sandman & Rosefielde-Keller, (BV) . . . 7101 Creedmoor Road, Suite 142
Sandquist, Susan J. '— '97
C.494 B.A., B.S. L.574 J.D. Mgr. Industry Resch., N.C. State Univ.
Sands, Alexander P., III, (AV) . . . '45 '71 C.228 A.B. L.575 J.D. [Womble C.S.&R.]
Sanford, Joanne . . . '50 '75 C.576 B.A. L.575 J.D. Chmn. Util. Comm.
Sanford Holshouser LLP, (AV) . . . 219 Fayetteville Street, Suite 1000 (⊙Pinehurst)
Santowasso, M. Rebecca, (BV) . . . '64 '90 C&L.575 B.A., J.D. [[A] Farrell&L.]
Saparilas, Nick, Law Offices of, (CV) '61 '95
C.575 B.A. L.615 J.D. 5 West Hargett Street, Suite 1010
Sar, David W., (BV) . . . '71 '96 C.228 B.A. L.976 J.D. [Brooks,P.M.H.&L.] ⊙
Sar, Robert A., (AV) . . . '68 '95 C.896 B.S. L.1345 J.D. [Ogletree,D,N.S.&S.]
Saravitz, David M. . . . '— '03 C.645 B.S. L.574 J.D. [[A] Alston&B.] (See Pat. Sect.)
Sarda, Peter J., (AV) . . . '45 '76 C.1070 B.S. L.896 J.D. [Wallace,N.&S.]
Sargent, William C., III . . . '44 '70 C.576 B.S. L.575 J.D. 4825 Rembert Dr.
Sarratt, John L., (AV) . . . '— '72 C.575 B.A. L.309 J.D. [Kennedy C.L.&H.]
Sartorio, Steven M., (AV) . . . '55 '81 C.575 B.A. L.896 J.D. [Smith,A.B.D.M.&J.]
Sasser, Jonathan D., (AV) . . . '56 '81 C&L.575 B.A., J.D. [Ellis&W.] (⊙Cary)
Sasser, Robert H., III, (AV) . . . '57 '83 C&L.896 B.S., J.D. [Womble C.S.&R.]

Sasser, Travis
(See Cary)

Satisky, Howard P., (AV) . . . '45 '69 C&L.575 B.S., J.D. [Satisky&S.]
Satisky, Keith A., (BV) . . . '67 '94 C.228 A.B. L.896 J.D. [Satisky&S.]

Satisky & Silverstein, LLP, (AV)
900 Ridgefield Drive Suite 250, 27609
Telephone: 919-790-9102 Telecopier: 919-790-1560
Howard P. Satisky; John M. Silverstein; Keith A. Satisky.
Commercial Real Estate, Eminent Domain, Corporate, Civil, Commercial and Business Litigation, Leasing, Construction Law, Municipal Law, Computer Law, Administrative.
See Professional Biographies, RALEIGH, NORTH CAROLINA

Saunders, Robert W., (AV) . . . '59 '87 C.575 B.A. L.893 J.D. [Brooks,P.M.H.&L.] ⊙
Savage, Warren Tobin, IV, (BV) . . . '64 '96 C.893 B.A. L.1228 J.D. [Bailey&D.]
Sawchak, Matthew W., (AV) . . . '62 '89 C.309 A.B. L.228 J.D. [Ellis&W.] (⊙Cary)
Saylor, Scott M. . . . '59 '85 C.575 B.S. L.574 J.D. 2809 Highwoods Boulevard
Sayre, Jeremy R. . . . '— '98 C.363 B.S. L.608 J.D. [Ward&S.] (⊙New Bern)
Scarzafava, Gary A. . . . '55 '80 C&L.744 B.A., J.D. 14460-149 New Falls of Neuse
Scarzafava Mediation Service, (BV⊕) . . . 12405 Schoolhouse St.
Schafer, C. Allison Brown, (AV) '58 '84
C.388 B.A. L.896 J.D. Legal Coun., N.C. Sch. Bds. Assoc.
Schafer, John C., (AV) . . . '59 '84 C.602 B.A. L.896 J.D. 4342 Mail Service Ctr.
Schenck, James S., IV, (AV) . . . '— '82 C&L.575 A.B., J.D. [Conner G.S.]
Schenk, Edward S., III . . . '78 '04 C.953 B.A. L.1228 J.D. [[A] Teague,C.D.&G.]
Schenk, Michael L., (BV) . . . '— '96 C.476 B.B.A. L.896 J.D. [[C] Kilpatrick S.]
Scherer, Elizabeth Brooks . . . '74 '00 C&L.280 B.S., J.D. [[A] Smith M.]
Scherer, John P., II . . . '67 '92 C.198 B.A. L.575 J.D. Jus. Dept.
Scherer, Sally H., (AV) . . . '40 '81 C.822 B.A. L.1218 J.D. [S.Scherer]

Scherer, Sally, Law Office of, (AV)
133 Fayetteville Street, Suite 200, P.O. Box 106, 27602
Telephone: 919-821-5393 Fax: 919-459-2727
Email: SSchererJD@aol.com
Sally H. Scherer. Associate: Angenette Stephenson.
Trial and Appellate Practice, Domestic and Family Law, Divorce, Custody, Mediation, Arbitration.
See Professional Biographies, RALEIGH, NORTH CAROLINA

Schilawski, Michael F., (AV) . . . '48 '82 C.575 B.A. L.1228 J.D. [Sokol M.S.O.L.P.]
Schilawski & Ingram, P.L.L.C., (BV) . . . 4350 Lassiter at North Hills Ave., Ste. 360
Schiller, Carol M. . . . '40 '85 C.1044 B.S. L.575 J.D. [Schiller&S.P.] ‡
Schiller, David G. . . . '70 '99 C.296 B.S. L.472 J.D. [Schiller&S.P.]
Schiller, Frank A., (AV) '61 '87
C.228 A.B. L.790 J.D. V.P. -Legal & Gen. Coun., Progress Energy
Schiller, Marvin, (AV) . . . '40 '75 C.472 B.A. L.228 J.D. [Schiller&S.P.]

Schiller & Schiller PLLC, (AV) [BB]
5540 Munford Road, Suite 101, 27612
Telephone: 919-789-4677 Fax: 919-789-4469
URL: http://www.schillerandschiller.com
Members of Firm: Marvin Schiller; Carol M. Schiller; David G. Schiller.
Appellate Practice, Automobile Accidents and Injuries, Business Disputes, Class Actions, Contracts, Deceptive Trade Practices, Defective Products, Defamation, Employment, Environment, Insurance Claims, Personal Injury, Property Damage, Retirement Benefits, Securities Fraud, Workers Compensation, Wrongful Death, Family Law, Divorce.
See Professional Biographies, RALEIGH, NORTH CAROLINA

Schmidlin, Walter A., III . . . '66 '99 C.198 B.S. L.1292 J.D. Asst. Dist. Atty.
Schmidt, Richard F. . . . '62 '87 C.576 B.A. L.1243 J.D. Soc. Sec. Admn.
Schmidt, Sorien K. . . . '62 '88 C&L.575 B.A., J.D. State Jus. Community Develop. Ctr.
Schneider, Alan Marc, (AV) . . . '64 '90 C.1349 B.A. L.1188 J.D. [Cheshire,P.S.B.&V.]
Schneider, Jason R. . . . '— '01 C.472 B.B.A. L.260 J.D. [[A] Helms M.&W.]
Schneiderman, F. Brian, (BV⊕) '65 '91 C&L.228 A.B., J.D.
(adm. in VA; not adm. in NC) [Troutman S.] (⊙Virginia Beach, VA)
Schofield, Robert M. . . . '60 '85 C.112 B.A. L.273 J.D. P.O. Box 28068
Schroer, Jonathan . . . '63 '90 C.1350 B.A. L.178 J.D. Hutchison & Assocs., Inc.
Schuette, Patrick J. . . . '66 '92 C.423 B.A. L.64 J.D. [Hodgdon&S.]
Schuhmacher, Robert E. '46 '77 C.174 B.A. L.790 J.D.
(adm. in SC; not adm. in NC) Sr. V.P., First-Citizens Bank & Trust Company
Schulze, Mindi L. . . . '80 '04 C.34 B.S. L.1228 J.D. [[A] Patterson,D.C.B.&A.]
Schwab, Carol A. . . . '53 '79 C.798 B.A. L.502 J.D. Assoc. Prof., N.C. State Univ.
Schwartz, Richard, (AV) . . . '53 '78 C.228 B.A. L.575 J.D. [Schwartz&S.]

Schwartz & Shaw, P.L.L.C., (AV)
Commerce Building, Suite 1000, 19 West Hargett Street, P.O. Box 2350, 27602
Telephone: 919-821-9011 Fax: 919-821-9015
URL: http://www.lawyers.com/schwartz-shaw
Members Of Firm: Richard Schwartz; Brian C. Shaw. Associates: Michael R. Delafield; Craig W. Noyes; Rachel B. Hitch.
Education Law, Employment Law, Civil Litigation.
Representative Clients: Moore County Board of Education; Guilford County Board of Education; Kannapolis City Board of Education; Dare County Board of Education; Pamlico County Board of Education; Avery County Board of Education; Asheville City Board of Education.
See Professional Biographies, RALEIGH, NORTH CAROLINA

Schwentker, Robert B., (AV) '48 '73 C.675 B.A. L.575 J.D.
Sr. V.P. & Gen. Coun., North Carolina Elec. Membership Corp.
Scoggin, William G., (AV) . . . '— '89 C.896 B.A. L.575 J.D. [Kennedy C.L.&H.]
Scott, Elizabeth Davenport, (AV) . . . '60 '86 C&L.575 B.A., J.D. [Maupin T.]
Scott, Grant J. . . . '62 '91 C.893 B.S.E.E. L.577 J.D. [Myers B.S.&S.] (See Pat. Sect.)
Scott, J. Brian, (AV) . . . '27 '51 C&L.896 LL.B. [Battle,W.S.&W.] ⊙
Scott, Nancy Lee Ebert . . . '42 '84 C&L.228 A.B., J.D. Asst. Atty. Gen.
Scott, Pamela A. . . . '65 '98 C&L.575 B.A., J.D. [[A] Poyner&S.]
Scott-Turrentine, Karlene . . . '64 '98 C&L.574 B.A., J.D. [Turrentine]
Scouten, Ellen B. . . . '43 '78 C&L.575 A.B., J.D. Atty. Gen.'s Off.
Scudder, Samuel Alan, (BV) . . . '59 '90 C.260 B.S. L.1228 J.D. [Scudder&H.]

Scudder & Hedrick, (BV)
1312 Annapolis Drive, Suite 203, 27608
Telephone: 919-828-7333 Fax: 919-828-1209
Email: shwcl@bellsouth.net
Partners: Samuel Alan Scudder (Board Certified Specialist in Workers' Compensation, North Carolina State Board of Legal Specialization); John A. Hedrick (Board Certified Specialist in Workers' Compensation, North Carolina State Board of Legal Specialization). Associate: Alice J. Tejada.
Languages: English, Spanish.
Workers Compensation, Serious Personal Injury, Mediation, Employment, Pharmacy Malpractice, Medical Malpractice.
See Professional Biographies, RALEIGH, NORTH CAROLINA

Scurfield, Scott A., (BV) . . . '63 '88 C&L.665 B.A., J.D. [Yates,M.&W.]
Searing, Adam S. G. . . . '67 '94 C.1169 B.A. L.575 J.D. State Health Policy Analyst
Seate, Jennifer H. . . . '— '96 C.1228 B.A. L.1345 J.D. [[A] Hardison&L.]
Seay, James Lee, (AV) . . . '28 '55 C.228 A.B. L.575 LL.B. [Seay&H.]
Seay & Horne, (AV) . . . 4934 Windy Hill Drive
Sedberry, Charles H., (AV) . . . '30 '59 C.576 B.Ch.E. L.893 LL.B. [Joslin,S.&L.]
Segars, Thomas H. . . . '75 '00 C.896 B.A. L.575 J.D. [[A] Ellis&W.] (⊙Cary)
Seiber, Ashleigh C. . . . '79 '03 C&L.575 B.A., J.D. 19 W. Hargett St., Ste. 406

Seibert, Gregory L., (BV) '50 '86 C.576 B.S.E. L.574 J.D.
117 Glenwood Avenue, 27603
Telephone: 919-546-0606 Fax: 919-546-0040
Email: seibert@seibert.com URL: http://www.seibert.com
Criminal Law, Driving While Intoxicated (DWI), Traffic Violations, Drug Crimes, Personal Injury, Automobile Accidents, Wrongful Death, Aviation Law.
See Professional Biographies, RALEIGH, NORTH CAROLINA

Seigle, Jeffrey M., (BV) . . . '55 '84 C.477 A.B.ed. L.1228 J.D. 234 Fayetteville St. Mall
Sellers, Dianne C. . . . '47 '76 C.438 B.A. L.896 J.D. Comr., NC Indus. Comm.
Setliff, Brian C. . . . '72 '99 C.34 B.A. L.1000 J.D. [[A] Boxley,B.G.&H.]
Sewell, Martha L., (AV) . . . '— '93 C.575 B.A. L.896 J.D. [Kilpatrick S.]
Sexton, Wendy I. . . . '73 '99 C.575 B.A. L.896 J.D. [[A] Ellis&W.] (⊙Cary)
Shaber, Steven Mansfield, (AV) . . . '51 '76 C.894 B.A. L.228 J.D. [Poyner&S.]
Shad, Kerry A., (AV) . . . '65 '91 C.259 B.S. L.575 J.D. [Smith,A.B.D.M.&J.]
Shanahan, Kieran Joseph, (AV) . . . '56 '82 C.232 B.S.B.A. L.575 J.D. [Shanahan]

Shanahan Law Group, (AV)
207 Fayetteville Street Mall, 27601
Telephone: 919-856-9494 Fax: 919-856-9499
Email: kieran@shanahanlawgroup.com URL: http://www.lawyers.com/shanahanlawgroup
Member: Kieran Joseph Shanahan. Associates: Robert Bruce Markworth; Steven K. McCallister. Of Counsel: Reef C. Ivey, II.
Business Formation and Financing, Complex Business Litigation, Federal Litigation, Regulatory Investigation, Professional Liability, Health Care Law, Business Litigation, Business Fraud, White Collar Crimes, Employment Law, Non Competes, Personal Injury, Insurance Matters, Trusts and Estates.
See Professional Biographies, RALEIGH, NORTH CAROLINA

Sharkey, Chad A. . . . '71 '00 C.576 B.A. L.201 J.D. [[A] Smith D.N.W.S.&M.]
Sharp, Leslee R. . . . '58 '85 C.267 B.A. L.900 J.D. [Sharp]
Sharp Law Offices . . . 316 W. Millbrook Rd., Ste. 113
Shaw, Barbara A., (BV) . . . '51 '83 C&L.575 B.A., J.D. Asst. Atty. Gen.
Shaw, Brian C., (BV) . . . '54 '80 C&L.309 B.A., J.D. [Schwartz&S.]
Shaw, John L., (AV) . . . '44 '69 C&L.575 B.S., J.D. [Poyner&S.]
Shaw, Robert W. . . . '77 '04 C.896 B.S. L.575 J.D. [[A] Maupin T.]
Shearon, David R., (AV) . . . '45 '70 C&L.575 B.S.B.A., J.D. 4038 Barrett Dr.
Sheffield, Walter L., III . . . '49 '74 C.228 B.A. L.880 J.D. [W.L.Sheffield,III]

Sheffield, Walter L., III, PLLC, Law Offices of
4505 Fair Meadow Lane, Suite 222, 27607
Telephone: 919-571-4398 Fax: 919-571-4368
Email: wsheffield@waltsheffield.com URL: http://www.waltsheffield.com
Walter L. Sheffield, III;—Erica A. Wehner.
Asset Protection, Long Term Care Planning, Estate Planning, Probate Avoidance, Elder Law, Guardianship, Wills, Trusts and Estates, Taxes, Maximize Income.
See Professional Biographies, RALEIGH, NORTH CAROLINA

Shekita, Melanie, (CV) . . . '72 '98 C.575 B.A. L.1345 J.D. Co. Dist. Atty. Off.
Shenton, William R., (AV) . . . '49 '79 C&L.575 B.A., J.D. [Poyner&S.]
Sheridan, Paul A., (BV) . . . '65 '92 C.81 B.S. L.1228 J.D. [Vann&S.]
Sherman, Anne C. . . . '72 '99 C.228 A.B. L.145 J.D. [[A] Poyner&S.]
Sherrill, Russell G., III . . . '44 '71 C.576 A.B. L.575 J.D. Dist. J.
Sherron, J. Kemp, III, (AV) . . . '58 '84 C.575 B.S. L.896 J.D. [Wyrick R.Y.&P.]
Shick, David B., (CV) . . . '68 '95 C.575 B.A. L.1228 J.D. [D.Shick]
Shick, David, (CV) . . . 1501 Hemphill Drive
Shields, Grady L., (AV) . . . '60 '85 C.228 B.A. L.575 J.D. [Wyrick R.Y.&P.]
Shipley, Curtis J. . . . '63 '90 C.597 B.S. L.352 J.D. [Ellis&W.] ⊙
Shipley, Nellie K., (AV) . . . '65 '94 C.976 B.S. L.846 J.D. [Womble C.S.&R.]
Shirley, A. Graham, (AV) . . . '63 '88 C.885 B.A. L.945 J.D. [Shirley&A.]

Shirley & Adams, PLLC, (AV)
150 Fayetteville Street Suite 520, 27601
Telephone: 919-899-6278 Fax: 919-899-6279
URL: http://www.shirley-adamslaw.com
Ryan J. Adams; A. Graham Shirley.
Civil Trial Practice, Construction Law, Commercial Litigation, Business Litigation and Surety Law.
See Professional Biographies, RALEIGH, NORTH CAROLINA

Shuford, Forrest H., II . . . '23 '47 C&L.896 J.D. 1212 Bancroft St.‡
Shyllon, Mohamed M. . . . '48 '76 C.709 B.A. L.574 J.D. [Shyllon&S.]
Shyllon, Prince E. N., (BV) . . . '43 '77 C.778 B.A. L.574 J.D. [Shyllon&S.]
Shyllon & Shyllon, P.A., (BV) . . . 4002 Barrett Dr.
Sibley, Kenneth D., (AV) '56 '85
C.1047 B.A. L.228 J.D. [Myers B.S.&S.] (See Pat. Sect.)
Sieredzki, Kimberly Woodell '— '98
C.575 B.A. L.1228 J.D. Asst. Reporter Decisions, NC Supreme Ct.
Sigmon, C. Miller, (AV) . . . '47 '87 C.477 B.M. L.574 J.D. [Sigmon]
Sigmon Law Firm, The, P.A., (AV) . . . 1100 Navaho Drive, Suite 112
Silber, Frank E. . . . '72 '97 C.575 B.S. L.896 J.D. [Parker,P.A.&B.]
Silver, Carolyn D. . . . '— '97 C.1097 B.S. L.809 J.D. 231 Waterville St.

Silver, Hayden J., III, (AV) .... '— '81 C.198 B.A. L.893 J.D. [Kilpatrick S.]
Silverstein, Carol K., (AV) ....'48 '72 C.659 B.A. L.831 J.D. [Silverstein&C.]
Silverstein, John M., (AV) ....'46 '71 C.165 A.B. L.575 J.D. [Satisky&S.]

Silverstein & Cook, P.A., (AV)
4020 Westchase Boulevard, Suite 325, 27607
Telephone: 919-829-3811 NC Wats 800-458-7620 Fax: 919-664-8546
Email: silverstein&cook@silvercooklaw.com
Carol K. Silverstein; Terri L. Cook.
Corporate, Employee Benefits, Health Care Law, Estate Planning, Estate Administration, Tax and Probate Law.

Simmons, Edward Bardin, Jr. .... '78 '03 C.228 B.A. L.896 J.D. [Ⓐ Poyner&S.]

Simmons, Stephen Russell, Attorney and Counsellor at Law '56 '89 C.576 B.S. L.846 J.D.
19 West Hargett Street, Suite 202, 27601
Telephone: 919-839-5533 Fax: 919-839-0115 URL: http://www.srsimmonslaw.com
URL: http://www.srsimmons.com
Criminal Law, Traffic Violations, Driving While Intoxicated, Speeding Tickets, Driving While License Revoked.
See Professional Biographies, RALEIGH, NORTH CAROLINA

Simons, Claude Ernest, Jr., (AV) ..... '45 '71 C&L.896 B.A., J.D. [Smith,A.B.D.M.&J.]
Simpson, Bryan T., (BV) ....'68 '93 C.576 B.A. L.1228 J.D. [Teague,C.D.&G.]
Simpson, Dana E. .... '74 '00 C&L.575 B.A., J.D. [Ⓐ Smith,A.B.D.M.&J.]
Simpson, George L., IV ....'74 '00 C&L.575 B.A., J.D. [Cranfill,S.&H.]
Simpson, Steven D., (AV) ....'53 '78 C.317 B.A. L.896 J.D. [S.D.Simpson]

Simpson, Steven D., P.A., Law Offices of, (AV)
Landmark Center II, 4601 Six Forks Road, Suite 530, 27609
Telephone: 919-788-9677 Telefax: 919-788-0775
Email: s.simpsonlaw@verizon.net URL: http://www.ssimpsonlaw.com
Steven D. Simpson.
Taxation, Nonprofit and Charitable Organizations, Tax Exempt Organizations, Municipal Finance, Health Care Law.
See Professional Biographies, RALEIGH, NORTH CAROLINA

Sims, Genevieve C., (BV) .... '47 '87 C.576 B.A. L.574 J.D. [G.Sims]
Sims, Genevieve, Law Office of, (BV) .... 313 S. Blount St., Ste. 200C
Singer, Richard G., (BV) ....'43 '69 C&L.575 B.A., J.D. [Clifton&S.]
Sin-I Ma, Sandy .... '70 '97 C.367 B.A. L.446 J.D. Am. Civil Liberties Union of N.C.
Sink, Henry H., Jr., (AV) ....'47 '72 C&L.575 A.B., J.D. [Sink&P.]
Sink, Kevin L., (BV) ....'69 '94 C.576 B.A. L.575 J.D. [Nicholls&C.]

Sink & Potter, L.L.P., (AV)
115 South St. Mary's Street, P.O. Box 1471, 27602
Mailing Address: P.O. Box 1471, Raleigh, NC 27602
Telephone: 919-828-0684 Fax: 919-828-5386
URL: http://www.lawyers.com/sink&potter
Members of Firm: Henry H. Sink (1918-1989); Henry H. Sink, Jr.; William H. Potter, Jr.
Alcoholic Beverage Control Law, Legislative Representation, and Administrative Law, Estate Planning, Probate, and Trusts, Corporation Matters, Real Estate Law, Health Law.
Approved Attorneys: Lawyers Title Insurance Corp.
See Professional Biographies, RALEIGH, NORTH CAROLINA

Sitton, Clint W., (AVⓉ) '57 '83 C.1365 B.A. L.245 J.D.
(adm. in GA; not adm. in NC) [Martin&J.] (⊙Atlanta, GA)
Sizemore, Stephen G. ....'53 '91 C&L.575 B.A., J.D. Land Use Planner Attorney
Skidmore, Matthew W. .... '78 '04 C.576 B.S. L.575 J.D. [Ⓐ Teague,C.D.&G.]
Skinner, Jeffrey T. ....'— '96 C.228 A.B. L.575 J.D. [Kilpatrick S.]
Skinner, William P., Jr., (AV) .... '29 '56 C&L.575 A.B., J.D. [Manning,F.&S.]
Skiver, Robert E., (AV) ....'50 '81 C.870 B.S. L.569 J.D. Asst. U.S. Atty.
Skogland, John E., Jr. '45 '72 C.843 B.A. L.845 J.D.
Assoc. Gen. Cnsl, Martin Marietta Materials, Inc.
Sledge, Kristi L. ....'71 '96 C&L.575 B.A., J.D. 4038 Barrett Dr.
Slifkin, Anne R., (AV) .... '51 '76 C.1036 B.A. L.575 J.D. [Becton,S.&B.]
Small, A. Thomas ....'43 '69 C.228 A.B. L.896 J.D. U.S. Bkptcy. J.
Smalley, Stephen H. ....'70 '95 C.806 B.A. L.192 J.D. [Ogletree,D.N.S.&S.]
Smiley, Tiare Bowe, (AV) '48 '77
C&L.575 B.A., J.D. Spec. Dep. Atty. Gen., NC Dept. of Jus.
Smith, Christopher G., (AV) .... '65 '92 C&L.659 B.A., J.D. [Smith,A.B.D.M.&J.]
Smith, Donald L. ....'39 '64 C.1317 B.S. L.896 J.D. 837 Green Ridge Dr.‡
Smith, Eugene A. ....'33 '61 C&L.575 B.S., J.D. Sr. Dep. Atty. Gen.
Smith, Fred J., Jr., (AV) .... '42 '66 C&L.896 B.A., J.D. [Ⓒ Smith D.N.W.S.&M.]
Smith, James Peeler ....'44 '69 C&L.575 A.B., J.D. Spec. Dep. Atty. Gen.
Smith, Jeffrey M. ....'73 '98 C.210 B.A. L.228 J.D. [Ⓐ Wyrick R.Y.&P.]
Smith, Jessica '65 '92 C&L.659 B.A., J.D.
(adm. in CT; not adm. in NC) Law Clk., U.S. Dist. J.
Smith, Lee C., (AV) ....'26 '53 C&L.228 A.B., LL.B. [Smith,A.B.D.M.&J.]
Smith, Leigh Ann G., (AV) ....'69 '95 C.575 B.A. L.1228 J.D. [Cranfill,S.&H.]
Smith, Mary Elizabeth ....'70 '98 C.1365 B.A. L.280 J.D. [Ⓐ Womble C.S.&R.]
Smith, Robert E. '69 '95 C.1091 B.A. L.608 J.D.
(adm. in MI; not adm. in NC) Assoc. Gen. Coun., Progress Energy
Smith, Robert E., (AV) ....'35 '65 C.228 A.B. L.575 LL.B. [Smith]
Smith, Robert K. .... '44 '69 C.228 A.B. L.575 J.D. Asst. Atty. Gen.; Dept. of Justice
Smith, Roger W., (AV) .... '41 '67 C&L.575 A.B., J.D. [Tharrington S.]
Smith, Roger W., Jr., (AV) ....'69 '99 C.575 B.A. L.1345 J.D. [Ⓐ Tharrington S.]
Smith, Scott Hartwell ....'60 '86 C&L.575 A.B., J.D. Soc. Sec. Admin.
Smith, Sharon Leigh ....'67 '94 C&L.575 B.A., J.D. [Unti&L.]
Smith, Sherwood H., Jr., (AV) '34 '60 C&L.575 A.B., J.D.
Chmn. of the Bd. & CEO, Carolina Power & Light Co.
Smith, Stephen T., (AV) .... '47 '73 C.232 A.B. L.575 J.D. [McMillan,S.&P.]
Smith, T. Byron ....'57 '83 C&L.574 B.A., J.D. [Ⓐ Thigpen,B.S.&F.]
Smith, Wade M., (AV) ....'37 '63 C&L.575 A.B., J.D. [Tharrington S.]
Smith, William C., Jr., (AV) .... '61 '87 C&L.575 B.A., J.D. [Manning,F.&S.]

Smith, Anderson, Blount, Dorsett, Mitchell & Jernigan, L.L.P., (AV)
2500 First Union Capitol Center, P.O. Box 2611, 27602-2611
Telephone: 919-821-1220 Telecopier: 919-821-6800
Email: info@smithlaw.com URL: http://www.smithlaw.com
Of Counsel: W. Linville Roach; Philip R. Tracy; Dwight W. Allen. Members of Firm: Willis Smith (1887-1953); Oscar Leach (1887-1967); Willis Smith, Jr. (1921-1971); John H. Anderson (1907-1990); James K. Dorsett, Jr. (1916-2001); Lee C. Smith; James D. Blount, Jr.; Henry A. Mitchell, Jr.; John L. Jernigan; Samuel G. Thompson; Claude Ernest Simons, Jr.; Michael E. Weddington; Carl N. Patterson, Jr.; James K. Dorsett, III; Robert Marks Arnold; Walter R. Rogers, Jr.; Julian D. Bobbitt, Jr.; Robin Kenton Vinson; Steven M. Sartorio; Susan Milner Parker; Timothy P. Lehan; Amos U. Priester, IV; Gerald F. Roach; Francis C. Bagbey; R. Donavon Munford, Jr.; John D. Madden; Michael A. Ash; C. Steven Mason; Rosemary Gill Kenyon; Donald H. Tucker, Jr.; William H. Moss; Michael W. Hubbard; Kimberly J. Korando; William T. Barnett, Jr.; David Todd Buckingham; Byron B. Kirkland; Christopher B. Capel; William W. Nelson; B. Davis Horne, Jr.; Lee M. Kirby, Jr.; Michael W. Mitchell; Robert Joseph Morris; Robert E. Duggins; Peter J. Marino; Caryn Coppedge McNeill; Kerry A. Shad; Amy Meyers Batten; Stephen T. Parascandola; Michael P. Saber; Kirk G. Warner; Christopher G. Smith; Zebulon D. Anderson; Jason L. Martinez; Scott A. Miskimon; Martin H. Brinkley; Susan Haney Hargrove; David W. Berry; Deanna Davis Anderson;—Stephen G. Driggers;

(This Listing Continued)

Smith, Anderson, Blount, Dorsett, Mitchell & Jernigan, L.L.P. (Continued)
Sean A. Timmons; Michael R. Gordon; David B. Clement; Geoffrey William Adams; Wayne K. Maiorano; Kimberly Quarles Swintosky; Benji Taylor Jones; S. Nikole Mariencheck; Jamison H. Hinkle; Jackson W. Moore; Margaret N. Rosenfeld; Bradley J. Daves; J. Mitchell Armbruster; Dana E. Simpson; Rachel S. Betts; Miranda R. Miller; Bryan A. McGann; James S. Hanson; Jan L. Newman; Matthew D. Rhoad; Ellen M. Jernigan; Christopher R. Kiger; Kelly L. Podger; Bartley A. Norman; K. Alan Parry, Jr.; Jennifer B. Markham; Jamal A. Rhinehardt; Addie K.S. Ries; Amy S. Wallace; J. Travis Hockaday; Brian D. Meacham.
Administrative Hearings and Appeals, Administrative Law, Admiralty and Maritime, Agricultural Law, Alternative Dispute Resolution, Antitrust and Trade Regulation, Appellate Practice, Asset Based Finance, Aviation and Aerospace, Bankruptcy, Banks and Banking, Biotechnology, Blue Sky Law, Business Law, Capital Markets, Civil Practice, Civil Rights, Closely Held Business Law, Collections, Commercial Law, Commercial Real Estate, Communications and Media, Complex and Multi-District Litigation, Computers and Software, Construction Law, Contracts, Copyrights, Corporate Law, Creditors Rights, Disabilities, Eminent Domain, Employee Benefits, Employment Discrimination, Employment Law, Energy, Environmental Law, Equipment Finance and Leasing, ERISA, Fidelity and Surety, Finance, Franchises and Franchising, General Practice, Government, Health Care, Hospital Law, Insurance, Insurance Defense, Intellectual Property, International Law, International Trade, Internet Law, Investments, Joint Ventures, Labor and Employment, Leases and Leasing, Legal Ethics and Professional Responsibility, Libel, Slander and Defamation, Litigation, Lobbying, Media Law, Medical Malpractice, Medicare and Medicaid, Mergers, Acquisitions and Divestitures, Mortgages, Nonprofit and Charitable Organizations, Mortgage Securitization, Partnership Law, Personal Injury, Premises Liability, Privatizations, Probate, Products Liability, Professional Liability, Property Law, Real Estate, Real Property, Regulatory Law, Secured Transactions, Securities, Taxation, Technology and Science, Torts, Technology Joint Ventures, Trade and Professional Associations, Trade Secrets, Trademark Infringement, Trademark Licensing, Trademark Litigation, Trademark Registration, Trademarks, Trusts and Estates, Utility Law, Wills, Workers Compensation.
Representative Clients: Aetna Life and Casualty; Capitol Broadcasting Co., Inc.; Century American Insurance Co.; First Union National Bank of North Carolina; Motion Picture Association of America; North Carolina Medical Society; St. Paul Insurance Cos.
See Professional Biographies, RALEIGH, NORTH CAROLINA

Smith Debnam Narron Wyche Saintsing & Myers, L.L.P., (AV)
4601 Six Forks Road, Suite 400, 27609 ⊙
Telephone: 919-250-2000 Facsimile: 919-250-2211
Email: mail@smithdebnamlaw.com URL: http://www.smithdebnamlaw.com
Members of Firm: W. Thurston Debnam, Jr.; John W. Narron (Board Certified Specialist in Family Law, North Carolina State Board of Legal Specialization); N. Hunter Wyche, Jr. (Board Certified Specialist in Business and Consumer Bankruptcy Law, North Carolina State Board of Legal Specialization); Bettie Kelley Sousa; Jerry T. Myers; Rose H. Stout (Board Certified Specialist in Family Law, North Carolina State Board of Legal Specialization); Byron L. Saintsing; Franklin Drake; Gerald H. Groon, Jr.; Caren Davis Enloe; Jeff D. Rogers; Connie E. Carrigan; Cynthia V. McAlister (Board Certified Specialist in Family Law, North Carolina State Board of Legal Specialization); Krista F. Norstog Leonard. Associates: Thomas A. Gray (Not admitted in NC); Aaron N. Bailey; Pedro J. Zabala, II; Stephanie Fountain Bynum; Chad A. Sharkey; James David Dill; Chad L. Halliday; Lynn Wilson Lupton; Adam M. Gottsegen; Amanda B. Banat. Of Counsel: Fred J. Smith, Jr.; Elizabeth B. Godfrey; Tracy T. Debnam; John P. McNeill.
General and Appellate Practice in all State and Federal Courts. Corporation, Bankruptcy, Non-Judicial Workouts and Reorganizations, Corporate Reorganization, Construction, Equipment Leasing and Finance, Estate Planning and Administration, Commercial and Retail Collections and Litigation. Administrative and Regulatory, Government Contracts and Procurement, Health Care, Land Use and Zoning, Limited Liability Companies and Partnerships, Public Finance, Residential and Commercial Real Estate, Family Law and Equitable Distribution, Telecommunications, Plaintiff's Personal Injury.
Charlotte, North Carolina Office: 4201 Congress Street, Suite 460, 28209. Telephone: 704-643-3220. Fax: 704-643-3898.
See Professional Biographies, RALEIGH, NORTH CAROLINA

Smith Law Offices PC, (AV) .... P.O. Box 1069

Smith Moore LLP, (AV) BB
2800 Two Hanover Square, P.O. Box 27525, 27601 ⊙
Mailing Address: P.O. Box 27525, Raleigh, NC 27611
Telephone: 919-755-8700 Fax: 919-755-8800
Email: smith.moore@smithmoorelaw.com URL: http://www.smithmoorelaw.com
Partners: Denise S. Cline; J. Donald Cowan, Jr.; James L. Gale; Patricia A. Markus; George J. Oliver; Bradley M. Risinger; Samuel O. Southern; Robert L. Wilson, Jr. Associates: D. Todd Brosius; R. James Cox, Jr.; Matthew S. Cunningham; James R. Holland; Molly G. Huggins; Shannon R. Joseph; Laura Murray Loyek; John W. Mann; Elizabeth Brooks Scherer; William W. Stewart, Jr.; Marc C. Tucker. Counsel: Sidney S. Eagles, Jr.
General, Trial and Appellate Practice in All State and Federal Courts, Dispute Resolution, Corporate, Taxation, Securities Regulation, Real Property and Finance, Labor and Employment (Management) Law, Employee Benefits, International and Immigration, Antitrust and Trade Regulation, Negligence, Products Liability, Insurance Coverage, Media, Banking, Commercial, Bankruptcy, Administrative, Environmental, Hospital and Health Care, Public Authority and Public Finance, Estate Planning and Administration, Probate, Legislative, Intellectual Property, Education, and Sports Law.
Greensboro, North Carolina Office: Wachovia Tower, 300 North Greene Street, Suite 1400, P.O. Box 21927. Telephone: 336-378-5200. Fax: 336-378-5400.
Atlanta, Georgia Office: One Atlantic Center, Suite 3700, 1201 West Peachtree Street. Telephone: 404-962-1000. Fax: 404-962-1200.
Wilmington, North Carolina Office: 300 North Third Street, Suite 301. Telephone: 910-251-7001. Fax: 910-251-7007.
See Professional Biographies, RALEIGH, NORTH CAROLINA

Smyth, Theodore B., (AV) .... '56 '81 C.164 B.A. L.896 J.D. [Smyth&C.]
Smyth & Cioffi, LLP, (AV) ....3321 Blue Ridge Rd.
Smythe, Jessica C. ....'— '96 C.471 B.A. L.1228 J.D. [Ⓐ Hedrick E.G.&K.]
Snyder, Adam B. '74 '02 C.48 B.A. L.16 J.D.
(adm. in AL; not adm. in NC) [Ⓐ Poyner&S.]
Sokol, Marc W., (BV) ....'48 '80 C.994 B.A. L.1009 J.D. [Sokol M.S.O.L.P.]

Sokol McLamb Schilawski Oliver Ladd PLLC, (AV)
d/b/a Wake Family Law Group
4350 Lassiter at North Hills Avenue Suite 360, 27609
Telephone: 919-787-4040 Facsimile: 919-787-4811 URL: http://www.wakefamilylawfirmgroup.com
URL: http://www.wakefamilylawgroup.com
Marc W. Sokol; Catherine C. McLamb (Board Certified Specialist in Family Law, North Carolina State Board of Legal Specialization); Michael F. Schilawski (Board Certified Specialist in Family Law, North Carolina State Board of Legal Specialization); Helen M. Oliver; Suzanne R. Ladd; Jennifer M. Bradley.
Domestic Relations, Civil Litigation, Appellate Practice, Mediation, Arbitration, Family Mediation, Family Arbitration, Collaborative Law, Family Law, Divorce, Child Custody, Equitable Distribution.
See Professional Biographies, RALEIGH, NORTH CAROLINA

Soles, M. Janette .... '64 '92 C.296 A.B. L.1228 J.D. Assoc. Atty. Gen.
Soltys, Adam P. ....'78 '03 C.198 B.A. L.575 J.D. [Ⓐ Kurtz&B.]
Soo, Kenneth A., (BV) ....'58 '91 C.228 A.B. L.575 J.D. [Tharrington S.]
Sousa, Bettie Kelley, (AV) ....'56 '81 C.575 B.A. L.896 J.D. [Smith D.N.W.S.&M.]
Sousa, David P., (AV) '55 '81 C.383 B.A. L.896 J.D.
Sr. V.P. and Gen. Coun., Medical Mutual Ins. Co. of N.C.
Southern, Samuel O., (AV) .... '44 '69 C.228 A.B. L.575 J.D. [Smith M.]

Southwick, Julia B., (AV) '54 '82 C.34 B.M. L.575 J.D.
4024 Barrett Drive, 27609
Telephone: 919-782-8673 Fax: 919-781-7281
Email: jsouthwick@southwicklaw.com URL: http://www.lawyers.com/southwicklaw
Bankruptcy, Consumer Bankruptcy, Personal Bankruptcy, Residential Real Estate, Wills.
See Professional Biographies, RALEIGH, NORTH CAROLINA

Sowerby, Richard G., Jr. .... '59 '85 C&L.575 B.A., J.D. Asst. Atty. Gen.
Spainhour, Elizabeth E. .... '73 '05 C.197 B.A. L.575 J.D. [Brooks,P.M.H.&L.] ⊙

Spalding, Valerie B., (BV) '48 '87 C.999 B.A. L.1228 J.D. Spec. Dep. Atty. Gen., NC Atty. Gen. Off
Sparrow, Marvin R., (BV) ..... '46 '83 C.1128 B.A. L.574 J.D. N.C. Prisoner Legal Servs.
Sparrow, R. Michelle .... '61 '92 C.953 B.A. L.356 J.D. [Sparrow]

Sparrow Law Firm
19 West Hargett Street, Suite 501, 27601
Telephone: 919-835-3600 Fax: 919-835-3667 URL: http://www.michellesparrowlaw.com
Email: nclawyer@bellsouth.net URL: http://www.michellesparrowattorney.com
R. Michelle Sparrow.
General Civil and Criminal Law, Driving While Intoxicated, (DWI), Drug Crimes, Felonies, Homicide, Juvenile Law, Misdemeanors, Parole and Probation, Assault, Traffic Violations, Law Enforcement, Police, Personal Injury, Automobile Accidents, Medical Malpractice, Mediation and Arbitration.
See Professional Biographies, RALEIGH, NORTH CAROLINA

Spearman, Robert W., (AV) .... '43 '71 C.575 A.B. L.976 LL.B. [Parker,P.A.&B.]
Speas, Edwin Marion, Jr., (AV) .... '45 '71 C&L.896 B.A., J.D. [Poyner&S.]
Spence, Amanda .... '69 '94 C&L.575 B.A., J.D. P.O. Box 2625
Spencer, Aaron G. .... '74 '99 C.612 B.S. L.802 J.D. [Ⓐ Helms M.&W.]
Spencer, David W. ... '65 '94 C.576 B.A L.1228 J.D. 6801 Pleasant Pines Drive, Suite 101
Spiro, Robert B. .... '68 '95 C.1287 B.A. L.896 J.D. [Bashyam&S.]
Spivey, Marvin M., Jr., (AV) .... '58 '83 C&L.575 B.A., J.D. [Young M.&H.]
Sprain, Theresa M. .... '72 '97 C.950 B.A. L.896 J.D. [Ⓐ Womble C.S.&R.]
Sprouse, James W., Jr., (CV) .... '69 '99 C.1039 B.S. L.575 J.D. [Ⓐ Vann&S.]
Spruill, W. Murray, (AV) .... '54 '92 C.232 B.S. L.273 J.D. [Alston&B.] (See Pat. Sect.)
Spurlock, Heather L. .... '— '02 C.575 B.S. L.1194 J.D. [Ⓐ F.B.Brice,Jr.]
Stagner, Deborah R. .... '63 '97 C.378 B.G.S. L.575 J.D. [Ⓐ Tharrington S.]
Stallings, Joseph H., (AV) .... '50 '76 C&L.575 A.B., J.D. [Howard,S.F.&H.] ⊙
Stambaugh, Christopher R. '75 '04 C.228 B.S.E. L.262 J.D. (adm. in NY; not adm. in NC) [Ⓐ Hunton&W.]
Stanback, Shonnese D. .... '71 '00 C.575 B.A. L.574 J.D. 4101 Lake Boone Trail, Ste. 200
Stanek, Elizabeth A. ... '75 '00 C.576 B.S. L.575 J.D. [Ⓐ Myers B.S.&S.] (See Pat. Sect.)
Stanford, M. Denise, (AV) .... '61 '90 C&L.575 B.A., J.D. [Bailey&D.]

Stark Law Group, PLLC
(See Chapel Hill)

Starks, Samuel L. '66 '94 C.790 B.A. L.228 J.D. (adm. in DC; not adm. in NC) [Martin&J.] (⊙Atlanta, GA)
Starling, Ray A. .... '76 '02 C.576 B.S. L.575 J.D. [Ⓐ Hunton&W.]
Staton, Shawna Y., (BV) .... '66 '91 C&L.575 B.A., J.D. [Firm of Hutchens,S.&B.]
Stauffer, Iain Matthew .... '72 '01 C.1122 B.S. L.574 J.D. 1 West Morgan Street
Steed, Thomas W., Law Offices of '30 '54 C&L.575 B.S.B.A., J.D. 863 B Washington Street
Steel, Charles L., IV, (AV) '45 '70 C.198 A.B. L.880 J.D. [Maupin T.] (⊙Research Triangle Park)
Steelman, Sanford L., Jr., (AV) .... '51 '76 C.198 A.B. L.575 J.D. 1 W. Morgan St.
Stephens, Donald W. .... '45 '70 C&L.575 B.S., J.D. Co. Ct. J.
Stephens, Linda, (AV) .... '50 '79 C.790 B.A. L.575 J.D. [Teague,C.D.&G.]
Stephenson, Angenette .... '68 '04 C.1124 B.S. L.575 J.D. [Ⓐ S.Scherer]

Stephenson & Stephenson, LLP
(See Cary)

Stevens, Eric P., (BV) .... '65 '90 C.896 B.A. L.469 J.D. [Poyner&S.]
Stevens, Hugh, (AV) .... '44 '68 C&L.575 A.B., J.D. [Everett,G.H.&S.]
Stevens, Richard V., III .... '69 '95 C&L.575 B.A., J.D. [Ⓐ Yates,M.&W.]
Stevens, Richard Y. .... '48 '74 C&L.575 A.B., J.D. Co. Mgr.
Stewart, William W., Jr., (BV) .... '64 '94 C.496 B.S. L.356 J.D. [Millberg,G.&S.]
Stewart, William W., Jr. .... '69 '95 C.10 B.S. L.16 J.D. [Ⓐ Smith M.]
Stock, Paul H. .... '50 '74 C.228 A.B. L.575 J.D. N.C. Bankers Assn.
Stone, Mary Ann .... '63 '90 C&L.575 J.D. Dept. of Health & Human Srvs.
Stoothoff, Judith '33 '74 C.383 A.B. L.117 J.D. (adm. in OH; not adm. in NC) 3113 Charles B. Root Wynd‡
Story, Ashley H., (AV) .... '56 '82 C.896 B.A. L.1228 J.D. [Troutman S.]
Stott, E. Gregory, (BV) .... '47 '73 C.576 B.A. L.575 J.D. 5 West Hargett Street
Stout, Rose H., (AV) .... '60 '85 C&L.1228 B.A., J.D. [Smith D.N.W.S.&M.]
Strach, Phillip J. .... '73 '00 C.1228 B.A. L.575 J.D. [Ⓐ Ogletree,D.N.S.&S.]
Stradley, J. David .... '69 '95 C.896 B.A. L.228 J.D. [White&S.]
Stranahan, Robert P., III '60 '92 C&L.575 B.S., J.D. Spec. Coun., Admin. Off. of the Cts.
Strandberg, William N. .... '54 '80 C&L.575 B.S.B.A., J.D. 4101 Rowan St.
Stratas, Nicholas A., Jr., (AV) .... '57 '84 C.576 B.A. L.575 J.D. [Stratas&W.] ⊙
Stratas & Weathers, L.L.P., (AV) .... 1550 Glenwood Avenue (⊙Wilmington)
Strickland, Donald R., (AV) .... '56 '84 C.575 B.S. L.228 J.D. [Twiggs,B.S.&R.]
Strickland, R. Michael, (AV) .... '47 '72 C.228 A.B. L.896 J.D. [Young M.&H.]
Strickland, Robin Eason .... '77 '02 C.576 B.A. L.1228 J.D. [Brannon S.]
Stroud, Kevin W. .... '69 '94 C.576 B.A. L.575 J.D. [Ⓐ Monroe,W.&W.]
Stroud, William R., Jr. '62 '87 C.198 A.B. L.575 J.D. Structured Financial Associates, Inc.
Stroupe, Odes L., Jr., (AV) .... '46 '71 C.576 B.A. L.575 J.D. [Bode,C.&S.]
Stuart, Ann H., (AV) .... '— '78 C&L.575 B.A., J.D. [Ⓒ Troutman S.]
Stuart, Catherine R., (AV) .... '55 '82 C.575 B.A. L.861 J.D. [Stuart]
Stuart, James L., (AV) .... '50 '75 C.228 B.S.E. L.273 J.D. [Stuart]

Stuart Law Firm, PLLC, (AV)
1033 Wade Avenue, Suite 202, 27605-1155
Telephone: 919-787-6050 Fax: 919-787-9988
Email: main@stuartlawfirm.com URL: http://www.stuartlawfirm.com
Members of Firm: James L. Stuart; Catherine R. Stuart. Associates: Theresa S. Dew; Charles C. Kyles; Sandhya G. Patel.
Administrative Law, Bankruptcy, Business Law, Dispute Resolution/Mediation, Government Relations, Housing Finance, Insurance Regulatory, Intellectual Property, Municipal Bond Finance, Sports Law, Tax Exempt Organizations, Workers Compensation, Workers Compensation Self Insurance.
See Professional Biographies, RALEIGH, NORTH CAROLINA

Stubbs, Alice Carson .... '67 '92 C.198 B.A. L.575 J.D. Dist. J.
Stubbs, Trawick H., Jr., (AV) .... '42 '67 C.575 A.B. L.228 J.D. [Stubbs&P.] ⊙

Stubbs, Cole, Breedlove, Prentis & Biggs, P.L.L.C.
(See Durham)

Stubbs & Perdue, P.A., (AV)
Two Hannover Square, 434 Fayetteville Street Mall, Suite 1630, P.O. Box 1630, 27602-1630 ⊙
Telephone: 919-856-9400 Fax: 919-856-9300 URL: http://www.stubbsperdue.com
Email: law@stubbsperdue.com URL: http://www.lawyers.com/stubbsperdue
Gary R. Perdue, Sr. (1947-1997); Trawick H. Stubbs, Jr.; Laurie B. Biggs.
General Practice in all Courts. Probate, Real Estate, Personal Injury, Bankruptcy Reorganization, Domestic Relations, Corporation and Criminal Law, Environmental Law; Toxic Tort.
Approved Attorneys for: Lawyers Title Insurance Corp.
References: First Citizens Bank; Branch Banking & Trust Co.
New Bern, North Carolina Office: 310 Craven Street, P.O. Box 1654. Telephone: 252-633-2700. Fax: 252-633-9600. Email: law@stubbsperdue.com
See Professional Biographies, RALEIGH, NORTH CAROLINA

Sturgis, K.D., (AV) .... '53 '80 C.645 B.A. L.228 J.D. Asst. Atty. Gen.
Styers, M. Gray, Jr., (AV) .... '62 '89 C.896 B.A. L.575 J.D. [Blanchard,J.M.L.&S.]
Styles, Jack B., (BV) .... '46 '71 C&L.575 A.B., J.D. 211 Six Forks Rd., Ste. 204
Styron, Hannah G. .... '73 '02 C.575 B.A. L.1228 J.D. [Ⓐ Bailey&D.]
Sugg, Randolph Palmer, (AV) .... '63 '89 C&L.1228 B.A., J.D. [Broughton W.S.&T.]

Suhr, Paul A., (BV) '40 '89 C.1228 B.A. L.574 J.D.
1110 Navaho Drive, Suite 502, 27609
Telephone: 919-876-4707 Fax: 919-876-4237
Email: paulsuhr@bellsouth.net URL: http://www.lawyers.com/paulsuhr
Language: Korean.
Immigration and Naturalization, Visas, Deportation, Citizenship, Adoptions, Criminal Law, DWI, Misdemeanors, Traffic Violations, Personal Injury, Automobile Accidents, Business Law.
See Professional Biographies, RALEIGH, NORTH CAROLINA

Sullivan, Jeffrey M. .... '— '95 C.575 B.A. L.880 J.D. [DLPiper R.G.C.U.]
Sullivan, M. Todd .... '67 '95 C.393 B.A. L.188 J.D. [Ⓐ Womble C.S.&R.]
Sullivan, Mark E., (AV) .... '45 '71 C.385 A.B. L.893 J.D. [Sullivan&G.]
Sullivan, Terrence D. '45 '72 C&L.575 B.A., J.D. Dir. of Research, State Gen. Assembly
Sullivan, Timothy P., (AV) .... '57 '83 C&L.575 B.S., J.D. [Poyner&S.]

Sullivan & Grace, P.A., (AV)
600 Wade Avenue, 27605
Telephone: 919-832-8507 Fax: 919-833-2852
Email: LAW8507@aol.com URL: http://www.ncfamilylaw.com
Mark E. Sullivan (Board Certified Specialist in Family Law, North Carolina State Board of Legal Specialization); Nancy L. Grace (Board Certified Specialist in Family Law, North Carolina State Board of Legal Specialization);—Katie Hardersen King.
Family Law, Property Division, Separation Agreements, Child Custody, Child Support, Alimony, Divorce, Adoption, Domestic Violence, Premarital Agreements, Collaborative Family Law, Wills and Probate, Military Pension Division, Arbitration, Mediation and Family Law Appeals.
See Professional Biographies, RALEIGH, NORTH CAROLINA

Sumner, Lisa P., (BV) .... '69 '94 C.575 B.A. L.228 J.D. [Poyner&S.]
Sumner, Robert W., (AV) .... '44 '70 C&L.896 B.A., J.D. [Cranfill,S.&H.]
Sun, Paul K., Jr., (AV) .... '57 '89 C.967 B.A. L.228 J.D. [Ellis&W.] (⊙Cary)
Suttle, William W. .... '33 '58 C&L.575 LL.B. Gen. Coun., State Ins. Dept
Swaim, Thomas P. .... '54 '80 C.34 B.S. L.469 J.D. Asst. U.S. Atty.
Swinson, Gwynn T. .... '53 '76 C.33 B.A. L.1162 J.D. 1301 Mail Service Center
Swintosky, Kimberly Quarles .. '70 '98 C&L.575 B.S.B.A., J.D. [Ⓐ Smith,A.B.D.M.&J.]
Syger, Elizabeth S. .... '59 '84 C.575 B.A. L.260 J.D. 4101 Lake Boone Trail
Tadych, Michael J. .... '68 '97 C.347 B.A. L.930 J.D. [Everett,G.H.&S.]
Taggart, John C. '46 '78 C.101 B.A. L.911 J.D. (adm. in CA; not adm. in NC) V.P. & Assoc. Gen. Coun., GE Mortgage Insurance
Taibi, Anthony D. .... '60 '95 C.475 B.A. L.228 J.D. 1930-101 Eyrie Court‡
Tamsberg, M. Catherine .... '53 '86 C.577 B.S. L.575 J.D. E. Central Comm. Legal Servs.
Tanner, Kathleen P. .... '75 '01 C&L.575 B.A., J.D. [Ⓐ Tharrington S.]
Tanner, Michael D. .... '70 '96 C&L.228 B.A., J.D. [Ⓐ Wyrick R.Y.&P.]
Tanoury, Dahr Joseph .... '63 '00 C.354 B.S. L.574 J.D. Atty. Gen.'s Off.
Tart, Charlotte L. .... '70 '96 C.575 B.A. L.896 J.D. [Wyrick R.Y.&P.]
Tate, Larry I. .... '35 '63 C.532 B.A. L.477 LL.B. 5151 Glenwood Ave., Ste. 300
Tate, Sarah Lindsay .... '29 '54 C&L.575 A.B., LL.B. 520 Marlowe Rd.‡
Tatum, Brian Steed .... '— '97 C&L.280 A.B., J.D. [Ⓐ Morris,S.&P.] (⊙Atlanta, GA)
Tatum, Robert M. .... '68 '02 C.893 B.S. L.575 J.D. [Ⓐ Teague,C.D.&G.]
Tatum, Robin L., (AV) .... '61 '90 C.576 B.S. L.575 J.D. [Poyner&S.]
Taylor, Arles A., Jr. .... '68 '94 C.576 B.S.B.A. L.575 J.D. [Jenkins,W.&T.] (Pat.) ⊙
Taylor, Erika D. .... '— '03 C.1378 B.A. L.574 J.D. [Ⓐ Hedrick E.G.&K.]
Taylor, Erin Fleming .... '74 '99 C.577 B.A. L.1228 J.D. [Cranfill,S.&H.]
Taylor, Herman L. .... '19 '45 C.892 B.S. L.178 LL.B. 555 New Bern Avenue
Taylor, Marva M. '55 '85 C.1030 B.S. L.1252 J.D. (adm. in CT; not adm. in NC) Assoc. Gen. Coun., Florida Power Corp.
Taylor, Melissa H. .... '64 '92 C.575 B.A. L.574 J.D. 10705 Cambium Court
Taylor, Nathan J. .... '71 '99 C.896 B.A. L.1228 J.D. [Ⓐ Young M.&H.]
Taylor, Ollie H. .... '65 '91 C.790 B.A. L.574 J.D. N.C. Prisoner Legal Servs., Inc.
Taylor, Patricia Potter, (BV) .... '51 '89 C.953 B.A. L.1228 J.D. 2017 Carrbridge Way
Taylor, R. U. .... '18 '41 C&L.896 LL.B. 504 Oakland Dr.

Taylor, Raymond Mason, The Law Offices of, (AV) '33 '60 C&L.575 A.B., J.D.
503 Oberlin Road, Suite 203, 27605-1327
Telephone: 919-832-8440 Fax: 919-832-8447
URL: http://www.lawyers.com/raymondmasontaylor
Elder Law, Medicare and Medicaid, Wills, Trusts and Estates, Guardianships, Small Business.
See Professional Biographies, RALEIGH, NORTH CAROLINA

Taylor, Ritchie W. .... '— '99 C&L.101 B.S., J.D. [Manning,F.&S.]
Taylor, S. Nicole .... '70 '96 C.232 B.A. L.577 J.D. [Manning,F.&S.]
Taylor, Samuel M., (BV) .... '56 '92 C.576 B.S. L.575 J.D. 8804 Ross Court
Taylor, Travis R. .... '70 '96 C&L.575 B.A., J.D. 221 Glenwood Ave.
Taylor, Wanda Blanche .... '62 '87 C.228 B.A. L.575 J.D. Indus. Comm.
Taylor, William W., Jr., (AV) .... '12 '33 C.198 L.896 [Maupin T.] ‡

Taylor, Penry, Rash & Riemann, PLLC, (AV)
510 Glenwood Avenue, Suite 319, 27603 ⊙
Telephone: 919-833-9449 Fax: 919-833-9448
URL: http://www.tprr.com
J. Anthony Penry; Neil A. Riemann;—Cynthia A. O'Neal. Of Counsel: Michael L. Weisel.
Construction Law, Construction Litigation, Commercial Litigation, Securities Litigation, Mediation, Arbitration, Intellectual Property Litigation, Insurance Coverage Litigation, Government Relations and Administrative Litigation.
Charlotte, North Carolina Office: 2359 Perimeter Pointe Parkway, Suite 360, 28208. Telephone: 704-424-2900. Fax: 704-424-2999.
See Professional Biographies, RALEIGH, NORTH CAROLINA

Teague, C. Woodrow, (AV) .... '13 '34 C&L.896 LL.B. [Teague,C.D.&G.]
Teague, G. Mark, (BV) .... '67 '93 C.575 B.A. L.896 J.D. [Moore&A.] ⊙
Teague, George M., (AV) .... '45 '71 C.575 A.B. L.880 J.D. [Nelson M.R.&S.]

Teague, Campbell, Dennis & Gorham, L.L.P., (AV) BR
1621 Midtown Place, 27609 ⊙
Telephone: 919-873-0166 Facsimile: 919-873-1814
URL: http://www.tcdg.com
Members of Firm: C. Woodrow Teague; George W. Dennis III; Henry W. Gorham; Dayle A. Flammia; Linda Stephens; Thomas M. Clare; Robert C. Kerner, Jr.; John A. Tomei; Bruce A. Hamilton; George H. Pender; Donald F. Lively; Bryan T. Simpson; J. Matthew Little; Mallory T. Underwood; Jan N. Pittman; Melissa R. Cleary. Associates: Tracey L. Jones; Jennifer B. Milak; Tara D. Muller; Season D. Atkinson; Carla M. Cobb; Jacob H. Wellman; Robert M. Tatum; Christopher G. Lewis; John L. Tidball, V; Michael D. Moore; William A. Bulfer; Julia S. Hooten; Kathryn Deiter-Maradei; Courtney C. Britt; Edward S. Schenk, III; Matthew W. Skidmore; Bradley Inman. Of Counsel: John Wishart Campbell (Resident at Lumberton Office); Marilyn Ellison Tomei.
General Civil Defense Trial and Appellate Practice, including Automobile, and Trucking Liability, Premises and Product Liability, Medical, Nursing Home, Legal, Real Estate and other Professional Liability, Construction Law, Environmental Law, including Mold and other Toxic Torts, Corporate, Non-Profit and other Business Litigation, Governmental and Municipal Law, Life, Health and Employment Law, Insurance Coverage Disputes, Dram Shop Actions, Arson and Fraud, and Workers Compensation.

(This Listing Continued)

Teague, Campbell, Dennis & Gorham, L.L.P. (Continued)

Lumberton, North Carolina Office: 408 North Chestnut Street, P.O. Box 1424. Telephone: 910-738-8534.

See Professional Biographies, RALEIGH, NORTH CAROLINA

Tejada, Alice J. ....'— '97 C.605 A.B. L.904 J.D. [Ⓐ Scudder&H.]
Telfer, Philip A., (AV) ....'51 '80 C.575 B.A. L.861 J.D. Spec. Dep. Atty. Gen.
Tempest, Mark J. ....'49 '81 C.575 B.A. L.280 J.D. P.O. Box 20343
Temple, G. Henry, Jr. ....'— '74 C.575 B.A. L.790 J.D. [Temple]

Temple Law Firm, PLLC
615 Willard Place, 27603
Telephone: 919-832-5732 1-800-982-2126 Fax: 919-832-7732
URL: http://www.templelawfirm.com
G. Henry Temple, Jr.;—Russell David Babb; Edith R. Salmony.
Pharmaceutical and Defective Medical Devices (Fen-hen, Vioxx, Celebrex & Bextra), Environmental and Toxic Torts, Personal Injury, Products Liability, Wrongful Death, Civil Litigation.

See Professional Biographies, RALEIGH, NORTH CAROLINA

Tenney, Brian H. ....'48 '73 C.576 B.A. L.896 J.D. [Tenney&T.]
Tenney, Juliann ....'52 '80 C.575 B.A. L.228 J.D. Duke Univ. School of Law
Tenney, Walter D. ....'73 '02 C.576 B.A. L.1202 J.D. [Tenney&T.]

Tenney & Tenney, LLP
160 Wind Chime Court, 27615
Telephone: 919-841-4696 Fax: 919-841-4699
Email: tenneylaw@msn.com
Members of the Firm: Brian H. Tenney; Walter D. Tenney.
Wills, Estates, Probate, Trusts, Living Trusts, Business Law, Corporate Law, Small Business, Intellectual Property, Contracts, Personal Injury, Automobile Accidents, Slip and Fall, Civil Litigation, Real Estate, Residential Real Estate, Real Estate Closings, Family Law.

See Professional Biographies, RALEIGH, NORTH CAROLINA

Tepper, Maury M., III, (AV) ....'65 '91 C.896 B.A. L.150 J.D. [Womble C.S.&R.]
Terry, Robin H., (BV) ....'59 '90 C.953 B.A. L.1228 J.D. [Cranfill,S.&H.]
Tessener, Hoyt G., (AV) ....'— '88 C.575 B.S. L.228 J.D. [Martin&J.] (⊙Durham)

Tew, Allen R., P.A.
(See Clayton)

Tharrington, J. Harold, (AV) ....'37 '63 C&L.575 A.B., J.D. [Tharrington S.]

Tharrington Smith, (AV)
A Registered Limited Liability Partnership
209 Fayetteville Street Mall, P.O. Box 1151, 27602 ⊙
Telephone: 919-821-4711 Telecopier: 919-829-1583
Email: kgardner@tharringtonsmith.com URL: http://tharringtonsmith.com
Members of Firm: Carlisle W. Higgins (1887-1980); George T. Rogister, Jr. (1946-1995); Wade M. Smith; Roger W. Smith; Carlyn G. Poole (Board Certified Specialist in Family Law, North Carolina State Board of Legal Specialization); Douglas E. Kingsbery; Randall M. Roden; Michael Crowell; Ann L. Majestic; Melissa Hill; Daniel W. Clark; Jonathan A. Blumberg; Rod Malone; Jaye Powell Meyer (Board Certified Specialist in Family Law, North Carolina State Board of Legal Specialization); Kenneth A. Soo; Lynn P. Burleson; F. Hill Allen; Fred M. Morelock. Associates: Roger W. Smith, Jr.; Carolyn A. Waller; Kara Grice Acree; Jill Schnabel Jackson; Kristopher B. Gardner; Deborah R. Stagner; Kathleen P. Tanner. Retired: J. Harold Tharrington.
Civil and Criminal Trials and Appeals in all State and Federal Courts, Mediation and Alternative Dispute Resolution, Education Law, Constitutional Law, Employment Law, Family Law, Professional Licensure Proceedings, Personal Injury, Voting Rights, Local Government Law, Construction Contracts and Litigation, Business and Corporate Law, Commercial Litigation, Alcoholic Beverage Control Law, Administrative Law, Tax Litigation, Unfair Competition, Copyright, Legislative and Lobbying, Sports and Entertainment Law.

See Professional Biographies, RALEIGH, NORTH CAROLINA

Thibaut, Sylvia H. ....'50 '81 C.228 B.A. L.574 J.D. Asst. Atty. Gen.
Thigpen, Cressie H., Jr., (AV) ....'46 '73 C.574 B.S. L.705 J.D. [Thigpen,B.S.&F.]
Thigpen, Blue, Stephens & Fellers, (AV) ....205 Fayetteville Street Mall, Suite 300
Thissen, Brenda J. '61 '04 C.494 B.A. L.575 J.D.
(adm. in DC; not adm. in NC) [Ⓐ Maupin T.]
Thomas, Catherine L. ....'— '03 C.822 B.A. L.904 J.D. [Ⓐ Kilpatrick S.]
Thomas, Christopher M. ....'68 '03 C.25 B.A. L.280 J.D. [Ⓐ Nelson M.R.&S.]
Thomas, Erica Jona ....'— '04 C.198 B.A. L.692 J.D. [Cranfill,S.&H.]
Thomas, Fredrick Rossiter '55 '82 C.259 B.S. L.208 J.D.
(adm. in CO; not adm. in NC) Sr. V.P., Wheat First Union
Thomas, James A. ....'— '87 C.47 A.B. L.228 J.D. [Parker,P.A.&B.]
Thomas, Jason S., (BV) ....'54 '91 C.604 B.Mus. L.575 J.D. [Ⓐ Hunton&W.]
Thomas, Mark S., (AV) ....'52 '78 C&L.896 B.A., J.D. [Maupin T.]
Thomas, Mason P., Jr. ....'28 '51 C&L.575 B.S., LL.B. P.O. Box 28856
Thomas, Nicholas D. ....'62 '89 C.260 B.A. L.259 J.D. P.O. Box 6514
Thompson, Benjamin E., III, (BV) '71 '97 C.576 B.S. L.1228 J.D.
[Broughton W.S.&T.]
Thompson, Benjamin N., (AV) ....'54 '79 C&L.1228 B.A., J.D. [Wyrick R.Y.&P.]
Thompson, John D. ....'70 '98 C.872 B.A. L.1187 J.D. 1708 Trawick Rd., Ste. 111
Thompson, Mary Davis ....'51 '88 C.1036 B.A. L.575 J.D. N.C. Gen. Assembly
Thompson, Mary Penny, (BV) ....'68 '97 C.576 B.S. L.861 J.D. Asst. Atty. Gen.
Thompson, R. Bruce, II, (AV) ....'67 '94 C&L.896 B.A., J.D. [Parker,P.A.&B.]
Thompson, Samuel G., (AV) ....'43 '68 C&L.575 B.S., J.D. [Smith,A.B.D.M.&J.]
Thompson, Samuel G., Jr. ....'75 '04 C.575 B.A. L.1228 J.D. [Ⓐ Yates,M.&W.]
Thompson, Sanford W., IV, (AV) '55 '80 C&L.575 A.B., J.D.
4601 Six Forks Rd, Ste. 500
Thompson, William H. ....'34 '68 C.576 B.S. L.575 J.D. 4913 Quail Hollow Dr.
Thomson, J. Faison, Jr., (BV) ....'23 '52 C.575 A.B. L.896 LL.B. 1105 Blenheim Drive
Thoren, Janet B. ....'63 '88 C.1317 B.S. L.575 J.D. N.C. Real Estate Comm.
Thornburg, Alan Z. ....'67 '96 C.198 B.A. L.896 J.D. Ct. of App. J.
Thorne, Leigh W. ....'64 '01 C.188 B.S. L.228 J.D. [Ⓐ Alston&B.] (See Pat. Sect.)
Thornton, James C., (AV) ....'64 '89 C&L.383 B.S., J.D. [Parker,P.A.&B.]
Thornton, Karon B., (AV) ....'65 '90 C.138 B.A. L.383 J.D. [Maupin T.]
Thornton, Michael R. ....'— '95 C.575 A.B. L.276 J.D. [Kennedy C.L.&H.]
Thornton, W. Gerald, (AV) ....'42 '67 C&L.575 B.S., J.D. [Manning,F.&S.]
Thorp, Isaac L., (AV) ....'57 '87 C.1307 B.A. L.569 J.D. [Kirby&H.]
Tidball, John L., V, (BV) ....'67 '99 C.508 B.A. L.1228 J.D. [Ⓐ Teague,C.D.&G.]
Tigges, Linda B. ....'65 '99 C&L.575 B.S., J.D. [Ⓐ Kilpatrick S.]
Tiller, Robert H., (AV) ....'55 '89 C.604 B.A. L.893 J.D. [Helms M.&W.]
Tillman, Jesse M., III, (BV) ....'64 '99 C.575 B.A. L.1228 J.D. [Cranfill,S.&H.]
Timmons, Sean A., (BV) ....'67 '98 C.951 B.A. L.228 J.D. [Ⓐ Smith,A.B.D.M.&J.]
Timmons-Goodson, Patricia ....'54 '81 C&L.575 B.A., J.D. Assoc. J., Ct. of App.
Tindall, L. Diane, (AV) ....'55 '86 C.945 B.A. L.575 J.D. [Wyrick R.Y.&P.]
Tingen, Gerald A., (AV) ....'58 '84 C&L.575 B.A., J.D. [Maupin T.]
Tippett, Walter L., Jr. ....'69 '95 C&L.575 B.S.B.A., J.D. [Ragsdale L.]
Titchener, William R., (BV) ....'47 '79 C.575 B.A. L.1228 J.D. 4080 Barrett Drive
Tobin, Jay P., (BV) ....'64 '91 C&L.575 B.A., J.D. [Young M.&H.]
Todd, Jacob W. ....'32 '59 C.575 A.B. L.309 LL.B. Mag.
Toland, Paul F. ....'63 '93 C.85 B.A. L.818 J.D. [Ⓐ Wilson&R.]
Tolliver Meyer, Staci ....'61 '90 C.160 B.A. L.574 J.D. Off. of Atty. Gen., Dept. of Jus.
Tomei, John A., (BV) ....'62 '89 C&L.575 B.A., J.D. [Teague,C.D.&G.]
Tomei, Marilyn Ellison, (BV) ....'63 '87 C&L.575 B.S., J.D. [Ⓒ Teague,C.D.&G.]
Toms, Herbert L., Jr., (AV) '28 '58
C.999 O.D. L.575 LL.B. Chmn. & Sr. Coun., United Title Co.

Toms, Frederic E., & Associates, PLLC
(See Cary)

Totten, Vanessa N. ....'— '01 C&L.575 B.A., J.D. Asst. Atty. Gen.
Tower, Daniel T. ....'71 '98 C.228 B.A. L.896 J.D. [D.T.Tower]

Tower, Daniel T., P.A.
4700 Six Forks Road, Suite 150, 27609
Mailing Address: P.O. Box 13011, Raleigh, NC 27609
Telephone: 919-781-2217 Fax: 919-781-7727
Email: dtower@towerlawfirm.com URL: http://www.towerlawfirm.com
Daniel T. Tower.
Real Estate, Real Estate Development, Real Estate Litigation, Construction Law, Commercial Litigation.

See Professional Biographies, RALEIGH, NORTH CAROLINA

Trachtman, James B. ....'— '95 C.659 B.S.E. L.228 J.D. [Trachtman]

Trachtman Law Firm, P.L.L.C.
Carolina Corporate Centre, 5400 Glenwood Avenue Suite G-01, 27612
Telephone: 919-781-3404 Facsimile: 919-781-3405
Email: Info@TrachtmanLawFirm.com URL: http://www.TrachtmanLawFirm.com
James B. Trachtman.
Real Estate Litigation, Contract Disputes, Broker/Dealer Litigation, Derivative Actions, Securities Litigation, Business Torts, Director and Officer Liability Claims, Fiduciary Liability Claims, Intellectual Property Claims, Unfair Trade Practices, Non-competition Agreements, Employee Benefits Litigation, Catastrophic Personal Injury, Wrongful Death, Appeals.

See Professional Biographies, RALEIGH, NORTH CAROLINA

Tracy, Philip R. ....'42 '67 C.546 B.A. L.273 LL.B. [Ⓒ Smith,A.B.D.M.&J.]
Trahos, Elizabeth Carr, (BV) ....'72 '97 C&L.692 B.A., J.D. [Holt Y.M.&H.]
Trathen, Marcus W., (AV) ....'65 '90 C&L.575 B.A., J.D. [Brooks,P.M.H.&L.] ⊙
Trehy, Jerome P., Jr., (AV) ....'57 '83 C.228 B.A. L.575 J.D. [Ⓒ Twiggs,B.S.&R.]
Tripp, David A. '44 '69 C.1365 A.B. L.245 J.D.
(adm. in GA; not adm. in NC) P.O. Box 29502
Trippe, Melissa L., (AV) ....'59 '86 C.576 B.A. L.574 J.D. Asst. Atty. Gen.
Trivette, Robert P., (BV) '56 '89 C.999 B.A. L.575 J.D.
[Ⓐ Vandeventer B.] (⊙Kitty Hawk, NC; Norfolk, VA)
Trott, William M., (AV) ....'46 '71 C&L.575 A.B., J.D. [Young M.&H.]
Trotter, James R., (AV) ....'23 '53 C&L.575 B.S., J.D. 887 Washington Street‡

Troutman Sanders LLP, (AV)
434 Fayetteville Street Mall, Two Hannover Square Suite 1100, 27601 ⊙
Telephone: 919-212-4100 Fax: 919-212-4101
Email: info@troutmansanders.com URL: http://www.troutmansanders.com
Partners: F. Brian Schneiderman (Not admitted in NC); Ashley H. Story (Board Certified Specialist in Business and Bankruptcy Law, North Carolina State Board of Legal Specialization). Associates: John D. Bristow; Benjamin P. Fisher; Albert Chen-Huei Hwang; Kevin G. Meeks. Of Counsel: Ann H. Stuart.
Alternative Dispute Resolution, Bankruptcy, Commercial Development and Real Estate Investments, Commercial Leasing, Community Association Law, Compensation and Employee Benefits, Complex Litigation, Construction, Corporate and Securities, Energy, Environmental and Natural Resources, Financial Institutions, Governmental, Government Business Transactions, Healthcare, International, Labor and Employment, Lending and Structured Finance, Media and Entertainment, Multifamily Housing, Nuclear Regulation, Products Liability, Project Development and Finance, Public Finance, Real Estate Finance, Special Investigations, Tax, Technology and Intellectual Property, Technology and Intellectual Property Litigation, Telecommunications and E-Commerce, Tort Liability, Transportation, Trusts and Estates.
Atlanta, Georgia Office: 600 Peachtree Street, NE, Suite 5200, Atlanta, GA 30308-2216. Telephone: 404-885-3000. Facsimile: 404-885-3900.
Washington, D.C. Office: 401 Ninth Street, N.W., Suite 1000, Washington, D.C. 20004-2134. Telephone: 202-274-2950. Facsimile: 202-274-2994.
Richmond, Virginia Office: Troutman Sanders Building, 1001 Haxall Point, Richmond, VA 23219. Telephone: 804-697-1200. Facsimile: 804-697-1339.
Other Richmond, Virginia Office: 500 Libbie Avenue, Richmond, VA 23226. Telephone: 804-697-1200. Facsimile: 804-288-8366.
McLean Virginia Office: 1660 International Drive, Suite 600, McLean, VA 22102. Telephone: 703-734-4334. Facsimile: 703-734-4340.
Norfolk, Virginia Office: 150 West Main Street, Suite 1600, Norfolk, VA 23510. Telephone: 757-687-7700. Facsimile: 757-687-7701.
Virginia Beach, Virginia Office: 222 Central Park Avenue, Suite 2000, Virginia Beach, VA 23462. Telephone: 757-687-7500. Facsimile: 757-687-7510.
New York, New York Office: The Chrysler Building, 405 Lexington Avenue, New York, NY 10174. Telephone: 212-704-6000. Facsimile: 212-704-6288.
Hong Kong Office: Suite 3403 Two Exchange Square, 8 Connaught Place, Central, Hong Kong. Telephone: 011-852-2533-7888. Facsimile: 011-852-2533-7898.
London, England Office: Regina House, 6th Floor, 5 Queen Street, EC4N 1SW, London. Telephone: +44 (0) 20 7038 6650. Fax: +44 (0) 20 7038 6651.

See Professional Biographies, RALEIGH, NORTH CAROLINA

Trustman, Lauren R. ....'74 '01 C.103 B.A. L.575 J.D. [Ⓐ Jernigan]
Tucker, Donald H., Jr., (AV) ....'59 '84 C.228 B.A. L.575 J.D. [Smith,A.B.D.M.&J.]
Tucker, Linda W. ....'— '81 C.446 B.S. L.228 J.D. N.C. Legal Edu. Asst. Foundation
Tucker, Marc C. ....'— '97 C.94 B.A. L.215 J.D. [Ⓐ Smith M.]
Tung, Jennifer J. ....'— '05 C.813 B.A. L.1565 J.D. [Ⓐ Hunton&W.]
Turlington, J. Edwin, (AV) ....'57 '82 C.228 B.A. L.575 J.D. [Brooks,P.M.H.&L.] ⊙
Turlington, John E. ....'57 '82 C.228 B.A. L.575 J.D. P.O. Box 1800
Turner, Seth C. ....'80 '05 C&L.575 B.A., J.D. [Ⓐ Millberg,G.&S.]
Turrentine Group, The, P.L.L.C. .... P.O. Box 61082
Tuttle, Jason N. ....'73 '00 C.576 B.A. L.574 J.D. [Ⓐ Stratas&W.]
Twiddy, Kathryn Ficklin, (BV) ....'— '89 C&L.575 B.A., J.D. Misys Healthcare
Twiggs, Howard F., (AV) ....'32 '57 C&L.896 B.S., J.D. [Twiggs,B.S.&R.]

Twiggs, Beskind, Strickland & Rabenau, P.A., (AV)
Wachovia Capitol Center, 150 Fayetteville Street Mall, Suite 1100, P.O. Drawer 30, 27602-0030
Telephone: 919-828-4357 Fax: 919-833-7924
Email: nctrial@nctrial.com URL: http://www.nctrial.com
Howard F. Twiggs; Donald H. Beskind; Donald R. Strickland; Karen M. Rabenau. Of Counsel: Jerome P. Trehy, Jr.
Personal Injury, Products Liability, Business Torts, Medical and other Professional Negligence, Federal and State Tort Claims, Environmental Torts, Insurance Bad Faith, Aviation Law and Wrongful Death.

See Professional Biographies, RALEIGH, NORTH CAROLINA

Tyler, J. Robert, III ....'61 '89 C&L.692 B.S., J.D. [Hutchison&M.]
Tyndall, Jessica C. ....'77 '02 C.228 A.B. L.692 J.D. [Ⓐ Ragsdale L.]
Tyson, John M., (BV) ....'53 '80 C.953 B.A. L.1228 J.D. Court of Appeals J.
Ullman, Charles R., (CV) ....'68 '93 C.1228 B.A. L.575 J.D. [C.R.Ullman&Assoc.]

Ullman, Charles R., & Associates, (CV)
109 South Bloodworth Street, 27601
Telephone: 919-829-1006 Facsimile: 919-829-1078
Email: cullman@nc.rr.com
Charles R. Ullman.

(This Listing Continued)

Ullman, Charles R., & Associates (Continued)

Family Law, Adoptions, Child Custody, Child Support, Divorce, Domestic Violence, Premarital Agreements, Spousal Support, Alimony, Equitable Distribution, Property Division.

See Professional Biographies, RALEIGH, NORTH CAROLINA

Underwood, Mallory T., (BV) .... '71 '95 C.790 B.S. L.896 J.D. [Teague,C.D.&G.]
Underwood, Robert L., III, (BVⓉ) '46 '73 C.576 B.A. L.575 J.D.
(adm. in DC; not adm. in NC) [Underwood&R.] (⊙Orlando, FL; Lexington, KY)

Underwood & Roberts, PLLC, (BVⓉ)
A Professional Limited Liability Company Including A Professional Association
4000 Westchase Boulevard, Suite 410, 27607 ⊙
Telephone: 919-664-8803 Fax: 919-664-8975
Email: runderwood@rlulaw.com URL: http://www.rlulaw.com
Robert L. Underwood, III (Not admitted in NC); Jeffery G. Roberts. Of Counsel: Carl A. Bertoch (Not admitted in NC); David S. Cohen; Shannon L. Evans (Resident, Las Vegas, Nevada Office). Associates: Lincoln H. Jones (Not admitted in NC); Eric E. Pridgen.
Federal Taxation, Automobile Dealership Law, Business Negotiation and Planning, Estate Planning, Business Transactions.
Las Vegas, Nevada Office: 3230 S. Buffalo, Suite 108, 89117. Telephone: 702-699-7333. Fax: 702-699-7377.
Orlando, Florida Office: 5728 Major Boulevard, Suite 550, 32819. Telephone: 407-354-3420. Fax: 407-354-3840.
Lexington, Kentucky Office: 175 East Main Street, Suite 200, 40507. Telephone: 800-686-1615.

See Professional Biographies, RALEIGH, NORTH CAROLINA

Unti, Michael Lee, (AV) .... '50 '81 C&L.902 B.A., J.D. [Unti&L.]
Unti & Lumsden LLP, (AV) .... 4020 Westchase Boulevard, Suite 465
Vakani, S. Halle .... '72 '00 C.038 B.A. L.029 LL.B. [Ⓐ Wyrick R.Y.&P.]
Valois, Robert A., (AV) .... '38 '72 C.472 B.B.A. L.896 J.D. [Maupin T.]
Van Arnam, Robert C. .... '66 '02 C.216 B.A. L.577 J.D. [Ⓐ Hunton&W.]
Vanderberry, J. Greer, Jr. .... '72 '01 C.575 B.A. L.896 J.D. [Cranfill,S.&H.]
VanDerweert, Susan J. .... '— '02 C.489 B.A. L.575 J.D. [Ⓐ Hedrick E.G.&K.]

Vandeventer Black LLP, (AV)
Two Hannover Square, Suite 1530, 434 Fayetteville Street Mall, P.O. Box 2599, 27602-2599 ⊙
Telephone: 919-754-1171 Fax: 919-754-1317
Email: dferrell@vanblkral.com URL: http://www.vanblk.com
Partners: G. William Birkhead; Dean T. Buckius; Patrick A. Genzler; Richard S. Guy; Patrick W. Herman; Daniel D. Khoury (Partner, Kitty Hawk/Roanoke Island Offices) (Board Certified Specialists in Real Property Law-Business, Commercial and Industrial Transactions); Neil S. Lowenstein; Robert L. O'Donnell; Edward J. Powers; Norman W. Shearin, Jr. (Resident Partner, Kitty Hawk, North Carolina Office) (Board Certified Specialist in Real Property Law- Business, Commercial and Industrial Transactions, North Carolina State Board of Legal Specialization). Associates: Wyatt M. Booth; David P. Ferrell; Terry C. Frank (Resident, Kitty Hawk, North Carolina Office); Robert P. Trivette.
General Civil Practice and General Litigation in State and Federal Courts, Trials and Appeals, Civil and Business Litigation, Public Utilities, Landline and Mobile Communications, Corporation, Cooperative, Non-profit Organizations, Mediation, Administrative, Social Security Disability (Raleigh office only), Admiralty, Arbitration and Mediation, Aviation, Banking, Bankruptcy and Creditors' Rights, Commercial Transactions, Community Associations, Construction Law, Environmental Law, Estate Planning, General Litigation in State and Federal Courts, Government/Public Contracts, Health Care Law, Immigration Law, International, Intellectual Property, Insurance Defense, Labor and Employment Law, Land Use, Local Government/Municipal Law, Malpractice, Maritime, Mergers and Acquisitions, Products Liability, Public Utilities, Real Estate, Taxation, Technology, Workers' Compensation.
Norfolk, Virginia Office: 500 World Trade Center, 23510-1699. Telephone: 757-446-8600. Telecopier: 757-446-8670.
Richmond, Virginia Office: Eighth & Main Building, 707 East Main Street, P.O. Box 1558, 23218-1558. Telephone: 804-237-8800. Fax: 804-237-8801.
Kitty Hawk, North Carolina Office: Southern Shores Law Building, 6 Juniper Trail, P.O. Box 1042, 27949 (Dare Co.). Telephone: 252-261-5055. Fax: 252-261-8444.
Roanoke Island, North Carolina Office: 305 Essex Square, Sir Walter Raleigh Street. Telephone: 252-473-1888. Fax: 252-261-5374.
London, England Office: Blackwell House, 23 Guildhall Yard, EC2V 5AE. Telephone: 011 44 020 7917 6053. Facsimile: 011 44 020 7917 6054.

See Professional Biographies, RALEIGH, NORTH CAROLINA

vanDusen, Theron McK., (BV) '57 '91
C.659 B.A. L.228 J.D. [Maupin T.] (⊙Research Triangle Park)
Vann, James R., (AV) .... '63 '92 C.1228 B.A. L.192 J.D. [Vann&S.]

Vann & Sheridan, LLP, (AV)
1720 Hillsborough Street, Suite 200, 27605
Mailing Address: P.O. Box 2445, Raleigh, NC 27602-2445
Telephone: 919-510-8585 Fax: 919-510-8570
URL: http://www.vannattorneys.com
James R. Vann; Paul A. Sheridan;—Nancy Edmunds Hannah; Paige Chandler; James W. Sprouse, Jr.; Gilbert W. File, IV. Of Counsel: David R. Cockman.
Business and Civil Litigation practice, Commercial Collections, Estate Planning and Wills, Construction Law, Creditor Rights.

See Professional Biographies, RALEIGH, NORTH CAROLINA

Vanore, Andrew A., (AV) .... '38 '63 C&L.575 A.B., LL.B. Chf. Dep. Atty. Gen.
Vaughan, Charles, III .... '77 '05 C&L.575 B.A., J.D. [Ⓐ Ragsdale L.]
Vaughn, K. Matthew, (BV) .... '68 '93 C.575 B.S. L.846 J.D. [Everett,G.H.&S.]
Veasey, Westray Bunn, (AV) .... '68 '95 C.575 B.A. L.896 J.D. 2324 Lake Drive
Venable, David W. .... '71 '96 C&L.575 B.A., J.D. [D.Venable]
Venable, Jennifer .... '— '96 C.945 B.A. L.575 J.D. Corp. Atty., Red Hat, Inc.
Venable, David .... P.O. Box 2984
Verdon, Jane K. .... '43 '92 C.93 B.A. L.1049 J.D. [J.K.Verdon]
Verdon, J K, Attorney at Law .... 514 Daniels St., Ste. 181
Vernon, Eric A., (AV) .... '52 '80 C.198 B.A. L.575 J.D. [Wyrick R.Y.&P.]
Vesel, David A. '59 '88 C.1044 B.A. L.978 J.D.
(adm. in NJ; not adm. in NC) 8212 Creedmoor Rd., Ste. 101
Vick, Brian C. .... '72 '02 C.881 B.A. L.280 J.D. [Ⓐ Ellis&W.] (⊙Cary)
Vick, Larry D. '52 '77 C.103 B.S. L.705 J.D.
(adm. in NJ; not adm. in NC) 105 Dartmouth Rd.★
Vilas, Mary C., (BV) .... '56 '88 C.999 B.A. L.575 J.D. 2017 Nancy Ann Dr.
Vincent, Peggy S., (BV) .... '51 '88 C.502 B.S. L.575 J.D. [Howard,S.F.&H.]
Vinson, Robin Kenton, (AV) .... '54 '79 C&L.896 B.A., J.D. [Smith,A.B.D.M.&J.]
Vitale, Lorion Macrae .... '70 '95 C.683 B.A. L.896 J.D. [Cheshire,P.S.B.&V.]
Vitek, Richard P. .... '60 '85 C.813 B.S. L.477 J.D. [Myers B.S.&S.] (See Pat. Sect.)
Voight, Victoria L. .... '55 '80 C.575 B.A. L.896 J.D. P.O. Box 629
Voltz, Elizabeth W. .... '— '99 C.296 A.B. L.575 J.D. [Weatherspoon&V.]
Vtipil, David E., (BV) .... '66 '93 C.896 B.A. L.1345 J.D. [Younce,V.&B.]
Wagner, David E. .... '— '00 C.575 B.A. L.790 J.D. [Ⓐ Kennedy C.L.&H.]

Wake Traffic Center
107 Fayetteville Street Mall Suite 210, 27601
Telephone: 919.833.6388 Toll Free: 866-456-traffic Fax: 919-838-5299
URL: http://www.traffic-dwi.com
Anthony M. Brannon; Robert J. Lane, III.
Driving While Intoxicated, Traffic Violations, Automobile Accidents and Injuries.

See Professional Biographies, RALEIGH, NORTH CAROLINA

Walczyk, Christine M. .... '71 '95 C.93 B.S. L.575 J.D. [Grafstein&W.]
Walden, Gerald L., Jr. .... '74 '01 C.1378 B.A. L.574 J.D. North Carolina Ct. of App.
Waldorf, Angela S., (BV) .... '54 '79 C.576 B.A. L.575 J.D. Gen. Coun.
Wall, Ann B. .... '53 '78 C.471 B.A. L.575 J.D. Dir., State Dept. of Labor
Wall, F. Marshall, (BV) .... '74 '99 C.575 A.B. L.1228 J.D. [Cranfill,S.&H.]
Wall, Joseph E., (AV) .... '45 '72 C.228 A.B. L.575 J.D. [Jordan P.W.G.J.&C.]
Wall, Karen M. .... '60 '98 C.240 B.A. L.574 J.D. Gen. Coun., INC Research, Inc.
Wallace, Amy S. .... '75 '03 C.62 B.A. L.575 J.D. [Ⓐ Smith,A.B.D.M.&J.]
Wallace, J. Gregory, (BV) .... '48 '73 C.437 B.A. L.575 J.D. [Monroe,W.&W.]
Wallace, John R., (AV) .... '51 '76 C.575 B.A. L.260 J.D. [Wallace,N.&S.]
Wallace, Nordan & Sarda, L.L.P., (AV) .... Suite 240, 3605 Glenwood Avenue
Wallace-Smith, Sandra .... '56 '91 C&L.107 B.A., J.D. 217 W. Jones St.
Waller, Carolyn A. .... '68 '98 C.112 B.A. L.575 J.D. [Ⓐ Tharrington S.]
Walling McCray, Gena ...... '70 '03 C&L.790 B.A., J.D. 3200 Beechleaf Court., Suite 100
Wallis, Diane A., (BV) .... '44 '82 C.882 L.228 LL.B. [Wallis&M.]
Wallis, Kimberly Ann .... '69 '95 C.576 B.A. L.896 J.D. [Gailor,W.&H.]
Wallis & Morton, P.A., (BV) .... 8382 Six Forks Road, Suite 200
Walston, Martha K., (AV) .... '51 '76 C&L.575 A.B., J.D. Sr. Fiscal Analyst
Ward, Acie L., (BV) .... '43 '75 C.452 B.S. L.574 J.D. Asst. Atty. Gen.
Ward, David D., (AV) .... '50 '75 C&L.896 B.A., J.D. [Cranfill,S.&H.]
Ward, David L., Jr., (AV) .... '— '62 C.575 B.S. L.228 J.D. [Ward&S.] (⊙New Bern)
Ward, Frank P., Jr., (AV) .... '44 '71 C.976 A.B. L.228 J.D. [Maupin T.]
Ward, Henry C. .... '78 '05 C.576 B.S. L.575 J.D. [Ⓐ Wyrick R.Y.&P.]
Ward, Henry V., Jr. .... '49 '76 C.575 A.B. L.896 J.D. 4401 Creedmoor Rd.

Ward and Smith, P.A., (AV)
Suite 2400, Two Hannover Square, Fayetteville Street Mall, P.O. Box 2091, 27602-2091 ⊙
Telephone: 919-836-4260 Facsimile: 919-836-4277
Email: wardsmith@wardandsmith.com URL: http://www.wardandsmith.com
William Joseph Austin, Jr.; Albert R. Bell, Jr.; Stuart B. Dorsett (Board Certified Specialist in Estate Planning and Probate Law, North Carolina State Board of Legal Specialization); Donalt J. Eglinton; A. Charles Ellis; William R. Lathan, Jr.; Samuel H. Poole; E. Knox Proctor V; Gary J. Rickner; Jeremy R. Sayre; David L. Ward, Jr.; Kenneth R. Wooten.
General and Trial Practice. Admiralty Law; Bankruptcy; Banks and Banking; Business Law; Civil Rights; Commercial Law; Construction Law; Contracts; Copyrights; Corporate Law; Debtor and Creditor; Elder Law; Eminent Domain; Employee Benefits; Environmental Law; Family Law including Divorce; Finance; Franchise Law; Government; Government Contracts; Health Care Law; Immigration and Naturalization; Insurance; International Law; International Trade; Investments; Labor and Employment including Discrimination, Sexual Harassment, and Workers' Compensation; Landlord and Tenant; Litigation; Personal Injury including Automobile Accidents, Legal Malpractice and Medical Malpractice; Products Liability; Real Estate; Securities; Taxation; Technology and Science including Internet Law, Trademarks, and Patents; Trusts and Estates including Estate Planning and Wills and Probate; Zoning and Land Use.
Barnhill Contracting Company; Chubb Insurance; Daedong-USA, Inc.; First-Citizens Bank & Trust Company; First Flight Federal Credit Union; Fountain Powerboats, Inc.; NC State Firemen's Association; Potash Corp.; State of North Carolina; Weyerhaeuser Co.
New Bern, North Carolina Office: 1001 College Court, P.O. Box 867. Telephone: 252-672-5400. Facsimile: 252-672-5400.
Greenville, North Carolina Office: 120 West Fire Tower Road, P.O. Box 8088. Telephone: 252-215-4000. Facsimile: 252-215-4077.
Wilmington, North Carolina Office: University Corporate Center, 127 Racine Drive, P.O. Box 7068. Telephone: 910-794-4800. Facsimile: 910-794-4877.

See Professional Biographies, RALEIGH, NORTH CAROLINA

Warner, Kirk G., (AV) .... '58 '83 C.608 B.S. L.851 J.D. [Smith,A.B.D.M.&J.]
Warren, Scott W. .... '62 '87 C.575 B.A. L.896 J.D. Wake Co. Attorney's Off.

Washburn, Jeanne H., (BV) '— '94 C.575 B.A. L.1228 J.D.
3737 Glenwood Avenue, Suite 100, 27612
Telephone: 919-821-7555 Fax: 919-573-1893
Email: jwshbrn@aol.com URL: http://www.washburn-law.com
Language: Spanish.
Civil Litigation, Personal Injury, Automobile Accidents and Injuries, Wrongful Death, Medical Malpractice, Workers Compensation.

See Professional Biographies, RALEIGH, NORTH CAROLINA

Washburn, Michael W. .... '63 '93 C.198 B.A. L.1345 P.O. Box 1729
Washington, J. Yancey .... '76 '01 C.301 B.A. L.1228 J.D. [Ⓐ Rose R.] ⊙
Waters, Marvin R. .... '53 '93 C.999 B.A. L.574 J.D. 1505 Mail Service Ctr.
Waters, Rebecca A., (BV) .... '61 '87 C.198 B.A. L.575 J.D. Asst. Dist. Atty.
Watford, Yvonne V., (BV) .... '48 '81 C.518 B.A. L.912 J.D. Asst. U.S. Atty.
Watkins, Anita Stephenson '— '00
C.576 B.A. L.577 J.D. NC Dept. of Envir. & Nat. Resources
Watkins, James B. '50 '77 C.804 B.S. L.910 J.D.
(adm. in MO; not adm. in NC)
V.P. & Reg. Gen. Coun., Centex Homes Mid-Atlantic Region
Watkins, Reginald L. .... '51 '75 C.576 B.A. L.575 J.D. Sr. Dep. Atty. Gen.
Watson, Georg-Ann .... '46 '88 C.790 B.A. L.575 J.D. State Gen. Assembly
Watson, Louis Sam, Jr. .... '62 '92 C.576 B.S. L.128 J.D. Staff Atty.
Watson, Stacie S. .... '— '97 C.864 B.S. L.37 J.D. [Ⓒ Francis&A.]
Watts, Alissa A. .... '67 '01 C.128 B.S.N. L.575 J.D. [Ⓐ Yates,M.&W.]
Waylett, Kathleen M. ...... '54 '85 C.1044 B.A. L.575 J.D. Asst. Atty. Gen., Dept. of Jus.
Weathers, W. Samuel, (BV) .... '58 '83 C.575 B.A. L.1228 J.D. 720 W. Hargett St.
Weatherspoon, William H., Jr., (BV) '63 '88 C.198 A.B. L.575 J.D.
[Weatherspoon&V.]
Weatherspoon & Voltz LLP, (BV) .... 612 W. Lane Street
Weaver, Gaines M. .... '70 '95 C.575 B.A. L.16 J.D. 1 S. Wilmington St.
Weaver, Jennifer L. .... '71 '01 C.788 B.A. L.228 J.D. [Ⓐ Manning,F.&S.]
Weaver, Katie J. .... '— '04 C.575 B.A. L.1228 J.D. [Cranfill,S.&H.]
Weaver, Kurt D., (AVⓉ) .... '61 '87 C.317 A.B. L.602 J.D. [Womble C.S.&R.]
Weaver, Margaret Lynne .... '67 '92 C.228 A.B. L.309 J.D. Asst. Atty. Gen.
Weaver, Reagan Hale, (AV) .... '51 '84 C&L.575 B.A., J.D. [Capitol D.]
Webb, Camden R., (AV) .... '70 '95 C.692 B.A. L.575 J.D. [Maupin T.]
Webb, John .... '26 '53 C.575 L.178 LL.B. [Webb&W.]
Webb, Mary McHugh, (BV) ...... '66 '92 C.575 B.A. L.1228 J.D. [Patterson,D.C.B.&A.]
Webb, Virginia Dockery .... '72 '97 C.575 B.A. L.896 J.D. [Ⓐ Edmisten&W.]
Webb, William A., (BVⓉ) '43 '74 C&L.184 B.S., J.D.
(adm. in PA; not adm. in NC) U.S. Magistrate Judge
Webb, William D., II, (BV) .... '62 '89 C&L.575 B.A., J.D. [Webb&W.]
Webb, William Woodward, (AV) .... '45 '71 C.813 B.A. L.575 J.D. [Edmisten&W.]
Webb, William Woodward, Jr., (BV) .... '70 '99 C.575 B.A. L.692 J.D. [Edmisten&W.]
Webb & Webb, (BV) .... 19 West Hargett Street
Webbink, Mark H., (BV) '50 '94
C.679 B.A. L.574 J.D. Sr. V.P. & Gen. Coun., Red Hat, Inc.
Webster, J. Aldean, III, (AV) '57 '81
C.228 B.A. L.896 J.D. 3101 Glenwood Avenue, Suite 200
Weddington, Michael E., (AV) ..... '41 '73 C.260 B.S. L.228 J.D. [Smith,A.B.D.M.&J.]
Weeks, Ryan C. .... '65 '91 C.577 B.A. L.1228 J.D. Surety Land Title
Weese, Elizabeth J. .... '58 '89 C.896 B.A. L.575 J.D. Atty. Gen. Off.
Wehner, Erica A. .... '79 '04 C&L.352 B.A., J.D. [Ⓐ W.L.Sheffield,III]
Weisel, Michael L., (AV) .... '57 '80 C.296 B.S. L.1345 J.D. [Ⓒ Taylor,P.R.&R.]
Welborn, Judson A., (BV) .... '73 '98 C.575 B.A. L.1228 J.D. [Manning,F.&S.]

Welch, Edwin W. .... '43 '68 C.428 B.S. L.896 J.D. Spec. Dep. Atty. Gen.
Wellman, Jacob H. .... '77 '02 C.575 B.A. L.896 J.D. [A Teague,C.D.&G.]
Wellons, Robert Shawn .... '68 '95 C.228 A.B. L.896 J.D. [Wellons]

Wellons Law Firm, The
One Exchange Plaza, Suite 730, 27601
Telephone: 919-834-2712 Fax: 919-834-2713
Email: swellons@wellonslaw.com URL: http://www.wellonslawfirm.com
Member of Firm: Robert Shawn Wellons.
Corporate Law, Taxation, Employment Law, Family Law, Estate Planning, Estate Administration.
See Professional Biographies, RALEIGH, NORTH CAROLINA

Wells, Brady W., (BV) .... '65 '91 C&L.575 B.A., J.D. [Cranfill,S.&H.]
West, Christopher Mitchell .... '70 '00 C.232 B.S. L.645 J.D. [A Yates,M.&W.]
West, James P. .... '65 '91 C.659 B.A. L.575 J.D. [West]
West, Thomas R., (AV) .... '54 '80 C.575 B.A. L.228 J.D. [Poyner&S.]

West Law Offices, P.C.
Suite 1735, Two Hannover Square, 434 Fayetteville Street Mall, 27601
Telephone: 919-856-8800 Fax: 919-856-8801
Email: jpwest@westlawpc.com URL: http://www.westlawpc.com
James P. West.
Utility Law, Estate Planning, Business and Employment Law.
See Professional Biographies, RALEIGH, NORTH CAROLINA

Westbrook, Margaret Rose, (BV) .....'— '96 C&L.575 B.A., J.D. [A Kennedy C.L.&H.]
Wetherill, Susan Evans .... '67 '92 C.198 B.A. L.896 J.D. 2500 1st Union Capitol Ctr.
Wetsch, Laura J. .... '59 '85 C&L.585 B.A., J.D. [C J.L.Davis&Assoc.]
Weyher, Barbara B., (AV) .... '52 '78 C&L.575 B.A., J.D. [Yates,M.&W.]
Wharton, V. Lane, Jr., (AV) .... '47 '74 C.808 B.A. L.145 J.D. [Bode,C.&S.]
Wheaton, Craig B., (AV) .... '— '81 C.893 B.A. L.896 J.D. [Kilpatrick S.]
Whichard, Willis P. .... '40 '65 C&L.575 A.B., J.D. Assoc. Supm. Ct. Jus.
Whitaker, Joshua M. .... '76 '03 C.576 B.A. L.1228 J.D. 2032 Simpkins Road
Whitaker, Thomas S. .... '48 '74 C.125 A.B. L.896 J.D. N.C. Employ. Sec. Comm.
White, A. Bartlett, (BV) .... '54 '81 C.885 B.A. L.692 J.D. [Hatch,L.&B.]
White, James R. .... '75 '00 C.575 B.A. L.896 J.D. [A Nodell,G.&H.]
White, Katherine R., (AV) '49 '76 C.289 B.A. L.446 J.D.
Information Protection Consultant, Off. of Tech. Services, N.C. Gov.'s Office
White, Nancy P., (BV) .... '60 '87 C.575 B.A. L.574 J.D. [White&S.]

White & Stradley, LLP, (BV)
3105 Charles B. Root Wynd, 27612
Telephone: 919-844-0400 Fax: 919-845-9745 Toll-Free: 888-666-2446 URL: http://www.injurednc.com
URL: http://www.whiteandstradleylaw.com
Nancy P. White; J. David Stradley. Associate: Caryn Madison.
Personal Injury Litigation, Workers Compensation, Sports Agency Law, Sports Law, Products Liability, Medical Malpractice, Wrongful Death, Dog Bites, Automobile Accidents and Injuries.
See Professional Biographies, RALEIGH, NORTH CAROLINA

Whiteman, Andrew O., (AV) .... '55 '80 C.473 B.S. L.608 J.D. [Hartzell&W.]
Whitener, Claud R., III .... '48 '77 C.1309 B.S. L.574 J.D. Asst. Atty. Gen.
Whiteside, Dorothy Thompson ..... '54 '78 C.112 B.A. L.575 J.D. Admin. Off. of the Cts.
Whitford, Elaine M. .... '64 '89 C&L.575 B.A., J.D. [C Womble C.S.&R.]
Whitley, Benjamin H. .... '77 '03 C.575 B.A. L.356 J.D. [A Whitley,R.&W.]
Whitley, Robert E., (AV) '49 '74 C.232 B.S.B.A. L.896 J.D.
[Whitley,R.&W.] (☉Greenville, Jacksonville, Kinston)
Whitley, Rodgman & Whitley, (AV)
3605 Glenwood Avenue, Suite 350 (☉Greenville, Jacksonville, Kinston, New Bern)
Whitlock, J. Allan .... '51 '84 C.575 A.B. L.1209 J.D. 5834 Faringdon Place
Whitman, Lee M., (AV) .... '68 '93 C.602 B.A. L.575 J.D. [Wyrick R.Y.&P.]
Whitman, Mebane R. .... '68 '93 C.893 B.A. L.575 J.D. 2312 Fairview Road
Whitmeyer, Randall M. .... '63 '91 C.228 B.S. L.597 J.D. [Hutchison&M.]
Whitney, Frank D., (BV) .... '59 '87 C.896 B.A. L.575 J.D. U.S. Atty.
Whitson, Mark A., (BV) .... '65 '96 C&L.575 B.A., J.D. [A Maupin T.]★
Whitt, Samuel W. .... '63 '91 C.101 B.S. L.1209 J.D. [C Sanford H.]
Whittle, Daniel J. .... '62 '89 C.880 B.A. L.174 J.D. 2500 Blue Ridge Rd., Ste. 330
Wicker, Dennis A., (AV) .... '52 '78 C.575 B.A. L.896 J.D. [Helms M.&W.]
Wicker, Julia R. .... '77 '03 C&L.896 B.A., J.D. [A Wyrick R.Y.&P.]
Wicker, Robert A., (AV) .... '44 '69 C&L.575 A.B., J.D. [Helms M.&W.]
Wickham, Douglas Q. .... '41 '66 C&L.976 B.A., LL.B. [Hatch,L.&B.]
Wike, Antoinette R., (AV) '45 '74
C.296 A.B. L.575 J.D. Chf. Coun., North Carolina Utilities Comm.
Wiles, John Keating .... '50 '95 C.613 B.M. L.575 J.D. [Cheshire,P.S.B.&V.]
Wilke, David L. .... '67 '97 C.339 B.A. L.813 J.D. [Wyrick R.Y.&P.]
Wilkerson, Katherine B., (BV) .... '67 '92 C.788 A.B. L.575 J.D. [Lynch&E.]
Wilkins, Charles P., (AV) .... '44 '69 C&L.575 A.B., J.D. [Broughton W.S.&T.]
Wilkinson, Anne T. .... '58 '86 C.446 B.A. L.228 J.D. Clk. to Assoc. Supm. Ct. Jus.
Willard, Christopher, (BV) .... '66 '92 [Willard&W.]
Willard, Gail Gonya, (BV) .... '67 '92 C.1369 B.A. L.896 J.D. [Willard&W.]
Willard & Willard, L.L.P., (BV) .... 1000 Saint Albans Dr., Ste. 350
Williams, Anthony L. .... '71 '98 C.575 B.A. L.896 J.D. [A Wyrick R.Y.&P.]
Williams, Bradford A. .... '74 '99 C&L.575 B.A., J.D. [A Holt Y.M.&H.]
Williams, Brian M. .... '77 '02 C.575 B.A. L.1228 J.D. [A Yates,M.&W.]

Williams, Edward V., Attorney at Law '62 '99 C.608 B.A. L.574 J.D.
158 Mine Lake Court, Suite 100, 27615
Telephone: 919-844-2847 Fax: 919-844-2874
Email: nclaw@bellsouth.net URL: http://www.evwlaw.com
Traffic Violations, Criminal Law, Driving While Intoxicated, Domestic Violence.
See Professional Biographies, RALEIGH, NORTH CAROLINA

Williams, J. Gaston B. .... '51 '77 C&L.692 B.A., J.D. U.S. Attorney's Off.
Williams, James T., Jr., (AV) ...... '40 '66 C&L.896 B.A., LL.B. [Brooks,P.M.H.&L.] ☉
Williams, Kathryn A. .... '73 '00 C.576 B.A. L.574 J.D. 8382 6 Forks Rd., Ste. 200
Williams, Mary M. .... '73 '99 C.198 B.A. L.575 J.D. [A Wyrick R.Y.&P.]
Williamson, Elizabeth C. .... '— '97 C&L.259 B.S., J.D. [A Kilpatrick S.]
Williamson, John T., (AV) .... '45 '73 C.871 B.S. L.228 J.D. [Maupin T.]
Williford, Joseph W., (AV) .... '56 '81 C&L.896 B.A., J.D. [Young M.&H.]
Willis, Carlton G. .... '63 '93 C&L.575 B.A., J.D. 112 N. Person St.

Willis, Robert J., Law Offices of '53 '79 C.311 B.A. L.575 J.D.
5 West Hargett Street, 27601
Telephone: 919-821-9031 Fax: 919-821-1763
Email: bnorman@jwillis-law.com URL: http://www.rjwillislaw.com
Workers Compensation, Criminal Defense, Driving While Intoxicated, Traffic Violations, Automobile Accidents, Wage and Hour Disputes.
See Professional Biographies, RALEIGH, NORTH CAROLINA

Willoughby, C. Colon, Jr., (AV) .... '51 '79 C.575 B.S. L.1228 J.D. Dist. Atty.
Willson, L. Alfred, Jr. .... '32 '61 C.576 B.M.E. L.273 J.D. 3705 Stonehaven Dr. (Pat.)
Wilson, Bryn D. .... '79 '05 C.477 B.A. L.569 J.D. [A Poyner&S.]
Wilson, Carolyn E. .... '63 '90 C.575 B.A. L.896 J.D. 2204 St. Marys St.‡
Wilson, Donald H., III '46 '77 C.976 A.B. L.309 J.D.
V.P. & Gen. Coun., Endacea, Inc.‡
Wilson, Harry E. .... '46 '73 C&L.575 A.B., J.D. Dept. of Pub. Educ.
Wilson, Heather R. .... '75 '01 C.1128 B.A. L.1228 J.D. [A Patterson,D.C.B.&A.]
Wilson, Jeffrey L., (AV) .... '65 '90 C.575 B.A. L.1228 J.D. [Jenkins,W.&T.] (Pat.) ☉
Wilson, Kimberly R., (CV) .... '69 '95 C&L.923 B.A., J.D. [A Lewis&R.]
Wilson, Robert L., Jr., (AV) .... '54 '81 C.575 A.B. L.896 J.D. [Smith M.]
Wilson, Robert W., Jr., (AV) .... '39 '63 C&L.575 A.B., LL.B. [C Poyner&S.]
Wilson, Sharon Coull .... '64 '91 C.1365 B.S.N. L.896 J.D. U.S. Attorney's Off.
Wilson, Thomas J., (AV) .... '52 '84 C.575 B.S.B.A. L.1228 J.D. [Wilson&R.]

Wilson & Iseman, L.L.P.
(See Winston-Salem)

Wilson, James A.
(See Durham)

Wilson & Ratledge, (AV)
Professional Limited Liability Company
4600 Marriott Drive Suite 400, P.O. Box 31447, 27622
Telephone: 919-787-7711 Fax: 919-787-7710
URL: http://www.wilsonandratledgelaw.com
Thomas J. Wilson; James E. R. Ratledge; Lesley W. Bennett; Heather L. Hawn; Richard Charles Inlow; Perry J. Pelaez; Kristine L. Prati; Paul F. Toland.
Trusts and Estates, Workers Compensation.
See Professional Biographies, RALEIGH, NORTH CAROLINA

Winborne, Paul Faison S., (BV) .... '60 '88 C.1128 B.A. L.574 J.D. [Winborne]
Winborne, Vaughan S. .... '17 '41 C&L.575 B.S., LL.B. 2635 Lakeview Dr.‡
Winborne, Vaughan S., Jr., (BV) .... '58 '86 C.575 B.S. L.574 LL.B. [Winborne]
Winborne Law Office, P.A., (BV) .... P.O. Box 1636
Windham, Alan K. .... '69 '98 C.575 B.A. L.345 J.D. [A Womble C.S.&R.]
Winslow, Edward C., III, (AV) ... '46 '74 C.198 B.A. L.575 J.D. [Brooks,P.M.H.&L.] ☉
Winslow, Everette P. .... '— '97 C.329 B.A. L.352 J.D. [A J.L.Davis&Assoc.]
Winslow, Sarah E. .... '73 '98 C&L.228 B.S., J.D. [A Ragsdale L.]

Winston & Maher
(See Chapel Hill)

Winters, Michael G., (AV) .... '53 '78 C&L.575 B.S., J.D. [Ellis&W.] (☉Cary)
Wisz, David S., (BV) .... '69 '94 C.712 B.B.A. L.383 J.D. [Bailey&D.]
Wisz, Katherine E. Davenport .... '69 '94 C.311 B.A. L.383 J.D. 1305 Navaho Dr.
Wittmer, Cynthia Leigh, (AV) .... '53 '81 C.575 B.A. L.228 J.D. [Parker,P.A.&B.]
Witzel, Corey A. .... '59 '85 C.918 B.A. L.94 J.D. 4101 Lake Boone Trail
Wofford, William N. .... '67 '95 C&L.893 B.A., J.D. [Hutchison&M.]
Wolf, Mitchell A. .... '53 '93 C.575 B.A. L.574 J.D. 309 West Milbrook Road
Wolgin, Neal B. .... '— '99 C.401 B.S. L.575 J.D. [C Kennedy C.L.&H.] (Pat.)
Wolters, Robert M., (AV) '24 '51 C.679 B.S. L.146 J.D.
(adm. in IL; not adm. in NC; Pat.) 8840 Reigate Lane
Womble, Robert B., (AV) .... '— '79 C.896 B.A. L.902 J.D. [Kennedy C.L.&H.]

Womble Carlyle Sandridge & Rice, (AV) BR
A Professional Limited Liability Company
2100 First Union Capitol Center, 150 Fayetteville Street Mall, P.O. Box 831, 27602
☉
Telephone: 919-755-2100 Fax: 919-755-2150
Email: lawyers@wcsr.com URL: http://www.wcsr.com
Members of Firm: Thomas B. Anderson, Jr.; Sean E. Andrussier; Paul H. Billow; John C. Cooke; Susan Davis Crooks; Mark A. Davis; William A. Davis, II; Hampton Y. Dellinger; Donald A. Donadio; Charles A. Edwards; Robert E. Fields III; Marilyn R. Forbes; Christopher T. Graebe; James B. Hunt, Jr.; Sarah Anne Keefe; G. Thomas Lee; Johnny M. Loper; Heather K. Mallard; William C. Matthews, Jr.; Pressly M. Millen; Burley B. Mitchell, Jr.; Jeffrey A. Poley; Alexander P. Sands, III; Robert H. Sasser, III; Nellie K. Shipley; Maury M. Tepper, III; Kurt D. Weaver. Associates: Kimberly Brackett-Jones; Jennifer Long Collins; Kathryn M. Eyster; Douglas W. Hanna; Matthew S. Healey; Beth Tyner Jones; Kelly B. Jones; Matthew K. Lung; Catherine E. Otto; Vidalia Patterson; Garrett R. Perdue; Morgan E. Persinger; Kristen S. Provenza Benko; Melody C. Ray-Welborn; Sheri Roberson; Mary Elizabeth Smith; Theresa M. Sprain; M. Todd Sullivan; Alan K. Windham. Of Counsel: E. Lawrence Davis, III; Peter J. Duffley; Donald R. Esposito, Jr.; Mary Lynne Grigg; Jeffrey M. Hahn; Gwenda L. Laws; Elizabeth LeVan Riley; Elaine M. Whitford. Staff Attorneys: Melissa Dix Donahue; Kimberly S. Justus.
General Civil Practice, Trial and Appellate Litigation. Administrative, Antitrust, Aviation, Banking, Bankruptcy and Creditor's Rights, Bond Financing, Civil Rights, Commercial, Construction, Consumer Lending, Corporate, E-Commerce, Employee Benefits, Environmental, Estate Planning, Family, Government Relations, Health Care, Insurance, Intellectual Property, International, Labor and Employment, Municipal, Negligence, Probate, Product Liability, Real Estate, Retirement Plans, Securities, Taxation, Toxic Tort, Wills and Trusts Law.
Representative Clients: Aetna Casualty and Surety Co., Inc.; ALSCO/AmeriMark Building Products, Inc.; Aoki Corporation America, Inc.; Hackney Brothers, Inc.; Lawyers Mutual Liability Insurance Company of North Carolina; Meredith College; Regency Park Corp.; Wachovia Bank, N.A.
Charlotte, North Carolina Office: 3500 One Wachovia Center, 301 South College Street. Telephone: 704-331-4900. Fax: 704-331-4955.
Winston-Salem, North Carolina Office: One West Fourth Street, 27101. Telephone: 336-721-3600. Fax: 336-721-3660.
Research Triangle Park, North Carolina Office: 2530 Meridian Parkway, Suite 400 (Durham), 27713, P.O. Box 13069, Research Triangle Park, 27709. Telephone: 919-484-2300. Fax: 919-484-2340.
Greensboro, North Carolina Office: 300 North Greene Street. Telephone: 336-574-8030. Fax: 336-574-4520.
Atlanta, Georgia Office: One Atlantic Center, 1201 West Peachtree Street, Suite 3500. Telephone: 404-872-7000. Fax: 404-888-7490.
Other Atlanta, Georgia Office: Suite 404, 2296 Henderson Mill Road, N.E. Telephone: 770-492-9030. Fax: 770-492-9609.
Washington, D.C. Office: Suite 700, 1401 Eye Street. Telephone: 202-857-4400. Fax: 202-467-6910.
Greenville, South Carolina Office: 700 Poinsett Plaza, 104 South Main Street, P.O. Box 10208. Telephone: 864-255-5400. Fax: 864-255-5440.
Tysons Corner, Virginia Office: 8065 Leesburg Pike, Fourth Floor. Telephone: 703-790-3310. Fax: 703-790-2623.
Reviser of the North Carolina Law Digest for this Directory.
See Professional Biographies, RALEIGH, NORTH CAROLINA

Wood, Jason S. .... '71 '00 C.228 B.S. L.893 J.D. [A Wyrick R.Y.&P.]
Wood, T. B. .... '36 '63 C&L.575 A.B., J.D. Asst. Atty. Gen.
Wood, W. Swain .... '— '97 C.276 A.B. L.309 J.D. [A Kilpatrick S.]
Woodard, David L. .... '65 '92 C.576 B.A. L.1228 J.D. [Poyner&S.]
Woodard, Kenneth W. .... '49 '76 C&L.575 A.B., J.D. Staff J. Advocate
Woodlief, Alan D., Jr. .... '69 '94 C.575 B.A. L.1228 J.D. [C Francis&A.]
Woodsmall, Joan .... '54 '81 C.112 B.A. L.61 J.D. 7708 Audubon Dr.‡
Woodson, Stephen A. '64 '89 C.421 B.A. L.896 J.D.
N.C. Farm Bureau Federation, Inc.
Woodward, Dorothy Kibler, (AV) .... '61 '86 C.34 B.S. L.575 J.D. Assoc. City Atty.
Woodward, Thomas M., (CV☉) .... '56 '82 C&L.923 B.A., J.D. P.O. Box 629
Wooten, Kenneth R., (AV) '— '79
C.596 B.A. L.595 J.D. [Ward&S.] (☉Greenville, New Bern)
Wooten, Louis E., III .... '63 '88 C.575 B.A. L.896 J.D. [Everett,G.H.&S.]
Worley, Anna E. .... '71 '96 C&L.896 B.A., J.D. [A Herring M.M.&F.]
Worley, Harriet F., (BV) '48 '89 C.896 B.A. L.1345 J.D.
Asst. Atty. Gen., Atty. Gen. Off.
Worm, Kathleen Nowack .... '60 '91 C.683 B.A. L.245 J.D. [Hutchison&M.]

Worth, Randolph L., (AV) '46 '72 C.575 A.B. L.880 J.D.
3737 Glenwood Avenue, Suite 100, 27612
Mailing Address: P.O. Box 20825, Raleigh, NC 27619-0825
Telephone: 919-573-6163 Fax: 919-573-6064
Email: worthlaw@bellsouth.net
Trusts and Estates, Estate Planning and Administration, Estate Litigation, Guardianship, Wills, Probate, Taxation.

See Professional Biographies, RALEIGH, NORTH CAROLINA

Worth, Thomas C., Jr., (AV) ... '41 '69 C.575 A.B. L.228 J.D. 16 W. Martin St., Suite 700
Wright, Christopher Chance .... '72 '01 C.576 B.A. L.862 J.D. [Wright]
Wright, Donald M., (BV) .... '50 '76 C.575 B.A. L.574 J.D. Asst. Atty. Gen.
Wright, Melvin F., Jr., (AV) '45 '73 C.575 B.S. L.896 J.D.
Exec. Dir., Chf. Jus. Com. on Professionalism
Wright, Victoria S., (BV) .... '56 '94 C.597 B.S.S. L.896 J.D. [Brewer]
Wright Law Firm, The .... 4601 Six Forks Rd., Ste. 500
Wrobel, Alan E. .... '74 '99 C.475 B.A. L.575 J.D. [A Wyrick R.Y.&P.]
Wyche, N. Hunter, Jr., (AV) ..... '51 '80 C&L.1228 B.B.A., J.D. [Smith D.N.W.S.&M.]
Wyman, Roy H., Jr., (BV) '63 '93
C.937 B.A. L.477 J.D. [Maupin T.] (⊙Research Triangle Park)
Wyne, Christopher M., (AV) .... '45 '72 C.976 B.S. L.1066 J.D. [Monroe,W.&W.]
Wynn, James A. .... '54 '79 C.575 B.A. L.893 LL.M. Appl. Ct. J., Ct. of App.
Wyrick, Samuel T., III, (AV) .... '44 '69 C.309 B.A. L.228 J.D. [© Wyrick R.Y.&P.]

Wyrick Robbins Yates & Ponton LLP, (AV)
4101 Lake Boone Trail Suite 300, P.O. Drawer 17803, 27607
Telephone: 919-781-4000 Telecopier: 919-781-4865
Email: info@wyrick.com URL: http://www.wyrick.com
D. Caldwell Barefoot Jr.; Donald L. Beci; Heidi C. Bloom; Stephen C. Brissette; Madison E. Bullard, Jr. (Board Certified Specialist in Estate Planning and Probate Law, North Carolina State Board of Legal Specialization); Lisa K. Canfield; Alyssa M. Chen; Charles W. Clanton; James L.S. Cobb; Thomas H. Cook, Jr.; Michael D. DeFrank; Alexander M. Donaldson; Carolyn M. Dudzik; Christine S. Eatmon; Kenneth E. Eheman, Jr.; Carolyn L. Fitzmorris; James E. Furr, IV; Kelly D. Furr; John M. Fuscoe; Robert E. Futrell, Jr.; John R. Green, Jr.; Lisa D. Inman; Jeffrey J. Johnson; Sarah M. Johnson; Roger Weldon Knight; Emil William Kratt (Board Certified Specialist in Estate Planning and Probate Law, North Carolina State Board of Legal Specialization); Winston P. Lloyd; J. Christopher Lynch; W. David Mannheim; Christine F. Mayhew; Dean M. McCord; D. Donovan Merritt (Board Certified Specialist in Real Property Law: Residential Transactions, North Carolina State Board of Legal Specialization); Jennifer M. Miller; Joseph H. Nanney, Jr.; Robert A. Ponton, Jr. (Board Certified Specialist in Family Law, North Carolina State Board of Legal Specialization); Daniel S. Porper; Donald R. Reynolds; Larry E. Robbins; J. Kemp Sherron, III; Grady L. Shields; Jeffrey M. Smith; Michael D. Tanner; Charlotte L. Tart; Benjamin N. Thompson; L. Diane Tindall; S. Halle Vakani; Eric A. Vernon; Henry C. Ward; Lee M. Whitman; Julia R. Wicker; David L. Wilke; Anthony L. Williams; Mary M. Williams; Jason S. Wood; Alan E. Wrobel; James M. Yates, Jr. Of Counsel: Wiley F. Bowen; John L. Crill; Barbara B. Garlock; K. Edward Greene; Richard A. Rogers, Jr.; Samuel T. Wyrick, III.
Languages: Spanish, French and Gujarati.
Appellate Advocacy, Arbitration, Banking, Bankruptcy and Workouts, Biotechnology, Broker-Dealer/Investment Advisor Compliance and Defense, Business, Commercial Contracts and Litigation, Commercial Real Estate, Communications, Community Associations, Computer, Construction, Copyright Licensing, Litigation and Registration, Corporate, Corporate Finance, Credit Union, Creditors Rights, Elder, Election Law, Employee Benefits, Employment, Entrepreneurial Business Law, Environmental, Estate Planning and Probate, Family Law, Franchise, Government Contracting, Health, Intellectual Property Protection and Licensing, Internet and E-Commerce, Labor, Litigation in all State and Federal Courts, Mediation, Mergers, Acquisitions and Divestitures, Municipal, Partnerships and LLC's, Private Placements, Public Offerings, Securities Arbitrations and Mediations, Securities Law, Strategic Partnerships and Collaborations, Taxation, Tax-Exempt and Non-Profit Organizations, Technology and Venture Capital Law.

See Professional Biographies, RALEIGH, NORTH CAROLINA

Yacono, Judith Anne, (BVⓣ) '50 '79 C.1044 B.S. L.744 J.D.
(adm. in TX; not adm. in NC) [Scarzafava M.]
Yannello, Cheryl Annette .... '47 '81 C.428 B.A. L.607 J.D. [C.A.Yannello]
Yannello, Cheryl A., P.A. .... 7409 Valley Run Dr.

Yarborough Law Office
(See Chapel Hill)

Yates, James M., Jr., (AV) .... '54 '79 C&L.575 B.S., J.D. [Wyrick R.Y.&P.]

Yates, McLamb & Weyher, L.L.P., (AV) BR
One Hannover Square, 421 Fayetteville Street Mall Suite 1200, 27601
Mailing Address: P.O. Box 2889, Raleigh, NC 27602-2889
Telephone: 919-835-0900 Fax: 919-835-0910
URL: http://www.ymwlaw.com
Members of Firm: Joseph W. Yates, III (1944-2002); Barry S. Cobb; John T. Honeycutt; Michael C. Hurley; Dan J. McLamb; John W. Minier; Rodney E. Pettey; Scott A. Scurfield; Barbara B. Weyher. Associates: William T. Kesler, Jr.; Monica Langdon Lee; Jennifer D. Maldonado; Erin D. McNeil; John T. Molleur; James T. Newman, Jr.; Jason D. Newton; Edgar Moore Page; Sean T. Partrick; Richard V. Stevens, III; Samuel G. Thompson, Jr.; Alissa A. Watts; Christopher Mitchell West; Brian M. Williams. Of Counsel: Susan T. Fountain; Julie R. Hurley; Shirley Maring Pruitt.
Trial and Appellate Practice before all State and Federal Courts. Civil Defense Litigation including Medical Malpractice, Legal Malpractice, Pharmaceutical Liability, Construction Litigation, Construction Liability Litigation, Environmental, Personal Injury and Insurance Coverage.

See Professional Biographies, RALEIGH, NORTH CAROLINA

York, C. Allen .... '— '04 C&L.577 B.A., J.D. [A Kennedy C.L.&H.]
York, David L., (BV) .... '63 '89 C.576 B.S. L.1228 J.D. [Holt Y.M.&H.]
York, Guilford Mattern .... '67 '00 C&L.575 B.A., J.D. [A Helms M.&W.]
Younce, Robert C., Jr., (CV) .... '58 '85 C.101 B.S. L.575 J.D. [Younce,V.&B.]
Younce, Vtipil & Bradford, (BV) .... 4300 Six Forks Rd., Ste. 800
Young, Ashley Browning .... '70 '98 C.575 B.A. L.574 J.D. [A Kuniholm]
Young, Claude N., Jr. .... '53 '88 C.575 B.S. L.574 J.D. 9001 Mail Svc Ctr.
Young, Julia M. .... '73 '00 C.576 B.A. L.1228 J.D. [A Burns,D.&P.]
Young, Pamela Thorpe .... '59 '88 C.575 B.A. L.574 J.D. N.C. Indus. Comm.
Young, William D., IV, (BV) .... '63 '91 C.576 B.A. L.574 J.D. [Hatch,L.&B.]

Young Moore and Henderson, P.A., (AV)
3101 Glenwood Avenue, Suite 200, 27612
Mailing Address: P.O. Box 31627, Raleigh, NC 27622
Telephone: 919-782-6860 Telecopier: 919-782-6753
Email: attorney@ymh.com URL: http://www.ymh.com
Charles H. Young, Jr. (1947-1992); Joseph C. Moore, Jr. (1919-1988); B. T. Henderson, II (1928-2000); J. Clark Brewer (Board Certified Specialist in Real Property Law-Residential, Business, Commercial, and Industrial Transactions, North Carolina State Board of Legal Specialization); John N. Fountain; William M. Trott; R. Michael Strickland; William P. Daniell; Robert C. Paschal; Walter E. Brock, Jr.; Joseph W. Williford; Rudy L. Ogburn; Marvin M. Spivey, Jr.; David M. Duke; Joe E. Austin, Jr.; Dana H. Davis; Glenn C. Raynor; Jay P. Tobin; Christopher A. Page; Brian O. Beverly; Jeffrey T. Linder; Reed N. Fountain; Dawn Dillon Raynor;—Josephine R. Darden; Zachary C. Bolen; Alexander R. Atchison; Robert C. de Rosset; Nathan J. Taylor; Jennifer Terry Gottsegen; Michael W. Ballance; *Matthew J. Gray; Anne Elizabeth Croteau; Angela N. Farag; Matthew B. Davis*; Elizabeth P. McCullough; Matthew C. Litz; Elinor Johnsey; Shannon S. Frankel.
General Trial and Appellate Practice before all State and Federal Courts and Agencies. Corporate and Business Law including Litigation of Employment, Franchise, Trade Practices, Antitrust, Tax, Employment Discrimination and Labor. Insurance Law including Litigation of Regulation, Treaties, Suretyship and Bonds, Casualty and Life. Litigation of Environmental, Personal Injury, Professional Liability, Workers Compensation, Products Liability and Commercial Matters. Commercial Real Estate, Estate Planning, Probate and Taxation. Criminal Trials in State and Federal Courts.

See Professional Biographies, RALEIGH, NORTH CAROLINA

Youngman, Julia F., (AV) .... '65 '94 C&L.228 B.S., J.D. [Ellis&W.] (⊙Cary)
Youth, Michael D. .... '74 '00 C&L.575 B.A., J.D. Asst. Attorney General
Zabala, Pedro J., II .... '72 '00 C&L.260 B.A., J.D. [A Smith D.N.W.S.&M.]
Zander, Karin Kirksey '48 '73 C.112 B.A. L.976 J.D.
(adm. in MA; not adm. in NC) P.O. Box 98536‡
Zaytoun, Robert E., (AV) .... '49 '75 C&L.575 A.B., J.D. [Zaytoun&M.P.]

Zaytoun & Miller, PLLC, Law Offices of, (AV)
414 West Jones Street, 27603
Mailing Address: P.O. Box 307, Raleigh, NC 27602-0307
Telephone: 919-832-6690 Fax: 919-831-4793 Email: rzaytoun@zaytoun-miller.com Email: stacymiller@zaytoun-miller.com
URL: http://www.lawyers.com/zaytoun&miller
Robert E. Zaytoun; W. Stacy Miller, II;—Shiloh A. Daum.
Medical Negligence, Catastrophic Personal Injury, Wrongful Deaths, Product Liability, Civil Litigation, Health Care Fraud, Business Crimes, Major Criminal Litigation, Business Torts, Managed Care Litigation and Practice in all State and Federal Courts.

See Professional Biographies, RALEIGH, NORTH CAROLINA

Zechini, Richard A. '70 '97 C.576 B.S. L.902 J.D.
Dir., North Carolina Association of Realtors, Regulatory Affs.
Zeszotarski, Joseph E., Jr., (AV) .... '68 '94 C.529 A.B. L.896 J.D. [Poyner&S.]
Ziko, Thomas J., (AV) .... '53 '78 C.976 B.A. L.228 J.D. Spec. Dep. Atty. Gen.

RAMSEUR, 1,588, *Randolph Co.*

Albright, Benjamin Spence, (BV) .... '53 '85 C.34 B.S.B.A. L.575 J.D. 101 Weatherly Sq.

RED SPRINGS, 3,493, *Robeson Co.*

Griffin, Anthony D., (CV) .... '67 '00 C.1317 B.A. L.1345 J.D. [Griffin]

Griffin Law Office, (CV)
106 South Main Street, 28377
Telephone: 910-843-9600 Fax: 910-843-9701
Email: attorneyanthonydgriffin@yahoo.com URL: http://www.griffinlaw-office.com
Anthony D. Griffin.
Abuse and Neglect, Juvenile Law, Real Estate Transactions, Traffic, Traffic Violations, DWI, Criminal Law, Domestic and Family Law.

See Professional Biographies, RED SPRINGS, NORTH CAROLINA

Harris, J. Gates, (BV) .... '46 '74 C&L.575 A.B., J.D. 119 W. Third Ave.
McManus, James M. .... '29 '59 C.575 B.S. L.904 LL.B. E. 3rd Ave.‡

REIDSVILLE, 14,485, *Rockingham Co.*

Blitzer, Craig M., (BV) .... '65 '95 C.1333 B.S. L.45 J.D. 1509 Freeway Dr., Ste. 2

Deaton, W. Edward, (AV) '41 '70 C&L.575 B.S., J.D.
Suite 230, Wachovia Bank Building, 227 West Morehead Street, P.O. Box 2156, 27320
Telephone: 336-342-5714 Fax: 336-342-5764
General Civil Practice. Real Estate, Probate.
Counsel for: Rockingham County Airport Authority.
Representative Clients: B B & T; Wachovia Bank, N.A.; Commercial & Residential Real Estate; Carolina Farm Credit; FNB Southeast.

Deuterman Law Group, The, P.A.
(See Greensboro)

Farmer, R. Lee, P.L.L.C. Law Offices of
(See Yanceyville)

Farver, H. Craig, (AV) .... '54 '79 C.160 B.S. L.896 J.D. [Farver,S.&M.]
Farver, Skidmore and McDonough, L.L.P., (AV) .... 108 S. Main St.
Glidewell, Powell W., IV .... '69 '99 C.34 B.S. L.1228 J.D. 416 S. Main St.
Griffin, Hugh P., Jr., (AV) .... '26 '52 C&L.575 B.S., J.D. 2600 Flat Rock Rd.
Gwyn, Julius J., (AV) .... '27 '53 C&L.228 A.B., LL.B. [© Farver,S.&M.]
Hester, Hugh S. .... '34 '64 C.575 A.B. L.945 B.C.L. 109 W. Morehead St.
Holt, Clark M., (AV) .... '37 '64 C&L.896 B.A., LL.B. [Holt&W.]

Holt & Watt, (AV)
211 Gilmer Street, P.O. Box 728, 27320
Telephone: 336-342-2997 Fax: 336-342-9158
Email: hwxandra@bellsouth.net
Clark M. Holt; Robert L. Watt, III.
General Practice. Probate and Real Estate.
Representative Clients: Branch Banking & Trust Co. (BB&T); Bank of America; FNB Southeast.
Approved Attorneys for: Lawyers Title Insurance Corp.; Chicago Title Insurance Co.; First American Title Insurance Co.

See Professional Biographies, REIDSVILLE, NORTH CAROLINA

Light, C. Orville
(See Eden)

Maddrey Etringer & Smith, L.L.P.
(See Eden)

McDonough, Darren A. .... '73 '98 C.577 B.A. L.896 J.D. [Farver,S.&M.]
Rankin, Thomas M., (BV) .... '30 '58 C&L.575 A.B., LL.B. 232 Gilmer St.
Ross, Jason E. .... '70 '95 C.369 B.A. L.574 J.D. [J.Ross]
Ross, Jason, Law Office of .... P.O. Box 2523

Schell Bray Aycock Abel & Livingston P.L.L.C.
(See Greensboro)

Skidmore, Scott K., (BV) .... '63 '92 C.1128 B.S. L.192 J.D. [Farver,S.&M.]

Tuggle Duggins & Meschan, P.A.
(See Greensboro)

Watlington, Stuart N.
(See Yanceyville)

Watt, Robert L., III, (AV) .... '46 '74 C.301 B.S. L.575 J.D. [Holt&W.]
Wrenn, Benjamin R., (AV) .... '33 '59 C&L.896 B.A., LL.B. 408 Woodrow St.

RESEARCH TRIANGLE PARK, —, *Durham Co.*

Allen and Pinnix, P.A.
(See Raleigh)

Alston & Bird LLP
(See Raleigh)

Baddour, David B. .... '73 '02 C&L.577 A.B., J.D. [A Womble C.S.&R.]

Bailey & Dixon, L.L.P.
(See Raleigh)

Banks, Sherrod, (BV) .... '63 '88 C&L.577 B.A., J.D. [Banks]
Banks Law Firm, The, P.A., (BV) .... Bristol Place, Suite 110 4819 Emperor Boulevard
Barrett, William A. .... '66 '97 C.48 B.A. L.896 J.D. [© Moore&V.P.] (See Pat. Sect.)
Bartnik, Bryan C. .... '— '94 C.577 B.A. L.607 J.D. [© Womble C.S.&R.]
Bassinger, Kenneth D. '68 '01 C.420 B.S. L.280 J.D.
Intell. Prop. Coun., Sony Ericsson Mobile Communications (USA) Inc. (Pat.)

Bertolini, Gina Louise .... '— '00 C.209 B.F.A. L.1375 J.D. [🄰 Kennedy C.L.&H.]
Bolen, M. Christopher, (AV) ....'58 '85 C&L.802 B.S., J.D. [Womble C.S.&R.]
Bouren, Amy L. .... '68 '95 C.1349 B.A. L.823 J.D. Mngr., IBM
Bowers, John J. .... '63 '93 C.688 B.S. L.228 J.D. [Womble C.S.&R.]
Bradin, David S. .... '64 '95 C.967 B.A. L.1292 J.D. [Womble C.S.&R.] (Pat.)
Brani, G. Carol .... '— '00 C.893 B.A. L.902 J.D. [🄰 Womble C.S.&R.]
Braun, Eric M., (BV) '— '93 C.1369 B.S. L.896 J.D.
[🄲 Kennedy C.L.&H.] (⊙Raleigh)
Brian, William J., (AV) '— '89 C.910 A.B. L.228 J.D.
[Kennedy C.L.&H.] (⊙Raleigh)
Brink, Robert H. '55 '93 C.105 B.S.Ch. L.1035 J.D.
V.P., U.S., Intell. Prop., GlaxoSmithKline (Pat.)

Brooks, Pierce, McLendon, Humphrey & Leonard, L.L.P.
(See Raleigh)

Browder, Leslie E., (AV) .... '30 '54 C.228 A.B. L.896 LL.B. [Womble C.S.&R.]
Brown, Venel D. '61 '91 C.329 B.S. L.945 J.D.
(adm. in MD; not adm. in NC) Aast. Gen. Coun., GlaxoSmithKline
Buffett, Sarah E. .... '74 '00 C.645 B.A. L.188 J.D. [🄰 Moore&V.P.]
Burton, Dilcy G. '73 '00
C.575 B.S.B.A. L.574 J.D. Asst. Gen. Coun., Triangle Transit Auth.
Byassee, William Sam, (AV) ....'50 '82 C.838 B.A. L.880 J.D. [Maupin T.] (⊙Raleigh)
Byker, Patrick L., (BV) '— '92 C.114 B.A. L.575 J.D.
[🄲 Kennedy C.L.&H.] (⊙Raleigh)
Byrne, Michael J. .... '69 '96 C.602 B.A. L.575 J.D. [🄲 Moore&V.P.]
Caira, Richard J., Jr. ....'69 '98 C.1418 B.A. L.1218 J.D. [🄰 Womble C.S.&R.]
Calogero, Stephen A. '67 '94
C.705 B.S.E.E. L.446 J.D. Staff Coun., Intell. Prop., IBM Corp. (Pat.)
Campen, Virginia G. '— '92
C.1375 B.A. L.1068 J.D. Sr. Pat. Coun., GlaxoSmithKline (Pat.)
Capalbo, Kevin M., (BV) .... '63 '88 C.659 B.A. L.861 J.D. [🄲 Moore&V.P.]
Carrillo, Carla C. '63 '91 C.36 B.A. L.767 J.D.
(adm. in CA; not adm. in NC) Medco Research, Inc.
Carroll, Kenneth G., (AV) .... '52 '85 C&L.896 B.A., J.D. [Womble C.S.&R.]
Carter, Adrianna L. '— '81
C.801 B.S. L.597 J.D. V.P. & Assoc. Gen. Coun., GlaxoSmithKline
Castillo, Leonard '44 '76 C.932 B.B.A. L.912 J.D.
Chf. Bus. Coun. & Asst. Secy., Bayer CropScience LP
Charleston, R. Jonathan, (CV) .... '60 '86 C.329 B.B.A. L.575 J.D. [🄲 Banks]
Cheney, M. Lee, (AV) .... '51 '83 C.309 A.B. L.893 J.D. [Womble C.S.&R.]
Chiantera, Dominic J. '39 '74
C.1046 B.S.E.E. L.1048 J.D. [Moore&V.P.] (See Pat. Sect.)

Chocklett, Gregory P., Law Offices of
(See Raleigh)

Christopher, William L. '62 '93
C.593 B.S. L.575 J.D. Asst. Gen. Coun., GlaxoSmithKline
Clarke, James H., (AV) ....'54 '79 C&L.575 B.A., J.D. [Moore&V.P.]
Clay, A. Bruce '50 '87 C.870 B.S. L.221 J.D.
(adm. in TX; not adm. in NC; Pat.) Sr. Atty., IBM
Cohen, Andrew B., (BV) .... '63 '89 C.197 B.A. L.976 J.D. Sr. Counsel, Eisai Inc.
Conger, Michael M. '67 '97 C&L.101 B.S., J.D.
(adm. in UT; not adm. in NC; Pat.) Pat. Coun., GlaxoSmithKline
Conte, Salvatore R. '29 '59 C.749 B.S. L.276 J.D.
(adm. in VA; not adm. in NC; Pat.) 5 Moore Dr.
Cortina, A. Jose, (AVⓉ) .... '— '79 C.30 B.S. L.904 J.D. [Daniels D.&V.] (Pat.)
Crabill, Elizabeth F. ..... '66 '92 C.309 A.B. L.575 J.D. Gen. Coun. & Secy., MCNC - RDI
Crandall, Terry Lynn '— '92 C.105 B.A. L.575 J.D.
Ass't Gen. Coun., GlaxoSmithKline
Crean, Kathryn V. ....'21 '49 C.66 B.A. L.178 LL.B. 3030 Cornwallis Rd‡
Crowley, Colleen M. ....'— '98 C.1369 B.S. L.896 J.D. [🄰 Kennedy C.L.&H.]
Cullen, Marc ....'70 '99 C&L.575 B.S., J.D. Coun., GlaxoSmithKline
Dadswell, Charles E. '58 '91 C.252 B.S. L.1187 J.D.
V.P., U.S. Intell. Prop., GlaxoSmithKline (Pat.)
Daniels, Linda Markus, (AV) ....'53 '83 C&L.228 B.A., J.D. [Daniels D.&V.]
Daniels, Walter E., (AV) ....'52 '79 C&L.575 B.A., J.D. [Daniels D.&V.]

Daniels Daniels & Verdonik, P.A., (AV)
Suite 200, Generation Plaza, 1822 N.C. Highway 54 East, P.O. Drawer 12218, 27709-2218
Telephone: 919-544-5444 Fax: 919-544-5920
Email: lawinfo@d2vlaw.com URL: http://www.d2vlaw.com
Walter E. Daniels; Linda Markus Daniels; James F. Verdonik; A. Jose Cortina; Caroline Horton Rockafellow; Amalie L. Tuffin. Of Counsel: John C. Lindsey.
Business, Corporations, Venture Capital, Securities, Corporate Finance, Computers, Biotechnology, Telecommunications, Copyright, Trademark, Patent, Technology and Science, Intellectual Property, Management and Licensing, Domestic and International Taxation, Limited Liability Companies and Partnerships, Joint Ventures, International Trade and Investment, Immigration.
See Professional Biographies, RESEARCH TRIANGLE PARK, NORTH CAROLINA

Davis, Dale J. .... '70 '05 C.1213 B.S.M.E. L.574 J.D. [🄰 Moore&V.P.]
DeBaugh, Arthur J., (AV) ....'63 '88 C&L.575 B.A., J.D. [Moore&V.P.]
DeCarlucci, Guy R. ....'— '03 C.645 B.S. L.228 J.D. [🄲 Moore&V.P.]
DeGraaf, Lawrence G., (BV) '68 '96 C.31 B.A. L.893 J.D.
Sr. Coun., GlaxoSmithKline
Dellerman, Karen M., (BV) '60 '88
C.150 B.S. L.345 J.D. Asst. Gen. Coun., BASF Corp. (Pat.)
Deppenbrock, Bonnie L. '47 '77 C.199 B.S. L.229 J.D.
(adm. in PA; not adm. in NC; Pat.) Sr. Pat. Coun., GlaxoSmithKline
Dickens, Theresa McCarthy ....'70 '97 C.575 B.A. L.823 J.D. [🄰 Banks]
Diosegy, Arlene J., (AV) ....'49 '74 C.25 B.A. L.831 J.D. [Maupin T.] (⊙Raleigh)
Doudnikoff, Gregory M. '60 '85 C.367 B.A. L.446 J.D.
(adm. in MD; not adm. in NC; Pat.) Sr. Atty., Intell. Prop. Law, IBM Corp.
Duffield, Edward H. .... '43 '71 C.477 B.S.M.E. L.273 J.D. IBM Corporation (Pat.)
Dymond, James W. ....'75 '00 C.1044 B.S. L.577 J.D. [🄰 Moore&V.P.]
Easter, Susan M. ....'64 '93 C.575 B.S. L.692 J.D. [🄲 Womble C.S.&R.]
Edwards, Neill .... '68 '93 C&L.893 B.A., J.D. [Womble C.S.&R.]
Edwards, William K., (BV) '55 '88
C.893 B.A. L.575 J.D. Asst. Gen. Coun., GlaxoSmithKline
Embree, Edward L., III, (AV) .... '47 '72 C.198 A.B. L.575 J.D. [Moore&V.P.]
Evans, Charles L. .... '64 '94 C.576 B.S. L.575 J.D. [🄲 Moore&V.P.] (See Pat. Sect.)
Fako, J. Erik '64 '97 C.1349 B.S.E.E. L.1218 J.D.
(adm. in MA; not adm. in NC; Pat.) IP Lead-Wireline; IP Defense, Nortel Networks Inc.
Faucette, David H. '48 '76 C&L.575 B.S., J.D.
Sr. Pat., Lic. Offr. & Sr. Contract Negotiator, Research Triangle Institute
Ferguson, William G. '49 '76 C&L.602 B.A., J.D.
(adm. in IN; not adm. in NC) Div. Coun. & Asst. Secy., Bayer CropScience LP

Fernandez, Cristina M., (CV) '60 '85
C.576 B.A. L.280 J.D. V.P. & Assoc. Gen. Coun., GlaxoSmithKline
Fix, Amy Hackman '71 '97
C.576 B.S. L.1345 J.D. Sr. Pat. Coun., GlaxoSmithKline (Pat.)
Fletcher, Randolph M., (AV) ....'56 '84 C&L.575 B.S., J.D. [Moore&V.P.]
Flynn, John D. ....'60 '93 C.886 B.S. L.273 J.D. Site Coun., Intell. Prop. Law, IBM Corp.
Fox, David E., (AV) ....'56 '82 C&L.575 B.A., J.D. [Moore&V.P.]
Freeman, William E., (AV) ....'55 '80 C&L.575 B.S., J.D. [Moore&V.P.]
Gaegler, Patricia A. '62 '90 C.575 B.A. L.477 J.D.
(adm. in MD; not adm. in NC) Asst. Gen. Coun., GlaxoSmithKline
Galvin, Thomas F. '39 '73 C.433 B.S. L.276 J.D.
Coun., Intell. Prop. Law, IBM Corporation (Pat.)‡
Gersten, Garth A. ....'59 '86 C.112 A.B. L.1065 J.D. [🄲 Womble C.S.&R.]
Giamportone, Susan J. ....'63 '97 C.1312 B.A. L.896 J.D. [🄰 Womble C.S.&R.]
Gigliotti, Thomas A. '62 '92 C.158 B.S. L.1202 J.D.
(adm. in TX; not adm. in NC; Pat.)
Gen. Coun., Enterprise Networks & Global Servs., Nortel Networks Inc.
Gilliland, Lisa Jeffrey '58 '83 C.290 A.B. L.575 J.D.
V.P., Legal Affairs, Research Triangle Institute
Ginsburg, Eric O. ....'52 '92 C.112 B.S. L.574 J.D. U.S. Envir. Protec. Agcy.
Gitterman, Amy Kahn '69 '95 C.800 B.A. L.846 J.D.
Sr. Contracting Offr., Research Triangle Institute
Goodridge, George S. '45 '73 C.696 B.A. L.930 J.D.
(adm. in NY; not adm. in NC) Chf. Environ. & Site Coun., Bayer CropScience LP
(⊙Pitts., PA)
Grant, Cary M. '58 '85 C.831 B.A. L.893 J.D.
(adm. in PA; not adm. in NC) Asst. Gen. Coun., GlaxoSmithKline
Grassler, Frank P., (BVⓉ) '55 '83 C&L.174 B.S., J.D.
(adm. in CO; not adm. in NC; Pat.) V.P., U.S. Intell. Prop., GlaxoSmithKline
Green, Kelly I. ....'— '96 C.575 B.A. L.896 J.D. [🅂 Womble C.S.&R.]
Grosser, George E. '38 '73 C.401 B.S.E.E. L.128 J.D.
(adm. in VA; not adm. in NC; Pat.) IBM Corporation‡
Hallyburton, Elizabeth J., (AV) '63 '91
C.896 B.A. L.575 J.D. Sr. Coun., GlaxoSmithKline
Hanks, Arlene D. ....'53 '96 C.420 B.S. L.574 J.D. [Moore&V.P.]
Harrington, R. Cole '59 '91 C&L.575 B.A., J.D.
(adm. in NY; not adm. in NC; Pat.) Hybrizyme Corporation
Herndon, Jerry W. '40 '77 C.886 B.S.E.E. L.776 J.D.
(adm. in NJ; not adm. in NC; Pat.) IBM Corporation
Hewitt, Rondi Rauch ....'56 '83 C.477 B.A. L.228 J.D. Glaxo Inc.
Hill, Arthur L., IV ....'68 '93 C&L.575 B.S., J.D. Ericson Inc.
Hoke, Julia Renfrow '61 '86 C.575 B.A. L.896 J.D.
Asst. Dir., Gen. Coun. & Legal Affairs

Holt York McDarris & High, LLP
(See Raleigh)

Holthausen, Peter D. ....'68 '95 C.575 B.A. L.893 J.D. 3039 Cornwallis Rd.
Holton, Charles R., (AV) .... '50 '73 C.1 B.A. L.228 J.D. [Womble C.S.&R.]

Howard, Stallings, From & Hutson, P.A.
(See Raleigh)

Hylton, Deborah J., (AV) .... '58 '83 C.69 B.A. L.228 J.D. [Womble C.S.&R.]

Intellectual Property/ Technology Law
(See Chapel Hill)

Jenkins, Wilson & Taylor, P.A.
(See Durham)

Jensen, Eric P. '61 '91 C.97 B.S. L.1161 J.D.
(adm. in OH; not adm. in NC; Pat.) IP Defense Lead, Nortel Networks Inc.
Jenzano, Joyce W. ....'43 '96 C.575 B.S. L.574 J.D. [🄲 Moore&V.P.]
Johnson, Leigh R. ....'77 '02 C.138 B.A. L.383 J.D. [🄰 Womble C.S.&R.]
Johnson, W. H., III, (BV) .... '66 '94 C&L.228 A.B., J.D. [Womble C.S.&R.]
Johnston, Mary Beth, (AV) .... '— '86 C.575 A.B. L.1228 J.D. [Kennedy C.L.&H.]
Johnston, Michael G. .... '61 '92 C.602 B.S. L.574 J.D. [Moore&V.P.] (See Pat. Sect.)
Jones, Gene A., Jr. ....'69 '97 C.198 B.A. L.575 J.D. [🄰 Womble C.S.&R.]
Joyner, Charles T. ....'43 '92 C.886 B.S. L.574 J.D. Pat. Atty., Eli Lilly & Co. (Pat.)
Joyner, Joseph D., Jr., (AV) ....'54 '81 C&L.575 A.B., J.D. [Moore&V.P.]
Kakefuda, Mary S. '64 '96 C.966 B.S. L.831 J.D.
(adm. in NJ; not adm. in NC; Pat.) Patent Atty., Syngenta
Keating, Margaret F., (BVⓉ) '59 '86 C.597 B.A. L.276 J.D.
(adm. in MO; not adm. in NC) Div. Coun. & Asst. Secy., Bayer CropScience

Kennedy Covington Lobdell & Hickman, L.L.P., (AV)
P.O. Box 14210, 27709-4210 ⊙
Mailing Address: 2801 Slater Road, Suite 120, Morrisville, NC 27560
Telephone: 919-466-1190 Fax: 919-831-7040
URL: http://www.kennedycovington.com
Partners: William J. Brian; Mary Beth Johnston; Patricia T. Meador; Gary S. Qualls. Special Counsel: Eric M. Braun (Also at Raleigh, North Carolina Office); Patrick L. Byker; John E. (Jack) Markham, Jr. Associates: Gina Louise Bertolini; Colleen M. Crowley; Shawn A. McMillan; Carolyn Fixel Merritt; Candice M. Murphy-Farmer; Craigie D. Sanders.
Administrative Law, Alternative Dispute Resolution, Antitrust and Trade Regulation, Bankruptcy, Banks and Banking, Business Law, Commercial Law, Commercial Real Estate Development, Construction Law, Corporate Law, Debt and Equity Finance, Emerging Growth Companies, Employee Benefits, Employment Law, Entrepreneurial Business Law, Environmental Law, Family Law, Finance, Governmental, Health Care, Immigration and Naturalization, Intellectual Property, International Law, Labor and Employment, Land Sales, Land Use Regulation, Limited Liability Companies and Partnerships, Litigation, Medical Malpractice, Mergers, Acquisitions and Divestitures, Non-Profit and Charitable Organizations, Patents, Private Equity, Products Liability, Professional Liability, Public Utility Law, Real Estate Development, Real Estate Leasing, Real Estate Finance, Securities, Taxation, Technology Law, Trademarks, Trial Practice, Trusts and Estates, Utility Law, Venture Capital, Zoning, Planning and Land Use.
Charlotte, North Carolina Office: Hearst Tower, 214 North Tryon Street, 47th Floor, 28202. Telephone: 704-331-7400. Fax: 704-331-7598.
Raleigh, North Carolina Office: 434 Fayetteville Street Mall, 19th Floor, P.O. Box 1070, 27602-1070. Telephone: 919-743-7300. Fax: 919-743-7358.
Columbia, South Carolina Office: NBSC Building, Suite 850, 1122 Lady Street, 29201. Telephone: 803-251-2300. Fax: 803-251-2315.
Rock Hill, South Carolina Office: 140 East Main Street, Suite 220, P.O. Box 11429, 29731-1429. Telephone: 803-329-7600. Fax: 803-329-7677.
See Professional Biographies, RESEARCH TRIANGLE PARK, NORTH CAROLINA

King, William O., (AV) ....'37 '64 C.575 A.B. L.896 LL.B. [Moore&V.P.]

Kirby & Holt, L.L.P.
(See Raleigh)

Knott, Clark & Berger, L.L.P.
(See Raleigh)

Knowles, Andrew T. '57 '88 C.245 B.A. L.1059 J.D.
Sr. Coun., GlaxoSmithKline (Pat.)

Kreeger, David M. ....'72 '98 C.176 B.A. L.472 J.D. Sr. Atty., Lenovo Group Limited
Kring, Kristine '68 '97 C&L.790 B.S., J.D.
(adm. in SC; not adm. in NC) Coun., Bayer CropScience LP
Lemanowicz, John L. '52 '92 C.161 B.S. L.1003 J.D.
(adm. in OH; not adm. in NC; Pat.) Sr. Pat. Coun., GlaxoSmithKline
Leubuscher, Lynn A. ....'69 '96 C.645 B.A. L.228 J.D. Staff Atty., IBM Corp.
Licata, Kimberly ....'72 '96 C.893 B.A. L.575 J.D. [Ⓐ Womble C.S.&R.]
Lindsey, John C. ....'— '85 C.575 B.A. L.276 J.D. [Ⓒ Daniels D.&V.]
Liu, Catherine P. ....'62 '00 C.112 B.A. L.575 J.D. The Banks Law Firm, P.A.
Locklair, Tanya D. ....'71 '98 C.790 B.A. L.574 J.D. [Ⓐ Banks]
Luger, Laura B., (AV) ....'54 '81 C.104 A.B. L.1066 J.D. [Ⓒ Womble C.S.&R.]
Lyford, Stephanie Kristen ......'70 '97 C&L.575 B.A., J.D. Sr. Coun., GlaxoSmithKline
Machovec, Jennifer Buchanan ......'69 '94 C.294 B.A. L.228 J.D. Staff Coun., IBM Corp.
Mackintosh, Bruce A., (BVⓉ) '53 '78 C.893 B.A. L.896 J.D.
V.P., Gen. Coun. & Secy, Bayer CropScience LP
Mahoney, Molly C. ....'66 '98 C&L.851 B.B.A., J.D. Sr. Coun., GlaxoSmithKline
Malkin, Melissa ....'66 '96 C.1349 B.A. L.477 J.D. Research Triangle Institute
Mangel, Claudia Pap '59 '86
C.597 B.A. L.276 J.D. Assist. Gen. Coun., GlaxoSmithKline

Manning & Crouch
(See Raleigh)

Manning, Fulton & Skinner, P.A.
(See Raleigh)

Markham, John E. (Jack), Jr., (AV) '— '73
C&L.575 A.B., J.D. [Ⓒ Kennedy C.L.&H.] (⊙Raleigh)
Martinko, Jeanmarie .....'67 '93 C.30 B.A. L.831 J.D. Coun., Nortel Networks Limited

Maupin Taylor, P.A., (AV)
480 Beta Building, Headquarters Park Post Office Box 13646, 27709-3646 ⊙
Telephone: 919-361-4900 Telecopier: 919-361-2262
URL: http://www.maupintaylor.com
Arlene J. Diosegy; Theron McK. vanDusen; Charles L. Steel, IV; Roy H. Wyman, Jr.; William Sam Byassee. Of Counsel: W. Travis Porter.
Agribusiness, Administrative, Alcoholic Beverages, Alternative Dispute Resolution, Antitrust and Trade Regulation, Aviation Law, Bankruptcy, Banking Law, Business Litigation, Charitable Organizations, Collective Bargaining, Commercial Leases, Commercial Real Estate, Computers and Software, Construction Law, Copyrights, Corporate Finance, Corporate Law, Creditors' Rights, Employee Benefits, Employer Liability, Employment Discrimination, Employment Law, Employment Litigation, Environmental Law, Franchises and Franchising, Government Contracts, Governmental (State and Local) Law, Health Law, Hospital Law, Immigration and Naturalization, Industrial Accidents, Industrial Relations, Intellectual Property, Labor Arbitration, Labor Law, Labor Legislation, Labor Relations, Management Labor Law, Medical Malpractice Defense, Mergers and Acquisitions, Occupational Health and Safety, Patent Litigation, Products Liability, Real Estate Finance, Secured Lending, Securities Regulation, Sports Law, Taxation, Technology Law, Trademark, Trusts and Estates, Venture Capital, Zoning Law.
Raleigh, North Carolina: Highwoods Tower One, Suite 500, 3200 Beechleaf Court, P.O. Drawer 19764. Telephone: 919-981-4000. Telecopier: 919-981-4300.
Wilmington, North Carolina Office: Landfall Park North, 1985 Eastwood Road, Suite 200, 28403. Telephone: 910-256-5135. Telecopier: 910-256-6451.
See Professional Biographies, RESEARCH TRIANGLE PARK, NORTH CAROLINA

Mc Clain, Timothy J. '62 '87 C.475 B.A. L.477 J.D.
(adm. in MI; not adm. in NC) Site Coun., IBM Corp.
McConnell, Daniel E. ....'38 '65 C.228 B.S.M.E. L.273 J.D. IBM Corp. (Pat.)
McDaniels, Patricia A. '48 '86 C.608 B.S. L.818 J.D.
(adm. in MA; not adm. in NC; Pat.) Sr. Atty., BASF Corp.
McMillan, Shawn A. ....'— '02 C.160 B.A. L.575 J.D. [Ⓐ Kennedy C.L.&H.]
Meador, Patricia T., (AVⓉ) ......'— '82 C.880 B.S.N. L.421 J.D. [Kennedy C.L.&H.]
Merrell, J. Scott '58 '83
C.228 A.B. L.896 J.D. Sr. Dir. & Coun., Research Triangle Institute
Merricks, Julia Wesley '56 '84 C&L.575 B.A., J.D.
Asst. Gen. Coun., GlaxoSmithKline
Merritt, Carolyn Fixel ....'— '02 C.198 B.A. L.880 J.D. [Ⓐ Kennedy C.L.&H.]

Millberg, Gordon & Stewart, PLLC
(See Raleigh)

Mirkin, Mark H., (AVⓉ) ....'58 '85 C&L.228 B.A., J.D. [Moore&V.P.]
Moore, Charles L., Jr. ....'52 '87 C&L.836 B.S.E.E., J.D. [Moore&V.P.] (See Pat. Sect.)

Moore & Van Allen PLLC, (AV) BR
430 Davis Drive, Suite 500, P.O. Box 13706, 27709 ⊙
Telephone: 919-286-8000 Fax: 919-286-8199
URL: http://www.mvalaw.com
Resident Members: Dominic J. Chiantera; James H. Clarke; Arthur J. DeBaugh; Edward L. Embree, III; Randolph M. Fletcher; David E. Fox; William E. Freeman; Arlene D. Hanks; Michael G. Johnston; Joseph D. Joyner, Jr.; William O. King; Mark H. Mirkin; Charles L. Moore, Jr.; Steven B. Phillips; James M. Tatum, Jr.; Reich L. Welborn; Jeffrey M. Young. Resident Of Counsel: E. K. Powe. Resident Counsel: William A. Barrett; Michael J. Byrne; Kevin M. Capalbo; Guy R. DeCarlucci; Charles L. Evans; Joyce W. Jenzano; Ellen A. Rubel; Jennifer L. Skord; Gregory Stephens; Dennis J. Williamson; John A. Zaloom. Resident Associates: Sarah E. Buffett; Dale J. Davis; James W. Dymond; John E. Slaughter, III; James C. White; Matthew W. Witsil.
Admiralty, Banking, Bankruptcy, Commercial Finance, Conduit Lending, Construction, Corporate, Distressed Debt Trading, Employee Benefits, Employment, Energy, Environmental, ERISA, Estate Planning and Administration, Government Contracts, Health Care, Immigration, Information Technology and E-Commerce, Insurance, Intellectual Property, International, Leasing, Litigation, Lobbying and Legislative Representation, Patent and Copyright, Real Estate, Securities, Surety, Taxation, Tax Incentives, Trusts, Utilities and Venture Capital.
Charleston, South Carolina Office: 40 Calhoun Street, Suite 300. Telephone: 843-579-7000. Fax: 843-579-7099.
Charlotte, North Carolina Office: 100 North Tryon Street, Suite 4700. Telephone: 704-331-1000. Fax: 704-331-1159.
See Professional Biographies, RESEARCH TRIANGLE PARK, NORTH CAROLINA

Morgan, Lorie Ann '67 '93 C.953 B.A. L.575 J.D.
Sr. Pat. Coun., GlaxoSmithKline (Pat.)
Moulton, Susanne Glen ....'52 '77 C&L.575 B.A., J.D. Dir., Pub. Policy, Glaxo Inc.
Moye, Maricia L. ....'72 '98 C.575 B.A. L.94 J.D. [Ⓐ Banks]
Murphy-Farmer, Candice M. ......'— '99 C.500 B.A. L.345 J.D. [Ⓐ Kennedy C.L.&H.]

Myers Bigel Sibley & Sajovec, P.A.
(See Raleigh)

Nimmo, Dale Edward, (BV) '60 '89
C.1369 B.S. L.893 J.D. Asst. Gen. Coun., GlaxoSmithKline
Nowell, Margaret A., (AV) '— '86
C&L.896 B.A., J.D. Asst. Gen. Coun., GlaxoSmithKline
Obringer, Dave ....'62 '89 C.313 B.A. L.575 J.D. RTI

Olive and Olive, P.A.
(See Durham)

Otterson, Carla C. '63 '91 C.36 B.S. L.1355 J.D.
Director, Contract Admin. & Corporate Atty., King Pharmaceutical Research & Development Corp.
O'Tuel, John W., III ....'70 '97 C.575 B.A. L.896 J.D. Coun., GlaxoSmithKline

Owen, Arlene G. '55 '80 C&L.880 B.A., J.D.
(adm. in TN; not adm. in NC) Sr. Coun., Nortel Networks Ltd.
Phillips, Steven B. ....'62 '93 C.659 B.S.E. L.575 J.D. [Moore&V.P.] (See Pat. Sect.)

Pinna Johnston & Burwell, P.A.
(See Raleigh)

Pinsker, Diane B. ....'— '03 C.628 B.S. L.1228 J.D. Atty., Bayer CropScience
Pontaoe, Sheldon R. '66 '94
C.999 B.S. L.564 J.D. Dir. & Trademark Coun., GlaxoSmithKline
Porter, Gregory D., (AV) '56 '83 C&L.575 B.A., J.D.
VP, Chief Adminstrative Legal Officer, Secretary, Quintiles Transnational Corp.
Porter, W. Travis, (AV) ....'31 '60 C&L.575 A.B., J.D. [Ⓒ Maupin T.] (⊙Raleigh)
Powe, E. K., (AV) ....'21 '50 C&L.575 A.B., J.D. [Ⓒ Moore&V.P.]
Prus, Karen L., (BV) ..... '— '95 C.643 B.S. L.574 J.D. Sr. Pat. Coun., GlaxoSmithKline
Qualls, Gary S., (BV) ....'— '89 C.48 B.S. L.228 J.D. [Kennedy C.L.&H.]
Rabun, Yolanda W. '69 '94 C.321 L.93
(adm. in GA; not adm. in NC) IBM Corp.

Ragsdale Liggett PLLC
(See Raleigh)

Rajaratnam, Arjun '58 '90 C.800 M.S. L.426 J.D.
V.P., Compl. Offr.-Global Pharmaceuticals, GlaxoSmithKline
Raphun, Charles R. '63 '92 C.260 B.S. L.575 J.D.
Contracts-Telus & Canadian MSO's, Nortel Networks Inc.
Raybould, Patricia L. '55 '90 C.569 B.A. L.724 J.D.
(adm. in NJ; not adm. in NC) 3039 Cornwallis‡
Ray-Yarletts, Jeanine S. '63 '93 C.645 B.S. L.574 J.D.
Sr. Atty., Intell. Prop. Law, IBM Corporation (Pat.)
Reid, Scott W. ....'62 '95 C.896 B.A. L.574 J.D. Staff Atty., IBM Corp. (Pat.)
Richardson, Mark E., III, (AV) '58 '86
C.999 B.A. L.575 J.D. V.P. & Assoc. Gen. Coun., GlaxoSmithKline
Richman, Gordon B. '61 '87 C.446 B.S. L.273 J.D.
(adm. in VA; not adm. in NC; Pat.) Quality Strategy Dir., Glaxo Wellcome, Inc.
Riek, James P. '65 '91 C.477 B.S. L.365 J.D.
(adm. in IL; not adm. in NC; Pat.) Sr. Pat. Coun., GlaxoSmithKline
Rintoul, John W. '52 '78 C&L.378 B.A., J.D.
Sr. Contracting Offr., Research Triangle Institute
Rock, Martin E. '55 '86 C.477 B.S.E. L.280 J.D.
(adm. in GA; not adm. in NC)
V.P. & Gen. Coun., Palmetto Engg. & Surveying Co., Inc.
Rockafellow, Caroline Horton ....'68 '93 C.225 B.S. L.1218 J.D. [Daniels D.&V.] (Pat.)
Roddy, Richard J. '34 '75 C.215 B.E.E. L.776 J.D.
Sony Ericsson Mobile Communications (USA) Inc. (Pat.)
Rom, Frederick W., (AV) ....'54 '79 C.321 B.A. L.93 J.D. [Womble C.S.&R.]
Roper, Leighton P., III ....'68 '00 C.893 B.A. L.228 J.D. [Ⓐ Womble C.S.&R.]
Roseboro, John P. ....'73 '99 C.1378 B.A. L.575 J.D. [Ⓐ Banks]
Rosen, Ann K. '59 '84 C.207 B.A. L.188 J.D.
(adm. in WV; not adm. in NC) Asst. Gen. Coun., GlaxoSmithKline
Rubel, Ellen A. ....'61 '86 C.659 B.A. L.30 J.D. [Ⓒ Moore&V.P.]
Russell, J. Kenneth, (BV) '62 '91
C.839 B.S. L.575 J.D. Asst. Gen. Coun., GlaxoSmithKline
Rutter, Mark H. ....'51 '76 C.705 A.B. L.1292 J.D. Chf. Coun, U.S. Army Research Off.★
Sanders, Craigie D. ....'— '03 C.383 B.A. L.574 J.D. [Ⓐ Kennedy C.L.&H.] (⊙Raleigh)
Schwartz, Randee Suzanne '— '96 C&L.861 B.A., J.D.
(adm. in CO; not adm. in NC; Pat.) Patent Atty., Syngenta Biotechnology Inc.
Sembrat, Kevin A. '62 '94
C.119 B.S.E.E. L.1218 J.D. IP -Wireline, Nortel Networks Inc. (Pat.)
Shade, Sherrie L. '— '93 C.679 B.S. L.424 J.D.
(adm. in IL; not adm. in NC) Sr. Coun., GlaxoSmithKline
Shannon, Belinda R. '60 '92 C.257 B.S. L.912 J.D.
(adm. in MI; not adm. in NC) Asst. Gen. Coun., GlaxoSmithKline
Shelton, Kenneth N., (AV) ....'56 '82 C&L.575 B.S., J.D. [Womble C.S.&R.]
Shere, Pankaj Kashiram ....'75 '01 C.576 B.S. L.1509 J.D. [Ⓐ Womble C.S.&R.]
Shults, Theodore F. ....'53 '84 C.4 B.A. L.1009 J.D. Compu Chem Labs.
Skord, Jennifer L., (BV) '48 '80 C.98 B.A. L.209 J.D.
[Ⓒ Moore&V.P.] (See Pat. Sect.)
Slaughter, John E., III ...'71 '97 C.886 B.A. L.893 J.D. [Ⓐ Moore&V.P.] (See Pat. Sect.)
Smith, Robert J. ....'62 '94 C.20 A.B. L.477 J.D. Sr. Pat. Coun., GlaxoSmithKline (Pat.)
Smith, Robin Whitlock ....'73 '98 C.893 B.A. L.228 J.D. Glaxo Inc.
Smith, Sandell Lee '55 '88 C.1175 B.A. L.809 J.D.
(adm. in FL; not adm. in NC) Integrated Lab. Sys.

Smith, Anderson, Blount, Dorsett, Mitchell & Jernigan, L.L.P.
(See Raleigh)

Spagnardi, Joseph M. '63 '90 C.205 B.S. L.575 J.D.
(adm. in NY; not adm. in NC) Asst. Gen. Coun., GlaxoSmithKline

Stark Law Group, PLLC
(See Chapel Hill)

Steel, Charles L., IV, (AV) ....'45 '70 C.198 A.B. L.880 J.D. [Maupin T.] (⊙Raleigh)
Stephens, Debra Kolc '64 '93 C.886 B.S.E.E. L.1292 J.D.
(adm. in NJ; not adm. in NC; Pat.) Sony Ericsson
Stephens, Gregory '66 '95 C.886 B.S.E.E. L.1292 J.D.
[Ⓒ Moore&V.P.] (See Pat. Sect.)
Stevens, Lauren C., (AV) '50 '85
C.608 B.A. L.575 J.D. V.P. & Assoc. Gen. Coun., GlaxoSmithKline
Story, G. Edward '62 '87 C.896 B.A. L.1228 J.D.
Dir., Offr. of Research Contracts, Research Triangle Institute
Strickland, J. Michael '67 '99
C.277 B.Ch.E. L.228 J.D. Pat. Coun., GlaxoSmithKline (Pat.)
Strowd, Richard E. '52 '81 C.575 B.A. L.574 J.D.
Sr. Contracting Offr., Research Triangle Institute
Tatum, James M., Jr., (AV) ....'47 '74 C&L.575 B.A., J.D. [Moore&V.P.]
Terry, Jacqueline ....'65 '91 C.1374 B.A. L.1009 J.D. [Womble C.S.&R.]

Tharrington Smith
(See Raleigh)

Thelen, Timothy A. .....'65 '90 C&L.602 B.A., J.D. Asst. Gen. Coun., GlaxoSmithKline
Thomas, Steven D. ....'67 '98 C.1378 B.S. L.574 J.D. Coun., GlaxoSmithKline
Trevett, Jennifer Leahy ....'72 '98 C.645 B.S. L.1529 J.D. Coun., GlaxoSmithKline
Tuchman, Mitch ....'45 '02 C.605 B.A. L.904 J.D. [Ⓐ Womble C.S.&R.]
Tuffin, Amalie L. ....'— '92 C.309 A.B. L.1065 J.D. [Daniels D.&V.]

Twiggs, Beskind, Strickland & Rabenau, P.A.
(See Raleigh)

Vandeventer Black LLP
(See Raleigh)

vanDusen, Theron McK., (BV) '57 '91 C.659 B.A. L.228 J.D. [Maupin T.] (⊙Raleigh)

Venture Counsel
(See Raleigh)

Verdonik, James F., (AV) ....'— '78 C&L.262 B.A., J.D. [Daniels D.&V.]
Wade, Lena D., (BV) ....'68 '97 C.811 B.A. L.228 J.D. [🄰 Banks]
Walton, Debra P. ....'62 '98 C.803 B.S.E.E. L.574 J.D. 3039 Cornwallis Rd.
Ward, Zachary B. '75 '00 C.890 B.A. L.893 J.D. (adm. in GA; not adm. in NC) Coun., GlaxoSmithKline
Wardell, Bryan E., (BV) ....'64 '94 C.188 B.S. L.575 J.D. [🄰 Banks]
Welborn, Reich L., (AV) ....'45 '71 C&L.575 A.B., J.D. [Moore&V.P.]
Werner, S. Mark '53 '78 C.311 B.A. L.659 J.D. (adm. in IL; not adm. in NC) Sr. V.P., Legal Ops US & GMS, GlaxoSmithKline
White, James C. ....'58 '03 C.722 B.A. L.228 J.D. [🄰 Moore&V.P.]
Whitlock Smith, Robin K. .....'73 '98 C.893 B.A. L.228 J.D. Sr. Coun., GlaxoSmithKline
Williams, F. Bruce ....'57 '88 C.1111 B.A. L.228 J.D. [Womble C.S.&R.]
Williamson, Dennis J. '59 '90 C.339 B.S.G.E. L.209 J.D. [🄲 Moore&V.P.] (See Pat. Sect.)
Witcher, J. Richard (Rick), III '68 '94 C.576 B.S. L.953 J.D. (adm. in NY; not adm. in NC; Pat.) IP-Wireline, Nortel Networks Inc.
Witsil, Matthew W. ...... '65 '99 C.893 B.S. L.228 J.D. [🄰 Moore&V.P.] (See Pat. Sect.)

Womble Carlyle Sandridge & Rice, (AV)
A Professional Limited Liability Company
2530 Meridian Parkway, Suite 400 (Durham), 27713, P.O. Box 13069, 27709 ⊙
Telephone: 919-484-2300 Fax: 919-484-2340
Email: lawyers@wcsr.com URL: http://www.wcsr.com
Resident Members: M. Christopher Bolen; John J. Bowers; David S. Bradin; Leslie E. Browder; Kenneth G. Carroll; M. Lee Cheney; Neill Edwards; Charles R. Holton; Deborah J. Hylton; W. H. Johnson, III; Frederick W. Rom; Kenneth N. Shelton; Jacqueline Terry; F. Bruce Williams. Resident Associates: David B. Baddour; G. Carol Brani; Richard J. Caira, Jr.; Susan J. Giamportone; Leigh R. Johnson; Gene A. Jones, Jr.; Kimberly Licata; Leighton P. Roper, III; Pankaj Kashiram Shere; Mitch Tuchman. Resident Of Counsel: Bryan C. Bartnik; Susan M. Easter; Garth A. Gersten; Laura B. Luger. Staff Attorney: Kelly I. Green.
General Civil Practice, Trial and Appellate Litigation. Administrative, Antitrust, Aviation, Banking, Bankruptcy and Creditor's Rights, Bond Financing, Civil Rights, Commercial, Construction, Consumer Lending, Corporate, E-Commerce, Employee Benefits, Environmental, Estate Planning, Family, Government Relations, Health Care, Insurance, Intellectual Property, International, Labor and Employment, Municipal, Negligence, Probate, Product Liability, Real Estate, Retirement Plans, Securities, Taxation, Toxic Tort, Wills and Trusts Law.
Representative Clients: Aetna Casualty and Surety Co., Inc.; ALSCO/AmeriMark Building Products, Inc.; Aoki Corporation America, Inc.; DiMon International, Inc.; Hackney Brothers, Inc.; Lawyers Mutual Liability Insurance Company of North Carolina; Meredith College; Regency Park Corp.; Wachovia Bank, N.A.
Winston-Salem, North Carolina Office: One West Fourth Street, 27101. Telephone: 336-721-3600. Fax: 336-721-3660.
Raleigh, North Carolina Office: 2100 First Union Capitol Center, 150 Fayetteville Street Mall, P.O. Box 831. Telephone: 919-755-2100. Fax: 919-755-2150.
Charlotte, North Carolina Office: 3500 One Wachovia Center, 301 South College Street. Telephone: 704-331-4900. Fax: 704-331-4955.
Greensboro, North Carolina Office: 300 North Greene Street. Telephone: 336-574-8030. Fax: 336-574-4520.
Atlanta, Georgia Office: One Atlantic Center, 1201 West Peachtree Street, Suite 3500. Telephone: 404-872-7000. Fax: 404-888-7490.
Other Atlanta, Georgia Office: Suite 404, 2296 Henderson Mill Road, N.E. Telephone: 770-492-9030. Fax: 770-492-9609.
Washington, D.C. Office: Suite 700, 1401 Eye Street. Telephone: 202-857-4400. Fax: 202-467-6910.
Greenville, South Carolina Office: 700 Poinsett Plaza, 104 South Main Street, P.O. Box 10208. Telephone: 864-255-5400. Fax: 864-255-5440.
Tysons Corner, Virginia Office: 8065 Leesburg Pike, Fourth Floor. Telephone: 703-790-3310. Fax: 703-790-2623.
Reviser of the North Carolina Law Digest for this Directory.

See Professional Biographies, RESEARCH TRIANGLE PARK, NORTH CAROLINA

Woods, Gerald R. '41 '67 C.350 B.S.E.E. L.273 J.D. (adm. in VA; not adm. in NC; Pat.) Consulting Atty., IBM Corporation
Woodward, Dean T. '66 '97 C.701 B.S. L.575 J.D. Patent Atty., Research Triangle Institute
Wyman, Roy H., Jr., (BV) ....'63 '93 C.937 B.A. L.477 J.D. [Maupin T.] (⊙Raleigh)

Wyrick Robbins Yates & Ponton LLP
(See Raleigh)

Young, Jeffrey M., (AV) .... '69 '94 C.34 B.A. L.880 J.D. [Moore&V.P.]
Zaloom, John A. .... '68 '96 C.839 B.A. L.846 J.D. [🄲 Moore&V.P.]
Zoffer, William M., (AV) '61 '88 C&L.309 A.B., J.D. (adm. in PA; not adm. in NC) Asst. Gen. Coun., GlaxoSmithKline

RICHLANDS, 996, *Onslow Co.*

Bardill, Mark D., (BV) ....'58 '85 C&L.575 B.A., J.D. 116 W. Hargett St.
Cameron, William M., III ....'54 '80 C.576 B.A. L.1228 J.D. Dist. J.

Morgan, Victor H.E., Jr., Attorney at Law
(See Jacksonville)

Morgan, William J., P.A.
(See Jacksonville)

Popkin, Samuel Stuart
(See Jacksonville)

RICH SQUARE, 931, *Northampton Co.*

Culpepper, Luther B., IV, (CV) ....'68 '94 C.232 B.A. L.1345 J.D. 257 S Main St.
Harvey, Thomas M., (CV) ....'49 '83 C.576 B.A. L.575 J.D. [Harvey]
Harvey Law Office, (CV) ....P.O. Box 707
Slade, Charles M., Jr., (BV) ....'47 '72 C&L.575 B.S., J.D. 803 Bus St.
Warmack, A. Jackson, Jr., (BV) ....'49 '76 C&L.575 B.A., J.D. 257 S. Main St.

ROANOKE RAPIDS, 16,957, *Halifax Co.*

Alford, Laura Jean ....'65 '94 C.999 B.S. L.1345 J.D. 1101 Drake St.

Battle, Winslow, Scott & Wiley, P.A.
(See Rocky Mount)

Benton, Thomas I. ....'46 '71 C&L.575 A.B., J.D. P.O. Box 846
Chichester, Gilbert W., (AV) ....'47 '75 C.999 B.A. L.692 J.D. [Chichester&W.]

Chichester & Walker, (AV)
500 Jackson Street, 27870 ⊙
Mailing Address: P.O. Box 8574, Rocky Mount, NC 27804
Telephone: 252-535-4477 Fax: 252-537-8060
Email: marsiglilaw@earthlink.net URL: http://www.lawyers.com/marsiglilaw
Gilbert W. Chichester; James E. Paschal Walker.
Criminal Defense, Drug Crimes, Felonies, Misdemeanors, Traffic Violations, Driving While Intoxicated, Personal Injury, Automobile Accidents, Slip and Falls, Worker's Compensation, Wrongful Death, General Practice.

(This Listing Continued)

Chichester & Walker (Continued)
Rocky Mount Office: 105 Candlewood Road, Suite A, P.O. Box 8574, 27804. Telephone: 252-451-4055. Fax: 252-451-4088.

See Professional Biographies, ROANOKE RAPIDS, NORTH CAROLINA

Crew, Tonya J. ....'62 '99 C&L.575 B.A., J.D. 1929 Roanoke Ave.
Crew, W. Lunsford, (AV) ....'17 '41 C&L.575 A.B., LL.B. 100 Becker Drive

Dalton Law Firm, The, P.A.
(See Raleigh)

Dickens, William F., Jr., (AV) .... '41 '67 C&L.896 B.A., J.D. [Moseley,E.&D.]

Dudley, Janet B., Attorney at Law
(See Scotland Neck)

Elliott, Bradley A., (BV) ....'53 '81 C.1388 B.A. L.1228 J.D. [Moseley,E.&D.]
Graham, William G., (BV) ....'33 '91 C.576 B.S. L.574 J.D. 400 Riversude Trail
Hanudel, Robert A., (BV) ....'49 '74 C.851 B.B.A. L.228 J.D. 734 Roanoke Ave.
Harris, James G., (BV) ....'36 '80 C.999 B.A. L.574 J.D. 100 Becker Dr.

Hux, Livermon & Armstrong, L.L.P.
(See Enfield)

James, Wellman & White, (BV)
644 Roanoke Avenue, P.O. Box 2018, 27870
Telephone: 252-535-4545 Fax: 252-535-5959
Email: jwwrrlaw@charter.net
Members of Firm: John A. James (1923-1988); Thomas H. Wellman; William O. White, Jr. Associate: Holly N. Wilson.
General Civil Trial Practice in State and Federal Courts. Personal Injury, Corporation, Real Estate, Probate, Trust, Estates, Bankruptcy Law.
Reference: Branch Banking and Trust Company.

See Professional Biographies, ROANOKE RAPIDS, NORTH CAROLINA

Jones, Franklin L., Jr., Law Office of
(See Halifax)

LeonLaw Firm, The
(See Greenville)

Long, Nicholas ....'23 '50 C&L.575 B.S., J.D. Ret. Chf. Dist. J.
Moseley, Wendell C., (AV) .... '38 '63 C&L.575 B.S., B.L. [Moseley,E.&D.]

Moseley, Elliott & Dickens, L.L.P., (AV)
928 Roanoke Avenue, 27870
Telephone: 252-537-3534 Fax: 252-535-3063
URL: http://www.med-lawfirm.com
Members of the Firm: Wendell C. Moseley; Bradley A. Elliott; William F. Dickens, Jr.
Real Estate, Probate, Criminal Law, Misdemeanors, Traffic Violations, Domestic Relations, Family Law, Municipal Corporations, Corporate Law, Civil Litigation.

See Professional Biographies, ROANOKE RAPIDS, NORTH CAROLINA

Murphrey, Willis E., III, (BV) ....'28 '57 C&L.896 B.S., LL.B. 220 Old Farm Rd.
Pittard, Jesse F., (CV) ....'69 '97 C.896 B.A. L.1338 J.D. 307 Hunting Ridge Road
Rollins, M. Glynn, Jr., (BV) .... '55 '81 C&L.575 A.B., J.D. [Rollins&R.]
Rollins, Phyllis B., (BV) ....'49 '74 C.471 A.B. L.575 J.D. [Rollins&R.]
Rollins and Rollins, (BV) .... 14 East 11th St.
Stephenson, W. Turner, III, (BV) .... '59 '85 C.925 B.S. L.574 J.D. P.O. Box 1516
Walker, James E. Paschal, (BV) ....'67 '92 C.232 B.A. L.1345 J.D. [Chichester&W.]
Webb, Lenita M., (CV) ....'69 '98 C.943 B.A. L.574 J.D. [Webb]
Webb, Sammy D. ....'66 '00 C.577 B.A. L.574 J.D. [Webb]
Webb Law Firm, (CV) .... 1485 Highway 158 West
Wellman, Thomas H., (BV) ....'50 '76 C&L.575 A.B., J.D. [James,W.&W.]
Whitaker, Cary, (AV) ....'34 '63 C.228 A.B. L.575 LL.B. 1107 Hamilton St.
White, William O., Jr., (BV) ....'48 '74 C.296 A.B. L.575 J.D. [James,W.&W.]

Willey, Ralph G., P.A.
(See Rocky Mount)

Wilson, Holly N. ....'74 '99 C.576 B.A. L.1228 J.D. [🄰 James,W.&W.]

ROBBINS, 1,195, *Moore Co.*

Marley, Clifton F., (CV) ....'56 '85 C&L.575 B.A., J.D. 105-A S. Middleton St.
Smith, Dock G., Jr. ....'35 '60 C.232 B.S. L.575 J.D. 118 E. Salisbury St.‡
Thigpen, Frank C., (BV) ....'45 '72 C.316 A.B. L.575 J.D. 131 S. Middleton St.

ROBBINSVILLE, * 709, *Graham Co.*

Cody, Donna K., (BV) ....'60 '85 C&L.838 B.A., J.D. Main St., Collins Bldg.
McKinney, Zeyland G., Jr., (BV) ....'58 '83 C.575 B.A. L.574 J.D. [McKinney&T.]
McKinney & Tallant, P.A., (BV) ....40 Court Street
Tallant, Mack D., (CV) ....'67 '95 C.34 B.A. L.1059 J.D. [McKinney&T.]

ROCKINGHAM, * 9,672, *Richmond Co.*

Brewer, Scott T., (BV) ....'58 '85 C.575 B.A. L.1375 J.D. 1206 Carolina Dr.
Buckner, Richard G., (AV) .... '51 '77 C.576 B.S. L.575 J.D. [Sharpe&B.]
Cafferty, Maureen E. ..... '59 '96 C.776 B.S.N. L.930 J.D. Presbyterian Home and Services
Carroll, Melanie J., (BV) ....'64 '89 C.34 B.A. L.1228 J.D. [Saunders&C.]
Clayton, Tamela Gay, (BV) .... '59 '84 C&L.575 B.A., J.D. 310 E. Washington St.

Clodfelter Law Office
(See Wadesboro)

Crump, George E., III, (BV) .... '53 '77 C.576 B.A. L.896 J.D. 109 E. Franklin St.

Daniel, John R., Law Office of, (BV) '52 '82 C.925 B.S. L.1228 J.D.
501 East Broad Avenue, 28380
Telephone: 910-895-1929 Fax: 910-895-1996
Email: johndaniellaw@carolina.rr.com URL: http://www.johnrdaniel.com
Associate: John W. Roebuck, Jr.
General Civil Trial Practice in all State and Federal Courts and Administrative Agencies. Personal Injury, Workers Compensation, Social Security Disability, Real Estate and Traffic.

See Professional Biographies, ROCKINGHAM, NORTH CAROLINA

Davis, Joseph G., III, (BV) .... '65 '92 C.575 B.A. L.1228 J.D. [Pittman&D.]
Davis, Joseph G., Jr., (AV) ....'31 '55 C&L.575 A.B., LL.B. [Pittman&D.]
Dawkins, Donald M., (BV) ....'38 '74 C.576 B.S. L.744 J.D. [Dawkins&S.]
Dawkins and Sullivan, (BV) .... 126 S. Hancock St.
Deane, Charles B., Jr., (BV) ....'37 '62 C&L.896 B.A., LL.B. [Deane,W.&D.]
Deane, Jason T. .... '74 '00 C.576 B.S. L.1228 J.D. [Deane,W.&D.]
Deane, Williams and Deane, (BV) ....208 East Franklin Street
Eichorn, John F., (BV) ....'50 '76 C.93 B.A. L.245 J.D. 501 E. Broad Ave.
Futrell, Stephan R., (BV) .... '56 '81 C.896 B.A. L.276 J.D. [Kitchin,N.W.W.&F.] ⊙

Gordon, Horne, Hicks and Floyd, P.A.
(See Laurinburg)

Gunter, Woodrow W., II, (AV) '47 '72 C.575 A.B. L.896 J.D. 219 East Franklin Street P.O. Drawer 249
Kitchin, Henry L., (AV) ....'39 '63 C&L.896 B.A., LL.B. [Kitchin,N.W.W.&F.] ⊙

Kitchin, Neal, Webb, Webb & Futrell, P.A., (AV) ......111 Washington Street (⊙Hamlet)
Lee, Hugh A., (AV) ....'21 '49 C.575 B.S. L.228 LL.B. 217 E. Washington St.‡

Lindler, H. Bright, (BV) '58 '87 C.575 B.S. L.469 J.D.
107 Rockingham Road, 28379
Mailing Address: P.O. Box 669, Rockingham, NC 28380
Telephone: 910-997-7715 Fax: 910-997-7764
Email: bright@hbrightlindler.com
Social Security.

Neal, F. Brent, (AV) .... '44 '72 C&L.575 A.B., J.D. [Kitchin,N.W.W.&F.] ⊙
Nichols, R. Thomas, Jr., (BV) .... '50 '85 C.1317 B.A. L.1228 J.D. 210 E. Franklin
Page, John T., Jr., (AV) .... '24 '49 C.896 B.S. L.228 J.D. 723 Stanley Ave.‡
Pittman, Ira B., (BV) .... '64 '89 C&L.575 B.A., J.D. [Pittman&D.]
Pittman & Davis, (AV) ....212 E. Franklin St.

Poisson Poisson & Bower, PLLC
(See Wadensboro)

Prelipp, Paul S., (BV) .... '68 '95 C.966 B.S. L.1228 J.D. P.O. Box 873

Purcell & Griswold, LLP
(See Laurinburg)

Roebuck, John W., Jr. .... '71 '03 C.953 B.A. L.1228 J.D. [Ⓐ J.R.Daniel]
Saunders, W. Reece, Jr., (AV) .... '52 '77 C&L.896 B.A., J.D. [Saunders&C.]
Saunders & Carroll, LLP, (AV) ....217 East Washington Street
Scott, Todd G., (BV) .... '69 '95 C.575 B.A. L.1228 J.D. P.O. Box 873
Setzer, Sharon L. ....'74 '99 C.896 B.A. L.1360 J.D. Asst. Dist. Atty.
Sharpe, Benny S. .... '38 '64 C&L.575 A.B., J.D. [Sharpe&B.]
Sharpe & Buckner, PLLC, (AV) ....109 West Franklin Street, Suite 1
Sullivan, John Daniel, (BV) .... '52 '89 C.232 B.A. L.1228 J.D. [Dawkins&S.]
Webb, Alden B., (AV) ....'49 '74 C.575 A.B. L.896 J.D. [Kitchin,N.W.W.&F.]
Webb, William R., Jr., (BV) .... '53 '79 C&L.896 B.A., J.D. [Kitchin,N.W.W.&F.] ⊙
Williams, Kelly G., (BV) .... '59 '85 C.896 B.A. L.1228 J.D. [Deane,W.&D.]
Wilson, Amanda L. .... '73 '00 L.574 J.D. P.O. Box 818

ROCKWELL, 1,971, *Rowan Co.*

Wooten, Thomas S. '45 '92 C.999 L.1026 J.D.
(adm. in CA; not adm. in NC) P.O. Box 1488

ROCKY MOUNT, 55,893, *Edgecombe & Nash Cos.*

Adams, Randall R., (AV) ....'59 '85 C.473 B.A. L.912 J.D. [Poyner&S.]
Allen, Michael Lynn ....'48 '75 C&L.838 B.S., J.D. Centura Bank
Anderson, Albeon G., Jr. ....'41 '68 C.611 B.A. L.597 J.D. [Anderson&A.] ⊙
Anderson, Michael J., (AV) ....'43 '69 C.611 B.A. L.607 J.D. [Anderson&A.] ⊙
Anderson and Anderson, (AV) ....1605 West Thomas Street (⊙Raleigh)
Anthony, Patricia B., (CV) .... '42 '87 C.380 B.A. L.575 J.D. 950 Country Club Rd.
Bailey, Sarah Patterson ....'45 '71 C.53 A.B. L.575 J.D. Dist. Ct. J.
Baker, Ronald G., (AV) ....'49 '75 C&L.575 B.S., J.D. [Baker,J.D.M.C.&D.] ⊙

Baker, Jones, Daly, Murray, Carter & Daughtry, P.A., (AV)
140 North Franklin Street, P.O. Box 68, 27802-0068 ⊙
Telephone: 252-442-1977 Facsimile: 252-442-5175
Email: rockymount@bjjlawoffices.com
Ronald G. Baker; Robert C. Jenkins; W. Hugh Jones, Jr.; Roswald B. Daly, Jr.; Ernie K. Murray; Ernest R. Carter, Jr.; Kevin Neil Lewis; Bruce L. Daughtry.
General Insurance Defense Civil Practice. Trials. Real Estate, Estate Planning, Probate, Business, Personal Injury Defense, Professional Liability, Insurance, Workers Compensation and Collections.
Representative Clients: North Carolina Farm Bureau Mutual Insurance Co.; Nationwide Mutual Insurance Co.; Great American Insurance Cos.; Aetna Life and Casualty Insurance Co.; Penn National Mutual Casualty Insurance Co.; Integon Insurance Corporation; Grain Dealers Mutual Insurance Co.; Reliance Insurance Co.; Lawyers Mutual Insurance Company of North Carolina.
Ahoskie, North Carolina Office: 304 W. Sunset Street, P.O. Box 986. Telephone: 252-332-2181. Facsimile: 252-332-8354.
See Professional Biographies, ROCKY MOUNT, NORTH CAROLINA

Battle, Winslow, Scott & Wiley, P.A., (AV)
2343 Professional Drive, P.O. Box 7100, 27804-0100 ⊙
Telephone: 252-937-2200 Telecopier: 252-937-8100
Email: battlewinslow@bwsw.com
Kemp D. Battle (1888-1973); Francis E. Winslow (1888-1976); Herman S. Merrell (1908-1966); Robert Mason Wiley (1925-1998); J. Brian Scott; Samuel S. Woodley, Jr.; Leon Henderson, Jr.; Marshall Aubrey Gallop, Jr.; G. Vincent Durham, Jr.; Joseph Newton Callaway (Board Certified Specialist in Consumer Bankruptcy Law and Business Bankruptcy Law, North Carolina State Board of Legal Specialization); Randall B. Pridgen; M. Greg Crumpler; W. Dudley Whitley, III; J. McLain Wallace, Jr.; Curtis L. Bentz; Jacob Reid Parrott, III; Katherine Wiggins Fisher;—A. Scott McKellar. Of Counsel: Thomas L. Young; Thomas G. Dill.
Administrative, Alternative Dispute Resolution, Banking, Bankruptcy, Construction, Commercial, Corporate, Environmental, Estate Planning, General Trial and Appellate Practice in all State and Federal Courts. Health Care, Insurance, Insurance Defense, Labor and Employment, Local Government Law, Personal Injury, Probate and Estate Planning, Real Estate, Tax, Workers' Compensation.
General Counsel for: Nash County; Nash Health Care Systems; Rocky Mount Redevelopment Commission.
Raleigh, North Carolina Office: 3737 Glenwood Avenue, Suite 100, 27612. Telephone: 919-573-1877. Facsimile: 919-573-1878.
See Professional Biographies, ROCKY MOUNT, NORTH CAROLINA

Batts, Jeff. D., (AV) .... '30 '58 C&L.896 B.B.A., J.D. [Batts,B.&B.]
Batts, Jeffrey A., (BV) ....'59 '86 C&L.896 B.S., J.D. [Batts,B.&B.]
Batts, Michael S., (BV) .... '58 '88 C&L.896 B.A., J.D. [Batts,B.&B.]
Batts, Batts & Bell, L.L.P., (AV) .... 103 Candlewood Road
Bayless, Kim L., (AV) ....'52 '77 C.610 B.B.A. L.851 J.D. [Poyner&S.]
Bell, Braxton H., (CV) .... '42 '90 C.101 B.S. L.574 J.D. 2805 Sunset Avenue
Bell, Joseph Luther, Jr., (BV) .... '62 '91 C.575 A.B. L.896 J.D. [Batts,B.&B.]
Bennett, Spier L. (Buddy), III, (AV) ..... '53 '79 C.575 B.A. L.1228 J.D. [Knox,K.&B.]
Bentz, Curtis L., (BV) ....'50 '76 C.1070 B.S. L.930 J.D. [Battle,W.S.&W.]
Bernat, Mark A. .... '60 '94 C.894 B.A. L.347 J.D. 117 Warrington Court
Biggs, M. Alexander, Jr., (AV) .... '27 '57 C&L.896 B.A., J.D. 3068 Zebulon Rd.
Bishop, J. O. ....'16 '38 L.896 LL.B. J. C. Wheat & Co.

Boyd, W. Thomas, Jr., P.A., Law Offices of
(See Wilson)

Braswell, David C., Law Office of, (BV) '63 '90
C.232 B.A. L.1187 J.D. 2627 Sunset Avenue, Suite A
Britt, Sharon R., (BV) ....'64 '89 C.575 B.A. L.574 J.D. [S.R.Britt]

Britt, Sharon Rose, P.L.L.C., (BV)
3210 Zebulon Road, 27804
Telephone: 252-451-4422 Fax: 252-451-4322
Email: srbattorneyatlaw@earthlink.net
Sharon R. Britt.
Family Law, Divorce, Child Custody, Adoptions, Family Law Mediation.
See Professional Biographies, ROCKY MOUNT, NORTH CAROLINA

Brown, Anthony W., (BV) ....'52 '80 C.511 B.A. L.575 J.D. [A.W.Brown]
Brown, Anthony W., Attorney at Law, P.C., (BV) ....3300 Sunset Ave., Ste. B

Brumbaugh, Mu & King, P.A., (BV)
876 Country Club Road, 27804 ⊙
Telephone: 252-451-4090
URL: http://www.bmklaw.net
Kenneth W. King, Jr.
Practice Limited to Injury Cases. Automobile, Wrongful Death, Medical Malpractice, Workers' Compensation, Products Liability and Social Security Claims.
See Professional Biographies, ROCKY MOUNT, NORTH CAROLINA

Callaway, Joseph Newton, (AV) ....'58 '83 C&L.575 B.A., J.D. [Battle,W.S.&W.]
Camp, Gregory S., (BV) ....'66 '94 C.575 B.A. L.228 J.D. [Poyner&S.]
Carter, Ernest R., Jr., (BV) '59 '84 C.575 B.S.B.A. L.1228 J.D.
[Baker,J.D.M.C.&D.] ⊙
Chandler, Robert M., Jr., (BV) ....'33 '67 C.228 A.B. L.575 LL.B. [Early&C.]
Cheatham, James T., (BV) ....'35 '61 C&L.575 B.S., J.D. 130 S. Franklin St.
Cherry, Cleveland P. ....'41 '65 C&L.575 A.B., J.D. 418 Western Ave.

Chichester & Walker, (AV)
105 Candlewood Road, Suite A, 27804 ⊙
Mailing Address: P.O. Box 8574, Rocky Mount, NC 27804
Telephone: 252-451-4055 Fax: 252-451-4088
Email: marsiglilaw@earthlink.net URL: http://www.lawyers.com/marsiglilaw
Jeffrey A. Marsigli.
Criminal Defense, Drug Crimes, Felonies, Misdemeanors, Traffic Violations, Driving While Intoxicated, Personal Injury, Automobile Accidents, Slip and Falls, Worker's Compensation, Wrongful Death, General Practice.
Roanoke Rapids Office: 500 Jackson Street, 27870. Telephone: 252-535-4477. Fax: 252-537-8060.
See Professional Biographies, ROCKY MOUNT, NORTH CAROLINA

Colo, Michael S., (AV) ....'45 '70 C.575 A.B. L.902 J.D. [Poyner&S.]
Colston, Harold D., (AV) .... '37 '67 C.576 B.S.C.E. L.575 J.D. [H.D.Colston]

Colston, Harold D., P.A., (AV)
1701 Sunset Avenue, P.O. Box 8446, 27804-1446
Telephone: 252-985-1701 Fax: 252-985-1800
Email: hcolston@coastalnet.com
Harold D. Colston.
Practice limited to Real Property, Business and Commercial Law, Trusts and Estates, Wills and Probate.
See Professional Biographies, ROCKY MOUNT, NORTH CAROLINA

Cooper, Kristin B. ....'56 '82 C.623 B.S. L.1228 J.D. N.C. Gen. Assembly
Cooper, Roy A., Jr., (AV) ....'27 '56 C.896 B.S. L.575 J.D. [Fields&C.] ‡
Craft, Leslie Locke, (BV) .... '60 '85 C.576 B.A. L.1228 J.D. 3202 Sunset Avenue, Suite B
Crews, Nanette W. ....'70 '97 C.471 B.A. L.575 J.D. 121 Opossum Trot Ct.
Crumpler, M. Greg, (BV) ....'58 '84 C.575 B.A. L.1228 J.D. [Battle,W.S.&W.]
Daly, Roswald B., Jr., (BV) ....'51 '76 C&L.575 A.B., J.D. [Baker,J.D.M.C.&D.] ⊙
Daughtry, Bruce L., (BV) ... '66 '93 C.1228 B.B.A. L.1345 J.D. [Baker,J.D.M.C.&D.] ⊙

Davenport, John E., P.A.
(See Nashville)

Diab, George Stephen ....'64 '90 C&L.575 B.S.B.A., J.D. Franklin at Western
Dill, Thomas G., (AV) ....'22 '47 C&L.575 B.A., J.D. [Ⓒ Battle,W.S.&W.]

Dudley, Janet B., Attorney at Law
(See Scotland Neck)

Duffy, George Paul, Jr., (BV) ....'45 '74 C.55 B.S. L.575 J.D. [Keel,L.&D.]
Durham, G. Vincent, Jr., (AV) ....'51 '76 C.575 A.B. L.896 J.D. [Battle,W.S.&W.]
Duvoisin, Anne ....'51 '78 C.228 B.A. L.575 J.D. [Ⓒ Henson&F.]

Early & Chandler, P.A., (BV)
119 South Grace Street, 27804
Telephone: 252-442-0126 Fax: 252-442-1388 Watts Line: 800-343-8951
Walter J. Early (Deceased); Robert M. Chandler, Jr.
General Practice in all Courts, Estate Planning, Probate, Corporation, Taxation, Personal Injury, Workers Compensation, Social Security Disability Law.
References: RBC Centura Bank, Rocky Mount, North Carolina; Southern Bank, Rocky Mount, North Carolina.

Edelman, Elizabeth A., (AVⓉ) '55 '80 C.475 B.A. L.245 J.D.
(adm. in GA; not adm. in NC) P.O. Box 1220
Edmundson, James J. '42 '67 C&L.575 A.B., J.D.
Assoc. Gen. Coun., Centura Banks, Inc.
Edwards, Diane, (CV) ....'65 '90 C.576 B.A. L.574 J.D. 600 Sunset Ave.
Edwards, Roberta L. ....'54 '86 C.53 B.S.N. L.574 J.D. [R.L.Edwards]
Edwards, Roberta L., P.A. .... 4117 Sunset Avenue
Ellis, J. Nicholas, (AV) ....'60 '86 C.886 B.S. L.896 J.D. [Poyner&S.]
Exum, John B., Jr., (BV) ....'25 '53 C&L.575 B.S., J.D. P.O. Box 1677‡
Fairman, Elizabeth H., (BV) ....'61 '86 C.575 B.A. L.1228 J.D. [Fields&C.]

Falk, Nile K. "Nick", (BV) '47 '77 C.352 B.A. L.692 J.D.
Suite 143, Station Square, 27804
Telephone: 252-977-3577 Fax: 252-977-0762
Email: nkfalk@earthlink.net URL: http://www.nickfalk.com
General Civil and Criminal Practice. Social Security Disability, Criminal Trials, DWI, Traffic Offenses, Personal Injury, Automobile Accidents.
Representative Clients: Standard Electric Co.; SE&M Constructors, Inc., Tharrington Industries, Inc.; Golden East Crossing; Westgate and Carrolton Nursing Centers; House of Lights, Inc.
References: RBC Centura Bank; BB&T.
See Professional Biographies, ROCKY MOUNT, NORTH CAROLINA

Fields, Milton P., (AV) ....'26 '53 C.232 A.B. L.896 J.D. [Fields&C.] ‡

Fields & Cooper, PLLC, (AV)
422 Sunset Avenue, P.O. Box 4538, 27803-0538 ⊙
Telephone: 252-442-3115 Fax: 252-442-4170
Milton P. Fields (Retired); Roy A. Cooper, Jr. (Retired); John S. Williford, Jr. (Board Certified Specialist in Bankruptcy Law, North Carolina State Board of Legal Specialization); Elizabeth H. Fairman; Mark E. Edwards (Resident, Nashville Office); Mark C. Osterhout;—Michael D. Gaynor (Resident, Nashville Office).
General Civil and Trial Practice in State and Federal Courts. Personal Injury, Creditor Bankruptcy and Collections, Construction, Corporate, Business Law, Contracts, Trusts, Estates, Wills, Probate, Real Estate, Commercial and Residential, Municipal, Land Use, Zoning, Traffic and Elder Law.
Representative Clients: RBC Centura Bank; PYA/Monarch, LLC; U.S. Foodservice, Inc.; Bennette Paint Mfg. Co.; L&L Stores, Inc.; Barnes Farming Corp.; Dale Bone Farms, Inc.; Southern Loans, Inc.; Century Finance, Inc.; Towns of Bailey, Castalia, Middlesex and Spring Hope.
Approved Attorneys for: Lawyers Title Insurance Corp.
Nashville, North Carolina Office: 113 Court Street, P.O. Box 757, 27856. Telephone: 252-459-2121. Fax: 252-459-2123.
See Professional Biographies, ROCKY MOUNT, NORTH CAROLINA

Fisher, Katherine Wiggins, (BV) ...... '67 '92 C.575 B.A. L.1228 J.D. [Battle,W.S.&W.]
Fleming, John B., Jr., (BV) '49 '78
C.575 B.S. L.896 J.D. Asst. Gen. Coun., Centura Banks, Inc.
Fountain, Richard T., Jr., (AV) ....'28 '56 C&L.575 B.S., J.D. [Ⓒ Hoyle&S.]
Fuerst, Robert L., (AV) ....'48 '73 C&L.575 B.A., J.D. [Henson&F.] ⊙
Gallop, Marshall Aubrey, Jr., (AV) .....'45 '75 C.228 B.S. L.818 J.D. [Battle,W.S.&W.]
Gaynor, Michael D. ....'76 '02 C&L.1228 B.B.A., J.D. [Ⓐ Fields&C.] ⊙

Gibson, T. Stewart, (BV) .... '47 '73 C.896 B.B.A L.790 J.D. [T.S.Gibson]
Gibson, T. Stewart, PLLC, (BV) .... 1701 Sunset Avenue
Hart, Ericka Fitch .... '68 '97 C.302 B.S. L.574 J.D. 833 N. Fairview Rd.
Henderson, Leon, Jr., (AV) ....'38 '64 C.576 B.S. L.896 J.D. [Battle,W.S.&W.]
Henson, Carmaletta L. .... '74 '99 C&L.575 B.A., J.D. [A Henson&F.] ⊙
Henson, David S., (CV) .... '73 '98 C&L.575 B.A., J.D. [Henson&F.] ⊙
Henson, Thomas W., Jr., (BV) '65 '89
C&L.575 B.S.B.A., J.D. [Henson&F.] (⊙Asheville, Raleigh)

Henson & Fuerst, P.A., (AV) BR
2317 Sunset Avenue, P.O. Box 7008, 27804-2529 ⊙
Telephone: 252-443-2111 Fax: 252-443-9429
Email: henson-fuerst@lawmed.com URL: http://www.lawmed.com
Thomas W. Henson (Resident, Raleigh Office); Robert L. Fuerst (Board Certified Specialist in Family Law, North Carolina State Board of Legal Specialization); Thomas W. Henson, Jr.; David S. Henson;—Carmaletta L. Henson; Joseph S. Hodgin. Of Counsel: Anne Duvoisin.
Civil Trial Practice, Medical Malpractice Nursing Home Liability, Nursing Home Abuse and Neglect, Personal Injury, Automobile Accidents, Wrongful Death, Social Security Disability and Worker's Compensation.
Raleigh Office: 2501 Blue Ridge Road, Suite 390, 27607. Telephone: 919-781-1107. Fax: 919-781-8048.
See Professional Biographies, ROCKY MOUNT, NORTH CAROLINA

Herring, Bradley J., (AV) .... '64 '89 C.575 B.A. L.896 J.D. [Poyner&S.]
Hester, Joseph M., Jr., (BV) .... '47 '77 C&L.575 A.B., J.D. [Hester&M.]
Hester & Moore, PLLC, (BV) .... 3230 Zebulon Road
Hodgin, Joseph S. .... '76 '02 C.1228 B.A. L.607 J.D. [A Henson&F.] ⊙
Hoyle, William S., (AV) .... '40 '68 C&L.575 A.B., J.D. [Hoyle&S.]
Hoyle & Stroud, LLP, (AV) .... 3109 Zebulon Road
Jacula, Michael .... '50 '99 C.563 B.A. L.575 J.D. [A R.L.Edwards]
Johnson, Samuel W., (AV) .... '47 '72 C&L.228 B.A., J.D. [Poyner&S.]
Jones, W. Hugh, Jr., (BV) ....'54 '80 C.198 A.B. L.575 J.D. [Baker,J.D.M.C.&D.] ⊙
Joyner, C. Ray, (BV) .... '48 '74 C&L.575 A.B., J.D. 120 N. Franklin St., Suite K
Keel, James W., Jr., (AV) .... '15 '37 C&L.575 B.A., LL.B. [Keel,L.&D.]
Keel, Lassiter & Duffy, (AV) ....Suite A, 120 North Franklin Street
Kellum, Norman B., Jr., (AV) .... '37 '65 C&L.896 B.S., J.D. [Kellum] ⊙

Kellum Law Firm, (AV)
3250 Zebulon Road, 27804 ⊙
Telephone: 252-442-3975 Fax: 252-442-7309
Email: ckeenhold@kellumlawfirm.com URL: http://www.lawyers.com/kellumlawfirm
Norman B. Kellum, Jr.;—Russell L. Needell.
State and Federal Civil Trial Practice, Personal Injury Law, Wrongful Death, Workers' Compensation, Social Security, Defective Products, Mass Torts and Insurance Law.
See Professional Biographies, ROCKY MOUNT, NORTH CAROLINA

King, Kenneth W., Jr., (BV) ...... '61 '86 C.575 B.S. L.469 J.D. [Brumbaugh,M.&K.] ⊙
King, Thomas W., (BV) ....'54 '79 C&L.575 B.S., J.D. 3202 Sunset Avenue, Suite F
Knox, Howard A., Jr., (AV) .... '36 '61 C&L.575 B.A., J.D. [Knox,K.&B.]

Knox, Kornegay & Bennett, L.L.P., (AV) BR
531 Sunset Avenue, 27804
Mailing Address: P.O. Drawer 7666, Rocky Mount, NC 27804-7666
Telephone: 252-442-8037 Fax: 252-442-0052; 252-442-1540
Email: kkblaw@earthlink.net URL: http://www.lawyers.com/kkblawoffice
Howard A. Knox, Jr.; Robert D. Kornegay, Jr.; Spier L. (Buddy) Bennett, III.
General Civil and Criminal Trial Practice. Personal Injury, Wrongful Death, Family/Domestic, DWI and Traffic Offenses, Corporate and Business Law, Probate Law and Mediation.
See Professional Biographies, ROCKY MOUNT, NORTH CAROLINA

Kornegay, Judith L., (BV) .... '46 '76 C.471 B.A. L.574 J.D. 820 Nichole Lane
Kornegay, Robert D., Jr., (BV) ....'48 '73 C.896 B.A. L.421 J.D. [Knox,K.&B.]
Lacy, Graham G., Jr. ....'39 '64 C.198 B.A. L.228 LL.B. Secy., Texfi Industries, Inc.
Lane, Charles T., (AV) .... '31 '56 C&L.896 B.A., J.D. [C Poyner&S.]
Lassiter, Will H., III, (AV) ....'46 '72 C&L.575 B.S., J.D. [Keel,L.&D.]
Levin, Peggy S., (BV) .... '48 '85 C.1011 B.A. L.1228 J.D. 1701 Sunset Ave.
Lewis, Kevin Neil, (BV) .... '65 '92 C.1228 B.A. L.1345 J.D. [Baker,J.D.M.C.&D.] ⊙
Livermon, James Shields, III .... '69 '99 C.301 B.A. L.1228 J.D. [A Poyner&S.]
Ludwig, Carol E. ....'53 '83 C.575 B.A. L.1243 J.D. [A]★
Lynn, Allen Michael ....'— '75 Centura Bank Mc 00-001-0301
Mahmoud, Nana A., Atty. at law ....'73 '00 C.999 L.659 1701 Sunset Ave., Ste. 301
Marsigli, Jeffrey A. .... '74 '03 C.576 B.A. L.1228 J.D. [Chichester&W.]
Martin, James T., (BVⓣ) .... '42 '67 C&L.896 B.A., J.D. [C Poyner&S.]
Massey, Kenneth R.................. '69 '94 C.1228 B.B.A. L.575 J.D. [A R.L.Edwards]
Matthews, Jenny L. .... '79 '05 C&L.575 B.A., J.D. [A Poyner&S.]
Matthews, Tom H. .... '27 '52 C&L.575 B.S., J.D. Ret. Dist. J.
McKellar, A. Scott ....'75 '01 C&L.575 B.A., J.D. [A Battle,W.S.&W.]
Meadows, Frank P., Jr., (AV) ....'27 '56 C.575 B.S. L.896 J.D. [C Poyner&S.]
Moore, J. Edgar, (AV) ....'37 '63 C&L.575 B.S., LL.B. 512 West Thomas St.
Moore, Thomas J., II, (BV) ....'63 '91 C.575 B.A. L.1228 J.D. [Hester&M.]

Morrison Law Firm, P.L.L.C.
(See Wilson)

Murphy, Michael P., (BV) ....'58 '91 C.575 B.S. L.574 J.D. [M.P.Murphy]

Murphy, Michael P., P.A., (BV)
3072 - C Sunset Avenue, P.O. Box 8738, 27804
Telephone: 252-451-1200 Fax: 252-451-1201
Email: murphylawoffice@aol.com URL: http://www.rockymountattorney.com
Michael P. Murphy.
Commercial Collections, Wills, Trust Law, Estate Planning, Personal Injury, Automobile Accidents and Injuries, Truck Accidents, Bankruptcy Chapter 7, Bankruptcy Chapter 13, Corporate Law, Limited Liability Company Law, Business Law, Criminal Law, Traffic Violations.
See Professional Biographies, ROCKY MOUNT, NORTH CAROLINA

Murray, Ernie K., (BV) ....'52 '80 C.575 B.A. L.896 J.D. [Baker,J.D.M.C.&D.] ⊙
Needell, Russell L., (BV) ......'56 '81 C.1170 B.A. L.117 J.D. [A Kellum] (⊙Greenville)
Oettinger, David, Jr. .... '52 '77 C.576 B.S. L.575 J.D. P.O. Box 8346‡
O'Garro-Moore, Carolyn ....'56 '87 C.276 A.B. L.574 J.D. [O'Garro-Moore]

O'Garro-Moore Law Office
Sunset Towers, 164 Roundabout Court, 27804
Telephone: 252-443-1419 Fax: 252-443-1493
Email: ogarromoore@earthlink.net URL: http://www.lawyers.com/ogarro-moore
Member of Firm: Carolyn O'Garro-Moore.
Immigration Law, Criminal Law, Family Law.
See Professional Biographies, ROCKY MOUNT, NORTH CAROLINA

Osterhout, Mark C., (BV) ....'61 '88 C.1126 B.A. L.1228 J.D. [Fields&C.]
Parrott, Jacob Reid, III, (BV) ....'67 '92 C&L.575 B.A., J.D. [Battle,W.S.&W.]
Pearsall, Mack B. ....'37 '63 C&L.575 A.B., LL.B. P.O. Box 7246

Poyner & Spruill LLP, (AV)
130 S. Franklin Street, P.O. Box 353, 27802-0353 ⊙
Telephone: 252-446-2341 Telecopier: 252-972-7045
URL: http://www.poynerspruill.com

(This Listing Continued)

Poyner & Spruill LLP (Continued)
Members of Firm: Michael S. Colo; Richard J. Rose; Samuel W. Johnson; Kim L. Bayless; David M. Warren; Randall R. Adams; J. Nicholas Ellis; Steven A. Rowe; Bradley J. Herring; Gregory S. Camp; Timothy Wood Wilson. Resident Associates: Deborah E. Sperati; James Shields Livermon, III; Jenny L. Matthews. Resident Of Counsel: Frank P. Meadows, Jr.; Charles T. Lane; James T. Martin.
Comprehensive business and litigation practice including: Appellate, Arbitration, Banking, Bankruptcy/Creditors' Rights, Complex Business Litigation, Construction, Credit and Financial Services, Eminent Domain/Condemnation, Employment Benefits, Employment Practices, Entertainment Law, Environmental, Estate, Exempt Organizations, General Corporate, Governmental Relations, Health Care, Intellectual Property Law, International, Land Use and Zoning, Limited Liability Companies, Local Government, Mediation, Partnerships, Personal and Financial Planning, Probate, Product Liability, Professional Liability, Railroad, Real Estate, Regulatory and Municipal, Securities, Sports Law, Tax, Technology and Emerging Business, Tort Litigation and Insurance Defense, Transactional including Mergers and Acquisitions, Transportation, Utilities, White Collar Criminal Defense.
Raleigh, North Carolina Office: 3600 Glenwood Avenue, P.O. Box 10096, 27605-0096. Telephone: 919-783-6400. Telecopier: 919-783-1075.
Charlotte, North Carolina Office: One Wachovia Center, 301 South College Street, Suite 2300, 28202. Telephone: 704-342-5250. Telecopier: 704-342-5264.
Southern Pines, North Carolina Office: 135 West New Hampshire Avenue, 28388-0371. Telephone: 910-692-6866. Telecopier: 910-695-3036.
See Professional Biographies, ROCKY MOUNT, NORTH CAROLINA

Pridgen, Randall B., (AV) ....'57 '83 C&L.575 B.A., J.D. [Battle,W.S.&W.]
Rose, Richard J., (AV) .... '46 '72 C.198 A.B. L.575 J.D. [Poyner&S.]

Rose Rand Attorneys, P.A.
(See Wilson)

Rowe, Steven A., (AV) .... '62 '88 C&L.896 B.A., J.D. [Poyner&S.]
Ruggiero, Anthony J., Jr. '40 '65 C.860 A.B. L.94 LL.B.
(adm. in MA; not adm. in NC) 2315 Sunset Ave.‡
Scott, J. Brian, (AV) ....'27 '51 C&L.896 LL.B. [Battle,W.S.&W.] ⊙
Seagroves, Corrie R. ....'72 '97 C.575 B.A. L.880 J.D. 1608 Bridgedale Dr.★
Shaw, H. Devone '58 '96 C.1011 B.S. L.608 J.D.
(adm. in DC; not adm. in NC) 633 Weathervane Way
Simpson, George L., III, (AV) .... '45 '70 C.575 B.A. L.178 J.D. 130 S. Franklin St.
Solomon, William R., Jr. ....'78 '03 C.1378 B.S. L.1228 J.D. [A L.Wiggins]
Sosna, Michael B., (BV) .... '45 '71 C.597 B.A. L.724 J.D. 1208 Tavern Lndg.
Sperati, Deborah E. .... '74 '99 C&L.575 B.A., J.D. [A Poyner&S.]
Sperati, Matthew P. .... '74 '99 C.575 B.S. L.574 J.D. P.O. Box 4307
Spivey, W. Michael, (AV) '51 '79 C.232 B.A. L.1228 J.D.
120 N. Franklin Street Suite F
Steed, Thomas W., III, (BV) '57 '83 C.228 A.B. L.1228 J.D.
Exec. V.P. & Gen. Coun., The Nottingham Co.
Stroud, Steven R., (BV) .... '53 '91 C.999 B.A. L.1228 J.D. [Hoyle&S.]
Sumner, Quentin T. ....'50 '75 C&L.574 B.A., J.D. Sr. Res. Supr. Ct. J.
Tucker, Damian L., (BV) ....'73 '98 C.953 B.A. L.574 J.D. [Hester&M.]
Turnage, John F., (BV) ....'35 '61 C&L.896 B.S., LL.B. 149 N. Franklin St.
Wallace, J. McLain, Jr., (AV) ....'62 '88 C&L.896 B.A., J.D. [Battle,W.S.&W.]
Warren, David M., (AV) .... '59 '84 C&L.896 B.A., J.D. [Poyner&S.]
Wells, John J., III, (BV) .... '58 '83 C&L.575 B.S.B.A., J.D. 3303 Sunset Ave., Ste. A
Whitaker, George G., (BV) ....'44 '69 C&L.575 A.B., J.D. 2639 Sunset Ave.
Whitley, W. Dudley, III, (BV) .... '60 '86 C.576 B.A. L.1228 J.D. [Battle,W.S.&W.]
Wiggins, Lamont, Law Office of, (CV) '66 '94 C.576 B.A. L.574 J.D.
833 Fairview Road
Willey, Ralph G., III, (AV) ....'49 '74 C.576 B.A. L.575 J.D. [R.G.Willey]

Willey, Ralph G., P.A., (AV)
3202 Sunset Avenue, Suite A, P.O. Box 7846, 27804
Telephone: 252-443-1117 Fax: 252-443-5812
Ralph G. Willey, III (Board Certified Specialist in Workers' Compensation, North Carolina State Board of Legal Specialization).
Workers Compensation, Board Certified, Personal Injury, Civil and Criminal Trial Practice in all Courts, Traffic, Mediation, Arbitration.
See Professional Biographies, ROCKY MOUNT, NORTH CAROLINA

Williams, Jessica Creech .... '67 '93 C.575 B.A. L.1209 J.D. 4497 Sunset Ave.
Williford, John S., Jr., (AV) ....'48 '76 C&L.575 B.A., J.D. [Fields&C.]
Wilson, Timothy Wood, (BV) ....'68 '95 C.228 B.S. L.280 J.D. [Poyner&S.]
Wilson, Wendy P. .... '68 '00 C.1213 B.S. L.575 J.D. [A Batts,B.&B.]
Woodley, Samuel S., Jr., (AV) ....'39 '63 C&L.575 A.B., J.D. [Battle,W.S.&W.]
Young, Thomas L., (AV) ....'30 '54 C&L.575 B.S., J.D. [C Battle,W.S.&W.]

ROSEBORO, 1,267, *Sampson Co.*

Philip E. Williams, (BV) ....104 South Broad Street
Williams, Philip E., (BV) ....'51 '79 C.232 B.S. L.575 J.D. [Philip E.W.]

ROSE HILL, 1,330, *Duplin Co.*

Turner, Kenneth W. ....'27 '53 C.575 L.692 LL.B. Chf. Dist. J.

ROWLAND, 1,139, *Robeson Co.*

Price, Robert E., (BV) ....'54 '80 C&L.575 B.S., J.D. P.O. Box 369

ROXBORO, * 8,696, *Person Co.*

Brann, Luann W. ....'61 '99 C.575 B.A. L.574 J.D. P.O. Box 1143
Cates, J. Linwood .... '74 '99 C.575 B.A. L.896 J.D. [Hubbard&C.]
Cates, Walter Bradsher, (AV) .... '50 '79 C.232 B.S.B.A. L.1228 J.D. [Hubbard&C.]

Daniel, George B., P.A.
(See Yanceyville)

Daniel, William H., P.A.
(See Yanceyville)

Fitzgerald, Thomas L., (AV) ....'53 '78 C.575 B.S. L.896 J.D. [Jackson&F.]
Harrison, Pattie Sue .... '— '83 Dist. J.
Hicks, Alan S., (AV) ....'47 '73 C&L.575 B.A., J.D. [A.S.Hicks]

Hicks, Alan S., P.A., (AV)
3 Union Plaza, 205 North Main Street, 27573
Telephone: 336-599-4032 Fax: 336-599-3656
Email: ash@roxboro.net URL: http://www.alanhicksattorney.com
Alan S. Hicks.
Business, Probate, Trusts and Estates, Personal Injury, Civil Trials, Real Estate and Commercial Law.
See Professional Biographies, ROXBORO, NORTH CAROLINA

Hubbard, Charles E., (AV) ....'36 '66 C.575 A.B. L.902 LL.B. [Hubbard&C.]

Hubbard & Cates, (AV)
36 Court Street, P.O. Box 679, 27573
Telephone: 336-597-2251; 599-2443 Fax: 336-597-3042
Members of Firm: Charles E. Hubbard; Walter Bradsher Cates; J. Linwood Cates.
General Civil, Criminal Trial and Appellate Practice in all Courts. Corporate, Real Estate, Tort, Probate, Estate Planning, Administrative, Commercial, Family, Bankruptcy, Personal Injury, Automobile Accidents, Traffic Violations.
Representative Clients: Person Memorial Hospital; Camp Chemical Corp.; Person-Caswell Lake Authority.

(This Listing Continued)

Hubbard & Cates (Continued)

Approved Attorneys for: Branch Banking and Trust; First Union National Bank of North Carolina; Central Carolina Bank and Trust Co., N.A.
References: Wachovia Bank; Roxboro Savings Bank, SSB.
See Professional Biographies, ROXBORO, NORTH CAROLINA

Hutchinson, Forney, Jr. '12 '36 C.623 B.A. L.278 LL.B.
(adm. in OK; not adm. in NC) 224 Charles Cir.‡
Jackson, George W., (AV) .... '37 '66 C&L.575 A.B., LL.B. [Jackson&F.]
Jackson & Fitzgerald, (AV) .... 22 Court Street
King, Ronnie P., (AV) .... '46 '72 C.576 B.S. L.575 J.D. [King P.]
King Law Group PLLC, (AV) .... 300 S. Main St.
Long, James A. .... '41 '66 C.198 B.A. L.880 LL.B. [Ramsey&L.]
Long, Ursula P. .... '65 '98 C.240 B.S.B.A. L.574 J.D. [Ⓐ Long]
Long Law Offices, P.A. .... P.O. Box 1038
Ramsey, James E., (AV) .... '31 '58 C&L.575 A.B., LL.B. [Ramsey&L.]
Ramsey & Long, (AV) .... 25 Abbitt Ave.
Weinberger, Joe .... '56 '83 C&L.896 B.A., J.D. 114 North Main Street

RUTHERFORDTON, * 4,131, *Rutherford Co.*

Arledge, A. Jervis, (AV) .... '28 '50 L.896 J.D. [Arledge]
Arledge Law Firm, (AV) .... 120 East Court Street
Bowen, James M., (AV) .... '42 '67 C&L.896 B.A., J.D. [⊡ Hamrick,B.M.G.&L.]
Burgin, Deborah Morrison, (CV) .... '54 '88 C.1128 M.Ed. L.896 J.D. [D.Burgin]
Burgin, Deborah, Law Office, (CV) .... P.O. Box 1555
Byers, Garland F., Jr. .... '68 '00 C.790 B.S. L.574 J.D. [Byers,M.&W.]

Byers, Martelle & Williams, P.L.L.C., (CV)
226 North Main Street, Suite 2, P.O. Box 550, 28139
Telephone: 828-288-1844 Fax: 828-288-1840 URL: http://www.williamsandmartellelawfirm.com
URL: http://www.gbyerslaw.com
Members of Firm: Garland F. Byers, Jr.; Robert Kenneth Martelle; Richard Preston Williams.
General Civil and Criminal Trial Practice in all courts, Family Law, Real Property Law, Elder Law, Wills, Trusts and Estates, Corporate Law, and Municipal Law.
See Professional Biographies, RUTHERFORDTON, NORTH CAROLINA

Byrd, John H., (BV) .... '47 '76 C.575 B.A. L.623 J.D. 113 W. 2nd St.
Callahan, James C. .... '51 '77 C.575 B.A. L.896 J.D. 400 Charlotte Rd.
Dalton, Walter H., (AV) .... '49 '75 C&L.575 B.S., J.D. [Nanney,D.&M.]

Deaton, Biggers & Gulden, P.L.L.C.
(See Shelby)

Elkins & Elkins
(See Hendersonville)

Fletcher, William W. '22 '54 C.214 B.B.A. L.213 LL.B.
(adm. in MI; not adm. in NC) 180 Kings Grant Drive, Unit 202
Greenway, Bradley K., (BV) ..... '52 '83 C.575 A.B. L.1228 J.D. [Hamrick,B.M.G.&L.]
Grimes, S. Janson, (BV) .... '46 '72 C&L.575 B.A., J.D. [Grimes&T.] ⊙
Grimes & Teich, (BV)
365 Charlotte Road (⊙Asheville, Waynesville, NC; Greenville, SC)
Guice, Zoro J., Jr. .... '— '69 C.575 B.A. L.896 J.D. Sr. Resident Supr. Ct. J.

Hamrick, Bowen, Mebane, Greenway & Lloyd, L.L.P., (BV)
153 West Court Street, P.O. Drawer 790, 28139
Telephone: 828-286-9152 Fax: 828-287-9101
Email: hbmg@rfci.net
Members of Firm: Fred Delmar Hamrick, Jr. (1908-1982); Robert L. Mebane; Bradley K. Greenway; David A. Lloyd. Of Counsel: James M. Bowen.
General Trial and Appellate Practice in all State and Federal Courts, Business, Collections and Creditor's Rights, Commercial, Construction, Corporations, DWI, Traffic Offenses, Criminal, Family, Divorce, Equitable Distribution, Child Custody, Child Support, Domestic, Employment, Insurance, Personal Injury, Real Estate, Social Security, Trusts and Estates and Workers Compensation.
See Professional Biographies, RUTHERFORDTON, NORTH CAROLINA

Jolley, Maxie G., II '65 '98 C.575 B.A. L.790 J.D.
(adm. in SC; not adm. in NC) [Ⓐ Arledge]
Jones, Woodrow W. .... '14 '37 C.999 L.896 LL.B. U.S. Sr. Dist. J.
Lane, Peter E., (CV) .... '60 '87 C.861 B.A. L.896 J.D. 131 East Court Street
Leonard, Alan C., (BV) .... '47 '75 C&L.575 B.A., J.D. Dist. Atty.
Lloyd, David A., (BV) .... '65 '90 C.198 A.B. L.575 J.D. [Hamrick,B.M.G.&L.]
Lowe, M. Leonard .... '19 '41 L.895 LL.B. P.O. Box 70‡
Martelle, Robert Kenneth, (CV) .... '69 '95 C.1128 B.A. L.1345 J.D. [Byers,M.&W.]
Mebane, Robert L., (BV) .... '52 '80 C.575 B.A. L.192 J.D. [Hamrick,B.M.G.&L.]
Miller, Elizabeth T., (BV) .... '63 '88 C&L.575 B.A., J.D. [Nanney,D.&M.]
Moore, Faye Bornstein '46 '75 C.145 B.A. L.1000 J.D.
(adm. in GA; not adm. in NC) 122 Huntwood Lane
Nanney, Louis W., Jr., (AV) .... '48 '73 C&L.575 A.B., J.D. [Nanney,D.&M.]

Nanney, Dalton & Miller, L.L.P., (AV)
346 North Main Street, P.O. Box 800, 28139
Telephone: 828-286-8222 Fax: 828-286-8229
Email: bmiller@ndmlaw.com
Members of Firm: Louis W. Nanney, Jr.; Walter H. Dalton; Elizabeth T. Miller.
General Practice in all Federal and State Courts, Trials, Business Law, Real Estate, Probate, Insurance Law, Personal Injury, Auto Accidents, Wrongful Death, Trusts and Estates.
See Professional Biographies, RUTHERFORDTON, NORTH CAROLINA

Norris, David S., (BV) .... '69 '95 C.404 B.A. L.575 J.D. Courthouse
Owens, Hollis M., Jr. .... '23 '49 C.968 A.B. L.228 LL.B. Supr. Ct. J.
Powell, Laura A., (CV) .... '69 '94 C.575 B.A. L.280 J.D. P.O. Box 1451

Roberts Law Firm, The, P.A.
(See Gastonia)

Rogers, David William, (CV) .... '65 '91 C.1288 B.S. L.862 J.D. 222 N. Main
Walker, Edna Ruffin, Attorney at Law .... '70 '96 C&L.1228 B.B.A., J.D. 199 N. Main St.
Williams, Richard Preston, (CV) .... '69 '94 C&L.575 A.B., J.D. [Byers,M.&W.]

Yelton, Farfour, McCartney, Lutz & Craig, P.A.
(See Shelby)

ST. PAULS, 2,137, *Robeson Co.*

Canady, Paul Truett, II, (BV) .... '58 '83 C.896 B.A. L.1228 J.D. [Canady&C.]
Canady & Canady, (BV) .... 304 W. Broad Street
Regan, Cabell Jones .... '52 '79 C.575 A.B. L.1228 J.D. [C.J.Regan]
Regan, George D., (BV) .... '45 '72 C&L.575 A.B., J.D. 119 S. 2nd St.
Regan, Cabell J., P.A. .... P.O. Box 478

SALEMBURG, 409, *Sampson Co.*

Cox, Rita Holbert .... '56 '88 C&L.1228 B.A., J.D. Dept. of Jus.
Maggio, Angelo J. '16 '43 L.180 LL.B.
(adm. in DC; not adm. in NC) P.O. Box 22‡
Moore, Kathy Jean, (CVⓉ) .... '52 '85 C.232 B.A. L.192 J.D. P.O. Box 99

O'Neal, Patrick B. .... '45 '70 C.893 B.A. L.309 J.D. NC Jus. Academy
Smith, Marc K. .... '61 '88 C.34 B.S. L.896 J.D. N.C. Dept. of Justice

SALISBURY, * 26,462, *Rowan Co.*

Abramson, Andrew J. .... '70 '97 C.472 B.A. L.1206 J.D. [Ⓐ Woodson,S.L.S.P.&W.]
Acree, M. Reid, Jr., (BV) .... '60 '89 C&L.896 B.A., J.D. 315 North Main Street
Adams, Scott M., (CV) .... '71 '97 C.945 B.A. L.896 J.D. [Patterson&A.P.] ⊙
Adkins, Michael S., (BV) .... '62 '87 C.77 B.A. L.896 J.D. [Kluttz,R.H.R.&A.]
Arnold, Anthony M. '43 '69 C&L.280 A.B., J.D.
(adm. in GA; not adm. in NC) Pres., Material Sales Co.
Barnhill, Cynthia G. .... '67 '95 C.290 B.A. L.575 J.D. Dist. Atty. Off.

Basinger, John A., Attorney at Law '78 '04 C.125 B.A. L.1228 J.D.
113-A East Council Street, 28144
Telephone: 704-637-0094 Fax: 704-637-0106
Email: johnbasinger2003@yahoo.com URL: http://www.johnbasingerlaw.com
Criminal Law, Felonies, Misdemeanors, Drug Crimes, Driving While Intoxicated, DUI, Juvenile Criminal Law, Family Law, Divorce, Child Custody, Child Support, Adoption Law, Domestic Violence, Visitation Rights, Premarital Agreements, Personal Injury, White Collar Crime, Parole and Probation.
See Professional Biographies, SALISBURY, NORTH CAROLINA

Bingham, David Y. .... '51 '75 C&L.896 B.S., J.D. 113 W. Council St.
Blankenship, Malcolm B., Jr., Attorney at Law, (BV) '46 '74
C.575 A.B. L.896 J.D. 131 N. Main St.
Blanton, Mary R., (BV) .... '50 '81 C.896 B.A. L.276 J.D. [Blanton]
Blanton, Theodore A. (Ted), (BV) .... '50 '84 C.722 B.A. L.276 J.D. [Blanton]

Blanton Law Firm, P.A., (BV)
228 West Council Street, P.O. Box 2327, 28145-2327
Telephone: 704-637-1100 Fax: 704-637-1500
Email: mrb@blantonlawfirm.com URL: http://www.blantonlawoffice.com
Mary R. Blanton (Board Certified Specialist in Family Law, North Carolina State Board of Legal Specialization); Theodore A. (Ted) Blanton.
Family Law, Divorce, Collaborative Law, Child Custody, Child Support, Spousal Support, Criminal Law, Driving While Intoxicated (DWI), Drug Crimes, Felonies, Parole and Probation, Misdemeanors, Traffic Violations, Wrongful Death, Personal Injury, Real Estate, Civil Litigation, Contracts, Family Financial Mediation.
See Professional Biographies, SALISBURY, NORTH CAROLINA

Bowers, Ronald J. .... '43 '69 C.576 B.S. L.575 J.D. 310 N. Main St.
Bridges, Benjamin H., III, (BV) .... '47 '73 C.125 A.B. L.896 J.D. [Bridges]

Bridges Law Firm, (BV)
Salisbury Professional Center, 1809 Brenner Avenue, Suite 203, 28144
Telephone: 704-633-6693 Telecopier: 704-633-6889
Email: bbridges@bridgeslawfirm.com URL: http://www.bbridgeslaw.com
Benjamin H. Bridges, III.
Real Estate Law, Mortgages, Business Law, Contract Law, General Civil Practice, Estate Planning, Probate and Wills.
See Professional Biographies, SALISBURY, NORTH CAROLINA

Brown, Charles E. .... '65 '93 C.34 B.S. L.793 J.D. Chf. Dist. Ct. J.
Burke, George L., Jr., (AV) .... '08 '48 C.576 B.S. L.228 LL.B. 120 Shady Lane‡
Busby, Bonnie L., (BV) .... '45 '80 C.1044 B.S. L.896 J.D. Asst. Dist. Atty.
Busby, Robert F., (BV) .... '47 '75 C.367 B.E.S. L.884 J.D. 901 W. Henderson St.‡
Caddell, Thomas M., (AV) .... '35 '73 C.575 B.S. L.262 J.D. [Shuford,C.&F.]
Calvert, Jill N. .... '72 '97 C.339 B.A. L.280 J.D. [Ⓐ Wallace&G.]
Cameron, William (Bill) W., III .... '75 '04 C.198 B.A. L.16 J.D. [Sherrill&C.]
Carlton, Graham M., Jr., (BV) .... '57 '82 C.1128 B.S. L.896 J.D. 109 W. Council St.

Carter, James L., Jr. '70 '98 C.1128 B.A. L.383 J.D.
625 W. Innes Street, 28144
Telephone: 704-633-8857 Fax: 704-633-8620
Email: jlcarter@salisbury.net URL: http://www.jcarter-law.com
Real Estate, Corporate, Business Law, Small Business, Limited Liability, Traffic, Insurance, Trust and Estates, Wills, Probate, Estate Planning, Contract, Civil Litigation.
See Professional Biographies, SALISBURY, NORTH CAROLINA

Castor, Andrea Bryant .... '72 '99 C.125 B.A. L.607 J.D. [Whitley,C.&J.]
Cobb, Renee A. .... '63 '95 C.1318 B.A. L.574 J.D. Employ. Sec. Comm.
Corriher, James A., (BV) .... '45 '80 C.1128 B.S. L.1228 J.D. [Corriher&K.] ⊙
Corriher & Koontz, (BV) .... 425 N. Main St. (⊙Landis)
Coughenour, William C., (AV) .... '17 '40 C&L.575 A.B., J.D. 611 Wiltshire Village‡
Crowell, Dwight L., III, (BV) .... '49 '75 C.198 B.A. L.896 J.D. [Crowell&P.]
Crowell & Porter, (BV) .... 120 North Jackson Street
Curry, Barbara L., (BV) .... '59 '90 C.47 B.A. L.896 J.D. [Ⓐ Wallace&G.]
Davis, James A., (BV) .... '56 '91 C.125 B.A. L.1339 J.D. [Davis]
Davis, Robert M. .... '27 '50 C.1318 B.S. L.896 J.D. [Davis]

Davis, Amy S.
(See Concord)

Davis Law Firm, (BV) .... 215 North Main Street
Dees, John W. (Jay), II .... '66 '98 C.575 B.A. L.1228 J.D. [Ketner&D.]
Dixon, Beth Spencer .... '64 '89 C.185 B.A. L.790 J.D. Dist. Ct. J., Rowan Co.
Dixon, R. Glenn, Jr. .....'60 '89 C.575 B.A. L.790 J.D. V.P. Real Estate, Food Lion, LLC
Doran, Michael, (BV) .... '58 '83 C.198 B.A. L.896 J.D. [Doran,S.P.H.]
Doran, Shelby, Pethel, Hudson, P.A., (BV) .... 122 North Lee Street
Evans, G. Linn ..... '64 '91 C&L.575 B.S.B.A., J.D. . Gen. Coun., Delhaize America, Inc.
Faust, James Y. .... '77 '04 C.105 B.A. L.124 J.D. [Hancock,F.&N.]
Flynn, Jennifer B., (CV) .... '63 '89 C&L.896 B.A., J.D. [Ⓐ Kluttz,R.H.R.&A.]
Ford, Larry G. .... '35 '65 C.575 A.B. L.896 J.D. Supr Ct. Judge
Fraley, Lucinda L., (BV) .... '68 '95 C.125 B.A. L.1345 J.D. [Shuford,C.&F.]
Gaines, Nancy R. .... '56 '88 C.781 B.S. L.245 J.D. P.O. Box 4118
Goodrich, Alan O., (AVⓉ) .....'58 '84 C.893 B.A. L.802 J.D. Sr. Coun., Food Lion, LLC
Graham, William M., (BV) ......'60 '91 C.125 B.A. L.33 J.D. [Wallace&G.] (⊙Charlotte)
Gray, J. Stephen, (BV) .... '47 '72 C.125 B.A. L.896 J.D. 310 North Main Street
Hancock, R. Darrell, (BV) .... '53 '78 C&L.575 A.B., J.D. [Hancock,F.&N.]

Hancock, Faust and Nance, P.L.L.C., (BV)
316 North Main Street, 28144
Telephone: 704-636-2080 Fax: 704-637-7991
URL: http://www.hfn-law.com
Members of Firm: R. Darrell Hancock; George R. Hundley (1952-2003); James Y. Faust; Bradley J. Nance.
Real Estate, Probate, Estate Planning, Wills, Personal Injury, Traffic Violations, Civil Litigation, Corporate Law and Bankruptcy.
See Professional Biographies, SALISBURY, NORTH CAROLINA

Hartsell & Williams, P.A.
(See Concord)

Hayes, Glenn S., (BV) .... '53 '80 C&L.945 B.A., J.D. [Kluttz,R.H.R.&A.]
Hayes, Joseph A., III '62 '91 C.896 B.A. L.575 J.D.
Legal Affs. Dir. & Asst. Gen. Coun., Food Lion, LLC

Hickey, Christopher J. ....'63 '95 C.201 B.A. L.1003 J.D. [Ⓐ Wallace&G.]
Hinkle, Paul P., Jr. ....'46 '73 C&L.896 B.S., J.D. P.O. Box 2232‡

Holshouser, John L., Jr., (AV) '38 '63 C&L.575 A.B., LL.B. BR
309 North Main Street, Suite 1, 28144
Telephone: 704-637-7700 FAX: 704-633-8617
Email: john@salisbury.net URL: http://www.jholshouserlaw.com
General Civil Trial Practice in State and Federal Courts, County and Local Municipal Law, Real Estate and Business Litigation, Wills, Probate and Estates Administration.
Representative Clients: Rowan County; Farmers & Merchants Bank; Sharonview Federal Credit Union; Falcon Development Group, Inc.
See Professional Biographies, SALISBURY, NORTH CAROLINA

Hudson, John T., (BV) ....'60 '85 C.576 B.A. L.1228 J.D. [Doran,S.P.H.]
Huffman, Richard L., Jr., (AV) ....'49 '81 C.404 B.A. L.896 J.D. [Huffman]
Huffman Law Firm, PA, (AV) ....100 W. Innes St., Ste. 301
Inge, Robert L., (BV) ....'62 '87 C&L.1228 B.S., J.D. 111 W. Council St.
Johnson, Judith H. ....'44 '73 C.228 B.A. L.477 J.D. 1235 W. Henderson St.
Jones, Phyllis P. ....'56 '82 C.228 A.B. L.477 J.D. 1327 Glenwood Ave.
Jones, T. Gregory, (BV) ....'69 '95 C.575 B.S. L.1339 J.D. [Ⓐ Doran,S.P.H.]
Jordan, Darrin D. ....'65 '90 C.125 B.A. L.1228 J.D. [Whitley,C.&J.]
Kenerly, William D., (AV) ....'45 '73 C.228 A.B. L.575 J.D. Dist. Atty.
Kester, Ronald C. '37 '75 C.896 B.A. L.969 J.D.
(adm. in GA; not adm. in NC) 3610 Mooresville Rd.‡
Ketner, Glenn E., Jr., (AV) ....'38 '63 C&L.228 A.B., J.D. [Ketner&D.]

Ketner & Dees, P.A., (AV)
121 East Kerr Street, P.O. Box 1308, 28144
Telephone: 704-637-3434 Fax: 704-637-3449
Email: glenn@ketnerlaw.com URL: http://www.ketner-law.com
Glenn E. Ketner, Jr.; John W. (Jay) Dees, II.
General Civil Practice State and Federal Courts, Real Estate, Zoning, Planning and Land Use, Corporate and Business Law, Elder Law, Trusts and Estates, Estate Planning, Probate, Wills, Health Care Law.
See Professional Biographies, SALISBURY, NORTH CAROLINA

King, Thomas M., (BV) ....'53 '79 C.125 B.A. L.896 J.D. Asst. Dist. Atty.
Kluttz, William C., Jr., (AV) ....'46 '75 C.575 A.B. L.893 J.D. Dist. Ct. Judge

Kluttz, Reamer, Hayes, Randolph & Adkins, L.L.P., (AV) BR
131 North Main Street, P.O. Drawer 1617, 28145-1617
Telephone: 704-636-7100 Telecopier: 704-636-2284
Email: office@rowanlawyer.com URL: http://www.rowanlawyer.com
Wm. Clarence Kluttz (1917-1996); Lewis P. Hamlin, Jr. (1919-1988); Richard R. Reamer; Glenn S. Hayes; James D.K.F. Randolph; Michael S. Adkins. Associates: Nathan C. Prater; Jennifer B. Flynn.
General Civil Practice. Trials. Employment Law, Corporation, Taxation, Real Estate, Estate Planning, Probate and Trusts, Traffic, Criminal Law, Mediation, Personal Injury, Driving While Impaired, Workers Compensation.
Representative Clients: Duke Power Co.; General Electric Co.; North Carolina Farm Bureau Mutual Insurance Co.; The Papco Group, Inc.; Johnson Concrete, Inc.; Rowan Community College; Gerry Wood Automotive, LLC; The Salisbury Post.
See Professional Biographies, SALISBURY, NORTH CAROLINA

Koontz, Earle Allen ....'71 '99 C.575 B.A. L.1228 J.D. [Corriher&K.]
Lawther, Francis Rivers, Jr., (AV) '42 '72 C&L.575 A.B., J.D.
[Woodson,S.L.S.P.&W.]
Lester, Robert A., (BV) ....'— '92 C.140 A.B. L.575 J.D. 1236 W. Innes St.
Lyda, Kimberly A., (BV) ....'69 '94 C.999 B.S. L.896 J.D. Food Lion, LLC
Martin, Jean Sutton ....'67 '98 C&L.896 B.S., J.D. [Ⓐ Wallace&G.]
McKeny, Tripe ....'70 '03 C.437 B.A. L.851 J.D. [McKeny,W.T.]

McKeny, William Trippe
116 North Main Street, 28144
Telephone: 704-636-3700 Fax: 704-636-8060
URL: http://www.trippemckeny.com
Member of Firm: Trippe McKeny.
Bankruptcy, Criminal Law, Traffic Violations, Family Law, Personal Injury, Automobile Accidents.
See Professional Biographies, SALISBURY, NORTH CAROLINA

McLaughlin, Robert F., (BV) ....'47 '77 C.569 B.S. L.896 J.D. 122 N. Ellis Street

Monath, Robert A., (BV) '60 '85 C&L.575 A.B., J.D.
213 South Main Street, Suite 201, 28144
Mailing Address: P.O. Box 4506, Salisbury, NC 28145-4506
Telephone: 704-645-0630 Fax: 704-645-0790
Email: rob@robmonath.com
Copyright, Trademark, Entertainment and Business Law.
Representative Clients: Wachovia Corporation (Legal Division); Catawba College; Pain Relief Centers, P.A.; That's Music to My Ears, LTD; Hinshaw Music.
See Professional Biographies, SALISBURY, NORTH CAROLINA

Nance, Bradley J. ....'77 '03 C.125 B.A. L.607 J.D. [Hancock,F.&N.]
Oberle, Edwin F. ....'41 '66 C.743 B.A. L.215 J.D. 1055 Glenfield Dr.

Oxendine, James T. '65 '94 C.831 B.A. L.823 J.D.
111 West Council Street, 28144
Telephone: 704-636-1862; Toll Free: 877-367-0296 Fax: 704-636-3175
Email: oxendinelaw@velocenet.net URL: http://www.oxendine-law.com
Criminal Law, Driving While Intoxicated (DWI), Traffic Violations, Family Law, Separation, Divorce, Juvenile, Personal Injury, Auto Accidents, Business, Estate Administration and Guardianships.
See Professional Biographies, SALISBURY, NORTH CAROLINA

Parrott, S. Edward, (AV) ....'52 '78 C&L.575 B.S.B.A., J.D. [Woodson,S.L.S.P.&W.]
Patterson, Brent A., (BV) ....'67 '92 [Patterson&A.P.] ⊙

Patterson and Adams PLLC, (BV)
710 North Main Street, 28144 ⊙
Telephone: 704-795-4317 URL: http://www.patterson-adams.com
URL: http://www.pattersonadamslawoffice.com
Scott M. Adams; Brent A. Patterson.
Personal Injury, Automobile Accidents, Wrongful Deaths, Workers Compensation, Medical Malpractice.
Concord, North Carolina Office: 433 Church Street North, 28025. Telephone: 704-795-4317. Fax: 704-795-5738.
Gastonia, North Carolina Office: 1305 East Garrison Boulevard, 28054. Telephone: 704-867-1955. Fax: 704-853-1875.
See Professional Biographies, SALISBURY, NORTH CAROLINA

Pauley, Edward L. ....'66 '91 C&L.923 B.A., J.D. [Ⓐ Wallace&G.]
Pethel, Branson A., (BV) ....'63 '87 C.125 B.A. L.896 J.D. [Doran,S.P.H.]
Porter, J. Andrew, (BV) ....'47 '75 C&L.896 B.A., J.D. [Crowell&P.]
Prater, Nathan C., (BVⓉ) ....'70 '96 C.999 B.A. L.192 J.D. [Ⓐ Kluttz,R.H.R.&A.]
Pross, Michael B. ....'66 '97 C.107 B.A. L.1187 J.D. [Ⓐ Wallace&G.]
Randolph, James D.K.F., (BV) ....'61 '90 C.576 B.A. L.192 J.D. [Kluttz,R.H.R.&A.]
Reamer, Richard R., (AV) ....'45 '71 C.228 A.B. L.575 J.D. [Kluttz,R.H.R.&A.]
Rhodes, Gary C., (BV) ....'46 '72 C.1318 A.B. L.896 J.D. 109 W. Council St.
Sayers, Donald D., (AV) ....'43 '68 C&L.575 A.B., J.D. [Woodson,S.L.S.P.&W.]
Schulman, David A. '57 '83 C.477 B.A. L.245 J.D.
(adm. in GA; not adm. in NC) Lerner Shoes Inc.

Seay, Thomas W., Jr. ....'26 '52 C&L.228 A.B., LL.B. Emer.Supr. Ct. J.‡
Setzer, Kathryn C. ....'78 '03 C.575 B.A. L.1228 J.D. [Ⓐ Doran,S.P.H.]
Shelby, David Alan ....'66 '91 C.125 B.A. L.896 J.D. [Doran,S.P.H.]

Shelley, Mark E.
(See Concord)

Sherrill, Carlyle, (BV) ....'53 '81 C.198 B.A. L.64 J.D. [Sherrill&C.]

Sherrill & Cameron, (BV)
117 West Council Street, 28144
Telephone: 704-633-5723 FAX: 704-633-0150
URL: http://www.sherrillcameron.com
Carlyle Sherrill; William (Bill) W. Cameron, III.
Criminal Trial Practice State and Federal Courts, Driving While Intoxicated, Drug Crimes, Juvenile Crimes, Traffic Violations, Family Law, Divorce, Child Custody, Child Support, Visitation Rights, Personal Injury, Automobile Accidents, Wrongful Death, Real Estate, Construction, Environmental, Landlord and Tenant, Bankruptcy, Debt and Credit, Collections, Wills and Probate.
See Professional Biographies, SALISBURY, NORTH CAROLINA

Shoaf, Milton Bays, Jr. ....'42 '68 C&L.575 A.B., J.D. 315 N. Main St.‡
Shook, Glenn D., (CVⓉ) ....'— '91 C.1270 B.M.E. L.845 J.D. Sr. Coun., Food Lion, LLC
Short, Carl M., Jr., (AV) ....'50 '76 C&L.575 A.B., J.D. [Woodson,S.L.S.P.&W.]
Showfety, June E., (BVⓉ) ....'59 '84 C.1128 B.A. L.838 J.D. [J.E.Showfety]
Showfety, June E., PLLC, (BVⓉ) ....121 W. Council St., Ste. 206

Shuford, Caddell & Fraley, (AV)
205 Wachovia Bank Building, 130 South Main Street, 28144
Telephone: 704-636-8050
Members of Firm: W. T. Shuford (1905-1990); Thomas M. Caddell (Board Certified Specialist in Estate Planning and Probate Law); Lucinda L. Fraley.
Corporation, Taxation, Real Estate, Estate Planning, Trusts and Estates, Wills and Probate, Business Law.
Representative Clients: Wachovia Bank, N.A.; Taylor Clay Products; Rowan Corp.; Ironwood Development, Inc.; Rockwell Farms; Gardner Glass Products, Inc; Premtec, Inc.; Home Concrete Co.; J.H. Cook & Sons, Inc.; Central Carolina Insurance Agency, Inc.
See Professional Biographies, SALISBURY, NORTH CAROLINA

Smith, Douglas A., (CV) '67 '97 C.1063 B.A. L.793 J.D.
216 North Jackson Street, 28144
Telephone: 704-633-9000 Fax: 704-636-3000
Email: attorneysmith@bellsouth.net URL: http://www.lawyers.com/dougsmith
Criminal Law, Felonies, Misdemeanors, Family Law, Divorce, Child Custody, Child Support, Separation, Traffic Violations, Driving While Intoxicated, Construction Law, Children, Child Abuse and Neglect, Child Care, Grandparents Custody, Grandparents Visitation Rights, Juvenile Criminal Law, Step Parent Adoptions, Criminal Defense, Drivers License Suspension, Theft, Weapons Charges, Drug Crimes, Alimony, Domestic Violence, Equitable Distribution, Military Divorce, Name Changes, Paternity, Qualified Domestic Relations Orders, Separation Agreements, Spousal Support, Uncontested Divorce, Guardianship and Conservatorship, Guardian Ad Litem, Incompetency Proceedings, Personal Injury, Accidents, Automobile Accidents and Injuries, Motor Vehicle Accidents and Injuries, Pedestrian Injuries.
See Professional Biographies, SALISBURY, NORTH CAROLINA

Smith, Mary Beth ....'— '91 C&L.575 J.D. 117 S. Main St.
Trent, Lucretia, (CV) ....'47 '90 C.1128 B.A. L.575 J.D. 121 W. Council St., Ste. 103
Walker, Sean C., (BV) ....'71 '97 C.575 B.A. L.1345 J.D. [Woodson,S.L.S.P.&W.]
Wallace, Mona Lisa, (BV) ....'54 '79 C.575 B.A. L.896 J.D. [Wallace&G.] (⊙Charlotte)
Wallace and Graham, (BV) ....525 N. Main St.
Walser, Jason A. ....'71 '98 C&L.575 B.S.B.A., J.D. Land Trust for Central NC
Waters, Sally M. ....'69 '95 C.953 B.A. L.425 J.D. 315 North Main Street
Whitler, Matthew R. ....'71 '98 C&L.923 B.A., J.D. [Ⓐ Wallace&G.]
Whitley, Cecil L., (BV) ....'44 '73 C.125 B.A. L.896 J.D. [Whitley,C.&J.]

Whitley, Castor & Jordan, (BV)
305 North Main Street, 28144
Telephone: 704-637-1111 Fax: 704-642-0672
Members Of Firm: Cecil L. Whitley; Andrea Bryant Castor; Darrin D. Jordan.
Criminal Law, Domestic Law, Personal Injury, Traffic.
See Professional Biographies, SALISBURY, NORTH CAROLINA

Wilson, David B. '55 '84 C.34 B.A./B.S. L.896 J.D.
Rowan Cnty. Dept. of Soc. Services

Woodson, Sayers, Lawther, Short, Parrott & Walker, LLP, (AV)
225 North Main Street, Suite 200, P.O. Box 829, 28145-0829
Telephone: 704-633-5000 Fax: 704-637-2388
Email: woodlaw@carolina.rr.com
Members of Firm: Walter H. Woodson (1875-1964); J. Giles Hudson (1890-1973); James L. Woodson (1916-1992); James G. Hudson, Jr. (1921-1996).
Donald D. Sayers; Francis Rivers Lawther, Jr.; Carl M. Short, Jr.; S. Edward Parrott; Sean C. Walker. Associate: Andrew J. Abramson.
General Practice. Trials in all State and Federal Courts. Estate Planning, Probate and Taxation, Corporate, Municipal and Real Estate Law. Criminal, Family and Domestic Relations Law. Personal Injury.
Representative Clients: Rowan County Board of Education; American Mutual Fire Insurance Co.; First Union National Bank of North Carolina; Cincinnati Insurance Company; City of Salisbury; Catawba College.
Local Counsel for: Piedmont Farm Credit, ACA; Cincinnati Insurance Co.
See Professional Biographies, SALISBURY, NORTH CAROLINA

SALUDA, 488, *Polk Co.*

Atkins, S. Lee, (BV) ....'43 '73 C.576 B.A. L.575 J.D. [Atkins&C.]
Atkins & Craven, (BV) ....Hwy. 176
Craven, Susan S., (BV) ....'44 '71 C.683 A.B. L.846 J.D. [Atkins&C.]
Gordon, William M. '35 '86
(adm. in SC; not adm. in NC) P.O. Box 550
Lewis, Charles B. '28 '62 C&L.260 B.S.B.A., J.D.
(adm. in FL; not adm. in NC) Rte. 1 Box 190‡

SANFORD, * 23,220, *Lee Co.*

Bain, Buzzard & McRae, LLP
(See Lillington)

Basden, Beverly D., (CV) ....'47 '90 C.1228 B.A. L.574 J.D. 1503 Woodland Ave.
Boone, Elizabeth Myrick ....'67 '93 C.896 B.A. L.1228 J.D. 3108 Pine Lake Drive‡
Cabe, Paige C. ....'67 '97 C.575 B.S. L.1228 J.D. [Ⓐ Harrington,W.G.&W.]
Christian, William A. ....'46 '72 C&L.575 B.S., J.D. Chief Dist. J.
Davan, Richard A., Jr '65 '96 C.588 B.A. L.1370 J.D.
(adm. in CA; not adm. in NC) 4300 Oak Park
Davis, Stephanie C. ....'— '05 C.327 B.S. L.574 J.D. [Ⓐ Harrington,W.G.&W.]
Doster, W. Woods, (BV) ....'50 '76 C&L.575 B.A., J.D. [Staton,P.D.P.&S.]
Duncan, Lisa M. ....'61 '87 C.575 B.A. L.1228 J.D. Central Carolina Community College
Durham, Norman G., Attorney at Law ....'54 '84 C&L.1015 B.A., J.D. 315 McIntosh St.
Farrington, Palmer D. '18 '46 C.945 L.724 LL.B.
(adm. in NY; not adm. in NC) 8044 Canterbury Circle‡
Faulk, Tron D. ....'71 '98 C.1128 B.S.W. L.575 J.D. 318 Court Square, Suite D
Feindel, Susan M., (CV) ....'55 '84 C.575 B.A. L.574 J.D. [Ⓐ Harrington,W.G.&W.]

Gfoeller, Monica S. .... '61 '87 C.94 B.A. L.608 J.D. 1502 Woodland Ave.
Gilleland, Robert B., (AV) .... '50 '75 C&L.575 A.B., J.D. [Harrington,W.G.&W.]
Hager, Richard B., (BV) .... '52 '79 C.575 B.A. L.1228 J.D. [R.B.Hager]
Hager, Richard B., P.A., (BV) .... 1518 Elm Street

Harrington, Ward, Gilleland & Winstead, LLP, (AV)
1410 Elm Street, P.O. Box 1045, 27330
Telephone: 919-776-4131 Fax: 919-774-8943
URL: http://www.hwgwlaw.com
Members of Firm: J. Allen Harrington (1914-2005); F. Jefferson Ward, Jr.; Robert B. Gilleland; Eddie S. Winstead. Associates: Susan M. Feindel; Paige C. Cabe; Stephanie C. Davis.
General Practice. Trials in all Courts. Collections, Traffic Matters, Corporation, Probate, Real Estate, Insurance, Workers Compensation and Personal Injury Law.
Approved Attorneys for: Fidelity National, Investors, Chicago and Lawyers Title.
Representative Client: Carolina-Atlantic Distributors, Inc.; Capital Bank; Progressive Contracting Co.; The Keller Group.
References: Branch Banking & Trust Co.; Centura Bank; First Bank.

Holmes, John M. ....'78 '04 C.1111 B.A. L.1228 J.D. [Holmes]
Holmes Law Group, PLLC ....1310 Woodland Ave.
Hoyle, Kenneth R., (AV) ....'26 '51 C&L.575 B.S.C., J.D. Co. Atty.
Love, Jimmy L., (AV) ....'34 '60 C&L.575 A.B., LL.B. [Love&L.]
Love, Jimmy L., Jr., (BV) ....'61 '88 C.575 B.S. L.1345 J.D. [Love&L.]
Love & Love, P.A., (AV) .... 315 McIntosh St.
McPherson, James R. '53 '86
C.1011 B.S. L.276 J.D. Dist. Mgr., Carolina Power & Light Co.

Moore, G. Hugh, (BV) '53 '78 C.198 B.A. L.575 J.D.
1401 Woodland Avenue, P.O. Box 194, 27330
Telephone: 919-774-9536 Facsimile: 919-775-4098
Email: ghmoore05@alltel.net
General Civil, Traffic and Criminal Trial Practice in all Courts. Personal Injury, Workers Compensation, Family and Commercial Law.
See Professional Biographies, SANFORD, NORTH CAROLINA

Moretz, J. Douglas, (BV) .... '43 '72 C.576 B.S.E.E. L.575 J.D. [J.D.Moretz]
Moretz, J. Douglas, P.A., (BV) .... 1114 Winterlocken Dr.
Myles, Jeffery T. ....'45 '71 C&L.575 B.A., J.D. Corp. Atty., L. P. Cox Company, Inc.
Patterson, Susan C. .... '65 '91 C.1130 B.A. L.1228 J.D. City Atty.
Peace, Jeanette T. .... '61 '87 C.296 B.A. L.896 J.D. P.O. Box 2147
Penny, Ronald T., (AV) .... '42 '68 C&L.575 B.S., J.D. 1402 Woodland Ave.
Perkinson, Ronald L., (BV) .... '48 '74 C.575 A.B. L.896 J.D. [⊡ Staton,P.D.P.&S.]
Perry, Marcus S. ....'61 '93 C.999 B.S.B.A. L.221 J.D. 4078-D Chatham Church Rd.
Post, Norman C., Jr., (BV) .... '54 '82 C.232 B.S.B.A. L.1228 J.D. [Staton,P.D.P.&S.]
Raisig, Paul J., Jr., (BV) .... '32 '89 C.627 B.G.E. L.1128 J.D. 325 Mallard Rd.
Schlamp, Philip L. '24 '57 C.672 L.823
(adm. in NY; not adm. in NC) 587 Spyglass Ln.‡
Seymour, Woodrow W., Jr., (BV) .... '50 '75 C.198 A.B. L.896 J.D. [Seymour&S.]
Seymour & Seymour, (BV) .... 133-135 North Moore Street
Shaw, Gerald E., (BV) .... '44 '69 C&L.575 A.B., J.D. 306 McIntosh St.
Silverman, Jonathan, (BV) .... '58 '85 C.705 B.A. L.575 J.D. [Staton,P.D.P.&S.]
Staton, William Wayne, (AV) .... '16 '41 C&L.896 B.A., J.D. [Staton,P.D.P.&S.]
Staton, Perkinson, Doster, Post & Silverman, P.A., (AV) .... 205 Courtland Drive
Stephenson, April E., (CV) ....'59 '84 C.296 B.A. L.1228 J.D. [A.E.Stephenson]
Stephenson, April E., P.A., (CV) .... 1518 Elm
Toddy, Clayton J. '24 '51 C.602 B.S. L.276 J.D.
(adm. in DC; not adm. in NC; Pat.) 714 Darwin Ct.‡
Trageser, Marcella Barkley ....'70 '95 C.893 B.A.S. L.896 J.D. U.S. Dist. Atty.
Ward, F. Jefferson, Jr., (BV) ....'42 '68 C&L.575 A.B., J.D. [Harrington,W.G.&W.]
Ward, Raye .... '56 '98 C.172 B.S. L.1065 J.D. 106 Hillcrest Drive
Webb, Fred D., Jr., Law Offices of .... '57 '87 C.953 B.A. L.575 J.D. 341 Carthage St.
Whitaker, George, (BV) ....'50 '87 C.232 B.S. L.574 J.D. 1600 Elm St.
Wiessler, John C. '22 '50 C.477 B.S.M.E. L.602 J.D.
(adm. in IN; not adm. in NC; Pat.) 6014 Cypress Point‡
Williams, Joyce T. ....'63 '01 C.1044 B.S. L.574 J.D. 607 W. Chisholm St.
Winstead, Eddie S., (BV) .... '53 '82 C.576 B.A. L.1228 J.D. [Harrington,W.G.&W.]
Winstead, Lyda Tyson .... '41 '83 C.577 B.A. L.1228 J.D. Sanford High School
Wishart, Frank W., Jr. ....'64 '92 C.953 B.A. L.1228 J.D. [F.W.Wishart,Jr.]
Wishart, Frank W., Jr., Attorney At Law .... 1503 Elm St., Ste. B

SAPPHIRE VALLEY, —, *Jackson Co.*

Vogelsang, Herbert W. '23 '51 C.188 A.B. L.107 J.D.
(adm. in FL; not adm. in NC) 1600 US Hwy 64, W.‡

SCOTLAND NECK, 2,362, *Halifax Co.*

Dudley, Janet B., Attorney at Law '51 '00 C.228 B.A. L.574 J.D.
140 E. 10th Street, P.O. Box 280, 27874
Telephone: 252-826-5124 Fax: 252-826-5056
Email: jdudley83@aol.com URL: http://www.dudleyfamilylaw.com
Family Law, Divorce, Adoption Law, Child Custody, Child Support, Domestic Violence, Visitation Rights, Traffic Violations, Consumer Fraud, Warranties.
See Professional Biographies, SCOTLAND NECK, NORTH CAROLINA

SELMA, 5,914, *Johnston Co.*

Bryant, Robert W., Jr., (AV) ....'53 '82 C&L.575 B.S., J.D. [Lucas,B.D.&E.]
Denning, W. Robert, III, (BV) .... '54 '83 C&L.1228 B.B.A., J.D. [Lucas,B.D.&E.]
Edwards, Sarah E., (BV) ....'68 '93 C.758 B.M. L.1228 J.D. 208 N. Webb St.
Ellerbe, Sarah .... '68 '93 [Lucas,B.D.&E.]
Fleetwood, Wilson C., Jr. '40 '70 C.575 B.A. L.1049 J.D.
(adm. in CA; not adm. in NC) 405 W. Richardson‡
Godwin, J. Brent ....'49 '92 C.575 B.A. L.1345 J.D. 909 Dixie Dr.
Hewett, Alan Bryant "Chip", (BV) .... '64 '91 C&L.1228 B.A., J.D. [Hinton&H.]
Hinton, W. Kenneth, (BV) ....'40 '65 C&L.896 B.A., LL.B. [Hinton&H.]
Hinton and Hewett, (BV) ....P.O. Box 369
Jones, E. Craig, Jr., (BV) ....'25 '51 C&L.273 J.D. Town Atty.
Lucas, Robert V., (BV) .... '52 '78 C.232 B.A. L.192 J.D. [Lucas,B.D.&E.]
Lucas, Bryant, Denning & Ellerbe, P.A., (AV) ....208 N. Webb St.

SEVEN LAKES, —, *Moore Co.*

(See West End)

SHALLOTTE, 1,381, *Brunswick Co.*

Anderson, Mason H., (BV) .... '35 '67 C.160 B.S. L.575 J.D. P.O. Box 2245

Baxley, Douglas W., (AV) '46 '75 C&L.575 A.B., J.D.
114 Cheers Street, P.O. Box 36, 28459 ⊙
Telephone: 910-754-6582 Fax: 910-754-9272
Email: dwbaxley@shallotte.net
Real Estate, Probate, Corporate, Estate Planning, Civil Practice.
Calabash Office: 10164 Beach Drive, SW, 28467. Telephone: 910-575-6884. Fax: 910-575-6885.
See Professional Biographies, SHALLOTTE, NORTH CAROLINA

Baxley, Douglas W., (AV) '46 '75
C&L.575 A.B., J.D. 114 Cheers Street (⊙Calabash, Shallotte)

Brumbaugh, Mu & King, P.A., (BV)
143 Holden Beach Road Suite #6-A, 28459 ⊙
Telephone: 910-754-3660
URL: http://www.bmklaw.net
Kenneth W. King, Jr.
Practice Limited to Injury Cases. Automobile, Wrongful Death, Medical Malpractice, Workers' Compensation, Products Liability and Social Security Claims.
See Professional Biographies, SHALLOTTE, NORTH CAROLINA

Chandler, John Calvin, (BV) .... '72 '98 C.999 B.S. L.1228 J.D. [Chandler]
Chandler Law Firm, The, P.A., (BV) ....P.O. Box 662
Cox, Michael T., (BV) ....'57 '84 C.575 A.B. L.896 J.D. [M.T.Cox]
Cox, Michael T., P.A., (BV) ....4914 Main St.
Edwards, Sam H., (BV) .... '43 '72 C.835 B.S. L.575 J.D. P.O. Box 968
Floyd, Robert D. ....'56 '83 C.1318 B.A. L.575 J.D. P.O. Box 2861
Foy, Henry G., (AV) .... '42 '68 C&L.575 A.B., J.D. [Frink,F.&Y.]

Frink, Foy & Yount, P.A., (AV) BB
4646 Main Street, P.O. Box 3207, 28459
Telephone: 910-754-6934 Fax: 910-754-9224
Email: frinkfoy@infoave.net
S. Bunn Frink (1899-1989); Henry G. Foy (Retired); Stephen B. Yount.
General Civil and Criminal Practice in State and Federal Courts. Family Law, Trials, Trusts, Personal Injury, Real Estate, Corporate and Admiralty Law.
Local Counsel for: Seaboard Coast Line Railroad Co.
Representative Clients: United Carolina Bank; Pilot Life Insurance Co.; Jefferson Standard Life Insurance Co.; Reeves Telecom Corp.; Nationwide Insurance Co.
Approved Attorneys for: Lawyers Title Insurance Corp.; First Title Insurance Corp.
References: United Carolina Bank; Security Savings Bank S.S.B.
See Professional Biographies, SHALLOTTE, NORTH CAROLINA

Gentry, Ashley Beck, (CV) '69 '96 C&L.896 B.A., J.D.
(adm. in SC; not adm. in NC) [Hudson&G.] ⊙
Hewett, Mack L., Jr., (CV) ....'53 '99 C.575 B.S. L.1158 J.D. [Hewett]
Hewett Law Firm, (CV) ....632 Village Road
Hudson, J. Dwight, (BVⓉ) ....'44 '72 C.575 A.B. L.790 J.D. [Hudson&G.] ⊙
Hudson & Gentry, L.L.C., (BVⓉ)
5211 South Main Street Suite 511 (⊙Conway, Myrtle Beach, SC)

Jones, Greg, & Associates, P.A.
(See Wilmington)

King, Kenneth W., Jr., (BV) ...... '61 '86 C.575 B.S. L.469 J.D. [Brumbaugh,M.&K.] ⊙
Lewis, Mark A., (BV) .... '56 '81 C.276 A.B. L.228 J.D. [Ramos&L.]
MacCallum, James J., (AVⓉ) ....'45 '77 C.437 A.B. L.923 J.D. 4914 Main St.
McLamb, Sheila K. ....'57 '83 C.953 B.S. L.1228 J.D. 111 Pine St.
Payne, W. James, (BV) ....'60 '84 C&L.1228 B.S., J.D. [Powell&P.]
Powell, William A., (BV) ....'30 '58 C&L.575 B.S., J.D. [Powell&P.]
Powell & Payne, (BV) ....4434 Main St.
Ramos, Michael R., (AV) ....'50 '82 C.1317 B.A. L.1228 J.D. [Ramos&L.]

Ramos & Lewis, L.L.P., (AV)
5101-4 Sellers Street, Meadow Square, P.O. Box 2019, 28459
Telephone: 910-754-7557; 754-7447 Fax: 910-754-6229
Email: ramoslewis@infoave.net
Michael R. Ramos (Board Certified Specialist in Criminal Law, North Carolina State Bar Board of Legal Specialization); Mark A. Lewis.
Real Property, Wills, Trusts and Estates, Corporations, Domestic, Hospital, Criminal Defense, Municipal, Personal Injury, Administrative Law, Criminal and Civil Litigation in State and Federal Courts.
Counsel for: Town of Calabash; BB&T; Brunswick Community Hospital; Security Savings Bank; Bank of America; First Citizens Bank; UAW-Legal Services Plan; Farmers Home Administration.
See Professional Biographies, SHALLOTTE, NORTH CAROLINA

Trest, Roy D., (AV) ....'48 '77 C.575 B.S. L.500 J.D. 114 Cheers Street (⊙Calabash)

Tyson, H. Mac, II, (CV) '51 '77 C.575 B.A. L.574 J.D.
4647 Main Street, Suite 11, 28470
Telephone: 910-755-6600 Fax: 910-754-3800
Email: hmactyson2@atmc.net URL: http://www.lawyers.com/mactysonii
General Practice including General Civil Trial, Traffic Violations, Criminal Defense, Personal Injury, Corporate, Municipal, Military Law, Equitable Distribution, Domestic Law, Workers Compensation, Real Estate (Commercial and Residential), Probate, Wills and Estates, Taxation, Business Litigation, Zoning Law, Governmental Law and Ethics.
Approved Attorney for: Lawyers Title Insurance Co.; Chicago Title Insurance Co.; Investor's Title Insurance Corp.
Representative Clients: Systel Office Automation; Tire King of Jacksonville, Inc.; Chrysler Motor Co.
References: First Citizens Bank & Trust Co.; Branch Bank & Trust.
See Professional Biographies, SHALLOTTE, NORTH CAROLINA

Yount, Stephen B., (BV) ....'52 '80 C.232 B.A. L.574 J.D. [Frink,F.&Y.]

SHELBY, * 19,477, *Cleveland Co.*

Bednarik, Michael J., Law Offices of, (BV) '55 '81
C.896 B.A. L.809 J.D. 421 S. Lafayette St. (⊙Charlotte)
Biggers, A. Susan, (BV) ....'66 '91 C.896 B.A. L.575 J.D. [Deaton,B.&G.]

Bogle, Anthony & Leach, P.A.
(See Gastonia)

Bridges, Forrest Donald, (AV) ....'53 '77 C.1128 B.A. L.896 J.D. Judge
Bridges, Kenneth D. ....'30 '55 C&L.896 B.S., LL.B. P.O. Box 942★
Brown, Becky J., (BV) .... '63 '88 C.610 B.S.J. L.150 J.D. 211 S. De Kalb St.

Bumgardner, Don H.
(See Gastonia)

Cash, C. B., Jr., (AV) ....'25 '50 C&L.896 J.D. 224 Windsor Dr.‡
Cerwin, Todd R., (BV) ....'58 '84 C.966 B.S. L.1228 J.D. [Cerwin]

Cerwin Law Firm, (BV)
522 S. DeKalb Street, 28150
Telephone: 704-471-0808 Fax: 704-471-0878
Email: t_cerwin@bellsouth.net
Member of Firm: Todd R. Cerwin. Associate: Michael W. Miller.
Personal Injury, Workers Compensation, Social Security, Criminal, Traffic, Automobile Accidents, Family Law, Child Custody, Estate Contested.
See Professional Biographies, SHELBY, NORTH CAROLINA

Church, John D., (AV) ....'42 '67 C&L.575 A.B., J.D. [Church,P.&W.]
Church, Paksoy & Wray, (AV) ....205 S. Washington St.
Colley, A. Gordon, Jr. '14 '51 C&L.893 B.S., J.D.
(adm. in VA; not adm. in NC) 506 Corvair Lane‡
Craig, Sam B. ....'58 '00 C.160 B.S. L.790 J.D. [Yelton,F.M.L.&C.]
Craver, Adelaide A. ....'42 '67 C.228 A.B. L.575 J.D. First Natl. Bk. of Shelby
Craver, Richard D., (BV) ....'42 '67 C&L.575 B.A., J.D. 522 W. Marion St.
Deaton, W. Robinson, Jr., (AV) .... '51 '76 C.838 B.S. L.228 J.D. [Deaton,B.&G.]

Deaton, Biggers & Gulden, P.L.L.C., (AV)
402 East Graham Street, P.O. Box 458, 28150
Telephone: 704-482-7300 Fax: 704-481-9562
Email: robdeaton@bellsouth.net URL: http://www.lawyers.com/shelbylaw
W. Robinson Deaton, Jr.; A. Susan Biggers; Brian Donald Gulden.
General Civil Practice. Trials. Practice before all State and Federal Courts and Administrative Agencies, Real Estate, Business Law, Wills and Estates, Estate Planning, Personal Injury, Workers Compensation, Criminal Law.
See Professional Biographies, SHELBY, NORTH CAROLINA

Ditz, Paul J., (CV) .... '71 '97 C.823 B.A. L.896 J.D. [Flowers,M.M.&D.]
Farfour, Leslie A., Jr., (BV) .... '46 '72 C&L.575 A.B., J.D. [Yelton,F.M.L.&C.]
Flowers, Fred A., (AV) .... '39 '63 C&L.896 B.A., LL.B. [Flowers,M.M.&D.]

Flowers, Martin, Moore & Ditz, P.A., (AV)
212 South DeKalb Street, 28150
Telephone: 704-482-4441 Fax: 704-482-4872
Email: lawyers@flowersmartinmoore.com
L. T. Hamrick (1911-1989); Joe Mauney (Retired); Fred A. Flowers; Thomas W. Martin, Jr.; Timothy K. Moore; Paul J. Ditz.
Transaction and Litigation Practice. Civil and Criminal Trial Practice in State and Federal Courts. Banking, Business/Corporate Law, Entertainment Law, Real Estate, Estate Planning, Probate and Trusts, Family Law, Governmental Law, Education Law, Personal Injury, Social Security Disability, Workers Compensation, Traffic.
Approved Attorneys for: Lawyers Title Insurance Corp.
See Professional Biographies, SHELBY, NORTH CAROLINA

Foster, Dina F. .... '65 '91 C.797 B.A. L.469 J.D. Dist. J.
Gardner, O. Max, III, (AV) .... '45 '74 C&L.575 A.B., J.D. P.O. Box 1000

Garland, J. Boyce, Jr.
(See Gastonia)

Gray, Layton, Kersh, Solomon, Sigmon, Furr & Smith, P.A.
(See Gastonia)

Griffin, Michael H., (BV) .... '53 '79 C.575 B.A. L.192 J.D. [Griffin,M.H.]
Griffin, Michael H., P.A., (BV) .... 403 South Lafayette Street
Gulden, Brian Donald ....'— '00 C.48 B.S. L.801 J.D. [Deaton,B.&G.]
Hamrick, George W. .... '33 '58 C&L.896 B.S., J.D. Ret. Chf. Dist. J.
Horn, C. A., (BV) .... '33 '61 C&L.896 B.S., LL.B. 211 S. DeKalb St.

Hullender, David Mark
(See Kings Mountain)

Kaylor, Stephen D., (BV) .... '51 '79 C.232 B.A. L.1228 J.D. 512 Leander St.
Kennedy, Michael S., (BV) .... '41 '65 C&L.575 A.B., J.D. City Atty.
Lackey, Mark D., (BV) .... '58 '83 C&L.575 A.B., J.D. [Lackey&L.]
Lackey, Seth N., (CV) .... '65 '93 C.575 B.A. L.1228 J.D. [Lackey&L.]

Lackey & Lackey, (BV)
400 West Warren Street, P.O. Box 2544, 28150
Telephone: 704-487-4511 Fax: 704-487-4222
Email: lackeyandlackey@aol.com
Members of Firm: Mark D. Lackey; Seth N. Lackey.
General Practice. Trials in State and Federal Courts. Corporate, Personal Injury, Estates, Wills, Trusts and Real Property.
Representative Clients: Shelby Federal Savings and Loan Assn.; United States Fidelity & Guaranty Co.; PPG Industries, Inc.; Celanese Corp.; J. P. Stevens Co.; Martin-Marietta Corp.; Duke Power Co.; NationsBank; N.C. State Employees Credit Union; Grover Industries, Inc.
See Professional Biographies, SHELBY, NORTH CAROLINA

Leigh, Gary S., Law Offices of .... '74 '98 C.925 L.200 J.D. 222 S. Washington St.
Li, Leyi "Larry", (CV) .... '53 '89 C.999 B.A. L.1345 J.D. 816 Surrey Dr.
Lutz, Robert Howard, (BV) .... '63 '89 C.404 B.A. L.1059 J.D. [Yelton,F.M.L.&C.]
Martin, Thomas W., Jr., (BV) .... '51 '76 C&L.896 B.A., J.D. [Flowers,M.M.&D.]
Mauney, Joe, (AV) .... '31 '55 C&L.896 B.A., J.D. [Flowers,M.M.&D.] ‡
McCartney, Charles E., Jr., (BV) ..... '47 '72 C&L.896 B.A., J.D. [© Yelton,F.M.L.&C.]
McLain, Brenda S., (BV) .... '52 '79 C&L.575 B.A., J.D. 310-3 E. Graham St.
McWhirter, Colin P., (CV) .... '62 '90 C.999 B.S. L.1228 J.D. 201 W. Marion Street
Meekins, Ralph W., (BV) .... '60 '86 C.575 B.A. L.1228 J.D. 1219 Fallston Rd.
Miller, Michael W. .... '65 '97 C.1369 B.A. L.1339 J.D. [Ⓐ Cerwin]
Moore, Timothy K., (CV) .... '70 '95 C.575 B.A. L.616 J.D. [Flowers,M.M.&D.]

Mullen Holland & Cooper P.A.
(See Gastonia)

Muskus, Michael A. .... '67 '99 C.240 B.A. L.1252 J.D. 100 Justice Pl.
Pack, Terry L., (BV) .... '61 '91 C.34 B.A. L.192 J.D. 211 S. Dekalb
Paksoy, Ali, Jr., (BV) .... '48 '74 C.575 A.B. L.16 J.D. [Church,P.&W.]
Plowden, William E., Jr. '45 '78 C.606 B.A. L.969 J.D.
(adm. in GA; not adm. in NC) V.P. & Tr. Offr., First Natl. Bk. of Shelby
Radeker, Gwynn G., (BV) .... '44 '73 C.951 B.A. L.575 J.D. Asst. Dist. Atty.

Roberts Law Firm, The, P.A.
(See Gastonia)

Schweppe, David M., II, (BV) .... '71 '97 C.902 B.S. L.1228 J.D. [Schweppe&S.]
Schweppe, John V., Jr., (BV) .... '46 '72 C.901 B.A. L.575 J.D. [Schweppe&S.]
Schweppe & Schweppe, P.A., (BV) .... P.O. Box 1269
Sweat, Daniel W., (BV) '63 '92
C.278 B.B.A. L.469 J.D. Corp. Coun., Cleveland Reg. Med. Ctr.
Talbert, Daniel Russell .... '76 '01 C.575 B.S. L.1228 J.D. 1219 Fallston Road
Teddy, David Roy, (CV) .... '63 '88 C.838 B.S.B.A. L.1228 J.D. 1219 Fallston Road
Trammell, Jerry M., (CV) .... '42 '67 C.198 B.A. L.575 J.D. Asst. Dist. Atty.
Tutterow, Cynthia D., (BV) .... '67 '92 C&L.575 B.A., J.D. Off. of Dist. Atty.
West, J. A., (BV) .... '24 '50 C.896 B.S. L.228 LL.B. 211 S. De Kalb

Wilkie, Lynn Broadway, Law Office of
(See Lincolnton)

Wilson, Larry J. .... '56 '89 C.1128 B.S. L.575 J.D. Dist. J.
Wray, Charles W., Jr., (BV) .... '39 '65 C&L.896 A.B., J.D. 301 East Warren St.
Wray, Julian B., (BV) .... '43 '68 C&L.896 B.A., J.D. [Church,P.&W.]
Wright, Karen C., (BV) .... '62 '90 C.1128 B.A. L.1345 J.D. [Wright]
Wright Law Firm, (BV) .... 310-7 East Graham Street
Yelton, Robert W., (BV) .... '42 '67 C&L.896 B.A., J.D. [Yelton,F.M.L.&C.]

Yelton, Farfour, McCartney, Lutz & Craig, P.A., (BV)
Professional Mall, 211 South Washington Street, P.O. Box 1329, 28150
Telephone: 704-482-7718 Fax: 704-482-6747
Email: yeltonr@bellsouth.net URL: http://www.ymflawfirm.com
Robert W. Yelton; Leslie A. Farfour, Jr.; Robert Howard Lutz; Sam B. Craig. Of Counsel: Charles E. McCartney, Jr.
General Practice. Corporation, Estate Planning, and Personal Injury Law. Trial and appellate practice in all courts. Creditors'' Rights and Bankruptcy law. Domestic and Family Law.
Reference: The First National Bank of Shelby, Inc.
See Professional Biographies, SHELBY, NORTH CAROLINA

SILER CITY, 6,966, *Chatham Co.*

Atwater, William Bennett, Jr., (BV) .... '51 '76 C.575 A.B. L.896 J.D. [Edwards&A.]
Dark, L. T., Jr., (BV) .... '21 '49 C.797 L.896 J.D. 301 E. Raleigh St.
Edwards, Phil S., (BV) .... '38 '64 C&L.575 B.S., J.D. [Edwards&A.]
Edwards & Atwater, (BV) .... 122 S. Chatham Ave.
Hancock, Burnace M., Jr. .... '41 '68 C&L.896 B.A., J.D. P.O. Box 592‡
Moody, Jack A., (AV) .... '27 '55 C.240 A.B. L.692 J.D. [© Moody,W.&R.] ‡
Moody, Williams & Roper, (AV) .... 235 E. Raleigh St.
Paschal, Wade H., Jr. .... '38 '66 C&L.896 B.B.A., LL.B. 301 E. Raleigh St.
Roper, C. Todd, (BV) .... '63 '89 C.16 B.S.C./B.A. L.192 J.D. [Moody,W.&R.]
Ryan, Kathleen Anne .... '56 '91 C.352 B.A. L.46 J.D. 250 Wildflower Lane (Pat.)
Stone, J. Ed, (BV) .... '37 '62 C.896 B.B.A. L.575 J.D. 229 East Raleigh St.
Williams, J. Samuel (Sam), (AV) .... '44 '70 C.575 B.A. L.896 J.D. [Moody,W.&R.]

SKYLAND, 2,177, *Buncombe Co.*

Barnwell, Stephen, (BV) '49 '76
C.576 B.S. L.790 J.D. 2000 Hendersonville Rd. (Asheville)

SMITHFIELD, * 11,510, *Johnston Co.*

Anderson, Edward Lee, II '59 '84 C.88 B.A. L.880 J.D.
(adm. in TN; not adm. in NC) 817 S. Vermont St.
Armstrong, L. Lamar, Jr., (AV) .... '56 '81 C&L.575 A.B., J.D. [Armstrong&A.]
Armstrong, Marcia H., (AV) .... '58 '83 C.758 B.A. L.896 J.D. [Armstrong&A.]
Armstrong & Armstrong, P.A., (AV) .... 602 South Third Street
Ashley, Emery D., (BV) .... '61 '89 C&L.1228 B.B.A., J.D. 208 East Church Street
Ashley, Wallace, Jr., (AV) .... '28 '54 C&L.575 B.S., J.D. 208 E. Church St.
Beam, Michael S., III, (BV) .... '61 '89 C&L.575 B.S., J.D. Asst. Dist. Atty.
Berkau, Thomas S., (AV) .... '47 '74 C.838 B.S. L.575 J.D. 212 Church St.
Bowens, Stephon John '68 '94 C.576 B.A. L.574 J.D.
Staff Atty., East Central Community Legal Services

Breeden, Jonathan D.
(See Garner)

Britt, William Ross, (AV) .... '23 '48 C&L.575 A.B., LL.B. 108 Johnston St.
Coats, Jason H. .... '77 '03 C&L.1228 B.B.A., J.D. [Ⓐ Wilkins&W.]
Corbett, Albert A., Jr. .... '43 '69 C&L.896 B.A., J.D. Dist. J.
Daughtry, Kelly K. .... '69 '95 C.197 B.A. L.575 J.D. P.O. Box 1960
Dobson, Tyson Y., Jr. .... '30 '57 C&L.575 A.B., LL.B. Dist. J.
Doyle, Susan I., (BV) .... '68 '93 C.575 B.A. L.1345 J.D. Dist. Atty. Off.
Floors, James E., (CV) .... '36 '71 C.999 B.S. L.896 J.D. 141 N. Second St.‡
Fortner, Dionne Loy, (BV) .... '69 '95 C&L.575 B.A., J.D. [Woodruff,R.&F.]
Guy, Laura Jean, (BV) .... '47 '72 C.138 B.A. L.228 J.D. 141 East Market Street

Hales & Conaway, PLLC, The Law Offices of
(See Clinton)

Haygood, Erin H. .... '72 '97 C.577 B.A. L.896 J.D. Staff Atty.
Holland, W. A., Jr., (BV) .... '45 '72 C.575 A.B. L.421 J.D. 201 N. Second St.
Howerton, Joy .... '58 '87 C.576 B.A. L.575 J.D. 207 N. 2nd St.‡
Jenkins, Knox V., Jr. .... '34 '62 C&L.575 A.B., LL.B. Supr. Ct. J.
Jones, Joy A. .... '58 '89 C.575 B.S. L.347 J.D. [Ⓐ Narron,O.&W.]

Jones, Jesse W.
(See Lillington)

Kirby, Ann H., (BV) .... '58 '85 C.925 B.S. L.1228 J.D. State Atty. Off.
Knott, Brian R. .... '68 '95 C.475 B.S. L.45 J.D. [Ⓐ Spence&S.]
Levinson, James R., (BV) .... '44 '74 C.871 B.A./B.S. L.575 J.D. [Levinson&L.] ⊙
Levinson & Levinson, (BV) .... 219 Johnson Street (⊙Benson)
Lock, Thomas H., (AV) .... '56 '81 C&L.575 B.A., J.D. Dist. Atty.
Mast, Charles D., (BV) .... '61 '87 C&L.896 B.S., J.D. [Mast,S.M.M.S.&J.]
Mast, George B., (AV) .... '36 '60 C&L.896 B.S., LL.B. [Mast,S.M.M.S.&J.]
Mast, Schulz, Mast, Mills, Stem & Johnson, P.A., (AV) .... P.O. Box 119 (⊙Garner)
Mills, David F., (BV) .... '66 '91 C.1228 B.A. L.1345 J.D. [Mast,S.M.M.S.&J.]
Mobley, T. Marie .... '80 '05 C&L.1228 B.A., J.D. [Ⓐ Mast,S.M.M.S.&J.]
Morris, John W. .... '52 '81 C.576 B.S. L.259 J.D. Gaskin Building‡
Narron, James W., (AV) .... '48 '75 C.575 B.A. L.866 J.D. [Narron,O.&W.]

Narron, O'Hale & Whittington, P.A., (AV) BB
102 South Third Street, P.O. Box 1567, 27577 ⊙
Telephone: 919-934-6021 Fax: 919-934-6280
URL: http://www.nowlaw.com
James W. Narron (Board Certified Specialist in Estate Planning and Probate Law); John P. O'Hale (Board Certified Specialist in Criminal Law); O. Hampton Whittington, Jr. (Resident, Benson Office). Associates: Jason W. Wenzel; Joy A. Jones; E. Scott Tart.
Alternative Dispute Resolution, Asset Acquisition, Mergers, and Divestitures, Automobile Accidents and Injuries, Civil Litigation, Corporate Law, Criminal Law, Trial and Appeals in State and Federal Courts, DWI, Elder Law, Estate Planning, Estate and Trusts, Family Law, Personal Injury, Taxation, Real Property Law, Commercial and Residential Real Estate, Workers Compensation, Wrongful Death.
Representative Clients: Wachovia Bank, N.A.; First Citizens Bank and Trust; E.D. Parker Corp.; Benson Auto Supply, Inc.; Carroll's Plant Center; Etheridge Oil Co.
Approved Attorneys For: Lawyers Title Insurance Corp.; Key Title Insurance Co.; Fidelity National Title Insurance Co.; Investors Title Insurance Co.
Benson, North Carolina Office: 207 East Main Street, P.O. Box 457. Telephone: 919-894-8565. Fax: 919-894-1198.
See Professional Biographies, SMITHFIELD, NORTH CAROLINA

O'Connor, Jennifer S. .... '71 '98 C.34 B.A. L.1228 J.D. 201 N. Second Street
O'Hale, John P., (AV) .... '50 '75 C&L.575 A.B., J.D. [Narron,O.&W.]
Payne, John M., (BV) .... '56 '83 C&L.575 B.A., J.D. Co. Atty.
Pridgen, Elton C. .... '24 '54 C&L.575 A.B., LL.B. Ret. Dist. J.‡
Reece, Mary M. .... '69 '94 C.228 B.A. L.575 J.D. [Woodruff,R.&F.]
Reece, Michael J. .... '68 '94 C.576 B.S. L.575 J.D. [Woodruff,R.&F.]
Rose, Terry F. .... '59 '92 C.232 B.S.N. L.574 J.D. 212 Bridge Street

Rose Rand Attorneys, P.A.
(See Wilson)

Schulz, Bradley N., (BV) .... '59 '85 C.896 B.A. L.564 J.D. [Mast,S.M.M.S.&J.]

Smith and Strickland, PLLC
(See Goldsboro)

Spence, Robert A., (AV) .... '22 '48 C&L.575 B.S., LL.B. Town Atty.‡
Spence, Robert A., Jr., (AV) .... '49 '75 C.918 A.B. L.575 J.D. [Spence&S.]

Spence & Spence, P.A., (AV)
212 South Second Street, P.O. Box 1335, 27577
Telephone: 919-934-1149 Fax: 919-934-3635
Email: spence@sst-law.com URL: http://www.sstlaw.com
Robert A. Spence, Jr. (Board Certified Specialist in Real Property Law, Residential Transactions, North Carolina State Board of Legal Specialization);—Brian R. Knott.
Civil Trial Practice, Insurance Litigation, Real Property and Business Litigation Transactions, Personal Injury, Construction and Business Litigation, Municipal Law, Planning Litigation, Corporation, Real Estate, Family Law, Juvenile, Domestic Relations, Traffic Tickets.
Representative Clients: Town of Smithfield; Allstate Insurance Co.; Independent Builders Supply Assn., Inc.; Town of Pine Level.
See Professional Biographies, SMITHFIELD, NORTH CAROLINA

Starling, Luther D., Jr, (BV) .... '65 '90 L.896 J.D. 405 E. Market St.
Stem, Christi C., (BV) .... '64 '93 C.232 B.A. L.1228 J.D. [Mast,S.M.M.S.&J.]
Stevens, L. Austin, (AV) .... '33 '59 C&L.575 B.S., J.D. 139 E. Market St.‡
Stubbs, Robert D., (BV) .... '47 '82 C.228 B.A. L.575 J.D. Asst. Dist. Atty.
Suarez, Vilma, (BV) .... '46 '85 Staff Atty., East Central Community Legal Services
Tart, E. Scott .... '76 '01 C.1228 B.A. L.577 J.D. [Ⓐ Narron,O.&W.] ⊙
Twisdale, John W., (BV) .... '36 '61 C.576 L.575 LL.B. 1755 Buffalo Rd.
Wellons, Allen H., (BV) .... '49 '75 C.575 B.A. L.574 J.D. [Wilkins&W.]
Wellons, James A., Jr., (AV) .... '10 '38 C.228 B.B.A. L.575 J.D. N. 2nd St.
Wenzel, Jason W. .... '76 '02 C.20 B.A. L.896 J.D. [Ⓐ Narron,O.&W.]
Wheeler, Travis Nathanael .... '70 '00 C&L.1228 B.A., J.D. P.O. Box 1598
Whitley, John A., (BV) .... '52 '79 C.896 B.A. L.1228 J.D. 219 Johnston St.
Whittington, O. Hampton, Jr., (AV) .... '49 '75 [Narron,O.&W.]

Wilkins & Wellons, (BV)
141 East Market Street, 27577
Telephone: 919-934-0553 Fax: 919-934-4613
Allen H. Wellons. Associate: Jason H. Coats.
Personal Injury, Workers Compensation, Real Estate, Traffic Violations, Driving While Intoxicated, Corporate, Civil Litigation, Business Transactions, Automobile Accidents, Truck Accidents, Wrongful Death.
See Professional Biographies, SMITHFIELD, NORTH CAROLINA

Willis, Robert J., Law Offices of
(See Raleigh)

Woodard, Stephen C., Jr., (AV) .... '49 '76 C.575 A.B. L.574 J.D. P.O. Box 1960
Woodruff, Gordon C., (AV) .... '51 '76 C.575 B.A. L.896 J.D. [Woodruff,R.&F.]

Woodruff, Reece & Fortner, (AV)
1023 B West Market Street, P.O. Box 708, 27577
Telephone: 919-934-4000 Fax: 919-934-5884 URL: http://www.wrflaw.com
URL: http://www.lawyers.com/reecelawfirm
Gordon C. Woodruff; Michael J. Reece; Mary M. Reece; Dionne Loy Fortner.
General Practice, Civil Trial Practice, Criminal, Driving While Intoxicated, Traffic Violations, Personal Injury, Domestic Relations, Family Law, Bankruptcy.
See Professional Biographies, SMITHFIELD, NORTH CAROLINA

SNEADS FERRY, 2,248, *Onslow Co.*

Dunn, Janine W., (BV) .... '54 '80 C&L.896 B.A., J.D. P.O. Box 842

SNOW HILL, * 1,514, *Greene Co.*

Crutchfield, Karen M., (BV) .... '54 '79 C&L.896 B.A., J.D. [Horton&C.]
Davis, Delaina J. .... '74 '99 C.576 B.S. L.1228 J.D. [White&A.] ⊙
Fillippeli, David J., Jr., (BV) .... '60 '85 C.576 B.A. L.575 J.D. [White&A.] ⊙
Horton, I. Joseph, (AV) .... '23 '50 C.55 A.B. L.896 LL.B. [Horton&C.]
Horton & Crutchfield, P.A., (AV) ....Court House Square
Hulbert, Robert B., Jr., (BV) .... '51 '76 C&L.896 B.A., J.D. P.O. Box 187
Jenkins, William R. .... '36 '66 C.575 B.S. L.362 LL.B. P.O. Box 561
Manning, William E., Jr., (BV) .... '66 '91 C&L.575 B.S.B.A., J.D. [White&A.] ⊙
White & Allen, P.A., (AV) .... 109 South East Second Street (⊙Kinston)

SOUTHERN PINES, 10,918, *Moore Co.*

Adinolfi, David J., II '68 '94 C.867 B.A. L.1218 J.D.
(adm. in NY; not adm. in NC) 179 Hunter Trail
Blevins, Steven W., (BV) .... '63 '92 C.575 B.A. L.1228 J.D. [Stovall&B.]
Bowler, John E. '19 '49 L.262 LL.B.
(adm. in NY; not adm. in NC) 500 Waters Drive‡
Broughton, H. Chalk, Jr., (BV) .... '61 '88 C&L.575 B.A., J.D. [Poyner&S.]
Broughton, Howard C., (BV) .... '30 '58 C&L.575 B.S.B.A., LL.B. [Ⓒ Poyner&S.]

Clark, William E.
(See Fayetteville)

Clarke & Phifer, LLP
(See Pinehurst)

Costanza, Richard John, (BV) '69 '94
C&L.1228 B.A., J.D. Law Offices of Richard J. Costanza
Crews, William B., Jr., (BV) .... '35 '65 C.575 B.A. L.896 J.D. [W.B.Crews,Jr.]
Crews, William B., Jr., PLLC, (BV) .... 235 E. Pennsylvania Ave.
Crockett, David G., (BV) .... '45 '70 C&L.575 A.B., J.D. [D.G.Crockett]
Crockett, David G., Law Office of, (BV) ....135 W. Vermont Ave.
Cunningham, Bruce T., Jr., (AV) ... '47 '73 C.575 A.B. L.893 J.D. [Cunningham,D.P.&S.]
Cunningham, Dedmond, Petersen & Smith, (AV) .... 225 North Bennett Street
Dedmond, Richard E., (BV) .... '47 '77 C&L.575 B.S., J.D. [Cunningham,D.P.&S.]
Dow, Randolph C., (BV) .... '50 '81 C.879 B.S. L.836 J.D. [Ⓒ Gill&T.]
Gatti, Raymond R., (CV) .... '55 '86 C&L.896 B.A., J.D. P.O. Box 1843
Gaydica, J. Stephen, III, (BV) .... '49 '74 C&L.896 B.A., J.D. P.O. Box 547
Gill, Douglas R., (AV) .... '40 '65 C.228 B.A. L.309 LL.B. [Gill&T.]
Gill & Tobias, (AV) .... 225 North Bennett Street
Good, James W., Jr. '10 '35 C&L.597 A.B., J.D.
(adm. in IL; not adm. in NC) P.O. Box 1497‡
Hardison, Kenneth L., (BV) .... '56 '82 C&L.1228 B.S., J.D. [Hardison&L.] ⊙
Hardison & Leone, L.L.P., (AV)
235 E. Pennsylvania Avenue (⊙Charlotte, Dunn, Fayetteville, Greensboro, Raleigh, NC; Myrtle Beach, SC)
Hay, Carol A. '35 '79 C.838 B.A. L.494 J.D.
(adm. in MN; not adm. in NC) 20 Glen Devon Dr.‡
Hill, Peter A. '51 '78 C.813 A.B. L.945 J.D.
(adm. in VA; not adm. in NC) P.O. Box 1021★
Jordan, Wayne E. '38 '63 C&L.896 B.A., LL.B.
V.P. & Reg. Tr. Offr., First Union Nat. Bk. of N.C.
McDevitt, Noel B., Jr., (BV) '64 '89
C.896 B.A. L.469 J.D. 115 West Pennsylvania Avenue
McLeod, Katharine, (BV) .... '49 '78 C&L.896 B.A., J.D. P.O. Box 2212

Morris Law Office
(See Whispering Pines)

Patterson, Sandy G., (BV) .... '51 '77 C&L.896 B.A., J.D. 245 S.E. Broad St.

Poyner & Spruill LLP, (AV)
135 West New Hampshire Avenue, P.O. Box 371, 28388 ⊙
Telephone: 910-692-6866 Telecopier: 910-695-3036
URL: http://www.poynerspruill.com
Member: H. Chalk Broughton, Jr. (Board Certified Specialist in Estate Planning and Probate, North Carolina State Board of Legal Specialization). Resident Of Counsel: Howard C. Broughton.
Comprehensive business and litigation practice including: Appellate, Arbitration, Banking, Bankruptcy/Creditors' Rights, Complex Business Litigation, Construction, Credit and Financial Services, Eminent Domain/Condemnation, Employment Benefits, Employment Practices, Entertainment Law, Environmental, Estate, Exempt Organizations, General Corporate, Governmental Relations, Health Care, Intellectual Property Law, International, Land Use and Zoning, Limited Liability Companies, Local Government, Mediation, Partnerships, Personal and Financial Planning, Probate, Product

(This Listing Continued)

Poyner & Spruill LLP (Continued)
Liability, Professional Liability, Railroad, Real Estate, Regulatory and Municipal, Securities, Sports Law, Tax, Technology and Emerging Business, Tort Litigation and Insurance Defense, Transactional including Mergers and Acquisitions, Transportation, Utilities, White Collar Criminal Defense.
Raleigh, North Carolina Office: 3600 Glenwood Avenue, P.O. Box 10096, 27605-0096. Telephone: 919-783-6400. Telecopier: 919-783-1075.
Rocky Mount, North Carolina Office: 130 S. Franklin Street, P.O. Box 353, 27802-0353. Telephone: 252-446-2341. Telecopier: 252-972-7045.
Charlotte, North Carolina Office: One Wachovia Center, 301 South College Street, Suite 2300, 28202. Telephone: 704-342-5250. Telecopier: 704-342-5264.
See Professional Biographies, SOUTHERN PINES, NORTH CAROLINA

Quist, Marcelle Compton '54 '88
C.112 B.S. L.508 J.D. Staff Atty., Legal Aid of North Carolina‡
Rhoades, Jerry D., Jr., (CV) .... '62 '89 C&L.575 B.A., J.D. [D.G.Crockett]

Robbins May & Rich LLP
(See Pinehurst)

Smith, Marsh, (BV) .... '58 '89 C.228 B.S. L.575 J.D. [Cunningham,D.P.&S.]
Smith, S. Kent, (AV) .... '50 '75 C&L.575 B.A., J.D. [West&S.]
Stovall, J. Hunter, (CV) .... '55 '93 C.893 B.A. L.1345 J.D. [Stovall&B.]
Stovall & Blevins, (BV) .... 230 N. Bennett St.
Suggs, Robert V. .... '34 '64 C&L.896 B.S., LL.B. [R.V.Suggs] (⊙Pinehurst)‡
Suggs, Robert V., P.A., (BV) .... 194 Longleaf Road
Thompson, Herman G. .... '— '75 C.307 B.A. L.329 J.D. P.O. Box 1181
Thompson, Robert S., (BV) .... '48 '83 C.611 B.A. L.896 J.D. [R.S.Thompson]

Thompson, Hurley E., Jr.
(See Carthage)

Thompson, Robert S., P.A., (BV)
325 West Pennsylvania, Suite E, 28387
Telephone: 910-692-2244 Fax: 910-692-3080
Email: rthompson@pinehurst.net URL: http://www.lawyers.com/rthompson
Robert S. Thompson (Board Certified Specialist in Estate Planning and Probate Law, Real Property Law-Residential, Business, Commercial and Industrial Transactions, North Carolina State Board of Legal Specialization).
Estate Planning Law, Business Law, Corporate Law, Probate Law, Wills, Trusts and Estates, Commercial and Residential Real Estate Law.
See Professional Biographies, SOUTHERN PINES, NORTH CAROLINA

Tobias, Emily A., (BV) .... '65 '95 C.970 B.A. L.575 J.D. [Gill&T.]

Van Camp, Meacham & Newman, PLLC
(See Pinehurst)

Watts, Wendy Michelle .... '74 '00 C.228 A.B. L.1228 J.D. P.O. Box 185
West, Stanley W., (AV) .... '50 '75 C.575 B.S.B.A. L.896 J.D. [West&S.]

West & Smith, L.L.P., (AV)
140 West Vermont Avenue, P.O. Box 1140, 28388
Telephone: 910-693-3411 Fax: 910-693-7727
Email: ws@westandsmith.com URL: http://www.lawyers.com/west&smith
Stanley W. West; S. Kent Smith.
Personal Injury, Wrongful Death, Civil Litigation, Insurance Litigation, Contested Wills, Worker's Compensation, Social Security Disability, Land Condemnation, Commercial Litigation, Construction Litigation, Mediation and Arbitration.
See Professional Biographies, SOUTHERN PINES, NORTH CAROLINA

SOUTHERN SHORES, 2,201, *Dare Co.*

Archbell, Roy A., Jr.
(See Kitty Hawk)

Cox, Richard Michael .... '71 '99 C.232 B.S. L.574 J.D. [Ⓐ Twiford]

Hornthal, Riley, Ellis & Maland, L.L.P.
(See Elizabeth City)

Morrison, John S., (BV) .... '46 '72 C&L.575 A.B., J.D. [Twiford]
O'Neal, Edward A., (BV) .... '48 '86 C.232 B.S. L.1228 J.D. [Twiford]
Twiford, Russell E. .... '26 '52 C.575 A.B. L.896 LL.B. [Twiford] ‡
Twiford Law Firm, The, L.L.P., (BV) ....8 Juniper Trail (⊙Elizabeth City)
Vincent, Branch W. "Chip", (BV) .... '61 '86 C.301 B.A. L.1228 J.D. [Vincent]

Vincent Law Firm, The, PC, (BV)
8 Juniper Trail, 27949
Telephone: 252-261-5477 Fax: 252-261-1828
Email: bwvincent2@earthlink.net URL: http://www.ncworkerscompensationlaw.com
Branch W. "Chip" Vincent (Board Certified Specialist in Worker's Compensation, North Carolina State Board of Legal Specialization).
Workers Compensation, Personal Injury, Auto Accidents, Social Security Disability, Wrongful Death and Admiralty Longshores.
See Professional Biographies, SOUTHERN SHORES, NORTH CAROLINA

Williams, Herscal P., Jr., (BV) .... '50 '78 C.296 B.A. L.692 J.D. [Twiford]

SOUTHPORT, 2,369, *Brunswick Co.*

Aldridge, John E., Jr., (AV) .... '43 '69 C&L.575 A.B., J.D. P.O. Box 10817
Campbell, Kenneth R., (BV) .... '50 '84 C.576 B.S. L.1228 J.D. [Prevatte,P.&C.]
Darby, Sandra L., (CV) .... '49 '81 C.966 B.A. L.285 J.D. 1430 N. Howe St.

David and Associates, pllc
(See Wilmington)

Disbrow, Jason C., (BV) .... '72 '98 C.576 B.A. L.574 J.D. P.O. Box 11058
Elrod, Joseph E., III, (AV) .... '45 '71 C&L.575 B.S., J.D. P.O. Box 3021
Fairley, William F., (AV) .... '53 '78 C&L.575 A.B., J.D. [Fairley,J.I.&G.]
Fairley, Jess, Isenberg & Green, (AV) ....109 East Moore Street
Gore, Grover A. .... '31 '65 C.576 B.S. L.896 LL.B. 108 Davis St.
Green, Richard F., (BV) .... '51 '79 C.397 B.A. L.30 J.D. [Fairley,J.I.&G.]
Griffith, Robert S., II, (BV) .... '50 '81 C.902 B.A. L.1228 J.D. P.O. Box 11145
Harper, Judith C. .... '43 '87 C.882 B.A. L.184 J.D. 4190 Shearwater Way, S.E.
Iapalucci, Adrian, (CV) .... '72 '99 C.896 B.A. L.1228 J.D. 804 N. Howe St.
Isenberg, Michael R., (BV) .... '51 '76 C&L.575 B.S., J.D. [Fairley,J.I.&G.]

Jackson & Associates
(See Wilmington)

Jess, Elva L., (AV) .... '49 '77 C.1309 B.A. L.896 J.D. [Fairley,J.I.&G.]
Johnson, Edward A., II .... '70 '96 C.34 B.S. L.469 J.D. [Johnson&M.]

Johnson & Moore, P.A.
1424 N. Howe Street, 28461
Telephone: 910-457-6115 Fax: 910-457-6266
URL: http://www.johnsonmoore.com
Edward A. Johnson, II; Kimberly L. Moore.
Real Estate, Corporate Law, Estate Planning, Civil Litigation, Business Law, Commercial Litigation, Construction Law.
See Professional Biographies, SOUTHPORT, NORTH CAROLINA

Lawrence, Gary S., (AV) .... '45 '75 C.576 B.S. L.896 J.D. 1226 North Howe

Lewis, Ola M. .... '65 '90 C.1011 B.A. L.574 J.D. Supr. Ct. J.
Mauney, Michael E., (AV) .... '46 '77 C.576 B.S. L.575 J.D. P.O. Box 10266 (Pat.)
Moore, Kimberly L. .... '67 '95 C.893 B.S. L.469 J.D. [Johnson&M.] (⊙Wilmington)
Prevatte, Elias J., (BV) .... '11 '36 C&L.896 B.S., LL.B. [⊡ Prevatte,P.&C.]
Prevatte, James R., Jr., (BV) .... '44 '69 C&L.896 B.A., J.D. [Prevatte,P.&C.]
Prevatte, Prevatte & Campbell, PLLC, (BV) .... 601 North Howe Street

Robinson, Bruce H., Jr.
(See Wilmington)

Shipman, Mason & Wright, L.L.P.
(See Wilmington)

Thompson, Laura E., (BV) .... '68 '94 C.575 B.A. L.1345 J.D. [⊡ Fairley,J.I.&G.]

Tighe, Charles M.
(See Wilmington)

Turner, Jeffry F., (BV Ⓣ) .... '50 '85 C.608 B.S. L.117 J.D. P.O. Box 3076
Walton, Ray H., (AV) .... '21 '50 C.1027 B.S. L.896 LL.B. 212 Park Ave. Extension‡

SPARTA, * 1,817, *Alleghany Co.*

Adams, Edmund I., (BV) .... '33 '60 C&L.280 A.B., LL.B. 121 E. Doughton St.
Baker, Garland B., (BV) .... '57 '86 C.500 B.A. L.575 J.D. [Vannoy&R.] ⊙
Doughton, Richard L., (AV) .... '47 '71 C.575 A.B. L.896 J.D. Spec. Supr. Ct. J.
Folger, Worth B., (AV) .... '17 '48 C&L.575 A.B. N. Main St.
Murray, Dan R., (AV) .... '48 '73 C&L.575 B.A., J.D. 19 S. Grayson St.
Reeves, Jimmy D., (AV) .... '48 '73 C&L.896 B.A., J.D. [Vannoy&R.] ⊙
Reeves, John "Jak" B. .... '79 '04 C.575 B.A. L.1228 J.D. [⊡ Vannoy&R.] ⊙
Reeves, M. Alexandra .... '76 '01 C.575 B.A. L.896 J.D. [Vannoy&R.] ⊙

Shumate, Donna L., (BV) '68 '93 C.575 B.A. L.1228 J.D.
83 South Main Street, P.O. Box 816, 28675
Telephone: 336-372-8922 Fax: 336-372-2844
Email: dlsatty@skybest.com
Criminal Trial Practice including Real Estate, Traffic matters including DUI/DWI.

Vannoy & Reeves, PLLC, (AV)
A Professional Limited Liability Company
112 South Main Street, P.O. Box 249, 28675 ⊙
Telephone: 336-372-8740 Fax: 336-372-6114 Email: jim@vannoyandreeves.com Email: alex@vannoyandreeves.com Email: garland@vannoyandreeves.com Email: jak@vannoyandreeves.com
Email: garland@vannoyandreeves.com URL: http://www.vannoyandreeves.com
Members of Firm: Wade E. Vannoy, Jr. (1927-1991); Jimmy D. Reeves; Garland B. Baker; M. Alexandra Reeves. Associate: John "Jak" B. Reeves.
General Civil and Criminal Trial Practice in State and Federal Courts, Real Property, Estate Planning, Probate, Business and Corporate Law, Traffic, Family Law, Plaintiff's Personal Injury Matters and Collections.
West Jefferson, North Carolina Office: 202 East Main Street, P.O.Drawer 67, 28694. Telephone: 336-246-7172. Fax: 336-246-5966.
See Professional Biographies, SPARTA, NORTH CAROLINA

SPENCER, 3,355, *Rowan Co.*

Hart-Morrison, Rosalee .... '68 '93 C.48 B.A. L.880 J.D. [Hart-Morrison]
Hart-Morrison Law Office .... 125-A Fifth Street

SPINDALE, 4,040, *Rutherford Co.*

Mitchell, T. Eugene, (CV) .... '48 '74 C.575 B.S. L.469 J.D. P.O. Box 466
Tomblin, A. Clyde .... '26 '52 C.968 B.A. L.896 J.D. [Tomblin&P.]
Tomblin and Perry .... 421 West Main Street

SPRING HOPE, 1,221, *Nash Co.*

Alford, Terry W., (BV) .... '55 '80 C.576 L.1228 J.D. 19 Main Street
Prenda, Brian J. .... '61 '93 C.1260 B.A. L.999 J.D. P.O. Box 1635

SPRING LAKE, 8,098, *Cumberland Co.*

Britt, Carl L., Jr., Attorney at Law
(See Fayetteville)

Maxwell & Melvin
(See Fayetteville)

SPRUCE PINE, 2,010, *Mitchell Co.*

Bartlow, Robert T. '21 '48 C&L.477 A.B., J.D.
(adm. in MI; not adm. in NC) 115 Hickory Hill Circle‡
Buchanan, Brian A., (BV) .... '65 '90 C.34 B.A. L.896 J.D. 137 Broad St.
Harrison, Hal G., (BV) .... '52 '78 C.925 B.A. L.574 J.D. 340 Oak Ave.
Hise, Lloyd, Jr., (AV) .... '44 '69 C&L.986 B.A., J.D. [L.Hise,Jr.]
Hise, Lloyd, Jr., P.A., (AV) .... 208-A Oak Avenue
Holmes, D. Michael .... '75 '03 C.152 B.S. L.1228 J.D. [Holmes&H.]
Holmes, Elizabeth L. .... '79 '04 C&L.1228 B.B.A., J.D. [Holmes&H.]
Holmes & Holmes .... 167 Locust Ave., Ste. 204
Hunt, Charlie A., Jr., (BV) .... '51 '76 C&L.896 B.A., J.D. [Watson&H.]
Kivett, Gary B. .... '65 '89 C.925 B.S. L.575 J.D. P.O. Box 707
Poore, Michaelle, (BV) .... '66 '91 C.198 B.A. L.575 J.D. [M.Poore]
Poore, Michaelle, P.A., (BV) .... 340 Oak Street
Teller, Herbert J. '25 '52 C&L.472 LL.B.
(adm. in FL; not adm. in NC) Rt. 3, Box 417C‡
Watson & Hunt, P.A., (BV) .... 216 Oak Avenue

STANLEY, 3,053, *Gaston Co.*

Cash, Michael Thomas .... '59 '00 C.679 B.S. L.999 J.D. 7950 Sandestin Lane

STATESVILLE, * 23,320, *Iredell Co.*

Ashburn, James P., (AV) .... '42 '67 C.247 A.B. L.896 J.D. [Eisele,A.G.&C.]
Baity, Billy J., Jr., (CV) .... '68 '97 C.999 B.S. L.1187 J.D. [B.J.Baity,Jr.]
Baity, Bill J., Jr., PLLC, Law Offices of, (CV) .... 117 N. Kelly Street
Benbow, C. David, (BV) .... '44 '72 C&L.575 B.A., J.D. [Benbow&P.]
Benbow and Phillips, P.C., (BV) .... 309 Davie Ave.

Bolduc Law Firm, The, PLLC
(See Charlotte)

Brown, Deborah Pelone, Law Office of, (BV) '54 '84
C.1128 B.A. L.575 J.D. 119 N. Tradd St.
Cannon, E. Bedford, (AV) .... '46 '71 C.228 B.A. L.575 J.D. [Massey,C.&G.]
Carpenter, Alan G., (AV) .... '57 '83 C&L.575 B.S., J.D. [A.G.Carpenter]

Carpenter, Alan G., P.A., (BV)
1318 Davie Avenue, Suite C, 28677
Telephone: 704-872-6242 Fax: 704-872-6246 URL: http://www.alancarpenter.com
Email: statesville@bellsouth.net URL: http://www.tandclaw.com
Alan G. Carpenter (Board Certified Specialist in Real Property Law - Residential Transactions, North Carolina State Board of Legal Specialization).

(This Listing Continued)

Carpenter, Alan G., P.A. (Continued)
Residential Real Estate, Commercial Real Estate, Construction, Business Law, Limited Liability, Partnerships, Corporate, Wills and Estates.
See Professional Biographies, STATESVILLE, NORTH CAROLINA

Cathey, Samuel A. .... '45 '73 C.198 A.B. L.575 J.D. Dist. J., Chf.
Chamblee, Fred G., (AV) .... '21 '48 C&L.896 B.S., J.D. 232 Davie Ave.
Chapman, Russell W., Jr., (BV) .... '54 '91 C.499 B.S. L.896 J.D. [Eisele,A.G.&C.]
Collier, Christopher M., (BV) .... '63 '89 C.575 B.A. L.896 J.D. Judge; Supr. Ct.
Concepcion, James Dagoberto, (BV) '61 '88
C.1128 B.A. L.896 J.D. 130 North Tradd Street
Conley, Jessie A., (BV) .... '58 '84 C.228 B.A. L.896 J.D. [Pressly,T.&C.]

Corbett, William T., Jr., Law Office of
(See Mooresville)

Crosswhite, Joseph N., (BV) .... '62 '92 C.838 B.S. L.790 J.D. [Crosswhite,E.&C.]
Crosswhite, Robert N., (BV) .... '65 '94 C.838 B.A. L.1339 J.D. [Crosswhite,E.&C.]
Crosswhite, William E., (AV) .... '33 '61 C.125 A.B. L.896 J.D. [Crosswhite,E.&C.]
Crosswhite, Edwards & Crosswhite, P.A., (AV) .... 239 East Broad Street

Dalton, Judy
(See Troutman)

Darty, Kenneth B., (CV) .... '62 '94 C.709 B.S. L.896 J.D. [Darty,K.B.]
Darty, Kenneth B., PLLC, (CV) .... 210 E Water St.
Davidson, Daryl G., Sr. .... '69 '99 C.329 B.A. L.352 J.D. [D.G.Davidson,Sr.]

Davidson, Daryl G., Sr., PC, Law Office of
210 East Water Street, 28677
Telephone: 704-871-2213; 871-2214 Fax: 704-871-2215
Email: darylgdavidson@bellsouth.net URL: http://www.darylgdavidson.com
Daryl G. Davidson, Sr.
Family Law, Child Support, Child Custody, Divorce, Domestic Violence, Visitation Rights, Criminal Law, Driving While Intoxicated (DWI); Drug Crimes, Traffic Violations, Immigration, Automobile Accidents.
See Professional Biographies, STATESVILLE, NORTH CAROLINA

Dudley, L. Ragan, (BV) .... '66 '92 C.575 B.A. L.896 J.D. [Homesley,J.G.D.M.&D.]
Edwards, Andrea D., (BV) .... '55 '85 C.575 B.S. L.896 J.D. [Crosswhite,E.&C.]
Eisele, Douglas G., (AV) .... '36 '65 C&L.575 LL.B. [Eisele,A.G.&C.]

Eisele, Ashburn, Greene & Chapman, P.A., (AV)
320 West Broad Street, P.O. Box 1108, 28687-1108
Telephone: 704-878-6400 Fax: 704-871-2039; 704-924-9727
URL: http://www.lawyers.com/eagandclaw
Douglas G. Eisele; James P. Ashburn; John D. Greene; Russell W. Chapman, Jr.
General Civil Practice in State and Federal Courts. Real Property, Estate Planning, Taxation, Corporation and Construction Law.
Representative Client: NationsBank of North Carolina, N.A.
See Professional Biographies, STATESVILLE, NORTH CAROLINA

Foreman, Suzanne R. .... '44 '81 C.228 B.A. L.896 J.D. 325 N. Oakwood Dr.‡
Gaines, Edmund L., (AV) .... '46 '71 C&L.575 B.A., J.D. [Homesley,J.G.D.M.&D.]
Gourley, Robert H., Jr., (BV) .... '66 '92 C&L.575 B.A., J.D. P.O. Box 1023
Gourley, Robert H., Sr., (AV) .... '41 '68 C.513 B.A. L.575 J.D. P.O. Box 1023
Graham, L. Dale, (BV) .... '57 '83 C.893 B.A. L.896 J.D. J.
Greene, John D., (BV) .... '47 '89 C.576 B.S. L.896 J.D. [Eisele,A.G.&C.]
Griffin, Jonathan Dean .... '67 '01 C.1274 B.S. L.574 J.D. [Massey,C.&G.]

Hayes, Ray A., II, P.A.
(See Cornelius)

Hicks, Carole A., (CV) .... '57 '92 C.999 B.S. L.61 J.D. 210 E. Water St., Ste. 8
Homesley, Troy C., Jr., (AV) ... '34 '58 C&L.575 A.B., J.D. [Homesley,J.G.D.M.&D.] ⊙

Homesley, Jones, Gaines, Dudley, McLurkin & Donaldson, PLLC, (AV)
316 East Broad Street, P.O. Box 149, 28677 ⊙
Telephone: 704-873-2172 Fax: 704-924-2103; 704-873-5908 Real Estate Email: realestate@statesville.net
Email: hjgd@statesville.net URL: http://www.iredell-law.com
Members of Firm: Troy C. Homesley, Jr.; Edmund L. Gaines; L. Ragan Dudley;—Mitchell P. Johnson.
General Civil and Criminal Practice in all Domestic and Federal Courts. Probate, Real Estate, Personal Injury, Family, Corporation, Insurance, Negligence, Workers Compensation, Social Security and Appeals.
References: Branch Bank and Trust Co., Statesville, North Carolina; First Union National Bank, Mooresville, N.C.
Mooresville, North Carolina Office: 236 Raceway Drive, Suite 7, Lakeside Business Park, 28117. Telephone: 704-664-1127. Real Estate Telephone: 704-664-2145. Fax: 704-663-0939; 704-664-6596. URL: http://www.mooresvillelakelaw.com
See Professional Biographies, STATESVILLE, NORTH CAROLINA

Howes, Robert C., (BV) .... '65 '93 C.207 B.A. L.574 J.D. [Parker&H.]
Jenkins, Vickie Y. .... '59 '00 C.404 B.A. L.1187 J.D. P.O. Box 168
Johnson, Mitchell P. .... '75 '00 C.228 A.B. L.575 J.D. [⊡ Homesley,J.G.D.M.&D.]
Johnson, Robert W. .... '40 '71 C.210 B.A. L.365 J.D. Ret. Emergency J.‡
Keiger, Robert K. .... '34 '60 C.575 B.S. L.896 J.D. Emergency Dist. Ct. J.
Kennedy, William A. .... '52 '77 C.228 B.A. L.575 J.D. Elledge Group, Inc.
Kummer, Thomas L. .... '48 '73 C.152 B.A. L.896 J.D. P.O. Box 6364
Kutteh, Constantine H., II, (BV) .... '52 '76 C.896 B.A. L.228 J.D. [Pope,M.K.S.&P.]
Lassiter, T Michael, Jr., (BV) .... '62 '91 C.575 B.A. L.1228 J.D. 115 N. Center St.
Lewis, John G., Jr., (AV) .... '33 '58 C&L.575 A.B., LL.B. [Lewis&P.]
Lewis and Patterson, (AV) .... 301 N. Ctr. St.
Mallory, James B., III, (BV) .... '55 '84 C.902 B.A. L.896 J.D. 102 West Broad Street
Massey, John M., (AV) .... '43 '68 C&L.575 B.A., J.D. [Massey,C.&G.]

Massey, Cannon & Griffin, PLLC, (AV)
140 East Water Street, 28677-5228
Telephone: 704-872-7438 Fax: 704-872-0108
URL: http://www.lawyers.com/ebedfordcannon
E. Bedford Cannon; Jonathan Dean Griffin; John M. Massey.
Civil Litigation, Corporation, Real Estate, Wills, Estate Planning, Probate, Business Law, Contracts, Personal Injury, Automobile Accidents, Family Law.
See Professional Biographies, STATESVILLE, NORTH CAROLINA

Mattox, J. Pressly, (BV) .... '58 '83 C.575 B.A. L.990 J.D. [J.P.Mattox]

Mattox, J. Pressly, P.C., The Law Office of, (BV)
102 West Broad Street, 28687
Telephone: 704-872-8189 Fax: 704-873-1687
URL: http://www.mattoxlaw.net
Member of Firm: J. Pressly Mattox.
Personal Injury, Auto Accidents, Workers Compensation, Real Estate, Business, Traffic.
See Professional Biographies, STATESVILLE, NORTH CAROLINA

McMillan, William H., (AV) .... '38 '68 C&L.575 B.S., J.D. [Pope,M.K.S.&P.]
Minor, David W., Law Office of, (BV) .... '54 '80 C.301 B.A. L.896 J.D. 252 Davie Ave.
Moyer, Justin P. .... '79 '05 C.999 B.A. L.1228 J.D. [⊡ Pope,M.K.S.&P.]

Parker, David P., (BV) ....'54 '79 C&L.575 B.A., J.D. [Parker&H.]
Parker & Howes, L.L.P., (BV) ....242 East Broad Street
Patterson, Walter B., (BV) ....'36 '71 C.125 B.A. L.575 J.D. [Lewis&P.]
Phillips, Richard A., (BV) ....'60 '85 C&L.575 B.A., J.D. [Benbow&P.]
Pope, William P., (AV) ....'42 '68 C&L.575 B.S., J.D. [Pope,M.K.S.&P.]

Pope, McMillan, Kutteh, Simon & Privette, P.A., (AV)
113 North Center Street, Suite 200, P.O. Drawer 1776, 28687-1776
Telephone: 704-873-2131 Fax: 704-872-7629
URL: http://www.popemcmillan.com
William P. Pope; William H. McMillan; Constantine H. Kutteh, II; Pamela H. Simon (Board Certified Specialist in Family Law, North Carolina State Board of Legal Specialization); Anthony S. Privette;—Charles Arthur Schieck; Justin P. Moyer.
General Civil and Criminal Trial Practice in State and Federal Courts. Real Estate, Personal Injury, Probate, Corporation, Taxation, Estate Planning, Administrative Law, Domestic and Family Law, Zoning.
Representative Clients: Nationwide Insurance Co.; Aetna Life & Casualty Insurance Co.; NationsBank; Barium Springs Home for Children; Piedmont Bank Carolina Farm Credit Assn.; Allstate Insurance Co.; Travelers Insurance Co.; Iredell County; Iredell-Statesville Schools.
Approved Attorneys for: Lawyers Title Insurance Corp.; Farmers Home and Federal Land Bank Assn.

See Professional Biographies, STATESVILLE, NORTH CAROLINA

Pressly, Edwin A., (BV) ....'51 '76 C.247 B.A. L.896 J.D. [Pressly,T.&C.]
Pressly, Thomas & Conley, P.A., (BV) ....224 Harrill Street
Privette, Anthony S., (BV) ....'70 '97 C.1128 B.S. L.1228 J.D. [Pope,M.K.S.&P.]
Ralston, Carl Jason ....'75 '00 C.152 B.S. L.192 J.D. 130 N. Tradd St.
Rhasiatry, Cecelia M. ....'69 '97 C.8 B.S. L.7 J.D. P.O. Box 6132
Schieck, Charles Arthur ....'70 '01 C.801 B.S. L.1228 J.D. [A Pope,M.K.S.&P.]

Schwartz Law Firm, P.C.
(See Charlotte)

Setzer, Beth R., (BV) ....'63 '90 C.34 B.S. L.896 J.D. 924 Davie Ave.
Simon, Pamela H., (AV) ....'45 '84 C.112 B.A. L.575 J.D. [Pope,M.K.S.&P.]
Smith, Peter A., (BV) ....'56 '86 C.228 B.A. L.990 J.D. 1318-B Davie Ave.

Smith, Douglas A.
(See Salisbury)

Tate, Steven G., (AV) ....'54 '78 C&L.896 B.A., J.D. 212 Cooper Street
Taylor, Kimberly Susan ....'55 '81 C.228 B.A. L.575 J.D. P.O. Box 47
Teague, Philip M., (CV) ......'65 '91 C.1128 B.A. L.896 J.D. 1318 Davie Avenue, Suite C
Thomas, Gary Watson., (BV) ....'55 '81 C.575 A.B. L.896 J.D. [Pressly,T.&C.]

Walker, Rufus F., Jr.
(See Hickory)

Walser, Albert F., (BV) ....'42 '77 C.575 B.S.B.A. L.896 J.D. 337 Earlwood Rd.
West, L. Hugh, Jr., (AV) ....'32 '62 C.968 A.B. L.896 J.D. 307 Davie Ave.

Willis, William M., IV, Attorney at Law
(See Mooresville)

Winthrop, Samuel B., (BV) ....'63 '89 C.575 B.A. L.896 J.D. 112 Court St.
Winthrop, Warren A., (BV) ....'35 '62 C.475 B.S. L.575 LL.B. 112 Court St.
Young, Thomas R. ....'68 '95 C.999 B.A. L.221 J.D. Staff Atty.

STONEVILLE, 1,002, *Rockingham Co.*

Smith, Robert G. ....'34 '60 C.575 A.B. L.896 LL.B. 202 S. Glenn St.‡

STONY POINT, 1,380, *Alexander & Iredell Cos.*

York, Vickie R., Law Offices of ....'59 '00 C.404 L.1187 J.D. 787 New Sterling

SUGAR GROVE, —, *Watauga Co.*

Mast, Everett L. '28 '55 C.34 B.S. L.228 LL.B.
(adm. in FL; not adm. in NC) Rte. 1‡

SUMMERFIELD, 7,018, *Guilford Co.*

Colanero, Alfred J., (CV) ....'46 '92 C.724 B.A. L.1325 J.D. 7475 Strader Rd.
Eagle, Jerry L. ....'40 '65 C.125 B.A. L.896 7240 Strawberry Rd.‡
Hartman, Patti L., (CV) ....'61 '93 C.1111 B.A. L.1158 J,D. 5221 Paula Way
Hughes-Coons, Cynthia '57 '95 C.375 B.S. L.378 J.D.
(adm. in KS; not adm. in NC) 6744 Phillip Court
Lockhart, George G., (AV) ....'42 '72 C&L.575 B.S., J.D. 6105 Gwynedd Rd
McSwain, Lawrence C. ....'46 '79 C.1378 B.S. L.574 J.D. 6918 Polo Farms Dr.
Wright, Luke W., (AV) ....'14 '39 C&L.16 A.B., LL.B. 3062 Pleasant Ridge Rd.‡

SUNSET BEACH, 1,824, *Brunswick Co.*

Murray, Douglas P., (AV) ....'39 '68 C.575 A.B. L.896 J.D. 942 Elderberry Lane‡

SUPPLY, —, *Brunswick Co.*

David, G. Phillip ....'59 '88 C.232 B.S.B.A. L.574 J.D. [David&Assoc.] ⊙

David and Associates, pllc
Highway 17, 28462 ⊙
Telephone: 910-754-8465 Toll Free: 1-800-856-9927
Email: aeverhart@davidandassociates.com URL: http://www.wilmingtonpiattorneys.com
G. Phillip David.
Personal Injury, Medical Malpractice, Wrongful Death, Products Liability, Workers Compensation, Aviation, Airplane Crashes, Negligence, Class Actions, Maritime Accidents, Boating Accidents, Bicycle Accidents, Motorcycle Accidents, Truck Accidents, School Bus Accidents, Railroad Accidents, Dog Bites, Slip and Fall, Birth Trauma, Brain Injury, Spinal Injury, Head Injury, Catastrophic Injury, Vehicular Homicide, Personal Injury Mediation, Products Liability, Drug and Medical Device Litigation, Product Defects, Automobile Liability, Motorcycle Products Liability, Amusement Park Liability, Hotel Liability, Marina Liability, Sports Injury.
Jacksonville, North Carolina Office: 405-B Western Boulevard. 28546. Telephone: 910-219-4878.
Wilmington, North Carolina Office: 1516 Dawson Street. 28401. Telephone: 910-251-8088.
Wallace, North Carolina Office: 107 North Norwood Street. 28466. Telephone: 910-285-8777.
Clinton, North Carolina Office: 610 Beaman Street. 28328. Telephone: 910-592-8400.
Winston-Salem, North Carolina Office: 1100-A South Stratford Road. 27103. Telephone: 336-354-1040.
Greensboro, North Carolina Office: 529 College Road. Suite G. 27410. Telephone: 336-354-1040.

See Professional Biographies, SUPPLY, NORTH CAROLINA

SURF CITY, 1,393, *Onslow & Pender Cos.*

Biggar, Lee Craig ....'49 '97 C.575 B.A. L.574 J.D. P.O. Box 2728
Fairley, Mary C. ....'39 '86 C.521 B.S. L.665 J.D. 106 N. Topsail Dr.
Johnston, Thomas D. ....'29 '57 C&L.575 A.B., J.D. P.O. Box 2366‡
Parsons, Susan '54 '79 C.1097 B.A. L.112 J.D.
(adm. in CA; not adm. in NC) 606 N. Shore Dr.

SWANNANOA, 4,132, *Buncombe Co.*

Garlock, Victor C. ....'65 '92 C.165 B.A. L.982 J.D. [V.Garlock]
Garlock, Victor ....132 Halcyon Hill Road
Wasson, Rodger D. ....'43 '68 C.206 B.S. L.500 J.D. Co. J.

SWANQUARTER, * 500, *Hyde Co.*

Davis, Geo. Thomas, Jr., (AV) ....'54 '79 C.575 B.S. L.896 J.D. [Davis&D.]
Davis & Davis, (AV) ....Main Street

SWANSBORO, 1,426, *Onslow Co.*

Cockshoot, Bruce J. '51 '82 C&L.221 B.A., J.D.
(adm. in IA; not adm. in NC) Mil. Law Assoc.
Martin, Scott W. ....'61 '89 C&L.575 B.A., J.D. Assoc. Coun.

Morgan, William J., P.A.
(See Jacksonville)

Peck, John J. ....'49 '81 C.1126 B.A. L.1228 J.D. 115 Hilltop Dr.

SYLVA, * 2,435, *Jackson Co.*

Baker, Heather C., (BV) ....'68 '94 C&L.575 B.A., J.D. [Coward,H.&S.]
Bridgers, Ben Oshel, (AV) ....'39 '70 C.315 B.A. L.575 J.D. P.O. Box 248
Bryson, David H., Jr., (CV) ....'42 '95 C.925 B.S. L.574 J.D. 10 E. Main St.
Buckner, Andrew C. ....'70 '99 C.510 B.M.E.D. L.383 J.D. 705 West Main Street
Clapsaddle, Christina Buchanan, (BV) ....'59 '83 C.925 B.S. L.1228 J.D. Asst. Dist. Atty.
Clark, Robert W., (BV) ....'53 '79 C.696 B.A. L.362 J.D. 401 Grindstaff Cove Rd.
Coward, J. K., Jr., (BV) ....'55 '84 C.198 B.A. L.1228 J.D. [Coward,H.&S.]
Coward, Orville D., (AV) ....'25 '51 C&L.575 A.B. [Coward,H.&S.]

Coward, Hicks & Siler, P.A., (AV) BB
705 West Main Street, 28779 ⊙
Telephone: 828-586-2147 Fax: 828-586-2605
James Kent Coward (1929-1989); Orville D. Coward; Ralph L. Hicks (Resident, Cashiers Office); Robert F. Siler (Resident, Franklin Office); Thomas R. Crawford (Board Certified Specialist in Estate Planning and Probate Law, North Carolina State Board of Legal Specialization); Orville D. Coward, Jr. (Resident, Franklin Office); J. K. Coward, Jr.; William H. Coward (Resident, Cashiers Office); Kimberly R. Coward (Resident, Cashiers Office); Monty C. Beck (Board Certified Specialist in Family Law, North Carolina State Board of Legal Specialization) (Resident, Franklin Office); Richard K. Walker (Resident, Franklin Office); Heather C. Baker;—David D. Moore.
General Practice in all Courts. Trials, Eminent Domain, Personal Injury and Workers Compensation, Probate, Estate Planning, Real Estate, Corporations, Family Law.
Franklin, North Carolina Office: 43 West Main Street, 28734. Telephone: 828-524-6475. Fax: 828-524-9833.
Cashiers, North Carolina Office: 211 Cashiers School Road, P.O. Box 1918, 28717. Telephone: 828-743-2401. Fax: 828-743-2403.

See Professional Biographies, SYLVA, NORTH CAROLINA

Crawford, Thomas R., (AV) ....'47 '72 C.198 B.A. L.575 J.D. [Coward,H.&S.]
Duls, Thomas G., (BV) ....'47 '72 C.446 B.A. L.896 J.D. P.O. Box 187
Earwood, Kristina L. ....'78 '03 C.886 B.A. L.1339 J.D. [Ridenour,L.&E.]
Earwood, Nathaniel James ....'78 '03 C.925 B.S. L.1339 J.D. [A Melrose,S.&L.]
Foster, Pamela W. ....'63 '94 C.953 B.A. L.575 J.D. Maple St.
Goldstein, Barbara Allison, (BV) ....'42 '93 C.679 B.A. L.260 J.D. P.O. Box 1924
Haire, R. Phillip, (AV) ....'36 '61 C&L.575 A.B., LL.B. P.O. Box 727
Hamilton, Orman L. ....'19 '55 C.280 L.472 J.D. 2571 N. Fork Rd.
Harper, Patti Owen ....'56 '81 C.575 B.A. L.1228 J.D. 24 Oakwood Lane
Harper, Richard B., (BV) ....'53 '81 C.575 B.A. L.1228 J.D. 1336 Savannah Dr.
Holland, Max K. ....'37 '68 C&L.575 B.S., J.D. 163 Old Dillsboro Rd.
Holt, W. Paul, Jr., (AV) ....'29 '57 C&L.575 B.S., LL.B. [W.P.Holt,Jr.]

Holt, W. Paul, Jr., P.A., (AV)
702 West Main Street, P.O. Box 217, 28779
Telephone: 828-586-2121 Facsimile: 828-586-4005
Email: paulholt2@mchsi.com
W. Paul Holt, Jr.
General Civil Practice in State and Federal Courts. Real Property, Probate Law, Corporation Law, Tort Law, General Criminal Practice.

Hunter, William P., III, (BV) ....'49 '77 C&L.575 B.A., J.D. 28 Maple St.
Kirby, Gary E., (BV) ....'50 '76 C.296 B.A. L.192 J.D. 90 E. Main St., Ste. 1
Large, Raymond D., (BV) ....'49 '78 C.122 B.S. L.836 J.D. 28 Maple St.
Lay, J. Frank, II ....'67 '96 C.1011 B.A. L.574 J.D. [Ridenour,L.&E.]
Lay, Kimberly Carpenter, (BV) ....'70 '96 C.925 B.S. L.574 J.D. [Melrose,S.&L.]
Leslie, Monica H., (BV) ....'70 '95 C.575 A.B. L.276 J.D. Dist. Atty.'s Off.
Melrose, Mark R., (BV) ....'62 '90 C.925 B.S. L.575 J.D. [Melrose,S.&L.]
Melrose, Seago & Lay, P.A., (BV) ....2775 Highway 74 East
Moore, David D. ....'72 '00 C.34 B.A. L.836 J.D. [A Coward,H.&S.]
Nestler, Lawrence, (BV) ....'48 '78 C.705 L.574 J.D. Western N.C. Legal Servs.
Owen, Lester W. ....'18 '54 C&L.575 B.S., J.D. 63 Savannah Dr.‡
Ridenour, Eric B., (BV) ....'69 '95 C.378 B.A. L.900 J.D. [Ridenour,L.&E.]
Ridenour, Lay & Earwood, pllc, (BV) ....21 Colonial Square
Seago, Randal, (BV) ....'57 '85 C.198 B.A. L.421 J.D. [Melrose,S.&L.]
Sherrill, Diane E., (BV) ....'55 '92 C.925 B.A.B.A. L.1228 J.D. P.O. Box 365
Spiro, James M., (BV) ....'56 '81 C.1038 B.A. L.1228 J.D. [J.M.Spiro]
Spiro, James M., P.A., (BV) ....629 W. Main Street
Walker, Richard K., (BV) ....'50 '87 C.790 B.S. L.575 J.D. [Coward,H.&S.]

Wenzel & Wenzel, PLLC
(See Waynesville)

Whaley, Kelley A. ....'60 '86 C.94 B.S. L.575 J.D. Western N.C. Legal Servs.

Wijewickrama, David, Law Office of
(See Waynesville)

Williams, Kris V., Attorney at Law ....'70 '01 C.576 B.A. L.500 J.D. P.O. Box 1935

TABOR CITY, 2,509, *Columbus Co.*

Jolly, Jerry A. ....'49 '79 C.575 B.A. L.896 J.D. Dist. J.
Jorgensen, Ralph G., (AV) ....'37 '63 C&L.273 B.A., LL.B. 116 W. 4th St.
McGougan Law Firm, The, (AV) ....200 South Lewis Street (⊙Whiteville)
Phipps, William Winslow, (AV) ....'52 '78 C.232 B.A. L.790 J.D. [Soles,P.R.&P.]
Prince, Sherry Dew, (BV) ....'54 '87 C.1317 B.S. L.1228 J.D. [Soles,P.R.&P.]
Ray, Joseph Lane, (BV) ....'60 '87 C.575 B.A. L.1228 J.D. [Soles,P.R.&P.]
Soles, Robert C., Jr., (AV) ....'34 '59 C.896 B.S. L.575 J.D. [Soles,P.R.&P.]

Soles, Phipps, Ray & Prince, (AV)
108 Live Oak Street, P.O. Box 6, 28463
Telephone: 910-653-2015 Fax: 910-653-4371
URL: http://www.lawyers.com/vaida
Robert C. Soles, Jr.; William Winslow Phipps; Joseph Lane Ray; Sherry Dew Prince.
General Civil, Domestic and Criminal Practice. Real Estate, Probate and Personal Injury Law. Litigation.
References: Southern National Bank; United Carolina Bank; Cooperative Savings & Loan Assn.

See Professional Biographies, TABOR CITY, NORTH CAROLINA

Stanley, C. Franklin, Jr., (BV) ....'47 '73 C.576 B.A. L.896 J.D. 211 East Fifth Street
Worley, Dennis T., (BV) ....'56 '81 C.576 B.S. L.1228 J.D. [McGougan]
Wright, O. Richard, Jr., (AV) ....'44 '71 C&L.575 A.B., J.D. [McGougan]

TARBORO, * 11,138, *Edgecombe Co.*

Allen, H. Frank, (AV) ....'46 '75 C.34 B.S.B.A. L.575 J.D. [H.F.Allen]
Allen, Herbert Frank, (AV) ....118 E. St. James
Boney, Howard S., Jr., (BV) ....'47 '73 C&L.575 B.S., J.D. Dist. Atty.

Bourne, Joel K. ....'25 '59 C&L.575 A.B., LL.B. 618 Howard Circle‡
Boyette, Alison L. ....'61 '89 C.896 B.A. L.1228 J.D. [Rountree&B.]
Boyette, Wayne S., (BV) ....'61 '87 C.575 B.A. L.1228 J.D. [Bridgers,H.&B.]
Bridgers, Katharine B. ....'19 '50 C&L.575 A.B., LL.B. 612 Lucille Dr.‡
Bridgers, Horton & Boyette, (BV) .... 201 East Pitt Street
Britt, John M., (BV) ....'63 '89 C.575 B.S. L.574 J.D. Dist. Ct. J.
Brown, Frank R. ....'36 '61 C&L.575 A.B., LL.B. Supr. Ct. J.

Chichester & Walker
(See Roanoke Rapids)

Covolo, John J., (BV) ....'51 '86 C.790 B.A. L.575 J.D. Asst. Dist. Atty.
Cromartie, Martin L., Jr. ....'28 '56 C.228 A.B. L.575 LL.B. 219 Main St.
Davidson, Janice Watson, (CV) .... '54 '79 C&L.575 B.A., J.D. P.O. Box 549
DeLoatch, Mahlon W., Jr., (AV) ....'35 '68 C.228 A.B. L.896 J.D. [Taylor,B.&D.]
Fountain, L. H. ....'13 '36 C&L.575 B.A., LL.B. 1102 Panola St.‡
Godwin, Walter H., Jr., (BV) ....'48 '77 C.53 B.A. L.574 J.D. 114 E. St. James St.
Harper, Joseph John, Jr. ....'42 '73 C&L.575 B.S., J.D. Dist. Co. J.
Hopkins, Grover Prevatte, (BV) ....'33 '71 C.259 A.B. L.575 J.D. 212 Main St.
Horton, Marvin V., (BV) ....'28 '51 C&L.575 A.B., LL.B. [Bridgers,H.&B.]
Jenkins, T. Perry, (BV) ....'44 '70 C.575 B.S. L.790 J.D. 414 Main St.
Keel, Jimmie R., (BV) ....'52 '78 C.575 A.B. L.896 J.D. [Keel O.]
Keel O'Malley, LLP, (BV) ....511 St. Andrew Street
Marrow, James C., Jr., (AV) ....'47 '72 C.198 A.B. L.575 J.D. 400 Main St.

Murphy, Michael P., P.A.
(See Rocky Mount)

Murray, Carlos W., Jr., (BV) '42 '67 C.232 A.B. L.896 J.D.
200 Trade Street, Suite A207
Muse, Eugene W., (BV) ....'54 '79 C&L.896 B.A., J.D. P.O. Box 26
O'Malley, Susan M., (BV) ....'68 '94 C.1128 B.S. L.575 J.D. [Keel O.]
Philips, H. H., Jr., (AV) ....'18 '46 C&L.575 A.B., LL.B. 112 E. St. James St.‡
Rideout, Robert W., Jr., (BV) ....'73 '98 C.953 B.A. L.420 J.D. Dist. Atty.

Rose Rand Attorneys, P.A.
(See Wilson)

Rountree, Charles S., III, (BV) ....'51 '79 C.575 A.B. L.896 J.D. [Rountree&B.]
Rountree & Boyette LLP, (BV) .... 309 Main St.
Simmons, Edward B., (BV) ....'50 '76 C.228 B.A. L.896 J.D. 118 E. St. James St.

Taylor, Brinson & DeLoatch, (AV)
210 East St. James Street, P.O. Drawer 308, 27886
Telephone: 252-823-8108 Fax: 252-823-7390
Email: tbdlaw@aol.com
Members of Firm: Mahlon W. DeLoatch, Jr.; Herbert H. Taylor, Jr. (1911-2001); Z. Creighton Brinson (1930-2005).
General Practice, Civil Practice, Corporations, Municipal, Commercial, Probate, Estate Planning and Real Property Law.
Counsel for: Edgecombe County, Edgecombe Community College; Rocky Mount-Wilson Airport Authority; Edgecombe County ABC Board; Redevelopment Commission of Town of Tarboro.
Representative Clients: ATPC, LLC; Seahawk Investment Group, LLC; PRA Ventures, LLC.

Tunstall, Joseph P., III ....'75 '00 C.575 B.A. L.896 J.D. [Ⓐ Keel O.]

TAYLORSVILLE, * 1,799, *Alexander Co.*

Campbell, Jerry A., (AV) ....'33 '57 C&L.575 A.B., J.D. 202 Main Ave., S.E.
Childers, Martha D. '39 '85 C&L.209 B.A., J.D.
(adm. in IL; not adm. in NC) Rte. 5, Box 470‡
Davis, Mark T., (BV) ....'55 '81 C&L.575 B.S., J.D. P.O. Box 1087

Elliott, J. Bryan
(See Hickory)

Erkman, Larissa J. ....'67 '92 C.575 B.A. L.276 J.D. P.O. Box 115
Gwaltney, Richard L., (BV) ....'42 '68 C&L.575 B.S., J.D. P.O. Box 963

Harbinson, Joel C., (AV) '54 '79 C&L.575 B.A., J.D.
70 East Main Avenue, P.O. Box 400, 28681-0400
Telephone: 828-632-4264 Telefax: 828-632-8927
Email: jharbinson@charter.net URL: http://www.joelharbinson.com
Auto Accidents, Child Custody, Child Support, Criminal Law, Divorce, DWI, Family Law, Medical Malpractice, Personal Injury, Social Security, Traffic, and Workers Compensation.
See Professional Biographies, TAYLORSVILLE, NORTH CAROLINA

Hedrick, Edward L., IV, (BV) ....'65 '90 C&L.575 B.S., J.D. 22 W. Main Ave.
Jennings, Edward, Law Offices of ....'48 '73 83 South Center Street (⊙Winston-Salem)

TERRELL, 860, *Catawba Co.*

Lamm, Jan W., (CV) ....'54 '79 C.34 B.A. L.1228 J.D. 4060 Kiser Cove Ln.

THOMASVILLE, 19,788, *Davidson Co.*

Batten, W. Russell, Law Office of, (BV) ....'47 '74 C&L.575 B.S., J.D. 40 Salem St.
Boles, Misti L. ....'76 '02 C.575 B.S. L.1228 J.D. 38 Salem St.
Bollinger, Paul S., (BV) ....'53 '83 C.404 B.A. L.45 J.D. 201 W. Main St., Ste. 303

Butler, Ron
(See High Point)

Citrin, Josephine L., (BV) ....'48 '71 C.831 B.A. L.1294 J.D. 38 Salem St.
Cranford, Randy L., (BV) ....'50 '76 C&L.575 A.B., J.D. 40 Salem St.
Doherty, David Scott, (CV) ....'63 '92 C.645 B.A. L.896 J.D. 5 E. Main St.
Earnheart, Frank J. ....'24 '51 C.575 B.A. L.273 J.D. 614 Flick Circle (Pat.)‡
Elliott, Douglas B., (BV) ....'69 '93 C.576 B.A. L.575 J.D. [Plyler&E.]
Green, J. Frank, (BV) ....'46 '73 C&L.575 B.S., J.D. 24 W. Guilford St.
Hauser, John A., (BV) ....'61 '87 C&L.575 B.A., J.D. [Mills&H.]
Hooper, E. W. ....'24 '51 C&L.896 B.S., LL.B. 604 E. Guilford St.‡
Lambeth, Charles F., Jr., (AV) ....'25 '52 C&L.575 B.A., LL.B. [Ⓒ Lambeth,M.&W.]
Lambeth, McMillan and Weldon, (BV) ....38 Trade Street
Leonard, Larry E., (BV) ....'41 '72 C.925 B.S. L.896 J.D. 201 West Main St.
Lewis, Edward L. ....'45 '99 C&L.575 B.A., J.D. 1420 Yokley Rd.
McGuire, L. Daryl, (BV) ....'39 '67 C.316 A.B. L.896 J.D. 2 Salem St.
McGuire, Mark L., (BV) ....'67 '93 C.575 B.A. L.574 J.D. P.O. Box 67
McMillan, James B., Jr., (BV) ....'46 '72 C.198 B.A. L.575 J.D. [Lambeth,M.&W.]
McQueen, Joetta Irene, (CV) ....'54 '87 C.999 B.A. L.7 J.D. 32 Trade Street
Mills, William B., (BV) ....'28 '56 C.152 B.S. L.896 J.D. [Mills&H.]

Mills and Hauser, L.L.P., (BV)
48 Salem Street, P.O. Box 964, 27361-0964
Telephone: 336-475-8131 Fax: 336-475-6177
William B. Mills; John A. Hauser.
Language: German.

(This Listing Continued)

Mills and Hauser, L.L.P. (Continued)

General Civil and Criminal Trial Practice in all State Courts. Criminal Defense, Traffic (including DWI), Adoptions, Real Estate, Probate, Wills and Estates, Domestic/Family, Personal Injury, Workers Compensation and Social Security Litigation.

Mitchell, Paul Rush ....'53 '78 C.198 B.A. L.896 J.D. City Atty. (⊙Denton)
Peace, Jerome L., (BV) ....'45 '71 C&L.575 B.S., J.D. 2 Salem St., Ste. 201
Perez, David A. ....'63 '89 C.999 B.A. L.838 J.D. 32 Trade St., Ste. C
Plyler, Cranford O., III, (BV) .... '57 '82 C&L.575 B.A., J.D. [Plyler&E.]
Plyler & Elliott, (BV) ....604 East Guilford Street
Saintsing, George W., (BV) ....'30 '58 C.316 B.A. L.896 LL.B. 22 W. Guilford St.

Schell Bray Aycock Abel & Livingston P.L.L.C.
(See Greensboro)

Sheek, Dawn, Law Office of .... '71 '01 C.1128 B.A. L.896 J.D. 25 West Guilford St.
Weldon, Wilson O., Jr., (BV) ....'44 '73 C.228 B.A. L.575 J.D. [Lambeth,M.&W.]

Wyatt Early Harris Wheeler L.L.P.
(See High Point)

TRENTON, * 248, *Jones Co.*

Brock, Clare L. ....'— '91 C.471 B.S.B.A. L.575 J.D. 111 E Jones St
Davenport, Sheri M. ....'58 '82 C.471 B.A. L.896 J.D. 111 E. Jones St.
Foy, Louis F., Jr. ....'44 '73 C.160 B.A. L.790 J.D. Dist. J.
Hood, James R., (BV) ....'38 '62 C.575 A.B. L.228 J.D. Co. Atty.
Koonce, Darris W., (CV) .... '16 '55 L.192 LL.B. P.O. Box 37
Proctor, Jimmie C. ....'37 '65 C&L.575 A.B. 109 W. Jones St.

TRENT WOODS, 4,192, *Craven Co.*

Alexander, Karen A., (CV) ....'65 '90 C.575 B.S. L.1345 J.D. 3707 Darby Rd.

TRINITY, 6,690, *Randolph Co.*

Abram, Marian C. '58 '83 C&L.930 B.S., J.D.
(adm. in OH; not adm. in NC) Sr. Atty., Sealy, Inc.
Braswell, Jamila '73 '98 C.309 A.B. L.893 J.D.
(adm. in VA; not adm. in NC) Sealy, Inc. (Legal Department)
Walker, Kenneth L. '48 '75 C.162 B.A. L.352 J.D.
(adm. in OH; not adm. in NC) V.P., Gen. Coun. & Secy., Sealy, Inc.

TROUTMAN, 1,493, *Iredell Co.*

Barker, Constance T. ....'43 '67 C&L.500 B.A., J.D. 258 Apache Rd.‡

Dalton, Judy, (CV) '64 '91 C.198 B.A. L.1228 J.D.
403 N. Main Street, 28166
Telephone: 704-528-7788 Fax: 704-528-7373
Email: judydalton_86@msn.com URL: http://www.judydaltonlawfirm.com
Family Law, Child Custody, Child Support, Visitation Rights, Divorce, Property Distribution, Restraining Orders, Adoptions, Criminal Defense, Felonies and Misdemeanors, DWI, Traffic Violations, Drug Crimes, Probation Violations, Civil Litigation, Wills, Debt Collections.
See Professional Biographies, TROUTMAN, NORTH CAROLINA

TROY, * 3,404, *Montgomery Co.*

Atkinson, Carl W., Jr., (BV) ....'44 '73 C.575 B.A. L.896 J.D. [Hollers&A.]
Deaton, John K., Law Office of, (CV) .... '72 '00 C.576 B.A. L.574 J.D. 416 Wood Street
Fisher, Harry E. ....'46 '72 C.896 B.A. L.893 J.D. [H.E.Fisher]
Fisher, Harry E., P.A. .... 407 North Main Street
Garner, Max A., (BV) ....'54 '79 C.575 B.A. L.423 J.D. 120 N. Main St.
Hollers, Russell J., (AV) ....'39 '63 C&L.575 A.B., LL.B. [Hollers&A.]

Hollers & Atkinson, (AV)
110 North Main Street, P.O. Box 567, 27371
Telephone: 910-572-3638 Fax: 910-576-1577
Email: hollers-atkinson@carolina.net
Russell J. Hollers; Carl W. Atkinson, Jr.
General Practice. Real Property and Estate Planning Law. Criminal Law. Traffic Court.
Representative Clients: First Bank, Troy, North Carolina; Town of Troy; Montgomery Foods, Inc.; Jordan Lumber & Supply, Inc.
See Professional Biographies, TROY, NORTH CAROLINA

Sabiston, Michael A. ....'53 '82 C.577 B.S. L.896 J.D. Dist. J.
Trull, J. Kent, (CV) '63 '91 C.575 B.A. L.1345 J.D.
Staff Atty., Co. Dept. of Soc. Servs.

TRYON, 1,680, *Polk Co.*

Beresford, Scott F. '43 '70 C.1068 B.A. L.245 J.D.
(adm. in GA; not adm. in NC) 251 Trade‡

Byers, Martelle & Williams, P.L.L.C.
(See Rutherfordton)

Corley, Donald G. '29 '53 C&L.228 A.B., J.D.
(adm. in DC; not adm. in NC) P.O. Box 1559‡

Deutsch, Robert J., P.A.
(See Asheville)

Elkins & Elkins
(See Hendersonville)

Freeman, Don C. '22 '53 C.309 A.B. L.1003 J.D.
(adm. in OH; not adm. in NC) 109 Warrior Dr.‡
Harroun, Bernard M. '22 '51 C.494 B.S.L. L.1018 LL.B.
(adm. in MN; not adm. in NC) 212 Warrior Dr.‡

Haynes, R. Anderson, (AV) '47 '73 C.855 B.A. L.575 J.D.
78 Pacolet Street, P.O. Box 100, 28782
Telephone: 828-859-9145 Fax: 828-859-2252
Estate Planning, Elder Law, Estate Administration, Probate, Real Estate, Corporate Law.
Reference: Bank of America, N.A., Tryon, NC.
See Professional Biographies, TRYON, NORTH CAROLINA

Hovendon, John C. ....'67 '93 C.31 A.B. L.659 J.D. 425 S. Trade St.
Johnson, William L., (AVⓉ) ....'38 '64 C.339 B.S. L.260 J.D. 98 Pacolet Street
Key, Hugh L., (BV) ....'42 '66 C&L.896 B.A., J.D. 1 Tryon Place
McDermott, Renee R., (AVⓉ) ....'50 '78 C.1111 B.A. L.1119 J.D. 845 Fox Run Ln.
McFarland, William A., Jr., (BV) .... '57 '82 C.925 B.S. L.1228 J.D. [McFarland&M.]
McFarland, Wm. A., (AV) ....'23 '51 C.401 L.896 J.D. [McFarland&M.]
McFarland & McFarland, (AV) .... 39 S. Trade St.
Meanix, William H., Jr. '27 '78 C.871 B.S. L.1294 J.D.
(adm. in NH; not adm. in NC) 15 Page Rd.
Miller, William H., (AV) .... '35 '65 C&L.575 A.B., LL.B. 84 Pacolet St.
Nager, A. Bailey ....'60 '87 C.228 A.B. L.1068 J.D. 1700 New Market Rd.
Skadow, Ronald R. '42 '66 C&L.597 B.S., J.D.
(adm. in IL; not adm. in NC) London Capital Corp.

TUXEDO, —, *Henderson Co.*

McGrady, Charles W., (AVⓉ) '53 '78 C.806 B.A. L.469 J.D. Dir., Falling Creek Camp for Boys, Inc.

VALDESE, 4,484, *Burke Co.*

Blackwell, Hugh A., (BV) .... '44 '69 C.575 A.B. L.309 J.D. [Mitchell,B.&M.]
Dill, G. Redmond, Jr., (BV) .... '46 '73 C.575 A.B. L.896 J.D. 149 W. Main St.
Mitchell, Marcus W. H., Jr., (AV) .... '52 '77 C.575 B.S. L.896 J.D. [Mitchell,B.&M.]
Mitchell, W. Harold, (AV) '25 '51 C&L.896 B.A., LL.B. Town Atty. [Mitchell,B.&M.] ‡
Mitchell, Blackwell & Mitchell, P.A., (AV) .... 215 East Main Street
Sitton, Juleigh, (BV) .... '62 '87 C.198 A.B. L.575 J.D. 215 E. Main St.

VILAS, 150, *Watauga Co.*

Moffatt, William D. '48 '77 C.259 B.S. L.1206 J.D. (adm. in FL; not adm. in NC) RR 001, Box 217-1‡

WADESBORO, * 3,645, *Anson Co.*

Beale, Michael E. .... '50 '76 C.690 B.A. L.575 J.D. Supr. Ct. J., Supr. Ct. Judges Off.
Bower, George C., Jr., (AV) .... '51 '78 C.575 A.B. L.896 J.D. [Poisson P.&B.]
Brauns, Brian P., (CV) .... '65 '91 C.576 B.A. L.577 J.D. P.O. Box 1018

Brown, Richard L., Jr.
(See Monroe)

Clodfelter, T. Lynn, (BV) .... '68 '93 C.575 A.B. L.1228 J.D. [Clodfelter]

Clodfelter Law Office, (BV)
202 East Wade Street, P.O. Box 754, 28170
Telephone: 704-694-0195 Fax: 704-694-0182
Email: lynn_tlclaw@alltel.net URL: http://www.tlclawfirm.com
T. Lynn Clodfelter.
Criminal Law, Domestic, Family Law, Child Custody, Divorce, Personal Injury, Wrongful Death, Traffic Violations, Driving While Intoxicated.
See Professional Biographies, WADESBORO, NORTH CAROLINA

Collini, Charles Weaver, (AV) '48 '74 C&L.575 B.A., J.D.
Anson Professional Building, 115 East Wade Street, P.O. Box 1039, 28170
Telephone: 704-694-9311 Fax: 704-694-9312 Email:ccollini@carolina.rr.com
Email: ccollini@alltel.net URL: http://www.lawyers.com/collinilaw
General Trial Practice. Personal Injury, Wrongful Death, Criminal Law, and Family Law.
Reference: United Carolina Bank.
See Professional Biographies, WADESBORO, NORTH CAROLINA

Cornwell, A. Milton .... '30 '61 C&L.575 A.B., J.D. 403 S. Park Rd. (Pat.)

Daniel, John R., Law Office of
(See Rockingham)

Drake, Henry T., Law Office of ..... '43 '69 C.1126 A.B. L.575 J.D. 211 S. Rutherford St.
Hightower, E. Avery, P.A., (AV) .... '14 '36 C.575 L.896 LL.B. 119 E. Wade St.
Huffman, Donald R. .... '38 '71 C.576 B.S. L.575 J.D. Res. Supr. Ct. J.
Little, Robert E., III, (BV) .... '34 '58 C&L.575 B.S., LL.B. 204 E. Wade St.
Lowe, Mark T., (BV) .... '55 '80 C&L.575 B.S.B.A., J.D. 115 E. Wade St.
Mason, William L., (BV) .... '36 '73 C&L.575 B.A., J.D. Town Atty.
McLendon, Moran D., Jr., (AV) .... '25 '50 C&L.575 A.B., LL.B. 1944 Morven Rd.
Mills, F. Fetzer .... '32 '61 C&L.575 A.B., LL.B. Emergency Supr. Ct. J.‡
Poisson, E. Stewart .... '78 '04 C&L.577 B.A., J.D. [Ⓐ Poisson P.&B.]
Poisson, Fred D., Jr., (AV) .... '51 '76 C.48 B.A. L.896 J.D. [Poisson P.&B.]
Poisson, Fred D., Sr., (AV) .... '26 '66 C&L.575 B.A., LL.B. [Poisson P.&B.]

Poisson Poisson & Bower, PLLC, (AV)
The Wyatt House, 300 East Wade Street, 28170
Telephone: 704-694-5515 Fax: 704-694-9645 URL: http://www.poissonpoissonbowerlaw.com
Email: info@poissonlaw.com URL: http://www.poissonlaw.com
Fred D. Poisson, Sr.; Fred D. Poisson, Jr. (Board Certified Specialist in Workers' Compensation, North Carolina State Board of Legal Specialization); George C. Bower, Jr.;—E. Stewart Poisson.
Personal Injury, Wrongful Death, Workers' Compensation, Social Security, Real Estate, Probate, Corporate Law and Traffic Cases.
See Professional Biographies, WADESBORO, NORTH CAROLINA

Taylor, H. P., Jr., (AV) .... '24 '48 C&L.575 B.S., LL.B. 115 E. Wade St.
Taylor, Susan Chandler .... '52 '78 C&L.575 B.A., J.D. Dist. J.

WAGRAM, 801, *Scotland Co.*

Memory, John M. .... '43 '68 C&L.896 B.A., J.D. U.S. Army Resv.

WAKE FOREST, 12,588, *Wake Co.*

Amos, Fred B., II .... '70 '98 C.576 B.A. L.1345 J.D. [Ⓐ Warren,P.&A.]
Anthony, Sue E., (BV) .... '58 '83 C&L.966 B.A., J.D. [Warren,P.&A.]

Brinkley, Dewey P.
(See Raleigh)

Chapek, Carlos .... '59 '95 C.178 B.A. L.352 J.D. 9028 Cornwell Court
Daly, John P. '37 '76 C.1040 B.B.A. L.1009 J.D. (adm. in NY; not adm. in NC) 7805 Fairlake Drive‡
Derrick, Jack H. .... '47 '77 C.277 B.S. L.896 J.D. Sr. Atty., Sprint Inc.
Drake, Kathryn S., (BVⓉ) '55 '79 C.577 B.S. L.575 J.D. (adm. in KY; not adm. in NC) [Warren,P.&A.]
Eason, F. Jackson, Jr. '45 '75 C.228 B.A. L.426 J.D. (adm. in CA; not adm. in NC) P.O. Box 22‡
Harris, Malcolm E., (AV) .... '48 '75 C.575 B.A. L.574 J.D. [M.E.Harris]

Harris, Malcolm E., P.A., (AV)
822 South White Street, 27587, P.O. Box 1100, 27588-1100
Telephone: 919-554-0700 Facsimile: 919-554-8052
Email: malcolmharris@nc.rr.com
Malcolm E. Harris.
Commercial and Residential Real Estate, Wills and Estates, Business Formation Law.
See Professional Biographies, WAKE FOREST, NORTH CAROLINA

Harvey, George H. '47 '72 C.232 A.B. L.896 J.D. Dir., Develop., Southeastern Baptist Theological Seminary

Hopper Law Firm
(See Raleigh)

Lake, I. Beverly, Sr., (AV) .... '06 '28 C.896 B.S. L.309 LL.B. P.O. Box 1915‡
Ledo, Michele Ann .... '67 '95 C.197 B.A. L.276 J.D. [M.A.Ledo]
Ledo, Michele A., PLLC, The Law Offices of .... 1640 Oak Grove Church Road
Levy, David J. .... '47 '78 C.831 B.A. L.273 J.D. 1012 Missy Lane (Pat.)
Lunding, Peter H. .... '59 '85 C.112 B.A. L.1065 J.D. P.O. Box 1151
MacKay, Kelly J. .... '68 '93 C.232 B.S. L.575 J.D [Warren,P.&A.]
Mills, John G., (AV) .... '33 '60 C&L.896 B.S., J.D. [Mills] (Pat.)
Mills Law Firm, PLLC, (AV) .... 822 S. White St. (Pat.)

Narron, Angela R., (BV) .... '68 '93 C.228 A.B. L.575 J.D. [Warren,P.&A.]
Nassif, Ellis, (AV) .... '07 '29 C&L.896 A.B., LL.B. 115 Elm Ave.‡
Paschal, Catherine .... '12 '42 C&L.896 B.A., LL.B. 340 Durham Rd.
Paschal, Edward, (BV) .... '21 '48 C&L.896 B.A., LL.B. 340 Durham Rd.
Perry, Michael Kiah, (BV) .... '58 '83 C.575 B.A. L.1228 J.D. [Warren,P.&A.]
Rasmussen, Georgianna .... '73 '99 C.747 B.A. L.213 J.D. 8501 Eaton Square Ct.
Reed, Laura K., (CVⓉ) '67 '93 C.695 B.A. L.902 J.D. (adm. in VA; not adm. in NC) 8812 Murdock Cir.
Rich, John M. .... '44 '70 C&L.896 B.A., J.D. 1743 S. Main Street‡
Sachtjen, Peter D. '40 '68 C&L.966 B.S.M.E., J.D. (adm. in MI; not adm. in NC) [Mills]
Shackleford, Richard K., (BV) .... '70 '96 C&L.896 B.A., J.D. [Warren,P.&A.]

Tenney & Tenney, LLP
(See Raleigh)

Warren, James S., (BV) .... '47 '74 C&L.896 B.A., J.D. [Warren,P.&A.]
Warren, Perry & Anthony, PLLC, (BV) .... 343 S. White St.
Wright, James B. .... '44 '69 C&L.378 B.A., J.D. Sr. Atty., Sprint Inc.

WALKERTOWN, 4,009, *Forsyth Co.*

Crews, Harold Ray .... '69 '99 C.34 B.A. L.1345 J.D. 4165 Camp Betty Hastings Rd.
Kilpatrick, Joseph E. .... '48 '75 C.198 B.A. L.575 J.D. Asst. Dir.

WALLACE, 3,344, *Duplin Co.*

Burrows, Richard L., (AV) .... '38 '65 C&L.575 A.B., LL.B. [Burrows&H.]
Burrows & Hall, (AV) .... 331 North Norwood Street
David, G. Phillip .... '59 '88 C.232 B.S.B.A. L.574 J.D. [David&Assoc.] ⊙

David and Associates, pllc
107 North Norwood Street, 28466 ⊙
Telephone: 910-285-8777 Toll Free: 1-800-856-9927
Email: aeverhart@davidandassociates.com URL: http://www.wilmingtonpiattorneys.com
G. Phillip David.
Personal Injury, Medical Malpractice, Wrongful Death, Products Liability, Workers Compensation, Aviation, Airplane Crashes, Negligence, Class Actions, Maritime Accidents, Boating Accidents, Bicycle Accidents, Motorcycle Accidents, Truck Accidents, School Bus Accidents, Railroad Accidents, Dog Bites, Slip and Fall, Birth Trauma, Brain Injury, Spinal Injury, Head Injury, Catastrophic Injury, Vehicular Homicide, Personal Injury Mediation, Products Liability, Drug and Medical Device Litigation, Product Defects, Automobile Liability, Motorcycle Products Liability, Amusement Park Liability, Hotel Liability, Marina Liability, Sports Injury.
Jacksonville, North Carolina Office: 405-B Western Boulevard. 28546. Telephone: 910-219-4878.
Supply, North Carolina Office: Highway 17. 28462. Telephone: 910-754-8465.
Wilmington, North Carolina Office: 1516 Dawson Street. 28401. Telephone: 910-251-8088.
Clinton, North Carolina Office: 610 Beaman Street. 28328. Telephone: 910-592-8400.
Winston-Salem, North Carolina Office: 1100-A South Stratford Road. 27103. Telephone: 336-354-1040.
Greensboro, North Carolina Office: 529 College Road. Suite G. 27410. Telephone: 336-354-1040.
See Professional Biographies, WALLACE, NORTH CAROLINA

Hall, Fred, (BV) .... '56 '81 C.575 B.A. L.1228 J.D. [Burrows&H.]
Phillips, Graham A., Jr., (BV) .... '33 '58 C&L.896 B.A., J.D. 224 E. Main St.
Phillips, Mary Susan .... '62 '87 C&L.896 B.S., J.D. P.O. Box 696
Powers, Anita Ruth, (BV) .... '60 '84 C.1128 B.A. L.574 J.D. 312 East Hall Street

WALNUT COVE, 1,465, *Stokes Co.*

Gehring, Jane Elizabeth Keiger .... '45 '80 C.6 B.A. L.896 J.D. Main St.‡
Gehring, John Edward, (BV) .... '42 '68 C&L.575 B.S., J.D. Main St.
Linville, Inez I. .... '42 '90 C.699 B.S. L.365 J.D. 711 S. Main Street
Rutledge, Jerry, (AV) .... '44 '69 C&L.575 A.B., J.D. Main & Second Sts.

WANCHESE, 1,527, *Dare Co.*

Malarney, Amber Davis .... '66 '91 L.896 J.D. Dist. Ct. J.

WARRENTON, * 811, *Warren Co.*

Bagshawe, Euan N. .... '60 '94 C.575 B.S. L.574 J.D. 406 N. Main St.
Bagshawe, Rhonda W. .... '65 '90 C&L.575 B.S.B.A., J.D. 400 N. Main St.
Banzet, Frank, (AV) .... '07 '32 C&L.597 101 North Front Street‡
Banzet, Julius, III, (AV) .... '37 '62 C&L.575 A.B., LL.B. [Banzet,B.&T.]

Banzet, Banzet & Thompson, P.L.L.C., (AV) 🅱🅱
Court House Square, 101 North Front Street, P.O. Box 535, 27589
Telephone: 252-257-3166 Fax: 252-257-2053
Email: bbanzet@nc.rr.com
Members of Firm: Julius Banzet, III; Lewis A. Thompson, III; Mitchell G. Styers.
General Civil and Criminal Trial Practice. State and Federal Criminal Defense, Traffic, Personal Injury Litigation, Workers Compensation, Medical Malpractice, Probate, Wills and Estates, Real Estate and Title Searches.
Representative Clients: Branch Banking & Trust Co.; Town of Norlina; Warren County Board of Education; Town of Warrenton.
Approved Attorneys for: Federal Land Bank of Columbia; Lawyers Title Insurance Corp.; Chicago Title Insurance Co.; Commonwealth Land Title Insurance Co.; AMI Title Insurance Co.; Fidelity National Title Insurance Corp.
See Professional Biographies, WARRENTON, NORTH CAROLINA

Clayton, Theaoseus T., Sr., (BV) .... '30 '61 C.369 A.B. L.574 LL.B. [Clayton&C.]
Clayton and Clayton, P.A., (BV) .... 307 W. Franklin St.

Davis, Sturges & Tomlinson
(See Louisburg)

Jackson, Harvey D., Attorney at Law
(See Henderson)

Johnson, Charles T., Jr., (AV) .... '29 '56 C&L.896 B.S., LL.B. 130 North Main Street
Rooker, Marvin P., (BV) .... '49 '77 C.232 B.A. L.192 J.D. 108 S. Bragg St.
Styers, Mitchell G. .... '69 '97 C.576 B.A. L.574 J.D. [Banzet,B.&T.]
Thompson, Lewis A., III, (AV) .... '52 '77 C.579 B.A. L.896 J.D. [Banzet,B.&T.]
Thompson, Susan M., (BV) .... '52 '77 C.293 B.A. L.896 J.D. P.O. Box 333
White, Charles M., III .... '26 '57 C&L.575 A.B., LL.B. W. Macon St.‡
Williams, Michael Antoine .... '74 '01 C.575 B.A. L.574 J.D. 113 West Market Street
Williams, Rhonda J. .... '65 '90 C&L.575 B.S.B.A., J.D. 400 South Main Street

WARSAW, 3,051, *Duplin Co.*

Kenan, S. Reginald, (BV) .... '55 '80 C.296 A.B. L.1228 J.D. 115 West Hill Street
Ludlum, Hayes S. .... '80 '05 C.301 B.A. L.1228 J.D. [Ludlum]
Ludlum, J. Garrett, (BV) .... '47 '81 C&L.1228 B.S., J.D. [Ludlum]

Ludlum Law Firm, (BV)
404 North Pine Street, P.O. Box 711, 28398-0711
Telephone: 910-293-2000 Facsimile: 910-293-2200
Email: gludlum@ludlumlawfirm.com URL: http://www.lawyers.com/ludlaw-nc
J. Garrett Ludlum; Hayes S. Ludlum.
Driving While Intoxicated and Traffic Violations. Criminal Defense, Real Estate, Divorce and Family Law, Accidents and Personal Injury, Litigation, Wills, Commercial Transactions.
See Professional Biographies, WARSAW, NORTH CAROLINA

Mikitka, Susan Collins, (BV) .... '66 '92 C&L.575 B.A., J.D. 114 West Hill Street
Stevens, Henry L., IV, (BV) .... '— '97 C.575 B.A. L.1339 J.D. Dist. J.
Thompson, E. C., III, (AV) .... '36 '66 C.575 B.A. L.896 LL.B. [Thompson&T.]
Thompson, Kennedy L. ....'75 '01 C.575 B.A. L.1002 J.D. [Thompson&T.]

Thompson & Thompson, P.C., (AV)
114 W. Hill Street, P.O. Box 901, 28398
Telephone: 910-293-3124 Fax: 910-293-7171
Email: kennedythompson@yahoo.com URL: http://www.thompsonandthompsonlaw.com
Kennedy L. Thompson; E. C. Thompson, III.
Language: Spanish.
Criminal Law, Driving While Intoxicated, Traffic Violations, Civil Litigation, Medical Malpractice, Real Estate.

See Professional Biographies, WARSAW, NORTH CAROLINA

WASHINGTON, * 9,583, *Beaufort Co.*

Archie, Thomas E., (AV) .... '43 '68 C&L.575 A.B., J.D. [Carter,A.H.&S.]

Brown, Roddey M. III, & Angela H. Brown, P.A.
(See Greenville)

Brumbaugh, Mu & King, P.A., (BV)
110 West Third Street, P.O. Box 338, 27889 ⊙
Telephone: 252-946-0793
URL: http://www.bmklaw.net
Kenneth W. King, Jr.
Practice Limited to Injury Cases. Automobile, Wrongful Death, Medical Malpractice, Workers' Compensation, Products Liability and Social Security Claims.

See Professional Biographies, WASHINGTON, NORTH CAROLINA

Burch Law Office
(See Greenville)

Carter, William B., Jr., (AV) ....'39 '64 C&L.575 A.B., LL.B. [Carter,A.H.&S.]
Carter, Archie, Hassell & Singleton, LLP, (AV) .... 112 S. Respess St.
Cayton, Darrell B., Jr., (BV) .... '62 '87 C.575 B.S. L.1228 J.D. 155 N. Market St.
Coleman, Vicki Gregory ....'59 '84 C&L.575 B.A., J.D. State Dept. of Commerce
Drouin, Steven Gerard ....'63 '04 C.232 B.S.N. L.1228 J.D. [S.G.Drouin]
Drouin, Steven G., RN, Attorney at Law .... 317 W. 2nd St.
Easley, Henry A., III .... '49 '74 C.576 B.S. L.575 J.D. 615 E. 12th Street
Fountain, R. M., Jr. '40 '67 C&L.575 B.S., LL.B.
Pres. CEO, Chmn. of the Board, Fountain PowerBoat Industries, Inc.
Francisco, David C., (AV) ....'44 '75 C.1090 B.S. L.896 J.D. [Rodman,H.F.&P.]
Gaddy, Erin Suzanne, (BV) ....'72 '97 C.259 B.A. L.228 J.D. Asst. Dist. Atty.
Gaskins, Debra H., (BV) ....'50 '80 C.575 B.A. L.1228 J.D. [Gaskins&G.]
Gaskins, Herman E., Jr., (AV) .... '49 '75 C&L.575 B.A., J.D. [Gaskins&G.]
Gaskins and Gaskins, P.A., (AV) ....214 East Water Street
Graves, Stephen A., (BV) ....'45 '75 C&L.836 B.B.A., J.D. [S.A.Graves]
Graves, Stephen A., P.A., (BV) ....151 N. Market St.

Gray Legal Group
(See Greensboro)

Grimes, Samuel G. .... '43 '68 C.198 A.B. L.575 J.D. Dist. J.
Hackney, Keith D., (BV) .... '48 '73 C.576 B.S. L.575 J.D. 211 N. Market St.
Hardy, Edwin M. "Sandy", (CV) .... '61 '89 C.232 B.A. L.896 J.D. 206 N. Market St.
Hassell, Sidney J., Jr., (BV) .... '54 '78 C&L.575 A.B., J.D. [Carter,A.H.&S.]
Holloman, Michael Anthony '56 '92
C.999 B.S. L.574 J.D. 122 S. Washingrton Harbour Dr.
Holscher, Franz F., (CV) ....'70 '97 C.575 B.S. L.1228 J.D. [Rodman,H.F.&P.]
Holscher, Frederick Norman, (AV) ......'48 '73 C&L.575 A.B., J.D. [Rodman,H.F.&P.]
Jacobi, John J. '21 '51 C&L.436 B.S.B.A., LL.B.
(adm. in WI; not adm. in NC) 103 Creek View Lane‡
Johnson, Robert F., (BV) .... '48 '73 C&L.896 B.A., J.D. Asst. Dist. Atty.
Johnston, Franklin B., (BV) ....'45 '72 C.232 B.A. L.896 J.D. 117 W. 3rd
King, Kenneth W., Jr., (BV) ...... '61 '86 C.575 B.S. L.469 J.D. [Brumbaugh,M.&K.] ⊙
Knott, Lee E., Jr., (BV) .... '32 '64 C.575 B.S. L.228 J.D. P.O. Box 548
Kubicek, Robert E., (AVⓉ) '27 '58 C.588 B.B.A. L.1048 J.D.
(adm. in MA; not adm. in NC) 118 Fairway Dr.‡
Laughton, Norma S. .... '45 '95 C.575 A.B. L.228 J.D. P.O. Box 517

LeonLaw Firm, The
(See Greenville)

Lilly, S. Matthew, Jr., (CV) .... '62 '89 C.893 B.A. L.896 J.D. 206 N. Market St.
Mason, Keith B., Attorney at Law, (BV) ....'57 '82 C&L.575 B.A., J.D. 105 E. 2nd St.
Mayo, William P., (AV) ....'26 '53 C&L.575 A.B., J.D. Co. Atty. [Mayo&M.]
Mayo, William P., Jr., (BV) ....'65 '90 C.575 B.S.B.A. L.1345 J.D. [Mayo&M.]
Mayo & Mayo, (AV) .... 102 West Second Street
McLendon, Christopher B., (BV) .... '51 '80 C.575 A.B. L.1228 J.D. [C.B.McLendon]
McLendon, Christopher B., P.A., (BV) ....157 N. Market St.
McMullan, James B., (AV) .... '24 '50 C&L.575 A.B., J.D. 729 Short Dr.‡
Page, William H., Jr. ....'61 '86 C&L.575 B.A., J.D. Page Management Group
Partrick, Cornelius T., Jr., (BV) .... '52 '80 C.575 B.A. L.896 J.D. [C.T.Partrick,Jr.]
Partrick, Cornelius T., Jr., P.A., (BV) ....204 N. Market St.
Paul, Michael A. .... '56 '81 C.896 B.A. L.1228 J.D. Dist. J.
Peck, R. Brantley, Jr., (BV) ....'57 '83 C.575 B.S. L.896 J.D. [Rodman,H.F.&P.]
Privette, Sonia M. ....'60 '85 C.575 B.A. L.923 J.D. 110 S. Reapess Street
Rodman, Edward N., (AV) ...... '26 '55 C.576 B.S. L.575 LL.B. [▣ Rodman,H.F.&P.] ‡

Rodman, Holscher, Francisco & Peck, P.A., (AV)
320 North Market Street, P.O. Drawer 1747, 27889
Telephone: 252-946-3122 Fax: 252-946-3125
URL: http://www.rhfp.net
Frederick Norman Holscher; David C. Francisco; R. Brantley Peck, Jr.; Franz F. Holscher. Retired: Edward N. Rodman.
General Civil Practice, Insurance Defense, Personal Injury, Social Security, Family Law, Corporate, Trusts and Estates, Probate, Real Property, Municipal Law, Criminal Law and Defense.
Representative Clients: Bank of America; NewSouth Bank; City of Washington; PCS Phosphate, Inc.; Lee Chevrolet, Inc.; Town of Plymouth; Geico Insurance.

See Professional Biographies, WASHINGTON, NORTH CAROLINA

Sermons, Wayland J., Jr., (P.A.), (BV) ..... '55 '80 C.575 Bus. L.896 J.D. 100 E. Main St.
Singleton, H. Ranee, (BV) ....'59 '89 C.575 B.A. L.1228 J.D. [Carter,A.H.&S.]
Swain, Deanna F., Attorney at Law '77 '03 C.232 B.A.B.A. L.896 J.D.
141 N. Market St.
Vosburgh, James R. .... '32 '64 C.152 B.S. L.575 J.D. Spec. Supr. Ct. J.

WAXHAW, 2,625, *Union Co.*

Buckley, John C. ....'58 '89 C.645 B.S. L.790 J.D. 8902 Horsecroft Ct.
Dodge, Joseph Francis, (CVⓉ) ......'62 '88 C.1121 B.S. L.1187 J.D. 8501 Tintinhull Ln.
Lassiter, Edward A. .... '33 '57 C&L.896 B.S., J.D. 8700 Baraka Place Apt. K‡

WAYNESVILLE, * 9,232, *Haywood Co.*

Bartleson, J. Andrew '56 '86 C&L.260 B.S., J.D.
(adm. in FL; not adm. in NC) 868 Walker Rd.

Blanchard, Newman & Hayes
(See Hendersonville)

Brown, Gavin A., (BV) ....'47 '72 C&L.575 A.B., J.D. [Brown&P.]
Brown, Glenn W., (AV) .... '26 '50 L.896 LL.B. [Brown,W.&H.] ‡
Brown & Patten P.A., (BV) ....370 N. Main St., Ste. 206

Brown, Ward & Haynes, P.A., (AV) ▣
Suite 300, 370 North Main Street, P.O. Drawer 928, 28786-0928
Telephone: 828-456-9436 Fax: 828-456-4069
Glenn W. Brown (Retired); H.S. Ward, Jr. (Retired); Woodrow H. Griffin; Stephen G. Ellis; Frank G. Queen; William E. Cannon, Jr. Of Counsel: David J. Haynes.
General Practice in all Courts. Trials. Probate, Corporation, Real Estate, Business Law, Utility Law, Domestic Relations, Criminal, Traffic Offenses, Civil Litigation, Estate Planning, Appellate Practice
General Counsel for: Century South Bank; Haywood Builders Supply Co., Inc.
Local Counsel for: Haywood Elect. Membership Corporation.
Approved Attorneys for: Lawyers Title Insurance Corp.; Chicago Title Insurance Co.; Federal Land Bank of Columbia; Lawyers Title of North Carolina; Commonwealth Title Co.

See Professional Biographies, WAYNESVILLE, NORTH CAROLINA

Bryant, Steven J. ....'52 '77 C.473 B.A. L.910 J.D. Dist. J.
Cannon, William E., Jr., (AVⓉ) ......'52 '77 C.1365 B.A. L.280 J.D. [Brown,W.&H.] ‡
Clark, Keith L., (BV) .... '52 '77 C.575 B.S. L.896 J.D. [Clark]
Clark Law Firm, P.A., (BV) ....741 S. Haywood St.
Davis, Ann Hines, (BV) ....'55 '79 C.925 B.S. L.575 J.D. [Kersten&D.]
Davis, Danny E. .... '53 '79 C.925 B.S. L.1345 J.D. Dist. J.
Decker, C. Caleb ....'76 '03 C.925 B.S. L.4210 J.D. P.O. Box 1191
Dickson, Clarence H., III, Attorney at Law, (BV) '53 '78
C.228 B.A. L.575 J.D. 137 Hazel St.
Dove, Ira L. ....'68 '99 C.1063 B.A. L.575 J.D. 486 E Marshall St
Ellis, Stephen G., (BV) .... '49 '84 C&L.575 B.A., J.D. [Brown,W.&H.]

Ferikes & Bleynat, PLLC
(See Asheville)

Finger, Timothy L., (BV) ....'55 '80 C.575 A.B. L.574 J.D. 154 N. Main St.
Fraser, Judith C. ....'42 '77 C.258 B.A. L.796 LL.B. 89 Walnut St.‡
Griffin, Woodrow H., (AV) ....'48 '74 C.316 B.A. L.896 J.D. [Brown,W.&H.]
Grimes, S. Janson, (BV) ....'46 '72 C&L.575 B.A., J.D. [Grimes&T.] ⊙
Grimes & Teich, (BV)
385 N. Haywood Street (⊙Asheville, Rutherfordton, NC; Greenville, SC)
Haynes, David J., (AV) ....'39 '62 C.699 L.896 LL.B. [▣ Brown,W.&H.]
Highsmith, Mose L. ....'58 '96 C.1290 B.A. L.1228 J.D. Asst. Dist. Atty.
Hyatt, J. Marlene ....'53 '80 C&L.896 B.A., J.D. Sr. Resident Supr. Ct. J.
Jay, John I., (BV) ....'39 '67 C.420 B.A. L.838 J.D. 236 N. Main St.
Jones, William J., (CV) ....'72 '98 C.925 B.S.B.A. L.575 J.D. [Jones,B.J.]
Jones, Bill J., (CV) ....367 Dellwood Rd., Blvd. B
Jordan, T. Michael, (BV) ....'48 '75 C&L.575 A.B., J.D. 154 N. Main St.
Kersten, John C., (AV) .... '40 '65 C&L.472 B.A., J.D. [Kersten&D.]

Kersten & Davis, P.A., (AV)
95 Depot Street, P.O. Drawer 1260, 28786
Telephone: 828-452-5801 Fax: 828-456-4917
Email: attorneys@kdlawfirm.com
John C. Kersten; Ann Hines Davis.
Real Estate, Corporate Law, Probate, Trusts and Estates, Litigation, Personal Injury, Criminal Law, Local Government Law, Securities.

See Professional Biographies, WAYNESVILLE, NORTH CAROLINA

Kirkpatrick, James Weaver, III, (BV) '68 '95
C.125 B.A. L.1339 J.D. [J.W.Kirkpatrick,III]

Kirkpatrick, James Weaver, III, P.A., (BV)
95 Depot Street, P.O. Drawer 1260, 28786
Telephone: 828-452-0801 Fax: 828-456-4917
Email: kirk@jwklaw.net URL: http://www.kirkpatricklawfirm.com
James Weaver Kirkpatrick, III.
Residential Real Estate, Criminal Law, DWI, Drug Offenses, Personal Injury, Auto Accidents, Wrongful Death, Traffic Violations.

See Professional Biographies, WAYNESVILLE, NORTH CAROLINA

Leslie, William H., (BV) ....'57 '88 C.48 B.A. L.469 J.D. 34 Joyce St.
Letts, Bradley B., (CV) ....'66 '95 C.575 B.A. L.500 J.D. 258 N. Main St.
Martin, Stephen J., (BV) ....'46 '76 C.1222 B.A. L.260 J.D. 434 S. Main St.
Millar, Wm. I., (AV) ....'28 '51 C&L.228 A.B., LL.B. [W.I.Millar]
Millar, Wm. I., P.A., (AV) .... 144 Montgomery St.

Moore Law Firm, The
(See Asheville)

Morley, E.K., PLLC, Law Offices of
(See Hendersonville)

Norris, Jeffrey W., (BV) .... '64 '93 C.896 B.A. L.831 J.D. [J.W.Norris&Assoc.]

Norris, Jeffrey W., & Associates, PLLC, (BV)
Norris Professional Building, 177 North Main Street, 28786
Telephone: 828-452-2221 Toll Free: 1-800-410-0380 Fax: 828-452-3534
URL: http://www.norrisandassoc.com
Jeffrey W. Norris. Of Counsel: Larry T. Reida.
Commercial Litigation, Real Estate, Business Transactions, Local Government Law, Estate Planning and Family Law, IRC Exchanges.

See Professional Biographies, WAYNESVILLE, NORTH CAROLINA

Orgelfinger, Louis '15 '39 C.294 A.B. L.724 LL.B.
(adm. in NY; not adm. in NC) 304 Jackson Dr.‡
Pasch, William H. .... '35 '74 C.390 B.S.E.E. L.879 J.D. App. Ref.
Patten, Donald N., (BV) ....'58 '83 C.228 A.B. L.469 J.D. [Brown&P.]
Prevost, Phyllis R. ....'24 '51 C.912 L.215 LL.B. Pres., Parkway Inn, Inc.
Queen, Frank G., (BV) ....'51 '76 C&L.575 A.B., J.D. [Brown,W.&H.]
Reida, Larry T., (BV) ....'35 '60 C&L.352 B.S.C., J.D. [▣ J.W.Norris&Assoc.]

Sluder, Curtis Alan
(See Asheville)

Smith, Burton C., Jr., (BV) ....'48 '72 C.228 A.B. L.260 J.D. 154 North Main Street
Tanner, John R. '31 '78 C.608 B.A. L.1206 J.D.
(adm. in FL; not adm. in NC) 23 Alpine Lane
Thomas, N. John '24 '51 C.976 B.E. L.309 J.D.
(adm. in NY; not adm. in NC) 30 Mountain Mist Lane‡
Thornhill, Edward, III, P.A., (AV) ... '33 '73 C&L.228 A.B., J.D. 122 S. Main St., Suite D
Ward, H.S., Jr., (AV) ....'32 '56 C.198 L.575 LL.B. [Brown,W.&H.] ‡
Wenzel, Derek M. ....'76 '02 C.198 B.A. L.904 J.D. [Wenzel&W.]
Wenzel, Sarah P. ....'78 '03 C.276 B.S.B.A. L.30 J.D. [Wenzel&W.]

Wenzel & Wenzel, PLLC
160 North Main Street, Suite 12, 28786
Telephone: 828-452-9099 Fax: 828-452-9059
URL: http://www.wenzellawfirm.com
Derek M. Wenzel; Sarah P. Wenzel.
Wills and Probate, Trusts and Estates, Business, Bankruptcy, Real Estate, Buying or Selling a Home, Residential Real Estate, Real Estate Construction, Eminent Domain, Landlord Tenant Law, Civil Litigation, Workers Compensation, General Practice.
See Professional Biographies, WAYNESVILLE, NORTH CAROLINA

White, Gladys I. '14 '48 C.259 B.S. L.260 J.D.
(adm. in FL; not adm. in NC) 405 Wayneview Dr.‡

Wijewickrama, David, Law Office of '69 '03 C.790 B.S. L.900 J.D.
160 North Main Street, Suite 11, 28786
Telephone: 828-454-1999 Fax: 828-454-1990
Email: davidwije17@yahoo.com URL: http://www.dwlawpractice.com
Personal Injury, Family Law, Civil Litigation, Bankruptcy, Real Estate.
See Professional Biographies, WAYNESVILLE, NORTH CAROLINA

WEAVERVILLE, 2,416, *Buncombe Co.*

Barnes, William A., Jr., (BV) .... '48 '74 C&L.575 B.A., J.D. [W.A.Barnes]
Barnes, William A., P.A., (BV) .... 38 N. Main St.
Booth, James C. '55 '81 C.886 B.A. L.836 J.D.
(adm. in TN; not adm. in NC) 4 Packsaddle Trail
Lollis, Margret, (BV) .... '54 '87 L.575 J.D. [[A] W.Wadford]
Reed, Wallace B. '29 '64 C.659 B.S. L.352 J.D.
(adm. in IA; not adm. in NC) 11 High Bluff Dr.‡
Root, Allan P., (BV) .... '55 '81 C.197 B.A. L.893 J.D. [Root&R.]
Root, Louise Critz, (BV) .... '55 '82 C.296 B.A. L.575 J.D. [Root&R.]
Root & Root, P.L.L.C., (BV) .... P.O. Box 727
Wadford, Alvin W., Jr., (BV) .... '48 '78 C.885 L.577 38 N. Main St.
Wadford, Wilder, (BV) .... '48 '73 C.885 B.A. L.575 J.D. [W.Wadford]
Wadford, Wilder, P.A., (BV) .... 38 North Main Street

WEDDINGTON, 6,696, *Mecklenburg & Union Cos.*

Robinson Law Office
(See Charlotte)

Spina-Hampton, Lauren '62 '88 C.188 B.S. L.477 J.D.
(adm. in NY; not adm. in NC) 3045 Rockridge Pass

WELDON, 1,392, *Halifax Co.*

Collins, Ernest Terrell, (BV) ......'69 '94 C.302 B.A. L.574 J.D. 1001 Roanoke Rapids Rd.
Warrick, Bradley A. '64 '90 C.473 B.A. L.347 J.D.
(adm. in IL; not adm. in NC) Gen. Counsel, Coastal Lumber Company

WENDELL, 4,247, *Wake Co.*

Adams, R. L., PLLC
(See Wendell)

Burgess, Timothy C. '63 '95 C.1228 B.B.A. L.370 J.D.
(adm. in AL; not adm. in NC) P.O. Box 150
Cutler, Jeffrey M., (BV) .... '64 '89 C.576 B.S. L.1228 J.D. [Kirk,K.H.C.&T.]
Ewell, Sam E., Jr. .... '46 '71 C.575 A.B. L.896 J.D. P.O. Box 1507‡
Hill, James D. .... '43 '81 C.1128 B.A. L.896 J.D. 3501 Wendell Blvd.
Howell, Joseph T., (BV) .... '58 '84 C.576 B.A. L.574 J.D. [Kirk,K.H.C.&T.]
Kirk, Clarence M., Sr., (BV) .... '25 '57 C&L.896 B.S., LL.B. [Kirk,K.H.C.&T.]
Kirk, Philip G., (AV) .... '58 '84 C.1228 B.S. L.574 J.D. [Kirk,K.H.C.&T.]
Kirk, Kirk, Howell, Cutler & Thomas, L.L.P., (AV) .... 200 N. Pine St.
Tantum, John E., (AV) '48 '73
C&L.896 B.S., J.D. 3401 Wendell Boulevard (⊙Emerald Isle)
Thomas, C. Terrell, Jr., (AV) .... '69 '94 C.34 B.S. L.896 J.D. [Kirk,K.H.C.&T.]

WENTWORTH, * 2,779, *Rockingham Co.*

Allen, Stanley L., (BV) .... '57 '83 C.896 B.A. L.1228 J.D. P.O. Box 287
Bailey, Daniel K., Attorney at Law, (AV) '49 '74
C.576 B.S. L.575 J.D. 1046 NC Highway 65

Daniel, George B., P.A.
(See Yanceyville)

Daniel, William H., P.A.
(See Yanceyville)

Folger & Tucker, P.A.
(See Madison)

Foster, Belinda J., (BV) .... '57 '86 C.1298 B.A. L.575 J.D. Dist. Atty.
Harrington, Thomas S., (AV) ... '26 '56 C.228 L.575 LL.B. 2 Courthouse Square (⊙Eden)

Maddrey Etringer & Smith, L.L.P.
(See Eden)

McHugh, Peter M. .... '47 '74 C.188 B.A. L.575 J.D. Supr. Ct. J.
Morgan, Melzer A. (Pat), Jr. .... '40 '67 C&L.575 A.B., J.D. Supr. Ct. J.
Pell, Suzanne P. .... '43 '98 C.577 B.A. L.574 J.D. Off. of Dist. Atty.
Russell, W. Eugene, (BV) .... '50 '75 C&L.575 A.B., J.D. Co. Atty.
Stone, Richard W. .... '55 '81 C.577 B.A. L.575 J.D. Chf. Dist. Ct. J.

Walker & Melvin, LLP
(See Eden)

Wayne, Shireen Z. .... '70 '98 C.575 B.A. L.1228 J.D. Asst. DA
Wilkins, Frederick B., (AV) .... '48 '75 C.656 B.S. L.896 J.D. Dist. Ct. J.
Wilson, Edwin G., Jr., (BV) .... '66 '93 C.893 B.A. L.896 J.D. P.O. Box 97

WEST END, 800, *Moore Co.*

Bierbaum, Robert J. .... '— '02 C.1130 B.A. L.574 J.D. 6535 Seven Lakes Village
Burrell, Leo D., (BVⓉ) ..... '16 '41 C.222 A.B. L.262 LL.B. Exec. Ctr., Seven Lakes Dr.
Kelly, William P. .... '21 '47 C.228 LL.B. Seven Lakes Shop. Ctr.
Meyer, Robert A. '21 '48 C&L.145 J.D.
(adm. in IL; not adm. in NC) 6113 Seven Lakes, W.‡
Williams, Clawson L., Jr., (BV) .... '34 '59 C&L.575 A.B., J.D. 7 Lakes Shopping Ctr.

WEST JEFFERSON, 1,002, *Ashe Co.*

Baker, Garland B., (BV) .... '57 '86 C.500 B.A. L.575 J.D. [Vannoy&R.] ⊙
Hurley, Benjamin G., Jr., (BV) .... '64 '89 C.575 A.B. L.1228 J.D. [Kilby&H.]
Kilby, John T., (AV) .... '46 '75 C.34 B.S. L.574 J.D. [Kilby&H.]

Kilby & Hurley, (AV)
122 North Jefferson Avenue, P.O. Box 24, 28694
Telephone: 336-246-3144 Fax: 336-246-6346
Members of Firm: John T. Kilby; Benjamin G. Hurley, Jr.
General Civil and Criminal Law, DWI, Traffic Offenses, Real Estate, Probate, Domestic Relations, Personal Injury.

(This Listing Continued)

Kilby & Hurley (Continued)

Representative Clients: Ashe County; Fleetwood Falls, Inc.; First Citizens Bank of West Jefferson; Peoples Rexall Drug Stores; J.R. Vannoy & Sons Construction; Heritage Auto Group; Ashe County Builders; Asheland Insurance; Cardinal Stone, Inc.; Jefferson Landing, Inc.

Lisk, John F., (AVⓉ) .... '52 '77 C&L.472 B.B.A., J.D. 1557 Blue Ridge Church Rd.
Moore, Larry S., (AV) .... '13 '39 C&L.896 LL.B. P.O. Box 300‡
Reeves, Jimmy D., (AV) .... '48 '73 C&L.896 B.A., J.D. [Vannoy&R.] ⊙
Reeves, John "Jak" B. .... '79 '04 C.575 B.A. L.1228 J.D. [[A] Vannoy&R.] ⊙
Reeves, M. Alexandra .... '76 '01 C.575 B.A. L.896 J.D. [Vannoy&R.] ⊙

Vannoy & Reeves, PLLC, (AV)
A Professional Limited Liability Company
202 East Main Street, P.O. Drawer 67, 28694 ⊙
Telephone: 336-246-7172 Fax: 336-246-5966 Email: jim@vannoyandreeves.com Email: garland@vannoyandreeves.com Email: alex@vannoyandreeves.com Email: jak@vannoyandreeves.com URL: http://www.lawyers.com/vannoyandreeves
URL: http://www.vannoyandreeves.com
Members of Firm: Wade E. Vannoy, Jr. (1927-1991); Jimmy D. Reeves; Garland B. Baker; M. Alexandra Reeves. Associate: John "Jak" B. Reeves.
General Civil and Criminal Trial Practice in State and Federal Courts, Real Property, Estate Planning, Probate, Business and Corporate Law, Traffic, Family Law, Plaintiff's Personal Injury Matters and Collections.
Sparta, North Carolina Office: 112 South Main Street, P.O.Box 249, 28675. Telephone: 336-372-8740. Fax: 336-372-6114.
See Professional Biographies, WEST JEFFERSON, NORTH CAROLINA

WHISPERING PINES, 2,090, *Moore Co.*

Johnson, Daniel W. '14 '40 C.315 A.B. L.608 J.D.
(adm. in OH; not adm. in NC) 62B Pine Lake Dr.‡
Morris, Gary .... '46 '00 C.5 B.A. L.1370 J.D. [Morris]

Morris Law Office
7451 Suite C, NC Hwy 22, 28327
Telephone: 910-690-4595 Fax: 910-949-5587
Email: morrislawoffice@charter.net URL: http://www.gmorrislaw.com
Gary Morris.
Criminal Law, Felonies and Misdemeanors, Traffic Violations and Tickets, Trucks, Motorcycles, Driving While Intoxicated, DUI, Animal Law, Equine, Horse Rights and Trusts, Veterans Benefits and Appeals.
See Professional Biographies, WHISPERING PINES, NORTH CAROLINA

Watson, Philip B., Jr. '26 '50 C&L.421 B.Ch.E., LL.B.
(adm. in KY; not adm. in NC) 94 S. Lake Shore Dr.‡

WHITE LAKE, 529, *Bladen Co.*

Nichols, Heather D. Miller
(See Fayetteville)

WHITEVILLE, * 5,078, *Columbus Co.*

Aldridge, Thomas V., Jr. .... '47 '72 C.55 B.S. L.575 J.D. Dist. J.
Bullard, Kevin Jarrett, (BV) .... '66 '95 C.576 B.A. L.1228 J.D. [McGougan]
Burns, Robert H., Jr., (AV) .... '12 '33 C&L.896 206 Pinckney St.
Dorman, Scott C. .... '65 '91 [Dorman]
Dorman Law Firm .... 812 Pinckney St.
Ekster, Paul J. .... '73 '99 C.860 B.S. L.896 J.D. [[A] McGougan]
Garner, H. Griffith, (BV) .... '63 '88 C.797 B.A. L.838 J.D. 609 N. Madison St.
Gore, William C., Jr. .... '51 '77 C.575 A.B. L.574 J.D. Supr. Ct. J.
Harper, Willis H., Jr., (BV) .... '63 '90 C.446 B.A. L.575 J.D. [McGougan]
High, John Alan, (BV) .... '66 '92 C.575 B.S. L.1345 J.D. [Hill&H.]
Hill, James E., Jr., (BV) .... '46 '73 C.896 B.A. L.790 J.D. [Hill&H.]

Hill & High, L.L.P., (BV)
Courthouse Square, 28472
Telephone: 910-642-8136 Fax: 910-640-2101
Email: hillandhigh@whitevillenc.net URL: http://www.lawyers.com/hillandhigh
Members of the Firm: James E. Hill, Jr.; John Alan High.
Personal Injury, Medical Malpractice, Automobile Accidents, Criminal Law, Driving While Intoxicated, Traffic Violations, Family Law, Divorce, Real Estate, Estate Planning, Wills, Trusts, Social Security and Disability Law.
See Professional Biographies, WHITEVILLE, NORTH CAROLINA

Hooks, D. Jack, Jr. .... '54 '80 C.790 B.A. L.1228 J.D. Supr. Ct. J.

Jones, Greg, & Associates, P.A.
(See Wilmington)

Lee, Junius Bright, III, (AV) .... '53 '79 C&L.575 B.S., J.D. [Lee&L.]

Lee & Lee, (AV)
812 Pinckney Street, 28472
Telephone: 910-642-3708 Fax: 910-642-9058
Email: llg@weblnk.net
Member of Firm: Junius Bright Lee, III.
Business and Corporations, Business Formation, Corporation Formation, Criminal, Driving While Intoxicated, Traffic Violations, White Collar Crime, Personal Injury, Automobile Accidents, Employment Law, Workers Compensation, Social Security, Wills, Trusts and Estates, Real Estate, Family Law.
See Professional Biographies, WHITEVILLE, NORTH CAROLINA

McGougan Law Firm, The, (AV) .... 130 Jefferson Street (⊙Tabor City)
Meekins, Fred C., Jr., (BV) .... '55 '84 C&L.575 B.A., J.D. 130 Memory Plaza
Melville, Robert H. (Sam), Jr. .... '62 '89 C.953 B.A. L.1345 J.D. 908 Pinckney Street
Noecker, Lisa Carter .... '64 '92 C.160 B.S. L.575 J.D. Staff Atty., United Carolina Bk.
Pope, Harold G., (AV) .... '47 '83 C.34 B.S. L.574 J.D. [Pope,S.&S.]
Pope, Sessoms & Sasser, (AV) .... 706 N. Madison St.
Powell, J. Coburn, (BV) .... '60 '85 C.575 B.S. L.896 J.D. [Powell&P.]
Powell & Powell, P.C., (BV) .... 709 North Madison Street
Sasser, Douglas B., (BV) .... '67 '93 C.576 B.A. L.1345 J.D. [Pope,S.&S.]
Sauls, W. Lewis, (BV) .... '40 '69 C.1228 B.S. L.575 J.D. 107 Courthouse Sq.
Scott, C. Martin, II .... '71 '99 C.575 A.B. L.1228 J.D. 136 Washington Street
Sessions, T. Scott, (BV) .... '65 '91 C.576 B.S. L.1228 J.D. [[A] McGougan]
Sessoms, William H., Jr., (BV) .... '44 '72 C&L.575 A.B., J.D. [Pope,S.&S.]
Tedder, David S., Law Office, (BV) '54 '86 C.953 B.A. L.1345 J.D.
135 Washington St.
Tedder, Marvin J., (BV) .... '42 '75 C.953 B.A. L.574 J.D. 110 W. Nance St.
Thomas, David L. '47 '72 C.12 B.S. L.192 J.D.
(adm. in AL; not adm. in NC) Exec. V.P., United Carolina Bancshares Corporation
Viets, Don W., (AV) .... '50 '79 C.575 B.A. L.1228 J.D. 107 Jefferson Street
Walton, Benton H., III, (AV) .... '36 '63 C.228 A.B. L.575 J.D. [Williamson&W.]
Williamson, C. Greg, (AV) .... '50 '77 C.309 B.A. L.896 J.D. [Williamson&W.]
Williamson, Carlton F., (BV) .... '54 '80 C.575 B.S. L.896 J.D. [Williamson&W.]
Williamson, Edward L., (AV) .... '23 '53 C.896 B.S. L.228 J.D. [[B] Williamson&W.]
Williamson & Walton, L.L.P., (AV) .... 136 Washington Street
Willis, Michael W., (BV) .... '47 '81 C.576 B.S. L.574 J.D. 200 Jefferson St.

Wood, William E., (AV) ....'48 '73 C.165 A.B. L.902 J.D. 100 Courthouse Sq.
Wright, Terry C., (CV) ....'50 '77 C.575 B.A. L.790 J.D. [T.C.Wright]
Wright, T. Craig, (CV) .... P.O. Box 1129

WHITSETT, 686, *Guilford Co.*

Johnsen, Lawrence P. '51 '78 C.1031 B.A. L.564 J.D.
(adm. in NY; not adm. in NC) P.O. Box 2350‡

WHITTIER, 5,015, *Jackson Co.*

Smith, Hannah E., Law Office of '71 '00 C.232 B.S. L.560 J.D.
(adm. in NM; not adm. in NC) P.O. Box 359

WILKESBORO, * 3,159, *Wilkes Co.*

Adams, Stacy L., (BV) ....'68 '94 C.320 B.A. L.896 J.D. Dist. Atty. Off.
Ashburn, Michael A. .... '41 '69 C&L.575 A.B., J.D. Dist. Atty.
Bennett, Charlotte S. ....'39 '74 C.597 B.A. L.896 J.D. 203 W. Main St.‡
Brewer, Gregory J. ....'58 '86 C.575 B.A. L.896 J.D. [Brewer&B.]
Brewer, Joe O. ....'31 '62 C&L.575 B.S., LL.B. [Brewer&B.]
Brewer & Brewer ....204 E. Main St.
Bricker, Leigh C., (BV) ....'70 '96 C.575 B.A. L.192 J.D. Asst. Dist. Atty.
Brooks, William F., (BV) .... '53 '80 C.404 B.A. L.896 J.D. 107 East Main Street
Burke, William R. .... '64 '97 C.575 B.A. L.1228 J.D. [Ⓐ Willardson,L.&M.]
Byrd, David V. '60 '93 C.34 B.A. L.575 J.D.
(adm. in MO; not adm. in NC) Dist. J.
Crumpton, Robert J., (BV) ....'71 '97 C.577 B.A. L.896 J.D. [Ⓐ W.F.Brooks]
Cunningham, George G., (AV) ....'51 '75 C&L.896 B.A., J.D. [Cunningham&G.]

Cunningham & Gray, P.A., (AV)
105 West Main Street, P.O. Drawer 520, 28697-0520
Telephone: 336-838-7500 Fax: 336-838-7700
George G. Cunningham (Board Certified Specialist in Family Law, North Carolina State Board of Legal Specialization); William C. Gray, Jr.
Trials-Criminal, Traffic Court, DWI Defense, Family Law, Divorce, Personal Injury, Probate and Estate Planning, Corporate.
References: NCNB National Bank of North Carolina; First Citizens Bank and Trust.
See Professional Biographies, WILKESBORO, NORTH CAROLINA

Davis Elder & Disability Law
(See Lewisville)
Duncan, Michael D., (BV) ....'68 '93 C.34 B.S. L.192 J.D. [Ⓐ W.F.Brooks]

Ferree, Max F., (AV) '24 '49 C&L.228 A.B., LL.B.
Court Square, P.O. Drawer 979, 28697
Telephone: 336-667-9500; 667-5557 Fax: 336-667-8050
Email: maxferreelaw@aol.com
General Civil and Criminal Trial Practice. Probate, Real Estate, Personal Injury Law, Products Liability, Construction Law, Insurance Law, Automobile Accidents, Wrongful Death.
References: Bank of America; Wachovia Bank; Integrity Financial; First Citizens Bank & Trust.
See Professional Biographies, WILKESBORO, NORTH CAROLINA

Ferree, Russell F., Attorney at Law, (AV) ...... '50 '75 C&L.896 B.A., J.D. 101 Court Sq.
Freeman, Paul Wesley, Jr., (AV) .... '51 '76 C&L.575 A.B., J.D. 101 Court Sq.
Gray, William C., Jr., (AV) ....'51 '76 C.575 A.B. L.896 J.D. [Cunningham&G.]
Greene, Robert G., Jr., (BV) .... '66 '93 C.575 B.S. L.1345 J.D. 115 E. Main St.
Gregory, Edgar B. .... '46 '70 C.575 B.S. L.896 J.D. Dist. J.
Harding, M. Beirne Minor, (AV) ....'46 '73 C.822 B.A. L.896 J.D. Asst. Dist. Atty.
Helms, Michael E. .... '47 '78 C&L.575 A.B., J.D. Dist. J.
Horner, Thomas E., (BV) ....'63 '89 C.269 B.A. L.1228 J.D. Dist. Atty.
Joyce, Dennis R., (AV) ....'48 '73 C.383 B.B.A. L.575 J.D. 210 E. Main St.
Lipscomb, William F., (AV) ....'54 '80 C&L.896 B.A., J.D. [Willardson,L.&M.]
Luck, Gregory, (CV) .... '53 '82 C&L.896 B.A., J.D. 101 West Street
Miller, D. Sigsbee, (BV) ....'57 '83 C&L.896 B.A., J.D. [Willardson,L.&M.]
Osborne, Samuel L. ....'39 '67 C&L.575 B.A., LL.B. Dist. J.
Rousseau, Julius A., Jr. ....'30 '56 C&L.575 A.B., LL.B. Supr. Ct. J.

Vannoy, Colvard, Triplett & Vannoy, P.L.L.C.
(See North Wilkesboro)
Welborn, Timothy D., (BV) ....'67 '94 C.896 B.A. L.1228 J.D. 200 E. Main St.
Willardson, John S., (AV) ....'46 '72 C&L.575 A.B., J.D. [Willardson,L.&M.]
Willardson, Lipscomb & Miller, LLP, (AV) ....206 East Main Street

WILLIAMSTON, * 5,843, *Martin Co.*

Batchelor, James R., Jr., (BV) ....'55 '80 C.896 B.A. L.575 J.D. 118 E. Main St.
Brandon, Thomas B., III, (CV) ....'49 '79 C.576 B.S.Ch.E. L.896 J.D. Mayor
Griffin, William C., JR. ....'42 '67 C.575 B.S. L.1292 LL.B. Jud. Dist. J.
Hardison, James W. ....'39 '64 C&L.575 A.B., J.D. Chf. Dist. J.
James, Richard S., (BV) .... '52 '77 C&L.575 A.B., J.D. [Peel&J.]
Manning, Daniel A., (BV) ....'39 '65 C&L.575 B.A., LL.B. Town Atty.
Peel, Robert C. ....'63 '93 C.575 B.A. L.813 J.D. P.O. Box 187
Peel and James, (BV) ....Lawyers Bldg.
Skinner, John M., (CV) .... '48 '76 C&L.575 A.B., J.D. P.O. Box 150
Willey, Ralph G., P.A.
(See Rocky Mount)

WILMINGTON, * 75,838, *New Hanover Co.*

Akin, Stephanie Michelle ....'75 '05 C.347 B.A. L.1119 J.D. [Ⓐ J.S.Price]
Allard, James L., Jr., (AV) ....'60 '86 C.953 B.A. L.1228 J.D. [Hewlett,C.&A.]
Allen, Charlton Laramie, (CV) ....'70 '97 C&L.575 B.A., J.D. [Seay&A.]
Allen, L. Gleason, (AV) ....'25 '49 C&L.575 A.B., LL.B. [Allen,M.&D.] ‡

Allen, MacDonald & Davis, PLLC, (AV)
1508 Military Cutoff Road Suite 102, 28403
Telephone: 910-256-6558 Fax: 910-256-6538
Email: allenmac@bellsouth.net URL: http://www.macdonald-law.com
Members of Firm: L. Gleason Allen (Retired); James A. MacDonald; Dean R. Davis.
Real Estate, Residential Real Estate, Real Estate Closings, Commercial Real Estate, Estate Planning, Wills and Trusts, Probate, Collections, Creditors Rights, Commercial Law..
See Professional Biographies, WILMINGTON, NORTH CAROLINA

Alley, Grieg Robertson ....'73 '99 C.575 A.B. L.910 J.D. [Peters,R.&M.]
Anderson, Daniel & Associates
(See Wrightsville Beach)
Armstrong, John S. '41 '73 C.158 B.S. L.420 J.D.
(adm. in LA; not adm. in NC) Civil & Crim. Mag.
Armstrong, Matthew J. '16 '52 C.569 L.262 LL.B.
(adm. in NY; not adm. in NC) 609 Robert E. Lee Dr.‡
Armstrong, Robert L., (BV) '57 '88
C.420 B.A. L.564 J.D. 1904 Eastwood Road, Suite 306
Austin, Jeffery W. .... '65 '04 C.953 B.A. L.1228 J.D. [Austin&C.]

Austin & Cooke, PLLC
5725 Oleander Drive Suite C-3, 28403
Telephone: 910-332-4104 Fax: 910-332-4124 URL: http://www.austinprice.com
Email: info@austincooke.com URL: http://www.austincooke.com

(This Listing Continued)

Austin & Cooke, PLLC (Continued)
Jeffery W. Austin; Jennifer G. Cooke.
Languages: English and Spanish.
Estate Planning, Wills, Trusts and Estates, Real Estates, Residential Real Estate, Business Law, Limited Liability Company Law, Family Law, Divorce, Custody, Adoption, Juvenile, Criminal, Tickets, DWI, Contracts.
See Professional Biographies, WILMINGTON, NORTH CAROLINA

Averitt, Anna Johnson, (CV) .... '72 '00 C.806 B.A. L.1228 J.D. [Ⓐ Johnson,L.&B.]
Averitt, F. Murphy, III ....'72 '99 C.575 B.A. L.1228 J.D. [Marshall,W.&G.]
Bailey, Stephen '75 '03 C.34 B.S. L.469 J.D.
[Ⓐ Firm of Hutchens,S.&B.] (⊙Fayetteville)
Bain, Roy C., (BV) ....'44 '73 C&L.575 B.S., J.D. 2909 Market St.
Baker, H. Mitchell, III, (AV) ....'51 '76 C&L.896 B.S., J.D. [Baker&S.] ⊙
Baker, Jeffrey M., (CV) ....'79 '00 C.651 B.S. L.1017 J.D. [J.M.Baker]
Baker, Jeffrey R., (CV) ....'56 '82 C.575 B.A. L.896 J.D. [J.Baker]
Baker, Jeffrey, Law Offices of, (CV) ....105 S. Front St.
Baker, J.M., Attorney at Law, (CV) .... 720 North Third Street, Suite 202
Baker & Slaughter, P.A., (AV) ....705 Princess Street (⊙Elizabethtown)
Baldwin, Charles S., IV, (CV) ....'68 '93 C.575 B.A. L.30 J.D. [Rountree,L.&B.]
Ball, Stephen M., (CV) ....'63 '93 C.577 B.S. L.896 J.D. P.O. Box 1887
Ballantine, Lisa Marie, (CV) ......'66 '92 C.473 B.A. L.200 J.D. 6008 Forest Creek Circle
Barefoot, David C., (AV) ..... '36 '65 C&L.896 B.S., LL.B. 107 N. Second Street, Suite C
Barefoot, Napoleon B. ....'30 '58 C&L.896 B.S., LL.B. Sr. Res. Supr. Ct. J.
Barnhill, Maurice V., Jr., (AV) ....'13 '36 C&L.575 A.B., LL.B. 519 Market St.‡
Batchelor, W. T., II ....'62 '86 C.953 B.A. L.575 J.D. 107 Castle St.
Baucom, Tyler Paige .... '74 '00 C&L.575 B.S.N., J.D. [Ⓐ Patterson,D.C.B.&A.]
Baynard, Stephen C., (CV) .... '68 '93 C.575 B.A. L.1345 J.D. [Ennis,N.&B.]
Beaudoin, Adam M. .... '— '01 C.1369 B.A. L.692 J.D. [Ward&S.] (⊙New Bern)
Behm, Christopher K., (BV) .... '73 '98 C.296 A.B. L.896 J.D. [Ⓐ Block,C.&K.]
Bennington, Erik T. '78 '03
C.1228 B.B.A. L.896 J.D. [Ⓐ Firm of Hutchens,S.&B.] (⊙Fayetteville)
Bennington, Margaret S. ....'77 '02 C.575 B.A. L.896 J.D. [Cranfill,S.&H.]
Bentley, Gregory S. '49 '78
C.860 B.S. L.178 J.D. Exec. V.P. & Gen. Coun., aaiPharma, Inc.
Birrell, George A. '21 '48 C&L.976 B.A., LL.B.
(adm. in NY; not adm. in NC) 217 Beach Rd., N.
Blackmore, Rebecca W. ....'53 '83 C.953 B.A. L.575 J.D. Dist. J.
Blackwell, Jeffrey H., (BV) ....'— '86 C&L.575 B.S., J.D. [Hedrick E.G.&K.]
Blair, Terrie Haydu .... '76 '01 C&L.575 114 S. Front St.
Blanchard, Norwood P., III ....'68 '99 C.232 B.S.B.A. L.228 J.D. [Cranfill,S.&H.]
Block, Franklin L. ....'36 '76 C.152 B.S. L.896 J.D. [Block,C.&K.] ‡

Block, Crouch & Keeter, L.L.P., (AV)
310 North Front Street, P.O. Box 4, 28402
Telephone: 910-763-2727 Fax: 910-762-6429
URL: http://www.bcklawfirm.com
Franklin L. Block (Retired); Auley M. Crouch, III; Jeffrey P. Keeter;—Christopher K. Behm; Linda B. Sayed.
General Practice.
See Professional Biographies, WILMINGTON, NORTH CAROLINA

Blossom, William C., (AV) ....'31 '59 C&L.896 B.S., J.D. [Wells&B.]
Blythe, Jesse J. ....'— '05 C.769 B.A. L.1049 J.D. [Cranfill,S.&H.]
Bokar, Gregory M. ....'62 '95 C.161 B.S. L.1187 J.D. 2320 Scientific Park Dr.

Boney, William J., Jr., (AV) '50 '76 C.576 B.A. L.896 J.D.
406 Market Street, P.O. Box 1301, 28402
Telephone: 910-762-4403 Fax: 910-762-0499
Email: bboney@bizec.rr.com
Civil and Criminal Trials, Criminal Law, DWI, Traffic Offenses, Personal Injury, Automobile Accidents, Wrongful Death, Domestic Law, Family Law, Divorce, Separation Agreements, Child Custody, Child Support, Alimony, Equitable Distribution.
See Professional Biographies, WILMINGTON, NORTH CAROLINA

Bonner, James P., (CV) ....'60 '88 C.575 B.A. L.1228 J.D. P.O. Box 7517
Boseman, Julia ....'66 '93 C.953 B.S. L.574 J.D. [Boseman&Assoc.]

Boseman & Associates, LLP
115 North 6th Street, 28401
Telephone: 910-251-6975 Fax: 910-251-6976
URL: http://www.bosemanandassociateslaw.com
Member of Firm: Julia Boseman. Associate: Breanna W. Rutledge.
Criminal Law, Misdemeanors, Traffic Violations, Driving While Intoxicated, Felonies, Family Law, Real Estate, Buying and Selling a Home.
See Professional Biographies, WILMINGTON, NORTH CAROLINA

Boyette, Geannine M. ....'68 '98 C.953 B.A. L.574 J.D. [Boyette]

Boyette Law Firm, The
401 Chestnut Street, Suite H, 28401
Telephone: 910-251-9213 Fax: 910-251-8880
URL: http://www.boyettelawfirm.com
Geannine M. Boyette. Associate: Tracy W. Wilkinson.
Family Law, Divorce, Custody, Visitation, Child Support, Adoption, Criminal Law, Traffic, DUI, White Collar Crimes.
See Professional Biographies, WILMINGTON, NORTH CAROLINA

Boyles, M. Scott, (CV) .... '65 '91 C.575 B.A. L.574 J.D. 319-A N. 4th St.
Braun, Eric Andrew ....'77 '01 C&L.896 B.A., J.D. [E.A.Braun]
Braun, Eric Andrew, PLLC, Law Office of .... 5710 Oleander Dr., Ste. 208
Brawley, Daniel Lee, (AV) ....'42 '67 C&L.575 A.B., J.D. [Ⓒ Maupin T.] (⊙Raleigh)
Brisson, Tracie H. .... '— '98 C.575 B.A. L.1228 J.D. [Ⓐ Hedrick E.G.&K.]
Britt, Donald E., Jr., (AV) ....'46 '71 C&L.896 B.A., J.D. [Britt]

Britt Law Firm, (AV)
The Promenade, 720 North Third Street Suite 401, 28401
Telephone: 910-762-2697 Facsimile: 910-762-0231
Email: donbritt@brittlawfirm.com
Donald E. Britt, Jr.
General Civil, Asbestos Product Liability, Corporate, Real Estate, Estate Administration, Personal Injury, Wills & Trusts. North Carolina Certified Mediator.
Representative Client: Owens-Corning Fiberglas Corp.
Approved Attorneys for: Commonwealth Title Insurance Co.; The Title Company of North Carolina; Investors Title Insurance Co.
Reference: Branch Banking & Trust Co.
See Professional Biographies, WILMINGTON, NORTH CAROLINA

Brown, Maynard M., (BV) .... '57 '87 C.575 B.A. L.896 J.D. [Johnson,L.&B.]

Brumbaugh, Mu & King, P.A., (BV)
2018 South 16th Street, 28401 ⊙
Telephone: 910-763-2111
URL: http://www.bmklaw.net
Kenneth W. King, Jr.
Practice Limited to Injury Cases. Automobile, Wrongful Death, Medical Malpractice, Workers' Compensation, Products Liability and Social Security Claims.
See Professional Biographies, WILMINGTON, NORTH CAROLINA

Bryan, Russ C., (CV) ....'72 '97 C.953 B.A. L.1345 J.D. [Clark,N.E.&B.]
Bullard, Norman D., (BV) ....'63 '89 C&L.575 B.S., J.D. P.O. Box 10243
Bullard, Wayne A., (BV) ....'61 '87 C&L.575 B.S., J.D. [Hogue,H.J.N.&L.]
Burnett, Gilbert H. ....'25 '56 C.575 L.896 Chief Dist. Ct. J.‡
Burney, John J., Jr., (AV) ....'24 '51 C&L.896 B.S., LL.B. [Burney,B.&J.]
Burney, Louis A., (AV) ....'32 '59 C&L.896 B.S., LL.B. [Burney,B.&J.] ‡
Burney, Burney & Jones, (AV) .... 110 N. 5th Ave.

Burns, John K., (CV) '46 '84 C.575 A.B. L.896 J.D.
208 Princess Street, 28401
Telephone: 910-343-8776 Fax: 910-343-8832
Email: johnkburnsatty@bellsouth.net URL: http://www.johnkburns.com
Domestic Relations Law, Family Law, Divorce, Adoptions, Child Custody Agreements, Child Support, Personal Injury Law, Automobile Accidents, Truck Accidents, Wrongful Death, Slip and Fall, Workers Compensation Law, Employment Law, Wrongful Termination, Sexual Harassment, Criminal Law, DWI, Traffic Violations, Drug Crimes, Parole and Probation.
See Professional Biographies, WILMINGTON, NORTH CAROLINA

Burpeau, Kemp P., (BV) ....'58 '81 C&L.575 B.A., J.D. Dep. Co. Atty.
Butler, Algernon L., Jr., (BV) ....'40 '68 C&L.575 A.B., J.D. 111 N. 5th Ave.
Butler, Algernon Lee, III ....'68 '94 C&L.575 B.A., J.D. 111 N. Fifth Ave.
Butler, Jenna Fruechtenicht, (BV) '— '96 C&L.896 B.A., J.D.
[Ward&S.] (⊙New Bern)
Bynum, Peter A., (CV) ....'68 '96 C.198 B.A. L.893 J.D. [Murchison,T.&G.]
Calder, J. Keith, (BV) ....'54 '88 C.953 B.A. L.574 J.D. [Calder&C.]
Calder, Robert, (AV) ....'22 '49 C.797 B.A. L.575 LL.B. [Calder&C.] ‡
Calder, Robert, Jr., (BV) ....'50 '84 C.953 B.A. L.575 J.D. [Calder&C.] ⊙

Calder & Calder, (BV)
611 Princess Street, 28401-4153 ⊙
Telephone: 910-763-1683 Fax: 910-343-9444 URL: http://www.calderlawfirm.com
URL: http://www.calderlaw.com
Members of Firm: Robert Calder (Retired); Robert Calder, Jr.; J. Keith Calder. Associate: Matthew Peter Doyle.
General Civil Practice. Real Estate Law, Commercial Real Estate, Buying and Selling a Home, Title Examinations, Closings, Foreclosures, Zoning and Land Use, Estate Planning and Wills.
See Professional Biographies, WILMINGTON, NORTH CAROLINA

Campbell, Lisa S. ....'64 '01 C.232 B.A. L.1228 J.D. 313 Walnut Street
Carriker, John E., (AV) ....'45 '70 C&L.896 B.A., J.D. Asst. Dist. Atty.
Carter, James Oliver, (AV) ....'49 '74 C&L.896 A.B., J.D. [Carter&H.]
Carter, John F., III, (BV) ....'52 '77 C&L.575 A.B., J.D. [Jackson,M.&C.]
Carter, Mark F., (BV) ....'67 '92 C.575 B.S. L.1228 J.D. [Stevens,M.M.L.&T.]

Carter & Huffine, P.A., (AV) [BB]
408 Market Street, P.O. Box 2154, 28402-2154
Telephone: 910-763-3626; 910-251-1954 Fax: 910-343-8966 Fax: 910-251-8590 Email: jocc1@bellsouth.net
Email: dhuffine@bizec.rr.com
James Oliver Carter; David E. Huffine.
Commercial and Residential Real Estate, Corporate, Business Law, Medical Business Practice, Business and Real Estate Litigation, Mediation, Bankruptcy and Creditors Rights.
See Professional Biographies, WILMINGTON, NORTH CAROLINA

Cartwright, Charles B. '26 '50 C.228 L.472 LL.B.
(adm. in FL; not adm. in NC) P.O. Box 6086 Hanover Center‡
Casteen, J. Wesley .... '68 '94 C.896 B.S. L.1345 J.D. Carolina Legal Counsel
Cavagnaro, Albert N., (BV) '57 '89
C.228 A.B. L.575 J.D. Associate General Counsel, AAI Pharma Inc.
Chadwick, Gary W. .....'47 '75 C.953 B.A. L.575 J.D. Sr. V.P., The Title Co. of N.C., Inc.
Cherry, William Robert, Jr., (AV) ....'51 '77 C&L.575 B.A., J.D. [Marshall,W.&G.]
Chestnut, Austin M. ....'76 '02 C.576 B.S. L.1228 J.D. [A Webb&G.]
Chleborowicz, Christopher A. ....'71 '98 C&L.896 B.S./B.A., J.D. [Lea,R.R.&C.]
Clark, George T., Jr., (AV) ....'28 '52 C&L.575 A.B., LL.B. [Clark,N.E.&B.] ‡
Clark, Linda A. ....'48 '97 C.953 B.A. L.574 J.D. [Clark,C.&Assoc.]

Clark, Clarke and Associates, L.L.P., (BV⊤)
265 Racine Drive, Suite 101, 28403
Telephone: 910-452-3333 Fax: 910-452-4890
URL: http://www.wilmingtonnclawyers.com
Linda A. Clark; Susan E. Clarke.
Real Estate, Buying or Selling a Home, Construction, Business Law, LLC Formation, Trusts and Estates, Wills and Probate, Family Law, Divorce, Child Custody and Support, Equitable Distribution, Criminal Law, Traffic, DWI, DUI, Drug Crimes, Domestic Violence, Personal Injury, Automobile Accidents, Wrongful Death.
See Professional Biographies, WILMINGTON, NORTH CAROLINA

Clark, Newton, Evans & Bryan, L.L.P., (AV) [BB]
509 Princess Street, 28401
Telephone: 910-762-8743 Facsimile: 910-762-6206
Email: cneclaw@netscape.net URL: http://www.lawyers.com/lawyerscomcneclaw
George T. Clark, Jr. (Retired); John Richard Newton; Don T. Evans, Jr.; Russ C. Bryan.
General Trial and Appellate Practice in all State and Federal Courts, Admiralty, Business Transactions, Real Estate and Corporate Law, Estate Planning and Estate Administration.
Representative Clients: North Carolina Natural Gas; North Carolina Shipping Assn. P&I CLUBS: The Britannia Club; Liverpool & London P&I Club; London Steamship Mutual P&I; Standard Steamship P&I; The Swedish Club; The Gard; United Kingdom Club.
See Professional Biographies, WILMINGTON, NORTH CAROLINA

Clarke, Susan E., (BV⊤) ....'53 '80 C.1111 B.A. L.990 J.D. [Clark,C.&Assoc.]
Clyburn, James Albert, (BV) ....'63 '90 C.576 B.A. L.575 J.D. [J.A.Clyburn]

Clyburn, J. Albert, P.L.L.C., (BV)
502 Market Street, 28401
Telephone: 910-202-1077 Fax: 910-202-1075
Email: clyburn@clyburnlaw.com
James Albert Clyburn.
Family Law, Child Custody, Child Support, Divorce, Visitation Rights, Equitable Distribution.
See Professional Biographies, WILMINGTON, NORTH CAROLINA

Cobb, W. Allen, Jr. ....'52 '78 C.575 A.B. L.574 J.D. Supr. Ct. J.
Coble, John L., (BV) ....'57 '85 C.576 B.A. L.1228 J.D. [Marshall,W.&G.]
Coble, Stephen E. ....'72 '04 C.240 B.A. L.201 J.D. [A Hedrick&M.]
Coe, Larry M., (BV) ....'43 '69 C.347 B.M.E. L.851 J.D. P.O. Box 870
Coggins, Stephen D., (AV) ....'52 '78 C.575 A.B. L.896 J.D. [Rountree,L.&B.]
Coleman, G. Edward, III, (BV⊤) ....'69 '94 C&L.836 B.A., J.D. [Hogue,H.J.N.&L.]
Collier, Clay Allen, (BV) ....'59 '86 C.575 A.B. L.1228 J.D. [Crossley M.P.&C.]
Collins, Andy '59 '90 C.37 B.S. L.990 J.D.
(adm. in CA; not adm. in NC) 219 Racine Drive
Collins, David B., Jr. ....'63 '93 C.1128 B.S. L.790 J.D. [Collins]
Collins, John C., (AV) ....'50 '76 C.228 B.A. L.896 J.D. [Hewlett,C.&A.]
Collins, Robert Green, Jr. ....'74 '00 C.576 B.S. L.896 J.D. 219 Racine Drive
Collins Law Firm ....5725-F2 Oleander Drive
Collis, Colleen Shea, (CV) ....'71 '97 C.1128 B.A. L.1228 J.D. [Cranfill,S.&H.]
Cook, Alexander B. ....'38 '64 C.608 B.S. L.276 J.D. 313 Walnut St.
Cooke, Jennifer G. ....'75 '03 C.575 B.A. L.1228 J.D. [Austin&C.]

Copley, Wanda Milligan, (BV) ....'55 '82 C.790 B.A. L.836 J.D. Co. Atty.
Corpening, J. H., II ....'54 '79 C&L.896 B.A., J.D. Dist. J.
Council, Ashley C. ....'73 '01 C.575 B.A. L.1228 J.D. [Culbreth]
Cox, J. Thomas, Jr., (BV) ....'56 '81 C.575 B.S. L.1228 J.D. [Cox&T.]
Cox & Tillery, P.A., (BV) .... 4020 Oleander Drive, Suite 4
Coxe, Bradley A., (BV) ....'68 '95 C&L.575 B.S., J.D. [Hodges&C.]
Craige, Lawrence S., & Associates, P.A. '66 '98
C.945 B.A. L.575 J.D. [L.S.Craige&Assoc.]

Craige, Lawrence S., & Associates, P.A.
701 Market Street, 28401
Telephone: 910-815-0085 Fax: 910-815-1095
Email: mail@lsclawfirm.com URL: http://www.lawrencecraige.com
Lawrence S. Craige & Associates, P.A. Associate: Charlotte Noel Fox.
Estate Planning, Wills and Probate, Trusts, Estate Administration, Construction Law, Civil Litigation, Juvenile Law, Real Estate, Buying and Selling a Home, Zoning and Land Use, Commercial Real Estate, Eminent Domain, Corporate Law, Business Law.
See Professional Biographies, WILMINGTON, NORTH CAROLINA

Cranfill, Sumner & Hartzog, L.L.P., (AV)
1209 Culbreth Drive, Suite 200, 28405 ⊙
Telephone: 910-509-9778 Fax: 910-509-9676
URL: http://www.cshlaw.com
Members of the Firm: John Dearman Martin; Colleen Shea Collis; Norwood P. Blanchard, III; Regan S. Toups; Cameron D. Simmons; Robert B. Jones, Jr.; Nicole B. Slaughter; Jennifer D. Ray; Margaret S. Bennington; Jesse J. Blythe.
General Trial and Appellate Practice before all State and Federal Courts. Litigation of Insurance Law, Personal Injury, Medical Malpractice, Nursing Home Negligence, Professional Malpractice, Products Liability, Premises Liability, Municipal and Police Liability, Intentional Torts, Commercial Litigation, Workers' Compensation, Employment, Education, Construction and Land Condemnation Law.
Raleigh, North Carolina Office: Hillsborough Place, 225 Hillsborough Street, Suite 300, P.O. Box 27808. Telephone: 919-828-5100. Fax: 919-828-2277.
Charlotte, North Carolina Office: 227 West Trade Street, Suite 600. Telephone: 704-332-8300. Fax: 704-332-9994.
See Professional Biographies, WILMINGTON, NORTH CAROLINA

Criner, Sandra Ray ....'64 '91 C.1203 B.A. L.1228 J.D. 615 Princess St.
Criner, Sherman Lee, (BV) '66 '94 C.576 B.A. L.1228 J.D.
[WorkersCompensation] & [Hedrick,B.&C.] ⊙
Crossley, John F., (AV) ....'21 '49 C.575 L.896 J.D. 616 Market St.‡

Crossley McIntosh Prior & Collier, (AV) [BB]
2451 South College Road, 28412
Telephone: 910-762-9711 Fax: 910-251-0446/ 1-800-499-9711
URL: http://www.cmpc-law.com
Members of Firm: Douglas F. McIntosh; Francis B. Prior; Clay Allen Collier; H. Mark Hamlet; Samuel H. MacRae; Andrew Hanley; Ashley M. Edwards; Brian E. Edes. Associate: Christopher J. Skinner.
General Civil Trial Practice, Insurance Defense, Personal Injury, Workers Compensation, Admiralty, Longshore and Maritime Law, Professional Liability, Premises Liability, Products Liability, Municipal Litigation, Commercial/Business Transactions and Litigation, Criminal Defense, Construction Litigation, Labor and Employment Law, Sexual Harassment, Title VII Discrimination, Family and Medical Leave Act, Americans with Disabilities Act.
Representative Clients: Allstate Insurance Co.; American International Adjustment Co.; Atlantic Casualty Insurance Co.; CNA; Maryland Casualty; Siebels Bruce Inc.; State Auto Insurance Co.; USAA.
See Professional Biographies, WILMINGTON, NORTH CAROLINA

Crouch, Auley M., III, (AV) ....'44 '76 C.152 B.S. L.365 J.D. [Block,C.&K.]
Crouch, Melinda Haynie, (BV) '58 '84 C.575 B.A. L.1228 J.D.
311 North Second Street
Culbreth, Stephen E., (AV) ....'43 '68 C.953 B.A. L.575 J.D. [Culbreth]

Culbreth Law Firm, L.L.P., (AV) [BB]
514 Chestnut Street, P.O. Box 446, 28402
Telephone: 910-763-3416 Facsimile: 910-763-9975
Email: culbrethlaw@juno.com URL: http://www.culbrethlawfirm.com
Members of Firm: Stephen E. Culbreth; Ashley C. Council.
General Civil and Criminal Trial Practice in all State and Federal Courts, Personal Injury, Automobile Accidents, Trucking Accidents, Construction Accidents, Probate, Wrongful Death, Workers Compensation, Appellate Work and Insurance Litigation, Collections, Mediation.
See Professional Biographies, WILMINGTON, NORTH CAROLINA

Currin, Samuel T., (AV) ....'48 '74 C.896 B.A. L.575 J.D. [Currin] ⊙

Currin Law Firm, PLLC, (AV)
Goolsby Law Building, 620 Market Street, 28401 ⊙
Telephone: 910-763-3339 Fax: 910-763-1720 URL: http://www.currinlaw.com
URL: http://www.lawyers.com/currinlaw
Samuel T. Currin; Thomas C. Goolsby.
Federal and State Criminal Defense, Civil and Criminal Forfeitures, Serious Personal Injury/Wrongful Death, Medical Malpractice, Government Relations.
Raleigh, North Carolina Office: Currin Law Building, 20 Market Plaza, P.O. Box 269, 27602-0269. Telephone: 919-833-0888. Facsimile: 919-833-8171.
See Professional Biographies, WILMINGTON, NORTH CAROLINA

Dale, Alexander C. .... '— '01 C.577 B.A. L.228 J.D. [Ward&S.] (⊙New Bern)
Da Silva, Eugene H. '37 '87 C.563 B.M.E. L.564 J.D.
(adm. in NJ; not adm. in NC) 3610 Bohicket Way
Davenport, Fred B., Jr., (AV) '51 '77 C&L.575 A.B., J.D.
General Counsel, Pharmaceutical Product Development, Inc.
Davenport, Michael Stuart ....'65 '91 C.966 B.S. L.809 J.D. [M.S.Davenport]
Davenport, Michael Stuart, P.C., Law Office of, The .... 21 North Front Street
David, Ann M. ....'62 '93 C.471 B.A. L.574 J.D. [A David&Assoc.]
David, G. Phillip ....'59 '88 C.232 B.S.B.A. L.574 J.D. [David&Assoc.] ⊙

David and Associates, pllc
1516 Dawson Street, 28401 ⊙
Telephone: 910-251-8088 Toll Free: 1-800-856-9927 Fax: 910-251-8430
Email: aeverhart@davidandassociates.com URL: http://www.wilmingtonpiattorneys.com
G. Phillip David. Associates: Michael J. Rizzi; David F. Turlington; G. Andrew Everhart; Ann M. David.
Personal Injury, Medical Malpractice, Wrongful Death, Products Liability, Workers Compensation, Aviation, Airplane Crashes, Negligence, Class Actions, Maritime Accidents, Boating Accidents, Bicycle Accidents, Motorcycle Accidents, Truck Accidents, School Bus Accidents, Railroad Accidents, Dog Bites, Slip and Fall, Birth Trauma, Brain Injury, Spinal Injury, Head Injury, Catastrophic Injury, Vehicular Homicide, Personal Injury Mediation, Products Liability, Drug and Medical Device Litigation, Product Defects, Automobile Liability, Motorcycle Products Liability, Amusement Park Liability, Hotel Liability, Marina Liability, Sports Injury.
Jacksonville, North Carolina Office: 405-B Western Boulevard. 28546. Telephone: 910-219-4878.
Supply, North Carolina Office: Highway 17. 28462. Telephone: 910-754-8465.
Wallace, North Carolina Office: 107 North Norwood Street. 28466. Telephone: 910-285-8777.
Clinton, North Carolina Office: 610 Beaman Street. 28328. Telephone: 910-592-8400.
Winston-Salem, North Carolina Office: 1100-A South Stratford Road. 27103. Telephone: 336-354-1040.
Greensboro, North Carolina Office: 529 College Road. Suite G. 27410. Telephone: 336-354-1040.
See Professional Biographies, WILMINGTON, NORTH CAROLINA

Davis, Dean R., (BV) ....'44 '75 C.894 A.B. L.245 J.D. [Allen,M.&D.]
Davis, Eugene B., Jr. ....'65 '89 C.198 B.A. L.575 J.D. JAGC Atty., U.S. Navy★

Davis, R. Theodore, Jr., (BV) '50 '77 C.575 B.A. L.896 J.D.
8 South Sixth Street, P.O. Box 2535, 28402
Telephone: 910-763-6249 Fax: 910-762-5175
Email: tdavjr@bellsouth.net URL: http://www.tdavisjrlaw.com
Family Law including Adoptions, Domestic Violence, Separation Agreements, Divorce, Child Custody, Child Support, Spousal Support and Property Division. General Civil and Criminal Practice including Civil Litigation, Misdemeanor and Felony Criminal Violations, DWI and Traffic Offenses.
See Professional Biographies, WILMINGTON, NORTH CAROLINA

Day Lewis, LLC .... 5006 Carleton Dr., Unit 116
Day-Lewis, Kimberly '58 '83 C.103 A.B. L.659 J.D. (adm. in PA; not adm. in NC) [Day L.]
Deaver, Benjamin W., (CV) .... '67 '00 C.472 B.B.A. L.1187 J.D. P.O. Box 2233
Demcio, Paul '29 '59 C.724 B.A. L.1009 LL.B. (adm. in NY; not adm. in NC) 2096 Albert Circle‡
DeSilva, Michael G. .... '39 '71 C.705 B.A. L.776 J.D. Asst. Dist. Atty.
Diab, G. Stephen, (BV) ....'64 '90 C&L.575 B.S., J.D. [Murchison,T.&G.]
Dill, Matthew T., (AV) ....'61 '86 C.301 B.A. L.1228 J.D. [M.T.Dill]

Dill, Matthew T., P.L.L.C., (AV) BB
Attorney and Counsellor at Law
1430 Commonwealth Drive, Suite 206, 28403
Mailing Address: P.O. Box 1226, Wrightsville Beach, NC 28480
Telephone: 910-256-9700 Telecopier: 910-256-2529
Email: mtd@matthewtdill.com
Matthew T. Dill (Board Certified Specialist in Estate Planning and Probate Law, North Carolina State Board of Legal Specialization).
Wills, Estates and Estate Planning, Federal Income, Estate and Gift Taxation Law, Probate Law and Trust Administration.
References: Centura Bank; First Citizens Bank; First Union National Bank of North Carolina; Bank of America; N.A.; Wachovia Bank of North Carolina, N.A.
See Professional Biographies, WILMINGTON, NORTH CAROLINA

Dillow, Robert E., Jr., (BV) ....'51 '81 C.1128 B.A. L.1228 J.D. 709 Princess Street
Doyle, Matthew Peter .... '69 '01 C.880 B.A. L.896 J.D. [A Calder&C.]
Dulaney, William B. .... '— '04 C.821 B.A. L.831 J.D. [A Hedrick E.G.&K.]
Durkin, Catherine M. '15 '49 C.470 A.B. L.930 J.D. (adm. in OH; not adm. in NC) 1212 Smith Bay Circle W.‡
Edes, Brian E. .... '71 '98 C.953 B.A. L.1228 J.D. [Crossley M.P.&C.]
Edwards, Ashley M., (BV) ....'72 '98 C.953 B.S. L.1205 J.D. [Crossley M.P.&C.]
Edwards, Samantha G. ....'65 '91 C.575 B.A. L.1345 J.D. Asst. Dist. Atty.
Elkins, Lloyd S., Jr., (AV) .... '27 '51 C.228 L.575 LL.B. 244 Princess St., Suite 10
Embrey, Elizabeth Wright ....'78 '04 C&L.575 B.A., J.D. [A Fletcher R.&S.]
Ennis, Donald W., (BV) ....'60 '86 C.576 B.S. L.1228 J.D. [Ennis,N.&B.]

Ennis, Newton & Baynard, P.A., (BV)
105 Burke Avenue, Suite E, 28403
Mailing Address: P.O. Box 1327, Wrightsville Beach, NC 28480
Telephone: 910-256-3992 Fax: 910-256-3578
Email: enb@enblaw.net
Donald W. Ennis; Jacqueline A. Newton; Stephen C. Baynard.
General Insurance and Self Insured Defense Litigation, including Property, Casualty, Automobile, Personal Injury, Premises Liability, Coverage Opinions, Subrogation, Products Liability, Workers Compensation. Trials in all State and Federal Courts.
See Professional Biographies, WILMINGTON, NORTH CAROLINA

Epple, Kenneth Hall ....'57 '89 C.575 B.A. L.1228 J.D. P.O. Box 12007
Evans, Don T., Jr., (BV) ....'65 '92 C.575 B.A. L.1345 J.D. [Clark,N.E.&B.]
Everhart, G. Andrew ....'77 '04 C.896 L.208 J.D. [A David&Assoc.]
Everhart, Meredith T. .... '— '99 C.576 B.A. L.575 J.D. [A Hedrick E.G.&K.]
Evers, Pamela S. '56 '91 C.375 B.S. L.802 J.D. (adm. in TX; not adm. in NC) P.O. Box 12627
Fletcher, George L., (AV) ....'47 '78 C&L.260 B.A., J.D. [Fletcher R.&S.]

Fletcher Ray & Satterfield, L.L.P., (AV)
131 Racine Drive, Suite 201, 28403
Telephone: 910-251-9900 Fax: 910-251-9667
URL: http://www.fletcherlaw.com
Members of Firm: George L. Fletcher; David L. Ray; T. Michael Satterfield; R. Jay Short, Jr.;—Kiersten M. Gordon; Elizabeth Wright Embrey. Of Counsel: Kimberly L. Moore.
General Practice in all State and Federal Courts, Trials, Banking, Insurance, Negligence, Health Law, Medical Malpractice, Bankruptcy, Construction, Creditors Rights, Lender Liability, Collections, Municipal and Land Use Law, Employment Law and Administrative Law.
See Professional Biographies, WILMINGTON, NORTH CAROLINA

Foote, Valerie P., (BVⓉ) ....'— '87 C.1175 B.A. L.260 J.D. 404 S. 5th St.
Fox, Charlotte Noel .... '75 '04 C.896 B.A. L.1228 J.D. [A L.S.Craige&Assoc.]
Fox, Douglas A., (BV) .... '48 '74 C.296 B.A. L.192 J.D. [Yow,F.&M.]
Fox, James C. .... '28 '57 C&L.575 B.S., LL.B. Sr. U.S. Dist. J.
Freeman, George K., Jr., (AV) '— '55 C.575 B.S.B.A. L.309 LL.B. [Ward&S.] (⊙New Bern)
Friede, Sarah M. ......'69 '96 C.201 B.A. L.884 J.D. The Title Company of North Carolina
Fryar, Kurt B. .... '75 '02 C.953 B.S. L.575 J.D. [A Stevens,M.M.L.&T.]
Fullwood, Ernest B. .... '44 '72 C.953 B.A. L.574 J.D. Supr. Ct. J.
Fuss, William H., Law Office of, (BVⓉ) '53 '79 C.264 B.A. L.472 J.D. (adm. in PA; not adm. in NC) 1904 Eastwood Rd., Ste. 214
Gaines, Lori A., (BV) ....'63 '91 C.953 B.A. L.1345 J.D. P.O. Box 2532
Geiszler-Ludlum, Joan C. ....'53 '86 C.205 B.A.A.S. L.575 J.D. 2720 Columbia Avenue
Geschickter, Brian Andrew, (BVⓉ) '66 '92 C.893 B.A. L.1209 J.D. [A Shipman,M.&W.]
Gibson, Frank B., Jr., (BV) .... '45 '75 C.197 B.A. L.880 J.D. [Murchison,T.&G.]
Gillespie, James B., Jr. ....'49 '74 C.198 A.B. L.188 J.D. 415 Chestnut St.
Girdwood, Richard Scott ....'78 '04 C.576 B.A. L.1228 J.D. [Mako&Assoc.]
Glancy, Kathleen S., Law Office, (BV) '55 '80 C.112 B.A. L.770 J.D. 114 S. Front Street
Godwin, David M. ....'56 '88 C&L.1228 B.B.A., J.D. [Godwin]

Godwin Law Firm
130 N. Front Street, Suite 201, 28401
Telephone: 910-762-0410 Fax: 910-762-2591
Email: davidg@davidmgodwinlaw.com URL: http://www.davidgodwinlaw.com
Member: David M. Godwin.
Family Law, Divorce, Property Settlements, Child Custody, Child Support, Adoptions, Alimony, Spousal Support, Personal Injury, Workers Compensation, Social Security Disability, Civil Litigation.
See Professional Biographies, WILMINGTON, NORTH CAROLINA

Goolsby, Thomas C. ....'61 '92 C.152 B.S. L.575 J.D. [Currin] ⊙
Gordon, Kiersten M. .... '— '95 C.606 B.A. L.884 J.D. [A Fletcher R.&S.]
Gorham, A. Dumay, Jr., (AV) .... '37 '65 C&L.575 A.B., LL.B. [Marshall,W.&G.]
Gott, Melissa ....'77 '03 C.575 B.A. L.1228 J.D. [M.Gott&Assoc.]
Gott, Melissa, PLLC, & Associates ....2451 South College Road
Graves, Rick E., (BV) ....'69 '97 C.999 B.A. L.8 J.D. [Webb&G.]
Green, John Felix, II ....'65 '98 C.576 B.A. L.692 J.D. [Hall&H.]
Green, Michael A., (BV) ....'46 '91 C.1038 B.A. L.1345 J.D. [M.A.Green]

Green, Michael A., P.C., (BV)
1908 Eastwood Road, Suite 217, 28403
Telephone: 910-509-9966 Fax: 910-509-0707
Email: mgreen@mgreenlaw.com URL: http://www.mgreenlaw.com
Michael A. Green.
Business Law, Health Care, Commercial Law, Banking Law, Construction Law, Corporate Law, Local Government Law, Entertainment Law; Contracts; Zoning and Land Use, Admiralty and Maritime Law.
See Professional Biographies, WILMINGTON, NORTH CAROLINA

Guyton, Nancy M., (BV) '59 '85 C.788 A.B. L.575 J.D.
321 North Front Street, 28401
Telephone: 910-251-2190 Fax: 910-251-2191
Email: nancyguyton@guyton-law.com URL: http://www.lawyers.com/nancyguyton
Commercial Real Estate, Corporate, Small Business, Community Associations, Real Estate, Limited Liability Companies, Partnerships, Corporations, Buying and Selling of Businesses, Commercial Law, Joint Ventures, Real Estate Development.
See Professional Biographies, WILMINGTON, NORTH CAROLINA

Haas, Michael A. '45 '76 C.367 B.A. L.229 J.D. (adm. in PA; not adm. in NC) 4206 Stratton Village

Hager, Virginia R., (CV) '55 '84 C.25 B.A. L.945 J.D.
3808-B Park Avenue, P.O. Box 2184, 28402-2184
Telephone: 910-796-2044 Fax: 910-796-2041 URL: http://hager.lawoffice.com
Email: VRHager@aol.com URL: http://www.lawyers.com/hagerlaw
—Karen L. Simmons (Not admitted in NC).
Practice limited to Domestic Relations Litigation (Divorce, Child Custody, Child and Spousal Support and Domestic Violence) and Negotiation (Separation Agreements, Relationship Contracts), Family Mediation, Wills, Simple Estate Planning.
See Professional Biographies, WILMINGTON, NORTH CAROLINA

Hall, Alexander M., (AV) .... '48 '78 C.575 B.A. L.796 J.D. [Hall&H.]

Hall & Horne, L.L.P., (AV) BB
718 Market Street, 28401
Telephone: 910-343-8433 Fax: 910-343-8165
Email: ahall@hallandhorne.com
Alexander M. Hall; Roseanna C. Horne; John Felix Green, II; William R. Shell.
Personal Injury, Professional Negligence, Toxic Tort, Wrongful Death, Land Condemnation, Workers Compensation, Social Security, General Civil and Criminal Practice, Felonies, Drug Offenses, Driving While Impaired.
See Professional Biographies, WILMINGTON, NORTH CAROLINA

Hamlet, Fred T., (AV) '47 '73 C.575 A.B. L.309 J.D. 201 North Front Street, Suite 713 (⊙Greensboro)
Hamlet, H. Mark, (BV) .... '66 '93 C.896 B.A. L.1228 J.D. [Crossley M.P.&C.]
Handlan, Joseph M. '14 '46 C.434 A.B. L.893 LL.B. (adm. in WV; not adm. in NC) Chf. Cir. J.‡
Haney, Thomas M. ....'29 '59 C.262 A.B. L.724 J.D. 306 Foxhall Ct.
Hanley, Andrew, (BV) .... '63 '91 C.188 B.A. L.861 J.D. [Crossley M.P.&C.]
Harjo, Jennifer, (BV) ....'62 '88 C&L.862 B.S., J.D. One North 3rd St.
Harris, Jason R. ....'76 '01 C.10 B.A. L.896 J.D. [Rountree,L.&B.]
Hartman, Mark S., (BV) ....'73 '00 C.576 B.S. L.896 J.D. [A Helms M.&W.]
Hatcher, Kenneth B., (CV) ....'41 '78 C.951 B.A. L.575 J.D. P.O. Box 2103
Hatton, Sharon A. ....'49 '99 C.994 B.A. L.1040 J.D. 321 N. Front St.
Hayes, Melodi R. ....'54 '88 C.577 B.S. L.192 J.D. [M.R.Hayes]
Hayes, Melodi R., P.A. ....206 North Fourth Street, Suite 4
Hearne, Joseph C., II, (BV) ....'64 '91 C.575 B.A. L.896 J.D. [White&H.]
Hedrick, P. Scott, (BV) ....'56 '81 C.968 B.A. L.1228 J.D. [Hedrick&M.]

Hedrick Eatman Gardner & Kincheloe, L.L.P., (AV)
1508 Military Cutoff Road, Suite 202, 28403 ⊙
Telephone: 910-509-9664 Fax: 910-509-9630
URL: http://www.hedrickeatman.com
Partners: Erica B. Lewis (Resident); Jeffrey H. Blackwell. Associates: Tracie H. Brisson; William B. Dulaney; Meredith T. Everhart; Benton L. Toups; Tobias J. Weyer.
General Civil Litigation and Insurance Defense, Legal and Professional Malpractice, Motor Vehicle Negligence, Premises Liability, Product Liability, Construction, Insurance Coverage Disputes, Arson and Fraud, Employment Law, Trucking and Transportation and Worker's Compensation.
Representative Clients: Ace-USA; Carolinas Healthcare Systems; Chubb Group; Continental Tire; Liberty Mutual; Medical Mutual Insurance; PMA Group; St. Paul Travelers Insurance Co.; United Parcel Service; USAA; Wal-Mart Corp.
Charlotte, North Carolina Office: 6000 Fairview Road, Suite 1000, 28210. Mailing Address: P.O. Box 30397, 28230. Telephone: 704-366-1101. Fax: 704-366-6181.
Raleigh, North Carolina Office: 4011 Westchase Boulevard, Suite 300, 27607. Telephone: 919-832-9424. Fax: 919-832-9425.
Columbia, South Carolina Office: 1201 Main Street, Suite 1200, 29201. Mailing Address: P.O. Box 11267, 29211. Telephone: 803-727-1200. Fax: 803-727-1259.
See Professional Biographies, WILMINGTON, NORTH CAROLINA

Hedrick & Morton, L.L.P., (BV)
6317 Oleander Drive, Suite C, 28403
Telephone: 910-343-1432 Fax: 910-762-3132
Email: info@Hedricklaw.com URL: http://www.hedricklaw.com
P. Scott Hedrick (Board Certified Specialist in Workers Compensation, North Carolina State Board of Legal Specialization); B. Danforth Morton; G. Grady Richardson, Jr. Associate: Stephen E. Coble.
General Civil Practice. Negligence, Insurance, Insurance Defense, Products Liability, Malpractice, Workers' Compensation, Construction, Employment, Corporation, Admiralty and Maritime Law, Alternative Dispute Resolution, Real Estate Litigation, Mediation and Arbitration. Trials in all Courts.
See Professional Biographies, WILMINGTON, NORTH CAROLINA

Helms Mulliss & Wicker, PLLC, (AV)
127 Grace Street, P.O. Box 599 (28402), 28401 ⊙
Telephone: 910-254-3800 Fax: 910-254-3900
URL: http://www.hmw.com
Member of Firm: J. Dickson McLean (Resident). Associates: Mark S. Hartman; Henry L. Kitchin, Jr.
Banking, Finance, Corporate, Government Relations, Business Litigation, Tax, Securities, Real Property and Finance, Labor and Employment (Management) Law, Employee Benefits, International, Technology, Insurance Coverage, Media, Commercial Bankruptcy, Environmental, Public Finance, ERISA, Estate Planning and Administration, Education, Venture Capital, Intellectual Property.
Charlotte, North Carolina Office: 201 North Tryon Street, P.O. Box 31247 (28231). Telephone: 704-343-2000. Fax: 704-343-2300. Telex: 572460.
Raleigh, North Carolina Office: 2600 Two Hannover Square, P.O. Box 27507. Telephone: 919-755-6600. Fax: 919-755-6699.
See Professional Biographies, WILMINGTON, NORTH CAROLINA

Herlevich, Camilla M., (BV) ....'52 '78 C.228 B.A. L.94 J.D. 3806 Park Ave. Ste. 8

Hewlett, Collins and Allard, (AV) BB
515 Princess Street, P.O. Box 121, 28402
Telephone: 910-763-0156 Fax: 910-763-9998
Members of Firm: Addison Hewlett, Jr. (1912-1989); John C. Collins; James L. Allard, Jr.
Trials in all Federal & State Courts, Criminal Defense, Trials, Traffic Law, DWI Defense, Sexual Assaults, Drug Offenses, Misdemeanors, Felonies, Federal Criminal Law, White Collar Crime.
References: Centura Bank; North Carolina Troopers Assn. Inc.; North Carolina Police Benevolent Assn. Inc., Fraternal Order of Police.
See Professional Biographies, WILMINGTON, NORTH CAROLINA

Hickmon, Elizabeth D. '42 '81
C.577 B.S. L.1228 J.D. 1430 Commonwealth Drive, Suite 307-A
Hicks, Thomas S., (BV) ....'52 '80 C.575 B.A. L.896 J.D. [T.S.Hicks]

Hicks, Thomas S., PLLC, (BV)
419 Grace Street, 28401
Telephone: 910-762-1202 Fax: 910-762-1108
Email: thomas.hicks@wilmingtonlaws.com URL: http://www.wilmingtonlaws.com
Thomas S. Hicks.
Family Law, Divorce, Child Custody and Support, Domestic Violence, Pre and Postmarital Agreements, Spousal Support, Personal Injury, Auto Accidents, Wrongful Death, Slip and Fall, DWI, Criminal Law, Drug Crimes, Homicide, Misdemeanors, Felonies, Juvenile Law, Sexual Assault, Sexual Abuse, Parole and Probation, Traffic Violations, Divorce.
See Professional Biographies, WILMINGTON, NORTH CAROLINA

Hill, William F., P.A.
(See Greenville)

Hingson, Constantine C. ......'— '04 C.575 B.A. L.1228 J.D. [Ward&S.] (⊙New Bern)
Hinn, Helen Kelly, (BV) ......'35 '83 C.953 B.A. L.575 J.D. 1319CC Military Cutoff Rd.
Hockenbury, Jay Donald ....'47 '72 C.152 B.A. L.896 J.D. Supr. Ct. J.
Hodges, C. Wes, II, (CV) ....'69 '95 C.575 B.A. L.472 J.D. [Hodges&C.]
Hodges & Coxe, (BV) .... 3138 Wrightsville Ave
Hogan, Mason, (CV) ....'57 '82 C&L.575 B.A., J.D. 114 S. Front St.
Hogston, Chad E., (CV) ....'71 '96 C.1369 B.S. L.1345 J.D. 213 Princess St.
Hogue, Cyrus D., Jr., (AV) ....'21 '47 C&L.575 B.S., LL.B. [⊡ Hogue,H.J.N.&L.]

Hogue, Hill, Jones, Nash & Lynch, L.L.P., (AV) BB
101 S. Third Street, P.O. Drawer 2178, 28402
Telephone: 910-763-4565 Telecopier: 910-762-6687
Email: hhjnlllp@hoguehill.com
Members of Firm: Cyrus D. Hogue (1888-1960); William L. Hill, II (1931-2001); W. Talmage Jones; David A. Nash; William O. J. Lynch; James B. Snow III; Wayne A. Bullard; G. Edward Coleman, III. Of Counsel: Cyrus D. Hogue, Jr.
General Practice. Trials in all State and Federal Courts. Insurance, Corporations, Taxation, Probate, Real Estate, Personal Injury, Admiralty and Environmental Law, Education Law, Family Law.
Representative Clients: Bank of America, N.A.; International Paper Company; Lower Cape Fear Water & Sewer Authority; New Hanover County Board of Education; Kaiser Aluminum & Chemical Corporation; Wilmington Shipping Company; Clancy & Theys Construction Company; Cooperative Bank for Savings; Independence Mall Associates.
See Professional Biographies, WILMINGTON, NORTH CAROLINA

Holland, Haman W., Attorney at Law, (CV) '63 '91
C.1128 B.A. L.574 J.D. 110 1/2 N. 5th Ave.
Hollandsworth, Dean W., (BV) '64 '89
C.577 B.A. L.896 J.D. New Hanover County Dept. of Social Svcs.
Holt, Shelly ....'57 '81 C.381 B.A. L.1509 J.D. Dist. Ct. J.
Horgan, Richard A., Esq. ....'43 '68 C.976 B.S. L.1066 J.D. 2017 Seawind Lane
Horne, Roseanna C., (BV) ....'67 '92 C.953 B.A. L.575 J.D. [Hall&H.]
Hovdesven, Arne, (AVⓉ) '28 '57 C.586 B.A. L.477 J.D.
(adm. in NY; not adm. in NC) 1425 Regatta Dr.‡
Huffine, David E., (AV) ....'51 '77 C.198 B.A. L.575 J.D. [Carter&H.]
Huffman, Sharon Jackson, (BV) ....'56 '81 C.953 B.S. L.575 J.D. P.O. Box 4

Hutchens, Senter & Britton, P.A., The Law Firm of
Suite 210 1437 Military Cutoff Road, 28403 ⊙
Mailing Address: P.O. Box 12969, Wilmington, NC 28405
Telephone: 910-509-7480 Facsimile: 910-509-7448
Email: lawfirm@hutchensandsenter.com URL: http://www.hutchensandsenter.com
Associates: Erik T. Bennington (Also at Fayetteville, North Carolina Office); Stephen Bailey (Also at Fayetteville, North Carolina Office).
General Civil Practice, Trials in all State and Federal Courts, Creditor Bankruptcy, Foreclosures and Collection, Personal Injury, Wrongful Death, Worker's Compensation, Insurance Law, Corporation, Business and Real Estate.
Fayetteville, North Carolina Office: 4317 Ramsey Street, P.O. Box 2505. Telephone: 910-864-6888. Fax: 910-864-6848.
Raleigh, North Carolina Office: Suite 1540, Two Hanover Square. Telephone: 919-834-2688. Fax: 919-834-3373.
See Professional Biographies, WILMINGTON, NORTH CAROLINA

Ingham, Marc C. ....'67 '99 C.953 B.A. L.923 J.D. 7731 Monarch Dr.
Jackson, Bruce H., Jr., (BV) ....'47 '79 C.953 B.A. L.1228 J.D. [Jackson&Assoc.]

Jackson & Associates, (BV)
615 Princess Street, P.O. Box 1407, 28402-1407
Telephone: 910-763-1041 Facsimile: 910-763-9375 URL: http://www.jacksonandassociates.com
URL: http://www.attorneysyoucancounton.com
Bruce H. Jackson, Jr.
Personal Injury, Wrongful Death, Automobile Accidents and Injuries, Medical Malpractice, Worker's Compensation, Criminal Law, Driving While Intoxicated, Misdemeanors, Felonies, Traffic Violations.
See Professional Biographies, WILMINGTON, NORTH CAROLINA

Jackson, Mills & Carter, P.A., (AV) ....5710 Oleander Drive, Suite 112
Jans, Fred C., Jr. '27 '55 C.446 B.S. L.273 LL.B.
(adm. in DC; not adm. in NC) 327 Robert E. Lee Dr.‡
Jennings, Margaret A. ....'65 '96 C.381 B.S. L.8 J.D. [M.Jennings]
Jennings, Margaret .... 1501 S. 3rd St.
Johnsen, Robert U., Jr., (BV) ....'50 '75 C.478 A.B. L.945 J.D. 119 N. 6th St.
Johnson, Erma L., Law Office of ....'51 '87 C.577 B.S. L.575 J.D. 2803 Market Street
Johnson, Melissa E. ....'79 '04 C.953 B.A. L.1228 J.D. [🄰 Johnson,L.&B.]
Johnson, Robert White, (AV) ....'40 '66 C.280 B.B.A. L.575 J.D. [Johnson,L.&B.]
Johnson, Thomas H., Jr., (BV) ....'— '85 C&L.575 B.S., J.D. [Ward&S.] (⊙New Bern)

Johnson, Lambeth & Brown, (AV) BB
232 Princess Street, P.O. Box 660, 28402
Telephone: 910-763-0481 Fax: 910-251-1276
Members of Firm: Robert White Johnson; Carter Tate Lambeth; Maynard M. Brown. Associates: Anna Johnson Averitt; Melissa E. Johnson.
Civil and Criminal Trials in all Courts. Insurance, Municipal Corporations, Estates, Family Law, Corporate Law, General Practice, Admiralty and Appellate Practice.
References: BB & T; Bank of America.
See Professional Biographies, WILMINGTON, NORTH CAROLINA

Johnson & Moore, P.A.
(See Southport)

Jones, G. Frank, (AV) ....'60 '85 C.576 B.A. L.575 J.D. [Burney,B.&J.]
Jones, Gregory Lawing, (BV) ....'60 '85 C.999 B.A. L.575 J.D. [G.Jones&Assoc.]
Jones, John Alan, (AV) ....'56 '82 C&L.575 B.A., J.D. [Martin&J.] (⊙Raleigh)
Jones, Robert B., Jr. ....'— '97 C.198 B.A. L.1228 J.D. [Cranfill,S.&H.]
Jones, W. Talmage, (AV) ....'40 '66 C&L.575 B.A., LL.B. [Hogue,H.J.N.&L.]
Jones, Wesley S. ....'64 '94 C.575 B.S. L.1228 J.D [W.S.Jones]

Jones, Greg, & Associates, P.A., (BV)
3015 Market Street, 28403
Telephone: 910-251-2240 Fax: 910-251-1520 URL: http://www.gregjoneslaw.com
Email: greg@gregjoneslaw.com URL: http://www.lawyers.com/gregoryjones&associates
Gregory Lawing Jones;—Russell D. Nugent; Marlo L. Thaggard. Of Counsel: Franklin D. Pope.

(This Listing Continued)

Jones, Greg, & Associates, P.A. (Continued)
Personal Injury, Automobile Accidents, Brain Injury, Motorcycle Accidents, Wrongful Death, Medical Malpractice, Spinal Cord Injuries, Drug and Medical Device Litigation, Pharmacists Liability, Head Injuries, Products Liability, Medical and Nursing Home Negligence, Workers Compensation, Toxic Torts, Nursing Home Abuse, Stock Fraud.
See Professional Biographies, WILMINGTON, NORTH CAROLINA

Jones, Wesley S., P.C., Law Office of ....1442 Military Cutoff Rd., Ste. 28
Jordan, Elizabeth J., (CV) ....'53 '85 C.1378 B.A. L.574 J.D. Law Clk. to Dist. Ct. J.
Kaufman, James J., (AV) '39 '65 C.105 A.B. L.982 LL.B.
Landfall Park North, 1985 Eastwood Rd Ste 200
Keeter, Jeffrey P., (BV) ....'59 '85 C&L.1228 B.S., J.D. [Block,C.&K.]

Kendrick, Vaiden P., (AV) '44 '69 C.152 B.A. L.575 J.D.
310 North Front Street, Suite 250, 28401
Telephone: 910-343-9742 Fax: 910-343-9744
Email: vpklaw@bellsouth.net
Civil Litigation, Insurance Defense, Construction Litigation, Commercial Litigation, Legal Malpractice Defense, Appellate Practice.
See Professional Biographies, WILMINGTON, NORTH CAROLINA

Kiernan, Ellen Arnold, Law Office of, (BV) .....'65 '90 C&L.347 B.A., J.D. 15 N. 6th St.
Kimbro, Stephanie L. ....'— '04 C.138 B.A. L.201 J.D. [🄰 Shanklin&N.]
King, Kenneth W., Jr., (BV) ......'61 '86 C.575 B.S. L.469 J.D. [Brumbaugh,M.&K.] ⊙
Kitchin, Henry L., Jr., (BV) ....'71 '96 C.575 B.A. L.896 J.D. [🄰 Helms M.&W.]
Klein, Richard M. '44 '69 C.688 B.S. L.262 J.D.
Sr. Atty., Legal Servs. of the Lower Cape Fear
Kowal, Kathleen H., Attorney at Law, (CV) '45 '00
C.446 B.S. L.1398 J.D. 201 N. Front St., Ste. 308H
Kromke, Brian J. ....'73 '01 C.1372 B.A. L.574 J.D. [🄰 Patterson,D.C.B.&A.]
Laing, Harold ....'35 '68 C&L.575 B.S., J.D. 226 Princess St.
Laite, Gilbert C., III, (AV) '57 '84 C.1248 B.S.B.A. L.896 J.D.
[Maupin T.] (⊙Raleigh)
Lamb, Thomas J., (AV) ....'61 '88 C.945 B.A. L.273 J.D. [T.J.Lamb]

Lamb, Thomas J., P.A., Law Offices of, (AV)
1908 Eastwood Road, Suite 225, 28403
Telephone: 910-256-2971 Facsimile: 910-256-2972
Email: Info@LambLawOffice.com URL: http://www.LambLawOffice.com
Thomas J. Lamb.
Drug and Medical Device Litigation, Toxic Torts, Asbestos Litigation, Chemical Exposure, Occupational Cancer, Workers Compensation, Products Liability, Welding Products Liability, Medical Malpractice, Hospital Negligence, Pharmacists Liability, Personal Injury and Wrongful Death.
See Professional Biographies, WILMINGTON, NORTH CAROLINA

Lambeth, Carter Tate, (AV) ....'46 '71 C.797 B.A. L.575 J.D. [Johnson,L.&B.]
Larrick, James K., (BV) ....'42 '70 C&L.575 B.S., J.D. 421 Highgreen Dr.
Lasar, Daniel R. ....'— '98 C.575 B.A. L.1365 J.D. 102 N. Front Street
Latshaw, James W., (BV) ....'60 '85 C.188 B.A. L.477 J.D. [Murchison,T.&G.]
Lea, James W., III, (AV) ....'54 '80 C.575 B.A. L.1228 J.D. [Lea,R.R.&C.]

Lea, Rhine, Rosbrugh & Chleborowicz, P.L.L.C., (AV) BB
314 Walnut Street, Suite 1000 and 2000 New Hanover County, 28401
Telephone: 910-772-9960 Fax: 910-772-9062
Email: lrattorneys@lrlawfirm.com
James W. Lea, III; Joel R. Rhine; Lori Wiggins Rosbrugh; Christopher A. Chleborowicz. Associate: Carrie A. Orlikowski.
General Trial Practice in all Federal and State Courts. Personal Injury including Wrongful Death, Construction Law, Stucco Litigation, Mold Litigation, Civil Litigation and Family Law. Complex Commercial Litigation including Class Actions, Securities Arbitrations.
See Professional Biographies, WILMINGTON, NORTH CAROLINA

Lee, Kari A. ....'78 '03 C.890 B.A. L.896 J.D. [🄰 Patterson,D.C.B.&A.]
Lee, Michael V. ....'— '97 C.575 B.A. L.896 J.D. [Smith M.]
Lee, Phyllis M., (BV) ....'57 '87 C.696 B.A. L.309 J.D. PharmaResearch Corp.
Lefler, Lisa S. ....'66 '91 C.896 B.A. L.1228 J.D. [L.S.Lefler]
Lefler, Lisa S., PC .... P.O. Box 2532
Legrand, Terri E. '66 '93 C.350 B.S. L.896 J.D.
Care Mgr., Methodist Home for Children
Leidy, Lee L., (BV) ...'63 '90 C.896 B.A. L.575 J.D. Contract Atty., NC Coastal Land Tr.
Lennon, Alton Y., (BV) ....'42 '68 C&L.896 B.A., J.D. [Stevens,M.M.L.&T.]
Leonard, Christopher J. ....'74 '99 C&L.896 B.A., J.D. [Murchison,T.&G.]
Lewis, Erica B. ....'— '95 C.112 B.A. L.896 J.D. [Hedrick E.G.&K.]
Lewis, J. Scott, (BV) ....'70 '95 C.575 B.A. L.896 J.D. [Patterson,D.C.B.&A.]
Lewis, James Drury ....'74 '00 C.575 B.A. L.896 J.D. P.O. Box 352
Lewis, Owen D., Jr. '69 '94 C&L.896 B.A., J.D.
Corp. Coun., Charles River Laboratories
Lewis, William P., II, (BV) '59 '84 C.575 A.B. L.1228 J.D.
Sr. V.P. & Coun., Commonwealth Land Title Co. of N.C.
Lindau, Jules W. '37 '66 C.477 B.S. L.976 LL.B.
(adm. in SC; not adm. in NC) 3044 Weatherby Ct.‡
Lineberry, Charles M., (BV) ....'59 '85 C.34 B.S.B.A. L.1228 J.D. [Lineberry]
Lineberry Law Firm, The, PC, (BV) ....3602 Wrightsville Ave.
Ling, William ....'32 '78 811 Seabury Ct.
Longval, Mark Joseph ....'57 '90 C.472 B.S. L.1241 J.D. [Real L.]
Losee, Geoffrey A., (CV) ....'63 '94 C.871 B.S. L.1228 J.D. [Rountree,L.&B.]
Lovett, John C. '37 '65 C.350 B.S. L.352 J.D.
(adm. in IA; not adm. in NC) 8724 Sedgley Drive
Low, Aaron C. ....'76 '03 C.576 B.A. L.999 J.D. [🄰 Cox&T.]
Lucas, Jana S. ....'46 '89 C.953 B.A. L.575 J.D. 401 Chestnut St., Ste. F
Lux, Arthur E. .... '44 '70 C.476 B.S. L.213 J.D. [Lux&L.]
Lux, Donna Beck '45 '70 C.136 B.A. L.213 J.D.
(adm. in MI; not adm. in NC) [Lux&L.]
Lux & Lux .... 6501 Carmel Trail
Lynch, William O. J., (AV) ....'45 '72 C.953 B.A. L.896 J.D. [Hogue,H.J.N.&L.]

MacCord Mason PLLC, (AV)
1209 Culbreth Drive, Suite 103, 28405 ⊙
Telephone: 910-256-3557 Fax: 910-256-0523
Email: wmason@mmpatent.com URL: http://www.maccordmason.com
William J. Mason (Resident).
Patent, Trademark, Copyright and Unfair Competition. Trade Secret Practice before all Courts. Intellectual Property Law, Litigation.
Greensboro, North Carolina Office: 300 North Greene Street, Suite 1600, P.O. Box 2974. Telephone: 336-273-4422. Fax: 336-271-2830.
Raleigh, North Carolina Office: 510 Glenwood Avenue, Suite 321, 27611. Telephone: 919-664-8624. Fax: 919-664-8625.
See Professional Biographies, WILMINGTON, NORTH CAROLINA

MacDonald, James A., (AV) ....'49 '74 C.228 B.A. L.575 J.D. [Allen,M.&D.]
MacRae, Samuel H., (CV) ....'65 '91 C.575 B.A. L.574 J.D. [Crossley M.P.&C.]

Madison Pratt, Vivian L. '56 '81 C&L.425 B.A., J.D.
(adm. in LA; not adm. in NC)
Vice President of Strategic Product Management, Applied Analytical Industries, Inc.
Mahn, Daniel D., Attorney at Law, (BV) ......'60 '85 C.953 B.S. L.575 J.D. 19 N., 5th St.
Mako, Sue Elaine ....'44 '73 C.97 B.S.Ed. L.851 J.D. [Mako&Assoc.]

Mako & Associates, P.A.
3208 Oleander Drive, 28403
Telephone: 910-343-9920 Fax: 910-343-9921
Email: smako@makoandasociates.com URL: http://www.makoandrobinson.net
Members of Firm: Sue Elaine Mako; Richard Scott Girdwood.
Personal Injury, Automobile Accidents, Wrongful Death, Trucking Accidents, Head Trauma, Spinal Cord Injuries, Motorcycle Accidents, Workers Compensation, Mediation and Arbitration, Birth Trauma, Medical Malpractice, Construction Accidents, Nursing Home Negligence, Nursing Home Abuse and Neglect and Dog Bites.
See Professional Biographies, WILMINGTON, NORTH CAROLINA

Mannen, Jerry A., Jr., (BV) ....'61 '90 C.576 B.A. L.1345 J.D. [Yow,F.&M.]

Marshall, Williams & Gorham, L.L.P., (AV) BR
14 South Fifth Street, P.O. Drawer 2088, 28402-2088
Telephone: 910-763-9891 Telecopier: 910-343-8604
Email: attorneys@mwglaw.com URL: http://www.mwglaw.com
Members of Firm: Alan A. Marshall (1908-1979); Lonnie B. Williams; A. Dumay Gorham, Jr.; Jerry C. Woodell; William Robert Cherry, Jr.; Ronald H. Woodruff; Lonnie B. Williams, Jr.; Charles D. Meier; John L. Coble; F. Murphy Averitt, III.
Civil Practice. Trials in all State and Federal Courts. Civil Litigation, Arbitration, Construction Law, Professional Liability, Insurance Defense, Personal Injury, Insurance, Banking Law, Business Law, Mergers and Acquisitions, Corporate Law, Commercial Law, Contracts, Collections, Debtor and Creditor, Health Care, Hospital Law, Estate Planning, Probate, Wills and Real Estate Law.
Representative Clients: Hale Building Co.; Unitrin Ins. Co.; New Hanover Regional Medical Center; Government Employers Insurance Co.; St. Paul Travelers Ins. Co.; LS3P Associates Ltd.; Air Wilmington, Inc.; MHI Hotels, LLC; Lowes Companies, Inc.
See Professional Biographies, WILMINGTON, NORTH CAROLINA

Martin, John Dearman, (AV) ....'59 '85 C.896 B.A. L.1228 J.D. [Cranfill,S.&H.]
Martin, W. Daniel, III, (AV) ... '— '73 C.576 B.A. L.575 J.D. [Ward&S.] (⊙New Bern)

Martin & Jones, (AV)
1213 Culbreth Drive, Suite 121, 28405 ⊙
Telephone: 910-256-4005
URL: http://www.MartinandJones.com
John Alan Jones.
Asbestos Litigation, Bad Faith and Unfair Competition, Business Litigation, Construction Site Injuries, Inadequate Security, Medical Malpractice, Nursing/Rest Home Negligence, Personal Injury, Pharmaceutical and Medical Device Litigation, Product Liability, Social Security Disability, Toxic Torts, Trucking Accidents, Workers' Compensation and Wrongful Death, Land Condemnation, FELA (Federal Employers' Liability Act), Securities Fraud.
Raleigh, North Carolina Office: 410 Glenwood Avenue, 27603. Telephone: 919-821-0005.
Durham, North Carolina Office: University Towers, Suite 526, 3100 Tower Boulevard, 27707. Telephone: 919-544-3000.
Atlanta, Georgia Office: 3353 Peachtree Road, NE, Suite 510, 30326. Telephone: 404-257-1117.
See Professional Biographies, WILMINGTON, NORTH CAROLINA

Mason, Bruce A., (BV) ....'64 '89 C.923 B.S. L.575 J.D. [B.A.Mason]
Mason, Lorraine H. '44 '77 C&L.575 A.B., J.D.
V.P. & Tr. Offr.-Estate Planning Advsr., Wachovia Bk., N.A.
Mason, William J., (BV) '40 '68 C.834 B.S. L.273 J.D.
[MacCord M.P.] (See Pat. Sect.)
Mason, William Norton ....'51 '77 C.575 B.A. L.896 J.D. [Shipman,M.&W.]
Mason, B. A., (BV) .... 105 N. 6th St.

Maupin Taylor, P.A., (AV)
Landfall Park North, 1985 Eastwood Road, Suite 200, 28403 ⊙
Telephone: 910-256-5135 Telecopier: 910-256-6451
URL: http://www.maupintaylor.com
Gilbert C. Laite, III. Of Counsel: Daniel Lee Brawley.
Agribusiness, Administrative, Alcoholic Beverages, Alternative Dispute Resolution, Antitrust and Trade Regulation, Aviation Law, Bankruptcy, Banking Law, Business Litigation, Charitable Organizations, Collective Bargaining, Commercial Leases, Commercial Real Estate, Computers and Software, Construction Law, Copyrights, Corporate Finance, Corporate Law, Creditors' Rights, Employee Benefits, Employer Liability, Employment Discrimination, Employment Law, Employment Litigation, Environmental Law, Franchises and Franchising, Government Contracts, Governmental (State and Local) Law, Health Law, Hospital Law, Immigration and Naturalization, Industrial Accidents, Industrial Relations, Intellectual Property, Labor Arbitration, Labor Law, Labor Legislation, Labor Relations, Management Labor Law, Medical Malpractice Defense, Mergers and Acquisitions, Occupational Health and Safety, Patent Litigation, Products Liability, Real Estate Finance, Secured Lending, Securities Regulation, Sports Law, Taxation, Technology Law, Trademark, Trusts and Estates, Venture Capital, Zoning Law.
Representative Clients: American International Group; Blue Cross/Blue Shield of North Carolina; CSX Transportation, Inc.; Fluor Daniel Midland, Inc.; E & J Gallo Winery; Glaxo Wellcome; Northern Telecom Inc.; Reichhold Chemical Co. Inc.; Sampson Regional Medical Center; Smithfield Foods, Inc.; SouthTrust Bank, N.A.
Raleigh, North Carolina: Highwoods Tower One, Suite 500, 3200 Beechleaf Court, P.O. Drawer 19764. Telephone: 919-981-4000. Telecopier: 919-981-4300.
Research Triangle Park, North Carolina Office: 480 Beta Building, Headquarters Park, Post Office Box 13646, 27709-3646. Telephone: 919-361-4900. Telecopier: 919-361-2262.
See Professional Biographies, WILMINGTON, NORTH CAROLINA

McCauley, Cleyburn L. '29 '70 C.870 B.S. L.945 LL.D.
(adm. in VA; not adm. in NC) 402 S. Third St.
McCulley, Michael D., Jr., (CV) ......'68 '96 C.232 B.A. L.1194 J.D. [M.D.McCulley,Jr.]
McCulley, Michael D., Jr., P.A., (CV) ....4728 Long Leaf Hills Drive
McCurry, Todd E. .... '— '87 C.406 B.S. L.574 J.D. [T.E.McCurry]

McCurry, Todd E., P.A., Attorney at Law
207 1/2 Princess Street, 28401
Mailing Address: P.O. Box 1443, Wilmington, NC 28402
Telephone: 910-772-1254 Fax: 910-772-1274
Email: lawyertm@bellsouth.net URL: http://www.lawyers.com/toddmccurry
Todd E. McCurry.
Workers Compensation; On-the-Job Injuries; Personal Injury; Automobile Accidents; Wrongful Death; Family Law; Divorce; Child Custody; Child Support; Spousal Support; Premarital Agreements.
See Professional Biographies, WILMINGTON, NORTH CAROLINA

McDaniel Keelin, Susan, (BV) '67 '92
C.228 B.A. L.910 J.D. 1437 Military Cutoff Rd., Ste. 201
McDow, Lisa T., The Law Office of ....'— '93 C.881 A.B. L.574 J.D. P.O. Box 2541
McEachern, Edna Caroline, (CV) ....'62 '88 C.953 B.A. L.1228 J.D. [Peters,R.&M.]
McEachern, Mary Margaret, (CV) ....'70 '96 C.575 B.A. L.1228 J.D. 709 Princess St.
McGill, Rosalie Cannone '43 '77 C.705 B.A. L.776 J.D.
(adm. in NJ; not adm. in NC) 8409 Fazio Dr.
McGinness, James E. '— '87 C.665 B.S.E. L.229 J.D.
(adm. in PA; not adm. in NC) Sr. Intel. Prop. Coun., GE Nuclear Energy
McIntosh, Douglas F., (AV) ....'59 '84 C.1154 B.S. L.1228 J.D. [Crossley M.P.&C.]
McIntyre, Maria D. ....'— '96 C&L.575 B.S., J.D. P.O. Box 390
McLean, J. Dickson, (AV) ....'63 '89 C.198 B.A. L.575 J.D. [Helms M.&W.]
McVey, Andrew K., (BV) ....'68 '93 C&L.896 B.A., J.D. [Murchison,T.&G.]

Meier, Charles D., (BV) ....'59 '85 C&L.575 B.A., J.D. [Marshall,W.&G.]
Mills, Franklin Darryl, (AV) ....'54 '83 C&L.575 B.A., J.D. [Jackson,M.&C.]
Mills, Michael T. ....'59 '82 C&L.575 B.A., J.D. 12 South Sixth Street
Moore, Brian J., & Associates ...'70 '98 C.712 B.A. L.607 J.D. 707 Market Street, Suite 2
Moore, Edwin H., III ......'69 '96 C.575 B.A. L.383 J.D. Asst. Co. Atty., Off. of Co. Atty.
Moore, John G., (AVⓉ) '20 '51 C.262 B.S. L.1009 LL.B.
(adm. in NY; not adm. in NC) 3212 Grey Leaf Drive
Moore, Kimberly L. ..... '67 '95 C.893 B.S. L.469 J.D. [G Fletcher R.&S.] (⊙Southport)
Morgan, James B., Jr., (BV) ....'57 '83 C.232 B.S. L.1228 J.D. Barrister's Row II
Morgan, Richard M., (AV) ....'40 '65 C.198 A.B. L.228 LL.B. [Stevens,M.M.L.&T.]
Morgan, Thomas J. ....'50 '76 C.575 B.S. L.469 J.D. 19 N. Fifth Ave.
Morris, Jennifer L. ....'79 '05 C.758 B.A. L.1228 J.D. [A Patterson,D.C.B.&A.]
Morton, B. Danforth, (BV) ....'60 '85 C.228 B.A. L.575 J.D. [Hedrick&M.]
Moss, Nicole Jo ....'— '00 C.999 B.A. L.309 J.D. [A Shipman,M.&W.]
Mulligan, Patrick J., IV ....'70 '98 C.953 B.A. L.896 J.D. [P.J.Mulligan]
Mulligan, Patrick J., P.C. ....124 Cavalier Dr.
Murchison, Michael, (AV) .... '49 '75 C.31 B.A. L.188 J.D. [Murchison,T.&G.]

Murchison, Taylor & Gibson, PLLC, (AV) BR
16 North Fifth Avenue, 28401-4593
Telephone: 910-763-2426 Fax: 910-763-6561
Members of Firm: Wallace C. Murchison (Retired); Joseph O. Taylor, Jr.; Frank B. Gibson, Jr.; Michael Murchison; W. Berry Trice; G. Stephen Diab; James W. Latshaw; Andrew K. McVey; Peter A. Bynum; Christopher J. Leonard. Associates: Frances Youngblood Trask; Faison Gibson Sutton.
General Practice: Trials in State and Federal Courts. Corporation and Business, Mergers and Acquisitions, Real Estate, Buying and Selling a Home, Commercial Real Estate, Commercial Finance, Taxation, Estate Planning and Administration, Elder Law, Healthcare, Employment Law, Intellectual Property, Administrative, Environmental, Labor Law and Creditor and Bankruptcy Law, Zoning and Land Use.
See Professional Biographies, WILMINGTON, NORTH CAROLINA

Myers, Dennis P., (AV) ....'44 '73 C&L.575 A.B., J.D. Asst. Atty. Gen.
Nash, David A., (AV) ....'45 '70 C&L.575 A.B., J.D. [Hogue,H.J.N.&L.]
Newton, Jacqueline A., (BV) ....'57 '91 C.925 B.S.B.A. L.1228 J.D. [Ennis,N.&B.]
Newton, John Richard, (AV) ....'32 '65 C&L.575 A.B., LL.B. [Clark,N.E.&B.]
Newton, Louis K., (AV) ....'29 '57 C&L.575 A.B., J.D. [Newton&N.]
Newton, Paul A., (BV) ....'56 '87 C.999 B.A. L.1228 J.D. [Newton&N.]
Newton & Newton, (AV) .... 20 N. 5th St.
Nichols, Matthew A. ....'71 '96 C.383 B.A. L.575 J.D. [Shanklin&N.]
Noecker, Jeffrey E., (CV) ....'65 '92 C.893 B.A. L.575 J.D. 307 N. 5th St.
Nugent, Russell D. ....'76 '04 C.577 B.A. L.276 J.D. [A G.Jones&Assoc.]
Nunalee, Thomas Hervey, IV, (BV) ......'69 '94 C.576 B.A. L.575 J.D. [T.H.Nunalee,IV]
Nunalee, Thomas H., IV, P.L.L.C., (BV) ....5725 Oleander Drive, Suite D-1
O'Connell, Thomas J. '29 '83 C.1133 B.S. L.1019 J.D.
(adm. in NY; not adm. in NC) 314 Wimbledon Ct.‡
O'Donnell, Patrick L. '35 '70 C.336 B.S. L.424 J.D.
(adm. in IL; not adm. in NC) 1012 Deepwood Pl.‡
Olsen, Andrew ....'47 '75 C.668 B.A. L.276 J.D. 213 North Second St.
Oring, Christopher L. ....'70 '96 C.8 B.A. L.851 J.D. 705 Princess Street
Orlikowski, Carrie A. ....'78 '03 C.228 B.A. L.575 J.D. [A Lea,R.R.&C.]
Overholt, H. Scott, (BV) ....'64 '91 C&L.45 B.S., J.D. [Overholt]
Overholt Law Firm, The, PC, (BV) .... P.O. Box 1288
Owens, Richard S., III, (BV) ....'44 '72 C&L.896 B.A., J.D. 7517 Promontory Ct.
Page, Jeremy S. ....'78 '05 C.953 L.896 J.D. [A Patterson,D.C.B.&A.]
Parker, Robbie B. ....'— '03 C.232 B.S. L.1228 J.D. [A Webb&G.] ⊙

Patterson, Dilthey, Clay, Bryson & Anderson, L.L.P., (AV)
2516 Independence Boulevard, Suite 200, P.O. Box 2258, 28412 ⊙
Telephone: 910-452-2797; Toll Free: 877-731-5007 Facsimile: 910-452-4151
URL: http://www.pattersondilthey.com
Partner: J. Scott Lewis. Associates: Tyler Paige Baucom; Ellen J. Persechini; Justin D. Robertson; Jerry L. Wilkins (Resident); W. Walter Rapp; Kari A. Lee; Brian J. Kromke; Jennifer L. Morris; Jeremy S. Page.
Civil Trial Practice. Trials in all State and Federal Courts. Workers Compensation, Products Liability, Medical Malpractice, Premises Liability, Automobile Liability and Insurance Law.
Raleigh, North Carolina Office: 4020 WestChase Boulevard, Suite 550. Telephone: 919-821-4020. FAX: 919-829-0055.
See Professional Biographies, WILMINGTON, NORTH CAROLINA

Pawlowski, Kathleen D.H. ....'61 '89 C.93 B.A. L.276 J.D. 4306 Forwalt Place
Pennington, Ralph S., (BV) ....'54 '84 C.953 B.A. L.575 J.D. [Pennington&S.]

Pennington & Smith, (BV)
107 North Sixth Street, 28401
Telephone: 910-763-3340 Fax: 910-763-8034
Members of Firm: Ralph S. Pennington; Tamara Avis Smith.
Family Law, Divorce, Child Custody, Child Support, Alimony, Equitable Distribution, Civil Litigation.
See Professional Biographies, WILMINGTON, NORTH CAROLINA

Peregoy, William T. ....'56 '90 C.1011 B.A.B.S. L.574 J.D. 206 Princess Street
Persechini, Ellen J. ....'78 '02 C.838 B.A. L.896 J.D. [A Patterson,D.C.B.&A.]
Peters, Kevin J., (BV) ....'53 '85 C.953 B.A. L.575 J.D. [Peters,R.&M.]
Peters, Register & McEachern, (BV) ....401 Chestnut St.
Pollard, Thomas C., (AV) ....'50 '79 C.37 B.A. L.575 J.D. City Atty.
Pollock, Melissa Ann, (BV) ....'63 '91 C.631 B.S.N. L.117 J.D. 314 Walnut Street
Pope, Franklin D. .... '— '88 C.953 B.A. L.575 J.D. [G G.Jones&Assoc.] (⊙Jacksonville)
Pope, Robert W., (AV) ....'25 '62 C.896 B.S. L.575 LL.B. Off. of Co. Atty.
Porter, Jeffrey W., (BV) ....'61 '88 C.893 B.A. L.945 J.D. 711 Princess St.
Pratt, Vivian L. Madison '56 '81 C&L.425 B.A., J.D.
(adm. in LA; not adm. in NC) aaiPharma, Inc.

Price, James S. '70 '04 C.575 B.A. L.1228 J.D.
4018 B Shipyard Boulevard, Suite 3, 28406
Telephone: 910-791-9422 Fax: 910-791-0432
Email: jamespriceatty@bellsouth.net URL: http://www.jamessprice.com
—Stephanie Michelle Akin; Wesley Sheffield.
Real Estate.
See Professional Biographies, WILMINGTON, NORTH CAROLINA

Prickett, Carlton S., Jr., (AV) ....'43 '69 C.896 B.A. L.575 J.D. 7 S. 5th Ave.
Pridgen, Otto K., II, (CV) ....'28 '53 C&L.896 B.S., LL.B. 220 Princess St.
Prior, Francis B., (AV) ....'57 '83 C.576 B.A. L.1228 J.D. [Crossley M.P.&C.]
Ramirez, Roberto F. ....'62 '92 C.839 B.S. L.846 J.D. Staff J. Adv.
Randall, Samuel J., IV ....'69 '98 C.953 B.A. L.61 J.D. [S.J.Randall,IV]
Randall, Samuel J., IV, P.C., The Law Offices of ....210 Princess Street
Raney, William A., Jr., (AV) .... '47 '73 C&L.575 B.A., J.D. [Wessell&R.]
Rapp, W. Walter ....'75 '03 C.575 B.A. L.896 J.D. [A Patterson,D.C.B.&A.]
Ray, David L., (BV) ....'66 '91 C&L.575 B.A., J.D. [Fletcher R.&S.]
Ray, Jennifer D. ....'— '03 C.198 B.S. L.790 J.D. [Cranfill,S.&H.]
Ray, Nicole Molin ....'73 '98 C.575 B.A. L.1228 J.D. 105 North Sixth Street
Real Law ....547 Chattooga Place
Register, Anthony L., (BV) ....'58 '86 C.1027 B.S. L.575 J.D. [Peters,R.&M.]

Retchin, Daniel D. .... '23 '48 C&L.575 B.S., J.D. 1815 Hawthorne Rd.‡
Rhine, Joel R., (AV) .... '62 '88 C.825 B.A. L.896 J.D. [Lea,R.R.&C.]
Rice, Charles E., III, (AV) .... '45 '70 C.228 A.B. L.575 J.D. 401 Chestnut Street
Richards, Karen Florence .... '71 '99 C.790 B.S. L.607 J.D. 5111 Gate Post Lane
Richardson, G. Grady, Jr. .... '72 '98 C.953 B.A. L.1345 J.D. [Hedrick&M.]

Richardson, Terry B., (CV) '54 '81 C.574 B.A. L.575 J.D.
209 Princess Street, 28402
Telephone: 910-763-7420 Fax: 910-762-4176
Personal Injury, Wrongful Death, Automobile Accidents, Truck Accidents, Criminal Cases, Traffic Offenses, DWIs, Estates and Wills. Trials in all Courts.
See Professional Biographies, WILMINGTON, NORTH CAROLINA

Rivenbark, Christina, & Associates, (CV) '62 '87 C&L.575 B.A., J.D.
4009 Oleander Drive, 28403 ⊙
Telephone: 910-251-8080 Facsimile: 910-395-8391
Email: cr@christinarivenbark.com URL: http://www.christinarivenbarklaw.com/
Personal Injury, Automobile Accidents, Workers Compensation, Wrongful Death, Medical Malpractice, Slip and Fall, Criminal Law, Driving While Intoxicated, Traffic Violations, Drug Offenses, Misdemeanors, Felonies, Sexual Assaults, Assaults, Burglary, Motorcycle Accidents, Head Injuries.
Clinton, North Carolina Office: 603A Northeast Boulevard, 28328. Telephone: 1-800-777-5159.
Garner, North Carolina Office: 5533 NC Highway 42 West, 27529. Telephone: 1-800-561-9221.
See Professional Biographies, WILMINGTON, NORTH CAROLINA

Rivenbark, James B., (BV) .... '35 '63 C&L.575 B.S., J.D. 5751 Oleander Dr., Ste. 8
Rizzi, Michael J., (CV) .... '69 '94 C.105 B.A. L.1228 J.D. [[A] David&Assoc.]
Robertson, Justin D. .... '72 '98 C.1128 B.A. L.1228 J.D. [[A] Patterson,D.C.B.&A.]

Robinson, Bruce H., Jr. '44 '69 C.928 B.A. L.896 J.D.
401 Chestnut Street, Suite D, 28401
Telephone: 910-763-7446 Fax: 910-763-7466
Email: brucerobinsonjr@aol.com
Personal Injury, Medical Malpractice, Hospital Negligence, Nursing Home Abuse and Neglect, Spinal Injuries, Brain Injury, Birth Trauma, Wrongful Death, Automobile Accidents, Truck Accidents, Motorcycle Accidents, DWI, DUI, Workers Compensation, Misdiagnosis of Heart Condition, Negligence, Surgeons Liability, Domestic Relations, Family Law, Divorce, Interstate Child Custody, Commercial Litigation, Real Estate Litigation, General Civil Litigation, Criminal Law, Criminal Defense and Felonies in all State and Federal Courts.
See Professional Biographies, WILMINGTON, NORTH CAROLINA

Robinson, Robin Wicks, (BV) .... '61 '86 C.185 B.A. L.575 J.D. [R.W.Robinson]

Robinson, Robin Wicks, P.C., (BV)
701 Market Street, P.O. Box 135, 28402
Telephone: 910-763-3374 Fax: 910-763-4004
Email: rrspc@bellsouth.net
Robin Wicks Robinson (Board Certified Specialist in Family Law, North Carolina State Board of Legal Specialization).
Family Law, Civil Litigation and Mediation.
See Professional Biographies, WILMINGTON, NORTH CAROLINA

Rodzik, Todd A. .... '68 '92 C.790 B.A. L.575 J.D. 2909 Market Street
Rolquin, Monica D. .... '60 '84 C.999 LL.B. L.178 LL.M. 6321 Towles Rd.
Roney, Ben E., Jr., (BV) .... '41 '74 C.999 B.S. L.575 J.D. 6056 Cedar Ridge Dr.
Rosbrugh, Lori Wiggins, (CV) .... '65 '96 C.1111 B.A. L.260 J.D. [Lea,R.R.&C.]
Rountree, George, III, (AV) .... '33 '60 C&L.37 B.A., LL.B. [Rountree,L.&B.]

Rountree, Losee & Baldwin, L.L.P., (AV) [BB]
2419 Market Street, P.O. Box 1409, 28403
Telephone: 910-763-3404 Telecopier: 910-763-0320
URL: http://www.rlblawfirm.com
Members of Firm: George Rountree, Jr. (1904-1979); George Rountree, III; Geoffrey A. Losee; Charles S. Baldwin, IV; Stephen D. Coggins; Jason R. Harris.
General Practice in all Courts. Civil Litigation, Business/Corporation, Admiralty, Environmental Law Litigation, Insurance, International, Estate Planning and Real Estate Law.
Representative Clients: American International Marine Agency; Answerthink, Inc.; Fireman's Fund Insurance Cos.; The Japan Shipowners' Mutual Protection & Indemnity Assn., Ltd.; Time Warner Cable - Advance/Newhouse Partnership.
Approved Attorneys for: Chicago Title Insurance Co.; Commonwealth Land Insurance Co.; Investors Title Insurance Co.; Lawyers Title Insurance Corp.
References: Centura Bank; First Union National Bank of America.
See Professional Biographies, WILMINGTON, NORTH CAROLINA

Royce, Robert C., (AVⓉ) '39 '68 C.103 A.B. L.1017 J.D.
(adm. in NY; not adm. in NC) 1908 Inverness Lane‡
Rusch, Randall Gregory .... '50 '89 C.477 B.A. L.574 J.D. [R.G.Rusch]
Rusch, Randall G., Attorney .... 516 Market St.
Rutledge, Breanna W. .... '75 '01 C.679 B.A. L.910 J.D. [[A] Boseman&Assoc.]
Ryan, Jeffrey, (BV) .... '57 '95 C.1071 B.S. L.851 J.D. 401 Chestnut St.
Ryan, S. Sam, (BV) .... '66 '95 C&L.851 B.S., J.D. 401 Chestnut St., Ste. L
Saffo, Anthony A., (BV) .... '61 '87 C.575 B.A. L.1228 J.D. [Saffo]

Saffo Law Firm, P.C., (BV)
1508 Military Cutoff Road, Suite 203, 28403
Telephone: 910-256-3364 Fax: 910-256-3301
URL: http://www.lawyers.com/saffolaw
Anthony A. Saffo (Board Certified Specialist in Estate Planning and Probate Law, North Carolina State Board of Legal Specialization).
Trusts and Estates, Estate Planning, Asset Protection, Estate Administration, Taxation, Tax Planning, Real Estate, Buying or Selling a Home, Zoning and Land Use, Business Transactions.
See Professional Biographies, WILMINGTON, NORTH CAROLINA

Samples, Barbara Allen ...... '66 '91 C&L.896 B.A., J.D. 1985 Eastwood Road, Suite 200
Satterfield, T. Michael, (BV) .... '59 '85 C.953 B.A. L.575 J.D. [Fletcher R.&S.]
Sayed, Linda B., (BV) .... '57 '98 C.953 B.A. L.1345 J.D. [[A] Block,C.&K.]
Schaefer, Elmer A. '27 '57 C.150 M.S. L.1340 J.D.
(adm. in OH; not adm. in NC) 117 Tanbridge Rd.‡
Schenkel, Kent D., (BV) .... '60 '87 C.362 B.A. L.259 J.D. [K.D.Schenkel]
Schenkel, Kent D., PLLC, (BV) .... 1205 Culbreth Drive
Seay, James L., Jr., (BV) .... '56 '82 C.575 B.A. L.1228 J.D. [Seay&A.]

Seay and Allen, Attorneys and Counselors at Law, (BV)
519 Market Street, 28401
Telephone: 910-763-2525 Fax: 910-251-7878
Members of Firm: James L. Seay, Jr.; Charlton Laramie Allen.
General Civil Practice. Trials in all State and Federal Courts. Corporation, Business Law, Insurance, Probate, Real Estate, Buying and Selling Homes, Criminal Defense, Traffic Violations, Driving While Intoxicated, Drug Crimes, Collections, Creditors Rights, Personal Injury, Automobile Accidents and Wrongful Death.
See Professional Biographies, WILMINGTON, NORTH CAROLINA

Shanklin, Kenneth A., (AV) .... '48 '73 C.34 B.A. L.575 J.D. [Shanklin&N.]

Shanklin & Nichols, LLP, (AV) [BB]
214 Market Street, P.O. Box 1347, 28402-1347
Telephone: 910-762-9400 Fax: 910-251-1773
Email: shanklaw@earthlink.net URL: http://www.shanklaw.com
Kenneth A. Shanklin; Matthew A. Nichols;—Stephanie L. Kimbro.
Trial Practice in all Courts. Corporation, Real Estate, Appeals, Utilities, Condominium, Construction, Bankruptcy, Insurance, Municipal, Probate, zoning, Land Use, Estate Planning, Environmental, Personal Injury, Leasing and Admiralty.
See Professional Biographies, WILMINGTON, NORTH CAROLINA

Sheffield, Wesley .... '78 '04 C.367 B.S.E.E. L.896 J.D. [[A] J.S.Price]
Shell, William R. .... '43 '73 C&L.575 A.B., J.D. [Hall&H.]
Sherman, Scott G., (BV) .... '63 '90 C.999 B.S. L.1345 J.D. 3965-B Market St.
Shipman, Gary K., (AV) .... '56 '80 C.953 B.A. L.1228 J.D. [Shipman,M.&W.]

Shipman, Mason & Wright, L.L.P., (AV) [BB]
11 South Fifth Avenue, 28401
Telephone: 910-762-1990; 800-762-1990 Fax: 910-762-6752
URL: http://www.shipmanlaw.com
Members: Gary K. Shipman; William Norton Mason; William G. Wright. Associates: Nicole Jo Moss; Brian Andrew Geschickter.
Focused Trial Practice in all Federal and State Courts. Complex Commercial Litigation, Product Liability, EIFS Litigation, Medical Devices, Medical Malpractice, Catastrophic Personal Injury and Wrongful Death, Nursing Home Litigation, Toxic Torts, Mold Litigation, Construction Litigation, and Consumer Class Actions.
See Professional Biographies, WILMINGTON, NORTH CAROLINA

Short, R. Jay, Jr., (BV) .... '69 '95 C.1128 B.A. L.896 J.D. [Fletcher R.&S.]
Siegel, Steven F., (BV) .... '43 '74 C&L.94 B.S., J.D. 1908 Eastwood Rd., Ste. 320
Simmons, Cameron D., (BV) .... '71 '99 C&L.923 B.S., J.D. [Cranfill,S.&H.]
Simmons, Karen L. '— '96 C.788 B.A. L.1048 J.D.
(adm. in MA; not adm. in NC) [[A] V.R.Hager]
Skinner, Christopher J. .... '80 '05 C.576 B.S. L.1228 J.D. [[A] Crossley M.P.&C.]
Slaughter, Martin T. .... '65 '93 C.575 B.A. L.838 J.D. [Baker&S.]
Slaughter, Nicole B., (BV) .... '— '94 C.1015 B.B.A. L.838 J.D. [Cranfill,S.&H.]
Slaughter, Robert C., III, (BV) .... '52 '79 C&L.893 B.A., J.D. P.O. Box 2693
Sloan, John Reeves, (BV) .... '— '90 C&L.575 A.B., J.D. [Ward&S.] (⊙New Bern)
Smerko, Mary Elizabeth, (BV) ..... '64 '90 C.575 A.B. L.1345 J.D. 105 Quail Ridge Road
Smith, Arnold .... '26 '66 4529 W. Cascade Rd.‡
Smith, James D., Attorney at Law, (BV) ..... '48 '73 C&L.575 A.B., J.D. 105 S. Front St.
Smith, Jason W. .... '74 '01 C.885 B.A. L.192 J.D. [[A] Webb&G.]
Smith, John W. .... '47 '72 C.198 B.A. L.896 J.D. Dist. J.
Smith, Louis B. .... '65 '90 C.1419 B.S. L.1228 J.D. 3965 Market St.
Smith, Tamara Avis .... '74 '01 C.438 B.A. L.192 J.D. [Pennington&S.]
Smith, W. G., (AV) .... '22 '50 C.896 A.B. L.575 LL.B. [Smith&S.]
Smith, Walter M., (BV) .... '54 '80 C.575 B.A. L.1228 J.D. [Smith&S.]

Smith Moore LLP, (AV)
300 North Third Street, Suite 301, 28401 ⊙
Telephone: 910-251-7001 Fax: 910-251-7007
Email: smith.moore@smithmoorelaw.com URL: http://www.smithmoorelaw.com
Partner: Michael V. Lee.
General, Trial and Appellate Practice in All State and Federal Courts, Dispute Resolution, Corporate, Taxation, Securities Regulation, Real Property and Finance, Labor and Employment (Management) Law, Employee Benefits, International and Immigration, Antitrust and Trade Regulation, Negligence, Products Liability, Insurance Coverage, Media, Banking, Commercial, Bankruptcy, Administrative, Environmental, Hospital and Health Care, Public Authority and Public Finance, Estate Planning and Administration, Probate, Legislative, Intellectual Property, Education, and Sports Law.
Greensboro, North Carolina Office: Wachovia Tower, 300 North Greene Street, Suite 1400, P.O. Box 21927. Telephone: 336-378-5200. Fax: 336-378-5400.
Raleigh, North Carolina Office: 2800 Two Hannover Square, P.O. Box 27525. Telephone: 919-755-8700. Fax: 919-755-8800.
Atlanta, Georgia Office: One Atlantic Center, Suite 3700, 1201 West Peachtree Street. Telephone: 404-962-1000. Fax: 404-962-1200.
See Professional Biographies, WILMINGTON, NORTH CAROLINA

Smith and Smith, (AV) .... 1 N. 3rd St.
Sneeden, David G., (BV) .... '51 '79 C.575 B.S. L.1228 J.D. 519 Market St.
Snell, John Jeremy .... '75 '00 C&L.45 B.S.B.A., J.D. P.O. Box 1288
Snow, James B., III, (BV) .... '56 '82 C.659 B.A. L.575 J.D. [Hogue,H.J.N.&L.]
Snyder, James W., Jr. .... '69 '95 C&L.953 B.A., J.D. 114 S. Front St.
Spivey, Jerry L., (BV) .... '42 '67 C&L.575 B.S., J.D. Dist. Atty.
Stephens, H. Kenneth, II, (BV) .... '56 '83 C.575 B.A. L.896 J.D. 701 Princess Street

Stevens, McGhee, Morgan, Lennon & Toll, L.L.P., (AV) [BB]
602 Market Street, P.O. Drawer 59, 28402
Telephone: 910-763-3666 Fax: 910-251-9562
Members of Firm: John A. Stevens (1895-1990); Karl W. McGhee (1923-1981); Richard M. Morgan; Alton Y. Lennon; Alan E. Toll; Mark F. Carter. Associate: Kurt B. Fryar.
General Practice, Trials in all State and Federal Courts, Commercial Litigation, Eminent Domain, Corporation, Real Estate, Probate, Land Use and Zoning, Insurance, and Utilities.
See Professional Biographies, WILMINGTON, NORTH CAROLINA

Stilley, Van A. '31 '63 C.597 B.S. L.569 J.D.
(adm. in NY; not adm. in NC) 3812 Sweetbriar Road‡
Stokes, Samantha K. .... '77 '03 C.924 B.S. L.896 J.D. [[A] B.J.Moore&Assoc.]
Stone, Russell D. .... '16 '40 L.228 LL.B. 454 Wayne Dr.‡
Stratas, Nicholas A., Jr., (AV) .... '57 '84 C.576 B.A. L.575 J.D. [Stratas&W.] ⊙
Stratas & Weathers, L.L.P., (AV) .... 1904 Eastwood Road, Suite 315 (⊙Raleigh)
Struthers, Caroline J. '49 '74 C.438 A.B. L.575 J.D.
Asst. Dist. Coun., U.S. Army Corps of Engrs.
Suggs, Bertha J. '47 '80 C.627 B.S. L.546 J.D.
(adm. in NE; not adm. in NC) Cesaw-Ir, 69 Darlington Avenue★
Sullivan, Barbara J. .... '48 '75 C.478 B.A. L.273 J.D. 107 S. Fourth St.‡
Sullivan, Dennis H., Jr., (BV) .... '68 '94 C.576 B.A. L.1228 J.D. [Sullivan]

Sullivan Law Firm, The, P.C., (BV)
29 North Third Street, 28401
Telephone: 910-362-1809 Fax: 910-362-9925
Email: sullivan-law@bizec.rr.com URL: http://www.sullivantriallaw.com
Dennis H. Sullivan, Jr. (Board Certified Specialist in State and Federal Criminal Law, North Carolina State Board of Legal Specialization).
Criminal Law, Criminal Defense, White Collar Crime, Fraud, DWI, Drug Crimes, Felonies and Misdemeanors, Homicide, Sexual Assault, Parole and Probation, Traffic Violations, Personal Injury, Automobile Accidents, Wrongful Death.
See Professional Biographies, WILMINGTON, NORTH CAROLINA

Sutton, Faison Gibson .... '78 '04 C.228 B.A. L.575 J.D. [[A] Murchison,T.&G.]
Swart, John P., (BV) .... '— '81 C.835 B.S. L.838 J.D. [Ward&S.] (⊙New Bern)
Tayloe, Ryal W., (AV) .... '— '82 C.575 A.B. L.896 J.D. [Ward&S.] (⊙New Bern)
Taylor, Joseph O., Jr., (AV) .... '46 '71 C&L.575 A.B., J.D. [Murchison,T.&G.]
Terrell, Mark T. .... '62 '90 C.240 B.A. L.574 J.D. 100-B Eastwood Rd.
Thaggard, Marlo L. .... '80 '05 C&L.1228 B.A., J.D. [[A] G.Jones&Assoc.]
Thompson, Matthew W. .... '— '04 C.205 B.A. L.945 J.D. [Ward&S.] (⊙New Bern)
Thompson, Miriam Mason, (BV) '69 '95 C&L.575 B.A., J.D.
314 Walnut Street, Suite C

Tighe, Charles M., (AVⓉ) '34 '60 C&L.309 A.B., J.D. [BB]
5725 Oleander Drive, Suite E-3, 28403
Telephone: 910-794-4444 Fax: 910-794-4244 URL: http://www.tighelex.com
URL: http://www.charlestighe.com
General Practice, Civil Trials in all Courts, Corporate, Business Law, Intellectual Property, Commercial and Construction Law, Employment Law Discrimination, Employee Benefits, Sexual Harassment, Wrongful Termination, Civil Rights Discrimination, Land Use, Zoning, and Environmental Law, Decedents Estates, Wills, and Estate Planning.
See Professional Biographies, WILMINGTON, NORTH CAROLINA

Tillery, John Gregory, III, (CV) ...'67 '94 C.575 B.A. L.273 J.D. [Cox&T.]
Tillery, L. Bradford ...'23 '50 C&L.575 B.S., LL.B. Supr. Ct. J.
Tisdale, Edwin J. ...'62 '92 C.1090 B.S. L.575 J.D. [E.J.Tisdale]

Tisdale, Edwin J., Attorney at Law PLLC
609-A Piner Road, P.O. Box 323, 28409
Telephone: 910-343-4992 Fax: 910-343-4101
Email: edtisdale@yahoo.com URL: http://www.edwintisdale.com
Edwin J. Tisdale.
Family Law, Divorce, Child Support, Business Law, Copyrights and Trademarks, Estate Planning, Trusts and Estates, Wills, Probate, Real Estate, Environmental Law.
See Professional Biographies, WILMINGTON, NORTH CAROLINA

Tise, Allan Brandon, (BV) ...'55 '86 C.232 B.A. L.896 J.D. 224 Colquitt Dr.
Toll, Alan E., (BV) ...'54 '84 C.575 B.A. L.896 J.D. [Stevens,M.M.L.&T.]
Toups, Benton L. ...'— '00 C&L.420 B.A., J.D. [A Hedrick E.G.&K.]
Toups, Regan S. ...'74 '00 C.576 B.S. L.420 J.D. [Cranfill,S.&H.]
Tramonte, Alice ...'57 '90 C.577 B.A. L.574 J.D. P.O. Box 12483
Trask, D. Webster, (BV) ...'53 '76 C.953 B.A. L.896 J.D. 1202 Eastwood Rd.
Trask, Frances Youngblood, (BV) '37 '83 C.896 B.S. L.575 J.D.
[A Murchison,T.&G.]
Trice, W. Berry, (BV) ...'60 '87 C.576 B.A. L.1228 J.D. [Murchison,T.&G.]
Trotman, William H. ...'49 '80 C.575 B.A. L.896 J.D. P.O. Box 352
Tucker, Elton G. ...'44 '73 C.576 B.S.Ch.E. L.896 J.D. Dist. J.
Turlington, David F., (CV) ...'68 '93 C&L.575 B.A., J.D. [A David&Assoc.]
Umbaugh, Jennifer L., (BV) ...'62 '90 C.953 B.A. L.574 J.D. 7232 Wrightsville Avenue
Ventriglia, Denis L. ...'55 '83 C.273 B.A. L.128 J.D. P.O. Box 11000
von Euler, Barbara ...'58 '85 C.951 B.A. L.93 J.D. 4644 Mockingbird Lane
Walen, David P. ...'52 '94 C.1333 B.S. L.1228 J.D. [D.P.Walen]
Walen, David P., P.A. ...1418 S. 42nd St.
Wall, James J., (BV) ...'45 '73 C.968 A.B. L.575 J.D. Mng Atty.
Wallace, James E. '16 '40 C&L.260 A.B., J.D.
(adm. in FL; not adm. in NC) 1816 Jumpin Run Dr.‡

Ward and Smith, P.A., (AV)
University Corporate Center, 127 Racine Drive, P.O. Box 7068, 28406-7068 ⊙
Telephone: 910-794-4800 Facsimile: 910-794-4877
Email: wardsmith@wardandsmith.com URL: http://www.wardandsmith.com
Adam M. Beaudoin; Jenna Fruechtenicht Butler; Alexander C. Dale; George K. Freeman, Jr.; Constantine C. Hingson; Thomas H. Johnson, Jr.; W. Daniel Martin, III; John Reeves Sloan (Board Certified Specialist in Estate Planning and Probate Law, North Carolina State Board of Legal Specialization); John P. Swart; Ryal W. Tayloe; Matthew W. Thompson; A. Rexford Willis, III.
General and Trial Practice. Admiralty Law; Bankruptcy; Banks and Banking; Business Law; Civil Rights; Commercial Law; Construction Law; Contracts; Copyrights; Corporate Law; Debtor and Creditor; Elder Law; Eminent Domain; Employee Benefits; Environmental Law; Family Law including Divorce; Finance; Franchise Law; Government; Government Contracts; Health Care Law; Immigration and Naturalization; Insurance; International Law; International Trade; Investments; Labor and Employment including Discrimination, Sexual Harassment, and Workers' Compensation; Landlord and Tenant; Litigation; Personal Injury including Automobile Accidents, Legal Malpractice and Medical Malpractice; Products Liability; Real Estate; Securities; Taxation; Technology and Science including Internet Law, Trademarks, and Patents; Trusts and Estates including Estate Planning and Wills and Probate; Zoning and Land Use.
Barnhill Contracting Company; Chubb Insurance; Daedong-USA, Inc.; First-Citizens Bank & Trust Company; First Flight Federal Credit Union; Fountain Powerboats, Inc.; NC State Firemen's Association; Potash Corp.; State of North Carolina; Weyerhaeuser Co.
New Bern, North Carolina Office: 1001 College Court. P.O. Box 867. Telephone: 252-672-5400. Facsimile: 252-672-5477.
Greenville, North Carolina Office: 120 West Fire Tower Road, P.O. Box 8088. Telephone: 252-215-4000. Facsimile: 252-215-4077.
Raleigh, North Carolina Office: Suite 2400, Two Hannover Square, Fayetteville Street Mall, P.O. Box 2091. Telephone: 919-836-4260. Facsimile: 919-836-4277.
See Professional Biographies, WILMINGTON, NORTH CAROLINA

Ward-Burns, Alpha ...'49 '74 C.575 B.A. L.692 J.D. 7000 W. Creek Edge Dr.‡
Warren, Maria C. ...'69 '96 C.575 B.A. L.608 J.D. P.O. Box 7503
Washburn, Jonathan W., (BV) ...'57 '82 C.198 B.A. L.575 J.D. [J.W.Washburn]
Washburn, Jonathan W., P.C., (BV) ...5006 Carleton Dr., Unit 34
Webb & Graves, P.L.L.C., (BV) ...5725 Oleander Drive, Suite C-3 (⊙Aberdeen)
Weber, Neil D. ...'59 '86 C.1317 B.A. L.575 J.D. 401 Chestnut St., Ste. K, Barrister Row
Wells, Heather ...'70 '98 C.911 B.A. L.228 J.D. [A E.L.West,III]
Wells & Blossom, (AV) ...1023 Birch Creek Dr.
Wertz, Mary E. ...'59 '88 C.945 B.A. L.575 J.D. 7209 Gray Gables‡
Wessell, John C., III, (AV) ...'46 '76 C.575 B.A. L.896 J.D. [Wessell&R.]

Wessell & Raney, L.L.P., (AV)
107-B North 2nd Street, P.O. Box 1049, 28402
Telephone: 910-762-7475 Facsimile: 910-762-7557
Email: wrlaw@bellsouth.net
Members of Firm: John C. Wessell, III; William A. Raney, Jr.
General Civil Practice in all Courts. Corporation, Real Estate, Probate, Municipal, Environmental, Commercial, Collection Law and Zoning, Planning and Land Use Law.
Approved Attorneys for: The Title Company of North Carolina, Inc.; Lawyers Title Insurance Corp.; Chicago Title Insurance Co.
Reference: Branch Banking and Trust Co.
See Professional Biographies, WILMINGTON, NORTH CAROLINA

West, Edwin L., III, (BV) ...'70 '95 C.301 B.A. L.896 J.D. [E.L.West,III]
West, Edwin L., III, PLLC, (BV) ...616 Market Street
Weyer, Tobias J. ...'— '05 C.896 B.A. L.128 J.D. [A Hedrick E.G.&K.]
White, Harold M., Jr. ...'49 '75 C.896 B.A. L.472 J.D. Gen. Coun.
White, Woody, (BV) ...'69 '94 C.999 B.A. L.546 J.D. [White&H.]

White & Hearne, L.L.P., (BV)
265 Racine Drive, Unit 104, 28403
Telephone: 910-313-3336 Toll Free: 800-807-4783 Facsimile: 910-798-9294 URL: http://www.woodywhite.com
URL: http://www.whiteandhearne.com
Woody White; Joseph C. Hearne, II.
General Practice in all Courts concentrating in Federal and State Criminal Law, Residential and Commercial Real Estate, Zoning and Land Use, DWI, Traffic Violations, Wills, Business Law, Misdemeanors, Felonies, Assaults, Personal Injury, Automobile Accidents, Wrongful Death, Medical Malpractice, Insurance and Civil Litigation.
See Professional Biographies, WILMINGTON, NORTH CAROLINA

Wilkins, Jerry L. ...'73 '00 C.575 B.A. L.1228 J.D. [A Patterson,D.C.B.&A.]
Wilkinson, Tracy W. ...'69 '01 C.577 B.A. L.801 J.D. [A Boyette]
Williams, Albert Jerome, Jr. '42 '78
C&L.575 B.A., J.D. Sr. App. Ref. & Spec. Dep. Comr., E.NC
Williams, Dolores M., (CV⑦) ...'51 '78 C&L.420 B.S., J.D. City Atty. Off.
Williams, James W., III, (CV) '64 '95 C.934 B.A. L.862 J.D.
Underwriting Coun., Chicago Title Insurance Co., CTIC-NC
Williams, Lonnie B., (AV) ...'28 '53 C&L.896 B.S., LL.B. [Marshall,W.&G.]
Williams, Lonnie B., Jr., (BV) ...'56 '81 C&L.896 B.A., J.D. [Marshall,W.&G.]
Willis, A. Rexford, III, (AV) ...'— '80 C&L.575 B.S., J.D. [Ward&S.] (⊙New Bern)
Wilson, Charleene ...'44 '75 C.228 B.A. L.276 J.D. 206 N. 4th St. Ste. 1
Wolak, William E., (BV) ...'46 '87 C.953 B.A. L.574 J.D. Asst. City Atty.

Woodell, Jerry C., (AV) ...'44 '73 C&L.575 B.A., J.D. [Marshall,W.&G.]
Woodruff, Ronald H., (AV) ...'52 '77 C.679 B.A. L.896 J.D. [Marshall,W.&G.]

Workers Compensation Law Firm, The, (BV)
508 Market Street, 28401 ⊙
Mailing Address: P.O. Box 7275, Wilmington, NC 28406
Telephone: 910-251-0004 Fax: 910-251-0005
Email: scriner@twclf.com URL: http://www.twclf.com
Mr. Sherman Lee Criner.
Workers Compensation, Alternative Dispute Resolution.
See Professional Biographies, WILMINGTON, NORTH CAROLINA

Worsley, Gerald Killian '34 '65 C.575 B.S. L.51 LL.B.
(adm. in GA; not adm. in NC) 3836 Echos Farms Blvd.‡
Wright, Ben ...'51 '83 C&L.575 A.B., J.D. 3224 Shadow Court
Wright, William G. ...'69 '99 C.953 B.A. L.1228 J.D. [Shipman,M.&W.]
Yazgi, Rogih '50 '77 C.197 B.A. L.309 J.D.
(adm. in NY; not adm. in NC) Chemtex Intl., Inc.
York, Cindy ...'61 '88 C&L.575 B.S., J.D. 2030 Eastwood Rd., Ste. 7
Yow, Lionel L., (BV) ...'43 '68 C.953 B.A. L.790 J.D. [⊠ Yow,F.&M.]

Yow, Fox & Mannen, L.L.P., (BV)
102 North Fifth Avenue, P.O. Drawer 479, 28401
Telephone: 910-762-2421 Fax: 910-251-9247
Members of Firm: Edgar L. Yow (1902-1983); Cicero P. Yow (1914-1990); William Allen Cobb (1917-1999); Douglas A. Fox; Jerry A. Mannen, Jr. Of Counsel: Lionel L. Yow.
General Civil and Criminal Trial Practice in all State and Federal Courts. Personal Injury, Automobile Accidents, Wrongful Death, Probate, Estate Planning, Administration, Corporation and Business Law, Real Estate Law, Buying or Selling a Home, Landlord and Tenant, Zoning and Land Use, Workers Compensation, Appellate Work, Commercial Litigation, Collections, Construction Law.
Representative Client: General Motors Acceptance Corp.
References: Central Carolina Bank; First Union National Bank; NCNB National Bank of North Carolina; Southern National Bank; United Carolina Bank.
See Professional Biographies, WILMINGTON, NORTH CAROLINA

Zalph, David A. '58 '83 C&L.228 B.S., J.D.
(adm. in DC; not adm. in NC) 4015 E. Bishop Ct.‡
Zimmer, Herbert J., (AV) ...'45 '70 C.228 B.A. L.30 J.D. [Zimmer&Z.]
Zimmer, Jeffrey Lee, (BV) ...'57 '80 C.1365 B.B.A. L.1228 J.D. [Zimmer&Z.]
Zimmer and Zimmer, L.L.P., (AV) ...111 Princess Street

WILSON, * 44,405, *Wilson Co.*

Abney, James W., III, (BV) ...'50 '72 C&L.575 B.A., J.D. 703 W. Nash St., Ste. E
Abrams, Bobby G., (BV) ...'40 '72 C.55 B.A. L.575 J.D. P.O. Box 876
Abrams, Stanley Glenn, (BV) ...'— '94 C.92 B.A. L.575 J.D. [A Connor,B.R.&W.]
Babb, Henry C., Jr., (AV) '44 '69 C&L.575 A.B., J.D.
Vice President, Secretary & General Counsel, Standard Commercial Corporation
Beaman, Stephen L., (AV) ...'47 '74 C.232 B.S. L.575 J.D. [S.L.Beaman]
Beaman, Stephen L., P.A., (AV) ...304 W. Nash St.
Blake, Marlene Dixon, (BV) ...'62 '90 C.576 B.A. L.1228 J.D. P.O. Box 485
Blake, Paul N., III, (BV) ...'60 '90 C.55 B.S. L.1228 J.D. [Rose R.]
Boyd, Andrew R. ...'72 '97 C.575 B.A. L.1228 J.D. 113 E. Nash St.
Boyd, W. Thomas, Jr., (BV) ...'49 '74 C&L.575 A.B., J.D. [W.T.Boyd,Jr.]

Boyd, W. Thomas, Jr., P.A., Law Offices of, (BV)
2536 Ward Boulevard, 27893
Mailing Address: P.O. Box 66, Wilson, NC 27894-0066
Telephone: 252-243-8400 Fax: 252-243-5017
Email: tom@boydlawfirm.com URL: http://www.wthomasboyd.com
W. Thomas Boyd, Jr.
Commercial Real Estate, Real Estate, Corporate Law, Business Law.
See Professional Biographies, WILSON, NORTH CAROLINA

Boyette, William H., (BV) ...'53 '80 C.576 B.S. L.1228 J.D. [A Connor,B.R.&W.]
Brown, Joseph E., III, (BV) ...'67 '93 C.575 B.S. L.574 J.D. [Sallenger&B.]
Bunn, Turner B., III, (AV) ...'40 '67 C&L.575 B.S., J.D. [Connor,B.R.&W.]

Caldwell, Derek R., P.A., Law Office of
(See Raleigh)

Cauley, James P., III, (AV) ...'59 '87 C&L.1228 B.B.A., J.D. [Rose R.]

Chichester & Walker
(See Roanoke Rapids)

Connor, Bunn, Rogerson & Woodard, P.L.L.C., (AV) ⊞
P.O. Box 3299, 27895-3299
Telephone: 252-243-3136 Fax: 252-243-8293; 252-243-2558
Email: kjr@nc.rr.com
Henry Groves Connor (1911-1989); David M. Connor (1935-1994); Turner B. Bunn, III; James F. Rogerson; David W. Woodard; L. Patrick Fleming, Jr.;—Stanley Glenn Abrams; William H. Boyette.
General Trial and Appellate Practice in all State and Federal Courts. Corporate, Business and Limited Liability Company Law. Federal, State and Local Taxation. Tax Exempt Financing. Probate and Estate Planning. Commercial and Business Litigation. Personal Injury. Commercial and Residential Real Estate. Family and Domestic Law. Zoning.
General Counsel for: The Wilson Daily Times, Inc.; New Hope Development Corp.; Bunn & Co.; Southern Piping Co.; Nash Realty Co.; Williamson Thermo King Dealerships, Inc.; Boone's Antiques, Inc.; Southern Testing & Research Laboratories, Inc.
See Professional Biographies, WILSON, NORTH CAROLINA

Cozart, William T., (BV) ...'40 '65 C&L.575 B.S., J.D. 605 West Nash Street
Eagles, Benjamin L. ...'70 '99 C.575 B.A. L.1345 J.D. [Narron&H.]
Echols, Stephen L. '42 '70 C.893 B.A. L.902 J.D.
(adm. in VA; not adm. in NC) V.P., Tr. Dept., Branch Banking & Tr. Co.
Ellis, Susan K., (BV) ...'58 '87 C.575 B.S. L.896 J.D. [A Rose R.]
Farris, Caroline Lee, (CV) ...'68 '94 C.575 B.A. L.1345 J.D. 108 E. Nash St.
Farris, Charles P., Jr., (BV) ...'47 '74 C&L.575 B.A., J.D. [Thomas&F.]
Farris, Robert A., Jr., (BV) ...'46 '71 C&L.575 A.B., J.D. 108 E. Nash St.
Farris, William C. ...'53 '78 C&L.575 A.B., J.D. Dist. J.
Farris, William M. J. ...'75 '01 C.575 L.574 J.D. 108 E. Nash St.
Fleming, L. Patrick, Jr., (BV) ...'55 '80 C.575 B.A. L.896 J.D. [Connor,B.R.&W.]
Gibbons, L. H., (AV) ...'21 '48 C&L.575 B.S., LL.B. 701 West Nash Street
Graves, Millicent G. ...'71 '97 C&L.574 B.S., J.D. 2500-B West Nash Street
Grode, Wendy Lynn ...'64 '90 C.228 B.A. L.575 J.D. Wilson Tech. Comm. Coll.
Harrison, Reginald W., Jr., (AV) ...'42 '67 C&L.575 A.B., J.D. [Narron&H.]

Hill, William F., P.A.
(See Greenville)

Hinson, Walter L., (AV) ...'47 '73 C.232 B.S. L.896 J.D. [Hinson&R.]

Hinson & Rhyne, P.A., (AV)
2401-G Wooten Boulevard, P.O. Box 7479, 27895-7479
Telephone: 252-291-1746 Facsimile: 252-291-2521 Email: walterhinson@nc.rr.com
Email: johnrhyne@nc.rr.com
Walter L. Hinson (Board Certified Specialist in Bankruptcy Law, North Carolina State Board of Legal Specialization); John G. Rhyne.
Bankruptcy and Debtor Creditor Rights Law, Corporate Law, Uniform Commercial Code Law, Agribusiness Law, Civil Litigation, Perishable Agricultural Commodities Act Claims.
See Professional Biographies, WILSON, NORTH CAROLINA

Holdford, William H., (AV) .... '32 '60 C&L.575 B.A., LL.B. [Narron&H.]
Hughes, Randell, (BV) ....'50 '79 C.232 B.S.B.A. L.1228 J.D. 605 West Nash Street
Ivey, Ivan Joe, (AV) ....'51 '77 C&L.575 A.B., J.D. [Narron&H.]
James, David E. .... '47 '71 C&L.896 B.B.A., J.D. Pres., James Properties, Inc.
Jones, T. Douglass, III, (AV) ....'52 '78 C.301 B.A. L.575 J.D. 701 West Nash Street
Josephs, Ernest H., Jr. ....'43 '80 C.232 B.A. L.1345 J.D. Co. Ct.
Keller, John R. ....'61 '87 C.951 B.A. L.228 J.D. Eastern Carolina Legal Servs.
Kuhn, William O. ....'29 '57 C&L.575 A.B., LL.B. P.O. Box 2030
Lane, Wiley L., Jr., (BV) ....'19 '42 C&L.896 B.S., J.D. 203 E. Nash St.
Lee, Cyrus F., (AV) ....'17 '46 C.999 A.B. L.575 J.D. Wilson County Office Bldg.
Leonard, J. Rich ....'49 '76 C.575 A.B. L.976 J.D. U.S. Bkrptcy. J.

LeonLaw Firm, The
(See Greenville)

Lynch, Marjorie K. .... '61 '86 C.575 B.A. L.273 J.D. bkrptcy. Admn.
Morrison, B. Perry, Jr., (AV) ....'62 '89 C&L.575 A.B., J.D. [Morrison]

Morrison Law Firm, P.L.L.C., (AV)
4612 W. Nash Street, 27894-2046
Mailing Address: P.O. Box 2046, Wilson, NC 27894
Telephone: 252-243-1003 Fax: 252-243-1004
Email: pmorrison@nccomplaw.com URL: http://www.nccomplaw.com
B. Perry Morrison, Jr.
Litigation, Collections, Workers Compensation, Personal Injury Law, Creditor Rights and Bankruptcy.
See Professional Biographies, WILSON, NORTH CAROLINA

Murphy, Michael P., P.A.
(See Rocky Mount)

Narron & Holdford, P.A., (AV)
204 North Tarboro Street, P.O. Drawer 279, 27894-0279
Telephone: 252-237-3153 Telecopier: 252-243-1733
Talmadge L. Narron (1925-1976); William H. Holdford; Reginald W. Harrison, Jr. (Board Certified Specialist in Real Property Law - Residential Transactions); Thomas J. Rhodes; C. David Williams, Jr.; Ivan Joe Ivey; William L. O'Quinn, Jr.; Benjamin L. Eagles;—Thomas J. Rhodes, Jr.; Jonathan M. Vanden Bosch.
Civil and Criminal Trial and Appellate Practice. Personal Injury, Wrongful Death, Products Liability, Professional Liability, Construction Law, Business, Commercial and Corporate Law, Individual and Corporate Taxation, Limited Liability Companies and Partnerships, Employment Law, Tax Exempt Organizations, Estate Planning and Administration, Real Estate, Land Use and Zoning, Family Law, Creditor Rights and Bankruptcy.
Representative Clients: NationsBank, N.A.; Wachovia Bank & Trust Co., N.A.; Parkwood Development Co.; Imperial Tobacco Leaf Services, Inc.; Standard Commercial Corp.; Thompson Plumbing, Inc.; S.T. Wooten Corp.
Approved Attorneys for: Lawyers Title Insurance Corp.; Farmers Home Administration.
See Professional Biographies, WILSON, NORTH CAROLINA

Newton, Eldon Sharpe, III .... '68 '99 C.34 B.S. L.1345 J.D. P.O. Box 2047

O'Garro-Moore Law Office
(See Rocky Mount)

O'Quinn, William L., Jr., (BV) ....'68 '94 C.228 A.B. L.575 J.D. [Narron&H.]
Orcutt, David S., (AV) ....'42 '67 C&L.575 B.S., J.D. P.O. Box 8009
Orndorff, Terry S., (BV) ....'63 '94 C.999 B.S. L.1345 J.D. 5100 Country Club Dr. N.
Osborn, Preston, (CVⓉ) ....'64 '90 C.210 B.A. L.245 J.D. 1107 Kingswood Road
Page, Jason R. ....'73 '05 C.576 B.S. L.1228 J.D. [Ⓐ Rose R.]
Peavey, Michael P., (BV) .... '46 '74 C.152 B.A. L.228 J.D. [M.P.Peavey]
Peavey, Michael P., P.A., (BV) ....404 Broad St. W
Pridgen, J. Brian ....'77 '03 C&L.575 B.A., J.D. [Ⓐ Rose R.]
Quiett, Valerie M. ....'64 '95 C.1378 B.S. L.574 J.D. 409 N. Goldsboro St.
Quinn, Caroline F., (CV) ....'68 '94 C.575 B.A. L.1345 J.D. 108 E. Nash St.
Quinn, Joseph N., Jr., (CV) ....'69 '95 C.575 B.A. L.1345 J.D. 108 E. Nash St.
Rand, T. Slade, Jr., (CV) ....'61 '98 C.1128 B.A. L.1345 J.D. [Rose R.]
Rand, William R., (AV) ....'36 '63 [Rose R.] ‡
Rhodes, Thomas J., (AV) ....'47 '73 C&L.575 B.A., J.D. [Narron&H.]
Rhodes, Thomas J., Jr., (AV) ....'72 '97 C&L.896 B.S., J.D. [Ⓐ Narron&H.]
Rhyne, John G., (BV) ....'64 '90 C.216 B.A. L.896 J.D. [Hinson&R.]
Rogerson, James F., (AV) ....'45 '73 C&L.575 B.A., J.D. [Connor,B.R.&W.]

Rose Rand Attorneys, P.A., (AV)
2500 West Nash Street, Unit C, P.O. Drawer 2367, 27894-2367 ⊙
Telephone: 252-291-3848 Telecopier: 252-291-9555
William A. Lucas (1881-1967); Oliver G. Rand (1895-1967); Naomi E. Morris (1921-1986); Z. Hardy Rose (1913-1999); William R. Rand (Retired); James P. Cauley, III; Paul N. Blake, III; T. Slade Rand, Jr.;—Susan K. Ellis; J. Yancey Washington; J. Brian Pridgen; Jason R. Page.
General Practice, all Courts. Corporation, Labor and Insurance Law. Trials, including Personal Injury, Wrongful Death and Workers Compensation, Eminent Domain, Tax, Estate Planning and Administration, Municipal, Environmental, Real Estate, Bankruptcy.
Representative Clients: Progress Energy, Inc.; City of Wilson; Town of Hookerton; Town of Scotland Neck; Upper Coastal Plain Council of Governments; Barton College; Wilson-Green Mental Health Association; International Paper Co.; Global TransPark Development Commission; Paxton Bonded Storage, Inc.
Raleigh, North Carolina Office: Corporate Plaza Building, Suite 1508 333 Fayetteville Street, 27601. Telephone: 919-832-4040. Fax: 919-832-4050.
See Professional Biographies, WILSON, NORTH CAROLINA

Ruch, Cheri J. .... '61 '90 C.1090 B.S. L.1194 J.D. U.S. Bkrptcy. Admr. Off.
Sallenger, Thomas R., (AV) ....'55 '83 C.232 B.S.B.A. L.575 J.D. [Sallenger&B.]
Sallenger & Brown, LLP, (AV) ....701 West Nash Street
Schmidt, Kurt D., (BV) .... '64 '90 C.576 B.A. L.1345 J.D. [Thomas&F.]
Smith, Eliot F., (BV) .... '61 '93 C.228 B.A. L.1345 J.D. [Thomas&F.]
Smith, Page Thomas, (BV) ....'64 '92 C.575 B.S. L.1345 J.D. [Thomas&F.]
Stewart, William G., (BV) ....'49 '78 C&L.575 A.B., J.D. Asst. Dist. Atty.
Stronach, George T., III ....'40 '67 C.55 B.A. L.228 LL.B. P.O. Box 443
Taylor, W. Earl, Jr., (BV) .... '59 '86 C.232 B.S. L.575 J.D. [Taylor]
Taylor Law Office, (BV) .... 605 West Nash Street
Thomas, Albert S., Jr. ....'49 '75 C&L.575 A.B., J.D. Dist. J.
Thomas, Allen G., (AV) ....'37 '63 C&L.575 A.B., LL.B. [Thomas&F.]
Thomas, Tartt B., (BV) ....'68 '97 C.575 B.S. L.1345 J.D. [Ⓐ Thomas&F.]
Thomas & Farris, P.A., (AV) .... 104 West Nash Street
Vanden Bosch, Jonathan M. ....'74 '99 C.575 B.A. L.228 J.D. [Ⓐ Narron&H.]

Wallace, Morris, Barwick, Landis & Stroud, P.A.
(See Kinston)

Walter, Lisa M. '74 '05 C.604 B.A. L.228 J.D.
Staff Atty., Legal Aid of North Carolina- Wilson
Washington, J. Yancey ....'76 '01 C.301 B.A. L.1228 J.D. [Ⓐ Rose R.] ⊙
Watson, Dovey E., Jr. ....'51 '78 C.575 B.A. L.896 J.D. 1007 Branch St.

Weaver, George A., (AV) '39 '64 C&L.575 A.B., J.D.
113 East Nash Street, Suite 404, 27893
Telephone: 252-291-7232 Fax: 252-291-1442
Email: gweaver@wilson-co.com
Real Estate, Decedent's Estates/Probate, Wills, Business Law, Corporations, Civil Litigation, Family Law.

(This Listing Continued)

Weaver, George A. (Continued)
Representative Clients: Wilson County; Barnes Motor & Parts Company; Town of Elm City; Town of Black Creek; Town of Lucama.

White, Bobby D. .... '57 '97 C.999 B.A. L.574 J.D. Barton Coll.
Whitley, Andrew J. ....'69 '99 C.577 B.A. L.574 J.D [Ⓐ Taylor]
Whitley, John L. ....'33 '62 C&L.575 A.B., J.D. Dist. J.
Williams, C. David, Jr., (BV) ....'47 '71 C.48 B.A. L.575 J.D. [Narron&H.]
Williams, Julie Turner, (BV) ....'64 '89 C.575 B.S.Ed. L.1228 J.D. [Thomas&F.]
Woodard, David W., (AV) ....'49 '76 C&L.575 B.A., J.D. [Connor,B.R.&W.]

WINDSOR, * 2,283, *Bertie Co.*

Burch, Stephen R., (AV) ....'39 '63 C&L.575 A.B., J.D. [Pritchett&B.] ‡
Cooke, William L., (AV) ....'25 '50 C&L.575 A.B., J.D. 211 W. Gray St.‡
Gillam, M. Braxton, III, (BV) ....'52 '84 C.575 B.A. L.1228 J.D. [Gillam&G.]
Gillam, Moses B., Jr., (AV) ....'16 '39 C&L.575 A.B., J.D. [Gillam&G.]

Gillam and Gillam, (AV)
201 Dundee Street, P.O. Box 547, 27983
Telephone: 252-794-2233 Fax: 252-794-5007
Email: gillamandgillam@coastalnet.com
Members of Firm: Sarah Starr Gillam (1912-1996); Moses B. Gillam, Jr.; M. Braxton Gillam, III.
General Civil and Criminal Practice. Probate, Real Estate and Corporation Law. Trials.
References: Southern Bank & Trust Co.; Wachovia.
See Professional Biographies, WINDSOR, NORTH CAROLINA

Huddleston, Jonathan E., (BV) ....'68 '94 C.880 B.S. L.896 J.D. [Pritchett&B.]
Missé, Maria ....'57 '95 C.728 B.A. L.831 J.D. [Ⓐ Pritchett&B.]
Pritchett & Burch, PLLC, (AV) ....203 Dundee Street
Ruffin, Tonza Demetria ....'71 '00 C.232 B.A. L.1059 J.D. P.O. Box 602
Simonsen, Lars P., (BV) ....'65 '90 C&L.953 B.A., J.D. [Pritchett&B.]
Skinner, Melissa L., (CV) ....'68 '93 C.575 B.A. L.500 J.D. [Pritchett&B.]
Smallwood, Teresa L., (CV) ....'59 '86 C.575 B.A. L.574 J.D. 117 N. King St.
Smith, Lloyd C., Jr., (AV) ....'50 '75 C&L.575 B.A., J.D. [Pritchett&B.]

Willey, Ralph G., P.A.
(See Rocky Mount)

WINSTON-SALEM, * 185,776, *Forsyth Co.*

Ackenbom-Kelly, Beatrice L., (BV) ....'40 '86 C.924 B.A. L.896 J.D. 4240 Bower Ln.
Adams, Alfred G., (AV) ....'42 '73 C&L.896 B.A., J.D. [Womble C.S.&R.]
Adams, Jean Taylor, (AV) ....'50 '85 C&L.228 B.A., J.D. [Womble C.S.&R.]
Adams, Reid C., Jr., (AV) ....'56 '81 C&L.896 B.A., J.D. [Womble C.S.&R.]
Addison, Robert Martin ....'68 '98 C.1185 B.S. L.896 J.D. [Craige B.L.&W.]
Aderhold, Mark T. ....'69 '96 C.575 B.A. L.1345 J.D. [Meadows&A.]
Alemanni, John C. ....'— '96 C.577 B.S. L.896 J.D. [Ⓐ Kilpatrick S.] (Pat.)
Alexander, Abner ....'29 '57 C.296 A.B. L.896 LL.B. Ret. Chf. Dist. J.
Alexander, Charles J., II, (AV) ....'46 '72 C&L.896 B.A., J.D. [Morrow A.&P.]
Alexander, Shonna Renee ....'74 '99 C.896 B.A. L.574 J.D. 2131 Hollyrood St.
Allen, Patrick M. ....'69 '93 C.228 B.A. L.575 J.D. [Womble C.S.&R.]
Allman, C. Edwin, III, (AV) ....'53 '79 C.1128 B.A. L.896 J.D. [Allman S.L.&C.]
Allman, M. Joseph, (AV) .... '60 '86 C&L.896 B.A., J.D. [Allman S.L.&C.]

Allman Spry Leggett & Crumpler, P.A., (AV)
Suite 700, 380 Knollwood Street, Drawer 5129, 27113-5129
Telephone: 336-722-2300 Telecopier: 336-721-0414
C. Edwin Allman (1926-1991); W. Dennie Spry (1912-2000); R. Bradford Leggett; Donald M. VonCannon (Board Certified Specialist in Real Property Law-Residential, Business, Commercial, and Industrial Transactions, North Carolina State Board of Legal Specialization); C. Edwin Allman, III (Board Certified Specialist in Bankruptcy Law, North Carolina State Board of Legal Specialization); Thomas T. Crumpler; Edward E. Raymer, Jr. (Board Certified Specialist in Estate Planning and Probate Law, North Carolina State Bar Board of Legal Specialization); M. Joseph Allman; Walter R. Hinnant; George T. "Ted" Mann; Scott Thomas Horn; Jeffrey B. Watson; Heather J. Bowen; Karen B. Malay; Karen H. Chapman.
General Civil Practice, Litigation in all State and Federal Courts. Tax, Probate, Trust, Estate Planning, Corporation, Partnership, Bankruptcy and Creditors Rights, Real Estate, Securities and Insurance Law.
Representative Clients: Highwoods Properties, Inc.; Krispy Kreme Doughnut Corporation; Malayan United Industries Behrad; Laura Ashley, Inc.; The Shelton Companies; Forsyth Technical Community College; Re: Source NC, SC, & GA; Bob Neill Pontiac, Inc.; Sara Lee Credit Union; Piedmont Aviation Credit Union.
See Professional Biographies, WINSTON-SALEM, NORTH CAROLINA

Allred, Amy Elizabeth ....'73 '99 C.575 B.S. L.862 J.D. [A.Allred]
Allred, Amy, P.C. ....1416 W. First St., Ste. B
Alston, Reginald D. ....'66 '97 C.1378 B.S. L.896 J.D. 8 W. Third St., Ste. 260
Anderson, Carol Boyles, (AV) '53 '81
C&L.228 B.A., J.D. Clinical Prof. of Law, Wake Forest Univ.

Anderson Korzen & Associates, P.C.
(See Kernersville)

Anthony, Daniel B., (CV) ....'— '94 C.473 B.A. L.575 J.D. [D.B.Anthony]

Anthony, Daniel B., PC, The Law Practice of, (CV)
1416 W. 4th Street, Suite B, 27101
Mailing Address: P.O. Box 20517, Winston-Salem, NC 27120-0517
Telephone: 336-917-0037 Fax: 336-917-0038
Email: daniel-b-anthony@bellsouth.net URL: http://www.dananthonylaw.com
Daniel B. Anthony.
Workers Compensation, Personal Injury, Criminal Defense, Disability Claims, Civil Litigation.
See Professional Biographies, WINSTON-SALEM, NORTH CAROLINA

Archenbronn, Michael ....'60 '90 C.259 B.S. L.896 J.D. 300 S. Main Street
Archer, David T., (AV) '64 '90
C.198 B.A. L.790 J.D. U.S. Treas. Dept., Estate & Gift Tax Atty.
Archer, Julia C., (BV) ....'66 '92 C.198 B.A. L.790 J.D. [Enns&A.]
Arias, Elizabeth K. ....'74 '00 C.575 B.A. L.1228 J.D. [Ⓐ Womble C.S.&R.]
Armentrout, James W., (AV) '44 '69
C.945 A.B. L.893 LL.B. Pres. & Gen. Coun., Ramey, Inc.
Armstrong, J. Douglas, (BV) '66 '93
C.999 B.S. L.896 J.D. Staff Atty., Legal Aid Soc. NW NC

Arneke, Gail C., (BV) '50 '75 C.228 B.A. L.575 J.D.
301 N. Main Street, Suite 2455, 27101
Telephone: 336-760-1434 Fax: 336-760-6149
Email: garneke@garneke.com URL: http://www.newsouthlaw.net
Bankruptcy, Consumer Bankruptcy, Business Bankruptcy, Foreclosures.
See Professional Biographies, WINSTON-SALEM, NORTH CAROLINA

Arnelle, H. Jesse, (AVⓉ) '33 '68 C.645 B.A. L.1017 LL.B.
(adm. in PA; not adm. in NC) [© Womble C.S.&R.]
Arundale, Matthew F. ....'77 '04 C.999 B.A. L.896 J.D. [Ⓐ Bell,D.&P.]
Ashe-Card, Alison Y. ....'67 '92 C.811 B.A. L.904 J.D. [Ⓐ Womble C.S.&R.]
Ashford, Kenneth R. ....'62 '94 C.860 B.A.B.S. L.569 J.D. [Ⓐ Womble C.S.&R.]
Atkinson, Mark T. ....'70 '98 C.575 B.S.B.A. L.896 J.D. 1416 W. First St.

Atkinson, Nathan B. ....'75 '01 C.896 B.A. L.469 J.D. [Ⓐ Blanco T.C.&M.]
Avram, Gabriel A., (AV) ....'32 '59 C.390 B.A. L.188 LL.B. [Finger,P.A.&R.]
Babb, R. Kenneth, (BV) ....'41 '67 C.838 B.S. L.575 J.D. 315 N. Spruce St.
Babcock, John W., (AV) ....'59 '86 C.477 B.S.A. L.896 J.D. [Bell,D.&P.]
Babcock, Jolinda J., (BV) ....'67 '92 C.754 B.S. L.575 J.D. [Robinson&L.]
Badgett, Richard G., (AV) ....'27 '59 C.576 L.575 LL.B. 200 West First Street
Bailey, David W., Jr., (AV) ....'57 '82 C.228 B.A. L.575 J.D. [Bailey&T.]
Bailey, J. Dennis, (AV) ....'60 '85 C.240 B.A. L.896 J.D. [Carruthers&B.]
Bailey, Stacey D. ....'70 '01 C.893 B.A. L.896 J.D. [Ⓐ Pharr&B.]
Bailey, Wesley, (AV) ....'31 '55 C&L.896 B.S., LL.B. [Bailey&T.]

Bailey & Thomas, P.A., (AV)
3069 Trenwest Drive, Suite 100, P.O. Box 52, 27102-0052
Telephone: 336-725-8366 Fax: 336-725-9206
Email: bailey1law@aol.com
Wesley Bailey; George S. Thomas; David W. Bailey, Jr.; John R. Fonda.
General Civil and Criminal Practice. Trials in all State and Federal Courts. Probate, Real Estate and Property Law. Wills, Trust and Estate Planning, Corporation, Insurance Law and Personal Injury Law.
Representative Client: Yarbrough Transfer Co.
Approved Attorneys for: Southern National Bank; Piedmont Federal Savings & Loan Association.
See Professional Biographies, WINSTON-SALEM, NORTH CAROLINA

Baker, Brian T. ....'75 '00 C&L.896 B.A., J.D. [Ⓐ Comerford&B.]
Baker, Crystal B. ....'74 '02 C&L.896 B.A., J.D. [Ⓐ Nelson M.R.&S.]
Baldwin, Janice C., (AV) ....'60 '85 C.1369 B.A. L.896 J.D. [Womble C.S.&R.]
Barber, John L., (AV) ....'46 '72 C.575 B.A. L.896 J.D. [Wells,J.L.&J.P.]
Barnes, David S. '52 '78 C.228 B.A. L.862 J.D.
(adm. in OK; not adm. in NC)
Sr. V.P. & Assoc. Gen. Coun., Branch Banking and Trust Company
Barnette, Carolyn Reid ....'60 '86 C.575 B.A. L.896 J.D. Integon Corp.
Barnhill, H. Grady, Jr., (AV) ....'30 '58 C.55 L.896 LL.B. [Womble C.S.&R.]
Barnhill, Jimmy H., (AV) ....'40 '65 C&L.896 A.B., LL.B. [Womble C.S.&R.]
Baron, Elizabeth A. ....'65 '96 C.918 B.A. L.575 J.D. Legal Aid Soc. NW NC
Barrett, C. Daniel, (AV) ....'— '85 C&L.896 J.D. 150 S. Stratford Rd., Ste. 340
Barrett, William Thomas '52 '76 C&L.902 B.A., J.D.
(adm. in DE; not adm. in NC) Wake Forest Univ. Sch. of Law
Beach, Shannon Warf, (BV) ....'66 '92 C.290 B.S. L.1228 J.D. [Davis&H.]
Beal, Christopher L., (BV) ....'53 '82 C&L.1228 B.S., J.D. [Metcalf&B.]
Beamguard, Nathan D. ....'72 '97 C.269 B.A. L.896 J.D. Law Clk., Dist. Ct.
Beaty, James A., Jr. ....'49 '74 C.925 B.A. L.575 J.D. U.S. Dist. J.
Beck, Lori Herndon '65 '90 C.1377 B.A. L.469 J.D.
(adm. in GA; not adm. in NC)
Asst. Gen. Coun. & V.P., Branch Banking and Trust Company
Becker, Joshua E. T. ......'73 '01 C.338 B.S. L.146 J.D. 370 Knollwood Street, Suite 310
Bedsworth, George A., (BV) ....'48 '78 C.232 B.A. L.896 J.D. 415 N. Trade St.
Beechler, Christopher A. ....'72 '01 C.152 B.A. L.896 J.D. [C.A.Beechler]
Beechler, Christopher A., P.C., Law Offices of ....200 Brookstown Avenue, Suite 304
Behan, Austin C., (BV) ....'45 '84 C.651 B.S. L.896 J.D. 415 N. Trade St.
Behan, Mary Jean, (BV) ....'51 '77 Asst. Dist. Atty.
Bell, Frank M., Jr., (AV) ....'37 '63 C.228 B.A. L.575 LL.B. [Bell,D.&P.]
Bell, George M., II ....'39 '66 C&L.896 B.A., LL.B. Vet. Admn.
Bell, Ranlet S., (AV) ....'48 '89 C.881 A.B. L.896 J.D. [Ⓖ Womble C.S.&R.]
Bell, Richard G. ....'28 '51 C.383 A.B. L.930 J.D. 104 Belle Vista Court‡

Bell, Davis & Pitt, P.A., (AV) BB
Century Plaza, Suite 600, 100 North Cherry Street, 27101 ⊙
Mailing Address: P.O. Box 21029, Winston-Salem, NC 27120
Telephone: 336-722-3700 Fax: 336-748-5890
URL: http://www.belldavispitt.com
William D. Harper (1943-1995); Frank M. Bell, Jr.; William K. Davis; Walter W. Pitt, Jr.; James R. Fox; Stephen M. Russell; D. Anderson Carmen; John W. Babcock; Stephen D. Poe; Amy K. Smith; Charlot F. Wood; Elizabeth M. Repetti; Alan M. Ruley; Mallory M. Oldham; Robin J. Stinson (Board Certified Specialist in Family Law, North Carolina State Board of Legal Specialization); John A. Cocklereece, Jr.; Daniel C. Bruton; G. Emmett McCall; Donald M. Nielsen; Kevin G. Williams; Anne H. Shelburne;—Galen G. Craun, III; Jenna B. Thomas; Daniel P. Quesnel; Jennifer I. Oakes; Bradley C. Friesen; Alexander P. Ryan; Monica R. Guy; Edward B. Davis (Resident, Charlotte Office); Matthew F. Arundale; Michael D. Phillips. Of Counsel: James T. Lambie.
General Practice in State and Federal Court Trials. Banking and Commercial Law. Corporation and Labor Law, Federal, State and Local Taxation, Estate Planning, Probate and Real Estate Law.
Charlotte, North Carolina Office: Carillon Building, Suite 2160, 227 West Trade Street, 28202. Telephone: 704-227-0400. Fax: 704-227-0178.
See Professional Biographies, WINSTON-SALEM, NORTH CAROLINA

Bennett, Joshua H. ....'77 '04 C.198 B.A. L.577 J.D. [Bennett&G.P.]
Bennett, Richard V., (AV) ....'45 '74 C&L.896 B.A., J.D. [Bennett&G.P.]

Bennett & Guthrie PLLC, (AV) BB
1560 Westbrook Plaza Drive, 27103-1328
Telephone: 336-765-3121 Fax: 336-765-8622
URL: http://www.bennett-guthrie.com
Richard V. Bennett; Rodney A. Guthrie; Franklin Scott Templeton; Roberta B. King; Joshua H. Bennett.
Civil Litigation in State and Federal Courts, Medical Malpractice (Defense), Employment Law, Personal Injury, Construction Litigation, Commercial Litigation, Insurance Defense, Business Law.
Representative Clients: American Home Assurance Company; GMAC Insurance; St. Paul Fire and Marine Insurance Co.; Novant Health, Inc.; Royal Sun Alliance; Mag Mutual Insurance Co.; State Farm Ins. Co.; Farmers Insurance Group; N.C. Farm Bureau Insurance Companies; U.S. Liability Group.
See Professional Biographies, WINSTON-SALEM, NORTH CAROLINA

Bennette, Tiffany Kay ....'75 '00 C.347 B.A. L.896 J.D. Dist. Atty's. Off.

Benson & Marshall, L.L.P.
(See Greensboro)

Berlin, Stephen R., (AV) ....'— '84 C&L.896 B.A., J.D. [Kilpatrick S.]
Beron, Celeste, (BV) ....'46 '80 C.569 B.S. L.818 J.D. [Beron]
Beron Firm, The, (BV) ....1261 North Peace Haven Road
Berry, John E., Jr. '50 '89
C.446 B.S. L.1218 J.D. Off. of Reg. Coun., Dept. of Vet. Affairs
Besse, Daniel V. ....'54 '80 C&L.575 B.A., J.D. P.O. Box 15306
Biggs, Loretta C. ....'54 '79 C.811 B.A. L.329 J.D. [Davis&H.]
Billings, Rhoda B. ....'37 '66 C.77 A.B. L.896 J.D. Wake Forest Univ.
Bircher, Amy L. ....'62 '95 C.1128 B.S. L.896 J.D. [Womble C.S.&R.]
Bissette, Thomas A. ....'72 '97 C&L.896 B.A., J.D. [Ⓐ Womble C.S.&R.]
Blancato, William A., (AV) ....'57 '83 C.994 B.A. L.228 J.D. [Blancato,D.&H.]

Blancato, Doughton & Hart, PLLC, (AV) BB
Suite 150, 633 West Fourth Street, 27101
Telephone: 336-725-9416 Fax: 336-725-5129
William A. Blancato; Thomas J. Doughton; Andrew D. Hart.
General Civil Practice. Corporate and Limited Liability Company Law, Real Estate, Wills, Estates and Probate, Commercial and Business Transactions, Litigation (Trials and Appeals in State and Federal Court), Insurance, Professional Liability, Governmental Liability, Construction Law, Mediation, Arbitration.

(This Listing Continued)

Blancato, Doughton & Hart, PLLC (Continued)
References: RBC Centura Bank; Chicago Title Insurance Co.; Lawyers Title Insurance Corp.
See Professional Biographies, WINSTON-SALEM, NORTH CAROLINA

Blanco, David B., (AV) ....'41 '66 C&L.228 A.B., LL.B. [Blanco T.C.&M.]

Blanco Tackabery Combs & Matamoros, P.A., (AV) BB
110 South Stratford Road, 5th Floor, P.O. Drawer 25008, 27114-5008
Telephone: 336-293-9000 Facsimile: 336-293-9030
URL: http://www.btcmlaw.com
David B. Blanco; Neal E. Tackabery; Reginald F. Combs; Ronald A. Matamoros; Gene B. Tarr; Steven C. Garland; Peter J. Juran; Brian L. Herndon; Bowen C. Houff; George E. Hollodick; Charles D. Luckey; Mary Margaret Ogburn; Jeffrey D. Patton; Deborah L. McKenney; Ashley S. Rusher;—Stephen C. Minnich; James E. Creamer, Jr.; Carolyn W. Scogin; Nathan B. Atkinson; Jeanette M. Stark; Amy C. Lanning; Melynda G. Broomfield; Linda L. McCarty; Susan M. Clapp.
General, Trial and Appellate Practice in all State and Federal Courts. Corporation, Partnership, Taxation, Commercial, Real Estate, Probate, Securities, Intellectual Property Registration, Intellectual Property Licensing, Intellectual Property Protection, Employment, Environmental, Bankruptcy and White Collar Crime.
References: Branch Banking and Trust Company, Winston-Salem, North Carolina; Allegacy Federal Credit Union, Winston-Salem, North Carolina; Southern Community Bank and Trust, Winston-Salem, North Carolina.
See Professional Biographies, WINSTON-SALEM, NORTH CAROLINA

Blixt, Charles A., (AV) '51 '77 C&L.339 B.S., J.D.
Exec. V.P. & Gen. Coun., R.J. Reynolds Tobacco Co.
Blynn, Guy M. '45 '71 C.659 B.S. L.309 J.D.
V.P. & Dep. Gen. Coun., R.J. Reynolds Tobacco Co.
Boggs, James M. ....'— '99 C.160 B.S. L.1218 J.D. [Ⓐ Kilpatrick S.]
Bomar, J. Chad, (BV) ....'75 '99 C.999 B.S. L.1228 J.D. [Ⓐ Wilson&I.]
Booker, Keith C. ....'72 '96 C.945 B.A. L.896 J.D. 1001 W. 4th St.
Booth, Samuel M., (AV) ....'36 '61 C&L.575 B.S., LL.B. [Frye&B.]
Borschke, August J. '54 '82 C.031 B.S. L.213 J.D.
(adm. in MI; not adm. in NC; Pat.) Sr. Coun., R.J. Reynolds Tobacco Co.
Bost, Alison R., (BV) ....'70 '97 C.296 B.S. L.896 J.D. [Ⓐ Womble C.S.&R.]
Bost, S. Fraley, (AV) ....'47 '79 C.301 B.S. L.896 J.D. [Womble C.S.&R.]
Bowden, Teresa G., (BV) ....'50 '78 C&L.896 B.A., J.D. [Wilson,D.&M.]
Bowen, Heather J. ....'73 '99 C.228 B.A. L.469 J.D. [Ⓐ Allman S.L.&C.]
Boyce, Stephen A., (BV) ....'55 '99 C.1129 B.A. L.896 J.D. P.O. Box 24786
Boyles, Laurel O., (BV) ....'43 '68 C&L.896 B.A., J.D. [L.O.Boyles]
Boyles, Susan Holdsclaw, (AV) ....'— '94 C&L.575 B.A., J.D. [Kilpatrick S.]
Boyles, Laurel O., P.A., (BV) ....315 N. Spruce St., Ste. 250
Boynton, Mark D., (BV) ....'68 '97 C.893 B.A. L.896 J.D. [Pharr&B.]
Brackney, William A. ....'28 '59 C.228 B.A. L.851 J.D. 1001 W. 4th St.
Bradburn, Julie B. ....'74 '03 C.576 B.A. L.1228 J.D. [Ⓐ Womble C.S.&R.]
Bradford, Bruce O. '71 '97 C.339 B.S. L.477 J.D.
(adm. in IL; not adm. in NC) Atty., Sara Lee Corporation
Bradshaw, Penni P., (AV) ....'54 '80 C.682 A.B. L.575 J.D. [Constangy,B.&S.]
Brett, Anthony H., (AV) ....'53 '79 C.976 B.A. L.228 J.D. [Womble C.S.&R.]
Bringle, Kathryn L. ....'54 '81 C&L.575 B.A., J.D. Chapter 13 Standing Trustee
Britt, Clifford, (AV) ....'60 '86 C&L.896 B.A., J.D. [Comerford&B.]
Brock, Stuart A. ....'67 '00 C.896 B.S. L.574 J.D. [Ⓐ Womble C.S.&R.] (⊙Charlotte)
Brock, Thomas E. ....'64 '96 C.575 B.A. L.896 J.D. [Brock&S.]
Brock & Scott, PLLC ....1315 Westbrook Plaza Dr.
Broomfield, Melynda G., (BVⓉ) .....'70 '96 C.319 B.A. L.93 J.D. [Ⓐ Blanco T.C.&M.]

Brotherton Ford Yeoman & Worley, PLLC
(See Greensboro)

Broughton, David Popham ....'— '97 C&L.575 B.A., J.D. [Ⓐ Kilpatrick S.]
Browder, Bannister R., Jr., (BV) ....'22 '47 C&L.228 A.B., LL.B. 111 Gloria Ave.
Brown, B. Ervin, II, (AV) ....'44 '71 C&L.575 B.A., J.D. [Handler&B.]
Brown, Larry T. ....'47 '78 C.870 B.S. L.1049 J.D. 8025 N Point Blvd★
Brown, Robert M., (BV) ....'46 '74 C.793 B.A. L.623 J.D. Hall of Jus.
Brown, Tadelro L. ....'77 '04 C&L.896 B.A., J.D. Offr., Wachovia Corporation
Bruce, David R. '42 '76 C.112 A.B. L.61 J.D.
(adm. in CA; not adm. in NC) 1227 Martin St.‡
Brunstetter, Peter S., (AV) ....'— '84 C.861 B.A. L.893 J.D. [Kilpatrick S.]
Bruton, Daniel C., (BV) ....'69 '95 C.198 B.A. L.896 J.D. [Bell,D.&P.]
Bryant, Matthew H., (BV) ....'63 '95 C.575 B.A. L.896 J.D. [Hendrick&B.]
Bryner, William M., (BV) ....'— '96 C.101 B.A. L.228 J.D. [Ⓐ Kilpatrick S.]
Buckland, Jason B. ....'77 '02 C.886 B.S. L.896 J.D. [Ⓐ Womble C.S.&R.]

Buie, Donald R., (CV) '56 '81 C.240 B.A. L.574 J.D.
8 West 3rd Street, Suite 100, 27101
Mailing Address: P.O. Box 20031, Winston-Salem, NC 27120
Telephone: 336-773-1398 Fax: 336-773-1505 URL: http://www.donald-buielaw.com
Email: drbuie@bellsouth.net URL: http://www.donaldrbuie.com
Serious Automobile Accidents, Tractor Trailer Accidents, Wrongful Death, Personal Injury, Consumer Bankruptcy, Driving Under the Influence, Traffic, Wills and Estates.
See Professional Biographies, WINSTON-SALEM, NORTH CAROLINA

Bunch, Ralph L., (BV) ....'64 '89 C.404 B.A. L.896 J.D. [Bunch&Assoc.]
Bunch & Associates, PLLC, (BV) ....514 South Stratford Road, Suite 315
Burge, D. Barrett, (BV) ....'49 '75 C.575 B.A. L.896 J.D. 2599 Reynolda Rd.
Burke, Charles A., (BV) ....'62 '87 C&L.575 B.A., J.D. [Womble C.S.&R.]
Burke, Logan T. ....'61 '86 C.511 B.A. L.574 J.D. Co. J.
Burns, W. Joseph, (AV) '49 '74 C&L.896 B.A., J.D.
415 North Trade Street, Second Floor
Byers, J. Darren, (BV) ....'67 '94 C.152 B.A. L.896 J.D. [J.D.Byers]
Byers, J. Darren, The Law Offices of, (BV) ....105 West Fourth St. Suite 400
Byrd, Jones P., Jr. ....'76 '02 C&L.896 B.A., J.D. [Ⓐ White&C.]
Caffey, David H., (BV) ....'50 '78 C&L.575 A.B., J.D. P.O. Box 20575

Calaway, Stephen G., (AV) '40 '64 C&L.896 B.A., LL.B.
1330 Ashley Square, Ashleybrook Lane, 27103
Telephone: 336-760-6420 Fax: 336-760-8811
Email: SCalawayAtty@aol.com
General Civil Practice, Residential Real Estate, Commercial Real Estate, Zoning and Land Use, Commercial Leasing, Construction.
References: Bank of America; Branch Bank and Trust Co.
See Professional Biographies, WINSTON-SALEM, NORTH CAROLINA

Caldwell, Anna E., (BV) ....'50 '86 L.896 J.D. [A.Caldwell&Assoc.]
Caldwell, Lisa J. ......'61 '86 C.575 B.S.B.A. L.896 J.D. R.J. Reynolds Tobacco Company
Caldwell, William E. '31 '55 C&L.838 B.S., J.D.
(adm. in TN; not adm. in NC) 400 Stoneleigh Court
Caldwell, Anna, & Associates, (BV) ....380 Knollwood Street, Suite 560
Calkins, Charles W., (AV) ......'— '85 C.453 S.B.Ch.E. L.94 J.D. [Kilpatrick S.] (Pat.)
Calvert, Ian A. ....'39 '62 C.691 B.A. L.326 LL.B. [Ⓖ Womble C.S.&R.] (Pat.)
Campbell, Robert B. ....'16 '40 C&L.896 B.S., J.D. 422 N. Hawthorne Rd.‡
Canady, Jack F., (AV) ....'22 '49 C&L.896 B.S., LL.B. 2599 Reynolda Road
Cannon, Craig D. ....'74 '01 C&L.352 B.A., J.D. [Ⓐ Womble C.S.&R.]

Cannon, Glen E. '51 '78 C.575 B.S. L.896 J.D. Tax Manager, Cannon & Company, L.L.P.
Carey, Karen Estelle, (AV) ... '43 '81 C.898 B.M.E. L.228 J.D. [Womble C.S.&R.]
Carlisle, Robert M., Jr. '31 '58 C.968 A.B. L.790 LL.B. (adm. in SC; not adm. in NC) 812 Sylvan Road‡
Carlson, Kenneth P., Jr., (AV) ... '— '90 C.575 B.A. L.896 J.D. [Constangy,B.&S.]
Carmen, D. Anderson, (AV) ... '57 '82 C.576 B.A. L.896 J.D. [Bell,D.&P.]
Carmon, Angela Ingram, (BV) ... '62 '87 C.329 B.A. L.575 J.D. Asst. City Atty.
Carroll, John F. '35 '76 C.870 B.S. L.1190 J.D. (adm. in CA; not adm. in NC) 2090 Royall Dr.
Carruthers, Catharine R. ... '54 '81 C.575 B.A. L.896 J.D. U.S. Bkrptcy. J.
Carruthers, Joseph T., (AV) ... '52 '77 C.228 B.A. L.896 J.D. [Carruthers&B.]

Carruthers & Bailey, P.A., (AV)
155 Sunnynoll Court, Suite 102, 27106
Telephone: 336-714-1220 Facsimile: 336-722-1993
Email: jcarruthers@carruthersbailey.com URL: http://www.lawyers.com/carruthers&bailey
Joseph T. Carruthers; J. Dennis Bailey.
Medical Malpractice, Products Liability, Personal Injury, Wrongful Death, Insurance Law, Premises Liability, Corporate Law, Employment Law.
See Professional Biographies, WINSTON-SALEM, NORTH CAROLINA

Cartledge, Kevin B., (CV) ... '71 '97 C.575 B.A. L.896 J.D. [Wilson&I.]
Cash, A. Lee, Jr. ... '68 '94 C&L.910 A.B., J.D. 3447 Robinhood Road, Suite 210
Cash, Clyde R., (BV) ... '58 '85 C&L.896 B.A., J.D. [Wells,J.L.&J.P.]
Castleman, Don R. ... '41 '68 C.394 B.S. L.838 J.D. Prof. of Law, Wake Forest Univ.
Celio, Christopher M. ... '63 '88 C.156 B.A. L.184 J.D. 101 N. Cherry St.
Chapman, Karen H. ... '77 '05 C&L.575 B.A., J.D. [Ⓐ Allman S.L.&C.]
Charnes, Adam H., (AV) ... '— '93 C.674 A.B. L.309 J.D. [Kilpatrick S.]
Christiansen, Susan L., (BV) '52 '77 C&L.575 A.B., J.D. VP & Gen. Coun., Taylor House Enterprises Ltd.
Clapp, Chad R. ... '72 '98 C.576 B.A. L.896 J.D. Trust Advsr., Wachovia Bk., N.A.‡
Clapp, Susan M. ... '79 '04 C&L.896 B.A., J.D. [Ⓐ Blanco T.C.&M.]
Clare, Jane C. ... '58 '82 C.34 BSCJ L.896 J.D. Trial Ct. Admr., Admn. Off. of the Cts.
Clark, Joseph P. ... '66 '93 C.575 B.S. L.574 J.D. Gen. Coun., Truliant Fed. Credit Union
Clark, Terry A. ... '60 '86 C.269 B.A. L.192 J.D. [Constangy,B.&S.]
Clark, Willie L., Jr. '40 '67 C.511 B.S. L.329 LL.B. (adm. in DC; not adm. in NC) N.L.R.B.
Clay Stuart Law Firm ... 2366 Fairway Dr.
Cleland, George M. ... '38 '68 C.871 L.861 J.D. One Salem Twr.
Cleland, George M., IV, (BV) ... '63 '90 C.896 B.A. L.575 J.D. 119 Brookstown Ave.
Clifton, Christopher R., (BV) ... '— '95 C.576 B.A. L.896 J.D. [Grace H.T.&C.]
Clifton, Michelle B., (BV) ... '— '95 C.576 B.S. L.896 J.D. [Ⓖ Grace H.T.&C.]
Clinard, Keith A., (AV) ... '54 '79 C&L.896 B.A., J.D. [Womble C.S.&R.]
Clodfelter, Robert F. ... '25 '49 C.1129 L.228 LL.B. 1011 Paschal Dr.‡
Clough, Mirielle P. ... '— '01 C.228 B.A. L.896 J.D. [Ⓐ Grace H.T.&C.]
Cocklereece, John A., Jr., (AV) ... '54 '79 C&L.902 B.A., J.D. [Bell,D.&P.]
Cofer, William L., (AV) ... '40 '65 C&L.896 B.A., LL.B. [W.L.Cofer]
Cofer, William L., P.A., (AV) ... 110 Oakwood Drive, Suite 410
Coffey, Larry B., (AV) ... '40 '65 C.894 A.B. L.1119 J.D. 2449 Ardmore Manor
Coffey, Tamura D., (BV) ... '68 '93 C&L.896 B.A., J.D. [Wilson&I.]
Cogdill, Jason M. ... '76 '01 C&L.896 B.A., J.D. [J.Cogdill]
Cogdill, Jason ... 2640 Reynolds Road
Collier, Lizabeth Cooper ... '60 '89 C.339 B.A. L.245 J.D. 1600 1 Triad Park
Colvin, Bruce E., (BV) ... '45 '77 C.1100 B.A. L.896 J.D. Dep. Co. Atty.
Combs, Reginald F., (AV) ... '53 '78 C&L.896 B.A., J.D. [Blanco T.C.&M.]
Comerford, W. Thompson, Jr., (AV) ... '49 '74 C&L.896 A.B., J.D. [Comerford&B.]

Comerford & Britt, L.L.P., (AV)
250 West First Street Suite 300, 27101
Telephone: 336-631-8510 Fax: 336-631-8228
Email: @comerfordbritt.com URL: http://www.comerfordbritt.com
Members of Firm: W. Thompson Comerford, Jr.; Clifford Britt. Associates: Terre Thomas Yde; Kevin J. Williams; Brian T. Baker; Alan Ronald Dickinson.
Aviation, Medical Malpractice, Products Liability, Personal Injury, Wrongful Death, Complex Civil Litigation.
See Professional Biographies, WINSTON-SALEM, NORTH CAROLINA

Conger, W. Mark, (AV) ... '— '91 C.301 B.A. L.896 J.D. [Kilpatrick S.]
Connor, Jerome F. ... '37 '59 C.94 B.S. L.273 LL.B. Natl. Labor Rel. Bd.
Conrad, Anita M., (BV) '58 '83 C.8 B.A. L.896 J.D. Corp. Coun., Wake Forest University, Legal Dept.

Constangy, Brooks & Smith, LLC, (AV)
100 North Cherry Street, Suite 300, 27101 ⊙
Telephone: 336-721-1001 Charlotte Telephone: 704-344-1040 Fax: 336-748-9112
URL: http://www.constangy.com
Members: Penni P. Bradshaw; Kenneth P. Carlson, Jr.; Terry A. Clark; Jill S. Cox; John J. Doyle, Jr.; W. Randolph Loftis, Jr.; Charles P. Roberts III; Robin E. Shea. Associates: Kristine M. Howard; Jeanette K. Phelan; Candice Sylvette Wooten.
Labor Relations, Employment Litigation, Employee Benefits Law, Wage and Hour, OSHA Law, Business Immigration, Affirmative Action.
Asheville, North Carolina Office: 80 Peachtree Road, Suite 208. Telephone: 828-277-5137. Fax: 828-277-5138.
Atlanta, Georgia Office: 230 Peachtree Street, N.W., Suite 2400. Telephone: 404-525-8622. Fax: 404-525-6955.
Austin, Texas Office: 111 Congress Avenue, Fourth Floor. Telephone: 512-391-4989. Fax: 512-391-6821.
Birmingham, Alabama Office: 1901 Sixth Avenue North, Suite 1410. Telephone: 205-252-9321. Fax: 205-323-7674.
Columbia, South Carolina Office: 1301 Gervais Street, NationsBank Tower, Suite 810. Telephone: 803-256-3200. Fax: 803-256-6277.
Fairfax, Virginia Office: 4100 Monument Corner Drive, Suite 520. Telephone: 571-522-6100. Fax: 571-522-6101.
Jacksonville, Florida Office: 200 West Forsyth Street, Suite 1610. Telephone: 904-356-8900. Fax: 904-356-8200.
Kansas City, Missouri Office: 2600 Grand Avenue, Suite 300. Telephone: 816-472-6400. Fax: 816-472-6401.
Macon, Georgia Office: 577 Mulberry Street, Suite 710. Telephone: 478-750-8600. Fax: 478-750-8686.
Nashville, Tennessee Office: Vanderbilt Plaza, Suite 925, 2100 West End Avenue. Telephone: 615-320-5200. Fax: 615-321-5891.
San Antonio, Texas Office: The Forum, 8000 IH 10 West, Suite 600. Telephone: 210-525-7977. Fax: 210-525-7978.
Tampa, Florida Office: 100 North Tampa Street, Suite 3350. Telephone: 813-223-7166. Fax: 813-223-2515.
See Professional Biographies, WINSTON-SALEM, NORTH CAROLINA

Cook, James C. ... '47 '73 C.790 B.S. L.896 J.D. Wake Forest Univ.
Copenhaver, W. Andrew, (AVⓉ) ... '46 '72 C.228 A.B. L.575 J.D. [Womble C.S.&R.]
Corbett, Leon H., Jr., (AV) ... '37 '61 C.198 B.A. L.896 J.D. P.O. Box 1013 Paschal Dr.
Covington, I. Boyce, III ... '43 '69 C.198 A.B. L.575 J.D. Wake Forest Univ. Sch. of Law
Cox, Jill S., (AV) ... '68 '93 C.1130 B.A. L.896 J.D. [Constangy,B.&S.]

Craige Brawley Liipfert & Walker LLP, (AV)
110 Oakwood Drive, Suite 300, 27103-1958
Telephone: 336-725-0583 Fax: 336-725-4677
URL: http://www.craigebrawley.com
Members of Firm: Cowles Liipfert (Board Certified Specialist in Estate Planning and Probate Law, North Carolina State Board of Legal Specialization); William W. Walker; B. Bailey Liipfert, III; John A. Keiger (Board Certified Specialist in Estate Planning and Probate Law, North Carolina State Bar Board of Legal Specialization); Brent W. Stephens; Robert Martin Addison. Associates: Aimee L. Smith; Rebecca L. Smitherman; Susan J. Ryan; Julian P. Robb. Of Counsel: H. David Niblock.
General Practice in State and Federal Courts. Taxation, Estate and Trust Administration, Estate Planning, Fiduciary Law, Guardianships, Elder Law, Long Term Care Planning, Special Needs Trust Planning and Administration, Real Property, Corporation, Commercial, Domestic, Collections and Personal Injury Law.
See Professional Biographies, WINSTON-SALEM, NORTH CAROLINA

Craun, Galen G., III ... '68 '99 C.682 B.A. L.896 J.D. [Ⓐ Bell,D.&P.]
Craven, David Leigh, (BV) '53 '78 C.198 B.A. L.896 J.D. Sr. V.P. & Assoc. Gen. Coun., Branch Banking and Trust Company
Craven, Frederick T., Jr ... '40 '69 C.902 B.A. L.575 J.D. Mediation
Craven, Mary Nell, (BV) ... '71 '96 C.575 B.A. L.896 J.D. [Ⓐ Womble C.S.&R.]
Craven, Thorns ... '40 '69 C.902 B.A. L.575 J.D. Mediation, Inc.
Craver, C. Penn, Jr., (AV) ... '— '66 C.198 A.B. L.575 J.D. [Kilpatrick S.]
Crawford, David R., (BV) ... '54 '80 C.339 B.A. L.896 J.D. 1 N. Marshall St.
Creamer, Amanda H. ... '70 '97 C.1369 B.A. L.896 J.D. [Ⓐ Tash&K.]
Creamer, James E., Jr., (BV) ... '67 '97 C.893 B.A. L.896 J.D. [Ⓐ Blanco T.C.&M.]
Crosby, Grady L., (BV) '66 '91 C.329 B.A. L.896 J.D. Secretary & General Counsel, National Textiles, L.L.C
Crumpler, Fred G., Jr., (AV) ... '31 '57 C.296 B.A. L.896 J.D. [White&C.]
Crumpler, Thomas T., (AV) ... '50 '75 C.575 B.S. L.896 J.D. [Allman S.L.&C.]
Cunningham, Charles T., (BVⓉ) ... '51 '77 C&L.923 B.A., J.D. 102 S. Cherry St.
Cunningham, James Calvin (Cal), III ... '— '00 C&L.575 B.A., J.D. [Ⓐ Kilpatrick S.]
Curtis, Michael K., (AV) '42 '69 C.797 A.B. L.575 J.D. Assoc. Prof. of Law, Wake Forest Univ.
Daggett, David D., (AV) ... '60 '85 C.346 B.A. L.896 J.D. [Lewis&D.]
Dale, Suzanne ... '53 '93 C.69 B.S. L.896 J.D. 1001 W. 4th St.
Dalton, Neil C. '52 '85 C.477 A.B. L.912 J.D. (adm. in MI; not adm. in NC) Wachovia Bldg.‡
Daly, Rachel E. ... '74 '01 C.890 B.A. L.896 J.D. [Ⓐ Womble C.S.&R.]
Daniel, Christopher G. ... '66 '92 C.112 B.S.M.E. L.861 J.D. [Ⓐ Womble C.S.&R.]
David, Benjamin R., (BV) ... '70 '95 C.260 B.S. L.896 J.D. 1001 W. 4th St.
David, G. Phillip ... '59 '88 C.232 B.S.B.A. L.574 J.D. [David&Assoc.] ⊙

David and Associates, pllc
1100-A South Stratford Road, 27103 ⊙
Telephone: 336-354-1040 Toll Free: 1-800-856-9927
Email: aeverhart@davidandassociates.com URL: http://www.wilmingtonpiattorneys.com
G. Phillip David.
Personal Injury, Medical Malpractice, Wrongful Death, Products Liability, Workers Compensation, Aviation, Airplane Crashes, Negligence, Class Actions, Maritime Accidents, Boating Accidents, Bicycle Accidents, Motorcycle Accidents, Truck Accidents, School Bus Accidents, Railroad Accidents, Dog Bites, Slip and Fall, Birth Trauma, Brain Injury, Spinal Injury, Head Injury, Catastrophic Injury, Vehicular Homicide, Personal Injury Mediation, Products Liability, Drug and Medical Device Litigation, Product Defects, Automobile Liability, Motorcycle Products Liability, Amusement Park Liability, Hotel Liability, Marina Liability, Sports Injury.
Jacksonville, North Carolina Office: 405-B Western Boulevard. 28546. Telephone: 910-219-4878.
Supply, North Carolina Office: Highway 17. 28462. Telephone: 910-754-8465.
Wallace, North Carolina Office: 107 North Norwood Street. 28466. Telephone: 910-285-8777.
Clinton, North Carolina Office: 610 Beaman Street. 28328. Telephone: 910-592-8400.
Wilmington, North Carolina Office: 1516 Dawson Street. 28401. Telephone: 910-251-8088.
Greensboro, North Carolina Office: 529 College Road. Suite G. 27410. Telephone: 336-354-1040.
See Professional Biographies, WINSTON-SALEM, NORTH CAROLINA

Davis, Gregory ... '49 '76 C.575 B.A. L.574 J.D. Fed. Pub. Def. Off.
Davis, H. Glenn ... '36 '60 C&L.574 B.A., LL.B. 301 N. Main St., Ste. 2221
Davis, H. Lee, Jr., (AV) ... '52 '77 C.576 B.S. L.896 J.D. [Davis&H.]
Davis, James A. ... '49 '85 C.381 B.A. L.607 J.D. 150 Strattford Road
Davis, Joslin, (AV) ... '51 '77 C.280 B.A. L.896 J.D. [Davis&H.]
Davis, Linwood L., (AV) ... '40 '67 C.674 A.B. L.228 J.D. [Womble C.S.&R.]
Davis, Ronald R., (AVⓉ) '58 '87 C.198 B.A. L.575 J.D. [Womble C.S.&R.] (⊙Greensboro)
Davis, Terrie A. ... '45 '79 C.758 B.A. L.896 J.D. 2815 Bartram Rd.‡
Davis, William K., (AV) ... '39 '66 C.198 A.B. L.896 LL.B. [Bell,D.&P.]

Davis Elder & Disability Law
(See Lewisville)

Davis & Hamrick, L.L.P., (AV)
635 West Fourth Street, P.O. Drawer 20039, 27120-0039
Telephone: 336-725-8385 Telecopier: 336-723-8838
Email: info@davisandhamrick.com URL: http://www.davisandhamrick.com
Members of Firm: H. Lee Davis, Jr.; Kent L. Hamrick; Shannon Warf Beach (Board Certified Specialist in Workers' Compensation, North Carolina State Board of Legal Specialization); James G. Welsh, Jr.;—Ann C. Rowe; R. Andrew Keever.
General Civil Practice in North Carolina and Federal Courts. Insurance Defense, Labor and Employment Law, Personal Injury, Workers' Compensation, Trucking, Real Estate, Traffic and Transportation Law.
Local Counsel for: State Farm Insurance Co.; Liberty Mutual Insurance Co.; Safeco Ins. Co.; St. Paul Insurance Companies; Metropolitan Property and Casualty Company; Allstate Ins. Co.; The Hartford.
See Professional Biographies, WINSTON-SALEM, NORTH CAROLINA

Davis & Harwell, P.A., (AV)
101 South Stratford Road Suite 200, 27104-4224
Telephone: 336-722-1534 Fax: 336-722-2382
Email: info@davisharwell.com URL: http://www.davisharwell.com
Fred R. Harwell, Jr.; Joslin Davis (Board Certified Specialist in Family Law, North Carolina State Board of Legal Specialization); Loretta C. Biggs; Mark H. Hoppe; John A. McMillen; Deborah S. Halvorsen (Board Certified Specialist in Family Law, North Carolina State Board of Legal Specialization); Caleigh H. Evans.
General Civil and Criminal Trial Practice in State and Federal Courts. Commercial, Business and Corporate, Personal Injury and Tort Litigation, Family Law, Wills and Estate Planning, and Employment Law.
See Professional Biographies, WINSTON-SALEM, NORTH CAROLINA

Dawson, Sherry R., (BV) '60 '85 C.886 B.A. L.896 J.D. Assoc. Coun., Partners Natl. Health Plans of N.C., Inc.
Dawson, Willie C. ... '46 '76 C&L.575 B.A., J.D. Legal Aid Soc. of Northwest N.C., Inc.
Deal, R. Brandt, (BV) ... '48 '73 C.301 B.S. L.896 J.D. [Hatfield,M.D.V.&M.]
Deem, Tonya R. ... '— '96 C.896 B.A. L.575 J.D. [Kilpatrick S.]
DeGraw, William R., Jr., (BV) ... '47 '75 C.659 B.A. L.896 J.D. [Wilson,D.&M.]
DeRamus, Judson D., Jr. ... '45 '68 C.228 B.A. L.575 J.D. Supr. Ct. J.

Deuterman Law Group, The, P.A.
(See Greensboro)

Dickerson, Robert W. '64 '92 C.610 B.G.S. L.896 J.D. The Northwestern Mut. Life. Ins. Co.

Dickinson, Alan Ronald ... '76 '01 C.896 B.A. L.228 J.D. [[A] Comerford&B.]
Dillard, Roger Lee, Jr. ... '45 '72 C.575 A.B. L.327 J.D. [Orbock R.&D.]
Dills, Jonathan S., (BV) ... '65 '91 C&L.575 B.S., J.D. [J.S.Dills]
Dills, Jonathan S. The Law Offices of, P.A., (BV) ... 411 N. Cherry St.
Divine, Hugh W. ... '09 '51 C.278 B.S. L.245 J.D. 3602 Dewsbury Rd.‡
Doherty, Louis W., (AV) ... '— '90 C.228 B.A. L.575 J.D. [Kilpatrick S.]
Donahue, Bonnie Kay, (AV) ... '51 '79 C.259 B.A. L.896 J.D. [Womble C.S.&R.]
Donahue, Daniel W. '42 '68 C&L.575 B.A., J.D.
Sr. V.P. & Dep. Gen. Coun., R.J. Reynolds Tobacco Co.
Doughton, Thomas J., (BV) ... '61 '89 C.269 B.A. L.896 J.D. [Blancato,D.&H.]
Douglas, Charles T., (BV) '60 '85 C.198 B.A. L.896 J.D.
V.P. & Gen. Coun., Douglas Battery Manufacturing Company
Douglas, Christina U., (AV) ... '68 '93 C.500 B.A. L.1015 J.D. [Womble C.S.&R.]
Douglas, George Walker, (BV) '62 '88 C.198 B.A. L.896 J.D.
Secy. & Assoc. Gen. Coun., Douglas Battery Manufacturing Company
Doyle, John J., Jr., (AV) ... '42 '66 C&L.575 A.B., LL.B. [Constangy,B.&S.]
Drew, Ellis B., III, (AV) ... '59 '84 C.896 B.A. L.902 J.D. [Wells,J.L.&J.P.]
Drye, Michael L., (AV) ... '— '90 C.1175 B.S.B.A. L.575 J.D. [Kilpatrick S.]
DuBois, Kathleen Quinn ... '— '03 C.602 B.B.A. L.896 J.D. 1100 A South Stratford Rd.
Du Buisson, Charles D. ... '42 '75 C.434 A.B. L.575 J.D. Winston-Salem Sentinel
Dummit, E. Clarke ... '61 '86 C.880 B.A. L.896 J.D. [Dummit]
Dummit Law Firm, The, (BV) ... 213 West 6th Street
Durham, Richard M., (BV) ... '54 '82 C.1128 B.A. L.575 J.D. 8 W. 3rd St., Ste. 360
Eagle, Shana L. ... '72 '99 C&L.896 B.A., J.D. Med. Litigation Analyst, FirmLogic

Early, James H., Jr., (AV) '39 '64 C&L.896 B.A., J.D.
1320 Westgate Center Drive, 27103-2933
Telephone: 336-768-2546 Fax: 336-765-9193
Email: jim@jimearly.com
Limited Civil Practice, Personal Injury, Malpractice, Employment Claims, Corporate and Business Law and Family Law. Trials in all Courts.
See Professional Biographies, WINSTON-SALEM, NORTH CAROLINA

Ebel, Deanne M. '68 '93 C.520 B.C.J L.221 J.D.
(adm. in IA; not adm. in NC) Tr. Officer, Wachovia Bank, N.A.
Ebersole, Daniel P. ... '— '04 C.446 B.S.M.E. L.577 J.D. [[A] Kilpatrick S.]
Edwards, Robert L., (AV) ... '— '65 C.232 A.B. L.575 LL.B. [Kilpatrick S.]
Edwards, W. David, (BV) ... '57 '82 C.575 B.S. L.228 J.D. [Womble C.S.&R.]
Ehlinger, Timothy J., (AV) ... '59 '85 C.1044 B.S. L.575 J.D. [Vaughn P.E.M.&S.]
Eldridge, William B. '29 '51 C&L.838 B.S., J.D.
(adm. in TN; not adm. in NC) Partner, Cannon & Company, L.L.P.
Eliason, Russell A. ... '44 '70 C.976 B.A. L.494 J.D. U.S. Mag. J.
Eller, John D., Jr., (AV) ... '29 '57 C.674 A.B. L.575 J.D. 808 Pine Valley Rd.‡
Elliot, Robert M., (AV) ... '— '77 C.575 B.A. L.896 J.D. [Elliot P.M.]

Elliot Pishko Morgan, P.A., (AV)
426 Old Salem Road, 27101-5283
Telephone: 336-724-2828 Fax: 336-724-3335
Email: jgmorgan@epmlaw.com URL: http://www.epmlaw.com
David C. Pishko (Board Certified Specialist in Family Law, North Carolina State Board of Legal Specialization); Robert M. Elliot; J. Griffin Morgan (Board Certified Specialist in Workers' Compensation, North Carolina State Board of Legal Specialization).
Civil Practice in State and Federal Courts. Negligence, Civil Rights, Family, Labor, Employment, Workers' Compensation and Commercial Litigation.
See Professional Biographies, WINSTON-SALEM, NORTH CAROLINA

Ellison, Eric ... '70 '99 C.475 B.S. L.1187 J.D. [Ellison]

Ellison Law Firm, The
515 W. 2nd Street, 27101
Telephone: 336-723-7370 Fax: 336-723-7372
Email: ellison@earthlink.net
Eric Ellison.
Real Estate, Landlord Tenant, Criminal Law, Traffic Violations, Divorce.
See Professional Biographies, WINSTON-SALEM, NORTH CAROLINA

Elster, J. Robert, (AV) ... '— '64 C.691 A.B. L.228 J.D. [Kilpatrick S.]
Engram, Jonathan M., (AVⓉ) ... '57 '83 C.797 B.A. L.280 J.D. [Womble C.S.&R.]
Enns, Rodrick J., (AV) ... '55 '79 C.911 B.A. L.309 J.D. [Enns&A.]

Enns & Archer LLP, (AV)
939 Burke Street, 27101
Telephone: 336-723-5180 Fax: 336-723-5181
URL: http://www.ennsandarcher.com
Partners: Rodrick J. Enns; Julia C. Archer.
Trademarks, Advertising and Marketing, Promotion Law and Sweepstakes, Copyrights, Trade Secrets, Intellectual Property Licensing, Intellectual Property Litigation, Antitrust and Trade Regulation, Commercial Law, Distribution Agreements, Dealer and Distributor Termination, Computers and Software, Internet Law, Federal Civil Litigation, Appellate Practice.
See Professional Biographies, WINSTON-SALEM, NORTH CAROLINA

Eppley, Marc Hunter ... '54 '01 C.575 B.A. L.896 J.D. [[A] Hatfield,M.D.V.&M.]

Ernest, Jodi A., Law Office of
(See Greensboro)

Erwin, Richard C. ... '23 '51 C.369 B.A. L.329 LL.B. Sr. U.S. Dist. J.
Eshelman, David F. ... '46 '73 C.381 B.S. L.7 J.D. Salem Logistics, Inc.
Esleeck, Robert E., (AV) ... '53 '79 C&L.575 B.S., J.D. Salem College
Evans, Caleigh H. ... '74 '01 C.34 B.S. L.280 J.D. [[A] Davis&H.]
Evans, George K., Jr., (AV) ... '46 '71 C.797 B.A. L.893 J.D. [© Womble C.S.&R.]
Ewing, Robert W., Law Offices of, (BV) '69 '94
C.576 B.A. L.1228 J.D. 2200 Silas Creek Pkwy., Ste. 5A
Exline, Christopher Perry ... '56 '84 C.577 B.A. L.575 J.D. One West Fourth St.
Fagerli, Thomas A., (BV) ... '56 '82 C.404 B.A. L.896 J.D. 3911 Univ. Pkwy.
Farr, H. Bartow, Jr. '21 '48 C.674 A.B. L.178 LL.B.
(adm. in NY; not adm. in NC) 1020 Kent Rd. W.‡
Feiereisel, Michael John ... '73 '01 C.1297 B.S. L.64 J.D. [M.J.Feiereisel]
Feiereisel, Michael J., Attorney at Law, PLLC ... 3325-A Healy Drive
Felsenburg, Miriam E. (Miki) '47 '91
C.208 B.A. L.896 J.D. Wake Forest Univ. School of Law
Fine, Lawrence J. ... '55 '82 C.264 B.A. L.896 J.D. Dist. J.
Finger, Parker, Avram & Roemer, L.L.P., (AV) ... 204 Northgate Park Drive (⊙Jonesville)
Fischer, J. Clark, (AV) ... '55 '80 C.880 B.A. L.896 J.D. [Randolph&F.]
Fitzgerald, Andrew ... '77 '02 C.896 B.A. L.893 J.D. [[A] Womble C.S.&R.]
Fitzgerald, John E., (BV) ... '65 '90 C&L.896 B.A., J.D. [Fitzgerald&H.]

Fitzgerald & Hunter, (BV)
114 South Spruce Street, 27101
Telephone: 336-777-1090 Fax: 336-723-8433
URL: http://www.fitzgeraldhunterlaw.com
Members of Firm: John E. Fitzgerald; Robert C. Hunter.
Criminal Law, Driving While Intoxicated (DWI), Drug Crimes, Parole and Probation, Traffic Violations, White Collar Crimes.
See Professional Biographies, WINSTON-SALEM, NORTH CAROLINA

Fitzner, James R. ... '46 '75 C.228 B.A. L.896 J.D. 1600 One Triad Pk.
Fleeson, Anne ... '— '02 C.228 B.A. L.896 J.D. [[A] Womble C.S.&R.]
Flynt, Fred P., III, (BV) ... '53 '80 C.576 B.A. L.1228 J.D. 105 W. 4th St.
Fonda, John R., (BV) ... '61 '87 C.575 B.A. L.896 J.D. [Bailey&T.]
Ford, Kent Conrad ... '67 '92 C.1128 B.A. L.896 J.D. [Orbock R.&D.]
Fothergill, David M. ... '77 '03 C.953 B.A. L.896 J.D. [[A] Wilson&I.]
Foushee, Wayne H., (BV) ... '40 '68 C.575 B.S. L.896 J.D. 315 N. Spruce St.
Fox, Christopher C., (BV) '67 '93
C.954 B.A. L.896 J.D. Asst. Coun., Sara Lee Branded Apparel
Fox, James R., (AV) ... '46 '71 C&L.228 A.B., J.D. [Bell,D.&P.]
Fradenburg, James J. ... '68 '93 C.1381 B.S. L.896 J.D. [[S] Womble C.S.&R.]
Francisco, George, (BV) ... '49 '83 C.34 B.A. L.1345 J.D. [G.Francisco]

Francisco, George, PC, (BV)
2000 West First Street, Suite 501, 27104
Telephone: 336-722-5088 Fax: 336-722-5118
Email: George@GeorgeFranciscoLaw.com URL: http://www.GeorgeFranciscoLaw.com
George Francisco (Board Certified Specialist in Workers Compensation Law, North Carolina State Board of Legal Specialization).
Civil Trial Practice including Personal Injury, Workers' Compensation, Insurance Claims, Business Torts, Investment Losses.
See Professional Biographies, WINSTON-SALEM, NORTH CAROLINA

Frankel, Gusti W., (AV) ... '46 '84 C.112 B.A. L.228 J.D. [Womble C.S.&R.]
Frazier, Daniel A. ... '49 '73 C&L.896 B.A., J.D. 202 Northgate Park Dr.
Freedman, David B., (AV) ... '56 '82 C&L.575 B.A., J.D. [White&C.]
Freedy, Barbara L. '59 '84 C&L.608 B.A., J.D.
(adm. in OH; not adm. in NC) Novant Health, Inc.
Freeman, William H. ... '45 '74 C&L.896 B.A., J.D. Ret. Supr. Ct. J.‡
Friende, Billy D., (BV) ... '50 '76 C.329 B.S.E.E. L.245 J.D. 548 N. Main St.
Friesen, Bradley C. ... '77 '02 C.937 B.A. L.378 J.D. [[A] Bell,D.&P.]
Frye, Leslie G., (BV) ... '35 '59 C.125 A.B. L.896 LL.B. [Frye&B.]
Frye & Booth, (AV) ... 1171 West Fourth Street
Fuller-Andrews, Lynnette ... '67 '91 C&L.575 B.S., J.D. Sara Lee Corp.
Furr, Jeffrey L., (AV) ... '56 '87 C.923 B.S. L.896 J.D. [Womble C.S.&R.]
Fus, Elliot Alexander, (CV) ... '— '97 C.575 A.B. L.896 J.D. [[A] Kilpatrick S.]
Galinski, Todd W. ... '— '01 C.37 B.S. L.896 J.D. [[A] Kilpatrick S.]
Gallagher, Celeste E. ... '62 '88 C.273 B.A. L.124 J.D. NC Baptist Hosp.
Gamble, Mary Caroline, (BV) '54 '79
C.575 B.S. L.896 J.D. In-House Coun., Slick Enterprises
Gardner, Steven, (AV) ... '— '94 C.1128 B.S.E.E. L.896 J.D. [Kilpatrick S.] (Pat.)
Garland, Steven C., (AV) ... '53 '80 C.228 B.A. L.896 J.D. [Blanco T.C.&M.]
Gates, Bryan E., Jr., (BV) '65 '94
C.575 B.A. L.896 J.D. 1 North Marshall Street, Suite 100
Gattalaro, Donald R. '47 '88 C.1044 B.S. L.896 J.D.
4035 University Parkway, Suite 200
Gatto, Joseph J., (BV) ... '53 '79 C.874 B.A. L.896 J.D. [Gatto]

Gatto Law Offices, P.A., (BV)
501 Harvey Street, 27103
Telephone: 336-768-2345 Telecopier: 336-768-2622
Email: jgatto@triad.rr.com URL: http://www.gattolawoffices.com
Joseph J. Gatto (Board Certified Specialist in Family Law, North Carolina State Board of Legal Specialization).
Family Law, Domestic Relations, Divorce, Equitable Distribution, Child Custody, Child Support, Premarital Agreements, Spousal Agreements.
See Professional Biographies, WINSTON-SALEM, NORTH CAROLINA

Gee, M. Elizabeth, (AV) ... '47 '75 C.228 A.B. L.276 J.D. 6026 Rittenhouse Rd.
Geis, Christopher J. ... '66 '98 C.925 B.A. L.896 J.D. [[A] Womble C.S.&R.]
Geraghty, Maureen, (BV) ... '60 '89 C.454 B.A. L.273 J.D. [Geraghty]
Geraghty Law Firm, The, (BV) ... 426 Old Salem Road
Gerber, Andrew J., (BV) ... '63 '89 C.259 B.S. L.896 J.D. [Horton,S.&G.]
Gerber, Nils E., (BV) ... '64 '90 C&L.896 B.A., J.D. 200 Brookstown Ave., Ste. 304
Gibbs, James S., Jr. ... '68 '97 C.910 B.A. L.178 J.D. [MacKenzie] & [© Moore&B.]
Gibson, William B., Attorney at Law, (BV) '44 '78
C.197 B.A. L.575 J.D. 8 W. 3rd St., Ste. 610
Gilley, James H., Jr. ... '47 '84 C.955 B.A. L.896 J.D. 6220 University Pkwy.
Gitter, Allan R., (AV) ... '36 '63 C.902 B.A. L.477 J.D. [Womble C.S.&R.]
Glass, Deborah M. '50 '79 C.577 B.A. L.896 J.D.
Asst. Univ. Coun., Winston-Salem State Univ.
Goble, Jacqueline M. ... '70 '96 C&L.1228 B.A., J.D. [[A] Womble C.S.&R.]
Godfrey, Brant H., (BV) ... '51 '83 C.759 B.A. L.896 J.D. 2631 Reynolda Road

Gold, Denise M. '68 '99 C.404 B.A. L.896 J.D.
1404 W. First Street, 27101
Telephone: 336-722-5950 Fax: 336-722-5951
Email: dmgoldattorney@aol.com URL: http://www.dmgoldattorney.com
General Civil Litigation, Criminal Law, DWI, Drug Crimes, Misdemeanors, Child Custody, Child Support, Divorce, Personal Injury, Adoption Law, Juvenile Law.
See Professional Biographies, WINSTON-SALEM, NORTH CAROLINA

Goodale, Ralph E. ... '18 '59 C.790 L.896 524 Harper St.‡
Gordon, Lawrence G., Jr., (BV) ... '43 '70 C.1130 B.A. L.896 J.D. 402 Upton St.
Gottlieb, Richard S., (BV) ... '— '96 C.1365 B.A. L.575 J.D. [Kilpatrick S.]

Goulder Immigration Law Firm
(See Greensboro)

Grace, Michael A., (AV) ... '— '77 C.48 B.A. L.896 J.D. [Grace H.T.&C.]

Grace Holton Tisdale & Clifton P.A., (AV)
301 N. Main Street, Suite 100, 27101
Telephone: 336-725-9428 Fax: 336-721-1176
URL: http://www.graceholtontisdalecliftonlaw.com
Michael A. Grace; Walter C. Holton, Jr.; Donald K. Tisdale, Sr.; Christopher R. Clifton; D. Kenneth Tisdale, Jr.;—Mirielle P. Clough. Of Counsel: Michelle B. Clifton.
Criminal Law in all State and Federal Courts. Traffic Violations, White Collar Crime.
See Professional Biographies, WINSTON-SALEM, NORTH CAROLINA

Graham, William T., Jr., (BV) ... '59 '90 C.228 A.B. L.1187 J.D. 200 N. Main St.
Grantham, C. Ray, Jr., (BV) ... '57 '88 C.870 B.S. L.575 J.D. [Robinson&L.]
Gray, Susan H., (BV) ... '53 '78 C.880 B.A. L.838 J.D. [Wells,J.L.&J.P.]
Greason, Murray C., III, (AV) ... '63 '97 C.174 B.A. L.508 J.D. [[A] Womble C.S.&R.]
Greason, Murray C., Jr., (AV) ... '36 '62 C&L.896 B.S., J.D. [Womble C.S.&R.]
Green, Charles C., Jr., (BV) '47 '72
C.198 B.A. L.575 J.D. Asst. City Atty., City Atty. Off.
Green, Edward R., (AV) ... '35 '62 C.575 A.B. L.896 J.D. [Nelson,B.N.&G.]
Green, Stanley B. ... '70 '98 C.575 B.A. L.1194 J.D. [[A] Womble C.S.&R.] (⊙Charlotte)
Greer, Laura A. ... '— '03 C.437 B.S. L.896 J.D. [[A] Kilpatrick S.]
Gregg, Ellen M., (AV) ... '61 '86 C&L.1228 B.A., J.D. [Womble C.S.&R.]
Griffis, John W., Jr. ... '— '67 C&L.896 A.B., J.D. 315 North Spruce Street, Suite 250
Griggs, Edward ... '77 '03 C.896 B.S. L.790 J.D. [[A] Womble C.S.&R.]

Grimes & Grimes of North Carolina, P.A.
(See Greensboro)

Groce, Holly, (BV) .... '70 '95 C.575 B.S.B.A. L.1228 J.D. [A Price]
Grogan, Alice Washington, (BV) ..... '56 '84 C.886 B.S. L.575 J.D. Wachovia Bank, N.A.
Groves, John S. .... '31 '60 C&L.896 B.S., LL.B. 3801 Northriding Rd.
Gruendel, Amy L. Cox .... '72 '00 C.477 B.A. L.93 J.D. Legal Aid Soc. NW NC
Gsteiger, Urs R., (AV) .... '55 '82 C.260 B.A. L.896 J.D. [Horton&G.]
Guia, Lucretia D., (AV) .... '63 '89 C.893 B.S. L.896 J.D. [C Womble C.S.&R.]
Gunter, Dale E., (BV) .... '62 '89 C.444 B.S. L.896 J.D. St. Staff Atty., Integon Corp.
Gunter, Denise M., (AV) .... '64 '89 C.597 B.A. L.273 J.D. [Nelson M.R.&S.]
Gunter, Michael D., (AV) .... '47 '72 C.896 B.A. L.575 J.D. [Womble C.S.&R.]
Gupton, Janet L. .... '62 '88 C&L.896 B.A., J.D. 1600 1 Triad Park
Guthrie, Rodney A., (BV) .... '52 '80 C.362 B.A. L.896 J.D. [Bennett&G.P.]
Guy, Monica R. .... '77 '03 C.259 B.S. L.896 J.D. [A Bell,D.&P.]
Gyves, Christopher J. .... '77 '04 C.198 L.896 J.D. [A Womble C.S.&R.]
Hairston, Bonita J. '72 '97 C&L.896 B.A., J.D.
Asst. Univ. Atty., Winston-Salem State Univ. Off. of Legal Affairs
Hall, David L., (BV) .... '62 '90 C.577 B.A. L.896 J.D. Asst. Dist. Atty.
Halsey, Hardin G., (AV) '55 '83
C.886 B.S. L.383 J.D. [Womble C.S.&R.] (⊙Greensboro)
Halstead, Stephen P. '54 '79 C.575 B.S. L.896 J.D.
Asst. V.P., Property & Cas. Div., Integon Corp.
Halvorsen, Deborah S., (BV) .... '73 '98 C.741 B.A. L.896 J.D. [A Davis&H.]
Hamilton, Donna Harper, (BV) '46 '84 C.225 A.B. L.896 J.D.
Coun., Wake Forest University (Legal Department)
Hamrick, Claude M., (AV) .... '26 '50 C&L.896 LL.B. 115 W. Third St.‡
Hamrick, Kent L., (AV) .... '58 '83 C.896 B.A. L.575 J.D. [Davis&H.]
Handler, Eric P., (AV) .... '46 '73 C&L.228 A.B., J.D. [Handler&B.]

Handler & Brown, P.L.L.C., (AV)
1014 West Fifth Street, 27101-2522
Telephone: 336-723-7966 Fax: 336-723-1035
Members of Firm: Eric P. Handler; B. Ervin Brown, II.
Business Law, Commercial Law, Insurance Premium Finance Law, Factoring, Leasing, Licensing, Franchise Law, Intellectual Property Law, Trademarks, Copyrights, Unfair Competition, Real Estate, Condominium Law, Association Law, Land Use, Environmental Law, Commercial Litigation, Unfair Trade Practice Law, Creditors Rights, Civil Trial Practice, Appellate Practice, Arbitration, Class Actions, Constitutional Law, Professional Liability, Medical Malpractice, Products Liability, Personal Injury, Civil Rights, Labor and Employment, Wrongful Discharge and Discrimination Law.
See Professional Biographies, WINSTON-SALEM, NORTH CAROLINA

Harrill, James A., Jr. .... '37 '66 C.575 A.B. L.896 LL.B. Chf. Dist. J.
Harrington, John M., (AV) .... '— '68 C.576 B.S. L.790 J.D. [Kilpatrick S.] (Pat.)
Harris, Celeste M., (BV) .... '59 '91 C.502 B.S.N. L.734 J.D. [Maynard&H.]
Harris, Jessica R. .... '— '04 C.1524 B.A. L.880 J.D. [A Kilpatrick S.]
Harris, Louise E., Law Office of '51 '90 C.228 B.A. L.574 J.D.
301 N. Main St., Ste. 2223
Harris, S. Ranchor, III, (BV) .... '68 '94 C.575 B.A. L.1148 J.D. [Wilson&I.]
Harris, Thomas A. .... '46 '72 C&L.228 A.B., J.D. Legal Aid Soc. of Northwest N.C., Inc.
Harrison, John S., (BV) .... '56 '82 C.575 B.A. L.228 J.D. 123 South Sunset Drive
Hart, Andrew D. .... '69 '97 C.576 B.A. L.896 J.D. [Blancato,D.&H.]
Hartsfield, Denise S. .... '54 '91 C.811 B.A. L.896 J.D. Law Clk., Chief U.S. Dist. J.
Hartsoe, R. Anthony, (BV) .... '65 '94 C.1288 B.A. L.910 J.D. [Hartsoe&Assoc.]
Hartsoe & Associates, P.C., (BV) .... 1068 West Fourth Street
Harwell, Fred R., Jr., (BV) .... '44 '73 C&L.575 A.B., J.D. [Davis&H.]
Hatfield, Weston P., (AV) .... '20 '47 C.896 B.A. L.309 LL.B. [Hatfield,M.D.V.&M.]

Hatfield, Mountcastle, Deal, Van Zandt & Mann, L.L.P., (AV)
Suite 605, Bethesda Oaks, 2990 Bethesda Place, 27103
Telephone: 336-768-1842 Fax: 336-768-1773; 336-768-5051
URL: http://www.h-mlawyers.com
Members of Firm: Weston P. Hatfield; George C. Mountcastle; R. Brandt Deal; John P. Van Zandt, III; John R. Mann. Associate: Marc Hunter Eppley.
General Civil Practice in all State and Federal Courts, Real Estate, Estate Planning, Probate, Taxation, Corporation and Estate Law.
Representative Clients: Bassett-Walker, Inc.; Johnston Mills Co.; Vulcan Materials Co.; NationsBank of North Carolina; Young-Phillips.
See Professional Biographies, WINSTON-SALEM, NORTH CAROLINA

Haulsee, Hada V., (AV) .... '50 '81 C.945 B.A. L.575 J.D. [Womble C.S.&R.]
Hayes, Roland H. .... '31 '71 C.955 B.S. L.574 J.D. Dist. Ct. J.
Healy, Joan M., (BV) '55 '80 C.276 B.S.N. L.128 J.D.
Corp. Coun., Novant Health, Inc.
Hearn, Jerry Carlyle "Carl", III .... '67 '00 C.404 B.A. L.209 J.D. [A Womble C.S.&R.]
Hefferan, James J., Jr. .... '— '03 C.477 B.A. L.896 J.D. [A Kilpatrick S.]
Helms, Howard Brent, (BV) .... '66 '92 C&L.896 B.S., J.D. [Robinson&L.]
Helms, Linda L., (BV) .... '67 '92 C.316 B.A. L.896 J.D. [Wilson&I.]
Hendrick, T. Paul, (AV) .... '48 '73 C.1318 B.A. L.896 J.D. [Hendrick&B.]

Hendrick & Bryant, L.L.P., (AV)
723 Coliseum Drive Suite 101, 27106-5326
Telephone: 336-723-7200 Fax: 336-723-7201
URL: http://www.hendricklawfirm.com
T. Paul Hendrick; Matthew H. Bryant; Phyllis E. Mendel; Timothy Nerhood; Kelly E. Motycka;—Kenneth C. Otis, III (Casey).
General Business and Corporation Practice including Civil Trial and Appellate Practice. Business Start-Ups, Business Transactions, Closely Held Business Law, Professional Sports Law, Corporate Commercial Law, Corporate Litigation, Real Estate and Banking, Merger and Acquisition, Sports, Automotive, Unfair Competition, Federal, State and Local Taxation, Construction, Insurance, Estate Planning and Bankruptcy.
See Professional Biographies, WINSTON-SALEM, NORTH CAROLINA

Henninger, Ursula M., (AV) .... '67 '92 C.34 B.A. L.896 J.D. [Womble C.S.&R.]
Henson, Jackson W. '51 '76 C.34 B.S. L.896 J.D.
Sr. Coun., R.J. Reynolds Tobacco Co.
Herndon, Brian L., (BV) .... '58 '86 C.576 B.A. L.192 J.D. [Blanco T.C.&M.]
Herring, Jerone C., (AV) '38 '63 C.198 B.A. L.228 LL.B.
Exec. V.P., Secy. & Gen. Coun., Branch Banking and Trust Company
Hicks, Jason C. '75 '01 C.893 B.A. L.896 J.D.
(adm. in VA; not adm. in NC) [A Womble C.S.&R.]
Hier, Teresa, (BV) .... '64 '92 C.1083 B.A. L.896 J.D. [Frye&B.]
Hinnant, Lori Privette, (BV) .... '61 '87 C&L.896 B.A., J.D. [Womble C.S.&R.]
Hinnant, Walter R., (BV) .... '61 '89 C&L.896 B.A., J.D. [Allman S.L.&C.]
Hinnegan, Ambrose J. .... '21 '50 C.728 B.S. L.831 J.D. 3124 Gladstone St.‡
Hinshaw, Robert D., (BV) ...... '50 '77 C&L.896 B.A., J.D. 185 Kimel Park Dr., Ste. 200
Hodges, Warren C., (BV) .... '51 '77 C&L.896 B.A., J.D. 3548 Summerfield Lane
Hollodick, George E., (BV) .... '59 '89 C.575 B.A. L.896 J.D. [Blanco T.C.&M.]
Holloway, Mark C. '60 '86 C.308 B.A. L.896 J.D.
(adm. in PA; not adm. in NC) 310 W. 4th St.
Holsapple, Henry T. '12 '39 C&L.309 A.B., LL.B.
(adm. in NY; not adm. in NC) 3142 Bonhurst Dr.‡

Holton, Martin L., III, (AV) '57 '82 C&L.575 B.A., J.D.
R.J. Reynolds Tobacco Company
Holton, Walter C., Jr., (AV) .... '55 '84 C.575 B.A. L.896 J.D. [Grace H.T.&C.]
Hoots, John Henry .... '26 '57 C.575 B.A. L.896 LL.B. 3328 York Rd.
Hoppe, Mark H., (BV) .... '57 '83 C.228 B.S. L.802 J.D. [Davis&H.]
Horn, Scott Thomas .... '64 '00 C.758 B.S.B.A. L.896 J.D. [A Allman S.L.&C.]
Horton, Elizabeth, (AV) .... '54 '87 C.999 B.S. L.896 J.D. [Horton&G.]
Horton, Hamilton C., Jr., (AV) .... '31 '56 C&L.575 A.B., LL.B. [Horton,S.&G.]
Horton and Gsteiger, P.L.L.C., (AV) .... 1365 Westgate Center Drive, Suite D
Horton, Sloan & Gerber, PLLC, (AV) .... 328 North Spring Street
Houff, Bowen C., (BV) .... '57 '88 C&L.575 B.A., J.D. [Blanco T.C.&M.]

Hough, David B., (AV) '44 '70 C.197 A.B. L.228 J.D.
301 North Main Street, Suite 2303, 27101
Telephone: 336-724-5987 Fax: 336-724-3980
Email: dhough@triad.rr.com URL: http://www.dhoughlaw.com
Divorce, Family Law, Personal Injury, Breach of Contract, Jury Trials, Prenuptial Agreements, Construction Law, Spousal Support, Premarital Agreements, Mediation, Lemon Law, Unfair Trade Practice, Child Custody, Traffic Violations, Consumer Law.
See Professional Biographies, WINSTON-SALEM, NORTH CAROLINA

House, Don R., (AV) .... '41 '66 C&L.228 A.B., LL.B. [House&T.]
House, Kay B., (BV) ...... '53 '79 C&L.575 B.A., J.D. Exec. Dir., Legal Aid Soc. NW NC

House & Tippett, PLLC, (AV)
3325 Healy Drive, 27103
Telephone: 336-768-2225 Fax: 336-768-3369 URL: http://www.lawyers.com/houseandtippett
Email: info@housetippett.com URL: http://www.housetippett.com
Don R. House; Scott K. Tippett.
Practice limited to Business Law, Taxation, Securities, Wills, Trusts, Probate and Commercial Real Estate.
See Professional Biographies, WINSTON-SALEM, NORTH CAROLINA

Howard, Jeffrey C., (AV) '54 '79 C.228 B.A. L.862 J.D.
Salem Investment Conselors, Inc
Howard, Kristine M. .... '73 '98 C.893 B.A. L.692 J.D. [A Constangy,B.&S.]
Howell, Julius A. .... '14 '35 C&L.896 B.S., LL.B. 480 Forsyth Med. Pk.‡
Howington, Richard B., (AV) .... '44 '69 C&L.896 B.S., J.D. [Nelson M.R.&S.]
Howland, Jeffrey C., (AV) .... '58 '82 C.896 B.A. L.790 J.D. [Womble C.S.&R.]
Hudson, Howard V., Jr., (BV) '45 '70 C.575 A.B. L.896 J.D.
Sr. V.P. & Assoc. Gen. Coun., Branch Banking and Trust Company
Humphrey, Dudley, (AV) .... '— '61 C.228 A.B. L.575 J.D. [Kilpatrick S.]
Humphrey, George D., Jr .... '33 '61 C.228 B.A. L.575 J.D. 1001 West Fourth St.
Hunter, Robert C. .... '60 '86 C.597 B.A. L.228 J.D. [Fitzgerald&H.]
Hutcherson, James P., (AV) '61 '89 C&L.896 B.A., J.D.
Chief Legal Officer, Luwa, Inc.
Hutchins, Fred S., Jr., (AV) .... '32 '59 C.575 B.S. L.896 LL.B. [C White&C.]
Hutchins, Laurie .... '56 '83 C.575 B.A. L.896 J.D. Dist. J.
Hutto, H. Marie, (BV) .... '67 '97 C.444 B.A. L.1345 J.D. [H.M.Hutto]

Hutto, H. Marie, P.C., (BV)
8 West Third Street, Suite 500, 27101
Telephone: 336-721-1060 Fax: 336-721-9102
Email: huttolaw2@hotmail.com URL: http://www.huttolawyer.com
H. Marie Hutto.
Criminal Law, Driving While Intoxicated, Drug Crimes, Felonies, Misdemeanors, Traffic Violations, Family Law, Separation Agreements, Collaborative Law, Divorce, Child Custody and Child Support, Spousal Support, Adoptions, Personal Injury.
See Professional Biographies, WINSTON-SALEM, NORTH CAROLINA

Hyde, Lisa, (AV⊤) '59 '85 C&L.69 B.B.A., J.D.
(adm. in TX; not adm. in NC) 335 Fairfax Drive
Ingersoll, Marc W., (BV) .... '64 '91 C.92 B.S. L.896 J.D. [Ingersoll&Assoc.]

Ingersoll & Associates, PLLC, (BV)
1590 Westbrook Plaza Drive, Suite 203, 27103
Telephone: 336-794-2278 Fax: 336-794-2281
URL: http://www.ingersollfirm.com
Marc W. Ingersoll;—Joel M. Williams.
Wills, Estate Planning, Trusts and Estates, Probate, Elder Law, Business Law, Corporate Law, Commercial Real Estate, Tax Law, Collections.
See Professional Biographies, WINSTON-SALEM, NORTH CAROLINA

Inman, Stephen T. .... '— '99 C.902 B.A. L.880 J.D. [A Kilpatrick S.]
Irvin, David A., (AV) .... '39 '66 C.198 B.A. L.575 LL.B. [Womble C.S.&R.]
Iseman, James M., Jr., (AV) .... '51 '77 C.228 A.B. L.575 J.D. [Wilson&I.]
Jackson, Jane C., (AV) .... '58 '83 C.896 B.S. L.893 J.D. [Robinson&L.]
James, Paul M., III, (BV) .... '59 '85 C.228 B.A. L.575 J.D. 811 W. 5th. St., Ste. 102
James, Randolph M., (BV) .... '53 '81 C.576 B.E.D.A. L.896 J.D. [R.M.James]

James, Randolph M., P.C., (BV)
116 North Spruce Street, P.O. Box 20069, 27101
Telephone: 336-724-7707 Fax: 336-724-9722
Email: rmjames@rmjameslaw.com URL: http://www.rmjameslaw.com
Randolph M. James.
Civil Litigation Practice in State and Federal Courts. Personal Injury, Workers Compensation, Employment, Products Liability, Professional Malpractice, Medical Malpractice, Legal Malpractice, Commercial and Construction Litigation, Unfair and Deceptive Trade Practices, Class Actions, Discrimination, Sexual Harassment, Automobile Accidents, Dog Bites, Sexual Abuse, Slip and Fall, Wrongful Death.
See Professional Biographies, WINSTON-SALEM, NORTH CAROLINA

Jeannette, Michael W. '57 '88 C.929 B.S. L.1356 J.D.
(adm. in VA; not adm. in NC) Nat. Labor Relations Bd.
Jenkins, Gordon W., (AV) .... '45 '74 C.228 A.B. L.575 J.D. [Wells,J.L.&J.P.]
Jenkins, Rebecca Jo '50 '76 C.392 A.B. L.1003 J.D.
(adm. in OH; not adm. in NC) Branch Banking and Trust Company

Jennings, Edward, Law Offices of, (BV) '48 '73 C&L.896 B.A., J.D.
3333 Brookview Hills Boulevard, Suite 206, 27103-5661 ⊙
Telephone: 336-760-3421 Fax: 336-659-6048
Email: lawyeroncall@aol.com URL: http://www.edwardjenningslaw.com
(Also Associated with Kirschbaum, Nanney & Brown, P.A., Raleigh).
Languages: English.
Civil and Criminal Trials and Appeals in all State and Federal Courts. Personal Injury, Family Law, Divorce, Child Custody, Estates, Real Estate, Workers Compensation, Social Security.
Taylorsville, North Carolina Office: 83 South Center Street, 28681. Telephone: 828-632-5869. Facsimile: 828-632-5764.
See Professional Biographies, WINSTON-SALEM, NORTH CAROLINA

Jernigan, Katherine B. .... '75 '00 C.228 L.896 J.D. Wachovia Bank, NA
Jernigan, Trent E. .... '75 '00 C.575 B.A. L.896 J.D. [A Womble C.S.&R.]
Jessup, Debra Ragin, (BV) .... '60 '89 C.276 B.A. L.896 J.D. [Jessup&P.]
Jessup & Probst, (BV) .... P.O. Box 11413
Johnson, Ana Davis '72 '97 C.472 B.B.A. L.569 J.D.
(adm. in NY; not adm. in NC) [A Womble C.S.&R.]
Johnson, Bradley R. .... '70 '98 C.506 B.A. L.1035 J.D. [A Womble C.S.&R.]

Johnson, Daniel S., (BV) .... '50 '75 C&L.896 B.A., J.D. 3910 White Hawk Lane
Johnson, John J. ..... '32 '60 C&L.896 B.S., J.D. V.P., Gen. Coun. & Secy., Integon Corp.
Johnson, Michael O., (AV) '46 '75 C.198 A.B. L.790 J.D.
V.P., Dep. Gen. Coun. & Secy., R. J. Reynolds Tobacco Co.
Johnson, Sarah M. .... '45 '79 C&L.896 B.A., J.D. [🄲 Womble C.S.&R.]
Johnson, Stephen A., (AV) '58 '84 C&L.893 B.A., J.D.
Sr. Coun. & Asst. Secy., Krispy Kreme Doughnut Corp.
Johnston, Daniel R., (BV) .... '47 '96 C.575 A.B. L.896 J.D. [Wood,R.&J.]
Jolly, Robert J. .... '57 '84 C.896 B.A. L.575 J.D. [🅂 Womble C.S.&R.]
Jones, G. Scott .... '45 '72 C&L.896 B.A., J.D. 1300 Brookstown Ave

Jordan, Jerry D. '65 '97 C.43 B.S. L.1187 J.D.
8 W. Third Street, Suite 610, 27101
Telephone: 336-725-5656 Fax: 336-725-5657
Email: JdjLaw@aol.com URL: http://www.jerryjordanlaw.com
Criminal, Drug Crimes, DWI, Traffic Violations, Family Law, Child Custody, Child Support.
See Professional Biographies, WINSTON-SALEM, NORTH CAROLINA

Joyner, George William, III .... '69 '96 C.674 A.B. L.896 J.D. [Womble C.S.&R.]
Juran, Peter J., (AV) .... '61 '86 C.165 B.A. L.228 J.D. [Blanco T.C.&M.]
Kadlec, Keith Daniel .... '69 '94 C&L.575 A.B., J.D. 3741 Derbyshire Rd.
Kangur, Tonu T., Jr., (BV) .... '65 '92 C.896 B.A. L.1345 J.D. 1340 Westgate Ctr. Dr.
Karr, Stephen P. .... '49 '76 C.966 B.A. L.896 J.D. R.J. Reynolds Tobacco Co.
Kearns, Phil H. .... '65 '94 C.896 B.A. L.1187 J.D. Staff Atty., Integon Corp.
Keever, R. Andrew .... '73 '04 C.575 B.A. L.1345 J.D. [🄰 Davis&H.]
Keiger, John A., (BV) .... '60 '89 C&L.575 B.A., J.D. [Craige B.L.&W.]
Keiger, R. Kason .... '34 '60 C.575 B.S. L.896 LL.B. Dist. J.
Keith, Thomas J., (AV) ...... '44 '70 C.575 A.B. L.896 J.D. Forsyth Cnty. Hall of Justice
Kelly, James H., Jr., (AV) .... '— '68 C.198 A.B. L.228 J.D. [Kilpatrick S.]
Kelly, Laurie Schlossberg, (BV) .... '66 '95 C.941 B.A. L.988 J.D. [White&C.]
Kendrick, Anne Catherine '75 '01 C.198 B.A. L.192 J.D.
Asst. VP, Wachovia Corporation
Kennedy, Annie Brown, (AV) ..... '24 '52 C.811 A.B. L.329 J.D. 310 W. 4th St., Ste. 710
Kennedy, Harold L., III, (AV) '52 '78 C.575 B.A. L.477 J.D.
301 N. Main St., Ste. 2000
Kennedy, Harvey L., (AV) ..... '52 '77 C.575 B.A. L.309 J.D. 301 N. Main St., Ste. 2000
Kennedy, Willie May Alexander, (BV) .... '39 '82 C.999 B.S. L.896 J.D. P.O. Box 11362
Keshian, Richard J., (AV) .... '— '83 C.228 A.B. L.880 J.D. [Kilpatrick S.]

Kilpatrick Stockton LLP, (AV)
1001 West Fourth Street, 27101-2400 ⊙
Telephone: 336-607-7300 Facsimile: 336-607-7500
Email: info@KilpatrickStockton.com URL: http://www.KilpatrickStockton.com
Members of Firm: Stephen R. Berlin (Resident); Susan Holdsclaw Boyles; Peter S. Brunstetter (Resident); Charles W. Calkins (Resident); Adam H. Charnes (Resident); W. Mark Conger (Resident); C. Penn Craver, Jr. (Resident); Tonya R. Deem; Louis W. Doherty (Resident); Michael L. Drye (Resident); Robert L. Edwards (Resident); J. Robert Elster (Resident); Steven Gardner (Resident); Richard S. Gottlieb; John M. Harrington (Resident); Dudley Humphrey (Resident); James H. Kelly, Jr. (Resident); Richard J. Keshian (Resident); Jeffrey T. Lawyer (Resident); George L. Little, Jr. (Resident); David C. Smith (Resident); Daniel R. Taylor, Jr. (Resident); Danielle Thompson Williams; William E. Wright (Resident). Resident Associates: John C. Alemanni; James M. Boggs; David Popham Broughton; William M. Bryner; James Calvin (Cal) Cunningham, III; Daniel P. Ebersole; Elliot Alexander Fus; Todd W. Galinski; Laura A. Greer; Jessica R. Harris; James J. Hefferan, Jr.; Stéphen T. Inman; J. Jason Link; Corena A. Norris-McCluney; Ryan B. Opel; Andrew A. Roppel (Not admitted in NC); Cynthia B. Rothschild; T. Benjamin Schroeder (Not admitted in NC); C. Edward Teague, III; Mark D. Tolman; Andrew H. Veach; J. Clinton Wimbish; Bret T. Winterle.
Civil Trial and Appellate Practice in all State and Federal Courts, Federal State and Local Taxation, Probate, Trust and Estate Planning, Real Estate, Environmental, Corporate, Corporate Reorganization, Securities, Banking Commercial, Antitrust, Labor, Employment, Administrative, Bankruptcy, Construction, Healthcare, Intellectual Property, Professional Malpractice, Products Liability and Negligence Law, Domestic Law and Equitable Distribution, Employee Benefits and Executive Compensation, Entrepreneurial Development, Franchising, Insurance Defense, Sports and Entertainment, State Agency and Lobbying Practice.
Atlanta, Georgia Office: Suite 2800, 1100 Peachtree Street. Telephone: 404-815-6500. Facsimile: 404-815-6555. Telex: 54-2307.
Augusta, Georgia Office: 699 Broad Street, Suite 1400, 30903-2043. Telephone: 706-724-2622. Facsimile: 706-722-0219.
Charlotte, North Carolina Office: Suite 2500, 214 North Tryon Street, 28202. Telephone: 704-338-5000. Facsimile: 704-338-5125.
London, England Office: 39th Floor, One Canada Square, London E145 NZ. Telephone: 44 (0)20 7154 6000. Facsimile: 44 (0)20 7154 6100.
New York, New York Office: 805 Third Avenue, 20th Floor, 10022. Telephone: 212-912-3527.
Raleigh, North Carolina Office: Suite 400, 3737 Glenwood Avenue, 27612. Telephone: 919-420-1700. Facsimile: 919-420-1800.
Stockholm, Sweden Office: Box 5421, SE-114 84. Telephone: 46-8-505-646-00. Facsimile: 46-8-505-646-99.
Washington, D.C. Office: Suite 900, 607 14th Street, N.W., 20005-2018. Telephone: 202-508-5800. Facsimile: 202-508-5858.
See Professional Biographies, WINSTON-SALEM, NORTH CAROLINA

King, Roberta B. .... '75 '03 C&L.896 B.A., J.D. [Bennett&G.P.]
Kitzman, Eleanor L. '56 '86 C.326 B.A. L.796 J.D.
(adm. in TX; not adm. in NC) V.P., Govt. Rel., Integon Corp.
Koontz, John K. .... [🄰 Lewis&D.]
Kreiner, Christopher A. .... '69 '94 C&L.575 B.S., J.D. [Womble C.S.&R.]
Kurtz, Jon Brenner, (BV) .... '68 '94 C.16 B.A. L.575 J.D. [Tash&K.]
Lambie, James T. .... '42 '70 C.122 B.S. L.273 J.D. [🄲 Bell,D.&P.]
Landers, James E., Jr. .... '27 '52 C&L.896 B.S., LL.B. 2832 Loch Dr.‡
Lang, Robert A., (AV) .... '59 '85 C.207 B.A. L.896 J.D. Off. of U.S. Atty.
Lanning, Amy C. .... '75 '04 C.1128 B.A. L.896 J.D. [🄰 Blanco T.C.&M.]
Latham, William E., II, (BV) .... '68 '93 C.228 A.B. L.420 J.D. [Womble C.S.&R.]
Lawing, Robert J., (AV) .... '46 '73 C.232 A.B. L.896 J.D. [Robinson&L.]
Laws, Robert B., (BV) .... '57 '85 C.575 B.A. L.896 J.D. 101 Charlois Blvd., Ste. 102
Lawyer, Jeffrey T., (AV) .... '— '86 C.259 B.S. L.228 J.D. [Kilpatrick S.]
Leach, Mark A., (CV) .... '71 '96 C.1349 B.A. L.896 J.D. [Orbock R.&D.]
Lee, Kelly Scott .... '62 '98 C.1097 B.A. L.896 J.D. [Teeter]
Lee, Robert E., Jr. .... '34 '60 C&L.896 B.S., LL.B. Vet. Admn.
Lefevre, Margaret L. .... '73 '00 C.902 B.A. L.896 J.D. [🄲 Womble C.S.&R.]
Lefkowitz, Victor M., (BV) .... '43 '77 C.688 B.E.E. L.896 J.D. 105 W. 4th St.
Leggett, R. Bradford, (AV) .... '44 '69 C&L.896 B.A., J.D. [Allman S.L.&C.]
Lemmerman, Richard D., Jr., (BV) '57 '82 C.896 B.A. L.1228 J.D.
V.P. Asst. & Gen. Coun., ACS Benefit Servs., Inc.
Leon, Christopher E., (AVⓉ) ..... '58 '84 C.597 B.S.I.E. L.896 J.D. [Womble C.S.&R.]
Leonard, Jonathan William Bain .... '73 '00 C.896 B.A. L.201 J.D. [Leonard]
Leonard, R. Michael, (AV) .... '53 '78 C&L.575 A.B., J.D. [Womble C.S.&R.]
Leonard Law Firm .... 100 S. Marshall St., Ste. 1
Levenson, Mary B. .... '62 '90 C.575 B.A. L.896 J.D. Sr. Atty., Integon
Lewis, Michael J., (AV) .... '45 '70 C&L.896 B.A., J.D. [Lewis&D.]
Lewis & Daggett, P.A., (AV) .... 285 Executive Park Blvd.
Ligon, Roddey M., Jr., (AV) .... '24 '51 C&L.575 B.S., J.D. [Womble C.S.&R.]
Liipfert, B. Bailey, III, (BV) .... '61 '91 C.575 A.B. L.1228 J.D. [Craige B.L.&W.]
Liipfert, Cowles, (AV) .... '38 '64 C&L.575 A.B., LL.B. [Craige B.L.&W.]
Liner, David V., (BV) .... '41 '69 C&L.896 B.S., J.D. One N. Marshall St.

Link, J. Jason, (BV) ....'— '98 C.576 B.S. L.575 J.D. [🄰 Kilpatrick S.]
Little, George L., Jr., (AV) .... '— '67 C.198 A.B. L.575 J.D. [Kilpatrick S.]
Lloyd, Emma M. .... '77 '02 C.260 B.S.B.A. L.896 J.D. Asst. Gen. Coun., Inmar, Inc.
Loftis, W. Randolph, Jr., (AV) .... '47 '71 C.968 B.A. L.896 J.D. [Constangy,B.&S.]

Long, C. R. "Skip", Jr., (BV) '50 '82 C.232 B.A. L.896 J.D.
2000 Frontis Plaza Boulevard, Suite 100, 27103
Telephone: 336-768-7772 Fax: 336-774-9914
Email: skiplong@triad.rr.com URL: http://www.lawyers.com/skiplong
(Board Certified Specialist in Family Law, North Carolina State Board of Legal Specialization).
Board Certified Specialist in Family Law; Certified Equitable Distribution Mediator, Equitable Distribution, Child Custody and Support, Alimony, Divorce, Personal Injury and Major Insurance Claims, Domestic and other Civil Appeals, Mediation and Arbitration.
See Professional Biographies, WINSTON-SALEM, NORTH CAROLINA

Long, L. Donald, Jr., (BV) '53 '78 C.198 B.A. L.896 J.D.
119 Brookstown Ave., Rm. 301
Lucas, Philip E., (AV) .... '18 '41 C&L.575 B.A., LL.B. [🄲 Wells,J.L.&J.P.]
Luckey, Charles D., (BV) .... '55 '85 C.893 B.A. L.184 J.D. [Blanco T.C.&M.]
Luckey, Julie M. .... '63 '90 C&L.575 B.A., J.D. [🄰 Price]
Lundquist, David R. '50 '77 C&L.352 B.A., J.D.
V.P. & Reg. Tr. Spec., First Union National Bank of North Carolina
Lupton, Harvey A. .... '09 '33 C.228 L.896 LL.B. Emergency J., Supr. Ct.
MacKenzie, Heather A. '61 '90 C&L.228 B.A., J.D.
(adm. in PA; not adm. in NC) [MacKenzie]
MacKenzie Law Firm, The .... 407 Summit Street
Madigan, Michael Joseph '64 '89
C.602 B.B.A. L.424 J.D., R.J. Reynolds Tobacco Company
Madonia, Marc P. .... '74 '01 C.264 B.A. L.776 J.D. 285 Executive Park Blvd.
Magers, Bruce, (BV) .... '45 '74 C.613 B.A. L.896 J.D. 2990 Bethesda Pl.
Magers, Michael B. ...... '45 '74 C.613 B.A. L.896 J.D. 2990 Bethesda Place, Suite 604-C
Malay, Karen B. .... '80 '05 C&L.1228 B.A., J.D. [🄰 Allman S.L.&C.]
Mann, George T. "Ted" .... '49 '74 C.893 B.A. L.880 J.D. [Allman S.L.&C.]
Mann, John R., (BV) .... '54 '81 C.575 B.S. L.896 J.D. [Hatfield,M.D.V.&M.]
Mann, Kim Kelly, (AV) .... '58 '85 C.577 B.A. L.1228 J.D. [Womble C.S.&R.]
Marcotullio, Richard J. '41 '67 C.276 A.B. L.724 J.D.
(adm. in NY; not adm. in NC) R.J. Reynolds Tobacco Intl., Inc.
Maready, William F., (AV) .... '32 '58 C&L.575 A.B., J.D. [Firm of W.F.Maready]
Maready, William F., The Law Firm of, (AV) .... 1076 West Fourth Street, Suite 100
Marsch, Darryl R. '66 '91 C&L.846 B.A., J.D.
RJ Reynolds Tobacco Co., RJ Reynolds Tobacco Co.
Marshburn, G. Wriston, Jr .... '67 '97 C.269 B.A. L.192 J.D. [🄰 Womble C.S.&R.]
Martin, Bobby G. .... '34 '65 C&L.896 B.A., LL.B. [B.G.Martin] ‡
Martin, Davida W., (BV) .... '53 '78 C.1378 B.S. L.896 J.D. Co. Atty.
Martin, Jennifer M., (BV) .... '74 '99 C&L.896 B.A., J.D. Dist. Atty.'s Off.
Martin, B. G. .... 3880 Vest Mill Rd.
Marty, Dina J. '73 '98 C.221 B.A. L.896 J.D.
Asst. Coun., Wake Forest University (Legal Department)
Mason, Robert D., Jr. .... '74 '00 C.228 A.B. L.902 J.D. [🄰 Womble C.S.&R.]
Massey, Carl B., Jr. .... '64 '97 C.896 B.S. L.94 J.D. [🄰 Womble C.S.&R.] (Pat.)
Mast, David P., Jr., (AV) .... '31 '55 C&L.896 B.S., LL.B. [Sapp&M.]
Matamoros, Ronald A., (AV) .... '50 '75 C.1365 B.A. L.245 J.D. [Blanco T.C.&M.]
Maxwell, Lylton E. .... '14 '39 C&L.228 A.B., LL.B. P.O. Box 11106‡
Maynard, C. Douglas, Jr., (BV) .... '63 '92 C.228 B.A. L.896 J.D. [Maynard&H.]

Maynard & Harris, Attorneys At Law, PLLC, (BV)
514 South Stratford Road, Suite 321, 27103
Telephone: 336-777-1411 Facsimile: 336-777-8882 URL: http://www.maynardharris.com
Email: maynlaw@aol.com URL: http://www.lawyers.com/maynard&harris
C. Douglas Maynard, Jr.; Celeste M. Harris.
Plaintiff Trial Practice, Personal Injury, Automobile and Tractor Trailer Accidents, Workers Compensation, Social Security, Wrongful Death, Nursing Home Liability, Insurance Claims.
See Professional Biographies, WINSTON-SALEM, NORTH CAROLINA

Mazza, David J. .... '62 '95 C.723 B.S. L.734 J.D. [🄰 Womble C.S.&R.]
McCall, G. Emmett, (AV) .... '43 '69 C&L.383 B.A., J.D. [Bell,D.&P.]
McCarty, Linda L. .... '72 '02 C.763 B.A. L.1202 J.D. [🄰 Blanco T.C.&M.]
McCloskey, Steven A., (CV) .... '52 '99 C.886 B.S. L.574 J.D. 240 Natalie Dr.
McDonald, Roy Lawrence, II .... '68 '00 C.296 B.S. L.896 J.D. 411 N. Cherry Street
McDougald, Lisa B. '59 '85 C.953 B.A. L.575 J.D.
Sr. V.P. & Assoc. Gen. Coun., Branch Banking and Trust Company
McElroy, C. Eugene .... '38 '63 C&L.896 B.A., LL.B. P.O. Box 5393‡
McFadden, Jeffrey R., (BV) ..... '58 '85 C.896 B.S. L.128 J.D. [Womble C.S.&R.] (Pat.)
McGee, Lawrence U., (AV) '53 '80
C.63 B.S. L.896 J.D. Sr. V.P. & Gen. Coun., Novant Health, Inc.
McIver, Roderick T., (BV) .... '68 '93 C.955 B.S. L.896 J.D. P.O. Box 21574
McKenney, Deborah L. .... '70 '95 C&L.477 A.B., J.D. [Blanco T.C.&M.]
McKim, Thomas F. '53 '78 C.453 S.B. L.145 J.D.
(adm. in DC; not adm. in NC) Asst. Gen. Coun., R.J. Reynolds Tobacco Co.
McMillen, John A., (BV) .... '63 '91 C.659 B.A. L.910 J.D. [Davis&H.]
McNames, Dennis W., (AV) .... '47 '72 C.575 B.S. L.896 J.D. [Womble C.S.&R.]
Meadows, John A., (BV) .... '48 '78 C.1287 B.B.A. L.201 J.D. [Meadows&A.]
Meadows & Aderhold, P.A., (BV) .... 2596 Reynolda Road, Suite C
Meeks, Nicole Marie '69 '94 C.575 B.A. L.128 J.D.
(adm. in MD; not adm. in NC) Jud. Law Clk., U.S. Dist. Ct.
Mendel, Phyllis E., (BV) .... '55 '95 C.577 B.S. L.896 J.D. [Hendrick&B.]
Menefee, Lisa V.L. .... '56 '82 C.228 B.A. L.1202 J.D. Dist. Ct. J.
Menzel, Kenneth E. .... '79 '05 C.282 B.A. L.896 J.D. [🄰 Pharr&B.]
Metcalf, W. Eugene, (BV) .... '54 '81 C.48 B.S. L.896 J.D. [Metcalf&B.]

Metcalf & Beal, L.L.P., (BV)
380 Knollwood Street, Suite 450, 27103
Telephone: 336-777-0067 Fax: 336-748-0375
Email: metcalf@metcalfandbeal.com URL: http://www.metcalfandbeal.com
W. Eugene Metcalf; Christopher L. Beal (Board Certified Specialist in Family Law, North Carolina State Board of Legal Specialization).
General Civil and Criminal Practice in State and Federal Courts. Family Law, Adoptions, Child Custody, Child Support, Divorce, Equitable Distribution, Visitation Rights, Criminal Law, Driving While Intoxicated (DUI), Drug Crimes, Parole and Probation, White Collar Crime, Traffic Violations, Personal Injury, Automobile Accidents, Slip and Fall, Wrongful Death, Medical Malpractice, Nursing Home Abuse, Workers Compensation, Real Estate, Eminent Domain, Employment, Wrongful Termination, Trust and Estates, Wills, Probate.
See Professional Biographies, WINSTON-SALEM, NORTH CAROLINA

Mewhinney, Kate, (AV) '51 '78 C.860 B.A. L.588 J.D.
Clinical Prof. & Mang. Atty., Wake Forest Univ., Elder Law Clinic
Michael, Kenneth R. .... '57 '94 C&L.260 B.Design, J.D. [Womble C.S.&R.]
Millar, John L. .... '45 '72 C.1115 A.B. L.923 J.D. 401 N. Main Street
Miller, Gordon A., (BV) .... '50 '75 C.381 B.A. L.896 J.D. [Wilson,D.&M.]
Miller, Kevin L., (AV) .... '59 '84 C.228 A.B. L.575 J.D. [Robinson&L.]
Miller, Mark Williams .... '57 '95 C.968 B.A. L.790 J.D. P.O. Box 84

Miller, Rebecca H. . . . . . '74 '00 C.606 B.A. L.280 J.D. [Ⓐ Robinson&L.]
Minnich, Stephen C., (BV) . . . . . '70 '96 C.294 B.A. L.930 J.D. [Ⓐ Blanco T.C.&M.]
Mitchell, Beverly R., (BV) . . . . . '42 '79 C.709 B.S. L.896 J.D. P.O. Box 20184
Mitchell, Eddie C., (AV) . . . . . '41 '68 C.232 A.B. L.575 J.D. [E.C.Mitchell]

Mitchell, Eddie C., P.A., (AV)
110 Oakwood Drive, Suite 410, 27103
Telephone: 336-725-9597 Fax: 336-725-6662
Eddie C. Mitchell.
Civil and Criminal Practice in all State Courts. Family Law, Divorce, Traffic, Driving While Impaired (DWI), Personal Injury, Mediation, Family Financial and Superior Court Mediation.
References: Wachovia Bank & Trust Co., N.A.; First Citizens Bank and Trust Company.
See Professional Biographies, WINSTON-SALEM, NORTH CAROLINA

Mohr, Philip J., (BV) . . . . . '70 '97 C&L.602 B.A., J.D. [Ⓐ Womble C.S.&R.]
Molitoris, Theodore M., (BV) . . . . . '52 '77 C.705 B.A. L.896 J.D. 823 W. 5th St.
Montaquila, Susan R. '51 '76 C.575 B.A. L.896 J.D.
Prof. of Legal Writing & Dir. of Mas. of Law Prog., Wake Forest Univ. Sch. of Law
Montecalvo, Michael . . . . . '69 '94 C.882 B.A. L.228 J.D. [Ⓐ Womble C.S.&R.]
Moore, Thomas W., Jr., (AV) . . . . . '37 '63 C&L.896 B.A., J.D. 115 W. 3rd St.‡
Moose, Robert M. . . . . . '26 '78 C.404 A.B. L.896 J.D. 3117 Kinnamon Rd.‡
Morgan, J. Griffin, (AV) . . . . . '50 '76 C.207 B.A. L.033 J.D. [Elliot P.M.]
Morgan, J. Reid, (AV) '53 '79 C&L.896 B.A., J.D.
V.P. & Gen. Coun., Wake Forest University (Legal Department)
Morgan, James R., Jr., (AV) . . . . . '58 '84 C&L.896 B.S., J.D. [Womble C.S.&R.]

Morgan, Herring, Morgan, Green, Rosenblutt & Gill, LLP
(See High Point)

Morris, John B., (BV) '67 '95
C.577 B.A. L.477 J.D. Asst. Gen. Counsel, Novant Health, Inc.

Morris York Williams Surles & Barringer, L.L.P.
(See Charlotte)

Morrow, John F., (AV) . . . . . '40 '65 C&L.896 B.B.A., J.D. [Morrow A.&P.]
Morrow, John F., Jr., (AV) . . . . . '70 '96 C.575 B.S. L.896 J.D. [Ⓐ Womble C.S.&R.]

Morrow Alexander & Porter, PLLC, (AV)
3890 Vest Mill Road, 27103-1302
Mailing Address: P.O. Box 25226, Winston-Salem, NC 27114-5226
Telephone: 336-760-1400 Fax: 336-760-4520
Email: info@morrowalexander.com URL: http://www.morrowalexander.com
John F. Morrow (Board Certified Specialist in Family Law, North Carolina State Board of Legal Specialization); Charles J. Alexander, II (Board Certified Specialist in Criminal Law, North Carolina State Board of Legal Specialization); Benjamin D. Porter (Board Certified Specialist in Criminal Law, North Carolina State Board of Legal Specialization).
Personal Injury, Domestic Relations, Equitable Distribution, Custody, Criminal Defense, Federal Criminal Law, DWI, Drug Crimes, Traffic, Mediation, Arbitration.
See Professional Biographies, WINSTON-SALEM, NORTH CAROLINA

Morton, J. Kevin, Attorney at Law, (BV) '57 '83 C.198 B.A. L.575 J.D.
1604 W. First St.
Moser, Kenneth A., (AV) . . . . . '42 '68 C&L.896 B.A., J.D. [Womble C.S.&R.]
Motycka, Kelly E. . . . . . '77 '02 C.679 B.A. L.896 J.D. [Hendrick&B.]
Mountcastle, George C., (AV) . . . . . '32 '61 C.575 A.B. L.896 J.D. [Hatfield,M.D.V.&M.]
Moxley, Marcus L., (AV) . . . . . '62 '89 C&L.575 B.S., J.D. [Vaughn P.E.M.&S.]
Murphrey, W. E., (BV) . . . . . '58 '84 C&L.896 B.A., J.D. [W.E.Murphrey]
Murphrey, W. E., PLLC, (BV) . . . . . 301 North Main Street, Suite 2452
Murphy, Frank '47 '72 C.198 A.B. L.880 J.D.
Exec. V.P., Gen. Coun. & Secy., Krispy Kreme Doughnut Corporation
Myers, Douglas K., (CV) . . . . . '51 '94 C.63 B.S. L.896 J.D. 301 South Liberty Street
Myers, Grover M. '40 '68 C.497 B.S. L.500 J.D.
Asst. Gen. Coun. & Chf. Pat. Coun., R.J. Reynolds Tobacco Co. (Pat.)
Myers, William C., (AV) . . . . . '36 '64 C.309 A.B. L.896 LL.B. 3511 Buena Vista Rd.
Nagle, Carl B. . . . . . '65 '93 C&L.280 B.B.A., J.D. [Nagle&Assoc.]

Nagle & Associates, P.A.
380 Knollwood Street Suite 320, 27103
Telephone: 336-723-4500 Fax: 336-723-1219
URL: http://www.lawyers.com/nagleandassociates
Carl B. Nagle.
Plaintiff Personal Injury.
See Professional Biographies, WINSTON-SALEM, NORTH CAROLINA

Neely, Joyce Riddle, (BV) . . . . . '44 '75 C.320 A.B. L.896 J.D. Ray Len Vineyards, Inc.
Nelson, William L., (BV) '32 '60
C.198 B.A. L.575 LL.B. [Nelson,B.N.&G.] & [Ⓒ CraigeB.L.&W.]
Nelson, Boyles, Niblock and Green, (AV) . . . . . 101 Charlois Blvd.

Nelson Mullins Riley & Scarborough LLP, (AV)
The Knollwood, 380 Knollwood Street, Suite 530, 27103 ⊙
Telephone: 336-774-3300 Fax: 336-774-3299
URL: http://www.nelsonmullins.com
Partners: Denise M. Gunter; Mark A. Stafford; Richard B. Howington. Associates: Crystal B. Baker; Donald R. Pocock. Of Counsel: Goran P. Stojkovich.
Health Care.
Atlanta, Georgia Office: 999 Peachtree Street, N.E., Suite 1400, 30309-3964. P.O. Box 77707, 30357-0707. Telephone: 404-817-6000. Telecopy: 404-817-6050.
Charleston, South Carolina Office: Liberty Center, Suite 600, 151 Meeting Street, 29401-2239. P.O. Box 1806, 29402-1806. Telephone: 843-853-5200. Telecopy: 843-722-8700.
Charlotte, North Carolina Office: Bank of America Corporate Center, Suite 2400, 100 North Tryon Street, 28202-4007. Telephone: 704-417-3000. Telecopy: 704-377-4814.
Columbia, South Carolina Office: Meridian, 17th Floor, 1320 Main Street, 29201, P.O. Box 11070, 29211-1070. Telephone: 803-799-2000. Telecopy: 803-256-7500.
Greenville, South Carolina Office: Poinsett Plaza, 104 South Main Street, Suite 900, 29601. P.O. Box 10084, 29603-0084. Telephone: 864-250-2300. Telecopy: 864-232-2925.
Myrtle Beach, South Carolina Office: Founders Centre, Suite 301, 2411 North Oak Street, 29577-3165. P.O. Box 3939, 29578-3939. Telephone: 843-448-3500. Telecopy: 843-448-3437.
Raleigh, North Carolina Office: GlenLake One, Suite 200, 4140 Parklake Avenue, 27612. Telephone: 919-877-3800. Telecopy: 919-877-3799.
Washington, D.C. Office: 101 Constitution Avenue, NW, Suite 900, 20001. Telephone: 202-712-2800. Fax: 202-712-2860.
See Professional Biographies, WINSTON-SALEM, NORTH CAROLINA

Nerhood, Timothy . . . . . '72 '98 C&L.575 B.S.B.A., J.D. [Hendrick&B.]
Newman, Joel S. '46 '72 C.103 A.B. L.145 J.D.
(adm. in NY; not adm. in NC) Prof., Wake Forest Univ. School of Law
Newman, John T., VI, (BV) . . . . . '58 '83 C.1318 B.A. L.896 J.D. 3511 Buena Vista Rd.
Newton, George D., Jr., (AV) . . . . . '31 '58 C.309 A.B. L.976 LL.B. 2818 Lazy Lane‡
Newton, T. Lawson, (BV) . . . . . '54 '81 C&L.896 B.S., J.D. [Wells,J.L.&J.P.]
Niblock, H. David, (BV) '54 '81
C.1130 B.A. L.1228 J.D. [Ⓒ Craige B.L.&W.] & [Nelson,B.N.&G.]
Nielsen, Donald M., (AV) . . . . . '57 '90 C.299 A.B. L.228 J.D. [Bell,D.&P.]
Nifong, Norman L., (BV) . . . . . '41 '68 C&L.896 B.A., J.D. 207 N. Poplar St.
Norris-McCluney, Corena A. . . . . . '— '00 C.576 B.A. L.896 J.D. [Ⓐ Kilpatrick S.]

North, Jane P. '49 '84 C.1236 B.A. L.838 J.D.
(adm. in TN; not adm. in NC) Natl. Labor Rel. Bd.
Oakes, Jennifer I. . . . . . '77 '02 C.228 A.B. L.1228 J.D. [Ⓐ Bell,D.&P.]
Ogburn, Mary Margaret, (BV) . . . . . '51 '94 C.576 B.S. L.228 J.D. [Blanco T.C.&M.]

Oldaker, Guy B., III '50 '96 C.893 B.A. L.923 J.D.
3410 Healy Drive, Suite 115, 27103-1403
Telephone: 336-725-2346 Facsimile: 336-760-0922
Email: oldakerg@bellsouth.net URL: http://www.oldakerlaw.com
Family Law, Child Custody, Child Support, Divorce, Separation Agreements, Visitation Rights, Criminal Law, Driving While Intoxicated, (DWI), Drug Crimes, Traffic Violations, Personal Injury, Automobile Accidents and Injuries, Wrongful Death, Lemon Law, Toxic Torts.
See Professional Biographies, WINSTON-SALEM, NORTH CAROLINA

Oldham, Christopher H. . . . . . '66 '95 C.951 B.A. L.174 J.D. [Ⓐ Womble C.S.&R.]
Oldham, Mallory M., (AV) . . . . . '57 '81 C.577 B.A. L.896 J.D. [Bell,D.&P.]
Oneill, James Roderick, (BV) '65 '95 C.228 B.A. L.564 J.D.
Forsyth Co. Dist. Atty. Off.
Opel, Ryan B. . . . . . '— '02 C.896 B.A. L.228 J.D. [Ⓐ Kilpatrick S.]
Orbock, Maureen Tierney, (AV) . . . . . '44 '87 C.758 B.A. L.896 J.D. [Orbock R.&D.]

Orbock Ruark & Dillard, PC, (AV)
1590 Westbrook Plaza Drive, Suite 102, 27103
Telephone: 336-760-8848 Fax: 336-760-5903
Email: thomaslaw@triad.rr.com URL: http://www.ordlawfirm.com
Maureen Tierney Orbock; Roger Lee Dillard, Jr.; Barbara E. Ruark; Kent Conrad Ford; Mark A. Leach;—Stacey Dawn Rubain.
Workers Compensation, Personal Injury Defense.
See Professional Biographies, WINSTON-SALEM, NORTH CAROLINA

Osborn, Malcolm E., (AV) . . . . . '28 '56 C.431 B.A. L.94 J.D. [M.E.Osborn]
Osborn, Malcolm E., P.A., (AV) . . . . . 3639 Kirklees Road
Oser, Diane Brock, (BV) . . . . . '41 '76 C.950 B.A. L.596 J.D. [Ⓒ Ross]
Otis, Kenneth C., III (Casey) . . . . . '72 '01 C.198 B.A. L.896 J.D. [Ⓐ Hendrick&B.]
Palmiter, Alan R. '54 '80 C.608 B.S. L.477 J.D.
(adm. in DC; not adm. in NC) Wake Forest Univ.
Panetti, Eleanor, (BV) . . . . . '64 '89 C&L.575 B.A., J.D. [Stroud&P.]
Pape, Julie Barker, (BV) . . . . . '72 '99 C.880 B.A. L.262 J.D. [Ⓐ Womble C.S.&R.]
Papoulias, Maria C. . . . . . '76 '01 C.575 B.A L.896 J.D. [Ⓐ Wilson&I.]
Parker, Deborah L., (AV) '52 '83 C.577 B.A. L.896 J.D.
Dir., Legal Resch. & Writing, Wake Forest Univ. Sch. of Law
Parker, G. Edgar, (AV) . . . . . '46 '71 C&L.896 B.A., J.D. [White&C.]
Parker, J. Wilson . . . . . '52 '77 C.976 B.A. L.228 J.D. Prof. of Law, Wake Forest Univ.
Parker, Marian F. . . . . . '47 '78 C.577 B.A. L.896 J.D. Wake Forest Univ.
Parker, Vance R. . . . . . '62 '92 C&L.846 B.A., J.D. Univ. of N. C.
Parrish, Carl F., (BV) . . . . . '49 '74 C.232 B.A. L.896 J.D. 250 Exec. Park Blvd.
Pasternak, Joel H. '43 '68 C.184 B.S. L.94 J.D.
(adm. in MA; not adm. in NC)
V.P. and House Coun., Republic Mortgage Insurance Company
Pate, Wanda L. . . . . . '53 '79 C.925 B.S. L.575 J.D. N.L.R.B.
Patterson, Kelly T., (BV) . . . . . '70 '98 C.260 B.A. L.896 J.D. [K.Patterson]
Patterson, Kelly, Law Office of, (BV) . . . . . 8 W. Third St., Ste. 220
Patton, David V. . . . . . '69 '99 C&L.608 B.S., J.D. [Ⓐ Womble C.S.&R.]
Patton, Jeffrey D., (BV) . . . . . '69 '94 C.945 B.A. L.896 J.D. [Blanco T.C.&M.]
Pauca, Janet F., (BV) . . . . . '41 '83 C&L.896 B.A., J.D. 102 West Third Street, Suite 210
Peck, W. Mark . . . . . '68 '01 C.205 B.A. L.896 J.D. [Ⓐ Robinson&L.]
Peebles, Stafford R., Jr., (BV) . . . . . '41 '71 C.240 B.A. L.575 J.D. [Peebles&S.]
Peebles, Todd M., (CV) . . . . . '63 '91 C.575 B.A. L.1228 J.D. [Peebles&S.]
Peebles & Schramm, P.C., (BV) . . . . . 102 S. Cherry St.
Peed, Charles O., and Associates, (BV) '44 '72
C.198 A.B. L.575 J.D. 200 West First Street
Peeples, Ralph A. . . . . . '51 '76 C.198 A.B. L.569 J.D. Prof., Wake Forest Univ. Sch. of Law
Pegram, Marshall L. . . . . . '30 '61 C.296 A.B. L.896 LL.B. Vet. Admn.
Penney, A. Carl . . . . . '41 '68 C.576 B.S.E. L.575 J.D. 301 S. Liberty Street

Peraldo, Jeffrey K., P.A., The Law Offices of
(See Greensboro)

Perkinson, John R., Jr., (AV) . . . . . '48 '81 C&L.896 B.A., J.D. [Vaughn P.E.M.&S.]
Perlah, Philip M. '45 '70 C.102 B.S. L.262 J.D.
(adm. in NY; not adm. in NC) 1000 East Hanes Mill Road
Pfefferkorn, William Gottholdt, (AV) . . . . . '37 '62 C.575 B.A. L.145 J.D. [W.G.Pfefferkorn]
Pfefferkorn, William G., P.A., (AV) . . . . . 204 W. 3rd St.
Pharr, Steve M., (AV) . . . . . '53 '85 C.198 A.B. L.893 J.D. [Pharr&B.]

Pharr & Boynton, PLLC, (AV)
2720 Georgetown Drive, 27106
Telephone: 336-721-2400 Fax: 336-721-0039
Email: lwray@pharrlaw.com URL: http://www.lawyers.com/pharr&boynton
Steve M. Pharr; Mark D. Boynton. Associates: Stacey D. Bailey; Kenneth E. Menzel.
Litigation, Construction, Products Liability, Professional Liability, Real Estate Litigation in State and Federal Courts.
See Professional Biographies, WINSTON-SALEM, NORTH CAROLINA

Phelan, Jeanette K. . . . . . '63 '94 C.260 B.A. L.362 J.D. [Ⓐ Constangy,B.&S.]
Phillips, Eugene H. . . . . . '19 '40 C&L.896 LL.B. 355 Roslyn Rd.‡
Phillips, James K., (AV) . . . . . '51 '77 C&L.896 B.S., J.D. [Womble C.S.&R.]
Phillips, Michael D. . . . . . '68 '03 C.684 B.A. L.896 J.D. [Ⓐ Bell,D.&P.]
Phipps, Melissa Perrell . . . . . '67 '94 C&L.575 B.A., J.D. Corp. Coun, Novant Health, Inc.
Pierce, Robert S., (AV) . . . . . '50 '80 C.454 B.A. L.575 J.D. [Womble C.S.&R.]
Pinkston, Frank George, Jr., (CV) . . . . . '60 '99 C.511 L.574 J.D. P.O. Box 30361
Pipes, Matthew D. '74 '99 C.260 B.S. L.228 J.D.
(adm. in TX; not adm. in NC) [Ⓐ Womble C.S.&R.]
Pishko, David C., (AV) . . . . . '50 '77 C&L.228 B.A., J.D. [Elliot P.M.]
Pitt, Walter W., Jr., (AV) . . . . . '45 '71 C.575 A.B. L.896 J.D. [Bell,D.&P.]
Pocock, Donald R. . . . . . '74 '00 C&L.896 B.A., J.D. [Ⓐ Nelson M.R.&S.]
Poe, Sheena E., (AV) '62 '87
C.576 B.A. L.1345 J.D. V.P., Gen. Coun. & Secy., Integon Corp.
Poe, Stephen D., (AV) . . . . . '51 '76 C.896 A.B. L.575 J.D. [Bell,D.&P.]
Poole, Patricia F., (BV) . . . . . '59 '86 C.296 B.S. L.896 J.D. [Ⓐ Womble C.S.&R.]
Poovey, Mark N., (AV) . . . . . '56 '80 C&L.896 B.A., J.D. [Womble C.S.&R.]
Porter, Benjamin D., (BV) . . . . . '70 '95 C.473 B.S. L.896 J.D. [Morrow A.&P.]
Porter, Robert W., (AV) . . . . . '40 '66 C.198 B.A. L.896 LL.B. [Wells,J.L.&J.P.]
Powell, Harrell, Jr., (AV) . . . . . '35 '60 C.125 B.A. L.896 J.D. 514 Stratford Rd.
Price, P. Eugene, Jr., (AV) . . . . . '39 '64 C.228 A.B. L.896 J.D. Co. Atty.
Price, Robert E., Jr., (AV) . . . . . '56 '80 C.197 A.B. L.893 J.D. [Price]
Price, Ronald M. . . . . . '45 '70 C.296 A.B. L.896 J.D. Wake Forest Univ. Law Sch.

Price Law Office, (AV)
1144 West Fourth Street, 27101
Telephone: 336-724-7030 Facsimile: 336-724-7047
Email: info@replegal.com URL: http://www.repcollect.com

(This Listing Continued)

Price Law Office (Continued)

Robert E. Price, Jr. (Board Certified Specialist in Bankruptcy Law, North Carolina State Board of Legal Specialization);—Holly Groce; Julie M. Luckey.
Bankruptcy, Creditors Rights, Collections, Debtor/Creditor, Commercial Litigation.

See Professional Biographies, WINSTON-SALEM, NORTH CAROLINA

Probst, Robert E., (BV) ... '62 '88 C.64 B.S. L.896 J.D. [Jessup&P.]
Pueschel, John E. ... '70 '01 C.575 B.A. L.896 J.D. [Ⓐ Womble C.S.&R.]
Pullen, Edwin T., (AV) ... '32 '57 C.198 B.S. L.575 J.D. 3030 University Dr.‡
Punger, Douglas, (AV) '47 '72 C&L.896 B.A., J.D.
Gen. Coun., Winston-Salem/Forsyth Co. Bd. of Educ.
Quander, James E., (BV) ... '72 '98 C&L.896 B.A., J.D. 200 Brookstone Avenue
Quesnel, Daniel P., (BV) ... '73 '99 C.48 B.A. L.896 J.D. [Ⓐ Bell,D.&P.]
Quick, Elizabeth L., (AV) ... '48 '74 C.228 A.B. L.575 J.D. [Womble C.S.&R.]
Quick, Robert L., (AV) ... '46 '74 C.1154 B.A. L.575 J.D. [Womble C.S.&R.]
Rabil, S. Mark, (AV) ... '55 '80 C.198 B.A. L.575 J.D. Asst. Captl. Def.
Rabil, Vincent F., (AV) ... '53 '84 C.198 A.B. L.575 J.D. Asst. Dist. Atty.
Rabil, William E., Jr., (AV) ... '49 '74 C&L.575 A.B., J.D. [Wood,R.&J.]
Ragland, George A., (AV) ... '43 '78 C.893 B.S. L.902 LL.B. [Womble C.S.&R.]
Ramm, Peter H. ... '36 '65 C.198 B.A. L.893 J.D. Sr. Coun., R.J. Reynolds Tobacco Co.
Ramsey, Richard D., (AV) ... '50 '77 C.575 A.B. L.896 J.D. 250 Executive Park Blvd.

Randolph & Fischer, (AV)
200 Brookstown Avenue, Suite 304, 27101
Telephone: 336-724-3513 Fax: 336-725-6330
Email: clarkf@randolphfischerlaw.com URL: http://www.randolphfischerlaw.com
J. Clark Fischer (Board Certified Specialist in Criminal Law including Appellate Practice, North Carolina State Board of Legal Specialization).
Criminal Trials, Felonies, Homicide, Drug Crimes, Appellate Practice, Family Law, Divorce, Custody, Litigation.

See Professional Biographies, WINSTON-SALEM, NORTH CAROLINA

Rascoe, Robert B. '42 '70
C.575 A.B. L.896 J.D. Pres., Commonwealth Land Title Co. of N.C.
Rawlings, Charles E. ... '58 '02 C.228 M.D. L.896 J.D. [Ⓐ MacKenzie]
Ray, Michael E., (AV) ... '49 '78 C.269 B.A. L.790 J.D. [Womble C.S.&R.]
Raymer, Edward E., Jr., (AV) ... '47 '74 C.575 B.S. L.896 J.D. [Allman S.L.&C.]
Read IV, Oliver M., (CV) ... '55 '00 C.871 B.S. L.896 J.D. [Ⓐ Robinson&L.]
Rector, Lloyd K. ... '29 '53 C&L.896 B.S., J.D. Wake Forest Univ. Sch. of Law
Redden, Charles R. ... '40 '69 C.316 B.S. L.896 J.D. 122 Fayette St.
Reeder, I'Ans ... '62 '88 C.575 B.S. L.896 J.D. [Ⓐ Womble C.S.&R.]
Remsburg, F. Raine '41 '67 C.575 A.B. L.228 J.D.
Assoc. Group Coun., Personal Prods., Sara Lee Corp.
Repetti, Elizabeth M., (AV) ... '55 '86 C.174 B.S. L.896 J.D. [Bell,D.&P.]
Reynolds, Suzanne '49 '77 C.471 B.A. L.896 J.D.
Prof., Wake Forest Univ. Sch. of Law
Rice, Richard T., (AV) ... '51 '77 C.228 B.A. L.896 J.D. [Womble C.S.&R.]
Rickert, Robert D. ... '25 '51 C.228 A.B. L.309 LL.B. 137 Westhaven Circle‡
Rinne, Susan R. ... '61 '94 C.218 B.A. L.309 J.D. 1001 W. 4th. St.
Robb, Julian P. ... '72 '98 C.575 B.A. L.896 J.D. [Ⓐ Craige B.L.&W.]
Roberts, Charles P., III, (BV) ... '53 '79 C.576 B.S. L.575 J.D. [Constangy,B.&S.]
Roberts, Parks, (BV) ... '32 '58 C&L.575 B.S., LL.B. 200 Liberty Walk
Roberts, Patricia '46 '76 C&L.608 B.A., J.D.
(adm. in OH; not adm. in NC) 2731 Regency Dr.‡
Roberts, Stephanie U., (BV) ... '70 '98 C.1365 B.A. L.260 J.D. [Ⓐ Womble C.S.&R.]
Robinson, Michael L., (AV) ... '55 '80 C.198 B.A. L.575 J.D. [Robinson&L.]
Robinson, Norwood, (AV) ... '25 '52 C.870 B.S. L.228 J.D. [Robinson&L.]
Robinson, Stephen, (BV) ... '62 '91 C.77 B.A. L.575 J.D. [Ⓐ Robinson&L.]

Robinson & Lawing, L.L.P., (AV)
370 Knollwood Street, Suite 600, 27103-1835
Telephone: 336-631-8500 Fax: 336-631-6999
URL: http://www.robinson-lawing.com
Members of Firm: Norwood Robinson; Robert J. Lawing; Michael L. Robinson; Jane C. Jackson; Kevin L. Miller; C. Ray Grantham, Jr. (Board Certified Specialist in Family Law, North Carolina State Board of Legal Specialization); John N. Taylor, Jr.; Jolinda J. Babcock; Karen M. Wilson; Howard Brent Helms; Kurt A. Seeber. Associates: Stephen Robinson; Oliver M. Read IV; W. Mark Peck; Rebecca H. Miller; Adam R. Smart.
General Civil and Complex Litigation in All Courts. Business, Corporate, Antitrust and Trade, Intellectual Property, Products Liability, Personal Injury, Professional Malpractice, Workers Compensation, Bankruptcy, Family Law, Wrongful Death, Insurance, Employee Benefits Law, Employment and Labor Law, Business Law, Estate and Tax Law.
Representative Clients: American Furniture Manufacturers Assn.; Amoco Corp.; Bernhardt Furniture Industries; Brown & Williamson Tobacco Corp.; Pine State Knitwear Co.

See Professional Biographies, WINSTON-SALEM, NORTH CAROLINA

Roemer, H. C., (AV) ... '24 '51 C.309 A.B. L.178 LL.B. 341 Arbor Rd
Roemer, Henry C., III, (BV) ... '56 '90 C.902 B.A. L.896 J.D. [Finger,P.A.&R.]
Roemer, Victoria Lane ... '53 '86 C&L.896 B.A., J.D. Dist. J.
Roppel, Andrew A. '— '95 C.276 B.S.B.A. L.1209 J.D.
(adm. in VA; not adm. in NC) [Ⓐ Kilpatrick S.]
Ross, C. Thomas, (AV) ... '41 '70 C.280 B.B.A. L.880 J.D. [Ross]
Ross, Sarah P. '46 '72 C.813 A.B. L.1065 J.D.
(adm. in CA; not adm. in NC) 781 Arbor Rd.‡
Ross Law Firm, (AV) ... 301 N. Main St.
Roth, Thomas M., III, (BV) ... '61 '86 C.198 A.B. L.896 J.D. 940 Fox Hall Drive
Rothschild, Cynthia B., (BV) ... '— '99 C.893 B.A. L.896 J.D. [Ⓐ Kilpatrick S.]
Rowe, Ann C., (CV) ... '74 '99 C.228 A.B. L.575 J.D. [Ⓐ Davis&H.]
Ruark, Barbara E., (AV) ... '62 '87 C&L.896 B.A., J.D. [Orbock R.&D.]
Rubain, Stacey Dawn ... '75 '99 C.823 B.A. L.896 J.D. [Ⓐ Orbock R.&D.]
Ruch, Susan Gwin ... '62 '87 C&L.228 A.B., J.D. 1220 Wilmar Place Ct.
Rucker, Richmond W. ... '38 '67 C.198 A.B. L.309 LL.B. 2520 Greenbrier Rd.‡
Rucker, Thomas J. '43 '70 C.797 B.A. L.575 J.D.
Sr. Coun., R. J. Reynolds Tobacco Co.
Ruley, Alan M., (BV) ... '59 '87 C.228 B.A. L.813 J.D. [Bell,D.&P.]
Rusher, Ashley S., (BV) ... '62 '87 C.383 B.A., J.D. [Blanco T.C.&M.]
Russell, Stephen M., (AV) ... '50 '80 C.232 B.S. L.896 J.D. [Bell,D.&P.]

Rutledge, Dean B., (AV) '54 '82 C.575 B.A. L.896 J.D. BB
1 North Marshall Street Suite 101, 27101
Telephone: 336-722-7000 Fax: 336-722-9011
Email: dbrutledge@aol.com URL: http://www.deanrutledge.com
(Board Certified Specialist in Family Law, North Carolina State Board of Legal Specialization).
Family Law, Adoptions, Child Custody, Child Support, Divorce, Equitable Distribution, Premarital Agreements, Spousal Support, Mediation, Felonies, Misdemeanors, Drug Crimes, Traffic Violations.

See Professional Biographies, WINSTON-SALEM, NORTH CAROLINA

Ryan, Alexander P. ... '73 '01 C.1122 B.A. L.896 J.D. [Ⓐ Bell,D.&P.]
Ryan, Susan J. ... '54 '05 C.945 B.A. L.896 J.D. [Ⓐ Craige B.L.&W.]
Salley, Brunson M., III ... '65 '99 C.1128 B.A. L.896 J.D. 3018 Cambridge Rd.
Sanai, Mitra ... '76 '01 C.1375 B.A. L.896 J.D. [Ⓐ Wells,J.L.&J.P.]
Sanders, W. Kirk, (BV) ... '70 '95 C.576 B.A. L.896 J.D. 846 West 4th Street
Sandridge, W. P., Jr., (AV) ... '34 '61 C.575 A.B. L.893 LL.B. [Womble C.S.&R.]
Sapp, Richard S. ... '32 '61 C.575 B.S. L.896 LL.B. 1832 Buddingbrook Lane
Sapp, Robert H., (BV) ... '30 '57 C&L.575 B.S., J.D. [Sapp&M.]
Sapp & Mast, (AV) ... 102 W. Third St.
Scales, Archibald H., II ... '16 '37 C&L.575 A.B. 2912 Robin Hood Rd.‡
Scales, Donald J., (BV) ... '53 '81 C.296 B.A. L.1228 J.D. [Ⓐ Womble C.S.&R.]
Scarlett, John D. '23 '51 C.125 B.A. L.309 LL.B.
(adm. in NY; not adm. in NC) Dean Emeritus & Prof., Wake Forest Univ. Law Sch.
Schell, A. Gregory ... '69 '99 C.101 B.A. L.896 J.D. 3000 Bethesda Place, Ste. 702

Schell Bray Aycock Abel & Livingston P.L.L.C.
(See Greensboro)

Schiro, Gregory W., (BV) '46 '70 C.228 A.B. L.896 J.D.
2200 Silas Creek Pkwy., Ste. 5A
Schneider, Nancy C., (BV) ... '65 '90 C&L.893 B.A., J.D. 1001 W. 4th St.
Schollander, Wendell L. ... '43 '72 C.659 B.S. L.228 J.D. 2000 W. 1st, Suite 308
Schollander, Wendell L., III ... '74 '01 C.575 B.A. L.896 J.D. [Ⓐ W.L.Schollander]
Schoonmaker, Meyressa H., (BV) ... '40 '68 C&L.896 B.A., J.D. 2090 Royall Drive
Schramm, John J., Jr., (BV) ... '42 '70 C.1126 B.A. L.896 J.D. [Peebles&S.]
Schroeder, Katherine M. ... '54 '81 C.758 B.A. L.896 J.D. 1825 Robinhood Road
Schroeder, T. Benjamin '— '02 C.966 B.S. L.1209 J.D.
(adm. in VA; not adm. in NC; Pat.) [Ⓐ Kilpatrick S.]
Schroeder, Thomas D., (AV) ... '59 '84 C.378 B.S.B.A. L.602 J.D. [Womble C.S.&R.]
Scogin, Carolyn W. ... '74 '99 C.280 B.A. L.896 J.D. [Ⓐ Blanco T.C.&M.]
Scott, Gregory A. ... '66 '97 C.645 B.S. L.896 J.D. [Brock&S.]
Searcy, Philip E., (BV) ... '55 '81 C.575 B.S. L.896 J.D. [Wells,J.L.&J.P.]
Seawell, Samuel G. ... '29 '59 C.198 B.S. L.575 LL.B. P.O. Box 25654
Seeber, Kurt A., (BV) ... '66 '93 C.576 B.A. L.896 J.D. [Robinson&L.]
Seeber, Ronald G., (BV) ... '40 '68 C.299 B.A. L.228 LL.B. City Atty.
Sharpe, Margaret Land ... '34 '78 C.577 B.A. L.896 J.D. Dist. J.
Shea, Robin E., (AV) ... '55 '88 C.575 B.A. L.896 J.D. [Constangy,B.&S.]
Shearin, Lisa Richardson ... '60 '90 C&L.575 B.S., J.D. N.L.R.B.
Shelburne, Anne H., (BV) ... '58 '84 C.138 B.A. L.421 J.D. [Bell,D.&P.]
Shelburne, Timothy O., (BV) '57 '84 C.853 B.A. L.421 J.D.
Sr. V.P. & Assoc. Gen. Coun., Branch Banking and Trust Company

Shepard, Paul C., (BV) '48 '76 C.881 B.A. L.896 J.D.
8 West Third Street, Suite 245, 27101
Telephone: 336-727-1364 Fax: 336-727-1365
Email: PaulCShepard@abanet.org URL: http://www.lawyers.com/paulcshepardattorney
(Board Certified Specialist in Family Law, North Carolina State Board of Legal Specialization).
Child Custody, Divorce, Family Law, Social Security Disability, Automobile Accidents and Personal Injury, Wills and Probate, Workers Compensation, Real Estate, Zoning and Land Use, Traffic Violations.

See Professional Biographies, WINSTON-SALEM, NORTH CAROLINA

Shipley, Edward T., III ... '77 '04 C.575 B.S. L.896 J.D. [Ⓐ Wilson&I.]
Shirlen, David A., (BV) ... '61 '86 C.296 B.A. L.280 J.D. [Womble C.S.&R.]
Shores, David F. '41 '67 C&L.352 B.B.A., J.D.
(adm. in IA; not adm. in NC) Prof., Wake Forest Univ. School of Law
Short, Ronald J., (BV) ... '46 '85 C.575 B.A. L.896 J.D. 110 S. Spruce St.
Shuler, Griffis Clark ... '68 '94 C.387 B.A. L.896 J.D. [Ⓐ Lewis&D.]
Sinal, Paul A., (BV) ... '45 '75 C&L.896 B.A., J.D. Asst. Co. Atty
Sink, Deborah A., (BVⓉ) '57 '82 C.893 B.S. L.886 J.D.
(adm. in WV; not adm. in NC) Branch Banking and Trust Company
Sizemore, James E. ... '25 '52 C.835 B.S. L.896 LL.B. Prof. of Law, Wake Forest Univ.
Slaydon, Roger J. '49 '79 C&L.260 B.A., J.D.
(adm. in FL; not adm. in NC) 1624 Caspian Way Lane‡

Small, Christopher J., (AV) '53 '78 C.125 B.A. L.896 J.D.
1078 West Fourth Street, 27101
Telephone: 336-722-0333 Fax: 336-722-0334
Email: cjsmall@cjsmallatty.com URL: http://www.cjsmallatty.com
Collections and Creditors' Rights enforced in all Courts.
Reference: Wachovia Bank and Trust Co.

See Professional Biographies, WINSTON-SALEM, NORTH CAROLINA

Smart, Adam R. ... '77 '03 C&L.575 B.A., J.D. [Ⓐ Robinson&L.]
Smith, Aimee L. ... '72 '02 C.577 B.A. L.896 J.D. [Ⓐ Craige B.L.&W.]
Smith, Amy K., (AV) ... '63 '88 C.925 B.S. L.869 J.D. [Bell,D.&P.]
Smith, David C., (AV) ... '— '84 C&L.896 B.A., J.D. [Kilpatrick S.]
Smith, Eddie D. '20 '58 C&L.912 A.B., LL.B.
(adm. in MI; not adm. in NC) N.L.R.B.
Smith, Greg L., (AV) ... '56 '82 C.103 A.B. L.188 J.D. [Womble C.S.&R.]
Smith, W. Read '35 '63 C&L.45 B.A., LL.B.
(adm. in AR; not adm. in NC) 2011 Greenbrier Road
Smitherman, Rebecca L. ... '76 '02 C.575 B.A. L.896 J.D. [Ⓐ Craige B.L.&W.]
Southerland, Larry K., (CV) ... '57 '98 C&L.896 B.A., J.D. 3000 Bethesda Pl., Ste. 703
Sparrow, Warren, (BV) ... '36 '65 C.228 B.S.C.E. L.896 J.D. 8 W. 3rd St., Suite 585

Spaugh, Robert G., (BV) '62 '90 C.198 A.B. L.896 J.D.
1352 Ashley Brook Lane, 27103
Telephone: 336-659-9450 Fax: 336-659-4570
Email: Spaughlaw@aol.com URL: http://www.rspaughlaw.com
Family Law, Child Support, Child Custody, Separation, Separation Agreements, Divorce, Visitation Rights, Domestic Violence, Marital Property, Equitable Distribution, Pre-Marital Agreements, Spousal Support, Workers Compensation, On the Job Injuries, Personal Injury, Automobile Accidents, Traffic Violations, Trusts and Estates, Wills and Probate.

See Professional Biographies, WINSTON-SALEM, NORTH CAROLINA

Speaks, William M., Jr., (BV) ... '46 '76 C&L.575 A.B., J.D. 301 N. Main St.
Spence, David L., (BV) ... '55 '80 C.1081 B.S. L.896 J.D. Asst. Dist. Atty.
Spivey, Cynthia G., (BV) ... '59 '85 C.575 B.S. L.896 J.D. [Ⓐ Womble C.S.&R.]
Spivey, Ronald E. ... '59 '85 C.576 B.A. L.896 J.D. Supr. Ct. J.
Splawn, Charles R. ... '61 '89 C.1128 B.A. L.896 J.D. Asst. V.P., Litigation, Integon Corp.
Springer, Randel S. ... '62 '90 C.347 B.A. L.352 J.D. [Womble C.S.&R.] (Pat.)
Spry, William D., Jr., (AV) ... '46 '72 C&L.575 A.B., J.D. 200 W. 2nd St.‡
Stafford, Mark A., (AV) ... '62 '89 C&L.575 A.B., J.D. [Nelson M.R.&S.]
Stakeman, Kurt C., (BV) ... '49 '74 C.269 B.A. L.575 J.D. [Ⓒ Womble C.S.&R.]
Stark, Jeanette M. ... '77 '03 C.945 B.B.A. L.896 J.D. [Ⓐ Blanco T.C.&M.]
Staton, Erin S. ... '78 '04 C.575 B.A. L.276 J.D. [Ⓐ Womble C.S.&R.]
Stephens, Brent W. ... '70 '96 C.575 B.A. L.1228 J.D. [Craige B.L.&W.]

Stephens, Herman L., (BV) '45 '70 C&L.575 A.B., J.D.
200 West First Street, 27101
Telephone: 336-722-7126 Fax: 336-631-8702
Email: lawstephens@bellsouth.net URL: http://www.lawstephens.com
Civil Litigation in all State and Federal Courts, Unfair Business Practice, Business Lawsuits, Workers Compensation, Personal Injury, Automobile Accidents, Consumer Protection, Lemon Law, Consumer Fraud.

See Professional Biographies, WINSTON-SALEM, NORTH CAROLINA

Stewart, Scott Michael '64 '89 C&L.734 B.A., J.D.
Compliance Offr., Wachouia Operational Services Corporation
Still, John R. .... '61 '93 C.577 B.S. L.356 J.D. [A Womble C.S.&R.]
Stinson, Robin J., (AV) .... '59 '84 C.228 B.A. L.575 J.D. [Bell,D.&P.]
Stockton, Robert Gray, (AV) .... '23 '49 C&L.575 B.S., J.D. 1001 W. 4th St.‡
Stogner, Kimberly H., (AV) .... '64 '94 C&L.896 B.A., J.D. [Vaughn P.E.M.&S.]
Stojkovich, Goran P. .... '65 '97 C.339 B.S. L.146 J.D. [C Nelson M.R.&S.] (Pat.)
Stowers, L. Jayne, (BV) .... '58 '87 C.896 B.A. L.575 J.D. [L.J.Stowers]
Stowers, L. Jayne, P.A., (BV) .... 811 W. 5th St., Ste. 102
Strauch, Jack M., (BV) .... '66 '95 C.197 B.A. L.602 J.D. [A Womble C.S.&R.]
Stroud, J. Keith, (BV) .... '55 '81 C.575 B.A. L.896 J.D. [Stroud&P.]

Stroud and Panetti, P.C., (BV)
102 West Third Street, Suite 650, 27101
Telephone: 336-724-2600 Telecopier: 336-724-6950
URL: http://www.stroudandpanetti.com
J. Keith Stroud; Eleanor Panetti.
Business Law, Business Litigation, Planning, Buying and Selling of Businesses, Limited Liability Company Law, Family Law, Adoptions, Child Custody, Child Support, Divorce, Domestic Violence, Premarital Agreements, Visitation Rights, Criminal Law, Driving While Intoxicated, (DWI), Drug Crimes, Felonies, Misdemeanors, Traffic Violations, Personal Injury, Automobile Accidents, Slip and Fall, Wrongful Death, Real Estate, Mortgages, Bankruptcy, Elder Law.
Approved Attorneys for: Lawyers Title Insurance Corp.; Wachovia Bank and Trust Co., N.A.
Representative Clients: Provided Upon Request.
Reference: Branch Banking and Trust Company.
See Professional Biographies, WINSTON-SALEM, NORTH CAROLINA

Stuart, Richard C. .... '77 '02 C.575 B.A. L.896 J.D. [Clay S.]
Styers, Robt. L., (CV) .... '28 '51 C&L.228 A.B., LL.B. 215 N. Broad St.
Sugg, Ann G. .... '55 '81 C.188 B.S. L.1017 J.D. [C Wells,J.L.&J.P.]
Sullivan, William B., (AV) .... '45 '70 C.893 B.A. L.309 J.D. [Womble C.S.&R.]
Summers, Cecil C., (BV) '54 '81 C.955 B.A. L.1228 J.D.
4265 Brownsboro Rd., Ste. 111
Surratt, John R., (AV) .... '28 '51 C.575 B.S. L.228 J.D. [Surratt&T.]

Surratt & Thompson, PLLC, (AV) BB
Wachovia Center, 100 N. Main Street, Suite 1500, 27101
Telephone: 336-725-8323 Facsimile: 336-722-5218
Email: firm@sandtpllc.com
John R. Surratt; Bryan C. Thompson.
General Civil Practice in all State and Federal Courts. Corporate Law, Business Law, Collections, Wills, Probate, Trusts and Estates, Taxation, Real Estate, Commercial Law, Bankruptcy, Family Law and Litigation.
See Professional Biographies, WINSTON-SALEM, NORTH CAROLINA

Tackabery, Neal E., (AV) .... '49 '76 C.597 B.S. L.228 J.D. [Blanco T.C.&M.]
Talley, Hannah C.E. Yonan .... '58 '86 C.294 B.A. L.896 J.D. [S Womble C.S.&R.]
Tally, Robert, (BV) .... '48 '76 C&L.228 A.B., J.D. [R.Tally]
Tally, Robert, A Professional Corporation, (BV) .... 2200 Silas Creek Parkway, Suite 4
Tanis, David R., (BV) .... '41 '76 C.401 B.A. L.896 J.D. 300 Friendship Cir.
Tarr, Gene B., (AV) .... '51 '83 C.999 B.A. L.1228 J.D. [Blanco T.C.&M.]
Tart, James K., (AV) .... '61 '86 C.575 B.A. L.574 J.D. [J.K.Tart]
Tart, J. Keith, The Law Office of, (AV) .... 3524 Yadkinville Road
Tash, Gary B., (AV) .... '46 '71 C.893 B.A. L.896 J.D. [Tash&K.]

Tash & Kurtz, PLLC, (AV) BB
3305 Healy Drive, 27103
Telephone: 336-768-1515 Fax: 336-768-1550
URL: http://www.lawyers.com/tashkurft
Gary B. Tash (Board Certified Specialist in Family Law, North Carolina State Board of Legal Specialization); Jon Brenner Kurtz (Board Certified Specialist in Family Law, North Carolina State Board of Legal Specialization);—Amanda H. Creamer.
Family Law, Divorce, Equitable Distribution, Child Custody, Child Support, Alimony, Domestic Violence, Visitation Rights, Appellate Practice, Mediation, Estate Planning.
See Professional Biographies, WINSTON-SALEM, NORTH CAROLINA

Tate, David K. '39 '73 C.475 B.S. L.215 J.D.
(adm. in MI; not adm. in NC) Sr. Coun., R. J. Reynolds Tobacco Co.
Taylor, Charles H. .... '26 '50 C&L.896 B.S., LL.B. Wake Forest Univ. Sch. of Law
Taylor, Daniel R., Jr., (AV) .... '— '76 C.870 B.S. L.896 J.D. [Kilpatrick S.]
Taylor, James, Jr. '27 '49 C&L.575 A.B., J.D.
Prof. of Law & Assoc. Dean, Wake Forest Univ.
Taylor, John N., Jr., (AV) .... '63 '88 C&L.896 B.A., J.D. [Robinson&L.]
Teague, C. Edward, III .... '— '02 C.575 B.A. L.896 J.D. [A Kilpatrick S.]
Teeter, Carol L., (Mr.), (BV) .... '33 '60 C&L.896 A.B., LL.B. 315 N. Spruce St.
Teeter, Carroll L. .... '33 '60 C&L.896 B.A., J.D. [Teeter]
Teeter, Stuart L., (BV) .... '63 '89 C.232 B.A. L.896 J.D. [Teeter]

Teeter Law Firm, (BV)
315 N. Spruce Street, Suite 275, 27101
Telephone: 336-725-8376 Fax: 336-722-5680
URL: http://www.teeterlawfirm.com
Members of Firm: Carroll L. Teeter; Stuart L. Teeter; Kelly Scott Lee.
Appellate Practice, Criminal Law, Civil Litigation, Domestic Relations, Personal Injury, Trusts and Estates and Wills.
See Professional Biographies, WINSTON-SALEM, NORTH CAROLINA

Temple Law Firm, PLLC
(See Raleigh)

Templeton, Franklin Scott .... '61 '89 C.577 B.S.B.A. L.896 J.D. [Bennett&G.P.]
Thomas, George S., (BV) .... '41 '66 C&L.575 B.S., J.D. [Bailey&T.]
Thomas, Jenna B. .... '70 '96 C.575 B.S. L.896 J.D. [B Bell,D.&P.]
Thompkins, Renita O., (BV) .... '58 '83 C.574 B.B.A. L.329 J.D. 205 West Third Street
Thompson, Bryan C., (BV) .... '75 '99 C.34 B.S. L.1228 J.D. [Surratt&T.]
Thornton, Jack Ewald, Jr., (AV) '49 '74 C&L.575 B.A., J.D.
185 Kimel Park Dr., Ste. 200
Thrift, Ashley O., (AV) .... '46 '73 C.575 A.B. L.790 J.D. [Womble C.S.&R.]
Timmins, Patricia L. '48 '74 C.94 A.B. L.818 J.D.
(adm. in MA; not adm. in NC) Reg. Atty.
Tippett, Scott K. .... '61 '87 C.228 B.A. L.575 J.D. [House&T.]
Tisci, Michael A. '60 '85 C.846 B.A. L.862 J.D.
(adm. in AZ; not adm. in NC)
Sr. V.P. & Assoc. Gen. Coun., Branch Banking and Trust Company
Tisdale, D. Kenneth, Jr. .... '— '97 C.576 B.A. L.896 J.D. [Grace H.T.&C.]
Tisdale, Donald K., Sr., (BV) .... '42 '68 C&L.896 B.A., J.D. [Grace H.T.&C.]
Tollie, Stacy O. .... '66 '93 C.105 B.A. L.982 J.D. Off. of the Mag.
Tolman, Mark D. .... '— '04 C.1085 B.S. L.577 J.D. [A Kilpatrick S.]
Tornow, W. McNair, (AV) .... '44 '69 C&L.896 B.A., J.D. 1340 Westgate Ctr. Dr.
Tucker, Elizabeth D. .... '73 '04 C.659 B.A. L.228 J.D. [A Womble C.S.&R.]
Tucker, Lennard D. .... '53 '86 C.1378 B.S. L.904 J.D. 8 West Third Street, Suite 600

Tuggle Duggins & Meschan, P.A.
(See Greensboro)

Turner, Julia Hines, (AV) '54 '81 C.471 B.A. L.896 J.D.
Asst. V.P., Asst. Gen. Coun. & Asst. Secy., Triad Guaranty Insurance Corporation
Vale, Patrick G., Law Offices of, (BV) '55 '88 C.988 B.A. L.896 J.D.
3737 Burbank Lane
Valenziano, Nicholas J., Jr., (BV) '62 '91
C.339 B.S. L.597 J.D. Asst. Coun., Intell. Prop., Sara Lee Corp.
Vandiver, Shannon L. .... '75 '00 C.575 B.A. L.1228 J.D. [A Womble C.S.&R.]
Van Zandt, John P., III, (AV) .... '48 '73 C&L.896 B.A., J.D. [Hatfield,M.D.V.&M.]
Vasudevan, Helen S. .... '56 '93 C&L.896 B.A., J.D. P.O. Box 25684
Vaughan, James E., (AV) .... '59 '84 C.97 B.S. L.607 J.D. [J.E.Vaughan]
Vaughan, Keith W., (AV) .... '50 '75 C.896 B.A. L.280 J.D. [Womble C.S.&R.]

Vaughan, James E., Attorney At Law, P.C., (AV)
206 North Spruce Street, Suite 2A, 27101
Telephone: 336-725-7772 Telecopier: 336-725-7737
Email: jvaughanlaw@earthlink.net URL: http://www.lawyers.com/jvaughan
James E. Vaughan.
Creditors Rights, Commercial Bankruptcy, Consumer Bankruptcy, Business Litigation, Commercial Litigation, Collections.
See Professional Biographies, WINSTON-SALEM, NORTH CAROLINA

Vaughn, Robert C., Jr., (AV) .... '31 '55 C&L.575 B.S., J.D. [Vaughn P.E.M.&S.]

Vaughn Perkinson Ehlinger Moxley & Stogner, (AV)
4505 Country Club Road, P.O. Box 25715, 27114
Telephone: 336-794-6000 Fax: 336-760-1625
Members of the Firm: Robert C. Vaughn, Jr.; John R. Perkinson, Jr.; Timothy J. Ehlinger; Marcus L. Moxley (Board Certified Specialist in Estate Planning and Probate Law, North Carolina State Board of Legal Specialization); Kimberly H. Stogner.
Probate, Trusts and Estates, Taxation, Estate Planning, Wills.
See Professional Biographies, WINSTON-SALEM, NORTH CAROLINA

Veach, Andrew H., (BV) .... '— '99 C.198 B.A. L.896 J.D. [A Kilpatrick S.]
Velasco, Francisco '71 '95 L.999 J.D.
(adm. in NY; not adm. in NC) Latin America Coun., Sara Lee Corporation
Venable, Charles H. .... '32 '60 C.925 B.A. L.575 LL.B. 500 W. 5th St.‡
Vestal, Randy G. .... '60 '86 C.574 B.A. L.575 J.D. [S Womble C.S.&R.]
Vickers, C. Wallace .... '14 '55 C.575 B.S. L.228 LL.B. 1244 Arbor Rd.‡
VonCannon, Donald M., (AV) .... '44 '71 C&L.896 B.A., J.D. [Allman S.L.&C.]
Vreeland, Douglas R., (BV) .... '70 '98 C.576 B.A. L.896 J.D. [A Womble C.S.&R.]
Vrsecky, Anthony J. .... '49 '74 C&L.575 B.A., J.D. 2000 Frontis Plz. Blvd., Ste. 100
Wagner, David H., Jr. .... '26 '68 C.1378 B.S. L.896 J.D. P.O. Box 21177‡
Wagner, Wake A., Law Offices of '76 '01 C.577 B.A. L.896 J.D.
225 North Spring Street
Walden, Daniel S., (BV) .... '49 '75 C.347 B.A. L.192 J.D. [Walden&W.]
Walden, Margaret D., (BV) .... '44 '75 C.896 B.A. L.192 J.D. [Walden&W.]
Walden & Walden, (BV) .... 102 West Third Street, Suite 503
Walker, Gary J. .... '47 '74 C.232 B.S. L.896 J.D. 2338 N. Liberty St.
Walker, George K. .... '38 '67 C.16 B.A. L.880 LL.B. Prof., Wake Forest Univ. Law Sch.
Walker, William W., (AV) .... '48 '77 C.282 A.B. L.896 J.D. [Craige B.L.&W.]
Wall, Earl F. '57 '82 C&L.896 B.A., J.D.
Senior Vice President, Secretary & General Counsel, Triad Guaranty Insurance Corporation
Wall, James David, (AV) .... '63 '89 C.945 B.B.A. L.893 J.D. [Wall]

Wall Law Firm, P.C., (AV)
1076 West Fourth Street, Suite 100, 27101
Telephone: 336-722-2900 Fax: 336-722-2906 URL: http://www.walllawoffice.com
Email: jwall@wallfirm.com URL: http://www.wallfirm.com
James David Wall.
Health Care, Corporate Law, Commercial Transactions, Bankruptcy, Mediation.
See Professional Biographies, WINSTON-SALEM, NORTH CAROLINA

Wallace, David A., (BV) .... '46 '76 C&L.896 B.A., J.D. 846 W. 4th St.
Walsh, Robert K. '42 '67 C.676 B.A. L.309 J.D.
(adm. in CA; not adm. in NC) Dean, Wake Forest Univ., School of Law
Ward, Mary E., (AV) '45 '79
C.228 A.B. L.896 J.D. Sr. Coun., R.J. Reynolds Tobacco Co.
Warren, John C. '48 '76 C.228 A.B. L.575 J.D.
Sr. V.P. & Assoc. Gen. Coun., Branch Banking and Trust Company
Warren, Reba H., (AV) .... '58 '87 C.329 B.A. L.228 J.D. Coun., R.J. Reynolds Co.
Waters, Joann A. .... '72 '00 C&L.1228 B.A., J.D. [A Womble C.S.&R.]
Watson, Jeffrey B., (BV) .... '66 '98 C.577 B.A. L.1228 J.D. [A Allman S.L.&C.]
Weidemann, Bradley J., (BV) .... '72 '96 C.27 B.A. L.896 J.D. [Weidemann]

Weidemann Law Firm, P.C., (BV)
102 West 3rd Street, Suite 485, 27101
Telephone: 336-725-8557 Fax: 336-725-8571
URL: http://triadlawyer.com
Bradley J. Weidemann.
Criminal Law, Driving While Intoxicated (DWI), Drug Crimes, Felonies, Juvenile Law, Misdemeanors, Parole and Probation, Traffic Violations, Family Law, Adoptions, Child Custody, Child Support, Divorce, Premarital Agreements, Spousal Support, Visitation Rights, Collections, Estate Planning, Wills and Probate.
See Professional Biographies, WINSTON-SALEM, NORTH CAROLINA

Weiss, Randi B. .... '58 '00 C.659 B.A. L.896 J.D. [A Womble C.S.&R.]
Welch, Joseph T. '54 '90 C.1044 B.A. L.1194 J.D.
(adm. in VT; not adm. in NC) N.L.R.B.
Wells, Dewey W., (AV) .... '29 '54 C&L.896 B.S., LL.B. [C Womble C.S.&R.]
Wells, R. Michael, (AV) .... '49 '74 C.893 B.A. L.896 J.D. [Wells,J.L.&J.P.]
Wells, R. Michael, Jr. .... '— '05 C.893 B.A. L.896 J.D. [A Wells,J.L.&J.P.]

Wells, Jenkins, Lucas & Jenkins PLLC, (AV)
155 Sunnynoll Court, Suite 200, 27106
Telephone: 336-725-2900 Fax: 336-724-1226
Email: youlaw.com URL: http://www.wellsjenkins.com
R. Michael Wells; Gordon W. Jenkins (Board Certified Specialist in Estate Planning and Probate Law, North Carolina State Board of Legal Specialization); John L. Barber; Clyde R. Cash; Ellis B. Drew, III; Philip E. Searcy (Board Certified Specialist in Real Property Law, Residential, Business, Commercial and Industrial Transactions, North Carolina State Board of Legal Specialization); Susan H. Gray (Board Certified Specialist in Family Law, North Carolina State Board of Legal Specialization); T. Lawson Newton; Robert W. Porter;—R. Michael Wells, Jr.; Mitra Sanai. Of Counsel: Ann G. Sugg; F. Gaither Jenkins (1910-2001); Philip E. Lucas (Retired).
Business Transactions, Mergers and Acquisitions, Nursing Home Litigation, Elder Law, Medicaid Planning, Business Transactions, Corporate Law, Limited Liability Company Law, Franchise Law, Commercial, Construction and Civil Litigation, Residential Real Estate, Commercial Real Estate, Personal Injury, Workers Compensation, Wills, Trusts, Estates, Bankruptcy, Traffic, Family Law, Equitable Distribution, Alimony, Child Support.
See Professional Biographies, WINSTON-SALEM, NORTH CAROLINA

Welsh, James G., Jr., (BV) .... '65 '97 C&L.896 B.A., J.D. [Davis&H.]

Weltz, Scott A. .... '60 '94 C.585 B.A. L.896 J.D. [▣ Womble C.S.&R.]
West, William E., Jr., (BV) .... '50 '78 C.575 B.S. L.896 J.D. 3000 Bethesda Pl.
Wettach, Jane R., (AV) .... '54 '81 C&L.575 B.A., J.D. 216 W. 4th St.
Whitaker, Garry, (BV) .... '59 '83 C&L.896 B.A., J.D. [G.Whitaker]
Whitaker, Garry, P.C., Attorney at Law, (BV) .... One North Marshall Street, Suite 350

White and Crumpler, (AV) ▣
301 N. Main Street, Suite 1100, 27101
Telephone: 336-725-1304 Fax: 336-761-8845
URL: http://www.whiteandcrumpler.com
Members of Firm: James G. White (1924-1974); Frank M. Armstrong (1900-1979); Clyde C. Randolph, Jr. (1928-1995); Barbara C. Westmoreland (1929-2000); Fred G. Crumpler, Jr. (Board Certified Specialist in Family Law, North Carolina State Board of Legal Specialization); G. Edgar Parker (Board Certified Specialist in Family Law); David B. Freedman (Board Certified Specialist in Federal and State Criminal Law); Dudley A. Witt; Laurie Schlossberg Kelly. Associate: Jones P. Byrd Jr. Of Counsel: Fred S. Hutchins, Jr.
General Civil and Criminal Practice. Trials in State and Federal Courts. Domestic Relations, Family Law, Equitable Distribution, Divorce, Complex Civil Law, Complex Business Law, Medical Malpractice, Personal Injury, White Collar Criminal Defense, Appellate Practice.
See Professional Biographies, WINSTON-SALEM, NORTH CAROLINA

Whitehurst, William R., (AV) '56 '82
C.896 B.A. L.575 J.D. [Womble C.S.&R.] (⊙Charlotte)
Whitley, Elise Morgan .... '74 '01 C.575 B.A. L.896 J.D. 3890 Vest Mill Road
Wiggins, Thomas F. '57 '86 C.575 B.S. L.896 J.D.
V.P., First Citizens Bank & Trust Co.
Wiley, C. Mark, (AV) .... '63 '88 C&L.896 B.S., J.D. [Womble C.S.&R.]
Wilkins, William Y. .... '16 '46 C.575 B.S. L.276 J.D. 706 First Ctr. Bldg.
Williams, Charles E., Jr. .... '26 '54 C&L.896 B.S., LL.B. Vet. Admn.
Williams, Danielle Thompson, (BV) .... '— '96 C.575 B.A. L.896 J.D. [Kilpatrick S.]
Williams, Erin, (BV) .... '72 '98 C.477 B.A. L.896 J.D. [Dummit]
Williams, Joel M. .... '— '04 C&L.352 B.B.A., J.D. [▣ Ingersoll&Assoc.]
Williams, Kevin G., (BV) .... '71 '98 C.575 B.S. L.896 J.D. [Bell,D.&P.]
Williams, Kevin J., (BV) .... '71 '96 C.228 A.B. L.896 J.D. [▣ Comerford&B.]
Williams, Michael P. .... '72 '98 C.575 B.A. L.574 J.D. [▣ Lewis&D.]
Williard, Dannielle D. .... '68 '00 C.999 B.A. L.896 J.D. [▣ Womble C.S.&R.]
Wilson, David L., Jr., (BV) .... '49 '75 C.575 B.S. L.896 J.D. [Wilson,D.&M.]
Wilson, G. Gray, (AV) .... '51 '76 C.198 B.A. L.228 J.D. [Wilson&I.] ⊙
Wilson, James C. .... '28 '55 C&L.575 B.S., LL.B. Chmn., Bocock-Stroud Co.‡
Wilson, Karen M., (AV) .... '60 '85 C&L.896 B.S., J.D. [Robinson&L.]
Wilson, Robert B., Jr., (AV) .... '22 '53 C&L.896 B.S., LL.B. 5315 Rosebriar Lane
Wilson, William T., III .... '54 '80 C.228 A.B. L.896 J.D. Pres., Highwoods/Forsyth
Wilson, DeGraw & Miller, L.L.P., (BV) .... 3911 University Pkwy.

Wilson & Iseman, L.L.P., (AV)
110 Oakwood Drive, Suite 400, 27103 ⊙
Telephone: 336-631-8866 Telefax: 336-631-9770
URL: http://www.wilsonandiseman.com
Members of Firm: G. Gray Wilson; James M. Iseman, Jr.; Tamura D. Coffey; S. Ranchor Harris, III; Linda L. Helms; Kevin B. Cartledge. Associates: J. Chad Bomar; Maria C. Papoulias; David M. Fothergill; Edward T. Shipley, III.
General Civil Practice, including Civil Trial and Appellate Work in all State and Federal Courts, Administrative, Aviation, Commercial, Construction, Corporate, Employee Benefits and Executive Compensation, Employment, Criminal, Federal, State and Local Taxation, Insurance Defense, Personal Injury, Probate, Wills, Trusts and Estate Planning, Products Liability and Negligence Law, Professional Malpractice and Real Estate.
Charlotte Office: 435 East Morehead Street, 28202. Telephone: 704-331-9585. Fax: 704-331-0773.
See Professional Biographies, WINSTON-SALEM, NORTH CAROLINA

Wimbish, J. Clinton .... '— '03 C&L.575 B.S., J.D. [▣ Kilpatrick S.] (Pat.)
Windham, G. Criston, (BV) .... '50 '76 C&L.896 B.A., J.D. [Womble C.S.&R.]
Wine, Jeanne S. .... '46 '82 C.1365 B.A. L.30 J.D. Gen. Atty., Veterans Admn.
Winfree, Frank W. .... '27 '51 C&L.575 A.B., LL.B. 1794 Silas Creek Pkwy.
Winterle, Bret T. .... '— '03 C.350 B.S. L.893 J.D. [▣ Kilpatrick S.] (Pat.)
Withrow, Robyn B., (BV) .... '71 '97 C&L.577 B.S., J.D. 840 W. 4th St.
Witt, Dudley A., (AV) .... '58 '83 C&L.896 B.A., J.D. [White&C.]
Wolfe, Laura M., Law Offices of .... '65 '97 C.846 B.A. L.896 J.D. 8 W. 3rd Street
Womble, Calder W., (AV) .... '22 '47 C&L.228 A.B., LL.B. [Womble C.S.&R.]
Womble, Erna A. P., (AV) .... '55 '86 C.140 B.A. L.790 J.D. [Womble C.S.&R.]
Womble, William F., (AV) .... '16 '39 C&L.228 A.B., J.D. [Womble C.S.&R.]
Womble, William F., Jr., (AV) .... '42 '67 C&L.228 A.B., J.D. [Womble C.S.&R.]

Womble Carlyle Sandridge & Rice, (AV) ▣
A Professional Limited Liability Company
One West Fourth Street, 27101 ⊙
Telephone: 336-721-3600 Fax: 336-721-3660
Email: lawyers@wcsr.com URL: http://www.wcsr.com
Resident Members: B. S. Womble (1882-1976); Irving E. Carlyle (1896-1971); W. Pendleton Sandridge (1904-1982); Leon L. Rice Jr. (1912-1987); Alfred G. Adams (Board Certified Specialist in Real Property Law, Residential, Business, Commercial and Industrial Transactions, North Carolina State Board of Legal Specialization); Jean Taylor Adams; Reid C. Adams, Jr.; Patrick M. Allen; Janice C. Baldwin; H. Grady Barnhill, Jr.; Jimmy H. Barnhill; Amy L. Bircher; S. Fraley Bost; Anthony H. Brett; Charles A. Burke; Karen Estelle Carey; Keith A. Clinard; W. Andrew Copenhaver; Linwood L. Davis; Ronald R. Davis (Also at Greensboro Office); Bonnie Kay Donahue; Christina U. Douglas; W. David Edwards; Jonathan M. Engram; Gusti W. Frankel; Jeffrey L. Furr; Allan R. Gitter; Murray C. Greason, Jr.; Ellen M. Gregg; Michael D. Gunter; Hardin G. Halsey (Also at Greensboro Office); Hada V. Haulsee; Ursula M. Henninger; Lori Privette Hinnant; Jeffrey C. Howland; David A. Irvin; George William Joyner, III; Christopher A. Kreiner; William E. Latham II; Christopher E. Leon; R. Michael Leonard; Roddey M. Ligon, Jr.; Kim Kelly Mann; Jeffrey R. McFadden; Dennis W. McNames; Kenneth R. Michael; James R. Morgan, Jr.; Kenneth A. Moser; James K. Phillips; Robert S. Pierce; Mark N. Poovey; Elizabeth L. Quick; Robert L. Quick; George A. Ragland; Michael E. Ray; Richard T. Rice; W. P. Sandridge, Jr.; Thomas D. Schroeder; David A. Shirlen; Greg L. Smith; Randel S. Springer; William B. Sullivan; Ashley O. Thrift; Keith W. Vaughan; William R. Whitehurst (Also at Charlotte, North Carolina Office); C. Mark Wiley; G. Criston Windham; Calder W. Womble; Erna A. P. Womble; William F. Womble; William F. Womble, Jr. Resident Associates: Elizabeth K. Arias; Alison Y. Ashe-Card; Kenneth R. Ashford; Thomas A. Bissette; Alison R. Bost; Julie B. Bradburn; Stuart A. Brock (Also at Winston-Salem, North Carolina Office); Jason B. Buckland; Craig D. Cannon; Mary Nell Craven; Rachel E. Daly; Christopher G. Daniel; Andrew Fitzgerald; Anne Fleeson; Christopher J. Geis; Jacqueline M. Goble; Murray C. Greason, III; Stanley B. Green (Also at Charlotte, North Carolina Office); Edward Griggs; Christopher J. Gyves; Jerry Carlyle "Carl" Hearn, III; Jason C. Hicks (Not admitted in NC); Trent E. Jernigan; Ana Davis Johnson (Not admitted in NC); Bradley R. Johnson; G. Wriston Marshburn, Jr; Robert D. Mason, Jr.; Carl B. Massey, Jr.; David J. Mazza; Philip J. Mohr; Michael Montecalvo; John F. Morrow, Jr.; Christopher H. Oldham; Julie Barker Pape; David V. Patton; Matthew D. Pipes (Not admitted in NC); Patricia F. Poole; John E. Pueschel; I'Ans Reeder; Stephanie U. Roberts; Donald J. Scales; Cynthia G. Spivey; Erin S. Staton; John R. Still; Jack M. Strauch; Elizabeth D. Tucker; Shannon L. Vandiver; Douglas R. Vreeland; Joann A. Waters; Randi B. Weiss; Bradley O. Wood. Members Of Counsel: H. Jesse Arnelle (Not admitted in NC); Ranlet S. Bell; Ian A. Calvert; George K. Evans, Jr.; Lucretia D. Guia; Kurt C. Stakeman; Dewey W. Wells. Senior Counsel: Scott A. Weltz. Counsel: Sarah M. Johnson; Margaret L. Lefevre; Dannielle D. Williard. Staff Attorneys: Robert J. Jolly; Hannah C.E. Yonan Talley; James J. Fradenburg; Randy G. Vestal.
General Civil Practice, Trial and Appellate Litigation. Administrative, Antitrust, Aviation, Banking, Bankruptcy and Creditor's Rights, Bond Financing, Civil Rights, Commercial, Construction, Consumer Lending, Corporate, E-Commerce, Employee Benefits, Environmental, Estate Planning, Family, Government Relations, Health Care, Insurance, Intellectual Property, International, Labor and Employment, Municipal, Negligence, Probate, Product Liability, Real Estate, Retirement Plans, Securities, Taxation, Toxic Tort, Wills and Trusts Law.

(This Listing Continued)

Womble Carlyle Sandridge & Rice (Continued)
Representative Clients: Brad Ragan, Inc.; Brenner Companies; Food Lion, Inc.; Hanes Companies, Inc.; North Carolina Baptist Hospitals, Inc.; R.J. Reynolds Tobacco Co.; Wachovia Corp.; Wake Forest University.
Charlotte, North Carolina Office: 3500 One Wachovia Center, 301 South College Street. Telephone: 704-331-4900. Fax: 704-331-4955.
Raleigh, North Carolina Office: 2100 First Union Capitol Center, 150 Fayetteville Street Mall, P.O. Box 831. Telephone: 919-755-2100. Fax: 919-755-2150.
Research Triangle Park, North Carolina Office: 2530 Meridian Parkway, Suite 400 (Durham), 27713, P.O. Box 13069, Research Triangle Park, 27709. Telephone: 919-484-2300. Fax: 919-484-2340.
Greensboro, North Carolina Office: 300 North Greene Street. Telephone: 336-574-8030. Fax: 336-574-4520.
Atlanta, Georgia Office: One Atlantic Center, 1201 West Peachtree Street, Suite 3500. Telephone: 404-872-7000. Fax: 404-888-7490.
Other Atlanta, Georgia Office: Suite 404, 2296 Henderson Mill Road, N.E. Telephone: 770-492-9030. Fax: 770-492-9609.
Washington, D.C. Office: Suite 700, 1401 Eye Street. Telephone: 202-857-4400. Fax: 202-467-6910.
Greenville, South Carolina Office: 700 Poinsett Plaza, 104 South Main Street, P.O. Box 10208. Telephone: 864-255-5400. Fax: 864-255-5440.
Tysons Corner, Virginia Office: 8065 Leesburg Pike, Fourth Floor. Telephone: 703-790-3310. Fax: 703-790-2623.
Reviser of the North Carolina Law Digest for this Directory.
See Professional Biographies, WINSTON-SALEM, NORTH CAROLINA

Wood, B. Jeffrey, (BV) .... '51 '78 C.575 B.A. L.896 J.D. [Wood,R.&J.]
Wood, Bradley O. .... '70 '95 C.896 B.A. L.575 J.D. [▣ Womble C.S.&R.]
Wood, Charlot F., (AV) .... '55 '89 C.471 B.A. L.869 J.D. [Bell,D.&P.]
Wood, William Z., Jr. .... '47 '72 C&L.575 A.B., J.D. Supr. Ct. J.
Wood, Rabil & Johnston, LLP, (AV) .... 3600 Country Club Road, Suite 100
Woods, Gloria L., (BV) .... '47 '93 C.1309 B.A. L.1228 J.D. 704 Hall of Justice
Woods, Stephanie B. .... '73 '98 C.1128 B.A. L.574 J.D. 4814 Tiffany Ave.
Wooten, Candice Sylvette .... '76 '01 C&L.577 B.A., J.D. [▣ Constangy,B.&S.]
Wooten, Nancy L., (BV) .... '39 '83 C.955 B.S. L.896 J.D. 102 W. 3rd St.
Wraight, Justin B. .... '78 '03 C.239 B.A. L.896 J.D. [A.Caldwell&Assoc.]
Wright, A. Bruce '10 '35 C&L.813 A.B., LL.B.
(adm. in CA; not adm. in NC) P.O. Box 3099‡
Wright, Ronald F., Jr. '59 '85 C.945 B.A. L.976 J.D.
(adm. in GA; not adm. in NC) Assoc. Prof., Wake Forest Univ. School of Law
Wright, William E., (AV) .... '— '84 C.855 B.A. L.228 J.D. [Kilpatrick S.]
Yde, Terre Thomas .... '69 '00 C.1111 B.A. L.923 J.D. [▣ Comerford&B.]
Yeatts, James C., III .... '42 '68 C.692 B.A. L.896 J.D. Asst. Dist. Atty.
Yett, Wesley Meredith .... '74 '01 Krispy Kreme Doughnut Corporation
Yokley, D. Blake, (AV) .... '38 '63 C&L.896 A.B., LL.B. [D.B.Yokley]

Yokley, D. Blake, P.A., (AV)
230 Town Run Lane, 27101
Telephone: 336-721-4772 Fax: 336-722-8589
Email: d105@bellsouth.net URL: http://www.dbyokley-law.com
D. Blake Yokley.
General Civil and Criminal Trial Practice in all State and Federal Courts. Personal Injury, Automobile Accidents, Workers Compensation, Domestic/Family Law, Divorce, Child Custody, Child Support, Real Estate, Probate and Estates, Criminal Defense, Traffic and DWI/DUI Defense.
See Professional Biographies, WINSTON-SALEM, NORTH CAROLINA

Zick, Kenneth A., II .... '49 '77 C.20 A.B. L.912 J.D. Prof. of Law, Wake Forest Univ.

WINTERVILLE, 4,791, *Pitt Co.*

Lassiter, E. Keen, (BV) .... '62 '90 C&L.896 B.A., J.D. P.O. Box 2636
Stocks, Lubie M. .... '22 '50 C&L.575 A.B., LL.B. P.O. Box 375‡

WINTON, 956, *Hertford Co.*

Burleson, L. Frank, Jr., (AV) .... '37 '64 C&L.896 B.A., LL.B. Town Atty.

WOODLAND, 760, *Northampton Co.*

Flythe, Joseph J., (AV) .... '30 '58 C.316 B.A. L.575 LL.B. P.O. Box 177
Vaughan, Charles J., (AV) .... '39 '65 C&L.575 B.S., LL.B. Co. Atty.

WRIGHTSVILLE BEACH, 2,593, *New Hanover Co.*

Anderson, Henry L., Jr., (AV) .... '43 '68 C&L.575 A.B., J.D. [Anderson,D.&Assoc.]
Anderson, John H., Jr. .... '75 '02 C.576 B.S. L.575 J.D. [▣ Anderson,D.&Assoc.]

Anderson, Daniel & Associates, (AV) ▣
232 Causeway Drive, P.O. Box 1309, 28480
Telephone: 910-256-6896 Fax: 910-256-3472
Email: janderson@attorneysada.com URL: http://www.attorneysada.com
Henry L. Anderson, Jr.; A. L. Butler Daniel:—D. Stuart Smith; John H. Anderson, Jr.
Medical Malpractice, Birth Injury, Cerebral Palsy, Personal Injury, Nursing Home Neglect, Products Liability, Professional Misconduct, Legal Malpractice, Complex Civil Litigation.
See Professional Biographies, WRIGHTSVILLE BEACH, NORTH CAROLINA

Brooks, Charles A. .... '47 '74 C.184 B.A. L.564 J.D. P.O. Box 1375
Daniel, A. L. Butler, (CV) .... '65 '93 C.232 B.S. L.1228 J.D. [Anderson,D.&Assoc.]

Ennis, Newton & Baynard, P.A.
(See Wilmington)

Fonvielle, W. Alex, Jr. .... '18 '46 C&L.575 A.B., LL.B. 8 E. Raleigh St.
Lanier, Russell J. .... '24 '51 C&L.896 B.S., LL.B. Ret. Supr. Ct. J.
Marks, Richard C. '37 '76 C&L.188 B.A., J.D.
(adm. in NY; not adm. in NC) 2305 North Lumina Aveune, Suite E
O'Quinn, Robert A., (AV) .... '46 '76 C.575 B.A. L.896 J.D. 530 Causeway Dr., Ste. C

Price, James S.
(See Wilmington)

Sherrill, John W., (BV) .... '49 '77 C.575 B.A. L.896 J.D. Asst. Dist. Atty.
Smith, D. Stuart .... '75 '01 C.575 B.A. L.1228 J.D. [▣ Anderson,D.&Assoc.]
Toms, Kelly Marlaine, Law Offices of .... '69 '98 C.304 B.A. L.107 J.D. P.O. Box 374

YADKINVILLE, * 2,818, *Yadkin Co.*

Graham, James Lee, (BV) .... '39 '68 C.576 B.S. L.896 J.D. Co. Atty.
Greene, Lora B., (BV) .... '64 '89 C.34 B.S. L.1345 J.D. 106 N. Jackson St.
Harding, Benjamin H., Jr., (AV) .... '42 '73 C&L.896 B.A., J.D. [Shore H.&H.]
Hudspeth, N. Lawrence, III, (AV) .... '52 '76 C&L.575 B.A., J.D. [Shore H.&H.]
Randleman, Richard N., (AV) .... '38 '62 C&L.896 B.A., LL.B. [R.N.Randleman]
Randleman, Richard N., P.A., (AV) .... 112 S. State St.
Shore, Henry B., (AV) .... '41 '69 C.576 B.S.C.E. L.896 J.D. [Shore H.&H.]
Shore Hudspeth & Harding, PA, (AV) .... 201 E. Main St.

Teeter Law Firm
(See Winston-Salem)

Terrell, Donna Shore, (BV) .... '60 '85 C.296 B.S. L.1228 J.D. [▣ Shore H.&H.]
Zachary, Frank Curry, Sr., (BV) .... '51 '76 C.575 B.A. L.574 J.D. [Zachary&Z.]
Zachary, Valerie Johnson, (BV) .... '62 '88 C.475 B.A. L.309 J.D. [Zachary&Z.]
Zachary, W. Lee, Jr., (AV) .... '46 '75 C&L.575 A.B., J.D. [Zachary&Z.]

Zachary and Zachary, (AV) .... Courthouse Sq.

YANCEYVILLE, * 2,091, *Caswell Co.*

Allen, Phillip W. .... '46 '72 C&L.575 A.B., J.D. Dist. J.
Blackwell, Robert R. .... '27 '52 C.1129 L.896 J.D. P.O. Box 146‡
Daniel, George B., (BV) .... '51 '76 C.576 B.S. L.896 J.D. [G.B.Daniel]
Daniel, William H. .... '53 '85 C.692 B.S. L.356 J.D. [W.H.Daniel]

Daniel, George B., P.A., (BV)
139 East Main Street, P.O. Box 999, 27379
Telephone: 336-694-4363 Fax: 336-694-6601
URL: http://www.danielthomaslaw.com
George B. Daniel; John M. Thomas.
Criminal Law, Felonies, Misdemeanors, Traffic Violations, Driving While Intoxicated, Automobile Accidents, Truck Accidents, Personal Injury, Wrongful Death, Civil Litigation, Real Estate, Residential Real Estate, Commercial Real Estate, Real Estate Litigation, Workers Compensation, Estate Planning, Estate Administration, Drug Crimes.
See Professional Biographies, YANCEYVILLE, NORTH CAROLINA

Daniel, William H., P.A.
118 West Main Street, 27379
Telephone: 336-694-5882 Fax: 336-694-4888
Email: attorney@williamhdaniel.com URL: http://www.williamdaniellaw.com
William H. Daniel.
Criminal Law, Felonies, Misdemeanors, Traffic Violations, Driving While Intoxicated, Drug Crimes, Personal Injury, Automobile Accidents, Truck Accidents, Motorcycle Accidents, Wrongful Death, Workers Compensation, Real Estate, Wills, Estate Administration.
See Professional Biographies, YANCEYVILLE, NORTH CAROLINA

Farmer, R. Lee, (AV) '48 '73 C.240 B.A. L.896 J.D.
[R.L.Farmer] (⊙Bald Head Island)

Farmer, R. Lee, P.L.L.C. Law Offices of, (AV) BB
21 Main Street West, P.O. Box 1600, 27379-1600 ⊙
Telephone: 336-694-4361; 694-6549 FAX: 336-694-5448
Email: caswelllaw@adelphia.net
R. Lee Farmer. Of Counsel: Bill T. Walker (Not admitted in NC); Sandra S. Pugh.
General Civil and Criminal Practice in all State and Federal Courts. Probate, Real Estate, Personal Injury, Commercial, Construction, Administrative and Corporation Law.
General Counsel for: Town of Yanceyville; Ronco, Inc.; A. D. Swann Trucking Co., Inc.; Gregory Pallet Co.
Representative Clients: Wachovia Bank of North Carolina, N.A.; Duke Power Co.; Brauch Banking and Trust Co.

(This Listing Continued)

Farmer, R. Lee, P.L.L.C. Law Offices of (Continued)

Approved Attorneys for: Lawyers Title Insurance Corp.; Rural Development, U.S.D.A.
Bald Head Island, North Carolina Office: 19 Ibis Roost, 28461.
Granite City, Illinois Office: 3388-B Maryville Road, 62040.
See Professional Biographies, YANCEYVILLE, NORTH CAROLINA

Gentry, Lloyd Michael, (CV) .... '47 '76 C&L.575 B.S., J.D. Co. Ct. J.
Johnson, Bruce C. .... '52 '84 C.674 A.B. L.150 J.D. Co. Atty.
Pressley, Theresa K., Law Office of .... '60 '92 C.436 B.S. L.896 J.D. P.O. Box 1045
Pugh, Sandra S. .... '44 '83 C.575 B.A. L.1228 J.D. [© R.L.Farmer]
Thomas, John M., (BV) .... '55 '89 C.232 B.F.A. L.574 J.D. [G.B.Daniel]
Walker, Bill T. '48 '78 C.240 A.B. L.1194 J.D.
(adm. in IL; not adm. in NC) [© R.L.Farmer] (⊙Granite City, IL)

Watlington, Stuart N., (AV) '54 '81 C.575 A.B. L.1228 J.D. BB
114 Court Square, 27379
Mailing Address: P.O. Box 1776, Yanceyville, NC 27379
Telephone: 336-694-1155 Fax: 336-694-1057
Email: snwatlaw@earthlink.net URL: http://www.swatlingtonlaw.com
General Civil and Criminal Practice in all State and Federal Courts. DWI, Traffic Violations, Personal Injury, Wrongful Death, Probate, Real Estate.
See Professional Biographies, YANCEYVILLE, NORTH CAROLINA

YOUNGSVILLE, 650, *Franklin Co.*

Riley, Barbara Peters .... '53 '81 C.575 B.A. L.1228 J.D. Dept. of Jus.

ZEBULON, 4,046, *Wake Co.*

Doyle, Howard G. .... '31 '63 C&L.575 B.A., J.D. P.O. Box 632
Gay, Andy W. .... '52 '80 C.55 B.S. L.1228 J.D. [Gay&S.]
Gay & Stroud, L.L.P., (BV) .... 305 N. Arendell Ave.
Jackson, Darren, (BV) .... '70 '96 C.575 B.A. L.228 J.D. [A Gay&S.]
Lloyd, Sean Kent .... '73 '00 C.576 B.S. L.862 J.D. 305 North Arendell Avenue
Pople, Deborah Ann '54 '94 C.720 B.A. L.446 J.D.
(adm. in MD; not adm. in NC) 284 Mallie Pearce Rd.
Stroud, Donna S., (BV) .... '64 '88 C&L.1228 B.A., J.D. [Gay&S.]
Watts, Sandra Denise .... '77 '02 C.471 B.S. L.574 J.D. [A J.M.Weeks]
Weeks, J. Michael, (BV) .... '46 '72 C.576 B.A. L.575 J.D. [J.M.Weeks]
Weeks, J. Michael, P.A., (BV) .... 221 N. Arendell Ave.

NORTH DAKOTA

CAPITAL: BISMARCK

The State Bar Association of North Dakota
P.O. Box 2136
Bismarck, North Dakota 58502-2136
Telephone: 701-255-1404
Fax: 701-224-1621

Index of Towns and Cities Listed by County

*Indicates County Seat

Adams County
* Hettinger

Barnes County
* Valley City

Benson County
* Minnewaukan

Billings County
* Medora

Bottineau County
* Bottineau

Bowman County
* Bowman

Burleigh County
* Bismarck

Cass County
Casselton
* Fargo
Leonard
West Fargo

Cavalier County
* Langdon

Dickey County
* Ellendale
Oakes

Divide County
* Crosby

Dunn County
Halliday
Killdeer

Eddy County
* New Rockford

Emmons County
* Linton
Strasburg

Foster County
* Carrington

Golden Valley County
* Beach

Grand Forks County
* Grand Forks
Larimore
Northwood
Thompson

Grant County
* Carson
Elgin

Griggs County
Binford
* Cooperstown

Hettinger County
* Mott
Regent

Kidder County
* Steele

La Moure County
Edgeley
* La Moure

Logan County
* Napoleon

McHenry County
* Towner

McIntosh County
* Ashley
Wishek

McKenzie County
* Watford City

McLean County
Garrison
* Washburn

Mercer County
Beulah
Hazen
* Stanton

Morton County
Hebron
* Mandan

Mountrail County
New Town
Parshall
* Stanley

Nelson County
* Lakota

Oliver County
* Center

Pembina County
* Cavalier
Hamilton
Walhalla

Pierce County
* Rugby

Ramsey County
* Devils Lake

Ransom County
Enderlin
* Lisbon

Renville County
* Mohall

Richland County
Hankinson
* Wahpeton

Rolette County
* Rolla

Sargent County
* Forman

Sheridan County
* McClusky

Sioux County
* Fort Yates

Stark County
* Dickinson

Stutsman County
* Jamestown

Towner County
* Cando

Traill County
Hatton
* Hillsboro
Mayville

Walsh County
* Grafton
Park River

Ward County
Burlington
Kenmare
* Minot

Wells County
Harvey

Williams County
Tioga
* Williston

ASHLEY, * 882, *McIntosh Co.*

Gross, Sidney A., (CV) .... '48 '84 C.583 B.S. L.585 J.D. [Gross]
Gross Law Office, (CV) .... 214 West Main
Kretschmar, B. E., (AV) .... '16 '41 L.911 States Atty. [Kretschmar&K.]
Kretschmar, William E., (BV) .... '33 '61 C.755 B.S. L.494 LL.B. [Kretschmar&K.]
Kretschmar & Kretschmar, (AV) .... Court House
Weisser, Frank J. .... '55 '88 C.579 B.S. L.585 J.D. P.O. Box 100

BEACH, * 1,205, *Golden Valley Co.*

Keohane, Brian W. .... '34 '60 C&L.585 Ph.B., LL.B. P.O. Box 369
Mackoff Kellogg Law Firm, (AV) .... 41 Central Avenue, South (⊙Dickinson)
Peterson, Charles J., (BV) .... '58 '83 C.581 B.A. L.508 J.D. [Mackoff K.] ⊙

BEULAH, 3,152, *Mercer Co.*

Hagen, Raymond M., (BV) .... '27 '57 C&L.585 B.S.C., J.D. 121 W. Main
Quast, Larry W., (BV) .... '45 '73 C.581 B.A. L.585 J.D. 420 W. Main Street
Solem, Scott T., (BV) .... '67 '93 C.999 B.A. L.585 J.D. [Solem]
Solem Law Office, (BV) .... 123 W. Main

BINFORD, 233, *Griggs Co.*

Coplen, Joel .... '15 '37 C&L.585 J.D., J.D. P.O. Box 37‡

BISMARCK, * 55,532, *Burleigh Co.*

Adams, John E. .... '29 '53 C&L.585 B.S.L., LL.B. 511 N. 13th St.
Addo, Kate '49 '88 L.999 LL.B.
(adm. in NY; not adm. in ND) Medcenter One Health Systems
American Legal Services, P.C., (CV) .... 1710 Burnt Boat Drive
Anderson, Sonna Marie .... '58 '85 C.585 B.S. L.208 J.D. Dist. J.
Anderson, Tag Christian, (BV) .... '63 '91 C.579 B.S. L.585 J.D. Atty. Gen. Off.
Anderson, Wayne J. .... '44 '69 C&L.585 B.A., J.D. Human Servs. Dept.
Anderson & Anderson, P.C. .... P.O. Box 2574
Andrews, Michael T., (BV) .... '66 '98 C.579 B.A. L.585 J.D. [Vogel]
Ansley, Robert John .... '64 '95 C.999 B.A. L.585 J.D. U.S. Ct.
Armstrong, Mitchell .... '— '03 C&L.585 B.B.A., J.D. [⊡ Smith B.O.P.&W.]
Atkinson, Myron H., Jr., (BV) .... '27 '51 C&L.585 B.S.C., J.D. 400 E. Broadway‡
Austin, Timothy J., (BV) .... '53 '79 C.584 B.A. L.221 J.D. 2000 Schafer St.
Baird, LaRoy, III, (AV) .... '48 '80 C.172 B.S. L.585 J.D. [L.Baird]
Baird, LaRoy, P.C., (AV) .... 109 N. 4th St., Suite 300
Bakke, Randall J. .... '57 '82 C&L.585 B.A., J.D. [Smith B.O.P.&W.]
Balaban, Steven, (BV) .... '64 '94 C&L.585 B.S., J.D. 418 East Rosser Avenue, Suite 102
Bard, Stuart F. .... '59 '84 C&L.585 B.S.B.A, J.D. 1101 E. Interstate Ave.★
Bauer, Arthur .... '25 '50 C&L.585 LL.B. 2035 Catherine Dr.
Baumstark, Beth Angus .... '46 '81 C.585 Ph.B. L.383 J.D. 1022 E. Divide Ave.
Beauclair, Leo J., (AV) .... '34 '58 C&L.585 Ph.B., LL.B. 919 S. 7th St., Ste. 207
Bender, Lawrence, (P.C.), (BV) .... '— '82 C.579 B.A. L.585 J.D. [Pearce&D.]
Bennett, Robert P., (AV) .... '49 '74 C.958 B.S. L.585 J.D. Asst. Atty. Gen.
Berg, Vivian Elaine .... '37 '79 C.584 B.S. L.585 J.D. 515 1/2 E. Bdwy
Bergeson, Brian L., (BV) .... '69 '94 C.585 B.B.A. L.494 J.D. P.O. Box 2196
Binek, William W. .... '41 '71 C&L.585 B.S., J.D. Chf. Coun., Pub. Serv. Comm.
Bitz, Steven M. .... '76 '03 C.999 B.A. L.585 J.D. [⊡ Bucklin,K.&M.]
Bjella, Brian R., (BV) .... '52 '79 C&L.585 B.A., J.D. [Fleck,M.&S.]
Bjornson, Jodi Billing .... '70 '96 C.579 B.A. L.585 J.D. 500 East Front Ave
Blazer, Brenda L., (AV) .... '52 '84 C&L.585 B.A., J.D. [Vogel]
Boeck, David .... '50 '75 C.492 B.A. L.585 J.D. 400 E. Bway. Ave., Ste. 616
Boeckel, Craig A., (BV) .... '61 '88 C&L.585 B.S.B.A., J.D. [Tschider&B.]
Bolinske, Robert, (CV) .... '74 '00 C&L.585 B.A., J.D. 515 N. 4th St.
Bolinske, Robert V., (BV) .... '44 '69 C.585 Ph.B. L.309 J.D. 515 N. 4th St.
Bormann, Clark J., (BV) .... '53 '78 C&L.793 B.A., J.D. [Bormann&M.]
Bormann & Myerchin, LLP, (BV) .... 418 E. Bway. Ave., Ste 240
Boschee, Larry L., (BV) .... '60 '85 C.583 B.S. L.585 J.D. [Pearce&D.]
Bowlinger, Paul J., (CV) .... '60 '88 C.182 B.A. L.585 J.D. [Bowlinger]
Bowlinger Law Office, (CV) .... 120 N. 3rd St., Ste. 100
Brady, Robert P. .... '43 '69 L.585 J.D. Admin. Law J.
Brown, Malcolm H., (AV) .... '40 '67 C&L.585 Ph.B., J.D. [M.H.Brown]

Brown, Malcolm H., P.C., (AV)
209 East Broadway Avenue, P.O. Box 2692, 58502-2692
Telephone: 701-224-8825 Fax: 701-224-8820
Email: mhblaw@btinet.net
Malcolm H. Brown.
Business Law, Real Estate, Commercial Law, Estate Planning, Probate, Condemnation, Eminent Domain, Bankruptcy, General Civil Trial before all State and Federal Courts.
See Professional Biographies, BISMARCK, NORTH DAKOTA

Bruggman, Colette Nicolson, (BV) '62 '87 C&L.585 B.B.A., J.D.
600 E. Boulevard Ave.
Bucklin, Leonard H., (AV) .... '33 '57 C&L.494 B.S.L., J.D. [⊡ Bucklin,K.&M.]

Bucklin, Klemin & McBride, P.C., (BV)
Wells Fargo Bank Building, Suite 500, 400 East Broadway Avenue, 58502-0955
Telephone: 701-258-8988 Fax: 701-258-8486
Email: lawyers@bkmpc.com URL: http://www.bkmpc.com
Lawrence R. Klemin; Karen L. McBride; David Schweigert. Associate: Steven M. Bitz. Of Counsel: Leonard H. Bucklin.
Products Liability, Environmental Law, Asbestos, Insurance Defense, Personal Injury, Natural Resources, Commercial Law, Civil Litigation, Corporate, Bankruptcy, Real Estate, Family Law, Domestic Relations, Divorce, Child Custody, Adoptions, Workers Compensation, Social Security, Health Law, Commercial Litigation, Administrative Law, Insurance Law, Estate Planning, Probate, Wills, Business Law.
See Professional Biographies, BISMARCK, NORTH DAKOTA

Buringrud, Jay E. .... '47 '72 C.579 B.S. L.585 J.D. State Legis. Council
Burke, Patricia L., (BV) .... '56 '79 C.585 B.A. L.629 J.D. P.O. Box 4050
Byers, Jonathan R., (BV) .... '61 '88 C&L.585 B.A., J.D. Atty. Gen. Off., Consumer Div.
Carlson, Christopher A., (BV) .... '52 '77 C.491 B.A. L.585 J.D. 414 E. Main St.
Carpenter, Deborah J., (CV) .... '58 '82 C.579 B.S. L.585 J.D. [Carpenter]
Carpenter, Kerry J., (BV) .... '56 '81 C.490 B.S. L.585 J.D. [⊡ Carpenter]
Carpenter Law Offices, (CV) .... 523 N. 4th St.
Catalano, Linda A., (BV) '48 '74
C.527 B.A. L.585 J.D. Exec. Dir., Legal Assistance of North Dakota
Chapman, Charles L., (BV) .... '50 '77 C.579 B.A. L.585 J.D. [Chapman&C.]
Chapman & Chapman, P.C., (BV) .... P.O. Box 1258
Cichy, Joseph J., (BV) .... '49 '81 C.579 B.A. L.585 J.D. [⊡ J.J.Cichy]

Cichy, Joseph J., P.C., (BV)
115 North 4th Street, Suite 2, 58501
Telephone: 701-223-4524 Fax: 701-223-0855
Email: jcichy@midconetwork.com
Joseph J. Cichy.

(This Listing Continued)

Cichy, Joseph J., P.C. (Continued)
Real Estate, Business Law, Corporate Law, Administrative Law, Association Management, Water Law, Lobbying, Family Law, Personal Injury.
See Professional Biographies, BISMARCK, NORTH DAKOTA

Clayburgh, Richard (Rick) S. .... '60 '94 C.182 B.A. L.585 J.D. State Tax Comr.
Coles, James J., (BV) .... '52 '77 C&L.585 B.S., J.D. [Coles]
Coles Law Firm, (BV) .... P.O. Box 2162
Conmy, Patrick A. .... '34 '59 C.309 B.A. L.276 J.D. U.S. Dist. J.
Cook, Maurice E., (AV) .... '36 '63 C&L.585 Ph.B., J.D. [Cook W.&W.P.]
Cook Wegner & Wike PLLP, (AV) .... 811 E. Interstate Ave.
Daley, Michael F., (BV) .... '56 '80 C&L.585 B.A., J.D. [Wheeler W.]
Dalsted, G. Leonard .... '15 '60 C.579 B.S. L.981 LL.B. 1128 Pioneer Dr.‡
Davison, Kathleen K. .... '52 '80 C&L.585 B.A., J.D. 1029 W Ave. C‡
Dawson, Timothy J. .... '69 '94 C&L.585 B.A., J.D. Legal Coun., Legislative Council
Dickson, Thomas A., (BV) .... '54 '81 C.999 B.A. L.802 J.D. 107 W. Main Ave., Ste. 150
Dietz, Kathryn L., (BV) .... '51 '75 C.579 B.A. L.585 J.D. [Dietz&L.]
Dietz & Little, (BV) .... 2718 Gateway Ave.
Dillinger, Michael Paul .... '74 '99 C.999 B.S. L.585 J.D. Supm. Ct.
Disselhorst, Thomas M., (CV) '47 '76
C.112 B.A. L.1066 J.D. 311 E. Thayer Ave., Suite 110
Dockter, Dennis D. .... '55 '82 C&L.585 B.A., J.D. Staff Atty., Supm. Ct.
Dodson, Christopher Thomas '64 '90
C.112 B.A. L.1066 J.D. Exec. Dir., ND Catholic Conf.
Dohrmann, Rebekah Ann Solberg .... '66 '93 C.182 B.A. L.585 J.D. P.O. Box 5511
Donlin, Charles L. .... '26 '50 C.723 L.494 LL.B. 226 W. Boulevard Ave.‡
Dopson, Lawrence A., (BV) .... '49 '75 C.358 B.S. L.597 J.D. [Zuger K.&S.]
Durick, B. Timothy, (AV) .... '45 '71 C.602 B.A. L.494 J.D. [Pearce&D.]
Durick, Patrick W., (AV) .... '40 '73 C.1070 B.S. L.190 J.D. [Pearce&D.]
Dwyer, John W., (BV) .... '48 '73 C.747 B.A. L.585 J.D. 1016 E. Owens Ave.
Dyer, Edwin W. F., III, (BV) .... '46 '74 C.454 B.S. L.94 J.D. [Dyer&S.]

Dyer & Summers, P.C., (BV)
418 East Broadway, Suite 246, P.O. Box 2261, 58502
Telephone: 701-223-2099 Fax: 701-223-4889
Email: dyersums@gcentral.com URL: http://www.lawyers.com/dyersums
Edwin W. F. Dyer, III; Anne E. Summers.
General Civil Practice in State, Federal, and Tribal Courts, Divorce and other Family Law, Consumer Bankruptcy, and Social Security Disability.
See Professional Biographies, BISMARCK, NORTH DAKOTA

Edison, Chris A., (BV) .... '66 '95 C.491 B.S. L.585 J.D. [Storslee]
Engel, Austin G., (BV) .... '28 '85 C.429 B.A. L.585 J.D. 418 East Rosser Avenue
Erickson, Edward E., (BV) .... '65 '90 C.427 B.A. L.494 J.D. Asst. Atty. Gen.
Espeseth, Ross, (BV) .... '56 '82 C.579 B.A. L.585 J.D. 109 N. 4th St., Ste. 300
Evenson, Jerry W., P.C., (AV) .... '49 '80 C&L.585 B.A., J.D. [Zuger K.&S.]
Feland, Cynthia M., (BV) '65 '90 C&L.585 B.A., J.D.
Burlington Co. Asst. States. Atty.
Fleck, Arnold V., (BV) .... '58 '83 C.579 B.S. L.585 J.D. [Fleck]

Fleck Law Office, (BV)
314 East Thayer Avenue, Suite 220, P.O. Box 6178, 58506-6178
Telephone: 701-258-5256 Fax: 701-258-5626
Email: arnfleck@usa.net
Arnold V. Fleck.
Personal Injury, Automobile Accidents, Wrongful Death, Medical Malpractice, Family Law, Divorce, Collections, Estate Planning, Probate, Civil Litigation.
See Professional Biographies, BISMARCK, NORTH DAKOTA

Fleck, Mather & Strutz, Ltd., (AV)
Sixth Floor, Wells Fargo Bank Building, 400 East Broadway, Suite 600, P.O. Box 2798, 58502-2798
Telephone: 701-223-6585 Facsimile: 701-222-4853
Email: fms@flecklaw.com URL: http://www.flecklaw.com
Ernest R. Fleck (1921-1995); Russell R. Mather (Retired); William A. Strutz (Retired); Gary R. Wolberg; Paul W. Summers; Brian R. Bjella; John W. Morrison, Jr.; Curtis L. Wike; Craig Cordell Smith; Shane A. Hanson; Michael C. Waller. Associate: Petra H. Mandigo.
Corporation, Real Estate, Labor and Employment Relations, Insurance, Legal Malpractice Litigation, Defense Litigation, Dental Malpractice, Medical Devices, Medical Malpractice, Oil and Gas and Mining Law. Trials and Appeals. General Civil Practice before all Courts and Administrative Boards.
See Professional Biographies, BISMARCK, NORTH DAKOTA

Fleming, James Conner, (BV) .... '68 '94 C.585 B.S. L.602 J.D. Asst. Atty. Gen.
Foss, Marilyn K., (BV) .... '51 '78 C&L.585 B.A., J.D. [M.Foss]
Foss, Mark D., (BV) '52 '78 C&L.585 B.A., J.D.
Gen. Coun., Dakota Gasification Company and Dakota Coal Company
Foss, Marilyn, Law Office of, (BV) .... P.O. Box 2216
Fox, John J., (BV) .... '52 '79 C.492 B.E.S. L.585 J.D. Asst. Atty. Gen.
Fraase, Paul H., (BV) .... '50 '77 C.182 B.A. L.585 J.D. Asst. City Atty.
Freed, Robert A. .... '59 '84 C.723 B.S. L.585 J.D. Ref. Dist. Ct.
Geiermann, Michael, (BV) .... '59 '84 C&L.585 B.S., J.D. [Rolfson S.&L.]
Germolus, Paul C., (CV) .... '67 '97 C.579 B.S. L.585 J.D. [Germolus]

Germolus Law Office, (CV)
Regency Business Center, 3333 E. Broadway Avenue, Suite 1215, 58501-3395
Telephone: 701-255-2010 Fax: 701-255-1980
Email: germoluslaw@bis.midco.net URL: http://www.lawyers.com/germoluslaw
Member of Firm: Paul C. Germolus.
Natural Resources Law, Agricultural Law, Fish and Wildlife Law, Real Property Law, Administrative Law.
See Professional Biographies, BISMARCK, NORTH DAKOTA

Gilbertson, Joel W., (BV) .... '49 '76 C.182 B.A. L.585 J.D. [Vogel]
Glaser, Gerald .... '32 '56 C&L.585 B.P.H., J.D. [⊡ Schmitz&S.]
Graff, Benny A. .... '38 '64 C&L.585 B.S.Ch.E., J.D. Dist. J.
Grindberg, Alan K., (BV) .... '32 '66 C&L.585 B.S.C.E., J.D. Law Clk., Dist. Ct. J.
Grinolds, Shawn Arlin, (CV) .... '67 '96 C&L.585 B.A., J.D. [⊡ Smith B.O.P.&W.]
Grinsteiner, John Wendelin, (CV) .... '72 '98 C&L.585 B.A., J.D. [Grinsteiner]
Grinsteiner Law Office, (CV) .... P.O. Box 285
Gross, Richard J. .... '47 '72 C.436 B.A. L.585 J.D. Governor's Coun.
Guler, Mary Maichel .... '61 '86 C&L.585 B.B.A., J.D. U.S. Bank
Gunderson, Gerry A., (BV) '58 '83 C.358 B.A. L.585 J.D.
Investment Center Group, Inc.
Gunkel, Lynde David, (BV) '50 '77
C.579 B.A. L.221 J.D. Dir., Central Legal Staff, N. Dak. Supm. Ct.
Hagburg, Michael .... '60 '95 C.494 B.A. L.585 J.D. Staff Atty., Supm. Ct.
Hager, Marvin M., (BV) .... '41 '72 C&L.585 B.A., J.D. 2207 E. Main
Hagerty, Gail .... '53 '78 C&L.585 B.A., J.D. Dist. J.
Hall, Kathleen J., (CV) .... '57 '92 C&L.585 B.B.A., J.D. [⊡ Carpenter]
Hanson, Earl J., (AV⊤) '41 '68 C.506 B.S. L.508 J.D.
(adm. in MT; not adm. in ND) V.P., Admin. & Coun., JTL Grp., Inc.
Hanson, Shane A., (BV) .... '70 '96 C.358 B.A. L.585 J.D. [Fleck,M.&S.]

Hauer, Melissa A., (CV) '68 '93 C.585 B.A. L.285 J.D.
Dir., Legal Advsry. Unit, Dept. of Human Servs.
Hausauer, Albert R. ... '23 '52 C&L.585 B.S.C., LL.B. 1101 Fairview Pl.‡
Hayden, Cameron W., (BV) ... '57 '82 C&L.585 B.A., J.D. Asst. U.S. Atty.
Hill, James S., P.C., (AV) ... '49 '74 C&L.585 B.A., J.D. [Zuger K.&S.]
Hinman, Michael J., (BV) '43 '73
C&L.585 B.A., J.D. Gen. Coun., Basin Elec. Power Coop.
Hjelmstad, Jerald A. '53 '78
C.999 B.A. L.585 J.D. Asst. Dir., North Dakota League of Cities
Hoberg, Allen C. ... '50 '77 C&L.585 B.A., J.D. Dir.
Hoberg, Mary N., (BV) ... '52 '77 C.705 A.B. L.585 J.D. 2023 Catherine Dr.
Hochhalter, Clare R., (BV) ... '57 '84 C.358 B.A. L.585 J.D. 220 E. Rosser Ave.
Hoffman, Michael R., (BV) ... '55 '80 C.579 B.A. L.802 J.D. 120 N. 3rd St., Ste. 100
Hofland, Constance N. ... '58 '00 C&L.585 B.S., J.D. [Ⓐ Zuger K.&S.]
Hogan, Christine A., (BV) ... '49 '75 C.579 B.S. L.585 J.D. Executive Dir.
Holloway, Douglas Lawrence ... '67 '93 C.579 B.A. L.585 J.D. 600 E. Boulevard Ave.
Hopgood, Tom K., (AVⓉ) '54 '79 C.506 B.A. L.285 J.D.
Assoc. Gen. Coun., MDU Resources Group, Inc.
Horner, Wayne J., (BV) ... '64 '90 C&L.585 B.B.A., J.D. [Rausch]
Hovland, Daniel L. '54 '79 C.182 B.S. L.585 J.D.
U.S. Dist. Ct. J., Dist. of North Dakota
Huettl, Damian J., (CV) ... '72 '97 C.491 B.A. L.585 J.D. [Wheeler W.]
Hummel, Krista Lyn ... '74 '98 C&L.585 B.A., J.D. Coun.
Humphrey, Bonnie Paradis, (CV) ... '60 '92 C.491 M.L.A. L.585 J.D. P.O. Box 2419
Isaac, Lance E. ... '59 '92 C.878 B.A. L.585 J.D. Jud. Law Clk., Supm. Ct.
Isakson, Charles R., (BV) ... '50 '77 C.358 B.A. L.585 J.D. [Ⓐ Chapman&C.]
Jacobson, Paul W., (BV) ... '48 '73 C.579 B.A. L.494 J.D. Disciplinary Coun., Supm. Ct.
Jeffcoat-Sacco, Illona A. ... '52 '76 C.431 B.A. L.585 J.D. Dir.

Jeffries, Olson & Flom, P.A.
(See Fargo)

Johnson, Kimberly A. ... '67 '92 C&L.585 B.A., J.D. Spec. Asst. to States Atty.
Johnson, Mary Ann, (AV) '49 '77 C&L.585 B.A., J.D.
V.P., Admn. & Asst. Secy., MDU Resources Group, Inc.
Johnson, Tiffany L. ... '77 '05 C.491 B.A. L.585 J.D. [Ⓐ Pearce&D.]
Johnston, Joy P. ... '62 '87 C.679 B.A. L.585 J.D. P.O. Box 2639
Jorgensen, Donald L. ... '44 '70 C&L.585 Ph.B., J.D. Dist. J. (☉Linton)
Kapsner, Carol Ronning ... '47 '77 C.713 B.A. L.174 J.D. Supm. Ct. Jus.
Kapsner, John C., (AV) ... '47 '73 C.723 B.A. L.1119 J.D. [Vogel]
Kautzmann, DeNae H. M., (BV) '53 '77
C.579 B.A. L.585 J.D. Appeals Supv., State Dept. of Human Servs.
Kautzmann, Dwight C. H. ... '45 '71 C.579 B.A. L.585 J.D. P.O. Box 1578‡

Kelsch Kelsch Ruff & Kranda
(See Mandan)

Kettleson, Jerome C., (BV) ... '46 '73 C.723 B.A. L.585 J.D. [Pearce&D.]
King, Lawrence E., (AVⓉ) ... '48 '75 C.679 B.S.E.E. L.851 J.D. 500 E. Front Ave.
King, Lawrence E., P.C., (BV) ... '65 '92 C&L.585 B.A., J.D. [Zuger K.&S.]
Kirmis, Lyle W., (BV) ... '49 '74 C&L.494 B.Ch.E., J.D. [Zuger K.&S.]
Klemin, Lawrence R., (BV) ... '45 '78 C&L.585 B.A., J.D. [Bucklin,K.&M.]
Koebele, Courtney M. ... '66 '91 C&L.585 B.S., J.D. [Wheeler W.]
Kolb, Tracy Vigness, P.C., (CV) ... '63 '95 C.584 B.A. L.585 J.D. [Zuger K.&S.]
Kraft, Carlan J., (BV) ... '45 '74 C.870 B.S. L.585 J.D. 1833 E. Bismarck Expwy., Ste. 1
Krenz, Julie A., (BV) ... '58 '85 C.494 B.A. L.585 J.D. Asst. Atty. Gen.
Lane, Robert E., (BV) ... '46 '72 C.446 B.S. L.585 J.D. Atty. Gen.
Larson, Gregory C., (BV) ... '52 '80 C.585 B.S. L.285 J.D. [Wheeler W.]
Latham, Steven L., (BV) ... '51 '76 C&L.585 B.A., J.D. [Wheeler W.]
Lee, David O. ... '47 '74 C&L.585 Ph.B., J.D. Dir.
Leer, David K. O. ... '35 '70 C.585 412 Mason Ave.
Levchak, Deborah Fohr, (AV) '51 '76 C&L.585 J.D.
Staff Coun., Basin Elec. Power Coop.
Levi, Bruce T. ... '57 '83 C&L.585 B.S.B.A., J.D. Leg. Coun.
Lewis Latimer, Nancy J ... '65 '92 C&L.585 B.S.Ed., J.D. Asst. Atty. Gen.
Liepitz, Karl A. ... '78 '03 C.489 B.A. L.1018 J.D. MDU Resources Group, Inc.

Lindell Law Office
(See Washburn)

Little, Stephen D., (BV) ... '50 '76 C.1101 B.A. L.585 J.D. [Dietz&L.]
Lucas, A. William, (BV) ... '39 '63 C&L.585 B.S.B.A., J.D. [Lucas]
Lucas Law Office, (BV) ... 314 E. Thayer Ave., Ste. 230
Magnusson, Keith C. ... '46 '74 C.585 B.S. L.900 J.D. State Dept. of Transp.
Maichel, Joseph R. ... '34 '59 C&L.585 B.S.B.A., J.D. 725 Bell St.‡
Malloy, Harry L. ... '29 '56 C&L.585 J.D. P.O. Box 1811
Mandigo, Petra H. ... '76 '03 C.694 B.A. L.190 J.D. [Ⓐ Fleck,M.&S.]
Maring, David S., (AV) ... '49 '74 C.579 B.S. L.585 J.D. [Maring W.] ☉
Maring, Mary Muehlen ... '51 '75 C.999 B.A. L.585 J.D. Supm. Ct. Jus.

Maring Williams Law Office, P.C., (AV)
400 East Broadway Suite 307, 58501 ☉
Telephone: 701-224-0430 Fax: 701-224-0454
Email: mwlo@maringlaw.com URL: http://www.maringlaw.com
David S. Maring.
Automobile Accidents, Wrongful Death, Personal Injury, NeuroLaw, Commercial Litigation, Professional Liability, Products Liability, Negligence, Civil Rights and Torts, Family Law, Civil Litigation. Trial Practice in all Courts.
Fargo, North Dakota Office: 1220 Main Avenue, Suite 105, P.O. Box 2103. 58107-2103. Telephone: 701-241-4141. Fax: 701-235-2268.
Detroit Lakes, Minnesota Office: 714 Lake Avenue, Suite 101. 56501. Telephone: 218-847-2257.
See Professional Biographies, BISMARCK, NORTH DAKOTA

Mather, R. Russell, (AV) '53 '78
C&L.585 B.A., J.D. Staff Coun., Basin Elec. Power Coop.
Mather, Russell R., (AV) ... '27 '52 C.906 L.174 J.D. [Fleck,M.&S.] ‡
Maxon, Mandy R. ... '77 '02 C.584 B.S. L.585 J.D. [Ⓐ Vogel]

Maxson Law Office, P.C.
(See Minot)

Mayer, Thomas A., (BV) ... '37 '61 C&L.602 B.S., LL.B. Asst. Atty. Gen.
McBride, Karen L., (BV) ... '45 '84 C.584 B.S. L.585 J.D. [Bucklin,K.&M.]
McCabe, Chad R. ... '69 '96 C&L.585 B.S.P.A., J.D. 523 N. Fourth Street
McCray, Loren Cay ... '66 '94 C.358 B.A. L.585 J.D. [L.McCray]
McCray, Loren ... 419 E. Broadway
McDonald, Jack, (BV) ... '40 '70 C&L.585 B.A., J.D. [Wheeler W.]
Miller, Penny L. ... '59 '90 C&L.585 B.A., J.D. Clk., Supm. Ct.
Miller, Scott A., (BV) ... '67 '94 C.585 B.B.A. L.950 J.D. Atty., Off. of the Atty. Gen.
Mills, William R. ... '20 '47 L.208 LL.B. 2904 Langer Lane‡
Moore, Sherry M., (AV) ... '51 '79 C.72 B.A. L.585 J.D. [S.M.Moore]
Moore, Sherry Mills, Attorney at Law, (AV) ... P.O. Box 4144

Morley Law Firm, Ltd.
(See Grand Forks)

Morris, Robert W. ... '64 '92 C.560 M.S. L.494 J.D. State Workers Comp. Bd.
Morrison, John W., Jr., (AV) ... '54 '78 C.999 B.S. L.585 J.D. [Fleck,M.&S.]
Morrow, Kent M. ... '53 '78 C.579 B.A. L.585 J.D. [Severin,R.&M.]
Murry, Bruce Douglas, (CV) ... '68 '95 C&L.585 B.S., J.D. 6100 Magnolia Dr.
Murry, C. Emerson ... '24 '50 C&L.585 B.S., J.D. Army Maj. Gen.‡
Myerchin, Paul Henry, (BV) ... '72 '97 C&L.585 B.S., J.D. [Bormann&M.]
Neubauer-Zoller, Brenda, (BV) ... '68 '94 C.999 B.A. L.585 J.D. [Severin,R.&M.]
Neumann, William A. ... '44 '69 C.585 B.S.B.A. L.813 J.D. Dist. J.
Nodland, Chad C., (BV) ... '66 '93 C&L.585 B.A., J.D. [Ⓐ Nodland]
Nodland, Irvin B., (AV) ... '35 '64 C.581 B.S. L.976 LL.B. [Nodland]
Nodland Law Offices, (AV) ... 109 N. 4th St., Suite 300
Nordwall, Blaine L., (BV) ... '48 '77 C&L.585 B.S., J.D. Dir. of Legal Advsr.
Norland, Cynthia J., (BV) '54 '82 C.584 B.S. L.585 J.D.
Assoc. Gen. Coun., MDU Resources Group, Inc.
Oliver, Leslie Bakken, (BV) ... '52 '91 C.207 B.A. L.585 J.D. [Vogel]
Olson, Claire M., (Mr.) '48 '75
C.584 B.S. L.585 J.D. Asst. Gen. Coun., Basin Elec. Power Coop.
Olson, John M., (BV) ... '47 '72 C.182 B.A. L.585 J.D. 115 North Fourth St.
Olsrud, John D. ... '41 '67 C&L.585 B.S., LL.B. Dir., State Legis. Council
Oster, Daniel H., (CV) ... '65 '91 C&L.585 B.A., J.D. 105 E. Broadway, Ste. 3
Pagel, Rodney E., (BV) ... '68 '93 C.1207 B.A. L.585 J.D. [Pagel W.]
Pagel Weikum, PLLP, (BV) ... 1715 Burnt Boat Drive
Pearce, William P., (AV) ... '40 '71 C&L.597 B.A., J.D. [Pearce&D.]

Pearce & Durick, (AV)
314 East Thayer Avenue, P.O. Box 400, 58502
Telephone: 701-223-2890 Fax: 701-223-7865
Email: law.office@pearce-durick.com URL: http://www.pearce-durick.com
Members of Firm: William R. Pearce (1910-1978); William P. Pearce; Patrick W. Durick; B. Timothy Durick; Gary R. Thune; David E. Reich; Jerome C. Kettleson; Larry L. Boschee; Lawrence Bender (P.C.); Jonathan P. Sanstead;—Tiffany L. Johnson.
Products Liability Defense, Oil and Gas, Mining, Insurance Defense, Negligence, Real Estate, Corporate Law, Taxation, Business Law, Commercial Law, Banking, Estate Planning, Probate, Wills, Public Utilities, Education Law, Intellectual Property, Employment Law, Appeals, Civil Litigation before all Courts and Administrative Agencies.
Representative Clients: American Insurance Assn.; Cigna-INA Insurance Co.; Deere & Co.; Emerson Electric Co.; Ford Motor Co.; General Motors Corp.; Kowasaki Motor Corp., U.S.A.; MDU Resources Group, Inc.; Royal Insurance Co.
See Professional Biographies, BISMARCK, NORTH DAKOTA

Persinger, Roger E. ... '28 '55 C&L.585 Ph.B., LL.B. P.O. Box 2751‡
Peterson, David L., (AV) ... '42 '68 C&L.585 B.S.B.A., J.D. Asst. U.S. Atty.
Petrik, John J., (BV) ... '54 '82 C.475 B.A. L.494 J.D. [Vogel]
Pierce, Rhonda R., (CV) '68 '94 C&L.585 B.A., J.D.
Spec. Asst. States Atty., Reg. Child Support Enforcement Unit
Pomeroy, Earl R., III ... '52 '79 C&L.585 B.S., J.D. State Ins. Comm.
Porsborg, Scott K. ... '66 '91 C&L.585 B.A., J.D. [Smith B.O.P.&W.]
Purdon, Timothy Q., (BV) ... '68 '95 C.491 B.A. L.300 J.D. 107 W. Main, Ste. 150
Purdy, James N. ... '31 '55 C.584 L.508 LL.B. Jud. Ref., Dist. Ct.
Rausch Law Office, The, (BV) ... 1620 S. Reno Dr.
Reich, David E., (BV) ... '56 '82 C&L.585 B.A., J.D. [Pearce&D.]
Reid, Shawnda R., (CV) ... '74 '99 C.585 B.A. L.546 J.D. [Ⓐ Zuger K.&S.]
Richter, Vonette Joy ... '59 '93 C&L.585 B.S.Ed.,B.A., J.D. 600 E. Blvd. Ave.
Riha, Richard J. ... '56 '82 C&L.585 B.A., J.D. State's Atty.
Ringsak, Marnell, (CV) ... '51 '79 L.585 J.D. [Severin,R.&M.]
Riskedahl, Burt L. ... '40 '73 C.358 B.A. L.1035 J.D. Dist. J.
Rogneby, Monte L., (BV) ... '66 '92 C.491 B.A. L.494 J.D. [Vogel]
Rolfson, Calvin N., (AV) ... '41 '66 C.182 B.A. L.585 LL.B. [Rolfson S.&L.]
Rolfson Schulz & Lervick, P.C., (AV) ... 425 North Fifth Street
Runge, Christianne Y., (BV) '54 '92
C.710 B.A. L.585 J.D. Exec. Dir., State Pub. Employees Assn.
Runge, Gregory Ian, (CV) ... '50 '89 C&L.585 B.S.P., J.D. 912 E. Owens Ave., Ste. 5
Rysavy, Don L. ... '55 '81 C&L.585 B.A., J.D. Staff Atty., Supm. Ct.
Saefke, Fred E., Jr. ... '21 '51 C.579 L.585 J.D. 411 N. 4th St.‡
Sagsveen, Matthew Arnold, (BV) '73 '99
C.182 B.A. L.585 J.D. Asst. Atty. Gen., Atty. Gen. Off.
Sand, Rosellen M., (BV) ... '55 '81 C&L.585 B.S., J.D. Dept. of Pub Instr.
Sanderson, Paul R. ... '74 '01 C&L.585 B.B.A., J.D. [Ⓐ Zuger K.&S.]
Sandness, Paul K., (BV) '54 '79 C.583 B.S. L.585 J.D.
Gen. Coun. & Secy., MDU Resources Group, Inc.
Sandstrom, Dale V. ... '50 '75 C.579 B.A. L.585 J.D. Supm. Ct. J.; ND Supm. Ct.
Sanstead, Jonathan P., (BV) ... '— '95 C.492 B.A. L.1035 J.D. [Pearce&D.]
Sasse, Brandi ... '73 '00 C.999 B.A. L.585 J.D. 514 E. Thayer Ave.
Sattler, Todd A. ... '63 '90 C.723 B.A. L.494 J.D. 600 E. Blvd. Ave., Dept. 125
Schlosser, James D., (BV) '37 '62 C.723 B.A. L.585 J.D.
Exec. V.P., N.D. Bankers Assn.
Schmidt, Cletus J. ... '24 '67 C.584 BS 2022 N. 3rd St.‡
Schmidt, Susan ... '— '95 C.839 B.S. L.585 J.D. [Ⓐ Severin,R.&M.]
Schmidt, William D., (BV) ... '50 '76 C&L.585 B.A., J.D. [Schmitz&S.]
Schmitz, Orell D., (AV) ... '47 '73 C.579 B.A. L.585 J.D. [Schmitz&S.]
Schmitz & Schmidt, A Professional Corporation, (AV) ... 314 E. Thayer Avenue
Schneider, Lea Ann, (BV) ... '59 '89 C.579 B.A. L.494 J.D. Asst. Atty. Gen.
Schneider, Scott J. ... '53 '78 C.210 B.A. L.585 J.D. 220 E. Rosser Ave.
Schreiner, Lance D., P.C., (AV) ... '50 '79 C.1142 B.A. L.585 J.D. [Zuger K.&S.]
Schultz, Alfred C. ... '20 '53 C.999 L.585 LL.B. 1708 N. Griffin St.‡
Schulz, Douglas W., (BV) '46 '74 C&L.585 B.A., J.D.
Assoc. Gen. Coun., MDU Resources Group, Inc.
Schulz, Norlyn E., (AV) ... '44 '69 C.584 B.A. L.585 J.D. [Rolfson S.&L.]
Schweigert, David, (BV) ... '67 '93 C.358 B.A. L.585 J.D. [Bucklin,K.&M.]
Schweigert, Suzanne M. ... '69 '96 C.358 B.A. L.585 J.D. [Smith B.O.P.&W.]
Seado, Paul, (BV) ... '56 '89 C.491 B.A. L.585 J.D. Gen. Coun., State Dept. of Trans.
Seaworth, Hugh Patrick ... '50 '78 C.585 B.S. L.910 J.D. 600 E. Blvd Ave.
Severin, William C., (BV) ... '50 '77 C.629 B.S. L.585 J.D. [Severin,R.&M.]
Severin, Ringsak & Morrow, (BV) ... 411 N. 4th St.
Shanahan, Donald E. '24 '51 C.723 B.S.L. L.748 LL.B.
(adm. in MN; not adm. in ND) Ret. Dist. J.
Smith, Craig Cordell, (BV) ... '63 '88 C.585 B.A. L.862 J.D. [Fleck,M.&S.]
Smith, Sean O., (P.C.), (AV) ... '57 '81 C&L.585 B.S.B.A., J.D. [Tschider&S.]
Smith, Sheldon A., (BV) ... '58 '83 C&L.585 B.S.B.A., J.D. [Smith B.O.P.&W.]
Smith Bakke Oppegard Porsborg & Wolf, (AVⓉ)
116 N. 2nd Street (☉Moorhead, MN; Fargo, ND)
Smith-Heinert, Amber L. ... '77 '02 C&L.585 B.A., J.D. [Ⓐ Tschider&S.]
Soggie, Marnie '74 '00 C&L.585 B.A., J.D.
Bismarck Reg. Child. Support Enforce. Unit

Spears, Lawrence D. '42 '72
C.813 B.A. L.145 J.D. Exec. Dir., N.D. Consensus Coun., Inc.
Stockman, Becky Bowen, (AVⓉ) '54 '80 C.896 B.A. L.575 J.D.
(adm. in TX; not adm. in ND) 723 Aspen Ave.‡
Stockman, Mark William '53 '80 C.886 B.S.C.E. L.93 J.D.
(adm. in TX; not adm. in ND) 1862 Montego Dr.
Storslee, Steven A., (AV) .... '51 '76 C.182 B.A. L.585 J.D. [Storslee]

Storslee Law Firm, P.C., (AV)
P.O. Box 4007, P.O. Box 1802 Allison Drive, 58502-4007
Telephone: 701-222-1315 Fax: 701-222-1373
Email: sstorslee@storsleelaw.com URL: http://www.lawyers.com/storsleelaw
Steven A. Storslee; Chris A. Edison.
Insurance Defense, Products Liability, Professional Liability Defense, Insurance Coverage, Property Damage Subrogation.

See Professional Biographies, BISMARCK, NORTH DAKOTA

Strutz, William A., (AV) .... '34 '59 C.578 B.A. L.585 J.D. [Fleck,M.&S.]
Suhr, Lloyd C., (CV) ....'71 '97 C.358 B.A. L.585 J.D. State Dept. of Human Servs.
Summers, Anne E., (BV) .... '47 '82 C&L.585 B.A., J.D. [Dyer&S.]
Summers, Paul W., (BV) .... '52 '78 C.358 B.A. L.990 J.D. [Fleck,M.&S.]
Tabor, Sandra L. ....'54 '81 C&L.585 B.S., J.D. Exec. Dir., State Bar Assn.
Thiele, David L. ....'59 '86 C&L.585 B.S.B.A., J.D. 500 E. Front Ave.
Thiem, Rebecca S., P.C., (AV) .... '50 '80 C.879 B.A. L.585 J.D. [Zuger K.&S.]
Thomas, L. A. ....'57 '83 C.025 Mus. Bac. L.300 J.D. Legis. Coun.
Thompson, Maury C., (BV) .... '45 '73 C&L.585 B.S.B.A., J.D. 1720 Burnt Boat Dr.
Thune, Gary R., (AV) ....'42 '74 C.584 B.S. L.585 J.D. [Pearce&D.]
Traynor, J. Patrick ....'65 '91 C&L.585 B.A., J.D. State Workers Comp. Bur.
Tschider, David A., (BV) .... '59 '84 C&L.585 B.S.B.A., J.D. [Tschider&S.]
Tschider, Gregory W., Jr., (BV) .... '47 '71 C&L.585 B.S., J.D. [Tschider&B.]
Tschider, Ivan A., (BV) .... '52 '76 C&L.585 B.S.B.A., J.D. 316 N. 5th St., Ste. 106
Tschider, Morris A., (P.C.), (AV) .... '33 '58 C&L.585 B.S., J.D. [Tschider&S.]
Tschider & Boeckel, (BV) ....316 N. 5th Street, Suite 106

Tschider & Smith, (AV) BR
A Partnership including Professional Corporations
Professional Building - Suite 200, 418 East Rosser Avenue, 58501
Telephone: 701-258-4000 Fax: 701-258-4001
Email: ssmith@tschider-smithlaw.com
Members of Firm: Morris A. Tschider (P.C.); Sean O. Smith (P.C.); David A. Tschider. Associate: Amber L. Smith-Heinert.
General Civil Practice before all State and Federal Courts. Litigation, Real Estate, Taxation, Banking, Commercial, Partnership, Corporation, Bankruptcy, Personal Injury, Estate Planning and Probate Law, Health Care Law.
Representative Clients: Agri Bank, FCB; Farm Credit Services of Mandan, FLCA; Farm Credit Services of Mandan, P.C.A.; Twin City Implement, Inc.; First Bank Bismarck; N.D. Independent Insurance Agents; Western Steel & Plumbing; Froelich Oil Co.; Bismarck Eagles; St. Alexius Medical Center.

See Professional Biographies, BISMARCK, NORTH DAKOTA

Tudor, Thomas B., (BV) '43 '72
C.585 B.S. L.494 J.D. Exec. Dir., N. Dak. Mun. Bond Bk.
Turner, Tyrone ....'66 '00 C.35 B.S. L.585 J.D. Courthouse
Vande Walle, Gerald W. ....'33 '58 C&L.585 B.S.C., J.D. Chf. Jus., Supm. Ct.
Van Sickle, Bruce M. .... '17 '41 C&L.494 B.S.L., J.D. U.S. Sr. Dist. J.‡
Varvel, Mary Ellen Thompson, (BV) '46 '81 C.378 B.A. L.585 J.D.
State Dept. of Transp.
Ver Weyst, Katherine Chester .....'51 '79 C&L.585 B.S., J.D. Legal Coun., Legis. Council
Vinje, Ralph A., (BV) .... '42 '77 C.490 B.S. L.585 J.D. 523 N. 4th St.
Vogel, Sarah M., (BV) ....'46 '71 C.585 B.A. L.569 J.D. 1022 E. Divide Ave.

Vogel Law Firm, (AV)
U.S. Bank Building, 200 N. 3rd Street, Suite 201, P.O. Box 2097, 58502-2097 ⊙
Telephone: 701-258-7899
URL: http://www.vogellaw.com
H. Patrick Weir; John C. Kapsner; John J. Petrik; Brenda L. Blazer; Leslie Bakken Oliver; Monte L. Rogneby; Michael T. Andrews; Joel W. Gilbertson;—Mandy R. Maxon.
Insurance Defense, Personal Injury, Products Liability, Professional Malpractice, Corporate, Labor and Employment, Probate, Tax Law, Health Law, Real Estate, Bankruptcy, Construction Law, Public Utilities, Securities and Antitrust, Arbitration and Mediation. Family Law, Criminal Law, Environmental Law, Intellectual Property, Ecommerce. Trials and Appeals in all Courts.
Representative Clients: Associated General Contractors of North Dakota; Blue Shield of North Dakota; Cass County Electric Cooperative, Inc.; Clark Equipment Co.; Forum Communications Company; Merit Care Medical Group; Northern Improvement Co.; Dakota Clinic Ltd.; United Parcel Service; Gateway Chevrolet, Inc.
Fargo, North Dakota Office: 218 N.P. Avenue, 58107. Telephone: 701-237-6983. Fax: 701-356-6395. Moorhead, Minnesota Office: 215 North 30th Street, P.O. Box 1977, 56561-1077. Telephone: 218-236-6462. Fax: 218-236-9873.

See Professional Biographies, BISMARCK, NORTH DAKOTA

Vogelpohl, Steven L., (BV) ....'51 '76 C.182 B.A. L.585 J.D. [S.Vogelpohl]
Vogelpohl, Steven, Law Office, (BV) ....400 E. Broadway, Ste. 501
Vukelic, James M. ....'50 '78 C&L.585 B.S., J.D. 916 W. Ave. C.
Wagner, Michael L., (BV) .... '63 '88 C&L.585 B.A., J.D. [Wagner]
Wagner Law Firm, PC, (BV) .... 1533 N. 12th Street
Wahl, Al. ..... '42 '67 C&L.585 B.S.P.A., LL.B. Admin. Law J., Off. of Admin. Hearings
Wald, Donnita A., (BV) .... '61 '91 C.579 B.A. L.585 J.D. Spec. Asst. Atty. Gen.
Waller, Michael C., (BV) ....'57 '85 C.585 B.S.Ed. L.336 J.D. [Fleck,M.&S.]
Walstad, John M. .... '52 '78 C.584 B.A. L.585 J.D. Code Revisor
Ward, Patrick J., (AV) .... '52 '79 C.238 B.A. L.585 J.D. [Zuger K.&S.]
Webb, Aaron K. ....'77 '03 C.999 B.S. L.585 J.D. [Ⓐ Zuger K.&S.]
Webster, Melvin L., (BV) ....'37 '84 C.584 B.S. L.585 J.D. 418 East Rosser Avenue
Wefald, Robert O. .... '42 '70 C.585 B.A. L.477 J.D. Dist. J.
Wegner, Scott D., (BV) ....'63 '91 C.182 B.A. L.900 J.D. [Cook W.&W.P.]
Weikum, Jeffrey S., (CV) .... '70 '95 C&L.585 B.B.S., J.D. [Pagel W.]
Weir, H. Patrick, (AV) .... '39 '64 C.723 B.S. L.602 LL.B. [Vogel]
Wezelman, Joy L., (BV) ....'49 '80 C.477 B.A. L.273 J.D. P.O. Box 7274

Wheeler Wolf Law Firm, (AV)
220 North 4th Street, P.O. Box 2056, 58502-2056
Telephone: 701-223-5300 Fax: 701-223-5366
Albert A. Wolf; Jack McDonald; Gregory C. Larson; Steven L. Latham; Michael F. Daley; Courtney M. Koebele; Damian J. Huettl.
Civil Trial Practice in all Courts and Administrative Agencies, Corporate Law, Administrative Law, Public Utilities, Taxation, Estate Planning, Probate, Wills, Elder Law, Banking, Real Estate, Commercial Law, Lobbying, Communications Law, Construction Law, Labor Relations, Collections, Personal Injury, Negligence, Workers Compensation, Social Security, Criminal Law, Bankruptcy, Agricultural Law.
Counsel for: North Dakota Board of Medical Examiners; The Independent Community Banks of North Dakota; North Dakota Newspaper Assn.; United Bank of Bismarck; BHS Long Term Care Association; Continental Western Insurance Co.; John Deere Co.

See Professional Biographies, BISMARCK, NORTH DAKOTA

Whitman, Charles C., (BV) ....'56 '82 C&L.585 B.S.B.A., J.D. City Atty.
Wike, Curtis L., (BV) .... '60 '85 C&L.585 B.S., J.D. [Fleck,M.&S.]
Wike, Jaclin M. ....'59 '87 C&L.585 B.S.B.A., J.D. [Cook W.&W.P.]
Wirtz, Robert W. .... '42 '67 C.813 A.B. L.585 J.D. Chief Coun., State Tax Dept.
Witham, Lyle, (BV) .... '56 '83 C.747 B.A. L.494 J.D. State Capitol
Wolberg, Gary R., (BV) .... '47 '76 C.581 B.A. L.585 J.D. [Fleck,M.&S.]
Wolf, Albert A., (AV) .... '31 '56 C.1268 B.A. L.1035 LL.B. [Wheeler W.]
Wolf, Debra Carney '61 '01 C.665 B.A. L.229 J.D.
(adm. in SD; not adm. in ND) Atty. Advsr.
Worthington, William C., Jr. .... '43 '76 C.260 B.A. L.1338 J.D. [Worthington]
Worthington Law Firm .... 1004 East Central Avenue
Zimmerman, Theresa L., (CV) ....'65 '92 C.763 B.S. L.464 J.D. [American]
Zuger, John A., P.C., (BV) ....'40 '67 C&L.494 B.A., J.D. [Ⓒ Zuger K.&S.]
Zuger, William P., (AV) .... '46 '72 C&L.494 B.A., J.D. 615 W. Thayer Ave.‡

Zuger Kirmis & Smith, (AV) BR
A Partnership including Professional Corporations
316 North Fifth Street, P.O. Box 1695, 58502-1695
Telephone: 701-223-2711 Fax: 701-223-7387; 701-223-9619
Email: zkslaw@zkslaw.com URL: http://www.zkslaw.com
Thomas O. Smith (1944-2001); Lyle W. Kirmis; Lance D. Schreiner, P.C.; James S. Hill, P.C.; Patrick J. Ward; Rebecca S. Thiem, P.C.; Jerry W. Evenson, P.C.; Lawrence A. Dopson; Lawrence E. King, P.C.; Tracy Vigness Kolb, P.C. Associates: Shawnda R. Reid; Constance N. Hofland; Paul R. Sanderson; Aaron K. Webb. Of Counsel: John A. Zuger, P.C.
Tort and Commercial Litigation. Insurance, Products Liability, Corporation, Malpractice, Real Estate, Labor Law, Public Utilities and Administrative Law, Probate, Natural Resources.
Representative Clients: American Family Insurance; Burlington Northern Railroad Co.; Knife River Coal Mining Company; Medcenter One Health Systems; Microsoft Corporation; Mor-Gran-Sou Electric Cooperative, Inc.; National Bank of Harvey; North Dakota Workers Compensation Bureau; Qwest; R.J. Reynolds Tobacco Companies.

See Professional Biographies, BISMARCK, NORTH DAKOTA

BOTTINEAU, * 2,336, *Bottineau Co.*

Benson, A. Swain, (BV) .... '50 '77 C.579 B.A. L.585 J.D. [Benson]
Benson, Anthony, (CV) ....'70 '00 C.579 B.S. L.585 J.D. [Benson]
Benson Law Office, (BV) .... 616 Main St.
Gregg, John R., (BV) .... '51 '76 C.477 B.A. L.585 J.D. 416 Sinclair St.
Ketterling, Lester S. ....'40 '64 C&L.585 B.Ph., LL.B. Dist. J.
Schell, Roger D. ....'38 '64 C&L.585 B.S.B.A., J.D. 116 W. 5th St.‡

BOWMAN, * 1,600, *Bowman Co.*

Anderson, Zane .... '51 '78 C&L.585 B.A., J.D. Dist. J.
Sadowsky, Timothy A., (BV) .... '51 '79 C.579 B.A. L.585 J.D. [Sadowsky&W.]

Sadowsky and Wild, Law Offices, P.C., (BV)
20 East Divide Street, P.O. Box 260, 58623
Telephone: 701-523-3112 Fax: 701-523-3019
Email: swlawpc@ndsupernet.com
Timothy A. Sadowsky; Steven J. Wild.
Probate, Real Estate, Estate Planning, Tax, Oil and Gas, Collections, Debtor-Creditor, Agricultural Law.
Representative Clients: Bowman County; City of Rhame; City of Scranton; City of Bowman; Scranton Equity Exchange; Dakota Western Bank; Cenex of Bowman; Southwest Healthcare Services, Inc.
References: Wells Fargo Bank, Bowman, ND; Dakota Western Bank of Bowman.

Wild, Steven J., (BV) ....'58 '83 C&L.585 B.S.B.A., J.D. [Sadowsky&W.]

BURLINGTON, 1,096, *Ward Co.*

Gilje, Brent .... '— '96 C.584 B.S. L.585 J.D. P.O. Box 301
Hays, Denise C., (CV) .... '66 '92 C.585 B.A. L.705 J.D. [Hays]
Hays, Mark R., (CV) .... '63 '92 C.1365 B.A. L.585 J.D. [Hays]
Hays Law Firm, P.C., (CV) ....1911 76th St., N.W.

CANDO, * 1,342, *Towner Co.*

Gibbens, J. Bruce, (BV) ....'57 '83 C.579 B.S. L.585 J.D. [Gibbens]
Gibbens, Lisa Beckstrom, (BV) .....'59 '84 C.489 B.A. L.585 J.D. State's Atty. [Gibbens]
Gibbens Law Office, (BV) ....P.O. Box 708

CARRINGTON, * 2,267, *Foster Co.*

Aljets, Thomas J., (AV) ....'53 '78 C&L.585 B.A., J.D. [Heinley&A.]
Heinley, R. C., (AV) ....'28 '56 C&L.585 Ph.B., J.D. [Heinley&A.]
Heinley & Aljets, (AV) ....700 4th Ave. S.
Noack, Fabian E., (AV) ....'30 '57 C&L.585 B.S.C., J.D. City & States Atty.

CARSON, * 383, *Grant Co.*

Peterson, Kenneth W. ....'27 '52 L.585 LL.B. 222 North Main

CASSELTON, 1,855, *Cass Co.*

Strehlow, Wm. Monty, (BV) .... '24 '49 C&L.585 J.D. 10 6th Ave., N.

CAVALIER, * 1,508, *Pembina Co.*

Askew, Stuart John .... '60 '96 C&L.585 B.A., J.D. [Askew]
Askew Law Office ....200 Park Street
Butler, Thomas D., (AV) ....'20 '51 C&L.585 J.D. 206 Dakota St., W.
DuBois, Lawrence D., (BV) ....'52 '79 C&L.585 B.A., J.D. [Fleming&D.]
Fleming, Neil W., (BV) ....'43 '68 C&L.585 Ph.B., J.D. [Fleming&D.]
Fleming, Robert C., (CV) ....'70 '99 C&L.585 B.A., J.D. [Ⓐ Fleming&D.]
Fleming & DuBois, (BV) .... 208 W. 2nd Ave., S.
Metelmann, Thomas K. .... '51 '76 C&L.585 B.A., J.D. Dist. J.
Robbins, William A., (BV) ....'38 '64 C&L.37 B.A., J.D. 211 W. Main St.
Whelan, Barbara L., (BV) ....'63 '90 C.182 B.A. L.64 J.D. Pemdina Co. State Off.

CENTER, * 678, *Oliver Co.*

Mahoney, Ann C., (BV) ....'53 '78 C&L.585 B.A., J.D. [Mahoney&M.]
Mahoney, John J., (BV) ....'51 '78 C&L.585 B.S., J.D. [Mahoney&M.]
Mahoney & Mahoney, (BV) ....P.O. Box 355

COOPERSTOWN, * 1,053, *Griggs Co.*

Lenaburg, Fitzner, Nelson, Hooper & Cruff, PLLP
(See Valley City)

Ratcliffe, Phyllis A., (BV) ....'33 '58 C&L.585 B.A., J.D. City Atty.

CROSBY, * 1,089, *Divide Co.*

Forsgren, F. Leslie, (BV) .... '21 '45 L.585 LL.B. 112 S. Main St.

Stefonowicz, Michel W., (AV) '43 '68 C&L.585 Ph.B., J.D.
115 South Main Street, P.O. Box 289, 58730-0289
Telephone: 701-965-6036 Telecopier: 701-965-6428
Email: mstefonowicz@steflaw.com
General Civil Practice in all Courts. Insurance, Real Estate, Business Law, Probate, Negligence and Oil and Gas Law.

(This Listing Continued)

Stefonowicz, Michel W. (Continued)

Representative Clients: Farmers Union Oil Company of Crosby; St. Lukes Hospital; City of Crosby; First National Bank & Trust Co. of Williston - Crosby Office; Noonan Farmers Telephone. Reference: Farmers State Bank of Crosby.

DEVILS LAKE, * 7,222, *Ramsey Co.*

Broden, Douglas L., (BV) .... '60 '85 C&L.585 B.S.B.A., J.D. [Broden]
Broden, Leo, (BV) .... '30 '59 C&L.585 Ph.B., LL.B. [Broden]
Broden Law Office, (BV) .... 505 5th Ave. S.
Buttz, Robert A. .... '12 '36 C&L.585 B.A., LL.B. 1023 4th St.‡
Christianson, Melvin, (AV) .... '23 '49 C&L.585 Ph.B., J.D. [Foughty,C.W.E.&B.]
Christofferson, Lee A. .... '46 '83 C.585 B.S. L.823 J.D. Dist. J.
Foughty, Donovan .... '55 '83 C&L.585 B.A., J.D. Dist. J., Ramfuy Co. Dist. Ct.
Foughty, Francis E., (AV) .... '19 '49 C&L.585 B.S., J.D. [Foughty,C.W.E.&B.]
Foughty, Christianson, White Eagle & Berg, (AV) .... 411 4th Ave.
Frith, John W., (CV) .... '44 '69 C&L.585 B.S., J.D. [Frith&S.]
Frith & Steffan, (BV) .... 609 4th Avenue
Goulding, Douglas A., (BV) .... '55 '87 C.585 B.A. L.174 J.D. 505 5th Ave. S.
Halbach, Maren H., (BV) .... '59 '84 C.585 B.S. L.1035 J.D. [Haugland,H.&H.]
Halbach, Peter K., (BV) .... '60 '85 C.494 B.A. L.1035 J.D. [Haugland,H.&H.]
Haugland, John C., (AV) .... '20 '50 C.585 B.S. L.748 J.D. [Haugland,H.&H.]
Haugland, Halbach & Halbach, (AV) .... P.O. Box 918
Heen, Douglas B. .... '20 '47 C&L.585 LL.B. Ret. Dist. J.
Heustis, Evan F. .... '45 '72 C&L.585 B.A., J.D. Admin. Suite, 300 4th St.

Moosbrugger, Carter & McDonagh, P.L.L.P.
(See Grand Forks)

Olson, Lonnie, (BV) .... '62 '87 C&L.585 B.A., J.D. State's Atty

Pearson Christensen Cahill & Clapp, PLLP
(See Grand Forks)

Steffan, Michael N., (BV) .... '52 '77 C.585 B.S.B.A. L.300 J.D. [Frith&S.]
Thompson, Neil, (AV) .... '26 '55 C.579 B.S. L.585 LL.B. [Thompson&T.]
Thompson, Scott R., (BV) .... '52 '77 C&L.585 B.S., J.D. [Thompson&T.]
Thompson & Thompson, (AV) .... 501 3rd. St.
Traynor, Daniel M., (BV) .... '70 '97 C&L.585 B.A., J.D. [Traynor]
Traynor, J. Thomas, Jr., (AV) .... '55 '80 C&L.585 B.A., J.D. [Traynor]
Traynor, John T., (AV) .... '26 '51 C&L.585 B.A., J.D. [Traynor]

Traynor Law Firm, P.C., (AV)
Attorneys at Law since 1897
509 5th Street NE, Suite 1, P.O. Box 838, 58301
Telephone: 701-662-4077 Fax: 701-662-7537 Toll Free: 877-872-9667 URL: http://www.traynorlawoffice.com
Email: dantraynor@traynorlaw.com URL: http://www.traynorlaw.com
Members of Firm: John T. Traynor (Retired); J. Thomas Traynor, Jr.; Daniel M. Traynor.
Insurance Defense, Insurance Coverage, Insurance Bad Faith, Personal Injury, Wrongful Death, Real Estate, Corporate Law, Banking, Estate Planning, Probate and Trusts, Collections, Subrogation, Title Insurance, Tribal Law, Civil Trial Practice before all State and Federal Courts.
Representative Clients: Dakota Fire Insurance Co.; Nodak Mutual Insurance Co.; Farm Credit Services, Grand Forks, N.D.; Leevers Foods, Inc., Devils Lake, N.D.; Great West Casualty Co.; Grinnell Mutual Reinsurance Group; City of Devils Lake; Bremer Bank of Devils Lake, N.D.; Ramsey National Bank and Trust Co., Devils Lake, N.D.; Western State Bank, Devils Lake, N.D.

See Professional Biographies, DEVILS LAKE, NORTH DAKOTA

Waller, John D. .... '70 '97 C.585 B.A. L.494 J.D. Lake Reg. Child Sup.

DICKINSON, * 16,097, *Stark Co.*

Bogner, Jon, (BV) .... '50 '78 C.581 B.S. L.585 J.D. [Kubik,B.R.&S.]
Bruhschwein, Glen R., (BV) .... '61 '87 C&L.585 B.A., J.D. [Mackoff K.]
Buresh, Eugene F., (BV) .... '50 '79 C.723 B.A. L.585 J.D. P.O. Box 1224

Dyer & Summers, P.C.
(See Bismarck)

Dynes, George T., (BV) .... '29 '56 C.581 B.S. L.585 J.D. 34 E. 1st St.
Ebeltoft, Paul F., Jr., (AV) .... '49 '76 C.285 A.B. L.273 J.D. [Mackoff K.]
Ficek, Vince H., (BV) .... '49 '76 C&L.585 B.A., J.D. [Ficek]
Ficek Legal Services, (BV) .... 41 First Ave. West
Freed, Howard A. .... '26 '53 C.755 B.S. L.436 J.D. 926-7th Ave. W.‡
Galloway, Gerald D., (BV) .... '40 '66 C&L.585 B.S.B.A., LL.B. 140 1st Avenue W.
Greenwood, Dann E., (AV) .... '52 '77 C&L.585 B.S.B.A., J.D. [Greenwood&R.]
Greenwood, Mark L., (BV) .... '51 '76 C.581 B.A. L.585 J.D. [M.Greenwood]

Greenwood, Mark, Law Office, (BV)
30 First Avenue East, P.O. Box 327, 58602-0327
Telephone: 701-227-3607 Fax: 701-483-3631
Email: mlglaw@ndsupernet.com URL: http://www.lawyers.com/mgreenwood
Mark L. Greenwood.
Criminal Defense, Felonies, Misdemeanors, Homicides, Sex Crimes, DUI, Family Law, Divorce, Support, Custody, Adoptions.

See Professional Biographies, DICKINSON, NORTH DAKOTA

Greenwood & Ramsey, P.L.L.P., (AV)
30 First Avenue East, P.O. Box 1157, 58602-1157
Telephone: 701-225-6074 Fax: 701-225-0492 URL: http://www.greenwoodramseylaw.com
URL: http://www.lawyers.com/greenwood&ramsey
Dann E. Greenwood; Gary D. Ramsey; Brenda L. Selinger.
Personal Injury, Auto Accidents, Family Law, Divorce, Adoptions, Probate, Bankruptcy, Creditors Rights, Collections, Real Estate, Criminal Defense, Civil Litigation.

See Professional Biographies, DICKINSON, NORTH DAKOTA

Hardy, Albert J., (BV) .... '42 '67 C&L.378 B.A., J.D. [Hardy,M.&N.]
Hardy, Maus & Nordsven, P.C., (BV) .... 137 First Avenue West
Henning, Tom, (BV) .... '50 '79 Asst. States Atty.
Herauf, William A., (BV) .... '57 '82 C&L.585 B.S.B.A., J.D. [Reichert&H.]
Heth, William G., (BV) .... '43 '68 C.581 B.S. L.585 J.D. [W.Heth]
Heth, William, (BV) .... 112 3rd St. W.
Hilden, Ronald L. .... '45 '76 C&L.585 B.A., J.D. S.W. Juv. Ct.
Hope, James A., (BV) .... '54 '79 C&L.585 B.A., J.D. Asst. State's Atty.
Howe, Bruce R. .... '32 '58 C&L.508 B.A., LL.B. [Howe&H.]
Howe, Carmi L., (CV) .... '60 '92 C.182 B.A. L.585 J.D. [Howe&H.]
Howe & Howe, (CV) .... 150 West Villard, Suite #3
Hunke, Maurice R. .... '39 '63 C.581 B.A. L.585 J.D. Dist J.‡
Keogh, Robert A., (BV) .... '46 '71 C.579 B.S. L.585 J.D. 141-3rd Street West
Kloster, Paul G., (AV) .... '35 '59 C&L.585 B.S., J.D. [Mackoff K.]
Kolling, Matthew R. .... '75 '01 C.585 B.A. L.494 J.D. [Ⓐ Mackoff K.]
Kubik, Bogner, Ridl & Selinger, L.L.P., (BV) .... 26 East 3rd Street
Kuntz, Sandra K., (BV) .... '69 '94 C&L.585 B.S.P.A., J.D. [Mackoff K.]

Mackoff Kellogg Law Firm, (AV)
(Mackoff, Kellogg, Kirby & Kloster, P.C.)
46 West Second Street, P.O. Box 1097, 58601 ⊙
Telephone: 701-227-1841 Fax: 701-227-4739
Email: firm@mackoff.com URL: http://www.mackoff.com

(This Listing Continued)

Mackoff Kellogg Law Firm (Continued)

H. A. Mackoff (1888-1963); Theodore Kellogg (1904-1990); Ward M. Kirby (1922-1993); Paul G. Kloster (Retired); John L. Sherman (Retired); Gordon W. Schnell; Paul F. Ebeltoft, Jr.; Timothy A. Priebe; Charles J. Peterson; Glen R. Bruhschwein; Randall N. Sickler; Sandra K. Kuntz. Associates: Matthew R. Kolling; N. Bob Pesall; Jessica L.Z. Pesall.
Estate Planning, Probate, Wills, Trusts, Real Estate, Foreclosures, Insurance Defense, Corporate Law, Personal Injury, Oil and Gas, Natural Resources, Environmental Law, Business Law, Creditor Bankruptcy, Banking, Contracts, Municipal Law, Administrative Law, Health Care, Taxation, Employee Benefits, Employment Law, Commercial Litigation, Medical Malpractice, Workers Compensation, Family Law, Mediation, Arbitration, Appeals, Civil Litigation in all State and Federal Courts.
Beach, North Dakota Office: 41 Central Avenue, South. Telephone: 701-872-3731. Fax: 701-872-4695.

See Professional Biographies, DICKINSON, NORTH DAKOTA

Magelky, Nancy K. .... '64 '89 C&L.585 B.B.A., J.D. 825 Park Ave.‡
Maus, Michael J., (BV) .... '49 '78 C.585 B.A. L.494 J.D. [Hardy,M.&N.]
McCabe, Kevin .... '63 '00 C.581 B.S. L.585 J.D. 1580 11th St. W.
Mehrer, Owen, (BV) .... '49 '79 C.581 B.A. L.585 J.D. States Atty.
Melbye, Diane F., (BV) .... '50 '80 C.182 B.S. L.585 J.D. 229 1st St. W.
Meyer, Nici Sue .... '75 '01 C.491 B.S. L.585 J.D. Dist. Ct.
Murtha, Thomas F., (BV) .... '34 '66 208 1st Ave., E.
Nordsven, Mary E., (BV) .... '49 '81 C.581 B.S. L.174 J.D. [Hardy,M.&N.]
Pesall, Jessica L.Z. .... '79 '04 C&L.793 B.A., J.D. [Ⓐ Mackoff K.]
Pesall, N. Bob .... '75 '04 C.791 B.S. L.793 J.D. [Ⓐ Mackoff K.]
Peterson, Charles J., (BV) .... '58 '83 C.581 B.A. L.508 J.D. [Mackoff K.] ⊙
Priebe, Timothy A., (BV) .... '61 '86 C.579 B.S. L.585 J.D. [Mackoff K.]
Ramsey, Gary D., (BV) .... '54 '85 C&L.585 B.S.B.A., J.D. [Greenwood&R.]
Reichert, Ronald A., (AV) .... '44 '73 C&L.585 B.S.B.A., J.D. [Reichert&H.]
Reichert & Herauf, P.C., (AV) .... 34 E. 1st St.
Ridl, David J., (BV) .... '54 '79 C.285 B.S. L.585 J.D. [Kubik,B.R.&S.]
Schmalenberger, Allan L. .... '46 '73 C&L.585 B.S.B.A., J.D. S.W. Juv. Ct.
Schnell, Gordon W., (BV) .... '40 '65 C&L.585 B.S.L., LL.B. [Mackoff K.]
Selinger, Brenda L., (BV) .... '58 '84 [Greenwood&R.]
Selinger, Bruce A., (BV) .... '56 '86 C.581 B.S. L.585 J.D. [Kubik,B.R.&S.]
Sherman, John L., (AV) .... '37 '66 C&L.585 B.S.B.A., J.D. [Mackoff K.]
Sickler, Randall N., (BV) .... '63 '89 C&L.585 B.S., J.D. [Mackoff K.]

Wheeler Wolf Law Firm
(See Bismarck)

EDGELEY, 680, *La Moure Co.*

Dukatz, Victoria A. .... '— '97 C.912 B.A. L.477 J.D. 519 W. 2nd St.

ELGIN, 659, *Grant Co.*

Weikum, Ronald J., (BV) .... '46 '74 C.585 B.A. L.972 J.D. [Weikum]
Weikum Law Office, (BV) .... 304 N. Main

ELLENDALE, * 1,559, *Dickey Co.*

Goodman, Ronald E. .... '47 '81 C.723 B.A. L.585 J.D. Dist. J.

ENDERLIN, 997, *Ransom Co.*

Myhre, Russell J. .... '48 '74 C.579 B.S. L.585 J.D. 210 3rd Ave.

FARGO, * 90,599, *Cass Co.*

Aakre, Steven K., (AV) .... '53 '81 C.585 B.A. L.494 J.D. [Serkland]
Aamodt, Paul R., (BV) '55 '82
C.352 B.B.A. L.300 J.D. Sr. Staff Atty., Amer. Fam. Ins. Grp.
Aarestad, Bruce, (CV) .... '43 '71 C&L.585 B.A., J.D. 2525 Broadway
Adams, Beverley L., (BV) .... '69 '95 C.011 B.A. L.585 J.D. [Ⓐ Serkland]
Adams, Jerilynn Brantner, (BV) .... '68 '93 C.182 B.A. L.585 J.D. [Vogel]
Albrecht, Kristy L., (BV) .... '61 '95 C.358 B.A. L.352 J.D. [Dorsey&W.]
Aldrich, Leslie Johnson, (BV) .... '57 '83 C.492 B.S. L.585 J.D. [Johnson]
Allen, John I. .... '— '88 C&L.585 B.S., J.D. [Weerts A.]
Anderson, Jacqueline S., (BV) '62 '95
C.491 B.A. L.585 J.D. [Nilles,I.S.P.&S.] (⊙Moorhead, MN)
Anderson, Jonathan H.P. .... '73 '00 C.393 B.A. L.585 J.D. 3503 46th Ave. S.
Anderson, Norman G., (AV) .... '50 '82 C&L.585 B.A., J.D. Asst. U.S. Atty.
Anderson, Richard P., (AV) .... '43 '68 C.585 B.A. L.208 J.D. [Anderson&B.]
Anderson, Wayne T., (AV) .... '47 '72 C.494 B.A. L.585 J.D. [Anderson]
Anderson & Bottrell, (AV) .... 3100 13th Avenue, S.W.
Anderson Law Office, (AV) .... 2108 S. University Dr., Ste. 103
Ankers, Alisha Lynn .... '67 '92 C.300 B.S. L.585 J.D. 114 Broadway, Ste. S1
Annear, Harold G., (AV) .... '33 '60 C&L.585 Ph.B., LL.B. 1st Asst. U.S. Atty.
Anthony, Eugene K. '27 '51 C&L.585 Ph.B., LL.B.
Ret. Admin Law J., U.S. Dept. of Health & Human Serv.
Astrup, Odell M. .... '30 '59 C&L.585 B.S.B.A., J.D. 2484 Lilac Ln.
Backes, Norman J. .... '37 '66 C.584 L.585 J.D. Dist. J.
Bader, Mary Beth Juelke '56 '84 C.585 B.S.B.A. L.436 J.D.
(adm. in WI; not adm. in ND) 1534 S. 9th St.‡
Bailey, Susan L., (BV) .... '63 '97 C&L.585 B.S., J.D. Asst. Cass Cty. State Atty.
Bailly, David R., (BV) ... '50 '76 C&L.585 B.S.B.A., J.D. Corp. Coun., 1st Intl. Bk. & Tr.
Beaton, Timothy J. '49 '75 C.579 B.S. L.585 J.D.
Sr. V.P., Community First National Bank of Fargo
Beauchene, Mark A., (BV) .... '54 '79 C.579 B.S. L.585 J.D. [Wold J.]
Beckstrom, James C. '37 '61 C&L.494 B.S.L., LL.B.
Part-Time Exec. Dir., N. Dakota Life and Health Ins. Guaranty Assn.‡
Bender, Christel .... '75 '00 C.585 B.B.A. L.221 J.D. Advsr.
Benson, Paul .... '18 '49 C.585 B.S.C. L.273 LL.B. U.S. Sr. Dist. J.
Berg, Bradley W., (AV) .... '51 '76 C.182 B.A. L.585 J.D. 5426 12th St., S.‡
Bergian, Cheryl F., (CV) .... '61 '88 C&L.585 B.A., J.D. 118 Broadway
Block, Lynn, (BV) .... '57 '96 C.579 B.A. L.585 J.D. [Dorsey&W.]
Boechler, Jeanette, (BV) .... '54 '79 C.584 B.A. L.585 J.D. P.O. Box 1932

Bossart, David R., (AV) '42 '65 C&L.585 B.A., LL.B.
1220 Main Avenue, Suite 105, 58103
Telephone: 701-271-8030 Fax: 701-271-6849
Email: david@bossartlaw.com URL: http://www.bossartlaw.com
Personal Injury Law, Wrongful Death, General Litigation.

See Professional Biographies, FARGO, NORTH DAKOTA

Bottrell, Lowell P., (AV) .... '55 '83 C.579 B.S. L.585 J.D. [Anderson&B.]
Boulger, John V., (AV) .... '49 '74 C.491 B.A. L.585 J.D. [Wold J.]
Brakke, Jon R., (BV) .... '54 '79 C.597 B.A. L.494 J.D. [Vogel]
Brantner, Jerry O., (AV) .... '35 '60 C&L.494 B.B.A., LL.B. [Ⓐ Vogel] ‡
Breitling, Duane R., (AV) ...... '38 '65 C&L.585 Ph.B., J.D. [Ohnstad T.] (⊙West Fargo)
Bright, Myron H. .... '19 '47 C&L.494 B.S.L., LL.B. Sr. U.S. Cir. J.
Brothers, James R., (BV) .... '50 '75 C.579 B.A. L.585 J.D. [Wold J.]
Brust, Kim E., (AV) .... '54 '79 C.579 B.A. L.585 J.D. [Conmy F.]
Bueide, Daniel A., (BV) .... '65 '90 C&L.585 B.B.A., J.D. [Vogel]
Bullis, James R., (CV) .... '66 '92 C&L.585 B.B.A., J.D. 4802 Amber Valley Pkwy.

Bye, Kermit Edward ....'37 '62 C&L.585 B.S., J.D. U.S. Ct. App. J.
Byrnes, George T. '44 '82 C.424 B.S. L.734 J.D.
(adm. in MO; not adm. in ND) Assoc. Dir., VA Med. Reg. Off. Ctr.

Camrud, Maddock, Olson & Larson, Ltd.
(See Grand Forks)

Carlson, Bruce H., (AV) ....'53 '78 C.182 B.A. L.585 J.D. [McNair,L.&C.]
Carlson, Jay D., (BV) ....'54 '79 C.723 B.A. L.800 J.D. P.O. Box 448
Carlson, Kyle L., (BV) ....'72 '98 C&L.579 B.A., J.D. [Anderson&B.]
Carlson, Wayne W., (BV) ....'65 '91 C.579 B.S. L.494 J.D. [Vogel]
Carter, Virginia G. ....'54 '97 C&L.579 B.B.A., J.D. The Mutual Group
Cleveland, Constance L., (BV) .... '60 '88 C&L.585 B.S.Ed., J.D. Asst. States Atty.
Combs, Jeanne, (BVⓉ) ....'58 '93 C&L.793 B.S., J.D. [Ⓐ Tax]
Conmy, E. T., Jr., (AV) ....'12 '35 C&L.585 A.B., LL.B. [Ⓒ Conmy F.] ‡
Conmy, E. Thomas, III, (AV) ....'37 '73 C.579 B.S. L.585 J.D. [Nilles,I.S.P.&S.]

Conmy Feste Ltd., (AV)
200 Wells Fargo Center, 406 Main Avenue, P.O. Box 2686, 58108-2686
Telephone: 701-293-9911 Fax: 701-293-3133
Email: firm@conmylaw.com URL: http://www.conmylaw.com
Paul M. Hubbard (Real Property Specialist Certified by the Real Property Section, Minnesota State Bar Association); Wickham Corwin; Kim E. Brust; Michael M. Thomas; Robert J. Schultz. Associates: Jeremy D. Holmes; Stephannie N. Stiel. Retired: E. T. Conmy, Jr.; Charles A. Feste.
General Civil Practice in State and Federal Courts. Banking, Creditor Bankruptcy, Commercial, Corporate, Insurance Defense, Insurance, Personal Injury, Wrongful Death, Products Liability, Trusts and Estates, Estate Planning, Title Insurance, Employment Law and Family Law.

See Professional Biographies, FARGO, NORTH DAKOTA

Conrad, Daniel R. ....'70 '96 C.491 B.A. L.585 J.D [Ⓐ Vogel]
Conroy, Erin M. ....'74 '03 C.182 B.A. L.585 J.D. [Ⓐ Jeffries,O.&F.]
Cooke, Donald J. ....'40 '64 C&L.585 B.S.B.A., J.D. Ret. Co. J.
Corwin, Wickham, (AV) ....'50 '76 C.878 B.S. L.585 J.D. [Conmy F.]
Craft, Dale J. .... '37 '70 C.723 B.A. L.878 J.D. 1111 Westrac Drive, Suite 108
Crary, Peter B. ....'47 '72 C.579 B.S. L.585 J.D. 629 9th St. S.
Crothers, Daniel J., (AV) ....'57 '82 C&L.585 B.A., J.D. [Nilles,I.S.P.&S.]
Cummings, Judith ....'53 '77 C.182 B.A. L.494 J.D. 1100 19th Ave. North., PMB 277
Davies, Heidi M. F., (CV) ....'69 '94 C&L.585 B.A., J.D. [Ⓐ Solberg,S.M.&J.]
Davies, Thomas A., (AV) ....'39 '63 C&L.585 B.S.B.A., LL.B. [T.A.Davies]
Davies, Thomas A., Ltd., A Professional Corporation, (AV) .... 1 2nd St. N., Ste. 118
DeBoer, Monte R. '65 '90 C.491 B.S. L.352 J.D.
(adm. in NE; not adm. in ND) 6943 Riverdale Dr.★
Deitz, Kevin J., (BV) ....'59 '86 C.491 B.A. L.585 J.D. 107 N. 8th St.
DeMars, David T., (AV) ....'41 '65 C&L.585 B.S.B.A., J.D. [DeMars&T.]

DeMars & Turman, Ltd., (AV)
15 Broadway, Suite 510, P.O. Box 110, 58107
Telephone: 701-293-5592 Fax: 701-293-8837
URL: http://www.demarsandturmanlaw.com
David T. DeMars; Joseph A. Turman;—Katrina A. Turman.
General Civil and Criminal Practice, Trials in State and Federal Courts, Business Bankruptcy, Business Reorganization, Commercial Law, Partnerships, Corporate, Banks and Banking, Agribusiness, Collections, Real Estate, Probate, Personal Injury, Family Law, Mediation and Arbitration.

See Professional Biographies, FARGO, NORTH DAKOTA

Dendy, Charles L. ....'76 '02 L.585 J.D. [Johnson,R.&L.]
Dexheimer, Gordon A. ....'51 '87 C&L.585 B.A., J.D. Legal Assistance of N.D.
Dietz, John A. ....'50 '74 C.579 B.S. L.585 J.D. Jud. Ref.
Donarski, Michelle M., (BV) ....'67 '95 C.510 B.S. L.585 J.D. [Anderson&B.]

Dorsey & Whitney LLP, (AV)
51 North Broadway, Suite 402, P.O. Box 1344, 58107-1344 ⊙
Telephone: 701-235-6000 Facsimile: 701-235-9969
URL: http://www.dorsey.com
Members of Firm: Sarah Andrews Herman (Resident); Jon E. Strinden; Todd E. Zimmerman; Kristy L. Albrecht. Resident Associates: Matthew Greenley; Nola A. McNeally. Of Counsel: Bradley J. Swenson. Attorney: Lynn Block.
Administrative Law, Antitrust and Trade Regulation, Business, Banking, Bankruptcy, Civil Litigation, Construction Law, Contracts, Labor and Employment Law, Health Law, Railroad Law, Real Estate, Structured Finance, Toxic Tort Law and Trade Secrets, Tax, Employee Benefits, Mergers and Acquisitions, Corporate, Securities.
Representative Clients: First Bank National Association (Formerly First National Bank of Minneapolis); The McKnight Foundation; Deluxe Corporation; Mayo Clinic.
Minneapolis, Minnesota Office: Suite 1500, 50 South Sixth Street, 55402-1498. Telephone: 612-340-2600.
Seattle, Washington Office: U.S. Bank Centre, 1420 Fifth Avenue, Suite 3400, 98101. Telephone: 206-903-8800.
New York, New York Office: 250 Park Avenue, 10177. Telephone: 212-415-9200.
Washington, D.C. Office: 1001 Pennsylvania Avenue, N.W., Suite 400 South, 20004. Telephone: 202-442-3000.
Denver, Colorado Office: 370 Seventeenth Street, Republic Plaza Building, Suite 4700, 80202-5647. Telephone: 303-629-3400.
London, England Office: 21 Wilson Street, EC2M 2TD. Telephone: 011-44-207-588-0800.
Hong Kong Office: Suite 3008, One Pacific Place, 88 Queensway. Hong Kong. Telephone: 011-852-252-65000. Fax: 011-852-252-43000.
Shanghai, China Office: Suite 6211-12, Plaza 66, No. 1266 Nanjing Xi Lu, Shanghai, 200040. Telephone: 86-21-6288-2323. Fax: 86-21-6288-3222.
Toronto, Ontario Office: BCE Place, 161 Bay Street, Suite 4310, P.O. Box 512, M5J 2S1. Telephone: 416-367-7370. Fax: 416-367-7371.
Vancouver, British Columbia Office: 666 Burrard Street, Suite 500, V6C 3P6. Telephone: 604-687-5151.
Anchorage, Alaska Office: 1031 West 4th Avenue, Suite 600, 99501-5907. Telephone: 907-276-4557.
Des Moines, Iowa Office: 801 Grand, Suite 3900, 50309. Telephone: 515-283-1000.
Salt Lake City, Utah Office: Wells Fargo Plaza, 170 South Main Street, Suite 900, 84101. Telephone: 801-933-7360.
Southern California Office: 38 Technology Drive, Irvine, 92618-5310. Telephone: 949-932-3600.
Great Falls, Montana Office: 507 Davidson Building, 8 Third Street North, P.O. Box 1566, 59401. Telephone: 406-727-3632.
Missoula, Montana Office: 125 Bank Street, Suite 600, 59802-4407. Telephone: 406-721-6025. Fax: 406-543-0863.
Paramus, New Jersey Office: 95 Route 17 South, Suite 203, 07652. Telephone: 201-291-8904. Fax: 201-712-9444.
Palo Alto, California Office: 1717 Embarcadero Road, 94303. Telephone: 650-857-1717.
San Francisco, California Office: 555 California Street, Suite 1000, 94104-1513. Telephone: 415-781-1989.

See Professional Biographies, FARGO, NORTH DAKOTA

Dunn, Daniel J., (AV) ....'65 '91 C.579 B.S. L.602 J.D. [Maring W.]
Dynes, Jane L., (BV) ....'59 '87 C.182 B.A. L.585 J.D. [Serkland]
Edison-Smith, Lisa Kay, (BV) ....'59 '96 C.579 B.S. L.300 J.D. [Vogel]
Elofson, Carl E. ....'32 '56 C.579 B.S. L.585 J.D. 118 Broadway, Ste. 804
Erickson, Alan C., Law Office of, (CV) ....'52 '77 C&L.585 B.A., J.D. P.O. Box 1447
Erickson, Kipley B. H. ....'52 '77 C&L.585 B.A., J.D. Warner & Co.
Erickson, Ralph R. ....'59 '84 C.358 B.A. L.585 J.D. Dist. J.
Fay, Jonathan (Jack) R., (AVⓉ) ...'55 '80 C.579 B.S. L.585 J.D. [J.Fay] (⊙St. Paul, MN)
Fay, Jonathan, P.C., (AVⓉ) ....51 Broadway
Feste, Charles A., (AV) ....'28 '56 C.182 B.A. L.585 J.D. [Ⓒ Conmy F.] ‡

Ficek, Gary A., (BV) '56 '81 C&L.585 B.A., J.D.
Alerus Financial Building, Suite 505, 15 Broadway, 58102-4907
Telephone: 701-241-8525 Fax: 701-241-8443. Toll Free: 1-800-786-8525
Email: ficeklaw@mcleodusa.net URL: http://www.ficeklaw.com
Social Security Disability, Social Security Appeals, Supplemental Security Income Disability, Administrative Hearings and Appeals, Workers' Compensation, Federal Employees Liability Act (FELA), Railroad Retirement Board, Federal Workers Compensation Appeals, Accidents and Civil Litigation.

See Professional Biographies, FARGO, NORTH DAKOTA

Fiebiger, Thomas D., (BV) ....'56 '84 C.747 B.A. L.585 J.D. 15 Broadway
Fisher, Dennis D. ....'44 '78 C.1016 B.A. L.424 J.D. [Stefanson L.]
Flom, Joel A., (BV) ....'53 '81 C.494 B.A. L.1035 J.D. [Jeffries,O.&F.]
Freeman, Russell F., (AV) ....'39 '64 C.293 A.B. L.597 J.D. [Nilles,I.S.P.&S.] ‡
Fremstad, Joel M., (CV) ....'73 '97 C.358 B.A. L.585 J.D. [Nilles,I.S.P.&S.]
Friese, Mark A., (BV) ....'69 '00 C.999 L.585 J.D. [Ⓐ Vogel]
Frissell, Anna M. '— '85 C.579 B.A. L.585 J.D.
V.P., Compliance & Ethics Offr., Blue Cross Blue Shield of N.D.
Garaas, David, (BV) ....'50 '75 C.579 B.S. L.585 J.D. [Garaas]
Garaas, Jonathan T., (BV) ....'48 '73 [Garaas]
Garaas Law Firm, (BV) ....1314 23rd St.,S.
Garrison, Michael J. '54 '79 C.579 B.A. L.585 J.D.
Asst. Law Prof., N. Dak. State Univ.
Gaughan, Thos. J. ....'30 '58 C&L.585 B.A., LL.B. 1129 5th Ave. S.‡
Geyer, James D. ....'43 '75 C.585 B.A. L.208 J.D. Admin. Law J., Soc. Sec. Admin.
Gigler, Douglas W., (BV) ....'59 '92 C.582 B.S. L.585 J.D. [Nilles,I.S.P.&S.]
Gjesdahl, Michael L., (BV) ....'59 '85 C&L.585 B.S., J.D. [Gjesdahl&Assoc.]
Gjesdahl & Associates, (BV) ....107 N. 8 St.
Gokey, Frank G., (BV) ....'57 '82 C.477 B.B.A. L.585 J.D. [Vogel]
Greenley, Matthew ....'77 '03 C.350 B.S. L.228 J.D. [Ⓐ Dorsey&W.]
Gregor, Shanon Marie '70 '99
C.579 B.A. L.585 J.D. [Nilles,I.S.P.&S.] (⊙Moorhead, MN)
Grimm, Wayne A. ....'17 '39 C&L.585 B.A., LL.B. 3115 Broadway‡
Grosz, John P. ....'25 '51 C.579 L.585 LL.B. 118 Broadway
Gullickson, Gregory B., (BV) '63 '89
C.491 B.S. L.585 J.D. Gen. Coun., Noridian Admin. Servs., LLC
Hagen, Leland F., (AV) ....'41 '65 C&L.585 B.A., J.D. [L.Hagen]
Hagen, Lee, Law Office, Ltd., (AV) ....902 28th Street South
Haggart, W. Todd, (AV) ....'50 '75 C&L.878 B.A., J.D. [Vogel]
Hamerlik, Michael F., (BV) '61 '88 C&L.585 B.B.A., J.D.
Sr. V.P. & Gen Coun., Blue Cross Blue Shield of N.D.
Hamm, Adam W. ....'71 '98 C.760 B.S. L.585 J.D. [Ⓐ Anderson&B.]
Hannig, Jean P., (BV) ....'52 '85 C.338 B.S.Ed. L.585 J.D. [Hannig&Assoc.]
Hannig, Jeffrey R., (BVⓉ) ....'54 '78 C&L.585 B.A., J.D. [Hannig&Assoc.]
Hannig & Associates, (BV) ....1 N. 2nd Street
Hansen, John Bill, (CV) ....'50 '77 C.182 B.A. L.585 J.D. 521 SouthWood Dr.‡
Hanson, Mark R., (BV) ....'64 '89 C.583 B.S. L.585 J.D. [Nilles,I.S.P.&S.]
Harrie, William P., (BVⓉ) ....'60 '86 C&L.585 B.S.B.A., J.D. [Nilles,I.S.P.&S.]
Hastings, Shon Kaelberer, (BV) .... '63 '93 C&L.585 B.S.B.A., J.D. U.S. Atty. Off.
Hauff, David J., (BV) ....'56 '84 C.491 B.S. L.1035 J.D. [Anderson&B.]
Healy, Richard L., (BV) ....'29 '52 C&L.585 B.S.C., J.D. P.O. Box 9075
Henderson, Jason J. ....'74 '00 C.182 B.A. L.585 J.D. [Ⓐ Tax]
Herman, Sarah Andrews, (AV) '52 '77
C.585 B.A. L.477 J.D. [Dorsey&W.] (⊙Mpls., MN)
Hill, Timothy P., (CV) ....'58 '87 C&L.585 B.A., J.D. [Hill]
Hill, William A. ....'46 '71 C&L.585 B.S.B.A., J.D. U.S. Bkrptcy. J.
Hill Law Office, (CV) ....1351 Page Dr., Ste. 104
Holloway, Donald R. ....'36 '65 C&L.585 Ph.B., J.D. Admin. Law J., Soc. Sec. Admn.
Holman, Maureen, (AV) ....'52 '83 C.546 B.A. L.585 J.D. [Serkland]
Holmes, Jeremy D. ....'74 '00 C.579 B.S. L.352 J.D. [Ⓐ Conmy F.]
Hourigan, Kirsti Broeder, (CV) ....'72 '00 C.188 B.S. L.896 J.D. [Nilles,I.S.P.&S.]
Hubbard, Paul M., (AV) ....'45 '73 C.491 B.A. L.793 J.D. [Conmy F.]
Hull, Daniel L., (BV) ....'56 '81 C.182 B.A. L.585 J.D. [Anderson&B.]
Hunke, Carlton J., (AV) ....'43 '67 C&L.585 Ph.B., J.D. [Vogel]
Hutchinson, Forrest, & Associates, (BVⓉ) '49 '76
C.494 B.A. L.1035 J.D. 1711 Gold Dr., Ste. 200
Ilvedson, Duane H., (AV) ....'40 '66 C.273 B.A. L.477 J.D. [Nilles,I.S.P.&S.]
Irby, John Charles, (BV) ....'56 '81 C.510 B.A. L.972 J.D. P.O. Box 2806
Jeffries, Richard N., (AVⓉ) ....'42 '70 C.491 B.A. L.585 J.D. [Jeffries,O.&F.]

Jeffries, Olson & Flom, P.A., (AVⓉ)
1325 23rd Street S.W., 58103
Telephone: 701-280-2300 Fax: 701-280-1880
URL: http://www.jeffrieslaw.com
Richard N. Jeffries; Thomas R. Olson (Civil Trial Specialist Certified by the Civil Litigation Section, Minnesota State Bar Association); Joel A. Flom (Civil Trial Specialist Certified by the Civil Litigation Section, Minnesota State Bar Association);—Erin M. Conroy.
General Insurance Defense, Trial and Appellate Practice in Minnesota and North Dakota State and Federal Courts. Medical and other Professional Malpractice, Civil Rights, Construction, Products Liability, Fire, Government and Municipalities, Errors & Omissions, Environmental Law, Health Law, Casualty, Negligence, Asbestos Litigation, Hazardous Waste, Toxic Substances, Pollution, No-Fault, Insurance Coverages, Employment, Liquor Liability, Automobile, Premises Liability, Commercial Litigation, Subrogation.
Representative Clients: American International Adjustment Co.; American States Safeco Insurance Co.; Farmers Insurance Group; Federated Mutual Insurance Co.; Fireman's Fund Insurance Co.; Hartford Insurance Co.; Midwest Medical Insurance Co.; Nodak Mutual Insurance Co.; St. Paul Fire & Marine Insurance Co.

See Professional Biographies, FARGO, NORTH DAKOTA

Jensen, Melody R.J. ....'57 '82 C.221 B.A. L.585 J.D. Clarica Life Insurance Co.
Jetvig, Chad S. ....'65 '02 C.579 B.S. L.585 J.D. 5424 S. 11th Street
Johnson, Bruce D., (BV) ....'45 '73 C.182 B.A. L.585 J.D. [Johnson,R.&L.]
Johnson, Craig E., (AV) ....'53 '80 C.579 B.S. L.585 J.D. [Johnson,R.&M.]
Johnson, David L., (AV) ....'50 '78 C&L.585 B.S., J.D. 51 Broadway, Suite 600
Johnson, Erik R., (BV) ....'57 '82 C.182 B.A. L.585 J.D. [Solberg,S.M.&J.]
Johnson, Gene P., Ltd., (BV) ....'34 '59 C.723 B.A. L.276 J.D. P.O. Box 2471‡
Johnson, J. Philip, (AV) ....'38 '62 C&L.585 Ph.B., J.D. [Wold J.]
Johnson, James L. ....'— '89 C&L.585 B.S.M.E., J.D. [Marsh F.&B.] (Pat.)
Johnson, Janice B., (BV) ....'37 '85 C.579 L.585 J.D. Ref. Supm. Ct.
Johnson, Rick D., (BV) ....'48 '77 C.579 B.A. L.585 J.D. Gen. Coun., ND State Univ.
Johnson, Steven A., (BV) ....'61 '88 C.510 B.S. L.585 J.D. [Vogel]
Johnson Law Office P.C., (BV) ....1018 1st. Ave. N.

Johnson, Ramstad & Mottinger, (AV)
15 9th Street, 58103-1830
Telephone: 701-235-7501 Fax: 701-235-8906
Members of Firm: Craig E. Johnson; Daylen D. Ramstad; Steven D. Mottinger.
General Practice in all Courts. Probate, Real Estate, Corporate, Commercial, Personal Injury and Negligence Law. Products Liability and Criminal Law.

See Professional Biographies, FARGO, NORTH DAKOTA

Johnson, Rodenburg & Lauinger, (BV)
107 Roberts Street, P.O. Box 2427, 58108
Telephone: 701-235-6411 Fax: 701-235-6678
URL: http://www.jrllawfirm.com
Members of Firm: Bruce D. Johnson; Clifton G. Rodenburg; Lisa Dawn Lauinger; Charles L. Dendy. Associate: Erin P.B. Zasada.
Creditors Rights, Commercial Law, Creditor Bankruptcy, Real Estate, Business Law, Corporate Law, Probate, Wills, Elder Law, Trusts, Estate Planning, Collections.
See Professional Biographies, FARGO, NORTH DAKOTA

Kadlec, Dale M. .... '69 '94 C.494 B.A. L.793 J.D. Atty., Microsoft Corp.
Kelly, Edward L. '50 '81 C.866 B.A. L.273 J.D. (adm. in CA; not adm. in ND) 3011 Elm St. N.‡
Kennelly, Christopher M., (BV) .... '71 '97 C.585 B.S. L.285 J.D. [Kennelly&O.]

Kennelly & O'Keeffe Ltd., (BV)
Alerus Financial Building, 15 Broadway, Suite 604, 58102
Telephone: 701-235-8000 Fax: 701-235-8023
URL: http://www.kennellylaw.com
Christopher M. Kennelly; Timothy M. O'Keeffe. Of Counsel: Max D. Rosenberg.
Business Law, Real Estate, Corporate Law, Estate Planning, Probate, Wills, Trusts, Elder Law, Commercial Litigation, Personal Injury, Automobile Accidents, Wrongful Death, Premises Liability, Bankruptcy, Municipal Law, Zoning, Planning, Land Use, Civil Litigation.
See Professional Biographies, FARGO, NORTH DAKOTA

Klein, Karen K. .... '49 '77 C.584 B.S. L.585 J.D. U.S. Mag. J.
Knoepfle, Terry W. .... '56 '81 C&L.585 B.S., J.D. [Knoepfle]
Knoepfle Law Office, P.C. ....4656 Amber Valley Pkwy., Ste. A
Knoll, Ronald J., (BV) ....'— '93 C.491 B.S. L.585 J.D. [A Anderson&B.]
Knox, Frank T., (AV) .... '19 '44 C&L.494 B.S., LL.B. 15 S. 9th St.‡
Koeck, George A., (AVⓉ) '52 '84 C.846 B.A. L.585 J.D. Corp. Secy. & Gen. Coun., Otter Tail Corp.
Korsmo, John T. ....'50 '75 C.494 B.A. L.276 J.D. Exec. V.P., Cass Co. Abstract Co.
Lamb, Raymond A. .... '40 '64 C.585 B.S.B.A. L.273 LL.B. 51 Bway.‡
Lamb, Steven F., (BV) '59 '85 C.670 B.S. L.585 J.D. Sr. Staff Atty., Amer. Fam. Ins. Grp.
Larsen, Paul D. '44 '85 C.813 B.A. L.112 J.D. (adm. in CA; not adm. in ND) 1120 28th Ave., N.‡
Larson, Jerry D., (BV) ....'45 '70 C.579 B.S., B.A. L.585 J.D. [McNair,L.&C.]
Lauinger, Lisa Dawn ....'71 '96 C.579 B.S. L.585 J.D. [Johnson,R.&L.]
Leahy, James E. ....'19 '49 C.579 L.585 LL.B. 322 Prairiewood Cir.‡
Leclerc, Lawrence A. .... '34 '66 C&L.585 B.A., LL.B. Dist. J.
Leibert-Hall, Linda A. ....'59 '85 C.910 B.S.B.A. L.734 J.D. [L.A.Liebert-H.]

Letnes, Marshall, Swanson & Warcup, Ltd.
(See Grand Forks)

Lewis, Barbara Anderson, (BVⓉ) '56 '84 C.1255 B.S. L.793 J.D. [A Smith B.O.P.&W.]
Liebert-Hall, Linda A., P.C. .... 2731 28th Ave. S.
Light, Robert M., (BV) ....'64 '90 C&L.585 B.S., J.D. [R.Light]
Light, Robert, Law Office, (BV) ....15 Broadway
Lillehaug, Duane A., (AVⓉ) ....'50 '75 C.579 B.A. L.585 J.D. [A Maring W.]
Linnerooth, Richard James, (CV) ....'58 '84 C.491 B.S. L.579 J.D. 921 2nd Ave., S.
Locken, Mary C., (BV) ....'62 '92 C&L.585 B.A., J.D. 406 Main Ave.
Lord, Angela Elsperger, (BV) ....'70 '95 C&L.585 B.A., J.D. [Vogel]
Madlom, Bruce L., (CV) ....'58 '89 C.579 B.S. L.585 J.D. P.O. Box 9693
Magill, Frank J. ....'27 '55 C&L.276 B.S.F.S., LL.B. U. S. Sr. Cir. J.
Mahler, Trent W. '67 '99 C.491 B.S. L.585 J.D. Asst. State Atty., Cass Co. State Atty. Off.
Manly, James A. .... '44 '72 C&L.585 B.A., J.D. Dir., Blue Cross Blue Shield of N.D.
Marcil, Jack G., (AV) ....'41 '68 C&L.585 B.S.B.A., J.D. [Serkland]
Maring, David S., (AV) ....'49 '74 C.579 B.S. L.585 J.D. [Maring W.] ⊙

Maring Williams Law Office, P.C., (AV)
1220 Main Avenue, Suite 105, P.O. Box 2103, 58107-2103 ⊙
Telephone: 701-241-4141 Fax: 701-235-2268
Email: mwlo@maringlaw.com URL: http://www.maringlaw.com
David S. Maring; Michael J. Williams; Daniel J. Dunn (Civil Trial Specialist Certified by the Civil Litigation Section, Minnesota State Bar Association); DeAnn M. Pladson;—Duane A. Lillehaug (Civil Trial Specialist Certified by the Civil Litigation Section, Minnesota State Bar Association); Anthony J. Weiler.
Automobile Accidents, Wrongful Death, Personal Injury, NeuroLaw, Commercial Litigation, Professional Liability, Products Liability, Negligence, Civil Rights and Torts, Family Law, Civil Litigation. Trial Practice in all Courts.
Detroit Lakes, Minnesota Office: 714 Lake Avenue, Suite 101. 56501. Telephone: 218-847-2257.
Bismarck, North Dakota Office: 400 East Broadway, Suite 307. 58501. Telephone: 701-224-0430. Fax: 701-224-0454.
See Professional Biographies, FARGO, NORTH DAKOTA

Marsh Fischmann & Breyfogle LLP
51 Broadway, Suite 502, 58102 ⊙
Telephone: 701-293-0301 Fax: 701-293-0286
URL: http://www.mfblaw.com
James L. Johnson.
Intellectual Property Law, Patent and Trademark Prosecution, Technology Transfer, Licensing and Due Diligence.
Aurora, Colorado Office: 3151 South Vaughn Way, Suite 411, 80014. Telephone: 303-338-0997. Fax: 303-338-1514.
Boulder, Colorado Office: 507 Canyon Boulevard, Suite 201, 80302. Telephone: 720-406-0506. Fax: 720-406-0520.
See Professional Biographies, FARGO, NORTH DAKOTA

McConn, Robert L., Jr., (BV) '58 '84 C&L.585 B.S.B.A., J.D. 3137 32nd Ave., S.W., Ste. 212
McCormick, Maurice G., (AV) ....'46 '71 C&L.436 B.S., J.D. [Vogel]
McCrae, Nancy D. ....'74 '99 C.011 B.A. L.585 J.D. [A Solberg,S.M.&J.]
McEvers, Lisa Fair ....'62 '97 C&L.585 B.B.A., J.D. Tax Law Off. P.L.L.P., The

McLarnan, Hannaher & Skatvold
(See Moorhead, Minnesota)

McLean, Ronald H., (AV) ....'50 '75 C.966 B.A. L.585 J.D. [Serkland]
McNair, Michael D., (BV) ....'45 '70 C&L.494 B.S., J.D. [McNair,L.&C.]
McNair, Larson & Carlson, Ltd., (AV) ....51 Bway., Ste. 600
McNeally, Nola A. ....'68 '00 C.491 B.S. L.585 J.D. [A Dorsey&W.]
Meier, Telly J. ....'77 '02 C&L.585 B.A., J.D. [Nilles,I.S.P.&S.]
Mertz, Monty G., (BV) ....'56 '81 C&L.585 B.S.S.W., J.D. 1308 23rd St., S.
Miller, Mike, (BV) ....'51 '77 C&L.585 B.S.B.A., J.D. [Solberg,S.M.&J.]

Miller, Norman & Associates, Ltd.
(See Moorhead, Minnesota)

Minch, Roger J., (AV) ....'52 '78 C.579 B.A. L.585 J.D. [Serkland]
Mohagen, Rodger G., (BV) ....'50 '95 C&L.585 B.S., J.D. [Tax]
Molbert, Lauris N., (AV) '57 '83 C&L.585 B.S.B.A., J.D. 4334 18th Ave. S.W., Ste. 200
Molick, Tracy Jo ....'66 '96 C.491 B.A. L.585 J.D. Asst. State's Atty.
Monson, Patricia R. Ellingson, (AV) ......'51 '79 C&L.585 B.A., J.D. [Nilles,I.S.P.&S.]
Montgomery, Michael S., (BV) '67 '93 C.37 B.S.B.A. L.585 J.D. 4733 Amber Valley Parkway
Morley, Janice M Schroeder ....'54 '92 C&L.585 B.A., J.D. U.S. Atty. Off.

Morley Law Firm, Ltd.
(See Grand Forks)

Mottinger, Steven D., (BV) ....'52 '79 C.723 B.A. L.1035 J.D. [Johnson,R.&M.]
Nelson, Berly D. ....'78 '04 C&L.585 B.A., J.D. [A Serkland]
Nelson, Brian W. ....'37 '62 C&L.585 Ph.B., LL.B. 111 9th St., S.
Neustel, Michael S., (CV) ....'71 '97 C.579 B.S.E.E. L.793 J.D. [Neustel]
Neustel Law Offices, (CV) ....2534 S. University Dr.
Nichol, Rebecca R. ....'71 '97 C.182 B.A. L.585 J.D. Staff Coun.

Nilles, Ilvedson, Stroup, Plambeck & Selbo, Ltd., (AV) BB
1800 Radisson Tower, 201 North 5th Street, P.O. Box 2626, 58108 ⊙
Telephone: 701-237-5544 Facsimile: 701-280-0762
URL: http://www.nilleslaw.com
J. Gerald Nilles (1922-1990); Lyle W. Selbo (1926-1988); Donald R. Hansen (1922-2001); Russell F. Freeman (Retired 2001); Duane H. Ilvedson; Robert L. Stroup, II; E. Thomas Conmy, III; Stephen W. Plambeck; Gregory B. Selbo; Leo F. J. Wilking; Richard Henderson (Resident, Moorhead, Minnesota Office); Daniel J. Crothers; William P. Harrie; Mark R. Hanson; H. Malcolm Pippin (Resident, Williston Office); Douglas W. Gigler; Andrew L. B. Noah; Jacqueline S. Anderson; Joel M. Fremstad; Kirsti Broeder Hourigan; Shanon Marie Gregor (Resident, Moorhead, Minnesota Office); Patricia R. Ellingson Monson; Telly J. Meier.
Civil Litigation, Commercial Litigation, Insurance Law, Errors and Omissions Litigation, Tort, Product Liability, Personal Injury, Railroad, Construction Litigation, Appeals, Professional Liability, Business Law, Probate, Estate Planning, Real Estate, Commercial Law, Banking, Bankruptcy, Employment Law and Worker's Compensation.
State Counsel: Burlington Northern; Santa Fe Railway.
Counsel: U.S. Bank National Association; Blue Cross and Blue Shield of North Dakota; Nodak Mutual Insurance Co.; Pioneer Mutual Life Insurance Co.
Williston, North Dakota Office: 3-4th Street East, Suite 206, Plainsman Building, P.O. Box 1525. Telephone: 701-572-5544. Fax: 701-572-5561.
Moorhead, Minnesota Office: 1401 South 8th Street. Telephone: 218-233-7407. Fax: 218-233-5133.
Reviser of the North Dakota Law Digest for this Directory.
See Professional Biographies, FARGO, NORTH DAKOTA

Noack, Steven E., (BV) ....'60 '85 C.602 B.B.A. L.188 J.D. [Vogel]
Noah, Andrew L. B., (BV) ....'67 '93 C&L.585 B.B.A., J.D. [Nilles,I.S.P.&S.]
Norgard, Tami L., (BV) ....'70 '95 C.585 B.A. L.1194 J.D. [Vogel]
O'Day, Leo Patrick, Jr. ....'61 '92 C&L.585 B.S.B.A., J.D. [P.O'Day,Jr.]
O'Day, Patrick, Jr. ....1024-3rd Ave. S.
Ohnstad Twichell, P.C., (AV) 15 Broadway, Ste. 500 (⊙Hillsboro, Mayville, West Fargo)
O'Keeffe, Timothy M., (BV) ....'73 '98 C.358 B.A. L.300 J.D. [Kennelly&O.]
Olson, Arthur R., Jr. ....'36 '60 C&L.793 B.A., J.D. 406 Main
Olson, Mitchell ....'41 '65 C&L.585 B.S.B.A., J.D. Partner, Eide Bailly LLP
Olson, Thomas R., (AVⓉ) ....'52 '81 C.55 B.A. L.1035 J.D. [Jeffries,O.&F.]
Oppegard, Paul R., (AVⓉ) '54 '80 C.182 B.A. L.1035 J.D. [Smith B.O.P.&W.] (⊙Moorhead, MN)
Orseth, Robert W., (BV) '55 '81 C.585 B.A. L.494 J.D. Gen. Coun., Farm Credit Servs. of Fargo
Ottenbacher, Ron G. '55 '81 C.590 B.S. L.221 J.D. (adm. in IA; not adm. in ND) 700 S. 7th St.
Page, Adele, (BV) ....'56 '92 C.107 B.A. L.276 J.D. [Page]

Page Law Firm LLC, (BV)
118 Broadway, Suite 200, P.O. Box 2067, 58107-2067
Telephone: 701-237-3423 Fax: 701-237-3426
URL: http://www.pagelf.com
Adele Page.
Labor and Employment Law Representing Management.
See Professional Biographies, FARGO, NORTH DAKOTA

Paulson, Terence J., (BV) ....'48 '78 C.579 B.A. L.585 J.D. 1820 39th St., S.W.

Pearce & Durick
(See Bismarck)

Pearson Christensen Cahill & Clapp, PLLP
(See Grand Forks)

Peterson, Craig A., (BV) '57 '83 C.182 B.A. L.585 J.D. 2108 S. University Dr., Ste. 102B
Phillips, Daniel E., (BV) ....'58 '93 C.584 B.S. L.585 J.D. P.O. Box 1897
Pladson, DeAnn M., (BV) ....'67 '92 C.491 B.A. L.585 J.D. [Maring W.]
Plambeck, Stephen W., (AV) ....'50 '75 C&L.273 B.A., J.D. [Nilles,I.S.P.&S.]
Quick, Bruce D., (AV) ....'52 '78 C.579 B.A. L.585 J.D. [Vogel]
Quinton, Corey J., (BV) ....'69 '95 C.590 B.S. L.585 J.D. [A Smith B.O.P.&W.]
Racek, Frank L. ....'57 '82 C.723 B.A. L.585 J.D. Dist. J.
Rajkumar, Roshini A. '— '97 C.93 B.A. L.494 J.D. (adm. in MN; not adm. in ND) KVLY-TV
Ramstad, Daylen D., (BV) ....'55 '79 C.579 B.S. L.585 J.D. [Johnson,R.&M.]
Rasmussen, David L. '47 '77 C&L.793 M.B.A., J.D. (adm. in SD; not adm. in ND) V.P., Frontier Trust Co.
Raum, Michael ....'75 '00 C.182 B.A. L.585 J.D. 655 1st Ave. N., Ste. 410
Reichert, Kari R. ....'— '04 C.494 B.A. L.976 J.D. [A Vogel]
Reisenauer, Keith W., (BV) ....'57 '82 C&L.585 B.A., J.D. Asst. U.S. Atty.
Richard, Paul F., (AV) '52 '79 C.579 B.S. L.585 J.D. Gen. Coun. & Sr. Exec., MeritCare Health System
Richard, Timothy G., (BV) ....'69 '97 C.579 B.S. L.585 J.D. [A Serkland]
Riley, John M. ....'34 '58 C&L.585 Ph.B., LL.B. Pres., First Tr. Co. of N. Dak., N.A.
Rilling, John E., (BV) ....'22 '50 C.579 B.S. L.585 LL.B. 1225 Broadway, Apt. 202‡
Rodenburg, Clifton G., (BV) ....'49 '74 C.579 B.S. L.585 J.D. [Johnson,R.&L.]
Rohleder, Thomas J., (BV) '64 '91 C.755 B.A. L.494 J.D. Gen. Coun. & Secretary, Community First Bankshares, Inc.
Rosenberg, Max D., (BV) ....'30 '57 C&L.585 B.S.C., J.D. [C Kennelly&O.]
Rothe-Seeger, Cynthia Ann ....'48 '75 C&L.585 B.A., J.D. Dist. J.
Rothfusz, Mary B., (CV) ....'61 '89 C.297 B.A. L.585 J.D. 4020 Copperfield Ct.
Rude, Jeffrey Paul ....'63 '89 C.1209 B.S. L.585 J.D. 3210 35th Ave., S.★
Sanden, James M., (BV) ....'47 '73 C.579 B.A. L.585 J.D. [Anderson&B.]
Sandsmark, James D., Law Office of, (BV) '59 '84 C.579 B.A. L.585 J.D. 921 2nd Ave. S.
Saxowsky, David M. ...... '54 '79 C.579 M.S. L.608 J.D. Assoc. Prof., N. Dak. State Univ.
Schimmelpfennig, Jerel C., (BV) '50 '81 C&L.585 B.S.P.A., J.D. [J.C.Schimmelpfennig]
Schimmelpfennig, Jerel C., PC, (BV) ....1521 10th St. S.
Schlossman, William A., Jr., (AV) ....'51 '76 C.597 B.A. L.494 J.D. [Vogel]
Schneider, Mark G., (BV) ....'48 '74 C.579 B.A. L.585 J.D. 815 3rd Ave. S.
Schneider, Steven C., (BV) ....'53 '81 C.579 B.A. L.585 J.D. 815 3rd Ave. S.
Schultz, Robert J., (BV) ....'55 '87 C.963 B.S. L.585 J.D. [Conmy F.]

Schuster, Roderic E. ....'41 '72 C.579 B.S. L.585 J.D. 4790 10th. Ave.,S.‡
Schwandt, Daniel E., (BV) '52 '88 C.491 B.A. L.585 J.D.
V.P. & Gen. Coun., Blue Cross Blue Shield of N.D.
Selbo, Gregory B., (BV) ....'50 '75 C.802 B.B.A. L.585 J.D. [Nilles,I.S.P.&S.]

Serkland Law Firm, A Professional Corporation, (AV)
10 Roberts Street, P.O. Box 6017, 58108-6017
Telephone: 701-232-8957 Fax: 701-237-4049
Email: firm@serklandlaw.com URL: http://www.serklandlaw.com
Chester J. Serkland (1909-1996); Jack G. Marcil (Civil Trial Specialist Certified by the Civil Litigation section, Minnesota State Bar Association); Ronald H. McLean; Roger J. Minch; Steven K. Aakre; Maureen Holman; Brad A. Sinclair; Jane L. Dynes;—Beverley L. Adams; Timothy G. Richard; Joseph A. Wetch, Jr.; Berly D. Nelson.
Insurance Defense, Banking, Estate Planning and Probate, Real Estate, Personal Injury, Commercial Litigation, Family, Health Care, Taxation, Employment, Transportation, Landlord/Tenant, Agricultural, Product Liability, General Litigation, Construction, Creditors Rights in Bankruptcy, Secured Transaction, Loan Documentation, Workouts, Collections, Foreclosures, Medical Malpractice (Defense Law), Mediation/Arbitration and Alternative Dispute Resolution, Guardianships and Conservatorships, General Civil Practice in all State and Federal Courts, Trials and Appeals.
Representative Clients: American International Group; Cit Group/Sales Financing, Inc.; Citizens State Bank of Enderlin; Industrial Indemnity Company; State Bank & Trust of Fargo; CENEX/Land O'Lakes Agronomy Company; Farm Credit Services of Fargo, ACA.
See Professional Biographies, FARGO, NORTH DAKOTA

Shark, Myer R. ....'13 '36 C&L.494 J.D. 566 42nd St., S.W.‡
Sheppard, Alan J., (CV) ....'51 '78 C&L.585 B.A., J.D. 921 S. 2nd Ave.
Shook, Dale R. '75 '00
C.358 B.A. L.547 J.D. Staff Coun., Blue Cross Blue Shield of N.D.
Simonson, Jared S., (CV) ....'53 '96 C.182 B.A. L.585 J.D. P.O. Box 2723
Sinclair, Brad A., (AV) .... '58 '83 C.491 B.S. L.585 J.D. [Serkland]
Smestad, Jennifer Osgood '70 '98
C.870 B.S. L.846 J.D. Assoc. Gen. Coun., Ottertail Corp.

Smith Bakke Oppegard Porsborg & Wolf, (AVⓉ) BR
Alerus Bank Building, 3137 32nd Avenue SW, Suite 212, 58102 ⊙
Telephone: 877-233-2336
Email: poppegard@sbolaw.com URL: http://www.sbolaw.com
Members of Firm: Paul R. Oppegard (Civil Trial Specialist Certified by the Civil Litigation Section, Minnesota State Bar Association); Sheldon A. Smith (Resident, Bismarck Office); Randall J. Bakke (Resident, Bismarck Office); Scott K. Porsborg (Resident, Bismarck Office); Troy A. Wolf; Suzanne M. Schweigert (Resident, Bismarck Office);—Corey J. Quinton; Barbara Anderson Lewis; Shawn Arlin Grinolds (Resident, Bismarck Office); Mitchell Armstrong (Resident, Bismarck Office).
Products Liability Defense, Civil Litigation, Insurance Defense, Environmental Torts, Toxic Torts, Asbestos Personal Injury and Property Litigation, Medical Malpractice, Professional Liability, Personal Injury, Governmental and Municipal Liability, Fire Losses, Liquor and Dram Shop Liability, Labor and Employment Law, Insurance Coverage, Civil Trial Practice in all State and Federal Courts in Minnesota, North Dakota and South Dakota.
References: ANR Pipline Co.; Bismarck National Bank; Gate City Federal Savings Bank; North Dakota Insurance Reserve Fund (NDIRF); Pennzoil Exploration and Production Co.; The Hartford Insurance Group.
Moorhead, Minnesota Office: 1800 30th Avenue S., P.O. Box 657, 56561-0657. Telephone: 218-233-8105. Fax: 218-233-8620.
Bismarck, North Dakota Office: 116 N. 2nd Street, P.O. Box 460, 58502-0460. Telephone: 1-877-233-2336.
See Professional Biographies, FARGO, NORTH DAKOTA

Solberg, Wayne O., (AV) .... '32 '66 C.579 B.S.Arch.E. L.585 J.D. [Solberg,S.M.&J.]
Solberg, Stewart, Miller & Johnson, (AV) .... 1129 Fifth Avenue South
Spaeth, Sidney J., (BV) .... '60 '91 C.813 B.A. L.1066 J.D. [Vogel]
Stafne, Philip D. ....'43 '68 C.747 B.A. L.208 J.D. P.O. Box 1166
Stanley, Caren L. ....'75 '04 C.118 B.A. L.300 J.D. [Ⓐ Vogel]

Stefanson Law
A Professional Limited Liability Partnership
606 1st Avenue North, 58102 ⊙
Telephone: 701-280-0015
Email: spff@stefansonlaw.com. URL: http://www.stefansonlaw.com
Dennis D. Fisher.
Real Estate, Family Law, Divorce, Criminal Defense, Estate Planning, Probate, Wills, Business Law, Employment Law, Personal Injury, Automobile Accidents, Wrongful Death, Health and Hospital Law, Mediation, Arbitration, Civil Litigation.
Moorhead, Minnesota Office: 302 First Bank Building, 403 Center Avenue, PO Box 1287, 56561-1287. Telephone: 218-236-1925. Fax: 218-236-6697.
See Professional Biographies, FARGO, NORTH DAKOTA

Stephens, Robin Moug ....'63 '89 C&L.585 B.B.A., J.D. First Tr. Co. of N. Dak., N.A.
Stevens, Richard J. '43 '68 C.746 B.B.A. L.436 J.D.
(adm. in WI; not adm. in ND) I.R.S.
Stewart, Garylle B., (AV) ....'40 '67 C.491 B.A. L.585 J.D. [Solberg,S.M.&J.]
Stiel, Stephannie N. ....'78 '03 C.999 B.A. L.585 J.D. [Ⓐ Conmy F.]
Stockman, Jacque G. ....'23 '51 C&L.585 Ph.B., LL.B. P.O. Box 2964‡
Streich, Judith A., (BV) ......'49 '77 C.583 B.S. L.585 J.D. Dakota Bank Bldg., Suite 500
Strinden, Jon E., (BV) ....'57 '82 C&L.585 B.S.B.A., J.D. [Dorsey&W.]
Stroup, Robert L., II, (AV) ....'41 '67 C&L.585 B.A., J.D. [Nilles,I.S.P.&S.]
Stroup, Robert L., III, (BV) '61 '86 C.494 B.A. L.585 J.D.
Dep. Gen. Coun., Blue Cross Blue Shield of N.D./Noridian Mutual Ins. Co.
Sullivan, Lawrence P. ....'50 '75 C.491 B.S. L.585 J.D. The Sullivan Agcy., Ltd.
Sullivan, Roger L. '51 '76 C.579 B.S. L.585 J.D.
Sr. V.P., First Tr. Co. of N. Dak., N.A.
Swenson, Bradley J. ....'65 '92 C.579 B.A. L.208 J.D. [Ⓒ Dorsey&W.]
Tax Law Office, P.A., (BV) .... 1444 45th Street SW, Suite 201
Thomas, Benjamin E., (BV) ....'64 '89 C&L.585 B.S., J.D. [Wold J.]
Thomas, Michael M., (BV) ....'59 '84 C&L.585 B.S.B.A., J.D. [Conmy F.]
Thompson, Gregory L., (BV) ....'56 '81 C.494 B.A. L.585 J.D. [Anderson&B.]
Thompson, Jennifer L., (BV) .... '— '97 P.O. Box 2806

Thompson, David C., Attorney at Law, P.C.
(See Grand Forks)

Tjon, Stacey Elizabeth, (BV) ....'71 '96 C.491 B.A. L.585 J.D. [Ⓐ Solberg,S.M.&J.]
Trader, Keith J., (BV) ....'53 '83 C.583 B.S.Ed. L.585 J.D. 501 40th St. S.W.
Traynor, Paul Edward ....'63 '89 C&L.585 B.A., J.D. Nodak Mutual Ins. Group
Tronson, Stacey Catherine '69 '94 C.585 B.A. L.190 J.D.
Donor Srvcs. Dir., Fargo-Moorhead Area Foundation
Turman, Joseph A., (BV) ....'48 '73 C&L.585 B.S., J.D. [DeMars&T.]
Turman, Katrina A. .... '77 '05 [Ⓐ DeMars&T.]
Twomey, James F., (BV) ....'54 '79 C&L.585 B.A., J.D. Asst. States Atty.
Udland, Robert J., (AV) .... '48 '76 C&L.585 B.S., J.D. [Vogel]
Unhjem, Michael B. '53 '78 C.358 B.A. L.585 J.D.
Pres. & CEO, Blue Cross Blue Shield of N.D.
Van Osdel, Thomas J., (AV) ....'41 '68 C.182 B.S. L.585 J.D. [Van Osdel&M.]
Van Osdel & Miller, Ltd., (AV) ....8507 South University Drive
Vogel, C. Nicholas, (AV) ....'43 '68 C.399 A.B. L.145 J.D. [Vogel]
Vogel, Mart Daniel, (AV) ....'48 '74 C.399 A.B. L.966 J.D. [Vogel]
Vogel, Mart R., (AV) ....'11 '38 C.579 L.273 LL.B. [Ⓐ Vogel] ‡

Vogel Law Firm, (AV)
218 N.P. Avenue, 58107 ⊙
Telephone: 701-237-6983 Facsimile: 701-356-6395
Email: vogellaw@vogellaw.com URL: http://www.vogellaw.com
Carlton J. Hunke; C. Nicholas Vogel; Maurice G. McCormick; Mart Daniel Vogel; William A. Schlossman, Jr.; Jon R. Brakke; W. Todd Haggart; Frank G. Gokey; Steven A. Johnson; Bruce D. Quick; Robert J. Udland; Wayne W. Carlson; Daniel A. Bueide; Sidney J. Spaeth; Jerilynn Brantner Adams; Lisa Kay Edison-Smith; Angela Elsperger Lord; Tami L. Norgard; Steven E. Noack;—Mark A. Friese; Leah M. Warner; Mart R. Vogel (Retired); Jerry O. Brantner (Retired); Daniel R. Conrad; Kari R. Reichert; Caren L. Stanley.
Insurance Defense, Personal Injury, Products Liability, Professional Malpractice, Corporate, Labor and Employment, Probate, Tax Law, Health Law, Real Estate, Bankruptcy, Construction Law, Public Utilities, Securities and Antitrust, Arbitration and Mediation. Family Law, Criminal Law, Environmental Law, Intellectual Property, Ecommerce. Trials and Appeals in all Courts.
Representative Clients: Associated General Contractors of North Dakota; Blue Shield of North Dakota; Cass County Electric Cooperative, Inc.; Clark Equipment Co.; Forum Communications Company; Merit Care Medical Group; Northern Improvement Co.; Dakota Clinic Ltd.; United Parcel Service; Gateway Chevrolet, Inc.
Bismarck, North Dakota Office: U.S. Bank Building, 200 N. 3rd Street, Suite 201, PO Box 2097, 58502-2097. Telephone: 701-258-7899.
Moorhead, Minnesota Office: 215 North 30th Street, P.O. Box 1077, 56561-1077. Telephone: 218-236-6462. Fax: 218-236-9873.
See Professional Biographies, FARGO, NORTH DAKOTA

Vogel, Weir, Hunke & McCormick, Ltd.
(See Vogel Law Firm)

Warner, Leah M. .... '76 '01 C.182 B.A. L.1035 J.D. [Ⓐ Vogel]
Webb, Rodney S. ....'35 '59 C&L.585 B.S.B.A., J.D. Sr. U.S. Dist. J.
Webb, Wade Lykken ....'70 '95 C.182 B.A. L.585 J.D. Dist. J.
Weerts, Melinda Hanson ....'69 '96 C.585 B.A. L.188 J.D. [Weerts A.]
Weerts Allen, L.L.C. .... 606 First Avenue, Suite 203
Weiler, Anthony J. ....'69 '98 C&L.585 B.A., J.D. [Ⓐ Maring W.]
Wetch, Joseph A., Jr. ....'66 '01 C&L.585 B.A., J.D. [Ⓐ Serkland]
Wilking, Leo F. J., (AV) ....'53 '78 C.309 A.B. L.262 J.D. [Nilles,I.S.P.&S.]
Williams, Michael J., (AV) ....'54 '79 C&L.585 B.A., J.D. [Maring W.]
Wold, Thomas C., (AV) ....'37 '62 C&L.585 Ph.B., LL.B. [Wold J.]

Wold Johnson, P.C., (AV)
400 Gate City Building, P.O. Box 1680, 58107
Telephone: 701-235-5515 Fax: 701-232-2585
Email: office@woldlaw.com URL: http://www.woldlaw.com
Thomas C. Wold; J. Philip Johnson; John V. Boulger; James R. Brothers; Mark A. Beauchene; Benjamin E. Thomas.
Real Estate, Estate Planning, Wills and Trusts, Probate, Corporations, Limited Liability Companies, Employment Law, Wrongful Termination, Business Law, Commercial Litigation, Personal Injury, Car Accidents, Wrongful Death, Family Law, Divorce, Child Custody, Guardianships, Juvenile Law, Hospital Law, Land Use, Criminal Defense, DWI, Civil Litigation.
Representative Clients: Gate City Federal Savings Bank; Community First Bank; Red River Commodities, Inc.; First Realty, Inc.; United Mortgage Corporation; Great Plains Software, Inc.; Blue Cross Blue Shield of North Dakota; West River Regional Medical Center; TMG (US), Inc.; CUMIS Insurance.
See Professional Biographies, FARGO, NORTH DAKOTA

Wolf, David A. ....'18 '46 C.999 L.537 LL.B. 566 42nd St. SW‡
Wolf, Troy A., (CVⓉ) ....'61 '91 C.36 B.S. L.1035 J.D. [Smith B.O.P.&W.]
Wosick, Crystal Webb ....'63 '88 C&L.585 B.B.A., J.D. Asst. State's Atty.
Yuill, William D., (AV) ....'35 '59 C&L.585 Ph.B., LL.B. 414 Gate City Bldg.
Zasada, Erin P.B. ....'77 '03 C.011 B.A. L.585 J.D. [Ⓐ Johnson,R.&L.]
Ziegelmann, Kathleen M., (BV) ....'58 '84 C.750 B.A. L.1035 J.D. 211 S. 9th St.
Zimmerman, Todd E., (BV) ....'65 '90 C.585 B.B.A. L.494 J.D. [Dorsey&W.]

FORMAN, * 586, *Sargent Co.*

Bopp, Lyle R., (BV) ....'54 '79 C&L.585 B.A., J.D. State's Atty. [Case&B.]
Case, Robert A., (BV) .... '23 '49 C&L.585 B.S.C., J.D. [Case&B.]
Case & Bopp, (BV) .... 332 Main Street, S.

FORT YATES, * 183, *Sioux Co.*

Peterson, Bradley D., (BV) '66 '91
C.584 B.A. L.585 J.D. Mng. Atty., Dakota Plains Legal Servs.

GARRISON, 1,318, *McLean Co.*

Martin, Carl J. ....'47 '77 C.585 B.S.C.E. L.352 J.D. 122 N. Main St.
Sletten, Douglas D., (BV) ....'46 '80 C.182 B.A. L.585 J.D. [Sletten]
Sletten Law Office, (BV) ....................P.O. Box 68

GRAFTON, * 4,516, *Walsh Co.*

Brosseau, Jon H., (BV) ....'45 '70 C&L.585 B.S.P.A., J.D. [Ⓒ Hodny C.]
Burianek, Todd D., (BV) ....'63 '90 C&L.585 B.A., J.D. 53 W. 5th St.
Burke, Robert L., (AV) ....'09 '51 C&L.585 B.A., J.D. 817 Hill Ave.‡
Einarson, Darcie M., (BV) .... '65 '92 C&L.585 B.A., J.D. [Einarson]
Einarson Law Office, P.C., (BV) ....640 Hill Ave.
Ekman, Steven C., Attorney at Law, (CV) .... '66 '92 C.182 B.A. L.585 J.D. 910 Hill Ave.
Geiger, M. Richard ....'51 '79 C.579 B.A. L.585 J.D. Dist. J.
Hall, Nicholas B., (BV) ....'48 '75 C&L.585 B.A., J.D. [Hodny C.]
Hodny, Jake C., (AV) ....'26 '60 C&L.585 B.A., J.D. [Ⓒ Hodny C.]
Hodny Currie Lawyers, (BV) .... 710 Hill Avenue (⊙Park River)
Longie-Goodell, Mary E. '71 '97 C&L.585 B.A., J.D.
Jud. Law Clerk, N.E. Dist. Ct. of North Dako

Moosbrugger, Carter & McDonagh, P.L.L.P.
(See Grand Forks)

Petersen, David L., (BV) ....'46 '81 C.56 B.S. L.585 J.D. [Hodny C.]
Rice, Stephen J., (BV) .... '46 '73 C&L.585 B.A., J.D. Co. Atty.
Tisdale, Dana J. ....'65 '90 C&L.585 B.A., J.D. 905 Cooper Ave.

GRAND FORKS, * 49,321, *Grand Forks Co.*

Ahlen, Michael J. ....'43 '68 C.207 B.A. L.880 J.D. Prof. of Law, Univ. of N. Dak.
Alm, Diane F., (CV) .... '42 '90 C.490 B.S. L.585 J.D. [Ⓐ Johnson]
Alphson, Robert A., (BV) ....'24 '47 C&L.585 J.D. P.O. Box 5668
Anderson, Dennis L. ....'39 '82 C.582 B.S. L.585 J.D. [Anderson]
Anderson Law Office .... P.O. Box 5252
Armstrong, Kelly M. ....'76 '03 C.585 B.A. [Ⓐ Reichert]
Arnason, A. Fred, (BV) ....'27 '52 C&L.585 LL.B. Asst. State's Atty.
Arnason, Joel F., (BV) ....'55 '81 C.309 B.A. L.585 J.D. [Arnason]
Arnason Law Office, (BV) ....301 N. 3rd St., Ste. 301A
Autrey, Shawn Leonard ....'75 '01 C&L.585 B.C.J., J.D. [Ⓐ Johnson]
Barker, Darin B. ....'70 '96 C&L.585 B.A., J.D. 645 Mighty Acres Drive
Barron, Sarah Susan ....'53 '95 C.33 B.A. L.989 J.D. [Ⓐ Pearson C.C.&C.] ⊙
Bata, Linda E., (BV) ....'— '90 C.182 B.A. L.585 J.D. [Pearson C.C.&C.] ⊙
Beehler, Bradley J., (BV) ....'62 '95 C&L.585 B.B.A., J.D. [Morley]
Bohlman, Bruce E. ....'39 '69 C&L.585 B.S.B.A., J.D. Dist. J.

Bott, Alexander J. '36 '63 C.749 A.B. L.262 J.D.
(adm. in NJ; not adm. in ND) Prof. of Law, Univ. of N. Dak.
Boucher, Alvin O., (AV) ... '51 '84 C.585 B.A. L.560 J.D. [R.Vogel]
Braaten, Karen Kosanda, (AV) ... '52 '79 C&L.585 B.A., J.D. [K.K.Braaten]
Braaten, Karen K., Ltd., (AV) ... 2502 Chestnut Street
Bring, Mark B., (BV) '65 '92
C.510 B.A. L.276 LL.M. Staff Atty., Minnkota Power Coop., Inc.
Brown, J. E. Rick ... '46 '81 C&L.585 B.S., J.D. 124 S. 4th St.‡
Cahill, Barton J., (BVⓉ) ... '61 '86 C.182 B.S. L.300 J.D. [Pearson C.C.&C.] ⊙
Cahill, Steven J., (AVⓉ) ... '48 '76 C.493 B.A. L.1035 J.D. [Pearson C.C.&C.] ⊙
Caldis, Gordon, (CV) ... '20 '48 C&L.585 B.S.C., J.D. [Caldis,T.&T.]
Caldis, Tingum & Tingum, Ltd., (BV) ... 217 S. 4th St.
Camrud, Theodore M., (AV) '31 '59 C&L.585 B.S.C., J.D.
401 Demers Avenue, Suite 500

Camrud, Maddock, Olson & Larson, Ltd., (AV)
401 Demers Avenue, Suite 500, P.O. Box 5849, 58206-5849
Telephone: 701-775-5595 Fax: 701-772-3743
URL: http://www.camrudlaw.com
Patrick J. Maddock; Gordon W. Myerchin; Darrell E. Larson; Scott D. Jensen; Timothy R. Dittus; Randall S. Hanson; Russ J. Melland; Gerad C. Paul; Janel C. Frank;—Jodi Nelson Meyer; Janel C. Frank; Tara L. Troge.
Insurance, Insurance Defense, Healthcare, Hospital Law, Probate, Trusts, Estates, Labor, Employment, Taxation, Real Estate, Corporate Law, Mediation. General Civil and Appellate Practice in North Dakota and Minnesota State and Federal Courts.
Representative Clients: Altru Clinic; Alerus Financial; Altru Hospital; Community National Bank of Grand Forks; Peterson Construction Co.; Aetna Insurance Cos.; Hartford Accident and Indemnity Co.; St. Paul Cos.; Phico Insurance Co.
See Professional Biographies, GRAND FORKS, NORTH DAKOTA

Carter, Ralph F., (BV) ... '46 '76 C&L.45 B.A., J.D. [Moosbrugger,C.&M.]
Christensen, Douglas A., (BV) ... '47 '71 C.182 B.A. L.585 J.D. [Pearson C.C.&C.] ⊙
Clapp, Richard A., (AV) ... '48 '76 C&L.585 B.A., J.D. [Pearson C.C.&C.] ⊙
Clapp, Sonja, (BV) ... '48 '87 C&L.585 B.A., J.D. Off. of States Atty.
Clifford, Thomas J. ... '21 '48 C&L.585 B.S., J.D. 1125 Reeves Dr.
Conklin, El Marie ... '65 '92 C&L.585 B.S., J.D. Legal Aid Assn.
Davis, W. Jeremy '42 '70 C&L.208 B.S.B.A., J.D.
Dean & Prof. of Law, Univ. of N. Dak. School of Law
Dittus, Sandra B., (BV) ... '— '86 C&L.585 B.S.B.A., J.D. [Zimney F.]
Dittus, Timothy R., (BV) ... '59 '86 C.36 B.S. L.585 J.D. [Camrud,M.O.&L.]
Dyrud, Harlan M. ... '36 '78 C.491 B.S. L.300 J.D. 124 S. 4th St.
Eslinger, Henry J., (BV) ... '43 '85 C.581 B.S. L.585 J.D. 711 N. Washington St., Ste. 100
Evans, Charles David, (CV) ... '54 '91 C.579 B.S. L.585 J.D. Off. of the Gen. Council
Evans, Julie A., (CV) ... '47 '89 C.705 B.A. L.585 J.D. P.O. Box 8196
Farroh, Richard, (CV) ... '53 '94 C&L.585 B.S.A.S., J.D. 711 N. Washington St.
Fischer, Ronald F., (AV) ... '55 '80 C.999 B.S. L.585 J.D. [Pearson C.C.&C.] ⊙
Fisher, Patrick W., (AV) ... '35 '68 C&L.585 B.S., J.D. [Fisher,O.&J.]

Fisher, Olson & Juntunen, Ltd., (AV)
315 First Avenue North, P.O. Box 5788, 58206-5788
Telephone: 701-775-4688 Fax: 701-775-2440
Email: pfisher@rrv.net URL: http://www.lawyers.com/f&olaw
Patrick W. Fisher; Richard W. Olson; Michael E. Juntunen.
Insurance Defense, Property Damage, Personal Injury, Products Liability, Wrongful Death, Agricultural, Banking, Corporate, Estate Planning, and Probate, Taxation, Collections, Education and School Law, Negligence, Tort and Commercial Litigation, Real Estate, Wills and Trusts, Elder Law, General Civil, Trial and Appellate Practice in North Dakota and Minnesota State and Federal Courts.
Representative Clients: Alerus Financial; UND Aerospace Foundation; Grand Forks School District; CHUBB Ins.; CNA Insurance Cos.; CENEX; Frito-Lay, Inc.; Knight-Ridder, Inc.
See Professional Biographies, GRAND FORKS, NORTH DAKOTA

Flaten, Allen J., (BV) ... '— '82 C.579 B.S. L.585 J.D. [Zimney F.]
Foster, John S., (AV) ... '— '76 C.959 B.A. L.585 J.D. [Zimney F.]
Frank, Janel C. ... '60 '03 C.581 B.S. L.585 J.D. [A Camrud,M.O.&L.] ⊙
Frank, Janel C. ... '60 '03 C.581 B.S. L.585 J.D. [A Camrud,M.O.&L.] ⊙
Fry, Patricia B. '42 '71 C.999 L.809 J.D.
(adm. in CA; not adm. in ND) Prof. of Law, Univ. of N. Dak.
Gaines-Stoner, Kelly ... '58 '89 C.639 B.S. L.623 J.D. Univ. of North Dakota
Gaustad, Daniel L., (BV) ... '66 '94 C&L.585 B.A., J.D. [Pearson C.C.&C.] ⊙
Gregory, Janet M., (BV) ... '46 '86 C.184 B.A. L.585 J.D. 711 N. Washington St.
Grijalva, James M. '64 '91 C.154 B.A. L.1051 J.D.
(adm. in WA; not adm. in ND) Asst. Prof. of Law, Univ. of N. Dak.
Hamilton, R. Lee, (BV) ... '40 '64 C&L.585 B.S.B.A., J.D. 218 S. 3rd St.

Hammarback Dusek & Associates, PLC
(See East Grand Forks, Minnesota)

Hand, James S. ... '49 '80 C.112 B.A. L.585 J.D. State Rep.
Hansen, Kenneth A. ... '53 '83 C.607 B.A. L.345 J.D. Univ. of N. Dak.‡
Hanson, Randall S., (BV) ... '66 '91 C&L.585 B.S., J.D. [Camrud,M.O.&L.]
Hanson, Robert Gustav ... '37 '63 C.489 B.A. L.585 J.D. 3603 12th Ave. N.
Henry, Blair C. '53 '80 C.911 B.A. L.678 J.D.
(adm. in WA; not adm. in ND) 3438 Meadow Dr.
Hovey, James D., (CV) ... '64 '96 C&L.585 B.A., J.D. [Pearson C.C.&C.] ⊙
Howard, Tarek, (CV) ... '65 '91 C&L.585 B.A., J.D. 2251 32nd Avenue S.
Jahnke, Shirley L., (CV) ... '45 '91 C.579 B.S. L.585 J.D. 59 Sloping Hills Cv.
Jasmer, Faye A. ... '51 '96 C&L.585 B.S., J.D. 115 S. 5th Street

Jeffries, Olson & Flom, P.A.
(See Fargo)

Jenny, Ruth A., (BV) '51 '83 C.491 B.S. L.585 J.D.
Asst. Clinical Prof., Atty., Univ. of North Dakota
Jensen, Jon J., (BV) ... '— '90 C.490 B.S. L.585 J.D. [Pearson C.C.&C.] ⊙
Jensen, Scott D., (BV) ... '61 '85 C&L.585 B.A., J.D. [Camrud,M.O.&L.]
Johnson, Carol E., (AV) ... '— '83 C&L.585 B.S., J.D. [Zimney F.]
Johnson, Ward K., III, (CV) ... '60 '88 C&L.585 B.A., J.D. [Johnson]
Johnson, Warren D., Jr., (BV) ... '40 '85 C.363 B.S. L.585 J.D. Asst. States Atty.
Johnson Law Firm, (CV) ... 215 N. 3rd St., Ste. 208
Jones, David T., (BV) ... '54 '79 C.579 B.S. L.585 J.D. 124 S. 4th St.
Juntunen, Michael E., (BV) ... '51 '83 C&L.585 B.S.B.A., J.D. [Fisher,O.&J.]
Kennedy, Tracy A., (CV) ... '— '99 C.584 B.A. L.585 J.D. [Zimney F.]
Kerbeshian, Lynn A., (BV) ... '46 '91 C.914 A.B. L.585 J.D. 2575 S. 35th St.
Kessler, David, (BV) ... '23 '51 C&L.585 B.A., J.D. 600 DeMers Ave., Ste. 401
King, Richard L., (CV) ... '21 '49 C&L.585 LL.B. P.O. Box 98
Kleve, Robert E., (CV) ... '29 '55 C&L.585 B.S.C., LL.B. 1103 24th Ave., S. (Pat.)
Kleven, Debbie G. ... '58 '83 C&L.585 B.S., J.D. Dist. J.
Kloster, Sylvia N., (BV) ... '— '88 C&L.585 B.S., J.D. [A Shaft,R.&S.]
Kosanda, Frank J. ... '21 '53 C&L.585 Ph.B., J.D. Co. J.
Kraft, Larry ... '37 '59 C.358 B.S. L.585 J.D. Prof. of Law, Univ. of N. Dak.
Kuenzel, Byron K., (CV) ... '39 '79 C&L.585 B.A., J.D. 2017 10th Ave., N.‡
Kulas, Ludwik ... '22 '51 C&L.585 B.S.C., J.D. Univ. of N. D.
Labine, Robert J., (BV) ... '47 '74 C.494 B.A. L.500 J.D. [Labine]

Labine Law Firm, (BV)
US Bank Building, Suite 202, 600 Demers Avenue, P.O. Box 5010, 58206-5010
Telephone: 701-746-7338 Toll Free: 800-762-4284 Fax: 701-746-8692
Email: rjlabine@rrv.net URL: http://www.labinelaw.com
Robert J. Labine.
Personal Injury, Automobile Accidents, Premises Liability, Wrongful Death, Medical Malpractice and Criminal Defense, Civil Litigation.
See Professional Biographies, GRAND FORKS, NORTH DAKOTA

Landa, Scott J., (BV) ... '— '90 C&L.585 B.A., J.D. [Zimney F.]
Larson, Darrell E., (BV) ... '52 '77 C.491 B.A. L.285 J.D. [Camrud,M.O.&L.]
Leavitt, MaryAnn '68 '97 L.585 J.D.
Dir. Atty. Servs., Univ. N. Dak., Thormodsgard Law Libr.
LeBel, Paul A. '49 '77 C.273 A.B. L.260 J.D.
(adm. in FL; not adm. in ND) Dean, Univ. of ND Sch. of Law
Leeds, Stacy L. '71 '97 C.910 B.A. L.862 J.D.
(adm. in OK; not adm. in ND) P.O. Box 9003
Letnes, Daniel S., (AV) ... '11 '37 C&L.585 J.D. [Letnes,M.S.&W.] ‡

Letnes, Marshall, Swanson & Warcup, Ltd., (AV)
1397 Library Circle, Suite 202, P.O. Box 12909, 58208-2909
Telephone: 701-772-3407; 800-342-0139 Fax: 701-772-3833
Email: hswanson@letneslaw.com URL: http://www.lawyers.com/letneslaw
Daniel S. Letnes (Retired); F. John Marshall; Howard D. Swanson; John Alan Warcup.
Insurance Defense, Municipal Law, Real Estate, Casualty, Fire, Auto, Products Liability, Professional Liability, Negligence, Employment Law, Environmental Law, Dramshop, Subrogation, Estate Planning, Probate, Arbitration, Civil Litigation in all state and federal courts.
See Professional Biographies, GRAND FORKS, NORTH DAKOTA

Lill, Kathryn Ebenhahn, (CV) '63 '88
C&L.585 B.S.B.A., J.D. Probate Officer, First Natl. Bk.
Lockney, Thomas M. '45 '70 C.966 B.A. L.846 J.D.
Prof. of Law, Univ. of N. Dak., School of Law
Longmire, George, (AV) ... '15 '47 C.409 B.A. L.585 J.D. 3510 Cherry Street, Unit C-1
Lundberg, Stuart A. ... '32 '61 C&L.585 B.S., LL.B. Univ. of N. Dak.
Mack, Jerome J., (BV) ... '26 '57 C&L.585 B.S., J.D. 219 S. 3rd St.‡
Maddock, Patrick J., (AV) ... '38 '64 C&L.585 B.S.B.A., LL.B. [Camrud,M.O.&L.]
Maragos, Ted ... '33 '72 C&L.585 B.S., J.D. 300 N. 5th St.
Marshall, F. John, (BV) ... '37 '62 C&L.585 Ph.B., J.D. [Letnes,M.S.&W.]
Mason, Earl S. ... '35 '74 C&L.585 B.S.C.E., J.D. Prof., Univ. of N. Dak.
Matt, Nicholas J., (CV) ... '28 '55 C&L.585 LL.B. 321 DeMers Ave.
McConn, Robert L., (AV) ... '29 '57 C.813 A.B. L.585 J.D. 315 1st Ave. N.‡
McDonagh, Alan M. ... '72 '97 C&L.585 B.A., J.D. [Moosbrugger,C.&M.]
Medd, Joel D. ... '47 '75 C&L.585 B.A., J.D. Dist. J.
Melland, Russ J., (BV) ... '57 '91 C.1270 B.A. L.585 J.D. [Camrud,M.O.&L.]
Meyer, Bradley A. ... '— '01 C.358 B.A. L.585 J.D. [Zimney F.]
Meyer, Jodi Nelson, (CV) ... '74 '00 C&L.585 B.A., J.D. [A Camrud,M.O.&L.]
Moosbrugger, John H. ... '34 '65 C.723 B.A. L.585 LL.B. [C Moosbrugger,C.&M.]

Moosbrugger, Carter & McDonagh, P.L.L.P., (BV)
311 S. 4th Street, Suite 101, 58201-4782
Telephone: 701-775-8146 Fax: 701-780-9081
URL: http://www.gflawfirm.net
Ralph F. Carter; Alan M. McDonagh. Of Counsel: John H. Moosbrugger.
Business Law, Real Estate, Banking, Corporate Law, Commercial Litigation, Personal Injury, Automobile Accidents, Wrongful Death, Medical Malpractice, Family Law, Divorce, Criminal Law, Civil Litigation.
See Professional Biographies, GRAND FORKS, NORTH DAKOTA

Morley, Michael J., (BV) ... '53 '79 C&L.585 B.S.B.A., J.D. [Morley]
Morley, Patrick R., (AV) ... '50 '76 C&L.585 B.S.B.A., J.D. [Morley]
Morley, Troy R. ... '72 '05 C.549 B.A. L.585 J.D. [A Morley]

Morley Law Firm, Ltd., (AV)
1697 South 42nd Street, Suite 200, P.O. Box 14519, 58208-4519
Telephone: 701-772-7266 Toll Free: 800-450-7266 Fax: 701-772-7269
Email: morley@morleylawfirm.com URL: http://www.morleylawfirm.com
Patrick R. Morley; Michael J. Morley; Bradley J. Beehler; Lolita G. Romanick; Kraig A. Wilson;—Troy R. Morley.
Insurance Defense, Negligence, Personal Injury, Governmental Defense, Products Liability, Toxic Torts Defense, Insurance Coverage, Legal Malpractice, Dram Shop, Construction Litigation, Communications Law, Medical Malpractice, Complex Business Litigation, Complex Commercial Litigation, Civil Trial Practice in all Courts.
Reference: First Bank of Grand Forks.
See Professional Biographies, GRAND FORKS, NORTH DAKOTA

Muhlhauser, Tara Lea ... '57 '85 C&L.585 B.S.S.W., J.D. Univ. of N.D.
Myerchin, Gordon W., (BV) ... '47 '75 C.999 B.A. L.585 J.D. [Camrud,M.O.&L.]
Myers, Bradley Kevin '60 '95 C.112 B.S. L.629 J.D.
(adm. in OR; not adm. in ND) Univ. of ND Sch. of Law
Nelson, Carlton G. ... '16 '39 C&L.585 B.S., J.D. 2717 Belmont Rd.‡
North Dakota, P.C., Law Offices, (BV) ... 215 A South 4th St.
Odegard, James T., (BV) ... '36 '70 C.584 B.S. L.585 J.D. State's Atty.
O'Kelly, Marcia ... '34 '71 C.597 B.A. L.585 J.D. Prof. of Law, Univ. of N. Dak.
Olson, Richard W., (AV) ... '44 '74 C.579 B.S. L.585 J.D. [Fisher,O.&J.]
Olson, Robin L. ... '60 '91 C.582 B.S. L.585 J.D. 405 Bruce Ave., Ste. 100 A
Omdahl, Thomas V., (CV) ... '47 '91 C.112 B.A. L.585 J.D. [Omdahl]
Omdahl Law Office, (CV) ... 424 Demers Avenue
Paranica, Kristine J. ... '65 '91 C&L.585 B.S., J.D. Dir., Conflict Resolution Ctr.
Parrish, Bradley W. ... '— '05 C.906 B.A. L.585 J.D. [Zimney F.]
Paul, Gerad C., (BV) ... '70 '95 C.182 B.A. L.585 J.D. [Camrud,M.O.&L.]
Paulson, Pauline A. ... '45 '87 C.510 B.S.N. L.585 J.D. Univ. of N. Dak. Sch. of Law
Pearson, Garry A., (AV) ... '34 '58 C&L.585 B.S.B.A., J.D. [Pearson C.C.&C.] ⊙

Pearson Christensen Cahill & Clapp, PLLP, (AV)
24 North 4th Street, P.O. Box 5758, 58201 ⊙
Telephone: 701-775-0521 Fax: 701-775-0524
Email: rclapp@grandforkslaw.com URL: http://www.grandforkslaw.com
Linda E. Bata; Douglas A. Christensen; Steven J. Cahill; Richard A. Clapp; Jay H. Fiedler (1952-2004); Ronald F. Fischer; Daniel L. Gaustad; James D. Hovey; Jon J. Jensen; Garry A. Pearson; Barton J. Cahill. Associates: Scott M. Strand; Sarah Susan Barron.
Language: Russian.
Insurance Defense, Construction Litigation, Products Liability, Tax Litigation, Commercial Litigation, Criminal Defense, Family Law, Appeals.
Representative Clients: American Estates Insurance Farmers Alliance; North Dakota Guarantee Fund; Norstar Mutual Insurance Co.; Walle Mutual; Heritage Insurance.
Reference: First National Bank, Grand Forks, North Dakota.
Moorhead, Minnesota Office: 403 Center Avenue, P.O. Box 1238, 56561. Telephone: 218-236-4900. Fax: 218-236-4909.
See Professional Biographies, GRAND FORKS, NORTH DAKOTA

Pettit, Kristi S., (BV) ... '73 '98 C.585 B.S. L.900 J.D. Asst. City Pros.
Porterfield, Naomi N. '78 '03 C.329 B.A. L.846 J.D.
(adm. in TX; not adm. in ND) JAG, U.S. Air Force

Potter, Thomas A. '49 '74 C&L.174 B.S., J.D.
(adm. in CO; not adm. in ND) 3625 Chestnut St.‡
Reichert, Alexander F., (BV) .... '70 '96 C.494 B.S. L.585 J.D. [Reichert]
Reichert Law Office, (BV) .... 218 S. 3rd St.
Reis, Sharon M., (BV) .... '— '77 C.583 B.S. L.585 J.D. [Shaft,R.&S.]
Richards, Larry James, (CV) .... '73 '99 C&L.585 B.A., J.D. [Richards]
Richards Law Office, (CV) .... 711 N. Washington St.
Rivard, Dale Richard .... '58 '95 C&L.585 B.A., J.D. 151 S. 4th, Ste. N101
Roehl, Warren J. .... '— '01 C&L.585 B.A., J.D. [Zimney F.]
Romanick, Lolita G., (BV) .... '56 '84 C.585 B.S. L.336 J.D. [Morley]
Rosenquist, Kerry S., (CV) .... '55 '91 C.999 B.S. L.585 J.D. 301 N. 3rd St., Ste. 301A
Ruemmele, Henry G., (AV) .... '15 '39 C&L.585 Ph.B., LL.B. 209 Third St., S.‡
Scurry, Michael E. .... '76 '00 C.1419 B.A. L.585 J.D. 3895 Mulberry Dr.
Seaworth, Mary Ellen, (CV) .... '47 '83 C&L.585 B.S.B.A., J.D. 421 Demers Ave.
Senechal, Alice R., (AV) .... '55 '84 C.579 B.S. L.494 J.D. [R.Vogel]
Shaft, Grant H., (BV) .... '— '86 C.36 B.S. L.585 J.D. [Shaft,R.&S.]

Shaft, Reis & Shaft, Ltd., (BV)
Gate City Federal Building, 2850 24th Avenue South, Suite 302, P.O. Box 5116, 58206-5116
Telephone: 701-772-8156 Fax: 701-772-9564
Email: shaftreis@gfwireless.com
John G. Shaft (1927-1997); Sharon M. Reis; Grant H. Shaft;—Sylvia N. Kloster.
Real Estate, Title Insurance Law, Business Law, Corporate Law, Estate Planning, Probate, General Practice.
Representative Clients: Chicago Title Insurance Co.; University of North Dakota; First National Bank North Dakota; J.R. Simplot Co.; Gate City Savings Bank; Grand Forks Board of Realtors.
See Professional Biographies, GRAND FORKS, NORTH DAKOTA

Silverman, Sam S. .... '15 '39 C&L.585 B.A., J.D. 1122 Walnut St.‡
Simonson, Steven J., (CV) .... '61 '92 C.579 B.S. L.585 J.D. 5155 7th Ave. N.
Smith, Kirk B. .... '30 '57 C.579 Ph.B. L.585 J.D. Dist. J.
Sogard, David B., (BV) '49 '75
C&L.585 B.A., J.D. Gen. Coun., Minnkota Power Coop., Inc.
Spain, Larry R. .... '51 '76 C.352 B.A. L.190 J.D. P.O. Box 9003
Strand, Scott M. .... '76 '03 C&L.585 B.B.A., J.D. [Ⓐ Pearson C.C.&C.] ⊙
Sundling, Roger R., (BV) .... '42 '83 C.766 B.A. L.585 J.D. [R.Vogel]
Swanson, Howard D., (BV) .... '58 '83 C.585 B.S. L.300 J.D. [Letnes,M.S.&W.]
Thelen, John A., (BV) .... '52 '81 C&L.585 B.S., J.D. 115 S. 5th Street
Thompson, David C. .... '53 '83 C.431 B.A. L.585 J.D. [D.C.Thompson]

Thompson, David C., Attorney at Law, P.C.
321 Kittson Avenue, P.O. Box 5235, 58201
Telephone: 1-800-704-7012
Email: dct@rrv.net
David C. Thompson.
Personal Injury.
See Professional Biographies, GRAND FORKS, NORTH DAKOTA

Tingum, Janice L., (BV) .... '58 '83 C.582 B.S. L.585 J.D. [Caldis,T.&T.]
Tingum, Kirk A., (BV) .... '57 '82 C&L.585 B.S.B.A., J.D. [Caldis,T.&T.]

Traynor Law Firm, P.C.
(See Devils Lake)

Troge, Tara L. .... '74 '05 C.999 B.S. L.585 J.D. [Ⓐ Camrud,M.O.&L.]
Vaaler, Robert, (AV) .... '23 '46 C&L.585 LL.B. House Coun., Vaaled Insurance, Inc.
Vigeland, David Harold .... '47 '80 C.747 B.A. L.585 J.D. P.O. Box 6347

Vogel, Robert, Law Office, P.C., (AV)
106 North 3rd Street, Suite 202, P.O. Box 5576, 58206
Telephone: 701-775-3117 Fax: 701-775-6274
Email: rvlo@prodigy.net
Robert Vogel (1918-2005); Roger R. Sundling; Alvin O. Boucher; Alice R. Senechal.
Civil Litigation, Personal Injury, Professional Malpractice, Workers Compensation, Employment Law, and Health Care Law.
See Professional Biographies, GRAND FORKS, NORTH DAKOTA

Voglewede, Barbara E. .... '62 '88 C&L.585 B.S., J.D. Univ. of N. Dak. Sch. of Law
Warcup, John Alan, (BV) .... '67 '93 C&L.585 B.B.A., J.D. [Letnes,M.S.&W.]
Watson, William Dele '49 '92 C.1365 B.S. L.1522 J.D.
Univ. of North Dakota, School of Aerospace Science
Widdel, John E., Jr., (BV) .... '36 '71 C&L.585 B.S.B.A., J.D. [North D.]
Wilson, Kraig A., (CV) .... '72 '99 C.972 B.S. L.585 J.D. [Morley]
Wright, Boyd L. .... '43 '77 C&L.585 Ph.B., J.D. Univ. of N. Dak.
Yon, Nancy Darlene .... '74 '99 C.011 B.A. L.585 J.D. State's Atty. Off.
Zierdt, Candace M. '51 '77 C&L.378 B.A., J.D.
(adm. in MO; not adm. in ND) Assoc. Prof. of Law, Univ. of N. Dak.‡
Zimney, Thomas L., (AV) .... '— '70 C&L.585 B.S.B.A., J.D. [Zimney F.]

Zimney Foster P.C., (AV)
Bremer Financial Center, Suite 200, 3100 South Columbia Road, P.O. Box 13417, 58208-3417
Telephone: 701-772-8111 Fax: 701-772-7328
Email: firm@northdakotalaw.net URL: http://www.northdakotalaw.net
Thomas L. Zimney; John S. Foster; Carol E. Johnson; Sandra B. Dittus; Allen J. Flaten; Scott J. Landa; Tracy A. Kennedy; Warren J. Roehl; Bradley A. Meyer; Bradley W. Parrish.
Agricultural Law, Banking Law, Business Law, Commercial Law, Construction Law, Corporate Law, Debtor-Creditor Law, Eminent Domain, Employment Law, Family Law, Immigration Law, Indian Law and Tribal Financing, Insurance, Litigation, Mediation, Mergers and Acquisitions, Natural Resources, Personal Injury, Products Liability, Real Estate, Taxation, Toxic Torts, Trusts and Estates, Wills and Probate, and Zoning, Planning and Land Use.
Representative Clients: Bremer Bank, N.A.; Federal Deposit Insurance Co.; U.S. Bank, N.A.; Sioux Manufacturing Co.; Hobart Corp.
Representative Insurance Clients: Fireman's Fund; CIGNA; State Farm Insurance Cos.; Allied Group Insurance Co.; Lawyers Title Insurance Co.
See Professional Biographies, GRAND FORKS, NORTH DAKOTA

HALLIDAY, 288, *Dunn Co.*

Gunderson, Thomas J., (BV) .... '40 '72 C.1042 B.A. L.585 J.D. 851 BIA Route 20

HAMILTON, 74, *Pembina Co.*

Argue, Wes, (AV) .... '42 '66 C&L.585 B.S.B.A., LL.B. [W.Argue]

Argue, Wes, P.C., (AV)
1 Wall Street, 58238
Telephone: 701-265-8228 Fax: 701-265-3119
Email: wesargue@polarcomm.com
Wes Argue.
Estate Planning, Estate Administration and Tax Law.

HANKINSON, 1,038, *Richland Co.*

La Qua, Vincent A. .... '25 '54 C&L.585 B.S.C., LL.B. P.O. Box 402

HARVEY, 1,989, *Wells Co.*

Grosz, Clifford C., (CV) .... '38 '64 C&L.585 B.S.B.A., LL.B. 118 E. 8th St.

Seibel, Ted D., (BV) '51 '77 C&L.585 B.A., J.D.
708 Lincoln Avenue, P.O. Box 186, 58341
Telephone: 701-324-4668 Fax: 701-324-4669
Email: tdseibel@gondtc.com URL: http://www.seibellaw.com
Estate Planning, Wills, Probate, Trusts and Estates, Real Estate, Insurance, Business Law, Banking, Collections, Corporate Law, Municipal Law, Personal Injury, Criminal Defense, Family Law, Social Security, Civil Litigation.
See Professional Biographies, HARVEY, NORTH DAKOTA

Trosen, Kathleen Kay .... '68 '95 C.494 CLA L.585 J.D. [Trosen]
Trosen Law Firm .... 120 W. 9th Street

HATTON, 800, *Traill Co.*

Uglem, Jonal H., (Ms.) .... '55 '81 C.579 B.S. L.585 J.D. Co. Jus.

HAZEN, 2,457, *Mercer Co.*

Donovan, Patrick A., (BV) .... '49 '89 C.172 B.S. L.585 J.D. [Richardson,L.&D.]
Lange, Gregory L., (BV) .... '52 '78 C&L.585 B.A., J.D. [Richardson,L.&D.]
Richardson, John A., (AV) .... '27 '51 L.508 J.D. [Richardson,L.&D.]
Richardson, Lange & Donovan, PLLP, (AV) .... 206 Central Ave., N.

HEBRON, 888, *Morton Co.*

Draeb, August C., (BV) .... '27 '51 L.585 J.D. City Atty.

HETTINGER, * 1,307, *Adams Co.*

Clement, James A., (AV) .... '16 '41 C&L.494 B.S.L., LL.B. 510 3rd Ave., N.‡
Secrest, T. L., (BV) .... '27 '56 C&L.585 Ph.B., J.D. [Secrest]
Secrest Law Firm, (BV) .... Adams County Courthouse

HILLSBORO, * 1,488, *Traill Co.*

Bertsch, Daniel E., (BV) .... '62 '88 C.579 B.S. L.585 J.D. P.O. Box 847
Juelson, John A., (BV) .... '50 '76 C&L.585 B.A., J.D. [Ohnstad T.]
Keller, Ross V., (BV) .... '58 '91 C.579 B.S. L.585 J.D. [Ⓐ Ohnstad T.]
Larson, Stuart A., (BV) .... '50 '75 C.182 B.A. L.585 J.D. [S.A.Larson]
Larson, Stuart A., P.C., (BV) .... 1 N. Main
Ohnstad Twichell, P.C., (AV) .... West Caledonia Avenue (⊙Fargo, Mayville, West Fargo)
Viker, Dewel E., Jr. .... '40 '65 C.182 B.A. L.585 LL.B. R.R. 2, Box 116

JAMESTOWN, * 15,571, *Stutsman Co.*

Baumann, Eric Paul, (CV) .... '72 '99 C.508 B.A. L.585 J.D. 105 10th St. SE
Bensch, Harold P. '37 '61
C&L.585 B.S. in B.A., LL.B. Pres. & CEO, Stutsman County Abstract Co.
Birst, Aaron Grayson .... '76 '01 C.585 B.S. L.579 J.D. 511 2nd Avenue S.E.
Buchanan, Daniel E., (BV) .... '37 '68 C.358 B.A. L.585 J.D. [Buchanan]
Buchanan Law Offices, (BV) .... 110 1st Street, East
Dalsted, Kenneth L., (BV) .... '48 '75 C.446 B.S. L.585 J.D. [Gilje&D.]
Douglas, Mark Samuel .... '52 '84 C.45 B.A., M. A. L.1243 J.D. Staff Atty.
Fremgen, Frederick R. .... '65 '91 C.488 B.A. L.585 J.D. State's Atty.★
Gilje, Charles J., (BV) .... '42 '67 C.579 B.A. L.585 J.D. [Gilje&D.]
Gilje & Dalsted, P.C., (BV) .... 208 2nd Ave., SW
Greenwood, John E. .... '49 '75 C&L.585 B.S., J.D. Dist. Ct. J.

Jeffries, Olson & Flom, P.A.
(See Fargo)

Jungroth, James R., (AV) .... '25 '50 C&L.585 Ph.B., J.D. [Ⓒ Mackenzie&R.]
Kropp, Lawrence P., (CV) .... '59 '84 C&L.585 B.S., J.D. [Kropp]
Kropp Law Offices, P.C., (CV) .... 105 10th St. S.E.
Lefevre, Troy .... '74 '02 C&L.585 B.A., J.D. 228 5th Ave. S.E.
Mackenzie, Hendry K., (AV) .... '21 '48 C.494 L.228 LL.B. [Ⓒ Mackenzie&R.]
Mackenzie, William A., (BV) .... '48 '76 C&L.585 B.A., J.D. [Mackenzie&R.]
Mackenzie & Reisnour, (BV) .... 404 Second Avenue, S.E.
Merrick, Thomas E., (BV) .... '50 '83 C.851 B.A. L.585 J.D. [Merrick&S.]
Merrick & Schaar, P.C., (BV) .... Jamestown Mall, Ste. 200
Muske, Tracy Robin .... '64 '90 C.182 B.A. L.546 J.D. 509 5th St. S.E.
Nerison, R. G., (AV) .... '17 '52 C&L.585 LL.B. 412 2nd Ave. N.E.‡
Nething, David E., (BV) ..... '33 '63 C.358 B.S. L.585 J.D. 2411 South Highway, Ste. 281
Ottmar, Joanne Hager, (AV) .... '54 '79 C&L.585 B.A., J.D. [Ottmar&O.]
Ottmar, Timothy J., (BV) .... '54 '79 C.358 B.A. L.585 J.D. [Ottmar&O.]

Ottmar & Ottmar, (AV) BB
226 2nd Avenue S.W., P.O. Box 1397, 58402-1397
Telephone: 701-252-7229 Fax: 701-252-7461
Members of Firm: Timothy J. Ottmar; Joanne Hager Ottmar.
Estate Planning, Probate, Wills and Trusts, Family Law, Divorce, Real Estate, Bankruptcy (Creditors), Personal Injury, Social Security Disability, Mediation, Civil Trial Practice.
See Professional Biographies, JAMESTOWN, NORTH DAKOTA

Reisnour, James A., (BV) .... '51 '77 C&L.858 B.A., J.D. [Mackenzie&R.]
Schaar, Cynthia, (BV) .... '55 '90 C.581 B.A. L.585 J.D. [Merrick&S.]
Schmitz, Jay A. '62 '89 C.491 B.S. L.809 J.D.
(adm. in CA; not adm. in ND) 1731 5 1/2 Ave. N.E.

Traynor Law Firm, P.C.
(See Devils Lake)

KENMARE, 1,081, *Ward Co.*

Steinberger, John S., Jr., (BV) .... '49 '76 C&L.585 B.S., J.D. P.O. Box 566

KILLDEER, 722, *Dunn Co.*

Bergerud, Marshall T., (BV) .... '29 '55 C.585 B.S. L.436 LL.B. P.O. Box 549

Johnson & Sundeen, Ltd.
(See Watford City)

LAKOTA, * 781, *Nelson Co.*

Anderson, Jeffry D. .... '63 '91 C.802 B.S. L.494 J.D. 206 Main St.
Bergquist, Harold John, (CV) .... '34 '92 C.585 B.A. L.1035 J.D. P.O. Box 257B
Devine, Terence P., (BV) .... '37 '65 C&L.585 B.S.B.A., J.D. 120 Main St.
Locken, Idean M. .... '18 '49 C.585 B.S.C. L.508 LL.B. 125 Main St.‡
Manbeck, Douglas G., (BV) .... '51 '76 C.579 B.A. L.585 J.D. City Atty.

LA MOURE, * 970, *La Moure Co.*

Kessel, Theodore, Jr., (BV) .... '38 '62 C&L.585 B.S., J.D. [Kessel S.&N.]
Kessel, Theodore F., (AV) .... '12 '36 C&L.585 17 6th Ave., N.W.‡
Kessel Splitt & Narum, PC, (AV) .... 19 1st Avenue S.E.
Narum, Daniel Dean, (BV) .... '69 '99 C.579 B.S. L.585 J.D. [Kessel S.&N.]
Splitt, Ronald G., (AV) .... '34 '58 C&L.585 B.S.B.A., J.D. [Kessel S.&N.]

LANGDON, * 2,101, *Cavalier Co.*

Heigaard, William S., (AV) .... '38 '67 C&L.585 B.Ph., LL.B. P.O. Box 68‡
La Qua, John F. .... '22 '51 C&L.585 Ph.B., LL.B. P.O. Box 69

Price, Robert Q., (AV) ... '11 '36 C.585 B.A. L.352 J.D. Hwy. #5 West
Sillers, Cameron D., (BV) ... '48 '75 C&L.585 B.A., J.D. 908 3rd St.
Stewart, R. Scott, (BV) ... '55 '80 C&L.585 B.A., J.D. [Stewart]
Stewart Law Offices, (BV) ... 306 9th Ave.

LARIMORE, 1,464, *Grand Forks Co.*

Hager, Donald, (BV) ... '55 '86 C.582 J.D. L.585 J.D. 207 Towner Ave.

LEONARD, 310, *Cass Co.*

Anderson-Viken, Marianne Denise '63 '88 C&L.585 B.S.P.A., J.D.
4680 153rd Ave., SE‡

LINTON, * 1,410, *Emmons Co.*

Becker, Donald R., (BV) ... '47 '73 C.579 B.S. L.37 J.D. [Becker]
Becker Law Office, (BV) ... Courthouse
Grenz, Donavin L. ... '47 '73 C&L.585 B.S., J.D. Co. J.
Huizenga, Jerry W. ... '40 '71 C.590 B.S. L.585 J.D. 101 S. Broadway
Jorgensen, Donald L. ... '44 '70 C&L.585 Ph.B., J.D. Dist. J. (⊙Bismarck)
Rohrich, Francis C. ... '33 '62 C&L.585 B.S., J.D. P.O. Box 657

LISBON, * 2,292, *Ransom Co.*

Eppler, Don B., (BV) ... '56 '81 C.585 B.A. L.494 J.D. [Eppler&L.]
Eppler & Leadbetter, (BV) ... 7 4th Ave., W.
Jones, Wayne P., (BV) ... '38 '68 C.793 B.A. L.352 J.D. [W.P.Jones]
Jones, Wayne P., P.C., (BV) ... 316 Main St.
Leadbetter, Jeffrey K., (BV) ... '60 '85 C&L.585 B.A., J.D. [Eppler&L.]
Stetson, Donavon K., (BV) ... '30 '55 C&L.585 LL.B. [Ⓐ W.P.Jones]
Thomason, Lyle P. ... '63 '00 C.494 B.S. L.793 J.D. [Thomason]
Thomason Law Office, P.C. ... P.O. Box 1896
Tjon, Lowell O. ... '25 '48 C.182 L.585 LL.B. Co. J.‡

MANDAN, * 16,718, *Morton Co.*

Bair, Bruce B., (AV) ... '28 '52 C&L.585 B.S., J.D. [Bair,B.&G.]
Bair, Thomas B., (BV) ... '55 '85 C&L.585 B.S., J.D. [Bair,B.&G.]
Bair, Bair & Garrity, LLP, (AV) ... 210 First Avenue, N.W.
Bard, Dean F., (CV) ... '33 '68 C&L.585 Ph.B., J.D. 1604 River Dr.
Burns, Craig B., (CV) ... '64 '95 C.846 B.A. L.1128 J.D. 104 3rd Ave. N.W., Ste. 2B
Coghlan, Leah Kopseng, (CV) ... '74 '99 C&L.585 B.B.A., J.D. 3520 Falcon Road SE
Delmore, William J., (AV) ... '— '75 C.585 B.A. L.976 J.D. [Kelsch K.R.&K.]
Feldner, Rodney K. ... '55 '80 C&L.585 B.S., J.D. 310 6th Ave. N.W.‡
Gallagher, Sharon A., (BV) ... '51 '76 C.742 B.A. L.585 J.D. [Gallagher]
Gallagher Law Firm, (BV) ... 105 Third Avenue, N.W.
Garrity, Patricia E., (BV) ... '52 '90 C.999 B.S. L.585 J.D. [Bair,B.&G.]
Gosbee, John J. ... '49 '77 C.1036 B.A. L.744 J.D. [Gosbee]
Gosbee Law Office ... 103 3rd Ave., N.W.
Goulet, Wallace R., Jr., (AV) '48 '73 C.602 B.B.A. L.585 J.D.
V.P. & Gen. Coun., Nat'l. Information Solutions Cooperative
Grosinger, Brian David ... '59 '87 C.579 B.S. L.585 J.D. Morton Co. States Atty.'s Off.
Kelsch, Thomas D., P.C., (BV) ... '— '82 C&L.585 B.A., J.D. [Kelsch K.R.&K.]
Kelsch, Thomas F., (BV) ... '— '65 C.723 B.A. L.585 J.D. [Kelsch K.R.&K.]
Kelsch, William C., (AV) ... '32 '56 C.723 B.A. L.585 J.D. [Kelsch K.R.&K.] ‡

Kelsch Kelsch Ruff & Kranda, (AV) BB
"A Partnership including Professional Corporations"
103 Collins Avenue, P.O. Box 1266, 58554-7266
Telephone: 701-663-9818 Fax: 701-663-9810
URL: http://www.kelschlaw.com
Members of Firm: C. F. Kelsch (1890-1987); William C. Kelsch (Retired); Thomas F. Kelsch; Arlen M. Ruff, P.C.; Thomas D. Kelsch, P.C.; Todd D. Kranda, P.C.; William J. Delmore. Associates: Cynthia Wagner-Goulet; Daniel J. Nagle.
Estate Planning, Probate, Wills, Real Estate, Family Law, Divorce, Adoptions, Commercial Litigation, Personal Injury, Products Liability, Administrative Law, Environmental Law, Lobbying, Banking, Business Law, Bankruptcy, Corporate Law, Collections, Civil Litigation.
Representative Clients: L & H Manufacturing Co.; Cloverdale Foods Co.; Logan Hill Realty, Bismarck; Wells Fargo; 1st Southwest Bank; Rainbow Gas Co.; Canadian Pacific Railway; Western Wireless; Waste Management.
See Professional Biographies, MANDAN, NORTH DAKOTA

Koppy, Allen ... '56 '84 C&L.585 B.S.B.A., J.D. State's Atty.
Kranda, Todd D., P.C., (BV) ... '— '87 C.579 B.S. L.585 J.D. [Kelsch K.R.&K.]
Lawhead, Janice M. ... '58 '92 C.494 B.S. L.1035 J.D. Asst. State's Atty.
Liffrig, Michael G., (BV) ... '59 '85 C.585 B.A. L.477 J.D. 2815 28th St.
Lindquist, Dennis William ... '42 '92 C.581 B.S. L.585 J.D. [Lindquist]
Lindquist Law Offices ... P.O. Box 490
Nagle, Daniel J. ... '76 '04 C&L.585 B.B.A., J.D. [Ⓐ Kelsch K.R.&K.]
Paul, Jack D. ... '27 '57 C&L.585 B.S.L., J.D. 701 3rd Ave. N.W.‡
Renner, Jerome L., (BV) ... '46 '76 L.585 J.D. 8660 Willow Rd. N.E.
Robinson, Rauleigh D., (BV) ... '46 '71 C.584 B.S. L.174 J.D. P.O. Box 490
Ruff, Arlen M., P.C., (BV) ... '— '79 C.358 B.A. L.221 J.D. [Kelsch K.R.&K.]
Schlax, James A. '46 '82 C.339 B.S. L.209 J.D.
(adm. in IL; not adm. in ND) Fin. Dir.Servs., Amoco Oil Co.
Schneider, Thomas J. ... '50 '81 C&L.585 B.A., J.D. Dist. J.
Schnell, Richard L., (CV) ... '34 '61 C&L.585 Ph.B., LL.B. 400 9th Ave. N.W.
Tuntland, Tom, (BV) ... '45 '75 C&L.585 B.A., J.D. 104 3rd Ave., N.W., 3rd Fl.
Ulmer, Leland G. ... '22 '51 C&L.585 LL.B. 505 6th Ave. N.E.‡
Wagner-Goulet, Cynthia, (BV) ... '— '85 C.579 B.S. L.585 J.D. [Ⓐ Kelsch K.R.&K.]
Wheeler, R. W., (AV) ... '22 '49 C&L.585 B.S., LL.B. 42 Captain Marsh Dr.‡

MAYVILLE, 1,953, *Traill Co.*

Brudvik, William J., (BV) ... '46 '74 C&L.494 B.A., J.D. [Ohnstad T.]
Engelman, Jerald L., (BV) ... '47 '74 C&L.585 B.S.B.A., J.D. State Natl. Guard
Larson, Carl J. ... '13 '36 C&L.585 LL.B. 433 1st St., N.W.‡
Moe, Thomas R., (CV) ... '51 '81 C.582 B.S. L.585 J.D. Mun. J.
Ohnstad Twichell, P.C., (AV) ... 12 Third Street S.E. (⊙Fargo, Hillsboro, West Fargo)
Vinje, S. Lee, (AV) ... '43 '68 C.597 B.S. L.585 J.D. [Ohnstad T.]

McCLUSKY, * 415, *Sheridan Co.*

Lipp, Walter M., (CV) ... '46 '73 C&L.585 B.S., J.D. 208 S. Main St.

MEDORA, * 101, *Billings Co.*

Brovold, Jay V., (CV) ... '51 '76 C&L.585 B.A., J.D. States Atty.

Johnson & Sundeen, Ltd.
(See Watford City)

MINNEWAUKAN, * 401, *Benson Co.*

Ward, Steve ... '14 '40 C&L.585 Ph.B., LL.B. Hwy. 281‡

MINOT, * 36,567, *Ward Co.*

Alm, Elin S. ... '75 '03 C.999 L.585 J.D. [Ⓒ Maxson]
Armstrong, Phillip D., (CV) ... '43 '79 C.502 B.S. L.285 J.D. 13 1st Avenue, SW
Backes, Jon W., (BV) ... '60 '90 C.584 B.S. L.585 J.D. [McGee,H.B.&D.]
Backes, Orlin W., (AV) ... '35 '63 C.584 B.S. L.585 J.D. [McGee,H.B.&D.]
Benson, Allan ... '52 '82 C&L.585 B.S.B.A., J.D. 202 3rd. Ave.,S.E.
Bergman, William E., (CV) ... '57 '82 C&L.585 B.A., J.D. [Lamont&S.]
Berning, Wallace D. ... '35 '60 C&L.502 A.B., LL.B. Dist.J.
Bosard, McCutcheon & Rau, L.T.D., (CV) ... 102 Heritage Place
Bosch, Edward J. ... '26 '54 C.584 B.S. L.585 J.D. 305-7 E. Central Ave.
Boughey, Lynn M. ... '56 '83 C.293 B.A. L.300 J.D. [Boughey]
Boughey Law Firm ... 201 South Main
Burns, Mary P. ... '49 '74 C&L.494 B.A., J.D. [Olson B.L.]
Cantor, Paul A. ... '56 '91 C.604 B.A. L.911 J.D. In-House Coun., Northern Life Ins. Co.
Cresap, Todd L., (BV) ... '61 '86 C.584 B.A. L.585 J.D. [Kenner&C.]
Cunningham, Kathleen B., (BV) ... '44 '86 P.O. Box 1089‡
Diaz, Donovan P. '75 '02
C.378 B.A. L.900 J.D. Asst. Staff Judge Advocate, Chief of Claims
Dillon, Kelly A., (BV) ... '66 '95 C.999 B.A. L.585 J.D. 600 22nd Ave., N.W.
Dobrovolny, Collin P., (BV) ... '50 '76 C.584 B.S. L.585 J.D. [McGee,H.B.&D.]
Eaton, Jonathan C., Jr., (AV) ... '27 '53 C.597 B.S. L.813 LL.B. [Eaton,V.&W.]
Eaton, Van de Streek & Ward, (AV) ... 201 South Main, Suite 200
Farhart, Moody M., (BV) ... '26 '59 C&L.585 Ph.B., J.D. 600 22nd Avenue N.W.
Frantsvog, Dean A. ... '74 '00 C.579 B.S. L.300 J.D. [Ⓐ Olson B.L.]
Gense, Glen G. ... '26 '51 L.585 LL.B. 401 S. Main St.
Hagar, Richard L., (CV) ... '57 '89 C.1070 B.S. L.585 J.D. [Ⓐ Kenner&C.]
Hankla, Brian W., (BV) ... '59 '86 C.585 B.S./B.A. L.802 J.D. [McGee,H.B.&D.]
Hankla, Peter B., (BV) ... '65 '91 C&L.585 B.B.A., J.D. [McGee,H.B.&D.]
Herigstad, Roger O., (AV) ... '19 '51 C.623 B.S. [Ⓐ Pringle&H.] ‡
Hoffarth, Debra L., (CV) ... '73 '00 C&L.585 B.B.A., J.D. [Ⓐ Pringle&H.]
Hogue, David J., (BV) ... '62 '87 C.188 B.S.S. L.585 J.D. [Pringle&H.]
Holum, Gary A. ... '37 '71 C&L.585 B.S.B.A., J.D. Dist. J.
Howard, Judith E., (BV) ... '41 '78 C.584 B.S. L.585 J.D. [Howard]
Howard Law Firm, P.C., (BV) ... 7 3rd St. S.E., Ste. 202
Kenner, Harris P. ... '27 '52 C.579 L.585 J.D. [Kenner&C.] ‡
Kenner & Cresap, P.C., (BV) ... 615 South Broadway
Kerian, Jon R. ... '27 '57 C&L.585 Ph.B., J.D. Dist. J.
Knutson, K. M., (BV) ... '20 '42 C&L.585 LL.B. U.S. Mag.
Lamont, Robert J. ... '47 '76 C&L.16 B.S., J.D. [Lamont&S.] ‡
Lamont & Skowronek, (BV) ... 116 1st St., SW
Larson, Carol K., (BV) ... '56 '86 C.494 B.A. L.585 J.D. [Pringle&H.]
Larson, Mark V., (BV) ... '54 '79 C&L.585 B.A., J.D. [Larson]
Larson, Rozanna C., (CV) ... '62 '95 C.579 B.S. L.585 J.D. Asst. States Atty.
Larson Law Firm, P.C., (BV) ... 816 20th Avenue SW
Lee, Ervin J., (CV) ... '52 '85 C&L.585 B.S.B.A., J.D. P.O. Box 359
Lee, Gary H. ... '55 '80 C&L.585 B.A., J.D. Dist. J.
Louser, Diane R., (BV) ... '42 '82 C&L.585 B.S., J.D. [Louser&Z.]
Louser & Zent, P.C., (BV) ... 1015 South Broadway-Suite 15
Mattson, Douglas L., (CV) ... '55 '85 C&L.585 B.A., J.D. State's Atty.
Maxson, R. James, (AV) ... '47 '73 C.491 B.A. L.585 J.D. [Maxson]

Maxson Law Office, P.C., (AV) BB
Town & Country Center, 1015 S. Broadway, Suite 15, 58701
Telephone: 701-839-6704 Fax: 701-852-8782
Email: maxsonlaw@minot.com URL: http://www.maxsonlaw.com
R. James Maxson. Of Counsel: Elin S. Alm.
Estate Planning, Probate, Trusts, Wills, Business Planning, Corporate Law, Real Estate, Commercial Litigation, Civil Litigation.
See Professional Biographies, MINOT, NORTH DAKOTA

McGee, Richard H., II, (AV) ... '50 '77 C.584 B.A. L.585 J.D. [McGee,H.B.&D.]

McGee, Hankla, Backes & Dobrovolny, P.C., (AV)
Suite 305 Wells Fargo Bank Center, 15 Second Avenue Southwest, P.O. Box 998, 58702-0998
Telephone: 701-852-2544 Fax: 701-838-4724
URL: http://www.mcgeelaw.com
Richard H. McGee (1918-1992); Orlin W. Backes; Richard H. McGee, II; Brian W. Hankla; Collin P. Dobrovolny; Jon W. Backes; Peter B. Hankla; Jason R. Vendsel; Bryan Van Grinsven;—Jennifer M. Stanley.
Personal Injury, Auto Accidents, Medical Malpractice, Wrongful Death, Products Liability, Insurance Defense, Business Law, Business Litigation, Immigration Law, Probate, Guardianships, Estate Planning, Wills, Trusts, Banking Law, Real Estate Law, Commercial Litigation, Agricultural Law, Cooperative Law, School Law, Employment Law, Healthcare Law, Family Law, Construction Law, Civil Trial Practice in all courts.
See Professional Biographies, MINOT, NORTH DAKOTA

McLees, William W. ... '51 '76 C&L.585 B.A., J.D. Dist. J.
Mendelson, Jamie L. '75 '02 C.1494 B.S. L.813 J.D.
(adm. in CA; not adm. in ND) Asst. Staff Judge Adv.
Meschke, Herbert L. ... '28 '53 C.358 B.A. L.477 J.D. [Ⓒ Pringle&H.]
Negaard, Donald A., (BV) ... '53 '79 C.584 B.A. L.585 J.D. [Pringle&H.]
Nostdahl, James E., (BV) ... '56 '82 C&L.585 B.A., J.D. [Pringle&H.]
Olson, Everett N. ... '39 '65 C.581 B.A. L.585 LL.B. Dist. J.
Olson, Richard P., (BV) ... '49 '74 C.182 B.A. L.494 J.D. [Olson B.L.]
Olson Burns Lee, P.C., (BV) ... 17 1st Ave. S.E.
Palda, Robert W., Jr. ... '32 '63 C&L.585 B.A., LL.B. 14 Souris Court

Pearce & Durick
(See Bismarck)

Portscheller, Connie Sue, (BV) ... '63 '93 C.584 B.S. L.585 J.D. P.O. Box 5005
Pringle & Herigstad, P.C., (BV) ... 20 First Street S.W.
Probst, Paul Michael, (CV) ... '63 '95 C.584 B.S. L.585 J.D. 600 22nd Avenue Nw
Purdy, Mark F., (BV) ... '27 '57 C.584 B.S. L.585 LL.B. [Ⓐ Pringle&H.]
Rasmuson, Mark B., (BV) ... '43 '68 C.579 B.S. L.585 J.D. [Rasmuson]
Rasmuson Law Office, (BV) ... 204 Union National Annex
Rau, Robert, (CV) ... '48 '73 C.1044 B.A. L.585 J.D. [Bosard,M.&R.]
Schmidt, Channing T. ... '70 '01 C.585 B.A. L.300 J.D. [Ⓐ Olson B.L.]
Sebby, Jan M., (BV) ... '39 '64 C.755 B.A. L.494 LL.B. [Ⓐ Pringle&H.]
Sharp, Kim Howard, (CV) '54 '92
C.584 B.S. L.585 J.D. Admin. Hearing Offr.; Dept. of Transp.
Skowronek, John C., (BV) ... '54 '86 C.584 B.S.C. L.585 J.D. [Lamont&S.]
Slorby, Robert, (CV) ... '52 '76 C&L.585 B.S., J.D. 20 1st Ave. S.W., Ste. 201
Slorby, Tom P., (BV) ... '48 '73 C.999 B.S. L.585 J.D. 600 22nd Ave., N.W.
Soderstrom, Reed, (BV) ... '62 '90 C.582 B.S. L.585 J.D. [Pringle&H.]
Stanley, Jennifer M. ... '77 '03 C.584 B.A L.585 J.D. [Ⓐ McGee,H.B.&D.]
Sturdevant, Michael G., (BV) ... '49 '74 C.880 B.A. L.585 J.D. [M.G.Sturdevant]

Sturdevant, Michael G., P.C., (BV)
SW Plaza Building, 900 20th Avenue SW, P.O. Box 970, 58702
Telephone: 701-852-4118
Email: mgslaw@srt.com
Michael G. Sturdevant.

(This Listing Continued)

Sturdevant, Michael G., P.C. (Continued)
Business Organizations, Corporate Law, Business Planning, Real Estate, Estate Planning, Probate, Commercial Litigation.
See Professional Biographies, MINOT, NORTH DAKOTA

Thomas, Richard B., (BV) ....'33 '57 C&L.585 Ph.B., J.D. [Thomas&T.]
Thomas, Robert S., (BV) ....'60 '86 C&L.585 B.A., J.D. [Thomas&T.]
Thomas & Thomas, (BV) .... 13 1st Avenue SW Fifth Floor First Avenue Building

Traynor Law Firm, P.C.
(See Devils Lake)

Van de Streek, Nevin, (BV) ....'45 '70 C.813 A.B. L.477 J.D. [Eaton,V.&W.]
Van Grinsven, Bryan, (BV) ....'69 '95 C.585 B.A. L.494 J.D. [McGee,H.B.&D.]
Van Grinsven, John P., III, (AV) ....'49 '77 C.584 B.A. L.585 J.D. Asst. States Atty.
Vendsel, Jason R., (BV) ....'65 '91 C&L.585 B.S.B.A., J.D. [McGee,H.B.&D.]
Ward, Michael M., (BV) ....'42 '67 C&L.585 B.A., LL.B. [Eaton,V.&W.]
Wheeler, Robert A., (BV) ..... '31 '66 C&L.585 Ph.B., J.D. 15 Second Avenue Southwest

Wheeler Wolf Law Firm
(See Bismarck)

Wilhelm, Timothy C., (BV) ....'50 '82 C.585 B.A. L.300 J.D. Ward Co. Courthouse
Will, Robert G., (CV) .... '72 '97 C&L.585 B.A., J.D. 925 20th Ave., S.W.
Zent, Brenda M., (BV) ....'59 '85 C&L.585 B.S.P.A., J.D. [Louser&Z.]

MOHALL, * 812, *Renville Co.*

Madsen, Marvin K., (BV) ....'48 '79 C.584 B.S. L.585 J.D. 106 1st Ave. NE

Wolff, James G., Law Offices of '69 '97 C.722 B.A. L.629 J.D.
105 West Main, P.O. Box 8, 58761
Telephone: 701-756-7199 Fax: 701-756-6882
Email: jamesgwolff@wolfflawoffices.com URL: http://www.wolfflawoffices.com
General Practice.
See Professional Biographies, MOHALL, NORTH DAKOTA

MOTT, * 808, *Hettinger Co.*

Crane, David M., (BV) ....'53 '82 C.585 B.A. L.629 J.D. [Crane]
Crane Law Office, (BV) .... Brown Avenue & 3rd Street

NAPOLEON, * 930, *Logan Co.*

Kuhn, Gerald A., (BV) .... '42 '73 C.590 B.A. L.260 J.D. P.O. Box 50

NEW ROCKFORD, * 1,463, *Eddy Co.*

Bekken, James M. ....'48 '77 C&L.585 B.S., J.D. Dist. J.
Hovey, John D. ....'38 '64 C&L.585 B.S.B.A., LL.B. 904 Central Ave.‡
Manly, Robert E., (BV) .... '45 '73 C.742 B.A. L.190 J.D. 121 1st Ave. S.
Peterson, Travis S., (CV) ....'73 '98 C.579 B.S. L.221 J.D. [Peterson]
Peterson Law Offices, P.C., (CV) ....523 Central Avenue

NEW TOWN, 1,388, *Mountrail Co.*

Fitzsimmons, James P. '52 '77 C&L.585 B.S.B.A., J.D.
Exec. Dir., ND Legal Serv., Inc.
Hermanson, Valeska Anne, (CV) .... '69 '99 C.488 B.A. L.585 J.D. ND Legal Srvcs.

NORTHWOOD, 959, *Grand Forks Co.*

Johnson & Lawrence, P.C., (BV) ....8 N. Main
Kringlie, A. Roger, (BV) ....'27 '53 C&L.585 Ph.B., LL.B. 4 N. Main St.
Lawrence, Gary W., (BV) ....'43 '67 C&L.585 B.S.B.A., LL.B. [Johnson&L.]

OAKES, 1,979, *Dickey Co.*

McLean, Stephen M., (BV) .... '48 '73 C.579 B.A. L.585 J.D. [S.M.McLean]
McLean, Stephen M., Ltd., (BV) .... 606 Main Ave.
Stites, Thomas E. '45 '78 C.870 B.S. L.585 J.D.
(adm. in CA; not adm. in ND) 817 Kola Ave.‡

PARK RIVER, 1,535, *Walsh Co.*

Currie, Stephen L., (BV) ....'44 '68 C&L.585 B.S.B.A., J.D. [Hodny C.]
Hodny Currie Lawyers, (BV) ....................................P.O. Box 108 (©Grafton)
Welch, Wes R. ....'66 '92 L.585 J.D. 406 Briggs Ave. S.

PARSHALL, 943, *Mountrail Co.*

Woods, William E., Jr., (BV) .... '59 '84 C.584 B.S. L.585 J.D. Asst. Co. Atty.

REGENT, 268, *Hettinger Co.*

Gion, James D., (BV) ....'53 '82 C&L.585 B.A., J.D. [Gion]
Gion Law Office, (BV) .... 23 Main Avenue, South

ROLLA, * 1,417, *Rolette Co.*

Boyum, Arne F., (BV) .... '44 '72 C&L.585 B.A., J.D. P.O. Box 908
O'Donnell, Mary K., (BV) .... '43 '85 C&L.585 B.A., J.D. States Atty.
Stormon, J. Howard, (AV) ....'18 '47 C.585 124 Main Ave.‡

RUGBY, * 2,909, *Pierce Co.*

Butz, Mark J. .... '37 '63 C&L.585 B.S., LL.B. 126 2nd Ave., S.W.
Hartl, William Robert, (BV) ....'69 '94 C&L.585 B.B.A., J.D. 130 S. Main
Hovland, Robert J., (CV) .... '62 '88 C&L.585 B.A., J.D. Pres., Center Mut. Ins. Co.
Mack, Galen J., (BV) .... '59 '86 C.579 B.S. L.585 J.D. States Atty. [Mack]
Mack Law Offices, P.C., (BV) ....P.O. Box 196
McClintock, John C., Jr. ..... '61 '91 C&L.585 B.S.B.A., J.D. Co. J., Pierce Co. Courthouse
Orvik, Charles D. ....'36 '67 C&L.585 B.S.B.A., LL.B. P.O. Box 196

STANLEY, * 1,371, *Mountrail Co.*

Enget, Wade G., (BV) ....'59 '84 C.581 B.C.S. L.585 J.D. [Schulte&E.]
Holte, Robert W. ....'41 '71 C&L.585 B.S., J.D. Dist. J.
Schulte, Quentin R., (BV) ....'16 '42 C&L.508 LL.B. [Schulte&E.]
Schulte & Enget, P.C., Law Offices of, (BV) ....18 Railroad Avenue

STANTON, * 345, *Mercer Co.*

Berg, Weston L. .... '56 '84 C&L.585 B.S.B.A., J.D. P.O. Box 207‡
Duppler, Alan, (CV) ....'51 '77 C.182 B.A. L.585 J.D. States Atty.
Johnson, James O., (CV) ....'47 '82 C.579 B.S. L.585 J.D. P.O. Box 39

STEELE, * 762, *Kidder Co.*

Molbert, Ralph .... '15 '41 C&L.585 B.S., J.D. Pres., Bank of Steele

STRASBURG, 553, *Emmons Co.*

Wikenheiser, Frank J. .... '22 '79 C.1056 B.A. L.585 J.D. 707 S. 2nd St.‡

THOMPSON, 930, *Grand Forks Co.*

Rubin, Samuel ....'13 '36 C&L.585 R.R. 1, Box 22-A

TIOGA, 1,125, *Williams Co.*

Peterson, Comart M., (BV) ....'27 '52 C&L.585 B.S.C., LL.B. 112 N. Main St.

TOWNER, * 669, *McHenry Co.*

McIntee, Michael S. ....'49 '76 C&L.585 B.A., J.D. [McIntee]
McIntee Law Firm .... 207 Main Street South
Williams, Jas. H., (AV) ....'27 '53 C.584 L.585 LL.B. Pres., State Bk. of Towner

VALLEY CITY, * 6,826, *Barnes Co.*

Cruff, Bradley A., (BV) .... '64 '94 C.583 B.S. L.585 J.D. [Lenaburg,F.N.H.&C.]
Delaney, H. Jean, (BV) ....'62 '91 C.579 B.S. L.585 J.D. Asst. States Atty.
Fitzner, R. Jon, (BV) ....'40 '64 C&L.585 B.S.B.A., J.D. [Lenaburg,F.N.H.&C.]
Goven, Thomas E., (BV) .... '57 '83 C&L.585 B.A., J.D. 117-3rd St. N.W.
Hooper, Ralph E., (BV) .... '47 '79 C&L.585 B.S.B.A., J.D. [Lenaburg,F.N.H.&C.]
Huseby, Robin, (BV) ....'53 '78 C&L.585 B.A., J.D. State's Atty; County Atty.
Kringlie, Karen ....'68 '93 C.583 B.S. L.585 J.D. Juv. Ct.
Lenaburg, Dean E., (AV) ....'33 '61 C&L.585 B.S.B.A., LL.B. [Lenaburg,F.N.H.&C.]

Lenaburg, Fitzner, Nelson, Hooper & Cruff, PLLP, (AV)
First Community Credit Union Building, 149 4th Street, N.E., P.O. Box 330, 58072
Telephone: 701-845-2701 Fax: 701-845-4474
Dean E. Lenaburg (Retired); R. Jon Fitzner; Carol S. Nelson; Ralph E. Hooper; Bradley A. Cruff;— Nicholas J. Simonson.
General Civil Practice in State and Federal Courts, Real Estate, Tax, Elder Law, Estate Planning and Probate, Insurance Defense, Municipal Law, Domestic Relations, Family Law, Mediation, Agriculture Law.
Representative Clients: Wells Fargo Bank, N.A., Valley City; Valley City Barnes County Development Corp.; First Community Credit Union; Valley Tealty, Inc.; The City of Valley, City; Barnes Rural Water.

Nelson, Carol S., (BV) ....'47 '80 C.583 B.A. L.585 J.D. [Lenaburg,F.N.H.&C.]
Paulson, John T. ....'43 '67 C&L.585 B.S.B.A., J.D. Dist. J.
Paulson, William L. .... '13 '37 C.583 B.A. L.585 J.D. Sur. Jus., Supm. Ct.
Simonson, Mikal ....'47 '76 C.583 B.S. L.585 J.D. Dist. J.
Simonson, Nicholas J. .... '78 '04 C.260 L.585 [Ⓐ Lenaburg,F.N.H.&C.]
Stephan, Richard A., (BV) ....'49 '74 C&L.585 B.S.B.A., J.D. [Stephan]
Stephan Law Office, (BV) .... 108 N.E. 3rd St.
Thorson, John O., Jr. .... '35 '62 C&L.585 Ph.B., LL.B. 202 Centra Ave., S.‡
Walker, David E., (AV) ....'49 '76 C.583 B.S. L.585 J.D. 674 15th Ave. S.W.
Weisenburger, Roger R., (AV) .... '44 '69 C&L.585 B.A., J.D. 104 E. Main St.

WAHPETON, * 8,586, *Richland Co.*

Anderson, Christian M., (CV) ....'49 '74 C&L.585 B.A., J.D. 824 2nd Ave. N.
Bullis, John, (BV) ....'57 '83 C.579 B.S. L.585 J.D. [Lies&B.]
Butts, Jason R. .... '72 '03 C.358 B.A. L.585 J.D. [Ⓐ Smith,S.&F.]
Fredericksen, Janel B., (CV) .... '68 '95 C.182 B.S.B.A. L.585 J.D. [Smith,S.&F.]
Grosz, Richard W. ....'53 '84 C&L.546 B.S., J.D. Dist. J.

Jeffries, Olson & Flom, P.A.
(See Fargo)

Johnson, Samuel S., (BV) ....'63 '89 C&L.585 B.A., J.D. P.O. Box 5
Kragness, Duane Alan, (BV) ....'54 '79 C&L.585 B.S., J.D. [Kragness]
Kragness Law Office, Ltd., (BV) ....922 Dakota Ave.
Krassin, Don R., (BV) ....'48 '74 C.866 B.A. L.494 J.D. [Krassin]
Krassin Law Office, (BV) ....500 Dakota Ave., Ste. 240
Lewis, Bayard ....'18 '55 C&L.585 LL.B. Ret. Co. J.
Lies, Steven J., (AV) ....'47 '72 C&L.585 B.A., J.D. [Lies&B.]

Lies & Bullis, (AV)
610 Second Avenue North, P.O. Box 275, 58074
Telephone: 701-642-8055 Fax: 701-642-1449
URL: http://www.liesandbullislaw.com
Members of Firm: Steven J. Lies; John Bullis.
Personal Injury, Insurance Defense, Civil Litigation, Toxic Torts, Products Liability, Real Estate, Wills, Estate Planning, Probate, Family Law, Business Law, Collections, Construction Law, Governmental, Municipal Law.
Representative Clients: Norwest Bank North Dakota, N.A.-Wahpeton; First Community Credit Union, Wahpeton; Valley Realty; Cities of: Wahpeton, Hankinson, Fairmount, Great Bend, Mantador, Lidgerwood, Wyndmere, Abercrombie and Colfax; Plains Truck & Trailer Service Center.
See Professional Biographies, WAHPETON, NORTH DAKOTA

McBeth, Ronald W., (BV) '47 '79 C.584 B.A. L.585 J.D.
Asst. State Atty., Richland Co. State Atty., Pros. Off.
Meyer, Mark A., (BV) ....'59 '84 C.742 B.A. L.300 J.D. 205 N. 7th St.
Myers, Earl R., Jr., (BV) ....'38 '69 C.152 A.B. L.585 J.D. State's Atty.
Sandberg, Simone Marie, (BV) ....'52 '79 C.494 B.A. L.585 J.D. [Sandberg]
Sandberg Law Office Ltd., (BV) ....709 Dakota Ave., Ste. C
Smith, Richard E. T., (AV) ....'52 '77 C&L.190 B.A., J.D. [Smith,S.&F.]

Smith, Strege & Fredericksen, Ltd., (AV)
321 Dakota Avenue, P.O. Box 38, 58074
Telephone: 701-642-2668 Fax: 701-642-4729
Email: fredstrege@smithstrege.com URL: http://www.smithstrege.com
Richard E. T. Smith; Fred Strege; Janel B. Fredericksen;—Jason R. Butts.
Personal Injury, Automobile Accidents, Wrongful Death, Business Law, Mergers and Acquisitions, Taxation, Real Estate, Collections, Commercial Litigation, Estate Planning, Wills, Trusts and Probate, Elder Law, Banking Law, Family Law, Divorce, Support, Custody, Adoptions, Criminal Defense, Felonies, Misdemeanors, DUI, Bankruptcy, Construction Law, Mediation, Arbitration, Civil Litigation in all State and Federal Courts.
References: Community First National Bank of Wahpeton, N.D.; First Bank-Breckenridge, Mn.
See Professional Biographies, WAHPETON, NORTH DAKOTA

Stokes, A. W., (BV) ....'41 '69 C&L.585 B.S., J.D. [Stokes]
Stokes Law Office, (BV) .... 203 N. 7th St.
Strege, Fred, (AV) ....'52 '77 C&L.585 B.S.B.A., J.D. [Smith,S.&F.]

WALHALLA, 1,131, *Pembina Co.*

Schurman, Duane H. ....'49 '74 C.579 B.S. L.585 J.D. [Schurman]
Schurman Law Firm ....P.O. Box 678

WASHBURN, * 1,389, *McLean Co.*

Lindell, David A., (BV) ....'66 '94 C&L.585 B.B.A., J.D. [Lindell]
Lindell, William F., (BV) ....'34 '59 C.911 B.A. L.585 J.D. [Lindell]

Lindell Law Office, (BV)
709 Main Street, P.O. Box 427, 58577
Telephone: 701-462-8566 Fax: 701-462-3761
Email: dlindell@westriv.com
William F. Lindell; David A. Lindell; John E. Williams (1879-1973).
Estate Planning, Wills, Trusts, Probate, Real Estate, Business Law, Taxation, Collections, Commercial Litigation, Civil Practice in all State and Federal Courts.
Counsel for: Farmers Security Bank of Washburn; Bank of Turtle Lake; McLean Electric Cooperative; City of Wilton; City of Turtle Lake; City of Washburn; City of Max.
See Professional Biographies, WASHBURN, NORTH DAKOTA

Romanick, John, (BV) .... '21 '53 C&L.174 B.S., LL.B. 611 7th St.
Torkelson, Merle A. .... '41 '81 C&L.585 B.S., J.D. State's Atty.

WATFORD CITY, * 1,435, *McKenzie Co.*

Johnson, Dennis Edward, (BV) .... '56 '80 C&L.585 B.A., J.D. [Johnson&S.]

Johnson & Sundeen, Ltd., (BV)
Formerly, Dennis Edward Johnson, Ltd.
109 5th Street S.W., P.O. Box 1260, 58854
Telephone: 701-444-2211 Toll Free: 888-783-8447 Fax: 701-842-2847
Email: jslo@ruggedwest.com URL: http://www.johnsonandsundeen.com
Dennis Edward Johnson; Ross L. Sundeen.
Oil and Gas, Natural Resources, Probate, Real Estate, Collections, Personal Injury, Automobile Accidents, Professional Negligence, Wrongful Death, Medical Malpractice, Commercial Litigation, Corporate Law, Family Law, Estate Planning, Business Law, Wills and Probate, Tribal Law, Trials and Appeals.
Representative Clients: Byerly Computer Services, Ltd.; Northern States Fishing Tool Co., Inc.; Lakeside State Bank, New Town, North Dakota.
References: McKenzie County Bank, Watford City, North Dakota; Lakeside State Bank, New Town, North Dakota.
See Professional Biographies, WATFORD CITY, NORTH DAKOTA

McKennett Stenehjem Reierson Forsberg & Chapman, P.C., (AV)
P.O. Box 1469 (⊙Williston)
Reierson, Kent, (AV) .... '54 '80 C&L.585 B.S., J.D. [McKennett S.R.F.&C.] ⊙
Sundeen, Ross L., (BV) .... '64 '93 C.579 B.S. L.585 J.D. [Johnson&S.]
Taylor, James L. .... '18 '53 C.584 B.S. L.585 LL.B. 109 2nd Ave., N.E.

WEST FARGO, 14,940, *Cass Co.*

Breitling, Duane R., (AV) .... '38 '65 C&L.585 Ph.B., J.D. [Ohnstad T.] (⊙Fargo)
Demeterio, Arabella Rita .... '62 '96 C.999 B.A. L.585 J.D. 1687 Oakwood Dr.
Dosland, John P., (AVⓉ) .... '30 '57 C&L.494 B.A., J.D. [Ⓐ Ohnstad T.]
Ellison, Susan L., (BV) .... '54 '90 C&L.585 B.A., J.D. P.O. Box 458 (⊙West Fargo)
Ellison, Susan L., (BV) .... '54 '90 C&L.585 B.A., J.D. [Ohnstad T.] (⊙West Fargo)
Foyt, Brenda R., (CV) .... '65 '97 C&L.585 B.A., J.D. [Ⓐ Ohnstad T.]
Fujimoto, Leah, (BV) .... '55 '81 C.494 B.A. L.1035 J.D. 330 Edgewater Drive
Hoy, Robert G., (AV) .... '53 '78 C.477 B.S. L.585 J.D. [Ohnstad T.]
McCullough, Marshall William, (BV) .... '62 '87 C.585 B.B.A. L.208 J.D. [Ohnstad T.]
McCullough, Steven E., (BV) .... '62 '87 C.491 B.A. L.585 J.D. [Ohnstad T.]
Nelson, Michael D., (BV) .... '51 '76 C.972 B.A. L.585 J.D. [Ohnstad T.]
Neugebauer, Brian D., (AV) .... '51 '77 C.182 B.A. L.585 J.D. [Ohnstad T.]
Ohnstad Twichell, P.C., (AV) .... 901 13th Avenue East (⊙Fargo, Hillsboro, Mayville)
Overboe, David A. .... '43 '72 C.579 B.S. L.585 J.D. [Overboe]
Overboe Law Office .... 1042 14th Ave. E., Ste. 201
Rindy, Dean A., (BV) .... '58 '86 C.579 B.A. L.585 J.D. [Ohnstad T.]
Rosenvold, Robert E., (AV) .... '47 '72 C.79 B.S. L.585 J.D. [Ohnstad T.]
Twichell, Daniel R., (AV) .... '27 '52 L.585 J.D. [Ohnstad T.]
Wanner, David L., (AV) .... '47 '72 C.579 B.A. L.585 J.D. [Ohnstad T.]

WILLISTON, * 12,512, *Williams Co.*

Anseth, LeRoy P. .... '37 '62 C&L.585 B.S., LL.B. 417 1st Ave.‡
Armstrong, Lee Edwin .... '59 '92 C.508 B.A. L.585 J.D. Asst. States' Atty.
Beede, William M. .... '22 '49 C&L.585 B.S., J.D. Surrogate J.‡
Bjella, Arley, (AV) .... '16 '41 C&L.585 LL.B. 111 E. Broadway
Chapman, Kevin J., (CV) .... '65 '93 C&L.585 B.S.P.A., J.D. 417 1st Ave., E.

Crowley, Haughey, Hanson, Toole & Dietrich P.L.L.P., (AV)
111 East Broadway, P.O. Box 1206, 58801 ⊙
Telephone: 701-572-2200 Fax: 701-752-7072
Email: crowley@crowleylaw.com URL: http://www.crowleylaw.com
Partners: Shane Douglas Peterson; Fred C. Rathert; Garth H. Sjue. Associates: Kenneth G. Hedge. Of Counsel: Bruce A. Fredrickson; Fred E. Whisenand.
General Civil Practice. Litigation, Insurance, Workers Compensation, Personal Injury, Products Liability, Malpractice, Bankruptcy, Financing Transactions, Administrative, Immigration, Antitrust, Banking, Corporate, Commercial, Real Estate, Public Utilities, Securities, Tax, Municipal and Tax Exempt Bonds, Entertainment, Health Care, Agricultural, Estate Planning, Probate, Pension and Profit Sharing, Natural Resources including Oil and Gas, Mining, Environmental and Water Law, Employment Law, Indian Law and Intellectual Property.
Representative Clients: Montana Power Co.; First Interstate Bank of Commerce; MDU Resources Group, Inc.; Chevron U.S.A., Inc.; Noranda Minerals Corp.; United Parcel Service.
Insurance Clients: Farmers Insurance Group; New York Life Insurance Co.
Billings, Montana Office: 500 Transwestern Plaza II, 490 North 31st Street, P.O. Box 2529, 59103-2529. Telephone: 406-252-3441. Fax: 406-259-4159.
Helena, Montana Office: IBM Building, 100 North Park Avenue, Suite 300, 59601. Telephone: 406-449-4165. Fax: 406-449-5149.
Kalispell, Montana Office: 431 1st Avenue West, 59901. Telephone: 406-752-6644. Fax: 406-752-5108.
Bozeman, Montana Office: 45 Discovery Drive, Suite 200, P.O. Box 10969, 59715. Telephone: 406-556-1430. Fax: 406-556-1433.
Missoula, Montana Office: 700 S.W. Higgins Avenue, Suite 200, 59803. Telephone: 406-829-2732. Fax: 406-829-2722.
Reviser of the Montana Law Digest for this Directory.
See Professional Biographies, WILLISTON, NORTH DAKOTA

Eiken, Dwight C., (BV) .... '51 '76 C.579 B.S. L.585 J.D. [Neff C.E.&I.]
Forsberg, Laurel J., (BV) .... '60 '86 C&L.585 B.S.B.A., J.D. [McKennett S.R.F.&H.]
Fredrickson, Bruce A., (BVⓉ) '55 '86 C.579 B.S. L.585 J.D.
[Ⓒ Crowley,H.H.T.&D.P.]
Furuseth, Peter H., (BV) .... '58 '84 C&L.585 B.A., J.D. States Atty. [Imes&F.]
Hedge, Kenneth G., (BV) .... '73 '99 C.506 B.A. L.972 J.D. [Ⓐ Crowley,H.H.T.&D.P.]
Hennessy, Greg W., (BV) .... '52 '77 C&L.585 B.A., J.D. [Hennessy]

Hennessy Law Office, P.C., (BV)
417 1st Avenue East, Drawer 756, 58802-0756
Telephone: 701-572-8296 Fax: 701-572-9181
Email: integrated@nemontel.net URL: http://www.lawyers.com/hennessylawoffice
Greg W. Hennessy.
Professional Malpractice, Oil and Gas, Personal Injury, Automobile Accidents, Wrongful Death, Employment Law, Child Custody for Husband, Civil Trial Practice, Alternative Dispute Resolution.
See Professional Biographies, WILLISTON, NORTH DAKOTA

Hermanson, David T., (CV) .... '73 '99 C.999 B.S. L.585 J.D. [McKennett S.R.F.&H.]
Hermanson, Valeska A., (CV) ..... '69 '99 C.488 B.A. L.585 J.D. [McKennett S.R.F.&H.]
Imes, Andrew C., (CV) .... '51 '76 C&L.585 B.S., J.D. 3 4th St., E.
Imes, Kathleen E. Key, (BV) .... '55 '84 C&L.585 B.A., J.D. [Imes&F.]
Imes & Furuseth, P.C., (BV) .... 3 E. 4th Street, Suite 201

Johnson & Sundeen, Ltd.
(See Watford City)

Kaiser, Marvin L., (AV) .... '43 '69 C&L.585 B.S.B.A., J.D. 201 East 26th Street
MacMaster, John H., (BV) .... '48 '74 C&L.585 B.S.B.A., J.D. [MacMaster]
MacMaster Law Firm, Ltd., (BV) .... 123 East Broadway
McIntee, Michael R., (AV) .... '21 '53 C&L.585 B.S., J.D. 1208 4th Ave., E.‡
McKennett, Richard A., (AV) .... '44 '69 C&L.585 B.A., J.D. [McKennett S.R.F.&H.]
McKennett Stenehjem Reierson Forsberg & Hermanson, P.C., (AV)
314 First Avenue East (⊙Watford City)
Neff, Charles L., (BV) .... '57 '83 C.585 B.S.B.A. L.862 J.D. [Neff C.E.&I.]
Neff, Vern C., (AV) .... '27 '52 C&L.585 B.S.C., J.D. [Neff C.E.&I.]
Neff Cresap Eiken & Irigoin, P.C., (AV) .... 111 East Broadway (⊙Lambert, MT)
Nelson, David W. .... '51 '81 C&L.585 B.A., J.D. Dist. J.

Nilles, Ilvedson, Stroup, Plambeck & Selbo, Ltd., (AV)
Plainsman Building, 3 - 4th Street East, Suite 206, P.O. Box 1525, 58802-1525 ⊙
Telephone: 701-572-5544 Fax: 701-572-5561
URL: http://www.nilleslaw.com
H. Malcolm Pippin.
Civil Litigation, Commercial Litigation, Insurance Law, Errors and Omissions Litigation, Tort, Product Liability, Personal Injury, Railroad, Construction Litigation, Appeals, Professional Liability, Business Law, Probate, Estate Planning, Real Estate, Commercial Law, Banking, Bankruptcy, Employment Law and Worker's Compensation.
State Counsel: Burlington Northern, Inc.
General Counsel: First Bank of North Dakota (NA) Fargo; First Bank (fsb); Blue Cross and Blue Shield of North Dakota; Nodak Mutual Insurance Co.; Pioneer Mutual Life Insurance Co.
Fargo, North Dakota Office: 1800 Radisson Tower, 201 North 5th Street, P.O. Box 2626. Telephone: 701-237-5544. Fax: 701-280-0762.
Moorhead, Minnesota Office: 1401 South 8th Street. Telephone: 218-233-7407. Fax: 218-233-5133.
Reviser of the North Dakota Law Digest for this Directory.
See Professional Biographies, WILLISTON, NORTH DAKOTA

Peterson, Shane Douglas, (BV) ..... '69 '95 C&L.585 B.A., J.D. [Crowley,H.H.T.&D.P.]
Pippin, H. Malcolm, (BV) .... '63 '89 C&L.585 B.B.A., J.D. [Nilles,I.S.P.&S.]
Rathert, Fred C., (AV) .... '40 '65 C.747 B.A. L.508 LL.B. [Crowley,H.H.T.&D.P.]
Reierson, Kent, (AV) .... '54 '80 C&L.585 B.S., J.D. [McKennett S.R.F.&H.] ⊙
Rustad, Gerald .... '44 '69 C&L.585 B.A., J.D. Dist. J.
Rustad, Josh B., (BV) .... '72 '99 C&L.585 B.A., J.D. [Ⓐ Neff C.E.&I.]
Schmitz, Cathy Howe, (BV) .... '55 '79 C&L.585 B.S.B.A., J.D. [Schmitz]
Schmitz Law Office, P.C., (BV) .... 421 East 20th Street
Sjue, Garth H., (BV) .... '53 '82 C&L.585 B.S.B.A., J.D. [Crowley,H.H.T.&D.P.]
Sogard, Patrick O., (BV) '58 '86 C&L.585 B.S.G.E., J.D.
American State Bank & Trust Co., Trust Dept.
Stenehjem, Mark L., (AV) .... '48 '73 C.182 B.A. L.508 J.D. [McKennett S.R.F.&H.]
Suess, John A., (BV) .... '55 '80 C&L.585 B.S.B.A., J.D. [Suess]
Suess Law Firm, P.C., (BV) .... 222 Univ. Ave.
Thompson, Gordon C. .... '24 '54 C&L.585 B.S., J.D. Sr. Co. J.
Walters, William D., Jr., (BV) .... '52 '77 C.86 B.S. L.508 J.D. [Walters]
Walters Law Office, (BV) .... 1121 2nd Avenue West
Whisenand, Fred E., (AV) .... '29 '57 C&L.585 Ph.B., J.D. [Ⓒ Crowley,H.H.T.&D.P.]
Wilder, Charles .... '54 '87 C.579 B.S. L.585 J.D. State Atty.
Wilder, Marlyce A., (BV) .... '54 '93 C&L.585 B.B.A., J.D. [Ⓐ MacMaster]
Wilson, Bert L., Jr. .... '21 '49 L.585 J.D. Ret. Dist. J.
Winkjer, Dean, (AV) .... '23 '47 C&L.585 Ph.B., J.D. 1202 Hilcourt‡
Zander, Janet Holter, (BV) .... '55 '80 C&L.585 B.S.B.A., J.D. [Zander]
Zander Law Office, P.C., (BV) .... 501 E. Bway., Suite 100

WISHEK, 1,171, *McIntosh Co.*

Herr, Richard E. .... '29 '57 C.585 B.A. L.309 LL.B. 13 N. 6th St.
Hoberg, Gordon O. .... '29 '59 C.358 B.S. L.585 LL.B. 6771 41st Ave., S.E.‡
Ogren, David Neil .... '67 '95 C.579 B.S. L.585 J.D. P.O Box 825

OHIO

CAPITAL: COLUMBUS

Ohio State Bar Association
1700 Lake Shore Drive
P.O. Box 16562
Columbus, Ohio 43216-6562
Telephone: 800-282-6556
Fax: 614-487-1008

Index of Towns and Cities Listed by County

*Indicates County Seat

Adams County
* West Union

Allen County
Bluffton
Delphos
* Lima
Spencerville

Ashland County
* Ashland
Loudonville
Perrysville

Ashtabula County
Andover
Ashtabula
Austinburg
Conneaut
Geneva
* Jefferson
Kingsville
North Kingsville
Rome

Athens County
* Athens
Guysville
Nelsonville

Auglaize County
Minster
New Bremen
St. Marys
* Wapakoneta
Waynesfield

Belmont County
Barnesville
Bellaire
Bridgeport
Martins Ferry
* St. Clairsville
Shadyside

Brown County
Aberdeen
Fayetteville
* Georgetown
Mt. Orab
Ripley

Butler County
Fairfield
* Hamilton
Middletown
Monroe
Oxford
Ross
Sharonville
Trenton
West Chester

Carroll County
* Carrollton
Magnolia
Malvern
Minerva
Sherrodsville

Champaign County
Mechanicsburg
* Urbana

Clark County
Enon
New Carlisle
* Springfield

Clermont County
Amelia
* Batavia
Bethel
Chilo
Felicity
Loveland
Milford
New Richmond
Williamsburg

Clinton County
Blanchester
New Vienna
Sabina
* Wilmington

Columbiana County
Columbiana
Damascus
East Liverpool
East Palestine
Leetonia
* Lisbon
Minerva
New Waterford
Salem
Wellsville

Coshocton County
* Coshocton

Crawford County
* Bucyrus
Crestline
Galion

Cuyahoga County
Bay Village
Beachwood
Bedford
Bedford Heights
Bentleyville
Berea
Bratenahl
Brecksville
Broadview Heights
Brooklyn
Brooklyn Heights
Brook Park
Chagrin Falls
* Cleveland
Cleveland Heights
Euclid
Fairview Park
Garfield Heights
Gates Mills
Highland Heights
Highland Hills
Independence

Cuyahoga Co.—*Continued*
Lakewood
Lyndhurst
Maple Heights
Mayfield
Mayfield Heights
Mayfield Village
Middleburg Heights
Moreland Hills
Newburgh Heights
North Olmsted
North Royalton
Olmsted Falls
Orange Village
Parma
Parma Heights
Pepper Pike
Richmond Heights
Rocky River
Seven Hills
Shaker Heights
Solon
South Euclid
Strongsville
University Heights
Walton Hills
Warrensville Heights
Westlake
Woodmere

Darke County
Arcanum
* Greenville
Versailles

Defiance County
* Defiance
Hicksville

Delaware County
Columbus
* Delaware
Dublin
Galena
Lewis Center
Powell
Sunbury
Westerville

Erie County
Huron
Milan
* Sandusky
Vermilion

Fairfield County
Amanda
Baltimore
Bremen
Canal Winchester
Columbus
* Lancaster
Millersport
Pickerington
Pleasantville
Reynoldsburg

Fayette County
Bloomingburg
New Holland
* Washington C. H.

Franklin County
Bexley
Canal Winchester
* Columbus
Dublin
Gahanna
Galloway
Grandview Heights
Grove City
Groveport
Hilliard
New Albany
Pickerington
Reynoldsburg
Upper Arlington
Westerville
Whitehall
Worthington

Fulton County
Archbold
Delta
Fayette
Metamora
Swanton
* Wauseon

Gallia County
* Gallipolis

Geauga County
Bainbridge
Burton
* Chardon
Chesterland
Newbury
Novelty

Greene County
Beavercreek
Bellbrook
Cedarville
Fairborn
Wilberforce
* Xenia
Yellow Springs

Guernsey County
Byesville
* Cambridge
Cumberland

Hamilton County
Blue Ash
* Cincinnati
Cleves
Evendale
Glendale
Harrison
Loveland
Mariemont
Montgomery
Mt. Healthy
North Bend

Hamilton Co.—*Continued*
Norwood
Reading
Sharonville
Terrace Park
Wyoming

Hancock County
Bluffton
* Findlay
Fostoria

Hardin County
Ada
* Kenton

Harrison County
Adena
* Cadiz
Hopedale

Henry County
Deshler
* Napoleon

Highland County
Greenfield
* Hillsboro

Hocking County
* Logan
Rockbridge

Holmes County
Loudonville
* Millersburg
Mt. Hope

Huron County
Bellevue
Milan
Monroeville
New London
* Norwalk
Willard

Jackson County
* Jackson
Wellston

Jefferson County
Adena
Dillonvale
* Steubenville
Tiltonsville
Toronto
Wintersville

Knox County
Centerburg
Danville
Fredericktown
Gambier
Howard
* Mt. Vernon

Lake County
Concord
Eastlake
Fairport Harbor
Kirtland
Madison
Mentor
* Painesville
Perry
Waite Hill
Wickliffe
Willoughby
Willoughby Hills
Willowick

Lawrence County
Chesapeake
* Ironton
Proctorville
South Point

Licking County
Alexandria
Granville
Heath
Hebron
Johnstown
* Newark
Pataskala
Reynoldsburg
Utica

Logan County
* Bellefontaine
Degraff
Huntsville
Lakeview
Russells Point
West Liberty

Lorain County
Amherst
Avon
Avon Lake
Columbia Station
* Elyria
Grafton
Lagrange
Lorain
North Ridgeville
Oberlin
Sheffield Lake
Sheffield Village
Vermilion
Wellington

Lucas County
Curtice
Holland
Maumee
Monclova
Oregon
Ottawa Hills
Sylvania
* Toledo
Waterville
Whitehouse

Madison County
* London
Mt. Sterling
Plain City
West Jefferson

Mahoning County
Alliance
Austintown
Boardman
Campbell
Canfield
Columbiana
Damascus
Lake Milton
Mineral Ridge
New Middletown

Mahoning Co.—*Continued*
North Jackson
North Lima
Petersburg
Poland
Sebring
Struthers
* Youngstown

Marion County
* Marion
Morral
Prospect

Medina County
Brunswick
Hinckley
Lodi
* Medina
Rittman
Seville
Sharon Center
Wadsworth
Westfield Center

Meigs County
* Pomeroy
Reedsville

Mercer County
* Celina
Coldwater

Miami County
Conover
Covington
Piqua
Tipp City
* Troy
West Milton

Monroe County
* Woodsfield

Montgomery County
Brookville
Centerville
Clayton
* Dayton
Englewood
Germantown
Huber Heights
Kettering
Miamisburg
New Lebanon
Oakwood
Springboro
Trotwood
Vandalia
West Carrollton

Morgan County
* McConnelsville

Morrow County
Cardington
Marengo
* Mt. Gilead

Muskingum County
Chandlersville
New Concord
* Zanesville

Noble County
* Caldwell

Ottawa County
Curtice
Elmore
Genoa
Lakeside
Oak Harbor
* Port Clinton
Put-In-Bay

Paulding County
Antwerp
* Paulding

Perry County
Junction City
* New Lexington
New Straitsville
Somerset
Thornville

Pickaway County
Ashville
* Circleville
New Holland

Pike County
Beaver
Piketon
* Waverly

Portage County
Aurora
Brimfield
Diamond
Garrettsville
Hiram
Kent
Mantua
Mogadore
* Ravenna
Rootstown
Streetsboro
Tallmadge

Preble County
Camden
* Eaton
Lewisburg
West Alexandria

Putnam County
Columbus Grove
Leipsic
* Ottawa
Pandora

Richland County
Butler
Lexington
Lucas
* Mansfield
Shelby

Ross County
* Chillicothe
Kingston

Sandusky County
Bellevue
Clyde
* Fremont
Gibsonburg
Woodville

Scioto County
Lucasville
McDermott
Minford
New Boston
* Portsmouth
South Webster
Wheelersburg

Seneca County
Fostoria
* Tiffin

Shelby County
Fort Loramie
* Sidney

Stark County
Alliance
Beach City
Brewster
Canal Fulton
* Canton
East Canton
Hartville
Louisville
Magnolia
Massillon
Minerva
Navarre
North Canton
Uniontown

Summit County
* Akron
Barberton
Bath
Clinton
Copley
Cuyahoga Falls
Fairlawn
Hudson
Lakemore
Macedonia
Mogadore
Munroe Falls
Northfield
Northfield Center
Norton
Richfield
Sagamore Hills
Silver Lake
Stow
Tallmadge
Twinsburg

Trumbull County
Brookfield
Cortland
Girard
Hubbard
Kinsman
Masury
Mineral Ridge
Newton Falls
Niles
Vienna
* Warren
Youngstown

Tuscarawas County
Dover
Gnadenhutten
Mineral City
* New Philadelphia
Strasburg
Sugarcreek
Uhrichsville

Union County
Dublin
* Marysville
Milford Center
Plain City
Raymond
Richwood

Van Wert County
Delphos
Ohio City
* Van Wert

Vinton County
* McArthur

Warren County
Franklin
* Lebanon
Loveland
Maineville
Mason
Middletown

Warren Co.—*Continued*
Springboro
Waynesville

Washington County
Belpre
* Marietta

Wayne County
Dalton
Doylestown
Kidron
Orrville
Rittman
Shreve
West Salem
* Wooster

Williams County
* Bryan
Edon
Montpelier
Stryker

Wood County
* Bowling Green
Fostoria
Grand Rapids
North Baltimore
Northwood
Pemberville
Perrysburg
Rising Sun
Rossford
Walbridge
Wayne

Wyandot County
Carey
Sycamore
* Upper Sandusky

*Indicates County Seat

ABERDEEN, 1,603, *Brown Co.*

Shaw, Gerald W. .... '33 '68 C.383 A.B. L.1003 J.D. P.O. Box 615

ADA, 5,582, *Hardin Co.*

Benson, David J. '42 '71 C.475 B.A. L.823 J.D.
Prof. of Law, Ohio Northern Univ., College of Law
Biddinger, Michael J. .... '59 '87 C&L.607 B.M.Ed., J.D. Ohio Northern Univ.
Brant, Joanne C. '61 '86 C.188 A.B. L.930 J.D.
Assoc. Prof. of Law, Ohio Northern Univ.
Caw, Melanie J. .... '61 '86 C.607 B.A. L.880 J.D. P.O. Box 233
Christoff, John P. '43 '77 C.602 M.A. L.607 J.D.
Prof. of Law, Ohio Northern Univ., School of Law
Crago, David C., (AV) '52 '77 C.228 A.B. L.477 J.D.
Prof. of Law, Ohio Northern Univ., School of Law
Crider, Cecily A., (CV) '52 '93 C&L.607 B.A., J.D.
Dir., Legal Research & Writing, ONU Coll. of Law‡
Failor, Kenneth G. .... '40 '66 C&L.607 B.A., J.D. [K.G.Failor]
Failor, Kenneth George .... 127 S. Main St.
Fenton, Howard Nathan '50 '75
C&L.846 B.S., J.D. Prof., Ohio Northern Univ., School of Law
French, Bruce Comly '47 '75 C.30 B.A. L.1162 J.D.
Prof. of Law, Ohio Northern Univ., Col. of Law
Grimslid, Gregory, (BV) .... '56 '81 C&L.607 B.A., J.D. [Grimslid&H.]
Grimslid and Hood, (BV) .... 229 N. Main St.
Guy, Daniel S. .... '28 '52 C.611 B.A. L.607 J.D. Ohio Northern Univ., Col. of Law
Haight, Richard L. '41 '65 C.94 A.B. L.818 J.D.
(adm. in MA; not adm. in OH) Prof. of Law, Ohio Northern Univ.
Hanson, Eugene N. .... '17 '46 C.427 B.A. L.966 J.D. Ret. Co. J.‡
Hill, Kevin D. '50 '80 C.383 B.S. L.1161 J.D.
(adm. in KY; not adm. in OH) Prof. of Law, Ohio Northern Univ., Col. of Law
Hood, J. Michael, (BV) .... '56 '81 C&L.607 B.A., J.D. [Grimslid&H.]
Laughlin, Gregory K. '61 '86 C.804 B.A. L.502 J.D.
(adm. in MO; not adm. in OH)
Dir., Law Lib. & Asst. Prof. of Law, Ohio Northern Univ.
Lobenhofer, Louis F. '50 '75 C.945 A.B. L.174 J.D.
(adm. in CO; not adm. in OH) Prof. of Law, OH Northern Univ.
Manley, Victoria Anne '43 '78 C&L.608 B.S.C., J.D.
Asst. Prof., Ohio Northern Univ., Col. of Law
McNeal, Jan C., (BV) .... '41 '66 C&L.607 B.A., J.D. 231 1/2 N. Main St.
Previte, Peter A. .... '43 '78 C.999 B.SC. L.607 J.D. 405 N. Main St.
Raack, David W. '54 '79 C.378 B.A. L.986 J.D.
(adm. in MO; not adm. in OH) Prof. of Law, Ohio Northern Univ.
Shea, Jennifer L. '65 '90 C.473 B.A. L.966 J.D.
(adm. in WI; not adm. in OH) Ohio Northern Univ.
Streib, Victor L. '41 '70 C.10 B.S.I.E. L.1119 J.D.
(adm. in IN; not adm. in OH) Dean, Ohio Northern Univ., Col. of Law
Traster, Vernon L. '47 '73 C&L.221 B.S.B.A., J.D.
(adm. in IA; not adm. in OH) Prof. of Law, Ohio Northern Univ., Col. of Law

VanDyne, Charles, (AV) '30 '54 C&L.607 B.A., J.D.
Huber Building, 231 1/2 North Main Street, 45810
Telephone: 419-634-5791 Fax: 419-634-9242
General Practice in all Courts. Probate and Estate Planning, Corporation, Negligence, Real Estate Law, Banking and Insurance. Trials.
See Professional Biographies, ADA, OHIO

Vaubel, Claire Morris .... '40 '71 C.62 B.A. L.607 J.D. 328 W. Lima Ave.
Veltri, Stephen C. '55 '81 C.665 B.A. L.276 J.D.
(adm. in PA; not adm. in OH) Prof. of Law, Onio Northern Univ., Col. of Law
Wells, Mindi L. '— '98 C&L.607 B.S.B.A., J.D.
Asst. Dean, OH Northern Univ., Pettit Coll. of Law
Young, Sherry '60 '84 C.475 B.A. L.309 J.D.
Prof. of Law, Ohio Northern Univ., Col. of Law

ADENA, 815, *Harrison & Jefferson Cos.*

Figurski, George A. .... '57 '84 C.608 B.S. L.851 J.D. P.O. Box RD #1 Box 173

AKRON, * 217,074, *Summit Co.*

Aberth, Joel R., (BV) .... '42 '71 C.608 B.S. L.8 J.D. [Aberth&C.]

Aberth & Champion Co., LPA, (BV)
3296 West Market Street, Suite D, 44333-3355
Telephone: 330-865-7722 Fax: 330-865-9742 URL: http://www.aberth-champion.com
Email: thchampion@aberth-champion.com URL: http://www.lawyers.com/aberth&championlaw
Joel R. Aberth; Timothy H. Champion.
Trust Administration, Estate Administration, Estate Planning, Probate, Real Estate, Elder Law.
See Professional Biographies, AKRON, OHIO

Abramson, Susan H. .... '51 '84 C.1313 B.A. L.930 J.D. 794 Wye Road
Adams, Jason Thomas, (BV) '63 '89 C.8 B.A. L.7 J.D.
Judicial Asst., Summit County Court of Common Plees
Adams, John R., (BV) .... '55 '83 C.97 B.S. L.7 J.D. U.S. District J
Adams, Tanzie .... '50 '85 C.161 B.B.A. L.1003 J.D. Mgr., First Energy Corp.
Adamson, Paul F., (BV) .... '49 '82 C.8 B.S. L.7 J.D. [Burdon&M.]
Adinolfi, Karen D. .... '69 '01 C.851 B.A. L.8 J.D. [Ⓐ Roetzel&A.]
Afarin, Lisa Marie Barbacci .... '59 '87 C.8 B.S. L.7 J.D. Law Clk., U.S. Bkrptcy. J.
Ahonen, Robert M. ...... '55 '87 C.8 B.S. L.1003 J.D. Advanced Elastomer Systems, L.P.
Alberti, John Curtis, (BV) .... '50 '79 C.8 J.D. L.610 B.A. [J.C.Alberti]
Alberti, John Curtis, Co., L.P.A., (BV) .... 525 North Cleveland-Massillon Road
Albrecht, Fred I. .... '17 '51 C.165 B.A. L.7 LL.B. 458 St. Andrews Dr.‡
Albrecht, Sophie E. .... '49 '78 C&L.08 B.A., J.D. 650 Dan St.
Allan, Ronald C., (AV) .... '37 '65 C&L.477 A.B., J.D. [Buckingham,D.&B.]
Altier, Mary W. .... '27 '79 C.980 B.S. L.7 J.D. 534 Garnette Rd.
Altwies, Charles J., (BV) .... '47 '76 C.381 B.B.A. L.7 J.D. 80 S. Portage Path

Amer Cunningham Co., L.P.A., (AV)
Key Building, 159 South Main Street, Suite 1100, 44308-1322
Telephone: 330-762-2411 Telecopy: 330-762-9918
URL: http://www.amer-law.com
Bernard J. Amer (1896-1985); Ernest L. Cunningham (1897-1971); Joseph F. Cook, Jr.; Andrew R. Duff; Jack Morrison, Jr.; Michael S. Urban; Joseph F. Cook (1926-1998); Thomas M. Saxer; Theresa A. Tarchinski;—Thomas R. Houlihan; J. Francis Mackey; Lisa A. Fike; Mark Gerald Stasitis; Daniel L. Silfani (Resident Bath, Ohio); Sergio A. Carano; Suzanne M. Gradisher.
General Civil Trial and Appellate Practice. Real Estate, Zoning, Corporate, Taxation, Labor, Personal Injury, Public Law, Probate, Trust, Pension and Profit Sharing, Estate Planning Law and Workers' Compensation, Government, Municipal and Public Law, Health Care Law.
See Professional Biographies, AKRON, OHIO

Amonett, Landon P. .... '45 '76 C.8 B.A. L.7 J.D. 86 Pocan Tico Ave.
Amundsen, Richard S. .... '49 '74 C.893 B.A. L.608 J.D. Sr. V.P., National City Bank
Andreeff, Nickolas P., (AV) .... '31 '61 C&L.8 B.A., J.D. [Ⓒ Brennan,M.&D.]
Armbruster, Robert, (BV) .... '52 '78 C.8 B.S.I.M. L.7 J.D. [Armbruster,K.K.H.&B.]
Armbruster, Kelley, Kot, Honeck & Baker, (AV) .... 159 S. Main St.
Arnold, Suzanne E. .... '68 '98 C&L.8 B.A., J.D. Asst. V.P., National City Bank
Aronson, Stanley P. .... '41 '70 C.8 B.A. L.7 J.D. 3085 W. Market St.
Ashley, Richard W. .... '49 '74 C&L.8 B.A., J.D. [Ashley&Assoc.]
Ashley & Associates .... 88 North Miller Road
Assaf, Timothy P., (BV) .... '57 '83 C.699 B.A. L.7 J.D. 230 White Pond Dr., Ste. A
Atwell, D. Cheryl, (AV) .... '50 '80 C.502 B.M. L.930 J.D. [Ⓐ Reminger&R.]
Axner, E. Arthur, (BV) .... '38 '62 C&L.930 B.A., J.D. 80 S. Summit St.
Aydin, Pauline R. .... '63 '96 C.309 B.A. L.7 J.D. Corp. Coun., Aydin Co.
Aynes, Richard L. '49 '75
C.473 B.S. L.1003 J.D. Dean & Prof., Univ. of Akron, Sch. of Law
Bach, Lawrence R., (BV) .... '54 '84 C.201 A.B. L.930 J.D. [Roderick L.]
Bagdasarian, Richard C., (AVⓉ) .... '55 '83 C.318 B.A. L.8 J.D. [Bagdasarian&B.] ⊙
Bagdasarian & Briggs, (AVⓉ) .... 4367 State Road (⊙Boca Raton, FL)
Bagga, Rajesh .... '64 '97 C.659 B.S.E.E. L.930 J.D. [Brouse M.]
Baird, William R. .... '34 '59 C.31 A.B. L.930 LL.B. 161 South High Street
Baker, Michael D., (BV) .... '32 '61 C.8 B.A. L.94 LL.B. [Hardesty,K.&Z.]
Baker, Robert C., (AV) .... '51 '77 C.399 B.A. L.7 J.D. [Armbruster,K.K.H.&B.]
Balmert, F. Daniel, (AV) .... '51 '76 C.602 B.A. L.117 J.D. [Vorys,S.S.&P.]
Barber, Mark H. .... '55 '87 C&L.8 B.S., J.D. Cole Co., L.P.A.
Barker, Laura L., (BV) .... '65 '92 C&L.8 B.A., J.D. 75 E. Market St.
Barnes, Heather M. .... '72 '99 C.8 B.S. L.607 J.D. [Ⓐ Brouse M.] (Pat.)
Barnes, Philip G. .... '15 '53 C.8 L.7 LL.B. Chief of Police‡
Barnes, W. Stuart .... '25 '57 C.381 B.S. L.7 J.D. 49 Borton Ave.
Barnhart, Jacqueline Mary, (BV) .... '47 '81 C.608 B.A. L.7 J.D. Asst. Co. Pros.
Barnum, Anna Maria .... '43 '77 C.478 A.B. L.7 J.D. Prof., Univ. of Akron‡
Barrett, John R., (AV) .... '27 '53 C.8 B.A. L.930 LL.B. [Barrett&D.]
Barrett & Davis, (AV) .... 159 S. Main Street

Bartek, Dennis J., (AV) '46 '71 C&L.8 B.A., J.D.
2300 East Market Street Suite E, 44312
Telephone: 330-784-8580 Fax: 330-784-8434
Email: DJBARTEK@AOL.COM
Trial Litigation, Wrongful Death, Personal Injury, Medical Malpractice, Products Liability, Business Litigation, Insurance Law, Criminal Law.
See Professional Biographies, AKRON, OHIO

Bartilson, Thomas R. .... '70 '04 C.8 B.S. L.7 J.D. [Ⓐ Guy,L.&T.]
Bartilson, William R., Sr. '37 '72
C.608 B.S. L.7 J.D. Atty., The Goodyear Tire & Rubber Co.
Batchelder, Wm. G., III, (BV) .... '42 '67 C.611 B.A. L.608 J.D. Appls. Ct. J.
Battagline, Richard F., (AV) .... '45 '70 C.610 B.B.A. L.602 J.D. [Brouse M.]
Bauer, Roland H., (BV) .... '54 '80 C.896 B.A. L.608 J.D. The Cypress Cos., Inc.
Bayer, Edward A. .... '28 '61 C.8 B.A. L.930 J.D. 209 South High Street
Bean, Gregory R. '50 '77 C.8 B.A. L.7 J.D.
Sr. V.P. & Sr. Tr. Offr., First Natl. Bk. of Ohio
Becker, John W. .... '69 '95 C.27 B.A. L.930 J.D. [Roetzel&A.]
Becker, Robert James, (BV) .... '— '82 U.S. Atty. Off.
Becker, William C., (AV) '29 '57
C.309 A.B. L.477 J.D. Prof. Emeritus of Law, Univ. of Akron
Beidler, Craig W. .... '59 '86 C.381 B.A. L.930 J.D. [Ⓐ Roderick L.]
Beistel, Peggy S. .... '66 '99 C.1260 B.A. L.124 J.D. [Ⓐ Buckingham,D.&B.]
Beiting, Michael R. '51 '77 C.138 B.A. L.383 J.D.
Assoc. Gen. Coun., FirstEnergy Corp.
Belfance, Eve Virginia .... '62 '90 C.976 B.A. L.930 J.D. 1 Cascade Plz., Ste. 2100
Belfance, Kathryn A., (AV) .... '37 '77 C.8 B.A. L.7 J.D. [K.A.Belfance&Assoc.]
Belfance, Kathryn A., & Associates, L.L.C., (AV) .... One Cascade Plaza, Suite 2100
Bell, Bertram '51 '76 C&L.930 B.A., J.D.
Assoc. Gen. Coun., Goodyear Tire & Rubber Company, The
Bell, Daniel L., (BV) .... '63 '90 C.846 B.A. L.8 J.D. [Brouse M.]
Bell, Sam H. .... '25 '52 C.970 B.A. L.8 J.D. U.S. Sr. Dist. J.
Bennett, Timothy D. .... '60 '02 C&L.8 B.S., J.D. [Ⓐ Brouse M.]
Benz, Gary D., (AV) '59 '84 C.97 B.S. L.851 J.D.
Assoc. Gen. Coun., FirstEnergy Corp.
Berg, Sharon, (BV) .... '45 '76 C&L.8 B.A., J.D. [S.Berg]

Berg, Sharon, Co., LPA, (BV)
784 Kenmore Boulevard, 44314
Telephone: 330-745-1000 Fax: 330-745-2661
Email: attyberg@sbcglobal.net URL: http://www.sberglaw.com
Member of Firm: Sharon Berg.
Family Law, Divorce, Dissolution, Separation Agreements, Spousal Support, Premarital Agreements, Post Divorce Modification, Domestic Violence, Child Custody, Child Support, Visitation, Paternity, Grandparents' Rights, Collaborative Divorce, Juvenile Law.
See Professional Biographies, AKRON, OHIO

Berger, Joshua S. .... '70 '97 C.659 B.A. L.930 J.D. [Ⓐ Buckingham,D.&B.]
Berke, Aaron S. .... '— '00 C.659 B.A. L.477 J.D. [Ⓐ Vorys,S.S.&P.]
Bernard, Aretta K., (AV) .... '62 '87 C.385 B.A. L.7 J.D. [Roetzel&A.]

Bernard Law Firm, The
(See Cleveland)

Bernel, Bruce G., (CV) .... '49 '76 C.381 B.A. L.7 J.D. 41 Merz Blvd.
Bernlohr, Mark W., (BV) .... '62 '87 C.645 B.S. L.117 J.D. [Bernlohr W.]

Bernlohr Wertz, LLP, (BV)
The Nantucket Building, 23 South Main Street, 3rd Floor, 44308-1460
Telephone: 330-434-1000 Fax: 330-434-1001
Email: jack@b-wlaw.com URL: http://www.b-wlaw.com
Partners of Firm: Mark W. Bernlohr; George R. Wertz; Christopher J. Niekamp; John C. Weisensell.
Associates: Jennifer J. Jacquemain; Melissa R. Cox; Sarah B. Cavanaugh.
General Practice.
See Professional Biographies, AKRON, OHIO

Bernstein, David J. ... '58 '83 C.381 B.B.A. L.7 J.D. 3200 West Market Street, Suite 303★
Berry, James F., (AV) '51 '78 C.650 B.A. L.8 J.D.
Branch Coun. & N. Ohio Sales Coun., LandAmerica/Lawyers Title Ins. Co.
Bertsch, David P., (AV) .... '53 '78 C.608 B.A. L.813 J.D. [Buckingham,D.&B.]
Bertsch, E. Katherine .... '57 '85 C.8 B.S. L.930 J.D. Ref. Juv. Ct.

Bhakuni, Pravin S., Attorney At Law
(See Medina)

Bickett, William W., II .... '47 '72 C&L.8 B.A., J.D. 1484 Frederick Blvd.‡
Billow, Patricia McQuillen .... '55 '81 C.8 B.S.B.A. L.7 J.D. Univ. of Akron
Binns, Harold G., (CV) .... '13 '50 C.8 B.S. L.930 LL.B. 1826 S. Main St.
Bittel, Timothy M., (AV) .... '45 '71 C.124 B.S. L.1003 J.D. [Joondeph&B.]

Black McCuskey Souers & Arbaugh, A Legal Professional Association
(See Canton, Ohio)

Blakemore, Allison B., (BV) .... '60 '89 C.381-B.A. L.8 J.D. [Ⓒ Blakemore,M.&B.]

Blakemore, Robert W., (AV) ....'26 '54 C.381 B.A. L.7 LL.B. [Blakemore,M.&B.]
Blakemore, Meeker & Bowler, L.P.A., (AV) ....19 N. High St.
Bobak, Donald J., (AV) '43 '73 C&L.8 B.S., J.D.
[Renner,K.G.B.T.&W.] (See Pat. Sect.)
Bobinets, Deborah L. ....'60 '95 C.8 B.A. L.7 J.D. Law Librarian, Univ. of Akron
Bodnar, Martin J. ....'59 '84 C.477 B.A. L.7 J.D. City Law Dir.
Boecker, Gary J., (BV) ....'53 '83 C.645 B.S. L.7 J.D. 520 S. Main St., Ste. 2515
Bogdanoff, Philip, (BV) ....'56 '81 C.658 B.S.Ed. L.7 J.D. Sr. Asst. Pros. Atty.
Bond, Jane ....'47 '76 C.610 B.S.J. L.7 J.D. Comm. Pleas J.
Bonetti, A. Edward, Jr., (BV) ....'61 '87 C.657 B.S. L.8 J.D. 411 Wolf Ledges, #304
Booher, Debra E. ....'69 '95 C.294 B.A. L.209 J.D. [D.E.Booher]
Booher, Debra E., Law Offices of, P.C. ....1 Cascade Plz.
Boose, Clyde R. ....'24 '55 C.8 B.S. L.7 LL.B. 560 Beaverbrook Drive
Borowski, Paul A., (CV) ....'31 '59 C.608 B.S. L.7 LL.B. 717 Lakewood Blvd.
Botnick, Ellen Witt, (BV) ....'51 '76 C.475 B.A. L.213 J.D. 4805 Stone Gate Blvd.
Bower, Terry L. ....'42 '71 C&L.8 B.S.A., J.D. [T.L.Bower]
Bower, Terry L., Company, L.P.A. ....437 Quaker Square
Bowler, Michael B., (BV) ....'45 '73 C.150 B.B.A. L.7 J.D. [Blakemore,M.&B.]
Box, Susan S., (AV) ....'60 '85 C&L.608 B.S., J.D. [Roetzel&A.]
Bozeka, George Angelo ....'55 '81 C.8 B.A. L.7 J.D. Asst., Dir. of Law
Bozzelli, Karen A., (AV) ....'59 '87 C.473 B.A. L.7 J.D. Sr. V.P., National City Bank
Bradley, Kate M. ....'75 '01 C.8 B.A. L.124 J.D. [Ⓐ Brouse M.]
Bradshaw, Duard D. ....'43 '73 C.537 L.7 J.D. [Roderick L.]

Breen, Kevin J., (BV) '58 '86 C.434 B.A. L.1003 J.D.
The Hermes Building, 43 E. Market Street Suite 202, 44308
Telephone: 330-374-9444 Fax: 330-762-2936
Email: kevin.j.breen@sbcglobal.net URL: http://www.home.att.net/~kevin.j.breen
Trial Litigation, Contracts Law and Business Representation including Small Business Law, Noncompetition Agreements, Employment Law, Franchise Law, Construction, Product Liability, Appellate Practice.
Representative Clients: Ryan Homes, Inc.; LaJolla Capital Corp.; Physician Weightloss Centers of America, Inc.; Jetfast Enterprises, Inc.; Chance Industries; Lafarge Corp.; Kemper Insurance Company.
See Professional Biographies, AKRON, OHIO

Brennan, Ann Amer, (BV) ....'33 '82 C.128 B.A. L.8 J.D. 159 S. Main Street
Brennan, David L., (AV) ....'31 '57 C.608 B.Sc. L.930 J.D. [Brennan,M.&D.]

Brennan, Manna & Diamond, LLC, (AV)
75 East Market Street, 44308 ⊙
Telephone: 330-253-5060 Fax: 330-253-1977
Email: lswalko@bmdllc.com URL: http://www.bmdllc.com
David L. Brennan; Anthony S. Manna; Jack T. Diamond; Lee S. Walko; Matthew A. Heinle; John B. Schomer; John F. Martin; Richard W. Burke; Frank Thomas Sossi; John N. Childs; Frank A. Lettieri; Scott P. Sandrock;—George F. Voinovich; Michael P. Morley; Joseph A. Shoaff; Darrin R. Toney; Priscilla A. Grant; Eric J. Stecz; Jason A. Butterworth; Leigh A. Maxa; Lisa Marie Clark; Stephen J. Yeargin. Of Counsel: Nickolas P. Andreeff.
Corporate Law, Business Law, Business Litigation, Mergers and Acquisitions, Finance, Commercial Lending, Taxation, Real Estate.
Jacksonville, Florida Office: 76 South Laura Street, Suite 2110, 32202. Telephone: 904-366-1500. Fax: 904-366-1501.
Bonita Springs Office: 3301 Bonita Beach Road Suite 202, 34134. Telephone: 239-992-6578 Fax: 239-992-9328
See Professional Biographies, AKRON, OHIO

Briggs, R. David, (BV) ....'54 '83 C.1044 B.A. L.7 J.D. [Bagdasarian&B.] ⊙
Briggs, Robert W. (Rob), Esq., (AV) '41 '66
C.228 B.A. L.608 J.D. [Buckingham,D.&B.]

Brightbill, James E., (CV) '49 '87 C.608 B.S. L.7 J.D.
One Cascade Plaza, Suite 710, 44308
Telephone: 330-374-0300 Fax: 330-374-0433
Email: jebright@brightbill.org URL: http://www.brightbilllaw.com
Family Law, Domestic Law, Divorce, Dissolutions, Child Custody, Bankruptcy, Personal Injury, Child Support, Auto Accidents, DUI, Criminal Law.
See Professional Biographies, AKRON, OHIO

Brooks, Ellen M., (AV) ....'47 '87 C.477 B.A. L.1003 J.D. [Ⓒ Slater,Z.&G.]

Brouse McDowell, A Legal Professional Association, (AV)
388 S. Main Street Suite 500, 44311 ⊙
Telephone: 330-535-5711 Toll Free: 800-837-5711 Facsimile: 330-253-8601
URL: http://www.brouse.com
Shareholders: Rajesh Bagga; Richard F. Battagline; Daniel L. Bell; Lisa S. Delgrosso; Clair E. Dickinson; Roger D. Emerson; Stanley E. Everett; John C. Fairweather; John C. Fickes; Richard H. Harris III; Jeffrey T. Heintz; David M. Hunter; Linda B. Kersker; Sallie Conley Lux; Shawn M. Lyden; Marc B. Merklin; David F. Raynor; Robert P. Reffner; Paul A. Rose; John M. Skeriotis; Michael A. Sweeney; Christopher F. Swing; Jerry F. Whitmer; Thomas J. Wiencek;—Heather M. Barnes; Timothy D. Bennett; Kate M. Bradley; Nicholas P. Capotosto; Deron A. Cook; Brandon L. Ford; Joy D. Kosiewicz; Amanda M. Leffler; Joy Ames Moxon; Hans A. Nilges; Nicole Swearingen-Hilker; Daniel A. Thomson; Jennifer D. Towell; Karen S. Walter; Nora J. Whitten. Of Counsel: Robert S. Burns; Richard T. Cunningham; Frank H. Harvey, Jr.; Joseph M. Holden; Oscar A. Hunsicker, Jr.; Charles R. Iden; Frederick K. Lacher; Mary T. Link (Not admitted in OH); M. Terrell Menefee; Frank E. Quirk; Jay G. Volk.
Administrative, Bankruptcy, Business, Business Litigation, Commercial, Corporation, Creative Technologies, Creditors' Rights, E-Commerce, Environmental, Estate Planning, Federal Securities, General Civil, Health Care, Immigration, Insurance, Intellectual Property, Labor and Employment, Litigation, Mediation, Mergers and Acquisitions, Municipal and Bond, OSHA Compliance, Probate, Real Estate, Succession Planning, Tax, Trademarks, Trial and Appellate Practice, Venture Capital.
Cleveland, Ohio Office: 1001 Lakeside Avenue, Suite 1600. Telephone: 216-830-6830. Toll Free: 877-837-5711. Facsimile: 216-830-6807.
See Professional Biographies, AKRON, OHIO

Brown, James E., (BV) ....'54 '83 C.381 B.A. L.8 J.D. [Ⓐ Slater,Z.&G.]

Brown, Robert H., (AV) '40 '65 C.8 B.S. L.150 J.D.
407 Quaker Square, 120 East Mill Street, 44308-1721
Telephone: 330-376-3000 Fax: 330-376-2906
Email: rhbrownlaw@yahoo.com
Family Law, Domestic Relations, Divorce.
See Professional Biographies, AKRON, OHIO

Bruggeman, Amie L., (AV) ....'— '82 C.508 B.A. L.7 J.D. [Roetzel&A.]

Buckingham, Doolittle & Burroughs, LLP, (AV)
50 South Main Street, P.O. Box 1500, 44309-1500 ⊙
Telephone: 330-376-5300; Toll Free: 1-800-686-2825 Fax: 330-258-6559
Email: bdb@bdblaw.com URL: http://www.bdblaw.com
Gillum H. Doolittle (1883-1973); Edmund Burroughs (1890-1981); Charles F. Scanlon (1906-1985); Lisle M. Buckingham (1895-1992); James C. Herndon (1918-1998). Managing Partner: Patrick J. Keating. Shareholders: Ronald C. Allan; David P. Bertsch; Robert W. (Rob) Briggs, Esq.; Edward V. Buehrle; Peter T. Cahoon; William L. Caplan; Steven A. Dimengo; David L. Drechsler; James L. Fisher; Nicholas T. George; Cathy Carter Godshall; Stephen M. Hammersmith; David W. Hilkert; David Kern; James D. Kraus; David J. Lewis; Frederick M. Lombardi; Robert W. Malone; Craig S. Marshall; Patricia A. Pacenta; Orville L. Reed, III; John L. Reyes; Susan C. Rodgers; George H. Rosin; Mark J. Skakun, III; Michelle A. Smithern; Thomas R. Trotter; Eleanor J. Tschugunov; Louis F. Wagner; Patrick J. Weschler; Philip R. Wiese; David W. Woodburn. Partner: Richard P. Rohrich. Of Counsel: Richard A. Chenoweth; Christine Amer Mayer; Duane Morris; Jean Van Ness. Associ-

(This Listing Continued)

Buckingham, Doolittle & Burroughs, LLP (Continued)
ates: Peggy S. Beistel; Joshua S. Berger; Matthew R. Duncan; Christopher C. Esker; David J. Hrina; Clay Kenneth Keller; Michael J. Matasich; Hillary B. McLean; Henry (Hank) F. Meyer; Marietta M. Pavlidis; Adam R. Van Rees.
Appellate, Bankruptcy, Business Law, Closely Held Companies, Commercial Law, Complex Litigation, Computer Law, Construction Law, Copyrights, Corporate Law, Creditors Rights, White Collar Crime or White Collar Criminal Defense, Employee Benefits, Employment Law, Environmental Law, Estate Planning, Family Law, Finance Law, Franchise, Health Care, Immigration Law, Insurance Defense, Intellectual Property, Labor, Land Use, Medical Malpractice Defense, Mergers and Acquisitions, Nonprofit Organizations Law, Patents, Private Foundations, Probate, Public Law, Publicly Held Companies, Real Estate, School Law, Securities, Service Marks, Succession Planning, Taxation, Toxic Tort, Trademarks, Trade Secrets, Trial, Trusts, Workers' Compensation, Zoning Law.
Canton, Ohio Office: 4518 Fulton Drive Northwest, P.O. Box 35548, 44735-5548. Telephone: 330-492-8717. Toll Free: 800-811-2825. Fax: 330-492-9625.
Cleveland, Ohio Office: 1375 East Ninth Street, Suite 1700, 44114. Telephone: 216-621-5300. Toll Free: 888-843-2825. Fax: 216-621-5440.
Columbus, Ohio Office: 191 West Nationwide Boulevard, 43215-3506. Telephone: 614-221-8448. Toll Free: 888-686-2825. Fax: 614-221-8590.
Boca Raton, Florida Office: 2500 North Military Trail, Suite 480, 33431. Telephone: 561-241-0414. Toll Free: 800-682-2825. Fax: 561-241-9766.
See Professional Biographies, AKRON, OHIO

Buehrle, Edward V., (BV) ....'64 '93 C.317 B.A. L.8 J.D. [Buckingham,D.&B.]
Bulford, Robert E., (AV) ....'51 '76 C.873 B.A. L.7 J.D. Asst. U.S. Atty.
Burdon, James L., (AV) ....'39 '67 C.694 B.A. L.8 J.D. [Burdon&M.]
Burdon & Merlitti, (AV) ....137 S. Main St.
Burgess, Thomas C. ....'52 '86 C.688 B.S.,E.P.E. L.8 J.D. 76 S. Main St.
Burk, James W. ....'60 '86 C.63 B.S. L.345 J.D. Sr. Atty., FirstEnergy Corporation
Burke, Richard W., (AV) ....'58 '83 C.608 B.S. L.8 J.D. [Brennan,M.&D.]
Burns, Robert S. ....'60 '85 C&L.8 B.A., J.D. [Ⓒ Brouse M.]
Bussman, James R. ....'47 '72 C.97 B.S.B.A. L.8 J.D. 915 Lynnhaven Lane‡
Butler, Brian J. ....'69 '01 C.999 B.S. L.8 J.D. [Ⓐ Hanna,C.&P.]
Butterworth, Jason A. ....'74 '00 C.608 B.A. L.7 J.D. [Ⓐ Brennan,M.&D.]
Buzzi, Paul F., (CV) ....'41 '68 C.201 B.S. L.1340 J.D. 631 W. Exchange St., 1st Fl.
Cable, Howard W., Jr. ....'37 '63 C.893 B.A. L.8 J.D. 50 S. Main St.
Cabral, Allen M. ....'44 '75 C.28 B.S. L.8 J.D. Prof., Univ. of Akron
Cady, William James, (AV) ....'20 '56 C.381 A.B. L.7 J.D. [Knowlton,S.]
Caesar, C. Douglas ....'43 '80 C.150 B.S. L.7 J.D. Hearing Off., Industrial Comm. of OH
Cahoon, Peter T., (AV) ....'53 '77 C.569 B.A. L.7 J.D. [Buckingham,D.&B.]
Calderone, Andrew J., (BV) ....'28 '73 C.381 B.S.Ed. L.7 J.D. 511 N. Main St.
Calderone, Kenneth A., (BV) ....'65 '90 C&L.8 B.S., J.D. [Hanna,C.&P.]
Calhoun, Howard L., (AV) '27 '51
C&L.608 B.B.S., J.D. [Calhoun,W.&H.] & [Ⓒ RoderickL.]
Calhoun, Waddell & Hunt, (AV) ....159 S. Main St.
Callahan, Lynne Lambert ....'57 '84 C.8 B.A. L.7 J.D. J., Akron Mun. Ct.
Callahan, Michael T., (AV) ....'57 '82 C.294 B.A. L.7 J.D. [Callahan,G.R.&S.]

Callahan, Greven, Rilley and Sinn, LLC, (AV)
7 West Bowery Street, Suite 907, 44308
Telephone: 330-376-9260 Fax: 330-376-9307
URL: http://www.cgrslaw.com
Michael T. Callahan; John William Greven; Scott A. Rilley; Jonathan Todd Sinn.
Criminal Law, DUI, Felonies, Driving While Intoxicated, Drug Crimes, Juvenile Crimes, Parole and Probation, Traffic Violations, Personal Injury, Domestic, Juvenile Law, Divorce, Family Law.
See Professional Biographies, AKRON, OHIO

Camilletti, George P. ....'45 '74 C.1323 B.S. L.7 J.D. U.S. Treas. Dept.
Campbell, James M., (BV) ....'59 '84 C.8 B.A. L.7 J.D. 500 Portage Lakes Drive
Campbell, Robert P., (CV) ....'51 '77 C.935 B.A. L.665 J.D. Chicago Title Ins. Co.
Campbell, Timothy C., (AV) ....'54 '82 C.8 B.S.I.M. L.7 J.D. [Hanna,C.&P.]
Caplan, William L., (AV) ....'51 '80 C.608 B.S. L.150 J.D. [Buckingham,D.&B.]
Capotosto, Nicholas P. ....'72 '03 C.1048 B.A. L.8 J.D. [Ⓐ Brouse M.]
Capriolo, Ralph A., (BV) ....'49 '74 C&L.8 B.S.B.A., J.D. [Ⓐ Mentzer&M.]
Carano, Sergio A., (BV) ....'61 '89 C&L.8 B.S., J.D. [Ⓐ Amer C.]
Carro, J. Dean ....'52 '78 C.1373 B.A. L.8 J.D. Univ. of Akron
Carroll, Helen S., (BV) ....'52 '92 C&L.8 B.A., J.D. [Whalen&C.]
Carroll, Michael E., (BV) ....'47 '72 C&L.8 B.S., J.D. Asst. Co. Pros.
Casalinova, G. Jerry, (BV) ....'26 '54 C.8 L.7 LL.B. 4 Merz Blvd.
Casolari, Samuel G., Jr. ....'— '86 C.294 B.A. L.8 J.D. [Marshall,D.W.C.&G.]
Cassetty, Michael T. ....'— '93 C.381 B.S. L.8 J.D. 1655 W. Market St., Ste. 400
Casto, Jeffrey J., (AV) ....'54 '81 C.608 B.A. L.930 J.D. [Roetzel&A.]
Catanzarite, Jeffrey A. ....'52 '79 C.8 B.S.I.M. L.7 789 W. Market St.
Cavanaugh, Mark C., (BV) ....'49 '75 C.381 B.B.A. L.7 J.D. 1745 W. Market St.
Cavanaugh, Sarah B. ....'79 '04 C.645 L.884 J.D. [Ⓐ Bernlohr W.]
Cek, Derek, Law Office of ....'73 '00 C&L.8 B.A., J.D. 137 South Main Street
Champion, Timothy H., (BV) ....'62 '88 C.973 B.A. L.7 J.D. [Aberth&C.]
Chenoweth, Richard A., (AV) '25 '48 C.309 A.B. L.930 LL.B.
[Ⓒ Buckingham,D.&B.]
Cherpas, Christopher T. ....'24 '52 C.8 L.1003 J.D. [Teodosio,C.&M.] ‡
Chester, David M., Law Offices of ....'68 '95 C.97 B.A. L.989 J.D. 137 S. Main Street
Chicatelli, Joy ....'67 '00 C.999 B.A. L.989 J.D. [Ⓐ Goldman&R.]
Childs, John N., (AV) ....'46 '74 C&L.8 B.S., J.D. [Brennan,M.&D.]
Chlysta, John R., (BV) ....'66 '92 C.381 B.A. L.930 J.D. [Ⓐ Hanna,C.&P.]
Choate, Cortlandt C., Jr. '59 '88 C.1046 B.A. L.1187 J.D.
(adm. in PA; not adm. in OH) Atty., FirstEnergy Corporation
Chris, William G., (AV) ....'60 '85 C.7 B.A. L.851 J.D. [Roderick L.]
Christie, William E. ....'76 '01 C.8 B.A. L.7 J.D. Staff Atty.
Chuparkoff, Karen M., (BV) ....'57 '84 C.472 B.A. L.7 J.D. 1655 W. Market St., Ste. 430
Chuparkoff, Theodore, (BV) '31 '62
C.980 B.Mech.E. L.8 J.D. 1655 West Market St., Ste. 430
Church, Chas. ....'19 '51 C.8 L.7 LL.B. 1602 E. Market St.
Ciccolini, Elio, (BV) ....'21 '53 C&L.8 LL.B. [Germano,R.&C.]
Ciccolini, Michael E., (BV) ....'59 '84 C.97 B.S. L.7 J.D. [Germano,R.&C.]
Ciccolini, Thomas A., (BV) ....'45 '73 C.8 B.A. L.1003 J.D. [Germano,R.&C.]
Ciccolini, Vincent N. ....'63 '91 C&L.8 B.S., J.D. 1144 E. Market St., Dept. 638‡
Cich, Frank A. ....'44 '74 C.1323 B.A. L.7 J.D. 1144 E. Market St.
Clark, George A., (AV) ....'33 '66 C.381 B.S. L.7 J.D. [G.A.Clark&Assoc.]
Clark, Lisa Marie ....'59 '89 C.381 B.S.N. L.8 J.D. [Ⓐ Brennan,M.&D.]
Clark, Robert J. ....'66 '93 C.608 B.S.M.E. L.8 J.D. [Ⓐ Hahn L.&P.] (See Pat. Sect.)
Clark, G. A., & Associates, (AV) ....875 North Cleveland-Massillon Road
Cody, Daniel S. ....'48 '90 C.608 B.A. L.8 J.D. 17 S. Main St.
Cole, Dana K., (BV) ....'56 '86 C.150 B.A. L.201 J.D. 302 Buchtel Mall
Cole, James L., (BV) ....'66 '91 C.674 A.B. L.665 J.D. 222 South Main Street
Cole, Leland D., (BV) ....'39 '69 C.378 B.A. L.608 J.D. [Cole]
Cole Co., L.P.A., (BV) ....863 N. Cleveland-Massillon Rd.
Collins, Gregory H., (BV) ....'— '88 C.318 B.A. L.930 J.D. [Davis&Y.]
Collins-Berger, Susan M. ....'52 '87 C.381 B.B.A. L.7 J.D. 159 South Main Street
Colopy, Conchita M. ....'41 '66 C.856 A.B. L.93 LL.B. 1980 Braewick Dr.
Colopy, Robert H. ....'26 '66 C.321 B.S. L.94 LL.B. Mun. Ct. J.

Comanor, Lawrence B., (BV) '44 '73
C.390 B.A. L.8 J.D. 161 South High Street, Suite 3011
Compton, G. Frederick, Jr., (AV) '48 '73 C.705 B.A. L.7 J.D. [Whalen&C.]
Conlin, James M., Jr. '42 '68 C&L.838 J.D. Goodyear Tire & Rubber Co.
Conner, James W. '41 '67 C.610 B.S.B.A. L.8 J.D. Roadway Express, Inc.
Conrad, Bruce R., (BV) '52 '79 C.608 B.A. L.8 J.D. [Burdon&M.]
Conway, Thomas, (BV) '61 '90 C&L.8 B.A., J.D. [D'Andrea&C.]
Cook, Deron A. '74 '00 C.477 B.S. L.966 J.D. [Ⓐ Brouse M.] (Pat.)
Cook, Joseph F., Jr., (AV) '56 '82 C.608 B.S.B.A. L.8 J.D. [Amer C.]
Cook, Lawrence J., (BV) '51 '77 C.8 B.A. L.1003 J.D. 563 Hampton Ridge Dr.
Coombs, W. Dick, (BV) '33 '66 C.473 B.S. L.8 J.D. 1226 Maryland Ave.
Cooper, Gary G., (BV) '51 '78 C.381 B.B.A. L.7 J.D. [Cooper&P.]
Cooper & Pachell, (BV) 525 N. Cleveland-Massillon Rd.
Cooperman, Jonathan M. '56 '94 C.446 B.S. L.8 J.D. Rehab. and Health Ctr., Inc.
Corgan, William Hillary, III '72 '01 C&L.8 B.S., J.D. 120 E. Mill St., Ste. 437
Corns, Frederick S., (AV) '36 '67 C.951 A.B. L.7 J.D. [Ⓒ Roderick L.]
Corzin, Christine K. '52 '00 C.381 B.A. L.7 J.D. 304 N. Cleveland-Massillon Road
Corzin, Harold A., (AV) '46 '75 C.8 B.A. L.851 J.D.
304 North Cleveland-Massillon Road
Cosgrove, Patricia Ann '51 '78 C&L.8 B.A., J.D. Comm. Pleas Ct.
Costello, Anthony James '56 '82 C.231 B.A. L.7 J.D. [A.Costello]
Costello, Anthony, Law Offices 2666 South Arlington Road
Costigan, William J. '48 '75 C&L.8 B.A., J.D. 183 W. Market St.‡
Coven, Christine L. '46 '74 C.381 B.A. L.8 J.D.
Lockheed Martin Defense Systems-Akron
Cox, Melissa R. '68 '99 C.1529 B.A. L.8 J.D. [Ⓐ Bernlohr W.]
Cox, Steven St. Leger, (BV) '66 '94 C.608 B.A. L.8 J.D. [Roetzel&A.]
Coyne, John M., III, (AV) '68 '95 C.838 B.S. L.1003 J.D. [Roetzel&A.]
Cramer, William T. '71 '97 C.150 B.A. L.930 J.D. Law Clk., Ct. App.
Crane, Robyn L. '51 '77 C.473 B.A. L.7 J.D. The Goodyear Tire & Rubber Co.
Creveling, Michael A., (BV) '65 '94 C.646 B.A. L.8 J.D. [Creveling&C.]
Creveling, Wendy S., (BV) '72 '95 C.999 L.L.B. L.8 J.D. [Creveling&C.]
Creveling & Creveling, (BV) 88 South Portage Path, Suite 306
Crimaldi, Joseph J. '— '95 C.473 B.S. L.1003 J.D. [Ⓐ Roetzel&A.] (Pat.)
Crocker, Robin G. '57 '96 C.659 B.A. L.8 J.D. Co. Ct. of Com. Pleas
Croft, M. Kathryn '32 '75 C.117 B.S. L.7 J.D. 945 Morningstar Dr.‡
Crookes, Thomas Richard, (BV) '60 '87 C.477 A.B. L.215 J.D. [Ⓒ Vorys,S.S.&P.]
Crooks, W. Edward '71 '02 C.608 B.S. L.7 J.D. [Ⓐ Hahn L.&P.]
Culbertson, David E., (BV) '36 '65 C.124 B.S.M.E. L.7 J.D. 2447 Manchester Rd.
Culver, Kathryn Frazzini, (BV) '57 '82 C.980 B.A. L.8 J.D. 120 E. Mill St., Ste. 415
Cunniff, John J. '62 '99 C.347 B.S. L.7 J.D. [Ⓐ Hahn L.&P.] (See Pat. Sect.)
Cunningham, Daniel P., (AV) '49 '78 C.1260 B.A. L.7 J.D.
Akron General Medical Center
Cunningham, Richard T., (AV) '30 '53 C.930 L.339 LL.B. [Ⓒ Brouse M.]
Cunningham, Robert T., Jr. '38 '65
C.679 B.S.M.E. L.893 J.D. The Goodyear Tire & Rubber Co.
Curtin, G. Michael, (BV) '56 '83 C.276 B.S. L.930 J.D. [Curtin&Assoc.]
Curtin & Associates, (BV) 159 S. Main St., Ste. 920
Dacoros, Carol L. '72 '97 C.521 B.A. L.930 J.D. Atty., FirstEnergy Corp.
Daily, John A. '38 '63 C&L.8 B.S., J.D. [Daily&H.]
Daily & Haskins, (BV) 7 W Bowery Street, Suite 604
Dalayanis, Tony '69 '97 C.8 B.S. L.7 J.D. 12 East Exchange Street
Daly, Brendan J. '73 '99 C.107 B.S. L.8 J.D. Sr. Tax Consultant, Ernst & Young
D'Andrea, Patrick J., (BV) '56 '81 C&L.8 B.S.B.A., J.D. [D'Andrea&C.]
D'Andrea & Conway, (BV) 697 West Market Street Suite 200
D'Arcy, Charles J. '44 '70 C.573 B.A. L.107 J.D.
V.P. & Sr. Trust Offr., Bank One Trust Co., N.A.
Davidson, Elaine S., (BV) '52 '78 C.8 B.A. L.7 J.D. Asst. Law Dir.
Davidson, John H., Jr., (BV) '24 '53 C&L.980 J.D. P.O. Box 5464
Davidson, Roger K., (BV) '50 '77 C.347 B.S. L.7 J.D.
441 Wolf Ledges Pkwy., Ste. 302
Davies, Lee Clarke, (BV) '29 '56 C.381 L.608 LL.B. 159 S. Main St.
Davies, Richard, (BV) '53 '80 C.970 B.A. L.608 J.D. [Ⓐ Kastner W.&W.]
Davis, Clifford L. '23 '62 C.8 B.S. L.7 J.D. 255 Swartz Rd.‡
Davis, Donald W., Jr., (BV) '58 '85 C.97 B.S. L.7 J.D. [Guy,L.&T.]
Davis, Elizabeth N., (AV) '53 '84 C.980 B.A. L.7 J.D. [Roetzel&A.]
Davis, Gerald L., (AV) '31 '56 C.477 A.B. L.930 LL.B. 430 Society Bldg.
Davis, James E., (BV) '34 '61 C.608 B.A. L.1003 LL.B. [Ⓒ Roderick L.]
Davis, Kevin G., (BV) '54 '79 C.8 B.A. L.7 J.D. 12 E. Exchange St., 8th Fl.
Davis, Rhonda Gail, (BV) '64 '91 C.43 B.A. L.500 J.D. [Zavarello&D.]
Davis, Thomas E., (AV) '55 '80 C.207 B.A. L.8 J.D. [Barrett&D.]

Davis & Young, (AV)
A Legal Professional Association
National City Center, One Cascade Plaza, Suite 800, 44308 ⊙
Telephone: 330-376-1717 Fax: 330-376-1797
URL: http://www.davisyoung.com
Gregory H. Collins; David G. Utley; Ann Marie O'Brien;—James Patrick Salamone.
General Trial and Appellate Practice, Products Liability, General Tort, Insurance Coverage, Personal Injury, Toxic Torts, Complex Mass Tort Claims, Legal and Medical Malpractice, Municipal Liability, Civil Rights, Employment Practices Liability, and Environmental and Commercial Liability.
Cleveland, Ohio Office: 1700 Midland Building, Suite 1700, 44115. Telephone: 216-348-1700. Fax: 216-621-0602.
Youngstown, Ohio Office: The Commerce Building, 201 East Commerce Street, Suite 100, 44503. Telephone: 330-743-1717.
Warren, Ohio Office: 108 Main Street, SW, Suite 1000, 44481. Telephone: 330-373-1717. Fax: 330-395-0610.
See Professional Biographies, AKRON, OHIO

Davison, E. Larry '43 '77 C.8 B.S. L.7 J.D. 59 Shiawassee Ave.
de Bruin, Walter E., (AV) '05 '28 C&L.608 A.B., J.D. 262 Winston Rd.‡
DeCarlo, Michael, (BV) '60 '86 C.97 B.S. L.7 J.D. [Roderick L.]
DeHaven, Darren W. '70 '95 C.381 B.A. L.7 J.D. [Ⓐ Blakemore,M.&B.]
Deitle, Chas. M., (BV) '21 '50 C&L.608 B.S., J.D. 120 Menlo Park Dr.
Delgrosso, Lisa S., (BV) '70 '95 C&L.8 B.A., J.D. [Brouse M.]
Delino, Lawrence L., Jr., (CV) '48 '84 C.980 A.B. L.7 J.D. 1 Cascade Plaza, Suite 700
Del Medico, Michael J., (AV) '55 '80 C.103 B.A. L.201 J.D. [Scanlon&G.]
DeLong, John D. '59 '00 C.475 B.S. L.7 J.D. 1144 E. Market Street (Pat.)
Derivan, Sharon Katherine '49 '87 L.128 J.D. Law Clk., U.S. Dist. Ct.
DeSantis, Vicki L. '56 '02 C.381 B.S.N. L.7 J.D. [Ⓐ Edminister&Assoc.]
DeSaussure, Hamilton '21 '48 C.976 A.B. L.309 LL.B.
(adm. in MA; not adm. in OH) Prof. Emeritus, Univ. of Akron Law School
DeSaussure, Hamilton, Jr., (AV) '57 '83 C.385 B.A. L.896 J.D. [Oldham&D.]
Detweiler, William J., (BV) '61 '87 C.8 B.A. L.930 J.D. [Roderick L.]
Devanney, Katharina Eileen '69 '98 C.150 B.A. L.930 J.D. 1894 Thornhill Drive
Deveny, Thomas A., III '30 '57 C&L.923 A.B., LL.B.
The Goodyear Tire & Rubber Co.
Dezso, Carol Jean '54 '80 C.8 B.A. L.989 J.D. Domestic Rela. J.
Dhinojwala, Duriya A. '68 '02 C.999 B.F.A. L.8 J.D. [Ⓐ Guy,L.&T.]
Diamond, Jack T., (AV) '56 '83 C.973 B.S.B.A. L.930 J.D. [Brennan,M.&D.]
Diamond, John Tiffin '56 '83 L.930 J.D. 75 E. Market St.
Dickinson, Clair E. '51 '77 C.665 B.A. L.161 J.D. [Brouse M.]
Dickos, Harry F. '27 '57 C.271 B.S. L.7 J.D. 2300 Burnham Rd.‡
Dietrich, George A., (AV) '43 '68 C.473 B.A. L.477 J.D. [Roetzel&A.]
DiFiore, David V., (BV) '70 '96 C.473 B.S. L.8 J.D. 120 East Mill Street
Dimengo, Steven A., (AV) '61 '86 C.8 B.A. L.7 J.D. [Buckingham,D.&B.]
Dion, Marc R., Sr. '42 '83 C.550 B.S. L.8 J.D. The Goodyear Tire & Rubber Co. (Pat.)

Dismuke, Daniel K. '77 '01 C.645 B.A. L.8 J.D.
P.O. Box 995, 44223
Telephone: 330-762-0080 Fax: 330-762-0720
Email: dismuke@attorneydismuke.com URL: http://www.neohiorealestatelawyer.com
Real Estate, Business Law, Litigation, Trusts and Estates, Family Law.
See Professional Biographies, AKRON, OHIO

Djordjevic, Michael M., (AV) '52 '77 C.25 B.A. L.930 J.D. [M.M.Djordjevic]
Djordjevic, Michael M., Co. LPA, (AV)
17 South Main Street at Maiden Lane Suite 201
Dobbins, Elizabeth A. '72 '03 C.880 B.A. L.7 J.D.
Ridgewood Centre Ste 105, 1000 S Cleveland Massillon Rd
Dobbins, Richard E., (AV) '48 '77 C.381 B.S. L.7 J.D. [Dobbins&Assoc.]
Dobbins & Associates, (AV) 1000 S. Cleveland Massillon Rd.

Dohner, John M., (AV) '55 '86 C&L.8 B.S., J.D.
407 Quaker Square, 120 East Mill Street, 44308
Telephone: 330-376-6300 Fax: 330-376-2906
Email: dohnerlaw@aol.com URL: http://www.lawyers.com/johndohnerlaw
(Certified Specialist in Family Relations Law, Ohio State Bar Association).
Trial Practice, Divorce, Dissolution, Child Custody, Child Support, Business Valuation for Divorce, Adoption, Premarital Agreements, Special Education Law.
See Professional Biographies, AKRON, OHIO

Dougherty, Diane Lynn '59 '88 1655 W. Market Street, Suite 400
Dowd, David D., Jr. '29 '54 C.970 B.A. L.477 J.D. U.S. Sr. Dist. J.
Dowling, William D., Jr., (AV) '53 '80 C.608 B.S. L.976 J.D. [Oldham&D.]
Dratler, Jay, Jr. '45 '78 C.112 A.B. L.309 J.D.
(adm. in CA; not adm. in OH) 302 Buchtel Mall
Drechsler, David L., (AV) '63 '89
C.608 B.S. L.930 J.D. [Buckingham,D.&B.] (⊙Cleveland)
Drenski, Tama L. '56 '03 C.607 B.A. L.8 J.D.
[Ⓐ Renner,K.G.B.T.&W.] (See Pat. Sect.)
Drew, David P., (CV) '63 '91 C.380 B.S. L.8 J.D. 611 W. Market St.
Duff, Andrew R., (AV) '54 '79 C.473 B.A. L.8 J.D. [Amer C.]
Dumas, David M., (BV) '66 '91 C.197 B.A. L.602 J.D.
Sr. Coun. - Litig., Bridgestone/Firestone Tech. Co.
Duncan, Matthew R. '75 '03 C.938 B.A L.124 J.D. [Ⓐ Buckingham,D.&B.]
Dunseath, Frances, (BV) '53 '94 C.068 B.A. L.8 J.D.
441 Wolf Ledges Parkway, Suite 302
Dutt, Janet L. Muntean '65 '92 C.610 B.B.A. L.7 J.D. Jud. Asst., Comm. Pleas Ct.
Easter, Felicia '74 '01 C&L.608 B.A., J.D. Pros. Off.
Eastman, David R., (BV) '61 '88 C.827 B.A. L.896 J.D. 2745 Nesbitt Avenue
Eastman, Fred E., (BV) '30 '54 C&L.608 B.S., J.D. 2745 Nesbitt Avenue
Eckberg, Barbara Susan '64 '90 C.8 B.A. L.608 J.D. P.O. Box 27171
Eckert, Phillip W. '49 '82 C.851 B.S. L.7 J.D. 76 South Main Street
Edminister, Michael Edward, (AV) '55 '87 C&L.8 B.A., J.D. [Edminister&Assoc.]
Edminister & Associates, (AV) 159 South Main Street
Egan, Richard J., (AV) '24 '53 C.251 B.E.E. L.1003 J.D. 1225 W. Market St. (Pat.)
Eisen, Hermine G., (BV) '39 '81 C.930 B.A. L.1003 J.D. [Eisen&W.] ⊙
Eisen & Westfall, LLP, (BV)
304 North Cleveland - Massillon Road (⊙Cleveland, Columbus)
Ekonomon, Deborah Ann '64 '90
C.967 B.A. L.8 J.D. Hearing Offr., State Industrial Comm.
Elias, Eugene M., (BV) '51 '94 C&L.8 B.S.B.A., J.D. 2483 S. Main St.

Elk & Elk Co., L.P.A.
(See Cleveland)

Elliott, Michael J., (BV) '68 '98 C.610 B.A. L.930 J.D. [Ⓐ Tipping]
Emershaw, George J., (BV) '40 '68 C.1113 B.A. L.8 J.D. [Emershaw,M.&S.]
Emershaw, Mushkat & Schneier, (BV) 120 E. Mill St.
Emerson, Roger D., (BV) '58 '87 C&L.8 B.S.M.E., J.D. [Brouse M.] (Pat.)
Eoff, Craig M. '72 '99 C&L.8 B.S., J.D. 12 E. Exchange St., 8th Fl.
Ephlin, Laura A., (BV) '64 '91 C.679 B.A. L.608 J.D. [Ⓐ Roetzel&A.]
Erisey, Catherine Kemp '67 '94 C.473 B.A. L.608 J.D.
76 South Main Street, Suite 1512
Esker, Christopher C., (BV) '— '88 C.8 B.A. L.7 J.D. [Ⓐ Buckingham,D.&B.]
Evanchan, Nicholas L., (AV) '51 '79 C.980 B.E. L.7 J.D. [Evanchan&P.]
Evanchan & Palmisano, (AV) One GOJO Plaza
Evans, Todd William '67 '93 C.532 B.A. L.989 J.D. OH Civil Rights Comm.
Everett, Stanley E., (AV) '44 '81 C&L.101 B.A., J.D. [Brouse M.]
Evers, Linda R. '66 '91 C.597 B.S. L.339 J.D. Atty., FirstEnergy Corporation
Fahey, Bruce H., (AV) '55 '80 C.81 B.A. L.7 J.D. [Kastner W.&W.]
Fairweather, John C., (AV) '52 '77 C.174 B.A. L.930 J.D. [Brouse M.]
Fallis, Stephen A., (BV) '48 '74 C.381 B.A. L.8 J.D. [Ⓐ Blakemore,M.&B.]
Fanelly, Angelo A. '22 '55 C.381 L.7 LL.B. 930 Society Bldg.‡
Farolino, Shane A., (AV) '62 '88 C.107 B.A. L.851 J.D. [Roetzel&A.]
Farris, George L., (BV) '46 '81 C.8 B.S.B.A. L.7 J.D. [Sawan&F.]
Farris, Julie A. '73 '01 C.938 B.A. L.1202 J.D. [Ⓐ Kaufmann&K.]
Faust, Laura (Megan), (BV) '66 '92 C.970 B.A. L.1003 J.D. [Roetzel&A.]
Feeney, Kate Marie '75 '01 C.8 B.A. L.930 J.D. Brouse McDowell
Feinberg, Kenneth S., (BV) '61 '87 C.97 B.S./B.A. L.930 J.D. 3465 S. Arlington Rd.
Feld, Stephen L. '49 '77
C.665 B.S. L.1017 J.D. Assoc. Gen. Coun., FirstEnergy Corporation
Ferguson, David H., (BV) '43 '70 C.8 B.A. L.7 J.D. [Ferguson&H.]
Ferguson, William R., (AV) '26 '56 C.472 B.B.A. L.7 LL.B. 159 South Main Street
Ferguson & Hanlon, (BV) 120 E. Mill St.
Fetzer, Robert J., (AV) '24 '55 C.608 B.M.E. L.1003 J.D. 1225 W. Market St. (Pat.)
Fickes, John C., (BV) '55 '85 C.363 B.A. L.930 J.D. [Brouse M.]
Fike, Lisa A. '66 '91 C.432 B.A. L.347 J.D. [Ⓐ Amer C.]
Finley, Michael J. '48 '81 C.8 B.A. L.7 J.D. V.P., National City Bank
Finn, Terrence S., (AV) '62 '87 C.980 B.E. L.851 J.D. [Roetzel&A.]
Fiocca, Carl J., (AV) '50 '76 C.8 B.A. L.7 J.D. 1003 East Turkeyfoot Lake, Suite C
Firestine, David L. '74 '00 C.62 B.A. L.8 J.D. [Witschey W.&F.]
Fisher, James L., (AV) '44 '71 C&L.8 B.S.C.E., J.D. [Buckingham,D.&B.]
Fitch, Susan Marie '62 '87 C.161 B.S. L.7 J.D.
Staff Atty., Western Reserve Legal Servs.
Flannery, Harry A. '47 '72 C.611 B.A. L.607 J.D. Atty., FirstEnergy Corporation
Flower, Nancy J., (BV) '60 '92 C&L.8 B.A., J.D. [Burdon&M.]

Ford, Brandon L. .... '— '04 C.124 B.S.N. L.7 J.D. [Ⓐ Brouse M.]
Fort, W. Howard, (AV) ....'15 '47 C&L.608 B.S., J.D. 80 S. Summit St.‡
Fortney, Michael L., (AV) ....'55 '86 C.838 B.S. L.161 J.D. [Fortney&K.]

Fortney & Klingshirn, (AV) BB
4040 Embassy Parkway Suite 280, 44333
Telephone: 330-665-5445 Telefax: 330-665-5446
Email: fortney@fklaborlaw.com URL: http://www.fklaborlaw.com
Members of Firm: Michael L. Fortney; Neil E. Klingshirn (Certified Specialist, Labor and Employment Law, Ohio State Bar Association).
Employment and Construction Law, Commercial Litigation. Trial and appellate practice in all state and federal courts. Construction practice includes claims and disputes, competitive bidding, and mechanics liens involving commercial projects. Employment practice includes discrimination, retaliation and harassment claims, Family Medical Leave Act, ERISA, Fair Labor Standard Act and non-competition litigation.
See Professional Biographies, AKRON, OHIO

Fox, Robert Roe ....'64 '89 C.207 B.A. L.8 J.D. [Ⓐ Parker L.H.&R.]
Frantz, William G. ....'55 '80 C.473 B.S. L.7 J.D. 1700 I Cascade Plaza‡
Freedman, Bruce R., (BV) '54 '81
C.472 B.S.B.A. L.608 J.D. 304 North Cleveland-Massillon Road
Frentz, John C., (AV) ....'26 '50 C.970 A.B. L.930 LL.B. 2367 Chatham Rd.‡
Fricke, Lori A., (BV) ....'64 '92 C.1285 B.A. L.7 J.D. [Ⓐ Hanna,C.&P.]
Friedman, David, (BV) ....'33 '58 C.608 B.S. L.930 LL.B. [Hardesty,K.&Z.]
Frisina, Dominic A. ....'72 '04 C.1062 B.S. L.4210 J.D. [Ⓐ Roetzel&A.] (Pat.)
Fuchs, Michael J. ....'78 '03 C.473 B.A. L.8 J.D. [Ⓐ Roetzel&A.]
Funk, Stephen W., (AV) ....'66 '92 C.473 B.A. L.309 J.D. [Roetzel&A.]
Furry, Thelma C. ....'10 '41 L.7 LL.B. 915 Witner Ave.‡
Gallas, James S. ....'27 '55 C.81 A.B. L.161 LL.B. U.S. Mag. J.
Galvin, Kelly Lynn ....'68 '93 L.117 J.D. Pros. Off.
Gamache, Elisa A. ....'66 '94 C&L.8 B.A., J.D. 233 Ely Rd.
Gardner, James E., (BV) ....'65 '91 C.608 B.A. L.930 J.D. 628 W Market St
Gargasz, Scott Steven '67 '94 C.97 B.A. L.1003 J.D.
Plastic Surgery Fellow, Akron General Medical Center
Garlock, Paul R. ....'48 '75 C.528 B.A. L.902 J.D. Progressive Ins. Co.
Garrett, Jean Cooper ....'53 '78 C.532 B.A. L.7 J.D. 546 Lovers Lane
Gasparovic, John J. '57 '82 C.912 B.A. L.597 J.D.
Vice President & General Counsel, Roadway Express, Inc.
Gates, Susan Poulos ....'60 '98 C&L.7 B.S.I.M., J.D. Summit Cty. Pros., Tax Div.
Gatts, Ronald Thomas, (BV) ....'71 '98 C&L.8 B.S., J.D. [R.T.Gatts]
Gatts, Ronald T., (BV) ....137 S. Main St., Ste. 206
Gaum, R. Eric, (AV) ...'66 '96 C.150 B.S.E.E.T. L.07 J.D. [Hahn L.&P.] (See Pat. Sect.)
Gearinger, Bradford M., (AV) ....'40 '65 C.797 B.A. L.880 J.D. [Ⓒ Scanlon&G.]
Genetin, Bernadette Bollas, (AV) '59 '88
C.602 B.A. L.608 J.D. Univ. of Akron School of Law
Gentilcore, Laura J., (BV) '53 '86
C.930 B.A. L.1003 J.D. [Ⓐ Renner,K.G.B.T.&W.] (See Pat. Sect.)
George, David R. ....'41 '66 C.363 B.S. B.A. L.608 LL.B. 533 W. Market St.‡
George, Joyce J. ....'36 '66 C.8 B.A. L.7 J.D. 3597 Sparrow Pond Cir.
George, Michael E., (BV) '70 '95
C.473 B.S.B.A. L.7 J.D. 76 South Main Street, Suite 1512
George, Nicholas T., (AV) ....'44 '70 C.8 B.A. L.7 J.D. [Buckingham,D.&B.]
Germano, Jacqueline J. ....'42 '82 C&L.8 B.S., J.D. P.O. Box 2104
Germano, Sal ....'06 '29 C.608 L.607 J.D. 4752 Manchester Rd.‡
Germano, Rondy & Ciccolini Co., L.P.A., (BV) ....2715 Manchester Rd.
Gerney, Blake R., (BV) ....'68 '95 C.839 B.S. L.08 J.D. [Oldham&D.]
Gerspacher, James A. ....'43 '69 C.117 B.S. L.930 J.D. Spalding Assoc.
Gertz, Marc P., (AV) ....'52 '77 C&L.608 B.S., J.D. [Goldman&R.]
Giannantonio, Rick C., (AV) '58 '85
C.161 B.B.A. L.1003 J.D. Sr. Atty., FirstEnergy Corporation
Gibbs, Harold J. ....'50 '83 C.8 B.A. L.7 J.D. Stark Technical College
Gibbs, Mary M. ....'51 '86 C.608 B.S. L.930 J.D. 716 Springwater Drive‡
Gigliotti, Louis J., Jr., (BV) ....'62 '91 C.610 B.B.A. L.1003 J.D. [Slater,Z.&G.]
Gilbert, Edward L., (BV) ....'51 '80 C.970 B.S. L.7 J.D. [Slater,Z.&G.]
Gill, James J. ....'24 '54 C.201 B.S. L.7 J.D. Ref., Dom. Rel. Ct.
Gingo, Joseph M. ....'44 '71 C.930 B.S. L.7 J.D. 618 Victoria Ave.‡
Gingrich, Mitchell L., (BV) ....'61 '88 C.8 B.A. L.7 J.D. 39 E. Market St.
Gippin, Robert M., (AV) ....'48 '73 C.197 A.B. L.309 J.D. [Goldman&R.]
Glassman, Ronald R., (BV) ....'42 '79 C.4 B.B.A. L.7 J.D. 106 S. Main St.
Glenn, John M., (AV) '31 '57 C.696 B.A. L.309 LL.B.
V.P., Gen. Coun. & Secy., Roadway Express, Inc.
Glick, S. Mark, (BV) ....'— '57 41 Merz Blvd.
Glick, Sidney ....'42 '72 C.1016 B.S. L.1049 J.D. [Glick]
Glick Law Firm ....2666 South Arlington Road
Glinsek, Gerald J., (BV) ....'39 '67 C&L.8 B.A., J.D. [Glinsek&H.]
Glinsek & Higham, (BV) ....88 Portage Path S.
Godshall, Cathy Carter, (AV) ....'51 '76 C.385 A.B. L.930 J.D. [Buckingham,D.&B.]
Godshall, Douglas N., (AV) ....'47 '76 C.831 B.A. L.930 J.D. [Hanna,C.&P.]

Goldman & Rosen, Ltd., (AV)
11 South Forge Street, 44304
Telephone: 330-376-8336 Telecopier: 330-376-2522
Email: Goldman@Goldman-Rosen.com
Samuel Goldman (1948-2000); Bernard I. Rosen; George P. Tsarnas; Michael B. Hendler; Robert M. Gippin; Marc P. Gertz; Gary M. Rosen; Irving B. Sugerman; Michael A. Steel;—Stacey Tsarnas Hackenberg; Joy Chicatelli. Of Counsel: Frank E. Steel, Jr.
Business Corporation, Bankruptcy, Civil Litigation, Criminal, Family Law, Divorce, Child Support, Visitation Rights, Adoption Law, Alimony, General Practice, Business, Civil Rights, Employment, Estate Planning, Probate, Commercial, Wills, Criminal Law, Driving While Intoxicated, Drug Crimes, Sexual Assault, Homicide, Inheritance, Bankruptcy Chapter 7, Bankruptcy Chapter 11, Bankruptcy Chapter 13, Insurance Defense, Zoning, Real Estate, Consumer Law, Appeals.
References: First National Bank of Ohio; National City Bank, Akron.
See Professional Biographies, AKRON, OHIO

Goldsmith, Richard L., Jr., (BV) '44 '69
C.473 B.S. L.7 J.D. Law Dir., City of Munroe Falls
Goldstein, Dana A. '57 '83 C.472 B.Phil. L.608 J.D.
Staff Atty., Community Legal Aid Services., Inc.
Gomberg, Steven L. ....'47 '72 C.930 B.A. L.1003 J.D. 3368 Dowling Dr.
Gordon, Amanda E., (AV) ....'65 '90 C.8 B.S. L.930 J.D. [Roetzel&A.]
Gore, William B., (AV) ....'38 '63 C.610 B.S.C. L.608 LL.B. 441 Wolf Ledges Pkwy.
Gorman, Joseph F., (BV) ....'65 '94 C.116 B.A. L.8 J.D. [Gorman,M.&P.]
Gorman, Malarcik & Pierce, (BV) ....1 Cascade Plz., Fl. 20
Gradisher, Suzanne M. ....'61 '04 C.549 B.S.B.A. L.8 J.D. [Ⓐ Amer C.]

Graham-Hurd, Melissa, (BV) '56 '84 C.8 B.A. L.7 J.D.
704 Landmark Building, 7 West Bowery Street, 44308-1149
Telephone: 330-996-4099 Telecopier: 330-376-3291 330-643-0732
Email: GrahamHurd@aol.com URL: http://www.ohiodrlaw.com
(This Listing Continued)

Graham-Hurd, Melissa (Continued)
Family Law including Child Support, Custody, Visitation, Grandparent Rights, Paternity, Divorce, Spousal Support, Marital Property Settlements, Post Divorce Modification, Premarital Agreements, and Mediation.
See Professional Biographies, AKRON, OHIO

Grant, Charles L., (BV) ....'30 '65 C.611 B.A. L.7 J.D. 239 North Highland Avenue
Grant, Paul Michael, Law Office of '62 '95 C.444 B.S. L.8 J.D.
441 Wolf Ledges Parkway
Grant, Priscilla A. ....'72 '97 C.318 B.A. L.8 J.D. [Ⓐ Brennan,M.&D.]
Grant, Richard L. ....'41 '67 C.659 B.S. L.813 J.D. [Ⓒ Tipping]
Graske, Leslie S., (BV) ....'57 '83 C.719 B.A. L.146 J.D. 333 S. Main St.
Green, Thomas E. ....'70 '02 C.980 B.S. L.989 J.D. [Ⓐ Kastner W.&W.]
Greene, Charles L. ....'38 '77 Asst. Dean, Stu. Life Dept., Kent State Univ.
Greene, Don H. ....'37 '64 C.475 B.A. L.477 LL.B. 1144 E. Market St.
Greene, Neil B. ....'36 '64 C.930 B.B.A. L.8 J.D. V.P., Mutual Oil & Gas Co.
Greive, Edward G., (AV) '42 '67
C.879 B.S.E.E. L.930 J.D. [Renner,K.G.B.T.&W.] (See Pat. Sect.)
Greven, John William, (BV) ....'64 '94 C.1457 B.S. L.989 J.D. [Callahan,G.R.&S.]
Grisi, Charles E., (AV) ....'45 '70 C&L.8 B.S., J.D. [Grisi&R.]

Grisi & Riegler, (AV) BB
159 South Main Street, Suite 1030, 44308
Telephone: 330-535-8171 Fax: 330-535-0106 Email: ejriegler@rieglerlaw.com
Email: grisi@nls.net
Charles E. Grisi; Edward J. Riegler.
Personal Injury, Medical Malpractice, Divorce, Probate and Estates, Municipal Zoning, Corporate.
See Professional Biographies, AKRON, OHIO

Guanciale, Christopher M. '59 '85
C.657 B.A. L.607 J.D. 121 South Main Street, Suite 200
Gugliotta, John D., Law Offices of, (BV) ....'62 '94 137 S. Main Street, Suite 202
Gui, Janice ....'41 '78 C.178 B.A. L.7 J.D. Mag., Dom. Rel. Ct.
Guran, John M. ....'52 '83 C.188 A.B. L.8 J.D. Time Warner Cable
Guster, Richard E., (AV) ....'28 '55 C.207 B.S. L.930 J.D. 50 S. Main St.
Gutbrod, James J., (BV) ....'57 '86 C.385 A.B. L.8 J.D. 4367 State Rd.
Guy, John J., (AV) ....'42 '70 C.381 B.B.A. L.8 J.D. [Guy,L.&T.]

Guy, Lammert & Towne, (AV)
2210 First National Tower, 106 S. Main Street, 44308-1419 ⊙
Telephone: 330-535-2151 Fax: 330-535-9048
Email: guylaw2210@aol.com URL: http://www.glt-law.com
Members of Firm: John J. Guy; Thomas E. Lammert (Resident, Canton, Ohio Office); Ronald N. Towne; E. Jane Taylor; Donald W. Davis, Jr. Associates: Ann Lynn Wehener; Duriya A. Dhinojwala; Thomas R. Bartilson.
Bankruptcy, Banking, Business Torts, Corporation, Commercial Litigation, Creditors Rights and Reorganization Law. Employment Law, Probate, Personal Injury, Trial Practice, Malpractice and Products Liability Law. General Litigation.
Representative Clients: Beacon Journal Publishing Company; Bunnell Printing Corp.; CIT Financial Services; Charter Express, Inc.; FCC National Bank; Ford Consumer Credit Company; Keybank National Association; Ohio Edison Co.; Second National Bank.
Canton, Ohio Office: P.O. Box 6426. Telephone: 330-452-1818 Fax: 330-535-9048
See Professional Biographies, AKRON, OHIO

Gwin, James S. ....'54 '79 C.385 A.B. L.8 J.D. U.S. Dist. J.
Haas, Paula Dale ....'68 '97 C.201 B.A. L.8 J.D. Summit Co. Probate Ct.
Hackenberg, Stacey Tsarnas ....'71 '96 C.473 B.A. L.117 J.D. [Ⓐ Goldman&R.]

Hahn Loeser & Parks LLP, (AV)
One Gojo Plaza Suite 300, 44311-1076 ⊙
Telephone: 330-864-5550; 1-877-HAHNLAW Facsimile: 330-864-7986
Email: inquiry@hahnlaw.com URL: http://www.hahnlaw.com
Resident Members: R. Eric Gaum; Scott M. Oldham; Mark A. Watkins. Resident Of Counsel: Louis F. Kreek, Jr. Resident Associates: Robert J. Clark; W. Edward Crooks; John J. Cunniff; Bret A. Hrivnak; Michael H. Minns; Amanda H. Wilcox.
Business, Corporate and Securities, Litigation, Taxation and Employee Benefits, Estate Planning, Probate, Real Estate, Labor, Creditors Rights, Reorganization and Bankruptcy, Intellectual Property and Technology, Environmental, Patent, Trademark and Copyright Law, Telecommunications Law, Government Relations, Public Utility and Regulatory Law, Health Care, Construction Law.
Reference: Star Bank, Akron, Ohio.
Cleveland, Ohio Office: 3300 BP Tower, 200 Public Square, 44114-2301. Telephone: 216-621-0150. Fax: 216-241-2824.
Columbus, Ohio Office: 65 East State Street, Suite 1400, 43215. Telephone: 614-221-0240. Fax: 614-221-5909.
Naples, Florida Office: 3301 Bonita Beach Road, Suite 308, Bonita Springs, 34134. Telephone: 239-949-6989. Fax: 239-949-6687.
See Professional Biographies, AKRON, OHIO

Hail, Gregory Lee ....'66 '92 C.970 B.A L.7 J.D. [Holland&M.]
Haley, E. Wm., Jr. ....'21 '50 C.701 B.S. L.7 J.D. [Haley]
Haley, Robert Scott ....'53 '82 C.381 B.S. L.8 J.D. [Haley]
Haley Law Offices, Co., L.P.A. ....867 Moe Drive, Suite G
Hall, Daniel N. ....'36 '73 C.197 A.B. L.776 J.D. 1200 Firestone Pkwy. (Pat.)‡
Hall, James A., (BV) '50 '76
C.473 B.A. L.7 J.D. Secy. & Coun., Great Northern Svgs. Co.
Hammersmith, Stephen M., (AV) ......'56 '81 C&L.608 B.A., J.D. [Buckingham,D.&B.]
Haneline, Kenneth M., (BV) ....'58 '86 C.930 B.S. L.1003 J.D. [Kastner W.&W.]
Hanlon, Deidre A., (BV) ....'52 '79 [Ferguson&H.]
Hanna, David J., (AV) ....'54 '79 C.882 B.A. L.930 J.D. [Hanna,C.&P.]
Hanna, Joseph E., (BV) ....'52 '78 C.8 B.A. L.930 J.D. 2745 Nesbitt Avenue
Hanna, Timothy H., (AV) ....'58 '85 C&L.8 B.S.B.A., J.D. [Parker L.H.&R.]
Hanna, Campbell & Powell, LLP, (AV) ....3737 Embassy Parkway
Harbin, Marty, (CV) ....'49 '90 C&L.8 B.A., J.D. State Dept. of Human Servs.
Hardesty, Stephen D., (BV) ....'45 '73 C.207 B.A. L.8 J.D. [Hardesty,K.&Z.]
Hardesty, Kaffen & Zimmerman, (AV) ....Suite 500 520 South Main Street
Hardman, Kevin P., (AV) ....'60 '85 C&L.608 B.A., J.D. [Scanlon&G.]
Haridakis, Paul M. ....'57 '84 C&L.8 B.A., J.D. Roadway Express, Inc.
Harkins, L. James, (BV) ....'24 '53 C.381 A.B. L.7 J.D. 3318 Manchester Road
Harnak, Brian K. ....'69 '94 C.608 B.A. L.7 J.D. [Ⓐ Roderick L.]
Harpst, Todd A., (BV) ....'69 '96 C.645 B.A. L.7 J.D. [Ⓐ Roetzel&A.]
Harrill, James F. ....'55 '84 C.8 B.A. L.7 J.D. Asst. Dir. City of Law
Harris, Richard H., III, (AV) ....'54 '80 C.385 B.A. L.8 J.D. [Brouse M.]
Harrison, Joseph R. ....'47 '75 C.8 B.S. L.7 J.D. [J.R.Harrison]
Harrison, Joseph R., Company, L.P.A. ....310 N. Cleveland Massillon Rd.
Hart, Patrick J., (AV) ....'50 '75 C.8 B.S. L.7 J.D. [Scanlon&G.]
Harvey, Frank H., Jr., (AV) ....'30 '55 C.674 A.B. L.930 LL.B. [Ⓒ Brouse M.]
Harvey-Williams, Lynda Euphemia, (BV) .....'47 '89 C.381 B.S. L.8 J.D. 106 S. Main St.
Harvie, C. Thomas, (AV) '43 '69 C.813 A.B. L.976 LL.B.
(adm. in NY; not adm. in OH)
Sr. V.P. & Gen. Coun., Goodyear Tire & Rubber Co., The
Haskins, Thomas F., Jr., (BV) ....'50 '76 C.8 B.S. L.7 J.D. [Daily&H.]
Haslinger, Connie J., (BV) ....'65 '91 C.381 B.S. L.8 J.D. Asst. Co. Pros.
Hathaway, Robert E. ....'32 '77 C.611 A.B. L.7 J.D. 76 S. Main St.

Hatzakis, P. Nicole ....'68 '97 C.207 B.S. L.7 J.D. Asst. Pros. Atty., Admin. Hearing Div.
Hayes, Andrew T. .... '73 '02 C.999 B.S. L.8 J.D. [Parker L.H.&R.]
Hayes, Timothy A. ....'58 '87 C.97 B.A. L.1003 J.D. Atty., FirstEnergy Corporation
Head, Elisa B. ....'71 '98 C.381 B.A. L.7 J.D. Law Clk., Co. Ct.
Hebert, Halle M. ....'75 '00 C.608 B.S. L.161 J.D. [Oldham&D.]
Heinle, Matthew A., (BV) ....'70 '95 C.473 B.S. L.608 J.D. [Brennan,M.&D.]
Heintz, Jeffrey T., (AV) ....'49 '75 C.610 B.A. L.8 J.D. [Brouse M.]
Heinzerling, Barbara M., (BV) .... '40 '79 C.608 B.S. L.7 J.D. 166 E. Market Street, #205
Heiser, Edward N., (BV) ....'26 '55 C&L.8 B.A., LL.B. 1999 Ganyard Rd.
Hendler, Michael B., (AV) ....'38 '63 C.8 B.A. L.608 J.D. [Goldman&R.]
Hendricks, Bruce J. '56 '81 C.924 B.A. L.117 J.D.
Assoc. Gen. Coun., The Goodyear Tire & Rubber Co. (Pat.)

Henning & Yost, L.P.A.
(See Canton)

Henretta, J. Thomas, (AV) ....'45 '75 C.8 B.A. L.7 J.D. [Henretta]

Henretta Law Offices, (AV)
400 Key Building, 159 S. Main Street, 44308
Telephone: 330-376-7800 Fax: 330-376-7854
Email: henrettalaw@neo.rr.com URL: http://www.henrettalaw.com
Member of Firm: J. Thomas Henretta.
Medical Malpractice, Legal Malpractice, Nursing Home Litigation, Insurance Litigation, Automobile Accidents and Injuries and Wrongful Death.
See Professional Biographies, AKRON, OHIO

Henshaw, James M., (BV) '56 '81
C.608 B.S.Econ. L.8 J.D. 1000 S. Cleveland Massillon Rd.
Herbaugh, Phillip L., (BV) '65 '95
C.779 R.B.A. L.7 J.D. 1655 West Market Street, Suite 400
Herman, John F., (BV) ....'43 '68 C.602 A.B. L.608 J.D. [J.F.Herman]
Herman, John F., Co., L.P.A., (BV) ....1800 First National Tower
Hewitt, William B., (BV) ....'32 '63 C.433 B.E.E. L.8 J.D. 4020 Stonebridge Blvd.
Heyne, Michael A. ....'45 '76 C.870 B.S. L.477 J.D. Dir., SS&G Invest. Servs. LLC
Hickman, Jason E., (BV) ....'69 '95 C.08 B.A. L.851 J.D. [Roderick L.]
Higham, Robert W., (BV) ....'40 '69 C.381 B.A. L.8 J.D. [Glinsek&H.]
Hilkert, David W., (AV) ....'49 '74 C.8 B.A. L.608 J.D. [Buckingham,D.&B.]
Hilkert, Mark, (AV) ....'50 '76 C.8 B.A. L.930 J.D. [Scanlon&G.]
Hill, John F., (AV) ....'62 '88 C.1062 B.A. L.93 J.D. [Scanlon&G.]
Hill, Patricia A. '— '80 C.657 B.S. L.7 J.D.
Mng. Atty., Community Legal Aid Services., Inc.
Hilston, Thomas A. '47 '77 C.161 B.C.E. L.1003 J.D.
Dir. of Opers. Support, FirstEnergy
Himmel, Gary L., (AV) ....'55 '80 C.381 B.A. L.7 J.D. 80 S. Summit Street
Hinton, Belinda Joyce ....'54 '81 P.O. Box 783
Hinton, James R. ....'32 '56 C.611 B.A. L.608 J.D. [J.R.Hinton] ‡
Hinton, James R., Co., L.P.A. ....4240 W. Bath Road
Hobson, Steven R., II, (BV) ....'71 '98 C.381 B.A. L.7 J.D. [Parker L.H.&R.]
Hodgkiss, Tim A. '73 '03
C.610 B.S.E.E. L.7 J.D. [Renner,K.G.B.T.&W.] (See Pat. Sect.)
Hofer, Keith R., (BV) ....'61 '89 C&L.8 B.A., J.D. 2745 Nesbitt Avenue
Hoff, George L., (BV) ....'54 '85 C.8 B.S. L.94 J.D. 529 Stratford Avenue
Hogan, Thomas Christopher .... '70 '01 C.97 B.A. L.117 J.D. Cincinnati Insurance Co.
Holcomb, John E. ....'48 '74 C.62 B.A. L.7 J.D. Mun. J.

Holda, Sheri L. '57 '01 C&L.8 B.S., J.D.
1699 King Drive, P.O. Box 308, 44309-0308
Telephone: 330-607-0438 Fax: 330-896-6496
Email: attorneyholda@neo.rr.com
Divorce, Child Custody, Adoption, Bankruptcy, Personal Bankruptcy, Wills.
See Professional Biographies, AKRON, OHIO

Holden, Joseph M., (AV) ....'27 '52 C.309 A.B. L.930 LL.B. [Brouse M.]
Holland, J. Jeffrey ....'61 '87 C.207 B.A. L.1218 J.D. [Holland&M.] ⊙
Holland & Muirden .... 55 South Miller Road, Suite 103 (⊙Sharon Center)
Hollinger Peeples, Brandie H. ....'— '03 C.302 B.A. L.8 J.D. [Roetzel&A.]
Holloway, Donald P. ....'28 '55 C.610 B.S. L.7 J.D. 601 Nome Ave.‡
Holmes, Karen M. ....'61 '85 C.851 B.A. L.8 J.D. Goodyear Tire & Rubber
Holub, Jerome L., (AV) ....'22 '51 C.608 L.607 J.D. 912 Society Bldg.
Honeck, Richard D., (BV) ....'53 '79 C&L.8 B.S.A., J.D. [Armbruster,K.K.H.&B.]
Horbus, Craig S. ....'78 '04 C.62 B.A. L.989 J.D. [Witschey W.&F.]
Horton, Harland B., Jr. '42 '72 C.674 A.B. L.7 J.D.
Gen. Coun., Litig., Bridgestone/Firestone Tech. Co.
Horwitz, Stuart M., (AV) ....'59 '85 C&L.608 B.S., J.D. [Horwitz]

Horwitz Group, The, LLC, (AV)
130 Springside Drive Suite 106, 44333
Telephone: 330-670-5300 Fax: 330-670-5355
URL: http://www.thehorwitzgroup.com
Stuart M. Horwitz.
Federal, State and Local Taxation, Corporate Law, ERISA, Estate Planning.
See Professional Biographies, AKRON, OHIO

Houlihan, Thomas R., (BV) ....'71 '98 C.528 B.A. L.8 J.D. [Amer C.]
Houston, Alma Faye '44 '80 C&L.45 B.A., J.D.
(adm. in AR; not adm. in OH) Akron Child Guidance Ctr.‡
Howard, William E., (BV) ....'44 '68 C&L.930 A.B., J.D. [Howard&G.]
Howard & Gaffney Co., L.P.A., (BV) ....76 S. Main St.
Hrina, David J. ....'70 '00 C.980 B.E.C.E. L.8 J.D. [Buckingham,D.&B.] (Pat.)
Hrivnak, Bret A. ....'70 '04 C&L.8 B.S., J.D. [Hahn L.&P.] (See Pat. Sect.)
Hudak, Daniel Joseph ....'73 '99 C.8 B.S. L.7 J.D. Hudak & Shunk Co., Lpa
Hudak, Michael J., (BV) ....'— '87 C.980 B.S. L.7 J.D. [Roetzel&A.]
Hulthen, Amy McKee, (BV) ....'63 '88 C.294 B.A. L.8 J.D. 867 Moe Dr.
Humphrys, Dawn Addie '74 '98
C.8 B.A. L.1003 J.D. Jud. Atty., Summit Co. Ct. of Com. Pleas
Hunsicker, J. Bruce, (AV) ....'54 '80 C.608 B.A. L.8 J.D. [Vorys,S.S.&P.]
Hunsicker, Oscar A., Jr., (AV) ....'22 '48 C.8 A.B. L.930 J.D. [Brouse M.]
Hunt, Robert C., (BV) ....'50 '76 C.8 B.S.I.M. L.7 J.D. [Calhoun,W.&H.]
Hunter, David M., (AV) ....'50 '75 C.674 A.B. L.8 J.D. [Brouse M.]
Huntley, Daphne W. ....'58 '94 C.10 B.S. L.8 J.D. 75 E. Market St.
Huston, Charles M. ....'37 '70 C.381 B.S.B.A. L.8 J.D. Huston Legal Servs.
Iden, Charles R., (AV) ....'14 '38 C&L.930 A.B., LL.B. [Brouse M.]
Incorvati, Robert A., (BV) ....'63 '90 C&L.8 B.S., J.D. [Germano,R.&C.]
Inman, James E. ....'41 '71 C.62 B.A. L.8 J.D. Prof. of Bus. Law, Univ. of Akron
Irvin, Richd. W. ....'16 '53 C.930 A.B. L.7 LL.B. 925 Canyon Trail‡
Ivey, Timothy C., (BV) ..... '62 '87 C.851 B.B.A. L.930 J.D. [Roetzel&A.] (⊙Cleveland)
Jaballas, Roderick Rosca ....'65 '93 C.201 B.A. L.884 J.D. 450 Grant St.
Jackson, Paul L., (AV) ....'63 '88 C&L.8 B.S., J.D. [Roetzel&A.]
Jacquemain, Jennifer J. ....'— '98 C.161 B.A. L.7 J.D. [Bernlohr W.]
James, Frances White, (BV) ....'44 '81 C.25 B.A. L.8 J.D. 2550 Addyston Road
James, Jeffrey N., (BV) ....'56 '91 C.608 B.A. L.8 J.D. 7 W. Bowery St.
Jamison, Andrew D. ....'71 '98 C&L.8 B.A., J.D. [Reminger&R.]
Janos, Peter D., (BV) ....'66 '92 C.665 B.A. L.8 J.D. [Perantinides&N.]

Jeffries, Timothy J.
(See Canton)

Jenkins, David W. .... '59 '87 C.277 M.S. L.273 J.D. Sr. Atty., FirstEnergy Corp.
Jenkins, Donald M. ....'28 '64 C&L.7 B.A., J.D. Prof. of Law, Univ. of Akron
Jenkins, Hayes A., (AV) ....'33 '59 C.170 A.B. L.309 J.D. 1144 E. Market St.‡
Johnson, Allan, (AV) ....'25 '49 C&L.309 A.B., LL.B. 1799 Akron-Peninsula Rd.‡
Johnson, Eric W. ....'68 '94 C.475 B.S. L.7 J.D. [Holland&M.]
Johnstone, Russell R. '13 '36 C&L.585 LL.B.
(adm. in ND; not adm. in OH) 333 N. Portage Path‡
Jones, Crystal L. ....'55 '83 C.1044 B.S. L.326 J.D. 765 Stoner Ave.
Jones, Erik M. ....'75 '00 C.161 B.A. L.1003 J.D. [Mentzer&M.]
Jones, Jean M. ....'52 '86 C.8 B.A. L.7 J.D. State Farm Ins. Cos.
Jones, Julie Ann ....'59 '91 C.66 B.A. L.7 J.D. Staff Atty., Ninth Dist. Ct. of Appeals
Jones, Michael Alan ....'55 '87 C.107 B.A. L.325 J.D. State Indus. Comm.
Jones, Wayne M., (BV) ....'54 '89 C.8 B.S. L.117 J.D. [Roetzel&A.] (⊙Wash., DC)

Jones, Douglas D., Co., LPA
(See Canton)

Joondeph, Jerome J., (AV) ....'43 '68 C.381 B.A. L.608 J.D. [Joondeph&B.]

Joondeph & Bittel, LLP, (AV)
Suite 700 Akron Centre Plaza, 50 South Main Street, 44308-1881
Telephone: 330-762-2600 Facsimile: 330-762-2604 Cleveland Telephone: 216-348-1935
Email: JB1LAW@aol.com
Members of Firm: Jerome J. Joondeph; Timothy M. Bittel. Associates: Dale V. Wilson; Kevin T. Lyden.
Civil Trial and Appellate Practice in Federal and State Courts. Taxation, Corporate, Health Care, Administrative, Pension, Real Estate, Construction Litigation, Labor and Employment, Bankruptcy, Estate Planning, Probate Law and Boat Manufacturing Liability.
Reference: First Merit Bank, N.A.
See Professional Biographies, AKRON, OHIO

Jordan, William S., III '49 '74 C.813 B.A. L.477 J.D.
(adm. in MI; not adm. in OH) McDowell Prof. of Law, Univ. of Akron School of Law
Julius, Thomas Norbert, (AV) ....'49 '73 C.1062 B.S.B.A. L.8 J.D. [T.N.Julius]

Julius, Thomas N., (AV)
265 Steeplechase Lane, 44262
Telephone: 330-283-6480 Fax: 330-633-5313
Email: tnjulius@aol.com URL: http://www.lawyers.com/tjulius
Thomas Norbert Julius.
Securities, Tax Law, Corporate Law, Business Law, Estate Planning, Mergers and Acquisitions.
See Professional Biographies, AKRON, OHIO

Kades, Matthew D. ....'69 '96 C.326 B.A. L.930 J.D. Asst. Co. Pros.
Kaffen, Ronald O., (AV) ....'48 '74 C.473 A.B. L.930 J.D. [Hardesty,K.&Z.]

Kaforey, Ellen C., (BV) '53 '89 C&L.8 B.S.N., J.D.
1024 Key Building, 159 South Main Street, 44308
Telephone: 330-253-0719 Fax: 330-253-0722
Email: ekaforey@neo.rr.com
Estate Planning, Wills, Trust Law, Guardianship, Adoption Law.
See Professional Biographies, AKRON, OHIO

Kaforey, Melville ....'22 '53 C.8 A.B. L.7 LL.B. 159 S. Main St.
Kainec, Lisa A. ....'67 '93 C.161 B.B.A. L.930 J.D. [Kastner W.&W.]
Kaluza, Michael E., (AV) '45 '74 C.294 A.B. L.665 J.D.
(adm. in PA; not adm. in OH) Gen. Coun., Advanced Elastomer Systems, L.P.
Kaminski, Edward C., (AV) ....'31 '59 C.8 B.A. L.930 J.D. 159 S. Main Street
Kaplan, Michael J., (BV) ....'50 '76 C.1505 B.A. L.8 J.D. 395 Springside Dr.
Kastner, Harley M., (AV) ....'49 '73 C.8 B.A. L.7 J.D. [Kastner W.&W.]

Kastner Westman & Wilkins, LLC, (AV) BB
3480 West Market Street, Suite 300, 44333
Telephone: 330-867-9998 Fax: 330-867-3786
Email: kww@kwwlaborlaw.com URL: http://www.kwwlaborlaw.com
Harley M. Kastner; Dean E. Westman; James P. Wilkins; Kenneth M. Haneline; Keith L. Pryatel; John W. McKenzie; Lisa A. Kainec; Bruce H. Fahey. Associates: Thomas E. Green; Richard Davies. Of Counsel: Ted N. Kazaglis.
Employment Law, including Labor Relations, Equal Employment Opportunity, Public Sector Labor Law, OSHA, Arbitration, Wage and Hour, Workers Compensation Law, Claims Management, Affirmative Action, Employee Benefits, Human Resources Consulting, Site Selection Analysis.
See Professional Biographies, AKRON, OHIO

Kaszowski, Tammy Lynn .... '70 '00 C.665 B.A. L.7 J.D. City Law Dept., Civil Div.
Kaufmann, Philip S., (AV) ....'46 '71 C.424 B.A. L.8 J.D. [Kaufmann&K.]

Kaufmann & Kaufmann, (AV)
1200 First National Tower, 44308-1460
Telephone: 330-762-7655 Telecopier: 330-762-7537
Frank P. Kaufmann (1908-1994); Frank P. Devany (1920-1980); Amos H. Englebeck (1885-1952); Philip S. Kaufmann; Roy A. Krall;—Loma L. Swett; Steven P. Mutersbaugh; Julie A. Farris.
General Civil Practice in all Courts. Corporate Law, Real Estate, Probate, Federal Income, Estate and Gift Taxation, Estate Planning, Guardianships, Medicaid Planning, Elder Law, Estate Planning for the Disabled, Estate Planning for Parents of Disabled Children.
Representative Clients: Miller's Rental and Sales Co., Inc.; The Village of St. Edward; Blind & Sons, Inc.; King Machine of Akron, Inc.; J. Parker & Sons, Inc.
References: First National Bank of Akron; Bank One, Akron, NA.
See Professional Biographies, AKRON, OHIO

Kayuha, Thomas A. ....'41 '72 C.1027 B.S. L.345 J.D. 76 S. Main St. (Pat.)
Kazaglis, Ted N. ....'62 '87 C.381 B.B.A. L.8 J.D. [Kastner W.&W.]
Kazlouskas, Anthony ....'20 '54 C.8 L.7 LL.B. Co. Welfare Dept.
Keating, Patrick J., (AV) ....'54 '83 C.381 B.A. L.7 J.D. [Buckingham,D.&B.]
Keller, Clay Kenneth ....'69 '00 C.958 B.S. L.602 J.D. [Buckingham,D.&B.]
Kelley, Thomas, (BV) ....'52 '78 C&L.8 B.A., J.D. [Armbruster,K.K.H.&B.]
Kemp, Edward G., (AV) '42 '68
C.473 B.A. L.608 J.D. Human Resources Dept, 44 E Exchange St
Kennedy, Ryan P. ....'— '04 C.967 B.S. L.8 [Roetzel&A.]
Kenner, Phillip L., (AV) '35 '65
C.339 B.S. L.8 J.D. [Renner,K.G.B.T.&W.] (See Pat. Sect.)
Kern, David, (AV) ....'60 '90 C.861 B.S. L.117 J.D. [Buckingham,D.&B.]
Kerper, Robert E., Jr. ....'44 '74 C.139 A.B. L.831 J.D. 1 Cascade Plaza
Kersker, Linda B., (AV) ....'47 '72 C.207 B.A. L.477 J.D. [Brouse M.]
Killian, Timothy James ....'52 '76 C&L.8 B.A., J.D. [Killian,T.J.]
Killian, Timothy J. ....2064 Killian Road
Kinder, Richard Andrew ....'65 '93 C.967 B.A. L.8 J.D. 159 S. Main St., Ste. 830
King, David L. ....'48 '89 C.608 B.S. L.150 J.D. 1144 E. Market St. (Pat.)
Kinsinger, Richard E. ....'26 '71 C.8 B.A. L.7 J.D. Adult Prob. Dept.
Kipp, Jerald B., (BV) ....'52 '81 C.381 B.A. L.1003 J.D. 2803 Fort Island Dr.

Klein, Linda B. ....'48 '89 C.966 B.A. L.8 J.D. 560 Tamiami Trail‡
Klingshirn, Neil E., (BV) ....'61 '86 C.381 B.B.A. L.608 J.D. [Fortney&K.]
Klug, William F., IV '39 '66 C.846 B.B.A. L.665 LL.B.
(adm. in PA; not adm. in OH) Roadway Express, Inc.
Knoll, Jeffrey T., (BV) ....'66 '91 C.886 B.S. L.608 J.D. [Stark&K.]
Knoll, Thomas G., (AV) ....'39 '65 C.473 B.A. L.608 J.D. [Stark&K.]
Knowlton, Sanderson Law Offices, (AV) ....One Cascade Plaza
Koch, Matthew J., (BV) ....'35 '67 C.608 B.S. L.1003 J.D. [Koch&R.]
Koch & Regal, (BV) ....405 Quaker Sq.
Kodish, Joseph S., (AV) '36 '69
C.608 B.S. L.1003 J.D. 411 Wolf Ledges Parkway, Suite 300
Koehler, Ronald J., (BV) ....'60 '86 C&L.8 B.A., J.D. 3522 Manchester Road
Kolich, Kathy J. ....'57 '87 C&L.608 B.S., J.D. Sr. Atty., FirstEnergy Corp.
Kolk, J. Michael ....'60 '86 C.930 B.S. L.161 J.D. Cohen & Co.‡
Konstand, Dean, (BV) ....'53 '79 C.8 B.A. L.7 J.D. 2500 First Natl. Twr.
Konstand, Robert ....'21 '48 C.8 B.A. L.930 LL.B. 106 S. Main St.‡
Konstand, Robert G., (BV) ....'52 '77 C.8 B.A. L.7 J.D. 2500 First National Twr.
Koosed, Margery B. M. ......'48 '74 C.473 B.S. L.930 J.D. Prof. of Law, Univ. of Akron
Kopp, Ronald S., (AV) ....'54 '79 C.473 A.B. L.608 J.D. [Roetzel&A.]
Korkosz, Arthur E. '47 '74
C.688 B.S. L.276 J.D. Sr. Atty., FirstEnergy Corporation (Pat.)
Kosiewicz, Joy D. ....'73 '98 C.25 B.S. L.930 J.D. [A Brouse M.]
Kosik, John F. '42 '70 C.754 B.S. L.851 J.D.
V.P., Secy. & Gen. Coun., Kay Jewelers, Inc.
Kostoff, Peter M., (BV) ....'56 '82 C.8 B.A. L.1003 J.D. [Roetzel&A.]
Kot, Thomas Philip, (AV) ....'52 '79 C.8 B.A. L.7 J.D. [Armbruster,K.K.H.&B.]
Kovac, Frederick J. ....'30 '62 C&L.8 B.S.,M.S., J.D. 130 Hickory Road
Kovach, John Joseph ....'61 '87 C&L.8 B.S., J.D. Stroud Engineering Servs.

Kovach & Farling Co., LPA
(See Cleveland)

Koval, William J., Jr. ....'58 '90 C.602 BBA L.1003 J.D. 75 E. Market St.
Kozlowski, Timothy E., Jr. '65 '91 C.604 B.A. L.989 J.D.
Staff Atty., Community Legal Aid Services., Inc.
Krajewski, John K., (BV) ....'59 '85 C.573 B.B.A. L.930 J.D. [Stark&K.]
Krall, Roy A., (AV) ....'62 '89 C.659 B.A. L.930 J.D. [Kaufmann&K.]
Kramer, Reginald S., (BV) ....'52 '80 C.970 B.A. L.7 J.D. [Oldham&D.]
Kraus, James D., (AV) ....'56 '83 C&L.8 B.A., J.D. [Buckingham,D.&B.]
Kreek, Louis F., Jr. ....'28 '52 C.453 B.S. L.273 J.D. [C Hahn L.&P.] (See Pat. Sect.)
Kremer, Stephan C. ....'66 '93 C&L.8 B.S.I.M., J.D. [A Reminger&R.]
Kristoff, Michael, Sr. ....'24 '68 C.8 B.A. L.7 J.D. 288 Selden Ave.‡
Krohn, Mark E., (BV) '70 '96 C.160 B.A. L.930 J.D.
Chief Operations Off/Gen. Coun., White Hat Ventures
Kruger, Gary I. ....'46 '77 C.350 B.S. L.7 J.D. Goodyear Tire & Rubber
Kuhlman, Kathleen ....'51 '95 C.473 B.S. L.8 J.D. 1858 Brookshire Rd.
Kurek, James D., (AV) ....'55 '81 C.851 B.B.A. L.477 J.D. [Roetzel&A.]
Kuri, Phillip A. ....'67 '93 C.970 B.A. L.8 J.D. [A Reminger&R.]
Kutuchief, Richard P., (BV) ....'52 '78 C.528 B.A. L.607 J.D. 807 Key Bldg.
Lacher, Frederick K., (AV) ....'20 '50 C.119 B.S. L.8 J.D. [C Brouse M.] (Pat.)
Lambert, John D. ....'55 '79 C.8 B.S.B.A. L.7 J.D. 265 S. Main St.
La Monica, Alfred N. ....'17 '46 C.8 L.7 LL.B. 319 W. Market St.
LaSalvia, Anthony J. ....'37 '72 C.363 B.S.S. L.7 J.D. Simmons Hall 59
Lasher, Alvin W. ....'31 '59 C&L.930 A.B., LL.B. 209 S. Main St.‡
Laybourne, Robert B., (BV) ....'48 '73 C&L.607 B.A., J.D. 503 Society Bldg.
Layfield, L. DeWayne '63 '90 C.1061 B.S.Ch.E. L.846 J.D.
(adm. in TX; not adm. in OH) 1200 Firestone Pkwy.
Lazar, John P., (BV) ....'46 '83 C.381 B.G.S. L.8 J.D. [J.P.Lazar]
Lazar, John P., Co., LPA, (BV) ....310 N. Cleveland Massillon Rd.
LeBoeuf, Bradley S. ....'59 '86 C.347 B.A. L.851 J.D. 7 W. Bowery St., Ste. 604
Lee, Robert E., (BV) ....'46 '74 C.608 B.A. L.607 J.D. 2483 S. Main St.
Lee, Ronald B., (AV) ....'52 '78 C.8 B.S. L.7 J.D. [Roetzel&A.]
Leffler, Amanda M. ....'— '02 C.851 B.A. L.7 J.D. [A Brouse M.]

Leffler, Daniel J., Counselor at Law '67 '03 C&L.8 B.S., J.D.
Union Point, 190 Union Street, Suite 201, 44304
Telephone: 330-253-5996 Fax: 330-762-9743
Email: danielleffler@sbcglobal.net URL: http://www.djlnegotiations.com
Employment Law, Union Contract Negotiations, Union Labor Law, Civil Litigation.
See Professional Biographies, AKRON, OHIO

Leffler, Frederick W., (BV) ....'64 '90 C.294 B.A. L.8 J.D. [Roetzel&A.]
Leiby, Stephen P., (BV) ....'47 '73 C.1208 B.A. L.8 J.D. [Parker L.H.&R.]
Lembright, Ronald K., (AV) ....'39 '73 C.610 B.S.C. L.161 J.D. [Roderick L.]
Lenart, Lynn Marie ....'57 '00 C&L.8 B.A., J.D. Univ. of Akron, School of Law
Lepp, Aaron G., (BV) ....'69 '95 C.896 B.A. L.608 J.D. [Stark&K.]
Leslie, Mary Ellen ....'38 '01 C.117 B.A. L.7 J.D. 777 W. Market
Lettieri, Frank A., (AV) ....'47 '74 C.8 B.S. L.7 J.D. [Brennan,M.&D.]
Levin, Richard V., (BV) ....'42 '67 C&L.930 A.B., J.D. 3250 W. Market Street, Suite 307
Lewandowski, Thomas P. '39 '70 C&L.851 B.S.M.E., J.D.
Patent Attorney, Goodyear Tire & Rubber (Pat.)
Lewis, David J., (AV) ....'57 '87 C.381 B.B.A. L.1003 J.D. [Buckingham,D.&B.]
Leyerle, Albert H. ....'32 '60 C.608 B.S. L.930 J.D. 80 N. Portage Path
Lieberth, David A., (AV) ....'47 '77 C.8 B.A. L.7 J.D. [Lieberth/A.]
Lieberth/Anderson, A Legal Prof. Assoc., (AV) ....159 S. Main St., Ste. 517
Lincicome, David V. C. ....'45 '86 C.367 B.A. L.8 J.D. Divison By Zero, Inc.
Lindsay, James R. ....'24 '52 C.477 B.S.E. L.7 J.D. 257 Keith Ave.‡
Link, Mary T. '60 '90 C.436 B.S. L.424 J.D.
(adm. in IL; not adm. in OH) [C Brouse M.]
Link, Terrence H., II ....'73 '99 C.473 B.S. L.930 J.D. [A Roetzel&A.]
Linnen, Jerome T., Jr., (BV) ....'61 '87 C.610 B.B.A. L.7 J.D. 789 W. Market St
Linton, Robert F., (AV) ....'37 '60 C.8 A.B. L.608 J.D. [C Roderick L.]
Livick, Anthony '38 '80 C&L.8 B.S.B.A., J.D.
Legal Counsel/Project Manager, URS Corporation
Lloyd, Philip A., (AV) ....'47 '72 C.611 B.A. L.8 J.D. [C Vorys,S.S.&P.]
Lockshin, Mary Jo, (BV) ....'57 '81 C&L.607 B.A., J.D. [Stark&K.]
Lohr, Mary Alison ....'71 '99 C.608 B.A. L.7 J.D. Pros. Off.
Lohr, Richard A. .....'61 '99 C.610 B.A. L.8 J.D. Investigator, Ohio Civil Rights Comm.
Lombardi, David G., (BV) ....'62 '89 C.473 B.S. L.8 J.D. 7 W. Bowery St., Ste. 507
Lombardi, Donald E., (BV) ....'38 '68 C&L.8 B.S., J.D. 2745 Nesbitt Ave.
Lombardi, Frederick M., (AV) ....'37 '62 C.8 B.A. L.930 J.D. [Buckingham,D.&B.]
Longbrake, W. Bradford, (CV) ....'69 '95 C.970 B.A. L.930 J.D. [A Reminger&R.]
Looney, David A., (BV) ....'50 '74 C.8 B.A. L.7 J.D. [D.A.Looney]
Looney, David A., Co., LPA, (BV) .... 1735 South Main Street
Love, William E., II ....'51 '76 C.967 B.A. L.7 J.D. 739 Rextur Dr.
Lowrey, Charles E., (BV) ....'30 '61 C.381 A.B. L.7 LL.B. 1686 Juniaia Rd.

Lowrie, Scott R., (BV) .....'59 '84 C.608 B.S. L.851 J.D. 3700 Massillon Road, Suite 360
Lowry, Mora, (BV) ....'73 '99 C.347 B.A. L.8 J.D. 120 E. Mill Street, Suite 315
Lucht, Gregory J. ....'76 '02 C.294 B.A. L.7 J.D. [A Scanlon&G.]
Luck, Elaine ....'48 '82 C.8 B.S. L.7 J.D. P.O. Box 5473
Ludwig, Mark H., (BV) ....'49 '74 C&L.8 B.S.B.A., J.D. [A Cole]
Luecke, Marcia ....'42 '79 C.879 B.A. L.910 J.D. Mag., Co. Juv. Ct.
Luecken, John J., Jr., (BV) ....'61 '90 C.608 B.S. L.161 J.D. Atty., FirstEnergy Corp.
Lux, Sallie Conley, (BV) ....'52 '81 C&L.150 B.A., J.D. [Brouse M.]
Lyden, Kevin T. ....'56 '87 C.980 A.B. L.7 J.D. [A Joondeph&B.]
Lyden, Shawn M., (BV) ....'59 '84 C.207 B.A. L.930 J.D. [Brouse M.]
Lynch, M. Teri ....'52 '90 C&L.8 B.S., J.D. 665 W. Exchange St.
Lynett, John J., (AV) ....'32 '61 C&L.8 B.A., J.D. [C Roderick L.]
Lynett, John J., Jr., (BV) ....'56 '93 C.8 B.S.M.T. L.7 J.D. [Slater,Z.&G.]
Lynett, Thomas F. ....'27 '57 C.8 L.7 LL.B. Mag., Mun. Ct.
Lyons, James M., Jr., (AV) ....'57 '82 C.363 B.S. L.608 J.D. [Hanna,C.&P.]
Machan, Sandra J., (BV) ....'63 '91 C&L.8 B.S., J.D. [Machan&Assoc.]
Machan & Associates Co. LPA, (BV) ....565 Wolf Ledges Pkwy.
Mack, Monte E. ....'27 '58 C.381 B.A. L.7 J.D. Mun. J.
Mackey, J. Francis ....'70 '98 C.473 B.S.Ed. L.8 J.D. [A Amer C.]
Maffei, Rocco J. '49 '75 C.855 B.A. L.1294 J.D.
Vice President & General Counsel, Lockheed Martin Naval Electronics & Surveillance Systems
Mahoney, Edward J. ....'24 '50 C.8 A.B. L.930 LL.B. Ret. Ct. of App. J.
Maillis, Michael J. ....'69 '95 C.980 B.A. L.8 J.D. [A Perantinides&N.]
Maj, JoAnn M. ....'32 '56 C.8 B.A. L.150 LL.B. Industrial Comm. of Ohio
Malarcik, Donald J., Jr., (BV) ....'67 '93 C.381 B.A. L.8 J.D. [Gorman,M.&P.]
Mallo, George D., (BV) ....'47 '74 C.610 B.S. L.607 J.D. 2483 South Main Street
Mallo, Ted A. ....'45 '72 C&L.8 B.S., J.D. Gen. Coun. & Asst. Secy., Univ. of Akron
Malone, Brian J. ....'70 '97 C.602 B.B.A. L.472 J.D. [Trattner&M.]
Malone, Robert W., (AV) ....'51 '76 C.528 B.A. L.608 J.D. [Buckingham,D.&B.]
Manella, Michael J. '56 '96
C.381 B.S. L.8 J.D. Gen. Coun., Aircraft Braking Systems Corp.
Manes, Gregg A., (BV) ....'59 '84 C.610 B.B.A. L.7 J.D. 333 S. Main St., Ste. 401
Manes, Louis L. ....'05 '29 C.8 L.608 100 Brookmont Rd.
Manfull, Ashley M. ....'— '99 C.294 B.A. L.7 J.D. [A Vorys,S.S.&P.]
Manley, Timothy M., (BV) ....'25 '77 C.309 B.A. L.1003 J.D. 450 Grant St.
Manna, Anthony S., (AV) ....'60 '86 C.608 B.A. L.245 J.D. [Brennan,M.&D.]
Manos, Chris G., (BV) ....'58 '85 C.381 B.A. L.7 J.D. 2745 Nesbitt Ave.
Manos, Geo. T., (AV) ....'27 '54 C.8 B.A. L.150 J.D. [Teodosio,C.&M.]
Marczely, David W. ....'43 '91 L.1003 J.D. Dir., Environmental Design Group Inc.
Margolis, Matthew A. ....'28 '50 C.8 B.A. L.477 J.D. 3265 W. Market St.‡
Markling, Matthew John, (CV) ....'71 '97 C&L.608 B.A., J.D. [McGown&M.]
Marks, Donald L. ....'28 '53 C.381 L.607 LL.B. 1650 Home Ave.
Markulis, George John '53 '85 C.871 B.S.E.E. L.770 J.D.
(adm. in CA; not adm. in OH) 1204 Massillon Road
Maroon, Andrea .....'72 '05 C&L.8 B.A., J.D. Trust Compl. Offr., First Merit Bank, N.A.
Marsh Stormer, Elinore ....'56 '82 C.198 B.A. L.8 J.D. Mun. J.
Marshall, Craig S., (AV) ....'60 '86 C.8 B.S. L.7 J.D. [Buckingham,D.&B.]

Marshall, Dennehey, Warner, Coleman & Goggin
120 E. Mill Street, Suite 240, 44308 ⊙
Telephone: 330-255-0037 Fax: 330-255-0040
Email: marshalldennehey@mdwcg.com URL: http://www.marshalldennehey.com
Shareholder: Samuel G. Casolari, Jr. Resident Associates: John Christopher Reece; Martin H. Sitler.
Defense Litigation Practice before all State and Federal Courts and Administrative Agencies. Appellate Advocacy; Arson; Fraud Litigation; Automobile Liability; Automotive Products Liability; Bad Faith; Employment Law; Commercial Litigation; Environmental and Toxic Torts; General Liability; Health Care Liability; Insurance Coverage; Insurance Law; Intellectual Property; Life, Health & Disability; Liquor Liability; Long-Term Care Liability; Municipal Liability and Civil Rights; Construction Litigation; Medical Device and Pharmaceutical; Medical Malpractice; Products Liability; Professional Malpractice; Property Damage; Railroad Litigation; Retail Liability; Special Investigations Litigation; Amusement Park, Sports and Entertainment; Securities & Investments; Transportation Litigation; Trucking Litigation; Workers' Compensation; Technology.
Bethlehem, Pennsylvania Office: 1200 Martin Tower. Telephone: 484-895-2300. Fax: 484-895-0208.
Doylestown, Pennsylvania Office: 10 North Main Street. Telephone: 267-880-2020. Fax: 215-348-5439.
Erie, Pennsylvania Office: Renaissance Centre, 1001 State Street, 14th Floor. Telephone: 814-461-7800. Fax: 814-461-7818.
Harrisburg, Pennsylvania Office: 4200 Crums Mill Road, Suite B. Telephone: 717-651-3500. Fax: 717-651-9630.
King Of Prussia, Pennsylvania Office: 620 Freedom Business Center, Suite 300. Telephone: 610-354-8250. Fax: 610-354-8299; 610-354-8499.
Pittsburgh, Pennsylvania Office: 600 Grant Street, US Steel Tower, Suite 2900. Telephone: 412-803-1140. Fax: 412-803-1188.
Scranton, Pennsylvania Office: 401 Adams Avenue, Suite 400. Telephone: 570-496-4600. Fax: 570-496-0567.
Williamsport, Pennsylvania Office: 33 W. Third Street, Suite 200. Telephone: 570-326-9091. Fax: 570-326-5507.
Cherry Hill, New Jersey Office: Woodland Falls Corporate Park, 200 Lake Drive East, Suite 300. Telephone: 856-414-6000. Fax: 856-414-6077.
Wilmington, Delaware Office: 1220 North Market Street, 5th Floor. Telephone: 302-552-4300. Fax: 302-651-7905.
Roseland, New Jersey Office: 425 Eagle Rock Avenue, Suite 302. Telephone: 973-618-4100. Fax: 973-618-0685.
Tampa, Florida Office: 201 E. Kennedy Boulevard, Suite 1100. Telephone: 813-472-7800. Fax: 813-472-7811.
Orlando, Florida Office: Landmark Center One, 315 East Robinson Street, Suite 475. Telephone: 407-246-0668. Fax: 407-839-3008.
Fort Lauderdale, Florida Office: One East Broward Boulevard, Suite 500. Telephone: 954-847-4920. Fax: 954-627-6640.
Jacksonville, Florida Office: 200 West Forsythe Street, Suite 1400. Telephone: 904-358-4200. Fax: 904-355-0018.
See Professional Biographies, AKRON, OHIO

Martin, John F., (BV) ....'59 '84 C.473 B.A. L.608 J.D. [Brennan,M.&D.]
Martin, Ronald M., (BV) ....'41 '69 C&L.8 B.S.B.A., J.D. 1615 Akron Peninsula Rd.
Marting, Margaret L. ....'61 '92 C.610 B.A. L.8 J.D. [A Hanna,C.&P.]
Mastrantonio, Steven W., (BV) ....'67 '92 C.107 B.A. L.08 J.D. [A Roderick L.]
Matasich, Michael J. ....'— '04 C&L.8 B.A., J.D. [A Buckingham,D.&B.]
Matejkovic, John E., (BV) ....'52 '79 C&L.8 B.A., J.D. 3250 W. Market St., Ste. 307
Maurer, Steven A. ....'44 '69 C.31 B.A. L.494 J.D. [A Cole]
Maxa, Leigh A. ....'78 '03 C.97 B.S. L.7 J.D. [A Brennan,M.&D.]
Maxwell, MaryBeth Green, (BV) ....'57 '82 C.97 B.A. L.7 J.D. 7 W. Bowery St #507
Mayer, Christine Amer ....'71 '96 C.228 B.A. L.608 J.D. [C Buckingham,D.&B.]
Mazak, Edward P., Jr., (BV) ....'28 '81 C.8 B.M.E. L.7 J.D. [Smith&M.]
Mazgaj, Frank G., (AV) ....'61 '87 C.8 B.S.B.A. L.7 J.D. [Hanna,C.&P.]
Mazur, Louise M., (BV) ....'57 '82 C.381 B.S. L.7 J.D. [C Rupert]
Mazzola, Todd A. ....'67 '93 C.610 B.S.J. L.608 J.D. [C Roderick L.]

McCarroll, John J.
(See Cleveland)

McCarty, Alison ....'62 '87 C.937 B.A. L.896 J.D. Mun. J.
McCarty, Robert A., (BV) ....'61 '88 C&L.8 B.A., J.D. [Mentzer&M.]

McCarty, Thomas M., (BV) .... '55 '82 C.8 B.A. L.7 J.D. [T.M.McCarty]
McCarty, Thomas M., Co., LPA, (BV) ....230 White Pond Dr.
McClain, A. Bradley .... '48 '97 C.8 B.A. L.7 J.D. 209 S. Main Street, 8th Floor
McCue, Shannon V. '71 '98
C.608 B.S.M.E. L.8 J.D. [🄰 Renner,K.G.B.T.&W.] (See Pat. Sect.)
McGarrity, Steven J. '68 '96 C.1077 B.A. L.930 J.D.
Network Administrator, Community Legal Aid Services., Inc.
McGowan, Michael L., (BV) ....'22 '60 C.800 B.S. L.8 J.D. 646 Cliffside Dr.
McGowan, R. James, (BV) ..... '53 '78 C.611 B.A. L.607 J.D. 1799 Akron Peninsula Rd.
McGown, Susan, (BV) ....'52 '88 C.188 B.A. L.8 J.D. [McGown&M.]
McGown & Markling, Co., L.P.A., (BV) ....1894 N. Cleveland Massillon Rd.
Mcguiness, Robert L. '45 '70 C&L.724 B.B.A., J.D.
(adm. in NY; not adm. in OH) F.B.I.
McIntyre, John O., (BV) ....'22 '55 C.8 B.S. L.7 LL.B. 1914 Evergreen Avenue
McKenna, Gene H., (BV) .... '44 '78 C.608 B.A. L.8 J.D. [McKenna&M.]
McKenna & Modugno, (BV) ....4367 State Rd.
McKenney, Todd M. ....'63 '89 C.318 B.A. L.608 J.D. The Chapel
McKenzie, John W., (AV) .... '62 '92 C.896 B.A. L.930 J.D. [Kastner W.&W.]
McKinzie, Timothy Dale, (BV) ....'54 '93 C.347 B.A. L.8 J.D. [McKinzie&Assoc.]

McKinzie and Associates, (BV)
529 White Pond, 44320-1123
Telephone: 330-864-3100 Fax: 330-864-7753
Email: law@apk.net URL: http://www.mckinzieandassociateslaw.com
Timothy Dale McKinzie.
Business Law, Criminal Law, Construction, Personal Injury, Family Law and Civil Practice.
See Professional Biographies, AKRON, OHIO

McLaughlin, Kelly L., (BV) ....'62 '87 C&L.608 B.A., J.D. 411 Wolf Ledges Pkwy.
McLean, Hillary B. .... '71 '04 C.363 B.A. L.8 J.D. [🄰 Buckingham,D.&B.]
McNally, Harry D. .... '44 '71 C.608 B.S. in Bus. L.8 J.D. Roadway Express, Inc.
McNeil, Keith P. ....'56 '81 C.8 B.A.Ed. L.7 J.D. State Civil Rights Comm.
McQueen, Aaron E. .... '71 '97 C.161 B.B.A. L.930 J.D. [Roetzel&A.]
Meador, Carl E., (BV) ....'35 '66 C&L.8 B.S., J.D. [Meador]
Meador Law Office, (BV) ....2770 W. Market St.
Meeker, Robert C., (BV) ....'44 '69 C.602 B.A. L.7 J.D. [Blakemore,M.&B.]

Mendenhall, Warner, Law Office of, (BV) '62 '98 C&L.8 B.A., J.D.
190 North Union Street, 44304
Telephone: 330-535-9160; 877-764-2219 Fax: 330-762-9743
Email: warnermendenhall@hotmail.com URL: http://www.warnermendenhall.com
Language: Spanish.
False Claims Act, Whistleblower Litigation, Qui Tam Litigation, Employment Law, Government, Municipal Law, Litigation, Bankruptcy.
See Professional Biographies, AKRON, OHIO

Menefee, M. Terrell .... '68 '99 C.294 B.A. L.1003 J.D. [🄲 Brouse M.]
Mentzer, Howard E., (AV) ....'44 '69 C.352 B.A. L.7 J.D. [Mentzer&M.]
Mentzer, Linda B., (BV) .... '47 '83 C.1267 B.A. L.7 J.D. [Mentzer&M.]
Mentzer and Mygrant Ltd., (AV) ....1 Cascade Plaza, 20th Floor
Merkle, Emil A. ....'03 '50 C.597 L.7 LL.B. 994 Hampton Ridge Dr.‡
Merklin, Marc B., (AV) ....'60 '84 C&L.930 B.A., J.D. [Brouse M.]
Merlitti, James A., (BV) .... '48 '74 C.602 B.A. L.8 J.D. [Burdon&M.]
Meyer, Henry (Hank) F. ....'62 '99 C.8 B.S. L.7 J.D. [🄰 Buckingham,D.&B.]
Michael, Kathryn Ann '61 '86 C&L.8 B.A., J.D.
2500 First National Tower, 106 S. Main Street
Migdal, Stanley B., (BV) '32 '56 C&L.608 B.S., LL.B.
First National Tower, Suite 2500
Mikesell, William F., (BV) .....'— '84 C.980 B.S.B.A. L.7 J.D. 159 S. Main St., Ste. 400
Miller, Anthony E. '51 '77 C.207 B.A. L.608 J.D.
Ast. Gen. Coun., Goodyear Tire & Rubber Company, The
Miller, Don R. ....'26 '56 C.8 B.A. L.7 J.D. 1805 Stabler Rd.
Miller, Ebony L. ....'77 '03 C.901 B.A. L.902 J.D. FirstEnergy Corporation
Miller, John R. .... '50 '76 C.610 B.A. L.861 J.D. 3250 W. Market St.
Miller-Leonard, Allyson .... '64 '92 C.829 B.S. L.7 J.D. Summit Co. Sheriff's Off.
Milligan, Kerry Grace .... '68 '93 C.97 B.A. L.8 J.D. 529 White Pond Drive
Milo, Sophie M. .... '71 '97 C.025 B.A. L.8 J.D. [🄰 Tipping] (⊙Akron)
Minc, David C. .... '48 '73 C.1230 B.A. L.188 J.D. Gen. Coun., Flexsys America L.P.
Minns, Michael H., (BV) '50 '85
C.477 B.S.E. L.1003 J.D. [🄰 Hahn L.&P.] (See Pat. Sect.)
Mitsopoulos, Sophie ......'71 '97 C.025 B.A. L.8 J.D. 2200 One Cascade Plaza (⊙Akron)
Modugno, Vincent R., (BV) ....'47 '78 C.381 B.A. L.8 J.D. [McKenna&M.]
Mohler, Robert E., (BV) ....'12 '47 C.8 A.B. L.7 J.D. 7 W. Bowery St.
Molnar, Kelly A. ....'72 '00 C&L.8 B.S., J.D. [🄰 Witschey W.&F.]
Monegan, Theodora M. .... '47 '87 C.610 B.S. L.7 J.D. YMCA
Montana, Amy M. .... '— '01 C.980 B.S.A.S. L.8 J.D. [🄰 Witschey W.&F.]
Montgomery, Jerry F., (BV) ....'24 '54 C.8 L.7 LL.B. 560 Patterson Ave.
Moore, Brian J., (AV) .... '58 '84 C.1044 B.A. L.7 J.D. [Roetzel&A.]
Moore, Carla D. ....'52 '77 C.8 B.A. L.608 J.D. Mun. J.
Moore, Donald T., (CV) ....'18 '56 C.8 B.S. L.7 LL.B. 1084 Hampton Ridge Dr.
Moore, Marvin M. '33 '57
C.912 A.B. L.228 LL.B. Prof. of Law, Univ. of Akron School of Law
Moore, Randall J., (BV) ....'59 '84 C.1044 B.S. L.607 J.D. [Roetzel&A.]
Morgan, Glen B. ....'28 '54 C&L.930 B.B.A., J.D. Ret. Com. Pleas J.
Morgan, Richard G. .... '46 '74 C.474 B.S. L.7 J.D. 1742 Karg Dr.n.
Morley, Michael P., (BV) ....'61 '89 C.473 B.S.Ed. L.150 J.D. [🄰 Brennan,M.&D.]
Morris, C. Donald, (BV) ....'43 '70 C&L.8 B.A., J.D. Chf. Mag., Dom. Rel. Ct.
Morris, Duane, (AV) ....'27 '53 C.31 B.A. L.477 J.D. [🄲 Buckingham,D.&B.]
Morris, Glenn W., (AV) ....'31 '63 C&L.8 B.A., J.D. 76 S. Main St.
Morris, Joseph R., (BV) '70 '96 C.999 B.A. L.8 J.D.
V.P., Corp. Oper. & Gen. Coun., First Communications, LLC
Morrison, Jack, Jr., (AV) ....'52 '81 C.8 B.S.B.A. L.7 J.D. [Amer C.]
Morton, Andrew B. '62 '93
C.607 B.S.E.E. L.879 J.D. [Renner,K.G.B.T.&W.] (See Pat. Sect.)
Mosley, Mark A. ....'60 '87 C.8 B.S. L.7 J.D. V.P. & Trust Off., First Merit Trust
Moss, A. Edward, (BV) '58 '83
C.20 B.A. L.930 J.D. Sr. V.P. & Tr. Offr., First Merit Bk., N.A.
Moss, David T., (AV) .... '57 '82 C.294 B.S. L.930 J.D. [Hanna,C.&P.]
Moss, Robert D., (AV) .... '09 '33 C&L.930 A.B., J.D. 1006 Bunker Dr.‡

Motylinski, Michael, The Law Offices of
(See Broadview Heights)

Mowery, Chad L. ....'75 '00 C.600 B.A. L.276 J.D. [🄰 Roetzel&A.]
Moxon, George W., II ....'44 '72 C.446 B.S.Ch.E. L.128 J.D. [Roetzel&A.] (Pat.)
Moxon, Joy Ames ....'73 '99 C.473 B.A. L.8 J.D. [🄰 Brouse M.]
Mueller, Raymond C., (BV) ....'52 '88 C.610 B.A. L.8 J.D. [🄰 Oldham&D.]
Muirden, Marjorie Anne ....'61 '88 C.938 B.A. L.1218 J.D. [Holland&M.] ⊙
Mullen, Thomas T., & Company, (BV) '51 '87
C.381 B.A. L.8 J.D. 3500 West Market Street, Suite 4
Muller, William G. '47 '82 C.691 B.A. L.861 J.D.
(adm. in LA; not adm. in OH; Pat.) Advanced Elastomer Systems, L.P.
(⊙Machelen, Belgium)
Muntean, David A. .... '62 '87 C.1115 B.S. L.7 J.D. Asst. Dir. of Law, City of Akron
Murphy, James E. ....'32 '62 C.602 B.S.C. L.7 J.D. J., Com. Pleas Ct.
Musarra, Thomas M., (BV) ....'54 '84 C.8 B.A. L.7 J.D. 4367 State Rd.
Mushkat, Barbara S., (BV) .... '40 '70 C.823 B.A. L.7 J.D. [Emershaw,M.&S.]
Musitano, Dominic A., Jr., (BV) '33 '60 C.610 A.B. L.8 J.D.
[🄰 Sternberg,N.S.&Assoc.]
Mussig, Linda Mae ....'52 '89 C&L.8 B.S., J.D. 1525 Sand Run Rd.
Mutersbaugh, Steven P. ....'71 '02 C.253 B.A. L.8 J.D. [🄰 Kaufmann&K.]
Myers, Minor ....'14 '40 C.165 B.A. L.930 LL.B. 777 N. Hametown Rd.‡
Mygrant, John W., (AV) .... '52 '77 C.97 B.A. L.608 J.D. [Mentzer&M.]
Nass, Terri L. ....'63 '89 C.62 B.A. L.8 J.D. One GOJO Plaza
Neiman, Maurice P., (BV) ....'30 '53 C.608 B.S. L.930 LL.B. 3200 W. Market St.
Neiman, Michelle L. ....'67 '96 C.393 B.A. L.7 J.D. Jud. Atty., Com. Pleas Ct.
Neman, Patrick J. .... '40 '67 C.381 B.A. L.7 J.D. 2045 Stabler Rd.
Neubauer, Deborah Ann, (AV) '57 '87
C.8 B.A. L.7 J.D. Attorney, Goodyear Tire & Rubber
Newman, Dianne R., (AV) ....'41 '79 C&L.8 B.A., J.D. [Sternberg,N.S.&Assoc.]
Newman, Herbert, (AV) .... '39 '65 C.608 B.S. L.8 J.D. [H.Newman]
Newman, Herbert, Co., L.P.A., (AV) .... 730 Market St., W.
Nicely, Judith A. .... '38 '77 C.608 B.S. L.7 J.D. 209 S. High St.
Nichol, David S. ....'62 '92 C.381 B.S. L.1187 J.D. [🄰 Roderick L.]
Niekamp, Christopher J., (BV) .... '65 '90 C.473 B.S. L.930 J.D. [Bernlohr W.]
Nielsen, Olaf ....'23 '57 C.860 B.S.M.E. L.7 J.D. 679 N. Revere Rd. (Pat.)
Nilges, Hans A. ....'73 '02 C&L.851 B.A., J.D. [🄰 Brouse M.]
Nilsson, Nils E. ....'48 '86 C.150 B.S.E.E. L.8 J.D. 76 S. Main St.
Nolan, Chris T., (AV) .... '47 '73 C.608 B.A. L.8 J.D. [Perantinides&N.]
Norris, Andrea L., (BV) ....'58 '85 C.381 B.A. L.7 J.D. [Norris&N.]
Norris, R. C., (AV) ....'27 '53 C.980 A.B.A. L.7 LL.B. [Norris&N.]
Norris & Norris, (AV) .... 4367 State Street
Nott, David Lauran ....'66 '92 C.381 B.A. L.276 J.D. Summit County Executive
Nukes, S. Samuel, (AV) ....'27 '57 C.8 B.A. L.930 J.D. 1 Cascade Plz., 12th Fl.
Obenour, Malcolm D. ....'33 '59 C.608 B.A. L.1003 LL.B. 2070 East Ave.‡
O'Brien, Ann Marie, (BV) ....'— '91 C.318 B.A. L.8 J.D. [Davis&Y.]
O'Brien, Kerry M., (BV) ....'47 '75 C.8 B.S.I.M. L.7 J.D. [Thomson&O.]
O'Brien, Tamara A., (BV) .... '66 '92 C.8 B.A. L.161 J.D. [Roderick L.]
Oby, Matthew W., (AV) ....'55 '87 C.970 B.A. L.7 J.D. [Oldham&D.]
Ochmann, Patricia M. .... '70 '01 C.381 B.S. L.8 J.D. [🄰 Vorys,S.S.&P.]
Ochsenhirt, Timothy J., (AV) ....'46 '71 C.8 B.A. L.893 J.D. [Roetzel&A.]
Ockerman, Michael, (BV) ....'57 '91 C&L.8 B.S., J.D. [Hanna,C.&P.]
O'Connor, Kandi Sue ....'69 '97 C.381 L.989 J.D. Jud. Atty.
Oelschlager, James D. '42 '68 C.207 B.A. L.597 J.D.
(adm. in IL; not adm. in OH) 1000 Woodhaven Blvd.‡
Oestreicher, Eugene L. .... '34 '58 C.8 B.S. L.930 LL.B. 152 Tecumseh Lane
Okey, Deborah A. '57 '87 C&L.8 B.A., J.D.
Assoc. Gen. Coun.-Litig., The Goodyear Tire & Rubber Co.
Olah, Michael J. ....'57 '85 C&L.8 B.A., J.D. 799 Weber Avenue
Oldfield, Joy Malek ....'75 '00 C.363 B.A. L.8 J.D. [🄰 Scanlon&G.]
Oldham, Jon A. ....'77 '02 C.610 B.S. L.8 J.D. [🄰 Oldham&D.]
Oldham, Joseph K., (BV) ....'70 '95 C.473 B.A. L.8 J.D. [Oldham&D.]
Oldham, Peter D., (BV) .... '46 '72 C.207 B.A. L.8 J.D. 159 S. Main St.
Oldham, Scott M., (BV) .... '61 '91 C.171 B.S. L.8 J.D. [Hahn L.&P.] (See Pat. Sect.)
Oldham, William M., (AV) ....'42 '67 C&L.8 B.A., J.D. [Oldham&D.]

Oldham & Dowling, (AV) BB
195 South Main Street Suite 300, 44308
Telephone: 330-762-7377 Telecopier: 330-762-7390
Email: wdowling@oldham-dowling.com URL: http://www.lawyers.com/oldham&dowling
Partners: William M. Oldham; William D. Dowling, Jr.; Hamilton DeSaussure, Jr.; Reginald S. Kramer; Matthew W. Oby; Joseph K. Oldham; Blake R. Gerney. Associates: Raymond C. Mueller; Halle M. Hebert; Colin G. Skinner; Jon A. Oldham; Mark J. Scarpitti; Cara L. Staley. Of Counsel: Donald S. Varian, Jr.
Civil Litigation, Insurance Defense, Personal Injury, Product Liability, Probate & Estate Planning, Administration, Family Law, Adoption.
Representative Clients: State Farm Mutual Automobile Insurance Co.; State Farm Mutual Fire Insurance Co.; Ohio Casualty Group Insurance Companies; The Step2 Company; WCI Steel Inc.; Safeco/American States Insurance Co.; May Company Department Stores; National City Bank, Masco; Liberty Mutual.
Reference: Key Bank.
See Professional Biographies, AKRON, OHIO

Oliver, Joseph E. .... '55 '83 C.8 B.S. L.7 J.D. 230 White Pond Dr., Ste. A
Pacenta, Patricia A., (AV) .... '46 '77 C&L.436 B.A., J.D. [Buckingham,D.&B.]
Pachell, James T. ....'58 '84 C.980 B.S. L.8 J.D. [Cooper&P.]

Pagano, Wilson, Thomarios, Gillissie & Lenahan LLC
(See Cleveland)

Paige, R. Douglas, (BV) ....'35 '68 C.790 A.B. L.8 J.D. Pub. Def. Off.
Palazzo, Lisa M. .... '69 '94 C.473 B.A. L.930 J.D. 75 E. Market St.
Palma, Maria G. Damascus '59 '85 C.884 B.A. L.1040 J.D.
(adm. in NY; not adm. in OH) Summa Health Sys.
Palmisano, Ralph J., (BV) ....'47 '73 C.8 B.A. L.1003 J.D. [Evanchan&P.]
Pantages, Pamela ....'55 '90 C.318 B.S. L.8 J.D. [🄰 M.M.Djordjevic]
Papas, Katerina C., (BV) ....'63 '89 C.381 B.A. L.8 J.D. 1650 W. Market St.
Pappas, Carol L. .... '58 '85 C&L.8 B.S., J.D. Hearing Offr., Indus. Comm. of Ohio
Pappas, George C., (BV) .... '49 '86 C.999 B.S. L.7 J.D. 159 S. Main St., Ste. 1002
Pappas, Stephanie .... '47 '74 C.608 B.A. L.8 J.D. 577 Rotunda Dr.★
Parikh, Lopa B., (CV) ....'68 '92 C.8 B.S. L.608 J.D. Asst. Co. Pros.
Park, Andrea Hae-Jhin, (BV) '74 '99
C.124 B.S. L.7 J.D. Asst. Pros., Summit Co. Pros. Off.
Parke, Charles D. ....'31 '57 C.309 A.B. L.608 J.D. Mun. Ct. Ref.
Parker, Harold G. .... '41 '69 C&L.7 B.A., J.D. 154 Birdwood Rd.
Parker, Thomas M., (AV) ....'54 '79 C.473 A.B. L.930 J.D. [Parker L.H.&R.]

Parker Leiby Hanna & Rasnick, LLC, (AV)
388 S. Main Street, Suite 402, 44311
Telephone: 330-253-2227 Fax: 330-253-1261
Email: main@neolaw.biz URL: http://www.neolaw.biz
Members of Firm: Thomas M. Parker; Stephen P. Leiby; Timothy H. Hanna; John F. Rasnick. Associates: Donald S. Plum; Robert Roe Fox; Steven R. Hobson, II; Andrew T. Hayes. Of Counsel: Cheryl L. Ramsburg.
Civil Litigation, Civil Appeals, Toxic Torts Litigation, Products Liability Litigation, Real Estate Brokers and Agents Liability, Commercial Real Estate, Residential Real Estate, Personal Injury, Medical Malpractice, Insurance Liability, Estate Planning, Probate, Corporate Law and Family Law.

(This Listing Continued)

Parker Leiby Hanna & Rasnick, LLC (Continued)
Representative Clients: Medtronic, Inc.; Shell Oil Co.; ChevronTexaco; PPG Industries, Inc.; Monsanto Co.; The Dow Chemical Co.
See Professional Biographies, AKRON, OHIO

Parms, Edwin L., (BV) ....'37 '65 C&L.8 B.A., J.D. [E.L.Parms]
Parms, Rebecca, (CV) ....'51 '77 C.8 B.A. L.174 J.D. 1354 Greenwood Ave.
Parms, Edwin L., Law Firm, (BV) ....209 S. Main St.
Parrish, Thomas E., (BV) '47 '77
C.967 B.A. L.7 J.D. Pres., Johnson & Parrish Title Agency, Inc.
Parsons, Dwight, (AV) ....'12 '38 C.674 A.B. L.309 J.D. 251 Overwood Rd.‡
Parsons, Joseph Donald ....'50 '87 C&L.7 B.S., J.D. 17 S. Main St., Ste. 401
Patrino, Anthony V. ....'21 '50 C.8 B.A. L.7 LL.B. 265 S. Main St.
Patterson, Barbara J. ....'47 '85 C.8 B.A. L.7 J.D. Ref., Com. Pleas Ct.
Patton, Terry E., (AV) '48 '75 C.381 B.S. L.7 J.D.
Sr. V.P., Secy. & Coun., First Natl. Bk. of Ohio

Paul, Dennis E.
(See Medina)

Pavick, Dean G., (BV) ....'50 '80 C.608 B.A. L.607 J.D. 159 S. Main St., Ste. 522
Pavick, Michael J., (BV) ....'23 '50 C&L.608 B.A., J.D. 4384 Idlebrook Dr.
Pavlidis, Marietta M. ....'71 '97 C.381 B.A. L.1003 J.D. [Ⓐ Buckingham,D.&B.]
Paxton, William A. ....'62 '89 C&L.8 B.A., J.D. 567 East Turkeyfoot Lake Road
Payne, James E., (AV) ....'44 '79 C.161 B.B.A. L.7 J.D. 797 Cliffside Dr.
Payne, Paul D., II '47 '77 C.473 B.A. L.8 J.D.
Staff Atty., Community Legal Aid Services., Inc.
Payntor, Carl S. '44 '73 C.63 B.S. L.345 J.D.
Computer Law Atty., Goodyear Tire & Rubber
Peck, Andrew F., (CV) ....'60 '85 C&L.8 B.A., J.D. [Ⓐ Whalen&C.]
Perantinides, Paul G., (AV) ....'44 '69 C.980 B.A. L.8 J.D. [Perantinides&N.]

Perantinides & Nolan Co., L.P.A., (AV) BR
300 Courtyard Square, 80 South Summit Street, 44308-1736
Telephone: 330-253-5454 Telecopier: 330-253-6524
Email: pn@perantinides.com URL: http://www.perantinides.com
Paul G. Perantinides; Chris T. Nolan;—Peter D. Janos; Antonios P. Tsarouhas; Michael J. Maillis.
General Civil Trial and Appellate Practice. Negligence, Products Liability, Medical Legal, Malpractice, Construction, Toxic Tort and Commercial Law. Insurance, Environmental, Aviation, Wrongful Death and Civil Rights.
References: Charter One Bank; National City Bank, Akron.
See Professional Biographies, AKRON, OHIO

Perduk, David C. ....'69 '96 3603 Darrow Road
Pere, John G. ....'17 '57 C.608 L.7 J.D. 2143 Pressler Rd. (Pat.)
Perris, Alex C. ....'50 '94 C.8 B.A. L.7 J.D. First National Tower, Suite 2500
Petersen, Lee, (BV) ....'46 '81 C.8 B.A. L.7 J.D. P.O. Box 13118
Petti, Gary M. ....'68 '95 C.8 B.A. L.7 J.D. [Slater,Z.&G.]
Pfeister, Alison Jean Russell '48 '85
C.608 B.S. L.7 J.D. Staff Coun., Cincinnati Insurance Co.
Pierce, Brian M., (BV) ....'68 '94 C.645 B.S. L.8 J.D. [Gorman,M.&P.]
Pierson, John C., Attorney at Law, (AV) '47 '82 C.309 A.B. L.7 J.D.
1221 W. Market St.
Pietrowski, Moira H., (BV) ....'72 '97 C.597 B.A. L.365 J.D. [Ⓐ Roetzel&A.]
Pietrykowski, Robert J. ....'56 '84 C.161 B.A. L.989 J.D. Summa Health System
Pignatelli, Francis M., (BV) ....'63 '88 C.8 B.S. L.930 J.D. 120 East Mill St.
Piotrowski, Michael W. '64 '94
C.999 B.A. L.930 J.D. Frat. Order of Police Ohio Labor Council
Pitchford, Marshal M., (BV) ....'74 '99 C.473 B.A. L.7 J.D. [Ⓐ Roetzel&A.]
Pitts, Thomas R., (BV) '46 '79
C.8 B.A. L.7 J.D. Landmark Bldg., 7 W. Bowery St., 10th Fl.
Pizzino, Elisa P. ....'63 '89 C.97 B.A. L.823 J.D. Legal Consult. Servs., Inc.
Platt, Marvin S. ....'30 '77 C.446 B.S. L.7 J.D. 85 N. Summit St.
Plesich, Gregory T., (BV) ....'45 '73 C.1323 B.S. L.8 J.D. 1615 Akron Peninsula Rd.
Plum, Donald S., (CV) ....'63 '88 C.893 B.A. L.477 J.D. [Ⓐ Parker L.H.&R.]
Porter, Jay P., (AV) ....'53 '78 C.294 B.A. L.945 J.D. [Ⓒ Vorys,S.S.&P.]
Porter, Michael L., Sr. ....'37 '81 C.346 B.S. L.7 J.D. 844 Bridlewood Dr.

Porter Wright Morris & Arthur LLP
(See Cleveland)

Portman, Irving A. ....'29 '55 C.381 B.S. L.608 J.D. 159 S. Main St.
Potenza, Rocco D., Jr., (BV) ....'64 '92 C.567 B.S. L.851 J.D. [Hanna,C.&P.]
Poth-Wypasek, Angela Kay ....'75 '01 C.999 B.A. L.7 J.D. Summit Co. Juv. Ct.
Poulos, Larry G., (AV) ....'47 '73 C&L.8 B.A., J.D. 209 South High Street
Powel, William A., III, (AV) '57 '83 C.813 A.B. L.902 J.D.
V.P., Legal Servs. & Gen. Coun., Summa Health System
Powell, Donald A., (AV) ....'40 '65 C.97 B.A. L.930 J.D. [Hanna,C.&P.]
Powell, Georgene B., (BV) ....'54 '79 C.381 B.S. L.7 J.D. [Powell&P.]
Powell, Joseph A., (BV) ....'53 '78 C.8 B.S. L.7 J.D. [Powell&P.]
Powell and Powell, (BV) ....655 S. Broadway
Powley, Douglas J., (BV) ....'49 '79 C.339 B.S. L.7 J.D. Chf. City Pros.
Prentice, Sally A. ....'53 '82 C.161 B.A. L.1003 J.D. 2209 Round Rock Dr.
Price, William J. ......'73 '99 C.213 B.S.B.A. L.475 J.D. 159 South Main Street, Suite 920
Pritchard, Susan K., (BV) ....'56 '80 C.8 B.A. L.7 J.D. [Whited&P.]
Pruneski, Stephen J., (BV) ....'60 '85 C.980 B.A. L.7 J.D. [Roderick L.]
Pryatel, Keith L., (AV) ....'61 '86 C.973 B.S.B.A. L.1003 J.D. [Kastner W.&W.]
Pullekins, Edward C., (BV) ....'50 '75 C.8 B.A. L.7 J.D. [Slater,Z.&G.]
Pullen, John R. ....'27 '55 C&L.8 B.A., J.D. 2652 Albrecht Ave.‡
Purnell, Norman, (BV) ....'28 '58 C.608 B.S. L.7 LL.B. 333 S. Main St.
Quillin, Daniel B. ....'30 '56 C.8 B.A. L.930 LL.B. Ct. of App. J.
Quinn, John P., Jr., (BV) ....'49 '76 C&L.608 B.A., J.D. 2295 Woodpark Rd.
Quirk, Frank E., (AV) ....'32 '59 C&L.608 B.S.Ed., J.D. [Ⓒ Brouse M.]
Ragon, Stacy A., (BV) ....'69 '96 C.999 B.A. L.201 J.D. [Roetzel&A.]
Ramsburg, Cheryl L. ....'58 '96 C.999 B.A. L.7 J.D. [Ⓒ Parker L.H.&R.]
Ranftl, James R., (BV) ....'51 '76 C.421 B.S. L.8 J.D. [Burdon&M.]
Rankins, Milton C. ....'64 '91 C.575 B.A. L.8 J.D. 50 South Main Street, 4th Fl.
Rasnick, John F., (BV) ....'56 '82 C.1260 B.A. L.7 J.D. [Parker L.H.&R.]
Rawlings, Thomas E., (BV) ....'50 '77 C.8 B.S. L.7 J.D. 2411 Sourek Rd.
Ray, Nathan A., (BV) ....'60 '89 C&L.8 B.A., J.D. 137 S. Main St., Ste. 201
Raynor, David F., (AV) ....'50 '76 C.611 B.A. L.930 J.D. [Brouse M.]
Reaven, Saul D. ....'13 '41 C.8 L.161 J.D. 66 Goodhue Dr.‡
Reece, John Christopher, (BV) ....'— '89 C&L.8 B.S., J.D. [Ⓐ Marshall,D.W.C.&G.]
Reece, John W. ....'33 '61 C.8 B.A. L.7 LL.B. Dist. Ct. of App. J.
Reed, Carl L., Co. (L.P.A.), (BV) ....'31 '66 C&L.608 B.S., LL.B. 2745 Nesbitt Ave.
Reed, Evan J. ....'09 '33 C&L.477 B.A., J.D. Ret. Com. Pleas J.
Reed, Joel D., (BV) ....'69 '96 C&L.8 B.A., J.D. 650 Dan Street
Reed, Orville L., III, (AV) ....'47 '73 C.999 B.A. L.602 J.D. [Buckingham,D.&B.]
Reese, Holly L. ....'72 '99 C.699 B.A. L.7 J.D. Asst. Pros. Atty.
Reffner, Robert P., (AV) ....'50 '77 C.8 B.S.E.E. L.930 J.D. [Brouse M.]
Regal, Edwin M., (BV) ....'37 '70 C.8 B.S. L.7 J.D. [Koch&R.]
Regallis, Caroline ....'— '02 C.8 B.S. L.124 J.D. [Ⓐ Roetzel&A.]
Reginelli, Arthur M. '69 '95
C.363 B.S. L.989 J.D. [Renner,K.G.B.T.&W.] (See Pat. Sect.)
Reich, Jacob L. ....'20 '51 C.8 B.A. L.7 LL.B. 159 S. Main St.
Reminger & Reminger Co., L.P.A., (AV)
80 S. Summit St. (⊙Covington, KY; Cin., Cleve., Columbus, Sandusky, Toledo, Youngstown, OH)
Rench, James L., (AV) ....'47 '74 C.473 B.S. L.608 J.D. [Stark&K.]

Renner, Kenner, Greive, Bobak, Taylor & Weber, A Legal Professional Association, (AV)
4th Floor, First National Tower, 44308-1456
Telephone: 330-376-1242 Facsimile: 330-376-9646
Email: patlaw@rennerkenner.com URL: http://www.rennerkenner.com
Phillip L. Kenner; Edward G. Greive; Donald J. Bobak; Ray L. Weber; Rodney Lee Skoglund; Andrew B. Morton; Arthur M. Reginelli; Laura J. Gentilcore; Shannon V. McCue; Mark L. Weber; Tama L. Drenski; Tim A. Hodgkiss.
U.S. and Foreign Patent, Trademark and Copyright Law and Licensing. Antitrust and Unfair Competition Law. Litigation.
Reference: Key Bank.
See Professional Biographies, AKRON, OHIO

Reyes, John L., (AV) ....'53 '78 C.8 B.S. L.880 J.D. [Buckingham,D.&B.]
Rich, William D. '53 '78 C.696 B.A. L.208 J.D.
(adm. in CO; not adm. in OH) Assoc. Prof. of Law, Univ. of Akron School of Law
Richards, Beverly J. ....'62 '98 C.999 B.R.E. L.8 J.D. Juv. Ct.
Richert, Paul ....'48 '77 C.339 A.B. L.861 J.D. Prof. of Law, Univ. of Akron
Rickett, William G. ....'52 '86 C.608 B.S.Ed. L.7 J.D. Univ. of Akron School of Law
Rickman, Michael R. .....'62 '87 C.879 B.A. L.910 J.D. Attorney, Goodyear Tire & Rubber
Riegler, Edward J., (AV) ....'44 '74 C&L.8 B.A., J.D. [Grisi&R.]
Riemenschneider, John K., (BV) ....'39 '69 C.381 B.S. L.7 J.D. [Ⓐ Roderick L.]
Rigrish, James W. ....'22 '50 C.608 B.S. L.309 LL.B. 1485 Wade Park Ave.‡
Rilley, Scott A., (BV) ....'66 '93 C.8 B.A. L.124 J.D. [Callahan,G.R.&S.]
Rimmel, Brad A. ....'70 '99 C.381 B.A. L.7 J.D. [Ⓐ Roetzel&A.]
Roberto, Carmen V. ....'48 '73 C.184 B.S. L.8 J.D. [Vasko,R.&E.]
Robinson, David J. ....'37 '76 C.8 B.S.E.E. L.7 J.D. 1615 Centerview Dr.
Robinson, H. Jeffrey ....'58 '84 C.840 B.B.A. L.862 J.D. Summit Co. Pros. Off.
Robinson, Michael L., (BV) ......'52 '77 C.679 B.S.Eng. L.7 J.D. 750 Springwater Drive‡
Robison, Richard A. ....'50 '84 C&L.8 B.A., J.D. Ohio Civil Rights Comm.
Rochford, Bernard A. ....'57 '90 C&L.8 B.A., J.D. Oriana House, Inc.

Roderick Linton, LLP, (AV)
One Cascade Plaza, 15th Floor, 44308
Telephone: 330-434-3000 Telecopier: 330-434-9220
Email: rodericklinton@neo.rr.com URL: http://www.rodericklinton.com
Members of Firm: Kurt R. Weitendorf; Timothy J. Truby; Stephen J. Pruneski; William J. Detweiler; Michael DeCarlo; Tamara A. O'Brien; Duard D. Bradshaw; William G. Chris (Resident, Akron Office); Lawrence R. Bach; Ronald K. Lembright;—John K. Riemenschneider; David S. Nichol; Rodd A. Sanders; Steven W. Mastrantonio; Jason E. Hickman; Craig W. Beidler; Brian K. Harnak. Of Counsel: Robert F. Linton; Todd A. Mazzola; Howard L. Calhoun; Frederick S. Corns; James E. Davis; John J. Lynett.
General Civil Trial Practice. Banking, Business, Commercial, Corporate, Probate, Workers Compensation, Administrative, Taxation, Insurance, Real Estate, Bankruptcy and Securities Law, Estate Planning, Zoning.
Counsel for: National City Bank, Ohio Edison Co.; K-Mart; The Prudential Insurance Co. of America; Maryland Casualty Co.; Summit County Medical Society; Federated Mutual Insurance Cos.; Motorists Insurance Group.
See Professional Biographies, AKRON, OHIO

Rodgers, Susan C., (BV) ....'66 '91 C.608 B.A. L.150 J.D. [Buckingham,D.&B.]

Roetzel & Andress, A Legal Professional Association, (AV) BR
222 South Main Street, 44308 ⊙
Telephone: 330-376-2700 Telecopier: 330-376-4577
Email: inquiries@ralaw.com URL: http://www.ralaw.com
Partners: Lewis W. Adkins, Jr. (Resident, Cleveland Office); R. Bruce Anderson (Resident, Naples, Florida Office); John W. Becker; Aretta K. Bernard; Robert E. Blackham (Certified Specialist in Workers' Compensation Law, Ohio State Bar Association) (Resident Partner, Cleveland Office); John T. Blakely (Board Certified Civil Trial Lawyer, Florida Bar Board of Legal Specialization and Education) (Resident, Naples, Florida Office); Susan S. Box; Wilbur E. Brewton (Resident, Tallahassee, Florida Office); Eric G. Bruestle (Certified Specialist in Workers' Compensation Law, Ohio State Bar Association) (Managing Partner, Cincinnati Office); Amie L. Bruggeman; Anthony J. Calamunci, Sr. (Resident, Toledo Office); Anna Moore Carulas (Resident, Cleveland Office); Robert B. Casarona (Resident, Cleveland Office); Jeffrey J. Casto; M. Brian Cheffer (Resident, Fort Myers, Florida Office); Steven St. Leger Cox; John M. Coyne, III; Clayton W. Crevasse (Resident, Fort Myers, Florida Office); Elizabeth N. Davis; David J. Demers (Resident, Columbus Office); George A. Dietrich; Thomas A. Dillon (Managing Partner, Columbus Office); Carl J. Dyczek (Resident, Cleveland Office); Steven M. Falk (Resident, Naples, Florida Office); Shane A. Farolino; Laura (Megan) Faust; Terrence S. Finn; Jon D. Fishbane (Resident, Naples, Florida Office); Jeffrey E. Fromson (Resident, Columbus Office); Patricia B. Fugée (Resident, Toledo Office); Stephen W. Funk; Stanley H. Goldschmidt (Resident, Washington, DC Office); Amanda E. Gordon; Beverly Grady (Board Certified City, County and Local Government Lawyer, Florida Bar Board of Legal Specialization and Education) (Resident, Fort Myers, Florida Office); Robert B. Graziano (Resident, Columbus Office); C. Neil Gregory (Board Certified Real Estate Lawyer, Florida Bar Board of Legal Specialization and Education) (Resident, Naples, Florida Office); David H. Gunning II (Resident, Cleveland Office); Michael J. Haas (Resident, Cleveland Office); David R. Harbarger (At Washington, D.C. and Cleveland, Ohio Offices); Denise M. Hasbrook (Resident, Toledo Office); Erika L. Haupt (Resident, Columbus Office); Joseph E. Herbert (Resident, Cleveland Office); Edward C. Hertenstein (Certified Specialist in Federal Tax Law, Ohio State Bar Association) (Resident, Columbus Office); Paul K. Heuerman (Resident, Naples, Florida Office); Daniel G. Hilson (Resident, Columbus Office); Steven W. Hubbard (Resident Managing Partner, Fort Myers, Florida Office); Michael J. Hudak; Timothy C. Ivey; Paul L. Jackson (Certified Specialist in Labor & Employment Law, Ohio State Bar Association); Kenneth A. Jones (Resident, Fort Myers, Florida Office); Peter Lawson Jones (Resident, Cleveland Office); R. Mark Jones (Resident, Cleveland Office); Stephen D. Jones (Resident, Columbus Office); Wayne M. Jones; Douglas M. Kennedy (Resident, Columbus Office); Ingrid A. Kinkopf-Zajac (Resident, Cleveland Office); Ronald S. Kopp (Managing Partner, Akron Office); Peter M. Kostoff; James D. Kurek (Certified Specialist in Labor and Employment Law, Ohio State Bar Association); Kenneth M. Lapine (Resident, Cleveland Office); Douglas G. Leak (Resident, Cleveland Office); Ronald B. Lee; Frederick W. Leffler; Judith D. Levine (Resident, Columbus Office); G. Carson McEachern (Board Certified Real Estate and Wills, Trusts and Estates Lawyer, Florida Bar Board of Legal Specializations and Education) (Resident, Naples, Florida Office); Mark P. McGrievy (Resident, Cleveland Office); Aaron E. McQueen; Robert G. Menzies (Resident, Naples, Florida Office); Russell R. Miller (Resident, Toledo Office); Richard S. Mitchell (Resident, Cleveland Office); Brian J. Moore; Randall J. Moore; George W. Moxon, II; Richard S. Mulligan (Resident, Columbus Office); Douglas S. Musick (Resident, Cleveland Office); Basil J. Musnuff (Resident, Cleveland Office); Peter K. Newman (Resident, Cincinnati Office); Cheryl A. O'Brien (Resident, Cleveland Office); Timothy J. Ochsenhirt; William R. O'Neill (Resident, Naples, Florida Office); Kevin J. Osterkamp (Resident, Columbus Office); Kelly B. Plante (Resident, Tallahassee, Florida Office); Kenneth J. Plante (Resident, Tallahassee, Florida Office); Richard A. Plewacki (Resident, Cleveland Office); Michael A. Poe (Resident, Columbus Office); Mark J. Price (Board Certified Real Estate Lawyer, Florida Bar Board of Legal Specialization and Education) (Resident Managing Partner, Naples, Florida Office); Robert D. Pritt (Board Certified City, County and Local Government Lawyer, Florida Bar Board of Legal Specialization and Education) (Resident, Naples, Florida Office); Stacy A. Ragon; Cathy S. Reiman (Board Certified Business Litigation Lawyer, Florida Bar Board of Legal Specialization and Education) (Resident, Naples, Florida Office); George W. Rooney, Jr. (Resident, Cleveland Office); Mark A. Ropchock; Thomas L. Rosenberg (Resident, Columbus Office); Albert N. Salvatore (Resident, Cleveland Office); Beverly A. Sandacz (Resident, Cleveland Office); George R. Sarkis; Mark L. Sarlson (Resident, Cleveland Office); Donald S. Scherzer (Resident, Cleveland

(This Listing Continued)

Roetzel & Andress, A Legal Professional Association (Continued)

Office); Bruce R. Schrader, II; James C. Scott (Resident, Cleveland Office); Jeffrey S. Shoskin (Resident, Cincinnati Office); Thomas M. Skove; Charles D. Smith (Resident, Columbus Office); Bradley L. Snyder (Resident, Columbus Office); Douglas E. Spiker (Certified Specialist in Workers' Compensation, Ohio State Bar Association) (Resident, Toledo Office); Gary W. Spring (Certified Specialist in Labor & Employment Law, Ohio State Bar Association); Roger J. Stevenson; Mark C. Terzola; Diana M. Thimmig (Resident, Cleveland Office); Stephen E. Thompson (Board Certified Real Estate Lawyer, Florida Bar Board of Legal Specialization and Education) (Resident, Naples, Florida Office) (Managing Partner, Florida Offices); Thomas A. Treadon; Timothy J. Webster (Certified Specialist in Workers' Compensation Law, Ohio State Bar Association); Steven I. Winer (Resident, Fort Myers, Florida Office); Alisa Labut Wright; Bradley A. Wright; Michael S. Yashko (At Columbus, Ohio and Fort Myers, Florida Offices); Joseph D. Zaks (Board Certified Wills, Trusts and Estates Lawyer, Florida Bar Board of Legal Specialization and Education) (Resident, Naples, Florida Office); Thomas S. Zaremba (Resident, Toledo Office). Of Counsel: Janice A. Isakoff (Resident, Cleveland Office); Teresa E. Purtiman (Resident, Cleveland Office); Gary A. Weiss (Resident, Cleveland Office); Charles E. Zumkehr;—Karen E. Adinolfi; Chad Arfons (Resident, Cleveland Office); Ryan E. Bonina (Resident, Columbus Office); Jeffrey S. Braun (Resident, Columbus Office); Eric S. Bravo (Resident, Columbus Office); Amy L. Butler (Resident, Toledo Office); Ricardo J. Cardenas (Resident, Cleveland Office); Tammi J. Carter (Resident, Cleveland Office); Sharon Cason-Adams (Resident, Columbus Office); Stephenie L. Conde (Resident, Cleveland Office); Joseph J. Crimaldi; Scot C. Crow (Resident, Columbus Office); Tamir D. Damari (Resident, Washington, DC Office); Kimberly A. Davis (Resident, Fort Myers, Florida Office); Julie A. Douglas (Resident, Toledo Office); Sean M. Ellis (Resident, Fort Myers Office); Laura A. Ephlin; James D. Fox (Resident, Naples, Florida Office); Dominic A. Frisina; Michael J. Fuchs; Lynn A. Gross (Resident, Cleveland Office); Todd A. Harpst; Melissa R. Hoeffel (Resident, Columbus Office); Brandie H. Hollinger Peeples; Pam Ellen Hudson (Resident, Naples, Florida Office); Marc A. Huling (Resident, Naples, Florida Office); Christine M. Kattola (Resident, Cleveland Office); Ryan P. Kennedy; Gregory S. Kessler (Resident, Cincinnati Office); Hugh S. Kinast (Resident, Cleveland Office); Lauren K. Kinkopf (Resident, Cleveland Office); David A. Kotnik (Resident, Cleveland Office); Douglas A. Lewis (Resident, Naples, Florida Office); Joseph L. Lindsay (Resident, Naples, Florida Office); Brian H. Linick (Resident, Cleveland Office); Terrence H. Link, II; Ashley D. Lupo (Resident, Naples, Florida Office); Rachel K. Mathoslah (Resident, Cleveland Office); Adam C. Miller (Resident, Cleveland Office); Lori L. Moore (Resident, Fort Myers Office); Chad L. Mowery; James P. Myers (Resident, Cleveland Office); Lisa Palm-Kuebler (Resident, Toledo Office); Moira H. Pietrowski; Marshal M. Pitchford; Eric M. Pizzuti (Resident, Cleveland Office); Caroline Regallis; Brad A. Rimmel; Kyle S. Scheatzle; Beth Ann Schenz (Resident, Cleveland Office); John J. Schriner, Jr. (Resident, Cleveland Office); Elizabeth Shaffer (Resident, Cincinnati Office); Mariam Alikhan Shah; Jennifer L. Souza; Jamison S. Speidel (Resident, Columbus Office); Vincent J. Squillace, III (Resident, Columbus Office); Tana D. Storey (Resident, Tallahassee, Florida Office); Nathan F. Studeny; Brian A. Tarian (Resident, Columbus Office); Sean J. Urvan; Tara L. Van Ho (Resident, Columbus Office); Daniel K. Weidenbruch (Resident, Naples, Florida Office); Jerome G. Wyss; E. Mark Young (Resident, Cleveland Office).

General Corporate and Business Law, Banking and Finance, Mergers, Acquisitions and Divestitures, Securities Law, Real Estate Law, Real Estate Development/Syndication/Condominium Law, Tax Law, Intellectual Property Law, Computer Law, Hospital and Health Care Law, Public Law and Finance, Governmental Relations, School Law, Commercial/Bankruptcy Law, Employment Law, Pension, Employee Benefits, Workers' Compensation, OSHA, Business and Commercial Litigation, Complex and Multidistrict Litigation, Antitrust Law, RICO, Federal Court Practice, Product Liability, Environmental Law/Toxic Torts, Insurance Law, Information Technology Law, Medical Malpractice Defense, Asbestos Litigation, Construction Law, 1st Amendment/Media Law, White Collar Criminal Defense, Railroad and FELA, Trucking and Transportation Law, Probate and Estate Planning, Utility Law, International Law, Trial and Appellate Practice.

Representative Clients: Akron City Hospital; Bank One; Beacon Journal Publishing Co.; Capital University; Chessie Systems Railroads; General Motors Corp.; Pentair, Inc.; Seaman Corp.; State of Ohio; United States Fidelity & Guaranty Co.

Columbus, Ohio Office: National City Center, 155 E. Broad Street, 12th Floor. Telephone: 614-463-9770. Telecopier: 614-463-9792.

Naples, Florida Office: 850 Park Shore Drive, Trianon Centre, 3rd Floor. Telephones: 239-649-6200; 800-535-7239. Telecopier: 239-261-3659.

Cleveland, Ohio Office: One Cleveland Center, 1375 East Ninth Street, 9th Floor. Telephone: 216-623-0150. Telecopier: 216-623-0134.

Cincinnati, Ohio Office: 250 East Fifth Street, 310 Chiquita Center. Telephone: 513-361-0200. Telecopier: 513-361-0335.

Fort Myers, Florida Office: 2320 First Street, Suite 1000. Telephone: 239-337-3850. Telecopier: 239-337-0970.

Toledo, Ohio Office: One SeaGate, 9th Floor. Telephone: 419-242-7985. Facsimile: 419-242-0316.

Tallahassee, Florida Office: 225 South Adams Street, Suite 250, P.O. Box 10369. Telephone: 850-222-7718. Telecopier: 850-222-8222.

Washington, D.C. Office: 1025 Connecticut Avenue, NW, Suite 220. Telephone: 202-625-0600. Telecopier: 202-338-6340.

See Professional Biographies, AKRON, OHIO

Rogers, Justin T. ....'29 '54 C.674 A.B. L.477 J.D. 370 Delaware Ave.‡
Rohrich, Richard P., (AV) ....'49 '73 C.967 B.A. L.228 J.D. [Buckingham,D.&B.]
Romano, Joan G., (BV) '33 '74 C.822 B.A. L.7 J.D.
Legal Coun., Dept of Human Servs.
Rondy, James A., (BV) ....'25 '51 C.1323 L.607 J.D. P.O. Box 2104
Rooney, George W., (AV) ....'15 '49 C.966 B.A.Sc. L.608 J.D. 75 E. Market St.
Ropchock, Mark A., (BV) ....'60 '85 C.607 B.A. L.930 J.D. [Roetzel&A.]
Rose, Paul A., (AV) ....'56 '82 C.623 B.A. L.608 J.D. [Brouse M.]
Rosebrough, Christina A. ......'69 '94 C&L.8 B.S., J.D. Jud. Law Clk., Domestic Rel. Div.
Rosen, Bernard I., (AV) ....'18 '47 C.8 B.A. L.930 LL.B. [Goldman&R.]
Rosen, Gary M., (BV) ....'53 '78 C.860 B.A. L.273 J.D. [Goldman&R.]
Rosin, George H., (AV) ....'51 '76 C.967 B.A. L.608 J.D. [Buckingham,D.&B.]
Rosner, Michael J. ....'52 '77 C.679 B.S. L.345 J.D. Goodyear Tire & Rubber
Ross, John M., (AV) .... '31 '57 C.976 B.A. L.831 LL.B. 1144 E. Market St.‡
Ross, Susan Baker ....'65 '91 C&L.8 B.S., J.D. Pros. Off.
Rossi, Gregory T., (AV) ....'62 '90 C&L.8 B.S., J.D. [Hanna,C.&P.]
Rote, Frank C., (AV) '27 '62 C.848 B.S. L.229 LL.B.
(adm. in PA; not adm. in OH; Pat.) 7 W. Bowery St.
Roth, Kathleen E. '71 '97 C.1329 B.S.G.A. L.945 J.D.
Sr. Coun. Litig., Bridgestone Americas Holding, Inc.
Roth, Michael J. ....'72 '97 C.610 B.S. L.7 J.D. 2745 S. Arlington Rd.
Roth, William '43 '68 C.112 B.A. L.1068 J.D.
(adm. in CA; not adm. in OH) Mayor
Rothal, Max, (AV) ....'32 '57 C.381 L.8 LL.B. City Law Dir.
Roubenes, Jerry G., (BV) ....'34 '65 C&L.8 B.S., J.D. 1st National Twr.
Roush, Carrie M. ....'74 '99 C.294 B.A. L.8 J.D. 76 South Main Street, Suite 1512
Rowland, Richd. W., (BV) ....'21 '49 C.8 A.B. L.930 LL.B. 1st Nat. Twr.
Rowlands, Mary Margaret, (BV) ....'58 '89 C.980 B.S. L.8 J.D. 190 N. Union Street
Royer, Robert A., (AV) ....'59 '84 C.25 B.A. L.608 J.D. [Scanlon&G.]
Rozmajzl, James A. ... '34 '64 C.679 B.Ch.E. L.8 LL.B. The Goodyear Tire & Rubber Co.
Rozmajzl, Michael F., C.P.A. '71 '01 C.473 B.A. L.124 J.D.
2295 W. Market St., Ste. G
Rubino, Sandy James '54 '78 C.8 B.A. L.7 J.D.
Chf. Asst. Pros., Civil Div., Co. Pros. Off.
Ruby, Deborah L. ....'60 '99 C.7 B.S. L.8 J.D. 697 W. Market St., Suite 200
Rucinski, Keith L., (BV) ....'65 '94 C&L.8 B.A., J.D. 2955 Millbrook Ave.
Ruffner, Keith C., II, (BV) ....'52 '88 C.473 B.S. L.7 J.D. 209 S. Main St., Ste. 201
Ruport, Scott H., (AV) ....'49 '74 C.97 B.S.B.A. L.7 J.D. [Ruport]

Ruport Co., L.P.A., (AV)
3700 Embassy Parkway, Suite 200, 44333
Telephone: 330-666-5555 Telecopier: 330-666-7272
URL: http://www.lawyers.com/ruportlaw
Scott H. Ruport (Board Certified, Civil Trial Specialist by the National Board of Trial Advocacy). Of Counsel: Louise M. Mazur.

(This Listing Continued)

Ruport Co., L.P.A. (Continued)

Complex Litigation. Civil Trial and Appellate Practice in Federal and State Courts. Construction, Banking, Commercial, Surety, Business, Corporate, Real Estate Law and Litigation.

See Professional Biographies, AKRON, OHIO

Ryan, Anne J. '64 '97 C.477 B.A. L.989 J.D.
Staff Atty., Community Legal Aid Services., Inc.
Sager, Rex E. ....'21 '54 C.8 B.B.A. L.7 LL.B. 120 E. Mill St.
Sahl, Joann '61 '86 C.608 B.A. L.8 J.D.
Staff Atty., Community Legal Aid Services., Inc.
Sahl, John Patrick '51 '82 C.93 B.A. L.1194 J.D.
Dep. Dean & Prof., Univ. of Bridgeport School of Law
Salamone, James Patrick ....'— '00 C.528 B.A. L.365 J.D. [A Davis&Y.]
Samad, Stanley A. ....'20 '48 C&L.150 A.B., LL.B. 633 Mardon Ave.‡
Sandberg, Robt. L. ....'19 '49 C.659 B.S. L.7 LL.B. 1940 Stockbridge St.
Sanders, Rodd A. ....'67 '94 C.532 B.S. L.8 J.D. [A Roderick L.] (Pat.)
Sanderson, R. Bruce .... '19 '47 C.8 A.B. L.537 LL.B. [Knowlton,S.] ‡
Sandrock, Scott P., (AV) ....'53 '78 C.602 B.A. L.608 J.D. [Brennan,M.&D.]
Sanislo, Kevin R., (BV) .....'55 '79 C.97 B.A. L.7 J.D. 304 N. Cleveland-Massillon Road
Sansonetti, Jos. P., (BV) ....'21 '58 C.8 L.7 LL.B. 41 Merz Blvd.
Sarkis, George R., (AV) ....'55 '80 C.103 A.B. L.930 J.D. [Roetzel&A.]
Satterfield, John L. ....'36 '74 C.8 B.S. L.7 J.D. 3289 Soureh Rd.
Savalan, Thomas L., (CV) ....'31 '61 C&L.8 B.A., J.D. 1655 W. Market St.
Sawan, Edmund M., (BV) ....'50 '76 C.8 B.A. L.7 J.D. [Sawan&F.]
Sawan & Farris, (BV) ....362 S. Main St.
Saxer, Thomas M., (BV) ....'66 '91 C.381 B.B.A. L.8 J.D. [Amer C.]
Scanlon, John T., (BV) ....'68 '94 C.201 B.A. L.1003 J.D. [Scanlon&G.]
Scanlon, Lawrence J., (AV) ....'51 '78 C.8 B.A. L.7 J.D. [Scanlon] ⊙
Scanlon, Maura E., (BV) ....'63 '88 C.321 B.A.Econ. L.930 J.D. [A Scanlon&G.]
Scanlon, Michael C., (BV) ....'40 '66 C.321 B.A. L.607 J.D. 106 South Main Street
Scanlon, Terence E., (AV) ....'45 '75 C.321 B.A. L.912 J.D. [B.H.Wilson]
Scanlon, Timothy F., (AV) ....'37 '62 C.321 A.B. L.477 J.D. [Scanlon&G.]

Scanlon & Co., L.L.C., (AV)
159 South Main Street, Suite 400 Key Building, 44308 ⊙
Telephone: 330-376-1440 Telecopier: 330-376-0257 URL: http://www.scanlonco.com
Email: ljscanlon@scanlonco.com URL: http://www.lawyers.com/scanlonco
Lawrence J. Scanlon (Board Certified Civil Trial Lawyer, Florida Bar Board of Legal Specialization and Education).
Civil Trial and Appellate Advocacy, Products Liability, Professional Liability and Wrongful Death Law, Insurance Law Litigation, Aviation Law, Highway Design Law, Personal Injury, Airplane Crashes, Automobile Accidents, Construction Site Accidents, Medical Malpractice, Nursing Home Abuse and Neglect, Railroad Accidents and Injuries, Slip and Fall, Unsafe Products, Wrongful Death, Contested Wills, Investor and Securities Litigation.
Reference: First Merit Bank.
Boca Raton, Florida Office: Scanlon & Croyle, LLP: 370 West Camino Gardens Boulevard, Suite 300. 33432-5817. Telephone: 561-368-4408. Fax: 561-368-4309.

See Professional Biographies, AKRON, OHIO

Scanlon & Gearinger Co., L.P.A., (AV)
50 South Main Street, Suite 1200, 44308
Telephone: 330-376-4558 Telecopier: 330-376-3550
URL: http://www.scangearlaw.com
Of Counsel: Timothy F. Scanlon; Bradford M. Gearinger. Partners: Michael J. Del Medico; Mark Hilkert; Patrick J. Hart; Robert A. Royer; Kevin P. Hardman; John F. Hill; John T. Scanlon;—Maura E. Scanlon; Melinda E. Smith; Joy Malek Oldfield; Gregory J. Lucht.
General Civil Trial and Appellate Practice. Negligence, Personal Injury, Products Liability, Medical Malpractice, Legal Malpractice, Litigation.

See Professional Biographies, AKRON, OHIO

Scarpitti, Mark J. ....'73 '02 C.97 B.A. L.8 J.D. [A Oldham&D.]
Schachter, Patti Michelle, (BV) ....'— '79 C.347 B.S. L.7 J.D. Legal Def. Off.
Schafer, Julie A. ....'57 '02 L.8 J.D. 755 White Pond Dr., Ste. 403
Schafer, Victoria E. ....'53 '83 C.8 B.A. L.7 J.D. 1003 E Turkeyfoot Lake Rd
Scheatzle, Kyle S. ....'76 '02 C.381 B.A. L.608 J.D. [A Roetzel&A.]
Scherf, Holly Lynn ....'72 '99 C.62 B.A. L.1003 J.D. [A D.E.Booher]
Schiller, Glenn M. ....'53 '98 C.188 B.S. L.796 J.D. [G.M.Schiller]
Schiller, Glenn M., Co., LLC .... 611 W. Market Street, Suite C
Schinker-Kuharich, Dynele L. ....'72 '98 C.980 A.B. L.7 J.D. 1 Cascade Plz.
Schneider, Edward M., (BV) '42 '95 C.453 B.S. L.8 J.D.
Mag., Common Pleas Ct., Domestic Rel. Div.
Schneiderman, Stan B., (AV) '30 '54
C.381 B.S. L.608 J.D. 585 White Pond Drive Suite D
Schneiderman, Ted ....'32 '56 C.381 B.S. L.608 J.D. Com. Pleas J.
Schneier, Bernard, (BV) ....'35 '62 C.381 B.S. L.7 J.D. [Emershaw,M.&S.]
Schobert, Jeffrey E., (AV) ....'56 '85 C.608 B.S. L.7 J.D. [Hanna,C.&P.]
Schoenewald, Michael A., (BV) ....'58 '88 C.610 B.S. L.1003 J.D. Chicago Title Co.
Schomer, John B., (AV) ....'66 '91 C.103 B.A. L.930 J.D. [Brennan,M.&D.]
Schott, John F. ....'22 '51 C.8 A.B. L.930 J.D. 7 W. Bowery St.
Schrader, Alfred E., (BV) '53 '78
C.381 B.A. L.608 J.D. 441 Wolf Ledges Pkwy., Suite 400
Schrader, Bruce R., II, (AV) ....'63 '87 C.8 B.A. L.150 J.D. [Roetzel&A.]
Schultz, William E., (BV) ....'16 '48 C.321 A.B. L.7 J.D. Asst. Pros. Atty.
Schwab, Harry W. ....'27 '54 C.150 B.B.A. L.8 J.D. 1021 Bunker Dr.
Schwartz, Bernard M. ....'40 '67 C&L.8 B.A., J.D. Ref. Juv. Ct.
Scott, Kimble Hale, (BV⑦) '62 '88
C.484 B.A. L.734 J.D. V.P. & Gen. Coun., Roberts Express, Inc.
Seeberger, Terrence L., (BV) ....'54 '78 C.293 B.A. L.910 J.D. [Stark&K.]
Segedy, Alan G., (BV) ....'43 '72 C&L.8 B.S., J.D. 105 E. Market St., Ste. 204
Seiberling, John F. ....'18 '50 C.309 A.B. L.178 LL.B. Univ. of Akron‡
Seikel, Louis A., Jr. ....'35 '60 C.608 B.S.B.A. L.607 LL.B. 686 W. Market St.
Sellers, Gary ....'47 '90 C.656 B.A. L.8 J.D. Univ. of Akron
Sermersheim, Michael D., (BV) '48 '73 C.8 B.A. L.7 J.D.
Assoc. Gen. Coun. & Dir., Claims Def. & Prop. Admn.
Sethna, Farhad, (BV) ....'65 '91 C&L.8 M.B.A., J.D. 17 South Main Street, Suite 201
Shah, Mariam Alikhan ....'76 '02 C.477 B.A L.276 J.D. [A Roetzel&A.]
Shapiro, Marvin A. ....'38 '65 C.8 B.A. L.7 J.D. Mun. J.
Sharp, John W. ....'42 '81 C.8 B.A. L.276 J.D. 1166 Marcy St.
Shea-Stonum, Marilyn, (AV) ....'47 '75 C.112 A.B. L.930 J.D. 2 S. Main St.
Sheck, Robert E. ....'14 '41 C.381 B.A. L.608 J.D. 100 Brookmont Rd.‡
Sheppard, Ray C., (BV) ....'27 '55 C.8 L.7 B.L. 583 Grant St.
Shifrin, Debra S., (BV) ....'56 '81 C.30 B.A. L.930 J.D. [Sternberg,N.S.&Assoc.]
Shoaff, Joseph A. ....'62 '99 C.980 B.S.A.S L.7 J.D. [A Brennan,M.&D.]
Shoemaker, John H. ....'40 '71 C&L.7 B.A., J.D. Mag., Ct. of Com. Pleas
Shumaker, Thomas A., (BV) ....'46 '74 C&L.8 B.A., J.D. 265 S Main Street, 1st Floor
Siegfried, Elayne M. '58 '94 C.656 B.A. L.7 J.D.
Pro Bono Coord., Community Legal Aid Services., Inc.
Siff, Alan L. '32 '63 C.309 A.B. L.150 J.D.
Chmn. of the Bd. & Gen. Coun., Widmann Siff & Co.
Silfani, Daniel L. ....'73 '99 C.8 BS./B.A. L.124 J.D. [A Amer C.]

Simon, Patrick O. .... '25 '53 C&L.421 B.A., J.D. 1201 Massilon Rd.
Simpson, Helen Mae Martin .... '63 '89 C&L.8 B.A., J.D. Assoc., First Merit Corp.
Singletary, Gary S., (BV) .... '50 '86 C.839 B.B.A. L.608 J.D. [A Hanna,C.&P.]
Sinn, Jonathan Todd .... '68 '94 C.980 B.A. L.8 J.D. [Callahan,G.R.&S.]
Sinopoli, Debra L. .... '64 '92 C.381 B.A. L.8 J.D. [Sinopoli&S.]
Sinopoli, Vito F. .... '60 '92 C&L.8 B.S., J.D. [Sinopoli&S.]
Sinopoli & Sinopoli, Co., L.P.A. .... 1717 Saddlewood Ave.
Sitler, Martin H. .... '— '92 C.608 B.S. L.793 J.D. [A Marshall,D.W.C.&G.]
Skakun, Mark J., III, (AV) .... '50 '74 C.602 B.A. L.930 J.D. [Buckingham,D.&B.]
Skeriotis, John M., (BV) .... '65 '97 C&L.8 B.S., J.D. [Brouse M.] (Pat.)
Skidmore, Archie W., (AV) .... '26 '54 C.381 L.7 LL.B. [Skidmore&Assoc.]
Skidmore, Brian K., (BV) .... '57 '84 C.528 B.A. L.896 J.D. [Skidmore&Assoc.]
Skidmore, Eric E., (BV) .... '60 '89 C.528 B.A. L.607 J.D. [Skidmore&Assoc.]
Skidmore, Thomas A., (BV) .... '61 '88 C.607 B.A. L.8 J.D. [T.A.Skidmore]

Skidmore & Associates, A Legal Professional Association, (AV)
National City Center, One Cascade Plaza, 12th Floor, 44308
Telephone: 330-253-1550 Medina: 330-721-4452 Telecopier: 330-253-9657
Email: info@skidmorelaw.com URL: http://www.skidmorelaw.com
Archie W. Skidmore; Spiros Vasilatos, Jr.; Brian K. Skidmore; Eric E. Skidmore.
General Civil Practice in all State and Federal Courts. Complex Litigation, Business, Commercial, Real Estate, Condominium, Construction, Banking, Corporation, Domestic Relations, Probate, Savings and Loan, Personal Injury and Tort Law. Bankruptcy and Corporate Reorganization. Trials and Appeals.

See Professional Biographies, AKRON, OHIO

Skidmore, Thomas A., Co., LPA, (BV) .... 1 Cascade Plaza, 12th Floor
Skinner, Colin G. .... '63 '95 C.645 B.S.B.A. L.8 J.D. [A Oldham&D.]
Skoglund, Rodney Lee '65 '91
C.532 B.A. L.8 J.D. [Renner,K.G.B.T.&W.] (See Pat. Sect.)
Skove, Thomas M., (AV) .... '51 '77 C.31 B.A. L.930 J.D. [Roetzel&A.]
Slabaugh, William F. .... '36 '71 C&L.8 B.S.B.A., J.D. Roadway Express, Inc.
Slaby, Lynn C., (BV) .... '38 '72 C&L.8 B.S.B.A., J.D. 9th Dist. Ct. of App.
Slater, James W., (BV) .... '43 '70 C.184 A.B. L.276 J.D. [Slater,Z.&G.] ⊙

Slater, Zurz & Gilbert, (BV)
One Cascade Plaza, 44308-1135 ⊙
Telephone: 330-762-0700 Toll Free: 800-297-9191 Fax: 330-762-3923
Email: s-z@ix.netcom.com URL: http://www.slater-zurz-gilbert.com
James W. Slater; Richard V. Zurz, Jr.; Louis J. Gigliotti, Jr.; Edward C. Pullekins; John J. Lynett, Jr.; Gary M. Petti; Edward L. Gilbert. Associates: E. Lee Wagoner, Jr.; James E. Brown; Michael J. Wright. Of Counsel: Ellen M. Brooks.
Personal Injury, Wrongful Death, Commercial Litigation, Corporate, Business, Real Estate, Business Organization, Domestic Relations, Construction Litigation.
Canton, Ohio Office: 4450 Belden Village Street, N.W., Suite 301, 44718. Telephone: 330-864-2999.

See Professional Biographies, AKRON, OHIO

Sloan, Jerry .... '45 '71 C&L.8 B.A., J.D. Admr. for Co.
Smith, Dean E., (BV) .... '33 '72 C&L.8 B.S.B.A., J.D. [Smith&M.]
Smith, Edward T., (CV) .... '56 '92 C&L.8 B.A., J.D. 577 Madison Ave.
Smith, Ivan L. .... '13 '38 C&L.608 B.A., J.D. 1254 S. Hometown Rd.‡
Smith, Katherine C. Hart, (AV) .... '53 '88 C.381 B.S. L.8 J.D. [A K.A.Belfance&Assoc.]
Smith, Melinda E. .... '74 '99 C.294 B.A. L.7 J.D. [A Scanlon&G.]
Smith, Russell, (AV) .... '36 '61 C&L.608 B.A., J.D. [R.Smith]
Smith, Scott F. .... '72 '98 C.381 B.A. L.8 J.D. [Sternberg,N.S.&Assoc.]
Smith & Mazak Co., L.P.A., (BV) .... 777 West Market Street

Smith, Russell, Attorney at Law, (AV) BB
503 Key Building, 159 South Main Street, 44308
Telephone: 330-434-7167; 877-434-7167 Fax: 330-434-7195
Email: smithar@bright.net URL: http://www.russsmithlaw.com
Russell Smith.
Personal Injury, Products Liability, Malpractice and Civil Litigation.

See Professional Biographies, AKRON, OHIO

Smithern, Michelle A., (AV) .... '59 '86 C.8 B.S. L.7 J.D. [Buckingham,D.&B.]
Snitchler, Todd A. .... '70 '02 C.294 B.A. L.8 J.D. 76 S. Main St., Suite 1512
Sokol, Maurice C., (CV) .... '18 '54 C.8 L.7 LL.B. 1881 Cromwell Dr.
Solomon, John W., (BV) .... '44 '73 C.188 A.B. L.477 J.D. [C Vorys,S.S.&P.]
Sommerfeld, Barbara Inge .... '51 '99 C.381 B.S. L.7 J.D. 264 South Arlington
Sossi, Frank Thomas, (CV) .... '52 '78 C.363 B.A. L.851 J.D. [Brennan,M.&D.]
Souza, Jennifer L., (CV) .... '72 '98 C.363 B.A. L.930 J.D. [A Roetzel&A.]
Spahr, Kenneth G., Jr. .... '39 '74 C.381 B.A. L.8 J.D. 650 Dan St.
Spetrino, Michael J., (BV) .... '55 '80 C.385 A.B. L.117 J.D. 50 S. Main St.
Spicer, Mary F. .... '37 '65 C.313 B.A. L.7 J.D. Com. Pleas J.
Spicer, Willard F. .... '42 '72 C&L.7 B.A., J.D. Com. Pleas J.
Sponseller, Alan W., (AV) '53 '80
C.980 A.B. L.117 J.D. V.P. & Gen. Coun., Cedarwood Companies
Spring, Gary W., (AV) .... '54 '79 C.8 B.A. L.608 J.D. [Roetzel&A.]
Squires, Thomas B., (BV) .... '64 '90 C.381 B.A. L.8 J.D. 451 S. Messner Rd.
Sremack, William M., (BV) .... '49 '75 C.8 B.A. L.7 J.D. [W.M.Sremack,Sr.]
Sremack, William M., Co., L.P.A., (BV) .... 2745 S. Arlington Road
Stachowiak, Robert W. .... '30 '69 C.494 B.S. L.7 J.D. 1685 Far View Rd.‡
Staehle, Richard W. .... '37 '72 C.8 B.S.A. L.7 J.D. 717 Lakewood Blvd.
Staley, Cara L. .... '79 '04 C.97 B.A. L.8 J.D. [A Oldham&D.]

Stanceu, James T.
(See Cleveland)

Stark, Michael L., (AV) .... '36 '61 C.473 B.S. L.1119 J.D. [Stark&K.]
Stark, Wendy E. .... '72 '97 C.373 B.A. L.477 J.D. Assoc. Gen. Coun., FirstEnergy Corp.

Stark & Knoll Co., L.P.A., (AV)
76 South Main Street, Suite 1512, 44308-1824
Telephone: 330-376-3300 Telecopier: 330-376-6237
URL: http://www.stark-knoll.com
Michael L. Stark; Thomas G. Knoll; James L. Rench; John K. Krajewski; John P. Susany; Jeffrey T. Knoll; Ronald K. Starkey; Aaron G. Lepp; Michael L. Wear; Mary Jo Lockshin; Terrence L. Seeberger.
Corporate Transactions, Real Estate and Commercial Leasing; Business Succession Planning, Taxation, Commercial Lending, Healthcare, Non-Profit Organizations, E-Commerce, Litigation, Labor and Employment, Estate Planning and Probate.
References: Bank One Akron; Key Bank of Akron.

See Professional Biographies, AKRON, OHIO

Starkey, Ronald K., (BV) .... '67 '92 C.8 B.A. L.930 J.D. [Stark&K.]
Stasitis, Mark Gerald .... '74 '01 C.381 B.A. L.7 J.D. [A Amer C.]
Stauffenger, Leonard W., (BV) .... '58 '83 C.608 B.S.B.A. L.7 J.D. 460 White Pond Dr.
Stecz, Eric J. .... '71 '96 C.363 B.A. L.930 J.D. [A Brennan,M.&D.]
Steel, Frank E., Jr., (BV) .... '38 '63 C.712 B.B.A. L.608 J.D. [C Goldman&R.]
Steel, Michael A., (BV) .... '67 '00 C.473 B.S. L.7 J.D. [Goldman&R.]
Stein, Ernest R., (BV) .... '27 '51 C.8 B.A. L.930 J.D. 92 E. Mill St.
Steiner, Judith A., (AV) '62 '87 C.8 B.A. L.930 J.D.
Assoc. Legal Coun., First National Bank of Ohio

Steinhauer, John S., **(AV) '43 '69 C&L.608 B.A., J.D.**
159 South Main Street, Suite 530, 44308-1300
Telephone: 330-535-1010 Fax: 330-535-1531
Email: jss530@sbcglobal.net
Mergers and Acquisitions, Corporate Law, Real Estate, Finance, Commercial and Business Law.

See Professional Biographies, AKRON, OHIO

Steinhauer, Susan Kelly .... '73 '98 C.473 B.S. L.345 J.D. Jud. Atty.
Sternberg, Richard, (AV) .... '28 '52 C.145 B.A. L.930 LL.B. [Sternberg,N.S.&Assoc.]
Sternberg, Newman, Shifrin & Associates, Inc., (AV)
411 Wolf Ledges Parkway, Suite 300
Sterner, Steven L. .... '59 '85 C.901 B.A. L.1003 J.D. Industrial Commission of Ohio
Stevenson, Diana Marie .... '66 '92 C&L.8 B.A., J.D. Summit Co. Prob. Ct.
Stevenson, Roger J., (AV) .... '52 '81 C.381 B.A. L.7 J.D. [Roetzel&A.]
Stevenson, Scot A., (BV) .... '66 '92 C&L.8 B.A., J.D. 441 Wolf Ledges Parkway
Stewart, Richard M. .... '21 '50 C.381 B.A. L.150 J.D. 903 Hampton Ridge Dr.‡
Stich, Janet I., (CV) .... '55 '86 C.970 B.A. L.7 J.D. 185 Schocalog Rd
Stile, David .... '55 '94 C.381 B.A. L.8 J.D. Stile Realty Co.
Stiller, Robin Rose, Law Office of .... '57 '00 C.608 B.S. L.8 J.D. 50 South Main Street
Stimler, James T., (BV) .... '52 '77 C.473 B.A. L.7 J.D. [Stimler]
Stimler, Kathleen E., (BV) .... '54 '80 C.318 B.A. L.8 J.D. [Stimler]
Stimler Law Offices, (BV) .... 50 S. Main Street, Suite 703
Stimler Law Offices, (BV) .... 50 S. Main St., Ste. 703
Stith, Michael R. .... '49 '79 C.870 B.S. L.7 J.D. Engr. & Gen. Coun.
Stormer, Elinore Marsh .... '56 '82 C.198 B.A. L.8 J.D. Com. Pleas J.
Strattan, Sara E. '51 '87 C.318 B.A. L.1003 J.D.
Exec. Dir., Community Legal Aid Services., Inc.
Strecker, Richard E. .... '26 '52 L.7 LL.B. V.P. & Title Offr., Chicago Title Ins. Co.
Striegel, Bernard M., Jr. .... '57 '84 C.602 A.B. L.851 J.D. 3299 Morewood Dr.
Studeny, Nathan F. .... '78 '04 C.473 B.A. L.989 J.D. [A Roetzel&A.]
Sugerman, Irving B., (BV) .... '56 '82 C.434 B.A. L.7 J.D. [Goldman&R.]
Susany, John P., (BV) .... '62 '87 C.610 A.B. L.477 J.D. [Stark&K.]
Swearingen-Hilker, Nicole .... '77 '03 C&L.8 B.A., J.D. [A Brouse M.]
Sweeney, Michael A., (BV) .... '47 '76 C.161 B.A. L.1003 J.D. [Brouse M.]
Swett, Loma L. .... '55 '80 C.362 B.A. L.7 J.D. [A Kaufmann&K.]
Swing, Christopher F., (BV) .... '65 '91 C.381 B.B.A. L.930 J.D. [Brouse M.]
Swyrydenko, Nicholas, (BV) .... '50 '89 C.381 B.A. L.8 J.D. [A Dobbins&Assoc.]
Syracopoulos, Nicholas C. .... '13 '39 C.8 B.A. L.273 LL.B. 897 Delia Ave.‡
Szabo, Carol Crimi, (BV) .... '49 '80 C.201 B.A. L.7 J.D. Evergreen Consol.
Taggart, J. William .... '43 '75 C.980 B.S. L.8 J.D. Prof., Univ. of Akron
Tarchinski, Theresa A., (BV) .... '63 '89 C.477 B.A. L.930 J.D. [Amer C.]
Tass, Morris H., (BV) .... '20 '74 C.8 B.E.E. L.7 J.D. 890 Shullo Dr.
Taylor, E. Jane, (AV) .... '54 '81 C.381 B.A. L.7 J.D. [Guy,L.&T.]
Taylor, Elizabeth Grooms, (BV) .... '66 '91 C.610 B.S. L.8 J.D. [A Whalen&C.]
Taylor, Merle E. .... '18 '62 C&L.8 B.A., LL.B. 1718 Summit Lake Blvd.‡
Taylor, Perry Reese, Jr. .... '35 '62 C.8 B.A. L.124 J.D. First National Tower, 4th Floor
Teodosio, Alexander E., (BV) .... '24 '53 C.569 L.1009 LL.B. [Teodosio,C.&M.]
Teodosio, Linda Tucci, (AV) .... '56 '82 C&L.8 B.S., J.D. Co. J.
Teodosio, Cherpas & Manos, (AV) .... 7 W. Bowery St.
Terjesen, Barry E., (BV) .... '41 '73 C.970 B.A. L.7 J.D. 4067 Shore Drive
Tersigni, Vincent J., (AV) .... '63 '88 C.473 A.B. L.930 J.D. [C Vorys,S.S.&P.]
Terzola, Mark C., (BV) .... '70 '96 C.602 B.S. L.8 J.D. [Roetzel&A.] (Pat.)
Thomas, David A., (AV) '38 '64 C.970 B.A. L.7 J.D.
Exec. V.P., Secy, Gen. Coun. & Chief Comp. Off., Bridgestone/Firestone Tech. Co. (Pat.)
Thomas, Robert Samual, II .... '70 '97 C.1356 B.A. L.904 J.D. [Thomas,T.&M.]
Thomas, Trattner & Malone, LLC, (BV) .... One South Main St. - 2nd Fl.
Thomasson, James S. .... '41 '69 C&L.8 B.S.B.A., J.D. 159 S. Main St., Ste. 317
Thompson, Dennis R., (BV) .... '53 '85 C&L.8 B.S., J.D. 2719 Manchester Rd.
Thompson, Parke G. .... '18 '42 C&L.930 A.B., LL.B. 252 Canton Rd.
Thomson, Daniel A. .... '71 '98 C.259 B.S. L.608 J.D. [A Brouse M.]
Thomson, Robert M., (BV) .... '36 '68 C.381 B.S. L.1003 J.D. [Thomson&O.]
Thomson & O'Brien, (BV) .... 159 S. Main St.
Timmons, Joseph F. .... '61 '87 C.631 B.A. L.608 J.D. 75 E. Market St.
Tipping, Christopher A., (BV) .... '70 '95 C.273 B.A. [Tipping]
Tipping, Harry A., (AV) .... '44 '71 C.1062 B.A. L.7 J.D. [Tipping]

Tipping Co., L.P.A., A Legal Professional Association, (AV)
Sanctuary Professional Building - Suite 207, 525 North Cleveland-Massillon Road, 44333
Telephone: 330-670-8400 Fax: 330-670-8454
Harry A. Tipping; Christopher A. Tipping;—Sophie M. Milo; Michael J. Elliott. Of Counsel: Dominic A. Olivo (1908-1997); Richard L. Grant.
General Civil Trial and Appellate Practice, Negligence, Personal Injury, Business, Commercial, Corporate, Probate, Workers Compensation, Administrative, Insurance, Real Estate, Bankruptcy, Estate Planning, Labor/Employment, Zoning, Municipal Law and Social Security Disability Law.

See Professional Biographies, AKRON, OHIO

Tipton, Robert L. .... '39 '73 C.8 B.S.B.A. L.7 J.D. 168 W. Caston Rd.‡
Toles, Dawn-Lorraine Sheri .... '73 '00 C.025 B.A. L.7 J.D. Lexis Nexis
Toney, Darrin R., (CV) .... '68 '95 C.206 B.S. L.7 J.D. [A Brennan,M.&D.]
Torch, Glenn F. .... '48 '74 C.381 B.S. L.1003 J.D. 650 Beaverbrook Dr.
Towell, Jennifer D. .... '— '00 C.473 B.S. L.608 J.D. [A Brouse M.]
Towne, Ronald N., (AV) .... '44 '69 C.980 B.A. L.7 J.D. [Guy,L.&T.]
Trattner, Robert B., (BV) .... '67 '93 C.473 B.S. L.851 J.D. [Thomas,T.&M.]
Trattner & Malone, LLC .... One South Main St. - 2nd Fl.
Treadon, Thomas A., (AV) .... '43 '75 C.1070 B.S. L.7 J.D. [Roetzel&A.]
Treier, J. Bret, (AV) .... '60 '85 C.97 B.S. L.930 J.D. [C Vorys,S.S.&P.]

Trivers & Dickerson, LLC
(See Cleveland)

Trotter, Thomas R., (AV) .... '49 '75 C.610 B.A. L.861 J.D. [Buckingham,D.&B.]
Troy, Frank J., Sr. .... '32 '67 C.980 B.S. L.8 J.D. 1200 Firestone Pkwy. (Pat.)
Truby, Timothy J., (BV) .... '46 '72 C.381 B.A. L.7 J.D. [Roderick L.]
Tsarnas, George P., (BV) .... '38 '63 C.8 B.A. L.608 J.D. [Goldman&R.]
Tsarouhas, Antonios P., (BV) .... '67 '94 C.377 B.A. L.607 J.D. [A Perantinides&N.]
Tschantz, Mary Myers .... '51 '78 C.8 B.A. L.7 J.D. 336 Melbourne Ave.
Tschugunov, Eleanor J., (BV) .... '55 '79 C.313 B.A. L.8 J.D. [Buckingham,D.&B.]
Tuccillo, Anthony, (BV) .... '33 '59 C&L.608 B.S., J.D. [A.Tuccillo]
Tuccillo, Anthony, Company, L.P.A., (BV) .... 1000 Society Building
Tucker, Jonathan D., (BV) .... '72 '97 C&L.8 B.A., J.D. [Daily&H.]
Tucker, Robert L., (AV) .... '58 '84 C.893 B.S. L.7 J.D. [Hanna,C.&P.]
Turowski, Kenneth L., (CV) .... '58 '83 C.8 B.A. L.7 J.D. 88 S. Portage Path Ste. 301

Umbaugh, David G.
(See Hudson)

Urban, Deborah K. .... '61 '87 C.381 B.A. L.608 J.D. 500 1st Nat. Twr.‡
Urban, Michael S., (BV) .... '57 '87 C.381 B.A. L.608 J.D. [Amer C.]

Urvan, Sean J. ... '77 '03 C.381 B.S. L.8 J.D. [A Roetzel&A.]
Utley, David G., (BV) ... '— '87 C.381 B.A. L.930 J.D. [Davis&Y.]
Vadas, Kathryn A. ... '71 '97 C.980 B.S.A.S. L.161 J.D. [A Hanna,C.&P.]
Vance, Patricia A., (BV) ... '37 '67 C&L.8 B.A., J.D. 544 White Pond Drive, Suite E
Van Ness, Jean ... '53 '79 C.976 B.A. L.893 J.D. [C Buckingham,D.&B.]
Van Oosterhout, Peter D. ... '32 '55 C&L.352 B.A., J.D. 3811 Granger Rd.‡
Van Rees, Adam R. ... '76 '02 C.610 B.B.A. L.124 J.D. [A Buckingham,D.&B.]
Van Winkle, Neil ... '52 '79 C.608 B.A. L.117 J.D. Roadway Express, Inc.
Varian, Donald S., Jr., (AV) ... '45 '70 C.8 B.A. L.904 J.D. [C Oldham&D.]
Vasilatos, Spiros, Jr., (BV) ... '58 '84 C.8 B.S. L.7 J.D. [Skidmore&Assoc.]
Vasko, George B., (BV) ... '31 '61 C.874 B.A. L.93 J.D. [Vasko,R.&E.]
Vasko, Roberto & Evans, Co., L.P.A., (BV) ... 137 S. Main St., Ste. 206
Veletean, Kory ... '75 '00 C.150 B.A. L.117 J.D. [A Bagdasarian&B.] ⊙
Venesy, Barbara Ann, (BV) ... '50 '91 C&L.8 B.S., J.D. [B.A.Venesy]
Venesy, Barbara A., The Law Office of, (BV) ... 2741 Foxwood Drive
Vengrow, Jeffrey S. ... '49 '74 C.454 B.A. L.7 J.D. P.O. Box 991
Venizelos, James C. ... '59 '91 C.967 B.A. L.1003 J.D. Goodyear Tire & Rubber Co.
Verity, Neal, (BV) ... '39 '71 C.610 B.S. L.7 J.D. Chf. Ref., Juv. Ct.
Vespoli, Leila ... '59 '84 C.473 B.S. L.930 J.D. Sr. V.P. & Gen. Coun., FirstEnergy Corp.
Victor, William H. ... '13 '37 C.8 A.B. L.930 LL.B. 1531 Triplett Blvd.
Vlosky, Edward F., (CV) '48 '86
C.1349 B.A. L.8 J.D. Exec. V.P. & Assoc. Coun., Cedarwood Cos.
Vogel, Walter J., (BV) ... '30 '60 C.885 A.B. L.472 LL.B. First Natl. Twr.
Voinovich, George F. ... '63 '90 C.150 B.A. L.930 J.D. [A Brennan,M.&D.]
Volk, Jay G., (AV) ... '68 '93 C.473 B.A. L.228 J.D. [C Brouse M.]

Vorys, Sater, Seymour and Pease LLP, (AV)
First National Tower, 106 South Main Street, Suite 1100, 44308 ⊙
Telephone: 330-208-1000 Fax: 330-208-1001
URL: http://www.vssp.com
Partner: F. Daniel Balmert. Associates: Ashley M. Manfull; Aaron S. Berke; Patricia M. Ochmann; Amanda J. Zaremba. Of Counsel: Philip A. Lloyd; John W. Solomon; Jay P. Porter; J. Bruce Hunsicker; J. Bret Treier; Thomas Richard Crookes; Vincent J. Tersigni.
Alternative Dispute Resolution, Antitrust, Trade Regulation, Customs, Banks and Banking, Finance, Bankruptcy, Biotechnology, Business Law, Civil Rights, Debtors and Creditors Rights, Computers and Software, Congressional Investigations, Construction Law, Contracts, Copyrights, Disabilities, Election, Campaign and Political Law, Employee Benefits, Environmental Law, Probate, Guardianship and Conservatorship, General Practice, Health Care, Labor, Employment, Occupational Safety and Health, Workers Compensation, Corporate Law, Securities, Energy, Natural Resources, Franchises and Franchising, Government Contracts, Hospital Law, Immigration and Naturalization, Insurance, Intellectual Property, International Law, International Trade, Legal Ethics and Professional Responsibility, Litigation, Media Law, Medicare and Medicaid, Mergers, Acquisitions and Divestitures, Municipal Law, Telecommunications, Personal Injury, Products Liability, Railroad Law, Real Estate, RICO, Sports Law, Taxation, Technology and Science, Torts, Toxic Torts, Trade Secrets, Transportation, Trusts and Estates, Unfair Competition, Utility Law, White Collar Defense, Wills, Zoning, Planning and Land Use.
Representative Client: Honda of America Mfg., Inc.
Local Counsel: Abbott Laboratories; Anheuser-Busch, Inc.; Anthem Insurance Compnies, Inc.; Bob Evans Farms, Inc.; Borden, Inc.; Connecticut General Life Insurance Co.; Coopers & Lybrand; Eaton Corporation; General Motors Corp.
Columbus, Ohio Office: 52 East Gay Street, P.O. Box 1008, 43216-1008. Telephone: 614-464-6400. Facsimile: 614-464-6350.
Washington, D.C. Office: 1828 L Street, N.W., 20036-5109. Telephone: 202-467-8800. Facsimile: 202-467-8900.
Cleveland, Ohio Office: 2100 One Cleveland Center, 1375 East Ninth Street, 44114-1724. Telephone: 216-479-6100. Facsimile: 216-479-6060.
Cincinnati, Ohio Office: Suite 2000, Atrium Two, 221 East Fourth Street, P.O. Box 0236, 45201-0236. Telephone: 513-723-4000. Facsimile: 513-723-4056.
Alexandria, Virginia Office: 277 South Washington Street, Suite 310, 22314. Telephone: 703-837-6999. Facsimile: 703-549-4492.

See Professional Biographies, AKRON, OHIO

Vuillemin, Lawrence W., (AV) ... '48 '73 C.602 B.A. L.7 J.D. [Mentzer&M.]
Wack, Patrick J., (BV) ... '44 '73 L.7 J.D. 41 Merz Blvd.
Waddell, David E., (AV) ... '28 '60 C.8 B.A. L.930 LL.B. [Calhoun,W.&H.]
Waechter, Thomas C. ... '42 '67 C.611 A.B. L.597 J.D. 1144 E. Market St.
Wagner, James L. ... '47 '76 C.165 B.A. L.7 J.D. 529 White Pond Dr.‡
Wagner, Louis F., (AV) ... '52 '84 C.901 B.A. L.8 J.D. [Buckingham,D.&B.] (Pat.)
Wagoner, E. Lee, Jr., (BV) ... '52 '87 C.473 B.A. L.1340 J.D. [A Slater,Z.&G.]
Waite, Eric Ramsey ... '61 '97 C.611 B.A. L.8 J.D. [A Hardesty,K.&Z.]
Walko, Lee S., (BV) ... '64 '93 C.532 B.A. L.930 J.D. [Brennan,M.&D.]
Waller, John T., Law Offices of, (BV) '46 '72 C.8 B.A. L.7 J.D.
23 S. Main St., Ste. 301
Walpole, Daniel M., (BV) ... '52 '85 C.260 B.S. L.7 J.D. 120 E. Mill Street, Suite 411
Walsh, Lawr. J. ... '26 '55 C.8 B.S. L.7 LL.B. 345 S. Rose Blvd.‡
Walsh, Sherri Bevan, (BV) ... '60 '85 C.473 B.A. L.179 J.D. Pros. Atty.
Walsh, Timothy Joseph ... '57 '83 C.8 B.S. L.7 J.D. Pros. Off.
Walter, James E., (BV) ... '27 '62 C.602 B.A. L.8 J.D. 599 Reynolds Ave.
Walter, Karen S. ... '66 '96 C.124 B.S.Ch.E. L.8 J.D. [A Brouse M.]
Walters, Jeffery A. ... '56 '84 C.8 B.S. L.7 J.D. S & S business Services, Inc.
Walton, Howard J., (AV) ... '45 '71 C.823 B.A. L.7 J.D. 405 Quaker Sq.
Ward, Barry M., (BV) ... '59 '84 C.107 B.A. L.7 J.D. 1 Cascade Plaza
Wasick, W. M. ... '47 '85 C&L.8 B.S., J.D. 76 S. Main St.
Waszak, Ralph R., Jr., (CV) '68 '93
C.97 B.S. L.930 J.D. 76 South Main Street, Suite 1512
Watkins, Mark A., (AV) ... '60 '88 C.607 B.S. L.7 J.D. [Hahn L.&P.] (See Pat. Sect.)
Wear, Michael L. ... '69 '95 C&L.8 B.S., J.D. [Stark&K.]
Weber, Douglas J. ... '59 '88 C.97 B.S. L.1003 J.D. Sr. Atty., FirstEnergy Corp.

Weber, Edward C., (BV) '44 '72 C.737 B.A. L.8 J.D.
159 South Main Street, Suite 1002, 44308-1318
Telephone: 330-535-6185 Fax: 330-996-4014
Email: edweazer@aol.com URL: http://www.edwardcweberlaw.com
Trials and Appeals in all Courts. Criminal, DUI, Traffic Violations, Personal Injury, Defense, Probate and Estates Drug Crimes, Assault, Domestic Violence.

See Professional Biographies, AKRON, OHIO

Weber, Mark L. ... '74 '99 C.823 B.S. L.8 J.D. [A Renner,K.G.B.T.&W.] (See Pat. Sect.)
Weber, Ray L., (AV) '45 '72
C.8 B.S.E.E. L.7 J.D. [Renner,K.G.B.T.&W.] (See Pat. Sect.)
Webster, Timothy J. ... '59 '87 C.201 B.A. L.1003 J.D. [Roetzel&A.]
Wehener, Ann Lynn ... '68 '94 C.1208 B.S. L.117 J.D. [A Guy,L.&T.]
Weiner, Matthew Cooper '71 '98 C.976 B.A. L.893 J.D.
(adm. in FL; not adm. in OH) Cooper Management Co.

Weiner, Keith D., & Associates Co., L.P.A.
(See Cleveland)

Weisensell, John C., (BV) ... '58 '85 C.970 B.A. L.1003 J.D. [Bernlohr W.]
Weisman, Mark S., (BV) ... '60 '85 C.659 B.S. L.94 J.D. 109 North Union
Weiss, Lucinda '50 '73 C.970 B.A. L.336 J.D.
(adm. in ID; not adm. in OH) The Goodyear Tire & Rubber Co.
Weissfeld, Randall D., (BV) ... '55 '79 C.318 B.A. L.608 J.D. 614 E. Market St.
Weisz, Louis J. ... '26 '58 C.608 B.S. L.1003 J.D. 156 South Main Street, Suite 808 (Pat.)

Weitendorf, Kurt R., (AV) ... '55 '80 C.608 B.A. L.7 J.D. [Roderick L.]
Wendelken, Richard J., (BV) ... '39 '70 C.717 B.A. L.8 J.D. 1615 Akron Peninsula Road
Werren, Nola, (CV) ... '62 '89 C.980 B.A. L.8 J.D. 80 S. Summit St., Suite 100
Wertz, George R., (BV) ... '50 '79 C.980 B.S. L.8 J.D. [Bernlohr W.]
Weschler, Patrick J., (BV) ... '56 '81 C.470 B.A. L.893 J.D. [Buckingham,D.&B.]
Wessell, Kelly M. ... '69 '94 C.207 B.A. L.117 J.D. Sr. Staff Atty., Summa Health System
Westfall, James W. ... '51 '77 C.150 B.A. L.930 J.D. [Eisen&W.] ⊙
Westman, Dean E., (AV) ... '53 '78 C.228 B.A. L.880 J.D. [Kastner W.&W.]
Whalen, Dennis M., (AV) ... '38 '66 C.970 B.A. L.7 J.D. [Whalen&C.]

Whalen & Compton, A Legal Professional Association, (AV)
565 Wolf Ledges Parkway, P.O. Box 2020, 44309-2020
Telephone: 330-376-1112; 1-800-376-1112 in Ohio Telecopier: 330-376-3200
URL: http://www.whalenandcompton.com
Dennis M. Whalen; G. Frederick Compton, Jr.; Helen S. Carroll;—Elizabeth Grooms Taylor; Mari Alice Zacharyasz; Andrew F. Peck.
General Civil Trial and Appellate Practice. Educational and School Law, Labor Law, Management, Civil Rights and Equal Employment Law. Real Estate regarding University and School Law.
Reference: Bank One Akron.

See Professional Biographies, AKRON, OHIO

Wheaton, Carolyn White ... '44 '89 C.914 B.A. L.930 J.D. Law Clk. to U.S. Sr. Cir. J.
Whitaker, William T., (BV) ... '44 '72 C.381 B.A. L.7 J.D. 190 N. Union St.
White, Harold F. ... '20 '52 C.610 B.S.C. L.7 LL.B. Ret. U.S. Bkrptcy. J.
Whited, James R., (BV) ... '44 '75 C.8 B.S. L.7 J.D. [Whited&P.]
Whited & Pritchard, (BV) ... 168 E. Market St.
Whitmer, Jerry F., (AV) ... '35 '60 C.381 B.A. L.930 J.D. [Brouse M.]
Whitmore, Beth ... '45 '82 C.293 B.A. L.8 J.D. Ct. App. J.
Whitney, Lawrence J., (AV) ... '48 '74 C.201 B.A. L.8 J.D. [Burdon&M.]
Whitten, Nora J. ... '56 '01 C.8 B.A./B.S. L.7 J.D. [A Brouse M.]
Whittington, Robert M., Jr., (BV) ... '56 '81 C.473 B.A. L.608 J.D. 1023 Society Bldg.
Wiencek, Thomas J., (AV) ... '56 '85 C.165 B.A. L.213 J.D. [Brouse M.]
Wiese, Philip R. ... '66 '96 C.970 B.A. L.607 J.D. [Buckingham,D.&B.]
Wiesen, Marilyn R. ... '53 '90 C.8 B.A. L.309 J.D. 75 E. Market St.
Wigley, Edmund A. ... '26 '55 C.381 B.A. L.7 LL.B. 511 N. Main St.
Wilcox, Amanda H. ... '76 '01 C.473 B.S. L.851 J.D. [A Hahn L.&P.] (See Pat. Sect.)
Wilkins, James P., (AV) ... '57 '83 C.970 B.A. L.273 J.D. [Kastner W.&W.]
Williams, Brian J. ... '52 '79 C.150 B.A. L.7 J.D. 611 W. Market St., Ste. C
Williams, Caroline ... '50 '77 C.8 B.A. L.7 J.D. Edwin Shaw Hosp.
Williams, Elizabeth Merryweather ... '65 '97 C.381 B.A. L.930 J.D. Pros. Off.
Williams, James R. ... '33 '65 C&L.8 B.A., J.D. Com. Pleas J.
Williams, Kenneth C. ... '43 '69 C&L.597 B.A., J.D. 1144 E. Market St.
Williams, Orlando J., (BV) ... '57 '86 C.97 B.A. L.851 J.D. 209 S Main St

Williams, Sennett & Scully Co., L.P.A.
(See Twinsburg)

Williger, Richard L., (BV) ... '53 '82 C.381 B.A. L.7 J.D. [R.L.Williger]
Williger, Richard L., Co., L.P.A., (BV) ... 2070 East Ave.
Willis, John ... '49 '86 C.36 B.A. L.879 J.D. Research Atty., Mun. Ct.
Willis, Todd L., (BV) ... '72 '98 C.276 B.A. L.8 J.D. 670 West Market Street

Wilson, Bruce H., (AV) '— '64 C.124 B.S. L.8 J.D.
789 West Market Street, 44303
Telephone: 330-253-8300
Email: BruceWilsonEsq@aol.com
Of Counsel: Terence E. Scanlon.
Antitrust, Deceptive Trade Practices, Commercial Litigation, Intellectual Property Litigation, Unfair Competition.

See Professional Biographies, AKRON, OHIO

Wilson, Dale V., (BV) ... '45 '83 C.381 B.A. L.8 J.D. [A Joondeph&B.]
Wilson, David H., (AV) ... '21 '48 C.31 A.B. L.930 LL.B. 50 S. Main St.‡
Wilson, Douglas A. ... '44 '75 C.659 B.S. L.7 J.D. Roadway Express, Inc.
Wilson, J. Robt. ... '14 '46 C.966 Ph.B. L.7 LL.B. 1195 Yellow Creek Ln.‡
Wilson, James D. ... '25 '54 C.790 B.S. in E.E. L.276 J.D. 76 S. Main St.
Wilt, David B. ... '44 '70 C.8 B.S. L.7 J.D. 1602 E. Market St.
Windon, Jeffrey David '49 '74 C.97 B.S. L.8 J.D.
Branch Coun. & N. Ohio Sales Coun., LandAmerica/Lawyers Title Ins. Co.
Winick, Bernard S., (BV) '33 '64 C.608 B.S.B.A. L.7 J.D.
Assoc. Law Prof. Emeritus, Akron Mediation Ctr.
Winston, David S. ... '66 '96 C.188 B.A. L.608 J.D. Atty., FirstEnergy Corp.
Winter, James P. ... '28 '55 C.999 L.7 LL.B. Ret. Com. Pleas J.‡
Witschey, Frank J., (BV) ... '66 '92 C.97 B.A. L.8 J.D. [Witschey W.&F.]
Witschey, Jeffrey T., (BV) ... '66 '92 C.97 B.A. L.8 J.D. [Witschey W.&F.]

Witschey Witschey & Firestine Co., L.P.A., (BV)
405 Rothrock Road Suite 103, 44321-3125
Telephone: 330-665-5117 Fax: 330-665-7615
Email: witschey@witscheylaw.com URL: http://www.witscheyandwitschey.com
Frank J. Witschey; Jeffrey T. Witschey; David L. Firestine;—Kelly A. Molnar; Craig S. Horbus; Amy M. Montana.
Corporate and Business Law, Real Estate, Zoning, Condominium and Construction Law, Oil and Gas Law, Probate, Estate and Business Succession Planning, Elder Care, Tax Law, Civil Litigation involving the above practice areas.

See Professional Biographies, AKRON, OHIO

Woerner, Daniel E. ... '47 '81 C.608 B.S.A.A.E. L.7 J.D. P.O. Box 991
Wolf, Barbara A. ... '55 '80 C.94 B.A. L.930 J.D. 3443 Hammond Blvd.
Wolfe, James D. '20 '52 C.38 B.S. L.862 J.D.
(adm. in OK; not adm. in OH; Pat.) 1225 W. Market St.
Wolfe, John L., Law Offices, (BV) '26 '53
C.8 A.B. L.477 J.D. 1 Cascade Plaza, Suite 1222
Wolfe, Michael G. ... '54 '81 Atty., FirstEnergy Corp.
Wolfe, Terry W. ... '41 '73 C.97 B.S. L.7 J.D. 1826 S. Main St.
Woodall, Shelby L., (BV) ... '— '94 C&L.8 B.S., J.D. 1305 Marcy St.
Woodburn, David W., (BV) ... '71 '97 C.473 B.S. L.8 J.D. [Buckingham,D.&B.]
Worhatch, S. David, Law Offices of ... '54 '79 C.229 B.A. L.602 J.D. 4920 Darrow Road
Wright, Alisa Labut, (BV) ... '68 '93 C.8 B.A. L.608 J.D. [Roetzel&A.]
Wright, Bradley A., (BV) ... '64 '90 C.473 B.A. L.608 J.D. [Roetzel&A.]
Wright, David J. ... '70 '96 C.645 B.A. L.608 J.D. 4000 Embassy Pkwy., Ste. 100
Wright, Michael J. ... '77 '02 C.201 B.A. L.7 J.D. [A Slater,Z.&G.]
Wyss, Jerome G. ... '75 '01 C.1105 B.A. L.124 J.D. [A Roetzel&A.]
Yeargin, Rocco P., (BV) ... '70 '96 C.318 B.A. L.7 J.D. 507 Canton Rd.
Yeargin, Stephen J. ... '— '04 C.999 B.A. L.8 J.D. [A Brennan,M.&D.]
York, Stephanie H., (CV) ... '70 '95 C.610 B.S. L.8 J.D. Asst. Law Dir., City Law Dept.
Young, Henry C., Jr. ... '35 '63 C.453 B.S. L.7 LL.B. 1144 E. Market St. (Pat.)
Young, Ralph C. ... '20 '51 C.8 B.S. L.7 J.D. 282 E. Dresden Ave.‡
Young, Robert Milton '25 '67
C.608 B.Ch.E. L.8 J.D. Assoc. Coun., Intl. Chemical Wkrs. Union
Zacharyasz, Mari Alice ... '61 '00 C.62 B.A. L.1003 J.D. [A Whalen&C.]
Zaremba, Amanda J. ... '79 '04 C.473 B.A. L.150 J.D. [A Vorys,S.S.&P.]

Zavarello, A. William, (AV) .... '37 '64 C.8 B.A. L.7 J.D. [Zavarello&D.]

Zavarello and Davis, Co., L.P.A., (AV)
313 South High Street, Corner South High and Buchtel, 44308-1532
Telephone: 330-762-9700 Fax: 330-762-1680 Email: RhDavis3205@netlink.net
Email: wzavarello@netlink.net
A. William Zavarello; Rhonda Gail Davis.
General Civil, Trial and Appellate Practice. Negligence, Medical, Legal Malpractice, Product Liability.
References: First National Bank of Ohio; National City Bank, Akron.
See Professional Biographies, AKRON, OHIO

Zerebniak, Harry M. .... '53 '83 C.8 B.A. L.7 J.D. 159 S. Main St., Ste. 400
Zerrusen, Kenneth M. .... '71 '99 C.1082 B.S. L.8 J.D. 3085 W. Market St., Suite 130
Ziegler, Deborah A., (BV) .... '55 '85 C.8 B.A. L.7 J.D. [Emershaw,M.&S.]
Zimmerman, Terry D., (BV) .... '49 '75 C.385 B.A. L.930 J.D. [Hardesty,K.&Z.]
Zindle, Charles W. .... '44 '70 C.381 B.S. L.8 J.D. 136 S. Rose Blvd.
Zugrave, George V., Jr. .... '55 '87 C.381 B.A. L.7 J.D. 310 N. Cleveland-Massillon Rd.
Zumkehr, Charles E., (AV) .... '38 '64 C.610 B.A. L.930 J.D. [Roetzel&A.]
Zurz, Richard V. .... '30 '53 C.381 L.607 LL.B. [Blakemore,M.&B.]
Zurz, Richard V., Jr., (BV) .... '57 '82 C.97 B.S. L.7 J.D. [Slater,Z.&G.]

ALEXANDRIA, 85, *Licking Co.*

Roggenkamp, David C. .... '30 '59 C.608 B.S.B.A. L.266 J.D. 7308 Sadie Thomas Rd., N.
Trimble, Kathy Miller .... '63 '88 C.294 B.A. L.665 J.D. 4470 Raccoon Valley Rd.
Turk, Thomas E., (BV) .... '37 '66 C.97 B.S. L.1003 J.D. 4255 Raccoon Valley Rd.

ALLIANCE, 23,253, *Mahoning & Stark Cos.*

Amsden-Michel, Alissa A. .... '68 '01 C.381 B.A. L.8 J.D. [Geiger,T.S.&H.]
Beaumont, William F. .... '22 '52 C&L.930 B.A., LL.B. 1st Natl. City Bk. of Alliance
Byrd, Wilbert .... '45 '76 C.8 B.A. L.7 J.D. P.O. Box 2293★
Casale, Joseph A., (BV) .... '23 '59 C.36 L.948 LL.B. [Casale&C.]
Casale, Ned J., (BV) .... '45 '84 C.610 B.G.S. L.7 J.D. [Casale&C.]
Casale & Casale, (BV) .... 1021 W. State St.
Clunk, Dennis R., (BV) .... '57 '82 C.363 B.A. L.7 J.D. [Clunk]
Clunk Law Office, (BV) .... 2040 S. Union Ave.
Collins, John C., (BV) .... '57 '82 C.473 B.A. L.8 J.D. [J.C.Collins]
Collins, John C., L.P.A., (BV) .... 2040 S. Union Ave.
England, Daniel L. .... '51 '80 C.8 B.A. L.7 J.D. 520 West Cambridge Street
Farmer, Kristin Grace .... '74 '01 C.884 B.S. L.930 J.D. City of Alliance, Law Dir.'s Off.
France, William I. .... '20 '50 C.528 A.B. L.930 LL.B. 475 E. Beech St.‡
Francis, Philip L., (BV) '58 '83
C.528 B.A. L.930 J.D. V.P. & Tr. Offr., United National Bk. & Tr.
Geiger, Teeple, Smith & Hahn, P.L.L., (AV) .... 1844 West State Street, #A
Goldthorpe, Christopher J., (BV) .... '45 '72 C.434 B.A. L.930 J.D. [Lundgren,G.&Z.] ⊙
Hahn, B. Scott, (BV) .... '54 '80 C.528 B.A. L.7 J.D. [Geiger,T.S.&H.]
Haupt, Fred J., (AV) .... '41 '67 C.528 B.A. L.930 J.D. [Krugliak,W.G.&D.] (⊙Canton)
Hunter, Robert R., Jr., (BV) .... '46 '75 C.150 B.S.C.E. L.276 J.D. [Hunter&H.]
Hunter, Robert R., Sr., (BV) .... '19 '50 C.528 A.B. L.948 LL.B. [Hunter&H.]
Hunter & Hunter, (BV) .... 520 E. Main St., Ste. 200
James, Robert N., (BV) .... '41 '67 C.1260 B.A. L.930 J.D. P.O. Box 3753
Krash, Allan Leonard .... '34 '61 C&L.124 B.A., LL.B 1001 Parkside Drive

Krugliak, Wilkins, Griffiths & Dougherty Co., L.P.A., (AV)
KeyBank Building, 960 West State Street, 44601 ⊙
Telephone: 330-823-9262 Facsimile: 330-821-2447
Email: legal@kwgd.com URL: http://www.kwgd.com
Fred J. Haupt.
Corporate Law, Mergers and Acquisitions, Labor and Employment (Private and Public Sector), Employee Benefits, Real Estate, Taxation, Complex Litigation, Contracts, Insurance Defense, Estates and Trusts, Probate, Elder Law, Commercial Litigation, Oil and Gas, Occupational Safety and Health, Environmental Law, Health Care Law, Hospital Law, Bankruptcy, Banks and Banking, Securities, Construction Law, Family Law, Education Law, Workers Compensation, Personal Injury Litigation, Collections, Debtor and Creditor, Government, Media Law and Electronic Commerce.
Canton, Ohio Office: 4775 Munson Street N.W. Telephone: 330-497-0700.
New Philadelphia, Ohio Office: 158 N. Broadway Street. Telephone: 330-364-3472.
See Professional Biographies, ALLIANCE, OHIO

Laslo, Tracey A. .... '— '99 C.528 B.A. L.7 J.D. [T.A.Laslo]
Laslo, Tracey A., LLC .... 325 E. Main Street
Lundgren, David J., (BV) .... '47 '76 C.967 B.A. L.930 J.D. [Lundgren,G.&Z.] ⊙
Lundgren, Goldthorpe & Zumbar, (BV) .... 526 East Main Street (⊙Hartville)
Luther, Brant A. .... '74 '02 C.317 B.A. L.8 J.D. 770 N. Lincoln Ave.
McAlister, Don E. .... '26 '64 C.528 B.A. L.8 LL.B. Clem Lumber & Distr. Co.
Morris, Evan W., (AV) .... '42 '65 C.528 B.A. L.607 J.D. 960 West State Street, Suite 130
Morris, John D., (BV) .... '50 '75 C.569 B.A. L.930 J.D. 1610 S. Union Ave.
Moushey, Thomas P., (BV) .... '51 '77 C.611 B.A. L.851 J.D. [Geiger,T.S.&H.]
Murray, Michael F. .... '40 '69 C.602 B.S. L.8 J.D. Atty., McDermott, Inc.
Ogline, Michael A., (AV) .... '52 '78 C.473 B.A. L.930 J.D. [Geiger,T.S.&H.]
Puckett, James P., (BV) .... '37 '69 C.381 B.A. L.8 J.D. 360 Overlook Dr.
Randall, T. Keith, (BV) .... '41 '68 C.312 B.B.A. L.608 J.D. [Geiger,T.S.&H.]
Robertson, Alex J., (BV) .... '64 '91 C.363 B.A. L.201 J.D. 2210 S. Union Avenue
Robertson, Alexander J., (BV) .... '30 '55 C.528 B.A. L.276 LL.B. 2210 S. Union Avenue
Robertson, Shawn Owen, (BV) .... '68 '93 C.363 B.A. L.8 J.D. 2210 South Union Avenue
Russell, Ronald L. .... '33 '64 C.528 B.A. L.7 J.D. 740 S. Union Ave.‡
Shetler, William B., (BV) .... '48 '73 C.381 B.B.A. L.1003 J.D. [Shetler&S.]
Shetler & Spalding, (BV) .... 950 S. Sawburg Ave.
Shuster, Elwood H., (BV) .... '28 '54 C.528 L.948 LL.B. 120 S. Union Ave.
Smith, Bruce E., (BV) .... '49 '75 C.381 B.A. L.7 J.D. [Geiger,T.S.&H.]
Spalding, David B., (BV) .... '56 '80 C.610 B.B.A. L.1003 J.D. [Shetler&S.]
Spiker, William J. .... '59 '84 C.528 B.A. L.607 J.D. Dir., Develop., Mt. Union Coll.
Stone, D. Stephen, Jr., (BV) .... '48 '73 C.528 B.A. L.930 J.D. 981 W. State St.
Stone, Donald S., (BV) .... '25 '62 C.528 B.A. L.8 J.D. 981 W State‡
Stone, Robert Henry, Jr. .... '65 '91 C.608 B.A. L.8 J.D. 643 West State Street
Tangi, Michael A. .... '27 '55 C.381 B.A. L.608 J.D. Mun. Ct. J.
Tangi, Thomas J., (BV) .... '56 '86 C.990 B.A. L.1187 J.D. 2040 S. Union Ave.
Tarian, Brian, (BV) .... '18 '49 C.528 A.B. L.930 LL.B. 22109 State Rte. 62
Tarian, Joseph, Jr. .... '15 '41 C.528 A.B. L.309 LL.B. 4210 S. Union Ave.‡
Teeple, John N., (AV) .... '25 '51 C&L.608 B.S., J.D. [Geiger,T.S.&H.]
Whitaker, Mark A. .... '54 '79 C.528 B.A. L.851 J.D. 2031 Ridgewood
Witte, Wylan W., (BV) .... '43 '73 C.162 B.A. L.607 J.D. 950 S. Sawburg Ave.
Zumbar, Andrew L., (BV) .... '67 '92 C.528 B.A. L.930 J.D. [Lundgren,G.&Z.] ⊙

AMANDA, 729, *Fairfield Co.*

Lunn, John P. .... '42 '78 C.424 B.S. L.117 J.D. 8498 Bowers Rd., S.W.

AMELIA, 2,752, *Clermont Co.*

Bevington, Maria D. .... '73 '98 C.973 B.S. L.150 J.D. Corp. Coun., Midland Co., The
Blomer, Philip J., (BV) .... '48 '77 C.973 B.A. L.1340 J.D. 1166 W. Ohio Pike
Brizzolara, Paul T. '57 '82 C.973 B.S.B.A. L.150 J.D.
Exec. V.P. & Chf. Legal Offr., Midland Co., The
Dinnen, Jeffrey A. .... '56 '98 C.607 B.A. L.150 J.D. Corp. Coun., The Midland Co.
Flowers, Michael L. '52 '78 C&L.383 B.S.B.E., J.D.
(adm. in KY; not adm. in OH) V.P., Asst. Secy. & Chf. Coun., The Midland Co. (⊙Cincinnati)
Gill, Nancy J., (AV) .... '51 '79 C.473 B.A. L.150 J.D. Corp. Coun., The Midland Co.
Griffith, Charles S., III '65 '97 C.150 B.B.A. L.1161 J.D.
Corp. Coun., The Midland Co.

Hennekes, Jason
(See Cincinnati)

Kiessling, Kurt M. .... '67 '92 C.952 B.A. L.1340 J.D. 7000 Midland Boulevard
Rapp, William Joseph, (BV) .... '61 '87 C&L.150 B.A., J.D. 1 E. Main Street
Reed, Kate .... '73 '99 C.610 B.A. L.150 J.D. Corp. Coun., The Midland Co.
Waldner, Linda D. .... '47 '82 C&L.150 B.B.A., J.D. 2030 Laurel Oak Drive
Whittle, James T., Jr. '57 '80 C.383 B.A. L.1340 J.D.
Legal Specialist, Midland Co., The
Wilson, T. Patrick .... '61 '88 C.973 B.S.B.A. L.150 J.D. The Midland Co.
Zugelter, Carl W., Law Office of, (AV) '49 '75
C.473 B.A. L.1340 J.D. 1285 W. Ohio Pike
Zuk, W. Kenneth, (BV) .... '47 '72 C.973 B.S. L.1340 J.D. [W.K.Zuk]
Zuk, W. Kenneth, Co., LPA, (BV) .... 325 W. Ohio Pike, Suite 102

AMHERST, 11,797, *Lorain Co.*

Anderson, Alan W., (BV) .... '46 '72 C.607 A.B. L.851 J.D. 238 Church St.
Bradley, Sam R., (BV) .... '62 '87 C.608 B.A. L.251 J.D. [S.R.Bradley]
Bradley, Sam R., Co., LPA, (BV) .... 1958 Kresge Dr.
Brosky, Robert E. '43 '69 C.473 B.S. L.607 J.D.
Pres., First Federal Sav. & Loan Assoc.
Chadwick, Geneva C., (CV) .... '45 '83 C.475 B.A. L.1003 J.D. 199 N. Leavitt Rd.
Conry, Martin J., (BV) .... '49 '74 C.608 B.S. L.851 J.D. 141 Park Ave.
Dworkin, Jonathan S., (BV) .... '36 '62 C&L.930 A.B., LL.B. 101 Park Ave.
Goldthorpe, David R. .... '15 '43 C.251 L.161 J.D. 659 Autumn Dr.‡
Gray, Russell W. .... '61 '87 C.319 B.A. L.930 J.D. 209 South Main Street
Janik, Frank J., (CV) .... '26 '54 C.608 B.S. L.161 J.D. 248 Park Ave.
Keressi, John S., Jr., (BV) .... '53 '79 C.381 B.A. L.7 J.D. 49561 Rt. 113
Nicol, Wayne Robert .... '79 '04 C.363 B.S.B.A. L.989 J.D. 1958 Kresge Dr.

Ramsey, Richard S. '77 '03 C.117 B.A. L.1003 J.D.
238 Church Street, 44001
Telephone: 440-988-3300 Fax: 440-988-9521
Email: RichardSRamsey@hotmail.com URL: http://www.ramseylawfirm.net
Domestic Relations, Family Law, Divorce, Child Custody, Criminal Law, Business Law, Landlord and Tenant Law, Civil Litigation.
See Professional Biographies, AMHERST, OHIO

Sheerer, Benjamin B., (BV) .... '34 '65 C.299 B.A. L.608 LL.B. 133 N. Leavitt Road
Torma, Mary D. .... '56 '92 C.741 B.A. L.1003 J.D. 6464 Balsam Dr.

ANDOVER, 1,216, *Ashtabula Co.*

Kotila, Richard B., (BV) .... '55 '80 C.210 B.A. L.1003 J.D. [McCombs&K.]
McCombs, David L., (BV) .... '48 '74 C&L.607 B.A., J.D. [McCombs&K.]
McCombs & Kotila, (BV) .... 100 Public Sq.
West, Joseph A. .... '17 '52 C&L.37 LL.B. 145 S. Main St.‡

ANTWERP, 1,677, *Paulding Co.*

Clemens, Tim A. .... '54 '79 C&L.607 B.S., J.D. P.O. Box 391‡

ARCANUM, 2,076, *Darke Co.*

Blinn, Caroline Rochelle .... '76 '01 C.608 B.A. L.117 J.D. P.O. Box 100
Cox, Robt. J. .... '23 '51 C&L.607 A.B., LL.B. 8903 State Rte. 571‡
Dynes, Craig A. .... '53 '79 C.608 B.A. L.851 J.D. [C.A.Dynes]
Dynes, Craig A., LLC .... P.O. Box 100
Garbig, Phillip R., (BV) .... '52 '85 C.608 B.S.B.A. L.117 J.D. 2840 Alt St Rt 49

ARCHBOLD, 4,290, *Fulton Co.*

Hagans, Mark D., (BV) .... '66 '94 C.611 B.A. L.851 J.D. [Plassman,R.S.&H.]
McQuade, Daniel P., (AV) .... '42 '67 C.424 B.S. L.608 J.D. [McQuades] ⊙
McQuades Co., The, L.P.A., (AV) .... 200 N. Defiance St. (⊙Swanton, Whitehouse)
Plassman, Harold H., (AV) .... '29 '57 C.117 A.B. L.477 J.D. [Plassman,R.S.&H.]

Plassman, Rupp, Short & Hagans, (AV)
302 North Defiance Street, P.O. Box 178, 43502-0178
Telephone: 419-445-8815 Fax: 419-445-1080
Email: attorneys@prshlaw.com
Members of Firm: Owen Rice (1900-1978); Harold H. Plassman; David P. Rupp, Jr.; Peter D. Short; Mark D. Hagans.
General Civil Practice in all Courts. Corporation, Probate and Estate Planning, Insurance Law, Personal Injury, Real Estate, Taxation, Municipal Law, Family/Domestic Relations and Trials.
Counsel for: The Farmers & Merchants State Bank; Sauder Woodworking Co.; Sauder Manufacturing Co.; Miller Bros. Const., Inc.; Lugbill Bros., Inc.; Archbold Medical Group, Inc.
Local Counsel for: Michigan Millers; United Ohio Insurance Co.; German Mutual Insurance Co.
See Professional Biographies, ARCHBOLD, OHIO

Rupp, David P., Jr., (AV) .... '41 '65 C&L.608 B.S.B.A., J.D. [Plassman,R.S.&H.]
Short, Peter D., (BV) .... '53 '78 C.607 B.S. L.150 J.D. [Plassman,R.S.&H.]
Winzeler, Brent L., (BV) .... '54 '79 C&L.117 B.A., J.D. 201 Vine St.

ASHLAND, * 21,249, *Ashland Co.*

Akers, Eric J., (CV) .... '47 '73 C&L.607 A.B., J.D. 46 W. Main St.
Anderson, C. Duane, (BV) .... '30 '59 C.49 L.607 J.D. [Wilson&A.]
Boyd, Bruce W. '57 '85 C.478 B.A. L.145 J.D.
(adm. in IL; not adm. in OH) V.P., Expert Corp.
Budd, Thomas J., II, (BV) .... '53 '78 C.62 B.A. L.8 J.D. 128 Church St.
Chorpening, Paul L. .... '20 '49 C.221 L.607 J.D. 246 E. Fourth St.‡

Critchfield, Critchfield & Johnston, Ltd.
(See Wooster)

DeSanto, Robert P., (BV) .... '46 '77 C.610 B.S.Ed. L.1003 J.D. Pros. Atty.
Dustin, David C. .... '63 '92 C.130 B.A. L.201 J.D. Off. of Pros. Atty.
Findley, Daniel G. .... '71 '97 C.49 B.S.B.A. L.7 J.D. 60 W. Second St.
Forsthoefel, Ronald P., Attorney at Law, (CV) '58 '83 C&L.607 B.A., J.D.
46 W. Main St.
Fridline, Jacob M. .... '38 '67 C.930 B.A. L.1003 J.D. Mun. J.
Galonski, John F. .... '67 '93 C&L.8 B.A., J.D. Dept. of Human Servs.
Ginty, J. Robert .... '24 '50 C.608 B.S. L.930 LL.B. [Halligan&G.]
Halligan, Brian J., (BV) .... '57 '83 C.473 B.A. L.851 J.D. [Halligan&G.]
Halligan & Ginty, (BV) .... 43 West Main Street

Harpster, Russell L., (BV) .... '34 '58 C.49 B.S. L.607 J.D. 60 W. Second St.
Henderson, Robert E. .... '27 '51 C.62 A.B. L.930 LL.B. Com. Pleas J.‡
Kearns, Joseph P., Jr. .... '67 '94 C.608 B.A. L.190 J.D. [Mason,M.&K.]

Keyser, George R.
(See Mansfield)

Lett, Robt. W. .... '15 '38 C.49 L.608 LL.B. 273 Sandusky St.
Lett, Sam J., (CV) .... '50 '77 C.385 B.A. L.851 J.D. P.O. Box 219
Locke, Gregory F., (BV) .... '48 '78 C.97 B.S. L.7 J.D. [Nordstrom&L.]
Locke, Nancy Nordstrom, (BV) .... '52 '77 C.945 B.A. L.150 J.D. [Nordstrom&L.]
Lutz and Oxley, (BV) .... 100 W. Main St.
Lytle, Diane S. '49 '92 C.610 B.S. L.117 J.D.
Human Resources Mgr., Allied Signal, Inc.
Mason, Josiah L., (BV) .... '35 '60 C.970 B.A. L.930 LL.B. [Mason,M.&K.]
Mason, Thomas L., (CV) .... '64 '89 C.970 B.S. L.608 J.D. [Mason,M.&K.]
Mason, Mason & Kearns, (BV) .... 153 W. Main St.
Murray, O. Joseph, (BV) .... '37 '62 C.385 B.A. L.477 LL.B. 10 E. Main St.
Nordstrom, Kenneth J., (AV) .... '16 '41 C&L.477 A.B., J.D. [Nordstrom&L.]
Nordstrom & Locke, (AV) .... 34 West Second Street
Oxley, Fred M., (BV) .... '48 '73 C.473 B.S. L.608 J.D. [Lutz&O.]
Oxley, William T., (BV) .... '25 '51 C.253 L.607 J.D. [Lutz&O.]
Potts, Timothy E. .... '71 '97 C.434 B.A. L.7 J.D. 60 W. Second St.

Richard Law Office, LLC
(See Wooster)

Rogers, Ramona Francesconi, (BV) '57 '82
C.363 B.A. L.8 J.D. Asst. Co. Pros., Ashland Pros. Off.
Runyan, Jeffrey L., (BV) .... '54 '79 C.97 B.S. L.608 J.D. 1494 State Rte 511
Samsel, David A., (CV) .... '45 '72 C&L.608 B.S., J.D. 107 E. Main St., Ste. 2
Shafer, Philip H., (BV) .... '36 '65 C.611 B.A. L.902 J.D. 10 E. Main St.
Sidwell, Robert C. .... '29 '56 C.475 B.A. L.477 J.D. 1646 Twp. Rd. 1323‡
Siverling, A. Ross .... '09 '33 C&L.607 J.D. 400 Orange St.
Sullivan, Michael, Attorney at Law, (CV) .... '56 '87 C.49 B.S. L.8 J.D. 10 E. Main St.
Troth, Hugh I., (AV) .... '23 '50 C.611 B.A. L.150 J.D. [Troth&V.]
Troth & Van Tilburg, (AV) .... 245 Sandusky Street
Tunnell, Christopher Rodney .... '73 '00 C.923 B.A. L.124 J.D. Asst. Pros. Atty.
Vanosdall, John A., (BV) .... '53 '78 C.49 B.S.B.A. L.607 J.D. 60 W. Second St.
Van Tilburg, William D., (AV) .... '37 '62 C.970 B.A. L.477 J.D. [Troth&V.]
Vercillo, Damian J., (AV) .... '49 '77 C&L.608 B.A., J.D. Juv. Ct. J.
Wilson, William Joseph .... '27 '53 C.8 A.B. L.930 J.D. [Wilson&A.] ‡
Wilson & Anderson, (BV) .... 46 W. Main St.

Wirth, David
(See Columbus)

Wolfe, Richard P., II, (CV) .... '47 '73 C.294 B.A. L.607 J.D. Dir. of Law
Woodward, Deborah Elizabeth .... '62 '89 Co. Juv. Ct. J.

ASHTABULA, 20,962, *Ashtabula Co.*

Altier, Christopher, (CV) .... '63 '89 C.970 B.A. L.8 J.D. [C.Altier]
Altier, Samuel L., (CV) .... '56 '82 C.608 B.S. L.7 J.D. [S.L.Altier]
Altier, Christopher, Co., L.P.A., (CV) .... 3503 Carpenter Road
Altier, Samuel L., Ltd., (CV) .... 1027 Lake Avenue
Andrews, Mark W., (BV) .... '50 '76 C.608 B.S. L.1003 J.D. [Andrews&P.]

Andrews & Pontius LLC, (BV)
4817 State Road Suite 100, P.O. Box 10, 44005-0010
Telephone: 440-998-6835 Fax: 440-992-6336
URL: http://www.andrewspontius.com
David E. Pontius; Mark W. Andrews; Jeffrey A. Ford; Pamela D. Houston;—Philip E. Cordova; Duane J. Dubsky.
General and Trial Practice. Civil Litigation, Corporation and Business Law, Personal Injury, Medical Malpractice, Complex Tort, Commercial Litigation, Municipal Law, Insurance Defense, Labor and Employment, School Law, Domestic Relations and Family Law, Real Estate Probate and Estate Planning.
Reference: Key Bank.
See Professional Biographies, ASHTABULA, OHIO

Bashein & Bashein Co., L.P.A.
(See Cleveland)

Bernardo, Katherine S. .... '74 '00 C.188 B.A. L.377 J.D. [Ⓐ Warren&Y.]
Camplese, Albert S. .... '58 '85 C.607 B.A. L.1003 J.D. Mun. J.
Cantagallo, Phillip J. .... '22 '52 C.930 B.B.A. L.608 J.D. 4029 Lake Ave.
Cardinal, John G. .... '18 '49 C.528 A.B. L.930 LL.B. Ret. Com. Pleas J.
Cimorell, Bret J., (BV) .... '59 '85 C.381 B.A. L.930 J.D. 4366 Main Street, Suite 102
Colin, John A., (AV) .... '14 '41 C.608 L.161 LL.B. 355 Prospect St.
Cordell, Stuart W., (AV) .... '56 '81 C.188 A.B. L.930 J.D. [Warren&Y.]
Cordova, Philip E. .... '67 '01 C.381 B.S. L.8 J.D. [Ⓐ Andrews&P.]
Coxon, Jeffrey L., (BV) .... '66 '92 C.473 B.S. L.608 J.D. [Warren&Y.]
Downey, L. E. .... '15 '46 C&L.980 J.D. 1411 Westminister‡
Downey, Pauline C. .... '21 '47 C.610 A.B. L.980 J.D. 1411 Westminster Dr.‡
Dubsky, Duane J., (AV) .... '47 '73 C.610 B.A. L.1003 J.D. [Ⓐ Andrews&P.]
Ellis, Ryan M. .... '79 '04 C.97 B.S. L.124 J.D. [Ⓐ Warren&Y.]
Field, Jon T., (BV) .... '48 '81 C.62 B.A. L.607 J.D. 4366 Main Ave.
Ford, Jeffrey A., (BV) .... '56 '82 C&L.608 B.S., J.D. [Andrews&P.]
Franklin, Michael, (BV) .... '57 '81 C&L.607 B.A., J.D. 2135 Walnut Blvd.
Hamilton, Terry Lee .... '48 '76 C.1365 B.A. L.904 J.D. Lighthouse Legal Ministries
Hawn-Jackson, Jane Ann .... '56 '83 C.883 B.A. L.607 J.D. [J.Hawn-Jackson]
Hawn-Jackson, Jane .... 4717 Park Ave.
Hough, Edith Marie .... '63 '91 C.599 B.A. L.7 J.D. Mag., Juv. Ct.
Houston, Pamela D. .... '70 '99 C.8 B.A. L.1003 J.D. [Andrews&P.]
Humphrey, Ralph L. '36 '74 C.401 B.S.M.E. L.276 J.D.
Owner, Humphrey Insurance Agency Inc. (Pat.)

Klein & Carney Co., L.P.A.
(See Cleveland)

Kobelak, William A., (BV) .... '47 '80 C.385 B.A. L.1003 J.D. 4366 Main Avenue
Larson, Bernadette T., (BV) .... '49 '77 C.161 B.A. L.1003 J.D. 4717 Park Ave.
Lesko, Jane L., (CV) .... '69 '96 C.851 B.S. L.117 J.D. 4717 Park Ave.
Liviola, George, Jr. .... '33 '64 C.381 B.S. L.1003 J.D. 6604 Hiram Ave.
Mahoney, John P., (AV) .... '16 '48 C.602 A.B. L.930 LL.B. P.O. Box 460
Meaney, Michael Patrick .... '62 '87 C.381 B.S. L.608 J.D. 2nd National Bk.
Muller, Carl F., (AV) .... '47 '72 C.293 B.A. L.188 J.D. [Warren&Y.]
O'Day, Tracey Kyle .... '60 '88 C.611 B.A. L.124 J.D. Case Law Editor, Lexis Nexis
Olsen, John E. .... '22 '48 C&L.930 A.B., J.D. Ret. Mun. J.
Pertz, Julianne Pistone, (AV) .... '56 '84 C.385 B.A. L.978 J.D. 4951 Rockwell Road
Pontius, David E., (BV) .... '52 '79 C.608 B.A. L.851 J.D. [Andrews&P.]
Reid, Dennis Michael .... '35 '73 C.608 B.S. in B.A. L.1003 J.D. Co. Pub. Def.
Riedel, William E., (AV) .... '42 '69 C&L.930 B.B.A., J.D. [Warren&Y.]

Sartini, James J. .... '65 '91 C.1062 B.S. L.117 J.D. [Sartini]
Sartini Law Firm .... 4717 Park Avenue
Sernik, Craig F. .... '71 '97 C.25 B.A. L.930 J.D. [Ⓐ Warren&Y.]

Sheldon, David C., (CV) '45 '73 C.473 B.A. L.893 J.D.
4109 Lake Avenue, P.O. Box 1152, 44005-1152
Telephone: 440-998-6923 Fax: 440-998-3442
Email: dcshel@alltel.net URL: http://www.lawyers.com/davidcsheldon
Personal Injury, Automobile Accidents and Injuries, Wills, Estates, Probate, Criminal, Family Law, Divorce, Domestic Relations, Commercial Transactions.
See Professional Biographies, ASHTABULA, OHIO

Shiflet, Hobart, (CV) .... '53 '82 C.913 B.A. L.1003 J.D. 217 Park Plaza
Simon, Thomas J. .... '50 '81 C.381 L.1003 J.D. 1105 Bridge Street

Spotts, David M., (AV) '49 '75 C.1027 B.S. L.1003 J.D.
6847 Lake Road West, P.O. Box 3046, 44005-3046
Telephone: 440-964-6466 Fax: 440-964-6502
Email: admiral@maritimelaw.com URL: http://www.maritimelaw.com
Admiralty, General Civil Practice in all State and Federal Courts, Personal Injury, Insurance, Products, Environmental, Liability Law, Trials/and Appeals.
See Professional Biographies, ASHTABULA, OHIO

Topalof, Dean F. .... '70 '96 C.473 B.A. L.8 J.D. 4920 State Road
Varckette, Francis A., (BV) .... '27 '53 C&L.608 B.Sc., LL.B. 4366 Main Avenue
Varckette, Ronald G. .... '29 '52 C&L.608 LL.B. Ret. Prob. & Juv. Ct. J.
Vermilya, Randy A. .... '58 '99 C.377 B.S. L.124 J.D. [Ⓐ Warren&Y.]
Warren, E. Terry, (AV) .... '30 '56 C&L.188 A.B., LL.B. 355 West Prospect Road

Warren and Young PLL, (AV)
134 West 46th Street, P.O. Box 2300, 44005-2300
Telephone: 440-997-6175 Facsimile: 440-992-9114
URL: http://www.warrenyoung.com
Theodore E. Warren (1897-1969); Myron H. Young (1910-1971); William E. Riedel; Carl F. Muller; Stuart W. Cordell; Jeffrey L. Coxon;—Craig F. Sernik; Randy A. Vermilya; Katherine S. Bernardo; Ryan M. Ellis.
General and Trial Practice. Corporation and Business Law, Labor and Employment Law, Insurance Defense, Civil Litigation, Real Estate, Probate and Estate Planning Law.
See Professional Biographies, ASHTABULA, OHIO

ASHVILLE, 3,174, *Pickaway Co.*

Gussler, Stephen S., (BV) .... '40 '66 C&L.608 B.A., J.D. 50 Bortz St.
Hall, Leo, (BV) .... '41 '65 C&L.608 B.A., J.D. 50 Bortz St.
Hosterman, John W., (BV) .... '49 '74 C.197 A.B. L.608 J.D. 50 Bortz St.
Sedlak, Alan F., (BV) .... '49 '75 C.597 B.A. L.608 J.D. Asst. Pros.

ATHENS, * 21,265, *Athens Co.*

Allshouse, Beth A., (CV) .... '66 '91 C.970 B.A. L.150 J.D. Dept. of Human Servs.
Annarino, Louise .... '49 '78 C.608 B.S. L.150 J.D. Asst. Dir., Legal Affs., Ohio Univ.
Baer, David G., (CV) .... '55 '80 C.967 B.A. L.117 J.D. 8 North Court
Beck, Amanda Marie .... '75 '00 C.999 L.150 J.D. Southeastern Ohio Legal Services
Bell, Kelli Lavonne .... '66 '99 C.610 B.B.A. L.150 J.D. Ohio University
Bennett, Douglas J. .... '49 '75 C.610 B.A. L.607 J.D. Mun. J.
Berry, Clair E. .... '25 '52 C.610 B.S.C. L.150 LL.B. 38 Graham Dr.‡
Biddlestone, William R., Jr., (CV) ...... '51 '84 C.610 B.A. L.1003 J.D. [Biddlestone&W.]
Biddlestone & Winkelmann Co., LPA, Attorneys & Counselors at Law, (CV)
8 N. Court St., Ste. 308
Bradford, Melinda K., (BV) .... '67 '97 C.608 B.S.N. L.179 J.D. 18 West State Street
Bridgewater, Erle, (AV) .... '19 '46 C.610 B.S. L.608 J.D. 14 W. Washington St.‡
Burns, John F. .... '44 '69 C.473 B.S. L.477 J.D. Dir., Legal Affs., Ohio Univ.
Carson, Herman A., (BV) .... '55 '80 C.607 B.A. L.608 J.D. [Sowash,C.&F.]

Colley Shroyer & Abraham Co., L.P.A.
(See Columbus)

Cornn, Thomas L., (BV) .... '47 '73 C.610 B.B.A. L.607 J.D. 8 N. Court St.
Cornwell, Foster B., (AV) .... '10 '35 C.610 A.B. L.608 J.D. 14 W. Washington St.‡
Driscoll, Robert Patrick .... '61 '93 C.608 B.S. L.117 J.D. Asst. Pros
Eliason, Lisa Ann, (BV) .... '54 '87 C.610 B.S.Ed. L.201 J.D. City Prosecutors Office
Eslocker, Thomas E., (BV) .... '51 '76 C.610 B.A. L.910 J.D. [Eslocker&O.]
Eslocker & Oremus, Co., L.P.A., (BV) .... 16 W. State St.
Ferrier, Beth B., (CV) .... '58 '85 C.472 A.B. L.930 J.D. [Sowash,C.&F.]
Foran, Timothy J. .... '51 '76 C.608 B.A. L.117 J.D. S.E. OH Legal Servs.
Gall, Cherie Hill, (BV) .... '55 '81 C.893 B.A. L.945 J.D. [Mollica,G.S.&S.]
Goldsberry, L. Alan .... '44 '69 C.610 B.A. L.228 J.D. Com. Pleas J.
Grim, William A., (BV) .... '47 '74 C&L.608 B.A., J.D. Mun. Ct. J.
Harvey, Karen M. .... '38 '89 C.791 B.A. L.117 J.D. Dom. Rel. Ref.
Hedges, Richard Houston, Law Office of ..... '52 '95 C.383 B.A. L.117 J.D. [R.H.Hedges]
Hedges, Richard H., Law Office of .... 8 North Court St., Suite 507
Huff, Debra K. .... '55 '83 C.381 B.S. L.7 J.D. 5131 Wooten Rd.‡
Huff, Michael Ray, (BV) .... '55 '83 C.63 B.S. L.7 J.D. Pros. Atty. Off.
Hunter, Garry E., (BV) .... '49 '74 C.610 B.B.A. L.851 J.D. [G.E.Hunter]
Hunter, Garry E., Law Offices, Inc, L.P.A., (BV) .... 26S. Congress St.
Kaufman, Beth F. .... '58 '99 C.610 B.A. L.608 J.D. Ohio Public Defender Commission
Lavelle, Francis (Frank) A., (BV) .... '55 '82 C.610 B.A. L.179 J.D. [Lavelle] ⊙
Lavelle, John P., (BV) .... '56 '82 C.837 B.B.A. L.192 J.D. [Lavelle&Assoc.]
Lavelle, William A., (AV) .... '25 '52 C.610 B.S.C. L.608 J.D. 1149 East State St.
Lavelle and Associates, (BV) .... 207 Columbus Rd., Ste. B

Lavelle Law Offices, L.P.A., (BV)
8 North Court Street, 2nd Floor, P.O. Box 661, 45701-0661 ⊙
Telephone: 740-593-3347 Fax: 740-592-6656
Email: flavelle@eurekanet.com
Francis (Frank) A. Lavelle.
Personal Injury, Real Estate, Oil and Gas Law, Custody, Divorce, Domestic Relations, Probate, Estate Planning, Public Sector, Administrative Agencies, Juvenile Law, Criminal Defense, Insurance Defense.
Meigs County Office: 66717 State Route 124, Reedsville, 45772. Telephone: 740-378-6456. Fax: 740-592-6656.
See Professional Biographies, ATHENS, OHIO

Malloy, Susan Elizabeth '71 '97 C.608 B.A. L.117 J.D.
Law Clk., Fourth Dist. Ct. of App.
Marinelli, Arthur J., Jr. ...... '42 '67 C.610 B.A. L.608 J.D. Prof. of Bus. Law, Ohio Univ.
McCarthy, George P., (BV) .... '65 '90 C.550 B.A. L.607 J.D. City Pros. Atty.
McGuire, Thomas R. ..... '47 '75 C.150 B.Ch.E. L.608 J.D. Southeastern Ohio Legal Servs.
Miller, Robert A. .... '64 '89 C.999 B.S. L.117 J.D. [Sowash,C.&F.]
Mollica, Andrew J., (BV) .... '63 '89 C&L.608 B.A., J.D. [Mollica,G.S.&S.]
Mollica, Anthony C. .... '58 '83 C.610 B.S.Ed. L.608 J.D. 10695 Rosewood Ln.‡
Mollica, Gerald A., (AV) .... '38 '63 C&L.608 B.A., J.D. [Mollica,G.S.&S.]
Mollica, Gall, Sloan & Sillery Co., L.P.A., (AV) .... 35 North College Street
Noftz, Brenda A. '56 '82 C.610 B.S.Ed. L.608 J.D.
Assoc. Dir., Ohio Univ. Police Dept.

Oliver Law Office
(See Columbus)

Oremus, Frederick L., (BV) .... '48 '73 C.967 B.A. L.117 J.D. [Eslocker&O.]
Pettey, Sky .... '72 '00 C.604 B.A. L.608 J.D. [Ⓐ Lavelle&Assoc.]

Plymale Partnership LLP, The
(See Columbus)

Rambo, Madeline, (BV) .... '54 '91 C.610 B.S. L.608 J.D. [Sowash,C.&F.]
Robe, Edward S. .... '36 '63 C.610 A.B. L.228 LL.B. Com. Pleas J., Prob. & Juv. Divs.
Robe, Scott M., (BV) .... '62 '89 C&L.999 A.B., J.D. [Robe]
Robe Law Offices, (BV) .... 14 W Washington St.
Roberson, Jessie C. .... '53 '80 C.674 A.B. L.477 J.D. Assoc. Prof., OH Univ.

Rourke & Blumenthal, LLP
(See Columbus)

Rubin, Anne Sessums .... '52 '81 1005 E. State Street, Suite 10
Schaffer, Jennifer D. .... '68 '96 C.025 B.A. L.117 J.D. Asst. Pub. Def.
Shostak, Robert J., (BV) .... '46 '71 C.97 B.A. L.665 J.D. [Shostak]
Shostak Law Office, (BV) .... 18 West State Street, Suite 101
Shumaker, James F., (BV) .... '19 '48 C.631 L.608 LL.B. P.O. Box 2470
Sillery, James D., (AV) .... '48 '73 C.1208 B.A. L.608 J.D. [Mollica,G.S.&S.]
Sloan, Steven T., (AV) .... '48 '73 C.20 B.A. L.930 J.D. [Mollica,G.S.&S.]

Slowik & Robinson, LLC
(See Columbus)

Sowash, Jonathan, (BV) .... '54 '80 C.97 B.A. L.608 J.D. [Sowash,C.&F.]

Sowash, Carson & Ferrier, (BV)
39 North College Street, P.O. Box 2629, 45701
Telephone: 740-594-8388 Fax: 740-593-6490
Email: scf@eurekanet.com
Members of Firm: Jonathan Sowash; Herman A. Carson; Beth B. Ferrier; Madeline Rambo; Robert A. Miller.
Criminal and Traffic Practice. Domestic Relations and Family Law, Labor and Employment Law, General Civil Trial and Appellate Practice, Nonprofit and Charitable Organizations, Business Law, Personal Injury, Wrongful Death, Historic Preservation Law, Employee Benefits, Agricultural Law, Zoning, Probate, Estate Planning, Intellectual Property Licensing, Technology Transfer.
See Professional Biographies, ATHENS, OHIO

Stewart, Robert W., (BV) ...... '49 '74 C.610 B.B.A. L.851 J.D. Athens Co. Prob. Juv. Ct.
Walker, Brian R., (BV) .... '56 '85 C.610 B.F.A. L.851 J.D. [Ⓐ Walker&W.]
Walker, William R., (BV) .... '50 '78 C.610 A.B. L.851 J.D. [Walker&W.]

Walker & Walker Co., L.P.A., (BV)
211 Columbus Road, P.O. Box 2470, 45701
Telephone: 740-594-8228 Fax: 740-593-5456
Email: walker@walkerlawlpa.com URL: http://www.walkerlawlpa.com
Wm. Parker Walker (1917-1985); William R. Walker;—Brian R. Walker.
General Civil and Criminal Practice. Probate and Real Estate Law. School Law, Elder Law. Insurance Defense. Personal Injury. Family and Domestic Law. Corporate and Business Law. Oil and Gas, Coal and Mineral Law.
References: Mutual Federal Savings & Loan; Bank One of Athens, N.A.
See Professional Biographies, ATHENS, OHIO

Wallace, James A. .... '52 '81 C.610 B.G.S. L.608 J.D. 11 E. Washington Street
Ward, Michael W. .... '46 '71 C.473 B.A. L.608 J.D. Com. Pleas J.
Westfall, James M., (BV) .... '54 '79 C.610 B.G.S. L.861 J.D. Pub. Def.
Wiens, Keith M., (CV) .... '55 '98 C.83 B.S. L.117 J.D. P.O. Box 2628
Wines, Larry D., (BV) .... '64 '97 C.112 B.A. L.117 J.D. [Ⓐ Mollica,G.S.&S.]
Winkelmann, David J. .... '55 '89 C.218 B.A. L.352 J.D. [Biddlestone&W.]
Yanity, Joseph Blair, (AV) .... '25 '53 C.235 B.A. L.902 J.D. P.O. Box 748

AURORA, 13,556, *Portage Co.*

Benjamin, David M., (BV) .... '52 '77 C.94 A.B. L.930 J.D. 199 South Chillicote Road
Christley, Norman L., (BV) .... '42 '68 C.62 B.S. L.1003 J.D. [Christley,H.&P.]
Christley, Herington & Pierce, (BV) .... 215 W. Garfield Rd., Ste. 230
Disantis, John P. .... '39 '75 C.381 B.A. L.1003 J.D. 105 Chesterton Lane
Friedman, Donald .... '26 '54 C.608 B.C.E. L.1003 J.D. 500-3 Pond Run
Gleisser, Marcus D. .... '23 '58 C.930 B.A. L.1003 LL.B. 647 Grand View Lane‡
Habowski, Ronald J., (BV) .... '48 '85 C.381 B.A. L.8 J.D. [Christley,H.&P.]
Hawke, Constance S., (AV) .... '52 '78 C.97 B.A. L.1003 J.D. 565 Club Dr.
Herington, Leigh E., (BV) .... '45 '76 C.381 B.B.A. L.7 J.D. [Christley,H.&P.]
Hermann, Philip J. .... '16 '42 C.608 B.A. L.930 LL.B. 615 Acadia Point‡
Huston, Robert K. .... '16 '46 C&L.16 B.S., LL.B. 26376 John Rd.‡
Kaiser, George B. .... '21 '52 C.645 B.S. L.659 LL.B. 229 Fox Run Trail (Pat.)‡
Kimmel, Roger A., Jr., (BV) .... '43 '72 C.610 B.S. L.1003 J.D. 443-21 Doe Trail
Kobyljanec, William .... '54 '81 C.930 B.S. L.1003 J.D. 1150 Crackle Rd.
Mayer, Charles H. F. .... '60 '90 C&L.665 B.A., J.D. 691 Deepwoods Dr.
Miller, Richard A. .... '27 '54 C.930 B.B.A. L.309 LL.B. 464-9 Deer Path
Mitchell, Robert J. .... '30 '60 C.608 B.S. L.1003 LL.B. 305 Chelmsford Dr.
Moroney, Carole Jo Hanzes .... '37 '64 C.436 B.S. L.1003 J.D. 629 W. Acadia Pt.
O'Connell-Burton, Kathleen, Law Firm of '43 '80 C.599 B.S. L.1003 J.D.
7781 Lori Ln.
Paul, Douglas K., (CV) .... '68 '95 C.62 B.A. L.607 J.D. [Ⓐ Christley,H.&P.]
Reitz, Thomas L. .... '69 '97 C.97 B.A. L.117 J.D. [Christley,H.&P.]
Reitz, Thomas Richard, (CV) .... '57 '88 C.274 B.A. L.879 J.D. 215 W. Garfield Rd.
Romans, C. Scott .... '47 '85 C.381 B.S. L.8 J.D. [Christley,H.&P.]
Seals, Thomas C. .... '40 '89 C.1042 B.S. L.930 J.D. P.O. Box 277
Shorr, Alan I., (BV) .... '44 '70 C.610 B.B.A. L.1003 J.D. [Ⓐ Christley,H.&P.]
Silver, James R., (BV) .... '54 '80 C.381 B.A. L.7 J.D. [Christley,H.&P.]
Thal, Michael L., (BV) .... '38 '65 C.930 B.B.A. L.1003 J.D. 10607 Crossings Drive
Tomasko, Elizabeth Straw .... '51 '91 C.473 B.S. L.989 J.D. [E.S.Tomasko]
Tomasko, Elizabeth S., Attorney at Law .... 240 Harmon Road
Tressler, Karen L. .... '66 '96 C.930 B.S.Ch.E L.8 J.D. 215 Chatham Dr.
Turell, Russell B., (AV) .... '44 '70 C.645 B.S. L.1003 J.D. 529 Treetop Court
Weber, Edward P., III .... '67 '96 C.97 B.A. L.1340 J.D. 204 N. Park Drive
Williams, Robert T. .... '27 '54 C&L.980 J.D. 181 Ben Shaw Rd.
Wolfson, Donald .... '26 '53 C.999 B.B.A. L.930 LL.B. 466/10 Deer Path‡
Wolkov, Leonard A., (BV) .... '43 '67 C.665 B.A. L.930 J.D. 237 Chelsea Ct.

AUSTINBURG, 600, *Ashtabula Co.*

Cooper, Hal D., (AV) .... '34 '63 C.350 B.S.M.E. L.273 J.D. 3561 Clay Street (Pat.)
McKay, Ellis H., (AV) .... '23 '55 C.25 A.B. L.659 LL.B. 930 Tote Rd.‡

AUSTINTOWN, 31,627, *Mahoning Co.*

Hepfner, Donald C., (BV) .... '61 '89 C.980 B.A. L.8 J.D. 21 N. Wickliffe Circle
Lefoer, Dominic S., (CV) .... '36 '65 C.381 B.S. L.607 J.D. 4374 Mahoning Ave.
Lilly, Jeffrey Alan .... '72 '99 C.381 B.A. L.8 J.D. UAW-GM Legal Serv. Plan
Paczelt, Anna Elizabeth '48 '86
C.608 B.A. L.7 J.D. Staff Atty., UAW-GM Legal Servs. Plan

Pritchard, Warren Godfrey .... '56 '82 C.313 B.A. L.7 J.D. 296 North Niles-Canfield Road
Regginello, John A. .... '54 '99 C.980 B.A. L.1003 J.D. 120 Westchester Dr., Ste. A
Sheftel, Lynn A., Mr., (CV) ... '41 '66 C&L.851 B.B.A., J.D. 1570 S. Canfield-Niles Road

AVON, 11,446, *Lorain Co.*

Altieri, Mark P., (BV) .... '52 '80 C.610 B.S. L.989 J.D. [Wickens,H.P.C.&B.]
Amendola, Mark A. .... '64 '89 C.363 B.S.B.A. L.1003 J.D. 33478 Vineyard Park
Ashar, Linda C., (BV) .... '— '85 C.532 B.A. L.7 J.D. [Wickens,H.P.C.&B.]
Barker, James E. .... '60 '85 C.851 B.A. L.1003 J.D. 33278 Mills Road
Batista, Daniel P., (AV) .... '34 '59 C.473 B.A. L.930 LL.B. [Wickens,H.P.C.&B.]
Belardo, Lee E. .... '67 '95 C.980 B.S. L.989 J.D. [L.E.Belardo]

Belardo, L.E., LLC
36368 Detroit Road, Suite A, P.O. Box 419, 44011-0419
Telephone: 440-934-2199 Fax: 440-934-2289
Email: belardo@centurytel.net URL: http://www.belardolaw.com
Member of Firm: Lee E. Belardo.
Family Law, Divorce, Child Custody, Child Support, Visitation Rights, Wills and Probate, Criminal Law, Drug Crimes, DUI/DWI, Juvenile Crimes, Parole and Probation, Traffic Violations, Real Estate, General Practice.
See Professional Biographies, AVON, OHIO

Brown, Deborah Janco, (BV) .... '55 '83 C&L.930 B.A., J.D. 3918 Jaycox Rd.
Collett, Marsha L., (BV) .... '50 '80 C.608 B.A. L.930 J.D. [Wickens,H.P.C.&B.]
Cook, Daniel A., (AV) .... '43 '68 C.105 B.S.B.A. L.477 J.D. [Wickens,H.P.C.&B.]
Ellis, Robert P., Jr., (AV) .... '49 '75 C.453 B.S. L.608 J.D. [Wickens,H.P.C.&B.]
Eversman, Erica L. .... '64 '93 C.915 B.A. L.1003 J.D. 32304 Stoney Brook Drive
Gasior, John A. .... '54 '84 C.930 L.1003 J.D. [Stringer,S.&G.]
Gemelas, James S. .... '69 '97 C.608 B.A. L.989 J.D. 3920 Case Road
Herzer, David L., (AV) .... '45 '70 C.976 B.A. L.309 J.D. [Wickens,H.P.C.&B.]
Kolis, William F., Jr., (BV) .... '55 '80 C&L.930 B.A., J.D. [Wickens,H.P.C.&B.]
Lefelar, Donald E. .... '42 '74 C.945 B.A. L.1003 J.D. 2018 Nottingham Pkwy
Leroux, Clayton G., Jr. .... '45 '71 C.602 B.S. L.1003 J.D. 4224 Lake Harbour Way
Marta, Wayne P., (BV) .... '52 '77 C.62 B.A. L.930 J.D. [W.P.Marta]
Marta, Wayne P., Co., L.P.A., (BV) .... 37106 Hunters Trl.
McBride, Dennis M. .... '— '89 C.161 B.A. L.1003 J.D. 2161 Lake Pointe Dr.
Moennich, James W., (BV) .... '51 '77 C.608 B.S. L.930 J.D. [Wickens,H.P.C.&B.]
Naegele, Richard A., (AV) .... '51 '79 C.610 B.A. L.930 J.D. [Wickens,H.P.C.&B.]
Nakon, Matthew W., (BV) .... '63 '88 C.62 B.A. L.1003 J.D. [Wickens,H.P.C.&B.]
Niederbaumer, Michael R. .... '70 '00 C.473 B.S. L.124 J.D. [Ⓐ Wickens,H.P.C.&B.]
Panza, Richard D., (AV) .... '47 '73 C.1044 B.A. L.1003 J.D. [Wickens,H.P.C.&B.]
Pawlukiewicz, Charles J., (AV) .... '46 '83 C.531 B.S. L.1003 J.D. [Wickens,H.P.C.&B.]
Peters, James Edward .... '71 '97 C.610 B.B.A. L.8 J.D. [Wickens,H.P.C.&B.]
Phillips, Gerald Wayne .... '50 '77 C.161 B.B.A. L.989 J.D. 35955 Detroit Road
Pillari, Thomas, (AV) .... '47 '73 C.1070 B.S. L.145 J.D. [Wickens,H.P.C.&B.]
Prescott, William P. .... '— '89 C.161 B.B.A. L.1003 J.D. [Wickens,H.P.C.&B.]
Rothman, Jason .... '77 '03 C.608 B.S.B.A. L.989 J.D. [Ⓐ Wickens,H.P.C.&B.]
Rutman, Rennie Caryn .... '72 '01 C.363 B.A. L.930 J.D. [Wickens,H.P.C.&B.]
Ryan, Spencer A. .... '76 '01 C.646 B.A. L.607 J.D. [Wickens,H.P.C.&B.]
Rybarczyk, John D., (BV) .... '62 '87 C.363 B.S. L.1003 J.D. [Wickens,H.P.C.&B.]
Schrader, Todd A. .... '65 '96 C.124 B.A. L.1003 J.D. [Wickens,H.P.C.&B.]

Spike & Meckler Law Firm, The, LLP
(See Elyria)

Stefanik, Thomas J., Jr. .... '69 '96 C.970 B.A. L.1003 J.D. [Ⓐ Wickens,H.P.C.&B.]
Stringer, Anthony R., (BV) .... '35 '67 C.321 A.B. L.1003 J.D. [Stringer,S.&G.]
Stringer, Daniel P., (BV) .... '36 '63 C.363 A.B. L.1003 J.D. [Stringer,S.&G.]
Stringer, Stringer & Gasior, (BV) .... 36815 Detroit Rd.
Timm, Richard M., Jr. .... '66 '95 C.473 B.A. L.989 J.D. Gen. Coun., Chemtron Corp.
Urban, Daniel C. .... '70 '96 C.976 B.A. L.1003 J.D. [Ⓐ Wickens,H.P.C.&B.]
Violand, James P. .... '52 '79 C.97 B.A. L.1003 J.D. 39004 Stallion Ct.

Wickens, Herzer, Panza, Cook & Batista, A Legal Professional Association, (AV) BR
35765 Chester Road, 44011-1262
Telephone: 440-930-8000 Facsimile: 440-937-4466 Cleveland Direct Line: 216-447-4418 Cleveland Facsimile: 216-447-0998
Email: pdahm@wickenslaw.com URL: http://www.wickenslaw.com
D. A. Cook (1883-1968); Dan K. Cook (1915-1976); William G. Wickens (1905-2002); Daniel P. Batista; Daniel A. Cook; David L. Herzer; Richard D. Panza; Robert P. Ellis, Jr.; David C. Wiersma (Certified Specialist in Estate Planning, Trust and Probate Law, Ohio State Bar Association); James W. Moennich; Thomas Pillari (Certified Specialist in Estate Planning, Trust and Probate Law, Ohio State Bar Association); Richard A. Naegele; Marsha L. Collett; William F. Kolis, Jr.; Charles J. Pawlukiewicz; Mark P. Altieri; Linda C. Ashar; John D. Rybarczyk; Matthew W. Nakon; William P. Prescott; Rachelle Kuznicki Zidar; Michael R. Niederbaumer; Rennie Caryn Rutman; Spencer A. Ryan; James Edward Peters; Todd A. Schrader; Daniel C. Urban; Thomas J. Stefanik, Jr.; Jason Rothman.
General Civil Practice. Corporate, Taxation, Professional Corporations, Pension, Profit Sharing, Employee Benefits, ERISA, Partnership, Real Estate, Environmental, Labor and Employment Relations; Health Care and Hospital, Public Law, Municipal Bonds, Libel and Media Law, Probate and Estate Planning Law, Insurance Defense, Trials and Appeals, Banking, Bankruptcy.
Representative Clients: Ross Environmental Services, Inc. (hazardous waste treatment facility); North Ohio Heart Center, Inc.; Community Health Partners of Ohio; Stow Dental Group; The Lorain National Bank; Ohio Edison Co.; Drs. Russell, Berkebile and Associates, Radiologists; South Shore Transportation Co.; Industrial Nut Corp; Liberty Ford Lincoln-Mercury, Inc.
See Professional Biographies, AVON, OHIO

Wiersma, David C., (BV) .... '47 '76 C.665 B.A. L.1003 J.D. [Wickens,H.P.C.&B.]
Zidar, Rachelle Kuznicki, (CV) '71 '96 C.97 B.A. L.1003 J.D.
[Ⓐ Wickens,H.P.C.&B.]

AVON LAKE, 18,145, *Lorain Co.*

Ban, Woodrow W. '47 '81 C.124 B.S.Ch.E. L.1003 J.D.
Sr. Coun. & Asst. Secy., PolyOne Corp. (Pat.)
Barnard, Dale E. .... '24 '57 C.313 B.A. L.1003 J.D. 525 Avon Belden Rd.‡
Bonds, William T. '38 '64
C.610 B.S.C. L.575 LL.B. Secy. & Treas., Helical Line Products Co.
Brusnahan, Kreig J., (BV) .... '55 '81 C.1356 B.S. L.1003 J.D. 158-A Lear Road
DeGeeter, Pamela A. .... '71 '97 C.473 B.A. L.989 J.D. [Ⓐ Smith&S.]
Everson, John H. .... '58 '86 C.608 B.S. L.851 J.D. 31781 Leeward Court
Frankel, Kenneth P., (AV) .... '50 '75 C.659 B.S.B.A. L.273 J.D. [Ⓐ Smith&S.]
Gentile, Leslie A. .... '53 '96 C.62 B.M.E. L.7 J.D. [Ⓐ Smith&S.]
Gibbons, Timothy J. .... '60 '89 C.161 B.A. L.1003 J.D. [Ⓐ Smith&S.]
Givler, Michael Dean '51 '78 C.602 B.A. L.178 J.D.
(adm. in NY; not adm. in OH) [Givler,M.D.]
Givler, Michael D. .... 32602 Carriage Ln.
Hahn, Richard E., (AV) '45 '71
C.970 B.A. L.930 J.D. Sr. Coun. & Asst. Secy., PolyOne Corp.
Hallett, Matthew H. .... '72 '98 C.1208 B.A. L.1003 J.D. [Ⓐ Smith&S.]
Hampole, Gowri V. .... '54 '97 C.999 B.A. L.1003 J.D. 330 Cheyenne Falls
Hornickel, John H. '53 '78 C.198 B.S. L.896 J.D.
Sr. Intell. Prop. Coun. & Asst. Secy., PolyOne Corp. (Pat.)

Isbell, Robert H., (BVⓉ) '44 '78 C.184 B.A. L.161 J.D.
(adm. in PA; not adm. in OH) 444 Long Pointe Dr.
Kerner, James B. .... '66 '94 C.363 B.A. L.1003 J.D. [J.B.Kerner]
Kerner, William J., Sr. .... '43 '69 C.363 B.A. L.724 J.D. 525 Avon Belden Road
Kerner, James B., Co., L.P.A. .... 525 Avon Belden Road, Rear Suite
Kuebler, Christopher D. .... '55 '82 C.97 B.S. L.1003 J.D. 32565 Lake Rd.
Lang, William P., (BV) .... '53 '79 C.607 B.A. L.1003 J.D. 110 Moore Road
Lastovka, Terri A. .... '64 '96 C.381 B.A. L.1003 J.D. 251 Parsons Drive
Mackin, John F., (BV) .... '32 '61 C.363 B.S. L.1003 J.D. 33463 Lake Rd.
Mackin, Patrick C., (CV) .... '61 '87 C.381 B.B.A. L.602 J.D. 33463 Lake Rd.
McClure, Richard D., (BV) .... '47 '72 C.597 B.A. L.930 J.D. [Ⓐ Smith&S.]
O'Rear-Lassen, Lisa Ellen '59 '85 C.210 B.A. L.910 J.D.
Northeastern Prof. Family Serv.
Petto, Peter John, III ...... '52 '85 C.597 B.A. L.1003 J.D. Arrow Aluminum Castings Co.
Pincura, John D., III, (BV) .... '37 '65 C.532 B.A. L.607 J.D. 158 Lear Rd., Ste. A
Rabold, C. Steven, (BV) .... '55 '80 C.97 B.A. L.201 J.D. [C.S.Rabold]
Rabold, C. Steven, Co., LPA, (BV) .... 110 Moore Road
Sanchez, Alfonso P. .... '33 '68 C.339 B.S. L.1003 J.D. 333 Champions Ct.
Shiba, Wendy C., (AVⓉ) '50 '80 C.475 B.S. L.831 J.D.
V.P., Chf. Legal Offr. and Secy., PolyOne Corp.
Shumaker, Jody L., (CV) .... '66 '92 C.608 B.A. L.1003 J.D. 110 Moore Rd.
Smith, Geoffrey Randall .... '58 '83 C.800 B.A. L.124 J.D. 110 Moore Road
Smith, Gerald M., (AV) .... '33 '61 C.746 B.S. L.1003 J.D. [Smith&S.]
Smith, James Joseph .... '59 '88 C.161 B.B.A. L.989 J.D. [Ⓐ Smith&S.]
Smith, Timothy T., (AV) .... '44 '69 C.1024 B.A. L.930 J.D. [Smith&S.] ⊙
Smith and Smith, (AV) .... 110 Moore Road (⊙Vermilion)

Smith, Stourton Scott, Co., LPA
(See Cleveland)

Spike & Meckler Law Firm, The, LLP
(See Elyria)

Stuart, Richard P., (BV) .... '58 '90 C.980 B.S., B.A. L.930 J.D. 110 Moore Road
Vandenbossche, Achille Craig .... '61 C.161 B.A. L.930 J.D. 525 Avon Belden Rd.
Walters, Susan M. .... '56 '80 C.62 B.A. L.276 J.D. 112 Westwind Dr.

BAINBRIDGE, 3,417, *Geauga Co.*

Sahli, Richard C. .... '54 '80 C.930 B.A. L.608 J.D. Asst. Atty. Gen.

BALTIMORE, 2,971, *Fairfield Co.*

England, Dale R., Jr., (BV) .... '47 '72 C.607 B.A. L.117 J.D. 719 W. Market St.
Hummell, Chester H. .... '19 '53 C.610 B.Sc. L.608 J.D. 3900 Blacklick Rd.‡
Jackson, G. Gene, (AV) .... '27 '51 C.435 L.608 LL.B. 719 W. Market St.
Keller, James L., (BV) .... '50 '75 C.610 A.B. L.117 J.D. 107 N. Main St.

BARBERTON, 27,899, *Summit Co.*

Bantz, William L., (CV) .... '15 '45 C.611 B.A. L.7 J.D. 545 Parker Ave.
Benedict, Lucius C., (BV) .... '12 '37 C.8 A.B. L.7 J.D. 480 W. Tuscarawas Ave.
Benedict, Robert L., (BV) '52 '77 C.62 B.A. L.7 J.D.
480 W. Tuscarawas Ave., Ste. 101
Boley, Thomas R., (BV) .... '49 '74 C&L.8 B.A., J.D. 682 W. Tuscarawas Ave.
Deibel, John W., (BV) .... '38 '63 C.973 B.S. L.215 LL.B. 103 5th St. S.E., Ste. M
Deuber, Fred J., (BV) .... '31 '61 C.608 B.Sc. L.273 LL.B. 480 W. Tuscarawas Ave.
Dool, Carl D. ..... '44 '71 C.610 A.B. L.930 J.D. Corp. Atty., Babcock & Wilcox Co., The
Dziewisz, John '65 '92 C.473 B.S. L.8 J.D.
Senior Attorney, The Babcock & Wilcox Company
Fish, David Edward .... '58 '84 C.861 B.A. L.8 J.D. City of Barberton Law Dept.
Gadanac, Adam, Jr. .... '23 '56 C&L.8 B.A., J.D. Ret. Mun. J.
Gingo, Michael J. .... '52 '81 C&L.8 B.S., J.D. Corp. Atty., Babcock & Wilcox Co.
Gipson, Thomas B., (BV) .... '52 '80 C.8 B.A. L.1003 J.D. Mag.
Grady, Michael J. ...... '53 '86 C.665 B.A. L.117 J.D. Mng. Atty., Babcock & Wilcox Co.
Harnden, Thomas L. '46 '76
C.607 B.A. L.7 J.D. Asst. Gen. Coun., Babcock & Wilcox Co.
Hood, Terry W. .... '53 '85 C.1301 B.B.A. L.7 J.D. Babcock & Wilcox
Howdyshell, Donald E. '47 '86 C.381 B.B.A. L.8 J.D.
Mng. Atty., Babcock & Wilcox Co.
Hurt, John P. .... '54 '79 C.381 B.A. L.608 J.D. Corp. Atty., Babcock & Wilcox Co.
Johnson, Edw. A., (BV) .... '23 '50 C.473 B.S. L.150 LL.B. 105 5th St. S.E.
Klingensmith, Robert D. '47 '79
C.607 B.S.M.E. L.7 J.D. Sr. Atty., Babcock & Wilcox Co.
Lysenko, John .... '70 '99 C.999 B.S. L.989 J.D. [J.Lysenko]
Lysenko, John, Co., L.P.A. .... P.O. Box 487
Marich, Eric .... '55 '85 C&L.8 B.S.M.E., J.D. Mng. Atty., Babcock & Wilcox Co.
May, Bruce J., (BV) .... '54 '85 C.25 B.S. L.8 J.D. [B.J.May]
May, Bruce J., LPA, (BV) .... 480 W. Tuscarawas Ave., Ste. 102
McNulty, Michael J., (AV) .... '49 '74 C.8 B.A. L.7 J.D. 576 West Park Avenue
Miller, Lisa Okolish .... '66 '91 C.49 B.S. L.8 J.D. Dir. of Human Res., City of Barberton
Naumoff, Mitchell A., Attorney at Law '50 '76
C.970 B.A. L.7 J.D. 564 W. Tuscarawas Ave., Ste. 306
Phillips, Florence J., (AVⓉ) '48 '84
C.1264 B.A. L.174 J.D. Sr. Coun., BWX Technologies, Inc.‡
Puglisi, Salvatore P., (BV) .... '50 '75 C.8 B.S. L.7 J.D. 103 Fifth St., S.E.
Radanof, R. Gary, (BV) .... '44 '69 C.610 B.B.A. L.7 J.D. 682 W. Tuscarawas Ave.
Weigand, Michael L. .... '42 '71 C.363 B.S.B.A. L.7 J.D. Mun. J.
Weigand, Richard G. .... '35 '68 C.363 B.S.B.A. L.7 J.D. 682 W. Tuscarawas Ave.‡
Winchell, Dennis R. .... '48 '76 C.8 B.S. L.7 J.D. 384 Newell St.

BARNESVILLE, 4,225, *Belmont Co.*

Chaney, William E., (AV) .... '27 '53 C.611 A.B. L.608 J.D. 111 E. Main St.
Hampton, Thomas A., (BV) .... '50 '83 C.952 B.A. L.608 J.D. [T.Hampton]
Hampton, Thomas, Law Offices, (BV) .... 160 E. Main St.
Hoffman, Grace L., (CV) .... '56 '91 C.920 B.A. L.229 J.D. 160 E. Main St.
Jefferis, Paul B., (CV) .... '52 '80 C.608 B.A. L.8 J.D. 58884 Wright Rd.
Koerber, Barry L. .... '58 '90 C.1115 B.A. L.8 J.D. 351 S. Chestnut St.

BATAVIA, * 1,700, *Clermont Co.*

Abrams, Kevin R. .... '56 '82 C.31 B.A. L.608 J.D. 3979 Hockstock Rd.
Anderson, William H., (AV) '38 '69 C&L.150 B.A., J.D.
Senior Vice President & General Counsel, Sportsman's Market Inc.
Arbaugh, Anne McClain .... '64 '91 C.393 B.A. L.201 J.D. Child. Protective Servs.

Arnold, James S., & Associates
(See Cincinnati)

Backscheider, Clifford Ralph .... '45 '79 2018 Plumb Lane
Ball, Douglas A., Attorney at Law, (CV) '64 '90
C&L.150 B.F.A., J.D. 233 E. Main Street, Suite 3
Birck, Mary Lynne, (BV) '66 '94
C.145 B.A. L.150 J.D. Asst. Pros. Atty., Clermont Co. Pros. Off.
Blust, Thomas L., (AV) .... '48 '73 C.473 A.B. L.150 J.D. 101 E. Main Street

Bossin, Phyllis G., Co., L.P.A.
(See Cincinnati)

Bradford, Douglas J., (BV) .... '46 '74 C.802 B.B.A. L.150 J.D. [Burreson,B.&H.]
Brock, Anthony W., (BV) .... '68 '93 C.973 B.A. L.150 J.D. Asst. Pros. Atty.

Buechner, Haffer, O'Connell, Meyers, Healey & Koenig Co., L.P.A.
(See Cincinnati)

Burreson, Allen L., (AV) .... '36 '64 C.879 B.A. L.150 J.D. [Burreson,B.&H.]
Burreson, Bradford & Hill, (AV) .... 40 S. 3rd Street
Carlier, Lawrence W. .... '32 '59 C.473 L.150 LL.B. Market & North Streets
Carroll, Rebecca Ruth .... '64 '89 C.1161 B.A. L.1340 J.D. Child Supp. Enforcement
Carter, David E., (BV) .... '55 '91 C.150 B.B.A. L.1340 J.D. [Nichols,S.&N.]

Chalfie & Farley, Co., L.P.A.
(See Cincinnati)

Daugherty, Kendra L., (BV) .... '56 '82 C&L.150 B.A., J.D. 10 S. 3rd St.
Davis, Rebecca Carroll .... '64 '89 C.1161 B.A. L.1340 J.D. Child Support Enforce. Agcy.
Dean, John R., (CV) .... '51 '79 C.150 B.A. L.1340 J.D. Clermont Co. Dom. Rel. Ct.
Decatur, Caitlin .... '56 '87 C.861 B.A. L.150 J.D. 196 E. Main St., Ste. C
Durkee & Uhle, (BV) .... 97 Main Street (⊙Cincinnati)
Edwards, Allan Lee .... '61 '87 C.473 B.S. L.150 J.D. 101 East Main St.
Ely, Rex E., (AV) .... '36 '61 C&L.150 A.B., LL.B. [Ely&T.]
Ely and True, (AV) .... 322 Main Street
Erhardt, Christian, (AV) .... '36 '62 C&L.150 B.A., LL.B. [C.Erhardt]
Erhardt, John D., (AV) .... '25 '52 C&L.150 B.A., LL.B. 285 Main St.‡
Erhardt, Chris, Law Offices, (AV) .... 65 N. 2nd St., Ste. 200
Faris, Corinne M. .... '55 '80 C.161 B.A. L.851 J.D. 2110 Carriage Staion Dr.
Faris, D. Vincent, (BV) .... '55 '80 C.383 B.A. L.851 J.D. [Burreson,B.&H.]
Ferenc, Richard P., (BV) .... '50 '77 C.150 B.B.A. L.1340 J.D. [Ely&T.]
Finney, Michael J. .... '52 '79 C.473 B.A. L.608 J.D. Dom. Rel. Ct. J.
Flessa, Thomas H., (BV) .... '55 '82 C&L.150 B.A., J.D. [Nichols,S.&N.]
Frey, David J., (AV) .... '50 '75 C&L.150 B.A., J.D. [Nichols,S.&N.]
Greer, Gary R., (CV) .... '52 '78 C.473 B.A. L.1340 J.D. [G.R.Greer]
Greer, Gary R., Co., LPA, (CV) .... 55 W. Main Street
Hannon, R. Daniel, (BV) .... '50 '77 C.973 A.B. L.150 J.D. Pub. Def.
Hauck, Stephen L., (BV) .... '51 '77 C.473 B.A. L.1340 J.D. 210 Main St.
Hawkins, Darrell Curtiss, (CV) '49 '89
C&L.150 B.S., J.D. Pros. Atty.; Clermont Co. Prosecutor Off.
Hein, Jonathan A. .... '71 '98 C.473 B.A. L.150 J.D. Staff Atty./Mag., Com. Pleas Ct.
Henderson, James C., (BV) .... '51 '76 C.207 B.A. L.150 J.D. [Ely&T.]

Hennekes, Jason
(See Cincinnati)

Herberth, Gretta M. .... '76 '03 C.473 B.A. L.150 J.D. Asst. Pub. Def.
Herman, Thomas R. .... '49 '78 C.150 B.B.A. L.1340 J.D. Mun. J.
Hill, Ralph A., (AV) .... '24 '49 C.473 B.A. L.150 J.D. [Burreson,B.&H.]
Hoffmann, David Henry, (BV) ...... '58 '84 C&L.150 B.B.A., J.D. 123 North Third Street
Hollenbach, Melissa W. .... '67 '97 C.138 B.A. L.151 J.D. Law Clk., Ct. of Com. Pleas
Hondorf, Sherrill P., (BV) .... '51 '87 C.150 B.A. L.1340 J.D. 4490 Hartman Ln.
Hunt, James A., (AV) .... '45 '74 C&L.150 B.A., J.D. 97 Main St.
Johnson, Laura C. .... '70 '95 C.112 B.A. L.800 J.D. Ct. Med., Com. Pleas Ct.
Kennedy, Michael Anthony, (BV) '47 '78
C.1118 B.A. L.1340 J.D. Rodenberg & Kennedy Ltd.
Korfhagen, John C., (BV) ... '57 '82 C&L.150 B.S., J.D. Mag., Juv. Ct. [Burreson,B.&H.]

Lopez, Hodes, Restaino, Milman & Skikos, A Law Corporation
(See Cincinnati)

Manley Burke, A Legal Professional Association
(See Cincinnati)

McBride, Jerry R. .... '51 '77 C&L.150 B.A., J.D. Com. Pleas J.
Meurer, Gregory J., (AV) '49 '74 C.262 B.A. L.178 J.D.
V.P. Fin. & Gen. Coun., Diversified Glass, Inc.
Miles, Kevin Todd .... '69 '99 C.1161 B.A. L.1340 J.D. Pros. Off.
Miller, Darren D., (BV) .... '64 '97 C.999 B.S. L.150 J.D. Asst. Pros.

Mills, Tina R., LLC, The Law Firm of
(See Cincinnati)

Montgomery, George P. .... '57 '90 C&L.150 B.S., J.D. 45 N. Market St.
Nichols, James G., (BV) .... '39 '68 C.473 A.B. L.150 J.D. [Nichols,S.&N.]

Nichols, Speidel & Nichols, (AV)
Hamilton Building, 237 Main Street, 45103-2979
Telephone: 513-732-1420 FAX: 513-732-0357
Email: nicholslaw@fuse.net URL: http://www.nsnlaw.com
Members of Firm: James G. Nichols; Donald W. White; David J. Frey; Thomas H. Flessa; Todd S. Stoffel; David E. Carter.
General Civil Practice. Wrongful Death and Personal Injury, Family, Corporate, Banking, Probate, Real Estate, Taxation, Divorce, Insurance Law. Trials and Appeals in all Courts, Litigation, Business, Trusts and Estates.
General Counsel for: Williamsburg Building & Loan Co.
Local Counsel for: Cincinnati Gas & Electric Co.

See Professional Biographies, BATAVIA, OHIO

O'Donnell, Priscilla S., (BV) .... '37 '77 C.150 B.A. L.1340 J.D. 202 Main St.
Osborne, Edward B. .... '19 '49 C.952 B.S. L.150 LL.B. P.O. Box 103‡
Ostendarp, Gary D., (AV) .... '45 '71 C.973 B.A. L.150 J.D. [Ely&T.]

Pattison, George E., (BV) '44 '72 C.608 B.S. L.150 J.D.
285 East Main Street, 45103
Telephone: 513-732-3800 Fax: 513-732-6003
Email: gepattison@aol.com URL: http://www.lawyers.com/pattisonlaw
Probate, Real Estate, Trusts and Estates, Wills, Estate Planning, Social Security, Disability, General Practice, Family Law, Adoptions, Child Custody, Child Support, Divorce, Domestic Violence, Premarital Agreements, Zoning Law, Elder Law, Eminent Domain, Condemnation, Criminal Law, Business Law, Family Business Law, Small Business Law, Contracts, Driving While Intoxicated, Drug Crimes, Felonies, Homicide, Juvenile Law, Misdemeanors, Parole and Probation, Sexual Assault, Traffic Violations.

See Professional Biographies, BATAVIA, OHIO

Purdy & Ring
(See Georgetown)

Ringland, Robert P. .... '45 '71 C.608 B.A. L.150 J.D. Com. Pleas J.
Rodenberg, Albert J., Jr. .... '48 '81 C&L.150 B.S., J.D. Co. Sheriff‡
Rogus, Claire V. .... '70 '95 C.347 B.A. L.150 J.D. 4591 Greensbury Court
Rosenhoffer, Chris .... '13 '51 C.151 B.S.C. L.1340 LL.B. 97 Main St.‡

Rosenhoffer, Gary A., (BV) ... '51 '79 C.473 B.A. L.1340 J.D. 190 Main Street
Rowe, Carol A. ... '67 '01 C.929 B.A. L.150 J.D. Clermont Co. Pros. Off.
Sacks, Arrianna S. ... '78 '03 C.880 B.A. L.1161 J.D. Staff Atty.
Schwartz, Jeffrey S., (BV) ... '49 '76 C.973 B.S. L.1340 J.D. 97 Main St.
Shriver, James Allen ... '56 '82 C&L.150 B.S., J.D. Mun. Ct. J.
Snyder, Terrell B., (BV) ... '58 '83 C.385 B.A. L.608 J.D. 196 E. Main St.
Stagnaro, Gene A., (CV) ... '60 '86 C.150 B.A. L.190 J.D. 2185 U.S. Hwy. 50
Stearns, William A., (BV) ... '45 '71 C.880 B.A. L.1340 J.D. 202 Main Street
Stoffel, Todd S., (BV) ... '64 '89 C.1161 B.A. L.150 J.D. [Nichols,S.&N.]
Stoner-Barone, Denise, (CV) ... '— '92 C.347 B.A. L.1340 J.D. 385 North St.
True, J. Robert, (AV) ... '38 '63 C.532 A.B. L.150 J.D. [Ely&T.]
Uhle, D'Anne D., (BV) ... '58 '83 C.383 B.M. L.150 J.D. [Durkee&U.]
Uhle, Richard B., Jr., (BV) ... '58 '83 C.967 B.A. L.150 J.D. [Durkee&U.] ⊙
Viney, Lauri D. ... '69 '98 C.150 B.A. L.1340 J.D. Off. of Pub. Def.
Voris, Michael J. ... '37 '68 C.610 A.B. L.1340 J.D. Com. Pleas J., Dom. Rel. Div.

Waite, Schneider, Bayless & Chesley Co., L.P.A.
(See Cincinnati)

Walker, Gayle A., (CV) '48 '83
C&L.150 B.S., J.D. Clermont Co. Child Support Enforcement
Walker, Lawrence, (BV) ... '42 '68 C.150 B.A. L.1340 J.D. 60 N. 4th St.
Walker, William ... '48 '73 C&L.150 B.A., J.D. Com. Pleas J., Gen. Div.
White, Donald W., (BV) ... '46 '73 C.150 B.B.A. L.1340 J.D. [Nichols,S.&N.]
Wyler, Stephanie A. ... '54 '78 C&L.150 B.S., J.D. Prob. J. & Juv. Ct. J.

BATH, 7,552, *Summit Co.*

Brzuziewski, Glenn E. ... '62 '97 C.97 B.S.B.A. L.1008 J.D. 1625 Orchard Dr.
Gaffney, Frank J., III, (BV) '27 '57
C.757 B.A. L.930 LL.B. 1911 North Cleveland-Massillon
Zeile, G. David, Jr., (AV) '26 '51 C.610 B.A. L.930 LL.B.
Pres., Ricwil Piping Systems Div. of Intergy Inc.

BAY VILLAGE, 16,087, *Cuyahoga Co.*

Anthony, Richard G. ... '44 '83 C.161 B.E.E. L.1003 J.D. 482 Elmwood Rd.
Biesterfeldt, John P. ... '65 '99 C.910 B.A. L.930 J.D. [J.Biesterfeldt]
Biesterfeldt, John ... 30305 Lake Rd.
Blenkhorn, Amy E. ... '59 '84 C.161 B.A. L.1003 J.D. 28008 Lincoln Road
Brantley, Scott, Jr. ... '47 '75 C&L.836 B.A., J.D. U.S. Dept. of Jus.
Frye, Robert Owen ... '— '94 C.645 B.S. L.1003 J.D. 28304 W. Oakland Rd.
Henry, C. J., Jr. '19 '50 C&L.659 A.B., LL.B.
(adm. in MD; not adm. in OH) 30200 Windsor Dr.‡
Honicky, David A. ... '63 '94 C.473 B.S. L.7 J.D. 31312 Carlton Dr.

Hunt & Cook LLC
(See Westlake)

Mahall, Kim ... '46 '94 C.381 B.B.A. L.989 J.D. P.O. Box 40504
Miller, Thomas E. ... '26 '69 C.8 B.S. L.161 J.D. 25926 Lake Rd.‡
Parker, John H., (BV) ... '35 '65 C.207 B.A. L.930 J.D. 31300 Lake Rd.
Pitts, Morris W. ... '23 '52 C.228 A.B. L.930 LL.B. 25770 Wolf Rd.‡
Toepfer, Robert A., (AV) ... '20 '43 C&L.150 A.B., J.D. 304 Apple Blossom Ln.‡
Trenta, Louis S. ... '66 '02 C.608 B.A. L.124 J.D. [Trenta]
Trenta Law Firm, The ... 30234 Westlawn Dr.
Woodlock, Donald F. ... '40 '70 C.97 B.S. L.1003 J.D. Lakewood Dairy Queen, Inc.

BEACH CITY, 1,137, *Stark Co.*

Cunningham, Priscilla J., Law Offices of, (CV) '67 '95
C.8 M.T. L.1003 J.D. 404 3rd Ave. S.W.

BEACHWOOD, 12,186, *Cuyahoga Co.*

Abbuhl, David W., (BV) ... '55 '81 C.509 B.A. L.930 J.D. [D.W.Abbuhl] (⊙Cleveland)
Abbuhl, David W. Co., L.P.A., (BV) ... 23230 Chagrin Boulevard
Abdullovski, Doreen M. '67 '95
C.1107 A.B. L.1048 J.D. The Prs Group, Credit General Ins. Co.
Arnoff, Fred J., (AV) ... '50 '75 C.473 B.S. L.7 J.D. [Persky,S.&A.]
Bendau, James M., (BV) ... '46 '72 C.608 B.S. L.1003 J.D. 23200 Chagrin Blvd.
Bennett, Stanley ... '33 '60 C.930 B.B.A. L.1003 J.D. 2652 Edgewood Road‡

Bernard & Haffey Co., L.P.A.
(See Cleveland)

Birne, Kenneth A., (BV) ... '56 '81 C.608 B.A. L.930 J.D. 23230 Chagrin Blvd., Ste. 715
Bohm, Lori Beckman ... '60 '85 C.608 B.S. L.1003 J.D. Mgr., Taxes, Austin Powder Co.‡
Bohm, Marvin William ... '52 '77 C.610 B.B.A. L.608 J.D. [M.Bohm]
Bohm, Marvin ... 24800 Chagrin Blvd., Ste. 301
Bonaguro, Mark N., (AV) '61 '90 C.436 B.S. L.365 J.D.
V.P. & Gen. Coun., Tyco Suppression Systems
Brokaw, Kevin M. ... '74 '00 C.97 B.A. L.1003 J.D. [Ⓐ Levy&D.]
Brooks, Jeffrey M. ... '41 '69 C.473 B.S.B.A. L.1003 J.D. 23215 Commerce Park Rd.
Budish, Armond D., (AV) ... '53 '77 C.821 B.A. L.569 J.D. [Budish&S.]
Budish & Solomon, Ltd., (AV) ... 23240 Chagrin Boulevard, Suite 450
Byrnes, Lawrence I., (AV) ... '24 '49 C&L.930 A.B., J.D. The Lamson & Sessions Co.
Carmen, Fred N., (BV) ... '55 '81 C.930 B.A. L.1003 J.D. 27800 Cedar Road
Chesler, Steven B., (BV) ... '56 '84 C.608 B.A. L.7 J.D. 23611 Chagrin Blvd., Ste. 120
Christy, Chastity ... '78 '03 C.648 B.A L.124 J.D. [Ⓐ Zipkin W.]
Chyun, Edward H. ... '77 '03 C.800 B.A. L.608 J.D. [Ⓐ Levy&D.]
Cornrich, Neil M., (AV) ... '57 '83 C.477 B.S. L.608 J.D. [Cornrich&C.]
Cornrich, Sidney M., (AV) ... '28 '51 C&L.608 J.D. [Cornrich&C.]
Cornrich & Cornrich, Co., L.P.A., (AV) ... 2000 Auburn Dr., Ste. 315
Costello, William L., (BV) ... '63 '88 C.473 B.S. L.930 J.D. [W.L.Costello]
Costello, William L. Co., L.P.A., (BV) ... 3401 Enterprise Pkwy.
Cyncynatus, Jerry M., (AV) '57 '83 C.608 B.A. L.851 J.D.
Developers Diversified Realty
Deckman, Adrienne L., (BV) ... '53 '78 C.873 A.B. L.608 J.D. [Deckman]
Deckman Law Office, (BV) ... 26613 Annesley Road
Dettelbach, Thomas L., (AV) '37 '66 C.608 B.S. L.1003 J.D.
3733 Park East Dr., Ste. 200
Donnem, Roland W., (AV) ... '29 '58 C.976 B.A. L.309 J.D. 3609 Park E.
Dowd, Robert E., (BV) ... '20 '75 C.602 B.S.C. L.161 J.D. 24609 Duffield Road
Dubyak, Robert J., (BV) ... '67 '92 C.473 B.A. L.930 J.D. [Levy&D.]
Duda, John E., (AV) ... '38 '61 C&L.608 B.A., J.D. 2101 Richmond Rd.
Eastman, Mark ... '60 '88 C&L.352 B.S., J.D. 25550 Chagrin Blvd., Suite 300
Elconin, Gene ... '38 '66 C.473 B.S. L.1003 J.D. 23200 Chagrin Blvd.
Eli, David A., (CV) ... '52 '79 C.381 B.G.S. L.7 J.D. Gen. Coun., Chase Properties
Erenrich, Alan L. ... '48 '87 C.119 B.S.C.E. L.1209 J.D. 2449 Beachwood Blvd.
Feder, Jeffrey S. ... '46 '71 C.608 B.S.B.A. L.930 J.D. P.O. Box 22538
Feldman, Daniel W. ... '24 '67 C.477 B.S.M.E. L.1003 J.D. 23213 Fairmount Blvd.‡
Fine, Michael L. ... '— '92 C.170 B.A. L.809 J.D. [Ⓐ Zipkin W.]
Fine, Philip R. ... '44 '69 C&L.477 B.A., J.D. 3681 Green Rd., Ste. 410
Finkelstein, Tracy K., (BV) '66 '92 C.477 B.A. L.1003 J.D.
23611 Chagrin Rd., Ste. 225
Fisher, Stanley M., (AV) ... '28 '53 C.604 B.A. L.477 J.D. [Ⓒ Budish&S.]
Foster, Torrey N. ... '34 '61 C.976 B.A. L.910 J.D. 27600 Chagrin Blvd.
Friedman, Mitchell Jay ... '57 '01 C.607 B.S. L.161 J.D. C.V.S.
Friedman, Robert G. ... '69 '94 C.608 B.A. L.1003 J.D. [Krantz,P.&F.]
Fromet, Avery H., (BV) '45 '72 C.381 B.B.A. L.1003 J.D.
Chagrin-Richmond Plz., 25550 Chagrin Blvd., Ste. 403
Gaynor, Donald A. ... '24 '50 C.659 B.S. L.930 LL.B. Three Commerce Pk. Sq.
Gilchrist, Amy Scott '63 '91 C.478 B.A. L.930 J.D.
Legal Counsel, PRS Management Group, Inc.
Goldstein, Jerrold L., (AV) ... '41 '67 C.608 B.S.B.A. L.930 J.D. [Persky,S.&A.]
Goldstein, Michael S., (BV) ... '45 '74 C.475 B.A. L.1003 J.D. [M.S.Goldstein]
Goldstein, Michael S., Co., L.P.A., (BV) ... 21625 Chagrin Boulevard, Suite 240
Groger, Herbert R. ... '28 '53 C&L.930 B.A., LL.B. Groger Travel Bureau
Hacala, Martin G. '61 '86 C&L.734 A.B., J.D.
(adm. in MO; not adm. in OH) Genesis Professional Liability Underwriters
Handelman, James M., (BV) ... '42 '78 C.477 M.A. L.1003 J.D. 23611 Chagrin Blvd.
Hawkins, Paula L. ... '63 '90 C.628 B.A. L.8 J.D. [Ⓐ Budish&S.]
Henck, John C. ... '67 '96 C.207 B.A. L.930 J.D. 23240 Chagrin Blvd., Ste. 535
Hogg, Kathleen A. '53 '79 C&L.477 B.B.A., J.D.
(adm. in NY; not adm. in OH) 19870 Chagrin Blvd.
Holzheimer, Edward T. '43 '69 C.276 B.S.B.A. L.1003 J.D.
Managing Partner, Amex. Tax and Bus. Servs.
Horwitz, Jos. ... '14 '40 C&L.608 B.S., J.D. 23811 Chagrin Blvd.
Hurst, Jonathan R. ... '76 '01 C.197 B.A. L.930 J.D. [Ⓐ Cornrich&C.]
Jacobs, Andrea Kanter, (AV) ... '55 '80 C.860 B.A. L.94 J.D. 26900 Cedar Rd.
Jaffe, Donald N., (BV) ... '38 '61 C&L.930 A.B., J.D. [Ⓒ Persky,S.&A.]
Jaffery, Sheldon R., (BV) ... '34 '64 C.608 B.A. L.930 J.D. 23834 Wendover Dr.
Kabat, Gary B., (BV) ... '40 '65 C.597 B.S. L.930 J.D. [Kabat,M.&S.]
Kabat, Mielziner & Sobel, (AV) ... 25550 Chagrin Boulevard, Suite 403
Kackley, Debra L., (BV) '55 '91 C.318 B.A. L.1003 J.D.
V.P., Gen. Coun. & Secy., Scott Technologies, Inc.

Karberg, Kurant, Wachter & Turner Co., L.P.A.
(See Cleveland)

King, David M., (AV) ... '47 '72 C.966 B.A. L.273 J.D. 24500 Chagrin Blvd.
Kraemer, Lisa R., (BV) ... '54 '79 C.309 A.B. L.150 J.D. 23200 Chargrin Boulevard
Krantz, Howard J. ... '60 '86 C.608 B.S. L.1003 J.D. [Krantz,P.&F.]
Krantz, Powers & Friedman, P.L.L., (BV) ... 23240 Chagrin Boulevard, Suite 180
Krasovec, Frank C., Jr., (AV) ... '58 '83 C.161 B.B.A. L.930 J.D. [Budish&S.]
Kraus, Alan H., (AV) ... '55 '81 C.1275 B.A. L.1003 J.D. [Lazzaro&K.]
Kraus, David P., (BV) ... '59 '88 C.161 B.A. L.1003 J.D. P.O. Box 22154
Krone, Norman Bernard ... '38 '64 C.930 L.362 LL.B. 2101 Richmond Rd.
Ladanyi, Albert Louis, II ... '52 '83 L.1003 J.D. Of Coun., Noral, Inc.
Lash, David L. ... '51 '77 C.610 B.A. L.1003 J.D. 23811 Chagrin Blvd., Ste. 228
Laudani, Anthony ... '29 '54 C&L.930 B.B.A., LL.B. Entrust Inc.
Lazzaro, Michele M., (AV) ... '56 '81 C.696 B.A. L.1003 J.D. [Lazzaro&K.]
Lazzaro and Kraus, (AV) ... 25700 Science Park Drive Suite 250
Leskovec, Mark, (BV) ... '61 '86 C.980 A.B. L.930 J.D. [Ⓐ Levy&D.]
Lester, Esther C. '29 '89
C.381 B.S.Ed. L.1003 J.D. 3715 Warrensville Center Rd., Apt. 307
Levin, Paul F., (AV) ... '47 '73 C.930 B.A. L.178 J.D. Asst. Dir. of Law
Levine, Allan L. ... '26 '49 C&L.930 A.B., LL.B. 24760 Albert Lane‡
Levy, Gregg S., (AV) ... '66 '91 C.347 B.S. L.608 J.D. [Levy&D.]

Levy & Dubyak, (AV)
25200 Chagrin Boulevard, Suite 310, 44122
Telephone: 216-896-5600 Fax: 216-896-5601
URL: http://www.ldlawfirm.com
Partners: Gregg S. Levy; Robert J. Dubyak. Associates: Aileen S. Sexton; Mark Leskovec; Kevin M. Brokaw; Timothy J. Weyls, Jr.; Edward H. Chyun. Of Counsel: Robert D. Schwartz.
Real Estate, Corporate Law, Business Law, Business Litigation, Finance, Employment Law, Commercial Law, Contracts, Mergers and Acquisitions, Real Estate Litigation.
See Professional Biographies, BEACHWOOD, OHIO

Longo, Charles V., (AV) ... '59 '85 C.363 B.S.B.A. L.1003 J.D. [C.V.Longo]
Longo, Charles V., Co., L.P.A., (AV) ... 25550 Chagrin Blvd., Ste. 320
Lukas, Anne L. ... '52 '86 C.610 B.F.A. L.1003 J.D. 2164 Campus Rd.
Madorsky, Larry I., (BV) ... '40 '67 C.608 B.S. L.150 J.D. [Madorsky&Assoc.]
Madorsky & Associates, L.P.A., (BV) ... 2101 Richmond Rd.
Mamich, Samuel J. ... '38 '73 C.381 B.A. L.989 J.D. [Ⓐ Zipkin W.]
Marshek, Ronald S., (BV) ... '44 '73 C.251 B.B.A. L.1003 J.D. [R.S.Marshek]
Marshek, Ronald S., Co. L.P.A., (BV) ... 27600 Chagrin Boulevard, Suite 160
McCamley, Janet, (BV) ... '56 '81 C&L.930 B.A., J.D. [Robert F.R.]
McGraw, Shawn M. ... '69 '94 C.473 B.A. L.930 J.D. Coun., Tremco, Inc.
McMillan, Kevin R. ... '73 '98 C.318 B.A. L.608 J.D. [Ⓐ Kabat,M.&S.]
Mielziner, Bruce L., (AV) ... '40 '67 C.473 B.A. L.1003 J.D. [Kabat,M.&S.]
Miller, Robert L., (BV) ... '46 '71 C.910 A.B. L.1003 J.D. 25550 Chagrin Blvd., Ste. 108
Mintz, Carl A. ... '09 '35 C.659 B.S. L.161 J.D. 23305 Chagrin Blvd.
Misra, Anand N. ... '57 '83 C&L.999 B.S., LL.B. [Misra] ‡
Misra Law Firm, LLC ... 3659 Green Road, Suite 100
Neff, James A., (BV) ... '57 '86 C.473 B.S. L.1003 J.D. 21625 Chagrin Blvd.
Occhionero, Michael J., (AV) ... '49 '74 C.602 A.B. L.1003 J.D. [M.J.Occhionero]
Occhionero, Michael J., L.P.A., (AV) ... 28601 Chagrin Blvd Ste 450
Palay, Alfred ... '11 '33 C&L.930 A.B., J.D. 27050 Cedar Rd.‡
Papa, Nicholas Anthony ... '66 '92 C.381 B.S. L.607 J.D. 29325 Chagrin Blvd., Ste. 305
Peck, Jennifer E. ... '68 '93 C.363 B.A. L.1003 J.D. [Budish&S.]
Peltz, Richard B., (BV) ... '42 '68 C.608 B.S. L.150 J.D. 23230 Chagrin Blvd., Ste. 715

Persky, Shapiro & Arnoff Co., L.P.A., (AV)
Signature Square II, 25101 Chagrin Boulevard, Suite 350, 44122
Telephone: 216-360-3737 Telecopier: 216-593-0921
Ezra Z. Shapiro (1902-1977); Joseph H. Persky (1914-1987); Sherman S. Hollander (1920-1987); Edward N. Salim (Retired); Paul Y. Shapiro; Fred J. Arnoff; Jerrold L. Goldstein; Stewart D. Roll; Michael J. Shapiro;—Paul R. Rosenberger; Mary Ann Schleimer. Of Counsel: Donald N. Jaffe; Patricia M. Ritzert.
General Practice, Corporate Law, Real Estate, Finance, Health Care, Taxation, Professional Corporations, Trusts and Estates, Estate Planning, Probate Law, Employee Benefits, Antitrust, Litigation, Family Law, Bankruptcy and Debtor and Creditor.
See Professional Biographies, BEACHWOOD, OHIO

Pfundstein, Joseph A., (BV) '66 '91
C.93 B.S. L.930 J.D. 24100 Chagrin Boulevard Suite 330
Powers, Laurence J., (BV) ... '58 '87 C.473 B.S. L.1003 J.D. [Krantz,P.&F.]
Quinn, Maria E., (AV) ... '48 '79 C.392 B.S. L.161 J.D. [M.E.Quinn]
Quinn, Maria E., Co., LPA, (AV) ... 25550 Chagrin Blvd., Ste. 320
Relman, Craig W., (BV) ... '61 '90 C.30 B.A. L.1003 J.D. [C.W.Relman]
Relman, Harvey M. ... '28 '52 C.260 L.472 J.D. 2465 Sittingbourne La.‡

Relman, Craig W., Co., L.P.A., (BV) 23875 Commerce Pk.
Reuven, David William, Law Office of '66 '92 C.608 B.S.B.A. L.989 J.D. [D.W.Reuven]
Reuven, David W., Law Office of 3681 Green Rd., Ste. 410
Rickel, Alice, & Associates, (BV) '47 '74 C.930 B.A. L.161 J.D. 3690 Orange Place
Risman, Robt. R. '28 '53 C.472 B.B.A. L.930 LL.B. Pres., Realtek Industries, Inc.‡
Ritzert, Patricia M., (BV) '52 '77 C.8 B.A. L.7 J.D. [C Persky,S.&A.]
Rocker, Michael D. '39 '66 C.930 B.B.A. L.1003 J.D. 9 Salem Court
Roll, Stewart D., (AV) '49 '78 C.610 B.G.S. L.285 J.D. [Persky,S.&A.]
Rosenbaum, Robert F., (BV) '45 '72 C.150 B.B.A. L.851 J.D. [C Robert F.R.] ‡
Rosenbaum & McCamley, Co., L.P.A., (BV) 24100 Chagrin Blvd.
Rosenberger, Paul R. '72 '98 C.597 B.A. L.608 J.D. [A Persky,S.&A.]
Rubin, Neil S. '— '98 C.608 B.S. L.989 J.D. [A Zipkin W.]
Sable, Marvin E. '46 '72 C.30 B.S. L.1003 J.D. 2176 Halcyon Road
Sack, Mark J. '58 '97 C.1036 B.A. L.1003 J.D. 3928 E. Ash Lane
Sadugor, Irving '13 '40 C&L.930 B.A., LL.B. 26300 Village Lane‡
Salim, Edward N., (AV) '12 '41 C.124 B.S. L.161 J.D. [Persky,S.&A.] ‡
Scalise, Justin T. '77 '03 C.645 B.A. L.1003 J.D. [A C.V.Longo]
Scharfeld, Leonard B. '26 '51 C&L.607 J.D. 26300 Village Ln., Ste. 209‡
Schleimer, Mary Ann '51 '02 C.62 B.A. L.989 J.D. [A Persky,S.&A.]
Schonfeld, Jay M. '45 '70 C.966 B.B.A. L.930 J.D. 20820 Chagrin Blvd., Ste. 302
Schumacher, James T. '— '90 C.201 B.A. L.989 J.D [A Zipkin W.]
Schuster, Linda B. '67 '93 C.473 B.S. L.1003 J.D. 3690 Orange Place
Schwartz, Robert D. '70 '96 C.1365 B.A. L.989 J.D. [C Levy&D.]
Sexton, Aileen S. '72 '99 C.363 B.A. L.124 J.D. [A Levy&D.]
Shapiro, Michael J., (AV) '68 '94 C.473 B.A. L.930 J.D. [Persky,S.&A.]
Shapiro, Paul Y., (AV) '38 '63 C&L.930 A.B., J.D. [Persky,S.&A.]
Shaver, Elizabeth A. '64 '89 C.880 B.A. L.188 J.D. Genesis Professional Liability Underwriters
Simon, Harlan M. '31 '54 C&L.608 B.S., LL.B. 24825 Hilltop Dr.
Smith, Michael L., (BV) '48 '76 C.608 B.S. L.1003 J.D. 23611 Chagrin Blvd.
Sobel, Jonathan F., (AV) '54 '79 C.165 B.A. L.228 J.D. [Kabat,M.&S.]
Soclof, Richard Lewis '72 '98 C.978 B.A. L.94 J.D. Robert L. Stark Enterprises, Inc.
Socrates, Christine Sabio, Attorney at Law '67 '93 C.93 B.A. L.1003 J.D. 2000 Auburn Dr., Ste. 200
Solomon, Michael L., (AV) '51 '76 C.679 B.S. L.276 J.D. [Budish&S.]
Steiner, Laurie G., (AV) '57 '89 C.970 B.A. L.1003 J.D. [Budish&S.]
Stern, Arthur J., (AV) '15 '39 C&L.930 B.A., J.D. 22655 Chagrin Blvd.‡
Stillman, Saul G. '10 '34 C&L.309 A.B., J.D. 27020 Cedar Rd.‡
Sweeney, Mary Elizabeth '58 '92 C.222 B.A. L.930 J.D. Genesis Prof. Liability Underwriters
Taylor, Suzanne Schulze '62 '89 C.951 B.A. L.94 J.D. Imperial Home Decor Grp., LLC
Thomas, Andrew R., Law Offices of, (AVⓉ) '56 '90 C.381 B.S. L.425 J.D. 3201 Enterprise Pkwy., Ste. 460
Tierney, James L., II, (AV) '61 '93 C.161 B.A. L.1003 J.D. V.P., Gen. Coun. & Asst. Secy., Tremco Inc.

Toerek Co., LPA
(See Cleveland)

Vavruska, Stasia M. '61 '86 C.930 B.A. L.273 J.D. Sr. V.P. & Gen. Coun., Resource Intl., Inc.
Veneziano, Anne D. '52 '95 C.823 B.A. L.930 J.D. 24100 Chagrin Boulevard, Suite 270
Weberman, Philip, (AV) '55 '85 C.912 B.A. L.213 J.D. 23611 Chagrin Blvd., Ste. 225
Weyls, Timothy J., Jr. '72 '98 C.381 B.A. L.930 J.D. [A Levy&D.]
Whitehead, George W. '22 '53 C.608 B.A. L.1003 LL.B. 24819 Wimbledon Road
Zartman, Michael B. '58 '84 C.604 B.A. L.477 J.D. Claims Mgr., Genesis Professional Liability Underwriters
Zipkin, Lewis A. '— '64 C.473 B.S. L.930 LL.B. [Zipkin W.]

Zipkin Whiting Co., L.P.A.
The Zipkin Whiting Building, 3637 South Green Road, 44122-5717
Telephone: 216-514-6400 Fax: 216-514-6406
Email: info@zipkinwhiting.com URL: http://www.zipkinwhiting.com
Lewis A. Zipkin;—Samuel J. Mamich; James T. Schumacher; Chastity Christy; Neil S. Rubin; Michael L. Fine.
Age Discrimination, Bankruptcy, Discrimination, Race Discrimination, Sex Discrimination, Criminal Law, Disability Discrimination, Americans With Disabilities Act, Family Law, Divorce, Consumer Violations, Nursing Home Abuse and Neglect, Employment Law, Employment Age Discrimination, Employment Disability Discrimination, Employment Discrimination, Harassment, National Origin Discrimination, Negligent Hiring, Retaliatory Discharge, Sexual Harassment, Title VII Discrimination, Wrongful Termination, Medical Malpractice, Personal Injury, Accidents, Automobile Accidents and Injuries, Wrongful Death.
See Professional Biographies, BEACHWOOD, OHIO

BEAVER, 464, *Pike Co.*

Salisbury, Mark A. '60 '85 C&L.608 B.S., J.D. V.P. & Coun., D.G.M., Inc.

BEAVERCREEK, 37,984, *Greene Co.*

Batka, Catherine M. '41 '84 C.741 B.A. L.200 J.D. 1465 Bills Dr.
Cloud, Darrel Gene '50 '88 C.1208 B.A. L.201 J.D. [Joe C.]
Dugmore, Kent C. '39 '64 C&L.878 B.S., J.D. (adm. in UT; not adm. in OH) 3268 Southfield Dr.
Hammond, Richard H., (BV) '43 '68 C&L.608 B.A., J.D. [Hammond,S.&S.]
Hammond, Stier & Stadnicar, (BV) 3836 Dayton-Xenia Rd.
Hart, Tracy L. '61 '94 C&L.201 B.S., J.D. 2828 Legend Falls Ct.
Hidy, Joseph D. '69 '96 C&L.790 B.A., J.D. Gen. Coun., Hidy Honda
Huber, John B. '41 '67 C.201 B.S. L.607 J.D. 2930 Stauffer Drive
Joe Cloud Law Office 3973 Dayton-Xenia Rd.
Kieffaber, Megan Alaine '75 '01 C.63 B.A. L.201 J.D. 2625 Commons Blvd
McNamee, Cynthia P. '64 '91 C&L.150 B.B.A., J.D. 2625 Commons Blvd.
McNamee, Michael P. '57 '90 C.923 B.S. L.150 J.D. 2625 Commons Blvd.

Pickrel, Schaeffer & Ebeling
(See Dayton)

Reid, Marilyn J., (BV) '41 '66 C.339 B.A. L.607 J.D. State Rep. [Reid&Assoc.]
Reid & Associate, (BV) 3866 Indian Ripple Rd.
Rutledge, Lois V. '62 '93 C.473 B.A. L.201 J.D. 1826 Shady Lane Dr.‡
Schumann, Ronald Gary '45 '70 C.823 A.B. L.1068 J.D. 2153 Crab Tree Dr.★
Simms, Thomas W. '47 '72 C&L.608 B.S., J.D. Legal Coun., Universal 1 Credit Union, Inc.
Stadnicar, Joseph W., (BV) '63 '90 C.363 B.S.B.A. L.608 J.D. [Hammond,S.&S.]
Stier, Charles H., Jr., (BV) '50 '77 C.1208 B.A. L.201 J.D. [Hammond,S.&S.]
Stokely, Elizabeth S. '59 '86 C.706 B.A. L.1029 J.D. 299 Redwood Boulevard

BEDFORD, 14,214, *Cuyahoga Co.*

Barnabee, Randi A. '60 '97 C.999 B.S. L.446 J.D. 934 Archer Rd.
Carson, Robert Otto, (BV) '48 '73 C.608 B.A. L.1003 J.D. [Carson&Assoc.]
Carson & Associates, (BV) 653 Broadway Avenue
Junkin, Peter J. '47 '72 C.373 B.A. L.930 J.D. Mun. J.
Lecso, Madeleine L. '53 '89 C.381 B.A. L.1003 J.D. 21 Mapledale Ave.
Melling, Blair N., (AV) '55 '80 C.611 B.A. L.607 J.D. 31 Columbus Rd.
Pidala, Joseph P., (BV) '22 '58 C.251 L.1003 LL.B. [Pidala&P.]
Pidala, Sherry A., (BV) '55 '85 C.97 B.S. L.8 J.D. [Pidala&P.]
Pidala & Pidala, (BV) 650 Broadway Ave.
Smith, Deborah A. '64 '88 C&L.145 A.B., J.D. 934 Archer Rd.
Stewart, Charles C. '37 '66 C.363 B.S. L.989 J.D. 714 Bway. Ave.

BEDFORD HEIGHTS, 11,375, *Cuyahoga Co.*

Bierman, Victor J., III '67 '99 C.602 B.B.A. L.851 J.D. [Roth B.]
Butera, Hayley L. '79 '05 C.880 B.A. L.446 J.D. [A Roth B.]
Chapman, Howard S. '46 '71 C.610 B.B.A. L.608 J.D. Gen. Coun., TransCon Builders, Inc.
Fisher, Vincent E. '70 '99 C.116 B.A. L.851 J.D. [Roth B.]
Jackson, Warner L. '33 '71 C.288 B.A. L.1003 J.D. Mag., Mun. Ct.
Kinstlinger, Marvin J. '44 '69 C.473 B.S. L.608 J.D. Regal Carpet Co.
Klein, Arthur '22 '54 C.930 B.S. L.1003 J.D. 6000 Bear Creek Drive‡
L'Hommedieu, Mary L. '68 '96 C.741 B.A. L.8 J.D. [S Roth B.]
Medford, Cecil L. '43 '72 C.1147 B.S. L.862 J.D. Pres., Halex Div., The Scott Fetzer Co.
Murphy, Linda M. '63 '91 C.62 B.A. L.930 J.D. Corp. Coun., Riser Foods Co.
Rosenbaum, Beth Stoller '63 '89 C.473 B.A. L.1003 J.D. [A Roth B.]
Roth, Dennis A., (AV) '41 '67 C.608 B.S. L.1003 J.D. [Roth B.]

Roth Bierman LLP, (AV)
5196 Richmond Road, 44146
Telephone: 216-595-0071 Fax: 216-595-0073 URL: http://www.darothlaw.com
Email: dar@rothbierman.com URL: http://www.rothbierman.com
Dennis A. Roth; Victor J. Bierman, III; Vincent E. Fisher;—Beth Stoller Rosenbaum; Jackson R. Williams; Hayley L. Butera; Mary L. L'Hommedieu.
Health Care Law, Strategic Planning, Financial, Corporate Law, Business Litigation.
See Professional Biographies, BEDFORD HEIGHTS, OHIO

Sabatine, Jeffrey P. '61 '87 C.980 B.A. L.930 J.D. Gen. Coun., Riser Foods Co.
Shellito, Christopher J. '70 '97 C.665 B.A. L.8 J.D. Nextel Communications
Shore, Sanford M., (AV) '29 '59 C.608 B.S. L.1003 J.D. The Dms Group, Inc.
Williams, Jackson R. '78 '03 C.201 B.A. L.851 J.D. [A Roth B.]

BELLAIRE, 4,892, *Belmont Co.*

Banker, Alan, (AV) '32 '57 C&L.608 B.A., J.D. [Banker&W.] ⊙
Banker, Megan, (CV) '57 '94 C.608 B.A. L.117 J.D. [A Banker&W.]
Banker & White, (AV) 3201 Belmont Street (⊙St. Clairsville)
Bonfini, Emilio M., (BV) '23 '50 C&L.608 B.S., J.D. Bank One Bldg.
Frizzi, Daniel L., Jr., (BV) '52 '77 C.610 B.B.A. L.607 J.D. [Frizzi]
Frizzi Law Offices, (BV) 224-32nd St.
Lancione, Richard L., (AV) '41 '66 C&L.608 B.S., J.D. [Lancione&L.]

Lancione & Lloyd Law Office, Co., L.P.A., (AV)
The Professional Complex, 3800 Jefferson Street, Suite 101, P.O. Box 560, 43906
Telephone: 740-676-2034 Fax: 740-676-3931
Email: richardlancione@comcast.net URL: http://www.lancionelloyd.com
Richard L. Lancione; Tracey J. Lloyd; Scott Alan Lloyd.
Auto Accidents, Trial Practice. Personal Injury, Medical Malpractice, Workers Compensation, Wrongful Death, Corporation Law, Insurance, Real Estate, Probate and Wills.
Reference: F & M National Bank.
See Professional Biographies, BELLAIRE, OHIO

Lloyd, Scott Alan, (CV) '63 '91 C.657 B.S. L.117 J.D. [Lancione&L.]
Lloyd, Tracey J., (CV) '65 '90 C.608 B.A. L.117 J.D. [Lancione&L.]
Schramm, David Earl '35 '71 C.434 B.A. L.30 J.D. [D.E.Schramm]
Schramm, D.E. P.O. Box 264
White, Harry W., (AV) '47 '73 C.610 A.B. L.608 J.D. [Banker&W.] ⊙

BELLBROOK, 7,009, *Greene Co.*

Boland, Amy S., Law Office of, (CV) '56 '81 C.201 B.A. L.150 J.D. 45 W. Franklin
Martin, Cynthia Grubart '63 '92 C.350 B.A. L.201 J.D. 90 East Franklin Street

BELLEFONTAINE, * 13,069, *Logan Co.*

Beck, Ann E., (BV) '51 '86 C.737 B.A. L.607 J.D. [Beck,B.&H.]
Beck, John R. '21 '48 C.253 L.607 LL.B. [Beck,B.&H.]
Beck, Beck and Hale, (BV) 709 North Main Street
Bennett, Daniel '72 '00 C.117 B.A. L.608 J.D. 111 S. Madriver St.
Billiar, Amy Jane Peterson '50 '93 101 S. Main St., Ste. 18
Brady, Michael L. '51 '82 C.194 B.A. L.201 J.D. Bellefontaine Co. Fam. Ct.
Chamberlain, C. Douglas, (BV) '43 '69 C&L.607 B.A., J.D. 111 S. Madriver St.
DeSomma, Peter K., (CV) '52 '94 C.1044 B.A. L.607 J.D. 105 High Avenue
Dougherty, Edwin '56 '91 C.651 B.A. L.607 J.D. [Dougherty]
Dougherty, Kathryn Cayton '57 '93 C&L.607 B.A., J.D. Mng. Atty.
Dougherty Law Office 113 West Columbus Avenue
Dunlap, Robert E., (AV) '29 '57 C.473 B.A. L.608 J.D. [Thompson,D.H.M.W.&T.]
Dyer, Garofalo, Mann & Schultz, A Legal Professional Association, (AV) 1709 South Main Street (⊙Richmond, IN; Dayton, Huber Heights, Lima, Middletown, Piqua, Springfield, Troy, Wilmington, Xenia, OH)
Finefrock, Richd. H. '19 '42 C.611 B.A. L.188 LL.B. Ret. Com. Pleas J.‡
Goslee, William Thomas, (BV) '53 '89 C.608 B.A. L.607 J.D. [Goslee&G.]

Goslee & Goslee, (BV)
114 South Main Street, P.O. Box 416, 43311
Telephone: 937-593-8075 Fax: 937-592-4806
Members of Firm: James R. Goslee (1911-1997); William Thomas Goslee.
General Civil Practice. Corporation, Negligence, Probate, Commercial and Commercial Collections, Insurance, Family and Domestic Relations Law, Construction Law. Trials and Appeals.
Reference: The Huntington National Bank of Bellefontaine.
See Professional Biographies, BELLEFONTAINE, OHIO

Hale, Alan N., (BV) '38 '91 C.197 B.A. L.607 J.D. [Beck,B.&H.]
Hanna, Dane M., (BV) '66 '91 C.91 B.A. L.61 J.D. [Thompson,D.H.M.W.&T.]
Haushalter, B. Joan, Law Office of '64 '89 C.502 B.S.E.E. L.215 J.D. 228 Bent Pine Court
Hawkins, Bridget Denise, (CV) '58 '91 C.959 B.S. L.607 J.D. 709 North Main Street
Heaton, Gerald, (BV) '52 '77 C.20 B.A. L.607 J.D. Co. Pros. Atty.
Hemphill, Richard A., (BV) '54 '85 C&L.607 B.A., J.D. 412 E. Columbus Ave.
Heydinger, Thomas A., (AV) '32 '58 C&L.608 J.D. [Thompson,D.H.M.W.&T.]
Kelly, John B., (AV) '25 '51 C&L.608 B.S., LL.B. 116 East Court Street
Lawrence, John T., (CV) '42 '67 C&L.607 A.B., J.D. 110 E. Court Ave.
MacDonald, Robert B., Jr., (AV) '50 '75 C.608 B.A. L.607 J.D. [Thompson,D.H.M.W.&T.]
MacGillivray, Douglas D., (BV) '36 '65 C.347 B.S. L.607 J.D. 325 N. Main Street
Miller, Edgar L. '23 '51 C.253 B.S. L.607 J.D. 1155 Allison Rd.‡

Minahan, W. Thomas, (BV) '53 '88 C.608 B.S. L.607 J.D. Mag., Com. Pleas Ct.
Montgomery, William R., (AV) '42 '68 C.610 A.B. L.608 J.D. [Smith,S.&M.]
O'Connor, Mark S. '44 '69 C.363 A.B. L.608 J.D. Com. Pleas J.

Oliver Law Office
(See Columbus)

Paulig & Singer
(See Urbana)

Ross, Chad A. '71 '96 C.473 B.S. L.880 J.D. [Thompson,D.H.M.W.&T.]
Ross, John L. '47 '74 C.610 B.A. L.608 J.D. Mun. J.
Schultz, Ronald E., (AV) '42 '67 C.610 B.S. L.608 J.D. [Dyer,G.M.&S.] (⊙Dayton, Huber Heights, Lima, Middletown, Piqua, Springfield)
Smith, Douglas M., (BV) '65 '92 C.597 B.A. L.851 J.D. [Smith,S.&M.]
Smith, J. MacAlpine, (AV) '41 '66 C.597 B.A. L.608 J.D. [Smith,S.&M.]
Smith, Smith & Montgomery, (AV) 112 North Main Street
Snapp, Jeffrey C., (BV) '64 '90 C.607 B.A. L.228 J.D. 5346 Tr. 55
Stolly, Terrence G. '70 '01 C.97 B.S. L.179 J.D. [Thompson,D.H.M.W.&T.]
Stoner, Linda, (BV) '62 '89 C.97 B.M. L.607 J.D. 325 N. Main St.
Thompson, Dunlap, Heydinger, MacDonald, Watkins & Traul, Ltd., (AV) 1111 Rush Avenue
Traul, Howard A., II, (BV) '51 '76 C.97 B.S. L.607 J.D. [Thompson,D.H.M.W.&T.]
Triplett, Marc S., (BV) '52 '77 C.205 B.A. L.192 J.D. 332 S. Main Street
Watkins, David R., (BV) '50 '76 C.608 B.S. L.607 J.D. [Thompson,D.H.M.W.&T.]
West, Jas. B. '23 '51 C&L.607 B.A., J.D. Ret. Prob. J.
West, John D., (BV) '30 '61 C.347 B.S. L.266 J.D. 111 S. Madriver St.
Wolf, Deborah Kay '57 '83 C&L.607 B.A., J.D. Mag., Logan Co. Prob. Juv. Ct.

BELLEVUE, 8,146, *Huron & Sandusky Cos.*

Aigler, Thomas L., (BV) '57 '83 C.477 B.A. L.851 J.D. [Aigler&P.]
Aigler, William F., (AV) '16 '43 C&L.477 B.A., J.D. [Ⓒ Aigler&P.] ‡
Aigler and Paul, (BV) 202 W Main St
Butz, Walter H., (BV) '23 '49 C.97 L.228 LL.B. 507 Northwest St.
Fox, Kenneth P. '36 '67 C.608 B.S. L.1003 J.D. 106 Northwest St.
Meyers, John E., (BV) '44 '69 C.1064 B.A. L.851 J.D. Co. Pros. Atty. [Meyers&W.]
Meyers & Wallingford, (BV) 117 W. Main St.
Paul, Roger D., (BV) '44 '72 C.117 B.A. L.608 J.D. [Aigler&P.]
Sliter, Charles F., (AV) '24 '51 C.363 L.215 LL.B. 223 N. West St.
Smith, Ronald R., (BV) '40 '74 C.313 B.A. L.1003 J.D. [R.R.Smith]
Smith, Ronald R., Law Firm, (BV) 203 Northwest Street
Wallingford, David A., (BV) '52 '77 C.675 B.A. L.339 J.D. [Meyers&W.]

BELPRE, 6,660, *Washington Co.*

Emrick, Gregg M., (BV) '52 '77 C.838 B.S. L.608 J.D. [McCauley,W.&E.] ⊙
Fox, Jim D., (BV) '45 '73 C.610 B.B.A. L.608 J.D. 2002 Washington Blvd.
McCauley, James H., (BV) '45 '69 C&L.923 B.S.J., J.D. [McCauley,W.&E.] ⊙
McCauley, Webster & Emrick, (BV) 1710 Washington Boulevard (⊙Marietta)
Webster, Thomas P., (BV) '50 '75 C.381 B.S. L.608 J.D. [McCauley,W.&E.] ⊙

BENTLEYVILLE, 947, *Cuyahoga Co.*

Borman, Bonnie M. '53 '79 C.56 B.A. L.273 J.D. 65 Quail Rdg.
Cavell-Howard, Tara J. '67 '93 C.107 B.A. L.1357 J.D. 5620 Park Wood Circle
Thomas, Anne B. '54 '94 C&L.8 B.S., J.D. 590 Solon Rd.

BEREA, 19,051, *Cuyahoga Co.*

Berena, John P., (BV) '42 '67 C.62 B.A. L.930 J.D. [J.P.Berena]
Berena, John P., Co., L.P.A., (BV) 28 Parkview Dr.
Berry, Ralph A., Jr., (BV) '— '73 C.607 B.A. L.1003 J.D. [Largent,B.P.&J.] ⊙
Bever, John H., (BV) '11 '41 C.608 L.161 J.D. 357 Prospect Street
Bobinsky, Syl F., (BV) '20 '49 C.62 B.A. L.930 J.D. 31 E. Bridge St.
Calabrase, Mark, (BV) '59 '86 C.62 B.A. L.1003 J.D. 2 Berea Commons, Ste. 1
Cipollo, Todd Donald '72 '98 C.97 B.S. L.1003 J.D. OH Patrolmen's Benevolent Assn.
Colabianchi, James, Jr. '71 '99 C.62 B.A. L.1003 J.D. 407 Front St.
Comstock, Mark A., (AV) '54 '79 C.967 B.A. L.285 J.D. Mun. Ct. J.
Conrad, Earl W. '47 '83 C.999 B.S. L.851 J.D. 90 Ellen Dr.‡
Coury, John M. '65 '90 C.851 B.B.A. L.930 J.D. Management Fiscal Services Corp.
Demer, John A., (BV) '47 '71 C.967 B.S. L.930 J.D. 2 Berea Commons, Ste. 200
Forstner, Gerald C., Jr. '42 '67 C.97 B.S.S. L.930 J.D. 140 Sheldon Rd.
French, Richard H., Jr., (BV) '52 '79 C.800 B.A. L.809 J.D. [French]
French Firm Co., The, L.P.A., (BV) 101 Seminary St.
Frost, Robert R., (BV) '37 '70 C.97 B.S. L.1003 J.D. [Frost&Assoc.]
Frost & Associates, Inc., (BV) 140 Sheldon Rd.
Fusco, Mark, (BV) '56 '88 C.318 B.A. L.930 J.D. [Wargo&W.]
James, Lyndall G., (BV) '32 '71 C.610 A.B. L.1003 J.D. 125 Barberry Dr.
Jamison, Neal M., (AV) '— '83 C.161 B.A. L.1003 J.D. [Largent,B.P.&J.]
Jeske, Kendra J. '70 '97 C.473 B.S. L.1003 J.D. P.O. Box 37
Jones, Barbara L., (AV) '59 '89 C.8 B.A. L.1003 J.D. Asst. City Pros. Atty.
Kavanaugh, Paul K. '20 '54 C.201 L.607 J.D. 43 E. Bridge St., Ste. 101
Kraus, Thomas J. '— '84 C.49 B.A. L.1003 J.D. [Ⓐ Largent,B.P.&J.]

Largent, Berry, Preston & Jamison Co., L.P.A., (AV)
1 Berea Commons, Suite 216, 44017 ⊙
Telephone: 440-816-0600 Toll Free: 888-891-4263 Fax: 440-816-0604; URL: http://www.lbpj.com
Email: lawyers@lbpj.com URL: http://www.largentberryprestonandjamison.com
Jeffrey W. Largent (1946-2004); Ralph A. Berry, Jr.; Kevin M. Preston; Neal M. Jamison;—Thomas J. Kraus; Denio A. Leone; Matthew J. Selby. Of Counsel: Kenneth G. Preston.
Medina, Ohio Office: 232 North Court Street, 44256. Telephone: 330-723-8828. Fax: 330-723-8898.

See Professional Biographies, BEREA, OHIO

Leone, Denio A., (BV) '— '84 C.608 B.A. L.930 J.D. [Ⓐ Largent,B.P.&J.]
Madzy, Matthew J. '73 '99 C.381 B.A. L.161 J.D. 276 Oakdale
Mahoney, William F. '28 '75 C.930 B.B.A. L.1003 J.D. [Ⓒ Wargo&W.]
Marniella, Marisa A. '70 '95 C.610 B.S. L.989 J.D. Mag.
McGrath, James C., (BV) '31 '58 C.973 B.S. L.930 LL.B. 31 E. Bridge St.
Miesse, Timothy S. '54 '79 C.62 B.A. L.607 J.D. P.O. Box 1102
Powers, Kevin Patrick '55 '93 C.161 B.A. L.1003 J.D. Patrolmen's Benevolent Assoc.

Powers & Groh-Wargo
(See Cleveland)

Preston, Kenneth G., (AV) '33 '60 C.930 B.S. L.1003 J.D. [Ⓒ Largent,B.P.&J.]
Preston, Kevin M., (BV) '— '81 C.105 B.A. L.1003 J.D. [Largent,B.P.&J.]
Rady, Marie M., (BV) '61 '90 C.313 B.S. L.8 J.D. [Wargo&W.]
Riemenschneider, Walter E., (BV) '32 '59 C.62 B.A. L.1003 J.D. 31 E. Bridge Street, Suite 302
Rooney, John James '58 '84 C.161 B.A. L.1003 J.D. [Rooney&S.]
Rooney & Smith 493 Front Street
Rosenfeld, Donald M. '44 '76 C.608 B.A. L.930 J.D. 78 Adams St.‡
Selby, Matthew J. '— '03 C.363 B.A. L.989 J.D. [Ⓐ Largent,B.P.&J.]

Smith, Anthony Joseph '59 '84 C.363 B.A. L.989 J.D. [Rooney&S.]
Spangler, Craig D. '— '79 C.62 B.A. L.1003 J.D. P.O. Box 261
Sponseller, Gregory M. '55 '82 C.611 B.A. L.989 J.D. 43 East Bridge Street, Suite #101
Walczak, Michael Alan '49 '81 C.20 B.A. L.1003 J.D. Baldwin-Wallace College
Walters, James N., III, (BV) '45 '73 C.608 B.A. L.1003 J.D. 343 West Bagley Road, Suite 101
Wargo, John J., Jr., (BV) '48 '75 C.97 B.S. L.1340 J.D. [Wargo&W.]
Wargo and Wargo Co., L.P.A., (BV) 30 Park Drive
Wilson, Hilary B., (Mr.) '39 '86 C.62 B.A. L.161 J.D. Baldwin-Wallace Coll.

BETHEL, 2,637, *Clermont Co.*

Ferguson, Jeffry D., (BV) '59 '85 C.184 B.S. L.150 J.D. 424 West Plane Street
Gregory, Patrick L., (BV) '50 '79 C.150 B.S. L.1340 J.D. P.O. Box 378
Leicht, George P., (AV) '45 '72 C.973 B.S. L.150 J.D. 202 E. Plane St.
West, West and Yelton, (AV) 424 W. Plane Street
Yelton, Paul R., (AV) '31 '56 C&L.150 A.B., LL.B. [West,W.&Y.]

BEXLEY, 13,203, *Franklin Co.*

Adjoua, Hakim B. '53 '79 C&L.477 B.S., J.D. [H.Adjoua]
Adjoua, Hakim, Law Offices of 2681 E. Main St., Ste. B
Kamin-Meyer, Tami '64 '91 C.150 B.A. L.117 J.D. 2599 East Main Street‡
Levine, Cathy J. '49 '77 C.569 B.A. L.1202 J.D. Natl Health Care
McGraw, Richard Withrow '59 '89 C.608 B.S.B.A. L.851 J.D. (adm. in IL; not adm. in OH) 714 Francis Ave.‡
Meyer, Jeffrey D. '66 '91 C.1365 B.A. L.608 J.D. President & General Counsel, Hummel Title Agency
Wasserman, Susan S. '49 '77 C.608 B.A. L.161 J.D. [Wasserman]
Wasserman Law Office 735 Euclaire Ave.

BLANCHESTER, 4,220, *Clinton Co.*

Campbell, Michael T. '73 '98 C.973 B.S. L.851 J.D. [Ⓐ Rose&D.] (⊙Sabina)
Dunlap, Brenda N., (BV) '50 '79 C.473 B.A. L.150 J.D. 212 W. Main
Goettke, Richard L., (BV) '51 '76 C.453 B.S. L.150 J.D. 213 N. Broadway
Kornman, Sharon A. '58 '94 C.284 B.A. L.602 J.D. 212 E. Main St.
McHenry, Ronald J., (BV) '47 '72 C&L.150 B.A., J.D. 212 W. Main
Porter, John S. '70 '96 C.385 B.A. L.608 J.D. [Rose&D.]
Rose, Gordon L., (BV) '51 '80 C.952 B.A. L.117 J.D. [Rose&D.] (⊙Sabina)
Rose & Dobyns Co., L.P.A., (BV) 212 East Main Street (⊙Sabina, Wilmington)

BLOOMINGBURG, 874, *Fayette Co.*

Pontious, Victor D., Jr., (BV) '49 '79 C.473 B.S. L.117 J.D. 5427 White Oak Road

BLUE ASH, 12,513, *Hamilton Co.*

Brown, Brian T. '55 '84 C.927 B.A. L.209 J.D. (adm. in IL; not adm. in OH) 4375 Chidester Ln.‡

Clements, Mahin & Cohen, LPA Co.
(See Cincinnati)

Gale, Marcus D. '72 '00 C.235 B.S. L.1340 J.D. (adm. in KY; not adm. in OH) [Gale,K.&B.]
Gale, King & Bleile, PLC 10999 Reed Hartman, Suite 229 (⊙Covington, KY)
King, Stephen R. '60 '96 C.1208 B.S.E.E. L.150 J.D. [Gale,K.&B.]
Liggett, Dennis A., (BV) '36 '64 C&L.150 B.A., J.D. 4725 Cornell Rd.
Schwegmann, Francis X. '18 '47 C.973 Ph.B. L.150 LL.B. 9279 Fidelis Dr.‡
Surkamp, Richard E., Jr. '64 '89 C.973 B.S.B.A. L.608 J.D. Asst. V.P./Title & Closing Counsel, Midland Title Security, Inc.

BLUFFTON, 3,896, *Allen & Hancock Cos.*

Diller, Samuel W., (BV) '34 '60 C.91 A.B. L.607 LL.B. 138 N. Main
Kingsley, Mitchell L., (CV) '49 '84 C.91 B.S. L.424 J.D. 138 N. Main St.
Romey, John H., (AV) '15 '42 C&L.608 B.Sc., J.D. [Romey&V.]
Romey and Vandemark, (AV) 138 N. Main St. (⊙Lima)
Staley-Burley, Gina C., (CV) '64 '92 C.97 B.S. L.607 J.D. Asst. Co. Pros.

BOARDMAN, 37,215, *Mahoning Co.*

Ausnehmer, John E., (BV) '54 '80 C.608 B.S. L.201 J.D. 120 Marwood Cir
Bernard, Elizabeth A., (BV) '62 '88 C.980 B.A. L.7 J.D. [Harshman&B.] ⊙
Bricker, T. Robert, (CV) '69 '00 C.532 B.A. L.989 J.D. [Ⓐ Osborne,D.S.&R.]
Broyles, Bruce M., (CV) '64 '89 C.967 B.A. L.608 J.D. [Ⓐ Osborne,D.S.&R.]
Chermely, Diane L., (CV) '62 '89 C.980 B.S.,B.A. L.150 J.D. 945 Windham Ct.
DeLaurentis, Dominic J., Jr., (BV) '61 '88 C.980 B.S.A.S. L.8 J.D. [Osborne,D.S.&R.]
Granito, A. James '38 '65 C&L.930 211 Griswold Dr.
Harlan, Michael D. '68 '98 C.980 B.A. L.8 J.D. [Ⓐ Harshman&B.] (⊙Warren, OH; Sharon, PA)
Harshman, Michael S., (BV) '40 '66 C.608 B.A. L.846 J.D. [Harshman&B.] ⊙
Harshman & Bernard LLC, (BV) 850 Boardman-Canfield Road (⊙Warren, Youngstown, OH; Sharon, PA)
Kmetz, Kimberlee J., (CV) '69 '94 C.980 B.A. L.8 J.D. [Ⓐ Harshman&B.] ⊙
Osborne, Glenn R., (BV) '61 '87 C.980 B.A. L.8 J.D. [Osborne,D.S.&R.]
Osborne, DeLaurentis, Sontich & Rafidi, Co. L.P.A., (BV) 100 Marwood Circle
Pecchio, Robert A., (BV) '56 '84 C.980 B.S.B.A. L.1187 J.D. 819 McKay Court
Rafidi, Mark A. '73 '98 C.610 B.B.A. L.851 J.D. [Osborne,D.S.&R.]
Rohrbaugh, Robert J., II, (CV) '73 '99 C.717 B.S. L.989 J.D. 4800 Market Street, Suite A
Schmidt, George A., (AV Ⓣ) '47 '72 C.188 B.A. L.930 J.D. DeBartolo Properties Mgmt., Inc.
Smith, Paul H., (BV) '24 '52 C&L.980 J.D. 8255 South Ave.
Sontich, Joseph P., Jr., (BV) '60 '86 C&L.93 A.B., J.D. [Osborne,D.S.&R.]
Sontich, Joseph P., Sr., (AV) '23 '49 C.980 A.B. L.930 J.D. [Osborne,D.S.&R.]
Tusek, Tim, (BV) '58 '83 C.980 B.A. L.150 J.D. 945 Windham Court, Suite 3
Vaughn, Jack R., (BV) '49 '77 C.294 B.A. L.7 J.D. 120 Marwood Cir
Wloch, Vincent J., (BV) '49 '74 C.107 B.S. L.8 J.D. 412 Boardman-Canfield Road
Zuckerman, Zvi Ariel '64 '91 Zuckerman Properties

BOWLING GREEN, * 29,636, *Wood Co.*

Bachman, Evelyn, (BV) '38 '62 C&L.607 B.A., J.D. 242 S. Main St.
Bachman, James W. '36 '63 C.97 B.A. L.607 J.D. Ret. Mun. J.‡
Baird, James A. '26 '57 C.477 B.A. L.851 J.D. 8505 Scotch Ridge‡
Bakies, Gregory Edward '60 '85 C.97 B.S. L.602 J.D. 224 E. Wooster St.
Baldwin, Allen R., (BV) '47 '78 C.97 B.A. L.851 J.D. P.O. Box 48
Bamburowski, Thomas J. '44 '75 C.97 B.S. L.851 J.D. 133 N. Prospect Street
Best, Norma Hatfield '18 '44 C&L.273 A.B., LL.B. 12698 Newton Rd.‡
Bevelhymer, Darlene P. '50 '87 C.610 B.S. L.851 J.D. 914 N. Prospect St.
Bishop, Gary Dean '59 '87 C.97 B.S. L.851 J.D. Chf. Asst. Pros. Atty.
Burton, Julie A. '70 '95 C.473 B.A. L.851 J.D. [Ⓐ Stearns&H.]

Calderon, Reina A. '58 '86 C.604 B.A. L.93 J.D.
(adm. in CT; not adm. in OH) Calderon Energy Co.
Callejas, Esteban R., (BV) ....'63 '89 C.1295 B.A. L.150 J.D. 1180 N. Main St.
Campbell, Craig W. ....'54 '90 C.203 B.S. L.851 J.D. Mag., Probate and Juv. Ct.
Cavitt, Valencia Grace ....'60 '96 C&L.851 B.A., J.D. P.O. Box 2595
Cheetwood, John S., (AV) ....'44 '69 C.228 A.B. L.608 J.D. [Cheetwood]

Cheetwood Law Offices, (AV)
300 North Main Street, 43402
Telephone: 419-352-4659 Fax: 419-354-4550
Email: Cheetwood.law@wcnet.org URL: http://www.wcnet.org/~jcheet/
John S. Cheetwood.
General Civil, Personal Injury, Probate, Estate Planning, Real Estate
Reference: Huntington National Bank.

See Professional Biographies, BOWLING GREEN, OHIO

Cody, David A., (CV) ....'55 '81 C.851 B.A. L.790 J.D. 224 E. Wooster St.
Coggin, Betty F., (BV) ....'43 '86 C.418 B.A. L.851 J.D. 406 Donbar Dr.
Coon, Scott T., (BV) ....'59 '84 C.150 B.A. L.607 J.D. [Rayle,M.&C.]
Crowley, Patrick, (BV) ....'28 '54 C.97 B.A. L.150 J.D. 133 N. Prospect St.
Davies, R. Nigel, (AV) ....'49 '76 C.051 L.851 J.D. [Davies&R.] ⊙

Davies & Ruck, PLL, (AV)
441 Frazee Avenue, Suite C, 43402 ⊙
Telephone: 419-287-3233 Fax: 419-287-3215
Email: ndaviesruck@aol.com URL: http://www.lawyers.com/davies&ruck
Members of Firm: R. Nigel Davies; J. Douglas Ruck.
General Civil Trial Litigation in all Local Courts, Estate and Tax Planning, Probate, Trusts, Real Estate Law and Development, Business Law, Corporations and Partnerships, Family Law, Personal Injury, Criminal Law and Traffic Violations.
Pemberville, Ohio Office: 427 W. College Ave., P.O. Box 412. Telephone: 419-287-3233. Fax: 419-287-3215.
Woodville, Ohio Office: 109 W. Main Street, 43469. Telephone: 419-849-2583. Fax: 419-849-3211.

See Professional Biographies, BOWLING GREEN, OHIO

DeCessna, Donald A. ....'28 '54 C&L.608 B.S., J.D. Com. Pleas J.
de la Serna, Arlen B. ....'65 '96 C.662 L.851 J.D. Comm. Pleas Ct.
DiMarzio, Dennis D. '52 '76 C.589 B.A. L.146 J.D.
(adm. in IL; not adm. in OH) Prof. of Law, Bowling Green Univ.
Dunipace, H. Richard, (BV) ....'20 '49 C.97 A.B. L.608 J.D. 415 W. Wooster St.
Dunipace, John M., (AV) ....'50 '75 C.97 B.S. L.851 J.D. [Marcin&D.]

Eastman & Smith Ltd.
(See Toledo)

Fech & Fech, L.L.C.
(See Toledo)

Footer, Nancy S. ....'57 '83 C.846 B.A. L.326 J.D. 308 McFall Center
Geer, Norman J., (AV) ....'44 '71 C.473 A.B. L.188 J.D. [Halleck&G.]
Halleck, Michael J., (AV) ....'44 '71 C.532 B.A. L.608 J.D. [Halleck&G.]
Halleck, Peter T., (BV) ....'46 '73 C.253 B.S. L.607 J.D. [Halleck]
Halleck & Geer, (AV) .... 105 North Main Street
Halleck Law Office, (BV) .... 107 E. Court St.
Hamm, Kathleen M., (BV) '58 '83
C.602 B.A. L.851 J.D. Chf. Pub. Def., Wood Co. Pub. Def. Off.
Hammer, James A., (BV) ....'58 '86 C.97 B.A. L.851 J.D. [Stearns&H.]
Hanna, Drew A., (BV) ....'47 '72 C.597 B.S. L.851 J.D. [Hanna&H.]
Hanna, Harold M., (AV) ....'46 '71 C.597 B.S. L.851 J.D. [Hanna&H.]

Hanna & Hanna, (AV)
Hanna Law Building, 700 North Main Street, P.O. Box 25, 43402-0025
Telephone: 419-352-6501 Fax: 419-352-7008
URL: http://www.hannaandhanna.com
Members of Firm: S. W. Bowman (1876-1957); Martin L. Hanna (1909-1994); Martin Shad Hanna (1940-2001); Harold M. Hanna; Drew A. Hanna.
General Civil Trial Litigation, Eminent Domain, Condemnation, Personal Injury, Wrongful Death, Automobile Accidents, Corporation, Wills and Probate, Trusts and Estates, Estate Planning, Medical and Legal Malpractice, Insurance, Real Estate Law, Family Law.
Local Counsel for: Dow Jones & Co., Inc. (Wall Street Journal); Norfolk & Southern Railway; Union Oil Co. of California; General Telephone Co. of Ohio; Nationwide Insurance Co.; Prudential Insurance Co.; Transamerica Insurance Group; Auto-Owners Insurance Co.; Mid-American National Bank & Trust Co.; Goodyear Tire & Rubber Co.

See Professional Biographies, BOWLING GREEN, OHIO

Heineman, Norman A. ....'48 '79 C.97 B.L.S. L.851 J.D. Asst. Pros Atty.
Hennessy, Nicholas J., (BV⊕) '57 '83 C.532 B.S. L.608 J.D.
(adm. in FL; not adm. in OH) 440 Student Servs. Bldg.‡
Heringhaus, Pamela A. Kaufman, (BV) .....'53 '81 C.259 B.A. L.851 J.D. [☒ Stearns&H.]
Hock, Jerome ....'30 '58 C.97 L.607 J.D. 130 E. Washington
Holmes, Linda F., (CV) '47 '83 C.945 A.B. L.851 J.D.
Chf. Civil Asst. Pros. Atty., Wood Co. Pros. Off.
Howe-Gebers, Gwen K., (BV) ....'63 '89 C.610 B.S. L.851 J.D. Asst. Co. Pros.
Huffman, Diane Rausch, (BV) ....'52 '82 C.473 B.S. L.851 J.D. [Spitler,H.Y.&N.]
Huffman, Rex H., (BV) ....'53 '79 C.473 B.S. L.851 J.D. [Spitler,H.Y.&N.] ⊙
Jones, Wendell R., (CV) ...... '32 '86 C.608 B.S. Ed. L.851 J.D. 1308 Bourgogne Avenue
Kelley, Michael B. ....'70 '98 113 N. Main St.
Kelsey, Reeve W. ....'48 '76 C.902 B.A. L.228 J.D. Com. Pleas J.
Kremer, Erica H. ....'70 '96 C.910 B.A. L.930 J.D. Jud. Law Clk., Com. Pleas Ct.
Kurfess, Charles F. ....'30 '58 C.97 B.A. L.608 J.D. Com. Pleas J.
Latta, Robert E., (CV) ....'56 '81 C.97 B.A. L.851 J.D. State Sen.
Lee, Jerry W., (CV) ....'44 '78 C.97 B.S.Ed. L.851 J.D. 121 Wooster St.
Marcin, Chester H., (BV) ....'44 '69 C&L.851 B.B.A., J.D. [Marcin&D.]
Marcin & Dunipace, (AV) .... 440 E. Poe Rd.
Marsh, C. Richard, (AV) ....'— '55 C.97 B.S. L.150 J.D. [Marsh&M.] ⊙
Marsh, Michael J., (AV) ....'— '79 C.97 B.B.A. L.608 J.D. [Marsh&M.]

Marsh & Marsh, (AV)
249 South Main Street, 43402-0347 ⊙
Telephone: 419-352-2518
C. Richard Marsh; Michael J. Marsh.
General Civil Practice. Commercial, Corporation, Banking, Probate and Estate Planning, Real Estate Law. Abstracting.
Representative Client: Sky Bank; Thayer Chevrolet-Toyota, Inc.; Village of Grand Rapids; Palmer Brothers Concrete, Inc.; City of Bowling Green; Eagle Ridge Development Co.; Preferred Properties Co.; Great Lakes Ford.
Agent and Approved Attorneys for: The Ohio Bar Title Insurance Co.; Port Lawrence Title & Trust Co.

See Professional Biographies, BOWLING GREEN, OHIO

Matthews, Frederic E., (BV) ....'55 '80 C.1505 B.A. L.851 J.D. [Rayle,M.&C.]
Maurer, Robert W., (BV) ....'43 '68 C.97 B.S. L.851 J.D. 445 E. Wooster St.
Mayberry, Alan R., (BV) ....'54 '79 C.97 B.S. L.851 J.D. Pros. Atty.
McOmber, Robert A. ....'51 '76 C.97 B.S. L.477 J.D. 420 Knollwood Dr.
Middleton, Staten T., (CV) ....'64 '93 C.97 B.A. L.1194 J.D. [Middleton,R.&N.]
Middleton, Thomas S., (AV) ....'37 '63 C.97 L.607 J.D. [Middleton,R.&N.]
Middleton, Roebke & Nelson, (AV) .... 521 N. Main St.
Mota, Sue Ann ....'57 '83 C.97 B.A. L.851 J.D. Bowling Green State Univ.‡
Moyer, Donald W. ....'29 '78 C.124 B.S. L.851 J.D. 14611 Sand Ridge Rd.‡
Nelson, Jeffrey A., (BV) ....'52 '79 C.207 B.A. L.477 J.D. [Middleton,R.&N.]
Newlove, John F., (BV) ....'59 '84 C.607 B.A. L.201 J.D. 224 E. Wooster St.
Newlove, Megan E., (BV) ....'70 '95 C.473 B.S. L.851 J.D. [Spitler,H.Y.&N.]
Ohanian, Aram Matthew ....'68 '94 C.475 B.S. L.851 J.D. Co. Pub. Def.
Peters, Lora Dawn ....'72 '97 C.207 B.A. L.150 J.D. Common Pleas Ct. 4
Pollex, Robert C. ....'47 '74 C&L.851 B.S., J.D. Com. Pleas J.
Pomeroy, Todd A., Law Offices of ...... '68 '98 C.27 B.A. L.607 J.D. 113 N. Main Street
Potter, Albert L., II, (BV) ....'52 '82 C.97 B.S.B.A. L.851 J.D. 107 E. Oak St.
Rayle, Max E., (AV) ....'49 '76 C.253 B.A. L.851 J.D. [Rayle,M.&C.]
Rayle, Matthews & Coon, (AV) .... 100 S. Main St.
Reddin, Evelyn ....'24 '49 C.604 A.B. L.477 J.D. P.O. Box 796‡
Reisner, John Richard ....'52 '81 C&L.851 B.A., J.D. 221 South Church St.

Ritter, Robinson, McCready & James
(See Toledo)

Roebke, Harry G., (AV) ....'15 '42 C.97 A.B. L.477 J.D. [Middleton,R.&N.] ‡
Ruck, J. Douglas ....'67 '97 C.97 B.S. L.851 J.D. [Davies&R.] (⊙Pemberville)
Schmidt, Richard A., (BV) ....'55 '86 C.97 B.A. L.851 J.D. 133 N. Prospect St.
Shultz, Jacqueline M. '71 '97
C.201 B.A. L.608 J.D. Asst. Co. Pros. Atty., Wood Co. Pros. Off.
Smith, C. J. Keller '67 '98 C.477 B.S. L.602 J.D.
(adm. in MI; not adm. in OH) Asst. Coun., Sky Financial Group, Inc.
Souder, W. Granger, Jr., (BV) '60 '86 C.967 B.A. L.851 J.D.
Exec. V.P. & Gen. Coun., Sky Financial Grp., Inc.
Spengler, Patricia Wise ....'61 '85 C.97 B.A.C. L.851 J.D. Sr. V.P., Mid Am, Inc.
Spitler, Daniel T., (AV) ....'39 '65 C.608 B.S. L.607 J.D. [Spitler,H.Y.&N.]
Spitler, Robert E., (AV) ....'49 '74 C.608 B.A. L.276 J.D. [Spitler,H.Y.&N.]
Spitler, Steven L., (CV) ....'67 '96 C.610 B.A. L.607 J.D. [Spitler,H.Y.&N.]

Spitler, Huffman, Yoon & Newlove, LLP, (AV)
131 East Court Street, 43402-2495 ⊙
Telephone: 419-352-2535 Fax: 419-353-8728
Email: svh@shynlaw.com URL: http://www.shynlaw.com
Emmett V. Spitler (1911-1995). Members of Firm: Daniel T. Spitler; Robert E. Spitler; Rex H. Huffman; Diane Rausch Huffman; Steven L. Spitler; Mimi S. Yoon; Megan E. Newlove.
General Civil Practice in all Courts. Corporation, Business, Personal Injury, Wrongful Death, Product Liability, Medical Malpractice, Probate and Estate Planning, Administrative and Real Estate Law, Public Utility, Trials and Appeals, Bankruptcy, Criminal Defense, Family Law, Criminal Law.
Representative Clients: First Federal Bank; Prudential Insurance Company of America; The Mutual Benefit Life Insurance Co.; John Hancock Mutual Life Insurance Co.; Equitable Life Assurance Society of the U.S.; Minnesota Mutual Life Insurance Co.; Wood County Regional Water and Sewer District.
Rossford, Ohio Office: 932 Dixie Highway. Telephone: 419-666-7130.

See Professional Biographies, BOWLING GREEN, OHIO

Stearns, Jodie L., (BV) ....'58 '84 C&L.608 B.S., J.D. [Stearns&H.]
Stearns & Hammer, (BV) .... 112 East Oak Street

Steltenpohl, James & Menacher, Co., LPA
(See Toledo)

Stevens, Bruce B. ....'73 '99 C.91 B.A. L.607 J.D. [☒ Middleton,R.&N.]
Teet, Thomas E., (BV) ....'59 '88 C&L.851 B.B.A., J.D. P.O. Box 523
Tolles, Mark D., (CV) ....'57 '81 C&L.851 B.A., J.D. 920 1/2 N. Main St.
Weinandy, James R., (CV) ....'61 '89 C.608 B.S. L.150 J.D. 1180 N. Main St.
Williamson, Gale E. ....'28 '64 C.97 B.S. L.851 J.D. Ret. Com. Pleas J.‡
Woessner, David E. ....'59 '85 C.97 B.A. L.851 J.D. Juv. Ct. J.
Yoon, Mimi S. ....'66 '92 C.788 B.A. L.608 J.D. [Spitler,H.Y.&N.]
Zografides, Christopher Adam .... '72 '00 C.980 B.S.A.S. L.607 J.D. [☒ T.A.Pomeroy]

BRATENAHL, 1,356, *Cuyahoga Co.*

Chancellor, Carl E., (AV) ....'29 '54 C.608 B.A. L.930 LL.B. One Bratenahl Pl.‡
Coghill, George J. ....'46 '75 C.363 B.S. L.1003 J.D. 10211 Lakeshore Blvd. (Pat.)
Schneider, Beverly, (BV) ....'34 '61 C&L.800 B.A., LL.B. 2 Bratenahl Pl.
Tyler, Thomas Scott ....'64 '88 C.97 B.A. L.1003 J.D. U.S. Dept. of Defense

BRECKSVILLE, 13,382, *Cuyahoga Co.*

Abookire, Charles A., Jr. ....'40 '67 C.610 A.B. L.930 J.D. 12929 Chippewa Road
Adams, Gary S., (BV) '53 '83
C.528 B.A. L.1003 J.D. Greater Cleveland Auto Dealers' Assn.
Baker, Wm. Joseph ....'74 '00 C.591 B.S. L.1003 J.D. 8223 Brecksville Rd., Ste. 201
Balzano, Laura A., (BV) ....'55 '80 C.161 B.A. L.1003 J.D. 8927 Brecksville Rd.

Baran, Piper, Tarkowsky, Fitzgerald & Theis Co., L.P.A., (AV)
8748 Brecksville Road, Suite 200, 44141 ⊙
Telephone: 440-746-1177 Fax: 440-746-9637
URL: http://www.baranlaw.com
John P. Calandra; Janet L. Miggins; Rose A. Patti.
General Civil Practice. Trials in all Courts. Insurance Defense, Corporate, Family Law, Estate Planning, Personal Injury, Products Liability and Construction Law. Commercial Litigation. Suretyship. Environmental and Governmental Liability. Professional Liability, Worker's Compensation.

See Professional Biographies, BRECKSVILLE, OHIO

Beck, Janet R., (AV) ....'52 '77 C.228 A.B. L.930 J.D. 7650 Chippewa Road
Berman, Bernard '46 '96 C.415 A.B. L.36 J.D.
(adm. in AZ; not adm. in OH; Pat.) Patent Coun., Promerus, LLC

Bernard Law Firm, The
(See Cleveland)

Calandra, John P., (BV) ....'39 '64 C.930 B.A. L.477 LL.B. [Baran,P.T.F.&T.]
Carson, Gayle Joan, (BV) ....'49 '76 C.608 B.A. L.1003 J.D. 7023 Mill Rd.
Castro, Michael M. ....'55 '80 C.97 B.S.B.A. L.608 J.D. Pres., MM Castro and Assoc.
Clark, Stanley M. ....'16 '46 C.124 B.S. L.930 LL.B. 8049 Robin Ln. (Pat.)‡
Clegg, Christopher R. ....'57 '84 C.112 B.A. L.276 J.D. Noveon Inc.
Collins, Forrest L. ....'45 '73 C.959 B.S. L.436 J.D. P.O. Box 41040 (Pat.)
Dacek, James S., (BV) ....'51 '76 C.97 B.L.S. L.1003 J.D. 6696 Farview Rd.
Day, William J., (BV) .....'47 '79 C.610 B.B.A. L.161 J.D. 8748 Brecksville Rd., Ste. 227
Donaldson, Michael R. ....'56 '85 C.150 B.A. L.1003 J.D. 4330 East Boston Road
Einhart, V. Jay, (AV) ....'22 '48 C&L.930 B.B.A., LL.B. 4516 East Royalton Road
Eldridge, Wendell Craig ....'62 '88 C.363 B.A. L.608 J.D. 8221 Brecksville Road
Fittipaldi, Frank N., Jr. ....'24 '52 C.608 B.A. L.930 LL.B. 11523 Cherokee Ln.
Guarnieri, William T., (BV) '38 '62 C&L.608 B.S., J.D.
8180 Brecksville Road (RTE 21) (⊙Cleveland)
Hogan, Douglas J. ....'54 '88 C.363 B.A. L.851 J.D. 6896 Miller Road
Kovacs, Julius E., (AV) ....'39 '67 C.381 B.S. L.1003 J.D. [J.E.Kovacs&Assoc.]
Kovacs, Julius E., & Associates Co., L.P.A., (AV) .... 8227 Brecksville Road
Laurie, Charles R., Jr., (BV) ....'49 '74 C.201 B.A. L.1003 J.D. 8180 Brecksville Rd.
Lukas, Henry F., Jr. ....'27 '60 C.951 B.A. L.1003 LL.B. 6600 Farview Rd.
Malone, Laurie A. ....'63 '97 C.161 B.S. L.1003 J.D. [Malone M.]
Malone Mediation .... 8180 Brecksville Road

Marczely, Bernadette A. '45 '95
C.848 B.A. L.1003 J.D. Corp. Coun., Education Personnel Services
McBride, Judith Bliss '59 '86 C.363 B.A. L.930 J.D. 7886 Cambridge Dr.
Miggins, Janet L. '47 '81 C.8 B.A. L.161 J.D. [Baran,P.T.F.&T.]
Motiska, Robert J. '44 '69 C.659 B.S. L.276 J.D. 9300 Mercer Ln.
Nemer, Charles Anthony '58 '83 C&L.734 B.A., J.D. [C.A.Nemer]
Nemer, Charles A., Co., LPA 8180 Brecksville Road
Onders, Kathleen Donovan '69 '94 C.97 B.S.B.A. L.1003 J.D. 9994 Gatewood Dr.
Patti, Rose A., (BV) '49 '91 C.161 B.A. L.1003 J.D. [Baran,P.T.F.&T.]
Pesek, Fred A. '29 '59 C.610 B.S.C. L.1003 LL.B. 9068 Highland Dr.
Ronyak, David M., (AV) '46 '75
C.930 B.S.Ch.E. L.8 J.D. Sr. Coun., Intell Prop., Goodrich Corp. (Pat.)
Shively, Arlene T. '64 '90 C.973 A.B. L.201 J.D. Cleveland Reg. Coun., Vet. Adm.
Shurell, Carolyn J. '44 '80 C.381 B.G.S. L.7 J.D. 10000 Brecksville Rd.
Wadsworth, Roger A., (AV) '37 '63 C.610 B.S. L.607 LL.B. 8927 Brecksville Rd.
Weiler, Kevin P., (AV) '48 '79 C.436 A.B. L.1003 J.D. [Weiler&Assoc.]
Weiler and Associates, (AV) 8920 Brecksville Rd.

BREMEN, 1,265, *Fairfield Co.*

Mowry, Kathy S., (BV) '52 '81 C.610 B.A. L.117 J.D. Spec. Asst. Pros. Atty.

BREWSTER, 2,307, *Stark Co.*

Callison, William A. '45 '77 C.813 B.A. L.276 J.D.
(adm. in IL; not adm. in OH)
Vice President Law & Government Relations, Wheeling & Lake Erie Railway Co.

BRIDGEPORT, 2,186, *Belmont Co.*

Archer, Kelley, (AV) '22 '50 C.674 A.B. L.309 LL.B. 332 Main St.
Davies, Albert E., III, (BV) '63 '92 C.473 B.S. L.851 J.D. [Thomas,F.M.H.&D.]
Fregiato, Frank A., (BV) '52 '77 C&L.608 B.A., J.D. [Thomas,F.M.H.&D.]
Gagin, Christopher J., (BV) '67 '94 C.477 B.G.S. L.7 J.D. [Ⓐ Thomas,F.M.H.&D.]
Sustersic, Edward G. '43 '69 C.610 B.B.A. L.229 J.D. [Sustersic]
Sustersic, Jean R. M. '44 '69 C&L.229 B.A., J.D. [Sustersic]
Sustersic Law Offices 894 Nat. Rd.
Thomas, Michael R., (AV) '18 '52 C.608 B.A. L.477 J.D. [Thomas,F.M.H.&D.] ‡
Thomas, Fregiato, Myser, Hanson & Davies, (BV) 320 Howard Street
Winzenreid, James Ernest '51 '87 C.920 A.B. L.229 J.D.
(adm. in PA; not adm. in OH) 47 Overbrook Dr.

BRIMFIELD, 3,248, *Portage Co.*

Salerno, Mark A. '58 '83 C.381 B.A. L.7 J.D. 330 Tallmadge Rd.
Weill, Leo '29 '72 C.4 B.S. L.8 J.D. 3853 Morley Drive

BROADVIEW HEIGHTS, 15,967, *Cuyahoga Co.*

Amari, Raymond R. '26 '54 C.62 B.A. L.1003 J.D. 1495 Windrow Lane‡
Bates, James C. '72 '97 C.473 B.A. L.8 J.D. 20 Eagle Valley Ct.
Boulas, James Emmanouel '71 '98 C.161 B.A. L.1003 J.D. [Boulas,J.E.]
Boulas, James E., Co., LPA 7914 Broadview Road
Burke, James F., Jr., (AV) '49 '77 C.610 B.B.A. L.1003 J.D. [Burke&H.]
Burke & Horrigan, (AV) 3505 E Royalton Rd
Conlon, James E., (AV) '51 '86 C.875 B.A. L.1003 J.D. Secy. & Gen. Coun., Stein Inc.
Hammer, Lisa A. '71 '98 C&L.851 B.A., J.D. 20 Eagle Valley
Horrigan, John J., (AV) '48 '75 C.116 B.S. L.1003 J.D. [Burke&H.]
Jackson, Dennis C. '57 '81 C.97 B.L.S. L.851 J.D. [D.C.Jackson]
Jackson, Dennis C., Co., L.P.A. 20 Eagle Valley
Kennedy, James David '63 '91 C.363 B.S.B.A. L.989 J.D. [Ⓐ D.C.Jackson]
Kluge, Graig E. '72 '97 C.528 B.A. L.930 J.D. [G.E.Kluge]
Kluge, Graig E., Co., L.P.A 1000 W. Wallings Rd., Ste. A
Kozelka, Frank C., (BV) '10 '37 C.363 B.S. L.607 LL.B. [Kozelka&K.]
Kozelka, Kay J., (BV) '51 '78 C.599 B.A. L.7 J.D. [Kozelka&K.]
Kozelka & Kozelka, (BV) 2207 E. Wallings Rd.
Kucha, Helen Anne, (BV) '44 '76 C.381 B.S. L.7 J.D. 180 E. Royalton
Landoll, Richard Wayne '64 '95 C.97 M.A. L.930 J.D. [R.W.Landoll]
Landoll, Richard W. 3505 E. Royalton Road, Suite 165
Leneghan, David M., Esq., Law Offices of '67 '93
C&L.930 B.A., J.D. 200 Treeworth Blvd., Ste. 200
Mauk, Cecil P. '11 '45 C.251 B.B.A. L.161 LL.B. 1401 W. Wallings Rd.‡
McGraw, Amanda R. '77 '05 C.347 B.A. L.989 J.D. [Ⓐ M.Motylinski]
Motylinski, Michael '76 '01 C.8 B.A. L.124 J.D. [M.Motylinski]

Motylinski, Michael, The Law Offices of
1000 West Wallings Road, Suite A, 44147
Telephone: 440-746-1000 Fax: 440-746-1003 URL: http://www.motylinskilaw.com
Email: mm@motylinski-law.com URL: http://www.motylinski.com
Michael Motylinski;—Amanda R. McGraw.
Business Law, Real Estate, Estate Planning, Collections, Criminal.

See Professional Biographies, BROADVIEW HEIGHTS, OHIO

Nosan, Bernard J. '37 '73 C.608 B.S. L.1003 J.D. P.O. Box 275
O'Connor, Debra Lynn '70 '95 C.1208 B.A. L.201 J.D. 1010 Orchard Ln.
Pollock, Ross H. '56 '88 C.8 B.A.Ed. L.7 J.D. 2069 Valley Park Circle
Ruffa, Vincenzo, (CV) '70 '94 C.754 B.A. L.425 J.D. 1000 Wallings Rd., Ste. A
Shearer, Mark Stephen '70 '96 C.363 B.A. L.1003 J.D. 8193 Avery Rd., Ste. 201
Tararin, Alexander A. '59 '98 L.124 J.D. 1518 W. Royalton Rd., Unit 6

BROOKFIELD, 1,288, *Trumbull Co.*

Hoffman, James E., III, (BV) '51 '76 C.608 B.A. L.7 J.D. [Hoffman&W.]
Hoffman and Walker Co., L.P.A., (BV) 7553 Warren Sharon Rd.
Kokor, Robert Charles '68 '93 C.934 B.A. L.851 J.D. [R.C.Kokor]
Kokor, Robert C. 394 St. Rt. 7, S.E.
O'Brien, James A., (BV) '40 '65 C.894 B.A. L.597 J.D. 7337 Warren-Sharon Road
Paroz, Roger C., (CV) '36 '80 C.980 B.S. L.7 J.D. P.O. Box 67
Walker, Elwood M., (BV) '44 '78 C.980 A.B. L.607 J.D. [Hoffman&W.]

BROOKLYN, 11,586, *Cuyahoga Co.*

Beyerle, John J. '22 '50 C&L.602 B.S., J.D. 4664 Southwood Dr.‡
Gibbons, Jason Matthew '65 '91
C.62 B.A. L.1003 J.D. Corp. Coun., Arrow International, Inc.
Graves, Marco E. '50 '92 C.381 B.A. L.1003 J.D. 4758 Ridge Rd., Ste. 116

BROOKLYN HEIGHTS, 1,558, *Cuyahoga Co.*

Holder, Timothy D. '42 '77 C.608 B.A. L.930 J.D. UAW-GM Legal Servs. Plan
Janco, David J. '60 '89 C.161 B.A. L.1003 J.D. UAW Legal Servs. PLAN
Keenon, Una H. R. '33 '75 C.832 B.A. L.161 J.D. UAW-GM Legal Servs. Plan
Moses, Barry W., (AV) '55 '81
C.610 B.A. L.851 J.D. Gen. Coun., Safeguard Properties, Inc.
Robusto, Michael A. '55 '79 C.363 A.B. L.1003 J.D. UAW-GM Legal Servs. Plan
Salemi, Alexandria Elizabeth '68 '99
C.161 L.7 General Counsel, Safeguard Properties, Inc.
Wenneman, Ann F. '55 '82 C.363 B.A. L.1003 J.D. UAW-GM Legal Servs. Plan

BROOK PARK, 21,218, *Cuyahoga Co.*

Arciaga, Arthur A. '49 '81 C.124 B.S. L.161 J.D. P.O. Box 42104
Chrostowski-Otto, Rebecca '74 '99 C.62 B.A. L.989 J.D. 6434 Edgehurst Dr.
Krantz, Timothy J., (AV) '54 '81 C.1260 B.A. L.1003 J.D. 5600 Henry Ford Blvd.
Mason, Cynthia Aleksa '50 '77 C&L.930 B.A., J.D. Ford Motor Co.
Mudry, Joey J. '64 '97 C.62 B.A. L.608 J.D. 6215 Sylvia Dr.
O'Connor, Adina C. '69 '97 C.161 B.A. L.1003 J.D. City Comr.
Otto, Louis A., Jr. '10 '36 C.201 A.B. L.930 J.D. 6360 Elmdale Rd.
Perry, Leonard C. '26 '51
C.930 B.A. L.1003 J.D. CEO, Aerospace Design & Fabrication, Inc.
Ramos, Anita M., (BV) '55 '91 C.62 B.A. L.989 J.D. 5600 Henry Ford Blvd.
Zielinski, Vernon J. '56 '83 C.851 B.B.A. L.1003 J.D. 6068 Middlebrook Blvd.

BROOKVILLE, 5,289, *Montgomery Co.*

Gilbert, B. Eugene '48 '92 C.235 B.S. L.117 J.D. 475 Arlington Road
Guenther, Vanessa L., (BV) '41 '84 C.1208 B.S. L.201 J.D. 715 Arlington Road

BRUNSWICK, 33,388, *Medina Co.*

Brobst, Lorie K., (CV) '64 '94 C.930 B.A. L.1003 J.D. 3695 Center Rd.
Clark, Amy L. '67 '92 C.823 B.A. L.608 J.D. 51 Clearwater Dr.
Conway, Michael Terrence, Esq., Attorney and Counselor at Law '61 '92
C.1119 B.S. L.8 J.D. 180 Aster Place
Deliman, Scott M. '69 '98 C.62 B.A. L.1003 J.D. [Ⓐ R.Tinl&Assoc.]
Edmunds, J. Timothy '48 '82 C.381 B.B.A. L.161 J.D. 1080 Sub Station Rd. T
Faber, Edward M. '42 '74 C.215 B.Ch.E. L.1003 J.D. 4626 Aldersyde Cir.
Hay, Walter '28 '59 C.8 L.7 LL.B. 719 Hadcock Road
Hopkins, Russell A. '67 '94 C.463 B.A. L.161 J.D. 3660 Center Rd., Ste. 359
Kaminsky, Michael P. '53 '79 C.62 B.A. L.1003 J.D. 1149 Krndia Ct.
Kray, Paul J., (CV) '65 '91 C.97 B.S.B.A. L.930 J.D. [Laribee,H.&K.] (⊙Medina)
Laribee, Hertrick & Kray, (BV) 111 Pearl Rd. (⊙Lodi, Medina)
McKinney, Karin Haas '57 '86 C.161 B.B.A. L.1003 J.D. 4628 Dogwood Dr.
Neely, Kermit K. '18 '61 C.363 L.1003 J.D. 1583 S. Carpenter Rd.‡
Porter, John N., Law Office, (CV) '48 '75 C.1062 B.A. L.1003 J.D. 1212 Pearl Road
Relic, Grant D., (BV) '53 '78 C.970 B.A. L.1003 J.D. 3511 Center Rd.

Riehl, David S., (BV) '48 '74 C.608 B.A. L.1003 J.D.
3695 Center Road, 44212
Telephone: 330-273-3450 Telecopier: 330-225-9770
Email: dsr@davidsriehlatty.com URL: http://www.lawyers.com/davidsriehlatty
Domestic Relations, Family Law, Divorce, Child Custody, Adoption Law, Premarital Agreements, Real Estate, Commercial Real Estate, Residential Real Estate, Small Business Law, Business Organization, Contracts, Probate, Estate Planning, Trust Law, Wills, Elder Care, Personal Injury, Automobile Accidents and Injuries, Negligence, Criminal Law, Driving While Intoxicated, Traffic Violations, Civil Practice.

See Professional Biographies, BRUNSWICK, OHIO

Tinl, Robert T., (BV) '49 '75 C.608 B.S. L.1003 J.D. [R.Tinl&Assoc.]
Tinl, Robert, & Associates, (BV) 3695 Center Road

BRYAN, * 8,348, *Williams Co.*

Ames, Herbert K. '12 '37 C.472 L.608 1112 Westfield Ave.‡
Bird, Steven R. '53 '84 C.72 B.A. L.201 J.D. Prob. & Juv. Ct. J.
Bish, William A., (BV) '40 '65 C&L.602 B.A., J.D. [Bish,R.B.&T.]
Bish, Roth, Butler & Thompson, Ltd., (AV) 1210 West High Street
Boehk, Robert P. '60 '85 C.607 B.A.B.S. L.851 J.D. Erie Construction Co.
Breininger, Ryan S. '72 '99 C.313 B.S. L.851 J.D. [Newcomer,S.S.&B.]
Butler, Charles C., (BV) '63 '92 C.347 B.S. L.851 J.D. [Bish,R.B.&T.]
Duggan, Paul H., (CV) '59 '93 C.602 B.A. L.851 J.D. [Duggan]
Duggan Law Office Co. LPA, (CV) 1426 E. High Street
Gallagher, Karen K., (BV) '61 '86 C.97 B.S. L.851 J.D. [Gallagher,S.&Y.]
Gallagher, Ralph W., (AV) '41 '70 C.608 B.S. L.851 J.D. [Gallagher,S.&Y.]

Gallagher, Stelzer & Yosick, Ltd., (AV)
216 South Lynn Street, 43506
Telephone: 419-636-3166 Fax: 419-636-5743
URL: http://www.nwohiolaw.com
Members of Firm: Frederick R. Parker (1907-1980); Gibson L. Fenton (1904-1994); Ralph W. Gallagher; J. T. Stelzer; Karen K. Gallagher; Kirk E. Yosick.
General Trial Practice. (Personal Injury, Wrongful Death and Commercial), Corporate, Probate and Estate Planning, Real Estate, Criminal Law, Domestic Relations, Trials and Appeals, Mediation.

See Professional Biographies, BRYAN, OHIO

Gretick, Anthony L. '36 '64 C&L.597 A.B., J.D. Com. Pleas J.
Grocki, Dale M., (CV) '57 '91 C&L.851 B.B.A., J.D. 233 W. Wilson
Hollin, Kimberly Joann Saylor, (CV) '62 '89 C.973 B.S. L.150 J.D. 117 W. Butler St.
Kiacz, Joseph R. '46 '73 C.201 B.A. L.1340 J.D. Mun. J.
Newcomer, Arthur S., (AV) '17 '41 C.317 B.S. L.607 LL.B. 117 W. Maple St.‡
Newcomer, David C., (AV) '47 '73 C.373 B.A. L.1065 J.D. [Newcomer,S.S.&B.]
Newcomer, Shaffer, Spangler & Breininger, (AV)
117 West Maple Street (⊙Montpelier)
Parker, Frederick B. '37 '64 C&L.477 B.A., J.D. Ret. Mun. J.
Query, Cecil A. '32 '62 C&L.879 A.B., LL.B.
(adm. in IN; not adm. in OH) 307 Orchard Hills Dr.‡
Rigdon, Harry J. '31 '66 C.473 B.S.B.A. L.851 J.D. Prob. J.
Roth, Craig L., (AV) '51 '76 C.203 B.A. L.851 J.D. [Bish,R.B.&T.]
Shaffer, John S. '57 '81 C.607 B.A. L.608 J.D. [Newcomer,S.S.&B.]
Shaffer, Michael A., (BV) '65 '90 C.97 B.S. L.851 J.D. [Newcomer,S.S.&B.]
Shaffer, Wayne E., (AV) '22 '49 C&L.607 A.B., LL.B. [Newcomer,S.S.&B.]
Spangler, Michael W., (BV) '59 '86 C.395 B.A. L.790 J.D. [Newcomer,S.S.&B.] ⊙
Stelzer, J. T., (BV) '55 '81 C.608 B.S. L.150 J.D. [Gallagher,S.&Y.]
Thompson, Ryan S. '74 '04 C.97 B.S. L.851 J.D. [Bish,R.B.&T.]
Thompson, Thomas A., (CV) '72 '97 C.999 B.B.A. L.851 J.D. [Bish,R.B.&T.]
Wilson, Robert G. '26 '53 C.477 A.B. L.851 J.D. Ret. Com. Pleas J.‡
Yosick, Kirk E., (CV) '65 '98 C&L.851 B.B.A., J.D. [Gallagher,S.&Y.]

BUCYRUS, * 13,224, *Crawford Co.*

Brown, Robert L. '20 '48 C.477 A.B. L.930 LL.B. 221 S. Poplar St.‡

Brown, Bemiller, Murray, McIntyre, Vetter & Heck, L.L.P.
(See Mansfield)

Cory, David R., (BV) '56 '82 C&L.607 B.A., J.D. [Cory&C.]
Cory, Richard L., (BV) '27 '51 C&L.607 LL.B. [Cory&C.]
Cory & Cory, P.L.L., (BV) 221 S. Poplar St.
Eckstein, Steven D. '46 '72 C&L.607 B.A., J.D. Prob.-Juv. Ct. J.
Flegm, Stanley E., (BV) '48 '73 C.608 B.S. L.117 J.D. Crawford Co. Pros. Off.
Gernert, Terry L., (BV) '53 '79 C.313 B.S. L.851 J.D. [Kennedy,P.H.&G.]

Griebling, Eric H., (BV) .... '55 '79 C.97 B.A. L.150 J.D. [Spurlock,S.P.G.&M.]
Hoeffel, Paul E., (BV) .... '45 '73 C.97 B.S. L.851 J.D. [Kennedy,P.H.&G.]
Holm, Mary Shafer, (BV) .... '50 '77 C.737 B.A. L.607 J.D. Mag., Com. Pleas Ct.
Kennedy, Michael A., (BV) .... '41 '66 C&L.607 B.S., J.D. 107 E. Mansfield
Kennedy, Purdy, Hoeffel & Gernert, LLC, (AV)
107 Washington Square The Farmers Citizens Bank Building
Kimerline, Nelfred G. .... '35 '64 C.117 A.B. L.37 LL.B. Com. Pleas J.
Leuthold, Sean E. .... '66 '95 C.91 B.A. L.7 J.D. 1317 E. Mansfield St.
Leuthold, Shane M. .... '69 '98 C.91 B.A. L.8 J.D. 1317 E. Mansfield St.
McBride, G. Scott, (BV) .... '61 '86 C.610 B.A. L.607 J.D. [Spurlock,S.P.G.&M.]
Murphy, Patrick T., (BV) .... '55 '80 C.608 B.S. L.851 J.D. 153 Washington Sq.
Neff, Robert Clark, (BV) .... '21 '50 C.970 A.B. L.607 LL.B. Law Dir. [Neff]
Neff, Robert Clark, Jr., (AV) .... '56 '83 C.381 B.A. L.851 J.D. [Neff]
Neff Law Firm, The, Ltd., (AV) .... 840 South Sandusky Avenue
Nicholson, Thomas G. .... '56 '88 C.1044 B.A. L.161 J.D. 438 E. Lucas St.
Pry, James W., II .... '45 '71 C.611 B.A. L.607 J.D. [Spurlock,S.P.G.&M.]
Sears, John D., Jr., (BV) .... '24 '50 C&L.607 LL.B. [Spurlock,S.P.G.&M.]
Sharrock, Kennedy Clare .... '40 '74 C.608 B.A. L.851 J.D. Mun. J.
Spiegel, John L., (CV) .... '49 '75 C.608 B.A. L.930 J.D. 222 W. Charles
Spurlock, Sears, Pry, Griebling & McBride, (BV) .... 120 North Lane Street
Starkey, Brad S., (BV) .... '62 '87 C.607 B.A. L.851 J.D. [Starkey&S.]
Starkey & Stoll, Ltd., (BV) .... 208 S. Walnut St.
Stoll, Geoffrey L., (BV) .... '58 '87 C.608 B.S.L.A. L.851 J.D. [Starkey&S.]
Strauch, C. Randolph .... '41 '73 C.608 B.C.E. L.117 J.D. Courthouse‡
Walker, Steven Hunter .... '49 '76 C.885 B.A. L.607 J.D. Crawford Co. CSEA
Wead, Edward R. .... '40 '66 C.97 B.S. L.851 J.D. 107 E. Mansfield Street
Whitaker, Lowell D. '50 '86 C.608 B.S. L.117 J.D.
Corp. Coun. & V.P.-Legal Affairs, Ohio Mutual Ins. Group
Wiseman, Russell B., (BV) .... '46 '75 C.608 B.S. L.117 J.D. Pros. Atty.

BURTON, 1,450, *Geauga Co.*

Cook, Jerold S., (BV) .... '29 '54 C.659 B.S. L.930 LL.B. Cook Legal Clinic
Ford, Robert B. .... '21 '49 C.608 A.B. L.930 LL.B. Ret. Com. Pleas J.
Forstag, Harvey Lewis .... '46 '80 C.608 B.A. L.179 J.D [Forstag F.]
Forstag Funds .... 11480 Robin Wood Ln.
Fuhry, David L., Law Office of, (BV) .... '51 '77 C.381 B.A. L.608 J.D. P.O. Box 345
Fuhry, Kenneth A., Law Office of, (BV) ..... '52 '78 C.473 B.A. L.930 J.D. P.O. Box 345

BYESVILLE, 2,435, *Guernsey Co.*

Keith, Mary Beth .... '75 '01 C.532 B.A. L.608 J.D. [M.B.keith]
keith, Mary B. .... P.O. Box 82

CADIZ, * 3,308, *Harrison Co.*

Beetham, Mark, (BV) .... '51 '75 C.608 B.S. L.976 J.D. [Beetham]
Beetham Law Offices, (BV) .... 146 S. Main Street
Collica, Raymond C., II .... '71 '96 C.896 B.A. L.608 J.D. Asst. Pros.
Hervey, Thomas S., (CV) .... '72 '97 C.608 B.S.Ed. L.851 J.D. Asst. Co. Pros.
Hutyera, Andrew, (BV) .... '43 '69 C&L.930 B.S., J.D. 105 Jamison Avenue
Mosser, Edw. D. .... '19 '49 C.528 A.B. L.228 J.D. Ret. Com. Pleas J.
Mosser, Geoffrey B., (BV) .... '46 '71 C.388 B.A. L.150 J.D. [Mosser&T.]
Mosser & Tabacchi, (BV) .... P.O. Box 265
Nunner, Michael K., (BV) .... '52 '77 C&L.608 B.A., J.D. 105 Jamison Ave.
Puskarich, Matthew P., (BV) .... '65 '91 C.631 B.A. L.896 J.D. Pros. Atty.
Savage-Dylewski, Mary Catherine, (BV) '64 '92 C.381 B.B.A. L.8 J.D.
111 W. Warren St.
Spiker, William E. .... '33 '60 C.528 A.B. L.607 J.D. P.O. Box 291‡
Tabacchi, John O., (BV) .... '48 '76 C.473 B.A. L.607 J.D. [Mosser&T.]
Van Tassel, Sherrilyn Farkas, Law Offices of '61 '96 C.1115 B.A. L.229 J.D.
(adm. in WV; not adm. in OH) 79300 Hurford Road
Werren, Robert B. .... '30 '60 C.528 A.B. L.607 J.D. Com. Pleas J.

CALDWELL, * 1,956, *Noble Co.*

Blakeslee, Jack A., (BV) .... '48 '76 C.973 B.S.B.A. L.7 J.D. [J.A.Blakeslee]
Blakeslee, Jack A., Co., L.P.A., (BV) .... 421 West St.
Fox, Fred F., (BV) .... '16 '50 C.610 L.607 J.D. 405 N. St.
Nau, John W. .... '49 '76 C.759 B.S. L.608 J.D. Com. Pleas J.
Paxton, Robert C., (BV) .... '19 '66 C.610 B.S.C.E. L.607 J.D. 425 1/2 Main St.
Tanner, Sharon L. .... '56 '83 C.610 B.A. L.607 J.D. 421 West St.
Young, Lucien C., III, (CV) .... '56 '83 C.434 B.A. 508 North St.
Young, Lucien C., Jr., Attorney at Law, (BV) '31 '59 C.611 B.A. L.607 J.D.
508 North St.

CAMBRIDGE, * 11,520, *Guernsey Co.*

Adams, John E. .... '31 '84 C.446 B.S. L.117 J.D. Com. Pleas Mag.
Baker, Richard A., (BV) .... '42 '67 C.201 B.S. L.608 J.D. [DeSelm&B.]
Bennett, David B., (BV) .... '60 '85 C.201 B.S. L.117 J.D. [Knowlton&B.]
Bennett, William Mark, (BV) .... '51 '77 C.97 B.A. L.607 J.D. [Knowlton&B.]
Biegler, Kent D., (BV) .... '56 '82 C.532 B.A. L.166 J.D. [Ⓐ Tribbie,S.P.&P.]
Booth, Russell H., Jr., (BV) .... '29 '57 C&L.608 B.S., LL.B. 745 Steubenville Ave.
Brown, Donald D., (BV) .... '51 '76 C.608 B.S. L.117 J.D. 803 Steubenville Ave.
Caldwell, Mary Ellen .... '64 '89 C.532 B.A. L.8 J.D. Asst. City Law Dir. / Pros.

Cultice & Brown
(See Zanesville)

Dayton, Lee H. .... '62 '92 C.867 B.S. L.201 J.D. 7 Hillcrest Lane

Denmead Law Office
(See Columbus)

DeSelm, David H., (AV) .... '40 '65 C.385 B.A. L.893 LL.B. [DeSelm&B.]
DeSelm & Baker, (AV) .... 819 Steubenville Avenue
Ellwood, David A. .... '43 '74 C.610 B.B.A. L.117 J.D. Com. Pleas J.
Eyen, Stephen, Law Offices of .... '54 '80 C.309 A.B. L.608 J.D. P.O. Box 1521
Ferguson, William H., (BV) .... '59 '85 C.1260 B.A. L.608 J.D. [Heine&F.]
Granitsas, James G. .... '26 '53 C.532 A.B. L.477 J.D. 123 W. 8th St.
Heine, Stephen C., (BV) .... '45 '74 C.967 A.B. L.930 J.D. [Heine&F.]
Heine and Ferguson, (BV) .... 803 Steubenville Avenue
Hollins, Marcia A., (BV) .... '50 '92 C.610 B.S. L.117 J.D. Mag.
Jones, Gerald L., (BV) .... '51 '76 C.610 B.B.A. L.608 J.D. 114 Southgate Pkwy.

Kincaid, Taylor & Geyer
(See Zanesville)

Knowlton & Bennett, (BV)
126 North 9th Street, 43725
Telephone: 740-439-2719 Fax: 740-432-4937
URL: http://www.lawyers.com/knowlton&bennett
William Mark Bennett; David B. Bennett; Daniel D. Knowlton (1924-2002).
Banks and Banking, Aged and Aging, Foreclosures, Juvenile Law, Commercial Real Estate, Criminal Law, Family Law, Probate, Wills, Trusts and Estates, Real Estate, Business Law, Creditors Rights, Collections, Divorce, Driving While Intoxicated, Traffic Violations.

(This Listing Continued)

Knowlton & Bennett (Continued)

Representative Clients: Eastern Ohio Mutual Fire & Tornado Insurance Co.; The Guernsey Bank; Peoples Bank; National City Bank.
Approved Attorneys for: Veterans Administration; Farmers Home Administration; Lawyers Title Land America; First American Titile Insurance Company.
References: Peoples Bank, Cambridge, Ohio; National City Bank, Cambridge, Ohio; The Guernsey Bank, Worthington, Ohio.

See Professional Biographies, CAMBRIDGE, OHIO

Lloyd, Thos. R. .... '20 '47 C.532 A.B. L.228 J.D. 1350 Edgeworth Ave.
McClure, Frank A., (CV) .... '47 '75 C.901 B.A. L.607 J.D. [F.A.McClure]
McClure, Frank A., Co., LPA, (CV) .... 213 N. 8th Street
McKnight, Charles E., (CV) .... '59 '89 C.610 B.B.A. L.117 J.D. 820 N. 8th St.
Mitchell, Stephanie L. .... '73 '01 C.532 B.A. L.117 J.D. [Ⓐ Tribbie,S.P.&P.]
Moll, Jeanette M. .... '65 '96 C.602 B.A. L.608 J.D. Mag., Com. Pleas Ct.
Nicholson, John M. .... '53 '83 C.976 B.A. L.607 J.D. Mun. J.
Nicholson, William T. .... '42 '85 C.608 B.S. L.607 J.D. 217 North Eighth Street
Nicolozakes, William A. '68 '95 C.608 B.A. L.117 J.D.
V.P. & Gen. Coun., Nicolozakes, Trucking & Construction
Padden, Daniel G., (BV) .... '61 '87 C&L.607 B.S.B.A., J.D. [Tribbie,S.P.&P.]
Plummer, C. Keith, (BV) .... '55 '81 C.608 B.A. L.117 J.D. [Tribbie,S.P.&P.]
Raptis, Sam L., (CV) .... '49 '77 C.608 B.S. L.999 J.D. 123 W. 8th St.
Scott, James R., (AV) .... '32 '62 C.473 B.S. L.608 J.D. [Tribbie,S.P.&P.]
Smith, Matthew T., (BV) .... '59 '85 C.473 A.B. L.150 J.D. Advantage Bank
Tingle, Lewis M., (BV) .... '45 '71 C.473 B.S. L.150 J.D. 138 N. 7th St.
Tostenson, Neal S. .... '34 '58 C&L.608 B.S., J.D. 7077 Glenn
Tribbie, Thomas L., (AV) .... '26 '52 C&L.608 B.A., J.D. [Tribbie,S.P.&P.]

Tribbie, Scott, Plummer and Padden, (AV)
139 Court House Square, P.O. Box 640, 43725-0640
Telephone: 740-432-6322 Fax: 740-439-1795
Email: tspp@verizon.net URL: http://www.tsppl aw.com
Members of Firm: Thomas L. Tribbie; James R. Scott; C. Keith Plummer; Daniel G. Padden;—Kent D. Biegler; Stephanie L. Mitchell.
General Civil Trial Practice. Corporation, Real Estate, Negligence, Insurance Defense, Insurance and Probate Law. Family Law, Divorce, Child Custody, Child Support.
Represent: Allstate Insurance Co.; State Farm Insurance Co.; The Westfield Cos.; Grange Insurance Co.; The Dailey Jeffersonian Co. (Newspaper).

See Professional Biographies, CAMBRIDGE, OHIO

Warhola, Andrew J., Jr., (BV) .... '54 '79 C.528 B.A. L.161 J.D. 110 N. 7th St.
Wilson, Melissa M. .... '77 '03 C.967 B.A. L.201 J.D. 213 N. 8th St.

Wirth, David
(See Columbus)

CAMDEN, 2,210, *Preble Co.*

Lambert, H. E. '38 '68 C.436 A.B. L.276 J.D.
(adm. in DC; not adm. in OH)
Vice President & Corporate Counsel, E-Z Serve Corporation

CAMPBELL, 9,460, *Mahoning Co.*

Jakubek, John T. .... '29 '57 C.381 A.B. L.608 J.D. 54 Courtland Ave.‡
Kolmacic, Joseph M. .... '23 '54 C&L.128 A.B., LL.B. Mun. J.

CANAL FULTON, 5,061, *Stark Co.*

Fellmeth, Eugene M. .... '24 '51 C.967 A.B. L.1003 J.D. 625 Circle Dr.‡
Lynch, Joseph M., Jr. .... '53 '80 C.8 B.A. L.7 J.D. P.O. Box 5017
Wilson, Randy K. .... '51 '76 C.150 B.A. L.851 J.D. 6010 Erie Ave. N.
Zahirsky, Linda B. .... '49 '85 C&L.8 B.A., J.D. 413 Milan St.S.

CANAL WINCHESTER, 4,478, *Fairfield & Franklin Cos.*

Dean, Martha F., (CV) .... '41 '84 C.347 B.A. L.117 J.D. 9646 Sharron Dr. N.W.
Dolin, Jason M. .... '54 '80 C.1019 B.A. L.823 J.D. Mid-American Waste Systems
Harman, Kenneth C., (BV) .... '44 '69 C.608 B.S. L.309 J.D. 45 N. High St.
Jolley, Elizabeth M. .... '68 '94 C.475 B.A. L.215 J.D. UAW - GM Legal Servs.
Kingery, Nathan A. .... '57 '82 C.647 B.S. L.229 J.D. 7725 Basil W. Rd.‡
Leininger, Robert E. '51 '77 C.475 B.S. L.424 J.D.
(adm. in IL; not adm. in OH) Sr. Legal Coun., Waste Management, Inc.
Lucas, Barbara D. .... '49 '89 C.610 B.S. L.117 J.D. 5071 Ebright Rd.
McNemar, Joseph G. .... '53 '78 C.608 B.A. L.597 J.D. 5802 Elder road
Stauffer, John H. '22 '62 C.610 A.B. L.802 J.D.
(adm. in TX; not adm. in OH) 225 E. Hocking St.‡
Stevenson, William W., (BV) .... '20 '56 C&L.266 A.B., J.D. Village Solr.
Weaver, Roger L. .... '60 '88 C.97 B.A. L.117 J.D. 3 S. High St.
Wedemeyer, Louis H., (BV) .... '18 '52 C.608 L.266 J.D. 20 S. High St.
Wortman, Mary, Law Office, (CV) .... '— '82 C.440 B.A. L.608 J.D. 20 S. High Street

CANFIELD, 7,374, *Mahoning Co.*

Allen, Kurt R., (CV) .... '62 '90 C.980 B.S. L.896 J.D. 150 Neff Ct.
Beck, James H., (BV) '35 '59
C.967 A.B. L.893 J.D. Olde Courthouse Building 7 Court Street
Brannigan, Mary Ellen, (CV) .... '55 '90 C.980 B.S.N. L.8 J.D. 3870 Starr Centre Dr.
Bresko, Andrew G., (BV) .... '49 '75 C.980 B.A. L.607 J.D. 3810 Starrs Centre Dr.
Brott, Gary N., (CV) .... '51 '83 C.980 A.B. L.607 J.D. 6600 Summit Dr.
Bryan, W. Burton '26 '52 C&L.352 B.S.C., J.D.
(adm. in IA; not adm. in OH) 4095 Sugarbush Dr.‡
Burke, Charlene E. .... '53 '89 C.980 B.A. L.8 J.D. Trust Offr., Bank One Trust Co., N.A.
Burky, Elton B., (BV) .... '14 '37 C&L.608 B.A., J.D. 3465 W. Western Reserve Rd.
Coniglio, Shirley J., (CV) .... '60 '89 C.980 A.B. L.930 J.D. Olde Courthouse Bldg.
Coope, Fred, (AV) .... '15 '47 C.611 A.B. L.980 J.D. 17 Court St.‡
Davis, Henry W. .... '20 '55 C.610 B.S. L.980 J.D. [Davis&D.]
Davis, James H., (BV) .... '52 '79 C.967 B.A. L.607 J.D. [Davis&D.]
Davis & Davis, (BV) .... 6715 Tippecanoe Rd., Ste. A103
DeFazio, John T., (AV) '45 '69 C.262 A.B. L.893 LL.B.
Administrative Trial Attorney, Nationwide Mutual Insurance Company
Dugic, Melody Gazda, (BV) .... '64 '90 C.436 B.A. L.680 J.D. 3810 Starrs Centre Dr.
Dunlap, Charles E., (BV) .... '47 '77 C&L.607 B.A., J.D. 3855 Starrs Centre Dr.
Elliott, Rush E., (BV) .... '42 '68 C.610 B.B.A. L.607 J.D. P.O. Box 37
Evans, James C., (AV) .... '42 '76 C.980 B.S. L.607 J.D. 6600 Summit Drive
Ferrante, Joseph A., (BV) .... '51 '88 C.97 B.A. L.1003 J.D. 6715 Tippecanoe
Ferris, Dean F., (BV) .... '27 '51 C&L.607 J.D. 106 S. Broad St.
Fox, Eugene B., (AV) .... '28 '52 L.607 J.D. 6630 Seville Dr.
Gardner, Joseph W., (BV) .... '52 '77 C.473 B.A. L.7 J.D. 4280 Boardman-Canfield Rd.
Goldberg, Martin S., (AV) .... '24 '52 C&L.608 B.S., J.D. [M.S.Goldberg] ⊙‡
Goldberg, Steven M., (BV) .... '62 '89 C.36 B.A. L.117 J.D. [Goldberg,S.M.] ⊙
Goldberg, Martin S., Co., L.P.A., (AV) .... 6600 Summit Dr. (⊙Palm Desert, CA)
Goldberg, Steven M., Co., L.P.A., (BV) .... 6600 Summit Dr. (⊙Solon)

Hafiz, Ishraq A., (CV) .... '58 '83 C.318 B.A. L.608 J.D. P.O. Box 1075
Hunter, Scott D., (BV) .... '63 '88 C.980 B.S. L.150 J.D. [Davis&D.]
Johnson, Eric C., (BV) ....'58 '83 C.608 B.S. L.150 J.D. [Johnson&J.]
Johnson, Nils P. .... '22 '50 C&L.608 LL.B. 3651 Mercedes Place
Johnson, Nils P., Jr., (AV) ....'50 '76 C.197 B.A. L.93 J.D. [Johnson&J.]
Johnson & Johnson, (AV) .... 12 West Main Street
Joseph, Jeffrey A. .... '67 '98 C.980 B.S.B.A. L.8 J.D. 6071 Deer Spring Run
Kalasky, William G., (BV) .... '53 '78 C.276 B.A. L.608 J.D. 106 S. Broad St.
Kannensohn, Fredric A., (AV) .... '39 '64 C.659 B.S. L.477 J.D. [Millstone&K.] ⊙
Kay, Charles J., (BV) .... '66 '93 C.103 A.B. L.930 J.D. [Davis&D.]
Kish, William J., (BV) ....'41 '70 C.980 B.S.B.A. L.8 J.D. 73 N. Broad St.
Longenhagen, Je Anne D. ....'55 '80 C.401 B.A. L.607 J.D. 5431 Bay Hill Dr.
Loshinsky, James R. ....'25 '59 C&L.980 B.A., J.D. 10609 Leffingwell Rd.
Machuga, Richard William ....'61 '87 C.980 B.S. in B.A. L.150 J.D. Mag.
Maruca, Christopher A. ....'68 '96 C.321 B.A. L.229 J.D. P.O. Box 129
Mercer, Jeralyn Goldberg, (CV) ....'54 '93 C.980 B.S. L.7 J.D. [Mercer,J.G.]
Mercer, Jeralyn G., (CV) ....6600 Summit Drive
Millstone & Kannensohn, (AV) ....53 South Champion Street (⊙Youngstown)
Modarelli, Jas. M., Jr. ....'16 '41 C.473 B.A. L.608 LL.B. 3736 Fairway Dr.
Morris, Patricia Anne, (CV) .... '54 '89 C.980 B.S.B.A. L.08 J.D. [P.A.Morris]
Morris, Patricia A., Law Office of, (CV) .... 4280 Boardman Canfield Rd.
Motosko, Linda Anne, (BV) ....'54 '80 C.980 B.S. L.608 J.D. 3679 Mercedes Pl.
Mumaw, Daniel J., (BV) ....'53 '86 C.935 B.A. L.7 J.D. 3810 Starrs Centre Dr.
Ortenzio, Albert J., (AV) ....'26 '51 C.980 B.A. L.477 J.D. 6600 Summit Dr.
Prassinos, Constant A., (BV) ....'42 '71 C.980 B.A. L.426 J.D. 6715 Tippecanoe Rd.
Rimmel, James E., (BV) ....'41 '74 C.913 B.A. L.229 J.D. [J.E.Rimmel]
Rimmel, James E., Co., L.P.A., (BV) ....P.O. Box 477
Rinehart, James P., (BV) ......'51 '80 C.980 B.S.B.A. L.1003 J.D. 3770 Starrs Centre Dr.
Rusu, Robert N., Jr., (BV) ....'67 '93 C.980 B.A. L.1187 J.D. 65B N. Broad St.
Sofranko, George Bernard, Jr., (CV) .....'55 '83 C.980 B.S. L.117 J.D. Admin. Clk. of Ct.
Stevens, Robert L. .... '47 '74 C.980 B.S. L.7 J.D. 6715 Tippecanoe Road

Toot, Douglas M., (BV) '47 '73 C.228 A.B. L.608 J.D.
106 South Broad Street, 44406
Telephone: 330-533-9810 Fax: 330-533-2124
Email: dougtoot@zoominternet.net URL: http://www.dougtootlawoffices.com
(Certified Specialist in Estate Planning, Trust and Probate Law, Ohio State Bar Association).
Wills and Trusts, Estate Planning, Probate, Elder Law, Business Planning, Corporate and Business Law, Real Estate.

See Professional Biographies, CANFIELD, OHIO

Travers, Thomas J., Jr., (BV) ......'49 '76 C.609 B.A. L.608 J.D. 3870 Satrr Centre Drive
Tyrrell, Emmet J., (CV) .... '37 '62 C&L.602 B.S., J.D. 132 S. Broad, Suite 301
White, David R., (BV) ....'41 '68 C.980 B.S.B.A. L.8 J.D. 106 S. Broad St.
Zellers, Richard G., (BV) ....'48 '74 C.631 B.A. L.117 J.D. 3810 Starrs Centre Dr.

CANTON, * 80,806, *Stark Co.*

Abel, Michael A. ....'65 '95 C.999 B.A. L.8 J.D. Colonial Title Agcy.
Abood, Ernest N. ....'14 '41 C.528 B.A. L.948 LL.B. 716 Renkert Bldg.
Ailes, William C. ....'11 '37 C.528 B.S. L.930 LL.B. 1119 Hawthorn Avenue, S.W.‡
Ake, David S., (BV) ....'45 '72 C.607 B.A. L.7 J.D. Asst. Co. Pros.
Ake, J. Whitney ....'41 '66 C&L.607 B.A., J.D. 401 Central Trust Twr.‡
Ake, Sherwood, (AV) ....'08 '32 C&L.477 B.A., LL.B. 260 Ironwood St. SW‡
Albrecht, Kirk T., (CV) '56 '82 C.8 B.A. L.7 J.D.
320 Citizens Building, 110 Central Plaza South
Albu, Thomas P., (BV) ....'47 '75 C.970 B.A. L.608 J.D. 2223 Fulton Rd., NW
Aman, Geo. J. ....'30 '54 C.97 A.B. L.608 J.D. 1101 Bank One Tower
Amiet, Ralph D., (AV) ....'41 '67 C&L.608 B.S.B.A., J.D. [Buckingham,D.&B.]
Amrhein, Christine B., (BV) '61 '87
C.25 B.A. L.665 J.D. Sr. Corp. Atty., The Timken Co.
Andrews, Eugene ....'23 '55 C.608 L.948 LL.B. 4808 Munson St., N.W.‡
Andrews, Timothy G., (BV) ....'48 '73 C.363 A.B. L.851 J.D. Asst. Pros.
Anthony, John F., (BV) ....'51 '77 C.473 B.A. L.7 J.D. 4450 Belden Village St., N.W.
Archer, John P. ....'75 '01 C.207 B.A. L.608 J.D. [Ⓐ Day K.]
Armatas, Steven A., (AV) ....'59 '84 C&L.309 B.A., J.D. [Buckingham,D.&B.]
Arnold, Richard W., (CV) ....'63 '94 C.97 B.S.B.A. L.7 J.D. [Day K.]
Ayers, Charles Stephen ....'46 '87 C.117 B.A. L.8 J.D. [C.S.Ayers]
Ayers, C. Stephen, Law Office ....4884 Dressler Road, N.W.
Baasten, Cornelius J., (AV) ....'48 '73 C.602 B.B.A. L.893 J.D. [Green H.S.]
Baasten, Jason M. ....'74 '99 C.602 B.A. L.150 J.D. [Ⓐ Krugliak,W.G.&D.]
Badger, William B., (BV) .... '37 '61 C.207 L.608 J.D. [Day K.]
Bailey, Nathan D. '67 '93 C&L.665 B.A., J.D.
(adm. in PA; not adm. in OH) Corp. Atty., The Timken Co.

Baker, Gerald L., Law Offices of, (BV) '43 '68 C.97 B.A. L.608 J.D.
3711 Whipple Avenue, N.W., 44718-2933
Telephone: 330-492-1001 Fax: 330-492-4577
Email: jbaker3094@aol.com
Corporate Law, Commercial Litigation, Environmental Law, Secured Transactions, Probate Law.

See Professional Biographies, CANTON, OHIO

Baker, Dublikar, Beck, Wiley & Mathews
(See North Canton)

Barnhart, Gene, (AV) .... '28 '53 C.923 L.150 J.D. [Ⓒ Black M.S.&A.L.&Assoc.]
Batchelder, James T. ....'56 '82 C.473 B.S. L.150 J.D. Pres., M. K. Morse Co., The
Batista, Roy H., (BV) .... '40 '65 C.473 B.A. L.477 J.D. 4808 Munson Street, N.W.
Baumoel, Lynn R., (BV) '65 '90 C.383 B.A. L.150 J.D.
Supv. Atty., Community Legal Aid Services, Inc.
Bell, Catherine Margarete Wegner ....'72 '99 C.473 B.S. L.7 J.D. [Bell,C.M.W.]
Bell, Lee J., (AV) .... '47 '73 C.1044 B.S. L.1119 J.D. [Buckingham,D.&B.]
Bell, Catherine M.W. ....610 Market Avenue North
Benson, Don M., (BV) .... '40 '65 C.532 B.A. L.607 J.D. [Herbert&B.]
Beoglos, Laura L. ....'65 '92 C&L.8 B.A., J.D. [Sand&S.]
Bergert, Jennifer Lynne Schandel '74 '01 C.381 B.A. L.8 J.D.
116 Cleveland Avenue, NW
Bing, Richard George, (BV) .... '29 '56 L.948 LL.B. 116 Cleveland Ave., N.
Bixler, Bruce M. ....'24 '52 C.528 A.B. L.930 LL.B. P.O. Box 35426‡
Black, Sheila Markley, (AV) ....'47 '72 C.518 B.A. L.228 J.D. [Day K.] (⊙Canton)

Black McCuskey Souers & Arbaugh, A Legal Professional Association, (AV)
220 Market Avenue South, Suite 1000, 44702 ⊙
Telephone: 330-456-8341; 877-656-8341 Fax: 330-456-5756; 877-456-5746
Email: info@bmsa.com URL: http://www.bmsa.com
Anthony E. Efremoff; Robert I. Friedman; Arnold R. Shifman; Victor R. Marsh; Daniel M. Jonas; Randolph L. Snow (Managing Director); Terrence P. Kessler; James R. Strawn; Joel K. Dayton; Gust Callas (Certified Specialist in Ohio Workers' Compensation Law and Labor and Employment Law, Ohio State Bar Association); Bruce M. Soares; James P. Kamerer (Certified Specialist in Estate Planning, Trust and Probate Law, Ohio State Bar Association); Richard D. Dodez; Mary E. Reynolds (Certified Specialist in Ohio Workers' Compensation Law, Ohio State Bar Association); John J. Rambacher; Thomas W. Connors; David M. Hanhart (Dover Office); C. Jason Deeds (Dover Office);

(This Listing Continued)

Black McCuskey Souers & Arbaugh, A Legal Professional Association (Continued)
Erick L. Bauer (Dover Office); Francis G. Centrone; Todd S. Bundy; Gordon D. Woolbert, II; Brian R. Mertes;—John L. Juergensen; Chrysanthe E. Vassiles; Kristin R. Zemis (Dover Office); Faith R. Dylewski; Daniel R. Griffith; Robert B. Preston, III; Robert J. Murphy. Of Counsel: Charles J. Tyburski (Certified Specialist in Estate Planning, Trust and Probate Law, Ohio State Bar Association); Gene Barnhart; Richard M. Hanhart.
General Civil Practice in all State and Federal Courts. Administrative, Acquisitions, Antitrust, Banking, Bankruptcy, Commercial, Construction, Corporate, Divorce, Environmental, Estate Planning and Trusts, Estate Administration, Family Law, Government, Health Care Law, Insurance, Labor, Litigation, Oil and Gas, Personal Injury, Real Estate, Securities, Taxation Law, Workers' Compensation and Wrongful Death and Zoning.
Representative Clients: The Hoover Co.; Diebold, Inc.; Travelers Insurance Co.
Dover, Ohio Office: Black McCuskey Hanhart Deeds & Bauer, A Legal Professional Association, 130 W. Third Street, 44622. Telephone: 330-364-6553. Fax: 330-364-2739.

See Professional Biographies, CANTON, OHIO

Blake, James R., (AV) .... '48 '73 C.228 B.A. L.608 J.D. [Day K.]
Blank, Norma Hudson ....'37 '84 C.318 B.A. L.7 J.D. Fam. Ct. Mag.
Boettler, Louis A., (AV) .... '31 '55 C.381 A.B. L.608 J.D. [Ⓒ Day K.]
Bogdan, Michael J. ....'79 '04 C.363 B.A. L.608 J.D. [Ⓐ Krugliak,W.G.&D.]
Boggins, John F. .... '32 '58 C.381 B.A. L.608 J.D. Judge
Boggins, John Vincent .... '58 '86 C&L.8 B.A., J.D. [J.V.Boggins]
Boggins, John V. ....1428 Market Avenue North
Bogniard, John, (AV) ....'47 '72 C.25 B.A. L.608 J.D. [Krugliak,W.G.&D.]
Bonta, Darlene B. '51 '94 C.150 B.S. L.8 J.D.
Staff Atty., Community Legal Aid Services, Inc.
Borcoman, Tom A., (BV) ....'46 '74 C.381 B.S. L.7 J.D. 5438 Island Dr., N.W.
Borden, David N. ....'24 '57 C.546 B.S. L.948 LL.B. P.O. Box 80039‡
Boske, Michael A., (BV) ....'68 '95 C.381 B.A. L.7 J.D. 122 Central Plaza North
Brannen, John H., (BV) ....'49 '75 C.610 B.A. L.477 J.D. [Day K.]
Braun, Dianne Blocker, (AV) ......'51 '76 C.347 B.A. L.1119 J.D. [Buckingham,D.&B.]
Bridenstine, David M., (BV) .... '49 '80 C.999 B.S. L.7 J.D. Asst. Pros. Atty.
Brooker, James K., (AV) .... '38 '62 C&L.608 LL.B. [Day K.]
Brown, Charles E., (AV) ....'42 '67 C.197 A.B. L.930 J.D. Co. Ct. J.
Brown, Larry R., (AV) ....'35 '60 C&L.608 B.S.B.A., J.D. [Ⓒ Day K.]
Brunn, Richard C., (AV) ..... '35 '59 C.611 B.A. L.477 LL.B. 4809 Munson Street, N.W.

Buckingham, Doolittle & Burroughs, LLP, (AV)
4518 Fulton Drive, Northwest, P.O. Box 35548, 44735-5548 ⊙
Telephone: 330-492-8717; Toll Free: 888-811-2825 Fax: 330-492-9625
Email: bdb@bdblaw.com URL: http://www.bdblaw.com
Managing Partner: Jeffrey A. Halm. Shareholders: Ralph D. Amiet; Steven A. Armatas; Lee J. Bell; David Patrick Dureska; William W. Emley, Sr.; Joseph J. Feltes; Mark D. Frasure; Stephen P. Griffin; Christopher S. Humphrey; Richard J. Lolli; Robert C. Meyer; Richard S. Milligan; Tod T. Morrow (Certified Specialist in Workers' Compensation Law, Ohio State Bar Association); Paul J. Pusateri; John C. Ross; John P. Van Abel. Partners: Dianne Blocker Braun; Thomas R. Himmelspach; Philip E. Howes; Barbara A. Knapic. Of Counsel: Arthur S. Leb. Associates: Karen D. Butera; G. Brenda Coey; Denise A. Gary; Justin S. Greenfelder; Kristina M. Harless; Edward T. Kennedy; Shila J. Nalawadi; Susan Chae Rank.
Appellate, Closely Held Companies, Commercial Law and Litigation, Computer and Technology, Construction Law, Copyrights, Corporate and Business, Creditors Rights/Bankruptcy, Criminal Law, Employment Law, Environmental, Estate Planning, Family Law, Finance and Public Law, Franchise, Health Care, Immigration Law, Insurance Defense, Intellectual Property, Labor and Employment, Land Use and Zoning, Medical Malpractice Defense, Mergers and Acquisitions, Patents, Probate, Publicly Held Companies, Real Estate, School Law, Securities, Succession Planning, Taxation and Employee Benefits, Toxic Tort/Complex Litigation, Trademarks/Service Marks, Trade Secrets, Trial, Trusts and Estates, Venture Capital/Emerging Companies, Workers' Compensation.
Akron, Ohio Office: 50 South Main Street, P.O. Box 1500, 44309-1500. Telephone: 330-376-5300. Toll Free: 800-686-2825. Fax: 330-258-6559.
Cleveland, Ohio Office: 1375 East Ninth Street, Suite 1700, 44114. Telephone: 216-621-5300. Toll Free: 888-843-2825. Fax: 216-621-5440.
Columbus, Ohio Office: 191 West Nationwide Boulevard, 43215-3506. Telephone: 614-221-8448. Toll Free: 888-686-2825. Fax: 614-221-8590.
Boca Raton, Florida Office: 2500 North Military Trail, Suite 480, 33431. Telephone: 561-241-0414. Toll Free: 800-682-2825. Fax: 561-241-9766.

See Professional Biographies, CANTON, OHIO

Bules, Raymond T., (BV) .... '56 '81 C.970 B.A. L.945 J.D. [Day K.]
Bump, Mark William, (BV) .... '56 '83 C&L.8 B.S., J.D. Corp. Atty., The Timken Co.
Bundy, Todd S., (AV) .... '54 '80 C.184 B.A. L.117 J.D. [Black M.S.&A.L.&Assoc.]
Burick, Elizabeth A., (BV) ....'60 '84 C&L.8 B.S., J.D. [E.Burick]
Burick, Elizabeth, Co., L.P.A., (BV) ....1428 N. Market
Burkhart, William R. '65 '90 C.260 B.A. L.309 J.D.
(adm. in PA; not adm. in OH) Sr. VP & Gen. Coun., The Timken Co.
Burns, Thomas A., (BV) '47 '75
C.610 B.B.A. L.1003 J.D. 116 Cleveland Ave., N.W., Ste. 717
Butera, Constance D., (BV) ....'36 '82 C.1260 B.A. L.7 J.D. 110 Central Plaza S.
Butera, Karen D. ....'— '99 C.999 B.A. L.08 J.D. [Ⓐ Buckingham,D.&B.]
Butz, David E., (BV) ....'61 '87 C.81 B.A. L.930 J.D. [Krugliak,W.G.&D.]
Calabretta, Joseph W., (BV) .... '44 '71 C.608 B.S. L.7 J.D. [J.W.Calabretta]
Calabretta, Joseph W., Co., L.P.A., (BV) ....4571 Stephens Circle, N.W.
Caldwell, Jacqueline Bollas, (BV) ....'59 '85 C.602 B.A. L.608 J.D. [Krugliak,W.G.&D.]
Caldwell, Ronald Mark, (BV) .... '57 '85 C.645 B.A. L.608 J.D. Asst. Pros.Atty.
Callas, Gust, (AV) .... '53 '78 C&L.8 B.S., J.D. [Black M.S.&A.L.&Assoc.]
Campbell, Kristen E., (CV) ....'71 '96 C.229 B.A. L.608 J.D. [Ⓐ Pelini&Assoc.]
Caplea, Nicholas G. ....'12 '35 C&L.607 LL.B. 620 Renkert Bldg.
Centrone, Francis G., (AV) ... '43 '68 C.229 B.A. L.607 J.D. [Black M.S.&A.L.&Assoc.]
Cerrone, Gary David, (BV) ....'53 '81 C.381 B.A. L.7 J.D. 5235 Lindford Ave. NE
Cespedes, Anthony J. ....'53 '78 C&L.8 B.S.B.A., J.D. 437 Market Ave. N.
Chessler, Craig ....'57 '83 C.631 B.S. L.7 J.D. Asst. Law Dir.
Christ, Roger Arthur ....'49 '87 C.1024 B.A. L.607 J.D. Nationwide Ins. Co.
Clark, John D. ....'71 '97 C.385 B.A. L.245 J.D. [Krugliak,W.G.&D.]
Cleaver, Sandra Watkins, (BV) ....'46 '88 C.8 B.A. L.7 J.D. [Simmons&C.]
Cline, William S., (BV) ....'49 '78 C.385 A.B. L.930 J.D. [Day K.]
Clunk, R. R. Denny .... '30 '55 C.528 B.S. L.930 LL.B. Co. Prob. J.
Cochrane, William, Jr. ....'15 '50 L.948 LL.B. 237 Grandview Ave., N.W.
Coey, G. Brenda ....'— '03 C.645 B.S. L.7 J.D. [Ⓐ Buckingham,D.&B.]
Collum, James J. .... '74 '99 C.260 B.S.B.A. L.608 J.D. 4571 Stephen Circle, NW
Conley, Craig T., (BV) ....'49 '83 C.8 B.A. L.7 J.D. 220 Market Ave. S.
Connors, Thomas W., (BV) '52 '78 C.363 B.A. L.1003 J.D.
[Black M.S.&A.L.&Assoc.]
Conrad, Eugene B., (CV) .... '30 '57 C.150 B.B.A. L.161 J.D. 3603 Cleveland Ave., S.
Contie, Leroy J., Jr. .... '20 '48 C&L.477 A.B., J.D. U.S. Ct. App. J.
Contini, James F., II, (BV) '67 '92
C.8 B.S. L.930 J.D. [Krugliak,W.G.&D.] (⊙New Philadelphia)
Cooper, Jack B., (BV) ....'62 '92 C.8 B.A. L.608 J.D. [Day K.]
Cope, Leland H., (CV) ....'29 '53 C.528 B.A. L.309 J.D. 224 44th St Nw
Cordova, Michelle L., (BV) ....'70 '96 C.610 A.B. L.8 J.D. Asst. Pros. Atty.
Corroto, Gary A., (BV) ....'65 '91 C.935 B.A. L.8 J.D. [Tzangas,P.M.&R.]

Coury, John S., (AV) '52 '77 C&L.608 B.A., J.D. 116 Cleveland Avenue, N.W., Suite 717
Craig, Steven L., (BV) ....'59 '84 C.610 B.B.A. L.7 J.D. 437 Market Ave., N.
Cranston, Thomas K. ....'51 '76 C.610 B.S. L.607 J.D. [Cranston]
Cranston Law Office, LLC ....1369 Market Ave. N.
Crawford, G. Ian, (BV) ....'59 '84 C.608 B.A. L.8 J.D. 101 Central Plaza South
Cross & Rose Co., L.P.A., (BV) .... 2884 Whipple Ave., N.W.
Crowell, Lawrence .... '43 '70 C.128 B.A. L.930 J.D. Nationwide Mut. Ins. Co.
Cunningham, Clay C. '62 '97 C.577 B.A. L.665 J.D. (adm. in PA; not adm. in OH; Pat.) [Sand&S.]
Curati, Jennifer E. ....'72 '00 L.8 J.D. P.O. Box 35548
Cusma, Patrick Louis ....'56 '96 C.1208 B.S. L.201 J.D. [P.L.Cusma]
Cusma, Patrick L. .... 315 W. Tuscarawas St., Ste. 301
Cutler, Jay L., (BV) ....'53 '83 C.608 B.S. L.8 J.D. 4618 Dressler Rd., NW
Cyperski, Nancy L., (BV) '51 '84 C.381 B.A. L.8 J.D. Assoc. Benefits Servs., The Timken Company
Cyperski, Robert H., (BV) ....'56 '84 C.509 B.S. L.8 J.D. 1201 30th St., N.W.
Daane, Robert B., (AV) ....'47 '75 C.228 A.B. L.930 J.D. [R.B.Daane]
Daane, Robert B., LLC, Law Office of, (AV)..........4429 Fulton Ave. N.W., Ste. 200
D'Atri, E. Lang, (AV) ....'38 '63 C.103 A.B. L.150 J.D. 220 Market Ave., S.
Davidson, George M., Jr. ....'18 '48 C.611 A.B. L.930 LL.B. 215-19th Street, N.W.‡
Davis, David ....'78 '03 C.124 B.A. L.608 J.D. [A Day K.]
Davis, Richard E., (AV) ....'50 '76 C.970 B.A. L.800 J.D. [Krugliak,W.G.&D.]
Dawkins, Karen A. ....'66 '91 C&L.608 B.S., J.D. Asst. Pros.

Day Ketterer Ltd., (AV)
Millennium Centre, Suite 300, 200 Market Avenue North, P.O. Box 24213, 44701-4213
Telephone: 330-455-0173 Telecopier: 330-455-2633 URL: http://www.dayketterer.com
URL: http://www.day-ketterer.com
Members of Firm: John R. Werren; William B. Badger; James K. Brooker; J. Sean Keenan; Wayne C. Kyhos; Sheila Markley Black; James R. Blake; John H. Brannen; Richard A. Princic; Tim A. Powell; Alicia M. Wyler; William S. Cline; Daniel A. Minkler; Matthew Yackshaw; Raymond T. Bules; John A. Murphy, Jr.; Merle D. Evans III; Robert E. Roland; Jill C. McQueen; J. Curtis Werren; Thomas E. Hartnett; Richard W. Arnold; Jack B. Cooper; Robert J. McBride; Stephen E. Matasich. Associates: John P. Archer; Joanne G. Paulino; John M. Prelac; R. Clint Zollinger; John S. Kaminski; David Davis; Steven D. Shandor. Of Counsel: Larry R. Brown; Louis A. Boettler; Robert J. Newbold.
General Civil Practice in all the Courts. General Business, Corporation, Insurance, Antitrust, Banking, Labor Law, Commercial Transactions, Bankruptcy, Environmental, Occupational Safety and Health, Workers Compensation, Estate Planning, Real Estate, Taxation, Family Law and Probate Law. Trials and Appeals in all Courts. Administrative Law.
Representative Clients: Bank One, N.A.; Canton Drop Forge; Detroit Diesel Corp.; National City Bank, N.E.; The Timken Co.
See Professional Biographies, CANTON, OHIO

Dayton, Joel K., (AV) .... '52 '77 C.1085 B.S. L.608 J.D. [Black M.S.&A.L.&Assoc.]
Deal, Geo. L. ....'14 '49 C.604 A.B. L.948 LL.B. 2974 Midvale Rd., N.W.‡
Dean, Michael P. '55 '81 C.20 B.A. L.215 J.D. (adm. in MI; not adm. in OH) 1107 Lake Breeze Dr.‡
de Forest, Benjamin B., (BV) .....'57 '84 C.1044 B.A. L.607 J.D. [C Krugliak,W.G.&D.]
DeHoff, Harold E. ....'24 '50 C.381 L.607 J.D. Ret. Com. Pleas J.
DeLaCruz, Christopher P., (BV) ....'53 '79 C.197 B.A. L.608 J.D. [C.P.DeLaCruz]
De La Cruz, Christopher Paul, (BV) ....437 Market Ave. N.
Demchak, Michael D., (BV) '52 '77 C.97 B.S. L.851 J.D. 116 Cleveland Avenue North, Suite 717

Denmead Law Office
(See Columbus)

Depasquale, David F., (CV) '61 '88 C.97 B.S.B.A. L.607 J.D. 4942 Higbee Avenue, N.W.
Dick, Paul Anthony, Jr. ....'53 '83 C.201 B.S. L.7 J.D. Leo A. Dick & Sons
Dickes, Don D. ....'31 '64 C.967 B.A. L.7 LL.B. 200 Market Ave., N.
Dickson, William H. ....'38 '72 C.62 B.S. L.8 J.D. 1845 Glenmont Dr., N.W.
Dingwell, David L., (BV) ....'67 '92 C.378 B.A. L.8 J.D. [Tzangas,P.M.&R.]
DioGuardi, Anthony M., II, (BV) '61 '86 C.1024 B.A. L.607 J.D. 4150 Belden Village St.
Dodez, Richard D., (BV) ....'42 '69 C&L.608 B.S., J.D. [Black M.S.&A.L.&Assoc.]
Dodson, Richard S., Jr., (BV) ....'52 '77 C.381 B.A. L.608 J.D. [Cross&R.]
Dossi, Jacquelyn Marks ....'73 '98 C.294 B.A. L.8 J.D. 115 Central Plaza N.
Dougherty, Ronald W., (AV) ......'32 '60 C.197 A.B. L.893 LL.B. [Krugliak,W.G.&D.]
Dressler, Donald J. ....'44 '73 C.8 B.A. L.7 J.D. 126 Central Plaza, North
Duffrin, Vivianne Whalen '67 '93 C.608 B.S. L.8 J.D. 116 Cleveland Ave., N.W., Ste. 717
Dureska, David Patrick, (BV) ...'58 '87 C&L.608 B.S., J.D. [Buckingham,D.&B.] (Pat.)
Dylewski, Faith R. ....'72 '02 C.381 B.A. L.8 J.D. [A Black M.S.&A.L.&Assoc.]
Eberly, Donald A., (BV) '09 '38 C.970 A.B. L.948 LL.B. Belden-Whipple Bldg.-Ste. #606, 4150 Belden Village Street, NW
Eckinger, Robert W., (CV) '59 '95 C&L.8 B.CH.E., J.D. 1201 30th St., N.W., Ste. 101B
Efremoff, Anthony E., (AV) .... '38 '63 C&L.477 A.B., J.D. [Black M.S.&A.L.&Assoc.]
Efremoff, Sarah Anne Kahn ....'39 '63 C&L.477 B.A., J.D. Stark Co. Fam. Ct.
Eisenbrei, Barbara Waltz, (CV) '40 '88 C.381 B.A. L.7 J.D. 4150 Belden Village Street, N.W., Suite 108

Elk & Elk Co., L.P.A.
(See Cleveland)

Elsass, Carrolyn M. ....'31 '58 C.608 B.Sc. L.7 LL.B. 5475 Tyro St., N.E.‡
Emley, William W., Sr., (BV) ......'45 '71 C.674 A.B. L.1066 J.D. [Buckingham,D.&B.]
Ergazos, John W. ....'24 '52 C.381 L.948 LL.B. 315 Tuscarawas St., W.
Eshelman, C. Richard, (BV) ....'37 '68 C.656 B.S. L.7 J.D. [Eshelman] ⊙
Eshelman, Robert P., (AV) ....'16 '41 C.604 A.B. L.930 J.D. 121 Cleveland Ave. S.‡
Eshelman Legal Group, (BV) 116 Cleveland Avenue, N.W. (⊙Cleveland, Cuyahoga Falls, Youngstown)
Espenschied, Diana ....'52 '86 C.999 B.A. L.1003 J.D. 317 Donald Pl., SW
Evans, Cari Fusco, (BV) ....'69 '93 C.532 B.S. L.930 J.D. [Fischer,E.&R.]
Evans, Merle D., III, (BV) ....'57 '83 C.228 B.A. L.930 J.D. [Day K.]
Falletta, Salvatore J. ....'42 '67 C.363 B.A. L.597 J.D. 4150 Belden Village St.
Fallon, Martin J., (BV) ....'64 '89 C.93 A.B. L.124 J.D. 4535 Dressler Road
Fals, Mary M. ....'47 '91 C.381 B.S. L.8 J.D. Mag., Prob. Ct.
Farmer, Sheila G. ....'45 '70 C.449 B.A. L.930 J.D. Ct. App. J.
Feisthamel, Toni Beth Schnellinger ....'74 '00 C&L.8 B.A., J.D. Stark Co. Prosecutor
Feltes, Joseph J., (AV) ....'48 '78 C.363 A.B. L.276 J.D. [Buckingham,D.&B.]
Ferrell, David B., (BV) ....'53 '78 C.97 B.S. L.851 J.D. 220 Market Avenue S.
Ferruccio, Samuel J., Jr., (BV) ....'52 '79 C.97 B.A. L.607 J.D. [S.J.Ferruccio,Jr.]
Ferruccio, Samuel J., Jr., Co., L.P.A., (BV) ..... 220 Market Ave. S. 400 Unizan Bank Plaza
Fickes, Jeffrey A. ....'67 '01 C.8 B.S. L.608 J.D. [A Krugliak,W.G.&D.]
Fidler, James G. ....'51 '75 C&L.831 B.A., J.D. FBI
Figler, Ronald G. ....'42 '71 C.473 B.S. L.7 J.D. [C Lesh,C.&M.]
Firestone, Eric A. ....'53 '78 C.608 B.S.B.A. L.8 J.D. 2800 Market Ave., N.
Fischer, Mark F., (BV) ....'60 '88 C.602 B.B.A. L.608 J.D. [Fischer,E.&R.]

Fischer, Evans & Robbins, Ltd., (BV)
4505 Stephen Circle NW Suite 100, 44718
Telephone: 330-244-0997 Fax: 330-244-8966
URL: http://www.fer-law.com
Members of Firm: Mark F. Fischer; Cari Fusco Evans; Donald L. Robbins, Jr.
Civil Trial and Appellate Practice in all State and Federal Courts, Litigation, Insurance Defense, Insurance Coverage, Products Liability Defense, Political Subdivisions, Premises Liability.
See Professional Biographies, CANTON, OHIO

Fitzpatrick, Lauren E., (BV) ....'57 '83 C.381 B.S. L.8 J.D. 4942 Higbee Ave.
Fladen, Sharon V., Attorney at Law, (BV) '53 '78 C.1365 B.A. L.117 J.D. Strawberry Sq., 15th Fl., Ste. 108
Flood, Michael E. ....'42 '82 C.676 B.S. L.8 J.D. Dir., Timken Co.
Foltz, Jeremy J. ....'73 '99 C.97 B.S. L.8 J.D. [Foltz]
Foltz, Joseph W. '43 '73 C.611 B.A. L.665 J.D. (adm. in PA; not adm. in OH) Sr. Legal Coun.-Europe, The Timken Co.
Foltz Law Offices, LLC .... 122 Central Plaza, North
Fowler, Douglas Todd ....'69 '95 C.970 B.A. L.930 J.D. [D.T.Fowler]
Fowler, Douglas T. .... 316 Grandview Avenue N. W.
Fox, Dennis J., (AV) ....'44 '71 C.1260 B.A. L.7 J.D. [Lesh,C.&M.]
Frame, Gary ....'67 '93 C.381 B.B.A. L.7 J.D. Indus. Comm. of OH
Frame, Kenneth Willliam ....'70 '96 C&L.851 B.A., J.D. 200 W. Tuscarawas St., Ste. 200
Frank, Michael ....'49 '90 C.976 B.A. L.930 J.D. Emer. Medicine Physicians, Ltd.
Frasure, Mark D., (AV) ....'47 '74 C.275 B.A. L.608 J.D. [Buckingham,D.&B.]
Friedman, Robert I., (AV) ... '39 '64 C.347 B.A. L.608 J.D. [Black M.S.&A.L.&Assoc.]
Fuchs, Lorrie E., (CV) ....'61 '86 C.473 B.A. L.7 J.D. P.O. Box 35787
Gaitanos, Mario, (BV) ....'58 '84 C.608 B.S. L.117 J.D. 437 Market Ave. N.
Gary, Denise A. ....'72 '98 C.8 B.A. L.930 J.D. [A Buckingham,D.&B.]
Geiser, Julie A., (BV) ....'68 '94 C.976 B.A. L.37 J.D. [A Pelini&Assoc.]
Genetin, Judee L. ....'54 '79 C.604 B.A. L.930 J.D. 220 East Tuscarawas Street
Genshaft, Steven M., (CV) ....'52 '77 C.608 B.A. L.930 J.D. 1103 Kenwood Cir., N.E.
Georges, William H., (Co., L.P.A.) ...... '39 '69 C.970 B.A. L.7 J.D. 220 Market Ave., S.
Giua, John R. ....'52 '77 C.645 B.A. L.7 J.D. 220 S. Market Ave., Ste. 400
Glantz, Arnold F., (CV) ....'60 '86 C.923 B.S. L.201 J.D. 4883 Dressler Road, N.W.
Golub, Gerald B. ....'48 '73 C.608 B.A. L.150 J.D. 306 Market Avenue, North
Goutras, Gust, (AV) ....'48 '85 C.381 B.A. L.7 J.D. Chief Dep. Mag.
Graham, Wayne E., Jr., (AV) .....'58 '85 C.999 B.S. L.8 J.D. 4571 Stephens Circle N.W.
Graves, Arthur C., (BV) ....'39 '64 C.385 A.B. L.608 J.D. [C Zwick] (⊙Columbus)
Green, Lemuel R., (BV) ....'43 '69 C.318 B.A. L.276 J.D. Mun. Ct. Ref.
Green Haines Sgambati Co., L.P.A., (AV) .....4150 Belden Village Street (⊙Youngstown)
Greenfelder, Justin S. ....'78 '04 C.207 B.A. L.8 J.D. [A Buckingham,D.&B.]
Gregg, James R., (BV) ....'39 '64 C.473 A.B. L.608 J.D. 4808 Munson Street, N.W.
Griffin, Stephen P., (BV) ....'60 '88 C.294 B.A. L.7 J.D. [Buckingham,D.&B.]
Griffith, Daniel R. ....'77 '02 C.528 B.A. L.608 J.D. [A Black M.S.&A.L.&Assoc.]
Griffiths, Raymond E., (AV) ....'32 '57 C.81 B.A. L.930 LL.B. [Krugliak,W.G.&D.]

Grisi & Riegler
(See Akron)

Gutierrez, Roy, (BV) ....'31 '61 C.381 B.A. L.8 J.D. 217-2nd St., N.W.

Guy, Lammert & Towne, (AV)
P.O. Box 6426, 44706-0426 ⊙
Telephone: 330-452-1818 Fax: 330-535-9048
Email: guylaw2210@aol.com
Resident Member: Thomas E. Lammert.
Bankruptcy, Banking, Business Torts, Corporation, Commercial Litigation, Creditors Rights and Reorganization Law. Domestic Relations, Employment Law, Probate, Personal Injury, Taxation, Trial Practice, Malpractice and Products Liability Law. General Litigation.
Akron, Ohio Office: 2210 First National Tower. Telephone: 330-535-2151. Fax: 330-535-9048
See Professional Biographies, CANTON, OHIO

Gwin, W. Scott, (AV) '51 '76 C.363 B.A. L.7 J.D. 100 Central Plaza, 3rd Floor, Citizens Savings Bldg.
Haines, Dennis, (AV) ....'37 '62 C.610 B.S.C. L.273 LL.B. [Green H.S.] ⊙
Hall, Charles D., III, (BV) ....'57 '83 C.1260 B.A. L.7 J.D. [Hall]
Hall, Rosemarie A., (BV) ....'57 '92 C.1260 B.A. L.8 J.D. 610 Market Ave., N.
Hall Law Firm, (BV) ....610 Market Ave. N.
Halm, Jeffrey A., (AV) ....'47 '73 C.207 B.A. L.608 J.D. [Buckingham,D.&B.]
Hamann, William J., (BV) ....'38 '68 C&L.608 B.A., J.D. 2404 University Ave. NW
Hardesty, Lee Patrick ....'69 '98 C.381 B.A. L.8 J.D. Nationwide Insurance Co.
Hardy, Charlene Selinsky ....'42 '96 C.381 B.S. L.8 J.D. Asst. Pros. Atty.
Harless, Kristina M. ....'67 '99 C.890 B.A. L.8 J.D. [A Buckingham,D.&B.]
Harrison, Stephen J., (CV) ....'55 '80 C.8 B.A. L.7 J.D. 1400 Market Street North
Hartnett, Chryssa N., (BV) ....'66 '95 C.575 B.S. L.150 J.D. Stark Co. Pros. Off.
Hartnett, Thomas E., (BV) ....'66 '93 C.882 B.A. L.150 J.D. [Day K.]
Hastings, Scott G. ....'75 '05 C.999 B.A. L.8 J.D. [A Krugliak,W.G.&D.]
Haupt, Fred J., (AV) ....'41 '67 C.528 B.A. L.930 J.D. [Krugliak,W.G.&D.] (⊙Alliance)
Haupt, Jason F. ....'76 '02 C.473 B.S. L.124 J.D. [A Krugliak,W.G.&D.]
Haupt, Jeffrey D., Office, (BV) ....'54 '85 C.528 B.A. L.8 J.D. 4884 Dressler Road N.W.
Hauritz, Tyrone D., (BV) '64 '90 C.608 B.S.B.S. L.607 J.D. 218 Cleveland Avenue, S.W., 7th Floor
Haut, Annette Ruth Ciavarella, Attorney at Law '62 '92 C.980 B.A. L.1003 J.D. 5656 Gray Fox Dr., N.W.‡
Heath, Taryn L., (BV) ....'57 '82 C.473 B.A. L.8 J.D. 315 W. Tuscarawas St.
Heichel, William S., (BV) ....'35 '60 C.62 A.B. L.309 J.D. 306 Market Ave. N.
Heinbach, Charles C., Jr. ....'54 '83 C.381 B.A. L.7 J.D. 128 Linwood Ave., N.W.
Henning, Richard L., (CV) ....'49 '76 C.608 B.S. L.7 J.D. [Henning&Y.]
Henning, Sally D., (BV) ....'50 '78 C.446 B.A. L.8 J.D. [Henning&Y.]

Henning & Yost, L.P.A., (BV)
5022 Yukon Street, Suite D, 44708
Telephone: 330-479-9825 Fax: 330-479-9827
Email: henninglaw@neo.rr.com URL: http://www.henninglaw.com
Richard L. Henning; Sally D. Henning.
Employment Law, Human Resource Management, Civil Litigation.
See Professional Biographies, CANTON, OHIO

Herbert, David L., (BV) ....'48 '74 C.381 B.B.A. L.8 J.D. [Herbert&B.]

Herbert & Benson, (BV)
4571 Stephen Circle, N.W., 44718
Telephone: 330-499-1016 Fax: 330-499-0790
Email: herblegal@aol.com URL: http://www.lawyers.com/herblegal
Members of Firm: David L. Herbert; Don M. Benson; Joseph L. Piccin. Of Counsel: James J. Collum; Warren R. Price; Lynn A. Zondorak.
Insurance, Malpractice and Products Liability Defense, Commercial and Corporate Law, Business Law, Buying and Selling of Businesses, Family Business Law, Limited Liability Company Law,

(This Listing Continued)

Herbert & Benson (Continued)

Partnership Law, Professional Practices, Small Business Law, Family Law, Franchises and Franchising, General Practice, Health Care, Real Estate, Wills and Probate, Contested Wills, Trusts and Estates. Trial and Appellate Practice.

See Professional Biographies, CANTON, OHIO

Hervey, Paul B., (BV) .... '69 '94 C.264 B.A. L.930 J.D. 101 Central Plz. S.
Hess, Jacob F., Jr., (AV) .... '26 '50 C.309 A.B. L.188 J.D. [Lesh,C.&M.]
Higley, Roberta C., (BV) .... '43 '79 C.317 B.A. L.930 J.D. Family Ct. Mag.
Himmelspach, Thomas R., (BV) ..... '51 '87 C.610 B.G.S. L.7 J.D. [Buckingham,D.&B.]
Hoffman, John R., Jr. .... '45 '70 C.381 B.A. L.930 J.D. Com. Pleas J.
Hoffman, William B. .... '51 '76 C.970 B.A. L.7 J.D. Ct. App. J.
Holland, Darrell W., Jr., (BV) .... '56 '82 C.999 B.A. L.8 J.D. [D.Holland&Assoc.]
Holland, Darrell, and Associates, (BV) .... 4200 Munson Street N.W.
Hollingsworth, Jon M., (BV) .... '51 '76 C.607 B.A. L.7 J.D. 1400 N. Market Ave.
Hontas, Jerry P. .... '22 '49 C.608 L.948 LL.B. 2564 Marsh Ave., N.W.
Hornbrook, John H., (CV) .... '57 '82 C.49 B.S. L.7 J.D. 1400 N. Market St.
Horowitz, Robert D., (AV) .... '46 '72 C.246 B.A. L.7 J.D. Pros. Atty.
Hossler, Jerome H., (BV) .... '25 '49 C&L.930 B.B.A., LL.B. 315 W. Tuscarawas St.
Houston, Denise K., (BV) .... '69 '95 C.210 B.A. L.8 J.D. [Ⓐ Tzangas,P.M.&R.]
Howes, Philip E., (AV) .... '35 '60 C.645 B.S. L.930 LL.B. [Buckingham,D.&B.]
Humphrey, Christopher S. .... '— '93 C.92 B.A. L.8 J.D. [Buckingham,D.&B.]
Hunt, Randall C., (BV) .... '53 '78 C.528 B.A. L.930 J.D. [Krugliak,W.G.&D.]
Huryn, Christopher M., (BV) .... '67 '93 C.473 B.A. L.8 J.D. [Tzangas,P.M.&R.]
Iams, Bradley Richard, (BV) .... '56 '81 C.381 B.A. L.930 J.D. [Iams,B.]
Iams, Bradley, (BV) .... 220 Market Ave. S., Ste. 400
Inboden, Marc B. '48 '73
C.631 B.A. L.608 J.D. V.P. & Tr. Offr., United Natl. Bk. & Tr. Co.
Ionno, John M., Law Office of, (BV) '44 '72
C.608 B.S. L.7 J.D. 2223 Fulton Road, N.W., Suite 206
James, Jim D. .... '58 '83 C&L.117 B.A., J.D. Fam. Ct. J.

Jeffries, Timothy J. '74 '00 C&L.608 B.A., J.D.
437 Market North, 44702
Telephone: 330-456-0061 Fax: 330-456-1344
Email: tjeffries@sbcglobal.net
Business Litigation, Real Estate, Commercial Real Estate, Landlord and Tenant Law, Residential Real Estate, Zoning Law, Land Use, Business Law, Business Acquisitions, Business Sales, Bankruptcy, Business Formation, Business Planning, Business Taxation, Collections, Contracts, Corporate, Partnership Law, Family Business Law, Franchise Law, Estate Planning.

See Professional Biographies, CANTON, OHIO

John, Michael L. .... '58 '83 C.610 A.B. L.7 J.D. 4607 Yale Ave. N.W.
Johnson, Mark D. '64 '92 C.338 B.A. L.589 J.D.
(adm. in IL; not adm. in OH) [Johnson] ⊙

Johnson Law Group
44718 ⊙
Telephone: 877-333-2889 Fax: 309-827-3991
Email: johnson.law@verizon.net
Mark D. Johnson (Not admitted in OH); P. Steven Maasz (Resident).
Languages: Japanese and Greek.
Felonies, Murder, White Collar Crime, Drugs, Domestic Violence, DWI.
Okemos, Michigan Office: 3474 Alaiedon Parkway, 47764. Telephone: 877-333-2889.
Bloomington, Illinois Office: 115 W. Front Street, 61701. Telephone: 309-827-3670.
South Bend, Indiana Office: 218 W. Washington Street, 46601. Telephone: 877-333-2889.

See Professional Biographies, CANTON, OHIO

Jonas, Daniel M., (AV) .... '41 '68 C&L.930 A.B., J.D. [Black M.S.&A.L.&Assoc.]
Jones, Douglas D. .... '55 '80 C.1288 B.A. L.8 J.D. [D.D.Jones]

Jones, Douglas D., Co., LPA
2867 Sharonwood Avenue NW, 44708
Telephone: 330-477-5570 Fax: 330-477-4744
Email: djones@neo.rr.com URL: http://www.dougdjones.com
Douglas D. Jones.
Languages: German, Hebrew, Greek.
Wills, Probate, Trusts and Estates, Family Law, Bankruptcy, Real Estate, Property Law, Personal Injury, Torts, Automobile Accidents, Adoptions, Divorce, Child Custody, Child Support, Debtor and Creditor, Estate Planning, Medical Malpractice and Products Liabilities.

See Professional Biographies, CANTON, OHIO

Juergensen, John L. .... '70 '99 C.967 B.B.A. L.7 J.D. [Ⓐ Black M.S.&A.L.&Assoc.]
Kahn, Bernard L. .... '23 '51 C.846 B.A. L.608 J.D. 1000 Market Ave. N.
Kamerer, James P. .... '49 '74 C.381 B.A. L.8 J.D. [Black M.S.&A.L.&Assoc.]
Kaminski, John S. .... '77 '03 C.597 B.A. L.1119 J.D. [Ⓐ Day K.]
Kanakaredes, Aretta H. .... '62 '87 C.385 B.A. L.7 J.D. Jud. Clk., Ct. of App. J.
Kandel, James R., (BV) .... '41 '72 C.528 B.A. L.607 J.D. [J.R.Kandel]
Kandel, James R., Co., L.P.A., (BV) .... 401 Bank One Tower
Kaplanis, Anthony T., (BV) '64 '89 C&L.608 B.A., J.D.
808 Courtyard Center, 116 Cleveland Avenue, N.W.
Kattman, Jeffrey C., Law Office ... '53 '81 C.610 B.A. L.161 J.D. 4429 Fulton Drive, NW
Keenan, J. Sean, (AV) .... '42 '67 C.999 B.A. L.602 LL.B. [Day K.]
Kendig, Russ, (BV) .... '57 '84 C.597 B.S. L.608 J.D. 201 Cleveland Ave. S.W.
Kennedy, Edward T. .... '67 '00 C.980 B.E. L.201 J.D. [Ⓐ Buckingham,D.&B.] (Pat.)
Kessler, Alan .... '47 '75 C.563 B.S. L.117 J.D. 301 Cleveland Ave., S.W.
Kessler, Terrence P., (AV) ... '50 '75 C.976 B.A. L.608 J.D. [Black M.S.&A.L.&Assoc.]
Kettler, J. Scott .... '50 '76 C.1260 B.A. L.7 J.D. Tr. Dept., Harter Bk. & Tr. Co.
Kirchner, Aric Howard .... '71 '98 C.150 B.A. L.930 J.D. 5046 Beechgrove Ave.
Klapp, Victoria Zwick, (BV) .... '49 '75 C.381 B.A. L.7 J.D. [Zwick]
Klide, Harry E. .... '30 '55 C.381 B.A. L.930 LL.B. Com. Pleas J.
Knapic, Barbara A., (AV) .... '— '86 C.381 B.A. L.8 J.D. [Buckingham,D.&B.]
Knight, Darci M. ... '73 '99 C.1260 B.A. L.1003 J.D. Community Legal Aid Services, Inc.
Knudsen, Nancy S., (CV) '52 '82 C&L.8 B.A., J.D.
Dir. Organizational Advancement, The Timken Company
Kodak, George .... '25 '57 C.381 B.A. L.150 LL.B. 729 Maryland Ave., S.W.‡
Kotnik, Donald Patrick, (BV) .... '64 '90 C.97 B.A. L.365 J.D. [Lesh,C.&M.]
Kovach, Linda Katherine .... '62 '91 C&L.8 B.S., J.D. Industrial Comm.

Krugliak, Wilkins, Griffiths & Dougherty Co., L.P.A., (AV) BB
4775 Munson Street, N.W., P.O. Box 36963, 44735-6963 ⊙
Telephone: 330-497-0700 Fax: 330-497-4020
Email: legal@kwgd.com URL: http://www.kwgd.com
F. Stuart Wilkins (Retired); Raymond E. Griffiths; Ronald W. Dougherty; David L. Simiele; Fred J. Haupt; John Bogniard; Michael A. Thompson; William G. Williams; Richard E. Davis (Certified Specialist in Estate Planning, Trust and Probate Law, Ohio State Bar Association); Randall C. Hunt; Sam O. Simmerman; Terry A. Moore; Paul H. Malesick II; Karen Soehnlen McQueen; Jacqueline Bollas Caldwell; David E. Butz; Leslie Iams Kuntz; Charles E. Ringer; Edward D. Murray (Certified Specialist in Workers' Compensation Law, Ohio State Bar Association); James F. Contini II (Certified Specialist in Estate Planning, Trust and Probate Law, Ohio State Bar Association); John M. Tucker; John D. Clark (Certified Specialist in Estate Planning, Trust and Probate Law, Ohio State Bar Association); Michael A. Warkall; Matthew P. Mullen; Scott R. Miller;—Gregory D. Swope; Scott M. Zurakowski; Jason M. Baasten; Jeffrey A. Fickes; Jason F. Haupt; Owen J. Rarric; Michael J. Bogdan; Nathan D. Vaughan; Jessica A. Morrison; Scott G. Hastings; Jennifer L. Lile. Of Counsel: Benjamin B. de Forest.

(This Listing Continued)

Krugliak, Wilkins, Griffiths & Dougherty Co., L.P.A. (Continued)

Corporate Law, Mergers and Acquisitions, Labor and Employment (Private and Public Sector), Employee Benefits, Real Estate, Taxation, Complex Litigation, Contracts, Insurance Defense, Estates and Trusts, Probate, Elder Law, Commercial Litigation, Oil and Gas, Occupational Safety and Health, Environmental Law, Health Care Law, Hospital Law, Bankruptcy, Banks and Banking, Securities, Construction Law, Family Law, Education Law, Workers Compensation, Personal Injury Litigation, Collections, Debtor and Creditor, Government, Media Law and Electronic Commerce.
Alliance, Ohio Office: KeyBank Building, 960 West State Street. Telephone: 330-823-9262.
New Philadelphia, Ohio Office: 158 N. Broadway Street. Telephone: 330-364-3472.
Sugarcreek, Ohio Office: 233 Factory Street, Suite 4. Telephone: 330-852-3355.

See Professional Biographies, CANTON, OHIO

Kuhn, Richard R., Attorney at Law, (BV) '51 '80
C.970 B.A. L.7 J.D. 1428 Market Ave. N.
Kuntz, Leslie Iams, (BV) .... '61 '86 C.473 B.A. L.8 J.D. [Krugliak,W.G.&D.]
Kyhos, Wayne C., (BV) .... '44 '69 C.210 B.A. L.7 J.D. [Day K.]

Lally, Thomas William '39 '73 C.381 B.A. L.8 J.D.
Belpar Law Center, 4571 Stephen Circle, N.W., 44718-3629
Telephone: 330-499-5474 Fax: 330-433-1313
Email: TLally4571@sbcglobal.net URL: http://www.lawyers.com/tlally4571
General Civil Trial Practice in State and Federal Courts.

See Professional Biographies, CANTON, OHIO

Lammert, Thomas E., (BV) .... '47 '76 C.665 B.S. L.7 J.D. [Guy,L.&T.]
Lancaster, Judith E., (CV) '40 '94 C.382 B.S. L.8 J.D.
116 Cleveland Ave., N.W., Ste. 300
Lancianese, Frank W. .... '58 '84 C.8 B.A. L.7 J.D. [Ⓐ Cross&R.]
Lattavo, Philip E., (BV) .... '41 '67 C.602 B.A. L.930 J.D. Pres., Lattavo Brothers Inc.
Leb, Arthur S., (AV) .... '30 '55 C.178 A.B. L.930 LL.B. [Ⓒ Buckingham,D.&B.]
Lee, Cheryl S. .... '48 '02 C.980 B.S. L.8 J.D. [Ⓐ Tzangas,P.M.&R.]
Lee, Joan Cook .... '29 '76 C&L.383 B.A., J.D. 196 E. Main St.
Leedy, Christopher D. .... '59 '85 C.1323 B.S. L.8 J.D. ATL Consulting Co.
Lesh, Casner & Miller, A Legal Professional Association, (AV)
4150 Belden Village Street, N.W.
Lile, Jennifer L. .... '68 '00 C.381 B.S. L.8 J.D. [Ⓐ Krugliak,W.G.&D.]
Lioi, Sara .... '60 '87 C.97 B.A. L.608 J.D. Com. Pleas J.
Little, Donald R. .... '38 '66 C.610 B.F.A. L.8 J.D. 1400 Market Ave., N.
Lolli, Richard J., (BV) .... '51 '76 C.276 B.S. L.930 J.D. [Buckingham,D.&B.]
Lombardi, Thomas J., (BV) .... '41 '66 C.363 B.S. L.608 J.D. [Lesh,C.&M.]
Lonas, Webster M., Jr. .... '34 '65 C.207 B.A. L.8 J.D. 1810 36th St., N.W.
Longbrake, Suzanne T. .... '64 '95 C.725 B.A. L.930 J.D. Ct. App.
Lowry, Derek J., (BV) .... '71 '98 C.381 B.B.A. L.7 J.D. 101 Central Plz. S., Ste. 300
Lucas, Cynthia G. .... '54 '81 C&L.117 B.M., J.D. 3880 Croydon Drive NW
Lucas, Frank, (AV) .... '14 '52 C.381 L.948 LL.B. P.O. Box 35656
Lunich, Dana Lynne .... '57 '85 C.381 B.A. L.7 J.D. Pub. Def. Off.
Maasz, P. Steven .... '66 '91 C.610 B.A. L.94 J.D. [Johnson]
Machan, Mitchell A., (CV) .... '55 '81 C.967 B.A. L.7 J.D. [M.Machan]
Machan, Mitchell, (CV) .... 3810 Tuscarawas St. W.
Mackall, Donald C. .... '22 '52 C.528 B.A. L.930 LL.B. 1545 Stayman St. S.W.
Madden, Jean A., (BV) .... '52 '90 C.528 B.A. L.8 J.D. 200 Tuscarawas Street, West
Majors, Shirley F. .... '34 '78 C.381 B.S. L.8 J.D. 5999 Canterbury, N.W.‡
Malesick, Paul H., II, (BV) .... '55 '81 C.381 B.A. L.7 J.D. [Krugliak,W.G.&D.]
Mannos, James G., (BV) .... '50 '77 C.97 B.A. L.607 J.D. [Tzangas,P.M.&R.]
Maragas, Douglas John .... '64 '92 C.967 B.A. L.7 J.D. Asst. Pros. Atty.
Markley, Sheila M., (AV) '47 '72
C.518 B.A. L.228 J.D. 200 Market Avenue North (⊙Canton)
Marsh, Bobbie L., (BV) .... '57 '89 C.999 B.A. L.930 J.D. 111 2nd St., N.W.
Marsh, Victor R., (AV) ...... '40 '66 C.174 B.A. L.608 J.D. [Black M.S.&A.L.&Assoc.]
Martuccio, Joseph ...... '53 '81 C.980 B.A. L.285 J.D. Asst. Law Dir., Canton Law Dept.
Matasich, Stephen E. .... '69 '96 C.8 B.A. L.1003 J.D. [Day K.]
McBride, Robert J., (BV) .... '66 '95 C.201 B.A. L.602 J.D. [Day K.]
McCall, John S., Jr., (BV) .... '46 '74 C.973 M.B.A. L.7 J.D. [Lesh,C.&M.]
McCallin, Alfred D., (BV) '57 '82
C.999 B.A. L.851 J.D. 116 Cleveland Avenue, N.W. Suite 500
McFarren, Randy ...... '49 '74 C.528 B.A. L.7 J.D. 220 Market Avenue, South Suite 1140
McGinnis, William F. .... '57 '92 C.381 B.A. L.7 J.D. [Puterbaugh&M.]
McHugh, James M., (BV) .... '60 '90 C.47 B.A. L.8 J.D. [Tzangas,P.M.&R.]
McIlwain, Jeaneen J. .... '60 '84 C.1147 B.S. L.7 J.D. 1835 Dueser Ave., SW, GNE-24‡
McKinley, Kathleen A. '47 '84 C.205 B.A. L.1066 J.D.
4150 Belden Village St., Ste. 604
McNulty, Mary F. .... '19 '56 C.599 B.A. L.948 LL.B. 7300 Beverly Ave. N.E.
McQueen, Jill C., (BV) .... '61 '86 C.930 B.A. L.608 J.D. [Day K.] (⊙Canton)
McQueen, Karen Soehnlen, (AV) '59 '84
C.607 B.S.B.A. L.608 J.D. [Krugliak,W.G.&D.]
Mehosky, Brian Lee '56 '86 C.610 B.S. L.989 J.D.
Sr. Intell. Prop. Atty., The Timken Co.
Mertes, Brian R., (BV) .... '70 '95 C.201 B.S. L.8 J.D. [Black M.S.&A.L.&Assoc.]
Mestel, Mariella, (BV) .... '40 '77 C.8 B.A. L.7 J.D. City Law Dept.
Meyer, Robert C., (AV) .... '53 '78 C.967 B.A. L.851 J.D. [Buckingham,D.&B.]
Miller, Donald M., (BV) .... '47 '74 C.999 B.A. L.7 J.D. 1400 N. Market Ave.
Miller, Rex W., (BV) .... '45 '70 C.607 B.A. L.930 J.D. [Lesh,C.&M.]
Miller, Scott R. .... '70 '97 C.381 B.A. L.8 J.D. [Krugliak,W.G.&D.]
Milligan, Richard S., (AV) .... '54 '80 C.385 A.B. L.7 J.D. [Buckingham,D.&B.]

Millisor & Nobil, A Legal Professional Association, (AV)
4117 Whipple Avenue NW, 44718 ⊙
Telephone: 330-493-8525; 888-867-6869 Telefax: 330-493-8606
Email: laborlaw@millisor.com URL: http://www.millisor.com
John R. Slater.
Employment Law including Labor Relations, Equal Employment Opportunity, Public Sector, OSHA, Arbitration Law, Litigation, Workers Compensation Law, Human Resources Consulting and Employee Benefit Law.
Cleveland, Ohio Office: 9150 South Hills Boulevard, Suite 300, 44147-3599. Telephone: 440-838-8800. Telefax: 440-838-8805.
Columbus, Ohio Office: 300 East Broad Street, Suite 190, 43215. Telephone: 614-221-2234. Telefax: 614-221-1278.

See Professional Biographies, CANTON, OHIO

Mills, Daniel M. .... '59 '86 C.963 B.S. L.607 J.D. P.O. Box 35656
Minkler, Daniel A., (AV) .... '52 '79 C.336 B.S. L.1003 J.D. [Day K.]
Mokodean, Michael J., Jr. '23 '55 C.381 B.S. L.948 J.D.
2607 Charing Cross Rd. N.W.‡
Moore, Edgar M., Jr., (BV) .... '51 '77 C&L.8 B.A., J.D. [E.N.Moore,Jr.]
Moore, Laureen M. '58 '84 C.201 B.S. L.607 J.D.
Mng. Atty., Community Legal Aid Services, Inc.
Moore, Terry A., (BV) .... '55 '80 C.980 B.A. L.150 J.D. [Krugliak,W.G.&D.]
Moore, Edgar N., Jr., Attorney at Law, (BV) .... 4200 Munson St. N.W.
Morris, Jonathan Eugene, (BV) .... '66 '94 C.611 B.A. L.893 J.D. [Redinger&M.]
Morrison, Jessica A. .... '79 '04 C.150 B.B.A. L.8 J.D. [Ⓐ Krugliak,W.G.&D.]

Morrow, Tod T., (BV) .... '61 '89 C.528 B.A. L.608 J.D. [Buckingham,D.&B.]
Mullen, Matthew P., (BV) .... '69 '94 C.8 B.A. L.7 J.D. [Krugliak,W.G.&D.]
Murphy, John A., Jr., (BV) .... '56 '81 C.851 B.B.A. L.861 J.D. [Day K.]
Murphy, Robert J. .... '79 '04 C.385 B.A. L.124 J.D. [Ⓐ Black M.S.&A.L.&Assoc.]
Murray, Edward D., (BV) .... '65 '91 C&L.608 B.A., J.D. [Krugliak,W.G.&D.]
Myers, Janel M., (BV) .... '64 '94 C&L.8 B.A., J.D. 4775 Munson St. N/W
Myers, Kenneth A. .... '57 '83 C&L.608 B.A., J.D. F.B.I.
Mylett, Robert E. .... '24 '52 C.381 L.948 LL.B. Com. Pleas J.
Nalawadi, Shila J. .... '— '01 C.528 B.S. L.124 J.D. [Ⓐ Buckingham,D.&B.]
Neal, M. Diane, (BV) '52 '77 C.610 B.A. L.930 J.D.
V.P., Admin. & Corp. Coun., Peoples Services, Inc.
Newbold, Robert J., (BV) .... '63 '89 C.528 B.A. L.8 J.D. [Ⓒ Day K.]
Nicodemo, John L., (BV) .... '47 '72 C.381 B.B.A. L.930 J.D. 124 15th St., N.W.
Nicodemo, Richard A., (BV) .... '57 '84 C.610 B.S. L.117 J.D. [Okey]
Oberholtzer, Matthew W., (BV) .... '61 '89 C&L.8 B.A., J.D. 116 Cleveland Ave., N.W.
O'Byrne, Eugene Donald, IV, (CV) .... '71 '98 C.790 B.S. L.8 J.D. Crim. Prosecutor
Okey, Eugene Paul, (AV) .... '23 '59 C.381 L.948 J.D. [Okey]
Okey, Mark D., (AV) .... '51 '76 C.381 B.A. L.607 J.D. [Okey]
Okey, Steven P., (AV) .... '62 '87 C.381 B.G.S. L.7 J.D. [Okey]
Okey Law Firm, The, L.P.A., (AV) .... 337 Third Street, N.W.
Osler, Tammie Marie .... '74 '01 C.528 B.A. L.8 J.D. City Pros. Off.
O'Toole, Linda A. .... '65 '99 C.999 B.S. L.989 J.D. Pub. Def.'s Off.
Otto, Jill F., (BV) .... '61 '86 C.930 B.A. L.608 J.D. 200 Market Avenue North (⊙Canton)
Paar, Louis H. .... '28 '58 C.381 B.S. L.7 LL.B. 2204 Monument Rd. N.W.‡
Pac-urar, Mary Lynn, (BV) '56 '89 C.381 B.A. L.7 J.D.
100 30th Street, N.W., Suite #107
Parker, Gerald M. .... '44 '71 C.313 B.A. L.607 J.D. 5120 Limerick N.W.
Pastore, Catherine A., (CV) .... '62 '87 C.437 B.S. L.7 J.D. 6370 Mt. Pleasant St. N.W.
Paulino, Joanne G. .... '70 '96 C&L.8 B.S., J.D. [Ⓐ Day K.]
Pearl, Blaine H. .... '14 '42 C.124 B.S. L.948 LL.B. 1007 Milford St., N.E.‡
Pelini, Craig G., (AV) .... '58 '84 C.901 B.A. L.665 J.D. [Pelini&Assoc.]

Pelini & Associates LLC, (AV)
Bretton Commons, Suite 400, 8040 Cleveland Avenue, N.W. (North Canton), 44720
Telephone: 330-305-6400 Fax: 330-305-0042
URL: http://www.lawyers.com/pelini&associates
Craig G. Pelini;—Julie A. Geiser; Kristen E. Campbell; Eric J. Williams; Randall M. Traub.
Litigation, Insurance Defense, Medical Malpractice Defense, Products Liability Defense, Political Subdivision Representation, Tort and Business Litigation, Construction Litigation, Insurance Coverage Litigation, Labor and Employment Law.
See Professional Biographies, CANTON, OHIO

Perlman, Marjorie R., Attorney at Law, (BV) '48 '77
C.788 A.B. L.94 J.D. 5502 Market Ave. N., Ste. B
Peshek, Linda M., (CV) .... '57 '86 C.381 B.A. L.7 J.D. 4775 Munson Street, N.W.
Piccin, Joseph L. .... '74 '00 C.473 B.S. L.8 J.D. [Herbert&B.]
Pidcock, William S. .... '56 '82 C.610 B.A. L.608 J.D. [Robertson,Z.&P.]
Piepho, Scott R., (BV) .... '64 '92 C.970 B.A. L.893 J.D. Asst. Pros. Atty.
Plakas, Leonidas E., (AV) .... '51 '76 C.8 B.S. L.7 J.D. [Tzangas,P.M.&R.]
Pontius, Robert A. .... '22 '57 C.608 L.948 LL.B. Suite 300, 111 2nd Street, N.W.‡
Poole, Doreen Smith .... '16 '43 C.381 B.S. L.948 LL.B. 2800 Market Ave., N.‡
Poulos, John A., (BV) .... '53 '81 C&L.8 B.A., J.D. 218 Cleveland Ave. N.W.
Powell, Barbara E. '54 '83 C.381 B.A. L.124 J.D.
Supv. Atty., Community Legal Aid Services, Inc.
Powell, Tim A., (BV) .... '42 '76 C.597 B.A. L.117 J.D. [Day K.]
Prelac, John M., (BV) .... '59 '84 C.528 B.A. L.8 J.D. [Ⓐ Day K.]
Preston, Robert B., III .... '70 '04 C.161 B.A. L.7 J.D. [Ⓐ Black M.S.&A.L.&Assoc.]
Price, Warren R. .... '72 '04 C.999 B.A. L.8 J.D. [Ⓒ Herbert&B.]
Princic, Richard A., (AV) .... '50 '76 C.25 B.A. L.608 J.D. [Day K.]
Procario, Gary J., (BV) .... '— '69 C.608 B.Sc. L.7 J.D. 4450 Belden Village St.
Proctor, James P., (BV) .... '52 '80 C.608 B.S. L.8 J.D. [Zwick]
Pusateri, Paul J., (CV) .... '64 '91 C.1260 B.A. L.930 J.D. [Buckingham,D.&B.]
Puterbaugh, Michael R., (BV) .... '61 '88 C.528 B.A. L.930 J.D. [Puterbaugh&M.] ⊙
Puterbaugh & McGinnis L.L.C., (BV) .... 111 Second Street NW
Putman, Timothy J., (CV) .... '54 '85 C.608 B.A.B.S. L.8 J.D. Putman Properties Inc.
Quinlan, Karen Ross, (BV) .... '59 '92 C.381 B.B.A. L.930 J.D. 4429 Fulton Dr. N.W.
Raies, Elizabeth A., (BV) .... '59 '87 C&L.923 B.S., J.D. [Tzangas,P.M.&R.]
Rambacher, John J., (BV) .... '60 '86 C.8 B.S. L.7 J.D. [Black M.S.&A.L.&Assoc.]
Rank, Susan Chae .... '— '98 C.659 B.A. L.770 J.D. [Ⓐ Buckingham,D.&B.]
Rarric, Owen J. .... '76 '02 C.318 B.A. L.7 J.D. [Ⓐ Krugliak,W.G.&D.]
Reader, W. Don, Jr. .... '27 '58 C.216 A.B. L.7 LL.B. Ret. Ct. App. J.‡
Recupero, James R., (BV) .... '56 '86 C&L.8 B.A., J.D. [J.R.Recupero]
Recupero, James R., Attorney at Law, LLC, (BV) .... 4051 Whipple Avenue NW, Suite C
Redinger, Ivan L., Jr., (BV) .... '61 '85 C.97 B.A. L.608 J.D. [Redinger&M.]
Redinger & Morris, L.L.P., (BV) .... 116 Cleveland Avenue, N.W., Suite 300
Reese, David D., Jr. .... '62 '94 C.1027 B.S. L.851 J.D. Asst. Co. Pros.
Reese, Robert Glenn .... '48 '93 C.651 B.A. L.8 J.D. [R.G.Reese]
Reese, Robert G. .... 4450 Belden Village St., NW
Regas, Steve G. .... '30 '64 C.97 B.S. L.7 LL.B. 2633 8th St. N.E.
Regula, Ralph S., (AV) .... '24 '52 C.528 B.A. L.948 LL.B. (M. C.)
Reinbold, Richard David, Jr. .... '46 '74 C.473 B.A. L.7 J.D. Com. Pleas Ct. J.

Renner, Kenner, Greive, Bobak, Taylor & Weber, A Legal Professional Association
(See Akron)

Reynolds, Mary E., (BV) .... '53 '83 C.381 B.A. L.7 J.D. [Black M.S.&A.L.&Assoc.]
Ringer, Charles E., (BV) .... '62 '89 C.8 B.A. L.608 J.D. [Krugliak,W.G.&D.]
Rinier, Alton L., (BV) .... '20 '48 C.608 B.S. L.930 LL.B. 116 Cleveland Ave., N.
Robbins, Donald L., Jr. .... '66 '02 C&L.8 B.S., J.D. [Fischer,E.&R.]
Robertson, James T., (BV) .... '45 '74 C.381 B.A. L.7 J.D. [Robertson,Z.&P.]
Robertson, Zeglen & Pidcock, (BV) .... 4690 Munson Street, N.W. Suite C
Rockenfelder, Wendy J. .... '54 '79 C.610 A.B. L.8 J.D. 5502 Market Ave. N., Ste. B
Roderick, Morgan W., Jr. .... '26 '54 C.381 B.A. L.608 LL.B. 4600 Castlebar St., N.W.‡
Roland, Deborah N. .... '61 '89 C.910 B.A. L.608 J.D. Ct. of Appeals
Roland, Robert E. .... '59 '85 C.473 B.A. L.608 J.D. [Day K.]
Rose, Mark N. .... '54 '92 C.291 B.A. L.477 J.D. V.P., Legal Affairs
Ross, John C. .... '57 '82 C.610 A.B. L.608 J.D. [Buckingham,D.&B.]
Ross, Ralph W. .... '21 '49 C.381 L.607 LL.B. 1250 Brushmore Ave. N.W.‡
Rothermel, Nancy J., (BV) .... '60 '86 C.381 B.B.A. L.7 J.D. 4180 Holiday Street, NW
Rubin, Robert G. .... '43 '68 C.367 B.A. L.930 J.D. 315 W. Tuscarawas St.
Rubin, Rosemary Gross, (BV) .... '49 '74 C.643 B.A. L.7 J.D. [Rubin&S.]

Rubin, Stanley R., (AV) '51 '76 C&L.930 B.A., J.D.
437 Market Avenue, North, 44702-1423
Telephone: 330-455-5206 Fax: 330-455-5200
Email: srrubin22@aol.com
Personal Injury Law, Medical Negligence Law, Insurance Bad Faith Litigation, Domestic Relations Law, Business Litigation, Commercial Litigation.
See Professional Biographies, CANTON, OHIO

Rubin and Selby, Co., LPA, (BV) .... 1428 Market Avenue, North
Rudebock, David Thomas '64 '91
C.8 B.S. L.851 J.D. Dep. Dir., Co. Dept. of Human Servs.
Rufo, Gregory J., (CV) .... '54 '83 C.363 B.A. L.7 J.D. [Rufo]

Rufo Law Firm, The, (CV)
Bank One Tower, 101 Central Plaza South, Suite 900, 44702
Mailing Address: P.O. Box 36793, Canton, OH 44735
Telephone: 330-456-8389 Fax: 330-456-5328 URL: http://www.divorcesource.com/OH/pages/kenandrea.html
Email: grufolaw@yahoo.com URL: http://www.grufolaw.com
Gregory J. Rufo.
Criminal Law, Domestic Relations, Business Law, Family Law, Divorce, Marriage Dissolution, Child Support, Child Custody, Visitation Rights, Alimony, Spousal Support, Criminal Defense, Misdemeanors, Felonies, DUI, Traffic Violations, Drug Crimes, Incorporation, Partnerships, Dissolution of Business, Business Contracts, Business Litigation, Collections.
See Professional Biographies, CANTON, OHIO

Sales, Gary N. .... '55 '80 C.150 B.S. L.608 J.D. 6491 Friarsgate Dr., N.W.
Sand, Michael, (AV) .... '38 '69 C.610 B.S.E.E. L.7 J.D. [Ⓒ Sand&S.] (Pat.)
Sand & Sebolt, A Legal Professional Association, (BV) .... 4940 Munson St., NW (Pat.)
Savan, Cheryl '67 '91 C&L.260 B.S., J.D.
(adm. in FL; not adm. in OH) 1474 Whittier St. N.E.‡
Saylor, Timothy B., (BV) .... '60 '89 C.97 B.A. L.8 J.D. 236 3rd Street S.W.
Schandel, Phillip D., (BV) .... '41 '67 C.363 B.S.S. L.608 J.D. [P.D.Schandel]
Schandel, Phillip D., Co., L.P.A., (BV) .... 709 Courtyard Center, Suite 709
Scherff, Scott Alan, (AV) '54 '79 C&L.608 B.A., J.D.
Corp. Sec. & Asst. Gen Coun., The Timken Co.
Schmuck, H. W., (AV) .... '15 '40 C.528 B.A. L.188 LL.B. 401 Central Trust Twr.
Schulman, Allen, Jr., (AV) .... '47 '75 C.473 B.A. L.7 J.D. 236 Third St. S.W.
Schultz, Stanley M. .... '46 '75 C.385 A.B. L.7 J.D. P.O. Box 8163‡
Scott, Frederic R., (BV) .... '67 '92 C&L.602 B.A., J.D. 1428 Market Avenue North
Sebolt, Joseph A., (BV) .... '67 '92 C.665 B.S.M.E. L.7 J.D. [Sand&S.] (Pat.)
Sekula, Mary Lou, (CV) .... '50 '96 C.18 B.S.N. L.8 J.D. 220 Market Ave., S.
Selby, Joan Patricia .... '53 '78 C.611 B.A. L.608 J.D. [Rubin&S.]
Selegean-Dostal, Sue Ellen .... '66 '96 C.8 B.A. L.124 J.D. 116 Cleveland Ave., N.W.
Severs, Drew H. .... '55 '83 C.231 A.B. L.8 J.D. Consumer Direct Inc.
Shandor, Steven D. .... '73 '04 C.980 B.A. L.608 J.D. [Ⓐ Day K.]
Shea-Moore, Laureen .... '58 '84 C.201 B.S. L.607 J.D. 306 N. Market Ave., Ste. 730
Sheehan, Earl C., (AV) .... '27 '52 C.528 B.A. L.930 LL.B. 220 South Market Street
Shifman, Arnold R., (AV) .... '40 '64 C&L.608 B.A., J.D. [Black M.S.&A.L.&Assoc.]
Silagy, Anne Piero, (BV) .... '60 '85 C&L.8 B.A., J.D. 220 Market Avenue S.
Simiele, David L., (BV) .... '36 '63 C.608 B.S. L.930 LL.B. [Krugliak,W.G.&D.]
Simmerman, Sam O., (BV) .... '53 '79 C.381 B.A. L.608 J.D. [Krugliak,W.G.&D.]
Simmons, David J., (AV) .... '56 '82 C.8 B.A. L.930 J.D. [Simmons&C.]
Simmons & Cleaver, LLP, (AV) .... 4690 Munson St. N.W.
Sinclair, V. Lee, Jr., (AV) .... '51 '76 C.381 B.A. L.7 J.D. Com. Pleas J.
Skakun, John M. .... '25 '58 C.381 L.948 LL.B. 4119 Whipple Ave., N.W.‡
Slater, James W., (BV) .... '43 '70 C.184 A.B. L.276 J.D. [Slater&Z.] ⊙
Slater, John R., (BV) .... '46 '81 C&L.608 B.A., J.D. [Millisor&N.] (⊙Cleveland)
Slater & Zurz, (BV) .... 4450 Belden Village Street, N.W. (⊙Akron)
Smith, Corey Lonjay Minor .... '74 '01 C.97 B.A. L.851 J.D. Co. Pros. Off.
Smith, Warren G., (AV) .... '10 '36 C.528 A.B. L.930 LL.B. 4430 Plain Center Road, N.E.
Snow, Randolph L., (AV) .... '46 '71 C.970 B.A. L.608 J.D. [Black M.S.&A.L.&Assoc.]
Soares, Bruce M., (AV) .... '55 '80 C.676 B.A. L.930 J.D. [Black M.S.&A.L.&Assoc.]
Sokolowski, Sue Ann .... '67 '01 C.1115 B.A. L.7 J.D. [Ⓐ Simmons&C.]
Solomon, Aurel .... '27 '52 C.381 A.B. L.607 LL.B. 652 Citizens Svgs. Bldg.
Souers, Loren E., Jr. .... '47 '74 C.207 B.A. L.930 J.D. 220 Market Ave. S.
Sparks, William R., (AV) '52 '77
C.294 A.B. L.602 J.D. 3930 Fulton Drive, N.W., Suite 106
Sponseller, John N., (BV) .... '31 '65 C.528 B.A. L.1003 J.D. 4180 Holiday Street NW
Steffy, Willis .... '15 '54 C.432 A.B. L.948 P.O. Box 80277
Stein, Donald M. .... '16 '49 C.477 A.B. L.948 LL.B. Pres., National Iron & Metal Co.
Strawn, James R., (BV) .... '51 '76 C.967 A.B. L.930 J.D. [Black M.S.&A.L.&Assoc.]
Stucki, David E. .... '59 '85 C.8 B.A. L.7 J.D. Fam. Ct. J.
Sweeney, Robert M. .... '38 '67 C.473 B.S. L.8 J.D. P.O. Box 24190
Swope, Gregory D., (BV) .... '63 '95 C.381 B.A. L.7 J.D. [Ⓐ Krugliak,W.G.&D.]
Tarr, David T., (BV) .... '37 '66 C.363 B.S.S. L.8 J.D. 1400 Market Avenue, N.
Thompson, Michael A., (BV) .... '48 '74 C.867 B.A. L.930 J.D. [Krugliak,W.G.&D.]

Tipping Co., L.P.A. A Legal Professional Association
(See Akron)

Totten, Albert S. .... '28 '56 C.381 L.948 LL.B. 140 Santa Clara, N.W.
Traub, Randall M. .... '67 '99 C.1111 B.A. L.8 J.D. [Ⓐ Pelini&Assoc.]
Trifelos, Geo. H. .... '31 '54 C.381 A.B. L.930 LL.B. 4450 Belden Village Ave., N.W.
Tscholl, Robert J., (BV) .... '51 '76 C.610 B.B.A. L.7 J.D. 220 Market Ave., S.
Tucker, John M., (BV) .... '71 '96 C.472 B.S. L.930 J.D. [Krugliak,W.G.&D.]
Tyburski, Charles J., (AV) '34 '64 C.611 B.A. L.608 J.D.
[Ⓒ Black M.S.&A.L.&Assoc.]
Tzangas, George J. .... '30 '57 C.610 B.Sc. L.902 LL.B. [Tzangas,P.M.&R.] ‡
Tzangas, Plakas, Mannos & Raies, (AV) .... 220 Market Ave. S., Fl. 8
Urban, George, (BV) .... '66 '94 C.381 B.G.S. L.8 J.D. 101 Central Plz. Ste. 3
Vaccaro, Michael F., (CV) .... '30 '57 C.381 B.A. L.930 LL.B. 6372 Groton St. N.W.
Vagotis, Angela T., (BV) .... '63 '90 C.97 B.S.N. L.8 J.D. [A.T.Vagotis]
Vagotis, Angela T., Co., L.P.A., (BV) .... 220 Market Avenue S.
Van Abel, John P., (AV) .... '32 '59 C.528 B.A. L.608 J.D. [Buckingham,D.&B.]
Vance, Joseph Edward .... '75 '99 C.610 B.A. L.7 J.D. Asst. Pros., Stark Co. Pros. Off.
Variola, John, (BV) .... '54 '79 C.473 B.S. L.608 J.D. 1024 Renkert Bldg.
Vassiles, Chrysanthe E., (BV) '71 '96
C.381 B.A. L.608 J.D. [Ⓐ Black M.S.&A.L.&Assoc.]
Vaughan, Nathan D. .... '79 '04 C.608 B.S. L.8 J.D. [Ⓐ Krugliak,W.G.&D.]
Vitale, Lisa Michelle .... '72 '97 C.610 B.A. L.7 J.D. Stark Co. Legal Aid Soc.
Wakser, Barry T., (BV) .... '66 '92 C.381 B.A. L.8 J.D. 200 Tuscarawas Street, West
Waldeck, John J. .... '21 '51 C.924 L.948 LL.B. 804 AmeriTrust Bldg.
Warkall, Michael A., (BV) .... '68 '94 C.381 B.A. L.851 J.D. [Krugliak,W.G.&D.]
Washam, Scott A., (BV) .... '62 '87 C.381 B.A. L.7 J.D. [Okey]
Weltman, Jeffrey H., (BV) .... '54 '79 C.294 B.A. L.8 J.D. 4819 Munson St., N.W.
Werren, J. Curtis, (CV) .... '67 '92 C.294 B.A. L.608 J.D. [Day K.]
Werren, John R., (AV) .... '37 '61 C.294 A.B. L.930 LL.B. [Day K.]
Whitticar, Ruth M. .... '13 '43 C.599 A.B. L.948 LL.B. 325 6th St. S.W.‡
Wilkins, F. Stuart, (AV) .... '— '52 C&L.477 A.B., J.D. [Krugliak,W.G.&D.] ‡
Wilkof, Jeffrey S., (AV) .... '47 '80 C.610 B.S. L.7 J.D. 124 15th Street, N.W.
Williams, Eric J., (CV) .... '73 '00 C.381 B.A. L.8 J.D. [Ⓐ Pelini&Assoc.]
Williams, James H. .... '34 '58 C.381 B.A. L.608 J.D. U.S. Bkrptcy. J.
Williams, William G., (AV) .... '50 '75 C.1323 B.A. L.161 J.D. [Krugliak,W.G.&D.]
Willoughby, John A. .... '48 '73 C.611 B.A. L.930 J.D. Republic Engineered Steels, Inc.
Wilson, Brian R., (BV) .... '62 '87 C.381 B.A. L.7 J.D. [Okey]
Wilson, Elwood C. .... '19 '50 C.930 A.B. L.948 LL.B. 222 Valleyview Avenue NW

Wilson, R. P. ....'07 '31 C&L.607 A.B., J.D. Ret. Mun. J.
Wirtz, John B., (BV) .... '48 '73 C.734 B.A. L.930 J.D. 220 Market Ave. S., Ste. 600
Wise, John W. .... '51 '79 C.97 B.A. L.607 J.D. Com. Pleas J.
Woolbert, Gordon D., II, (CV) '70 '97
C.813 B.A. L.880 J.D. [Black M.S.&A.L.&Assoc.]
Wyler, Alicia M., (AV) .... '46 '78 C.8 B.A. L.7 J.D. [Day K.]
Yackshaw, Matthew, (BV) .... '53 '79 C.363 B.A. L.608 J.D. [Day K.]
Zeglen, Joseph M., (CV) .... '59 '85 C.8 B.S. L.7 J.D. [Robertson,Z.&P.]
Zemis, Kristin R. .... '67 '93 C.245 B.A. L.201 J.D. [A Black M.S.&A.L.&Assoc.]
Zimmerman, Brian L., (BV) .... '62 '89 C.473 B.A. L.8 J.D. 236 3rd Street S.W.
Zink, Larry A., (BV) .... '51 '75 C.381 B.A. L.930 J.D. [Zink,Z.&Z.]

Zink, Zink & Zink Co., L.P.A., (BV)
3711 Whipple Avenue, N.W., 44718
Telephone: 330-492-2225 Fax: 330-492-3956
Email: lazohio@aol.com
Edward J. Zink (1921-1996); Larry A. Zink.
General Civil Practice. Corporation and Business Law. Real Estate, Probate, Contract, Environmental, Commercial and Construction Litigation. Federal and State Trial Practice.
Hillsboro Beach, Florida Office: 1198 Hillsboro Mile, Suite 244, 33062. Telephone: 945-428-3672.
See Professional Biographies, CANTON, OHIO

Zirpolo, Michael P., (BV) .... '50 '75 C.1260 B.A. L.607 J.D. 1101 Bank One Tower
Zollinger, R. Clint .... '70 '99 C.901 B.A. L.7 J.D. [A Day K.]
Zondorak, Lynn A. .... '77 '03 C.608 B.A. L.124 J.D. [C Herbert&B.]
Zugravu, Leroy V. '16 '53 C.381 L.472 LL.B.
(adm. in FL; not adm. in OH) 4840 South Blvd., N.W.‡
Zurakowski, Scott M., (CV) .... '72 '98 C.528 B.A. L.607 J.D. [A Krugliak,W.G.&D.]
Zwick, Leander P., III, (AV) .... '50 '75 C.473 B.A. L.607 J.D. [Zwick]
Zwick Law Offices Co., L.P.A., (AV) .... 1500 Market Ave. N., On the Triangle

CARDINGTON, 1,770, *Morrow Co.*

Ray, Thomas E., (BV) .... '30 '57 C&L.608 B.S., J.D. [T.E.Ray]
Ray, Thomas E., Co., Ltd., (BV) .... 107 South Marion Street

CAREY, 3,901, *Wyandot Co.*

Beck, Linden J., (BV) .... '47 '73 C&L.608 B.A., J.D. 102 E. Findlay St.
Burson, Paul A., (BV) .... '21 '49 C.112 B.S.B.A. L.608 J.D. Supm. Ct.
Maison, Robert T., (BV) .... '44 '73 C&L.851 B.B.A., J.D. 103 E. South St.

CARROLLTON, * 3,190, *Carroll Co.*

Allmon, Wm. T. .... '21 '50 C.611 L.948 LL.B. Co. Law Libr.
Benson, Paul F. .... '25 '50 C.62 L.948 LL.B. 219 Timberline Ln.‡
Burns, Donald Ralph, Jr. .... '54 '88 C.8 L.7 J.D. Pros. Atty.
Campbell, John S., (CV) '50 '76 C.8 B.S. L.362 J.D.
(adm. in FL; not adm. in OH) 130 Public Sq.
Chapman, Martin A., (CV) .... '44 '85 C.608 B.S. L.8 J.D. Co. Law Libr.
Childers, John C., (BV) .... '50 '78 C.610 B.S. L.117 J.D. [Childers&S.]
Childers and Smith, (BV) .... 70 Pub. Sq.
Falconer, Christine Lynn .... '72 '98 P.O. Box 508
Johnston, Charles A. .... '50 '77 C.935 B.A. L.607 J.D. Co. J.
Martin, William J. .... '47 '72 C.608 B.A. L.930 J.D. Com. Pleas J.
Olivito, Dominick E., Jr., (CV) .... '53 '78 C.97 B.A. L.7 J.D. Co. Law Libr.
Rice, Scott Edward .... '72 '99 C.608 B.A. L.161 J.D. Co. Pros.
Rumbaugh, Richard L., (CV) .... '41 '72 C&L.8 B.S., J.D. 63 E. Main St.
Saltsman, John K., (BV) .... '31 '58 C.528 B.A. L.608 J.D. 968 Thomas Ave. N.W.
Smith, Sean R.H. .... '56 '81 C.970 B.A. L.7 J.D. [Childers&S.]
Stoneman, Kathleen Ann Almon .... '56 '82 C.528 B.A. L.7 J.D. 63 Second St.
Weyand, John H. .... '45 '72 C.318 B.A. L.7 J.D. Prob. J.

CEDARVILLE, 3,828, *Greene Co.*

Gentry, Daniel J. .... '69 '95 C&L.201 B.A., J.D. Applied Sciences, Inc.

CELINA, * 10,303, *Mercer Co.*

Bernstein, J. Michael .... '42 '71 C&L.607 B.A., J.D. Mag., Com. Pleas Ct.
Boley, Leisa R. .... '60 '94 C&L.608 B.S., J.D. 4590 Miller Road
Chapel, Matthew W. .... '58 '95 C.92 B.A. L.930 J.D. One Insurance Sq.
Dean, Rebecca Lynn .... '66 '98 C.610 B.S.J. L.117 J.D. Celina Insurance Grp.

Drucker, Jacquelin F., Arbitration Offices of, Esq., (AV(T)) '54 '81 C&L.608 B.A., J.D.
806 Harbor Point Drive, 45822 ⊙
Telephone: 800-810-4174
Email: jdrucker@aol.com URL: http://www.druckerarbitration.com
Arbitration, Labor and Employment Law and Commercial Disputes.
New York, N.Y. Office: 432 East 58th Street, Suite 2. Telephone: 212-688-3919. Fax: 212-935-1870.
See Professional Biographies, CELINA, OHIO

Gilmore, Matthew L., (BV) .... '68 '94 C.608 B.A. L.607 J.D. 118 W. Market St.
Hinders, Andrew J., (BV) .... '52 '81 C.473 B.A. L.201 J.D. Asst. Co. Pros.
Hinders, John J., (AV) .... '25 '50 C&L.128 B.A., LL.B. 110 W. Market St.‡
Hirschfeld, Fred G. .... '32 '72 C.608 B.S. L.607 J.D. 116 E. Market St.‡
Hogan, James P., (BV) .... '41 '72 C&L.607 B.S., J.D. 409 Myers Rd.
Ikerd, Amy B. .... '70 '96 C.473 B.A. L.94 J.D. Co. Pros. Off.
Ingraham, Jeffrey R. .... '50 '75 C.967 B.A. L.607 J.D. Co. J.
Klosterman, Mark V. .... '30 '60 C.215 B.C.E. L.477 J.D. Com. Pleas J., Prob. & Juv. Div.
Knapke, Jeffrey Patrick, (BV) .... '66 '93 C.608 B.A. L.117 J.D. [Knapke]
Knapke, Murph, (BV) .... '47 '72 C.608 B.A. L.117 J.D. [Knapke]
Knapke Law Office, (BV) .... 115 N. Walnut St.
Lammers, Thomas D., (AV) .... '51 '77 C.610 B.S. L.608 J.D. [Purdy,L.&S.]
Luth, Thomas E., (BV) .... '52 '77 C.1208 B.A. L.607 J.D. [Meikle,T.&L.]
McKirnan, Kevin M., (BV) .... '51 '76 C.679 B.A. L.607 J.D. City Law Dir.
Meikle, William, (AV) .... '33 '59 C&L.477 B.B.A., J.D. [Meikle,T.&L.]
Meikle, Tesno & Luth, (AV) .... 100 N. Main St. at Market St.
Mielke, Steven P. .... '69 '95 C.608 B.A. L.117 J.D. [Mielke]
Mielke Law Office .... 116 E. Market St.
Montgomery, William W. '50 '86 C.210 B.A. L.607 J.D.
(adm. in IN; not adm. in OH) Pres. & CEO, Celina Ins. Grp.
Myers, Daniel, (BV) .... '50 '76 C.838 B.S. L.607 J.D. [Myers]
Myers Law Office, (BV) .... P.O. Box 230
Nolan, Gary L. .... '53 '80 C.1208 B.S. L.607 J.D. [Nolan]
Nolan Law Office .... 445 Johnson Ave.
Post, Donna M., (BV) .... '61 '86 C.1208 B.A. L.607 J.D. P.O. Box 126
Purdy, Don M., (AV) .... '23 '49 C.976 L.607 J.D. [Purdy,L.&S.] ‡
Purdy, Lammers & Schiavone, (AV) .... 113 East Market Street
Sacher, John W., (BV) .... '42 '68 C.201 B.A. L.607 J.D. Acting Mun. J.
Scheer, James J. .... '48 '75 C.1208 B.S. L.608 J.D. Mun. J.
Schiavone, Louis J., (BV) .... '59 '84 C.63 B.A. L.201 J.D. [Purdy,L.&S.]
Tesno, James A., (BV) .... '50 '75 C.608 B.S. L.607 J.D. [Meikle,T.&L.]
Van Arsdel, Peter R., (BV) .... '52 '82 C.1208 B.A. L.607 J.D. P.O. Box 298

Whitmer, Lewis W. .... '17 '51 C.201 L.150 J.D. Ret. Prob. J.
Zitter, Mary Pat, (BV) '47 '83 C.1208 B.A. L.201 J.D.
Co. Child Support Enforce. Agcy.

CENTERBURG, 1,432, *Knox Co.*

Cooper, Thom L. .... '45 '83 C.25 B.A. L.117 J.D. [T.L.Cooper]

Cooper, Thom L., Co., LPA
36 West Main Street, P.O. Box 747, 43011
Telephone: 740-625-5215 Toll-Free: 1-800-798-5297 Fax: 740-625-6881
Email: tlc@cooperelderlaw.com URL: http://www.cooperelderlaw.com
Thom L. Cooper;—Christopher Lavin.
Estate Planning, Estate Administration, Elder Law, Nursing Home Planning, Medicaid and Medicare, Disability Planning, Long Term Care, Guardianships, Conservatorships, Estate and Gift Tax Planning, Fiduciary Administration, Inter Vivos, Decedent's Estate Administration, Fiduciary Tax Administration, Trusts and Estates, Charitable Remainder Trusts, Insurance Trusts, Supplemental Care Trusts, Living Wills, Living Trusts.
See Professional Biographies, CENTERBURG, OHIO

Lavin, Christopher .... '68 '98 C.973 B.S.B.A. L.201 J.D. [A T.L.Cooper]
Wirth, David
(See Columbus)

CENTERVILLE, 23,024, *Montgomery Co.*

Altick & Corwin Co., L.P.A.
(See Dayton)

Billingham, Katherine L. '58 '82 C.1044 B.A. L.362 J.D.
7985 Washington Wood Drive

Chalker, Brad A., (BV) '50 '81 C.871 B.S. L.472 J.D.
848-C East Franklin St., 45459
Mailing Address: P.O. Box 750726, Dayton, OH 45475-0726
Telephone: 937-436-1893 Fax: 937-436-1894
Email: BAC@chalkerlaw.com URL: http://www.chalkerlaw.com
General Civil Practice, Employment Law, Workers' Compensation Defense, OSHA, Product Liability and Civil Litigation.
See Professional Biographies, CENTERVILLE, OHIO

Coughlin, Edward J., Jr. .... '29 '56 847 Revere Village Ct.
Deutsch, David M., Co., L.P.A.
(See Dayton)

Dundon, Jeffrey R., (BV) .... '51 '78 C.529 A.B. L.1358 J.D. 156 East Spring Valley Road
Garner, Gregory P., (BV) .... '57 '87 C.1208 B.A. L.150 J.D. Leonard Smell Developer
Gibson, Gregory C., Co., L.P.A.
(See Dayton)

Green, Christopher C. .... '70 '02 C.1208 B.A. L.1541 J.D. [A C.T.Matthews&Assoc.]
Gross, J. Robert .... '29 '53 L.608 J.D. P.O. Box 751893
Hawkins, H. Donald .... '28 '53 C&L.477 A.B., J.D. 6496 Seton Hill (⊙Dayton)
Lehman, Barbara Leinbach .... '51 '76 C.91 B.A. L.1119 J.D. 9515 Sheehan Road
Manning, Thomas J., (BV) .... '68 '92 C.696 B.A. L.201 J.D. [T.J.Manning]
Manning, Thomas J., Co., LPA, (BV) .... 800 E. Franklin St.
Matthews, Craig T., (BV) .... '52 '78 C.473 B.A.Chem. L.201 J.D. [C.T.Matthews&Assoc.]
Matthews, Craig T., and Associates, LPA, (BV) .... 376 Regency Ridge Dr.
Maurer, Ronald J., (BV) .... '69 '94 C.631 B.A. L.201 J.D. [Maurer]

Maurer Law Offices, LLC, (BV)
800 East Franklin Street, 45459
Telephone: 937-291-3400 Fax: 937-291-0757 URL: http://www.maurerlaw.com
Email: rmaurer@maurerlaw.com URL: http://www.maurerlawoffices.com
Member of Firm: Ronald J. Maurer.
Criminal Law, Driving While Intoxicated, Drug Crimes, Traffic Violations, White Collar Crime, Insurance, Personal Injury, Automobile Accidents and Injuries, Dog Bites, Sexual Abuse, Slip and Fall, Wrongful Death, Family Law, Divorce, Child Custody, Child Support, Domestic Violence, Visitation Rights, Employment Law, Disabled Access, Discrimination, Sexual Harassment, General Practice.
See Professional Biographies, CENTERVILLE, OHIO

Moland, William W. .... '31 '58 C.62 B.A. L.608 J.D. 5005 Rhine Way
Patterson, Reid E., (AV) .... '16 '44 C.178 B.A. L.150 J.D. 154 East Franklin Street
Phillips, Thomas M., Attorney at Law .... '60 '87 C.210 B.A. L.1003 J.D. 7970 Clyo Rd.
Podsedly, Susan V. .... '61 '87 C&L.201 B.S., J.D. 2033 Meadow Side Lane★
Root, Frank M., (AV) .... '26 '51 C&L.608 B.A., J.D. 6816 Cranford Drive
Sherrets Law Offices, LLC
(See Kettering)

Soltau, Hans H., (BV) .... '48 '73 C&L.150 B.A., J.D. [H.H.Soltau]
Soltau, Hans H., Co., L.P.A., (BV) .... 6776 Loop Road
Waggoner, Donald E. .... '31 '65 C.103 A.B. L.1340 J.D. 7765 Park Creek Dr.‡
Wagner, Albert J., (BV) .... '51 '77 C.1323 B.S. L.201 J.D. Co. Auditor
Yarema-Dubel, Julia Beth .... '59 '86 C.1208 B.A. L.608 J.D. 6818 Loop Road
Zwayer, Ted .... '50 '76 C&L.608 B.S., J.D. 205 Laura Ave.

CHAGRIN FALLS, 4,024, *Cuyahoga Co.*

Bagley, Donald B., III .... '68 '93 C.473 B.A. L.1003 J.D. [C Weiss&F.]
Barr, O. O., Jr. .... '22 '54 C&L.477 B.B.A., J.D. 55 Maple Hill Dr.‡
Brown, Don P., (AV) .... '36 '61 C.207 B.A. L.930 LL.B. [D.P. .R.H.B.Brown]
Brown, Richard H., (AV) .... '43 '68 C.610 B.B.A. L.930 J.D. [D.P. .R.H.B.Brown]

Brown, Don P., Richard H. Brown, (AV)
10 Center Street, 44022
Telephone: 440-247-9100 Fax: 440-247-9109 URL: http://www.immigrationohio.com Email: rhbrown@ameritech.net
Email: dpbrown@ameritech.net URL: http://www.dpbrownlaw.com
Don P. Brown; Richard H. Brown.
Probate Law, Estate Law, Estate Planning, Estate and Gift Taxation, Successions, Trusts, Wills, Probate Administration, Elder Care, Corporate Law, Immigration, Real Estate, Business Law.
See Professional Biographies, CHAGRIN FALLS, OHIO

Bruner, Henry B., (AV) .... '32 '58 C.918 A.B. L.930 LL.B. 200 Industrial Pkwy.
Burroughs, Nancy Haas .... '57 '82 C.207 B.A. L.1003 J.D. 7496 Chagrin Rd.
Buss, Dennis A. .... '46 '74 C.97 B.S. L.851 J.D. V.P. & Gen. Coun., Van Dorn Co.
Caimi, Paul A., (BV) .... '59 '86 C.309 A.B. L.94 J.D. [P.A.Caimi]
Caimi, Paul A., Co., L.P.A., (BV) .... 46 Chagrin Plaza Suite 106
Callaghan, Thomas O., (AV) '47 '73
C.93 B.S.B.A. L.188 J.D. 40 E. Washington St., Ste. 1
Corcoran, Dan'l R. .... '24 '52 C.631 A.B. L.1003 J.D. 5 S. Franklin St.
Crosley, Marianne .... '58 '85 C.165 B.A. L.608 J.D. 186 Kenton Rd.
Daniel, Clarence H. .... '17 '50 C.119 B.S. L.1003 J.D. 45050 Mather Ln.‡
Davis, James B., (AV) .... '30 '59 C.31 B.A. L.309 LL.B. 67 E. Washington St.
Dolan, Eva Haas, (CV) .... '33 '84 C.741 B.S. L.161 J.D. 516 E. Washington St.
Ferguson, Mark A. .... '61 '86 C.970 B.A. L.904 J.D. Bearware, Inc.

Fisher, Jeffrey Michael .... '53 '84 C.62 B.A. L.161 J.D. [J.M.Fisher]
Fisher, Jeffrey M. .... 8356 Canterbury Ct.
Freedman, Howard J., (AV) .... '45 '70 C.861 B.A. L.930 J.D. [Weiss&F.]
Fried, Lorna J. .... '67 '92 C.347 B.A. L.1003 J.D. [Ⓐ S.G.Thomas&Assoc.]
Fruchter, Murray .... '22 '53 C.251 B.B.A. L.1003 LL.B. 8505 Tanglewood Trail‡
Gorretta, Laura J., (BV) .... '50 '86 C.318 B.A. L.930 J.D. 50 E. Washington St.
Griffiths, David E., (AV) .... '30 '57 C.611 B.A. L.930 LL.B. [Woodward&G.]

Gruber, James P.
(See Cleveland)

Hale, Kathleen M. .... '57 '84 C.930 B.A. L.608 J.D. 280 Grey Fox Run
Hardacre, Lynn L. ......'67 '93 C.608 B.A. L.1003 J.D. Coun., The Medical Protective Co.
Heavilin, Albert M., (AV) .... '17 '40 C&L.930 B.A., J.D. 35 Highland Lane‡
Herrick, Craig W. ....'65 '91 C.31 B.A. L.280 J.D. 7181 Chagrin Rd., Ste. 240
Holtz, Mark A. .... '55 '84 C.294 B.S.M.E. L.1003 J.D. 100 Waverly Ln.
Hopkins, Gregory Lee .... '62 '89 105 Edgewood Court
Horn, Christopher, (BV) .... '51 '76 C.276 B.S.B.A. L.930 J.D. Township Trustee
Johnson, Geoffrey M. .... '— '00 C.293 B.A. L.145 J.D. 33 River St.
Jones, Brooks M., (AV) ....'17 '47 C.674 A.B. L.976 LL.B. 37300 Fairmount Blvd.‡
Kaber, Steven C. .... '51 '84 C.62 B.A. L.1003 J.D. Mogul Corp.
Kadis, Suellen S. .... '56 '81 C.823 B.A. L.930 J.D. 120 W. Juniper Ln.‡
Ketchel, Edwin J., (BV) .... '27 '53 C.251 B.B.A. L.1003 J.D. 8246 Tulip Lane
King, Douglas A., (BV) .... '53 '78 C.608 B.A. L.930 J.D. 34 S. Main St.
King, Julie Mitrovich, Law Office of .....'69 '94 C.273 B.A. L.1003 J.D. P.O. Box 23626
Klammer, Martin A., (BV) .... '54 '85 C.161 B.I.E. L.1003 J.D. 9744 Bainbridge Rd.
Klein, Roger D. ....'61 '98 C.930 B.A. L.976 J.D. 33800 Jackson Road
Kleinman, Richard E., (AV) .... '31 '56 C&L.930 A.B., LL.B. 170 Glen Rd.‡
Kramer, Nancy W. .... '54 '79 C.97 B.S. L.930 J.D. 57 E. Washington St.
Kriz, Judith Anne .... '48 '79 C.610 B.S. L.1003 J.D. Mogul Corp.
Lamanna, Michael A. .... '49 '75 C.111 B.S. L.982 J.D. 17119 Northbrook Trial
Lawrence, Phillip A., (BV) .... '30 '60 C.608 B.B.A. L.1003 J.D. 26 S. Franklin St.
Lee, Karen E., (BV) .... '57 '82 C.97 B.A. L.1003 J.D. [Ⓐ McSherry]
Lentz, Mary A., (AV) .... '— '73 C.876 B.A. L.1003 J.D. [M.A.Lentz]

Lentz, Mary A., Co., L.P.A., (AV)
100 North Main Street, Suite 210, 44022-2766
Telephone: 440-247-8701 Fax: 440-247-8741
URL: http://www.lawyers.com/lentz
Mary A. Lentz.
Public School Law, Private Education Law, Personal Policies, Appeals, Administrative Hearings, Child Abuse and Neglect, Child Sexual Abuse.
See Professional Biographies, CHAGRIN FALLS, OHIO

Lewis-Gellen, Karen .... '63 '94 C.112 B.S. L.1003 J.D. 19133 Ridgeview Trl.
Liber, John R., II, (AV) ....'65 '90 C.840 B.S. L.930 J.D. 100 N. Main St., Ste. 350
Lieberman, Gary L., (BV) .... '54 '81 C.608 B.S. L.1003 J.D. 35 River Street
Lybarger, Leonard F., (AV) ....'37 '63 C.477 B.A. L.1003 J.D. P.O. Box 23428
Lynch, Matthew Joseph DuMont, (BV) '51 '80 C.363 B.A. L.1003 J.D.
[Lynch&Assoc.]
Lynch & Associates, (BV) .... P.O. Box 23279
Mac Iver, Elizabeth Anne .... '53 '83 C.161 B.S.Ed. L.1003 J.D. P.O. Box 505
Magyaros, Anne Schaefer, (BV) ......'65 '90 C.97 B.S. L.930 J.D. 1188 Bell Rd., Ste. 105
Maistros, David M., (AV) ....'64 '90 C.97 B.S. L.1003 J.D. 50 East Washington Street
McCrystal, Thomas W., (AV) ....'52 '80 C.363 B.S.B.A. L.930 J.D. 53 Cascades Dr.
McLeod, Edward A., (AV) .... '22 '49 C.309 S.B. L.930 LL.B. 231 Manorbrook Dr.‡
McSherry, James C. .... '55 '87 C.893 B.A. L.1003 J.D. [McSherry]
McSherry & Company ....178 E. Washington
Menefee, Donald Ray .... '48 '01 L.1003 J.D. [D.R.Menefee]
Menefee, Donald R., Dr. .... P.O. Box 23671
Miller, Cherrie N. ....'49 '78 C.381 B.S. L.607 J.D. 4180 Chagrin River Rd
Musallam-Martin, Yasmina Tadjera ....'61 '01 C.1154 B.A. L.161 J.D. 126 Leaview Lane
Naylor, Wendy Hoge .... '57 '85 C.732 B.A. L.896 J.D. 92 E. Washington St.
Norwick, Robert J. .... '21 '58 C.477 A.B. L.1003 J.D. 90 Skyline Dr.‡
Papesh, Amy L. .... '74 '00 C.363 B.A. L.161 J.D. Assoc., McSherry & Co.
Patton, Steven E. .... '57 '84 C.473 B.A. L.851 J.D. 178 E. Washington St.
Paulett-Toumert, Mary Jo .... '56 '87 C.473 B.A. L.608 J.D. 178 E. Washington St.
Prasse, Frederick C. .... '18 '48 C.381 B.S. L.930 LL.B. 8110 Chagrin Mills Rd.‡
Redmond, William K. .... '55 '83 C.93 A.B. L.989 J.D. [W.K.Redmond]
Redmond, William K., Co., LPA ....16700 Brigadoon Drive
Robinson, Gregory C. '46 '72 C.679 B.S.I.M. L.1119 J.D.
(adm. in IN; not adm. in OH) Pres., Custom Materials, Inc.
Schwartz, Stanley G. .... '48 '74 C.608 B.A. L.7 J.D. P.O. Box 359
Searby, Edmund W. .... '64 '90 C.197 A.B. L.477 J.D. 33 River Street
Simon, Lynn Beth, (BV) ....'50 '80 C.205 L.930 J.D. 3130 Topping Lane
Smith, Gilbert L., Jr. .... '11 '41 C.31 B.A. L.365 LL.B. 371 Hickory Hill Rd.‡
Snyder, James L. '41 '71 C.544 B.A. L.546 J.D.
(adm. in NE; not adm. in OH) 58 Potomac Dr.‡
Speece, Janet L. .... '— '87 C.599 B.A. L.1003 J.D. P.O. Box 23016
Stearns, Jon D. '47 '72 C&L.966 B.B.A., J.D.
(adm. in WI; not adm. in OH) 9110 Lake In The Woods Trail‡
Stevenson, Ernest B. .... '22 '49 C.930 A.B. L.1003 J.D. 17593 Walnut Trail‡
Strasshofer, Roland H., Jr., (AV) ....'24 '50 C&L.930 B.A., J.D. 34110 Chagrin Blvd.
Teagno, Joseph R. .... '16 '44 C.854 B.S. L.912 LL.B. 219 Manorbrook Dr.
Thomas, Stephen G., (AV) .... '47 '77 C.478 A.B. L.930 J.D. [S.G.Thomas&Assoc.]
Thomas, Stephen G. & Assocs., Co., L.P.A., (AV) ....35 River St.
Todd, Walker F. .... '45 '75 C.880 B.A. L.94 J.D. 1164 Sherbrook Dr.
Turnock, Lawr. C., Jr. ....'19 '48 C.453 S.M. L.930 LL.B. 270 Pheasant Run Dr.‡
Vogt, Peter W., (AV) ....'49 '74 C&L.659 B.S., J.D. Gen. Coun., MultiMedia Mgmt., Inc.
Weber, William M. .... '39 '66 C.228 A.B. L.1003 J.D. 3200 Roundwood Rd.‡
Weiss, Roger J., (AV) .... '40 '66 C.165 B.A. L.1003 J.D. [Weiss&F.]
Weiss & Freedman, LLP, (AV) ....35 River Street
Wilson, Robert D. .... '59 '84 C.930 B.S. L.1003 J.D. [R.D.Wilson]
Wilson, Robert D., Co., LPA .... 16716 Chillicothe Rd., Ste. 100
Woodward & Griffiths, (AV) .... 41 N. Main St.
Ziegler, Richard P., (BV) '46 '75
C.318 B.A. L.989 J.D. 17800 Chillicothe Road, Suite 270
Zucker, Dale P., (BV) .... '49 '74 C.608 B.S. L.607 J.D. [D.P.Zucker]
Zucker, Dale P., Co., L.P.A., (BV) ....512 East Washington Street

CHANDLERSVILLE, —, *Muskingum Co.*

Conley, Robert .... '43 '83 C.659 B.A. L.117 J.D. 6755 Sugargrove Rd.‡

CHARDON, * 5,156, *Geauga Co.*

Bender, Mary K., (BV) .... '47 '81 C.97 B.A. L.930 J.D. [M.K.Bender]

Bender, Mary K., Co., L.P.A., (BV)
Village Station Bldg. 4A, 401 South Street, 44024
Telephone: 440-285-4332 Fax: 440-285-9562
URL: http://www.lawyers.com/marybender

(This Listing Continued)

Bender, Mary K., Co., L.P.A. (Continued)
Mary K. Bender.
General Civil Trial Practice, Trials and Appeals in all Courts, Family, Custody and Support, Domestic Relations, Divorce, Juvenile, Real Estate.
See Professional Biographies, CHARDON, OHIO

Binder, Rudolph .... '24 '71 C.999 L.1003 J.D. 12793 Taylor-Wells Rd.‡
Bond, Daniel Earl, (BV) ....'50 '75 C.381 B.B.A. L.608 J.D. 109 Main St.
Borland, David G., (BV) .... '48 '73 C&L.930 A.B., J.D. 213 Turner Dr.
Brice, Edward T., (BV) ....'49 '74 C.201 B.A. L.1003 J.D. 214 East Park Street
Brooks, Keith K., (BV) .... '43 '69 C.95 B.A. L.188 J.D. [Ⓒ Petersen&I.]
Brown, Douglas B. .... '53 '85 C.477 B.G.S. L.117 J.D. 13715 Clover Lake Drive
Burt, Forrest W. .... '45 '76 C.608 B.S. L.1003 J.D. Com. Pleas J.
Carey, Lisa J., (BV) .... '67 '93 C.81 B.A. L.150 J.D. [Ⓐ Svete,M.&C.]
Carrabine, James P., (BV) .... '55 '84 C.363 B.S. L.1003 J.D. [Svete,M.&C.]
Cisan, Heidi M., (BV) .... '59 '89 C.608 B.A. L.930 J.D. [Thrasher,D.&D.]
Collier, William C., (CV) ....'38 '66 C.251 B.B.A. L.1003 J.D. 203 Main St.
Cooper, Patricia A., (BV) ....'51 '76 C.25 B.A. L.229 J.D. 12154 Fowlers Mill Rd.

Cooper & Forbes
(See Painesville)

Day, C. Lynne, (BV) .... '68 '93 C.967 B.A. L.608 J.D. [Petersen&I.]
Dolan, Lawrence J., (AV) .... '31 '57 C&L.602 A.B., LL.B. [Thrasher,D.&D.] ‡
Dolan, Matthew J., (BV) ....'65 '90 C.93 A.B. L.930 J.D. [Thrasher,D.&D.]

Driggs, Hogg & Fry Co., LPA
(See Willoughby Hills)

Eardley, David J., (AV) .... '32 '57 C&L.602 B.S., J.D. 109 Court Street
Flaiz, James R. .... '77 '02 C.608 B.A. L.989 J.D. [Ⓐ Svete,M.&C.]
Flynn, J. Jaredd ....'76 '03 C.473 B.S. L.124 J.D. [Ⓐ Thrasher,D.&D.]
Gargiulo, Dawn Marion .... '61 '92 211 Main Street
Green, Frederick H., (BV) .... '47 '75 C&L.608 B.A., J.D. [F.Green]
Green, Frederick, (BV) ....209 Center St., Ste. J
Hanus, Ronald B., (BV) .... '47 '74 C.610 B.B.A. L.1003 J.D. [R.B.Hanus]
Hanus, R.B., (BV) .... 107 N. Hambden St.
Hassett, Mark J., (BV) .... '49 '75 C.976 B.A. L.930 J.D. [M.J.Hassett]
Hassett, Mark J., Co., L.P.A., (BV) ....117 South Street, Suite 110
Heffter, Sarah L., Law Office, (CV) ....'52 '95 C.381 B.F.A. L.1003 J.D. 151 Main St.
Hicks, Todd C., (BV) .... '69 '94 C.150 B.A. L.608 J.D. [Thrasher,D.&D.]
Hofstetter, Edwin T. .... '18 '52 C.608 B.S. L.1003 J.D. Ret. Ct. App. J.‡

Hofstetter, William C., (BV) '50 '75 C.608 B.A. L.1003 J.D.
155 Main Street, 44024
Telephone: 440-285-2247 Fax: 440-285-4140
Email: wchofstetter@aol.com URL: http://www.lawyers.com/hofstetter
Civil Practice, Real Estate, Estate Planning, Wills, Trusts and Estates, Estate Administration, Probate, Banking Law.
See Professional Biographies, CHARDON, OHIO

Hollingsworth, Jay A., (AV) ....'30 '56 C.381 B.S. L.930 LL.B. 10771 Mayfield Rd.
Ibold, Dennis J., (BV) .... '48 '73 C.436 B.A. L.1003 J.D. [Petersen&I.]
Ibold, Michael G., (BV) .... '55 '80 C.967 B.A. L.1003 J.D. [Petersen&I.]
Inderlied, H. F., Jr. .... '40 '65 C.37 B.S. L.930 J.D. Com. Pleas J.
Jevnikar, David W., (CV) ....'50 '81 C.207 B.A. L.851 J.D. 214 East Park Street
Joyce, David Patrick, (BV) .... '57 '82 C&L.201 B.S., J.D. Pros. Atty.
Lavrich, Frank G. .... '24 '52 C.363 A.B. L.1003 J.D. Prob. J.
Leary, Pearce, (BV) .... '49 '74 C&L.930 B.S.E.E., J.D. 401 South St.
Lee, Dorothy H. ....'55 '94 C.318 B.A. L.1003 J.D. 100 Short Court
Lloyd, Scott Andrew, (BV) '59 '90
C.611 B.A. L.1003 J.D. Gen. Coun., ELTECH Systems Corp.
Lowe, David E., (AV) .... '37 '70 C.363 A.B. L.1003 J.D. [Thrasher,D.&D.]
Lubecky, David .... '62 '87 C.49 B.A. L.150 J.D. Mag., Prob. & Juv.
Markowitz, Dale H., (AV) ....'50 '75 C.608 B.S. L.1003 J.D. [Thrasher,D.&D.]
McGee, David A., (BV) .... '52 '82 C.262 A.B. L.1003 J.D. [Svete,M.&C.]
McGregor, Emanuel H., (CV) .... '20 '48 C.608 L.930 LL.B. 203 Main Street
Moser, L. Gordon, Law Office of, (CV) '57 '82
C.473 B.A. L.851 J.D. 11905 Fowlers Mill Rd.
Navatsyk, Donald A., (BV) .... '53 '80 C.604 B.A. L.930 J.D. 12444 Woodin Rd.
Newman, Paul A., (BV) ....'48 '77 C.930 B.A. L.1003 J.D. 214 East Park Street
O'Brien, Casey P. .... '75 '00 C.1260 B.A. L.989 J.D. [Petersen&I.]
Ondrey, David M., (BV) .... '51 '80 C.473 B.A. L.1003 J.D. [Thrasher,D.&D.]
O'Reilly, D. Kevin, (BV) ....'42 '68 C.980 B.S.B.A. L.1003 J.D. [D.K.O'Reilly]
O'Reilly, D. Kevin, Co., L.P.A., (BV) ....109 Court St.
Orndorff, Jeffrey T., (BV) ....'52 '77 C.610 A.B. L.851 J.D. 117 South Street, Ste. 110
Penhallurick, Kent W., (BV) .... '51 '76 C.390 A.B. L.930 J.D. U.S. Dist. Atty.
Petersen, Jerry A., (AV) ....'38 '66 C.381 B.S. L.608 J.D. [Petersen&I.]
Petersen, Todd E., (CV) ....'70 '96 C.119 B.S. L.608 J.D. [Petersen&I.]

Petersen & Ibold, (AV)
401 South Street, 44024-1495
Telephone: 440-285-3511 Telecopier: 440-285-3363
Email: p&i@peteribold.com URL: http://www.lawyers.com/peteribold
Jerry A. Petersen; Dennis J. Ibold; Michael G. Ibold; C. Lynne Day; Todd E. Petersen; Casey P. O'Brien. Associate: Robin Stanley. Of Counsel: Keith K. Brooks; Susan E. Peterson.
Personal Injury, Real Estate and Zoning, Family Law, Criminal, Wills, Probate, Estate Planning and Elder Law, Corporate, Business and Labor Law, Bankruptcy, School Law and Workers Compensation.
See Professional Biographies, CHARDON, OHIO

Peterson, Susan E. .... '71 '97 C.980 B.A. L.989 J.D. [Ⓒ Petersen&I.]
Reardon, James W., (CV) .... '66 '92 C.473 A.B. L.930 J.D. [Svete,M.&C.]
Riddle, Wanda P. .... '38 '75 C.999 B.A. L.1003 J.D. 10219 Wilson Mills Rd.‡
Seymour, Christine M. Simon, (CV) ....'59 '90 C.392 B.A. L.1003 J.D. 109 Main St.
Skrabec, David J. .... '42 '75 C.251 B.E.E. L.161 J.D. 100 Seventh Ave.
Slattery, Kelly A. .... '77 '02 C.602 B.A. L.124 J.D. [Ⓐ Thrasher,D.&D.]
Smalheer, Bruce C. .... '45 '72 C.976 B.A. L.813 J.D. [Zulandt&S.]
Smith, Ced L. .... '23 '51 C.363 B.S. L.1003 LL.B. P.O. Box 107‡
Stanley, Robin .... '78 '03 C.313 B.S. L.8 J.D. [Ⓐ Petersen&I.]

Sternberg & Zeid Co., L.P.A.
(See Mentor)

Svete, Joseph T., (AV) .... '37 '64 C.124 B.S. L.1003 J.D. [Svete,M.&C.]

Svete, McGee & Carrabine Co., L.P.A., (AV)
100 Parker Court, 44024-1141
Telephone: 440-286-9571 Fax: 440-286-7504
Joseph T. Svete; David A. McGee; James P. Carrabine; James W. Reardon;—Lisa J. Carey; James R. Flaiz.
Insurance Defense, Personal Injury, Products Liability, Professional Malpractice, Commercial, Governmental Construction and General Negligence Litigation, Automobile Accidents, Wrongful Death, Medical Negligence, Real Estate and Zoning, Contracts, Deeds, Easements, Leases, Family Law,

(This Listing Continued)

Svete, McGee & Carrabine Co., L.P.A. (Continued)

Divorce, Dissolution, Child Custody and Support, Paternity, Adoption, Child Abuse and Neglect, Criminal Defense, Felonies, Misdemeanors, Juvenile and Traffic Offenses, D.U.I., Wills, Probate, Estate Planning, Elder Law, Trusts, Powers of Attorney, Living Wills, Guardianships, Asset Preservation, Medicare/Medicaid Planning, Litigation, Corporate and Business Law, Partnerships, Limited Liability Companies, Buying and Selling of a Business.

See Professional Biographies, CHARDON, OHIO

Thrasher, Dinsmore & Dolan, A Legal Professional Association, (AV)
100 7th Avenue, Suite 150, 44024-1079
Telephone: 440-285-2242 Cleveland Line: 440-942-1034 Facsimile: 440-285-9423
Ray K. Thrasher (1906-1973); James W. Dinsmore (1916-1975); Lawrence J. Dolan (Retired); David E. Lowe; Dale H. Markowitz; Joseph R. Znidarsic; David M. Ondrey; Heidi M. Cisan; Todd C. Hicks; Matthew J. Dolan;—J. Jaredd Flynn; Kelly A. Slattery.
General Civil and Criminal Practice. Corporation, Probate, Municipal, Communication Law, Real Estate, Taxation, Zoning, Banking and Insurance Law. Estate Planning. Trials and Appeals. Labor Law. Domestic and Creditors Rights.

See Professional Biographies, CHARDON, OHIO

Umholtz, R. Robert, (BV) .... '51 '84 C.999 B.A. L.1003 J.D. Co. Pub. Def.
Veit, Hans R. .... '30 '60 C.477 A.B. L.1003 J.D. Ret. Com. Pleas J.
Wantz, Robert R., (BV) .... '32 '62 C.318 B.A. L.1003 J.D. 100 7th Avenue, Suite 150
Weber, Robert F. .... '21 '59 C.97 B.S.B.A. L.1003 LL.B. 454 N. Hambden St.‡
Wharton, Lawrence M., (CV) .... '69 '94 C.473 B.A. L.1003 J.D. Co. Pros.
Wheatley, Myron Daniel, (CV) .... '53 '87 C&L.101 B.A., J.D. 145 Main Street
Znidarsic, Joseph R., (BV) .... '51 '76 C.97 B.S. L.930 J.D. [Thrasher,D.&D.]
Zulandt, Robert E., Jr., (BV) .... '47 '73 C.935 B.A. L.161 J.D. [Zulandt&S.]
Zulandt & Smalheer, (BV) .... 114 East Park Street

CHESAPEAKE, 842, *Lawrence Co.*

Kaiser, J. Stewart, (BV) .... '36 '64 C.277 B.S. L.608 J.D. 411 Rockwood Ave.
Meyers, Richard B., (BV) .... '41 '67 C.473 B.S. L.150 J.D. 220 4th St.
Neville, Brenda K., (CV) .... '54 '93 C.790 B.A. L.117 J.D. 220 4th St.

CHESTERLAND, 2,646, *Geauga Co.*

Bender, Mary K., Co., L.P.A.
(See Chardon)

Bertolo, Peter F. '55 '86 C.251 B.ME. L.1003 J.D.
The Cleveland Elec. Illuminating Co.
Blageff, Lillian V. .... '62 '91 C&L.930 B.A., J.D. Business Laws, Inc.
Bloom, Robert M. .... '48 '73 C.473 B.A. L.930 J.D. Pres., Bloom Bros. Supply, Inc.
Chaloupka, Robert S. '75 '01 C&L.124 B.A., J.D.
Assoc. Ed., Business Laws, Inc. (Legal Department)
Doles, Edward A. .... '53 '84 C.161 B.B.A. L.989 J.D. 8130 Wedgewood Dr.
Ebersbacher, Susan M. .... '58 '83 C.607 B.A. L.1003 J.D. 12110 Privacy Ln.
Fant, John F., Jr. .... '21 '56 C.659 B.S. L.1003 LL.B. 13271 Caves Rd.
Gardner, Robert E. .... '24 '65 C.608 M.D. L.1003 J.D. 13178 W. Geauga Trail‡
Gibson, Tammy G. .... '65 '96 C.161 B.A. L.989 J.D. [T.G.Gibson]
Gibson, Tammy G., Co., LPA .... 8228 Mayfield Road
Griffith, Thomas J. .... '59 '90 C.880 B.A. L.930 J.D. V.P.-Legal, Business Laws, Inc.
Hancock, William A. .... '42 '66 C.861 B.S. L.930 J.D. Pres., Business Laws, Inc.
Hanover, Stanley Ira .... '47 '78 C.309 B.A. L.930 J.D. Ohio Dispute Resolution
Holland, Mara Jill .... '65 '95 C.472 B.A. L.1206 J.D. Assoc. Ed., Business Laws, Inc.
Irvin, Carol, (CV) .... '48 '75 C.610 B.A. L.1003 J.D. 11401 Willow Hill Dr.
Kadis, Gary M. .... '57 '83 C.381 B.S.Ed. L.1003 J.D. 12963 Lynn Dr.
Kancelbaum, Joshua J., (AV) .... '36 '60 C&L.930 B.A., LL.B. 8228 Mayfield Rd.
Kassen, Elizabeth A. Kruse .... '52 '79 C.161 B.A. L.1003 J.D. 11000 Walnut Ridge
Kassen, William J. .... '44 '78 C.453 B.S. L.1003 J.D. 11000 Walnut Ridge Rd.
Korosec, Jason A. .... '68 '97 C.696 B.A. Consul., Orgin Tech.
Korosec, Kenneth D., (BV) .... '43 '67 C.930 B.A. L.1003 J.D. 12573 Chillicothe Road
Larrick, Scott A. .... '62 '90 C.8 B.A. L.1187 J.D. 8442 Mayfield Road
Lindsay, Anne W. .... '34 '77 C.823 B.A. L.1003 J.D. 8180 Sherman Rd.
Makowski, Pamela W. .... '57 '81 C.97 B.A. L.851 J.D. 8228 Mayfield Rd., Ste. 6B
Malik, David B. .... '53 '79 C.318 B.A. L.1003 J.D. 8437 Mayfield Road
Norton, John F., (AV) .... '32 '59 C.363 A.B. L.930 LL.B. 8251 Mayfield Rd.
Patete, Nancy Fioritto .... '47 '86 C.381 B.S.Ed. L.989 J.D. P.O. Box 895
Payton, Janet G. .... '54 '88 C.930 B.A. L.1003 J.D. Business Laws, Inc.
Purdy, Dorrit W., (BV) .... '33 '78 C.518 B.A. L.1003 J.D. 8970 Wilson Mills Rd.
Rushworth, Kim R., (CV) .... '41 '76 C.473 B.A. L.161 J.D. 8228 Mayfield Rd.
Schiemann, Jeffrey J. .... '56 '88 C.607 B.A. L.124 J.D. P.O. Box 934
Sos, Emil F., Jr., (BV) .... '41 '70 C.645 B.S. L.1003 J.D. [E.Sos]
Sos, Emil, (BV) .... 12690 Opalocka Dr.
Wang, William P. '48 '80 C.659 B.A. L.818 J.D.
(adm. in MA; not adm. in OH) P.O. Box 8‡
Weiss, Joseph H., Jr., (BV) .... '43 '70 C.363 A.B. L.1003 J.D. 8228 Mayfield Rd.

CHILLICOTHE, * 21,796, *Ross Co.*

Ater, Michael M., (CV) .... '64 '94 C.608 B.A. L.930 J.D. [Nusbaum,A.&W.]
Barrington, Deborah Douglas, (BV) ...... '47 '77 C.608 B.S. L.117 J.D. 134 S. Paint Street
Barrington, James E., (BV) .... '44 '74 C.608 B.A. L.117 J.D. 41 E. 4th St.
Benson, J. Jeffrey, (BV) .... '57 '82 C.631 B.A. L.117 J.D. 36 S. Paint St.
Blair, John G., (BV) .... '33 '59 C&L.608 J.D. 6 W. Main St.
Boulger, James T. .... '50 '79 C.1230 B.A. L.884 J.D. 2 West Fourth Street

Boulger, William C., (AV) '24 '51 C.309 A.B. L.150 LL.B.
45 West Fourth Street, P.O. Box 204, 45601
Telephone: 740-774-1625 Fax: 740-774-1625
General Practice. Probate and Tax Law. Trials.

See Professional Biographies, CHILLICOTHE, OHIO

Brown, Edward J., (BV) .... '46 '74 C.201 B.A. L.607 J.D. 97 West Main Street
Bugg, Clifford N., (BV) .... '58 '92 C.437 B.A. L.851 J.D. [Phillips&S.]
Bunch, Thomas E., (BV) .... '49 '80 C.201 B.S. L.851 J.D. Mun. Ct. J.
Bunstine, Edward R., (BV) .... '56 '81 C.473 B.S. L.607 J.D. [Bunstine]
Bunstine Law Office, (BV) .... 32 S. Paint St.

Calig & Handelman, LPA
(See Columbus)

Childers, Pamela Christine .... '67 '97 C&L.560 B.A., J.D. [P.C.Childers]
Childers, Pamela C., Law Offices of .... 133 1/2 W. Main St.

Colley Shroyer & Abraham Co., L.P.A.
(See Columbus)

Cutright, James K., (BV) .... '60 '84 C.473 A.B. L.608 J.D. [Cutright&C.]
Cutright, James M., (AV) .... '27 '50 C.473 A.B. L.150 J.D. [Cutright&C.]
Cutright & Cutright, (AV) .... 76 West Second Street
DiCesare, John Charles .... '59 '86 C.97 B.S. L.851 J.D. Mag. J.
Drake, Claire Fried, (CV) .... '68 '96 C.608 B.A. L.228 J.D. [⊠ Mann&P.]
Eddy, Toni Lee .... '58 '00 C.608 B.S. L.117 J.D. 20 E. 2nd St.
Evans, Gary Lou .... '42 '89 C.610 A.B. L.7 J.D. Ross Co. Child Support Enforce.
Fleshman, Gary Alan .... '61 '94 C.608 B.A. L.851 J.D. [Fleshman,G.A.]
Fleshman, Gary A. .... 63 N. Paint St.
Fuchsman, Rita S., (BV) .... '53 '77 C.446 B.A. L.1003 J.D. 26 W. 4th St.
Fuller, Don E., (BV) .... '28 '55 C.608 B.A. L.117 J.D. 19 W. 2nd St.
Greenwald, Tammy Lynn '73 '00 C.138 B.A. L.602 J.D.
Southeastern Ohio Legal Services
Henthorne, Christine B., (BV) .... '55 '80 C.63 B.S. L.117 J.D. 72 N. Paint St.

Hess, Robert C., (BV) '48 '74 C.973 B.A. L.734 J.D.
Room 2 - Foulke Block, 14 South Paint Street, 45601
Telephone: 740-774-6152 Fax: 740-774-6153
Wills and Probate, Estates, Trusts, Elder Law, Real Estate, Personal Injury and Civil Litigation.

See Professional Biographies, CHILLICOTHE, OHIO

Hine, Katherine .... '49 '77 C.608 B.S. L.851 J.D. 80 Wissler Ave.
Hirsch, Carl P., Jr., (BV) .... '43 '74 C.608 B.A. L.770 J.D. [Hirsch,S.]
Hirsch, Stanhope & Co., L.P.A., (BV) .... 55 E. Second St.
Holmes, Nicholas H., Jr. .... '42 '69 C.951 B.A. L.150 J.D. Com. Pleas J.
Horne, Benjamin Dodge .... '67 '00 C.118 B.A. L.602 J.D. S.E. OH Legal Servs.
Jones, Carl Wendell .... '38 '64 C&L.608 B.S., J.D. 36 South Print Street
Kear, J. G., (AV) .... '23 '49 C.473 A.B. L.150 J.D. P.O. Box 1609

Livorno & Arnett Co., LPA
(See Columbus)

Malek & Malek
(See Columbus)

Mann, James L., (AV) .... '43 '68 C.610 A.B. L.597 J.D. [Mann&P.]
Mann & Preston, LLP, (AV) .... 18 E. 2nd St.
Martin, Jane Spring, (BV) .... '54 '78 C.610 A.B. L.608 J.D. 176 W. Water St.
McMahon, Paige J., (BV) .... '63 '88 C&L.608 B.S., J.D. 42 E. 5th St.
Miller, Jason .... '76 '01 C.610 B.A. L.607 J.D. 72 N. Paint St.
Moore, William B. .... '30 '71 C.610 B.A. L.117 J.D. 315 W. 4th St.‡
Motes, Joseph E., (BV) .... '63 '96 C.610 B.B.A. L.1339 J.D. 13 S. Paint St.
Napier, Shawn Patrick ...... '75 '01 C.1175 B.A. L.117 J.D. 4th Dist. Ct. of Appeals, Ohio
Nusbaum, Scott W., (BV) .... '53 '78 C.967 B.A. L.990 J.D. [Nusbaum,A.&W.]
Nusbaum, Ater and Wissler, (BV) .... 72 North Paint Street

Oliver Law Office
(See Columbus)

Phillips, David M., (BV) .... '25 '52 C.276 B.S. L.477 LL.B. [Phillips&S.]
Phillips & Street, (AV) .... 37 N. Paint St.

Plymale Partnership LLP, The
(See Columbus)

Preston, Mark A., (BV) .... '51 '80 C.434 B.A. L.1003 J.D. [Mann&P.]
Radcliffe, Gerald E. .... '23 '50 C.610 A.B. L.150 J.D. Ret. Prob. & Juv. J.‡
Rainsberger, Ben Allen, (CV) .... '56 '81 C.631 B.A. L.608 J.D. State Pub. Def. Off.
Rittinger, Martha Gerber .... '33 '85 C.610 B.A. L.117 S. D. 23597 State Rte. 104‡
Rovins, Arthur '49 '78 C.390 B.A. L.421 J.D.
(adm. in CT; not adm. in OH) Mgr., YSK Corp.
Rutherford, Sherri K. .... '— '98 C.610 B.S. L.117 J.D. 95 W. Main Street
Scherff, John Matthew, (CV) .... '62 '89 C.1271 B.A. L.607 J.D. 291 Mill St.
Silcott, Daniel Lynn, (BV) .... '50 '84 C.473 B.A. L.117 J.D. Co. Pub. Def. Off.
Sladoje, Douglas, Attorney at Law, (AV) '62 '88
C&L.608 B.S., J.D. 38 South Paint Street (⊙Columbus)
Spetnagel, Thomas M., (AV) .... '49 '75 C.608 B.S. L.150 J.D. 42 E. 5th St.
Stout, Cherita E. .... '— '94 55 E. 2nd St.
Street, John B. .... '56 '81 C.896 B.A. L.902 J.D. Mun. J.
Street, John S., Jr., (AV) .... '28 '54 C&L.228 A.B., J.D. [Phillips&S.]
Sulzer, Joseph, (CV) .... '47 '82 C.610 B.G.S. L.117 J.D. [Sulzer]
Sulzer Law Office, (CV) .... 38 S. Paint St.
Sutton, Linda I. .... '53 '87 C.610 B.S. L.608 J.D. Southeastern Ohio Legal Servs.

Twyford & Donahey, P.L.L.
(See Columbus)

Van de Carr, Charles R., IV, (BV) .... '45 '76 C.679 B.S.I.M. L.607 J.D. Supvr. Atty.
Ward, Richard G., (BV) .... '42 '68 C.229 B.A. L.884 J.D. Co. Pros.

CHILO, 130, *Clermont Co.*

Jackson, Chas. W. .... '21 '51 C.151 L.1340 LL.B. Ret. Com. Pleas J.

CINCINNATI, * 331,285, *Hamilton Co.*

Aaron, Marjorie Corman '56 '81 C.674 B.A. L.309 J.D.
(adm. in MA; not adm. in OH) Univ. of Cincinnati Coll. of Law
Abaray, Janet G., (AV) '57 '82
C&L.150 B.A., J.D. [Lopez,H.R.M.&S.] (⊙Newport Beach, CA)
Abare, Terri Reyering, (AV) .... '54 '83 C.473 B.A. L.276 J.D. [Vorys,S.S.&P.]
Abbott, David L. .... '56 '84 C.150 B.M. L.665 J.D. Dir., Aircraft Engine Lic.
Abel, F. Bruce, (AV) .... '39 '64 C.976 B.A. L.309 LL.B. 885 Greenville Avenue
Abernethy, William S., Jr., (AV) .... '42 '67 C&L.150 B.A., J.D. [Strauss&T.]
Abes, Alan H. .... '68 '93 C.608 B.A. L.597 J.D. [Dinsmore&S.]
Abrams, Laura A. .... '65 '91 C.201 B.A. L.150 J.D. [Sirkin P.&S.]
Abreu, Steven A. .... '79 '04 C.339 L.608 [⊠ Dinsmore&S.]
Acciani, Henry D., (BV) .... '49 '79 C.150 B.A. L.1340 J.D. [O'Connor,A.&L.]
Acheson, Edwin R., Jr., (BV) '55 '80 C.502 B.S. L.228 J.D.
[Frost B.T.] (See Pat. Sect.)
Adams, Deborah S., (AV) .... '55 '82 C.150 B.A. L.309 J.D. [Frost B.T.]
Adams, Donald C., Jr., (AV) .... '57 '82 C.473 B.A. L.150 J.D. [Rendigs,F.K.&D.]
Adams, E. Stanley '49 '76 C&L.150 B.A., J.D.
(adm. in KY; not adm. in OH) Formica Corp.
Adams, Edmund J., (AV) .... '38 '63 C.973 A.B. L.602 LL.B. [⊠ Frost B.T.]
Adams, Gregory L., (AV) .... '51 '77 C.894 B.A. L.1340 J.D. [Croswell&A.]
Adams, Gregory P., (AV) .... '54 '79 C.478 A.B. L.818 J.D. [Dinsmore&S.]
Adams, James R., (AV) .... '38 '63 C.207 A.B. L.597 J.D. [⊠ Frost B.T.]
Adams, Thomas A. '71 '98 C.340 B.A. L.608 J.D.
(adm. in IN; not adm. in OH; Pat.) Corp. Coun., The Procter & Gamble Co.
Adams, William R. .... '55 '87 C.679 B.A. L.150 J.D. 121 W. 9th St.

Adams, Stepner, Woltermann & Dusing, P.L.L.C.
(See Covington, Kentucky)

Adelman, Denise E. '63 '93 C.728 B.A. L.705 J.D.
(adm. in PA; not adm. in OH) Coun., Commercial Operations GE Transportation
Agar, Elizabeth E., (BV) .... '53 '80 C.475 B.S. L.150 J.D. [Croswell&A.]
Ahlers, Donald B., (BV) .... '29 '53 C.973 L.150 LL.B. 6045 Budmar Ave.
Ahlers, Edward C., (BV) .... '56 '82 C.973 B.A. L.150 J.D. 414 Walnut St., Ste. 707
Ahlers, Laurie K. .... '56 '95 C.98 B.S. L.150 J.D. 2345 Ashland Ave.
Ahlrichs, Jas. W., (AV) .... '29 '56 C.973 B.S. L.150 LL.B. [Ahlrichs&A.]

Ahlrichs, Susan M., (BV) '58 '85 C.473 B.Ph. L.770 J.D. [Ahlrichs&A.]
Ahlrichs & Ahlrichs, (AV) 4037 Glenway Ave.
Ahrens, Gregory F., (BV) '61 '87
C.846 B.S.Ch.E. L.966 J.D. [Wood,H.&E.] (See Pat. Sect.)
Ahrens, Megan C. '77 '03 C.347 B.A. L.150 J.D. [Ⓐ Schroeder,M.B.&P.]
Akin, Edward P. '63 '01 C.810 B.A. L.602 J.D. [Ⓐ Aronoff,R.&H.]
Albainy-Jenei, Stephen R., (BV) '64 '95
C.201 B.S. L.150 J.D. [Frost B.T.] (See Pat. Sect.)
Albrecht, David S. '72 '98 C.608 B.S. L.117 J.D. [Lutz,C.&M.]
Albrinck, Daniel E. '65 '96 C.1118 L.151 Univ. of Cincinnati Med. Assoc.
Albrinck, J. Jeffrey '61 '87 C.150 B.S. L.851 J.D. [Lutz,C.&M.]
Alexander, Henry G., Jr., (AV) '49 '75 C&L.150 B.A., J.D. [Graydon H.&R.]
Alexander, Tony M. '59 '00 C.1208 B.S. L.608 J.D. [Ⓐ Lerner,S.&R.]
Algenio, Rebecca N. '73 '01 C.881 B.A. L.588 J.D. [Ⓐ Freking&B.]
Algie, Glenn E., (CVⓉ) '63 '88 C&L.383 B.A., J.D. [Weltman,W.&R.]
Allaer, Paul, (AV) '60 '86 C&L.999 B.A., J.D. [Thompson H.]
Allen, Claudia G., (AV) '48 '79 C.1044 B.F.A. L.107 J.D. [Strauss&T.]
Allen, Eric P. '62 '87 C.610 B.A. L.851 J.D. [O'Connor,A.&L.]
Allen, Nadine Lovelace '49 '77 C.608 B.A. L.117 J.D.
1000 Main St., Rm. 164, Ste. 205
Allen, William R. '57 '00 C.244 B.S. L.838 J.D. [Ⓐ Wood,H.&E.]
Allf, Rebecca Jane '59 '86 C.347 B.S. L.201 J.D. 8970 Winton Road
Allison, Jon B. '70 '01 C.477 B.A. L.150 J.D. [Ⓐ Dinsmore&S.]
Allison, Kreg T. '76 '03 C.880 B.A. L.608 J.D. Chf. Legal Offr.
Allman, Bruce M., (AV) '43 '74 C&L.150 B.S., J.D. [Thompson H.]
Alsfelder, Deborah T., Attorney at Law '57 '91 C.610 B.S. L.150 J.D. 3700 Center St.
Alsfelder, Robert F., Jr., (BV) '53 '81 C.347 B.A. L.150 J.D. [R.F.Alsfelder]
Alsfelder, Robert F., (BV) 3700 Center St.
Altenau, Michael J. '60 '88 C.973 B.A. L.607 J.D.
Western & Southern Life Ins. Co., The
Alter, Joseph C. '77 '02 C.473 B.A. L.1049 J.D. [Ⓐ Keating M.&K.]
Altman, D. David, (AV) '46 '74 C&L.150 B.A., J.D. [D.D.Altman&Assoc.]
Altman, John M. '63 '90 C.908 B.A. L.285 J.D.
(adm. in WA; not adm. in OH) Treas. Dept., I.R.S.

Altman, D. David, Co., A Legal Professional Association, (AV) BR
15 East Eighth Street, Suite 200W, 45202
Telephone: 513-721-2180 Fax: 513-721-2299 URL: http://www.environlaw.com
Email: daltman@one.net URL: http://www.lawyers.com/environlaw
D. David Altman;—Amy J. Leonard; Amy M. Beiersdorfer.
Environmental Law, Toxic Torts. Local Governmental and Municipality, Environmental Representation, Class Actions. General Litigation. Art Agency.
See Professional Biographies, CINCINNATI, OHIO

Aluotto, Christopher J. '67 '92 C.30 B.A. L.201 J.D. [Rendigs,F.K.&D.]
Alvaro, Jay R. '64 '95 C.473 B.S. L.151 J.D. Coun., Cinergy Corp.
Alves, Judy '51 '77 C.705 B.A. L.607 J.D. 9000 Plainfield Rd.
Ammer, Timothy C. '71 '98 C.575 B.S.B.A. L.150 J.D. [Ⓐ Montgomery,R.&J.]
Amrine, Kimberly S. '71 '00 C.597 B.A. L.273 J.D. [Ⓐ Frost B.T.]
Anderson, P. Richard, Jr., (AVⓉ) '47 '73 C.446 B.A. L.945 J.D.
[Greenebaum D.&M.] (⊙Atlanta, GA; Covington, Frankfort, Lexington, Louisville, KY; Nashville, TN)
Anderson, Robert N. '37 '67 C.1044 A.B. L.982 LL.B. 675 Watch Hill Ln.‡
Anderson, William H., (AV) '26 '52 C&L.150 LL.B. 511 Walnut St., Suite 1900
Andes, William S. '64 '92 C&L.201 B.M.E., J.D.
Intellectual Prop. Coun., General Electric Co. (Pat.)
Andrew, Marcia Voorhis, (BV) '62 '88 C.951 B.A. L.893 J.D. [Taft,S.&H.]
Andrews, J. Robert, (BV) '51 '80 C.381 B.A. L.1340 J.D. [Schuh&G.]
Anness, Harold L., (AV) '53 '78 C.473 B.S. L.607 J.D. [Griffin -F.]
Anstaett, Jennifer Griffin '75 '01 C.138 B.A. L.902 J.D. [Ⓐ Beckman W.S.]
Antaki, Vincent P. '69 '00 C.976 B.A. L.1340 J.D. [Ⓐ Reminger&R.]
Antell, Barbara Brigham, (BV) '52 '77 C.347 B.A. L.345 J.D. [Brigham&B.]
Anthony, Brenda Ann '49 '99 C&L.150 B.M., J.D. Co. Juv. Ct.
Anthony, Lori Ann '66 '97 C.967 B.A. L.1194 J.D. Asst. Atty. Gen.
Anthony, Thomas D., (AV) '52 '77 C.473 B.S. L.930 J.D. [Frost B.T.]
Aplin, Kenneth L. '35 '59 C&L.150 B.A., LL.B. Prof. of Law, Univ. of Cinn.
Appel, John H., (AV) '49 '74 C.150 B.A. L.309 J.D. [Frost B.T.]
Applegarth, Barbara F. '52 '79 C.183 A.B. L.930 J.D. [Ⓒ Frost B.T.]
Applegate, James Edward '28 '54 C&L.150 LL.B. [Masters] ‡
Applegate, John S. '57 '81 C.311 B.A. L.309 J.D.
(adm. in DC; not adm. in OH) 2624 Clifton Ave.
Appleton, William, (AV) '49 '78 C.665 B.A. L.569 J.D. [Baker&H.]
Arenstein, Hal R., (AV) '54 '79 C.207 B.A. L.930 J.D. [Arenstein&G.]
Arenstein & Gallagher, Law Offices of, (AV) 114 East Eighth Street
Argo, Susan M. '71 '96 C.707 B.A. L.221 J.D. [Ⓒ Graydon H.&R.]
Armstead, Thaddeus J., (BV) '41 '75
C.410 B.S. L.734 J.D. Asst. Corp. Coun., Cincinnati Milacron Inc.
Armstrong, Jody H., (BV) '— '92
C.352 B.A. L.209 J.D. [Ⓐ Dinsmore&S.] (See Pat. Sect.)
Armstrong, Kelly A. '77 '02 C.383 B.A. L.966 J.D. [Ⓐ Freund,F.&A.]
Arnett, Bradley C. '64 '95 C.1161 B.S. L.151 J.D. Coun., Cinergy Corp.

Arnold, James S., & Associates '65 '93 C.501 B.A. L.1340 J.D.
9737 Loveland Madeira Road, 45140
Telephone: 513-984-8313 Fax: 513-984-8480 URL: http://www.jarnoldlaw.com
Email: jarnold@rLtagency.com URL: http://www.jalawfirm.com
Associate: Gregory E. Smith.
General Practice, focusing on Driving Under the Influence, Driving while Intoxicated, DUI, DWI, OVI, Personal Injury, Wrongful Death, Medical Malpractice, Real Estate, Domestic Relations, Bankruptcy and Probate.
See Professional Biographies, CINCINNATI, OHIO

Arnold, Jason Douglas '70 '96 C.249 B.S. L.201 J.D. [J.D.Arnold]
Arnold, John J., (BV) '53 '78 C.97 B.A. L.150 J.D. 7265 Kenwood Rd., Ste. 150
Arnold, Jason D., Law Office 7901 Vine Street

Arnzen, Wentz, Molloy, Laber & Storm, P.S.C.
(See Covington, Kentucky)

Aronoff, Stanley J., (AV) '32 '57 C&L.309 A.B., LL.B. [Aronoff,R.&H.]

Aronoff, Rosen & Hunt, A Legal Professional Association, (AV)
2200 U.S. Bank Tower, 425 Walnut Street, 45202
Telephone: 513-241-0400 Telecopier: 513-241-2877
Irwin I. Aronoff (1905-1987); Stanley J. Aronoff; Stephen R. Hunt; Mark W. Reis; Richard A. Paolo; Patrick M. O'Neill;—Edmonde P. DeGregorio; Valerie L. Van Valkenburg; Tina M. Donnelly; Edward P. Akin. Of Counsel: Irving H. Rosen.
Real Estate, Construction, Mechanic's Lien, Corporate, Estate Planning, Probate, Trusts, Administrative and Zoning, Taxation and Civil Litigation.

(This Listing Continued)

Aronoff, Rosen & Hunt, A Legal Professional Association (Continued)

Representative Clients: Hunkar Laboratories, Inc.; United Radio, Inc.; Capital Management Corp.; William Cargile Contractor, Inc.; Metropolitan Tile Co. Inc.; H. Passman & Son, Inc.; Old Reliable Beauty & Barber Supply Co., Inc.
See Professional Biographies, CINCINNATI, OHIO

Asbury, Mary, (BV) '51 '75 C.855 B.A. L.94 J.D. 901 Elm St.
Ash, Linda A. '55 '91 C.37 B.A. L.1340 J.D. [Dinsmore&S.]
Ash, Patricia Tighe, (AV) '53 '79 C&L.150 B.A., J.D. Atty., Kroger Company, The
Ash, Reuel D., (BV) '57 '91 C.813 A.B. L.150 J.D. [Ⓐ Ulmer&B.]
Ashcraft, Raymond R. '33 '70 C.77 B.A. L.1340 J.D. 139 E. 4th St.
Ashdown, Charles C., (AV) '61 '86 C.262 B.A. L.602 J.D. [Strauss&T.]
Ashdown, Philomena Saldanha, (AV) '58 '86 C.1383 B.S. L.602 J.D. [Ⓒ Strauss&T.]
Ashton, Amy C. '71 '00 C.473 B.A. L.893 J.D. [Ⓐ Taft,S.&H.]
Aspinall, Brian E. '37 '62 C&L.150 B.B.A., LL.B. P.O. Box 599‡
Atkins, Charles G., (AV) '35 '62 C&L.150 B.A., J.D. [Ⓒ Strauss&T.]
Atkins, Katrina R. '75 '03 C.150 B.S.W. L.1340 J.D. [Ⓐ Dinsmore&S.]
Atkins, Thomas P., (AV) '47 '72 C.902 B.A. L.150 J.D. 1775 E. McMillan St.‡
Attenborough, Bruce W., (BV) '47 '84 C.1208 B.A. L.150 J.D. 617 Vine St.
Atwood, Daniel C. '63 '89 C.150 B.S. L.117 J.D. 7722 Hamilton Ave.
Aubin, A. Norman, (AV) '54 '83 C.588 B.S. L.201 J.D. [Faulkner&T.]
Auerbach, Boris, (AV) '31 '54 C&L.145 A.B., J.D. 7 West 7th Street
Aug, J. Vincent, (AV) '14 '39 C.477 B.A. L.150 LL.B. 5555 Drake Rd.‡
Aug, J. Vincent, Jr. '46 '73 C.276 B.A. L.150 J.D. U.S. Bkrptcy. J.
Auttonberry, Sheri E. '74 '99 C.418 B.a. L.880 J.D. [Ⓐ Katz,T.B.&H.]
Averbeck, Linda R. '70 '98 C.472 B.A. L.1340 J.D. 312 Elm St.
Avery, C. Richard '41 '65 C.269 B.A. L.245 J.D. 36 East 7th Street, Suite 2525
Ayers, G. Randall, (BV) '62 '88 C.231 A.B. L.608 J.D. [Frost B.T.]
Babb, Brian M., (BV) '56 '86 C.608 B.S. L.117 J.D. [Keating M.&K.]
Babinec, Gehl P. '42 '67 C.973 B.S.B.A. L.150 J.D. [Ⓒ Keating M.&K.]
Bacevich, Michael P. '71 '96 C&L.201 B.S., J.D. Mng. Dir., Virgin Ventures Fund
Bach, Michael B. '61 '87 C&L.150 B.A., J.D. [DeHaan&B.]
Bachman, Michael L., (AV) '58 '84 C.973 B.S.B.A. L.151 J.D. Co. Prosecutor's Off.
Backs, William B. '11 '41 L.1340 LL.B. 4756 Happiness Way
Backsman, Mary G., (BV) '34 '58 C.473 A.B. L.150 LL.B. 630 Vine St., 10th Fl.
Backus, W. William '51 '76 C.201 B.A. L.94 J.D. 6206 Edwood
Bacon, John C. '17 '46 C.608 L.273 LL.B. Ret. Com. Pleas J.
Baechtold, William J., (AV) '47 '72 C.973 B.S.B.A. L.150 J.D. [Graydon H.&R.]
Bagliore, Jayma C., (BV) '54 '80 C.608 B.A. L.150 J.D. [Ⓐ O'Connor,A.&L.]
Bahlman, William T., Jr., (AV) '20 '47 C&L.976 B.A., LL.B. 312 Walnut St.‡
Bailes, Michael S., (AV) '64 '90 C.1349 B.A. L.94 J.D. Tr. Coun., The Fifth Third Bk.
Bailey, Ann K., (AV) '50 '76 C&L.347 B.A., J.D.
Assoc. Gen. Coun., The Procter & Gamble Co.
Bailey, Donyetta D. '75 '00 C.339 B.A. L.117 J.D. [Ⓐ Keating M.&K.]
Bailey, Melanie S. '71 '97 C.1161 B.A. L.151 J.D. [Ⓐ Lopez,H.R.M.&S.]
Bailey, Stephen A., (AV) '45 '71 C.973 B.S. L.150 J.D. [Martin&B.]
Bailey, Todd H., (AV) '51 '76 C.473 B.A. L.228 J.D. [Ⓒ White,G.&M.] (Pat.)
Bailey-Newell, Susan Marie '67 '94 C.973 B.A. L.1340 J.D.
Dir. of Legal Servs. & HR, Cinci. Metro. Housing Auth.
Bajwa, Loveleen K. '— '02 C.973 B.A. L.1187 J.D. [Bajwa]
Bajwa Law Offices 5948 Glenway Avenue
Baker, Joan M. '52 '77 C.99 B.A. L.383 J.D.
(adm. in KY; not adm. in OH) N.L.R.B.
Baker, Neal D., (AV) '57 '84 C.1044 B.A. L.1292 J.D. [Dinsmore&S.]

Baker & Hostetler LLP, (AV)
312 Walnut Street Suite 3200, 45202-4074 ⊙
Telephone: 513-929-3400 Telecopier: 513-929-0303 To contact an attorney on the Internet use first initial and surname followed by @bakerlaw.com
URL: http://www.bakerlaw.com
Office Managing Partner: William Appleton. Partners: Michael F. Bigler; Martiné R. Dunn; Eric J. Geppert; Robin E. Harvey; David G. Holcombe; Thomas W. Kahle; Ted T. Martin. Associates: Benjamin G. Dusing; Robert F. Morwood; Eleni V. Stratigeas. Staff Attorney: Angela Hayden.
General Practice.
In Cleveland, Ohio: 3200 National City Center, 1900 East Ninth Street. Telephone: 216-621-0200.
In Columbus, Ohio: Capitol Square, Suite 2100, 65 East State Street. Telephone: 614-228-1541.
In Costa Mesa, California: 600 Anton Boulevard, Suite 900. Telephone: 714-754-6600.
In Denver, Colorado: 303 East 17th Avenue, Suite 1100. Telephone: 303-861-0600.
In Houston, Texas: 1000 Louisiana, Suite 2000. Telephone: 713-751-1600.
In Los Angeles, California: 333 South Grand Avenue, Suite 1800. Telephone: 213-975-1600.
In Orlando, Florida: SunTrust Center, Suite 2300, 200 South Orange Avenue. Telephone: 407-649-4000.
In Washington, D. C.: Washington Square, Suite 1100, 1050 Connecticut Avenue, N.W. Telephone: 202-861-1500.
In New York, N.Y.: 666 Fifth Avenue. Telephone: 212-589-4200.
See Professional Biographies, CINCINNATI, OHIO

Bakst, Jeffrey S., & Associates, (BV) '58 '83 C.150 B.A. L.291 J.D. 2406 Auburn Ave.
Balash, Paul E., (BV) '50 '76 C.973 B.S.B.A. L.1340 J.D. [Burke,F.B.&B.]
Baldrate, Eugene J. '45 '82 C.971 B.S.E.E. L.1029 J.D.
(adm. in CT; not adm. in OH) 3907 Brigadoon Dr.‡
Baldwin, Aine M. '75 '02 C.198 B.A. L.150 J.D. [Ⓐ Graydon H.&R.]
Baldwin, Gerald L., (AV) '46 '69 C.1118 A.B. L.150 J.D. [Frost B.T.]
Baldwin, Thomas A., (AV) '47 '75 C.475 B.A. L.150 J.D. P.O. Box 6129
Baldwin, William D.G. '67 '97 C.966 B.A. L.1161 J.D. [Vorys,S.S.&P.]
Bales, John W. '26 '60 C.967 B.A. L.477 J.D. 8626 Zenith Court‡
Bamber, Jeffrey V. '57 '84 C.150 B.S.C.E. L.608 J.D. The Procter & Gamble Co. (Pat.)
Banker, Marcia A. '57 '84 C.896 B.A. L.150 J.D. Ct. of App.
Banks, Andrew K. '67 '95 C.973 B.S.B.A. L.383 J.D.
Gen. Electric Aircraft Engines Grp.
Banner, John G. '51 '77 C.339 B.S. L.276 J.D. 139 E. 4th St.
Barber, Raymond P., (BV) '47 '73 C.973 B.S. L.1340 J.D. 5115 Delhi Rd.
Barbiere, Lawrence E., (AV) '51 '77 C.341 A.B. L.150 J.D. [Schroeder,M.B.&P.]
Bardach, Robert A. '63 '89 C.477 B.A. L.851 J.D. [Statman,H.S.&E.]
Barker, Jason C. '70 '96 C.475 B.A. L.215 J.D. Manager, Market Policy, Cinergy Corp.
Barker, Peggy Murphy, (CVⓉ) '66 '93 C.235 B.A. L.1340 J.D. [Kohnen&P.]
Barlow, Anthony M., (BV) '59 '90 C&L.150 B.A., J.D. [Strauss&T.]
Barnes, John E., (AV) '56 '81 C.734 B.A. L.150 J.D. [Dinsmore&S.]
Barnes, Michael David '62 '87
C.679 B.S.I.M. L.910 J.D. V.P., & Tr. Coun., Johnson Trust Company
Barnett, Michael N. '63 '90 C.262 B.A. L.608 J.D. Western & Southern Life Ins. Co.
Barresi, James J. '66 '91 C.27 B.A. L.896 J.D. [Squire,S.&D.]
Barrett, C. Francis, (AV) '46 '71 C.973 B.S. L.150 J.D. [Barrett&W.]
Barrett, Michael R., (AV) '51 '77 C&L.150 B.A., J.D. [Barrett&W.]
Barrett, Tina J. '62 '04 C.473 B.A. L.150 J.D. [Ⓐ Wolfe,P.]

Barrett & Weber, A Legal Professional Association, (AV) BR
500 Fourth & Walnut Centre, 105 East Fourth Street, 45202
Telephone: 513-721-2120 Facsimile: 513-721-2139
URL: http://www.barrettweber.com

(This Listing Continued)

Barrett & Weber, A Legal Professional Association (Continued)

C. Francis Barrett; H. Patrick Weber (Certified Specialist in Estate Planning, Trust and Probate Law, Ohio State Bar Association); Michael R. Barrett; M. Michele Fleming; Janet L. Bell;—Kenneth J. Eling; Karri K. Haffner; Stephanie K. Bowman; Thomas W. Breidenstein.
General Civil Practice including Commercial, Condominium, Construction, Corporate, Eminent Domain, Estate and Gift Taxation, Estate Planning, Federal and State Income Tax, Land Use and Planning, Local Government, Negligence, Probate, Real Estate, Tax Valuation of Real Estate, Title Insurance and Zoning. Administrative, Trial and Appellate Practice.
See Professional Biographies, CINCINNATI, OHIO

Barron, Carrie Atkins, (BV) . . . '66 '93 C.347 B.A. L.345 J.D. [A Freking&B.]
Barron, Dennis P. . . . '60 '85 C.477 B.A. L.150 J.D. P.O. Box 8090‡
Barron, Michael S. . . . '65 '90 C.477 B.A. L.880 J.D. [Barron,P.B.&S.]
Barron, Norman I., (AV) . . . '35 '60 C&L.150 B.B.A., LL.B. [Barron,P.B.&S.]
Barron, Peck, Bennie & Schlemmer, Co., L.P.A., (AV) . . . 3074 Madison Road
Barsman, Marvin J., (BV) . . . '27 '50 C&L.150 LL.B. 607 2nd Nat. Bldg.
Barth, David L., (AV) . . . '54 '78 C.973 H.A.B. L.1340 J.D. [Cors&B.] ⊙
Bartlett, William T., (AV) . . . '45 '74 C.645 B.S.I.E. L.1340 J.D. [Bartlett&W.]

Bartlett & Weigle Co., L.P.A., (AV)
Suite 1100 Tri-State Building, 432 Walnut Street, 45202 ⊙
Telephone: 513-241-3992 Fax: 513-241-1816
Email: bartlettlaw@fuse.net URL: http://www.bartlettlaw.com
William T. Bartlett; Douglas S. Weigle;—Darrell S. Wright; Matthew L. Benson.
General Civil and Criminal Law. Estate Planning, Real Estate and Corporate Franchise Law. Immigration and Naturalization Law. Business Bankruptcy. Trials and Appeals in all Courts.
Reference: Starbank of Cincinnati.
Covington, Kentucky Office: 211 East Fourth Street. Telephone: 859-491-1122.
See Professional Biographies, CINCINNATI, OHIO

Barty, Lawrence J., (AV) . . . '42 '73 C.259 B.A. L.228 J.D. [Taft,S.&H.]
Basil, Beth L. '57 '91 C.383 B.A. L.1340 J.D.
Corp. Vice President, Secretary & Legal Counsel, Intrieve, Incorporated
Basil, Mark A. . . . '57 '83 C.967 B.A. L.150 J.D. 4557 Montgomery Road, Suite 206
Baskett, William D., (AV) . . . '39 '64 C&L.309 B.A., LL.B. [B Frost B.T.]
Bass, Herbert, (AV) . . . '23 '49 C&L.150 LL.B. [B Schwartz,M.&R.]
Bassett, Kenneth B., (AV) . . . '31 '56 C.207 B.A. L.150 LL.B. [B Cors&B.]
Bassin, Jeffrey L. . . . '52 '78 C.959 B.A. L.966 J.D. Reg. Coun., I.R.S.
Bassler, Thomas B. . . . '42 '76 1351 William Howard Taft Road, Mail Location CK3-050
Batchelder, Alice M. . . . '44 '71 C.611 B.A. L.7 J.D. Ct. of App. J.
Bauer, H. Clifford . . . '17 '64 C.235 L.1340 LL.B. 4316 Fairdale Ct.‡
Bauer, John C., (BV) . . . '45 '72 C.384 A.B. L.1340 J.D. 5319 Delhi Avenue
Bauer, Nicholas . . . '08 '30 C.150 L.1340 LL.B. [Bauer,M.&H.]
Bauer, Morelli & Heyd Co., L.P.A., (AV) . . . 1029 Main St.

Bauernschmidt, Karen H., Co., LPA
(See Cleveland)

Baunach, Christi G. '68 '92
C&L.421 B.A., J.D. Staff Atty., American Legal Publishing Corp.
Baus, Jeanette . . . '60 '86 C.150 B.A. L.1340 J.D. U.S. Dept of Labor

Bavely, E. Hanlin, (AV) '38 '64 C&L.150 B.A., J.D.
850 Tri State Building, 432 Walnut Street, 45202-3914
Telephone: 513-621-6621 Fax: 513-721-4129
Bankruptcy, Debtor/Creditor, Commercial Collections, Civil Litigation, Probate.
See Professional Biographies, CINCINNATI, OHIO

Bazell, Haskell . . . '24 '50 C.145 L.150 B.L. P.O. Box 15588
Beach, Richard G. . . . '62 '99 C.473 B.A. L.1340 J.D. Coun., Cinergy Servs.
Beacock, Kathy A., (AV) . . . '53 '79 C&L.150 B.A., J.D. 2444 Madison Road, Suite 102
Beall, Augustus, III '26 '55 C.150 L.1340 LL.B.
Chmn. of the Bd., Arlington Memorial Gardens
Beatty, John W., (AV) . . . '36 '65 C.884 B.Ch.E. L.602 J.D. [B Dinsmore&S.]
Bechhold, Christopher M., (AV) . . . '54 '80 C.976 B.A. L.124 J.D. [Thompson H.]
Beck, Bradley D. . . . '— '88 C.150 B.S.A.E. L.1340 J.D. [B Wood,H.&E.] (See Pat. Sect.)
Beck, Raymond D. . . . '56 '82 C.1161 B.A. L.1340 J.D. Sr. V.P., Star Bank, N.A.
Beck, Walter P. . . . '12 '37 C.967 B.A. L.150 LL.B. 3315 Evergreen Ridge Dr.‡
Becker, Gary E., (AV) . . . '58 '84 C.879 B.A. L.150 J.D. [Dinsmore&S.]
Becker, Lawrence G. '33 '60 C.475 B.A. L.477 LL.B.
(adm. in IL; not adm. in OH) 1 E. 4th St.
Beckjord, Walter E., (AV) . . . '22 '49 C&L.976 B.S., LL.B. 3683 Kroger Ave.
Beckman, Vincent H., (AV) . . . '15 '41 C.973 B.A. L.309 LL.B. [Beckman W.S.] ‡

Beckman Weil Shepardson LLC, (AV)
1200 Mercantile Center, 120 East 4th Street, 45202-4010
Telephone: 513-621-2100 Telecopier: 513-621-0106
URL: http://www.beckman-weil.com
Vincent H. Beckman (Retired). Members of Firm: Sidney Weil; W. Philip Shepardson, Jr.; David E. Hathaway; Richard M. Hopple; Peter L. Cassady; Joseph H. Feldhaus; Margaret A. Hilvert; Janet Eileen Pecquet; Brian G. Dershaw. Associates: Brian R. Redden; Jennifer Griffin Anstaett; Laurie A. Lamb; Kristen M. Myers.
General Practice. Civil Litigation, Corporation, Domestic Relations, Employment, Tax, Labor, Trademark, Real Estate, Insurance, Medical Malpractice, Hospital, Health Care, Probate, Estate Planning, Elder Law, Medicaid and University Law. Trials and Appeals.
Representative Clients: Cincinnati Financial Corp.; Cincinnati Insurance Co.; Xavier University; University of Cincinnati.
See Professional Biographies, CINCINNATI, OHIO

Beckwith, Sandra S. . . . '43 '69 C&L.150 B.A., J.D. Chf. U.S. Dist. Ct. J.
Bedall, Thomas G. . . . '51 '78 C&L.8 B.A., J.D. Staff Atty., Pro Seniors, Inc.
Bedell, Christopher Jon . . . '63 '95 C.228 B.S.E. L.150 J.D. 300 Pike St.
Bedree, Kathleen Kernan, (AV) '58 '84
C&L.150 B.A., J.D. 1900 Chemed Center, 255 E. Fifth Street
Bedree, Melvin A., (AV) . . . '59 '84 C.210 B.A. L.150 J.D. [Vorys,S.S.&P.]
Bee, Gregory W. . . . '73 '02 C.610 A.B. L.477 J.D. [A Taft,S.&H.]
Beech, Joseph, III, (AV) . . . '45 '73 C.31 B.A. L.150 J.D. [Kohnen&P.]
Beerck, Daniel Robert '57 '94 C&L.150 B.F.A., J.D.
Assoc. Gen. Coun., 1st Grp. Amer.
Beers, Janet Ellen . . . '76 '04 C.473 B.A. L.150 J.D. [A Wolfe,P.]
Beiersdorfer, Amy M. . . . '72 '02 C.592 B.S. L.1194 J.D. [A D.D.Altman&Assoc.]
Beirne, Patrick J. . . . '71 '96 C.473 B.A. L.1161 J.D. [A Lawrence] ⊙
Beirne & Wirthlin, Co., L.P.A., (AV) . . . 1745 Madison Rd.
Bell, James R. . . . '42 '84 C.150 B.S. L.1340 J.D. 6700 Chestnut Street
Bell, Janet L., (BV) . . . '48 '84 C.30 B.A. L.1340 J.D. [Barrett&W.]
Bell, John Ashley . . . '58 '84 C.473 B.A. L.150 J.D. [J.A.Bell]
Bell, Ronald A. . . . '67 '94 C.667 B.S.A.E. L.608 J.D. [Squire,S.&D.]
Bell, Susan R. . . . '57 '98 C&L.150 B.Mus., J.D. [Cors&B.]
Bell, William D., Sr., (BV) . . . '50 '76 C&L.339 B.S., J.D. 830 Main St., #604
Bell, John A. . . . 9000 Plainfield Rd.
Bella, Ronald T., (AV) . . . '53 '79 C.150 B.B.A. L.201 J.D. 9545 Kenwood Rd.
Bellamy, Glenn D., (AV) . . . '62 '88 C&L.150 B.S., J.D. [B Greenebaum D.&M.] (Pat.)
Bence, David S., (AV) . . . '65 '90 C.477 A.B. L.608 J.D. [Frost B.T.]

Bender, Edward D., (AV) . . . '68 '95 C.150 B.A. L.1340 J.D. [A Wood&L.]
Benedict, Ronald L. '42 '68 C.150 B.A. L.1340 J.D.
Corp. V.P., Secy. & Coun., The Ohio Natl. Life Ins. Co.
Benintendi, Christopher A. . . . '65 '90 C.967 B.A. L.201 J.D. [Dinsmore&S.]
Benintendi, Robert F., (CV) . . . '64 '92 C.967 B.A. L.201 J.D. P.O. Box 44053
Benjamin, John A., (AV) . . . '14 '40 C.608 B.A. L.976 J.D. [Benjamin,Y.&H.]
Benjamin, Marva Kinley . . . '69 '96 C.150 B.B.A. L.1340 J.D. Co. Pub. Def. Off.

Benjamin, Yocum & Heather, LLC, (AV)
312 Elm Street Suite 1850, 45202-2740
Telephone: 513-721-5672 Fax: 513-562-4388
Email: info@byhlaw.com URL: http://www.byhlaw.com
Members of Firm: John A. Benjamin; Thomas R. Yocum; Timothy P. Heather; Anthony J. Iaciofano; Lisa Marie Bitter. Associates: Christopher J. Mulvaney; Bradford C. Weber; Richard O. Hamilton, Jr.; Brian A. Lee; Charles F. Hollis, III.
General Civil Practice. Insurance, Construction Law, Personal Injury, Employment Relations and Labor Law, Estate Planning, Probate, Litigation, Business, Corporate, Bankruptcy Law, and Creditors' Rights.
See Professional Biographies, CINCINNATI, OHIO

Bennett, Clyde, II . . . '65 '92 C.150 B.S. L.201 J.D. [Dinsmore&S.]
Bennett, Earl M., (AVⓉ) '50 '81 C.309 A.B. L.1292 J.D.
(adm. in NJ; not adm. in OH) Formica Corp. ⊙
Bennett, Lawrence T. . . . '44 '71 C.30 B.A. L.904 J.D. [Katzman,L.H.&B.]
Benson, Matthew L. . . . '77 '03 C.383 B.S. L.1340 J.D. [A Bartlett&W.]
Beraha, Stephen C. '70 '97 C.910 B.A. L.150 J.D.
Sr. Corp. Coun., Great American Insurance Co.
Berg, Bertram H. . . . '11 '43 C.150 L.1340 LL.B. 4413 Brazee
Berg, John L., (BV) . . . '51 '76 C.608 B.A. L.851 J.D. [B Katzman,L.H.&B.]
Berger, Andrew R., (AV) . . . '55 '78 C.546 B.A. L.188 J.D. [Katz,T.B.&H.]
Berger, Daniel O., (AV) . . . '45 '73 C.207 B.A. L.477 J.D. [Thompson H.]
Bergeron, Jennifer Paschen . . . '73 '02 C.138 B.A. L.150 J.D. [A Ulmer&B.]
Bergeron, Pierre H. . . . '74 '99 C.138 B.A. L.893 J.D. [A Squire,S.&D.]
Bergman, Thomas H., (AV) . . . '52 '78 C.659 B.A. L.150 J.D. [T.H.Bergman&Assoc.]
Bergman, Thomas H., & Associates, LLC, (AV) . . . 5710 Wooster Pike, Ste. 212
Bergmann, Michael J., (BV) . . . '57 '82 C.473 B.A. L.150 J.D. [M.J.Bergmann]
Bergmann, Michael J., LLC, (BV) . . . 6020 Cheviot Road
Beridon, Thomas Olivier . . . '72 '99 C.610 B.S. L.150 J.D. Pub. Def.
Beringhaus, Beth Niehaus, (BV) . . . '54 '81 C.473 B.A. L.1340 J.D. 914 Main St., 5th Fl.
Berliant, Mark H., (AV) . . . '32 '56 C&L.893 B.A., LL.B. [Strauss&T.]
Bernard, Kathryn, (BV) . . . '53 '79 C&L.150 B.A., J.D. CBS Pers. Servs.
Bernat, Richard A., (BV) . . . '46 '75 C.846 B.A. L.1340 J.D. 1000 Main St., Rm. 585
Bernat, Stephen M. . . . '71 '98 C.610 B.B.A. L.1161 J.D. [McCaslin,I.&M.] ⊙
Bernens, Robert E., (BV) . . . '21 '48 C.973 Ph.B. L.150 LL.B. 14 Garfield Pl.
Berner, Milton T., (BV) . . . '39 '74 C.999 B.A. L.1340 J.D. Probate & Juv. Ct. Mag.
Bernhard, Dale H., (BV) . . . '48 '77 C.150 B.S. L.1340 J.D. 3646 Glenmore Ave.
Berninger, Paul R., (AV) . . . '43 '71 C.973 B.S. L.1340 J.D. [Wood&L.]
Berquist, Lynn Marie '67 '01 C&L.477 B.S., J.D.
(adm. in MN; not adm. in OH) Staff Physician, VAMC
Bettman, Marianna Brown, (AV) '44 '77
C&L.150 B.A., J.D. Univ. of Cincinnati, College of Law
Betts, Carolyn A. . . . '— '84 C.104 A.B. L.1340 J.D. [B Dinsmore&S.]
Bevan, P. Michelle, (BV) '64 '90
C.383 B.A. L.150 J.D. Ass't Corp. Coun., Cincinnati Milacron Inc.
Bever, Mark S. . . . '59 '84 C.602 B.A. L.851 J.D. [Graf&S.&M.]
Bezney, Michael A. '64 '89 C.846 B.B.A. L.659 J.D.
Sr. V.P. & Gen. Coun., Catholic Healthcare Partners
Bibus, Thomas Wm., (BV) . . . '49 '76 C.150 B.A. L.1161 J.D. 2962 Harrison Ave.
Bickley, John J. . . . '22 '52 C.62 B.A. L.161 J.D. 6213 Coachlite Way‡
Bieler, Cole Alan, (BV) . . . '52 '78 C&L.150 B.A., J.D. 432 Walnut St., Tri-State Bldg.
Bigler, Michael F., (AV) . . . '57 '83 C.150 B.A. L.602 J.D. [Baker&H.]
Billing, Bernadette M. . . . '72 '97 C.1161 B.A. L.150 J.D. Asst. Co. Pros.
Bilott, Robert A., (AV) . . . '65 '90 C.1275 B.A. L.608 J.D. [Taft,S.&H.]
Bishop, Jerome C. . . . '69 '02 C&L.276 B.A., J.D. [A Katz,T.B.&H.]
Bison Jacobson, Barbara, (AV) . . . '48 '75 C.473 B.A. L.608 J.D. [B Vorys,S.S.&P.]
Bissinger, Charles C., Jr., (AV) . . . '55 '79 C.477 B.A. L.309 J.D. [Vorys,S.S.&P.]
Bissinger, Julie F., (BV) . . . '58 '84 C.294 B.A. L.831 J.D. Personal Dir.
Bissinger, Mark C., (AV) . . . '57 '83 C.679 B.S.C.E. L.150 J.D. [Dinsmore&S.]
Bitter, Lisa Marie, (BV) . . . '61 '91 C.610 B.S. L.150 J.D. [Benjamin,Y.&H.]
Blachman, Gary D. . . . '65 '95 C.705 B.A. L.365 J.D. [A Thompson H.]
Black, David D. . . . '68 '94 C.531 B.A. L.151 J.D. [Dinsmore&S.]
Black, Robert L., Jr. . . . '17 '46 C.976 A.B. L.309 LL.B. Ret. Ct. App. J.
Black, Stephen L., (AV) . . . '48 '74 C&L.309 A.B., J.D. [Graydon H.&R.]
Black, Timothy S., (AV) . . . '53 '83 C.309 A.B. L.1340 J.D. J., Hamilton Co. Mun. Ct.
Blackburn, Kenneth L. . . . '71 '03 C&L.383 B.S., J.D. Coun., Proctor & Gamble
Blackburn, Troy A. . . . '67 '92 C.228 A.B. L.150 J.D. 1 Paul Brown Stadium
Blair, Linda A., (BV) . . . '61 '86 C&L.608 B.A., J.D. 10726 Escondido Dr.
Blandford, Colleen M. . . . '69 '93 C&L.150 B.A., J.D. [Kohnen&P.]
Blank, Cynthia F., (AV) . . . '25 '56 C.930 A.B. L.1340 J.D. [B Taft,S.&H.]
Blank, Thomas J. . . . '29 '59 C.973 B.S.B.A. L.1340 J.D. 5735 Eaglesridge Ln.

Blank Rome LLP, (AV)
PNC Center, 201 East Fifth Street, Suite 1700, 45202 ⊙
Telephone: 513-362-8700 Fax: 513-362-8787
Email: webmaster@BlankRome.com URL: http://www.BlankRome.com
Partners: Michael L. Cioffi; Matthew J. Siembieda (Not admitted in OH); Sharon J. Zealey. Senior Counsel: Nathaniel R. Jones. Associate: William M. Huse.
Administrative Law, Administrative Adjudications; Administrative Agency Practice, Administrative Hearings and Appeals, Administrative Litigation, Federal Administrative Law, Professional Licensing, Professional Licensing Regulation, Public Law, Admiralty and Maritime Law, Marine Law, Maritime Contracts, Maritime Finance, Maritime Law, Maritime Liens, Ship Sales and Mortgages, Aged and Aging, Age Discrimination, Elder Care, Elder Law, Agency and Distributorships, Distribution Agreements, International Distribution, Alcoholic Beverages, Liquor Licensing, Alternative Dispute Resolution, Arbitration, International Arbitration, International Dispute Resolution, Mediation, Antitrust and Trade Regulation, Antitrust, Business Combinations, Competition, Covenants Not To Compete, Deceptive Trade Practices, Noncompetition and Non-Solicitation Agreements, Price-Fixing, Restrictive Covenants, Trade Regulation, Unfair Trade, Appellate Practice, Civil Appeals, Art Law, Artists Rights, Museum Law, Asset Protection, International Asset Protection, Aviation and Aerospace, Aircraft Finance and Leasing, Aircraft Sales, Airline Labor Law, Aviation Law, Aviation Defense, Aviation Insurance, Aviation Litigation, Aviation Products Liability, Aviation Regulation, Bankruptcy, Bankruptcy Arbitration, Bankruptcy Chapter 7, Bankruptcy Chapter 11, Bankruptcy Chapter 12, Bankruptcy Chapter 13, Bankruptcy Collections, Bankruptcy Litigation, Bankruptcy Mediation, Bankruptcy Reorganization, Bankruptcy Taxation, Bankruptcy Trustees Rights, Commercial Bankruptcy, Commercial Foreclosure, Commercial Insolvency, Commercial Recovery, Commercial Workouts, Foreclosures, Fraudulent Conveyance, Insolvency, International Bankruptcy, International Insolvency, Liquidations, Out of Court Debt Restructuring, Pre-Bankruptcy Workouts, Receiverships, Repossessions, Workouts, Workouts Taxation, Banks and Banking, ATM Networks, Bank Collections, Bank Directors and Officers Liability, Bank Foreclosures, Bank Mergers and Acquisitions, Banking Antitrust, Banking Law, Banking Litigation, Commercial Banking, Commercial Credit, Commercial Loans, Consumer Banking, Credit Card Law, Credit Finance, Credit Law, Electronic Banking, Fair Lending, Financial Law, Interest and Usury, International Banking Law, International Loans, Lender Law, Lender Liability, Lender Regulation, Lenders Rights, Letters of

(This Listing Continued)

Blank Rome LLP (Continued)

Credit, Loan Restructuring, Loan Workouts, Loans, Savings and Loan Law, Secured Lending, Truth in Lending, Biotechnology, Biomedical Technology, Biotechnology Licensing, Business Law, Business Arbitration, Business Associations Law, Business Crimes, Business Development, Business Dissolutions, Business Estate Planning, Business Formation, Business Fraud, Business Litigation, Business Mediation, Business Organization, Business Planning, Business Regulation, Business Reorganization, Business Sales, Business Succession Planning, Business Successions, Business Syndication, Business Taxation, Business Torts, Business Transactions, Business Transfers, Business Trusts, Business Valuation, Buying and Selling of Businesses, Capital Formation, Closely Held Business Estate Planning, Closely Held Business Law, Closely Held Business Taxation, Complex Business Litigation, Emerging Business Law, Emerging Growth Companies, Entrepreneurial Business Law, Family Business Law, Family Business Mediation, Family Business Successions, International Business Law, International Joint Ventures, Joint Ventures, Limited Liability Company Law, Privatization, Professional Practices, Small Business Law, Sole Proprietorships, Strategic Alliances, Chancery and Equity, Chancery Practice, Children, Child Custody, Child Support, Civil Practice, Federal Civil Practice, Sex Discrimination, Commercial Collections, Post Judgment Collections, Commercial Law, Commercial Litigation, Complex Commercial Litigation, Secured Transactions, Uniform Commercial Code, Commercial Real Estate, Commercial Real Estate Acquisitions, Commercial Real Estate Development, Commercial Real Estate Finance, Commercial Real Estate Foreclosure, Commercial Real Estate Sales, Commercial Real Estate Syndication, Commercial Real Estate Workouts, Industrial Real Estate Law, Shopping Center Acquisitions, Shopping Center Development, Shopping Center Law, Complex and Multi-District Litigation, Computers and Software, Computer Contracts, Computer Law, Computer Security, Computer Software Law, Computer Technology, Electronic Commerce, Information Technology, Information Technology Contracts, Information Technology Licensing, International Computer Law, Internet Law, Software Copyright, Software Licensing, Software Protection, Year 2000 Computer Conversion, Constitutional Law, First Amendment Law, Construction Law, Construction Finance, Construction Litigation, Construction Workouts, Environmental Construction Law, International Construction Law, Public Construction Law, Consumer Law, Consumer Arbitration, Consumer Class Actions, Consumer Credit, Consumer Credit Compliance, Consumer Finance, Consumer Fraud, Consumer Litigation, Consumer Protection, Consumer Rights, Fair Credit Reporting Act, Contracts, Breach of Contract, Commercial Contracts, Contract Fraud, Contract Litigation, International Commercial Contracts, International Contracts, Copyrights, Copyright Infringement, Copyright Litigation, Copyright Prosecution, Copyright Protection, Copyright Registration, International Copyright Law, Corporate Law, Closely Held Corporations, Corporate Banking Law, Corporate Commercial Law, Corporate Contracts, Corporate Control Contests, Corporate Criminal Law, Corporate Dissolutions, Corporate Ethics, Corporate Fiduciary Law, Corporate Finance, Corporate Formation, Corporate Governance, Corporate Income Tax, Corporate Insurance, Corporate Insurance Defense, Corporate Investigations, Corporate Litigation, Corporate Organization, Corporate Partnerships, Corporate Planning, Corporate Real Estate, Corporate Reorganization, Corporate Successions, Corporate Tax Controversies, Corporate Tax Planning, Corporate Taxation, Corporate Trusts, Corporate Workouts, Family Corporations, Foreign Sales Corporations, Hostile Takeovers, Incorporation, International Corporate Finance, International Corporate Law, International Corporate Taxation, Nonprofit Corporations, Offshore Corporations, Professional Corporations; Proxy Contests, Public Corporations, S Corporations, Securitization, Small Business Corporations, Takeovers, Tender Offers, Transfer Pricing, Criminal Law, Debtor and Creditor, Creditor Bankruptcy, Creditors Rights, Creditors Rights in Bankruptcy, Debtor and Creditor Bankruptcy, Debtor and Creditor Collections, Debtor and Creditor Remedies, Debtor and Creditor Reorganization, Debtor and Creditor Rights, Debtor and Creditor Workouts, Debtor Bankruptcy, International Creditors Rights, Secured Creditors Rights, Unsecured Creditors Rights, Disabilities, Americans with Disabilities Act, Academic Employment, College and University Law, Administrative Lobbying, Executive Lobbying, Legislative Lobbying, Lobbying, Eminent Domain, Employee Benefits, COBRA, Deferred Compensation, Employee Benefit Taxation, Employee Benefit Trusts, Employee Compensation, Employee Stock Ownership Plans, ERISA, Executive Compensation, Executive Compensation Taxation, Flexible Benefit Plans, Multi-Employer Benefits, Multi-Employer Pensions, Non-Qualified Benefits, Pension and Profit Sharing Plans, Pension Plans, Pension Taxation, Profit Sharing, Public Pension Plans, Qualified Retirement Plans, Retirement Benefit Plans, Taft-Hartley Plans, Unemployment Compensation, Music Copyright, Environmental Law, Environmental Compliance, Environmental Liability, Environmental Litigation, Environmental Mediation, International Environmental Law, Equipment Finance and Leasing, Equipment Finance, Equipment Leasing, Vehicle Leasing, Family Law, Divorce, Matrimonial Law, Finance, Asset Based Finance, Financial Institution Reorganization, Financial Institutions Law, Financial Institutions Taxation, Financial Restructuring, International Commercial Finance, International Finance, Franchises and Franchising, Franchise Law, Franchise Licensing, Franchise Litigation, Franchise Taxation, International Franchising, General Practice, Federal Practice, Government, County Government Law, Federal Government Law, Government Affairs, Government Agency Practice, Government Relations, Legislative Practice, Local Government Law, Public Policy, Qui Tam Litigation, State Government Law, State Legislative Practice, Township Law, Government Contracts, Government Construction Contracts, Government Contract Arbitration, Government Contract Fraud, Government Procurement, International Government Contracts, Local Government Contracts, Public Bidding, Public Contract Law, Public Works Contracts, Guardianship and Conservatorship, Health Care, Alternative Health Care Delivery System, Certificates of Need, Health Care Administration, Health Care Contracts, Health Care Corporate Law, Health Care Facility Licensing, Health Care Facility Regulation, Health Care Finance, Health Care Fraud, Health Care Legislation, Health Care Licensing, Health Care Mergers and Acquisitions, Health Care Regulation, Health Care Reimbursement, Health Care Taxation, Health Insurance, Health Insurance Coverage, Health Insurance Defense, Health Insurance Trusts, Health Law, Health Maintenance Organizations, Integrated Health Care Delivery Systems, Long Term Care, Managed Care, Managed Care Contracts, Medical Antitrust, Mental Health Law, Nursing Home Regulation, Pharmacy Law, Physicians Contracts, Hospital Law, Hospital Administration, Medical Staff Contracts, Medical Staff Credentialing, Housing Law, Affordable Housing, Apartment Projects, Housing Finance, Insurance, Commercial Insurance, Insurance Company Taxation, Insurance Litigation, Insurance Defense, Intellectual Property, Artistic Property, Chemical Intellectual Property, Electrical Intellectual Property, Intellectual Property Infringement, Intellectual Property Licensing, Intellectual Property Litigation, International Intellectual Property, International Licensing, Mechanical Intellectual Property, Medical Intellectual Property, Pharmaceutical Intellectual Property, Piracy, Proprietary Rights, Taxation of Intellectual Property, International Law, International Trade, Antidumping, Countervailing Duties, Customs Law, Export Regulation, Import and Export Law, International Trade Regulation, Latin America Trade, Russia Trade, Investments, Financial Services Law, Financial Services Regulation, Foreign Investment, Foreign Investment in the United States, International Investment, Investment Banking Law, Investment Company Law, Investment Partnerships, Investment Regulation, Labor and Employment, Affirmative Action, Collective Bargaining, Employee Drug Testing, Employer Liability, Employment at Will, Employment Contracts, Employment Discrimination, Employment Litigation, Employment Mediation, Executive Employment Law, Executive Severance Contracts, Fair Labor Standards, Family and Medical Leave Act, Federal Employment Law, Harassment, International Employment Contracts, International Labor Law, Labor Arbitration, Management Labor Law, National Labor Relations Act, Personnel Policies, Public Sector Collective Bargaining, Public Sector Labor Relations, Sexual Harassment, Unfair Labor Practices, Union Contract Negotiations, Union Elections, Union Organization, Wage and Hour Law, WARN Act, Workplace Violence, Wrongful Termination Defense, Leases and Leasing, Commercial Leasing, International Leasing, Landlord and Tenant Law, Lease Finance, Leasing, Leveraged Leasing, Office Leasing, Retail Leasing, Shopping Center Leasing, Legal Ethics and Professional Responsibility, Legal Ethics, Litigation, Civil Litigation, Complex Litigation, Defense Litigation, Federal Civil Litigation, Federal Litigation, International Litigation, Long-Arm Litigation, Trial Practice, U.S. Supreme Court Litigation, Newspaper Contracts, Publishing Contracts, Medical Malpractice, Medicare and Medicaid, Medicaid Planning, Medicare and Medicaid Reimbursement, Medicare Fraud and Abuse, Mergers, Acquisitions and Divestitures, Business Acquisitions, Business Divestitures, International Mergers and Acquisitions, Leveraged Acquisitions, Leveraged Buyouts, Merger Reorganization, Mergers and Acquisitions, Mergers and Acquisitions Finance, Mortgages, Commercial Mortgages, Mortgage Banking Law, Mortgage Bankruptcy, Mortgage Finance, Mortgage Foreclosure, Mortgage Insurance, Mortgage Lien Foreclosure, Mortgage Refinancing, Mortgage Securitization, Mortgage Tax, Mortgage Workouts, Secondary Mortgage Market, Municipal Bonds, Municipal Bonds Taxation, Municipal Contracts, Municipal Corporation Law, Municipal Derivative Products, Municipal Finance, Municipal Labor Law, Municipal Leasing, Municipal Pension Law, Municipal Redevelopment, Municipal Securities, Municipal Taxation, Tax Increment Finance, Natural Resources, Nonprofit and Charitable Organizations, Charitable Limited Partnerships, Charitable Organizations Law, Charitable Trusts and Foundations, Nonprofit Organizations Law, Nonprofit Tax Law, Private Foundations, Tax Exempt Organizations, Occupational Safety and Health, OSHA, Partnership Law, Family Limited Partnerships, Family Partnerships, Limited Liability Partnerships, Limited Partnerships, Partnership Dissolution, Partnership Formation, Partnership Organization, Partnership Syndication, Partnership Taxation, Patents, Biochemical Patents, Biotechnology Patent Prosecution, Biotechnology Patents, Chemical Patent Prosecution, Chemical Patents, Computer and Software Patents, Design Patents, Electrical Patent Prosecution, Electrical Patents, Electronic Patents, International Patents, Mechanical Patent Prosecution, Mechanical Patents, Medical Patents, Metal-

(This Listing Continued)

Blank Rome LLP (Continued)

lurgical Patents, Molecular Biology Patents, Patent Applications, Patent Infringement, Patent Interference Practice, Patent Licensing, Patent Litigation, Patent Prosecution, Patent Protection, Pharmaceutical Patents, Personal Injury, Premises Security, Probate, Ancillary Probate, International Probate, Probate Administration, Probate Litigation, Probate Taxation, Products Liability, Drug and Medical Device Defense, Firearms Products Liability, Professional Liability, Public Finance, Bond Finance, Economic Development, Housing and Urban Development, Industrial Development, International Economic Development, International Project Finance, Project Finance, Public Authority Finance, Public Finance Taxation, Public-Private Development, Tax Exempt Bonds, Tax Exempt Finance, Railway Labor Law, Real Estate, Condominium Association Law, Condominium Conversions, Condominium Development, Condominium Law, Conveyancing, Cooperative Association Law, Cooperative Conversions, Cooperative Housing Law, Easements, International Real Estate, Land Acquisitions, Land Sales, Land Trusts, Planned Unit Development Law, Real Estate Acquisitions, Real Estate Arbitration, Real Estate Banking Law, Real Estate Bankruptcy, Real Estate Brokers Licensing, Real Estate Contracts, Real Estate Development, Real Estate Finance, Real Estate Foreclosure, Real Estate Investment, Real Estate Investment Taxation, Real Estate Investment Trusts, Real Estate Joint Ventures, Real Estate Leasing, Real Estate Litigation, Real Estate Mediation, Real Estate Partnerships, Real Estate Restructuring, Real Estate Sales, Real Estate Secured Lending, Real Estate Securities, Real Estate Settlements, Real Estate Syndication, Real Estate Tax Appeals, Real Estate Tax Assessment, Real Estate Taxation, Real Estate Title, Real Estate Transfers, Real Estate Valuation, Real Estate Workouts, Real Property, Real Property Acquisitions, Real Property Development, Real Property Finance, Residential Real Estate, Residential Real Estate Development, Waterfront Development, Regulatory Law, Drug and Medical Device Regulation, Federal Regulatory Law, Regulated Industries, Regulatory Agency Practice, Regulatory Investigations, Religious Nonprofit Corporation Law, RICO, Securities, Bank Securities, Broker-Dealer Arbitration, Broker-Dealer Regulation, Initial Public Offerings, Private Placement, Private Placement Syndication, Public Offerings, SEC Enforcement, Securities Arbitration, Securities Litigation, Securities Offerings, Securities Registration, Securities Regulation, Shareholder Agreements, Shareholder Disputes, Tax Exempt Securities, Sports Contracts, Sports Licensing, Taxation, Employment Tax, Estate and Gift Taxation, Federal Income Tax, Federal Tax Controversies, Federal Taxation, Fiduciary Income Tax, Income Tax, Individual Taxation, International Tax Controversies, International Taxation, Like Kind Exchanges, Local Taxation, Low Income Housing Tax Credits, Property Tax Abatement, Property Tax Appeals, Sales and Use Tax, State Taxation, Tax Appeals, Tax Audits, Tax Collection, Tax Deferred Exchanges, Tax Planning, Tax Shelters, Trusts and Estates Taxation, Electronics, High Technology Contracts, Semiconductor Technology, Technology Contracts, Technology Licensing, Technology Protection, Technology Transfers, Torts, Trade Association Law, Toxic Torts, Trade Secrets, Theft of Trade Secrets, Trademarks, International Trademarks, Trade Dress, Trade Names, Trademark Arbitration, Trademark Infringement, Trademark Licensing, Trademark Litigation, Trademark Prosecution, Trademark Protection, Trademark Registration, Transportation, Common Carrier Law, Mass Transit Law, Public Transportation Law, Transit Labor, Trusts and Estates, Decedents Estates, Estate Administration, Estate Litigation, Estate Planning, Family Trusts, Family Wealth Transfer, Fiduciary Law, Fiduciary Liability, Fiduciary Litigation, Financial Planning, International Estate Planning, International Trusts, Living Trusts, Offshore Trusts, Personal Planning, Retirement Planning, Trust Administration, Trust Law, Trust Litigation, Trust Planning, Wealth Preservation, Unfair Competition, Utility Law, Utility Acquisitions, Utility Contracts, Utility Taxation, White Collar Crime, Embezzlement, White Collar Criminal Defense, White Collar Fraud, Wills, Contested Wills, Inheritance, Living Wills, Successions, Zoning, Planning and Land Use, Building and Public Safety Codes, Cemetery Law, Environmental Land Use, Fire Districts, Improvement Districts, Land Conservation, Land Development, Land Entitlement, Land Use, Land Use Litigation, Land Use Permitting, Land Use Regulation, Rezoning, Special Districts, Subdivisions, Water Districts, Zoning Law, Zoning Variances, Retail Industry Development.

Philadelphia, Pennsylvania Office: One Logan Square, 18th & Cherry Streets, 19103-6998. Telephone: 215-569-5500. FAX: 215-569-5555.

Media, Pennsylvania Office: Rose Tree Corporate Center, 1400 N. Providence Road, Building 1, Suite 301, 19063. Telephone: 610-891-7800. FAX: 610-891-7804.

Cherry Hill, New Jersey Office: 210 Lake Drive East, Woodland Falls Corporate Park, Suite 200, 08002-1164. Telephone: 856-779-3600. FAX: 856-779-7647.

Boca Raton, Florida Office: 1200 North Federal Highway, Suite 417, 33432. Telephone: 561-417-8100. FAX: 561-417-8101.

Allentown, Pennsylvania Office: 1620 Pond Road, Suite 200, 18104-2255. Telephone: 610-706-4300. FAX: 610-706-4343.

Wilmington, Delaware Office: Chase Manhattan Centre, 1201 Market Street, Suite 800, 19801. Telephone: 302-425-6400. FAX: 302-425-6464.

Washington, D.C. Office: Watergate, Eleventh Floor, 600 New Hampshire Avenue N.W., 20037. Telephone: 202-772-5800. Fax: 202-772-5858.

Trenton, New Jersey Office: 200 West State Street, 08608. Telephone: 609-278-2320. FAX: 609-278-2323.

Baltimore, Maryland Office: 1 North Charles Street, Suite 1905, 21201. Telephone: 410-659-3939. FAX: 410-659-3969.

New York, New York Office: The Chrysler Building, 405 Lexington Avenue, 10174. Telephone: 212-885-5000. FAX: 212-885-5001.

See Professional Biographies, CINCINNATI, OHIO

Blankenship, Randy J. . . . . '61 '86 C.1161 B.A. L.1340 J.D. [Robbins,K.P.&T.]
Blaske, Nathan H. . . . .'78 '03 C.383 B.B.A. L.1340 J.D. [Ⓐ Wood&L.]
Blasky, Aaron E. . . . . '37 '73 C.150 B.B.A. L.1340 J.D. Int. Rev. Serv.
Blatt, P. Andrew . . . .'66 '98 C.1333 B.S. L.150 J.D. [Ⓐ Wood,H.&E.] (See Pat. Sect.)
Blatt, Robert . . . . '31 '64 C.494 B.A. L.1340 J.D. 10925 Reed Hartman Hwy.
Bley, Kellie Sue . . . .'71 '97 C.150 B.A. L.117 J.D. Pros. Off.
Blickensderfer, Matthew C., (AV) . . . .'70 '95 C.597 B.A. L.309 J.D. [Frost B.T.]
Bloch, Randal S., (AV) . . . .'49 '73 C.966 B.A. L.1009 J.D. [Wagner&B.]
Block, Patricia K. . . . .'73 '98 C.607 B.A. L.117 J.D. [Ⓐ Lerner,S.&R.]
Block, Robert G. . . . . '50 '75 C.150 B.A. L.607 J.D. [Droder&M.]
Blomeke, Stacy Christman . . . . '— '00 C.973 B.S. L.201 J.D. [Ⓐ Frost B.T.]
Blumberg, Gerald . . . . '30 '54 C&L.150 A.B., LL.B. 1940 River Rd.
Bodley, James C. . . . . '47 '78 C.150 B.B.A. L.1340 J.D. [Ⓐ Griffin -F.]
Boehm, David F., (AV) . . . .'44 '72 C.973 B.S. L.150 J.D. [Boehm,K.&L.]
Boehm, Kurt J. . . . . '77 '02 C.174 B.A. L.910 J.D. [Ⓐ Boehm,K.&L.]
Boehm, Paul J., (BV) . . . .'24 '50 C&L.150 B.S., LL.B. 4812 Vine St.

Boehm, Kurtz & Lowry, (AV)
Suite 1510, URS Center, 36 East Seventh Street, 45202
Telephone: 513-421-2255 Telecopier: 513-421-2764
Email: KIUC@AOL.COM
Members of Firm: David F. Boehm; Michael L. Kurtz; John P. Lowry. Associate: Kurt J. Boehm. Public Utility, Electricity, Natural Gas, Water, Estate Planning and Corporate Law.

See Professional Biographies, CINCINNATI, OHIO

Boggs, Danny J. . . . .'44 '69 C.309 A.B. L.145 J.D. Chief J., Ct. of App.
Boggs, Paula Yasuyo '74 '03 C.383 B.S.B.A. L.150 J.D.
(adm. in KY; not adm. in OH) [Ⓐ Keating M.&K.]
Bogner, Eugene P. . . . . '37 '66 C.581 B.S. L.585 LL.B. 906 Main St.
Bohlen, Monica R., (BV) . . . .'49 '74 C&L.150 B.A., J.D. 36 E. 7th St., Ste. 2020
Bolam, Brian M. '66 '93 C.201 B.S. L.128 J.D.
Sen. Coun., Pats., The Procter & Gamble Co. (Pat.)
Bolce, Louis H., II . . . . '25 '50 C&L.150 LL.B. 2429 Gilbert Ave.
Bolin, James H., Jr. '67 '94 C.145 A.B. L.976 J.D.
Asst. Gen. Coun., Current Communications Services
Bolin, Linda S. . . . . '49 '85 C.97 B.A. L.1340 J.D. 15 E. 8th St.
Boll, Edward J., III . . . .'77 '00 C.150 B.A. L.200 J.D. [Ⓐ Lerner,S.&R.]
Bollhauer, Raymond G. . . . '64 '90 C&L.150 B.A., J.D. Editor, American Legal Pub. Corp.
Bolotin, Jay A. . . . . '69 '95 C.347 B.A. L.472 J.D. [Young,R.&N.]
Bolsinger, Hiram C., Jr., (BV) . . . .'06 '28 L.1340 LL.B. 5945 Ridge Ave.
Bond, Cole D. . . . .'73 '99 C.378 B.A. L.880 J.D. [Ⓐ Keating M.&K.]
Bond, Dianna K. '61 '90 C&L.150 B.A., J.D.
Asst. Atty. Gen., State of Ohio, Atty General's Off.

Bond, Kasey ....'73 '98 C.383 B.A. L.880 J.D. [A Frost B.T.]
Bonhaus, Laurence A. ....'49 '76 C&L.150 B.S., J.D. 948 Dana Ave.
Borchelt, Joseph ....'76 '02 C.970 B.A. L.7 J.D. [A Reminger&R.]
Borders, Patrice Baughman '64 '92 C.824 B.A. L.608 J.D.
Global Lead Mgmt. Consulting
Borland, Cheryl L. ....'62 '94 C.1161 B.S. L.1340 J.D. [A Katz,G.&N.]
Borne, Troy Allen ....'70 '95 C.1118 B.A. L.151 J.D. Coopers & Lybrand, LLP
Bortz, Arnold L. ....'46 '74 C.309 A.B. L.276 J.D. Towne Properties
Bortz, Lee, (BV) ....'25 '50 C&L.150 B.B.A., LL.B. 1821 Summit Rd.
Bortz, Milton H. ....'30 '55 C&L.150 B.B.A., J.D. 1550 Shenandoah Ave.
Bossin, Phyllis G., (AV) ....'50 '77 C.150 B.A. L.1340 J.D. [P.G.Bossin]

Bossin, Phyllis G., Co., L.P.A., (AV)
Suite 1210, 36 East Fourth Street, 45202
Telephone: 513-421-4420 Fax: 513-421-0691 URL: http://www.bossinlaw.com
Email: PBossin@bossinlaw.com URL: http://www.lawyers.com/phyllisbossin
Phyllis G. Bossin (Certified Specialist in Family Relations Law, Ohio State Bar Association);— Shannon F. Eckner.
Domestic Relations and Family Law. Child Custody, Support, Divorce, Premarital Agreements.
See Professional Biographies, CINCINNATI, OHIO

Boster, B. Scott, (BV) ....'59 '85 C.473 B.S. L.150 J.D. [Ulmer&B.]
Bouffard, Alison J. ....'79 '04 C.347 B.A. L.150 J.D. [A Keating M.&K.]
Bowers, Andrew D. ....'73 '99 C.967 B.A. L.608 J.D. [A Keating M.&K.]
Bowling, John C. ....'31 '57 C&L.150 B.A., LL.B. Pres., Bowling Portfolio Mgmt., Inc.
Bowman, Stephanie K. ....'74 '00 C.339 B.A. L.209 J.D. [A Barrett&W.]
Boyd, David Henry ....'69 '95 C.390 A.B. L.150 J.D. 324 Reading Rd.
Boyd, David J., (BV) ....'38 '64 C.973 B.A. L.150 J.D. 7 W. 7th St.
Boydston, Richard, (AV) ....'— '77 C.309 A.B. L.659 J.D. [Greenebaum D.&M.]
Boykin, Yvette S. ....'69 '97 C.150 B.B.A. L.151 J.D. Off. of Pub. Def.
Boylan, Michael J., (AV) ....'46 '76 C.973 B.S. L.128 J.D. [Cohen,T.K.&S.]
Boyle, John J. '53 '85 C.597 B.A. L.209 J.D.
(adm. in IL; not adm. in OH) I.R.S.‡
Boynton, Richard J. '44 '69 C.659 B.S. L.966 J.D.
(adm. in WI; not adm. in OH) Pres., Stoner & Assocs.
Brabenec, Susan E. ....'75 '02 C.259 B.A. L.150 J.D. [C Mezibov&J.]

Bradford, Sara '— '96 C&L.383 B.S., J.D.
407 Vine Street, Suite 146, 45202
Telephone: 513-381-5094 Fax: 513-861-2932
Estate Planning, Wills, Trust, Elder Law, Real Estate.
See Professional Biographies, CINCINNATI, OHIO

Brady, Robert M. ....'31 '74 C.679 B.S.M.E. L.1340 J.D. 36 Andover Rd.
Brady, Robert M. '37 '62 C&L.602 B.S., LL.B.
Dir., U.S. Tax Operations, Procter & Gamble Company, The
Brammer, Matthew V., (BV) ....'59 '93 C.608 B.S. L.150 J.D. [Ulmer&B.]
Branch, Jennifer L. ....'61 '87 C.569 B.A. L.930 J.D. 617 Vine St., Ste. 1409
Brand, Jack Irwin ....'49 '83 C.477 B.A. L.1066 J.D. 6530 Hudson Pkwy.
Brandser, Kristin J. ....'62 '87 C.352 B.A. L.145 J.D. 4 Emery Lane
Brann, Amy ....'66 '91 C.1161 B.S. L.1340 J.D. Legal Editor, Anderson Publishing Co.
Brant, Joel S. ....'68 '97 C.197 B.A. L.276 J.D. [A Katz,T.B.&H.]
Brant, Joseph A., (AV) ....'37 '61 C&L.150 B.A., J.D. [C Katz,T.B.&H.]
Brant, Robert E., (AV) ....'49 '74 C.150 B.A. L.813 J.D. [Katz,T.B.&H.]
Braun, Joseph J. ....'73 '98 C.383 B.A. L.851 J.D. [A Strauss&T.]
Brautigam, Michael G. '60 '89 C.645 B.Ph. L.994 J.D.
(adm. in CT; not adm. in OH) [A G.Mesh&Assoc.]
Braxton, Patricia D. ....'61 '90 C.563 B.A. L.201 J.D. [A Taft,S.&H.]
Breed, Thomas J., (AV) ....'49 '74 C.347 A.B. L.1119 J.D. [Wood&L.]
Breen, Timothy P. ....'60 '86 C.201 B.S. L.260 J.D. 201 East Fourth Street‡
Breidenstein, Thomas W., (CV①) ....'62 '93 C.473 B.A. L.1340 J.D. [A Barrett&W.]
Breitenbach, Thomas A., (AV) ....'61 '90 C.602 B.B.A. L.608 J.D. [Graydon H.&R.]
Breitholle, Howard F., (BV) ....'24 '50 C&L.150 LL.B. [C Katzman,L.H.&B.]
Breitkreutz, Brenda M. ....'71 '98 C.912 B.S. L.477 J.D. [A Taft,S.&H.]
Brendamour, Reeta H. ....'58 '96 C.303 B.A. L.150 J.D. [C White,G.&M.]
Brennan, Mary Anne ....'42 '67 C.737 B.A. L.608 J.D. 2 Walsh Lane‡
Brennan, Thomas A., (AV) ....'38 '66 C&L.608 B.A., J.D. [Graydon H.&R.]
Brenneman, Deborah S. ....'62 '93 C.610 B.S. L.150 J.D. [Thompson H.]
Brenton, Dean T. ....'12 '42 C.784 B.S. L.1340 LL.B. Ohio Farmers Ins. Co.
Bretz, Charles G., Jr. ....'41 '71 C.150 M.B.A. L.161 J.D. 4725 Cornell Road
Brewer, Kevin R. ....'72 '97 C.201 B.S. L.150 J.D. [A Katz,G.&N.]
Brewer, Stephen J., (AV) ....'— '77 C.1118 B.A. L.1340 J.D. [Buckley K.]
Bride, Nancy J. ....'70 '97 C.95 B.A. L.602 J.D. [A Greenebaum D.&M.]
Bridge, Wade '68 '97 C.502 B.A. L.1340 J.D.
(adm. in KY; not adm. in OH) 221 E 4th St.
Bridgeland, James R., Jr., (AV) ....'29 '57 C&L.309 A.M., LL.B. [Taft,S.&H.] ‡
Brigham, Charles A., III, (BV) ....'60 '85 C.607 B.S.B.A. L.930 J.D. [Brigham&B.]
Brigham, Charles A., Jr., (AV) ....'24 '50 C&L.150 B.A., J.D. 2909 Ebenezer Rd.‡
Brigham & Brigham, A Legal Professional Association, (BV) ....4977 Delhi Ave.
Brinker, John R., (BV) ....'62 '87 C.150 B.B.A. L.602 J.D. 414 Walnut St., Ste. 1220
Brinker, Stephen G., (BV) ....'46 '77 C.1024 B.A. L.1340 J.D. [Haverkamp,B.R.&R.]
Brinkman, David H. ....'61 '94 C.860 B.S.E.E. L.201 J.D. [Wood,H.&E.] (See Pat. Sect.)
Brinkman, Karen Riestenberg, (BV) ....'58 '84 C.973 A.B. L.608 J.D. [Brinkman&Assoc.]
Brinkman, Michael R. ....'58 '84 C.1118 B.A. L.1340 J.D. [A Lerner,S.&R.]
Brinkman and Associates, (BV) ....119 E. Court St.
Brinn, Stuart C., (AV) ....'51 '76 C.659 B.S. L.150 J.D. [Strauss&T.]
Britt, Curtis D. ....'52 '99 C.678 B.A. L.150 J.D. [A Reisenfeld&Assoc.]
Britt, Kent A. ....'70 '97 C.347 B.S. L.150 J.D. [A Vorys,S.S.&P.]
Brittingham, J. David, (BV) ....'65 '93 C.500 B.F.A. L.151 J.D. [Dinsmore&S.]
Brock, Louise Sadowsky ....'71 '96 C.339 B.A. L.477 J.D. [Dinsmore&S.]
Brocker, Nanci H. ....'68 '98 C.999 B.F.A. L.150 J.D. Off. of Pub. Def.
Brockman, James F., (AV) ....'52 '81 C&L.150 B.S., J.D. [Lindhorst&D.]
Brockman, John P. ....'13 '53 C.973 A.B. L.1340 J.D. 7384 Timberknoll Dr.‡
Broderick, Dennis J., (AV) '48 '76 C.602 B.A. L.276 J.D.
Sr. V.P., Gen. Coun. & Secy., Federated Dept. Stores, Inc.
Broeman, Dwight W. ....'17 '53 C.150 B.A. L.472 J.D. 441 Vine St.
Brokamp, Lawrence J. ....'68 '97 5710 Wooster Pike, Ste. 212
Brom, Joseph P. '35 '63 C&L.966 B.S., LL.B.
(adm. in MN; not adm. in OH)
Exec. V.P. & Chief Investment Offr., Ohio Nat'l Financial Svcs.‡
Bromberg, Barbara Schwartz, (AV) ....'41 '65 C.107 B.A. L.178 LL.B. [Dinsmore&S.]
Bromberg, Robert S., (AV) ....'35 '60 C&L.178 A.B., LL.B. 1144 Rookwood Dr.
Bronson, Michael J. ....'76 '01 C.207 B.A. L.880 J.D. [A Vorys,S.S.&P.]

Brooking, Moeves & Halloran
(See Fort Wright, Kentucky)

Brooks, Kyle C., (BV) ....'62 '88 C.1155 B.S. L.150 J.D. [Barron,P.B.&S.]
Brooks, Stephen G. ....'50 '84 C.1118 B.A. L.607 J.D. 1672 Robinway Dr.

Bross, David Joseph ....'78 '04 C.383 B.B.A. L.1340 J.D. [A Kohnen&P.]
Brothers, Ronald J. '50 '72 C.679 B.S. L.345 J.D.
(adm. in IN; not adm. in OH) Assoc. Gen. Coun., Cinergy Servs.
Brown, Albert T., Jr., (BV) ....'42 '66 C.473 A.B. L.1340 J.D. [Brown&W.]
Brown, Barbara M. ....'36 '80 C.150 B.S. L.151 J.D. [B.Brown]
Brown, Caleb, Jr., (BV) ....'44 '74 C.1023 B.A. L.150 J.D. 527 Linton St.
Brown, Catherine U. '69 '98 C.150 B.S. L.1187 J.D.
Pat. Atty., Miami Valley Lab. (Pat.)
Brown, Charles H., III, (BV) '57 '87
C.893 B.S.M.E. L.945 J.D. [Dinsmore&S.] (See Pat. Sect.)
Brown, Marianne Mandell '49 '82 C.339 B.A. L.208 J.D.
(adm. in PA; not adm. in OH) 7815 Hartford Hill Lane‡
Brown, Michael H., (BV①) ....'58 '81 C.973 B.S.B.A. L.602 J.D. [Greenebaum D.&M.]

Brown, Phyllis E., Law Offices of, (AV) '39 '86 C.788 B.A. L.150 J.D.
119 East Court Street, 45202
Telephone: 513-412-7681 Fax: 513-412-7683
Email: pebrown@fuse.net
False Claims Act, Complex Litigation, Representation of Charter Schools, Education of Individuals with Disabilities, Disciplinary Issues.
See Professional Biographies, CINCINNATI, OHIO

Brown, Richard T., III '46 '73 C&L.446 B.A., J.D.
Sr. Coun., Labor & Employ. Law, GE Aircraft Eng.
Brown, Robert F., (AV) ....'63 '88 C.473 B.S. L.608 J.D. [Rendigs,F.K.&D.]
Brown, Robert S, (AV) ....'43 '67 C&L.150 B.A., J.D. [Brown]
Brown, Ronald D. '53 '78 C.150 B.B.A. L.201 J.D.
V.P. & Chf. Fin. Offr., Cincinnati Milacron Inc.
Brown, Scott R. ....'56 '95 C.150 B.A. L.1340 J.D. [Frost B.T.]
Brown, Timothy R., (AV) ....'62 '87 C.973 B.S.B.A. L.245 J.D. [Thompson H.]
Brown, Barbara ....868 Waycross Rd., Ste. A
Brown Firm Inc., The, L.P.A., (AV) ....2199 Victory Parkway
Brown and Warnock, (BV) ....1014 Vine Street
Brownfield, Matthew, (AV) ....'57 '84 C.201 B.A. L.150 J.D. [M.Brownfield]
Brownfield, Matthew, Co., LPA, (AV) ....1 Financial Way
Browning, James A. '78 '03 C.138 B.S. L.1161 J.D.
(adm. in KY; not adm. in OH) [A Dinsmore&S.]
Bruch, Charles A. ....'60 '03 C.610 B.B.A. L.150 J.D. [A Dinsmore&S.]
Bruckner, John H. ....'20 '51 C.151 L.1340 LL.B. 7892 Mitchell Farm Lane‡
Brueneman, A. J., Jr. ....'13 '41 C.150 B.Lit. L.1340 LL.B. 4129 La Crosse Ave.‡
Bruestle, Eric G., (AV) ....'53 '77 C&L.150 B.Mus., J.D. [Roetzel&A.]
Brumleve, Wilson L., (AV) ....'14 '45 C.150 L.1340 [C Barron,P.B.&S.]
Brun, James H., (AV) ....'51 '76 C.1024 B.A. L.150 J.D. [Keating M.&K.]
Bruns, Jeanne Marie ....'68 '99 C.436 B.A. L.276 J.D. [A Taft,S.&H.]
Bruns, Julie M. Tomlinson ....'74 '99 C.473 B.A. L.150 J.D. [A Frost B.T.]
Bruns, Robert T., (AV) ....'50 '75 C&L.150 B.B.A., J.D. [Peck,S.&W.]
Bruns, Thomas B., (AV) ....'65 '90 C.473 B.A. L.150 J.D. [Freund,F.&A.]
Brunsman, Theresa M., (BV) '60 '84 C.150 B.A. L.273 J.D.
Asst. Couns., Union Central Life Insurance Company
Bryant, Herman V. ....'17 '60 C.922 B.S. L.151 J.D. 6566 Montgomery Rd.‡
Bryson, Craig M. ....'74 '01 C.473 B.A. L.608 J.D. [A Frost B.T.]
Bryson, Gary A. '49 '78 C.150 B.A. L.1340 J.D.
V.P. & Assoc. Gen. Coun., The Union Central Life Ins. Co.
Bucciere, Robert L., (BV) ....'39 '66 C.150 B.S. L.1161 J.D. 8044 Montgomery Rd.
Buchanan, Beth A., (BV) ....'64 '97 C.608 B.S.B.A. L.201 J.D. [A Frost B.T.]
Buchert, Christopher B. '71 '98
C.473 B.S. L.1340 J.D. Trial Coun., Juv./Dom. Rel., Pub. Def. Off.
Buck, Matthew K. ....'68 '96 C.152 B.A. L.831 J.D. [Keating M.&K.]
Buckley, Daniel J., (AV) ....'49 '74 C.611 B.A. L.150 J.D. [Vorys,S.S.&P.]

Buckley King, A Legal Professional Association, (AV)
1420 PNC Center, 201 East Fifth Street, 45202-4182
Telephone: 513-412-5400 National Watts Line: 800-255-2825 Telecopier: 513-412-5401
Email: bkb-cincinnati.com URL: http://www.buckleyking.com
Dale A. Stalf; Stephen J. Brewer;—Jack S. Healy; Wm. Eric Minamyer; Timothy E. Rogus; Melissa Campbell Subit.
Corporate, Litigation, Commercial, Estate Planning, Banking and Finance, Real Estate, Merger and Acquisition, Appellate, Bankruptcy, Professional and Executive (Directors and Officers) Liability, Insurance Law, Products Liability, Health Care, Hospital Law, Medical Malpractice Defense, Immigration and Naturalization, Toxic and Hazardous Materials, ERISA, Taxation, Environmental, Labor and Litigation for Management, Public Employment Relations, Employee Benefits and NLRB Matters.
Cleveland, Ohio Office: 1400 Fifth Third Center. Telephone: 216-363-1400. Telecopier: 216-579-1020.
Columbus, Ohio Office: One Columbus, 10 West Broad Street, Suite 1300. Telephone: 614-461-5600. Telecopier: 614-461-5630.
Atlanta, Georgia Office: Suite 1220 Lennox Building, 3399 Peachtree Road. Telephone: 404-816-7791. Telecopier: 404-816-9786.
See Professional Biographies, CINCINNATI, OHIO

Budde, John E. ....'59 '88 C.472 B.S. L.150 J.D. Dist. Couns.
Budinger, Carrie L. ....'59 '88 C.150 B.A. L.1340 J.D. Allstate Staff Coun.

Buechel & Conley
(See Covington, Kentucky)

Buechner, Robert W., (AV) '47 '74 C.674 B.S.E. L.477 J.D.
[Buechner,H.O.M.H.&K.]

Buechner, Haffer, O'Connell, Meyers, Healey & Koenig Co., L.P.A., (AV)
105 East Fourth Street Suite 300, 45202
Telephone: 513-579-1500 Fax: 513-977-4361
URL: http://www.bhomhlaw.com
Robert W. Buechner; Gloria S. Haffer; Edward M. O'Connell, Jr.; Robert J. Meyers; Roger W. Healey; Francis X. Marnell; Peter E. Koenig; Stephen B. Hoffsis; David Randolph Valz;—Michael E. Neiheisel; Laurie M. Harmon.
General Practice. Estate and Gift Taxation, Probate, Family Law, Corporate, Negligence, Medical Legal Products Liability, Real Estate, Construction, Land Use, Zoning and Eminent Domain Law. Trials and Appeals, Pension and Profit Sharing, Federal Income.
See Professional Biographies, CINCINNATI, OHIO

Bueckman, Lynn A., The Law Offices of '58 '00 C.684 B.S. L.117 J.D.
The Bueckman Law Building, 7124 Vine Street, 45216
Telephone: 513-821-4844
Email: bueckmanlaw@cinci.rr.com URL: http://www.bueckmanlawfirm.com
Bankruptcy, Immigration, DUI, Business Law, Corporate Law, Contracts, Consumer Law.
See Professional Biographies, CINCINNATI, OHIO

Buffington, Carolyn Brown, (BV) '57 '85 C.473 B.A. L.150 J.D.
Law Clk., U.S. Dist. Ct.
Buford, Calvin D., (AV) ....'59 '85 C.597 B.A. L.309 J.D. [Dinsmore&S.]
Buhring, Debra '66 '90 C.388 B.A. L.145 J.D.
(adm. in IL; not adm. in OH) Asst. Gen. Coun., Chiquita Brands, LLC
Bullock, Roddy M. '57 '97 C&L.846 B.S.M.E., J.D.
Coun., Procter & Gamble Co. (Pat.)

Bumiller, Carl L. ... '05 '32 C&L.150 LL.B. 1113 Leaftree Ct.‡
Bunch, Nicholas E., (AV) ... '53 '80 C.608 B.S. L.201 J.D. [White,G.&M.]
Bunke, Norbert J., (AV) ... '27 '50 C.973 L.150 LL.B. [Ⓒ Haverkamp,B.R.&R.] ‡
Bunyan, George W., Jr., (BV) ... '22 '51 C.511 A.B. L.94 J.D. 30 East Central Parkway
Burdsall, Theo. F. ... '21 '50 C.475 L.150 LL.B. 8001 Kenwood Rd.
Burger, Thomas J., (AV) '60 '86 C&L.602 B.S.E.E., J.D. [Wood,H.&E.] (See Pat. Sect.)
Burgin, Cynthia R. ... '60 '85 C.910 B.S.B.A. L.930 J.D. The Ohio Natl. Life Ins. Co.
Burgin, Lester J., (BV) ... '56 '82 C.1365 B.A. L.150 J.D. [Harris&B.]
Burke, Daniel E., (AV) ... '62 '88 C.602 B.A. L.150 J.D. [Graydon H.&R.] ⊙
Burke, Daniel F., Jr., (AV) ... '49 '77 C.150 B.B.A. L.1161 J.D. 906 Main St., Ste. 308
Burke, Edward A., (AV) ... '20 '48 C.973 A.B. L.150 LL.B. [Burke,F.B.&B.]
Burke, James E., (AV) ... '53 '78 C.976 B.A. L.150 J.D. [Keating M.&K.]
Burke, Kim K., (AV) ... '55 '80 C.651 B.S. L.665 J.D. [Taft,S.&H.]
Burke, Patrick J. ... '55 '80 C.201 B.S. L.150 J.D. Mng. Partner, Burke and Co.
Burke, Rachel E. ... '71 '96 C.473 B.S. in B.A. L.945 J.D. [Ⓐ Porter W.M.&A.]
Burke, Tara K. ... '— '00 C.973 B.A. L.150 J.D. [Ⓐ Vorys,S.S.&P.]
Burke, Timothy M., (AV) ... '48 '73 C.973 A.B. L.150 J.D. [Manley B.]
Burke, Fitzgerald, Burns & Balash, (AV) ... 817 Main Street, Suite 8
Burks, Margaret A. ... '55 '85 C.150 B.A.B.S. L.1340 J.D. Chap. 13 Trustee
Burleigh, David W., (BVⓉ) ... '68 '95 C.210 B.A. L.150 J.D. [Deters,B.&L.] ⊙
Burnham, Ralph E. ... '64 '91 C.846 B.A. L.1341 J.D. [Montgomery,R.&J.]
Burns, Andrea L. ... '72 '97 C.610 B.A. L.607 J.D. [Ⓐ Harris&B.]
Burns, Faith B., (CVⓉ) '58 '87 C.47 A.B. L.421 J.D. (adm. in KY; not adm. in OH) Director, Wallace Law Reg.
Burns, Joseph S. ... '75 '02 C.1161 B.A. L.1340 J.D. [Ⓐ Cors&B.]
Burns, Nancy J. ... '58 '95 C&L.1161 B.A., J.D. [Ⓐ Graf&S.&M.]
Burns, Robert E. ... '37 '65 C.454 B.S. L.93 LL.B. 4730 North Edgewood Avenue
Burns, Robert Wall, (BV) ... '49 '74 C.473 B.S. L.880 J.D. [Burke,F.B.&B.]
Burr, Peter A., (BV) ... '62 '88 C.198 A.B. L.945 J.D. [Ⓐ Barron,P.B.&S.]
Burrell, Peter M., (AV) ... '59 '84 C.611 B.A. L.602 J.D. [Wood&L.]
Burton, Shawn P. ... '77 '04 C.967 B.A. L.851 J.D. [Ⓐ Dinsmore&S.]
Busacker, Bret F. ... '70 '00 C.1335 B.A. L.608 J.D. [Ⓐ Thompson H.]
Buse, Jennifer Dietz ... '67 '92 C.473 B.S. L.150 J.D. Procter & Gamble Co.
Busemeyer, William A., (BV) ... '40 '65 C.602 A.B. L.150 J.D. [W.A.Busemeyer]
Busemeyer, William A. Co., LPA, (BV) ... 3805 Edwards Dr., Ste. 105
Busse, Robert L. ... '57 '84 C.309 A.B. L.228 J.D. 9720 Tall Timber Dr.
Butkovich, John E., (BV) ... '41 '68 C.602 B.S.E.E. L.1340 J.D. [Ⓒ Butkovich,S.S.&G.]
Butkovich, Joseph A., (AV) ... '66 '93 C.602 B.A. L.117 J.D. [Butkovich,S.S.&G.]
Butkovich, Schimpf, Schimpf & Ginocchio, A Legal Professional Association, (AV) 36 East Seventh Street
Butler, Robert T., (BV) ... '62 '90 C.1201 B.A. L.972 J.D. [Ⓐ Donnellon,D.&M.]
Butler, Stephen J., (AV) ... '52 '77 C.1024 B.A. L.150 J.D. [Thompson H.]
Buttress, Christine A., (AV) ... '53 '79 C.363 B.S. L.150 J.D. [Graydon H.&R.] ⊙
Byrne, Kenneth L., (BV) '44 '71 C.973 B.S. L.150 J.D. Gen. Coun., Cincom Systems, Inc.
Byrne, Mark J., (AV) ... '58 '83 C&L.150 B.B.A., J.D. [Jacobs,K.S.&M.]
Cadwallader, William Rayburn ... '— '59 C&L.150 B.B.A., D.J.P. Credo, Inc.
Cain, Charles C. ... '54 '80 C.608 B.A. L.1340 J.D. Insured Land Title Agency
Calardo, Stephen P., (AV) ... '55 '81 C&L.150 B.A., J.D. 5608 Harrison Ave.
Calaway, Wendy R. ... '73 '98 C&L.150 B.A., J.D. [Ⓒ Mezibov&J.]
Calder, Thomas S., (AV) '32 '57 C&L.602 A.B., LL.B. [Ⓒ Dinsmore&S.] (See Pat. Sect.)
Calderhead, David C., (AV) '61 '87 C.827 B.A. L.1003 J.D. [Triona C.&L.] & [Calderhead] (⊙Milford)
Caldwell, Steven W. '68 '02 C.383 B.S. L.823 J.D. (adm. in NY; not adm. in OH; See Pat. Sect.) [Ⓐ Frost B.T.]
Calico, Paul B., (AV) ... '54 '80 C.929 B.S. L.383 J.D. [Strauss&T.]
Callan, Sean P. ... '68 '93 C.197 A.B. L.150 J.D. [Dinsmore&S.]
Callinan, Maureen ... '54 '91 C.710 B.A. L.1187 J.D. 3757 Chimney Hill Drive
Callow, Amy Gasser ... '69 '94 C.473 B.S. L.150 J.D. [Ⓒ Wood&L.]
Callow, Joseph M., Jr., (BV) ... '68 '93 C.473 B.A. L.150 J.D. [Keating M.&K.]
Calloway-Campbell, Marsha ... '60 '85 C&L.150 B.A., J.D. [Ⓐ Freking&B.]
Cambron, Robyn W. ... '70 '99 C.208 B.A. L.424 J.D. Pub Def.
Camden, Bonnie G., (AV) ... '50 '89 C.928 B.A. L.150 J.D. [Dinsmore&S.]
Cameron, Phillip F., (BV) ... '45 '71 C.303 B.A. L.150 J.D. 4400 Carew Tower
Camp, Jason J. '71 '98 C&L.608 B.S., J.D. Sr. Coun., The Procter & Gamble Co., Intell. Prop. Div.
Campbell, Charles W. ... '24 '51 C&L.966 B.A., J.D. Admin. Law J., U.S. Dept. of Labor
Campbell, David W., II, (BV) ... '45 '75 C.210 B.A. L.150 J.D. 6988 5 Mile Rd.
Campbell, Hugh Kolb ... '53 '84 C.929 B.S. L.1340 J.D. [H.K.Campbell]
Campbell, Janet B., (AV) ... '52 '79 C.228 B.A. L.150 J.D. [Ⓐ Cohen,T.K.&S.]
Campbell, Jill A. ... '65 '90 C.645 B.A. L.655 J.D. 312 Walnut Street, 14th Floor
Campbell, John L., (AV) ... '48 '77 C.170 B.A. L.150 J.D. [Kohnen&P.]
Campbell, Hugh K., PSC ... 2011 Madison Road
Canary, Thomas L., Jr., (AVⓉ) '59 '84 C&L.383 B.S., J.D. [Mapother&M.] (⊙Lexington, Louisville, KY; Huntington, WV)
Candito, Joseph, (BV) ... '54 '86 C.610 B.A. L.201 J.D. 9403 Kenwood Road
Cantleberry, Jill C. ... '59 '84 C.97 B.S.B.A. L.930 J.D. 1055 St. Paul Place
Canton, Doreen, (AV) ... '48 '88 C.116 B.A. L.150 J.D. [Taft,S.&H.]
Caplinger, Candace C., (AV) '— '82 C.698 A.B. L.150 J.D. Hamilton Co. Ct. of Common Pleas, Domestic Relations Div.
Cappel, Harry W. ... '70 '96 C&L.150 B.A., J.D. [Graydon H.&R.] ⊙
Carey, Robert P. ... '43 '80 C.150 B.S.M.E. L.1340 J.D. 7189 Grantham Way
Cariappa, Padma Tatta '55 '82 C&L.999 B.A., LL.B. Oper. V.P. & Asst. Gen. Coun., Federated Dept. Stores, Inc.
Carmody, Katherine S. ... '— '01 C.508 B.A. L.823 J.D. [Ⓐ Sanders&Assoc.]
Carpenter, Robert A. ... '70 '95 C.303 B.A. L.150 J.D. [Dinsmore&S.]
Carr, Michael Gerard ... '58 '01 C.150 M.B.A. L.1340 J.D. [M.G.Carr&Assoc.]
Carr, Michael H. '56 '82 C.1161 B.S. L.1340 J.D. (adm. in KY; not adm. in OH) Coun., GE Aviation Services, Inc.
Carr, Michael G., & Associates, LPA ... 5582 Penway Court
Carroll, Courtney R. ... '69 '96 C.910 B.A. L.276 J.D. P.O. Box 5578
Carroll, James J., (AV) ... '46 '78 C.150 B.B.A. L.1340 J.D. [Ⓒ Cors&B.]
Carroll, Karen A., (AV) ... '54 '87 C.523 B.S.N. L.150 J.D. [Kohnen&P.]
Carroll, Patrick F., (BV) ... '51 '84 C.1161 B.A. L.1340 J.D. 324 Reading Rd.
Carroll, Scott A. ... '67 '93 C&L.150 B.S., J.D. [Vorys,S.S.&P.]
Carson, Cheryl Lynn ... '65 '90 C.973 B.S. L.150 J.D. [Carson]
Carson Law Offices ... 2576 Eastern Avenue
Carter, Jandá M. ... '— '02 C.679 B.S.E. L.201 J.D. [Ⓐ Frost B.T.]
Carter, Karen Elisha ... '62 '94 C.150 B.A. L.1340 J.D. Ohio Cas.
Carter, Melody '54 '93 C.1118 B.S L.1340 J.D. (adm. in KY; not adm. in OH) The Christ Hospital‡
Cartolano, Fredk. J. ... '27 '52 C&L.150 A.B., J.D. Com. Pleas J.
Caruso, Anthony J., (AV) ... '62 '88 C.150 B.A. L.608 J.D. [Kohnen&P.]
Carville, Christopher R. ... '72 '97 C.973 B.S.B.A. L.150 J.D. [Rendigs,F.K.&D.]
Casey, Deborah A. '62 '94 C.473 B.A. L.117 J.D. Asst. Co. Pros., Hamilton Co. Pros. Off.
Cash, Albert D., (AV) ... '34 '59 C.973 A.B. L.477 LL.B. 432 Walnut St.
Cash, Joshua N. '71 '96 C.138 B.S. L.421 J.D. Coun., Litigation & Preventive Law, GE (⊙Fairfield, CT)
Casper, Paul W., Jr., (BV) ... '46 '81 C.757 B.A. L.200 J.D. [Frost B.T.]

Casper and Casper, (AV)
119 East Court Street, Fourth Floor, Suite 410, 45202 ⊙
Telephone: 513-381-7096
Rebecca L. Wilkinson.
Personal Injury, Workers Compensation and Social Security Disability Law. Products Liability Litigation. Trials.
Middletown, Ohio Office: Gas and Electric Building, One North Main Street, P.O. Box: 510, 45042. Telephone: 513-424-2401.
Dayton, Ohio Office: First National Plaza Building, 130 West Second Street, Suite 1950, 45402. Telephone: 937-224-1122.
Hamilton Office: 2 South 3rd Street, Suite 360, 45011. Telephone: 513-892-2560.
See Professional Biographies, CINCINNATI, OHIO

Cassady, Michael C. ... '51 '76 C.610 A.B. L.117 J.D. U.S. Ct. of App.
Cassady, Peter L., (AV) ... '47 '74 C.321 B.A. L.94 J.D. [Beckman W.S.]
Cassidy, Mary Margaret Gorman ... '55 '92 C.339 B.S.N. L.1340 J.D. 1 Moyer Pl., Ste. 1
Cassinelli, Tracy A. ... '69 '94 C.473 B.S. L.383 J.D. [Reminger&R.] (⊙Covington, KY)
Castañeda, Janet Y. ... '59 '96 C.62 B.S. L.851 J.D. [Ⓐ Wood&L.]

Castelli, Anthony D., (AV) '51 '81 C.150 B.S. L.1340 J.D.
11085 Montgomery Road, Suite 200, 45249
Telephone: 513-621-2345 Fax: 513-621-2519 URL: http://www.castellilaw.com
Email: tony@castellilaw.com URL: http://www.lawyers.com/castellilaw
(Certified Specialist in Workers' Compensation Law, Ohio State Bar Association).
Automobile Accidents, Workers Compensation, Personal Injury, Social Security Disability, Wrongful Death, Product Liability, Dog Bites.
See Professional Biographies, CINCINNATI, OHIO

Castellini, Richard A., (AV) ... '32 '64 C.602 B.S. L.1340 J.D. City Solr.
Casterline, C. Scott ... '— '01 C.8 B.S. L.7 J.D. [Ⓐ Lerner,S.&R.]
Cater, Lyndsey R. ... '79 '04 C.473 B.S. L.150 J.D. [Ⓐ Graydon H.&R.]
Cathey, Christopher D. ... '73 '99 C.260 B.A. L.150 J.D. [Ⓐ Ulmer&B.]
Cavanaugh, Natasha M. ... '77 '02 C.813 B.A. L.893 J.D. [Ⓐ Taft,S.&H.]
Cawood, James M., III ... '72 '99 C.383 B.A. L.1340 J.D. [Ⓐ Freund,F.&A.]
Cayot, Dale L. '45 '72 C.63 B.S. L.345 J.D. (adm. in IN; not adm. in OH) Asst. Chf. Coun., Bur. of Alcohol, Tobacco & Firearms
Cettel, Robert W., (BV) '47 '74 C.473 B.F.A. L.1340 J.D. 7265 Kenwood Road, Suite 175
Chabot, Steven J., (BV) ... '53 '78 C.945 B.A. L.1340 J.D. Co. Comr.
Chacksfield, Roger R. ... '23 '49 C&L.150 LL.B. 9801 Tollgate Lane
Chaiken, Frank D., (AV) ... '60 '87 C.309 A.B. L.93 J.D. [Thompson H.]
Chain, Donald J. ... '56 '80 C.473 B.A. L.150 J.D. 36 East 7th Street
Chalfie, James J., (AV) ... '41 '66 C.1036 L.150 J.D. [Chalfie&F.]
Chalfie, Samuel L., (AV) ... '11 '36 C.608 B.S. L.150 J.D. 7300 Dearwester Drive‡

Chalfie & Farley, Co., L.P.A., (AV)
36 East Seventh Street, Suite 1600, 45202
Telephone: 513-381-8616 Fax: 513-381-8619
Email: jimc@one.net URL: http://www.chalfielaw.com
James J. Chalfie; Katrina Z. Farley.
Probate Litigation, Probate Administration, Estate Planning, Trials and Appeals, Estate and Gift Tax, Trusts, Estates, Wills, Family Law, Negligence, Wrongful Death, Will Contests, Living Trusts and Automobile Collisions.
See Professional Biographies, CINCINNATI, OHIO

Chambers, J. Robert, (AV) '45 '72 C.608 B.Met.E. L.912 J.D. [Wood,H.&E.] (See Pat. Sect.)
Chang, Nadya ... '51 '88 C.145 A.B. L.945 J.D. [M.E.a.C.N.Clancey]
Chapman, Brian E., (BV) ... '62 '87 C.383 B.B.A. L.1340 J.D. [Ⓐ Weltman,W.&R.]
Charles, Mark Anthony '— '01 C.838 B.S. L.228 J.D. Atty., Intel. Prop. Div., The Procter & Gamble Company (Pat.)
Charls, Joseph E., (BV) ... '34 '71 C.150 B.S. L.1340 J.D. 3165 Harrison Ave.
Chasar, Matthew R. ... '76 '02 C.473 B.S. L.150 J.D. [Ⓐ Strauss&T.]
Chatfield, Melancthon W. ... '58 '84 C.150 B.A. L.500 J.D. [Chatfield&C.]
Chatfield, William H., (BV) ... '47 '72 C.575 A.B. L.150 J.D. [Chatfield&C.]
Chatfield & Chatfield, (BV) ... 7 W. 7th St., Ste. 1800
Chesley, Stanley M., (AV) ... '36 '60 C&L.150 B.A., LL.B. [Waite,S.B.&C.]
Chester, Victoria L. ... '59 '92 C&L.150 J.D. Sr. V.P & Secy., Globe Business Resources
Chewning, John B. ... '22 '73 C.659 M.D. L.1340 J.D. 7765 Graves Rd.‡
Chiaro, Cynthia M. ... '61 '96 C.623 B.B.A. L.150 J.D. [Ⓐ Rendigs,F.K.&D.]
Chick, Catherine Irene '61 '90 C.201 B.S. L.150 J.D. Asst. Corp. Coun., Community Mutual Insurance Company
Childs, Erin C. ... '77 '02 C.734 B.A. L.150 J.D. [Ⓐ Thompson H.]
Chin, Gabriel J. '64 '88 C.918 B.A. L.477 J.D. (adm. in MA; not adm. in OH) Prof. of Law, Univ. of Cincinnati, Coll. of Law‡
Chin, Nee Fong, (AV) ... '59 '87 C&L.150 B.A., J.D. Chf. Asst. Pros., Co. Pros. Off.
Christenson, Gordon A. '32 '56 C&L.878 B.S.L., J.D. (adm. in UT; not adm. in OH) 3465 Principio Ave.‡
Christian, Ronald C., (AV) ... '62 '87 C.531 B.S. L.1340 J.D. [Taft,S.&H.]
Christopher, John E., Jr. ... '67 '94 C.383 B.S. L.151 J.D. [Dinsmore&S.]
Christy, Diana R. ... '74 '01 C.953 B.A. L.1340 J.D. [Ⓐ Frost B.T.]
Chumley, Mark J. ... '66 '96 C.477 B.A. L.150 J.D. [Keating M.&K.]
Church, Arthur C., (BV) ... '42 '67 C&L.150 B.A., J.D. [A.C.Church]
Church, Arthur C., Co., L.P.A., (BV) ... 601 Main St.
Ciclet, Donna R. '69 '93 C.806 B.S. L.880 J.D. Asst. Coun., Federated Dept. Stores, Inc.
Cioffi, Michael L., (AV) ... '53 '79 C.602 B.A. L.150 J.D. [Blank R.]
Cissell, James C., (AV) ... '40 '66 C.973 A.B. L.150 J.D. 230 East 9th Street Floor 10
Clancey, Michael E. ... '63 '88 C.431 B.A. L.945 J.D. [M.E.a.C.N.Clancey]
Clancey, Michael E. and Chang, Nadya ... 7200 Paddison Road
Clark, Craig S. ... '33 '63 C.999 B.S.C. L.1340 J.D. [Ⓐ Hammond]
Clark, Eric S. ... '74 '99 C.363 B.S. L.150 J.D. [Ⓐ Thompson H.]
Clark, George W., (AV) ... '45 '71 C.973 B.S. L.1340 J.D. 4343 Marcrest Dr.
Clark, Karen F. ... '58 '88 Procter & Gamble Co.
Clark, Lisa M. ... '72 '97 C.945 B.B.A. L.1161 J.D. [Ⓐ Butkovich,S.S.&G.]
Clark, Megan E. ... '69 '95 C.321 B.A. L.347 J.D. [Ⓐ Freking&B.]
Clark, Ravert Jerome, (BV) ... '63 '89 C.156 B.A. L.150 J.D. 114 East 8th Street
Clark, Raymond H. ... '27 '54 C.150 L.1340 LL.B. 7226 Green Farms Dr.‡
Clark, Tiffany Reece ... '73 '99 C.896 B.A. L.150 J.D. [Ⓐ Ulmer&B.]
Clarke, Deanne E. ... '73 '98 C.150 B.A. L.424 J.D. [Ⓐ Frost B.T.]
Clarke, Jeffrey M. ... '69 '99 C.150 B.A. L.124 J.D. [Ⓐ Thompson H.]
Clarke, Naima Rasheen ... '— '95 C.610 B.B.A. L.608 J.D. Nat'l Labor Rel. Bd.

Clary, Daniel K. . . . . '58 '84 C.150 B.A. L.1340 J.D. 1446 Sigma Cir.
Class, Maribeth . . . . '— '94 C.610 B.S. L.150 J.D. Asst. Pros.Atty.
Clay, Eric Lee . . . . '48 '72 C.575 B.A. L.976 J.D. U.S. Ct. of App. J.
Claybon, Stanley, (BV) . . . . '45 '71 C.150 B.B.A. L.383 J.D. 11499 Lippelman Rd.
Claycomb, Gregory J., (BV) . . . . '60 '89 C&L.150 B.A., J.D. [A Kircher,R.&W.]
Claymon, Allan W., (AV) . . . . '37 '63 C&L.352 B.B.A., J.D. 914 Main St.
Clements, William E., (AV) . . . . '53 '79 C.473 B.A. L.150 J.D. [Clements,M.&C.]

Clements, Mahin & Cohen, LPA Co., (AV) BB
The Executive Building, 35 East Seventh Street, Suite 710, 45202-4009
Telephone: 513-721-6500 Facsimile: 513-763-6415 URL: http://www.cmclawyers.com
Email: info@cmclawyers.com URL: http://www.lawyers.com/cmclawyers
Members of Firm: William E. Clements (Certified Specialist in Workers' Compensation Law, Ohio State Bar Association); John E. Mahin; Edward Cohen; Catharin R. Taylor (Certified Specialist in Workers' Compensation Law, Ohio State Bar Association). Associate: Lane N. Cohen (Certified Specialist in Workers' Compensation Law, Ohio State Bar Association).
Civil Litigation, Workers Compensation, Personal Injury, Products Liability, Medical Malpractice, Legal Malpractice, Appellate Practice, Social Security.
See Professional Biographies, CINCINNATI, OHIO

Clemons, Michelle L. . . . . '70 '97 C.1111 B.S. L.117 J.D. [A Lindhorst&D.]
Cleves, Joseph A., Jr., (BV(T)) . . . . '55 '78 C.1118 B.A. L.734 J.D. [Deters,B.&L.] ⊙
Cliffe, David W., (CV) . . . . '66 '92 C.976 B.A. L.150 J.D. [A Weltman,W.&R.]
Cline, Claudia, (BV) . . . . '54 '86 C.112 B.A. L.800 J.D. V.P., Legal, Convergys Corp.
Clum, Lewis L. . . . . '31 '58 C.378 B.S. L.477 LL.B. 7780 Indian Hill Rd.
Cobey, John G., (AV) . . . . '43 '69 C.188 B.S. L.150 J.D. [Cohen,T.K.&S.]
Cochran, Janine G. . . . . '67 '96 C.473 B.S. L.201 J.D. Natl. Underwriter Publishing Co.
Cody, Thomas G., (AV) '41 '67 C.999 B.A. L.724 LL.B.
(adm. in NY; not adm. in OH)
Exec. V.P., Legal and Human Res., Federated Dept. Stores, Inc.
Coffaro, Joseph M., (BV) . . . . '38 '69 C.150 B.S. L.1340 J.D. 3537 Epley Lane‡
Coffaro, Steven C., (AV) . . . . '70 '95 C.473 B.A. L.150 J.D. [Keating M.&K.]
Coffey, Shirley A., (AV) . . . . '59 '92 C&L.150 B.Mus., J.D. [A Shea&Assoc.]
Cohen, Alfred M., (AV) . . . . '29 '53 C.473 A.B. L.150 LL.B. [C Cohen,T.K.&S.]
Cohen, Edward, (AV) . . . . '54 '82 C&L.150 B.A., J.D. [Clements,M.&C.]
Cohen, Gregory A., (BV) . . . . '57 '93 C.473 B.A. L.851 J.D. The Citadel, 114 E. 8th St.
Cohen, Harvey Jay, (AV) . . . . '60 '87 C.276 A.B. L.150 J.D. [Dinsmore&S.]
Cohen, Jason M. . . . . '73 '99 C.309 A.B. L.813 J.D. [A Keating M.&K.]
Cohen, Lane N., (AV) . . . . '51 '87 C.150 B.A. L.201 J.D. [A Clements,M.&C.]

Cohen, Todd, Kite & Stanford, LLC, (AV)
250 East Fifth Street, Suite 1200, 45202-4139
Telephone: 513-421-4020 Fax: 513-241-4490
URL: http://www.ctks.com
Members of Firm: Stanley L. Stanford; John G. Cobey; Terrence A. Mire; Marc W. Rubin; Michael J. Boylan; Richard D. Nelson; Robert S. Rubin; Stanton H. Vollman (Certified Specialist in Estate Planning, Trust and Probate Law, Ohio State Bar Association); Michael R. Schmidt; Kevin C. McDonough; Donald J. Rafferty; John L. O'Shea; Richard M. Stone; Matthew McD. Kite; Curtis E. Kissinger. Senior Attorney: Janet B. Campbell. Associates: Heidi A. Selden; Jeffrey S. Vollman; Joseph M. Hutson; Monica V. Kindt; Angela M. Hughes. Of Counsel: Alfred M. Cohen; John W. Kilcoyne; Thomas C. Kilcoyne.
Banking, Bankruptcy and Reorganization, Corporate and Business, Employee Benefits, Estate Planning and Probate, Litigation, Real Estate and Taxation, General and White Collar Criminal Defense, and Juvenile Delinquency Defense.
Counsel For: JP Morgan Chase Bank, NA; CamVic Corporation; Hoeweler Group, Inc.; Cities of St. Bernatrd and Deer Park; Cincinnati Sub-Zero Products, Inc.; Frishch's Restaurants, Inc.; MAE Holding Company; Florence Freedom Baseball Team; Casual Restaurant Concepts, Inc.; R.G. Properties, Inc.
See Professional Biographies, CINCINNATI, OHIO

Colbert, Andrea Smith . . . . '70 '96 C.608 B.A. L.200 J.D. Pros. Off.
Colbert, John P. . . . . '71 '96 C.610 B.S. L.201 J.D. [A Thompson H.] (Pat.)
Cole, Douglas G., (AV) . . . . '21 '48 C.604 A.B. L.150 J.D. 150 E. 4th St.‡
Cole, R. Guy, Jr. . . . . '51 '75 C.860 B.A. L.976 J.D. U.S. Cir. J.
Colebrook, Mary Joann '58 '00 C.1161 B.A. L.1340 J.D.
(adm. in KY; not adm. in OH) The David J. Joseph Co.
Coleman, John K. . . . . '68 '99 C.1229 B.S.M.S. L.150 J.D. 230 East 9th Street, Suite 3000
Coletti, Robert E., (AV) . . . . '57 '82 C.473 B.S. L.150 J.D. [Keating M.&K.]
Collett, Thomas E. . . . . '48 '75 C.49 B.S. L.1340 J.D. V.P., Invesmart of Cincinnati, Inc.
Collier, Julia Ann . . . . '61 '87 C.201 B.S. L.150 J.D. 125 E. Court St.
Collins, Edward J., (BV) . . . . '51 '77 C.973 B.A. L.150 J.D. [Droder&M.]
Collins, Marcus L. '68 '97
C.122 B.A. L.1340 J.D. Asst. Coun., The Ohio Natl. Life Ins. Co.
Collins, Rebecca Lynn . . . . '71 '01 C.1161 B.A. L.150 J.D. Hamilton Co. Pros. Office
Collins, Regina Adelle . . . . '63 '97 C.518 L.608 J.D. 119 E. Court Street
Collins, Wilbur L., (AV) . . . . '30 '54 C&L.608 B.S., J.D. [Taft,S.&H.] ‡
Colston, Gregory A. '59 '86 C.1161 B.S. L.383 J.D.
(adm. in KY; not adm. in OH) Soc. Sec. Admin., Off. of Hearing & Appeals
Colvin, Adam D. . . . . '77 '03 C.309 A.B. L.1494 J.D. [A Katz,T.B.&H.]
Colvin, Sterling W. . . . . '69 '95 C.383 B.S. L.151 J.D. [Dinsmore&S.]
Combs, Ann Ruley, (AV) . . . . '52 '77 C.477 B.S.N. L.802 J.D. [Kohnen&P.]
Combs, Claire Grandpré, (AV) '56 '88 C.473 B. Ph. L.150 J.D.
Sr. V.P. & Gen. Coun., Mercy Health Partners of S.W. Ohio
Cômbs, Eric K. . . . . '71 '96 C.473 B.A. L.966 J.D. [Taft,S.&H.]
Combs, Mark E. . . . . '51 '77 C.150 B.A. L.151 J.D. Ct. Adm. & Trial Ref.
Comey, Margaret Walker, (AV) . . . . '52 '77 C.207 B.A. L.150 J.D. [C F.O.Kiel]
Comodeca, James A., (AV) . . . . '62 '87 C.473 A.B. L.7 J.D. [Dinsmore&S.]
Concannon, John P., (AV) . . . . '49 '76 C.973 B.S. L.1340 J.D. [C McCaslin,I.&M.] ⊙
Condit, James J., (AV) . . . . '30 '62 C.973 B.S.B.A. L.1340 J.D. 9403 Kenwood Rd.
Conkin, Elizabeth . . . . '60 '86 C.210 B.A. L.146 J.D. [Gonzalez,S.&H.]
Connaughton, Joseph J., (AV) . . . . '26 '54 C.201 B.S. L.150 LL.B. 201 E. Fifth St.
Conners, Thos. J. . . . . '25 '50 C&L.150 B.B.A., LL.B. 125 Calhoun St.‡
Conrad, Jeannette M. '72 '03 C.999 B.S. L.4210 J.D
(adm. in KY; not adm. in OH) [A Weltman,W.&R.]
Conrad, Ralph J. . . . . '62 '87 C.607 B.S.B.A. L.7 J.D. [A Schwartz,M.&R.]
Consalvi, Genina, (BV) '50 '80
C.383 B.A. L.930 J.D. Sr. Corp. Coun., Great Amer. Ins. Co.
Conte, Jason P. . . . . '73 '99 C.602 B.A. L.880 J.D. [A Ulmer&B.]
Conway, Patrick J. . . . . '49 '80 C.477 B.A. L.213 J.D. [Legal H.]
Coogan, James H., (AV) . . . . '37 '61 C&L.150 B.A., J.D. [Drew&W.]
Cook, Allyson True, (BV(T)) '64 '89 C&L.383 B.A., J.D.
(adm. in KY; not adm. in OH) [A Graydon H.&R.] ⊙
Cook, Barbara J. . . . . '52 '77 C&L.477 B.A., J.D. 917 Main St.
Cook, Brant C. . . . . '68 '93 Coun., Pats., The Procter & Gamble Co.

Cook, Cathy R., (AV) '57 '82 C.473 B.A. L.150 J.D. BB
114 East Eighth Street, 45202-1103
Telephone: 513-241-4029 Fax: 513-723-8634
Email: cathy.cook@cathycooklaw.com URL: http://www.cathycooklaw.com
Criminal Law, Criminal Appeals, Criminal Defense, Drivers License Suspension, Felonies, Homicide, Manslaughter, Misdemeanors, Murder, Sex Crimes, Sexual Assault, Theft, Traffic Violations. Family Law-Alimony, Cohabitation Agreements, Divorce, Domestic Relations, Domestic Violence, Equitable

(This Listing Continued)

Cook, Cathy R. (Continued)
Distribution, Marital Property Distribution, Marital Property Law, Marital Property Settlements, Matrimonial Law, Non-Traditional Family Law, Paternity, Post-Divorce, Premarital Agreements, Separation Agreements, Spousal Support.
See Professional Biographies, CINCINNATI, OHIO

Cook, David M., (AV) . . . . '53 '78 C.347 A.B. L.150 J.D. [D.M.Cook]
Cook, Deborah L. . . . . '52 '78 C.8 B.A. L.7 J.D. U.S. Cir. App. J.
Cook, Melynda W. . . . . '71 '96 C.476 B.S. L.150 J.D. [Schad&C.]
Cook, Michael Alan . . . . '58 '83 C.150 B.A. L.201 J.D. 2406 Auburn Ave.
Cook, Stanley C. . . . . '21 '49 C&L.150 B.B.A., J.D. 6545 Apache Cir.‡

Cook, David M., LLC, (AV)
22 W. Ninth Street, 45202
Telephone: 513-721-7500 Fax: 513-721-1178
Email: dcook@dmcllc.com URL: http://www.davidmcookllc.com
David M. Cook. Associates: Stephen A. Simon; Robert E. Rickey.
COBRA, Employee Benefit Trusts, Litigation, Employee Stock Ownership Plans, ERISA, Class Actions, Litigation Health Benefits, Multi Employer Benefits, Multi Employer Pensions, Pension Plans, Profit Sharing, Taft-Hartley, 401k Plans, Unemployment Compensation, Wrongful Termination, Family Medical Leave Act, Labor Law, Arbitration, Union Organization, Union Contracts, Sexual Harassment, Labor and Employment, Employee Benefits, Toxic Torts, representing Labor Organizations and Labor Unions.
See Professional Biographies, CINCINNATI, OHIO

Cooney, J. Michael, (AV) . . . . '50 '75 C.974 A.B. L.477 J.D. [Dinsmore&S.]
Cooney, Kevin L. . . . . '69 '97 C.679 B.S. L.910 J.D. [Frost B.T.]
Cooper, Jeffrey R. '51 '77 C.94 B.A. L.472 J.D.
Chf. Compliance Officer, V.P., Great Amer. Finan. Resources, Inc.
Cooper, Todd L., (AV) . . . . '55 '81 C.31 A.B. L.602 J.D. [Peck,S.&W.]
Copeland, David A. '41 '79 C.846 B.S. L.796 J.D.
(adm. in TX; not adm. in OH) Assoc. Coun., Millenium Petrochemicals Inc.
Copeland, William M., (BV) . . . . '37 '78 C.1196 B.A. L.1340 J.D. [Copeland&Assoc.]
Copeland & Associates LLC, (BV) . . . . 4701 Creek Road
Corcoran, T. Jeffrey . . . . '47 '94 C.1118 B.A. L.201 J.D. 6177 State Route 132
Cordes, William H., (AV) . . . . '45 '73 C&L.477 B.B.A., J.D. [Thompson H.]
Cornetet, John B., (BV) . . . . '60 '87 C.150 B.B.A. L.201 J.D. [Lutz,C.&M.]
Cornett, Curtis L., (BV) . . . . '62 '93 C.16 B.M. L.150 J.D. [Cors&B.]
Cors, L. Barry, (AV) . . . . '32 '61 C&L.150 B.A., LL.B. [Cors&B.]

Cors & Bassett, LLC, (AV)
537 East Pete Rose Way, Suite 400, 45202-3502 ⊙
Telephone: 513-852-8200 Fax: 513-852-8222
URL: http://www.corsbassett.com
Members of Firm: L. Barry Cors; Paul R. Moran; William G. Kohlhepp; Richard J. Valleau; Joseph H. Vahlsing; Robert J. Hollingsworth; David L. Barth; Michael L. Gay; Elizabeth A. Horwitz; Jeffrey J. Harmon; Stephen S. Holmes; Katharine C. Weber; Hans M. Zimmer; Janet L. Houston; David J. Schmitt; Kevin R. Feazell; Curtis L. Cornett; Tracy Byrd Jamison; Sara Straight Wolf; Victor C. Halpin; Susan R. Bell; Andrew C. Emmert. Associates: Kenneth H. Kinder II; Joseph S. Burns; R. Scott Hughes. Of Counsel: Kenneth B. Bassett; James W. Halloran; D. Lynn Spraetz; Michelle A. Mullee; James J. Carroll; Hal F. Franke; David P. Heidrich (Not admitted in OH); Robert Gray Edmiston; David H. Todd.
General Practice. Corporation, Securities, Labor Relations and Employment Law, Transportation, Environmental, Energy, Land Use Planning and Zoning, International Law, Taxation, Bankruptcy, Estate Planning, Probate, Domestic Relations, Products Liability, Negligence, Franchising, Real Estate Law, Construction Contract and Claims Litigation, and E-Commerce. Trial and Appellate Practice in State and Federal Courts.
Representative Clients: Roadway Express, Inc.; The Hillman Group, Inc.; Pomeroy Computer Resources, Inc.; Kenwood Dealer Group; The Midland Company; Citizens Bank of Northern Kentucky; R & L Carriers; Hyatt Hotels; Dugan & Meyers Construction Co.; The Bistro Group, Inc.
Ft. Wright, Kentucky Office: 1881 Dixie Highway, Suite 350, 41011. Telephone: 859-331-6440.
See Professional Biographies, CINCINNATI, OHIO

Corwin, Melanie S., (AV) . . . . '62 '90 C.235 B.A. L.1340 J.D. [A Waite,S.B.&C.]
Cosgrove, Kristen A. . . . . '74 '01 C.966 J.B.A. L.150 J.D. [A Reisenfeld&Assoc.]
Cosgrove, Paul J. (P.J.) . . . . '73 '99 C.608 B.A. L.1292 J.D. [A Ulmer&B.]
Cosgrove, Terrence R., (AV) . . . . '51 '76 C.602 A.B. L.150 J.D. Chief Pros.
Coston, P. Casey '64 '93 C.373 B.A. L.273 J.D.
(adm. in MI; not adm. in OH) [A Squire,S.&D.]
Cottingham, John . . . . '— '02 C.477 B.S.E. L.569 J.D. [A Thompson H.]
Coulter, Lisa Weekley, (BV) . . . . '61 '88 C.434 B.A. L.608 J.D. [C Frost B.T.]
Covatta, Anthony G., Jr., (AV) . . . . '44 '79 C.1150 B.A. L.150 J.D. [Drew&W.]
Cover, Melissa Kurzhals . . . . '73 '00 C&L.150 B.S., J.D. [A Taft,S.&H.]
Cowan, Grant S., (AV) . . . . '59 '85 C.893 B.A. L.150 J.D. [Frost B.T.]
Cox, J. Stephen, (AV) . . . . '57 '91 C.150 B.F.A. L.1340 J.D. [Martin&B.]
Cox, Lance S., (BV) . . . . '40 '70 C.679 B.S. L.1340 J.D. [L.S.Cox]
Cox, Lance S., Co., L.P.A., (BV) . . . . 480 Ohio Pike
Coyle, Timothy L., (BV) . . . . '57 '87 C.383 B.S. L.1340 J.D. [C Squire,S.&D.]
Coyne, Kenneth P. . . . . '72 '98 C.473 B.S. L.245 J.D. [A Haverkamp,B.R.&R.]
Coz, Thomas A., (BV) . . . . '53 '79 C.973 A.B. L.150 J.D. P.O. Box 5039

Crabbe, Brown & James LLP, (AV)
30 Garfield Place, Suite 740, 45202 ⊙
Telephone: 513-784-1525 Fax: 513-784-1250
Email: info@cbjLawyers.com URL: http://www.cbjLawyers.com
Brian E. Hurley; Robert J. Gehring. Associate: Beth Wayne.
General Insurance Defense, Product Liability, Professional Malpractice, Premises Liability, Environmental and Toxic Tort Claims, Employment and Labor Law, Tax Matters, General Business and Corporate Law and Litigation, Banking and Securities, Real Estate, Probate and Estate Planning, Criminal Law, Administrative, Regulatory and Governmental Law, Workers Compensation, Intellectual Property, Fire, Arson and Fraud, Fidelity and Surety Life, Accident and Health, Insurance Coverage Law, Construction Claims, Health and Hospital Law, Oil, Gas and Energy Law, Transportation Law, Automobile Dealer Law, Zoning, International Practice and Domestic Law, Land Use Planning, and Eminent Domain.
Columbus, Ohio Office: 500 South Front Street, Suite 1200. Telephone: 614-228-5511. Fax: 614-229-4559.
Cleveland, Ohio Office: 1280 W. Third Street. Telephone: 216-574-9312.
Lancaster, Ohio Office: 111 South Broad Street, Suite 209, 43130. Telephone: 740-689-1743. Fax: 740-689-1746.
Urbana, Ohio Office: 118 Scioto Street. Telephone: 937-652-4000.
See Professional Biographies, CINCINNATI, OHIO

Crafton, Constance J.D.C. . . . . '69 '95 C.347 B.A. L.1119 J.D. Becker Gallagher
Craig, L. Clifford, (AV) . . . . '38 '64 C&L.228 A.B., LL.B. [Taft,S.&H.]
Crase, Charles Shane . . . . '72 '04 C.871 B.S. L.1340 J.D. [A Dinsmore&S.]
Crawford, Robert W., (AV) . . . . '30 '57 C&L.150 B.B.A., LL.B. 312 Walnut St.‡
Craycraft, Kenneth R., Jr. . . . . '62 '01 C.999 B.A. L.228 J.D. [A Squire,S.&D.]
Creahan, David J. . . . . '16 '75 C.150 B.B.A. L.1340 J.D. 6600 Corbly Rd.‡
Creative Counsel . . . . 4523 Hector Ave.
Creighton, Richard L., Jr., (AV) . . . . '48 '73 C.973 B.A. L.734 J.D. [Keating M.&K.]
Cremeens-Strong, Sally L. . . . . '61 '87 C.674 A.B. L.94 J.D. 225 W. Court St.
Crisler, Scott A. . . . . '65 '95 C.280 B.B.A. L.623 J.D. [A Dinsmore&S.]
Croall, David T., (AV) . . . . '55 '81 C.945 A.B. L.309 J.D. [Porter W.M.&A.]
Cronin, Patrick J., (BV) . . . . '52 '77 C.207 B.A. L.150 J.D. [C Spraul,V.&D.]
Croog, Charles F. . . . . '68 '94 C.976 B.A. L.659 J.D. Financial Stocks, Inc.

Crooks, Scott B., (AV) ....'43 '68 C&L.477 B.A., J.D. [Thompson H.]
Croskery, Robert F. ....'56 '95 C&L.150 B.G.S., J.D. [Croskery]

Croskery Law Offices, (AV)
7746 Beechmont Avenue, 45255
Telephone: 513-232-LAWS (5297) Fax: 513-701-5528
Email: rcroskery@croskerylaw.com URL: http://www.croskerylaw.com
Robert F. Croskery; Melinda E. Knisley.
Sexual Harassment, Wrongful Death, Serious Personal Injury, Auto Accidents, Small Business Representation.
See Professional Biographies, CINCINNATI, OHIO

Cross, Anita .... '55 '91 C.399 B.A. L.1340 J.D. Assoc. Gen. Coun., Cincinnti Bell
Cross, C. Thomas ....'26 '54 C.150 Ch.E L.912 J.D. 2324 Madison Rd. (Pat.)‡
Cross, Wende C. ....'66 '93 C.473 B.A. L.1340 J.D. [Cross,S.&Assoc.]
Cross, Smith & Associates Co., L.P.A. ....3460 Reading Road
Crosthwaite, Daryl A., (AV) ....'60 '89 C.235 B.A. L.1340 J.D. 9545 Kenwood Rd.
Croswell, R. Scott, III, (AV) .... '47 '74 C.275 B.S. L.1340 J.D. [Croswell&A.]
Croswell & Adams Co., L.P.A., (AV) ....1208 Sycamore St.
Crouse, Candace C. ....'75 '00 C.923 B.A. L.608 J.D. [Ⓐ Sirkin P.&S.]
Crowe, James J., (AV) ....'35 '63 C.980 B.A. L.276 J.D. [Ⓒ Thompson H.]
Crowley, James C., IV, (AV) ....'49 '76 C.93 B.S. L.150 J.D. [Crowley,F.&A.]
Crowley, Frank & Ahlers, Co., LPA, (AV) ....414 Walnut Street, Suite 707
Crush, Thomas H. ....'34 '61 C.973 B.A. L.276 J.D. Com. Pleas Ct. J.
Cruze, John J., (AV) .... '43 '70 C.473 B.A. L.1340 J.D. # 270, 6470 Glenway Ave
Culbertson, Wm. S. ....'23 '50 C.151 L.1340 LL.B. 3236 Harrison Ave.
Cummings, Philip R. ....'63 '89 C.608 B.S. L.150 J.D. Asst. Pros. Atty.
Cummins, James R., (AV) .... '42 '67 C.674 A.B. L.150 J.D. [Ⓐ Waite,S.B.&C.]
Cummins, John R., (BV) ....'60 '86 C.597 B.A. L.608 J.D. [Slovin&C.] ⊙
Cuni, Thomas L., (AV) ....'47 '75 C&L.150 B.A., J.D. [Cuni,F.&L.]

Cuni, Ferguson & LeVay Co., L.P.A., (AV)
10655 Springfield Pike, 45215-1120
Telephone: 513-771-6768 Fax: 513-771-6781
Thomas L. Cuni; Amy Schott Ferguson; Helen Fanz LeVay. Associates: Mark A. Wilder; Joseph V. Pitstick.
Real Estate, Corporate, Community and Condominium Association (including Foreclosure), Estate Planning and Probate, and Civil Litigation.
See Professional Biographies, CINCINNATI, OHIO

Cunningham, James R. '17 '47 C&L.838 A.B., J.D.
(adm. in TN; not adm. in OH) 3761 Harvard Acres‡
Cunningham, Penelope R. ....'48 '87 C&L.150 B.A., J.D. Com. Pleas J.
Cunningham, Pierce E., (AV) ....'34 '60 C.321 A.B. L.276 LL.B. [P.E.Cunningham]
Cunningham, William D., (BV) ....'47 '75 C.973 B.A. L.851 J.D. 9000 Plainfield Rd.
Cunningham, Pierce E., Co., LPA, The Law Offices of, (AV)
312 Walnut Street, Suite 3250
Curran, Charles E., III '46 '72 C&L.339 B.S., J.D.
(adm. in IL; not adm. in OH) Sr. V.P., Mktg., Comair, Inc.
Cussen, Michael P. ....'69 '95 C.973 B.A. L.1340 J.D. [McCaslin,I.&M.] ⊙
Cussen, William M., (AV) .... '43 '69 C.973 B.S. L.1340 J.D. [McCaslin,I.&M.]
Custis, Douglass L. ....'43 '67 C.610 B.S. L.150 J.D. Admin. Law J., Soc. Sec. Admn.
Cutcher, Timothy R., (BV) ....'46 '74 C.608 B.A. L.150 J.D. 1019 Main Street
Czanik, Kara A. ....'— '02 C.967 B.A. L.150 J.D. [Ⓐ Graydon H.&R.]
Dada, Pamela V. '67 '93 C.823 B.A. L.477 J.D.
Asst. Coun., Federated Dept. Stores, Inc.
D'Addesa, Danielle M. ....'77 '03 C.699 B.A. L.150 J.D. [Ⓐ Keating M.&K.]
Daggett, John K., (AV) ....'55 '82 C.432 B.S. L.1340 J.D. [Moore,M.&M.]
Dahl, Elisabeth A. ....'62 '88 C.197 A.B. L.910 J.D. 400 Broadway
Dailey, Michael G. ....'66 '99 C.473 B.S. L.150 J.D. [Ⓐ Dinsmore&S.]
Dalal, Amy R. ....'78 '04 C.1365 B.A. L.150 J.D. [Ⓐ Hammond]
Dale, Kenneth P. '46 '72 C.112 A.B. L.1068 J.D.
(adm. in CA; not adm. in OH) I.R.S.
Dale, Myron L., (AV) ....'49 '75 C.976 B.A. L.276 J.D. [Frost B.T.] ‡
Dallob, Naomi C. ....'54 '79 C&L.150 B.A., J.D. Corp. V.P. & Secy., Chemed Corp.
Daly, Hugh F. "Trey" ....'63 '87 C.973 B.A. L.383 J.D. Legal Aid Soc.
D'Amelio, Michael J. '58 '91
C.454 B.S.M.E. L.36 J.D. Pat. Coun., The Procter & Gamble Co. (Pat.)
Dameron, Jonathan P., (BV) ....'62 '91 C.1161 B.S. L.1340 J.D. [Schuh&G.]
Dameron, Nancy Jane ....'67 '93 C.473 B.A. L.347 J.D. 914 Main Street, Suite 200
Danehy, James S. ....'38 '85 C.602 B.B.A. L.201 J.D. P.O. Box 54482
Daniel, Stephanie B. '76 '04 C.835 B.S. L.838 J.D.
(adm. in TN; not adm. in OH) [Ⓐ Dinsmore&S.]
Darlington, Frederick Lee '56 '83 C.383 B.S. L.1340 J.D.
V.P. & Sr. Coun., Provident Financial Group, Inc.
Darner, Thomas A. ....'43 '68 C&L.378 B.S., J.D. U.S. Envir. Protect. Agency
Darrow, Helana A. ....'72 '98 C.510 B.A. L.150 J.D. [Ⓐ Dinsmore&S.]
Daughtrey, Martha Craig ....'42 '68 C&L.880 B.A., J.D. U.S. Cir. J.
Dauterman, Steven L. .....'54 '78 C.532 B.A. L.608 J.D. Sr. Tr. Offr., The Fifth Third Bk.
Davidson, James P. ....'60 '86 C.608 B.S.E.E. L.851 J.D. 10250 Alliance Road (Pat.)
Davidson, Kristi L. ....'71 '97 C.930 B.S. L.201 J.D. [Ⓐ Wood,H.&E.] (See Pat. Sect.)
Davis, Charles J., (AV) ....'49 '77 C.321 B.A. L.121 J.D. One West Fourth Street
Davis, David P. ....'40 '72 C.510 B.A. L.1340 J.D. Com. Pleas J.
Davis, Frank G., (AV) ....'18 '42 C&L.150 A.B., J.D. [Davis&H.]
Davis, Gary J., (BV) ....'54 '79 C.1161 B.S. L.1340 J.D. [Wood&L.]
Davis, John P. ....'64 '95 C.679 B.S.E.E. L.1339 J.D. [Ⓐ Wood,H.&E.]
Davis, Myron Y., Jr., (BV) ....'69 C.610 B.S.Ed. L.1340 J.D. 700 Walnut
Davis, Norma J. Holt .....'49 '82 C.864 B.S.Chem. L.150 J.D. 1205 Pendleton St., Ste. 1
Davis, Perry, Jr., (BV) ....'60 '87 C.1023 B.S. L.803 J.D. [Harmon,D.&K.]
Davis, Robert L., (AV) ....'28 '58 C.150 B.A. L.1340 J.D. 3600 Carew Tower
Davis, Sherry L., (BV) ....'50 '85 C.150 B.A. L.1340 J.D. 307 Wyoming Avenue
Davis, Stephen E. ....'42 '68 C.210 A.B. L.345 J.D. Admin. Law J., Soc. Sec. Admin.
Davis, Steven C., (BV) ....'61 '86 C.1111 B.A. L.260 J.D. [Barron,P.B.&S.]
Davis and Hengelbrok, (AV) ....830 Main St.
Dawson, Phyllis I. ....'62 '94 C.150 B.S. L.201 J.D. S&S Healthcare Strategies
Day, John L., Jr., (AV) ....'49 '81 C.383 B.A. L.1340 J.D. [Ⓐ Weltman,W.&R.]
Day, Stephanie M. ....'69 '00 C.63 B.S. L.1340 J.D. [Ⓐ Goodson]
Deabler, Christopher A. ....'74 '02 C.825 B.A. L.597 J.D. [Ⓐ Squire,S.&D.]
Deardorff, Julie A., (BV) ....'49 '87 C&L.150 B.B.A., J.D. 2936 Observatory Ave.
Deardorff, Timothy J. ....'51 '79 C.973 B.A. L.1340 J.D. [Deardorff&Assoc.]
Deardorff & Associates, (BV) ....2645 Erie Avenue
Debbeler, J. Michael, (AV) ....'55 '80 C.383 B.A. L.150 J.D. [Graydon H.&R.] ⊙
Debbeler, Lisa Maechling, (AV) ......'55 '80 C.973 A.B. L.150 J.D. 1242 Rookwood Dr.
DeBlasis, Rick D., (AV) ....'54 '80 C&L.150 B.A., J.D. [Lerner,S.&R.]
DeCenso, William A., (AV) ....'53 '79 C.93 A.B. L.150 J.D. [Santen&H.]
Decker, Randy L., (AVⓉ) '55 '84 C.965 B.A. L.300 J.D.
Sr. V.P. & Dep. Gen. Coun., Provident Financial Group, Inc.
Dedischew, Carol L. ....'46 '84 C.893 B.S.N. L.1340 J.D. 49 E. 4th Street
Deering, Jennifer K. ....'70 '96 C.473 B.A. L.1340 J.D. Asst. Pros. Atty.

DeFusco, Robert G., (CVⓉ) '48 '79 C.510 B.A. L.1340 J.D.
(adm. in KY; not adm. in OH) 525 Vine St.
DeGraffenreid, Stacey Leigh ......'69 '00 C.421 B.S.B.A. L.150 J.D. [S.L.DeGraffenreid]
DeGraffenreid, Stacey L., L.P.A. ....260 Northland Blvd., Ste. 312A
DeGregorio, Edmonde P., (AV) ....'52 '77 C.178 B.A. L.150 J.D. [Ⓐ Aronoff,R.&H.]
DeHaan, Elizabeth Slone, (AV) .....'51 '76 C.692 B.A. L.150 J.D. [Ⓐ Robbins,K.P.&T.]
DeHaan, Peter R., (BV) ....'45 '74 C.645 B.S. L.1340 J.D. [DeHaan&B.]
DeHaan & Bach, Co., L.P.A., (BV) ....11256 Cornell Park Drive, Suite 500
Dehan, Paula J. ....'63 '03 C.973 B.A. L.1340 J.D. [Ⓐ Taft,S.&H.]
Dehner, Joseph J., (AV) ....'48 '73 C.674 A.B. L.309 J.D. [Frost B.T.]
Delev, Gregory D., (BV) ....'61 '91 C.608 B.S. L.851 J.D. [Delev&W.]
Delev & Williams, L.L.C., (BV) ....432 Walnut Street
DeLong, Deborah, (AV) ....'50 '75 C.880 B.A. L.150 J.D. [Dinsmore&S.]
De Marco, Paul M., (AV) ....'59 '84 C.970 B.A. L.464 J.D. [Ⓐ Waite,S.B.&C.]
Demmerle, Daniel H., II, (AV) ....'48 '73 C.207 B.A. L.880 J.D. [Strauss&T.]
Dempsey, Fredrick Russell '73 '01 C.437 B.A. L.117 J.D.
(adm. in WV; not adm. in OH) Gen. Coun., d.e. Foxx & Associates, Inc.
Denham, Robert E. '42 '70 C.951 A.B. L.569 J.D.
(adm. in NY; not adm. in OH) Assoc. Coun., Millennium Petrochemicals Inc.
Denicola, Ronald J., (BV) ....'41 '67 C.973 A.B. L.150 J.D. [Denicola]

Denicola & Co., L.P.A., (BV)
36 East Seventh Street, Suite 2020, 45202
Telephone: 513-621-9660 Fax: 513-345-3900
Email: rdenicola@fuse.net URL: http://www.denicolalaw.com
Ronald J. Denicola.
Corporation and Business Law, Civil Litigation, Commercial Litigation and Collections, Subrogation, Probate, Real Estate, Transportation, Motor Carrier Law, Personal Injury, Automobile Accidents.
See Professional Biographies, CINCINNATI, OHIO

Denlinger, Rosenthal & Greenberg, A Legal Professional Association, (AV) BB
425 Walnut Street, Suite 2310, 45202-3918
Telephone: 513-621-3440 Fax: 513-621-4449
URL: http://www.drgfirm.com
Dean E. Denlinger (1929-2000); Daniel G. Rosenthal (Certified Specialist in Labor and Employment Law, Ohio State Bar Association); Gary L. Greenberg; John W. Fischer, II; Mark E. Lutz; James A. Mills;—Jill Stanforth Tauber; Emily J. Gelhaus; Michael P. Majba.
Labor and Employment Law.
Representative Clients: Columbia Sussex Corp.; Duro Bag Manufacturing Co.; Georgia-Pacific Corp.; The City of Kettering; The Kroger Co.; Moraine Materials Co.; The Ohio Masonic Home; The Standard Textile Co.; Trimble Navigation Ltd.
See Professional Biographies, CINCINNATI, OHIO

Denmead Law Office
(See Columbus)

Denney, Mark A. ....'64 '95 C.973 B.A. L.201 J.D. [Ⓐ Wood&L.]
Dennis, Douglas R. ....'63 '95 C.870 B.S. L.150 J.D. [Ⓐ Frost B.T.]
Denton, D. Brock ....'74 '00 C.383 B.S. L.1340 J.D. [Ⓐ Keating M.&K.]
Dershaw, Brian G. ....'75 '00 C.117 B.A. L.150 J.D. [Beckman W.S.]
Desai, Deepak K. ....'68 '93 C.1161 B.A. L.1340 J.D. [Ⓐ Santen&H.]
Desmond, William J. '49 '78 C.973 B.A. L.1340 J.D.
Dir., S.W. Ohio Reg. Transit Auth.
DeStigter, Mitchell L. '67 '93 C.132 B.A. L.352 J.D.
Dir., Legal Servs., Catholic Healthcare Partners

Deters, Benzinger & LaVelle, P.S.C., (BV)
3500 Carew Tower, 441 Vine Street, 45202-3007 ⊙
Telephone: 513-241-4110 Telecopier: 513-241-4551
URL: http://www.dbllaw.com
Joseph A. Cleves, Jr.; Alan J. Hartman; William J. Moran, Jr.; David W. Burleigh. Associates: Carla M. Venhoff (Not admitted in OH); Peter A. Schmid. Of Counsel: Pierce E. Cunningham.
General Practice. Trials and Appeals. Banking, Health Care, Corporate, Personal Injury, Real Estate, Insurance, Labor and Employee Relations, Media, Antitrust, Employee Benefits, Family, Adoption, Collections, Internet, Computer, Information Technology, International, Equine, Probate, Estate Planning, Administrative, Workers' Compensation, Taxation, Zoning, Commercial, Agricultural, Bankruptcy, Construction, Eminent Domain and Criminal Law.
Covington, Kentucky Office: Thomas More Park, 207 Thomas More Parkway. Telephone: 859-341-1881. Telecopier: 859-341-1469.
See Professional Biographies, CINCINNATI, OHIO

Deutch, Joel, (CV) ....'67 '93 C.347 B.S. L.213 J.D. 9000 Plainfield Rd.
DeVita, David, (AV) ....'52 '78 C.602 B.A. L.608 J.D. [DeVita&H.]

DeVita & Howe, LLP, (AV)
117 East Court Street, 45202-1203
Telephone: 513-632-5332 Fax: 513-241-7434
Members of Firm: David DeVita; William D. Howe.
General Business, Real Estate, Tax, Estate Planning and Probate.
See Professional Biographies, CINCINNATI, OHIO

Dewan, Margaret Wood '53 '78
C.608 B.A. L.150 J.D. Sr. Coun., The Procter & Gamble Co.
DeWine, R. Patrick ....'68 '95 C.473 B.A., B.S. L.477 J.D. [Ⓒ Keating M.&K.]
Deye, Thomas E., (BV) ....'52 '79 C.93 A.B. L.201 J.D. 6975 Presidio Ct.
Diamond, Harvey S. ....'29 '54 C&L.150 B.B.A., LL.B. 315 W. 5th St.
Dias, Monica L. ....'62 '01 C.929 B.A. L.1340 J.D. [Ⓐ Frost B.T.]
Dickey, Patricia L. ....'58 '89 C.207 B.A. L.851 J.D. 813 Broadway, 1st Fl.
Dickman, H. Brunner ....'12 '37 C&L.150 B.A., LL.B. 5005 S. Ridge Dr.‡
Diedrichs, Frank M., (AV) ....'43 '76 C.150 A.B. L.1340 J.D. [Rice&D.]
Dieffenbach, Roxann H., (BV) '46 '78
C.289 B.A. L.1340 J.D. Suite 100, 13 East Court Street
Dierks, Mark N., (BV) ....'63 '88 C.381 B.A. L.150 J.D. [Ⓐ Lerner,S.&R.]
Diersing, George A., Jr., (BV) ....'50 '76 C.150 B.A. L.1340 J.D. 632 Vine St.
Dietz, Christopher P. ....'55 '79 C.659 B.A. L.150 J.D. Sr. Staff Atty., Ct. of App.
Dietz, John H. '36 '60 L.215 LL.B.
(adm. in MI; not adm. in OH) 8 Linden Ln.‡
Dill, Stephanie A. ....'72 '99 C.473 B.S. L.150 J.D. [Ⓐ Strauss&T.]
Diller, Edward D., (AV) ....'47 '76 C.91 B.A. L.309 J.D. [Taft,S.&H.]
Dilts, Joseph L., (AV) ....'56 '81 C&L.150 B.A., J.D. [Kohnen&P.]
DiMauro, Caroline M. ....'69 '99 C.1119 B.A. L.150 J.D. [Ⓐ Keating M.&K.]
Dimling, Robert A., (AV) ....'41 '66 C.97 B.A. L.477 J.D. [Frost B.T.]
Dinardo, Nicholas J. .....'71 '98 C&L.150 B.A., J.D. Legal Aid Soc. of Greater Cincinnati
Dine, Jennifer D. ....'77 '03 C.477 B.A. L.150 J.D. [Ⓐ Montgomery,R.&J.]
Dinkelacker, Patrick T. ....'53 '79 C.973 B.A. L.201 J.D. Com. Pleas J.

Dinsmore & Shohl LLP, (AV) BB
255 East Fifth Street, Suite 1900, 45202-4700 ⊙
Telephone: 513-977-8200 FAX: 513-977-8141
Email: info@dinslaw.com URL: http://www.dinslaw.com
Frank F. Dinsmore (1891-1962); Walter M. Shohl (1908-1970). Members of Firm: Jerome H. Kearns; Clifford A. Roe, Jr.; Lawrence R. Elleman; John M. Kunst, Jr.; Thomas J. Sherman; Vincent B. Stamp; Frank C. Woodside, III; Mark L. Silbersack; Gerald V. Weigle, Jr.; Michael W. Hawkins; Mark A. Vander Laan; William M. Freedman; Paul R. Mattingly; J. Michael Cooney (Certified Specialist in Estate Planning, Trust and Probate Law, Ohio State Bar Association); Michael S.

(This Listing Continued)

Dinsmore & Shohl LLP (Continued)

Glassman; Nancy A. Lawson; Michael D. Eagen; Paul A. Ose; Charles F. Hertlein, Jr.; Joanne M. Schreiner; John D. Luken; Deborah R. Lydon; George H. Vincent; Lynda E. Roesch; George B. Wilkinson; John E. Jevicky; Jerry S. Sallee; Mark C. Bissinger; Gary E. Becker; Neal D. Baker; Charles M. Roesch; K. C. Green; M. Gabrielle Hils; Stephen G. Schweller; Steven H. Schreiber; Calvin D. Buford; Gregory A. Harrison; Ben F. Wells; Holly D. Kozlowski; Frederick M. Erny; Timothy A. Tepe; Harvey Jay Cohen; James A. Comodeca; Joseph (Jay) L. Sallee, Jr.; Joan M. Verchot (Certified Specialist in Workers Compensation Law, Ohio State Bar Association); Kim Martin Lewis; John E. Barnes; Charles H. Brown, III; Brian S. Sullivan; Colleen P. Lewis; Susan B. Zaunbrecher (Chair, Banking and Financial Institutions Practice Group); Christopher A. Benintendi; William A. Sherman, II; Jeffrey P. Hinebaugh; Clyde Bennett, II; Martin J. Miller; Mary-Jo Middelhoff; Bonnie G. Camden (Certified Specialist in Estate Planning, Trust and Probate Law, Ohio State Bar Association); Deborah DeLong; Alan H. Abes; Michael A. Manzler; Barbara Schwartz Bromberg; Mary J. Healy (Certified Specialist in Estate Planning, Trust and Probate Law, Ohio State Bar Association); Richard B. Tranter; John J. Schmidt; Sean P. Callan; Brian J. O'Connell; Brian P. Perry (Certified Specialist in Workers Compensation Law, Ohio State Bar Association); Steven H. Ray; Robert J. Reid (Certified Specialist in Labor and Employment Law, Ohio State Bar Association); Linda A. Ash; David D. Black; J. David Brittingham; John E. Christopher; Sterling W. Colvin; Jason B. Sims; Lee M. Stautberg; A. Scott Fruechtemeyer; Louise Sadowsky Brock; Robert A. Carpenter; John V. Harmeyer; Gregory P. Adams; Douglas Halpert. Associates: G. Franklin Miller; Christine L. McBroom; Richard D. Porotsky, Jr.; Steve N. Siegel; Robert H. Hoskins; Bryan E. Pacheco; Christopher L. Muzzo; Matthew D. Shuler; Helana A. Darrow; Neal A. Frink; Daniel L. Jones, Jr.; David P. Fornshell; Michael G. Dailey; Noah J. Stern; H. Toby Schisler; Jennifer O. Mitchell; Christopher R. McDowell; Becky Barlow Fitzsimmons; Melissa L. Korfhage; Suzanne Cahill McNabb; Amanda P. Lenhart; David S. Sullivan; James A. Marx; Scott A. Crisler; Jon B. Allison; Clayton L. Kuhnell; Joshua A. Lorentz; M. Dave O'Guinn, III; Eric M. Robbins; Lori S. Drasnin; Alicia L. Wilhelmy; Donald W. Mallory; Tracy Rottner Yu; Geoffrey L. Oberhaus; Allyson B. Handler; James M. Wherley, Jr.; Douglas J. Feichtner; Peter J. Georgiton; Andrew R. Kwiatkowski; Susan M. Luken; Margaret M. Maggio; Emerson C. Moser; Michael J. Newman; Jennifer K. Swartz; Katrina R. Atkins; Jessica S. Hylander; Sarah V. Lewis; Pete S. Singer; David A. Whaley; Brian K. Groemminger; Mary E. Widdowson; Charles A. Bruch; Polly Rickard Patel; Alison N. Sackenheim; Steven A. Abreu; Shawn P. Burton; Charles Shane Crase; Shana N. Eaton; Ben Gerlach; Nicholas J. Kemphaus; Angelina N. Jackson; Toby D. Merchant; David J. Myers; James T. Sutton; Andrew J. Wamsley; Jody H. Armstrong; Clare M. Iery; Jeffrey A. Willis; Gwendolyn M. Odmark; James A. Browning (Not admitted in OH); Dawne McKenna Parrish; Jeremy A. Klotz (Not admitted in OH); Max V. Langenkamp; Matthew A. Whitlow; John P. Sellers, III; Peter A. Draugelis; Carrie W. Ryan; Stephanie B. Daniel (Not admitted in OH). Of Counsel: Carolyn A. Betts; Harris K. Weston; Powell McHenry; John E. McDowell; Harry L. Riggs, Jr.; Thomas S. Calder; Harold S. Freeman; John W. Beatty; Kathryn K. Przywara; Thomas J. Westerfield; John B. Persiani.

General Practice: Antitrust, Aviation Law, Banking, Bankruptcy, Business Crimes Law, Computers, Construction, Corporations, Creditors' Rights, Drug and Medical Device, Employee Benefits, Environmental, ERISA, Estate Planning, Franchising, Healthcare, Hospitals, Intellectual Property, International, Immigration, Insurance Law, Labor and Employment Law, Litigation, Medical Malpractice Defense, Mergers and Acquisitions, OSHA, Probate, Products Liability, Real Estate, Securities, State and Local Government Law, Taxation, Transportation Law, Trial and Appellate Practice in State and Federal Courts, Trusts, Workers' Compensation, Zoning.

Dayton, Ohio Office: One Dayton Centre, One South Main Street, Suite 1300, 45402. Telephone: 937-449-6400. FAX: 937-449-6405.

Columbus, Ohio Office: 10th Floor, 175 South Third Street, 43215-5134. Telephone: 614-628-6880. FAX: 614-628-6890.

Lexington, Kentucky Office: Lexington Financial Center, 250 West Main Street, Suite 1400, 40507. Telephone: 859-425-1000. FAX: 859-425-1099.

Louisville, Kentucky Office: 1400 PNC Plaza, 500 West Jefferson Street, 40202. Telephone: 502-540-2300. FAX: 502-585-2207.

Pittsburgh, Pennsylvania Office: The Grant Building, 330 Grant Street, Suite 2415, 15219. Telephone: 412-281-5000. FAX: 412-281-5055.

Charleston, West Virginia Office: 900 Lee Street, Huntington Square, Suite 600, 25301. Mailing Address: P.O. Box 11887, 25339. Telephone: 304-357-0900. FAX: 304-357-0919.

See Professional Biographies, CINCINNATI, OHIO

DiPuccio, John M., (AV) .... '38 '67 C.973 B.S. L.1340 J.D. Asst. U.S. Atty.
Dittmeier, Anthony T., (BV) .... '21 '51 C.421 L.93 J.D. 2375 Twigwood Lane
Dix, Robert Charles .... '— '01 C.610 B.A. L.546 J.D. [Lerner,S.&R.]
Dixon, Gertrude Priscilla '51 '97
C.150 B.S. L.201 J.D. Crim. Pros., City of Cincinnati Pros. Off.
Dixon, Joseph A., (BV) .... '41 '71 C.973 B.S. L.1340 J.D. 5804 Rapid Run Rd.
Dizenhuz, Robert S., (BV) .... '65 '91 C.311 B.A. L.150 J.D. Sr. Coun., Anthem, Inc.
Dlott, Susan J. .... '49 '73 C.659 B.A. L.94 J.D. U.S. Dist. J.
Doan, Charles H., (BV) .... '45 '72 C.611 B.A. L.150 J.D. 830 Main St., Ste. 1115
Doan, Rupert A. .... '33 '58 C.611 B.A. L.150 LL.B. Appeals Ct. J.
Doering, Edw. A. .... '12 '37 C.973 A.B. L.276 J.D. 7303 Willowbrook Lane
Doggett, Robert Irvin, (BV) ..... '32 '58 C&L.150 A.B., J.D. 1014 Vine Street, Suite 2416
Dolle, Robert E., (BV) .... '17 '43 C.151 L.1340 LL.B. [Dolle,R.&M.]
Dolle, Robert H. .... '48 '73 C.97 B.S. L.150 J.D. [Dolle,R.&M.] ‡
Dolle, Rueger & Mathews Co., L.P.A., (AV) .... 817 Main St.
Dolman, Charles M. .... '29 '55 C&L.150 B.A., J.D. 830 Main St.‡
Donenfeld, Jack A., (AV) .... '51 '76 C.597 B.A. L.93 J.D. [J.A.Donenfeld]

Donenfeld, Jack A., A Legal Prof. Assn., Law Offices of, (AV)
119 East Court Street, 45202
Telephone: 513-632-5311 Fax: 513-721-1213 URL: http://www.donenfeldlawoffice.com
URL: http://www.donenfeldlawfirm.com
Email: JAD@DonenfeldLaw.com URL: http://www.donenfeldlawoffices.com
Jack A. Donenfeld. Of Counsel: Robert W. Edler (Not admitted in OH); Bruce S. Fenton (Not admitted in OH).
Securities, Closely Held Corporations, Limited Liability Companies, Partnerships, Business Planning, Mergers and Acquisitions, Corporate Finance, Franchising and Real Estate, Asset Protection, International Asset Protection, Business Law, Business Formation, Business Succession Planning, Joint Ventures, Profession Practices, Small Business Law, Strategic Alliances, Corporate Law, Corporate Formation, Corporate Governance, Incorporation, Offshore Corporations, Private Finance, Investments, International Investments, Partnerships, Private Equity, Syndication, Venture Capital, Leverage Buyouts, Partnership Law, Real Estate Investments, Private Residence Clubs, Blue Sky Law, Private Placement, Securities Offerings, Securities Registration, Trusts and Estates, Estate Planning.

See Professional Biographies, CINCINNATI, OHIO

Donnellon, Daniel J., (AV) .... '61 '86 C.97 B.A. L.150 J.D. [Keating M.&K.]
Donnellon, Edward J. .... '24 '51 C.150 L.1340 J.D. [Donnellon,D.&M.]
Donnellon, Terrence M., (AV) .... '54 '79 C&L.150 B.A., J.D. [Donnellon,D.&M.]
Donnellon, Thomas E., (AV) .... '50 '76 C.150 B.A. L.1340 J.D. [Donnellon,D.&M.]

Donnellon, Donnellon and Miller, A Legal Professional Association, (AV)
9079 Montgomery Road, 45242
Telephone: 513-891-7087 Fax: 513-891-7125
Thomas E. Donnellon; Terrence M. Donnellon; R. Douglas Miller;—Robert T. Butler. Of Counsel: Edward J. Donnellon.
Negligence, Insurance, Family, Probate, Criminal, Real Estate Corporations, Taxation and Municipal Law. Trials.

See Professional Biographies, CINCINNATI, OHIO

Donnelly, Matthew Jon ...... '75 '01 C.1457 B.A. L.201 J.D. 1 West 4th Street, Suite 1800
Donnelly, Tina M. .... '— '00 C.150 B.A. L.1340 J.D. [Aronoff,R.&H.]
Donnett, David D., (BV) .... '49 '80 C.473 B.A. L.1340 J.D. 1212 Sycamore
Donoghue, Michelle L. .... '76 '01 C&L.383 B.S., J.D. [Freund,F.&A.]
Donovan, Corey A. .... '77 '02 C&L.150 B.A., J.D. [Vorys,S.S.&P.]
Donovan, Mary Jill H. .... '62 '01 C.999 B.A. L.150 J.D. [Donovan L.]

Donovan Law
910 Race Street, 45202
Telephone: 513-362-2190 Fax: 513-651-4937
Email: mjdonovan@irowco.com URL: http://www.donovan-law.com
Mary Jill H. Donovan; Michael P. McCafferty; Rene B. Heinrich (Not admitted in OH).
Criminal Defense, Driving While Intoxicated, Family Law, Divorce, Civil Litigation, Juvenile Law, Real Estate, Personal Injury, Auto Accidents.

See Professional Biographies, CINCINNATI, OHIO

Donson, G. Jack, Jr., (AV) .... '46 '71 C.608 B.A. L.150 J.D. [Taft,S.&H.]
Doppes, Michael J. .... '57 '82 C.1161 B.S. L.1340 J.D. 432 Walnut St.
Doppes, Paul J. .... '15 '54 C.973 B.A. L.1340 LL.B. 5889 Calmhaven Dr.
Dorger, Paul D., (BV) .... '65 '92 C.602 B.A. L.150 J.D. [Keating M.&K.]
Dornette, William Stuart, (AV) .... '51 '75 C.951 B.A. L.893 J.D. [Taft,S.&H.]
Dorr, James W., (AV) .... '30 '55 C.973 A.B. L.477 LL.B. 2638 Kipling Avenue
Dorsey, Edward S., (AV) .... '52 '77 C.276 A.B. L.128 J.D. [Lindhorst&D.]
Dorton, David Wesley .... '67 '01 C.886 M.S.M.E. L.201 J.D. [Wood,H.&E.]
Douglas, Flach, (BV) .... '31 '57 C&L.150 A.B., LL.B. [Drew&W.] (⊙Milford)
Dourson, Martha Culler, (BV) .... '52 '83 C.967 A.B. L.150 J.D. [M.C.Dourson]
Dourson, Martha C., Attorney at Law, (BV) ....4303 Kirby Ave.
Dowling, Kerry B. .... '64 '91 C.150 B.B.A. L.1340 J.D. Law Clk., Com. Pleas J.
Doyle, James R., Jr., (BV) ...... '47 '72 C.602 B.B.A. L.150 J.D. 4955 Western Hills Ave.
Drasnin, Lori S. .... '76 '01 C.477 B.A., B.A. L.245 J.D. [Dinsmore&S.]
Draugelis, Peter A. .... '73 '00 C.608 B.A. L.201 J.D. [Dinsmore&S.]
Draut, James W. .... '50 '77 C.679 B.S. L.208 J.D. Palm Beach Co.
Drennen, Mary Louise '51 '83 C.97 B.A. L.564 J.D.
(adm. in NY; not adm. in OH) Off. of Reg. Coun., Dept. of Vet. Affs.
Dressing, John W., (BV) '37 '70
C.150 B.S. L.1340 J.D. 1172 West Galbraith Road, Suite 211
Dressman, Marianne '70 '99
C.973 B.S. L.1161 J.D. Coun., Pats., The Procter & Gamble Co.
Drew, George Raymond, (AV) .... '18 '40 C.178 L.818 LL.B. [Drew&W.]

Drew & Ward, A Legal Professional Association, (AV)
24th Floor, Fourth & Vine Tower, One West Fourth Street, 45202
Telephone: 513-621-8210 Telecopier: 513-621-5444
Email: info@drewlaw.com URL: http://www.drewlaw.com
Richard H. Ward; James H. Coogan; Frederic L. Goeddel; Anthony G. Covatta, Jr.; Ruth I. Rounding (Certified Specialist, Estate Planning, Trust and Probate Law, Ohio State Bar Association); Richard J. Ruebel; Michael D. McNeil; Robert M. Smyth; Richard G. Ward; William C. Sulau; Mark W. Jordan; Sybil B. Mullin; James R. Schaefer (Certified Specialist in Residential Real Estate Law, Ohio State Bar Association). Of Counsel: George Raymond Drew; Flach Douglas.
General Practice. Civil Trial Litigation. Corporation, Employee Benefits, Family Law, Estate Planning, Franchise Law, Negligence, Probate, Real Estate, Tax, Zoning and Planning Law.
Representative Clients: AAA Allied Group, Inc.; American National Life Insurance Co.; Baxter Precast, Inc.; Cardiology Associates of Cincinnati, Inc.; Cheviot Savings Bank; Cincinnatus Savings & Loan, Co.; Cinfield Federal Credit Union; Fraternity Printing Co.; Gardner Publications, Inc.; G. C. Fuller Mfg. Co., Inc.

See Professional Biographies, CINCINNATI, OHIO

Dreyer, Kevin T., (BV) .... '61 '87 C.1161 B.A. L.1340 J.D. 11501 Northlake Drive
Droder, Eugene J., III .... '78 '04 C.473 B.A. L.201 J.D. [Frost B.T.]
Droder & Miller Co., L.P.A., (AV) ....125 West Central Parkway
Duesing, Jerome A. .... '30 '62 C.150 B.S. L.1340 J.D. 617 Vine St.
Dugan, Ellen R. '42 '75 C.813 M.A. L.16 J.D.
(adm. in IN; not adm. in OH)
Oper. V.P. & Asst. Gen. Coun., Federated Dept. Stores, Inc.
Dugan, Leah Austing ....'52 '78 C.1161 B.S. L.1340 J.D. Admin. Mag., Co. Juv. Ct.
Dumbacher, John P., (AV) .... '38 '63 C.973 B.S. L.150 J.D. 9157 Montgomery Rd.
Duncan, Julie Lippert .... '64 '91 C.929 B.S. L.383 J.D. 1034 Paxton Ave.‡
Dunn, Dolores A. .... '41 '75 C.473 B.A. L.1340 J.D. Anderson Publishing Co.
Dunn, Martiné R., (AV) .... '59 '85 C.597 B.S. L.477 J.D. [Baker&H.]
Dupuis, C. Thomas, (AV) .... '38 '68 C.390 B.S. L.150 J.D. [Rendigs,F.K.&D.]
Dupuis, Fay Danner, (AV) .... '44 '69 C.228 B.A. L.150 J.D. City Solr.
Duran, Samuel M., (AV) .... '56 '84 C.477 B.A. L.608 J.D. [Taft,S.&H.]
Durben, Annette M. .... '70 '99 C.967 B.A. L.150 J.D. U.S. Bankruptcy Ct., S.D. OH
Durham, Corbett Q., Jr. .... '45 '76 C.150 B.A. L.1340 J.D. Chicago Title Ins. Co.
Durham, Leona L., (BV) .... '30 '77 C.942 B.A. L.352 J.D. 117-121 E. Court St.

Durham, M. Freeman, (AV) '58 '83 C.880 B.A. L.597 J.D.
2725 Johnstone Place, 45206-1822
Telephone: 513-651-4900
Email: freeman.durham@usa.net
Trusts and Estates, Employee Benefits, Taxation.

See Professional Biographies, CINCINNATI, OHIO

Durkee & Uhle, (BV) .... 9000 Plainfield Rd. (⊙Batavia)
Durkin, Cynthia Lowe, (BVⓉ) '68 '93
C&L.383 B.A., J.D. Coun., Litig., GE Aviation Services, Inc.
Dusing, Benjamin G. .... '75 '02 C.276 B.S. L.383 J.D. [Baker&H.]
Dusterberg, Richard B., (BV) '38 '66
C.207 B.A. L.150 J.D. 9157 Montgomery Road, Suite 203
Dutro, Daniel G., Jr. .... '66 '94 C.976 B.A. L.150 J.D. [Keating M.&K.]
Dwight, George, II .... '58 '85 C.228 B.A. L.178 J.D. Sr. Coun., Cinergy Servs.
Dziech, Robert W., II .... '70 '96 C.967 B.A. L.151 J.D. Pros. Off.
Eagen, Michael D., (AV) .... '46 '74 C.321 A.B. L.477 J.D. [Dinsmore&S.]
Earl, Jack J., (AV) .... '31 '61 C.679 B.S. L.1119 LL.B. 7618 Carriage Ln.‡
Eaton, Shana N. .... '77 '04 C.347 B.A. L.276 J.D. [Dinsmore&S.]
Eberly, Stephen S., (AV) .... '45 '73 C.966 B.B.A. L.477 J.D. [Vorys,S.S.&P.]
Ebling, Louis K. .... '61 '87 C.20 A.B. L.477 J.D. [Greenebaum D.&M.] (Pat.)

Ebner & Riker, L.L.P., (AV)
1900 Kroger Building, 1014 Vine Street, 45202-1141
Telephone: 513-621-2888; 800-699-6446 Fax: 513-345-4449 URL: http://www.erlaw.org
URL: http://www.lawyers.com/ebner&riker
J. Timothy Riker;—Sharon M. J. Shartzer.
Civil Litigation, Personal Injury, Small Business and Corporate Law, Insurance Defense, Probate, Trusts and Estates, Domestic Relations.

See Professional Biographies, CINCINNATI, OHIO

Eby, C. Richard .... '41 '68 C.150 B.S. L.1340 J.D. [Wood,H.&E.] (See Pat. Sect.)
Eby, Gary Moore, (AV) .... '51 '76 C&L.150 B.A., J.D. [Manley B.]
Eccles, Pamela J. .... '66 '91 C&L.150 B.A., J.D. 8050 Hosbrook Rd.
Eckert, Charles A., II, (AV) .... '32 '55 C&L.150 A.B., J.D. [Eckert,E.&E.]
Eckert, John C. .... '65 '92 C.150 B.B.A. L.607 J.D. [Eckert,E.&E.]
Eckert, Roger C. .... '43 '91 C.610 B.S.J. L.150 J.D. 121 W. 9th St.
Eckert, Eckert & Eckert .... Suite 200, 3723 Glenmore Avenue
Eckner, Shannon F. .... '— '03 C&L.150 B.A., J.D. [P.G.Bossin]
Eckstein, Timothy A. '72 '02 C.1070 B.S.E.E. L.150 J.D.
Coun., Procter & Gamble Co.
Eddy, Marilyn M. .... '53 '88 C.610 B.S. L.378 J.D. 431 Ohio Pike
Eder, William H., Jr., (BV) .... '38 '63 C&L.150 B.A., J.D. [Wood&L.]
Edler, Robert W., (AVⓉ) '36 '62 C.210 B.A. L.813 LL.B.
(adm. in IL; not adm. in OH) [J.A.Donenfeld] (⊙Chgo., IL)

Edmiston, James P., (AV) '45 '75 C.1024 B.A. L.1340 J.D.
119 E. Court Street, Suite 412
Edmiston, Robert Gray, (AV) '54 '81 C&L.383 B.A., J.D. [C Cors&B.]
Edwards, Ryan C. '77 '02 C&L.383 B.A., J.D. [A Taft,S.&H.]
Edwards, Tawanda J. '72 '00 C&L.150 B.A., J.D. [A Katz,G.&N.]
Egan, Shannon O'Connell '71 '98 C.421 B.A. L.420 J.D.
(adm. in KY; not adm. in OH) [A Lerner,S.&R.]

Eichel & Krone Co., L.P.A., (AV)
302 Gwynne Building, 602 Main Street, 45202
Telephone: 513-241-1234 Fax: 513-241-2731
Email: bak@baklaw.com
Lawrence E. Eichel (1908-1981); Paul W. Krone (1925-1995); Bruce A. Krone.
Trusts and Estates, Wills, Probate, Real Estate, Taxation, Business Law, Charitable Trusts and Foundations, Private Foundations and Tax-Exempt Organizations.
References: Star Bank N.A.; PNC Bank N.A.
See Professional Biographies, CINCINNATI, OHIO

Eichner, Claire Seltz '65 '90 C.910 B.A. L.597 J.D. [A Frost B.T.]
Eidlin, Michael B. '46 '92 C.259 B.S. L.1051 J.D. V.P., Parsons Brinckerhoff
Eifrig, Eric W. '56 '03 C.207 B.A. L.150 J.D. 8070 Beechmont Ave.
Eiler, Janis E. '55 '97 C.432 B.A. L.1340 J.D. 2752 Erie Ave.‡
Eilers, John W., Jr., (AV) '39 '67 C.434 B.A. L.1340 J.D. [Wood&L.]

Einspanier, Anne
(See Anne Einspanier Krehbiel, Lebanon, Ohio)

Eisele, Thomas D. '48 '73 C.966 B.A. L.309 J.D.
(adm. in IL; not adm. in OH) Prof. of Law, Univ. of Cincinnati
Eiselein, Albert C., Jr., (AV) '30 '54 C&L.150 B.B.A., LL.B. 5 W. 4th St.
Eling, Kenneth J. '64 '93 C.973 B.S. L.151 J.D. [A Barrett&W.]

Elk & Elk Co., L.P.A.
(See Cleveland)

Elleman, Lawrence R., (AV) '40 '66 C&L.608 B.S., J.D. [Dinsmore&S.]
Ellerman, Paige L. '74 '99 C.383 B.A. L.1340 J.D. [A Taft,S.&H.]
Elliff, Brian E. '63 '90 C.208 B.S. L.339 J.D. 7919 Asbury Hills Dr.
Ellington, Sarah B. '77 '03 C.472 B.A. L.150 J.D. [A Wood&L.]
Elliott, Lori K. '59 '84 C&L.665 B.A., J.D. 901 Elm St.
Ellis, Lisa M. '66 '91 C.473 B.A. L.150 J.D. [A Katz,G.&N.]
Ellis, Ralph F. '25 '59 C&L.150 Ph.B., LL.B. 6285 Kenwood Hills Dr.‡
Ellis, William R., (AV) '49 '75 C.201 B.A. L.229 J.D. [Wood&L.]
Elsener, Mark E., (AV) '54 '80 C&L.150 B.A., J.D. [Porter W.M.&A.]
Elswick, Christopher '— '02 C.383 B.S. L.608 J.D. [A Thompson H.] (Pat.)
Emden, Milton M. '07 '33 12 Towne Commons Way
Emmert, Andrew C., (AV) '59 '88 C&L.150 B.B.A., J.D. [Cors&B.]
Emmert, Marianne Scott, (AV) '59 '84 C&L.150 B.A., J.D. 2936 Alpine Ter.
Emmrich, Joseph Lawrence '47 '72
C.201 B.A. L.608 J.D. Sr. Trial Coun., Hamilton Co. Pub. Def. Off.
Engeman, William K., (AV) '39 '65 C.103 A.B. L.893 LL.B. [Taft,S.&H.] ‡

Engle, John H., Attorney and Counselor at Law, (BV) '43 '68 C&L.188 A.B., J.D.
Federated Building Suite 1800, 7 West 7th Street, 45202
Telephone: 513-241-7332; 513-241-0572 Fax: 513-621-5410
URL: http://www.jenglelaw.com
Insurance Defense, Arson, Insurance Fraud, Personal Injury, Subrogation, Construction, Casualty Insurance and Commercial Litigation.
See Professional Biographies, CINCINNATI, OHIO

Englender, Saml. '14 '42 L.150 2 Belshaw Pl.
Englert, James J., (AV) '53 '90 C.93 B.A. L.150 J.D. [Rendigs,F.K.&D.]
Ennis, William J., (AV) '35 '66 C.973 B.S. L.1340 J.D. [Ennis,R.&F.] ⊙
Ennis, Roberts and Fischer, A Legal Professional Association, (AV)
121 W. 9th St. (⊙Harrison)
Ent, Robert W., (Co., L.P.A.) '29 '58 C&L.150 B.A., LL.B. 944 Pavilion St.
Epling, John A. '31 '57 C.823 B.A. L.608 J.D. 202 Williamsburg Rd.
Eppstein, Steven D., Law Office of, (AV) '49 '74
C.880 B.A. L.836 J.D. 4526 Montgomery Rd.
Erhart, Sue A. '71 '96 C.973 B.S. L.150 J.D. [Keating M.&K.]
Erickson, Richard J., (AV) '46 '71 C.207 B.A. L.880 J.D. [Frost B.T.]
Erickson, Robert M. '49 '74 C.611 B.A. L.880 J.D. 38 Fountain Sq. Plz.
Ernst, Matthew T. '68 '96 C.150 B.B.A. L.851 J.D. [M.Ernst]
Ernst, Tina I. '60 '91 C.1208 B.A. L.1340 J.D. 800 Broadway
Ernst, Matthew 114 E. 8th St.
Erny, Frederick M. '61 '87 C.665 B.A. L.229 J.D. [Dinsmore&S.]
Erven, Thomas P., (BV) '57 '83 C.473 B.A. L.608 J.D. [Young&A.]
Espohl, Frank E. '26 '52 C.973 L.1340 LL.B. 1137 Meredith Circle‡
Espohl, Frank Eric '65 '96 C.930 B.S. L.150 J.D. 1241 Nagel Rd.
Espohl, Virginia B. '26 '54 L.1340 J.D. 1137 Meredith Dr.‡
Essig, Ellen, (AV) '50 '86 C.608 B.S. L.1340 J.D. [Katz,G.&N.]
Estenfelder, Regina L. '65 '94 C.1161 B.S. L.150 J.D. Summer Hill, Inc.
Evans, David N. '54 '79 C.383 B.B.A. L.851 J.D. Eagle-Picher Industries, Inc.
Evans, Jack G., (AV) '08 '34 C&L.608 B.S., J.D. 7320 Tangleridge Ln.‡
Evans, James E., (AV) '46 '72 C.475 B.A. L.608 J.D.
Dir., Sr. V.P. & Gen. Coun., Amer. Premier Underwriting, Inc. & Amer. Fin. Corp., Inc.
Evans, Lisa May '63 '94 C.150 B.A. L.1340 J.D. [C Thompson H.]
Evans, Marquette D., (BV) '54 '77 C&L.608 B.A., J.D. [Garvin,L.H.&E.]
Evans, Richard H., (AV) '33 '58 C.674 A.B. L.309 LL.B. 2700 Carew Tower (Pat.)
Evans, Ross M., (AV) '60 '86 C&L.150 B.A., J.D. [Katz,G.&N.]
Evans, Thomas M., (AV) '60 '86 C.174 B.A. L.150 J.D. [Rendigs,F.K.&D.]
Eynon, Ernest A., II, (BV) '44 '69 C.951 B.A. L.150 J.D. 312 Walnut St.
Eyrich, David J., (AV) '46 '73 C.611 B.A. L.150 J.D. [Statman,H.S.&E.]
Eyrich, George C., (AV) '18 '47 C.611 A.B. L.150 LL.B. 2811 Dunaway Avenue‡
Ezenagu, Samuel O., Law Office of '— '98
C.1208 B.S. L.117 J.D. 917 Main Street, Suite 200
Faaborg, Karen Kramer '41 '84 C.383 B.A. L.150 J.D. Univ. of Cincinnati
Fabe, George, (BV) '21 '81 C&L.150 B.A., J.D. [C Manley B.]
Fagel, Barry F., (BV) '65 '91 C.973 B.S. L.150 J.D. [Lindhorst&D.]
Fagel, Stephen J., (BV) '54 '80 C.608 B.A. L.150 J.D.
Asst. City Solr., City of Cincinnati Dept. of Law
Fairweather, Neil '68 '95 C.303 B.A. L.383 J.D. [A Graydon H.&R.] ⊙
Fairweather, Sarah B. '— '02 C.973 B.A. L.150 J.D. [A Vorys,S.S.&P.]

Faller, Raymond T., (AV) '50 '76 C.973 A.B. L.150 J.D.
The Kroger Building, 1014 Vine Street, Suite 1450, 45202-1116
Telephone: 513-579-1266
Email: rfall@aol.com URL: http://www.rtfaller.com
Criminal Law, DUI, Felonies, Misdemeanors, Homicide, Theft, Drug Crimes, Driving Suspensions, Domestic Violence, Assault, Drug Offenses.
See Professional Biographies, CINCINNATI, OHIO

Faller, Susan Grogan, (AV) '50 '75 C.150 B.A. L.477 J.D. [Frost B.T.]

Falter, Karen K. '68 '96 C.473 B.A. L.365 J.D. Asst. Pros. Atty.
Fannin, Donald E., (BV) '47 '73 C.472 B.S. L.1340 J.D. 2647 Pancoast Ave.
Farley, Bobbie W. '44 '78 C.437 A.B. L.923 J.D. 6075 Redbird Hollow Lane
Farley, Katrina Z., (BV) '63 '92 C.63 B.S. L.1340 J.D. [Chalfie&F.]
Farrell, Thomas M. '40 '72 C.150 B.S.M.E. L.1340 J.D.
Chf. Intell. Prop. Coun., Cincinnati Machine/A Unova Co. (Pat.)
Farrell, William I., (AV) '63 '89 C.473 B.A. L.150 J.D. [Finkelmeier&F.]
Farrish, Kelly, (BV) '46 '79 C.150 B.B.A. L.1340 J.D. [K.Farrish]
Farrish, Kelly, L.P.A., (BV) 601 Main Street, Third Floor
Fath, Harry J., Jr. '41 '69 C.602 B.B.A. L.150 J.D. 255 E. 5th St.‡
Fatora, Jerome F. '25 '63 C.321 A.B. L.602 J.D. Staff Hearing Off., Indus. Comm.
Faulkner, Laura R. '74 '99 C.473 B.A. L.201 J.D. [A Weltman,W.&R.]

Faulkner & Tepe, LLP, (AV)
2200 Fourth and Vine Tower, 1 West Fourth Street, 45202-3606
Telephone: 513-421-7500 Fax: 513-421-7502
URL: http://www.faulknertepe.com
Members of Firm: David P. Faulkner (1929-1999); R. Edward Tepe (1939-2003); John C. Scott; A. Norman Aubin; Joseph T. Mordino. Associate: Ann E. Walter.
Insurance Defense, General Practice, Bankruptcy, Insolvency, Negligence, Probate, Litigation, Complex Litigation, Construction and Surety Law and Criminal Defense.
Reference: Fifth Third Bank.
See Professional Biographies, CINCINNATI, OHIO

Fausz, Daniel E. '61 '90 C.597 B.A. L.569 J.D. [Taft,S.&H.]
Favret, Bruce A., (BV) '50 '77 C.973 B.S. L.1340 J.D. 2631 Erie Avenue
Fayette, Thibault '72 '00 Of Coun., The Proctor & Gamble Co.
Fazio, Cynthia A., (BV) '59 '88 C&L.150 B.B.A., J.D. Co. Pros. Atty.
Fealko, Jill L. '75 '00 C.532 B.A. L.124 J.D. [A Lerner,S.&R.]
Feazell, Kevin R., (BV) '60 '92 C&L.150 B.A., J.D. [Cors&B.]
Fecher, William B., (BV) '62 '87 C.108 B.A. L.201 J.D. [A Statman,H.S.&E.]
Feichtner, Douglas J. '77 '02 C.473 B.A. L.150 J.D. [A Dinsmore&S.]
Fein, Ronald J. '44 '75 C.999 B.A. L.1340 J.D. Mag.
Feldhaus, Joseph H., (AV) '51 '79 C.150 B.S. L.809 J.D. [Beckman W.S.]
Feldkamp, Joseph F., Jr., (BV) '40 '66 C.973 B.S. L.150 J.D. 14 Garfield Pl.
Feldmann, Donald Joseph '49 '75 C.602 B.A. L.1340 J.D. 8044 Montgomery Road
Feldmann, Steven M. '66 '89 C.1118 B.A. L.383 J.D.
Corp. Atty., Student Loan Funding Resources, Inc.
Feldmeier, John P. '66 '91 C.737 B.A. L.117 J.D. [A Sirkin P.&S.]
Feldmeier, Melissa M. '72 '97
C.473 B.A. L.150 J.D. Cinergy Services (Legal Department)
Felix, Jeffrey A., (BV) '61 '91 C.384 B.A. L.1340 J.D. [Lane,F.&R.]
Fellerhoff, Matthew W., (BV) '66 '94 C.473 B.A. L.1340 J.D. [Manley B.]
Felson, Cynthia C., (BV) '55 '93 C.150 B.A. L.151 J.D. [A Taft,S.&H.]
Felson, Edward J., (BV) '56 '89 C.999 B.A.A. L.150 J.D. 36 E. Seventh St., Ste. 1650

Felson, Stephen R., (BV) '41 '66 C.309 B.A. L.150 J.D.
617 Vine Street, Suite 1401, 45202
Telephone: 513-721-4900 Fax: 513-639-7011
Email: steveF8953@aol.com URL: http://www.cincylawyer.com
Consumer Class Actions, Appellate Practice, Civil Litigation, Employment Law, Credit Fraud, Auto Fraud, Consumer Fraud, Civil Rights, Lemon Law, Landlord Tenant Law, Medical Malpractice, Personal Injury.
See Professional Biographies, CINCINNATI, OHIO

Fenton, Bruce S. '46 '70 C.976 B.A. L.309 J.D.
(adm. in NY; not adm. in OH) [C J.A.Donenfeld]
Fenton, John H. '70 '95 C.309 A.B. L.228 J.D. Fin. Planner, Lincoln Financial Advisors
Ferestad, Mark Allen '65 '92 C.506 B.A. L.285 J.D. [M.Ferestad]
Ferestad, Mark, Law Firm 30 Garfield Pl., Ste. 430
Ferrell, Richard L., III '69 '94 C.316 B.A. L.8 J.D. [A Taft,S.&H.]
Ferris, James K., (BV) '60 '85 C.117 B.A. L.150 J.D. 6124 Corbly Rd.
Fershtman, Alan S. '66 '94 C.473 B.S. L.150 J.D. [Keating M.&K.]
Fettner, Saul A. '40 '65 C&L.150 A.B., J.D. 10 W. 9th St.
Feuer, Sherri L. '56 '81 C.473 B.A. L.150 J.D. I.R.S.
Ficke, Gregory C. '52 '90 C.473 B.S. L.1340 J.D. 139 E. 4th St.
Fiddes, Richard C. '45 '70 C.388 B.A. L.597 J.D.
Oper. V.P. & Asst. Gen. Coun., Federated Dept. Stores, Inc.
Fidler, Edward, (BV) '13 '37 C&L.150 A.B., LL.B. 830 Main St.
Field, Eileen K., (AV) '56 '82 C&L.150 B.A., J.D. 36 East Fourth Street
Filiatraut, Renee S., (AV) '63 '88 C.477 A.B. L.1044 J.D. [Thompson H.]
Finch, Linda B. '55 '80 C.273 B.A. L.150 J.D. Nat. Labor Relations Board
Fingerman, Albert R., (AV) '20 '48 C&L.150 LL.B. [C M.F.Gehrig] ‡
Fink, Jerold A., (AV) '41 '66 C&L.228 A.B., LL.B. [Taft,S.&H.]
Finkbeiner, Mae Louise '25 '51 C.787 B.A. L.150 LL.B. 7669 Thompson Rd.
Finke, Harry J., IV, (AV) '55 '82 C.103 A.B. L.228 J.D. [Graydon H.&R.]
Finke, Nicholas D. '41 '80 C.93 A.B. L.309 J.D. P.O. Box 210142
Finkelmeier, Louis J., (AV) '43 '68 C&L.150 B.A., J.D. [Finkelmeier&F.]

Finkelmeier & Farrell, (AV)
36 East Seventh Street, Suite 1660, 45202-4461
Telephone: 513-621-9921 Fax: 513-621-9923
Email: finkelmeier@fuse.net
Louis J. Finkelmeier (Board Certified Specialist, Ohio Workers' Compensation Law, Ohio State Bar Association); William I. Farrell (Board Certified Specialist, Ohio Workers' Compensation Law, Ohio State Bar Association).
Workers Compensation, Sports Injury and Social Security Disability.
See Professional Biographies, CINCINNATI, OHIO

Finn, Janet C., (BV) '51 '86 C.276 B.A. L.150 J.D. 560 Evanswood Pl.
Finney, Christopher P., (BV) '61 '87 C.973 A.B. L.1340 J.D. 2623 Erie Ave., Ste. 8804
Finnigan, John J., Jr., (AV) '55 '79 C&L.150 B.A., J.D. Sr. Coun., Cinergy Corp.
Finocharo, John J. '58 '84 C.473 B.A. L.608 J.D.
Sr. Coun., The Procter & Gamble Co.
Finucane, Michael E. '58 '88 C.1074 B.S. L.150 J.D. [A Reisenfeld&Assoc.]
Fiocca, John A., Jr., (BV) '50 '75 C.473 B.A. L.930 J.D. [A Smith,R.&S.]
Fiorenza, Robert O. '56 '98 C.624 B.S. L.1340 J.D. 10490 Adventure Lane
Fischer, J. Michael, (AV) '44 '70 C.321 A.B. L.150 J.D. [Ennis,R.&F.]
Fischer, John W., II, (AV) '56 '81 C.150 B.B.A. L.930 J.D. [Denlinger,R.&G.]
Fischer, John W., III, (AV) '43 '68 C&L.477 B.A., J.D. [Peck,S.&W.]
Fischer, Joseph M. '54 '80
C.321 B.A. L.150 J.D. Asst. Coun., The Ohio Natl. Life Ins. Co.
Fischer, Patrick F., (AV) '57 '83 C.309 A.B. L.1565 J.D. [Keating M.&K.]
Fischer, Susan Kelly '52 '82 C.818 B.S. L.150 J.D. Law Clk., U.S. Bkruptcy. J.
Fischer, Timothy A., Law Office of, (AV) '44 '71 C.276 A.B. L.150 J.D.
3507 Aultwoods
Fish, B. David '45 '72 C.150 B.B.A. L.1340 J.D. 119 E. Court St. #510
Fitch, Mark R. '58 '87 C&L.150 B.A., J.D. [Fitch&S.]
Fitch & Spegal 3752 Edwards Road, Suite 1
FitzGerald, Timothy J. '63 '91 C.150 B.B.A. L.1340 J.D. 5102 Carthage Ave.
Fitzgerald, William F., (BV) '35 '62 C&L.150 B.A., LL.B. [Burke,F.B.&B.]

Fitzpatrick, Matthew P. '69 '96
C.893 B.S.N.E. L.446 J.D. Coun., The Procter & Gamble Co.
Fitzsimmons, Becky Barlow ... '68 '00 C.928 B.A. L.446 J.D. [Dinsmore&S.]
Fjord, Hilliard J., (AV) ... '24 '50 C.210 A.B. L.477 J.D. 6725 Wooster Pike‡
Flacks, Kenneth B., (AV) ... '48 '73 C.473 B.S. L.150 J.D. [Rendigs,F.K.&D.]
Flagel, Todd J. ... '70 '96 C.473 B.S. L.201 J.D. One Financial Way
Flamm, Justin D. ... '74 '99 C.473 B.A. L.902 J.D. [Taft,S.&H.]
Flanagan, John A., (AV) ... '42 '68 C.352 B.A. L.276 J.D. [Graydon H.&R.]
Flax, William E., (BV) ... '34 '59 C.604 A.B. L.150 LL.B. 414 Walnut St.
Fledderman, Anne M. ... '— '86 C.383 B.A. L.1340 J.D. 1411 Sycamore St.
Flege, John Blain, Jr. ... '29 '93 C.383 B.S. L.150 J.D. 4 Granoin Ln.
Fleischer, Neil Ian ... '75 '00 C.319 A.B. L.117 J.D. [R.I.Fleischer&Assoc.]

Fleischer, Richard I., & Associates, (AV) '44 '71 C.150 B.B.S. L.383 J.D.
917 Main Street, 45202
Telephone: 513-977-4209 Fax: 513-977-4238
Email: fleischer@immigrate2usa.com URL: http://www.immigrate2usa.com
Associate: Neil Ian Fleischer.
Practice Limited to Immigration Law.

See Professional Biographies, CINCINNATI, OHIO

Flemer, Lawrence A., (AV) ... '51 '80 C.150 B.A. L.1340 J.D. [Statman,H.S.&E.]
Fleming, M. Michele, (AV) ... '53 '79 C.679 B.S. L.150 J.D. [Barrett&W.]
Fleming, Rose Ann, (BV) ... '32 '89 C.523 B.A. L.1340 J.D. [R.A.Fleming]
Fleming, Rose Ann, Professoinal Corporation, (BV) ... 3855 Ledgewood Dr.
Flessa, John H., (BV) ... '57 '82 C&L.150 B.A., J.D. 114 E. 8th St.
Fletcher, Michael C., (AV) ... '44 '69 C.473 B.A. L.150 J.D. [Griffin -F.]
Floth, Kathleen Annear ... '76 '01 C.421 B.S. L.150 J.D. Natl. Labor Rel. Brd.
Flottman, Anne B. ... '57 '01 C.383 B.A. L.150 J.D. 2345 Ashland Avenue
Flowers, Laura J. ... '70 '96 C.108 B.A. L.221 J.D. Trust Corp. Coun., Alderwoods Group
Flowers, Michael L. '52 '78 C&L.383 B.S.B.E., J.D.
(adm. in KY; not adm. in OH) V.P. & Secy., Amer. Modern Home Ins. Co. (⊙Amelia)
Flynn, John M., (AV) ... '42 '68 C.602 B.A. L.930 J.D. Kroger Company, The
Flynn, Kevin R., (AV) ... '60 '87 C&L.150 B.A., J.D. [Griffin -F.]
Flynn, Thomas J. ... '50 '76 C.150 B.A. L.1202 J.D. Chf. Mag., Co. Juv. Ct.
Flynn, Thomas W., (AV) '33 '63 C.790 B.S. L.273 J.D.
[Wood,H.&E.] (See Pat. Sect.)
Flynn, William K., (AV) ... '60 '85 C.473 B.A. L.150 J.D. [Strauss&T.]
Fogelman, Adam R. ... '— '01 C.150 B.A. L.851 J.D. [Lerner,S.&R.]
Foley, Michael P., (BV) ... '66 '93 C.973 B.A. L.607 J.D. [Rendigs,F.K.&D.]
Foote, Carl F. ... '49 '75 C.381 B.A. L.150 J.D. Assoc. Prof., Univ. of Cincinnati
Forbes, Jeffrey D. ... '72 '01 C.610 B.S.Ed. L.150 J.D. [Wood&L.]
Ford, Ashley L. ... '39 '63 C.674 A.B. L.976 LL.B. P.O. Box 599‡
Ford, William W., III, (AV) ... '59 '85 C.118 B.A. L.228 J.D. Sr. Atty., Convergys Corp.
Forman, Keith Christopher ... '69 '01 C.973 B.S. L.201 J.D. Pros. Off.
Forney, Ferdinand A., (BV) ... '28 '54 C.973 B.S. L.150 LL.B. 7725 Hartfield Pl.
Fornshell, David P. ... '73 '99 C.610 B.B.A. L.1117 J.D. [Dinsmore&S.]
Foster, Philip Ashton ... '53 '80 C.303 B.A. L.1340 J.D. Fifth 3rd Bank
Foster, Robin W., Attorney at Law ... '66 '00 C.473 B.A. L.1340 J.D. 3009 Fairfield Ave.
Foster, Thomas C., (BV) ... '31 '60 C&L.150 B.B.A., LL.B. [Rich,P.W.F.&M.]
Foster, Ty L., (BV) ... '56 '81 C.608 B.A. L.150 J.D. 830 Main St., Suite 1105
Foster, Walter N. ... '16 '60 C.150 B.S. L.1340 J.D. 2778 Eugenie Lane‡
Foureman, William C. '49 '84
C.855 B.A. L.477 J.D. Sr. Coun., The Procter & Gamble Co.
Fowler, Byron T. '51 '82
C.1070 B.S. L.893 J.D. Assoc. Coun., Federated Dept. Stores, Inc.
Fox, Bernard C., (AV) ... '22 '50 C.973 Ph.B. L.1340 LL.B. [Fox&F.]
Fox, Bernard C., Jr., (BV) ... '48 '78 C.150 B.S. L.1340 J.D. [Fox&F.]
Fox, Peter M., (BV) ... '55 '85 C.116 B.A. L.150 J.D. [Kircher,R.&W.]
Fox, Randy F. ... '57 '87 C&L.150 B.S., J.D. 1513 Central Trust Twr.
Fox, Romi T. ... '53 '86 C.381 B.A. L.8 J.D. [Lerner,S.&R.]
Fox & Fox, A Legal Professional Association, (AV) ... 2407 Ashland Ave.
Franckewitz, Stephanie P. ... '65 '01 C.923 B.S., B.A. L.1161 J.D. [Triona C.&L.]
Frank, Jerome, (AV) ... '25 '50 C&L.150 LL.B. [Crowley,F.&A.] ‡
Frank, Kevin K. ... '70 '97 C.112 B.A. L.767 J.D. [Wood&L.]
Frank, William Nelson ... '53 '78 C.97 B.S. L.851 J.D. [Frank,W.N.]
Frank, William N. ... 3050 Harrison Ave.
Franke, Carolyn Mussio, (BV) ... '58 '83 C.473 B.A. L.910 J.D. 3411 Michigan Ave.
Franke, Gary F., (BV) ... '60 '85 C.973 B.S.B.A. L.200 J.D. [G.F.Franke]
Franke, Hal F. ... '28 '53 C.973 L.150 LL.B. [Cors&B.]
Franke, Gary F., Co., LPA, (BV) ... 120 East Fourth Street, Suite 560
Frankel, Edward M. '54 '77 C.659 B.S.Econ. L.477 J.D.
Sr. V.P., Chf. Admin. Offr., Secy. & Treas., Standard Textile Co., Inc.
Frankel, Jan M., (AV) ... '51 '78 C.1322 B.A. L.1340 J.D. [Wood&L.]
Frankel, Reneé S., (BV) ... '42 '84 C.608 B.S. L.150 J.D. [Goodman&G.]
Franklin, David E. ... '62 '95 C.378 B.S.E.E. L.734 J.D. [Frost B.T.] (See Pat. Sect.)
Frankowski, Norman J., II ... '68 '93 C.851 B.S. L.608 J.D. One Financial Way
Frantz, Robert W. '50 '77 C&L.705 B.S., J.D.
(adm. in NJ; not adm. in OH) Gen. Mgr. & Coun., GE Engine Services
Franz, Paul A., (AV) '51 '81 C.150 B.A. L.1068 J.D.
Assoc. Gen. Coun., The Procter & Gamble Co.
Frasca, James J. ... '52 '80 C&L.608 B.A., J.D. 801-B W. 8th St.
Freedman, William M., (AV) ... '46 '73 C.118 B.A. L.309 J.D. [Dinsmore&S.]
Freemal, Beth ... '68 '97 C.597 B.S. L.146 J.D. [Thompson H.]
Freeman, Harold S., (AV) ... '33 '60 C.143 B.S. L.150 LL.B. [Dinsmore&S.]
Freeman, Herbert E., (AV) ... '47 '73 C.973 B.S. L.1340 J.D. 114 E. 8th St.
Freeman, John A. ... '43 '74 C&L.851 B.A., J.D. U.S. Treasury
Frei, Donald F., (AV) ... '38 '65 C.188 B.M.E. L.276 J.D. [Wood,H.&E.] (See Pat. Sect.)
Freiberg, Albert M. ... '10 '34 C&L.309 A.B., J.D. 7100 E. Aracoma Dr.‡
Freking, Randolph H., (AV) ... '57 '82 C.201 B.A. L.608 J.D. [Freking&B.]
Freking & Betz, (AV) ... 215 E. Ninth St., 5th Fl.
French, Eric S. ... '55 '99 C.1118 B.B.A. L.1340 J.D. Coun., Cinergy Servs.
French, Gregory S., Law Offices of '51 '76
C&L.879 B.A., J.D. 1244 Paddock Hills Avenue

Freund, Freeze & Arnold, A Legal Professional Association, (AV)
Fourth and Walnut Centre, 105 East Fourth Street Suite 1400, 45202-4006 ⊙
Telephone: 513-665-3500 Telecopier: 513-665-3503
Email: ffalawci@ffalaw.com URL: http://www.ffalaw.com
Thomas B. Bruns; Mark A. MacDonald; Dee Sheriff-MacDonald; Timothy B. Schenkel; Jennifer K. Nordstrom; John J. Garvey, III; David A. Shearer, Jr.;—Judd R. Uhl; David W. Zahniser; James M. Cawood, III; Michelle L. Donoghue; Kelly A. Armstrong; Ilona I. Katrus; Poul H. Lemasters; Jason A. Mosbaugh; Ruth T. Kelly.
Civil Litigation including Commercial Litigation, Employment Defense, Professional Malpractice Defense, Employer Intentional Torts, Construction Litigation, Civil Rights Defense, Local Government Defense, Nursing Home Defense, Environmental Litigation and Insurance Defense.
Local Counsel for: Auto-Owners Insurance Co.; CNA Insurance Co.; Crum and Foster Underwriters; Employers Reinsurance Corp.; Farmers Insurance Group; Lloyds of London; Medical Protective; Midwestern Group; State Farm Mutual Automobile Insurance Co.

(This Listing Continued)

Freund, Freeze & Arnold, A Legal Professional Association (Continued)

Special Trial Counsel for: City of Dayton.
Dayton, Ohio Office: One Dayton Centre, One South Main Street, Suite 1800, 45402-2017. Telephone: 937-222-2424. Telecopier: 937-222-5369. Email: ffalawda@ffalaw.com.
Columbus, Ohio Office: Capitol Square Office Building, 65 East State Street, Suite 800, 43215. Telephone: 614-827-7300. Telecopier: 614-827-7303. Email: ffalawco@ffalaw.com.
Covington, Kentucky Office Suite: RiverCenter, 50 East RiverCenter Boulevard, Suite 408, 41011. Telephone: 859-292-2088. Telecopier: 859-292-2514. Email: ffalawky@ffalaw.

See Professional Biographies, CINCINNATI, OHIO

Friedman, Benjamin S. '74 '01
C.1349 B.A. L.339 J.D. 270 Northland Boulevard, Suite 216
Friedman, Jerry M. ... '26 '51 C.608 L.150 LL.B. 3728 Mantell Ave.‡
Friedman, Penny, (AV) ... '51 '77 C&L.477 A.B., J.D. Bartlett & Co.
Friedman, Tedd H. ... '67 '92 C.966 B.S. L.150 J.D. [Katz,T.B.&H.]
Friedmann, Roger E., (BV) '51 '76 C&L.150 B.A., J.D.
Asst. Pros. Atty. [Loeb,V.H.&F.]
Frink, Neal A. ... '63 '99 C.119 B.S. L.1161 J.D. [Dinsmore&S.] (See Pat. Sect.)
Friskney, Stephen H. '52 '80 C.150 B.S.M.E. L.1340 J.D.
I.P. Coun., GE Aircraft Engines (GEAE Legal Operation) (Pat.)
Fritz, Matthew J. '55 '79 C.973 A.B. L.383 J.D.
(adm. in KY; not adm. in OH) Reg. Coun., I.R.S.
Froncek, Theodore J., (BV) ... '55 '80 C.473 B.A. L.150 J.D. 1208 Sycamore St.
Fronduti, John S. ... '72 '98 C.602 B.B.A. L.150 J.D. [Keating M.&K.]
Frooman, Thomas E., (AV) ... '67 '94 C&L.151 B.S.B.A., J.D. Cintas Corp.

Frost Brown Todd LLC, (AV)
2200 PNC Center, 201 East Fifth Street, 45202-4182 ⊙
Telephone: 513-651-6800 Telecopier: 513-651-6981
Email: info@fbtlaw.com URL: http://www.frostbrowntodd.com
Members: Edwin R. Acheson, Jr.; Deborah S. Adams; Stephen R. Albainy-Jenei; Thomas D. Anthony; John H. Appel; G. Randall Ayers; Gerald L. Baldwin; David S. Bence; Matthew C. Blickensderfer; Scott R. Brown; Paul W. Casper, Jr.; Kevin L. Cooney; Grant S. Cowan; Myron L. Dale; Joseph J. Dehner; Robert A. Dimling; Richard J. Erickson; Susan Grogan Faller; Henry G. Frost (1875-1951); Neil Ganulin; Joanne Wissman Glass; Richard M. Goehler; Ronald E. Gold; Steven J. Goldstein; D. Scott Gurney; Christopher S. Habel; Walter E. Haggerty; Adam P. Hall; Jack B. Harrison; Douglas E. Hart; Stephen N. Haughey; Carl M. Jacobs (1886-1967); Frederick W. Kindel; John C. Krug; Lori A. Landrum; Patricia D. Laub; James K. L. Lawrence; P. Reid Lemasters; Douglas L. Lutz; Frederick J. McGavran; Bernard L. McKay; Kevin N. McMurray; Martin E. Mooney; Katherine Cook Morgan; Beth Schneider Naylor; Raymond D. Neusch; Sandra L. Nunn; E. Richard Oberschmidt; Michael J. O'Grady; David C. Olson; Scott D. Phillips; T. Stephen Phillips; Ann Gallagher Robinson; Jeffrey S. Rosenstiel; Jeffery R. Rush; David E. Schmit; Charles E. Schroer; Samuel M. Scoggins; Robert D. Shank; David A. Skidmore, Jr.; Kevin S. Sprecher; William C. Strangfeld; Jeffrey R. Teeters; Douglas D. Thomson; Jill Meyer Vollman; James S. Wachs; H. Lawson Walker, II; W. Russell Wilson; George E. Yund; Hilla M. Zerbst (Certified Specialist in Workers' Compensation Law, Ohio State Bar Association). Senior Associates: Kimberly S. Amrine; Stacy Christman Blomeke; Kasey Bond; Julie M. Tomlinson Bruns; Craig M. Bryson; Steven W. Caldwell (Not admitted in OH); Diana R. Christy; Deanne E. Clarke; Douglas R. Dennis; David E. Franklin; Mary M. Godar; Kyle R. Grubbs; Colleen M. Haas; Maureen P. Haney; John S. Higgins; Kevin K. Malof; Christina M. Sprecher; Steven M. Wesloh. Associates: Beth A. Buchanan; Jandá M. Carter; Monica L. Dias; Eugene J. Droder, III; Claire Seltz Eichner; Jennifer Fuller; Stephen M. Gracey; Chelsea C. Green; Melissa Green; Murray W. Griess; Erin N. Halenkamp; Catherine Ann Heitchue Reed; Nicolette R. Hudson; Andrew R. Kaake; Allison Hiltz Kropp; Bridget Gannon McGraw; Joel F. McGuire; Kelly P. Moore; Rodger W. Moore; William S. Morriss; Monica H. Norris; Jennifer A. O'Guinn; Bill J. Paliobeis; Scott Richardson; Ria Farrell Schalnat; Karlyn A. Schnapp, Ph.D; James D. Schoeny; Yvette R. Simpson; Jud B. Sims; Rita M. Stolper; Joseph A. Tomain; Andrew B. Ulmer; Vance V. VanDrake, III; Joshua L. Vineyard; David W. Walulik; Clint C. Watson; Kristin K. Whitaker; Janice Baker Whitlow; Jeffrey L. Zackerman. Counsel: Edmund J. Adams; James R. Adams; Barbara F. Applegarth; William D. Baskett; Lisa Weekley Coulter; William E. Gallagher; Albert E. Heekin, III; James A. Katsanis; Linda M. Keck; James M. Kipling; Karen Ecker Kratz; Lawrence H. Kyte, Jr.; Kimberly K. Mauer; Vincent E. Mauer; Karen M. McLaughlin; David J. McPherson; Victor C. Moreno; Ljubomir Nacev (Not admitted in OH); John K. Rose; Carla Haunz Rusconi; Mary Ann Schenk; Jane Hils Shea.
Alternative Dispute Resolution, Bankruptcy and Reorganization, Business Acquisitions, Business and Corporate, Commercial Finance, Commercial Litigation, Commercial/Real Estate, Construction, Copyright, Corporate Responsibility and Defense, Employee Benefits, Energy and Natural Resources, Entrepreneurial, Environmental, Equine, Estate Planning and Administration, Financial Institutions, Fire and Explosion, Health Care, Immigration, International, Intellectual Property, International Business, Internet and Electronic Commerce, Labor and Employment Law, Litigation, Media, Mold and Water Intrusion, Multi-District Litigation, Patent Litigation, Personal Planning and Family Business, Privacy and Information Security, Product Liability, Public Finance, Securities, Tax, Tort & Insurance Law, Trademark, Venture Capital, General Trial Practice in all State and Federal Courts.
Representative Clients: American Home Products Corporation; Anchor Hocking Glass Company; AK Steel Corporation; Arthur Andersen LLP; Bethesda Hospital, Inc; B. F. Goodrich Hilton Davis Inc.; Broadwing Inc.; Champion International Corporation; Chevron U.S.A., Inc.; Chiquita Brands International Inc.
Columbus, Ohio Office: One Columbus, 10 West Broad Street, 43215-3467. Telephone: 614-464-1211. Telecopier: 614-464-1737.
Middletown, Ohio Office: 300 North Main Street, Suite 200, 45042-1919. Telephone: 513-422-2001. Telecopier: 513-422-3010.
Lexington, Kentucky Office: 250 West Main Street, Suite 2700, 40507-1742. Telephone: 859-231-0000. Telecopier: 859-231-0011.
Louisville, Kentucky Office: 400 West Market Street, 32nd Floor, 40202-3363. Telephone: 502-589-5400. Telecopier: 502-581-1087.
Nashville, Tennessee Office: 424 Church Street, Suite 1600, 37219-2308. Telephone: 615-251-5550. Telecopier: 615-251-5551.
New Albany, Indiana Office: 120 West Spring Street, Suite 400, 47150-3655. Telephone: 812-948-2800. Telecopier: 812-948-7994.

See Professional Biographies, CINCINNATI, OHIO

Frost & Jacobs LLP
(See Frost Brown Todd LLC)

Fruechtemeyer, A. Scott ... '69 '95 C.477 B.A. L.494 J.D. [Dinsmore&S.]
Fry, Sallee Maureen, (AV) ... '63 '89 C.150 B.A. L.1340 J.D. [S.M.Fry]
Fry, W. Roger, (AV) ... '40 '66 C.150 B.A. L.1340 J.D. [Rendigs,F.K.&D.]
Fry, Sallee M., Law Office of, (AV) ... 2345 Ashland Avenue
Fuchs, Jack F., (AV) ... '52 '82 C.145 B.A. L.150 J.D. [Thompson H.]
Fuller, Gerald W. '28 '57 C.228 A.B. L.383 LL.B.
(adm. in KY; not adm. in OH) Int. Rev. Serv.
Fuller, Jennifer ... '— '04 C.804 B.S. L.608 J.D. [Frost B.T.]
Furlong, Kathleen A., (AV) '54 '80 C.973 B.A. L.150 J.D.
Op. V.P. & Asst. Gen. Coun., Federated Dept. Stores, Inc.
Furnier, Robert R., (AV) ... '56 '83 C.473 B.A. L.150 J.D. [Furnier&T.]
Furnier & Thomas, LLP, (AV) ... 1 Financial Way
Gabelman, Thomas L., (AV) ... '58 '84 C&L.150 B.A., J.D. [Vorys,S.S.&P.]
Gack, Bruce M. '56 '81 C.347 B.S. L.1119 J.D.
(adm. in IN; not adm. in OH) Sr. Atty., Kroger Company, The
Gaier, Thomas M., (AV) ... '49 '75 C&L.150 B.A., J.D. [Robbins,K.P.&T.]
Gainer, James B. ... '59 '86 C.97 B.A. L.200 J.D. Assoc. Gen. Coun., Cinergy Servs.
Gaines, Terry D., (AV) ... '40 '69 C.531 B.S. L.1340 J.D. First Asst. Co. Pros.
Galasso, Michael A. ... '70 '00 C.235 B.A L.1161 J.D. [Robbins,K.P.&T.]
Gallagher, Brenda Ann ... '58 '89 C.610 B.S. L.150 J.D. 525 Vine Street, Suite 900
Gallagher, William E. ... '62 '92 C.645 B.S.M.E. L.665 J.D. [Frost B.T.]
Gallagher, William R., (BV) ... '62 '87 C.405 B.B.A. L.146 J.D. [Arenstein&G.]
Gambill, Barbara Fruehling ... '55 '85 C.597 B.A. L.1119 J.D. Sr. Coun., Cinergy Servs.
Gann, Erica D. ... '— '04 C&L.150 B.A., J.D. [Vorys,S.S.&P.]

Ganulin, Neil, (AV) '48 '73 C.150 B.A. L.477 J.D. [Frost B.T.]
Garber, David W. ... '47 '75 C.473 B.A. L.1340 J.D. V.P. & Tr. Offr., The Fifth Third Bk.
Garber, Deanna R. '66 '90 C.610 B.A. L.150 J.D. [Ⓐ Haverkamp,B.R.&R.]
Garcia, Dineen E. McDonald '68 '95
C.415 B.A. L.564 J.D. Asst. Coun., Federated Dept. Stores, Inc.
Gardner, Don R., (AV) '35 '60 C.150 B.A. L.602 J.D. [Keating M.&K.]
Gardner, J. Neal, (AV) '44 '69 C.602 B.S.M.E. L.276 J.D. [Keating M.&K.]
Garfinkel, Jane E., (AV) '52 '80 C.938 B.A. L.477 J.D. [Thompson H.]
Garner, Dean L. '65 '91 C.446 B.S. L.904 J.D. 5063 Lake Forest Ln (Pat.)
Garner, Douglas A. '66 '91 C&L.150 B.A., J.D. 1745 Madison Road
Garrigan, Terrence D. '29 '54 C.31 B.A. L.976 LL.B. 8051 Witts Mill Lane
Garrigan, Terrence M., (BV) '59 '87 C.973 B.B.A. L.150 J.D. 6680 Tupelo Ln.
Garry, Bruce S., (BV) '46 '71 C&L.150 B.A., J.D. Sr. Asst. Pros. Atty.
Garry, Patrick J., (BV) '64 '91 C.93 B.A. L.150 J.D. 1019 Main St.
Garry, Timothy A., (AV) '36 '61 C.973 A.B. L.930 J.D. [Keating M.&K.]
Garry, Timothy A., Jr., (BV) '60 '86 C.276 B.A. L.150 J.D. [Ⓐ Wood&L.]
Garry, Victoria Davidson, (BV) '59 '86 C.473 B.A. L.1340 J.D. [Garry&G.]
Garry & Garry Co., L.P.A., (BV) 600 Vine Street
Garvey, John J., III, (BV) '66 '91 C.973 A.B. L.151 J.D. [Freund,F.&A.]
Garvey, Robert A. '69 '94 C.473 B.A. L.150 J.D. 425 Walnut St.‡
Garvin, James R., (BV) '67 '95 C.610 B.A. L.1187 J.D. [Garvin,L.H.&E.]
Garvin, Kathleen M. '68 '93 C.93 B.A. L.424 J.D. 6735 Ken Arbre Dr.‡
Garvin, Lippert, Heile & Evans, (AV) 7 W. 7th Street
Gast, Stephen P. '58 '86 C.97 B.A. L.117 J.D. [Ⓐ Butkovich,S.S.&G.]
Gatch, Lewis G., (AV) '34 '61 C.674 A.B. L.477 J.D. [L.G.Gatch]
Gatch, Lewis G., Co., L.P.A., (AV) 8050 Hosbrook Rd. Ste. 10
Gates, Robt. G. '20 '50 C.973 L.1340 LL.B. 5408 Sanrio Ct.‡
Gaunt, Karen Kreider '71 '97 C.207 B.A. L.150 J.D. [Keating M.&K.]
Gay, Michael L., (AV) '52 '77 C.608 B.A. L.150 J.D. [Cors&B.]
Gaynor, William T., Jr. '54 '81 C.966 B.A. L.209 J.D.
(adm. in IL; not adm. in OH) Loyal America Life Ins. Co.
Gearding, Monica L. '65 '98 C.608 B.A. L.930 J.D. [Ⓐ Taft,S.&H.]
Gebhart, David E. '36 '61 C.313 B.A. L.477 J.D. 264 Ludlow Avenue

Gehrig, Michael F., (AV) '47 '74 C.608 B.A. L.1340 J.D.
1140 Bartlett Building, 36 East Fourth Street, 45202-3811
Telephone: 513-421-9010 Fax: 513-421-4464
Email: gehriglaw@zoomtown.com URL: http://www.lawyers.com/gehriglaw
Albert R. Fingerman (Retired).
Negligence, Trial Practice, Personal Injury, Professional Liability and Product Liability.
Reference: U.S. Bank.
See Professional Biographies, CINCINNATI, OHIO

Gehring, Robert J., (AV) '54 '80 C.473 B.A. L.1340 J.D. [Crabbe,B.&J.]
Geiger, Lee P. '75 '00 C.473 B.A. L.851 J.D. [Ⓐ Graydon H.&R.]
Geiger, Michael B. '48 '74 C.197 A.B. L.352 J.D.
(adm. in IA; not adm. in OH) Supervisory Atty. Advsr., Off. of Hearings & App.
Geiler, Geri Hernandez, (BV) '64 '89
C.846 B.A. L.150 J.D. 801 Plum, City Hall, Rm. 214
Geisen, William G., (AV) '58 '83 C.973 H.A.B. L.383 J.D.
(adm. in KY; not adm. in OH) [Graydon H.&R.] ⊙
Geiser, Edward J. '60 '89 C.973 B.S.B.A. L.201 J.D. [Ⓐ Smith,R.&S.]
Gelhaus, Emily J. '78 '03 C&L.150 B.A., J.D. [Ⓐ Denlinger,R.&G.]
Gellenbeck, Lynne '49 '75 C.228 A.B. L.284 J.D. Kroger Company, The
Gelwicks, Joseph W., (AV) '49 '76 C.1161 A.B. L.1340 J.D. [Rendigs,F.K.&D.]
Gelwicks, Thomas A., (AV) '51 '82 C.30 B.A. L.1340 J.D. [Gelwicks,T.]
Gelwicks, Thomas, The Law Offices of, (AV) 10945 Reed Hartman Hwy., Ste. 212
Gemmato, Anthony J., Jr. '62 '87 C.381 B.A. L.930 J.D. [Ⓐ Lerner,S.&R.]
Geoppinger, Jean M., (AV) '65 '90 C.473 B.A. L.150 J.D. [Ⓐ Waite,S.B.&C.]
Geoppinger, Jeffrey '75 '01 C.93 B.A. L.150 J.D. [Ⓐ Ulmer&B.]
Georgiton, Peter J. '76 '02 C.967 B.A. L.608 J.D. [Ⓐ Dinsmore&S.]
Gephardt, Stephanie M. '62 '88
C.210 B.A. L.608 J.D. Sr. Coun., Anthem Blue Cross/Blue Shield
Gephart, John F. '49 '79 C.1323 B.A. L.117 J.D.
2nd V.P., Advanced Sales, The Union Central Life Ins. Co.
Geppert, Eric J. '63 '88 C.354 B.S. L.273 J.D. [Baker&H.]
Gerard, David A. '44 '67 C&L.107 B.A., J.D.
(adm. in NY; not adm. in OH) Admin. Law J.
Gerhardstein, Alphonse A., (AV) '51 '76 C.72 B.A. L.569 J.D. [Laufman,R.&G.]
Gerhardt, Charles H., III, (AV) '59 '86 C.602 B.B.A. L.734 J.D. [Ⓒ Keating M.&K.]
Gerlach, Ben '74 '04 C.421 B.A. L.150 J.D. [Ⓐ Dinsmore&S.]
Germain, Kenneth B., (AV) '45 '70 C.705 A.B. L.569 J.D. [Thompson H.]
Gerner, David E., (AV) '60 '83 C.1118 B.A. L.1340 J.D. 215 W. 9th St.
Gershuny, Pamela '59 '95 C.347 B.S. L.477 J.D. Univ. of Cincinnati
Gerwin, Ann W., (AV) '49 '79 C.611 B.A. L.1340 J.D. [Strauss&T.]
Geygan, Thomas J., (BV) '38 '63 C.973 B.A. L.150 J.D. 8050 Hosbrook Rd.
Geygan, Thomas James, Jr. '64 '98 C.973 B.S. L.1340 J.D.
8050 Hosbrook Rd., Ste. 107
Ghassomian, Kevin R. '73 '99 C.383 B.A. L.880 J.D. [Ⓐ Greenebaum D.&M.]
Ghiz, Leslie E. '69 '94 C.923 B.A. L.117 J.D. [Ⓐ Kohnen&P.]
Giannella, Andrew R. '70 '96 C.165 B.A. L.150 J.D. [Ulmer&B.]
Gibbons, Julia S. '50 '75 C.880 B.A. L.893 J.D. U.S. Cir. J.
Gibson, Cynthia L., (AV) '64 '89 C.896 B.A. L.893 J.D. [Katz,T.B.&H.]
Gibson, Whitney C. '— '04 C.645 B.S. L.150 J.D. [Ⓐ Vorys,S.S.&P.]
Gierl, John R., (AV) '58 '83 C.473 B.S. L.608 J.D. [Katz,T.B.&H.]
Giglio, Augustine, (AV) '45 '70 C&L.150 B.S., J.D. 3 Cypress Garden
Gilbert, Scott T. '74 '03 C.556 B.A. L.1509 J.D. 215 West Ninth Street
Gilday, Anne L. '78 '03 C.140 B.A. L.1340 J.D. [Ⓐ Lawrence] ⊙
Gilday, Bernard J., Jr. '23 '49
C.973 A.B. L.150 LL.B. Admin. Law J., U.S. Dept. of Labor
Gilday, Michael D., (AV) '48 '77 C.150 B.S. L.1340 J.D. 110 E. 8th St.
Giles, Brian T. '74 '00 C.473 B.A. L.383 J.D. [Ⓐ Statman,H.S.&E.]
Gill, David L. '49 '82 C.608 B.A. L.1340 J.D. Oxford Financial Grp.
Gill, Eric J. '48 '94 C.150 B.A. L.151 J.D. Natl. Labor Relations Bd.
Gillam, Marcheta L., (AV) '52 '79 C.112 B.A. L.809 J.D. 901 Elm
Gillen, Stephen E., (AV) '53 '80 C.473 B.S.B.A. L.151 J.D.
[Greenebaum D.&M.] (Pat.)
Gilligan, Louis F., (AV) '43 '68 C.754 B.S. L.150 J.D. [Keating M.&K.] (Pat.)
Gilligan, Mary Kathleen '56 '81 C.93 B.A. L.150 J.D. 120 E. 4th St., Ste. 800‡
Gillum, Amy L. '76 '03 C.510 B.A. L.1340 J.D. [Ⓐ Lerner,S.&R.]
Gilman, Ronald Lee '42 '67 C.453 S.B. L.309 J.D. U.S. Cir. J.
Ginocchio, Deborah Nellis, (BV) '54 '79
C.610 A.B. L.150 J.D. Conference Atty., Cir. Ct. of App.
Ginocchio, James S., (BV) '45 '79
C.973 B.S. L.1340 J.D. Asst. City Solr. [Deardorff&Assoc.]
Ginocchio, Ralph P., (AV) '48 '77 C.276 A.B. L.1340 J.D. [Butkovich,S.S.&G.]

Ginsburg, Pamela '55 '90 C.1524 B.A. L.880 J.D. [Ⓐ Ulmer&B.]
Gittinger, Steven C., (BV) '57 '84 C.235 B.A. L.1340 J.D. Classics Title Services
Glass, Gary M., (AV) '64 '86 C.165 B.A. L.602 J.D. [Thompson H.]
Glass, Joanne Wissman '69 '94 C.973 B.A. L.151 J.D. [Frost B.T.]
Glass, Thomas P. '64 '93 C.1208 B.A. L.201 J.D. [Strauss&T.]
Glassman, Michael S., (AV) '51 '76 C&L.150 B.A., J.D. [Dinsmore&S.]
Glassman, Thomas F., (BV) '66 '93 C.150 B.A. L.1340 J.D. [Smith,R.&S.]
Glazer, Richard H. '44 '70 C.150 B.B.A. L.608 J.D. [R.H.Glazer]

Glazer, Richard H., Co., L.P.A.
8180 Corporate Park Drive Suite 300, 45242
Telephone: 513-489-7200 Fax: 513-489-4044
Email: glazerlaw@fuse.net URL: http://www.lawyers.com/glazerlaw
Richard H. Glazer.
Personal Injury, Wrongful Death, Medical Malpractice, Civil Litigation and Eminent Domain, Taking of Property by Appropriation & Condemnation Proceedings.
See Professional Biographies, CINCINNATI, OHIO

Gleeson, Francis M., II '26 '56 C.973 B.S. L.1340 LL.B. 9888 Winton Rd.
Glueck, Neal Jay '54 '80
C.150 B.B.A. L.1340 J.D. V.P., Tax, Federated Dept. Stores, Inc.‡
Godar, Mary M. '70 '95 C.679 B.A. L.464 J.D. [Ⓐ Frost B.T.]
Godbey, Mark E., & Associates, (BV) '63 '89
C.1260 B.A. L.8 J.D. 914 Main Street, Suite 200
Godby, Marissa L. '63 '94 [Ⓐ O'Connor,A.&L.]
Goderre, Diane M. '71 '98 C&L.150 B.A., J.D. [Ⓐ Thompson H.]
Goeddel, Frederic L., (AV) '48 '73 C.207 B.A. L.150 J.D. [Drew&W.]
Goehler, Richard M., (AV) '56 '82 C.473 B.A. L.602 J.D. [Frost B.T.]
Goering, Eric W., (AV) '67 '93 C.207 B.A. L.151 J.D. [Goering&G.]
Goering, Robert A., (AV) '35 '62 C.976 B.A. L.1340 J.D. [Goering&G.]
Goering, Robert Albert, (AV) '60 '86 C.207 B.A. L.1340 J.D. [Goering&G.]
Goering, Ruth F. '30 '59 C.150 M. Ed. L.151 J.D. 128 S. 6th St.
Goering & Goering, (AV) 220 W. 3rd St.
Gold, Ronald E., (AV) '64 '89 C.477 B.A. L.665 J.D. [Frost B.T.]
Goldberg, Abe D. '10 '34 L.1340 LL.B. 2134 Madison Rd.

Goldberg, Brian M., (AV) '60 '85 C.150 B.A. L.851 J.D.
4300 Carew Tower, 441 Vine Street, 45202
Telephone: 513-721-3111 Fax: 513-721-3077
Email: rgoldbri@aol.com URL: http://www.riverfrontsportsmanagement.com
Sports Law. Athlete Representation and Contract Negotiation.
See Professional Biographies, CINCINNATI, OHIO

Goldberg, John A., (AV) '41 '73 C.424 B.A. L.1340 J.D. [Lindhorst&D.]
Goldberg, Mitchell B., (AV) '44 '68 C&L.150 B.A., J.D. [Ⓒ Strauss&T.]
Goldberg, Richard, (AV) '48 '75 C.150 B.S. L.1340 J.D. [Schuh&G.]
Golden, Jason A. '70 '95 C.347 B.S. L.861 J.D. [Ⓐ Montgomery,R.&J.]
Goldenberg, Jeffrey S. '65 '94 C&L.347 B.A., J.D. [Murdock G.S.&G.]
Goldman, Edward R., (AV) '43 '73 C.150 B.S. L.1340 J.D. [Rendigs,F.K.&D.]
Goldman, Fern E., (AV) '57 '97 C.1036 B.A. L.569 J.D. [Ⓐ Statman,H.S.&E.]
Goldman, Gary S. '51 '94 C.1118 B.E.S. L.1340 J.D. 7 W. Seventh St.
Goldsmith, Katherine D. .... '71 '96 C&L.608 B.A., J.D. Sr. Atty., Ohio Natl. Life Ins. Co.
Goldstein, Steven J., (AV) '51 '75 C.453 B.S. L.94 J.D. [Frost B.T.] (See Pat. Sect.)
Goldwasser, Brian D. '66 '93 C.473 B.S. L.1003 J.D. [Ⓐ Reminger&R.]

Gonzalez, Saggio & Harlan, L.L.P., (BV)
Carew Tower, 441 Vine Street, Suite 3615, 45202 ⊙
Telephone: 513-651-3456 Fax: 513-651-3446
Email: main@gshllp.com URL: http://www.gshllp.com
John J. Williams; Elizabeth Conkin.
Business and Corporate Law, Civil Litigation, Insurance Defense Law, Equal Opportunities and Employment, School Law, Municipal Finance, Business and Commercial Litigation, Patents, Trademarks, Copyrights, Intellectual Property Licensing, Real Estate, Construction, Condemnation Law, Environmental, Taxation, Utilities Law, Trials and Appeals, Government Relations.
Representative Clients: Accenture; Alliant Energy; Bear, Stears & Co.; Chubb Insurance Company; City of Milwaukee; CNH Global N.V.; Darden Restaurants, Inc.; Denny's; Eastman Kodak Company; E.I. du Pont de Nemours and Company.
Indianapolis, Indiana Office: 201 North Illinois Street, Suite 1900, 46204. Telephone: 317-686-9800. Fax: 317-686-9821.
West Des Moines, Iowa Office: 1501 42nd Street, Suite 465, 50266. Telephone: 515-453-8509. Fax: 515-267-1408.
Milwaukee, Wisconsin Office: 225 East Michigan, 4th Floor, 53202-4900. Telephone: 414-277-8500. Fax: 414-277-8521.
Chicago, Illinois Office: 208 LaSalle Street, Suite 1460, 60604. Telephone: 312-236-0475. Facsimile: 312-236-1750.
See Professional Biographies, CINCINNATI, OHIO

Good, Martha H. '49 '85 C.787 B.A. L.150 J.D. 3532 Herschel View Way‡
Goode, Joshua L. '82 '03 C&L.150 B.A., J.D. [J.Goode]
Goode, Joshua, Law Office of 917 Main St., 2nd Fl.
Goodin, Steven P. '69 '99 C.473 B.A. L.150 J.D. Asst. Pros. Atty.
Goodman, Barry A. '42 '67 C.150 B.A. L.608 J.D. 7269 Willowbrook Lane★
Goodman, Farrell J. '58 '85 C.472 B.M. L.990 J.D. 2035 Reading Rd.
Goodman, Jeffrey S., (BV) '59 '85 C.477 A.B. L.880 J.D. [Goodman&G.]
Goodman, Richard Lanahan, Law Office of, (AV) '46 '74
C.973 B.S. L.1161 J.D. 3706 Broadview Drive
Goodman, Ronald J., (BV) '37 '62 C&L.150 A.B., J.D. [Ⓒ Goodman&G.]
Goodman, Stanley, (AV) '31 '55 C&L.150 B.A., J.D. [Goodman&G.]
Goodman, Terrence L., (AV) '58 '84 C.20 B.A. L.902 J.D. [Ⓐ Waite,S.B.&C.]
Goodman & Goodman, A Legal Professional Association, (AV) .....123 East Fourth Street
Goodson, Brett C., (AV) '51 '76 C.610 B.G.S. L.1049 J.D. [Goodson]
Goodson, Stephen M., (AV) '55 '80 C.150 B.B.A. L.276 J.D. [Keating M.&K.]

Goodson & Company, Ltd., (AV)
110 East Eighth Street Suite 200, 45202
Telephone: 513-621-5631 Fax: 513-621-3855 URL: http://www.goodsonandcompany.com
Email: brettgoodson@goodsonandcompany.com URL: http://www.lawyers.com/goodsonandcompany
Brett C. Goodson;—Stephanie M. Day.
Personal Injury, Insurance Law, Professional Negligence, Trials and Appeals, Wrongful Death, Products Liability.
See Professional Biographies, CINCINNATI, OHIO

Goodwin, Jonathon T. '49 '84 C.381 B.S. L.8 J.D. 324 Reading Rd.
Gora, Felix J., (AV) '55 '80 C.473 A.B. L.150 J.D. [Rendigs,F.K.&D.]
Gores, Guido J. '17 '41 C.674 A.B. L.309 LL.B. Pres., Queen City Financial
Gores, H. Drewry '54 '01 C.188 B.A. L.1340 J.D. [Ⓐ Kohnen&P.]
Goret, Ronald J., (AV) '37 '64 C.150 B.B.A. L.1340 J.D. [Katz,T.B.&H.]
Gorman, Robert Herancourt '35 '60
C.103 A.B. L.150 LL.B. Ct. of App. J., 1st Appl. Dist. of OH
Gortsas, Alex, (BV) '33 '58 C&L.150 B.A., LL.B. 441 Vine Street
Gothard, Jennifer K. '67 '92 C.851 B.A. L.150 J.D. Kroger Co.
Gottesman, & Associates 36 E 7th Street, Suite 2121
Gottesman, Zachary '66 '92 C.210 B.A. L.201 J.D. [Gottesman]

Gould, Thomas M., (BV) ... '45 '74 C.150 B.A. L.477 J.D. Co. Ct. Clk.
Gourlay, Thomas H., Jr. '55 '78 C.800 A.B. L.464 J.D.
(adm. in CA; not adm. in OH) U.S. Army Corps of Engrs.
Graber, Sarah Otte ... '72 '97 C.347 B.A. L.201 J.D. [Ⓐ Wood,H.&E.]
Gracey, Stephen M. ... '76 '03 C.178 B.A. L.150 J.D. [Ⓐ Frost B.T.]
Grady, Karla J. ... '54 '80 Mun. J.
Graeter, Richard A., II ... '64 '89 C.473 B.S. L.150 J.D. Gen. Coun., Graeter's Inc.
Graf, Andrew D. ... '72 '97 C.201 B.A. L.880 J.D. [Ⓐ Griffin -F.]
Graf, William R., (AV) ... '50 '76 C.207 B.A. L.608 J.D. [Graf&S.&M.]

Graf | Stiebel | Moyers, A Legal Professional Association, (AV) BR
Suite 2400, U.S. Bank Tower, 425 Walnut Street, 45202
Telephone: 513-618-7800 Fax: 513-618-7801
URL: http://www.grafstiebel.com
William R. Graf (Certified Specialist in Estate Planning, Trust and Probate Law, Ohio State Bar Association); Mark A. Stiebel; Michael K. Moyers; Debbe A. Levin; Mark S. Bever;—Nancy J. Burns; Sean K. Mangan.
Closely-Held Business Law, Taxation, Estate Planning, Probate and Trust Administration, Employee Benefits, Retirement Distribution Planning, Litigation of Tax, Probate, and Trust Matters.

See Professional Biographies, CINCINNATI, OHIO

Grafe, Karl J., (AV) '60 '85 C&L.150 B.A., J.D.
Asst. Gen. Coun. & Asst. Secy., Amer. Fin. Grp., Inc.
Graff, Milton B., IV '42 '80 C.188 B.Ch.E. L.1340 J.D.
The Procter & Gamble Co. (Pat.)
Graham, Elizabeth Ann '56 '79 C.383 B.A. L.421 J.D
(adm. in KY; not adm. in OH) Medic One, Inc.
Grant, Cheryl D., (BV) ... '44 '73 C&L.150 B.A., J.D. 3766 Ashworth Dr.
Grant, James A., (AV) ... '59 '85 C.303 B.A. L.1340 J.D. [Beirne&W.]
Grant, Marvin F. ... '27 '55 C.973 B.S. L.1340 J.D. 4123 Delhi Pike
Gravitt, Cassius B., Jr. '20 '50 C&L.383 A.B., LL.B.
(adm. in KY; not adm. in OH) 439 Flemridge Ct.‡
Gray, Victoria M. ... '57 '93 C.150 B.A. L.1340 J.D. [Moore,M.&M.]

Graydon Head & Ritchey LLP, (AV) BR
1900 Fifth Third Center, 511 Walnut Street, P.O. Box 6464, 45202-3157 ⊙
Telephone: 513-621-6464 Fax: 513-651-3836
Email: info@graydon.com URL: http://www.graydon.com
Partners: Henry G. Alexander, Jr.; William J. Baechtold; Stephen L. Black; Thomas A. Breitenbach; Thomas A. Brennan; Daniel E. Burke (Certified Specialist in Workers' Compensation Law, Ohio State Bar Association); Christine A. Buttress (Certified Specialist in Estate Planning, Trust and Probate Law, Ohio State Bar Association); Harry W. Cappel; J. Michael Debbeler; Harry J. Finke IV; John A. Flanagan; William G. Geisen (Not admitted in OH); John C. Greiner; Jeffrey M. Hendricks; Daniel C. Heyd; Michael A. Hirschfeld; Bruce A. Hoffman; Michael S. Jones; Joseph E. Kane; Monica Donath Kohnen; Robert L. Kreidler; John J. Kropp; Richard T. La Jeunesse; J. Jeffrey Landen; Michael R. Miller; Gerald F. O'Connell, Jr.; Eric C. Okerson; Bruce I. Petrie, Jr.; John B. Pinney; Thomas A. Prewitt; Karen J. Renz; Michael A. Roberts; Richard L. Robinson (Not admitted in OH); Jeffrey L. Rohr; Robert R. Saelinger; Richard G. Schmalzl; Jamie D. Scott; Mark E. Sims; Peter M. Slater; David S. Warren; Kent Wellington; A. Christian Worrell III. Associates: Paul Alley (Resident, Fort Mitchell, Kentucky Office); Aine M. Baldwin; Lyndsey R. Cater; Allyson True Cook (Not admitted in OH); Kara A. Czanik; Neil Fairweather; Lee P. Geiger; Everett L. Greene; Christopher Allen Griffin; Matthew B. Lake; Katherine M. Lasher; Amy E. Lippert; Sharon S. Parsley; Jennifer S. Pearson; Daniel E. Reitz; Ann K. Schooley; Michael C. Surrey; Brian C. Thomas; Hans M. Tinkler. Of Counsel: Susan M. Argo.
Antitrust, Banking, Bankruptcy, Computer, Construction, Corporate, Creditors' Rights, Employee Benefits, Employment, Environmental, Equine, Estate Planning, Finance, Health Care, Human Resources, Intellectual Property, International, Internet Commerce, Labor Relations, Legislative, Litigation, Media Law, Mergers and Acquisitions, Probate, Products Liability, Real Estate, Securities, Succession Planning, Tax, Trial and Appellate Practice in State and Federal Courts, Workers' Compensation.
Fort Mitchell, Kentucky Office: 2500 Chamber Center Drive, Suite 300, P.O. Box 17070, 41017. Telephone: 859-282-8800. Fax: 859-525-0214.

See Professional Biographies, CINCINNATI, OHIO

Grayson, Deborah R. ... '52 '77 C.383 B.A. L.273 J.D. [Meizlish&G.]
Green, Chelsea C. ... '68 '00 C.473 B.S. L.150 J.D. [Ⓐ Frost B.T.]
Green, F. Harrison, (BV) ... '46 '72 C.500 A.B. L.421 J.D. [F.H.Green]
Green, K. C., (AV) ... '58 '84 C.930 B.A. L.893 J.D. [Dinsmore&S.]
Green, Leonard ... '47 '72 C.150 B.A. L.477 J.D. Clk., U.S. Ct. of Apps.
Green, Melissa ... '— '04 C.475 B.A. L.477 J.D. [Ⓐ Frost B.T.]

Green, F. Harrison, Co., L.P.A., (BV)
4015 Executive Park Drive, Suite 130, 45241-4017
Telephone: 513-769-0840 Fax: 513-563-2953
Email: fhgreen@ix.netcom.com URL: http://www.lawyers.com/f_harrison_green_co-lpa
F. Harrison Green;—Douglas A. Mackinnon.
Litigation, Family Law, Personal Injury, Medical Malpractice, Workers Compensation, Employment Law, Civil Rights, Wills and Trust Law.
Representative Clients: Thomas Products Co.; King International, Inc.; Access Benefits Corp.; Aluxier Trucking & Excavating; Peoples Trust Company.

See Professional Biographies, CINCINNATI, OHIO

Greenberg, Bradley J., (AV) ... '66 '91 C.608 B.A. L.893 J.D. 230 E. Ninth St.
Greenberg, Gary L., (AV) ... '53 '78 C.659 B.A. L.477 J.D. [Denlinger,R.&G.]
Greenberg, Gerald S., (AV) ... '51 '77 C.216 B.A. L.309 J.D. [Taft,S.&H.]
Greenberg, Matthew Lawrence '58 '00
C.429 B.A. L.150 J.D. Hamilton Co., OH Pub. Def. Comm.
Greenberger, Jeffrey J., (BV) ... '66 '92 C.473 B.S. L.201 J.D. [Katz,G.&N.]
Greenberger, Mark Alan, (AV) ... '40 '66 C&L.150 B.A., J.D. [Katz,G.&N.]
Greene, Everett L. ... '47 '04 C.871 B.S. L.329 J.D. [Ⓐ Graydon H.&R.]
Greene, Gordon C., (AV) ... '35 '60 C&L.150 B.A., J.D. [Ⓒ Rendigs,F.K.&D.]

Greenebaum Doll & McDonald PLLC, (AV)
2800 Chemed Center, 255 East Fifth Street, 45202-4728 ⊙
Telephone: 513-455-7600 Fax: 513-455-8500
Email: lrv@gdm.com URL: http://www.greenebaum.com
Members of Firm: S. L. Greenebaum (1902-1973); Edward L. McDonald (1870-1961); Angus W. McDonald (1912-1980); W. VanMeter Alford (1916-1981); Laramie L. Leatherman (1932-1994); Wm. T. (Bill) Robinson III; John A. West; Mark H. Longenecker; Richard Boydston; P. Richard Anderson, Jr.; C. Christopher Muth; William L. Montague; Mark T. Hayden; Louis K. Ebling; Michael H. Brown; Philip J. Schworer; Robert D. Hudson; Suzanne P. Land; Steven R. Smith; Stephen E. Gillen; Mikio Nishizu. Of Counsel: Glenn D. Bellamy. Associates: Nancy J. Bride; Kevin R. Ghassomian; W. Ashley Hess; Lori E. Krafte.
General Civil Trial and Appellate Practice in all Courts, Litigation, Corporate Law, Business Law, Commercial Law, Securities, Mergers and Acquisitions, Finance, Electronic Commerce, Economic Development, Banks and Banking, Commercial Credit, Bankruptcy, Health Care, Insurance, Environmental Law, Natural Resources, Mining Law, Oil and Gas Law, Labor and Employment, Employee Benefits, Taxation, Probate, Trusts and Estates, Real Estate, Zoning, Planning and Land Use, Intellectual Property Law, Trademark Law, Patent Law, International Trade, Immigration and Naturalization, Antitrust and Trade Regulation, Franchises and Franchising, Equine, Products Liability Defense, Professional Liability Defense, Alternative Dispute Resolution, Administrative Law, Workers Compensation.
Representative Clients: Ashland Inc.; Humana Inc.
Louisville, Kentucky Office: 3300 National City Tower, 101 S. Fifth Street. Telephone: 502-589-4200. Fax: 502-587-3695.
Lexington, Kentucky Office: Suite 1100, 300 West Vine Street. Telephone: 859-231-8500. Fax: 859-255-2742.
Covington, Kentucky Office: 50 East RiverCenter Boulevard. Telephone: 859-655-4200. Fax: 859-655-4239.

(This Listing Continued)

Greenebaum Doll & McDonald PLLC (Continued)
Frankfort, Kentucky Office: Suite 101, 229 West Main Street. Telephone: 502-875-0050. Fax: 502-875-0850.
Nashville, Tennessee Office: 700 Two American Center, 3102 West End Avenue. Telephone: 615-760-7100. Fax: 615-760-7300.
Atlanta, Georgia Office: 1175 Peachtree Street, N.E., 100 Colony Square, Suite 780. Telephone: 404-879-2170. Fax: 404-879-2180.
Washington, D.C. Office: 1146 19th Street, N.W., Suite 250. Telephone: 202-293-7000. Fax: 202-293-9700.

See Professional Biographies, CINCINNATI, OHIO

Greenwood, Scott T., (BV) ... '63 '89 C.473 A.B. L.145 J.D. P.O. Box 54400
Gregg, John W. '46 '79
C.383 B.S.E.E. L.1340 J.D. Pat. Coun., Cincinnati Milacron Inc. (Pat.)
Greiner, Carey (Allen) '75 '00 C.770 B.S. L.112 J.D.
Coun., Lit. & Preventive Law, GE Aircraft Engines (GEAE Legal Operation)
Greiner, John C., (AV) ... '58 '83 C.473 B.A. L.602 J.D. [Graydon H.&R.]
Greiwe, Nancy S., (AV) ... '57 '81 C.910 A.B. L.94 J.D. [Markovits&G.]
Gressel, Gerard Stephen ... '57 '92 C.475 B.S. L.1161 J.D. Johnson & Johnson
Greulich, John E. '41 '69 C.973 A.B. L.1340 J.D.
Sr. Coun., Fluor Daniel Fernald Corp.
Gribbell, Frederick H. '50 '90
C.150 B.S.E.E. L.1340 J.D. 10250 Alliance Road, Suite 120 (Pat.)
Gribler, Michael A. ... '47 '75 C.631 B.A. L.117 J.D. Cinergy Corp.
Grieme, Rosemary E. ... '43 '82 C.522 A.B. L.1340 J.D. Sr. Coun., Cinergy Servs.
Griess, Murray W. ... '65 '95 C.604 B.A. L.477 J.D. [Ⓐ Frost B.T.]
Griffin, Christopher Allen ... '76 '03 C.383 B.B.A. L.362 J.D. [Ⓐ Graydon H.&R.]

Griffin - Fletcher, LLP, (AV) BR
3500 Red Bank Road, 45227
Telephone: 513-421-1313 Fax: 513-421-1118 Email: ltcincy.com
Email: griffin-fletcher.com
Earl W. Griffin (1890-1970); Edward P. Hackett (1922-1989); John R. Fletcher (1920-2004). Members of Firm: Michael C. Fletcher; Karen L. Mastruserio, L.P.A.; Richard D. Herndon; Kevin R. Flynn; Harold L. Anness. Associates: James C. Bodley; Andrew D. Graf; David L. Huprich; Bruce G. Hopkins.
General Practice, General Business, Real Estate, Probate, Estate Planning, Real Estate Litigation.
Representative Clients: Lawyers Title Insurance Corp.; Fifth Third Bank; Cincinnati Federal Savings & Loan Association; Eagle Savings Bank; Miami Savings & Loan; Winton Savings & Loan; Foundation Savings Bank; Park National Bank.

See Professional Biographies, CINCINNATI, OHIO

Griffith, Stephen M., Jr., (AV) ... '53 '81 C.597 B.A. L.945 J.D. [Taft,S.&H.]
Grigsby, Donald E. ... '42 '69 C.201 B.A. L.150 J.D. U.S. Treas. Dept.
Grimmer, Ronald G. ... '36 '70 C.150 A.B. L.151 J.D. Assoc. Chf., App. Div., I.R.S.
Groemminger, Brian K. ... '— '03 C&L.346 B.S., J.D. [Ⓐ Dinsmore&S.]
Groenke, David A., (AV) ... '56 '81 C.477 A.B. L.880 J.D. [Vorys,S.S.&P.]
Groh, Theresa L., (AV) ... '60 '85 C.473 B.A. L.150 J.D. [Murdock G.S.&G.]
Groneman, Raymond C., (BV) ... '48 '73 C.973 B.S. L.734 J.D. Asst. Pros. Atty.
Gronotte, Sharon E. ... '75 '99 C.1118 B.A. L.383 J.D. [Ⓐ Ulmer&B.]
Groshoff, David A. ... '72 '96 C.347 B.S. L.608 J.D. V.P., J.P. Morgan
Grosser, Theodore D., (AV) ... '52 '77 C.150 B.A. L.902 J.D. [Porter W.M.&A.]
Grossman, Kurt L., (AV) '55 '81
C.150 B.S.E.E. L.273 J.D. [Wood,H.&E.] (See Pat. Sect.)
Grossmann, David E. ... '28 '52 C&L.150 A.B., LL.B. 800 Broadway, 14th Floor
Grossmann, Thomas E., (AV) ... '56 '82 C.473 B.A. L.150 J.D. [Taft,S.&H.]
Grote, Jane M. ... '52 '76 C.201 B.A. L.602 J.D. 602 Main Street, Suite 307
Grote, Leo F., (BV) ... '56 '84 C.980 A.B. L.150 J.D. 4555 Lake Forest Drive
Grubbs, Kyle R. ... '76 '01 C.1118 B.A. L.150 J.D. [Ⓐ Frost B.T.]
Gruber, John P. ... '62 '89 C.973 A.B. L.608 J.D. American Financial Resources Co. Inc.
Gruber, Joseph C., (BV) ... '61 '86 C.602 B.A. L.150 J.D. [McCaslin,I.&M.] ⊙
Gruber, Thomas J., (AV) ... '54 '79 C.973 B.A. L.150 J.D. [McCaslin,I.&M.] ⊙
Gruenschlaeger, Jeanne E. '51 '76 C&L.150 B.B.A., J.D.
8050 Hosbrook Road Ste. 400‡
Guckenberger, Guy C. ... '44 '69 C&L.150 B.A., J.D. Mun. Ct. J.
Guckenberger, Herman J., Jr., (AV) '14 '46 C.150 B.A. L.1340 J.D.
5343 Hamilton Ave.
Guenthner, Carla A. ... '63 '90 C.973 B.S. L.692 J.D. Co. Juv. Ct.
Guethlein, Albert ... '29 '57 6378 Hillside Ave.
Guggenheim, Richard E. ... '13 '37 C.477 B.A. L.307 LL.B. 2470 Grandin Road
Guilfoyle, Catherine T., (BV) ... '59 '84 C.1118 B.A. L.150 J.D. 2323 Park Ave.
Gunderson, Eric J., (BV) ... '67 '92 C.321 B.A. L.608 J.D. 5257 Montgomery Rd.
Gurney, D. Scott, (BV) ... '61 '86 C.347 B.A. L.1119 J.D. [Frost B.T.]
Gustafson, Derek, (BV) ... '58 '84 C.249 B.S. L.150 J.D. 1014 Vine St.
Gustafson, Jill ... '58 '90 C.608 B.S.N. L.8 J.D. [Ⓐ Lawrence] ⊙
Gustin, James W., (AV) ... '30 '55 C.973 B.S. L.150 LL.B. [J.W.Gustin]
Gustin, James W., Co., L.P.A. and Associates, (AV) ... Suite 800, 830 Main St.
Guttag, Eric W. ... '— '77 C.118 B.A. L.1509 J.D. [Jagtiani&G.] (Pat.)
Gutzwiller, Robert H., (BV) ... '47 '73 C.437 B.S. L.245 J.D. 36 E. 4th Street, #1208
Guy, Ralph B., Jr. ... '29 '54 C&L.477 A.B., J.D. Sr. U.S. Cir. J.
Haas, Bradley G., (AV) ... '60 '86 C&L.150 B.B.A., J.D. [Katz,T.B.&H.]
Haas, Colleen M. ... '70 '97 C&L.602 B.B.A., J.D. [Ⓐ Frost B.T.]
Haas, Herbert J. ... '49 '81 C.150 B.A. L.1161 J.D. 114 E. Eighth St.
Habel, Christopher S., (BV) ... '69 '95 C.150 B.S.C.E. L.608 J.D. [Frost B.T.]
Hadden, Richard R., (BV) ... '32 '76 C.150 B.A. L.309 J.D. [R.R.Hadden]
Hadden, Richard R., L.P.A., (BV) ... 3900 Rosehill Ave.
Haders, William D., (BV) ... '50 '75 C&L.150 B.A., J.D. Atty. Gen.
Haffer, Gloria S., (AV) ... '41 '77 C.150 B.A. L.1340 J.D. [Buechner,H.O.M.H.&K.]
Haffner, Karri K. ... '70 '94 C.699 B.A. L.150 J.D. [Ⓐ Barrett&W.]
Hageman, Jennifer Bouchard ... '70 '96 C.973 B.A. L.150 J.D. [Ulmer&B.]
Hagerstrand, Eric C., (BV) '47 '74
C.967 B.A. L.150 J.D. Chmn., Superior Pharmaceutical Co.
Haggerty, Walter E., (AV) ... '51 '78 C.973 B.S.B.A. L.1340 J.D. [Frost B.T.]
Hagopian, Gary, (AV) '50 '76 C.602 B.S. L.494 J.D.
V.P. & Gen. Coun.-Global Beauty Care, The Procter & Gamble Co. (Pat.)
Hahl, Neil M. '48 '77 C.674 A.B. L.309 J.D.
(adm. in NY; not adm. in OH) 7807 Greenbriar Lane
Haines, Richard M., (BV) ... '50 '76 C.207 B.A. L.150 J.D. [Kohnen&P.]
Hair, Deidra L. ... '45 '74 C.150 B.A. L.1340 J.D. Mun. J.
Hair, Roberta Ann, (AV) ... '42 '69 C&L.150 B.A., J.D. 7554 Wooster Pike
Hake, Carol C., (BV) ... '36 '75 C.207 B.S. L.151 J.D. 7194 Hamilton Hills Drive
Halaby, Dennis E., (BV) ... '50 '77 C&L.150 B.A., J.D. Asst. City Solr.
Halaby, Edward K., (AV) ... '18 '50 C&L.150 B.A., J.D. 6280 Glade Ave.‡
Halenkamp, Erin N. ... '77 '02 C.853 B.A. L.1340 J.D. [Ⓐ Frost B.T.]
Hall, Adam P., (AV) ... '64 '89 C.608 B.A. L.930 J.D. [Frost B.T.]
Hall, Jan C. ... '33 '77 C&L.150 B.A., J.D. 2nd Fl., Legal, 201 East 5th St.
Hall, Michael S., (BV) ... '58 '84 C.150 B.A. L.201 J.D. [M.S.Hall&Assoc.]

Hall, Michael S., Offices of, Legal Professional Association, (BV) 432 Walnut St., Ste. 1000
Hallenbeck, Prentiss W., Jr. ....'55 '98 C&L.893 B.A., J.D. [Ⓐ Ulmer&B.]
Halloran, James W., (AV) .... '34 '60 C.674 A.B. L.893 LL.B. [Ⓒ Cors&B.]
Halper, Steven D., (BV) ....'50 '75 C.608 B.S. L.276 J.D. [Katzman,L.H.&B.]
Halpert, Douglas, (AV) ....'62 '89 C.145 B.A. L.262 J.D. [Dinsmore&S.]
Halpin, Victor C. .... '69 '97 C&L.150 B.B.A., J.D. [Cors&B.]
Haman, William Douglas ....'72 '98 C.473 B.S. L.150 J.D. [D.Haman]
Haman, Douglas, Law Office of ....4107 Allston, Ste. 2
Hambley, William C. ....'52 '78 C.347 B.A. L.345 J.D. Staff Atty., Pro Seniors, Inc.
Hamilton, Frederick Nichols '53 '92
C.150 B.S. L.1340 J.D. Assoc. Gen. Coun., Univ. of Cinci. Med. Ctr.
Hamilton, Louis G. ....'54 '82 C.150 B.A. L.1340 J.D. 9464 Montgomery Rd.
Hamilton, Renell M. ...... '46 '78 C.963 B.S. L.150 J.D. American Legal Publishing Corp.
Hamilton, Richard O., Jr. ....'68 '00 C.999 B.S. L.1340 J.D. [Ⓐ Benjamin,Y.&H.]
Hammelrath, W. Smith, (BV) .... '38 '65 C.303 B.A. L.1340 J.D. [Siebold&H.]
Hammer, Vickie L. ....'55 '80 C.91 B.A. L.150 J.D. Internal Rev. Estate & Gift
Hammond, Michael F., (AV) ....'64 '89 C.130 B.A. L.150 J.D. [Hammond]

Hammond Law Group, LLC, (AV)
3311 Carew Tower, 441 Vine Street, 45202
Telephone: 513-381-2011 Fax: 513-381-2227
URL: http://www.hammondlawfirm.com
Michael F. Hammond; Sherry L. Neal; Christopher T. Musillo; Harlan Simon (Not admitted in OH);—Craig S. Clark; Peter Long Le; Cindy J. Unkenholt (Not admitted in OH); Amy R. Dalal; Judith M. Pendergast (Not admitted in OH).
Immigration and Nationality Law.
See Professional Biographies, CINCINNATI, OHIO

Hanauer, Richd. H. ....'30 '55 C&L.150 B.A., LL.B. 38 Fountain Square Plaza‡
Hancock, John W. .... '30 '68 C.976 B.S. L.1003 J.D. 7910 Shawnee Run Rd.
Handler, Allyson B. ....'71 '96 C.659 B.A. L.276 J.D. [Ⓐ Dinsmore&S.]
Handler, David P. '71 '96 C.659 B.A. L.273 J.D.
(adm. in MD; not adm. in OH) Coun., GE Aircraft Engines
Hands, John M., (AV) ....'61 '88 C.473 B.A. L.150 J.D. [Ulmer&B.]
Haney, Maureen P. ....'73 '99 C.473 B.A. L.608 J.D. [Ⓐ Frost B.T.]
Haney, Richard D., (BV) ....'27 '52 C.473 A.B. L.150 LL.B. 6725 Whitehall Ave.‡
Hankins, Scott H. '55 '80 C.605 A.B. L.813 J.D.
(adm. in CA; not adm. in OH) Fin. Coun., GE Aviation Services, Inc.
Hanna, David B., Law Offices of ....'61 '95 C.494 B.S. L.796 J.D. 7106 Royalgreen Drive
Hardin, David E. ....'67 '96 C.608 B.A. L.851 J.D. [Ⓐ Hardin,L.L.&M.]
Hardin, Donald E., (AV) ....'34 '63 C.608 B.A. L.1340 J.D. [Hardin,L.L.&M.]
Hardin, Jim L. ....'66 '91 C&L.150 B.A., J.D. P.O. Box 6491
Hardin, Lefton, Lazarus & Marks, LLC, (AV) .... 30 Garfield Place
Hardy, William R., (AV) ..... '34 '63 C.674 A.B. L.309 J.D. 432 Walnut Street, Suite 206
Hargreaves, Jeanette .... '66 '95 C.383 B.B.A. L.150 J.D. [Ⓐ Ulmer&B.]
Harmeyer, John V. ....'69 '96 C.201 B.S.E.E. L.150 J.D. [Dinsmore&S.] (See Pat. Sect.)
Harmon, Arthur W., Jr., (BV) .... '52 '81 C&L.150 B.A., J.D. [Harmon,D.&K.]
Harmon, Jeffrey J., (AV) ....'58 '81 C.973 A.B. L.273 J.D. [Cors&B.]
Harmon, Laurie M. ....'67 '92 C.473 B.S. L.117 J.D. [Ⓐ Buechner,H.O.M.H.&K.]
Harmon, Davis & Keys, A Legal Professional Association, (BV) ....1200 Cypress St.
Harper, James W., (AV) '45 '74
C.473 B.A. L.150 J.D. Chf. Asst. Co. Pros. [Loeb,V.H.&F.]
Harpster, Linda Marie .... '45 '78 C.1142 B.A. L.1340 J.D. University of Cincinnati
Harrell, Dennis O. ....'45 '75 C.894 B.A. L.150 J.D. U.S. Cir. Ct. of App.
Harrington, John P. .... '24 '53 C.197 A.B. L.1340 LL.B. [J.P.Harrington]
Harrington, John P., Co., L.P.A. .... 8404 Eustis Farm Rd.
Harris, Irving, (AV) .... '27 '51 C&L.150 LL.B. 441 Vine Street, Suite 3801‡
Harris, Jeffrey P., (AV) ....'51 '76 C.856 B.A. L.94 J.D. [Statman,H.S.&E.]
Harris, Jerald David, (AV) ....'47 '72 C.473 A.B. L.150 J.D. [Harris&B.]
Harris, Robt. J., (BV) .... '13 '37 L.150 LL.B. 632 Vine St.
Harris, Ronald C., Law Offices of, (BV) '32 '78
C.150 B.S. L.1340 J.D. 6218 Thompson Road
Harris & Burgin, (AV) .... 9545 Kenwood Rd.
Harrison, Gregory A., (AV) ....'61 '85 C.97 B.S.B.A. L.201 J.D. [Dinsmore&S.]
Harrison, Jack B., (AV) ....'55 '93 C.143 B.A. L.150 J.D. [Frost B.T.]
Harrison, James B., (AV) ....'57 '83 C.383 B.A. L.1340 J.D. [Wood&L.]
Harrison, William K. ....'33 '59 C.880 B.A. L.893 J.D. 5495 Windridge Court
Harrod, Robert C. ....'47 '84 C.265 B.A. L.1340 J.D. 9830 Tollgate Ln.
Hart, Douglas E., (AV) ....'58 '82 C.347 B.A. L.477 J.D. [Frost B.T.]
Hart, Lashawn Cheriss .... '74 '01 C.276 B.S.E.S. L.150 J.D. Hamilton Co. Pros. Off.
Hart, Robert R., Jr. ....'58 '85 C.893 B.A. L.1340 J.D. 1019 Main St.
Hartke, James R. ....'48 '73 C.973 B.A. L.150 J.D. 917 Main St.
Hartleb, David F. ....'44 '74 C.150 B.A. L.1340 J.D. Provost, Univ. of Cincinnati
Hartmann, Dennis P., (BV) .....'44 '73 C&L.150 B.B.A., J.D. 630 Vine Street, Suite 1000
Hartmann, Gregory P. ....'67 '97 C.902 B.A. L.990 J.D. Asst. Co. Pros. Atty.

Harvey, Anne Catherine, (BV) '61 '85 C&L.201 B.S., J.D.
Tri-State Building, 432 Walnut Street, Suite 1001, 45202 ⊙
Telephone: 513-721-2960 Fax: 513-621-3017
Email: lawyeranneharvey@yahoo.com URL: http://www.lawfirmanneharvey.com
Languages: Sign Language.
Trials, Appeals, Federal, State and Municipal Criminal Defense, Divorce, Dissolution, Child Custody, Military Domestic Relations Law.
Dayton Office: 5335 Far Hills Avenue, Suite 313, 45429. Telephone: 937-439-5708. Fax: 937-439-5710.
See Professional Biographies, CINCINNATI, OHIO

Harvey, Robin E., (AV) ....'52 '78 C.1168 B.A. L.1162 J.D. [Baker&H.]
Hassebrock, Richard J. .... '70 '98 C.472 B.A. L.1340 J.D. IRS Dist. Coun.
Hastings, Deborah C. ....'57 '94 C.1161 B.A. L.150 J.D. 22 W. 9th St
Hastings, Kerry P. ....'71 '96 C.477 B.A. L.309 J.D. [Taft,S.&H.]
Hastings, Robert R., Jr., (AV) .... '46 '73 C.207 B.A. L.150 J.D. [Reed,T.&H.]
Haswell, Andrew J., Jr., (AVⓉ) '37 '63 C.674 A.B. L.309 LL.B.
(adm. in OK; not adm. in OH) Coun. Devlp. Dept., Children's Hospital Medical Center
Hatcher, John Randolph .... '71 '98 C.473 B.P. L.150 J.D. Off. of Pub. Def.
Hathaway, David E., (BV) ....'44 '72 C.473 B.S. L.608 J.D. [Beckman W.S.]
Hathaway, Diane Duty ......'47 '72 C&L.608 B.S., J.D. Prof. of Law, Univ. of Cincinnati
Hattersley, Thomas J. ....'49 '77 C.207 B.S. L.1340 J.D. 7967 Cooper Road
Hauer, Wm. S., (BV) ....'27 '49 C&L.150 B.A., LL.B. 14 Garfield Pl.
Haughey, Stephen N., (AV) ....'55 '84 C.1208 B.S. L.201 J.D. [Frost B.T.]
Haupt, Keith R., (AV) .....'63 '92 C.880 B.E. L.608 J.D. [Wood,H.&E.] (See Pat. Sect.)
Haverkamp, Gary J., (AV) ....'38 '63 C.608 B.S. L.150 J.D. [Haverkamp,B.R.&R.]
Haverkamp, Michael F., (AV) '48 '74
C.150 B.B.A. L.608 J.D. V.P. & Coun., The Ohio Natl. Life Ins. Co.
Haverkamp, Brinker, Rebold & Riehl Co., L.P.A., (AV) ....5856-5900 Glenway Ave.
Haverkos, Harry C. ....'18 '50 C.999 A.B. L.150 LL.B. 5697 Candlelite Terr.‡
Hawkins, Douglas N. .... '61 '87 C.973 B.S. L.150 J.D. 1300 Chiquita Center‡
Hawkins, Lawrence C., Jr., (BV) ....'44 '75 C.150 B.A. L.1340 J.D. 3909 Reading Rd.
Hawkins, Melissa N. ....'78 '03 C.97 B.A. L.245 J.D. [Ⓐ Peck,S.&W.]
Hawkins, Michael W., (AV) ....'47 '72 C&L.383 B.B.A., J.D. [Dinsmore&S.]
Hawkins, Tracy L. ....'71 '00 C.249 B.S. L.1340 J.D. [Ⓐ Statman,H.S.&E.]
Hawkins, William H., II, (AV) ....'48 '78 C.150 B.S. L.1340 J.D. 600 Vine Street
Haycox, Rolanda Moore '64 '92 C&L.347 B.S.N., J.D.
(adm. in IN; not adm. in OH) Coun., Anthem Ins. Cos., Inc.
Hayden, Angela ....'72 '99 C.523 B.A. L.7 J.D. [Ⓢ Baker&H.]
Hayden, Mark T., (BVⓉ) .... '61 '86 C.347 B.A. L.1119 J.D. [Greenebaum D.&M.]
Hayden, William T., (AV) ....'54 '79 C.207 B.A. L.150 J.D. [Katz,T.B.&H.]
Hayes, Ronald C. '43 '73 C.942 B.A. L.900 J.D.
(adm. in KS; not adm. in OH)
Asst. V.P., Assoc. Gen. Coun. & Asst. Secy., Great Amer. Ins. Co.
Hayes, Thomas A., (AV) .... '43 '68 C.973 B.S. L.477 J.D. [Ⓒ Keating M.&K.]
Hayes, William D., (AV) ....'61 '86 C.207 B.A. L.117 J.D. [Vorys,S.S.&P.]
Hayhow, Stephen F. .... '44 '70 C.150 B.A. L.1340 LL.B. 917 Main St., Ste. 2
Headley, James G., (AV) ......'11 '36 C.31 A.B. L.150 LL.B. 201 E. 5th St.,P.N.C Center‡
Healey, Roger W., (BV) ....'49 '76 C.610 B.A. L.150 J.D. [Buechner,H.O.M.H.&K.]
Healy, Jack S., (BV) ....'— '73 C.901 B.A. L.150 J.D. [Ⓐ Buckley K.]
Healy, Mary J., (AV) ....'52 '78 C.150 B.A. L.1340 J.D. [Dinsmore&S.]
Heather, Timothy P., (AV) .... '55 '80 C&L.150 B.F.A., J.D. [Benjamin,Y.&H.]
Heckerman, Arthur R., (AV) .... '15 '40 C&L.150 A.B., J.D. 201 E. 5th St.
Heekin, Albert E., III, (AV) ....'40 '65 C.602 B.B.A. L.150 J.D. [Ⓒ Frost B.T.]
Heekin, Christopher R., (BV) ....'62 '89 C.856 B.A. L.94 J.D. [Heekin&H.]
Heekin, Thomas D., (AV) ....'37 '62 C.951 A.B. L.477 J.D. [Taft,S.&H.]
Heekin, Thomas Donald, Jr., (BV) ....'60 '88 C.170 B.A. L.150 J.D. [Heekin&H.]
Heekin, William C. ....'54 '84 C.973 B.A. L.1340 J.D. 120 E. Fourth St., Ste. 425

Heekin & Heekin, (BV)
817 Main Street, Suite 200, 45202
Telephone: 513-345-5560 Fax: 513-345-5565 Fax: 1-800-300-3210
Email: attorneys@heekinattorneys.com URL: http://www.heekinattorneys.com
Members of the Firm: Thomas Donald Heekin, Jr.; Christopher R. Heekin.
Civil Litigation, Financial Institutions, Commercial Law, Real Estate Law, Personal Injury, Wrongful Death, Landlord and Tenant Law, Mortgages, Criminal Law, DUI, Driving While Intoxicated, Drug Crimes, Felonies, Homicide, Juvenile Law, Misdemeanors, Parole and Probation, Sexual Assault, Traffic Violations.
See Professional Biographies, CINCINNATI, OHIO

Hegge, Colleen M., (AV) ....'62 '87 C.510 B.S. L.1340 J.D. [Ⓒ Statman,H.S.&E.]
Heggland, Roy T. '51 '80 C.1033 B.S. L.705 J.D.
(adm. in NJ; not adm. in OH) Senior Vice President & General Counsel, CBIS
Heidrich, David P. '59 '83 C.973 B.S.B.A. L.1340 J.D.
(adm. in KY; not adm. in OH) [Ⓒ Cors&B.]

Heilbrun, John L., (BV) '51 '77 C.1350 B.A. L.150 J.D.
3536 Edwards Road, Suite 100, 45208-1368
Telephone: 513-321-3940 Fax: 513-321-3929 URL: http://www.johnheilbrun.com
Email: heilbrun@one.net. URL: http://www.heilbrunlaw.com
Plaintiffs' Personal Injury, Automobile/Motor Vehicle Accidents and Injuries, Automobile Insurance, Catastrophic Injuries, Head Injuries, uninsured and Underinsured Motorists, Wrongful Death, Collaborative Family Law, Child Custody, Divorce, Domestic Relations, Criminal Defense, Driving While Intoxicated, Domestic Violence, Search and Seizure, Felonies and Misdemeanors.
See Professional Biographies, CINCINNATI, OHIO

Heile, C. Donald, (AV) .... '36 '62 C.973 B.S. L.150 LL.B. [Garvin,L.H.&E.]
Hein, William J. '41 '66 C.602 B.B.A. L.1119 J.D.
Sr. Coun., The Procter & Gamble Co.‡
Heinichen, Jeffrey K., (BV) '52 '78
C.840 B.B.A. L.1340 J.D. Gen. Coun., Gen. Polymers Corp.
Heinrich, Rene B. '73 '00 C.235 B.A. L.1340 J.D.
(adm. in KY; not adm. in OH) [Donovan L.]
Heis, Forest S., (AV) .... '44 '69 C.150 B.B.A. L.309 J.D. [Heis&W.]
Heis, Jennifer Snyder ....'76 '01 C.385 B.A. L.245 J.D. [Ⓐ Ulmer&B.]
Heis & Wenstrup Co., L.P.A., (AV) .... 817 Main St., Ste. 800
Heiser, Stacey M. ....'69 '94 C.207 B.A. L.150 J.D. Counsel, Kendle International
Heitchue Reed, Catherine Ann ....'78 '03 C&L.477 A.B., J.D. [Ⓐ Frost B.T.]
Heldman, James G., (AV) ....'49 '75 C.309 A.B. L.273 J.D. [Strauss&T.]
Heldman, Paul W., (AV) '51 '77 C.94 B.S. L.150 J.D.
Sr. V.P., Secy. & Gen. Coun., Kroger Company, The
Helfrich, Loretta Marie, Attorney at Law '61 '89 C.1118 B.A. L.150 J.D.
119 E. Court St.
Helmer, James B., Jr., (AV) ....'50 '75 C.207 B.A. L.150 J.D. [Helmer,M.R.&P.]

Helmer, Martins, Rice & Popham Co., L.P.A., (AV)
1900 Fourth and Walnut Centre, 105 East Fourth Street, 45202-4009
Telephone: 513-421-2400 513-421-7902
Email: support@fcalawfirm.com URL: http://www.fcalawfirm.com
James B. Helmer, Jr.; Paul B. Martins; Robert M. Rice; Julie Webster Popham;—Donald G. Stiens, Jr.; Jennifer L. Lambert. Of Counsel: Robert Clark Neff, Jr.
Civil Trial and Appellate Practice; False Claims Act Litigation.
Reference: Huntington National Bank.
See Professional Biographies, CINCINNATI, OHIO

Helmick, Bertha Garcia ....'54 '95 C&L.150 B.M.E., J.D. 1014 Vine St.
Helmick, Dennis S. ....'47 '72 C.973 B.S. L.150 J.D. Mun. J.
Helmling, Margaret R., (Mrs.) ....'28 '59 C.973 A.B. L.1340 J.D. 3939 Creek Rd.‡
Helwig, Nancy C. ....'50 '80 C.473 B.A. 272 Parkway Ave.
Hemingway, Ronald L. ....'35 '68 C.150 B.S. L.1340 J.D. 5366 Dickens Dr. (Pat.)‡
Hemminger, David G. ....'37 '65 C.363 B.S.S. L.602 J.D. P.O. Box 599‡
Henderson, Stephen P. '49 '74 C.906 B.A. L.629 J.D.
(adm. in OR; not adm. in OH) Sr. Coun., GE Aviation Services, Inc.
Henderson, Thomas L. ....'56 '88 C.610 B.S. L.117 J.D. [Ⓐ Lerner,S.&R.]
Hendon, Sylvia S. ....'44 '75 C.999 B.A. L.1340 J.D. Ct. of App. J.
Hendricks, Jeffrey M. ....'71 '96 C.973 B.A. L.150 J.D. [Graydon H.&R.] ⊙
Hendricks, Louis J., Jr. ....'25 '58 C.611 B.A. L.151 J.D. 4557 Montgomery Rd.
Hendrickson, Nora C., Law Office of '59 '86
C.347 B.A. L.1119 J.D. 230 Northland Boulevard, Suite 231
Hengehold, Steven D., (AV) ...... '59 '85 C.973 B.S.B.A. L.150 J.D. [Rendigs,F.K.&D.]
Hengelbrok, James W., (AV) ....'21 '48 C.973 B.A. L.150 J.D. [Davis&H.]
Henkel, Mary C., (AV) ....'54 '79 C.973 B.A. L.309 J.D. [Ⓒ Vorys,S.S.&P.]

Hennekes, Jason '77 '02 C.150 B.S. L.1161 J.D.
830 Main Street, 45202
Telephone: 513-721-2850 Fax: 513-241-0584
Email: jayhennekes@hotmail.com URL: http://www.jasonhennekes.com
Criminal Law, Driving While Intoxicated, Felonies, Misdemeanors, Homicide, Theft, Drug crimes, Traffic Violations, Domestic Violence, Assault.
See Professional Biographies, CINCINNATI, OHIO

Hensley, Douglas L., (BV) ....'68 '93 C.967 B.A. L.150 J.D. General Electric Co.
Herbert, John D. '30 '57 C.674 A.B. L.477 J.D.
Corp. Legal Coun. & Secy., Ace Doran Hauling & Rigging Co.
Hermann, Julie R.L. ....'67 '93 C.473 B.A. L.851 J.D. Alderwoods Group, Inc.
Herndon, Richard D., (AV) ....'61 '86 C&L.150 B.A., J.D. [Griffin -F.]

Herrell, Robin L. ....'56 '84 C.339 B.S. L.880 J.D. State Dist. Coun. Off. for I.R.S.
Hersh, Gail C., Jr., (BV) ....'64 '92 C.385 B.A. L.150 J.D. [Ⓐ Weltman,W.&R.]
Hersko, Bart S. '55 '85 C&L.966 B.S.Ch.E., J.D.
Coun., Patents, The Procter & Gamble Co. (Pat.)
Hertlein, Charles F., Jr., (AV) ....'55 '80 C.150 B.A. L.477 J.D. [Dinsmore&S.]
Hertz, Giles T., (BVⓉ) '59 '89 C.383 B.A. L.1340 J.D.
(adm. in KY; not adm. in OH) 2623 Erie Avenue
Hertzman, Glenda Morgan, (BV) ....'46 '79 C.532 B.A. L.117 J.D. [White,G.&M.]
Hery, Mary Jane, (AV) ....'48 '79 C&L.150 B.A., J.D. 2444 Madison Rd.
Hess, Andrew C., (BV) '54 '82 C&L.878 B.S., J.D.
Sr. IP Coun. & Engineering Coun., GE Aviation Services, Inc. (Pat.)
Hess, Otis R., Jr. '39 '64 C.902 A.B. L.150 J.D.
V.P. & Coun., Great Amer. Surplus Lines Ins. Co.
Hess, W. Ashley ....'73 '98 C.893 B.A. L.902 J.D. [Ⓐ Greenebaum D.&M.]
Heuck, Robert, II, (AV) ....'56 '85 C.685 B.A. L.629 J.D. [Ⓐ Waite,S.B.&C.]
Hewitt, Harry Leon ....'57 '00 C.477 B.S. L.201 J.D. 7374 Reading Rd., Ste 117
Hext, Stephen R. ....'47 '72 C.602 A.B. L.150 LL.B. 14 Garfield Pl.
Heyd, Charles G., (AV) ....'35 '61 C.973 B.S. L.1340 J.D. [Bauer,M.&H.]
Heyd, Daniel C., (AV) ....'61 '86 C.973 B.S.B.A. L.150 J.D. [Graydon H.&R.]
Heyd, Joseph D., (AV) '63 '89 C.608 B.A. L.893 J.D.
Prod. Safety Coun., GE Aviation Services, Inc.
Hickey, Timothy A., (AV) ....'45 '71 C.276 B.A. L.1340 J.D. 1014 Vine Street
Hickman, Ingrid Nada ....'— '99 C.277 B.I.E. L.273 J.D. Procter & Gamble Co.
Hicks, Drew M. ....'76 '03 C.228 B.A. L.150 J.D. [Ⓐ Keating M.&K.]
Hicks, Steven R., (AV) ....'52 '89 C.150 B.A. L.201 J.D. [S.R.Hicks]
Hicks, Steven R., Inc., The Law Offices of, (AV) ....10999 Reed Hartman Highway
Hidy, Richard J., (AV) '62 '88
C.276 B.A. L.178 J.D. Sr. V.P. & Dep. Gen. Coun., U.S. Bancorp.
Higgins, James A. ....'43 '69 C&L.150 B.A., J.D. Cir. Exec., U.S. Cts. of App.
Higgins, John S. ....'66 '97 C.150 B.S. L.1003 J.D. [Ⓐ Frost B.T.]
High, Theodore K., (AV) ....'28 '58 C.347 A.B. L.976 J.D. P.O. Box 42235
Hight, James S., (AV) ....'17 '52 C.150 L.1340 LL.B. 839 Old Orchard Rd. (Pat.)‡
Hild, Guy M., (AV) ....'37 '62 C&L.150 A.B., J.D. [Katz,T.B.&H.]
Hill, James D. '58 '85 C.30 B.S. L.982 J.D.
(adm. in NY; not adm. in OH) I.R.S.
Hill, Thomas C., (AV) ....'46 '73 C.930 A.B. L.145 J.D. [Taft,S.&H.]
Hiller, Robert S., (AV) ....'51 '77 C.347 A.B. L.838 J.D. [Schroeder,M.B.&P.]
Hillerich, Laura I. ....'77 '02 C.967 B.A. L.150 J.D. [Ⓐ Rendigs,F.K.&D.]
Hillman, Harry D. ....'18 '53 C.151 L.1340 LL.B. Asst. City Solr.
Hils, M. Gabrielle, (AV) ....'59 '84 C.1118 B.A. L.383 J.D. [Dinsmore&S.]
Hils, Mary Elizabeth, (BV) '55 '80 C.1118 B.A. L.602 J.D.
V.P. & Sr. Corp. Coun., Provident Financial Group, Inc.
Hilton, Robert W., Jr., (AV) '16 '41 C.902 A.B. L.309 LL.B.
3983 Rosslyn Dr., Apt. 2002
Hilvert, Margaret A. ....'42 '89 C.523 B.A. L.150 J.D. [Beckman W.S.]
Hindert, Patrick J. ....'— '74 C.309 B.A. L.477 J.D. Benefit Designs, Inc.
Hinebaugh, Jeffrey P., (AV) ....'67 '92 C.294 B.A. L.477 J.D. [Dinsmore&S.]
Hinegardner, Laura A. ....'71 '96 C.383 B.A. L.150 J.D. [Katz,T.B.&H.]
Hines, G. Robert, (AV) ....'48 '75 C.645 B.A. L.1340 J.D. 1014 Vine St.
Hines, Jeffrey M. ....'70 '99 C.610 B.A. L.1161 J.D. [Ⓐ Kohnen&P.]

Hines, Dean Edward
(See Dayton)

Hinners, Jason R. ....'77 '03 C.473 B.S. L.201 J.D. [Ⓐ Robbins,K.P.&T.]
Hinners, Stacy ....'78 '03 C.611 B.A. L.201 J.D. [Ⓐ Mezibov&J.]
Hinson, Maureen S. ....'77 '03 C.473 B.A. L.150 J.D. [Ⓐ Lerner,S.&R.]
Hirsch, William C. ....'18 '46 L.879 J.D. 602 Main Street‡
Hirschfeld, Michael A., (AV) ....'51 '77 C.385 A.B. L.893 J.D. [Graydon H.&R.]
Hirsh, Ernest H. ....'51 '77 C.381 B.A. L.7 J.D. P.O. Box 779
Hoberg, Timothy E., (AV) ....'44 '70 C.608 B.E.E. L.893 J.D. [Taft,S.&H.]
Hochstrasser, Jennifer A. '64 '91 C.339 B.A. L.734 J.D.
(adm. in FL; not adm. in OH) Procter & Gamble Co.
Hock, Thomas P. ....'47 '73 C.602 B.B.A. L.150 J.D. Professional Transit Mgmt.
Hodge, Pamela Morgan, (BV) ....'62 '89 C.150 B.S. L.276 J.D. [Keating M.&K.]
Hodges, Jason L. ....'75 '00 C.138 B.A. L.383 J.D. [Ⓐ Vorys,S.S.&P.]
Hoefle, H. Fred, (AV) ....'38 '65 C.150 A.B. L.151 J.D. 30 E. Central Pkwy.
Hoehne, Jeffry M. ....'42 '70 C.210 B.A. L.150 J.D. 6613 Pownerfarm Dr.‡
Hoff, Louis A. '16 '61 C.151 B.S.C. L.1340 J.D.
V.P., Samuel W. Bell Home for Sightless, Inc.
Hoffheimer, Daniel J., (AV) ....'50 '76 C.309 A.B. L.893 J.D. [Taft,S.&H.]
Hoffheimer, Harry M., (AV) ....'12 '38 C.309 A.B. L.976 J.D. 600 Vine St.

Hoffheimer, Jon, (AV) '41 '65 C.165 B.A. L.597 J.D.
1200 Mercantile Library Building, 414 Walnut Street, 45202-3906
Telephone: 513-421-7666 Fax: 513-421-7693
Email: Jon@jonhoffheimer.com
(Certified Specialist in Estate Planning, Trust and Probate Law, Ohio State Bar Association).
Estate Planning, Probate Law, Wills, Trusts, General Practice.
See Professional Biographies, CINCINNATI, OHIO

Hoffman, Bridget C. ....'77 '02 C.973 B.A. L.150 J.D. [Ⓐ Taft,S.&H.]
Hoffman, Bruce A., (AV) ....'50 '75 C.207 B.A. L.188 J.D. [Graydon H.&R.]
Hoffman, Joseph V., (AV) ....'18 '53 C.674 A.B. L.150 LL.B. 6739 Fieldhouse Way‡
Hoffmann, Gary R., (AV) ....'47 '73 C&L.150 B.A., J.D. [G.R.Hoffmann]
Hoffmann, Gary R. Co., LPA, (AV) ....11935 Mason-Montgomery Road Suite 130
Hoffpauir, G. Todd ....'66 '95 C.808 B.S. L.425 J.D. [Montgomery,R.&J.]
Hoffsis, Stephen B., (BV) ....'61 '86 C.473 B.A. L.150 J.D. [Buechner,H.O.M.H.&K.]
Hoft, Thomas W., (BV) '57 '83
C.934 B.A. L.502 J.D. Legal Coun. & Secy., Senco Prods., Inc.
Hogan, Andrew J. ....'62 '87 C.105 B.A. L.930 J.D. [Kohnen&P.]
Hogan, Edward A., (AV) ...'24 '53 C.150 B.B.A. L.1340 J.D. 3518 Brookwood Meadow‡
Hogan, Kathryn H. '62 '88 C.201 B.A. L.421 J.D.
(adm. in IL; not adm. in OH) [Ⓐ Mason,S.&M.]
Hogan, Patricia B., (AV) ....'48 '89 C&L.150 B.A., J.D. [Keating M.&K.]
Hogan, Robert K. ....'— '82 C.865 B.A. L.930 J.D. [Javitch,B.&R.]
Hogan, Tara C. ....'74 '01 C.6 B.A. L.575 J.D. Coun., The Procter & Gamble, Co.
Hogan, Timothy S. ....'41 '73 C.201 B.A. L.1340 J.D. U.S. Mag. J.
Hohn, Michael, (BV) ....'48 '74 C.970 B.A. L.608 J.D. 3420 Beaumont Pl.
Hojnoski, Robert W. ....'73 '98 C.1062 B.S. L.201 J.D. [Ⓐ Reminger&R.]
Holcombe, David G., (BV) ....'55 '81 C.207 B.A. L.930 J.D. [Baker&H.]
Holifield, Johnathan M. ...'64 '96 C.923 B.A. L.150 J.D. 300 Carew Tower, 441 Vine St.
Hollingsworth, Robert J., (AV) ....'48 '73 C.973 A.B. L.150 J.D. [Cors&B.]
Hollis, Alysse E. '72 '00 C.172 B.A. L.1065 J.D.
(adm. in CO; not adm. in OH) [Ⓐ Peck,S.&W.]
Hollis, Charles F., III ....'71 '97 C.1161 B.A. L.150 J.D. [Ⓐ Benjamin,Y.&H.]
Holmes, Renée '52 '82 C.588 B.S. L.150 J.D.
(adm. in LA; not adm. in OH) Dep. Gen. Coun., Envir., Fluor Daniel Fernald, Inc.
Holmes, Stephen S., (AV) ....'57 '82 C.853 B.A. L.383 J.D. [Cors&B.]
Holschuh, John D., Jr., (AV) ....'55 '80 C.473 B.S. L.150 J.D. [Santen&H.]
Holschuh, Wendy G. ....'54 '83 C.645 B.S. L.150 J.D. 6896 Treeridge Dr.‡
Holtzman, Jan M. ....'46 '72 C.901 B.A. L.150 J.D. Asst. U.S. Atty.
Holzapfel, Eric C., (BV) ....'46 '72 C.207 B.A. L.245 J.D. [Wood&L.]
Holzman, Robert S., (BV) ....'36 '64 C&L.150 B.A., LL.B. [Holzman&H.]
Holzman, Wallace Ross, Jr., (BV) ....'36 '65 C&L.150 B.A., J.D. [Holzman&H.]
Holzman & Holzman, (BV) ....8425 Vine St.
Honerlaw, Joseph, (BV) ....'54 '80 C.385 B.A. L.117 J.D. [Honerlaw&H.]
Honerlaw, Michael J., (AV) ....'61 '86 C.602 B.A. L.117 J.D. [Honerlaw&H.]
Honerlaw & Honerlaw Co., L.P.A., (AV) ....9227 Winton Rd.
Hoopes, Robbin S. ....'62 '88 C.8 B.A. L.150 J.D. 14 East Interwood Place
Hopewell, Craig S., (AV) '55 '80 C.165 B.A. L.150 J.D.
Gen. Coun., Sentron Med., Inc.
Hopkins, Bruce G. ....'57 '90 C.976 B.A. L.1340 J.D. [Ⓐ Griffin -F.]
Hopper, George ....'13 '40 C.967 A.B. L.1340 LL.B. 7434 Jager Ct.‡
Hopper, Kevin J., (AV) ....'50 '78 C.150 B.S.M.E. L.1340 J.D. [Ⓒ Montgomery,R.&J.]
Hopping, Edwin N. '34 '61
C.473 B.S. L.150 LL.B. Sr. Coun., The Cincinnati Gas & Elec. Co.
Hopple, Richard M., (AV) ....'48 '73 C&L.150 B.A., J.D. [Beckman W.S.]
Hordes, Donald B., (BV) ....'44 '69 C.446 B.A. L.273 J.D. [Schwartz,M.&R.]
Horne, David J. ...'48 '74 C.454 B.A. L.188 J.D. Bureau of Alcohol, Tobacco & Firearms
Horner, James E. ....'34 '69 C.383 B.A. L.1340 J.D. N.L.R.B.
Horney, Kenneth A., (BV) ....'32 '60 C.973 L.150 LL.B. 3617 Ault Park Ave.
Horrell, Jack E., (AV) '51 '77
C.473 B.S. L.245 J.D. Prod. Mgmt. Coun., Great Amer. Ins. Co.‡
Horrell, Karen Holley, (AV) '52 '77 C.78 B.S. L.245 J.D.
Sr. V.P., Exec. Coun. & Corp. Secy., Great Amer. Ins. Co.
Horwitz, Elizabeth A., (AV) ....'51 '83 C.150 B.U.P. L.1340 J.D. [Cors&B.]

Horwitz Law Firm, The, P.S.C.
(See Crescent Springs, Kentucky)

Hoskins, Robert H. ....'64 '97 C.231 B.A. L.201 J.D. [Ⓐ Dinsmore&S.]
Houston, Daniel R., (BV) ....'41 '66 C.473 B.A. L.150 J.D. 8287 Winton Rd.
Houston, James ....'71 '00 C.473 B.A. L.201 J.D. [Ⓐ Thompson H.]
Houston, Janet L. ....'64 '89 C.623 B.B.A. L.150 J.D. [Cors&B.]
Howard, Barbara J., (AV) ....'54 '79 C.973 A.B. L.150 J.D. [B.J.Howard]
Howard, Catherine E. ....'78 '03 C.421 B.A. L.1340 J.D. [Ⓐ Taft,S.&H.]

Howard, Barbara J. Co., L.P.A., (AV)
960 Mercantile Center, 120 East Fourth Street, 45202
Telephone: 513-421-7300 Fax: 513-562-3532
Email: bjhowardco@aol.com
Barbara J. Howard (Certified Specialist in Family Relations Law, Ohio State Bar Association);—April Marie Payne.
Family Law, Divorce, Collaborative Law, Litigation.
See Professional Biographies, CINCINNATI, OHIO

Howard-Hodesh, Janine ....'54 '82 C.610 B.G.S. L.150 J.D. U.S. Ct. of App., 6th Cir.
Howe, Aaron C. ....'66 '91 C.973 B.A. L.990 J.D. [Ⓐ Smith,R.&S.]
Howe, Kenneth A. '41 '66 C&L.383 B.A., J.D.
(adm. in KY; not adm. in OH) Sr. Staff Atty., U.S. Ct. of App.
Howe, William D., (AV) ....'52 '77 C.973 B.A. L.150 J.D. [DeVita&H.]
Hoy, Judson, (AV) ....'30 '54 C.207 B.A. L.150 LL.B. 312 Walnut St.
Hubbard, James R., (AV) '58 '83
C.165 B.A. L.150 J.D. Sr. V.P. & Gen. Coun., Fifth Third Bank
Huber, Giselle K., (BV) ....'58 '86 C.973 B.A. L.201 J.D. 3507 Glenmore Ave.
Huber, John Christopher '68 '94
C.150 B.B.A. L.201 J.D. V.P. & Sr. Coun., Fifth Third Bank
Huddleson, William A., (AV) ....'46 '74 C.150 B.A. L.1340 J.D. [Huddleson&L.]
Huddleson & Lane Co., L.P.A., (AV) ....6061 Bridgetown Rd.
Hudec, Pamela A. ....'71 '96 C.528 B.A. L.930 J.D. [Ⓐ Lerner,S.&R.]
Hudson, Calvin Ransom ....'66 '93 C.10 B.S./B.A. L.880 J.D. Fed. Pub. Def. Off.
Hudson, Nicolette R. ....'72 '99 C.473 B.A. L.150 J.D. [Ⓐ Frost B.T.]
Hudson, Robert D., (BV) '62 '87
C&L.383 B.S., J.D. [Greenebaum D.&M.] (ⓒCovington, KY)
Huffman, Earl R., (AV) ....'30 '56 C.299 B.A. L.188 LL.B. Budco Grp., Inc.
Hughes, Angela M. ....'72 '04 C.347 B.S. L.200 J.D. [Ⓐ Cohen,T.K.&S.]
Hughes, Matthew W. ....'60 '84 C.150 B.S.C.E. L.383 J.D. 1 Neumann Way
Hughes, R. Scott ....'74 '99 C.1118 B.A. L.150 J.D. [Ⓐ Cors&B.]
Hughes, Richard Alan ....'55 '88 C.602 B.B.A. L.1340 J.D. One P & G Plaza
Huller, Mark J. '53 '82 C.150 B.F.A. L.383 J.D.
Sr. Coun. & Gen. Mgr., The Cincinnati Ins. Co.
Humbarger, Michael L. ....'68 '96 C&L.851 B.B.A., J.D. Ernst & Young
Humbert, Mark A., (BV) ....'55 '90 C.150 L.1340 J.D. 1014 Vine St.
Humbert, Vernon H. ....'14 '41 C.150 B.S. L.1340 J.D. 1217 Balmoral Dr.‡
Humphrey, Thomas W. '66 '93 C.453 B.S.E.E. L.309 J.D.
[Wood,H.&E.] (See Pat. Sect.)
Hunt, Marshall C., Jr., (BV) ....'42 '67 C&L.150 A.B., J.D. 66 E. Hollister St.
Hunt, Stephen R., (AV) ....'55 '80 C&L.150 B.B.A., J.D. [Aronoff,R.&H.]
Hunt, William E. ....'47 '72 C.347 A.B. L.608 J.D. Asst. U.S. Atty
Hunter, Bruce A., (AV) ....'54 '84 C&L.150 B.A., J.D. [Katz,T.B.&H.]
Huprich, David L. ....'33 '58 C.532 B.A. L.608 J.D. [Ⓐ Griffin -F.]
Hurd, John K., (AV) ....'43 '74 C.473 B.S. L.1340 J.D. [McCaslin,I.&M.] ⓒ
Hurlburt, Christopher H. ....'75 '00 C.973 B.A. L.150 J.D. [Ⓐ Lindhorst&D.]
Hurley, Brian E., (AV) ....'53 '79 C.363 B.A. L.608 J.D. [Crabbe,B.&J.]
Hurley, James M. '43 '72 C.276 A.B. L.209 J.D.
(adm. in IL; not adm. in OH) Sr. V.P., John Morrell & Co.
Hurley, Timothy J., (AV) ....'51 '76 C.973 A.B. L.734 J.D. [Taft,S.&H.]
Huse, William M. ....'— '03 C.679 B.S. L.150 J.D. [Ⓐ Blank R.]
Hust, John W., (AV) ....'49 '75 C.608 B.S. L.150 J.D. [Schroeder,M.B.&P.]
Huston, Larry L., (BV) '55 '87 C&L.851 M.S.M.E., J.D.
Sr. Coun., Patents, The Procter & Gamble Co. (Pat.)
Hutcherson, William H., Jr., (AV) '25 '54 C.207 A.B. L.893 LL.B.
[Rendigs,F.K.&D.] ‡
Hutson, Joseph M. ....'72 '98 C.610 B.A. L.150 J.D. [Ⓐ Cohen,T.K.&S.]
Hutton, Mary Ellyn LaBach '40 '76 C&L.383 B.A., J.D.
(adm. in KY; not adm. in OH) 6913 Fox Hill Ln.‡
Hutton, Thomas C. '50 '76 C.674 B.A. L.188 J.D.
(adm. in NY; not adm. in OH) Chemed Corp.
Hyland, Robert G., (AV) ....'47 '72 C.299 A.B. L.150 J.D. [Ritter&R.]
Hylander, Brian R. ....'73 '03 C.676 B.A. L.477 J.D. [Ⓐ Taft,S.&H.]
Hylander, Jessica S. ....'— '03 C.473 B.A. L.477 J.D. [Ⓐ Dinsmore&S.]
Hyle, Francis M., (BV) ....'48 '74 C.973 A.B. L.150 J.D. [Hyle&M.]
Hyle & Mecklenborg, Co., L.P.A., (BV) ....3050 Harrison Ave.
Hynden, Douglas S. ....'56 '81 C.210 B.A. L.383 J.D. Pres., Anchor Assocs., Inc.
Iaciofano, Anthony J., (BV) ....'60 '85 C.1118 B.A. L.201 J.D. [Benjamin,Y.&H.]

Ice, Andrew G. .... '68 '96 C.150 B.A. L.851 J.D. [Zegarski&I.]
Iery, Clare M. .... '— '01 C&L.150 B.A., J.D. [Ⓐ Dinsmore&S.] (See Pat. Sect.)
Imbus, Karen L. ....'62 '96 C.602 B.A. L.150 J.D. [Ⓐ Ulmer&B.]
Imm, Stephen E., (BV) ....'62 '87 C.150 B.A. L.276 J.D. [Katz,G.&N.]
Immell, Todd M. ... '71 '98 C&L.150 B.A., J.D. Sr. Tax Consultant, Ernst & Young, LLP
Immerman & Tobin, (BV) ....632 Vine Street, Suite 1010
Imwalle, Mark A. ....'72 '02 C.973 B.A. L.851 J.D. 7207 Wooster Pike
Infante, Renée A., (BV) ....'65 '91 C.473 B.A. L.608 J.D. [Ⓐ Waite,S.B.&C.]
Ingram, Harvey L. ....'21 '55 C.150 L.1340 1013 Thornfield Ln.
Ionna, Massimino M. ....'71 '00 C.383 B.A. L.1340 J.D. Mag., Hamilton Co. Juv. Ct.
Ipsaro, John R. ....'66 '93 C.107 B.S. L.201 J.D. [Ulmer&B.]
Ireton, Louis A., (AV) ....'32 '61 C.165 B.A. L.1340 LL.B. 4209 Erie Ave.‡
Irwin, Kevin E., (AV) ....'51 '77 C.473 B.A. L.1003 J.D. [Keating M.&K.]
Isaly, Charles W., (BV) ....'44 '69 C.473 A.B. L.229 J.D. [Reed,T.&H.]
Isidor, John M., (BV) .... '46 '84 C.150 B.A. L.1340 J.D. 4290 Glendale Milford Road
Issenmann, John K., (BV) ....'42 '67 C.201 B.A. L.150 J.D. 700 Walnut St.
Izenson, Daniel E., (AV) ....'64 '90 C.347 B.S. L.608 J.D. [Keating M.&K.]
Jackson, Angelina N.......................'75 '04 C.257 B.A. L.150 J.D. [Ⓐ Dinsmore&S.]
Jackson, Brian S. ....'70 '97 C.150 B.A. L.117 J.D. [Ⓐ Lerner,S.&R.]
Jackson, Christopher L. ....'74 '03 C.384 B.S. L.117 J.D. [C.L.Jackson]
Jackson, Kory A. ....'— '00 C&L.150 B.A., J.D. [Ⓐ Vorys,S.S.&P.]
Jackson, Randall S., Jr. .....'72 '98 C&L.734 B.A., J.D. [Ⓐ Wood,H.&E.] (See Pat. Sect.)
Jackson, Christopher L., LLC, Law Office of ....2115 Luray Avenue
Jacob, Nancy Vasileff, (BV) ....'56 '87 C&L.150 B.A., J.D. [N.V.Jacob]
Jacob, Nancy V., Attorney at Law, (BV) .... 4966 Glenway Ave., Ste. 103
Jacobs, Jon H., (AV) ....'36 '62 C.199 A.B. L.1340 J.D. [Jacobs&S.]
Jacobs, Mary Ann, (BV) ....'57 '82 C.473 B.A. L.150 J.D. [Ritter&R.]
Jacobs, Robert E., (AV) ....'26 '53 C.973 B.S.C. L.1340 LL.B. [Jacobs,K.S.&M.]
Jacobs, Thomas W. ....'57 '89 C&L.150 B.A., J.D. [Lutz,C.&M.]
Jacobs, Wayne L. ......'60 '90 C.839 B.S.M.E. L.421 J.D. [Wood,H.&E.] (See Pat. Sect.)
Jacobs, William R., (AV) ....'48 '73 C.910 A.B. L.150 J.D. [Strauss&T.]
Jacobs, Kleinman, Seibel and McNally, (AV) ....1014 Vine St., Ste. 2300
Jacobs & Startsman Co., L.P.A., (AV) .... 432 Walnut St.
Jacobson, Deborah '54 '80 C.604 B.A. L.665 J.D.
(adm. in PA; not adm. in OH) N.L.R.B.
Jacobson, Timothy A. .... '53 '93 C.870 B.S. L.1339 J.D. 9260 Village Green Dr.
Jaeger, Bruno G. ....'27 '56 C.383 L.150 LL.B. 3101 Stout Rd.

Jagtiani + Guttag
5332 Kindlewood Drive, West Chester, 45069 ⊙
Telephone: 513-856-7272
Eric W. Guttag (Resident).
Patents, Trademarks, Copyrights, Trade Secrets, International Trade, Litigation, Technology Transfer, Mergers and Acquisitions, Intellectual Property.
Fairfax, Virginia Office: 10363-A Democracy Lane, 22030. Telephone: 703-591-2664. Fax: 703-591-5907.
Charlottesville, Virginia Office: 300 Preston Avenue, Suite 300, 22902. Telephone: 703-591-2664.
See Professional Biographies, CINCINNATI, OHIO

Jahnke, Mark J., (AV) .... '54 '79 C.608 B.A. L.597 J.D. [Katz,T.B.&H.]
James, Thomas C., Jr. .... '66 '92 C.606 B.A. L.245 J.D. [Ⓐ Sanders&Assoc.]
Jameson, Kenneth D., (BV) ....'52 '79 C.608 B.A. L.150 J.D. 1029 Main St.
Jamison, Tracy Byrd .... '67 '93 C.313 B.S. L.150 J.D. [Cors&B.]
Janes, T. Andrew .... '56 '81 C.608 B.A. L.117 J.D. 425 Walnut Street, LOC 7196
Jansing, James M., (AV) .... '56 '82 C&L.150 B.S., J.D. [Keating M.&K.]
Janson, Julia Ann ....'64 '88 C.275 B.A. L.150 J.D. Cinery Corp.
Janszen, August T., (AV) ....'66 '93 C.734 B.A. L.201 J.D. [Strauss&T.]
Jarvis, Robin A. ....'61 '98 C.932 B.S. L.201 J.D. [R.A.Jarvis]
Jarvis, Robin A., Co., L.P.A. .... 7357 Brookcrest Drive

Javitch, Block & Rathbone L.L.P., (AV)
The Gwynne Building, 602 Main Street, Suite 500, 45202 ⊙
Telephone: 513-744-9600 Fax: 513-744-9602
URL: http://www.JBandR.com
Robert K. Hogan (Resident).
General Civil Practice. Collection, Commercial, Bankruptcy, Corporate, Landlord and Tenant, Family, Personal Injury, Real Estate and Probate Law. Trials and Appeals.
Representative Clients: General Motors Acceptance Corp.; Associated Estates Corp.; J.P. Morgan Chase; Bank of America; General Electric Capital Corp.; Household Finance Corporation; Key Bank; National City Corp.; Chrysler Financial Corp.; Bank One.
Cleveland, Ohio Office: Bond Court Building, 14th Floor, 1300 East Ninth Street. Telephone: 216-623-0000. Fax: 216-623-0190.
Columbus, Ohio Office: 33 North Third Street, Suite 500, 43215. Telephone: 614-228-9550. Fax: 614-228-2818.
See Professional Biographies, CLEVELAND, OHIO

Jefferies, David E. ....'70 '98 C.231 B.A. L.345 J.D. [Ⓐ Wood,H.&E.] (See Pat. Sect.)
Jefferson, Mina Jones, (BV) ...'65 '90 C.473 B.A. L.150 J.D. Univ. of Cinci. Coll. of Law
Jeffries, Lori E. .... '72 '97 C.473 B.S. L.1161 J.D. [Ⓐ Taft,S.&H.]
Jemison, Steven W., (AV) '51 '75
C.238 B.A. L.608 J.D. Corp. Sec., Proctor & Gamble Co.
Jenkins, Christian A. ....'69 '95 C.645 B.A. L.966 J.D. [Mezibov&J.]
Jensen, Carl M. ....'24 '50 C&L.150 LL.B. 3008 Glenmore Ave.
Jensen, Joel K., (CV) ....'56 '82 C.893 B.A. L.608 J.D. [Ⓐ Lerner,S.&R.]
Jevicky, John E., (AV) ....'54 '80 C.651 B.A. L.201 J.D. [Dinsmore&S.]
Johns, Michael D. '63 '97
C.813 B.S.B.A. L.150 J.D. Coun., The Procter & Gamble Co. (Pat.)
Johnson, Bonnie L. '48 '83 C.150 B.S.Ed. L.1340 J.D.
Assistant Vice President, Great American Life Insurance Co.
Johnson, David E. .... '67 '98 C&L.383 B.A., J.D. [Ⓐ Lerner,S.&R.]
Johnson, Ellsworth H., (AV) ....'11 '41 C&L.150 A.B., LL.B. 7483 Ross Ave.‡
Johnson, George H. .... '10 '35 C.951 B.A. L.150 J.D. 6701 E. Leeds Lane‡
Johnson, Inza E. ....'60 '88 C.610 B.S.C. L.150 J.D. 2323 Park Ave.
Johnson, James J., (AV) '46 '72
C.475 B.A. L.608 J.D. Chf. Legal Offr., The Procter & Gamble Co.
Johnson, James L., (BV) ....'45 '80 C&L.150 B.A., J.D. Chf. City Investigator
Johnson, Joseph F. ....'38 '62 C&L.424 LL.B. Exec. V.P., Campeau Develop. Corp.
Johnson, Kevin C. ....'65 '90 C&L.502 B.S.M.E., J.D. The Procter & Gamble Co.
Johnson, Linda F. ....'63 '88 C.973 B.A. L.150 J.D. Jud. Clk., Dist. Ct. App.
Johnson, Patrick G. ....'74 '03 C.911 B.A. L.893 J.D. [Ⓐ Taft,S.&H.]
Johnson, Richard H., (AV) ... '42 '68 C.679 B.S. L.150 J.D. 9902 Carver Road, 2nd Floor
Johnson, Robert P., (AV) ....'63 '88 C.945 B.A. L.880 J.D. [Thompson H.]
Johnson, Tracey M. ....'70 '97 C&L.150 B.S., J.D. [Ⓐ Lerner,S.&R.]
Johnston, Robert A. '26 '53
C.846 B.S.M.E. L.477 LL.B. 9403 Kenwood Road, Suite B-203
Johnstone, Robert H., Jr., (AV) ....'44 '71 C&L.150 B.A., J.D. Asst. City Solr.
Jones, B. Scott ....'73 '98 C.347 B.A. L.201 J.D. [Ⓐ Reminger&R.]
Jones, Daniel Lee, Jr. ....'67 '99 C&L.1161 B.O.S., J.D. [Ⓐ Dinsmore&S.]
Jones, Donald T., (BV) ....'47 '80 C.150 B.S. L.1340 J.D. 914 Main St.
Jones, J. Gregory '55 '84 C.929 B.A. L.1340 J.D.
(adm. in KY; not adm. in OH) U.S. Ct. of App.
Jones, Jeniece D. ....'— '02 C.923 B.S. L.1161 J.D. [Ⓐ Lerner,S.&R.]
Jones, Karen E. ....'66 '04 C.383 B.A. L.150 J.D. [Ⓐ Ulmer&B.]
Jones, Kevin ....'— '93 C.051 [Ⓒ O'Connor,M.&D.]
Jones, Kevin P. ....'45 '74 C.150 B.A. L.1161 J.D. 8035 Hosbrook Road
Jones, Melody A. '— '98 C.235 B.S. L.188 J.D.
Corp. Coun., Procter & Gamble Co. (Pat.)
Jones, Michael S. ....'65 '94 C.150 B.A. L.420 J.D. [Graydon H.&R.]
Jones, Nathaniel R. ....'26 '57 C&L.980 A.B., LL.B. [Ⓒ Blank R.]
Jones, Rick A. ....'55 '96 C.608 B.A. L.150 J.D. [R.A.Jones]
Jones, Robert R. ....'59 '85 C.201 B.S. L.989 J.D. [Ⓐ O'Connor,A.&L.]
Jones, Stephen Russell ....'63 '00 C.1302 B.S. L.1340 J.D. Gem City Tire Co.
Jones, Thomas W., Jr. ....'45 '71 C.880 B.A. L.477 J.D. 1227 Ida St.
Jones, Gary L., Co., L.P.A.
(See Columbus)
Jones, Rick A., Co., LPA ....7800 Cooper Rd., Ste. 101
Jonson, George D., (AV) ....'57 '83 C.473 B.A. L.150 J.D. [Montgomery,R.&J.]
Jordan, Joseph R., (BV) '42 '68 C.602 B.S. L.276 J.D.
[Ⓐ Wood,H.&E.] (See Pat. Sect.)
Jordan, Mark W., (AV) ....'55 '80 C.276 B.F.S. L.150 J.D. [Drew&W.]
Joseph, Jane E., (AVⓉ) '57 '85 C.604 B.A. L.1035 J.D.
[Ⓐ Lopez,H.M.&S.] (⊙Newport Beach, CA)
Joseph, Richard S. ....'65 '90 C.973 B.S.B.A. L.150 8733 Colerain Ave.‡
Josephic, David J., (AV) '35 '66 C.973 B.S.C. L.276 J.D.
[Wood,H.&E.] (See Pat. Sect.)
Jreisat, Wijdan ....'70 '94 C.138 B.A. L.893 J.D. [Katz,T.B.&H.]
Juenke, Timothy Robert ....'60 '93 C.276 B.A. L.1161 J.D. 215 E. Ninth St., Ste. 200
Julian, Frank G., (AV) '57 '82
C.383 B.S. L.602 J.D. Tax Coun., Federated Dept. Stores, Inc.‡
Jurs, Peter B. ....'72 '97 C.473 B.A. L.150 J.D. [Ⓐ Rendigs,F.K.&D.]
Jutze, Robert G. '66 '92 C.138 B.A. L.201 J.D.
Corp. Coun., Environmental Quality Management, Inc.
Kaake, Andrew R. ....'75 '00 C.1161 B.S. L.150 J.D. [Ⓐ Frost B.T.]
Kadish, Scott P., (AV) ....'60 '85 C.94 B.S.B.A. L.904 J.D. [Ulmer&B.]
Kadon, Karl P., (AV) ....'58 '84 C.473 A.B. L.1340 J.D. Hamilton Co. Pros. Off.
Kafker, Serena L. ....'33 '80 C.66 B.A. L.150 J.D. Univ. of Cinc., Coll. of Bus. Ad.
Kahle, Thomas W., (AV) ....'50 '75 C.201 B.A. L.608 J.D. [Baker&H.]
Kahmann, Kathleen E. ....'— '02 L.150 J.D. [Ⓐ Lerner,S.&R.]
Kahn, Marla Jean ....'55 '01 C.846 B.A. L.150 J.D. 1639 North Bend Road
Kaiser, Robert Daniel ....'48 '74 C&L.602 B.S., J.D. I.R.S. District Counsel
Kalafut, Christopher M. ....'59 '87 C.477 B.A. L.851 J.D. Industrial Comm.
Kallas, Hani R. ....'68 '94 C.473 B.S. L.150 J.D. [Vorys,S.S.&P.]
Kaltman, Sandra P. ....'55 '85 C.477 B.S.N. L.276 J.D. 4290 Glendale Milford Road
Kamine, Charles S., (AV) ....'52 '76 C.1036 B.A. L.208 J.D. [C.Kamine]
Kamine, Charles, (AV) .... 602 Main St., Ste. 1309
Kaminski, Gerald F., (AV) ....'46 '70 C.201 B.A. L.150 J.D. Sr. Litig. Coun.
Kammer, David D. ....'67 '93 C.602 B.A. L.150 J.D. [Tobias,K.&T.]
Kammer, Joseph C., (BV) ....'32 '55 C.973 B.S. L.276 J.D. 511 Walnut Street
Kamp, David P., (AV) ....'52 '81 C.1118 B.A. L.150 J.D. [White,G.&M.]
Kane, Joseph E. ....'43 '75 C.871 B.S. L.273 J.D. U.S. Admin. Law J.
Kane, Joseph E., (AV) ....'45 '70 C&L.602 B.A., J.D. [Graydon H.&R.]
Kane, Scott A. ....'69 '97 C.932 B.S. L.150 J.D. [Squire,S.&D.]
Kantor, Eric B. '65 '90 C.390 B.A. L.273 J.D.
(adm. in PA; not adm. in OH)
Div. Coun., Millt. Systems Opers. & Govt. Bus., GE Aviation Services, Inc.
Kaplan, Andrew M., (AV) ....'57 '83 C.31 B.A. L.276 J.D. [Vorys,S.S.&P.]
Kaplan, Bradley D., (AV) ....'61 '87 C.347 B.A. L.117 J.D. [Ulmer&B.]
Kapor, David W., (BV) ....'55 '80 C.473 B.S. L.365 J.D. 2306 Park Ave., Ste. 102
Karam, Ernest ....'09 '47 C.608 B.S.B.A. L.1340 J.D. Chief Mag., Ct. of Dom. Rel.
Karam, Gregory L. ....'— '82 C.608 M.A. L.1340 J.D. P.O. Box 43070
Karam, Suzanne W. ....'— '90 C.910 B.S. L.150 J.D. P.O. Box 43070
Kates, Darryl M., (BV) ....'66 '91 C.967 B.A. L.150 J.D. GE
Kates, Rick D. ....'70 '95 C.607 B.S.B.A. L.150 J.D. Mgr., Arthur Andersen‡
Katrus, Ilona I. ....'77 '03 C.973 B.S. L.150 J.D. [Ⓐ Freund,F.&A.]
Katsanis, James A., (AV) .... '31 '57 C&L.150 A.B., LL.B. [Ⓒ Frost B.T.]
Katz, Alfred B., (AV) ....'11 '35 C&L.150 B.A., LL.B. [Ⓒ Katz,G.&N.] ‡
Katz, Louis H., (BV) ....'49 '73 C.966 B.A. L.150 J.D. [Katz,G.&N.]
Katz, Reuven J., (AV) ....'24 '50 C.150 B.A. L.309 J.D. [Katz,T.B.&H.]

Katz, Greenberger & Norton, (AV) [BR]
105 East Fourth Street 4th Floor, 45202-4011
Telephone: 513-721-5151 Fax: 513-621-9285
Email: kgnlaw.com URL: http://www.kgnlaw.com
Mark Alan Greenberger; Louis H. Katz; Richard L. Norton; Steven M. Rothstein; Ellen Essig (Certified Specialist in Family Relations Law, Ohio State Bar Association); Ross M. Evans; Jeffrey J. Greenberger; Stephen E. Imm. Associates: Kevin R. Brewer; Christina S. Yager; Cheryl L. Borland; Lisa M. Ellis; Tawanda J. Edwards. Of Counsel: Alfred B. Katz (Retired).
General Practice. Corporate, Negligence, Labor, Tax, Probate and Immigration Law, Trials and Bankruptcy.
See Professional Biographies, CINCINNATI, OHIO

Katz, Teller, Brant & Hild, A Legal Professional Association, (AV) [BR]
255 East Fifth Street, Suite 2400, 45202-4787
Telephone: 513-721-4532 Telecopier: 513-721-7120
Email: ktbh@katzteller.com URL: http://www.katzteller.com
Reuven J. Katz; Jerome S. Teller; Guy M. Hild; Robert A. Pitcairn, Jr.; Robert E. Brant; Ronald J. Goret; Stephen C. Kisling; James F. McCarthy, III; Andrew R. Berger; Mark J. Jahnke; William F. Russo; William T. Hayden; John R. Gierl; Bruce A. Hunter; Bradley G. Haas; Daniel P. Utt; Cynthia L. Gibson; Tedd H. Friedman; Wijdan Jreisat; Laura A. Hinegardner;—Joel S. Brant; Tara A. Klee; Sheri E. Auttonberry; Jerome C. Bishop; Adam D. Colvin. Of Counsel: Joseph A. Brant.
General Civil Practice. Banking, Bankruptcy, Business Acquisitions, Business, Civil Litigation, Corporation, ERISA, Estate Planning, Family, Health Care and Hospital, Municipal Law and Zoning Law, Environmental Law, Labor and Employment Law, Pension and Profit Sharing, Probate, Real Estate, Securities, Sports and Entertainment, Tax and Tax Litigation.
See Professional Biographies, CINCINNATI, OHIO

Katzman, Amy, (BV) ....'52 '77 C.393 B.A. L.150 J.D. [Ⓐ Katzman,L.H.&B.]
Katzman, Irwin, (BV) ....'20 '49 C.838 L.150 LL.B. [Katzman,L.H.&B.]
Katzman, Logan, Halper & Bennett, (AV) .... 9000 Plainfield Rd.
Kaye, Rebecca K., (BV) ....'44 '78 C.313 B.A. L.1340 J.D. 1014 Vine St.
Kearney, Eric H., (AV) .... '63 '89 C.197 A.B. L.150 J.D. 354 Hearne Avenue
Kearns, George H., (BV) .... '38 '64 C.973 B.S. L.1340 J.D. 3028 Victory Pkwy.
Kearns, Jerome H., (AV) ....'41 '66 C.973 B.S. L.477 J.D. [Dinsmore&S.]
Kearns, Michael Allen .... '62 '94 C.150 B.A. L.1003 J.D. 3028 Victory Pkwy.
Kearns, Michael Scott ....'67 '93 C&L.1161 B.A., J.D. 215 W. 9th St.
Keating, Thomas T., (AV) ....'47 '74 C.425 B.A. L.1340 J.D. 8050 Hosbrook St., Ste. 200
Keating, William J., (AV) ....'27 '50 C&L.150 B.B.A., J.D. [Ⓒ Keating M.&K.]
Keating, William J., Jr., (AV) ....'53 '79 C&L.150 B.B.A., J.D. [Keating M.&K.]

Keating Muething & Klekamp PLL, (AV) BR
One East Fourth Street, Suite 1400, 45202
Telephone: 513-579-6400 Facsimile: 513-579-6457
URL: http://www.kmklaw.com
Members of Firm: John L. Muething; Donald P. Klekamp; Timothy A. Garry; Gary P. Kreider; Don R. Gardner; Louis F. Gilligan; Herbert B. Weiss; Joseph P. Rouse; Richard D. Siegel; Joseph L. Trauth, Jr.; James R. Whitaker; J. David Rosenberg; Robert W. Maxwell II; Richard D. Spoor; J. Neal Gardner; Richard L. Creighton, Jr.; Paul V. Muething; James E. Burke; Kevin E. Irwin; Timothy B. Matthews; William J. Keating, Jr.; William A. Posey; Joseph P. Mellen; Mark J. Weber; Gregory M. Utter; Robert E. Coletti; James M. Jansing; Patrick F. Fischer; David K. Montgomery; James R. Matthews; Edward E. Steiner; Stephen M. Goodson; Robert G. Sanker; Lisa Wintersheimer Michel; W. Keith Noel; Daniel J. Donnellon; Brian M. Babb; Daniel E. Izenson; Gail T. King; Kenneth P. Kreider; Gail Glassmeyer Pryse; Mary Ellen Malas; Michael L. Scheier; Jody T. Klekamp; Pamela Morgan Hodge; Paul D. Dorger; Mark A. Weiss; James H. Brun; Joseph M. Callow Jr.; Alan S. Fershtman; James J. McGraw, Jr.; Steven C. Coffaro; John F. Meisenhelder; Mark J. Chumley; Sue A. Erhart; F. Mark Reuter; Adrienne J. Roach; Rachael A. Rowe; Jill A. Weller; John S. Fronduti; Karen Kreider Gaunt; Matthew K. Buck; Patricia B. Hogan; E. Todd Wilkowski. Associates: John N. Winstead; Benjamin A. Schneider; Caroline M. DiMauro; Jamie M. Ramsey; D. Brock Denton; Thomas M. Tepe, Jr.; Michael J. Moeddel; Jason M. Cohen; Danielle M. D'Addesa; Drew M. Hicks; Brian P. Muething; Ari B. Redbord (Not admitted in OH); Cole D. Bond; Jason V. Stitt; Joseph C. Alter; Christy M. Nageleisen; William D. Spoor (Not admitted in OH); M. Scott McIntyre; Alison J. Bouffard; Brian A. Riddell; Steven W. Sebastian; Sean S. Suder; Jennifer K. Walwyn; David A. Meyer; Paula Yasuyo Boggs (Not admitted in OH); Daniel G. Dutro Jr.; Donyetta D. Bailey; Andrew D. Bowers; Jennifer J. Morales; W. Jeffrey Sefton. Of Counsel: William J. Keating; Gehl P. Babinec; Thomas A. Hayes; Charles H. Gerhardt, III; R. Patrick DeWine.
General Practice: Administrative, Banking, Bankruptcy, Corporations, Criminal, Employee Benefits Law, Environmental, ERISA, Estate Planning, Health Care, Immigration, Intellectual Property, Labor, Mergers and Acquisitions, Probate, Real Estate, Securities, Taxation, Trials and Appeals.
Representative Clients: American Financial Group; The Cincinnati Reds; Cincom Systems, Inc.; Cintas Corp.; Comair, Inc.; Fifth Third Bank; Great American Insurance Co.; Joseph Automotive Group; Kendle International; The Midland Co.

See Professional Biographies, CINCINNATI, OHIO

Keck, Linda M. .... '69 '96 C.276 B.S.L.A. L.339 J.D. [Ⓒ Frost B.T.]
Keefe, Daniel McGregor .... '51 '78 C.999 B.S. L.836 J.D. Great American Insurance Co.
Keegan, Mary Ellen, (BVⓉ) '54 '80
C.927 B.A. L.678 J.D. Atty., GE Aviation Services, Inc.
Keenan, Francis A. '39 '64 C.93 A.B. L.94 LL.B.
(adm. in MA; not adm. in OH) 841 Ludlow Ave.‡
Keeney, Kathleen Barlage .... '58 '83 C&L.150 B.A., J.D. Ct. of App.
Keffer, James D. '66 '92 C.347 B.S. L.150 J.D.
(adm. in KY; not adm. in OH) [Ⓐ Lerner,S.&R.]
Kehres, Julie Schimpf, (BV) .... '65 '92 C.201 B.A. L.117 J.D. [Ⓐ Butkovich,S.S.&G.]
Keiser, Howard T., (AV) '10 '39 C.679 B.S. L.276 J.D.
(adm. in DC; not adm. in OH) 2525 Ranchvale Dr.‡
Keith, Damon J. .... '22 '50 C.922 B.A. L.329 LL.B. Sr. Cir. J.
Keith, R. Fred '63 '90
(adm. in KY; not adm. in OH) 5710 Wooster Pike, Ste. 212
Keith, Robert F. .... '63 '90 C.235 B.B.A. L.1340 J.D. 5710 Wooster Park, Ste. 212
Keller, Aimee L. .... '66 '93 C&L.188 B.S., J.D. [Taft,S.&H.]
Keller, James F., (AV) .... '64 '92 C&L.150 B.S., J.D. [Ⓐ Gottesman]
Keller, James K. .... '56 '94 C.1006 B.A L.150 J.D. [Schwartz,M.&R.]
Keller, John T., (BV) .... '46 '75 C.150 B.A. L.151 J.D. 2345 Kemper Lane
Keller, Katherine A., (BV) .... '44 '73 C.523 B.S. L.150 J.D. 139 E. 4th St.
Kelley, John J., Jr., (BV) .... '23 '50 C&L.602 B.A., LL.B. 3468 Forest Oak Court
Kelley, John J., Jr., (AV) .... '36 '60 C.610 B.S.C. L.930 LL.B. [Kohnen&P.]
Kelley, Rebecca .... '71 '97 C.289 B.A. L.150 J.D. YMCA of Greater Cincinnati
Kelley, Stuart J. .... '31 '58 C.973 A.B. L.150 LL.B. 8156 Sagamore Dr.‡
Kelley, Terence J. '45 '76 C.734 A.B. L.502 J.D.
(adm. in MO; not adm. in OH) Div. Coun., Off. of Council U.S. Army Corps of Engrs.
Kelley, Terrence E. .... '72 '02 C.94 B.A. L.607 J.D. [Ⓐ Heis&W.]
Kellogg, Paul J. .... '67 '93 C.610 B.S. L.201 J.D. [Ⓒ Rendigs,F.K.&D.]
Kelly, Charles J., (AV) .... '40 '65 C.973 B.S. L.150 J.D. [Lindhorst&D.]
Kelly, Cornelius Joseph '32 '86 C.999 B.A. L.508 J.D.
(adm. in MT; not adm. in OH) V.P., Ethics, Sisters of Charity Health Care Systems, Inc.
Kelly, James M., (AV) .... '52 '76 C.973 A.B. L.150 J.D. [Robbins,K.P.&T.]
Kelly, Jeffrey B. .... '52 '78 C.429 B.A. L.144 J.D. Cincinnati Milacron Inc.
Kelly, John T., III ..... '39 '69 C.973 Litt.B. L.150 J.D. Admin. Law J., Soc. Sec. Admin.
Kelly, Robert G., (BV) .... '51 '77 C.973 B.S.B.A. L.1340 J.D. [R.G.Kelly]
Kelly, Ruth T. .... '78 '05 C.611 B.A. L.999 J.D. [Ⓐ Freund,F.&A.]
Kelly, Robert G., Co. LPA, (BV) .... 4353 Montgomery Road
Kelly-Schilling, Sandra D., (BV) .... '53 '79 C&L.150 B.A., J.D. Asst. City Solr.
Kemphaus, Nicholas J. .... '78 '04 C.1118 B.S. L.1340 J.D. [Ⓐ Dinsmore&S.]
Kendall, Dara M. '70 '97 C.1378 B.S. L.574 J.D.
Sr. Coun., The Procter & Gamble Co., IP Div. (Pat.)
Kendrick, Claborn L. .... '17 '58 C.150 L.1340 LL.B. 798 Clinton Springs
Kenkel, Kenneth R. '61 '93 C&L.383 B.A., J.D.
(adm. in KY; not adm. in OH) Staff Atty., Staff Atty. Off.
Kennedy, Cornelia G. .... '23 '47 C&L.477 A.B., J.D. Sr. U.S. Ct. App. J.
Kennedy, J. Terry, (BV) .... '54 '79 C.243 B.A. L.1003 J.D. [Kennedy&K.]
Kennedy, James C., (AV) '50 '76 C&L.150 B.B.A., J.D.
V.P. Secy. & Dep. Gen. Coun., Amer. Premier Underwriting, Inc. & Amer. Fin. Corp., Inc.
Kennedy & Kennedy Co., A Legal Professional Association, (AV)
10723 Montgomery Rd.
Kenney, Jeffrey T., (AV) .... '65 '91 C.608 B.A. L.1340 J.D. [Droder&M.]
Kenrich, John L. .... '29 '53 C.473 B.S. L.150 LL.B. 504 Abilene Trail‡
Kereiakes, Annette .... '55 '80 C&L.150 B.A., J.D. 14 Garfield Pl.
Kern, David Graham .... '73 '00 C.797 B.A. L.608 J.D. [Ⓐ Kohnen&P.]
Kern, David O. .... '67 '97 C.303 B.A. L.1161 J.D. One West Fourth Street
Kerr, David L., (BV) .... '47 '73 C&L.150 B.S., J.D. [Ⓐ Ritter&R.]
Kerschen, Marco R. '74 '01 L.055 J.D.
(adm. in NY; not adm. in OH) Sr. Coun., The Procter & Gamble Co.
Kessler, Gregory S. .... '66 '96 C&L.150 B.S.A.E., J.D. [Ⓐ Roetzel&A.]
Ketz, Roy .... '15 '45 C.150 L.1340 LL.B. 1861 Dalewood Pl.
Keyes, R. Michael .... '45 '72 C.945 A.B. L.930 J.D. 2nd Fl., Legal, 201 East 5th St.
Kiel, Frederick O., (AV) '42 '66 C.952 A.B. L.309 J.D.
1095 Nimitzview Drive Suite 103
Kilcoyne, John W., (AV) .... '08 '34 C.973 A.B. L.150 J.D. [Ⓒ Cohen,T.K.&S.]
Kilcoyne, Thomas C., (AV) .... '58 '84 C.197 A.B. L.150 J.D. [Ⓒ Cohen,T.K.&S.]
Kiley, Wm. A. .... '16 '50 C.973 B.S.C. L.150 LL.B. 873 North Bend Rd.‡
Kilgarriff, Mary E. .... '22 '66 C.151 B.Sc. L.1340 J.D. 2935 Erie Ave.‡
Killoran, William V., Jr. '52 '77 C.604 A.B. L.910 J.D.
(adm. in IL; not adm. in OH) Sr. Coun., Envir. Affairs Div., GE Aviation Services, Inc.

Killworth, Gottman, Hagan & Schaeff, L.L.P.
(See Dinsmore & Shohl LLP)

Kimball, Steven C. .... '54 '86 C.235 B.S. L.1340 J.D. KZF, Inc.
Kincaid, Daniel E. '66 '92 C.347 B.A. L.421 J.D.
(adm. in KY; not adm. in OH) Staff Atty., Community Mutual Insurance Company

Kindel, Frederick W., (AV) .... '52 '80 C.383 B.A. L.838 J.D. [Frost B.T.]
Kindel, Patricia A. '52 '80 C.383 B.A. L.838 J.D.
Potter Stewart, U.S. Courthouse 100 East 5th St.
Kinder, Kenneth H., II .... '69 '00 C.853 B.A. L.1340 J.D. [Ⓐ Cors&B.]
Kindleberger, David W. '26 '53 C.893 B.S. L.537 LL.B.
(adm. in DC; not adm. in OH) 8845 Raiders Run‡
Kindt, Monica V. .... '74 '99 C.747 B.A. L.1526 J.D. [Ⓐ Cohen,T.K.&S.]
King, Frederick G. '65 '91 C&L.608 B.S., J.D.
V.P., Gen. Coun. & Secy., Givaudan Flavors Corp.
King, Gail T., (AV) .... '64 '90 C&L.150 B.A., J.D. [Keating M.&K.]
King, Kathleen Connellan .... '46 '75 C.932 B.A. L.213 J.D. Mag.
King, Stephen M., (AV) .... '60 '85 C.902 B.A. L.608 J.D. [Thompson H.]
King, W. Gary, (AV) .... '37 '62 C.473 A.B. L.608 J.D. 2800 Gilbert Avenue
Kinnen, Jennifer .... '— '02 C.608 B.A. L.150 J.D. [Ⓐ Thompson H.]
Kinney, Ann Jouett '72 '97 C.138 B.A. L.383 J.D.
(adm. in KY; not adm. in OH) 201 E. Fourth Street, 102-890
Kinney, Jean M. .... '56 '85 C.602 B.S. L.1340 J.D. 401 Reily Rd.
Kinney and Schenk, (AV) .... 250 E. 5th St.
Kinsley, Jennifer M. .... '75 '99 C.260 B.A. L.228 J.D. [Ⓐ Sirkin P.&S.]
Kipling, James M. ..... '— '72 C.150 B.S.M.E. L.276 J.D. [Ⓒ Frost B.T.] (See Pat. Sect.)
Kircher, Thomas J., (AV) .... '40 '66 C.973 B.S. L.276 J.D. [Kircher,R.&W.]
Kircher, Robinson & Welch, (AV) .... 1014 Vine Street, Suite 2520
Kirila, Jill S. .... '72 '97 C.608 B.A. L.276 J.D. [Ⓐ Squire,S.&D.] (⊙Columbus)
Kirk, Roger W. .... '56 '82 C.150 B.A. L.201 J.D. 114 E. 8th St.
Kirkwood, Thomas J., (AV) .... '49 '74 C&L.150 B.A., J.D. [Thompson H.]
Kirschner, Leonard, (AV) .... '28 '50 C&L.150 A.B., LL.B. 10 W. 9th St.‡
Kirshner, Deborah M. .... '50 '78 C.1036 B.A. L.150 J.D. 1135 Edwards Road
Kirzner, Ryan D. .... '74 '00 C.472 B.A. L.150 J.D. [Ⓐ Barron,P.B.&S.]
Kisling, Stephen C., (AV) .... '51 '76 C.611 B.A. L.1170 J.D. [Katz,T.B.&H.]
Kissel, Larry E. .... '41 '69 C.150 B.S.C.E. L.1340 J.D. 139 E. 4th St.
Kissinger, Curtis E., (BV) .... '65 '90 C.150 B.A. L.201 J.D. [Cohen,T.K.&S.]
Kite, Matthew McD. .... '64 '95 C.170 B.A. L.117 J.D. [Cohen,T.K.&S.]
Klain, Jeffrey .... '67 '00 C.145 B.A. L.477 J.D. P.O. Box 8487
Klain, Nancy '— '98 C.145 A.B. L.477 J.D.
(adm. in MI; not adm. in OH) P.O. Box 8487
Klaine, Franklin A., Jr., (AV) .... '41 '67 C.321 B.S. L.150 J.D. [Strauss&T.]
Klee, Tara A. .... '72 '98 C.473 B.S. L.150 J.D. [Ⓐ Katz,T.B.&H.]
Klein, Joseph C. .... '68 '97 C&L.477 B.A., J.D. [Ⓐ Ulmer&B.]
Kleinhaus, Ferdinand Herman, (BV) '49 '75
C.973 A.B. L.1340 J.D. 830 Main St., Ste. 200
Kleinman, Marvin, (AV) .... '26 '53 C.151 B.S.C. L.1340 LL.B. [Ⓒ Jacobs,K.S.&M.]
Klekamp, Donald P., (AV) .... '32 '57 C.973 A.B. L.150 J.D. [Keating M.&K.]
Klekamp, Jody T., (BV) .... '65 '92 C.473 B.A. L.150 J.D. [Keating M.&K.]
Klineman, Susan B. .... '65 '93 C.679 B.A. L.345 J.D. [Ⓐ Weltman,W.&R.]
Klingler, Robert A., (AV) .... '52 '85 C.432 B.A. L.150 J.D. [R.A.Klingler]

Klingler, Robert A., Co., L.P.A., (AV) BR
525 Vine Street, Suite 2320, 45202-3124
Telephone: 513-665-9500 Fax: 513-621-3240
Email: rak@klinglerlaw.com URL: http://www.klinglerlaw.com
Robert A. Klingler;—Robert M. Lamb; Susan Marie Sauter.
Commercial and Business Litigation, Labor and Employment, Personal Injury, Medical Malpractice, Sexual Harassment.

See Professional Biographies, CINCINNATI, OHIO

Klocke, Dale W. .... '48 '73 C&L.150 B.B.A., J.D. 3572 Blue Rock Road
Kloos, Brenda M., (AV) .... '56 '82 C.27 B.A. L.201 J.D. [Thompson H.]
Klotz, Jeremy A. '73 '02 C.347 B.A. L.209 J.D.
(adm. in IN; not adm. in OH) [Ⓐ Dinsmore&S.]
Kluener, Thomas J., (BV) .... '53 '84 C.973 B.S.B.A. L.1340 J.D. 3507 Glenmore Avenue
Klusmeier, Harry T. .... '22 '49 C&L.150 B.A., LL.B. Ret. Ct. of App. J.
Klusmeier, Mark H., (AV) .... '58 '83 C&L.150 B.A., J.D. 2623 Erie Ave.
Knabe, Arthur T., (AV) .... '29 '58 C.150 B.B.A. L.1340 J.D. [Mack,M.&K.]
Knabe, Bruce D., (AV) .... '67 '94 C.473 B.A. L.151 J.D. [Ⓐ Mack,M.&K.]
Knapp, William C., (BV) .... '42 '78 C.929 B.S. L.1340 J.D. 8044 Montgomery Rd.
Knisley, Melinda E., (AV) .... '55 '84 C.473 B.A. L.150 J.D. [Croskery]
Knox, Scott E., (BV) .... '56 '85 C.693 B.A. L.150 J.D. 13 East Court Street, Suite 300
Kobasuk, Mark A., (AV) .... '57 '90 C.318 B.A. L.276 J.D. [Taft,S.&H.]
Koch, Elizabeth M. '61 '93 C.421 B.S.M.E. L.1206 J.D.
Sr. Coun., Procter & Gamble Co.

Koch, Ronald J.
(See Columbus)

Koenig, Darlene M. .... '53 '85 C.523 B.A. L.1340 J.D. Ct. of App.
Koenig, Donald E., Jr. '58 '84 C&L.273 B.A., J.D.
(adm. in PA; not adm. in OH) Corp. Dir. & Staff Coun., Catholic Healthcare Partners
Koenig, Kenneth J., Attorney at Law, (BV) '52 '77
C.276 A.B. L.262 J.D. 441 Vine St., Ste. 4400
Koenig, Peter E., (AV) .... '56 '81 C.610 B.A. L.930 J.D. [Buechner,H.O.M.H.&K.]
Koffler, Ian F. '77 '04 C.692 B.A. L.383 J.D.
(adm. in KY; not adm. in OH) [Ⓐ Peck,S.&W.] (⊙Covington, Louisville, KY)
Kohlhepp, William G., (AV) .... '41 '65 C.1118 A.B. L.383 LL.B. [Cors&B.]
Kohn, Michael G., (AV) .... '44 '75 C.1365 A.B. L.776 J.D. P.O. Box 8160
Kohnen, Monica Donath, (AV) ...... '60 '85 C.228 B.A. L.150 J.D. [Graydon H.&R.] ⊙
Kohnen, Ralph B., (AV) .... '35 '60 C.276 B.A. L.150 LL.B. [Kohnen&P.] ‡

Kohnen & Patton LLP, (AV)
PNC Center, Suite 800, 201 East Fifth Street, 45202 ⊙
Telephone: 513-381-0656 FAX: 513-381-5823
Email: info@kohnenpatton.com URL: http://www.kohnenpatton.com
Members of Firm: Ralph B. Kohnen (Retired); W. Andrew Patton; Mark J. Zummo; Joseph Beech, III; Joseph L. Dilts; John J. Kelley, Jr.; Keith D. Meyer; K. Roger Schoeni; Richard M. Haines; John L. Campbell; Jeffrey C. Shipp; Anthony J. Caruso; Ann Ruley Combs; Andrew R. Leeper; Terry E. Moore; Andrew J. Hogan; Karen A. Carroll; Colleen M. Blandford; Peggy Murphy Barker; Kimberly A. Mayer; Michael J. Stegman. Associates: Malinda L. Langston; Kimberly Kyle Zamary; H. Drewry Gores; Jeffrey M. Hines; David Graham Kern; Louis C. Schneider; David Joseph Bross; Leslie E. Ghiz. Of Counsel: John P. Tafaro.
Litigation, Insurance Law, Probate, Securities, Real Estate Law, Banking Law, Technology, Medical Malpractice Defense, Mediation, Corporate Law, Business Law, Estate Planning.
Representative Clients: American Loyalty Insurance Co.; Clermont Mercy Hospital; Cincinnati Insurance; Cottingham Retirement Community; Drake Center, Inc.; The Future Now, Inc.
Ft. Mitchell, Kentucky Office: 211 Grandview Drive, Suite 236 41017. Telephone: 859-341-0009. Facsimile: 859-341-0034.

See Professional Biographies, CINCINNATI, OHIO

Kolesar, Andrew L., (AV) .... '58 '91 C.885 B.S. L.276 J.D. [Thompson H.]
Kolesar, Geri Weiseman '57 '90 C.966 B.A. L.276 J.D.
(adm. in NY; not adm. in OH) 1304 Dillon Ave.
Kolstein, Marvin N. .... '28 '54 C&L.150 LL.B. 7 W. 7th Street‡

Koons, Patricia B. '23 '49 C.856 A.B. L.150 LL.B.
(adm. in ME; not adm. in OH) 7935 Annesedale‡
Korbee, Harold G., (AV) '39 '65 C.973 B.S. L.1340 J.D. [Wood&L.]
Korbee, Thomas C., (AV) '48 '77 C.973 B.S. L.150 J.D. [Ⓐ Lawrence] ⊙
Kordons, Uldis '41 '71 C.674 A.B. L.276 J.D. [Kordons]
Kordons & Co., L.P.A. 8238 Wooster Pike
Korfhage, Melissa L. '75 '00 C.1150 B.A. L.4210 J.D. [Ⓐ Dinsmore&S.]
Kotian, Manisha Bansal, Law Office of '68 '93
C.150 B.B.A. L.665 J.D. 9200 Montgomery Road
Kotlarsic, Liza A. '64 '89 C.161 B.B.A. L.150 J.D. 3949 East Kemper Road
Koustmer, Thomas R., (BV) '55 '80 C.610 B.A. L.880 J.D. 7 W. 7th St.
Kozimer, Kenneth G. '47 '82 C.434 B.S. L.969 J.D.
(adm. in GA; not adm. in OH) 6235 Cedar Crossing Lane
Kozlowski, Holly D., (AVⓉ) '58 '84
C.105 B.S.Ch.E. L.1209 J.D. [Dinsmore&S.] (See Pat. Sect.)
Kraft, Robt. S. '28 '50 C&L.150 B.A., LL.D. Com. Pleas J.
Krafte, Lori E. '55 '98 C.347 B.A. L.150 J.D. [Ⓐ Greenebaum D.&M.]
Krass, Marc S. '49 '76 C.604 A.B. L.597 J.D.
Assoc. Gen. Coun., The Procter & Gamble Co.
Krass, Norbert C. '23 '55 L.1340 LL.B. Fireman's Fund Amer. Ins. Cos.
Kratz, Karen Ecker '66 '92 C.201 B.A. L.602 J.D. [Ⓒ Frost B.T.]
Kraus, Christopher E. '60 '97 C.95 A.B. L.1340 J.D. 215 E. Ninth St.
Kraus, Marvin H., (AV) '29 '54 C.309 B.A. L.150 LL.B. [Tobias,K.&T.]
Krebs, Jay A. '61 '95 C.383 B.S.M.E. L.1340 J.D.
Sr. Coun., The Procter & Gamble Co.
Kreider, Gary P., (AV) '38 '64 C&L.150 B.A., J.D. [Keating M.&K.]
Kreider, Kenneth P., (AV) '64 '89 C.385 A.B. L.150 J.D. [Keating M.&K.]
Kreidler, Robert L., (AV) '37 '62 C.976 A.B. L.150 J.D. [Graydon H.&R.]
Kreiner & Peters Co., L.P.A., (BV)
2055 Reading Road, Suite 290 (⊙Cleveland, Columbus)
Kriete, Wilbur ... '36 '69 C.473 B.S. L.1340 J.D. Tax Admr., Federated Dept. Stores, Inc.‡
Krone, Bruce A., (AV) '54 '82 C.608 B.S. L.201 J.D. [Eichel&K.]
Kropp, Allison Hiltz '— '03 C&L.276 B.S.F.S., J.D. [Ⓐ Frost B.T.]
Kropp, John J., (AV) '46 '72 C.150 B.A. L.276 J.D. [Graydon H.&R.]
Krouse, James E. '29 '60 C&L.607 B.A., LL.B. 6355 Harrison Ave.‡
Krug, John C., (AV) '64 '89 C.659 B.A. L.273 J.D. [Frost B.T.]
Kruger, Jackie R. '— '04 C.1375 B.A. L.477 J.D. [Ⓐ Vorys,S.S.&P.]
Krumpelbeck, Gerald W., (AV) '50 '77
C.1118 B.A. L.1340 J.D. Sr. Asst. Pros. Atty., Hamilton Co. Pros. Off.
Kruse, Daniel A., (AV) '45 '70 C.973 A.B. L.602 J.D. [Bauer,M.&H.]
Kubicki, Charles J., Jr. '62 '93 C.608 B.A. L.1340 J.D. Com. Pleas J.
Kubicki, Margaret G. '68 '93 C.150 B.S. L.1340 J.D. [Ⓐ Lindhorst&D.]
Kuck, Richard W. '52 '77 C.473 B.S. L.608 J.D. 201 East Fourth Street‡
Kuhnell, Clayton L. '75 '01 C&L.150 B.S.Ch.E., J.D.
[Ⓐ Dinsmore&S.] (See Pat. Sect.)
Kulick, Susan Goldsmith '54 '79 C.477 B.A. L.912 J.D. Jewish Federation of Cinn.
Kuller, Barbara '35 '80 C.150 B.S. L.1340 J.D. Ref., Juv. Ct.
Kunst, John M., Jr., (AV) '41 '66 C.967 A.B. L.150 J.D. [Dinsmore&S.]
Kuprionis, M. Denise '56 '95 C&L.1161 B.B.A., J.D. The E.W. Scripps Co.
Kurlansky, Amy Lynn '73 '98 C.477 B.A. L.150 J.D. Pub. Def., GAL Div.
Kurlansky, Stephen E., (BV) '44 '69 C.1029 B.A. L.150 J.D. 6537 Ridge Cir.
Kurtz, Michael L., (AV) '59 '86 C.674 A.B. L.150 J.D. [Boehm,K.&L.]
Kwiatkowski, Andrew R. '76 '02 C&L.229 B.S., J.D. [Ⓐ Dinsmore&S.]
Kyte, Lawrence H., Jr., (AV) '38 '66 C.602 A.B. L.893 LL.B. [Ⓒ Frost B.T.]
Laber, Christopher T., (BV) '54 '79 C.967 B.A. L.150 J.D. 22 W. 9th Street
Labmeier, John F. '49 '75 C&L.150 B.A.B.S., J.D.
V.P., Assoc. Gen. Coun. & Asst. Secy., The Union Central Life Ins. Co.
Ladrigan, Terrence F., (BV) '45 '75 C.150 B.B.A. L.151 J.D. 2345 Kemper Ln.
Lafkas, David M. '74 '01 C.701 B.S. L.150 J.D. 7811 Laurel Avenue, Suite B (Pat.)
Laing, Michael A., (AVⓉ) '61 '86 C.10 B.S. L.16 J.D. [Taft,S.&H.]
Laite, David A., (AV) '65 '90 C.8 B.A. L.930 J.D.
U.S. Dept. of Labor [Garvin,L.H.&E.]
La Jeunesse, Richard T., (AV) '53 '80 C.973 B.S. L.477 J.D. [Graydon H.&R.]
Lake, Matthew B. '72 '99 C.347 B.S. L.150 J.D. [Ⓐ Graydon H.&R.]
Lakin, Thomas J. '42 '71 C.150 B.A. L.1340 J.D.
Exec. V.P. & Gen. Coun., Star Bank Corporation
Lamb, Laurie A. '78 '03 C.1161 B.S. L.1340 J.D. [Ⓐ Beckman W.S.]
Lamb, Robert M., (BV) '52 '82 C.150 B.A. L.477 J.D. [Ⓐ R.A.Klingler]
Lambert, Jennifer L. '70 '02 C.150 B.A. L.1161 J.D. [Ⓐ Helmer,M.&P.]
Lameier, Richard D., (AV) '41 '68 C&L.150 B.A., J.D. [Barron,P.B.&S.]
Lamm, Dennis J., (BV) '57 '83 C.1208 B.S. L.201 J.D. [Droder&M.]
Lampe, David J. '74 '00 C.150 B.B.A. L.608 J.D. 121 W. Ninth St.
Lampe, Gerald A., (AV) '46 '71 C&L.150 B.A., J.D. Asst. Pros. Atty.
Lampley, Nathaniel, Jr., (AV) '63 '89 C.201 B.A. L.150 J.D. [Vorys,S.S.&P.]
Land, Gregory E., (AV) '59 '84 C.150 B.A. L.608 J.D. Gen. Coun., CMC Properties
Land, Suzanne P., (AV) '64 '90 C.980 A.B. L.930 J.D. [Greenebaum D.&M.]
Landen, Everett E., (BV) '45 '73 C.210 B.A. L.150 J.D. 617 Vine St.
Landen, J. Jeffrey, (BV) '57 '82 C.138 B.A. L.383 J.D. [Graydon H.&R.] ⊙
Landers, Dawn R. '73 '00 C&L.608 B.S.N., J.D. [Ⓐ Taft,S.&H.]
Landon, Thomas W. '64 '97 C.150 B.S. L.1340 J.D. Mag., Prob. Ct.
Landrum, Lori A., (BV) '68 '93 C.967 B.A. L.150 J.D. [Frost B.T.]
Landrum, Rick J., (BV) '64 '93 C.1208 B.A. L.150 J.D. Atty., Kroger Company, The
Lane, David C., (AV) '53 '82 C.1118 B.A. L.1340 J.D. [Lane,F.&R.]
Lane, Donald A., (AV) '62 '87 C.97 B.S.B.A. L.608 J.D. [Droder&M.]
Lane, Patrick D., (AV) '55 '80 C.893 B.A. L.150 J.D.
Assoc. Gen. Coun., Pat. Lit., Procter & Gamble Co.
Lane, Sandra T. '69 '93 C.138 B.S. L.383 J.D. Gen. Coun., GovConnect, Inc.
Lane, Felix & Raisbeck, (AV) 4931 Delhi Pike
Lang, Andrew L. '40 '71 C&L.838 B.S., J.D.
(adm. in TN; not adm. in OH) N.L.R.B.
Langenbahn, Jay R., (AV) '50 '76 C.383 B.S. L.1340 J.D. [Lindhorst&D.]
Langenkamp, Max V. '74 '02 C.608 B.A. L.575 J.D. [Ⓐ Dinsmore&S.]
Langner, Kevan K. '45 '75 C&L.150 A.B., J.D.
Gen. Coun., Pentair Pool Products, Inc.
Langston, Malinda L. '71 '97 C.1065 B.S. L.201 J.D. [Ⓐ Kohnen&P.]
Lanier, Addison '24 '50 C&L.902 B.C., LL.B. Emery Grp., Inc.
Lape, Kathleen S. '— '92 C.383 B.A. L.1340 J.D. Law Clk. to Com. Pleas J.
Lape, Lynn A., Law Office of '63 '97 C.973 B.S.B.A. L.1340 J.D. 3533 Epley Lane
Lapp, Judith Anton '56 '83 C.608 B.A. L.150 J.D. Asst. Pros.
Larimer, John T., (BV) '33 '66 C.608 B.S.Ed. L.1340 J.D. [Skirvin&L.]
Larimer, Rae Skirvin, (BV) '36 '60 C&L.608 B.A., J.D. [Skirvin&L.]
Larsen, Bea V., (AV) '29 '69 C.33 B.A. L.151 J.D. 8 W. 9th St.
Lasher, Katherine M. '72 '99 C&L.150 B.A., J.D. [Ⓐ Graydon H.&R.]
Latter, Bruce E., (BV) '48 '75 C.473 B.S. L.1340 J.D. 2nd National Bldg.
Laub, Patricia D., (AV) '58 '83 C.201 B.A. L.150 J.D. [Frost B.T.]
Lauer, Richard T. '69 '94 C.454 B.A. L.150 J.D. [Ⓐ Robbins,K.P.&T.]
Laufman, Paul M. '70 '96 C.966 B.A. L.150 J.D. 617 Vine St.
Laufman, Robert F., (AV) '31 '61 C.871 B.S. L.151 J.D. [Laufman,R.&G.]
Laufman, Rauh & Gerhardstein, (AV) 617 Vine St.
Laumann, J. Michael, (BV) '50 '77 C.150 B.S.C.E. L.1340 J.D. 3505 Glenmore Ave.
Laurens, Jesse Sky '74 '01 C.696 B.A. L.150 J.D. 119 E. Court St.
Lausch, Connie Cline '61 '86 C&L.8 B.A., J.D. 324 Reading Rd.
Lausche, Louis F., (BV) '40 '65 C.610 A.B. L.150 J.D. 9526 Winton Rd.
Lautzenhiser, Roger E., (AV) '54 '79 C.813 A.B. L.1068 J.D. [Vorys,S.S.&P.]
Lawrence, James K. L., (AV) '40 '65 C&L.608 A.B., J.D. [Frost B.T.]
Lawrence, Jennifer L. '71 '96 C.608 B.A. L.151 J.D. [Ⓐ Lawrence] ⊙
Lawrence, Rebecca R. '62 '89 C.347 B.A. L.1119 J.D. Procter & Gamble
Lawrence, Richard D., (AV) '44 '71 C.150 B.A. L.1340 J.D. [Lawrence] ⊙

Lawrence Firm, The, L.P.A., (AV) BR
8804 Montgomery Road, Suite 700, 45236 ⊙
Telephone: 513-651-4130 Fax: 513-651-0525
Email: lawrence@lawrencefirm.com URL: http://www.lawrencefirm.com
Richard D. Lawrence;—Thomas C. Korbee; Jennifer L. Lawrence; Jill Gustafson; Patrick J. Beirne; Robert Donnelly Lewis Jr.; Anne L. Gilday.
Civil Litigation, Personal Injury, Medical Malpractice, Trucking Accidents, Automobile Accidents, Head and Spinal Injuries, Drug and Medical Device Litigation. Plaintiffs and Defense.
Northern Kentucky Office: The Lawrence Firm, PSC, 606 Philadelphia Street, Covington, Kentucky, 41011. Telephone: 859-578-9130. Facsimile: 859-578-1032.
See Professional Biographies, CINCINNATI, OHIO

Lawson, Jerry H., (AV) '44 '68 C.347 B.A. L.178 LL.B. 8 West 9th Street
Lawson, Kenneth L., (AV) '63 '89 C.967 B.A. L.150 J.D. [K.L.Lawson&Assoc.]
Lawson, Margaret Avril, (AV) '57 '82 C.197 B.A. L.309 J.D. [Taft,S.&H.]
Lawson, Mark Byron '65 '98 C.973 B.S. L.150 J.D. City Legal Aid Scoiety
Lawson, Nancy A., (AV) '— '75 C.787 B.A. L.851 J.D. [Dinsmore&S.]
Lawson, Kenneth L., & Associates, L.P.A., (AV) 808 Elm Street, Suite 100
Layton, Charles M. '36 '62 C.235 A.B. L.383 LL.B.
(adm. in KY; not adm. in OH) I.R.S.
Lazaron, Thos. F. '23 '52 C&L.150 B.A., LL.B. 2456 Fulbourne Dr.

Lazarus, David, (BV) '32 '82 C.309 A.B. L.150 J.D.
7 West Seventh Street, Suite 1850, 45202 ⊙
Telephone: 513-241-7460 Fax: 513-684-7777
Real Estate Tax Appeals, Governmental Law, Lobbying and General Civil Practice.
See Professional Biographies, CINCINNATI, OHIO

Lazarus, David, (BV) '32 '82 C.309 A.B. L.150 J.D. [Ⓒ Rubenstein&T.] (⊙Cincinnati)
Lazarus, Stephen S., (AV) '63 '89 C.855 B.A. L.150 J.D. [Hardin,L.L.&M.]
Le, Peter Long '73 '03 C.150 B.A. L.201 J.D. [Ⓐ Hammond]
Leach, Lori R. '67 '98 C.973 B.S.B.A. L.1340 J.D. [Ⓐ Lerner,S.&R.]
Leal, George '70 '03 C.846 B.S.M.E. L.326 J.D. Coun., Procter & Gamble
Learmonth, Doloris F., (AV) '43 '78 C.228 A.B. L.150 J.D. [Peck,S.&W.]
Lee, Brian A. '70 '00 C.1161 B.A. L.1340 J.D. [Ⓐ Benjamin,Y.&H.]
Lee, Edmund S. '26 '52 C.679 B.S.M.E. L.588 J.D. [Kinney&S.] ‡
Lee, Kathleen K. '— '96 C.112 B.S. L.150 J.D. Procter and Gamble
Lee, Tanya M. '— '01 C.674 A.B. L.329 J.D. Coun., Procter & Gamble Co., The
Leeper, Andrew R., (BV) '56 '83 C.970 B.A. L.608 J.D. [Kohnen&P.]
Leese, William F. '37 '73 C.244 B.A. L.1340 J.D. 9059 Long Ln.‡
Lefton, David H., (AV) '62 '87 C.98 B.S. L.201 J.D. [Hardin,L.L.&M.]
Lefton, Jimmy J. '68 '94 C.608 B.A. L.1187 J.D. [Ⓐ Barron,P.B.&S.]
Legal Helpers 1014 Vine Street
Lehmann, Terry W., (AV) '43 '72 C.275 B.A. L.1340 J.D. Asst. U.S. Atty.
Lehner, Lisa deHart, (BV) '66 '93 C.473 B.A. L.29 J.D. [Wood&L.] ⊙
Leis, Simon L., Jr., (AV) '34 '66 C.973 B.S. L.151 J.D. Sheriff
Leist, Nelson R. '30 '61 C.150 Ch.E. L.1340 LL.B. 8238 Winton Rd.
Lemasters, P. Reid, (AV) '46 '71 C.347 B.A. L.345 J.D. [Frost B.T.]
Lemasters, Poul H. '70 '04 C.999 B.S. L.1340 J.D. [Ⓐ Freund,F.&A.]
Lembke, Raymond W., (AV) '59 '83 C.597 B.A. L.880 J.D. [Ⓐ Taft,S.&H.]
Lemmink, Robert D. '39 '91 C.150 B.S. L.1340 J.D. Asst. Secy., Cincinnati Bell, Inc.
Lenhart, Amanda P. '75 '00 C.473 B.Phil. L.150 J.D. [Ⓐ Dinsmore&S.]
Lennertz, C. Robert '27 '77 C.679 B.S.C.E. L.1340 J.D. V.P., N.C. Nutting Co.
Lenox, Bryce A. '71 '98 C.602 B.B.A. L.201 J.D. [Ⓐ Thompson H.]
Lent, Krista R. '63 '91 C.473 B.A. L.1340 J.D. Asst. Prosec.
Leon, Gus, (BV) '57 '85 C.150 B.A. L.1340 J.D. 8293 Fawn Lake Ct.
Leonard, Amy J. '63 '88 C.838 B.A. L.861 J.D. [Ⓐ D.D.Altman&Assoc.]
Leonard, Geo. A., (AV) '24 '51 C&L.477 A.B., J.D. Comm., OH Elections Comm.
Leonard, William L., (BV) '27 '50 C&L.150 LL.B. 31 E. Observatory Hill
Lerman, Murray '29 '89 C.569 B.C.M.E. L.150 J.D. 1528 Spring Park Walk
Lerner, Donald M., (AV) '35 '60 C.473 B.S. L.976 LL.B. [Lerner,S.&R.]
Lerner, Stephen D., (AV) '60 '86 C&L.659 B.A., J.D.
[Squire,S.&D.] (⊙New York, NY)

Lerner, Sampson & Rothfuss, A Legal Professional Association, (AV)
120 East Fourth Street, Suite 800, 45202
Telephone: 513-241-3100 Fax: 513-241-4094
Email: info@lsrlaw.com
Donald M. Lerner; Kirk Sampson; Richard M. Rothfuss; Rick D. DeBlasis; Sara M. Petersmann;—Romi T. Fox; Craig A. Thomas; Carlos S. Ramirez; Melissa J. Whalen; Michael R. Brinkman; Brian S. Jackson; Susan E. Mandryk; Jon J. Lieberman; Christopher J. Siegel; Pamela S. Petas; Tracey M. Johnson; Andrew M. Top; Edward J. Boll, III; Patricia K. Block; Jill L. Fealko; Lori R. Leach; Joel K. Jensen; Robert Charles Dix; Cynthia M. Roselle; C. Scott Casterline; Adam R. Fogelman; Thomas L. Henderson; Kerri L. Nunley; Anita L. Maddix; David E. Johnson; Donald K. Swartz; Shannon O'Connell Egan (Not admitted in OH); Anthony J. Gemmato, Jr.; Kevin R. Walsh; James D. Keffer (Not admitted in OH); Matthew I. McKelvey; Kathleen E. Kahmann; Jeniece D. Jones; William L. Purtell; Susana E. Lykins; Robyn M. Regan; Jeremy M. Rettig (Not admitted in OH); Kristen J. Mudd (Not admitted in OH); Steven L. Sacks; Steven V. Sorg; Pamela A. Hudec; R. Mark Rothfuss, II (Not admitted in OH); Amy L. Gillum; Michael R. Proctor; Nathan L. Swehla; Jennifer K. Ross; Maureen S. Hinson; Michael H. Schlueter; Mark N. Dierks; Steven H. Patterson; S. Scott Martin; Tony M. Alexander; Diana V. Shanov; Mary E. Rauen.
Commercial Litigation and Real Estate Law. Commercial Bankruptcy Law, Commercial and Consumer Foreclosure. General Civil Practice.
Representative Clients: Bank of America; Chase Manhattan Mortgage Corporation; Citimortgage; Countrywide Home Loans; Federal Home Loan Mortgage Corporation; Federal National Mortgage Association; Fifth-Third Bank; GMAC Mortgage Corporation; National City Mortgage; Wells Fargo; U.S. Bank.

Lesser, Richard F., (BV) '49 '82 C.150 B.S. L.1340 J.D.
36 East Seventh Street, Suite 2020, 45202
Telephone: 513-621-9660 FAX: 513-345-3900
Email: rflesser@fuse.net URL: http://www.lesserlaw.com
Probate, Elder Law, Real Estate, Bankruptcy, Estate Planning, Trusts, Wills, Guardianship, Personal Injury, Auto Accidents, Collection.
See Professional Biographies, CINCINNATI, OHIO

Lester, Wilbur R. '15 '40 C.504 A.B. L.597 J.D. 1517 Hollywood Ave.‡
LeVay, Helen Fanz, (BV) '60 '85 C&L.608 B.A., J.D. [Cuni,F.&L.]

Levin, Debbe A., (AV) ... '54 '79 C.910 B.A. L.150 J.D. [Graf&S.&M.]
Levin, Peter F. ... '36 '61 C.951 B.A. L.477 LL.B. Bartlett & Co.
Levine, David S., (AV) '53 '78 C&L.150 B.A., J.D.
Sr. Corp. Coun. & Div. Asst. V.P., Great Amer. Ins. Co.
Levor, L. Ruth ... '45 '85 C&L.150 B.A., J.D. Univ. of Cinci. College of Law Library
Levy, Barry D., (BV) ... '51 '76 C.608 B.A. L.117 J.D. [O'Connor,A.&L.]
Levy, Howard Samuel ... '64 '89 C.608 B.S. L.94 LL.M. Phillips Law Firm
Levy, John M. ... '78 '04 C.882 B.A. L.150 J.D. [Ⓐ Strauss&T.]
Levy, Jonathan H. '58 '92 C.766 B.A. L.999 J.D.
(adm. in CA; not adm. in OH) 2181 Victory Pkwy.‡
Lewis, Colleen P., (BV) ... '59 '89 C.1161 B.S. L.1340 J.D. [Dinsmore&S.]
Lewis, Donald B. ... '50 '76 C.976 B.A. L.477 J.D. [Ⓒ Vorys,S.S.&P.]
Lewis, Kim Martin, (AV) ... '62 '87 C.63 B.S. L.810 J.D. [Dinsmore&S.]
Lewis, Robert Donnelly, Jr. ... '67 '97 C.473 B.A. L.150 J.D. [Ⓐ Lawrence] ⊙
Lewis, Sarah V. ... '— '03 C.210 B.A. L.945 J.D. [Ⓐ Dinsmore&S.]
Lewnard, Lawrence E. ... '28 '78 C.145 M.B.A. L.1340 J.D. Asst. Dir., Univ. of Cinci.
Liddy, J. Patrick, (AV) ... '51 '76 C.602 B.A. L.608 J.D. Asst. Coun., The Fifth Third Bk.
Lieberman, Bernard, (BV) ... '23 '52 C&L.150 B.A., LL.B. 2nd Fl. 216 E. 9th St.
Lieberman, Harold ... '21 '48 C&L.150 B.A., LL.B. 216 E. 9th St., 2nd Fl.‡
Lieberman, Jon J. ... '64 '92 C&L.150 B.A., J.D. [Ⓐ Lerner,S.&R.]
Lieberman, Sidney C., (BV) ... '42 '68 C&L.150 B.A., J.D. 415 Glensprings Dr.
Liebman, Robert L., (BV) ... '46 '73 C.473 B.A. L.1340 J.D. 1014 Vine St.
Lilley, Robert O. ... '21 '51 L.1340 LL.B. 607 2nd Nat. Bldg.
Lin, Michael M.J. ... '69 '96 C.1375 B.A. L.94 J.D. Sr. Coun., Procter & Gamble
Lindberg, Charles D., (AV) ... '28 '54 C.56 A.B. L.976 LL.B. [Ⓒ Taft,S.&H.]
Lindgren, Lawrence F. ... '49 '95 C.1347 B.A. L.999 J.D. 114 E. 8th Street

Lindhorst & Dreidame Co., L.P.A., (AV) BB
312 Walnut Street, Suite 2300, 45202-4091
Telephone: 513-421-6630 Telecopier: 513-421-0212
Email: info@lindhorstlaw.com URL: http://www.lindhorstlaw.com
Ambrose H. Lindhorst (1913-1997); Robert F. Dreidame (1914-1978); William J. Walsh (1919-1996); Leo J. Breslin (1928-2000). Members of Firm: James L. O'Connell; Charles J. Kelly; John A. Goldberg; James M. Moore; Jay R. Langenbahn; James H. Smith, III; Michael F. Lyon; Thomas E. Martin; James F. Brockman; Edward S. Dorsey; Barry F. Fagel;—Charles G. Skidmore; Margaret G. Kubicki; Michelle L. Clemons; Bradley McPeek; David Williamson; Edward Roberts; Laurie A. McCluskey; Christopher H. Hurlburt; Joshua J. Nolan; John D. Moschandreas.
General Civil Practice, including Insurance, Tort, Medical Legal, Admiralty, Corporate, Commercial, Real Estate, Labor, Taxation, Probate and Estate Planning. General Trial Practice in all State and Federal Courts.
See Professional Biographies, CINCINNATI, OHIO

Linman, E. Kelly '44 '72 C.911 B.S.M.E. L.1340 J.D.
Assoc. Gen. Coun., Procter & Gamble Co. (Pat.)
Linn, Cliff G. ... '57 '85 [Ⓐ O'Connor,A.&L.]
Linne, Sheryl M. ... '51 '79 C.679 B.S. L.347 J.D. 1 E. 4th St.
Linneman, J. Robert ... '— '01 C.473 B.A. L.1340 J.D. [Ⓐ Santen&H.]
Linnenberg, John William, (AV) ... '43 '69 C.894 A.B. L.150 J.D. 5971 Beechtop
Lippert, Amy E. ... '76 '01 C.477 B.A. L.150 J.D. [Ⓐ Graydon H.&R.]
Lippert, G. Mitchel, (BV) ... '40 '70 C.608 B.A. L.1340 J.D. 11137 Main Street
Lippert, James W., (AV) ... '44 '69 C.473 B.A. L.150 J.D. [Garvin,L.H.&E.]
Lippert, Richard H., (BV) '40 '65 C&L.150 B.A., J.D.
Asst. Atty. Gen. [Garvin,L.H.&E.]
Lipps, Thomas R. '50 '81 C.150 B.A. L.1340 J.D.
Ct. Admin. & Chf. Ref., Hamilton Co. Juv. Ct.
Lips, J. Alan, (AV) ... '38 '68 C&L.383 B.S., J.D. [Ⓒ Taft,S.&H.]
Lishawa, Allen C. ... '10 '38 C.150 L.151 J.D. 6141 Wasigo Dr.‡
Liss, William J. ... '71 '97 C.608 B.A. L.150 J.D. [Ⓐ Santen&H.]
Little, Darryl C. ... '62 '94 C&L.831 B.S., J.D. The Procter & Gamble Co.
Littner, Jay G., (BV) ... '61 '86 C.150 B.A. L.201 J.D. Asst. Pros. Atty.
Lockemeyer, David S. ... '55 '92 C.313 B.M. L.1003 J.D. [Triona C.&L.]
Lockhart, John M. '11 '38 C.597 B.S. L.146 LL.B.
(adm. in IL; not adm. in OH) Pres., Lockhart Co.‡
Lockwood, Bert B., Jr. ... '44 '81 C.732 B.A. L.823 J.D. Univ. of Cincinnati
Lodge, Harry L. ... '19 '53 C.271 B.A. L.1340 J.D. 8711 Long Lane‡
Loeb, Alvin M., (AV) ... '06 '30 C.608 L.150 LL.B. [Loeb,V.H.&F.]
Loeb, Vollman, Harper & Friedmann, (AV) ... 1014 Vine St.
Loftus, Matthew C. ... '76 '02 C.473 B.S. L.608 J.D. [Ⓐ Taft,S.&H.]
Logan, Philip A., (AV) ... '47 '72 C.347 B.S. L.150 J.D. [Katzman,L.H.&B.]
Long, Frank E., (BV) ... '30 '59 C.81 L.607 J.D. 5902 Meyers Drive
Longenecker, Mark H., (AV) ... '51 '75 C.207 B.A. L.309 J.D. [Greenebaum D.&M.]
Longi, Maria A. ... '66 '93 C.597 B.S.Ch.E. L.1340 J.D. 6775 Camaridge
Longtin, Lynne M. ... '71 '99 C.347 B.A. L.150 J.D. [Ⓐ Rendigs,F.K.&D.]

Lopez, Hodes, Restaino, Milman & Skikos, A Law Corporation, (AV)
312 Walnut Street, Suite 2090, 45202 ⊙
Telephone: 513-852-5600 Fax: 513-852-5611
Email: info@lopez-hodes.com URL: http://www.lopezhodes.com
Janet G. Abaray;—Jane E. Joseph (Resident, Cincinnati, Ohio Office); Beverly H. Pace; Calvin S. Tregre, Jr.; Melanie S. Bailey; Joseph M. Lyon.
Mass Tort Litigation, Medical Malpractice, Products Liability, Employment Law, Personal Injury and Elder Law.
Newport Beach, California Office: 450 Newport Center Drive, 92660. Telephone: 949-640-8222. Fax: 949-640-8294.
San Francisco, California Office: 625 Market Street, 11th Floor, 94105. Telephone: 415-956-5257. Fax: 415-956-4416.
Shorewood, Minnesota Office: 27995 Boulder Circle, 55331. Telephone: 952-401-4377. Fax: 425-963-3467.
Boston, Massachusetts Office: 95 Commercial Wharf, 02110. Telephone: 617-973-9777. Fax: 617-589-0789.
See Professional Biographies, CINCINNATI, OHIO

Lorentz, Joshua A. ... '75 '01 C.610 B.S., B.A. L.201 J.D. [Ⓐ Dinsmore&S.]
Loudermilk, Timothy Dudley ... '59 '91 C.608 B.S. L.1340 J.D. [T.D.Loudermilk]
Loudermilk, Timothy D. ... 311 Elm Street, Suite 200
Love, Ellsworth, (BV) ... '48 '74 C.608 B.A. L.309 J.D. 30 Garfield Pl., Ste. 730
Lovell, Kelly D. ... '50 '86 C.350 B.A. L.221 J.D. 400 Broadway
Lowery, Robert R. ... '34 '63 C&L.150 A.B., J.D. 6906 Plainfield Rd.
Lowry, John P., (BV) ... '60 '86 C.473 B.A. L.450 J.D. [Boehm,K.&L.]
Lowry, Patricia O., (AV) ... '47 '73 C.518 A.B. L.893 J.D. [Taft,S.&H.]
Lucas, John M. '51 '79 C.1161 B.S. L.1340 J.D.
(adm. in KY; not adm. in OH)
Asst. Coun. & Asst. to Secy., The Union Central Life Ins. Co.
Ludwig, James D. ... *'68 '95 C.886 B.S. L.150 J.D. 35 E. 7th St., Ste. 750*
Luebbers, Thomas A., (AV) ... '42 '66 C.602 A.B. L.976 LL.B. [Peck,S.&W.]
Lugbill, Ann, (AV) ... '54 '80 C.373 B.A. L.893 J.D. 2406 Auburn Avenue
Luken, Clement H., Jr., (AV) '56 '86
C.973 B.S.Chem. L.1340 J.D. [Wood,H.&E.] (See Pat. Sect.)
Luken, John D., (AV) ... '56 '81 C.597 B.A. L.813 J.D. [Dinsmore&S.]
Luken, Susan M. ... '69 '02 C&L.150 B.A., J.D. [Ⓐ Dinsmore&S.]
Luken, Thomas A. ... '25 '51 C.973 B.A. L.1340 J.D. 1513 Central Trust Twr.

Lukey, Paul E. ... '47 '75 C.1024 B.S. L.1340 J.D. 1538 Cedar Ave.
Lummanick, James F., (BV) '47 '80
C.608 B.A. L.1340 J.D. Secy. & Coun., Bartlett & Co.
Lundrigan, Nicole M. ... '77 '02 C.201 B.A. L.607 J.D. [Ⓐ Strauss&T.]
Lundrigan, W. Kelly ... '66 '92 C&L.150 B.A., J.D. [Ⓒ Manley B.]
Lunn, Gregory J., (AV) '55 '78 C.1118 B.A. L.383 J.D.
[Wood,H.&E.] (See Pat. Sect.)
Luttenegger, Jerry F., (AV) ... '44 '71 C.973 B.S.B.A. L.1340 J.D. Asst. City Solr.
Lutz, Douglas L., (AV) ... '65 '91 C.472 B.S. L.851 J.D. [Frost B.T.]
Lutz, James G., (AV) ... '33 '60 C&L.150 A.B., J.D. [Lutz,C.&M.]
Lutz, Mark E., (AV) ... '56 '81 C.381 B.A. L.145 J.D. [Denlinger,R.&G.]
Lutz, Cornetet & Meyer, Co., L.P.A., (AV) ... 130 Tri-County Parkway, Suite 208
Lydon, Deborah R., (AV) ... '55 '81 C&L.150 B.G.S., J.D. [Dinsmore&S.]
Lykins, Herbert C. ... '16 '43 C.150 L.1340 LL.B. Fireman's Fund Amer. Ins. Cos.
Lykins, Susana E. ... '— '02 C.150 B.A. L.201 J.D. [Ⓐ Lerner,S.&R.]
Lyman, Beverly A. ... '56 '96 C.999 B.S. L.1015 J.D. [Wood,H.&E.] (See Pat. Sect.)
Lynch, Edward J. ... '53 '78 C.973 A.B. L.150 J.D. 1282 Aldrich Ave.★
Lynch, John David ... '22 '49 C&L.477 A.B., J.D. 7635 Demar Rd.‡
Lynch, Teresa Perkins ... '62 '91 L.201 J.D. Pros. Off.
Lyon, Joseph M. ... '— '03 C.64 B.A. L.146 J.D. [Ⓐ Lopez,H.R.M.&S.]
Lyon, Michael F., (AV) ... '47 '75 C.973 B.A. L.1340 J.D. [Lindhorst&D.]
Lyons, James L., (AV) ... '25 '50 C.973 L.150 LL.B. [Lyons&F.]
Lyons, James W., (AV) ... '48 '75 C.150 B.A. L.1340 J.D. [Lyons&F.]
Lyons & Fries Co., L.P.A., (AV) ... 30 E. 7th St., Ste. 750
Maag, Marilyn J., (AV) ... '56 '86 C&L.150 B.S., J.D. [Strauss&T.]
MacConnell, Stephen T., (AV) ... '47 '72 C.473 A.B. L.150 J.D. 3095 Victoria Avenue
MacDonald, Mark A., (AV) ... '53 '80 C&L.150 B.A., J.D. [Freund,F.&A.]
Mace, Robert A. ... '22 '48 C&L.150 A.B., J.D. 2201 Sweetbriar Lane
Machol, Melynda J., (AV) '63 '88 C.19 B.A. L.150 J.D.
Asst. Pros. Atty., Hamilton Co. Dist. Atty. Off.
Mack, James R. ... '37 '64 C.973 B.S. L.1340 J.D. 139 E. 4th St.
Mack, Thomas A., (AV) ... '48 '79 C.150 B.B.A. L.1340 J.D. [Mack,M.&K.]
Mack McKay & Knabe, Co., LPA, (AV) ... 35 E. 7th St., Ste. 400
MacKay, Walter S. ... '32 '58 C&L.150 B.B.A., LL.B. Mag., Co. Prob. Ct.
Mackey, William R. '26 '54 C.882 B.A. L.569 J.D.
(adm. in NY; not adm. in OH) 8738 Apple Knoll Ln.‡
Mackinnon, Douglas A. ... '71 '01 C.473 B.S. L.1340 J.D. [Ⓐ F.H.Green]
MacLeid, Matthew T., (BV) ... '35 '63 C&L.150 B.S., J.D. 1348 Chapel St.
MacQueeney, Vincent Patrick ... '64 '89 C.893 B.A. L.945 J.D. OH Atty. Gen. Off.
Madden, Stephan D., (BV) ... '54 '80 C.473 A.B. L.1340 J.D. [S.D.Madden]

Madden, Stephan D., Co., LPA, (BV)
601 Main Street, 3rd Floor, 45202
Telephone: 513-621-8700 Fax: 513-241-1572
Email: madlaw@fuse.net URL: http://www.stevemaddenlaw.com
Stephan D. Madden.
Language: English.
Criminal Law, Family Law, Personal Injury, Driving While Intoxicated.
See Professional Biographies, CINCINNATI, OHIO

Maddix, Anita L. ... '77 '02 C.1161 B.A. L.607 J.D. [Ⓐ Lerner,S.&R.]

Magee, James V., Jr., (AV) '46 '74 C.1296 A.B. L.1161 J.D.
36 East 7th Street, Suite 2020, 45202
Telephone: 513-621-9660 Fax: 513-345-3900 URL: http://www.jamesvmageelaw.com
Email: jvmageejr@mageelaw.com URL: http://www.mageelaw.com
Real Estate Law, Litigation, Title Insurance Law, Commercial Litigation, Bankruptcy.
See Professional Biographies, CINCINNATI, OHIO

Magee, Linda Lee Barth ... '48 '73 C.235 A.B. L.150 J.D. 2184 Telegraph Court
Magee, Mark E., (AV) '48 '75 C.473 B.A. L.150 J.D.
Gen. Dep. Coun. & Secy., Provident Financial Group, Inc.
Maggio, Margaret M. ... '54 '02 C.424 B.S.N. L.1340 J.D. [Ⓐ Dinsmore&S.]
Magnus, Richard A., (BV) ... '58 '82 C.659 B.S. L.880 J.D. 4526 Montgomery Rd.
Mahany, Michael D. ... '53 '89 C.602 A.B. L.201 J.D. 268 W. Crest Dr.
Mahin, John E., (AV) ... '52 '77 C.436 B.A. L.201 J.D. [Clements,M.&C.]
Mahon, Stephen C., (AV) '64 '89 C&L.880 B.A., J.D.
[Squire,S.&D.] (⊙New York, NY)
Mahoney, Dennis C., (BV) ... '58 '90 C.150 B.B.A. L.1340 J.D. [Ⓐ O'Connor,A.&L.]
Maichl, Linda E., (BV) ... '58 '89 C&L.150 B.B.A., J.D. [Ulmer&B.]
Maiman, Earle Jay, (AV) ... '48 '81 C.610 B.S. L.150 J.D. [Thompson H.]
Main, David K. ... '48 '74 C&L.150 B.A., J.D. Pres., Hamilton Co. Develop. Co.
Maislin, Blake R. ... '— '97 C.107 B.A. L.151 J.D. [B.Maislin]
Maislin, Blake, Law Office of ... 214 E. 9th St., Fl. 5
Majba, Michael P. ... '78 '03 C.602 B.A. L.150 J.D. [Ⓐ Denlinger,R.&G.]
Major, Ronald D., (AV) ... '47 '74 C.383 B.A. L.1340 J.D. 30 Garfield Place
Makos, Susan Smith, (BV) '54 '79 C.385 B.A. L.1119 J.D.
Sen. V.P. & Gen. Coun., Catholic Healthcare Partners
Malas, Mary Ellen, (BV) ... '62 '91 C.150 B.A. L.1340 J.D. [Keating M.&K.]
Mallory, Donald W. ... '66 '99 C.150 B.B.A. L.1161 J.D. [Ⓐ Dinsmore&S.]
Malloy, Matthew M. '63 '95 C.871 B.S. L.893 J.D.
Assoc. Gen. Coun., The Procter & Gamble Co.
Malloy, Robert P., (AV) ... '43 '74 C&L.150 B.A., J.D. [Wood&L.]
Malof, Kevin K. ... '67 '00 C.473 B.S. L.1340 J.D. [Ⓐ Frost B.T.]
Malone, Kathleen Kelly '60 '87 C.201 B.A. L.150 J.D.
Sr. Atty., Legal Aid Soc. of Cinci.
Maltz, David S. '71 '96 C.477 B.B.A. L.273 J.D.
(adm. in MD; not adm. in OH) Sr. Coun., Cinergy Services, Inc.
Manahan Alkire, Erin M. ... '76 '01 C.160 B.A. L.945 J.D. [Ⓐ Thompson H.]
Mancino, David A. ... '65 '94 C.477 B.S.E.E. L.150 J.D. [Taft,S.&H.] (Pat.)
Mandryk, Susan E. ... '69 '97 C.473 B.S. L.1003 J.D. [Ⓐ Lerner,S.&R.]
Manes, Dennis L., (AV) ... '48 '73 C.381 B.A. L.851 J.D. [Ⓒ Schwartz,M.&R.]
Manes, Marlene Penny, (BV) ... '45 '70 C.608 B.S.B.A. L.904 J.D. 917 Main St.
Mangan, Sean K. ... '73 '02 C.602 B.A. L.893 J.D. [Ⓐ Graf&S.&M.]
Mangan, Timothy S. '70 '95 C.347 B.A. L.494 J.D.
Cinergy Services (Legal Department)
Mangels, Alfred J., (AVⓉ) ... '35 '64 C.667 B.M.E. L.1340 J.D. 4729 Cornell Rd. (Pat.)
Manley, Robert E., (AV) ... '35 '60 C.973 S.B. L.309 J.D. [Manley B.]

Manley Burke, A Legal Professional Association, (AV) BB
225 West Court Street, 45202
Telephone: 513-721-5525 Fax: 513-721-4268
Email: info@manleyburke.com URL: http://www.manleyburke.com
Robert E. Manley; Timothy M. Burke; Gary E. Powell; Robert H. Mitchell; Matthew W. Fellerhoff;—Emily T. Supinger; Daniel J. McCarthy; Nathan W. Sprong. Retired: William A. McClain. Of Counsel: George Fabe; George F. Moeller; Gary Moore Eby; Gerald David Prager; W. Kelly Lundrigan.

(This Listing Continued)

Manley Burke, A Legal Professional Association (Continued)

Litigation, Local Government Law, Land Use and Zoning Law, Civil Rights, Probate. Fraternal Law. Personal Injury, Labor Law, Workers Compensation, Employee Benefits and Professional Malpractice.

See Professional Biographies, CINCINNATI, OHIO

Mann, David S., (AV) . . . '39 '68 C&L.309 B.A., LL.B. [Mann&M.]
Mann, Michael T. . . . '67 '01 C.347 B.A. L.150 J.D. [Mann&M.]
Mann & Mann, LLC, (AV) . . . 1014 Vine Street
Mannheimer, Rita P. . . . '54 '85 C.245 B.A. L.446 J.D. 201 E. 5th Street
Manogue, Edward S., (AV) . . . '23 '49 C&L.150 A.B., LL.B. [Manogue&M.]
Manogue, Roy, Jr., (AV) . . . '17 '42 C&L.150 A.B., LL.B. [Manogue&M.]
Manogue & Manogue, (AV) . . . 5683 Annajoe Court
Manzler, Michael A., (BV) . . . '66 '92 C.976 B.A. L.145 J.D. [Dinsmore&S.]
Mapother, William R., (AVⓉ) . . . '38 '63 C.602 A.B. L.893 J.D. [Mapother&M.] ⊙
Mapother & Mapother, P.S.C., (AVⓉ)
1014 Vine Street (⊙Evansville, IN; Lexington, Louisville, KY; Huntington, WV)
Mara, Timothy G., (BV) . . . '49 '78 C.150 B.C.P. L.151 J.D. 250 E. 5th St., 15th Fl.
Marchese, Michael, III '64 '90 C.347 B.S. L.150 J.D.
A.V.P. - Dir., Tax Research & Plan., Western & Southern Financial Group
Marcum, Kent Eldon . . . '43 '82 C.383 B.B.A. L.1340 J.D. U.S. Treasury Dept.
Marinakis, George S. . . . '64 '91 C.150 B.A. L.201 J.D. [Marinakis&M.]
Marinakis, Marina . . . '66 '91 C.150 B.A. L.1340 J.D. [Marinakis&M.]
Marinakis & Marinakis . . . 605 Sycamore St.
Markesbery, Maria Agnes Saba '61 '86
C.973 B.S. L.150 J.D. Mercy Health Partners of Southwest Ohio
Markovits, W. B., (AV) . . . '57 '81 C.910 A.B. L.309 J.D. [Markovits&G.]
Markovits & Greiwe, Co., L.P.A., (AV) . . . 119 E. Court St.
Marks, Edward G., (AV) . . . '41 '67 C&L.150 B.F.A., J.D. [Hardin,L.L.&M.]
Marks, Jeffrey A., (AV) . . . '55 '81 C.608 B.A. L.150 J.D. [Ⓒ Squire,S.&D.]
Marlow, James R., (AV) . . . '41 '67 C.150 B.A. L.1340 J.D. 600 Vine St.
Marmer, Lynn, (AV) . . . '52 '86 C&L.150 B.S., J.D. Kroger Co., The
Marmer, Melvin E., (AV) . . . '33 '62 C.446 B.S. L.273 LL.B. [Thompson H.]
Marnell, Francis X., (AV) . . . '55 '82 C.813 A.B. L.945 J.D. [Buechner,H.O.M.H.&K.]
Marrero, Michael A., (AV) . . . '53 '77 C.973 A.B. L.477 J.D. [Ulmer&B.]
Marshall, Courtland E., (BV) . . . '19 '49 C&L.150 LL.B. 7 W. 7th St.
Marshall, Pamela . . . '65 '04 C.1161 B.S. L.1340 J.D. [Ⓐ Montgomery,R.&J.]
Marsick, Philip J. . . . '41 '72 C.973 B.S. L.1340 J.D. [McCaslin,I.&M.] ⊙
Marsland, Cindy L. . . . '62 '95 C.477 B.B.A. L.150 J.D. 7162 Reading Road
Martin, Boyce F., Jr. . . . '35 '63 C.198 A.B. L.893 LL.B. U.S. Ct. App. J.
Martin, Carol A., (AV) . . . '54 '82 C.976 B.A. L.150 J.D. 7645 Trailwind Dr.
Martin, James V. . . . '56 '87 C.150 B.S.M.E. L.1340 J.D. Ethicon, Inc.
Martin, Richard L., (BV) . . . '22 '49 C.973 A.B. L.150 LL.B. 120 W. 5th St.
Martin, Richard T., (BV) . . . '28 '61 C.930 B.B.A. L.1340 LL.B. 8650 Zenith St.
Martin, Robert C., (AV) . . . '26 '53 C.150 B.A. L.1340 J.D. [Martin&B.]
Martin, S. Scott . . . '71 '99 C.150 B.A. L.851 J.D. [Ⓐ Lerner,S.&R.]
Martin, Steven E., (BV) . . . '56 '82 C.347 B.S. L.1119 J.D. Co. Common Pleas Ct.
Martin, Ted T., (AV) . . . '56 '82 C.321 A.B. L.150 J.D. [Baker&H.]
Martin, Thomas E., (AV) . . . '54 '79 C.967 B.A. L.150 J.D. [Lindhorst&D.]
Martin, William L., Jr., (AV) . . . '46 '71 C.321 B.A. L.150 J.D. [Thompson H.]

Martin & Bailey, (AV)
Suite 420, 120 East Fourth Street, 45202
Telephone: 513-333-0990 Facsimile: 513-333-0066
Email: mblaw@one.net URL: http://www.martinbaileylaw.com
Members of Firm: J. Roger Blust (1938-1995); Robert C. Martin; Stephen A. Bailey; C. Curtis Walden; J. Stephen Cox; Douglas J. May.
Insurance Defense, Auto Accidents, Personal Injury, Product Liability, Uninsured, Underinsured Motorists, Malpractice Prevention Consulting, Arson and Property Damage, Insurance Coverage, Construction and Contractor Liability, Corporate Litigation, Contract Disputes, Litigation, Accidents, Worker's Compensation, Theft, False Arrest, Malicious Prosecution, Defamation, Probate, Tax Law.
Representative Clients: Alexsis; Arkansas Best Freight; Century Surety Co.; CNA Insurance Cos.; CNI Claims Service, Inc.; Chubb & Son, Inc.; Erie Insurance Group; General American Life Insurance Co.; Goodyear Tire & Rubber Co.; Indiana Insurance.

See Professional Biographies, CINCINNATI, OHIO

Martin Lewis, Kim . . . '62 '87 C.63 B.S. L.809 J.D. 201 E. 5th St.‡
Martinez, Jose A. '53 '93 C.178 B.S. L.150 J.D.
Asst. Atty. Gen., State of Ohio, Atty General's Off.
Martini, Elizabeth Ford '59 '84
C.607 B.A. L.150 J.D. Asst. Coun., The Union Central Life Ins. Co.
Martins, Paul B., (AV) . . . '54 '79 C.602 A.B. L.1049 J.D. [Helmer,M.R.&P.]
Marx, James A. . . . '64 '97 C.150 B.A. L.608 J.D. [Ⓐ Dinsmore&S.]
Mason, Jeremy R. . . . '74 '00 C.188 B.S. L.608 J.D. [Mason,S.&M.]
Mason, John L. . . . '21 '48 C&L.150 B.B.A., LL.B. Pres., Anderson Publishing Co.
Mason, Jonathan A., (AV) . . . '47 '73 C&L.150 B.A., J.D. [Mason,S.&M.] ⊙
Mason, Michael G. . . . '43 '68 C&L.150 B.B.A., J.D. 7919 Plainfield Rd.
Mason, Natalie A. '65 '91 C.249 B.S. L.74 J.D.
Sr. Corp. Coun., Great American Ins. Co.
Mason, Rachel J. . . . '77 '03 C.401 B.A. L.1017 J.D. [Ⓐ Mason,S.&M.]

Mason, Schilling & Mason Co., L.P.A., (AV) BR
11340 Montgomery Road, Suite 210, 45249-2313 ⊙
Telephone: 513-489-0829 800-840-3514 Fax: 513-489-0834
Email: msm@mason-law.com URL: http://www.mason-law.com
Jonathan A. Mason; Richard D. Schilling; Jeremy R. Mason;—Joseph M. Ruwe; Rachel J. Mason; Kathryn H. Hogan (Not admitted in OH). Of Counsel: Fred H. Summe (Not admitted in OH; Resident, Covington, KY Office); Richard L. Levine; Kristen D. VandeWater (Not admitted in OH).
Commercial, Creditors Rights, Bankruptcy, Collection, Banking and Financial Institution Law, Civil Litigation, Federal Consumer Law Litigation, Foreclosures, Automobile Deficiencies, Credit Cards, Medical Debts, Bad Checks, Business Loans/Commercial Debt, Vehicle and Property Repossessions, Landlord Representation/Evictions/Lease Litigation, Equipment Leasing.
Representative Clients: Fifth Third Bank and its affiliates; Citicorp and Citibank; Contel Credit Corp.; Borg Warner Acceptance Corp.; Park National Bank; U.S. Bancorp; Arcadia Health Services; Firstar Bank; Provident Bank; Information Leasing Corp.
Covington, Kentucky Office: Heritage International, Suite 203, P.O. Box 2158. Telephone: 513-489-0829. Fax: 513-489-0834.
Columbus Office: 460 E. Main Street. Telephone: 513-489-0829. Fax: 513-489-0834.
Dayton Office: 319 Liberty Tower. Telephone: 513-489-0829. Fax: 513-489-0834.
Lima Office: P.O. Box 937. Telephone: 513-489-0829. Fax: 513-489-0834.
Madison, Indiana Office: 201 East Main Street. Telephone: 513-489-0829. Fax: 513-489-0834.

See Professional Biographies, CINCINNATI, OHIO

Masters, Robert L., (BV) . . . '39 '71 C.337 B.S. L.151 J.D. [Masters]
Masters & Co., L.P.A., (BV) . . . 468 Batavia Pike
Mastruserio, Dominic . . . '42 '73 C.150 B.A. L.1340 J.D. [D.Mastruserio]
Mastruserio, Karen L., L.P.A., (BV) . . . '53 '86 C&L.150 B.A., J.D. [Griffin -F.]
Mastruserio, Dominic, Co. LPA . . . 306 E. 14th St.

Masuda, Funai, Eifert & Mitchell, Ltd.
(See Chicago, Illinois)

Mathews, S. Mark . . . '69 '99 C.607 B.S.B.A. L.1187 J.D. 4557 Montgomery Rd.
Mathews, S. Paul, (AV) . . . '14 '38 C&L.150 LL.B. 4557 Montgomery Rd.
Mathews, Stanley A., (AV) . . . '44 '68 C.477 B.A. L.150 J.D. 4557 Montgomery St.
Mathews, William S. . . . '26 '53 C&L.150 B.A., LL.B. Ret. Com. Pleas J.‡
Mathews, Wm. Stewart, II, (AV) . . . '50 '77 C.150 B.A. L.1161 J.D. [Dolle,R.&M.]
Matlock, Raymond H., (BV) '46 '73 C.150 B.A. L.838 J.D.
Assoc. Prof. of Legal Studies, Univ. of Cincinnati
Mattheis, David Kent . . . '59 '01 C.350 B.S. L.1161 J.D. The Proctor & Gamble Co.
Matthews, David W., (AV) . . . '32 '59 C.309 A.B. L.150 LL.B. 5520 Wasigo Dr.‡
Matthews, James R., (AV) . . . '60 '85 C&L.150 B.A., J.D. [Keating M.&K.]
Matthews, Kevin G. '61 '86 C.276 A.B. L.184 J.D.
Lit. Coun., GE Aviation Services, Inc.
Matthews, Timothy B., (AV) . . . '56 '81 C.309 A.B. L.1565 J.D. [Keating M.&K.]
Mattingly, Elizabeth B., (AV) . . . '50 '75 C.116 B.A. L.602 J.D. 7857 Thompson Rd.
Mattingly, Paul R., (AV) . . . '50 '75 C.201 B.A. L.602 J.D. [Dinsmore&S.]
Mauer, Kimberly K., (AV) . . . '59 '84 C.513 B.A. L.221 J.D. [Ⓒ Frost B.T.]
Mauer, Vincent E., (AV) . . . '58 '85 C.513 B.S. L.221 J.D. [Ⓒ Frost B.T.]
Maundrell, Michael E., (AV) . . . '46 '74 C.477 B.A. L.150 J.D. [Ⓒ Schroeder,M.B.&P.]
Maxwell, Robert W., II, (AV) . . . '43 '68 C.301 B.S. L.228 J.D. [Keating M.&K.]
May, Douglas J., (BV) . . . '63 '89 C.608 B.A. L.150 J.D. [Martin&B.]
Mayer, James J., (AV) . . . '38 '69 C.150 B.S.E.E. L.1340 J.D. [Ⓒ Taft,S.&H.]
Mayer, Kimberly A. . . . '66 '96 C.473 B.A. L.151 J.D. [Kohnen&P.]
Mayerson, Frederic H. . . . '46 '72 C.473 B.A. L.477 J.D. 7900 Spring Valley‡
Mazzei, Stephen S., (BV) . . . '55 '80 C.608 B.A. L.851 J.D. [Young,R.&N.]
McAdams, Ernest Fuller, Jr. . . . '52 '79 C.999 B.A. L.1161 J.D. City Pros.
McBeth, Steven J. . . . '65 '94 C.608 B.S. L.607 J.D. [D.W.Norris]
McBride, Mark R., (AV) . . . '58 '81 C.150 B.B.A. L.851 J.D. 8624-Winton Rd.
McBride, Michael L. . . . '57 '87 8624-B Winton Road
McBroom, Christine L., (AV) . . . '53 '81 C.608 B.S. L.201 J.D. [Ⓐ Dinsmore&S.]
McCafferty, Michael P. . . . '— '04 C.473 L.880 J.D. [Donovan L.]
McCarthy, Daniel J. . . . '77 '02 C.502 B.A. L.734 J.D. [Ⓐ Manley B.]
McCarthy, James F., III, (AV) . . . '52 '77 C.973 B.A. L.608 J.D. [Katz,T.B.&H.]
McCartney, Paul W., (AV) . . . '62 '88 C.385 B.A. L.608 J.D. [Rendigs,F.K.&D.]

McCaslin, Imbus & McCaslin, A Legal Professional Association, (AV)
The Provident Building, 632 Vine Street Suite 900, 45202-2442 ⊙
Telephone: 513-421-4646 Fax: 513-421-7929
URL: http://www.mimlaw.com
Philip J. Marsick; John K. Hurd; R. Gary Winters; Thomas J. Gruber; Joseph C. Gruber; Bernard W. Wharton; Michael P. Cussen; Ian R. Smith; Stephen M. Bernat; William M. Cussen. Of Counsel: John P. Concannon.
Alternative Dispute Resolution, Bonds, Business Law, Civil Rights, Civil Litigation, Contracts, Domestic Relations, Environmental Law, Guardianship and Conservatorship, Insurance, Labor and Employment, Legal Malpractice, Medical Malpractice, Personal Injury, Probate, Products Liability, Professional Liability, School Law, Trade Secrets; Trust and Estates, Workers' Compensation, Wills.
Representative Client: AETNA Casualty & Surety Co.
West Chester, Ohio Office: 7969 Cincinnati-Dayton Road, 45069. Telephone: 513-759-9123. Fax: 513-759-7688.

See Professional Biographies, CINCINNATI, OHIO

McCaw, Michael E. . . . '54 '79 C.608 B.S. L.770 J.D. Belcan Corp.
McClain, William A. . . . '13 '38 C.967 A.B. L.477 J.D. [Manley B.] ‡
McClure, John D., (AV) . . . '47 '72 C&L.150 B.A., J.D. 7 W. 7th St., Ste. 1800
McCluskey, Laurie A. . . . '73 '02 C.150 B.S.N. L.1340 J.D. [Ⓐ Lindhorst&D.]
McConnell, Martin Pitt . . . '39 '74 C.150 B.Mus. L.1161 J.D. Pros. Off.
McCord, Charles B., III . . . '66 '95 C.446 B.A. L.1340 J.D. 121 W. Ninth St.
McCord, Elizabeth A. . . . '52 '82 C.77 B.A. L.383 J.D. [Ⓒ Montgomery,R.&J.]
McCoy, John J., (AV) . . . '52 '77 C.973 B.S. L.145 J.D. [Taft,S.&H.]
McCracken, Wendy Reuter '57 '83 C.518 B.A. L.347 J.D.
(adm. in IN; not adm. in OH) 425 Walnut St.‡
McCrate, Mitchell D. . . . '55 '86 C.611 B.A. L.228 J.D. Gen. Coun. Off.
McCue, Richard G., (BV) . . . '43 '68 C&L.150 B.A., J.D. [R.G.McCue]
McCue, Richard G., Co., L.P.A., (BV) . . . 948 Old St., Rt. 74
Mccullough, C. Joseph . . . '73 '98 C.108 B.S. L.201 J.D. [Ⓐ White,G.&M.]
McCune, Francis P., (BV) . . . '56 '83 C.201 B.A. L.150 J.D. Eagle-Picher Inc.
McDaniel, James F., (AV) . . . '46 '78 C.604 B.A. L.477 J.D. 36 East Fourth Street
McDaniel, Scott F., (AVⓉ) . . . '53 '83 C.611 B.A. L.201 J.D. 36 E. 7th Street
McDaniel, Vernon W., (AV) . . . '15 '41 C.77 B.A. L.1340 LL.B. 906 Main St.
McDonough, Jas. P. . . . '13 '50 L.1340 LL.B. 1035 Pamela Dr.
McDonough, Kevin C. . . . '55 '89 C.973 B.S.B.A. L.150 J.D. [Cohen,T.K.&S.]
McDonough, Therese S. '63 '88
C.150 B.B.A. L.608 J.D. Assoc. Coun., The Ohio Natl. Life Ins. Co.
McDow-Dunham, Kelly L. . . . '70 '97 C.477 B.S.Ch. L.151 J.D. Procter & Gamble Co.
McDowell, Christopher R. . . . '69 '94 C.437 B.A. L.923 J.D. [Ⓐ Dinsmore&S.]★
McDowell, John E., (AV) . . . '27 '52 C.473 A.B. L.477 J.D. [Ⓒ Dinsmore&S.]
McElhinney, Paul A. . . . '— '85 V.P., GE Transportation
McFarland, Barbara A. . . . '52 '82 C.893 B.S. L.150 J.D. Univ. of Cincinnati
McGavran, Frederick J., (AV) . . . '43 '72 C.385 B.A. L.309 J.D. [Frost B.T.]
McGehee, John H. . . . '42 '80 C.309 B.A. L.150 J.D. P.O. Box 141453
McGrath, V. Brandon . . . '72 '00 C.383 B.S. L.150 J.D. [Ⓐ Wood&L.]
McGraw, Bridget Gannon . . . '78 '03 C.473 B.A. L.150 J.D. [Ⓐ Frost B.T.]
McGraw, James J., Jr., (AV) . . . '49 '74 C.602 B.B.A. L.7 J.D. [Keating M.&K.]
McGregor, Jane C. '— '84 C.1210 B.S. L.1218 J.D.
(adm. in NY; not adm. in OH; Pat.)
Assoc. Dir, Assoc. Gen. Coun., The Procter & Gamble Co.
McGuire, Joel F. . . . '71 '01 C.610 B.A. L.597 J.D. [Ⓐ Frost B.T.]
McHenry, Martin, (AV) . . . '57 '83 C.608 B.A. L.188 J.D. [Ⓒ Haverkamp,B.R.&R.]
McHenry, Powell, (AV) . . . '26 '51 C.150 A.B. L.309 LL.B. [Ⓒ Dinsmore&S.]
McIlwain, Carol Newell, (BV) . . . '43 '77 C.608 B.A. L.1340 J.D. 35 E. 7th St., Ste. 510
McIlwain, Douglas W., (BV) . . . '51 '79 C.473 B.A. L.1340 J.D. 35 E. 7th St.
McIlwain, Harry H., Jr., (BV) '48 '76 C.473 B.S. L.1340 J.D.
35 East 7th Street, Suite 510
McIntosh, A. Brian . . . '68 '95 C.150 L.1161 J.D. [McIntosh&M.]
McIntosh, Bruce B., (AV) . . . '34 '60 C.207 A.B. L.597 J.D. [McIntosh&M.]
McIntosh, Jill Valiton . . . '72 '97 C.973 B.S.B.A. L.851 J.D. The Kroger Co.
McIntosh, Michael Todd . . . '65 '93 C.150 B.A. L.1161 J.D. [McIntosh&M.]
McIntosh, Thomas G. . . . '76 '03 C&L.383 B.S., J.D. [Ⓐ Ulmer&B.]
McIntosh & McIntosh, P.L.L.C., (AV) . . . 15 East Eighth Street, Suite 300 W
McInturf, Lora N. . . . '77 '03 C.610 B.B.A. L.608 J.D. [Ⓐ Taft,S.&H.]
McIntyre, M. Scott . . . '75 '02 C.1118 B.A. L.383 J.D. [Ⓐ Keating M.&K.]
McKay, Bernard L., (AV) . . . '69 '94 C.510 B.B.A. L.1340 J.D. [Frost B.T.]
McKay, Timothy E., (BV) . . . '61 '88 C.393 B.A. L.1340 J.D. [Mack,M.&K.]
McKelvey, Matthew I. . . . '— '02 C.264 B.A. L.1202 J.D. [Ⓐ Lerner,S.&R.]
McKenna, Kevin R. '57 '83 C.602 B.A. L.146 J.D.
(adm. in IL; not adm. in OH) Container Corp. of Amer.
McKinney, Daniel H., (AV) . . . '29 '55 C.608 A.B. L.309 J.D. [McKinney&N.] ⊙

McKinney & Namei Co., L.P.A., (AV)
15 East Eighth Street, 45202 ⊙
Telephone: 513-721-0200 Fax: 513-632-5898
Email: firooz@zoomtown.com
Daniel H. McKinney; Firooz T. Namei. Associates: John Robert Natkevicius; Blake P. Somers.
General Civil and Criminal, Trial and Appellate Practice in all Courts. Business, Corporate, Personal Injury, Immigration, ERISA, Real Estate, Insurance, Family Law and Divorce. Alternative Dispute Resolution, Estate Planning, Probate, Employee Benefits, Pension and Profit Sharing and Federal and State Taxation.
Covington, Kentucky Office: 700 Scott Street, P.O. Box 120008, 41012-0008. Telephone: 513-721-0200. Fax: 513-632-5898.
See Professional Biographies, CINCINNATI, OHIO

McLaughlin, John F., (AV) . . . . '61 '87 C.1107 B.A. L.276 J.D. [Rendigs,F.K.&D.]
McLaughlin, Karen M., (BV) . . . .'51 '81 C.1118 A.B. L.1340 J.D. [Ⓒ Frost B.T.]
McLean, James E., Jr., (AV) . . . . '65 '90 C.967 B.A. L.150 J.D. [Rendigs,F.K.&D.]
McManus, John Francis . . . . '52 '80 C.150 B.A. L.1340 J.D. 800 Broadway
McMillan, Shelby M., (BV) . . . .'72 '97 C.835 B.S. L.201 J.D. [Ⓐ Reminger&R.]
McMullen, Martin Edwin, (BV) . . . . '41 '67 C.197 B.A. L.1340 J.D. Ref., Dom Rel. Ct.
McMurray, Kevin N., (AV) . . . . '63 '89 C&L.150 B.S.Ch.E., J.D. [Frost B.T.]
McMurry, Kyndle . . . .'64 '89 C.1322 B.B.A. L.150 J.D. Marwin Controls Inc.
McNabb, Suzanne Cahill . . . .'72 '00 C.855 B.A. L.880 J.D. [Ⓐ Dinsmore&S.]
McNair, Brian, (BV) . . . .'59 '86 C.473 B.S. L.201 J.D. 441 Vine Street
McNally, John Wm., Jr., (BV) . . . .'42 '74 C.150 B.S. L.1340 J.D. [Jacobs,K.S.&M.]
McNally, Robert A., (BV) . . . . '36 '66 C.973 B.S. L.1340 J.D. 3631 Parfore Court
McNeil, Michael D. . . . .'64 '91 C.896 B.A. L.150 J.D. [Drew&W.]
McPeek, Bradley . . . . '73 '99 C.602 B.A. L.150 J.D. [Ⓐ Lindhorst&D.]
McPherson, David J. . . . . '54 '86 C.97 B.S. L.150 J.D. [Ⓒ Frost B.T.] ‡
McSherry, Jeffrey P., (BV) . . . . '65 '91 C.97 B.S. L.201 J.D. [Wood&L.]
McTigue, Edward J. . . . .'51 '79 C.973 B.S.B.A. L.1340 J.D. 601 Main St., 3rd Fl.
Meagher, J. Kenneth, (AV) . . . .'33 '60 C&L.150 B.A., J.D. [Ⓒ Rendigs,F.K.&D.]
Mebs, Frederick W., (BV) . . . . '27 '52 C&L.665 B.S., J.D. 30 E. Central Pkwy.
Mechem, Charles S., Jr., (AV) '30 '55
C.473 A.B. L.976 LL.B. 1 East Fourth Street, 9th Floor
Mecklenborg, Robert P., (BV) . . . . '52 '78 C.610 B.A. L.150 J.D. [Hyle&M.]
Meckstroth, James J. . . . . '67 '94 C.973 B.S.B.A. L.150 J.D. 22 W. 9th St.
Meckstroth, John R., Jr., (BV) . . . . '54 '81 C.150 B.U.P. L.1187 J.D. 22 W. 9th St.
Medven, Ann-Dana . . . . '71 '99 C.6 B.A. L.150 J.D. [Ⓐ Harris&B.]
Meek, Patricia S. . . . .'52 '98 C.523 B.A. L.150 J.D. 4725 Cornell Rd.
Meeks, Lisa, (BV) . . . . '58 '93 C.868 B.M. L.1340 J.D. [Newman&M.]
Meguire, Catherine M. . . . . '55 '87 C.385 B.A. L.383 J.D. 3438 Zumstein Avenue
Mehas, Andrew G. . . . .'15 '41 C&L.150 A.B., LL.B. 3680 Traskwood Circle‡
Mehnert, Thomas P., (AV) '42 '67 C.207 B.A. L.145 J.D.
Vice President - Legal, Convergys Corporation
Meier, Aimee M. . . . . '59 '97 C.523 B.A. L.1340 J.D. [Meier&M.]
Meier, Carl Lore, (AV) . . . .'15 '38 C&L.150 A.B., LL.B. 3731 Merwin-Ten Mile Rd.‡
Meier, Robert C. . . . . '64 '97 C.150 B.A. L.1161 J.D. [Meier&M.]
Meier & Meier . . . . 7345 Southpointe Dr.
Meisenhelder, Jamie L. . . . . '75 '00 C.473 B.S. L.1340 J.D. 432 Ray Norrish Dr.
Meisenhelder, John F. . . . . '63 '91 C.608 B.S. L.150 J.D. [Keating M.&K.]
Meiser, Stephen Michael, (BV) . . . . '57 '86 C&L.150 B.F.A., J.D. [S.M.M.L.p.a.]
Meiser, Stephen M., Co., L.p.a., (BV) . . . . 4995 Glenway Ave.
Meister, Julia B. . . . . '69 '95 C.973 B.A. L.602 J.D. [Taft,S.&H.]
Meister, Thomas E. . . . . '20 '50 C.973 B.Sc. L.1340 LL.B. 1734 Emerald Glade Lane
Meizlish, Bruce H., (AV) . . . . '52 '77 C.608 B.A. L.273 J.D. [Meizlish&G.]
Meizlish & Grayson, (AV) . . . . .830 Main Street, Suite 999
Mellen, Joseph P., (AV) . . . . '49 '77 C.973 B.S. L.851 J.D. [Keating M.&K.]
Mellott, John T. . . . .'64 '89 C.473 B.A. L.273 J.D. The Brisben Companies
Melville, Charles H., (AV) . . . . '37 '62 C.674 A.B. L.150 LL.B. [Ⓒ Strauss&T.]
Melville, John W., (AV) . . . .'09 '35 C&L.150 M.E., J.D. 3113 Evergreen Ridge Dr.‡
Melvin, William H.J. . . . . '46 '83 C.188 B.S. L.150 J.D. Juv. Ct. Ref.-Mag.
Mendelsohn, Donald S., (AV) . . . .'49 '75 C.976 B.A. L.813 J.D. [Thompson H.]
Mendelsohn, Robert N. '53 '93
C.1083 B.A. L.201 J.D. 10979 Reed Hartman Hwy., Suite 201
Mendenhall, Robert J. . . . . '30 '59 C.150 B.B.A. L.151 J.D. 30 E. Central Pkwy.‡
Menke, David J. '56 '81 C.473 B.A. L.309 J.D.
Sr. Coun., Western & Southern Financial Group
Menninger, Henry E., Jr., (AV) . . . .'50 '77 C.150 B.A. L.1340 J.D. [Wood&L.]
Meranus, David . . . . '65 '91 C.473 B.A. L.851 J.D. The Sheakley Group. Inc.
Meranus, Leonard S., (AV) . . . . '28 '54 C.705 Litt.B. L.309 LL.B. [Ⓒ Thompson H.]
Merchant, Toby D. . . . . '78 '04 C.188 B.S. L.930 J.D. [Ⓐ Dinsmore&S.]
Mercurio, Michael T. . . . .'68 '00 C.150 B.A. L.1340 J.D. [Ⓐ Reisenfeld&Assoc.]
Mercurio, Vincent M., (BV) . . . .'10 '31 L.472 J.D. 5780 Eagles Ridge Ln.‡
Merkel, Edward W., (AV) . . . .'08 '32 C.197 A.B. L.309 LL.B. 4001 Rosslyn Dr.‡
Merling, Joseph C. '52 '77 C.973 B.A. L.150 J.D.
Superv. Staff Atty., 6th Cir. Ct. of App.
Merritt, Gilbert S., Jr. . . . . '36 '60 C.976 B.A. L.880 LL.B. Sr. U.S. Cir. J.
Mesh, Gene, & Associates, (AV) '31 '64 C.477 B.B.A. L.1340 J.D.
2605 Burnet Avenue
Messer, Earl K., (AV) . . . . '54 '91 C.999 B.S. L.1340 J.D. [Taft,S.&H.]
Metz, Jerome J., Jr., (AV) . . . .'50 '80 C.973 B.S. L.150 J.D. [Porter W.M.&A.]
Metz, John H., (AV) . . . .'52 '77 C.150 B.A. L.1218 J.D. 441 Vine St., 44th Fl.
Meyer, Charles M., (AV) . . . . '51 '77 C&L.93 A.B., J.D. [Santen&H.]
Meyer, David A. . . . . '69 '96 C.1118 B.S. L.1340 J.D. [Ⓐ Keating M.&K.]
Meyer, Joseph W. . . . . '66 '93 C.999 B.A. L.150 J.D. Industrial Commission of Ohio
Meyer, Karen P. . . . . '60 '92 C.473 B.S. L.150 J.D. [Lutz,C.&M.]
Meyer, Keith D., (AV) . . . .'55 '80 C&L.150 B.B.A., J.D. [Kohnen&P.]
Meyer, Marsha R. . . . .'48 '96 C.150 B.B.A. L.151 J.D. 8070 Beechmont Avenue
Meyer, Richard E., (BV) . . . .'30 '66 C.150 E.E. L.1340 J.D. 1231 Hollywood Ave.
Meyer, Ronald A., (AV) . . . .'44 '69 C.608 B.A. L.150 J.D. [White,G.&M.]
Meyer, Scott A. . . . .'61 '86 C.473 B.S. L.339 J.D. 11620 Timber Ridge Lane
Meyer, William D. . . . . '17 '43 C&L.150 B.B.A., LL.B. 2100 Central Trust Tower‡
Meyer, William F. . . . .'22 '53 C.976 Sc.B. L.309 J.D. 5557 Mapleridge Drive
Meyers, Eliot N., (BV) . . . . '65 '91 C&L.309 A.B., J.D. [Vorys,S.S.&P.]
Meyers, George W. . . . . '40 '65 C.659 B.S. L.150 J.D. 1200 Tri-State Bldg.
Meyers, Paul W., (BV) . . . . '52 '78 C.973 B.S. L.1340 J.D. Ref., Dom. Rel. Ct.
Meyers, Robert J., (BV) . . . . '50 '75 C.602 B.A. L.276 J.D. [Buechner,H.O.M.H.&K.]
Mezher, Kathleen, (BV) . . . . '59 '84 C.473 B.A. L.201 J.D. 1241 Nagel Rd.
Mezibov, Marc D., (AV) . . . . '45 '70 C.29 B.A. L.93 J.D. [Mezibov&J.]

Mezibov & Jenkins, LLP, (AV)
401 East Court Street, Suite 600, 45202
Telephone: 513-723-1600 Fax: 513-723-1620
Email: esteelman@mezibovjenkins.com URL: http://www.mezibovjenkins.com
Marc D. Mezibov; Christian A. Jenkins;—Stacy Hinners. Of Counsel: Wendy R. Calaway; Susan E. Brabenec.

(This Listing Continued)

Mezibov & Jenkins, LLP (Continued)
Employment Discrimination, Title VII Discrimination, Sexual Harassment, Civil Rights, Constitutional Law, Litigation, Employment Law, Class Actions.
See Professional Biographies, CINCINNATI, OHIO

Miano, Tamara A. . . . . '65 '01 C.188 B.S. L.1340 J.D. [Ⓐ Taft,S.&H.]
Michel, Lisa Wintersheimer, (AV) . . . . . .'63 '88 C.973 B.A. L.150 J.D. [Keating M.&K.]
Michel, Timothy A., (AV) . . . .'64 '88 C.473 B.S. L.150 J.D. [Haverkamp,B.R.&R.]
Middelhoff, Mary-Jo, (BV) . . . .'59 '91 C.973 B.S.N. L.150 J.D. [Dinsmore&S.]
Midei, Matt C., (BV) . . . . '58 '83 C.201 B.A. L.607 J.D. V.P., Marsh & McLennan, Inc.
Mikita, William H., (BV) . . . . '54 '83 C.150 B.A. L.607 J.D. [Ⓐ O'Connor,M.&D.]
Miller, A. Dennis, (AV) . . . . '47 '73 C.150 B.A. L.1340 J.D. [Droder&M.]
Miller, Ann B., (BV) . . . . . . '56 '84 C.276 B.S.F.S. L.201 J.D. 5710 Wooster Pike, Ste. 212
Miller, Floyd B. '27 '57 C.346 B.S. L.861 J.D.
(adm. in LA; not adm. in OH) 580 Walnut St., 7th Fl.
Miller, G. Franklin, (AV) . . . .'38 '63 C.178 B.A. L.477 J.D. [Ⓐ Dinsmore&S.]
Miller, Kenneth B. . . . . '39 '77 C.150 B.S.I.M. L.1340 J.D. Ethicon, Inc.
Miller, Martin J., (AV) . . . . .'63 '91 C.679 B.S. L.851 J.D. [Dinsmore&S.] (See Pat. Sect.)
Miller, Marvin A., (BV) . . . .'34 '66 C&L.150 B.B.A., J.D. [Rich,P.W.F.&M.]
Miller, Michael R. . . . .'57 '83 C.97 B.S. L.201 J.D. [Graydon H.&R.]
Miller, Orville J., (BV) . . . .'39 '70 C.150 B.S. L.1340 J.D. [Rich,P.W.F.&M.]
Miller, Peter J. . . . . '61 '88 C.976 B.A. L.150 J.D. 8513 Myrtlewood Ave.
Miller, R. Douglas, (BV) . . . . '55 '81 C.150 B.B.A. L.1340 J.D. [Donnellon,D.&M.]
Miller, Robert J. '50 '77 C.150 B.S.I.M. L.893 J.D.
Vice Pres. & Gen. Coun., The Procter & Gamble Co.
Miller, Sarah J. . . . .'50 '75 C&L.150 B.S., J.D. Admin. Law J.
Miller, Steven R. . . . .'69 '94 C.999 A.B. L.213 J.D. [Ⓢ Vorys,S.S.&P.]
Miller, Steven W. '59 '84 C&L.608 B.S.M.E., J.D.
Assoc. Gen. Coun., The Procter & Gamble Co. (Pat.)
Miller, W. Timothy, (BV) . . . .'67 '92 C.209 B.Mus. L.188 J.D. [Taft,S.&H.]
Mills, Elisa '68 '93 C.929 B.A. L.1340 J.D.
V.P. & Sr. Corp. Coun., Provident Financial Group, Inc.
Mills, James A., (AV) . . . .'55 '80 C.679 B.A. L.150 J.D. [Denlinger,R.&G.]
Mills, Tina Renee . . . .'72 '99 C.523 B.A. L.200 J.D. [Firm of T.R.Mills]

Mills, Tina R., LLC, The Law Firm of
4351 Gleneste Withamsville Road, 45245
Telephone: 513-732-9999 Fax: 513-735-2455
Email: mills@millslegal.com URL: http://www.millslegal.com
Tina Renee Mills.
Business Law, Buying and Selling of Businesses, Family Business Law, Limited Liability Company Law, Partnership Law, Small Business Law, Consumer Law, Corporate Law, Criminal Law, Debtor and Creditor, Collections, Creditors Rights, Nonprofit and Charitable Organizations, Charitable Giving, Landlord and Tenant Law, Trusts and Estates, Asset Protection, Estate Litigation, Estate Planning, Guardianship and Conservatorship, Wills and Probate.
See Professional Biographies, CINCINNATI, OHIO

Minamyer, Wm. Eric, (BV) . . . .'— '79 C.8 B.A. L.904 J.D. [Ⓐ Buckley K.]
Minutolo, James P., (BV) . . . . '58 '83 C.602 B.A. L.880 J.D. [J.P.Minutolo]
Minutolo, James P., Co., LPA, (BV) . . . . 2090 Florence Ave., Ste. 201
Mire, Terrence A., (AV) . . . . '47 '72 C.259 B.A. L.150 J.D. [Cohen,T.K.&S.]
Mire, Wm. N. . . . .'16 '49 C.150 B.B.A. L.1340 LL.B. 806 Main St.‡
Mitchell, Charles E., (BV) . . . .'50 '78 C.150 B.B.A. L.151 J.D. 6024 Harrison Ave.
Mitchell, Darryl '62 '93
C.178 B.A. L.150 J.D. Coun., Contracts, GE Aviation Services, Inc.
Mitchell, Darryl . . . . '52 '86 C.150 B.A. L.1340 J.D. Asst. City Solr.
Mitchell, Jennifer O. . . . .'73 '98 C.473 B.A. L.8 J.D. [Ⓐ Dinsmore&S.]
Mitchell, Patrick J., (AV) . . . . '51 '86 C.150 B.B.A. L.904 J.D. [Taft,S.&H.]
Mitchell, Robert H., (BV) . . . . '60 '86 C.894 B.A. L.150 J.D. [Manley B.]
Mitchell, William J. . . . .'71 '96 C.20 B.S. L.215 J.D. [Ⓐ G.R.Hoffmann]
Mitroussia, Antonia . . . . '61 '91 C&L.150 B.A., J.D. [Ⓐ Taft,S.&H.]
Mittendorf, Richard K. . . . . '24 '50 L.150 LL.B. 7128 Paddison Rd.
Mock, Russell J., II . . . . '69 '96 C.201 B.A. L.607 J.D. 11137 Main St.
Moeddel, Michael J. . . . .'78 '02 C.608 B.A. L.150 J.D. [Ⓐ Keating M.&K.]
Moeller, George F., (BV) . . . .'54 '85 C&L.150 B.B.A., J.D. [Ⓒ Manley B.]
Mohl, Douglas C. '39 '71 C.494 B.Ch.E. L.1340 J.D.
Associate General Counsel-Patents, Health Care, Procter & Gamble Company (Pat.)
Mohler, Jarrod M. . . . .'73 '00 C.347 B.S. L.150 J.D. [Ⓐ Robbins,K.P.&T.]
Mohnsam, Lisa Ellis . . . .'66 '91 C.473 B.A. L.150 J.D. 4328 Courageous Circle
Mohylsky, Katherine A. '53 '91 C.452 B.M. L.150 J.D.
Asst. Dean., Admin. Affrs., Univ. of Cin. Coll. Conservatory Music
Molinsky, George D., (AV) . . . . '66 '94 C&L.602 B.B.A., J.D. [Taft,S.&H.]
Mollaun, Terrance Tod . . . . '74 '00 C.473 B.S. L.201 J.D. 906 Main St., Ste. 500
Mongan, Thos. H., (BV) '21 '47 C&L.150 B.A., LL.B.
The Guarantee Title & Trust Co.
Monnie, Terrance R., (AV) '44 '74
C.645 B.A. L.1340 J.D. [O'Connor,M.&D.] (⊙Fort Mitchell, KY)
Monning, Virginia W. . . . .'28 '55 C.150 L.1340 LL.B. 1307 Hayward Ct.‡
Montague, William L., (AV) '57 '82
C.967 B.A. L.150 J.D. [Greenebaum D.&M.] (⊙Covington, KY)
Montfort, Donald G., (BV) . . . . '26 '51 C.151 B.S.C. L.1340 J.D. Pub. Def.
Montgomery, David . . . .'51 '79 C.910 A.B. L.477 J.D. LEXIS-NEXIS
Montgomery, David K., (AV) . . . .'58 '84 C.473 B.A. L.880 J.D. [Keating M.&K.]
Montgomery, James J., (AV) . . . .'48 '76 C.473 B.S.Ed. L.1340 J.D. [Montgomery,R.&J.]
Montgomery, Leanne R. . . . .'59 '01 C.610 B.S. L.150 J.D. [Ⓐ Freking&B.]
Montgomery, Matthew A. . . . . '71 '98 C&L.150 B.B.A., J.D. 6061 Bridgetown Rd.‡

Montgomery, Rennie & Jonson, (AV)
36 East Seventh Street, Suite 2100, 45202-4413
Telephone: 513-241-4722 Fax: 513-241-8775
Email: mrjlaw@mrj.cc
Members of Firm: James J. Montgomery; Douglas W. Rennie; George D. Jonson; Kelly Carbetta Scandy; Linda L. Woeber; Elizabeth P. Sherwood; Janet A. Self; Ralph E. Burnham; G. Todd Hoffpauir; Matthew E. Stubbs;—Kimberly Vanover Riley; Timothy C. Ammer; Jason A. Golden; Hope A. Smith; Jennifer D. Dine; Pamela Marshall. Of Counsel: Kevin J. Hopper; Elizabeth A. McCord.
Civil Trial and Appellate Practice in: Automotive, Aviation, Civil Rights, Commercial Construction, Consumer, Employment, Environmental, Motor Carrier Liability, Personal Injury, Premises Liability, Products Liability, Professional Malpractice.
Representative Clients: Ford Motor Co.; Navistar International Transportation Corp.; Chrysler Corp.; Toyota Motor Sales U. S. A., Inc.; United States Aviation Underwriters, Inc.; Transport Insurance Co.; Nissan Motor Corporation in U.S.A., Inc.; Powermatic, A Division of DeVlieg-Bullard, Inc.; Countrywide Services Corp.
See Professional Biographies, CINCINNATI, OHIO

Mooney, Donald J., Jr., (AV) . . . .'50 '75 C.602 B.A. L.150 J.D. [Ulmer&B.]
Mooney, Martin E., (AV) . . . .'52 '78 C.674 A.B. L.602 J.D. [Frost B.T.]
Moore, Christopher L., (BV) . . .'67 '93 C.973 B.S./B.A. L.851 J.D. [Schroeder,M.B.&P.]
Moore, Donald C., Jr., (BV) '54 '80
C.150 B.B.A. L.1340 J.D. 4355 Ferguson Dr., Ste. 200
Moore, Gregory A. . . . .'66 '91 C.1161 B.A. L.1340 J.D. 1014 Vine St., Ste. 1690

Moore, James M., (AV) ... '47 '72 C.190 A.B. L.150 J.D. [Lindhorst&D.]
Moore, Karen Nelson ... '48 '73 C.681 A.B. L.309 J.D. U.S. Ct. App. J.
Moore, Kelly P. ... '77 '02 C.879 B.S. L.1170 J.D. [[A] Frost B.T.]
Moore, Lisa Marie, (BV(T)) '66 '90 C.383 B.S. L.1340 J.D.
(adm. in KY; not adm. in OH) V.P. & Sr. Corp. Coun., Provident Financial Group, Inc.
Moore, Richard L., (AV) ... '65 '93 C.97 B.S. L.150 J.D. [Vorys,S.S.&P.]
Moore, Rodger W. ... '68 '01 C.45 B.S. L.245 J.D. [[A] Frost B.T.]
Moore, Terry E., (BV) ... '60 '86 C&L.150 B.B.A., J.D. [Kohnen&P.]
Moore, Moore and Moore, LLP, (AV) ... 7416 Jager Court
Moraites, John S. ... '24 '51 C.150 L.16 LL.B. P.O. Box 12365
Morales, Jennifer J. ... '78 '03 C.309 A.B. L.569 J.D. [[A] Keating M.&K.]
Moran, Joseph L. ... '27 '53 C.973 B.S. L.150 LL.B. 1 Walsh Ln.‡
Moran, Paul R., (AV) ... '33 '59 C.150 B.A. L.893 LL.B. [Cors&B.]
Moran, William J., Jr., (BV) ... '65 '92 C.973 B.S.B.A. L.117 J.D. [Deters,B.&L.] ⊙
Mordino, Joseph T., (BV) ... '71 '95 C.732 B.A. L.150 J.D. [Faulkner&T.]
Morehart, Douglas M., (BV) ... '61 '87 C.473 B.A. L.150 J.D. [Haverkamp,B.R.&R.]
Morelli, Arnold, (AV) ... '28 '55 C.150 B.A. L.309 LL.B. [Bauer,M.&H.]
Moreno, Victor C. ... '66 '95 C.608 B.S.M.E. L.150 J.D. [[C] Frost B.T.] (See Pat. Sect.)
Morgan, Amy Triplett ... '71 '99 C.437 B.A L.851 J.D. [[A] Weltman,W.&R.]
Morgan, Ann M., (BV) ... '52 '80 C.150 B.B.A. L.1340 J.D. 22 W. 9th St.
Morgan, Frederick M., Jr., (AV) '56 '83
C.207 B.A. L.150 J.D. [Volkema,T.M.B.S.&M.] ⊙
Morgan, Katherine Cook ... '69 '97 C.821 B.A. L.150 J.D. [Frost B.T.]
Morgan, Noel M. ... '42 '96 C.381 B.A. Legal Aid Soc. of Cincinnati
Morgeson, J. Allan ... '43 '69 C.150 B.A. L.1340 J.D. 105 West Fourth Street
Morgeson, Philip J. ... '75 '00 C.362 B.A. L.150 J.D. [Morgeson]
Morgeson Law Office, The, L.L.C. ... 105 W. Fourth St., Ste. 1115
Morris, Gwen M. ... '68 '94 C.473 B.Phil L.276 J.D. 38 Fountain Square Plaza
Morrison, Patricia W. ... '41 '76 C.914 B.A. L.150 J.D. 3740 Clifton Ave.‡
Morrisroe, Donald P., (AV) ... '54 '79 C.473 B.S. L.150 J.D. [Goodman&G.]
Morriss, William S. ... '— '05 C.800 B.S. L.276 J.D. [[A] Frost B.T.]
Morrissey, Wm. J., Jr. ... '21 '49 C.473 L.1340 LL.B. Sr. Com. Pleas J.
Morthorst, Michael E. ... '50 '77 C.973 B.A. L.1340 J.D. Asst. Pros. Atty.
Morton, W. Stanley '47 '74 C&L.608 B.S., J.D.
Assoc. Gen. Coun., Procter & Gamble Co.
Morton, William Stanley ... '47 '74 C&L.608 B.S., J.D. Procter & Gamble Co.
Morton, Wm. Stanley '47 '74 C&L.608 B.S., J.D.
Assoc. Gen. Coun., The IAM's Co., The Procter & Gamble Co.
Morwood, Robert F. ... '— '04 C&L.608 B.A., J.D. [[A] Baker&H.]
Mosbaugh, Jason A. ... '— '03 C.473 B.A. L.276 J.D. [[A] Freund,F.&A.]
Moschandreas, John D. ... '75 '03 C.118 B.A. L.945 J.D. [[A] Lindhorst&D.]
Moser, Emerson C. ... '76 '02 C.679 B.A./B.S. L.896 J.D. [[A] Dinsmore&S.]
Moskowitz, James H., (BV) ... '69 '94 C.608 B.A. L.1340 J.D. [Moskowitz&M.]
Moskowitz, Joel S., (AV) ... '40 '65 C&L.150 B.A., J.D. [Moskowitz&M.]
Moskowitz, Michael A., (BV) ... '64 '89 C.477 B.A. L.608 J.D. [Moskowitz&M.]

Moskowitz & Moskowitz, (AV) [BR]
4300 Carew Tower, 441 Vine Street, 45202
Telephone: 513-721-3111 Fax: 513-721-3077
URL: http://www.lawyers.com/mm-law
Members of Firm: Joel S. Moskowitz; Michael A. Moskowitz; James H. Moskowitz.
Domestic Relations, Civil Litigation, Appeals and Probate Law, Automobile Accidents and Injuries, Divorce, Post Divorce Modifications, Child Custody, Child Support, Visitation Rights, Business Litigation, Breach of Contract.
Representative Clients: ACE Exterminating Co.; Three Rivers Nursing and Rehabilitation Center, Inc.; Greenlon, Inc. of Cincinnati; Lighting EFX.
See Professional Biographies, CINCINNATI, OHIO

Mottley, J. Donald ... '54 '91 C.1208 B.A. L.1340 J.D. [[A] Taft,S.&H.]
Moyer, David M., (AV) '49 '80 C.732 B.A. L.818 J.D.
Assoc. Gen. Coun., Procter & Gamble Co., The
Moyers, Michael K., (BV) ... '66 '91 C&L.813 A.B., J.D. [Graf&S.&M.]
Mrozek, Ronald A. '44 '69 C&L.339 A.B., J.D.
(adm. in IL; not adm. in OH) GE Transp., Aircraft & Engines
Mudd, Kristen J. '74 '01 C.1161 B.A. L.421 J.D.
(adm. in KY; not adm. in OH) [[A] Lerner,S.&R.]
Mueller, John J., (AV) ... '52 '79 C.150 B.B.A. L.1340 J.D. [J.J.Mueller]
Mueller, John M., (BV) ... '70 '97 C.679 B.S. L.347 J.D. [[A] Taft,S.&H.] (Pat.)
Mueller, John J., A Limited Liability Company, (AV) ... 630 Vine St., Ste. 800
Muething, Brian P. ... '78 '03 C.473 B.A. L.150 J.D. [[A] Keating M.&K.]
Muething, John L., (AV) ... '21 '48 C.973 B.A. L.150 J.D. [Keating M.&K.]
Muething, Mark F., (AV) '59 '84 C.602 B.B.A. L.150 J.D.
Ex. V.P. & Gen. Coun., American Annuity Grp., Inc.
Muething, Paul V., (AV) ... '52 '77 C.973 B.A. L.150 J.D. [Keating M.&K.]
Mullee, Michelle A., (BV) ... '60 '85 C.602 B.A. L.93 J.D. [[C] Cors&B.]
Mullenix, Charles D., (BV) ... '39 '73 C&L.608 B.S., J.D. 1080 Nimitzview Dr Ste 30
Muller, Bradley K., (AV) ... '51 '78 C.608 B.S. L.1340 J.D. [Lyons&F.]
Mullin, Sybil B. ... '65 '95 C.207 B.A. L.1161 J.D. [Drew&W.]
Mullins, J. Scott, (BV) ... '60 '87 C&L.150 B.A., J.D. 36 East Seventh Street, Suite 2600
Mulvaney, Christopher J. ... '63 '97 C.608 B.A. L.1161 J.D. [[A] Benjamin,Y.&H.]
Mulvey, John J. ... '65 '94 C.973 B.S.B.A. L.1340 J.D. 2306 Park Ave., Ste. 104
Mulvey, William J., (BV) ... '48 '75 C.609 B.A. L.150 J.D. 35 E. 7th St.
Muncy, Jason Patrick ... '74 '00 C.138 B.A. L.383 J.D. Sr. Coun., Procter & Gamble Co.
Murdock, Jack A. ... '32 '57 615 Main St.
Murdock, John C., (AV) ... '64 '94 C.473 B.S. L.602 J.D. [Murdock G.S.&G.]
Murdock, Norman A., (AV) ... '31 '68 C.973 B.S. L.150 J.D. Suite 400 700 Walnut Street

Murdock Goldenberg Schneider & Groh, L.P.A., (AV)
35 East Seventh Street, Suite 600, 45202-2446
Telephone: 513-345-8291 Facsimile: 513-345-8294
Email: info@mgsglaw.com URL: http://www.mgsglaw.com
John C. Murdock; Jeffrey S. Goldenberg; Theodore J. Schneider; Theresa L. Groh; Todd B. Naylor.
Of Counsel: Norman A. Murdock.
Complex Civil Litigation, Class Actions, Consumer Law, Products Liability, Personal Injury, Wrongful Death, Commercial Litigation, Environmental Law, Toxic Torts, Corporate Law.
See Professional Biographies, CINCINNATI, OHIO

Murnane, Linda Strite ... '52 '81 C.945 B.A. L.150 J.D. 3877 Limerick Ave.★
Murphy, Eugene F. '36 '60 C.994 B.A. L.262 LL.D.
(adm. in NY; not adm. in OH) Pres. & CEO, G.E. Aerospace, General Electric Co.
Murphy, Ross A. ... '26 '90 C.1044 B.S.,P.S. L.1340 J.D. 7168 Beechmont Ave.
Murphy Kennedy, Sherri, (AV) ... '53 '79 C.610 B.A. L.161 J.D. [Kennedy&K.]
Murray, Michael C. ... '59 '89 C.973 B.A. L.1340 J.D. 705 Central Avenue
Musillo, Christopher T. ... '70 '98 C.884 B.S.B.A. L.150 J.D. [Hammond]
Muth, C. Christopher, (AV) ... '55 '80 C.150 B.B.A. L.146 J.D. [Greenebaum D.&M.]
Muto, Anthony J., (AV) '49 '78
C&L.201 B.S., J.D. V.P., Global Fastening Solutions, LLC
Muzzo, A. Lawrence ... '43 '70 C.105 B.S. L.150 J.D. Pres., F. L. Emmert Co.
Muzzo, Christopher L. ... '72 '97 C&L.597 B.A., J.D. [[A] Dinsmore&S.]

Myers, Beth A., (AV) ... '57 '82 C.473 A.B. L.150 J.D. Co. J.
Myers, David J. ... '78 '04 C.150 B.B.A. L.602 J.D. [[A] Dinsmore&S.]
Myers, James Y. '50 '95 C.973 B.S.B.A. L.1161 J.D.
Coun., Secy. & Corp., Loroco Industries, Inc.
Myers, Kelly Mulloy ... '68 '95 C.347 B.A. L.150 J.D. [[A] Freking&B.]
Myers, Kristen M. ... '— '04 C.318 B.A. L.150 B.A. [[A] Beckman W.S.]
Myers, Marcia J. ... '59 '85 C.97 B.A. L.608 J.D. [Schottenstein,Z.&D.]
Myers, Thomas R. ... '63 '88 C&L.150 B.A., J.D. [[A] Weltman,W.&R.]
Nacev, Ljubomir '52 '76 C.367 B.A. L.365 J.D.
(adm. in IL; not adm. in OH) [[C] Frost B.T.]
Nadel, Norbert A. ... '41 '65 C.150 A.B. L.1340 J.D. Com. Pleas J.
Naegel, Mark R., (BV) ... '49 '74 C&L.150 B.S., J.D. [[C] Crowley,F.&A.]
Nagel, Ellen L. ... '48 '87 C.652 B.S. L.150 J.D. Atty. Advsr., Soc. Sec. Admin.
Nageleisen, Christy M. ... '78 '03 C.1118 B.A. L.150 J.D. [[A] Keating M.&K.]
Nakao, Toshio ... '52 '84 C.999 B.A. L.228 J.D. [Taft,S.&H.]
Nalbandian, John B. ... '69 '97 C.659 B.S. L.893 J.D. [Taft,S.&H.]
Namanworth, Eli, Law Offices of, (BV) '38 '76
C.563 B.S. L.1340 J.D. 36 East Seventh Street
Namei, Firooz T., (BV) ... '41 '82 C&L.150 B.S., J.D. [McKinney&N.] ⊙
Napier, Mark W., (BV) ... '53 '78 C.608 B.S.B.A. L.607 J.D. [[A] Freking&B.]
Napolitano, Gregory A. ... '72 '97 C.974 B.A. L.229 J.D. [Lutz,C.&M.]
Narciso, David Lee '57 '90 C&L.101 B.S., J.D.
(adm. in CA; not adm. in OH) Pat. Coun., GE Aviation Services, Inc.
Nash, Sylvester M., Jr. ... '17 '49 C.383 L.1340 LL.B. Dept. of Health & Human Servs.
Natkevicius, John Robert ... '69 '02 C.363 B.A. L.851 J.D. [[A] McKinney&N.]
Navarra, Antoinette J. ... '19 '55 C.151 L.1340 LL.B. 1071 Celestial St.‡
Naylor, Beth Schneider, (AV) ... '61 '86 C.473 B.A. L.602 J.D. [Frost B.T.]
Naylor, Todd B. ... '72 '97 C.98 B.A. L.174 J.D. [Murdock G.S.&G.]
Neal, Sherry L. ... '69 '94 C.130 B.A. L.201 J.D. [Hammond]
Nechemias, Stephen M., (AV) ... '44 '69 C.608 B.S. L.150 J.D. [Taft,S.&H.]
Neiheisel, Jeffrey K. '70 '96 C.383 B.A. L.1161 J.D.
Corp. Coun., Alderwoods Group. Inc.
Neiheisel, Michael E., (BV) '44 '69 C.973 H.A.B. L.477 J.D.
[[A] Buechner,H.O.M.H.&K.]
Nelson, David A. ... '32 '58 C.299 A.B. L.309 LL.B. Sr. U.S. Cir. J.
Nelson, Frederick D. ... '58 '84 C.299 A.B. L.309 J.D. Hamilton Co. Ct. of Common Pleas
Nelson, Richard D., (AV) ... '49 '74 C.473 A.B. L.150 J.D. [Cohen,T.K.&S.]
Nelson, Ryan L. ... '71 '97 C.967 B.A. L.150 J.D. Asst. Co. Pros.
Nelson, Sara S. '68 '94 C.1365 B.A. L.893 J.D.
(adm. in NY; not adm. in OH) Asst. Prof., University of Cincinnati College of Law
Nelson, Steven Arthur, (BV) ... '52 '77 C.473 B.A. L.228 J.D. 209 Hosea Ave., Ste. 3
Nelson, William E., (AV) '44 '70 C.480 B.A. L.190 J.D.
(adm. in NE; not adm. in OH) Sr. Coun., Millennium Petrochemicals Inc.
Neubeck, Stephen J. '48 '76 C.321 A.B. L.818 J.D.
(adm. in MA; not adm. in OH) I.R.S.
Neuman, Larry A., (AV) ... '42 '67 C.861 B.A. L.383 J.D. [Strauss&T.]
Neusch, Raymond D., (AV) ... '47 '78 C.229 B.A. L.1340 J.D. [Frost B.T.]
Newbauer, Frank Lewis ... '54 '88 C.96 B.S. L.150 J.D. 221 E. Fourth Street, Ste. 300
Newberry, J. Stuart, (BV) ... '49 '82 C.705 B.A. L.831 J.D. [J.S.Newberry&Assoc.]
Newberry, Peter C., (BV) ... '56 '88 C.966 B.S. L.150 J.D. [[C] Heis&W.]
Newberry, J. Stuart, A Legal Professional Association, (BV) ... 1538 Cedar Ave.
Newbold Mcclain, Elizabeth ... '59 '84 C&L.150 B.B.A., J.D. Great Amer. Ins.
Newman, Donald A. '24 '49 L.150 LL.B.
Chmn. & Corp. Coun., Newman Brothers, Inc.
Newman, James O. ... '41 '66 C.276 A.B. L.150 J.D. Pres., Newman Leather Corp.‡
Newman, Mark L. ... '64 '89 C.347 B.S. L.150 J.D. 9545 Kenwood Rd.
Newman, Michael J. ... '60 '89 C.569 B.F.A. L.30 J.D. [[A] Dinsmore&S.]
Newman, Peter K., (BV) ... '— '80 C.473 B.A. L.276 J.D. [Roetzel&A.]
Newman, Robert B., (AV) ... '41 '67 C.575 B.A. L.245 J.D. [Newman&M.]
Newman & Meeks Co., L.P.A., (AV) ... 617 Vine St.
Newton, Robert Adam '— '01 C.347 B.A. L.880 J.D.
Sr. Coun., Procter & Gamble Co.
Ney, Arthur M., Jr. ... '26 '54 C.973 Ph.B. L.1340 LL.D. Com. Pleas J.
Ney, Peter L., (AV) ... '61 '87 C.602 B.S. L.150 J.D. [Rendigs,F.K.&D.]
Nicewander, Karen A. ... '73 '98 C.473 B.A. L.201 J.D. [[A] Wood&L.]
Nidich, Paul A., Attorney at Law, (BV) '48 '74
C&L.150 B.A., J.D. 4555 Lake Forest Dr., Ste. 365
Nieberding, J. R., (BV) ... '33 '63 C.150 B.A. L.1340 J.D. 914 Main St.
Nieberding, James L., (BV) ... '58 '87 C.473 A.B. L.150 J.D. 914 Main Street, Suite 500
Nieberding, Michael J. ... '68 '94 C.201 B.S.E.E. L.150 J.D. [Thompson H.] (Pat.)
Niehaus, Barron M., (BV) ... '49 '76 C.1115 B.S. L.1340 J.D. Asst. Atty. Gen.
Niehaus, Francis Joseph ... '50 '78 [F.J.Niehaus]
Niehaus, Maurice A. ... '15 '41 C.150 L.1340 J.D. 830 Main St.‡
Niehaus, Richard A. ... '44 '70 C.276 A.B. L.1340 J.D. Com. Pleas J.
Niehaus, Robt. L. ... '22 '49 C.973 Ph.B. L.150 LL.B. 7727 Compton Lake Dr.
Niehaus, Roccina S., (AV) ... '56 '81 C.973 B.A. L.150 J.D. [[A] Wood&L.]
Niehaus, Francis J., LLC ... 4820 Glenway Ave.
Niehoff, H. C. Buck, (AV) ... '47 '73 C.207 B.A. L.150 J.D. [[C] Peck,S.&W.]
Niekamp, Thomas J. ... '54 '87 C.1208 B.S. L.607 J.D. Dept. of the Treasury

Nielson & Sherry, PSC
(See Newport, Kentucky)

Nieman, Jos. B., (BV) ... '14 '39 C.973 B.A. L.150 LL.B. 5692 Eaglesridge Lane
Nieman, Joseph D., (BV) ... '29 '57 C.973 B.S. L.150 LL.B. [[A] Eckert,E.&E.]
Niemeyer, Clifford G., (BV) ... '21 '50 C&L.150 J.D. 5574 Jessup Rd.‡
Niemeyer, Jonathan D. '68 '93 C&L.383 B.A., J.D.
V.P. & Assoc. Gen. Coun., Western & Southern Financial Group
Niklas, Frank D. '53 '78 C.665 B.S. L.1137 J.D.
(adm. in CA; not adm. in OH) PMC Inc.
Nishizu, Mikio ... '44 '94 C.999 B.A. L.345 J.D. [Greenebaum D.&M.]
Noel, W. Keith, (BV) ... '62 '88 C.383 B.A. L.150 J.D. [Keating M.&K.]
Noggler, Clifford J. ... '33 '66 C.151 B.S.C. L.1340 J.D. 2103 Bluebell Dr.
Nolan, Gregory M., (BV) ... '50 '78 C.150 B.A. L.151 J.D. 3505 Glenmore Ave.
Nolan, James P., II, (BV) ... '53 '91 C.150 B.S. L.201 J.D. [[A] Smith,R.&S.]
Nolan, John J., (BV) ... '31 '56 C.1118 A.B. L.150 LL.B. 7707 Camargo Rd.
Nolan, Joshua J. ... '74 '04 C.851 B.A. L.150 J.D. [[A] Lindhorst&D.]
Nolan, Timothy P. ... '58 '84 C.894 B.A. L.150 J.D. 7754 Camargo Rd., Ste. 12
Nolen, Kay Cody, (AV) '52 '82 C.475 B.A. L.1340 J.D.
Dir., Legal Servs., Community Mutual Insurance Company
Nordstrom, Jennifer K. ... '71 '96 C.607 B.A. L.150 J.D. [Freund,F.&A.]
Nordstrom, Orrin B. ... '41 '69 C&L.608 B.S., J.D. 11610 Thistlehill‡
Norman, Mark A., (AV) ... '56 '83 C.273 B.A. L.276 J.D. [Vorys,S.S.&P.]
Norris, Alan E. ... '35 '60 C.631 B.A. L.569 LL.B. Sr. U.S. Cir. J.
Norris, Daniel W., (BV) ... '56 '87 C&L.150 B.A.F.A., J.D. [D.W.Norris]
Norris, Monica H. ... '74 '99 C.473 B.S. L.150 J.D. [[A] Frost B.T.]

Norris, D.W., Co., LPA, (BV) .... 2245 Gilbert Ave.
Norton, Esther Maria .... '75 '00 C.602 B.A. L.201 J.D. [Ⓐ Robbins,K.P.&T.]
Norton, Richard L., (AV) .... '39 '64 C&L.608 B.A., J.D. [Katz,G.&N.]
Norwine, John C. .... '48 '76 C.97 B.A. L.1340 J.D. Exec. Dir., Cincinnati Bar Association
Noser, Patrick E. .... '76 '02 C&L.150 B.A., J.D. [Ⓐ Taft,S.&H.]

Novakov, Linda S. & Associates, PLLC
(See Erlanger)

Novik, Jos., (BV) .... '17 '49 C&L.150 LL.B. 1263 Avon Dr.
Nuckols, Lori Gayle .... '60 '91 C.914 B.A. L.309 J.D. 1237 Paddock Hills Avenue
Nuckols, Gerald L., (BV) .... '52 '79 C.150 B.A. L.151 J.D. 324 Reading Rd.
Nuñez, Ramon E. .... '50 '85 C.280 B.S.Ed. L.464 J.D. Coun., Garrett Aviation Services
Nunley, Kerri L. .... '73 '01 C.384 B.S. L.1340 J.D. [Ⓐ Lerner,S.&R.]
Nunn, Sandra L. .... '55 '95 C&L.150 B.S., J.D. [Frost B.T.]
Nurre, Richard L., (BV) .... '23 '50 C.973 B.S.B.A. L.150 J.D. [Ⓑ Robbins,K.P.&T.]
Nurre, Thomas Charles .... '30 '57 C.973 B.S. L.150 LL.B. Com. Pleas J.
Nyktas, Anthony W., (AV) .... '45 '71 C.980 A.B. L.150 J.D. Tha U.S. Atty.
Oberhaus, Geoffrey L. '69 '98
C.215 B.Che.E. L.1292 J.D. [Ⓐ Dinsmore&S.] (See Pat. Sect.)
Oberklein, Daniel F. .... '75 '00 C.973 B.S. L.145 J.D. [Ⓐ Taft,S.&H.]
Oberschmidt, E. Richard, (AV) .... '53 '78 C.473 B.A. L.893 J.D. [Frost B.T.]
O'Brien, Thomas P., Jr., (BV) '37 '60
C&L.902 B.A., LL.B. Sr. Atty., Kroger Company, The
O'Brien, William F., (AV) '50 '80
C.602 B.S. L.1340 J.D. Gen. Coun., Winegardner & Hammons, Inc.
Ochstein, Daniel S. .... '52 '77 C.347 B.S. L.910 J.D. 12111 Champion Way
O'Connell, Brian J., (BV) .... '62 '92 C&L.201 B.A., J.D. [Dinsmore&S.]
O'Connell, Edward M., Jr., (AV) '47 '73
C.1115 B.S. L.150 J.D. [Buechner,H.O.M.H.&K.]
O'Connell, Gerald F., Jr., (AV) .... '59 '84 C.608 B.S. L.150 J.D. [Graydon H.&R.]
O'Connell, James L., (AV) .... '31 '58 C.973 A.B. L.150 J.D. [Lindhorst&D.]
O'Connor, John P. .... '39 '67 C.973 B.S. L.151 J.D. Com. Pleas. J.‡
O'Connor, Lynn C. .... '65 '91 C.602 B.A. L.665 J.D. Asst. Co. Pros.
O'Connor, Michael J., (BV) .... '59 '89 C.1139 B.S. L.117 J.D. [O'Connor,M.&D.]
O'Connor, Michael P., (BV) .... '55 '79 C.861 B.A. L.150 J.D. [O'Connor,A.&L.]
O'Connor, Acciani & Levy, LLC, (BV) .... 1014 Vine Street, Suite 2200
O'Connor, Mikita & Davidson LLC, (AV) .... 8035 Hosbrook Rd., Ste. 200
Odmark, Gwendolyn M. .... '73 '00 C.602 B.A. L.245 J.D. [Ⓐ Dinsmore&S.]
O'Donnell, Hugh C. '51 '77 C.611 B.A. L.150 J.D.
Sr. V.P. Gen. Coun., Sec., Cincinnati Milacron Inc.
O'Dowd, Jerome L., (BV) .... '43 '70 C.973 B.S. L.1340 J.D. 216 E. 9th St., 2nd Fl.
Oechsler, Michael C. '46 '78
C.973 B.S. L.1340 J.D. Sr. Legal Editor, Anderson Publishing Co.
Oestreicher, Michael R., (AV) .... '50 '76 C.473 A.B. L.94 J.D. [Thompson H.]
O'Flaherty, Thomas H. .... '34 '60 C&L.976 B.S., LL.B. 2502 Grandin Rd.‡
Ogg, Nancy Neubauer '48 '81
C.523 A.B. L.1340 J.D. Asst. Dir., Risk Mgmt. Dept., Jewish Hosp.
O'Grady, Erin Eileen ... '67 '93 C.477 B.S. L.150 J.D. Assoc. Dir., Proctor & Gamble Co.
O'Grady, Michael J., (BV) .... '70 '95 C.477 B.A. L.150 J.D. [Frost B.T.]
O'Guinn, Jennifer A. .... '— '03 C.373 B.A. L.602 J.D. [Ⓐ Frost B.T.]
O'Guinn, M. Dave, III .... '69 '01 C.210 B.S. L.602 J.D. [Ⓐ Dinsmore&S.]
Okerson, Eric C., (AV) .... '49 '80 C.94 B.A. L.861 J.D. [Graydon H.&R.]
O'Leary, Joseph P. '45 '76 C.563 B.A. L.262 J.D.
(adm. in NY; not adm. in OH) Asst. V.P., Advanced Sales, The Ohio Natl. Life Ins. Co.
Olinger, Philip S., (AV) .... '29 '55 C&L.150 B.B.A., LL.B. Chief Coun.
Olivas, Adolf, (CV) .... '56 '81 C&L.150 B.A., J.D. Mayor
Olson, Carol Duane, (AV) .... '46 '72 C.93 B.A. L.893 LL.B. [Peck,S.&W.]
Olson, David C., (AV) .... '49 '78 C.951 B.A. L.608 J.D. [Frost B.T.]
Olson, Robert W., (AV) '45 '71 C.951 B.A. L.893 J.D.
Sr. V.P., Gen. Coun. & Secy., Chiquita Brands Intl., Inc.
O'Neill, Patrick M. .... '61 '93 C.610 B.A. L.201 J.D. [Aronoff,R.&H.]
Oney, Jack Lee, JR. .... '71 '01 C.150 B.E. L.1340 J.D. Procter & Gamble Co., The
Orlet, Dimity V. '72 '97 C.475 B.A. L.150 J.D.
Asst. Coun. & Dir. CLE, Cincinnati Bar Association
Orner, Dan R., (BV) .... '52 '78 C&L.607 B.A., J.D. One Crowne Point
Ose, Paul A., (AV) .... '51 '77 C.347 A.B. L.477 J.D. [Dinsmore&S.]
O'Shea, Jill T., (BV) '60 '86
C.473 A.B. L.150 J.D. Assoc. Gen. Coun., Cinergy Serv., Inc.
O'Shea, John L., (BV) .... '60 '89 C.851 B.S. L.150 J.D. [Cohen,T.K.&S.]
Osmond, Charles D. .... '51 '84 C.207 B.A. L.1003 J.D. Union Central Life Ins. Co.
Oster, Wednesday .... '79 '04 C.853 B.A. L.150 J.D. [Ⓐ Wood&L.]
Osterlund, Anthony L. .... '67 '99 C.350 B.A. L.150 J.D. [Ⓐ Vorys,S.S.&P.]
Ostrander, Leslie L. .... '64 '89 C.477 B.A. L.150 J.D. 340 C Gest St.
O'Sullivan, Daniel F. '66 '93 C.999 B.A. L.201 J.D.
Coun., Antitrust & Competition Policy, GE Aviation Services, Inc.
Oti, George N. '61 '92 C.475 B.A. L.178 J.D.
(adm. in NY; not adm. in OH) [Ⓑ Squire,S.&D.] (⊙New York, NY)
Outcalt, Peter Louis, (BV) .... '54 '78 C.679 B.S. L.150 J.D. Mag., Co. Mun. Ct.
Overbey, Terry L., (AV) '49 '75 C.597 B.S. L.608 J.D.
V.P. & Associate General Counsel, The Procter & Gamble Co.
Overholt, Mary Ann, (AV) .... '35 '64 C.610 A.B. L.1340 J.D. 1876 Waycross Rd.‡

Owens, Amy L. '70 '94 C.999 B.A. L.150 J.D.
The Kroger Building, 1014 Vine Street, Suite 1525, 45202
Telephone: 513-381-5094 Fax: 513-396-6477
Commercial Law, Corporate Law.

See Professional Biographies, CINCINNATI, OHIO

Owens, Robert E., Jr., (BV) ...... '47 '74 C.973 B.A. L.1340 J.D. 230 E. 9th St., Ste. 2000
Owens, Ross Collins, III '47 '77
C.309 B.A. L.94 J.D. Sr. Atty., Legal Aid Society of Cinn.
Pace, Beverly H., (BV) '47 '86 C&L.150 B.A., J.D.
[Ⓐ Lopez,H.R.M.&S.] (⊙Newport Beach, CA)
Pacheco, Bryan E. .... '69 '97 C.8 B.A. L.150 J.D. [Ⓐ Dinsmore&S.]
Padro, Diego J., III .... '64 '99 C.4 B.A. L.150 J.D. Hamilton Co. Pub. Defender's Off.
Pahutski, Michael J. .... '60 '99 C.1271 M.B.A. L.1340 J.D. Coun., Cinergy Servs.
Painter, Jack W. .... '53 '78 C.347 B.S. L.893 J.D. 5820 Graves Lake Dr.
Painter, John Woodward .... '53 '78 C.347 B.S L.893 J.D. 5820 Graves Lake Drive
Painter, Mark P. ... '47 '73 C&L.150 B.A., J.D. Appl. Ct. J., The OH 1st Dist. Co. of App.
Palermo, Maria C. .... '65 '91 C&L.150 B.B.A., J.D. Cincinnati Bar Association
Paliobeis, Bill J. .... '69 '96 C.851 B.A. L.930 J.D. [Ⓐ Frost B.T.]
Palm, Irwin D., Jr. .... '46 '73 C.973 B.S. L.93 J.D. 139 E. 4th St.
Palmer, George H., (AV) .... '23 '49 C.473 A.B. L.150 LL.B. 201 E. 5th St.‡
Palmieri, Francis W. '26 '52 C.205 L.1009 LL.B.
(adm. in NY; not adm. in OH) 3590 Round Bottom Rd.‡
Palumbo, John P. .... '45 '70 C&L.608 B.S., J.D. Alderwoods Group, Inc.
Panioto, Ronald A. .... '35 '67 Hamilton Co. Dom. Rel. Ct.
Panos, Christine .... '25 '53 C.150 B.A. L.1340 J.D. 632 Vine St.
Pantel, Nicholas J., (BV) .... '43 '72 C.150 B.A. L.1340 J.D. Asst. U.S. Atty.
Paolo, Richard A., (AV) .... '56 '82 C&L.150 B.A., J.D. [Aronoff,R.&H.]
Paolucci, Michael A., (BV) .... '65 '91 C.1161 B.A. L.151 J.D. 120 E. Fourth
Papakirk, Maria J. .... '72 '97 C.347 B.A. L.201 J.D. Camp Washington Chili, Inc.
Papner, Donald F. .... '30 '60 C.610 B.S. L.1340 LL.B. 7854 Kimbee Dr.
Pappas, Harry J. .... '13 '53 C.790 B.S.C. L.1340 LL.B. 30 E. Central Pkwy.
Paradise, James C. .... '05 '28 C&L.569 B.S., J.D. 195 Wedgewood Ave.‡
Park, R. Gregory .... '50 '77 C.282 B.A. L.1202 J.D. 917 Main St.
Parker, Kenneth L. .... '— '97 C.864 B.S. L.1119 J.D. 1914 Freeman Ave.
Parker, R. Joseph, (AV) .... '44 '69 C.276 A.B. L.93 J.D. [Taft,S.&H.]
Parmele, Paul W. '62 '87 C.1369 B.S. L.893 J.D.
(adm. in GA; not adm. in OH) Kroger Company, The
Parrish, Dawne McKenna .... '69 '96 C.381 B.B.A. L.150 J.D. [Ⓐ Dinsmore&S.]
Parrish, Matthew S. .... '69 '94 C.381 B.A. L.150 J.D. 2535 Spring Grove Avenue
Parsley, Sharon S. .... '61 '04 C.973 B.S.B.A. L.1340 J.D. [Ⓐ Graydon H.&R.] ⊙
Patel, Ken K. '64 '90 C.679 B.S.Ch.Engr. L.150 J.D.
Assoc. Gen. Coun.-Intell. Prop., The Procter & Gamble Co.
Patel, Polly Rickard .... '76 '02 C.473 B.A. L.117 J.D. [Ⓐ Dinsmore&S.]
Patsfall, Stephen J., (BV) .... '55 '81 C.207 B.S. L.150 J.D. One W. Fourth St., Suite 1800
Patterson, Christine J. .... '48 '86 C.150 B.A. L.151 J.D. 2508 Kellerman Avenue
Patterson, Edwin W., III, (AV) '49 '78
C.473 B.A. L.851 J.D. Gen. Coun., Cincinnati Bar Association
Patterson, Geo. F., Jr. .... '22 '48 C&L.150 A.B., LL.B. 7707 Camargo Rd.‡
Patterson, Lisa L. .... '68 '96 C.025 B.A. L.117 J.D. [Ⓐ Taft,S.&H.] (⊙Dayton)
Patterson, Mark C., (AV) .... '49 '79 C.973 B.A. L.1340 J.D. [Robbins,K.P.&T.]
Patterson, Steven H. .... '70 '01 C&L.150 B.A., J.D. [Ⓐ Lerner,S.&R.]
Patton, James W., (AV) .... '47 '72 C.610 B.B.A. L.150 J.D. 2345 Kemper Lane
Patton, Jay D. .... '70 '97 C.63 B.S. L.150 J.D. [Ⓐ Schroeder,M.B.&P.]
Patton, M. Leigh-Anne '71 '98 C.973 B.A. L.150 J.D.
Assoc. Coun., The Fifth Third Bank
Patton, Sarah Mortensen '62 '87
C.970 B.A. L.945 J.D. Great American Financial Resources, Inc.
Patton, W. Andrew, (AV) .... '42 '68 C.473 A.B. L.150 J.D. [Kohnen&P.]
Paul, Andrew A. .... '70 '99 C.338 B.S. L.201 J.D. 11511 Reed Hartman Hwy.
Paxton, Beth Ann '73 '99 C&L.608 B.A., J.D.
Dept. of Labor, Off. of Admin. Law Judges
Payne, April Marie .... '71 '98 C.150 B.A. L.8 J.D. [Ⓐ B.J.Howard]
Pearson, Jennifer S. .... '77 '03 C&L.150 B.B.A., J.D. [Ⓐ Graydon H.&R.]
Pease, Elizabeth D. .... '59 '84 C.385 B.A. L.150 J.D. 1100 Rockwood Dr.‡
Peck, David Hamilton .... '59 '92 C.476 B.S. L.477 J.D. [Taft,S.&H.]
Peck, David W., (AV) .... '44 '70 C.475 B.A. L.1340 J.D. [Barron,P.B.&S.]
Peck, David Winchester, (AV) .... '39 '66 C.473 B.S. L.1340 J.D. [Rendigs,F.K.&D.]
Peck, Jeffrey F., (AV) .... '57 '82 C.473 B.A. L.150 J.D. [Ulmer&B.]
Peck, John Weld, (AV) .... '44 '69 C.473 B.S. L.150 J.D. [Peck,S.&W.]

Peck, Shaffer & Williams LLP, (AV)
201 E. 5th Street, Suite 900, 45202 ⊙
Telephone: 513-621-3394; 800-927-2663 Telecopier: 513-621-3813
Email: lawinfo@peck-shaffer.com URL: http://www.peck-shaffer.com
Members of Firm: Hiram D. Peck (1844-1914); Frank Holmes Shaffer (1857-1936); Floyd C. Williams (1884-1963); Bruce D. Agin (Not admitted in OH; Resident Member, Chicago, Illinois Office); Dirk M. Bedarff (Resident Member, Covington and Louisville, Kentucky Offices); Robert T. Bruns; George D. Buzard III (Resident Member, Chicago, Illinois Office); Richard A. Cardwell (Resident Member, Columbus, Ohio Office); Edward Cavezza (Resident Member, Columbus, Ohio Office); Todd L. Cooper; Mary S. Duffey (Resident Member, Columbus, Ohio Office); John W. Fischer III; Stephen P. Grassbaugh (Resident Member, Columbus, Ohio Office); Mary L. Groves (Resident Member, Denver, Colorado Office); Susan Pease Langford (Not admitted in OH; Resident Member, Atlanta, Georgia Office); Doloris F. Learmonth; Thomas A. Luebbers; Michael J. Melliere (Resident Member, Columbus, Ohio Office); John C. Merchant (Resident Member, Louisville, Kentucky Office); Carol Duane Olson; Sujyot S. Patel (Resident Member, Louisville, Kentucky Office); John Weld Peck; Roger L. Peterman (Resident Member, Covington and Louisville, Kentucky Offices); Jerry G. Peterson (Not admitted in OH; Resident Member, Atlanta, Georgia Office); Glendon B. Pratt (Resident Member, Columbus, Ohio Office); Bradley N. Ruwe; Dennis G. Schwallie (Resident Member, Columbus, Ohio Office); Abbot A. Thayer; Brenda K. Wehmer; Thomas A. Wilson (Resident Member, Columbus, Ohio Office). Of Counsel: H. C. Buck Niehoff; Mary W. Sullivan. Associates: Jennifer R. Blaser (Resident Associate, Columbus, Ohio Office); Jason L. George (Resident Associate, Columbus, Ohio Office); Melissa N. Hawkins; Alysse E. Hollis (Not admitted in OH); Marc Kamer (Resident Associate, Columbus, Ohio Office); Ian F. Koffler (Not admitted in OH); Nicolle Stallworth (Not admitted in OH; Resident Associate, Columbus, Ohio Office); Lona J. Valentine; Charles H. Waterman, IV (Resident Associate, Columbus, Ohio Office); David H. Williams, Jr. (Resident Associate, Atlanta, Georgia Office); Patrick Woodside.
Public Finance, Municipal Bonds, Municipal Bond Taxation, Municipal Securities. Tax Exempt Bonds, Housing and Urban Development, Health Care Finance, Tax Increment Finance, Municipal Leasing, Public Finance Taxation, Securities Finance, Blue Sky Law, Low Income Housing, Industrial Development Bonds, Municipal Bankruptcy, Public Construction Law.
Atlanta, Georgia Office: Peck, Shaffer & Williams LLP, Atlanta Financial Center, Suite M20, 3353 Peachtree Road, N.E. Telephone: 404-995-3850. Fax: 404-995-3851.
Chicago, Illinois Office: Peck, Shaffer & Williams LLP, 11 South LaSalle Street, Suite 2100. Telephones: 312-372-6060; 877-372-6060. Fax: 312-372-6085.
Columbus, Ohio Office: Peck, Shaffer & Williams LLP, 175 South Third Street, Suite 600, 43215. Telephone: 614-224-5205; 888-900-5205. Telecopier: 614-224-0069.
Covington, Kentucky Office: Peck, Shaffer & Williams LLP, 118 West 5th Street, 41011. Telephones: 859-431-7000; 888-431-7511. Telecopier: 859-431-0673.
Denver, Colorado Office: Peck, Shaffer & Williams LLP, 555 17th Street, Suite 845 South, 80202. Telephone: 303-296-3996; 877-296-0333. Fax: 303-296-0344.
Louisville, Kentucky Office: Peck, Shaffer & Williams LLP, 239 S. Fifth Street, Suite 1603, 40202. Telephone: 502-561-0054. Telecopier: 502-561-0058.

See Professional Biographies, CINCINNATI, OHIO

Pecquet, Janet Eileen, (BV) .... '55 '81 C.1042 B.A. L.809 J.D. [Beckman W.S.]
Peller, Kenneth E., Attorney at Law, (AV) '49 '76
C.607 B.A. L.1340 J.D. 700 Walnut St., Ste. 313
Pendergast, Judith M. '48 '92 C.1216 B.S.N. L.436 J.D.
(adm. in WI; not adm. in OH) [Ⓐ Hammond]
Pennak, Arthur F. .... '13 '48 C&L.150 C.E., LL.B. 3145 Rickbury St.‡
Pennekamp, Lisa A., (AV) '59 '84 C.473 B.A. L.150 J.D.
Asst. V.P. & Asst. Gen. Coun., Great Amer. Ins. Co.
Pennick, Edward C. .... '13 '56 C.214 L.1003 LL.B. I.R.S.
Pepper, David A. .... '71 '99 C&L.976 B.A., J.D. [Ⓐ Squire,S.&D.]
Pera, Marc G. .... '71 '96 C.297 B.A. L.608 J.D. 4355 Ferguson Dr., Ste. 200
Peraino, Vito C. .... '56 '81 C.912 B.A. L.477 J.D. 580 Walnut St., 11E
Perez, Robert Armand, Sr., (BV) ...... '51 '83 C.150 B.A. L.345 J.D. [Perez,L.&Assoc.]

Perez Law Firm Co., The, A Legal Professional Association, (BV)
7672 Montgomery Road, Suite 378, 45236-4204
Telephone: 513-891-8777 Fax: 513-891-0317
Email: rperez@perezfirm.com URL: http://www.perezfirm.com
Robert Armand Perez Sr.
Civil Litigation, Class Actions, Employee Benefit Litigation of Pension, Health and Disability, and Insurance Bad Faith.

See Professional Biographies, CINCINNATI, OHIO

Perin, Martha H. .... '21 '49 C&L.150 B.B.A., LL.B. 6823 Kenwood Rd.‡

Perr, Karolina F. ... '64 '89 C.347 B.A. L.201 J.D. [A Weltman,W.&R.]
Perrino, Dominic F., (BV) ... '33 '62 C.973 B.S. L.1340 J.D. 806 Main St.
Perrino, Nicholas A., (AV) ... '40 '69 C.973 B.S. L.1340 J.D. 830 Main St.
Perry, Brian P. ... '68 '93 C&L.150 B.A., J.D. [Dinsmore&S.]
Perry, David A. ... '60 '87 C.608 B.A. L.930 J.D. State Dept. of Taxation
Perry, James N., (AV) ... '35 '62 C.973 B.S. L.150 LL.B. 601 Main St., 3rd Fl.
Pershern, Judy L. '59 '84 C.97 B.S.B.A. L.150 J.D.
Dir. & Coun., Anthem Ins. Cos., Inc.
Persiani, John B. '— '89 C.1115 B.A. L.228 J.D.
(adm. in PA; not adm. in OH) [A Dinsmore&S.]
Peschke, Joel L. ... '72 '00 C.836 B.A. L.150 J.D. [A Triona C.&L.]
Petas, Pamela S. ... '61 '92 C.608 B.A. L.851 J.D. [A Lerner,S.&R.]
Peters, James M., (BV) ... '50 '76 C.363 B.S.B.A. L.1003 J.D. [Kreiner&P.] (⊙Columbus)
Peters, Robt. L. ... '15 '39 C&L.150 B.A., LL.B. 1652 Brunnerwood Dr.
Petersmann, Sara M. ... '66 '91 C.973 B.S. L.150 J.D. [Lerner,S.&R.]
Petrie, Bruce I., Jr., (AV) ... '54 '80 C.103 B.A. L.597 J.D. [Graydon H.&R.]
Pettit, Kenton K. ... '63 '95 C.966 B.B.A. L.228 J.D. 138 E. Court Street
Pfister, Betty D. ... '22 '48 C.597 B.S. L.976 LL.B. 7705 Indian Hill Rd.
Pflum, Joseph F., (AV) ... '64 '89 C.1161 B.S. L.1340 J.D. 1 W. 4th Street
Phalen, Thomas F., Jr. '38 '67 C.321 B.S. L.128 J.D.
U.S. Admin. Law J., Dept. of Labor
Phelps, Arthur E., Jr., (AV) ... '60 '85 C.207 B.A. L.930 J.D. [Rendigs,F.K.&D.]
Phillip, Harvey G. '66 '92 C&L.347 B.A., J.D.
(adm. in IN; not adm. in OH) 451 Ludlow Ave.‡
Phillips, John H. ... '58 '89 C.150 B.S.N.E. L.1035 J.D. [Phillips]
Phillips, Mary K. ... '65 '99 C.150 B.A. L.1161 J.D. 5537 Cheviot Road
Phillips, Scott D., (AV) ... '62 '89 C.802 B.B.A./B.A. L.30 J.D. [Frost B.T.]
Phillips, T. Stephen, (AV) ... '41 '66 C.210 A.B. L.288 LL.B. [Frost B.T.]
Phillips Law Firm ... 9521 Montgomery Road
Pieples, Gary J. '66 '96 C.150 B.A. L.347 J.D.
Sr. Atty., Legal Aid Society of Greater Cincinnati
Pierce, James R. ... '52 '81 C.150 B.A. L.1340 J.D. 800 Compton Rd.
Pierce, Mary E. '39 '82 C.388 B.A. L.329 J.D.
(adm. in MN; not adm. in OH) I.R.S.
Pierre, Kenya Thacker ... '74 '01 C.811 B.S. L.150 J.D. Procter & Gamble Co., The
Pikna, Raymond J., Jr., (AV) ... '54 '79 C.602 B.B.A. L.930 J.D. [A Wood&L.]
Pinales, Martin S., (AV) ... '42 '68 C.150 B.B.A. L.1340 J.D. [Sirkin P.&S.]
Pinney, John B., (AV) ... '47 '72 C.659 B.S.Econ. L.477 J.D. [Graydon H.&R.] ⊙
Pitcairn, Robert A., Jr., (AV) ... '48 '73 C.970 B.A. L.150 J.D. [Katz,T.B.&H.]
Pitocco, Joseph A., Law Offices, (BV) '51 '77 C.973 B.A. L.1340 J.D.
2134 Madison Rd.
Pitstick, Joseph V. ... '68 '93 C.381 B.A. L.150 J.D. [A Cuni,F.&L.]
Pittman, Geoffrey Wayne, (BV) ... '61 '91 C.150 B.A. L.1340 J.D. [G.W.Pittman]
Pittman, Geoffrey W. Co., LPA, Law Office of, (BV) ... 114 E. 8th St.
Pitzer, Philip E., (AV) ... '44 '71 C.608 B.A. L.383 J.D. 1009 Paradrome St.
Plotnick, Harry B., (BV) ... '44 '77 C.150 B.S. L.1340 J.D. [A Phillips]
Poe, Heather K. '67 '93 C.77 B.A. L.150 J.D.
(adm. in KY; not adm. in OH) 1 E. 4th St.‡
Poffenberger, J. Dwight, Jr. '64 '94
C.477 B.S.M.E. L.1209 J.D. [A Wood,H.&E.] (See Pat. Sect.)
Poffenberger, John D., (AV) '34 '61
C.608 B.S.I.E. L.273 LL.B. [C Wood,H.&E.] (See Pat. Sect.)
Polanco, Héctor A., Law Office of '68 '00
C.1134 B.S. L.145 J.D. 2124 Madison Road, Suite 2F
Polaniecki, Elliott, (BV) ... '51 '76 C&L.150 B.A., J.D. 9000 Plainfield Road
Polley, John E. '52 '78 C.197 B.A. L.309 J.D.
(adm. in IN; not adm. in OH) Sr. Coun., Cinergy Servs.
Pontius, Erica Strawman ... '73 '98 C.477 B.A. L.608 J.D. Kroger Co., The
Popham, Julie Webster ... '67 '92 C.1118 B.A. L.150 J.D. [Helmer,M.R.&P.]
Popp, Pamela ... '52 '84 C&L.150 B.S.N., J.D. 255 E. 5th St., Ste. 2800
Porotsky, Richard D., Jr. ... '70 '96 C&L.880 B.S., J.D. [A Dinsmore&S.]
Porter, Robert C., III, (AV) ... '54 '79 C.477 A.B. L.150 J.D. [Porter&P.]
Porter, Robert C., Jr., (AV) ... '27 '52 C.477 A.B. L.309 J.D. [Porter&P.]

Porter & Porter, (AV) BB
2100 Fourth & Vine Tower, One West Fourth Street, 45202
Telephone: 513-621-3993 Fax: 513-621-1746
Members of Firm: Robert C. Porter (1890-1954); Robert C. Porter, Jr.; Robert C. Porter, III.
General Civil Practice in all Courts. Estate Planning, Probate, Corporate, Federal and State Taxation, Bankruptcy, Negligence, Real Estate and Family Law. Trials and Appeals. Employee/Fringe Benefits, Charitable Foundations, Insurance Law.
See Professional Biographies, CINCINNATI, OHIO

Porter Wright Morris & Arthur LLP, (AV)
250 E. Fifth Street, Suite 2200, 45202-5117 ⊙
Telephone: 513-381-4700; (800-582-5813) Fax: 513-421-0991
Email: cincinnati@porterwright.com URL: http://www.porterwright.com
Resident Partners: David T. Croall; Mark E. Elsener; Theodore D. Grosser; Jerome J. Metz, Jr.; Michael G. Reed; David Reichert; R. Jeffrey Schlosser; John S. Stith; Christine S. Wheatley. Resident Of Counsel: Daniel W. Scharff. Resident Associate: Rachel E. Burke.
Alternative Dispute Resolution, Agricultural Law, Antitrust and Trade Regulation, Business and Corporate, Complex Litigation, Construction, Employee Benefits, Energy and Utilities, Environment, Federal Administrative Law, Federal Contracting and Procurement, Financial Institutions, General Practice, Governmental Affairs, Health Care, Insurance, Intellectual Property, International Business, Labor and Employment, Litigation, Public Law, Public Finance, Real Estate, Securities, Taxation, Technology, Trusts and Estates.
Columbus, Ohio Office: 41 South High Street, 43215-6194. Telephones: 614-227-2000; (800-533-2794). Fax: 614-227-2100. Internet: columbus@porterwright.com.
Dayton, Ohio Office: One Dayton Centre, One South Main Street, Suite 1600, 45402-2028. Telephones: 937-449-6810; (800-533-4434). Fax: 937-449-6820. Internet: dayton@porterwright.com.
Cleveland, Ohio Office: 925 Euclid Avenue, Suite 1700, 44115-1483. Telephones: 216-443-9000; (800-824-1980). Fax: 216-443-9011. Internet: cleveland@porterwright.com.
Washington, D.C. Office: 1919 Pennsylvania Avenue, N.W., Suite 500, 20006-3434. Telephones: 202-778-3000; (800-456-7962). Fax: 202-778-3063. Internet: washington@porterwright.com.
Naples, Florida Office: 5801 Pelican Bay Boulevard, Suite 300, 34108-2709. Telephones: 239-593-2900; (800-876-7962). Fax: 239-593-2990. Internet: naples@porterwright.com.
See Professional Biographies, CINCINNATI, OHIO

Posey, Webster W. ... '12 '53 C.150 B.A. L.1340 LL.B. 963 Marion Ave.‡
Posey, William A., (AV) ... '54 '79 C&L.150 B.A., J.D. [Keating M.&K.]
Postow, Charles Jay, (AV) ... '50 '75 C.446 B.S. L.904 J.D. [Strauss&T.]
Potter, Carolyn A. ... '66 '91 C&L.831 B.A., J.D. Loewen Group Intl. Inc.
Potter, John R. ... '78 '03 C.198 B.A. L.893 J.D. [A Taft,S.&H.]
Potthast, Elizabeth Shinkle '76 '04 C.97 B.S.Ed. L.608 J.D.
Staff Atty., Legal Aid Society of Greater Cincinnati
Powell, Bradley A., (BV) ... '61 '86 C.608 B.S. L.150 J.D. [Droder&M.]
Powell, Gary E., (AV) ... '58 '84 C&L.150 B.A., J.D. [Manley B.]
Powell, Jessica Leigh ... '77 '01 C.421 B.A. L.930 J.D. 215 E. 9th St., Ste. 200
Powell, Katharine ... '79 '03 C.827 B.A. L.910 J.D. 36 E. Fourth St., Ste. 1208
Power, Wallace M. ... '24 '48 C.893 L.150 LL.B. Asst. City Solr.

Powers, John A. ... '38 '92 C.209 B.Sc. L.150 J.D. Prof., Univ. of Cincinnati
Powers, Melissa Ann, (BV) ... '61 '91 C&L.150 B.A., J.D. 306 East Fourteenth Street
Powers, Todd M., (AV) ... '58 '84 C.608 B.A. L.150 J.D. [Schroeder,M.B.&P.]
Prager, Gerald David, (AV) ... '40 '93 C.378 B.S. L.326 J.D. [C Manley B.]
Pratt, Charles A., (BV) ... '40 '66 C.473 A.B. L.150 J.D. 3276 Daytona Ave.
Prem, David Lawrence, (BV) ... '60 '87 C.150 B.A. L.1340 J.D. 1019 Main St.
Prescott, Karen Comisar, (BV) ... '54 '83 C&L.150 B.A., J.D. 5725 Dragon Way
Pressler, Frederick D. ... '74 '03 C.150 B.A. L.1340 J.D. Attorney, Becker Gallagher
Pressman, Marianne ... '— '92 C.150 B.S. L.151 J.D. Asst. Atty. Gen.
Prewitt, Thomas A., (AV) ... '63 '88 C.610 B.A. L.383 J.D. [Graydon H.&R.] ⊙
Price, Edwin C., Jr., (AV) ... '30 '57 C.846 B.A. L.150 LL.B. [Price]
Price, Geo. Gerald '42 '67 C.602 B.A. L.260 J.D.
(adm. in FL; not adm. in OH) Cincinnati Milacron Inc.
Price, William C. '62 '90 C.210 B.A. L.1340 J.D.
V.P. & Coun., The Ohio National Life Insurance Company
Price Co., L.P.A., (AV) ... Dixie Terminal Bldg.
Pridemore, Katherine E. ... '73 '98 C&L.150 B.A., J.D. Asst. Atty. Gen.
Proctor, Michael R. ... '77 '02 C.650 B.A. L.150 J.D. [A Lerner,S.&R.]
Proietti, Louis D. '63 '91 C.477 B.A. L.424 J.D.
Dir. Legal Affs., Givaudan Flavors Corp.
Pryor, Patricia Anderson ... '73 '98 C.610 B.A. L.150 J.D. [A Taft,S.&H.]
Pryse, Gail Glassmeyer, (AV) ... '63 '88 C.610 B.A. L.602 J.D. [Keating M.&K.]
Przywara, Kathryn K., (AV) ... '57 '82 C.602 B.A. L.1119 J.D. [C Dinsmore&S.]
Pugh, Jason R. ... '73 '98 C.608 B.S L.989 J.D. 8044 Montgomery Rd., Suite 400
Pundzak, Lynn D., (BV) ... '61 '86 C&L.383 B.A., J.D. 830 Main St., Ste. 999
Purdue, Jas. C. ... '17 '50 C.150 L.1340 LL.B. 10484 Adventure Ln.
Purdy, Eugene K., (BV) ... '29 '53 L.1340 J.D. [E.K.Purdy]
Purdy, Eugene K., Co., L.P.A., (BV) ... 10776 Mill Rd.
Purtell, William L. ... '— '02 C.1118 B.A., 1999 L.150 J.D [A Lerner,S.&R.]
Puthoff, Tracey Chriske ... '66 '95 C.502 B.S.A.E. L.151 J.D. [Taft,S.&H.]
Putnick, Otto F., (AV) ... '25 '48 C.973 B.A. L.1340 LL.B. [O.F.Putnick]
Putnick, Otto F., (AV) ... 2134 Madison Road
Qualls, John ... '47 '77 C&L.150 B.A., J.D. General Counsel, Anderson Publishing Co.
Quinn, Timothy J., (AV) ... '47 '75 C.976 B.A. L.608 J.D. [Taft,S.&H.]
Rabkin, Morton, (BV) ... '36 '61 C.1036 B.A. L.477 J.D. 123 E. 4th St.
Rabourn, D. Arthur, (AV) ... '53 '79 C.510 A.B. L.1340 J.D. [A Waite,S.B.&C.]
Rack, Robert W., Jr. '47 '73
C.363 B.A. L.851 J.D. Sr. Conference Atty., 6th Cir. Ct. of App.
Rader, James A. ... '41 '79 C.608 B.S. L.151 J.D. 117-121 E. Ct. St.
Rafferty, Donald J., (AV) ... '62 '89 C.373 B.A. L.150 J.D. [Cohen,T.K.&S.]
Raisbeck, Thomas E. ... '66 '92 C.383 B.B.A. L.1340 J.D. [Lane,F.&R.]
Ramaswamy, V.G. '52 '98 C.999 B.Sc. L.1340 J.D.
Coun., IP, GE Aviation Services, Inc.
Rambo, Deborah Price, (BV) ... '56 '87 C.150 B.A. L.309 J.D. [W.C.Rambo] ‡

Rambo, William Cates, Law Office of, (AV) '48 '82 C.608 B.S. L.117 J.D.
414 Walnut Street, Suite 508, 45202-3913
Telephone: 513-768-8901 Fax: 513-768-8909
Email: bill@iplawrambo.com URL: http://www.iplawrambo.com
—Deborah Price Rambo.
Preparation and Prosecution of Domestic and Foreign Patents, Trademark and Copyright Registrations, Litigation and Licensing of Intellectual Property, Patent and Trademark Searches and Infringement Studies.
See Professional Biographies, CINCINNATI, OHIO

Ramey Kojetin, Erica ... '77 '04 C.108 B.S. L.896 J.D. Legal Coun., Fifth Third Bank
Ramirez, Carlos S. ... '70 '95 C.473 B.A. L.30 J.D. [A Lerner,S.&R.]
Rammes, Lisa M. ... '69 '96 C.473 B.A. L.150 J.D. [Wood&L.]

Ramos, G. Ernie, Jr., (AV) '46 '77 C.383 B.S. L.1340 J.D.
2115 Luray Avenue, 45206
Telephone: 513-221-8383 Fax: 513-221-4433
Email: ernieramos@fuse.net URL: http://www.ramoslawohio.com
General Trial Practice, Personal Injury, Insurance, Wills and Probate and Tort Law.

Ramsey, Jamie M. ... '74 '99 C&L.1161 B.S., J.D. [A Keating M.&K.]
Ramundo, Kimberly E. ... '71 '96 C.473 B.A. L.150 J.D. [Thompson H.]
Ran, Ronald S. ... '42 '69 C&L.150 B.S., J.D. I.R.S.
Ranaghan, William L., Jr., (AV) '52 '78 C.973 B.A. L.1340 J.D.
Spec. Asst. to Treasurer
Randall, Kevin C. '57 '82 C.473 A.B. L.477 J.D.
(adm. in TX; not adm. in OH)
Sr. Coun., Financing & Transactions, GE Aviation Services, Inc.
Randolph, Daniel P., (AV) ... '46 '77 C.973 B.S. L.1161 J.D. [Ritter&R.]
Randolph, Marc A. ... '72 '96 C.473 B.S. L.902 J.D. [A Ritter&R.]
Randolph, Peter J., (BV) '31 '59 C.973 B.S. L.150 LL.B.
30 E. Central Parkway, Suite 901
Ranz, David A. ... '56 '01 C.973 B.S.B.A. L.1340 J.D. 910 Race St.
Ranz, John H., (BV) ... '24 '50 C&L.150 B.S., J.D. 7186 Greenfringe Lane
Ranz, Robert James ... '53 '80 C.973 B.S.B.A. L.1161 J.D. [R.J.Ranz]
Ranz, Robert J., Law Office of ... 1071 Celestial Street
Rapien, Gerald J., (AV) '43 '68 C.973 A.B. L.602 LL.B.
[Taft,S.&H.] (⊙Covington, KY)
Rapp, W. C. ... '14 '39 C.150 L.1340 LL.B. 6336 Meis St.
Ratliff, Philip Q., (BV⊤) '60 '92 C.235 B.B.A. L.421 J.D.
(adm. in KY; not adm. in OH) [A Weltman,W.&R.]
Rauchman, Judith L., (BV) ... '55 '83 C.273 B.A. L.607 J.D. 7809 Laurel Ave., Ste. 9
Rauen, Mary E. ... '59 '99 C.1161 B.S. L.1340 J.D. [A Lerner,S.&R.]
Rauh, Trudy D., (AV) ... '29 '78 C&L.150 B.A., J.D. [Laufman,R.&G.]
Ray, Mary E. '68 '95 C.1161 B.A. L.1340 J.D.
(adm. in KY; not adm. in OH) Corp. Coun., Cincinnati Bell Inc.
Ray, Steven H. ... '61 '88 C.546 B.A. L.705 J.D. [Dinsmore&S.]
Raymer, Joel L. '57 '84 C.918 B.A. L.424 J.D.
(adm. in IL; not adm. in OH) Asst. Gen. Coun., Chiquita Brands Intl., Inc.
Reblin, Kelly L. ... '71 '97 C.62 B.A. L.744 J.D. [A Thompson H.]
Rebold, Peter M., (BV) ... '43 '68 C.973 B.S. L.276 J.D. [Haverkamp,B.R.&R.]
Recker, Frank R., (BV) ... '46 '81 C.973 B.S. L.1340 J.D. [F.R.Recker&Assoc.] ⊙
Recker, Frank R., & Assoc. Co., LPA, (BV) ... One West Fourth Street ⊙
Reckman, Mark S., (AV) ... '53 '79 C.882 B.A. L.150 J.D. [Wood&L.]
Reckman, Robert F., (AV) ... '22 '48 C.210 A.B. L.150 LL.B. [C Wood&L.]
Rector, Daniel G. ... '53 '84 C&L.150 B.A., J.D. I.R.S.
Redbord, Ari B. '74 '00 C.228 B.A. L.276 J.D.
(adm. in NJ; not adm. in OH) [A Keating M.&K.]
Redden, Brian R. ... '72 '99 C.973 B.A. L.1340 J.D. [A Beckman W.S.]
Reed, Mark Harold ... '59 '86 C&L.383 B.A., J.D. Ct. Admr., Hamilton Co. Juv. Ct.
Reed, Michael G., (AV) ... '56 '81 C.473 B.S. L.150 J.D. [Porter W.M.&A.]
Reed, Robert F., (BV) ... '35 '64 C.25 A.B. L.151 J.D. [Reed,T.&H.]
Reed, Tilton & Hastings, (AV) ... 22 W. 9th St.
Regan, Robyn M. ... '— '02 C.973 B.A. L.124 J.D. [A Lerner,S.&R.]

Regberg, Neil S. ... '51 '76 C&L.150 B.A., J.D. App. Offr., I.R.S.
Rehling, Beth L. ... '58 '85 C.523 B.A. L.607 J.D. 2761 Falconbridge Dr.‡
Rehme, Thomas F., (AV) ... '29 '54 C.276 B.S.S. L.976 LL.B. [🄰 Waite,S.B.&C.]
Reichert, David, (AV) ... '29 '54 C.97 B.A. L.150 LL.B. [Porter W.M.&A.]
Reichert, James A., (BV) ... '44 '73 C.150 B.A. L.796 J.D. 14 Garfield Pl., Ste. 300
Reichert, Robert C., (BV) '40 '84 C.150 L.999 J.D.
(adm. in CA; not adm. in OH) Pres Gen. Coun., Kenwood Dealer Grp., Inc.
Reid, Robert J., (BV) ... '67 '93 C.973 B.A. L.150 J.D. [Dinsmore&S.]
Reif, Robert Daniel ... '36 '70 C.150 B.B.A. L.999 J.D. Atty. Gen. Off.
Reik, Rose ... '11 '49 2515 Handasyde Ct.‡
Reilly, Timothy P., (AV) ... '53 '78 C.602 B.A. L.150 J.D. [Taft,S.&H.]
Reis, Mark W., (BV) ... '52 '83 C.434 B.S. L.150 J.D. [Aronoff,R.&H.]
Reisenfeld, Bradley A. ... '64 '90 C.608 B.A. L.117 J.D. [🄰 Reisenfeld&Assoc.]
Reisenfeld, Sylvan P., (AV) ... '33 '60 C&L.150 B.B.A., LL.B. [Reisenfeld&Assoc.]
Reisenfeld & Associates, (AV) ... 2355 Auburn Avenue
Reitz, Daniel E. ... '77 '01 C.473 B.A. L.150 J.D. [🄰 Graydon H.&R.]
Remaklus, Theodore R. '62 '93 C&L.150 B.S.M.E., J.D.
[Wood,H.&E.] (See Pat. Sect.)
Reminger, Richard T., (AV) '31 '57
C.930 A.B. L.1003 J.D. [Reminger&R.] (⊙Covington, KY)
Reminger & Reminger Co., L.P.A., (AV)
7 W. 7th St., Ste. 1990 (⊙Covington, KY; Akron, Cleve., Columbus, Sandusky, Toledo, Youngstown, OH)
Render, Leon M. ... '11 '46 C.389 B.S. L.1340 LL.B. 3940 Dickson Ave.‡
Render, M. Dale ... '32 '59 C.475 L.150 LL.B. 5956 Salem Rd.‡

Rendigs, Fry, Kiely & Dennis, L.L.P., (AV)
1 West Fourth Street, Suite 900, 45202
Telephone: 513-381-9200 FAX: 513-381-9206
Email: info@rendigs.com URL: http://www.rendigs.com
Partners of the Firm: August A. Rendigs, Jr. (1895-1988); Robert M. Dennis (1917-1973); William H. Fry (1905-1975); John A. Kiely (1899-1986); W. Roger Fry; David Winchester Peck; Paul F. Wenker; Edward R. Goldman; Joseph W. Gelwicks; Leonard A. Weakley, Jr.; Carolyn A. Taggart; Donald C. Adams, Jr.; Wilson G. Weisenfelder, Jr.; Steven D. Hengehold; Thomas M. Evans; Felix J. Gora; John F. McLaughlin; Peter L. Ney; Robert F. Brown; Kenneth B. Flacks; Paul W. McCartney; Jonathan P. Saxton; Arthur E. Phelps, Jr. (Certified Specialist in Workers' Compensation Law, Ohio State Bar Association); James J. Englert; James E. McLean, Jr.; Michael P. Foley; Christopher R. Carville; Christopher J. Aluotto. Retired Partner: William H. Hutcherson, Jr. Of Counsel: J. Kenneth Meagher; Gordon C. Greene; C. Thomas Dupuis; Paul J. Kellogg. Associates: Karen A. Rolcik; Cynthia M. Chiaro; Peter B. Jurs; Chad E. Willits; Lynne M. Longtin; George J. Zamary; Robert J. Thumann; Laura I. Hillerich.
Trial and General Practice, Appellate Practice, Products Liability, Insurance Litigation, Personal Injury, Medical Liability, Medical Malpractice, Nursing Home Litigation, Health Law, Hospital Law, Professional Liability, Construction Law, Mold Claims, Corporate Law, Business Law, Maritime Law, Aviation Law, Commercial Law, Taxation, Real Estate, Probate, Trusts and Estates, Wills, Bankruptcy, Family Law, Environmental Law, Transportation, Medical Devices, Civil Rights, Premises Liability, Premises Security, Labor Law, Employment Law, Employee Benefits, Criminal Law, Class Actions, Complex and Multi-District Litigation, Alternative Dispute Resolution, Legal Professional Liability, Workers' Compensation Defense, Zoning, Planning and Land Use.
Representative Clients: Medical Protective Co.; St. Paul Insurance Co.
See Professional Biographies, CINCINNATI, OHIO

Rennie, Douglas W., (AV) ... '52 '78 C.473 B.A. L.1340 J.D. [Montgomery,R.&J.]
Renz, Karen J. ... '64 '96 C.232 B.S.B.A. L.472 J.D. [Graydon H.&R.]
Resler, Mark L. ... '56 '82 C&L.150 B.A., J.D. Asst. Cty. Pros.
Resnick, Kenneth S. '55 '81
Sr. Coun., Litig. & Preventive Law, GE Aviation Services, Inc.
Rettig, Jeremy M. '— '02 C&L.1161 B.A., J.D.
(adm. in KY; not adm. in OH) [🄰 Lerner,S.&R.]
Reul, George Marvin, Jr. ... '72 '98 C.347 B.A. L.880 J.D. [🄰 Freking&B.]
Reuter, F. Mark ... '71 '96 C&L.602 B.A., J.D. [Keating M.&K.]
Reutter, Mary Joan Gertrude ... '59 '99 C.602 B.A. L.150 J.D. [M.J.Reutter]
Reutter, Mary Joan ... 6924 Plainfield Road
Reverman, Richard E., (BV) ... '55 '80 C.1118 B.A. L.150 J.D. [Young,R.&N.]
Reyering, William H., (AV) ... '22 '49 C.973 L.150 J.D. [🄲 Spraul,V.&D.]
Reynolds, Charles E., (AV) ... '54 '81 C.575 B.S. L.838 J.D. [Santen&H.]
Reynolds, Mark M. ... '20 '50 C&L.150 LL.B. N.L.R.B.
Reynolds, Paul L., (BV) ... '61 '86 C.1161 B.S. L.383 J.D. 38 Fountain Square Plaza
Rice, Clark H., Jr. ... '32 '58 C&L.608 B.S., J.D. 6643 Hitchingpost Lane‡
Rice, James K., (AV) ... '42 '67 C&L.150 B.B.A., J.D. [Rice&D.]
Rice, John David '36 '65 C.877 B.S. L.273 J.D.
Sr. Coun., Millennium Petrochemicals Inc. (Pat.)
Rice, Kenneth C. '64 '94 C&L.150 B.A., J.D.
Coun., Labor & Employment, GE Aviation Services, Inc.
Rice, Michael D. ... '61 '86 C.210 B.A. L.880 J.D. 49 E. 4th St.‡
Rice, Nancy G. ... '50 '80 C.8 B.A. L.607 J.D. 1424 Oak Knoll Dr.
Rice, Robert M. ... '68 '93 C.201 B.A. L.150 J.D. [Helmer,M.R.&P.]

Rice and Diedrichs, LLP, (AV)
3530 Edwards Road, 45208-1358
Telephone: 513-871-1545 Fax: 513-871-1545
URL: http://www.lawyers.com/rice&diedrichs
James K. Rice; Frank M. Diedrichs.
Federal, State and Local Taxation (Compliance and Planning), Estate Planning, Probate, Business and Real Estate.
See Professional Biographies, CINCINNATI, OHIO

Rich, Michael L. ... '78 '03 C.205 B.A. L.813 J.D. [🄰 Vorys,S.S.&P.]
Rich, Robert E., (AV) ... '44 '70 C.383 A.B. L.309 J.D. [Taft,S.&H.]
Rich, Pott, Wetherell, Foster & Miller, (BV) ... 830 Main St.
Richard, Arthur M., III ... '64 '93 C.477 B.A. L.851 J.D. 114 E. 8th Street, Suite 400
Richards, Gates T., (AV) ... '38 '69 C.885 B.A. L.280 LL.B. 5 Grandin Lane
Richards, Stuart L., (BV) ... '38 '62 C&L.150 B.A., LL.B. 906 Main St.
Richards, Thomas D., (BV) ... '50 '84 C.608 B.A. L.1340 J.D. [Richards&Assoc.]
Richards and Associates Co., LPA, A Legal Professional Association, (BV)
3322 Erie Avenue
Richardson, Eric W. ... '73 '96 C.1118 B.A. L.150 J.D. [Vorys,S.S.&P.]
Richardson, Scott ... '75 '02 C.999 B.S.M.E. L.201 J.D. [🄰 Frost B.T.]
Richey, Stephen L., (BV) ... '46 '93 C.973 B.A. L.151 J.D. [Thompson H.]
Richshafer, Howard L., (AV) ... '45 '75 C.150 B.A. L.1340 J.D. [Statman,H.S.&E.]
Richter, Melisa J. ... '61 '87 C.973 B.S. L.150 J.D. 2355 Auburn Ave.
Rickey, Robert E. ... '— '02 C.967 B.A. L.150 J.D. [🄰 D.M.Cook]
Riddell, Brian A. ... '77 '04 C.383 B.A. L.1340 J.D. [🄰 Keating M.&K.]
Riehl, Keith S., (BV) ... '56 '81 C.608 B.S. L.150 J.D. [Haverkamp,B.R.&R.]
Riehl, Nancy Kohli, (CV) ... '57 '82 C.473 B.A. L.150 J.D. 5856 Glenway Avenue
Riggs, Harry L., Jr., (AV) ... '30 '57 C.138 A.B. L.150 J.D. [🄲 Dinsmore&S.]
Riker, J. Timothy, (AV) ... '48 '77 C.62 B.A. L.117 J.D. [Ebner&R.]
Riley, Kimberly Vanover ... '73 '97 C&L.150 B.A., J.D. [🄰 Montgomery,R.&J.]
Rimedio, James (Jim) ... '38 '65 C.473 B.A. L.1340 J.D. 810 Matson Pl.
Rinear, Richard J., (BV) ... '58 '84 C.150 B.A. L.1340 J.D. [Droder&M.]
Rinear, Robert L., (BV) ... '32 '65 C.973 B.S.B.A. L.1340 J.D. 4820 Glenway Ave.

Rines, David A. ... '66 '95 C.602 B.S. L.893 J.D. [🄰 Thompson H.]
Ringenbach, Laura A., (AV) ... '53 '83 C.973 B.S. L.150 J.D. [🄲 Taft,S.&H.]
Rink, Thomas C., (AV) ... '45 '70 C&L.602 B.B.A., J.D. [Strauss&T.]
Ris, Cynthia Nitz ... '57 '82 C.839 B.A. L.477 J.D. 834 Strathcoma Dr.
Risch, Dennis S., (BV) ... '53 '79 C.1302 B.S. L.151 J.D. [🄰 Heis&W.]
Rittenhouse, Roger P. '51 '75
C.608 B.Sc. L.150 J.D. Soc. Sec. Admin., Off. of Hearings & App.
Ritter & Randolph, LLC, (AV) ... 105 East Fourth Street, Suite 1200
Rizer, Jo Jones '60 '85 C.1021 B.A. L.150 J.D.
Dir. Legal Servs., Bus. Opers., Community Mutual Insurance Company
Roach, Adrienne J. ... '71 '96 C.692 B.A. L.150 J.D. [Keating M.&K.]
Robbins, Eric M. ... '74 '01 C.602 B.S.E.E. L.150 J.D. [🄰 Dinsmore&S.]
Robbins, Fredric J., (AV) ... '49 '74 C.473 B.S. L.150 J.D. [Robbins,K.P.&T.] ⊙
Robbins, M. Kathleen, (BV) ... '52 '80 C.973 B.S.B.A. L.150 J.D. Asst. City Solr.

Robbins, Kelly, Patterson & Tucker, A Legal Professional Association, (AV)
The Federated Building, Suite 1400, 7 West Seventh Street, 45202-2417 ⊙
Telephone: 513-721-3330 Telecopier: 513-721-5001
URL: http://www.rkpt.com
Fredric J. Robbins; James M. Kelly; Mark C. Patterson; Jack L. Tucker; Thomas M. Gaier; Daniel J. Temming; Randy J. Blankenship; William D. Sherman; Barry A. Spaeth;—Richard T. Lauer; Elizabeth Slone DeHaan; Esther Maria Norton; Michael A. Galasso; Stephen M. Sager; Jarrod M. Mohler; Jason R. Hinners. Of Counsel: Richard L. Nurre.
Mason, Ohio Office: 315 West Main Street, 45040. Telephone: 513-336-7550. Fax: 513-336-7750.
See Professional Biographies, CINCINNATI, OHIO

Roberts, Douglas D. ... '63 '89 C.473 A.B. L.1068 J.D. [Thompson H.]
Roberts, Edward ... '64 '95 C.150 B.A. L.1340 J.D. [🄰 Lindhorst&D.]
Roberts, George E., III, (AV) ... '44 '69 C.473 B.A. L.150 J.D. [Ennis,R.&F.]
Roberts, Michael A., (AV) ... '63 '90 C&L.602 B.S., J.D. [Graydon H.&R.]
Roberts, Norton Brooke, (BV) '51 '93 C.150 B.B.A. L.1340 J.D.
Dir., Hamilton Co. Common Place Alt. Dispute Resol.
Robinette, Joseph A. '62 '87 C&L.201 J.D., J.D.
Gen. Coun., The U.S. Playing Card Co.
Robinson, Ann Gallagher ... '62 '94 C.602 B.S. L.1340 J.D. [Frost B.T.] (See Pat. Sect.)
Robinson, Gerald J. ... '32 '59 C.339 B.S. L.1340 LL.B. Pres., Kenko Corp.
Robinson, James B. ... '44 '70 C.309 B.A. L.659 J.D. [Kircher,R.&W.]
Robinson, Richard L., (BV) '58 '83 C.235 B.A. L.1340 J.D.
(adm. in KY; not adm. in OH) [Graydon H.&R.] ⊙
Robinson, Wm. T. (Bill), III, (AVⓉ) '45 '71
C.1118 A.B. L.383 J.D. [Greenebaum D.&M.] (⊙Covington, KY)

Robison, Stephen L., (AV) '60 '86 C&L.150 B.A., J.D.
4500 Cooper Road, Suite 305, 45242
Telephone: 513-412-3483 Fax: 513-412-3482 URL: http://www.robinsontaxlaw.com
Email: steve@robisiontaxlaw.com URL: http://www.stephenlrobison.com
(Certified Specialist in Federal Tax Law, Ohio State Bar Association).
Taxation, Estate Planning and Corporate Law, Like Kind Exchanges, Tax Planning, Tax Controversies.
See Professional Biographies, CINCINNATI, OHIO

Rodriguez Escalera, Manuel '49 '74 C.728 B.S. L.677 J.D.
(adm. in PR; not adm. in OH)
V.P., Govt. & Intl. Affs. & Corp. Respon. Offr., Chiquita Brands Intl., Inc.
Roe, Clifford A., Jr., (AV) ... '42 '67 C.973 B.S. L.602 J.D. [Dinsmore&S.]
Roelker, Daniella A., Law Office of ... '71 '97 C.608 B.A. L.150 J.D. 11137 Main Street
Roeller, Robert K., (BV) ... '36 '62 C&L.150 A.B., LL.B. 1029 Main St.
Roesch, Charles M., (AV) ... '58 '84 C.602 B.B.A. L.150 J.D. [Dinsmore&S.]
Roesch, Lynda E., (AV) ... '53 '79 C.602 B.S. L.851 J.D. [Dinsmore&S.] (See Pat. Sect.)

Roetzel & Andress, A Legal Professional Association, (AV) BR
310 Chiquita Center, 250 East Fifth Street, 45202 ⊙
Telephone: 513-361-0200 Telecopier: 513-361-0335
Email: inquiries@ralaw.com URL: http://www.ralaw.com
Partners: Eric G. Bruestle (Managing Partner) (Certified Specialist in Workers' Compensation Law, Ohio State Bar Association); Peter K. Newman; Jeffrey S. Shoskin;—Gregory S. Kessler; Elizabeth Shaffer.
General Corporate and Business Law, Banking and Finance, Mergers, Acquisitions and Divestitures, Securities Law, Real Estate Law, Real Estate Development/Syndication/Condominium Law, Tax Law, Intellectual Property Law, Computer Law, Hospital and Health Care Law, Public Law and Finance, Governmental Relations, School Law, Commercial/Bankruptcy Law, Employment Law, Pension, Employee Benefits, Workers' Compensation, OSHA, Business and Commercial Litigation, Complex and Multidistrict Litigation, Antitrust Law, RICO, Federal Court Practice, Product Liability, Environmental Law/Toxic Torts, Insurance Law, Information Technology Law, Medical Malpractice Defense, Asbestos Litigation, Construction Law, 1st Amendment/Media Law, White Collar Criminal Defense, Railroad and FELA, Trucking and Transportation Law, Probate and Estate Planning, Utility Law, International Law, Trial and Appellate Practice.
Akron, Ohio Office: 222 South Main Street. Telephone: 330-376-2700. Telecopier: 330-376-4577.
Columbus, Ohio Office: National City Center, 155 E. Broad Street, 12th Floor. Telephone: 614-463-9770. Telecopier: 614-463-9792.
Naples, Florida Office: 850 Park Shore Drive, Trianon Centre, 3rd Floor. Telephones: 239-649-6200; 800-535-7239. Telecopier: 239-261-3659.
Cleveland, Ohio Office: One Cleveland Center, 1375 East Ninth Street, 9th Floor. Telephone: 216-623-0150. Telecopier: 216-623-0134.
Fort Myers, Florida Office: 2320 First Street, Suite 1000. Telephone: 239-337-3850. Telecopier: 239-337-0970.
Toledo, Ohio Office: One SeaGate, 9th Floor. Telephone: 419-242-7985. Facsimile: 419-242-0316.
Tallahassee, Florida Office: 225 South Adams Street, Suite 250, P.O. Box 10369. Telephone: 850-222-7718. Telecopier: 850-222-8222.
Washington, D.C. Office: 1025 Connecticut Avenue, NW, Suite 220. Telephone: 202-625-0600. Telecopier: 202-338-6340.
See Professional Biographies, CINCINNATI, OHIO

Rogers, Brie S. ... '78 '02 C.10 B.A. L.150 J.D. [🄰 Taft,S.&H.]
Rogers, Donald K. '64 '89 C.608 B.S./B.A. L.851 J.D.
(adm. in IL; not adm. in OH) Sr. Trial Atty.
Rogers, Gregory Parker, (AV) ... '64 '89 C.473 B.S. L.245 J.D. [Taft,S.&H.]
Rogers, James E., Jr. ... '54 '79 C.999 B.A. L.851 J.D. I.R.S.
Rogers, John M. ... '48 '75 C.813 B.A. L.477 J.D. U.S. Ct. App. J.
Rogers, Thomas J. ... '46 '71 C&L.150 B.A., J.D. 6250 Beechmont Ave.
Rogus, Timothy E. ... '— '94 C.201 B.S. L.150 J.D. [🄰 Buckley K.]
Rohner, Nicholas K. ... '74 '01 C.473 B.A. L.150 J.D. [🄰 Weltman,W.&R.]
Rohr, Jeffrey L., (AV) ... '60 '85 C.473 B.S. L.276 J.D. [Graydon H.&R.]
Rolcik, Karen A. ... '61 '86 C.108 B.S. L.1119 J.D. [🄰 Rendigs,F.K.&D.]
Rolf, Donald H., Jr., (AV) ... '40 '67 C&L.150 B.A., J.D. 312 Walnut St.
Rolfes, Jerome F. ... '63 '89 C.150 B.A. L.607 J.D. [Smith,R.&S.]
Rollman, Jeffrey M., (AV) ... '45 '74 C.610 B.A. L.1340 J.D. [Wood&L.]
Romer, Clement T., Jr. ... '30 '56 C&L.602 B.S., LL.B. 1st Nat. Bk. Bldg.
Ronneau, Suzanne W. ... '45 '92 C.347 B.A. L.150 J.D. 9000 Plainfield Rd.
Roof, Carl J. ... '62 '92 C.354 B.A. L.823 J.D. The Procter & Gamble Co. (Pat.)
Rooney, Kevin G. ... '64 '92 C.150 B.S.M.E. L.273 J.D. [Wood,H.&E.] (See Pat. Sect.)
Rorer, Sara Simrall, (AV) ... '53 '88 C.473 B.A. L.150 J.D. [🄰 Taft,S.&H.]
Rosado, Raul, Jr. ... '64 '89 C.973 B.S. L.150 J.D. Gen. Coun., Cognis Corp.
Rose, Janet T., (Ms.), (CV) ... '35 '78 C&L.150 B.A., J.D. 2971 Ridgewood Ave.

Rose, John K., (AV) .... '29 '60 C.150 A.B. L.309 LL.B. [🄲 Frost B.T.]
Rose, John W., (BV) .... '55 '81 C.473 B.A. L.851 J.D. 632 Vine St.
Rose, Michael D. ... '42 '66 C.150 B.B.A. L.309 J.D. Exec. V.P., Weingardner Enterprises
Roselle, Cynthia M. .... '— '01 C.477 B.A. L.608 J.D. [🄰 Lerner,S.&R.]
Roselle, Louise M., (BV) .... '48 '72 C&L.608 B.S., J.D. [🄰 Waite,S.B.&C.]
Rosen, Eve Cutler, (AV) '52 '76 C.104 A.B. L.884 J.D.
(adm. in PA; not adm. in OH) Sr. V.P., Great Amer. Ins. Co.
Rosen, Irving H., (AV) .... '28 '57 C&L.150 B.A., J.D. [🄲 Aronoff,R.&H.]
Rosen, Steven J. '— '79 C.569 B.S.A.E. L.564 J.D.
(adm. in PA; not adm. in OH) 4729 Cornell Rd. (Pat.)
Rosenacker, Frank B. .... '52 '83 C.999 B.S. L.1340 J.D. [F.B.Rosenacker]
Rosenacker, Frank B. Co., L.P.A. .... 5537 Cheviot Road
Rosenbaum, Morton I., (BV) .... '23 '49 C&L.150 B.A., LL.B. 602 Main St., Ste. 1309
Rosenberg, Bernard L., (AV) .... '27 '50 C&L.150 LL.B. 2615 Central Trust Twr.
Rosenberg, Hilda .... '56 '90 C.1036 B.A. L.446 J.D. U.S. Dist. Ct.
Rosenberg, J. David, (AV) .... '49 '74 C.659 B.S. L.383 J.D. [Keating M.&K.]
Rosenberg, Jay A., (AV) .... '39 '66 C.659 B.S. L.477 J.D. [J.A.Rosenberg]
Rosenberg, Marvin .... '33 '57 C.473 L.150 LL.B. 1055 St. Paul Pl.

Rosenberg, Jay A., LPA, (AV)
One Financial Way, Suite 312, 45242
Telephone: 513-792-6729 Fax: 513-745-0747
Email: jrosenberg@fandtlaw.com URL: http://www.dodeeds.com
Jay A. Rosenberg (Also Of Counsel to Furnier & Thomas, LLP).
Real Estate, Title Insurance, Corporate.

See Professional Biographies, CINCINNATI, OHIO

Rosenstiel, Jeffrey S. .... '66 '96 C.382 B.A. L.1161 J.D. [Frost B.T.]
Rosenthal, Daniel G., (AV) .... '53 '77 C.967 B.A. L.228 J.D. [Denlinger,R.&G.]
Rosenwald, Peter, (AV) .... '45 '73 C.150 B.S. L.1340 J.D. 114 E. Eighth St.
Roser, Christopher P. .....'57 '90 C.150 B.S. L.1340 J.D. V.P., Donnellon McCarthy, Inc.
Rosnell, Tara M. '66 '91
C.201 B.A. L.150 J.D. Pat. Atty., The Procter & Gamble Co. (Pat.)
Rosner, Lisa Miner .... '56 '83 C.473 B.A. L.150 J.D. 9297 Witherbone Ct.‡
Ross, Jennifer K. ....'73 '03 C.473 B.A. L.150 J.D. [🄰 Lerner,S.&R.]
Ross, Lori A. ....'75 '00 C.473 B.A. L.150 J.D. [🄰 Strauss&T.]
Roszmann, Elisabeth Frey ....'64 '92 C.207 B.A. L.1340 J.D. Anderson Publishing Co.
Roth, Neil J., (CV) .... '55 '84 C.165 B.A. L.383 J.D. 414 Walnut Street
Rothchild, Eugene M. ....'31 '56 C&L.150 B.B.A., LL.B. 441 Vine St.
Rothfuss, R. Mark, II '77 '03 C&L.383 B.A., J.D.
(adm. in KY; not adm. in OH) [🄰 Lerner,S.&R.]
Rothfuss, Richard M., (AV) ....'51 '77 C.383 B.A. L.1340 J.D. [Lerner,S.&R.]
Rothstein, Debra ... '49 '76 C.107 B.A. L.1340 J.D. Sr. Atty., Legal Aid Soc. of Cincinnati
Rothstein, Steven M., (BV) .... '53 '77 C.473 A.B. L.150 J.D. [Katz,G.&N.]
Rottinghaus, Thomas J. .... '47 '73 C.1024 B.S. L.1340 J.D. Admr., Dist. Ct. of App.
Rounding, Ruth I., (AV) ....'52 '76 C.028 B.A. L.309 J.D. [Drew&W.]
Rouse, Joseph P., (AV) ....'44 '70 C.602 B.A. L.150 J.D. [Keating M.&K.]
Routh, Jeffrey S., Esq. .... '63 '89 C.893 B.A. L.608 J.D. 407 Vine Street, Suite 184
Rowe, Rachael A. ....'71 '96 C.473 B.A. L.150 J.D. [Keating M.&K.]
Rowland, James E., (BVⓉ) '49 '78 C.1118 B.A. L.1340 J.D.
(adm. in KY; not adm. in OH) 7265 Kenwood Road, Suite 315 (⊙Fort Thomas, KY)
Rozic, James P. .... '66 '92 C.473 B.A. L.1340 J.D. [🄰 J.Waite&Assoc.]
Rubenstein, Charles A., (BV) ...... '55 '81 C.608 B.B.A. L.201 J.D. Chf. Dep. Pros. Atty.
Rubenstein, Jack C., (AV) .... '42 '67 C.228 A.B. L.608 J.D. [Rubenstein&T.]
Rubenstein, Louis, (AV) ....'53 '78 C.150 B.A. L.201 J.D. 7 W. 7th Street
Rubenstein, Scott A. .... '73 '99 C.174 B.A. L.150 J.D. [Rubenstein&T.]
Rubenstein & Thurman, A Legal Prof. Assn., (AV) .... 7 W. 7th St., Ste. 1850
Rubin, Julian ....'28 '50 C&L.150 B.A., LL.B. 2355 Vera Ave.
Rubin, Marc W., (AV) .... '49 '74 C&L.150 B.A., J.D. [Cohen,T.K.&S.]
Rubin, Robert S., (AV) ....'54 '79 L.150 J.D. [Cohen,T.K.&S.]
Rubin, Walter I., (BV) .... '40 '66 C.150 B.A. L.1340 J.D. 3194 Dot Drive
Ruby, Stanley L., (AV) .... '37 '63 C&L.880 B.A., LL.B. [Schwartz,M.&R.]
Rucker, Fanon A. .... '71 '96 C.302 B.A. L.150 J.D. [🄰 Santen&H.]
Rudig, Robert H., (BV) ....'18 '58 C.150 B.Sc. L.1340 LL.B. 1332 Hollywood Ave.
Ruebel, Richard J., (AV) ....'48 '73 C.188 B.A. L.150 J.D. [Drew&W.]
Rueger, James M., (BV) ....'48 '77 C.679 B.S.I.M. L.1340 J.D. [Dolle,R.&M.]
Ruehlman, Robert P. ....'52 '77 C&L.150 B.S., J.D. Com. Pleas J.
Ruehlmann, Eugene P., (AV) ....'25 '50 C.150 A.B. L.309 LL.B. [🄲 Vorys,S.S.&P.]
Ruehlmann, Gregory A., (AV) ....'55 '81 C.597 B.A. L.880 J.D. [🄲 Squire,S.&D.]
Ruehlmann, Mark J., (AV) '61 '87
C.602 B.A. L.880 J.D. [Squire,S.&D.] (⊙New York, NY)
Ruger, James W. ....'55 '83 C.347 B.A. L.1340 J.D. Dist. Coun., I.R.S.
Ruh, Michael A., Jr., (AV) ....'68 '96 C.383 B.B.A. L.150 J.D. [Strauss&T.]
Rumberg, Orly R. .... '68 '93 C&L.930 B.A., J.D. [🄲 Schwartz,M.&R.]
Rummer, Keith A. ....'69 '94 C.207 B.A. L.608 J.D. Asst. VP, Fifth Third Bank
Rumpf, John M. '65 '89 C.893 B.S. L.477 J.D.
Coun., Environ. Affs., GE Aviation Services, Inc.
Rusche, Joseph F., (AV) .... '21 '49 C.973 B.S.C. L.150 LL.B. 830 Main St.
Rusconi, Carla Haunz ....'63 '88 C.602 B.A. L.893 J.D. [🄲 Frost B.T.]
Rush, D. Todd ....'67 '97 C.610 B.A. L.201 J.D. [Lutz,C.&M.]
Rush, Jeffery R., (AV) .... '50 '75 C.659 B.S. L.880 J.D. [Frost B.T.]
Russell, Allison S. .... '74 '99 C.210 B.A. L.930 J.D. [🄰 Taft,S.&H.]
Russo, William F., (AV) ....'55 '79 C&L.150 B.A., J.D. [Katz,T.B.&H.]
Rust, Mary L., (AV) .... '62 '87 C.473 B.S. L.150 J.D. [🄰 Taft,S.&H.]
Rust, Richard S., IV, (BV) .... '49 '74 C.276 A.B. L.150 J.D. Cinci. Metro Hous. Auth.
Rust, Richd. S., Jr. .... '18 '46 C.150 A.B. L.1340 LL.B. 7925 Graves Rd.
Ruttle, Timothy M. '55 '80 C.151 B.S. L.1340 J.D.
Administrative Trial Attorney, Nationwide Mutual Insurance Company
Ruwe, Bradley N. ....'70 '97 C.973 B.S.B.A. L.151 J.D. [Peck,S.&W.]
Ruwe, Joseph M. .... '65 '98 C&L.1161 B.A., J.D. [🄰 Mason,S.&M.]
Ruwe, Katherine A. ....'77 '02 C.201 B.A. L.150 J.D. [🄰 Taft,S.&H.]
Ruwe, Thomas J. ....'54 '83 C.973 B.S. L.1340 J.D. 5710 Wooster Road, Suite 203
Ryan, Carrie W. ....'71 '97 C.383 B.A. L.424 J.D. [🄰 Dinsmore&S.]
Ryan, James J., (AV) '31 '58
C.973 A.B. L.150 LL.B. 10999 Reed Hartman Highway, Suite 204
Ryan, James J., (AV) .... '29 '54 C.973 A.B. L.150 LL.B. [🄲 Taft,S.&H.]
Ryan, James L. ....'32 '57 C&L.215 B.A., LL.B. Sr. U.S. Cir. J.
Ryder, Ely M. T., II, (BV) ....'44 '71 C.473 A.B. L.150 J.D. Asst. City Solr.
Saba, Paul T., (BV) ....'68 '94 C.1208 B.A. L.851 J.D. 2623 Erie Ave.
Sachs, Lee H. .... '24 '55 C.150 Ch.E. L.1340 LL.B. 15 Muirfield Lane‡
Sack, Tamara S. ....'64 '99 C.800 B.A. L.150 J.D. Co. Pros. Off.
Sackenheim, Alison N. .... '78 '03 C.473 B.S. L.150 J.D. [🄰 Dinsmore&S.]
Sacks, Steven L. ....'— '03 C.347 B.A. L.1161 J.D. [🄰 Lerner,S.&R.]
Saelinger, Gina M., (BV) ....'69 '93 C.973 B.S. L.150 J.D, [🄲 Ulmer&B.]
Saelinger, Robert R., (AV) ....'57 '80 C.973 B.A. L.383 J.D. [Graydon H.&R.] ⊙
Safier, Kristen L. .... '77 '01 C.473 B.A. L.150 J.D. [🄰 Taft,S.&H.]
Sager, Stephen M. ....'72 '97 C.473 B.S. L.1340 J.D. [🄰 Robbins,K.P.&T.]
Sahlfeld, Linden C. ....'22 '53 C.973 B.S.C. L.1340 LL.B. 6230 Nuevelle Lane‡
St. Clair, Leslie .... '56 '81 C.381 B.A. L.424 J.D. 4785 Rumpke Rd.
Salinas, Vincent A., (BV) ....'48 '74 C.973 B.S.B.A. L.1340 J.D. 100 Merchant St.
Salinger, Ann J. .... '51 '82 C.103 B.A. L.150 J.D. Ref., Domestic Relations Ct.
Sallee, Jerry S., (AV) ....'54 '80 C.150 B.B.A. L.117 J.D. [Dinsmore&S.]
Sallee, Joseph (Jay) L., Jr., (AV) ....'55 '85 C.383 B.S. L.1340 J.D. [Dinsmore&S.]
Salmon, James L., (CVⓉ) ....'67 '94 C.845 B.A. L.150 J.D. [🄰 Ulmer&B.]
Salyer, Mary M. ....'51 '96 C.383 B.S. L.1161 J.D. 226 Fort Mitchell Ave.
Sambrook, Michael J. '78 '03 C&L.201 B.Ch.E., J.D.
Corp. Coun., The Procter & Gamble Co., P&G Beauty (Pat.)
Sampang, Jocelyn M. ....'68 '94 C.424 B.A. L.151 J.D. Asst. Pros.
Sampson, Kirk, (AV) ....'50 '75 C.473 B.A. L.150 J.D. [Lerner,S.&R.]
Sanders, M. Bradford, (AV) .... '54 '85 C.385 B.A. L.910 J.D. [Sanders&Assoc.]

Sanders & Associates, LPA, (AV)
9122 Montgomery Road, Suite 201, 45242
Telephone: 513-891-8900 Fax: 513-891-8937
Email: lawfirm@sandersassociates.net URL: http://www.sandersassociates.net
M. Bradford Sanders;—Thomas C. James, Jr.; Katherine S. Carmody.
General Civil and Trial Practice in all Courts. National Litigation Practice, Commercial Disputes, Insurance Coverage, Crop Insurance and Personal Injury.

See Professional Biographies, CINCINNATI, OHIO

Sanders Law Firm, The
(See Covington, Kentucky)

Sanker, Mary F. .... '52 '85 C.150 B.A. L.1340 J.D. 3190 Portsmouth Ave.
Sanker, Robert G., (AV) ....'62 '86 C.973 B.A. L.276 J.D. [Keating M.&K.]
Sanks, Julius F., (BV) .... '25 '82 C.151 B.S.C. L.1340 J.D. 30 East Central Parkway
Sansalone, Antonio M. ....'60 '87 C&L.150 B.A., J.D. 1008 Marshall Ave.
Sansone, A. J. ....'10 '40 C.150 A.B. L.1340 J.D. 2134 Madison Rd.
Santangelo, Scott Michael .... '60 '86 C.207 B.A. L.607 J.D. 3322 Erie Avenue
Santen, Edward E. '61 '88 C.170 B.A. L.150 J.D.
Legal Aid Society of Greater Cincinnati
Santen, William E., (AV) ....'28 '55 C.276 B.S. L.150 LL.B. [Santen&H.]
Santen, William E., Jr., (AV) ....'55 '84 C.150 B.A. L.1187 J.D. [Santen&H.]

Santen & Hughes, A Legal Professional Association, (AV)
Suite 3100, 312 Walnut Street, 45202
Telephone: 513-721-4450 Fax: 513-721-0109
URL: http://www.santen-hughes.com
William E. Santen; Charles M. Meyer; Charles E. Reynolds; John D. Holschuh, Jr.; James P. Wersching; C. Gregory Schmidt; William E. Santen, Jr.; William A. DeCenso; Sarah Tankersley;—Fanon A. Rucker; Deepak K. Desai; William J. Liss; J. Robert Linneman; Andrew Weisenberger.

See Professional Biographies, CINCINNATI, OHIO

Sapinsley, Thomas S., (BV) ....'55 '82 C.347 B.A. L.150 J.D. [Statman,H.S.&E.]
Sarra, Martha Cutright '63 '88
C.608 B.S.B.A. L.150 J.D. Sr. Coun. & Asst. Secy., The Kroger Co.
Sauers, Mark E. ....'51 '76 C.112 B.A. L.426 J.D. Co. Pros.
Sauter, Susan Marie .... '66 '91 C.608 B.A. L.150 J.D. [🄰 R.A.Klingler]
Sawyer, Edward, (BV) ....'29 '59 C&L.150 B.A., LL.B. 61 Wm. H. Taft Rd.
Saxton, Jonathan P., (AV) ....'64 '89 C.493 B.S. L.150 J.D. [Rendigs,F.K.&D.]
Sayre, Russell S., (AV) .... '64 '90 C.890 B.A. L.893 J.D. [Taft,S.&H.]
Scacchetti, David J., (BV) ....'56 '82 C&L.150 B.A., J.D. 601 Main St.
Scacchetti, Marcia G., (BV) ....'59 '83 C.608 B.A. L.150 J.D. 1009 Paradrome St.
Scahill, John P. .... '27 '52 C&L.150 B.A., J.D. 830 Main Street, Suite 1115
Scandy, Kelly Carbetta, (BV) ....'60 '86 C.97 B.A. L.150 J.D. [Montgomery,R.&J.]
Scanlon, John C. ....'19 '48 C.999 A.B. L.150 LL.B. 5662 Rapid Run Rd.
Schad, Brian ....'72 '98 C.608 B.A. L.989 J.D. [🄲 Schad&C.]
Schad, Kevin M. ....'68 '93 C.608 B.A. L.150 J.D. [Schad&C.]
Schad & Cook .... 8240 Beckett Park Drive
Schaefer, Christian J., (BV) ....'51 '76 C&L.150 B.A., J.D. Asst. Pros. Atty.
Schaefer, James J., (BV) ....'63 '89 C.973 A.B. L.150 J.D. Asst. Pros. Atty.
Schaefer, James R. ....'62 '92 C.608 B.A. L.117 J.D. [Drew&W.]
Schaefer, Jeffrey R., (AV) .... '55 '93 C.165 A.B. L.1340 J.D. [🄰 Ulmer&B.]
Schaefer, Kimberly J. .... '73 '98 C.473 B.S. L.228 J.D. [🄰 Vorys,S.S.&P.]
Schaefer, Laura Arline .... '65 '90 C.973 B.A. L.421 J.D. I.R.S.
Schaengold, Sol ....'48 '79 C.150 B.S. L.1340 J.D. Providence Hosp.
Schaeperklaus, Rae Ellen ...... '55 '80 C.1161 B.S. L.608 J.D. 3412 Fiddler's Green Road
Schafstall, Richard D. '42 '73 C.679 B.S. L.1340 J.D.
(adm. in KY; not adm. in OH) Sr. Coun., Cinergy Servs.
Schalnat, Ria Farrell ....'71 '99 C.1161 B.S. L.201 J.D. [🄰 Frost B.T.] (See Pat. Sect.)
Scharff, Daniel W. .... '59 '91 C.1161 B.S. L.1340 J.D. [🄲 Porter W.M.&A.]
Schatz, Brett A. ....'72 '00 C.150 B.S.M.E. L.1340 J.D [🄰 Wood,H.&E.]
Scheier, Michael L., (AV) ....'60 '91 C.319 B.A. L.150 J.D. [Keating M.&K.]
Schenck, Donald A., (BV) .... '35 '62 C.608 B.S. L.150 J.D. 2829 Whitehouse Ln
Schenk, John G., (AV) .... '26 '51 C.608 B.C.E. L.607 J.D. [Kinney&S.]
Schenk, Mary Ann, (AV) ....'51 '76 C.999 B.A. L.1340 J.D. [🄲 Frost B.T.]
Schenkel, Timothy B. ....'66 '92 C.201 B.S. L.1340 J.D. [Freund,F.&A.]
Scheper, James H., (AV) .... '42 '68 C.973 B.S. L.1340 J.D. [🄰 Shea&Assoc.] ‡
Scheper, Norbert J., (BV) .... '41 '74 C.973 B.S.B.A. L.1340 J.D. 100 Merchant Street
Scherer, Gordon M., (BV) .... '38 '66 C.150 B.A. L.1340 J.D. 5761 Sidney Rd.
Scheve, Thomas J., (BV) .... '50 '78 C.973 B.A. L.1161 J.D. Asst. Pros. Atty.
Schiff, Elizabeth York, (BV) ....'59 '86 C&L.228 B.A., J.D. 2 Forest Hill Dr.
Schilling, Richard D., (BV) .... '52 '77 C.675 B.A. L.150 J.D. [Mason,S.&M.]
Schilling, Ronald D., (BV) ....'52 '77 C.675 B.A. L.150 J.D. 602 Main St.
Schimanski, James R. .... '64 '91 C.912 B.A. L.150 J.D. 7 W. 7th St.
Schimpf, Jerome L., (BV) .... '31 '66 3861 Mt. Carmel Rd.
Schimpf, Richard J., (AV) ....'40 '67 C.602 B.A. L.1340 J.D. [Butkovich,S.S.&G.]
Schirmer, Albert W., (BV) ....'23 '57 C.973 B.S.C. L.1340 J.D. 607 2nd Nat. Bldg.
Schisler, H. Toby ....'72 '97 C.473 B.A. L.150 J.D. [🄰 Dinsmore&S.]
Schlemmer, Arthur H., (BV) ....'50 '76 C.347 B.A. L.1340 J.D. [Barron,P.B.&S.]
Schloemer, Jeffrey S., (AV) ....'58 '83 C.602 A.B. L.228 J.D. [Taft,S.&H.]
Schloneger, Mark R. ....'70 '96 C.288 B.A. L.150 J.D. U.S. Dept. of Labor
Schloss, Stuart A., Jr., (AV) ....'47 '72 C.174 B.A. L.477 J.D. [Ulmer&B.]
Schlosser, R. Jeffrey, (AV) ....'57 '83 C.138 B.A. L.1340 J.D. [Porter W.M.&A.]
Schlotman, James T. ......'53 '78 C&L.150 B.B.A., J.D. 3481 Central Parkway, Suite 100
Schlueter, Daniel Jeffrey, (BV) ....'48 '74 C.150 B.A. L.1340 J.D. Legal Affs. Admr.
Schlueter, Michael H. .... '77 '03 C.363 B.S.B.A. L.285 J.D. [🄰 Lerner,S.&R.]
Schmaltz, Kimberly A. .... '60 '99 C.523 B.A. L.1340 J.D. [🄰 Statman,H.S.&E.]
Schmalzl, Mary W., (BVⓉ) .... '59 '84 C.383 B.S. L.893 J.D. 1900 5th 3rd Ctr.
Schmalzl, Richard G., (AV) .... '56 '82 C.665 B.S. L.893 J.D. [Graydon H.&R.]
Schmerber, Donald E. .... '43 '74 C.150 B.B.A. L.1340 J.D. 1043 Hickok Lane
Schmid, Peter A. .... '73 '04 C.945 B.S. L.1340 J.D. [🄰 Deters,B.&L.]
Schmidt, C. Gregory, (BV) .... '55 '80 C.150 B.B.A. L.201 J.D. [Santen&H.]
Schmidt, C. J., III, (AV) ....'57 '83 C&L.150 B.S., J.D. [Wood&L.]
Schmidt, Dale G., (BV) ....'31 '65 C.151 B.S. L.1340 J.D. 1071 Celestial St.

Schmidt, Jerome C. .... '49 '73 C&L.150 B.A., J.D. V.P., The Union Central Life Ins. Co.
Schmidt, John J. ....'60 '92 C.973 B.A. L.150 J.D. [Dinsmore&S.]
Schmidt, Michael C. .... '72 '01 C.383 B.A. L.1340 J.D. [A Ulmer&B.]
Schmidt, Michael R., (AV) .... '51 '81 C.973 B.A. L.151 J.D. [Cohen,T.K.&S.]
Schmit, David E., (AV) '47 '75 C.150 B.S.E.E. L.1340 J.D. [Frost B.T.] (See Pat. Sect.)
Schmitt, David J. .... '62 '91 C.434 B.S. L.150 J.D. [Cors&B.]
Schnapp, Karlyn A., Ph.D ....'62 '00 C.150 B.S. L.1340 J.D. [A Frost B.T.]
Schneider, Benjamin A. ....'71 '00 C.473 B.A. L.1340 J.D. [A Keating M.&K.]
Schneider, Donald Edward, (BV) '49 '75 C.734 B.A. L.608 J.D. 1101 St. Gregory Street, Suite 350
Schneider, Hallie L. ....'78 '03 C.973 H.A.B. L.150 J.D. [A Schwartz,M.&R.]
Schneider, Harry Roy Stein .... '55 '80 C.608 B.S.B.A. L.8 J.D. Hills Developers, Inc.
Schneider, Kenneth J., (AV) .... '37 '66 C.973 B.S. L.1340 J.D. [Wood&L.]
Schneider, Louis C. ....'76 '03 C.473 B.S.B.A. L.150 J.D. [A Kohnen&P.]
Schneider, Richard J., (CV) ....'50 '77 C.1160 B.A. L.1340 J.D. Asst. Pros.
Schneider, Robert L. ....'37 '64 C.150 B.A. L.1340 J.D. 2324 Madison Rd.
Schneider, Theodore J., (BV) ...... '57 '92 C.1118 B.A. L.1340 J.D. [Murdock G.S.&G.]
Schneiderman, Diane, (AV) ....'47 '72 C.188 B.A. L.976 J.D. [G Strauss&T.]
Schober, George P. ....'49 '86 C.309 B.A. L.477 J.D. 344 Warren Avenue
Schoeni, K. Roger, (AV) ....'55 '82 C.97 B.S. L.494 J.D. [Kohnen&P.]
Schoeny, James D. ....'77 '03 C.424 B.A. L.150 J.D. [A Frost B.T.]
Schoettmer, Sara A. ....'— '82 C.150 B.A. L.851 J.D. Juv. Ct.
Schold, John D. ....'67 '92 C.502 B.A. L.910 J.D. Sr. Coun., Cognis Corp.
Scholer, Douglas A. ....'71 '00 C.602 B.S.E.E. L.1161 J.D. [A Wood,H.&E.]
Scholl, Lawrence E. ....'38 '64 C.473 A.B. L.145 J.D. P.O. Box 1460
Scholles, James R. ....'36 '77 C.608 B.S. L.930 J.D. [Scholles&S.]
Scholles, Jeffrey J. ....'61 '86 C.269 B.A. L.150 J.D. [Scholles&S.]
Scholles & Scholles .... 8970 Winton Rd.
Schooley, Ann K. ....'71 '99 C.150 B.B.A. L.347 J.D. [A Graydon H.&R.]
Schott, Donald L. ....'36 '67 C.150 B.A. L.1340 J.D. Ret. Com. Pleas J.
Schott Ferguson, Amy, (BV) .... '68 '92 C.150 B.S. L.930 J.D. [Cuni,F.&L.]

Schottenstein Zox & Dunn Co., LPA, (AV)
Bank One Towers, 8044 Montgomery Road, Suite 630, 45236-2926 ⊙
Telephone: 513-792-0792 Fax: 513-792-0803
Email: info@szd.com URL: http://www.szd.com
Marcia J. Myers.
Business (Corporate, Banking and Lending, Real Estate/Land Use, General Tax, State and Local Tax, Employee Benefits, Estate Planning, White Collar Crime, E-Commerce, Intellectual Property/Technology Protection, International); Labor and Employment Law, Litigation, Health Law, Construction Law, Bankruptcy Law, Environmental Law, Debtor/Creditor Rights, Workers' Compensation, Municipal Law, Government Affairs.
Columbus, Ohio Office: 250 West Street, 43215-2538. Telephone: 614-462-2700. Telecopier: 614-462-5135. Telex: 650 24 444 365.
Cleveland, Ohio Office: USBank Centre, 1350 Euclid Avenue, Suite 1400, 44115. Telephone: 216-621-6501. Fax: 216-621-6502.
See Professional Biographies, CINCINNATI, OHIO

Schreiber, Steven H., (AV) ....'48 '81 C&L.608 B.A., J.D. [Dinsmore&S.]
Schreiner, Joanne M., (AV) ....'54 '79 C.8 B.A. L.145 J.D. [Dinsmore&S.]
Schrider, John E. ....'49 '74 C.884 B.A. L.659 J.D. Legal Aid Soc.
Schroeder, William P., (AV) ......'42 '68 C.150 B.S. L.1340 J.D. [G Schroeder,M.B.&P.]

Schroeder, Maundrell, Barbiere & Powers, (AV)
11935 Mason Road, Suite 110, 45249
Telephone: 513-583-4200 Fax: 513-583-4203
Email: tpowers@smbplaw.com URL: http://www.smbplaw.com
Members of Firm: John W. Hust; Robert S. Hiller; Lawrence E. Barbiere; Todd M. Powers; Christopher L. Moore. Associates: Jay D. Patton; Derek W. Scranton; Megan C. Ahrens. Of Counsel: William P. Schroeder; Michael E. Maundrell.
Litigation.
See Professional Biographies, CINCINNATI, OHIO

Schroer, Charles E. ....'54 '79 C.276 A.B. L.734 J.D. [Frost B.T.]
Schrotel, Betty F. ....'26 '49 C.150 L.1340 J.D. 621 Mehring Way‡
Schrotel, Stanley R. ....'14 '50 C.150 L.1340 621 Mehring Way
Schuch, Paul W., (BV) '28 '53 C.207 B.A. L.150 LL.B. Provident Bank Building, Suite 1000
Schuck, Thomas R., (AV) ....'50 '76 C.210 B.A. L.309 J.D. [Taft,S.&H.]
Schuh, Arthur J., (BV) ....'25 '52 C.973 A.B. L.1340 LL.B. 2662 Madison Rd.
Schuh, John A., (AV) ....'51 '77 C.610 B.B.A. L.1340 J.D. [Schuh&G.]
Schuh, Stephen J., (AV) ....'52 '78 C.610 B.B.A. L.1340 J.D. [Schuh&G.]
Schuh & Goldberg, LLP, (AV) ....2662 Madison Road
Schulcz, Mary C. Torbeck ....'62 '87 C.201 B.A. L.851 J.D. Juv. Ct. Mag.
Schulman, Alan, (BV) ....'46 '72 C.966 B.A. L.477 J.D. 206 Hill Top Lane
Schulte, Deborah C. ....'57 '94 C.1161 B.A. L.150 J.D. 22 W. 9th St.
Schulte, Karen Louise, (BV) ....'50 '77 C.1038 B.A. L.1340 J.D. 426 Crestline Ave.
Schultz, John F. ....'49 '75 C.973 B.S.B.A. L.1340 J.D. Sr. V.P., Marsh, Inc.
Schultz, Susan E. ....'62 '99 C.249 B.A. L.1340 J.D. [Creative]
Schumacher, Thomas G. ....'43 '68 C&L.150 B.B.A., J.D. Sr. Auditor I.R.S.
Schumacher, William R., (BV) ....'25 '52 C.151 L.1340 LL.B. 5050 Kugler Mill Rd.
Schutte, Michael J. ....'68 '94 C.150 B.A. L.201 J.D. [A Beirne&W.]
Schwallie, David F. ...... '60 '84 C.201 B.S. L.150 J.D. Asst. Sr.V.P., Univ. of Cincinnati
Schwartz, Harry S., (BV) ....'12 '37 C.150 L.1340 J.D. 3542 Amberacres Dr.
Schwartz, Howard M., (AV) ....'48 '75 C.150 B.S.E.E. L.1340 J.D. [Sirkin P.&S.]
Schwartz, Jos. X., (BV) ....'11 '37 L.608 LL.B. 216 E. 9th St., 2nd Fl.
Schwartz, Michael G. ....'66 '92 C.659 B.S. L.150 J.D. [G Vorys,S.S.&P.]
Schwartz, Michael S., (BV) ....'44 '71 C.608 B.S. L.1340 J.D. [Schwartz&S.]
Schwartz, Richard M., (AV) ....'36 '62 C.994 B.S. L.94 LL.B. [Schwartz,M.&R.]
Schwartz, Robert L., (BV) ....'40 '66 C.608 B.A. L.1340 J.D. [Schwartz&S.]

Schwartz, Manes & Ruby, A Legal Professional Association, (AV)
2900 Carew Tower, 441 Vine Street, 45202-3090
Telephone: 513-579-1414 Telecopier: 513-579-1418
URL: http://www.smrfirm.com
Richard M. Schwartz; Stanley L. Ruby; Scott M. Slovin; Donald B. Hordes; William S. Wyler; James K. Keller. Associates: Ralph J. Conrad; Hallie L. Schneider. Of Counsel: Dennis L. Manes; Herbert Bass; Orly R. Rumberg.
Administrative Law, Business Planning, Civil Trial Practice, Taxation, Estate Planning, Employee Benefits, Real Estate, Intellectual Property, Mergers and Acquisitions, Probate, Securities, Personal Injury, Retirement Planning, Labor, Employment, Family Law, Information Technology, Copyright, Trademark, Corporate Partnerships, Trusts, Government Contracts, Health Care Law.
See Professional Biographies, CINCINNATI, OHIO

Schwartz & Schwartz, (BV) .... 906 Main St. (⊙Matawan, NJ)
Schwarz, Paul E. ....'64 '92 C.150 B.A. L.1340 J.D. U.S. Bank‡
Schwegman, Russell J. ....'54 '79 C.976 B.A. L.150 J.D. Dept. of Admn. Servs.
Schweiger, Scott M., (BV) '56 '83 C.150 B.A. L.201 J.D. 11085 Montgomery Road, Suite 202
Schweikert, Mark R. ....'52 '80 C.608 B.A. L.1161 J.D. Com. Pleas J.
Schweller, Stephen G. ....'59 '84 C.207 B.A. L.902 J.D. [Dinsmore&S.]
Schwierling, John T., (BV) ....'33 '57 C.973 B.S.B.A. L.276 LL.B. [Ritter&R.]
Schworer, Philip J., (AV) ....'55 '86 C.150 B.S. L.1161 J.D. [Greenebaum D.&M.]
Scoggins, Samuel M., (AV) ....'50 '75 C.207 B.A. L.893 J.D. [Frost B.T.]
Scott, Alexis Z. .... '57 '86 C.424 B.A. L.734 J.D. 11915 Kemper Springs Dr.
Scott, Bratton E. .... '71 '97 C.607 L.150 J.D. 11331 Grooms Rd.
Scott, Jamie D., (AV) ....'56 '83 C.150 B.B.A. L.101 J.D. [Graydon H.&R.]
Scott, John C., (AV) ....'60 '85 C.973 A.B. L.150 J.D. [Faulkner&T.]
Scranton, Derek W. ....'70 '02 C.610 B.A. L.150 J.D. [A Schroeder,M.B.&P.]
Scrivens, Kathleen M. ....'56 '88 C.608 B.S.N. L.150 J.D. Univ. of Cincinnati
Scrofano, Sal G., (BV) .... '48 '74 C&L.150 B.A., J.D. P.O. Box 62860
Seaton, Kim D. ....'64 '97 C.97 B.S. L.597 J.D. [A Squire,S.&D.]
Sebastian, Steven W. ....'69 '00 C.383 B.S. L.477 J.D. [A Keating M.&K.]
Secrest, Thomas Anthony ....'68 '94 C.188 B.S. L.201 J.D. 705 Central Ave., Ste. 500
Sefton, W. Jeffrey ....'70 '02 C.608 B.A. L.117 J.D. [A Keating M.&K.]
Segal, Andrew Lawrence .... '67 '98 C.608 B.A. L.1187 J.D. 120 E. 4th St., Ste. 1040
Segal, Kenneth C. ....'36 '64 C.608 B.S. L.1340 J.D. 1433 E. McMillan
Seibel, Kenneth F., (AV) ......'44 '69 C.973 B.S. L.150 J.D. 1014 Vine Street, Suite 2300
Seibel, Scott K. ....'73 '98 C.973 B.S. L.117 J.D. 1014 Vine Street, Suite 2300
Seiler, Stacie A., (BV) ....'60 '85 C.473 B.A. L.150 J.D. 312 Walnut St.
Seitz, K. G. .... '14 '50 C.659 B.S. L.1340 LL.B. 4321 Hamilton Ave.‡
Seitz, William J., III, (AV) ....'54 '78 C&L.150 B.A., J.D. [Taft,S.&H.]
Selak, Robert A., (AV) ....'54 '79 C.1115 B.S. L.309 J.D. [Thompson H.]
Selden, Heidi A. ....'70 '96 C.201 B.A. L.1243 J.D. [A Cohen,T.K.&S.]
Self, Janet A., (AV) ....'54 '88 C&L.150 B.A., J.D. [Montgomery,R.&J.]
Sellers, John P., III ....'55 '82 C.10 B.A. L.150 J.D. [A Dinsmore&S.]
Sellins, W. John, (BV) ....'48 '76 C.347 A.B. L.1340 J.D. [Droder&M.]
Sennett, William L., III '64 '88 C.631 B.A. L.608 J.D. Division Counsel, Cincinnati Machine
Serena, Terry, (BV) ....'49 '78 C.150 B.A. L.930 J.D. I.R.S.
Setterberg, Richard A., (BV) ....'47 '78 C&L.188 A.B., J.D. [R.A.Setterberg]
Setterberg, Richard A., Co., L.P.A., A Legal Prof. Assn., (BV) ....9872 Fawnrun Ct.
Settles, Brian S. ....'79 '04 C.473 B.S. L.383 J.D. [A Taft,S.&H.]
Shadley, Frederic X., (AV) ....'55 '81 C&L.602 B.S.E.E., J.D. [Ulmer&B.]
Shafer, Cynthia A. ....'60 '86 C.97 B.S. L.150 J.D. [G Vorys,S.S.&P.]
Shafer, Jeffrey A. .... '70 '96 C.1288 B.A. L.1339 J.D. 11175 Reading Rd., Ste. 103
Shaffer, Elizabeth ....'78 '03 C.138 B.A. L.150 J.D. [A Roetzel&A.]
Shaffer, Robert M.M. ....'68 '96 C.976 B.A. L.150 J.D. [A Vorys,S.S.&P.]
Shank, Robert D. ....'71 '96 C.973 B.A. L.880 J.D. [Frost B.T.]
Shanley, Sharon I. ....'61 '99 C&L.280 A.B., J.D. [A Taft,S.&H.]
Shanov, Diana V. ....'78 '04 C.974 B.S.B.A. L.150 J.D. [A Lerner,S.&R.]
Shapiro, Joshua A. ....'72 '99 C.150 B.A. L.1119 J.D. [A Taft,S.&H.]
Shartzer, Sharon M. J. ....'74 '04 C.835 B.A. L.1161 J.D. [A Ebner&R.]
Shaver, Thomas R. '34 '60 C.473 B.A. L.813 J.D. (adm. in IL; not adm. in OH) Recotr, All Saints Episcopal Church‡
Shaw, Gene R. ... '47 '75 C.150 B.S.I.M. L.1340 J.D. 7164 Beechmont Avenue, Suite 101
Shaw, Stephen K., (AV) ....'54 '79 C.970 B.A. L.150 J.D. 6476 Old Barn Ct.
Shea, Jane Hils, (AV) ....'53 '79 C.1024 B.A. L.150 J.D. [G Frost B.T.]
Shea, Joseph W., III, (AV) ....'47 '74 C.150 B.A. L.1340 J.D. [Shea&Assoc.]
Shea, Kevin M., (AV) '53 '79 C.363 A.B. L.150 J.D. V.P. & Sr. Corp. Coun., Provident Financial Group, Inc.

Shea & Associates, (AV) BR
444 Chiquita Center, 250 E. Fifth Street, 45202-4119
Telephone: 513-621-8333 Telecopier: 513-651-3272 Email: jshea@shea-associates.com Email: scoffey@shea-associates.com Email: jscheper@shea-associates.com
URL: http://www.shea-associates.com
Joseph W. Shea III. Associates: Shirley A. Coffey; James H. Scheper.
Civil Litigation, Catastrophic Personal Injury, Negligence Law, Medical Malpractice and Products Liability.
See Professional Biographies, CINCINNATI, OHIO

Shearer, David A., Jr., (CV) .... '68 '93 C.880 B.A. L.383 J.D. [Freund,F.&A.]
Sheeran, Thomas M. .... '24 '51 C.973 B.S. in B.A. L.150 J.D. 5781 Pandora Ave.
Sheffield, Wm. T., (BV) ....'20 '48 C.473 B.S. L.150 LL.B. 245 Ritchie Ave.
Sheldon, Henry E., (BV) ....'36 '63 C.894 A.B. L.150 J.D. 1618 Sycamore St.
Sheline, Miriam Hirsch, (BV) .... '61 '84 C.879 B.A. L.1340 J.D. Pro Seniors, Inc.
Shepardson, W. Philip, Jr., (AV) ....'45 '71 C&L.150 B.A., J.D. [Beckman W.S.]
Shepherd, Jason Wesley '65 '00 C.885 B.A. L.1161 J.D. (adm. in KY; not adm. in OH) Internal Rev. Serv.
Sheridan, Jacqueline R. ....'77 '03 C.679 B.A. L.602 J.D. [A Ulmer&B.]
Sheriff-MacDonald, Dee, (BV) .... '43 '84 C.1161 B.A. L.1340 J.D. [Freund,F.&A.]
Sherman, Adam C. ....'— '02 C.477 B.A. L.569 J.D. [A Vorys,S.S.&P.]
Sherman, Jack, Jr. ....'37 '69 C.608 B.Sc. L.1340 J.D. Ret. Mag.
Sherman, Thomas J., (AV) ....'44 '69 C&L.150 B.A., J.D. [Dinsmore&S.]
Sherman, William A., II, (AV) ....'60 '87 C.512 B.A. L.446 J.D. [Dinsmore&S.]
Sherman, William D. ....'68 '94 C.602 B.A. L.150 J.D. [Robbins,K.P.&T.]
Sherwood, Elizabeth P., (AV) ....'58 '87 C.143 B.S. L.150 J.D. [Montgomery,R.&J.]
Shick, Daniel S. '55 '83 C.974 A.B. L.150 J.D. 2nd V.P. & Couns., The Union Central Life Ins. Co.
Shipp, Jeffrey C., (BV) ....'59 '85 C.1161 B.A. L.1340 J.D. [Kohnen&P.]
Shoemaker, Kent A. ....'61 '92 C.473 B.A. L.228 J.D. Coun., GE Energy
Shook, Susan M. '68 '97 C.679 B.A/.B.S. L.347 J.D. Sr. Coun., Procter & Gamble Co., The
Shore, Carol L. '51 '80 C.446 B.A. L.273 J.D. (adm. in DC; not adm. in OH) Nat. Labor Rel. Bd.
Shore, John E. ....'37 '62 C.164 B.A. L.597 J.D. 10875 Indeco Dr.
Shoskin, Jeffrey S., (AV) ....'58 '83 C.294 B.A. L.831 J.D. [Roetzel&A.]
Shott, Andrew M., (AV) ....'55 '81 C&L.893 B.A., J.D. [Strauss&T.]
Shotten, Melvin S., (AV) ....'43 '68 C&L.477 B.S., J.D. [Taft,S.&H.]
Shuetts, Howard P., (BV) .... '18 '43 C&L.150 B.B.A., LL.B. 9933 Forestglen Dr
Shuler, Gary R., Jr. ....'72 '98 C.1019 B.A. L.7 J.D. Dist. Coun., I.R.S.
Shuler, Matthew D. ....'72 '98 C.608 B.S.B.A. L.1003 J.D. [A Dinsmore&S.]
Shuller, Donald J., (AV) ....'51 '76 C&L.893 B.S., J.D. [Vorys,S.S.&P.]
Siebold & Hammelrath Co., L.P.A., (BV) ....432 Walnut Street, Suite 850
Siegel, Christopher J. ....'69 '98 C.473 B.A. L.851 J.D. [A Lerner,S.&R.]
Siegel, Richard D., (AV) ....'44 '71 C&L.383 B.S., J.D. [Keating M.&K.]
Siegel, Robert H., (BV) ....'45 '75 C.150 B.A. L.1340 J.D. [Statman,H.S.&E.]
Siegel, Steve N. ....'50 '97 C.207 B.A. L.117 J.D. [A Dinsmore&S.]
Siegesmund, Jean D. ....'60 '85 C.207 B.A. L.597 J.D. 2900 Timberview Dr.
Siehl, Jeffrey D. ....'72 '98 C.473 B.A. L.608 J.D. [A Squire,S.&D.]
Siembieda, Matthew J., (AV Ⓣ) '45 '70 C.116 B.A. L.659 J.D. (adm. in PA; not adm. in OH) [Blank R.] (⊙Phila., PA)
Sieve, James E., (BV) ....'38 '64 C.276 B.A. L.150 J.D. P.O. Box 11076
Sigalov, Vlad, Law Offices of '71 '99 C.800 B.A. L.1187 J.D. 7374 Reading Road, Suite 121
Sigman, Gloria J., (BV) ....'— '90 C.1269 B.A. L.796 J.D. 3233 Cooper Road
Silbersack, Mark L., (AV) ....'46 '71 C.93 A.B. L.145 J.D. [Dinsmore&S.]

Siler, Eugene E., Jr. ... '36 '63 C.880 B.A. L.893 LL.B. Sr. U.S. Ct. App. J.
Silver, Susan M. ... '54 '81 C&L.150 B.F.A., J.D. Dir. of Admn., Co. Auditor's Off.

Silverman, Beth, (AV) '57 '84 C.473 B.S. L.150 J.D.
Suite 920, 30 Garfield Place, 45202
Telephone: 513-241-9844 FAX: 513-241-9908
Email: attybeth@aol.com URL: http://www.bethsilverman.com
Domestic Relations, Divorce, Custody, and Juvenile Law.

See Professional Biographies, CINCINNATI, OHIO

Silvers, Jane Fink, (AV) ... '61 '86 C.608 B.S.B.A. L.150 J.D. [J.F.Silvers]

Silvers, Jane Fink, Co., Ltd., (AV)
Suite 400-A, 1080 Nimitzview, 45230
Telephone: 513-624-6720 Fax: 513-624-6720
Email: jsilvers@silvers-law.com URL: http://www.lawyers.com/janefinksilvers
Jane Fink Silvers.
Business Estate Planning, Estate Planning, Business Transactions, Probate, Business Successions, Professional Practices, Limited Liability Company Law, Small Business Law, Family Limited Partnerships, Tax Law, Estate Administration, Trust Administration.

See Professional Biographies, CINCINNATI, OHIO

Simler, Francis L. ... '09 '51 C.347 A.B. L.151 J.D. 3914 Miami Rd.
Simmonds, Rasheed A. ... '68 '97 C.976 B.A. L.150 J.D. [Furnier&T.]
Simmons, Gerald W., (AV) ... '43 '67 C.276 A.B. L.976 LL.B. [Thompson H.]
Simon, Harlan '57 '86 C.170 B.A. L.569 J.D.
(adm. in CA; not adm. in OH) [Hammond]
Simon, Stephen A. ... '68 '97 C.477 B.A. L.150 J.D. [🄰 D.M.Cook]
Simpson, Yvette R. ... '78 '04 C.473 B.A. L.150 J.D. [🄰 Frost B.T.]
Sims, Jason B. ... '65 '94 C.1208 B.S. L.150 J.D. [Dinsmore&S.]
Sims, Jud B. ... '71 '99 C.473 B.S. L.930 J.D. [🄰 Frost B.T.]
Sims, Mark E., (AV) ... '55 '80 C&L.150 B.B.A., J.D. [Graydon H.&R.]
Singer, Pete S. ... '77 '03 C.473 B.A. L.201 J.D. [🄰 Dinsmore&S.]
Singer, William B., (AV) ... '42 '67 C.276 B.A. L.228 LL.B. [W.B.Singer]
Singer, William B., AAL, (AV) ... 621 E. Mehring Way, Apt. 1609
Sirkin, Alan L., (BV) ... '39 '70 C.150 B.A. L.273 J.D. 8075 Reading Road, Suite 400
Sirkin, H. Louis, (AV) ... '40 '65 C&L.150 A.B., J.D. [Sirkin P.&S.]

Sirkin Pinales & Schwartz LLP, (AV) BR
920 Fourth & Race Tower, 105 West Fourth Street, 45202-2726
Telephone: 513-721-4876 Telecopier: 513-721-0876
Email: hschwartz@sirkinpinales.com URL: http://www.sirkinpinales.com
Members of Firm: H. Louis Sirkin; Martin S. Pinales; Howard M. Schwartz; Laura A. Abrams. Associates: John P. Feldmeier; Jennifer M. Kinsley; Candace C. Crouse.
Criminal Law, First Amendment Law, Constitutional Law, Wills and Probate, Trusts and Estates, Township Law, Municipal Law, Appellate Practice, White Collar Criminal Defense, Trials and Appeals in all State and Federal Courts, Corporate Law, Business Law, Personal Injury, Civil Rights.
Reference: The Huntington National Bank.

See Professional Biographies, CINCINNATI, OHIO

Sizemore, Gregory Lee ... '57 '92 C.150 B.A. L.1161 J.D. [Sizemore]
Sizemore & Co. ... 4100 Executive Park Dr., Ste. 210
Skavdahl, Duane R., (BV) ... '46 '80 C.491 B.S. L.990 J.D. [Smith,R.&S.]
Skeens, Troy W., Jr., (BV) ... '54 '81 C.150 B.A. L.607 J.D. [🄰 Waite,S.B.&C.]
Skidmore, Charles G., (BV) ... '66 '92 C.210 B.B.A., J.D. [🄰 Lindhorst&D.]
Skidmore, David A., Jr. ... '65 '91 C.228 B.A. L.597 J.D. [Frost B.T.]
Skilken, Lynne, (AV) ... '47 '75 C.860 B.A. L.608 J.D. [Brown]
Skinkiss, Ralph J. '36 '70 C.665 B.S.M.E. L.734 J.D.
Senior Patent Attorney, International Paper Company (Pat.)
Skirvin, Rae ... '36 '60 C&L.608 B.A., J.D. 830 Main Street
Skirvin & Larimer, (BV) ... 830 Main St.
Skoog, Norma ... '50 '75 C&L.724 B.A., J.D. The Future Now, Inc.
Slater, Peter M. ... '65 '92 C.787 B.S. L.930 J.D. [Graydon H.&R.]
Slattery, James J., Jr. ... '47 '71 C.973 B.S. L.150 J.D. 230 E. Ninth St.
Slauson, John G., (AV) ... '40 '66 C&L.608 B.S., J.D. 119 East Court Street
Slocum, Lee R., (BV) ... '52 '78 C.150 B.A. L.1340 J.D. Asst. Pros. Atty.
Slovin, Randy T., (BV) ... '58 '83 C.347 B.A. L.150 J.D. [Slovin&C.] ⊙
Slovin, Scott M., (AV) ... '52 '77 C.347 B.S. L.150 J.D. [Schwartz,M.&R.]
Slovin, Sherri Goren, (AV) ... '54 '79 C&L.150 B.A., J.D. [S.G.Slovin]

Slovin & Cummins Co., LPA, (BV)
9435 Waterstone Boulevard, Suite 270, 45249 ⊙
Telephone: 513-683-9000 Fax: 513-683-9073
Email: sclpa@sclpa.com URL: http://www.attorneysonline.us/sclaw.htm
Randy T. Slovin; John R. Cummins.
Commercial Litigation, Collections, Bankruptcy, Landlord and Tenant Law, Federal Consumer Law, Compliance and Defense, Commercial Litigation, Consumer Litigation.
Crescent Springs, Kentucky Office: 2335 Buttermilk Crossing, Suite 330, 41017. Telephone: 513-683-900. Fax: 513-683-9073.

See Professional Biographies, CINCINNATI, OHIO

Slovin, Sherri Goren, Co., L.P.A., (AV)
30 Garfield Place, Suite 920, 45202-4322
Telephone: 513-241-9844 Fax: 513-241-9908
Email: sgslovin@slovinlaw.com URL: http://www.slovinlaw.com
Sherri Goren Slovin.
Domestic Relations, Collaborative Family Law, Mediation, Parenting and Child Related Issues, Child Support, Spousal Support, Family Law, Divorce, Dissolution, Visitation, Post-Divorce Matters, Collaborative Divorce.
Other Cincinnati Office (Field-Ertel): 9435 Waterstone Boulevard, Suite 270, 45249. Telephone: 513-241-9844.

See Professional Biographies, CINCINNATI, OHIO

Slowik & Robinson, LLC
(See Columbus)

Slutsky, June Clayton, (BV) ... '51 '91 C.608 B.A. L.201 J.D. [Slutsky&S.]
Slutsky, Norman L., (AV) ... '45 '70 C.454 B.A. L.150 J.D. [Slutsky&S.]
Slutsky & Slutsky Co., L.P.A., (AV) ... 4153 Crossgate Ln.
Slutz, Leonard D., (AV) ... '13 '37 C.611 A.B. L.150 LL.B. 105 W. 4th‡
Smart, Jerry D. '35 '65 C.623 B.A. L.802 LL.B.
(adm. in TX; not adm. in OH) Southwestern Ohio Seniors Servs., Inc.
Smith, Anne M., (CVⓉ) '63 '89
C.531 B.S. L.1340 J.D. [🄰 Weltman,W.&R.] (⊙Villa Hills, KY)
Smith, Brad H. '53 '83 C.101 B.A. L.910 J.D.
(adm. in NV; not adm. in OH) Sr. Coun., Fluor Daniel Fernald, Inc.
Smith, D. Shannon, (AV) ... '37 '71 C.602 B.A. L.1340 J.D. 601 Main St.
Smith, Denise M. ... '71 '96 C.421 B.A. L.1161 J.D. [🄰 Ulmer&B.]
Smith, Elliot M. ... '79 '04 C.999 B.T.L. L.446 J.D. [🄰 Squire,S.&D.]
Smith, Fred C. ... '20 '51 C&L.150 J.D. 7701 Moss Ct.
Smith, Gloria L. ... '63 '93 C.17 B.A. L.1340 J.D. [Cross,S.&Assoc.]
Smith, Gregory E. ... '79 '04 C.473 B.A. L.201 J.D. [🄰 J.S.Arnold&Assoc.]
Smith, Hope A. ... '76 '01 C.659 B.A. L.150 J.D. [🄰 Montgomery,R.&J.]
Smith, Ian R. ... '71 '97 C.385 B.A. L.150 J.D. [McCaslin,I.&M.] ⊙
Smith, James H., III, (AV) ... '50 '75 C.385 A.B. L.851 J.D. [Lindhorst&D.]
Smith, Jenny Namanworth ... '67 '92 C.385 B.A. L.1340 J.D. 2306 Park Ave., Ste. 103
Smith, Jonathan ... '63 '97 C.679 B.S. L.1187 J.D. 415 Glensprings Dr., Ste. 102
Smith, Julie C. '69 '98 C.945 B.A. L.776 J.D.
(adm. in NJ; not adm. in OH) [🄰 Ulmer&B.]
Smith, Kathryn E. ... '70 '96 C.385 B.A. L.851 J.D. [🄰 Wood,H.&E.]
Smith, Kimberly A. ... '64 '90 C.473 L.117 J.D. 201 E. Fifth St., Trust Div.
Smith, Linda E. ... '65 '95 C.97 B.A. L.201 J.D. Law Clerk
Smith, Marcella Kay ... '78 '04 C.473 B.A. L.94 J.D. [🄰 Taft,S.&H.]
Smith, Mark B., (AV) ... '59 '84 C&L.150 B.B.A., J.D. [M.B.Smith]
Smith, Matthew Jon, (BV) ... '58 '84 C.150 B.F.A. L.1340 J.D. [Smith,R.&S.]
Smith, Monte G. ... '64 '90 C&L.608 B.A., J.D. Jud. Clk. to U.S. Dist. Ct. J.
Smith, Philip S. ... '26 '53 C.976 B.A. L.477 J.D. Sr. V.P., Paine Webber Inc.
Smith, Phillip J. ... '68 '94 C.473 B.A. L.477 J.D. [Vorys,S.S.&P.]
Smith, Ronald G. ... '68 '98 C.473 B.S. L.150 J.D. [🄰 Ulmer&B.]
Smith, Sheila M., (AV) ... '58 '95 C.679 B.S.E.E. L.150 J.D. [🄰 Freking&B.]
Smith, Steven R., (BV) ... '— '84 C.150 B.A. L.201 J.D. [Greenebaum D.&M.]
Smith, Thomas R., (AV) ... '30 '57 C.973 A.B. L.150 LL.B. [🄲 Haverkamp,B.R.&R.]
Smith, Timothy A., (AV) ... '49 '77 C.473 B.A. L.150 J.D. 114 E. 8th St.
Smith, Verena, (AV) ... '28 '68 C.150 B.S. L.1340 J.D. 201 E. Fifth St.‡
Smith, Mark B., Co., L.P.A., (AV) ... 123 E. 4th St.
Smith, Rolfes & Skavdahl Co., L.P.A., (BV) ... 1014 Vine Street
Smith-Monahan, Richard W. ... '68 '95 C.259 B.A. L.356 J.D. 36 E. 7th St.
Smithson, Amy B. ... '72 '97 C&L.150 B.A., J.D. 414 Walnut St.
Smitson, Patricia Mann, (AV) ... '— '77 C&L.150 B.A., J.D. [Thompson H.]
Smyth, Robert M. ... '69 '94 C.473 B.A. L.150 J.D. [Drew&W.]
Snyder, Richard, (AV) '39 '64
C.608 B.S. L.150 J.D. [🄲 Rubenstein&T.] (⊙Fort Wright, KY)
Snyder, William D., (BV) ... '48 '76 C.150 B.B.A. L.1340 J.D. 2115 Luray Ave.
Sobers, Sharon ... '46 '85 C.607 B.A.M.A. L.150 J.D. [Tobias,K.&T.]
Solergibert, Jorge '63 '90 C.999 LL.B. L.659 LL.M.
(adm. in Costa Rica; not adm. in OH) Sr. Intl. Coun., Chiquita Brands Intl., Inc.
Solimine, Louis F., (AV) ... '52 '76 C.1208 B.A. L.150 J.D. [Thompson H.]
Solimine, Michael E. ... '56 '81 C.1208 B.A. L.597 J.D. Prof. of Law, Univ. of Cincinnati
Sollmann, William J. ... '45 '74 C.973 A.B. L.893 J.D. 1026 Kreis Lane
Somers, Blake P. ... '79 '04 C.974 B.A. L.150 J.D. [🄰 McKinney&N.]
Sommer, Rick J. ... '57 '99 C.1213 B.S. L.1340 J.D. [R.J.Sommer] ⊙
Sommer, Rick J., Law Offices of ... 4555 Lake Forest Drive, Suite 650 ⊙
Sorg, Steven V. ... '65 '91 C.235 B.A. L.1340 J.D. [🄰 Lerner,S.&R.]
Southard, Terence J. ... '— '83 C.235 M.B.A. L.1340 J.D. 36 E. 4th St.
Sova, Gregory, (BV) ... '51 '76 C.477 B.A. L.851 J.D. 38 Fountain Square Plaza
Spaeth, Barry A., (BV) ... '53 '94 C.1120 B.A. L.150 J.D. [Robbins,K.P.&T.]
Spain, John A., (AV) ... '23 '50 C.473 B.S. L.150 J.D. 9075 Old Indian Hill Rd.‡
Spaite, Paul W. ... '26 '64 C.608 B.Ch.E. L.1340 J.D. [P.W.Spaite]
Spaite, Paul W., Co., L.P.A. ... 6315 Grand Vista Ave.
Spegal, Karen L. ... '60 '92 C.235 B.B.A. L.1340 J.D. [Fitch&S.]
Sperber, Thomas S., (BV) ... '48 '73 C.602 B.A. L.150 J.D. 7265 Kenwood Rd., Ste. 175
Spiegel, S. Arthur ... '20 '48 C.150 B.A. L.309 LL.B. U.S. Sr. Dist. J.
Spiegel, Walter E. '59 '84 C.1365 B.A. L.477 J.D.
V.P. & Gen. Coun., Standard Textile Co., Inc.
Spiering, Kevin J., (BV) ... '65 '94 C.1290 B.A. L.150 J.D. 119 East Court Street
Spiller, Keith P. ... '— '89 C.473 B.A. L.896 J.D. [Thompson H.]
Spitzmueller, Lawrence J. ... '57 '84 C.150 B.B.A. L.228 J.D. Franklin Svgs.
Splain, John F. ... '56 '85 C.973 B.A. L.1340 J.D. 221 E. 4th St.
Spoelker, Ross K. ... '75 '04 C.383 B.S. L.1161 J.D. 917 Main Street
Spoor, Richard D., (AVⓉ) ... '44 '72 C.150 B.A. L.1565 J.D. [Keating M.&K.]
Spoor, William D. '79 '02 C.974 B.A. L.150 J.D.
(adm. in KY; not adm. in OH) [🄰 Keating M.&K.]
Spraetz, D. Lynn, (BV) ... '63 '88 C.473 B.S. L.608 J.D. [🄲 Cors&B.]
Spraul, Daniel G., (BV) ... '56 '82 C.473 B.S. L.150 J.D. [Spraul,V.&D.]
Spraul, Holly Doan, (BV) ... '64 '88 C.188 A.B. L.150 J.D. [Spraul,V.&D.]
Spraul, Veith & Doan Co., LPA, (BV) ... 830 Main St.
Sprecher, Christina M. ... '70 '96 C.347 B.A. L.879 J.D. [🄰 Frost B.T.]
Sprecher, Kevin S. ... '68 '95 C.679 B.S.I.E. L.879 J.D. [Frost B.T.] (See Pat. Sect.)
Springman, Ronald W., Jr., (BV) ... '63 '89 C.973 B.A. L.150 J.D. Asst. Pros. Atty.
Sprong, Nathan W. ... '72 '04 C.276 B.A. L.201 J.D. [🄰 Manley B.]
Spurr, Christin Popp '60 '93 C.473 B.S. L.1340 J.D.
(adm. in KY; not adm. in OH) 6435 Hunters Trail

Squire, Sanders & Dempsey L.L.P., (AV) BR
312 Walnut Street, Suite 3500, 45202-4036 ⊙
Telephone: 513-361-1200 Fax: 513-361-1201
URL: http://www.ssd.com
Partners - Cincinnati Office: James J. Barresi; Ronald A. Bell; Scott A. Kane; Stephen D. Lerner; Stephen C. Mahon; Mark J. Ruehlmann; Bryan J. Venesy. Of Counsel - Cincinnati Office: Timothy L. Coyle; Jeffrey A. Marks; George N. Oti (Not admitted in OH); Gregory A. Ruehlmann. Associates - Cincinnati Office: Pierre H. Bergeron; P. Casey Coston (Not admitted in OH); Kenneth R. Craycraft, Jr.; Christopher A. Deabler; Jill S. Kirila; David A. Pepper; Kim D. Seaton; Jeffrey D. Siehl; Elliot M. Smith; Ryan D. Walters; David L. Wheeler.
Bankruptcy and Reorganization, Chemicals, Communications, Construction and Engineering, Corporate Transactions and Securities Regulation, E-Commerce, Economic Regulation, Education, Energy, Environmental, Health and Safety, Financial Institutions and Services, Financial Services, Gaming and Casinos, Government and Administrative Agencies, Health Care and Hospitals, Health Sciences, Hospitality and Recreation, Insurance, Intellectual Property, International Dispute Resolution, Labor and Employment, Life Sciences, Litigation, Manufacturing, Media and Entertainment, Private Equity, Project Finance, Public Finance, Real Estate, Real Estate and Hospitality, Sports, Steel, Taxation, Technology, Transportation and Utilities.
The Americas Offices: Cleveland, Columbus, Houston, Los Angeles, Miami, New York, Palo Alto, Phoenix, San Francisco, Tallahassee, Tampa, Tysons Corner, Washington DC, West Palm Beach, Caracas, Santo Domingo, Rio de Janeiro.
European Offices: Bratislava, Brussels, Budapest, London, Madrid, Milan, Moscow, Prague, Warsaw.
Asia Offices: Beijing, Hong Kong, Shanghai, Tokyo.
Associated Offices: Bucharest, Dublin, Kyiv, Buenos Aires, Santiago.
Revisor of the Ohio and Texas Law Digests for this Directory

See Professional Biographies, CINCINNATI, OHIO

Staadeker, David ... '18 '51 C.150 B.B.A. L.151 LL.B. 1600 Central Pkwy.
Stachler, Robert G., (AV) ... '29 '57 C.201 B.S. L.150 LL.B. [🄲 Taft,S.&H.]
Stachler, Thomas L., (AV) ... '60 '89 C.138 B.S. L.150 J.D. [Strauss&T.]
Stagnaro, Eugene J., Jr., (BV) ... '37 '63 C.150 A.B. L.1340 J.D. 808 Main St.
Stagnaro, Jeffrey G., (AV) ... '64 '89 C.473 B.S. L.117 J.D. 2623 Erie Ave.
Stainton, Jeffrey L. ... '65 '97 C.597 B.A. L.150 J.D. [🄰 Thompson H.]
Staley, Jeffrey J., (BV) ... '50 '77 C.150 B.B.A. L.1340 J.D. 5510 W. Fork Rd.
Stalf, Dale A., (AV) ... '— '83 C.973 B.S. L.150 J.D. [Buckley K.]
Stallard, David S., (AV) ... '44 '68 C.275 B.S. L.421 J.D. [Wood,H.&E.] (See Pat. Sect.)
Stallworth, Nicolle '74 '04 C.302 B.S. L.262 J.D.
(adm. in NY; not adm. in OH) [🄰 Peck,S.&W.] (⊙Columbus)
Stamp, Vincent B., (AV) ... '44 '69 C.1150 A.B. L.602 J.D. [Dinsmore&S.]
Stanford, Stanley L., (AV) ... '30 '58 C.235 B.S. L.150 J.D. [Cohen,T.K.&S.]
Stanton, Jeanne F. ... '20 '54 C.150 B.A. L.1340 J.D. 3580 Shaw Ave.‡

Staples, D. Christian, III '68 '97 C.1161 B.S. L.421 J.D.
(adm. in KY; not adm. in OH) 38 Fountain Square Plaza
Stargel, Rogena, (BV) ...... '57 '82 C.518 A.B. L.150 J.D. 230 E. Ninth Street, 10th Floor
Starkey, J. Shane .... '69 '95 C.967 B.A. L.150 J.D. [Thompson H.]
Startsman, Daniel B., Jr., (BV) .... '48 '73 C.902 B.S. L.150 J.D. [Jacobs&S.]
Statman, Alan J., (AV) .... '58 '83 C.150 B.A. L.201 J.D. [Statman,H.S.&E.]

Statman, Harris, Siegel & Eyrich, LLC, (AV)
2900 Chemed Center, 255 East Fifth Street, 45202-2912
Telephone: 513-621-2666 Facsimile: 513-587-4477
Alan J. Statman; Jeffrey P. Harris; Robert H. Siegel; David J. Eyrich; Robert A. Bardach; Howard L. Richshafer; Thomas S. Sapinsley;—William B. Fecher; Fern E. Goldman; Thomas A. Wietholter; Tracy L. Hawkins; Brian T. Giles; Kimberly A. Schmaltz. Of Counsel: Lawrence A. Flemer; Colleen M. Hegge.
General Civil Trial and Appellate Practice in Federal and State Courts. Commercial Litigation, Bankruptcy, Banking, Personal Injury and Family Law. Corporate Acquisitions, Dispositions, Spin-Offs, Corporate Formation, Financings, Real Estate, Banking and Commercial Law, Reorganizations, Restructurings, Bankruptcy, Civil Litigation, General Business, Intellectual Property, Taxation, Estate Planning.
References: Bank One, Cincinnati, N.A.; Fifth Third Bank.
Dayton, Ohio Office: Fifth Third Center, 110 North Main Street, Suite 1520, 45402. Telephone: 937-222-1090. Fax: 937-222-1046.
Chicago, Illinois Office: 333 West Wacker Drive, Suite 1710, 60606. Telephone: 312-263-1070. Fax: 312-263-1201.
See Professional Biographies, CINCINNATI, OHIO

Stautberg, Elizabeth A. .... '65 '92 C.893 B.A. L.150 J.D. Children's Hosp. Med. Ctr.
Stautberg, Julia A. .... '66 '95 C.736 B.A. L.151 J.D. Hamilton Co. Com. Pleas Ct.
Stautberg, Lee M., (AV) .... '68 '93 C&L.608 B.S.B.A., J.D. [Dinsmore&S.]
Steffen, Carey K. .... '75 '00 C.1161 B.S. L.1340 J.D. [Ritter&R.]
Stegbauer, Joseph A. '68 '96 C.645 B.A. L.150 J.D.
Assoc. Dir. Assoc. Gen. Coun., P&G
Stegman, Michael J., (AV) .... '58 '83 C.602 B.A. L.569 J.D. [Kohnen&P.]
Steiden, Eric A. .... '66 '94 C.150 B.M. L.383 J.D. 830 Main Street, Suite 1105-1115
Stein, Jacob K., (AV) .... '31 '53 C.145 A.B. L.150 LL.B. 312 Walnut St.‡
Steinberg, Lisa Huwer .... '58 '84 C.608 B.A. L.201 J.D. 9050 Ambercreek Dr.
Steinberg, Robert A., (AV) .... '42 '67 C&L.608 B.A., J.D. [Waite,S.B.&C.]
Steiner, Edward E., (AV) .... '55 '83 C.893 B.A. L.976 J.D. [Keating M.&K.]
Steines, Ann Munson '65 '90
C.188 B.S. L.1068 J.D. Assoc. Coun., Federated Dept. Stores, Inc.
Steinher, Jan Hatcher .... '53 '86 C.97 B.A. L.150 J.D. 742 Watch Hill Ln.‡
Steinmanis, Karl S. '48 '73 C.197 A.B. L.1119 J.D.
Gen. Coun.-Global Baby Care Products, The Procter & Gamble Co.
Steltenpohl, Robert H., (BV) '44 '76 C.973 B.S.B.A. L.1340 J.D.
4100 Montgomery Road
Stenger, Mark G., (BV) .... '59 '84 C&L.150 B.A., J.D. 8572 St. Ives Place
Stepaniak, Mark J., (AV) .... '55 '80 C.1118 B.A. L.150 J.D. [Taft,S.&H.]
Stephan, Charles Michael, (AV) .... '49 '79 C.973 B.A. L.150 J.D. [Taft,S.&H.]
Stern, Noah J. .... '71 '99 C.1375 B.A. L.569 J.D. [Dinsmore&S.]
Stern, Ronald H., (BV) '43 '71
C.610 B.S. L.1340 J.D. CEO, Crown Management Corporation
Stevenson, David T., (BV) .... '55 '81 C&L.150 B.B.A., J.D. 230 E. 9th.
Stewart, Frank H., (AV) .... '31 '57 C.309 B.A. L.893 LL.B. [Taft,S.&H.] ‡
Stewart, Gwyneth G. '57 '83 C.1349 B.A. L.188 J.D.
(adm. in NY; not adm. in OH) Assoc. Coun., Federated Dept. Stores, Inc.
Stewart, Richard N. P. .... '41 '78 C.401 B.A. L.150 J.D. 211 Greendale Ave.‡
Stewart, Thomas H., (BV(T)) '60 '92
C.138 B.A. L.150 J.D. 1700 PNC Center, 201 East Fifth Street
Stich, Carl J., Jr., (AV) .... '53 '80 C&L.383 B.S., J.D. [White,G.&M.]
Stiebel, Mark A., (AV) .... '55 '80 C&L.150 B.B.A., J.D. [Graf&S.&M.]
Stiens, Donald G., Jr. .... '66 '03 C.473 B.A. L.150 J.D. [Helmer,M.R.&P.]
Stigler, Margaret M., (BV) '— '83 C.150 B.S. L.1161 J.D.
5725 Dragon Way, Suite 306

Stillpass, John E., (AV) '56 '81 C.659 B.S.E. L.930 J.D.
9545 Kenwood Road, Suite 103, 45242-6100
Telephone: 513-936-0800 Fax: 513-794-8800
Email: jstillpass@stillpass.com URL: http://www.stillpass.com
General Practice. Marine, Automobile Franchises and Dealerships, Admiralty and Maritime, Probate Law, Real Estate, Business and Commercial Law.
See Professional Biographies, CINCINNATI, OHIO

Stilz, Fay E., (AV) .... '51 '78 C.473 B.S. L.150 J.D. [Waite,S.B.&C.]
Stimson, Martha A. .... '16 '43 C.788 B.A. L.150 LL.B. 3983 Rosslyn DR.‡
Stinebruner, Scott A. '68 '93 C.910 B.S.E.E. L.494 J.D.
[Wood,H.&E.] (See Pat. Sect.)
Stineman, Jerome P. .... '44 '72 C.701 B.S.M.E. L.150 J.D. 2101 Grandin Road, Suite 601
Stith, John S., (AV) .... '39 '64 C.674 A.B. L.150 J.D. [Porter W.M.&A.]
Stitt, Jason V. .... '75 '02 C&L.383 B.A., J.D. [Keating M.&K.]
Stober, James .... '30 '61 9225 Silva Dr.
Stockdale, David C. .... '50 '76 C.610 A.B. L.150 J.D. Mun. J.
Stocker, David E. .... '44 '79 C.608 B.S. L.607 J.D. Assoc., Sallie Mae
Stoller, Harry, (BV) .... '30 '58 C&L.150 B.A., LL.B. 105 E. 4th Street
Stolper, Rita M. .... '54 '79 C.245 B.A. L.446 J.D. [Frost B.T.]
Stone, Richard M. .... '46 '71 C.390 B.S. L.659 J.D. [Cohen,T.K.&S.]
Stone, Robert L. .... '27 '63 C.608 B.S. L.1340 J.D. 645 Walnut St.
Stoner, Michael B. .... '63 '97 C&L.201 B.A., J.D. [Strauss&T.]
Story, Garlinn H. .... '48 '77 C.413 B.A. L.464 J.D. P.O. Box 5576
Stout, Gregory A. .... '71 '02 C&L.999 B.S., J.D. [Mapother&M.]
Stout, William A., Jr. .... '43 '81 C.473 B.S. L.1340 J.D. 2648 Lytham Ct.
Strain, Charles E., (BV) .... '52 '81 C.210 B.A. L.608 J.D. 830 Main Street, Suite 500
Strangfeld, William C., (AV) .... '45 '84 C.379 B.A. L.608 J.D. [Frost B.T.]
Strasser, Albert E., (AV) .... '24 '48 L.150 J.D. 201 E. 5th St. (Pat.)
Strasser, JoAnn M. .... '59 '94 C&L.150 B.U.P., J.D. [Thompson H.]
Stratigeas, Eleni V. .... '71 '98 C.878 B.A. L.880 J.D. [Baker&H.]
Strauss, Stephen D., (AV) .... '40 '66 C.347 B.S. L.309 J.D. 414 Walnut Street
Strauss, William V., (AV) .... '42 '67 C.309 A.B. L.659 J.D. [Strauss&T.]

Strauss & Troy, A Legal Professional Association, (AV)
The Federal Reserve Building, 150 East Fourth Street, 45202-4018
Telephone: 513-621-2120 Fax: 513-241-8259
Email: info@strausstroy.com URL: http://www.strausstroy.com
Lucien G. Strauss (1900-1982); Orville A. Troy (1896-1967); Kenneth D. Troy (1918-1993); Alan C. ***Rosser (1946-2001); Mark H. Berliant; William V. Strauss; Larry A. Neuman; William S. Abernethy,*** **Jr.; Thomas C. Rink; Franklin A. Klaine, Jr.; William R. Jacobs; Daniel H. Demmerle, II; James G. Heldman; Charles Jay Postow; Stuart C. Brinn; Martin C. Butler (Resident, Covington, Kentucky Office); R. Guy Taft; Ann W. Gerwin; Richard S. Wayne; Paul B. Calico; Andrew M. Shott; Claudia G. Allen; Timothy B. Theissen (Resident, Covington, Kentucky Office); William K. Flynn; Charles C. Ashdown; Marilyn J. Maag; Thomas L. Stachler; Anthony M. Barlow; Marshall K. Dosker (Resident, Covington, Kentucky Office); Shawn M. Young; August T. Janszen; Pete A. Smith (Resident, Covington, Kentucky Office); Thomas P. Glass; Michael A. Ruh, Jr.;—Michael B. Stoner; Joseph J. Braun; Stephanie A. Dill; Lori A. Ross; Jeremy A. Hayden (Resident, Covington, Kentucky Office);**

(This Listing Continued)

Strauss & Troy, A Legal Professional Association (Continued)
Matthew R. Chasar; Nicole M. Lundrigan; Jason D. Tonne; William O. Williamson; John M. Levy; Stephen G. Nesbitt (Resident, Covington, Kentucky Office). Of Counsel: Samuel M. Allen (Resident, Covington, Kentucky Office); Gordon H. Hood (Resident, Covington, Kentucky Office); Charles G. Atkins; Mitchell B. Goldberg (Certified Specialist in Labor and Employment Law, Ohio State Bar Association); Leon L. Wolf; Paul J. Theissen (Resident, Covington, Kentucky Office); Diane Schneiderman; Charles H. Melville; Philomena Saldanha Ashdown.
General Civil Practice, Litigation, Alternative Dispute Resolution, Corporate, Probate, Tax, Estate Planning, Real Estate, Securities, Employment Law, Trade Regulation, Antitrust, Patent and Trademark Litigation, Real Estate and Development Law, Housing and Urban Development, Syndication Law, Land Use and Zoning, Trials and Appeals, Pension and Profit Sharing Law, ERISA, Franchise Law, Hospitality and Lodging.
Representative Clients: BP Oil Co.; PNC Bank, N.A. (Ohio and Kentucky); Meijer, Inc.; Anderson Publishing Co.; US Bank National Association; Cincom Systems, Inc.; Corporex Companies, Inc.; Forest Pharmaceuticals.
Northern Kentucky Office: 50 East RiverCenter Boulevard, Covington, Kentucky, 41011. Telephone: 513-621-8900. Fax: 513-629-9444.
See Professional Biographies, CINCINNATI, OHIO

Streckfuss, James A. '51 '82 C.150 B.A. L.969 J.D.
(adm. in IN; not adm. in OH) WWI Aviation Historians League
Stridsberg, Roger C. .... '26 '49 C&L.150 A.B., LL.B. 914 Main Street, Suite 200
Strong, Michael H. .... '64 '92 C.608 B.S. L.851 J.D. 917 Main St.
Stroud, Robert R., Sr. '10 '31 C.36 L.37 J.D.
(adm. in AZ; not adm. in OH) 4003 Rosslyn Dr.‡

Strubbe, William B., (AV) '52 '79 C.629 B.A. L.150 J.D.
1525 Kroger Building, 45202
Telephone: 513-621-4775 Fax: 513- 621-4789
Email: wstrubbe@one.net URL: http://www.strubbelaw.net
Insurance Coverage and Defense Litigation, Product Liability, Commercial Litigation, Personal Injury, Copyright, Legal Malpractice.
See Professional Biographies, CINCINNATI, OHIO

Stubbs, Matthew E. .... '70 '96 C.608 B.A. L.150 J.D. [Montgomery,R.&J.]
Stuhlbarg, Steven F., (BV) .... '56 '92 C.769 B.A. L.150 J.D. 7809 Shadowhill Way
Suarez, Joseph P., (BV) '52 '82
C.401 B.A. L.831 J.D. Sr. Coun., The Procter & Gamble Co.
Subit, Melissa Campbell .... '— '99 C.1115 B.A. L.608 J.D. [Buckley K.]
Sucher, Mark L. '49 '74 C.1070 B.S. L.309 J.D.
Gen. Coun., Fluor Daniel Fernald, Inc.
Suder, Sean S. .... '78 '04 C&L.893 B.S., J.D. [Keating M.&K.]
Suffern, Michael J. .... '62 '90 C.602 B.A. L.424 J.D. [Ulmer&B.]
Suhre, Joseph B., IV .... '74 '99 C.973 B.S. L.150 J.D. 1014 Vine Street, Suite 1525
Suhrheinrich, Richard F. .... '36 '63 C.912 B.S. L.213 J.D. Sr. U.S. Ct. App. J.
Sulau, William C., (AV) .... '50 '81 C.207 B.A. L.1187 J.D. [Drew&W.]
Sullivan, Brian S., (AV) .... '64 '88 C&L.150 B.A., J.D. [Dinsmore&S.]
Sullivan, David S. .... '75 '00 C.294 B.A. L.383 J.D. [Dinsmore&S.]
Sullivan, James P., (AV) .... '51 '77 C.150 B.A. L.1340 J.D. [Sullivan&S.]
Sullivan, John J., (AV) .... '21 '51 C.150 A.B. L.174 J.D. [Sullivan&S.]
Sullivan, Lisa A. ..... '65 '93 C&L.150 B.A., J.D. Staff Atty., The Procter & Gamble Co.
Sullivan, Mary W., (AV) .... '56 '80 C.973 B.A. L.150 J.D. [Peck,S.&W.]
Sullivan, Timothy C., (AV) .... '61 '85 C.188 A.B. L.150 J.D. [Taft,S.&H.]
Sullivan, Wendall .... '24 '50 C.973 L.150 LL.B. 8006 Beechmont Ave.‡
Sullivan & Sullivan, (AV) .... 7184 Pippin Rd.
Summe, Kurt Andrew, (AV) '65 '91 C&L.150 B.S., J.D.
[Wood,H.&E.] (See Pat. Sect.)
Summers, Cynthia Porter, (BV) '49 '81
C.201 B.S. L.150 J.D. 800 Compton Road, Unit 37A Suite 107
Summers, Stuart G. '37 '64 C.197 A.B. L.184 LL.B.
Exec. V.P. & Gen. Coun., The Ohio Natl. Life Ins. Co.‡
Supinger, Emily T. .... '75 '01 C.610 B.S. L.8 J.D. [Manley B.]
Surber, Nell D., (BV) .... '28 '55 C.66 B.A. L.150 LL.B. 201 E. Fifth St.

Surdyk, Dowd & Turner, Co., L.P.A., Law Offices of
(See Dayton)

Surrey, Michael C. .... '— '98 C.138 B.S. L.383 J.D. [Graydon H.&R.]
Susskind, Stuart R., (AV) .... '44 '69 C&L.150 B.B.A., J.D. [Ulmer&B.]
Sutherland, William R. .... '29 '54 C&L.966 B.B.A., LL.B. 11203 Marlette Dr.
Sutton, James T. .... '79 '04 C.974 B.S.B.A. L.383 J.D. [Dinsmore&S.]
Sutton, Jeffrey S. .... '— '90 C.951 B.A. L.608 LL.B. U.S. Ct. App. J.
Suwanski, Jillian M. .... '77 '02 C.384 B.A. L.383 J.D. [Taft,S.&H.]
Swaney, Dennis .... '49 '76 C.880 B.A. L.117 J.D. 7217 Silver Crest Dr.‡
Swanton, Sandra L. ..... '60 '86 C.473 B.A. L.831 J.D. Law Clk., Ct. of Common Pleas J.
Swartz, Donald K. .... '70 '97 C.690 B.A. L.8 J.D. [Lerner,S.&R.]
Swartz, Jennifer K. .... '75 '00 C.97 B.A. L.221 J.D. [Dinsmore&S.]
Sway, Michael Andrew .... '69 '96 C.970 B.A. L.945 J.D. [Smith,R.&S.]
Sweeney, Patricia J., (BV) '40 '77
C.741 B.A. L.1340 J.D. Sr. Acct. Rep., West Publishing Company
Swehla, Nathan L. .... '75 '02 C.150 B.B.A. L.999 J.D. [Lerner,S.&R.]
Swenty, Peter W., (AV) .... '31 '55 C&L.150 B.A., LL.B. 30 E. Central Parkway
Swick, Kevin L., (BV) .... '56 '81 C.150 B.A. L.201 J.D. 8050 Hosbrook, Ste. 200
Swigert, J. Mack, (AV) .... '07 '35 C.293 S.B. L.309 LL.B. [Taft,S.&H.]
Swillinger, Bradley Micah, Law Office of '75 '01
C.269 B.A. L.851 J.D. 1014 Vine Street, Suite 1650
Syler, Keith Eric .... '68 '01 C.999 B.A. L.150 J.D. Law Clk., U.S. Dist. Ct.
Tafaro, John P. .... '55 '83 C.967 B.A. L.1340 J.D. [Kohnen&P.]
Taft, Dudley S. .... '40 '66 C.976 B.A. L.893 LL.B. Taft Bdcstg. Co.
Taft, R. Guy, (AV) .... '49 '76 C&L.150 B.A., J.D. [Strauss&T.]

Taft, Stettinius & Hollister LLP, (AV)
425 Walnut Street, Suite 1800, 45202-3957
Telephone: 513-381-2838 Facsimile: 513-381-0205
URL: http://www.taftlaw.com
Members of Firm: Robert A. Taft (1889-1953); John L. Stettinius (1882-1924); John B. Hollister (1890-1979); L. Clifford Craig; Robert J. Townsend; Jerold A. Fink; Thomas D. Heekin; Melvin S. Shotten; Gerald J. Rapien; Stephen M. Nechemias; Stephen M. O'Bryan†††; Robert E. Rich; R. Joseph Parker; Timothy E. Hoberg; G. Jack Donson Jr.; David L. Johnson†; Thomas C. Hill; Lawrence J. Barty; Margaret Anne Cannon†††; Thomas T. Terp; Lawrence D. Walker†; Roger A. Weber; Ross E. Wales; Timothy P. Nagy†; William Stuart Dornette; Timothy J. Quinn; Edward D. Diller; Daniel J. Hoffheimer; Timothy J. Hurley; John J. McCoy; Steven W. Weeks; Timothy P. Reilly; William J. Seitz III; Thomas R. Schuck; Michael J. Zavatsky; Kim K. Burke; Mark J. Stepaniak; John D. Brown†††; Joel A. Makee†††; Thomas J. Lee†††; Carl A. Murway†††; Charles Michael Stephan; Gerald S. Greenberg; Margaret Avril Lawson; Toshio Nakao; Robert B. Craig††; Stephen M. Griffith Jr.; Thomas E. Grossmann; Mark J. Valponi†††; Jeffrey S. Schloemer; Steven A. Marrer††††; Timothy C. Sullivan; Patrick J. Mitchell; Michael A. Byers†; Samuel M. Duran; Susan E. Wheatley; Bruce L. Waterhouse, Jr.†††; Doreen Canton; Gregory Parker Rogers; Mark A. Kobasuk; Ronald C. Christian; Marcia Voorhis Andrew; Robert A. Bilott; Russell S. Sayre; Patricia O. Lowry; Earl K. Messer; Robert P. McManus†††; Robert W. McAdams, Jr.†; Timothy B. Mitchell†; David H. Wallace†††; Peter M. Poulos†††; W. Timothy Miller; David Hamilton Peck; Daniel E. Fausz; George D. Molinsky; Donna M. Flammang†††; Mary Grace Balazs†††; Gregory J. O'Brien†††; Jill Friedman Helfman†††; David A. Mancino; Daniel R. Warncke; Tracey Chriske Puthoff; J. Steven Justice††††; Michael A. Laing; Hugh E. Wall, III††††; William J. Stavole†††; Daniel K. Wright, II†††; Bruce J.

(This Listing Continued)

Taft, Stettinius & Hollister LLP (Continued)

L. Lowe†††; John P. Curp†; David V. Allen†††; Aimee L. Keller; John B. Nalbandian; Timothy L. Zix†††; James B. Farmer†; Stephen H. Jett†††; Julia B. Meister; Eric K. Combs; Kerry P. Hastings; Charles A. Bowers†††. Of Counsel: J. Mack Swigert; Charles D. Lindberg; Robert G. Stachler; Fred J. Livingstone†††; James J. Ryan; Cynthia F. Blank; David E. Burke†††; James J. Mayer; Laura A. Ringenbach; George J. Dunn†††; Frank A. Titus†; Richard D. Tomsick†††; J. Alan Lips; Diane D. Reynolds†. Retired Partners: James R. Bridgeland Jr.; Frank H. Stewart; Wilbur L. Collins; William K. Engeman. Associates: Raymond W. Lembke; Patricia D. Braxton; Cynthia C. Felson; Mary L. Rust; Christine Lewanski†††; Lori E. Jeffries; Brenda M. Breitkreutz; Thomas P. Vergamini††; Antonia Mitroussia; Patricia Anderson Pryor; Jeanne Marie Bruns; Paige L. Ellerman; Justin D. Flamm; Allison S. Russell; Tracy T. Ward; James M. Zimmerman; Sara Simrall Rorer; Joshua A. Shapiro; Lisa L. Patterson††††; J. Donald Mottley; Robert B. Owen†††; Patrick J. Krebs†††; Amy C. Ashton; Shelli Turner Clark†; Melissa Kurzhals Cover; Dawn R. Landers; Daniel F. Oberklein; Sharon I. Shanley; J. Stephen Smith††; Richard L. Ferrell, III; Tamara A. Miano; Ryan L. Willis; Theresa H. Vella; Monica L. Gearding; Matthew T. Viola†††; Gregory W. Bee; Natasha M. Cavanaugh; Ryan C. Edwards; Bridget C. Hoffman; Matthew C. Loftus; Patrick E. Noser; Brie S. Rogers; Katherine A. Ruwe; Jillian M. Suwanski; Julia E. Tarvin; Rachel S. Zahniser; Heather L. Tonsing†††; John M. Mueller; Robert H. Fischer, Jr.†††; Majeed G. Makhlouf†††; Kimberlie L. Huff†††; Lawrence C. Davison†††; Paula J. Dehan; Catherine E. Howard; Brian R. Hylander; Lora N. McInturf; Benjamin J. Parsons†; LaQuita S. Wilson; Bryan E. Wise; Patrick G. Johnson; Patricia Fleming Krewson†††; Kristen L. Safier; Adam D. Cornett†††; Kristin R. Erenburg†††; John R. Potter; Gregory Turner††††; Brian S. Settles; Marcella Kay Smith; Matthew J. Wiles††††; Vanessa A. Wernicke; Kristi J. Kmetz†††; Ronn J. Gehring†††; Barbara A. McNeil†.
Antitrust, Bankruptcy and Debtor/Creditor Rights, Business and Finance, E-Business (Internet and E-Commerce), Employee Benefits/ERISA and Tax-Planning, Environmental Law, Family Law, Family Business Planning, Franchise, General Litigation, Health Care, Immigration, Institutional Finance, Intellectual Property and Technology Group, International, Japanese Practice, Labor and Employment, Mergers and Acquisitions, Nonprofit and Tax-Exempt Organizations, Product Liability and Personal Injury, Public Finance, Real Property, Securities, Tax, Probate and Estate Planning, Workers' Compensation.
Counsel for: Cincinnati Bengals; CINergy; Gibson Greetings, Inc.; Morton International, Inc.; Sisters of Charity Healthcare Systems, Inc.; Thiokol Corporation; U.S. Bancorp; U.S. Bank National Assn.
Columbus, Ohio Office: Twelfth Floor, 21 East State Street. Telephone: 614-221-2838.
Covington, Kentucky Office: 1717 Dixie Highway, Suite 340. Telephone: 859-331-2838; 513-381-2838.
Cleveland, Ohio Office: 3500 BP Tower, 200 Public Square. Telephone: 216-241-2838.
Dayton, Ohio Office: 110 North Main Street, Suite 900. Telephone: 937-228-2838.
†Columbus Office
††Covington, Kentucky Office
†††Cleveland Office
††††Dayton Office

See Professional Biographies, CINCINNATI, OHIO

Taggart, Carolyn A., (AV) ....'51 '78 C.473 B.S. L.150 J.D. [Rendigs,F.K.&D.]
Taggart, Georgana, (BV) ....'47 '80 C.303 A.B. L.1340 J.D. 8050 Hosbrook Rd.
Taliaferro, George W., Jr., (AVⓉ) ....'42 '67 C.674 A.B. L.893 LL.B. [P.E.Cunningham]
Taliaferro, Mehling, Shirooni, Carran & Keys, PLLC
(See Covington, Kentucky)
Tallarigo, Matthew ....'47 '73 C&L.150 B.A., J.D. 352 Thrall St.‡
Tamarkin, Ivan L., (BV) ....'42 '67 C.473 B.A. L.150 J.D. 830 Main St.
Tankersley, Sarah ....'69 '97 C.1161 B.A. L.383 J.D. [Santen&H.]
Tarvin, Julia E. ....'74 '02 C.1161 B.A. L.1340 J.D. [Ⓐ Taft,S.&H.]
Tate, Charles L. ....'62 '00 C&L.150 B.A., J.D. [Ⓐ Weltman,W.&R.]
Tate, John M. ....'44 '72 C&L.150 B.B.A., J.D. Chiquita Brands Int'l., Inc.
Tate, Mary Lynn ....'61 '99 C.945 B.S. L.383 J.D. [Ⓐ Ulmer&B.]
Tauber, Jill Stanforth ....'74 '01 C.973 B.S. L.150 J.D. [Ⓐ Denlinger,R.&G.]
Taylor, Catharin R., (BV) ....'66 '92 C&L.150 B.B.A., J.D. [Clements,M.&C.]
Taylor, Douglas C. ....'61 '86 C.150 B.B.A. L.990 J.D. Sr. Coun., Cinergy Corp.
Taylor, Thomas E. '46 '71 C.532 B.A. L.930 J.D.
General Counsel & Secretary, Broadwing Inc.
Taylor, Wayne F., (AV) '43 '68 C&L.880 B.A., J.D.
V.P., Gen. Coun. & Secy., Cincinnati Milacron Inc.
Teeters, Jeffrey R. ....'68 '93 C.201 B.A. L.150 J.D. [Frost B.T.]
Teller, Jerome S., (AV) ....'30 '53 C&L.150 B.A., J.D. [Katz,T.B.&H.]
Tellez, Raul E., (BV) '64 '92
C.421 B.S. L.150 J.D. Sr. Corp. Coun., Great American Ins. Co.
Temming, Daniel J., (AV) ....'51 '79 C.150 B.S. L.1340 J.D. [Robbins,K.P.&T.]
Tepe, Thomas M., (AV) ....'45 '71 C.973 B.S. L.734 J.D. 22 West Ninth Street
Tepe, Thomas M., Jr. ....'72 '99 C.608 B.A. L.475 J.D. [Ⓐ Keating M.&K.]
Tepe, Timothy A., (AV) ....'60 '87 C&L.150 B.A., J.D. [Dinsmore&S.]
Tepe, Timothy N. ....'56 '89 C.973 B.A. L.1340 J.D. V.P., Schiff, Kreidler-Shell, Inc.
Terp, Thomas T., (AV) ....'47 '73 C.20 B.A. L.945 J.D. [Taft,S.&H.]
Tewksbury, Linn A. ....'59 '87 C&L.150 B.S.I.E., J.D. 3314 Monteith Avenue (Pat.)
Thatch, John S. ....'07 '40 C.8 B.S. L.7 J.D. 7832 C Village Dr.‡
Thayer, Abbot A., (AV) ....'53 '80 C.309 B.A. L.150 J.D. [Peck,S.&W.]
Thiemann, Paul P., Jr. ....'27 '57 C.973 B.S.B.A. L.1340 LL.B. 6561 Devonwood Dr.
Thole, Lori D. ....'66 '93 C.930 B.A. L.989 J.D. 2763 Orchard Park Drive
Thole, Thomas J., Attorney at Law '47 '74 C.973 B.S. L.1340 J.D.
7803 Outlookridge Ln.
Thomas, Brian C. ....'76 '01 C.277 B.S. L.201 J.D. [Ⓐ Graydon H.&R.]
Thomas, Craig A. ....'61 '86 C&L.150 B.A., J.D. [Ⓐ Lerner,S.&R.]
Thomas, Ernest V., III, (BV) ....'58 '82 C.1118 B.A. L.150 J.D. [Thomas&T.] ⊙
Thomas, Ernest V., Jr., (BV) ....'35 '68 C.973 B.S.B.A. L.1340 J.D. [Thomas&T.]
Thomas, Evan David ....'69 '00 2323 Park Avenue
Thomas, Joseph P. ....'56 '88 C.906 Phar.B. L.1340 J.D. [Ulmer&B.]
Thomas, Leslie Fern, Co., L.P.A. ....'55 '95 [L.F.Thomas]
Thomas, Suja A. '66 '92 C.597 B.A. L.569 J.D.
Asst. Professor, University of Cincinnati College of Law
Thomas, Vincent E., (BV) ....'57 '87 C.1118 B.A. L.1340 J.D. [Thomas&T.]
Thomas, Leslie F., Co., L.P.A. ....1420 E. McMillan, Ste. Two
Thomas & Thomas, (BV) ....2323 Park Avenue (⊙Newport, KY; Cleve., Columbus, OH)
Thompson, Blair C. '51 '79
C.846 B.A. L.990 J.D. V.P., PNC Bank, Ohio, National Association
Thompson, Cory D. ....'76 '04 C&L.150 B.A., J.D. 2638 Victory Pkwy., Ste. 200
Thompson, James W., (AV) ....'41 '68 C.381 B.A. L.1340 J.D. [Thompson]
Thompson, Molly M. ....'66 '91 C.692 B.A. L.276 J.D. 10118 Humphrey Road

Thompson & Company, L.P.A., (AV)
Southampton Square, 7434 Jager Court, 45230-4344
Telephone: 513-232-7576 Fax: 513-232-7654
Email: thompson@colpa.com URL: http://www.lawyers.com/thompson
James W. Thompson.
General Civil Practice including Taxation, Business Organization, Real Estate, Business Acquisitions and Sales, Estate Planning and Probate Law and Commercial Litigation.
Reference: Bank One of Cincinnati.

See Professional Biographies, CINCINNATI, OHIO

Thompson Hine LLP, (AV)
312 Walnut Street, 14th Floor, 45202-4089 ⊙
Telephone: 513-352-6700 Fax: 513-241-4771
Email: info@ThompsonHine.com URL: http://www.ThompsonHine.com
Amos Burt Thompson (1871-1965); Charles P. Hine (1877-1942); Walter L. Flory (1880-1951); Michael L. Hardy (Partner-in-Charge, Cleveland); Patricia Mann Smitson (Partner-in-Charge, Cincinnati); Anthony C. White (Partner-in-Charge, Columbus); Robert M. Curry (Partner-in Charge,

(This Listing Continued)

Thompson Hine LLP (Continued)

Dayton); Nicholas J. DiMichael (Partner-in-Charge, Washington, DC); George J. Walsh III (Partner-in-Charge, New York City); Ludo Deklerck (Partner-in-Charge, Brussels); Walt A. Linscott (Partner-in-Charge, Atlanta). Partners: Paul Allaer; Bruce M. Allman; Christopher M. Bechhold; Daniel O. Berger; Deborah S. Brenneman; Timothy R. Brown; Stephen J. Butler; Frank D. Chaiken; William H. Cordes; Scott B. Crooks; Renee S. Filiatraut; Jack F. Fuchs; Jane E. Garfinkel; Kenneth B. Germain; Gary M. Glass; Robert P. Johnson; Stephen M. King; Thomas J. Kirkwood; Brenda M. Kloos; Andrew L. Kolesar; Earle Jay Maiman; Melvin E. Marmer; William L. Martin, Jr.; Donald S. Mendelsohn; Michael J. Nieberding; Michael R. Oestreicher (Member, Executive Committee); Kimberly E. Ramundo; Stephen L. Richey; Douglas D. Roberts; Robert A. Selak; Gerald W. Simmons; Patricia Mann Smitson (Partner-in-Charge); Louis F. Solimine; Keith P. Spiller; J. Shane Starkey; JoAnn M. Strasser; John H. Wendeln; Rodney M. Young; Deborah A. Youtsey. Associates: Gary D. Blachman; Bret F. Busacker; Erin C. Childs; Eric S. Clark; Jeffrey M. Clarke; John P. Colbert; John Cottingham; Christopher Elswick; Beth Freemal; Diane M. Goderre; James Houston; Jennifer Kinnen; Bryce A. Lenox; Erin M. Manahan Alkire; Kelly L. Reblin; David A. Rines; Jeffrey L. Stainton; Kimberly D. Wilcoxon; David Willbrand; M. Scott Young. Of Counsel: James J. Crowe; Lisa May Evans; Leonard S. Meranus. Senior Attorney: Lisa M. Wharton.
Administrative Law, Admiralty and Maritime Law, Agency and Distributorships, Antitrust and Trade Regulation, Aviation and Aerospace, Bankruptcy, Banks and Banking, Biotechnology, Business Law, Business Litigation, Business Regulation, Business Transactions, Closely Held Business Law, Joint Ventures, Class Actions, Commercial Law, Commercial Real Estate, Communications and Media, FCC Regulation, Computers and Software, Construction Law, Contracts, Copyrights, Corporate Law, Corporate Finance, Corporate Litigation, Corporate Tax Controversies, Debtor and Creditor, Employee Benefits, ERISA, Energy, Energy Regulation, Environmental Law, Finance, Commercial Finance, Franchises and Franchising, General Practice, Government, False Claims Act, Qui Tam Litigation, Government Contracts, Health Care, Insurance Coverage, Insurance Regulation, Intellectual Property, International Law, International Trade, Internet Law, Labor and Employment, Life Sciences, Litigation, Complex Litigation, Medicare Fraud and Abuse, Mergers, Acquisitions and Divestitures, Natural Resources, Nonprofit and Charitable Organizations, Occupational Safety and Health, OSHA, Partnership Law, Patents, Probate, Products Liability, Product Safety, Professional Liability, Public Finance, Railroad Law, Real Estate, Regulatory Law, Drug and Medical Device Regulation, Food and Drug Regulation, International Regulatory Law, Regulated Industries, Securities, Initial Public Offerings, Public Offerings, Taxation, Tax Controversies, Toxic Torts, Trade Secrets, Trademarks, Transportation, Trusts and Estates, Unfair Competition, Utility Law, White Collar Crime, Zoning, Planning and Land Use.
Cleveland, Ohio Office: 3900 Key Center, 127 Public Square, 44114-1291. Telephone: 216-566-5500. Fax: 216-566-5800. Email: info@ThompsonHine.com.
Columbus, Ohio Office: 10 West Broad Street, Suite 700, 43215-3435. Telephone: 614-469-3200. Fax: 614-469-3361. Email: info@ThompsonHine.com.
Dayton, Ohio Office: 2000 Courthouse Plaza, N.E., P.O. Box 8801, 45401-8801. Telephone: 937-443-6600. Fax: 937-443-6635. Email: info@ThompsonHine.com.
Washington, D.C. Office: 1920 N Street, N.W., Suite 800, 20036-1600. Telephone: 202-331-8800. Fax: 202-331-8330. Email: info@ThompsonHine.com.
New York, N.Y. Office: One Chase Manhattan Plaza, 58th Floor, 10005-1401. Telephone: 212-344-5680. Fax: 212-809-6890. Email: info@ThompsonHine.com.
Brussels, Belgium Office: Avenue Louise 375 - b8, 1050 Brussels, Belgium, Telephone: 011 (32-2) 626-3280. Fax: 011 (32-2) 626-3299. Email: info@ThompsonHine.com.
Atlanta, Georgia Office: Proscenium Center, Suite 1200, 1170 Peachtree Street, 30309-7673. Telephone: 404-541-2900. Fax: 404-541-2905. Email: info@ThompsonHine.com.

See Professional Biographies, CINCINNATI, OHIO

Thomson, Douglas D., (AV) ....'60 '86 C.210 B.A. L.896 J.D. [Frost B.T.]
Thomson, Stephanie Schrimpf, (AV) ....'62 '87 C.973 B.A. L.150 J.D. 1199 Edison Drive
Thumann, Robert J. ....'72 '02 C.150 B.A. L.1340 J.D. [Ⓐ Rendigs,F.K.&D.]
Thurman, Milton, Jr., (BV) ....'36 '61 C.473 B.A. L.150 LL.B. [Rubenstein&T.]
Tierney, Kevin Mckay ....'74 '00 C.201 B.S. L.150 J.D. Pros. Off.
Tierney, Mark R. ....'68 '95 C.610 B.S.C. L.151 J.D. Asst. Pros.

Tillar, Mark T., (CV) '55 '85 C.112 B.A. L.678 J.D.
105 East Main Street, Suite 202, 45040
Telephone: 513-770-0264 Fax: 513-770-0267
Email: info@marktillar.com URL: http://www.marktillar.com
Criminal Law, DUI/DWI, Entertainment, Sports and Leisure Law, White Collar Crimes, Domestic Violence.

See Professional Biographies, CINCINNATI, OHIO

Tilton, Fredric F., (AV) ....'42 '67 C.611 B.A. L.793 J.D. [Reed,T.&H.]
Timperman, Ernest J. ....'26 '58 C.150 E.E. L.1340 J.D. 3491 Mirror Lane
Ting, Jennifer J. ....'— '00 C.1097 M.B.A. L.734 J.D. The Procter & Gamble Company
Tinkler, Hans M. ....'68 '02 C.1070 B.S. L.150 J.D. [Ⓐ Graydon H.&R.] ⊙
Tittel, Bruce, (AV) ....'38 '63 C&L.880 B.A., LL.B. [Wood,H.&E.] (See Pat. Sect.)
Tobias, Charles H., Jr., (AV) '21 '49
C&L.309 A.B., LL.B. Potter Stewart, U.S. Courthouse‡
Tobias, Paul H., (AV) ....'30 '58 C&L.309 A.B., LL.B. [Tobias,K.&T.]
Tobias, Kraus & Torchia, (AV) ....414 Walnut St.
Tobin, Stuart, (BV) ....'42 '69 C.150 B.S. L.607 J.D. [Immerman&T.]
Todd, David H., (AV) ....'38 '63 C.207 B.A. L.150 J.D. [Ⓒ Cors&B.]
Tolbert, Steven M., (BV) ....'51 '78 C.150 B.A. L.1340 J.D. Chf. Asst. Co. Pros.
Tomain, Joseph A. ....'76 '01 C&L.602 B.A., J.D. [Ⓐ Frost B.T.]
Tomain, Joseph P. '48 '74 C.602 A.B. L.273 J.D.
(adm. in NJ; not adm. in OH) Dean & Prof. of Law, Univ. of Cincinnati
Tonne, Jason D. ....'77 '02 C&L.150 B.B.A., J.D. [Ⓐ Strauss&T.]
Toole, Daniel A. '47 '72 C.260 B.A. L.665 J.D.
(adm. in PA; not adm. in OH) Div. Coun., GE Aviation Services, Inc.
Top, Andrew M. ....'70 '98 C.967 B.A. L.201 J.D. [Ⓐ Lerner,S.&R.]
Torchia, David G., (AV) ....'59 '84 C.973 B.S.B.A. L.851 J.D. [Tobias,K.&T.]
Torok, Ruth M. ....'59 '85 C.381 B.A. L.150 J.D. [Ⓐ Triona C.&L.]
Toron, Moshe Y. ....'70 '99 C.999 B.A. L.1161 J.D. [Toron]
Toron Law Firm, The ....4555 Lake Forest Dr., Suite 650
Touchton, Robert E. '43 '74 C.952 A.B. L.37 J.D.
(adm. in KY; not adm. in OH) I.R.S.‡
Townsend, Robert J., (AV) ....'38 '64 C.476 B.A. L.309 LL.B. [Taft,S.&H.]
Tracey, Ann Marie ....'50 '75 C.741 B.A. L.150 J.D. William Coll. of Bus.
Trachsel, Gregory A., (BV) ....'59 '85 C.473 B.A. L.150 J.D. 11 Triangle Park Dr.
Trammell, Dennis L. '47 '77 C.437 B.A. L.150 J.D.
2nd V.P. & Assoc. Gen. Coun., The Union Central Life Insurance Company
Tranter, Richard B., (AV) ....'58 '85 C.276 B.A. L.201 J.D. [Dinsmore&S.]
Tranter, Terence M., (BV) ....'44 '69 C.276 A.B. L.150 J.D. 830 Main St., Ste. 806
Tranter, Terry William ....'71 '99 C.473 B.A. L.201 J.D. 830 Main St., Ste. 806
Trapp, Byron Edward, (BV) ....'37 '67 C.201 B.A. L.930 J.D. 1451 Coventry Woods Dr.
Trauth, Joseph L., Jr., (AV) ....'45 '73 C.973 B.S. L.150 J.D. [Keating M.&K.]
Trautmann, Richard S., (BV) ....'45 '74 C.973 B.S. L.1340 J.D. 5 W. 4th St.
Travis, Philip C., (BV) ....'43 '72 C.150 A.B. L.1340 J.D. 3040 Madison Rd.
Tregre, Calvin S., Jr. '74 '01 C.974 B.S. L.150 J.D.
[Ⓐ Lopez,H.R.M.&S.] (⊙Newport Beach, CA)
Tremain, Kenneth D. '34 '60 C.679 B.S.Ch.E. L.273 J.D.
(adm. in VA; not adm. in OH; Pat.) Chf. Pat. Coun., Natl. Distillers & Chem. Corp.
Trenz, Alan R., (BV) ....'56 '81 C&L.150 B.A., J.D. 700 Walnut Street, Suite 200
Triantafilou, Alexander M. ....'71 '96 C.150 B.A. L.1161 J.D. Anderson Publishing Co.
Triona, James P., (AV) ....'53 '77 C.275 B.A. L.608 J.D. [Triona C.&L.]

Triona Calderhead & Lockemeyer, (AV)
2909 Vernon Place, 45219 ⊙
Telephone: 513-569-9999 Fax: 513-569-9998

(This Listing Continued)

Triona Calderhead & Lockemeyer (Continued)

David C. Calderhead. Members of Firm: James P. Triona; David S. Lockemeyer (Resident). Associates: Stephanie P. Franckewitz; Joel L. Peschke; Ruth M. Torok (Resident).
Medical Malpractice Defense, Professional Liability, Appellate Practice, Civil Litigation, Insurance Defense, Health Care, Consumer Law Defense, Negligence Defense, Family Law, Criminal Law, Entertainment Law.
Milford, Ohio Office: 200 Techne Center Drive, Suite 100, 45150. Telephone: 513-576-1060.

See Professional Biographies, CINCINNATI, OHIO

Tripp, Douglas S., (BV) .... '57 '85 C.476 B.S. L.862 J.D. [Ⓑ Vorys,S.S.&P.]
Trogolo, Richard E. '46 '71 C.446 B.S. L.128 J.D.
(adm. in MD; not adm. in OH) Chief Coun., I.R.S., Dept. of Treasury
Trombetta, Patricia J. .... '55 '81 C.475 B.A. L.383 J.D. Co. Arbitrator [Ⓐ Smith,R.&S.]
Troutman, Jane M. .... '58 '92 L.692 J.D. Law Clerk
Trumbo, Steven R. '59 '87
C.896 B.A. L.1340 J.D. Asst. Coun., The Ohio Natl. Life Ins. Co.
Tucker, Jack L., (AV) .... '57 '83 C.275 B.S. L.150 J.D. [Robbins,K.P.&T.]
Tucker, Stacy Leigh .... '72 '00 C.323 B.A. L.150 J.D. Law Clk., 1st Dist. Ct. of App.
Tulch, Robert .... '28 '67 C.150 B.S. L.151 J.D. 28 Carpenters Rdg.‡
Turner, James L., (AV) '59 '84 C.63 B.S. L.345 J.D.
(adm. in IN; not adm. in OH) Sr. Coun., Cinergy Servs.
Turner, Richard Paul '73 '98 C.1161 B.A. L.1340 J.D.
10979 Reed Hartman H., Ste. 115
Turner, Wm. K., Jr. .... '23 '49 C&L.607 LL.B. P.O. Box 1118
Tytus, John B. .... '10 '35 C.976 B.A. L.150 LL.B. 8605 Indian Hill St.‡
Uhl, Jay J., (BV) .... '46 '74 C.321 B.A. L.150 J.D. 3814 West St.
Uhl, Judd R. .... '73 '99 C.473 B.A. L.8 J.D. [Ⓐ Freund,F.&A.]
Uhl, Leslee Moore .... '71 '98 C.880 B.A. L.7 J.D. Atty. Gen.'s Off.
Uhle, Richard B., Jr., (BV) .... '58 '83 C.967 B.A. L.150 J.D. [Durkee&U.] ⊙
Uhrig, Robert Francis, (AV) '62 '92
C.973 B.S. L.150 J.D. MPS Gen. Coun., Fifth Third Bk.
Ulmer, Andrew B. .... '77 '03 C.608 B.A. L.150 J.D. [Ⓐ Frost B.T.]

Ulmer & Berne LLP, (AV)
600 Vine Street, Suite 2800, 45202 ⊙
Telephone: 513-698-5000 FAX: 513-698-5001
Email: infocincinnati@ulmer.com URL: http://www.ulmer.com
Partners: B. Scott Boster; Matthew V. Brammer; Andrew R. Giannella; Jennifer Bouchard Hageman; John M. Hands; John R. Ipsaro; Scott P. Kadish; Bradley D. Kaplan; Linda E. Maichl; Michael A. Marrero; Donald J. Mooney, Jr.; Jeffrey F. Peck; Stuart A. Schloss, Jr.; Frederic X. Shadley; Michael J. Suffern; Stuart R. Susskind; Joseph P. Thomas. Of Counsel: Gina M. Saelinger. Senior Attorney: Reuel D. Ash. Associates: Jennifer Paschen Bergeron; Christopher D. Cathey; Tiffany Reece Clark; Jason P. Conte; Paul J. (P.J.) Cosgrove; Jeffrey Geoppinger; Pamela Ginsburg; Sharon E. Gronotte; Prentiss W. Hallenbeck, Jr.; Jeanette Hargreaves; Jennifer Snyder Heis; Karen L. Imbus; Karen E. Jones; Joseph C. Klein; Thomas G. McIntosh; James L. Salmon; Jeffrey R. Schaefer; Michael C. Schmidt; Jacqueline R. Sheridan; Denise M. Smith; Julie C. Smith (Not admitted in OH); Ronald G. Smith; Mary Lynn Tate; Traci L. Wallace.
Antitrust; Banking and Commercial Lending; Broker/Dealer and Securities Litigation; Business Law; Business Litigation; Business Restructuring; Class Action Defense; Construction Law; Corporate Finance; Corporate Restructuring and Creditors' Rights; Corporate Succession Planning; Emerging Businesses; Employee Benefits; Employment and Labor; Environmental; Fair Housing; Financial Institution Compliance; General Counsel Services; Health Care; Income Tax; Insurance Coverage; Intellectual Property and Technology; Joint Ventures; Liability Defense; Mass Torts; Mergers, Acquisitions and Divestitures; Nonprofit; OSHA; Pharmaceutical; Product Liability; Public Law; Real Estate; Securities; Securities Regulatory Compliance; Subrogation; Tax; Technology Transactions; Toxic Tort Defense; Trade Secrets/Unfair Competition; Trusts and Estates; Venture Capital; Workers' Compensation; Trial and Appellate Practice in All Courts.
Cleveland, Ohio Office: Skylight Office Tower, 1660 West 2nd Street, Suite 1100. Telephone: 216-583-7000. FAX: 216-583-7001.
Columbus, Ohio Office: 88 East Broad Street, Suite 1600. Telephone: 614-229-0000. FAX: 614-229-0001.
Chicago, Illinois Office: One North Franklin Street, Suite 1825. Telephone: 312-324-8000. FAX: 312-324-8001.

See Professional Biographies, CINCINNATI, OHIO

Ultsch, Wm. F., (BV) .... '24 '50 C&L.150 LL.B. 3001 Ebenezer Rd.
Unkenholt, Cindy J. '71 '98 C.150 B.S. L.184 J.D.
(adm. in CT; not adm. in OH) [Ⓐ Hammond]
Urling, James Patrick .... '70 '99 C.608 B.A. L.1339 J.D. Pros. Atty. Off.
Utaski, Thomas J. .... '42 '77 C.597 B.A. L.813 J.D. 4555 Lake Forest Drive, Suite 365
Utt, Daniel P., (AV) .... '61 '86 C.97 B.S. L.201 J.D. [Katz,T.B.&H.]
Utter, Gregory M., (AV) .... '56 '81 C&L.150 B.B.A., J.D. [Keating M.&K.]
Utz, Eugene J. .... '23 '53 C.150 B.B.A. L.1340 J.D. Ret. Ct. of App. J.‡
Vahlsing, Joseph H., (BV) .... '47 '72 C.150 B.A. L.383 J.D. [Cors&B.]
Vale, Emil, (BV) .... '11 '36 C&L.150 A.B., LL.B. 10910 Brookgreen Ct.
Valentine, Frederick Lee .... '23 '55 C.150 B.B.A. L.597 J.D. 3814 West St.
Valentine, Lona J. .... '72 '00 C.1150 B.S. L.383 J.D. [Ⓐ Peck,S.&W.]
Valleau, Richard J., (AV) .... '36 '62 C.973 B.S. L.150 J.D. [Cors&B.]
Valz, David Randolph .... '68 '94 C.880 B.S. L.151 J.D. [Buechner,H.O.M.H.&K.]
Vance, James .... '30 '60 C.62 B.A. L.1003 J.D. 6600 Wyman Lane
Vander Laan, Mark A., (AV) .... '48 '73 C.323 A.B. L.477 J.D. [Dinsmore&S.]
VandeWater, Kristen D. '76 '02 C.347 D.Psych. L.421 J.D.
(adm. in IN; not adm. in OH) [Ⓑ Mason,S.&M.] (⊙Madison, IN)
VanDrake, Vance V., III .... '— '05 C.108 B.A. L.150 J.D. [Ⓐ Frost B.T.]
Van Horn, Ray A. .... '27 '77 C.665 B.A. L.150 J.D. 4509 Glenridge Dr.
Van Houten, Dennis W., (BV) .... '50 '76 C.347 B.A. L.1340 J.D. [Droder&M.]
Van Matre, James H. .... '20 '53 C.150 A.B. L.151 J.D. 4018 Carew Twr.
Van Sickle, R. Matthew '78 '03 C.896 B.A. L.1119 J.D.
(adm. in IN; not adm. in OH) [Ⓐ Weltman,W.&R.]
Van Valkenburg, Valerie L., (BV) .... '60 '86 C.523 B.A. L.150 J.D. [Ⓐ Aronoff,R.&H.]
Vardiman, Edwin L. '27 '54 C&L.421 A.B., LL.B.
(adm. in KY; not adm. in OH) U.S. Army Corps of Engineers
Vardiman, Edwin L., Jr. .... '65 '99 C.1161 B.A. L.1340 J.D. [Ⓐ Ritter&R.]
Varney, Kimberly .... '66 '91 C.235 B.A. L.1340 J.D. [Ⓐ Thomas&T.]
Vaske, Philip J. .... '46 '76 C.1118 B.A. L.1340 J.D. Tres., The Besl Transfer Co.
Veith, Patrick R. .... '76 '02 C.602 B.A. L.1340 J.D. [Ⓐ Spraul,V.&D.]
Veith, Terrence M., (BV) .... '50 '75 C.812 B.A. L.150 J.D. [Spraul,V.&D.]
Vella, Theresa H. .... '73 '99 C.1149 B.A. L.734 J.D. [Ⓐ Taft,S.&H.]
Venesy, Bryan J., (BV) ...... '63 '88 C.611 B.A. L.150 J.D. [Squire,S.&D.] (⊙Columbus)
Veneziano, Frank J., (BV) .... '59 '85 C.611 B.A. L.150 J.D. [Weltman,W.&R.]
Venhoff, Carla M. '74 '99 C.1118 B.A. L.4210 J.D.
(adm. in KY; not adm. in OH) [Ⓐ Deters,B.&L.] ⊙
Vennemann, Jerome A. '50 '79 C.150 B.A. L.607 J.D.
Actg. Gen. Coun. & Asst. Corp. Secy., Cinergy Servs.
Ventress, William W. .... '24 '54 C.150 B.A. L.802 LL.B. 9525 Whitegate Lane‡
Verchot, Joan M., (AV) .... '61 '86 C.446 B.A. L.117 J.D. [Dinsmore&S.]
Verkamp, Jennifer M. .... '70 '96 C.973 B.S. L.276 J.D. [Volkema,T.M.B.S.&M.] ⊙
Vernon, M. Catherine '58 '93
C.473 B.A. L.930 J.D. Asst. Gen. Coun., Formica Corporation
Verst, Edward C. .... '37 '63 C.1118 B.A. L.150 J.D. N. L. R. B.

Vick, Joe P. '20 '48 C&L.228 A.B., LL.B.
(adm. in NC; not adm. in OH) Int. Rev. Serv.
Victor, Irving W. .... '21 '55 C.679 B.S. L.1340 J.D. 3215 S. Whitetree Circle‡
Vincent, George H., (AV) .... '57 '82 C&L.477 B.A., J.D. [Dinsmore&S.]
Vineyard, Joshua L. .... '77 '04 C&L.150 B.S., J.D. [Ⓐ Frost B.T.]
Vitenberg, Vladimir '55 '95 C.999 B.S. L.150 J.D.
Sr. Coun., The Procter & Gamble Co.
Vizedom, Anita .... '71 '01 C.610 B.A. L.150 J.D. Hamilton Co. Pros.'s Off.
Vogel, Cedric, (AV) '09 '32
C&L.150 A.B., LL.B. 800 Main Professional Bldg., 817 Main St.‡
Vogel, Cedric W., (BV) .... '46 '72 C.976 B.A. L.309 J.D. [Ⓑ Heis&W.]
Vogel, E. Brian .... '68 '95 C.1118 B.A. L.150 J.D. 2915 Treevalley Court.
Vogele, James A., (BV) .... '47 '73 C&L.150 B.A., J.D. 2367 Chickasaw St.

Volkema, Thomas, Miller, Burkett, Scott & Merry, A Legal Professional Association, (AV)
700 Walnut Street, Suite 400, 45202-2015 ⊙
Telephone: 513-651-4400 Fax: 513-651-4405
Email: attorneys@vt-law.com
Frederick M. Morgan, Jr.; Jennifer M. Verkamp.
Qui Tam (Whistleblower), False Claims Act, Civil State and Federal Trial and Appellate Practice. Personal Injury. Malpractice, Nursing Home Negligence, HMO Liability, Class Actions, Wrongful Death, Automobile Accidents, Product Liability, Employee Benefits, Insurance Bad Faith, Aviation and Tort Law, ERISA.
Reference: Huntington National Bank.
Columbus, Ohio Office: 140 East Town Street, Suite 1100. 43215-5183. Telephone: 614-221-4400. Fax: 614-221-6010.

See Professional Biographies, CINCINNATI, OHIO

Vollman, Carl W., (BV) .... '24 '51 [Loeb,V.H.&F.]
Vollman, Jeffrey S. .... '71 '97 [Ⓐ Cohen,T.K.&S.]
Vollman, Jill Meyer .... '71 '96 C.522 B.A. L.151 J.D. [Frost B.T.]
Vollman, Mark C., (BV) .... '55 '81 C.321 B.A. L.1340 J.D. 1014 Vine Street
Vollman, Stanton H., (AV) .... '40 '66 C.973 B.S.B.A. L.1340 J.D. [Cohen,T.K.&S.]
Von Hagen, Frank J. .... '22 '55 C&L.1340 B.S.C., J.D. 11340 Kenn Rd.‡
Von Wahlde, Stephen '57 '82
C.201 B.A. L.150 J.D. Assoc. Coun., Federated Dept. Stores, Inc.
Voorhees, Michael R. .... '57 '87 C.1161 B.S. L.1340 J.D. 9521 Montgomery Rd.

Vorys, Sater, Seymour and Pease LLP, (AV) 🅱🅱
Atrium Two, Suite 2000, 221 East Fourth Street, P.O. Box 0236, 45201-0236 ⊙
Telephone: 513-723-4000 Facsimile: 513-723-4056
URL: http://www.vssp.com
Partners: Glenn V. Whitaker; Stephen S. Eberly; Daniel J. Buckley; Donald J. Shuller; Charles C. Bissinger, Jr.; Roger E. Lautzenhiser; David A. Groenke; Terri Reyering Abare; Andrew M. Kaplan; Mark A. Norman; Melvin A. Bedree; Thomas L. Gabelman; W. Breck Weigel; William D. Hayes; Nathaniel Lampley, Jr.; Eliot N. Meyers; Victor A. Walton, Jr.; Scott A. Carroll; Richard L. Moore; Hani R. Kallas; Phillip J. Smith; Eric W. Richardson; William D.G. Baldwin. Associates: Robert M.M. Shaffer; Kent A. Britt; Kimberly J. Schaefer; Anthony L. Osterlund; Tara K. Burke; Jason L. Hodges; Mr. Kory A. Jackson; Michael J. Bronson; Corey A. Donovan; Sarah B. Fairweather; Adam C. Sherman; Michael L. Rich; Ward B. Washington; Geoffrey M. White; Erica D. Gann; Mr. Whitney C. Gibson; Jackie R. Kruger. Of Counsel: Eugene P. Ruehlmann; Roger A. Yurchuck; Barbara Bison Jacobson; Donald B. Lewis; Mary C. Henkel; Douglas S. Tripp; Cynthia A. Shafer; Michael G. Schwartz; Rosemary D. Welsh. Staff Attorney: Steven R. Miller.
Banking, Civil/Commercial Litigation, Commercial Transactions/Bankruptcy, Environmental, Estate Planning/Probate, Health Care, Savings and Loan/Thrifts.
Columbus, Ohio Office: 52 East Gay Street, P.O. Box 1008, 43216-1008. Telephone: 614-464-6400. Facsimile: 614-464-6350.
Cleveland, Ohio Office: 2100 One Cleveland Center, 1375 East Ninth Street, 44114-1724. Telephone: 216-479-6100. Facsimile: 216-479-6060.
Washington, D.C. Office: 1828 L Street, N.W., Suite 1111, 20036-5104. Telephone: 202-467-8800. Facsimile: 202-467-8900.
Alexandria, Virginia Office: 277 South Washington Street, Suite 310, 22314. Telephone: 703-837-6999. Facsimile: 703-549-4492.
Akron, Ohio Office: First National Tower, 106 South Main Street, Suite 1100, 44308. Telephone: 330-208-1000. Facsimile: 330-208-1001.

See Professional Biographies, CINCINNATI, OHIO

Wachs, James S., (AV) .... '33 '58 C.150 B.A. L.309 LL.B. [Frost B.T.]
Wade, Martin, (BV) .... '49 '81 C.339 B.S. L.1340 J.D. 119 E. Court St.
Waggal, John G. .... '56 '83 C&L.607 B.A., J.D. 830 Main Street, Suite 1115
Wagner, Barbara, (AV) '51 '82 C.976 B.A. L.178 J.D.
Assoc. Gen. Coun. & Corp. Compl. Offr., Chiquita Brands Intl., Inc.
Wagner, Esther .... '15 '78 C&L.150 B.Sc., J.D. 2918 Hoadly Ct.‡
Wagner & Bloch, (AV) ....2345 Ashland Avenue
Waisblum, Phillip L. '25 '53 C&L.378 B.A., LL.B.
(adm. in KS; not adm. in OH) Chf. Admin. Law J., Soc. Sec. Admn.
Waite, C. Jeffrey, (BV) .... '55 '81 C.1353 B.A. L.608 J.D. [J.Waite&Assoc.]
Waite, Jeffrey, & Associates Co. LPA, (BV) ....830 Main Street, Suite 500

Waite, Schneider, Bayless & Chesley Co., L.P.A., (AV) 🅱🅱
1513 Fourth and Vine Tower, Fourth and Vine Streets, 45202
Telephone: 513-621-0267 Fax: 513-381-2375; 621-0262
Email: wsbclaw@aol.com URL: http://www.wsbclaw.com
Stanley M. Chesley;—James R. Cummins; Fay E. Stilz; Robert A. Steinberg; Louise M. Roselle; Thomas F. Rehme; D. Arthur Rabourn; Troy W. Skeens, Jr.; Paul M. De Marco; Terrence L. Goodman; Robert Heuck II; Jane Hanna Walker; Jean M. Geoppinger; Melanie S. Corwin; Renée A. Infante.
General Civil Practice. Aviation, Antitrust Litigation, Class Action, Commercial Litigation, Complex Litigation, Corporate Law, Federal Employees Liability, General Civil Trials and Appeals in all Courts, Insurance, Labor, Consolidated and Multi-district Litigation, Products Litigation, Securities Litigation and Wrongful Death.

See Professional Biographies, CINCINNATI, OHIO

Walden, C. Curtis, (AV) .... '59 '84 C&L.150 B.A., J.D. [Martin&B.]
Wales, Ross E., (AV) .... '47 '74 C.674 A.B. L.893 J.D. [Taft,S.&H.]

Walk, Rodger N., (BV) '48 '74 C&L.150 B.A., J.D.
The Nathaniel Ropes Building, 917 Main Street, Suite 400, 45202
Telephone: 513-977-4220 Fax: 513-977-4218
Email: rnwalklaw@fuse.net URL: http://www.lawyers.com/rnwalklaw
Catastrophic Injury and Loss, Wrongful Death, Medical Malpractice, Personal Injury, Complex Commercial Litigation, Collaborative Divorce, Business and Commercial Law, Family Law, Litigation and Appeals, Alternative Dispute Resolution, Employee Employment Law, Products Liability.

See Professional Biographies, CINCINNATI, OHIO

Walker, Bernice L. .... '— '93 C.970 B.A. L.1340 J.D. Dir., Small Business Develop.
Walker, Douglas A. .... '52 '79 C&L.150 B.B.A., J.D. V.P. of Opers., Chiquita Brands
Walker, H. Lawson, II, (BV Ⓣ) .... '49 '75 C&L.150 B.B.A., J.D. [Frost B.T.]
Walker, Jane Hanna, (AV) .... '57 '84 C.150 B.A. L.607 J.D. [Ⓐ Waite,S.B.&C.]
Walker, Janice L. .... '61 '95 C.640 B.S. L.151 J.D. Coun., Cinergy Servs.
Walker, Stephen W. .... '61 '89 C&L.150 B.S., J.D. Staff Atty., 1st Dist. Ct. of App.
Walker, Steven R. '58 '89 C&L.259 B.S., J.D.
(adm. in FL; not adm. in OH) V.P., Law, Alderwoods Group, Inc.
Wallace, David T. .... '63 '89 C.473 B.A. L.151 J.D. U.S. Cir. Ct. of App.
Wallace, Helen C. ..... '72 '00 C.150 B.A. L.273 J.D. Montgomery Cnty. Asst. Pros. Atty.

Wallace, John E. '66 '92
C.473 B.A. L.608 J.D. Staff Coun., U.S. Court of Appeals-6th Cir.
Wallace, Traci L. '68 '00 C.473 B.A. L.1340 J.D. [A] Ulmer&B.]
Walsh, Kevin R. '— '01 C.602 B.A. L.124 J.D. [A] Lerner,S.&R.]
Walter, Ann E. '73 '99 C.37 B.A. L.117 J.D. [A] Faulkner&T.]
Walter, Edward Lee '58 '87 C.63 B.S. L.151 J.D. I.R.S.
Walters, Ryan D. '76 '03 C.608 B.A. L.477 J.D. [A] Squire,S.&D.]
Walther, Chris B. '66 '91 C.138 B.A. L.383 J.D.
Assoc. Gen. Coun, The Procter & Gamble Co.
Walton, Victor A., Jr., (BV) '64 '91 C&L.276 B.S.F.S., J.D. [Vorys,S.S.&P.]
Walulik, David W. '71 '99 C&L.608 B.S.B.A., J.D. [A] Frost B.T.]
Walwyn, Jennifer K. '78 '03 C.188 B.S. L.1068 J.D. [A] Keating M.&K.]
Wamsley, Andrew J. '79 '04 C.94 B.A. L.276 J.D. [A] Dinsmore&S.]
Wang, Charleston '56 '82 C.205 B.E.B.S. L.1340 J.D. 6924 Plainfield Road
Ward, Dennis R. '50 '91 C.472 B.S. L.151 J.D. Dir., Andrew Jergens Co.
Ward, Jonathan D. '48 '78 C.30 B.S. L.1340 J.D. 10608 Merrick Ln.‡
Ward, Richard G. '55 '86 C.207 B.A. L.150 J.D. [Drew&W.]
Ward, Richard H., (AV) '23 '49 C.207 L.150 LL.B. [Drew&W.]
Ward, Tracy T. '69 '99 C&L.150 B.A., J.D. [A] Taft,S.&H.]
Wareham, Kristi A. '63 '99 C.97 B.S. L.851 J.D.
(adm. in NM; not adm. in OH) 7658 Coldstream Dr.
Warncke, Daniel R., (BV) '59 '93 C.446 B.A. L.150 J.D. [Taft,S.&H.]
Warnock, Frank E., (BV) '55 '87 C.531 B.S. L.1340 J.D. [Brown&W.]
Warren, David S., (AV) '63 '89 C.97 B.A. L.276 J.D. [Graydon H.&R.]
Washington, Ward B. '69 '03 C.039 B.A. L.228 J.D. [A] Vorys,S.S.&P.]
Wasserman, Frank J. '49 '75 C&L.273 B.S., J.D. Cinci. Legal Aid Soc.
Wasserman, Mark J., (BV) '44 '84 C.994 L.150 J.D. 1726 Young
Wassler, Jane Frances '54 '84 C.150 B.A. L.1340 J.D. City Public Schools
Watkins, Robert J. '30 '53 C&L.608 B.A., J.D. 22 Diplomat Dr.‡
Watson, Clint C. '79 '05 C.896 B.A. L.477 J.D. [A] Frost B.T.]
Watson, John L. '24 '50 C&L.150 LL.B. 3645 Hopper Ridge
Watts, Barbara G. '46 '78 C.679 B.A. L.150 J.D.
Assoc. Dean, Univ. of Cincinnati Coll. of Law
Watts, Susan E. '51 '85 C.8 B.A. L.851 J.D. Legal Aid Society of Greater Cin.
Wayne, Beth, (BV) '54 '89 C.880 B.S. L.150 J.D. [A] Crabbe,B.&J.]
Wayne, Richard S., (AV) '52 '79 C.150 B.A. L.201 J.D. [Strauss&T.]
Weakley, Leonard A., Jr., (AV) '46 '77 C.150 B.B.A. L.1340 J.D. [Rendigs,F.K.&D.]
Webb, Gary A. '52 '85 C.454 B.A. L.930 J.D.
Assoc. Coun., Federated Dept. Stores, Inc.
Weber, Arthur D., Jr., (BV) '47 '73 C.201 B.A. L.1340 J.D. [Wood&L.]
Weber, Bradford C. '70 '97 C.473 B.A. L.383 J.D. [A] Benjamin,Y.&H.]
Weber, Donald L., (AV) '31 '61 C.151 B.S.C. L.1340 J.D. 813 Broadway
Weber, Frank J., Jr. '28 '60 C.150 B.B.A. L.1340 LL.B. I.R.S.
Weber, H. Patrick, (AV) '49 '74 C&L.602 B.B.A., J.D. [Barrett&W.]
Weber, Herman J., Jr. '27 '52 C.631 B.A. L.608 J.D. Dist. J.
Weber, Katharine C. '65 '89 C.383 B.B.A. L.1340 J.D. [Cors&B.]
Weber, Mark F., (AV) '53 '78 C.473 B.S. L.150 J.D. 8044 Montgomery Rd., Ste. 120
Weber, Mark J., (AV) '54 '80 C.228 A.B. L.150 J.D. [Keating M.&K.]
Weber, Mary Helen '50 '76 C.914 B.A. L.150 J.D. Asst. Reg. Coun., I.R.S.
Weber, Michael L., (BV) '64 '89 C.124 B.S. L.273 J.D. 813 Broadway, 1st Floor
Weber, Roger A., (AV) '49 '73 C.608 B.A. L.309 J.D. [Taft,S.&H.]
Weber, Terry A. '51 '81 C.150 B.A. L.1340 J.D. 3907 N. Bend Rd.
Weed, Ithamar D. '14 '39 C.610 A.B. L.608 J.D. 3818 Miami Rd.‡
Weeks, Steven W., (AV) '50 '77 C.900 B.S. L.309 J.D. [Taft,S.&H.]
Wegner, Kenneth E., (BV) '56 '82 C.1036 B.A. L.608 J.D. 9200 Montgomery Rd.
Wehmer, Brenda K., (AV) '64 '91 C&L.150 B.A., J.D. [Peck,S.&W.]
Wehrman, Mary T. '76 '03 C.383 B.S. L.1340 J.D. Becker Gallagher
Weidner, Robert B. '32 '73 C.150 M.S. L.1340 J.D. 5779 Filview Cir.
Weigel, W. Breck, (AV) '60 '85 C.174 B.A. L.150 J.D. [Vorys,S.S.&P.]
Weigle, Douglas S., (AV) '50 '76 C.97 B.S. L.1340 J.D. [Bartlett&W.] ⊙
Weigle, Gerald V., Jr., (AV) '47 '71 C.597 B.S. L.477 J.D. [Dinsmore&S.]
Weil, Rex '51 '77 C.597 B.A. L.150 J.D. N.L.R.B.
Weil, Sidney, (AV) '26 '50 C&L.150 LL.B. [Beckman W.S.]
Weill, Neal J. '51 '78 C.4 A.B. L.150 J.D. Asst. U.S. Trustee
Weinstein, Gerald C., (BV) '42 '72 C.150 B.A. L.1340 J.D. 7 W. 7th St.
Weirich, David M. '68 '93
C.475 B.S. L.823 J.D. Coun., Patents, The Procter & Gamble Co.
Weisenberger, Andrew '77 '02 C.473 B.S. L.4210 J.D. [A] Santen&H.]
Weisenfelder, Wilson G., Jr., (AV) '53 '85 C.150 B.B.A. L.1340 J.D.
[Rendigs,F.K.&D.]
Weisensel, Michael D. '70 '97 C.1044 B.S. L.8 J.D. [A] O'Connor,A.&L.]
Weiss, Herbert B., (AV) '40 '65 C&L.150 B.A., J.D. [Keating M.&K.]
Weiss, Mark A., (AV) '66 '92 C.477 A.B. L.150 J.D. [Keating M.&K.]
Weisser, Mark B., (AV) '58 '83 C.473 B.A. L.930 J.D. 1014 Vine Street, Suite 1650
Welch, Robert J., Jr., (BV) '45 '75 C.973 B.S. L.1340 J.D. [Kircher,R.&W.]
Welker, Paula L. '54 '88 C&L.801 B.S., J.D. 230 E. 9th. St. 12th. Fl.
Weller, Jill A., (AV) '56 '81 C.276 A.B. L.180 J.D. [Keating M.&K.]
Wellington, Kent, (AV) '65 '91 C.385 B.A. L.608 J.D. [Graydon H.&R.]
Wells, Ben F., (AV) '58 '83 C&L.150 B.B.A., J.D. [Dinsmore&S.]
Wells, Frederick E. '30 '54 C&L.178 B.A., LL.B.
(adm. in AR; not adm. in OH) 1 Procter & Gamble Plz.‡
Welsh, Rosemary D. '49 '95 C.297 B.A. L.150 J.D. [C] Vorys,S.S.&P.]

Weltman, Weinberg & Reis Co., L.P.A., (AV)
525 Vine Street, Suite 800, 45202 ⊙
Telephone: 513-723-2200 Fax: 513-723-2239
Email: wwr@weltman.com URL: http://www.weltman.com
Frank J. Veneziano; Glenn E. Algie;—Brian E. Chapman; David W. Cliffe; Jeannette M. Conrad (Not admitted in OH); John L. Day, Jr.; Laura R. Faulkner; Gail C. Hersh, Jr.; Susan B. Klineman; Amy Triplett Morgan; Thomas R. Myers; Karolina F. Perr; Philip Q. Ratliff (Not admitted in OH); Nicholas K. Rohner; Anne M. Smith; Charles L. Tate; R. Matthew Van Sickle (Not admitted in OH).
Burlington, New Jersey Office: Telephone: 609-914-0437.
Deerfield, Illinois Office: Telephone: 847-940-9812.
Chicago, Illinois Office: Telephone: 312-786-9676.
Cleveland, Ohio Office: Telephone: 216-685-1000.
Columbus, Ohio Office: Telephone: 614-228-7272.
Philadelphia, Pennsylvania Office: Telephone: 215-599-1500.
Pittsburgh, Pennsylvania Office: Telephone: 412-434-7955.
Troy, Michigan Office: Telephone: 248-362-6100.

See Professional Biographies, CINCINNATI, OHIO

Wendel, Richard G., II, (BV) '67 '92 C.197 A.B. L.150 J.D.
441 Vine Street, Suite 4400
Wendeln, John H., (BV) '59 '84 C&L.201 B.S., J.D. [Thompson H.]
Wenker, Paul F., (AV) '42 '67 C.973 B.S. L.276 J.D. [Rendigs,F.K.&D.]
Wenstrup, Daniel J., (BV) '48 '76 C.602 A.B. L.1340 J.D. [Heis&W.]
Werden, George W. '49 '80
C.610 B.S.Ed. L.1340 J.D. Assoc. Gen. Coun., The U.S. Shoe Corp.
Werkman, Diana J. '74 '00 C.929 B.A. L.383 J.D. Law Clk.
Wernicke, Vanessa A. '76 '04 C.188 B.S. L.150 J.D. [A] Taft,S.&H.]
Wersching, James P., (AV) '55 '80 C.602 B.B.A. L.150 J.D. [Santen&H.]
Wesloh, Steven M. '71 '96 C.347 B.A. L.150 J.D. [A] Frost B.T.]
Wesner, James Ermal '— '92 Gen. Coun., Univ. of Cincinnati
Wessendarp, Edw. M. '10 '55 C.150 L.1340 LL.B. 2330 Kemper Ln.
West, John A., (AVⓉ) '40 '67
C.383 B.A. L.150 J.D. [Greenebaum D.&M.] (⊙Covington, KY)
Westendorf, Douglas L., (AV) '47 '74 C.262 B.A. L.178 J.D. [A] Wood&L.]
Westerbeck, David F., (AV) '45 '72 C&L.150 B.A., J.D.
Exec. V.P., Gen. Coun. & Secy., The Union Central Life Ins. Co.
Westerfield, Thomas J., (AV) '55 '81 C.602 B.A. L.150 J.D. [C] Dinsmore&S.]
Westermeyer, Daniella A. '71 '97 C.608 B.A. L.150 J.D. 105 W. 4th St.
Weston, Harris K., (AV) '18 '46 C&L.309 A.B., LL.B. [C] Dinsmore&S.]
Wetherall, Greg '68 '96 C&L.150 B.B.A., J.D. [G.Wetherall]
Wetherall, Greg, LPA, Law Office of 4030 Mt. Carmel Tobas, Suite 122
Wetherell, Raymond C., (AV) '16 '43 C&L.150 LL.B. 830 Main St.‡
Wettstein, Albert, (BV) '17 '41 C&L.150 B.A., LL.B. Solr.
Whalen, Melissa J. '67 '97 C.138 B.A. L.1340 J.D. [A] Lerner,S.&R.]
Whaley, David A. '78 '03 C&L.201 B.S., J.D. [A] Dinsmore&S.]
Whaley, Susan Street '74 '99 C.347 B.S. L.150 J.D. Sr. Coun., Procter & Gamble Co.
Wharton, Bernard W., (BV) '67 '94 C.668 B.A. L.150 J.D. [McCaslin,I.&M.] ⊙
Wharton, Lisa M., (BV) '56 '88 C.937 B.A. L.770 J.D. [A] Thompson H.]
Wheatley, Bryan C. '70 '97 720 E. Peter Rose Way, Suite 400
Wheatley, Christine S. '71 '96 C.602 B.A. L.608 J.D. [Porter W.M.&A.]
Wheatley, Susan E., (AV) '60 '86 C.976 B.A. L.597 J.D. [Taft,S.&H.]
Wheeler, David L. '67 '96 C.882 B.S.B.A. L.150 J.D. [A] Squire,S.&D.]
Wherley, James M., Jr. '74 '01 C.294 B.S. L.150 J.D. [A] Dinsmore&S.]
Whitaker, Glenn V., (AV) '47 '72 C.207 B.A. L.273 J.D. [Vorys,S.S.&P.]
Whitaker, James R., (AV) '46 '73 C.610 B.B.A. L.37 J.D. [Keating M.&K.]
Whitaker, Kristin K. '75 '02 C.692 B.A. L.1340 J.D. [A] Frost B.T.]
White, Alfred K., Jr. '29 '59 C.282 B.A. L.976 LL.B.
(adm. in NY; not adm. in OH) 885 Spooke Ridge Ln.‡
White, Byron E., (BV) '21 '48 C.207 A.B. L.150 J.D. One East Fourth St.
White, Geoffrey M. '78 '03 C.890 B.A. L.477 J.D. [A] Vorys,S.S.&P.]
White, Maurice O., (AV) '53 '78 C.893 B.S. L.150 J.D.
7 West Seventh Street, Suite 1850
White, Michael J. '58 '84 C.96 B.S. L.201 J.D. The Union Central Life Ins. Co.

White, Getgey & Meyer Co., L.P.A., (AV)
1700 Fourth & Vine Tower, 1 West Fourth Street, 45202-3621
Telephone: 513-241-3685 Fax: 513-241-2399
Ronald A. Meyer; Nicholas E. Bunch; David P. Kamp; Glenda Morgan Hertzman (Certified Specialist in Workers' Compensation Law, Ohio State Bar Association); Carl J. Stich, Jr.;—Leona Beth Zahneis; C. Joseph Mccullough. Of Counsel: Reeta H. Brendamour; Todd H. Bailey.
Civil Litigation, Personal Injury Law, Medical Malpractice Law, Workers Compensation Law, Appellate Practice.

See Professional Biographies, CINCINNATI, OHIO

Whitehurst, John R., II '48 '81 C.608 B.Sc. L.1340 J.D. 2302 Carew Twr.
Whiteley, Daniel E., Jr., (BV) '44 '75 C.150 B.A. L.1340 J.D. 3852 Burwood Ave.
Whitlow, Janice Baker '77 '03 C&L.201 B.S.E.E., J.D. [A] Frost B.T.]
Whitlow, Matthew A. '77 '03 C.383 B.S. L.201 J.D. [A] Dinsmore&S.]

Whitman, Bruce B., (AV) '51 '80 C&L.150 B.A., J.D.
3536 Edwards Road, Suite 100, 45208
Telephone: 513-321-3940 Fax: 513-321-3929
Email: bbwhits123@aol.com URL: http://www.whitmanlawoffice.com
Civil Litigation, Product Liability, Employment Law, Medical Malpractice, Wrongful Death, Criminal Defense and Personal Injury, Divorce/Dissolution, Business Litigation.

See Professional Biographies, CINCINNATI, OHIO

Whitman, Virginia Conlan, (AV) '49 '81 C&L.150 B.A., J.D.
One West Fourth Street, Suite 1700, 45202-3621
Telephone: 513-352-0401 FAX: 513-241-2399
Email: vwhitman@wgmlpa.com
General Civil Litigation in State and Federal Courts. Employment Discrimination, Employee Counseling, Business Litigation.

See Professional Biographies, CINCINNATI, OHIO

Whittaker, James A., (AV) '58 '85 C.960 B.S. L.851 J.D. [Butkovich,S,S.&G.]
Widdowson, Mary E. '68 '98 C.346 B.A. L.851 J.D. [A] Dinsmore&S.]
Wiethe, Barbara R., (BV) '39 '79 C.973 B.A. L.1340 J.D. 118 W. 6th St.
Wiethe, Donetta D., (AV) '52 '77 C.473 B.A. L.150 J.D. Asst. U.S. Atty.
Wiethe, John A. '12 '40 C.150 Ph.B. L.1340 LL.B. 7 W 7th St.

Wiethe, Michael J., (BV) '47 '72 C.734 B.A. L.150 J.D.
Suite 1800 Federated Building, 7 West Seventh Street, 45202
Telephone: 513-241-7332 Fax: 513-621-5410
Email: mjwiethe@fuse.net URL: http://www.mjwiethe.com
General Practice.

See Professional Biographies, CINCINNATI, OHIO

Wietholter, Thomas A., (CVⓉ) '51 '86 C.1161 B.S. L.1340 J.D. [A] Statman,H.S.&E.]
Wilcoxon, Kimberly D. '76 '01 C.473 B.A. L.150 J.D. [A] Thompson H.]
Wilder, Mark A. '65 '99 C&L.150 B.A., J.D. [A] Cuni,F.&L.]
Wilhelmy, Alicia L. '75 '01 C.974 H.B.A. L.150 J.D. [A] Dinsmore&S.]
Wilkerson, Conley G. '25 '55 C.853 A.B. L.383 LL.B.
(adm. in KY; not adm. in OH) Int. Rev. Serv.
Wilkins, Nancy Ellen, (BVⓉ) '48 '75
C.347 B.A. L.602 J.D. 4866 Cooper Road, Suite 103
Wilkinson, Carl E. '32 '58 C&L.150 B.B.A., LL.B. 29 Carpenter's Ridge‡
Wilkinson, George B., (AV) '51 '82 C.893 B.A. L.276 J.D. [Dinsmore&S.]
Wilkinson, Rebecca L. '58 '83 C.249 B.S. L.347 J.D. [Casper&C.] (⊙Middletown)
Wilkowski, E. Todd '67 '98 C.1070 B.S. L.1339 J.D. [Keating M.&K.]
Wilkowski, Heather Alisha '72 '98 C.473 B.A. L.1339 J.D. Co. Pros. Off.
Willacker, Terence M. '46 '76 C.201 B.A. L.1340 J.D. Legal Aid Soc.
Willbrand, David '70 '96 C.309 A.B. L.150 J.D. [A] Thompson H.]
Williams, John J., (BV) '63 '89 C.1380 B.A. L.107 J.D. [Gonzalez,S.&H.]
Williams, John M., (BV) '64 '94 C.608 B.A. L.1161 J.D. [Delev&W.]
Williams, John P., Jr., (AV) '41 '66
C.674 A.B. L.150 J.D. Cincinnati Chamber of Commerce
Williams, Melvin O., Jr. '24 '63 C.339 B.S. L.1340 J.D. 11340 Kenn Rd.‡
Williams, Tina '70 '01 C.150 B.S. L.192 J.D. Atty., Cincom Systems Inc.
Williamson, David '73 '99 C.303 B.A. L.1340 J.D. [A] Lindhorst&D.]
Williamson, Leonard A. '38 '73
C.1023 B.S. L.325 J.D. 10339 Giverny Boulevard, Suite 1 (Pat.)
Williamson, William O. '77 '04 C.8 B.S.B.A. L.150 J.D. [A] Strauss&T.] ⊙
Willis, Jeffrey A. '75 '02 C.97 B.S. L.150 J.D. [A] Dinsmore&S.]
Willis, Marisa B. '75 '03 C.117 B.A. L.150 J.D. Com. Pleas Ct.
Willis, Ryan L. '76 '01 C.701 B.S. L.201 J.D. [A] Taft,S.&H.] (Pat.)

Willits, Chad E. ... '69 '96 C.201 B.A. L.150 J.D. [Ⓐ Rendigs,F.K.&D.]
Willmann, Neal O. ... '44 '72 C.221 B.S. L.502 J.D. 9521 Montgomery Rd. (Pat.)
Wills, Teddy L. ... '50 '92 C.696 B.M. L.608 J.D. Ct. of App.
Wilson, Christopher J. '65 '91
C.1118 B.A. L.602 J.D. V.P. & Gen. Coun., Cincinnati Bell
Wilson, Danielle M. ... '79 '04 C.610 B.S. L.1003 J.D. [Ⓐ Wolfe,P.]
Wilson, Gregory R., (BV) ... '46 '78 C.150 B.B.A. L.1340 J.D. [G.R.Wilson]
Wilson, LaQuita S. ... '78 '03 C.383 B.A. L.150 J.D. [Ⓐ Taft,S.&H.]
Wilson, Raymond G. '20 '52 C.62 A.B. L.1003 J.D.
Asst. Secy. & Sr. Coun., Cincinnati Milacron Inc.
Wilson, Samuel S., (AV) ... '24 '61 C.674 A.B. L.150 LL.B. 1278 Dillon Ave.‡
Wilson, W. Russell, (AV) ... '57 '83 C.674 A.B. L.150 J.D. [Frost B.T.]
Wilson, Gregory R., Co., L.P.A., (BV) ... 1411 Sycamore Street
Winget, James L. '70 '95 C.473 B.S. L.150 J.D.
Coun., Coml Contracts, GE Aviation Services, Inc.
Wingo, Wm. T. ... '27 '54 C.150 L.1340 LL.B. 49 E. 4th St.
Winstead, John N. ... '67 '98 C&L.383 B.A., J.D. [Ⓐ Keating M.&K.]
Winters, R. Gary, (AV) ... '48 '76 C&L.150 B.A., J.D. [McCaslin,I.&M.] ⊙
Wirthlin, J. Stephen, (AV) ... '50 '79 C.150 B.A. L.1340 J.D. [Beirne&W.]
Wirthlin, John R., (AV) '58 '85
C&L.150 B.S., J.D. Corp. Coun., Provident Financial Group, Inc.
Wirthlin, John S., (AV) ... '24 '51 C.973 L.1340 J.D. [Beirne&W.] ‡
Wirthlin, Michael F., (BV) ... '54 '82 C.150 B.A. L.1340 J.D. [Beirne&W.]
Wise, Bryan E. ... '78 '03 C&L.602 B.A., J.D. [Ⓐ Taft,S.&H.]
Wissman, Brian Michael '73 '00
C&L.150 B.S., J.D. Bureau of Alcohol, Tobacco & Firearms
Witte, Monte D. ... '37 '74 C.623 B.S. L.1340 J.D. 3578 Tiffany Ridge Lane (Pat.)
Witte, Richard C., (AV) ... '29 '56 C.474 B.S. L.1119 J.D. 596 Abilene Trail‡
Woeber, Linda L., (AV) ... '62 '87 C.473 B.S. L.150 J.D. [Montgomery,R.&J.]
Woebkenberg, Thomas M., (AV) ... '60 '86 C.893 B.A. L.607 J.D. [Wood&L.]
Woeste, Ralph T. ... '26 '53 C.151 L.1340 LL.B. 1731 Norcol Ln.
Wolf, David A. ... '38 '66 C.150 B.S. L.1340 J.D. 10925 Reed Hartman Hwy.
Wolf, Leon L., (AV) ... '26 '50 C.610 L.150 LL.B. [Ⓒ Strauss&T.]
Wolf, Sara Straight, (AV) ... '47 '76 C.473 B.S.Ed. L.150 J.D. [Cors&B.]
Wolfe, Jennifer C. ... '71 '99 C.63 B.S. L.150 J.D. [Wolfe,P.]

Wolfe Practice, The, LPA
4445 Lake Forest Drive, Suite 420, 45242
Telephone: 513-618-8700 Fax: 513-618-8740
Email: jwolfe@twplaw.com URL: http://www.twplaw.com
Jennifer C. Wolfe;—Tina J. Barrett; Danielle M. Wilson; Janet Ellen Beers.
Banks and Banking, Business Law, Business Litigation, Business Transactions, Closely Held Business Law, Joint Ventures, Commercial Law, Commercial Real Estate, Communications and Media, Construction Law, Contracts, Copyrights, Corporate Law, Corporate Finance, Corporate Litigation, Environmental Law, Finance, Commercial Finance, Franchises and Franchising, General Practice, Health Care, Intellectual Property, Internet Law, Labor and Employment, Litigation, Mergers, Acquisitions and Divestitures, Nonprofit and Charitable Organizations, Partnership Law, Probate, Real Estate, Taxation, Trade Secrets, Trademarks, Trusts and Estates, Unfair Competition, Zoning, Planning and Land Use. Adoption, Cohabitation Agreements; Divorce Law; Domestic Relations Law; Marital Property Law; Matrimonial Law; Non-Traditional Family Law; Paternity Law; Post-Divorce Law; Premarital Agreements; Separation Agreements; Spousal Support Law.
See Professional Biographies, CINCINNATI, OHIO

Wolfgang, Rex A., The Law Office of
(See Hamilton)

Wolnitzek & Rowekamp, P.S.C.
(See Covington, Kentucky)

Wolper, David P. ... '46 '75 C.105 B.S. L.945 J.D. 8006 Deershadow Ln.
Wolske, Walter J., Jr., (AV) ... '32 '56 C&L.608 B.S., J.D. [Wolske&B.] ⊙
Wolske & Barclay, A Legal Professional Association, (AV)
655 Eden Park Drive, Suite 770 (⊙Columbus)
Wolter, Warren H. '48 '75 C&L.494 B.A., J.D.
(adm. in MN; not adm. in OH) 9854 Tall Timber Drive
Wood, Carol Schwetschenau ... '58 '88 C.473 A.B. L.150 J.D. [Ⓐ Freking&B.]
Wood, David R. ... '61 '87 C.97 B.S. L.117 J.D. Asst. Pros. Atty.
Wood, Frank E. ... '42 '67 312 Walnut, Suite #3550‡
Wood, Sean W. ... '51 '79 C.150 B.A. L.1187 J.D. Coopers & Lybrand
Wood, Walter S. ... '59 '84 C&L.383 B.S., J.D. Corp. Coun., Cincinnati Milacron Inc.

Wood, Herron & Evans, L.L.P., (AV) BB
2700 Carew Tower, 45202
Telephone: 513-241-2324 Fax: 513-421-7269
Email: info@whepatent.com URL: http://www.whepatent.com
Members of Firm: Edmund E. Wood (1868-1916); William R. Wood (1893-1935); Edmund P. Wood (1923-1968); Truman A. Herron (1935-1976); Edward B. Evans (1937-1971); Bruce Tittel; Donald F. Frei; David J. Josephic; David S. Stallard; J. Robert Chambers; Gregory J. Lunn; Kurt L. Grossman; Clement H. Luken, Jr.; Thomas J. Burger; Gregory F. Ahrens; Wayne L. Jacobs; Kurt Andrew Summe; Kevin G. Rooney; Keith R. Haupt; Theodore R. Remaklus; Thomas W. Humphrey; Scott A. Stinebruner; David H. Brinkman; Beverly A. Lyman. Senior Associates: Joseph R. Jordan; C. Richard Eby. Associates: J. Dwight Poffenberger, Jr.; Kathryn E. Smith; Kristi L. Davidson; P. Andrew Blatt; David E. Jefferies; William R. Allen; John P. Davis; Douglas A. Scholer; Brett A. Schatz; David Wesley Dorton; Sarah Otte Graber; Randall S. Jackson, Jr. Of Counsel: John D. Poffenberger; Thomas W. Flynn; Bradley D. Beck.
Intellectual Property and Related Litigation; Computer Law, Patents, Trademarks and Copyrights.
See Professional Biographies, CINCINNATI, OHIO

Wood & Lamping, L.L.P., (AV)
600 Vine Street, Suite 2500, 45202-2491 ⊙
Telephone: 513-852-6000 Fax: 513-852-6087
Members of Firm: Kenneth J. Schneider; William R. Ellis; Harold G. Korbee; Eric C. Holzapfel; Paul R. Berninger; Robert P. Malloy; Jeffrey M. Rollman; Mark S. Reckman; Jan M. Frankel; Gary J. Davis; James B. Harrison; Henry E. Menninger, Jr.; C. J. Schmidt, III; Thomas M. Woebkenberg; Arthur D. Weber, Jr.; Thomas J. Breed; John W. Eilers, Jr.; Lisa deHart Lehner; Peter M. Burrell; Jeffrey P. McSherry; Lisa M. Rammes. Of Counsel: Robert F. Reckman; William H. Eder, Jr.; Amy Gasser Callow. Associates: Douglas L. Westendorf; Raymond J. Pikna, Jr.; Roccina S. Niehaus; Timothy A. Garry, Jr.; Edward D. Bender; Mark A. Denney; Janet Y. Castañeda; Kevin K. Frank; Karen A. Nicewander; Jeffrey D. Forbes; V. Brandon McGrath; Nathan H. Blaske; Sarah B. Ellington; Wednesday Oster.
Civil and Commercial Litigation, Corporate and Business, including Mergers and Acquisitions, Tax, Labor and Employment, Workers Compensation, Real Estate, Municipal and Administrative, Admiralty, Products Liability Defense, Insurance Defense, Securities, Bankruptcy, Estate Planning, Probate, Family Law, Land Use and Zoning, Employee Benefits, Health and Hospital Law.
Lawrenceburg, Indiana Office: Wood, Lamping & Lehner, 208 Walnut Street, 47025. Telephone: 812-537-2375. Fax: 812-537-2368.
See Professional Biographies, CINCINNATI, OHIO

Woodard, Kevin S. ... '66 '91 C.473 B.A. L.150 J.D. 817 Main St., 8th Fl.
Woods, Harvey B., (BV) ... '23 '53 C.150 B.B.A. L.1340 LL.B. 900 American Bldg.
Woodside, Frank C., III, (AV) ... '44 '69 C&L.608 B.S., J.D. [Dinsmore&S.]
Woodside, Patrick ... '76 '05 C.178 B.S. L.608 J.D. [Ⓐ Peck,S.&W.]
Worrell, A. Christian, III, (AV) ... '51 '85 C.150 B.A. L.1340 J.D. [Graydon H.&R.] ⊙
Wright, Darrell S., (BV) ... '56 '85 C.1161 B.S. L.1340 J.D. [Ⓐ Bartlett&W.] ⊙
Wright, LaTonia Denise ... '71 '97 C.973 B.S.N. L.150 J.D. [L.T.D.Wright]
Wright, Roger ... '53 '82 C.836 B.A. L.1340 J.D. Univ. of Cincinnati
Wright, Ross A. ... '68 '94 C&L.150 B.B.A., J.D. Convergys Corp.
Wright, La Tonia Denise, RN, LLC, Law Office of ... P.O. Box 15756
Wunsch, Eric J. ... '— '96 C.473 B.S. L.597 J.D. Sr. Coun., Procter & Gamble Co., The
Wurster, Walter C., II, (BV) ... '47 '74 C.264 A.B. L.500 J.D. [W.C.Wurster]
Wurster, Walter C., Co., L.P.A., (BV) ... 8044 Montgomery Road
Wykoff, John R., (AV) ... '51 '79 C.150 B.B.A. L.201 J.D. 2337 Victory Parkway
Wyler, William S., (AV) ... '46 '72 C.30 B.A. L.150 J.D. [Schwartz,M.&R.]
Xanders, George L., (AV) ... '54 '80 C.967 B.S. L.1119 J.D. [Xanders&X.]
Xanders & Xanders Co., L.P.A., (AV) ... 808 Elm Street, Suite 200
Yaeger, Daniel A. ... '52 '81 C.973 B.S. Sr. Coun., Fluor Daniel Fernald Corp. (Pat.)
Yager, Christina S. ... '53 '99 C.608 B.S.S.W. L.1340 J.D. [Ⓐ Katz,G.&N.]
Yaros, Alma Proffitt, (BV) ... '49 '77 C.523 B.S. L.1340 J.D. Pro Seniors, Inc.
Yates, Irene W. ... '64 '96 C.473 B.S. L.1340 J.D. Grp. Mgr., Procter & Gamble Co., The
Yates, Janice E. ... '47 '82 C.347 A.B. L.1340 J.D. Chf. Dep. Clk., U.S. Ct. App.
Yeager, Stephen M., (AV) ... '54 '81 C.473 B.S. L.1340 J.D. 1 W. 4th St., Ste. 1800
Yelton, Donald George '52 '94 C&L.150 B.B.A., J.D.
Dir. of Fin. Planning, New England Financial
Yetter, Jerry J. ... '39 '73 C.679 B.S. L.1340 J.D. 6174 Seica Dr. (Pat.)‡
Yocum, Thomas R., (AV) ... '53 '79 C.608 B.A. L.150 J.D. [Benjamin,Y.&H.]
Youkilis, John C. ... '57 '85 C.103 A.B. L.893 J.D. Pres., The Victor Corp.
Young, Gregory E. '51 '78 C.705 A.B. L.851 J.D.
Coun., Govt. Compl., Lit.& Preventive Law, GE Aviation Services, Inc.
Young, M. Scott ... '67 '93 C.722 B.A. L.124 J.D. [Ⓐ Thompson H.]
Young, Martin M. ... '36 '59 C&L.150 B.A., J.D. [Young,R.&N.]
Young, Michael T. ... '56 '83 C.97 B.S. L.851 J.D. Springdale Title Agency
Young, Michele Lori ... '58 '91 C.012 B.A. L.276 J.D. 632 Vine St.
Young, Robert E. Lee ... '14 '37 C&L.150 LL.B. 1127 Ryland Ave.‡
Young, Rodney M. ... '60 '94 C.16 B.S.M.E. L.1340 J.D. [Thompson H.] (Pat.)
Young, Shawn M., (AV) ... '55 '87 C.1161 B.S. L.1340 J.D. [Strauss&T.]

Young & Alexander Co., L.P.A., (AV)
110 Boggs Lane, Suite 242, 45246 ⊙
Telephone: 513-326-5555 FAX: 513-326-5550
Thomas P. Erven.
Business Law. Environmental Law. Health Care. Insurance Law. Labor and Employment. Nonprofit and Charitable Organizations. Personal Injury. Products Liability. Real Estate. Toxic Torts. Trusts and Estates. Wills and Probate.
Counsel for: The Children's Medical Center, Dayton, Ohio; The Colonial Stair & Woodwork Co.; The Greater Dayton Area Hospital Assn.; Mike-Sell's Potato Chip Co.; Moorman Pontiac, Inc.
Local Counsel for: Colonial Penn Insurance Co.; John Hancock Mutual Life Insurance Co.; Hertz Corp.; State Farm Insurance Co.
Dayton, Ohio Office: 130 West Second Street, Suite 2000, 45402-0668. Telephone: 937-224-9291. Telecopier: 937-224-9679.
See Professional Biographies, DAYTON, OHIO

Young, Reverman & Napier Co., L.P.A., (BV) ... 1014 Vine Street
Youtsey, Deborah A. ... '— '85 C.385 A.B. L.1048 J.D. [Thompson H.]
Yu, Tracy Rottner ... '74 '99 C.602 B.A. L.150 J.D. [Ⓐ Dinsmore&S.]
Yund, George E., (AV) ... '52 '77 C.608 B.A. L.477 J.D. [Frost B.T.]
Yungblut, Gibson R., (AV) ... '33 '60 C.309 A.B. L.150 J.D. 201 E. 5th St. (Pat.)
Yurchuck, Roger A., (AV) ... '38 '62 C.597 A.B. L.309 J.D. [Ⓒ Vorys,S.S.&P.]
Zackerman, Jeffrey L. ... '63 '97 C&L.150 B.A., J.D. [Ⓐ Frost B.T.]
Zahneis, Leona Beth ... '71 '01 C.235 B.S. L.1340 J.D. [Ⓐ White,G.&M.]
Zahniser, David W., (CVⓉ) ... '65 '96 C.291 B.S. L.383 J.D. [Ⓐ Freund,F.&A.]
Zahniser, Rachel S. ... '72 '99 C.138 B.A. L.383 J.D. [Ⓐ Taft,S.&H.]
Zamary, George J. ... '72 '99 C.610 B.S. L.117 J.D. [Ⓐ Rendigs,F.K.&D.]
Zamary, Kimberly Kyle ... '75 '00 C.608 B.A. L.150 J.D. [Ⓐ Kohnen&P.]
Zaunbrecher, Susan B., (AV) ... '59 '90 C.861 B.A. L.150 J.D. [Dinsmore&S.]
Zavatsky, Kathleen Hanson, (AV) '47 '79
C&L.94 A.B., J.D. Assoc. Coun., Federated Dept. Stores, Inc.
Zavatsky, Michael J., (AV) ... '48 '80 C.608 B.A. L.150 J.D. [Taft,S.&H.]
Zavon, Dan A. ... '51 '76 C.94 A.B. L.150 J.D. 4020 Rose Hill Ave.‡
Zealey, Sharon J., (AV) ... '59 '84 C.974 B.S. L.150 J.D. [Blank R.]
Zegarski, Daniel S. ... '70 '95 C.201 B.A. L.200 J.D. [Zegarski&I.]

Zegarski & Ice Co., L.P.A.
700 Walnut Street, Suite 220, 45202
Telephone: 513-651-4226 Fax: 513-651-0224
Email: dzegarski@fuse.net
Daniel S. Zegarski; Andrew G. Ice.
Bankruptcy, Consumer Bankruptcy, Foreclosures, Family Law, Adoptions, Child Custody, Child Support, Divorce, Domestic Violence, Premarital Agreements, Spousal Support, Visitation Rights, Dissolution, Modifications, Garnishments, Harassment, Lawsuits, Alimony, Paternity, Personal Injury.
See Professional Biographies, CINCINNATI, OHIO

Zeinner, Lawrence Allen '60 '98 C.150 B.S. L.472 J.D.
Contract Compliance Consultant, The Ohio National Life Insurance Company
Zerbst, Hilla M., (AV) ... '49 '78 C.608 B.A. L.117 J.D. [Frost B.T.]

Ziegler & Schneider, P.S.C.
(See Covington)

Ziermaier, Klaus M. '45 '70 C&L.608 B.S., J.D.
Div. V.P. & Asst. Gen. Coun., Federated Dept. Stores, Inc.
Zigman, Andrea K. ... '56 '82 C.33 B.A. L.112 J.D. 901 Elm St.
Zimmer, Barry H., (BV) ... '54 '79 C&L.150 B.A., J.D. [Zimmer]
Zimmer, Christine M., (BV) '58 '84 C.930 B.A. L.575 J.D.
Univ. of Cinn. College of Law
Zimmer, Hans M., (AV) ... '62 '84 C&L.150 B.A., J.D. [Cors&B.]
Zimmer Law Firm, The, (BV) ... 4540 Cooper Rd., Ste. 300
Zimmerman, Donald J. '37 '61 C&L.608 B.A., J.D.
Sr. V.P., Ins. Opers., The Ohio Natl. Life Ins. Co.
Zimmerman, James M. ... '74 '99 C&L.880 B.A., J.D. [Ⓐ Taft,S.&H.]
Zummo, Mark J., (AV) ... '55 '80 C.893 B.A. L.150 J.D. [Kohnen&P.]
Zummo, Valerie Brown ... '56 '82 C&L.150 B.F.A., J.D. [Barron,P.B.&S.]

CIRCLEVILLE, * 13,485, *Pickaway Co.*

Adkins, John R. ... '44 '73 C.385 A.B. L.150 J.D. Mun. J.
Ammer, William ... '19 '47 C&L.608 B.S., J.D. 141 Pleasant St.
Archer, William L., Jr. '62 '88
C.473 B.S. L.150 J.D. Pickaway County Prosecutor's Office
Bennington, Kevin Gregory ... '71 '99 C.473 B.A. L.608 J.D. P.O. Box 682
Bennington, Roger E., (BV) ... '34 '64 C&L.608 B.S., J.D. 149 W. Franklin St.

Benson, Michael E.
(See Columbus)

Berger, Allan, (AV) ... '32 '59 C.610 A.B. L.608 J.D. [Berger]
Berger Law Office, (AV) ... 119B S. Court St.

Bowers, John E., (BV) ... '49 '79 C.608 B.S. L.607 J.D. 233 N. Court St.
Branham, Elisa M. ... '65 '93 C.383 B.B.A. L.608 J.D. Pickway Co. Common Pleas Ct.
Brown, Jennifer L., (CV) ... '63 '89 C&L.607 B.A., J.D. 119 S. Court St.

Calig & Handelman, LPA
(See Columbus)

Cline, Guy G. ... '15 '41 C&L.608 LL.B. Ret. Prob. J.

Colley Shroyer & Abraham Co., L.P.A.
(See Columbus)

Crowder-Dorsey, Kathy, Attorney at Law, (CV) '64 '89
C&L.117 B.A., J.D. 130 W. Franklin St.
Donahey, Richard S., (BV) ... '41 '68 C&L.608 B.C.E., J.D. [Twyford&D.] ⊙
Eyerman, Susan E. ... '54 '84 C.226 B.S. L.117 J.D. Staff Atty. & Mag., Ct.of Apps.
Farthing, John H., (BV) ... '45 '73 C.339 B.S. L.117 J.D. P.O. Box 541

Geary, William L.
(See Columbus)

Gerhardt, Richard L., (BV) ... '41 '66 C.607 B.A. L.276 J.D. 143 West Franklin Street

Goldman & Rosenthal
(See Columbus)

Greene, Patrick, (BV) ... '53 '84 C.610 B.S.C. L.117 J.D. [Greene&L.]
Greene and Lucks, L.P.A., (BV) ... 203 S. Scioto St.
Hill, James K., (BV) ... '45 '72 C.608 B.S. L.117 J.D. [Hill]
Hill Law Office, (BV) ... 408 East Main Street
Huffer, Robert H., (AV) ... '31 '56 C&L.608 B.A., J.D. [Huffer&H.]
Huffer, Roy H., Jr., (BV) ... '35 '64 C.608 A.B. L.266 J.D. [Huffer&H.]
Huffer and Huffer Co., L.P.A., (AV) ... 130 West Franklin Street

Kenney-Pfalzer, Susan
(See Columbus)

Kenworthy, Gary D., (BV) ... '54 '80 C&L.607 B.A., J.D. 443 North Court Street
Kingsley, James R., (BV) ... '47 '72 C.532 B.A. L.851 J.D. 157 W. Main St.
Kitchen, James Denny, (BV) ... '39 '70 C.610 B.B.A. L.608 J.D. [Kitchen,J.D.]
Kitchen, James D., (BV) ... 11841 Street, Rt. 56 E.
Kline, Roger L. ... '47 '78 C.610 B.B.A. L.117 J.D. Com. Pleas J., Prob. & Juv. Div.
Knece, P. Randall ... '55 '81 C&L.117 B.A., J.D. Com. Pleas Ct. J.

Lamkin, Van Eman, Trimble, Beals & Dougherty, LLC
(See Columbus)

Lemming, Stacey M. ... '70 '96 C.473 B.A. L.930 J.D. Law Clk., Ct. App.
Long, Jan Michael ... '52 '79 C.608 B.A. L.117 J.D. M.C. [🄲 Greene&L.]
Long, P. Eugene, II, (BV) ... '45 '74 C.610 B.B.A. L.851 J.D. Pros. Atty.
Lucks, Barbara J., (BV) ... '52 '76 C.238 B.A. L.117 J.D. [B.J.Lucks]
Lucks, Barbara J., L.P.A., (BV) ... P.O. Box 828
Marting, Rodger A. ... '45 '74 C.610 B.S. L.608 J.D. 414 S. Court St.‡
Noble, Ricky Duane, (CV) '66 '93 C.610 B.A. L.117 J.D.
Leg. Unit Coordinator, Child Supp. Enf. Agcy.

Oliver Law Office
(See Columbus)

Penn, Richard W., (BV) ... '21 '50 C.385 A.B. L.608 J.D. 503 Springhollow Rd.

Plymale Partnership LLP, The
(See Columbus)

Rogers, Ann Weiss '52 '79 C.1044 B.A. L.982 J.D.
(adm. in CA; not adm. in OH) 6440 Yankeetown Pike‡

Rourke & Blumenthal, LLP
(See Columbus)

Steely, Melody L., (BV) ... '54 '78 C.631 B.A. L.117 J.D. 151 West Franklin Street

Stumler, Rebecca J.
(See Columbus)

Tootle, Thomas F., (BV) ... '46 '73 C.611 B.A. L.607 J.D. 180 W. Franklin St.

Twyford & Donahey, P.L.L., (BV)
214 South Court Street, 43113 ⊙
Telephone: Toll Free: 1-800-686-1699 Fax: 614-849-0475
Email: help@twyforddonahey.com URL: http://www.twyforddonahey.com
Richard S. Donahey.
Personal Injury Litigation, Wrongful Death, Medical Malpractice, Products Liability, Automobile Accidents, Trucking Accidents, Head and Spinal Injuries, Motorcycle Accidents and Injuries, Uninsured Motorists, Insurance Law, Airplane Crash Litigation, Railroad Accidents, Slip and Fall, Dog Bites, Work Related Injuries, Birth Injuries, Nursing Home Abuse and Neglect.
References: The Huntington National Bank; Bank One of Columbus; BancOhio National Bank.
Columbus, Ohio Office: 495 South High Street, 43215-5058. Telephone: Toll Free: 1-800-686-1699. Email: help@twyforddonahey.com.
Delaware, Ohio Office: 163 N. Sandusky Street, Suite 103, 43015. Telephone: Toll Free: 1-800-686-1699. Email: help@twyforddonahey.com.
Lancaster, Ohio Office: 3794 Old Columbus, N.W., 43130. Telephone: Toll Free: 1-800-686-1699. Email: help@twyforddonahey.com.
Newark, Ohio Office: 137 West Main Street, Suite C., 43025. Telephone: Toll Free: 1-800-686-1699. Email: help@twyforddonahey.com.
London, Ohio Office: 25 West Fifth Street, 43140. Telephone: Toll Free: 1-800-686-1699. Email: help@twyforddonahey.com.

See Professional Biographies, CIRCLEVILLE, OHIO

Weldon and Wilburn, (BV) ... 210 S. Court St.
Wilburn, Bernard P., (CV) ... '57 '84 C.608 B.A. L.930 J.D. [🄰 Weldon&W.]
Wilburn, Charles W., (BV) ... '29 '64 C&L.608 B.S., J.D. [Weldon&W.]

CLAYTON, 13,347, *Montgomery Co.*

Beers, Janice I., (BV) ... '32 '80 C.518 A.B. L.201 J.D. 268 N. Diamond Mill Rd.
Office, Gerald S., Sr. ... '11 '37 C.201 A.B. L.309 LL.B. 6183 Par Ave.‡

CLEVELAND, * 478,403, *Cuyahoga Co.*

Abakumov, Georg, Law Offices of, (BV) '50 '77
C.930 B.A. L.1003 J.D. 1701 E. 12th St., Ste. 3G
Abbarno, Kenneth P. ... '66 '92 C.116 B.A. L.161 J.D. [🄰 Reminger&R.] (⊙Youngstown)
Abbuhl, David W., (BV) '55 '81
C.509 B.A. L.930 J.D. [🄲 Peckinpaugh&T.] (⊙Beachwood)
Abel, Jack W., (BV) ... '48 '74 C.608 B.A. L.575 J.D. [Abel&Z.]

Abel & Zocolo, LPA, (BV)
The Superior Building - Suite 1915, 815 Superior Avenue, 44114
Telephone: 216-621-6138 Fax: 216-241-5620
Email: lorizocolo@aol.com URL: http://www.lawyers.com/jackabellaw
Jack W. Abel; Lori A. Zocolo. Associate: Sharon R. Ditko-Bevione.
Family Law, Divorce, Custody, Interstate Custody, International Custody, Domestic Violence, Personal Injury, Divorce Taxation, Probate, Guardianship Law, Sports Law representing professional athletes in Family Law matters.

See Professional Biographies, CLEVELAND, OHIO

Abens, Matthew ... '77 '02 C.973 H.B.A. L.124 J.D. Judicial Staff Atty.
Abood, Mark S. ... '73 '98 C.363 B.S.B.A. L.1003 J.D. 9100 S. Hills Blvd. #300
Abramoff, Howard B., (AV) ... '51 '77 C.999 B.A. L.276 J.D. [Abramoff]
Abramoff Law Firm, (AV) ... 1500 S. Green Rd.
Acosta, Lori A. ... '63 '89 C.1048 B.S.B.A. L.930 J.D. 318 Solon Road
Acton, Shawn M. ... '75 '00 C.201 B.A. L.989 J.D. [🄰 Kelley&F.]
Adamo, Kenneth R. ... '— '75 C.688 B.S.Ch.E. L.982 J.D. [Jones D.] (See Pat. Sect.)
Adams, Albert T., (AV) ... '50 '77 C&L.309 B.A., J.D. [Baker&H.]
Adams, Beth M. ... '76 '02 C.62 B.A. L.989 J.D. [🄰 Brzytwa,Q.&M.]
Adams, Gregory J. ... '68 '98 C.608 B.S.E.E. L.930 J.D. 629 Euclid Ave., Ste. 1210 (Pat.)
Adams, Jennifer Lawry ... '70 '96 C.276 B.A. L.930 J.D. [Ulmer&B.]
Adams, Thomas W. ... '49 '92 C.59 B.A. L.161 J.D. [Renner,O.B.&S.] (See Pat. Sect.)
Adamson, Bryan, (BV) ... '63 '90 C.473 B.A. L.930 J.D. 11075 E. Blvd.
Adamson, Charles Z. ... '31 '57 C&L.94 A.B., LL.B. 815 Superior Avenue N.E.
Adelman, Harlin G. ... '65 '90 C&L.94 B.A., J.D. Univ. Hosp. of Clev.
Adelstein, Carol B., (BV) ... '62 '88 C.161 B.A. L.1003 J.D. [C.Adelstein]
Adelstein, Carol, (BV) ... 2043 Random Rd., Apt. 3
Adkins, Lewis W., Jr., (BV) ... '64 '93 C.563 B.S. L.8 J.D. [Roetzel&A.]
Adler, Charles F., (AV) ... '57 '83 C.473 B.S. L.161 J.D. [Schneider,S.R.&L.]
Adler, David F., (BV) ... '— '86 C.477 B.A. L.978 J.D. [Jones D.]
Adrine, Ronald B. ... '47 '73 C.254 B.A. L.1003 J.D. Assoc. Mun. J.
Agati, Andrew ... '70 '95 C.25 B.A. L.930 J.D. [Squire,S.&D.]
Aggers, David F. ... '47 '83 C.363 B.A. L.1003 J.D. [Aggers,J.&C.]

Aggers, Joseph & Cheverine Co., L.P.A., (BV)
Executive Commons East, 29525 Chagrin Boulevard, Suite 306, 44122-4601
Telephone: 216-765-8520 Fax: 216-765-8817
Email: ajc@ajclawfirm.com URL: http://www.ajclawfirm.com
David F. Aggers; Kathryn Theresa Joseph; Vincent L. Cheverine. Of Counsel: John V. Scharon, Jr.
Business Law, Commercial, Admiralty and Maritime, Environmental, Contracts, Corporate, Employment Law, Construction Law, Wills, Probate, Real Estate, State and Federal Litigation.

See Professional Biographies, CLEVELAND, OHIO

Agin, Bernard I., (BV) ... '46 '75 C.608 B.S. L.1003 J.D. [Agin&A.]
Agin, Sandra K., (BV) ... '48 '78 C.161 B.B.A. L.1003 J.D. [Agin&A.]

Agin and Agin Co. L.P.A., (BV)
5910 Landerbrook Drive Suite 200, 44124
Telephone: 440-460-1415 Fax: 440-446-1240
Email: bernieagin@aol.com URL: http://www.lawyers.com/agin&agin
Bernard I. Agin; Sandra K. Agin.
Business, Family and Probate Law, Personal Injury, Elder Care Law, General Civil Trials.
Reference: National City Bank.

See Professional Biographies, CLEVELAND, OHIO

Agopian, Richard, (BV) ... '46 '75 C.912 B.S. L.1003 J.D. 1415-1419 W. 9th Street
Agozzino, Leozino ... '— '85 C.604 B.A. L.608 J.D. [🄲 Jones D.] (See Pat. Sect.)
Ahern, Ann Marie ... '72 '98 C.201 B.A. L.989 J.D. [🄰 Simon]
Ahern, Terrance R., (BV) ... '55 '81 C.161 B.A. L.1003 J.D. 1500 W. 3rd St.
Ahonen, William D. ... '28 '53 C.318 A.B. L.477 J.D. 2815 Goldwood Dr.‡
Akers-Parry, Deborah, (Formerly Deborah Rowley Akers), (AV) '49 '76
C.910 A.B. L.1003 J.D. [Wolf&A.]
Alavi, Atossa M. ... '— '03 C.999 B.D.S. L.124 J.D. [🄰 Jones D.]
Alber, Alyson Suter ... '71 '98 C.188 B.S. L.893 J.D. 11075 East Boulevard
Albert, Steven W., (AV) ... '46 '71 C.30 B.A. L.851 J.D. [Ulmer&B.]
Albores, Oscar E. ... '77 '02 C.363 B.S. L.608 J.D. [🄰 Carlisle,M.R.K.&U.]
Alcox, Patrick J., (BV) ... '46 '76 C.161 B.B.A. L.1003 J.D. 75 Public Square, Suite 650
Alden, David B., (AV) ... '— '83 C.604 B.A. L.477 J.D. [Jones D.]
Aldrich, Anna ... '27 '52 C.178 B.A. L.569 J.S.D. U.S. Sr. Dist. J.
Aldrich, Thomas A., (AV) ... '56 '82 C.610 A.B. L.309 J.D. [Thompson H.]
Alexander, Andrew C., (BV) '64 '89 C.273 B.A. L.930 J.D.
Senior Vice President & General Counsel, Boykin Lodging Company
Alexander, Joseph P. ... '56 '81 C.8 B.S.B.A. L.7 J.D. [Rotatori,B.G.S.&A.]
Alexander, Louis P., Jr. ... '77 '03 C.473 B.S. L.989 J.D. [🄰 Shapiro&F.]
Alexandersen, Kevin C., (AV) ... '— '86 C.696 B.S. L.607 J.D. [Gallagher S.]
Alfred, Lynne B. ... '42 '76 C.477 A.B. L.930 J.D. BP American, Inc.
Alikhan, Cheryl A. ... '47 '89 C.381 B.A. L.851 J.D. 14427 Shireen Dr.
Allan, Sean P., (BV) ... '64 '89 C.473 B.A. L.1003 J.D. Coun., Cincinnati Fin. Corp.
Allbery, Scott E. ... '62 '87 C.610 B.S. L.930 J.D. Eaton
Allen, David V. ... '61 '87 C.62 B.A. L.7 J.D. [Taft,S.&H.]

Allen, Thomas F., (AV) '42 '68 C&L.976 B.A., LL.B.
1801 East Ninth Street, Suite 1300, 44114
Telephone: 216-771-4000 Fax: 216-771-0422
Tax and Business Law.

See Professional Biographies, CLEVELAND, OHIO

Allen, Thomas S. '54 '79 C.228 A.B. L.930 J.D.
V.P. & Tr. Dept. Mgr., Society Natl. Bk.
Allington, Frances F. ... '47 '97 C.62 B.A. L.1003 J.D. 17246 Park Lane Dr.
Allotta, John J. ... '75 '01 C.611 B.A. L.124 J.D. [🄰 Baker&H.]
Almond, Paul Martin '— '79
Sr. Coun., TRW Automotive Electronics, Birmingham, England
Alperin, Mitchell L., (BV) ... '51 '77 C.679 B.S. L.930 J.D. 3690 Orange Pl., Ste. 575
Alten, Heidi ... '— '97 C&L.178 B.A., J.D. [🄰 Duvin,C.&H.]
Alten, John M. ... '72 '99 C.597 B.S. L.930 J.D. [🄰 Ulmer&B.]
Alter, Janet L. ... '56 '90 C&L.150 B.A., J.D. [🄰 Walter&H.]
Althouse, Philip D. ... '54 '91 C.966 B.S.Ed. L.1003 J.D. 2012 W. 25th St.
Altmeyer, Susan Mary ... '64 '91 C.608 B.S. L.989 J.D. Cleveland Law Libr.
Alusheff, Charles P., (AV) ... '60 '85 C.608 B.A. L.1003 J.D. [Reminger&R.]
Amaddio, Mark D., (BV) ... '53 '89 C.161 B.S. L.930 J.D. [M.D.Amaddio]
Amaddio, Mark D., Co., L.P.A., (BV) ... 1801 E. Ninth St., Ste. 1710
Amato, Anthony J. ... '63 '92 C.363 B.A. L.1003 J.D. 6325 York Road
Amato, Thomas S. ... '58 '85 C.381 B.S. L.161 J.D. [🄰 Licata&Assoc.]
Amber, Joseph ... '41 '01 C&L.025 B.A., LL.B. [Taylor&A.] ⊙
Ambrose, Richard J. ... '53 '87 C.893 B.S. L.1003 J.D. Com. Pleas J.
Amer, Kathleen M. ... '— '04 C&L.602 B.B.A., J.D. [🄰 Jones D.]
Amer, Margaret E. ... '67 '94 C&L.930 B.A., J.D. 14402 Granger Road
Amin, Aarti Patel '74 '98 C.362 B.B.A. L.1365 J.D.
(adm. in PA; not adm. in OH) Coun., Parker-Hannifin Corporation
Amin, Himanshu S. ... '65 '95 C.608 B.S.E.E. L.930 J.D. [Amin&T.] (See Pat. Sect.)

Amin & Turocy, LLP
24th Floor, National City Center, 1900 East 9th Street, 44114
Telephone: 216-696-8730 Fax: 216-696-8731
URL: http://www.thepatentattorneys.com
Partners: Himanshu S. Amin; Gregory Turocy; Jeffrey R. Sadlowski; Deborah Corpus; Jeffrey D. Hale (Not admitted in OH); Eric D. Jorgenson. Associates: Daniel B. Bortnick; Carlos Garritano; David W. Grillo; John M. Ling; Michael J. Medley; James J. Pingor; Jeffrey N. Prulhiere; Vahid Sharifi (Not admitted in OH).

(This Listing Continued)

Amin & Turocy, LLP (Continued)
Patents, Patent Prosecution, Trademarks, Trademark Prosecution, Copyrights, Litigation, Intellectual Property.
See Professional Biographies, CLEVELAND, OHIO

Amini, Saeid Baradaran ... '54 '99 C.352 Ph.D. L.124 J.D. [S.Amini]
Amini, Saeid ... 13916 Cedar Rd.
Amirault, Leo P., (AV) ... '23 '52 C.800 L.94 J.D. [Amirault&R.]
Amirault & Rocco, A Professional Association, (AV) ... 25000 Euclid Ave.
Ammons, Linda L. '53 '87 C.999 B.A. L.608 J.D.
Cleveland Marshall Law Sch, 2121 Euclid Ave Lb 138
Ammons, Randal G. ... '67 '92 C.472 B.S. L.861 J.D. [Walter&H.]
Amos, Marc D. ... '73 '04 C.871 B.S. L.1187 J.D. [Ⓐ Sutter,O.&F.]
Amstadt, Nancy R. '68 '97 C.475 B.A. L.574 J.D.
(adm. in NC; not adm. in OH) Nat'l. City Corp.
Anastos, Thomas L., (AV) ... '59 '89 C.930 B.A. L.1565 J.D. [Ⓐ Ulmer&B.]
Andelman, Barbara F. '58 '86 C.188 B.A. L.608 J.D.
Admissions Asst. Dean, Franklin Thomas Backus Sch. of Law
Anderle, Catherine Criswell '66 '91 C.201 B.A. L.930 J.D.
(adm. in PA; not adm. in OH) Sr. Atty., U.S. Dept. of Educ.
Anderle, Robert D., (BV) ... '64 '90 C.473 B.A. L.930 J.D. [Porter W.M.&A.]
Anderson, Benjamin H. ... '64 '91 C.880 B.S. L.990 J.D. [Ⓐ Weisman,G.&W.]
Anderson, Laura R., (BV) ... '— '90 C.880 B.A. L.990 J.D. [Ⓐ Jones D.]
Anderson, Thomas W. '43 '80 C.353 B.A. L.201 J.D.
V.P., Case Western Reserve Univ.
Anderson, Timothy S. ... '74 '99 C.472 B.A. L.477 J.D. [Ⓐ Duvin,C.&H.]
Anderson, William J. '44 '69 C&L.352 B.A., J.D.
(adm. in IA; not adm. in OH) V.P. & Sr. Atty., Nat. City Corp.‡
Anderton, Michael ... '67 '93 C.473 B.S. L.930 J.D. [Ⓐ Tucker E.&W.]
Andorka, Frank H., (AV) ... '46 '75 C.610 A.B. L.188 J.D. [Baker&H.]
Andrachik, Roger A., (AV) ... '56 '84 C.62 B.A. L.1003 J.D. 19891 Beach Cliff Blvd.
Andrassy, Dana Rountree ... '64 '94 C&L.790 B.S., J.D. [Baker&H.]
Andreas, Frederick W. ... '60 '91 C.608 B.S. L.1003 J.D. 70 E. 208th Street
Andreini, Mark J. ... '— '94 C&L.494 B.M., J.D. [Ⓐ Jones D.]
Andrews, Barry W. ... '68 '95 C.976 B.A. L.602 J.D. [Baker&H.]
Andrews, Catherine V. ... '73 '99 C.861 B.A. L.930 J.D. [Ⓐ Hahn L.&P.]
Andrews, David T. ... '68 '93 C.610 B.A. L.893 J.D. [Ross,B.&S.]
Andrews, Douglas A. ... '56 '84 C.910 B.A. L.930 J.D. [Ⓒ Wilsman&S.]
Andrews, Oakley V., (AV) ... '40 '65 C.976 B.A. L.930 J.D. [Baker&H.]
Anenson, T. Leigh ... '67 '94 C.1042 B.A. L.8 J.D. 101 W. Prospect Ave., Suite 1400
Angelo, Michael J., (AV) ... '55 '84 C.980 B.S. L.7 J.D. [Johnson,A.&C.]
Angelotta, John L. ... '23 '52 C.930 A.B. L.1003 J.D. Com. Pleas J.
Angney, Jessica N. ... '75 '01 C.62 B.A. L.161 J.D. [Ⓐ Benesch,F.C.&A.]
Anhold, Gordon A. ... '46 '71 C&L.879 B.A., J.D. Sr. V.P., Society Natl. Bk.
Ankuda, Christopher J. ... '— '— [Ritzler,C.&S.]
Annos, George J. ... '58 '92 C.528 B.A. L.8 J.D. [Ⓐ Carlisle,M.R.K.&U.]
Ansberry, Sean M. ... '73 '99 C.473 B.S. L.150 J.D. [Ⓐ Hahn L.&P.]
Anselmo, Christopher A. ... '62 '89 C.363 B.S.B.A. L.161 J.D. [Anselmo]
Anselmo, Michelle B., (BV) ... '— '89 C.436 B.A. L.930 J.D. [Ⓐ Baker&H.]
Anselmo, Victor V., (BV) ... '63 '88 C.201 B.S. L.1003 J.D. [Ⓐ Armstrong,M.D.&Z.]
Anselmo Company ... 4161 Ridge Rd.
Antel, Harry C. ... '17 '58 C.930 B.A. L.161 J.D. 24470 Barret Rd.
Antolino, Dominick A., Jr. '53 '79 C.823 A.B. L.930 J.D.
1300 Union Commerce Bldg.‡
Antonelli, Dominic M. ... '62 '87 C.385 B.A. L.930 J.D. [Rieth&A.]
Antonelli, Mariellen M. ... '— '02 C.876 B.A. L.179 J.D. [Rieth&A.]
Antonelli, Patrick, Jr. ... '47 '72 C&L.276 B.S.B.A., J.D. 19615 Nottingham Rd.
Anway, Stephen P. ... '76 '02 C.97 B.A. L.608 J.D. [Ⓐ Squire,S.&D.]
Apelt, Ronald A., (BV) ... '65 '90 C.608 B.A. L.930 J.D. 1422 Euclid Avenue, Suite 717
Apicella, F. M., (AV) ... '30 '54 C&L.608 B.A., J.D. [Apicella&T.]

Apicella and Trapp, (AV) BR
1200 Penton Media Building, 1300 East Ninth Street, 44114-1503
Telephone: 216-696-3550 Fax: 216-696-3830
Email: aptrapp@msn.com
Members of Firm: F. M. Apicella; Mary Jane Trapp.
General Trial and Appellate Practice. Negligence, Federal Employers Liability, Railroad, Family, Professional Liability, Products Liability, Probate Litigation, Nursing Home Litigation.
Reference: Key Bank.
See Professional Biographies, CLEVELAND, OHIO

Appelbaum, Jeffrey R., (AV) ... '52 '77 C&L.188 B.A., J.D. [Thompson H.]
Apple, Lawrence E. ... '41 '67 C.178 A.B. L.976 LL.B. TransCon Builders, Inc.
Aquila, Frank D. ... '42 '90 L.1003 J.D. Prof., Cleveland State Univ.
Arbeznik, Leo J. '16 '50 C.363 B.S. L.1003 J.D.
Legal Coun., Meadowbrook Development Corp.
Archibald, Robert D., (AV) ... '31 '56 C.790 B.A. L.930 J.D. [Ⓒ McNeal,S.A.&B.]
Arendt, Michelle R. ... '72 '98 C.201 B.A. L.124 J.D. [Ⓐ Ulmer&B.]
Arfons, Chad ... '71 '97 C.8 B.A. L.861 J.D. [Ⓐ Roetzel&A.]
Arinze, Francis Morah ... '61 '98 C.1037 B.A. L.989 J.D. Co. Pub. Def.
Arison, Barbara J., (AV) ... '52 '75 C.8 B.A. L.893 J.D. [Frantz W.]
Arjani, Neville A. ... '51 '81 C.999 B.Sc. L.1292 J.D. Findley Davies
Armstrong, Barbara Lee ... '— '87 C.970 B.A. L.930 J.D. [Buckley K.]
Armstrong, Erin Adams ... '72 '97 C.602 B.A. L.608 J.D. [Ⓐ D.D.Briller]
Armstrong, Lester W., (AV) ... '60 '86 C.313 B.A. L.851 J.D. [Kahn K.]
Armstrong, Timothy J., (AV) ... '44 '72 C.363 B.A. L.930 J.D. [Armstrong,M.D.&Z.]
Armstrong, William E., (AV) ... '38 '67 C.610 B.S.C. L.608 J.D. [Deacon,H.&A.]

Armstrong, Mitchell, Damiani & Zaccagnini, (AV)
1725 Midland Building, 101 Prospect Avenue West, 44115-1091
Telephone: 216-566-0064 Fax: 216-566-0224
Members of Firm: Timothy J. Armstrong; William Mitchell; Louis C. Damiani; Bruce A. Zaccagnini.
Associates: Victor V. Anselmo; Maura Norton.
Personal Injury, Product Liability, Medical Malpractice, Wrongful Death, School Law, State and Federal Litigation and Appellate Practice, Federal, State and Local Taxation, Real Estate, Commercial Law, Administrative Law, Probate and Estate Planning, Labor Law, Attorney Disciplinary Law, Government Law and Criminal Law.
Reference: National City Bank of Cleveland.
See Professional Biographies, CLEVELAND, OHIO

Arnold, David, (AV) ... '41 '66 C&L.608 B.A., J.D. [Weston H.]
Arnold, Kemper D. ... '49 '80 C.207 B.S. L.1003 J.D. Vantage Financial Group Inc.
Arnold, Wanda Rembert ... '53 '80 C.696 B.A. L.1003 J.D. Gen. Ref., Probate Ct.
Arnold, William L. ... '52 '77 C.472 B.A. L.1003 J.D. [Ⓒ Baker&H.]
Aronoff, George N., (AV) ... '33 '58 C&L.930 A.B., LL.B. [Benesch,F.C.&A.]
Aronoff, James B., (AV) ... '59 '84 C.95 A.B. L.930 J.D. [Thompson H.]
Aronoff, Karen Feibel, (AV) ... '60 '85 C.860 B.S. L.930 J.D. 3142 Somerset Dr.
Aronoff, Steven K., (BV) ... '61 '86 C.901 B.A. L.930 J.D. 615 W. Superior Ave., 12th Fl.
Aronoff, Steven K. ... '43 '67 C.1138 B.A. L.1009 J.D. [S.K.Aronoff]
Aronoff, Steven K., PC ... 615 W. Superior Ave., 12th Floor
Arrighi, Amy L. ... '69 '98 C.999 B.S. L.989 J.D. [Ⓐ Strachan,M.O.&R.]
Arthur, Harry L., (BV) ... '56 '82 C.473 B.S. L.930 J.D. [Moriarty&J.]
Arvin, Ashley M. ... '71 '04 C.679 B.S. L.989 J.D. [Ⓐ Mansour,G.G.&M.]
Asam, Michael R. ... '— '01 C.385 A.B. L.228 J.D. [Ⓐ Jones D.] (See Pat. Sect.)
Asher, Kenneth D. ... '46 '91 C.611 B.A. L.1003 J.D. Tr. Offr., Society Natl. Bk.
Ashmus, Keith A., (AV) ... '49 '74 C.475 B.A. L.976 J.D. [Frantz W.]
Asman, Robert J. ... '24 '52 C.128 A.B. L.276 J.D. Asst. Co. Pros.
Assini, Frederick W., (AV) ... '43 '68 C.321 B.S. L.228 J.D. [Calfee,H.&G.] ‡
Aster, Dennis C. '53 '78 C.150 B.A. L.930 J.D.
1500 North Point Tower, 1001 Lakeside Avenue‡
Astrab, Michael K., Law Office of ... '71 '97 C.473 B.S. L.1003 J.D. 2000 E. 9th St.
Atkinson, Kathleen A. ... '73 '02 C.201 B.S. L.989 J.D. [Ⓐ Reminger&R.]
Auciello, Ernest W., Jr., (AV) ... '— '85 C.97 B.S. L.851 J.D. [Gallagher S.]
Audey, Susan Marie ... '57 '94 C.161 B.A. L.989 J.D. Jud. Clk., 8th Dist. Ct. of App.
Augustine, Katherine A. '69 '95
C.1134 B.A. L.608 J.D. Assoc., Third Federal Savings and Loan
Augustyn, Kevin Christopher ... '67 '92 C.363 B.A. L.880 J.D. Mag., Cuyahoga Co. Ct.
Aurelius, William E. ... '28 '56 C&L.930 B.A., J.D. Com. Pleas J.
Ausprunk, Karen S. ... '55 '85 C.777 B.A. L.1003 J.D. Community Fund Mgmt.
Aussem, James S., (AV) ... '— '75 C.62 B.A. L.1003 J.D. [Weston H.]
Austin, Arthur D., II '32 '64 C.893 B.S. L.861 J.D.
(adm. in VA; not adm. in OH) Prof. of Law, Case Western Reserve Univ.
Austin, Heather Aley ... '68 '93 C&L.665 B.A., J.D. [Ⓒ Thompson H.]
Austin, Jeffrey L. ... '72 '98 C.608 B.A. L.365 J.D. [Ⓐ Keis G.]
Austin, Nicholas A. ... '73 '98 C.201 B.S. L.608 J.D. [Petronzio S.]
Austria, Robert L. ... '62 '98 C.473 B.S. L.989 J.D. [Ⓐ Moscarino&T.]
Auvil, Steven M. ... '64 '94 C.608 B.S.M.E. L.251 J.D. [Benesch,F.C.&A.] (Pat.)
Avsec, Mark E. ... '54 '95 C.161 B.A. L.1003 J.D. [Ⓐ Benesch,F.C.&A.]
Awadallah, Saleh S. ... '69 '94 C.62 B.A. L.930 17602 Hilliard Road
Axel, Michael A., (AV) '57 '83 C.188 A.B. L.930 J.D.
Sr. V.P. & Managing Coun., KeyBank Natl. Assn.
Azoff, Elliot S., (AV) ... '46 '72 C.976 B.A. L.309 J.D. [Baker&H.]
Babbit, Harold W., (AV) ... '41 '67 C.352 B.A. L.976 LL.B. [Calfee,H.&G.]
Babbitt, Lindsay C. ... '76 '04 C.477 B.A. L.966 J.D. [Ⓐ Benesch,F.C.&A.]
Babcock, Cliff G. ... '55 '89 C.381 B.A. L.1003 J.D. [Babcock&W.]
Babcock & Wasserman Co., LPA, (BV) ... 55 Public Sq., Ste. 700
Babington, Margaret M. ... '59 '84 C.150 B.A. L.1003 J.D. 6988 N. Renwood Rd.
Babinski, Michael Thomas ... '72 '98 C.608 B.A. L.8 J.D. Jud. Law Clk.
Bacchus, Renee Arlene ... '66 '94 C.329 B.B.A. L.1003 J.D. Pros. Atty.'s Off.
Bacon, Brett K., (AV) ... '47 '72 C.226 B.A. L.597 J.D. [Frantz W.]
Baddeley, Jeffrey, (AV) ... '55 '83 C.145 A.B. L.124 J.D. [Baker&H.]
Bagnato, Elizabeth R. ... '57 '82 C.823 A.B. L.930 J.D. Mag. J.
Bailey, David B., (AV) ... '32 '57 C.25 B.A. L.976 LL.B. 1900 E. 9th St., 17th Fl.‡
Bain, Richard M., (BV) ... '— '79 C.473 B.A. L.930 J.D. [Buckley K.]
Baisden, W. Eric ... '— '91 C.49 B.S. L.930 J.D. [Ⓐ Calfee,H.&G.]
Bajorek, Christine Carol, (BV) ... '62 '89 C.608 B.A. L.1003 J.D. 28604 Chagrin Blvd.
Baker, Eric D. ... '72 '98 C.473 B.A. L.7 J.D. 600 Superior Ave. E.
Baker, James A., (AV) '44 '70 C.607 B.S.M.E. L.1003 J.D.
V.P., Dep. Gen. Coun. and Asst. Secy., Parker-Hannifin Corp. (Pat.)

Baker, Jason T. '74 '99 C&L.608 B.S.B.A., J.D.
55 Public Square, Suite 1330, 44113
Telephone: 216-771-3966 Fax: 216-771-4124
URL: http://www.jbakerlaw.com
Bankruptcy, Criminal Law, DUI, Drug Crimes, Traffic Violations, Divorce, Probate, Wills, Child Custody, Child Support.
See Professional Biographies, CLEVELAND, OHIO

Baker, John M., (AV) ... '42 '67 C.363 B.A. L.93 J.D. [Ⓒ Weston H.]
Baker, Kenneth B., (BV) ... '— '77 C.174 B.A. L.1003 J.D. [Javitch,B.&R.]
Baker, Lawrence M., Law Office of, (BV) '29 '61
C.608 B.Sc.B.A. L.1003 LL.B. 629 Euclid Ave.
Baker, Linda L. ... '48 '88 C.62 B.A. L.1003 J.D. Asst. Co. Pros.
Baker, Robert H., (AVⓉ) ... '42 '69 C&L.976 B.A., LL.B. 601 Lakeside Ave.
Baker, Stacie L. ... '74 '99 C.112 B.A. L.608 J.D. [Ⓐ Reminger&R.]
Baker, Stuart D. ... '77 '04 C.97 B.A. L.7 J.D. [Ⓐ Sutter,O.&F.]
Baker, Thomas W. ... '70 '99 C.62 B.A. L.1003 J.D. [Ⓐ Tucker E.&W.]
Baker, W. Joseph ... '74 '00 C.591 B.S. L.989 J.D. [Ⓐ Janik&D.]

Baker & Hostetler LLP, (AV) BR
3200 National City Center, 1900 East Ninth Street, 44114-3485 ⊙
Telephone: 216-621-0200 Telecopier: 216-696-0740 To contact an attorney on the Internet use first initial and surname followed by @bakerlaw.com
URL: http://www.bakerlaw.com
Newton D. Baker (1871-1937); Joseph C. Hostetler (1885-1958); Thomas L. Sidlo (1888-1955). Executive Partners: R. Steven Kestner; Alec Wightman (Resident, at Columbus Office). Office Managing Partner: Hewitt B. Shaw, Jr. Partners: Albert T. Adams; Frank H. Andorka; Dana Rountree Andrassy; Barry W. Andrews; Oakley V. Andrews; Elliot S. Azoff; Jeffrey Baddeley; Richard H. Bamberger; Brian A. Bash; Bruce O. Baumgartner; Mary M. Bittence; Maureen A. Brennan; Terry M. Brennan; Gary L. Bryenton; Phillip M. Callesen; Diane P. Chapman; Elaine A. Chotlos; Avery S. Cohen; Louis A. Colombo; Wayne C. Dabb, Jr.; Elizabeth A. Dellinger; John D. Drinko; Dennis E. Eckart; Steven A. Eisenberg; Paul P. Eyre (Managing Partner, New York Office); Michael K. Farrell; Paul H. Feinberg; José C. Feliciano; Charles J. French, III; Robert R. Galloway; John M. Gherlein; Wendy J. Gibson; Edward S. Ginsburg; Matthew R. Goldman; Matthew D. Graban; James B. Griswold; J. Richard Hamilton; Suzanne K. Hanselman; Jane T. Haylor; L. Dennis Hoffman Jr.; Richard R. Hollington, Jr.; Joseph F. Hutchinson, Jr.; Scott D. Irwin; Suzanne M. Jambe; Amy Elizabeth Kellogg; Tom A. King; Calvin B. Kirchick; Robert K. Lease; Todd H. Lebowitz; Earl M. Leiken; Melissa A. Leonard; Richard H. Leukart, II; John B. Lewis; Lawrence V. Lindberg; James A. Loeb; Robert M. Loesch; Thomas R. Lucchesi; Arthur H. Lundberg; Raymond M. Malone; Ruth Ann Maloney; David L. Marburger; Robert G. Markey; Mark R. Mazanec; John J. McGowan, Jr.; Michael P. McNamara, Jr.; Gregory V. Mersol; Wade A. Mitchell; Karen B. Newborn; Patricia J. O'Donnell; Ronald S. Okada; W. James Ollinger; Jeffrey H. Paravano; John D. Parker; Patrick J. Pauken; Stephen J. Petras, Jr.; Robert C. Petrulis (Certified Specialist in Labor & Employment Law, Ohio State Bar Association); Thomas J. Piatak; Patricia A. Poole; David A. Posner; Edward G. Ptaszek, Jr.; Kevin G. Robertson; McKinley Hobart Sauer III; Paula F. Seger; Thomas M. Seger; Thomas H. Shunk; Randall L. Solomon; James Spallino, Jr.; Ronald A. Stepanovic; David J. Strauss; Victor Strimbu, Jr.; Michelle Pierce Stronczer; John E. Sullivan; Stephen C. Sutton; Christopher J. Swift; Alexander J. Szilvas; Halle Fine Terrion; William M. Toomajian; Ernest E. Vargo, Jr.; R. Byron Wallace; Daniel R. Warren (Group Leader, Business Litigation); Thomas D. Warren; Robert A. Weible; Deborah A. Schaff Wilcox; James R. Wooley; Martin T. Wymer. Of Counsel: William L. Arnold; Chris Bator; Thomas S. Campanella; Victoria Johnson; Melinda L. Reynolds; Mary A. Wilson. Associates: John J. Allotta; Michelle B. Anselmo; Mathew B. Beredo; Bridget Meehan Brennan; Kimberly C. Brunner; Kelly S. Burgan; Wan Collier; Deanna M. Conrad; Emanuel J. Cotronakis; Andrea L. Csomos; William J. Culbertson; Anne M. Davet; Todd Dawson; Michael P. DeMinico; Patrick J. Egan; Bethany L. Fabian; (Guenther) Karl Fanter; Megan P. Frient; Ruth E. Hartman; Michelle M. Hervey; Scott C. Holbrook; F. Arthur Jones, II; Sean M. Kammer; Brandon E. Kepple; Kelly M. King; Andrew W. Kirkpatrick; David E. Kitchen; Melinda M. Kline; Deborah L. Koerwitz; Laurie G. Kosanovich; Rebecca C. Lutzko; Michael D. Mierau, Jr.; Tanya F. Miller; Jennifer A. Mills; Christina J. Moser; Michael E. Mumford; Andrew J. Murray; Edward D. Papp; Christopher D. Pelliccioni; Jason P. Perdion; David F. Proaño; Lora M. Reece; Timothy J. Richards; James H. Rollinson (Not admitted in OH); Aaron J. Rupert; Stephan J. Schlegelmilch; Karin M. Scholz; Douglas R. Sergent; Jeremy J. Sharp; James A. Slater; Janet A. Spreen; Kevin R. Talbot;

(This Listing Continued)

Baker & Hostetler LLP (Continued)

Matthew A. Tenerowicz; Roger G. Trim; Corinne M. Tyler; Margaret M. VanDeHey; Aaron M. VanderKaay; Peter W. Van Euwen, III; Michael A. VanNiel; Monica S. Verma; Brett A. Wall; Nathan F. Ware; Thomas M. Wearsch (Not admitted in OH). Staff Attorneys: Gina A. Beredo; Geraldine J. Butler; Lidia V. Carr; Melanie S. Corcoran; Joseph E. DiBaggio; Jennifer L. Eschedor; Diane L. Feigi; Julie E. Firestone; Kristin J. Jakiel; Lance T. Mason; Nichol M. Schoenfield; Diane D. Wilcox.
General Practice.
In Cincinnati, Ohio: 312 Walnut Street, Suite 3200. Telephone: 513-929-3400.
In Columbus, Ohio: Capitol Square, Suite 2100, 65 East State Street. Telephone: 614-228-1541.
In Costa Mesa, California: 600 Anton Boulevard, Suite 900. Telephone: 714-754-6600.
In Denver, Colorado: 303 East 17th Avenue, Suite 1100. Telephone: 303-861-0600.
In Houston, Texas: 1000 Louisiana, Suite 2000. Telephone: 713-751-1600.
In Los Angeles, California: 333 South Grand Avenue, Suite 1800. Telephone: 213-975-1600.
In Orlando, Florida: SunTrust Center, Suite 2300, 200 South Orange Avenue. Telephone: 407-649-4000.
In Washington, D.C.: Washington Square, Suite 1100, 1050 Connecticut Avenue, N.W. Telephone: 202-861-1500.
In New York, N.Y.: 666 Fifth Avenue. Telephone: 212-589-4200.

See Professional Biographies, CLEVELAND, OHIO

Balantzow, Robert S., (AV) ... '40 '65 C.659 B.S. L.930 J.D. [McCarthy,L.C.&L.]
Balazs, James A. '66 '99 C.188 B.S.M.E. L.1003 J.D. [🄰 Rankin,H.P.&C.] (See Pat. Sect.)
Balazs, Mary Grace, (AV) ... '53 '80 C.363 B.A. L.1003 J.D. [Taft,S.&H.]
Bales, Stephen M., (AV) ... '57 '83 C.697 B.A. L.161 J.D. [Ziegler,M.&M.]
Balin, Paulette F., (BV) '55 '78 C.930 B.A. L.910 J.D. 1422 Euclid Avenue, Suite 970 (⊙Mentor)
Ballard, Brent D., (AV) ... '55 '85 C.67 B.A. L.930 J.D. [Calfee,H.&G.]
Ballard, John F., (AV) ... '47 '78 C.309 B.A. L.930 J.D. [Buckingham,D.&B.]
Ballard, Mary Beth, (AV) ... '54 '78 C.161 B.A. L.124 J.D. V.P., Chicago Title Ins. Co.
Ballin, Stacy D., (AV) ... '58 '83 C.105 B.A. L.930 J.D. [Squire,S.&D.]
Ballou, Scott H., (BV) ... '53 '80 C.610 B.S. L.1003 J.D. 614 W. Superior Ave., Ste. 850
Balog, Joseph A. ... '48 '76 C&L.1003 B.S., J.D. Gen. Coun., Dalad Grp.
Balraj, Solomon F. ... '66 '92 C&L.930 B.A., J.D. Asst. Dir. of Law, City of Cleveland
Bamberger, Richard H., (AV) ... '45 '72 C.95 B.A. L.930 J.D. [Baker&H.]
Banchek, Melvin H., (Co., L.P.A.), (BV) ... '47 '73 C.473 B.A. L.150 J.D. 55 Pub. Sq.
Bancsi, Pamela Ward, (BV) ... '51 '76 C&L.930 B.A., LL.B. Beachcliff Financial Mgmt.
Bandy, Mark E., (BV) '62 '91 C.474 B.S.Ch.E. L.1003 J.D. [Fay,S.F.M.&M.] (See Pat. Sect.)
Bang, Jun Suk ... '72 '97 C.659 B.A. L.831 J.D. Field Atty., Natl. Labor Rel. Bd.
Bank, Malvin E., (AV) ... '30 '57 C.645 B.A. L.976 LL.B. [🄲 Thompson H.]
Banks, Kenneth E., Jr. '43 '73 C.363 B.A. L.930 J.D. Sr. Coun., Contracts & Real Estate

Banta, Michael E., (BV) '47 '73 C.608 B.A. L.930 J.D.
75 Public Square Suite 525, 44113
Telephone: 216-566-0770
General Civil and Criminal Trial Practice. DUI, Driving While Intoxicated; Traffic Violations, Personal Injury, Automobile Accidents, Domestic Relations Law, Family Law, Divorce. Wills and Probate.

See Professional Biographies, CLEVELAND, OHIO

Baraona, Robert C. ... '— '98 C.610 B.S. L.608 J.D. [🄰 McDonald H.]
Barbour, Mark E., (AV) ... '59 '88 C.967 B.A. L.1003 J.D. [Jeffries,K.F.&M.]
Baringer, Jennifer Hay ... '— '95 C.477 B.A. L.1187 J.D. [🅂 Jones D.]
Baringer, Randal S., (BV) ... '— '90 C.980 B.S. L.608 J.D. [Jones D.]
Barker, Pamela ... '— '82 C.385 B.A. L.608 J.D. [🄲 Davis&Y.]
Barmen, Bradley J. ... '72 '03 C.161 B.A. L.989 J.D. [🄰 Reminger&R.]
Barnard, Thomas H., (AV) ... '39 '64 C.678 B.A. L.178 LL.B. [Ulmer&B.]
Barnes, Austin B., III ... '65 '91 C.610 B.B.A. L.8 J.D. GLS Capital-Cuyahoga, Inc.
Barnes, Geoffrey K., (AV) ... '45 '73 C.207 B.A. L.930 J.D. [Squire,S.&D.]
Barnes, Kevin D., (AV) ... '54 '79 C&L.309 A.B., J.D. [Kahn K.]
Barnes, Nancy M. ... '68 '94 C.945 B.A. L.659 J.D. [Thompson H.]
Barnett, Kelley J. ... '73 '99 C.475 B.A. L.930 J.D. Asst. Pros. Atty.
Barnett, William A., (AV) '56 '81 C.597 B.S.S. L.930 J.D. State Industrial Products Corporation
Barney, Donald F., Jr. ... '54 '79 C.229 B.A. L.930 J.D. Sr. V.P., & Mng. Dir., KeyBank
Barnhizer, David R. '44 '69 C.532 A.B. L.608 J.D. Prof. of Law, Cleve.-Marshall Coll. of Law
Barni, Thomas A. ... '67 '95 C.161 B.A. L.1003 J.D. [Dinn,H.&P.]
Baron, Frederick M., (AVⓉ) '47 '71 C&L.846 B.A., J.D. (adm. in TX; not adm. in OH) [Baron&B.] (⊙Dallas, TX)
Baron, Nicole ... '74 '00 C.347 B.A. L.989 J.D. 614 W. Superior Ave.
Baron, Russell Z., (AV) ... '30 '55 C&L.930 B.B.A., LL.B. [Ticktin,B.K.]
Baron & Budd, A Professional Corporation, (AVⓉ)
7271 Engle Road, Suite 309 (⊙Glen Carbon, IL; Baton Rouge, LA; Monroe, OH; Dallas, TX)
Barr, Anthony S. ... '58 '02 C.161 B.A. L.989 J.D. [🄰 Strachan,M.O.&R.]
Barr, Douglas N., (AV) ... '— '72 C.478 B.A. L.930 J.D. [Buckley K.]
Barr, Lewis T., (AV) ... '42 '67 C.659 B.A. L.477 J.D. [Ulmer&B.]
Barr, Robert D., (AV) ... '71 '96 C.20 B.A. L.930 J.D. [Dettelbach,S.&B.]
Barragate, Brett P. ... '— '96 C.1033 B.A. L.161 J.D. [🄰 Jones D.]
Barragate, Phillip C. ... '66 '92 C.882 B.A. L.365 J.D. [🄰 Shapiro&F.]
Barrat, Elliott S., (BV) '57 '86 C.608 B.S.B.A. L.1003 J.D. 33840 Aurora Road, Suite 200
Barrett, Lisa M. ... '67 '92 C.27 B.A. L.930 J.D. [Norchi,B.&F.]
Barrows, Melissa E. ... '78 '03 C.999 L.161 J.D. [🄰 Schwarzwald&M.]
Barsoum, Marianne K. ... '73 '99 C.363 B.A. L.124 J.D. [🄰 Reminger&R.]
Bartell, Jonathan A. ... '70 '00 C.354 B.S. L.124 J.D. 700 West St. Clair, Suite 100
Bartell, Laurence A. ... '46 '72 C.473 B.S. L.1003 J.D. 1801 E. Ninth St., Ste. 920
Barthol, Britta, (BV) ... '63 '91 C.62 B.A. L.1003 J.D. Asst. Pub. Def.
Bartimole, Todd Welles ... '63 '93 C.610 B.A. L.1003 J.D. 1801 E. 9th St., Ste. 900
Bartman, Douglas V., (AV) ... '67 '93 C.477 A.B. L.310 J.D. [Kahn K.]
Barto, Victoria ... '74 '99 C.8 B.A. L.930 J.D. [🄰 Sutter,O.&F.]
Barz, Patricia, (AV) ... '53 '79 C.976 B.A. L.893 J.D. Dir. of Law, Cleveland Metropolis
Bash, Brian A. ... '49 '75 C&L.861 B.A., J.D. [Baker&H.]
Bashein, Richard W. ... '64 '89 C.608 B.A. L.1003 J.D. [Bashein&B.]
Bashein, W. Craig, (AV) ... '60 '86 C&L.608 B.A., J.D. [Bashein&B.]

Bashein & Bashein Co., L.P.A., (AV)
35th Floor Terminal Tower, 50 Public Square, 44113
Telephone: 216-771-3239; 800-771-4457 Fax: 216-781-5876 URL: http://www.basheinlaw.com
URL: http://www.lawyers.com/basheinlaw
W. Craig Bashein; Richard W. Bashein.
Product Liability, Automobile Accidents, Insurance Law, Appellate Practice, Personal Injury Defense, Medical Malpractice, Workers Compensation, Commercial Litigation. Labor and Employment, General Practice.

See Professional Biographies, CLEVELAND, OHIO

Basil, Autumn ... '63 '96 C.1086 B.A. L.930 J.D. Off. of Pub. Def.
Basil, David A. ... '53 '80 C.679 B.S. L.930 J.D. V.P. & Sr. Coun., KeyBank Natl. Assn.
Bassett, Benton ... '39 '64 C.674 A.B. L.477 J.D. Asst. Pros. Atty.
Bassett, Stephen Jay, (BV) ... '38 '65 C.930 B.B.A. L.1003 J.D. 23230 Chagrin Boulevard
Basta, Samuel W. ... '66 '95 C.150 B.S. L.8 J.D. 2189 Professor Avenue, Suite 100
Bator, Chris, (BV) ... '62 '87 C.363 B.A. L.930 J.D. [🄲 Baker&H.]
Batt, John Paul, (AV) ... '52 '78 C.951 B.A. L.930 J.D. [🄲 Calfee,H.&G.]
Baucco, Anthony A. ... '78 '03 C.201 B.A. L.989 J.D. [🄰 Ross,B.&S.]
Bauders, Robert Samuel ... '45 '70 C.674 A.B. L.608 J.D. 1370 Ontario St., Ste. 1700
Bauer, Fred D. '65 '90 C.659 B.A./B.S. L.309 J.D. V.P., Gen Coun. & Secy., Applied Industrial Technologies
Bauer, Gregory A. ... '— '97 C.363 B.A. L.608 J.D. [🄰 Jones D.]
Bauer, James P. ... '67 '93 C.475 B.A. L.608 J.D. [🄰 Nicola,G.&C.]
Bauernschmidt, Charles J., (AV) ... '47 '74 C.699 B.A. L.930 J.D. Asst. City Pros.
Bauernschmidt, Karen H., (BV) ... '51 '76 C.967 A.B. L.930 J.D. [K.H.Bauernschmidt]

Bauernschmidt, Karen H., Co., LPA, (BV)
700 West St. Clair Avenue, Suite 214, 44113
Telephone: 216-566-8500 Fax: 216-566-0942 URL: http://www.khbtaxlaw.com
Email: kbauerns@mindspring.com URL: http://www.ohiorealestatetax.com
Karen H. Bauernschmidt.
Real Estate Tax, Litigation, Appellate Practices and Procedure.

See Professional Biographies, CLEVELAND, OHIO

Baughman, R. Patrick, (BV) ... '38 '63 C&L.608 B.S., J.D. [🄲 Baughman&J.]

Baughman & Joyce, LLC
2500 Brook Park Road Suite E, 44134
Telephone: 216-687-1244 Fax: 216-621-4066
Eileen M. Joyce. Of Counsel: R. Patrick Baughman.
Civil Litigation and Appeals, Employment Law, Personal Injury, Products Liability, Construction Law, Workers' Compensation, Toxic Torts, Railroad (FELA) Law, Maritime Law, Administrative Law.
Representative Client: General Motors Corp.
Reference: National City Bank.

See Professional Biographies, CLEVELAND, OHIO

Baumbick, John Joseph ... '70 '98 First American Equity Loan Servs., Inc.
Baumgardner, Lorraine R., (AV) ... '55 '80 C.970 B.A. L.930 J.D. [Berkman,G.M.&D.]
Baumgart, Debra Andrea ... '55 '79 C.1349 B.A. L.608 J.D. 2434 Cedarwood‡
Baumgart, Richard A., (AV) ... '53 '78 C.696 B.A. L.608 J.D. [Dettelbach,S.&B.]
Baumgartner, Bruce O., (AV) ... '42 '67 C&L.597 B.A., J.D. [Baker&H.]
Bautista, Brooke Turner ... '74 '00 C.610 B.A. L.608 J.D. [🄰 McGlinchey S.]
Bautista, Philip R. ... '73 '01 C.228 B.S. L.608 J.D. [🄰 Kahn K.]
Baxter, Howard H., Law Offices of '31 '56 C.350 B.S. L.930 J.D. 815 Superior Avenue, N.E.
Baxter, Randolph ... '46 '76 C.864 B.S. L.7 J.D. Chf. J.
Bays, James C. ... '49 '74 C.197 A.B. L.893 J.D. V.P. & Gen. Coun., Ferro Corp.
Beal, David A., (BV) ... '45 '82 C.377 A.B. L.1003 J.D. 1801 E. 9th St.
Beasley, David E. ... '10 '56 C.329 B.S. L.1003 LL.B. 3150 Ludlow Rd.‡
Beatty, Richard H. ... '31 '58 C.197 A.B. L.477 LL.B. 896 Northboro Dr.
Beaudry, Stephen M. ... '— '03 C.363 B.A. L.608 J.D. [🄰 Gallagher S.]
Becker, Michael F., (AV) ... '49 '76 C.966 B.A. L.365 J.D. [Becker&M.]
Becker, Susan J., (AV) ... '55 '84 C.235 B.A. L.161 J.D. 1801 Euclid Ave.
Becker & Mishkind, Co. LPA, (AV) ... 1660 W. 2nd Street
Beckstrom, Sean C. ... '67 '95 C.610 A.B. L.1003 J.D. [🄰 Calfee,H.&G.]
Bedell, Richard J., Jr., (AV) ... '— '87 C.8 B.S.C.E. L.93 J.D. [Jones D.]
Beebe, Richard A. ... '48 '73 C.97 B.A. L.608 J.D. 1370 Ontario Street
Beg, Murad A. ... '69 '95 C.385 B.A. L.1040 J.D. [Calfee,H.&G.]
Beggs, Gordon J. ... '47 '74 C&L.659 B.A., J.D. Cleveland-Marshall College of Law
Beins, J. Christian ... '42 '78 C.973 B.S. L.851 J.D. Lewis Research Ctr.
Bekeny, Karl A. ... '77 '02 C.970 B.A. L.1171 J.D. [🄰 Tucker E.&W.]
Belasic, Mark A., (AV) ... '— '86 C.970 B.A. L.178 J.D. [Jones D.]
Belcher, Michael L., (BV) ... '52 '77 C.922 B.A. L.161 J.D. 75 Pub. Sq.
Belden, Thomas G., (AV) ... '44 '71 C.602 B.B.A. L.930 J.D. [Cavitch,F.D.&F.]
Belfiglio, Victoria ... '52 '84 C.608 B.A. L.930 J.D. N.L.R.B., Region 8
Belkin, Jeffrey A., (AV) ... '— '64 C.103 A.B. L.477 LL.B. [🄲 Duvin,C.&H.]
Bell, Alyssa J. ... '71 '02 C.473 B.S. L.124 J.D. [🄰 Calfee,H.&G.]
Bell, Douglas J. ... '57 '87 C.311 B.A. L.930 J.D. Fed. Process Comm.
Bell, Edward J. ... '58 '83 C.473 B.S. L.930 J.D. Gries Financ. LLC
Bell, Everett A., (BV) ... '35 '76 C.1023 B.S. L.1003 J.D. 20475 Farnsleigh Rd.
Bell, Irving ... '35 '59 C.930 A.B. L.178 LL.B. 1750 Standard Bldg.
Bell, Lawrence M., (AV) ... '35 '61 C.473 B.S. L.930 LL.B. [Benesch,F.C.&A.]
Bell, Steven D., (AV) ... '53 '79 C.602 B.A. L.7 J.D. [Simon]
Belman, Steven A. '49 '75 C.610 A.B. L.245 J.D. Manufacturers Wholesale Lumber Co.
Belman, Susan L. ... '51 '77 C.674 B.A. L.930 J.D. [🄰 Thompson H.]
Belzer, Geoffrey A. ... '65 '00 C.597 B.S.J. L.7 J.D. [🄰 Mazanec,R.&R.]
Bembenick, Brian G. ... '66 '98 C.1062 B.S. L.128 J.D. [Pearne&G.] (See Pat. Sect.)
Bemer, Andrew D., (AV) ... '48 '73 C.608 B.A. L.1003 J.D. [Seeley,S.&E.L.&Assoc.]
Bender, J. Timothy, (AV) ... '49 '78 C&L.8 B.S., J.D. [Rotatori,B.G.S.&A.]
Benedict, James Joseph, Jr. ... '64 '96 C.62 B.A. L.989 J.D. Cleveland Clinic Foundation

Benesch, Friedlander, Coplan & Aronoff LLP, (AV)
2300 BP Tower, 200 Public Square, 44114-2378 ⊙
Telephone: 216-363-4500 Facsimile: 216-363-4588
URL: http://www.bfca.com
Members of Firm: George N. Aronoff; Steven M. Auvil; Lawrence M. Bell; Gary B. Bilchik; Gregory G. Binford; Harry M. Brown; Thomas R. Brule; Maynard A. Buck, III; Thomas O. Crist; Leslie A. Drockton; Gregg A. Eisenberg; Pete C. Elliott; Irwin M. Feldman; James M. Friedman; Gregory K. Gale; Jeremy Gilman; Allan Goldner; Bernard D. Goodman; Joseph N. Gross; Norman W. Gutmacher; Douglas E. Haas; James M. Hill; Edward Kancler; Ira C. Kaplan; Peter N. Kirsanow; Ann E. Knuth; Howard A. Levy (Certified Specialist in Labor and Employment Law, Ohio State Bar Association); Richard G. Lillie; Ezio A. Listati; Kevin D. Margolis; David R. Mayo; Megan Lum Mehalko; David W. Mellott; Barry J. Miller; Mark A. Phillips; Michael A. Primrose; Anna K. Raske; Alan E. Schabes; William E. Schonberg; H. Jeffrey Schwartz; Peter K. Shelton; Howard A. Steindler; Michael K. Swearengen; Joseph G. Tegreene; Ronald J. Teplitzky; Richard F. Tracanna; Jeffry L. Weiler; Jeffrey J. Wild; Eric L. Zalud; Jeffrey D. Zimon. Senior Attorney: Sheila M. Ninneman. Associates: Jessica N. Angney; Mark E. Avsec; Lindsay C. Babbitt; Susan E. Clady; Jeffrey A. Crossman; Jacob Derenthal; John S. Gambaccini; W. Scott Harders; Ryan P. Hooper; Bryan Jaketic; Jeffrey P. Jones; Tamara L. Karel; Ross J. Kirchick; Rita Kline; Jean Kerr Korman; M. Casey Kucharson; Stuart A. Laven, Jr.; Nathan L. Lutz; Robert A. Marchant; Craig L. Moore; David M. Neumann; Julie M. Price; Robert C. Psaropoulos; Christopher P. Reuscher; William J. Shin; Nick D. Shofar; Todd L. Sladek; Edward J. Stoll, Jr.; Clare R. Taft; Mark D. Trainer; Theologos Verginis; Yanping Wang. Of Counsel: Mariann E. Butch; Robert C. Cross; Gretchen A. Holderman; Margaret A. Kennedy; Lisa C. Kimmel; Allan D. Kleinman; Deanna Coe Kursh; Richard D. Margolis; Ginger Fuller Mlakar (Certified Specialist in Estate Planning, Trust and Probate Law, Ohio State Bar Association); Robert M. Spira; Michael D. Zaverton. Retired Counsel: Alfred A. Benesch (1879-1973); Robert C. Coplan (1918-2003); Jerome M. Friedlander (1900-1993); Richard L. Phillips.
Bankruptcy, Bankruptcy Reorganization, Banks and Banking, Business Law, Casino and Gambling, Class Actions, Collections, Commercial Law, Commercial Real Estate, Complex and Multi-District Litigation, Construction Law, Consumer Law, Contracts, Copyrights, Corporate Law, Debtor and Creditor, Election Campaign and Political Law, Electronic Commerce, Employee Benefits, Environmental Law, Finance, Health Care, Immigration Law, Intellectual Property, Internet and Technology, Labor and Employment, Leases and Leasing, Mergers, Acquisitions, Divestitures, Mortgages, Patent,

(This Listing Continued)

Benesch, Friedlander, Coplan & Aronoff LLP (Continued)

Probate, Product Liability, Real Estate, Resort and Leisure, Securities, Taxation, Trademarks, Transportation, Trusts and Estates, Wills, Workers Compensation, Zoning, Planning and Land Use. Columbus, Ohio Office: 88 East Broad Street, Suite 900, 43215-3506. Telephone: 614-223-9300. Facsimile: 614-223-9330.

See Professional Biographies, CLEVELAND, OHIO

Benford, Sheryl Yvonne King '47 '80
C.943 B.S. L.1003 J.D. Greater Cleveland Reg. Transit Auth.
Benjamin, Lawrence S., (BV) .... '49 '74 C.473 B.A. L.1003 J.D. 23230 Chagrin Blvd.
Benjamin, Virginia D., (AV) ....'51 '76 C.788 A.B. L.94 J.D. [Calfee,H.&G.]
Bennett, Jennifer A. ....'68 '94 C.8 B.S. L.150 J.D. [A Ross,B.&S.]
Bennett, Rebecca J. ....'73 '98 C.608 B.A. L.1003 J.D. [A Frantz W.]
Benni, Todd A. '71 '99 C.679 B.S.I.E. L.665 J.D.
(adm. in PA; not adm. in OH; Pat.) [A McDonald H.]
Bentoff, Fred J., (AV) ....'35 '61 C&L.608 B.S., J.D. 526 Superior Ave.
Bentoff, Jerome L. ....'30 '54 C&L.608 LL.B. 230 Leader Bldg.‡
Bentoff & Spero Co., L.P.A., (AV) ....55 Public Sq., Ste. 1200
Benza, Michael J. ....'64 '93 C&L.930 B.A., J.D. [M.J.Benza]
Benza, Michael J., Inc., The Law Office of ....4403 St. Clair Ave.
Beranek, Steven B. ....'67 '96 C.25 B.A. L.8 J.D. 2001 Crocker Rd., Ste. 400
Beredo, Cipriano S., III ....'70 '99 C.473 B.A. L.347 J.D. [A Squire,S.&D.]
Beredo, Gina A. ....'74 '99 C.734 B.A. L.347 J.D. [S Baker&H.]
Beredo, Mathew B. ....'72 '98 C.976 B.A. L.477 J.D. [A Baker&H.]
Berenger, Lori A. .....'62 '93 C.161 B.S.N. L.1003 J.D. Consul., Watson Wyatt Worldwide
Beres, Susan Ann ....'55 '81 C.251 B.A. L.989 J.D. Atty. Gen. Off.
Beresh, Laura .... '— '00 C.967 B.A. L.8 J.D. [A Jones D.]
Berg, Aaron Philip ....'73 '01 C.967 B.A. L.989 J.D. 50 Public Square
Berger, Gayl Manes ....'61 '00 C.347 B.S. L.161 J.D. Pros. Off.
Berger, I. Joseph, (AV) ....'25 '50 C&L.930 B.B.A., J.D. [Berger&Z.]
Berger, Sanford J. ....'26 '52 C&L.930 B.A., LL.B. 1032 Som Center Rd.

Berger & Zavesky Co., L.P.A., (AV) [BB]
Rockefeller Building, Suite 1425, 614 W. Superior Avenue, 44113
Telephone: 216-830-9000 Toll Free in Ohio: 1-877-515-5677 Fax: 216-830-4200
Email: bergzav@earthlink.net URL: http://www.bergzal.com
I. Joseph Berger; Robert J. Zavesky;—Jeffrey D. Lojewski; Douglas L. Winston. Of Counsel: George W. White; Sam Thomas, III.
Personal Injury, Medical Malpractice, Pharmaceutical Drug and Medical Device Litigation, Automobile Accidents, Products Liability, Wrongful Death, Nursing Home Abuse and Neglect, Worker's Compensation, Employment Law, Sexual Harassment, Real Estate, Family Law, Child Abuse, Intentional Torts. Trial Practice in State and Federal Court.

See Professional Biographies, CLEVELAND, OHIO

Bergrin, Irving S., (AV) ....'50 '76 C.679 B.S.I.M. L.1003 J.D. 27600 Chargrin Blvd.
Berick, Daniel G., (AV) ....'62 '88 C.178 A.B. L.145 J.D. [Squire,S.&D.]
Berk, Gerald A., (AV) ....'43 '70 C.608 B.S. L.161 J.D. [Steuer,E.B.&B.]
Berk, Robert J., (BV) ....'43 '69 C.608 B.S. L.1003 J.D. [R.J.Berk]
Berk, Robert J., Co., L.P.A., (BV) ....75 Public Sq.

Berkman, Gordon, Murray & DeVan, (AV)
2121 The Illuminating Building, 55 Public Square, 44113-1949
Telephone: 216-781-5245 Fax: 216-781-8207
Email: bgmdclvld@aol.com URL: http://www.lawyers.com/berkmangordonmurray&devanlaw
Members of Firm: Bernard A. Berkman (1929-1985); J. Michael Murray; Mark R. DeVan; Lorraine R. Baumgardner; Jeremy A. Rosenbaum; Steven D. Shafron; Brooke F. Kocab. Associates: Erin L. Reiffer; Raymond Vasvari. Of Counsel: Larry S. Gordon.
Trial and Appellate Practice in Civil, Criminal and Constitutional Law. Labor, Civil Rights and Employment Law, Corporate, Personal Injury, Administrative, Family Law and General Practice. Reference: First National Bank of Ohio.

See Professional Biographies, CLEVELAND, OHIO

Berkson, Hugh D. ....'68 '94 C.846 B.B.A. L.930 J.D. [Hermann,C.&S.]
Berlin, Jennifer W. '— '97
C.473 B.S. L.209 J.D. COO & Gen. Coun., Berlin Financial, Ltd.
Berliner, Irv, (AV) .... '54 '79 C.473 B.A. L.608 J.D. [Kahn K.]
Berliner, Stacy R.C. ....'78 '03 C.970 B.A. L.989 J.D. [A Calfee,H.&G.]
Berman, Keevin, (BV) ....'51 '77 C.363 B.S.Ec. L.1003 J.D. Legal Aid Soc.
Bernard, Dale A., (AV) ....'59 '84 C.608 B.A. L.1003 J.D. [Bernard]

Bernard & Haffey Co., L.P.A., (AV)
Jefferson Centre, 5001 Mayfield Road #301, P.O. Box 24005, 44124-0005
Telephone: 216-291-3600 FAX: 216-291-0159
Email: bernardhaffey@sbcglobal.net URL: http://www.lawyers.com/bernard&haffey
Clifford H. Bernard (1907-1985); J. Ross Haffey, Jr.; Timothy P. Haffey; Kirk W. Liederbach.
General Civil and Criminal Practice. Corporate, Probate, Commercial Law, Bankruptcy, Trusts and Estates, Negligence, Family Law, Divorce, Juvenile, and Real Estate. Trial and Appellate Practice, Personal Injury.
Reference: National City Bank (Cleveland).

See Professional Biographies, CLEVELAND, OHIO

Bernard Law Firm, The, (AV) [BB]
Crown Centre Building, Suite 600, 5005 Rockside Road, 44131-6808
Telephone: 440-546-7500 Fax: 440-546-7501 URL: http://www.bernardlaw.com
Email: bernardlaw@aol.com URL: http://www.lawyers.com/bernardlaw
Dale A. Bernard.
Complex Business Litigation, Accountants Malpractice, Stockbroker Malpractice, Banking Litigation, Employment Litigation, Personal Injury, Wrongful Termination, Employment Discrimination, Race Discrimination, Sex Discrimination, Sexual Harassment, Americans with Disabilities, Age Discrimination in Employment, Employment Termination, Family and Medical Leave Act, Breach of Contract, Contract Litigation, Insurance, Class Actions, Securities Litigation, Shareholder Derivative Actions, Lender Liability, Antitrust, Consumer Litigation, Consumer Fraud, Construction Defects, Construction Accidents, Construction Law, Automobile Accidents and Injuries, Wrongful Death, Dog Bites, Slip and Fall, Nursing Home Litigation, Products Liability.

See Professional Biographies, CLEVELAND, OHIO

Berns, Jordan, (BV) ....'65 '90 C.477 A.B. L.608 J.D. [Berns,O.&G.]
Berns, Sheldon, (AV) ....'32 '60 C.608 B.S. L.930 LL.B. [Berns,O.&G.]

Berns, Ockner & Greenberger, LLC, (AV)
3733 Park East Drive Suite 200, 44122
Telephone: 216-831-8838 Fax: 216-464-4489
Members: Sheldon Berns; Jordan Berns; Benjamin J. Ockner; Paul M. Greenberger; Gary F. Werner; Timothy J. Duff.
Zoning, Land Use, Real Estate, Construction, Business Litigation, Insurance and Unfair Competition Law.

See Professional Biographies, CLEVELAND, OHIO

Berris, Richard J., (AV) ....'53 '80 C.608 B.A. L.1003 J.D. [Weisman,G.&W.]
Berry, D. Jeffrey '69 '98 C.1128 B.S. L.615 J.D.
(adm. in OK; not adm. in OH) Atty.-Agent, International Management Group
Berry, Patrick J. ....'64 '89 C.97 B.S. L.276 J.D. [McDonald H.]
Bersticker, Steven C. ....'61 '86 C.170 B.A. L.930 J.D. [Kohrman J.&K.]
Bertovich, Richard ....'53 '92 C.608 B.A. L.1003 J.D Asst. Dir., City Law Dept.
Bertram, Ricky Lee, (AV) ..... '59 '84 C.97 B.S. L.607 J.D. Asst. Gen. Coun., Park Corp.
Bertsch, John R., (AV) ....'29 '59 C.363 B.S. L.1003 LL.B. 1280 W. Third St.
Bertsch, Michael J., (AV) ....'56 '82 C.973 B.S.B.A. L.1003 J.D. [Moscarino&T.]
Besser, Barbara Kaye, (AV) ....'48 '73 C.1019 B.A. L.1003 J.D. [Elfvin&B.]
Besser, Matthew D. ....'73 '04 C.273 B.A. L.608 J.D. [A Vorys,S.S.&P.]
Bettasso, Katharine Lang, (CV) '54 '79 C.970 B.A. L.117 J.D.
466 Northfield Rd., 1st Fl.
Bettendorf, Edward L. ....'48 '81 C.976 B.A. L.597 J.D. Litig., SBC Corp.
Betts, James E., (AV) ....'33 '76 C.610 B.S.Comm. L.989 J.D. [C Walter&H.]
Betz, Thomas E., (AV) ....'42 '68 C.363 A.B. L.477 J.D. 1501 Euclid Avenue‡
Beus, Karl S., (AV) ....'64 '92 C.878 B.A. L.336 J.D. [Calfee,H.&G.]
Beyer, William D., (AV) ....'44 '69 C.611 B.A. L.930 J.D. [Wuliger,F.&B.]
Bialer, Bruce A., (BV) .... '45 '75 C.473 B.S. L.1003 J.D. 526 Superior Ave., Ste. 833
Bialosky, Herbert S., (AV) ....'17 '42 C.930 A.B. L.161 LL.B. 55 Public Sq.
Bianchi, Robert C., (BV) ....'48 '84 C.161 B.A. L.989 J.D. 6325 York Rd.
Biars, Mark M. ....'51 '77 C&L.930 B.A., J.D. Sr. V.P. & Chief Coun., Nat'l City Bk.
Bickerstaff, Linda L. ....'59 '91 C.363 B.A. L.1003 J.D. 1111 Superior Ave.
Bickett, James L., (BV) ....'51 '74 C.8 B.S. L.477 J.D. Asst. U.S. Atty.
Bidar, Mohammed J., (AV) ....'58 '84 C&L.930 B.S., J.D. [Cavitch,F.D.&F.]
Bidari, Jayashree Y. .....'58 '92 C.999 B.A. L.1003 J.D. 31031 Center Ridge Road, Suite 6
Bieganski, Walter R. ....'59 '85 C.161 B.B.A. L.608 J.D. 1300 Huntington Bldg.‡
Biernacki, John V. ....'— '95 C&L.215 B.Ch.E., J.D. [A Jones D.] (See Pat. Sect.)
Biggins, Brian P. ....'60 '96 C.473 B.S. L.1003 J.D. [B.P.Biggins&Assoc.]
Biggins, Brian P., & Associates Co., L.P.A. ....19071 Old Detroit Rd., Ste. 201
Bigler, Laura A. ....'— '01 C.363 B.S. L.161 J.D. [A Jones D.]
Bilchik, Gary B., (AV) ....'45 '71 C.610 B.B.A. L.608 J.D. [Benesch,F.C.&A.]
Bilfield, Murray D., (BV) ....'49 '74 C.610 B.A. L.8 J.D. [Bilfield&S.]
Bilfield & Sandel Co., L.P.A., (BV) ....1301 East Ninth Street
Billick, John T. ....'— '73 C.363 B.A. L.276 J.D. [Duvin,C.&H.]
Billingsley, Ann B. Voorhees '53 '80 C.112 B.S. L.930 J.D.
(adm. in NY; not adm. in OH) Pres., Hearth Publications Inc.
Billingsley, Henry E., II, (AV) ....'53 '78 C.178 B.A. L.930 J.D. [Tucker E.&W.]
Billington, Glenn E., (AV) .... '43 '70 C.188 A.B. L.161 J.D. [Billington,G.E.]
Billington, Glenn E., Co., LPA, (AV) ....1991 Lee Rd.
Binder, Paul L. ....'47 '72 C.973 B.S. L.602 J.D. U.S. Dept. of Jus.
Binford, Gregory G., (AV) .... '48 '73 C&L.930 A.B., J.D. [Benesch,F.C.&A.]
Binstock, Allen '47 '79 C.930 B.A. L.184 J.D.
(adm. in CT; not adm. in OH) N.L.R.B.
Binzley, Richard C., (AV) ....'37 '66 C.385 A.B. L.930 J.D. [Thompson H.]
Birch, Steven K. ....'47 '96 C.610 B.A. L.1003 J.D. V.P., Architect K.A., Inc.
Birch, Wanda Jordan ....'48 '91 C.788 B.A. L.930 J.D. Co. Probate Ct.
Bitonti, Marie Teresa '63 '98 C.105 B.A. L.823 J.D.
(adm. in NY; not adm. in OH) 8252 Findley Dr
Bittel, Patricia Thomas, (AV) '51 '76
C.1365 B.A. L.893 J.D. 30628 Detroit Rd., PMB 254
Bittence, Mary M., (AV) ....'52 '82 C&L.161 B.A., J.D. [Baker&H.]
Bittence, Stephen L. ....'— '04 C.608 B.S.C.E. L.161 J.D. [A Jones D.]
Bitterman, Eileen M. ....'69 '97 C.201 B.A. L.1003 J.D. [Weltman,W.&R.]
Bixenstine, Barton A., (AV) ....'50 '81 C.381 B.A. L.145 J.D. [Ulmer&B.]
Bixenstine, Kim F., (AV) '58 '82
C.478 B.A. L.145 J.D. V.P. & Chf. Litig. Coun., TRW Inc.
Black, Carl E. .... '— '98 C.610 B.S.E.D. L.608 J.D. [A Jones D.]
Blackburn, Douglas C., (BV) ....'50 '75 C.97 B.S. L.1003 J.D. 24441 Detroit Road
Blackford, Jason C., (AV) ....'38 '64 C.207 B.A. L.976 LL.B. [C Weston H.]
Blackham, Katherine S. ....'62 '87 C.473 B.A. L.1003 J.D. 1410 Terminal Twr.‡
Blackham, Robert E., (AV) ....'59 '87 C.608 B.A. L.1003 J.D. [Roetzel&A.]
Blackhurst, Scott D. ....'63 '90 C.645 B.S. L.659 J.D. Sr. Counsel, TRW Inc.
Blackie, William E., III, (AV) ....'54 '79 C.611 B.A. L.608 J.D. [C Millisor&N.]
Blackmon, Patricia A. ....'50 '76 C.852 B.A. L.1003 J.D. Ct. of App. J.
Blackwell, Joseph H. ....'28 '63 C.339 B.S. L.1003 J.D. 113 Saint Clair Avenue, N.E.
Blair, Becky, (AV) ....'60 '86 C.645 B.S. L.607 J.D. 815 Superior Ave., E
Blair, Mitchell G., (AV) ....'57 '82 C.867 B.A. L.945 J.D. [Calfee,H.&G.]
Blake, Christopher S.W. ....'70 '99 C.502 B.A. L.1003 J.D. [A Hahn L.&P.]
Blake, Martin C., (AV) ....'31 '57 C.473 B.B.S. L.930 LL.B. 23230 Chagrin Blvd.
Blake, William J. '56 '81 C.201 B.A. L.150 J.D.
Sr. V.P. & Assoc. Gen. Coun., KeyBank Natl. Assn.
Blake, William L. ....'27 '56 C.608 B.S. L.1003 J.D. 614 Superior Ave.
Blakely, Jonathan P. ....'63 '89 C.611 B.A. L.930 J.D. 23875 Commerce Park
Blakemore, Edward H. ....'74 '00 C.511 B.A. L.201 J.D. [A Sutter,O.&F.]
Blaschka, Francis L. .....'61 '86 C.629 B.S. L.178 J.D. 1500 West Third Street, Suite 410
Blattner, Robert A., (AV) ....'34 '59 C.597 B.S. L.930 LL.B. 30799 Pinetree Rd. # 415
Bliss, Thomas P., (BV) ....'51 '76 C.650 B.A. L.1003 J.D. [Bliss&H.]
Bliss & Hoty-Bliss, (BV) ....20899 Lorain Rd.
Bloch, Marc J., (AV) ....'43 '69 C.473 B.A. L.251 J.D. [Duvin,C.&H.]
Block, Brian C. ....'— '03 C.347 B.A. L.1003 J.D. 1300 East Ninth Street, 14th Floor
Block, Bruce A., (AV) ....'— '76 C.30 B.A. L.930 J.D. [Javitch,B.&R.]
Blocker, David S. ....'76 '02 C.473 B.A. L.124 J.D. [A Kohrman J.&K.]
Blomgren, Gilbert E. ....'69 '95 C.385 B.A. L.930 J.D. [A K.D.Weiner&Assoc.]
Bloom, Douglas E. ....'73 '01 C.608 B.A. L.989 J.D. [A Hahn L.&P.]
Bloom, Mark G., (AV) '61 '93 C.608 B.S. L.1218 J.D.
Chf. Patent and Licensing Coun., The Cleveland Clinic Foundation (Pat.)
Bloom, Richard S. ....'51 '77 C.150 B.A. L.607 J.D. I.R.S.
Bloom, Stephen E., (BV) ....'53 '85 C.150 B.A. L.1003 J.D. [S.E.Bloom]

Bloom, Stephen E., Co, L.P.A., (BV)
526 Superior Leader Building, 44114
Telephone: 216-575-9100
Email: seb216@sebloomlaw.com URL: http://www.lawyers.com/sebloomlaw
Stephen E. Bloom.
Personal Injury, Workers Compensation, Contracts, Auto Accidents, Nursing Home Abuse, Head and Spinal Cord Injuries, Wrongful Death, Medical Malpractice, Motorcycle Accidents, Slip and Fall, Dog Bites, Trucking Accidents.

See Professional Biographies, CLEVELAND, OHIO

Blumenthal, Don M. '52 '76 C.604 B.A. L.659 J.D.
(adm. in PA; not adm. in OH) Fed. Trade Comm.
Blumenthal, Michael R., (AV) .... '59 '89 C.608 B.S. L.1003 J.D. [Waxman B.]
Bluso, Linda L., (AV) ....'54 '82 C&L.161 B.A., J.D. [Brouse M.]
Blythe-Glaze, Amy M. ....'72 '99 C.607 B.A. L.7 J.D. [A Carlisle,M.R.K.&U.]
Boatwright, Joseph W., IV ....'80 '04 C.1356 B.A. L.945 J.D. [A Britton,S.P.&K.]
Bobka, Todd A. ....'73 '99 C.610 B.B.A. L.989 J.D. [A K.D.Weiner&Assoc.]
Bobrow, Howard J. ....'70 '96 C.473 B.A. L.930 J.D. [A Kahn K.]
Bobula, Marilyn A. ....'47 '77 C.608 B.A. L.1003 J.D. U.S. Dept. of Jus.
Bocciarelli, Marco G. ....'72 '03 C.381 B.S. L.7 J.D. [A Sutter,O.&F.]
Boddy, Carla Denine .....'70 '96 C.473 B.A. L.347 J.D. Asst. V.P. & Atty., Nat'l City Bk.
Bode, Hugh J., (AV) ....'52 '78 C.597 B.A. L.930 J.D. [A Remminger&R.]
Bodi, Robert F. ....'64 '00 C&L.8 B.S., J.D. [A Pearne&G.] (See Pat. Sect.)
Bodnar, Brenda T., (BV) ....'59 '84 C.161 B.A. L.1003 J.D. 880 East 185th Street
Boehlefeld, Heidi A. .... '61 '90 C&L.930 B.S., J.D. [Renner,O.B.&S.] (See Pat. Sect.)

Boehm, David H. ... '74 '00 C.610 B.A. L.989 J.D. [Ⓐ McLaughlin&M.]
Boise, April V. ... '68 '94 C.477 B.B.A. L.145 J.D. [Thompson H.]
Boisselle, Armand P., (AV) '31 '65
C.455 B.S.Ed. L.930 J.D. [Renner,O.B.&S.] (See Pat. Sect.)
Bokor, David B. ... '61 '93 C.610 B.B.A. L.989 J.D. [Ⓐ L.R.Kravitz]
Bolek, Cathleen M., (AV) ... '66 '92 C.823 B.A. L.124 J.D. [Cohen R.&K.]

Bolek, Joseph E., Jr. '41 '67 C.363 A.B. L.930 J.D.
3659 Green Road, Suite 200, 44122
Telephone: 216-831-0004 Fax: 216-831-5051 URL: http://www.josephbolekjr.com
Email: bolekslaw@adelphia.net URL: http://www.bolekslaw.com
Family Law, Divorce, Child Custody, Child Support, Alimony, Personal Injury.
See Professional Biographies, CLEVELAND, OHIO

Boles, Edgar H., (BV) ... '47 '73 C.611 B.A. L.930 J.D. [Ⓒ Moriarty&J.]
Bolinger, Brian W. ... '77 '02 C.851 B.S. L.930 J.D. [Ⓐ Tarolli,S.C.&T.] (See Pat. Sect.)
Bollin, Kip T. ... '70 '95 C.569 B.A. L.276 J.D. [Thompson H.]
Bolmeyer, Frank G., Jr., (AV) ... '56 '81 C.161 B.A. L.1003 J.D. [Sammon&B.]
Bomberger, Jeffrey A. ... '56 '84 C.400 B.S. L.659 J.D. [Ⓒ Squire,S.&D.]
Bombik, Richard John, (AV) ... '50 '78 C.161 B.B.A. L.1003 J.D. Asst. Pros. Atty.
Bonacci, Louis M., (BV) ... '48 '73 C.363 B.A. L.1003 J.D. Asst. Pros.
Bonaiuto, Frank F. ... '23 '57 C.999 B.A. L.1003 J.D. 7314 Creekwood Dr.
Bonder, Daniel L. ... '53 '84 C.363 B.S. L.365 J.D. V.P., Women's Fed. Svgs. Bk.
Bonezzi, William D., (AV) ... '45 '73 C.97 B.S. L.161 J.D. [Bonezzi S.M.&P.]

Bonezzi Switzer Murphy & Polito Co., L.P.A., (AV) BR
526 Superior Avenue, Suite 1400, 44114-1491
Telephone: 216-875-2767 Fax: 216-875-1570
Email: bsmp@bsmplaw.com URL: http://www.bsmplaw.com
William D. Bonezzi; Steven J. Hupp; Kevin O. Kadlec; Patrick J. Murphy; John S. Polito; Beth A. Sebaugh; Donald H. Switzer;—Peter A. Holdsworth; Lynette E. Kiss; Brett A. Miller; Bret C. Perry; Patrick J. Quallich; Susan M. Reinker; Timothy G. Sweeney; Kimberly A. Thomas.
Asbestos Litigation, Consumer Protection Law, Contract Law, Employment Law, General Insurance Defense, including Construction Litigation, Motor Vehicle Accidents, Premises Liability, Product Liability and Personal Injury, Hospital Defense, Hospital Risk Management, Medical Malpractice, Nursing Home Litigation, Pharmaceutical, Professional Negligence, Toxic Tort, Uninsured Motorist Law, UCC Law and Appellate Practice.
Representative Clients: Affiliated FM Insurance; AO Smith; AP Capital; ASE USA; Ashtabula General Medical Center; Baltimore Ennis Land Company; Brandon Drying Fabrics; California Insurance Guarantee Assoc.; Catholic Cemetaries; Catholic Charities Services Corporation.
See Professional Biographies, CLEVELAND, OHIO

Bonko, Robert J. ... '55 '93 C.8 B.A. L.161 J.D. [Ⓢ Calfee,H.&G.]
Bonner, Chet J. ... '66 '02 C.610 B.S. L.989 J.D. [Ⓐ Calfee,H.&G.] (See Pat. Sect.)
Boomer, John R. '61 '86 C.691 B.A. L.846 J.D.
(adm. in TX; not adm. in OH) Asst. Dean, Case Western Reserve Univ. Law Sch.
Boop, Gregory K. ... '— '97 C.161 B.A. L.1003 J,D, [Ⓐ Gallagher S.]
Borders, Keith Lenzie ... '74 '00 C.608 B.A. L.7 J.D. [Ⓐ Rauser,L.&Assoc.]
Borison, Susan R. ... '61 '90 C.1036 B.A. L.930 J.D. 23214 Ranch Rd.
Bork, Derek D. ... '71 '96 C.813 A.B. L.276 J.D. [Thompson H.]
Boron, Martin C., (AV) '53 '81
C.608 B.A. L.1003 J.D. V.P.& Sr. Coun., KeyBank Natl. Assn.
Borosh, Lawrence P. ... '38 '70 C.363 A.B. L.1003 J.D. Borosh Realty
Borowitz, Albert I., (AV) ... '30 '57 C&L.309 B.A., J.D. 901 Lakeside Ave.‡
Bortnick, Daniel B. ... '60 '00 C.161 B.S.E.E. L.1003 J.D. [Ⓐ Amin&T.] (See Pat. Sect.)
Bossin, Kenneth A., (BV) ... '43 '71 C.502 B.S. L.1003 J.D. 1392 SOM Center Road
Bostwick, John Murry, Jr., (BV) '43 '86 C.62 B.A. L.989 J.D.
[Ⓐ T.J.Kenneally&Assoc.]
Bouhall, Robert C., (AV) ... '31 '55 C.602 Ph.B. L.607 LL.B. [Conway,P.&B.]
Boukis, Christ, (AV) ... '39 '65 C.251 B.B.A. L.930 J.D. [Hohmann,B.&C.]
Boukis, Kenneth, (BV) ... '40 '66 C.251 B.B.A. L.930 J.D. [Hohmann,B.&C.]
Bowers, Charles A. ... '67 '94 C.390 B.A. L.930 J.D. [Taft,S.&H.]
Bowes, Robert C., (AV) '52 '78
C.273 B.A. L.1003 J.D. Sr. V.P. & Assoc Gen. Coun., KeyCorp.
Bowling, Chandra S. ... '64 '93 C.608 B.A. L.1161 J.D. [Ⓐ Squire,S.&D.]
Bownas, Pearson N. ... '— '97 C.473 B.A. L.424 J.D. [Ⓐ Jones D.]
Box, Gregory C. ... '59 '91 C.116 B.S L.8 J.D. [Macedonio&B.]
Boxer, Yelena ... '71 '99 C.473 B.S. L.930 J.D. [Ⓐ Ulmer&B.]
Boyce, Jennifer H. ... '— '96 C.679 B.A. L.665 J.D. [Ⓐ Jones D.]
Boyce, Kevin D. ... '— '96 C.679 B.A. L.94 J.D. [Ⓐ Jones D.]
Boyd, John W., (AV) ... '60 '85 C.25 B.A. L.930 J.D. V.P. & Sr. Atty., Nat'l City Bk.
Boyd, Robert A., (BV) ... '54 '80 C.602 B.A. L.1003 J.D. [Ⓐ Gibson,B.Z.&M.]
Boyd, William A., (AV) ... '46 '74 C&L.608 B.A., J.D. [Calfee,H.&G.] ‡
Boyko, Christopher A. ... '54 '79 C.528 B.A. L.1003 J.D. U.S. Dist. J.
Boyko, William ... '20 '54 C.363 B.S. L.1003 J.D. 3540 Ridge Rd.‡
Boyle, James P., (BV) ... '66 '91 C.473 B.A. L.930 J.D. [Young,G.&S.]
Boyle, Mary Jane ... '64 '89 C.354 B.A. L.1003 J.D. Com. Pleas J.
Boyle, Timothy E. '61 '86 C.207 B.A. L.228 J.D.
(adm. in MD; not adm. in OH) 1111 Superior Ave.
Brackett, Scott Douglas ... '59 '88 C.1102 B.S. L.7 J.D. Coopers & Lybrand
Bradbury, Petra J., (AV) '47 '88
C.1209 B.S. L.893 J.D. V.P. & Asst. Coun., KeyBank Natl. Assn.
Bradford, Matthew ... '71 '01 C.124 B.A. L.1003 J.D. [Ⓐ Thompson H.]
Bradley, Mary Louise ... '58 '00 C.610 B.S. L.161 J.D. [M.L.Bradley&Assoc.]
Bradley, Steven L., (BV) ... '64 '90 C.851 B.A. L.1003 J.D. 526 Superior Ave., Ste. 222
Bradley, Mary L., and Associates ... P.O. Box 43669
Brady, Catherine M. ... '58 '83 C.363 B.A. L.221 J.D. 3695 Rocky River Dr.
Bragg, Caprice H. ... '64 '89 C.604 B.A. L.569 J.D. 1422 Euclid Avenue
Bralliar, Thomas B., Jr. ... '68 '95 C.165 A.B. L.94 J.D. [T.B.Bralliar,Jr.]
Bralliar, Thomas B., Jr., Co., L.P.A. ... 691 Robin Drive
Branagan, James J., (AV) '43 '68 C.385 B.A. L.178 LL.B.
19801 Van Aken Boulevard Suite 203 (Shaker Heights)
Brandt, Alan C. ... '— '01 C.999 B.S. L.124 J.D. [Ⓐ Calfee,H.&G.] (See Pat. Sect.)
Brandt, Jean Marie ... '62 '89 C.161 B.S.W. L.608 J.D. [J.M.Brandt]
Brandt, Jean M. ... 1028 Kenilworth Avenue
Brantley, Sandra J., (AV) ... '50 '80 C.836 B.S. L.1003 J.D. V.P., Natl City Corp.
Brauer, Jeffrey A., (BV) ... '68 '94 C.597 B.S. L.880 J.D. [Hahn L.&P.]
Braun, Lillian M. ... '31 '80 C.161 B.A. L.930 J.D. 1223 West 6th Street
Braverman, Herbert L., (AV) ... '47 '72 C.659 B.S. L.309 J.D. [Walter&H.]
Bravo, Kenneth A., (AV) ... '42 '67 C.705 B.A. L.608 J.D. [Ulmer&B.]
Braxter, Milton J. ... '53 '80 C&L.930 B.A., J.D. 4028 E. 143rd St.
Brcak, Frank ... '21 '51 C&L.930 B.B.A., J.D. 4141 Rockside Rd.‡
Breitenbach, William H. ... '53 '80 C.602 A.B. L.1003 J.D. 25701 Science Park Drive
Brejt, Sara Naiman '57 '82 C.1149 B.S. L.94 J.D.
(adm. in NY; not adm. in OH) 3621 Severn Rd.
Brelo, Clayton E., (BV) ... '41 '67 C.705 B.A. L.1003 J.D. [Gibson,B.Z.&M.]
Brem, Joseph Michael ... '70 '98 C.363 B.S.B.A. L.7 J.D. Pricewaterhouse Coopers LLP
Brendel, John M. ... '71 '96 C.145 B.A. L.659 J.D. Dist. Ct., Jud. Law Clk.
Brennan, Bridget Meehan ... '74 '00 C.363 B.A. L.124 J.D. [Ⓐ Baker&H.]
Brennan, Kimberly A. ... '67 '93 C.473 B.A. L.930 J.D. [Ⓐ McCarthy,L.C.&L.]
Brennan, Maureen A., (AV) ... '49 '77 C.104 B.A. L.93 J.D. [Baker&H.]
Brennan, Michael D. ... '71 '96 C.97 B.A. L.1003 J.D. [Ⓐ Hermann,C.&S.]
Brennan, Terry M., (AV) ... '70 '95 C.473 B.A. L.347 J.D. [Baker&H.]
Brenner, Paul M. ... '60 '86 C.97 B.S. L.851 J.D. Key Tr. Co. of OH.
Brezic, Richard F. ... '41 '71 C.930 B.B.A. L.161 J.D. 1900 E. 9th St., Ste. 3500
Brice, John C. ... '62 '87 C.692 B.A. L.930 J.D. 1100 Superior Ave. E., Ste. 1700
Brick, Philip D. '30 '58 C&L.494 B.B.A., LL.B.
(adm. in MN; not adm. in OH) Dir., Envir. Affs., Cleveland-Cliffs Inc
Brick, Timothy T., (AV) ... '— '88 C.967 B.A. L.930 J.D. [Gallagher S.]

Bricker & Eckler LLP, (AV)
1375 East Ninth Street, Suite 1500, 44114-1718 ⊙
Telephone: 216-523-5405 Fax: 216-523-7071
Email: info@bricker.com URL: http://www.bricker.com
Partners: Alan J. Ross; Glenn S. Krassen; Richard M. Knoth; Suzanne Klensmith Saganich; Jayne L. Jakubaitis. Of Counsel: Breaden M. Douthett; Joel S. Heiser;—Maura L. Brozovic; Joshua M. Marks; Michael J. Montgomery.
Antitrust and Competitive Business Practices, Banking, Bankruptcy, Commercial, Construction, Corporate Governance, Corporation and Partnership, Cyberlaw, Creditor-Debtor, Education, Emerging Business, Employment Relations, Energy, Entertainment/Sports, Environmental, Federal Taxation, Governmental Agencies and Legislative Law, Health Care, Insurance, Intellectual Property, International Transactions, Litigation, Mental Retardation and Developmental Disabilities, Mergers and Acquisitions; Mortgage Lending, Oil and Gas, Pension and Employee Benefits, Public Finance, Public Utilities, OSHA, Real Estate, Securities, State and Local Taxation, Trusts and Estates, Workers' Compensation.
Columbus, Ohio Office: 100 South Third Street, 43215-4291. Telephone: 614-227-2300. Fax: 614-227-2390.
See Professional Biographies, CLEVELAND, OHIO

Brickner, Paul ... '40 '66 C.692 B.A. L.930 J.D. Admin. Law J., Soc. Sec. Admn.
Briggs, David J., (BV) ... '56 '81 C.363 B.S. L.1003 J.D. [Sammon&B.]
Briggs, Thomas A. ... '— '94 C.8 B.S.Ch.E. L.365 J.D. [Jones D.] (See Pat. Sect.)
Bright, James R., (AV) ... '49 '76 C.674 A.B. L.276 J.D. [Spieth,B.M.&N.]
Briller, David D. ... '49 '77 C.62 B.A. L.1003 J.D. [D.D.Briller]
Briller, David D., Co., L.P.A., The Law Offices of ... 7379 Pearl Rd.
Brink, Michael C. ... '76 '03 [Ⓐ Brouse M.]
Brinsky, Gabriel P. ... '17 '41 C.930 L.608 LL.B. 21465 Erie Rd.
Bristol, Jason R. ... '75 '00 C.96 B.A. L.989 J.D. [Cohen R.&K.]
Britt, Stephen T., (CV) ... '63 '89 C.1260 B.A. L.1003 J.D. McCauley & Associates
Brittain, Brian K., (BV) ... '— '81 C.528 B.A. L.930 J.D. [Ross,B.&S.]
Brittain, Michael E., (AV) ... '54 '79 C.610 A.B. L.930 J.D. [Calfee,H.&G.]
Britton, John E., (AV) ... '55 '81 C.879 B.A. L.851 J.D. [Britton,S.P.&K.]

Britton, Smith, Peters & Kalail Co., L.P.A., (AV) BR
Summit One, Suite 540, 4700 Rockside Road, 44131-6814
Telephone: 216-642-0323 Facsimile: 216-642-0747
URL: http://www.ohioedlaw.com
Members of the Firm: John E. Britton; David Kane Smith; Scott C. Peters; Karrie M. Kalail; Krista K. Keim; David H. Seed. Associates: Joseph W. Boatwright, IV; Sherrie D. Clayborne; Lori A. Kosakowski; David A. Rose; Michael E. Stinn.
Limited to the representation of boards of education in all aspects of Education Law, including School Law, Management Employment Law, Management Labor Law, Collective Bargaining, Employment Arbitration, School Board Defense, Defense Litigation, Special Education, Civil Rights Defense, General Liability Defense, Public Finance, Public Construction Law, Real Estate Valuation, Real Estate Tax Appeals, Workers' Compensation Defense.
See Professional Biographies, CLEVELAND, OHIO

Brizzolara, Anthony M. '58 '83 C&L.94 B.A., J.D.
(adm. in MA; not adm. in OH) Spec. Agent F.B.I.
Brobst, Claudia '51 '81 C.318 B.A. L.276 J.D.
Asst. Gen. Coun.-Benefits, Parker-Hannifin Corp.
Brodhead, Peter J., (AV) ... '54 '79 C.207 B.A. L.1003 J.D. [Spangenberg,S.&L.]
Brogan, Stephen J., (AV Ⓣ) '— '77 C.93 A.B. L.602 J.D.
(adm. in DC; not adm. in OH) [Jones D.] (⊙Wash., DC)
Brooks, Patrick J. ... '71 '98 C&L.8 B.A., J.D. [Ⓐ Squire,S.&D.]
Brooks, William H. ... '49 '76 C.197 A.B. L.477 J.D. Hyatt Legal Plans, Inc.
Broome, J. Scott, (AV) ... '63 '89 C.608 B.S. L.930 J.D. [Rotatori,B.G.S.&A.]
Brosse, Peter D., (BV) ... '59 '84 C.608 B.S. L.851 J.D. [Meyers,R.F.&L.]
Brouhard, Julia R., (AV) ... '47 '81 C.63 B.S. L.326 J.D. [Ray,R.C.&D.]

Brouse McDowell, A Legal Professional Association, (AV)
1001 Lakeside Avenue, Suite 1600, 44114 ⊙
Telephone: 216-830-6830 Toll Free: 877-837-5711 Telex: 216-830-6807
Email: brouse@brouse.com URL: http://www.brouse.com
Shareholders: Linda L. Bluso (Resident); Christopher J. Carney (Resident); Joseph T. Dattilo (Resident); Ms. Keven Drummond Eiber (Resident); Cathryn R. Ensign (Resident); Patricia A. Gajda (Resident); Thomas A. Gattozzi (Resident); Alan M. Koschik (Resident); David A. Lum (Resident); Charles D. Price (Resident); Jessica E. Price (Resident); Thomas J. Ubbing (Resident); Robert M. Walter; Timothy D. Wood (Resident);—Michael C. Brink (Resident); Michael P. O'Donnell. Of Counsel: Theodore A. Ward.
Administrative, Bankruptcy, Business, Business Litigation, Commercial, Corporation, Creative Technologies, Creditors' Rights, E-Commerce, Environmental, Estate Planning, Federal Securities, General Civil, Health Care, Immigration, Insurance, Intellectual Property, Labor and Employment, Litigation, Mediation, Mergers and Acquisitions, Municipal and Bond, OSHA Compliance, Probate, Real Estate, Succession Planning, Tax, Trademarks, Trial and Appellate Practice, Venture Capital.
Akron, Ohio Office: 388 S. Main Street, Suite 500. Telephone: 330-535-5711. Toll Free: 800-837-5711. Facsimile: 330-253-8601. URL: http://www.brouse.com.
See Professional Biographies, CLEVELAND, OHIO

Browarek, Matthew F. ... '52 '88 C.1529 B.A. L.989 J.D. 1370 Ontario St.
Brown, Anne Rachel '— '94 C.259 B.S. L.446 J.D.
(adm. in DC; not adm. in OH; Pat.) Sr. Dir. Intell. Prop., Athersys Inc.
Brown, Charles Thomas ... '60 '85 C.363 B.A. L.117 J.D. Cuyahoga Co. Prob. Ct.
Brown, Craig M., (AV) ... '54 '79 C.477 B.A. L.276 J.D. [Duvin,C.&H.]
Brown, David H. ... '73 '02 C.610 B.A. L.989 J.D. [Ⓐ Janik&D.]
Brown, Edward R., (AV) ... '33 '62 C.309 B.A. L.930 LL.B. 15901 Chadbourne Rd.
Brown, Ella Marie ... '45 '80 C&L.347 B.S., J.D. Defense Fin. & Acct. Serv.
Brown, Harry M., (AV) ... '47 '72 C.978 B.A. L.569 J.D. [Benesch,F.C.&A.]
Brown, James Mitchell, (AV) ... '46 '73 C.608 B.S. L.1003 J.D. [J.M.Brown]
Brown, Jaron R. ... '76 '02 C.1033 B.S. L.124 J.D. [Ⓐ Calfee,H.&G.]
Brown, John D., (AV) ... '42 '69 C.174 B.A. L.930 J.D. [Taft,S.&H.]
Brown, Leslie S. ... '— '96 The Lincoln Electric Co.
Brown, Lori E. ... '— '99 C.477 B.A. L.608 J.D. [Ⓐ Gallagher S.]
Brown, Michael C. ... '59 '88 C.930 B.A. L.8 23200 Chagrin Blvd.
Brown, Neil A. ... '56 '81 C.473 B.S. L.1003 J.D. H & I Advsrs., Inc.
Brown, Robert L., (AV) ... '48 '92 C.1266 B.A. L.989 J.D. [R.Brown]
Brown, T. Christopher ... '71 '97 C.477 B.A. L.608 J.D. [Ⓐ Walter&H.]
Brown, Troy R., (AV) ... '44 '72 C&L.966 B.S., J.D. [Singerman,M.D.&K.]
Brown, Virgil E., Jr., (BV) ... '45 '74 C.124 B.S. L.161 J.D. 2136 Noble Road
Brown, William D. ... '65 '91 C.97 B.S. L.930 J.D. [Steuer,E.B.&B.]
Brown, James Mitchell, L.P.A., (AV) ... Terminal Twr., Ste. 1420
Brown, Robert, LLC, (AV) ... 1468 W. 9th St., Ste. 210

Brown & Szaller Co., L.P.A., (AV)
14222 Madison Avenue, 44107-4510
Telephone: 216-228-7200 Fax: 216-228-7207 URL: http://www.lawandhelp.com
Email: atty@lawandhelp.com URL: http://www.lawyers.com/brownszaller
James F. Szaller; Kenneth J. Knabe.
General Civil Trial and Appellate Practice. Personal Injury, Accidents, Products Liability and Medical Malpractice Law.

See Professional Biographies, CLEVELAND, OHIO

Browne, J. Patrick '35 '60 C.363 B.S. L.215 LL.B. Prof. of Law, Cleveland State University
Browner, Jeremy Todd .... '75 '02 C.1333 B.S. L.1019 J.D. [Browner&H.]

Browner and Henderson LLC
The Leader Building, 526 Superior Avenue East, Suite 545, 44114
Telephone: 216-774-0000 Fax: 216-774-0493
URL: http://www.lawyers.com/brownerandhenderson
Members of Firm: Jeremy Todd Browner; Brandon Henderson.
Consumer Bankruptcy, Civil Litigation, Collections, Business Formation, Criminal Law, Real Estate.

See Professional Biographies, CLEVELAND, OHIO

Browning, Marc D. ....'— '98 C.473 B.S. L.893 J.D. [🄰 Jones D.]
Broyles, Phillip L. .... '55 '80 C.329 B.A. L.569 J.D. Reg. Dir., Fed. Trade Comm.
Brozovic, Maura L. ....'73 '00 C&L.124 B.A., J.D. [🄰 Bricker&E.]
Brule, Thomas R. ....'54 '80 C.651 B.S. L.421 J.D. [Benesch,F.C.&A.]
Bruml, Charles R. ....'12 '36 C&L.930 B.A., LL.B. 2992 Lincoln Rd.
Bruner, Harvey B. .... '50 '74 C.608 B.A. L.1003 J.D. 55 Public Sq.
Brunn, Thomas L., Jr., (AV) .... '64 '89 C.363 B.A. L.1003 J.D. [Brunn]
Brunn, Thomas L., Sr., (AV) ....'37 '67 C.363 B.S. L.1003 J.D. [Brunn]

Brunn Law Firm, The, Co., LPA, (AV)
700 West St. Clair Avenue, Suite 208, 44113-1230
Telephone: 216-623-7300 Fax: 216-623-7330
Email: brunn@core.com
Thomas L. Brunn, Sr.; Thomas L. Brunn, Jr.;—Alison D. Ramsey.
Medical Malpractice, Product Liability, Litigation.

See Professional Biographies, CLEVELAND, OHIO

Brunner, Kimberly C. ....'— '02 C.880 B.A. L.608 J.D. [🄰 Baker&H.]
Bryenton, Gary L., (AV) ....'39 '65 C.313 A.B. L.930 J.D. [Baker&H.]
Brzytwa, E. John, (AV) ....'43 '68 C.62 B.A. L.276 J.D. [Brzytwa,Q.&M.]

Brzytwa, Quick & McCrystal, LLC, (AV)
900 Skylight Office Tower, 1660 West Second Street, 44113-1411
Telephone: 216-664-6900 Fax: 216-664-6901
Email: METZLER@BQMLAW.COM URL: http://www.bqmlaw.com
Members of Firm: E. John Brzytwa; Harry T. Quick; James L. McCrystal, Jr.; Daniel F. Petticord. Associates: Robert E. Cahill; Beth M. Adams.
Litigation, Alternative Dispute Resolution, Appellate Practice, Torts, Toxic Tort Defense, Products Liability, Aviation Litigation, Medical Malpractice, Professional Malpractice, Legal Ethics, Personal Injury, Commercial Litigation, Trade Regulation, Banking Litigation, Business Law, Construction Law, Contracts, Intellectual Property Litigation, Insurance Litigation, Insurance Coverage and Constitutional Law.

See Professional Biographies, CLEVELAND, OHIO

Bucalo, John C. .... '65 '94 C.8 B.S.B.A. L.1003 J.D. [🄰 Wincek&D.]
Bucha, Stephen Michael, III .... '69 '95 C.124 B.S. L.989 J.D. Mag.
Buchanan, A. Deane, (AV) .... '46 '73 925 Euclid Ave.ve.
Buchmann, Alan P., (AV) ....'34 '60 C&L.976 B.A., LL.B. 127 Public Sq.
Buck, Frank W., (AV) .... '54 '80 C&L.477 B.A., J.D. [Duvin,C.&H.]
Buck, Maynard A., III, (AV) .... '58 '83 C.1208 B.A. L.851 J.D. [Benesch,F.C.&A.]

Buckingham, Doolittle & Burroughs, LLP, (AV)
1375 East Ninth Street, Suite 1700, 44114 ⊙
Telephone: 216-621-5300; Toll Free: 1-888-843-2825 Fax: 216-621-5440
Email: bdb@bdblaw.com URL: http://www.bdblaw.com
Managing Partner: Ronald M. Wilt. Shareholders: Gerald B. Chattman; Alan P. DiGirolamo; David L. Drechsler; Robert A. Hager; William B. Leahy; Douglas J. Paul; Dirk E. Riemenschneider; Deborah Sesek; John P. Slagter; Terry W. Vincent (Former Managing Partner, Cleveland); Ronald F. Wayne (Certified Specialist in Estate Planning, Trusts and Probate Law, Ohio State Bar Association); Grant M. Yoakum. Partners: John F. Ballard; Edward C. Coaxum, Jr.; Lisa M. deFilippis; Paul A. Dzenitis; Lawrence Friedlander; Dale A. Nowak; Henry I. Reder. Associates: Mark F. Craig; Christine M. Faranda; David J. Lindner; Walter A. (Scott) Lucas; Ryan J. Morley; Beth A. Nagel; Brian K. Nam; Timothy A. Spirko.
Appellate, Closely Held Companies, Commercial Law and Litigation, Computer and Technology, Construction Law, Copyrights, Corporate and Business, Creditors Rights/Bankruptcy, Criminal Law, Employment Law, Environmental, Estate Planning, Family Law, Finance and Public Law, Franchise, Health Care, Immigration Law, Insurance Defense, Intellectual Property, Labor and Employment, Land Use and Zoning, Medical Malpractice Defense, Mergers and Acquisitions, Patents, Probate, Publicly Held Companies, Real Estate, School Law, Securities, Succession Planning, Taxation and Employee Benefits, Toxic Tort/Complex Litigation, Trademarks/Service Marks, Trade Secrets, Trial, Trusts and Estates, Venture Capital/Emerging Companies, Workers' Compensation.
Akron, Ohio Office: 50 South Main Street, P.O. Box 1500, 44309-1500. Telephone: 330-376-5300. Toll Free: 800-686-2825. Fax: 330-258-6559.
Canton, Ohio Office: 4518 Fulton Drive Northwest, P.O. Box 35548, 44735-5548. Telephone: 330-492-8717. Toll Free: 888-811-2825. Fax: 330-492-9625.
Columbus, Ohio Office: 191 West Nationwide Boulevard, 43215-3506. Telephone: 614-221-8448. Toll Free: 888-686-2825. Fax: 614-221-8590.
Boca Raton, Florida Office: 2500 North Military Trail, Suite 480, 33431. Telephone: 561-241-0414. Toll Free: 800-682-2825. Fax: 561-241-9766.

See Professional Biographies, CLEVELAND, OHIO

Buckles, H. E. '47 '76 C.930 B.A. L.7 J.D. Sr. Assoc. Gen. Coun., Electrolux North America
Buckley, Brent M., (AV) ....'— '82 C.930 B.A. L.161 J.D. [Buckley K.]
Buckley, Thomas '37 '65 C.262 A.B. L.976 LL.B. (adm. in ND; not adm. in OH) 2121 Euclid Ave

Buckley King, A Legal Professional Association, (AV) 🅱🆁
1400 Fifth Third Center, 44114 ⊙
Telephone: 216-363-1400 National Watts Line: 800-255-2825 Telecopier: 216-579-1020
Email: bkb@bucklaw.com URL: http://www.buckleyking.com
Brent M. Buckley; Woods King III; Richard J. Disantis; Harry W. Greenfield; David C. Engle; Rosemary Sweeney; Daniel P. Carter; Barbara Lee Armstrong; Jeffrey C. Toole; Richard M. Bain; Theodore M. Dunn, Jr.; Paul Psota; Harold R. Rauzi; Douglas N. Barr; Kevin R. Keogh; Regina M. Massetti; Michael J. Spisak;—Lorraine Debose; Dov Y. Frankel; Eric D. Krajewski; Lindsay Maxwell; Heidi J. Milicic; James L. Miller; Jeffrey W. Ruple; Deborah D. Zielinski. Of Counsel: John A. Hallbauer; Elliot M. Kaufman.
Corporate, Litigation, Commercial, Estate Planning, Banking and Finance, Real Estate, Merger and Acquisition, Appellate, Bankruptcy, Professional and Executive (Directors and Officers) Liability, Insurance Law, Products Liability, Health Care, Hospital Law, Medical Malpractice Defense, Immigration and Naturalization, Toxic and Hazardous Materials, ERISA, Taxation, Environmental, Labor and Litigation for Management, Public Employment Relations, Employee Benefits and NLRB Matters.
Columbus, Ohio Office: One Columbus, 10 West Broad Street, Suite 1300. Telephone: 614-461-5600. Telecopier: 614-461-5630.
Cincinnati, Ohio Office: 1420 PNC Center, 201 East Fifth Street. Telephone: 513-412-5400. Telecopier: 513-412-5401.
Atlanta, Georgia Office: Suite 1220 Lennox Building, 3399 Peachtree Road. Telephone: 404-816-7791. Telecopier: 404-816-9786.

See Professional Biographies, CLEVELAND, OHIO

Buckman, Herbert, (AV) ....'15 '40 C&L.976 A.B., LL.B. [🄲 Weston H.]
Bucur, Nicholas A., (BV) ....'24 '51 C.363 B.S. L.1003 J.D. 10206 Clifton Blvd.
Budzik, James A. .... '60 '85 C.201 B.A. L.117 J.D. [🄰 Johnson,A.&C.]
Buelow, Edward Thomas .... '56 '82 C.161 B.A. L.989 J.D. City Pros. Off.
Buescher, Stephen L., (AV) ....'44 '69 C.25 B.A. L.930 J.D. [Thompson H.]
Buford, Thomas C., (AV) ....'47 '77 C.918 B.A. L.1003 J.D. 75 Public Sq., Ste. 650
Bugg, Mayme Carol .... '45 '78 C.254 B.A. L.989 J.D. Mag., Cuyahoga Co. Juv. Ct.
Bullard, Marcia J. ....'54 '84 C.62 B.A. L.1003 J.D. [🄲 Lasko&L.]
Buller, Carolyn J., (AV) ....'55 '81 C.604 B.A. L.930 J.D. [Squire,S.&D.]
Bulloch, John T. .... '52 '91 C.851 B.S.Ph. L.930 J.D. [🄰 Moscarino&T.]
Bulloch, Steven N., (AV) '46 '74 C.309 B.A. L.930 J.D. Sr. V.P. & Sr. Mng. Coun., KeyBank Natl. Assn.
Bulloff, Aaron H., (AV) ....'— '72 C.608 B.A. L.477 J.D. [Kadish,H.&W.]
Bulson, Don W., (AV) '51 '76 C.610 B.S.M.E. L.608 J.D. [Renner,O.B.&S.] (See Pat. Sect.)
Bumpass, T. Merritt, Jr., (AV) ....'43 '69 C.870 B.S. L.896 LL.B. [Frantz W.]
Bundy, Charlett A. ....'47 '91 C.446 B.A. L.930 J.D. 3655 Cummings Rd.

Bundy, Roger M. '71 '02 C.475 B.A. L.1003 J.D.
4766 Broadview Road, 44109
Telephone: 216-781-1720 Fax: 216-622-2714
Email: rbundy@rogerbundylaw.com URL: http://www.rogerbundylaw.com
Personal Injury Litigation, Automobile Accidents, Slip and Fall, Trucking Accidents, Consumer Bankruptcy, Litigation, Estate Planning, Probate, Wills, Trusts, Nursing Home Abuse, Sexual Abuse, Real Estate, Commercial Leasing, Consumer Law, Truth-in-Lending, Lemon Law, Consumer Fraud.

See Professional Biographies, CLEVELAND, OHIO

Bungo, Larissa L. .... '70 '96 C.352 B.A. L.930 J.D. Fed. Trade Comm.
Burchmore, David W. ....'52 '86 C.674 A.B. L.893 J.D. [Squire,S.&D.]
Burgan, Kelly S. ....'— '01 C.608 B.A. L.989 J.D. [🄰 Baker&H.]
Burge, David A., (AV) ....'43 '70 C.339 B.S.G.E. L.421 J.D. [D.A.Burge] (Pat.)

Burge, David A., Co., L.P.A., (AV) 🅱🆁
2901 South Park Boulevard, 44120-1842
Telephone: 216-921-8900 Fax: 216-921-0209
David A. Burge.
Patent and Trademark Practice.

See Professional Biographies, CLEVELAND, OHIO

Burger, Robert W. ....'63 '97 C.999 B.S. L.861 J.D. [🄰 Thompson H.]
Burger, Todd M. ....'77 '02 C.97 B.A. L.851 J.D. [🄰 Kohrman J.&K.]
Burgess, Julia E. ....'52 '80 C&L.028 B.A., LL.B. V.P., Natl City Bk.
Burgess, M. John ....'74 '02 C.150 B.A. L.989 J.D. [🄰 McDonald H.]
Burgess, Patricia A. ....'— '02 C.608 B.S. L.930 J.D. [🄰 Thompson H.]
Burkart, Gregory C. '63 '88 C.812 B.S. L.734 J.D. (adm. in IL; not adm. in OH) [🄲 Squire,S.&D.]
Burke, David E. ....'37 '64 C.201 B.A. L.930 LL.B. [🄲 Taft,S.&H.]
Burke, James P. ....'— '01 C.145 B.A. L.602 J.D. [🄰 Jones D.]
Burke, James W., Jr., (AV) ....'41 '70 C.381 B.S. L.1003 J.D. 22649 Lorain Rd.
Burke, Jerome L. ....'45 '71 C.602 A.B. L.1003 J.D. 4544 Rocky River Drive
Burke, John F., III, (BV) ....'65 '92 C.473 B.A. L.1003 J.D. [Mansour,G.G.&M.]
Burke, Joseph F. '32 '57 C.973 B.S. L.879 LL.B. (adm. in IL; not adm. in OH) Sr. V.P., Chicago Title Ins. Co.
Burke, Kathleen B., (AV) ....'— '73 C&L.724 B.A., J.D. [Jones D.]
Burke, Lillian W. ....'17 '51 C.608 B.S. L.1003 LL.B. Mun. J.
Burke, Matthew E. ....'68 '95 C.477 B.A. L.930 J.D. [🄰 Calfee,H.&G.]
Burke, Patrick J. ....'72 '03 C.608 B.S. L.161 J.D. [🄰 Squire,S.&D.]
Burlingame, Alexander G. ....'71 '98 C.862 B.A. L.930 J.D. [🄰 Squire,S.&D.]
Burney, Janet E. ....'52 '79 C.787 B.S. L.1003 J.D. Juv. Ct. J.
Burney, Nona M. .... '49 '82 C.597 B.S. L.1003 J.D. Admr., Cleveland Pub. Schools
Burnham, Francis N. '42 '68 C.188 B.S. L.930 J.D. Consultant, Watson Wyatt Worldwide
Burns, John J. ....'— '98 C.201 B.A. L.161 J.D. [🄰 Singerman,M.D.&K.]
Burns, Kenneth B., (BV) .... '32 '62 C.610 B.S.C. L.1003 J.D. [Gallup,B.&M.]
Burns, Robert J., (AV) ....'55 '80 C.1024 B.A. L.8 J.D. V.P. & Sr. Coun., KeyCorp
Burnside, Janet R. ....'46 '77 C&L.608 B.S., J.D. Com. Pleas J.
Burtzlaff, Kevin J. ....'58 '88 C.473 B.A. L.161 J.D. Clev. Bd. of Ed.
Busby, William Curtis ....'71 '99 C.967 B.A. L.117 J.D. Athersys, Inc.
Busch, Lawrence J. ...... '50 '76 C&L.879 B.A., J.D. 3401 Enterprise Parkway, Suite 340
Buser, Daniel C. .... '61 '88 C.851 B.A. L.7 J.D. [🄲 Lasko&L.]
Bush, Theodore J. .... '68 '94 C.93 B.A. L.930 J.D. 1300 E. 9th Street
Butch, Mariann E. .... '58 '96 C.477 B.A. L.930 J.D. [🄲 Benesch,F.C.&A.]
Butcher, Samuel V., (AV) ....'54 '84 C.607 B.S. L.1003 J.D. [Stewart&D.]
Butler, Annette G., (BV) ....'44 '73 C.930 B.A. L.161 J.D. Asst. U.S. Atty.

Butler, Charles S. '42 '67 C.659 B.S. L.477 J.D.
35 Severance Circle, Suite 809, 44118-1519
Telephone: 216-691-9404; 216-691-9959 Fax: 216-297-1972 URL: http://www.cbutlerjusticeforvictims.com
Email: cbutlerjustice@ameritech.net URL: http://www.lawyers.com/justiceforvictims
Sexual Harassment, Fired Unjustly, Discrimination, Labor and Employment, Malpractice, Personal Injury, Wrongful Death, Probate, Criminal.

See Professional Biographies, CLEVELAND, OHIO

Butler, Geraldine J. ....'71 '00 C.363 B.A. L.989 J.D. [🅂 Baker&H.]
Butler, Kevin M., Law Offices of ...'75 '01 C.473 A.B. L.251 J.D. 2401 Superior Viaduct
Butler, Michael Patrick, (BV) .... '49 '83 C.381 B.A. L.989 J.D. [M.P.Butler]
Butler, Michael P., (BV) .... 2401 Superior Viaduct
Butscher, Alisa C. .... '58 '96 C.62 B.S. L.1003 J.D. 1406 W. 6th St., Third Fl.
Button, David R. ....'66 '92 C&L.608 B.S.B.A., J.D. [Wegman,H.&V.]
Buzney, Sandra J. .... '51 '99 C.150 B.A. L.930 J.D. [Hickman&L.]
Byrd, Nailah K. ....'72 '00 C.178 B.A. L.1009 J.D. [🄰 Squire,S.&D.]
Byrne, James A. .... '62 '90 C.818 B.S. L.1003 J.D. [🄰 McMahon,D.H.&L.]
Cabral, Thomas J., (BV) ....'— '86 C.1260 B.A. L.7 J.D. [Gallagher S.]
Cada, Gregory A., (BV) ....'49 '78 C.124 B.S.E.E. L.1003 J.D. 3421 Prospect Ave. E.
Cadle, Amy L. ....'75 '02 C.318 B.A. L.902 J.D. [🄰 Squire,S.&D.]
Cahill, Robert E. .... '74 '00 C.602 B.A. L.124 J.D. [🄰 Brzytwa,Q.&M.]
Cahill, Thomas Michael ....'49 '94 C.161 B.B.A. L.1003 J.D. Co. Pros. Off.
Cahn, James S., (AV) ....'46 '73 C.659 B.A. L.608 J.D. [Hermann,C.&S.]
Cahn, Stephen J., (AV) .... '31 '61 C.260 B.S. L.1003 J.D. [Duvin,C.&H.]
Cain, Elizabeth A., (BV) ....'57 '82 C.473 A.B. L.150 J.D. Asst. Atty. Gen.
Cain, James Matthew .... '42 '72 C.608 B.S. in B.A. L.989 J.D. U.S. Atty.'s Off.
Caine, Steven Robert ....'59 '92 [S.R.Caine]
Caine, Steven R. .... 28601 Chagrin Blvd., Ste. 300
Cairns, J. Donald, (AV) .... '31 '58 C.309 A.B. L.608 J.D. [Spieth,B.M.&N.]
Cajacob, Kathleen D. .... '71 '98 C.473 B.S. L.823 J.D. Bus. Analyst, Key Bk. USA‡
Calabrese, Anthony O., III ....'72 '97 C.276 B.A. L.930 J.D. [🄰 Vorys,S.S.&P.]
Calabrese, Anthony O., Jr. .....'35 '61 C.363 B.S.S. L.1003 LL.B. 8th Dist. Ct. of Appeals
Calabrese, J. Philip ....'71 '00 C.321 B.A. L.309 J.D. [🄰 Squire,S.&D.]

Calatrello, Frederick J. '42 '70 C.588 A.B. L.818 J.D.
(adm. in MA; not adm. in OH) Reg Dir., N.L.R.B.
Calderas, Erica L. .... '68 '94 C.188 A.B. L.597 J.D. [Hahn L.&P.]
Calderone, Donald A. .... '34 '61 C.473 B.A. L.989 J.D. 6800 Mayfield Rd.
Caldwell, Carrie M. .... '77 '02 C&L.893 B.A., J.D. [Ⓐ Vorys,S.S.&P.]
Caldwell, Deborah A. ..... '— '98 C.381 B.S.N. L.1003 J.D. Dept of Child & Fam. Servs.
Caldwell, W. Wilson, (BV) .... '14 '42 C.532 B.A. L.161 J.D. 140 Public Sq.

Calfee, Halter & Griswold LLP, (AV) BR
1400 McDonald Investment Center, 800 Superior Avenue, 44114-2688 ⊙
Telephone: 216-622-8200 Telecopier: 216-241-0816 Telex: 980499
URL: http://www.calfee.com
Partners: Harold W. Babbit; Brent D. Ballard; Murad A. Beg; Virginia D. Benjamin; Karl S. Beus; Mitchell G. Blair; Michael E. Brittain; John R. Cernelich; Thomas A. Cicarella; John S. Cipolla; Peter J. Comodeca; Timothy J. Connors; William E. Coughlin; David J. Crandall; Mara E. Cushwa; Cheryl A. D'Amico (Certified Specialist in Estate Planning, Trust and Probate Law, Ohio State Bar Association); Anthea R. Daniels; Philip M. Dawson; Shelly G. Dedmon; John J. Eklund; Lynn M. Gattozzi; Richard P. Goddard; Guy F. Guinn; Arthur C. Hall III; Walter G. Harper; Julie A. Harris; Richard J. Hauer, Jr.; Maura L. Hughes; John J. Jenkins; Tracy Scott Johnson; Thomas A. Jorgensen; Joseph K. Juster; Tara A. Kastelic; Matthew J. Klaben; Brian E. Kondas; Stephen P. Kresnye; Anthony J. LaCerva; James F. Lang; James M. Lawniczak; Leonard L. Lewis; Charles B. Lyon; Michael F. Marhofer; Darlene Evans McCoy; Thomas F. McKee; Brian A. McMahon; Daniel J. McMullen; Thomas I. Michals; Robert A. Miller; JoEllen M. Minchak; John M. Mino; Gerald A. Monroe; Edward W. Moore; Sean T. Moorhead; Kimberly Moses; Douglas A. Neary; Ronald H. Neill; Todd F. Palmer (Certified Specialist in Labor & Employment Law, Ohio State Bar Association); Michael D. Phillips; William M. Phillips; Robert N. Rapp; Mary M. Reil; Sandra G. Rolitsky; Robert A. Ross; William L. S. Ross; Raymond Rundelli; Lawrence N. Schultz; Ronald C. Stansbury; James F. Streicher; James C. Vanderwist; Thomas E. Wagner; Mark I. Wallach; Marcia J. Wexberg; Cornelius J. Whitford; John T. Wiedemann; Christopher S. Williams; Scott R. Wilson. Retired Partners: Frederick W. Assini; William A. Boyd (Retired); Richard Cusick; Brian M. Eisenberg; Daniel L. Ekelman; Charles R. Emrick, Jr. (Retired); Dale C. LaPorte; F. Rush McKnight; Michael L. Miller; John L. Naylor, Jr.; Timothy J. Nolan; Richard N. Ogle; William A. Papenbrock; Kenneth R. Schmeichel; Joseph D. Sullivan (Retired); Kevin M. Sullivan; John D. Wheeler. Associates: W. Eric Baisden; Alyssa J. Bell; Stacy R.C. Berliner; Chet J. Bonner; Alan C. Brandt; Jaron R. Brown; Matthew E. Burke; Massimo Capretta (Not admitted in OH); Zoe K. Carlisle; S. Paige Christopher; Suzanne M. Conroy; Heather C. Corrigan; Tracy D. Crandall; Diane Hughes Dobrea; Ryan W. Falk; Kristin J. Frost; Alexander E. Gertsburg; Melissa M. Gleespen; James D. Graham; Gina K. Hagedorn; Warren M. Haines II; Shelly K. Hillyer; George Hoskins; Mark R. Hull; William A. Johnston; Laura K. Kendall; Deneen LaMonica; Jeffrey J. Lauderdale; Sharon A. Luarde; Scott C. Matasar; Laura C. McBride (Not admitted in OH); Stephen L. McCauley; Amy B. McGann; John J. McGuire; Ronald M. McMillan; Wesley C. Meinerding; Matthew M. Mendoza; Brian M. Murray; Thomas R. O'Donnell; Colleen Moran O'Neil; Nenad Pejic; Daniel P. Petrov; Gregory J. Phillips; Brent M. Pietrafese; Billy Carter Raulerson; Karla M. Rogers; Jennifer L. Roth; David A. Ruiz; Kenneth J. Smith; Kristofer K. Spreen; Varnesh Sritharan; Anthony F. Stringer; K. James Sullivan; Alexander N. Teeter; Jennifer L. Vergilii; Karen A. Visocan; Thomas M. Welsh; Nathan A. Wheatley; Jennifer L. Wick; Georgia E. Yanchar; Lisa M. Yerrace. Senior Attorneys: Sean C. Beckstrom; Peter A. Carfagna; Wade Douglass Clark; Corine R. Corpora; Pamela A. Docherty; Mary E. Golrick; Jean M. Hillman; Sheryl K. Kelly; Donald E. Lampert; Kenneth L. Lohiser; Ruth L. Lovett; John E. Miller, Jr.; Michael T. Mulcahy; Cynthia Krips Port; Gretchen Rogge; Cristin Rose Snodgrass; Jack R. Starkoff (Certified Specialist in Workers' Compensation Law, Ohio State Bar Association); Christopher M. Stevens (Not admitted in OH); Susan R. Strom; Magda B. Szabo; Paul E. Szabo; Christina Tait; Inna Vysman (Not admitted in OH); William E. Zitelli (Not admitted in OH). Staff Attorneys: Robert J. Bonko; Linda U. Elliott; David E. Gray, II. Senior Counsel: Marc L. Oberdorff. Of Counsel: John Paul Batt.
Antitrust and Trade Regulation, Banking and Bank Regulation, Bankruptcy and Creditors' Rights, Commercial Business and Finance, General Corporate, Corporate Succession Planning, Employee Benefits, Labor and Employment Relations, Environmental, Estate Planning and Administration, Executive Compensation, Federal Government Contracts and Agency Regulation, Franchise Law, Government Relations and Legislation, Healthcare, Information Technology, Intellectual Property and Technology, International, Litigation, Oil and Gas, Partnerships and Joint Ventures, Public Finance, Public Law, Real Estate, Securities, Tax.
Columbus, Ohio Office: 1100 Fifth Third Center, 21 East State Street. Telephone: 614-621-1500. Fax: 614-621-0010.

See Professional Biographies, CLEVELAND, OHIO

Calkins, Benjamin, (BV) .... '56 '82 C.309 A.B. L.477 J.D. [Spieth,B.M.&N.]
Callaghan, Greg J., (AV) .... '44 '69 C.602 B.A. L.608 J.D. 30000 Chagrin Boulevard
Callaghan, Thos. M. .... '25 '53 C.930 L.1003 LL.B. 2628 Detroit Ave.‡
Callahan, Michael William .... '64 '91 C.980 B.S. in B.A. L.851 J.D. [M.W.Callahan]
Callahan, Thomas J., (AV) .... '57 '85 C.228 B.S. L.930 J.D. [Thompson H.]
Callahan, Michael W. .... 5001 Mayfield Rd., Ste. 301
Callesen, Phillip M., (AV) .... '62 '87 C.97 B.A. L.930 J.D. [Baker&H.]
Calta, Diane A. .... '72 '99 C.741 L.879 J.D. [Ⓐ J.W.Diemert,Jr.&Assoc.]
Calvert, Joseph J. .... '07 '31 C&L.692 LL.B. 23311 Greenlawn Ave.‡
Cameron, David K. .... '52 '78 C.930 B.A. L.1003 J.D. [Cameron&C.]
Cameron, Denise R. .... '53 '79 C.604 A.B. L.339 J.D. Asst. Pros. Atty.
Cameron, Sandy R., (AV) .... '51 '76 C.150 B.B.A. L.1003 J.D. [S.R.Cameron]
Cameron & Cameron .... 925 Euclid Ave. (⊙Montgomery, AL)
Cameron, Sandy R., Co., LPA, (AV) .... 301 Chagrin Blvd., Ste. 300
Camino, Carmine, (BV) .... '50 '80 C.363 B.A. L.215 J.D. 1370 Ontario St.
Camino, Paula E. .... '66 '91 C.679 B.A. L.930 J.D. [Ⓐ Schmelzer&Assoc.]
Camp, Margaret .... '69 '95 C.693 B.A. L.989 J.D. 1370 W. Sixth, Ste. 213
Campana, Jeremy M. .... '73 '00 C.690 B.A. L.1292 J.D. [Ⓐ Thompson H.]
Campanella, Thomas S. .... '50 '77 C.610 B.A. L.1003 J.D. [Ⓖ Baker&H.]
Campanella, Vincent .... '42 '69 C.363 B.S. L.1003 J.D. Co. Comr.
Campbell, David A., III .... '71 '96 C&L.608 B.S.B.A., J.D. [Vorys,S.S.&P.]
Campbell, Jay R. ...... '62 '89 C.608 B.S.M.E. L.8 J.D. [Renner,O.B.&S.] (See Pat. Sect.)
Campbell, Laura R. .... '59 '93 C.161 B.S. L.1003 J.D. 1737 Euclid Ave.
Campbell, William P., (BV) .... '67 '93 C.81 B.A. L.201 J.D. [Ⓐ Schiff&D.]
Canala, Robert L. .... '— '86 C.923 B.S. L.8 J.D. [Jones D.]
Canaris, Jas. E., (BV) .... '28 '56 C.610 B.S.C. L.930 J.D. 614 Superior Ave.
Canda, Ronald J. .... '61 '86 C.1260 B.A. L.999 J.D. 50 Public Sq.
Canfield, Scott R. '59 '97 C.97 B.A. L.851 J.D.
(adm. in WV; not adm. in OH) US Bank Centre Fl 7, 1350 Euclid Ave
Cannon, Margaret Anne, (AV) .... '48 '73 C.604 A.B. L.124 J.D. [Taft,S.&H.]
Capers, Jean M. .... '13 '45 L.1003 J.D. 4614 Prospect Ave.
Capes, Hubbard C., (AV) .... '23 '51 C.251 B.B.A. L.1003 LL.B. 800 Superior Ave.‡
Caplea, Don E., (L.P.A.), (BV) .... '45 '72 C&L.607 B.A., J.D. [D.E.Caplea]
Caplea, Don E., Co., LPA, (BV) .... 116 Cleveland Avenue, N.W., Suite 500
Caporossi, Robert W. '55 '87 C.980 B.S. L.273 J.D.
(adm. in VA; not adm. in OH) MK-Ferguson Grp.
Cappel, Carolyn M., (AV) .... '52 '77 C.347 B.A. L.1003 J.D. [Weston H.]
Cappellazzo, Ronald L. .... '— '89 C.999 B.S. L.161 J.D. [Ⓑ Jones D.]
Capretta, Massimo '74 '00 C.145 A.B. L.477 J.D.
(adm. in IL; not adm. in OH) [Ⓐ Calfee,H.&G.]
Caputo, Diane J. .... '54 '80 C.608 B.A.S. L.1003 J.D. 20880 Stratford
Carabell, Robert S. .... '38 '67 C.188 A.B. L.7 J.D. 1900 Richmond Rd.
Caravona, Donald E., (AV) .... '46 '73 C.363 B.A. L.1003 J.D. [Caravona&C.]
Caravona & Czack, P.L.L., (AV) .... 50 Public Square, 19th Floor
Carbone, Joseph A., (AV) .... '49 '75 800 Standard Bldg.
Carbone, Rick J., (BV) .... '47 '72 C.363 B.A. L.930 J.D. 6690 Beta Dr. #E-106
Cardenas, Ricardo J. .... '68 '96 C.161 B.A. L.930 J.D. [Ⓐ Roetzel&A.]
Caresani, Ann M. .... '65 '94 C.161 B.B.A. L.1003 J.D. [Porter W.M.&A.]
Carfagna, Peter A., (AV) .... '53 '79 C.309 A.B. L.1565 J.D. [Ⓐ Calfee,H.&G.]
Cargle, A. Elizabeth .... '68 '98 C.381 B.A. L.8 J.D. [Ⓐ Weltman,W.&R.]
Cariglio, Terrence L., (BV) .... '54 '81 C.381 B.A. L.7 J.D. [Cariglio&Assoc.]
Cariglio & Associates Co., L.P.A., (BV) .... 75 Public Square, Suite 920
Carino, Philip J., (AV) '64 '90 C.27 B.A. L.188 J.D.
Coun., GE Consumer and Industrial
Carissimi, Mark M. .... '51 '76 C.608 B.A. L.161 J.D. Region 8 N.L.R.B.
Carkhuff, Denise A. .... '— '95 C.473 B.A. L.851 J.D. [Jones D.]
Carl, Herbert R. .... '37 '68 C.363 B.S.S. L.161 J.D. 2188 W. 100th St.
Carle, William D., III, (AV) .... '29 '55 C.473 B.S. L.1003 J.D. [Ⓒ Ray,R.C.&D.]
Carlin, Angela G., (AV) .... '30 '55 C.97 A.B. L.930 J.D. [Weston H.]
Carlini, Lawrence J., (BV) .... '49 '73 C.823 A.B. L.930 J.D. [Van Aken,W.&W.]
Carlisle, Gerald K., (AV) '34 '60 C.970 B.A. L.1003 LL.B.
[Carlisle,M.R.K.&U.] (⊙Middleburg Heights)
Carlisle, Zoe K. .... '79 '04 C.124 B.A. L.245 J.D. [Ⓐ Calfee,H.&G.]

Carlisle, McNellie, Rini, Kramer & Ulrich Co., L.P.A., (AV)
24755 Chagrin Boulevard, Suite 200, 44122-5690 ⊙
Telephone: 216-360-7200 FAX: 216-360-7210
URL: http://www.carlisle-law.com
Gerald K. Carlisle; Richard L. McNellie; William T. Rini; Herbert J. Kramer; Phyllis A. Ulrich;— Richard A. Utz (Resident at Columbus Office); James L. Sassano; Eric T. Deighton; Amy M. Blythe-Glaze; Mark A. Poland; Richard J. Feuerman; George J. Annos; Oscar E. Albores; Sandor W. Sternberg.
General Civil Practice. Real Estate, Mortgage, Corporation, Probate, Bankruptcy and Family Law. Trials.
Reference: First Merit Bank N.A.
Columbus, Ohio Office: Suite 200, 155 West Main Street. Telephone: 614-464-2704.

See Professional Biographies, CLEVELAND, OHIO

Carlozzi, Louis Joseph .... '65 '94 C.608 B.S. L.607 J.D. 1382 W. 9th St.
Carlson, Douglas C., (AV) .... '50 '75 C.381 B.B.A. L.930 J.D. [Hahn L.&P.]
Carlson, James R., (AV) .... '47 '75 C.604 B.A. L.309 J.D. [Thompson H.]
Carnahan, Anne Schiavone '55 '79 C.608 B.A. L.8 J.D.
Natl. City Bk. Privite Client Gp.
Carnahan, Timothy D. .... '54 '79 C.8 B.S.B.A. L.7 J.D. [Nicola,G.&C.]
Carnes, James S., (AV) .... '23 '50 C&L.930 A.B., LL.B. 820 Orchard Park Drive
Carney, Christopher J., (AV) .... '61 '86 C.363 B.A. L.930 J.D. [Brouse M.]
Carney, Christopher J., (BV) .... '67 '93 C.201 B.A. L.1003 J.D. [Klein&C.]
Carney, James A., (AV) .... '46 '73 C.188 B.S. L.930 J.D. [Carney&C.]
Carney, John James, (AV) .... '44 '69 C.951 B.A. L.178 J.D. [Carney&C.]
Carney, Joseph D., (AV) .... '52 '77 C.94 B.A. L.930 J.D. [J.D.Carney&Assoc.]
Carney & Carney, (AV) .... 2001 Crocker Road

Carney, Joseph D., & Associates, L.L.C., (AV)
2001 Crocker Road, Suite 440, 44145
Telephone: 440-899-1551 Fax: 440-892-4147
Email: info@jdcarney.com URL: http://www.jdcarneylaw.com
Joseph D. Carney. Associate: Bryan S. Mollohan.
Small, Medium and Large Business Counseling, Corporate Law, Litigation, Commercial and Residential Real Estate, Estate Planning, Employment Law Compliance, Securities Law, Capital Formation, Commercial Contracts, Mergers and Acquisitions, Financing Related Law, Employment Law, Construction, Regulatory, Liquor Law, Broker-Dealers, Insurance Law.

See Professional Biographies, CLEVELAND, OHIO

Carpinelli, Ralph R. .... '35 '66 C.608 B.A. L.1003 J.D. 614 Superior Ave., W.
Carr, Anthony P. .... '22 '50 C.608 B.S. L.1003 J.D. 526 Superior Ave.
Carr, Connie S. .... '61 '91 C.130 B.A. L.30 J.D. [Ⓐ Kohrman J.&K.]
Carr, George H. .... '— '98 C.608 B.Mus. L.989 J.D. [Ⓐ Gallagher S.]
Carr, Lidia V. .... '— '01 C.611 B.A. L.8 J.D. [Ⓢ Baker&H.]
Carr, Lindsey A. .... '75 '01 C.597 B.S. L.930 J.D. [Ⓐ Frantz W.]
Carrick, Kathleen M. .... '50 '77 C.229 B.A. L.1003 J.D. Admr., Case Law Sch.
Carroll, James J. .... '16 '41 C.363 Ph.B. L.930 LL.B. Ret. Com. Pleas. J.
Carroll, Matthew P. .... '64 '89 C.103 A.B. L.276 J.D. 1925 St. Clair
Carson, Drew A. .... '57 '86 C.604 B.A. L.930 J.D. [Goodman W.M.]
Carson, Jay R. .... '69 '97 C.62 B.A. L.608 J.D. [Ⓐ Frantz W.]
Carson, Van, (AV) .... '38 '66 C.528 B.A. L.228 LL.B. [Squire,S.&D.]
Carter, Daniel P., (AVⓉ) .... '— '74 C.728 B.S. L.884 J.D. [Buckley K.]
Carter, Leigh H. .... '60 '94 C.94 B.S. L.930 J.D. Trust and Invest. Offr., Natl. City Bank‡
Carter, Tammi J. .... '79 '04 C.1031 B.A. L.124 J.D. [Ⓐ Roetzel&A.]
Carulas, Anna Moore, (AV) .... '61 '86 C.27 B.A. L.602 J.D. [Roetzel&A.]
Cary, Judith D. '45 '96 C.838 B.S. L.1003 J.D.
Atty. Advr., Soc. Sec. Admin. Off. of Hearings & App.
Caryl, Christopher J. .... '71 '98 C.529 B.A. L.989 J.D. [Ⓐ Tucker E.&W.]
Casarona, Robert B., (AV) .... '60 '86 C.36 B.S. L.150 J.D. [Roetzel&A.]
Cascarilla, Ralph E., (AV) .... '49 '76 C.602 B.A. L.1187 J.D. [Walter&H.]
Casper, Michael J., (BV) .... '50 '75 C.659 B.A. L.930 J.D. Asst. Pros. Atty.
Cass, Edward J., (AV) .... '37 '62 C&L.608 B.S., J.D. 1501 Euclid Avenue‡
Cassaro, Charles T. .... '42 '70 C.363 B.S. L.1003 J.D. 1370 Ontario St.
Cassidy, Christopher L. '— '01 C.210 B.A. L.345 J.D.
(adm. in IN; not adm. in OH) 1300 East Ninth Street, 14th Floor
Cassidy, Paul W., (AV) .... '19 '47 C.363 L.1003 J.D. [Cassidy&R.]
Cassidy, William A. '53 '81
C.385 B.A. L.1003 J.D. 4900 Society Center, 127 Public Square
Cassidy & Reiman, (AV) .... 4700 Rockside Road
Castele, John T., (BV) .... '65 '92 C.93 B.A. L.930 J.D. 2401 Superior Via
Castrigano, Charles D. .... '46 '74 C.608 B.A. L.1003 J.D. 16130 Falmouth Drive
Castrodale, Joseph A., (AV) .... '58 '83 C.980 A.B. L.309 J.D. [Ulmer&B.]
Cathcart, David B., (AV) .... '50 '75 C.207 B.A. L.930 J.D. [Mansour,G.G.&M.]
Cathcart, Robert F. .... '70 '99 C.549 B.A. L.930 J.D. [Ⓐ Mazanec,R.&R.]
Caticchio, Michael J., (BV) .... '56 '82 C.473 B.A. L.1003 J.D. [Zimmerman,C.E.&M.]
Caticchio, Pat .... '28 '64 C.347 B.A. L.1003 J.D. 5001 Mayfield Rd.‡
Catz, Robert S. .... '44 '71 C.800 A.B. L.284 J.D. Prof. of Law, Cleveland State Univ.
Cavallo, Francis Joseph .... '72 '01 C.94 B.S. L.989 J.D. Pub. Def. Off.
Cavanaugh, Mary A., (AV) .... '64 '93 C.363 B.A. L.930 J.D. [Ⓐ Spangenberg,S.&L.]
Cavasinni, Joseph E. .... '65 '95 C.201 B.S. L.117 J.D. [Reminger&R.]
Cavitch, Zolman, (AV) .... '25 '51 C&L.477 A.B., J.D. [Cavitch,F.D.&F.] ‡

Cavitch, Familo, Durkin & Frutkin Co., L.P.A., (AV)
1717 East Ninth Street, Fourteenth Floor, 44114-2876
Telephone: 216-621-7860 Telecopier: 216-621-3415
Email: law@cfdf.com URL: http://www.cfdf.com
Harvey L. Frutkin; Thomas G. Belden; Robert M. Nelson; James Dickinson; Michael C. Cohan; Stephen E. Pigott; Douglas A. DiPalma; Thomas M. Cawley; Mohammed J. Bidar; Harold O. Maxfield, Jr.; Ronald D. Holman, II; Mark A. Trubiano; Alexander E. Goetsch. Retired Partners: Zolman Cavitch; Edward D. Familo. Of Counsel: George J. Durkin; Howard P. Kasdan;—Robert C. Heintel; Shannon L. McEaneney; Matthew E. Senra; Sara E. DeCaro; Rebecca S. Molyneaux; Jeffrey W. Gallup.
Business Law, Taxation, Estate Planning, Probate, Pension and Profit Sharing, Real Estate, Trial and Appellate Practice.

See Professional Biographies, CLEVELAND, OHIO

Cawley, M. Terence .... '— '90 C.385 B.A. L.575 J.D. [Ⓐ Duvin,C.&H.]

Cawley, Thomas M., (AV) ... '56 '82 C.294 B.A. L.930 J.D. [Cavitch,F.D.&F.]
Celebrezze, Frank D. ... '28 '57 C.62 B.S. L.1003 J.D. 123 W. Prospect Ave.
Centa, Emil J. ... '23 '54 C.363 B.B.A. 761 E. 185th St.
Centa, Ernest R. ... '23 '55 C.363 B.B.S. L.1003 LL.B. 763 E. 185th St.
Cergol, Frank J. ... '16 '45 C&L.930 A.B., LL.B. 12039 Edgewater Dr.
Cerio, Arthur R. ... '26 '55 C.251 B.B.A. L.1003 J.D. [A.R.Cerio]
Cerio, Arthur R., Co., L.P.A. ... 4545 Hinckley Parkway
Cermelj, Mary R. ... '63 '89 C.970 B.A. L.930 J.D. Law Clk. to Ct. of App. J.
Cernansky, Justin M. ... '— '04 C.602 B.A. L.1556 J.D. [A Jones D.]
Cernelich, John R., (AV) ... '59 '86 C.309 A.B. L.893 J.D. [Calfee,H.&G.]
Cerrezin, Richard M., (AV) ... '24 '49 C&L.930 A.B., J.D. 55 Pub. Sq.
Cesareo, Filomena Pascarella ... '64 '89 C.19 B.A. L.1029 J.D. 631 West St. Clair Ave.
Chaffee, Eric C. ... '— '02 C.608 B.A. L.659 J.D. [A Jones D.]
Chamberlain, Henry W., (AV) ... '64 '90 C.608 B.S. L.1003 J.D. [Weisman,G.&W.]
Chambers, John J. ... '67 '95 C.424 B.A. L.1003 J.D. 4007 Riveredge Rd.
Chandler, Johnny M. ... '52 '82 C.951 B.A. L.1003 J.D. Asst. Co. Pros.
Chandra, Meenakshi Morey '67 '93
C.161 B.A. L.989 J.D. U.S. Dept. of Ed., Off. of Civil Rts.
Chandra, Subodh ... '67 '95 C.813 A.B. L.976 J.D. 3006 Ludlow Rd.
Chapman, Diane P., (AV) ... '52 '78 C.229 B.A. L.1003 J.D. [Baker&H.]
Chapman, Frank H., II ... '67 '96 C.610 B.A. L.124 J.D. [Chapman]
Chapman, John S., (AV) '55 '84 C.860 B.A. L.930 J.D.
700 W. Saint Clair Ave., Ste. 300
Chapman Law Firm ... 123 W. Prospect Ave., Ste. 260
Chappell, Inajo Davis, (AV) ... '60 '88 C.976 B.A. L.178 J.D. [Ulmer&B.]
Charlton, Melody K. ... '66 '97 C.62 B.A. L.989 J.D. V.P. & Assoc. Coun., Key Bank
Charms, Stephen J., (AV) ... '55 '81 C.608 B.A. L.161 J.D. 200 Public Square
Chase, Beth Anne ... '64 '95 C.473 B.A. L.1003 J.D. Gidden Co., The
Chase, Edward J. ... '17 '51 C.381 B.S. L.1003 J.D. 7314 Craigmere Dr.‡
Chatfield, Hedy Schuster ... '67 '92 C.207 B.A. L.930 J.D. Dept. of Def.
Chattman, Gerald B., (AV) '42 '67
C.477 B.A. L.930 J.D. [Buckingham,D.&B.] (⊙Lorain)
Chattman, Gaines & Stern, (AV) ... 1350 Euclid Avenue (⊙Lorain)
Cheatham, Stephen V., (AV) '51 '77
C.976 B.A. L.893 J.D. Gen. Coun., Ohio Savings Bank
Chema, Thomas V., (AV) ... '46 '71 C.602 A.B. L.309 J.D. 925 Euclid Avenue
Chenault, D. Larkin '46 '78 C.853 A.B. L.421 J.D.
(adm. in KY; not adm. in OH) Exec. Dir., Cleveland Bar Assn.
Chenette, Frank A., (AV) ... '49 '76 C.363 B.S. L.1003 J.D. 55 Public Sq.
Chenin, Avery M. ... '63 '89 C&L.930 B.S., J.D. Asst. V.P. & Atty., Natl City Bk.
Cherchiglia, Dean K. '56 '84 C.610 B.B.A. L.930 J.D.
V.P., Asst. Secy. & Assoc. Coun., Ohio Savings Financial Corp.
Cherkala, Brian L. '53 '78 C.97 B.S. L.7 J.D.
V.P. & Dept. Mgr., Key Trust Co. of Ohio, N.A.
Chernak, John A. ... '29 '56 C.103 A.B. L.597 J.D. 13700 Broadway‡
Chernett, Robert I., (AV) ... '46 '72 C.608 B.S. L.1003 J.D. [Chernett W.Y.&P.]
Chernett Wasserman Yarger & Pasternak LLC, (AV) ... 1301 E. 9th Street, Suite 3300
Chesler, Howard I., (BV) ... '17 '48 C.607 L.1003 LL.B. 2112 Acacia Park Dr.
Chesney, Michael N., (AV) ... '66 '92 C.228 A.B. L.602 J.D. [Frantz W.]
Cheung, Jeremy G. ... '— '04 C.836 B.A. L.201 J.D. [A Gallagher S.]
Cheverine, Vincent L., (BV) ... '63 '90 C&L.893 B.A., J.D. [Aggers,J.&C.]
Childs, Ishmael C. ... '15 '56 C.14 B.S. L.1003 J.D. 7918 Quincy Ave.
Childs, Miller & Associates, LPA ... 24600 Detroit Road, Suite 240

Chin, James '50 '76 C.597 B.A. L.930 J.D.
745 Leader Building, 526 Superior Avenue, East, 44114-1402
Telephone: 216-241-0646; 800-653-7161 Telefax: 216-241-4246
Email: JimmyChin@aol.com URL: http://www.lawyers.com/oh-immigration
Business, Immigration, Labor Certifications, Real Estate, Civil Litigation, International Laws Corporation.
See Professional Biographies, CLEVELAND, OHIO

Chinni, Benjamin T. ... '45 '70 C&L.608 B.S., J.D. U.S. Dept. of Labor Solr. Off.
Chisling, Stephanie A. ... '65 '91 C.608 B.A. L.365 J.D. Emerald Health Network
Chisolm, Laura Brown, (AV) ... '48 '81 C&L.930 B.A., J.D. 11075 East Blvd.
Chitlik, Edward ... '19 '42 C&L.930 A.B., J.D. Prof. of Law, Cleve. State Univ.
Chlarson, Kevin L. ... '71 '03 C.36 B.A. L.37 J.D. [A Kohrman J.&K.]
Chmielewski, Dawn M. ... '73 '04 C.8 B.S.N. L.989 J.D. [A Climaco,L.P.W.&G.]
Chockley, F. Wilson, Jr., (AV) ... '23 '49 C.659 B.S. L.930 LL.B. 1300 Terminal Twr.
Chodosh, Hiram E. '62 '92 C.918 B.A. L.976 J.D.
(adm. in NY; not adm. in OH) Prof. of Law, Case Western Reserve Univ.
Choe, Iva Y. ... '70 '95 C.178 A.B. L.608 J.D. Field Atty., Nat'l Labor Relations Bd.
Chotlos, Elaine A., (BV) ... '58 '83 C.150 B.A. L.608 J.D. [Baker&H.]
Christ, Paula, (AV) ... '63 '91 C.659 B.S. L.930 J.D. Sr. Coun., TRW Inc.
Christie, John R. ... '70 '97 C.363 B.A. L.8 J.D. 55 Public Sq., Ste. 850
Christman, Leif B. ... '72 '98 C.436 B.A. L.1003 J.D. 1370 Ontario St., Ste. 2000
Christopher, S. Paige ... '68 '95 C.228 B.A. L.365 J.D. [A Calfee,H.&G.] (See Pat. Sect.)
Christopher, Stanley '34 '58 C&L.893 LL.B.
(adm. in MO; not adm. in OH) Admin. Law J., Soc. Sec. Admin.
Chriszt, James R., (AV) ... '56 '87 C.602 B.B.A. L.1003 J.D. [C Nicola,G.&C.]
Chu, Howard W. ... '— '04 C.473 B.S. L.608 J.D. [A Jones D.]
Chudakoff, Robert E., (AV) ... '62 '87 C.472 B.A. L.930 J.D. [Ulmer&B.]
Chudner, Richard ... '— '98 C.161 B.S. L.989 J.D. 3715 W. 139th St.
Chung, Elizabeth Holmes ... '65 '91 C.62 B.A. L.1003 J.D. 24525 Detroit Rd.
Chunyo, Jennifer J. ... '— '96 C.62 B.A. L.851 J.D. [S Jones D.]
Chylla, Heidi P. ... '69 '93 C.280 B.A. L.1206 J.D. [Hermann,C.&S.]
Ciano, Mario C., (AV) ... '42 '68 C&L.930 B.A., J.D. [R Reminger&R.]

Cibella, Mary L., (AV) '56 '84 C.381 B.S. L.1003 J.D.
614 West Superior Avenue Suite 1300, 44113
Telephone: 216-344-9220 Facsimile: 216-664-6999
Disciplinary Defense, Legal Malpractice Defense, Pre-Admission Licensure, Ethics Advisory Opinions, The Grievance Process.
See Professional Biographies, CLEVELAND, OHIO

Cicarella, Thomas A., (AV) ... '49 '74 C.347 A.B. L.345 J.D. [Calfee,H.&G.]
Cicerchi, Kent B. ... '58 '86 C.363 B.S. L.1003 J.D. 4720 Autumn Ln.
Cicero, Michael E. ... '65 '92 C.473 B.S. L.1003 J.D. [A Nicola,G.&C.]
Cinnamond, Clyde A. ... '20 '71 C.732 B.A. L.1003 J.D. 123 W. Prospect Ave.‡
Cipolla, John S., (AV) ... '63 '89 C.97 B.S. L.161 J.D. [Calfee,H.&G.] (See Pat. Sect.)
Citeroni, Maria A. ... '67 '01 C.999 B.S. L.1003 J.D. [A Ulmer&B.]
Citrino, Diane E., (AV) ... '57 '82 C.103 B.A. L.1066 J.D. The Housing Advocates, Inc.
Ciulla, Joseph F. ... '25 '65 C.381 L.1003 6972 Windward Hls‡
Clady, Susan E. ... '71 '96 C&L.608 B.A., J.D. [A Benesch,F.C.&A.]
Claflin, Beecher N. ... '19 '47 C.473 A.B. L.178 LL.B. 29980 Bolingbrook Rd.‡
Clancy, Daniel T. '36 '62 C.602 B.S. L.930 J.D.
Asst. V.P., Univ. Alumni Affs., Case Western Reserve Univ.

Clapp, R. Jack, (BV) '49 '90 C.150 B.S. L.1003 J.D.
[R.J.Clapp&Assoc.] (⊙Wash., DC)

Clapp, R. Jack, & Assoc. Co., L.P.A., (BV)
One Cleveland Center Suite 2420, 1375 East Ninth, 44114 ⊙
Telephone: 800-334-8500 Fax: 216-861-1401
Email: info@rjackclapp.com URL: http://www.rjackclapp.com
R. Jack Clapp.
Wrongful Death, Personal Injury, Medical Malpractice, Professional Malpractice, Defective Products, Automobile Accidents, Aviation Law, Nursing Home Negligence, Commercial Vehicle Liability, Tourist Injuries, Farm Equipment Liability.
Washington, D.C. Office: 444 North Capital Street, N.W. Hall of States Building, Suite 828. 20001. Telephone: 888-334-8500.
Mentor, Ohio Office: 7784 Reynolds Road. Telephone: 216-946-1100. Fax: 216-946-1756.
See Professional Biographies, CLEVELAND, OHIO

Clark, Charles B. ... '27 '57 C.930 B.B.A. L.1003 LL.B. 12951 Lake St.‡
Clark, Daniel J. ... '54 '85 C.373 B.A. L.1003 J.D. 6140 Parkland Blvd., Ste. 300
Clark, Janet C. '64 '94 C.477 B.F.A. L.930 J.D.
V.P. & Asst. Coun., KeyBank Natl. Assn.
Clark, Kenneth A. '58 '86 C.161 B.Met.E. L.1003 J.D.
[Rankin,H.P.&C.] (See Pat. Sect.)
Clark, Wade Douglass ... '54 '80 C.980 B.A. L.7 J.D. [A Calfee,H.&G.]
Clarke, Charles F., (AV) ... '16 '40 C.902 B.A. L.477 LL.B. [Squire,S.&D.]
Clay, Darrell A., (BV) ... '68 '94 C.1111 B.A. L.861 J.D. [Walter&H.]
Clay, Pamela S. ... '61 '96 C.381 B.G.S. L.1003 J.D. 2307 Allison Rd.
Clayborne, Sherrie D. ... '69 '96 C.970 B.A. L.608 J.D. [A Britton,S.P.&K.]
Clayton, Michael E. ... '49 '77 C.161 B.A. L.1003 J.D. Legal Aid Soc.
Cleary, Michael Francis ... '58 '84 C.363 B.S. L.200 J.D. 6200 Rockside Road
Cleary, Timothy R., (BV) ... '47 '75 C.363 B.A. L.1003 J.D. [Cleary&Assoc.]
Cleary & Associates Co., L.P.A., (BV) ... 6000 Lombardo Center Drive
Clemens, Charles A. '42 '69 C.725 B.A. L.345 J.D.
(adm. in IN; not adm. in OH) 1400 Ohio Svgs. Plz.‡
Clements, Arthur L. (Tim), III ... '57 '85 C.976 B.A. L.608 J.D. [C Nicola,G.&C.]
Cleveland, Phyllis E. ... '58 '89 C&L.930 B.A., J.D. Asst. Pros. Atty.
Clifford, Gregory F., (BV) ... '49 '81 C.610 B.S.Ed. L.161 J.D. Dep. Chf. Mag., Mun. Ct.
Climaco, John R., (AV) ... '41 '67 C.608 B.S. L.930 J.D. [Climaco,L.P.W.&G.]

Climaco, Lefkowitz, Peca, Wilcox & Garofoli Co., L.P.A., (AV)
1220 Huron Road, Suite 1000, 44115-1711 ⊙
Telephone: 216-621-8484 Telecopier: 216-771-1632
Email: japeca@climacolaw.com URL: http://www.climacolaw.com
John R. Climaco; John A. Peca; Dennis R. Wilcox; Thomas J. Tarantino; David M. Cuppage; Keith T. Vernon; David W. Neel; Paul S. Lefkowitz (Retired); Anthony J. Garofoli (1936-2003); Jack D. Maistros (1956-2001);—John F. Corrigan; Margaret M. Metzinger; Scott D. Simpkins; Jennifer L. Stueber; Joseph P. Fegen; P. Wesley Lambert; Lisa Ann Gorshe (Not admitted in OH); Dawn M. Chmielewski; Terri A. Lightner.
General Civil, Corporate, Environmental, Government and Labor Law. E.R.I.S.A., Litigation. Bankruptcy, Real Estate, Criminal, Securities, Public Utility, Municipal, Class Actions, Mass Torts, Securities Litigation, Personal Injury, Workers Compensation, Family, Public Employment Relations, Commercial and Public Financing, Entertainment, Television (CATV), School and Intellectual Property.
References: National City Bank; Security Federal Savings & Loan.
Washington, D.C. Office: 818 Connecticut Avenue, N.W., Suite 857, 20006. Telephone: 202-887-4777. Fax: 202-887-4778.
See Professional Biographies, CLEVELAND, OHIO

Climer, James A., (AV) ... '54 '80 C.473 B.A. L.851 J.D. [Mazanec,R.&R.]
Cline, Guy Grover, Jr. ... '52 '78 C&L.608 B.S.M.E., J.D. Lincoln Electric Co., The
Cline, Jerry P. ... '69 '02 C.705 B.A. L.117 J.D. [A Ross,B.&S.]
Cline, Richard W. ... '69 '97 C.705 B.A. L.260 J.D. [A McDonald H.]
Cloonan, William P. '53 '92
C.363 B.A. L.1003 J.D. V.P. & Asst. Coun., KeyBank Natl. Assn.
Clough, John A., III, (BV) ... '50 '77 C.999 B.A. L.1003 J.D. Asst. Co. Pros.
Coakley, George S., (AV) ... '49 '75 C.597 B.A. L.930 J.D. [A Reminger&R.]
Coates, Lisa L. ... '67 '94 C.97 B.S.B.A. L.930 J.D. U.S. Dept. of Vet. Affairs
Coaxum, Edward C., Jr., (AV) ... '— '71 C.951 B.A. L.94 J.D. [Buckingham,D.&B.]
Cobb, Arthur L., (AV) ... '49 '75 C&L.188 A.B., J.D. [Hahn L.&P.]
Cobb, Craig S., Law Offices of, (AV) '55 '82
C.473 B.A. L.161 J.D. 815 Superior Ave., Ste. 1605
Coburn, Howard E., (AV) '53 '84
C.363 A.B. L.930 J.D. V.P. & Sr. Coun., KeyBank Natl. Assn.
Cochran, David B. ... '— '96 C.339 B.S. L.161 J.D. [C Jones D.] (See Pat. Sect.)
Cochran, James C., (AV) ... '53 '78 C.201 B.A. L.1003 J.D. [Cochran,N.&P.]
Cochran, Naso & Porter, (AV) ... 9100 South Hills Boulevard Suite 300
Codinach, Maria J. ... '44 '76 C.416 A.B. L.608 J.D. 4900 Society, Ctr., 127 Public Sq.
Coffey, Ronald J. '36 '61
C.973 A.B. L.150 LL.B. Case Western Reserve Univ. Law School
Coffey, Thomas W., (BV) ... '59 '87 C&L.150 B.M., J.D. 925 Euclid Ave.
Coghlan, Scott ... '67 '92 C.97 B.S. L.930 J.D. [A Ross,B.&S.]
Cohan, Michael C., (AV) ... '52 '77 C.93 A.B. L.425 J.D. [Cavitch,F.D.&F.]
Cohen, Avery S., (AV) ... '36 '61 C.930 A.B. L.309 J.D. [Baker&H.]
Cohen, David R. ... '59 '91 C.477 B.A. L.930 J.D. Sr. Law Clerk
Cohen, Hyman ... '32 '60 C.563 B.A. L.569 LL.B. [H.Cohen]
Cohen, Joshua R., (AV) ... '59 '84 C&L.846 B.A., J.D. [Cohen R.&K.]
Cohen, Ronald B. ... '34 '61 C.608 B.S. L.1003 J.D. 1300 E. Ninth St.
Cohen, Hyman, Co., L.P.A. ... P.O. Box 22360

Cohen Rosenthal & Kramer LLP, (AV)
The Western Reserve Building - Suite 705, 1468 West Ninth Street, 44113
Telephone: 216-781-7956 Fax: 216-781-8061
URL: http://www.crklaw.com
Joshua R. Cohen; James B. Rosenthal; Ellen Maglicic Kramer; Jason R. Bristol; Cathleen M. Bolek.
Trial Practice, Appellate Practice, Complex Litigation, Complex Civil Litigation, Class Action, Securities Litigation, Antitrust, Corporate Law, Shareholders Rights, Contract Law, Commercial Litigation, Fraud, Bankruptcy.
See Professional Biographies, CLEVELAND, OHIO

Cohn, Howard M. ... '43 '69 C.446 B.S.M.E. L.904 J.D. [H.M.Cohn] (Pat.)‡
Cohn, Mark B., (AV) ... '47 '74 C&L.608 B.S., J.D. [McCarthy,L.C.&L.]

Cohn, Howard M., Patent Attorney, LLC
21625 Chagrin Boulevard, Suite 220, 44122-5335
Telephone: 216-752-0955 Fax: 216-752-0957 URL: http://www.cohnpatents.com
Email: howard.cohn@cohnpatents.com URL: http://www.lawyers.com/howardmcohn
Howard M. Cohn.
Patents, Trademarks, Copyrights, Licensing, Intellectual Property.
See Professional Biographies, CLEVELAND, OHIO

Colabianchi, Nicholas A. ... '61 '86 C.62 B.A. L.930 J.D. 5725 Broadway
Colacarro, Robert J. ... '— '02 C.363 B.S.B.A L.93 J.D. [A Jones D.]
Colaluca, Thomas L., (AV) ... '47 '78 C.712 B.A. L.1003 J.D. [Johnson,A.&C.]
Cole, Allison E. '74 '00
C.473 B.A./B.A. L.989 J.D. Atty., The Sherwin-Williams Company

Cole, Francine R. . . . . '50 '92 C.610 B.S.Ed. L.161 J.D. V.P., Society Natl. Bk.
Cole, Kevin P. . . . . '53 '80 C.363 B.A. L.1003 J.D. Fed. Reserve Bk.of Celevland
Cole, Michael L. . . . . '70 '00 C.528 B.A. L.8 J.D. [Ⓐ S.S.Keller&Assoc.]
Cole, R. Michael '43 '68 C.976 B.A. L.477 J.D.
(adm. in DC; not adm. in OH) Dir., Jewish Community Federation of Cleveland
Cole, Randall A. . . . . '— '73 C.902 B.A. L.930 J.D. [Ⓑ Jones D.]
Coleman, Deborah A., (AV) . . . . '51 '76 C.681 A.B. L.309 J.D. [Hahn L.&P.]
Coleman, L. Christopher . . . . '77 '02 C.383 B.A. L.8 J.D. [Ⓐ Steuer,E.B.&B.]
Coleman, Rodney V., (BV) . . . . '32 '57 C&L.608 A.B., J.D. 2250 E. 105th St.
Coletta, Dominic J. . . . . '78 '04 C.473 B.A. L.1003 J.D. [Ⓐ Synenberg&Assoc.]
Collet Stanisic, Eileen M. '70 '97 C.741 B.A. L.345 J.D.
(adm. in IN; not adm. in OH) KPMG, LLP
Collier, Wan . . . . '71 '98 C&L.188 B.A., J.D. [Ⓐ Baker&H.]
Collier-Williams, Cassandra, Law Offices of '57 '91
C.473 B.A. L.1003 J.D. P.O. Box 94062
Colligan, Owen M. '66 '91 C.107 B.S. L.569 J.D. 925 Euclid Avenue
Collin, James M. . . . . '49 '78 C.381 B.A. L.30 J.D. Litig. Coun., Oglebay Norton
Collin, James Mitchell . . . . '— '95 1240 E. 9th Street, #2083
Collin, Thomas J., (AV) . . . . '49 '75 C.494 B.A. L.276 J.D. [Thompson H.]
Collins, Daisy G. '37 '70 C.608 B.S.B.A. L.329 J.D.
Admin. Law J., Dept. of Health & Human Svcs, SSA
Collins, Daniel E., (AVⓉ) . . . . '42 '70 C.112 B.A. L.1067 J.D. 29323 Regency Cir.
Collins, Patrick S. '56 '84 C.62 B.A. L.607 J.D. Coun., Lottery Comm.
Collins, Tim L., (AV) . . . . '57 '86 C.62 B.A. L.1003 J.D. [Collins&S.]

Collins & Scanlon LLP, (AV)
Formerly Donahue & Scanlon
3300 Terminal Tower, 50 Public Square, 44113-2294
Telephone: 216-696-0022 Telecopier: 216-696-1166
Email: lawyers@collins-scanlon.com URL: http://www.collins-scanlon.com
Members of Firm: Tim L. Collins; Russell David Kornblut; Harvey Labovitz; Thomas J. Scanlon; M. Scott Wilson. Associate: Kristie Marie Weibling.
General Civil Practice. Corporate, Business, Securities, Real Estate, Condominium, Taxation, Secured Transactions, Commercial, Probate, Trust and Estate Planning Law. Trials.
Reference: Huntington Bank.

See Professional Biographies, CLEVELAND, OHIO

Collister, Scott E. . . . . '— '99 C.610 B.A. L.150 J.D. 1300 East Ninth Street, 14th Floor
Colombo, Louis A., (AV) . . . . '47 '73 C.475 B.A. L.477 J.D. [Baker&H.]
Colovas, Dean A., (BV) . . . . '61 '86 C.161 B.A. L.1003 J.D. 55 Public Sq.
Comella, John S. '39 '75 C.201 B.S. L.1003 J.D.
U.S. Treasury Dept., Internal Revenue Service
Comodeca, Peter J., (AV) . . . . '54 '84 C.870 B.S. L.309 J.D. [Calfee,H.&G.]
Conde, Stephenie L. . . . . '69 '94 C.97 B.A. L.989 J.D. [Ⓐ Roetzel&A.]
Condeni, Joseph A., (AV) . . . . '56 '82 C.97 B.L.S. L.161 J.D. [Smith&C.]
Coniam, Robert T., (AV) . . . . '48 '86 C.607 B.S.M.E. L.161 J.D. [Ray,R.C.&D.]
Connally, C. Ellen . . . . '45 '71 C.97 B.S. L.1003 J.D. Mun. J.
Connell, Daniel . . . . '— '04 C.276 B.A. L.124 J.D. [Ⓐ Duvin,C.&H.]
Connell, Michele L. . . . . '72 '03 C.276 B.S. L.124 J.D. [Ⓐ Squire,S.&D.]
Conner, Larry W. . . . . '71 '97 C.347 B.S. L.930 J.D. [Ⓐ Frantz W.]
Conner, William H., (AV) . . . . '40 '67 C.473 A.B. L.477 J.D. [Squire,S.&D.]
Connick, Michael J. . . . . '57 '90 C.363 B.S.B.A. L.1003 J.D. [Ⓑ Wilsman&S.]
Connick, Thomas J. . . . . '— '99 C.363 B.A. L.1003 J.D. [Ⓐ Davis&Y.]
Connor, Thomas S. . . . . '62 '91 C.161 B.A. L.1003 J.D. [Sanislo&Assoc.]
Connors, Timothy J. . . . . '64 '89 C.475 B.A. L.477 J.D. [Calfee,H.&G.]
Conomy, Christopher P. . . . . '70 '00 C.354 B.A. L.1003 J.D. [Ⓐ Mazanec,R.&R.]
Conrad, Deanna M. . . . . '76 '04 C.66 B.A. L.930 J.D. [Ⓐ Baker&H.]
Conrad, Jane K. . . . . '— '00 C.381 B.A. L.7 J.D. [Ⓐ Hermann,C.&S.]
Conroy, James P., (AV) . . . . '49 '74 C&L.608 B.A., J.D. [Walter&H.]
Conroy, Suzanne M. . . . . '69 '95 C.610 B.S. L.1003 J.D. [Ⓐ Calfee,H.&G.]
Consiglio, Charles J., (BV) . . . . '32 '61 C.973 A.B. L.930 LL.B. 801 Citizens Bldg.
Consolo, Jeffrey P., (AV) . . . . '53 '78 C.929 B.S. L.421 J.D. [McDonald H.]
Consolo, Patricia Daley . . . . '50 '79 C.260 B.A. L.161 LL.M. Ameritrust Bk.
Conte, Richard M. . . . . '55 '82 C.608 B.S. L.1003 J.D. 31200 Gaes Mills Blvd
Conti, Patricia S., (AV) . . . . '— '95 C.363 B.A. L.989 J.D. [Ⓐ Duvin,C.&H.]
Conway, James J., (AV) . . . . '28 '55 C.381 L.1003 LL.B. [Ⓑ Karberg,K.W.&T.]
Conway, James P. '23 '61
C.363 B.S.B.A. L.1003 J.D. Assoc. to V.P., Case Western Reserve Univ.
Conway, John F., (AV) . . . . '18 '50 C.363 B.A. L.1003 J.D. [Conway,P.&B.]
Conway, John J., (AV) . . . . '18 '43 C&L.930 B.B.A., J.D. 127 Public Sq.
Conway, Kara . . . . '75 '02 C.321 B.A. L.930 J.D. [Ⓐ Hawkins]
Conway, Patton & Bouhall, (AV) . . . . 925 Euclid Ave.
Cook, Craig D. . . . . '65 '91 C.532 B.A. L.930 J.D. Pres., Precision Production, Inc.
Cook, David J., (BV) '29 '58 C.124 B.S. L.930 LL.B.
Secy., Treas. & Gen. Coun., HY-Level Industries, Inc.
Cook, Francis X., (BV) . . . . '42 '79 C.999 A.B. L.1003 J.D. [Payne P.&C.]
Cook, Jerome W., (AV) . . . . '58 '86 C.930 B.A. L.1003 J.D. [McDonald H.]
Coolbaugh, Stephen P. . . . . '— '01 C.276 B.S.F.S. L.1529 J.D. [Ⓐ Jones D.]
Cooley, Sheila P. '42 '76 C.228 B.A. L.608 J.D. 1370 Ontario Street
Cooney, Colleen Conway . . . . '55 '81 C&L.930 B.S., J.D. City Mun. Ct.‡
Cooney, John G. . . . . '52 '79 C&L.188 B.A., J.D. Ct. of App.
Cooney, Patrick J., III, (BV) . . . . '66 '91 C.472 B.S. L.1003 J.D. 1370 Ontario St., Ste. 800
Cooper, Gerald F., (AV) . . . . '31 '57 C.363 A.B. L.1003 J.D. [Cooper,S.&W.]
Cooper, Jonathan R., (AV) . . . . '60 '86 C.25 B.A. L.1003 J.D. 925 Euclid Ave.
Cooper, Lawrence D., (BVⓉ) '54 '83 C.1021 B.A. L.744 J.D.
(adm. in NY; not adm. in OH) V.P. & Asst. Coun., KeyBank Natl. Assn.
Cooper, Lorri W. . . . . '— '95 C.1048 B.S. L.184 J.D. [Ⓐ Jones D.] (See Pat. Sect.)
Cooper, Margaret E. . . . . '71 '00 C.608 B.S. L.161 J.D. 55 Public Square, Suite 650
Cooper, Richard A., (AV) . . . . '52 '77 C.608 B.A. L.145 J.D. [Nicola,G.&C.]
Cooper, Richard S., (AV) . . . . '56 '81 C.823 A.B. L.276 J.D. [McDonald H.]
Cooper, Robert A. . . . . '70 '97 C.1033 B.A. L.989 J.D. [Ⓑ Hahn L.&P.]
Cooper, William J. '70 '98 C.610 B.S.E.E. L.8 J.D.
629 Euclid Avenue, Suite 1210 (Pat.)
Cooper, Spector & Weil Co., L.P.A., (AV) . . . . 50 Public Sq.
Cope, Kevin L. '77 '04 C.608 B.A. L.597 J.D.
(adm. in IL; not adm. in OH) Law Clk. to the Hon. James S. Gwin
Copeland, Terence E., (AV) . . . . '48 '74 C.951 B.A. L.309 J.D. Coun. for Opportunities
Coquillette, William H., (AV) . . . . '— '75 C.976 B.A. L.309 J.D. [Jones D.]
Corcoran, James I. W. . . . . '41 '66 C&L.309 B.A., LL.B 2915 Fairfax Rd.
Corcoran, Melanie S. . . . . '55 '91 C.381 B.A. L.1003 J.D. [Ⓑ Baker&H.]
Corder, Bradley S. . . . . '63 '90 C.381 B.B.A. L.930 J.D. 2189 Professor Ave.
Corea, Charles . . . . '49 '87 C.610 B.S. L.989 J.D. 6202 Thoreau Dr.
Coreno, Terese M. . . . . '74 '99 C.363 B.A. L.989 J.D. [Ⓐ Reid,B.M.&W.]
Corman, Lawrence W., (AV) . . . . '43 '69 C.473 B.A. L.1003 J.D. 55 Public Square
Cormier, Shawn A. . . . . '— '98 C.607 B.A. L.989 J.D. [Ⓐ Davis&Y.]
Cornely, John P. . . . . '68 '95 C.363 B.S. L.608 J.D. [Fay,S.F.M.&M.] (See Pat. Sect.)
Cornett, Adam D. . . . . '75 '04 C.970 B.A. L.989 J.D. [Ⓐ Taft,S.&H.]
Cornett, Harry D., Jr., (AV) . . . . '45 '71 C.473 B.A. L.608 J.D. [Tucker E.&W.]
Corpora, Corine R. . . . . '63 '92 C.161 B.B.A. L.930 J.D. [Ⓐ Calfee,H.&G.]
Corpus, Christopher A. . . . . '70 '00 C.49 B.S. L.124 J.D. [Ⓐ Wegman,H.&V.]
Corpus, Deborah . . . . '— '00 C.112 B.S. L.124 J.D. [Amin&T.] (See Pat. Sect.)
Corpus, Deborah Liu . . . '— '00 C.112 B.S. L.124 J.D. 1900 E. 9th Street, 24th Floor (Pat.)
Corrado, David A., Law Office of '57 '91
C.381 B.B.A. L.930 J.D. 1660 W. Second St., Ste. 410
Corrado, Paul J., (AV) . . . . '51 '86 C.299 A.B. L.930 J.D. 2000 East Ninth Street
Corrigall, Amy K. . . . . '75 '01 C.381 B.A. L.8 J.D. [Ⓐ Sutter,O.&F.]
Corrigan, Anne T. . . . . '63 '92 C.363 B.S. L.390 J.D. [McDonald H.]
Corrigan, Brian J. . . . . '51 '84 C.201 B.E.E. L.989 J.D. Com. Pleas J.
Corrigan, Brian T. '62 '94 C.150 B.A. L.1003 J.D. [Ⓐ R.E.Sweeney]
Corrigan, Eddie . . . . '22 '49 C.976 A.B. L.930 LL.B. Mun. J.
Corrigan, Heather C. . . . . '73 '01 C.381 B.A. L.989 J.D. [Ⓐ Calfee,H.&G.]
Corrigan, James, (BV) . . . . '54 '81 C.472 B.S.B.A. L.1003 J.D. 3134 Somerset St.
Corrigan, James J. '24 '66 C.363 L.1340 LL.B.
(adm. in MI; not adm. in OH) 1360 W. 9th St.‡
Corrigan, John E. . . . . '36 '69 C.973 B.S.,B.A. L.1003 J.D. Prob. J.
Corrigan, John F., (BV) . . . . '61 '86 C.363 B.A. L.1003 J.D. [Ⓐ Climaco,L.P.W.&G.]
Corrigan, John V. . . . . '20 '48 C.363 A.B. L.930 LL.B. (Ret.) App. Ct. J.
Corrigan, Karen J. . . . . '— '93 C.363 B.A. L.161 J.D. [Ⓢ Jones D.]
Corrigan, Michael J. . . . . '49 '74 C.93 B.A. L.1003 J.D. Com. Pleas J.
Corrigan, Peter J. . . . . '62 '96 C.103 A.B. L.1003 J.D. Asst. Co. Prosecutor
Corrigan, Thomas D., (AV) '51 '75
C.276 B.S.F.S. L.930 J.D. 55 Public Square, Suite 1500
Corsaro, Joseph G. . . . . '57 '82 C.885 B.A. L.1003 J.D. [Corsaro&Assoc.]
Corsaro & Associates Co., L.P.A. . . . . 2001 Crocker Road, Gemini Tower II, Ste. 400
Corsi, Mary Joan Reilly . . . . . . '34 '93 C.521 B.S. L.989 J.D. Standard Bldg., 1370 Ontario
Corso, Jennifer A. . . . . '68 '94 C.476 B.A. L.1003 J.D. [Ⓐ Wegman,H.&V.]
Corso, Joseph J. . . . . '42 '69 C.610 B.S.Ch.E. L.8 J.D. [Pearne&G.] (See Pat. Sect.)
Coscarelli, Dianne S., (AV) . . . . '52 '78 C.610 A.B. L.767 J.D. [Thompson H.]
Cosentino, Leonard M. . . . . '62 '87 C.294 B.A. L.930 J.D. [McDonald H.]
Cosgrove, Timothy J., (AV) . . . '61 '87 C&L.161 B.A., J.D. [Squire,S.&D.] (ⓞColumbus)
Cosiano, Ralph V., (AV) . . . . '33 '59 C.610 A.B. L.930 LL.B. 155 Panorama Dr.
Cossler, Christine Tomko . . . . '71 '02 C.980 B.E. L.124 J.D. [Ⓐ Squire,S.&D.]
Costanzo, Anthony J., (BV) . . . . '39 '65 C.610 B.S.Ed. L.930 J.D. 1300 W. Blvd.
Coticchia, Lori A. '63 '88 C.116 B.A. L.602 J.D. [Ⓑ Reminger&R.]
Cotronakis, Emanuel J. . . . . '— '98 C.960 B.A. L.276 J.D. [Ⓐ Baker&H.]
Cottle, Cullen J. . . . . '74 '00 C.473 B.A. L.124 J.D. [Ⓐ Lavelle&L.]
Cottle, Lisa A. . . . . '— '00 C.477 B.A. L.124 J.D. [Ⓐ Duvin,C.&H.]
Cotton, Anthony J. . . . . '21 '55 C.930 B.B.A. L.1003 LL.B. 12903 Euclid Ave.‡
Coughlin, Barring, (AV) . . . . '13 '39 C.674 B.A. L.309 J.D. 3900 Society Ctr.‡
Coughlin, Thomas M., Jr., (BV) . . . . '65 '91 C.477 B.A. L.1003 J.D. [Ritzler,C.&S.]
Coughlin, Timothy J., (AV) . . . . '59 '84 C.602 B.B.A. L.930 J.D. [Thompson H.]
Coughlin, William E., (AV) . . . . '56 '83 C&L.276 A.B., J.D. [Calfee,H.&G.]
Couhig, Stephanie S. . . . . . '— '02 C.201 B.S.C.E. L.602 J.D. [Ⓐ Jones D.] (See Pat. Sect.)
Courtney, Michael M., (BV) . . . . '50 '75 C.610 B.S. L.1003 J.D. [Rapoport,S.F.&C.]
Covell, Calvin G., (AV) '36 '66
C.477 B.S.M.E. L.276 J.D. [Tarolli,S.C.&T.] (See Pat. Sect.)
Covey, Christine C., (AV) . . . . '55 '80 C.97 B.A. L.1003 J.D. [Duvin,C.&H.]
Cowan, Dale H., (AV) . . . . '38 '81 C.309 A.B. L.930 J.D. 6100 W. Creek Rd.
Cowan, Elmer G., (AV) . . . . '24 '52 C.980 L.1003 LL.B. 2639 Wooster Road
Cowden, Gerald W., (AV) . . . . '49 '75 C.901 B.A. L.7 J.D. [Cowden,H.N.&L.]

Cowden, Humphrey, Nagorney & Lovett Co., L.P.A., (AV)
1414 Terminal Tower, 50 Public Square, 44113-2204
Telephone: 216-241-2880 Telecopier: 216-241-2881
URL: http://www.cowdenlaw.com
Gerald W. Cowden; Robert M. Humphrey; Mary Forbes Lovett (Certified Specialist in Business, Commercial and Industrial Real Property Law, Ohio State Bar Association); Frank P. Nagorney; James S. Hogg; Terrence J. Steel; Debora S. Lasch (Certified Specialist in Business, Commercial and Industrial Real Property Law, Ohio State Bar Association); Karl E. May; Frederic P. Schwieg;—Matthew J. Lenhard; John Storey; Phillip A. Helon.
Outsourced general counsel, Corporate and international, Corporate formation and structure, Finance and capital formation, Securities, mergers and acquisitions, Lender and borrower representation, Real estate and Urban Development, Business succession counseling, Bankruptcy and creditors rights.

See Professional Biographies, CLEVELAND, OHIO

Cox, Andrew H. . . . . '72 '99 C&L.352 B.A., J.D. [Ⓐ Thompson H.]
Cox, Diane E. '73 '98 C.62 B.S. L.1003 J.D.
Asst. Gen. Coun., NE Ohio Reg. Sewer Dist.
Cox, Duane E. . . . . '53 '79 C.381 B.A. L.7 J.D. 1422 Euclid Ave.
Coyle, Martin A., (AV) . . . . '41 '66 C.611 B.A. L.608 J.D. Exec. V.P., TRW Inc.
Coyne, Anthony J., (AV) . . . . '60 '87 C.363 B.A. L.1003 J.D. [Mansour,G.G.&M.]
Coyne, Dennis M., (BV) . . . . '57 '85 C.201 B.A. L.607 J.D. 1428 Hamilton Avenue
Coyne, John P., (AV) . . . . '31 '56 C&L.602 Ph.B, J.D. 1459 Hamilton Ave.
Coyne, Loretta A., (BV) . . . . '44 '70 C.599 B.A. L.1003 J.D. 7055 Engle Rd., Ste. 606
Coyne, Lorraine . . . . '57 '96 C.62 B.S. L.1003 J.D. Asst. Pros.
Coyne, Michael P., (AV) . . . . '52 '79 C.611 B.A. L.930 J.D. [W.Coyne]
Coyne, Richard T. . . . . '64 '89 C.201 B.A. L.930 J.D. [Wegman,H.&V.]
Coyne, Thomas J., (AV) . . . . '59 '85 C.321 B.A. L.602 J.D. [Thompson H.]
Coyne, William J. . . . . '34 '64 C.363 B.S.S. L.1003 J.D. Com. Pleas J.
Cozean, Ronald J., Jr. '63 '91 C&L.976 B.A., J.D.
Secretary & General Counsel, Park-Ohio Industries, Inc.
Cozza, Michael E. . . . . '18 '52 C.930 B.B.A. L.1003 J.D. Standard Bldg.

Crabbe, Brown & James LLP, (AV)
1280 W. Third Street, 44113 ⊙
Telephone: 216-574-9312
Email: info@cbjLawyers.com URL: http://www.cbjLawyers.com
Of Counsel: Brian R. McGraw.
General Insurance Defense, Product Liability, Professional Malpractice, Premises Liability, Environmental and Toxic Tort Claims, Employment and Labor Law, Tax Matters, General Business and Corporate Law and Litigation, Banking and Securities, Real Estate, Probate and Estate Planning, Criminal Law, Administrative, Regulatory and Governmental Law, Workers Compensation, Intellectual Property, Fire, Arson and Fraud, Fidelity and Surety Life, Accident and Health, Insurance Coverage Law, Construction Claims, Health and Hospital Law, Oil, Gas and Energy Law, Transportation Law, Automobile Dealer Law, Zoning, International Practice and Domestic Law, Land Use Planning, and Eminent Domain.
Columbus, Ohio Office: 500 South Front Street, Suite 1200. Telephone: 614-228-5511. Fax: 614-229-4559.
Cincinnati, Ohio Office: 30 Garfield Place, Suite 740, 45202. Telephone: 513-784-1525. Fax: 513-784-1250.
Lancaster, Ohio Office: 111 South Broad Street, Suite 209, 43130. Telephone: 740-689-1743. Fax: 740-689-1746.
Urbana, Ohio Office: 118 Scioto Street. Telephone: 937-652-4000.

See Professional Biographies, CLEVELAND, OHIO

Craig, Mark F. . . . . '— '02 C.999 B.A. L.8 J.D. [Ⓐ Buckingham,D.&B.]
Craig, Mary Robin . . . . '53 '79 C.103 A.B. L.930 J.D. 4070 Mayfield Rd.

Cramer, Roger A., (BV) .... '38 '66 C.930 L.1003 LL.B. 5885 Landerbrook Dr.
Crandall, David J. .... '66 '91 C.25 B.S. L.823 J.D. [Calfee,H.&G.]
Crandall, Tracy D. .... '72 '97 C.105 B.A. L.1003 J.D. [Ⓐ Calfee,H.&G.]
Crane, James M. .... '67 '98 C.690 B.A. L.930 J.D. [Ⓐ Ulmer&B.]
Crane, Jonathan O. .... '54 '81 C.473 B.A. L.1003 J.D. Society Natl. Bk.
Crane, Robert P. ....'68 '94 C.477 B.A. L.1003 J.D. [Ⓐ R.Frederick&Assoc.]
Crawford, Stephen J. .... '68 '94 C&L.107 B.A., J.D. [Ⓐ Squire,S.&D.]
Creagan, J. Michael, (BV) ....'— '85 C.602 A.B. L.1003 J.D. [Ⓒ Davis&Y.]
Creger, Michelle B., (AV) '55 '81 C.190 B.A. L.930 J.D.
Asst. Gen. Coun., Litig. & Employ., Amer. Greetings Corp.
Crehore, Charles A. .... '46 '76 C.967 B.A. L.7 J.D. [Ⓒ Ulmer&B.] (Pat.)
Crespy, Gregory Paul ....'59 '87 C.645 B.S. L.117 J.D. Soc. Sec. Admn.
Crisafi, Frank R. .... '33 '71 C.930 B.B.A. L.1003 J.D. 31220 Roxbury Pk. Dr.‡
Crisafi, Marilyn Miller, (AV) .... '64 '92 C.893 B.S.N. L.1003 J.D. 925 Euclid Avenue
Crisci, George S., (BV) ....'58 '83 C.970 B.A. L.930 J.D. [Ulmer&B.]
Crist, Edward C. .... '43 '73 C.610 B.S.M.E. L.1003 J.D. 9973 Gatewood Dr.
Crist, Paul G., (AV) ....'— '74 C.546 B.A. L.569 J.D. [Jones D.]
Crist, Thomas O., (AV) ....'70 '95 C.608 B.A. L.117 J.D. [Benesch,F.C.&A.]
Cristallo, Paul J., (CV) ....'67 '93 C.8 B.A. L.1003 J.D. [Mazanec,R.&R.]
Crone, Chester F. .... '43 '70 C&L.930 B.A., J.D. Cleveland Wire Cloth & Mfg.
Crosby, Elizabeth A., (AV) ....'57 '89 C.8 B.A. L.1003 J.D. 55 Public Sq., Ste. 1475
Crosby, James P. '— '81 C.205 B.S. L.1509 J.D.
V.P.-Office Mktg. & Leasing, Forest City Commercial Group, Inc.
Crosley, John C. ....'23 '57 C.930 B.A. L.1003 J.D. 55 Public Square
Cross, Carolyn C. ....'57 '86 C.999 B.A. L.07 J.D. Navy Finance Ctr.
Cross, Robert C. ....'56 '87 C.930 B.A. L.339 J.D. [Ⓒ Benesch,F.C.&A.]
Crossman, Darryl H. ....'52 '93 C.251 B.C.E. L.989 J.D. [Ⓐ Reid,B.M.&W.]
Crossman, Jeffrey A. .... '72 '01 C.528 B.A. L.989 J.D. [Ⓐ Benesch,F.C.&A.]
Crowther, Lawrence S., (AV) .... '58 '84 C.732 B.A. L.902 J.D. [Wegman,H.&V.]
Crump, Robert J., (AV) ....'43 '68 C.611 B.A. L.930 J.D. [Walter&H.]
Crystal, Larry, (AV) ....'38 '65 C.930 B.B.A. L.1003 J.D. [McCarthy,L.C.&L.]
Csikos, Debra ....'67 '94 C.381 B.A. L.608 J.D. [Ⓐ Tucker E.&W.]
Csomos, Andrea L. ....'— '01 C&L.851 B.A., J.D. [Ⓐ Baker&H.]
Cubar, John C., (AV) .... '52 '78 C.473 A.B. L.1003 J.D. [McNeal,S.A.&B.]
Cuellar, Michael M. '58 '92
C.229 B.S.B.A. L.1003 J.D. Sr. Tax Coun., Danaher Corporation
Cuilli, Leonard A. .... '66 '97 C.608 B.A. L.989 J.D. [Ⓐ K.D.Weiner&Assoc.]
Culbertson, William J. ....'66 '95 C.67 B.A. L.930 J.D. [Ⓐ Baker&H.]
Cullen, James P., (BV) ....'58 '85 C.719 B.A. L.1003 J.D. [Rego,C.&H.]
Cullen, Jean M., (BV) ....'54 '91 C.713 B.A. L.930 J.D. [Ⓐ Singerman,M.D.&K.]
Cullen, John L., (AV) ....'65 '93 C.999 B.A. L.1003 J.D. [Cullen]

Cullen Co. LPA, (AV) [BB]
The Superior Building, 815 Superior Avenue, Suite 1210, 44114
Telephone: 216-621-2090 Fax: 216-621-2062
URL: http://www.ohioelaw.com
John L. Cullen.
Civil Litigation, Employment Law, Wrongful Termination, For Labor Standards Act, Age Discrimination, Sexual Harassment, Racial Discrimination, Personal Injury, Medical Malpractice, Nursing Home Malpractice, Class and Collective Actions, Municipal Laws.
See Professional Biographies, CLEVELAND, OHIO

Culler, M. Patricia, (AV) ....'54 '85 C.602 B.A. L.1003 J.D. [Ⓒ Hahn L.&P.]
Cullers, Michael A. .... '70 '95 C.473 B.S. L.930 J.D. [Ⓐ Squire,S.&D.]
Cullers, Romney B., (AV) .... '65 '91 C.1310 B.A. L.930 J.D. [R.Cullers]
Cullers, Romney, Co., LPA, (AV) ....55 Public Square, Suite 1700
Culum, Kevin C. ....'64 '90 C.602 B.A. L.508 J.D. Trial Attorney
Cummins, Michael Timothy .... '58 '83 C.161 B.A. L.930 J.D. Sherwin-Williams Co.
Cupar, David B. ....'74 '99 C&L.930 B.S., J.D. [Ⓐ McDonald H.] (Pat.)
Cuppage, David M., (BV) .... '64 '90 C.381 B.A. L.1003 J.D. [Climaco,L.P.W.&G.]
Curatolo, Joseph G. ....'52 '77 C.363 B.S. L.8 J.D. [Curatolo S.] (Pat.)

Curatolo Sidoti, A Legal Professional Association
24500 Center Ridge Road Suite 280, 44145
Telephone: 440-808-0011 Fax: 440-808-0657
Email: cleveland@patentandtm.com URL: http://www.patentandtm.com
Joseph G. Curatolo; Salvatore A. Sidoti. Associate: James E. Oehlenschlager.
Intellectual Property Law.
See Professional Biographies, CLEVELAND, OHIO

Curran, Thomas P. ....'36 '62 C.608 B.A. L.930 J.D. Com. Pleas J.
Currie, William E. .... '21 '83 C.971 B.S.M.E. L.161 J.D. 1172 Berwick Ln.
Currivan, John D. ....'— '78 C&L.188 B.S., J.D. [Jones D.]
Curry, Earl M., Jr. '33 '64 C&L.923 B.S., J.D.
Assoc. Prof. of Law, Cleve.-Marshall Coll. of Law
Curry, Matthew P. .... '74 '04 C.980 B.A. L.1003 J.D. [Ⓐ K.D.Weiner&Assoc.]
Curtin, John D. ....'— '03 C.1049 B.A. L.823 J.D. [Ⓐ Jones D.]
Curtis, Jack, (AV) ....'58 '85 C.381 B.A. L.1003 J.D. [Hohmann,B.&C.]
Curtis-Patrick, Saundra Jayne '54 '80
C.881 B.A. L.124 J.D. 1200 Ontario Street, 8th Floor
Cushing, Mary T., (AV) .... '56 '81 C.381 B.A. L.930 J.D. The LTV Corp.
Cushion, R. Paul, II '57 '86 C.381 B.S. L.1003 J.D.
615 West Superior Avenue, 12thFloor-State Office Bldg.
Cushwa, Mara E. ....'65 '90 C.602 B.A. L.930 J.D. [Calfee,H.&G.]
Cusick, Mark A. .... '48 '75 C.229 B.A. L.893 J.D. [Squire,S.&D.] (⊙London, England)
Cusick, Richard, (AV) .... '31 '55 C.363 B.S. L.930 LL.B. [Calfee,H.&G.] ‡
Cusimano, Joseph J., (BV) .... '66 '92 C.478 B.A. L.930 J.D. 50 Public Sq.
Cuthbertson, Jennifer L. ....'79 '04 C.228 B.A. L.124 J.D. [Ⓐ Frantz W.]
Cuthbertson, Patricia Casey, (AV) '55 '90 C.38 B.S.N. L.1003 J.D.
[Ⓐ Moscarino&T.]
Cvetkovic, Adrienne N. ....'79 '04 C.318 B.A. L.930 J.D. [Ⓐ Schneider,S.R.&L.]
Cweiber, Bruce E. '62 '88 C.446 B.A. L.64 J.D.
(adm. in MD; not adm. in OH) Precision Title Agency, Inc.
Cybulski, Donald, (AV) ....'51 '75 C.659 B.S. L.930 J.D. [Ⓒ Lowe E.W.&M.]
Cyphert, Michael A., (AV) ....'48 '73 C&L.930 B.A., J.D. [Walter&H.]
Czack, Michael W., (AV) ....'59 '84 C.97 B.S. L.1003 J.D. [Caravona&C.]
Dabb, Wayne C., Jr., (AV) ....'46 '71 C.878 B.S. L.477 J.D. [Baker&H.]
Daddona, David Scott, (BV) ....'58 '83 C.473 B.A. L.930 J.D. [Ⓐ Lasko&L.]
Dahl, Sherri L. ....'68 '01 C.684 B.S. L.608 J.D. [Ⓐ McDonald H.]
Daiker, Paul B., (BV) .... '67 '93 C.880 B.A. L.1003 J.D. [Zukerman,D.&L.]
Daiker-Middaugh, Pamela Ann '62 '89
C.1365 B.A. L.1003 J.D. Cleveland Marshall Coll. of Law
Dakin, Carol F., (AV) ....'43 '69 *C.518 A.B. L.161 J.D. [Squire,S.&D.]*
Dakin, Robert F. .... '38 '65 C.309 B.A. L.659 LL.B. V.P., Natl City Bk.
Daloia, Andrea B. ....'74 '01 C.470 B.A. L.989 J.D. [Ⓐ Thompson H.]
Dalton, Jamie Manning ....'51 '80 C.800 B.A. L.767 J.D. 1501 Euclid Avenue‡
Damelio, Marillyn Fagan, (AV) '53 '78 C.1044 B.A. L.607 J.D.
Managing Trial Attorney-N.E. Ohio, Nationwide Mutual Insurance Company
Damiani, Louis C., (BV) .... '53 '79 C.608 B.A. L.1003 J.D. [Armstrong,M.D.&Z.]

D'Amico, Ann M., (BV) .... '57 '88 C.473 B.A. L.1003 J.D. [Zimmerman,C.E.&M.]
D'Amico, Cheryl A. ....'— '96 C.62 B.A. L.161 J.D. [Calfee,H.&G.]
Dampeer, John L., (AV) ....'16 '46 C&L.309 S.B., LL.B. 127 Public Sq.‡
D'Angelo, Patrick A., (AV) ....'51 '77 C.363 A.B. L.1003 J.D. [P.A.D'Angelo]
D'Angelo, Patrick A., LLC, (AV) .... 1370 Ontario St., Ste. 2000
Daniels, Anthea R., (BV) ....'64 '89 C.207 B.A. L.930 J.D. [Calfee,H.&G.]
Daniels, E. Kent, Jr., (AV) '32 '59
C.923 B.S.M.E. L.273 LL.B. [Ⓒ Fay,S.F.M.&M.] (See Pat. Sect.)
Daniels, Stephen H., (BV) .... '53 '78 C.967 B.A. L.267 J.D. [McMahon,D.H.&L.]
Daniels, Thomas C. ....'— '86 C.381 B.Mus. L.8 J.D. [Jones D.]
Dannenhirsh, Moses .... '40 '74 C.930 B.A. L.1003 J.D. U.S. Dept. of Labor
Danvers, Garet H. '51 '84 C.999 B.S.B.A. L.229 J.D.
(adm. in PA; not adm. in OH) Ernst & Young L.L.P.
Danzig, Allen J., (AV) '55 '80 C.659 B.A. L.1292 J.D.
Assoc. Gen. Coun., Environ., The Sherwin-Williams Co.
Darlington, Stephen M., (AV) .... '42 '67 C.207 B.A. L.930 J.D. [Ziegler,M.&M.]
Daroff, Charles, II, (BV) ....'61 '88 C&L.930 B.A., J.D. [Hurtuk&D.]
Dattilo, Joseph T., (AV) ....'48 '73 C.381 B.A. L.608 J.D. [Brouse M.]
Dauscher, Raymond G. .... '29 '58 C.610 B.S. L.1003 J.D. 11770 Berea Rd.
Davet, Anne M. ....'— '04 C.363 B.A. L.602 J.D. [Ⓐ Baker&H.]
Davey, Karen A., (AV) ....'55 '80 C.363 A.B. L.989 J.D. [Weston H.]
Davidson, Gerry, (BV) ....'45 '72 C.610 B.B.A. L.1003 J.D. 800 Standard Bldg.
Davidson, Virginia Ann ....'59 '84 C.436 B.A. L.94 J.D. 1111 Superior Ave., E.
Davies, David G., (AV) ....'33 '62 C&L.477 B.S.E., J.D. [Ⓒ Ray,R.C.&D.]
Davis, Andrea Y. ....'62 '95 C.674 B.A L.930 J.D. Travelers Ins. Co.
Davis, Audrey H. ....'53 '77 C.887 B.A. L.150 J.D. 1468 W. 9th St.
Davis, C. LeAnn '75 '03 C.228 B.A. L.260 J.D.
(adm. in FL; not adm. in OH) [Ⓐ Thompson H.]
Davis, Catherine A. ....'70 '98 C.1208 B.A. L.851 J.D. [Ⓐ Janik&D.]
Davis, Dwight E. ....'49 '77 C.217 B.A. L.1003 J.D. [Davis,W.]
Davis, Leonard, (BV) ....'32 '66 C.607 B.S. L.1003 J.D. 1370 Ontario St.
Davis, Marilyn Tamaren ....'50 '82 25 W. Prospect Ave., Ste. 1100
Davis, Mary, (BV) .... '52 '88 C.1183 B.A. L.930 J.D. [Seeley,S.&E.L.&Assoc.]
Davis, Michael H. '46 '75 C.605 B.A. L.1019 J.D.
(adm. in CO; not adm. in OH) Cleveland Marshall Law Sch, 2121 Euclid Ave Lb 138
Davis, Renee L. ....'69 '03 C.392 B.S. L.989 J.D. [Ⓐ Thompson H.]
Davis, Robert E. ....'46 '77 C.999 B.S. L.1003 J.D. [R.E.Davis]
Davis, Steven S., (AV) ....'50 '75 C.696 B.A. L.161 J.D. [S.S.Davis]
Davis, Robert E., Co., L.P.A. ....55 Public Sq., Ste. 1500

Davis, Steven S., Co., L.P.A., (AV)
450 Standard Building, 1370 Ontario Street, 44113
Telephone: 216-781-3311 Fax: 216-781-3312
Email: sdavis@epitrustee.com URL: http://www.rabbanddavis.com
Steven S. Davis.
Bankruptcy, Bankruptcy Chapter ll, Bankruptcy Chapter 13, Bankruptcy Chapter 7, Debtor and Creditor, Commercial.
See Professional Biographies, CLEVELAND, OHIO

Davis, Williams & Co., L.P.A., (BV) ....1370 Ontario St.

Davis & Young, (AV) [BB]
A Legal Professional Association
1700 Midland Building, 44115 ⊙
Telephone: 216-348-1700 Fax: 216-621-0602
Email: atty@davisyoung.com URL: http://www.davisyoung.com
Rees H. Davis, Sr. (1892-1965); Fred J. Young (1889-1946); George W. Lutjen; C. Richard McDonald; Paul D. Eklund; Jan L. Roller; Thomas W. Wright; David J. Fagnilli; William Vance; Patrick F. Roche; Dennis R. Fogarty; Richard M. Garner. Associates: Thomas J. Connick; Shawn A. Cormier; Kristi L. Haude; Shannon M. Pietrafese; Patrick M. Roche; Jennifer Sardina; Ronald J. Ziehm. Of Counsel: Martin J. Murphy; Henry A. Hentemann; J. Michael Creagan; R. Emmett Moran; Pamela Barker.
General Trial and Appellate Practice, Products Liability, General Tort, Insurance Coverage, Personal Injury, Toxic Torts, Complex Mass Tort Claims, Legal and Medical Malpractice, Municipal Liability, Civil Rights, Employment Practices Liability, and Environmental and Commercial Liability.
Counsel for: Westfield Companies; Cincinnati Insurance Co.; University Hospitals of Cleveland; Central Mutual Insurance Co.; St. Paul Insurance Co.; State Farm Insurance Cos.; Progressive Insurance Cos.; Erie Insurance Group; Motorists Mutual Insurance Group; SYSCO Food Services of Cleveland, Inc.
Akron, Ohio Office: National City Center, One Cascade Plaza, Suite 800, 44308. Telephone: 330-376-1717. Fax: 330-376-1797.
Youngstown, Ohio Office: The Commerce Building, 201 East Commerce Street, Suite 100, 44503. Telephone: 330-743-1717.
Warren, Ohio Office: 108 Main Street, SW, Suite 1000, 44481. Telephone: 330-373-1717. Fax: 330-395-0610.
See Professional Biographies, CLEVELAND, OHIO

Davison, John F. ....'28 '68 C.608 L.1003 J.D. 2322 E. 88th St.‡
Davison, Lawrence C. .... '66 '91 C.201 B.S.B.A. L.930 J.D. [Ⓐ Taft,S.&H.]
Dawson, Chester C., Jr. ....'40 '69 C.573 B.A. L.107 J.D. Mgr., Indus. Rel., BP Oil Co.
Dawson, Philip M., (AV) ....'45 '72 C.473 B.A. L.245 J.D. [Calfee,H.&G.]
Dawson, Todd ....'73 '98 C.980 B.A. L.228 J.D. [Ⓐ Baker&H.]
Deacon, Robert F., (BV) .... '49 '79 C.97 B.S. L.607 J.D. [Deacon,H.&A.]
Deacon, Harwood & Armstrong, LTD, (AV) .... 127 Public Square
Dean, Charles F., Jr. .... '26 '62 C.251 B.B.A. L.1003 LL.B. 5810 Orchard Ave.
Dean, Jeffrey L., (BV) ....'50 '80 C.381 B.A. L.1003 J.D. [Malek D.&Assoc.]
Dean, Jonathan .... '44 '70 C.309 B.A. L.145 J.D. Attorney, Goodyear Tire & Rubber
Dean, Richard A., (AVⓉ) ....'48 '73 C.210 B.A. L.1119 J.D. [Tucker E.&W.]
DeBaggis, Henry F., II, (AV) .... '56 '81 C.381 B.A. L.1003 J.D. 55 Publis Sq.
DeBaltzo, Michelle M. '70 '97
C.363 B.A. L.1003 J.D. Trial Atty., U.S. Dept. of Lab, Solr. Off.
Debaltzo, Nicholas J., Jr. .... '72 '99 C.363 B.A. L.1003 J.D. [Ⓐ Johnson,A.&C.]
Debevec, Rhonda Baker .... '71 '97 C.385 B.A. L.930 J.D. [Ⓐ Spangenberg,S.&L.]
Debitetto, Rocco I. .... '76 '01 C.201 B.A. L.150 J.D. [Ⓐ Hahn L.&P.]
DeBord, David L. ....'— '03 C.611 B.A. L.880 J.D. [Ⓐ Jones D.]
Debose, Lorraine ....'— '03 C.1365 B .A. L.124 J.D. [Ⓐ Buckley K.]
Debski, Christopher R. ....'71 '97 C.477 B.A. L.8 J.D. [Ⓐ Ross,B.&S.]
DeCaro, Sara E. .... '74 '00 C.62 B.A. L.989 J.D. [Ⓐ Cavitch,F.D.&F.]
Decensi, Patricia Marie Bunn '61 '87 C.201 B.A. L.930 J.D.
Sr. Assoc. Corp. Coun., Medical Mutual of Ohio
De Chant, Thomas H., (AV) ....'32 '58 C.215 Ph.B. L.930 LL.B. [Stewart&D.]
DeCosky, Richard L., Jr. .... '47 '78 C.608 B.S. L.464 J.D. 10109 Burton Ave.
Dedmon, Shelly G. .... '61 '88 C.1322 B.A. L.352 J.D. [Calfee,H.&G.]
Deegan, F. Timothy, (AV) .... '40 '72 C.973 B.S. L.1003 J.D. [Deegan&M.]
Deegan, Hallie Maureen ....'71 '02 C.473 B.A. L.1003 J.D. Jud. Law Clk.
Deegan, Joseph Edward ......'69 '94 C.20 B.A. L.602 J.D. Sr. Consultant, Ernst & Young
Deegan & McGarry, (AV) ....1468 W. 9th St.
Deese, James L., (AV) '53 '80 C.604 A.B. L.1003 J.D.
20325 Center Ridge Rd., Ste. 512
deFilippis, Lisa M. .... '55 '86 C.893 B.A. L.818 J.D. [Buckingham,D.&B.]
DeFoy, Ernest D., (BV) ....'61 '88 C.472 B.A. L.930 J.D. [Douglass&D.]

De Franco, Ralph T., (BV) ... '43 '73 C.363 A.B. L.1003 J.D. 75 Public Square
De Gennaro, Susanne ... '68 '04 C.999 B.F.A. L.989 J.D. [Ⓐ Walter&H.]
DeGrandis, Ronald L. ... '46 '73 C.276 B.S.B.A. L.1003 J.D. 10001 Lakeside Ave., E.
DeGross, Charles M., (BV) ... '48 '94 C.161 B.Com. L.1003 J.D. 1400 E. Schaaf Rd.
DeGulis, Gregory J., (AV) ... '60 '90 C.477 B.A. L.930 J.D. [McMahon,D.H.&L.]
Deighton, Eric T. ... '73 '99 C.1115 B.A. L.930 J.D. [Ⓐ Carlisle,M.R.K.&U.]
Deioma, David B., (AV) '40 '65 C.930 B.S.E.S. L.276 J.D.
[Pearne&G.] (See Pat. Sect.)
Delahunty, Martin S., (BV) ... '62 '87 C.472 B.A. L.161 J.D. 6110 Parkland Boulevard
Delaney, Timothy J., (BV) ... '51 '76 C.385 B.A. L.851 J.D. [Scully&D.]
Del Balso, Colleen R. ... '— '02 C.611 B.A. L.989 J.D. [Ⓐ Gallagher S.]
Delchin, Steven A. ... '71 '97 C.363 B.A. L.930 J.D. [Ⓐ Squire,S.&D.]
Del Col, John J. '63 '98 C.608 B.S.M.E. L.850 J.D.
[Ⓐ Renner,O.B.&S.] (See Pat. Sect.)
DeLeon, Jose Enrique ... '51 '93 P.O. Box 93318
della Volpe, Dean A., (BV) ... '54 '85 C.161 B.A. L.1003 J.D. 1228 Euclid Ave.
Dellinger, Elizabeth A., (BV) ... '61 '87 C.385 A.B. L.930 J.D. [Baker&H.]
Del Monaco, Maria ... '61 '87 C.860 B.A. L.309 J.D. [Ulmer&B.]
Delon, Evana C. ... '79 '04 C.607 B.A. L.989 J.D. [Ⓐ Babcock&W.]
Deluca, Amy L. ... '76 '03 C.8 B.A. L.989 J.D. [Ⓐ Porter W.M.&A.]
Demanelis, Ernie K., (AV) ... '56 '81 C&L.923 B.A., J.D. [Squire,S.&D.]
DeMarchi, Darvin, Jr., (AV) ... '38 '62 C&L.976 B.A., LL.B. 901 Lakeside Ave.
DeMarco, Daniel A., (AV) ... '58 '83 C.145 B.A. L.477 J.D. [Hahn L.&P.]
DeMarr, Edward M. ... '43 '73 C.930 B.A. L.1003 J.D. I.R.S.
DeMarr, Jean A. ... '— '83 C.62 B.A. L.1003 J.D. East Ohio Gas Co.
Demaske, Susan J. '59 '84 C&L.930 B.S., J.D.
V.P. & Asst. Gen. Coun., J.P. Morgan Trust Co. N.A.
DeMelto, Vincent K., (BV) ... '37 '71 C.436 B.S. L.930 J.D. 425 Lakeside Ave., Ste 100
Demer, Adrian J., (BV) ... '50 '74 C.62 B.A. L.930 J.D. 18660 Bagley Road, Suite 203
Demer, Gregory W., (BV) ... '45 '76 C.62 B.A. L.1003 J.D. 18660 Bagley Rd.
Demeter, Thomas P. ... '36 '69 C.8 B.S.B.A. L.1003 J.D. V.P., Society Natl. Bk.
DeMetz, Kathleen S. ... '52 '77 C.1036 B.A. L.602 J.D. Legal Aid Soc.
Demian, Simon P. ... '66 '92 C.264 B.A. L.1003 J.D. [Ⓐ Wegman,H.&V.]
DeMinico, Michael P. ... '75 '03 C.945 B.A. L.273 J.D. [Ⓐ Baker&H.]
Demitrack, Thomas, (AV) ... '— '79 C.1033 B.Mus. L.608 J.D. [Jones D.]
Dempsey, Bourne P., (AV) ... '30 '55 C.976 B.A. L.309 LL.B. 925 Euclid Avenue
Dempsey, Louise Pomeroy '44 '82 C.012 B.A. L.1003 J.D.
Asst. Dean, Cleveland-Marshall College of Law
Dempsey, Wm. F. ... '23 '54 C.363 B.S. L.1003 J.D. Sales Rep., Champion Rivet Co., The
Demsey, Richard L., (AV) ... '53 '82 C.610 B.F.A. L.930 J.D. [R.L.Demsey]

Demsey, Richard L., Co., L.P.A., (AV)
1350 Euclid Avenue, 44115
Telephone: 216-263-7900 Fax: 216-263-7901
Email: rdemseylaw.com URL: http://www.demseylawoffice.com
Richard L. Demsey.
Construction Accidents, Nursing Home Negligence, Obstetric Malpractice, Wrongful Death, Automobile Accidents, Brain Injury, Catastrophic Injury, Motorcycle Accidents and Injuries, Plaintiff's Personal Injury, Severe Burns, Spinal Injury, Railroad Accidents and Injuries, Railroad Crossing Accidents, Aviation Law, Trucking Accidents, Medical Malpractice, Sexual Harassment, Premise Liability, Product Liability.

See Professional Biographies, CLEVELAND, OHIO

Denkewalter, J. Kurt, (BV) ... '56 '90 C.1208 B.S. L.201 J.D. [Thompson H.]

Denmead Law Office
(See Columbus)

Denny, Douglas R., (AV) ... '47 '74 C.1027 B.S. L.608 J.D. [Ray,R.C.&D.]
Dent, George W., Jr. '47 '74 C&L.178 B.A., J.D.
(adm. in NY; not adm. in OH) 11075 E. Blvd.
Dent, Rebecca Holloway, (AV) ... '47 '76 C.66 B.A. L.178 J.D. [Spieth,B.M.&N.]
DeNuzzo, Noreen ... '— '86 C.1156 B.S. L.930 J.D. [Ⓢ Jones D.]
DePerro, Dayna M. ... '79 '04 C.473 B.A. L.989 J.D. [Ⓐ Kelley&F.]
DePiero, Daniel R. ... '58 '94 C.62 B.A. L.1003 J.D. 1648 Hanna Bldg.
DeRaedt, Kathleen M. ... '70 '95 C.30 B.A. L.851 J.D. Linderlake Corp.
DeRamus, Monica D. ... '61 '01 L.989 J.D. [M.D.DeRamus]
DeRamus, Monica D., LLC ... 850 Euclid Avenue, Suite 728
Derenthal, Jacob ... '77 '05 C.477 B.A. L.724 J.D. [Ⓐ Benesch,F.C.&A.]
DeRienzo, Elizabeth M. ... '78 '04 C.608 B.S.B.A. L.989 J.D. [Ⓐ Ulmer&B.]
Derkin, William Scott, (BV) ... '45 '73 C.363 B.S. L.930 J.D. Allstate Ins. Co.
DeRoche, James A. ... '65 '91 C.696 B.A. L.930 J.D. 1600 Rockefellar Bldg.
DeRosa, Joseph C., (AV) ... '54 '79 C.608 B.S. L.1003 J.D. [Wincek&D.]
Derrick, William A., Jr., (BV) '43 '69
C.363 A.B. L.329 J.D. Mng. Dir., Derrick Commodities
Dertouzos, Nicholas J. ... '73 '99 C.475 B.A. L.930 J.D. [Ⓐ Nicola,G.&C.]
Dertouzos, Nicole Burns '74 '99 C.318 B.A. L.930 J.D.
Pub. Def., Legal Aid. Soc. of Cleveland, Crim. Div.
DeSantis, Fedele, (AV) ... '58 '84 C.363 B.S. L.1003 J.D. Atty. Gen. Off
DeSantis, Frank R., (AV) ... '51 '80 C.470 B.A. L.285 J.D. [Thompson H.]
De Santis, Lynette S. '59 '84 C.980 B.S. L.1003 J.D.
Sr. Tax Coun., White Consolidated Industries, Inc.
Desberg, Gary S., (AV) ... '60 '85 C.477 A.B. L.930 J.D. [Singerman,M.D.&K.]
Deseran, Sophia M. ... '57 '92 C.970 B.A. L.1003 J.D. [Walter&H.]
Desmond, Richard K., (AV) ... '28 '52 C&L.608 B.A., J.D. 127 Public Sq.‡

Dettelbach, Sicherman & Baumgart, A Legal Professional Association, (AV)
1100 Ohio Savings Plaza, 1801 East 9th Street, 44114-3169
Telephone: 216-696-6000 Telecopier: 216-696-3338
Email: dsb@dsb-law.com
Arthur H. Dettelbach (1904-1972); Marvin A. Sicherman; Richard A. Baumgart; Robert D. Barr;—Lisa A. Vardzel.
Bankruptcy, Chapter 11 Reorganization, Commercial Bankruptcy and Transactions, Corporate, Insolvency, Uniform Commercial Code, Real Estate, Commercial. General Civil Trial and Appellate Practice.

See Professional Biographies, CLEVELAND, OHIO

DeVan, Mark R., (AV) ... '48 '74 C.49 B.A. L.161 J.D. [Berkman,G.M.&D.]
Dever, A. Steven, (AV) ... '58 '85 C.249 B.S. L.1003 J.D. 13363 Madison Ave.
Devine, Sara C. ... '78 '02 C.381 B.A. L.124 J.D. [Ⓐ Hawkins]
DeVito, Christopher Michael, (BV) '65 '90
C.602 B.B.A. L.608 J.D. [Morganstern,M.&D.]
DeVore, Tara C. ... '— '02 C&L.8 B.S., J.D. [Ⓐ McDonald H.]
Dezort, Robert E., (BV) ... '66 '92 C.945 B.A. L.989 J.D. [Millisor&N.]
Diamant, Michael H., (AV) ... '46 '71 C.930 B.S. L.309 J.D. [Kahn K.]
Diamond, Rand J. ... '59 '87 C.95 B.A. L.262 J.D. Cleve. Law Library
Diaz, Derek E. ... '73 '98 C.363 B.A. L.608 J.D. [Ⓐ Hahn L.&P.]
Diaz, Robert J. ... '65 '93 C.550 B.A. L.966 J.D. [Ⓐ Hahn L.&P.] (Pat.)
DiBaggio, Joseph E. ... '— '02 C.201 B.A. L.1003 J.D. [Ⓢ Baker&H.]
Dickerson, Denise A. ... '67 '95 C.831 B.S. L.1003 J.D. [Sutter,O.&F.] ⊙
Dickinson, James, (AV) ... '48 '73 C.902 B.A. L.893 J.D. [Cavitch,F.D.&F.]
Dickson, Blake A., (BV) ... '67 '92 C.228 A.B. L.930 J.D. [Schiff&D.]
Diehl, Paul A. ... '14 '37 L.150 LL.B. 4106 Rocky River Dr.‡
Diemert, Joseph W., Jr., (AV) ... '46 '72 C.602 B.A. L.276 J.D. [J.W.Diemert,Jr.&Assoc.]
Diemert, Joseph W., Jr. & Associates, Co., L.P.A., (AV) ... 1360 S.O.M. Ctr. Rd.
Digges, Randolph E., III, (BV) '64 '92
C.608 B.A. L.851 J.D. [Rankin,H.P.&C.] (See Pat. Sect.)
DiGirolamo, Alan P., (BV) ... '63 '89 C.36 B.S. L.930 J.D. [Buckingham,D.&B.]
Dileno, Jon M., (AV) ... '62 '88 C.62 B.A. L.861 J.D. [Duvin,C.&H.]
DiLisi, Richard A. ... '64 '89 C&L.930 B.A., J.D. 323 Lakeside Ave., W.
Dillman, Jennifer Lynn ... '71 '00 C.508 B.A. L.851 J.D. [Ⓐ Thompson H.]
Di Marco, Victor T. ... '64 '00 C.62 B.S. L.989 J.D. [Ⓐ Weston H.]
DiMassa, Pasquale, Jr. ... '75 '01 C.62 B.A. L.124 J.D. [Ⓐ Hahn L.&P.]
Dimitrijevs, James A. ... '67 '94 C.363 B.A. L.1003 J.D. [McDonald H.]
Dimond, Douglas A. '54 '80 C.150 B.A. L.608 J.D.
Gen. Coun., All Erection & Crane Rental Corp.
Dingus, Titee M. ... '58 '92 C.216 B.A. L.1003 J.D. Staff Atty., U.S. Dist. Ct.
Dinn, Irwin J., (AV) ... '39 '64 C&L.477 A.B., LL.B. [Dinn,H.&P.]

Dinn, Hochman & Potter, LLC, (AV) BR
5910 Landerbrook Drive, Suite 200 (Mayfield Heights), 44124
Telephone: 440-446-1100 Fax: 440-446-1240
Email: dhp@dhplaw.com URL: http://www.dhplaw.com
Members of Firm: Irwin J. Dinn; David B. Hochman; Steven B. Potter; Thomas A. Barni. Associates: Renee S. Pienta; Ryan L. Rivchun. Of Counsel: Michael C. Hennenberg; Irwin M. Frank.
General Civil Practice. Corporate Law, Business Law, Civil Litigation, Commercial, Real Estate, Telecommunications, Probate, Estate Planning, Family Law, Workers Compensation and Administrative Agencies.

See Professional Biographies, CLEVELAND, OHIO

Dinner, Gary L., (AV) ... '48 '73 C.665 B.S. L.188 J.D. [Ⓒ Tucker E.&W.]
DiPalma, Douglas A., (AV) ... '55 '80 C.602 B.A. L.930 J.D. [Cavitch,F.D.&F.]
DiPalma, Joy A. ... '— '00 C.473 B.A. L.1003 J.D. [Ⓐ McGlinchey S.]
Di Petta, Deanna Lynn, (AV) ... '58 '87 C.161 B.A. L.1003 J.D. [Ⓐ Zashin&R.]
DiPuccio, Dominic A., (BV) ... '64 '90 C.973 B.S. L.930 J.D. [Kahn K.]
Disantis, Richard J., (AV) ... '— '66 C.385 A.B. L.477 J.D. [Buckley K.]
Di Silvio, Marilena ... '67 '95 C.659 B.S.N. L.1003 J.D. [Ⓐ Reminger&R.]

Dismuke, Daniel K.
(See Akron)

Ditchey, Timothy John ... '64 '00 C.1245 B.A. L.1003 J.D. [T.J.Ditchey]
Ditchey, Timothy J., LLC ... 1148 Euclid Ave., Ste. 405
Ditko-Bevione, Sharon R. ... '75 '04 C.161 B.A. L.124 J.D. [Ⓐ Abel&Z.]
DiVenere, Anthony J., (AV) ... '41 '67 C.363 A.B. L.608 J.D. [McDonald H.]
Dixon, James T. ... '68 '97 C.207 B.A. L.124 J.D. [Ⓐ Frantz W.]
Dixon, Robert A., (BV) ... '56 '81 C.999 B.A. L.1003 J.D. 4403 Saint Clair Avenue
Doan, James N. ... '46 '71 C.475 B.A. L.477 J.D. Coun., Eaton Corp.
Dobrea, Diane Hughes ... '64 '94 C&L.124 B.A., J.D. [Ⓐ Calfee,H.&G.] (See Pat. Sect.)
Dobronos, Michael G. ... '66 '91 C.608 B.A. L.117 J.D. Dist. Hearing Offr.
Docherty, Pamela A. ... '44 '94 C.903 B.S. L.8 J.D. [Ⓐ Calfee,H.&G.] (See Pat. Sect.)
Dodd, Stephen D. ... '74 '00 C.92 B.S. L.124 J.D. [Ⓐ Karberg,K.W.&T.]
Dodrill, Joyce Marot ... '56 '84 C.169 B.A. L.1003 J.D. Co. Pros. Off.
Doerner, Maureen A., (BVⓉ) ... '51 '81 C.1102 B.A. L.190 J.D. Charter One Bank, N.A.
Doganiero, Mara Grame ... '55 '80 C.62 B.S. L.930 J.D. Law Clk., to U.S. Bkrptcy. J.
Doheny, John T., (AV) ... '48 '74 C.363 B.S.B.A. L.1003 J.D. [Tucker E.&W.]
Dolejs, Richard F. ... '29 '67 C.251 B.A. L.1003 J.D. 1444 Primrose Dr.,#2
Dolin, Lawrence S. ... '43 '69 C&L.930 B.A., J.D. Pres., Front Row Theater
Doman, Paul M. '69 '95 C.930 B.A. L.1003 J.D.
V.P. & Gen. Coun., First American Equity Loan Servs., Inc.
Domanovic, Dieter ... '52 '81 C.161 B.B.A. L.1003 J.D. 14805 Detroit Avenue, Suite 490
Domiano, Joseph C., (AV) ... '28 '57 C.930 B.B.A. L.161 J.D. [Friedman,D.&S.] ⊙
Donahey, William F., (AV) ... '28 '56 C.103 B.A. L.930 LL.B. 401 Euclid Ave.‡
Donahue, James R. '30 '57 C.381 A.B. L.930 LL.B.
1 Lakeside Avenue, N.W., Room 252
Donahue, Mary E. ... '58 '94 C.201 B.S. L.1003 J.D. [Ⓐ Mansour,G.G.&M.]
Donchess, James M., (BV) '63 '88 C.610 B.B.A. L.1051 J.D.
Asst. Gen. Coun., Parker-Hannifin Corporation
Donnelly, Kathleen ... '57 '89 C.611 B.A. L.1003 J.D. 526 Sprior Ave E Ste 1030
Donnelly, Nancy Howe, (BV) ... '66 '91 C.207 B.A. L.930 J.D. 1400 Bank One Ctr.
Donnersbach, Sara M. ... '72 '98 C.313 B.S. L.1003 J.D. [Weltman,W.&R.]
Doran, James M. ... '73 '98 C.473 B.S. L.989 J.D. [Ⓐ Weltman,W.&R.]
Doris, Alan S., (AV) ... '47 '72 C.473 A.B. L.309 J.D. [Squire,S.&D.]
Dorman, Andrew J. ... '67 '94 C.97 B.S.B.A. L.1003 J.D. [Janik&D.]
Dorrell, John S., (AV) ... '46 '75 C.473 B.S. L.851 J.D. Medical Mutual of Ohio
Dottore, Domenico G., (BV) ... '26 '54 C.930 B.B.A. L.1003 J.D. 140 Public Sq.
Doubrava, Brenda W. ... '45 '78 C.25 B.A. L.161 J.D. Fed. Trade Comm.
Dougherty, James P. ... '— '99 C.1372 B.A. L.1068 J.D. [Ⓐ Jones D.]
Dougherty, Paul V. ... '23 '52 C.436 L.161 J.D. 321 E. 280th
Dougherty, Veronica M. '55 '87
C.81 B.A. L.309 J.D. Assoc. Prof., Cleveland Marshall Law Sch.
Doughten, David L., (AV) ... '54 '81 C.611 B.A. L.930 J.D. [D.L.Doughten]
Doughten, David L., Co., LPA, (AV) ... 4403 Saint Clair Ave.
Douglas, Malcolm C., (AV) '30 '57
C.299 A.B. L.930 LL.B. Asst. Dir. of Law, City of Cleveland
Douglas, Sue Marie, (AV) ... '— '81 C.276 B.A L.904 J.D. [Duvin,C.&H.]
Douglass, James R., (BV) ... '54 '80 C.970 B.A. L.1003 J.D. [Douglass&D.]
Douglass & DeFoy, (BV) ... 630 Leader Building
Douthett, Breaden M. ... '66 '91 C.207 B.A. L.608 J.D. [Ⓒ Bricker&E.]
Dove, Valerie Denise ... '69 '95 C.207 B.S. L.1003 J.D. [Ⓐ Forbes,F.&Assoc.]
Dover, Thomas E., (AV) ... '— '80 C&L.201 B.S., J.D. [Gallagher S.] ⊙
Dowling, Joseph P. ... '53 '80 C.477 B.G.S. L.1003 J.D. 14533 Alger Rd.
Downey, Brian P., (BV) ... '63 '89 C.201 B.S. L.1003 J.D. [Schwartz,D.]
Downing, Timothy J., (AV) ... '63 '88 C.25 B.A. L.930 J.D. [Ulmer&B.]
Downs, Paul B. ... '50 '75 C.347 B.A. L.161 J.D. V.P., Society Natl. Bk.
Doyle, William T. ... '45 '72 C.1115 B.S.Ec. L.161 J.D. 1370 Ontario St., Ste. 2000
Drago, Christian R. ... '76 '01 C.607 B.S.E.E. L.851 J.D. [Ⓐ Tucker E.&W.] (Pat.)
Drain, John M., (AV) ... '15 '40 C.363 A.B. L.930 LL.B. 3331 Kenmore Rd.
Drasner, Lawrence S. ... '67 '92 C.91 B.S. L.477 J.D. 801 W. Superior Ave.
Draucker, Carl A. ... '51 '77 C.318 B.A. L.607 J.D. [Squire,S.&D.]
Drechsler, David L., (AV) '63 '89 C.608 B.S. L.930 J.D.
[Buckingham,D.&B.] (⊙Akron)
Dreher, Joseph D. ... '65 '91 C.201 B.E.E. L.930 J.D. [Fay,S.F.M.&M.] (See Pat. Sect.)
Dreis, Michael E. ... '70 '97 C.608 B.S.B.A. L.1003 J.D. Ernst & Young
Dresp, Donna M. ... '61 '95 C.62 B.A. L.1003 J.D. [Ⓐ Wegman,H.&V.]
Dresser, Rebecca Susan '52 '79 C.347 B.A. L.309 J.D.
(adm. in WI; not adm. in OH) 11075 E. Blvd.
Dreyfuss, Daniel W., (AV) ... '53 '78 C.610 B.G.S. L.608 J.D. [D.W.Dreyfuss]
Dreyfuss, Daniel W., Co., L.P.A., (AV) ... 1801 E. 9th Street, Suite 740

Driggs, Hogg & Fry Co., LPA
(See Willoughby Hills)
Drinko, Donald G. ....'— '93 C.161 B.A. L.1003 J.D. [Ⓐ Gallagher S.]
Drinko, John D., (AV) ....'21 '45 C.437 B.A. L.608 J.D. [Baker&H.]
Drockton, Leslie A. ....'60 '86 C.183 B.A. L.930 J.D. [Benesch,F.C.&A.]
Drozdowski, James M., (AV) ....'70 '95 C.150 B.A. L.930 J.D. [Hahn L.&P.]
Drucker, David H. ....'59 '84 C.608 B.S. L.930 J.D. [D.H.Drucker]
Drucker, Richard H., (BV) ....'57 '81 C.608 B.A. L.161 J.D. 27500 Cedar Rd.
Drucker, David H., Co., L.P.A. .... 1370 Ontario Street, Suite 330
Drushel, Kelly E. ....'64 '90 C.363 B.A. L.930 J.D. 7000 Fitzwater Road, Suite 202
D'Souza, Gerard I. ....'60 '96 C.999 B.S. L.1003 J.D. [Ⓒ J.L.Madorsky] ⊙
Dub, Stanley M., (BV) ....'— '75 C.608 B.S. L.930 J.D. [Gallagher S.]
DuBay, Roger L. '36 '61 C.363 B.A. L.930 LL.B.
Sr. Atty., The Cleveland Elec. Illuminating Co.
Duber, Michael J., (BV) ....'47 '73 C.608 B.S. L.150 J.D. 526 Superior Ave. E., Ste. 230
Dubin, Gary W., (BV) ....'39 '65 C&L.930 B.B.A., J.D. [Dubin&J.]
Dubin, Jeffrey E. ....'— '97 C.107 B.A. L.1003 J.D. [Javitch,B.&R.]
Dubin & Joseph, (BV) .... 75 Public Sq.
Ducatman, Robert P., (AV) ....'— '80 C&L.161 B.A., J.D. [Jones D.] (See Pat. Sect.)
DuChez, Neil A., (AV) '46 '72
C.251 B.Ch.E. L.161 J.D. [Renner,O.B.&S.] (See Pat. Sect.)
Ducoff, Ronni Elise, (BV) ....'55 '87 C.241 B.S. L.912 J.D. 1200 Ontario, 9th Fl.
Duddy, Suzanne ....'75 '00 C.473 B.A. L.608 J.D. [Ⓐ Ulmer&B.]
Dudley, Vincent B. ....'60 '97 C&L.574 B.A., J.D. Dep. Dir., Enforcement Svcs.
Duff, Timothy J., (BV) ....'64 '90 C.207 B.A. L.930 J.D. [Berns,O.&G.]
Duffy, Kevin T. ....'46 '76 C&L.161 B.A., J.D. V.P., Natl City Bk.
Duffy, Mary Beth ....'— '89 C.473 B.S.B.A. L.1003 J.D. [Ⓐ Kadish,H.&W.]
Dugan, Matthew P. '67 '00
C.980 B.E.M.E. L.989 J.D. [Ⓐ Fay,S.F.M.&M.] (See Pat. Sect.)
Dugan, Patrick J., (AV) ....'57 '82 C.97 B.S. L.608 J.D. [Squire,S.&D.] (⊙Columbus)
Duggar, Raymond E. ....'47 '99 C.107 B.A. L.989 J.D. [Ⓐ Gurney,M.&M.]
Dugovics, Jill T. ....'56 '84 C.381 B.A. L.1003 J.D. Asst. V.P., Society Natl. Bk.
Duhamel, Marcel C., (AV) ....'68 '93 C.930 B.A. L.145 J.D. [Ⓐ Vorys,S.S.&P.]
Dukes, Patrick M., (AV) ....'64 '91 C.980 B.A. L.608 J.D. 323 Lakeside Ave., W.
Dulabon, David W. ....'— '01 C.645 B.A. L.880 J.D. [Ⓐ Jones D.]
Dunbar, Sandra ....'47 '72 C.381 B.A. L.8 J.D. NLRB
Duncan, Ed E., (AV⊤) ....'48 '74 C.604 B.A. L.597 J.D. [Tucker E.&W.]
Duncan, William A. ....'— '87 C.1260 B.A. L.8 J.D. [Kadish,H.&W.]
Dunford, Oliver J. ....'73 '01 C.201 B.A. L.989 J.D. [Ⓐ Thompson H.]
Dunlap, Jeffrey S. ....'63 '89 C.188 B.S. L.309 J.D. [Ulmer&B.]
Dunn, Carrie ....'77 '03 C.608 B.A. L.665 J.D. [Ⓐ Vorys,S.S.&P.]
Dunn, George J., (AV) ....'35 '60 C.976 B.S. L.309 LL.B. [Ⓒ Taft,S.&H.]
Dunn, Howard A. ....'51 '78 C.473 B.A. L.607 J.D. 34840 Sherwood Dr.
Dunn, James J. ....'44 '84 C.363 B.S. L.989 J.D. 1300 Ontario
Dunn, John P., (AV) ....'— '74 C.436 B.A. L.276 J.D. [Jones D.]
Dunn, Milton, (Co., L.P.A.), (AV) ....'18 '48 C.608 B.S. L.930 J.D. P.O. Box 21752
Dunn, Richard W. ....'29 '63 C.251 L.1003 J.D. 55 Public Sq.‡
Dunn, Theodore M., Jr., (AV) ....'— '82 C.473 B.A. L.161 J.D. [Buckley K.]
Dunn, William P. ....'72 '99 C.699 A.B. L.861 J.D. [Ⓐ Frantz W.]
Dunson, James A., Jr., (BV) ....'53 '78 C&L.851 [Dunson&D.]
Dunson, Jas. A. ....'16 '47 C.381 L.161 J.D. [Dunson&D.]
Dunson & Dunson, (BV) .... 21851 Center Ridge Rd.
Durchslag, Melvyn R., (AV) '40 '65 C&L.597 B.S., J.D.
Prof. of Law, Case Western Reserve Law Sch.
Durkin, Elizabeth M. '49 '74
C.604 B.A. L.930 J.D. Asst. Staff Coun., Women's Fed. Svgs. Bk.
Durkin, George J., (AV) ....'34 '62 C.602 B.B.S. L.930 LL.B. [Ⓒ Cavitch,F.D.&F.]
Dus, Kathleen G. ....'57 '88 C.62 B.A. L.1003 J.D. 1100 Huntington Bldg.
Duvin, Robert P., (AV) ....'37 '61 C.347 B.A. L.1119 J.D. [Duvin,C.&H.]

Duvin, Cahn & Hutton, A Legal Professional Association, (AV) BB
Erieview Tower, 20th Floor, 1301 East Ninth Street, 44114
Telephone: 216-696-7600 Facsimile: 216-696-2038
Email: attorneys@duvin.com URL: http://www.duvinlaw.com
Robert P. Duvin; Stephen J. Cahn; Lee J. Hutton; Marc J. Bloch; Andrew C. Meyer; Martin S. List; Craig M. Brown; Frank W. Buck; Neal B. Wainblat; John T. Billick; Kenneth B. Stark; Robert M. Wolff; Sue Marie Douglas; Stephen J. Sferra; Christine C. Covey; Jon M. Dileno; Suellen Oswald; Janette McCarthy Louard; Kathleen M. Kordeleski; Kenneth D. Schwartz; Bradley A. Sherman; Barry Y. Freeman; Lessie Milton Jones;—Lisa Froimson Mann; M. Terence Cawley; Jonathan S. Forman; Teresa R. Pofok; Patricia S. Conti; Fredrick W. Englehart; Heidi Alten; Shannon K. Patton; Timothy S. Anderson; Bonnie L. Kristan; Lisa A. Cottle; James P. Smith; Patrick H. Lewis; Stephanie Seeley; Sherrie M. Mikhail; Lisa Orlando; Richard D. Porter; Meredith A. Lobritz; Kathy Scadden; Daniel Connell; Emily Fiftal; Julia G. Wainblat. Of Counsel: Jeffrey A. Belkin; Mark V. Webber; Linda Hauserman Harrold.
Labor Relations Law and Litigation. Public Employment Relations, Civil Trial and Appellate Practice in all State and Federal Courts, Employee Benefit and Equal Opportunity Law, OSHA, Workers' Compensation Law and Commercial Litigation.
Representative Clients: Ameritech; B.F. Goodrich Aerospace; Cleveland-Akron-Canton Supermarket Industry; The Scott Fetzer Co.; B.P. America; Electronic Data Systems Corporation.
See Professional Biographies, CLEVELAND, OHIO

Dvorin, David M. ....'71 '97 C.473 B.A. L.608 J.D. 1301 East Ninth Street, Suite 3300
Dwyer, John J., (AV) ....'17 '45 C.210 B.A. L.309 LL.B. 127 Public Sq.‡
Dyczek, Carl J., (AV) ....'54 '80 C.107 B.A. L.161 J.D. [Roetzel&A.]
Dyke, Lori Anne E. ....'69 '98 C.363 B.A. L.161 J.D. Asst. Pros. Atty.
Dysert, David C. ....'55 '90 C.381 B.S. L.8 J.D. Ernst & Young, Llp
Dzenitis, Paul A. ....'67 '94 C.674 B.A. L.383 J.D. [Buckingham,D.&B.]
Earp, Robert H., III ....'70 '96 C&L.201 B.S., J.D. [McDonald H.]
Easley, Leesa M. '60 '89
C.473 B.A. L.1003 J.D. V.P. & Assoc. Coun., KeyBank Natl. Assn.
Ebert, Gary A., (AV) ....'50 '78 C.49 B.S. L.1003 J.D. [Seeley,S.&E.L.&Assoc.]
Eby, Gary L. ....'50 '76 C.608 B.M. L.1003 J.D. 12900 Lake Ave., Suite 1828
Eckart, Dennis E. ....'50 '74 C.973 B.A. L.1003 J.D. [Baker&H.] (⊙Wash., DC)
Eddington, Isaac J. ....'73 '00 C.1335 B.A. L.309 J.D. [Ⓐ Ulmer&B.]
Eddy, Robert H., (AV) ....'— '79 C.602 B.A. L.851 J.D. [Gallagher S.]
Edelman, Mark S., (AV) ....'61 '86 C.477 B.A. L.608 J.D. [McGlinchey S.]

Edelstein, Robert, (BV) '58 '83 C.861 B.A. L.930 J.D.
23825 Commerce Park Suite A, 44122-5834
Telephone: 216-514-4981 Fax: 216-514-4987
Email: RECUBE@AOL.com URL: http://www.edelsteincollectionlaw.com
Language: Spanish
General Business Practice, Commercial Collections, Debtor and Creditor, Bankruptcy, Landlord and Tenant Law, Litigation.
See Professional Biographies, CLEVELAND, OHIO

Edgehouse, Gregory J. '54 '79
C.930 B.A. L.188 J.D. V.P.& Sr. Coun., KeyBank Natl. Assn.
Edwards, Michelle Caryn ....'55 '92 C&L.930 B.A., J.D. Pros. Off.
Edwards, Paul N., (AV) ....'53 '79 C.608 B.S. L.1003 J.D. [McDonald H.]
Edwards, William D. ....'67 '94 C.967 B.A. L.930 J.D. [Ulmer&B.]
Edwards, William J. ....'44 '69 C.434 B.A. L.930 LL.B. First Asst. U.S. Atty.
Egan, Patrick J. ....'— '01 C.509 B.A. L.229 J.D. [Ⓐ Baker&H.]
Egleston, James D. ....'68 '94 C.8 B.S.B.A. L.607 J.D. [Ⓐ W.Coyne]
Ehrenreich, Leonard, (AV) ....'47 '73 C.8 B.A. L.930 J.D. [Ehrenreich&Assoc.]
Ehrenreich & Associates, (AV) .... 1130 Leader Building
Ehrman, James W., (AV) ....'48 '74 C.309 A.B. L.659 J.D. [Porter W.M.&A.]
Ehrnfelt, Walter F., III, (AV) ....'52 '88 C.967 B.A. L.1003 J.D. [W.Coyne]
Eiber, Keven Drummond, (AV) ....'58 '83 C.339 B.A. L.904 J.D. [Brouse M.]
Eide, Randolph S. ....'45 '70 C.611 B.A. L.930 J.D. 45 Erieview Plz.
Eidnier, Robert J., (AV) ....'57 '82 C.473 B.S. L.893 J.D. [Squire,S.&D.]
Eilers, S. Stuart, (AV) ....'38 '63 C.951 B.A. L.477 J.D. [Thompson H.]
Einhorn, Theodore ....'69 '97 C.855 B.A. L.128 J.D. [Ⓐ Kahn K.]
Eisen, Brian N., (AV) ....'66 '92 C&L.309 A.B., J.D. [Greene&M.]
Eisen, Hermine G., (BV) ....'39 '81 C.930 B.A. L.1003 J.D. [Eisen&W.] ⊙
Eisen, Saul, (AV) ....'35 '59 C&L.930 B.A., LL.B. 200 Public Square
Eisen & Westfall, LLP, (BV) .... 75 Public Square, Suite 1005 (⊙Akron, Columbus)
Eisenberg, Brian M., (AV) ....'42 '67 C.659 B.S. L.477 J.D. [Calfee,H.&G.]
Eisenberg, Gregg A. ....'71 '97 C.696 B.A. L.608 J.D. [Benesch,F.C.&A.]
Eisenberg, Hyman ....'31 '67 C.608 B.S. L.1003 J.D. 6917 Carnegie Ave.
Eisenberg, Richard D., (BV) ....'37 '63 C.608 B.A. L.930 LL.B. [Zimmerman,C.E.&M.]
Eisenberg, Steven A. ....'70 '95 C.473 B.S. L.1003 J.D. [Baker&H.]
Eisenhardt, Howard A., III, (AV) ....'56 '82 C.216 B.A. L.117 J.D. 1215 Superior Ave.
Eisner, Gary W., (BV) ....'46 '73 C&L.1003 B.B.A., J.D. 3241 Superior Ave.
Eisner, Michael L. ....'68 '95 C.319 B.A. L.1003 J.D. [Ⓐ Friedman,D.&S.]
Ekelman, Daniel L., (AV) ....'26 '52 C.611 A.B. L.930 LL.B. [Calfee,H.&G.] ‡
Eklund, Claudia Rieth, (AV) ....'51 '79 C.161 B.A. L.1003 J.D. [Lowe E.W.&M.]
Eklund, John J., (AV) ....'55 '80 C.867 B.A. L.902 J.D. [Calfee,H.&G.]
Eklund, Paul D., (AV) ....'— '78 C.473 A.B. L.930 J.D. [Davis&Y.]
Elfvin, Bruce B., (AV) ....'47 '72 C.597 B.A. L.161 J.D. [Elfvin&B.]
Elfvin & Besser, (AV) .... 4070 Mayfield Road
Elhamshari, Muhammad Kamal, The Law Office of '72 '01
C&L.124 B.A., J.D. 7450 Baldwin Creek Dr.
Elk, Arthur M. ....'47 '73 C.930 B.A. L.161 J.D. [Elk&E.] ⊙
Elk, David J., (BV) ....'39 '65 C&L.930 B.B.A., J.D. [Elk&E.] ⊙

Elk & Elk Co., L.P.A., (BV)
Landerhaven Corporate Center, 6100 Parkland Boulevard, 44124-4187 ⊙
Telephone: 888-355-6446
Email: kthompson@elkandelk.com URL: http://www.elkandelklaw.com
David J. Elk; Arthur M. Elk.
Automobile Accidents, Product Defects, Nursing Home Neglect, Medical Malpractice, Personal Injury.
Columbus, Ohio Office: Fifth Third Center, Capital Square, 21 East State Street, Suite 320, 43215. Telephone: 1-888-ELK-OHIO.
See Professional Biographies, CLEVELAND, OHIO

Ellerin, Jerome M., (AV) ....'31 '56 C&L.930 B.B.A., J.D. [J.M.Ellerin]
Ellerin, Jerome M., Co., L.P.A., (AV) .... 1301 E. 9th St.
Elliott, Linda U. ....'— '91 C.161 B.A. L.1001 J.D. [Ⓒ Calfee,H.&G.]
Elliott, Michael E. ....'53 '80 C.385 B.A. L.930 J.D. [Tucker E.&W.]
Elliott, Pete C., (AV) ....'59 '84 C.216 B.A. L.930 J.D. [Benesch,F.C.&A.]
Ellis, John R. ....'53 '79 C.107 B.A. L.990 J.D. I.R.S.
Ellis, Michael A., (AV) ....'54 '77 C.659 B.A. L.228 J.D. [Porter W.M.&A.]
Ellis, Nicole Marie ....'74 '99 C.97 B.S.B.A. L.989 J.D. Crim. Pros.
Ellis, Stephen C., (AV) ....'47 '72 C.207 B.A. L.930 J.D. [Tucker E.&W.]
Ellsworth, Jeffrey S. '68 '00 C&L.1335 B.S., J.D.
(adm. in CA; not adm. in OH) [Ⓐ Wegman,H.&V.]
Elzeer, Bradley E., II ....'64 '91 C.62 B.A. L.930 J.D. [B.E.Elzeer]
Elzeer, Jeffrey M. ....'66 '91 C.62 B.A L.930 J.D. [Ⓐ Rodgers]
Elzeer, Kimrey D. ....'67 '96 C.62 B.A. L.989 J.D. [Elzeer,K.D.]
Elzeer, Bradley E. .... 55 Public Sq., Ste. 2222
Elzeer, Kimrey Denise .... 625 Rockefeller Building
Embleton, Jeffrey M., (AV) ....'50 '75 C.610 B.A. L.930 J.D. [Mansour,G.G.&M.]
Emerson, Frank D. ....'16 '40 C.8 A.B. L.930 LL.B. Prof. of Law, Cleveland State Univ.
Emery, Steven ....'— '02 C.860 B.A. L.930 J.D. [Ⓐ Weltman,W.&R.]
Emrick, Charles R., Jr., (AV) ....'29 '58 C.610 B.S.C. L.1003 J.D. [Calfee,H.&G.] ‡
Endress, Jeffrey C., (BV) ....'54 '80 C.347 B.A. L.930 J.D. [Endress&E.]
Endress & Endress Co., L.P.A., (BV) .... 17119 Madison Ave.
Engle, David C. ....'— '81 C.608 B.S. L.8 J.D. [Buckley K.]
Englehart, Fredrick W. ....'— '97 C.766 B.A. L.930 J.D. [Ⓐ Duvin,C.&H.]
English, Brent L., Law Offices of, (BV) '50 '80
C.608 B.A. L.930 J.D. 1500 W. 3rd Street, Suite 470
English, Lawrence K. ....'61 '89 C.930 B.S. L.1003 J.D. N.E. OH Reg. Sewer Dist.
English, Matthew D. ....'72 '99 C.475 B.A. L.124 J.D. [Ⓐ Vorys,S.S.&P.]
Ensign, Cathryn R., (AV) ....'54 '86 C.161 B.A. L.1003 J.D. [Brouse M.]
Ensign, Gregory M., (BV) '49 '75 C.611 B.A. L.117 J.D.
V.P.-Admin., Secy. & Gen. Coun., Kirkwood Industries, Inc.
Entin, Jonathan L. '47 '82 C.103 A.B. L.597 J.D.
(adm. in DC; not adm. in OH) Prof. of Law & Poli. Sci., Case Western Reserve Univ.
Entis, Robert ....'15 '53 C.251 L.1003 J.D. 4500 Rockside Rd.
Epp, Henry C., (BV) ....'45 '72 C.381 B.B.A. L.930 J.D. 55 Public Sq.
Epstein, Robert E. ....'49 '76 C.608 B.A. L.7 J.D. 2421 Allen Blvd.
Erb, L. William ....'60 '00 C.385 B.A. L.989 J.D. [Ⓐ Porter W.M.&A.]
Erenburg, Kristin R. ....'74 '04 C.477 B.A. L.989 J.D. [Ⓐ Taft,S.&H.]
Ernewein, Michael E., (BV) ....'48 '73 C.93 B.A. L.569 J.D. [Kolick,G.&E.]
Erney, Jeffry J. ....'60 '88 C.161 B.S. L.930 J.D. [Thompson H.]
Ernst, Christopher M., (AV) ....'66 '91 C.860 B.A. L.930 J.D. [Weston H.]
Ertle, John Beardsley, Jr., (BV) ....'62 '87 C.722 B.A. L.1003 J.D. [Ertle,J.B.]
Ertle, John B., Jr., (BV) .... 21300 Lorain Rd.
Esborn, Theodore J., (BV) ....'52 '79 C.901 B.A. L.930 J.D. [McDonald H.]
Eschbach-Hall, Patricia ....'— '99 C.385 B.A. L.608 J.D. [Ⓐ Jones D.]
Eschedor, Jennifer L. ....'67 '93 C.97 B.A. L.608 J.D. [Ⓑ Baker&H.]
Eschweiler, Thomas G. ....'67 '97 C.475 B.S.E.E. L.802 J.D. [Eschweiler&Assoc.]
Eschweiler & Associates, LLC .... 629 Euclid Ave., Ste. 1210
Escovar, Thomas J., (AV) ....'40 '69 C.573 B.A. L.1003 J.D. [Steuer,E.B.&B.]
Eshelman, C. Richard, (BV) ....'37 '68 C.656 B.S. L.7 J.D. [Eshelman] ⊙
Eshelman Legal Group, (BV)
5005 Rockside Road, Suite 600 (⊙Canton, Cuyahoga Falls, Youngstown)
Eterovich, Janet M. ....'35 '60 C.251 B.B.A. L.1003 J.D. 1116 Englewood Dr.‡
Ettinger, Steven Z. '60 '84 C&L.978 B.S., J.D.
(adm. in NJ; not adm. in OH) Tax Atty., BP America, Inc.
Eva, W. Allan, III ....'60 '87 C.860 B.A. L.930 J.D. 9601 Corporate Cir.
Evanick, Barbara A. ....'67 '95 C.201 B.S.B.A. L.1003 J.D. Atty., Bur. of Workers Comp.
Evans, Christina D'Eramo ....'— '91 C.473 B.A. L.930 J.D. [Hahn L.&P.]
Evans, Neil K., (AV) ....'36 '64 C.696 B.A. L.659 LL.B. [Ⓒ Hahn L.&P.]
Evans, Susan M. ....'66 '93 C.970 B.A. L.1003 J.D. [Lustig,E.&L.]

Everett, Margaret Dodane, (AV) ...... '60 '85 C.473 A.B. L.930 J.D. [A Vorys,S.S.&P.]
Ewers, John J. ...... '20 '51 C&L.724 LL.B. 6730 Stafford Dr.
Ext, Traci L. ...... '73 '98 C.691 B.A. L.309 J.D. Legal Aid Soc. of Cleveland
Eyman, Culver F., III ...... '55 '80 C&L.161 B.A., J.D. 267 E. 197
Eyre, Paul P., (AV) ...... '47 '75 C&L.966 B.A., J.D. [Baker&H.] (⊙New York, NY)
Ezolt, Russell A. ...... '40 '71 C.999 B.M.E. L.1003 J.D. Dist.Coun., Immig. & Nat. Serv.
Fabens, Andrew L., III, (AV) ...... '42 '67 C.976 A.B. L.145 J.D. [Thompson H.]
Fabian, Bethany L. ...... '— '02 C.999 B.A. L.276 J.D. [A Baker&H.]
Fabian, Ernest E. ...... '24 '55 C.610 B.S.C. L.1003 J.D. 8511 Pin Oak Dr.
Fabian, John D. ...... '74 '02 C.813 B.A. L.276 J.D. [A McDonald H.]
Fadel, William I., (BV) ...... '43 '69 C&L.930 B.A., J.D. [Wuliger,F.&B.]
Faeges, Jay R., (BV) ...... '60 '91 C.161 B.S. L.1003 J.D. [Goodman W.M.]
Fafrak, Kenneth W., Jr. '64 '03
C.161 B.E.E. L.989 J.D. [A Renner,O.B.&S.] (See Pat. Sect.)
Fagan, Christopher B., (AV) '37 '65
C.602 B.S.M.E. L.276 J.D. [B Fay,S.F.M.&M.] (See Pat. Sect.)
Fagnilli, David J., (AV) ...... '86 C.999 B.A. L.1003 J.D. [Davis&Y.]
Fahrer, Clare, (AV) ...... '14 '49 C.203 A.B. L.150 J.D. 1370 W. 6th St.
Falin, William H., (AV) ...... '61 '87 C.610 A.B. L.1003 J.D. [Moscarino&T.]
Falk, Arthur V. ...... '24 '54 C.930 A.B. L.1003 J.D. [Falk&S.]
Falk, Bryan H. ...... '72 '97 C.473 B.A. L.930 J.D. [McDonald H.]
Falk, Patricia J. '57 '86 C.867 B.A. L.546 J.D.
(adm. in NE; not adm. in OH) Assoc. Prof. of Law, Cleveland Marshall Coll. of Law
Falk, Ryan W. ...... '77 '03 C.8 B.S. L.930 J.D. [A Calfee,H.&G.] (See Pat. Sect.)
Falk & Scrivens, (BV) ...... 2628 Detroit Ave.
Fallon, Brian M. ...... '55 '80 C.276 B.S.B.A. L.930 J.D. [B.M.Fallon]
Fallon, Christine A. ...... '66 '91 C.1149 B.A. L.608 J.D. 1640 Standard Bldg.
Fallon, Dominic J., (AV) ...... '33 '59 C.381 A.B. L.930 LL.B. 1640 Standard Bldg.
Fallon, James C. ...... '64 '94 C.602 B.A. L.262 J.D. Atty., Sherwin-Williams Co.
Fallon, Brian M., Co., L.P.A. ...... 1370 Ontario Street
Familo, Edward D., (AV) ...... '21 '48 C&L.930 A.B., LL.B. [Cavitch,F.D.&F.]
Fanger, Jeffrey J. ...... '66 '92 C.273 B.A. L.608 J.D. [Fanger]
Fanger Law Office ...... 600 Superior Ave. E., Ste. 1300
Fanos, William R., (AV) '53 '80 C.980 B.A. L.1003 J.D.
V.P., Key Tr. Co. of Ohio N.A.
Fanter, (Guenther) Karl ...... '— '02 C.97 B.A. L.309 J.D. [A Baker&H.]
Faranda, Christine M. ...... '— '96 C.161 B.B.A. L.989 J.D. [A Buckingham,D.&B.]
Farchione, Joseph A., Jr., (AV) ...... '62 '87 C.107 B.A. L.930 J.D. [Sutter,O.&F.]
Farkas, Bryan J. ...... '— '00 C.112 B.A. L.930 J.D. [A Vorys,S.S.&P.]
Farkas, David S ...... '74 '03 C.1539 B.A. L.446 J.D. [A Ross,B.&S.]
Farkas, Gregory R. ...... '72 '98 C.475 B.A. L.477 J.D. [A Frantz W.]
Farley, Donald W., (AV) ...... '30 '57 C.363 B.S.S. L.930 LL.B. 2401 Superior Viaduct
Farling, Harold E., (AV) ...... '66 '91 C.385 B.A. L.930 J.D. [Kovach&F.]
Farmer, James P., Jr., (AV) ...... '51 '81 C.610 B.S. L.1003 J.D. [Schneider,S.R.&L.]
Farnan, Brian P. ...... '76 '02 C.679 B.S. L.723 J.D. [A Ulmer&B.]
Farnan, John G., (AV) ...... '61 '87 C.276 B.A. L.602 J.D. [Weston H.]
Farrall, William P., (AV) ...... '45 '72 C.532 B.A. L.1003 J.D. [A Reminger&R.]
Farrell, Charles J., Jr. ...... '66 '92 C.321 A.B. L.30 J.D. [A W.Coyne]
Farrell, Elise Louise ...... '54 '79 C.912 B.A. L.930 J.D. Legal Aid Soc. of Cleve.
Farrell, Michael F., Law Office of, (AV) '51 '76
C.363 A.B. L.930 J.D. 614 W. Superior Ave., Ste. 1300
Farrell, Michael K., (AV) ...... '62 '88 C.473 B.A. L.930 J.D. [Baker&H.]
Farrell, Patrick M., (BV) ...... '57 '83 C.97 B.S.B.A. L.1003 J.D. [Hildebrand,W.&F.]
Farren, Anthony S. ...... '69 '96 L.1003 J.D. [A Bilfield&S.]
Farroni, Mark B. ...... '— '83 C.201 B.A. L.93 J.D. [B Jones D.]
Fatica, John A., (BV) ...... '63 '91 C.473 B.S. L.1003 J.D. [B M.C.Hennenberg]
Faulkner, David G. ...... '46 '86 C.381 B.S. L.1003 J.D. [Faulkner,M.&P.]
Faulkner, George H. ...... '51 '80 C.381 B.S. L.589 J.D. [Faulkner,M.&P.]
Faulkner, Muskovitz & Phillips, LLP, (AV) ...... 820 West Superior Avenue, Ninth Floor
Faust, Geo. H. ...... '15 '54 C.45 M.A. L.1003 LL.B. 615 Leader Bldg.
Fauvie, Lori L. ...... '74 '03 C.610 B.S. L.989 J.D. [A Vorys,S.S.&P.]
Faxon, Robert S. ...... '— '92 C.880 B.A. L.930 J.D. [Jones D.]
Fay, Regan J., (AV) ...... '— '74 C.456 B.S. L.273 J.D. [Jones D.] (See Pat. Sect.)

Fay, Sharpe, Fagan, Minnich & McKee, LLP, (AV) BR
1100 Superior Avenue, Seventh Floor, 44114
Telephone: 216-861-5582 FAX: 216-241-1666
Email: fs@faysharpe.com URL: http://www.faysharpe.com
Members of Firm: Mark E. Bandy; John P. Cornely; Joseph D. Dreher; Jude A. Fry; Steven M. Haas; Michael E. Hudzinski; Richard M. Klein; Thomas E. Kocovsky, Jr.; Sandra M. Koenig; Scott Andrew McCollister; Jay F. Moldovanyi; Philip J. Moy, Jr.; Timothy E. Nauman; Patrick R. Roche; James E. Scarbrough; Ann M. Skerry; Mark S. Svat; Brian E. Turung; Gregory S. Vickers; Robert V. Vickers. Associates: Matthew P. Dugan; Patrick D. Floyd; Colleen Flynn Goss; Karl William Hauber; Eric M. Highman; Erik J. Overberger†; Sue Ellen Phillips; Robert A. Sidoti; Robert M. Sieg; Scott M. Slaby; Joseph E. Waters†; Jonathan A. Withrow; Jeffrey N. Zahn; Marina V. Zalevsky; John S. Zanghi. Of Counsel: E. Kent Daniels, Jr.; Christopher B. Fagan; James W. McKee; Richard J. Minnich; Thomas E. Young.
Providing a complete range of Domestic and International Intellectual Property Law services including Patents, Trademarks, Copyrights, Trade Secrets, Licensing Matters, Unfair Competition Law and Litigation.
†Member: Cleveland, Ohio State and American Bar Associations; Cleveland Intellectual Property Law Association; American Intellectual Property Law Association.
See Professional Biographies, CLEVELAND, OHIO

Fazio, Catherine ...... '— '04 C.276 B.A. L.124 J.D. [A Gallagher S.]
Fazio, John C. '38 '65 C&L.930 B.A., J.D.
Pres. & Mng. Editor, Justinian Publishing Co.
Fazio, Stephen M. ...... '72 '03 C.454 B.S. L.124 J.D. [A Squire,S.&D.]
Fazio, Tyrone Charles ...... '50 '79 C.161 B.A. L.989 J.D. [T.C.Fazio]
Fazio, Timothy C., Law Offices of ...... 55 Public Square, Suite 2200
Feagan, Glenn D. ...... '62 '89 C.383 B.S.B.A. L.1340 J.D. [G.D.Feagan]
Feagan, Glenn D., PSC, Law Offices of ...... 6200 Rockside Rd.
Federman, Jerry I., Law Offices of, (BV) '47 '76
C.381 B.S.Ed. L.1003 J.D. 526 Superior Ave., E.
Feeling, F. Drexel ...... '— '95 C.659 B.S. L.608 J.D. [Jones D.] (See Pat. Sect.)
Fegen, Joseph P. ...... '69 '95 C.201 B.A. L.117 J.D. [A Climaco,L.P.W.&G.]
Feher, Thomas L., (AV) ...... '60 '87 C.381 B.S. L.1003 J.D. [Thompson H.]
Feighan, Ann M. ...... '58 '92 C.161 B.A. L.1003 J.D. Asst. Pros. Atty.
Feighan, Joseph E., Jr., (AV) ...... '30 '60 C.201 B.A. L.1003 J.D. 11009 Edgewater Drive
Feigi, Diane L. ...... '72 '98 C.8 B.A. L.989 J.D. [B Baker&H.]
Fein, Alvin A. ...... '16 '57 C.608 L.1003 J.D. 21825 Chagrin Blvd.
Fein, Robert A., (AV) ...... '46 '70 C.608 B.S. L.161 J.D. [Ulmer&B.]
Fein, Robert U., (AV) ...... '63 '88 C&L.608 B.S.B.A., J.D. [B Kahn K.]
Feinberg, Melvin E. ...... '41 '69 C.930 B.A. L.1003 J.D. N.L.R.B.
Feinberg, Paul H., (AV) ...... '38 '65 C.659 A.B. L.309 LL.B. [Baker&H.]

Felber, Mark B., (BV) '58 '84 C.1036 B.A. L.930 J.D.
1525 Leader Building, 526 Superior Avenue N.E., 44114
Telephone: 216-363-3900 Fax: 216-241-2286
Email: m.felber.esq@att.net URL: http://www.lawyers.com/felberlaw
General Civil and Criminal Practice, Drug Crimes, Juvenile Crimes, Parole and Probation, Litigation, Family Law, Divorce, Child Custody, Spousal and Child Support, Domestic Violence, Visitation Rights, Personal Injury, Head and Spinal Injuries, Sexual Abuse, Slip and Fall, Trucking Accidents, Automobile Negligence, Wrongful Death, Nursing Home Litigation, Social Security Disability, Dog Bites, Workers' Compensation, Trusts and Estates, Estate Planning, Guardianship, Wills and Probate, DWI, Bankruptcy, Admiralty, Maritime Injuries, Aviation, Airplane Crashes, Consumer Law, Consumer Fraud, Lemon Law, Unsafe Products, Warranties, Education, Employment Law, Sexual Harassment, Wrongful Termination, Medical Malpractice, Products Liability, Drugs and Medical Devices, Real Estate, Buying or Selling a Home, Business Law, Debt and Credit, Collections, Creditor's Rights, Contracts, Lawsuits, Starting a Business.
See Professional Biographies, CLEVELAND, OHIO

Feldman, Irwin M., (AV) ...... '39 '64 C&L.966 B.B.A., J.D. [Benesch,F.C.&A.]
Feldman, Marvin J., (AV) ...... '30 '55 C&L.930 B.B.A., J.D. 815 Superior Ave., N.E.
Feldman, Rubin ...... '26 '53 C.477 B.B.A L.1003 LL.B. Sr. V.P., Amer. Greeting Corp.
Feldman, Steven M. ...... '66 '93 C.478 B.A. L.1194 J.D. Capstone Realty Advsr.
Feliciano, José C., (AV) ...... '50 '75 C.363 B.A. L.1003 J.D. [Baker&H.]
Feliciano, Santiago, Jr. ...... '51 '77 C.363 B.A. L.989 J.D. 1422 Euclid Ave., Ste. 1162
Felker, Nathan A. ...... '72 '02 C.273 B.B.A. L.930 J.D. [A Hurtuk&D.]
Felty, Kriss D., (AV) ...... '54 '83 C.930 B.A. L.8 J.D. [Shapiro&F.]
Fenn, David R. ...... '58 '98 C.970 B.A. L.1003 J.D. [A Mazanec,R.&R.]
Fenner, Kathryn Braun '— '84
C&L.161 B.A., J.D. V.P. & Sr. Coun., KeyBank Natl. Assn.
Fenske, Audrey A. ...... '62 '89 C.966 B.A. L.893 J.D. Ernst & Young
Feran, Amy Rollason ...... '53 '79 C.103 A.B. L.893 J.D. 5650 Hawthorne Dr.
Ferguson, Rhonda S. ...... '69 '94 C.597 B.S. L.930 J.D. Asst. Gen. Coun., Ferro Corp.
Fernandez, Susan E. ...... '57 '87 C.608 B.S. L.7 J.D. N.L.R.B.
Fernengel, Gregory ...... '75 '03 C.608 B.S. L.124 J.D. [A Pearne&G.] (See Pat. Sect.)
Ferrante, Jason P. ...... '73 '04 C.610 B.A. L.989 J.D. [A Sutter,O.&F.]
Ferraro, Adrienne M. ...... '— '03 C.970 B.A. L.608 J.D. [A Jones D.]
Ferraro, James L., (AV⊕) ...... '57 '83 C&L.472 B.B.A., J.D. [Kelley&F.] (⊙Miami, FL)
Ferreri, Robert A. ...... '49 '80 C.945 B.S. L.1003 J.D. 820 W. Superior Ave., Ste. 310
Fertel, Robert M. ...... '47 '72 C&L.608 B.A., J.D. [A Zashin&R.]
Fetzek, Raymond, (AV) ...... '26 '52 C.472 L.607 5566 Pearl Rd.
Feudo, Vincent A. ...... '39 '65 C.610 B.S.J. L.1003 J.D. [B Nicola,G.&C.]
Feuer, Charles E. ...... '58 '89 C.381 B.B.A. L.1003 J.D. 405 Longspur Rd.
Feuerman, Richard J. ...... '72 '99 C.608 B.A. L.1003 J.D. [A Carlisle,M.R.K.&U.]
Fidler, J. Paul ...... '71 '96 C.645 B.S. L.608 J.D. [Schneider,S.R.&L.]
Fields, Darrell A. ...... '58 '83 C.967 B.A. L.329 J.D. [A Forbes,F.&Assoc.]
Fifner, Greta E. ...... '56 '86 C.577 B.F.A. L.1003 J.D. Jud. Ref.
Fiftal, Emily ...... '— '04 C.587 B.A. L.124 J.D. [A Duvin,C.&H.]
Figelman, Jacob M. ...... '78 '04 C.446 B.A. L.124 J.D. [A Urban&P.]
Fiktus, Richard D. ...... '53 '78 C.610 B.B.A. L.161 J.D. [Rolf&G.]
Filak, John J. ...... '30 '56 C.152 A.B. L.930 LL.B. Asst. Coun., Women's Fed. Svgs. Bk.
Fillo, Nicholas J., (AV) ...... '38 '63 C.363 B.S.S. L.930 J.D. [Fillo]
Fillo Law Firm, (AV) ...... 1360 W. 9th Street
Fincun, Jeffrey D., (AV) ...... '46 '73 C.105 B.S. L.930 J.D. [Weston H.]
Finer, Joel J. '38 '64 C.563 B.B.A. L.976 LL.B.
(adm. in DC; not adm. in OH) 1801 Eculid Ave.‡
Finerman, Scott C. ...... '60 '87 C.477 B.B.A. L.1003 J.D. 1300 E. Ninth St.
Fingerhut, Lloyd J. ...... '31 '59 C.608 B.S. L.1003 J.D. 16645 Granite Rd.‡
Fink, Franklin E. ...... '62 '89 C.881 B.A. L.188 J.D. Asst. Gen. Coun., AG Properties
Fink, Joseph J., (BV) ...... '52 '79 C.473 L.851 J.D. 11221 Pearl Rd.
Fink, Kevin H. ...... '— '02 C.473 B.S. L.124 J.D. [A Jones D.]
Fink, Scott D. ...... '72 '98 C.473 B.A. L.124 J.D. [A Weltman,W.&R.]
Finley, Bonnie S. ...... '69 '95 C.228 B.A. L.910 J.D. [A Walter&H.]
Finley, David G., (BV) ...... '59 '84 C.902 B.A. L.930 J.D. [D.G.Finley]
Finley, David G., Co., L.P.A., (BV) ...... 25 Prospect Avenue, NW, 704-L
Finnerty, Audrine Piasecki ...... '63 '92 C.1356 B.A. L.1003 J.D. 5700 Pearl Road
Fiore, Rose Marie L. ...... '70 '95 C&L.930 B.A., J.D. [Hahn L.&P.]
Fiorella, Andrew G. ...... '— '03 C.107 B.A. L.1556 J.D. [A Jones D.]
Firestone, Julie E. ...... '70 '96 C.473 B.S. L.930 J.D. [B Baker&H.]
Firstenberg, Barbara A., (AV) ...... '44 '81 C.4 M.A. L.1003 J.D. [B.A.Firstenberg&Assoc.]
Firstenberg, Barbara A., & Associates Co., LPA, (AV) ...... 20133 Farnsleigh Rd.
Fischbein-Cohen, Ruth Rose, (BV) ...... '40 '89 C.161 B.A. L.1003 J.D. 3552 Severn Rd.
Fischer, Henry B., (AV) ...... '36 '64 C.597 B.S.Ch.E. L.161 J.D. [H.B.Fischer] (Pat.)
Fischer, Julie A. ...... '71 '99 C.381 B.A. L.1003 J.D. [A McDonald H.]
Fischer, Lynne C. ...... '— '96 C&L.161 B.A., J.D. [B Jones D.]
Fischer, Michelle K. ...... '— '89 C.976 B.A. L.145 J.D. [Jones D.]
Fischer, Rebecca Kucera ...... '74 '99 C.62 B.A. L.930 J.D. [A Porter W.M.&A.]
Fischer, Robert H., Jr. ...... '73 '99 C.610 B.A. L.880 J.D. [A Taft,S.&H.]

Fischer, Henry B., Co., L.P.A., (AV)
26111 Brush Avenue, Suite 400, P.O. Box 32644, 44132-0644
Telephone: 216-731-3535 Fax: 216-261-5252
Email: HBFCoLPA@cs.com URL: http://www.lawyers.com/henryfischerlaw
Henry B. Fischer.
Civil Litigation and Appeals, Construction, Business, General Practice, Municipal, Real Estate Law, Probate, Trusts and Wills.
See Professional Biographies, CLEVELAND, OHIO

Fishel, Ralph J. ...... '23 '54 C.930 L.1003 J.D. 21817 Halburton Rd.
Fisher, Christopher P. ...... '60 '97 C.945 B.S. L.846 J.D. [A Ulmer&B.]
Fisher, Damaris G. ...... '— '00 C.67 B.A. L.878 J.D. [A Thompson H.]
Fisher, Donald J., (AV) ...... '48 '76 C.318 B.A. L.930 J.D. [Porter W.M.&A.]
Fisher, Kenneth J., (AV) ...... '51 '76 C.608 B.A. L.1003 J.D. [K.J.Fisher]
Fisher, Lee I., (AV) '51 '76
C.604 B.A. L.930 J.D. Pres./CEO, Ctr. for Families and Children
Fisher, Ryan H., (AV) ...... '64 '89 C.97 B.A. L.1003 J.D. 75 Public Sq., Suite 914
Fisher, Stanley M. ...... '21 '50 C.930 A.B. L.1003 LL.B. Com. Pleas J.‡
Fisher, Virginia Egan, (BV) ...... '53 '82 C.161 B.B.A. L.1003 J.D. Atty. Gen Off.
Fisher, Kenneth J., Co., L.P.A., (AV) ...... 50 Public Square
Fishman, Aaron A. ...... '72 '99 C&L.851 J.D. [Pearne&G.] (See Pat. Sect.)
Fishman, Gary S., (BV) ...... '52 '82 C.381 B.B.A. L.851 J.D. 75 Public Sq.
Fishman, Lawrence R. '44 '69 C.608 B.S. L.930 J.D.
Assoc. Gen. Coun., Forest City Enterprises, Inc.

Fishman, Mark S., Law Offices of, (BV) '56 '81 C&L.608 B.A., J.D.
The Leader Building, 526 Superior Avenue, Suite 853, 44114
Telephone: 216-781-4800 Fax: 216-621-4121
Email: msf1400@aol.com URL: http://www.markfishman.com
Personal Injury, Automobile Accidents, Worker's Compensation, Dog Bites, Insurance Law.
See Professional Biographies, CLEVELAND, OHIO

Fistek, Thomas G. '76 '04
C.446 B.S.M.E. L.989 J.D. [A Renner,O.B.&S.] (See Pat. Sect.)
Fister, Anna S. ...... '— '03 C.318 B.A. L.201 J.D. [A Gallagher S.] ⊙

FitzGerald, Claudia P., Law Office of, (BV) '53 '80
C.381 B.S. L.1003 J.D. 1370 Ontario St., Ste. 450
Fitzgerald, Edward .... '68 '93 C.608 B.A. L.1003 J.D. 55 Public Sq., Ste. 2222
FitzGerald, Timothy F. .... '50 '77 C.201 B.A. L.1003 J.D. I.R.S.
Fitzgerald, Timothy J., (AV) .... '— '89 C.436 B.S. L.1003 J.D. [Gallagher S.] ⊙
Fitzpatrick, Jon, (AV) .... '36 '77 C.608 B.S.B.A. L.1003 J.D. [🄲 McCarthy,L.C.&L.]
Fitzpatrick, Michael D. '55 '87
C.1062 B.S. L.1003 J.D. Assoc. Coun., The Cincinnati Insurance Co.
Fitzsimmons, Matthew T., (AV) .... '53 '80 C.602 A.B. L.201 J.D. [Nicola,G.&C.]
FitzSimons, Brian W., (AV) .... '46 '74 C.436 A.B. L.930 J.D. [Tucker E.&W.]
Flaherty, James T. .... '28 '64 C&L.93 B.S., J.D. Prof. of Law, Cleveland State Univ.
Flammang, Donna M. .... '51 '75 C.20 B.A. L.161 J.D. [Taft,S.&H.]
Flanagan, Patrick M., (BV) .... '46 '73 C.611 B.A. L.1003 J.D. [Flanagan]
Flanagan, Timothy M. '46 '71
C.610 B.B.A. L.1003 J.D. Comm. Pleas Ct., J. Domestic Relations Div.
Flanagan LLC, (BV) .... 20102 Center Ridge Rd.
Flannery, Sarah C. .... '— '02 C.363 B.S. L.989 J.D. [🄰 Thompson H.]
Fleck, Robert E., (AV) '31 '58 C.930 A.B. L.309 J.D.
1400 Midland Bldg, 101 Prospect Ave., West
Fleming, Charles W. .... '28 '56 C.381 L.1003 LL.B. Presiding & Admin. Mun. J.
Fleming, Jennifer A. Lesny .... '68 '93 C.473 B.A. L.880 J.D. [Thompson H.]
Fleming, Linda K. '66 '92
C.477 B.A. L.893 J.D. V.P & Assoc. Coun., KeyBank Natl. Assn.
Fleshler, David, (AV) .... '57 '85 C.477 A.B. L.93 J.D. 1100 Huntington Bldg.
Flinker, Jon C., (AV) '38 '65 C.188 B.S. L.569 LL.B.
Suite 202, 25550 Chagrin Boulevard (Beachwood)
Flowers, Paul William, (AV) .... '64 '90 C.383 M.A. L.608 J.D. [P.W.Flowers]

Flowers, Paul W., Co., L.P.A., (AV)
Terminal Tower, 35th Floor, 50 Public Square, 44113-2216
Telephone: 216-344-9393 Fax: 216-344-9395
Email: pwf@pwfco.com URL: http://www.pwfco.com
Paul William Flowers.
Civil Litigation, Civil Appeals, Administrative Hearings and Appeals, Business Litigation, Insurance Litigation, Civil Liability, Corporate Law, Real Estate, Estate Planning and Probate Administration.
See Professional Biographies, CLEVELAND, OHIO

Floyd, Lawrence Richard '61 '92
C.347 B.S. L.1003 J.D. Pros. Off., Cuyahoga Co. [L.R.Floyd]
Floyd, Mark S., (AV) .... '58 '83 C.813 A.B. L.178 J.D. [Thompson H.]
Floyd, Patrick D. '63 '93 C.150 B.S.E.E. L.851 J.D.
[🄰 Fay,S.F.M.&M.] (See Pat. Sect.)
Floyd, Lawrence R. .... 3955 Euclid Avenue
Flynn, Jas. P., Jr. .... '10 '49 C.363 A.B. L.1003 J.D. 15513 Fernway St.‡
Flynn, Joan '59 '89 C.293 B.A. L.569 J.D.
(adm. in IL; not adm. in OH) N.L.R.B.
Fogarty, Dennis R., (AV) .... '— '91 C.363 B.A. L.1003 J.D. [Davis&Y.]
Fogarty, Robert J., (AV) .... '52 '77 C&L.150 B.A., J.D. [Hahn L.&P.]
Foley, Dianne, (AV) .... '47 '76 C.93 B.A. L.776 J.D. [Spieth,B.M.&N.]
Foley, Margaret R., (BV) .... '36 '85 C.856 B.A. L.161 J.D. 2500 Terminal Twr.
Folkman, Debra Lynne '65 '91 C&L.124 B.A., J.D.
Rating Specialist, Dept. of Vet. Affs.
Folland, Robert C. .... '70 '95 C.97 B.A. L.607 J.D. [Thompson H.]
Follen, Joseph L., (BV) .... '18 '51 C.363 B.B.A. L.989 LL.B. [🄲 Rhoa,F.&R.]
Foos, James Reed, Jr., Attorney at Law, (AV) '53 '80
C.150 B.S. L.1003 J.D. 17138 Lorain Ave., Ste. 211
Forbes, George L. .... '31 '62 C.62 L.161 J.D. [Forbes,F.&Assoc.]
Forbes, Helen M. .... '59 '85 C.811 B.A. L.329 J.D. [Forbes,F.&Assoc.]
Forbes, Lisa Babish, (AV) .... '63 '92 C.188 B.S. L.930 J.D. [Vorys,S.S.&P.]
Forbes, Steven J., (AV) .... '62 '89 C.31 A.B. L.273 J.D. [Norchi,B.&F.]
Forbes, Forbes & Associates .... 614 Superior Ave., N.W.
Ford, Anne Owings .... '— '89 C.477 B.A. L.880 J.D. [🄰 Jones D.]
Ford, J. Scott .... '63 '90 C.385 A.B. L.880 J.D. Lottery Comm.
Ford, Joan A., (BV) .... '51 '83 C.62 B.A. L.1003 J.D. 2005 Sperrys Forge Trail
Ford, Robert B., (AV) .... '44 '68 C.976 B.A. L.477 J.D. [Thompson H.]
Forman, Jonathan S. .... '68 '94 C.477 B.A. L.150 J.D. [🄰 Duvin,C.&H.]
Forrest, Audrey P. .... '54 '78 C.62 B.A. L.1003 J.D. [A.P.Forrest]
Forrest, David A., (AV) .... '54 '79 C.62 B.A. L.161 J.D. [Jeffries,K.F.&M.]
Forrest, Audrey P., Co., LPA .... 101 Prospect Ave., W.
Forrester, Traci L. .... '71 '02 Corp. Atty., Cleveland-Cliffs Inc.
Forrester and Kovanda, (AV) .... 140 Public Sq.
Forristal, John T. .... '73 '05 C.262 B.A. L.124 J.D. [🄰 Kelley&F.]
Forte, David F., (AV) .... '41 '86 C.309 A.B. L.178 J.D. 1801 Eculid Ave.
Fortunato, Christopher R., (BV) '62 '87
C.363 A.B. L.1003 J.D. 13400 Shaker Blvd., Apt. 506
Fortunato, Theresa A., (BV) .... '67 '92 C.363 B.A. L.930 J.D. [Weltman,W.&R.]
Fosnight, William D. '59 '84 C.473 B.A. L.930 J.D.
V.P. & Assoc. Gen. Coun., Federal Reserve Bk. of Cleveland
Foster, Ivan V. .... '46 '76 C&L.1003 B.A., J.D. 3614 Tolland Rd.
Foust, Jerry L. .... '43 '68 C.276 A.B. L.930 J.D. V.P., Huntington Trust Co., N.A.‡
Fout, Karen .... '59 '04 C.1057 B.A. L.989 J.D. [🄰 Keis G.]
Foy, Patrick M., (AV) .... '— '87 C&L.161 B.A., J.D. 55 Public Square, Suite 850
Fraelich, Timothy P. .... '— '93 C.980 B.A. L.188 J.D. [Jones D.]
Franey, Martin T., (AV) .... '53 '78 C.363 B.A. L.930 J.D. 55 Public Sq., Ste. 850
Frangos, Gus, Law Offices of, (BV) ... '54 '82 C.8 B.A. L.161 J.D. 1325 Carnegie Avenue
Frank, Ian H. .... '71 '96 C.62 B.A. L.1003 J.D. [Frantz W.]
Frank, Irwin M., (BV) '47 '72
C.473 B.S. L.1003 J.D. 5910 Landerbrook Dr. (⊙Cleveland)
Frank, Irwin M., (BV) .... '47 '72 C.473 B.S. L.1003 J.D. [🄲 Dinn,H.&P.] (⊙Cleveland)
Frank, John J. .... '— '98 L.989 J.D. 1300 East Ninth Street, 14th Floor

Frank, Mark S., (BV) '56 '81 C.150 B.A. L.161 J.D.
323 West Lakeside Avenue, Suite 450, 44113
Telephone: 216-621-5661 Fax: 216-241-5670
Email: markfrank@lawyers.com URL: http://www.lawyers.com/markfranklaw
Personal Injury, Medical Malpractice, Trial Litigation, Municipal, Collections, Probate Law, Bankruptcy and Criminal Defense Law. General Practice, Driving While Intoxicated, Traffic Violations, Automobile Accidents, Wrongful Death, Premises Liability, Premises Security, Dog Bites, Animal Bites, Torts, Negligence and Insurance Law.
Representative Client: Crown Carpet USA, Inc.
Reference: National City Bank.
See Professional Biographies, CLEVELAND, OHIO

Frank, Theobald .... '27 '51 C&L.930 B.A., LL.B. 2718 Sulgrave St.
Frankel, Donald M. .... '23 '51 C&L.930 B.A., LL.B. 3270 Warrensville
Frankel, Dov Y. .... '69 '94 C.999 B.A. L.446 J.D. [🄰 Buckley K.]
Frankel, Thomas D. .... '49 '76 C.363 B.A. L.607 J.D. The Travelers Shoppes
Franklin, Earl R. .... '43 '68 C.145 A.B. L.659 J.D. V. P. & Sec., Eaton Corp.
Frankovich, George S. .... '53 '80 C&L.8 B.S.A., J.D. Coopers & Lybrand

Franks, Jennifer R. .... '76 '02 C.741 B.A. L.8 J.D. [🄰 Shapiro&F.]
Frantz, Michael J., (AV) .... '51 '76 C.602 B.A. L.276 J.D. [Frantz W.]

Frantz Ward LLP, (AV)
2500 Key Center, 127 Public Square, 44114-1230
Telephone: 216-515-1660 Fax: 216-515-1650
Email: attorneys@frantzward.com URL: http://www.frantzward.com
Members of Firm: Barbara J. Arison; Keith A. Ashmus; Brett K. Bacon; T. Merritt Bumpass, Jr.; Michael N. Chesney; Ian H. Frank; Michael J. Frantz; Stephen F. Gladstone; Carl H. Gluek; Patrick F. Haggerty; Ralph P. Higgins, Jr.; Joel R. Hlavaty; Brian J. Kelly; Christopher C. Koehler; John F. Kostelnik, III; Maris J. McNamara; Colleen C. Murnane; Andrew J. Natale; Bernard H. Niehaus; James B. Niehaus; M. Neal Rains; Mark L. Rodio; Marc A. Sanchez; Michael E. Smith; Daniel A. Ward. Of Counsel: Michael M. Hughes. Associates: Rebecca J. Bennett; Lindsey A. Carr; Jay R. Carson; Larry W. Conner; Jennifer L. Cuthbertson; James T. Dixon; William P. Dunn; Gregory R. Farkas; Travis F. Jackson; Melissa A. Jones; Christopher G. Keim; Hans L. Larsen; Kelly Summers Lawrence; Anthony J. Lazzaro; Edward J. Leader; Brian A. Maciak; Matthew H. Matheney; Jenifer E. Novak; Julie L. Pietrzen; Brian E. Roof; Jennifer L. Whitney; Steven R. Yoo.
Corporate Law, Business Law, Litigation, Labor and Employment, Construction Law, College and University Law, Banking Law, Health Care, Worker's Compensation, Antitrust Law, Telecommunications Law, Estate Planning, Probate, Products Liability, Real Estate, Civil Rights, OSHA, Trade Regulation, ERISA, Creditors' Rights, Bankruptcy, Alternative Dispute Resolution Services, Insurance, Taxation.
See Professional Biographies, CLEVELAND, OHIO

Franz, Paul E. .... '— '99 C.579 B.S.E.E. L.988 J.D. [🄰 Jones D.] (See Pat. Sect.)
Fraunfelder, William A., Jr., (AV) ...... '43 '68 C.970 B.A. L.597 J.D. Trial Ref., Juv. Ct.
Frederick, Ronald Ira .... '56 '94 C.473 B.A. L.8 J.D. [R.Frederick&Assoc.]
Frederick, Ronald, & Associates LLC .... 55 Public Square, Suite 1300
Freeburg, Antoinette E. .... '74 '99 C.161 L.1003 J.D. [🄰 C.P.Kasunic]
Freeburg, David A. .... '— '99 C.107 B.A. L.161 J.D. [🄰 McFadden&Assoc.]
Freed, Robt. E. .... '31 '56 C&L.930 A.B., LL.B. N.A.S.A.
Freedman, Leland S. .... '29 '56 C.930 B.A. L.1003 LL.B. [L.S.Freedman]
Freedman, Steven A., (BV) '51 '76 C.610 B.B.A. L.930 J:D.
5525 Warrensville Center Rd.
Freedman, Leland Sidney .... 3797 Hillbrook Rd.
Freeman, Barry Y., (AV) .... '67 '93 C.145 A.B. L.477 J.D. [Duvin,C.&H.]
Freeman, Bryan Scott .... '69 '99 C.93 B.A. L.989 J.D. [Schiff&D.]
Freeman, Kenneth J. .... '57 '81 C.597 B.S. L.930 J.D. [K.J.Freeman]
Freeman, Kevin C. .... '57 '88 C.381 B.A. L.7 J.D. 5108 Denison Ave.
Freeman, Mark T. .... '69 '97 C.473 B.A. L.1119 J.D. Assoc. Coun., KeyCorp.
Freeman, Michelle M. .... '73 '99 C.473 B.A. L.608 J.D. The Sherwin-Williams Co.
Freeman, Thomas J., (BV) .... '57 '82 C.528 B.A. L.8 J.D. 1215 Superior Ave.
Freeman, Kenneth J., Co., L.P.A. .... 526 Superior Avenue
Freimuth, Marc W., (AV) '— '71 C&L.494 B.A., J.D.
Sr. V.P., Gen. Coun. & Secy., Ohio Savings Financial Corporation
French, Charles J., III, (AV) .... '51 '78 C.161 B.A. L.1003 J.D. [Baker&H.]
French, James H., (AV) .... '45 '74 C.999 B.A. L.1003 J.D. [French&F.]
French, Jo Anne, (BV) .... '43 '88 C.161 B.A. L.1003 J.D. 1370 Ontario St., Ste. 330
French, Michael K. .... '74 '01 C.276 B.S. L.989 J.D. [🄰 Schneider,S.R.&L.]

French & French, (AV)
820 West Superior Avenue, Suite 510, 44113
Telephone: 216-621-4260 Fax: 216-621-4262
Email: frenchandfrench@msw.com
Members of Firm: James H. French; Ralph F. French (1908-2001).
General Civil Trial Practice, Workers Compensation, Probate Law, Social Security Disability and Personal Injury Law.
See Professional Biographies, CLEVELAND, OHIO

Frenden, John A., & Associates, Law Offices of, (BV) '35 '64
C.62 B.B.A. L.930 LL.B. 724 Leader Building, Suite 724
Frey, Louis Christopher, (BV) .... '52 '87 C&L.161 B.A., J.D. 165 E. 190th St.
Fricke, Wade M., (AV) .... '61 '89 C.674 A.B. L.902 J.D. [Spieth,B.M.&N.]
Fried, Adam M., (BV) .... '69 '95 C.608 B.A. L.930 J.D. [🄰 Reminger&R.]
Friedberg, Ronald P., (BV) .... '65 '91 C.477 B.B.A. L.930 J.D. [Meyers,R.F.&L.]
Friedell, Katherine A., (BV) .... '45 '92 C.477 B.A. L.930 J.D. [🄰 Walter&H.]
Friedland, Carolyn B. .... '43 '78 C.645 B.A. L.1003 J.D. Com. Pleas J.
Friedland, Dale R., (AV) .... '48 '76 C.608 B.A. L.117 J.D. [Rapoport,S.F.&C.]
Friedlander, Daniel A., (AV) '58 '83
C.477 B.A. L.930 J.D. Vice President & Attorney, Natl. City Bank
Friedlander, Jody E. .... '— '85 C.881 A.B. L.472 J.D. Sherwin Williams Company
Friedlander, Lawrence, (AV) ...... '40 '65 C.1036 A.B. L.930 J.D. [Buckingham,D.&B.]
Friedman, Avery S., (AV) .... '45 '73 C.421 A.B. L.161 J.D. 850 Euclid Avenue
Friedman, Frederic A., (BV) .... '38 '63 C.473 B.B.A. L.930 J.D. 3494 Berkeley Rd.
Friedman, Gordon S., (AV) .... '42 '68 C.473 B.A. L.273 J.D. [Friedman&G.]
Friedman, Harold E., (AV) .... '34 '59 C.608 B.S. L.930 LL.B. [Ulmer&B.]
Friedman, James M., (AV) .... '41 '66 C.197 A.B. L.309 J.D. [Benesch,F.C.&A.]
Friedman, Jeffrey H., (AV) .... '47 '73 C.363 B.A. L.930 J.D. [Friedman,D.&S.] ⊙
Friedman, Laurence A. .... '68 '93 C.976 B.A. L.893 J.D. [🄲 M.Levin]
Friedman, Lisa S. .... '69 '94 C.608 B.A. L.1003 J.D. [🄰 Schulman,S.&M.]
Friedman, Nelson .... '12 '39 C.930 B.A. L.161 J.D. 55 Public Sq.
Friedman, Paul M., (AV) .... '52 '77 C.610 B.A. L.851 J.D. 1148 Euclid Ave.
Friedman, Peter B., (P.C.) '59 '85 C.103 A.B. L.477 J.D.
(adm. in NY; not adm. in OH) 11075 E. Blvd.
Friedman, Richard L., (BV) .... '50 '82 C.36 B.S. L.930 J.D. 614 Superior Ave NW
Friedman, Robert E. .... '47 '75 C&L.986 B.A., J.D. F.B.I.
Friedman, Steven A. .... '67 '92 C.604 B.A. L.145 J.D. [Squire,S.&D.]
Friedman, Stuart A. .... '44 '70 C.659 B.A. L.477 J.D. Com. Pleas J.

Friedman, Domiano & Smith Co., L.P.A., (AV) 🄱🄱
Sixth Floor, Standard Building, 1370 Ontario Street, 44113-1701 ⊙
Telephone: 216-621-0070; 1-800-280-0070 Fax: 216-621-4008
Email: fds@fdslaw.com URL: http://www.fdslaw.com
Jeffrey H. Friedman; Joseph C. Domiano; M. David Smith;—Stephen S. Vanek; Michael L. Eisner; Kevin L. Lenson; Donna Taylor Kolis; Daina B. Van Dervort; Christine M. LaSalvia.
Products Liability, Negligence, Wrongful Death, Medical Malpractice, General Civil Practice. Trials, Personal Injury, Insurance Law, Automobile Accidents.
Marco Island, Florida Office: 1141 Swallow Building 4, 34145. Telephone: 941-642-0252.
See Professional Biographies, CLEVELAND, OHIO

Friedman & Gilbert, (AV)
1700 Standard Building, 1370 Ontario Street, 44113
Telephone: 216-241-1430 Fax: 216-621-0427
URL: http://www.friedmanandgilbert.com
Members of Firm: Gordon S. Friedman; Terry H. Gilbert.
State and Federal Criminal and Civil Trial and Appellate Practice. Negligence, Civil Rights Law.
Reference: National City Bank.
See Professional Biographies, CLEVELAND, OHIO

Friel, Thomas J., L.P.A., (AV) .... '26 '49 C&L.436 B.S., J.D. 448 Leader Bldg.
Frient, Megan P. .... '73 '98 C.201 B.A. L.930 J.D. [🄰 Baker&H.]
Friesen, Brendon P. .... '77 '03 C.605 B.A. L.608 J.D. [🄰 Mansour,G.G.&M.]
Frishe, Charles F. .... '42 '73 C.381 B.A. L.1003 J.D. Pres., Plastran, Inc.
Fritz, Bryan Joseph .... '54 '78 C.363 B.A. L.161 J.D. Pros. Off.

Frodyma, Scott F. .... '— '98 C.478 B.A. L.273 J.D. [Ⓐ Jones D.]
Froelich, Georgia A. .... '— '84 C.161 B.A. L.1003 J.D. First Natl. Bk. of Ohio
Froelich, Raymond R., Jr., (BV) .... '48 '73 C.96 B.S. L.930 J.D. [R.R.Froelich]
Froelich, Raymond R., (BV) .... 2100 Salem Pkwy.
Fromhercz, Stephen .... '56 '82 C.973 B.S.B.A. L.424 J.D. 1300 Union Com. Bank Bldg.‡
Fromson, A. Scott, (BV) .... '61 '87 C.477 B.A. L.851 J.D. 23240 Chagrin Boulevard
Fromson, Richard A., (BV) .... '30 '55 C.251 B.B.A. L.930 LL.B. [Sonkin,F.K.&K.]
Frost, Corey Wade, (BV) .... '62 '87 C.161 B.A. L.930 J.D. [Kelley&F.]
Frost, Kristin J. .... '72 '01 C.1347 B.S. L.608 J.D. [Ⓐ Calfee,H.&G.] (See Pat. Sect.)
Frutkin, Harvey L., (AV) .... '45 '72 C.610 A.B. L.477 J.D. [Cavitch,F.D.&F.]
Fry, Jude A. .... '61 '91 C.980 B.E. L.1003 J.D. [Fay,S.F.M.&M.] (See Pat. Sect.)
Fry, Sherry L. .... '58 '97 C.381 B.A. L.161 J.D. 127 Public Square, Oh 01-27-1607
Fuerst, Gerald E. .... '34 '59 C&L.930 B.A., LL.B. Clk., Com. Pleas Ct.
Fuerst, Norman A. .... '25 '53 C.363 A.B. L.1003 LL.B. Com. Pleas J.
Fuerst, Robert A., (AV) .... '53 '79 C.174 B.S. L.930 J.D. [Kahn K.]
Fuhrer, Eryn Ace .... '75 '00 C.363 B.S. L.7 J.D. Atty., The Sherwin-Williams Co. (Pat.)
Fuller, Adam D. .... '— '03 C.473 B.S. L.124 J.D. [Ⓐ Thompson H.]
Fuller, J. H. .... '— '20 12618 Woodside St.
Fulton, Arlishea L. .... '71 '99 C.257 B.S. L.930 J.D. [Ⓐ Ulmer&B.]
Fulton, Burt J., (AV) .... '25 '51 C&L.352 B.A., J.D. 1501 Euclid Avenue‡
Fulton, John M. .... '34 '63 C.31 B.A. L.1003 J.D. Sr. V.P., Society Natl. Bk.
Fulton, William H., (BV) .... '— '72 C.970 B.A. L.930 J.D. [Ⓖ Gallagher S.]
Fumich, William M., Jr., (BV) .... '51 '76 C.611 B.A. L.930 J.D. 600 Superior Ave. E.
Fumich, Wm. M. .... '19 '49 C&L.608 B.S., J.D. 600 Superior Ave.
Funkhouser, Liza M. .... '75 '00 C.665 B.A. L.124 J.D. [Ⓐ Karberg,K.W.&T.]
Furio, Catherine A. .... '42 '91 C.737 B.S. L.1003 J.D. 1621 Euclid Ave.
Fusco, David M., (AV) .... '59 '84 C.273 B.A. L.1003 J.D. [Schwarzwald&M.]
Fuss, Gregory C. .... '46 '78 C.276 B.S. L.1003 J.D. Ref., Dom. Rel. Div.
Gabinet, Leon .... '27 '55 C&L.145 B.A., J.D. 11075 E. Blvd.
Gabinet, Sarah, (AV) .... '53 '82 C.604 B.A. L.930 J.D. [Kohrman J.&K.]
Gabriel, D. Bruce, (AV) .... '54 '80 C.162 B.A. L.597 J.D. [Squire,S.&D.]
Gabriel, Gary V., (BV) .... '48 '84 C.363 B.A. L.1003 J.D. Pros. Off.
Gagliano, Bill J., (AV) .... '55 '80 C.363 B.S.B.A. L.930 J.D. [Ulmer&B.]
Gagnon, Suzanne B. .... '— '00 C.201 B.E.E. L.608 J.D. [Ⓐ Pearne&G.] (See Pat. Sect.)
Gaines, Clarence L. .... '16 '56 C.930 B.B.A. L.1003 J.D. 1111 Superior Ave.
Gaines, George L. .... '50 '88 C&L.161 B.S., J.D. 1111 Superior Ave.
Gaj, Brian L., (BV) .... '59 '84 C.930 B.A. L.188 J.D. [Ⓖ Thompson H.]
Gajda, Patricia A. .... '65 '90 C.363 B.S.B.A. L.930 J.D. [Brouse M.]
Galaska, Edward J., (BV) .... '57 '82 C.161 B.A. L.1003 J.D. 930 Leader Bldg.
Gale, Gregory K. .... '70 '94 C.475 B.A. L.945 J.D. [Benesch,F.C.&A.]
Galin, M. David .... '68 '96 C.277 B.E.E. L.930 J.D. [Renner,O.B.&S.] (See Pat. Sect.)
Galin, Sharon M. '72 '97 C.910 B.A. L.930 J.D.
Jewish Commmunity Federation of Cleveland
Gallagher, Candace Monty .... '48 '75 C.124 B.A. L.161 J.D. 1801 East 12th Street
Gallagher, Eileen Anna, (AV) .... '56 '87 C.737 B.A. L.1003 J.D. 46 Pond Dr.
Gallagher, Francis Patrick .... '47 '75 C.976 B.S. L.161 J.D. [F.P.Gallagher]
Gallagher, Jean M. .... '56 '86 C.610 B.S.J. L.1003 J.D. Asst. Pub. Def.
Gallagher, M. Colette .... '60 '85 C.363 B.S.B.A. L.930 J.D. 21911 Avalon Dr.
Gallagher, Michael R., (AV) .... '22 '49 C.381 A.B. L.477 J.D. 1501 Euclid Avenue‡
Gallagher, Patrick F. .... '18 '55 C.930 A.B. L.1003 LL.B. 614 S. Superior Ave., Ste. 1300
Gallagher, Timothy J. .... '63 '92 C.161 B.A. L.1003 J.D. [Schwarzwald&M.]
Gallagher, Francis P. .... 1801 East 12th Street

Gallagher Sharp, (AV) BB
(Formerly Hauxhurst, Sharp, Mollison & Gallagher)
Bulkley Building, Sixth Floor, 1501 Euclid Avenue, 44115 ⊙
Telephone: 216-241-5310 Telecopier: 216-241-1608
URL: http://www.gallaghersharp.com
Members of Firm and Senior Attorneys: Kevin C. Alexandersen; Ernest W. Auciello, Jr.; Timothy T. Brick; Thomas J. Cabral; Thomas E. Dover; Stanley M. Dub; Robert H. Eddy; Timothy J. Fitzgerald; William F. Gibson; Larry C. Greathouse; Mark A. Greer; Todd M. Haemmerle; Julie L. Juergens; James F. Koehler; Eric H. Mann; Sheila A. McKeon; Margaret Mary Meko; Daniel J. Michalec; Lynn L. Moore; John T. Murphy; Gary L. Nicholson; Forrest A. Norman III; Joseph W. Pappalardo; Alan M. Petrov; Jay Clinton Rice; Timothy Patrick Roth; Monica A. Sansalone; Joseph J. Santoro; Paul J. Schumacher, Jr.; John A. Simon; Alton L. Stephens, Jr.; D. John Travis; James T. Tyminski, Jr.; John A. Valenti;—Stephen M. Beaudry; Gregory K. Boop; Lori E. Brown; George H. Carr; Jeremy G. Cheung; Colleen R. Del Balso; Donald G. Drinko; Catherine Fazio; Anna S. Fister; Abby Gardner; Leah M. Hohenberger; J. Colin Knisely; Elena N. Lougovskaia; Jennifer L. McKeegan; Colleen A. Mountcastle; Thomas F. Naughton; John N. Neal; Holly Olarczuk-Smith; Martin J. Pangrace; Stephen T. Persia; Michael J. Pike; Richard C.O. Rezie; Theresa A. Richthammer; Paul Kohl Schneider; Pamela S. Schremp; Mark M. Turner; Kristin L. Wedell; Darlene E. White; Deborah W. Yue. Staff Attorney: Jamie L. Manning. Of Counsel: William H. Fulton.
General Civil Practice. Insurance, Product Liability, Aviation, Railroad, Professional Negligence, Mass Tort, Drugs and Devices, Construction, Environmental, Corporation, Securities, Probate Law, Workers' Compensation, Appellate.
Representative Clients Available Upon Request.
Toledo, Ohio Office: 420 Madison Avenue, Suite 1250, 43604. Telephone: 419-241-4860. Telecopier: 419-241-4866.

See Professional Biographies, CLEVELAND, OHIO

Gallick, Donald Michael .... '69 '01 C.610 B.A. L.8 J.D. Pros. Off.
Gallo, Charles J., (BV) .... '28 '55 C.177 B.A. L.1003 J.D. 55 Public Sq.
Gallo, Charles J., Jr., (BV) .... '62 '89 C.967 B.A. L.1003 J.D. [C.J.Gallo]
Gallo, Charles J., Co., L.P.A., (BV) .... 55 Public Sq.
Galloway, Robert R., (BV) .... '63 '88 C.299 B.A. L.930 J.D. [Baker&H.]
Gallucci, Anthony .... '69 '96 C.473 B.A. L.1003 J.D. [Kelley&F.]
Gallucci, Frank Lewis, III .... '75 '00 C.93 B.S. L.989 J.D. [Plevin&G.]
Gallup, David B., (BV) .... '49 '79 C.608 B.A. L.1003 J.D. [Gallup,B.&M.]
Gallup, Jeffrey W. .... '72 '03 C.94 B.S. L.124 J.D. [Ⓐ Cavitch,F.D.&F.]
Gallup, Burns & Mills, (BV) .... 815 Superior Ave., E.
Galvin, Martin T., (BV) .... '69 '91 C.904 B.A. L.608 J.D. [Ⓐ Reminger&R.]
Gambaccini, John S. .... '75 '00 C.8 B.A. L.273 J.D. [Ⓐ Benesch,F.C.&A.]
Gamiere, Dorothy Sue .... '27 '75 C.599 B.A. L.365 J.D. 27000 Lakeshore Blvd.
Gammie, Sandra E. .... '— '86 C.446 B.S. L.276 J.D. [Ⓖ Jones D.]
Gandal, Robt. '28 '55 C.930 B.B.A. L.1003 J.D.
V.P., Secy. & Corp. Coun., Management Recruiters International, Inc.
Ganger, Milton E., Jr. .... '28 '62 C.610 A.B. L.1003 LL.B. Pres., Etched Metal Co.
Ganske, Lyle G., (AV) .... '— '84 C.97 B.S.B.A. L.608 J.D. [Jones D.]
Gard, Stephen William '47 '73 C.210 B.A. L.347 J.D.
Cleveland Marshall Law Sch, 2121 Euclid Ave Lb 138
Gardner, Abby .... '— '98 C.611 B.A. L.1003 J.D. [Ⓐ Gallagher S.]
Gardner, Francis X., (AV) .... '52 '79 C.602 B.S. L.930 J.D. [Ⓐ Reminger&R.]
Gardner, G. Andrew .... '70 '96 C.970 B.A. L.608 J.D. [McDonald H.]
Gardner, Gary T. .... '58 '97 C.381 B.B.A. L.8 J.D. [Ⓐ Ulmer&B.]
Gardner, John N., (BV) .... '24 '64 C.363 L.1003 LL.B. 614 W. Superior Ave.

Gardner, Mark, Attorney and Counselor at Law, (AV) '64 '93 C.999 B.S. L.930 J.D.
526 Superior Avenue, Suite 1130, 44114
Telephone: 216-696-9800 Fax: 216-696-2200

(This Listing Continued)

Gardner, Mark, Attorney and Counselor at Law (Continued)
Criminal Law, Driving While Intoxicated, Traffic Violations, Personal Injury, Wrongful Death, Negligence, Slip and Fall, Small Business Law, Litigation.

See Professional Biographies, CLEVELAND, OHIO

Gardner, Michael Bruce .... '55 '93 C.610 B.S. L.930 J.D. 22132 Westchester Road
Gardner, Steven L., (AV) .... '50 '76 C&L.608 B.S., J.D. [McDonald H.]
Garfield, Robert E., (AV) .... '37 '63 C.930 B.A. L.188 J.D. [Ⓖ Keevican&W.]
Garfinkel, Gregg D. .... '77 '04 C.1457 B.A. L.1003 J.D. [Ⓐ Synenberg&Assoc.]
Garfinkel, Howard M. .... '50 '75 C.473 B.A. L.608 J.D. Pres., Superior Tool Co.
Gargiulo, William C., (BV) '36 '69
C.610 A.B. L.1003 J.D. 27801 Euclid Avenue, Suite 500
Gariepy, Stephen H., (AV) .... '52 '77 C.930 B.A. L.608 J.D. [Hahn L.&P.]
Garlock, Peter D. '39 '74 C&L.976 B.A., J.D.
(adm. in NY; not adm. in OH) Cleveland Marshall Law Sch, 2121 Euclid Ave Lb 138
Garner, Richard M., (AV) .... '— '93 C&L.608 B.A., J.D. [Davis&Y.]
Garnett, Robert O'Neil .... '37 '77 C.381 B.A. L.8 J.D. 20475 Farnsleigh Road
Garred, John X., (AV) .... '59 '84 C.1062 B.E.E. L.1003 J.D. [Tucker E.&W.] (Pat.)
Garrett, Glen H. .... '69 '95 C.610 B.B.A. L.161 J.D. [Ⓐ Ziegler,M.&M.]
Garritano, Carlos .... '— '04 C.124 B.S. [Ⓐ Amin&T.]
Garry, Robert D. .... '25 '59 C.363 B.B.A. L.1003 LL.B. 131 E. 200th St.
Garson, Brian K., (AV) .... '44 '74 C.608 B.S. L.1003 J.D. 17 Hanna Ln.
Garson, Peter K., (BV) .... '37 '65 C.31 A.B. L.1003 J.D. 25550 Chagrin Blvd.
Garson, Stuart I., (BV) .... '49 '76 C.608 B.A. L.1003 J.D. [Garson&Assoc.]
Garson & Associates Co., L.P.A., (BV) .... 614 West Superior Avenue
Garver, Jonathan N. .... '48 '74 C.30 B.A. L.94 J.D. 4403 St. Clair Avenue
Garvey, Mary Anne, (AV) ... '55 '80 C.363 B.A. L.930 J.D. U.S. Dept. of Labor Solr. Off.
Garvey, Michael W. .... '62 '91 C.602 B.S.E.E. L.945 J.D. [Pearne&G.] (See Pat. Sect.)
Garvin, Michael J., (AV) .... '58 '84 C.473 B.S. L.945 J.D. [Hahn L.&P.]
Gasbarre, Lisa M. '61 '92 C.363 B.A. L.1002 J.D.
Gen. Coun., Catholic Charities Health & Human Servs., Diocese of Cleveland
Gates, Lisa B. .... '— '88 C.645 B.S. L.665 J.D. [Ⓐ Jones D.]
Gattozzi, Lynn M., (AV) .... '62 '87 C.602 B.A. L.930 J.D. [Calfee,H.&G.]
Gattozzi, Thomas A. .... '68 '94 C.659 B.A. L.930 J.D. [Brouse M.]
Gaughan, Patricia A. .... '53 '78 C.741 B.A. L.602 J.D. Dist. J., U.S. Fed. Ct.
Gaul, Daniel .... '53 '81 C.161 B.A. L.117 J.D. Com. Pleas J.
Gavin, Michael T., (AV) .... '28 '55 C.363 B.S.S. L.930 LL.B. [Mansour,G.G.&M.]
Gavin-Wuertz, Maribeth, (AV) .... '55 '84 C.97 B.S. L.1003 J.D. [Millisor&N.]
Gawlik, Denise L. .... '75 '01 C.973 B.A. L.989 J.D. [Ⓐ Thompson H.]
Gawlik, Gregory J. .... '— '01 C.97 B.A. L.989 J.D. [Ⓐ Thompson H.]
Gaynor, Bruce E., (AV) .... '45 '72 C.97 B.S. L.161 J.D. [Kahn K.]
Gechter, Maureen F. .... '60 '89 C.161 B.A. L.1003 J.D. [Davis,W.]
Gedeon, Richard L. .... '55 '85 C.161 B.A. L.1003 J.D. Cuyahoga Co. Probate Ct.
Gee, Kathleen E. .... '72 '02 C.381 B.B.A. L.989 J.D. [Ⓐ Moscarino&T.]
Geffert, Alexandra J. .... '76 '03 C.207 B.A. L.124 J.D. [Ⓐ Thompson H.]
Gehring, Ronn J. .... '77 '03 C.97 B.A. L.8 [Ⓐ Taft,S.&H.]
Geib, Richard P. .... '65 '95 C.608 B.A. L.8 J.D. [Ⓐ Tucker E.&W.]
Geier, Deborah A. '57 '87 C.62 A.B. L.930 J.D.
(adm. in NY; not adm. in OH) Cleveland Marshall Law Sch, 2121 Euclid Ave Lb 138
Geiger, Richard S. .... '— '99 C.509 B.A. L.161 J.D. [Ⓢ Jones D.]
Geise, Steven N. .... '— '96 C.201 B.A. L.607 J.D. [Jones D.]
Gellman, Paula .... '53 '78 C.604 B.A. L.94 J.D. Legal Aid Soc. of Cleveland
Gelman, Sheldon '46 '73 C&L.705 A.B., J.D.
(adm. in NY; not adm. in OH) Cleveland Marshall Law Sch, 2121 Euclid Ave Lb 138
Gemind, Linda S. .... '58 '90 C.381 B.A. L.260 J.D. [Ⓐ Schottenstein,Z.&D.]
Gemperline, Richard B., (BV) '54 '80
C.973 A.B. L.1003 J.D. Claims Legal Coun., Nationwide Ins. Co.
Geneva, F. Scott B. .... '73 '00 C.473 B.A. L.608 J.D. [Ⓐ Meyers,R.F.&L.]
Geneva, Louis B., (AV) .... '47 '73 C.473 B.A. L.818 J.D. [Ⓖ Meyers,R.F.&L.]
Gentry, Eldred A. .... '20 '59 C.251 B.S.I.E. L.1003 J.D. [Gentry&G.]
Gentry, James E. .... '50 '78 C.367 B.A. L.1003 J.D. [Gentry&G.]
Gentry & Gentry Co., L.P.A. .... 14701 Detroit Ave.
George, Gene B., (AV) .... '49 '74 C.97 B.A. L.477 J.D. [Ray,R.C.&D.]
George, Leslie M. .... '13 '57 C.608 B.S. L.1003 J.D. 1760 Detroit Ave.
George, Susan F. .... '79 '04 C&L.124 B.A., J.D. [Ⓐ McDonald H.]
George, Warren S., (AV) .... '64 '89 C.161 B.A. L.1003 J.D. [Keis G.]
Georgeadis, Philip N., (BV) .... '44 '70 C.62 B.A. L.1003 J.D. [Kolick,G.&E.]
Geraci, Victor T., (AV) .... '63 '88 C&L.930 B.A., J.D. [McDonald H.]
Gerak, John .... '70 '02 C.645 B.S. L.665 J.D. [Ⓐ Vorys,S.S.&P.]
Gerber, Ramona L. .... '57 '92 C.313 B.A. L.930 J.D. Jud. Law Clk., Comm. Pleas Ct.
Gerber, Susan M. .... '— '99 C&L.08 A.A.B., J.D. [Ⓐ Jones D.]
Gerberry, Robert A. .... '69 '97 C.602 B.A. L.1003 J.D. 2100 Bank 1 Ctr.
Gerbick, Amy E. .... '— '02 C.967 B.A. L.161 J.D. [Ⓐ Jones D.]
Gerhardt, Michael J. '56 '85 C.976 B.A. L.145 J.D.
(adm. in GA; not adm. in OH) 11075 E. Blvd.
Gerhart, Peter M. '45 '72 C.597 B.A. L.178 J.D.
(adm. in NY; not adm. in OH) 11075 E. Blvd.
Gerlack, Julius R., (AV) .... '36 '62 C.610 B.S.C. L.930 LL.B. [Mansour,G.G.&M.]
Gerlack, Lisa M., (BV) .... '64 '89 C.967 B.A. L.1003 J.D. [Ⓐ Keis G.]
Gerred, Michelle Marie .... '66 '01 C.150 B.S. L.8 J.D. Gen Coun., NCS
Gertsburg, Alexander E. .... '75 '01 C.473 B.A. L.989 J.D. [Ⓐ Calfee,H.&G.]
Gervinski, Nancy Lee '53 '78 C.97 B.A. L.851 J.D.
Greater Cleveland Regional Transit Authority
Gest, Kristen Lau .... '— '03 C.945 B.A. L.124 J.D. [Ⓐ Jones D.]
Gherlein, Gerald L., (AV) .... '38 '63 C.608 B.S. L.477 J.D. 1111 Superior Ave.‡
Gherlein, John H., (AV) .... '26 '51 C.611 B.A. L.930 LL.B. 127 Public Sq.‡
Gherlein, John M., (AV) .... '55 '80 C.105 B.A. L.930 J.D. [Baker&H.]
Ghezzi, Karen B. .... '46 '89 C.96 B.S L.1003 J.D. 6055 Rockside Woods Blvd.
Gibbon, Christopher L., (AV) .... '50 '77 C.118 B.A. L.1003 J.D. [Walter&H.]
Gibbon, John H., (AV) .... '43 '72 C.604 B.A. L.930 J.D. [Walter&H.]
Gibbons, John B., (AV) .... '49 '75 C.436 B.A. L.1003 J.D. 1370 Ontario Street
Gibbons, Joseph P., (AV) .... '54 '79 C.363 B.A. L.1003 J.D. [Ⓖ Schneider,S.R.&L.]
Gibbons, M. Colette, (AV) .... '51 '76 C.363 A.B. L.1003 J.D. [Schottenstein,Z.&D.]

Gibbons, William P., (AV) '42 '73 C.363 B.S.B.A. L.1003 J.D. BB
1525 Leader Building, 44114
Telephone: 216-623-8000; 241-2500 Facsimile: 216-241-2286
Email: wpgibbonsesq@aol.com
Business and Corporate Law, Business Acquisitions, Development and Organizations, Closely Held Businesses, Federal Income Taxation Law, Estate Planning and Litigation Related to All of the Foregoing.

See Professional Biographies, CLEVELAND, OHIO

Gibbs, Arthur E., III .... '69 '96 C.262 B.A. L.930 J.D. [Ⓐ Hahn L.&P.]
Giblin, Stephen Q., (AV) .... '— '80 C.902 B.A. L.228 J.D. [Jones D.]
Gibson, Joseph, (AV) .... '42 '72 C.381 B.B.A. L.1003 J.D. [Gibson,B.Z.&M.]
Gibson, L. Todd .... '68 '97 C.207 B.A. L.930 J.D. [Ⓐ Squire,S.&D.]

Gibson, Warren A. '41 '73 C.347 B.S. L.1119 J.D.
(adm. in MI; not adm. in OH) 601 Lakeside Ave., City Hall
Gibson, Wendy J., (AV) . . . . '53 '79 C.675 B.A. L.569 J.D. [Baker&H.]
Gibson, William F., (BV) . . . . '— '73 C.237 B.A. L.1003 J.D. [Gallagher S.]
Gibson, Brelo, Zicarelli & Martello, (AV) . . . . 55 Public Sq., Ste. 2075
Gideon, Antoinette F., (AV) . . . . '61 '87 C.201 B.A. L.851 J.D. [Wegman,H.&V.]
Giesze, Craig R. '58 '87 C.973 B.A. L.276 J.D.
(adm. in NY; not adm. in OH) CRG Enterprises, Inc.
Giffen, Karen L., (AV) . . . . '58 '89 C.161 B.A. L.1003 J.D. [Giffen&K.]

Giffen & Kaminski, LLC, (AV) [BB]
1717 East Ninth Street, Suite 2100, 44114-2876
Telephone: 216-621-5161 Telecopier: 216-621-2399
URL: http://www.thinkgk.com
Members of the Firm: Karen L. Giffen; Kerin Lyn Kaminski. Associates: Steven R. Malynn; Tracy A. Turoff; Emily Allegretti Vlasich; Kathleen Nitschke; Jeffrey T. Peters.
Commercial Litigation, Employment Litigation, Real Estate Litigation, Securities Litigation and Arbitration, Creditors Rights, Probate and Trust Litigation, Banking Litigation, Management Labor Relations, Products Liability.
See Professional Biographies, CLEVELAND, OHIO

Gilbert, Terry H., (AV) . . . . '48 '73 C.473 B.A. L.1003 J.D. [Friedman&G.]
Gilbertson, Glen G. '53 '79 C.161 B.A. L.1003 J.D.
Mgr., Human Resources, Birmingham Steel Corp.‡
Gilbride, Michael P. . . . . '68 '93 C.884 B.S. L.930 J.D. [Ⓐ Reminger&R.]
Gilchrist, Thomas C. . . . . '57 '91 C.67 B.A. L.930 J.D. Law Clk., U.S. Dist. J.
Gill, Anita A. . . . . '65 '90 C.610 B.B.A. L.117 J.D. I.R.S.
Gill, John J., (BV) . . . . '32 '62 C.381 L.1003 J.D. 1370 Ontario Street
Gill, Thomas P., (AV) . . . . '44 '73 C.363 B.S.B.A. L.1003 J.D. 2401 Superior Via
Gillespie-Mobley, Ricky L. . . . . '56 '88 C.299 B.A. L.94 J.D. [R.L.Gillespie-Mobley]
Gillespie-Mobley, Ricky Lee . . . . 711 East 105th Street
Gillespy, Robert H., (AV) . . . . '26 '50 C.437 L.150 LL.B. One Cleveland Ctr., 20th Fl.
Gillissie, Rebecca R. . . . . '73 '01 C.473 B.A. L.161 J.D. [Pagano,W.T.G.&L.]
Gillombardo, Carl F., Jr., (AV) . . . . '42 '67 C.363 A.B. L.930 J.D. 1370 Ontario Street
Gilman, Jeremy, (AV) . . . . '55 '83 C.176 A.B. L.930 J.D. [Benesch,F.C.&A.]
Gilmartin, Matthew T., (CV) . . . . '56 '82 C.363 B.A. L.8 J.D. [Ⓐ J.M.Smaili]
Gilmore, Robert S. . . . . '61 '86 C.150 B.A. L.608 J.D. [Kohrman J.&K.]
Gimbel, Adam H. . . . . '69 '95 C.347 B.S. L.472 J.D. [Weston H.]
Ginley, Richard B., (BV) . . . . '29 '55 C.363 B.S. L.1003 J.D. 1510 Standard Bldg.
Ginn, Walter P. . . . . '48 '73 C.401 B.A. L.569 J.D. Standard Oil Co.
Ginn, William D., (AV) . . . . '23 '50 C.67 A.B. L.976 LL.B. [Ⓒ Thompson H.]
Ginsberg, Jamie F. . . . . '72 '05 C.477 B.A. L.989 J.D. [Ⓐ Walter&H.]
Ginsburg, Edward S., (AV) . . . . '48 '75 C.1044 B.A. L.608 J.D. [Baker&H.]
Gisser, Sheldon M., (AV) . . . . '38 '63 C.197 A.B. L.145 J.D. 17000 S Waterloo Rd.
Giuliani, Albert A., (AV) . . . . '54 '83 C.610 B.G.S. L.161 J.D. 526 Superior Ave.
Gladstone, Stephen F., (AV) . . . . '50 '81 C.973 A.B. L.930 J.D. [Frantz W.]
Glaser, Robert E., (AV) . . . . '35 '60 C.973 B.S.B.A. L.150 LL.B. 925 Euclid Avenue
Glavinos, George, Jr., (AV) . . . . '44 '71 C.608 B.A. L.1003 J.D. 1965 E. 6th St., Ste. 507
Glazer, Jeffrey Stuart, (BV) . . . . '46 '71 C.659 B.S.E. L.930 J.D. 28815 Aurora Rd.
Gleason, Melissa '68 '94 C.473 B.A. L.7 J.D.
Assoc. Coun., The Cleveland Clinic Foundation
Gleason, Michael J. . . . . '— '01 C.567 B.A. L.188 J.D. [Ⓐ Jones D.]
Gleespen, Melissa M. . . . . '68 '00 C.309 A.B.A. L.588 J.D. [Ⓐ Calfee,H.&G.]
Glenn, Douglas H., (BV) . . . . '41 '71 C.381 B.B.A. L.1003 J.D. 4403 Saint Clair Ave
Glenn, Peter G. . . . . '43 '70 C.478 B.A. L.659 J.D. 901 Lakeside Ave.
Glenn-Katzakis, Joan '57 '93 C.608 B.S.B.A. L.1003 J.D.
Asst. Gen. Coun., Forest City Enterprises, Inc.
Glesius, Amy S. . . . . '71 '96 C.473 B.A. L.930 J.D. [A.S.Glesius]
Glesius, Amy S., LLC, The Law Office of . . . . 1220 W. Sixth St., Ste. 307
Glick, Gregory R. . . . . '48 '73 C&L.930 B.A., J.D. [Ⓒ Lichko&S.]
Glickman, Robert T. . . . . '66 '92 C.577 B.A. L.930 J.D. [McCarthy,L.C.&L.]
Glorioso, Russell J., (BV) '40 '67 C.999 B.A. L.1003 J.D.
11125 Cheyenne Trail, Apt. 104
Glowacki, James L., (AV) . . . . '50 '80 C.381 B.A. L.1003 J.D. 510 Leader Bldg., Ste. 510
Gluek, Carl H., (AV) . . . . '59 '85 C.164 B.A. L.930 J.D. [Frantz W.]
Gluntz, Kevin P. . . . . '59 '95 C.381 B.B.A. L.8 J.D. [Spieth,B.M.&N.]
Goddard, Richard P., (AV) . . . . '52 '79 C.604 B.A. L.902 J.D. [Calfee,H.&G.]
Goetsch, Alexander E. . . . . '69 '95 C.313 B.A. L.1003 J.D. [Cavitch,F.D.&F.]
Goetz, Daniel P. . . . . '66 '95 C.473 B.S. L.930 J.D. [Ⓐ Weisman,G.&W.]
Goff, Robert E., Jr. . . . . '72 '98 C.201 B.S. L.1003 J.D. [Ⓐ Weston H.]
Goffman, Ira S., (AV) . . . . '56 '81 C.1044 B.S. L.851 J.D. [Rolf&G.]
Goggins, Bari E., (BV) . . . . '49 '80 C.1023 B.A. L.161 J.D. [Ⓐ Ulmer&B.]
Goheen, John C., (AV) . . . . '51 '79 C.197 A.B. L.276 J.D. [Ulmer&B.]
Goins, Frances Floriano, (AV) . . . . '50 '77 C.999 B.Mus. L.930 J.D. [Ulmer&B.]
Gold, Erin S. . . . . '72 '97 C.1366 B.A. L.665 J.D. [Ⓐ Reminger&R.]
Gold, Gerald S., (AV) . . . . '31 '54 C&L.930 A.B., J.D. [Gold&P.]
Gold, Roger M. . . . . '65 '91 C.95 B.A. L.569 J.D. [Ⓐ Squire,S.&D.]

Gold and Pyle, LPA, (AV)
526 Superior Avenue E, Suite 1140, 44114
Telephone: 216-696-6122 Fax: 216-696-3214
Gerald S. Gold; John S. Pyle.
General, Criminal and Civil Trial and Appellate Practice in all State and Federal Courts. Business Litigation, Labor and Employment, Employment Discrimination, Real Estate and Construction Law, Professional Liability and Malpractice, Professional Discipline, Education Law, Arbitration and Mediation.
See Professional Biographies, CLEVELAND, OHIO

Goldberg, David . . . . '43 '69 C.608 B.S. L.930 J.D. 1801 E. 9th St.‡
Goldberg, Gerald, (BV) '40 '66
C.608 B.S.B.A. L.1003 J.D. Ohio Savings Financial Corporation
Goldberg, James R., (AV) . . . . '38 '64 C.608 B.S. L.930 J.D. [Weisman,G.&W.]
Goldberg, Michael J., (BV) '63 '88
C.150 B.A. L.608 J.D. 323 W. Lakeside Avenue, Suite 450
Goldberg, Paul M. '39 '68 C.197 A.B. L.911 J.D.
(adm. in MA; not adm. in OH) Flagship Properties
Goldberg, Scott E. . . . . '61 '85 C.1365 B.B.A. L.608 J.D. 5866 Broadview Rd.
Goldblatt, Jay A. '58 '83 C.150 B.A. L.930 J.D.
Assoc. Gen. Coun. & Asst. Sec., Pubco Corporation
Goldenberg, Warren, (AV) . . . . '57 '81 C.1044 B.A. L.477 J.D. [Hahn L.&P.]

Goldense, David W., (AV) '51 '77 C.207 B.A. L.851 J.D.
Terminal Tower, Suite 920, 50 Public Square, 44113
Telephone: 216-241-0300 Fax: 216-241-2731
Email: DWGoldense@aol.com URL: http://www.davidwgoldenselaw.com
Automobile Accidents, Medical Malpractice, Employment Discrimination, Personal Injury, Dog Bites, Employment Law.
See Professional Biographies, CLEVELAND, OHIO

Goldfarb, Bernard S., (AV) . . . . '17 '40 C&L.930 B.A., J.D. 55 Public Square, Suite 1500

Goldfarb, Gary M., (BV) '47 '72 C.610 B.B.A. L.930 J.D.
2000 Standard Building, 1370 Ontario Street, 44113
Telephone: 216-579-1117; 216-363-6066 Fax: 216-363-6013; 216-363-6010
Email: gar4law@aol.com URL: http://www.lawyers.com/garygoldfarb
General, Civil Trial, Personal Injury, Workers Compensation, Domestic Relations, Corporate Law, Automobile Accidents, Divorce, Child Custody, Child Support, Wrongful Death, Medical Malpractice.
See Professional Biographies, CLEVELAND, OHIO

Goldfarb, Joanne D. . . . . '50 '75 C.930 B.A. L.607 J.D. 2000 Auburn Dr., Ste. 200
Goldfarb, Steven A., (AV) . . . . '60 '85 C.347 B.A. L.608 J.D. [Hahn L.&P.]
Golding, Michael L. . . . . '68 '93 C.105 B.A. L.276 J.D. [Ⓐ Norchi,B.&F.]
Goldman, Donald L. '37 '60 C.604 A.B. L.477 J.D.
V.P. & Gen. Coun., Management Recruiters Intl., Inc.
Goldman, Matthew R., (AV) . . . . '52 '79 C.1044 B.A. L.659 J.D. [Baker&H.]
Goldman Scarlato & Karon, P.C., (AV Ⓣ)
55 Public Square, Suite 1100 (ⒸConshohocken, PA)
Goldner, Allan, (AV) . . . . '47 '73 C.610 A.B. L.161 J.D. [Benesch,F.C.&A.]
Goldsmith, James A., (AV) . . . . '55 '80 C.208 B.S.B.A. L.930 J.D. [Ulmer&B.]
Goldstein, Heidi B. . . . . '70 '95 C.608 B.S. L.930 J.D. [Thompson H.]
Goldstein, Joyce, (AV) . . . . '56 '83 C.881 A.B. L.923 J.D. 526 Superior Ave., E.
Goldstein, Michael D. . . . . '77 '02 C.608 B.S. L.966 J.D. [Goldstein&G.]
Goldstein, Susan S. . . . . '51 '77 C.454 B.S. L.215 J.D. 5 Country Lane
Goldstein, William Melvin . . . . '39 '69 C.608 B.S. L.1003 J.D. [Goldstein&G.]
Goldstein & Goldstein Co. L.P.A. . . . . 55 Public Sq., Ste. 650
Goldston, David B. '51 '77 C.145 A.B. L.273 J.D.
(adm. in DC; not adm. in OH) V.P. & Asst. Gen. Coun., TRW Inc.
Goldwasser, Gary H., (AV) . . . . '41 '67 C.473 B.A. L.1003 J.D. [Ⓐ Reminger&R.]
Goldwood, Jack J. . . . . '70 '98 C.477 B.A. L.930 J.D. [Ⓐ Tucker E.&W.]
Goler, Michael D., (AV) . . . . '52 '77 C.867 B.A. L.930 J.D. [Goodman W.M.]
Golish, Matthew Doyle . . . . '74 '99 C.602 B.B.A. L.989 J.D. Co. Pros. Off.
Goloboff, Barry D., (BV) . . . . '38 '63 C.473 B.A. L.930 LL.B. 3659 Green Rd.
Golovan, Kathleen Rose '69 '94
C.970 B.A. L.930 J.D. Assoc. Corp. Coun., Medical Mutual of Ohio
Golrick, Mary E., (BV) '57 '85 C.161 B.S. L.1003 J.D.
[Ⓐ Calfee,H.&G.] (See Pat. Sect.)
Gonda, Diane M. . . . . '57 '92 C.381 B.A. L.1003 J.D. [Gonda&Assoc.]
Gonda, Richard F., (BV) . . . . '25 '52 C.930 A.B. L.1003 LL.B. 75 Public Sq.
Gonda & Associates Co., LPA . . . . 75 Public Square
Gonyer, Todd E. . . . . '72 '98 C.610 B.A. L.378 J.D. [Ⓐ Walter&H.]
Gonzalez, Vincent F. . . . . '47 '74 C.589 B.A. L.1003 J.D. 2159 W. Boulevard
Good, Amy Leizman . . . . '65 '90 C.477 B.A. L.608 J.D. Atty. Advisor, U.S. Dept. of Jus.
Good, Darcy M. . . . . '71 '97 C.602 B.A. L.930 J.D. Terminal Twr. 50 Pub. Sq.
Good, Jonathan A., (BV) . . . . '69 '95 C.197 B.A. L.1003 J.D. [Ⓐ Thompson H.]
Goodluck, James R. . . . . '54 '89 C.161 B.A. L.1003 J.D. 3517 St. Albans Rd.
Goodman, Alan I., (BV) . . . . '42 '69 C.608 B.S. L.161 J.D. [A.I.Goodman]
Goodman, Alan M. . . . . '40 '73 C.381 B.S.B.A. L.1003 J.D. 55 Public Sq., Ste. 1616
Goodman, Bernard D., (AV) . . . . '35 '60 C.477 A.B. L.930 LL.B. [Benesch,F.C.&A.]
Goodman, David S., (AV) . . . . '52 '77 C.604 B.A. L.309 J.D. [Squire,S.&D.]
Goodman, Eric R. . . . . '— '03 C.323 B.A. L.477 J.D. [Ⓐ Jones D.]
Goodman, Grant Adam '70 '95 C.150 B.A. L.179 J.D.
(adm. in WI; not adm. in OH) [G.A.Goodman]
Goodman, John L., (BV) . . . . '42 '70 C.473 B.A. L.1003 J.D. [Ⓒ R.E.Sweeney]
Goodman, Jonathan R. . . . . '74 '98 C.477 B.A. L.180 J.D. [Ⓐ Walter&H.]
Goodman, Robert A., (AV) . . . . '35 '60 C.197 B.A. L.930 LL.B. [Ⓒ Goodman W.M.]
Goodman, Alan I., Co., L.P.A., (BV) . . . . 55 Public Square, Suite 1300
Goodman, Grant A., Attorney at Law . . . . 1300 E. Ninth St., Ste. 1717

Goodman Weiss Miller LLP, (AV) [BB]
100 Erieview Plaza, 27th Floor, 44114-1882
Telephone: 216-696-3366 Telecopier: 216-363-5835
Email: gwm@goodmanweissmiller.com URL: http://www.goodmanweissmiller.com
Members of Firm: Steven J. Miller; Jay R. Faeges; Michael D. Goler; Drew A. Carson. Associates: Deborah J. Michelson; David A. Kunselman; Sarah H. Kostura. Of Counsel: Robert A. Goodman; Ronald I. Weiss.
Business and Complex Litigation. Corporation, Securities, Taxation, Real Estate, Banking, Commercial Finance, Antitrust, International, Computer and Employment Law. Trials and Appeals in Federal and State Courts. Litigation of Restrictive Covenants, Emergency Injunction and Equity Practice, Securities, Business Torts, Warranty, and Franchise Litigation, Creditors Rights; Health Care Law; Intellectual Property Rights.
Reference: National City Bank.
See Professional Biographies, CLEVELAND, OHIO

Goodwin, Paula Rae, (BV) '53 '77 C.183 B.A. L.930 J.D.
820 W. Superior Ave., Ste. 510
Goots, Thomas R. . . . . '— '96 C.610 B.S. L.8 J.D. [Ⓐ Jones D.]
Gorczynski, Linda M. . . . . '69 '99 C.363 B.A. L.8 J.D. 101 W. Prospect Ave., Suite 1400
Gordillo, Gregory A. . . . . '61 '94 C.597 B.S. L.161 J.D. 1370 Ontario St.
Gordon, Charles B., (AV) '22 '50 C.674 B.S.E. L.309 LL.B.
[Pearne&G.] (See Pat. Sect.)
Gordon, David J., (AV) '52 '78 C&L.930 B.A., J.D.
Assoc. Gen. Coun., Forest City Enterprises, Inc.
Gordon, Harlan M., (AV) . . . . '43 '68 C&L.930 A.B., J.D. [Nurenberg,P.H.&M.]
Gordon, Howard D. '44 '71
C.679 B.S.I.E. L.161 J.D. Gen. Pat. Coun., Eaton Corp. (Pat.)
Gordon, Jonathan Charles . . . . '59 '86 C.176 B.A. L.178 J.D. 11075 E. Blvd.
Gordon, Larry S., (AV) . . . . '31 '56 C&L.930 B.A., LL.B. [Ⓒ Berkman,G.M.&D.]
Gordon, Michael Scot . . . . '— '86 C.893 B.A. L.273 J.D. [Ⓐ Vorys,S.S.&P.]
Gordon, Rochelle Louise '52 '82 C.1183 B.A. L.365 J.D.
Legal Aid Society of Cleveland
Gordon, Sean . . . . '— '01 C.260 B.A.B.S. L.124 J.D. [Ⓐ Thompson H.]
Gordon, William J., Jr. '38 '73 C.363 B.S.B.A. L.1003 J.D.
30285 Bruce Industrial Pkwy.
Gore, George, (AV) . . . . '39 '64 C.602 A.B. L.930 J.D. [Tucker E.&W.]
Gore, Janet S., (AV) . . . . '47 '86 C.105 B.A. L.1003 J.D. [Ⓒ Tucker E.&W.]
Gorjanc, Laura T. . . . . '75 '04 C.161 B.A. L.930 J.D. Tax Atty., The Sherwin-Williams Co.
Gorman, Jennifer Hays '64 '89 C.473 B.A. L.161 J.D.
Sr. Atty., State Industrial Products Corporation
Gorman, Joseph T., Jr. . . . . '61 '87 C.611 B.A. L.930 J.D. Colliers Intrn'l.
Gormley, Darryl Edward '— '97 C.62 B.A. L.1003 J.D.
1300 East Ninth Street, 14th Floor
Gornik, James T. . . . . '46 '73 C.363 B.S. L.930 J.D. 30883 Lytham Cir.‡
Gorom, Stanley R., III, (AV) . . . . '63 '93 C.347 B.S. L.209 J.D. [Hahn L.&P.]
Gorshe, Lisa Ann '69 '97 C.55 B.A. L.1158 J.D.
(adm. in FL; not adm. in OH) [Ⓐ Climaco,L.P.W.&G.]
Gorski, Jeffrey A. . . . . '68 '94 C.436 B.A. L.930 J.D. [Singerman,M.D.&K.]
Goshien, David B. '37 '62 C.103 B.A. L.145 J.D.
Prof. of Law, Cleveland-Marshall Coll. of Law
Goshien, Deborah Purcell . . . . '41 '70 C.145 B.A. L.1003 J.D. [D.P.Goshien]
Goshien, Deborah Purcell, Co., L.P.A. . . . . 3391 Superior Park Dr.

Goss, Colleen Flynn, (AV) ... '55 '80 C.860 B.A. L.930 J.D. [(A) Fay,S.F.M.&M.]
Goss, Geoffrey S. ... '69 '98 C.901 B.A. L.608 J.D. [(A) Meyers,R.F.&L.]
Gottfried, R. Mark ... '60 '87 C.802 B.A. L.124 J.D. [(A) Stefanski&Assoc.] ⊙
Goulder, Richard A., (AV) ... '34 '60 C.473 B.S. L.930 LL.B. [R.A.Goulder]
Goulder, Richard A., Co. L.P.A., (AV) ... 15887 Snow Rd.
Gourash, Daniel F., (AV) ... '57 '83 C.1156 B.A. L.228 J.D. [Porter W.M.&A.]
Gowan, James G., (AV) ... '38 '65 C.363 B.S. L.930 J.D. 1501 Euclid Avenue‡
Graban, Matthew D. ... '71 '97 C.8 B.S. L.930 J.D. [Baker&H.]
Grable, Jason P. ... '77 '03 C.608 B.A. L.607 J.D. [(A) Keis G.]
Grabow, Rachel J. ... '70 '97 C.321 B.A. L.128 J.D. [(A) Vorys,S.S.&P.]
Gragel, Susan L., (AV) ... '55 '80 C.251 B.A. L.1003 J.D. [Rotatori,B.G.S.&A.]
Graham, James D. ... '65 '95 C.318 B.A. L.930 J.D. [(A) Calfee,H.&G.]
Graham, Sarah Sheida '74 '99 C.1062 B.A. L.1003 J.D.
232240 Chagrin Blvd., Suite #180
Graham, Sulaiman Roy ... '56 '99 C.911 B.A. L.989 J.D. 3250 East 116 Street
Graham-Oliver, Heather D. ... '57 '84 C.103 A.B. L.930 J.D. Chief Trial Coun.
Graines, Stuart J. ... '47 '72 C.273 B.A. L.930 J.D. 4645 Richmond Rd.
Gran, Julianne Schumacher ... '64 '90 C&L.747 B.A., J.D. 35050 Ada Dr.
Grant, David L., (AV) ... '51 '76 C.608 B.S. L.7 J.D. [Grant&O.]
Grant, David Robert, (AV) ... '69 '95 C.1529 B.A. L.1003 J.D. 1801 E. 9th St., Ste. 900
Grant, Elizabeth R. ... '63 '95 C.930 B.S. L.1003 J.D. [(A) Forbes,F.&Assoc.]
Grant & O'Malley, (AV) ... 1148 Euclid Ave., Ste 300
Grassi, Carl J., (AV) ... '59 '84 C.363 B.S.B.A. L.1003 J.D. [McDonald H.]
Grauer, Tami Irene ... '57 '82 C.207 B.A. L.1003 J.D. 3845 W Surrey Court
Gravens, Terrance P., (AV) ... '50 '77 C.276 A.B. L.1003 J.D. 55 Public Sq., Ste. 850
Gray, David E., II ... '70 '99 C.437 B.A. L.989 J.D. [(S) Calfee,H.&G.]
Gray, Jeffrey S., (AV) ... '57 '85 C.31 B.A. L.930 J.D. Oglebay Norton
Gray, Louis, (BV) ... '17 '42 C&L.608 B.A., J.D. Standard Bldg.

Gray, R. Benton, & Company, (AV) '51 '83 C.385 A.B. L.228 J.D.
55 Public Square, Suite 900, 44113
Telephone: 216-579-0800 Facsimile: 216-781-3066 Email: bengray@bengraylaw.com
Email: rbgraylaw@sbcglobal.net URL: http://www.bengraylaw.com
Litigation, Employment Law, Equal Employment Opportunity Law, Sexual Harassment, Wrongful Termination, Executive Employment Law, Non-Compete Agreements, Employment Retention and Severance Agreements, Civil Practice, Civil Appeals.
See Professional Biographies, CLEVELAND, OHIO

Gray, Susan M. '49 '82 C.145 B.A. L.1358 J.D.
21330 Center Ridge Rd., 44116
Telephone: 440-331-3949 Fax: 440-331-8160
Email: smgray@smgraylaw.com URL: http://www.lawyers.com/susangraylaw
Bankruptcy, Consumer Law, Consumer Fraud, Foreclosures, Debtor and Creditor, Fair Credit Reporting Act, Fair Debt Collection Practices Act.
See Professional Biographies, CLEVELAND, OHIO

Gray, Todd A. ... '70 '99 C.476 B.S. L.851 J.D. [Mannion&G.]
Greathouse, Larry C., (AV) ... '— '83 C.608 B.A. L.1003 J.D. [Gallagher S.]
Greco, Frank J. ... '46 '85 C.161 B.EE. L.989 J.D. NASA
Greco, Karen L., (BV) ... '57 '82 C.363 B.A. L.1003 J.D. [Kohrman J.&K.]
Greco, Melissa A. ... '79 '05 C.318 B.A. L.124 J.D. [(A) D.W.Leopold&Assoc.]
Green, Brian J. ... '69 '94 C.347 B.S. L.910 J.D. [Shapero&G.]
Green, Donald ... '56 '87 C.288 B.A. L.309 J.D. Legal Aid Soc.
Green, Lynda Pegram ... '51 '86 C.161 B.A. L.1003 J.D. 19450 Lorain Rd., Apt. 302
Green, Richard A. ... '56 '80 C.608 B.A. L.930 J.D. [(C) McMahon,D.H.&L.]
Green, Stanley, (BV) ... '43 '69 C.473 B.S. L.8 J.D. [(A) Weltman,W.&R.]
Greenberg, Barbara C. ... '48 '94 C.608 B.A. L.1003 J.D. Ste 1240, 526 Superior Ave
Greenberg, Jonathan D., (AV) ... '57 '83 C.429 B.A. L.930 J.D. [Walter&H.]
Greenberg, Sheldon J. ... '35 '64 C.473 B.S. L.930 J.D. 1370 Ontario Street, Suite 1310
Greenberger, Paul M., (AV) ... '49 '75 C.608 B.S.Ch.E. L.273 J.D. [Berns,O.&G.]
Greenblatt, Ronald Harvey ... '45 '74 C&L.608 [R.H.Greenblatt]
Greenblatt, Ronald H. ... 101 W. Prospect Ave., Ste. 1835
Greene, William Martin, (AV) ... '46 '72 C.608 B.A. L.930 J.D. [Greene&M.]
Greene, Wm. M., (AV) ... '30 '55 C&L.930 A.B., LL.B. 56 Pub. Sq. Bldg.
Greene & Eisen Co., L.P.A., (AV) ... 1801 Bond Ct. Bldg.
Greenfeld, Rena Hofmann ... '52 '77 C.107 B.A. L.446 J.D. 2549 Lafayette Dr.‡
Greenfield, Harry W., (AV) ... '— '70 C.610 B.B.A. L.161 J.D. [Buckley K.]
Greenlee, Gary S. ... '59 '97 C.97 B.A. L.930 J.D. [(A) Ulmer&B.]
Greenlee, Mark B. '58 '83 C.25 B.S. L.117 J.D.
(adm. in PA; not adm. in OH) Coun., Federal Reserve Bk. of Cleveland
Greenspan, Ronald B., (AV) ... '47 '74 C.665 B.A. L.831 J.D. 700 Standard Bldg.
Greenwald, Leonard S., (BV) ... '41 '69 C.608 B.S.B.A. L.1003 J.D. [L.S.Greenwald]
Greenwald, Robert M., (AV) ... '54 '84 C.381 B.B.A. L.1003 J.D. 32125 Solon Road
Greenwald, Leonard S., Co., L.P.A., (BV) ... 526 Superior Avenue
Greenwell, Matthew D. ... '77 '04 C.851 B.S. L.989 J.D. [(C) Wuliger,F.&B.]
Greer, Mark A., (BV) ... '— '86 C.150 B.A. L.930 J.D. [Gallagher S.]
Gregory, Earnest B. ... '— '04 C.1208 B.S. L.1565 J.D. [(A) Jones D.]
Gregory, Herman Edward, III '58 '87
C.385 A.B. L.608 J.D. Sr. Staff Atty., Legal Aid Society
Greiner, Ted R., (BV) ... '38 '62 C&L.607 B.A., LL.B. 1370 W. 6th St., Suite 203
Gresko, Gary E. ... '50 '97 C.99 B.A. [(A) Lasko&L.]
Gretter, Craig ... '71 '02 C.198 B.A. L.124 J.D. [(A) Tucker E.&W.]
Greve, Thomas F., (AV) ... '56 '81 C.611 B.A. L.1003 J.D. [Rademaker,M.M.&G.]
Grieco, Paul, (BV) ... '64 '89 C.882 B.A. L.930 J.D. [Landskroner G.M.]
Griffin, Burt W. ... '32 '59 C.31 B.A. L.976 J.D. Com. Pleas J.
Griffith, Calvin P. ... '— '88 C&L.608 B.S., J.D. [Jones D.] (See Pat. Sect.)
Griffith, James A., (AV) ... '33 '58 C&L.930 B.B.A., J.D. [McDonald H.]
Griffith, Nancy L. ... '64 '90 C.182 B.A. L.930 J.D. 11001 Euclid Avenue
Grillo, David W. ... '— '03 C.608 B.A. L.989 J.D. [(A) Amin&T.]
Grinham, Jill A. ... '76 '02 C.935 B.S. L.1040 J.D. [(A) Squire,S.&D.]
Grisko, Jerome P., Jr. ... '61 '87 C.381 B.B.A. L.930 J.D. 1900 E. 9th St., Suite 3200
Griswold, James B., (AV) ... '46 '74 C.309 A.B. L.477 J.D. [Baker&H.]
Groedel, Caryn Markowitz '58 '86
C.273 B.A. L.1209 J.D. Exec. Dir., Womens Law Fund, Inc.
Groedel, Howard M., (AV) ... '57 '82 C.473 A.B. L.273 J.D. [Ulmer&B.]
Groedel, Marc W., (AV) ... '54 '79 C.025 B.A. L.930 J.D. [(A) Reminger&R.]
Groh-Wargo, Frank J., (BV) ... '51 '80 C&L.201 B.A., J.D. [Powers&G.]
Gross, Alan D., (AV) ... '48 '74 C.385 A.B. L.880 J.D. 1750 Euclid Avenue
Gross, Gary L., (AV) ... '52 '77 C.910 A.B. L.1003 J.D. 14300 Ridge Rd.
Gross, Joan M., (AV) ... '50 '76 C.94 B.S. L.930 J.D. [(C) Hahn L.&P.]
Gross, Joseph N. ... '51 '91 C.502 B.S.I.E. L.1003 J.D. [Benesch,F.C.&A.]
Gross, Judd H., (BV) ... '22 '67 C.251 B.B.A. L.1003 J.D. 2115 Campus Dr.
Gross, Lynn A. ... '74 '00 C.475 B.A. L.124 J.D. [(A) Roetzel&A.]
Gross, Melvin M. ... '40 '67 C.930 A.B. L.1003 J.D. 55 Public Sq.
Gross, Michael A. ... '74 '00 C.659 B.A. L.930 J.D. [(A) Ulmer&B.]
Gross, Robert Lawrence ... '68 '93 C.608 B.A. L.930 J.D. 22901 Millcreek Blvd., Ste. 395
Gross, Sanford, (AV) ... '40 '66 C&L.930 B.B.A., J.D. 22901 Millcreek Blvd., Ste. 395
Gross, Seymour, (BV) ... '27 '52 C&L.930 B.B.A., J.D. 450 Standard Bldg.

Grossman, Theodore M., (AV) ... '— '75 C&L.188 A.B., J.D. [Jones D.]
Grove, Elizabeth A., (AV) ... '— '90 C.381 B.A. L.930 J.D. [(A) Jones D.]
Grove, James H. ... '62 '88 C.475 B.S. L.930 J.D. [Nicola,G.&C.]
Grube, Brian K. ... '— '97 C.610 B.B.A. L.145 J.D. [(A) Jones D.]
Gruber, James P., (BV) ... '58 '88 C.174 B.A. L.930 J.D. [J.P.Gruber]
Gruber, William M. Ondrey ... '55 '82 C.276 B.A. L.930 J.D. Chief Asst. Dir. of Law

Gruber, James P., (BV)
50 East Washington Street, 44022
Telephone: 440-893-9686 Fax: 440-247-1031
URL: http://www.jpglawfirm.com
James P. Gruber.
Probate, Wills, Trusts, Estate Planning, Business, Corporations, Partnerships, LLC's, Business Succession Planning, Tax and Real Estate.
See Professional Biographies, CLEVELAND, OHIO

Gruenspan, Charles, (BV) ... '48 '82 C.679 B.S.I.E. L.161 J.D. [C.Gruenspan]
Gruenspan, Charles, Co., L.P.A., (BV) ... 23230 Chagrin Blvd. Ste. 900
Grugle, Scott D. ... '70 '95 C.473 B.S. L.1003 J.D. Coopers & Lybrand
Gruhin, Gloria S. ... '52 '93 C.161 B.S. L.989 J.D. 1468 W. 9th St.
Gruhin, Lois A. ... '47 '71 C.705 B.A. L.421 J.D. [(A) Zashin&R.] ⊙
Gruhin, Michael H., (BV) ... '51 '76 C.608 B.A. L.1003 J.D. 1468 W. 9th St., Ste. 750
Grundstein, Nathan D. '13 '53
C.608 B.A. L.273 LL.B. Prof. of Law, Case Western Reserve Univ.
Grunick, Rebecca J., (AV) '55 '85 C.381 B.A. L.8 J.D.
Sr. V.P. & Assoc. Gen. Coun., KeyBank Natl. Assn.
Guarnieri, William T., (BV) '38 '62
C&L.608 B.S., J.D. 815 Superior Avenue (⊙Brecksville)
Gudbranson, Robert N., (AV) ... '32 '61 C.197 A.B. L.930 LL.B. [Nicola,G.&C.]
Guenther, Ralph A. '23 '50 C&L.930 A.B., J.D.
900 Bank One Center, 600 Superior Avenue East
Guest, James W., Jr. ... '41 '70 1441 West 25th Street
Guidubaldi, David J., (AV) ... '45 '72 C.980 B.S. L.161 J.D. [Young,G.&S.]
Guinn, Guy F. ... '49 '75 C.228 A.B. L.477 J.D. [Calfee,H.&G.]
Gullia, Theodore A., Jr., (BV) ... '32 '66 C.363 B.B.A. L.1003 J.D. Huntington Bldg.
Gundy, John M., Jr. ... '66 '92 C.696 B.A. L.930 J.D. [,J.Gundy,Jr.]
Gundy, John, Jr., Ltd. ... 30100 Chagrin Blvd., Ste. 301
Gunn, John W. '51 '74 C.839 B.B.A. L.846 J.D.
(adm. in TX; not adm. in OH) 5545 Miller Rd.‡
Gunning, David H., II, (BV) ... '67 '94 C.393 B.A. L.1003 J.D. [Roetzel&A.]
Gunning, Gina K. ... '— '95 C&L.602 B.A., J.D. [(A) Jones D.]
Gupta, Manju ... '— '03 C.363 B.S. L.989 J.D. 1300 East Ninth Street, 14th Floor
Gurbst, Richard S., (AV) ... '46 '71 C.1036 B.A. L.659 J.D. [Squire,S.&D.]
Gurney, Neil W., (AV) ... '52 '78 C&L.608 B.A., J.D. [Ulmer&B.]
Gurney, Miller & Mamone, (BV) ... 75 Public Square, Suite 525
Gurnick, Ray ... '22 '53 C.124 B.S.,M.S. L.1003 J.D. 15807 Stillwood Ave.
Gusley, Mark R. ... '65 '91 C.62 B.A. L.1003 J.D. [M.R.Gusley&Assoc.]
Gusley, Mark R., & Associates Co., LPA ... 6600 Park Ave.
Gustafson, Davin Randal ... '58 '86 C.97 B.S. L.1003 J.D. Key Corp.
Gutkoski, Brian R. ... '78 '03 C.62 B.A. L.989 J.D. [(A) Shapiro&F.]
Gutmacher, Norman W., (AV) ... '46 '71 C.608 B.S. L.150 J.D. [Benesch,F.C.&A.]
Guttman, Rubin, (AV) ... '52 '77 C.102 B.A. L.1003 J.D. [R.Guttman&Assoc.]

Guttman, Rubin, & Associates, L.P.A., (AV)
55 Public Square Suite 1860, 44113-1998
Telephone: 216-696-4006 Fax: 216-696-2778
Email: GUTTLAW@AOL.COM URL: http://www.guttlaw.com
Rubin Guttman;—Ann Marie Stockmaster.
Language: Hebrew.
Plaintiffs Personal Injury, Medical Malpractice, Negligence, Business, Corporate and Real Estate Litigation, Employment Defense, Cable Television and Communication Litigation and Commercial Litigation, Appellate Practice.
See Professional Biographies, CLEVELAND, OHIO

Gymer, Ronald G. ... '39 '69 C&L.930 B.A., J.D. Pres., McDonald Trust Co.
Haas, Douglas E., (AV) ... '50 '77 C.860 B.A. L.910 J.D. [Benesch,F.C.&A.]
Haas, Gary C., (AV) ... '44 '69 C.610 A.B. L.930 J.D. [(C) Perry&O.]
Haas, Michael J., (AV) ... '68 '94 C.823 B.A. L.1003 J.D. [Roetzel&A.]
Haas, Patricia J. ... '69 '99 C.381 B.A. L.989 J.D. [(A) McDonald H.]
Haas, Steven M. ... '69 '94 C.150 B.S.C.S. L.8 J.D. [Fay,S.F.M.&M.] (See Pat. Sect.)
Habat, John L. '54 '83 C.905 B.A. L.161 J.D.
V.P., Govt. Rels., Greater Cleveland Growth Assn.
Haber, Richard C., (AV) ... '65 '90 C.696 B.A. L.930 J.D. [(A) Reminger&R.]
Haber, Richd. M. ... '19 '47 C.309 A.B. L.976 LL.B. 13900 Shaker Blvd.‡
Hackerd, Richard E., (BV) ... '65 '91 C.97 B.S. L.1003 J.D. 2000 Standard Building
Hacking, Timothy J. ... '— '01 C.878 B.S. L.124 J.D. 1300 East Ninth Street, 14th Floor
Hackwelder, Scott W. ... '— '04 C.228 B.S.E. L.823 J.D. [(A) Jones D.] (See Pat. Sect.)
Hadi, Laila M. ... '66 '91 C.347 B.A. L.421 J.D. Staff Atty.
Hadji, Serge B. ... '42 '68 C.107 B.A. L.213 J.D. 1900 Richmond Road
Haemmerle, Todd M. ... '— '93 C.473 B.S. L.851 J.D. [Gallagher S.]
Haffey, J. Ross, Jr., (AV) ... '38 '64 C.363 B.S.S. L.1003 J.D. [Bernard&H.]
Haffey, Timothy P., (BV) ... '59 '89 C.363 B.A. L.1003 J.D. [Bernard&H.]
Haffke, Christopher W. '70 '95
C.165 B.A. L.1365 J.D. Asst. Gen. Coun., Amer. Greetings Corp.
Haffke, E. William, Jr., (BV) ... '43 '70 C.187 A.B. L.228 J.D. 7055 Engle Rd., Suite 403
Hagan, Brian F., (BV) ... '56 '81 C.717 B.S. L.1003 J.D. [Rego,C.&H.]
Hagedorn, Gina K. ... '77 '04 C.473 B.S. L.124 J.D. [(A) Calfee,H.&G.]
Hagen, Daniel C. ... '— '80 C.62 B.A. L.893 J.D. [Jones D.]
Hager, Robert A., (AV) ... '62 '88 C.363 B.A. L.1003 J.D. [Buckingham,D.&B.]
Haggerty, John J. ... '67 '92 C.264 B.A. L.831 J.D. [Ulmer&B.]
Haggerty, Patrick F., (AV) ... '55 '85 C.012 B.A. L.1003 J.D. [Frantz W.]
Haggins, Edward T. ... '29 '66 C.922 B.S.B.A. L.1003 J.D. 3030 Euclid Ave.‡
Hahn, Victor H., (AV) ... '25 '50 C.62 A.B. L.930 J.D. [Hahn,S.&P.]

Hahn Loeser & Parks LLP, (AV)
3300 BP Tower, 200 Public Square, 44114-2301 ⊙
Telephone: 216-621-0150 FAX: 216-241-2824/1-877-HAHNLAW
Email: inquiry@hahnlaw.com URL: http://www.hahnlaw.com
Members of Firm: Jeffrey A. Brauer; Erica L. Calderas; Douglas C. Carlson; Arthur L. Cobb; Deborah A. Coleman; Daniel A. DeMarco; James M. Drozdowski; Christina D'Eramo Evans (Certified Specialist in Estate Planning, Trust and Probate Law, Ohio State Bar Association); Rose Marie L. Fiore; Robert J. Fogarty; Stephen H. Gariepy; Michael J. Garvin; Warren Goldenberg; Steven A. Goldfarb; Stanley R. Gorom III; Kathleen B. Havener; Candace M. Jones; Arthur M. Kaufman; Stephen J. Knerly, Jr.; Alan S. Kopit; Robert D. Markus; John E. Mellyn, Jr.; David J. Michalski; Gregory M. Nolfi; F. Ronald O'Keefe; Lawrence E. Oscar; Stephen P. Owendoff; Andrew S. Pollis; Lee D. Powar; Richard T. Prasse; Royce R. Remington; Dennis R. Rose; Michael P. Shuster; Steven H. Sneiderman; Mark E. Staib; Mark F. Swary; Edward A. Weinstein; Craig Owen White. Of Counsel: M. Patricia Culler (Certified Specialist in Estate Planning, Trust and Probate Law, Ohio State Bar Association); Joan M. Gross; Randy J. Hart; N. Herschel Koblenz; Barbara H. Levine; Harry D. Mercer. Counsel: Robert A. Cooper; Neil K. Evans. Associates: Catherine V. Andrews; Sean M. Ansberry; Christopher S.W. Blake; Douglas E. Bloom; Rocco I. Debitetto; Derek E. Diaz; Robert J. Diaz; Pasquale DiMassa, Jr.; Arthur E. Gibbs, III; Dawn T. Haynes; Herbert Hotchkiss; Eric B.

(This Listing Continued)

Hahn Loeser & Parks LLP (Continued)

Levasseur; Yuri R. Linetsky; Bradley C. Link; James W. May; Christopher W. Peer; Robert B. Port; Sonja C. Rice; Steven E. Seasly; Cathryn A. Sussman; Joni Todd; Nancy A. Valentine; Christopher B. Wick; Ann C. Ziegler. Columbus, Ohio Resident Members: Stephen E. Chappelear; Marc J. Kessler; Thomas J. Riley; Arland T. Stein; Jeffrey W. Stiltner. Resident Associates: Julie E. Brigner; Dawn-Rae Grauel; Anthony J. Miller; Erica K. Williams; Jeffrey A. Yeager. Akron, Ohio Resident Members: R. Eric Gaum; Scott M. Oldham; Mark A. Watkins. Resident Of Counsel: Louis F. Kreek, Jr. Resident Associates: Robert J. Clark; W. Edward Crooks; John J. Cunniff; Bret A. Hrivnak; Michael H. Minns; Amanda H. Wilcox. Bonita Springs, Florida Resident Members: Jeffrey M. Folkman; Kim M. Hastings; Andrew J. Krause (Not admitted in OH). Resident Associate: Starling N. Hendriks.

Business, Corporate and Securities, Litigation, Taxation and Employee Benefits, Estate Planning, Probate, Real Estate, Labor, Creditors Rights, Reorganization and Bankruptcy, Intellectual Property and Technology, Environmental, Patent, Trademark and Copyright Law, Telecommunications Law, Government Relations, Public Utility and Regulatory Law, Health Care, Construction Law.

Representative Clients: City of Cleveland; Prudential-Bache Securities, Inc.; Safeco Insurance Companies of America; Shell Oil Co.; The CIT Group; The Cleveland Museum of Art; Tishman Midwest Management Corp.

Columbus, Ohio Office: 65 East State Street, Suite 1400, 43215. Telephone: 614-221-0240. Fax: 614-221-5909.

Akron, Ohio Office: One Gojo Plaza, Suite 300, 44311-1076. Telephone: 330-864-5550. Fax: 330-864-7986.

Naples, Florida Office: 3301 Bonita Beach Road, Suite 308, Bonita Springs, 34134. Telephone: 239-949-6989. Fax: 239-949-6687.

See Professional Biographies, CLEVELAND, OHIO

Hahn, Swadey & Pollock, (AV) ... 820 W. Superior Ave., Ste. 510
Haiman, Irwin S., (AV) ... '16 '41 C.930 A.B. L.1003 J.D. [McCarthy,L.C.&L.]
Haines, Jacque M. ... '32 '58 C&L.930 A.B., LL.B. 3820 Monticello Blvd.
Haines, Jeffrey D. '61 '92 C.528 B.A. L.1003 J.D.
Gen. Coun., Prospect Title Agcy., Inc.
Haines, Warren M., II '— '95 C.378 B.S. L.229 J.D.
[Calfee,H.&G.] (See Pat. Sect.)
Hairston, Craig A. ... '73 '99 C.610 B.S. L.117 J.D. [Rieth&A.]
Halbritter, Marc A. '55 '80 C&L.923 B.S.B.A., J.D.
(adm. in WV; not adm. in OH) General Counsel, East Ohio Gas Company
(⊙Clarksburg, WV)
Hale, Jeffrey D. '65 '97 C.502 B.S.E.E. L.1218 J.D.
(adm. in NY; not adm. in OH; See Pat. Sect.) [Amin&T.]
Hales, David K. ... '69 '96 C.1349 B.S. L.94 J.D. [McDonald H.]
Haley, Donald C. ... '28 '63 C.339 B.S. L.1003 J.D. 1111 Superior Ave.
Halfon, Ellen E. ... '— '88 C.342 B.A. L.426 J.D. [Jones D.]
Hall, Arthur C., III ... '62 '93 C.264 B.A. L.602 J.D. [Calfee,H.&G.]
Hall, Barbara S., (AV) ... '47 '79 C.215 B.A. L.1003 J.D. Com. Pleas-Dom. Rel. J.
Hall, Charles M. ... '46 '79 C.197 B.A. L.930 J.D. The Capital Creation Co., Inc.
Hall, Eric J. ... '73 '01 C&L.260 B.A., J.D. [Walter&H.]
Hall, Lindsey I. ... '— '02 C.161 B.A. L.1003 J.D. 1300 East Ninth Street, 14th Floor
Hall, Michael J. ... '73 '04 C.130 B.A. L.910 J.D. [Ulmer&B.]
Hall, Stephen K. ... '71 '97 C&L.608 B.A., J.D. [McDonald H.] (⊙Columbus)
Hallbauer, John A., (AV) ... '— '66 C.20 B.A. L.930 J.D. [Buckley K.]
Halliday, Brian J. ... '66 '01 C.610 B.S. L.989 J.D. [Rosner&Assoc.]
Halpern, Marvin N. ... '— '61 C.477 B.A. L.930 J.D. [M.N.Halpern]
Halpern, Marvin N., Co., L.P.A. ... 815 Superior Ave.
Hamed, Michael R. ... '72 '98 C.473 B.A L.659 J.D. [Kushner&R.]
Hamilton, J. Richard, (AV) ... '29 '56 C.610 B.S.C. L.608 J.D. [Baker&H.]
Hamilton, Thomas A. ... '— '93 C.477 B.A. L.930 J.D. [Jones D.]
Hamm, George E., Jr. ... '52 '92 C.691 B.A. L.930 J.D. 1380 E. Sixth Street
Hammer, Daniel W., (AV) ... '32 '59 C&L.602 B.S., LL.B. [Thompson H.] ‡
Hammond, Carl M. ... '50 '77 C.930 B.A. L.1003 J.D. Admin. Law J., E.E.O.C.
Hammond, Kim M. ... '67 '93 C.107 B.A. L.989 J.D. [K.D.Weiner&Assoc.]
Hammond, Richard W., (AV) '38 '67
C.645 B.S. L.477 J.D. Pres. & CEO, University Mednet
Hanculak, Thomas M., (AV) ... '49 '75 C.602 A.B. L.879 J.D. [J.W.Diemert,Jr.&Assoc.]
Hanna, Harry A., (AV) ... '40 '64 C.363 B.S. L.930 J.D. 1200 Ontario St.
Hanna, Robert J., (AV) ... '59 '86 C.611 B.A. L.1003 J.D. [Tucker E.&W.]
Hanna, W. Michael, (AV) ... '54 '80 C.283 B.A. L.923 J.D. [Squire,S.&D.]
Hanna, William R. ... '65 '97 C.473 A.B. L.989 J.D. [Walter&H.]
Hannan, Tracy ... '76 '03 C.477 B.A. L.94 J.D. [Thompson H.]
Hanninen, John H., (AV) '20 '50
C.869 B.S. L.1003 J.D. Coun., Great Lake Protective Assn.
Hanover, Pamela Iddings ... '55 '80 C.347 B.A. L.608 J.D. [Squire,S.&D.]
Hanselman, Suzanne K. ... '63 '91 C.473 B.A. L.608 J.D. [Baker&H.]
Hansen, William R. '46 '73 C.1042 B.A. L.145 J.D.
(adm. in MD; not adm. in OH) V.P. & Gen. Coun., The Richard E. Jacobs Group, Inc.
Hanson, Jay S. ... '60 '85 C.62 B.A. L.1003 J.D. [Weston H.]
Haran, Craig ... '75 '00 C.363 B.A. L.124 J.D. [Rolf&G.]
Harbarger, David R., (BV) ... '45 '75 [Roetzel&A.] (⊙Wash., DC)
Harbottle, Scott A. '56 '82
C.198 B.A. L.945 J.D. V.P. & Assoc. Coun., KeyBank Natl. Assn.
Harders, W. Scott ... '64 '97 C.602 B.S.E.E. L.1049 J.D. [Benesch,F.C.&A.] (Pat.)
Hardiman, James L., (AV) ... '41 '68 C.62 B.A. L.1003 J.D. 75 Public Square
Hardin, Charles W., Jr. ... '— '87 C.607 B.A. L.608 J.D. [Jones D.]
Harding, Frank I., III ... '44 '69 C.477 B.A. L.930 J.D. Pres., Society Natl. Bk.
Harding, James N., (BV) ... '47 '73 C.373 B.A. L.930 J.D. 31 Columbus St.
Hardin-Levine, Peter S., (AV) ... '59 '84 C.597 B.A. L.477 J.D. [Thorman&H.]
Hardy, Michael L., (AV) ... '47 '72 C.363 A.B. L.477 J.D. [Thompson H.]
Hardy, Richard G., (AV) ... '53 '78 C.352 B.A. L.930 J.D. [Ulmer&B.]
Hargate, Edwin V., III ... '57 '83 C.294 B.A. L.1003 J.D. 1055 Eastlawn Dr.
Hargitai, Zoltan ... '75 '04 C.161 B.A. L.1003 J.D. U.S. Dist. Ct., Northern Dist. of OH
Harkins, Laurie N. ... '54 '80 C.623 B.S. L.862 J.D. Asst. Coun., Society Natl. Bk.
Harlow, Kathryn ... '57 '88 C.37 B.A. L.178 J.D. Cleveland Works, Inc.
Harmody, Richard M., (BV) ... '30 '60 C.251 B.B.A. L.930 LL.B. 4824 W. 14th St.
Harp, Malinda D. ... '51 '89 C.62 B.A. L.930 J.D. 4250 Lee Road
Harper, Sara J. ... '27 '52 C&L.930 B.S., LL.B. Ct. App. J.
Harper, Walter G., (AV) ... '44 '74 C.870 B.S. L.880 J.D. [Calfee,H.&G.]
Harrington, Michael P. ... '51 '77 C.93 A.B. L.930 J.D. 3649 W. 159th St.★
Harris, Alan B., Law Offices of '47 '74
C.363 B.A. L.989 J.D. 614 W. Superior Ave., Suite 804
Harris, Arthur I. ... '57 '82 C.188 A.B. L.477 J.D. 201 Superior Ave.
Harris, Beverly A., (BV) ... '44 '78 C.876 B.A. L.989 J.D. [Weston H.]
Harris, Cecille Caluya ... '65 '95 C.473 B.A. L.329 J.D. Ohio Attorney General
Harris, Christopher P. '65 '97
C.1109 B.S.E.E. L.1003 J.D. [Tarolli,S.C.&T.] (See Pat. Sect.)
Harris, Julie A. ... '70 '95 C.97 B.L.S. L.276 J.D. [Calfee,H.&G.]
Harris, Leodis ... '34 '63 C.930 L.1003 J.D. 2163 E. 22nd Street
Harris, Michael F., (AV) ... '52 '77 C.477 B.A. L.930 LL.B. [Tucker E.&W.]
Harrold, Linda Hauserman, (AV) ... '— '79 C.293 A.B. L.930 J.D. [Duvin,C.&H.]
Hart, Randy J., (AV) ... '63 '90 C.608 B.S. L.1003 J.D. [Hahn L.&P.]
Hart, Robert D. ... '36 '63 C&L.880 B.E., LL.B. 15700 Van Aken Blvd.
Hartman, Alan S., (BV) ... '39 '65 C&L.930 A.B., J.D. [A.S.Hartman]
Hartman, Anthony J., (AV) ... '43 '68 C.608 B.S. L.930 J.D. [Hermann,C.&S.]
Hartman, Dale M. ... '58 '87 C.597 B.A. L.930 J.D. 27600 Chagrin Boulevard, Suite 340
Hartman, Franklin L. ... '34 '66 C.352 B.A. L.477 J.D. 1385 Burlington Rd.‡
Hartman, Robert W. ... '77 '04 C.25 B.A. L.124 J.D. [Zashin&R.]
Hartman, Ruth E. ... '— '05 C.966 B.A. L.477 J.D. [Baker&H.]
Hartman, Sheldon R. '45 '71 C.610 B.B.A. L.1003 J.D.
Sr. V.P. & Assoc. Gen. Coun., KeyBank Natl. Assn.
Hartman, Allen S., LLC, (BV) ... 27600 Chagrin Blvd.
Hartwig, Jeffrey R. ... '— '05 C.766 B.A. L.665 J.D. [Thompson H.]
Harvey, Elizabeth A. ... '60 '92 C.27 B.A. L.1187 J.D. [Ulmer&B.]
Harvey, Henry C., (AV) ... '15 '40 C&L.976 B.A., LL.B. 2489 Arlington Rd.‡
Harvey, Michael P., (AV) ... '57 '87 C.463 B.S. L.1003 J.D. [M.P.Harvey]
Harvey, R. Scot, (BV) ... '63 '90 C.823 B.A. L.608 J.D. [Millisor&N.]
Harvey, Thomas F. ... '38 '64 C.951 B.A. L.150 J.D. Sr. V.P., Natl. City Bk.

Harvey, Michael P., Co., L.P.A., (AV)
311 Northcliff Drive, 44116-1344
Telephone: 440-356-9108 Fax: 440-356-9128
Email: mpharveyco@aol.com
Michael P. Harvey.
Small Business, Employment, Commercial Litigation and Trade Secrets, Labor and Employment, Business Law, Litigation, Unfair Competition, Corporate, Civil Rights, Commercial Law, Computers and Software, Contracts, Disabilities, Franchises and Franchising, Trial and Appellate.
See Professional Biographies, CLEVELAND, OHIO

Harwood, Peter R., (AV) ... '38 '65 C.674 A.B. L.477 LL.B. [Deacon,H.&A.]
Hasenflue, Oliver W. ... '19 '43 C.970 A.B. L.930 LL.B. 19800 Ctr. Ridge Rd.
Hassell, Charles D. ... '— '72 C&L.569 B.E., J.D. [Jones D.]
Hastings, Susan C., (AV) ... '59 '85 C&L.352 B.A., J.D. [Squire,S.&D.]
Hatch, Lawrence H., (AV) ... '59 '86 C.976 B.A. L.893 J.D. 1130 Hanna
Hatina, Joseph D. ... '— '99 C.97 B.S. L.161 J.D. [Jones D.]
Hauber, Karl William '63 '01
C.161 B.I.E. L.989 J.D. [Fay,S.F.M.&M.] (See Pat. Sect.)
Haude, Daniel R. ... '69 '97 C.980 B.A. L.8 J.D. [Reminger&R.]
Haude, Kristi L. ... '— '02 C.381 B.A. L.989 J.D. [Davis&Y.]
Hauer, Richard J., Jr. ... '50 '75 C.93 B.A. L.930 J.D. [Calfee,H.&G.]
Haumann, Theresa R. '61 '88
C.150 B.A. L.161 J.D. Atty., Brush Engineered Materials, Inc.
Hauser, Laura A., (AV) ... '64 '88 C.608 B.A. L.930 J.D. [Thompson H.]
Havach, James M., (AV) ... '46 '74 C.363 B.S.B.A. L.902 J.D. [Spieth,B.M.&N.]
Havener, Kathleen B., (AV) ... '54 '91 C.812 B.A. L.309 J.D. [Hahn L.&P.]
Havener, Thomas G., (BV) ... '61 '87 C.608 B.A. L.930 J.D. [Squire,S.&D.]
Havens, Hunter S., (AV) ... '54 '84 C.930 B.A. L.1003 J.D. [Hermann,C.&S.]
Haverstick, Rebecca Wistner ... '71 '96 C.473 B.A. L.930 J.D. [Squire,S.&D.]
Havighurst, Alan W. ... '45 '77 C.31 B.A. L.150 J.D. 3071 Huntington Rd.
Hawal, William, (AV) ... '53 '80 C.610 B.A. L.1003 J.D. [Spangenberg,S.&L.]
Hawk, George W., Jr. '56 '87 C.207 B.S. L.930 J.D.
Assist. Gen. Couns. and Assist. Secy., Cleveland-Cliffs Inc. (Legal Department)
Hawk, Morris L. ... '67 '95 C.610 B.A. L.930 J.D. [Walter&H.]
Hawkins, Ann Marie, (AV) ... '54 '80 C.602 B.B.A. L.436 J.D. [Hawkins]
Hawkins, Edward C., (AV) ... '27 '54 [Hawkins] ‡
Hawkins, John T. ... '60 '87 C.973 B.S.B.A. L.1003 J.D. [Hawkins]
Hawkins & Co., L.P.A., (AV) ... 1267 West Ninth Street, Suite 500
Hawley, Barbara L., (AV) ... '50 '77 C.145 A.B. L.930 J.D. [Squire,S.&D.]
Hawranko, George E. '54 '82 C.665 B.S.E.E. L.229 J.D.
(adm. in PA; not adm. in OH)
Sr. Assoc. Gen. Coun., Electrolux North America (Legal Department)
Hawrylak, Richard S. '57 '88
C.161 B.B.A. L.1003 J.D. V.P. & Assoc. Coun., KeyBank Natl. Assn.
Hay, Doris Hogan ... '49 '81 C.930 B.A. L.1003 J.D. 15803 Oakhill Rd.
Haygood, Sebraien M., & Associates, (BV) '54 '88
C.207 B.A. L.1162 J.D. 1422 Euclid Avenue
Haylor, Jane T. ... '46 '86 C&L.930 B.S., J.D. [Baker&H.]
Haymond, Daniel M. ... '62 '93 C&L.608 B.S., J.D. [Thompson H.]
Haynes, Cheryl A. '59 '87 C.881 B.A. L.329 J.D.
Assoc. Coun., Admin. & Labor Law, Greater Cleveland Reg. Transit Auth.
Haynes, Dawn T. ... '74 '01 C.124 B.S. L.1003 J.D. [Hahn L.&P.]
Hazelwood, James Michael '46 '83
C.392 B.S. L.989 J.D. 1801 East Ninth Street, Suite 1710
Hazelwood, Michael, (BV) ... '46 '83 C.392 B.S. L.161 J.D. [Hazelwood&K.]
Hazelwood & Kasle, (BV) ... 1801 E. Ninth St., Ste. 730
Head, David A. ... '77 '02 C.49 B.A. L.161 J.D. [Weltman,W.&R.]
Headen, Raymond C. '60 '87 C.951 B.A. L.659 J.D.
[Schottenstein,Z.&D.] (⊙Columbus)
Healy, Jeffrey A., (AV) ... '62 '92 C.197 B.A. L.93 J.D. [Tucker E.&W.]
Heard, Arthur B. ... '24 '63 C.251 L.1003 J.D. 3751 E. 154th St.
Hearey, Bruce G., (AV) ... '50 '75 C.918 B.A. L.262 J.D. [Spieth,B.M.&N.]
Heasley, Howard N. ... '18 '48 C&L.930 M.A., LL.B. 2919 Litchfield Rd.‡
Heavenrich, John D. ... '43 '71 C.197 A.B. L.477 J.D. Reg. V.P., Creative Capital, Inc.
Heben, Edward J., Jr. ... '50 '75 C.161 B.S. L.1003 J.D. [Heben&Assoc.]
Heben & Associates ... 3740 Euclid Avenue
Hecht, Emanuel H., (AV) ... '17 '41 C&L.477 B.A., J.D. P.O. Box 21564
Hecht, Roger D. ... '45 '71 C.96 B.S. L.188 J.D. Pres., Allwaste Recycling Inc.
Heckman, Karl W. '46 '72 C.264 B.A. L.659 J.D.
(adm. in DC; not adm. in OH) The LTV Corp.
Heddesheimer, Don J. ... '48 '74 C.62 B.A. L.1003 J.D. Hearing Offr., State of Ohio
Heddesheimer, Walter J., (AV) ... '10 '35 C.611 B.A. L.309 LL.B. 17668 Ridge Creek Rd.
Hedman, Kent S. ... '— '75 C&L.575 A.B., J.D. [Kadish,H.&W.]
Hedrick, Hal C., Jr. '45 '70 C.684 B.A. L.228 J.D.
(adm. in TX; not adm. in OH) 200 Public Sq.
Heer, John A. ... '65 '91 C.347 B.A. L.930 J.D. [Walter&H.]
Heffernan, Thomas A., (AV) ... '35 '64 C&L.930 B.A., J.D. 127 Public Sq.‡
Heideloff, Glenn F. ... '20 '53 C.251 B.Met.E. L.1003 LL.B. 1038 Parkside St.
Heidorf, Travis M. ... '— '03 C.965 B.B.A. L.494 J.D. [Jones D.]
Heiman, David G., (AV) ... '— '71 C&L.150 B.B.A., J.D. [Jones D.]
Heindel, Edward M. ... '64 '90 C.381 B.S. L.8 J.D. 1370 Ontario St., Ste. 450
Heine, William J. '53 '81
C.473 B.S. L.1003 J.D. Dist. Hearing Offr., Industrial Comm. of OH
Heinke, Lowell L., (AV) '32 '60 C.124 B.S. L.273 LL.B.
[Pearne&G.] (See Pat. Sect.)
Heintel, Robert C. ... '71 '96 C.363 B.S.B.A. L.124 J.D. [Cavitch,F.D.&F.]
Heise, Michael R. '60 '87 C.813 A.B. L.145 J.D.
(adm. in IL; not adm. in OH) Prof. of Law, Case Western Reserve University
Heiser, Joel S. ... '66 '94 C.30 B.S.B.A. L.1187 J.D. [Bricker&E.]
Helfman, Jill Friedman, (AV) ... '62 '87 C.477 A.B. L.930 J.D. [Taft,S.&H.]

Heller, Irving L. ... '28 '57 C.930 B.B.A. L.1003 LL.B. Peat, Marwick, Mitchell & Co.

Heller, Maurice L., (AV) ... '31 '56 C.477 B.A. L.597 J.D. [Nurenberg,P.H.&M.]

Heller, Nancy J., (BV) ... '64 '88 C&L.569 B.A., J.D. [Petronzio S.]

Hellner, Leigh A. '71 '96 C.597 B.A. L.659 J.D. (adm. in IL; not adm. in OH) [A Kahn K.]

Helon, Phillip A. ... '78 '04 C.608 B.S.B.A. L.124 J.D. [A Cowden,H.N.&L.]

Hemann, Patricia A. ... '42 '80 C.339 B.A. L.1003 J.D. Mag.

Henderson, Brandon ... '76 '02 C.610 B.A. L.124 J.D. [Browner&H.]

Henderson, Harold W., (AV) ... '48 '76 C.869 B.S. L.1003 J.D. [Thompson H.]

Henderson, Louis G., (AV) '44 '81 C.161 B.A. L.1003 J.D. Pub. Def. Office [A Gibson,B.Z.&M.]

Henes, Samuel E., (AV) ... '37 '62 C.188 A.B. L.309 LL.B. 13605 Shaker Blvd.

Henkel, Oliver C., Jr., (AV) ... '36 '64 C&L.976 B.A., LL.B. [Thompson H.]

Henkin, Howard A., (BV) ... '45 '71 C.124 A.B. L.930 J.D. [Henkin&S.]

Henkin, Merrill Howard ... '46 '78 55 Public Square, Ste. 1300

Henkin & Seewald, (BV)
1220 W. 6th Street, Suite 205, 44113
Telephone: 216-781-8288 Fax: 216-781-1273
Email: howardhenkin2@aol.com URL: http://www.henkinandseewald.com
Members of Firm: Howard A. Henkin; J. Gary Seewald.
Estate Planning, Wills and Trusts, Insurance, Medical Malpractice, Probate and Liquor Law.

See Professional Biographies, CLEVELAND, OHIO

Hennenberg, Michael C., (AV) '48 '74 C.608 B.S. L.1003 J.D.
Landerbrook Corporate Center, 5910 Landerbrook Drive, Suite 200, 44124-6500 ⊙
Telephone: 440-544-2000 Fax: 440-544-2002
Email: Hennenberg@aol.com URL: http://www.hennenberg.com
—John A. Fatica.
Criminal Defense, Trial and Appellate Practice, State and Federal Courts, White Collar Defense, Health Care Fraud, Antitrust Defense, Regulatory Investigations, Tax Fraud, Complex Civil Fraud, Attorney Discipline, Legal Malpractice Defense.

See Professional Biographies, CLEVELAND, OHIO

Hennenberg, Michael C., (AV) '48 '74 C.608 B.S. L.1003 J.D. [C Dinn,H.&P.] (⊙Cleveland)

Hennig, Janet L. ... '55 '86 C.161 B.S. L.1003 J.D. V.P., Natl. City Bk.

Henretta Law Offices
(See Akron)

Henrikson, Kirk R. ... '65 '91 C.473 B.A. L.1003 J.D. [Rademaker,M.M.&G.]

Henry, Alice Katherine, (BV) ... '36 '65 C.930 B.B.A. L.1003 J.D. 5001 Mayfield Road

Henry, Deirdre G., (AV) ... '53 '77 C.97 B.S. L.851 J.D. [Weston H.]

Henry, Laura A. ... '58 '83 C.97 B.A. L.161 J.D. NASA

Henry, M. Diane ... '44 '72 C.381 B.A. L.1003 J.D. 6800 Day Dr.

Hentemann, Henry A., (AV) ... '— '63 C.363 A.B. L.1003 J.D. [C Davis&Y.]

Herbert, Joseph E., (AV) ... '65 '92 C.473 B.S. L.851 J.D. [Roetzel&A.]

Herman, Richard T., & Associates, (AV) '64 '93 C.150 B.A. L.124 J.D. 815 Superior Ave., Ste. 1910

Hermann, Gary D., (AV) '46 '71 C.318 B.A. L.597 J.D. [Hermann,C.&S.] (⊙Big Sky, MT)

Hermann, Cahn & Schneider, LLP, (AV) BR
Suite 500, 1301 East Ninth Street, 44114
Telephone: 216-781-5515 Facsimile: 216-781-1030 Email: hcs@hcsattys.com
Email: hcs@en.com URL: http://www.hcsattys.com
Members of Firm: Gary D. Hermann; James S. Cahn; Kent B. Schneider; Anthony J. Hartman; Robert Warren, Jr.; Kerry S. Volsky; Peter J. Krembs; Jay H. Salamon; Hunter S. Havens; Hugh D. Berkson; Heidi P. Chylla. Associates: Jeffrey S. Moeller; Jonetta J. Kapusta-Dorogi; Michael D. Brennan; James L. Lane; Jane K. Conrad; Alicia L. Mazzi. Of Counsel: Charles Kampinski; Henry V. Kerr.
General Practice, Civil Litigation in all Courts. Complex Litigation, Trial Practice, Asbestos Litigation, Insurance Defense, Products Liability, Environmental, Employment and Trade Practice Litigation, Personal Injury Law, Domestic Relations, Corporate and Business Law, Securities Law, Fidelity and Surety Law, Franchise Law, Taxation, Pension and Profit Sharing Law.

See Professional Biographies, CLEVELAND, OHIO

Herrington, David W. ... '60 '86 C.160 B.A. L.608 J.D. [Wegman,H.&V.]

Herrmann, Mark, (AV) ... '— '83 C.674 A.B. L.477 J.D. [Jones D.]

Herron, David L. ... '71 '96 C.473 B.A. L.930 J.D. Asst. Gen. Coun.

Herron, Mark P., (CV) ... '64 '91 C.128 B.A. L.1003 J.D. 1801 E. 12th St.

Hervey, Michelle M. ... '72 '00 C&L.124 B.S., J.D. [A Baker&H.]

Herzberger, William A. ... '— '87 C.473 B.S. L.608 J.D. [Jones D.]

Hess, Erin Siebenhar ... '75 '01 C.97 B.A. L.1003 J.D. [A Reminger&R.]

Hessler, David J., (AV) ... '43 '68 C&L.879 B.A., J.D. [Wegman,H.&V.]

Hessler, Nathan E. ... '70 '95 C&L.879 BA, JD [A Wegman,H.&V.]

Hessler, Peter A., (AV) ... '53 '78 C&L.879 B.A., J.D. [Wegman,H.&V.]

Hetfield, James I., II ... '63 '95 C.659 B.A. L.468 J.D. [C Taylor&A.] (⊙Elizabeth, NJ)

Heutsche, John V., (BV) ... '46 '73 C.363 B.A. L.1003 J.D. [J.V.Heutsche]

Heutsche, John V., Co., LPA, (BV)
310 Lakeside Avenue W., Suite 500, 44113-1069
Telephone: 216-241-1000 Fax: 216-241-1093 URL: http://www.heutschelaw.com
Email: johnvheutsche@heutschelaw.com URL: http://www.heutsche.com
John V. Heutsche; Gail A. Hurd.
Family Law, Domestic Relations, Child Custody, Divorce, Mediation, Separation Agreements, Spousal Support.
Reference: First Merit Bank, Cleveland, OH.

See Professional Biographies, CLEVELAND, OHIO

Hewitt, Christopher J. ... '— '95 C.851 B.B.A. L.276 J.D. [Jones D.]

Heyink, Marian Louise '— '92 C.161 B.A. L.1003 J.D. Dir., Soc. Work& Risk Mgmt., St. Vincent Hosp. & Health Ctr.

Hibbs, Lisa A. ... '72 '98 C.610 B.S. L.8 J.D. Fiduciary Offr., Natl. City Bk.

Hickey, Theresa Ann ... '61 '86 C.851 B.S. L.161 J.D. 3794 Pearl Rd.

Hickman, Franklin J., (AV) ... '46 '73 C.128 B.A. L.659 J.D. [Hickman&L.]

Hickman & Lowder Co., L.P.A., (AV)
1370 Ontario Street, Suite 1620, 44113-1743
Telephone: 216-861-0360 Fax: 216-861-3113
URL: http://www.lawyers.com/h&lcolaw
Franklin J. Hickman; Janet L. Lowder; Elena Lidrbauch; Sandra J. Buzney; Judith C. Saltzman;—Mary Bresnicky McKee.
Administrative Law, Civil Rights, Disability Law, Special Education Law, Elder Law, Estate Planning, Probate, Public Law, Social Security Law, SSI, Special Needs Trusts.

See Professional Biographies, CLEVELAND, OHIO

Hicks, George R., Jr. ... '54 '88 C.871 B.S. L.1003 J.D. [Weltman,W.&R.]

Hidek, Christina Tuggey ... '75 '00 C.383 B.A. L.124 J.D. [A Sutter,O.&F.]

Higerd, Jeffrey J., (AV) ... '48 '75 C.611 B.A. L.930 J.D. [Moriarty&J.]

Higgins, Ralph P., Jr., (AV) ... '55 '80 C&L.602 B.B.A., J.D. [Frantz W.]

Highman, Eric M. ... '62 '97 C.161 B.S. L.1003 J.D. [A Fay,S.F.M.&M.] (See Pat. Sect.)

Hilbert, Peter G. ... '— '03 C.823 B.A. L.659 J.D. [A Jones D.]

Hildebrand, John P., (BV) ... '42 '70 C.608 B.S. L.1003 J.D. [Hildebrand,W.&F.]

Hildebrand, Williams & Farrell, (BV) ... 21430 Lorain Road

Hill, Edwin V., Jr. ... '42 '67 C.945 B.A. L.930 J.D. Rockwell Automation

Hill, James M., (AV) ... '53 '79 C.352 B.A. L.976 J.D. [Benesch,F.C.&A.]

Hill, Stephen A., (AV) '47 '74 C.453 B.S. L.930 J.D. [Rankin,H.P.&C.] (See Pat. Sect.) ⊙

Hiller, David P., (AV) ... '41 '69 C.8 A.B. L.477 J.D. [Millisor&N.] (⊙Columbus)

Hillman, Jean M. ... '60 '94 C.62 B.A. L.1003 J.D. [A Calfee,H.&G.]

Hillyer, Shelly K. ... '— '94 C.608 B.A L.831 J.D [A Calfee,H.&G.]

Hilow, Henry Joseph, (AV) ... '56 '81 C.473 B.A. L.1003 J.D. 614 W. Superior Ave.

Himmel, Albert F., (BV) ... '24 '52 C.930 A.B. L.1003 J.D. 25035 Twickenham Dr.

Hindel, Joanne E. ... '57 '84 C.161 B.B.A. L.989 J.D. FirstMerit Bk., N.A.

Hines-Crook, Sheila K. ... '59 '92 C.657 B.S. L.8 J.D. 1111 Superior Ave. E.

Hinkel, Kevin M., (AV) ... '— '80 C.363 B.S.B.A. L.161 J.D. [Kadish,H.&W.]

Hinkle, Steven D., (AV) ... '59 '84 C&L.608 B.A., J.D. Society Natl. Bk.

Hinton, Jennifer Nock ... '66 '98 C.150 B.S.E.E. L.930 J.D. [A Watts H.] (See Pat. Sect.)

Hirshman, Ellen Hobbs, (AV) ... '57 '82 C.363 B.A. L.1003 J.D. [Linton&H.]

Hirth, Alan N., (AV) ... '48 '73 C.563 B.A. L.1003 J.D. [Meyers,R.F.&L.]

Hiser, Ted S., (AV) ... '— '85 C.313 B.A. L.161 J.D. [C Jones D.]

Hisrich, Kelly Rachel ... '73 '98 C.69 B.S. L.930 J.D. McDonald Invests.

Hlavaty, Joel R., (AV) ... '55 '83 C.363 B.A. L.7 J.D. [Frantz W.]

Hlavka, John R. ... '49 '76 C.930 B.S.M.E. L.1003 J.D. [Watts H.] (See Pat. Sect.)

Hoag, Joan ... '49 '77 C.161 B.A. L.1003 J.D. 15316 Shiloh Rd.

Hobt, Stephen D., (AV) ... '52 '78 C.602 B.A. L.1003 J.D. 1370 Ontario Street

Hochberg, D. Peter, (AV) '— '69 C.188 B.M.E. L.276 J.D. [D.P.Hochberg] (See Pat. Sect.)

Hochberg, D. Peter, Co., L.P.A., (AV)
Baker Building, Sixth Floor, 1940 East Sixth Street, 44114
Telephone: 216-771-3800 Fax: 216-771-3804 1-800-776-8166
Email: dphochberg@aol.com
D. Peter Hochberg;—Katherine R. Vieyra; Sean F. Mellino. Of Counsel: Piero G. Ruffinengo (Not admitted in OH); James A. Rich (Not admitted in OH).
Patent, Trademark, Copyright, Unfair Competition and Trade Secrets Law, Trials.

See Professional Biographies, CLEVELAND, OHIO

Hochheiser, Alan C., (AV) ... '63 '89 C.1044 B.A. L.930 J.D. [Weltman,W.&R.]

Hochman, David B., (AV) ... '49 '74 C.608 B.S. L.1003 J.D. [Dinn,H.&P.]

Hochman, Kenneth G., (AV) ... '— '73 C.107 B.A. L.178 J.D. [Jones D.]

Hodous, David F. ... '44 '76 C.607 B.A. L.1003 J.D. [C Childs,M.&Assoc.]

Hoen, Benjamin N. ... '76 '04 L.989 J.D. [A Weltman,W.&R.]

Hoerner, Robert J., (AV) ... '31 '60 C.187 B.A. L.477 J.D. 901 Lakeside Ave.‡

Hofelich, James A., (AV) ... '43 '69 C.967 B.S. L.930 J.D. [Hofelich&H.] ⊙

Hofelich, James J. ... '73 '00 C.967 B.A. L.989 J.D. [C Hofelich&H.]

Hofelich & Hofelich, (AV) ... 600 Superior Avenue, East (⊙Westlake)

Hoffer, Christine S. ... '61 '87 C&L.8 B.S., J.D. Sherwin-Williams Co., The

Hoffman, Gary H., (BV) ... '51 '76 C.659 B.S. L.930 J.D. 27970 Chagrin Blvd., Ste. 200

Hoffman, Joseph C., Jr. ... '65 '91 C.381 B.A. L.8 J.D. [Faulkner,M.&P.]

Hoffman, L. Dennis, Jr. ... '68 '97 C.477 B.G.S. L.1003 J.D. [Baker&H.]

Hoffman, Mark Allan ... '54 '80 C.970 B.A. L.8 J.D. Natl. City Bk.

Hoffman, W. Andrew, III, (AV) ... '54 '79 C.679 B.A. L.1003 J.D. [Hoffman]

Hoffman Legal Group, LLC, (AV)
23230 Chagrin Boulevard, Suite 232, 44122-5495
Telephone: 216-292-5200 Fax: 216-292-8766
URL: http://www.hoffmanlegalgroup.net
W. Andrew Hoffman, III;—Douglas S. Hunter.
General Practice.

See Professional Biographies, CLEVELAND, OHIO

Hogan, James A. ... '72 '99 C.602 B.A. L.150 J.D. [A Vorys,S.S.&P.]

Hogan, Michael W. ... '50 '77 C.321 B.A. L.262 J.D. [A R.E.Sweeney]

Hogg, James S., (AV) ... '52 '78 C.373 B.A. L.477 J.D. [Cowden,H.N.&L.]

Hohenberger, Leah M. ... '— '02 C.363 B.A. L.989 J.D. [A Gallagher S.]

Hohler, Kathleen ... '— '80 C.473 B.A. L.276 J.D. [C Jones D.]

Hohmann, William T., (AV) ... '39 '65 C.381 B.A. L.930 J.D. [Hohmann,B.&C.]

Hohmann, Boukis & Curtis Co., L.P.A., (AV)
1370 Ontario Street Suite 520, 44113-1701
Telephone: 216-696-1076 Fax: 216-696-2317
Email: hbc@clevelandlawyers.cc
William T. Hohmann; Kenneth Boukis; Christ Boukis; Jack Curtis.
General Civil, Trial and Appellate Practice. Corporation, Commercial, Reorganization, Bankruptcy, Probate, Taxation and Real Estate Law. Commercial Collections. Estate Planning. International Transactions.
Reference: National City Bank.

See Professional Biographies, CLEVELAND, OHIO

Hojnacki, Kathleen A. '58 '84 C.567 B.A. L.107 J.D. (adm. in NY; not adm. in OH) V.P. & Sr. Coun., KeyBank Natl. Assn.

Hoke, Matthew M. ... '68 '95 C.201 B.A. L.1003 J.D. Law Clk. to Ct. of Com. Pleas

Hoke, S. Candice '55 '84 C.320 B.A. L.976 J.D. (adm. in MA; not adm. in OH) Assoc. Prof. of Law, Cleveland-Marshall College of Law

Holbrook, Amy Clum ... '72 '02 C.607 B.A. L.8 J.D. [A Weltman,W.&R.]

Holbrook, Scott C. ... '75 '00 C.611 B.A. L.893 J.D. [A Baker&H.]

Holderman, Gretchen A. ... '64 '92 C.610 B.A. L.1003 J.D. [C Benesch,F.C.&A.]

Holdsworth, Peter A. ... '75 '02 C.150 B.S. L.989 J.D. [A Bonezzi S.M.&P.]

Holecek, Christopher A., (AV) ... '61 '88 C.363 B.A. L.1003 J.D. [Wegman,H.&V.]

Holecek, Tanja M., (BV) ... '64 '89 C.363 B.S. L.1003 J.D. [Wegman,H.&V.]

Holland, David R. ... '62 '97 C.607 B.S.B.A. L.1003 J.D. 614 W. Superior Ave.

Hollander, Jason S. ... '74 '99 C.910 B.A. L.930 J.D. [A Ulmer&B.]

Hollander, Lisa E. ... '59 '84 C.910 B.A. L.846 J.D. 3826 Euclid Ave.

Hollingsworth, Jack L., (AV) ... '28 '57 C.97 B.S. L.1003 LL.B. P.O. Box 19040

Hollington, Richard R., Jr., (AV) ... '32 '57 C.951 B.A. L.309 LL.B. [Baker&H.]

Hollister, Terry R., (AV) '49 '74 C.381 B.A. L.8 J.D. Gen. Coun. & Sec., MTD Products Inc

Holman, Ronald D., II ... '59 '86 C.197 B.A. L.178 J.D. [Cavitch,F.D.&F.]

Holmes, Clarence H. ... '26 '53 C&L.930 A.B., LL.B. 3048 Keswick Rd.

Holmes, Thomas Charles ... '76 '01 C.473 B.A. L.930 J.D. 5005 Rockside Rd., Ste. 260

Holmgren, Cedar R. ... '— '03 C.260 B.A. L.494 J.D. [A Jones D.]

Holt, Nicole M. ... '75 '02 C.476 B.S. L.124 J.D. [A Rademaker,M.M.&G.]

Holtz, Gregory T. ... '51 '77 C.973 A.B. L.930 J.D. V.P., Society Natl. Bk.

Holzer, Walter S. ... '— '95 C.608 B.S. L.117 J.D. [Jones D.]

Hom, Harold L., Co., LPA, (BV) '62 '88 C.608 B.S.Ch.E. L.930 J.D.
1991 Crocker Road Suite 600, Gemini Tower 1, 44145
Telephone: 440-892-3374 Fax: 440-892-3375 URL: http://www.HomLaw.net
Email: harold@HomLaw.net URL: http://www.haroldhomlawfirm.com
Estate Planning, Probate, Business Law, Intellectual Property and Immigration Law.

See Professional Biographies, CLEVELAND, OHIO

Homolak, Gloria Rowland ... '56 '81 C.528 B.A. L.930 J.D. 6515 Olde York Road

Homolak, John R. ... '55 '80 C.528 B.A. L.930 J.D. Mag., Ct. Majestry

Hong, Laura Kingsley, (AV) ... '59 '85 C.604 B.A. L.930 J.D. [Squire,S.&D.]

Honohan, Kathleen R. '61 '91 C.477 B.A. L.1003 J.D.
Tr. Offr., Huntington Bk. Tr. Dept.
Hooker, David J., (AV) '50 '75 C.207 B.A. L.813 J.D. [Thompson H.]
Hooper, Ryan P. '76 '01 C.201 B.A. L.276 J.D. [🄰 Benesch,F.C.&A.]
Hoover, Valoria C., (BV) '64 '92 C.473 B.A. L.201 J.D. [Kohrman J.&K.]
Hoppe, Herbert J., Jr., (AV) '28 '53 C.347 B.S. L.930 J.D. [🄰 W.Coyne]
Hopps, Lisa R. '65 '93 C.145 B.A. L.893 J.D. Corp. Coun., Forest City Enterprises, Inc.
Hopson, Harvey A., Jr. '47 '75 C.62 B.A. L.930 J.D. 10108 Olivet Ave.★
Horbaly, Robert S., (AV) '45 '70 C.608 B.S. L.851 J.D. [Walter&H.]
Horbaly, Will G. '29 '57 C.381 B.A. 50 Public Sq.
Horejs, Edward R., Jr. '51 '76
C.165 B.A. L.365 J.D. Assoc. Reg. Coun., Chicago Title Ins. Co.
Horkay, Joan Butler '42 '77 C.118 B.A. L.1003 J.D. Staff Coun., Amer. Taxi Serv. Ltd.
Horn, Byron J. '64 '89 C.385 B.A. L.930 J.D. [🅂 Thompson H.]
Horn, Debra J., (AV) '59 '89 C&L.494 B.A., J.D. [Meyers,R.F.&L.]
Horn, Melissa E. '— '03 C.827 B.A. L.161 J.D. [🄰 Jones D.]
Horn, Michael D., (AV) '52 '77 C.8 B.A. L.851 J.D. Asst. Co. Pros.
Horning, Gerald R., (AV) '53 '84 C.473 B.A. L.161 J.D. 1419 West 9th Street
Horrigan, Suzanne Kennedy '50 '75
C.734 A.B. L.989 J.D. 50 Public Square, Suite 400 Terminal Tower
Horst, J. Robert, (AV) '43 '68 C&L.930 A.B., J.D. V.P. & Gen. Coun., Eaton Corp.
Horton, Brett Earle '68 '94 C.511 B.A. L.930 J.D. 1111 Superior Ave.
Horton, Debbie K. '61 '86 C.999 B.A. L.1003 J.D. [Davis,W.]
Horvath, David J. '65 '91 C.930 B.S. L.851 J.D.
7100 E. Pleasant Valley Road Suite 100
Horvath, Joan E. '32 '57 C&L.930 B.S., J.D. 22582 Vine Ct.‡
Horvath, Richard F. '52 '77 C.276 B.A. L.930 J.D. Asst. Dir. of Law
Horvitz, Michael J., (AV) '— '75 C.659 B.S. L.893 J.D. [🄲 Jones D.]
Horwitz, Martin S., (BV) '53 '79 C.150 B.S. L.7 J.D. P.O. Box 22750
Hoskins, George '72 '98 C.145 B.A. L.608 J.D. [🄰 Calfee,H.&G.]
Hotchkiss, Herbert '70 '96 C.92 B.A. L.989 J.D. [🄰 Hahn L.&P.]
Hoty-Bliss, Diane, (BV) '50 '82 C.650 B.A. L.1003 J.D. [Bliss&H.]
Hotz, Gary A., (BV) '46 '77 C.608 B.A. L.161 J.D. 24461 Detroit Rd.
House, Linda L. '54 '93 C.477 B.A. L.1003 J.D. [🄲 Lasko&L.]
House, Robert N. '54 '80 C.97 B.S.B.A. L.930 J.D. Coun., GE Consumer and Industrial
Housel, Robert V., (AV) '44 '73 C.363 B.S.B.A. L.161 J.D. [R.V.Housel]
Housel, Robert V., Co., L.P.A., (AV) 55 Public Square, Suite 11600
Howard, Joseph L., Jr. '43 '68 C&L.945 A.B., J.D. 1223 West 6th Street
Howard, Kristin K. C. '74 '99 C.914 B.A. L.1565 J.D. [🄰 McDonald H.]
Howard, Timothy J., (BV) '42 '68 C.608 B.S. L.1003 J.D.
1406 W. 6th Street, Suite 400
Hoza, Michele L. '71 '01 C.381 B.A. L.989 J.D. [🄰 Kohrman J.&K.]
Hubbard, Kenneth W. '66 '96 C.879 B.A. L.1003 J.D. [🄰 Thompson H.]
Hubbard, William J. '— '03 C.970 B.A. L.93 J.D. [🄰 Thompson H.]
Hubbert, Christopher J. '66 '91 C.477 B.A. L.930 J.D. [Kohrman J.&K.]
Huber, Mary Elizabeth '— '96 C.741 B.B.A. L.602 J.D. [🄰 Jones D.]
Hudak, David J. '68 '99 C.207 B.S. L.1003 J.D. [🄰 Sutter,O.&F.]

Hudak, James A., (AV) '40 '74 C.124 B.S.E.E. L.1003 J.D.
29425 Chagrin Boulevard, Suite 304, 44122-4602
Telephone: 216-292-3900 Fax: 216-292-3930
Email: hudakjames@aol.com
Patent, Trademark, Copyright and Unfair Competition Law.
See Professional Biographies, CLEVELAND, OHIO

Hudson, Timothy M. '— '04 C.945 B.A. L.228 J.D. [🄰 Jones D.]
Hudzinski, Michael E. '61 '89
C.161 B.E.E. L.1003 J.D. [Fay,S.F.M.&M.] (See Pat. Sect.)
Huff, Kimberlie L. '75 '00 C.879 B.A. L.339 J.D. [🄰 Taft,S.&H.]
Huff, Leslye Maria '50 '99 C.161 B.S. L.1003 J.D. [Huff]
Huff Law Group, LLC 4403 Saint Clair Ave. N.E.
Hufford, Allen C. '76 '02 C.679 B.S. L.124 J.D. 4040 Mayfield Rd.
Huggins, Emily S. '78 '04 C.893 B.A. L.602 J.D. [🄰 Thompson H.]
Hughes, Kathleen Marie '69 '95
C.602 B.A. L.124 J.D. Cleveland Municipal School District
Hughes, Maura L., (AV) '67 '93 C.103 A.B. L.309 J.D. [Calfee,H.&G.]
Hughes, Michael M., (AV) '37 '62 C.276 B.S.S.S. L.477 J.D. [🄲 Frantz W.]
Hughes, Michael M., Jr., (BV) '63 '89
C.276 A.B. L.930 J.D. Asst. Coun., Cleve. Bar Assn.
Huhn, Wilson Ray '50 '77 C.976 B.A. L.188 J.D. 29475 Bryce Rd.
Hull, Allan, (AV) '13 '38 C.604 A.B. L.309 J.D. [Hull&H.]
Hull, Grover A., (BV) '45 '70 C.970 B.A. L.930 J.D. [🄲 Hull&H.]
Hull, Jonathan '52 '78 C.970 B.A. L.930 J.D. [Hull&H.]
Hull, Mark R. '68 '04 C.645 B.S. L.8 J.D. [🄰 Calfee,H.&G.] (See Pat. Sect.)
Hull and Hull, (AV) 6505 Wilson Mills Road
Hulme, Roy A., (AV) '54 '79 C.117 B.A. L.930 J.D. [🄰 Reminger&R.]
Hultin, Pamela N., (AVⓉ) '45 '73 C.207 B.F.A. L.174 J.D. [McCarthy,L.C.&L.]
Humphrey, Robert M. '54 '82 C.455 B.A. L.818 J.D. [Cowden,H.N.&L.]
Hungerford, James M., (BV) '53 '80 C.1349 B.A. L.1003 J.D. 2424 Broadview Rd.
Hunt, Karen S. '54 '84 C.81 B.A. L.8 J.D. U.S. Dept. of Labor
Hunt, R. Todd, (AV) '54 '84 C.651 B.A. L.930 J.D. [Walter&H.]
Hunt, Thomas Joseph '70 '96 C.363 B.A. L.989 J.D. 1540, Leader Building
Hunter, Christopher H. '64 '89 C.105 B.S. L.930 J.D.
Asst. Gen. Coun., Intel. Prop., Parker-Hannifin Corp. (Pat.)
Hunter, Douglas S. '75 '00 C.851 B.S. L.607 J.D. [🄰 Hoffman]
Huntsberger, Jeffrey R., (AV) '54 '80 C.879 B.A. L.930 J.D. [McDonald H.]
Hupertz, Lawrence R., (BV) '58 '83
C.885 B.A. L.1003 J.D. 925 Euclid Avenue, Suite 1995
Hupp, Diane H. '65 '89 C.62 B.A. L.161 J.D.
Sr. Corp. Coun., The Sherwin-Williams Co.
Hupp, Steven J., (AV) '63 '88 C.363 B.A. L.1003 J.D. [Bonezzi S.M.&P.]
Hurd, Calvin F., Jr., (AV) '35 '61 C.610 B.S. L.930 LL.B. 1750 Standard Bldg.
Hurd, Gail A. '59 '85 C.385 B.A. L.930 J.D. [J.V.Heutsche]
Hurlbut, Chris L. '58 '88 C.161 B.A. L.1003 J.D.
Corp. Coun., Litig., The Sherwin-Williams Co.
Hurst, John P., (BV) '54 '79 C.473 B.A. L.1003 J.D.
Asst, General Counsel, Progressive Insurance Company

Hurt, Marcia, (AV) '46 '81 C.161 B.S. L.930 J.D.
18201 Shelburne, 44118
Telephone: 216-321-2775 Fax: 216-321-3375
Email: mehurt@mindspring.com
Products Liability, Labor and Employment Law, Litigation, Civil Appeals.

Hurtuk, Edward A., (AV) '53 '79 C.930 B.A. L.608 J.D. [Hurtuk&D.]
Hurtuk & Daroff Co., L.P.A., (AV) 6120 Parkland Boulevard, Suite 100
Hurwitz, Raymond '13 '35 C&L.608 2331 Allison St.
Hutchings, Mary P. '— '51 C.403 A.B. L.1003 LL.B. 3039 Becket Rd.‡

Hutchins, Sara E. '78 '03 C.608 B.A. L.117 J.D. [🄰 Squire,S.&D.]
Hutchinson, Joseph F., Jr., (AV) '49 '74 C.477 B.A. L.608 J.D. [Baker&H.]
Hutchinson, Trudy '47 '83 C.502 B.S. L.1003 J.D. 1983 East 24th Street
Huth, Jeffrey A. '55 '89 C.381 B.G.S. L.1003 J.D. 2000 E. 9th St., Ste. 700
Hutton, Lee J., (AV) '50 '75 C.610 A.B. L.477 J.D. [Duvin,C.&H.]
Hyatt, Hudson '14 '39 C&L.930 B.A., LL.B. 2648 Euclid Hts. Blvd.‡
Hyatt, Susan M. '50 '81 C.150 B.S. L.930 J.D.
(adm. in MO; not adm. in OH) Hyatt Legal Servs.
Hyde, Alan L., (AV) '28 '53 C.31 A.B. L.309 J.D. 127 Public Sq.‡
Hyland, Leo J. '27 '56 C.679 B.S. L.1003 J.D. 1836 Maywood St.
Hyman, Jonathan T. '73 '97 C.999 B.A. L.930 J.D. [🄰 Reminger&R.]
Hyre, Rexford C. '40 '64 C&L.930 A.B., J.D. V.P., Society Natl. Bk.
Ibold, Charles J., (BV) '52 '82 C.150 B.A. L.1003 J.D. 5340 Avion Pk. Dr.
Icove, Edward A., (AV) '51 '77 C.610 B.G.S. L.851 J.D. 1801 E. 9th Street, Ste. 900
Iddings, Sarah L. '78 '03 C.610 B.A. L.124 J.D. [🄰 Walter&H.]
Igel, Peter A., (AV) '60 '86 C.473 B.S. L.608 J.D. [🄲 Kahn K.]
Ikuma, Kaya A. '71 '99 C.323 B.A. L.851 J.D.
Asst. Co. Prosecutor, Cuyahoga Co. Prosecutor's Off.
Iler, Don C., (AV) '29 '60 C.608 B.S. L.1003 LL.B. [Iler&I.]
Iler, Nancy C., (AV) '60 '87 C.8 B.S.N. L.1003 J.D. [Iler&I.] (Pat.)

Iler & Iler, (AV)
1640 Standard Building, 44113
Telephone: 216-696-5700
Email: nancyiler@ameritech.net URL: http://www.ilerlawoffice.com
Don C. Iler; Nancy C. Iler.
General Practice.
See Professional Biographies, CLEVELAND, OHIO

Immormino, Mark, (AV) '56 '80 C.161 B.A. L.1003 J.D. [M.Immormino]
Immormino, Mark, Co., L.P.A., (AV) 1370 Ontario St., Ste. 1000
Incorvaia, Santo T., Law Office '57 '88
C.161 B.A. L.930 J.D. 5005 Rockside Road, Suite 600
Ingersoll, John David '58 '85 C.165 B.A. L.989 J.D.
526 Superior Avenue East, Suite 458
Ingersoll, Robert M., (AV) '52 '81 C.197 B.A. L.930 J.D. Asst. Pub. Def.
Inglis, David S., (AV) '57 '82 C.597 B.A. L.477 J.D. 1300 E. 9th St.
Insul, Donald A., (AV) '44 '68 C.966 B.S. L.930 J.D. 6 Hinting Hollow Dr.
Ipavec, Charles F., (AV) '21 '51 C.152 B.A. L.1003 J.D. 1215 Superior Ave.

Ireland-Phillips, Karen S., Attorney At Law '58 '96 C.161 B.A. L.989 J.D.
Rockefeller Building, 614 West Superior Avenue, Suite 1448, 44113
Telephone: 216-696-5530 Fax: 216-696-5531 URL: http://www.irelandpnillipslaw.com
Email: ksiplaw@hotmail.com URL: http://www.ireland-phillips-law.com
Family Law, Workers Compensation, Civil Litigation, Probate, Wills, Social Security, Personal Injury.
See Professional Biographies, CLEVELAND, OHIO

Irwin, Scott D. '— '92 C.381 B.A. L.608 J.D. [Baker&H.]
Isakoff, Andrew H. '61 '86 C.97 B.A. L.851 J.D. The Progressive Corp.
Isakoff, Janice A. '60 '86 C.253 B.A. L.851 J.D. [🄲 Roetzel&A.]
Isquick, Margaret Oshuns '49 '85 C.608 B.S. L.1003 J.D. 1849 Prospect, Ste. 222
Israel, Rachael L. '73 '00 C.967 B.A. L.124 J.D. [🄰 Kushner&R.]
Isroff, Brian D. '63 '88 C.473 B.S. L.188 J.D. V.P., Natl. City Bk.
Isroff, Ronald H., (AV) '43 '67 C.94 B.S.B.A. L.608 J.D. [Ulmer&B.]
Itani, Stuart Yusuf '77 '02 C.659 B.A. L.273 J.D. [🄰 Tucker E.&W.]
Ivey, Timothy C., (BV) '62 '87 C.851 B.B.A. L.930 J.D. [Roetzel&A.] (☉Akron)
Izanec, Peter E. '— '01 C.951 B.A. L.309 J.D. [🄰 Jones D.]
Jablonski, Richard W. '69 '94 C.363 B.A. L.161 J.D. Law Clk. to Com. Pleas J.
Jablonski, Robert C. '42 '66 C.863 A.B. L.930 J.D. 3805 E. 71st St.★
Jackson, Denise A. '61 '94 C.597 B.M. L.1065 J.D. [🄰 Squire,S.&D.]
Jackson, Iverson Matthew '74 '03 C.150 B.A. L.124 J.D./M.B.A. [🄰 Norchi,B.&F.]
Jackson, John V., II, (AV) '47 '72 C.610 B.A. L.1003 J.D. [Sutter,O.&F.]
Jackson, Leo A. '20 '50 C.511 A.B. L.1003 LL.B. Ret. Ct. of App. J.
Jackson, Michael E., (AV) '44 '75 C.610 B.A. L.46 J.D. [Schwarzwald&M.]
Jackson, Robert H. '36 '61 C.339 B.A. L.930 LL.B. [Kohrman J.&K.]
Jackson, Todd G. '60 '85 C.381 B.B.A. L.989 J.D. [Weston H.]
Jackson, Travis F. '74 '99 C.620 B.A. L.602 J.D. [🄰 Frantz W.]
Jacobs, Brian D. '72 '97 C.473 B.S. L.8 J.D. Ernst & Young LLP
Jacobs, Christopher B. '69 '95
C&L.608 B.S.M.E., J.D. [Renner,O.B.&S.] (See Pat. Sect.)
Jacobs, Gregory A., (AV) '52 '77 C.674 A.B. L.178 J.D. 2230 Euclid Avenue
Jacobs, James K. '55 '80 C.608 B.S. L.1003 J.D. 29555 Shaker Blvd.
Jacobs, Leslie W., (AV) '44 '68 C.597 B.S. L.309 J.D. [Thompson H.]
Jacobs, Mark R. '73 '99 C.910 A.B. L.608 J.D. [🄰 Kahn K.]
Jacobs, Thomas L., (BV) '34 '59
C&L.930 A.B., LL.B. Western Reserve Building, Suite 220
Jacobs, William G. E. '43 '69 C.477 A.B. L.608 J.D.
Assoc. Gen. Coun. & Asst. Secy., Electrolux North America
Jacobs, William W., (AV) '51 '76 C.475 B.A. L.930 J.D. [Thompson H.]
Jacobs Thomas, Joan '56 '84 C.92 B.A. L.989 J.D. 23850 Center Ridge Road
Jacobson, Arthur E. '39 '75 C.627 B.G.E. L.585 J.D.
(adm. in NC; not adm. in OH) Admin. Law J.
Jacobson, William S., (AV) '57 '84 C.901 B.A. L.930 J.D. [Nurenberg,P.H.&M.]
Jacono, Anthony T. '— '00 C.930 B.S.; B.A. L.494 J.D. [🄰 Jones D.]
Jaffe, Ari H., (AV) '60 '87 C.1036 B.A. L.930 J.D. [Kohrman J.&K.]
Jaffe, Daniel A. '60 '89 C&L.178 B.A., J.D. [🄰 Squire,S.&D.]
Jaffe, David I., (BV) '56 '81 C.385 B.A. L.1003 J.D. 5157 Crofton Avenue
Jaketic, Bryan '76 '04 C.188 B.S. L.273 J.D. [🄰 Benesch,F.C.&A.]
Jakiel, Kristin J. '73 '98 C.608 B.A. L.30 J.D. [🅂 Baker&H.]
Jakubaitis, Jayne L. '57 '92 C.602 B.A. L.1003 J.D. [Bricker&E.]
Jakubs, Michele L. '70 '99 C.608 B.S. L.989 J.D. [🄰 Zashin&R.]
Jambe, Suzanne M., (AV) '60 '93 C.893 B.A. L.851 J.D. [Baker&H.]
James, Bernard F. '19 '60 C.930 B.B.A. L.161 J.D. 9540 Cove Dr.
James, Patricia S. '40 '73 C.597 B.A. L.30 J.D.
(adm. in IA; not adm. in OH) Case Western Reserve Univ. Sch. of Law
Jamieson, Daniel J., (BV) '52 '80 C.161 B.A. L.1003 J.D. 75 Public Square, Suite 1200
Jamieson, Sally A. '63 '00 C.363 B.A. L.1003 J.D. [🄰 Ulmer&B.]
Janecek, Radek '73 '98 C.516 J.D. L.273 LL.M. 4900 Key Tower, 127 Public Square
Janik, Steven G., (AV) '51 '76 C.207 B.A. L.1003 J.D. [Janik&D.]

Janik & Dorman, L.L.P., (AV) 🄱🅁
9200 South Hill Boulevard, Suite 300, 44147-3521
Telephone: 440-838-7600 Fax: 440-838-7601
Email: scott.cerny@janiklaw.com URL: http://www.janiklaw.com
Partners: Steven G. Janik; Andrew J. Dorman; Jonathan Philipp; Jason D. Winter. Associates: Brian D. Spitz; Barry Ronald Murner; David H. Brown; Stacy N. Lilly; Lori Ross Tark; Charles C. Spagnoli; Christopher J. Van Blargan; Crystal L. Nicosia; Eric J. Weiss; Matthew M. Nee; Mark E. Kremser; Kelly H. Rogers; Michael J. Stanuszek; Catherine A. Davis; W. Joseph Baker. Of Counsel: Thomas D. Lambros; Ellyn B. Mehendale; Christopher L. Parker.

(This Listing Continued)

Janik & Dorman, L.L.P. (Continued)

Litigation. Insurance Coverage and Defense, Corporate and Commercial Defense and Labor and Employment. Professional Liability, Casualty, Products Liability, Aviation, Toxic Tort and Environmental Law.

See Professional Biographies, CLEVELAND, OHIO

Janke, Ronald R., (AV) .... '— '74 C.967 B.A. L.228 J.D. [Jones D.]
Janovitz, Barbara Bellin, (AV) .... '58 '83 C.659 B.S. L.569 J.D. [[A] Reminger&R.]
Janusz, John M. .... '72 '98 C.107 B.A. L.989 J.D. [[A] Weston H.]
Jaquay, Robert B. .... '55 '81 C.363 B.S.B.A. L.161 J.D. George Gund Found.
Jaras, William P. .... '35 '60 C&L.930 A.B., LL.B. Pres., Capital Planning Corp.
Jarmusch, Robert T. .... '22 '51 C.930 B.B.S. L.7 LL.B. 20863 Farnsleigh Rd.‡
Jaros, Stanley T., (AV) .... '45 '73 C.103 A.B. L.930 J.D. [Moriarty&J.]
Jaros, Susan Stevens, (AV) '47 '73
C.207 B.A. L.930 J.D. Assoc. V.P., Case Western Reserve Univ.
Jarrett, Rita M. .... '— '92 C.161 B.B.A. L.1003 J.D. [[A] Kadish,H.&W.]
Jasper, Mabel M. .... '— '77 C.381 B.S. L.1003 J.D. Mun. J.
Javitch, Victor M., (AV) .... '— '62 C.477 B.A. L.930 LL.B. [Javitch,B.&R.]

Javitch, Block & Rathbone L.L.P., (AV)
1300 East Ninth Street, 14th Floor, 44114-1503 ⊙
Telephone: 216-623-0000 Fax: 216-623-0190
Email: bblock@JBandR.com URL: http://www.JBandR.com
Victor M. Javitch; Bruce A. Block; Joel H. Rathbone; Marc A. Melamed; Kenneth B. Baker; Michele Polito Soucie; Michael D. Linn; Michael D. Slodov; Jeffrey E. Dubin; Robert N. Lurie; Theodore A. Konstantinopoulos.
Bankruptcy, Commercial, Corporate, Collection, General Civil Practice, Landlord-Tenant, Real Estate, Trials and Appeals.
Representative Clients: General Motors Acceptance Corp.; Associated Estates Corp.; J.P. Morgan Chase; Bank of America; General Electric Capital Corp.; Household Finance Corporation; Key Bank; National City Corp.; Chrysler Financial Corp.; Bank One.
Cincinnati, Ohio Office: 602 Main Street, Suite 500, 45202. Telephone: 513-774-9600. Fax: 513-744-9602
Columbus, Ohio Office: 33 North Third Street, Suite 300, 43215. Telephone: 614-228-9550. Fax: 614-228-2818.

See Professional Biographies, CLEVELAND, OHIO

Jeffers, John W., (AV) .... '36 '64 C.309 A.B. L.659 J.D. [Weston H.]

Jeffries, Kube, Forrest & Monteleone Co., L.P.A., (AV)
1650 Midland Building, 44115
Telephone: 216-771-4050 Fax: 216-771-0732
Email: attys@jkfmlaw.com URL: http://www.jkfmlaw.com
Salvatore P. Jeffries (1930-1992); J. Michael Monteleone; David A. Forrest; M. Jane Rua; Mark E. Barbour; Bradford D. Zelasko; Michael R. Kube (Retired).
Personal Injury, Wrongful Death, Medical Malpractice and Products Liability Law. General Civil, Trial and Appellate Practice.
Reference: First Merit Bank, N.A.

See Professional Biographies, CLEVELAND, OHIO

Jenkins, James A., (BV) .... '54 '85 C.679 B.A. L.1003 J.D. 2000 Standard Bldg.
Jenkins, Jay T. '54 '84 C.1044 B.A. L.107 J.D.
(adm. in NY; not adm. in OH) 26180 Curtiss Wright Pkwy.
Jenkins, John J. .... '62 '86 C.116 B.A. L.893 J.D. [Calfee,H.&G.]
Jenkins, Lindsay C. .... '— '02 C.473 B.S. L.161 J.D. [[A] Jones D.]
Jenks, Carl M., (AV) .... '— '82 C.118 B.A. L.309 J.D. [Jones D.]
Jennings, Colin R. .... '71 '97 C.25 B.A. L.930 J.D. [[A] Squire,S.&D.]
Jennings, James Kieran, III .... '67 '94 C.651 B.Acct. L.989 J.D. 30195 Chagrin Blvd.
Jennrich, Terry, (BV) .... '— '83 C.8 B.A. L.1003 J.D. 1370 Ontario St.
Jenny, Leslie Moore .... '72 '96 C.62 B.A. L.1003 J.D. [[A] Reminger&R.]
Jenovic, Joanne D'Emilia '63 '89
C.363 B.A. L.989 J.D. Jud. Law Clk., U.S. Dist. Ct., N. Dist. of OH
Jensen, Erik M. '45 '80 C.453 S.B. L.188 J.D.
(adm. in NY; not adm. in OH) Prof. of Law, Case Western Reserve U. Sch. of Law
Jerdonek, Elizabeth A. .... '72 '97 C.62 B.A. L.989 J.D. [[A] Ulmer&B.]
Jereb, Brian J. .... '58 '83 C.363 B.A. L.851 J.D. [McDonald H.]
Jerome, Joseph B., (AV) .... '50 '75 C.97 B.S.B.A. L.1003 J.D. [J.B.Jerome&Assoc.]
Jerome, Joseph B., and Associates, (AV) .... 55 Public Square
Jerse, Edward S., (AV) .... '58 '83 C.276 B.A. L.309 J.D. [[A] Moscarino&T.]
Jerse, Shannon Fogarty, (AV) '62 '88
C.363 B.A. L.1003 J.D. Asst. Gen. Coun., Meridia Health Sys.
Jett, Stephen H., (BV) .... '62 '90 C&L.383 B.A., J.D. [Taft,S.&H.]
Jewitt, John R., Jr., (BV) .... '22 '49 C.385 A.B. L.930 LL.B. 2500 Terminal Twr. Bldg.
Jobe, Lisa (Schworm) .... '73 '98 C.930 B.A. L.273 J.D. Officemax, Inc.
Johanek, Mary Ann Sabol, (AV) .... '31 '80 C.599 B.S. L.1003 J.D. 24950 Chagrin Blvd.
Johnson, Andrew L., Jr., (AV) '31 '60 C.597 B.S. L.1003 J.D.
1205 W. 110th St., Apt. 16
Johnson, Brenda M. .... '62 '93 C.381 B.G.S. L.251 J.D. [[A] Nurenberg,P.H.&M.]
Johnson, Christopher A. .... '50 '78 [Tetlow&J.]
Johnson, Christopher R. .... '75 '00 C.124 B.A. L.273 J.D. [[A] Thompson H.]
Johnson, Clarence .... '30 '60 C.381 B.S. L.1003 LL.B. 16115 Delrey Ave.
Johnson, Eric J. .... '75 '00 C.207 B.A. L.228 J.D. [[A] Squire,S.&D.]
Johnson, Gary C., (AV) .... '41 '80 C.693 B.A. L.930 J.D. [Johnson,A.&C.]
Johnson, Gary W., (AV) .... '54 '79 C.276 B.S.B.A. L.851 J.D. [Weston H.]
Johnson, Ila W. .... '18 '43 C&L.477 A.B., LL.B. 4320 Mayfield St.‡
Johnson, Lance B., (AV) .... '44 '69 C&L.94 B.A., J.D. 23420 Lakeland Boulevard
Johnson, Linda L. .... '58 '96 C.174 B.S.C.E. L.161 J.D. [[A] Mansour,G.G.&M.]
Johnson, Marcia Walker, (AV) '51 '76
C&L.930 B.A., J.D. Chf. Civil Div.; U.S. Atty. Off. Dept. of Jus.
Johnson, Mark C. .... '74 '00 C.436 B.E. L.124 J.D. [[A] Renner,O.B.&S.] (See Pat. Sect.)
Johnson, Melissa S. .... '70 '96 C.62 B.A. L.930 J.D. Navisource
Johnson, Nelli .... '58 '84 C.347 B.A. L.608 J.D. 815 Superior Ave. E., Ste. 1920
Johnson, Pamela M. '66 '91 C.363 B.S.B.A. L.608 J.D.
Tax Coun., Sherwin Williams Co.
Johnson, Richard G. .... '64 '90 C&L.930 B.A., J.D. [R.G.Johnson]
Johnson, Robert A. .... '33 '61 C&L.976 B.A., LL.B. BP America, Inc.
Johnson, Ronald V. .... '70 '05 C.161 L.8 J.D. KeyBank Natl. Assn.
Johnson, Timothy D., (AV) .... '48 '74 C.973 B.S.B.A. L.930 J.D. [Weston H.]
Johnson, Tom L., (BV) .... '52 '81 C.930 B.A. L.1003 J.D. 4403 St. Clair Ave.
Johnson, Tracy Scott .... '63 '95 C.871 B.S. L.1338 J.D. [Calfee,H.&G.] (See Pat. Sect.)
Johnson, Victoria .... '— '90 C.62 B.A. L.930 J.D. [[B] Baker&H.]
Johnson, Angelo & Colaluca, L.L.C., (AV) .... 1001 Lakeside Avenue, Suite 1700
Johnson, Richard G., Co., L.P.A. .... 955 West St. Clair Avenue
Johnston, William A. .... '66 '99 C.645 B.S. L.989 J.D. [[A] Calfee,H.&G.] (See Pat. Sect.)
Joliet, Leo J. .... '25 '49 C.363 A.B. L.930 LL.B. 21761 Gatehouse Lane
Jones, Bruce P., (AV) .... '48 '73 C.165 B.A. L.976 J.D. [Squire,S.&D.]
Jones, Candace M., (AV) .... '— '92 C.30 B.A. L.930 J.D. [Hahn L.&P.]
Jones, F. Arthur, II .... '77 '03 C.309 A.B. L.276 J.D. [[A] Baker&H.]
Jones, Garlandine, (CV) .... '44 '86 C.608 B.A. L.1003 J.D. One Lakeside Avenue
Jones, Gary L. .... '58 '97 C.161 B.A. L.1003 J.D. [[A] Kohrman J.&K.]
Jones, Gretchen Corps., (AV) .... '56 '82 C.611 B.A. L.930 J.D. Case Western University

Jones, Jeffrey P. .... '64 '93 C.112 B.A. L.464 J.D. [[A] Benesch,F.C.&A.]
Jones, Larry J. .... '— '02 C.161 B.A. L.1003 J.D. [[A] Thompson H.]
Jones, Lessie Milton .... '— '85 C.381 B.A. L.989 J.D. [Duvin,C.&H.]
Jones, Melissa A. .... '74 '02 C.608 B.A. L.989 J.D. [[A] Frantz W.]
Jones, Peggy Foley, (AV) .... '58 '85 C.429 B.A. L.161 J.D. Co. J.
Jones, Peter Lawson, (AV) .... '52 '80 C&L.309 A.B., J.D. [Roetzel&A.]
Jones, R. Mark, (AV) .... '57 '83 C.174 B.A. L.930 J.D. [Roetzel&A.]

Jones Day, (AV)
North Point, 901 Lakeside Avenue, 44114-1190 ⊙
Telephone: 216-586-3939 Telecopier: 216-579-0212
Email: counsel@jonesday.com URL: http://www.jonesday.com
Members of Firm in Cleveland: Stephen J. Brogan (Not admitted in OH); Kenneth R. Adamo; David F. Adler; David B. Alden; Randal S. Baringer; Richard J. Bedell, Jr.; Mark A. Belasic; Thomas A. Briggs; Kathleen B. Burke; Robert L. Canala; Denise A. Carkhuff; William H. Coquillette; Paul G. Crist; John D. Currivan; Thomas C. Daniels; Thomas Demitrack; Robert P. Ducatman; John P. Dunn; Robert S. Faxon; Regan J. Fay; F. Drexel Feeling; Michelle K. Fischer; Timothy P. Fraelich; Lyle G. Ganske; Steven N. Geise; Stephen Q. Giblin; Calvin P. Griffith; Theodore M. Grossman; Daniel C. Hagen; Thomas A. Hamilton; Charles W. Hardin, Jr.; David G. Heiman; Mark Herrmann; William A. Herzberger; Christopher J. Hewitt; Kenneth G. Hochman; Walter S. Holzer; Ronald R. Janke; Carl M. Jenks; Stephen J. Kaczynski; Robert C. Kahrl; Sanjiv K. Kapur; Christopher M. Kelly; Dennis M. Kelly; Paul D. Koethe; David A. Kutik; Dennis W. LaBarre; Richard P. Layman; Jeffrey S. Leavitt; Patrick J. Leddy; Heather Lennox; Irvin A. Leonard; Barbara J. Leukart; Mary D. Maloney; Michael G. Marting; Bernadette Mihalic Mast; Stephen C. Mixter; Anthony R. Moore; Dennis L. Murphy; John M. Newman, Jr.; Timothy J. O'Hearn; Zachary T. Paris; William T. Plesec; Joseph D. Pollack; David P. Porter; Rachel L. Rawson; Robert H. Rawson, Jr.; John A. Rego; Richard L. Reppert; Jeanne M. Rickert; Geoffrey J. Ritts; Lisa A. Roberts-Mamone; Louis Rorimer; James A. Rydzel; John M. Saada, Jr.; Edward J. Sebold; Steven E. Sigalow; David W. Sloan; Stephen G. Sozio; Stephen J. Squeri; John L. Strauch; Richard G. Stuhan; Brian F. Toohey; Jeffery D. Ubersax; Michael W. Vary; Robert S. Walker; James L. Wamsley, III; Robert C. Weber; Richard B. Whitney; Paula Batt Wilson; James E. Young. Senior Partner: Patrick F. McCartan. Senior Of Counsel: George J. Moscarino. Of Counsel: David B. Cochran; Michael J. Horvitz; Richard H. Sayler. Counsel: Leozino Agozzino; Randall A. Cole; Sandra E. Gammie; Ellen E. Halfon; Charles D. Hassell; Ted S. Hiser; Kathleen Hohler; Charles M. Kennedy; J. Joseph Korpics; Kathy P. Lazar; Stephen D. Scanlon; Marc A. Silverstein; Charles M. Steines; H. Duane Switzer; Rose Mary Wenstrup. Associates: Atossa M. Alavi; Kathleen M. Amer; Laura R. Anderson; Mark J. Andreini; Michael R. Asam; Brett P. Barragate; Gregory A. Bauer; Laura Beresh; John V. Biernacki; Laura A. Bigler; Stephen L. Bittence; Carl E. Black; Pearson N. Bownas; Jennifer H. Boyce; Kevin D. Boyce; Marc D. Browning; James P. Burke; Justin M. Cernansky; Eric C. Chaffee; Howard W. Chu; Robert J. Colacarro; Stephen P. Coolbaugh; Lorri W. Cooper; Stephanie S. Couhig; John D. Curtin; David L. DeBord; James P. Dougherty; David W. Dulabon; Patricia Eschbach-Hall; Adrienne M. Ferraro; Kevin H. Fink; Andrew G. Fiorella; Anne Owings Ford; Paul E. Franz; Scott F. Frodyma; Lisa B. Gates; Susan M. Gerber; Amy E. Gerbick; Kristen Lau Gest; Michael J. Gleason; Eric R. Goodman; Thomas R. Goots; Earnest B. Gregory; Elizabeth A. Grove; Brian K. Grube; Gina K. Gunning; Scott W. Hackwelder; Joseph D. Hatina; Travis M. Heidorf; Peter G. Hilbert; Cedar R. Holmgren; Melissa E. Horn; Mary Elizabeth Huber; Timothy M. Hudson; Peter E. Izanec; Anthony T. Jacono; Lindsay C. Jenkins; A. Gregory Junge; Salim A. Kafiti; Gus Kallergis; Dainius A. Krivinskas; Lea J. Krivinskas; Lisa K. Kunkle; Kabir A. Lalchandani; Lisa S. Lathrop; Jonathan B. Leiken; Jennifer C. Lewis; John Q. Lewis; Nathan T. Lewis; Arthur P. Licygiewicz; Burkhart R. Lindahl; Shoshana E. Litt; Julia Ann Love; Sheryl H. Love; John Paul Lucci; Karl M. Maersch; David M. Maiorana; Jeffrey R. A. Manghillis; Sasha Markovic; John E. Mazey; Philip W. McCarty; Ryan B. Mccrum; Dawn E. McFadden; Daniel A. Messeloff; Heather Varley Miller; Nicholas M. Miller; David E. Mills; Kimberley P.H. Mitchell; Isaac A. Molnar; Anna L. Moscioni; Eric H. Mosier; Cassandra G. Mott; Adam D. Munson; Melissa J. Nandi; Josephine S. Noble; Patrick J. Norton; Aidana K. Nurgaliyeva; R. Jason Oblander; Michael S. Owendoff; Johanna F. Parker; Theodore C. Parsons; Vipul B. Patel; Stephen R. Penrod; Shane T. Pfleiderer; Christine M. Przybysz; Charles W. Pugh; Kimberly J. Pustulka; Mark B. Radefeld; Dustin B. Rawlin; Meggan A. Rawlin; Brian E. Ray; Robert F. Rivera; Julie W. Rogers; Ryan T. Routh; Jeffrey Saks; Joseph M. Sauer; Stefan K. Schnopp; Asha B. Scielzo; Katherine M. Serevitch; Paula G. Shakelton; Jenny L. Sheaffer; Matthew P. Silversten; John L. Sinatra, Jr.; Amanda M. Snyder; Brad A. Sobolewski; Michael J. Solecki; Nicole D. Stanger; Tracy K. Stratford; Jessica E. Trilling; Henry E. Turner Jr.; Wade R. Wagatsuma; Christopher J. Wagner; Andrew M. Walker; James W. Walworth, Jr.; Stephen L. Washington; Brooke D. Werner; Meredith M. Wilkes; Caroline M. Williams; Thomas A. Wilson; Jonathan P. Witmer-Rich. Senior Staff Attorneys: Jennifer Hay Baringer; Karen J. Corrigan; Mark B. Farroni; Michael S. Martis. Staff Attorneys: Ronald L. Cappellazzo; Jennifer J. Chunyo; Noreen DeNuzzo; Lynne C. Fischer; Richard S. Geiger; Jeffrey D. Roush.
Languages: Chinese (Mandarin), French, German, Greek, Hindi, Japanese, Lithuanian, Portuguese and Spanish.
Full-Service Civil Practice, Antitrust and Competition Law, Business Restructuring and Reorganization, Capital Markets, Complex Commercial and Multijurisdictional Litigation, Corporate Criminal Investigations, Employee Benefits and Executive Compensation, Energy Delivery and Power, Government Regulation, Health Care, Intellectual Property and Technology, International Litigation and Arbitration, Issues and Appeals, Labor and Employment, Lending/Structured Finance and Derivatives, Life Sciences, Mergers and Acquisitions, Oil and Gas, Private Equity, Products Liability, Personal Injury Torts and Health Litigation, Real Estate and Environment, Securities and Shareholder Litigation, Tax.
In Columbus, Ohio: 325 John H. McConnell Boulevard, Suite 600. Telephone: 614-469-3939. Telecopier: 614-461-4198.
In Atlanta, Georgia: 1420 Peachtree Street, N.E., Suite 800. Telephone: 404-521-3939. Telecopier: 404-581-8330.
In Beijing, China: 3201 China World Tower 1, No. 1 Jianguomenwai Avenue. Telephone: 86-10-5866-1111. Telecopier: 86-10-5866-1122.
In Brussels, Belgium: Boulevard Brand Whitlocklaan 165, 1200 Brussels. Telephone: 32-2-645-14-11. Telecopier: 32-2-645-14-45.
In Chicago, Illinois: 77 West Wacker. Telephone: 312-782-3939. Telecopier: 312-782-8585.
In Dallas, Texas: 2727 North Harwood Street. Telephone: 214-220-3939. Telecopier: 214-969-5100.
In Frankfurt, Germany: Hochhaus am Park, Grüneburgweg 102, 60323 Frankfurt am Main. Telephone: 49-69-9726-3939. Telecopier: 49-69-9726-3993.
In Hong Kong, China: 31st Floor, Edinburgh Tower, The Landmark, 15 Queen's Road, Central. Telephone: 852-2526-6895. Telecopier: 852-2868-5871.
In Houston, Texas: 717 Texas, Suite 3300. Telephone: 832-239-3939. Telecopier: 832-239-3600.
In Irvine, California: 3 Park Plaza, Suite 1100. Telephone: 949-851-3939. Telecopier: 949-553-7539.
In London, England: 21 Tudor Street. Telephone: 44-20-7039-5959. Telecopier: 44-20-7039-5999.
In Los Angeles, California: 555 South Flower Street, Fiftieth Floor. Telephone: 213-489-3939. Telecopier: 213-243-2539.
In Madrid, Spain: Velázquez 51, 4th Floor. Telephone: 34-91-520-39-39. Telecopier: 34-91-520-39-38.
In Menlo Park, California: 2882 Sand Hill Road, Suite 240. Telephone: 650-739-3939. Telecopier: 650-739-3900.
In Milan, Italy: Via Turati, 16/18. Telephone: 39-02-7645-4001. Telecopier: 39-02-7645-4400.
In Moscow, Russia: Smolenskaya Square 3, 9th Floor, 121099 Moscow. Telephone: 7-095-980-6769. Telecopier: 7-095-980-6765.
In Munich, Germany: Prinzregentenstr. 11, 80538 Munich. Telephone: 089-20 60 42-200. Telecopier: 089-20 60 42-293.
In New York, New York: 222 East 41st Street. Telephone: 212-326-3939. Telecopier: 212-755-7306.
In Paris, France: 120, rue du Faubourg Saint-Honoré. Telephone: 33-1-56-59-39-39. Telecopier: 33-1-56-59-39-38.
In Pittsburgh, Pennsylvania: 500 Grant Street, One Mellon Bank Center, 31st Floor. Telephone: 412-391-3939. Telecopier: 412-394-7959.
In San Diego, California: 12750 High Bluff Drive, Suite 300. Telephone: 858-314-1200. Telecopier: 858-314-1150.
In San Francisco, California: 555 California Street, 26th Floor. Telephone: 415-626-3939. Telecopier: 415-875-5700.
In Shanghai, China: 30th Floor, Shanghai Kerry Centre, 1515 Nanjing Road West. Telephone: 86-21-2201-8000. Telecopier: 86-21-5298-6569.
In Singapore, Singapore: 30 Cecil Street, #29-01 Prudential Tower. Telephone: 65 6 538 3939. Telecopier: 65 6 536 3939.
In Sydney, Australia: Australia Square, Level 38, 264-278 George Street. Telephone: 61-2-8272-0500. Telecopier: 61-2-8272-0599.
In Taipei, Taiwan: 6th Floor, 2 Tun Hwa South Road, Section 2. Telephone: (886-2) 2704-6808 or (886-2) 7712-3399. Telecopier: (886-2) 2704-6791.
In Tokyo, Japan: Shiroyama MT Building, 6th Floor, 1-17 Toranomon 4-chome, Minato-ku, Tokyo 105-0001. Telephone: 81-3-3433-3939. Telecopier: 81-3-5401-2725.

(This Listing Continued)

Jones Day (Continued)

In Washington, D.C.: 51 Louisiana Avenue, N.W. Telephone: 202-879-3939. Telecopier: 202-626-1700.

See Professional Biographies, CLEVELAND, OHIO

Jones, Gary L., Co., L.P.A.
(See Columbus)

Jontz, Jennifer C. ... '67 '92 C.477 B.A. L.347 J.D. Parker-Hannifin Corporation

Joondeph & Bittel, LLP
(See Akron)

Jordan, Anthony David ... '65 '96 C.511 B.A. L.329 J.D. City of Cleveland, Law Dept.
Jordan, Michael J., (AV) ... '54 '79 C.611 B.A. L.273 J.D. [Walter&H.]
Jorgensen, Matthew W. ... '70 '96 C&L.608 B.A., J.D. [Keller&K.]
Jorgensen, Thomas A., (AV) ... '43 '68 C.178 A.B. L.228 LL.B. [Calfee,H.&G.]
Jorgenson, Eric D. ... '51 '02 C.491 B.A. L.1363 J.D. [Amin&T.] (See Pat. Sect.)
Jorgenson, Mary Ann, (AV) ... '41 '75 C.6 B.A. L.930 J.D. [Squire,S.&D.]
Joseph, James G., (BV) ... '46 '73 C.608 B.A. L.1003 J.D. [Dubin&J.]
Joseph, Kathryn Theresa, (BV) ... '60 '86 C.696 B.A. L.930 J.D. [Aggers,J.&C.]
Joseph, Steven W., (AV) ... '46 '72 C.659 B.A. L.477 J.D. Deloitte & Touche
Joseph, William R., (AV) ... '46 '72 C&L.178 B.A., J.D. [Weston H.]
Josselson, Stanley L. ... '36 '66 C.383 B.S. L.117 J.D. [S.L.Josselson]
Josselson, Stanley L., Company, L.P.A. ... 1276 W. 3rd
Jouannet, Francis L., Jr. ... '27 '54 C.228 A.B. L.1003 LL.B. Pres., Auto Bolt & Nut Co.
Joyce, Eileen M. ... '69 '98 C.161 B.B.A. L.930 J.D. [Baughman&J.]
Juergens, Julie L. ... '— '96 C.712 B.A. L.930 J.D. [Gallagher S.]
Julian, Christine M. ... '67 '93 C.381 B.A. L.608 J.D. [Julian&J.]
Julian, Linda M. ... '63 '91 C.161 B.A. L.1003 J.D. [Julian&J.]
Julian & Julian, LLC ... 1836 Euclid Avenue, Suite 308
Juliano, L. James, Jr., (AV) ... '50 '77 C&L.930 B.A., J.D. [Nicola,G.&C.]
Junge, A. Gregory ... '— '04 C.385 B.A. L.273 J.D. [🄰 Jones D.]
Junger, Peter D. '33 '59 C&L.309 A.B., LL.B.
(adm. in NY; not adm. in OH) 11075 E. Blvd.
Jurczenko, Alexander, (BV) ... '46 '73 C.831 B.A. L.1003 J.D. 1415 W. 9th St.
Juster, Joseph K., (BV) ... '57 '85 C.951 B.A. L.94 J.D. [Calfee,H.&G.]
Kabat, Andrew A. ... '69 '94 C.347 B.S. L.1003 J.D. [🄰 Reminger&R.]
Kabb, Kenneth S., (BV) ... '39 '69 C.610 B.S.M.E. L.1003 J.D. [K.S.Kabb]
Kabb, Kenneth S., Co., L.P.A., (BV) ... P.O. Box 18558
Kacenjar, Allen A. ... '74 '99 C.473 B.S. L.930 J.D. [🄰 Squire,S.&D.]
Kacenjar, Laura E. ... '76 '01 C.473 B.S. L.477 J.D. [🄰 Squire,S.&D.]
Kachmarik, Ronald M. ... '63 '94 C.8 B.S. L.1003 J.D. [Pearne&G.] (See Pat. Sect.)
Kaczanowski, Christine ... '52 '85 C.476 B.S. L.215 J.D. Staff Atty., Vet. Admn.
Kaczynski, Stephen J., (AV) ... '— '79 C&L.724 B.A., J.D. [Jones D.]
Kadish, Matthew F., (AVⓉ) ... '— '87 C.951 B.A. L.930 J.D. [Kadish,H.&W.]
Kadish, Stephen L., (AV) ... '— '64 C.951 B.A. L.178 LL.B. [Kadish,H.&W.]

Kadish, Hinkel & Weibel, A Legal Professional Association, (AV)
1717 East Ninth Street, Suite 2112, 44114
Telephone: 216-696-3030 Telecopier: 216-696-3492
URL: http://www.khwlaw.com
Stephen L. Kadish; Kevin M. Hinkel; David G. Weibel; Aaron H. Bulloff; William A. Duncan; James H. Rownd; Dean M. Rooney; Matthew F. Kadish;—Mary Beth Duffy; Kent S. Hedman; Jeffrey J. Platko; Rita M. Jarrett.
General Civil Practice. Federal Taxation, Corporation, Business, Real Estate, Trust, Probate, Estate Planning and Pension and Profit Sharing Law. Health Care, State and Local Taxation, Litigation.
See Professional Biographies, CLEVELAND, OHIO

Kadlec, Kevin O. ... '56 '87 C.161 B.A. L.1003 J.D. [Bonezzi S.M.&P.]
Kaesgen, Derek ... '67 '93 C.170 B.A. L.930 J.D. Corp. Coun., MTD Products Inc.
Kafiti, Salim A. ... '— '01 C.473 B.A. L.930 J.D. [🄰 Jones D.]
Kahan, David D., Law Offices of '32 '64 C.608 A.B. L.1003 J.D.
3486 Rolling Hills Dr.
Kahan, Julian ... '26 '59 C.999 L.1003 1717 Illuminating Bldg.
Kahan, Steven E., (BV) ... '58 '83 C.473 A.B. L.930 J.D. 4469 Renaissance Pkwy.
Kahn, Craig Anthony ... '— '94 C.172 B.A. L.1194 J.D. [Kahn&Assoc.]
Kahn, Ronald L., (AV) ... '46 '73 C.659 B.S.E. L.477 J.D. [Ulmer&B.]
Kahn, Scott H., (BV) ... '55 '82 C.363 B.S.B.A. L.1003 J.D. [McIntyre,K.&K.]
Kahn, Shepard L. ... '45 '79 C.608 B.A. L.150 J.D. 31229 S. Woodland Rd.

Kahn & Associates, L.L.C.
55 Public Square, Suite 650, 44113
Telephone: 216-621-6101; 888-536-6671 Fax: 216-621-6006
Email: help@kahnandassociates.com URL: http://www.kahnandassociates.com
Craig Anthony Kahn.
Lemon Law, Warranty Law, Consumer Bankruptcy, Debt Resolution, Personal Injury, Credit Reporting Violations and Repair.
See Professional Biographies, CLEVELAND, OHIO

Kahn Kleinman, (AV) BB
2600 Erieview Tower, 1301 East 9th Street, 44114-1824
Telephone: 216-696-3311 Telecopiers: 216-623-4912; 216-696-1009
URL: http://www.kahnkleinman.com
Lester W. Armstrong; Kevin D. Barnes; Douglas V. Bartman; Irv Berliner; Michael H. Diamant; Dominic A. DiPuccio; Robert A. Fuerst; Bruce E. Gaynor; Neil Kurit; Stuart L. Larsen; Marc H. Morgenstern; Steven M. Moss; Richard S. Rivitz; Richard A. Rosner; David R. Tavolier; Robert J. Valerian; Missia H. Vaselaney; Robert A. Zimmerman;—Philip R. Bautista; Howard J. Bobrow; Leigh A. Hellner (Not admitted in OH); Theodore Einhorn; Mark R. Jacobs; Peter Nealis; Mark E. Owens; Mark J. Stockman; Michael R. Tucci; Deborah A. Weisman; Elizabeth Marie Zoller. Senior Counsel: Bennett Yanowitz. Of Counsel: Robert U. Fein; Peter A. Igel.
Corporation, Securities, Venture Capital, Real Estate, Bankruptcy, Computer & Technology, Labor and Employment, Litigation, Taxation, Trust and Estate Planning.
Reference: National City Bank.
See Professional Biographies, CLEVELAND, OHIO

Kahrl, Robert C., (AV) ... '— '75 C.674 A.B. L.608 J.D. [Jones D.] (See Pat. Sect.)

Kainski, Dale F., (AV) '50 '75 C.97 B.S. L.602 J.D.
55 Public Square, Suite 2020, 44113-1901
Telephone: 216-574-9500 Telefax: 216-241-2920
Federal and State Trial and Appellate Litigation, Business, Commercial, Municipal, Civil Rights, Insurance Defense.
See Professional Biographies, CLEVELAND, OHIO

Kaiser, Gordon S., Jr., (AV) ... '48 '73 C.62 B.A. L.930 J.D. [Squire,S.&D.]
Kaiser, Thomas Joseph, (BV) '57 '82
C.363 B.S. L.161 J.D. Chf. Trial Coun., Cleveland Law Dept.
Kalail, Karrie M. ... '63 '88 C.610 B.A. L.8 J.D. [Britton,S.P.&K.]
Kalbrunner, Roger J., (BV) ... '48 '73 C.385 A.B. L.930 J.D. 3630 Trowbridge Ave.
Kalette, Stephen R., (AV) '50 '74
C.608 B.A. L.930 J.D. V.P. & Gen. Coun., Pubco Corporation
Kalk, Daniel L., (BV) ... '58 '83 C.161 B.B.A. L.1003 J.D. 32100 Solon Rd.
Kall, David M. ... '67 '93 C&L.608 B.A., J.D. [McDonald H.]
Kall, Matthew B. ... '71 '96 C.188 B.S. L.477 J.D. U.S. Atty. Off.
Kallergis, Gus ... '— '99 C.976 B.A. L.602 J.D. [🄰 Jones D.]

Kalnay, John "JT" ... '61 '98 C.018 B.A. L.930 J.D. [🄰 McDonald H.] (Pat.)
Kálnoki, Anikó Trombitás ... '44 '91 C.608 B.S.Ed. L.1003 J.D. [Sharon&K.]
Kaman, David W., (AV) ... '55 '80 C.363 B.A. L.1003 J.D. 600 Terminal Twr.
Kamat, Deborah L. ... '53 '82 C.502 B.A. L.1003 J.D. Def. Finance & Accounting Sev.
Kaminski, Kathleen ... '61 '91 C.381 B.S.N. L.930 J.D. 10803 Lake Ave.
Kaminski, Kerin Lyn, (AV) ... '58 '85 C.49 B.A. L.1003 J.D. [Giffen&K.]
Kammer, Karl D., (AV) ... '26 '53 C.930 B.A. L.1003 LL.B. 75 Public Sq.
Kammer, Sean M. ... '80 '04 C.972 B.A. L.228 J.D. [🄰 Baker&H.]
Kammer, Stanley L., (BV) ... '23 '50 C.610 B.S.C. L.930 LL.B. 1208 Standard Bldg.
Kampani, Dharminder L., (BV) ... '46 '75 C.999 B.Sc. L.161 LL.M. [D.Kampani]
Kampani, Dharminder, Law Office, (BV) ... 17140 Lorain Ave.
Kampinski, Charles, (AV) ... '47 '74 C&L.608 B.A., J.D. [🄲 Hermann,C.&S.]
Kampman, Joseph W. ... '54 '80 C.161 B.B.A. L.1003 J.D. [Ziegler,M.&M.]
Kanareff, Alexander ... '28 '56 C.610 B.S. L.930 LL.B. 28901 Clemens Rd.
Kancler, Edward, (AV) ... '39 '64 C.610 A.B. L.930 J.D. [Benesch,F.C.&A.]
Kangesser, Hedy ... '60 '85 C.659 B.A. L.930 J.D. Asst. Pub. Def.
Kantz, Mary Kay ... '41 '82 C.876 A.B. L.1003 J.D. Case Western Reserve Univ.
Kaplan, Ira C., (AV) ... '54 '79 C.696 B.A. L.273 J.D. [Benesch,F.C.&A.]
Kaplan, Morton L., (BV) ... '36 '67 C.645 B.A. L.1003 J.D. Standard Bldg.
Kaplow, Richard J., Attorney at Law, (BV) '45 '73
C.473 B.A. L.930 J.D. 614 Superior Ave. N.W., Ste. 808
Kaprosy, David V. '46 '73 C.608 B.A. L.851 J.D.
Sr. V.P. & Sr. Underwriting Coun., Midland Title Security, Inc.
Kapur, Sanjiv K., (BV) ... '— '85 C&L.309 A.B., J.D. [Jones D.]
Kapusta-Dorogi, Jonetta J. ... '63 '92 C.930 B.A. L.1003 J.D. [🄰 Hermann,C.&S.]
Karakul, Kurt, (AV) ... '51 '79 C.385 B.A. L.930 J.D. [Weston H.]
Karas, Kimon P., (AV) ... '52 '78 C.473 A.B. L.607 J.D. [McCarthy,L.C.&L.]
Karberg, Bruce K., (AV) ... '45 '75 C.161 B.A. L.1003 J.D. [Karberg,K.W.&T.]

Karberg, Kurant, Wachter & Turner Co., L.P.A., (AV)
Suite 300, Pepper Pike Place, 30195 Chagrin Boulevard, 44124-5703
Telephone: 216-292-3300 Telecopier: 216-292-3340
Email: lawfirm@lawkkwt.com URL: http://www.conwaymarken.com
Jeffrey G. Wyner; Bruce K. Karberg; Jack Kurant; Mark I. Wachter; Peter Turner;—Neil S. Sarkar; Stephen D. Dodd; Liza M. Funkhouser. Of Counsel: A. R. (Bud) Mays; James J. Conway; Howard A. Marken.
Business and Corporate, Mergers and Acquisition, Employment Litigation, Real Estate, Taxation, Probate, Estate Planning, Litigation in all Courts.
See Professional Biographies, CLEVELAND, OHIO

Karel, Tamara L. ... '70 '05 C.97 B.S. L.161 J.D. [🄰 Benesch,F.C.&A.]
Karl, Nelson G. ... '26 '53 C.930 A.B. L.1003 J.D. Admin. Law J., Hearings & App.
Karlgaard, Jill M. H. ... '76 '02 C.585 B.A. L.494 J.D. [🄰 Thompson H.]
Karlovec, Lucien B., Jr., (BV) ... '36 '62 C.105 B.S. L.161 J.D. 2935 Prospect Ave.
Karnatz, William E., Jr. ... '67 '92 C.201 B.A. L.1003 J.D. National City Bk.
Karnatz, William E., Sr., (AV) ... '37 '62 C.363 B.B.A. L.930 J.D. [Thompson H.]
Karner, Cheryl S. ... '45 '70 C.930 A.B. L.597 J.D. 1 Lakeside‡
Karnes, William M., (BV) ... '45 '71 C.363 B.A. L.1003 J.D. [W.M.Karnes]
Karnes, William M., Co., L.P.A., (BV) ... 13604 Lorain Ave.
Karol, Brian Keith ... '56 '83 C.980 A.B. L.1003 J.D. 4579 Whitehall Dr.
Karon, Daniel R., (AVⓉ) ... '66 '91 C.347 B.A. L.608 J.D. [Goldman S.&K.] ⊙
Karp, Harlan Daniel ... '64 '89 C&L.659 B.A., J.D. 2000 E. 9th St., Suite 710
Karp, Marvin L., (AV) ... '34 '58 C&L.976 B.A., LL.B. [Ulmer&B.]
Karp, Sheldon, (BV) ... '40 '67 C.610 B.S.C. L.608 J.D. [S.Karp]
Karp, Sheldon Co., L.P.A., (BV) ... 101 Prospect Ave., W.
Karpinski, Diane Joan ... '35 '81 C.608 B.A. L.1003 J.D. 1 Lakeside Ave
Karr, Bernard L., (AV) ... '47 '73 C.97 B.S. L.608 J.D. [McDonald H.]
Kasdan, Howard P. ... '45 '69 C.610 A.B. L.930 J.D. [🄲 Cavitch,F.D.&F.]
Kaselak, Dennis J., (AV) ... '47 '74 C.381 B.A. L.161 J.D. [🄲 Lasko&L.]
Kasik, George B. ... '17 '47 C.124 B.S. L.930 LL.B. 24901 Lakeview Dr.‡
Kasle, Andrew R. ... '56 '89 C.473 B.A. L.851 J.D. [Hazelwood&K.]
Kastelic, Tara A. ... '65 '91 C&L.851 B.S.C.S.E., J.D. [Calfee,H.&G.] (See Pat. Sect.)
Kastelic, Thomas James '51 '82 C.602 B.A. L.161 J.D.
901 Lakeside Avenue, North Point
Kasunic, Carl P., (BV) ... '55 '86 C.161 B.A. L.1003 J.D. [C.P.Kasunic] ⊙
Kasunic, Carl P., Co., L.P.A., (BV) ... 1370 Ontario Street (⊙Willoughby)
Kattola, Christine M. ... '79 '04 C.213 B.A. L.608 J.D. [🄰 Roetzel&A.]
Katz, Daniel M. ... '69 '96 C.659 B.A. L.1003 J.D. 842 Terminal Twr.
Katz, David A., (AV) ... '40 '65 C.610 A.B. L.930 J.D. [D.A.Katz]
Katz, Howard E. '54 '77 C.930 B.A. L.309 J.D.
Dir. of Strategic Planning, Co. Treas. Off.
Katz, Lewis R. ... '38 '63 C.680 A.B. L.1119 J.D. Prof. of Law, Case Western Res. Univ.
Katz, Mark D., (BV) ... '49 '74 C.107 B.A. L.930 J.D. [Ulmer&B.]
Katz, David A., Co., L.P.A., (AV) ... Terminal Tower, Suite 842
Kaufman, Arthur M., (AV) ... '50 '83 C.608 B.S.Ed. L.1003 J.D. [Hahn L.&P.]
Kaufman, David A., (AV) ... '15 '40 C.608 B.A. L.930 LL.B. 692 Alpha Road
Kaufman, Elliot M., (AV) ... '— '64 C&L.608 B.S.B.A., J.D. [🄲 Buckley K.]
Kaufman, Jack ... '32 '56 C.966 B.A. L.930 LL.B. Vice Chmn., Hildebrandt, Int'l.‡
Kaufman, Jules L. ... '27 '50 C&L.893 B.A., LL.B. 2856 Chadbourne Rd.
Kaufman, Paul M., (AV) ... '49 '74 C.385 A.B. L.880 J.D. 801 Terminal Tower, Suite 801
Kaufman, Roy M. ... '30 '71 C.930 B.A. L.1003 J.D. Leader Boulding
Kaufman, Steven S., (AV) ... '50 '75 C.165 A.B. L.930 J.D. [Thompson H.]

Kaufman & Cumberland Co., L.P.A.
(See Thompson Hine LLP)

Kauntz, Edmund G., (BV) ... '62 '87 C&L.930 B.S., J.D. [Singerman,M.D.&K.]
Kavuru, Joan A. ... '63 '92 C.879 B.S.N. L.930 J.D. [🄰 Squire,S.&D.]
Kay, Abraham, (BV) ... '50 '79 C.930 B.A. L.262 J.D. 55 Public Square, Suite 1200
Kay, Jeffrey T. ... '72 '98 C.49 B.S. L.1003 J.D. [🄰 Mazanec,R.&R.]
Kazdin, Gary A., (AV) ... '36 '62 C.930 B.A. L.1003 J.D. [G.A.Kazdin]
Kazdin, Gary A., Co., L.P.A., (AV) ... 75 Public Square, Suite 1020
Kealy, John C., (BV) ... '44 '70 C.276 B.A. L.930 J.D. 123 W. Prospect Ave.
Keane, Michael J. '41 '75 C.743 A.B. L.276 J.D.
(adm. in DC; not adm. in OH) U.S. Dept. of Justice, Antitrust Div.
Kearney, Keith J. ... '68 '98 C.1115 B.A. L.989 J.D. [🄰 Mansour,G.G.&M.]
Keco, Laurie A. ... '71 '96 C.473 B.S. L.930 J.D. 925 Euclid Ave.
Kedzior, John D., (AV) ... '55 '81 C.161 B.A. L.1003 J.D. [Wegman,H.&V.]
Keefe, F. Barry, (AV) ... '42 '73 C.707 B.A. L.930 J.D. [Squire,S.&D.]
Keen, Paul R. '49 '74 C.409 B.A. L.383 J.D.
(adm. in KY; not adm. in OH) V.P., Gen. Coun. & Secy., Argo-Tech Corp.
Keenan, Martin James ... '51 '77 C.884 B.S. L.1003 J.D. 11510 Buckeye Rd.
Keenan, Thomas J. ... '22 '52 C.363 B.S. L.1003 J.D. [🄲 Rhoa,F.&R.]
Keevican, Leo A., Jr., (AVⓉ) ... '49 '75 C.976 B.A. L.94 J.D. [Keevican&W.] ⊙
Keevican & Weiss, Professional Corporation, (AV)
200 Public Square (⊙Wash., DC; Troy, MI; Harrisburg, Pitts., PA)

Kehn, James M., (BV) ... '44 '71 C.608 B.Sc. L.1003 J.D. 5555 Mayfield Road
Kehoe, Robert D., (AV) ... '56 '82 C.363 A.B. L.831 J.D. [Keller&K.]
Kehres, Robert A. ... '24 '55 C.893 B.S. L.1003 LL.B. Cleveland Trencher Co.
Keim, Christopher G. ... '71 '96 C.608 B.S. L.930 J.D. [Ⓐ Frantz W.]
Keim, Krista K. ... '71 '96 C.473 B.A. L.930 J.D. [Britton,S.P.&K.]
Keiper, Jeffrey B., (AV) ... '64 '92 C.970 B.A. L.608 J.D. [McDonald H.]
Keis, William H., Jr., (BV) ... '55 '82 C.161 B.A. L.1003 J.D. [Keis G.]

Keis / George LLP, (AV)
55 Public Square, Suite 800, 44113
Telephone: 216-241-4100 Fax: 216-771-3111
Email: info@keisgeorge.com URL: http://www.keisgeorgellplaw.com
Members of Firm: William H. Keis, Jr.; Warren S. George; Herbert L. Nussle. Associates: Patrick J. O'Malley; Lisa M. Gerlack; Jeffrey L. Austin; Timothy L. Sprague; Carole A. Lohr; Scott T. Knowles; Karen Fout; Jason P. Grable.
Personal Injury, Insurance Subrogation, Insurance Defense, Construction Law, Products Liability, Insurance, Health Care Subrogation, Automobile Accidents, Medical Malpractice.
See Professional Biographies, CLEVELAND, OHIO

Kelleher, Jeffry F., (AV) ... '46 '75 C.385 A.B. L.1003 J.D. [J.F.Kelleher&Assoc.]
Kelleher, Sean F., (BV) ... '63 '92 C.549 B.A. L.1003 J.D. 5579 Pearl Rd., Ste. 203
Kelleher, Jeffry F., & Associates Co., (AV) ... 526 Superior Ave.
Keller, C. Reynolds, (AV) ... '38 '63 C.674 A.B. L.477 LL.B. [Ⓒ Ulmer&B.]

Keller, Ellen Holland, (AV) '40 '79 C.473 B.A. L.1003 J.D.
55 Public Square, Suite 1510, 44113
Telephone: 216-771-4830 Fax: 216-771-4615
Email: holland@gwis.com
Consumer Law, Bankruptcy, Business Law, Commercial Law, Mediation.
See Professional Biographies, CLEVELAND, OHIO

Keller, Stanley S., (AV) ... '33 '58 C.381 A.B. L.930 LL.B. [S.S.Keller&Assoc.] ⊙
Keller & Kehoe LLP, (AV) ... 1940 East Sixth Street

Keller, Stanley S., & Associates Co., LPA, (AV) [BR]
Suite 330 The Hanna Building, 1422 Euclid Avenue, 44115-1901 ⊙
Telephone: 216-566-7100 Fax: 216-566-5430
Email: sskeller@en.com
Stanley S. Keller; Walter H. Krohngold; Martin T. Powers; Michael L. Cole.
General Practice.
Reference: Bank One, Cleveland.
Lorain County, Ohio Office: 5455 Detroit Road, Sheffield Village, 44054. Telephone: 440-930-4039. Fax: 440-934-7205.
See Professional Biographies, CLEVELAND, OHIO

Kelley, Elizabeth, (BV) ... '— '94 C.483 B.A. L.124 J.D. [E.Kelley]
Kelley, Kevin ... '68 '04 C.436 B.S. L.161 J.D. [Ⓐ Porter W.M.&A.]
Kelley, Kevin E. ... '49 '77 C.321 A.B. L.1003 J.D. 27631 Whitehill Circle
Kelley, Lawrence Patrick ... '15 '54 C.363 Ph.B L.1003 J.D. 16213 Marquis Ave.‡
Kelley, Lynn Arko ... '55 '85 C.901 B.A. L.1003 J.D. [Ⓒ Kelley&F.]
Kelley, Michael V., (BV) ... '51 '82 C.930 B.A. L.1003 J.D. [Kelley&F.]
Kelley, Thomas G., (BV) ... '45 '72 C.363 B.S. L.161 J.D. 75 Public Sq., Ste. 700
Kelley, Elizabeth, L.P.A., Inc., (BV) ... 1422 Euclid Ave., Ste. 1504

Kelley & Ferraro LLP, (AV) [BR]
1300 East Ninth Street, Suite 1901, 44114
Telephone: 216-575-0777; Toll Free: 1-888-839-8479 Fax: 216-575-0799
Email: k&f@kelley-ferraro.com URL: http://www.kelley-ferraro.com
James L. Ferraro; Michael V. Kelley; John A. Sivinski; Thomas M. Wilson; Anthony Gallucci; Corey Wade Frost; John Martin Murphy; Sandra Becher Sommers;—Shawn M. Acton; Lori Ann Luka; Robert A. Marcis, II; Jaeson L. Taylor; William Edward Uzl; Catherine J. Testa; Jennifer L. Mancino; Dayna M. DePerro; Eric C. Wiedemer; Jennifer L. Rozic; John T. Forristal. Of Counsel: Lynn Arko Kelley.
Products Liability, Toxic Tort, Wrongful Death, Personal Injury, Medical Malpractice, Asbestos Litigation, Silica Litigation, Welding Road Litigation, Vioxx, Workers Compensation, Sports Law, Entertainment Law, Family Law and Probate Law
See Professional Biographies, CLEVELAND, OHIO

Kelley, Jasons, McGuire & Spinelli, L.L.P.
629 Euclid Avenue, Suite 1037, 44114 ⊙
Telephone: 216-902-4444 Fax: 216-902-4447
John A. Kristan, Jr.; Steven M. Lichtig.
Philadelphia, Pennsylvania Office: Centre Square West, Suite 1500, 1500 Market Street, 19102. Telephone: 215-854-0658. Fax: 215-854-8434.
Wilmington, Delaware Office: 800 Delaware Avenue, P.O. Box 194, 19899. Telephone: 302-652-8560. Fax: 302-652-8405.
See Professional Biographies, CLEVELAND, OHIO

Kellogg, Amy Elizabeth, (AV) ... '62 '86 C.851 B.B.A. L.608 J.D. [Baker&H.]
Kellon, Anthony J. ... '60 '89 C.1023 B.A. L.1003 J.D, Asst. Prosecutor
Kelly, Amy Collini ... '68 '94 C.477 B.A. L.823 J.D. Medical Mutual of Ohio
Kelly, Brian J. ... '69 '94 C&L.477 B.A., J.D. [Frantz W.]
Kelly, Christopher M., (AV) ... '— '88 C.116 B.A. L.228 J.D. [Jones D.]
Kelly, Constance R. ... '50 '79 C.970 B.A. L.930 J.D. 2666 N. Moreland Rd., 2nd Fl.
Kelly, Dennis M., (AV) ... '— '68 C.363 A.B. L.602 J.D. [Jones D.]
Kelly, Edwin ... '48 '86 C.610 B.S.Ed. L.1003 J.D. [Ⓢ Trivers&D.]
Kelly, R. Patrick (Pat) '45 '73
C.318 B.A. L.1003 J.D. 1100 Huntington Bldg., 925 Euclid Avenue
Kelly, Sandra Maurer, (AV) ... '60 '86 C.608 B.S. L.990 J.D. [Ray,R.C.&D.]
Kelly, Scott J. ... '73 '98 C.97 B.S.B.A. L.608 J.D. [Ⓐ Tucker E.&W.]
Kelly, Sean S. ... '71 '02 C.381 B.A. L.989 J.D. [Ⓐ R.E.Sweeney]
Kelly, Sheryl K. ... '56 '80 C.8 B.A. L.7 J.D. [Ⓐ Calfee,H.&G.]
Kelly, William Bradley ... '48 '84 C.318 B.A. L.1003 J.D. 1335 Warren Rd.
Kemme, David A. ... '56 '81 C.363 B.S. L.1003 J.D. National City Bank‡
Kempke, Robert E. ... '42 '71 C.161 B.B.A. L.1003 J.D. 9 Chippenham Ct.‡
Kendall, Laura K. ... '77 '04 C.8 B.A. L.124 J.D. [Ⓐ Calfee,H.&G.]
Kender, Frank A. '27 '54 C.124 B.S. L.1003 LL.B.
The Cleveland Elec. Illuminating Co.
Kendis, Alvin M., (AV) ... '18 '42 C&L.930 A.B., LL.B. 600 Superior Ave.‡
Kendis, James D., (AV) ... '41 '66 C&L.930 A.B., J.D. [Kendis&Assoc.]
Kendis, L. S. ... '16 '40 C&L.930 B.A., LL.B. 1765 Cumberland Rd.
Kendis, Robert D., (AV) ... '44 '69 C&L.930 B.A., J.D. 614 W. Superior Ave.
Kendis & Associates Co. L.P.A., (AV) ... 614 Superior Ave. N.W., 15th Fl.
Kenneally, Sean ... '69 '98 C.201 B.A. L.989 J.D. [Ⓐ T.J.Kenneally&Assoc.]
Kenneally, Terrence J., & Associates, (AV) '48 '78
C.161 B.A. L.8 J.D. 20595 Lorain Rd., Terrace
Kennedy, Charles M. ... '— '80 C.294 B.A. L.145 J.D. [Ⓒ Jones D.]
Kennedy, Edwin A., (AV) ... '31 '56 C.124 L.1003 J.D. 925 Euclid Avenue‡
Kennedy, Margaret A., (AV) ... '46 '76 C.190 B.S. L.930 J.D. [Ⓒ Benesch,F.C.&A.]
Kennedy, R. Eric, (AV) ... '55 '80 C.732 B.A. L.930 J.D. [Weisman,G.&W.]
Kennedy, Robin M. ... '45 '70 C.602 A.B. L.930 J.D. Legal Aid Soc.
Kennedy, Stephanie E. ... '73 '98 C.174 B.A. L.930 J.D. [Ⓐ Ulmer&B.]
Kennedy, Terence M. ... '65 '90 C.973 B.S.B.A. L.930 J.D. Tax Mgr., Ernst & Young
Kennedy, Thos. M. ... '23 '49 C.363 B.S. L.930 LL.B. 13926 Lake Ave.‡

Kennedy Reeve & Knoll
75 Public Square, Suite 1300, 44113 ⊙
Telephone: 216-771-5511 Facsimile: 216-771-5511
URL: http://www.krkattorneys.com/
Associate: Patrick M. Watts.
Sexual Harassment, Americans with Disability Act, Age Discrimination in Employment Act, Title VII Race and Gender Discrimination, Family Medical Leave Act, National Origin Discrimination, Civil Service, State and Federal Civil Rights Litigation, Religion Discrimination, Representation to the Equal Employment Opportunity Commission and Ohio Civil Rights Commission, Administrative Law, Unemployment, Worker's Compensation Retaliation, Whistleblower Statute, Intentional Tort, Equal Protection and Due Process Violations, Employee Benefits, Wrongful Termination, Public Policy, Severance Package Review and Negotiation, Contract Review, Negotiation and Litigation, Small Business Start-Up and Consulting.
Columbus, Ohio Office: 98 Hamilton Park, 43203. Telephone: 614-228-2050. Facsimile: 614-228-3320.
See Professional Biographies, CLEVELAND, OHIO

Kennemuth, Jerald ... '50 '78 C.62 B.A. L.150 J.D. N.A.S.A.
Kenney, Mary Anne, (BV) ... '50 '87 C.201 B.S. L.1003 J.D. 1801 E. 9th St., Ste. 740
Kenney, Richard C., Jr., (AV) ... '49 '79 C.201 B.A. L.1003 J.D. [R.C.Kenney,Jr.]
Kenney, Richard C., Jr., Co., L.P.A., (AV) ... 55 Public Sq., Ste. 1550
Kenny, Maureen Sheridan ... '71 '98 C.97 B.A. L.161 J.D. [Ⓐ Squire,S.&D.]
Kenny, Robert E., III ... '55 '82 C.363 B.S. L.161 J.D. P.O. Box 22356
Kent, Stanley B., (AV) '23 '50 C.477 A.B. L.930 LL.B.
Chief Legal Clk., Cuyahoga Co. Com. Pleas Ct.
Keogh, Kevin R., (BV) ... '— '83 C.62 B.A. L.161 J.D. [Buckley K.]
Kepple, Brandon E. ... '78 '03 C.473 B.S. L.608 J.D. [Ⓐ Baker&H.]
Kerek, Wayne Lewis, (CV) ... '54 '83 C.62 B.A. L.1003 J.D. P.O. Box 360678
Kerester, Charles J., (AV) ... '27 '52 C&L.608 B.S., J.D. 11075 East Blvd.
Kerka, Kathryn A., (BV) ... '61 '85 C.161 B.A. L.1003 J.D. [Ⓐ Rodgers]
Kern, Anna M. ... '73 '98 C.999 B.S. L.930 J.D. [Ⓐ Masters&Assoc.]
Kern, Heather M. ... '76 '04 C.599 B.A. L.124 J.D. [Ⓐ McDonald H.]
Kern, Keith W. ... '51 '75 C.475 B.S. L.608 J.D. [Ⓒ Wilsman&S.]
Kerr, Henry V. ... '37 '63 C.546 B.A. L.724 LL.B. [Ⓒ Hermann,C.&S.]
Kersey, James M., (AV) ... '43 '73 C.152 B.A. L.930 J.D. 1148 Euclid Avenue, Suite 300
Kess, Stephanie S. ... '61 '88 C.608 B.S. L.117 J.D. [Sonkin,F.K.&K.]
Kessler, Amanda A. '78 '03 C&L.734 B.A., J.D.
(adm. in MO; not adm. in OH) [Ⓐ Thompson H.]
Kessler, Jonathan L. ... '58 '85 C.807 B.A. L.228 J.D. Fed. Trade Comm.
Kestner, R. Steven, (AV) ... '54 '79 C.611 B.A. L.608 J.D. [Baker&H.]
Ketler, Suzanne K. ... '67 '01 C&L.597 B.A., J.D. [Ⓐ Squire,S.&D.]
Keyes, Robt. L., (AV) ... '30 '54 C&L.608 B.S., J.D. 55 Public Sq.
Keyse-Walker, Irene C., (AV) ... '55 '81 C.691 B.A. L.228 J.D. [Tucker E.&W.]
Khayat, Clark H. I. ... '71 '96 C.197 A.B. L.659 J.D. Natcity Investments, Inc.
Khorzad Adi, Mehta, Esq. ... '79 '04 C.608 B.A L.124 J.D. [Ⓐ D.W.Leopold&Assoc.]
Kidder, Richelle W. '71 '00 C.608 B.A. L.326 J.D.
(adm. in TX; not adm. in OH) [Ⓐ Tucker E.&W.]
Kidder, Stephen J. ... '— '76 C.112 B.A. L.809 J.D. 2692 Sulgrave Road
Kiefer, Daran P. ... '69 '94 C.138 B.A. L.930 J.D. [Kreiner&P.] (ⓒColumbus)
Kiffner, Kent C. ... '79 '04 C.62 B.A. L.823 J.D. [Ⓐ McDonald H.]
Kilbane, Catherine M., (AV) '63 '87 C&L.930 B.A., J.D.
Sr. V.P., Gen. Coun. & Secy., American Greetings Corp.
Kilbane, Thomas B. ... '69 '96 C.363 B.A. L.1003 J.D. [Ⓐ Reminger&R.]
Kilbane, Thomas S., (AV) ... '41 '66 C.363 B.A. L.597 J.D. [Squire,S.&D.]
Kilbane-Koch, Judith ... '38 '76 C.161 B.A. L.1003 J.D. Com. Pleas J.
Kilcoyne, James F. ... '33 '62 C.363 B.S.S. L.1003 J.D. 12700 Lake Avenue, Suite 2409
Killeen, Eugene M. ... '63 '88 C.436 B.A. L.276 J.D. [Tucker E.&W.]
Kilpatrick, Todd D., (BVⓉ) '64 '90 C.970 B.A. L.1003 J.D.
(adm. in NY; not adm. in OH) [Ⓐ Squire,S.&D.]
Kilpeck, Lori ... '75 '02 C.161 B.A. L.989 J.D. [Ⓐ Ziegler,M.&M.] (ⓒPainesville)
Kim, Eduardo ... '— '00 C&L.188 B.A., J.D. [Ⓐ Thompson H.]
Kimble, David E. '43 '68 C.922 B.A. L.923 J.D.
(adm. in WV; not adm. in OH)
Dir. of Corp. Develop. & Gen Coun., Middough Assoc., Inc.
Kimmel, Lisa C., (AV) ... '60 '86 C.105 B.A. L.930 J.D. [Ⓒ Benesch,F.C.&A.]
Kimmel, Robert M. ... '05 '28 C&L.930 B.A., J.D. 140 Public Sq.‡
Kinast, Hugh S. ... '77 '04 C.74 B.A. L.124 J.D. [Ⓐ Roetzel&A.]
Kinder, Gordon D., (AV) '48 '77
C&L.930 B.S.M.E., J.D. [Renner,O.B.&S.] (See Pat. Sect.)
King, Chaundra C. ... '77 '04 C.309 B.A. L.178 J.D. [Ⓐ Squire,S.&D.]
King, David M., (AV) ... '63 '91 C.97 B.A. L.1003 J.D. Asst. Pub. Def.
King, Henry T., Jr. ... '19 '43 C&L.976 B.A., J.D. [Ⓒ Squire,S.&D.]
King, Kelly M. ... '— '03 C.473 B.A. L.124 J.D. [Ⓐ Baker&H.]
King, R. Reed '57 '85 C.602 B.A. L.188 J.D.
Manager, Real Estate Legal Services, BP Amoco Corporation
King, Sheryl '47 '80 C.943 B.S. L.1003 J.D.
Asst. Dean, Cleveland-Marshall Coll. of Law
King, Tom A. ... '54 '90 C.25 B.A. L.1003 J.D. [Baker&H.]
King, Woods, III, (AV) ... '— '83 C.902 B.A. L.161 J.D. [Buckley K.]
Kinkopf, Charles W. ... '63 '94 C.381 B.S. L.8 J.D. [Ⓐ Rademaker,M.M.&G.]
Kinkopf, Lauren K. ... '— '92 C.999 B.S. L.989 J.D. [Ⓐ Roetzel&A.]
Kinkopf-Zajac, Ingrid A., (BV) ... '61 '96 C.540 B.A. L.930 J.D. [Roetzel&A.]
Kirchick, Calvin B., (AV) ... '46 '72 C&L.477 B.A., J.D. [Baker&H.]
Kirchick, Ross J. ... '74 '00 C.477 B.A. L.608 J.D. [Ⓐ Benesch,F.C.&A.]
Kirk, C. Scott ... '73 '98 C.491 B.A. L.161 J.D. 13317 Madison
Kirkpatrick, Andrew W. ... '75 '03 C.174 B.A. L.904 J.D. [Ⓐ Baker&H.]
Kirsanow, Peter N. ... '53 '79 C.188 A.B. L.161 J.D. [Benesch,F.C.&A.]
Kirschenbaum, Dan G., (BV) ... '55 '84 C.608 B.A. L.607 J.D. [Kirschenbaum]
Kirschenbaum, David, (BV) ... '25 '50 C.608 L.607 J.D. [Kirschenbaum]

Kirschenbaum Law Offices Co., L.P.A., (BV)
1919 East 13th Street, 44114
Telephone: 216-621-0890 Toll Free in Ohio: 1-877-822-4402 Fax: 216-621-3590 URL: http://www.kirschenbaumlaw.com
Email: kirschenbaumlaw@aol.com URL: http://www.lawyers.com/kirschenbaumlaw
David Kirschenbaum; Dan G. Kirschenbaum; Robert W. Todt.
Personal Injury, Medical Malpractice, Workers' Compensation, Products Liability, Employment Law and Discrimination, Labor Management Relations, Wage and Hour, Real Estate (HUD), Health and Elder Care Law, Family Law, Bankruptcy. Civil Trials and Appeals in all Courts.
See Professional Biographies, CLEVELAND, OHIO

Kirshner, Adrienne B. ... '76 '02 C.145 B.A. L.124 J.D. [Ⓐ McLaughlin&M.]
Kisatsky, Michele ... '62 '88 C.93 B.A. L.930 J.D. 1801 E. 9th St.
Kiss, Lynette E. ... '74 '00 C.201 B.A. L.124 J.D. [Ⓐ Bonezzi S.M.&P.]
Kitchen, Charles W., (AV) ... '26 '50 C&L.930 B.A., J.D. 600 Superior Ave. E.‡
Kitchen, David E. ... '77 '04 C.101 B.S. L.145 J.D. [Ⓐ Baker&H.]
Klaben, Matthew J. ... '69 '95 C.116 B.A. L.188 J.D. [Calfee,H.&G.]
Klaric, Betty ... '31 '84 C.608 B.A. L.1003 J.D. U.S. Dept. of Labor
Klayman, Larry E. '51 '77 C.228 A.B. L.245 J.D.
(adm. in FL; not adm. in OH) [Walter&H.]

Klein, Ann M. ....'52 '94 C.999 R.N.,B.S.N. L.851 J.D. [Ⓐ D.W.Dreyfuss]
Klein, Jonathan I. ....'51 '80 C.930 B.A. L.1003 J.D. 22899 Byron Rd.
Klein, Larry S., (BV) .... '53 '80 C.94 B.A. L.1003 J.D. [Klein&C.]
Klein, Richard C., (AV) .... '32 '64 C.97 B.S. L.1003 J.D. 18091 E. 9th St.
Klein, Richard M. ....'58 '85 C.608 B.S. L.930 J.D. [Fay,S.F.M.&M.] (See Pat. Sect.)
Klein, Shana F. ....'76 '01 C.608 B.A. L.597 J.D. [Ⓐ Thompson H.]

Klein & Carney Co., L.P.A., (BV)
55 Public Square, Suite 1200, 44113
Telephone: 216-861-0111 Toll Free: 1-800-360-2889 Fax: 216-861-8203
Email: kleinandcarney@aol.com URL: http://www.kleinandcarney.com
Larry S. Klein; Christopher J. Carney.
Personal Injury, Medical Malpractice, Insurance Law, Wrongful Death, Motor Vehicle Accidents, Nursing Home Negligence, Workers Compensation.

See Professional Biographies, CLEVELAND, OHIO

Kleinman, Allan D., (AV) ....'26 '52 C&L.930 B.B.A., LL.B. [Ⓒ Benesch,F.C.&A.]
Kleinman, Bennet, (AV) ......'19 '47 C.161 B.B.A. L.1003 LL.B. The Tower at Erieview‡
Kleinman, Kenneth W., (AV) ....'46 '74 C.188 B.S. L.276 J.D. [Ⓒ Kohrman J.&K.]
Kleinman, Lenore ....'50 '86 C.608 B.S. L.1003 J.D. U.S. Trustee Off., Dept. of Jus.
Kleinman, Roger L., (AV) ....'51 '84 C.608 B.A. L.1003 J.D. [McDonald H.]
Klepach, Anne M. ....'77 '03 C.473 B.S. L.608 J.D. [Ⓐ Ulmer&B.]
Kleppel, Kenneth J. ....'79 '05 C&L.602 B.B.A., J.D. [Ⓐ Porter W.M.&A.]
Kleri, Jon C. '34 '73 C.930 B.A. L.1003 J.D.
(adm. in FL; not adm. in OH) 15521 Galemore Dr.‡
Klimek, Amy ....'67 '93 C.806 B.A. L.608 J.D. [Ⓐ McMahon,D.H.&L.]
Klimek, Mark D. ....'63 '93 C.473 B.S. L.608 J.D. [McDonald H.]
Kline, James N. ....'59 '84 C.477 B.A. L.608 J.D. [Ulmer&B.]
Kline, Melinda M. ....'— '04 C.696 B.A. L.930 J.D. [Ⓐ Baker&H.]
Kline, Rita ....'74 '00 C.363 B.S. L.161 J.D. [Ⓐ Benesch,F.C.&A.]
Kline, Stuart F., (AV) .... '45 '73 C.659 B.S.Econ. L.564 J.D. 25825 Science Park Dr.
Klink, Bradley J. ....'79 '04 C.201 B.A. L.124 J.D. [Ⓐ Walter&H.]
Klonowski, Daniel J., (BV) ....'53 '78 C.610 B.A. L.608 J.D. 5001 Turney Rd.
Klopf, Charles H. ....'41 '66 C&L.309 A.B., LL.B. Pres., Arrow Publicity Co.
Klug, Paul S., (AV) ....'50 '75 C.25 B.A. L.930 J.D. [Ziegler,M.&M.]
Kluznik, John S., (AV) .... '50 '77 C.610 B.A. L.976 J.D. [Weston H.]
Kmetz, Kristi J. ....'77 '03 C.980 B.A. L.607 J.D. [Ⓐ Taft,S.&H.]
Kmiec, Thomas D. ....'34 '71 C.363 B.S. L.1003 J.D. 1558 Temple Ave.
Kmiecik, Robert E., (AV) .... '59 '84 C.381 B.S. L.1003 J.D. 50 Public Square
Knabe, Kenneth J., (AV) ....'54 '79 C.150 B.A. L.1003 J.D. [Brown&S.]
Knecht, Denise J., (AV) ....'48 '81 C.8 B.S. L.1003 J.D. 75 Public Sq.
Knerly, Stephen J., Jr., (AV) ....'49 '76 C.95 A.B. L.930 J.D. [Hahn L.&P.]
Knevel, Mark H. ....'51 '77 C.602 B.A. L.930 J.D. [Knevel&Assoc.]

Knevel & Associates Co. LPA
629 Euclid Avenue, Suite 519, 44114
Telephone: 216-523-7800 Fax: 216-523-7801
URL: http://www.lawyers.com/knevel&associates
Mark H. Knevel.
Bankruptcy.

See Professional Biographies, CLEVELAND, OHIO

Knisely, J. Colin ....'— '97 C.25 B.A. L.930 J.D. [Ⓐ Gallagher S.]
Knoth, Richard M., (AV) ....'58 '83 C.93 A.B. L.209 J.D. [Bricker&E.]
Knott, Paul ....'65 '92 C.161 B.A. L.1003 J.D. [T.Repicky]
Knowles, David R., (AV) .... '47 '74 C.161 B.B.A. L.1003 J.D. [Wegman,H.&V.]
Knowles, Scott T. ....'— '04 C.201 B.S. L.851 J.D. [Ⓐ Keis G.]
Knox, Frank H. ....'25 '58 C.930 B.S. L.161 J.D. 26250 Euclid Ave.
Knuth, Ann E. ....'63 '93 C.565 B.S. L.930 J.D. [Benesch,F.C.&A.]
Koach, Jules N., (BV) ....'41 '66 C.473 A.B. L.930 J.D. [Ⓒ Monroe&Z.]
Kobal, Cindy L. ....'73 '00 C&L.8 B.S., J.D. [Ⓐ Stewart&D.]
Kobasic, Dena M. ....'63 '89 C.599 B.A. L.602 J.D. [Thompson H.]
Koberg, Jeffrey L. ....'65 '90 C.347 B.S. L.930 J.D. [Ⓐ Ziegler,M.&M.]
Koberna, Mark R., (AV) ....'61 '87 C.363 B.A. L.930 J.D. [Sonkin,F.K.&K.]
Koblentz, Richard S., (AV) ....'50 '75 C.608 B.S.Ed. L.1003 J.D. [Koblentz&K.]
Koblentz, Steven B., (BV) '51 '81
C.608 B.S.B.A. L.161 J.D. 5910 Landerbrook Dr., Ste. 200

Koblentz & Koblentz, (AV) BB
55 Public Square, Suite 1170, 44113
Telephone: 216-621-3012 Fax: 216-621-6567
Richard S. Koblentz;—Craig J. Morice; Bryan L. Penvose; Marvin A. Koblentz (1922-1995).
Legal Ethics and Discipline Law. General Practice of Law, including Small Business, Corporate Real Estate, Criminal Defense, Civil Litigation, Domestic Relations, Probate and White Collar Criminal Defense.

See Professional Biographies, CLEVELAND, OHIO

Koblenz, N. Herschel, (AV) ....'34 '60 C.188 A.B. L.976 J.D. [Ⓒ Hahn L.&P.]
Kocab, Brooke F., (BV) ....'60 '85 C.999 B.S. L.1003 J.D. [Berkman,G.M.&D.]
Koch, Suzana Krstevski ....'76 '01 C.1260 B.A. L.608 J.D. [Ⓐ Porter W.M.&A.]
Koch, Ronald J.
(See Columbus)
Kochis, Joseph A., (BV) ....'53 '78 C.97 B.A. L.930 J.D. [J.A.Kochis]
Kochis, Rob M. ....'63 '90 C.8 B.S. L.930 J.D. Townsend Grp.
Kochis, Joseph A., Co., L.P.A., (BV) ....1468 West 9th Street
Kocian, Jeffrey, (BV) ....'42 '66 C.62 B.A. L.607 J.D. 25360 Westwood Rd.
Kocinski, Joseph J., Jr. ....'45 '77 C.124 B.S.E. L.930 J.D. Machine Improvement Co.
Kocovsky, Thomas E., Jr. '47 '75
C.188 B.S. L.273 J.D. [Fay,S.F.M.&M.] (See Pat. Sect.)
Kodish, Joan Allyn .... '51 '79 C.119 B.A. L.7 J.D. [J.A.Kodish]
Kodish, Joan Allyn, Co., L.P.A. ....815 Superior Ave. E., Ste. 1620
Koehler, Christopher C., (AV) ....'67 '92 C.321 B.A. L.930 J.D. [Frantz W.]
Koehler, James F., (AV) ....'— '73 C.970 B.A. L.930 J.D. [Gallagher S.]
Koenig, James C. ....'58 '87 C.363 B.S.B.A. L.930 J.D. [Thompson H.]
Koenig, John Paul '52 '82 C.161 B.A. L.1003 J.D.
Sr. Assoc. Coun., Def. Fin. & Accounting Serv.
Koenig, Sandra M. '60 '87 C.161 B.Ch.E. L.1003 J.D.
[Fay,S.F.M.&M.] (See Pat. Sect.)
Koepper, Engeline H., (BV) ....'38 '67 C.161 B.A. L.1003 J.D. [Ticktin,B.K.]
Koerwitz, Deborah L. ....'71 '99 C.473 B.S. L.910 J.D. [Ⓐ Baker&H.]
Koesel, Margaret M., (AV) ....'50 '89 C.62 B.A. L.161 J.D. [Porter W.M.&A.]
Koeth, Robert J., (BV) ....'52 '82 C.161 B.A. L.1003 J.D. [Koeth,R.&L.]

Koeth, Rice & Leo Co., L.P.A., (AV)
(Formerly Bertsch, Millican & Winslow Co., L.P.A.)
1280 West Third Street, 44113
Telephone: 216-696-1433 Telecopier: 216-696-1439
Email: info@krplpa.com URL: http://www.krplpa.com
Richard M. Bertsch (1926-1995); Robert J. Koeth; Clark D. Rice; Ann Leo;—Shawn W. Schlesinger. Of Counsel: Jeffrey H. Spiegler.
Civil Trial and Appellate Practice. Insurance, Labor and Employment, Environmental Law, Personal Injury, Products Liability, Medical Malpractice.

(This Listing Continued)

Koeth, Rice & Leo Co., L.P.A. (Continued)

Representative Clients: Home Insurance Co.; Surplus Lines Adjusting Co.; Lloyds of London. Reference: Society Bank.

See Professional Biographies, CLEVELAND, OHIO

Koethe, Paul D. .... '— '86 C.105 B.S.B.A. L.930 J.D. [Jones D.]
Kohn, Andrew ....'48 '74 C.696 B.A. L.930 J.D. Hyatt Legal Plans
Kohn, Meyer J. ....'22 '52 C.930 B.B.A. L.1003 J.D. 23215 Commerce Park Dr.
Kohrman, S. Lee, (AV) ....'27 '53 C&L.309 A.B., LL.B. [Kohrman J.&K.]

Kohrman Jackson & Krantz P.L.L., (AV) BB
One Cleveland Center, 20th Floor, 1375 East Ninth Street, 44114
Telephone: 216-696-8700 Telecopier: 216-621-6536
URL: http://www.kjk.com
Members of Firm: S. Lee Kohrman; Robert H. Jackson; Byron S. Krantz; Kevin T. O'Connor; Alan M. Rauss; Sarah Gabinet; Marc C. Krantz; Steven C. Bersticker; Christopher J. Hubbert; Ari H. Jaffe; Robert S. Gilmore; Valoria C. Hoover; David R. Posteraro; Karen L. Greco; Brett S. Krantz; Mark B. Schildhouse; Mary K. Whitmer;—Gary L. Jones; Connie S. Carr; Michele L. Hoza; Mark S. O'Brien; Kevin L. Chlarson; Todd M. Burger; Jon J. Pinney; Laura L. Volpini; David S. Blocker. Of Counsel: Kenneth W. Kleinman; Stephen C. Weingrad; Marc I. Strauss; Stephen D. Richman.
Automotive Franchise and Dealership, Bankruptcy, Banks and Banking, Broker Dealer Arbitration, Business Law, Commercial Litigation, Commercial Real Estate, Computers and Software, Complex Litigation, Corporate Law, E Commerce, Employment Contracts, Employment Termination, Executive Compensation, Family Law, Finance, Health Care, Leveraged Buyouts, Local Government Law, Litigation, Mergers, Acquisitions and Divestitures, Partnership Law, Private Equity, Labor and Employment, Probate, Real Estate, Securities, Securities Class Actions, Software Licensing, Taxation Law, Trusts and Estates, Venture Capital, Wills and Wrongful Termination.
Representative Clients: Ceres Group; Concord Hotels; Developers Diversified; Hawk; Kings Medical; Merrill Lynch; Ohio Department of Development; Rexam Beverage; Starbak Communications; Rostra Companies.

See Professional Biographies, CLEVELAND, OHIO

Kola, Arthur A., (AV) .... '39 '64 C.197 A.B. L.228 LL.B. 6100 Oak Tree Boulevard
Kolesar, Michael P., (BV) ....'44 '72 C.161 B.A. L.1003 J.D. Asst. Pros. Atty.
Koletsky, Carol J., (AV) ....'59 '84 C.477 B.A. L.930 J.D. 31089 Shaker Blvd.
Kolick, David, (AV) ....'48 '74 C.321 B.A. L.930 J.D. [Kolick,G.&E.]
Kolick, Georgeadis & Ernewein, (AV) ....55 Public Sq.
Kolis, Donna Taylor, (BV) ....'54 '84 C.999 B.A. L.161 J.D. [Ⓐ Friedman,D.&S.]
Kollar, John ....'30 '56 C&L.930 B.A., LL.B. Nat. Labor Rel. Bd.
Komorowski, James J., (BV) ....'47 '71 C.381 B.B.A. L.1003 J.D. [Ⓒ Fillo]
Kondas, Brian E. .....'65 '95 C.477 B.S.E.E. L.1003 J.D. [Calfee,H.&G.] (See Pat. Sect.)
Konet, Thomas J., Law Offices, (CV) '42 '72
C.930 B.A. L.1003 J.D. 1370 Ontario Street, Suite 2000
Konkol-Myers, Kim R. ....'59 '85 C.161 B.A. L.1003 J.D. 32906 Lisa Lane
Konkoly, Anthony D. ....'— '86 [McDonald H.]
Konstantinopoulos, Theodore A. ....'— '95 C&L.8 J.D. [Javitch,B.&R.]
Koosed, Lee A., (BV) ....'49 '74 C.473 A.B. L.930 J.D. [Stotter&K.]
Kopek, Richard A. '51 '78 C.321 B.A. L.477 J.D.
(adm. in NY; not adm. in OH) V.P. & Sr. Coun., KeyBank Natl. Assn.
Kopit, Alan S., (AV) ....'52 '77 C.860 B.A. L.145 J.D. [Hahn L.&P.]
Kopkas, Andrew J. '22 '59 C.251 B.B.A. L.1003 J.D.
Room 615 Leader Bldg., East 6th & Superior Avenue
Koplow, James B., (BV) ....'30 '56 C.608 L.1003 J.D. 75 Public Sq.
Kopp, William J., (AV) ....'46 '80 C.871 B.S. L.930 J.D. Asst. U.S. Atty.
Kordas, Anne M. ....'58 '95 C.97 B.S.N. L.1003 J.D. [Ⓐ Tucker E.&W.]
Kordeleski, Kathleen M., (AV) ....'60 '86 C.851 B.B.A. L.1003 J.D. [Duvin,C.&H.]
Korey, Frederick A. ....'25 '55 C.363 A.B. L.1003 J.D. West Tech. High Sch.

Korey, Philip J., (AV) '52 '80 C.363 B.S. L.1003 J.D. BB
Suite 410, Leader Building, 526 Superior Avenue, East, 44114
Telephone: 216-771-7030 FAX: 216-771-2421
Email: pjkoreylaw@sbcglobal.net URL: http://www.lawyers.com/philipjkorey
General Criminal and Personal Injury Trial and Appellate Practice in State and Federal Courts.

See Professional Biographies, CLEVELAND, OHIO

Korff, Christopher .... '66 '03 C.688 B.S. L.124 J.D. [Ⓐ Rankin,H.P.&C.] (See Pat. Sect.)
Korman, Jean Kerr ....'58 '90 C.608 B.S. L.161 J.D. [Ⓐ Benesch,F.C.&A.]
Kornblut, Russell David, (AV) ....'60 '85 C.347 B.A. L.1003 J.D. [Collins&S.]
Korpics, J. Joseph ....'— '91 C.602 B.S. L.839 J.D. [Ⓒ Jones D.]
Korpowski, Scott T. ....'67 '93 C.97 B.S. L.851 J.D. [Richardson&S.]
Korte, Peter B. ....'64 '93 C.608 B.S.B.A. L.930 J.D. 30575 Bainbridge Road
Kosakowski, Lori A. ....'78 '03 C.62 B.A. L.879 J.D. [Ⓐ Britton,S.P.&K.]
Kosanovich, Laurie G. ....'72 '97 C.970 B.A. L.930 J.D. [Ⓐ Baker&H.]
Koschik, Alan M. ....'61 '89 C&L.477 B.A., J.D. [Brouse M.]
Kosek, Kelly A. ....'77 '02 C.25 B.A. L.945 J.D. [Ⓐ Thompson H.]
Kosinski, Charles Edward '69 '95 C.645 B.S.E.E. L.665 J.D.
(adm. in MI; not adm. in OH; Pat.) Eaton Corp.
Kosko, John R., (AV) ....'56 '81 C&L.161 B.A., J.D. Co. Pros. Off.
Kosmin, Martin A. ....'40 '68 C.923 B.A. L.585 J.D. Al/Ko Creative Retirement Planners
Kostelnik, John F., III, (AV) .... '56 '81 C.473 B.S. L.608 J.D. [Frantz W.]
Kostritsky, Juliet P. '54 '81 C.309 A.B. L.966 J.D.
(adm. in NY; not adm. in OH)
John Homer Kapp Prof. of Law, Case Western Reserve Univ.
Kostura, Bryan T. ....'78 '05 C.363 B.A. L.989 J.D. [Ⓐ Weltman,W.&R.]
Kostura, Sarah H. .... '04 C.363 B.A. L.124 J.D. [Ⓐ Goodman W.M.]
Kotulic, Irene M. ....'24 '55 C.930 B.S. L.1003 J.D. 7425 Dartworth Dr.‡
Kovac, James E., (BV) ....'39 '77 C.363 B.S.S. L.1003 J.D. 1370 Ontario St.
Kovach, Christopher M. ....'70 '95 C.610 B.A. L.930 J.D. [Ⓐ Shapiro&F.]
Kovach, Thomas G. ....'64 '90 C.385 B.A. L.608 J.D. [Kovach&F.]

Kovach & Farling Co., LPA, (AV)
925 Leader Building, 526 Superior Avenue East, 44114
Telephone: 216-357-3301 Fax: 216-357-3304
Email: tkovach@kflpa.com URL: http://www.kovachandfarling.com
Thomas G. Kovach; Harold E. Farling.
Commercial Contract Disputes, Business Litigation, Trade Secret Litigation, Business Tort Litigation, Takeover Litigation, Class Action Litigation, Securities Litigation, Restrictive Covenant Litigation, Shareholder Derivative.

See Professional Biographies, CLEVELAND, OHIO

Kovacs, George C. ....'50 '77 C.161 B.A. L.608 J.D. 445 Richmond Park W.
Kovanda, Ralph D., (AV) ....'24 '50 C.309 A.B. L.930 LL.B. [Forrester&K.]
Kowalski, Kenneth J. ....'49 '81 C.930 B.A. L.608 J.D. [Kramer&Assoc.]
Kozlowski, Kenneth S. ....'57 '91 C.8 B.A. L.1003 J.D. Cleveland Law Libr. Assn.
Kracht, Robert R., (BV) ....'51 '83 C.912 B.Ph. L.1003 J.D. [McIntyre,K.&K.]
Krafcik, Jamie R. ....'62 '95 C.651 B.S. L.1003 J.D. 7200 Langerford Dr.
Kraguljac, Peter ....'66 '94 C.608 B.S.C.S. L.989 J.D. [McDonald H.] (Pat.)
Kraig, Jerry B., (AV) ....'37 '63 C.381 B.A. L.1003 J.D. 614 Superior, W.
Krajewski, Eric D. ....'— '04 C.96 B.S. L.989 J.D. [Ⓐ Buckley K.]
Kramer, Edward G., (AV) ....'50 '75 C.381 B.S.Ed. L.930 J.D. [Kramer&Assoc.]
Kramer, Ellen Maglicic ....'66 '91 C.363 B.A. L.608 J.D. [Cohen R.&K.]
Kramer, Eugene L., (AV) ....'39 '64 C.363 A.B. L.602 LL.B. 1422 Euclid Ave.

Kramer, Fredric E., (AV) ... '37 '62 C.363 B.S. L.930 LL.B. [McNeal,S.A.&B.]
Kramer, Herbert J. ... '58 '84 C.363 B.S.B.A. L.1003 J.D. [Carlisle,M.R.K.&U.]
Kramer, John F. ... '64 '90 C.276 B.A. L.608 J.D. Sr. Atty., The Sherwin-Williams Co.
Kramer & Associates, (AV) ... 3214 Prospect Ave., E.
Krantz, Brett S. ... '63 '90 C.197 A.B. L.145 J.D. [Kohrman J.&K.]
Krantz, Byron S., (AV) ... '35 '62 C.197 A.B. L.930 J.D. [Kohrman J.&K.]
Krantz, Marc C., (AV) ... '60 '86 C.197 A.B. L.659 J.D. [Kohrman J.&K.]
Krantz, Michele L.S. '61 '87 C.188 B.S. L.659 J.D.
Asst. Gen. Coun., Meridia Health Sys.
Krasnicki, Suzana ... '74 '01 C.470 B.A. L.989 J.D. [A K.D.Weiner&Assoc.]
Krasovec, Jay E., (BV) ... '70 '98 C&L.8 B.A., J.D. [A Schottenstein,Z.&D.]
Krassen, Glenn S., (AV) ... '55 '80 C.273 B.A. L.608 J.D. [Bricker&E.]
Kratt, Peter G. ... '40 '66 C.473 A.B. L.930 J.D. 917 Euclid Avenue
Kratus, Eugene A., (AV) ... '51 '76 C.602 B.B.A. L.1003 J.D. [Spieth,B.M.&N.]
Kraus, Edward H., (BV) '— '86
C.608 B.A. L.1003 J.D. 1300 East Ninth Street, 14th Floor
Kraus, William J., (AV) ... '13 '34 C&L.930 A.B., LL.B. 1801 E. Ninth Street
Kraus, William M., (AV) ... '23 '50 C&L.930 A.B., LL.B. 4491 University Pkwy.‡
Krause, Andrew J., (AVⓉ) '54 '81 C.136 B.S.B.A. L.1187 J.D.
(adm. in FL; not adm. in OH) [Hahn L.&P.] (⊙Bonita Springs, FL)
Krause, Christopher W. ... '62 '93 C.62 B.A. L.608 J.D. [A Wegman,H.&V.]
Krause, David H. ... '73 '99 C.1113 B.A. L.124 J.D. [A Reminger&R.]
Krause, Dawn Marie ... '60 '85 C.970 B.A. L.117 J.D. Atty. I.R.S.
Krause, Douglas R. '67 '92 C.363 B.A. L.879 J.D.
Asst. Coun., The Richard E. Jacobs Group, Inc.
Kraushaar, Richard H., (AV) ... '37 '62 C.210 B.A. L.930 LL.B. 10832 Partridge Tr.‡

Kravitz, Lee R., (BV) '55 '80 C.610 B.A. L.1003 J.D.
4508 State Road, 44109
Telephone: 216-749-0808 Fax: 216-749-5389
Email: leekravitz@adelphia.net URL: http://www.leekravitzlaw.com
Associate: David B. Bokor.
Bankruptcy Law, Chapter 7, Chapter 13, Consumer Bankruptcy.
See Professional Biographies, CLEVELAND, OHIO

Krawczak, Kenneth F. ... '51 '77 C.926 A.B. L.608 J.D. [Swartz C.]
Krebs, Martha H., (AV) ... '43 '79 C.161 B.A. L.1003 J.D. 55 Public Sq., Ste. 1717
Krebs, Patrick J. ... '75 '00 C.884 B.A. L.124 J.D. [A Taft,S.&H.]
Kreiner, Fred J., (BV) ... '37 '64 C.424 B.S. L.1003 J.D. [Kreiner&P.] (⊙Columbus)
Kreiner, Frederick J. ... '60 '96 C.363 B.A. L.989 J.D. [F.J.Kreiner]
Kreiner, Frederick J., Co., L.P.A. ... 1401 Terminal Tower 50 Public Square
Kreiner & Peters Co., L.P.A., (BV) ... P.O. Box 6599 (⊙Cincinnati, Columbus)
Krembs, Andrew P., (AV) ... '50 '76 C.966 B.A. L.930 J.D. [A.P.Krembs&Assoc.]
Krembs, Peter J., (AV) ... '44 '73 C.966 B.S. L.930 J.D. [Hermann,C.&S.]
Krembs, Andrew P., & Associates Co., L.P.A., (AV) ... 55 Public Square, Suite 1700
Kremser, Mark E. ... '71 '96 C.97 B.A. L.930 J.D. [A Janik&D.]
Krent, Eugene P., (AV) ... '23 '52 C.381 A.B. L.930 LL.B. 1708 Rustic Trail‡
Kresnye, Stephen P., (AV) ... '49 '77 C.363 B.S.B.A. L.477 J.D. [Calfee,H.&G.]
Krewson, Patricia Fleming ... '79 '03 C.97 B.A. L.930 J.D. [A Taft,S.&H.]
Kriessler, Lynn A. ... '65 '91 C.914 B.A. L.930 J.D. [Meyers,R.F.&L.]
Kristan, Bonnie L. ... '70 '98 C.473 B.S., B.A. L.665 J.D. [A Duvin,C.&H.]
Kristan, John A., Jr. ... '72 '98 C.1113 B.A. L.665 J.D. [A Kelley,J.M.&S.]
Krivinskas, Dainius A. ... '— '03 C.228 A.B. L.477 J.D. [A Jones D.]
Krivinskas, Lea J. ... '— '05 C.228 A.B. L.1565 J.D. [A Jones D.]
Kriynovich, Wayne S. ... '52 '88 C.161 B.A. L.1003 J.D. Asst. Atty. Gen.
Krizman, Frederick E. ... '16 '53 C.363 B.B.A. L.1003 LL.B. 25900 Euclid Ave.‡
Krock, Earl J. ... '11 '37 C.363 B.A. L.989 J.D. 4367 Rocky River Dr.‡
Krohngold, Walter H., (BV) ... '56 '83 C.696 B.A. L.930 J.D. [A S.S.Keller&Assoc.]
Krol, Kenneth H. ... '55 '81 C.161 B.A. L.1003 J.D. 4437 W. 11th St.
Kronenberg, Jacob A. H., Law Office of, (BV) '51 '74
C.385 A.B. L.273 J.D. 4403 St. Clair Ave., N.E.
Krongold, Gerald ... '52 '77 C&L.659 B.A., J.D. 11075 E. Blvd.
Krosin, Donald N. ... '32 '58 C.124 B.B.A. L.989 J.D. 1700 East 13th St., Suite 20-s
Krotinger, Myron N., (AV) ... '14 '37 C.569 B.A. L.178 LL.B. [Van Aken,W.&W.]
Krueger, Jeffrey W. ... '60 '85 C.97 B.S. L.930 J.D. [Wegman,H.&V.]
Kruppa, Andrew R. ... '75 '00 C.164 B.A. L.608 J.D. [A Squire,S.&D.]
Kruse, Mark F., (BV) ... '60 '85 C.97 B.S. L.1003 J.D. [McIntyre,K.&K.]
Krymowski, John J. ... '25 '56 C.754 L.537 LL.B. 7716 Ridge Rd.
Kryshtalowych, Helen Z. '45 '80
C.608 B.A. L.1003 J.D. [C Squire,S.&D.] (⊙Moscow, Russia)
Kryszak, Michele T. ... '76 '03 C.207 B.A. L.124 J.D. [A Thompson H.]
Kube, Michael R., (AV) ... '41 '67 C.62 B.A. L.930 J.D. [Jeffries,K.F.&M.] ‡
Kucharson, M. Casey ... '79 '04 C.473 B.S. L.8 J.D. [A Benesch,F.C.&A.]
Kuechle, Gerrit C. ... '41 '69 C.72 B.A. L.1003 J.D. Pres., National Assocs., Inc.
Kuenzi, Hans C., (BV) ... '57 '83 C.477 B.A. L.1003 J.D. [H.C.Kuenzi]
Kuenzi, Hans C., Co., L.P.A., (BV) ... 1660 W. 2nd Street
Kuepper, Richard R., (AV) ... '41 '80 C.161 B.A. L.1003 J.D. 1660 W. 2nd St.
Kugelman, Harvey ... '58 '84 C.94 B.A. L.1003 J.D. 1370 Ontario St.
Kuhlman, Gina A. ... '70 '96 C&L.930 B.S., J.D. [A Johnson,A.&C.]
Kukuca, Kathleen Ende ... '53 '83 C.161 B.A. L.1003 J.D. William Silverman & Co.
Kundtz, John Andrew, (AV) '33 '58 C.276 B.S. L.930 LL.B.
3550 Lander Road, Suite 140
Kunkle, Lisa K. ... '— '94 C.473 B.S. L.851 J.D. [A Jones D.]
Kunselman, David A. ... '76 '01 C.865 B.A. L.124 J.D. [A Goodman W.M.]
Kurant, Jack, (AV) ... '46 '72 C.608 B.A. L.930 J.D. [Karberg,K.W.&T.]
Kurit, Neil, (AV) ... '40 '64 C.473 B.S. L.930 J.D. [Kahn K.]
Kurland, Gerald, Law Office of, (BV) '30 '68
C&L.930 B.B.A., J.D. 1 Bratenahl Pl., Ste. 704
Kursh, Deanna Coe, (AV) ... '42 '74 C.608 B.S. L.930 J.D. [C Benesch,F.C.&A.]
Kurtz, John C. ... '38 '68 C.363 B.S. L.1003 J.D. 4843 Gleeton Rd.
Kurtz, William A. ... '47 '72 C.602 B.A. L.608 J.D. Co. Admr., Juv. Ct.
Kushner, Philip S., (AV) ... '59 '85 C.976 B.A. L.145 J.D. [Kushner&R.]

Kushner & Rendon Co., L.P.A., (AV)
2860 BP Tower, 200 Public Square, 44114
Telephone: 216-696-6700 Fax: 216-696-6772
Members of the Firm: Philip S. Kushner; Carole Schwartz Rendon; Michael R. Hamed;—Rachael L. Israel.
Civil Litigation, Criminal Litigation, Family Law.
See Professional Biographies, CLEVELAND, OHIO

Kusner, Andrew T. '61 '94 C.161 B.A. L.1003 J.D.
Consultant, Watson Wyatt Worldwide
Kutash, Henry, (AV) ... '07 '29 C&L.930 B.A., LL.B. 23305 Chagrin Blvd.‡
Kutik, David A., (AV) ... '— '80 C.165 A.B. L.930 J.D. [Jones D.]
Kutsko, Douglas A. ... '69 '97 C.381 B.A. L.1003 J.D. [A B.P.Biggins&Assoc.]
Kvale, Craig P. ... '66 '91 C.967 B.A. L.117 J.D. [Webster W.K.]
Kwarciak, Richard F. ... '68 '94 C.659 B.A. L.1003 J.D. 1375 E. 9th Street

LaBarre, Dennis W., (AV) '— '68 C.597 B.A. L.893 J.D.
[Jones D.] (⊙New York, NY)
Labes, Robert D., (AV) ... '62 '88 C&L.477 B.A., J.D. [Squire,S.&D.]
Labovitz, Harvey, (AV) ... '44 '69 C.473 A.B. L.1066 J.D. [Collins&S.]
LaCerva, Anthony J., (AV) ... '59 '86 C.381 B.A. L.851 J.D. [Calfee,H.&G.]
Lachman, Roy E., (BV) '45 '77 C.659 B.A. L.94 J.D.
Asst. Gen. Coun. & V.P., Ohio Savings Financial Corporation
Lacivita, Richard J. ... '75 '00 C.473 B.S. L.608 J.D. [A Shapiro&F.]
LaCivita, Robert J. ... '77 '02 C.473 B.S. L.989 J.D. [A Shapiro&F.]
Lacks, Monica L., (BVⓉ) ... '65 '90 C.367 B.A. L.1565 J.D. [C McGlinchey S.]
Laderman, Samuel, (BV) ... '22 '55 C.608 B.S.B.A. L.1003 J.D. 845 Leader Bldg.
Lafave, Arthur J., Jr. ... '33 '58 C.951 B.A. L.976 LL.B. Intl. Mgmt. Grp.
Lafferty, Scott W. '55 '80
C.970 B.A. L.930 J.D. Sr. Assoc. Coun., Def. Fin. & Acct. Serv.
LaFond, Thomas J., (AV) ... '41 '66 C.363 B.S.B.A. L.930 J.D. [Schneider,S.R.&L.]
Laino, Kenneth J., (AV) ... '53 '79 C.363 A.B. L.477 J.D. [Schneider,S.R.&L.]
Lake, Andrew C. ... '64 '99 C.970 B.A. L.7 J.D. [A Wegman,H.&V.]
Lalak, Lori Ann ... '70 '95 C.318 B.A. L.904 J.D. Sr. Atty-Editor, West Group
Lalchandani, Kabir A. ... '— '04 C.188 B.S. L.1556 J.D. [A Jones D.]
Lallo, Ernest A., (BV) ... '54 '79 C.363 A.B. L.1003 J.D. 55 Public Sq., Ste. 1616
Lally, Charles J., (BV) ... '46 '81 C.381 B.A. L.8 J.D. Ct. of App. J.
Lally, Elizabeth Nunziato '62 '89 C.363 B.S. L.1003 J.D.
(adm. in CT; not adm. in OH) Banks Baldwin Law Pub. Co.
Lally, Robert J., (BV) '61 '88
C.602 B.B.A. L.724 J.D. Gen. Coun., Middough Consulting Co.
Lally, Robt. J. ... '28 '53 C&L.602 Ph.B., LL.B. 16803 Euclid Ave.‡
Lally Spicer, Meegan ... '68 '93 C.97 B.S. L.251 J.D. [A Squire,S.&D.]
La Marca, Thos. J., (BV) ... '26 '53 C.930 B.B.A. L.1003 J.D. 1370 Ontario St.
Lamb, Brian J., (AV) ... '65 '91 C.970 B.A. L.178 J.D. [Thompson H.]
Lambert, David G., (BV) ... '53 '85 C.610 B.A. L.1003 J.D. 2112 E. Ohio Bldg.
Lambert, P. Wesley ... '78 '03 C.608 B.S. L.124 J.D. [A Climaco,L.P.W.&G.]
Lambros, Thomas D., (AV) ... '30 '52 C.250 L.161 J.D. [C Janik&D.]
LaMonica, Deneen ... '— '01 C.161 B.A. L.1003 J.D. [Calfee,H.&G.]
Lamos, Philip D. ... '67 '96 C.363 B.A. L.1003 J.D. Off of the Chap. 13 Trustee
Lampert, Donald E., (AV) ... '48 '86 C.665 B.A. L.930 J.D. [A Calfee,H.&G.]
Lancione, John A., (AV) ... '62 '88 C.207 B.A. L.930 J.D. [Lancione&L.]
Lancione, John G., (AV) ... '35 '59 C.610 B.S.C. L.608 LL.B. [Lancione&L.]

Lancione & Lancione, PLL, (AV) [BB]
200 Public Square, Suite 2955, 44114
Telephone: 216-623-4949 Fax: 216-623-3975
Email: jgl@lancionelaw.com URL: http://www.lancioneandlancione.com
John G. Lancione; John A. Lancione.
Medical Malpractice, Personal Injury, Automobile Accidents, Hospital Liability, Negligence, Wrongful Death.
See Professional Biographies, CLEVELAND, OHIO

Landever, David ... '70 '95 C.473 B.A. L.930 J.D. [A Weisman,G.&W.]
Landskroner, Jack, (AV) ... '67 '92 C.94 B.A. L.1003 J.D. [Landskroner G.M.]
Landskroner, Lawrence, (AV) ... '27 '50 C.207 L.880 J.D. 55 Public Square, Suite 1040
Landskroner Grieco Madden, Ltd., (AV) ... 1360 W. 9th St., Suite 200
Lane, Aimee W. ... '74 '99 C.434 B.A. L.124 J.D. [A Walter&H.]
Lane, James L. ... '73 '99 C.610 B.B.A. L.7 J.D. [A Hermann,C.&S.]
Lang, Daniel Patrick, (BV) ... '61 '86 C.1115 B.A. L.1003 J.D. 5579 Pearl Rd., Ste. 203
Lang, James F. ... '63 '92 C.896 B.A. L.893 J.D. [Calfee,H.&G.]
Lang, Jeffrey R. ... '75 '02 C.201 B.A. L.1003 J.D. [A Weston H.]
Lang, Paul A. ... '67 '92 C.473 B.A. L.930 J.D. [Rolf&G.]
Lang, Thomas J. '56 '82 C.276 B.S.F.S. L.128 J.D.
(adm. in DC; not adm. in OH) 2800 Scarborough Rd.‡
Lange, Jill J. ... '42 '87 C.645 B.S. L.1003 J.D. Sr. Atty., Legal Aid Soc.
Langer, Carlton E. '54 '79
C.20 A.B. L.1003 J.D. Sr. V.P. & Asst. Gen. Coun., Natl. City Bk.
Langer, Philip E., (AV) ... '48 '73 C&L.608 B.A., J.D. [Porter W.M.&A.]
Langhenry, Barbara A., (AV) ... '57 '87 C.602 A.B. L.930 J.D. 601 Lakeside Ave.
Lansdowne, Dennis R., (AV) ... '55 '81 C.161 B.A. L.1003 J.D. [Spangenberg,S.&L.]
Lanz, John E., Jr. '42 '71 C.397 B.A. L.262 J.D.
(adm. in CT; not adm. in OH) V.P., TRWInc.
Lanza, Robt. F. ... '17 '50 C.363 L.1003 LL.B. 13354 Cedar St.
Lapine, Kenneth M., (AV) ... '42 '67 C.197 A.B. L.477 J.D. [Roetzel&A.]
LaPorte, Dale C., (AV) ... '42 '66 C.602 B.S. L.930 J.D. [Calfee,H.&G.] ‡
Lardakis, Terry E., (BV) ... '49 '77 C&L.8 B.A., J.D. [Millisor&N.]

Largent, Berry, Preston & Jamison Co., L.P.A.
(See Berea)

Larissey, Michele L. ... '70 '97 C.502 B.A. L.208 J.D. [A Swartz C.]
Larsen, Hans L. ... '59 '92 C.871 B.S. L.893 J.D. [A Frantz W.]
Larsen, Lynn Rowe ... '63 '91 C.317 B.A. L.896 J.D. [T.F.Sweeney]
Larsen, Stuart L., (BV) ... '64 '93 C.161 B.B.A. L.608 J.D. [Kahn K.]
Larson, John S., (AV) ... '51 '77 C.197 A.B. L.659 J.D. [Squire,S.&D.]
Larson, Leslie L. '47 '75 C.339 B.S. L.145 J.D.
(adm. in IL; not adm. in OH) BP Oil Co.
Larson, Robert L., (AV) ... '29 '56 C.339 B.A. L.309 J.D. 127 Public Sq.‡
LaSalvia, Christine M. ... '76 '03 C.608 B.S. L.1003 J.D. [A Friedman,D.&S.]
LaSalvia, Shelly R. ... '78 '04 C.363 B.S. L.989 J.D. [A Novak,R.P.&S.]
Lasch, Debora S., (AV) ... '58 '88 C.473 B.A. L.161 J.D. [Cowden,H.N.&L.]
Lasko, John J., Jr. ... '52 '77 C.363 B.S.B.A. L.930 J.D. 614 Superior Ave., N.W.‡
Lasko, Ronald H., (BV) ... '48 '76 C.608 B.A. L.1003 J.D. [Lasko&L.]
Lasko & Lind, A Legal Professional Association, (BV) ... 1406 W. 6th Street
Laszcz, Joseph S. ... '52 '81 C.608 B.A. L.851 J.D. Staff Hearing Offr., Indus. Comm.
Lathrop, Lisa S. ... '— '01 C.136 B.S. L.602 J.D. [A Jones D.]
Laubenthal, Thomas J. ... '54 '80 C.150 B.B.A. L.1003 J.D. Ernst & Young
Lauderdale, Jeffrey J. ... '75 '02 C.610 A.B. L.608 J.D. [A Calfee,H.&G.]
Laundy, Henry H. ... '13 '49 C.597 B.S. L.1003 LL.B. 489 Lake Forest Dr.
Lavelle, Neal P., (BV) ... '35 '60 C&L.930 B.A., J.D. [Lavelle&L.]
Lavelle, Patrick S. ... '67 '93 C.150 B.A. L.161 J.D. 123 West Prospect Avenue
Lavelle & Lavelle Co., L.P.A., (BV) ... 526 Superior Ave. East
Laven, Stuart A., (AV) ... '43 '70 C.659 A.B. L.930 J.D. [Ulmer&B.]
Laven, Stuart A., Jr. ... '72 '99 C.273 B.S. L.608 J.D. [A Benesch,F.C.&A.]
Lavey, David B. ... '62 '87 C.674 B.A. L.280 J.D. [C Squire,S.&D.]
Lavey, Wendlene M. ... '63 '89 C.216 B.A. L.930 J.D. [Squire,S.&D.]
Lavin, Sean T. ... '76 '01 C.363 B.A. L.989 J.D. [A McLaughlin&M.]
Lavllo, Frank Joseph ... '57 '84 C.611 B.A. L.1003 J.D. 3787 Princeton Blvd.
Lavrisha, Anton M., (BV) ... '53 '79 C.161 B.A. L.1003 J.D. 18975 Villaview Rd.‡
Lawko, Wm. A. ... '21 '50 C.251 B.B.A. L.1003 LL.B. 11711 Lorain Ave.
Lawniczak, James M., (AV) ... '51 '77 C&L.477 B.A., J.D. [Calfee,H.&G.]
Lawrence, Kelly Summers ... '75 '02 C.473 B.A. L.989 J.D. [A Frantz W.]

Lawrence, William B., (AV) '44 '70
C.381 B.A. L.930 J.D. Exec. V.P. & Gen. Coun., TRW Inc.
Lawry, Robert P. '41 '67 C.262 B.A. L.659 J.D.
(adm. in PA; not adm. in OH) Prof. of Law, Case Western Reserve Univ.
Lawson, Douglas E. '53 '80 C.381 B.A. L.823 J.D. Tremont W. Develop. Corp.
Lawson, Scott E. '62 '94 C.1457 B.A. L.1003 J.D. [Lawson]

Lawson Firm, The, LLC
Plaza West Executive Center, 20220 Center Ridge Road, Suite 320, 44116
Telephone: 440-409-0303 Fax: 440-409-0323
Email: slawson@lawsonfirm.net URL: http://www.lawsonfirm.net
Member of Firm: Scott E. Lawson.
Insurance Law, Insurance Regulation, Internet Law, General Corporate Law, Business Law, Intellectual Property.

See Professional Biographies, CLEVELAND, OHIO

Lawther, Jennifer L. '71 '96 C.608 B.S.B.A. L.1003 J.D. 55 Public Sq.
Lawther, Robert M. '27 '53 C.970 B.A. L.930 LL.B. Com. Pleas J.
Layman, Richard P., (AV) '— '80 C.607 B.A. L.477 J.D. [Jones D.]
Layne, Judith L. '66 '91 C.381 B.A. L.1003 J.D. P.O. Box 771252
Lazar, Kathy P., (AV) '— '82 C.381 B.A. L.930 J.D. [Ⓒ Jones D.]
Lazarus, Stephen R. '39 '65
C.951 A.B. L.309 LL.B. Assoc. Prof. of Law, Cleve. State Univ.
Lazich, Trish D. '63 '91 C.381 B.S. L.117 J.D. [Ⓐ Ulmer&B.]
Lazzaro, Anthony J. '79 '04 C.880 B.A. L.989 J.D. [Ⓐ Frantz W.]
Lazzaro, Lynn A., (AV) '50 '75 C.317 A.B. L.1003 J.D.
101 W. Prospect Ave., Ste. 1700
Lazzaro, Patrick G. '27 '57 C.930 L.1003 J.D. Adm. Law J., Soc. Sec. Admn.‡
Leach, John C. '52 '02 C.473 B.A. L.8 J.D. [Ⓐ Sutter,O.&F.]
Leader, Edward J. '72 '97 C&L.602 B.A., J.D. [Ⓐ Frantz W.]
Leahy, William B., (AV) '43 '68 C&L.608 B.A., J.D. [Buckingham,D.&B.]
Leak, Douglas G., (AV) '62 '88 C.94 B.A. L.989 J.D. [Roetzel&A.]
Lear, S. Michael '62 '89 C.608 B.A. L.930 J.D. [Zukerman,D.&L.]
Lease, Robert K., (AV) '48 '76 C.197 A.B. L.184 J.D. [Baker&H.]
Leatherberry, Wilbur C. '43 '68 C&L.930 A.B., J.D.
Assoc. Dean, Academic Affrs. & Prof. of Law, Case Western Reserve Univ.
Leavitt, Jeffrey S., (AV) '— '73 C.188 A.B. L.930 J.D. [Jones D.]
Lebold, John W., (AV) '57 '82 C.473 B.A. L.930 J.D.
Assoc. Gen. Coun. Litig., The Sherwin-Williams Co.
Lebovitz, James R., (AV) '56 '82 C.161 B.A. L.1003 J.D. [Nurenberg,P.H.&M.]
Lebowitz, Todd H. '72 '97 C&L.477 B.A., J.D. [Baker&H.]
Lechnowsky, Orest J. '59 '85 C.1122 B.A. L.107 J.D.
(adm. in NY; not adm. in OH)
V.P. & Asst. Gen. Coun., Chase Manhattan Financial Corp.
Leddy, Patrick J., (AV) '— '90 C.161 B.B.A. L.1003 J.D. [Jones D.]
Lee, Martha Cole 50 '76 C.788 A.B. L.930 J.D. 13800 Shaker Blvd. #808
Lee, Thomas J., (AV) '52 '77 C.967 B.A. L.930 J.D. [Taft,S.&H.]
Leece, Robert L. '41 '70 C.97 B.A. L.930 J.D. 9840 Lorain Ave.
Leece, Wilson A., II, (BV) '43 '69 C.894 B.A. L.930 J.D. 9840 Lorain Ave.
Leeders, Lawrence D., Law Offices of '54 '80
C.473 B.A. L.161 J.D. 1991 Crocker Road, Suite 600
Lefelar, Scott A. '69 '94 C.29 B.A. L.930 J.D. [Millisor&N.]

Leffler, Daniel J., Counselor at Law
(See Akron)

Lefkowitz, James E., (AV) '47 '73 C.608 B.S. L.472 J.D. 1111 Superior Ave Ste 900‡
Lefkowitz, Paul S., (AV) '49 '74 C&L.930 B.A., J.D. [Climaco,L.P.W.&G.] ‡
Legenza, Richard A. '59 '84 C&L.507 B.S.B.A., J.D.
Assoc. Gen. Coun. Corp., The Sherwin-Williams Co.
Legerski, Mary L. '58 '94
C.876 B.S.N. L.1003 J.D. Risk Mgr. & Staff Atty., MetroHealth Sys.
Legin, Joel L. '52 '78 C.902 B.A. L.64 J.D.
(adm. in MD; not adm. in OH) Contracts Mgr., Northrop Grumman Corp.
Lehecka, William B. '20 '51 C.385 A.B. L.1003 J.D. Asst. Dir. of Law
Leiken, Earl M., (AV) '42 '67 C&L.309 B.A., LL.B. [Baker&H.]
Leiken, Jonathan B. '— '97 C.1036 B.A. L.659 J.D. [Ⓐ Jones D.]
Leikin, Jeffrey A., (AV) '59 '85 C.174 B.A. L.1003 J.D. [Nurenberg,P.H.&M.]
Leizman, William S., (AV) '26 '51 C.930 B.B.A. L.1003 LL.B.
Leader Building, Suite 833
Lembright, Mark R. '62 '89 C.610 B.A. L.7 J.D. [Shapiro&F.]
Lenahan, Christopher Richards '67 '00 C.436 B.A. L.989 J.D. [Pagano,W.T.G.&L.]
Leneghan, Christine T. '64 '91 [Leneghan&L.]
Leneghan, Patrick P., JR, (BV) '64 '89 C.436 B.S. L.930 J.D. [Leneghan&L.]
Leneghan & Leneghan, (BV) 9500 Maywood Ave.
Lenhard, John E. '39 '66 C.973 B.A. L.150 J.D.
V.P., Secy. & Gen. Coun., Cleveland-Cliffs Inc.
Lenhard, Matthew J. '74 '99 C.602 B.A. L.880 J.D. [Ⓐ Cowden,H.N.&L.]
Lenhardt, Fred P. '64 '94 C.608 B.A. L.999 J.D. 1419 West 9th Street
Lenhart, Thomas E., (AV) '55 '88 C&L.608 B.S., J.D. N.E. Ohio Reg. Sewer Dist.
Lennox, Heather, (AV) '— '92 C.363 B.A. L.276 J.D. [Jones D.]
Lenson, Kevin L. '70 '96 C.966 B.A. L.851 J.D. [Ⓐ Friedman,D.&S.]
Lenson, Murray K., (AV) '42 '68 C.473 B.A. L.851 J.D. [Ulmer&B.]
Leo, Ann, (BV) '53 '79 C.161 B.A. L.1003 J.D. [Koeth,R.&L.]
Leo, Victor J., (BV) '54 '79 C.473 A.B. L.1003 J.D.
Counsel-Litigation, Eaton Corporation
Leonard, Irvin A., (AV) '— '67 C.665 B.A. L.569 J.D. [Jones D.]
Leonard, Melissa A. '69 '95 C.473 B.S. L.477 J.D. [Baker&H.]
Leonetti, Albert F., (BV) '41 '66 C&L.930 A.B., J.D. 13111 Shaker Sq.
Leonetti, Ellen M. '60 '86 C.363 B.A. L.1003 J.D. Mag., Co. Juv. Ct.
Leonetti, Frank, III, (BV) '56 '82 C.597 B.A. L.930 J.D. [Ⓐ Reminger&R.]
Leonti, Joseph R. '71 '00 C.161 B.B.A. L.989 J.D. [Ⓐ Tucker E.&W.]
Leopard, Amy, (AV) '60 '96 C.10 B.S. L.930 J.D. [Walter&H.]
Leopold, David W., (AV) '58 '85 C.477 A.B. L.930 J.D. [D.W.Leopold&Assoc.]

Leopold, David Wolfe, & Associates Co., LPA, (AV)
2000 East Ninth Street, Suite 300, 44115
Telephone: 216-696-4676 Fax: 216-696-8268 URL: http://www.immvisa.com
Email: info@immvisa.com URL: http://www.dwllawfirm.com
David W. Leopold;—Mehta Khorzad Adi, Esq.; Melissa A. Greco.
Immigration, Visa and Citizenship Law.

See Professional Biographies, CLEVELAND, OHIO

Lepene, Alan R., (AV) '46 '71 C.610 B.A. L.477 J.D. [Thompson H.]
Lepene, Scott '75 '03 C.610 B.S. L.880 J.D. [Ⓐ Porter W.M.&A.]
Lerner, Rachel D. '— '96 C.260 B.A. L.251 J.D.
Assoc. Gen. Coun., AG Properties, Inc.
Lesco, Richard A., (AV) '36 '61 C&L.930 B.B.A., LL.B. [Snyder]
Lesher, Greta '49 '79 C.970 B.A. L.1003 J.D. 3570 Eldorado Dr.
Leslie, Timothy C. '59 '94 C.473 A.B. L.188 J.D. Assoc. Gen. Coun., Degussa Corp.

Lester, David L., (AV) '58 '83 C.170 B.A. L.930 J.D. [Ulmer&B.]
Leukart, Barbara J., (AV) '— '75 C.66 B.A. L.930 J.D. [Jones D.]
Leukart, Richard H., II, (AV) '42 '67 C.197 A.B. L.477 J.D. [Baker&H.]
Leung, Diane S. '— '92 C.970 B.A. L.1003 J.D. [Ⓐ Thompson H.]
Levasseur, Eric B. '76 '02 C.165 B.A. L.124 J.D. [Ⓐ Hahn L.&P.]
Levin, Daniel J. '64 '91 C.472 B.S. L.1003 J.D. [M.Levin]
Levin, Dennis P. '52 '78 C.473 B.S. L.851 J.D. 5910 Landerbrook Dr., Ste. 200
Levin, Frank K. '07 '32 C.477 B.A. L.608 LL.B. 6415 Detroit Ave.‡
Levin, James A., (BV) '53 '79 C.477 B.A. L.930 LL.B 6415 Detroit Ave.
Levin, Joel, (AV) '51 '77 C.145 B.A. L.94 J.D. [Levin&Assoc.]
Levin, Morris '26 '52 C.679 B.S. L.309 J.D. [M.Levin]
Levin, Morton Q., (AV) '41 '66 C&L.477 B.A., J.D. 1505 Ohio Svgs. Plaza

Levin & Associates Co., L.P.A., (AV)
Tower at Erieview, Suite 1100, 1301 East 9th Street, 44114
Telephone: 216-928-0600 Fax: 216-928-0016 URL: http://www.levinandassociates.com
URL: http://www.lawyers.com/levinlaw
Joel Levin;—Aparesh Paul; Christopher M. Vlasich.
Commercial Litigation, Medical Malpractice, Personal Injury, Product Liability.

See Professional Biographies, CLEVELAND, OHIO

Levin, Morris, Co., L.P.A. 55 Public Sq., Ste. 940
Levine, Alan S., (AV) '52 '79 C.608 B.A. L.1003 J.D. 55 Public Square Suite 1200
Levine, Barbara H., (AVⓉ) '50 '77 C.705 B.A. L.831 J.D. [Ⓒ Hahn L.&P.]
Levine, David L., (AV) '29 '53 L.1003 J.D. 55 Public Sq., Ste 1200
Levine, Gary H., (AV) '49 '76 C.608 B.A. L.161 J.D. 55 Public Square
Levy, Donald M., (BV) '40 '65 C.475 B.A. L.930 J.D. 55 Public Sq.
Levy, Howard A., (AV) '44 '73 C.385 B.A. L.930 J.D. [Benesch,F.C.&A.]

Levy & Dubyak
(See Beachwood)

Lewanski, Christine '70 '96 C.320 B.A. L.124 J.D. [Ⓐ Taft,S.&H.]
Lewis, David M. '67 '00 C.161 B.A. L.124 J.D. [Ⓐ Porter W.M.&A.]
Lewis, David Paul '56 '87 C.645 B.S. L.1003 J.D. V.P., Natl. City Bk.
Lewis, Franklin C. '39 '63 C.930 B.A. L.608 J.D. Asst. Law Dir.
Lewis, H. Donal '60 '86 C.848 B.A. L.607 J.D. [Ⓐ Reid,B.M.&W.]
Lewis, Jennifer C. '— '95 C.363 B.A. L.930 J.D. [Ⓐ Jones D.]
Lewis, John B., (AV) '47 '72 C&L.502 B.A., J.D. [Baker&H.]
Lewis, John F., (AV) '32 '58 C.31 B.A. L.477 J.D. [Ⓒ Squire,S.&D.]
Lewis, John Q. '— '96 C.373 B.A. L.229 J.D. [Ⓐ Jones D.]
Lewis, Kenneth James '73 '00 C.608 B.A. L.124 J.D. 323 Lakeside Avenue
Lewis, Leonard L. '54 '84 C.602 B.S.E.E. L.161 J.D. [Calfee,H.&G.] (See Pat. Sect.)
Lewis, Martin H., (AV) '51 '79 C.976 B.A. L.273 J.D. [Tucker E.&W.]
Lewis, Nathan T. '— '04 C.437 B.S. L.608 J.D. [Ⓐ Jones D.]
Lewis, Patrick H., (AV) '— '85 C.930 B.A. L.1003 J.D. [Ⓐ Duvin,C.&H.]
Lewis, Patrick T. '79 '04 C.945 A.B. L.1565 J.D. [Ⓐ Porter W.M.&A.]
Lewis, Robert Lee '44 '72 C.824 B.A. L.352 J.D. Legal Aid Soc.
Lewis, Robert S. '76 '02 C.215 B.A. L.930 J.D. [Ⓐ Thompson H.]
Lewis, Robt. J. '15 '50 C.943 B.S. L.1003 LL.B. 18668 Parkland Dr.
Lewis, Scott M., (AV) '59 '84 C.477 B.A. L.145 J.D. [Meyers,R.F.&L.]
Liber, John D., (AV) '38 '63 C.679 B.S. L.608 J.D. [Ⓒ Spangenberg,S.&L.]
Licata, Louis J., (AV) '58 '83 C.161 B.A. L.893 J.D. [Licata&Assoc.]
Licata & Associates Co., L.P.A., (AV)
6480 Rockside Woods Boulevard South, Suite 390
Lichko, Gregory M., (AV) '47 '75 C.610 A.B. L.930 J.D. [Lichko&S.]

Lichko & Schechter, (AV)
1600 Illuminating Building, 55 Public Square, 44113
Telephone: 216-928-1503 Fax: 216-619-9846
URL: http://www.lichkoschechter.com
Members of Firm: Gregory M. Lichko; Roy J. Schechter. Of Counsel: Gregory R. Glick.
Civil Litigation at the Trial and Appellate Levels in State and Federal Courts, Business Litigation, Construction Litigation, Corporate Law, Real Estate and Securities.

See Professional Biographies, CLEVELAND, OHIO

Lichtig, Steven M. '65 '92 C.150 B.A. L.201 J.D. [Ⓐ Kelley,J.M.&S.] (ⓒPhila., PA)
Lichtman, Corey '— '02 C.94 B.A. L.1003 J.D. [Ⓐ Chernett W.Y.&P.]
Lichtman, Jeffrey E. '45 '71 C.473 B.A. L.161 J.D. U.S. Dist. Ct.
Licygiewicz, Arthur P. '— '97 C.602 B.S. L.823 J.D. [Ⓐ Jones D.]
Lidrbauch, Elena '59 '99 C.161 B.A. L.7 J.D. [Hickman&L.]
Liebson, Matthew E. '74 '99 C.207 B.A. L.309 J.D. [Ⓐ Thompson H.]
Liederbach, Kirk W. '60 '92 L.989 J.D. [Bernard&H.]
Liffman, Kenneth B., (AV) '54 '79 C.473 B.S. L.1003 J.D. [McCarthy,L.C.&L.]
Light, Jeffrey H. '61 '86 C.473 B.S. L.1003 J.D. The Sherwin-Williams Co.
Lightbody, Jennifer L. '66 '92 C.923 B.A. L.117 J.D. U.S. Dist. Ct.

Lightbody, William S. '50 '77 C.81 B.S. L.569 J.D.
32600 Fairmount Boulevard, Atrium Suite, 100, 44124
Telephone: 216-621-7337 Fax: 216-621-7393
URL: http://www.williamlightbodylaw.com
Litigation, Intellectual Property, Patent, Trademark, Copyright, Unfair Competition, Trade Secrets.

See Professional Biographies, CLEVELAND, OHIO

Lightner, Terri A. '— '04 C.876 B.S.N. L.989 J.D. [Ⓐ Climaco,L.P.W.&G.]
Lill, Abby K. '79 '04 C.124 B.A. L.1003 J.D. [Ⓐ Shapero&R.]
Lillie, Richard G., (AV) '50 '79 C.161 B.A. L.1003 J.D. [Benesch,F.C.&A.]
Lilly, John C. '50 '77 C.373 B.A. L.608 J.D. Charter One Bk., F.S.B.
Lilly, Stacy N. '75 '00 C.610 B.A. L.851 J.D. [Ⓐ Janik&D.]
Lim, Gene M. '65 '92 C.611 B.A. L.1003 J.D. [Petronzio S.]
Lincoln, Erik C. '66 '91 C.763 B.S. L.8 J.D. Ernst & Young‡
Lind, John K., (BV) '59 '89 C.178 B.A. L.262 J.D. [Lasko&L.]
Lindahl, Burkhart R. '— '00 C.97 B.A. L.851 J.D. [Ⓐ Jones D.]
Lindberg, Lawrence V., (AV) '47 '73 C.970 B.A. L.569 J.D. [Baker&H.]
Linden, Michael J., (AV) '50 '75 C.608 B.S. L.161 J.D. [M.J.Linden]

Linden, Michael J., Co., LPA, (AV)
(An Association of Independently Practicing Lawyers)
Suite 400 Park Plaza Building, 1111 Chester Avenue, 44114
Telephone: 216-621-0590 Fax: 216-621-5665
Email: michael.linden@lindenlpa.com
Michael J. Linden.
Mortgages, Real Estate, Banking, Foreclosures and related Bankruptcy, Financial Institutions, Secured Transactions, Condominium and Real Estate Development Law.
References: National City Bank; Ohio Savings Assn.

See Professional Biographies, CLEVELAND, OHIO

Lindner, Daniel F., (CV) '68 '94 C.477 B.A. L.124 J.D. [Lindner W.C.]
Lindner, David J. '73 '01 C&L.608 B.A., J.D. [Ⓐ Buckingham,D.&B.]
Lindner Weaver Crane LLP, (CV) 55 Public Square, Suite 1600
Linehan, Paul W. '69 '98 C.602 B.B.A. L.930 J.D. [Ⓐ McDonald H.]
Linetsky, Yuri R. '— '00 C&L.930 B.A., J.D. [Ⓐ Hahn L.&P.]
Ling, Daniel R. '78 '03 C.477 B.S.C.E. L.124 J.D. [Ⓐ Renner,O.B.&S.] (See Pat. Sect.)

Ling, John M. ... '73 '00 C.477 B.A. L.37 J.D. [Ⓐ Amin&T.]
Ling, Wendy Asma '56 '91 C.114 B.A. L.477 J.D.
(adm. in MI; not adm. in OH) 1 Lakeside Ave
Linick, Brian H. ... '— '05 C.608 B.S. L.1003 J.D. [Ⓐ Roetzel&A.]
Link, Bradley C. ... '72 '04 C.1359 B.A. L.989 J.D. [Ⓐ Hahn L.&P.]
Linn, Martin Paul ... '55 '82 C.97 B.S.B.A. L.1003 J.D. Intl. Mgmt. Grp.
Linn, Michael D., (CV) ... '— '86 C.381 B.A. L.1003 J.D. [Javitch,B.&R.]
Linton, Robert F., Jr., (AV) ... '59 '84 C.610 B.S. L.930 J.D. [Linton&H.]
Linton & Hirshman, (AV) ... 700 W. St. Clair Ave.
Linville, Timothy H. ... '76 '03 C.937 B.A. L.228 J.D. [Ⓐ Thompson H.]
Lipcsik, Robert N. '65 '96 C.930 B.S.M.E. L.989 J.D.
[Ⓐ Tarolli,S.C.&T.] (See Pat. Sect.)
Lippe, Stuart H. ... '43 '75 C.363 B.S.B.A. L.1003 J.D. 526 Superior Ave.
Lipski, Christopher ... '64 '89 C.651 B.S. L.201 J.D. Ernst & Young
Lipson, Alan Gordon ... '43 '68 C&L.477 B.B.A., J.D. Pres., Lipson, Inc.‡
Lipson, Ronald M., (BV) ... '34 '58 C&L.930 B.B.A., LL.B. 55 Public Sq.
List, Martin S., (AV) ... '50 '75 C.188 B.S. L.705 J.D. [Duvin,C.&H.]
Listati, Ezio A. ... '65 '90 C.363 B.S. L.930 J.D. [Benesch,F.C.&A.]
Litt, Shoshana E. ... '— '03 C.311 B.A. L.904 J.D. [Ⓐ Jones D.]
Litzow, Joan M., (AV) ... '42 '84 C.879 B.A. L.930 J.D. [J.M.Litzow]
Litzow, Joan M., Co., LPA, (AV) ... 55 Public Sq., Ste. 1600
Liu, Margaret ... '68 '95 C.477 A.B. L.831 J.D. Asst. V.P., Natl. City Bk.
Livingstone, Fred J., (AV) ... '26 '50 C.930 L.309 LL.B. [Ⓐ Taft,S.&H.]
Lobo, Alfred D., (BV) ... '33 '64 C.477 B.S.Ch.E. L.1003 J.D. [A.D.Lobo] (Pat.)
Lobo, Alfred D., L.P.A., Company, (BV) ... 526 Superior Avenue, Suite 456 (Pat.)
Lobritz, Meredith A. ... '— '03 C&L.608 B.S., J.D. [Ⓐ Duvin,C.&H.]
Locke, Kevin J. ... '65 '90 C&L.8 B.S., J.D. [Ⓐ Pepple&W.]
Locke, Susan S., (AV) '48 '74 C.104 B.A. L.831 J.D.
Sr. V.P.& Assoc. Gen. Coun., KeyBank Natl. Assn.
LoConti, Dennis N., (BV) ... '56 '82 C.161 B.A. L.1003 J.D. [Ⓐ Forbes,F.&Assoc.]
Lodge, James M. '54 '81 C.311 B.A. L.309 J.D.
(adm. in MD; not adm. in OH) Assoc. Jewish Charities & Welfare Fund
Loeb, James A., (AV) ... '63 '88 C&L.608 B.A., J.D. [Baker&H.]
Loesch, Robert M. ... '64 '92 C.1030 B.A. L.930 J.D. [Baker&H.]
Loesel, Pamela E. ... '54 '95 C.879 B.A. L.8 J.D. [Weston H.]
Logan, Heather C. ... '71 '97 C.967 B.A. L.124 J.D. [Ⓐ Tucker E.&W.]
Lohiser, Kenneth L. ... '63 '88 C.608 B.A. L.150 J.D. [Ⓐ Calfee,H.&G.]
Lohr, Carole A. ... '71 '00 C.576 B.A. L.989 J.D. [Ⓐ Keis G.]
Lojewski, Jeffrey D., (BV) ... '57 '82 C.473 A.B. L.1003 J.D. [Ⓐ Berger&Z.]
Lokiec, Benjamin Kenneth ... '74 '01 C.473 B.S. L.930 J.D. West Group
Lombardi, Maria T., (AV) ... '61 '92 C.565 B.S. L.1003 J.D. [McMahon,D.H.&L.]
Lombardo, Vincent J., (BV) ... '— '82 C&L.161 B.M.E., J.D. 614 Superior Ave.
Lombardo, Vincent T., (AV) ... '56 '81 C.659 B.A. L.1003 J.D. OH Atty. Gen.
Lonardo, Angelo F., (BV) ... '50 '79 C.608 B.S. L.1003 J.D. [Yelsky&L.]
London, James D., (AV) ... '42 '67 C&L.608 B.S., J.D. Legal Aid Soc.
Long, Ronald J. ... '56 '83 C.798 B.S. L.502 J.D. Tax Atty., BP America, Inc.
Long, Ryan L. ... '79 '04 C.610 B.A. L.124 J.D. [Ⓐ Zashin&R.]
Longano, Robert F., (AV) ... '19 '43 C&L.930 B.A., J.D. 600 Superior Ave.‡
Longino, Nicole Christina ... '56 '83 C.414 B.S. L.989 J.D. [N.C.Longino]
Longino, Nicole C. ... 11811 Shaker Boulevard, Suite 420
Longley, Earl T., (BV) ... '27 '54 C.930 A.B. L.1003 LL.B. 10511 Fitzwater Rd.
Lonjak, George F., (AV) ... '55 '82 C.1260 B.A. L.1003 J.D. [G.F.Lonjak]
Lonjak, George F., Inc., (AV) ... 1280 W. 3rd St.
LoPresti, Charles A. ... '71 '96 C.161 B.A. L.851 J.D. [Ⓑ Vorys,S.S.&P.]
LoPresti, Joseph J., Jr., (AV) ... '47 '73 C.602 B.B.A. L.608 J.D. [McDonald H.]
LoPresti, Salvatore J., (AV) ... '44 '73 C.381 B.A. L.1003 J.D. [Willacy&L.]
Lord, Frank H., (BV) ... '29 '58 C&L.930 B.A., J.D. [Lord&L.]
Lord, Kimberly M., (BV) ... '58 '85 C.317 A.B. L.607 J.D. [Lord&L.]
Lord & Lord, (BV) ... 1100 Rockefeller Bldg.
Lorentzen, Lee A. ... '54 '79 C.608 B.A. L.7 J.D. V.P. & Sr. Coun., KeyBank Natl. Assn.
Losh, Thos.C. ... '27 '53 C.97 L.1003 J.D. 5755 Granger Rd.
Louard, Janette McCarthy ... '61 '86 C.914 B.A. L.178 J.D. [Duvin,C.&H.]
Loucka, Sharon L. '50 '95 C.161 B.S. L.1003 J.D.
1100 Huntington Building, 925 Euclid Avenue
Lougovskaia, Elena N. ... '— '00 C.207 B.S. L.124 J.D. [Ⓐ Gallagher S.]
Louttit, Kathryn Hale '64 '94 C.473 B.S. L.851 J.D.
(adm. in PA; not adm. in OH) V.P. & Asst. Coun., KeyBank Natl. Assn.
Love, Julia Ann ... '— '95 C.94 B.A. L.276 J.D. [Ⓐ Jones D.]
Love, Sheryl H. ... '— '95 C.178 B.A. L.884 J.D. [Ⓐ Jones D.]
Lovequist, Sarah E. ... '76 '01 C.876 B.A. L.989 J.D. 127 Public Sq., 52nd Fl.
Lovett, Mary Forbes, (AV) ... '53 '85 C.608 B.S. L.1003 J.D. [Cowden,H.N.&L.]
Lovett, Ruth L. ... '50 '85 C.1047 B.A. L.930 J.D. [Ⓐ Calfee,H.&G.]
Lovinger, Daniel L., (BV) '42 '67 C.473 B.S. L.930 J.D.
1370 Ontario Street, Suite 2000
Lowder, Janet L. ... '52 '92 C.62 B.A. L.1003 J.D. [Hickman&L.]
Lowe, Bruce J. L., (AV) ... '49 '79 C.051 B.A. L.999 [Taft,S.&H.]
Lowe, James A., (AV) ... '45 '72 C.659 B.A. L.161 J.D. [Lowe E.W.&M.]

Lowe Eklund Wakefield & Mulvihill Co., L.P.A., (AV)
Tower City Center 610 Skylight Office Tower, 1660 West Second Street, 44113-1454
Telephone: 216-781-2600 Fax: 216-781-2610
Email: lew@lewm.com URL: http://www.lewm.com
James A. Lowe; Claudia Rieth Eklund; Mark L. Wakefield; Dennis P. Mulvihill;—Gregory S. Scott; Sara S. Ravas. Of Counsel: Donald Cybulski.
Products Liability, Personal Injury, Medical Malpractice, Commercial Litigation, Wrongful Death, Business Litigation.

See Professional Biographies, CLEVELAND, OHIO

Lowenkamp, Cynthia D. ... '45 '96 C.999 B.A. L.989 J.D. 9197 Willowbrook Court
Lowry, Van M. ... '54 '82 C.574 B.S. L.930 J.D. 1422 Euclid Ave.
Lowy, Geo., (BV) ... '24 '50 C.930 L.472 LL.B. Standard Bldg.
Lu, David S. ... '67 '95 C.309 A.B. L.959 J.D. [Ⓐ Tucker E.&W.]
Luarde, Sharon A. ... '64 '95 C&L.347 B.A., J.D. [Ⓐ Calfee,H.&G.]
Lubbe, Timothy P. ... '69 '98 C.201 B.A. L.607 J.D. [Ⓐ W.Coyne]
Lucarelli, Robert R., (BV) ... '59 '86 C.161 B.B.A. L.1003 J.D. 1300 E. 9th St., Ste. 1202
Lucas, Matthew Harris ... '65 '91 C.970 B.A. L.1003 J.D. [Lustig,E.&L.]
Lucas, Paul H. ... '72 '97 C.385 B.A. L.1003 J.D. 1200 Ontario St., 11th Fl.
Lucas, Sandra C. ... '75 '00 C.363 B.A. L.124 J.D. [Ⓐ Schneider,S.R.&L.]
Lucas, Walter A. (Scott) ... '71 '97 C.62 B.A. L.1003 J.D. [Ⓐ Buckingham,D.&B.]
Lucchesi, Thomas R., (AV) ... '59 '84 C&L.477 A.B., J.D. [Baker&H.]
Lucci, John Paul ... '— '03 C&L.124 B.A., J.D. [Ⓐ Jones D.]
Luikart, Loyal E., Jr., (BV) ... '25 '54 C.62 B.A. L.1003 J.D. 18975 Villaview Dr.
Luka, Lori Ann ... '73 '00 C.980 B.S. L.989 J.D. [Ⓐ Kelley&F.]
Luke, Saralee K. '39 '88 C.914 B.A. L.930 J.D.
(adm. in IL; not adm. in OH) 13901 Shaker Blvd.‡
Lukich, Richard A. ... '54 '82 C.161 B.A. L.1003 J.D. 1111 Superior Avenue, Suite 630
Lum, David A. ... '69 '94 C.860 B.A. L.930 J.D. [Brouse M.]
Lundberg, Arthur H. ... '66 '94 C.93 B.S. L.930 J.D. [Baker&H.]
Lundin, Thomas M. ... '68 '98 C.930 B.S. L.1003 J.D. Marconi Med. Syst., Inc. (Pat.)
Luo, Li-Hua '66 '92 C.999 B.S. L.260 J.D.
(adm. in PA; not adm. in OH) Sr. Coun., Intell. Prop., GE Consumer and Industrial
Lurie, Leonard N. ... '43 '69 C.608 B.S. L.1003 J.D. 3677 Stoer Rd.
Lurie, Robert N. ... '— '94 C.966 B.A. L.1003 J.D. [Javitch,B.&R.]
Luskin, John P., & Associates ... '53 '88 C.363 B.A. L.1003 J.D. P.O. Box 24237
Lusnia, Kenneth J., (AV) ... '48 '74 C.321 A.B. L.818 J.D. Dir., Ct. Servs., Co. Juv. Ct.
Lusnia, Kristen Louise ... '73 '99 C.999 B.A. L.989 J.D. Cuyahoga Co. Pros. Off.
Lustig, Arthur F., (AV) ... '29 '60 C.251 A.B. L.1003 LL.B. [Lustig,E.&L.]
Lustig, Robert M., (AV) ... '36 '60 C&L.930 A.B., LL.B. [Lustig,E.&L.]
Lustig, Evans & Lucas, L.P.A., (AV) ... 526 Superior Ave. E., Ste. 615
Lutjen, George W., (AV) ... '— '64 C.363 B.S. L.1003 J.D. [Davis&Y.]
Lutz, Nathan L. ... '73 '02 C.608 B.S. L.145 J.D. [Ⓐ Benesch,F.C.&A.]
Lutzko, Rebecca C. ... '71 '98 C.94 B.A. L.276 J.D. [Ⓐ Baker&H.]
Lynch, Anne Kennedy, (BV) ... '59 '91 C.363 B.A. L.1003 J.D. [Lynch&L.]
Lynch, George F. ... '31 '58 C&L.477 B.S., J.D. 127 Public Sq.‡
Lynch, John Kennedy, (AV) ... '11 '36 C.867 A.B. L.276 J.D. [Lynch&L.]
Lynch, Robert Patrick, Jr. ... '73 '00 C.381 B.A. L.823 J.D. City of Cleveland Law Dept.
Lynch & Lynch, Co., L.P.A., (AV) ... 526 Superior Avenue East
Lynd, Tamara Siegel ... '68 '97 C.679 B.A. L.608 J.D. Fed. Pub. Def.
Lyon, Charles B., (AV) '44 '71
C.623 B.S.M.E. L.273 J.D. [Calfee,H.&G.] (See Pat. Sect.)
Lyon, Donald M. '52 '89 C.972 B.A. L.285 J.D.
(adm. in WA; not adm. in OH) Trial Atty., U.S. Dept. of Jus.
Lytle, Erika Ritt ... '71 '96 C.473 B.A. L.930 J.D. Asst. Co. Pros.
MacAdams, Pamela J., (BV) ... '58 '84 C.62 B.A. L.1003 J.D. [Morganstern,M.&D.]
Macdonald, George W., (BV) ... '50 '79 C.97 B.A. L.1003 J.D. 848 Rockefeller Building
MacDougall, Irene M., (AV) ... '58 '83 C&L.930 B.A., J.D. [Porter W.M.&A.]
Mace, Damond R., (AV) ... '59 '84 C.967 B.A. L.309 J.D. [Squire,S.&D.]
Macedonio, Rosemary A., (BV) ... '54 '80 C.452 B.A. L.930 J.D. [Macedonio&B.]
Macedonio & Box, P.L.L., (BV) ... 29525 Chagrin Boulevard Suite 208
Macek, Stephen G., (BV) '52 '82
C.381 B.A. L.1003 J.D. Sr. Staff Atty., Charter One Bank, N.A.
Maciag, Kimberly Dawn '73 '99 C.20 B.A. L.215 J.D.
(adm. in MI; not adm. in OH) Thomson West
Maciak, Brian A. ... '75 '00 C.381 B.A. L.823 J.D. [Ⓐ Frantz W.]
Mack, Richard W. ... '53 '78 C&L.608 B.S., J.D. P.O. Box 5756
Mackey, James M., (AV) ... '49 '74 C.363 B.A. L.161 J.D. [Walter&H.]
Mackin, Maura C. ... '— '89 L.1003 J.D. Hearing & Appeals Off.
Maclean, Timothy Michael ... '71 '98 C.161 B.A. L.1003 J.D. 2000 E. 9th St.
Madden, Justin F., (AV) ... '64 '93 C.732 B.A. L.607 J.D. [Landskroner G.M.]
Madden, Michael I., (BV) ... '58 '85 C.473 B.A. L.1003 J.D. [D.Seaman&Assoc.]
Madorsky, Harold A. '50 '81 C.454 B.A. L.94 J.D.
Executive Vice President, Research Environmental Industries, Inc.
Madorsky, J. Lewis, (BV) ... '54 '84 C.610 B.A. L.1003 J.D. [J.L.Madorsky] ⊙
Madorsky, J. Lewis, Co., L.P.A., (BV)
3934 Washington Blvd. (⊙Dar Es Salaam, Tanzania)
Maersch, Karl M. ... '— '02 C.679 B.S.M.E. L.365 J.D. [Ⓐ Jones D.] (See Pat. Sect.)
Maestle, Shawn W. ... '68 '94 C.161 B.A. L.607 J.D. [Weston H.]
Magid, Wm. H. ... '30 '54 C&L.608 B.A., LL.B. 13610 Cedar Rd.‡
Magner, Caitlin ... '— '02 C.771 B.A. L.989 J.D. [Ⓐ Rosner&Assoc.]

Maguire & Schneider LLP, (AV)
1370 Ontario Street, Suite 1700, 44113 ⊙
Telephone: 800-600-1222 Fax: 216-274-9808
Email: msandhu@ms-lawfirm.com
Associate: Manbir S. Sandhu.
Business Litigation, Labor and Employment, Insurance Defense, Directors Liability Errors and Omissions Defense, Real Estate Malpractice Claims, Real Estate, Corporate, Commercial Litigation, Health Care Law, Health Care Fraud and Abuse, Banking Law, Probate and Estate Planning, Family Law, Adoptions, Mediation, White Collar Crime, Criminal Defense, Consumer Law, Administrative Law, Creditor's Rights Law, Financial Institution Law, Intellectual Property, Internet Law, Lemon Law, Product Liability, and Worker's Compensation.
Columbus, Ohio Office: 250 Civic Center Drive, Suite 500, 43215. Telephone: 614-224-1222. Fax: 614-224-1236.

See Professional Biographies, CLEVELAND, OHIO

Maher, Christopher S. '66 '91 C.473 B.A. L.117 J.D.
Cuyahoga Co. Pub. Def. Off., Felony Trial Div.
Maher, Edward J., (AV) ... '39 '64 C&L.276 B.S., J.D. [E.J.Maher]
Maher, Edward J., Co., L.P.A., (AV) ... Suite 1548 Standard Building
Mahoney, Michael J. '54 '79 C.276 A.B. L.309 J.D.
Dir., Regul. Affairs and Coun., CGI Info. Systems & Manage. Consult., Inc.
Maier, Barbara Arnold '51 '76 C&L.966 B.A., J.D.
(adm. in WI; not adm. in OH) Fed. Trade Comm.
Maier, John P. ... '67 '98 C.152 B.S. L.8 J.D. Chf. Coun.
Maimbourg, Rita Ann, (AV) ... '56 '81 C.665 B.A. L.930 J.D. [Ⓒ Tucker E.&W.]
Maimona, Cheryl T. ... '49 '75 C.608 B.A. L.117 J.D. [Ⓐ Pepple&W.]
Maiorana, David M. ... '— '99 C.893 B.S. L.904 J.D. [Ⓐ Jones D.] (See Pat. Sect.)
Maiwurm, James J., (AV Ⓣ) '48 '74 C.970 B.A. L.477 J.D.
[Squire,S.&D.] (⊙Wash., DC; Tysons Corner, VA)
Majernik, Meghan D. ... '78 '02 C.62 B.A. L.1003 J.D. [Ⓐ Schottenstein,Z.&D.]
Majeski, Colleen A. ... '70 '97 C.201 B.A. L.1003 J.D. Com. Pleas Ct.
Majka, Susan Louise ... '51 '95 C.1057 B.A. L.989 J.D. 8th Dist. Ct. of App.
Makee, Dan L., (AV) ... '60 '85 C.207 A.B. L.124 J.D. [McDonald H.]
Makee, Joel A., (AV) ... '44 '69 C.967 B.A. L.930 J.D. [Taft,S.&H.]
Makhlouf, Majeed G. ... '77 '01 C.318 B.A. L.608 J.D. [Ⓐ Taft,S.&H.]
Makofsky, Michael ... '74 '99 C.184 B.A. L.930 J.D. [Ⓐ McDonald H.]
Makowski, Richard J., (BV) ... '52 '77 C.973 A.B. L.930 J.D. Asst. Atty. Gen.
Malaker, Albert Deane ... '32 '60 C&L.347 B.S., LL.B. 17600 Detroit Avenue, Suite 214
Malbasa, Stephanie H. ... '53 '79 C.607 B.A. L.161 J.D. 13405 Lake Shore Boulevard
Malek, Nate N. ... '71 '96 C.575 B.A. L.1003 J.D. [Malek D.&Assoc.]
Malek Dean & Associates LLC, (BV) ... 113 Saint Clair Ave. N.E., Ste. 305
Malemud, Franklin C. ... '72 '97 C.608 B.A. L.124 J.D. [Ⓐ Reminger&R.]
Malkin, Jennifer ... '61 '86 C&L.930 B.A., J.D. V.P., Natl. City Bk.
Malloy, Amy J. ... '63 '95 C.363 B.S.B.A. L.161 J.D. Premier Farnell Corp.
Malloy, Mary A. ... '45 '92 C.599 B.A. L.1003 J.D. 1524 Grace Avenue
Malloy, Sean D. ... '68 '92 C.472 B.A. L.893 J.D. [McDonald H.]
Malnar, Patti Jo ... '66 '91 C.901 B.A. L.930 J.D. [Ⓐ Reminger&R.]
Malone, James L., (AV) ... '45 '70 C.602 B.A. L.150 J.D. [Ⓐ Reminger&R.]
Malone, John P., Jr., (AV) ... '44 '71 C.321 A.B. L.930 J.D. 614 Superior Ave. N.W.
Malone, Raymond M., (AV) ... '57 '82 C.473 B.S. L.930 J.D. [Baker&H.]
Maloney, Mary D., (AV) ... '— '87 C.8 B.S. L.1003 J.D. [Jones D.]
Maloney, Michael Patrick ... '61 '87 C.161 B.A. L.1003 J.D. 24461 Detroit Rd.
Maloney, Ruth Ann ... '58 '90 C.608 B.S. L.851 J.D. [Baker&H.]
Maloof, George M., (BV) ... '21 '78 C.882 L.1003 J.D. 2115 Ontario St.

Malumphy, Christopher Robin .... '52 '88 801 Superior Avenue
Malynn, Steven R. .... '59 '96 C.112 B.A. L.602 J.D. [A Giffen&K.]
Mamone, Edward J., (BV) .... '61 '87 C.210 B.A. L.930 J.D. [A Gurney,M.&M.]
Mamone, Joseph A., (BV) .... '35 '61 C.608 B.A. L.930 LL.B. [Gurney,M.&M.]
Mamrack, Edward .... '20 '50 C&L.930 A.B., LL.B. 623 St. Clair Ave., N.W.‡
Mancino, Brett M. .... '71 '99 C.728 B.A. L.930 J.D. [McIntyre,K.&K.]
Mancino, James P., (BV) .... '39 '65 C.610 A.B. L.608 J.D. Asst. Atty. Gen.
Mancino, Jennifer L. .... '76 '04 C.379 B.A. L.8 J.D. [A Kelley&F.]
Mancino, Paul, III '66 '92 C.597 B.A. L.1003 J.D.
Dir., Legal Affairs & Sr. Corp. Coun., Medical Mutual of Ohio
Mancino, Paul A., Jr., (BV) .... '38 '63 C&L.930 A.B., LL.B. 615 Superior Avenue, N.W.
Mancuso, John H., (AV©) '44 '76 C.93 A.B. L.823 J.D.
(adm. in NY; not adm. in OH) Sr. V.P. & Dep. Gen. Coun., KeyBank Natl. Assn.
Mandel, Bruce P., (AV) .... '51 '76 C.608 B.S. L.930 J.D. [Ulmer&B.]
Mandell, Ellen .... '52 '78 C.930 B.A. L.1003 J.D. 55 Public Sq.
Mangano, Basil W. .... '70 '96 C.1149 B.A. L.1003 J.D. [A Masters&Assoc.]
Manghillis, Jeffrey R. A. .... '— '00 C.608 B.A. L.309 J.D. [A Jones D.]
Manghillis, Katherine G. .... '78 '04 C.970 B.A. L.7 J.D. [A Schottenstein,Z.&D.]
Maniker, Howard B., (BV) .... '42 '68 C.608 B.S.B.A. L.1003 J.D. 1370 Ontario St.

Manley • Deas • Kochalski LLC
(See Columbus)

Manly, Cornelius A. .... '42 '73 C.30 B.A. L.904 J.D. Cleveland Legal Aid Soc.
Mann, Eric H., (BV) .... '— '80 C.381 B.A. L.930 J.D. [Gallagher S.]
Mann, Kent L., (AV) .... '51 '76 C.197 A.B. L.228 J.D. [C Thompson H.]
Mann, Kevin E. '65 '91 C.999 B.S. L.1049 J.D.
(adm. in CA; not adm. in OH) Assoc. Gen. Coun., Degussa Corp.
Mann, Lisa Froimson, (BV) .... '56 '80 C.347 B.A. L.930 J.D. [A Duvin,C.&H.]
Mann, Robert J. '63 '88 C.473 B.A. L.608 J.D.
[C Shihab&Assoc.] (⊙Wash., DC; Columbus, OH)
Mann, Theodore M., Jr., (AV) .... '48 '76 C.25 B.A. L.930 J.D. [T.M.Mann,Jr.]

Mann, Theodore M., Jr., Law Firm, (AV)
644 Huntington Building, 925 Euclid Avenue, 44115-1493
Telephone: 216-621-6147 FAX: 216-621-6149
Email: mannlawoffice@ameritech.net URL: http://www.lawyers.com/tmannlaw
Theodore M. Mann, Jr. Of Counsel: Theodore M. Mann (1921-1999).
Alternative Dispute Resolution, Mediation, Appellate Practice, Business Law, Business Litigation, Contracts, Corporate Law, Elder Law, Franchises and Franchising, Fraud, General Practice, Labor and Employment, Litigation, Negligence, Personal Injury, Probate, Real Estate, Real Estate Litigation, Residential Real Estate, Torts, Trade Secrets Trusts and Estates, Estate Planning, Trust Administration, Wills.
Reference: Huntington Bank.
See Professional Biographies, CLEVELAND, OHIO

Manning, Jamie L. .... '— '80 C.800 B.A. L.1355 J.D. [S Gallagher S.]
Manning, Janice .... '— '83 C.97 B.A./M.A. L.851 J.D. Gen. Coun., Garland Co., Inc.
Manning, Timothy E. '67 '98
C.363 B.S. L.1003 J.D. [A Renner,O.B.&S.] (See Pat. Sect.)
Mannion, Thomas P., (BV) .... '63 '93 C.97 B.S. L.8 J.D. [Mannion&G.]

Mannion and Gray Co., L.P.A., (BV)
1300 East 9th Street, Suite 1625, 44114
Telephone: 216-344-9422 Fax: 216-344-9421
URL: http://www.manniongray.com
Members of Firm: Thomas P. Mannion; Todd A. Gray. Associate: Ryan K. Rubin.
Catastrophic Injuries, Medical Malpractice, Products Liability, Medical Device and Class Action, Professional Liability, and Consumer Law.
See Professional Biographies, CLEVELAND, OHIO

Manolis, Chris E. .... '73 '03 C.608 B.A. L.851 J.D. [A Shapiro&F.]
Manoloff, Richard D. .... '64 '92 C.674 A.B. L.976 J.D. [Squire,S.&D.]
Manos, Eli, (AV) .... '31 '58 C&L.309 B.A., LL.B. [Mansour,G.G.&M.]
Manos, John M. .... '22 '50 C.124 B.S. L.1003 J.D. U.S. Sr. Dist. J.
Mansour, Ernest P., (AV) .... '31 '55 C.717 B.A. L.930 LL.B. [Mansour,G.G.&M.]
Mansour, Robert G., (BV) .... '61 '86 C.967 B.A. L.1003 J.D. 3500 Terminal Tower

Mansour, Gavin, Gerlack & Manos Co., L.P.A., (AV) BR
55 Public Square, Suite 2150, 44113-1994
Telephone: 216-523-1500 Telecopier: 216-523-1705
URL: http://www.mggmLPA.com
Ernest P. Mansour; Michael T. Gavin; Julius R. Gerlack; Eli Manos; Dale E. Markworth; Jeffrey M. Embleton; Anthony J. Coyne; David B. Cathcart; Samuel R. Martillotta; John F. Burke, III; Bruce G. Rinker;—Edward O. Patton; Bradford J. Patrick; Linda L. Johnson; Mary E. Donahue; Amy L. Phillips; William J. Muniak; Michael Patrick Quinlan; Keith J. Kearney; Brendon P. Friesen; Ashley M. Arvin.
General Civil Practice. Corporate, Insurance, Real Estate, Labor, Employment, Wrongful Discharge, Discrimination, Municipal, Probate and Condemnation Law, Litigation, Product and Hospital Liability, Environmental Litigation.
Representative Clients: Invacare Corp.; Michigan Mutual Liability Insurance Co.; Swagelok Co.; Zurich Insurance Co.
See Professional Biographies, CLEVELAND, OHIO

Mantione, Lianne .... '74 '03 C.392 B.S. L.161 J.D. [A Squire,S.&D.]
Manuszak, Michael J. .... '51 '77 C.215 A.B. L.1003 J.D. 2905 Paxton Rd.
Marburger, David L., (AV) .... '54 '83 C.823 B.S. L.665 J.D. [Baker&H.]
Marchant, Robert A. .... '72 '01 C.1335 B.S. L.950 J.D. [A Benesch,F.C.&A.]
Marcis, Robert A., II .... '73 '98 C.228 A.B. L.896 J.D. [A Kelley&F.]
Marein, Mark B., (BV) .... '57 '82 C.608 B.A. L.1003 J.D. 526 Superior Ave., Ste. 222
Marek, Edward F., (AV) .... '40 '65 C.610 B.S.C. L.930 J.D. 1100 Haverston Road
Marek, Robert J. .... '44 '69 C.610 B.S.B.A. L.930 J.D. 615 W. Superior Ave.
Margolis, Daniel M. '67 '96 C.118 B.A. L.1194 J.D.
323 West Lakeside Avenue Suite 450
Margolis, Kenneth R. '50 '76
C.112 B.A. L.930 J.D. Case Western Reserve Univ. Sch. of Law
Margolis, Kevin D., (AV) .... '63 '89 C.597 B.A. L.930 J.D. [Benesch,F.C.&A.]
Margolis, Loren J., (BV) '58 '83
C.608 B.S.B.A. L.1003 J.D. Gen. Coun., M. Weingold & Co.
Margolis, Richard D., (AV) .... '38 '63 C.659 B.S.E. L.976 J.D. [C Benesch,F.C.&A.]
Margolius, Andrew L., (AV) .... '58 '83 C.1365 B.A. L.124 J.D. 55 Public Sq.
Margulies, Jeffrey J., (AV) .... '46 '73 C&L.352 B.A., J.D. [Squire,S.&D.]
Margulies, Susan C. .... '66 '91 C.473 B.A. L.930 J.D. 18 Country Ln.
Marhofer, Michael F. .... '65 '91 C.473 B.S. L.8 J.D. [Calfee,H.&G.]
Marken, Howard A., (AV) .... '24 '50 C.608 B.Sc. L.477 J.D. [C Karberg,K.W.&T.]
Markey, Robert G., (AV) .... '39 '64 C.103 A.B. L.930 J.D. [Baker&H.]
Markovic, Sasha .... '— '04 C&L.161 B.S., J.D. [A Jones D.]
Markowski, Lucille .... '48 '89 C.999 B.S. L.1003 J.D. [A Weltman,W.&R.]
Marks, Erin Elizabeth .... '77 '04 C.608 B.A. L.930 J.D. [A Squire,S.&D.]
Marks, Jeffrey B. .... '39 '69 C.473 B.A. L.930 J.D. Asst. Dir. of Law
Marks, Joshua M. .... '70 '96 C.610 B.A. L.1003 J.D. [A Bricker&E.]

Marks, Seth B., (BV) '45 '71 C.473 B.A. L.930 J.D.
3637 Green Road, 44122
Telephone: 216-292-2600 Fax: 216-464-7866 Toll Free: 888-514-4600
Email: sethb123@aol.com URL: http://www.lawyers.com/sethmarkslaw
Residential Real Estate, Wills, Commercial Collections, Trusts, Leases, For Sale By Owner, Deeds, Landlord/Tenant.
See Professional Biographies, CLEVELAND, OHIO

Markstrom, Wilbur J., (AV) .... '30 '59 C&L.477 B.A., J.D. 1620 Oakwood Drive‡
Marksz, John A., (AV) .... '40 '65 C&L.930 B.A., J.D. 11200 Edgewater Dr.
Markulin, Katica Katarina .... '64 '89 C.980 A.B. L.124 J.D. 18975 Villaview Road
Markus, Egidijus, (AV) .... '53 '77 C.128 B.A. L.930 J.D. 877 E. 185th St.
Markus, Robert D., (AV) .... '40 '67 C.966 B.S. L.930 J.D. [Hahn L.&P.]
Markus, Stephen A., (AV) .... '54 '79 C&L.930 B.A., J.D. [Ulmer&B.]
Markworth, Dale E., (AV) .... '48 '73 C.207 B.A. L.910 J.D. [Mansour,G.G.&M.]
Marmaros, Peter W., (AV) .... '55 '83 C.62 B.A. L.1003 J.D. [P.W.Marmaros]
Marmaros, Peter W., Co., LPA, (AV) .... 323 W. Lakeside Ave., Ste. 450
Marnecheck, Philip A., (BV) .... '56 '81 C&L.608 B.S.B.A., J.D. 1468 W. 9th St.
Marolt, Evelyn Rose .... '30 '87 1370 Ontario Street, Suite 1130
Marrer, Steven A., (AV) .... '58 '83 C.597 B.A. L.930 J.D. [Taft,S.&H.]
Marron, John Edward .... '68 '95 C.436 B.A. L.989 J.D. 8th App. Dist. Ct. of Appeals
Marshall, Bernadette, (CV) .... '52 '85 C.381 B.A. L.989 J.D. [Reid,B.M.&W.]
Marshall, Christina J. .... '71 '98 C.734 B.A. L.8 J.D. [A Sutter,O.&F.]
Marshall, G. Timothy .... '49 '78 C.381 L.1003 J.D. 1267 W. 9th St., 2nd Fl.
Marshall, Kent, Jr., (CV) .... '51 '79 C.207 B.A. L.930 J.D. 2189 Professor Ave.
Marshall, Wentworth J., Jr., (AV) .... '31 '56 C.951 B.A. L.930 J.D. [Smith M.]
Marshall, William Porter .... '50 '77 C.659 B.A. L.145 J.D. 11075 E. Blvd.
Martahus, Craig R., (AV) .... '54 '79 C.651 B.S. L.659 J.D. [Thompson H.]
Martello, James P., (BV) .... '47 '74 C.201 B.A. L.1003 J.D. [Gibson,B.Z.&M.]
Martillotta, Samuel R., (AV) .... '51 '80 C.611 B.A. L.1003 J.D. [Mansour,G.G.&M.]
Martin, Adam W. .... '71 '04 C.608 B.A. L.7 J.D. [A Sutter,O.&F.]
Martin, Aric D. .... '70 '95 C.473 B.A. L.608 J.D. [Rolf&G.]
Martinez, Richard D., (BV) .... '28 '62 C.473 A.B. L.1003 LL.B. 14701 Detroit Ave.
Marting, Michael G., (AV) .... '— '74 C&L.976 B.A., J.D. [Jones D.]
Martinsek, Amanda, (AV) .... '62 '91 C.604 B.A. L.569 J.D. [Vorys,S.S.&P.]
Martis, Charles G. .... '31 '55 C&L.608 B.A., J.D. P.O. Box 5756
Martis, Michael S. .... '— '85 C.608 B.A. L.161 J.D. [S Jones D.]
Maruster, Robert F. .... '38 '75 C.97 B.A. L.1003 J.D. 2939 S. Bay Dr.
Marvar, Raymond J., (AV) '54 '79 C.97 B.S. L.602 J.D.
V.P. & Gen. Coun., Cleveland Clinic Health Sys-W Reg
Marvinney, Craig A., (AV) .... '57 '82 C&L.930 B.A., J.D. [Ulmer&B.]
Marvinney, Michelle Powe, (AV) .... '55 '84 C.473 B.S. L.930 J.D. [A Porter W.M.&A.]
Masch, Clifford C., (BV) .... '58 '83 C.207 B.A. L.1003 J.D. [A Reminger&R.]
Mason, Lance T. .... '— '92 C.970 B.A. L.477 J.D. [S Baker&H.]
Mason, Thomas A., (AV) .... '36 '62 C.385 A.B. L.930 LL.B. [Thompson H.]
Massetti, Regina M., (AV) .... '— '81 C.62 B.A. L.1003 J.D. [Buckley K.]
Mast, Bernadette Mihalic, (AV) .... '— '88 C.608 B.S. L.930 J.D. [Jones D.]
Masters, John M., (AV) .... '58 '85 C.8 B.S.L.E. L.930 J.D. [Masters&Assoc.]
Masters, William N. .... '58 '83 C.679 B.S. L.7 J.D. [Winters&M.]
Masters & Associates, A Legal Professional Association, (AV) .... 1111 Superior Avenue
Mastrangelo, Mark Evan .... '54 '82 C.608 B.S. L.161 J.D. Atty. Gen.
Matasar, Scott C. .... '70 '96 C.178 B.A. L.94 J.D. [A Calfee,H.&G.]
Matejczyk, David M., (AV) .... '58 '89 C.1072 B.S. L.930 J.D. [Vozar,R.&M.]
Matejka, Marcella M. .... '21 '60 C.930 B.A. L.1003 J.D. 4808 Gifford Ave.‡
Matejkovic, Margaret Andreeff, (AV) '58 '92
C&L.8 B.A., J.D. 9150 South Hills Boulevard, Suite 300
Matheney, Matthew H. .... '71 '98 C.970 B.A. L.1003 J.D. [A Frantz W.]
Mather, Jason N. .... '— '00 C.880 B.A. L.1565 J.D. Law Clerk
Mathews, Tyler L. .... '68 '94 C.20 B.A. L.1003 J.D. [McDonald H.]
Matia, David T., Jr., (AV) .... '64 '90 C.473 B.S. L.930 J.D. 2274 Demington Dr.
Matia, Paul R. .... '37 '62 C.930 B.A. L.309 J.D. [Porter W.M.&A.]
Matile, Michael W. .... '72 '00 C.383 B.B.A. L.851 J.D. [A Moscarino&T.]
Matty, David J., (AV) .... '54 '79 C.363 B.A. L.1003 J.D. [Rademaker,M.M.&G.]
Mausar, Donald A., (BV) .... '63 '95 C.161 B.A. L.1003 J.D. [Weltman,W.&R.]
Mausser, Cynthia B. .... '66 '91 C.97 B.A. L.930 J.D. Hearing Offr., State Parole Bd.
Maxfield, Harold O., Jr., (BV) .... '61 '86 C.62 B.A. L.1003 J.D. [Cavitch,F.D.&F.]
Maxton, Reginald .... '48 '93 C.1162 B.A. L.1003 J.D. [S Trivers&D.]
Maxwell, Lindsay .... '— '93 C.207 B.A. L.851 J.D. [A Buckley K.]
May, James Dean .... '69 '96 C.309 A.B. L.124 J.D. Pros. Off.
May, James W. .... '76 '04 C.797 B.A. L.577 J.D. [A Hahn L.&P.]
May, Karl E., (AV) .... '49 '74 C.607 B.A. L.608 J.D. [Cowden,H.N.&L.]
Mayer, Kristen L. .... '67 '91 C.648 B.A. L.665 J.D. [C Tucker E.&W.]
Mayer, Richard M. '66 '96
C.674 A.B. L.608 J.D. Vice President, Lakeside Construction Co.
Mayernik, Thomas J., (BV) .... '63 '89 C.62 B.A. L.1003 J.D. [A Gibson,B.Z.&M.]
Maynard, Angela L. '65 '89 C.27 B.A. L.215 J.D.
(adm. in MI; not adm. in OH) V.P. & Sr. Coun., KeyBank Natl. Assn.
Mayo, David R., (AV) .... '51 '76 C.473 B.S. L.1003 J.D. [Benesch,F.C.&A.]
Mays, A. R. (Bud), (AV) .... '31 '56 C.381 B.S.B.A. L.228 LL.B. [C Karberg,K.W.&T.]
Mays, Anita Laster .... '64 '92 C.608 B.S.B.A. L.1003 J.D. Mun. Ct. J.
Mays, Thomas Charles .... '61 '86 C.161 B.S. L.989 J.D. [Obral&M.&Assoc.]
Mazanec, Daniel C. .... '79 '04 C.602 B.A. L.893 J.D. [A Squire,S.&D.]
Mazanec, David T., (BV) .... '47 '76 C.103 B.A. L.1003 J.D. 34305 Solon Rd.
Mazanec, Mark R. .... '61 '88 C.602 B.S. L.477 J.D. [Baker&H.]
Mazanec, Richard O., (AV) .... '51 '76 C.973 A.B. L.734 LL.B. [Reed,M.&W.]
Mazanec, Thomas S., (AV) .... '49 '76 C.973 B.S.B.A. L.1003 J.D. [Mazanec,R.&R.]

Mazanec, Raskin & Ryder Co., L.P.A., (AV)
100 Franklin's Row, 34305 Solon Road, 44139 ⊙
Telephone: 440-248-7906 Fax: 440-248-8861
Email: mrr1aw.com URL: http://www.mrrlaw.com
Thomas S. Mazanec; Todd M. Raskin; Edward M. Ryder; John T. McLandrich; James A. Climer; Joseph F. Nicholas, Jr.; Patrick W. Winslow; Paul J. Cristallo;—Timothy R. Obringer; Natasha A. Wells-Niklas; David R. Fenn; Edward A. Proctor; Jeffrey T. Kay; Robert F. Cathcart; Geoffrey A. Belzer; Christopher P. Conomy; David James Sipusic; Frank H. Scialdone; Steven J. Moody; Julius E. Trombetto; Martin James O'Connell.
Civil Litigation, Insurance Defense, Construction Law, Negligence, Professional Negligence, Municipal Law, Civil Rights, Real Estate, Business Law, Probate, Estate Planning.
Representative Clients: Colonial Insurance Co.; Crawford & Co.; Farmers Insurance Group; Leader National Insurance Co.; Liberty Mutual Insurance Co.; National Casualty Insurance Co.; Progressive Casualty Insurance Co.; Scottsdale Insurance Co.; State Farm Fire & Casualty Company; Utica Mutual Insurance Co.
Columbus, Ohio Office: Suite 400, 250 Civic Center Drive. 43215. Telephone: 614-228-5931. Fax: 614-228-5934.
See Professional Biographies, CLEVELAND, OHIO

Mazey, John E. .... '— '98 C&L.161 B.A., J.D. [A Jones D.]
Mazurkiewcz, Janice L. .... '53 '79 C.161 B.A. L.930 J.D. P.O. Box 94189 1640
Mazza, Margaret M., (BV) .... '34 '63 C.876 L.1003 J.D. 2235 Valleyview Dr.

Mazzi, Alicia L. .... '77 '02 C.363 B.A. L.930 J.D. [🄰 Hermann,C.&S.]
McAllister, Ralph A. .... '28 '56 C.381 B.S. L.1003 J.D. Ret. Com. Pleas J.‡
McBride, Brian A. .... '58 '83 C&L.770 B.S.C., J.D. 2069 W. 3rd St.
McBride, Laura C. '74 '03 C.970 B.A. L.273 J.D.
(adm. in CA; not adm. in OH) [🄰 Calfee,H.&G.]
McBride, Robert D. .... '48 '73 C.381 B.B.A. L.930 J.D. Pres., The Kirby Co.
McCabe, Peter J. '63 '88 C.473 B.S. L.608 J.D.
Gen. Coun., Snider-Blake Bus. Serv., Inc.
McCafferty, Bridget M. .... '66 '91 C.473 B.A. L.1003 J.D. 1200 Ontario St.
McCafferty, Joseph P. .... '61 '86 C.381 B.B.A. L.8 J.D. [J.P.McCafferty]
McCafferty, Joseph P., Co., LPA .... 2000 East Ninth Street
McCaffrey, John F., (AV) .... '61 '87 C.363 B.A. L.930 J.D. [McLaughlin&M.]
McCall, Peter L. .... '48 '85 C.910 B.A. L.1003 J.D. Case Western Res. Univ.
McCallum, Allison .... '74 '99 C.363 B.A. L.1003 J.D. [🄰 Spieth,B.M.&N.]
McCann, Donald B., (AV) .... '25 '51 C.930 B.A. L.1003 J.D. 200 Public Sq.‡

McCarroll, John J. '44 '89 C.972 B.A. L.1003 J.D.
516 Standard Building, 1370 Ontario Street, 44113
Telephone: 216-861-6655; 877-861-6655 Fax: 216-861-6653
Email: mccarrol@apk.net URL: http://www.usavisalaws.com
Victims Rights, Personal Injury, Bankruptcy, Business Law, Probate, Criminal Defense, Immigration Law.

See Professional Biographies, CLEVELAND, OHIO

McCartan, Patrick F., (AV) .... '— '60 C&L.602 A.B., LL.B. [Jones D.]
McCarthy, Daniel R., (AV) .... '24 '54 C.930 B.B.A. L.1003 J.D. [McCarthy,L.C.&L.]
McCarthy, Ellen M., (AV) .... '62 '90 C.1290 B.A. L.161 J.D. [Nurenberg,P.H.&M.]
McCarthy, John J., (AV) .... '26 '55 C.381 B.S.B.A. L.1003 LL.B. [Nurenberg,P.H.&M.]
McCarthy, Mark F., (AV) .... '51 '76 C&L.276 A.B., J.D. [Tucker E.&W.]

McCarthy, Lebit, Crystal & Liffman Co., L.P.A., (AV) 🄱🅁
1800 Midland Building, 101 Prospect Avenue, West, 44115
Telephone: 216-696-1422 Fax: 216-696-1210
Email: tfa@mccarthylebit.com URL: http://www.mccarthylebit.com
Daniel R. McCarthy; Edward A. Lebit (1936-1988); Larry Crystal; Irwin S. Haiman; Kenneth B. Liffman; Mark B. Cohn; John S. Seich (Certified Specialist in Federal Tax Law, Ohio State Bar Association); Robert S. Balantzow; Kimon P. Karas (Certified Specialist in Federal Tax Law, Ohio State Bar Association); David A. Schaefer; David L. Rosenzweig; Pamela N. Hultin; Richard A. Rabb; Stuart A. Mintz; Charles P. Royer; Glenn R. Wilson; Robert T. Glickman; E. Roger Stewart;—Ellen R. Stein; Leslie Erin Wargo; Kimberly A. Brennan; Katherine E. Wensink; Matthew B. Murphy; Eric C. Powell. Of Counsel: Wilton S. Sogg; Jon Fitzpatrick.
Corporate and General Business, Real Estate, Taxation, Litigation, Commercial Banking, Estate Planning and Probate, Domestic Relations, Bankruptcy and Creditors Rights, Intellectual Property and Information Technology.

See Professional Biographies, CLEVELAND, OHIO

McCarty, Philip W. .... '— '03 C.918 B.A. L.966 J.D. [🄰 Jones D.]
McCauley, Stephen L. .. '60 '93 C.381 B.S. L.608 J.D. [🄰 Calfee,H.&G.] (See Pat. Sect.)
McClatchey, John F., (AV) .... '29 '57 C.976 B.A. L.309 LL.B. 127 Public Sq‡
McClelland, James Scott .... '28 '57 C.930 B.A. L.1003 J.D. 7120 Southfield Ave.
McClelland, Robert C., (AV) .... '52 '80 C.207 B.A. L.1003 J.D. [Rademaker,M.M.&G.]
McClelland, Warren Lester, Jr. .... '50 '81 C.161 B.A. L.851 J.D. Cuyahoga Co. Pub. Def.
McClendon, Mark A. '62 '89 C.959 B.A. L.436 J.D.
(adm. in WI; not adm. in OH) Assoc. Gen. Coun., Degussa Corp.
McCollister, Scott Andrew '64 '89
C.679 B.S. L.930 J.D. [Fay,S.F.M.&M.] (See Pat. Sect.)
McCollum, Rathuel L. .... '24 '61 C.511 B.S. L.1003 J.D. 16512 Invermere Avenue
McConnell, Donald J. '54 '90 C.62 B.A. L.1003 J.D.
Corp. Coun., Environ., The Sherwin-Williams Co.
McConville, Celestine Richards '65 '91 C.94 B.A. L.276 J.D.
(adm. in IL; not adm. in OH) Law Clk., Dist. J.‡
McCormac, Orville Theodore '42 '73
C.318 B.A. L.161 J.D. 1660 West 2nd Street, Suite 310
McCormack, Scott B. .... '57 '84 C.818 B.A. L.1097 J.D. Intl. Mgmt. Grp.
McCormack, Tim .... '44 '72 C.473 B.A. L.1003 J.D. State Sen.
McCormick, Timothy P. .... '56 '82 C.276 B.A. L.1292 J.D. Com. Pleas J.
McCoy, Darlene Evans, (AV) .... '53 '79 C.381 B.G.S. L.7 J.D. [Calfee,H.&G.]
McCoy, Patricia A. '54 '84 C.604 B.A. L.1375 J.D.
(adm. in DC; not adm. in OH)
Assoc. Prof., Cleve.-Marshall Coll. of Law, Cleveland State Univ.
McCracken, Christopher C., (AV) .... '51 '77 C.97 B.A. L.930 J.D. [Ulmer&B.]
McCracken, Matthew J. .... '77 '04 C.881 B.S. L.124 J.D. [🄰 Simon]

McCray, Muzilla, Smith & Meyers Co., L.P.A.
(See Elyria)

McCreary, Sherry Maurice Frazier '43 '78
C.533 B.S. L.1003 J.D. 8th Fl., 1200 Ontario St.
McCreery, R. Douglas .... '52 '86 C&L.930 B.A., J.D. [🄰 Spieth,B.M.&N.]
Mccrum, Ryan B. .... '— '99 C.367 B.S. L.930 J.D. [🄰 Jones D.]
McCrystal, James L., Jr., (AV) .... '48 '73 C.363 A.B. L.602 J.D. [Brzytwa,Q.&M.]
McDonald, C. Richard, (AV) .... '— '73 C.210 B.A. L.930 J.D. [Davis&Y.]
McDonald, Robert E. '49 '79
Assoc. Gen. Coun., Pats. & Trademarks, The Sherwin-Williams Co. (Pat.)
McDonald, T. D., (AV) '28 '53
C.210 A.B. L.608 LL.B. Gen. Coun., The Dickey-Grabler Co.
McDonald, Thomas L., Jr., (BV) .... '51 '75 C.363 B.A. L.930 J.D. P.O. Box 43445

McDonald Hopkins Co., LPA, (AV)
600 Superior Avenue, E. Suite 2100, 44114-2653 ⊙
Telephone: 216-348-5400 Telecopier: 216-348-5474
Email: info@mcdonaldhopkins.com URL: http://www.mcdonaldhopkins.com
Scott R. Austin (Resident, West Plam Beach, Florida Office); Peter M. Bernhardt (Resident, West Plam Beach, Florida Office); Patrick J. Berry; Jeffrey P. Consolo; Jerome W. Cook; Richard S. Cooper; Anne T. Corrigan; Leonard M. Cosentino; James A. Dimitrijevs; Anthony J. DiVenere; Robert H. Earp, III; Paul N. Edwards; Theodore J. Esborn; Bryan H. Falk; Richard C. Farrin (Resident, Columbus, Ohio Office); G. Andrew Gardner; Steven L. Gardner; Victor T. Geraci; Carl J. Grassi; James A. Griffith; David K. Hales; Jeffrey R. Huntsberger; Brian J. Jereb; David M. Kall; Bernard L. Karr; Jeffrey B. Keiper; Roger L. Kleinman; Mark D. Klimek; Anthony D. Konkoly; Peter Kraguljac; Joseph J. LoPresti, Jr.; Dan L. Makee; Sean D. Malloy; Tyler L. Mathews; George L. McGaughey, Jr.; Michael J. Meaney; John T. Metzger (Board Certified Real Estate Lawyer, Florida Bar Board of Legal Specialization and Education)(Resident, West Palm Beach, Florida Office); John T. Mulligan; William J. O'Neill; Scott N. Opincar; R. Jeffrey Pollock; Michael G. Riley; Shawn M. Riley; Jean R. Robertson; Douglas B. Schnee; Roger L. Shumaker; Michele Smolin; Michael L. Snyder; Glenn D. Southworth; James E. Stief; James M. Stone; Dale R. Vlasek; Kenneth J. Walsh; David D. Watson; John M. Wirtshafter; Michael W. Wise; Jane Marie Pine Wood (Resident, Dennis, Massachusetts Office); Thomas M. Zaino; Charles B. Zellmer;—Robert C. Baraona; Todd A. Benni (Not admitted in OH); M. John Burgess; Richard W. Cline; David B. Cupar; Maura S. Curran (Resident, West Plam Beach, Florida Office); Sherri L. Dahl; Tara C. DeVore; John D. Fabian; Julie A. Fischer; Susan F. George; Maria-Alexa Pilar Guevara (Resident, West Plam Beach, Florida Office); Patricia J. Haas; Stephen K. Hall; Kristin K. C. Howard; John "JT" Kalnay; Heather M. Kern; Kent C. Kiffner; Paul W. Linehan; Michael Makofsky; Patrick W. Maraist (Resident, West Plam Beach, Florida Office); Adam D. Marshall (Resident, West Plam Beach, Florida Office); Grant A. Monachino; Nicole M. Monachino; David T. Movius; Vincent J. Nardone; Lucy K. O'Shaughnessy; Lynette M. Papushak; Andrew S. Perry; Mark E. Porter; Matthew R. Rechner; Katayoon Sadre May; R.

(This Listing Continued)

McDonald Hopkins Co., LPA (Continued)
Christopher Salata; Matthew A. Salerno; Richard D. Summers; Andrew J. Von Gustedt (Resident, West Plam Beach, Florida Office); David E. Weisblatt.
General Civil Trial and Appellate Practice. Corporate, Taxation, Pension and Profit Sharing, Professional Corporations, Insurance, Securities, Estate Planning, Probate, Real Estate, Family Law, Banking, Partnership, Employment and Labor Relations, Equipment Leasing, Bankruptcy, Communications, Computer Law, Health and Hospital Law.
West Palm Beach, Florida Office: McDonald Hopkins Co., PA, One Clearlake Centre, 250 Australian Avenue S., Suite 700, 33401-5007. Telephone: 561-472-7510. Fax: 561-472-2975.
Dennis, Massachusetts Office: 956 Main Street, 02638. Telephone: 508-385-5227. Fax: 508-385-4355.
Columbus, Ohio Office: 41 South High Street, Suite 3650, 43215. Telephone: 614-458-0025. Fax: 614-458-0028.

See Professional Biographies, CLEVELAND, OHIO

McDonnell, Daniel P., (BV) .... '24 '52 C.363 B.S. L.1003 LL.B. 75 Public Sq., Ste. 700
McDonnell, James J., (BV) .... '56 '82 C.976 B.A. L.1003 J.D. 75 Public Sq., Ste. 700
McDonnell, Nancy Rose .... '59 '85 Co. Ct. of Comm. Pleas
McDougal, Larry E. .... '43 '85 C.631 B.S.Ed. L.1003 J.D. [L.E.McDougal]
McDougal, Larry E., Co., LPA .... 21360 Center Ridge Road, Suite 301
McDowell, Alicia M. '73 '98 C.811 B.A. L.930 J.D.
Christian Mediation & Legal Consulting Serv(s).
McEaneney, Shannon L. .... '72 '98 C.363 B.A. L.1003 J.D. [🄰 Cavitch,F.D.&F.]
McElhaney, James W. '37 '62 C&L.228 B.A., LL.B.
(adm. in WI; not adm. in OH) Prof., Case Western Reserve Univ. Sch. of Law
McFadden, Dawn E. .... '— '03 C.97 B.A. L.124 J.D. [🄰 Jones D.]
McFadden, Donald P., (BV) .... '— '73 C.734 B.A. L.930 J.D. [McFadden&Assoc.]

McFadden & Associates Co. LPA, (BV)
1370 Ontario Street, Suite 1700, 44113
Telephone: 216-622-0850 Fax: 216-622-0854
Email: mcfadden@mcfaddenlaw.us
Donald P. McFadden;—David A. Freeburg; Bradley P. Toman.
Language: Spanish.
Real Estate, Residential Real Estate, Commercial Real Estate, Industrial Real Estate Law, Litigation, Business Enterprises.

See Professional Biographies, CLEVELAND, OHIO

McFaul, Kevin Thomas .... '58 '86 C.62 B.A. L.1003 J.D. [K.T.McFaul]
McFaul, Kevin T., Co., L.P.A. .... 1566 East 36th
McGaffick, Jeffrey M. .... '61 '86 C.97 B.S. L.1003 J.D. 3740 Euclid Avenue
McGann, Amy B. .... '76 '01 C.93 B.S. L.930 J.D. [🄰 Calfee,H.&G.]
McGann, Regis E., (AV) .... '49 '75 C.276 B.A. L.161 J.D. 1370 Ontario St.
McGarry, James J., (BV) .... '26 '63 C.381 A.B. L.1003 J.D. [Deegan&M.]
McGarry, Timothy L., (BV) .... '66 '91 C.608 B.S.B.A. L.597 J.D. [🄲 Nicola,G.&C.]
McGaughey, George L., Jr., (AV) .... '45 '75 C.976 B.A. L.930 J.D. [McDonald H.]
McGill, Danielle M. .... '77 '03 C.161 M.B.A. L.989 J.D. [Ritzler,C.&S.]
McGinness, Joseph T., (AV) .... '42 '69 C&L.930 A.B., J.D. P.O. Box 221031
McGinness, Neil, (AV) .... '39 '69 C.276 A.B. L.930 J.D. 1900 Superior Ave., Ste. 230
McGinty, John P. .... '25 '58 C.363 A.B. L.1003 J.D. 1039 Kirtland Lane
McGinty, Timothy J. .... '51 '81 C.313 B.A. L.1003 J.D. Com. Pleas J.
McGinty, William T., (AV) .... '52 '80 C.611 B.A. L.1003 J.D. 614 W. Superior Ave.

McGlinchey Stafford, PLLC, (AV)
25550 Chagrin Boulevard Suite 406, 44122-4640 ⊙
Telephone: 216-378-9905 Fax: 216-378-9910
URL: http://www.mcglinchey.com
Members of Firm: Mark S. Edelman; David W. Thompson; Arthur J. Rotatori; Barbara Friedman Yaksic. Associates: Brooke Turner Bautista; Joy A. DiPalma; Kimberly Y. Smith. Of Counsel: Eugenia M. Schmidley; Monica L. Lacks; James S. Wertheim.
General Practice in the State and Federal Courts. Admiralty/Maritime Law, Agricultural, Antitrust and Trade Regulation, Aviation, Banking and Financial Institutions, Bankruptcy/Reorganization/ Creditors' Rights, Business Litigation, Collection Law, Commercial Finance/Asset-Based Lending, Construction, Consumer Financial Services Law and Regulation, Corporate and General Business, Employee Benefits/ERISA/Executive Compensation, Gaming Law and Regulation, Energy Law and Regulation, Environmental Law and Regulation, General Litigation and Insurance Defense, Governmental Relations and Legislation, Health Care Law and Regulation, Housing and Housing Finance, Manufactured Housing and Manufactured Housing Finance, Insurance Law and Regulation, Intellectual Property, International Law and Business Transactions, Labor and Employment, Products Liability, Professional Liability/Director and Officer Liability, Project and Structured Finance, Public Finance, Public Law and Finance, Public Utilities Law and Regulation, Real Estate, Securities Law and Regulation, Taxation and Tax Litigation, Trusts/Estate Planning and Administration.
New Orleans, Louisiana Office: 643 Magazine Street, 70130-3477. Telephone: 504-586-1200. Fax: 504-596-2800. TDD: 504-596-2728. Telex: 584327.
Houston, Texas Office: 1001 McKinney, Suite 1500, 77002. Telephone: 713-520-1900. Fax: 713-520-1025.
Dallas, Texas Office: 2711 N. Haskell, Suite 2700 LB25, 75204. Telephone: 214-257-1700. Fax: 214-257-1717.
Baton Rouge, Louisiana Office: One American Place, 14th Floor, 301 Main Street, 70825. Telephone: 504-383-9000. Fax: 504-343-3076.
Jackson, Mississippi Office: Suite 1100 South, City Centre, 200 South Lamar Street, 39201. Telephone: 601-960-8400. Fax: 601-960-8406.
Monroe, Louisiana Office: 1811 Tower Drive, Suite A, 71201. Telephone: 318-651-0807. Fax: 318-651-0809.
Albany, New York Office: 194 Washington Avenue, 6th Floor, 12210. Telephone: 518-432-1200. Fax: 518-432-8711.

See Professional Biographies, CLEVELAND, OHIO

McGowan, Harvey J. .... '53 '83 C.161 B.A. L.1003 J.D. 1245 E. 135th St., E. Cleveland
McGowan, John J., Jr. .... '56 '84 C&L.851 B.B.A., J.D. [Baker&H.]
McGrath, Brian T. .... '50 '87 C.390 A.B. L.1003 J.D. 1 American Road‡
McGrath, Mary Helen, (AV) .... '58 '89 C.201 B.S. L.1003 J.D. Cuyahoga Co. Pros. Off.
McGrath, Michele Angele '69 '96 C.610 B.B.A. L.989 J.D.
McDonald Invts Inc./Keybank
McGraw, Brian R., (AV) .... '57 '86 C.385 A.B. L.1003 J.D. [🄲 Crabbe,B.&J.]
McGraw, Mary Haas .... '57 '84 C.363 B.A. L.989 J.D. [McGraw&M.C.]
McGraw, Richard J., (AV) .... '30 '56 C&L.930 A.B., J.D. 55 Public Sq.‡
McGraw, Robert E. .... '47 '80 C.930 B.A. L.1003 J.D. 13613 Ardoon Ave.
McGraw & McGraw CO., LPA .... 1280 W. 3rd Street
McGregor, Erica E. .... '73 '98 C.477 B.A. L.94 J.D. [🄰 Spieth,B.M.&N.]
McGrew, Steven D. .... '58 '01 C.97 B.A. L.124 J.D. [🄰 Ulmer&B.]
McGrievy, Mark P. .... '63 '90 C.529 B.A. L.1003 J.D. [Roetzel&A.]
McGuire, Daniel J. .... '62 '88 C.970 B.A. L.930 J.D. 1900 E. 9th St.
McGuire, James J. .... '45 '74 C.62 B.A. L.1003 J.D. Exec. V.P., Society Natl. Bk.
McGuire, John J. .... '73 '98 C.659 B.A. L.930 J.D. [🄰 Calfee,H.&G.]
McGuire, Thomas D., (BV) .... '— '83 C.970 B.A. L.930 J.D. Asst. Atty. Gen.
McHargh, Kelly-Marie .... '67 '98 C.381 B.A. L.1003 J.D. U.S. Dept. of Educ.
McIntyre, Patrick J. .... '— '89 C.645 B.A. L.1003 J.D. [Weston H.]
McIntyre, Robert W. .... '44 '75 C.317 B.S. L.1003 J.D. [McIntyre,K.&K.]
McIntyre, Kahn, & Kruse, (BV) .... 1301 E. Ninth St., Ste 2200
McKay, Hugh E., (AV) .... '56 '82 C.103 B.A. L.659 J.D. [Porter W.M.&A.]
McKee, James W., (AV) '42 '69
C.1229 B.M.E. L.930 J.D. [🄲 Fay,S.F.M.&M.] (See Pat. Sect.)
McKee, Mary Bresnicky .... '60 '85 C.976 B.A. L.602 J.D. [🄰 Hickman&L.]
McKee, Thomas F., (AV) .... '48 '75 C.477 A.B. L.930 J.D. [Calfee,H.&G.]

McKeegan, Jennifer L. ... '— '97 C.446 B.A. L.1003 J.D. [▣ Gallagher S.]
McKeon, Sheila A., (BV) ... '— '84 C.93 B.A. L.930 J.D. [Gallagher S.]
McKew, Walter M. '48 '72 C.602 A.B. L.150 J.D.
Assoc. Gen. Coun., Washington Tru Solutions LLC
McKinley, Stacey L. ... '60 '97 C.611 B.A. L.1003 J.D. [▣ Ulmer&B.]
McKinney, Louise E. W., (BV) '42 '78 C.313 B.A. L.930 J.D.
Prof., Case Western Reserve Univ. Sch. of Law

McKinzie and Associates
(See Akron)

McKnight, F. Rush, (AV) ... '29 '55 C&L.930 A.B., LL.B. [Calfee,H.&G.] ‡
McLandrich, John T., (AV) ... '57 '83 C.363 B.S.Ec. L.930 J.D. [Mazanec,R.&R.]
McLaughlan, Kathleen A. ... '79 '04 C.262 B.A. L.124 J.D. [▣ Ziegler,M.&M.]
McLaughlin, Carol A. ... '48 '85 C.777 B.S. L.930 J.D. 1100 Huntington Bldg.
McLaughlin, John B. ... '47 '72 C.602 A.B. L.851 J.D. 11800 River Moss Rd.
McLaughlin, Lynn A. ... '64 '89 C.62 B.A. L.930 J.D. Asst. City Pros.
McLaughlin, Patrick M., (AV) ... '46 '76 C.610 B.G.S. L.930 J.D. [McLaughlin&M.]

McLaughlin & McCaffrey, LLP, (AV)
Eaton Center, Suite 1350, 1111 Superior Avenue, 44114-2500
Telephone: 216-623-0900 Fax: 216-623-0935
Email: law@paladin-law.com URL: http://www.lawyers.com/paladin-law
Patrick M. McLaughlin; John F. McCaffrey; Dennis P. Zapka. Associates: Anthony R. Petruzzi; David H. Boehm; Adrienne B. Kirshner; Sean T. Lavin.
Federal and State Trials and Appeals, White Collar Criminal Defense and Complex Civil Litigation.
See Professional Biographies, CLEVELAND, OHIO

McMahon, Brian A. ... '67 '94 C&L.608 B.S.B.A., J.D. [Calfee,H.&G.]
McMahon, Carl G., Attorney and Counsellor at Law, (BV) '48 '73
C.201 B.S. L.930 J.D. 526 Superior Avenue
McMahon, Louis L. ... '63 '96 C.363 B.A. L.1003 J.D. [Thompson H.]
McMahon, Michael S., (AV) ... '55 '81 C.363 B.A. L.178 J.D. [McMahon,D.H.&L.]
McMahon, Rebecca Ruppert ... '67 '93 C.788 B.A. L.608 J.D. KeyBank Natl. Assn.
McMahon, Seamus J. ... '78 '03 C.124 B.A. L.1003 J.D. [▣ Moscarino&T.]

McMahon, DeGulis, Hoffmann & Lombardi LLP, (AV)
The Caxton Building - Suite 650, 812 Huron Road, 44115-1126
Telephone: 216-621-1312 Telecopier: 216-621-0577 URL: http://www.mdhl.net
Email: envlaw@mdhl.net URL: http://www.lawyers.com/mdh
Members of Firm: Michael S. McMahon; Gregory J. DeGulis; Maria T. Lombardi; Stephen H. Daniels. Associates: Suzanne Wiery; Erick C. Smith; Evan J. Palik; James A. Byrne; Amy Klimek. Of Counsel: Richard A. Green.
Environmental Law and Litigation.
See Professional Biographies, CLEVELAND, OHIO

McManamon, Joseph F. ... '19 '50 C.363 B.A. L.1003 LL.B. Com. Pleas J.
McManus, Robert P., (AV) ... '53 '78 C.602 B.B.A. L.608 J.D. [Taft,S.&H.]
McMenamin, Michael, (AV) ... '43 '68 C.930 B.A. L.659 LL.B. [Walter&H.]
McMillan, Ronald M. ... '68 '00 C.251 B.A. L.161 J.D. [▣ Calfee,H.&G.]
McMonagle, Christine T., (AV) ... '49 '74 C.597 B.A. L.930 J.D. Legal Aid Society
McMonagle, James J. ... '44 '70 C.276 B.S./B.A. L.1003 J.D. [▣ Vorys,S.S.&P.]
McMonagle, Richard J. ... '41 '67 C.884 B.S. L.930 J.D. Com. Pleas J.
McMonagle, Timothy E. ... '45 '74 C.201 B.A. L.1003 J.D. Ct. of App. J.
McMullen, Daniel J., (AV) ... '56 '83 C&L.309 B.A., J.D. [Calfee,H.&G.]
McMunigal, Kevin C., (AV Ⓣ) '50 '79 C.813 B.A. L.1066 J.D.
(adm. in CA; not adm. in OH) 11075 E. Blvd.
McNair, Eben O., IV, (AV) ... '50 '80 C.732 B.A. L.188 J.D. [Schwarzwald&M.]
McNamara, Maris J. ... '67 '93 C.116 B.A. L.8 J.D. [Frantz W.]
McNamara, Michael P., Jr. ... '71 '96 C.128 B.A. L.930 J.D. [Baker&H.]
McNamee, L. J. ... '13 '37 C.363 B.A. L.309 LL.B. 18777 Lookout Circle‡

McNeal, Schick, Archibald & Biro Co., L.P.A., (AV)
Van Sweringen Arcade, 123 West Prospect Avenue, Suite 250, 44115
Telephone: 216-621-9870 Fax: 216-522-1112
Email: msab@apk.net URL: http://www.msablaw.com
Harley J. McNeal (1911-1996); Thomas Schick (1923-1997); Albert J. Biro (1926-1995); Paul W. Ziegler; Fredric E. Kramer; John C. Cubar; Marilyn J. Singer; Brian T. Winchester. Associates: Kristina M. Packard; Dawn E. Snyder. Of Counsel: Robert D. Archibald.
General Civil Trial and Appellate Practice in all State and Federal Courts. Admiralty, Architects and Engineers, Commercial, Corporation, Environmental, Insurance, Malpractice, Products Liability and Toxic Substances Law.
Representative Clients: Allstate Insurance Co.; Auto-Owners Insurance Co.; GEICO.
See Professional Biographies, CLEVELAND, OHIO

McNeeley, Patrick H. ... '29 '60 C.363 B.S. L.1003 LL.B. 1240 East 9th Street
McNellie, Richard L., (AV) ... '48 '75 C.930 B.A. L.1003 J.D. [Carlisle,M.R.K.&U.]
McPhillips, Michael D. '60 '90
C.363 B.S.B.A. L.1003 J.D. Tax Mgr., Hausser & Taylor, CPA's
McQuade, Rachel ... '70 '95 C&L.150 B.A., J.D. [▣ Tucker E.&W.]
McWilliams, Douglas A. ... '60 '94 C.604 B.A. L.112 J.D. [Squire,S.&D.]
Meade, Karen K. ... '56 '83 C.381 B.A. L.1003 J.D. [K.K.Meade&Assoc.]

Meade, Karen K., & Associates Co. LPA
1370 West 6th Street, Suite 208, 44113
Telephone: 216-696-3327 Fax: 216-621-8609
Email: immigration_atty@yahoo.com
Karen K. Meade.
Languages: Spanish, French, German, Greek, Farsi (Persian).
Immigration and Nationality Law.
See Professional Biographies, CLEVELAND, OHIO

Meadows, Jennifer Jenkins '76 '03 C.896 B.A. L.145 J.D.
(adm. in GA; not adm. in OH) [▣ Squire,S.&D.]
Meadows, William A., (AV) ... '61 '86 C.97 B.S. L.7 J.D. [▣ Reminger&R.]
Meaney, Michael J., (AV) ... '52 '77 C.276 A.B. L.608 J.D. [McDonald H.]
Meaney, Thomas P., Jr., (AV) ... '29 '53 C.363 A.B. L.602 LL.B. 600 Superior Ave.‡
Mearns, Edward A., Jr. '30 '58 C.976 B.S. L.893 LL.B.
(adm. in VA; not adm. in OH) 11075 E. Blvd.‡
Medley, Michael J. ... '— '04 C.610 B.S. [▣ Amin&T.]
Meehan, Ellen K., (AV) ... '49 '92 C.523 B.A. L.161 J.D. [▣ Squire,S.&D.]
Meehan, Michael J., (AV) '49 '81 C.363 A.B. L.851 J.D.
Asst. Secy. & Assoc. Coun., Cleveland Clinic Foundation, The
Meeker, Brian A. ... '64 '94 C.381 B.S. L.8 J.D. [▣ Reminger&R.]
Mehalko, Megan Lum ... '65 '90 C.105 B.A. L.930 J.D. [Benesch,F.C.&A.]
Mehendale, Ellyn B. ... '69 '94 C.473 B.S. L.1003 J.D. [▣ Janik&D.]
Mehlman, Maxwell J. '48 '75 C.685 B.A. L.976 J.D.
Prof. of Law & Dir., Case Western Reserve Univ.
Mehok, George K. ... '31 '65 C.930 B.A. L.1003 J.D. The Richard E. Jacobs Grp.
Meimaris, James George ... '47 '87 C.1029 B.S.B.A. L.8 J.D. [Meimaris,J.G.]
Meimaris, James G. ... 1801 East Ninth Street, Suite 730
Meinerding, Wesley C. ... '74 '02 C.602 B.S.M.E. L.851 J.D. [▣ Calfee,H.&G.]
Meissner, Joseph P., (AV) ... '42 '66 C.973 A.B. L.309 LL.B. Legal Aid Soc.
Meissner, Michael G., (AV) ... '54 '79 C.602 B.A. L.309 J.D. [Squire,S.&D.]

Meko, Margaret Mary, (BV) ... '— '84 C.273 B.A. L.161 J.D. [Gallagher S.]
Melamed, Marc A., (AV) ... '— '77 C.910 A.B. L.1003 J.D. [Javitch,B.&R.]
Mellino, Christopher M., (AV) ... '59 '84 C.161 B.A. L.1003 J.D. [Mellino]
Mellino, Gaynel F., (Ms.) ... '59 '84 C.473 B.A. L.1003 J.D. 25425 Center Ridge Rd.
Mellino, Sean F. ... '76 '01 C.216 B.S. L.124 J.D. [▣ D.P.Hochberg] (See Pat. Sect.)

Mellino Law Firm LLC, (AV)
55 Public Square, Suite 1260, 44113
Telephone: 216-621-8348 Fax: 216-621-8378
Email: cmm@mellinolaw.com URL: http://www.christophermellino.com
Member: Christopher M. Mellino. Associate: Paige H. Platten.
Negligence, Insurance, Products Liability, Medical Malpractice, Nursing Home Negligence.
See Professional Biographies, CLEVELAND, OHIO

Mellott, David W., (AV) ... '53 '78 C.473 B.A. L.608 J.D. [Benesch,F.C.&A.]
Mellyn, John E., Jr., (AV) ... '45 '73 C.93 A.B. L.893 J.D. [Hahn L.&P.]
Melnick, Phyllis, (BV) ... '33 '84 C.188 B.A. L.1003 J.D. 23500 S. Woodland Road‡
Melnyk, Stephanie Katherine '70 '99 C.763 B.A. L.608 J.D.
City of Cleveland, Law Dept.
Melsher, Gary W., (AV) ... '39 '64 C.608 B.S. L.930 J.D. [▣ Singerman,M.D.&K.]
Mendenhall, John M. '50 '76 C.276 A.B. L.107 J.D.
(adm. in NY; not adm. in OH) Reg. Dir., Fed. Trade Comm.

Mendenhall, Warner, Law Office of
(See Akron)

Mendes, Scott Michael ... '64 '89 C.473 B.S. L.94 J.D. Todd Org. of Cleve.
Mendoza, Matthew M. ... '70 '97 C.381 B.A. L.608 J.D. [▣ Calfee,H.&G.]
Mentrek, Joseph Michael ... '60 '85 C&L.607 B.S.B.A., J.D. Meaden & Moore, Ltd.
Menuez, Jonathan M. ... '69 '95 C.608 B.S.B.A. L.8 J.D. [Sutter,O.&F.]
Menz, David F. '65 '91 C.188 B.S. L.309 J.D.
(adm. in NY; not adm. in OH) Sr. Coun., Sec. & Fin., TRW Inc.
Menzalora, William M. ... '67 '92 C.363 B.A. L.124 J.D. [Faulkner,M.&P.]
Menzies, John Whitley, Jr. '48 '75
C.973 B.A. L.1340 J.D. Mag., Ct. of Com. Pleas, Juv. Div.
Meraglio, Russell J., Jr., (AV) ... '57 '83 C.62 B.A. L.1003 J.D. [▣ Reminger&R.]
Mercer, Harry D., (AV) ... '42 '67 C&L.659 B.A., LL.B. [▣ Hahn L.&P.]
Mercer, Kathryn Lynn '56 '83
C.228 A.B. L.930 J.D. Prof., Case Western Reserve Univ. Law Sch.
Mericle, Denise A. ... '68 '93 C.347 B.S. L.345 J.D. The Robertson Agcy., Inc.
Meros, John C., (AV) ... '50 '80 C.161 B.A. L.1003 J.D. [Schulman,S.&M.]
Merriam, Stephen C., (BV) ... '57 '85 C.103 A.B. L.930 J.D. [Ulmer&B.]
Merrick, Patrick P. ... '68 '04 C.980 B.S. L.124 J.D. [▣ Steuer,E.B.&B.]
Merriman, Thomas Conley, (BV) ... '61 '88 C.602 B.A. L.309 J.D. Dep. Atty. Gen.
Mersol, Gregory V., (AV) ... '60 '85 C&L.930 B.A., J.D. [Baker&H.]
Merz, Stuart O. H., (AV) ... '30 '58 C&L.188 B.S., LL.B. 901 Lakeside Ave.
Mesch, Lester D. ... '25 '54 C.608 B.S. L.1003 J.D. 2421 Allen Blvd.
Mesel, Kathleen L. ... '65 '97 C.477 A.B. L.930 J.D. 17800 Royalton Road
Mesi, Douglas P. ... '62 '88 C&L.930 B.A. J.D 592 Strumbly Dr.
Messeloff, Daniel A. ... '— '03 C.910 B.A. L.262 J.D. [▣ Jones D.]
Messerman, Gale S., (AV) ... '42 '69 C.472 B.S. L.802 J.D. [Messerman&M.]
Messerman, Gerald A., (AV) ... '36 '61 C&L.930 B.A., LL.B. [Messerman&M.]
Messerman & Messerman Co., L.P.A., (AV) ... 127 Public Square
Messinger, Donald H., (AV) ... '43 '68 C.165 A.B. L.228 J.D. [Thompson H.]
Mester, Jonathan D. ... '70 '98 C.823 B.A. L.608 J.D. [Nurenberg,P.H.&M.]
Mester, Thomas, (BV) ... '44 '69 C.363 B.A. L.930 J.D. [Nurenberg,P.H.&M.]
Meszaros, Magdalene H. ... '— '78 L.1003 J.D. V.P., Natl. City Bk.
Metcalf, J. Seth ... '79 '04 C.608 B.A. L.188 J.D. [▣ Squire,S.&D.] (⊙Columbus)
Metz, Carol K. ... '70 '00 C.8 B.S.B.A. L.124 J.D. [▣ Weston H.]
Metzenbaum, Howard M., (AV) ... '17 '41 C&L.608 B.A., J.D. U.S. Sen.
Metzger, Robert L., (AV) ... '37 '62 C&L.477 A.B., LL.B. [Ziegler,M.&M.]
Metzinger, Margaret M. ... '65 '95 C.318 B.A. L.1003 J.D. [▣ Climaco,L.P.W.&G.]
Meyer, Andrew C., (AV) ... '52 '76 C.610 A.B. L.930 J.D. [Duvin,C.&H.]
Meyer, Arnold R. ... '29 '53 C&L.930 A.B., LL.B. 3589 Strandhill St.
Meyer, Donna J. '70 '95 C.30 B.A. L.930 J.D.
Assoc. Coun., Cleveland Clinic Foundation, The
Meyer, G. Christopher, (AV) ... '48 '73 C.378 B.A. L.659 J.D. [Squire,S.&D.]
Meyer, Thomas L., (BV) '55 '79 C.97 B.S. L.477 J.D.
V.P. Law, Dep. Gen. Coun. & Asst. Secy., Parker-Hannifin Corporation
Meyers, Anne L., (AV) ... '51 '77 C.608 B.A. L.117 J.D. [Meyers,R.F.&L.]

Meyers, Roman, Friedberg & Lewis, A Legal Professional Association, (AV)
28601 Chagrin Boulevard, Suite 500, 44122
Telephone: 216-831-0042 Fax: 216-831-0542 URL: http://www.meyerslamannarandroman.com
Email: attys@meyersroman.com URL: http://www.meyersroman.com
Members of Firm: Anne L. Meyers; Barbara K. Roman; Ronald P. Friedberg; Scott M. Lewis; Peter D. Brosse; Alan N. Hirth; Debra J. Horn; Lynn A. Kriessler; Debra A. Perelman. Associates: F. Scott B. Geneva; Matthew E. Parkins; Kennee B. Switzer; Geoffrey S. Goss; Jenifere M. Reichard; Stephen M. Nowak. Of Counsel: Louis B. Geneva.
Surety and Insurance Defense Law, Business and Corporate Law, Estate Planning, Business Succession, Environmental Law, Commercial Litigation, Construction and General Litigation, Probate, Family Law, Employment Law and Real Estate Law.
See Professional Biographies, CLEVELAND, OHIO

Meyerson, David ... '59 '84 C.608 B.A. L.1003 J.D. 5601 Walworth Avenue
Mezacapa, Victor A. ... '59 '91 C.363 B.S.B.A. L.1003 J.D. 55 Public Square, Suite 2200
Michalec, Daniel J., (BV) ... '— '89 C.381 B.S. L.8 J.D. [Gallagher S.]
Michals, Thomas I. ... '56 '88 C.134 B.S. L.930 J.D. [Calfee,H.&G.]
Michalski, David J., (BV) ... '66 '94 C.966 B.A. L.93 J.D. [Hahn L.&P.]
Michel, David S., (BV) ... '58 '84 C.477 B.A. L.930 J.D. [▣ Shapero&G.]
Michel, Lisa Hall ... '59 '84 C.860 B.A. L.124 J.D. Key Bk., N.A.
Michelson, Deborah J., (BV) ... '63 '88 C.597 B.A. L.930 J.D. [▣ Goodman W.M.]
Michelson, Michael B., (AV) ... '41 '71 C.569 B.S. L.724 J.D. [Stege&M.]
Middleton, Fred D., Jr. ... '47 '73 C&L.329 B.A., J.D. 526 Superior Avenue, N.E.
Midian, Kathleen Lucille ... '46 '82 C.381 B.S. L.201 J.D. U.S. Attorney's Off.
Miehls, Donald E. ... '59 '84 C.757 B.A. L.724 J.D. 1801 East Ninth Street
Mierau, Michael D., Jr. ... '— '98 C.8 B.A. L.989 J.D. [▣ Baker&H.]
Miguel, Melanie V. ... '68 '95 C.363 B.A. L.1003 J.D. 614 Superior Ave., 15th Fl.
Mihelich, Jos. A. ... '30 '56 C&L.930 B.A., LL.B. 1370 Ontario St.
Mihet, Horatio ("Harry") G. ... '— '02 C.260 B.A. L.228 J.D. [▣ Thompson H.]
Mika, Karin ... '62 '90 C.62 B.A. L.1003 J.D. Asst. Dir., Cleveland-Marshall Coll. of Law
Mikhail, Sherrie M. ... '76 '01 C.363 B.A. L.124 J.D. [▣ Duvin,C.&H.]
Milan, Irene M. ... '54 '85 C.161 B.A. L.8 J.D. Law Libr., U.S. Cts.
Milano, Jay, (AV) ... '51 '81 C.608 B.A. L.1003 J.D. [Milano W.&a.&Assoc.]
Milano, Jerome P. ... '28 '55 C.381 L.1003 J.D. 410-34 Meadview Dr.‡

Milano Weiser, Attys. & Counselors at Law, A Legal Prof. Assoc., (AV)
Milano Law Building, 2639 Wooster Road, 44116
Telephone: 440-356-2828 Fax: 440-356-2873
Email: inquire@milanolaw.com URL: http://www.milanolaw.com
Jay Milano; Rachel M. Weiser;—Tikvah Shachter.

(This Listing Continued)

Milano Weiser, Attys. & Counselors at Law, A Legal Prof. Assoc. (Continued)
Criminal Defense, White Collar Crime, Wrongful Death, Medical Malpractice, Nursing Home Negligence, Internet Law, Consumer Law.
See Professional Biographies, CLEVELAND, OHIO

Milenkovich, Milosh D. '41 '75 C.930 B.S. L.1003 J.D. 7986 N. Wright Rd.
Miley, Kathryn M. '71 '96 C.712 B.A. L.494 J.D. [🄰 Wilkerson&Assoc.]
Milgrom, Michael '48 '73 C.145 A.B. L.494 J.D. Fed. Trade Comm.
Milicic, Heidi J. '— '96 C.475 B.A. L.930 J.D. [🄰 Buckley K.]
Milkes, Robert A. '56 '88 C.1349 B.A. L.161 J.D. 3955 Euclid Avenue, #301-E
Miller, Adam C. '65 '94 C.608 B.A. L.117 J.D. [🄰 Roetzel&A.]
Miller, Alan L. '50 '77 C.8 B.S.B.A. L.7 J.D. V.P., Admin., Cardinal Amer. Corp.
Miller, Amy L. '75 '04 C.216 B.A. L.124 J.D. 1422 Euclid, Ste. 248
Miller, Anne Marie '67 '96 C.112 B.A. L.472 J.D.
(adm. in CO; not adm. in OH) Asst. V.P. & Asst. Coun., KeyBank Natl. Assn.
Miller, Barry J., (AV) '54 '83 C.473 B.S. L.930 J.D. [Benesch,F.C.&A.]
Miller, Brett A. '74 '01 C.97 B.A. L.989 J.D. [🄰 Bonezzi S.M.&P.]
Miller, Catherine L. '73 '01 C.602 B.B.A. L.124 J.D. [🄰 Thompson H.]
Miller, Chas. R., (AV) '23 '47 C.659 A.B. L.976 LL.B. 1228 Euclid Ave.
Miller, Craig S., (AV) '45 '71 C.228 B.A. L.273 J.D. [Ulmer&B.]
Miller, David H. '38 '63 C.473 A.B. L.477 J.D. 32415 Brighton Park Blvd.‡
Miller, Heather Varley '— '03 C.156 B.A. L.823 J.D. [🄰 Jones D.]
Miller, Ivan L., (AV) '14 '38 C&L.930 B.A., J.D. 925 Euclid Avenue‡
Miller, James L. '— '96 C.608 B.S. L.161 J.D. [🄰 Buckley K.]
Miller, Jeffrey C. '71 '97 C.381 B.A. L.602 J.D. [🄰 Johnson,A.&C.]
Miller, John E., Jr. '44 '70
C.679 B.S.Chem.E. L.276 J.D. [🄰 Calfee,H.&G.] (See Pat. Sect.)
Miller, John J. '35 '66 C.608 B.S. L.1003 J.D. [Childs,M.&Assoc.]
Miller, Mark J., (BV) '55 '83 C.608 B.A. L.1003 J.D. 1954 Clague Road
Miller, Michael L., (AV) '41 '66 C.610 A.B. L.228 LL.B. [Calfee,H.&G.] ‡
Miller, Nancy Herbst '52 '83 C.473 B.A. L.1003 J.D. 3131 Oakwood Lane
Miller, Nicholas M. '71 '98 C.161 B.A. L.1003 J.D. [🄰 Jones D.]
Miller, Ralph A., (BV) '22 '48 C.970 A.B. L.930 J.D. [Gurney,M.&M.]
Miller, Richd. H., (BV) '31 '55 C&L.602 B.A., J.D. [Miller&M.]
Miller, Robert A., (BV) '— '82 C.970 B.A. L.930 J.D. [Calfee,H.&G.]
Miller, Robert G., (AV) '— '73 C.1003 B.A. L.94 J.D. [Strachan,M.O.&R.]
Miller, Ross P. '76 '01 C.94 B.A. L.124 J.D. [🄰 Shapiro&F.]
Miller, Scott D. '53 '79 C.645 B.A. L.607 J.D.
Sr. V.P. & Sr. Mng. Coun., KeyBank Natl. Assn.
Miller, Steven J., (AV) '56 '81 C.103 A.B. L.930 J.D. [Goodman W.M.]
Miller, Tanya F. '73 '99 C&L.930 B.A., J.D. [🄰 Baker&H.]
Miller & Miller, (BV)
1700 E. 13th St. (⊙L.A., CA; Balt., MD; Pearl, MS; Seneca Falls, NY)
Milles, James G. '56 '91 C&L.734 B.A., J.D.
(adm. in MO; not adm. in OH)
Law Libr., Case Western Reserve University School of Law
Millet, David G. '72 '98 C.610 B.S. L.989 J.D. Financial Planner, The Financial Group
Millet, Paul L., (AV) '44 '70 C.608 B.S. L.1003 J.D. [P.L.Millet&Assoc.]
Millet, Paul L., and Associates, A Legal Prof. Assn., (AV) 25550 Chagrin Blvd.
Millican, James T., II, (AV) '42 '67 C.894 B.A. L.930 J.D. [🄲 Weston H.]
Millisor, Kenneth R., (AV) '37 '61 C.611 B.A. L.608 J.D. [Millisor&N.]
Millisor, Richard A., (AV) '64 '90 L.1165 J.D. [Millisor&N.]

Millisor & Nobil, A Legal Professional Association, (AV)
9150 South Hills Boulevard, Suite 300, 44147-3599 ⊙
Telephone: 440-838-8800; 800-800-8806 Telefax: 440-838-8805
Email: laborlaw@millisor.com URL: http://www.millisor.com
Kenneth R. Millisor; Steven M. Nobil; Thomas D. Rooney; David E. Schreiner; David P. Hiller; Maribeth Gavin-Wuertz; Michael J. Reidy; John R. Slater; Richard A. Millisor (Certified Specialist in Labor and Employment Law, Ohio State Bar Association); Terry E. Lardakis; Paul C. Morrison; Robert E. Dezort; R. Scot Harvey; Daniel P. O'Brien; Scott A. Lefelar; Jennifer A. Welfley. Associates: Melanie L. Webber; Carol D. Strassman (Certified Specialist in Workers' Compensation Law, Ohio State Bar Association); Monica M. Weber; Jeffrey D. Smith; Robert C. Pivonka, II. Of Counsel: William E. Blackie, III.
Employment Law including Labor Relations, Equal Employment Opportunity, Public Sector, OSHA, Arbitration Law, Litigation, Workers Compensation Law, Human Resources Consulting and Employee Benefit Law.
Counsel for: Anderson-Dubose Co.; Case Foods; Goodrich Corp.; May Department Stores; McDonald Steel Corporation; Ohio Turnpike Commission; PolyOne Corp.; Rock & Roll Hall of Fame and Museum, Inc.; Sekely Industries, Inc.; TJX Companies, Inc.
Columbus, Ohio Office: 300 East Broad Street, Suite 190, 43215. Telephone: 614-221-2234. Telefax: 614-221-1278.
Canton, Ohio Office: 4117 Whipple Avenue NW, 44718. Telephone: 330-493-8525; 888-867-6869. Telefax: 330-493-8606.
See Professional Biographies, CLEVELAND, OHIO

Mills, David E. '— '02 C.165 B.A. L.477 J.D. [🄰 Jones D.]
Mills, David M. '54 '91 C.161 B.A. L.1003 J.D. [Gallup,B.&M.]
Mills, Jennifer A. '68 '96 C.150 B.S. L.608 J.D. [🄰 Baker&H.]
Mills, Osborne, Jr., (AV) '47 '75 C.197 A.B. L.930 J.D. [Squire,S.&D.]
Mills, William M., (AV) '50 '75 C.197 A.B. L.188 J.D. [Singerman,M.D.&K.]
Millstone, David J., (AV) '46 '71 C.367 A.B. L.923 J.D. [Squire,S.&D.]
Milner, Irvin M., (AV) '16 '40 C&L.930 B.A., J.D. 1370 Ontario St.
Miltner, Lawrence J. '52 '78
C.381 B.A. L.1003 J.D. Gen. Coun., Cuyahoga Community College
Minahan, Kathleen M. '70 '95 C.611 B.A. L.930 J.D. [🄰 Thompson H.]
Minchak, JoEllen M. '60 '85 C.318 B.A. L.309 J.D. [Calfee,H.&G.]
Mineff, George, Jr., (BV) '59 '84 C.790 B.A. L.1003 J.D. 1370 Ontario Street
Mingus, Ronald A. '64 '90 C.363 B.S.B.A. L.930 J.D. [🄰 Reminger&R.]
Minichiello, Alfred C. '22 '55 C.251 B.B.A. L.1003 LL.B. P.O. Box 33152
Minney, R. Brent, (AV) '53 '78 C.607 B.A. L.201 J.D. 5005 Rockside Rd., Ste. 260
Minnich, Richard J., (AV) '33 '65
C.381 B.S. L.1003 J.D. [🄲 Fay,S.F.M.&M.] (See Pat. Sect.)
Mino, John M., (AV) '59 '84 C&L.276 B.S.F.S., J.D. [Calfee,H.&G.]
Minshall, Kent R. '19 '48 C&L.930 B.A., LL.B. 21690 River Oaks Dr.
Minshall, Kent R., Jr., (BV) '51 '79 C.207 B.A. L.930 J.D. [Minshall]
Minshall Law Offices, (BV) 2189 Professor Ave., Ste. 100
Mintz, Gary Lee '52 '79 [Mintz&Assoc.]
Mintz, Stuart A., (BV) '53 '78 C.610 B.A. L.1003 J.D. [McCarthy,L.C.&L.]
Mintz & Associates Co. LPA 5533 State Road
Miraldi, Leslee W. '— '76 C.610 B.A. L.608 J.D. [Thompson H.]
Mischka, Cash H. '63 '91 C.178 B.A. L.930 J.D. [🄰 Ulmer&B.]
Mishkind, Howard D., (AV) '55 '80 C.150 B.B.A. L.1003 J.D. [Becker&M.]
Mitchell, John R. '70 '96 C.608 B.A. L.117 J.D. [🄰 Thompson H.]
Mitchell, Kimberley P.H. '— '02 C.475 B.A. L.188 J.D. [🄰 Jones D.]
Mitchell, Lu Ann '— '83 C.150 J.D. L.893 J.D. P.O. Box 08531
Mitchell, Marla L. '58 '84 C.980 B.S. L.7 J.D. 11075 East Blvd.
Mitchell, Michael D., (AV) '26 '59 C.436 L.1003 LL.B. 19462 Coffinberry Blvd.
Mitchell, Richard N. '34 '60 C&L.930 B.A., LL.B. 1481 Warrensville Center Rd.
Mitchell, Richard S., (AV) '59 '84 C.861 B.S. L.930 J.D. [Roetzel&A.]
Mitchell, Sheila Noonan, (BV) '57 '92 C.207 B.S. L.8 J.D. 595 Miner Road
Mitchell, Wade A., (AV) '54 '85 C.869 B.S. L.273 J.D. [Baker&H.]
Mitchell, William, (AV) '49 '78 C.610 B.S. L.1003 J.D. [Armstrong,M.D.&Z.]
Mitchell, Willie Lee '67 '95 C.165 B.A. L.161 J.D. City Law Dept.
Mixter, Stephen C. '— '86 C.608 B.A. L.228 J.D. [Jones D.]
Mizer, Susan L. '67 '93 C&L.930 B.A., J.D. [Tucker E.&W.] (Pat.)
Mlakar, Ginger Fuller, (AV) '63 '92 C&L.608 B.S.B.A., J.D. [🄲 Benesch,F.C.&A.]
Mock, Clay, (AV) '27 '54 C.477 A.B. L.608 J.D. 925 Eulcid Ave.‡
Modica, Donald A., (AV) '42 '70 C.602 B.A. L.930 J.D. [Zimmerman,C.E.&M.]
Moeller, Jeffrey S. '65 '89 C.473 B.A. L.575 J.D. [🄰 Hermann,C.&S.]
Moffet, Beverly L. '37 '75
C.429 B.A. L.1003 J.D. Mag., Common Pleas Ct., Dom. Rel. Div.
Mog, Cynthia C. '68 '93 C.473 B.S. L.597 J.D. [🄰 Squire,S.&D.]
Moldovanyi, Jay F., (AV) '48 '79
C.930 B.S.M.E. L.608 J.D. [Fay,S.F.M.&M.] (See Pat. Sect.)
Mollohan, Bryan S. '72 '98 C.62 B.A. L.161 J.D. [🄰 J.D.Carney&Assoc.]
Molnar, Edward S., (BV) '39 '64 C.973 B.S.B.A. L.734 J.D. 920 Terminal Twr.
Molnar, Isaac A. '— '99 C&L.608 B.Sc., J.D. [🄰 Jones D.] (See Pat. Sect.)
Molnar, John A., Jr. '64 '92 C.980 B.E. L.608 J.D.
Asst. Gen. Coun., Intel. Prop., Parker-Hannifin Corp. (Pat.)
Molyneaux, Rebecca S. '76 '02 C&L.823 B.S., J.D. [🄰 Cavitch,F.D.&F.]
Monachino, Grant A. '— '03 C.528 B.A. L.989 J.D. [🄰 McDonald H.]
Monachino, Nicole M. '78 '03 C.318 B.A. L.602 J.D. [🄰 McDonald H.]
Monastra, Carl C., (BV) '53 '81 C.161 B.A. L.1003 J.D. 75 Public Square, Suite 1000
Mondalek, Allyson '78 '04 C.608 B.S. L.124 J.D. [🄰 Porter W.M.&A.]
Mondello, Joseph T., (BV) '35 '61 C.363 B.S. L.930 LL.B. 55 Public Sq.
Monica, John C., Jr. '64 '91 C.597 B.A. L.273 J.D. [Porter W.M.&A.]
Monihan, M. Elizabeth, (AV) '57 '84 C.363 B.S. L.161 J.D. [Spieth,B.M.&N.]
Monnin, Robert D., (AV) '41 '68 C.473 A.B. L.1003 J.D. [Thompson H.]
Monroe, Gerald A. '64 '92 C.597 B.S.J. L.1003 J.D. [Calfee,H.&G.]
Monroe, John W., (BV) '68 '93 C.1030 B.A. L.273 J.D. [Walter&H.]
Monroe, Robert William '60 '85 C.321 B.A. L.930 J.D. [Hawkins]
Monroe, Thomas W., (BV) '59 '92 C.599 B.B.A. L.1003 [🄰 Monroe&Z.]
Monroe, William T., (AV) '26 '53 C.363 B.S. L.1003 J.D. [Monroe&Z.]
Monroe & Zucco, (AV) 1525 Leader Building
Monteleone, J. Michael, (AV) '49 '74 C.363 B.A. L.1003 J.D. [Jeffries,K.F.&M.]
Montgomery, Michael J. '74 '99 C&L.608 B.A., J.D. [🄰 Bricker&E.]
Montie, William J. '32 '56 C.604 A.B. L.930 LL.B. 25550 Chagrin Blvd.‡
Montville, Julanne '— '02 C.1012 B.A. L.930 J.D. [🄰 Thompson H.]
Monty, Jennifer M. '78 '03 C.210 B.A. L.608 J.D. [🄰 Weltman,W.&R.]
Moody, Lizabeth A., (AV) '34 '59
C.66 A.B. L.976 LL.B. Prof. of Law, Cleveland State Univ.
Moody, Steven J. '62 '02 C.161 B.A. L.1003 J.D. [🄰 Mazanec,R.&R.]
Mooney, Paul Joseph '63 '88 C.812 B.A. L.989 J.D. One Bratenahl
Mooney, William D. '51 '76 C.188 B.S. L.930 J.D. 14058 Wilma Dr.‡
Moore, Anthony R., (AV) '— '75 C.309 A.B. L.893 J.D. [Jones D.]
Moore, Craig L. '66 '94 C.150 B.A. L.251 J.D. [🄰 Benesch,F.C.&A.]
Moore, Edward W., (BV) '57 '82 C.473 B.A. L.930 J.D. [Calfee,H.&G.]
Moore, George W. '18 '49 C.852 A.B. L.209 J.D.
(adm. in IL; not adm. in OH) U.S. Vet. Admn.
Moore, James M., (AV) '48 '88 C.8 B.S.E.E. L.1003 J.D. [Pearne&G.] (See Pat. Sect.)
Moore, Kathy L., (AV) '52 '79 C.381 B.A. L.930 J.D. Dep. Pub. Def.
Moore, Kenneth C., (AV) '47 '73 C.318 B.A. L.309 J.D. [Squire,S.&D.]
Moore, Lynn L., (AV) '— '84 C.610 B.S. L.1003 J.D. [Gallagher S.]
Moore, Mary Beth Salem '74 '00 C.610 B.A. L.989 J.D.
Co. Comm. Mental Health Brd.
Moore, William D. '30 '60 C.864 B.S. L.329 LL.B. 620 Leader Building
Moore, Zoe Ann '61 '86 C.62 B.A. L.1003 J.D. Soc. Sec. Admn.
Moore-Hewitt, Sheilarayne '51 '86
C.381 B.S. L.161 J.D. Sr. Human Res. Atty., Cleveland-Cliffs Inc
Moorhead, Russell A. '— '85 C.8 B.S.B.A. L.7 J.D. 614 W. Superior Ave., Ste. 860
Moorhead, Sean T. '64 '93 C.477 B.S.E. L.608 J.D. [Calfee,H.&G.] (See Pat. Sect.)
Moorman, Scott A. '64 '89 C&L.602 B.A., J.D. Erieview Twr., 20th Fl.
Moran, Glenn J. '47 '72 C.645 B.A. L.831 J.D.
(adm. in PA; not adm. in OH) Sr. V.P., Gen. Coun. & Secy., The LTV Corp.
Moran, Mary Ansbro '54 '80 C.705 B.S. L.910 J.D.
Sr. Title Atty., Chicago Title Ins. Co.
Moran, R. Emmett, (AV) '— '77 C.215 B.A. L.1003 J.D. [🄲 Davis&Y.]
Moran, Susan J. '70 '96 C.610 B.B.A. L.1003 J.D. Jud. Clk., Ct. of App.
Moravick, Robert J. '41 '70 C.363 B.S.B.A. L.1003 J.D. 2042 Aldersgate Dr.
Morell, Dan A., Jr., (BV) '57 '86 C.8 B.A. L.7 J.D. 6060 Rockside Woods Boulevard
Morell, Karen M., (CV) '62 '88
C.62 B.A. L.930 J.D. The Bevelin House, 2913 Clinton Ave.
Morelli, Matthew J. '69 '94 C.97 B.A. L.930 J.D. [Ulmer&B.]
Morelli, Theresa E. '62 '89 C&L.8 B.A., J.D. Forest City Enterprises
Morford, James Leroy '56 '84 C.25 B.A. L.117 J.D. Off. of U.S. Atty.
Morford, Joseph J., (AV) '— '91 C.602 B.A. L.424 J.D. [Tucker E.&W.]
Morgan, Christopher H. '51 '77 C.623 B.S. L.846 J.D.
Assoc. Gen. Coun., Parker-Hannifin Corp. (Pat.)
Morgan, Hugh J., (AV) '53 '78 C.363 B.S.B.A. L.1003 J.D.
6611 Rockside Rd., Ste. 225
Morgan, Jeffrey Lyle '58 '92 C.207 B.A. L.8 J.D. OH Savings Bk.
Morgan, Patrick J., (AV) '44 '70 C.363 A.B. L.161 J.D. [Zeisler&M.]
Morgan, Terry A. '— '88 C&L.966 B.M., J.D.
(adm. in WI; not adm. in OH) N.L.R.B.
Morganstern, Stanley, (AV) '41 '67 C.608 B.S. L.1003 J.D. [Morganstern,M.&D.]

Morganstern, MacAdams & DeVito Co., L.P.A., (AV)
623 West St. Claire Avenue, 44113
Telephone: 216-621-4244; 216-687-1212 Fax: 216-621-2951
URL: http://www.mmd-law.com
Stanley Morganstern (Certified Specialist in Family Law, Ohio State Bar Association); Pamela J. MacAdams (Certified Specialist in Family Relations Law, Ohio State Bar Association); Christopher Michael DeVito;—Michael A. Partlow.
Civil Trial Practice with Emphasis on Family Law, Juvenile Law, Adoption, Custody, Business Litigation and Commercial Litigation.
See Professional Biographies, CLEVELAND, OHIO

Morgenstern, Conrad J., (BV) '24 '49 C&L.930 A.B., LL.B. U.S. Trustee (Region 9)
Morgenstern, Marc H., (AV) '50 '75 C.976 B.A. L.94 J.D. [Kahn K.]
Morgenstern-Clarren, Pat E. '52 '77 C.477 A.B. L.930 J.D. 201 Superior Ave.
Morhard, Albert J., (AV) '29 '56 C.930 B.A. L.188 J.D. [🄰 Rhoa,F.&R.]
Moriarty, Matthew P., (AV) '55 '81 C.276 A.B. L.930 J.D. [Tucker E.&W.]
Moriarty, Richard J., (AV) '21 '49 C.363 B.B.A. L.1003 J.D. [Moriarty&J.]

Moriarty & Jaros, P.L.L., (AV)
30000 Chagrin Boulevard, Suite 200, 44124
Telephone: 216-360-2124 Telecopier: 216-360-2199
Email: info@moriartyjaros.com URL: http://www.moriartyjaros.com
Members of Firm: Richard J. Moriarty; Stanley T. Jaros; Jeffrey J. Higerd; Harry L. Arthur; David R. Riley. Of Counsel: Edgar H. Boles.
General Civil Practice. Corporate, Probate, Real Estate, Administrative, Taxation Law. Estate Planning. Litigation.
See Professional Biographies, CLEVELAND, OHIO

Morice, Craig J. '64 '95 C.734 B.A. L.1003 J.D. [Ⓐ Koblentz&K.]
Morley, Ryan J. '76 '01 C.473 B.A. L.1252 J.D. [Ⓐ Buckingham,D.&B.]
Moroney, John Kevin '53 '80 2639 Wooster Rd., Ste. 1
Moroscak, Richard J. '38 '70 C.363 B.S. L.1003 J.D. P.O. Box 24635
Morrical, Glenn E., (AV) '52 '77 C.608 B.A. L.309 J.D. [Tucker E.&W.]
Morris, Melissa A. '— '00 C.473 B.A. L.851 J.D. 1300 East Ninth Street, 14th Floor
Morris, R. Crawford, (AV) '16 '41 C.674 B.A. L.309 LL.B. 925 Euclid Ave.‡
Morrison, Donald W., (AV) '26 '50 C.911 B.S. L.813 LL.B. 925 Euclid Avenue
Morrison, Harvey S., (BV) '37 '62 C.608 B.Sc. L.477 J.D. 75 Public Sq. Bldg.
Morrison, Paul C., (AV) '39 '64 C.25 B.A. L.930 J.D. [Millisor&N.]
Morriss, Andrew P. '60 '85 C.674 A.B. L.846 J.D.
(adm. in TX; not adm. in OH) 11075 E. Blvd.
Morscher, Roy C. '66 '92 C.930 B.A. L.1003 J.D. [Morscher&S.]
Morscher & Straka 11711 Lorain Ave.
Morse, Andrew R. '51 '78 C&L.930 B.A., J.D. Ohio Awning & Manufacturing Co.
Morse, Stephen S. '47 '75 C.473 B.A. L.161 J.D. 1810 West 25th
Morsek, Leslie A. '76 '01 C.473 B.S. L.8 J.D. [Ⓐ Squire,S.&D.]
Morton, J. Alex '48 '75 C&L.930 B.A., J.D. 2000 Auburn Drive, Ste. 200
Moscarino, George J., (AV) '— '58 C.610 A.B. L.930 LL.B. [Ⓒ Jones D.]
Moscarino, George M., (AV) '58 '83 C.207 B.A. L.930 J.D. [Moscarino&T.]

Moscarino & Treu, L.L.P., (AV)
The Hanna Building, 1422 Euclid Avenue, Suite 630, 44115
Telephone: 216-621-1000 Fax: 216-622-1556
Email: gmoscarino@mosctreu.com URL: http://www.lawyers.com/moscarino&treu
George M. Moscarino; Kris H. Treu; Michael J. Bertsch; William H. Falin;—Edward S. Jerse; Patricia Casey Cuthbertson; John T. Bulloch; Robert L. Austria; Sean M. Sweeney; Michael W. Matile; Carol J. Moskowitz; Kathleen E. Gee; Mary E. White; Seamus J. McMahon.
General Civil Trial and Appellate Practice. Civil Litigation in all Courts. Complex Litigation, Medical Legal, Product Liability, Business, Banking and Commercial Litigation, Personal Injury and Employment Litigation, White Collar Criminal Defense.
See Professional Biographies, CLEVELAND, OHIO

Moscioni, Anna L. '— '00 C.97 B.A. L.930 J.D. [Ⓐ Jones D.]
Moser, Barbara J., (BV) '56 '82 C.392 B.A. L.608 J.D. 815 Superior Road
Moser, Christina J. '73 '98 C.610 B.S. L.1117 J.D. [Ⓐ Baker&H.]
Moses, Kimberly '58 '85 C.856 B.A. L.1003 J.D. [Calfee,H.&G.]
Mosesson, Bernard, (Co., L.P.A.), (BV) '19 '50 C.473 B.A. L.1003 J.D. 1370 Ontario
Mosher, Louise H., (BV) '42 '74 C.381 B.A. L.1003 J.D. 1370 Ontario St.
Mosier, Eric H. '— '97 C.309 A.B. L.188 J.D. [Ⓐ Jones D.]
Mosinski, Jos. A. '08 '42 C.363 B.S. L.161 J.D. [Mosinski&M.]
Mosinski & Moss 6400 Fordham Dr.
Moskowitz, Carol J. '61 '02 C.477 B.S.N. L.989 J.D. [Ⓐ Moscarino&T.]
Moskowitz, Jan S., (BV) '41 '68 C.473 B.S. L.1003 J.D. 1703 Brookpark Rd.
Moskowitz, Leah '60 '86 C.597 B.A. L.309 J.D.
Asst. Legal Coun., Cleveland State Univ.
Moskowitz, Suzann R. '77 '04 C.188 B.S. L.813 J.D. [Ⓐ Ulmer&B.]
Moss, Frank, (AV) '27 '51 C&L.178 B.A., LL.B. [Ⓒ Waxman B.]
Moss, James E., (CV) '64 '93 C.473 B.A. L.1003 J.D. 1200 Ontario St.
Moss, Jerald Lee, (BV) '56 '83 C.161 B.A. L.1003 J.D. 2806 Payne Ave.
Moss, Karen Gabriel '62 '89 C.473 B.A. L.146 J.D. [Ⓐ Rosner&Assoc.]
Moss, Ralph J. '24 '53 C.363 B.S.S. L.1003 J.D. [Mosinski&M.]
Moss, Steven M. '63 '91 C.354 B.S. L.161 J.D. [Kahn K.]
Mott, Cassandra G. '— '99 C.607 B.A. L.608 J.D. [Ⓐ Jones D.]
Motta, Patricia A. '70 '99 C.473 B.A. L.436 J.D.
(adm. in WI; not adm. in OH) Amer. Greetings Corp.
Mottl, Ronald M., (BV) '34 '57 C&L.602 B.S., LL.B. 2525 Brookpark Road
Mountcastle, Colleen A. '— '98 C.201 B.A. L.930 J.D. [Ⓐ Gallagher S.]
Mountcastle, Jennifer Mingus '75 '00 C.97 B.A. L.989 J.D. [Ⓐ Thompson H.]
Mounts, Mia M. '73 '98 C&L.8 B.A., J.D. [Walter&H.]
Movius, David T. '73 '98 C.678 B.A. L.30 J.D. [Ⓐ McDonald H.]
Mowls, Robert L. '45 '74 C&L.608 B.A., J.D. One Erieview Plaza, Suite 500
Moy, Philip J., Jr., (BV) '54 '84 C.197 A.B. L.273 J.D.
[Fay,S.F.M.&M.] (See Pat. Sect.)
Moyar, Bert W., (AV) '41 '65 C.665 B.A. L.477 J.D. Pres., Moyar Enterprises Inc.
Moyar, David W. '67 '94 C&L.976 B.A., J.D.
(adm. in CT; not adm. in OH) Pres., MEI Develop. Co.
Mozola, John M. '49 '77 C.608 B.S.B.A. L.201 J.D. BP America, Inc.
Mrohaly, Clayton J. '24 '49 C.659 B.S. L.930 LL.B. 30014 Winsor
Mueller, Wally '61 '90 C.150 B.A. L.209 J.D.
Assoc. Coun., Labor & Employment Law, GE Consumer and Industrial
Mugnano, John A. '69 '01 C.473 B.S. L.989 J.D. [Ⓐ Porter W.M.&A.]
Mulac, Carol A. '60 '86 C.339 B.A. L.930 J.D.
Asst. Gen. Coun., Parker-Hannifin Corp.
Mulcahy, Michael T. '51 '76 C.97 B.S. L.1003 J.D. [Ⓐ Calfee,H.&G.]
Mull, Donald P., Co. (L.P.A.) '26 '52 C.608 B.S. L.896 J.D. 614 Superior Ave., N.W.
Mull, W. Clifford '78 '05 C.210 B.A. L.124 J.D. [Ⓐ Walter&H.]
Mulligan, John T., (AV) '46 '74 C.602 A.B. L.930 J.D. [McDonald H.]
Mullin, Gregory K. '61 '86 C.97 B.S. L.1003 J.D. Asst. Pub. Def.
Mulvihill, Dennis P. '66 '94 C.385 B.A. L.1003 J.D. [Lowe E.W.&M.]
Mumford, Michael E. '— '01 C&L.124 B.A., J.D. [Ⓐ Baker&H.]
Muniak, William J., (BV) '67 '92 C.97 B.L.S. L.1003 J.D. [Ⓐ Mansour,G.G.&M.]
Muñoz-Hurwitz, Amy Margaret '69 '93 C.911 B.S. L.659 J.D. West Grp.
Munson, Adam D. '— '01 C.201 B.A. L.228 J.D. [Ⓐ Jones D.]
Mural, Walter V. '19 '50 C.381 B.S. L.1003 J.D. 10534 Tanger Tr.

Murman & Associates
(See Lakewood)

Murnane, Colleen C. '67 '95 C.93 B.A. L.608 J.D. [Frantz W.]
Murner, Barry Ronald '69 '98 C.150 L.989 [Ⓐ Janik&D.]
Murphy, Cynthia S. '60 '88 C.277 B.M.E. L.1003 J.D.
[Renner,O.B.&S.] (See Pat. Sect.)
Murphy, Dennis L., (AV) '— '91 C.1113 B.A. L.930 J.D. [Jones D.]
Murphy, Donald Richard '38 '72 C.943 B.A. L.564 J.D. Civil Rights Comm.
Murphy, James P., (AVⓉ) '44 '69 C.602 A.B. L.477 J.D.
[Squire,S.&D.] (⊙Wash., DC)
Murphy, John F. '49 '80 C.392 B.S. L.1003 J.D. [J.F.Murphy]
Murphy, John Martin '70 '96 C.679 B.A. L.1187 J.D. [Kelley&F.]
Murphy, John T., (BV) '— '90 C.475 B.S. L.1003 J.D. [Gallagher S.]
Murphy, Martin J., (AV) '— '63 C.363 B.S.S. L.930 LL.B. [Ⓒ Davis&Y.]
Murphy, Matthew B. '73 '02 C.161 B.A. L.1003 J.D. [Ⓐ McCarthy,L.C.&L.]
Murphy, Patrick J., (AV) '49 '74 C.884 A.B. L.930 J.D. [Bonezzi S.M.&P.]
Murphy, Rebecca S. '55 '82 C.970 B.A. L.1003 J.D. 7055 Engle Rd.
Murphy, Thomas O., (AV) '23 '50 C.385 A.B. L.930 LL.B.
Dir. of Claims & Litig., Univ. Hospitals of Cleveland
Murphy, John F., Inc., L.P.A. 6000 Freedom Square Dr.
Murray, Andrew J. '72 '98 C&L.608 B.S., J.D. [Ⓐ Baker&H.]
Murray, Brian M. '74 '99 C&L.930 B.A., J.D. [Ⓐ Calfee,H.&G.]
Murray, David J., (BV) '29 '57 C.363 B.B.A. L.1003 LL.B. 14701 Detroit Ave.
Murray, J. Michael, (AV) '50 '76 C.602 B.A. L.1003 J.D. [Berkman,G.M.&D.]
Murray, Jan E. '52 '78 C.882 B.A. L.124 J.D. [Squire,S.&D.]
Murray, Patrick J. '56 '89 C&L.930 B.S., J.D. BP Amer. Inc.
Murray, Peter Allen, (BV) '59 '84 C.970 B.A. L.1003 J.D. 1496 Arthur Ave.
Murtaugh, John P., (AV) '52 '78 C.602 B.A. L.477 J.D. [Pearne&G.] (See Pat. Sect.)
Murway, Carl A., (AV) '58 '83 C.604 B.A. L.966 J.D. [Taft,S.&H.]
Musallam, Samer M. '77 '04 C.025 B.A. L.124 J.D. [Ⓐ Thompson H.]
Musca, Anthony J. '33 '59 C.363 B.S.S. L.930 LL.B. 1300 E. 9th St.
Muscarella, Lawrence G., (AV) '58 '83 C.475 B.A. L.851 J.D.
Assoc. Gen. Coun., Electrolux North America
Musick, Douglas S., (AV) '67 '92 C.477 B.A. L.930 J.D. [Roetzel&A.]
Muskovitz, Susannah, (AV) '59 '84 C.012 A.B. L.930 J.D. [Faulkner,M.&P.]
Musnuff, Basil J., (AV) '64 '89 C.311 B.A. L.188 J.D. [Roetzel&A.]
Muto, Andrea M. '66 '95 C.608 L.1003 J.D. 55 Public Sq.‡
Myer, John David '73 '01 C.604 B.A. L.477 J.D. [Ⓐ Thompson H.]
Myers, James P. '76 '02 C.896 B.A. L.124 J.D. [Ⓐ Roetzel&A.]
Myers, Kenneth D., (BV) '58 '91 C.597 B.A. L.161 J.D. 75 Public Sq., Ste. 1300
Myerson, Anita L. '— '81 C.293 B.A. L.124 J.D. Legal Aid Soc. of Cleveland
Myles, Tina L. '68 '96 C.473 B.A. L.930 J.D. Asst. City Dir.
Nader, Joyce E. '29 '56 C.930 B.S. L.1003 J.D. 5981 North View Dr.
Naeem, Tariq Mahmood '71 '00 C.473 B.A. L.124 J.D. [Ⓐ Tucker E.&W.]
Naffah, Eli Thomas, (BV) '23 '51 C.757 B.S. L.128 J.D. [E.T.Naffah]
Naffah, Eli Thomas, Co., L.P.A., (BV) 7533 Amber Ln.
Naftzinger, David J., (AV) '48 '73 C.659 B.S. L.228 J.D. [Thompson H.]
Nagel, Beth A. '— '97 C.8 B.S.N. L.1003 J.D. [Ⓐ Buckingham,D.&B.]
Nager, David E., (BV) '63 '90 C.381 B.A. L.1003 J.D. 425 Lakeside.
Nagorney, Frank P., (AV) '50 '75 C.930 B.S. L.569 J.D. [Cowden,H.N.&L.]
Nagy, Joseph J. '32 '60 C.318 B.A. L.1003 LL.B. 19120 Detroit Rd.
Nahra, Joseph J. '27 '52 C.930 B.A. L.309 J.D. Ret. Ct. of App. J.‡
Nam, Brian K. '75 '04 C.30 B.A. L.608 J.D. [Ⓐ Buckingham,D.&B.]
Nance, Frederick R., (AV) '53 '78 C.309 B.A. L.477 J.D. [Squire,S.&D.]
Nandi, Melissa J. '— '98 C.712 B.A. L.982 J.D. [Ⓐ Jones D.]
Nardone, Vincent J., (BV) '70 '96 C.229 B.S. L.179 J.D.
[Ⓐ McDonald H.] (⊙Columbus)
Nash, Carl, (BV) '31 '60 C.610 B.S. L.1003 J.D. [Nash&N.]
Nash, David E., (AV) '55 '81 C.896 B.A. L.228 J.D. [Thompson H.]
Nash, Jean K., (BV) '32 '77 C.610 B.S.Ed. L.1003 J.D. [Nash&N.]
Nash, Joel A. '61 '93 4325 Mayfield Rd.
Nash & Nash, (BV) 683 Parkside Blvd
Naso, Carmen '53 '78 C.381 B.A. L.989 J.D. [Cochran,N.&P.]
Natale, Andrew J., (AV) '64 '89 C.201 B.A. L.150 J.D. [Frantz W.]

Naticchia, A. Dale '52 '86 C.363 B.A. L.989 J.D.
4141 Rockside Road, Suite 230, 44131
Telephone: 216-520-5297 Fax: 216-642-5355
Email: dale@naticchia.com URL: http://www.naticchialaw.com
Driving While Intoxicated, Traffic Violations, Juvenile Law, Drivers License Suspension, DUI, Estate Planning, Wills and Probate Law, Contested Wills, Felonies and Collections.
See Professional Biographies, CLEVELAND, OHIO

Naughton, John D. '28 '57 C.608 B.A. L.1003 J.D. David N. Myers Coll.
Naughton, Thomas F., (BV) '— '94 C.608 B.A. L.213 J.D. [Ⓐ Gallagher S.] ⊙
Nauman, Timothy E. '58 '83
C.602 B.S.C.E. L.201 J.D. [Fay,S.F.M.&M.] (See Pat. Sect.)
Nave, Michele Garrick, (BV) '48 '82 C.392 B.S. L.1003 J.D. 3374 Rumson Road
Naylor, John L., Jr., (AV) '27 '51 C.894 A.B. L.477 J.D. [Calfee,H.&G.] ‡
Nazette, Adam R. '— '03 C.473 B.S. L.930 J.D. [Ⓐ Thompson H.]
Neal, John N. '— '02 C.473 B.A. L.124 J.D. [Ⓐ Gallagher S.]
Nealis, Peter '75 '00 C.164 B.A. L.608 J.D. [Ⓐ Kahn K.]
Neary, Douglas A., (AV) '60 '85 C.477 B.A. L.94 J.D. [Calfee,H.&G.]
Nee, Matthew M. '— '00 C.867 B.A. L.607 J.D. [Ⓐ Janik&D.]
Neel, David W., (AV) '58 '86 C.385 B.A. L.989 J.D. [Climaco,L.P.W.&G.]
Negrelli, William E., (BV) '36 '66 C.363 B.S. L.1003 J.D. 1360 W. 9th St. Ste 420
Neill, Ronald H., (AV) '44 '69 C.970 B.A. L.288 J.D. [Calfee,H.&G.]
Nelson, Alison L. '61 '88 C.893 B.A. L.124 J.D. 2163 E. 22nd Street
Nelson, Delos T. '19 '48 C&L.930 A.B., J.D. 19901 Van Aken Blvd.
Nelson, Douglas M., II '67 '96 C.645 B.S. L.1003 J.D. [Ⓐ Spieth,B.M.&N.]
Nelson, George A., (AV) '26 '52 C.930 B.B.A. L.161 J.D. [Sanislo&Assoc.] ‡
Nelson, Robert B., (AV) '35 '61 C&L.477 A.B., J.D. 901 Lakeside Ave.‡
Nelson, Robert M., (AV) '46 '71 C.363 B.S. L.930 J.D. [Cavitch,F.D.&F.]
Nemer, Laura Bancroft '— '96 C.393 B.A. L.424 J.D. [Ⓐ Thompson H.]
Nemeth, Laura D. '63 '89 C&L.608 B.S.B.A., J.D. [Squire,S.&D.]
Nemeth, Richard H. '55 '84 C.124 B.A. L.989 J.D. [Nemeth&Assoc.]
Nemeth & Associates Co., L.P.A. 526 Superior Avenue N.E., Suite 410
Nerren, Guy V., (BV) '44 '71 C.363 B.S.B.A. L.1003 J.D. 2401 Superior Viaduct
Neth, Spencer '39 '64 C.473 A.B. L.309 LL.B.
Prof. of Law, Case Western Reserve Law Sch.
Neubecker, Mark Forrest '52 '78 C.930 B.A. L.608 J.D. Field Atty., N.L.R.B.
Neuger, Charles J. '26 '54 C.608 B.S.B.A. L.1003 LL.B. Leader Bldg.
Neumann, David M. '67 '97 [Ⓐ Benesch,F.C.&A.]
Neville, John A., (AV) '42 '68 C.473 B.S. L.1003 J.D. [Ⓐ Reminger&R.]
Nevins, Patrick A. '46 '77 C.46 B.S.E.E. L.209 J.D.
(adm. in IL; not adm. in OH) Prin., Towers & Perrin
Newborn, Karen B., (AV) '44 '76 C.289 B.A. L.161 J.D. [Baker&H.]
Newell, Sterling, Jr., (AV) '21 '49 C.311 B.S. L.569 LL.B. [Spieth,B.M.&N.]
Newman, John M., Jr., (AV) '— '70 C.276 B.A. L.309 J.D. [Jones D.]
Neylon, Benjamin J. '71 '99 C.610 L.1003 J.D. [Ⓐ F.P.Ramos&Assoc.]
Nicastro, Deborah J. '54 '79 C.161 B.A. L.930 J.D. Mun. J.
Nicholas, Joseph F., Jr. '61 '87 C.201 B.A. L.1003 J.D. [Mazanec,R.&R.]
Nicholson, Gary L., (BV) '— '84 C.608 B.A. L.851 J.D. [Gallagher S.]

Nicola, Gudbranson & Cooper, LLC, (AV)
Republic Building, Suite 1400, 25 W. Prospect Avenue, 44115-1048
Telephone: 216-621-7227 FAX: 216-621-3999 URL: http://www.nicola.com
URL: http://www.nicolalaw.com
K. V. Nicola (1906-1994). Members of Firm: Robert N. Gudbranson; Richard A. Cooper; John D. Sayre; Timothy D. Carnahan; Matthew T. Fitzsimmons; L. James Juliano, Jr.; James H. Grove; Richard G. Witkowski. Associates: Michael E. Cicero; Ronald C. Yingling; James P. Bauer; Nicholas

(This Listing Continued)

Nicola, Gudbranson & Cooper, LLC (Continued)

J. Dertouzos; Brenda L. Wolff; Becky M. Scheiman. Of Counsel: Vincent A. Feudo; Anthony R. Troia; James D. Roseman; James R. Chriszt; Timothy L. McGarry; Arthur L. (Tim) Clements, III.
Corporations, Transactions, Taxation, Real Estate, Estate Planning, Probate and Trusts, Business and Commercial Litigation and Appeals, Employment Law, Municipal Law, School Law, Products Liability, Health Care Law, Real Estate Ad Valorem Tax Litigation.
References: National City Bank; Key Bank, N.A.

See Professional Biographies, CLEVELAND, OHIO

Nicols, Howard J.C., (AV) '56 '81 C.1044 B.A. L.188 J.D. [Squire,S.&D.]
Nicosia, Crystal L. '79 '03 C.1529 B.A. L.201 J.D. [Ⓐ Janik&D.]
Niehaus, Bernard H., (AV) '30 '55 C.363 B.S.S. L.930 LL.B. [Frantz W.]
Niehaus, James B., (AV) '58 '83 C&L.602 B.A., J.D. [Frantz W.]
Niehaus, Stephanie E. '77 '02 C.276 B.A. L.602 J.D. [Ⓐ Squire,S.&D.]
Niermann, Dennis J., (BV) '46 '81 C.363 B.A. L.161 J.D. [D.J.Niermann]
Niermann, Dennis J., Co., LPA, (BV) 4070 Mayfield Road
Nigro, Suzanne M., (AV) '40 '83 C.876 B.A. L.1003 J.D.
123 W. Prospect Ave., Van Sweringen Arcade
Niklas, Christian Eric '71 '96 C.381 B.A. L.851 J.D. [Ⓐ Shapiro&F.]
Nimrick, Sandra L. '63 '89
C.103 A.B. L.309 J.D. Asst. Atty. Gen., Atty. Gen. Jim Petro Off.
Nimrod, Alfred F. '28 '57 C.381 B.A. L.930 LL.B. P.O. Box 10051
Ninneman, Sheila M. '59 '89 C.201 B.A. L.1003 J.D. [Ⓐ Benesch,F.C.&A.]
Nischwitz, Jeffrey L., (AV) '59 '84 C.607 B.S. L.608 J.D. CBIZ, Inc.‡
Nissen, Walter I., Sr. '17 '55 C.650 B.S. L.1003 LL.B. 6659 Pearl Rd.
Nissenbaum, Robert J. '52 '80 C.273 B.A. L.1048 J.D.
(adm. in MA; not adm. in OH) Assoc. Prof. of Law, Cleveland State Univ.
Nitschke, Kathleen '— '01 C.363 B.S. L.213 J.D. [Ⓐ Giffen&K.]
Nittskoff, David '45 '70 C.381 B.A. L.930 J.D. [Nittskoff]
Nittskoff Law Firm 4491 Mayfield Rd.
Noall, Nancy A., (AV) '57 '81 C.363 B.A. L.930 J.D. [Walter&H.]
Nobil, Steven M., (AV) '47 '72 C.62 B.A. L.608 J.D. [Millisor&N.]
Nobili, David L., (AV) '44 '71 C.473 B.S. L.1003 J.D. 5579 Pearl Rd., Ste. 203
Noble, David D., (AV) '41 '67 C.970 B.A. L.228 LL.B. [Ⓒ Walter&H.]
Noble, Josephine S. '— '04 C.309 A.B. L.107 J.D. [Ⓐ Jones D.]
Noble, Scott A. '63 '88 C.201 B.S. L.276 J.D. 5507 Avion Park Dr.
Nolan, John M. '58 '87 C.62 B.A. L.930 J.D. 3200 Nat. City Ctr.
Nolan, Timothy J., (AV) '— '67 C.610 B.B.A. L.608 J.D. [Calfee,H.&G.]
Nolfi, Gregory M., (AV) '50 '77 C.980 B.S. L.851 J.D. [Hahn L.&P.]
Norchi, Kevin M., (AV) '59 '86 C.262 A.B. L.930 J.D. [Norchi,B.&F.]

Norchi, Barrett & Forbes LLC, (AV) BB
Commerce Park IV, 23240 Chagrin Boulevard, Suite 600, 44122
Telephone: 216-514-9500 Fax: 216-514-4304
Email: kmn@norchilaw.com
Kevin M. Norchi; Lisa M. Barrett; Steven J. Forbes; Michael L. Golding; Iverson Matthew Jackson.
Medical Negligence Defense, Health Care Litigation, Employment Law, Insurance Defense.
REPRESENTATIVE CLIENTS: University Hospital Health Systems; Summa Health Systems; St. Paul Insurance Co.; The Doctors Company; ACE USA Insurance Co.; U.S. Liability Insurance Co.; National Guardian Risk Retention; Case Western Reserve University; Laurelwood Hospitals & Counseling Centers; Philadelphia Insurance Companies.

See Professional Biographies, CLEVELAND, OHIO

Norcross, Scott A. '74 '01 C.472 B.A. L.851 J.D. [Ⓐ Ziegler,M.&M.]
Norfus, Natalie E. '80 '04 C.30 B.A. L.273 J.D. [Ⓐ Squire,S.&D.]
Norman, Dennis O., (BV) '42 '69 C&L.8 B.S., J.D. 11216 Lake Ave.
Norman, Forrest A., (AV) '29 '54 C&L.930 B.B.A., J.D. 1501 Euclid Avenue‡
Norman, Forrest A., III, (AV) '— '92 C&L.930 B.A., J.D. [Gallagher S.]
Norman, Matthew Tyler '73 '99 C.97 B.S. L.1003 J.D. City Pros. Off.
Normington, Dale A. '44 '69 C&L.8 B.A., J.D.
Assoc. Gen. Coun., Complex Litig., The Sherwin-Williams Co.
Norton, Margaret M. '47 '83 C.446 B.A. L.1003 J.D. 8952 Spring Crest Dr.
Norton, Maura '65 '91 C.363 B.A. L.930 J.D. [Ⓐ Armstrong,M.D.&Z.]
Norton, Patrick J. '— '98 C.597 B.S. L.930 J.D. [Ⓐ Jones D.]
Norton, Susan Linda '49 '00 C.33 B.A. L.930 J.D. City of Cleveland, Dept. of Law
Novak, Jenifer E. '70 '99 C.381 B.A. L.1003 J.D. [Ⓐ Frantz W.]
Novak, William J., (AV) '49 '73 C&L.94 B.S.B.A., J.D. [Novak,R.P.&S.]

Novak, Robenalt, Pavlik & Scharf, LLP, (AV)
Skylight Office Tower, Tower City Center, 1660 West Second Street, Suite 950, 44113-1498
Telephone: 216-781-8700 Facsimile: 216-781-9227 URL: http://www.ohiomedicalmalpractice.com
Email: nrps@nrpslaw.com URL: http://www.ohiodebtrelief.com
Partners: William J. Novak; Thomas D. Robenalt; Thomas C. Pavlik; Scott H. Scharf;—Colin P. Sammon; Shelly R. LaSalvia.
Medical Malpractice, Birth Trauma, Automobile Accident, Personal Injury, FELA, Products Liability, Debtor-Creditor Law, Personal and Business Bankruptcy and Workouts, Business Law, Real Estate, General and Civil Trial Practice, Litigation.

See Professional Biographies, CLEVELAND, OHIO

November, Raymond R., (BV) '35 '62 C&L.930 B.B.A., J.D. 470 Lynden Dr.
Novinc, Raymond C. '49 '76 C.610 A.B. L.1003 J.D. 1st Amer. Midwest Exch.
Novotney, George C., (BV) '50 '81 C.381 B.Arch. L.1003 J.D. [Potts&N.]
Nowak, Dale A., (AV) '53 '80 C.161 B.A. L.1003 J.D. [Buckingham,D.&B.]
Nowak, Stephen M. '77 '04 C.201 B.A. L.989 J.D. [Ⓐ Meyers,R.F.&L.]
Nuccio, Anthony J., (BV) '29 '56 C.251 B.B.A. L.930 LL.B. [A.J.Nuccio]
Nuccio, Anthony J., L.P.A., (BV)
The Standard Building, 1370 Ontario Street-Suite #950
Nudelman, Marc S. '60 '90 C.477 B.A. L.930 J.D. Ernst & Young
Nugent, Donald C. '48 '74 C.973 A.B. L.1003 J.D. U.S. Dist. J.
Nurenberg, Marshall I., (AV) '25 '53 C&L.930 B.B.A., LL.B. [Nurenberg,P.H.&M.]

Nurenberg, Plevin, Heller & McCarthy Co., L.P.A., (AV) BB
1370 Ontario Street Suite 100, 44113-1792
Telephone: 216-621-2300; Toll Free: 1-800-562-7438 Fax: 216-771-2242
Email: nphm@nphm.com URL: http://www.nphm.com
A. H. Dudnik (1905-1963); S. F. Komito (1902-1984); Marshall I. Nurenberg (Retired); Maurice L. Heller (Retired); John J. McCarthy (Retired); Thomas Mester; Harlan M. Gordon; David M. Paris; James R. Lebovitz; William S. Jacobson; Jeffrey A. Leikin; Ellen M. McCarthy; Kathleen J. St. John; Jonathan D. Mester;—Robert S. Zeller; Brenda M. Johnson; Andrew R. Young.
Plaintiff Personal Injury and Wrongful Death Litigation, Airplane Crash Litigation, Aviation Litigation, Civil Litigation, Commercial Litigation, Construction Accidents, Medical and Hospital Negligence, Product Liability, Premises Liability, Railroad Accidents and Injuries, FELA, Class Action Litigation, Appellate Practice, Vehicular Accident Law.
Reference: Society Key Corp.

See Professional Biographies, CLEVELAND, OHIO

Nurgaliyeva, Aidana K. '— '04 C.308 B.A. L.107 J.D. [Ⓐ Jones D.]
Nussle, Herbert L. '— '94 C.608 B.A. L.1003 J.D. [Keis G.]
Nwabara, Chisara Sandra '53 '85 C.136 B.S. L.930 J.D. [C.S.Nwabara]
Nwabara, Chisara Sandra, L.P.A. 3347 Central Avenue
Nyerges, George L. '25 '51 C.930 B.S. L.1003 LL.B. United Off. Bldg.
Nyerges, Louis S. '24 '55 C.124 L.1003 J.D. 11602 Edgewater Drive
Nykulak, Nick A. '76 '03 C.161 B.A. L.989 J.D. [Ⓐ Ross,B.&S.]
Oakar, James L., (AV) '36 '62 C.363 B.B.A. L.276 J.D. 1000 W. Wallings Rd.
Oakley, David G. '70 '97 C.7 B.A. L.930 J.D. [Ⓐ Kramer&Assoc.]
Oakley, Eric M., (AV) '42 '67 C.309 A.B. L.893 LL.B.
4900 Society Ctr., 127 Public Sq.
O'Bell, Frank G. '12 '36 L.607 J.D. Ret. Mun. J.
Oberdick, William J. '41 '76 C.743 B.A. L.262 J.D.
(adm. in NY; not adm. in OH) Dept. of Jus.
Oberdorff, Marc L., (AV) '53 '80 C.674 A.B. L.276 J.D. [Ⓒ Calfee,H.&G.]
Obert, Lisa M., (BV) '62 '87 C.473 B.A. L.1003 J.D. 6500 Creekside Tr.
Oblander, R. Jason '— '00 C.375 B.A. L.893 J.D. [Ⓐ Jones D.]
Obral, Mark Joseph '56 '84 C&L.161 B.A., J.D. [Obral&M.&Assoc.]

Obral & Mays & Associates
Standard Building, 1370 Ontario Street, 44113
Telephone: 216-696-4421 Fax: 216-696-3228
Email: tmays@lawmjo.com
Mark Joseph Obral; Thomas Charles Mays.
Personal Injury, Medical Malpractice, Automobile Accidents, Workers Compensation, Wrongful Death, Truck Accidents, Nursing Home Abuse, Products Liability, Dog Bites, Slip and Fall, Criminal Law.

See Professional Biographies, CLEVELAND, OHIO

O'Brien, Cheryl A., (BV) '59 '89 C.876 B.S.N. L.1003 J.D. [Roetzel&A.]
O'Brien, Daniel P. '59 '84 C.20 B.A. L.930 J.D. [Millisor&N.]
O'Brien, Gregory E., (AV) '60 '86 C.1260 B.A. L.608 J.D. [Weston H.]
O'Brien, Gregory J. '66 '94 C.851 B.B.A. L.251 J.D. [Taft,S.&H.]
O'Brien, Mark S. '65 '00 C.608 B.A. L.989 J.D. [Ⓐ Kohrman J.&K.]
O'Brien, Michael J., (AV) '56 '83 C.321 B.A. L.1003 J.D. [Perry&O.]
O'Brien, Timothy F., (AV) '42 '69
C.128 A.B. L.1003 J.D. 700 West St. Clair Avenue, Suite 210
O'Brien, William J. '33 '80 C&L.161 B.B.A., J.D. [W.J.O'Brien]
O'Brien, William J. Co., L.P.A. 3401 Enterprise Pkwy.
Obringer, Timothy R. '65 '91 C.608 B.A. L.851 J.D. [Ⓐ Mazanec,R.&R.]
O'Bryan, Keely J. '73 '99 C.93 B.a. L.1194 J.D. [Ⓐ Thompson H.]
O'Bryan, Stephen M., (AV) '44 '69 C.97 B.A. L.930 J.D. [Taft,S.&H.]
Ochocki, Gregory J. '67 '94 C.712 B.S. L.1003 J.D. Rent-Way, Inc.
Ockington, William J., (AV) '40 '74
C.608 B.S.B.A. L.1003 J.D. 29325 Chagrin Boulevard
Ockner, Benjamin J., (BV) '60 '86 C.473 A.B. L.276 J.D. [Berns,O.&G.]
O'Connell, Martin James '53 '03
C.150 B.A. L.989 J.D. [Ⓐ Mazanec,R.&R.] (©Shaker Heights)
O'Connell, Matthew C., (AV) '57 '83 C.966 B.A. L.930 J.D. [Sutter,O.&F.]
O'Connor, Bryan P. '66 '94 C.446 B.A. L.128 J.D. 526 Superior Ave. E.
O'Connor, Donald J., (AV) '29 '60 C.363 B.S. L.1003 J.D. 820 Rockefeller Building
O'Connor, Kevin T., (AV) '50 '77 C.276 B.S. L.1003 J.D. [Kohrman J.&K.]
O'Donnell, Michael P. '— '04 C.363 B.S.B.A. L.989 J.D. [Ⓐ Brouse M.]
O'Donnell, Patricia J., (AV) '48 '82 C.161 B.A. L.1003 J.D. [Baker&H.]
O'Donnell, Thomas P., (AV) '54 '84
C.150 B.B.A. L.1003 J.D. 3700 Northfield Road, Suite 11
O'Donnell, Thomas R. '— '96 C.363 B.A. L.1003 J.D. [Ⓐ Calfee,H.&G.]
Oehlenschlager, James E. '68 '01 C&L.8 B.S., J.D. [Ⓐ Curatolo S.] (Pat.)
O'Flaherty, Sharon L. '55 '82 C.97 B.S. L.930 J.D. Eaton Corp.
Ogle, Richard N., (AV) '36 '61 C.967 A.B. L.145 J.D. [Calfee,H.&G.] ‡

Ogne, Alberts & Stuart, P.C.
(See Troy, Michigan)

OH, James W. '— '99 C.930 B.A. L.1003 J.D. 1300 East Ninth Street, 14th Floor
O'Hearn, Timothy J. '— '84 C.150 B.S.M.E. L.8 J.D. [Jones D.] (See Pat. Sect.)
Ohly, Robert S. '60 '85 C.473 A.B. L.930 J.D. 4403 St. Clair Avenue
Oiffer, Michael C., (BVⓉ) '58 '85 C.102 B.A. L.1325 J.D.
(adm. in WA; not adm. in OH) V.P. & Sr. Coun., KeyBank Natl. Assn.
Okada, Ronald S. '60 '85 C.118 B.A. L.477 J.D. [Baker&H.]
O'Keefe, F. Ronald, (AV) '50 '77 C.276 A.B. L.1003 J.D. [Hahn L.&P.]
Okek, Ann Marie '74 '99 C.601 B.A. L.588 J.D.
(adm. in MD; not adm. in OH) U.S. Dept. of Justice, Antitrust Division
Oker, Michael R., (BV) '42 '71 C.381 B.S. L.930 J.D. Ameritech Ohio
Okun, Jill G., (AV) '58 '83 C.860 B.A. L.93 J.D. [Ⓒ Squire,S.&D.]
Olarczuk-Smith, Holly '— '00 C.645 B.A. L.989 J.D. [Ⓐ Gallagher S.]
Oldknow-Marshall, Sharon L. '59 '97 C.967 B.A. L.776 J.D. Asst. Pros. Atty.
O'Leary, Ronald Joseph '70 '97 C.473 B.A. L.124 J.D. City of Cleve., Dept. of Law
Olender, Robert J., (AV) '51 '76 C.264 B.A. L.1003 J.D. [Strachan,M.O.&R.]
Oliss, Philip M. '70 '96 C.608 B.A. L.150 J.D. [Ⓐ Squire,S.&D.]
Oliver, James P., (AV) '44 '69 C.97 B.S. L.150 J.D. [Squire,S.&D.]
Oliver, Randall C. '51 '79 C.8 B.A. L.1003 J.D. 15008 Lorain Ave., Ste. 6
Oliver, Solomon, Jr. '47 '73 C.970 B.A. L.569 J.D. U.S. Dist. J.
Ollinger, W. James, (AV) '43 '68 C.117 B.A. L.930 J.D. [Baker&H.]
O'Loughlin, Daniel J., (AV) '25 '51 C.363 B.S. L.477 LL.B. [Squire,S.&D.]
Olsavsky, Charles R., Jr., (AV) '56 '87 C.980 B.E. L.8 J.D. [Ⓒ Ulmer&B.]
Olson, Robert K. '68 '96 C.20 B.A. L.188 J.D. The Sherwin-Williams Co.
Olson, Russell A., (AV) '29 '54 C.210 A.B. L.930 J.D. 200 Public Sq., 35th Fl.‡
Olsztyn, Christopher E. '77 '04 C.477 B.A. L.930 J.D. [Ⓐ Weltman,W.&R.]
O'Malley, Anthony J., (AV) '58 '84 C.363 B.A. L.930 J.D. [Vorys,S.S.&P.]
O'Malley, Joseph P. '66 '92 C.363 B.A. L.1003 J.D. 2401 Superior Via
O'Malley, Kathleen McDonald '56 '82 C.385 A.B. L.930 J.D.
U.S. Dist. J., OH Dist. Ct. House Eastern Div.
O'Malley, Michael P. '54 '80 C.150 B.B.A. L.1003 J.D. [Grant&O.]
O'Malley, Patrick J. '69 '95 C.1082 B.S. L.1003 J.D. [Ⓐ Keis G.]
O'Malley, Thomas F., Jr., (AV) '58 '86 C.201 B.S. L.117 J.D. 2401 Superior Viaduct
Omerza, Raphael J. '67 '94 C.93 B.A. L.1194 J.D. [Ⓐ Squire,S.&D.]
Ondak, Robert C., Jr. '73 '98 C.1030 B.A. L.930 J.D. [Ⓐ Hurtuk&D.]
O'Neal, R. Michael, (AV) '48 '77 C.821 B.A. L.1003 J.D. 815 Superior Avenue
O'Neil, Colleen Moran '70 '96 C.363 B.A. L.1003 J.D. [Ⓐ Calfee,H.&G.]
O'Neil, John '65 '94 C.473 B.S. L.365 J.D. [Ⓐ Reminger&R.]
O'Neil, Michael W. '62 '94
C.712 B.B.A. L.1003 J.D. 820 Superior Avenue N.W., 10th Floor
O'Neill, Brian M., (AV) '61 '87 C.608 B.S. L.1003 J.D. [Ulmer&B.]
O'Neill, Kevin F., (AV) '55 '85 C.766 B.A. L.930 J.D. Cleveland Sch. of Law
O'Neill, Laura Elizabeth '75 '00 C.276 B.A. L.930 J.D. [Ⓐ Webster W.K.]
O'Neill, Mark, (AV) '25 '52 C&L.309 A.B., J.D. [Weston H.]
O'Neill, William J., (AV) '60 '85 C.1107 B.A. L.608 J.D. [McDonald H.]
O'Neill, William J., Jr. '33 '58 C.276 B.S.S. L.309 LL.B. U.S. Bkrptcy. J.
O'Neill, William M. '47 '80 C.610 B.S. L.1003 J.D. Asst. Atty. Gen.
Onusko, Thomas J., (AV) '52 '77 C.602 B.A. L.188 J.D. [Ⓒ Vorys,S.S.&P.]
Onysko, Peter, (BV) '20 '51 C&L.608 B.A., LL.B. 1208 Standard Bldg.

Opett, Edward J., (BV) '49 '75
C.229 B.A. L.161 J.D. Coun., Greater Cleveland Reg. Transit Auth.
Opincar, Scott N. '68 '94 C.8 B.A. L.1003 J.D. [McDonald H.]
Oppenheimer, David Arthur '69 '94 C.381 B.A. L.608 J.D. Atty. Gen. Off.
Opsincs, Katherine H. '79 '04 C.970 B.A. L.930 J.D. [Ⓐ Powers&G.]
Oreh, John Paul '59 '85 C.161 B.A. L.989 J.D. 925 Euclid Ave., Ste. 1995
Orkin, Louis H., (AV) '30 '54 C.610 L.94 J.D. 26600 George Zeiger Dr.
Orlando, Lisa '— '02 C.93 B.S. L.124 J.D. [Ⓐ Duvin,C.&H.]
Orloff, Jeffrey K. '63 '89 C.477 B.A. L.930 J.D. Intl. Mgmt. Grp.
Ornstein, Stanley E., (AV) '42 '68
C.604 A.B. L.145 J.D. C/O Tarolli, 1111 Leader Bldg. (Pat.)
Ornstein, Warren K., (AV) '28 '52 C.197 B.A. L.477 LL.B.
Assoc. Gen. Coun., Forest City Enterprises, Inc.
O'Rourke, Timothy J. '56 '95 C&L.790 B.S., J.D.
(adm. in SC; not adm. in OH)
Assoc. Gen. Coun., Electrolux North America (Legal Department)
Oroz, Helena J. '— '02 C.207 B.A. L.989 J.D. [Ⓐ Zashin&R.]
Orr, Michelle F. '65 '91
C.97 B.A. L.1003 J.D. V.P. & Assoc. Coun., KeyBank Natl. Assn.
Orris, Harry A. '45 '80 C.608 B.S. L.1003 J.D. Reg. Dir., U.S. Dept. of Education
Ortman, Bradley L. '69 '96 C.477 B.A. L.273 J.D. [Ⓐ Rosner&Assoc.]
Osborne, Frank R., (AV) '46 '73 C.363 A.B. L.1003 J.D. [Ⓒ Tucker E.&W.]
Oscar, Lawrence E., (AV) '56 '81 C.659 B.S. L.569 J.D. [Hahn L.&P.]
O'Shaughnessy, Lucy K. '64 '99 C.967 B.A. L.124 J.D. [Ⓐ McDonald H.]
O'Shaughnessy, Timothy J., (BV) '59 '85 C.930 B.S. L.1003 J.D. 1593 Beethoven Dr.
O'Shea, Michael J., (CV) '61 '87 C.473 B.A. L.851 J.D. [O'Shea&Assoc.]
O'Shea & Associates, Co., LPA, (CV) 323 Lakeside Ave., Ste. 450
O'Stafy, Stacey A. '— '99 C&L.851 B.A., J.D. [Ⓐ Strachan,M.O.&R.]
Ostrowski, Thomas W. '66 '93 C.107 B.A. L.1003 J.D. [Ulmer&B.]
Ostry, Randi Marie '61 '89 C.97 B.S. L.1003 J.D. 2300 BP Tower, 200 Public Square
Oswald, Suellen, (AV) '59 '90 C.650 B.A. L.930 J.D. [Duvin,C.&H.]
O'Toole, Charles J., (AV) '32 '64 C.363 B.S. L.1003 J.D. [Ⓒ Tucker E.&W.]
O'Toole, John K. '41 '67 C.999 B.A. L.1003 J.D. 1370 Ontario Street, Suite 1314
O'Toole, Thomas E., Law Offices of '53 '78 C.602 B.S. L.930 J.D.
2401 Superior Viaduct
Ott, Steven M., (AV) '55 '80 C.611 B.A. L.1003 J.D. [Ott&Assoc.]

Ott & Associates Co., L.P.A., (AV)
55 Public Square, Suite 1250, 44113
Telephone: 216-771-2600 Fax: 216-830-8939
Email: steven.ott@ottesq.com URL: http://www.lawyers.com/ottesq
Steven M. Ott.
Corporate Law, Real Estate, Condominium Law, Probate, Civil Litigation, Internet Law.
See Professional Biographies, CLEVELAND, OHIO

Otto, Donald L., (AV) '36 '64
C.350 B.S.M.E. L.273 LL.B. [Renner,O.B.&S.] (See Pat. Sect.)
Ousley, Bobette Smiley '50 '75 C&L.329 B.A., J.D. Cleveland Mun. Ct.
Overberger, Erik J. '73 '00
C.610 B.S.M.E. L.117 J.D. [Ⓐ Fay,S.F.M.&M.] (See Pat. Sect.)
Oviatt, Richard A., (AV) '42 '67 C.207 B.A. L.930 J.D. 1370 Ontario St.g.
Oviatt, Richard B. '13 '38 C.188 A.B. L.161 LL.B. 24600 Hazelmere St.
Owen, Robert B. '67 '00 C.318 B.A. L.989 J.D. [Ⓐ Taft,S.&H.]
Owendoff, Michael S. '— '96 C.201 B.S. L.161 J.D. [Ⓐ Jones D.]
Owendoff, Stephen P., (AV) '43 '69 C.381 B.A. L.276 J.D. [Hahn L.&P.]
Owens, Mark E. '68 '97 C.473 B.A. L.608 J.D. [Ⓐ Kahn K.]
Ozanne, Dominic L., (BV) '53 '79 C.94 B.A. L.309 J.D. 1635 E. 25th St.
Pace, Stanley Dan, (AV) '47 '75 C.207 B.A. L.851 J.D. [Spieth,B.M.&N.]
Pacernick, Craig P. '69 '94 C.477 B.A. L.1019 J.D.
(adm. in MA; not adm. in OH) Coun., TRW Inc. (Legal Department)
Packard, Kristina M. '73 '00 C.363 B.A. L.989 J.D. [Ⓐ McNeal,S.A.&B.]
Paffilas, Steven John '60 '86 C.259 B.A. L.989 J.D. U.S. Atty.'s Off.
Pagano, Joseph V. '70 '01 L.989 J.D. [Pagano,W.T.G.&L.]

Pagano, Wilson, Thomarios, Gillissie & Lenahan LLC
1370 Ontario Street Suite 1240, 44113
Telephone: 216-685-9940 Fax: 216-685-9942
Joseph V. Pagano; Rachel C. Wilson; Elizabeth A. Thomarios; Rebecca R. Gillissie; Christopher Richards Lenahan.
Criminal Law, Employment Defense, Personal Injury, Workers Compensation, Social Security Disability, Probate, Estate Planning, Family Law, Business Law, Collections.
See Professional Biographies, CLEVELAND, OHIO

Paglia, Michael A. '65 '99 C.8 B.S. L.1003 J.D. [Ritzler,C.&S.]
Pahys, Thomas R., (BV) '47 '73 C.930 B.A. L.904 J.D. 18123 Sloane Ave
Palda, George W., (AV) '46 '76 C.930 B.A. L.1003 J.D. 55 Public Square, Suite 2121
Palik, Evan J. '60 '85 C.473 B.S. L.8 J.D. [Ⓐ McMahon,D.H.&L.]
Palinkas, Laura T. '55 '88 C.161 B.A. L.1003 J.D. 4431 S. Meadow Ln.

Palkovitz, Herbert, (AV) '42 '69 C.901 B.A. L.1003 J.D. BB
1600 Standard Building, 44113
Telephone: 216-771-3777 FAX: 216-771-1950
Email: palkovlaw@aol.com URL: http://www.lawyers.com/palkovlaw
Associate: Adam J. Thurman.
Divorce, Domestic Relations, Family Law. Trials. Arbitration.
References: National City Bank; Society National Bank.
See Professional Biographies, CLEVELAND, OHIO

Pallam, John J. '40 '65 C.930 A.B. L.608 J.D.
V.P. & Gen. Coun., Brush Engineered Materials Inc.
Paller, Aaron R. '30 '56 C.930 B.B.A. L.1003 J.D. 26300 Village Ln.‡
Palmer, Berthina E. '27 '54 C.930 B.A. L.1003 J.D. AFL-CIO Federation of Labor
Palmer, Jeffrey G. '72 '99 C.1377 B.A. L.285 J.D. [Ⓐ Weston H.]
Palmer, John A. '45 '76 C.679 B.S.M.E. L.1003 J.D. Pres., Repko Machine Inc.
Palmer, Stacey A. '— '04 C.62 B.A. L.989 J.D. [Ⓐ Thompson H.]
Palmer, Todd F. '65 '90 C.473 B.A. L.608 J.D. [Calfee,H.&G.]
Palmeri, Charles J., Esq., (AV) '52 '77 C.363 B.A. L.201 J.D. [C.J.Palmeri]

Palmeri, Charles J., Co., L.P.A., (AV) BB
Suite 207, Corporate Circle, 30100 Chagrin Boulevard, 44124-5705
Telephone: 216-831-7338 Toll Free: 800-274-7067 Facsimile: 216-504-0240
Email: cjpalmeri@cjpalmeri.com URL: http://www.cjpalmeri.com
Charles J. Palmeri, Esq.
Creditors' Rights, Real Estate Foreclosure, Creditor Bankruptcy, Secured Creditor Rights, Secured Collections and Loan Workouts.
See Professional Biographies, CLEVELAND, OHIO

Palmieri, Anthony G., Jr., (BV) '50 '75 C.659 B.A. L.1003 J.D. [A.G.Palmieri,Jr.]
Palmieri, Anthony G., Jr., Co., L.P.A., (BV) 700 W. St. Clair Avenue, Suite 210
Palombo, Anthony N. '65 '95 C.381 B.A. L.1003 J.D. [Young,G.&S.]
Paluf, Timothy G., (BV) '53 '78 C.602 B.B.A. L.1003 J.D. 526 Superior Ave.
Pandurevic, Branislav '59 '87 C.161 B.A. L.1003 J.D. 31031 Lake Road
Pangrace, Martin J. '— '01 C.119 B.A. L.124 J.D. [Ⓐ Gallagher S.]
Panzica, Cathy B. '62 '86 C.477 B.A. L.608 J.D. [Ⓒ Thompson H.]
Paolano, Mary J., (BV) '42 '74 C.477 B.A. L.161 J.D. P.O. Box 99101
Papajcik, Dale E. '57 '86 C.8 B.S.C.E. L.7 J.D. [Squire,S.&D.]
Papandreas, John G., (AV) '27 '54 C.913 B.S. L.930 LL.B. 1370 W. 6th St.
Papenbrock, William A., (AV) '38 '63 C.473 B.S. L.930 LL.B. [Calfee,H.&G.] ‡
Papp, Edward D. '71 '97 C.363 B.A. L.608 J.D. [Ⓐ Baker&H.]
Pappalardo, Joseph W., (AV) '— '80 C.930 B.A. L.608 J.D. [Gallagher S.]
Papushak, Lynette M. '71 '98 C.62 B.A. L.608 J.D. [Ⓐ McDonald H.]
Parasiliti, Mary F. '68 '95 C.1365 B.A. L.188 J.D.
(adm. in GA; not adm. in OH) 4167 W. 220th St,
Paravano, Jeffrey H. '66 '91 C.363 B.S.B.A. L.276 J.D. [Baker&H.] (⓪Wash., DC)
Parham, David L., (AV) '45 '74 C.124 B.S. L.930 J.D. [Thompson H.]
Paris, David M., (AV) '52 '78 C.608 B.A. L.1003 J.D. [Nurenberg,P.H.&M.]
Paris, E. Tasso '60 '87 C.161 B.S. L.1003 J.D. [Paris&P.]
Paris, John Thomas '59 '85 C.97 B.B.A. L.1003 J.D. [Paris&P.]
Paris, Michelle Louise, (BV) '53 '84 C.607 B.S. L.1003 J.D. Chf. Ref. Mun. Ct.
Paris, Scott W. '73 '03 C.608 B.A. L.7 J.D. 1422 Euclid Ave., Ste. 1510
Paris, Thomas, (BV) '24 '53 C.528 B.A. L.930 J.D. [Paris&P.]
Paris, Zachary T., (AV) '— '73 C&L.976 B.A., J.D. [Jones D.]
Paris & Paris, LPA, (BV) 55 Public Square, Suite 1275
Parker, Alan B., (BV) '56 '81 C.608 B.A. L.861 J.D. [Ⓐ Reminger&R.]
Parker, Anthony T. '72 '97 L.1003 J.D. 614 Superior Ave., N.W.
Parker, Christopher L., (BV) '66 '91 C.473 B.S. L.201 J.D. [Ⓒ Janik&D.]
Parker, Elton L. '73 '99 C.107 B.S. L.930 J.D. [Ⓐ Squire,S.&D.]
Parker, Johanna F. '— '99 C.602 B.A. L.930 J.D. [Ⓐ Jones D.]
Parker, John D., (AV) '58 '83 C.97 B.A.C. L.930 J.D. [Baker&H.]
Parkes, Wright C. '42 '83 C.952 A.B. L.1003 J.D. 1932 Woodward Ave.
Parkins, Matthew E. '74 '00 C.610 B.A. L.117 J.D. [Ⓐ Meyers,R.F.&L.]
Parobek, Drew T., (AV) '57 '84 C&L.880 B.A., J.D. [Vorys,S.S.&P.]
Parrino, Thos. J. '17 '42 C&L.607 A.B., LL.B. Ret. Ct. of App. J.
Parsons, Theodore C. '72 '98 C.608 B.S. L.228 J.D. [Ⓐ Jones D.] (See Pat. Sect.)
Partlow, Michael A. '56 '86 C.8 L.7 J.D. [Ⓐ Morganstern,M.&D.]
Paspek, Andrea Marie '62 '89 C.363 B.S. L.989 J.D. Law Dept., City of Cleveland
Pasterak, Helene Kamenar '14 '68 C.608 D.D.S. L.1003 J.D. 1579 Maywood Rd.‡
Pasternak, Michael B., (CV) '67 '92 C.363 L.1003 [Chernett W.Y.&P.]
Patel, Ami J. '— '04 C.610 B.A. L.124 J.D. [Ⓐ Schuster&S.]
Patel, Vipul B. '— '03 C.124 B.S. L.178 J.D. [Ⓐ Jones D.]
Paton, Brian A. '65 '91 C.473 B.A. L.659 J.D. Sr. Coun., TRW Automotive
Patrick, Bradford J. '68 '99 C.201 B.S. L.930 J.D. [Ⓐ Mansour,G.G.&M.]
Patrick, John '65 '93 C.980 B.S. L.8 J.D. [Ⓐ Reminger&R.]
Patronite, Gerald J., (BV) '47 '73 C.608 B.A. L.1003 J.D. [G.J.Patronite]
Patronite, Gerald J., Company, L.P.A., (BV) 34950 Chardon Rd.
Patterson, Jill S. '73 '98 C.363 B.A. L.989 J.D. [Ⓐ Weston H.]
Patterson, John P. '70 '99 C.976 B.A. L.378 J.D. [Ⓐ Tucker E.&W.]
Patterson, Neal J. '59 '84 C.602 B.A. L.188 J.D.
(adm. in IN; not adm. in OH) BP America, Inc.
Patton, Edward O., (BV) '64 '89 C.973 B.A. L.1003 J.D. [Ⓐ Mansour,G.G.&M.]
Patton, John T. '29 '58 C.161 B.B.A. L.1003 J.D. Ct. of App. J.
Patton, Norman T., (AV) '17 '50 C.930 L.1003 LL.B. [Conway,P.&B.]
Patton, Shannon K. '72 '98 C.473 B.A. L.608 J.D. [Ⓐ Duvin,C.&H.]
Pauken, Margaret M. '63 '90 C.473 B.A. L.930 J.D. 1468 West 9th, Suite 700
Pauken, Patrick J., (AV) '52 '78 C.610 B.G.S. L.930 J.D. [Baker&H.]
Paul, Aparesh '72 '03 C.880 B.A. L.124 J.D. [Ⓐ Levin&Assoc.]
Paul, Douglas J., (AV) '49 '74 C.367 B.A. L.930 J.D. [Buckingham,D.&B.]
Paul, Ross R. '58 '90 C.161 B.A. L.1003 J.D. 3860 Jeanne Dr.
Pavlik, Thomas C., (AV) '41 '66 C.602 A.B. L.930 J.D. [Novak,R.P.&S.]
Pavlovic, Nevenka '— '00 C.150 B.A. L.607 J.D. 1300 East Ninth Street, 14th Floor
Pawlicki, Clarence F. '30 '60 C.251 B.B.A. L.1003 J.D.
Dir., Taxes, Cleveland-Cliffs Inc
Pawlik, James D. '58 '84 C.608 B.A. L.309 J.D. Jud. Law Clk., Cir. U.S. Appl. J.
Paxton, Jeffrey C. '59 '90 C.97 B.A. L.1003 J.D. Coun., Dollar Bk., Fed. Svgs. Bk.
Payne, Frederick J., (AV) '21 '48 C.602 B.S. L.930 J.D. [Payne P.&C.]
Payne, Kevin F. '55 '81 C.363 B.A. L.1003 J.D. 6100 Oak Tree Boulevard
Payne, William A. '53 '84 C.363 B.S.B.A. L.607 J.D. [Payne P.&C.]
Payne Payne & Cook, (AV) 6100 Oak Tree Boulevard
Peacock, Bruce E., (AV) '50 '75 C.1316 B.S. L.851 J.D. [Wegman,H.&V.] (Pat.)
Pearlman, Samuel S., (AV) '42 '67 C&L.659 A.B., LL.B. [Squire,S.&D.]

Pearne & Gordon LLP, (AV)
1801 East 9th Street Suite 1200, 44114-3108
Telephone: 216-579-1700 Facsimile: 216-579-6073
Email: ip@pearnegordon.com URL: http://www.pearnegordon.com
Members of Firm: John F. Pearne (1912-1981); Charles B. Gordon; Thomas P. Schiller; David B. Deioma; Joseph J. Corso; Howard G. Shimola; Jeffrey J. Sopko; John P. Murtaugh; James M. Moore; Michael W. Garvey; Richard A. Sharpe; Ronald M. Kachmarik; Paul A. Serbinowski; Brian G. Bembenick; Aaron A. Fishman. Associates: Stephen S. Wentsler; Robert F. Bodi; Suzanne B. Gagnon; Una Schumacher; Steven J. Solomon; Gregory Fernengel. Of Counsel: Lowell L. Heinke; Thaddeus A. Zalenski (Not admitted in OH).
Patent, Trademark, Copyright, Trade Secret, Unfair Competition, and Related Intellectual Property Law.
See Professional Biographies, CLEVELAND, OHIO

Pearson, Benita Y. '63 '95 C.276 B.S. L.161 J.D. Asst. U.S. Atty.
Peca, John A., (AV) '52 '77 C.363 B.S. L.930 J.D. [Climaco,L.P.W.&G.]
Pecenka Cullen, Danielle '73 '98 C.608 B.A. L.117 J.D. [Ⓐ Weltman,W.&R.]
Peckinpaugh, Roger T., (AV) '45 '70 C.611 B.A. L.608 J.D. [Peckinpaugh&T.]
Peckinpaugh & Thornton, (AV) 23230 Chagrin Blvd., Ste. 605
Pederson, Jeffrey W. '42 '80 C.8 B.A. L.1137 J.D. 3305 Beechwood Ave.
Peer, Christina Henagen '73 '99 C.473 B.A. L.910 J.D. [Ⓐ Squire,S.&D.]
Peer, Christopher W. '— '03 C.611 B.A. L.989 J.D. [Ⓐ Hahn L.&P.]
Pejic, Nenad '67 '96 C.608 B.S. L.161 J.D. [Ⓐ Calfee,H.&G.] (See Pat. Sect.)
Pelagalli, Rodger A. '60 '86 C.970 B.A. L.201 J.D. 6659 Pearl Road
Pellegrin, Joan K., (BV) '55 '80 C.381 B.A. L.1003 J.D. 3323 W. 130th St.
Pelliccioni, Christopher D. '76 '03 C.800 B.A. L.930 J.D. [Ⓐ Baker&H.]
Penca, Gerald F., (BV) '43 '71 C.381 B.B.A. L.1003 J.D. Terminal Twr.
Pence-Lavy, M. Melissa '— '98 C&L.608 B.S., J.D. Coun., Abbott Labs.
Pendergast, John R., Jr., (BVⓉ) '59 '85 C&L.966 B.A., J.D.
(adm. in WI; not adm. in OH) Assoc. Gen. Coun., Degussa Corp.
Penrod, Stephen R. '— '00 C.970 B.A. L.161 J.D. [Ⓐ Jones D.]
Penttila, Jane Eileen '53 '92 C.161 B.A. L.930 J.D.
Assoc. Gen. Coun. & Dir. Claims & Litig., University Hospitals of Cleveland
Pentz, Joel R. '72 '99 C.470 B.A. L.930 J.D. [Ⓐ Chernett W.Y.&P.]
Penvose, Bryan L. '75 '01 C.901 B.A. L.989 J.D. [Ⓐ Koblentz&K.]
Peppard, Sean T. '73 '01 C.976 B.A. L.477 J.D. [Ⓐ Squire,S.&D.]
Pepple, William C., (AV) '49 '82 C.97 B.S. L.7 J.D. [Pepple&W.]
Pepple & Waggoner, (AV) 5005 Rockside Rd., Ste. 960

Perantinides & Nolan Co., L.P.A.
(See Akron)
Perdion, Jason P. '70 '98 C.608 B.S.N.R. L.851 J.D. [A Baker&H.]
Perelman, Debra A. '63 '89 C.473 B.S. L.124 J.D. [Meyers,R.F.&L.]
Perillo, Danl. R. '28 '54 C.475 B.S. L.1003 LL.B. Div. Pres., Kirkwood Industries, Inc.
Perisutti, Stephen J. '62 '88
C.8 B.S. L.7 J.D. Sr. Corp. Coun., The Sherwin-Williams Co.
Perl, Elizabeth Ann '71 '97 C.734 B.A. L.94 J.D. City Legal Aid Soc.
Perl, Warren Robert '53 '78 C.608 B.A. L.1003 J.D. 1836 Euclid Avenue, Suite #335
Perla, Randall M., (AV) '49 '74 C.97 B.A. L.1003 J.D. BB
19443 Lorain Road, 44126
Telephone: 440-333-2503 Fax: 440-333-9650 URL: http://www.randallperla.com
Email: theperlas5@aol.com URL: http://www.perlalaw.com
Domestic Relations, Family Law, Divorce, Personal Injury, Automobile Accidents and Injuries, Probate, Child Custody.
See Professional Biographies, CLEVELAND, OHIO
Perlmuter, Jeffrey A. '49 '75 C.861 B.A. L.30 J.D. [C Schottenstein,Z.&D.]
Perrette, John E. '50 '76 C.161 B.B.A. L.1003 J.D. Tax Atty., Natl. City Corp.
Perrico, Daniel E. '74 '99 C.62 B.A. L.201 J.D. [A Sutter,O.&F.]
Perrin, Ronald J. '23 '54 C.118 B.A. L.1003 LL.B. 2860 Bonny Blvd.
Perris, Terrence G., (AV) '47 '72 C.851 B.A. L.477 J.D. [Squire,S.&D.]
Perry, Allen L. '20 '66 C.329 B.S. L.1003 J.D. 3832 Woodridge Rd.
Perry, Andrew S. '68 '00 C.608 B.S. L.179 J.D. [A McDonald H.]
Perry, Bret C. '72 '01 C.97 B.S. L.989 J.D. [A Bonezzi S.M.&P.]
Perry, Dominic V., (AV) '55 '80 C.608 B.S. L.930 J.D. [Perry&O.]
Perry, George W. '26 '53 C.976 B.A. L.893 LL.B. 1801 E. 12th St.‡
Perry, Karla Louise '67 '93 C.967 B.A. L.879 J.D. Legal Aid
Perry, Samuel S., (AV) '20 '55 C.930 B.B.A. L.1003 J.D. [S.S.Perry&Assoc.]
Perry, Stephen F. '29 '54 C.174 B.A. L.477 LL.B. 21810 Addington Blvd.‡
Perry & O'Brien LLP, (AV) 627 W. Saint Clair Ave.
Perry, Samuel S., and Associates, (AV) 17626 Van Aken Blvd.
Pershing, Lenore M. '60 '85 C.108 B.S. L.930 J.D. 2665 W. ST. James Pkwy.
Persia, Stephen T. '— '04 C.160 B.A. L.851 J.D. [A Gallagher S.]
Persing, Brenda Lynn '72 '98
Trust Officer, McDonald Financial Group, Key Bank, M.A.
Persky, Shapiro & Arnoff Co., L.P.A.
(See Beachwood)
Pesuit, Jo Ann D. '44 '95 C.599 B.A. L.989 J.D. 719 National City Bank Bldg.
Peters, George Elias, IV '66 '93 C.393 B.A. L.930 J.D. City Atty.
Peters, Jeffrey T. '— '99 C.97 B.S.B.A. L.989 J.D. [A Giffen&K.]
Peters, Scott C., (AV) '67 '92 C.385 A.B. L.930 J.D. [Britton,S.P.&K.]
Petersen, Susan E. '71 '98 C.980 B.F.A. L.989 J.D. [A Spangenberg,S.&L.]
Peterson, Natalie L. '68 '97 C.119 B.A. L.813 J.D. Asst. Dir. of Law
Peterson, Robert J. '56 '82 C.363 B.S. L.161 J.D.
Vice President & General Counsel, Park Corporation
Peterson, Robin J. '62 '92
C.381 B.A. L.161 J.D. 6060 Rockside Woods Boulevard, Suite 250
Peto, Terri M. '52 '88 C.599 B.A. L.930 J.D. 25435 Wimbeldon Rd.
Petras, Stephen J., Jr., (AV) '54 '79 C.967 B.A. L.930 J.D. [Baker&H.]
Petrello, Colleen H., (BV) '50 '89 C.876 B.A. L.1003 J.D. [A Sutter,O.&F.]
Petrey, Katherine G., (AV) '48 '74 C&L.383 B.A., J.D. [C Squire,S.&D.]
Petrik, Joe '24 '54 C.313 B.A. L.1003 LL.B. 1827 Brookview Blvd.
Petrinovic, Peter '54 '79 C.930 B.A. L.1003 J.D. 6576 Edgemoor Ave.
Petroff, D. James '63 '89 C.608 B.A. L.200 J.D. [A Faulkner,M.&P.]
Petronelli, Jack L., (BV) '54 '80 C.381 B.B.A. L.1003 J.D. [A Johnson,A.&C.]
Petronzio, Anna M. '67 '93 C.128 B.A. L.818 J.D. [Petronzio S.]
Petronzio Schneier Co., L.P.A., (AV) 5001 Mayfield Road, Suite 201
Petrov, Alan M., (AV) '— '74 C.705 A.B. L.930 J.D. [Gallagher S.]
Petrov, Daniel P. '76 '01 C.178 B.A. L.124 J.D. [A Calfee,H.&G.]
Petrulis, Richard D., (AV) '51 '77 C.363 B.A. L.1003 J.D.
Sr. V.P. & Sr. Mng. Coun., KeyBank Natl. Assn.
Petrulis, Robert C., (AV) '61 '88 C.930 B.A. L.477 J.D. [Baker&H.]
Petruzzi, Anthony R. '71 '98 C.610 A.B. L.1003 J.D. [A McLaughlin&M.]
Petry, Samuel Richard, II '42 '67 C&L.930 A.B., J.D.
Senior Counsel - International, Eaton Corporation
Petticord, Daniel F., (AV) '68 '92 C.105 B.A. L.1003 J.D. [Brzytwa,Q.&M.]
Pettinelli, Joan E. '64 '90 C.576 B.A. L.575 J.D. [Wuliger,F.&B.]
Peyton, Jennifer I. '71 '98 C.855 B.A. L.930 J.D. 2012 W. 25th Street
Pfaff, Robert E. '60 '86 C.477 B.A. L.608 J.D. [C Reed,M.&W.]
Pfleiderer, Shane T. '— '03 C&L.851 B.B.A., J.D. [A Jones D.]
Pharis, Stewart Shaw '57 '93 C.597 B.Mus. L.1065 J.D. Law Clk., U.S. Bkrptcy. J.
Phelan, Harold Anthony, (AV) '34 '58 C.276 B.S. L.930 J.D. 55 Public Sq.‡
Philipp, Jonathan '64 '89 C.222 B.A. L.273 J.D. [Janik&D.]
Phillips, Amy L. '73 '98 C.381 B.A. L.1003 J.D. [A Mansour,G.G.&M.]
Phillips, Cynthia L. '53 '84 C.381 B.S. L.7 J.D. 3260 Green Rd.
Phillips, David G. '65 '90 C.161 B.A. L.879 J.D. 2000 E. 9th St., Ste. 710
Phillips, Gregory J. '70 '98 C.674 A.B. L.893 J.D. [A Calfee,H.&G.]
Phillips, Mark A., (AV) '52 '90 C.610 B.A. L.1003 J.D. [Benesch,F.C.&A.]
Phillips, Michael D. '51 '71 C.893 B.A. L.945 J.D. [Calfee,H.&G.]
Phillips, Richard L., (AV) '26 '55 C.608 B.S. L.1003 J.D. [C Benesch,F.C.&A.] ‡
Phillips, Richard W. '53 '84 C.472 B.A. L.1003 J.D. 10910 Thrush Ave.‡
Phillips, Robert M., (AV) '40 '70 C.999 B.S. L.1003 J.D. [Faulkner,M.&P.]
Phillips, Sue Ellen '58 '85 C.610 B.S. L.1003 J.D. [A Fay,S.F.M.&M.] (See Pat. Sect.)
Phillips, William M. '57 '83 C.473 B.S. L.608 J.D. [Calfee,H.&G.]
Piatak, Thomas J., (AV) '64 '89 C.930 B.A. L.477 J.D. [Baker&H.]
Piazza, Anthony M., (BV) '51 '77 C.381 B.A. L.607 J.D. 1370 Ontario St.
Picker, Jane M. '35 '61 C.821 A.B. L.976 LL.B. Prof. of Law, Cleve. State Univ.
Picker, Sidney I., Jr. '34 '60 C.197 A.B. L.813 LL.B.
Prof. & Dir., Russian Legal Studies Prog., Case Western Reserve Univ.
Pickus, Albert P., (AV) '31 '58 C.477 A.B. L.930 J.D. 127 Public Sq.
Pienta, Renee S. '75 '01 C.473 B.S. L.124 J.D. [A Dinn,H.&P.]
Pierpont, Christine Murphy, (AV) '58 '83 C.381 B.A. L.1248 J.D. [A Squire,S.&D.]
Pietch, Richard S. '53 '80 C.8 B.A. L.1003 J.D.
Sr. V.P. & Gen. Coun., Electrolux North America
Pietrafese, Brent M. '78 '03 C.473 B.S. L.930 J.D. [A Calfee,H.&G.]
Pietrafese, Shannon M. '80 '04 C.97 B.A. L.930 J.D. [A Davis&Y.]
Pietrzen, Julie L. '74 '04 C.20 B.A. L.124 J.D. [A Frantz W.]
Pigott, Stephen E., (AV) '54 '80 C.645 B.S. L.608 J.D. [Cavitch,F.D.&F.]
Pike, Michael J. '— '01 C.1030 B.S. L.124 J.D. [A Gallagher S.]
Pikus, James X. '48 '85 C.161 B.A. L.8 J.D. 880 E. 185th St.
Pilat, George V., (BV) '62 '87 C.611 B.A. L.930 J.D. [McIntyre,K.&K.]
Pilloff, Benson Dale '41 '66 C.473 B.S. L.930 J.D. 4 Longmeadow Ln.‡
Pinchak, George L., Jr., (AV) '56 '91
C.161 B.I.E. L.1003 J.D. [Watts H.] (See Pat. Sect.)
Pingor, James J. '66 '98 C.665 B.S. L.117 J.D. [A Amin&T.] (See Pat. Sect.)
Pinjuh, Lori '70 '97 C.880 B.S. L.823 J.D. 3150 Chester Ave., Ste. 200
Pinkney, Betty K. '35 '77 C.1023 A.B. L.1003 J.D. Sr. Atty., East Ohio Gas Co.
Pinney, Jon J. '75 '00 C.363 B.S. L.989 J.D. [A Kohrman J.&K.]
Pinto, Libert, (AV) '54 '80 C.967 B.A. L.1003 J.D. 920 Terminal Twr.
Piraino, Katherine D. Wood '55 '82 C.477 B.A. L.930 J.D. 2749 Southington
Piraino, Thomas A., Jr., (AV) '49 '74 C.25 B.A. L.188 J.D.
V.P., Gen. Coun. & Secy., Parker-Hannifin Corp.
Piscitelli, Frank E., Jr., (AV) '67 '93 C.161 B.A. L.1003 J.D. [F.Piscitelli]
Piscitelli, Frank, Co., L.P.A., (AV)
Suite 900, The Halle Building, 1228 Euclid Avenue, 44115
Telephone: 216-931-7000 Fax: 216-931-9925
URL: http://www.piscitellilaw.com
Frank E. Piscitelli, Jr.
Automobile Accidents, Personal Injury, Medical Malpractice and Class Action Litigation.
See Professional Biographies, CLEVELAND, OHIO
Pitcock, Charles L., (BV) '42 '67 C.611 B.A. L.477 J.D.
Assoc. Gen. Coun., Forest City Enterprises, Inc.
Pitcock, Danielle '73 '98 C.610 B.B.A. L.989 J.D. [A Cleary&Assoc.]
Pittman, Darryl E., & Associates '48 '73 C&L.178 A.B., J.D.
2940 Noble Road, Suite 202, 44121
Telephone: 216-291-1005 Fax: 216-382-8580
Email: dpittman@stratos.net URL: http://www.pittmanalexanderattorneys.com
Consumer Law, Bankruptcy, Lead Poisoning.
See Professional Biographies, CLEVELAND, OHIO
Pittman, Lori A. '— '04 C.980 B.S. L.7 J.D. [C Thompson H.]
Pitzer, Gary J. '69 '95 C.608 B.S.E.E. L.472 J.D. [Tarolli,S.C.&T.] (See Pat. Sect.)
Pivonka, Robert C., II '68 '96 C.436 B.A. L.930 J.D. [A Millisor&N.]
Pla, Jorge Luis '59 '99 C.608 B.S. L.989 J.D. [J.L.Pla]
Pla, Jorge Luis, L.L.C. 1700 East 13th Street, Suite 13FE
Plagens, John F. '56 '84 C.608 B.A. L.1003 J.D. 24308 Bruce Rd.
Planas, Melvin '67 '01 C.260 B.A. L.1340 J.D. Pros. Off.
Plank, Paul E. '49 '78 C.930 B.S. L.1003 J.D. V.P., James B. Oswald Company, The
Plant, Thomas A., (AV) '48 '74
C.24 B.A. L.7 J.D. Sr. V.P. & Asst. Gen. Coun., Natl. City Bk.
Platko, Jeffrey J. '— '97 C.107 B.S. L.1003 J.D. [A Kadish,H.&W.]
Platt, Jonathan A. '61 '97 C&L.930 B.S., J.D. [Renner,O.B.&S.] (See Pat. Sect.)
Platten, Paige H. '67 '04 C.124 B.S.N. L.1202 J.D. [A Mellino]
Plesec, William T., (AV) '— '71 C.363 A.B. L.1003 J.D. [Jones D.]
Plevin, Leon M., (AV) '32 '57 C.923 A.B. L.1003 J.D. [Plevin&G.]
Plevin & Gallucci Company, L.P.A., (AV)
The Illuminating Building, 55 Public Square, Suite 2222, 44113
Telephone: 216-861-0804 Fax: 216-861-5322
Email: FGallucci@PGlawyer.com URL: http://www.plevinandgallucci.com
Leon M. Plevin; Frank Lewis Gallucci III.
Personal Injury, Workers' Compensation, Medical Malpractice; Airplane Crash Litigation; Construction Accidents, Nursing Home Negligence; Insurance Litigation, Birth Trauma; Obstetric Malpractice; Nursing Malpractice; Wrongful Death; Automobile Accidents; Brain Injury; Catastrophic Injury; Motor Vehicle Accidents and Injuries; Railroad Accidents and Injuries; Railroad Crossing Accidents.
See Professional Biographies, CLEVELAND, OHIO
Plewacki, Richard A., (AV) '48 '80 C.97 B.A. L.7 J.D. [Roetzel&A.]
Podboy, Alvin M., Jr. '47 '72 C.610 A.B. L.930 J.D. 3200 National City Ctr.
Podor & Associates
(See Solon)
Poe, Jeanne Early '60 '87 C&L.502 B.S.Ed., J.D.
(adm. in MO; not adm. in OH) V.P. & Sr. Coun., KeyBank Natl. Assn.
Pofok, Teresa R. '— '94 C.381 B.A. L.1292 J.D. [A Duvin,C.&H.]
Pogue, Richard W., (AV) '28 '53 C.188 B.A. L.477 J.D. 1301 E. 9th St.‡
Pohl, Irwin P., (BV) '13 '38 C&L.930 B.A.; LL.B. 3141 Green Rd.
Poklar, Michael A., Law Offices of, (AV) '47 '73
C.201 B.A. L.1003 J.D. 3555 Rolling Hills Dr.
Poklar, Robert A., (AV) '53 '78 C.602 B.B.A. L.1003 J.D. [R.A.Poklar&Assoc.]
Poklar, Robert A., & Associates, L.L.P., (AV) 10100 Brecksville Rd.
Pokorny, Michael D., (BV) '55 '83 C.363 B.A. L.1003 J.D. Co. Dist. Bd. of Health
Poland, Mark A. '70 '00 C.150 B.B.A. L.989 J.D. [A Carlisle,M.R.K.&U.]
Poling, Brant E. '68 '94 C&L.117 B.A., J.D. [Sutter,O.&F.]
Polinko, John A. '72 '01 C.608 B.A. L.8 J.D. [A Shapiro&F.]
Polito, John A. '47 '73 C&L.161 B.A., J.D. Ref., Prob. Ct.
Polito, John S., (AV) '52 '77 C.973 B.A. L.1003 J.D. [Bonezzi S.M.&P.]
Polito, LuAnn A. '67 '89 C.973 B.S. L.1003 J.D. City Law Dept.‡
Polito, Michael G., (BV) '65 '91 C.215 B.A. L.1003 J.D. [Polito&R.]
Polito & Russo, LLP, (AV) 21300 Lorain Rd.
Polk, Shannon J. '75 '00 C.323 B.A. L.124 J.D. [A Reminger&R.]
Pollack, Joseph D. '— '84 C.97 B.B.A. L.8 J.D. [Jones D.] (See Pat. Sect.)
Pollack, Lawrence D., (AV) '64 '89 C.473 B.A. L.608 J.D. [Ulmer&B.]
Pollina, Daniel T. '68 '94 C.473 B.S. L.1003 J.D. Moskal Klein, Inc.
Pollis, Andrew S., (AV) '64 '90 C.103 A.B. L.309 J.D. [Hahn L.&P.]
Pollock, Candace M. '— '87 C.62 B.A. L.1003 J.D. [Hahn,S.&P.]
Pollock, R. Jeffrey, (AV) '46 '76 C.210 B.A. L.588 J.D. [McDonald H.]
Polster, Dan A. '51 '76 C&L.309 A.B., J.D. U.S. Dist Ct., Northern Dist. of OH
Polster, Harold '43 '69 C.930 B.B.A. L.1003 J.D. BP America, Inc.
Pomerantz, David I., (BV) '60 '85 C.477 B.A. L.608 J.D. [Pomerantz&C.]
Pomerantz, Norman S., (BV) '31 '59 C.608 B.S. L.930 LL.B.
20676 Southgate Park Blvd.
Pomerantz and Crosby Co., L.P.A., (BV) 20676 Southgate Park Blvd.
Pompeani, Fred J., (AV) '57 '82 C.473 B.A. L.930 J.D. [Porter W.M.&A.]
Pona, Charles G., (AV) '60 '87 C.97 B.S. L.989 J.D. [Weltman,W.&R.]
Ponick, Franklin J. '19 '52 C&L.930 B.B.A., LL.B. P.O. Box 5756
Poole, Donza M. '60 '87 C.823 B.S. L.930 J.D. I.R.S.
Poole, Patricia A. '54 '91 C.97 B.S.N. L.1003 J.D. [Baker&H.]
Poore, Gregory R. '45 '72 C.207 B.A. L.608 J.D.
V.P. & Sr. Coun., KeyBank Natl. Assn.
Pophal, Joseph J. '66 '92
C.679 B.S.M.E. L.347 J.D. Coun., Parker-Hannifin Corporation (Pat.)
Popson, James M. '66 '00 C.814 B.S. L.8 J.D. [A Sutter,O.&F.]
Porcaro, James G. '72 '99 C.8 B.A. L.823 J.D. [A Schwarzwald&M.]
Port, Cynthia Krips '69 '98 C.446 B.A. L.904 J.D. [A Calfee,H.&G.]
Port, Robert B. '66 '04 C.223 B.S. L.124 J.D. [A Hahn L.&P.]
Porter, Anne L. '58 '83 C&L.793 B.A., J.D.
(adm. in SD; not adm. in OH) U.S. Dept. of Jus.
Porter, David P., (AV) '— '81 C.112 B.S. L.930 J.D. [Jones D.]
Porter, Elliott Vaughn '48 '76 C.161 B.A. L.124 J.D. U.S. Equal Empoy. Opp. Comm.
Porter, Gerald M., (AV) '37 '63 C.363 A.B. L.477 LL.B. [Cochran,N.&P.]

Porter, James M. ....'31 '57 C.363 A.B. L.477 J.D. Appl. Ct. J.
Porter, John B. C. ....'76 '02 C.967 B.A. L.608 J.D. [A Weltman,W.&R.]
Porter, Mark E. ....'62 '00 C.871 B.S. L.1292 J.D. [A McDonald H.]
Porter, Mary Robenalt '61 '89
C.473 B.A. L.161 J.D. Gen. Coun., Northstar Title Services, LLC
Porter, Richard D. ....'— '02 C.528 B.A. L.608 J.D. [A Duvin,C.&H.]
Porter, Wayne D., Jr., (AV) '47 '75
C.923 B.S.A.E. L.276 J.D. [Rankin,H.P.&C.] (See Pat. Sect.)

Porter Wright Morris & Arthur LLP, (AV)
925 Euclid Avenue, Suite 1700, 44115-1483
Telephone: 216-443-9000; (800-824-1980) Fax: 216-443-9011
Email: cleveland@porterwright.com URL: http://www.porterwright.com
Partners: Robert D. Anderle; Ann M. Caresani; James W. Ehrman; Michael A. Ellis; Donald J. Fisher; Daniel F. Gourash; Margaret M. Koesel; Philip E. Langer; Irene M. MacDougall; Hugh E. McKay; Paul R. Matia; John C. Monica, Jr.; Fred J. Pompeani; Patricia A. Screen; Leo M. Spellacy, Jr.; Ralph Streza; David C. Tryon; Tracey L. Turnbull; Jeffrey J. Weber; William R. Weir; Alan D. Wright. Resident Associates: Amy L. Deluca; L. William Erb; Rebecca Kucera Fischer; Kevin Kelley; Kenneth J. Kleppel; Suzana Krstevski Koch; Scott Lepene; David M. Lewis; Patrick T. Lewis; Michelle Powe Marvinney; Allyson Mondalek; John A. Mugnano; Nicole J. Quathamer; Natalie H. Rauf; Howard G. Strain; Charles W. Zepp. Of Counsel: Lisa A. Reid.
Alternative Dispute Resolution, Agricultural Law, Antitrust and Trade Regulation, Business and Corporate, Complex Litigation, Construction, Employee Benefits, Energy and Utilities, Environment, Federal Administrative Law, Federal Contracting and Procurement, Financial Institutions, General Practice, Governmental Affairs, Health Care, Insurance, Intellectual Property, International Business, Labor and Employment, Litigation, Public Law, Public Finance, Real Estate, Securities, Taxation, Technology, Trusts and Estates.
Columbus, Ohio Office: 41 South High Street, 43215-6194. Telephones: 614-227-2000; (800-533-2794). Fax: 614-227-2100. Internet: columbus@porterwright.com.
Dayton, Ohio Office: One Dayton Centre, One South Main Street, Suite 1600, 45402-2028. Telephones: 937-449-6810; (800-533-4434). Fax: 937-449-6820. Internet: dayton@porterwright.com.
Cincinnati, Ohio Office: 250 E. Fifth Street, Suite 2200, 45202-5117. Telephones: 513-381-4700; (800-582-5813). Fax: 513-421-0991. Internet: cincinnati@porterwright.com.
Washington, D.C. Office: 1919 Pennsylvania Avenue, N.W., Suite 500 20006-3434. Telephones: 202-778-3000; (800-456-7962). Fax: 202-778-3063. Internet: washington@porterwright.com.
Naples, Florida Office: 5801 Pelican Bay Boulevard, Suite 300, 34108-2709. Telephones: 239-593-2900; (800-876-7962). Fax: 239-593-2990. Internet: naples@porterwright.com.
See Professional Biographies, CLEVELAND, OHIO

Porterfield, Michael C., (BV) ....'49 '76 C.608 B.A. L.930 J.D. Terminal Tower
Portnoy, Libby, (BV) ....'37 '87 C.831 B.A. L.8 J.D. V.P., Natl. City Bk.
Posner, David A., (BV) ....'64 '89 C.347 B.S. L.930 J.D. [Baker&H.]
Post, Robert E. ....'24 '66 C.976 B.E. L.1003 J.D. N.A.S.A.
Posteraro, David R., (AV) ....'52 '81 C.262 B.A. L.930 J.D. [Kohrman J.&K.]
Potash, Erica L. ....'80 '04 C.473 B.S. L.161 J.D. Asst. Gen. Coun., OverDrive, Inc.

Potash, Lester S., Law Offices of, (BV) '50 '75 C.473 B.A. L.930 J.D.
55 Public Square, Suite 1717, 44113
Telephone: 216-771-8400 Fax: 216-771-8404
Email: lsp@potashlaw.com
General Practice, Social Security, Personal Injury, Automobile Accidents, Criminal Law, Drunk Driving, Probate, Litigation, Medical Malpractice, Legal Malpractice.
See Professional Biographies, CLEVELAND, OHIO

Potash, Loree E. ....'51 '80 C.608 B.A. L.1003 J.D. 8555 Sweet Valley Dr.
Potter, Steven B., (AV) ....'56 '81 C.188 A.B. L.930 J.D. [Dinn,H.&P.]
Potts, Timothy J., (AV) ....'42 '67 C.363 B.A. L.930 J.D. [Potts&N.]
Potts & Novotney, (AV) ....600 Standard Building
Poulos, Peter M. ....'65 '90 C.910 B.S.E.E. L.930 J.D. [Taft,S.&H.]
Powar, Lee D., (AV) ....'38 '63 C.188 B.A. L.477 J.D. [Hahn L.&P.]
Powell, David T. ....'— '03 C.980 B.S. L.608 J.D. 1300 East Ninth Street, 14th Floor
Powell, Eric C. ....'75 '01 C.608 B.A. L.607 J.D. [A McCarthy,L.C.&L.]
Powers, Dale D., (AV) ....'31 '60 C.381 B.S.B.A. L.1003 J.D. 720 Leader Bldg.‡
Powers, Donald H., (AV) ....'30 '55 C.294 B.A. L.597 J.D. [Powers&G.]
Powers, Donna J. ....'62 '88 C.25 B.A. L.678 J.D. [Powers&G.]
Powers, Martin T. ....'62 '91 C.161 B.A. L.8 J.D. [A S.S.Keller&Assoc.]

Powers & Groh-Wargo, (AV)
2 Berea Commons, Suite 215 (Berea), P.O. Box 1059, 44017
Telephone: 440-243-2955 Facsimile: 440-243-2967
URL: http://www.pgwohio.com
Donald H. Powers; Frank J. Groh-Wargo; Donna J. Powers; Melinda L. Ruschak; Katherine H. Opsincs.
Real Estate Leasing, Land Use and Acquisition, Condominiums, Construction, Estate Planning and Administration, Corporate Law, Domestic Relations, Civil Litigation.
See Professional Biographies, CLEVELAND, OHIO

Powlen, David M., (AV(T)) '53 '78 C&L.309 A.B., J.D.
(adm. in IN; not adm. in OH)
Co-Manager, Restructuring Group, McDonald Investments Inc.
Pozzuto, Bridgette D. ....'68 '94 C.611 B.A. L.831 J.D. [Urban&P.]
Prado Wittica, Camilo ....'76 '99 Atty, TRW Inc. (Legal Department)
Prasse, Richard T., (AV) ....'53 '81 C.228 B.A. L.930 J.D. [Hahn L.&P.]
Prehn, Diana J. ....'— '02 C.49 B.S. L.201 J.D. 1300 East Ninth Street, 14th Floor
Prekop, Joseph Emil ....'58 '83 C&L.851 B.B.A., J.D. Electrolux North America
Prendergast, Maurice E. ....'32 '62 C.363 B.S.B.A. L.1003 J.D. 3430 Warren Rd.‡
Presti, Geralyn M., (AV) '55 '89 C.610 B.Mus. L.930 J.D.
Sr. V.P. & Gen. Coun., Forest City Enterprises, Inc.
Prestrud, Jack E. '37 '72 C&L.911 B.A., J.D.
(adm. in WA; not adm. in OH) I.R.S.
Prewitt-Stanley, Jocelyn N. ....'77 '03 C.293 B.A. L.352 J.D. [A Vorys,S.S.&P.]
Price, Andrea K. '— '83
C.161 B.A. L.1003 J.D. Sr. Staff Atty., Legal Aid Soc. of Cleveland
Price, Charles D. ....'69 '95 C.201 B.S. L.930 J.D. [Brouse M.]
Price, Jessica E. ....'72 '97 C.473 B.A. L.607 J.D. [Brouse M.]
Price, John T., (BV) ....'48 '73 C.973 B.A. L.150 J.D. 1370 Ontario Street, Suite 1218
Price, Julie M. ....'74 '99 C.97 B.S. L.161 J.D. [A Benesch,F.C.&A.]

Primes, Marlon A. '64 '90 C.610 B.S.J. L.276 J.D.
Carl B. Stokes Federal Courthouse, Suite 400, 801 West Superior Avenue, 44113
Telephone: 216-622-3684 Fax: 216-522-4982
Email: marlon.primes@usdoj.gov
Civil Practice.
See Professional Biographies, CLEVELAND, OHIO

Primrose, Michael A. ....'60 '89 C.1341 B.A. L.477 J.D. [Benesch,F.C.&A.]
Prince, John J., (BV) ....'30 '55 C.215 Ph.B. L.930 J.D. 15613 Waterloo Rd.
Prince, Troy S. ....'— '04 C.124 B.S. L.989 J.D. [A Thompson H.] (Pat.)
Privitera, Angela Marie ....'72 '98 C.107 B.A. L.989 J.D. [A Wegman,H.&V.]
Proaño, David F. ....'76 '05 C.114 B.S. L.1565 J.D. [A Baker&H.]
Proctor, Edward A. ....'68 '98 C.363 B.S. in B.A. L.608 J.D. [A Mazanec,R.&R.]
Prugh, Leigh Suzanne ....'75 '00 C.473 B.A. L.930 J.D. City of Cleveland Dept. of Law
Prulhiere, Jeffrey N. ....'57 '84 C&L.8 B.S.E.E., J.D. [A Amin&T.]
Pryatel, Steven E., (BV) ....'60 '86 C.973 B.S. L.1003 J.D. [Wegman,H.&V.]
Przybysz, Christine M. ....'— '04 C.611 B.A. L.124 J.D. [A Jones D.]

Psaropoulos, Robert C. ....'70 '96 C.608 B.S.B.A. L.161 J.D. [A Benesch,F.C.&A.]
Psota, Paul, (BV) ....'— '89 C.62 B.A. L.1003 J.D. [Buckley K.]
Ptaszek, Edward G., Jr., (AV) ....'50 '78 C.97 B.S. L.930 J.D. [Baker&H.]
Puckett, Kathryn ....'51 '77 C&L.597 B.S., J.D. 2158 Belvoir Blvd.
Pugh, Charles W. ....'— '04 C.385 B.A. L.569 J.D. [A Jones D.]
Purcell, Kevin, (BV) ....'52 '81 C.363 B.A. L.1003 J.D. [K.Purcell]
Purcell, Mary Eileen ....'— '94 C.97 B.S. L.851 J.D. [S Vorys,S.S.&P.]

Purcell, Kevin, Co., L.P.A., (BV)
19109 Old Detroit Road, 44116
Telephone: 440-331-5883 Fax: 440-331-9125
Email: kevintrust@stratos.net URL: http://www.ohioestateplanninglaw.com
Kevin Purcell.
Elder Law, Trusts and Estates, Asset Protection, Estate Planning, Guardianship, Wills, Probate, Medicaid Eligibility, Revocable Trusts, Living Trusts, Charitable Giving, Living Will, Health Care Power of Attorney.
See Professional Biographies, CLEVELAND, OHIO

Purtiman, Teresa E. ....'— '01 C.608 B.A. L.8 J.D. [C Roetzel&A.]
Pusey, Mark E. ....'62 '90 C.473 B.S. L.930 J.D. Keybank
Pustulka, Kimberly J. ....'— '00 C.107 B.S. L.309 J.D. [A Jones D.]
Pyle, John S., (AV) ....'48 '74 C.318 B.A. L.930 J.D. [Gold&P.]
Quade, Loretta C. ....'49 '75 C.494 B.A. L.930 J.D. 2865 Winthrop
Quallich, Patrick J. ....'71 '99 C.150 B.S. L.989 J.D. [A Bonezzi S.M.&P.]
Quartell, Robert J. ....'52 '98 C.339 A.B. L.1003 J.D. Law Clk., U.S. Dist. Ct.
Quathamer, Nicole J. ....'73 '99 C.608 B.A. L.989 J.D. [A Porter W.M.&A.]
Quick, Harry T., (AV) ....'39 '65 C.363 B.S. L.930 J.D. [Brzytwa,Q.&M.]
Quinlan, Michael Patrick ....'71 '96 C.201 B.S. L.989 J.D. [A Mansour,G.G.&M.]
Quintrell, Thomas A., (AV) ....'20 '48 C.674 A.B. L.309 LL.B. 925 Euclid Avenue
Rabb, Richard A., (AV) ....'63 '90 C.608 B.A. L.1003 J.D. [McCarthy,L.C.&L.]
Rabin, Julie E., (AV) ....'56 '81 C.597 B.S.J. L.569 J.D. [Rabin&R.]
Rabin, Kathy S., (AV) ....'58 '84 C.976 B.A. L.309 J.D. 55 Public Sq., Ste. 1510
Rabin, Mary Ann (Mickey), (AV) ....'34 '78 C.910 A.B. L.930 J.D. [Rabin&R.]

Rabin & Rabin Co., L.P.A., (AV)
55 Public Square, Suite 1510, 44113
Telephone: 216-771-8084 Fax: 216-771-4615
Email: jrabin@rabinandrabin.com URL: http://www.lawyers.com/rabin&rabin
Mary Ann (Mickey) Rabin; Julie E. Rabin.
Bankruptcy, Real Estate, Probate, Commercial Litigation, Creditors Rights, Debtors Rights, Consumer Bankruptcy, Chapter 7, Chapter 11, Chapter 13.
See Professional Biographies, CLEVELAND, OHIO

Racey, Susan L., (AV) ....'63 '89 C.201 B.S. L.930 J.D. [Tucker E.&W.]
Radefeld, Mark B. ....'— '03 C.25 B.A. L.8 J.D. [A Jones D.]
Radel, Victor D. ....'65 '02 C.161 B.A. L.1003 J.D. [Chernett W.Y.&P.]
Rademaker, Dennis A., (AV) ....'50 '77 C.161 B.A. L.1003 J.D. [Rademaker,M.M.&G.]

Rademaker, Matty, McClelland & Greve, (AV)
55 Public Square, Suite 1775, 44113
Telephone: 216-621-6570 Fax: 216-621-1127
URL: http://www.rmmglaw.com
Members of Firm: Dennis A. Rademaker (Certified Specialist in Workers' Compensation Law, Ohio State Bar Association); David J. Matty; Robert C. McClelland; Thomas F. Greve; Kirk R. Henrikson (Certified Specialist in Workers' Compensation Law, Ohio State Bar Association). Associates: Jennifer L. Whitt; Nicole M. Holt; Charles W. Kinkopf.
General Civil Trial and Appellate Practice before State and Federal Courts and Administrative Agencies, Workers' Compensation Defense, Municipal Law, Personal Injury and Products Liability and Insurance Defense, Banking, Corporation, Partnership, Estate Planning, Probate, Real Estate, Labor and Employment Practices Defense.
Reference: First National Bank of Ohio.
See Professional Biographies, CLEVELAND, OHIO

Rader, Elizabeth Anne, (AV) '61 '87
C.608 B.A. L.976 J.D. Gen. Coun., LOCUM Medical Group
Rae, Michael Thomas ....'56 '84 C.130 B.A. L.989 J.D. U.S. Postal Inspection Service
Raeder, James A. ....'48 '75 C.734 B.A. L.1003 J.D. 31825 Bayview Dr.
Rains, M. Neal, (AV) ....'43 '68 C.352 B.A. L.597 J.D. [Frantz W.]
Rains, Robert N., (AV) ....'45 '70 C&L.930 B.A., J.D. 1300 W. 9th Street, Suite 1
Rajki, Sonja C. '76 '02 C.399 B.A. L.124 J.D.
(adm. in IA; not adm. in OH) [A Schneider,S.R.&L.]
Raker, Keith H., (AV) ....'66 '92 C.692 B.A. L.608 J.D. [Tucker E.&W.]
Ralls, Nancy E. ....'— '86 C.161 B.B.A. L.1003 J.D. 34805 Bridle Trail Lane
Ramm, Brian N., (BV) ....'62 '87 C.473 B.A. L.851 J.D. [Ulmer&B.]
Ramos, Edgar A., (BV) ....'48 '77 C.608 B.A. L.930 J.D. 19152 Coffinberry Blvd.
Ramos, Fred P., (BV) ....'52 '78 C&L.201 B.A., J.D. [F.P.Ramos&Assoc.]
Ramos, Fred P., and Associates Co., L.P.A., (BV)
4700 Rockside Road, Suite 650 (Independence)
Ramsey, Alison D. ....'76 '04 C.477 B.A. L.124 J.D. [A Brunn]
Randazzo, Thomas M. ....'62 '88 C.25 B.A. L.851 J.D. N.L.R.B.
Ranke, Daniel R. ....'62 '90 C.363 B.A. L.1003 J.D. Ct. of Appeals

Rankin, Hill, Porter & Clark LLP, (AV)
925 Euclid Avenue, Suite 700, 44115-1405
Telephone: 216-566-9700 Fax: 216-566-9711
Email: info@rankinhill.com URL: http://www.rankinhill.com
Members of Firm: Stephen A. Hill; Wayne D. Porter, Jr.; Kenneth A. Clark; David E. Spaw; Randolph E. Digges, III. Associates: James A. Balazs; Christopher Korff.
Patent, Trademark, Copyright, Unfair Competition Law and Antitrust Law.
Lake County, Ohio Office: 4080 Erie Street, 44094-7836. Telephone: 216-566-9700. Fax: 216-566-9711.
See Professional Biographies, CLEVELAND, OHIO

Ranney, Phillip Allyn, (AV) ....'36 '61 C.197 B.A. L.930 LL.B. [Schneider,S.R.&L.]
Ransom, William H., (AV) ....'38 '64 C&L.477 A.B., J.D. 127 Public Sq.‡
Rapoport, Alan J., (AV) ....'49 '75 C.385 A.B. L.930 J.D. [Rapoport,S.F.&C.]
Rapoport, Kenneth J. ....'51 '77 C.608 B.A. L.930 J.D. 5496 Lansbury Ln.
Rapoport, Spitz, Friedland & Courtney, (AV) ....55 Public Sq.
Rapp, Adrienne L. ....'78 '04 C.473 B.A. L.608 J.D. [A Ulmer&B.]
Rapp, Robert N., (AV) ....'47 '72 C&L.930 B.A., J.D. [Calfee,H.&G.]
Raske, Anna K. ....'71 '96 C.473 B.A. L.201 J.D. [Benesch,F.C.&A.]
Raskin, Todd M., (AV) ....'50 '80 C.381 B.S. L.1003 J.D. [Mazanec,R.&R.]
Rasmussen, Frank M., (AV) ....'34 '60 C.894 A.B. L.309 LL.B. 127 Public Sq.
Rassi, Christopher M. ....'— '03 C&L.930 B.A., J.D. [A Thompson H.]
Rathbone, Joel H., (AV) ....'— '79 C.575 B.A. L.1003 J.D. [Javitch,B.&R.]
Rathbone, Kimberly Lamson '— '01
C.608 B.A. L.989 J.D. 1300 East Ninth Street, 14th Floor
Rathke, Sarah K. ....'76 '01 C.276 B.A. L.477 J.D. [A Squire,S.&D.]
Ratliff, Elizabeth A. ....'77 '02 C.945 B.A. L.893 J.D. [A Vorys,S.S.&P.]
Ratner, Charles A. ....'41 '66 C.165 B.A. L.569 LL.B. 50 Public Sq.

Ratner, Ilana Horowitz, (AV) '50 '78 C.289 B.A. L.564 J.D. 23811 Chagrin Boulevard‡
Rauf, Natalie H. '75 '01 C.340 B.A. L.124 J.D. [Ⓐ Porter W.M.&A.]
Raulerson, Billy Carter '70 '01 C.1111 B.S.C.S. L.201 J.D. [Ⓐ Calfee,H.&G.] (See Pat. Sect.)
Rauser, Victor Paul '68 '93 C.473 B.S. L.930 J.D. [Rauser,L.&Assoc.]
Rauser & Associates, Legal Clinic Co., L.P.A. 614 W. Superior
Rauss, Alan M., (AV) '44 '72 C.659 B.S. L.477 J.D. [Kohrman J.&K.]
Rauzi, Harold R., (BV) '— '89 C.018 B.A. L.930 J.D. [Buckley K.]
Ravas, Sara S. '78 '03 C.1115 B.A. L.124 J.D. [Ⓐ Lowe E.W.&M.]
Rawlin, Dustin B. '— '00 C.93 B.A. L.228 J.D. [Ⓐ Jones D.]
Rawlin, Meggan A. '— '01 C.674 B.A. L.228 J.D. [Ⓐ Jones D.]
Rawlin, Ronald V., (AV) '45 '72 C.97 B.S. L.930 J.D. [Rhoa,F.&R.]
Rawson, Rachel L. '— '91 C.385 B.A. L.178 J.D. [Jones D.]
Rawson, Robert H., Jr., (AV) '— '71 C.674 A.B. L.309 J.D. [Jones D.]
Ray, Brian E. '— '01 C.602 B.A. L.608 J.D. [Ⓐ Jones D.]

Ray, Robinson, Carle & Davies P.L.L., (AV)
1717 East 9th Street, Suite 1650, 44114-2878
Telephone: 216-861-4533 Facsimile: 216-861-4568
Email: rayrob@rayrobcle.com URL: http://www.rayrobcle.com
Members of Firm: Douglas R. Denny; Gene B. George; Julia R. Brouhard; Robert T. Coniam; Sandra Maurer Kelly; Thomas More Wynne. Of Counsel: Lucian Y. Ray (1903-1987); Theodore C. Robinson (1916-2002); William D. Carle, III; David G. Davies.
General Civil Practice in all State and Federal Courts. Trials and Appeals.
Representative Clients: The Cleveland-Cliffs Iron Co.; Bethlehem Steel Corp., Great Lakes Steamship Division; Canada Steamship Lines, Ltd.; Canadian Shipowners Assn.; Interlake Steamship Co.; Ispat Inland, Inc.; Amoco Oil Co.; Container Port Group, Inc.; Euclid Universal Corp.
See Professional Biographies, CLEVELAND, OHIO

Raymond, Robert G. '45 '72 C&L.107 B.A., J.D. (adm. in NY; not adm. in OH) Standard Oil Co.
Rea, John S., (AV) '24 '51 C.604 A.B. L.1003 LL.B. 815 Superior Avenue, N.E.
Read, Deborah Zider, (AV) '57 '82 C.610 A.B. L.94 J.D. [Thompson H.]
Read, John Winship, (AV) '47 '72 C.597 B.A. L.911 J.D. [Vorys,S.S.&P.]
Reader, Harold (Kip), (AV) '49 '74 C.103 A.B. L.930 J.D. [Ulmer&B.]
Ready, John J., Law Offices of '62 '88 C.363 B.A. L.930 J.D. 310 Lakeside Ave. W.
Reagan, John J. '68 '96 C.49 B.A. L.1003 J.D. [Ⓐ Reminger&R.]
Reali, Colleen Ann '72 '00 C.262 B.A. L.724 J.D. Pros. Off.
Rechner, Matthew R. '76 '01 C.602 B.A. L.930 J.D. [Ⓐ McDonald H.]
Rechtin, George A. '09 '32 C&L.973 LL.B. (adm. in KY; not adm. in OH) 28925 Fall River Dr.‡
Redeker, John E., (AV) '49 '74 C.207 B.A. L.1003 J.D. [Ziegler,M.&M.]
Reder, Henry I., (AV) '50 '79 C.381 B. Arch. L.1003 J.D. [Buckingham,D.&B.]
Redmond, Charles C. '17 '39 C&L.607 J.D. 1422 Euclid Ave.‡
Redmond, Hope E. '76 '01 C.294 B.A. L.602 J.D. [Ⓐ Thompson H.]
Redmond, Ian M. '75 '02 C.1105 B.A. L.602 J.D. Jud. Staff Atty.
Reece, Lora M. '— '02 C.576 B.A. L.477 J.D. [Ⓐ Baker&H.]
Reed, Robert C., (AV) '49 '75 C.363 B.A. L.930 J.D. [Reed,M.&W.]
Reed, Stephanie R. '69 '94 C.811 B.A. L.607 J.D. Co. Metro Housing Auth.
Reed, Mazanec & Wheeler, Ltd., (AV) 1801 E. 9th St., Ste. 1710
Reeder, Harold C., (AV) '57 '82 C.259 B.S. L.1003 J.D. 1370 Ontario Street
Rees, Harry D., (AV) '19 '50 C&L.930 B.B.A., J.D. [Ⓒ Lasko&L.]
Reese, Olan R. '55 '84 C.161 B.A. L.1003 J.D. 1375 E. 9th St.
Reeve, Mary E. '46 '82 C.8 B.A. L.7 J.D. Sr. Atty., Federal Reserve Bk. of Cleveland
Rego, John A., (AV) '— '88 C.813 B.S. L.893 J.D. [Jones D.]
Rego, Lucian C., (AV) '44 '71 C.973 B.S. L.1003 J.D. [Rego,C.&H.]
Rego, Cullen & Hagan Co., L.P.A., (AV) 55 Public Sq., Ste. 1550
Reichard, Jenifere M. '78 '98 C.884 B.A. L.989 J.D. [Ⓐ Meyers,R.F.&L.]
Reichard, William E., (AV) '38 '68 C.321 B.S. L.569 J.D. 25109 Detroit Road Suite 300
Reichek, Edward Russ, (AV) '33 '57 C&L.608 B.A., J.D. [E.R.Reichek]
Reichek, Edward R., (AV) 75 Public Sq., Rm. 2336
Reichenbach, Dorothy Foster '41 '75 C.910 B.A. L.124 J.D. Cuyahoga Co. Pros. Atty.
Reid, Christine '67 '93 C.425 B.A. L.1003 J.D. [Ⓐ Reminger&R.]
Reid, Jas. S., Jr. '26 '51 C&L.309 A.B., LL.B. Pres., Standard Products Co.
Reid, Lisa A., (BV) '61 '88 C.363 B.S. L.1003 J.D. [Ⓒ Porter W.M.&A.]
Reid, Timothy T., (AV) '44 '71 C.610 B.B.A. L.930 J.D. [Reid,B.M.&W.]
Reid, Berry, Marshall & Wargo, (AV) 55 Public Sq., Ste. 2000
Reidy, John J., Jr. '32 '57 C.602 A.B. L.930 LL.B. [Ⓒ Ziegler,M.&M.]
Reidy, Michael J., (AV) '52 '78 C.8 B.S. L.930 J.D. [Millisor&N.]
Reiffer, Erin L. '78 '04 C.114 B.A. L.124 J.D. [Ⓐ Berkman,G.M.&D.]
Reil, Mary M., (AV) '56 '82 C.472 B.A. L.276 J.D. [Calfee,H.&G.]
Reiman, Donald L., (AV) '49 '79 C.381 B.A. L.1003 J.D. [Cassidy&R.]
Reinker, Robb F., (BV) '45 '77 C.970 B.A. L.161 J.D. Ferry Cap & Set Screw Co.
Reinker, Susan M., (BV) '— '79 C.161 B.A. L.930 J.D. [Ⓐ Bonezzi S.M.&P.]
Reitman, Robert S. '33 '58 C.923 B.S. L.930 LL.B. Chmn. & CEO, Tranzonic Companies, The
Rekstis, Walter J., III, (AV) '45 '72 C&L.150 B.B.A., J.D. [Ⓒ Squire,S.&D.]
Reminger & Reminger Co., L.P.A., (AV) 101 Prospect Ave., Ste. 1400 (ⓒCovington, KY; Akron, Cin., Columbus, Sandusky, Toledo, Youngstown, OH)
Remington, Royce R., (AV) '61 '88 C.1213 B.S. L.1003 J.D. [Hahn L.&P.]
Rendon, Carole Schwartz '62 '89 C&L.597 B.A., J.D. [Kushner&R.]
Renkert, Richard C., (AV) '25 '50 C.473 A.B. L.930 LL.B. 901 Lakeside Ave.‡
Renner, John W., (AV) '29 '54 C.81 B.S. L.930 LL.B. [Ⓒ Renner,O.B.&S.] (See Pat. Sect.)

Renner, Kenner, Greive, Bobak, Taylor & Weber, A Legal Professional Association
(See Akron)

Renner, Otto, Boisselle & Sklar, LLP, (AV) BB
Nineteenth Floor, 1621 Euclid Avenue, 44115-2183
Telephone: 216-621-1113 Fax: 216-621-6165
Email: mailroom@rennerotto.com URL: http://www.rennerotto.com
John F. Oberlin (1880-1971); Edwin E. Donnelly, Jr. (1925-1976). Members of Firm: Donald L. Otto; Armand P. Boisselle; Warren A. Sklar; Neil A. DuChez; Don W. Bulson; Gordon D. Kinder; Jay R. Campbell; Mark D. Saralino; Cynthia S. Murphy; Christopher B. Jacobs; Jonathan A. Platt; Heidi A. Boehlefeld; Thomas W. Adams; M. David Galin; Todd R. Tucker. Associates: John J. Del Col; Jason A. Worgull; Mark C. Johnson; Kenneth W. Fafrak, Jr.; Daniel R. Ling; Timothy E. Manning; Marisa J. Zink; Thomas G. Fistek; Michele M. Tyrpak. Of Counsel: John W. Renner.
Patent, Trademark, Copyright, Unfair Competition and Related Antitrust Law.
See Professional Biographies, CLEVELAND, OHIO

Rennillo, Irene Holyk '59 '83 C.610 B.A. L.1003 J.D. 1301 E. 9th St.‡
Repicky, Thomas G., (AV) '53 '79 C.363 B.A. L.1003 J.D. [T.Repicky]
Repicky, Thomas, Co., L.P.A., (AV) 526 Superior Avenue
Repko, David V. '52 '78 C.645 B.A. L.229 J.D. (adm. in PA; not adm. in OH) Towers Perrin Consultants
Reppert, Richard L., (AV) '— '74 C.401 B.A. L.884 J.D. [Jones D.]
Reuscher, Christopher P. '75 '02 C.999 B.A. L.8 J.D. [Ⓐ Benesch,F.C.&A.]
Reynolds, Melinda L. '62 '97 C.161 B.B.A. L.930 J.D. [Ⓒ Baker&H.]
Rezie, Richard C.O. '— '99 C.1374 B.A. L.124 J.D. [Ⓐ Gallagher S.]
Reznick, Morris M., (AV) '23 '51 C.610 B.S.C. L.1003 J.D. 815 Superior Avenue, Suite 1001
Rhoa, Albert J., (AV) '24 '49 C&L.930 A.B., LL.B. [Rhoa,F.&R.]
Rhoa, Patrick J., (BV) '60 '90 C.150 B.S. L.1003 J.D. [Ⓐ Sullivan&S.]
Rhoa, Follen & Rawlin Co., L.P.A., (AV) 55 Public Sq., Ste. 850
Rhodes, Tina Y. '61 '86 C.161 B.A. L.574 J.D. Jud. Clk. for Ct. of App.
Ricco, David C. '68 '04 C.8 B.S. L.930 J.D. 1220 West 6th St.
Rice, Clark D., (AV) '55 '80 C.81 B.A. L.1003 J.D. [Koeth,R.&L.]
Rice, Jay Clinton, (AV) '— '79 C&L.930 B.A., J.D. [Gallagher S.]
Rice, John P., Jr. '29 '57 C.363 B.S.S. L.930 LL.B. 1300 Terminal Twr.
Rice, Sonja C. '70 '01 C.604 B.A. L.124 J.D. [Ⓐ Hahn L.&P.] ‡
Rice, Weldon H. '— '03 C.434 B.A. L.989 J.D. [Ⓒ Vorys,S.S.&P.]
Rich, James A. '38 '71 C.688 B.S.M.E. L.276 J.D. (adm. in NY; not adm. in OH; See Pat. Sect.) [Ⓒ D.P.Hochberg]
Rich, Jodi B. '75 '00 C.537 B.A. L.124 J.D. [Ⓐ Ulmer&B.]
Rich, Jonathan A., (BV) '66 '93 C.608 B.S. L.1003 J.D. [Zashin&R.]
Rich, Lauren '51 '76 C.608 B.A. L.930 J.D. N.L.R.B.
Rich, Lawrence J., (BV) '41 '67 C.608 B.S. L.1003 J.D. [Ⓒ Zashin&R.]
Rich, Linda M., (BV) '52 '77 C.161 B.A. L.1003 J.D. 25000 Euclid Ave.
Richard, Renee Tramble '54 '88 C.381 B.B.A. L.1003 J.D. [Ⓐ Squire,S.&D.]
Richards, Daniel A., (AV) '67 '92 C.473 B.S. L.1003 J.D. [Weston H.]
Richards, Joseph V., Jr. '48 '76 C.150 B.B.A. L.8 J.D. Ernst & Young
Richards, Timothy J. '76 '04 C.918 B.A. L.608 J.D. [Ⓐ Baker&H.]
Richardson, Donald J. '67 '97 C.604 B.A. L.930 J.D. [Ⓐ Ulmer&B.]
Richardson, Glen S., (AV) '54 '81 C.827 B.A. L.1003 J.D. [Bentoff&S.]
Richardson, Jeffrey S. '64 '93 C.608 B.S. L.1003 J.D. [Richardson&S.]
Richardson, Nita Kay '69 '94 C.861 B.A. L.930 J.D. [Ⓐ Ulmer&B.]
Richardson, Scott A., (CV) '66 '96 C.7 B.S.I.M. L.8 J.D. [Ⓐ Tucker E.&W.]
Richardson & Schneiberg Co., L.P.A. 1419 West Ninth Street
Richman, Ellen '42 '90 C.793 B.S. L.1003 J.D. 627 W. Saint Clair Ave.
Richman, Stephen D. '57 '86 C.473 B.B.A. L.1003 J.D. [Ⓒ Kohrman J.&K.]
Richthammer, Theresa A. '— '97 C.475 B.A. L.989 J.D. [Ⓐ Gallagher S.]
Rickert, Jeanne M., (AV) '— '80 C.188 B.A. L.930 J.D. [Jones D.]
Ricotta, John J., (BV) '55 '80 C.602 B.A. L.161 J.D. 425 W. Lakeside Ave., Ste. DN
Rider, William H., (BV) '47 '74 C.610 B.S.I.T. L.1003 J.D. [Ⓐ Gibson,B.Z.&M.]
Riebe, Radd L. '52 '78 C.970 B.A. L.930 J.D. V.P., Society Natl. Bk.
Riehl, Charles T., III, (AV) '44 '71 C.165 B.A. L.930 J.D. [Walter&H.]
Riek, F. Benjamin, III, (BV) '52 '78 C&L.124 B.A., J.D. [Riek&Assoc.]
Riek & Associates Co., L.P.A., (BV) 75 Public Square, Suite 1010
Riemenschneider, Dirk E., (AV) '66 '91 C.62 B.A. L.1003 J.D. [Buckingham,D.&B.]
Riester, Jennifer A. '71 '99 C.161 B.S. L.1003 J.D. [Ⓐ Weston H.]
Rieth, Janice Edgehouse, (AV) '53 '78 C.610 B.A. L.930 J.D. [Schneider,S.R.&L.]
Rieth, Richard C. '53 '79 C.161 B.A. L.1003 [Rieth&A.]

Rieth & Antonelli Co.
BP Office Tower, 200 Public Square, Suite 2940, 44114
Telephone: 216-861-2222 Fax: 216-861-2220
Email: dantonelli@riethantonelli.com URL: http://www.riethantonellilaw.com
Members of Firm: Richard C. Rieth; Dominic M. Antonelli; Craig A. Hairston; Mariellen M. Antonelli.
Family Law, Divorce, Collaborative Divorce, Child Custody, child Support, Visitation Rights, Premarital Agreements, Collaborative Law, Family Relations Law.
See Professional Biographies, CLEVELAND, OHIO

Riley, Brian P. '74 '00 C.1381 B.S. L.989 J.D. [Ⓐ Weston H.]
Riley, Christine Sommer '60 '90 C.363 B.A. L.161 J.D. AcroMed Corp.
Riley, David R. '48 '80 C.103 A.B. L.930 J.D. [Moriarty&J.]
Riley, Michael G., (AV) '56 '87 C.321 B.A. L.823 J.D. [McDonald H.]
Riley, Patrick '53 '80 C.825 B.A. L.1003 J.D. BP Oil Co.
Riley, Ronald K. '40 '73 C.502 B.S. L.161 J.D. 1240 W. 6th Street
Riley, Shawn M., (AV) '61 '86 C.381 B.A. L.930 J.D. [McDonald H.]
Rilley, Sue A. '68 '93 C.528 B.A. L.930 J.D. 2112 E. Ohio Bldg.
Rini, Gusty A. '44 '71 C.602 B.B.A. L.1003 J.D. Legal Aid Soc.
Rini, Mary Ann O., (AV) '47 '79 C.599 B.A. L.1003 J.D. Asst. Atty. Gen., State Atty. Gen. Off.
Rini, William T., (AV) '49 '75 C.62 B.A. L.1003 J.D. [Carlisle,M.R.K.&U.]
Rinker, Bruce G., (AV) '51 '77 C.299 B.A. L.930 J.D. [Mansour,G.G.&M.]

Rippner, Schwartz & Carlin
(See Weston Hurd L.L.P.)

Rischitelli, Robert J., Jr '70 '95 C.381 B.A. L.8 J.D. [Ⓒ Sullivan&S.]
Risman, Robert G. '59 '84 C.861 B.A. L.472 J.D. (adm. in FL; not adm. in OH) Exec. V.P., Realtek Industries, Inc.
Risman, Wm. B. '25 '50 L.472 LL.B. (adm. in FL; not adm. in OH) 2701 Park Driveway‡
Rispo, Ronald A., (AV) '43 '67 C.321 A.B. L.477 J.D. [Weston H.]
Ristau, Timothy P., (AV) '42 '66 C.98 B.A. L.930 J.D. [Weston H.]
Ritchey, John J. '47 '73 C.62 B.A. L.608 J.D. V.P., National City Corp.
Ritter, Marin K. '65 '96 C.604 B.A. L.930 J.D. [Rosner&Assoc.]
Ritts, Geoffrey J., (AV) '— '93 C&L.976 B.A., J.D. [Jones D.]
Ritz, Steven W. '62 '88 C.161 B.B.A. L.1003 J.D. 1200 Ontario St.
Ritzenberg, Marvin '27 '52 C.930 B.B.A. L.608 LL.B. 23451 Bryden St.
Ritzler, Joseph G., (BV) '64 '91 C.980 B.S. L.1003 J.D. [Ritzler,C.&S.]
Ritzler, Coughlin & Swansinger, Ltd., (BV) 1001 Lakeside Avenue
Rivchun, Ryan L. '— '02 C.1044 B.S. L.124 J.D. [Ⓐ Dinn,H.&P.]
Rivera, Robert F. '— '03 C.980 B.S. L.608 J.D. [Ⓐ Jones D.]
Rivitz, Richard S., (AV) '42 '67 C.188 A.B. L.309 J.D. [Kahn K.]
Roach, Jennifer S. '75 '01 C.228 A.B. L.597 J.D. [Ⓐ Thompson H.]
Robenalt, James D., (AV) '56 '81 C.473 A.B. L.608 J.D. [Thompson H.]
Robenalt, Thomas D., (BV) '65 '91 C.473 B.A. L.607 J.D. [Novak,R.P.&S.]
Roberson, Christopher W. '55 '80 C.97 B.S. L.1003 J.D. Co. Pub. Def. Off.
Roberts, Glenna M., (BV) '62 '87 C.973 A.B. L.930 J.D. [Vozar,R.&M.]
Roberts, Kevin T., (BV) '57 '86 C.309 A.B. L.930 J.D. [Roberts]
Roberts, Megan K. '75 '02 C.62 B.A. L.1003 J.D. [Ⓐ Ulmer&B.]
Roberts, Tommy, Jr. '52 '84 C.161 B.E.E. L.989 J.D. 3611 Prospect Ave.
Roberts Law Firm, The, (BV) 323 Lakeside Ave. W., Ste. 450
Roberts-Mamone, Lisa A. '— '88 C.294 B.A. L.930 J.D. [Jones D.]
Robertson, Darnella Tracy '69 '96 C.473 B.A. L.1003 J.D. Law Dept.
Robertson, Heidi Gorovitz '64 '90 C.860 B.A. L.966 J.D. 1801 Euclid Ave.
Robertson, Jean R., (AV) '65 '90 C&L.608 B.A., J.D. [McDonald H.]
Robertson, Kevin G., (AV) '60 '84 C&L.930 B.S., J.D. [Baker&H.]

Robey, Gregory Scott '65 '91 C.967 B.A. L.692 J.D.
14402 Granger Road, 44137
Telephone: 216-581-8200 Fax: 216-581-2822 URL: http://www.gregoryscottrobey.com
Email: robeylaw@aol.com URL: http://www.robey-law.com
(Also Member, Robey & Robey).
Associate: Margaret A. Robey.
Federal Criminal Cases, Drug Cases, DUI/DWI, Sex Offenses, Homicide, Weapons, White Collar Crime, Arson, Traffic Offenses, Appeals, Juvenile Cases, Defense of Police Officers.
See Professional Biographies, CLEVELAND, OHIO

Robey, Margaret A. .... '67 '94 C&L.124 B.A., J.D. [G.S.Robey]
Robey, Richard M., (BV) .... '39 '64 C.363 B.S. L.930 J.D. 14402 Granger Rd.
Robinson, Kenneth F. .... '61 '86 C.188 A.B. L.930 J.D. 4101 Fulton Parkway
Robinson, Loreen M. .... '53 '88 C.597 B.S.J. L.46 J.D. 820 W. Superior Ave., Ste. 900
Robinson, Marquettes D. .... '— '01 C&L.309 B.A., J.D. [Vorys,S.S.&P.]
Robinson, Ronald .... '41 '85 C.8 B.A. L.161 J.D. 1276 W. 3rd St., Ste. 424
Robinson, Scott Joseph .... '76 '01 C.930 B.A. L.161 J.D. [Wilkerson&Assoc.]
Rocco, Kenneth A. .... '39 '65 C.610 A.B. L.930 J.D. 1 Lakeside Ave.
Rocco, Patrick R., (BV) .... '43 '69 C.602 A.B. L.251 J.D. [Amirault&R.]
Roche, Patrick F., (AV) .... '— '76 C.1019 B.B.A. L.1003 J.D. [Davis&Y.]
Roche, Patrick M. .... '— '99 C.201 B.S. L.1003 J.D. [Davis&Y.]
Roche, Patrick R., (AV) '52 '78
C.602 B.S.E.E. L.1003 J.D. [Fay,S.F.M.&M.] (See Pat. Sect.)
Rodak, Andrew N. .... '52 '83 C.161 B.A. L.1003 J.D. Staff Atty., Ct. of App.
Roddy, John J. .... '32 '59 C.363 B.S. L.1003 LL.B. 11510 Buckeye Road
Rode, Michael K. .... '55 '80 C.967 B.A. L.930 J.D. Management Recruiters Intl., Inc.
Rodgers, Joseph P. .... '72 '98 C.970 B.A. L.1003 J.D. [Squire,S.&D.]
Rodgers, Lynnette L. .... '70 '01 C.161 B.A. L.1003 J.D. [Ulmer&B.]
Rodgers, Walter A., (AV) .... '44 '70 C.648 B.S. L.161 J.D. [Rodgers]

Rodgers and Co., L.P.A., (AV)
1600 Guildhall, Landmark Office Towers, 45 Prospect Avenue, West, 44115
Telephone: 216-861-6191 Fax: 216-861-4699
Email: attys@rodgersandcolpa.com URL: http://www.lawyers.com/rodgersandco
Walter A. Rodgers;—Jeffrey M. Elzeer; Kathryn A. Kerka.
General Civil Trial and Appellate Practice in all Courts. Complex Litigation, Professional Liability Defense, Commercial, Construction, Personal Injury, Employment, General Insurance Defense, Toxic Tort, ERISA and Insurance Coverage Litigation, Life and Health Insurance, Environmental Law, Real Estate Law, Alternative Dispute Resolution, Products Liability.
See Professional Biographies, CLEVELAND, OHIO

Rodio, Mark L. .... '69 '95 C.930 B.S. L.659 J.D. [Frantz W.]
Rodriguez, Oscar Eduardo .... '74 '01 C.124 B.S.E. L.989 J.D. Asst. Pros.
Roessler, Kirk W., (AV) .... '63 '88 C.385 A.B. L.608 J.D. [Strachan,M.O.&R.]

Roetzel & Andress, A Legal Professional Association, (AV)
One Cleveland Center, 1375 East Ninth Street, 9th Floor, 44114
Telephone: 216-623-0150 Telecopier: 216-623-0134
Email: inquiries@ralaw.com URL: http://www.ralaw.com
Partners: Lewis W. Adkins, Jr. (Resident); Robert E. Blackham (Certified Specialist in Workers' Compensation Law, Ohio State Bar Association); Anna Moore Carulas (Resident); Robert B. Casarona; Carl J. Dyczek; David H. Gunning II; Michael J. Haas (Resident); David R. Harbarger; Joseph E. Herbert (Resident); Timothy C. Ivey; Peter Lawson Jones (Resident); R. Mark Jones (Resident); Ingrid A. Kinkopf-Zajac (Resident); Kenneth M. Lapine (Resident); Douglas G. Leak (Resident); Mark P. McGrievy; Richard S. Mitchell (Resident); Douglas S. Musick (Resident); Basil J. Musnuff; Cheryl A. O'Brien; Richard A. Plewacki (Resident); George W. Rooney, Jr. (Resident); Albert N. Salvatore; Beverly A. Sandacz (Resident); Mark L. Sarlson; Donald S. Scherzer (Resident); James C. Scott; Diana M. Thimmig. Of Counsel: Janice A. Isakoff; Teresa E. Purtiman; Gary A. Weiss (Also at Columbus Office);—Chad Arfons; Ricardo J. Cardenas; Tammi J. Carter; Stephenie L. Conde; Lynn A. Gross (Resident); Christine M. Kattola; Hugh S. Kinast; Lauren K. Kinkopf; Brian H. Linick; Adam C. Miller; James P. Myers; Beth Ann Schenz; John J. Schriner, Jr. (Resident); E. Mark Young.
General Corporate and Business Law, Banking and Finance, Mergers, Acquisitions and Divestitures, Securities Law, Real Estate Law, Real Estate Development/Syndication/Condominium Law, Tax Law, Intellectual Property Law, Computer Law, Hospital and Health Care Law, Public Law and Finance, Governmental Relations, School Law, Commercial/Bankruptcy Law, Employment Law, Pension, Employee Benefits, Workers' Compensation, OSHA, Business and Commercial Litigation, Complex and Multidistrict Litigation, Antitrust Law, RICO, Federal Court Practice, Product Liability, Environmental Law/Toxic Torts, Insurance Law, Information Technology Law, Medical Malpractice Defense, Asbestos Litigation, Construction Law, 1st Amendment/Media Law, White Collar Criminal Defense, Railroad and FELA, Trucking and Transportation Law, Probate and Estate Planning, Risk Management, Utility Law, International Law, Trial and Appellate Practice.
Akron, Ohio Office: 222 South Main Street. Telephone: 330-376-2700. Telecopier: 330-376-4577.
Columbus, Ohio Office: National City Center, 155 E. Broad Street, 12th Floor. Telephone: 614-463-9770. Telecopier: 614-463-9792.
Naples, Florida Office: 850 Park Shore Drive, Trianon Centre. Telephones: 239-649-6200; 800-535-7239. Telecopier: 239-261-3659.
Cincinnati, Ohio Office: 250 East Fifth Street, 310 Chiquita Center. Telephone: 513-361-0200. Telecopier: 513-361-0335.
Fort Myers, Florida Office: 2320 First Street, Suite 1000. Telephone: 239-337-3850. Telecopier: 239-337-0970.
Toledo, Ohio Office: One SeaGate, 9th Floor. Telephone: 419-242-7985. Facsimile: 419-242-0316.
Tallahassee, Florida Office: 225 South Adams Street, Suite 250, P.O. Box 10369. Telephone: 850-222-7718. Telecopier: 850-222-8222.
Washington, D.C. Office: 1025 Connecticut Avenue, NW, Suite 220. Telephone: 202-625-0600. Telecopier: 202-338-6340.
See Professional Biographies, CLEVELAND, OHIO

Rogers, Julie W. .... '— '05 C&L.228 A.B., J.D. [Jones D.]
Rogers, Karla M. .... '70 '97 C.8 B.S. L.1003 J.D. [Calfee,H.&G.]
Rogers, Kelly H. .... '79 '05 C.20 B.A. L.477 J.D. [Janik&D.]
Rogge, Gretchen .... '69 '97 C.597 B.A. L.94 J.D. [Calfee,H.&G.]
Rogo, Patricia Anne .... '54 '79 C.363 B.A. L.1003 J.D. Law Clk., Com. Pleas Ct.
Rokakis, Alexander Alexandros .... '56 '82 C.161 B.A. L.989 J.D. U.S. Atty. Off.
Rolf, Carol, (AV) .... '52 '76 C.930 B.A. L.161 J.D. [Rolf&G.]

Rolf & Goffman Co., L.P.A., (AV)
350 Corporate Circle, 30100 Chagrin Boulevard, 44124-5705
Telephone: 216-514-1100 Telecopier: 216-514-0030
Email: info@rolfgoffman.com URL: http://www.rolfgoffman.com
Carol Rolf; Ira S. Goffman (Board Certified Health Law Lawyer, Florida Bar Board of Legal Specialization and Education); Richard D. Fiktus; Aric D. Martin; Paul A. Lang; Scott Salsbury;—Christopher M. Tost; Craig Haran.
Health Care Law, Labor and Employment, General Civil Litigation in all State and Federal Courts, Administrative, Business, Corporate, Banking, Real Estate, Estate Planning and Probate Law.
Reference: Ohio Health Care Assn.
See Professional Biographies, CLEVELAND, OHIO

Rolitsky, Sandra G. .... '54 '80 C.477 B.A. L.215 J.D. [Calfee,H.&G.]
Roller, Jan L., (AV) .... '— '80 C.207 B.A. L.930 J.D. [Davis&Y.]
Rollinson, James H. '69 '98 C.692 B.S. L.1556 J.D.
(adm. in NY; not adm. in OH) [Baker&H.]
Rollocks, Mildred V. Rucker '32 '61
C.930 A.B. L.329 J.D. World Peace and Progress Foundation, Inc.
Romaine, Daniel A. .... '71 '96 C.381 B.B.A. L.1003 J.D. 425 Lakeside Ave., Ste. 100
Roman, Barbara K., (AV) .... '50 '77 C.608 B.A. L.989 J.D. [Meyers,R.F.&L.]
Romanchek, Catherine Ziroli .... '78 '03 C.602 B.A. L.477 J.D. [Squire,S.&D.]

Romanowski, Esther Barbara .... '51 '79 C.97 B.S. L.989 J.D. Soc. Sec. Admin.
Rome, Peter A., (AV) .... '59 '84 C.860 B.A. L.273 J.D. [Ulmer&B.]
Roof, Brian E. .... '71 '99 C&L.602 B.A., J.D. [Frantz W.]
Rooney, Dean M., (AV) .... '— '83 C.161 B.A. L.1003 J.D. [Kadish,H.&W.]
Rooney, George W., Jr., (AV) .... '49 '74 C.893 B.S.M.E. L.608 J.D. [Roetzel&A.] (Pat.)
Rooney, Thomas D., (BV) .... '47 '72 C.610 B.B.A. L.608 J.D. [Millisor&N.]
Roosa, James K. .... '58 '87 C.604 B.M. L.930 J.D. [Roosa]
Roosa Co., LPA .... 3723 Pearl Road
Roosevelt, James M. '43 '71 C.855 B.S. L.477 J.D.
(adm. in CA; not adm. in OH) 1900 Richmond Road
Rorimer, Louis, (AV) .... '— '75 C.309 A.B. L.930 J.D. [Jones D.]
Roscoe, George Dennis '51 '81 C.980 B.M.Ed. L.1003 J.D.
Advsr., Soc. Sec. Admin., Off. of Hearings & Apps.
Rose, Bruce R., The Law Offices of, (BV) '48 '75
C.94 A.B. L.1003 J.D. 1991 Lee Rd., Ste. 203
Rose, Clark M. .... '47 '73 C.910 A.B. L.597 J.D. Pres., S. Rose Inc.
Rose, Dana A., (AV) .... '59 '84 C.276 B.S.F.S. L.930 J.D. [Weston H.]
Rose, David A. .... '75 '01 C.676 B.A. L.851 J.D. [Britton,S.P.&K.]
Rose, Dennis R., (AV) .... '56 '87 C&L.161 B.S., J.D. [Hahn L.&P.]
Rose, Joseph B., III .... '45 '71 C&L.930 A.B., J.D. 55 Pub. Sq. Bldg., 22th Fl.
Rose, Michael Benjamin '48 '88 C.112 B.A. L.229 J.D.
(adm. in PA; not adm. in OH) Fed. Trade Comm.
Rose, Richard C., Jr. .... '42 '68 C&L.930 B.B.A., J.D. 9570 Park Pl. Dr.‡
Rose, Sam L. .... '23 '51 C&L.930 3718 Silsby Rd.
Rose, Timothy F., (BV) .... '53 '82 C.62 B.A. L.1003 55 Public Sq. Blvd.
Roseman, James D. .... '47 '72 C.610 B.A. L.930 J.D. [Nicola,G.&C.]
Rosen, Allard J. .... '22 '51 C&L.930 B.B.A., LL.B. 1422 Euclid Ave.
Rosenbaum, Emily Raemore .... '75 '03 C.902 B.S. L.124 J.D. 1500 W. Third St., Ste. 460
Rosenbaum, Jacob I., (AV) .... '27 '51 C&L.560 J.D. [Tucker E.&W.]
Rosenbaum, Jeremy A. .... '58 '85 C.150 B.A. L.1003 J.D. [Berkman,G.M.&D.]
Rosenberg, Todd O., (BV) .... '61 '86 C.473 B.A. L.930 J.D. 6110 Parkland Blvd.
Rosenfeld, Robert T., (AV) .... '33 '58 C.103 A.B. L.930 LL.B. 31853 Cedar Rd.
Rosenfeld, Ronald A. .... '39 '64 C.659 B.S. L.309 LL.B. Pres., Multiplex, Inc.
Rosenfield, Ronald L., (BV) .... '43 '70 C.608 B.S.B.A. L.1003 J.D. [Spero&R.]
Rosenthal, Barbara S. .... '35 '87 C.914 B.A. L.1003 J.D. 13800 Shaker Blvd.
Rosenthal, James B., (AV) .... '62 '90 C.976 B.A. L.276 J.D. [Cohen R.&K.]
Rosenthal, Scott S. .... '71 '98 C.473 B.S. L.1003 J.D. [Wilsman&S.]
Rosenzweig, David L., (AV) .... '39 '68 C.980 B.S. L.930 J.D. [McCarthy,L.C.&L.]

Rosman, Barbara Goldberg, (BV) '51 '88 C.831 B.A. L.930 J.D.
Landmark Centre, Suite 360, 25700 Science Park Drive, 44122
Telephone: 216-831-7300 Fax: 216-831-7361
Email: BGRLaw@sbcglobal.net URL: http://www.lawyers.com/barbaragoldbergrosman
Criminal Defense, Civil Practice, Family Law, Divorce, Child Custody, Health Care, Juvenile Law, Medical Collections, Collections, Medical Law, Mediation, Collaborative Law, Debt Collection, Collections, Residential Real Estate, Small Business, Contract Law.
See Professional Biographies, CLEVELAND, OHIO

Rosman, Warren, (AV) .... '51 '76 C.367 B.A. L.930 J.D. [Weston H.]
Rosner, Richard A., (AV) .... '39 '64 C&L.930 B.B.A., J.D. [Kahn K.]
Rosner, William R., (AV) .... '46 '82 C.610 B.A. L.1049 J.D. [Rosner&Assoc.]
Rosner & Associates, L.L.C., (AV) .... 812 Huron Road
Rospert, Anthony J. .... '— '03 C.363 B.A. L.1194 J.D. [Thompson H.]
Ross, Alan G., (AV) .... '49 '75 C.477 B.A. L.1003 J.D. [Ross,B.&S.]
Ross, Alan J., (AV) .... '47 '75 C.161 B.C.E. L.1003 J.D. [Bricker&E.] (Pat.)
Ross, David, (AV) .... '51 '76 C.597 B.A. L.1003 J.D. [Reminger&R.]
Ross, Harold A., (AV) .... '31 '56 C.930 A.B. L.309 J.D. [Ross&K.]
Ross, Richard G., (BV) .... '58 '83 C.696 B.A. L.930 J.D. [Wuliger,F.&B.]
Ross, Robert A., (AV) .... '60 '85 C.473 B.S. L.276 J.D. [Calfee,H.&G.]
Ross, William L. S., (AV) .... '56 '82 C.893 B.A. L.945 J.D. [Calfee,H.&G.]

Ross, Brittain & Schonberg Co., L.P.A., (AV)
6000 Freedom Square Drive, Suite 540, 44131
Telephone: 216-447-1551 Telecopier: 216-447-1554
URL: http://www.rbslaw.com
Alan G. Ross; Brian K. Brittain (Certified Specialist, Workers' Compensation Law, Ohio Bar Board of Legal Specialization and Education); Evelyn P. Schonberg (Certified Specialist, Labor and Employment Law, Ohio Bar Board of Legal Specialization and Education); David T. Andrews;—Anthony A. Baucco; Jennifer A. Bennett; Jerry P. Cline; Scott Coghlan; Christopher R. Debski; David S Farkas; Nick A. Nykulak; Meredith L. Ullman; Thomas R. Wyatt.
Practice Limited to the Representation of Management in all aspects of Labor Law, Employment Relations and Workers Compensation Matters.
See Professional Biographies, CLEVELAND, OHIO

Ross & Kraushaar Co., L.P.A., (AV) .... 1370 Ontario St.
Rossen, Howard M., (AV) .... '36 '64 C.665 A.B. L.1003 J.D. [Rossen&R.]
Rossen, Marc D. .... '68 '94 C.477 B.A. L.1003 J.D. [Rossen&R.]
Rossen & Rossen, (AV) .... 16781 Chagrin Blvd., Ste. 108
Rossi, Assunta .... '59 '89 C.608 B.A. L.117 J.D. Gen. Coun., Victoria Financial Corp.
Rossman, Alan C., (BV) .... '53 '81 C.999 M.A. L.1003 J.D. 75 Public Sq., Ste. 1325
Rotatori, Arthur J. .... '56 '81 C.930 B.A. L.597 J.D. [McGlinchey S.]
Rotatori, Robert J., (AV) .... '37 '62 C&L.930 B.A., J.D. [Rotatori,B.G.S.&A.]

Rotatori, Bender, Gragel, Stoper & Alexander Co. L.P.A., (AV)
800 Leader Building, 526 Superior Avenue East, 44114-1498
Telephone: 216-928-1010 Fax: 216-928-1007
URL: http://www.rotatori.com
Robert J. Rotatori; J. Timothy Bender; Susan L. Gragel; Richard L. Stoper, Jr.; Joseph P. Alexander; J. Scott Broome;—Cara L. Santosuosso.
Employment Law, Civil Practice, Trial Practice, Appellate Practice, Labor Law, Domestic Relations, Antitrust, Securities Litigation, Trade Secrets, White Collar Criminal Defense, Taxation, Business Law, Civil and Criminal Tax Controversy.
See Professional Biographies, CLEVELAND, OHIO

Roth, Arnold A. .... '18 '55 C.608 L.1003 J.D. 1111 Rochefeller Bldg.
Roth, Carole A., (AV) .... '53 '78 C.665 B.A. L.1003 J.D. 3162 Huntington Rd.
Roth, Jennifer L. .... '74 '02 C.608 B.S. L.124 J.D. [Calfee,H.&G.]
Roth, Lad J., (AV) .... '26 '50 C.251 B.B.A. L.930 J.D. [Hahn,S.&P.]
Roth, Lisa J. .... '72 '01 C.97 B.A. L.989 J.D. [Ziegler,M.&M.]
Roth, Randolph Richard .... '58 '94 C.62 B.A. L.1003 J.D. 6000 Freedom Square Drive
Roth, Ronald J. .... '41 '65 C.145 B.S. L.930 J.D. 2200 Kerwin Rd.‡
Roth, Timothy Patrick .... '— '94 C.262 B.A. L.930 J.D. [Gallagher S.]

Roth Bierman LLP
(See Bedford Heights)

Rothenberg, Larry R., (AV) .... '53 '78 C.610 B.B.A. L.608 J.D. [Weltman,W.&R.]
Rothenbuecher, H. Alan, (BV) .... '64 '89 C.477 A.B. L.930 J.D. [Schottenstein,Z.&D.]
Rothschild, Edmund W., (AV) .... '29 '58 C.347 A.B. L.930 J.D. 3681 S. Green Rd.
Round, Edmund .... '45 '75 C.103 A.B. L.930 J.D. Admin. Law J., Soc. Sec. Admin.
Roush, Jeffrey D. .... '— '02 C.851 B.A. L.477 J.D. [Jones D.]
Routh, Ryan T. .... '— '99 C.611 B.A. L.477 J.D. [Jones D.]
Rowan, Maria A. .... '76 '03 C.610 B.A. L.124 J.D. [Weltman,W.&R.]

Rowinski, Gregory B. ....'52 '77 C.602 B.A. L.1003 J.D. 1200 Ontario Street
Rowland, Ann Catherine ....'51 '76 C&L.124 B.A., J.D. Asst. U.S. Atty.
Rowles, Kami Davis ....'73 '99 C.473 B.A. L.150 J.D. [Ⓐ Schuster&S.]
Rownd, James H. ....'— '89 C.967 B.A. L.347 J.D. [Kadish,H.&W.]
Rowthorn, David L., (BV) ....'50 '76 C&L.930 B.A., J.D. [Lavelle&L.]
Royer, Charles P., (BV) ....'61 '86 C.651 B.A. L.665 J.D. [McCarthy,L.C.&L.]
Rozic, Jennifer L. ....'77 '05 C.610 B.B.A. L.989 J.D. [Ⓐ Kelley&F.]
Rua, M. Jane, (AV) ....'58 '86 C.851 B.S.N. L.608 J.D. [Jeffries,K.F.&M.]
Ruben, Alan M. '31 '57 C&L.659 A.B., J.D.
Prof. of Law, Cleveland Marshall Coll. of Law
Ruben, Susan Grody, (AV) ....'55 '83 C.1380 B.F.A. L.1065 J.D. 30799 Pinetree Rd.
Rubenstein, Ronald M., (AV) '33 '57
C.477 B.A. L.930 J.D. 1660 West Second Street, Tower City Center
Rubin, Karen E., (AV) ....'53 '85 C.161 B.A. L.1003 J.D. [Ⓐ Thompson H.]
Rubin, Ryan K. ....'78 '04 C.473 B.A L.930 J.D. [Ⓐ Mannion&G.]
Rubinstein, Richard E., (AV) ....'39 '63 C.102 B.A. L.178 LL.B. [Ulmer&B.]
Ruda, Lisa Marie ....'69 '94 C.97 B.A. L.930 J.D. Cleveland Mun. School Dist.
Rudland, William P. '37 '60 C.994 B.A. L.178 LL.B.
(adm. in NY; not adm. in OH) 1111 Superior Avenue
Rudnick, Elizabeth S. ....'72 '98 C.659 B.A. L.930 J.D. [Ⓐ Ulmer&B.]
Rudy, Mark T., (BV) ....'63 '90 C.259 B.S. L.1003 J.D. 11510 Buckeye Rd.
Ruffinengo, Piero G. '44 '75 C.37 B.S. L.878 J.D.
(adm. in UT; not adm. in OH; See Pat. Sect.) [Ⓒ D.P.Hochberg]
Ruggeri, Robert A., (AV) ....'41 '68 C.152 B.A. L.1003 J.D. 55 Public Sq.
Ruiz, David A. ....'73 '00 C&L.608 B.A., J.D. [Ⓐ Calfee,H.&G.]
Rukovena, George ....'43 '72 C.980 B.S. L.1003 J.D. 25751 Woodpath Trail
Rule, Hilary W. ....'— '88 C.1365 B.A. L.94 J.D. Coun., TRW Inc.
Rundelli, Raymond ....'60 '85 C.473 A.B. L.477 J.D. [Calfee,H.&G.]
Rupert, Aaron J. ....'76 '02 C.970 B.A. L.477 J.D. [Ⓐ Baker&H.]
Ruple, Jeffrey W. ....'— '97 C.207 B.A. L.201 J.D. [Ⓐ Buckley K.]
Ruppelt, Ronna F. '60 '85 C.381 B.S. L.1003 J.D.
Litigation Manager, Progressive Insurance Company
Ruschak, Melinda L. ....'61 '86 C.608 B.A. L.117 J.D. [Powers&G.]
Ruschel, Brian G. ....'61 '90 C.161 B.B.A. L.1003 J.D. 925 Euclid Avenue, Suite 660
Rush, Daryl P. ....'57 '85 C.150 B.A. L.329 J.D. 1956 W 25th St. Suite 200
Rush, Scott R. ....'65 '90 C.631 B.A. L.607 J.D. Ernst & Young
Russ, Christopher J., (BV) .....'57 '83 C.602 B.A. L.851 J.D. 1200 Ontario Street, Floor 8
Russell, Carolyn C. ....'61 '99 C.668 B.A. L.477 J.D. [Ⓐ Tucker E.&W.]
Russell, Delisa Y. ....'69 '01 C.801 B.S. L.345 J.D. [Ⓐ Thompson H.]
Russell, James F. ....'32 '66 C.475 B.S. L.1003 J.D. 3400 W. 123rd. St.
Russell, Shawn R. ....'58 '86 C.347 B.A. L.161 J.D. [Ⓒ Squire,S.&D.]
Russin, Rodion ....'32 '60 C.1028 A.B. L.1003 J.D. [Rutter&R.]
Russo, Angelo ....'73 '02 C.161 B.S. L.989 J.D. [A.Russo]
Russo, John J., (AV) ....'65 '92 C.363 B.A. L.161 J.D. [Polito&R.]
Russo, Nancy M. ....'56 '82 C.920 A.B. L.1003 J.D. Com. Pleas J.
Russo, Angelo, & Co., LLC ....820 W. Superior Ave., Ste. 310
Rusyn, Daria H. ....'50 '78 C.49 B.A. L.607 J.D. 7650 Plumwood Ln.
Rutherford, Guy D. ....'64 '96 C.161 B.A. L.1003 J.D. 614 Superior Avenue, Suite 940
Rutkowski, Robert W., (AV) ....'66 '91 C.8 B.A. L.124 J.D. [Weltman,W.&R.]
Rutsky, Bruce S., (AV) ....'57 '83 C.347 B.A. L.608 J.D. [Petronzio S.]
Rutter, Robert P., (AV) ....'54 '79 C.608 B.S. L.930 J.D. [Rutter&R.]
Rutter & Russin, (AV) ....4700 Rockside Road Suite 650
Ryan, Anne M. ....'61 '86 C.161 B.A. L.1003 J.D. 1991 Crocker Rd. Ste. 550
Ryan, Daniel J. ....'45 '73 C.363 B.A. L.161 J.D. [D.J.Ryan]
Ryan, Jody P. ....'65 '91 C.532 B.A. L.124 J.D. [Ⓐ Licata&Assoc.]
Ryan, Kate E. ....'— '97 C.97 B.S. L.989 J.D. [Ⓐ Ulmer&B.]
Ryan, Michael John ....'71 '96 C.25 B.A. L.989 J.D. City Pros. Off.
Ryan, Miles F., Jr. ....'19 '48 C&L.930 B.A., J.D. 26376 John Rd.‡
Ryan, Robert E. ....'42 '68 C&L.930 B.A., J.D. 4403 Saint Clair Ave.
Ryan, Terrance L., (AV) ....'47 '76 C&L.851 B.A., J.D. [Shanahan] ⊙

Ryan, Daniel J., LPA
1370 Ontario Street, Suite 2000, 44113
Telephone: 216-363-6082 Fax: 216-696-1718
Email: offdanryan@msn.com URL: http://www.lawyers.com/lawyerscomdanieljryan
Daniel J. Ryan.
Personal Injury, Auto Accidents, Civil Litigation, Industrial Injuries, Medical Malpractice, Professional Malpractice, Business Litigation, Employment Law, Wrongful Termination.
See Professional Biographies, CLEVELAND, OHIO

Rybka, Edward W., (BV) '55 '81 C.363 B.A. L.1003 J.D.
Councilman, City of Cleveland
Rybka, Robert S., (BV) ....'57 '84 C.967 B.A. L.930 J.D. 6302 Fleet Ave.
Ryder, Edward M., (AV) ....'48 '77 C.161 B.A. L.1003 J.D. [Mazanec,R.&R.]
Rydzel, James A., (AV) ....'— '72 C.734 B.A. L.228 J.D. [Jones D.]
Ryhal, James L., Jr., (AV) ....'24 '52 C&L.930 A.B., J.D. 1501 Euclid Avenue‡
Rymond, Richard J., (BV) ....'56 '82 C.429 B.A. L.930 J.D. [Ⓐ Reminger&R.]
Saada, John M., Jr. ....'— '93 C.363 B.S. L.930 J.D. [Jones D.]
Saba, Ruth Hakaim '55 '80 C.611 B.A. L.1003 J.D.
Gen. Atty., Dept. of Veterans Affairs
Sable, Theresa E. ....'68 '96 C.608 B.A. L.930 J.D. P.O. Box 241127
Sabroff, Brett M. .....'49 '77 C.608 B.S. L.1003 J.D. 23230 Chagrin Boulevard, Suite 720
Sacco, Joel F. ....'56 '83 C.188 A.B. L.1003 J.D. Mag., Com. Pleas Ct.
Saccogna, Patrick J., (BV) ....'— '90 C.381 B.B.A. L.930 J.D. [Ⓒ Thompson H.]
Sadd, George J., (AV) ....'42 '67 C.363 B.S.S. L.930 J.D. 2001 Crocker Rd.
Sadlowski, Jeffrey R. ....'63 '90 C.192 B.S. L.161 J.D. [Amin&T.] (See Pat. Sect.)
Sadre May, Katayoon ....'78 '04 C.893 B.A. L.575 J.D. [Ⓐ McDonald H.]
Saffold, Shirley Strickland ....'51 '77 C.1023 B.A. L.1003 J.D. Com. Pleas J.
Saganich, John M. ....'57 '84 C&L.930 B.A., J.D. [Vorys,S.S.&P.]
Saganich, Suzanne Klensmith, (AV) ....'61 '87 C.373 B.A. L.930 J.D. [Bricker&E.]
Sage, Victoria M. ....'55 '88 C.66 B.A. L.1003 J.D. 22649 Lorain Road
Saggio, Joseph A. ....'36 '67 C.610 B.S.M.E. L.1003 J.D. 1816 Halls Carriage Path
St. John, Kathleen J., (BV) ....'56 '82 C.610 B.A. L.1003 J.D. [Nurenberg,P.H.&M.]
Saks, Jeffrey ....'— '97 C.94 B.A., B.S. L.262 J.D. [Ⓐ Jones D.]
Saks, William M. ....'55 '91 C.273 A.B. L.930 J.D. 2511 Overlook Rd.
Salamon, Jay H., (AV) ....'54 '80 C.381 B.S. L.930 J.D. [Hermann,C.&S.]
Salata, R. Christopher ....'76 '01 C.602 B.S. L.124 J.D. [Ⓐ McDonald H.]
Salatka, Michael A. '57 '92 C.37 B.S. L.607 J.D.
(adm. in WI; not adm. in OH) Medical Mutual of Ohio
Salerno, Matthew A. ....'74 '99 C.608 B.A. L.930 J.D. [Ⓐ McDonald H.]
Salisbury, David W., (AV) ....'56 '84 C.228 B.A. L.880 J.D. [Thompson H.]
Salisbury, George A. ....'25 '72 C&L.161 B.B.S., J.D. 8191 Broadview Rd.
Salsbury, Scott, (BV) ....'62 '87 C.381 B.A. L.608 J.D. [Rolf&G.]
Saltzman, Barbara E., (AV) ....'46 '77 C.679 B.A. L.930 J.D. 75 Public Sq.
Saltzman, Judith C. ....'49 '74 C.918 B.A. L.588 J.D. [Hickman&L.]
Saltzman, Michael J. ....'45 '70 C.679 B.S. L.124 J.D. [Saltzman&Assoc.]

Saltzman and Associates Co., LPA ....1370 Ontario Street
Salvatore, Albert N., (AV) ....'54 '82 C.363 B.S.B.A. L.1003 J.D. [Roetzel&A.]
Sammon, Albert C., (AV) ....'56 '85 C.973 B.S. L.989 J.D. [Sammon&B.]
Sammon, Colin P. ....'76 '03 C.473 B.S. L.607 J.D. [Ⓐ Novak,R.P.&S.]
Sammon & Bolmeyer Co., L.P.A., (AV) ....614 Superior Avenue N.W.
Sampliner, Thomas A., (BV) ....'46 '71 C.608 B.A. L.477 J.D. 2651 Kerwick Rd.
Sanborn, Elizabeth M., (AV) ....'55 '81 C.173 B.A. L.1228 J.D. [Ⓐ Squire,S.&D.]
Sanchez, Marc A., (AV) ....'66 '91 C.228 A.B. L.813 J.D. [Frantz W.]
Sandacz, Beverly A., (AV) ....'60 '94 C.876 B.S.N. L.1003 J.D. [Roetzel&A.]
Sandel, Martin L., (BV) ....'47 '73 C.937 B.A. L.607 J.D. [Bilfield&S.]
Sander, Richard W. ....'43 '71 C.679 B.S. L.1003 J.D. Pres. & CEO, St. Claire Co.
Sanders, Robert B. '42 '68
C.473 B.A. L.1003 J.D. Sr. V.P. Dir. Mktg., Maxus Investment Grp.
Sandhu, Manbir S. ....'— '00 C.8 B.A. L.1187 J.D. [Ⓐ Maguire&S.] ⊙
Sandler, Alan G. ....'35 '59 C.610 B.S.C. L.930 LL.B. 50 Pub. Sq.
Sands, John F. ....'30 '56 C.930 L.1003 LL.B. 5001 Buttonbush Ln.
Sanislo, Paul S., (AV) ....'27 '61 C.62 B.A. L.1003 J.D. [Ⓒ Stewart&D.]
Sanislo & Associates Co., L.P.A., (AV) ....1370 Ontario St.
Sansalone, Monica A. ....'— '95 C.424 B.A. L.1003 J.D. [Gallagher S.]
Sanson, Michael A., (AV) ....'49 '74 C.363 B.S.B.A. L.1003 J.D. 1640 Standard Building
Santoli, David M. ....'63 '88 C.930 B.A. L.893 J.D. 614 Superior Ave., N.W.
Santoro, Joseph J. ....'— '97 C.363 B.S. L.851 J.D. [Gallagher S.]
Santosuosso, Cara L. ....'73 '98 C.363 B.A. L.1003 J.D. [Ⓐ Rotatori,B.G.S.&A.]
Saralino, Mark D. ....'61 '89 C&L.7 B.S.E.E., J.D. [Renner,O.B.&S.] (See Pat. Sect.)
Sardina, Jennifer ....'73 '00 C.116 B.A. L.989 J.D. [Ⓐ Davis&Y.]
Sargent, John DeVore '46 '71 C.381 B.A. L.150 J.D.
U.S. Equal. Employ. Oppt. Comm.
Sargent, Lynn S. '63 '89 C.861 B.A. L.659 J.D.
(adm. in VA; not adm. in OH) 2180 S. Overlook Rd.‡
Sarkar, Neil S. ....'71 '97 C.145 B.A. L.930 J.D. [Ⓐ Karberg,K.W.&T.]
Sarkar, Richik ....'71 '98 C.477 B.A. L.124 J.D. [Ⓐ Ulmer&B.]
Sarlson, Mark L., (AV) ....'61 '86 C.893 B.A. L.608 J.D. [Roetzel&A.]
Sassano, James L. ....'64 '93 C.97 B.S.B.A. L.1003 J.D. [Ⓐ Carlisle,M.R.K.&U.]
Sasse, Benjamin C. ....'75 '00 C.231 B.A. L.124 J.D. [Ⓐ Tucker E.&W.]
Satola, James W. ....'61 '89 C.608 B.S. L.930 J.D. [Ⓐ Squire,S.&D.]
Satullo, Nicholas D., (AV) ....'54 '85 C.161 B.A. L.1003 J.D. [Ⓐ Reminger&R.]
Sauer, Joseph M. ....'— '99 C.923 B.S.E.E. L.229 J.D. [Ⓐ Jones D.] (See Pat. Sect.)
Sauer, McKinley Hobart, III, (AV) ....'60 '87 C.8 B.S. Acct. L.608 J.D. [Baker&H.]
Sauvain, Timothy W., (BV) ....'44 '70 C.363 B.S.B.A. L.161 J.D. 27900 Chagrin Blvd.
Savage, Jennifer A., (AV) ....'65 '90 C.691 B.A. L.930 J.D. [Thompson H.]
Savage, Mark J. ....'73 '98 C.62 B.A. L.251 J.D. [Ⓐ Squire,S.&D.]
Savidge, Keith A., (AV) ....'46 '72 C.930 B.A. L.989 J.D. [Seeley,S.&E.L.&Assoc.]
Savren, Clifford ....'53 '79 C.696 B.A. L.930 J.D. 505 Terminal Tower‡
Savren, Joy B., (BV) ....'57 '82 C.966 B.A. L.161 J.D. 1422 Euclid Ave.
Sayler, John Liston ....'56 '81 C.607 B.A. L.1003 J.D. 1662 Parkwood Rd.
Sayler, Richard H., (AV) .....'— '70 C.197 A.B. L.477 J.D. [Ⓒ Jones D.] (See Pat. Sect.)
Sayoc, Jeffrey A. ....'72 '00 C.97 B.A. L.851 J.D. [Ⓐ Singerman,M.D.&K.]
Sayre, John D., (AV) ....'50 '77 C.210 B.A. L.930 J.D. [Nicola,G.&C.]
Scadden, Kathy ....'— '03 C.508 B.S. L.989 [Ⓐ Duvin,C.&H.]
Scalish, Rachel Nigro ....'63 '90 C&L.602 B.A., J.D. Cleveland City Coun.
Scanlon, Stephen D. ....'— '85 C.567 B.S. L.150 J.D. [Ⓒ Jones D.] (See Pat. Sect.)
Scanlon, Thomas J., (AV) ....'38 '63 C.363 B.S. L.1003 J.D. [Collins&S.]
Scarbrough, James E. '64 '97
C.645 B.S.M.E. L.930 J.D. [Fay,S.F.M.&M.] (See Pat. Sect.)
Scarlato, Antonio J. ....'74 '01 C&L.851 B.S., J.D. [Ⓐ Shapiro&F.]
Schabes, Alan E., (AV) ....'57 '81 C.229 B.S. L.1019 J.D. [Benesch,F.C.&A.]
Schaefer, Charles R., (AV) ....'43 '69 C.401 B.A. L.930 J.D. [Walter&H.]
Schaefer, David A., (AV) ....'48 '74 C.473 B.S. L.930 J.D. [McCarthy,L.C.&L.]
Schafer, Cynthia C., (AV) ....'58 '86 C.597 B.S. L.893 J.D. Coun., Ameritech Corp.
Scharf, Scott H., (BV) ....'64 '90 C.608 B.A. L.930 J.D. [Novak,R.P.&S.]
Scharf, Stephen L. '64 '91 C&L.477 B.S.E., J.D.
Asst. Gen. Coun., Intell. Prop., Amer. Greetings Corp.
Scharon, John V., Jr., (AV) ....'53 '78 C.8 B.A. L.930 J.D. [Ⓒ Aggers,J.&C.]
Schatz, William B., (AV) ....'46 '73 C&L.930 B.B.A., J.D. 3826 Euclid Ave.
Schaul, Louis R. ....'43 '78 C.951 B.A. L.1003 J.D. Pres., David Advertising, Inc.
Schaut, Jos. W. ....'28 '53 C&L.276 B.S.S., J.D. V.P., Society Natl. Bk.
Schechter, Roy J., (BV) ....'58 '86 C.36 B.S. L.930 J.D. [Lichko&S.]
Schecter, Sheldon D., (AV) ....'26 '53 C&L.930 B.A., LL.B. 113 St. Clair
Schedlbauer, Kara M. ....'78 '03 C.25 B.A. L.124 J.D. [Smith M.]
Scheiman, Becky M. ....'72 '98 C.901 B.A. L.436 J.D. [Ⓐ Nicola,G.&C.]
Schenck, Brett A. '64 '92 C.679 B.S.E.E. L.879 J.D.
[Ⓐ Tarolli,S.C.&T.] (See Pat. Sect.)
Schenz, Beth Ann ....'70 '01 C.973 B.S. L.989 J.D. [Ⓐ Roetzel&A.]
Scherzer, Donald S., (AV) ....'49 '75 C.97 B.S. L.930 J.D. [Roetzel&A.]
Scheufler, Alan W., (AV) ....'58 '83 C.473 B.A. L.930 J.D. [Ulmer&B.]
Schiau, Daniel Louis ....'63 '91 55 Public Square, Suite 800
Schieman, Nancy Eileen ....'59 '91 C.161 B.A. L.930 J.D. Ct. of App.
Schiff, Marvin H., (BV) ....'59 '84 C.184 B.A. L.930 J.D. [Schiff&D.]
Schiff & Dickson, L.L.C., (BV) ....1370 Ontario Street
Schifko, Robert F. ....'30 '64 C.97 B.S. L.930 LL.B. Asst. Law Dir.
Schildhouse, Mark B. ....'52 '80 C.150 B.A. L.1003 J.D. [Kohrman J.&K.]
Schiller, James J., & Associates, (AV) '33 '62
C.124 B.S. L.477 J.D. 13224 Shaker Square, Suite 210
Schiller, John E., (AV) ....'57 '84 C.893 B.A. L.930 J.D. [Ⓐ Walter&H.]
Schiller, Thomas P., (AV) ....'34 '60 C.124 B.S. L.930 J.D. [Pearne&G.] (See Pat. Sect.)
Schiopota, Eugene ....'26 '64 C.608 B.M.E. L.1003 J.D. 5723 Gateway Ln.
Schlegelmilch, Stephan J. ....'74 '00 C&L.124 B.A., J.D. [Ⓐ Baker&H.]
Schleimer, G. N. ....'17 '42 C.930 L.989 J.D. 2016 W. Schaaf Rd.
Schlesinger, Shawn W. ....'73 '98 C.610 B.A. L.1003 J.D. [Ⓐ Koeth,R.&L.]
Schmeichel, Kenneth R. ....'47 '73 C.238 B.A. L.145 J.D. [Calfee,H.&G.] ‡
Schmelzer, Thomas ....'51 '77 C&L.930 B.A., J.D. [Schmelzer&Assoc.]
Schmelzer & Associates ....55 Public Sq., Ste. 2200
Schmidley, Eugenia M. ....'52 '78 C.822 B.A. L.262 J.D. [Ⓒ McGlinchey S.]
Schmidt, David G., (AV) ....'45 '70 C.429 B.A. L.350 J.D. [Schmidt]
Schmidt, Robert N. '48 '81 C.688 B.S.M.E. L.1003 J.D.
Pres., Orbital Research Inc. (Pat.)
Schmidt Legal Group, (AV) ....614 West Superior Avenue, Suite 1500
Schmitz, Joseph P., (BV) ....'53 '79 C&L.608 B.A., J.D. Asst. U.S. Atty.
Schmitz, Thomas M. ....'38 '67 C.124 B.S. L.1003 J.D. 925 Euclid Ave. (Pat.)
Schmitz, William F. ....'49 '85 C.381 B.S. L.161 J.D. [Ⓐ Johnson,A.&C.]
Schnee, Douglas B., (AV) ....'69 '94 C.861 B.A. L.930 J.D. [McDonald H.]
Schneiberg, Jerald A. ....'66 '93 C.610 B.A. L.989 J.D. [Richardson&S.]
Schneider, Hubert H., (AV) ......'02 '27 C.611 A.B. L.309 LL.B. 1111 Superior Ave. E.‡

Schneider, Joseph G., (AV) '33 '57 C.800 A.B. L.930 LL.B. 1900 East Ninth Street
Schneider, Kent B., (AV) '51 '76 C.608 B.A. L.1292 J.D. [Hermann,C.&S.]
Schneider, Paul Kohl '— '92 C.602 B.S. L.989 J.D. [A Gallagher S.]

Schneider, Smeltz, Ranney & LaFond P.L.L., (AV)
1111 Superior Avenue, Suite 1000, 44114
Telephone: 216-696-4200 Telecopier: 216-696-7303
URL: http://www.ssrl.com
Members of Firm: John E. Smeltz; Phillip Allyn Ranney; Thomas J. LaFond; James D. Vail; Janice Edgehouse Rieth; James P. Farmer, Jr.; Charles F. Adler (Certified Specialist in Estate Planning Trust and Probate Law, Ohio State Bar Association); Jonathan L. Stark; Kenneth J. Laino; J. Paul Fidler;—Sonja C. Rajki (Not admitted in OH); Sandra C. Lucas; Michael K. French; Adrienne N. Cvetkovic. Of Counsel: Joseph P. Gibbons.
General Practice, Corporate, Estate Planning and Probate, Real Estate, Taxation, Domestic Relations, Employment Law, Civil Litigation, Health Care.
References: National City Bank; KeyBank.
See Professional Biographies, CLEVELAND, OHIO

Schneier, Jamie B. '63 '93 C.608 B.S.B.A. L.809 J.D. [Petronzio S.]
Schnopp, Stefan K. '— '97 C.608 B.A. L.851 J.D. [A Jones D.]
Schoby, Maurice '53 '79 C.970 B.A. L.276 J.D.
Case Western Reserve Univ. Law School
Schoenfield, Nichol M. '70 '96 C.605 B.A. L.608 J.D. [S Baker&H.]
Scholz, Karin M. '— '03 C.473 B.A. L.1003 J.D. [A Baker&H.]
Schonberg, Evelyn P. '55 '81 C.30 B.S. L.1003 J.D. [Ross,B.&S.]
Schonberg, William E., (AV) '54 '79 C.610 B.G.S. L.1003 J.D. [Benesch,F.C.&A.]
Schooler, Scott H., (BV) '57 '84 C.569 B.A. L.930 J.D. [A Forbes,F.&Assoc.]
Schoonover, John E., (AV) '58 '84 C.604 B.A. L.930 J.D. [Wilsman&S.]

Schottenstein Zox & Dunn Co., LPA, (AV)
USBank Centre, 1350 Euclid Avenue, Suite 1400, 44115 ⊙
Telephone: 216-621-6501 Fax: 216-621-6502
Email: info@szd.com URL: http://www.szd.com
M. Colette Gibbons; Raymond C. Headen; H. Alan Rothenbuecher; Robert M. Stefancin; Matthew J. Stockslager;—Linda S. Gemind; Jay E. Krasovec; Meghan D. Majernik; Katherine G. Manghillis. Of Counsel: Jeffrey A. Perlmuter.
Business (Corporate, Banking and Lending, Real Estate/Land Use, General Tax, State and Local Tax, Employee Benefits, Estate Planning, White Collar Crime, E-Commerce, Intellectual Property/Technology Protection, International); Labor and Employment Law, Litigation, Health Law, Construction Law, Bankruptcy Law, Environmental Law, Debtor/Creditor Rights, Workers' Compensation, Municipal Law, Government Affairs.
Columbus, Ohio Office: 250 West Street, 43215-2538. Telephone: 614-462-2700. Telecopier: 614-462-5135. Telex: 650 24 444 365.
Cincinnati, Ohio Office: Bank One Towers, 8044 Montgomery Road, Suite 630, 45236-2926. Telephone: 513-792-0792. Fax: 513-792-0803.
See Professional Biographies, CLEVELAND, OHIO

Schrader, Thomas C., (AV) '40 '66 C&L.215 B.A., J.D. [G Walter&H.]
Schreiber, Svetlana J., (AV) '50 '82 C.705 B.A. L.1003 J.D. 1370 Ontario Street
Schreiner, David E., (AV) '48 '73 C.103 A.B. L.930 J.D. [Millisor&N.]
Schremp, Pamela S. '— '98 C.97 B.S.N. L.1003 J.D. [A Gallagher S.]
Schriner, John J., Jr. '73 '99 C.597 B.A. L.608 J.D. [A Roetzel&A.]
Schroeder, Michael Samuel '70 '95 C.97 B.S. L.124 J.D. 1360 W. 9th St.
Schroeder, Oliver, Jr. '16 '41 C.930 A.B. L.309 J.D. 1890 E. 107th St.‡
Schron, Jack H., Jr. '48 '75 C.258 B.S. L.607 J.D. Corp. Coun., Jergens Inc.
Schulman, Howard A., (AV) '45 '72 C.197 B.A. L.309 J.D. [Schulman,S.&M.]
Schulman, Jack M., (AV) '42 '67 C.197 B.A. L.309 LL.B. [Schulman,S.&M.]
Schulman, Schulman & Meros, L.P.A., (AV) 1370 Ontario St.
Schultz, Lawrence N., (AV) '48 '79 C.607 B.A. L.1003 J.D. [Calfee,H.&G.]
Schultz, Richard F. '56 '91 C.473 B.A. L.161 J.D. West Group
Schultz, Stephen J. '50 '77 C.1044 B.S. L.966 J.D. [Watts H.] (See Pat. Sect.)
Schulz, Isaac, (AV) '41 '71 C&L.477 B.A., J.D. [Ulmer&B.]
Schulz, James H., Jr. '57 '83 C.473 B.A. L.150 J.D. 1370 Ontario St., Ste. 1520
Schumacher, James T. '61 '90 C.201 B.A. L.1003 J.D. 1370 Ontario St., 1st Fl.
Schumacher, Paul J., Jr., (AV) '— '83 C.201 B.A. L.1003 J.D. [Gallagher S.]
Schumacher, Una '— '02 C.473 L.989 J.D. [A Pearne&G.] (See Pat. Sect.)
Schuman, Kenneth A. '72 '97 C.363 B.S.E.C. L.1003 J.D. 5306 Transportation Blvd.
Schuster, Nancy C., (AV) '33 '68 C.966 B.S. L.161 J.D. [Schuster&S.]

Schuster & Simmons Co., A Legal Professional Association, (AV)
The Bevelin House, 2913 Clinton Avenue, 44113
Telephone: 216-348-1100 FAX: 216-348-0013
Email: ss@apk.net
Nancy C. Schuster;—Kami Davis Rowles; Ami J. Patel.
Business and Commercial Matters including Federal and State Litigation. White Collar Criminal Defense, Labor and Employment.
See Professional Biographies, CLEVELAND, OHIO

Schwab, Richard B. '51 '76 C.150 B.B.A. L.117 J.D. V.P. & Sr. Atty., Natl. City Bk.
Schwartz, Diane, (BV) '46 '79 C.502 B.A. L.930 J.D. 2699 Wicklow Rd.
Schwartz, H. Jeffrey, (AV) '54 '80 C&L.161 B.A., J.D. [Benesch,F.C.&A.]
Schwartz, Jennifer E., (BV) '66 '91 C&L.608 B.A., J.D. [Schwartz,D.]
Schwartz, Kenneth D. '— '91 C.381 B.A. L.339 J.D. [Duvin,C.&H.]
Schwartz, Mark B. '42 '67 C.28 B.A. L.930 J.D. 30100 Chagrin Blvd.
Schwartz, Niki Z., (AV) '38 '64 C&L.608 B.A., J.D. [Schwartz,D.] & [Gold&P.]
Schwartz, Richard W., (AV) '37 '62 C.477 B.A. L.930 J.D.
55 Public Square, Suite 2500

Schwartz, Downey & Co., L.P.A., (AV)
Guild Hall Building, 45 West Prospect, Suite 1616, 44115
Telephone: 216-696-7100 Fax: 216-696-7210
Members of Firm: Niki Z. Schwartz; Brian P. Downey; Jennifer E. Schwartz.
Complex Civil and Criminal Litigation in State and Federal Courts. Mediation and Arbitration.
See Professional Biographies, CLEVELAND, OHIO

Schwarzwald, Melvin S., (AV) '37 '62 C&L.309 A.B., J.D. [Schwarzwald&M.]

Schwarzwald & McNair LLP, (AV)
616 Penton Media Building, 1300 East Ninth Street, 44114-1503
Telephone: 216-566-1600 Fax: 216-566-1814
Email: smcn@smcnlaw.com
Melvin S. Schwarzwald; Eben O. McNair, IV; Michael E. Jackson; David M. Fusco; Todd M. Smith; Timothy J. Gallagher;—Daniel S. White; James G. Porcaro; Melissa E. Barrows.
Union Side and Employee Labor and Employment Law. Practice and Trials and Appeals before all Courts and Administrative Agencies. Labor Law, ERISA Law, ERISA Litigation, and Bankruptcy Law, Personal Injury and Medical Malpractice.
Reference: Dollar Bank, Cleveland, Ohio.

Schwieg, Frederic P., (AV) '— '85 C&L.930 B.A., J.D. [Cowden,H.N.&L.]
Schwotzer, Tracy R. '75 '02 C&L.608 B.S., J.D.
Staff Atty., Common Pleas Ct. of Cuyahoga Cnty.
Scialdone, Frank H. '70 '02 C.540 B.A. L.989 J.D. [A Mazanec,R.&R.]
Scielzo, Asha B. '— '99 C.659 B.A. L.276 J.D. [A Jones D.]

Scola, Ralph J., (AV) '— '69 C.223 B.S. L.884 J.D.
2628 Courtland Boulevard, 44118-4738
Telephone: 216-321-3562 Fax: 216-371-2093
Email: Ralphscola@aol.com URL: http://www.lawyers.com/scola
(This Listing Continued)

Scola, Ralph J. (Continued)
Business Law, Corporate Law, Commercial Law, Civil Litigation, Health Care, Intellectual Property, International Trade, Non-Profit and Charitable Organizations, Mergers, Acquisitions and Divestitures, Trusts and Estates, Antitrust and Trade Regulation, Entertainment and the Arts.
Representative Clients: The Consolidated Core Company; The Consolidated Metals Company, Inc.; The Fasola Family Racing Stables, LLC; The Handel Company; HLR Systems, Inc.; The Internal Medicine Foundation of St. Luke's Medical Center; The St. Luke's Surgical Foundation, Inc.; Strike Force Sales & Supply, Inc.; The Surgical Foundation of St. Luke's Medical Center, Inc.
See Professional Biographies, CLEVELAND, OHIO

Scott, Gregory S. '69 '96 C.604 B.A. L.1003 J.D. [A Lowe E.W.&M.]
Scott, James C. '61 '91 C.323 B.S. L.930 J.D. [Roetzel&A.] (Pat.)
Scott, John R., (AV) '44 '70 C&L.352 B.A., J.D.
1400 Midland Bldg, 101 Prospect Ave., West
Scott, Joseph Francis, (CV) '58 '85 C.602 B.A. L.7 J.D.
Chf. Asst. Dir. of Law, City of Cleveland Law Dept.
Scott, Maialisa Ann '73 '99
C.1331 B.A. L.911 J.D. Legal Aid Soc. of Cleveland-Crim. Div.
Scott, Stuart E. '68 '95 C.63 B.S. L.608 J.D. [A Spangenberg,S.&L.]
Screen, Patricia A., (AV) '56 '85 C.1083 B.A. L.893 J.D. [Porter W.M.&A.]
Scrivens, Scott L., (BV) '55 '81 C.97 B.A. L.1003 J.D. [Falk&S.]
Scully, Lawrence B., (BV) '34 '67 C.363 B.S.S. L.161 J.D. [Scully&D.]
Scully, William F., Jr., (AV) '50 '75 C.602 B.A. L.930 J.D. [W.F.Scully Jr.]
Scully & Delaney, (BV) 614 Superior Ave. W.
Scully, William F., Jr. Co., L.P.A., (AV) 113 St. Clair Building, Suite 430
Seacrist, Susan M. '66 '92 C.201 B.S. L.1003 J.D. [A Reminger&R.]
Seaholm, Reidar H. '21 '60 C.251 B.B.A. L.1003 LL.B. 5001 Mayfield Rd.‡
Seaman, Dennis, (BV) '42 '67 C&L.608 B.A., J.D. [D.Seaman&Assoc.]
Seaman, Richard F. T. '13 '39 C&L.930 A.B., LL.B. 2181 Ambleside Dr.‡
Seaman, Dennis, & Associates Co., L.P.A., (BV) 614 Superior Ave., N.W.
Seasly, Steven E. '70 '99 C.97 B.S. L.1003 J.D. [A Hahn L.&P.]
Sebaugh, Beth A., (AV) '54 '80 C.610 B.S.E. L.1003 J.D. [Bonezzi S.M.&P.]
Sebold, Diane Sheehy '65 '90 C&L.477 B.A., J.D.
Director of Career Servs., Case Western Reserve School of Law
Sebold, Edward J. '— '94 C.363 B.A. L.477 J.D. [Jones D.]
Secrist, Robert V., Jr. '47 '72 C&L.608 B.A., J.D.
Assoc. Coun., Cleveland Clinic Foundation, The
Seed, David H. '68 '96 C.385 A.B. L.161 J.D. [Britton,S.P.&K.]
Seeley 600 Superior Ave. E.
Seeley, Glenn J., (BV) '26 '55 C.930 B.B.A. L.1003 J.D. 600 Superior Avenue, East
Seeley, Gregory D., (AV) '47 '72 C.385 B.A. L.30 J.D. [Seeley,S.&E.L.&Assoc.]
Seeley, Matthew K. '71 '97 C.385 B.A. L.8 J.D. [Seeley]
Seeley, Stephanie '76 '01 C.25 B.A. L.823 J.D. [A Duvin,C.&H.]

Seeley, Savidge & Ebert, Co., A Legal Professional Association, (AV)
Fifth Third Center - Suite 800, 600 Superior Avenue, East, 44114-2655
Telephone: 216-566-8200 Fax-Telecopier: 216-566-0213
URL: http://www.sse-law.com
Gregory D. Seeley; Keith A. Savidge; Gary A. Ebert; Andrew D. Bemer; Mary Davis; Douglas P. Whipple.
Civil Trial /Corporate Commercial Law, Securities, Employment, Labor, Health Care, Real Estate, Environmental, Litigation, Appellate Practice, Insurance Defense, Construction, Municipal, Estate Planning.
Reference: KeyBank.
See Professional Biographies, CLEVELAND, OHIO

Seewald, Amanda M. '69 '95
C&L.930 B.A., J.D. Corp. Coun., Forest City Enterprises, Inc.
Seewald, J. Gary, (BV) '46 '71 C&L.930 A.B., J.D. [Henkin&S.]
Seger, Paula F., (AV) '54 '79 C.347 A.B. L.608 J.D. [Baker&H.]
Seger, Thomas M., (AV) '46 '72 C.473 B.A. L.1565 J.D. [Baker&H.]
Seibert, Henry E., IV, (AV) '42 '68 C.674 A.B. L.228 J.D. [Spieth,B.M.&N.]
Seibert, Mark E. '57 '97 C.201 B.S. L.1003 J.D. 45 Erieview Plz.
Seich, John S., (AV) '49 '82 C.608 B.S. L.930 J.D. [McCarthy,L.C.&L.]
Seifert, Patricia L. '59 '89 C.437 B.A. L.1003 J.D. 55 Public Square
Seifert, Patricia Lynn '70 '99 C.980 B.A. L.7 J.D. Pros. Off.
Seink, Daniel P. '67 '92 C.363 B.A. L.1003 J.D. [D.P.Seink]
Seink, Daniel P., Co., Ltd. 5005 Rockside Road, Suite 600
Seitz, Charles R. '50 '92 C.116 B.A. L.1003 J.D. 1370 Ontario St., Ste. 2000
Seleman, Fred '68 '93 C.347 B.A. L.930 J.D. [Ulmer&B.]
Selker, Eugene I., (AV) '29 '53 C&L.930 B.B.A., LL.B. [Selker&Assoc.]

Selker & Associates LLC, (AV)
34305 Solon Road, Suite 100, 44139
Telephone: 440-248-7906 FAX: 440-248-8861
Email: eselker@mrrlaw.com
Member of Firm: Eugene I. Selker.
General Civil Practice in all State and Federal Courts, Real Estate, Civil Litigation, Business Law.
See Professional Biographies, CLEVELAND, OHIO

Selvidge, Barry E. '58 '88 C&L.838 B.S., J.D.
V.P., Regulatory Affs. & Gen. Coun., Communications Central Inc.

Seminatore, Kenneth F., Law Offices of, (AV) '47 '71 C.930 A.B. L.309 J.D.
The Superior Building, Suite 1715, 815 Superior Avenue, N.E., 44114
Telephone: 216-344-3838 Fax: 216-344-0515
General Practice, Corporate and Commercial Transactions, Civil Litigation, Health Care and Insurance.
See Professional Biographies, CLEVELAND, OHIO

Senich, Kevin J. M. '52 '84 C.477 A.B. L.1003 J.D. 4438 Pearl Rd.
Sennett, James C., (AV) '25 '54 C.363 B.B.A. L.161 LL.B. 901 Lakeside Ave.
Senra, Matthew E. '71 '00 C.696 B.M. L.989 J.D. [A Cavitch,F.D.&F.]
Senturia, Harris A. '69 '93 C.691 B.A. L.178 J.D. [Squire,S.&D.]
Serbinowski, Paul A. '67 '94 C.24 B.S.C.E. L.1338 J.D. [Pearne&G.] (See Pat. Sect.)
Serevitch, Katherine M. '— '04 C.884 B.S. L.124 J.D. [A Jones D.]
Sergent, Douglas R. '66 '99 C.930 B.A. L.1003 J.D. [A Baker&H.]
Serra, Wayne M. '67 '97 C.454 B.S. L.94 J.D. [A Ulmer&B.] (Pat.)
Serrano, Mariela F. '48 '80 C.1086 B.A. L.1003 J.D. 5530 State Rd., Ste. 9
Serrat, Jaime P., (AV) '55 '83 C.528 B.A. L.1003 J.D. 1370 Ontario St., Ste. 1630
Sesek, Deborah, (AV) '50 '76 C.201 B.A. L.1003 J.D. [Buckingham,D.&B.]
Sesnowitz, Douglas K. '69 '94 C.910 B.A. L.608 J.D. [Ulmer&B.]
Sevcik, Wilma A. '23 '48 C&L.930 A.B., LL.B. Legal Aid Soc.
Sexton, Sheila M. '68 '97 C.363 B.A. L.1003 J.D. Penton Media, Inc.
Sexton, William J., (Co., L.P.A.), (BV) '29 '58
C.363 B.B.S. L.1003 J.D. 800 Standard Bldg.
Seymour, Carolyn K. '60 '85
C.165 B.A. L.477 J.D. Case Western Reserve Univ., Sch. of Law
Sferra, Stephen J., (AV) '61 '86 C.97 B.S. L.930 J.D. [Duvin,C.&H.]
Sgro, Valentina '54 '80 C.363 B.S.B.A. L.477 J.D. SGRO Consulting
Shachter, Tikvah '75 '01 [A Milano W.&a.&Assoc.]

Shackelford, William M. .... '61 '96 C.999 B.A. L.7 J.D. [Ⓐ Weltman,W.&R.]
Shafron, Steven D., (AV) .... '62 '87 C.477 B.A. L.930 J.D. [Berkman,G.M.&D.]
Shagrin, Michael B., (AV) .... '39 '64 C&L.930 B.B.A., J.D. 75 Public Square, Suite 650
Shaheen, Matthew M. .... '68 '97 C&L.8 B.S.M.T., J.D. [Tarolli,S.C.&T.] (See Pat. Sect.)
Shakarian, Melanie A. '77 '03 C.363 B.A. L.124 J.D.
Dir. of Develop., The Legal Aid Soc. of Cleveland
Shakelton, Paula G. .... '— '04 C.602 B.A. L.245 J.D. [Ⓐ Jones D.]
Shaklee, William V. .... '76 '02 C.690 B.A. L.608 J.D. [Ⓐ Squire,S.&D.] (Pat.)
Shamberg, Stefen K. .... '70 '00 C.381 B.A. L.989 J.D. 3421 Prospect Avenue
Shanahan, Brien W., (BV) '53 '79
C.602 B.A. L.607 J.D. Dir., Legal Affs., Medical Mutual of Ohio
Shanahan, J. Kearney, (AV) .... '44 '72 C.674 A.B. L.276 J.D. [Shanahan] ⊙
Shanahan, Karen F. .... '45 '72 C.706 B.A. L.276 J.D. BP Oil Co.
Shanahan Law Firm, The, LLC, (AV) .... 925 Euclid Avenue (⊙Wash., DC; Toledo, OH)
Shane, Barbara Kanter .... '57 '82 C.205 B.A. L.245 J.D. 39425 Cortina Cir.
Shane, Michael, (AV) .... '27 '53 C&L.608 B.A., LL.B. 1460 Illuminating Bldg.
Shanker, Morris G. '26 '52 C.679 B.S.E.E. L.477 J.D.
Prof. of Law, Case Western Reserve U. Sch. of Law
Shannon, James F., (BV) .... '46 '74 C.161 B.B.A. L.1003 J.D. 75 Public Sq., Ste. 700
Shapero, James I. .... '33 '59 C.902 B.S. L.930 LL.B. 16025 Van Anken Blvd.
Shapero, Michael I., (AV) .... '44 '71 C.608 B.S. L.1003 J.D. [Shapero&G.]
Shapero, Neal E., (AV) .... '58 '84 C.381 B.S. L.7 J.D. [Shapero&R.]

Shapero & Green, LLC, (AV)
Signature Square II, Suite 220, 25101 Chagrin Boulevard, 44122-5656
Telephone: 216-831-5100 Toll Free 1-877-404-6300 Fax: 216-831-9467
Members of Firm: Michael I. Shapero; Brian J. Green;—David S. Michel; Jennifer Stakes.
Personal Injury, Medical Malpractice, General Civil, Business Litigation, Corporate Law, Banking, Real Estate, Domestic Relations, Probate.
See Professional Biographies, CLEVELAND, OHIO

Shapero & Roloff Co., L.P.A., (AV)
1350 Euclid Avenue, Suite 1550, 44115-1828
Telephone: 216-781-1700; 800-321-9199 Fax: 216-781-1972
Email: nshapero@shaperoroloff.com URL: http://www.shaperoroloff.com
Neal E. Shapero;—Abby K. Lill.
Plaintiffs Personal Injury, Wrongful Death, Medical Malpractice, Nursing Home Negligence, Products Liability, FELA, Premises Liability, Class Actions, Employment Law, Employment Discrimination, Wrongful Discharge, Sexual Harassment, Civil Rights, Union Labor Law.
See Professional Biographies, CLEVELAND, OHIO

Shapiro, Daniel Lawrence, (BV) .... '65 '92 C.363 B.S.B.A. L.161 J.D. [Shapiro,S.&S.]
Shapiro, Fred D., (AV) .... '26 '54 C.608 B.A. L.309 LL.B. 526 Superior Avenue
Shapiro, Geoffrey Jerome, (BV) .... '61 '88 C.112 B.A. L.93 J.D. [Shapiro,S.&S.]
Shapiro, Gerald M. '43 '69 C.597 B.S. L.209 J.D.
(adm. in IL; not adm. in OH) [Shapiro&F.] (⊙Fairfax, VA)
Shapiro, Philip .... '48 '75 C.161 B.A. L.1003 J.D. 55 Public Sq.

Shapiro & Felty, L.L.P., (AV) [BR]
1500 West Third Street, Suite 400, 44113-9873
Telephone: 216-621-1530 Fax: 216-621-7646
Email: shapfelt@logs.com
Gerald M. Shapiro (Not admitted in OH); Kriss D. Felty; David S. Kreisman (Not admitted in OH); Mark R. Lembright;—Christopher M. Kovach; Phillip C. Barragate; Daniel Spirko; Christian Eric Niklas; Ross P. Miller; Robert J. LaCivita; John A. Polinko; Richard J. Lacivita; Antonio J. Scarlato; Jennifer R. Franks; Louis P. Alexander, Jr.; Brian R. Gutkoski; Martha R. Spaner; Chris E. Manolis.
Foreclosure, Bankruptcy, Landlord and Tenant, Real Estate Litigation, Closing and Title Services, Creditor and Collection Services, Probate and Estate Planning, Business and Corporate Law.
See Professional Biographies, CLEVELAND, OHIO

Shapiro, Shapiro & Shapiro Co., L.P.A., (BV) .... 4469 Renaissance Parkway
Sharb, Michael L. .... '66 '96 C.610 B.B.A. L.174 J.D. [Squire,S.&D.]
Sharifi, Vahid '— '00 C.597 M.S. L.424 J.D.
(adm. in IL; not adm. in OH; See Pat. Sect.) [Ⓐ Amin&T.]
Sharon, Michael H., (AV) .... '58 '82 C.95 A.B. L.930 J.D. [Sharon&K.]
Sharon & Kálnoki LLC, (AV) .... 55 Public Square, Suite 750
Sharp, Debra L. '57 '82 C.259 B.S. L.1003 J.D.
Admin. Law J., Equal Employ. Opportunity Comm.
Sharp, Jeremy J. .... '— '99 C.945 B.A. L.608 J.D. [Ⓐ Baker&H.]
Sharpe, Calvin W. '45 '74 C.155 B.A. L.597 J.D.
(adm. in IL; not adm. in OH) Case Western Reserve Univ. Law Sch.
Sharpe, Richard A., (AV) .... '65 '92 C.631 B.S. L.904 J.D. [Pearne&G.] (See Pat. Sect.)
Shaughnessy, Thomas M. .... '33 '64 L.1003 LL.B. 11510 Buckeye Rd.
Shaw, Christopher J. .... '61 '86 C.645 B.A. L.273 J.D. 1276 W. 3rd St.
Shaw, Hewitt B., Jr., (AV) .... '55 '80 C.294 A.B. L.930 J.D. [Baker&H.]
Shaw, Laura J. .... '66 '91 C.659 B.A. L.178 J.D. 127 Public Square, Floor 2
Shaw, Nancy A., (AV) .... '55 '80 C&L.352 B.A., J.D. 1900 Richmond Road
Shaw, Russell C., (AV) .... '40 '65 C&L.608 B.S., J.D. [Walter&H.]
Shea, Christopher R. .... '66 '93 C.385 A.B. L.893 J.D. [Ⓐ Squire,S.&D.]
Sheaffer, Jenny L. .... '— '98 C.565 B.S. L.823 J.D. [Ⓐ Jones D.] (See Pat. Sect.)
Sheehan, John J., Jr., (AV) .... '41 '67 C.363 B.S.S. L.930 J.D. Hanna Bldg., Ste. 422
Sheehan, Michelle J., (CV) .... '68 '93 C.473 B.A. L.1003 J.D. [Ⓐ Reminger&R.]
Sheehan, Thomas F., (BV) .... '44 '72 C.363 A.B. L.161 J.D. 1422 Euclid Ave.
Sheehan, Thomas John .... '70 '98 C.363 B.A. L.989 J.D. Atty. Gen. Off.
Sheeran, Timothy J., (AV) .... '48 '75 C.608 B.A. L.309 J.D. [Squire,S.&D.]
Sheir, Jonathan E. .... '— '98 C.930 B.A. L.124 J.D. [Ⓐ Kramer&Assoc.]
Shelby, James D., (BV) .... '45 '73 C.318 B.A. L.1003 J.D. 3153 Fairmount Blvd.
Shelley, Howard A., Jr. .... '24 '66 C.124 B.S. L.1003 J.D. 2329 Walden Rd.‡
Shelley, John F., (AV) .... '43 '68 C&L.309 A.B., LL.B. [Squire,S.&D.]
Shelley, John S. .... '— '03 C.881 B.A. L.124 J.D. 1300 East Ninth Street, 14th Floor
Shelton, Peter K. .... '61 '93 C.174 B.A. L.161 J.D. [Benesch,F.C.&A.]
Shelton, William R. .... '56 '86 C.381 B.S. L.1003 J.D. Medimetrix Consulting
Shemisa, Jenann Othman .... '67 '99 C.97 B.A. L.1003 J.D. KeyBank Natl. Assn.
Shenyey, Peter F., (BV) .... '49 '76 C.930 A.B. L.161 J.D. Res. Sq., 1701 E. 12th St.
Shepard, Robert, (AV) .... '54 '80 C.273 B.A. L.930 J.D. 3740 Carnegie Avenue
Shepherd, John B., Jr., (AV) .... '52 '78 C.473 A.B. L.1003 J.D. [Short&S.]
Shepherd, John E., (BV) .... '36 '61 C.602 B.A. L.930 LL.B. P.O. Box 16151
Sheppard, Donald J. .... '21 '56 L.1003 J.D. 313 Buckner Dr.‡
Sheridan, James P. .... '67 '99 C.161 B.A. L.989 J.D. [J.P.Sheridan]
Sheridan, Michael P. .... '67 '01 C.97 B.A.C. L.989 J.D. Ohio Savings Bank
Sheridan, James P., LLC .... 75 Public Sq., Ste. 1225
Sherman, Bradley A., (AV) .... '68 '94 C.597 B.A. L.930 J.D. [Duvin,C.&H.]
Sherman, Charna E., (AV) .... '58 '85 C.309 B.A. L.276 J.D. [Squire,S.&D.]
Sherman, Dennis H., & Associates .... '39 '66 C.608 B.C.E. L.1003 J.D. 3681 Green Road
Shibley, Cathy M. .... '57 '82 C.473 B.A. L.851 J.D. [Ⓐ B.A.Firstenberg&Assoc.]
Shihab, Gus M., (BV) '61 '93 C.608 B.S.C.E. L.117 J.D.
[Shihab&Assoc.] (⊙Wash., DC; Columbus, OH)
Shihab, Sam M., (BV) .... '62 '94 C.608 B.S.C.E. L.117 J.D. [Shihab&Assoc.] ⊙
Shihab & Associates, (BV)
600 Superior Avenue East, Suite 1300 (⊙Wash., DC; Columbus, OH)

Shillman, David B. .... '35 '61 C&L.309 A.B., LL.B. 8437 Mayfield Road
Shimko, Timothy A., (AV) .... '51 '76 C.93 A.B. L.7 J.D. [T.A.Shimko&Assoc.]
Shimko, Timothy A., & Associates, Co., L.P.A., (AV) .... 925 Euclid Avenue
Shimola, Howard G., (AV) '42 '70
C.124 B.S.M.E. L.1003 J.D. [Pearne&G.] (See Pat. Sect.)
Shin, William J. .... '77 '02 C.228 A.B. L.602 J.D. [Ⓐ Benesch,F.C.&A.]
Shlensky, William '38 '63 C.659 B.S.E. L.145 J.D.
(adm. in IL; not adm. in OH) Dir., Admn., Bellefaire
Shlonsky, Patricia A., (AV) .... '59 '84 C.473 B.A. L.608 J.D. [Ulmer&B.]
Shofar, Nick D. .... '53 '87 C.94 B.A. L.1003 J.D. [Ⓐ Benesch,F.C.&A.]
Shopneck, Craig H. '53 '84 C.604 A.B. L.851 J.D.
Sr. Vice President & General Counsel, Dynamic Telcom Engineering, L.L.C.
Shore, Michael A., (AV) .... '31 '59 C.659 B.S. L.1003 J.D. [M.A.Shore]
Shore, Michael A., Co., LPA, (AV) .... 23230 Chagrin Blvd., Ste. 900
Shorr, Randall B., (AV) .... '58 '86 C.161 B.A. L.930 J.D. 6314 Franklin Blvd., N.W.
Short, Dale W., (AV) .... '50 '77 [Short&S.]
Short & Shepherd, (AV) .... 24461 Detroit Rd.
Shroge, Michael David .... '70 '00 C.161 B.A. L.989 J.D. [Ⓐ Reminger&R.]
Shucofsky, Joseph F., (BV) '61 '86
C.201 A.B. L.930 J.D. 526 Superior Avenue, Suite 1525
Shulman, Zinaida .... '71 '99 C.473 B.S. L.1003 J.D. Key Corp.
Shumaker, Roger L., (AV) .... '50 '76 C.432 B.A. L.930 J.D. [McDonald H.]
Shumay, Robert G. .... '64 '89 C.477 A.B. L.608 J.D. The Kirby Co.
Shunk, Thomas H., (AV) .... '54 '79 C.976 B.A. L.178 J.D. [Baker&H.]
Shuster, Michael P., (AV) .... '67 '92 C.602 B.B.A. L.608 J.D. [Hahn L.&P.]
Shuzman, William I. '51 '77 C.994 B.A. L.1019 J.D.
(adm. in NY; not adm. in OH) N.L.R.B.
Sicherman, Marvin A., (AV) .... '34 '60 C&L.930 B.A., J.D. [Dettelbach,S.&B.]
Sidoti, Robert A. '71 '98 C.37 B.S.M.E. L.1003 J.D.
[Ⓐ Fay,S.F.M.&M.] (See Pat. Sect.)
Sidoti, Salvatore A. .... '70 '99 C.318 B.A. L.989 J.D. [Curatolo S.] (Pat.)
Sieg, Robert M. .... '69 '05 C.161 B.S. L.1003 J.D. [Ⓐ Fay,S.F.M.&M.] (See Pat. Sect.)
Siegel, Edward F., Law Offices of, (AV) '46 '74
C.178 B.A. L.930 J.D. 5910 Landerbrook Drive
Siegel, Fred, (AV) .... '31 '55 C.610 B.S.C. L.930 LL.B. 30195 Chagrin Boulevard
Siegel, John M. '48 '74 C&L.893 B.A., J.D.
(adm. in VA; not adm. in OH) Asst. U.S. Atty.
Siegel, Nessa G. .... '43 '86 C.473 B.S. L.161 J.D. 4070 Mayfield Road
Siegel, Richard H., (AV) .... '35 '61 C.930 B.A. L.145 J.D. [R.H.Siegel]
Siegel, Richard H., Co., L.P.A., (AV) .... 1846 Coventry Rd.
Siegfried, Kurt S. .... '68 '94 C.980 B.A. L.1003 J.D. [Ⓐ Ulmer&B.]
Sieman, Harold, (BV) .... '12 '44 C.980 L.989 J.D. 825 Nat. City Bank Bldg.
Sierk, Carroll H. '31 '53 C&L.744 B.B.A., J.D.
(adm. in TX; not adm. in OH) Prof., Cleve.-Marshall Coll. of Law
Sigalow, Steven E., (BV) .... '75 C.608 B.A. L.930 J.D. [Jones D.]
Sigmier, Harry, (AV) .... '55 '80 C.262 B.A. L.930 J.D. [Weston H.]
Sikora, J. William .... '50 '76 C.999 A.B. L.608 J.D. Chief Coun., NASA
Sikora, Peter, (AV) .... '51 '80 C.62 B.A. L.930 J.D. Co. J.
Silk, Thomas J., (AV) .... '59 '85 C.97 B.A. L.1003 J.D. 50 Public Sq.
Silliman, Kenneth G. .... '52 '78 C.930 B.A. L.575 J.D. City of Cleveland Dept. of Law
Silverman, Brent Samuel .... '67 '93 C.473 B.A. L.209 J.D. [Ⓐ Reminger&R.]
Silverman, Martin '27 '61 C.930 A.B. L.1003 J.D.
Sr. Consultant, National Assocs., Inc.
Silveroli, Genevieve A. '69 '97 C.608 B.S. L.1003 J.D.
Asst. Gen. Coun., Electrolux North America (Legal Department)
Silverstein, Marc A., (AV) .... '— '80 C.103 Sc.B. L.309 J.D. [Ⓒ Jones D.]
Silversten, Matthew P. .... '— '02 C.896 B.A. L.608 J.D. [Ⓐ Jones D.]
Simakis, George K., (BV) .... '38 '72 C.161 B.A. L.1003 J.D. P.O. Box 609102
Simek, Douglas R. .... '76 '03 C.201 B.A. L.989 J.D. [Ⓐ Sutter,O.&F.]
Simmons, George R. .... '46 '87 C.381 B.A. L.1003 J.D. 2913 Clinton Ave‡
Simmons, Kenneth D. .... '48 '74 C.150 B.S. L.930 J.D. Cleveland Cliffs, Inc.
Simmons, Thomas R. .... '66 '93 C&L.930 B.A., J.D. [Tucker E.&W.]
Simms, Edward P. .... '71 '98 C.381 B.A. L.161 J.D. [Ⓐ Ulmer&B.]
Simms, Joseph S. .... '71 '96 C.608 B.A. L.1003 J.D. [Ⓐ Ulmer&B.]

Simon, David O., (AV) '49 '75 C.97 B.S.B.A. L.1003 J.D.
1370 Ontario Street, Suite 450, 44113-1744
Telephone: 216-621-6201 Telecopier: 216-575-1405
Email: dsimon@epiqtrustee.com
Bankruptcy and Commercial Law.
See Professional Biographies, CLEVELAND, OHIO

Simon, Declan Joseph .... '52 '91 C.161 B.A. L.8 J.D. U.S. Dist. Ct.
Simon, Ellen S., (AV) .... '69 '95 C.1036 B.A. L.818 J.D. [Simon]
Simon, George T. .... '42 '67 C.608 B.A. L.930 J.D. V.P., Natl. City Bk.
Simon, John A. .... '— '90 C.363 B.S. L.1003 J.D. [Gallagher S.]
Simon, Sunny M., (BV) .... '63 '88 C.363 B.A. L.930 J.D. 1660 W 2nd Street

Simon Law Firm, The, LLP, (AV)
Suite 1717 Penton Media Building, 1300 East Ninth Street, 44114-1503
Telephone: 216-575-1002 Fax: 216-575-1556
Email: mail@esimonlaw.com
Steven D. Bell; Ellen S. Simon;—Ann Marie Ahern; Matthew J. McCracken.
Employment Law, Discrimination, Harassment, Civil Litigation.
See Professional Biographies, CLEVELAND, OHIO

Simonetta, Paulette .... '64 '89 C.161 B.A. L.1003 J.D. West Group
Simpkins, Scott D. .... '70 '96 C.611 B.A. L.117 J.D. [Ⓐ Climaco,L.P.W.&G.]
Sims, Richard J. .... '51 '78 C.1044 B.A. L.94 J.D. CEO, Tranzonic Companies
Sinatra, John L., Jr. .... '— '97 C&L.107 B.A., J.D. [Ⓐ Jones D.]

Sindell, Lowe & Guidubaldi
(See Lowe Eklund Wakefield & Mulvihill Co., L.P.A.)

Sindyla, Robert J., (BV) .... '42 '71 C.1072 B.A. L.1003 J.D. 7425 Royalton Rd.
Singer, Marilyn J., (AV) .... '55 '79 C.104 A.B. L.930 J.D. [McNeal,S.A.&B.]
Singerman, Egon P. .... '63 '88 C.608 B.A. L.930 J.D. 3681 Green Rd.
Singerman, Paul J., (AV) .... '58 '83 C&L.930 B.A., J.D. [Singerman,M.D.&K.]

Singerman, Mills, Desberg & Kauntz, (AV) [BR]
3401 Enterprise Parkway, Suite 200, 44122
Telephone: 216-292-5807 Fax: 216-292-5867
URL: http://www.smdklaw.com
Paul J. Singerman; William M. Mills; Gary S. Desberg; Edmund G. Kauntz; Troy R. Brown; Jeffrey A. Gorski. Of Counsel: Gary W. Melsher. Associates: Michael R. Stavnicky; Jean M. Cullen; John J. Burns; Jeffrey A. Sayoc.
Banks and Banking, Secured Lending, Corporate Law, Real Estate, Bankruptcy, Taxation, Limited Liability Company Law, Partnership Law, Estate Planning, Probate, Trusts and Estates, Litigation, Commercial Law, Construction Law.
See Professional Biographies, CLEVELAND, OHIO

Singhal, Dheeraj K. '75 '01 C&L.112 B.S., J.D.
(adm. in CA; not adm. in OH) [Ⓐ Squire,S.&D.] (⊙L.A., CA)
Sipusic, David James .... '— '01 L.989 J.D. [Ⓐ Mazanec,R.&R.]
Sirvaitis, Algis, (BV) .... '39 '66 C.363 B.S.S. L.1003 J.D. 880 E. 185 St. (⊙Mentor)
Siskovic, Carole N., (AV) .... '40 '83 C.599 A.B. L.1003 J.D. 1360 W. 9th Street
Sitko, Richard L. .... '28 '66 C.363 B.B.A. L.1003 J.D. Cleveland Pneumatic Tool Co.
Sivinski, John A., (AV) .... '59 '86 C.363 B.S. L.930 J.D. [Kelley&F.]
Sizemore, Cheryl Alleyne ..... '63 '01 C.1015 B.S. L.1003 J.D. Natl. Labor Relations Bd.
Skall, David W. .... '70 '97 C.347 B.A. L.930 J.D. [Ⓐ Sutter,O.&F.]
Skaryd, Drue M. .... '74 '99 C.610 B.A. L.124 J.D. [Ritzler,C.&S.]
Skeans, David W. .... '62 '95 C&L.8 B.A., J.D. 4000 E. 116th St. (Pat.)
Skerry, Ann M. .... '56 '97 C.999 B.Sc. L.930 J.D. [Fay,S.F.M.&M.] (See Pat. Sect.)
Skiljan, David R. .... '64 '96 C.97 B.S.B.A. L.1003 J.D. V.P., Marsh USA Inc.
Skillen, Richard, Jr. '31 '61
C.475 B.S. L.1003 LL.B. Asst. V.P., Bank One Ohio Tr. Co., N.A.
Skingle, Ronald A. .... '69 '94 C.608 B.A. L.161 J.D. 2450 St. Clair Ave., Ste. 12
Skirbunt, James R., (AV) .... '49 '74 C.276 B.S. L.93 J.D. [Skirbunt&S.]
Skirbunt, Sharon A., (BV) .... '54 '86 C.381 B.S. L.930 J.D. [Skirbunt&S.]
Skirbunt & Skirbunt Co., L.P.A., (AV) .... 55 Public Square, Suite 1310
Sklar, Warren A., (AV) '44 '71
C.124 B.S.E.E. L.273 J.D. [Renner,O.B.&S.] (See Pat. Sect.)
Skoczen, Danielle A. ...... '73 '99 C.607 B.S.M.E. L.1003 J.D. [Ⓐ Wegman,H.&V.] (Pat.)
Skutnik, Carol M. .... '64 '92 C.97 B.S. L.1003 J.D. Asst. Co. Pros.
Slaby, Scott M. ...... '73 '03 C.363 B.S. L.1003 J.D. [Ⓐ Fay,S.F.M.&M.] (See Pat. Sect.)
Sladek, Todd L. .... '56 '04 C.602 B.A. L.8 J.D. [Ⓐ Benesch,F.C.&A.]
Slagter, John P., (AV) .... '66 '91 C.363 B.A. L.930 J.D. [Buckingham,D.&B.]
Slater, James A. .... '— '02 C.532 B.S. L.608 J.D. [Ⓐ Baker&H.]
Slater, John R., (BV) .... '46 '81 C&L.608 B.A., J.D. [Millisor&N.] (⊙Canton)
Sleibi, Jalal T. .... '76 '03 C.161 B.A. L.124 J.D. 4040 Mayfield Rd., Ste. 1
Slive, Harriet Weinmann .... '51 '84 C.124 B.A. L.989 J.D. [Slive&S.]
Slive, Steven H., (BV) .... '50 '76 C.610 B.G.S. L.1003 J.D. [Slive&S.]
Slive & Slive Co., LPA, (BV) .... 526 Superior, Suite 935
Slivka, John M., (AV) .... '53 '81 C.161 B.B.A. L.1003 J.D. [Spieth,B.M.&N.]
Sliwinski, Teddy, (BV) .... '51 '76 C&L.161 B.A., J.D. [Sliwinski]
Sliwinski Center, (BV) .... 5800 Fleet Ave.
Sloan, David W., (AV) .... '— '74 C.674 A.B. L.309 J.D. [Jones D.]
Slodov, Michael D., (BV) .... '— '91 C.161 B.A. L.930 J.D. [Javitch,B.&R.]
Slomak, Michael J. .... '51 '76 Chmn. of the Bd. & CEO, Hair Care Harmony, Inc.
Slough, J. Helen '08 '29 C.876 Litt.B. L.161 J.D.
21010 Center Ridge Rd., Suite 803 (Pat.)

Slowik & Robinson, LLC
(See Columbus)

Smaili, Jihad M. .... '71 '98 C.851 B.A. L.989 J.D. [J.M.Smaili]

Smaili, Jihad M., Esq., L.L.C., Attorneys & Counselors at Law
The Western Reserve Building South Wing, 1468 West 9th Street, Suite 330, 44113
Telephone: 216-685-9500 Fax: 216-685-9685 URL: http://www.smaililaw.com
Email: jihad@smaililaw.com URL: http://www.smaililawfirm.com
Jihad M. Smaili;—Matthew T. Gilmartin.
Languages: English, Spanish and Arabic.
Criminal Defense, Immigration, Business Formation and Transactions, Civil Litigation, Civil Rights, Contracts, Employment Discrimination, Personal Injury, Medical Malpractice, Workers Compensation, Bankruptcy, Probate, Trusts, Wills and Estates.
See Professional Biographies, CLEVELAND, OHIO

Smakula, Michael J., (BV) .... '51 '76 C.161 B.A. L.1003 J.D. [Ⓐ Reid,B.M.&W.]
Small, Robert E., (BV) .... '32 '61 C.363 B.S. L.1003 J.D. [R.E.Small]
Small, Robert E., Co., L.P.A., (BV) .... 16249 Oakhill Road
Smearman, R. Eric, (BV) .... '68 '93 C&L.930 B.A., J.D. [Smith M.]
Smeltz, John E., (AV) .... '22 '48 C.970 B.A. L.930 LL.B. [Schneider,S.R.&L.]
Smilanick, Diane, (BV) .... '56 '83 C.161 B.A. L.1003 J.D. Asst. Co. Pros.
Smirnoff, Tracy W. .... '72 '97 C.105 B.A. L.1003 J.D. Coun., GE Consumer and Industrial
Smith, Aliceia J. .... '78 '04 C&L.124 B.A., J.D. [Ⓐ Ulmer&B.]
Smith, Bernard A. .... '57 '82 C.201 B.A. L.477 J.D. Asst. U.S. Atty.
Smith, David Kane, (AV) .... '47 '84 C.930 B.A. L.1003 J.D. [Britton,S.P.&K.]
Smith, Drew Allen .... '70 '98 C.823 M.A. L.124 J.D. Co. Pros. Off.
Smith, Erick C. .... '63 '88 C.1372 B.A. L.930 J.D. [Ⓐ McMahon,D.H.&L.]
Smith, Geri M. '53 '81 C.910 B.A. L.161 J.D.
Clk. of Ct., U.S. Dist. Ct., N. Dist. of Ohio
Smith, James A., (AV) .... '30 '61 C.930 A.B. L.178 LL.B. 127 Public Sq.
Smith, James M., (AV) .... '27 '52 C&L.477 B.B.A., J.D. 629 Elucid Ave, Ste 1000‡
Smith, James P. .... '76 '01 C.976 B.A. L.150 J.D. [Ⓐ Duvin,C.&H.]
Smith, Jeffrey D. .... '79 '04 C.62 B.S. L.930 J.D. [Ⓐ Millisor&N.]
Smith, Kenneth J. ...... '72 '00 C.851 B.S. L.989 J.D. [Ⓐ Calfee,H.&G.] (See Pat. Sect.)
Smith, Kestra J. .... '51 '90 C.604 B.A./B.Mus. L.150 J.D. Co. Pros. Off.
Smith, Kimberly Y. .... '65 '96 C.827 B.A. L.930 J.D. [Ⓐ McGlinchey S.]
Smith, M. David, (BV) .... '44 '70 C.608 B.S. L.1003 J.D. [Friedman,D.&S.] ⊙
Smith, Maria A. .... '58 '84 C.502 A.B. L.893 J.D. Housing Ct. Mag.
Smith, Mark A., (AV) .... '25 '53 C.976 A.B. L.1003 LL.B. P.O. Box 5756
Smith, Michael E. .... '64 '89 C.602 B.A. L.930 J.D. [Frantz W.]
Smith, N. Lindsey, (BV) .... '50 '76 C.97 B.S. L.851 J.D. [Smith&C.]
Smith, Scott C., (AV) .... '62 '87 C.20 B.A. L.930 J.D. [Weston H.]
Smith, Stanford S. .... '19 '58 C.864 B.S. L.1003 J.D. 1380 E. 13th St.
Smith, Stephen Lee .... '61 '89 C.604 B.A. L.930 J.D. Nat. City Corp.
Smith, Steven Scott .... '51 '82 C.161 B.A. L.989 J.D. West Group
Smith, Stourton Scott .... '69 '95 C.610 B.A. L.879 J.D. [S.S.Smith] ⊙
Smith, Susan Ferraro .... '55 '81 C.901 B.A. L.229 J.D. [Ⓐ W.Coyne]
Smith, Todd M., (CV) .... '46 '91 C.674 A.B. L.124 J.D. [Schwarzwald&M.]
Smith, William H. .... '47 '77 C.411 B.S. L.1003 J.D. [W.H.Smith&Assoc.]
Smith, William K., (AV) .... '53 '78 C.902 B.A. L.893 J.D. [Ⓒ Ulmer&B.]
Smith and Condeni, Co., L.P.A., (AV) .... 1801 E. 9th St.

Smith Marshall, LLP, (AV)
500 National City East Sixth Building, 1965 East Sixth Street, 44114
Telephone: 216-781-4994 Telecopier: 216-781-9448
Email: law@smithmarshall.com URL: http://www.smithmarshall.com
Richard C. Green (1910-1967); Melvin M. Roberts (1911-1971); John M. Cronquist (1931-1993); Jack F. Smith (1917-1996); Wentworth J. Marshall, Jr.; Philip J. Weaver, Jr.; Frederick P. Vergon, Jr.; R. Eric Smearman; Kara M. Schedlbauer.
General Civil Practice. Business and Corporate, Commercial, Construction, Environmental, Insurance, Negligence, Probate, Product Liability, Real Estate Law. Trials and Appeals.
See Professional Biographies, CLEVELAND, OHIO

Smith, Stourton Scott, Co., LPA
75 Public Square, Suite 800, 44113 ⊙
Telephone: 216-344-9338 Fax: 216-344-9337
Email: stourtonsmith@sbcglobal.net URL: http://www.aggressivelegalrep.com
Stourton Scott Smith.
Criminal Law, DWI, Bankruptcy, Personal Injury, Divorce, Family Law.

(This Listing Continued)

Smith, Stourton Scott, Co., LPA (Continued)
Elyria, Ohio Office: 633 West Broad Street, Suite 200, 44035. Telephone 440-284-0101. Fax: 440-322-5509.
See Professional Biographies, CLEVELAND, OHIO

Smith, William H., & Associates .... 614 Superior Avenue, NW
Smits, Anthony M. .... '72 '99 C.436 B.A. L.150 J.D. [Ⓐ Squire,S.&D.]
Smolin, Michele, (AV) .... '60 '92 C.521 B.A. L.930 J.D. [McDonald H.]
Smyers, Robyn M. .... '69 '98 C.309 A.B. L.976 J.D. [Ⓐ Thompson H.]
Sneiderman, Lisa N. .... '68 '94 C.608 B.A. L.930 J.D. [Ⓐ Reid,B.M.&W.]
Sneiderman, Steven H., (AV) .... '66 '91 C.347 B.S. L.608 J.D. [Hahn L.&P.]
Snipes, Alonzo, Jr., (BV) .... '29 '68 C.922 B.S. L.1003 J.D. 3815 Lee Road
Snodgrass, Cristin Rose .... '77 '03 C.608 B.A. L.124 [Ⓐ Calfee,H.&G.]
Snow, David A. .... '48 '73 C.597 B.A. L.930 J.D. 1370 Ontario St.
Snow, David F. .... '32 '61 C.197 B.A. L.309 J.D. U.S. Bkrptcy. J.
Snow, Renee Lee .... '47 '97 C.882 B.A. L.124 J.D. 1200 Ontario St.
Snyder, Amanda M. .... '— '03 C.901 B.A. L.1541 J.D. [Ⓐ Jones D.]
Snyder, David V. '66 '91 C.976 B.A. L.861 J.D.
(adm. in LA; not adm. in OH) Cleve. Marshall College‡
Snyder, Dawn E. .... '78 '04 C.25 B.A. L.989 [Ⓐ McNeal,S.A.&B.]
Snyder, Laurence R. .... '59 '86 C.161 B.A. L.1003 J.D. [Snyder]
Snyder, Lloyd B. .... '44 '70 C&L.659 B.S., J.D. Prof. of Law, Cleveland State Univ.
Snyder, Michael L. .... '61 '88 C.101 B.A. L.273 J.D. [McDonald H.]
Snyder, William F., (AV) .... '22 '49 C.309 A.B. L.477 J.D. [Snyder]
Snyder Associates, (AV) .... 20800 Center Ridge Rd.
Sobel, Ryan A. .... '— '04 C.473 B.A. L.124 J.D. [Ⓐ Thorman&H.]
Sobolewski, Brad A. .... '— '00 C.276 B.A. L.602 J.D. [Ⓐ Jones D.]
Soeten, Jan, Jr. .... '44 '69 C.184 B.A. L.930 J.D. Legal Aid Soc.
Sogg, Nancy Walsh, (BV) '48 '75
C.477 B.A. L.930 J.D. Sr. V.P. & Coun., Meridia Health System
Sogg, Wilton S., (AV) .... '35 '60 C.197 A.B. L.309 J.D. [Ⓒ McCarthy,L.C.&L.]
Sokolowski, Jeffrey J. .... '73 '00 C.602 B.A. L.989 J.D. [Ⓐ J.W.Diemert,Jr.&Assoc.]
Solecki, Michael J. .... '— '98 C.228 A.B. L.893 J.D. [Ⓐ Jones D.]
Solganik, Vivian L., (AV) '38 '70 C.930 B.A. L.1003 LL.B.
Assoc. Coun., Ohio Savings Financial Corporation
Sollitto, Sharmon .... '48 '77 C.66 B.A. L.1003 J.D. 2849 Fairfax
Solomon, Lanny M., (BV) .... '51 '76 C.473 B.S. L.1003 J.D. 1800 Standard Bldg.
Solomon, Randall L., (AV) .... '48 '73 C.1208 B.A. L.930 J.D. [Baker&H.]
Solomon, Steven J. .... '75 '03 [Ⓐ Pearne&G.] (See Pat. Sect.)
Sommers, Sandra Becher .... '59 '85 C.610 A.B. L.117 J.D. [Kelley&F.]
Somogyi, Robert E. .... '67 '93 C.608 B.A. L.1003 J.D. [Ⓐ H.C.Kuenzi]
Sondik, Kenneth I. .... '63 '90 C.107 B.A. L.930 J.D. 1370 Ontario Street
Sonkin, Loren M. .... '58 '89 C.679 B.S. L.930 J.D. 1 Lakeside Avenue, Suite 208
Sonkin, Rick D., (AV) .... '62 '87 C&L.608 B.S., J.D. [Sonkin,F.K.&K.]
Sonkin, Shale S., (AV) .... '28 '53 C.610 B.S. L.930 LL.B. [Sonkin,F.K.&K.]
Sonkin, Yvette B. .... '31 '90 C.930 B.A. L.1003 J.D. 55 Public Sq.
Sonkin, Fromson, Kess & Koberna Co., L.P.A., (AV) .... 55 Public Sq.
Sopko, Jeffrey J., (AV) ...... '48 '75 C.201 B.T. L.1003 J.D. [Pearne&G.] (See Pat. Sect.)
Sorin, Marvin .... '24 '59 C.659 B.S. L.1003 LL.B. 5767 Mayfield Rd.
Sosin, Jeremy S. .... '— '97 C.347 B.A. L.879 J.D. [Ⓐ Thompson H.]
Soucie, Michele Polito, (AV) .... '— '82 C.62 B.A. L.1003 J.D. [Javitch,B.&R.]
Soukup, Christopher E. '48 '75
C.608 B.A. L.124 J.D. [Ⓐ Ziegler,M.&M.] (⊙Pepper Pike)
Southworth, Ann '60 '86 C&L.813 B.A., J.D.
(adm. in CA; not adm. in OH) Prof., Case Western Reserve Law School
Southworth, Glenn D., (AV) .... '65 '91 C.446 B.S. L.30 J.D. [McDonald H.]
Sozio, Stephen G., (AV) .... '— '83 C.645 B.A. L.1003 J.D. [Jones D.]
Spagnoli, Charles C. .... '69 '95 C.976 B.A. L.309 J.D. [Ⓐ Janik&D.]
Spain, Charles H., Jr. ...... '44 '73 C.411 A.B. L.178 J.D. V.P. & Sr. Atty., Natl. City Bk.
Spallino, James, Jr. .... '59 '93 C.229 B.S. L.8 J.D. [Baker&H.]
Spanagel, Kenneth R. .... '50 '75 C.597 B.S. L.930 J.D. Mun. J.
Spaner, Martha R. .... '— '02 C.610 B.S. L.1003 J.D. [Ⓐ Shapiro&F.]
Spangenberg, Shibley & Liber LLP, (AV)
1900 East Ninth Street 2400 National City Center
Spanos, Paul G. .... '72 '98 C.161 B.A. L.930 J.D. Trial Atty., U.S. Dept. of Labor
Spaw, David E. ...... '65 '91 C.161 B.E.E. L.1003 J.D. [Rankin,H.P.&C.] (See Pat. Sect.)
Spechalske, Richard A. .... '55 '80 C&L.930 B.S., J.D. 22034 Lake Shore Blvd.
Specian, Patricia A. .... '63 '98 C.608 B.S.N. L.1003 J.D. 614 W. Superior Ave.
Spector, Gary M., (AV) .... '35 '61 C&L.608 B.S., LL.B. [Cooper,S.&W.]
Spellacy, Kevin Matthew, (AV) '63 '89 C.116 L.989 J.D.
614 W. Superior Ave., Ste. 1300
Spellacy, Leo M. .... '34 '59 C.276 B.S. L.930 LL.B. Ct. of App. J.
Spellacy, Leo M., Jr. .... '69 '96 C.363 B.A. L.1003 J.D. [Porter W.M.&A.]
Spencer, Leslie Y. .... '61 '90 C.385 B.A. L.1003 J.D. P.O. Box 24373
Spero, Keith E., (AV) .... '33 '56 C&L.930 B.A., J.D. [Spero&R.]
Spero, Scott A., (BV) .... '64 '89 C.347 B.S. L.1003 J.D. [Bentoff&S.]
Spero & Rosenfield Co., L.P.A., (AV) .... 526 Superior Avenue
Spiegler, Jeffrey H., (BV) .... '48 '74 C.608 B.S.B.A. L.1003 J.D. [Ⓒ Koeth,R.&L.]

Spieth, Bell, McCurdy & Newell Co., L.P.A., (AV)
2000 Huntington Building, 925 Euclid Avenue, 44115-1496
Telephone: 216-696-4700 Fax: 216-696-2706
Email: law@spiethbell.com URL: http://www.spiethbell.com
Clyde E. Williams, Jr.; Sterling Newell, Jr.; J. Donald Cairns (Certified Specialist in Estate Planning, Trust and Probate Law, Ohio State Bar Association) (Board Certified Wills, Trusts and Estates Lawyer, Florida Bar Board of Legal Specialization and Education); Eugene Stevens; Richard T. Watson; Henry E. Seibert, IV; Frederick I. Taft; James M. Havach; Stanley Dan Pace; Bruce G. Hearey; J. Talbot Young, Jr.; Dianne Foley; James R. Bright; Rebecca Holloway Dent; Eugene A. Kratus; John M. Slivka; Benjamin Calkins; M. Elizabeth Monihan; Kristin L. Ubersax; Wade M. Fricke; Timothy G. Warner; Kevin P. Gluntz;—R. Douglas McCreery; Douglas M. Nelson, II; Erica E. McGregor; Allison McCallum.
Business Law, Corporate Law, Real Estate Law, Taxation, Trusts and Estates, Wills, Probate, Nonprofit and Charitable Organizations, Litigation, Labor and Employment, Alcoholic Beverage Control.
Representative Clients: Astrup Co.; Baldwin Wallace; Cavaliers Operating Company, LLC; Cleveland Institute of Art; Dougherty-Hanna Resources Co.; Enpac Corporation; Elevation Motorsports, LLC; Cumberland Development, LLC.
See Professional Biographies, CLEVELAND, OHIO

Spike & Meckler Law Firm, The, LLP
(See Elyria)

Spinks, Thomas F., (BV) .... '45 '74 C.1024 B.A. L.851 J.D. 5700 Pearl Road
Spira, Robert M., (AV) .... '47 '72 C.473 B.A. L.930 J.D. [Ⓒ Benesch,F.C.&A.]
Spirko, Daniel .... '72 '00 C.608 B.S.B.A. L.989 J.D. [Ⓐ Shapiro&F.]
Spirko, Timothy A. .... '71 '99 C.645 B.A. L.1003 J.D. [Ⓐ Buckingham,D.&B.]
Spisak, Michael J., (BV) .... '— '94 C.930 B.A. L.1003 J.D. [Buckley K.]
Spitz, Brian D. .... '71 '97 C.30 B.A. L.124 J.D. [Ⓐ Janik&D.]
Spitz, James E., (AV) .... '43 '69 C.473 B.A. L.1003 J.D. [Rapoport,S.F.&C.]

Spoke, Nicholas M. .... '13 '39 C&L.477 A.B., J.D. 3564 Palmerston Rd.
Spotts, David M.
(See Ashtabula)
Spotz, Richard T., Jr., (AV) .... '48 '73 C.473 B.S. L.1003 J.D. [Ziegler,M.&M.]
Sprague, Charles Edward .... '50 '82 C.25 B.A. L.1003 J.D. Juv. Ct. Mag.
Sprague, Madelon, (AV) ...... '43 '77 C.966 B.B.A. L.776 J.D. 20600 Chagrin Boulevard
Sprague, Timothy L. .... '72 '99 C.608 B.A. L.989 J.D. [Ⓐ Keis G.]
Spreen, Janet A. .... '— '99 C.608 B.A. L.276 J.D. [Ⓐ Baker&H.]
Spreen, Kristofer K. .... '74 '99 C.911 B.A. L.276 J.D. [Ⓐ Calfee,H.&G.]
Spring, Herbert A., Jr., (AV) ..... '20 '48 C.951 B.A. L.930 LL.B. 19300 South Park Blvd.
Spring, William L., (AV) .... '42 '67 C.207 B.A. L.930 J.D. [Ziegler,M.&M.]
Squeri, Stephen J., (AV) .... '— '79 C.1019 B.A. L.602 J.D. [Jones D.]

Squire, Sanders & Dempsey L.L.P., (AV) BR
4900 Key Tower, 127 Public Square, 44114-1304 ⊙
Telephone: 216-479-8500 Fax: 216-479-8780
URL: http://www.ssd.com
Partners: Cleveland Office: Andrew Squire (1850-1934); William B. Sanders (1854-1929); James H. Dempsey (1859-1920); Andrew Agati; Stacy D. Ballin; Geoffrey K. Barnes; Daniel G. Berick; Carolyn J. Buller; David W. Burchmore; Van Carson; Charles F. Clarke; William H. Conner; Timothy J. Cosgrove; Mark A. Cusick (Also at London, England Office); Carol F. Dakin; Ernie K. Demanelis; Alan S. Doris; Carl A. Draucker; Patrick J. Dugan; Robert J. Eidnier; Steven A. Friedman; D. Bruce Gabriel; David S. Goodman; Richard S. Gurbst; W. Michael Hanna; Pamela Iddings Hanover; Susan C. Hastings; Thomas G. Havener; Barbara L. Hawley; Laura Kingsley Hong; Bruce P. Jones; Mary Ann Jorgenson; Gordon S. Kaiser, Jr.; F. Barry Keefe; Thomas S. Kilbane; Robert D. Labes; John S. Larson; Wendlene M. Lavey; Damond R. Mace; James J. Maiwurm; Richard D. Manoloff; Jeffrey J. Margulies; Douglas A. McWilliams; George M. von Mehren; Michael G. Meissner; G. Christopher Meyer; Osborne Mills, Jr.; David J. Millstone; Kenneth C. Moore; James P. Murphy; Jan E. Murray; Frederick R. Nance; Laura D. Nemeth; Howard J.C. Nicols; James P. Oliver; Daniel J. O'Loughlin; Dale E. Papajcik; Samuel S. Pearlman; Terrence G. Perris; Harris A. Senturia; Michael L. Sharb; Timothy J. Sheeran; John F. Shelley; Charna E. Sherman; R. Thomas Stanton; Dale E. Stephenson; Martha S. Sullivan; Dynda A. Thomas; James D. Thomas; James D. Troxell; Gregory J. Viviani; Robin G. Weaver; Jeffrey J. Wedel; David C. Weiner; Joseph C. Weinstein; David A. Zagore. Senior Counsel: Cleveland Office: Helen Z. Kryshtalowych; John F. Lewis; Walter J. Rekstis, III. Counsel: Cleveland Office: Jeffrey A. Bomberger; Katherine G. Petrey. Of Counsel: Cleveland Office: Gregory C. Burkart (Not admitted in OH); David B. Lavey; Jill G. Okun; Shawn R. Russell; Louis Stokes; Mitchell S. Thompson; Michael Wager. Consultant: Cleveland Office: Henry T. King Jr. Senior Attorneys: Cleveland Office: Roger M. Gold; Meegan Lally Spicer; James W. Satola; Christopher R. Shea. Associates: Cleveland Office: Stephen P. Anway; Cipriano S. Beredo, III; Chandra S. Bowling; Patrick J. Brooks; Patrick J. Burke; Alexander G. Burlingame; Nailah K. Byrd; Amy L. Cadle; J. Philip Calabrese; Michele L. Connell; Christine Tomko Cossler; Stephen J. Crawford; Michael A. Cullers; Steven A. Delchin; Stephen M. Fazio; L. Todd Gibson; Jill A. Grinham; Rebecca Wistner Haverstick; Sara E. Hutchins; Denise A. Jackson; Daniel A. Jaffe; Colin R. Jennings; Eric J. Johnson; Allen A. Kacenjar; Laura E. Kacenjar; Joan A. Kavuru; Maureen Sheridan Kenny; Suzanne K. Ketler; Todd D. Kilpatrick (Not admitted in OH); Chaundra C. King; Andrew R. Kruppa; Lianne Mantione; Erin Elizabeth Marks; Daniel C. Mazanec; Jennifer Jenkins Meadows (Not admitted in OH); Ellen K. Meehan; J. Seth Metcalf; Cynthia C. Mog; Leslie A. Morsek; Stephanie E. Niehaus; Natalie E. Norfus; Philip M. Oliss; Raphael J. Omerza; Elton L. Parker; Christina Henagen Peer; Sean T. Peppard; Christine Murphy Pierpont; Sarah K. Rathke; Renee Tramble Richard; Joseph P. Rodgers; Catherine Ziroli Romanchek; Elizabeth M. Sanborn; Mark J. Savage; William V. Shaklee; Dheeraj K. Singhal (Not admitted in OH); Anthony M. Smits; Catherine M. Swartz; Terence L. Thomas; Catherine Corrigan Tompkins; James A. Vollins; Dana B. Weiss; Kristine M. Wellman.
Bankruptcy and Reorganization, Chemicals, Communications, Construction and Engineering, Corporate Transactions and Securities Regulation, E-Commerce, Economic Regulation, Education, Energy, Environmental, Health and Safety, Financial Institutions and Services, Financial Services, Gaming and Casinos, Government and Administrative Agencies, Health Care and Hospitals, Health Sciences, Hospitality and Recreation, Insurance, Intellectual Property, International Dispute Resolution, Labor and Employment, Life Sciences, Litigation, Manufacturing, Media and Entertainment, Private Equity, Project Finance, Public Finance, Real Estate, Real Estate and Hospitality, Sports, Steel, Taxation, Technology, Transportation and Utilities.
The Americas Offices: Cincinnati, Columbus, Houston, Los Angeles, Miami, New York, Palo Alto, Phoenix, San Francisco, Tallahassee, Tampa, Tysons Corner, Washington DC, West Palm Beach, Caracas, Santo Domingo, Rio de Janeiro.
European Offices: Bratislava, Brussels, Budapest, London, Madrid, Milan, Moscow, Prague, Warsaw.
Asia Offices: Beijing, Hong Kong, Shanghai, Tokyo.
Associated Offices: Bucharest, Dublin, Kyiv, Buenos Aires, Santiago
Revisor of the Ohio and Texas Law Digests for this Directory
See Professional Biographies, CLEVELAND, OHIO

Sritharan, Varnesh .... '75 '01 C.454 B.A. L.339 J.D. [Ⓐ Calfee,H.&G.]
Stack, Charles M., (AV) .... '54 '82 C.373 B.A. L.930 J.D. 1300 E. 9th St.
Stadler, David P. .... '71 '01 C.665 B.A. L.989 J.D. [Ritzler,C.&S.]
Stafford, Joseph G., & Associates '60 '85 C.201 B.A. L.1003 LL.D.
323 W Lakeside Ave.
Stafford, Vincent A. .... '67 '92 C.201 B.A. L.1003 J.D. 323 W. Lakeside Ave.
Staib, A.M. Nancee .... '49 '77 C.223 B.S. L.1003 J.D. 2648 Berkshire Rd.
Staib, Mark E., (AV) .... '48 '73 C.363 A.B. L.893 J.D. [Hahn L.&P.]
Stakes, Jennifer .... '75 '02 C.876 B.A. L.7 J.D. [Ⓐ Shapero&G.]
Stanard, James J. .... '21 '49 C.321 A.B. L.930 LL.B. 55 Public Sq.‡

Stanceu, James T. '51 '79 C.608 B.A. L.276 J.D.
425 Western Reserve Building, 1468 W. Ninth Street, 44113
Telephone: 216-588-1001; 800-641-7989 Fax: 216-588-1003
Email: jtstanceu@neo.rr.com URL: http://www.jtstanceulaw.com
Personal Injury, Automobile Accidents and Injuries, Truck Accidents and Injuries, Wrongful Death, Medical Malpractice, Workers Compensation, Workers' Compensation Appeals.
See Professional Biographies, CLEVELAND, OHIO

Standish, Linda S. '52 '82 C&L.347 B.S., J.D.
(adm. in IN; not adm. in OH) V.P. & Corp. Sec., Ceres Group, Inc.
Stanford, Barbara J. .... '47 '80 C.119 B.F.A. L.1003 J.D. Lewis A. Zipkin & Co.
Stanger, Nicole D. .... '— '98 C.645 B.S. L.8 J.D. [Ⓐ Jones D.]
Stanisic, Eileen M. Collet '70 '97 C.741 B.A. L.345 J.D.
(adm. in IN; not adm. in OH) KPMG Peat Marwick LLP
Stanley, Forrest F. '51 '78 C.608 B.A. L.930 J.D.
Sr. V.P. & Assoc. Gen. Coun., KeyBank Natl. Assn.
Stanley, Hugh M., Jr., (AV) .... '44 '69 C.201 B.A. L.276 J.D. [Tucker E.&W.]
Stano, Paul J., (BV) .... '56 '81 C.97 B.A. L.1003 J.D. [P.J.Stano]
Stano, Paul J., Co., LPA, Law Offices of, (BV) .... 6650 Pearl Road, Suite 202
Stansbury, Ronald C., (AV) .... '48 '74 C&L.608 B.A., J.D. [Calfee,H.&G.]
Stanton, R. Thomas, (AV) '43 '69
C.388 B.A. L.597 J.D. [Squire,S.&D.] (⊙New York, NY)
Stanuszek, Michael J. .... '79 '04 C.136 B.S.B.A. L.838 J.D. [Ⓐ Janik&D.]
Star, Philip D. '47 '75 C.966 B.A. L.124 J.D.
Cleveland State University, Center for Neighborhood Development
Stark, J. Norman .... '29 '73 C.381 B.Arch. L.1003 J.D. [J.N.Stark]
Stark, Jonathan L. .... '67 '92 C.91 B.A. L.930 J.D. [Schneider,S.R.&L.]
Stark, Kenneth B., (AV) .... '48 '79 C.966 B.S.Ch.E. L.930 J.D. [Duvin,C.&H.]
Stark, J. Norman, Co., L.P.A. .... 1310 E. 49th Street, Suite 2
Starke, Sheldon Philip, (BV) '45 '71 C.608 B.A. L.1003 J.D.
232220 Chagrin Boulevard
Starkoff, Jack R. .... '69 '94 C.966 B.S. L.245 J.D. [Ⓐ Calfee,H.&G.]
Stauffer, Susan P., (AV) .... '44 '70 C&L.930 B.A., J.D. Legal Aid Soc.
Stavnicky, Michael R., (BV) .... '69 '94 C.610 B.S. L.1003 J.D. [Ⓐ Singerman,M.D.&K.]
Stavole, C. Anthony, (AV) .... '33 '61 C.363 B.S. L.1003 J.D. 5700 Pearl Rd., Ste. 202
Stavole, William J., (AV) .... '63 '88 C.385 B.A. L.608 J.D. [Taft,S.&H.]
Stealey, Patricia A. ...... '33 '80 C.161 B.B.A. L.1003 J.D. 9404 N. Church Dr., Apt. 302
Stearns, Roger S., (BV) .... '41 '67 C.930 B.A. L.1003 J.D. 4307 Groveland Rd.
Steeb, Cindy L. .... '63 '01 C.970 B.A. L.989 J.D. [Ⓐ Tucker E.&W.]
Steel, Terrence J., (AV) .... '46 '71 C&L.608 B.A., J.D. [Cowden,H.N.&L.]
Steely, Robert L., (AV) .... '43 '71 C.97 B.A. L.161 J.D. 8227 Brecksville Road
Stefancin, Robert M., (AV) .... '65 '90 C.901 B.A. L.930 J.D. [Schottenstein,Z.&D.]
Stefanova, Vania T. .... '65 '90 C.999 J.D. L.7 J.D. [Ⓐ R.T.Herman&Assoc.]
Stefanski, D. Kim, (BV) .... '54 '79 C&L.150 B.A., J.D. [Stefanski&Assoc.] ⊙
Stefanski & Associates LLC, (BV) .... 613 West Superior Avenue (⊙Youngstown)
Steffen, Wallace R. .... '26 '50 C.62 B.A. L.930 J.D. 1555 Queen Annes Gate
Stege, Edward Richard, (AV) .... '43 '68 C.165 A.B. L.966 J.D. [Stege&M.]

Stege & Michelson Co., L.P.A., (AV)
32nd Floor, BP America Building, 200 Public Square, Suite 3220, 44114
Telephone: 216-348-0700 Fax: 216-348-0803
Email: email@stege-law.com URL: http://www.stege-law.com
Edward Richard Stege; Michael B. Michelson;—Andrew J. Thompson. Of Counsel: Deborah A. Wainey; Thomas C. Wood, Jr.
Trial Practice in the State and Federal Courts including Personal Injury, Medical Malpractice, Nursing Home Abuse and Neglect, FELA/Railroad Law, Labor and Employment, Insurance Litigation, Commercial Litigation, Business Tort Litigation, Criminal Defense. Elder Law, Estate Planning and Probate Law.
See Professional Biographies, CLEVELAND, OHIO

Steiger, Sheldon G., (AV) .... '45 '72 C.608 B.A. L.1003 J.D. 75 Public Square, Suite 650
Stein, David J. '74 '02 C.608 B.S. L.124 J.D.
Pat. Atty., The Cleveland Clinic Foundation (Pat.)
Stein, Ellen R. .... '64 '98 C.608 B.S.B.A. L.1003 J.D. [Ⓐ McCarthy,L.C.&L.]
Stein, Laurel Green .... '74 '00 C.910 A.B. L.836 J.D. 623 W. St. Clair Ave.
Stein, Robert N. .... '61 '86 C.608 B.A. L.1003 J.D. [R.N.Stein]
Stein, Samuel L. .... '29 '51 C&L.930 B.A., LL.B. 27060 Cedar Rd.
Stein, Sheldon, (BV) .... '51 '76 C.930 B.A. L.1003 J.D. 400 Terminal Tower
Stein, Stanley E., (BV) .... '28 '62 C.930 B.S. L.1003 J.D. [S.E.Stein&Assoc.]
Stein, William H. .... '24 '51 C.210 A.B. L.930 LL.B. 7791 Brecksville Rd.‡

Stein, Robert N., Co., LPA
1450 Rockefeller Building, 614 Superior Avenue, N.W., 44113
Telephone: 216-781-8040 Fax: 216-781-9091
Email: robertnsteinesq@sbcglobal.net URL: http://www.lawyers.com/robertsteinlaw
Robert N. Stein.
Business Law, Contract Disputes, Corporate Law, Small Business Law, Litigation, Real Estate, Civil Trial, Personal Injury, Auto Accidents, Dog Bites, Premises Liability.
See Professional Biographies, CLEVELAND, OHIO

Stein, Stanley E., & Associates Co., L.P.A., (BV) .... 75 Public Sq., Suite 714
Steinberg, Gerald L., (AV) '46 '76 C.363 B.S.B.A. L.1003 J.D.
1370 Ontario St., Ste. 1020
Steindler, Howard A., (AV) .... '42 '67 C.473 B.S. L.608 J.D. [Benesch,F.C.&A.]
Steiner, Carolyn L. .... '57 '90 C.604 B.A. L.994 J.D. P.O. Box 20649
Steiner, William F., (AV) .... '25 '51 C.608 B.S. L.477 J.D. [Steiner&S.]
Steiner & Stern Co., L.P.A., (AV) .... 75 Public Sq.
Steines, Charles M. .... '— '77 C.473 B.S. L.117 J.D. [Ⓒ Jones D.]
Steinmetz, Arthur P., (AV) .... '25 '51 C&L.930 B.A., LL.B. [Ⓒ Walter&H.]
Stellato, Louis E. '50 '77 C.846 B.B.A. L.665 J.D.
(adm. in PA; not adm. in OH) V.P., Gen. Coun. & Secy., The Sherwin-Williams Co.
Steltenkamp, Gerald Lawrence '47 '73 C.150 B.A. L.1340 J.D.
Dir., State and Local Taxation, The Sherwin-Williams Co.
Stepan, Linda L. .... '— '91 C.161 B.A. L.1003 J.D. [Ⓐ Reminger&R.]
Stepanek, Walter .... '22 '58 C.930 B.B.A. L.1003 J.D. 6107 Biddulph Rd.
Stepanovic, Ronald A. .... '63 '88 C&L.930 B.S., J.D. [Baker&H.]
Stephens, Alton L., Jr., (AV) .... '— '75 C.839 B.S. L.1161 J.D. [Gallagher S.]
Stephenson, Dale E., (AV) '56 '82 C.999 B.A. L.477 J.D.
[Squire,S.&D.] (⊙Hous., TX)
Stephenson, James .... '74 '01 C.381 B.S L.989 J.D. [Ⓐ Reid,B.M.&W.]
Stern, Harold S., (AV) .... '27 '52 C.347 B.S. L.930 J.D. [Ⓒ Chattman,G.&S.]
Stern, Howard S., (AV) .... '29 '56 C.608 B.Sc. L.930 J.D. [Steiner&S.]
Stern, Jeffrey A. .... '— '77 C.930 B.A. L.1003 J.D. Trial Atty., U.S. EEO Comm.

Stern, Mitchell A., (AV) '52 '77 C.473 B.A. L.608 J.D.
55 Public Square, Suite 1717, 44113-1901
Telephone: 216-861-0006 Fax: 216-771-8404
Workers Compensation, Appeals, Personal Injury, Automobile Accidents, General Practice.
See Professional Biographies, CLEVELAND, OHIO

Stern, Robert W. .... '42 '69 C.608 B.S.B.A. L.1003 J.D. Pres., Short Sizes Inc.
Sternberg, Sandor W. .... '54 '84 C.161 B.A. L.607 J.D. [Ⓐ Carlisle,M.R.K.&U.]
Sternberg & Zeid Co., L.P.A.
(See Mentor)
Sternlicht, Melissa R. .... '— '90 C&L.930 B.A., J.D. Fed. Trade Comm.
Steuer, Arlene B. .... '27 '52 C.251 L.1003 J.D. Standard Bldg.
Steuer, Richard B. .... '25 '51 C.309 A.B. L.930 LL.B. [Steuer,E.B.&B.] ‡

Steuer, Escovar, Berk & Brown Co., L.P.A., (AV)
55 Public Square, Suite 1828, 44113-1977
Telephone: 216-771-8121 Fax: 216-771-8120 URL: http://www.sebblaw.com
Email: info@sebblaw.com URL: http://www.lawyers.com/steuerescovar&berk
Richard B. Steuer (Retired); Alfred L. Steuer (1892-1967); Thomas J. Escovar; Gerald A. Berk; William D. Brown;—L. Christopher Coleman; Patrick P. Merrick.
General Civil and Criminal Practice. Personal Injury, Negligence, Workers Compensation, Corporation, Mergers and Acquisitions, Taxation, Real Estate, Bankruptcy, Family, Probate and Commercial Law. Estate Planning, Trials and Medical Malpractice, Civil and Criminal Appellate Work, Insurance Defense, Business Law, Administrative Law.
See Professional Biographies, CLEVELAND, OHIO

Stevens, Anne K. .... '54 '79 C.264 B.A. L.930 J.D. Legal Aid Soc.
Stevens, Christopher M. '65 '91 C.94 B.A. L.823 J.D.
(adm. in CA; not adm. in OH) [Ⓐ Calfee,H.&G.]
Stevens, Eugene, (AV) .... '34 '58 C&L.930 B.B.A., LL.B. [Spieth,B.M.&N.]
Stevens, Fred A., (BV) .... '47 '73 C.363 B.A. L.930 J.D. 75 Public Sq., Ste. 1450
Stevens, Sam R. .... '30 '56 C.930 L.608 LL.B. 1187 Alpine Rd.‡
Stevens, Thomas C., (AV) '49 '74 C.1044 B.A. L.228 J.D.
Sr. Exec. V.P., Gen. Coun. & Secy., KeyBank Natl. Assn.
Stevenson, Anthony Mark .... '63 '96 C.436 B.A. L.989 J.D. 1240 E. Ninth Street
Stewart, E. Roger .... '51 '98 C.846 B.A. L.1003 J.D. [McCarthy,L.C.&L.]
Stewart, Heather B. .... '77 '02 C.207 B.A. L.424 J.D. Amer. Greetings Corp.
Stewart, Kirk .... '46 '76 C.902 B.A. L.1003 J.D. Lutheran Housing Corp.
Stewart, Lawrence E., (AV) .... '25 '50 C.610 B.Sc. L.930 J.D. [Stewart&D.]
Stewart, Melody J. '62 '89 C.150 B.M. L.1003 J.D.
Asst. Dean, Cleveland-Marshall College of Law
Stewart, Scott E., (AV) .... '51 '76 C.81 B.A. L.930 J.D. [Stewart&D.]
Stewart, William R., (AV) .... '43 '68 C.976 B.A. L.228 J.D. [Thompson H.]

Stewart and De Chant Co., L.P.A., (AV)
The Standard Building, 1370 Ontario Street, Suite 1440, 44113-1701
Telephone: 216-781-2258 Fax: 216-781-8210
Email: INFO@STEWARTDECHANT.COM URL: http://www.STEWARTDECHANT.COM
Lawrence E. Stewart; Thomas H. De Chant; Fred Wendel III; Scott E. Stewart; Samuel V. Butcher;— Cindy L. Kobal; Lawrence D. Wilson; Sheri A. Sweeney. Of Counsel: Paul S. Sanislo.
General Trial and Appellate Practice. Negligence, Products Liability, Malpractice, Medical Legal, Workers Compensation and Social Security Disability Law. Wrongful Death Law.
Reference: Keybank (Main Office).

See Professional Biographies, CLEVELAND, OHIO

Stewart-Johnson, Lynne .... '55 '84 C.161 B.A. L.1003 J.D. 1665 Wagar Ave.
Stickan, Christian H. .... '50 '75 C.363 B.A. L.345 J.D. Off. of U.S. Atty.
Stickney, John M., (AV) .... '26 '51 C&L.930 A.B., LL.B. [Stickney&S.]
Stickney, Thomas M. .... '69 '95 C.385 B.A. L.8 J.D. [Stickney&S.]
Stickney & Stickney, (AV) .... 50 Public Square
Stief, James E. .... '70 '97 C.363 B.S. L.602 J.D. [McDonald H.]
Stienecker, Andrew .... '71 '00 C.608 B.S. L.607 J.D. [Weston H.]
Stifel, Orville E., II, (BV) .... '46 '88 C.610 B.A. L.1003 J.D. [O.E.Stifel,II]
Stifel, Orville E., II, Co., LPA, (BV) .... 526 Superior Ave. E., Ste. 1140
Stinn, Michael E., (AV) .... '58 '84 C.276 B.S. L.1003 J.D. [Britton,S.P.&K.]
Stockman, Mark J. .... '61 '96 C.381 M.A. L.161 J.D. [Kahn K.]
Stockmaster, Ann Marie .... '58 '96 C.161 B.A. L.1003 J.D. [R.Guttman&Assoc.]
Stockslager, Matthew J., (BV) .... '66 '92 C.608 B.S. L.8 J.D. [Schottenstein,Z.&D.]
Stoken, Henry A., (BV) ...... '42 '81 C.161 B.A. L.1003 J.D. 7229 Parma Park Boulevard
Stokes, Louis, (AV) .... '25 '53 C.930 L.161 LL.B. [Squire,S.&D.] (Wash., DC)
Stolarsky, Lon D., (BV) .... '59 '84 C.608 B.A. L.1003 J.D. [L.Stolarsky]
Stolarsky, Lon, (BV) .... 1370 Ontario St., Ste. 1630
Stoll, Edward J., Jr. .... '66 '94 C.207 B.A. L.161 J.D. [Benesch,F.C.&A.]
Stoll, Myron S., (AV) '34 '60
C.610 B.A. L.930 LL.B. V.P., Communication Technologies Ltd.
Stolzer, Daniel R. '56 '83 C.105 B.A. L.1048 J.D.
(adm. in PA; not adm. in OH) Sr. V.P. & Assoc. Gen. Coun., KeyBank Natl. Assn.
Stone, James M., (AV) .... '52 '86 C.608 B.A. L.1003 J.D. [McDonald H.]
Stoper, Richard L., Jr., (BV) ...... '58 '84 C.608 B.A. L.1003 J.D. [Rotatori,B.G.S.&A.]
Storey, John .... '— '05 C.970 B.A. L.989 J.D. [Cowden,H.N.&L.]
Storie, Lloyd .... '46 '73 C.472 B.B.A. L.1068 J.D. [Rosner&Assoc.]
Stotter, Robert H., (BV) .... '48 '73 C&L.930 B.A., J.D. [Stotter&K.]
Stotter & Koosed, Co LPA, (BV) .... 75 Public Square, Suite 1200
Stovsky, Michael D., (AV) .... '64 '91 C.597 B.A. L.659 J.D. [Ulmer&B.]
Strachan, William R., (AV) .... '46 '72 C.532 B.A. L.930 J.D. [Strachan,M.O.&R.]
Strachan, Miller, Olender & Roessler, Co., L.P.A., (AV) .... 925 Euclid Avenue
Strain, Howard G. .... '64 '96 C.33 B.A. L.608 J.D. [Porter W.M.&A.]
Straka, Joseph J. .... '66 '92 C.610 B.A. L.1003 J.D. [Morscher&S.]
Stralka, Gregory T., (BV) .... '62 '87 C.967 B.A. L.823 J.D. 5005 Rockside Road
Strang, Carter E., (AV) .... '51 '84 C.381 B.S. L.1003 J.D. [Tucker E.&W.]
Strassfeld, Anne F. .... '55 '82 C.918 B.A. L.893 J.D. The Cleveland Clinic Foundation
Strassfeld, Robert N. '54 '85 C.918 B.A. L.893 J.D.
(adm. in MD; not adm. in OH) 11075 E. Blvd.
Strassman, Carol D., (AV) .... '55 '80 C.473 A.B. L.930 J.D. [Millisor&N.]
Stratford, Tracy K. .... '— '98 C&L.608 B.A., J.D. [Jones D.]
Stratton, Robert Brent .... '51 '92 C.381 B.B.A. L.989 J.D. Marsh, Inc.
Strauch, John L., (AV) .... '— '63 C.665 B.A. L.569 LL.B. [Jones D.]
Strauss, David J., (AV) .... '43 '67 C&L.352 B.B.A., J.D. [Baker&H.]
Strauss, Marc L., (BV) .... '61 '86 C.37 B.S.B.A. L.1003 J.D. [Kohrman J.&K.]
Streeter, Richard E., (AV) .... '34 '60 C&L.976 B.A., LL.B. 127 Public Sq.‡
Streicher, James F., (AV) .... '40 '66 C.608 B.A. L.930 J.D. [Calfee,H.&G.]
Streza, Ralph, (AV) .... '56 '82 C.473 B.A. L.1003 J.D. [Porter W.M.&A.]
Striefsky, Linda A., (AV) .... '52 '77 C.452 B.A. L.276 J.D. [Thompson H.]
Strimbu, Victor, Jr., (AV) .... '32 '60 C.313 B.A. L.178 J.D. [Baker&H.]
Stringer, Anthony F. .... '73 '99 C.262 B.A. L.608 J.D. [Calfee,H.&G.]
Stroh, Gary E. .... '54 '92 C.161 B.A. L.1003 J.D. Adult Prob. Dept.
Stroh, Thomas M., (BV) .... '45 '79 C.363 B.A. L.1003 J.D. 18123 Sloane Avenue
Strom, Susan R. .... '51 '78 C&L.150 B.A., J.D. [Calfee,H.&G.]
Stronczer, Michelle Pierce .... '58 '96 C&L.8 B.A., J.D. [Baker&H.]
Strunk, Wayne E. .... '46 '80 C.161 B.A. L.1003 J.D. Mag., Com. Pleas Ct., Juv. Div.
Studly, Paul A. .... '40 '70 C.610 B.B.A. L.161 J.D. Appeals Offr., I.R.S.
Studnicha, Cynthia H. .... '67 '92 C.363 B.A. L.1003 J.D. 1660 West 2nd Street
Stueber, Frederick G., (AV) '53 '80 C.951 B.A. L.309 J.D.
Sr. V.P., Gen. Coun. & Secy., Lincoln Electric Co., The
Stueber, Jennifer L. .... '69 '96 C.608 B.A. L.1003 J.D. [Climaco,L.P.W.&G.]
Stuhan, Richard G., (AV) .... '— '76 C.229 B.A. L.893 J.D. [Jones D.]
Stuhldreher, George W., (AV) .... '23 '51 C&L.608 B.A., J.D. 1501 Euclid Avenue‡
Stump, Kenneth A. .... '69 '94 C.94 B.S.B.A. L.1003 J.D. [Vorys,S.S.&P.]
Stupica, Terri L., (AV) .... '62 '88 C.363 B.A. L.1003 J.D. [T.L.Stupica]
Stupica, Terri L., Co., LPA, (AV) .... 6449 Wilson Mills Rd.
Stuplinski, Bernard J., (AV) '26 '52 C&L.930 B.B.A., J.D.
5432 Mayfield Road, Suite 103
Stuplinski, Linda A., The Law Office of '62 '94 C.62 B.A. L.1003 J.D.
75 Public Square
Sucher, Daniel M., (BV) .... '66 '91 C.363 B.A. L.1003 J.D. [Young,G.&S.]
Sukenik, Rosalyn K., (BV) .... '40 '79 C.597 B.A. L.1003 J.D. 18020 S. Woodland Rd.
Sullivan, Brian D. .... '69 '94 C.1349 B.A. L.1003 J.D. [Reminger&R.]
Sullivan, Joan F. .... '45 '73 C.1036 A.B. L.930 J.D. U.S. Dept. of Jus.
Sullivan, John E., (AV) .... '58 '84 C.207 B.A. L.880 J.D. [Baker&H.]
Sullivan, John E., III, (AV) .... '58 '85 C.93 B.A. L.846 J.D. [Sullivan&S.]
Sullivan, Joseph D., (AV) .... '31 '58 C.363 B.S. L.477 LL.B. [Calfee,H.&G.] ‡
Sullivan, Julia Ryan .... '61 '86 C&L.846 B.A., J.D. [Sullivan&S.]
Sullivan, K. James .... '76 '01 C.363 B.A. L.893 J.D. [Calfee,H.&G.]
Sullivan, Kevin M. .... '44 '74 C.321 B.S. L.930 J.D. [Calfee,H.&G.] ‡
Sullivan, Mark E., Law Offices of, (BV) '50 '82
C.893 B.A. L.1003 J.D. 75 Public Sq., Rm. 1016
Sullivan, Martha S. .... '67 '94 C.787 B.S. L.930 J.D. [Squire,S.&D.]
Sullivan, Michael A. .... '63 '89 C.602 B.A. L.262 J.D. Asst. Co. Pros.
Sullivan, Terrence P. .... '49 '86 C.161 B.A. L.1003 J.D. 448 Leader Bldg.

Sullivan & Sullivan, Ltd., (AV)
25201 Chagrin Boulevard Suite 350, 44122
Telephone: 216-896-0001 Fax: 216-896-0002
URL: http://www.sullivanandsullivan.com
John E. Sullivan, III; Julia Ryan Sullivan. Associate: Patrick J. Rhoa. Of Counsel: Robert J. Rischitelli, Jr.
Asset Protection Planning, Asset Recovery, Debtor/Creditor, Collections, Levy, Attachment, Bankruptcy and Workouts, Estate Planning, Oil & Gas, Commercial Litigation and Appellate.

See Professional Biographies, CLEVELAND, OHIO

Summers, Linda DelaCourt .... '68 '96 C.575 B.S.B.A. L.930 J.D. [Ulmer&B.]
Summers, Lisa D., (CV) ... '57 '87 C.392 B.A. L.1003 J.D. 526 Superior Ave. E., Ste. 440
Summers, Richard D. .... '71 '98 C.62 B.A. L.8 J.D. [McDonald H.]
Summers, Sylvester, Jr. '60 '89 C.951 B.A. L.930 J.D.
Bank One Center, 600 Superior Avenue Suite 1300
Summers, William L., (AV) .... '42 '69 C.381 B.A. L.161 J.D. [Summers&V.]
Summers & Vargas Co., LPA, (AV) .... 55 Public Square
Sundheim, Robert B., (AV) '36 '64
C.971 B.S. L.215 LL.B. [Tarolli,S.C.&T.] (See Pat. Sect.)
Sundheimer, Marlene, (BV) '52 '79 C.318 B.A. L.1003 J.D.
UAW-GM Legal Servs. Plan
Sussman, Cathryn A. .... '70 '98 C.610 B.S. L.1003 J.D. [Hahn L.&P.]
Suster, Ronald, (BV) .... '42 '67 C&L.930 B.A., J.D. Com. Pleas J.
Sutherland, Annette Tucker .... '59 '87 C.228 B.A. L.880 J.D. [A.T.Sutherland]
Sutherland, Annette Tucker, Co., L.P.A. .... 16817 Aldersyde Drive
Sutkus, Richard A. .... '69 '97 C&L.734 B.S., J.D. [Tarolli,S.C.&T.] (See Pat. Sect.)
Sutter, Lawrence A., (AV) .... '63 '89 C.283 B.A. L.7 J.D. [Sutter,O.&F.]
Sutter Hodgins, Grace '59 '91
C.608 B.S. L.8 J.D. Coun., Federal Reserve Bk. of Cleveland

Sutter, O'Connell & Farchione, (AV)
3600 Erieview Tower, 1301 East Ninth Street, 44114
Telephone: 216-928-2200 Fax: 216-928-4400
Email: LSutter@sutter-law.com URL: http://www.sutter-law.com
Members of Firm: Lawrence A. Sutter; Matthew C. O'Connell; Joseph A. Farchione, Jr.; Denise A. Dickerson; Jonathan M. Menuez; Joy D. Day (Resident Partner, Franklin, Tennessee Office); Brant E. Poling; John V. Jackson, II. Of Counsel: Thomas H. Terry, III. Associates: Colleen H. Petrello; Christina J. Marshall; David W. Skall; David J. Hudak; Daniel E. Perrico; Victoria Barto; Edward H. Blakemore; James M. Popson; J. Britt Phillips (Resident, Franklin, Tennessee Office); Christina Tuggey Hidek; Amy K. Corrigall; John C. Leach; Douglas R. Simek; Marco G. Bocciarelli; Marc D. Amos; Adam W. Martin; Jason P. Ferrante; Stuart D. Baker.
Trial Practice in all Courts: General and Automotive Product Liability, Medical Malpractice, Trucking/Transportation, Medical Device, Material Handling, Toxic Tort, General Liability, Professional Liability, Excess Insurance, and Class Action Defense.
Franklin, Tennessee Office: 217 Second Avenue, South, 37064-2622. Telephone: 615-791-1031. Fax: 615-791-9578.

See Professional Biographies, CLEVELAND, OHIO

Sutton, Betty .... '63 '91 C.381 B.A. L.8 J.D. [Faulkner,M.&P.]
Sutton, Lisa Duffett .... '68 '94 C.473 B.A. L.930 J.D. Eaton Corp.
Sutton, Stephen C. .... '66 '91 C.1044 B.A. L.1003 J.D. [Baker&H.]
Sutton, Thomas A. .... '60 '87 C&L.352 B.B.A., J.D. 2860 Detroit Ave.
Sutula, John D., (AV) .... '51 '76 C.424 A.B. L.1003 J.D. 920 Terminal Tower
Sutula, John J., (AV) .... '22 '53 C.930 B.B.A. L.1003 J.D. [Chattman,G.&S.]
Sutula, Kathleen A. .... '52 '86 C.608 B.S. L.1003 J.D. Com. Pleas. J.
Svat, Mark S. .... '59 '89 C.161 B.S.E.T. L.989 J.D. [Fay,S.F.M.&M.] (See Pat. Sect.)
Svec, Jennifer Sue .... '74 '99 C.1260 B.A. L.989 J.D. [Zashin&R.]

Svete, McGee & Carrabine Co., L.P.A.
(See Chardon)

Swadey, Robert J. .... '26 '50 C.363 L.608 J.D. [Hahn,S.&P.]
Swain, Maureen Redlin .... '70 '96 C.62 B.A. L.1003 J.D. 127 Public Square
Swain, William L. .... '58 '84 C.161 B.A. L.1003 J.D. 15705 Van Aken Blvd., Apt. 4
Swansinger, John .... '62 '89 C.97 B.S.B.A. L.7 J.D. [Ritzler,C.&S.]
Swanson, Charles A., (BV) .... '48 '75 C.49 B.A. L.161 J.D. 1800 Standard Building
Swartz, Catherine M. .... '76 '02 C.970 B.A. L.608 J.D. [Squire,S.&D.]
Swartz, Joseph B., (AV) .... '41 '70 C.478 A.B. L.188 J.D. [Weston H.]

Swartz Campbell LLC
55 Public Square, Suite 1120, 44113
Telephone: 216-685-9188 Fax: 216-685-9293
Email: webmaster@swartzcampbell.com URL: http://www.swartzcampbell.com
Resident Partner: Kenneth F. Krawczak. Associate: Michele L. Larissey.
General Civil and Trial Practice in State and Federal Courts including Insurance, Workers Compensation, Product Liability, Toxic Torts, Medical Malpractice, Legal Malpractice, and Commercial, Bankruptcy Defense, Employment and Labor Law.
Allentown, Pennsylvania Office: Suite 230, 5100 Tilghman Street. Telephone: 610-395-5903. Fax: 610-395-7097.
Bedminster, New Jersey Office: Bedminster Center, 90 Washington Valley Road. Telephone: 908-719-8932. Fax: 908-719-6005.
Fort Myers, Florida Office: World Plaza, 12585 New Brittany Boulevard, Suite 21E. Telephone: 239-790-7700. Fax: 239-332-5325.
Harrisburg, Pennsylvania Office: 1631 North Front Street, 2nd Floor. Telephone: 717-233-3515. Fax: 717-233-3468.
Media, Pennsylvania Office: 115 North Jackson Street. Telephone: 610-566-9222. Fax: 610-566-7351.
Mount Laurel, New Jersey Office: Bloom Court, Suite 101. 1300 Route 73. Telephone: 856-727-4777. Fax: 856-727-0464.
New York, New York Office: Suite 900, 132 Nassau Street. Telephone: 212-406-1282. Fax: 212-619-2340.
Orlando, Florida Office: Millenia Park One, 4901 Vineland Road, Suite 300. Telephone: 407-209-1000. Fax: 407-209-1001.
Philadelphia, Pennsylvania Office: 1601 Market Street, 34th Floor. Telephone: 215-564-5190. Telefax: 215-299-4301.
Pittsburgh, Pennsylvania Office: U.S. Steel Building, 47th Floor, 600 Grant Street. Telephone: 412-232-9800. Fax: 412-471-1106.
Scranton, Pennsylvania Office: Bank Towers, 11th Floor, 321 Spruce Street. Telephone: 570-343-0029. Fax: 570-343-1534.
West Chester, Pennsylvania Office: One South Church Street, Suite 400. Telephone: 610-692-9500. Fax: 610-692-4936.
Wilmington, Delaware Office: 300 Delaware Avenue, Suite 1130, P.O. Box 330. Telephone: 302-656-5935. Fax: 302-656-1434.

See Professional Biographies, CLEVELAND, OHIO

Swartzbaugh, Marc L., (AV) .... '37 '61 C.967 A.B. L.659 LL.B. 901 Lakeside Ave.‡
Swary, Mark F., (AV) .... '— '73 C.1024 B.A. L.930 J.D. [Hahn L.&P.]
Swearengen, Michael K., (AV) .... '60 '89 C.851 B.A. L.276 J.D. [Benesch,F.C.&A.]
Sweebe, Richard D., (AV) .... '51 '79 C.381 B.A. L.7 J.D. [Ulmer&B.] (Columbus)
Sweeney, Emily M. .... '48 '81 C.251 B.A. L.989 J.D. Office of the United States Attorney
Sweeney, James .... '30 '61 Ct. App. J.
Sweeney, James F., (AV) .... '32 '59 C.363 B.S. L.930 LL.B. 1501 Euclid Avenue‡
Sweeney, Kelley Ann .... '71 '97 C.363 B.S. L.989 J.D. Atty. Gen. Off.
Sweeney, Kristin W. .... '70 '95 C.473 B.A. L.930 J.D. Asst. Pub. Def.
Sweeney, Martin L. .... '22 '51 C.276 B.S. L.1003 J.D. 3605 Rocky River Drive
Sweeney, Mary Brigid .... '59 '89 C.93 B.A. L.1003 J.D. [R.E.Sweeney]
Sweeney, Patrick J., (AV) .... '58 '86 C.970 B.A. L.1003 J.D. [Thompson H.]
Sweeney, Robert E., (AV) .... '24 '51 C.62 L.161 J.D. [R.E.Sweeney]
Sweeney, Robert P., (AV) .... '50 '76 C.321 B.S. L.930 J.D. [R.E.Sweeney]
Sweeney, Rosemary, (AV) .... '— '87 C.363 B.S. L.930 J.D. [Buckley K.]
Sweeney, Sean M. .... '68 '99 C.150 B.A. L.1003 J.D. [Moscarino&T.]
Sweeney, Sheri A. .... '73 '02 C.381 B.A. L.989 J.D. [Stewart&D.]
Sweeney, Suzan Marie .... '58 '90 C.161 B.A. L.1003 J.D. Asst. Pub. Def.

Sweeney, Timothy F., Law Office of, (AV) '60 '87 C.602 A.B. L.608 J.D.
The 820 Building, 820 West Superior Avenue, Suite 430, 44113-1800
Telephone: 216-241-5003 Fax: 216-241-3138
Email: tim@timsweeneylaw.com
—Lynn Rowe Larsen.

(This Listing Continued)

Sweeney, Timothy F., Law Office of (Continued)

Litigation, including General Civil and Criminal Litigation in State and Federal Courts at the Trial and Appellate Levels; Arbitration; Commercial Litigation; Employment Litigation and Employment Matters; Insurance and Contract Litigation; Products Liability Litigation; Construction Litigation; Bankruptcy Litigation, including representing Creditors in Bankruptcy and Related Proceedings; Workouts; Corporate and Commercial Transactions; Criminal Defense; Criminal Appeals and Post-Conviction Proceedings; Federal Death Penalty Litigation.

See Professional Biographies, CLEVELAND, OHIO

Sweeney, Timothy G., (BV) ... '57 '84 C.608 B.A. L.1003 J.D. [🄰 Bonezzi S.M.&P.]
Sweeney, Timothy R., (AV) '35 '60 C.363 B.S. L.215 LL.B. 815 Superior Avenue, N.E.
Sweeney, Robert E., Co., L.P.A., (AV) ... 1220 W. 6th St., Ste. 303
Sweet, Joy A. ... '38 '83 C.161 B.B.A. L.930 J.D. 800 Brick Mill Run
Swift, Christopher J., (AV) ... '55 '80 C.611 B.A. L.608 J.D. [Baker&H.]
Switzer, Donald H., (AV) ... '50 '78 C.839 B.A. L.893 J.D. [Bonezzi S.M.&P.]
Switzer, H. Duane ... '— '64 C.474 B.S.C.E. L.276 LL.B. [🄲 Jones D.] (See Pat. Sect.)
Switzer, Kennee B. ... '53 '88 C.012 B.A. L.989 J.D. [🄰 Meyers,R.F.&L.]
Switzer, Stephanie N. '67 '94 C.604 B.A. L.94 J.D. Assoc. Coun., The Cleveland Clinic Foundation
Synenberg, Joan C. ... '57 '89 C.161 B.A. L.989 J.D Mun. Ct. J.
Synenberg, Roger M., (AV) ... '49 '77 C.30 B.S. L.1003 J.D. [Synenberg&Assoc.]

Synenberg & Associates, LLC, (AV)
55 Public Square Suite 1200, 44113
Telephone: 216-622-2727 Fax: 216-622-2707
Email: lawoffice@synenberg.com URL: http://www.synenberglaw.com
Roger M. Synenberg;—Gregg D. Garfinkel; Dominic J. Coletta.
Federal and State Criminal Defense. White Collar Crimes, Drug Crimes, Felonies, Misdemeanors, Driving While Intoxicated.

See Professional Biographies, CLEVELAND, OHIO

Syracuse, Vetus J. ... '45 '70 C.610 A.B. L.930 J.D. 26250 Euclid Ave.
Syroney, David J. ... '65 '94 C.207 B.A. L.1003 J.D. [🄰 J.B.Jerome&Assoc.]
Szabo, Gabriel S., Jr. ... '24 '53 C&L.930 A.B., LL.B. 5432 Mayfield Rd.
Szabo, John Z., (AV) ... '41 '69 C&L.930 B.A., J.D. 5432 Mayfield Rd.
Szabo, Magda B. ... '53 '77 L.989 J.D. [🄰 Calfee,H.&G.]
Szabo, Paul E., (AV) ... '53 '79 C.722 B.A. L.1003 J.D. [🄰 Calfee,H.&G.] (See Pat. Sect.)
Szaller, James F., (AV) ... '45 '75 C.161 B.A. L.1003 J.D. [Brown&S.]
Szilvas, Alexander J. ... '62 '87 C.602 B.B.A. L.276 J.D. [Baker&H.]
Szorady, Ernest A. ... '51 '82 C.161 B.A. L.1003 J.D. Co. Bd. of Comrs.
Szpalik, Peter R. ... '54 '91 C.161 B.B.A. L.1003 J.D. I.R.S.

Szuter, Gregory P., (AV) '45 '73 C.363 B.A. L.930 J.D.
730 Ohio Savings Plaza, 1801 East 9th Street, 44114 ⊙
Telephone: 216-861-0503; 1-877-301-0332 Fax: 216-696-6653
Email: gpsz@aol.com URL: http://www.lawyers.com/arbitration
(Certified Specialist in Labor and Employment Law, Ohio State Bar Association).
Alternative Dispute Resolution, Arbitration, Mediation.
Northbrook, Illinois Office: 500 Skokie Boulevard, Suite 350, 60062.

See Professional Biographies, CLEVELAND, OHIO

Tabac, William L. ... '40 '67 C.930 B.A. L.273 LL.B. Prof. of Law, Cleve. State Univ.
Taber, Edward E. ... '68 '96 C.477 B.A. L.150 J.D. [🄰 Tucker E.&W.]
Taddeo, Joseph H., (BV) ... '40 '69 C.602 B.S. L.1003 J.D. One Chagrin Highlands (Pat.)
Taft, Clare R. ... '78 '03 C.363 B.A. L.161 J.D. [🄰 Benesch,F.C.&A.]
Taft, Frederick I., (AV) ... '45 '72 C&L.976 B.A., J.D. [Spieth,B.M.&N.]

Taft, Stettinius & Hollister LLP, (AV) BR
3500 BP Tower, 200 Public Square, 44114-2302 ⊙
Telephone: 216-241-2838 Facsimile: 216-241-3707
URL: http://www.taftlaw.com
Resident Members: Stephen M. O'Bryan; Margaret Anne Cannon; John D. Brown; Joel A. Makee; Thomas J. Lee; Carl A. Murway; Mark J. Valponi; Steven A. Marrer; Bruce L. Waterhouse, Jr.; Robert P. McManus; David H. Wallace; Peter M. Poulos; Donna M. Flammang; Mary Grace Balazs; Gregory J. O'Brien; Jill Friedman Helfman; William J. Stavole; Daniel K. Wright, II; Bruce J. L. Lowe; David V. Allen; Timothy L. Zix; Stephen H. Jett; Charles A. Bowers. Of Counsel: Fred J. Livingstone; David E. Burke; George J. Dunn; Richard D. Tomsick. Resident Associates: Christine Lewanski; Robert B. Owen; Patrick J. Krebs; Matthew T. Viola; Heather L. Tonsing; Robert H. Fischer, Jr.; Majeed G. Makhlouf; Kimberlie L. Huff; Lawrence C. Davison; Patricia Fleming Krewson; Adam D. Cornett; Kristin R. Erenburg; Kristi J. Kmetz; Ronn J. Gehring.
Antitrust, Bankruptcy and Debtor/Creditor Rights, Business and Finance, E-Business (Internet and E-Commerce), Employee Benefits/ERISA and Tax-Planning, Environmental Law, Family Law, Family Business Planning, Franchise, General Litigation, Health Care, Immigration, Institutional Finance, Intellectual Property and Technology Group, International, Japanese Practice, Labor and Employment, Mergers and Acquisitions, Nonprofit and Tax-Exempt Organizations, Product Liability and Personal Injury, Public Finance, Real Property, Securities, Tax, Probate and Estate Planning, Workers' Compensation.
Cincinnati, Ohio Office: 425 Walnut Street, Suite 1800. Telephone: 513-381-2838.
Columbus, Ohio Office: Twelfth Floor, 21 East State Street. Telephone: 614-221-2838.
Covington, Kentucky Office: 1717 Dixie Highway, Suite 340. Telephone: 859-331-2838; 513-381-2838.
Dayton, Ohio Office: 110 North Main Street, Suite 900. Telephone: 937-228-2838.

See Professional Biographies, CLEVELAND, OHIO

Taft-Milby, Rosemary, (AV) ... '57 '83 C&L.421 B.A., J.D. [Weltman,W.&R.]
Taich, Harry H., (BV) ... '46 '73 C.608 B.S. L.161 J.D. 720 Leader Bldg., Ste. 720
Tait, Christina ... '64 '95 C.94 B.A. L.124 J.D. [🄰 Calfee,H.&G.]
Talaganis, Dean S., (BV) ... '62 '89 C.980 B.S.B.A. L.117 J.D. [🄰 Weltman,W.&R.]
Talbert, Richard C., (AV) ... '33 '65 C.473 B.S. L.1003 J.D. 101 W. Propect Avenue
Talbot, Kevin R. ... '— '01 C.116 B.A. L.602 J.D. [🄰 Baker&H.]
Talcott, Thomas J., (AV) ... '47 '75 C.602 A.B. L.569 J.D. 50 Public Sq., Ste. 3300
Tall, Christopher Taliferro '64 '92 C.381 B.B.A. L.930 J.D. Dir., Corp. Rel., Case Western Reserve Univ.
Talty, Francis J. ... '20 '46 C.363 Ph.B. L.930 LL.B. Prob. J.
Talty, Patrick E., (BV) ... '46 '87 C.201 B.S. L.989 J.D. 20325 Center Ridge Rd.
Tamburrino, Ron M., (AV) '58 '83 C.8 B.S. L.7 J.D. Sr. Corp. Coun., Litig., The Sherwin-Williams Co.
Tancredi, Dara A. ... '— '92 C.161 B.B.A. L.930 J.D. The T.W. Grogan Co.
Tanner, James R., Jr. ... '49 '92 C.1286 B.S. L.1003 J.D. Dom. Rel. Ct.
Tarantino, Thomas J. ... '63 '90 C.161 B.A. L.1003 J.D. [Climaco,L.P.W.&G.]
Tark, Lori Ross ... '69 '03 C.161 B.S. L.124 J.D. [🄰 Janik&D.]
Tarnow, Sara E. ... '75 '00 C.477 B.A. L.930 J.D. Jud. Staff Atty.
Tarolli, James L. ... '66 '91 C.608 B.S.M.E. L.930 J.D. [Tarolli,S.C.&T.] (See Pat. Sect.)
Tarolli, Thomas L., (AV) '35 '61 C.665 B.S. L.273 LL.B. [Tarolli,S.C.&T.] (See Pat. Sect.)

Tarolli, Sundheim, Covell & Tummino, L.L.P., (AV)
Leader Building, Suite 111, 526 Superior Avenue, 44114
Telephone: 216-621-2234 Telex: 980209 TSC CLV PAT Facsimile: 216-621-4072
Email: tarolli@tarolli.com URL: http://www.tarolli.com
Members of Firm: Thomas L. Tarolli; Robert B. Sundheim; Calvin G. Covell; Barry L. Tummino; James L. Tarolli; Richard S. Wesorick; Richard A. Sutkus; Matthew M. Shaheen; Gary J. Pitzer; Christopher P. Harris. Associates: Robert N. Lipcsik; Brett A. Schenck; Brian W. Bolinger.
Intellectual Property Law including Patent, Trademark, Copyright and Unfair Competition Law.

See Professional Biographies, CLEVELAND, OHIO

Tasse, Jeffrey L., (BV) ... '— '81 C.473 B.A. L.930 J.D. [Weston H.]
Tassi, Arthur J., (AV) ... '54 '79 C.93 B.A. L.930 J.D. 75 Public Sq.
Tatter, Rachel J. ... '75 '01 C.608 B.A. L.276 J.D. [🄰 Thompson H.]
Taubman, Bruce D. ... '48 '76 C.608 L.117 [B.D.Taubman]
Taubman, Bruce D., Co., LPA ... 55 Public Square, Suite 1670
Tavolier, David R., (AV) ... '61 '86 C.477 B.B.A. L.276 J.D. [Kahn K.]
Tayfel, Eric William ... '72 '97 C.851 B.B.A. L.1003 J.D. [🄰 Gibson,B.Z.&M.]
Taylor, Heather Ann ... '74 '00 C.608 B.A. L.989 J.D. Cleveland Mun. Housing Ct.
Taylor, Hilary S., (AV) ... '44 '77 C.1023 B.S. L.1003 J.D. [Weston H.]
Taylor, Jaeson L. ... '75 '01 C.901 B.A. L.124 J.D. [🄰 Kelley&F.]
Taylor, Jas. B. ... '10 '54 C.943 B.S. L.1003 LL.B. 10728 Gooding Ave., N.E.‡
Taylor, Randy L. ... '68 '98 C.1369 B.A. L.1003 J.D. [🄰 Weston H.]

Taylor & Amber
564 Downing Street, 44114 ⊙
Member: Joseph Amber; Mr. James I. Hetfield, II.
Intellectual Property, Copyrights, Patent Prosecution, Patent Litigation, Corporate Law, Bankruptcy. Trial and Appellate Practice in State and Federal Courts.
Toronto, Ontario Office: Chanlon Road, Building 1. M5H 1J9. Telephone: 416-595-5100.
Summit, New Jersey Office: 34 River Road, 100 Harper Plaza, P.O. Box 361, 07901. Telephone: 201-595-5100.
Somerville, New Jersey Office: 178 Rehill Street, P.O. Box: 5646, 08875. Telephone: 908-595-5100.
Elizabeth, New Jersey, USA Office: 217 Vine Street, Garden Center, 07201. Telephone: 908-595-5555.
New York, New York, USA Office: 123 Main Street, 10001. Telephone: 212-595-5100.

Teamor, Ricardo B., (BV) ... '46 '76 C.610 B.A. L.930 J.D. [Teamor&Assoc.]
Teamor & Associates, (BV) ... 1228 Euclid Ave., Ste. 840
Teeter, Alexander N. ... '75 '02 C.165 B.A. L.93 J.D. [🄰 Calfee,H.&G.]
Tegreene, Joseph G., (AV) ... '53 '84 C.385 B.A. L.1003 J.D. [Benesch,F.C.&A.]
TeGrotenhuis, Theodore A., (AV) '07 '37 C.8 B.S. L.161 J.D. 7315 Columbia Rd. (Pat.)‡
Teicher, Bruce J. '55 '81 C.31 B.A. L.178 J.D. (adm. in CA; not adm. in OH) 4347 Cranwood Pky.‡
Telich, Mark S. ... '52 '82 C.363 B.S. L.1003 J.D. 782 E. 185th Street
Temas, Jeffery David ... '61 '87 C.62 B.A. L.1003 J.D. P.O. Box 44123
Tenerowicz, Matthew A. ... '73 '98 C.611 B.A. L.608 J.D. [🄰 Baker&H.]
Teplitzky, Ronald J. ... '61 '87 C.610 A.B. L.930 J.D. [Benesch,F.C.&A.]
Terez, Dennis G., (AV) ... '59 '85 C.276 B.S.F.S. L.477 J.D. Fed. Def.
Termini, Mark M., (AV) ... '56 '84 C.930 B.A. L.1003 J.D. 8934 Brecksville Rd.
Terrion, Halle Fine ... '68 '93 C.477 A.B. L.930 J.D. [Baker&H.]
Terry, Thomas H., III, (AV) ... '50 '79 C.436 B.A. L.161 J.D. [🄲 Sutter,O.&F.]
Tessler, Harvey E. ... '44 '71 C.831 B.A. L.989 J.D. 850 Euclid Avenue, Suite 801
Testa, Catherine J. ... '76 '04 C.901 B.A. L.989 J.D. [🄰 Kelley&F.]
Tetlow, William J. ... '20 '48 C.528 A.B. L.930 LL.B. [Tetlow&J.]
Tetlow & Johnson ... 1340 Depot St.
Tew, Sheila ... '— '74 C.331 B.A. L.161 J.D. Legal Aid Soc.
Thacker, Michael J. '58 '84 C.473 B.S. L.608 J.D. V.P. & Assoc. Coun., KeyBank Natl. Assn.
Theis, Stuart H. ... '42 '68 C.705 B.A. L.273 J.D. Oglebay Norton
Theiss, Raymond E. '54 '85 C.381 B.A. L.1003 J.D. Exec. Vice President & General Counsel, Transtar Industries, Inc.
Thesling, William H., (BV) ... '34 '76 C.161 B.B.A. L.1003 J.D. 5566 Pearl Rd.
Thimmig, Diana M., (AV) ... '59 '83 C.363 B.A. L.1003 J.D. [Roetzel&A.]
Thomarios, Elizabeth A. ... '73 '99 C.385 B.A. L.989 J.D. [Pagano,W.T.G.&L.]
Thomas, Clyde E., (AV) ... '28 '56 C.363 B.S. L.1003 J.D. 315 Rockside Plz.
Thomas, David P. ... '67 '93 C.473 B.A. L.930 J.D. 50 Public Sq.
Thomas, Dynda A., (AV) ... '59 '86 C.473 B.A. L.150 J.D. [Squire,S.&D.]
Thomas, Ernest V., III, (BV) ... '58 '82 C.1118 B.A. L.150 J.D. [Thomas&T.] ⊙
Thomas, Gregory S. ... '63 '93 C.851 B.B.A. L.989 J.D. [G.S.Thomas]
Thomas, James D., (AV) ... '61 '87 C.5 B.A. L.851 J.D. [Squire,S.&D.]
Thomas, Kimberly A. ... '65 '04 C.876 B.S.N. L.989 J.D. [🄰 Bonezzi S.M.&P.] (Pat.)
Thomas, Mary Ann, (BV) ... '50 '84 C.161 B.S. L.1003 J.D. 12800 York Rd., Ste. 2
Thomas, Max W. ... '66 '03 C&L.124 B.A., J.D. [🄰 Ulmer&B.]
Thomas, Sam, III ... '47 '97 C.161 B.A. L.989 J.D. [🄲 Berger&Z.]
Thomas, Terence L. ... '62 '94 C.188 B.S. L.608 J.D. [🄰 Squire,S.&D.]
Thomas, Gregory S., LLC ... 1422 Euclid Avenue, Suite 1604
Thomas & Thomas, (BV) ... 629 Euclid Avenue (⊙Newport, KY; Cin., Columbus, OH)
Thompson, Adrian D. ... '61 '86 C.97 B.A. L.608 J.D. 1380 E. Sixth Street
Thompson, Andrew J. ... '62 '99 C&L.124 B.A., J.D. [🄰 Stege&M.]
Thompson, Darin G. ... '71 '96 C.390 B.A. L.930 J.D. Fed. Def. Off.
Thompson, David W., (BV) ... '65 '90 C.853 B.A. L.383 J.D. [McGlinchey S.]
Thompson, Ernest W. ... '24 '56 C.251 L.1003 J.D. 886 E. 130th St.
Thompson, Helen A. ... '70 '96 C.381 B.A. L.229 J.D. [Kreiner&P.] (⊙Columbus)
Thompson, Horace S. ... '21 '48 C&L.966 B.A., LL.B. Hearing Offr., State of Ohio
Thompson, Mitchell S. ... '63 '94 C.651 B.A. L.930 J.D. [🄲 Squire,S.&D.]
Thompson, Oliver A., (BV) ... '24 '52 C.930 B.B.A. L.161 J.D. [🄰 Rhoa,F.&R.]
Thompson, Paul J. ... '27 '53 C.33 A.B. L.930 LL.B. Progressive Cas. Ins. Co.
Thompson, William H. '53 '84 C.674 A.B. L.245 J.D. Gen. Coun., Seagate Investment Co.
Thompson, William J. '37 '62 C.473 B.S. L.608 LL.B. Pres., B. J. Thompson Assocs., Inc.
Thompson, William W., IV, (AV) ... '53 '80 C.161 B.A. L.1003 J.D. Pub. Def. Off.

Thompson Hine LLP, (AV)
3900 Key Center, 127 Public Square, 44114-1291 ⊙
Telephone: 216-566-5500 Fax: 216-566-5800 Telex: 980217 Cable Address: "Thomflor"
Email: info@ThompsonHine.com URL: http://www.ThompsonHine.com
Amos Burt Thompson (1871-1965); Charles P. Hine (1877-1942); Walter L. Flory (1880-1951); Michael L. Hardy (Partner-in-Charge, Cleveland); Patricia Mann Smitson (Partner-in-Charge, Cincinnati); Anthony C. White (Partner-in-Charge, Columbus); Robert M. Curry (Partner-in Charge, Dayton); Nicholas J. DiMichael (Partner-in-Charge, Washington, DC); George J. Walsh III (Partner-in-Charge, New York City); Ludo Deklerck (Partner-in-Charge, Brussels); Walt A. Linscott (Partner-in-Charge, Atlanta). Partners: Thomas A. Aldrich; Jeffrey R. Appelbaum (Group Leader, Construction); James B. Aronoff; Nancy M. Barnes; Richard C. Binzley; April V. Boise; Kip T. Bollin; Derek D. Bork; Stephen L. Buescher; Thomas J. Callahan; James R. Carlson; Thomas J. Collin; Dianne S. Coscarelli; Timothy J. Coughlin; Thomas J. Coyne; J. Kurt Denkewalter; Frank R. DeSantis; Jeffry J. Erney; S. Stuart Eilers; Andrew L. Fabens, III; Thomas L. Feher; Jennifer A. Lesny Fleming; Mark S. Floyd; Robert C. Folland; Robert B. Ford; Heidi B. Goldstein; Michael L. Hardy (Partner-in-Charge); Laura A. Hauser; Daniel M. Haymond; Harold W. Henderson; Oliver C. Henkel, Jr.; David J. Hooker (Managing Partner); Leslie W. Jacobs; William W. Jacobs; William E. Karnatz, Sr.; Steven S. Kaufman; Dena M. Kobasic; James C. Koenig; Brian J. Lamb; Alan R. Lepene; Craig R. Martahus; Thomas A. Mason; Louis L. McMahon; Donald H. Messinger; Leslee W. Miraldi; Robert D. Monnin (Group Leader, Product Liability Litigation); David J. Naftzinger; David E. Nash; Deborah Zider Read; James D. Robenalt; David W. Salisbury; Jennifer A. Savage; William R. Stewart (Group Leader, Tax); Linda A. Striefsky; Patrick J. Sweeney; Brian A. Troyer; Roy L. Turnell; Robert F. Ware Jr.; Stephen D. Williger; Elizabeth B. Wright; Daniel T. Young; Karen D. Youngstrom. Retired Partners: David L. Parham; Thomas F. Zych. Associates: Matthew Bradford; Patricia A. Burgess; Robert W. Burger; Jeremy M. Campana; Andrew H. Cox; Andrea B. Daloia; C. LeAnn Davis (Not admitted in OH); Renee L. Davis; Jennifer Lynn Dillman; Oliver J. Dunford; Damaris G. Fisher; Sarah C. Flannery; Adam D. Fuller; Denise L. Gawlik; Gregory J. Gawlik; Alexandra J. Geffert; Jonathan A. Good; Sean Gordon; Tracy Hannan; Jeffrey R. Hartwig; Kenneth W. Hubbard; William J. Hubbard; Emily S. Huggins; Christopher R. Johnson; Larry J. Jones; Jill M. H. Karlgaard;

(This Listing Continued)

Thompson Hine LLP (Continued)

Amanda A. Kessler (Not admitted in OH); Eduardo Kim; Shana F. Klein; Kelly A. Kosek; Michele T. Kryszak; Robert S. Lewis; Matthew E. Liebson; Timothy H. Linville; Horatio ("Harry") G. Mihet; Catherine L. Miller; Kathleen M. Minahan; John R. Mitchell; Julanne Montville; Jennifer Mingus Mountcastle; Samer M. Musallam; John David Myer; Adam R. Nazette; Laura Bancroft Nemer; Keely J. O'Bryan; Stacey A. Palmer; Troy S. Prince; Christopher M. Rassi; Hope E. Redmond; Jennifer S. Roach; Anthony J. Rospert; Karen E. Rubin; Delisa Y. Russell; Robyn M. Smyers; Jeremy S. Sosin; Rachel J. Tatter; Curtis L. Tuggle; Andrew L. Turscak, Jr.; Gary L. Walters; Mark A. Weintraub; Kate B. Wexler; Nicole K. Wilson; Robin M. Wilson; Audra J. Zarlenga. Of Counsel: Heather Aley Austin; Malvin E. Bank; Brian L. Gaj; William D. Ginn (Retired); Daniel W. Hammer; Kent L. Mann; Cathy B. Panzica; Patrick J. Saccogna. Senior Attorneys: Susan L. Belman; Diane S. Leung; Pamela Zarlingo. Staff Attorneys: Byron J. Horn; Lori A. Pittman.

Administrative Law, Admiralty and Maritime Law, Agency and Distributorships, Antitrust and Trade Regulation, Aviation and Aerospace, Bankruptcy, Banks and Banking, Biotechnology, Business Law, Business Litigation, Business Regulation, Business Transactions, Closely Held Business Law, Joint Ventures, Class Actions, Commercial Law, Commercial Real Estate, Communications and Media, FCC Regulation, Computers and Software, Construction Law, Contracts, Copyrights, Corporate Law, Corporate Finance, Corporate Litigation, Corporate Tax Controversies, Debtor and Creditor, Employee Benefits, ERISA, Energy, Energy Regulation, Environmental Law, Finance, Commercial Finance, Franchises and Franchising, General Practice, Government, False Claims Act, Qui Tam Litigation, Government Contracts, Health Care, Insurance Coverage, Insurance Regulation, Intellectual Property, International Law, International Trade, Internet Law, Labor and Employment, Life Sciences, Litigation, Complex Litigation, Medicare Fraud and Abuse, Mergers, Acquisitions and Divestitures, Natural Resources, Nonprofit and Charitable Organizations, Occupational Safety and Health, OSHA, Partnership Law, Patents, Probate, Products Liability, Product Safety, Professional Liability, Public Finance, Railroad Law, Real Estate, Regulatory Law, Drug and Medical Device Regulation, Food and Drug Regulation, International Regulatory Law, Regulated Industries, Securities, Initial Public Offerings, Public Offerings, Taxation, Tax Controversies, Toxic Torts, Trade Secrets, Trademarks, Transportation, Trusts and Estates, Unfair Competition, Utility Law, White Collar Crime, Zoning, Planning and Land Use.

Cincinnati, Ohio Office: 312 Walnut Street, 14th Floor, 45202-4089. Telephone: 513-352-6700. Fax: 513-241-4771. Email: info@ThompsonHine.com.

Columbus, Ohio Office: 10 West Broad Street, Suite 700, 43215-3435. Telephone: 614-469-3200. Fax: 614-469-3361. Email: info@ThompsonHine.com.

Dayton, Ohio Office: 2000 Courthouse Plaza, N.E., P.O. Box 8801, 45401-8801. Telephone: 937-443-6600. Fax: 937-443-6635. Email: info@ThompsonHine.com.

Washington, D.C. Office: 1920 N Street, N.W., Suite 800, 20036-1600. Telephone: 202-331-8800. Fax: 202-331-8330. Email: info@ThompsonHine.com.

New York, N.Y. Office: One Chase Manhattan Plaza, 58th Floor, 10005-1401. Telephone: 212-344-5680. Fax: 212-809-6890. Email: info@ThompsonHine.com.

Brussels, Belgium Office: Avenue Louise 375 - b8, 1050 Brussels, Belgium, Telephone: 011 (32-2) 626-3280. Fax: 011 (32-2) 626-3299. Email: info@ThompsonHine.com.

Atlanta, Georgia Office: Proscenium Center, Suite 1200, 1170 Peachtree Street, 30309-7673. Telephone: 404-541-2900. Fax: 404-541-2905. Email: info@ThompsonHine.com.

See Professional Biographies, CLEVELAND, OHIO

Thomson, Maynard F., (AV) .... '44 '71 C.94 B.A. L.930 J.D. 901 Lakeside Ave.‡
Thorman, Christopher P., (AV) .... '63 '91 C.385 A.B. L.930 J.D. [Thorman&H.]
Thorman, Lincoln R. .... '18 '51 C.367 B.S. L.1003 J.D. 28790 Chagrin Blvd.

Thorman & Hardin-Levine, (AV)
1220 West 6th Street, Suite 307, 44113
Telephone: 216-621-9767 Fax: 216-621-3422 URL: http://www.thllaw.com Email: plevine@thllaw.com
Email: cthorman@thllaw.com URL: http://www.lawyers.com/christopherthorman
Members of Firm: Christopher P. Thorman; Peter S. Hardin-Levine;—Ryan A. Sobel.
Employment Law, Civil Rights, Discrimination, Harassment, Job Termination.
See Professional Biographies, CLEVELAND, OHIO

Thornton, A. Clifford, Jr., (AV) .... '43 '69 C.1 B.A. L.608 J.D. [Peckinpaugh&T.]
Thurman, Adam J. .... '72 '97 C.363 B.A. L.1003 J.D. [Ⓐ H.Palkovitz]
Tiburzio, Terese M. '66 '92 C&L.608 B.A., J.D.
Asst. Co. Pros., Cuyahoga Co. Pros. Off.
Ticktin, Daniel S., (BV) ...... '57 '85 C.381 B.A. L.1003 J.D. 1621 Euclid Ave., Ste. 1700
Ticktin, Harold, (AV) .... '27 '53 C.608 B.A. L.930 LL.B. [Ticktin,B.K.]
Ticktin, Baron, Koepper & Co., L.P.A., (AV) .... 1621 Euclid Ave.
Tighe, James Michael .... '50 '77 C.608 B.A. L.94 J.D. [Ⓒ Kramer&Assoc.]
Tighe, Robert F. '46 '80 C.252 B.S. L.969 J.D.
(adm. in FL; not adm. in OH) 17000 Melgrave‡
Tiktin, Roger D., (BV) .... '49 '74 C.112 B.A. L.1003 J.D. 5005 Rockside Rd.
Tipping, Mary Jo, (AV) .... '63 '91 C.97 B.S. L.1003 J.D. 526 Superior Ave., Ste. 222

Tipping Co., L.P.A. A Legal Professional Association
(See Akron)

Tirey, Arthi K. '75 '00 C.473 B.S. L.989 J.D.
Patent Atty., The Sherwin-Williams Co. (Pat.)
Tocci, Dennis, (BV) '60 '85
C.161 B.A. L.1003 J.D. Sr. Corp. Coun., The Sherwin-Williams Co.
Tocco, David J., (AV) .... '60 '86 C.477 B.B.A. L.930 J.D. [Vorys,S.S.&P.]
Todd, Joni .... '74 '05 C.161 B.A. L.989 J.D. [Ⓐ Hahn L.&P.]
Todd, Michael D. .... '74 '05 C.870 B.S. L.124 J.D. [Ⓐ Ulmer&B.]
Todt, Robert W., (BV) .... '50 '86 C.161 B.A. L.1003 J.D. [Kirschenbaum]
Toerek, Sharon L., (CV) .... '63 '91 C.161 B.A. L.1003 J.D. [Toerek]

Toerek Co., LPA, (CV)
29525 Chagrin Boulevard, Suite 208, 44122
Telephone: 216-360-9919 Fax: 216-360-7450
Sharon L. Toerek.
Copyrights, Trademarks, Business Law.
See Professional Biographies, CLEVELAND, OHIO

Tolaro, Alfred J., (AV) '28 '59
C.251 B.B.A. L.1003 J.D. 800 Halle Building, 1228 Euclid Avenue
Toler, Lynn C., (AV) .... '59 '84 C.309 A.B. L.659 J.D. 1267 Oakridge Drive
Tolley, Kenneth J. .... '24 '55 C.62 B.A. L.1003 LL.B. 18175 Trailside Pl.‡
Tolliver, Stanley E. .... '25 '53 C.62 B.B.A. L.1003 J.D. 1464 E. 105th St.
Tolt, Lester T. .... '28 '63 C.930 B.B.A. L.1003 J.D. Ste 8, 3730 Rocky River Dr
Toman, Bradley P. .... '— '89 C.970 B.A. L.1003 J.D. [Ⓐ McFadden&Assoc.]
Tomaro, Robert B., (AV) .... '49 '74 C.207 B.A. L.930 J.D. [Tucker E.&W.]
Tomasello, Shirley Ann .... '62 '92 C.161 B.A. L.1003 J.D. 601 Lakeside Avenue
Tomon, Bert R. .... '42 '72 C.201 B.S. L.1003 J.D. 4772 Pearl Rd.
Tompkins, Catherine Corrigan .... '68 '95 C.276 A.B. L.930 J.D. [Ⓐ Squire,S.&D.]
Tomsick, Richard D., (AV) .... '59 '84 C&L.930 B.A., J.D. [Ⓒ Taft,S.&H.]
Tomson, William L., (BV) .... '45 '71 C.25 B.A. L.930 J.D. 14400 Pearl Rd.
Tomusko, Dale P. .... '48 '73 C.610 B.S. L.1003 J.D. 16458 Fox Hunt Dr.
Tonsing, Heather L. .... '72 '98 C.8 B.S. L.1003 J.D. [Ⓐ Taft,S.&H.]
Toohey, Brian F., (AV) .... '— '69 C.299 A.B. L.188 J.D. [Jones D.]
Toole, Jeffrey C., (BV) .... '— '85 C.385 B.A. L.188 J.D. [Buckley K.]
Toomajian, William M., (AV) .... '43 '68 C.299 B.A. L.477 J.D. [Baker&H.]
Torgerson, Kenneth A., (AV) .... '41 '66 C.197 B.A. L.597 J.D. [Weston H.]

Torres Williams Co. LPA
75 Public Square, Suite 800, 44113
Telephone: 216-771-6303 Fax: 216-771-6993
URL: http://www.torreswilliams.com
Jose A. Torres-Ramirez; Kathryn A. Williams.

(This Listing Continued)

Torres Williams Co. LPA (Continued)

Family Law, Divorce, Child Support, Immigration Law, Business Dissolutions, Business Successions, Personal Injury, Creditors Rights, Bankruptcy, Litigation, Wills, Probate, Trusts and Estates, Estate Planning, Criminal Law.
See Professional Biographies, CLEVELAND, OHIO

Torres-Ramirez, Jose A. .... '66 '94 C.1088 B.A. L.999 J.D. [Torres W.]
Tost, Christopher M. .... '73 '99 C.717 B.A. L.930 J.D. [Ⓐ Rolf&G.]
Toth, Barbara Breneman .... '49 '86 C.119 B.A. L.1003 J.D. 21831 Westchester Rd.
Tracanna, Richard F., (AV) .... '59 '84 C.602 B.B.A. L.575 J.D. [Benesch,F.C.&A.]
Traci, Robert V., (AV) .... '50 '75 C.321 B.S. L.930 J.D. 1370 W. Sixth St., Ste. 350
Trainer, Mark D. .... '77 '02 C.305 B.A. L.74 J.D. [Ⓐ Benesch,F.C.&A.]
Tramer, Neil M., (BV) .... '58 '83 C.473 B.S. L.930 J.D. 23775 Commerce Pk.
Trapp, Mary Jane, (AV) .... '56 '81 C.518 A.B. L.930 J.D. [Apicella&T.]
Trattner, Barry A., Attorney at Law, (BV) '41 '68
C.608 B.S.B.A. L.1003 J.D. Ontario St. at St. Clair Ave.
Trattner, Mary Lou, (BV) .... '47 '74 C.161 B.S. L.1003 J.D. [Ⓐ B.A.Trattner]
Traut, Ted Matthew .... '73 '00 C.381 B.S. L.150 J.D. P.O. Box 6599
Travaglini, Kristine Rae .... '71 '97 C.381 B.A. L.7 J.D. City Pros. Off.
Travis, D. John, (AV) .... '— '76 C&L.608 B.S., J.D. [Gallagher S.]
Treinish, Alan J., (AV) .... '49 '74 C.608 B.A. L.1003 J.D. [A.J.Treinish]
Treinish, Alan J., Co., L.P.A., (AV) .... 1370 Ontario St.
Treister, William R., (BV) .... '51 '76 C.659 B.S. L.1003 J.D. 800 Standard Bldg.
Trentes, John H. .... '62 '87 C.665 B.A. L.930 J.D. 866 E. 185th St.
Treu, Kris H., (AV) .... '57 '83 C.197 A.B. L.608 J.D. [Moscarino&T.]
Tricarichi, Carla M., (BV) '57 '83
C.860 B.A. L.930 J.D. 614 Superior Ave. N.W., Ste. 620
Tricarichi, Charles S., (AV) '23 '50
C&L.930 B.A., LL.B. 614 Superior Avenue N.W., Suite 1020
Trilling, Jessica E. .... '— '01 C.477 B.A. L.659 J.D. [Ⓐ Jones D.]
Trim, Roger G. .... '76 '04 C.477 B.B.A. L.124 J.D. [Ⓐ Baker&H.]
Tripi, Philip G. .... '21 '57 C.363 B.A. L.1003 J.D. Standard Bldg.
Trivers, Oscar .... '34 '60 C.318 B.A. L.930 LL.B. [Trivers&D.]

Trivers & Dickerson, LLC
55 Erieview Plaza, Suite 220, 44114
Telephone: 216-696-5444 Fax: 216-696-3937
URL: http://www.triversanddickersonlaw.com
Oscar Trivers; Emmanuel Eugene Dickerson (1919-2003). Attorneys: Edwin Kelly; Reginald Maxton.
Criminal Law, Family Law, Personal Injury, Divorce.
See Professional Biographies, CLEVELAND, OHIO

Troia, Anthony R., (AV) .... '38 '66 C.381 B.S. L.608 J.D. [Ⓒ Nicola,G.&C.]
Trombetta, I. Bernard .... '39 '63 C.363 B.S.S. L.930 LL.B. 30505 Bainbridge Rd.
Trombetto, Julius E. .... '76 '02 C.679 B.S. L.124 J.D. [Ⓐ Mazanec,R.&R.]
Trostle, W. M. .... '— '23 C.607 B.S. L.930 LL.B. 25935 Detroit Rd.‡
Troxell, James D. .... '46 '76 C&L.8 B.A., J.D. [Squire,S.&D.]
Troyer, Brian A. .... '— '92 C.970 B.A. L.309 J.D. [Thompson H.]
Trubiano, Mark A. .... '63 '88 C&L.930 B.S., J.D. [Cavitch,F.D.&F.]
Trudeau, Stephanie Dutchess, (AV) .... '— '82 C.851 B.A. L.209 J.D. [Ulmer&B.]
Trumbo, George W. .... '26 '53 C.608 B.S.B.A. L.930 LL.B. Mun. J.‡
Trump, Robert C. .... '21 '48 C.150 B.B.A. L.309 LL.B. 1300 Huntington Bldg.‡
Tryon, David C., (AV) .... '58 '85 C.101 B.S. L.477 J.D. [Porter W.M.&A.]
Tsang, Vivien Y. '59 '96 C.477 B.S. L.213 J.D.
Sr. Patent Atty., The Sherwin-Williams Co. (Pat.)
Tucci, Louis R. .... '20 '44 C&L.930 B.A., LL.B. 5028 S. Sedgewick Rd.
Tucci, Michael R. .... '67 '99 C.117 B.A. L.930 J.D. [Ⓐ Kahn K.]
Tucker, Catherine Pomeroy .... '64 '93 C.381 B.S. L.930 J.D. Pros. Off.
Tucker, Lawrence, (AV) .... '32 '57 C&L.930 A.B., LL.B. 407 Leader Bldg.
Tucker, Michael S., (BV) .... '61 '86 C.473 B.A. L.930 J.D. [Ulmer&B.]
Tucker, Robert C., (AV) .... '50 '76 C.951 B.A. L.608 J.D. [Tucker E.&W.]
Tucker, Todd R. .... '69 '95 C.352 B.S.E. L.200 J.D. [Renner,O.B.&S.] (See Pat. Sect.)
Tucker Ellis & West LLP, (AV) .... 925 Euclid Avenue (Pat.) (⊙L.A., San Fran., CA)
Tuckerman, John L. .... '29 '54 C&L.930 A.B., LL.B. 3120 Corydon Rd.
Tuffin, Paul J. .... '27 '57 C.999 B.S. L.1003 J.D. 1200 Ontario Street
Tuggle, Curtis L. .... '77 '04 C&L.608 B.A., J.D. [Ⓐ Thompson H.]
Tulley, Patrick J., (AV) .... '58 '94 C.608 B.A. L.1003 J.D. [Ⓐ Ulmer&B.]
Tuma, Robert L., (BV) .... '35 '64 8225 Brecksville Road
Tummino, Barry L., (BV) '50 '80
C&L.161 B.E.S., J.D. [Tarolli,S.C.&T.] (See Pat. Sect.)
Turek, James J., (BV) .... '57 '82 C.150 B.A. L.930 J.D. [Ⓐ Reminger&R.]
Turnbull, Tracey L. .... '69 '96 C.299 B.A. L.930 J.D. [Porter W.M.&A.]
Turnell, Roy L., (AV) .... '47 '74 C.976 B.A. L.966 J.D. [Thompson H.]
Turner, Franzetta Darlene .... '61 '87 C.25 B.A. L.823 J.D. Justice Center - 12th Floor
Turner, Henry E., Jr. .... '— '03 C.145 A.B. L.477 J.D. [Ⓐ Jones D.]
Turner, Mark M. .... '— '02 C.124 B.A. L.608 J.D. [Ⓐ Gallagher S.]
Turner, Peter, (AV) .... '56 '81 C.608 B.A. L.930 J.D. [Karberg,K.W.&T.]
Turocy, Gregory .... '63 '91 C.608 B.A. L.469 J.D. [Amin&T.] (See Pat. Sect.)
Turoff, Carole R. .... '— '70 C.28 B.A. L.1003 J.D. 20320 Farnsleigh Rd.
Turoff, Jack N., (BV) .... '33 '60 C&L.608 B.S., J.D. 629 Euclid Ave., Ste. 420
Turoff, Tracy A. .... '— '02 C.124 B.A. L.989 J.D. [Ⓐ Giffen&K.]
Turscak, Andrew L., Jr. .... '64 '01 C.980 B.A. L.989 J.D. [Ⓐ Thompson H.]
Turung, Brian E. ..... '63 '91 C.326 B.Ch.E. L.734 J.D. [Fay,S.F.M.&M.] (See Pat. Sect.)
Tweed, Guy E., II .... '49 '74 C.229 B.A. L.930 J.D. P.O. Box 181202
Twohig, Catherine B. .... '— '96 C.321 B.A. L.793 J.D. [Yulish,T.&Assoc.]
Twohig, Mark M., III, (BV) .... '45 '73 C.363 A.B. L.1003 J.D. 1419 W. 9th St.
Tylee, Mary C. .... '59 '85 C.734 B.A. L.161 J.D. Asst. Pub. Def.
Tyler, Barbara Jane .... '— '89 C.62 B.A. L.1003 J.D. Coll.
Tyler, Corinne M. .... '— '98 C.124 B.A. L.989 J.D. [Ⓐ Baker&H.]
Tyminski, James T., Jr. .... '— '99 C.363 B.A. L.1003 J.D. [Gallagher S.]
Tyrpak, Michele M. '65 '96 C.161 B.S. L.989 J.D.
[Ⓐ Renner,O.B.&S.] (See Pat. Sect.)
Ubbing, Thomas J. .... '57 '85 C.608 B.S. L.851 J.D. [Brouse M.]
Ubersax, Jeffery D., (AV) .... '— '84 C.31 B.A. L.309 J.D. [Jones D.]
Ubersax, Kristin L., (BV) .... '61 '87 C.976 B.A. L.309 J.D. [Spieth,B.M.&N.]
Ugan, James R., (BV) .... '16 '40 C&L.607 LL.B. 629 Euclid Ave.
Uhlig, Gael Edward '61 '96 C&L.184 B.A., J.D.
(adm. in FL; not adm. in OH)
V.P. & Title Coun. Coun., First American Equity Loan Servs., Inc.
Ullman, Meredith L. .... '77 '02 C.610 B.A. L.124 J.D. [Ⓐ Ross,B.&S.]

Ulmer & Berne LLP, (AV)
Skylight Office Tower, 1660 West 2nd Street, Suite 1100, 44113-1448 ⊙
Telephone: 216-583-7000 Fax: 216-583-7001
Email: infocleveland@ulmer.com URL: http://www.ulmer.com
Partners: Jennifer Lawry Adams; Steven W. Albert; Thomas H. Barnard; Lewis T. Barr; Barton A. Bixenstine (Certified Specialist in Labor & Employment Law, Ohio State Bar Association); Kenneth A. Bravo; Joseph A. Castrodale; Inajo Davis Chappell; Robert E. Chudakoff; George S. Crisci

(This Listing Continued)

Ulmer & Berne LLP (Continued)

(Certified Specialist in Labor and Employment Law, Ohio State Bar Association); Maria Del Monaco; Timothy J. Downing; Jeffrey S. Dunlap; William D. Edwards; Robert A. Fein; Harold E. Friedman; Bill J. Gagliano; John C. Goheen; Frances Floriano Goins; James A. Goldsmith; Howard M. Groedel; Neil W. Gurney; John J. Haggerty; Richard G. Hardy; Ronald H. Isroff; Ronald L. Kahn; Marvin L. Karp; Mark D. Katz; James N. Kline; Stuart A. Laven; Murray K. Lenson; David L. Lester; Bruce P. Mandel; Stephen A. Markus; Craig A. Marvinney; Christopher C. McCracken; Stephen C. Merriam; Craig S. Miller; Matthew J. Morelli; Brian M. O'Neill; Thomas W. Ostrowski; Lawrence D. Pollack; Brian N. Ramm; Harold (Kip) Reader; Peter A. Rome; Richard E. Rubinstein; Alan W. Scheufler; Isaac Schulz; Fred Seleman (Certified Specialist in Labor and Employment Law, Ohio State Bar Association); Douglas K. Sesnowitz; Patricia A. Shlonsky; Michael D. Stovsky; Richard D. Sweebe; Stephanie Dutchess Trudeau (Certified Specialist in Labor and Employment Law, Ohio State Bar Association); Michael S. Tucker; Michael N. Ungar; Jeffrey W. Van Wagner; F. Thomas Vickers; Frederick N. Widen; David D. Yeagley; Leonard D. Young. Of Counsel: Charles A. Crehore; C. Reynolds Keller; William K. Smith. Senior Counsel: Charles R. Olsavsky, Jr. Senior Attorneys: Thomas L. Anastos; Bari E. Goggins (Certified Specialist in Labor and Employment Law, Ohio State Bar Association). Associates: John M. Alten; Michelle R. Arendt; Yelena Boxer; Maria A. Citeroni; James M. Crane; Elizabeth M. DeRienzo; Suzanne Duddy; Isaac J. Eddington; Brian P. Farnan; Christopher P. Fisher; Arlishea L. Fulton; Gary T. Gardner; Gary S. Greenlee; Michael A. Gross; Michael J. Hall; Elizabeth A. Harvey; Jason S. Hollander; Sally A. Jamieson; Elizabeth A. Jerdonek; Stephanie E. Kennedy; Anne M. Klepach; Trish D. Lazich; Steven D. McGrew; Stacey L. McKinley; Cash H. Mischka; Suzann R. Moskowitz; Adrienne L. Rapp; Jodi B. Rich; Donald J. Richardson; Nita Kay Richardson; Megan K. Roberts; Lynnette L. Rodgers; Elizabeth S. Rudnick; Kate E. Ryan; Richik Sarkar; Wayne M. Serra; Kurt S. Siegfried; Edward P. Simms; Joseph S. Simms; Aliceia J. Smith; Linda DelaCourt Summers; Max W. Thomas; Michael D. Todd; Patrick J. Tulley; Kristin M. Walker; Jane F. Warner; Elizabeth M. Widman; Tanya L. Williams; Jake P. Yanchar (Not admitted in OH); Elin B. Young; Melissa L. Zujkowski; Robert E. Zulandt III.

Antitrust; Banking and Commercial Lending; Broker/Dealer and Securities Litigation; Business Law; Business Litigation; Business Restructuring; Class Action Defense; Construction Law; Corporate Finance; Corporate Restructuring and Creditors' Rights; Corporate Succession Planning; Emerging Businesses; Employee Benefits; Employment and Labor; Environmental; Fair Housing; Financial Institution Compliance; General Counsel Services; Health Care; Income Tax; Insurance Coverage; Intellectual Property and Technology; Joint Ventures; Liability Defense; Mass Torts; Mergers, Acquisitions and Divestitures; Nonprofit; OSHA; Pharmaceutical; Product Liability; Public Law; Real Estate; Securities; Securities Regulatory Compliance; Subrogation; Tax; Technology Transactions; Toxic Tort Defense; Trade Secrets/Unfair Competition; Trusts and Estates; Venture Capital; Workers' Compensation; Trial and Appellate Practice in All Courts.

Columbus, Ohio Office: 88 East Broad Street, Suite 1600. Telephone: 614-229-0000. FAX: 614-229-0001.

Cincinnati, Ohio Office: 600 Vine Street, Suite 2800. Telephone: 513-698-5000. FAX: 513-698-5001.

Chicago, Illinois Office: One North Franklin Street, Suite 1825. Telephone: 312-324-8000. FAX: 312-324-8001.

See Professional Biographies, CLEVELAND, OHIO

Ulrich, Phyllis A., (AV) .... '66 '91 C&L.8 B.A., J.D. [Carlisle,M.R.K.&U.]
Ungar, Michael N., (AV) ....'59 '84 C&L.94 B.A., J.D. [Ulmer&B.]
Union, Marvin L. .... '44 '69 C.124 B.S. L.930 J.D. Easton Corp.
Unverzagt, Anne '44 '73 C.207 B.A. L.1065 J.D.
(adm. in WI; not adm. in OH) 3065 Fairfax Rd.‡
Urban, Brian M., (AV) ....'54 '79 C.363 B.A. L.1003 J.D. [Urban&P.]

Urban & Pozzuto LLC, (AV)
600 Standard Building, 1370 Ontario Street, 44113
Telephone: 216-241-4244 Fax: 216-241-1677 URL: http://www.urbanfamilylaw.com
Email: brian@urbanfamilylaw.com URL: http://www.lawyers.com/urbanfamilylaw
Brian M. Urban (Certified Specialist in Family Relations Law, Ohio State Bar Association); Bridgette D. Pozzuto;—Jacob M. Figelman.
Domestic Relations, Family Law, Divorce, Child Custody, Child Support, Premarital Agreements.

See Professional Biographies, CLEVELAND, OHIO

Urbancic, Brano, (AV) .... '28 '56 C.276 B.S. L.930 J.D. 18975 Villaview Road
Uzl, William Edward ....'64 '90 C.528 B.A. L.930 J.D. [Ⓐ Kelley&F.]
Vaccarelli Mussman, Julie A. ....'77 '03 C.1529 B.A. L.1003 J.D. [Ⓐ Weltman,W.&R.]
Vadnal, Richard A., (AV) .... '63 '88 C.161 B.A. L.1003 J.D. [R.A.Vadnal]
Vadnal, Richard A., Co., L.P.A., (AV) ....35350 Curtis Blvd., Suite 330
Vagi, Jolán Barbara ....'57 '82 C.161 B.A. L.1003 J.D. Ref., Cleveland Mun. Ct.
Vail, James D., (AV) .... '53 '79 C&L.930 B.A., J.D. [Schneider,S.R.&L.]
Vail, Thomas V. H., Jr., (CV) ....'55 '84 C.276 B.A. L.893 J.D. 3957 Mayfield Road
Valenti, John A., (AV) ....'— '80 C.161 B.A. L.1003 J.D. [Gallagher S.]
Valentine, Nancy A. ....'72 '98 C.880 B.A. L.608 J.D. [Ⓐ Hahn L.&P.]
Valentino, Nicholas ....'47 '77 C.610 B.B.A. L.1003 J.D. Advisory Servs. Inc.
Valerian, Robert J., (AV) ....'43 '76 C.276 B.S. L.930 J.D. [Kahn K.]
Valins, Fred F. '46 '76 C.608 B.C.E. L.1003 J.D.
Sr. Envir. Specialist, BP Chemicals Inc.
Valis, William V., (AV) '43 '68 C.757 B.A. L.930 J.D.
1400 Midland Bldg, 101 Prospect Ave., West
Vallorz, Sonia Chopko ....'59 '84 C&L.602 B.A., J.D. Broadview Svgs. Bk.
Valore, A. Richard, (BV) .... '32 '59 C.381 B.B.A. L.930 LL.B. 6116 W. Creek Rd.
Valponi, Mark J., (AV) .... '52 '77 C.679 B.S.I.M. L.1003 J.D. [Taft,S.&H.]
Vana, Robert J., (AV) '49 '77
C.381 B.S. L.7 J.D. Chief Corporate Counsel, Charter One Bank
Van Aken, Withers & Webster, (AV) .... 629 Euclid Avenue
Van Blargan, Christopher J. ....'67 '96 C.363 B.S. L.8 J.D. [Ⓐ Janik&D.]
Vance, Victoria L., (AV) '58 '82 C.363 A.B. L.188 J.D.
Assoc. Coun./Dir. of Med. Litig., The Cleveland Clinic Foundation
Vance, William, (AV) ....'— '81 C.97 B.S. L.1003 J.D. [Davis&Y.]
VanDeHey, Margaret M. ....'— '99 C&L.966 B.A., J.D. [Ⓐ Baker&H.]
Vanderburg, Keith A., (BV) ....'53 '78 C.1304 B.A. L.879 J.D. [Wegman,H.&V.]
VanderKaay, Aaron M. ....'75 '01 C.188 B.S. L.608 J.D. [Ⓐ Baker&H.]
Van Dervort, Daina B. .... '55 '80 C.930 B.A. L.602 J.D. [Ⓐ Friedman,D.&S.]
Vanderwist, James C., (BV) ....'58 '83 C.228 B.A. L.276 J.D. [Calfee,H.&G.]
Van Deusen, Roger W., (AV) .... '43 '68 C.611 B.A. L.930 J.D. [VanDeusen&W.]
Van Deusen & Wagner, LLC, (AV) .... 1422 Euclid Avenue, Suite 1610
Vanek, Stephen S. .... '67 '92 C.62 B.A. L.1003 J.D. [Ⓐ Friedman,D.&S.]
Van Euwen, Peter W., III ....'73 '98 C.610 B.B.A. L.608 J.D. [Ⓐ Baker&H.]
VanGilder, Donald N. ....'70 '98 C.81 B.A. L.930 J.D. [Ⓐ Cariglio&Assoc.]
Van Iden, Byron D. ....'42 '72 C.930 B.B.A. L.1003 J.D. 55 Public Square, Suite 2200
Vanik, John Charles .... '55 '82 C.207 B.A. L.1003 J.D. Ochs & Vanik
VanNiel, Michael A. ....'— '01 C.608 B.A. L.851 J.D. [Ⓐ Baker&H.]
Vannucci, Dominic J., (BV) ....'48 '74 C.201 B.I.E. L.1003 J.D. 22649 Lorain Rd.
Van Stolk, Charlotte M. U. ....'26 '66 C.66 B.A. L.930 J.D. 14606 Larchmere Blvd.‡
Van Valkenburgh, Paul F. ....'62 '88 C.473 B.A. L.477 J.D. 10524 Euclid Avenue
Van Wagner, Jeffrey W., (AV) ....'53 '79 C.363 B.A. L.930 J.D. [Ulmer&B.]
Vara, Timothy J. ....'57 '82 C.103 A.B. L.608 J.D. Sr. V.P., Society Natl. Bk.
Vardzel, Lisa A. ....'78 '03 C.611 B.A. L.124 J.D. [Ⓐ Dettelbach,S.&B.]
Vargas, Edwin J. ....'64 '94 C.611 B.A. L.1003 J.D. [Summers&V.]
Varga-Sinka, Michael ....'49 '82 C.97 B.F.A. L.1003 J.D. 13749 Madison Ave.
Vargo, Ernest E., Jr. ....'60 '85 C.608 B.A. L.477 J.D. [Baker&H.]
Vargo, James A. .... '59 '83 C.8 B.A. L.1003 J.D. P.O. Box 30778
Varley, Nancy A. ....'50 '82 C.999 B.A. L.930 J.D. Asst. to the Comr.
Vary, Michael W., (AV) ....'— '82 C.363 B.S. L.930 J.D. [Jones D.] (See Pat. Sect.)
Vas, Rinda E. '71 '99 C.679 B.S.C.E. L.1003 J.D.
Corp. Coun., American Greetings Corp. (Pat.)

Vaselaney, Missia H., (AV) ....'61 '85 C.201 B.S. L.1003 J.D. [Kahn K.]
Vasvari, Raymond ....'65 '91 C.309 A.B. L.930 J.D. [Ⓐ Berkman,G.M.&D.]
Vavruska, Jeffrey A. .... '60 '86 C.161 B.B.A. L.1003 J.D. Cleveland-Cliffs Inc.
Vecchiarelli, Nancy A. .... '51 '77 C.473 B.A. L.150 J.D. Mag., U.S. Dist. Ct.
Vecchio, Robert J., (BV) .... '55 '82 C.260 B.A. L.1188 J.D. [R.J.Vecchio] ⊙
Vecchio, Robert J., Co., L.P.A., (BV) .... 526 Superior Avenue, East (⊙Mansfield)
Vedouras, Anna ....'60 '89 C.477 B.A. L.161 J.D. Dept. of Def.
Vega, Sharon Marie ....'72 '99 C.276 B.S.B.A. L.677 J.D. Deloitte & Touche
Veith, Sarah A. .... '— '02 C.269 B.A. L.1340 J.D. 1300 East Ninth Street, 14th Floor
Velisek, James C. .... '32 '61 C.251 B.B.A. L.1003 J.D. [Velisek&V.]
Velisek, Jos. J. .... '23 '51 C.251 L.1003 J.D. [Velisek&V.] ‡
Velisek & Velisek .... 4079 E. 71st St.
Vergilii, Jennifer L. ....'72 '97 C.321 B.A. L.930 J.D. [Ⓐ Calfee,H.&G.]
Verginis, Theologos ....'74 '02 C&L.8 B.S.W., J.D. [Ⓐ Benesch,F.C.&A.]
Vergon, Frederick P., Jr., (AV) .... '44 '69 C.207 B.A. L.930 J.D. [Smith M.]
Verma, Monica S. ....'— '93 C.999 B.A. L.124 LL.M. [Ⓐ Baker&H.]
Vernon, Keith T. .... '69 '96 C.728 B.S. L.425 J.D. [Climaco,L.P.W.&G.] ⊙
Vickers, F. Thomas, (AV) ....'55 '83 C.09 B.A. L.161 J.D. [Ulmer&B.]
Vickers, Gregory S. ....'63 '97 C.923 B.S. L.1003 J.D. [Fay,S.F.M.&M.]
Vickers, Robert V., (AV) '34 '61
C.999 B.M.E. L.273 J.D. [Fay,S.F.M.&M.] (See Pat. Sect.)

Vickers, Daniels & Young
(See Fay, Sharpe, Fagan, Minnich & McKee, LLP)

Victor, Jennifer A. '73 '98
C.610 B.S. L.930 J.D. Corp. Coun., Forest City Enterprises, Inc.
Vieyra, Katherine R. .....'52 '95 C.691 B.A. L.124 J.D. [Ⓐ D.P.Hochberg] (See Pat. Sect.)
Vilfroy, Ute Lindenmaier '50 '91
C.161 B.A. L.1003 J.D. Ct. Admr., Ct. of Appeals, 8th Dist.
Villa, Herbert J., (AV) ....'39 '66 C&L.494 B.A., LL.B. Asst. U.S. Atty.
Vincent, Musette T. '56 '81
C.788 A.B. L.930 J.D. V.P. & Practice Dept. Chmn., Natl. City Bk.
Vincent, Terry W. ....'55 '87 C&L.8 B.S., J.D. [Buckingham,D.&B.]
Vinocur, Peter A., (AV) '54 '79 C&L.607 B.A., J.D.
V.P., Gen. Coun. & Secy., Degussa Corp. (⊙Parsippany, NJ)
Viola, Anthony J., (AV) ....'32 '57 C&L.930 B.A., LL.B. [Walter&H.]
Viola, Matthew T. ....'73 '00 C.473 B.S.B.A. L.989 J.D. [Ⓐ Taft,S.&H.]
Visani, Hernan N. ....'58 '86 C.243 B.S.B.A. L.477 J.D. [Weston H.]
Visocan, Karen A., (AV) ....'— '93 C.610 B.S. L.117 J.D. [Ⓐ Calfee,H.&G.]
Vito, Virginia A. ....'57 '84 C.608 B.A. L.7 J.D. Asst. Atty. Gen.
Viviani, Gregory J., (AV) ....'59 '84 C.473 B.S. L.930 J.D. [Squire,S.&D.]
Vlasek, Dale R., (AV) ....'48 '82 C.161 B.A. L.352 J.D. [McDonald H.]
Vlasich, Christopher M. ....'77 '02 C.475 B.A. L.124 J.D. [Ⓐ Levin&Assoc.]
Vlasich, Emily Allegretti ....'— '02 C&L.124 B.A., J.D [Ⓐ Giffen&K.]
Vlasuk, Heather R. Baldwin ....'77 '04 C.97 B.A. L.989 J.D. [Ⓐ Weltman,W.&R.]
Vogel, Philip Z., (BV) ....'56 '82 C.1036 B.A. L.930 J.D. 601 Rockwell Ave.
Vogele, Allan W., (BV) '50 '75 C.124 B.S.E.E. L.930 J.D.
Sr. Coun., TRW Automotive Electronics (Pat.)
Vollins, James A. ....'68 '93 C.918 B.A. L.930 J.D. [Ⓐ Squire,S.&D.]
Volpini, Laura L. ....'77 '02 C.363 B.S.B.A. L.124 J.D. [Ⓐ Kohrman J.&K.]
Volsky, Kerry S., (AV) ....'54 '80 C.381 B.A. L.930 J.D. [Hermann,C.&S.]
Volsky, Mark R., (BV) .... '56 '81 C.608 B.S. L.161 J.D. 1301 E. 9th St.
von Boeselager, Kurt J., (AV⊕) ....'53 '78 C&L.608 B.A., J.D. [Hurtuk&D.]
von Mehren, George M., (AV) ....'50 '77 C&L.309 A.B., J.D. [Squire,S.&D.]
Voorhees, Andrew C. .... '78 '04 C&L.8 B.A., J.D. [Ⓐ Weltman,W.&R.]

Vorys, Sater, Seymour and Pease LLP, (AV)
2100 One Cleveland Center, 1375 East Ninth Street, 44114-1724 ⊙
Telephone: 216-479-6100 Facsimile: 216-479-6060
URL: http://www.vssp.com
Partners: John Winship Read; Anthony J. O'Malley; Drew T. Parobek; John M. Saganich; David J. Tocco; Amanda Martinsek; Lisa Babish Forbes; David A. Campbell III. Senior Attorney: Margaret Dodane Everett. Associates: Michael Scot Gordon; Marcel C. Duhamel; Anthony O. Calabrese III; Matthew D. English; James A. Hogan; Bryan J. Farkas; Marquettes D. Robinson; Elia O. Woyt; Carrie M. Caldwell; John Gerak; Elizabeth A. Ratliff; Carrie Dunn; Lori L. Fauvie; Jocelyn N. Prewitt-Stanley; Rachel J. Grabow; Matthew D. Besser. Of Counsel: James J. McMonagle; Thomas J. Onusko. Staff Attorneys: Jerome C. Webbs; Mary Eileen Purcell (Certified Specialist in Workers' Compensation Law, Ohio State Bar Association); Kenneth A. Stump; Charles A. LoPresti; Weldon H. Rice.
Civil Litigation, Commercial Transactions/Bankruptcy, Environmental, International, Labor and Employment, Product Liability, Workers Compensation.
Columbus, Ohio Office: 52 East Gay Street, P.O. Box 1008, 43216-1008. Telephone: 614-464-6400. Facsimile: 614-464-6350.
Cincinnati, Ohio Office: Suite 2000, Atrium Two, 221 East Fourth Street, P.O. Box 0236, 45201-0236. Telephone: 513-723-4000. Facsimile: 513-723-4056.
Washington, D.C. Office: Suite 1111, 1828 L Street, N.W., 20036-5104. Telephone: 202-467-8800. Facsimile: 202-467-8900.
Alexandria, Virginia Office: 277 South Washington Street, Suite 310, 22314. Telephone: 703-837-6999. Facsimile: 703-549-4492.
Akron, Ohio Office: First National Tower, 106 South Main Street, Suite 1100, 44308. Telephone: 330-208-1000. Facsimile: 330-208-1001.

See Professional Biographies, CLEVELAND, OHIO

Vozar, Thomas J., (BV) ....'55 '86 C.610 B.A. L.596 J.D. [Vozar,R.&M.]
Vozar, Roberts & Matejczyk, (AV) .... 3505 E. Royalton Rd.
Vysman, Inna '67 '94 C.999 B.S. L.262 J.D.
(adm. in CT; not adm. in OH) [Ⓐ Calfee,H.&G.]
Wachter, Mark I., (AV) ....'50 '77 C.477 A.B. L.904 J.D. [Karberg,K.W.&T.]
Wade, John E. .... '18 '42 C.253 A.B. L.607 J.D. Sr. V.P., First Natl. Supermarkets, Inc.
Wagatsuma, Wade R. .... '— '99 C.312 B.A. L.930 J.D. [Ⓐ Jones D.]
Wager, Michael, (BV) ....'51 '82 C.30 B.A. L.569 J.D. [Ⓒ Squire,S.&D.]
Waggoner, Glenn D., (BV) ....'49 '80 C.97 B.S. L.273 J.D. [Pepple&W.]
Wagner, Charles E. ....'61 '90 C.363 B.A. L.209 J.D. 5010 Mayfield Road, Suite 105
Wagner, Christopher J. ....'— '03 C.208 B.S. L.124 J.D. [Ⓐ Jones D.]
Wagner, Edwin J. .... '26 '67 C.97 B.S.Ed. L.1003 J.D. 6360 Manchester Rd.
Wagner, Erika Jordan, (BV) .... '41 '84 C.930 B.A. L.1003 J.D. [E.J.Wagner]
Wagner, Paul C., Jr., (AV) .... '28 '54 C&L.930 B.S., LL.B. 21761 Gatehouse Lane‡
Wagner, Thomas C., (AV) ....'49 '85 C.363 B.A. L.1003 J.D. [VanDeusen&W.]
Wagner, Thomas E., (AV) ....'44 '73 C.870 B.S. L.880 J.D. [Calfee,H.&G.]
Wagner, Wendy E. '60 '88 C.303 B.A. L.976 J.D.
(adm. in MI; not adm. in OH) 11075 E. Blvd.
Wagner, Erika J., (BV) .... 5530 State Rd., Ste. 9
Wahl, Cheryl Forino ....'69 '94 C.165 B.A. L.665 J.D. Ass. Gen. Coun.
Wainblat, Julia G. ....'— '92 C.473 B.A. L.161 J.D. [Ⓐ Duvin,C.&H.]
Wainblat, Neal B., (AV) ....'54 '81 C.696 B.A. L.930 J.D. [Duvin,C.&H.]
Wainey, Deborah A., (BV) ....'59 '91 C.62 B.A. L.1003 J.D. [Ⓒ Stege&M.]
Wakefield, Mark L., (AV) ....'56 '82 C.732 B.A./B.S. L.930 J.D. [Lowe E.W.&M.]
Waldeck, John W., Jr., (AV) .... '49 '77 C.363 B.S. L.989 J.D. [Walter&H.]
Waldheger, Ronald J., (AV) ....'51 '76 C.273 B.A. L.276 J.D. [W.Coyne]
Waldheger • Coyne, A Legal Professional Association, (AV) ....1991 Crocker Rd.

Waldron, Richard G., (AV) '59 '84 C.610 B.S. L.608 J.D.
Sr. Assoc. Corp. Coun., Medical Mutual of Ohio
Walk, Rochelle Friedman, (AV) ... '61 '86 C.165 A.B. L.930 J.D. Oglebay Norton
Walk, Steven M. ... '57 '82 C.1365 B.A. L.608 J.D. Navigent Grp.
Walker, Andrew M. ... '— '03 C.473 B.S.B.A. L.608 J.D. [[A] Jones D.]
Walker, Josephine ... '16 '54 C.930 M.A. L.1003 J.D. 2304 E. 89th St.‡
Walker, Kristin M. ... '74 '01 C.62 B.A. L.930 J.D. [[A] Ulmer&B.]
Walker, Robert S., (AV) ... '— '82 C.228 B.s. L.1003 J.D. [Jones D.]
Walker, Sandra L. ... '50 '84 C.381 B.S.N. L.1003 J.D. Asst. Co. Pros.
Walker, Stephen O., (BV) ... '47 '74 C.383 B.S.Ch.E. L.1003 J.D. 1340 Sumner Ct.

Walker, Wallace W., Jr., (AVⓉ) '41 '66 C.611 B.A. L.930 J.D. [BR]
7774 Oakhurst Circle, P.O. Box 470340, 44147-0340
Telephone: 440-526-4244 Fax: 440-526-8511
Email: wwwalker@adelphia.net
Bankruptcy, Commercial Law, Debtors' Rights.
See Professional Biographies, CLEVELAND, OHIO

Walkowiak, Robt. J. ... '13 '51 C.930 L.1003 J.D. 6731 Almond Walcott Ct., N.‡
Wall, Brett A. ... '71 '98 C&L.608 B.A., J.D. [[A] Baker&H.]
Wallace, David H. ... '61 '86 C.478 B.A. L.930 J.D. [Taft,S.&H.]
Wallace, Gail H. ... '59 '85 C.385 A.B. L.930 J.D. U.S. Dept. of Labor
Wallace, Jodi M. ... '68 '98 C.381 B.A. L.1003 J.D. Asst. Co. Pros. Atty.
Wallace, R. Byron, (AV) ... '45 '74 C.309 A.B. L.930 J.D. [Baker&H.]
Wallace-Curry, Virginia ... '51 '88 C.161 B.A. L.1003 J.D. 11075 East Blvd.
Wallach, Mark I., (AV) ... '49 '74 C.918 B.A. L.309 J.D. [Calfee,H.&G.]
Waller, Marcie R. ... '48 '84 C.477 B.A. L.930 J.D. 4014 Dogwood Circle
Walsh, Anthony A. ... '40 '71 C.381 B.A. L.930 J.D. 4403 Saint Clair Ave.
Walsh, Kenneth J., (AV) ... '45 '75 C.321 A.B. L.930 J.D. [McDonald H.]
Walsh, Mary Karen ... '47 '94 C&L.161 B.A., J.D. P.O. Box 26013
Walsh, Mary V. G., (BV) ... '39 '76 C.381 B.A. L.1003 J.D. 4403 Saint Clair Ave.
Walsh, Richard F., (BV) '39 '71
C.973 B.S. L.1003 J.D. 22255 Center Ridge Rd., Suite 208
Walter, Robert M. ... '47 '72 C.645 B.A. L.659 J.D. [Brouse M.]

Walter & Haverfield LLP, (AV) [BR]
The Tower at Erieview, 1301 East Ninth Street, Suite 3500, 44114
Telephone: 216-781-1212 Fax: 216-575-0911
Email: law@walterhav.com URL: http://www.walterhav.com
Managing Partner: Ralph E. Cascarilla. Partners of Firm: Paul W. Walter (1907-1992); D. Rusk Haverfield (1907-1993); Anthony J. Viola; Russell C. Shaw; Robert J. Crump; Michael McMenamin; Charles R. Schaefer; Robert S. Horbaly; Charles T. Riehl, III; Herbert L. Braverman; John H. Gibbon; Michael A. Cyphert; James P. Conroy; David W. Welty; James M. Mackey; Christopher L. Gibbon; John W. Waldeck, Jr.; Michael J. Jordan; Gary A. Zwick; Nancy A. Noall; Frederick W. Whatley; Jonathan D. Greenberg; R. Todd Hunt; Kenneth A. Zirm; Patricia F. Weisberg; Randal G. Ammons; Sophia M. Deseran; Susan M. Zidek; John W. Monroe; Amy Leopard; Darrell A. Clay; William R. Hanna; Mia M. Mounts; Larry E. Klayman (Not admitted in OH). Associates: John E. Schiller; Janet L. Alter; John A. Heer; Katherine A. Friedell; Bonnie S. Finley; Morris L. Hawk; T. Christopher Brown; Aimee W. Lane; Leslie G. Wolfe; Eric J. Hall; Todd E. Gonyer; Sarah L. Iddings; Susanne De Gennaro; Bradley J. Klink; Jamie F. Ginsberg; Jonathan R. Goodman; W. Clifford Mull. Of Counsel: Arthur P. Steinmetz; Sheldon M. Young; Thomas C. Schrader; David D. Noble; James E. Betts; Mark D. Weller.
General Practice (State and Federal Courts). Antitrust and Trade Regulation, Banking Law, Business Acquisitions, Commercial Law, Constitutional Law, Construction Law, Corporate Financing, Corporation Law, Employee Benefits, Employment Discrimination, Environmental Law, Estate Planning, Wills and Probate Law, Health Care, Labor Relations, Legislative Practice, Libel, Media Law, Municipal, Public Contract, School, Zoning and Related Public Law, Lender's Counsel, Products Liability, Property, Public Employment Relations and Related Labor Law, Real Estate Development, Taxation, Cable Television/Telecommunications and Related Business Law, International Business.
Representative Clients: A.J. Rose Manufacturing Co.; Edgepark Surgical, Inc.; Braden Sutphin Ink Co.; Morse Diesel International; WJW-TV (Cleveland).
See Professional Biographies, CLEVELAND, OHIO

Walters, Gary L. ... '56 '99 C.10 B.A. L.188 J.D. [[A] Thompson H.]
Walters, Richard E. ... '52 '86 C.801 B.S. L.1003 J.D. Gen. Coun., Western Reserve Assn.
Walters, Sally Sue ... '48 '93 C.381 B.A. L.930 J.D. Ohio Bureau of Workers' Comp.
Walters, Stephen D., (AV) ... '43 '68 C.276 A.B. L.608 J.D. [Weston H.]
Walters, Stephen E., (BV) ... '58 '83 C.161 B.A. L.1003 J.D. [[A] Reminger&R.]
Walton, Gerald R., (BV) ... '49 '80 C.705 B.S. L.1003 J.D. [G.R.Walton&Assoc.]
Walton, Gerald R., & Associates Co. L.P.A., (BV) ... 2800 Euclid Avenue, Suite 320
Walworth, James W., Jr. ... '— '01 C.894 A.B. L.188 J.D. [[A] Jones D.]
Wambsgans, Katherine L. ... '52 '87 C.138 B.A. L.930 J.D. I.R.S.
Wamsley, James L., III, (AV) '— '75
C.893 B.S.E.E. L.477 J.D. [Jones D.] (See Pat. Sect.)
Wamsted, Jan M. '56 '81 C&L.276 B.S.F.S., J.D.
(adm. in DC; not adm. in OH) West Group
Wang, Yanping ... '69 '92 C.999 LL.B. L.378 J.D. [[A] Benesch,F.C.&A.]
Ward, Daniel A., (AV) ... '52 '82 C.397 B.S. L.862 J.D. [Frantz W.]
Ward, P. Michael, (AV) ... '49 '75 C.97 B.S. L.930 J.D. [[A] Reminger&R.]
Ward, Theodore A., (AV) ... '46 '71 C.207 B.A. L.930 J.D. [[C] Brouse M.]
Ware, Karl E. ... '26 '59 C.473 B.A. L.1003 J.D. 11770 Berea Rd.‡
Ware, Nathan F. ... '74 '00 C&L.608 B.S., J.D. [[A] Baker&H.]
Ware, Robert F., Jr., (AV) ... '66 '91 C.893 B.A. L.477 J.D. [Thompson H.]
Wargo, Andrew M. ... '62 '92 C.381 B.A. L.1003 J.D. [Reid,B.M.&W.]
Wargo, Leslie Erin ... '75 '00 C.8 B.A. L.124 J.D. [[A] McCarthy,L.C.&L.]
Warner, Carlos ... '71 '97 C.648 B.A. L.8 J.D. Asst. Pub. Def.
Warner, Deborah P., (AV) ... '59 '85 C.1044 B.A. L.94 J.D. Sr. Coun., TRW Automotive
Warner, Jane F. ... '64 '02 C.876 B.S.N. L.989 J.D. [[A] Ulmer&B.]
Warner, John L. ... '20 '59 C.431 A.B. L.1003 J.D. 18012 Cornwall Rd.
Warner, Robert D., (BV) ... '52 '78 C.363 B.A. L.589 J.D. [[A] Reminger&R.]
Warner, Timothy G. ... '64 '93 C.651 B.A. L.823 J.D. [Spieth,B.M.&N.]
Warren, Daniel R., (AV) ... '56 '82 C.103 B.A. L.1375 J.D. [Baker&H.]
Warren, Robert, Jr., (AV) ... '49 '74 C&L.608 B.S., J.D. [Hermann,C.&S.]
Warren, Thomas D. ... '66 '92 C.309 A.B. L.813 J.D. [Baker&H.]
Warren, William M. '29 '52 C.608 A.B. L.930 LL.B.
Gen. Coun. Emeritus, Forest City Enterprises, Inc.
Warshawsky, Kittie D. '67 '95 C.103 B.A. L.276 J.D.
Case Western Reserve, Sch of Med.
Warshawsky, Laura Klopper ... '70 '96 C.184 B.A. L.989 J.D. Ct. of Appeals
Washington, Stephen L. ... '— '96 C.966 B.A. L.978 J.D. [[A] Jones D.]
Wasil, Jo Ann F. ... '53 '79 C.610 A.B. L.608 J.D. 75 Public Sq., Ste. 1230
Wasserman, Eric, (BV) ... '44 '69 C.473 B.A. L.930 J.D. [Babcock&W.]
Wasserman, Myron E., (AV) ... '21 '51 C.930 B.A. L.1003 J.D. 322 Leader Bldg.
Wasserman, Steven L., (AV) ... '53 '78 C.150 B.A. L.1003 J.D. [Chernett W.Y.&P.]
Waterhouse, Bruce L., Jr., (AV) ... '55 '82 C.477 B.S. L.904 J.D. [Taft,S.&H.]
Waters, Joseph E. ... '73 '00 C.363 B.S. L.124 J.D. [[A] Fay,S.F.M.&M.] (See Pat. Sect.)
Watkins, Frederick A. '40 '68 C.164 A.B. L.930 J.D.
Exec. V.P., National Tel. Supply Co.
Watson, C. Larry ... '46 '73 C.1023 B.S. L.1003 J.D. Reg. Atty., E.E.O.C.
Watson, David D., (AV) ... '— '94 C.309 A.B. L.276 J.D. [McDonald H.]
Watson, Jeffery Scott ... '64 '91 L.989 J.D. 1419 West Ninth Street, The Hilliard Building

Watson, Richard T., (AV) ... '33 '60 C&L.309 A.B., LL.B. [Spieth,B.M.&N.]
Watson, Scott M. '56 '81 C.597 B.A. L.930 J.D.
Field Off. Chief, U.S. Dept. of Jus., Antitrust Div.
Watson, Thos. S., (BV) ... '21 '51 C&L.930 A.B., LL.B. [Watson&W.]
Watson & Watson, (BV) ... 815 Superior Ave. E., Ste. 400 (⊙Orlando, FL)
Watts, Andrew W. '50 '75 C&L.902 B.A., J.D.
Sr. V.P. & Gen. Coun., Federal Reserve Bk. of Cleveland
Watts, Patrick M. ... '— '02 L.608 J.D. [[A] Kennedy R.&K.]

Watts Hoffmann Co., L.P.A., (AV)
Diamond Building, 1100 Superior Avenue East Suite 1750, 44114-2518
Telephone: 216-241-6700 Facsimile: 216-241-8151
Blythe D. Watts (1888-1984); Daniel J. Sammon (1934-1991); James T. Hoffmann (1900-2002); Thomas E. Fisher (1926-2005); John R. Hlavka; Stephen J. Schultz; George L. Pinchak, Jr.;—Jennifer Nock Hinton; John A. Yirga.
Intellectual Property Law including Patent, Trademark, Copyright and Unfair Competition Law. Trials and Appeals.
See Professional Biographies, CLEVELAND, OHIO

Wax, Harvey '28 '54 C.107 L.564 LL.B.
(adm. in NY; not adm. in OH) Dist. Coun., Vet. Adm.
Waxman, David B., (AV) ... '58 '86 C.608 B.A. L.851 J.D. [Waxman B.]

Waxman Blumenthal LLC, (AV) [BR]
29225 Chagrin Boulevard Suite 350, 44122
Telephone: 216-514-9400 Fax: 216-514-9401
URL: http://www.waxmanblumenthal.com
David B. Waxman; Michael R. Blumenthal. Of Counsel: Frank Moss.
Construction Law, Corporate Law, Environmental Law, General Civil, Trial and Appellate Practice, OSHA Law, Real Estate Development, Real Estate Finance, Real Estate Leasing, Zoning Law, Redevelopments and Brownfields.
See Professional Biographies, CLEVELAND, OHIO

Wayne, Ronald F., (AV) ... '53 '78 C.161 B.A. L.1003 J.D. [Buckingham,D.&B.]
Wearsch, Thomas M. '75 '02 C.309 A.B. L.893 J.D.
(adm. in NY; not adm. in OH) [[A] Baker&H.]
Weatherhead, Ann ... '56 '82 C.976 B.A. L.930 J.D. Mag., Com. Pleas Ct.
Weaver, Clark B., (AV) ... '34 '66 C.610 B.S.C. L.1340 J.D. 55 Public Sq., Ste. 1310
Weaver, Philip J., Jr., (AV) ... '47 '74 C.967 A.B. L.608 J.D. [Smith M.]
Weaver, Robert P. ... '45 '76 C&L.930 B.A., J.D. Fed. Trade Comm.
Weaver, Robin G., (AV) ... '48 '74 C.608 B.A. L.477 J.D. [Squire,S.&D.]
Webber, Mark V., (AV) ... '47 '74 C.178 B.A. L.93 J.D. [[C] Duvin,C.&H.]
Webber, Melanie L. ... '70 '99 C.161 B.A.A. L.1003 J.D. [[A] Millisor&N.]
Webbs, Jerome C. ... '55 '80 C.604 A.B. L.930 J.D. [[S] Vorys,S.S.&P.]
Weber, Jeffrey J. ... '62 '93 C.871 B.S. L.893 J.D. [Porter W.M.&A.]
Weber, Monica M. ... '79 '04 C.363 B.S.B.A. L.608 J.D. [[A] Millisor&N.]
Weber, Robert C., (AV) ... '— '76 C.976 B.A. L.228 J.D. [Jones D.]
Webster, Beth Brandon, (BV) ... '63 '90 C.597 B.A. L.930 J.D. [Webster W.K.]
Webster, David B., (AV) ... '62 '90 C.610 B.F.A. L.930 J.D. [Webster W.K.]
Webster, Stephen D., (AV) ... '44 '73 C.696 A.B. L.930 J.D. [Van Aken,W.&W.]
Webster Webster Kvale LLP, (AV) ... 1220 West Sixth Street
Wedel, Jeffrey J. ... '57 '83 C.216 B.A. L.1187 J.D. [Squire,S.&D.]
Wedell, Kristin L. ... '— '00 C.851 B.A. L.1211 J.D. [[A] Gallagher S.]
Weedon, John A. ... '33 '61 C.930 B.A. L.178 LL.B. Dept. of Jus.
Weeks, Charles M., (AV) '27 '53 C.31 B.A. L.309 LL.B.
1100 National City Bank Bldg.
Weeks, James A., (AV) ... '— '23 C.8 B.S. L.930 J.D. 127 Public Sq.‡

Wegman, Hessler & Vanderburg, A Legal Professional Association, (AV) [BR]
6055 Rockside Woods Boulevard, Suite 200, 44131
Telephone: 216-642-3342 Fax: 216-642-8826
Martin J. Wegman (1918-1977); David J. Hessler; Keith A. Vanderburg; Peter A. Hessler; David R. Knowles (Certified Specialist in Labor & Employment Law, Ohio State Bar Association); John D. Kedzior; Steven E. Pryatel; Richard T. Coyne; Lawrence S. Crowther; Bruce E. Peacock; Jeffrey W. Krueger; Christopher A. Holecek; David W. Herrington; Antoinette F. Gideon; David R. Button; Tanja M. Holecek;—Nathan E. Hessler; Simon P. Demian; Donna M. Dresp; Karl Robert Wetzel; Jennifer A. Corso; Lesley A. Weigand; Christopher A. Corpus; Angela Marie Privitera; Andrew C. Lake; Danielle A. Skoczen; Jeffrey S. Ellsworth (Not admitted in OH); Christopher W. Krause.
General Civil Practice in all Courts. Corporate, Labor/Employment, Personal Injury, Products Liability, Real Estate, Probate, Domestic Relations, Trials and Business and Estate Planning, Intellectual Property.
Reference: Key Bank of Cleveland.
See Professional Biographies, CLEVELAND, OHIO

Weibel, David G., (AV) ... '— '80 C.363 B.S.B.A. L.930 J.D. [Kadish,H.&W.]
Weible, Robert A., (AV) ... '53 '78 C.967 B.A. L.608 J.D. [Baker&H.]
Weibling, Kristie Marie ... '75 '01 C.980 B.S. L.989 J.D. [[A] Collins&S.]
Weick, Paul A. ... '55 '79 C.976 B.A. L.7 J.D. V.P. & Asst. Coun., KeyBank Natl. Assn.
Weigand, Kathleen A., (AV) '58 '88 C.1062 B.S. L.930 J.D.
V.P., Asst. Gen. Coun. & Asst. Secy., TRW Inc.
Weigand, Lesley A., (BV) ... '71 '96 C.473 B.S. L.8 J.D. [[A] Wegman,H.&V.]
Weiler, Jeffry L., (AV) ... '42 '70 C.472 B.S. L.1003 J.D. [Benesch,F.C.&A.]
Weinberg, Alan H., (AV) ... '50 '74 C.94 B.A. L.930 J.D. [Weltman,W.&R.]
Weinberg, Marilyn Orkin ... '58 '83 C&L.608 B.A., J.D. Asst. Pros. Atty.
Weinberg, Richard Michael '63 '88
C.608 B.S. L.365 J.D. 1801 East Ninth Street, Suite 920
Weinberg, Ronald E., Jr ... '67 '92 C.597 B.A. L.802 J.D. Weinberg Capital Corp.
Weinberger, Peter H., (AV) ... '50 '75 C.823 A.B. L.930 J.D. [Spangenberg,S.&L.]
Weiner, David C., (AV) ... '43 '68 C.150 B.B.A. L.276 J.D. [Squire,S.&D.]
Weiner, Keith D., (AV) ... '57 '82 C.107 B.A. L.161 J.D. [K.D.Weiner&Assoc.]
Weiner, Paul L. ... '49 '82 C.608 B.S. L.161 J.D. P.O. Box 21060

Weiner, Keith D., & Associates Co., L.P.A., (AV) [BR]
75 Public Square Fourth Floor, 44113
Telephone: 216-771-6500 Fax: 216-771-6540
Email: collections@weinerlaw.com URL: http://www.weinerlaw.com
Keith D. Weiner;—Kim M. Hammond; Gilbert E. Blomgren; Leonard A. Cuilli; Suzana Krasnicki; Todd A. Bobka; Matthew P. Curry.
Collections, Bankruptcy, Foreclosures, Evictions, Replevins, Mechanic Liens, Commercial Litigation, Post Judgment Collections.
See Professional Biographies, CLEVELAND, OHIO

Weingartner, Lucile Gray '53 '80 C.188 B.A. L.608 J.D.
Vice President, Law Division, Natl. City Bank
Weingrad, Stephen C., (AV) ... '41 '73 C.385 B.A. L.390 J.D. [[C] Kohrman J.&K.]
Weinmann Slive, Harriet, (BV) ... '51 '84 C.930 M.A. L.1003 J.D. 526 Superior Ave.
Weinstein, Alan C. '44 '78 C.659 B.A. L.1066 J.D.
(adm. in MA; not adm. in OH) Assoc. Prof., Cleveland-Marshall Coll. of Law
Weinstein, Edward A. ... '— '86 C.473 B.S. L.930 J.D. [Hahn L.&P.]
Weinstein, Joseph C., (AV) ... '58 '83 C&L.930 B.A., J.D. [Squire,S.&D.]
Weinstein, Norman H. ... '26 '52 C.604 B.A. L.930 LL.B. 14176 Cedar Road, Suite 103
Weinstein, Co., Harold, (L.P.A.), (BV) '20 '47
C&L.930 A.B., LL.B. 3271 Van Aken Blvd.

Weintraub, Craig T., Law Offices of '61 '87 C.608 B.A. L.989 J.D. 23220 Chagrin Blvd., Ste. 360
Weintraub, Edward A. '47 '73 C.910 A.B. L.537 J.D. Pres., Mantua Mfg. Co.
Weintraub, Julianne Louise '70 '96 C.930 B.A. L.1003 J.D. Pros. Off.
Weintraub, Mark A. '— '05 C.473 B.S. L.989 J.D. [Ⓐ Thompson H.]
Weir, William R., (AV) '59 '84 C.597 B.A. L.930 J.D. [Porter W.M.&A.]
Weisberg, Martin A. '51 '76 C.363 B.S.B.A. L.1003 J.D. V.P., Provident Bk.
Weisberg, Patricia F., (BV) '59 '86 C.966 B.A. L.1003 J.D. [Walter&H.]
Weisblatt, David E., (BV) '68 '94 C.860 B.A. L.608 J.D. [Ⓐ McDonald H.]
Weise, Robert L., Law Office of '68 '97 C.691 B.A. L.608 J.D. 4837 W. 220th St., Ste. A
Weiser, Rachel M. '75 '98 C.665 B.A. L.930 J.D. [Milano W.&a.&Assoc.]
Weisman, Deborah A. '69 '94 C.477 B.A. L.273 J.D. [Ⓐ Kahn K.]
Weisman, Fred, (AV) '26 '51 C&L.930 B.A., LL.B. [Weisman,G.&W.]
Weisman, Jed, (AV) '33 '66 C.611 B.A. L.1003 J.D. [Weisman,G.&W.]
Weisman, Mitchell A., (AV) '58 '83 C.1365 B.B.A. L.608 J.D. [Weisman,G.&W.]
Weisman, Goldberg & Weisman Co., L.P.A., (AV) Landmark Office Towers
Weiss, Dana B. '75 '03 C.846 B.J. L.161 J.D. [Ⓐ Squire,S.&D.]
Weiss, David E., (AV) '61 '86 C.477 B.A. L.608 J.D. 600 Superior Ave.
Weiss, David H. '52 '77 C.604 B.A. L.208 J.D. Pres., Better Business Bureau, Inc.
Weiss, Eric J. '74 '00 C.97 B.A. L.989 J.D. [Ⓐ Janik&D.]
Weiss, Gary A., (AV) '63 '90 C.8 B.A. L.851 J.D. [Ⓒ Roetzel&A.]
Weiss, Jerome F., (AV) '46 '72 C.823 A.B. L.930 J.D. 101 Prospect Avenue West
Weiss, Kathleen G. '57 '88 C.62 B.A. L.1003 J.D. Chf. Legal Coun., Ohio Lottery Comm.
Weiss, Leon A., (AV) '42 '66 C.105 B.S. L.930 J.D. [Ⓐ Reminger&R.]
Weiss, Michael Seth '54 '81 C.473 B.A. L.1003 J.D. Pres., A. & C. Auto Parts & Wrecking Co.
Weiss, Ronald I., (AV) '40 '65 C.659 B.S. L.930 J.D. [Ⓒ Goodman W.M.]
Weiss, Steven M., (AV) '54 '80 C.610 B.S.C. L.930 J.D. 1250 Illuminating Bldg., Ste. 1250
Weiss, William B. '— '77 C.608 B.A. L.999 J.D. Acct. Exec., Marvel Consultants, Inc.
Weissman, Esther S., (BV) '32 '61 C.831 L.1003 LL.B. [E.S.Weissman]
Weissman, Esther S., Co., L.P.A., (BV) 614 Superior Ave. W.
Welch, Robert L. '27 '58 C.381 B.S.B.A. L.7 LL.B. Sr. Assoc. Coun.
Welfel, Frederick M., (BV) '49 '92 C.494 M.H.A. L.1003 J.D. Asst. Gen. Coun., MetroHealth Sys.
Welfley, Jennifer A. '72 '97 C.381 B.S. L.851 J.D. [Millisor&N.]
Weller, Robert R., (AV) '46 '72 C.309 B.A. L.976 J.D. 3171 Coleridge Road
Welling, David A. '76 '03 C.608 B.S. L.8 J.D. [Ⓐ T.A.Shimko&Assoc.]
Wellman, Kristine M. '70 '95 C.477 A.B. L.930 J.D. [Ⓐ Squire,S.&D.]
Wells, John '62 '93 C.117 B.A. L.1003 J.D. 6300 Wilson Mills Rd.
Wells, Lesley Brooks '37 '75 C.643 B.A. L.1003 J.D. U.S. Dist. J.
Wells-Niklas, Natasha A. '71 '96 C.610 B.A. L.851 J.D. [Ⓐ Mazanec,R.&R.]
Welsh, Thomas M. '77 '03 C.473 B.A. L.930 J.D. [Ⓐ Calfee,H.&G.]
Weltman, Robert B., (AV) '37 '65 C.608 B.B.A. L.930 LL.B. [Weltman,W.&R.]
Weltman, Scott S., (AV) '64 '89 C&L.800 B.S., J.D. [Weltman,W.&R.]

Weltman, Weinberg & Reis Co., L.P.A., (AV)
323 W. Lakeside Avenue, Suite 200, 44113 ⊙
Telephone: 216-685-1000 Fax: 216-363-4121
Email: wwr@weltman.com URL: http://www.weltman.com
Robert B. Weltman; Alan H. Weinberg; Larry R. Rothenberg; Charles G. Pona; Alan C. Hochheiser; Scott S. Weltman; Rosemary Taft-Milby; Theresa A. Fortunato; Donald A. Mausar; Robert W. Rutkowski; George R. Hicks, Jr.; Sara M. Donnersbach; Eileen M. Bitterman;—A. Elizabeth Cargle; James M. Doran; Steven Emery; Scott D. Fink; Stanley Green; David A. Head; Benjamin N. Hoen; Amy Clum Holbrook; Bryan T. Kostura; Lucille Markowski; Jennifer M. Monty; Christopher E. Olsztyn; Danielle Pecenka Cullen; John B. C. Porter; Maria A. Rowan; William M. Shackelford; Dean S. Talaganis; Julie A. Vaccarelli Mussman; Heather R. Baldwin Vlasuk; Andrew C. Voorhees; Stacie H. Wittenberg; Matthew M. Young; Amanda Yurechko.
Creditors Rights, Collections, Creditor Bankruptcy, Foreclosure/Eviction, Title Insurance Law, Fair Debt Collections Practices Act, Probate/Deceased Collections, Subrogation, Credit Union Law, Banks and Banking, Creditor Defense, Complex Consumer and Commercial Litigation, Real Estate Title & Closing Services.
Burlington, New Jersey Office: Telephone: 609-914-0437.
Chicago, Illinois Office: Telephone: 312-782-9676.
Cincinnati, Ohio Office: Telephone: 513-723-2200.
Columbus, Ohio Office: Telephone: 614-228-7272.
Deerfield, Illinois Office: Telephone: 847-940-9812
Philadelphia, Pennsylvania Office: Telephone: 215-599-1500.
Pittsburgh, Pennsylvania Office: Telephone: 412-434-7955.
Troy, Michigan Office: Telephone: 248-362-6100.

See Professional Biographies, CLEVELAND, OHIO

Welton, Copani Marie '70 '01 C.610 B.A. L.989 J.D. National City Corp.
Welty, David W., (AV) '49 '74 C.473 B.S. L.930 J.D. [Walter&H.]
Wendel, Fred, III, (AV) '49 '74 C.165 B.A. L.930 J.D. [Stewart&D.]
Wensink, Katherine E. '74 '99 C.679 B.A. L.477 J.D. [Ⓐ McCarthy,L.C.&L.]
Wenstrup, Rose Mary '— '95 C.734 B.A. L.930 J.D. [Ⓒ Jones D.]
Wentsler, Stephen S. '67 '97 C.150 B.S.M.E. L.823 J.D. [Ⓐ Pearne&G.] (See Pat. Sect.)
Wentz, Robert C. '63 '89 C.161 B.A. L.1003 J.D. [R.C.Wentz]
Wentz, Robert C., Co., LPC 1370 Ontario Street
Werner, Brooke D. '— '04 C.125 B.A. L.982 J.D. [Ⓐ Jones D.]
Werner, Gary F., (AV) '62 '94 C.1494 B.A. L.1522 J.D. [Berns,O.&G.]
Werner, Ronald B. '30 '61 C.930 B.A. L.1003 J.D. 12300 Lorain Ave.
Wertheim, James S., (BV) '60 '85 C.477 B.A. L.608 J.D. [Ⓒ McGlinchey S.]
Wertheimer, Victor, (BV) '22 '48 C&L.477 B.A., LL.B. 1897 Winchester Rd.
Wesel, Michael E. '64 '90 C.608 B.S. L.930 J.D. Ernst & Young
Wesorick, Richard S. '66 '95 C.679 B.S.M.E. L.200 J.D. [Tarolli,S.C.&T.] (See Pat. Sect.)
Wessman, Carol A., (BV) '46 '78 C.599 B.A. L.1003 J.D. 23230 Chagrin Boulevard, Suite 740
West, John H., (BV) '57 '82 C.229 B.A. L.930 J.D. 6650 Pearl Rd.
West, William G., (AV) '44 '74 C.855 B.A. L.930 J.D. Sr. V.P. & Gen. Coun., MetroHealth Sys.
West, William N. '41 '67 C.473 B.S. L.930 J.D. Ptnr., Colliers Intl.
Westbrooks, Robert A. '51 '82 C.8 B.S.B.A. L.7 J.D. Chf. Coun., East Ohio Gas Co.
Westfall, James W. '51 '77 C.150 B.A. L.930 J.D. [Eisen&W.] ⊙

Weston Hurd LLP, (AV)
The Tower at Erieview, 1301 East 9th Street, Suite 1900, 44114-1882
Telephone: 216-241-6602; Ohio Toll Free: 800-336-4952 FAX: 216-621-8369
URL: http://www.westonhurd.com
S. Burns Weston (1904-1994); Frank Seth Hurd (1913-1990); Harold Fallon (1910-1989); Louis Paisley (1922-2002); Lee C. Howley (1910-1983). Members of Firm: David Arnold; James S. Aussem; Carolyn M. Cappel; Angela G. Carlin; Karen A. Davey; Christopher M. Ernst; John G. Farnan; Jeffrey D. Fincun; Adam H. Gimbel; Jay S. Hanson; Beverly A. Harris; Deirdre G. Henry; Todd G. Jackson; John W. Jeffers; Gary W. Johnson; Timothy D. Johnson; William R. Joseph; Kurt Karakul; John S. Kluznik; Pamela E. Loesel; Shawn W. Maestle; Patrick J. McIntyre; Gregory E. O'Brien; Mark O'Neill; Daniel A. Richards; Ronald A. Rispo; Timothy P. Ristau; Dana A. Rose; Warren Rosman;

(This Listing Continued)

Weston Hurd LLP (Continued)

Harry Sigmier; Scott C. Smith; Joseph B. Swartz; Jeffrey L. Tasse; Hilary S. Taylor; Kenneth A. Torgerson; Hernan N. Visani; Stephen D. Walters. Of Counsel: John M. Baker; Jason C. Blackford; Herbert Buckman; James T. Millican II. Associates: Victor T. Di Marco; Robert E. Goff, Jr.; John M. Janusz; Jeffrey R. Lang; Carol K. Metz; Jeffrey G. Palmer; Jill S. Patterson; Jennifer A. Riester; Brian P. Riley; Andrew Stienecker; Randy L. Taylor.
General Civil Practice in State and Federal Courts. Appellate, Banking and Finance, Bankruptcy, Business Law, Civil Litigation, Commercial Law, Commercial Litigation, Corporate Law, Construction Law, Creditors' Rights, Domestic Relations, Environmental Law, Family Law, Government Relations, Health Care, Insurance, Intellectual Property, Labor and Employment, Litigation, Long Term Care, Medical Malpractice, Mergers, Acquisitions and Divestitures, Municipal Law, Nonprofit and Charitable Organizations, Nursing Home Litigation, Probate, Products Liability, Professional Liability Defense, Real Estate, Securities, Taxation, Toxic Torts, Trademarks and Copyrights, Trusts and Estates.

See Professional Biographies, CLEVELAND, OHIO

Wetzel, Karl Robert '58 '84 C.97 B.A. L.1000 J.D. [Ⓐ Wegman,H.&V.]
Wetzel, Rebecca B. '63 '90 C.967 B.A. L.930 J.D. 1200 Ontario St., 11th Fl.
Wexberg, Marcia J., (AV) '53 '80 C.473 B.A. L.659 J.D. [Calfee,H.&G.]
Wexler, Kate B. '— '02 C.881 B.A. L.930 J.D. [Ⓐ Thompson H.]
Whatley, Frederick W., (AV) '49 '81 C.1208 B.S. L.1003 J.D. [Walter&H.]
Wheatley, Nathan A. '69 '00 C.381 B.A. L.8 J.D. [Ⓐ Calfee,H.&G.]
Wheeler, John D., (AV) '40 '64 C.25 B.S. L.930 J.D. [Calfee,H.&G.]
Wheeler, John D., (AV) '52 '77 C.97 B.A. L.1003 J.D. [Reed,M.&W.]
Wheeler, Morris H. '60 '89 C.454 B.A. L.976 J.D. (adm. in NY; not adm. in OH) Pres. & Chf. Oper. Offr., Clarion Mgmt., Ltd.
Whelan, Richard V., Jr., (AV) '33 '62 C.976 B.A. L.893 LL.B. 127 Public Sq.‡
Whipple, Douglas P., (AV) '53 '80 C.62 B.A. L.1003 J.D. [Seeley,S.&E.L.&Assoc.]
Whitaker, David W. '43 '82 L.1003 J.D. 1782 E. 65th St.
White, Craig Owen, (AV) '57 '83 C.951 B.A. L.893 J.D. [Hahn L.&P.]
White, Daniel S. '64 '90 C.473 B.A. L.608 J.D. [Ⓐ Schwarzwald&M.]
White, Darlene E. '— '00 C.363 B.A. L.989 J.D. [Ⓐ Gallagher S.]
White, Frederic '48 '73 C&L.178 B.A., J.D. Assoc. Dean, Cleveland State Univ.
White, George W. '31 '56 C.62 L.1003 LL.B. [Ⓒ Berger&Z.]
White, Mary E. '60 '03 C.97 B.S.N. L.1003 J.D. [Ⓐ Moscarino&T.]
White, Morley H. '36 '64 C.608 B.A. L.326 LL.B. Admin. Law J.
White, William T., (BV) '41 '67 C.573 B.A. L.1003 J.D. 1382 W. 9th St.
Whitehead, David W. '46 '73 C&L.1003 B.A., J.D. Gen. Coun., The Cleveland Elec. Illuminating Co.
Whitehead, Michael J. '74 '00 C.608 B.S.E.E. L.1218 J.D. (adm. in DC; not adm. in OH; Pat.) Chf. Coun., The Lincoln Electric Co., Legal Div.
Whitesell, Jeffrey M. '68 '97 C.97 B.S.B.A. L.1003 J.D. [Ⓐ Tucker E.&W.]
Whitford, Cornelius J. '64 '89 C.262 B.A. L.178 J.D. [Calfee,H.&G.]
Whitford, Timothy P. '65 '92 C.608 B.S. L.276 J.D. [Ritzler,C.&S.]
Whitman, Daniel J. '69 '00 C.679 B.S.M.E. L.8 J.D. Sr. Coun., Int'l Prop., Parker-Hannifin Corporation (Pat.)
Whitmer, Mary K., (AV) '51 '75 C&L.930 B.A., J.D. [Kohrman J.&K.]
Whitney, Jennifer L. '73 '99 C.611 B.A. L.989 J.D. [Ⓐ Frantz W.]
Whitney, Richard B., (AV) '— '73 C.866 B.A. L.930 J.D. [Jones D.]
Whitt, Jennifer L. '74 '02 C.528 B.A. L.7 J.D. [Ⓐ Rademaker,M.M.&G.]
Whittington, A. Daniel, (BV) '31 '66 C.608 B.B.A. L.1003 J.D. 55 Public Sq.
Wick, Christopher B. '75 '00 C&L.902 B.A., J.D. [Ⓐ Hahn L.&P.]
Wick, G. Michael '47 '89 C&L.161 B.A., J.D. Asst. Dist. Coun., U.S. Dept. of Jus.
Wick, Jennifer L. '76 '01 C&L.902 B.S., J.D. [Ⓐ Calfee,H.&G.]

Wickens, Herzer, Panza, Cook & Batista, A Legal Professional Association
(See Avon)

Wickline, Paul O., (BV) '55 '81 C.97 B.S.B.A. L.1003 J.D. Asst. Gen. Coun., Parker-Hannifin Corp.
Widen, Frederick N., (AV) '54 '81 C.161 B.B.A. L.1003 J.D. [Ulmer&B.]
Widman, Elizabeth M. '79 '04 C.610 B.A. L.8 J.D. [Ⓐ Ulmer&B.]
Wiedemann, John T., (AV) '52 '77 C.150 B.S. L.608 J.D. [Calfee,H.&G.] (See Pat. Sect.)
Wiedemer, Eric C. '77 '05 C.424 B.B.A. L.989 J.D. [Ⓐ Kelley&F.]
Wieder, David L. '13 '41 C.62 B.A. L.1003 J.D. Ref. Prob. Ct.
Wiener, June W., (AV) '32 '65 C.104 A.B. L.1003 J.D. City Chf. Asst. Dir. of Law
Wiener, Stanley B., (AV) '28 '53 C&L.930 A.B., J.D. 75 Public Sq.
Wiery, Suzanne '72 '98 C.363 B.S. L.1003 J.D. [Ⓐ McMahon,D.H.&L.]
Wieser, Molly Barbara '67 '98 C.381 B.A. L.124 J.D. The Racial Fairness Project
Wilcox, Deborah A. Schaff, (AV) '63 '87 C&L.966 B.A., J.D. [Baker&H.]
Wilcox, Dennis R., (AV) '51 '77 C.608 B.A. L.930 J.D. [Climaco,L.P.W.&G.]
Wilcox, Diane D. '57 '88 C.610 B.S.J. L.7 J.D. [Ⓢ Baker&H.]
Wild, Jeffrey J. '72 '97 C.978 B.A. L.1398 J.D. [Benesch,F.C.&A.]
Wilder, John H. '21 '52 C.610 B.S.C. L.1003 LL.B. 1422 Euclid Ave.
Wiley, Tossie, Jr., (BV) '46 '75 C.604 B.A. L.1003 J.D. [Ⓒ Davis,W.]
Wilkerson, Ernest L., Jr., (BV) '61 '86 C.597 B.A. L.659 J.D. [Wilkerson&Assoc.]
Wilkerson & Associates Co., L.P.A., (BV) 1422 Euclid Ave., Suite 248
Wilkes, Meredith M. '— '96 C.172 B.A. L.190 J.D. [Ⓐ Jones D.]
Willacy, Aubrey B., (AV) '45 '70 C.197 A.B. L.329 J.D. [Willacy&L.]
Willacy, Hazel M. '46 '76 C.788 B.A. L.930 J.D. Corp. Dir. Employment Policies & Labor Relations, Sherwin-Williams Company
Willacy & LoPresti, (AV) 1468 W. 9th St.
Williams, Brinley H., Jr. '36 '71 C.381 B.S. L.128 J.D. Fed. Trade Comm.
Williams, Caroline M. '— '04 C.207 B.A. L.477 J.D. [Ⓐ Jones D.]
Williams, Christopher S., (BV) '64 '90 C.473 B.A. L.376 J.D. [Calfee,H.&G.]
Williams, Clyde E., Jr., (AV) '19 '45 C.207 A.B. L.309 LL.B. [Spieth,B.M.&N.]
Williams, Cynthia L. '50 '86 C.684 B.A. L.1003 J.D. Forest City Capitol Corp.
Williams, Danny R., (AV) '53 '78 C.674 A.B. L.477 J.D. Co. Admin.
Williams, David R., (AV) '41 '66 C.165 A.B. L.930 J.D. Sr. Coun., Litig., TRW Inc.
Williams, Diane Rubin '47 '72 C.608 B.A. L.930 J.D. Law Clk., to U.S. Dist. J.
Williams, Donald C., (BV) '42 '73 C.97 B.A. L.1003 LL.B. [Davis,W.]
Williams, Harold L. '43 '76 C.999 B.A. L.128 J.D. Legal Aid Soc.
Williams, James C. '21 '50 C.943 B.S. L.930 LL.B. Ste. 12738‡
Williams, Kathryn A. '70 '98 C.659 B.A. L.930 J.D. [Torres W.]
Williams, Laura A. '49 '83 C.329 B.A. L.1003 J.D. 1200 Ontario-Justice Center, 12th Floor
Williams, Michael T., (BV) '67 '92 C.610 B.B.A. L.1003 J.D. 1801 East 9th St., Suite 740
Williams, Robert A. '23 '49 C.473 L.1003 LL.B. 3842 Parkdale Rd.‡
Williams, Robert H., (BV) '55 '80 C.313 B.A. L.1003 J.D. [Hildebrand,W.&F.]
Williams, Tabetha '70 '99 C&L.8 B.A., J.D. [Ⓐ Wilkerson&Assoc.]
Williams, Tanya L. '79 '04 C&L.575 B.S., J.D. [Ⓐ Ulmer&B.]
Williams, Warren J., Jr. '43 '71 C.610 B.B.A. L.1003 J.D. 19317 Telbir Ave.
Williams, Wayne Douglas '62 '88 C.97 B.A. L.930 J.D. Atty. Gen., Atty. Gen. Off.
Williams, William J. '28 '56 L.692 LL.B. Chmn. of the Bd., The Huntington Natl. Bk.

Williams, Sennett & Scully Co., L.P.A., (AV)
113 St. Clair Avenue N.E., Suite 430, 44114-1214 ⊙
Telephone: 216-771-8660 Fax: 216-771-8831
Email: attorneys@wsslaw.com URL: http://www.wsslaw.com
William F. Scully, Jr.
General Civil Trial and Appellate Practice in all Courts. Insurance, Casualty and Surety, Life, Accident and Health, Negligence Litigation, Medical-Legal, Products Liability, Labor and Employment Law and Commercial Litigation, Toxic Tort and Environmental Law, Professional Liability Defense.
Twinsburg, Ohio Office: 2241 Pinnacle Parkway. Telephone: 330-405-5061. Fax: 330-405-5586.
See Professional Biographies, CLEVELAND, OHIO

Williams-Alexander, Donna L. '— '87 C.97 B.A. L.608 J.D.
Sr. Trial Atty., U.S. Equal Employment Opp. Comm.
Williams-Hornh, Ma'Rion Deloris ...... '62 '99 C.381 B.G.S. L.930 J.D. P.O. Box 603783
Williger, Stephen D., (AV) .... '51 '82 C.610 B.A. L.989 J.D. [Thompson H.]
Willis, Craig E., (BV) .... '56 '83 C.674 A.B. L.477 J.D. 2984 Becket Rd.
Willis, James R., (AV) .... '26 '53 C.922 B.S. L.930 LL.B. 113 Saint Clair Ave., N.E.
Willis, Robert J. .... '67 '94 C.473 B.S. L.1003 J.D. [Petronzio S.]
Wills, Wendy I. .... '53 '83 C.161 B.A. L.1003 J.D. P.O. Box 91262
Willson, Irene Lowe .... '51 '82 C.911 B.A. L.930 J.D. Dept. of Vet. Affairs
Wilsman, James M., (AV) .... '39 '64 C.318 B.A. L.477 J.D. [Wilsman&S.]

Wilsman & Schoonover, L.L.C., (AV) BB
The Tower at Erieview, Suite 1420, 1301 East 9th Street, 44114
Telephone: 216-589-9600 Fax: 216-589-9800
Email: wslegal@sbcglobal.net
James M. Wilsman (Certified Specialist in Family Law, Ohio State Bar Association); John E. Schoonover (Certified Specialist in Family Law, Ohio State Bar Association). Associates: Scott S. Rosenthal; Moira A. Wopershall. Of Counsel: Keith W. Kern; Michael J. Connick; Douglas A. Andrews.
Family Law, General and Commercial Litigation, Credit Union Law, Manufacturers' Agents Law.
See Professional Biographies, CLEVELAND, OHIO

Wilson, Glenn R. .... '63 '90 C.97 B.A. L.851 J.D. [McCarthy,L.C.&L.]
Wilson, Hugh R. .... '41 '69 C.930 B.A. L.1003 J.D. 4901 Perkins‡
Wilson, James D., (AV) .... '62 '87 C.128 B.A. L.276 J.D. [J.D.Wilson]
Wilson, James R. '53 '78 C.651 B.A. L.659 J.D.
(adm. in PA; not adm. in OH) Off. of U.S. Atty.
Wilson, Lawrence D. .... '77 '03 C.893 B.A. L.124 J.D. [A Stewart&D.]
Wilson, M. Scott .... '52 '84 C.999 B.M. L.477 J.D. [Collins&S.]
Wilson, Mary A. .... '55 '81 C.1044 B.A. L.107 J.D. [© Baker&H.]
Wilson, Nicole K. .... '76 '02 C.999 L.228 J.D. [A Thompson H.]
Wilson, Paula Batt .... '— '95 C.103 A.B. L.930 J.D. [Jones D.]
Wilson, Rachel C. .... '71 '97 C.610 B.S. L.989 J.D. [Pagano,W.T.G.&L.]
Wilson, Robin M. .... '61 '96 C.610 B.S. L.1003 J.D. [A Thompson H.]
Wilson, Scott R., (AV) .... '51 '77 C.477 A.B. L.930 J.D. [Calfee,H.&G.]
Wilson, Sonali Bustamante '58 '86 C.94 B.A. L.276 J.D.
Off. of Univ. Legal Coun., Cleveland State Univ.
Wilson, Stewart S. '49 '79
C.610 B.G.S. L.1003 J.D. 7530 Lucerne Dr. (⊙Middleburg Heights)
Wilson, Thomas A. .... '— '03 C.674 A.B. L.1494 J.D. [A Jones D.]
Wilson, Thomas H. '38 '69 C.477 B.S. L.213 J.D.
(adm. in MI; not adm. in OH) V.P., M.A. Hanna Co.
Wilson, Thomas M. .... '56 '87 C.161 B.A. L.1003 J.D. [Kelley&F.]

Wilson, James D., LLC, (AV)
75 Public Square, Suite 1100, 44113
Telephone: 216-861-6393 Fax: 216-861-6394
Email: jwilson@wilsonlawyers.com
James D. Wilson.
Creditors Rights, Commercial Litigation, Bankruptcy, Construction Litigation, Creditors Bankruptcy.
See Professional Biographies, CLEVELAND, OHIO

Wilt, Ronald M., (AV) .... '65 '92 C.231 B.A. L.150 J.D. [Buckingham,D.&B.]
Wincek, Arthur T., (AV) .... '21 '49 C.363 A.B. L.930 J.D. [Wincek&D.]
Wincek, Christopher G., (BV) .... '57 '86 C.385 A.B. L.1003 J.D. [Wincek&D.]
Wincek & DeRosa Co., L.P.A., (AV) .... 1370 Ontario Street
Winchester, Brian T. .... '71 '98 C.973 B.A. L.1003 J.D. [McNeal,S.A.&B.]
Windham, Patricia Koch .... '64 '91 C.36 B.A. L.930 J.D. 17732 Scottsdale Boulevard
Winslow, Patrick W., (BV) .... '53 '77 C.659 B.S. L.161 J.D. [Mazanec,R.&R.]
Winston, Douglas L. .... '60 '86 C.930 B.A. L.608 J.D. [A Berger&Z.]
Winston, Robert M. .... '45 '76 C.823 B.S. L.262 J.D. [R.M.Winston]
Winston, Robert M., L.P.A. .... 1370 Ontario Street
Winter, Jason D. .... '74 '00 C.94 B.A. L.276 J.D. [Janik&D.]
Wintering, Mark, (BV) .... '51 '77 C.608 B.A. L.930 J.D. [R.E.Sweeney]
Winters, Christopher S. .... '56 '82 C.980 B.A. L.7 J.D. [Winters&M.]
Winters, Nancy C. .... '60 '89 C.161 B.A. L.1003 J.D. 31116 Carlton Drive
Winters & Masters, Co., L.P.A. .... 820 W. Superior Ave., Ste. 600
Wintner, Alix Ann .... '60 '85 3659 S. Green Road, Suite 100
Wireman, Kathy A. .... '54 '80 C.25 B.A. L.1003 J.D. Nat. Labor Rel. Bd.

Wirth, David
(See Columbus)

Wirtshafter, John M., (AV) .... '59 '84 C.347 B.S. L.930 J.D. [McDonald H.]
Wirtz, Amy .... '— '92 C.851 B.Ed. L.989 J.D. [© Skirbunt&S.]
Wise, Michael W. .... '62 '90 C.294 B.A. L.930 J.D. [McDonald H.]
Withers, Carl R., (AV) .... '24 '54 C.967 A.B. L.477 LL.B. [Van Aken,W.&W.]
Withrow, Jonathan A. .... '73 '02 C.608 B.S. L.161 J.D. [A Fay,S.F.M.&M.]
Witkowski, Richard G., (AV) .... '54 '85 C.473 B.B.A. L.1003 J.D. [Nicola,G.&C.]
Witmer-Rich, Jonathan P. .... '— '01 C.288 B.A. L.477 J.D. [A Jones D.]
Witt, C. David .... '47 '73 C.602 B.A. L.930 J.D. 1441 W. 25th Street
Wittenberg, Stacie H. .... '75 '00 C.477 B.A. L.851 J.D. [A Weltman,W.&R.]
Wohl, William M., Law Offices of, (BV) '39 '67
C.610 A.B. L.1003 J.D. 23230 Chagrin Boulevard, Suite 800
Wohlgemuth, Theresa A. .... '67 '92 C.363 B.A. L.930 J.D. Jud. Law Clk., Com. Pleas. Ct.
Wojcik, Waldemar J. .... '54 '80 C.478 B.A. L.930 J.D. 815 Superior Avenue, N.E.
Wolanin, John S., Law Office of .... '64 '91 C&L.930 B.A., J.D. 127 Public Sq., Ste. 4110
Wolf, Elizabeth M. .... '— '92 L.37 J.D. [E.M.Wolf]
Wolf, Marshall J., (AV) .... '41 '67 C.473 B.A. L.930 J.D. [Wolf&A.]
Wolf, Paul V., Law Offices of, (AV) '60 '87 C.161 A.B. L.1003 J.D.
920 Terminal Tower
Wolf, Seth M. '67 '94 C.112 B.A. L.930 J.D.
Assoc. Gen. Coun., University Hospitals Health System
Wolf, Thomas R. .... '58 '94 C.62 B.A.B.A. L.1003 J.D. [A Remminger&R.]

Wolf and Akers, A Legal Professional Association, (AV) BB
1717 East Ninth Street, Suite 1515, 44114
Telephone: 216-623-9999 Fax: 216-623-0629
Marshall J. Wolf; Deborah Akers-Parry (Formerly Deborah Rowley Akers).

(This Listing Continued)

Wolf and Akers, A Legal Professional Association (Continued)
Practice Limited to Domestic Relations Law.
See Professional Biographies, CLEVELAND, OHIO

Wolf, Elizabeth M., Co., LPA, Inc. .... 10524 Euclid Avenue
Wolfe, Leslie G. .... '71 '00 C.473 B.A. L.124 J.D. [A Walter&H.]
Wolfe, Mary Stavish .... '59 '90 C.81 B.A. L.1003 J.D. 5116 Eastover
Wolff, Brenda L. .... '65 '94 C.161 B.B.A. L.989 J.D. [A Nicola,G.&C.]
Wolff, Robert M., (AV) .... '55 '80 C.604 B.A. L.339 J.D. [Duvin,C.&H.]
Wolf-Maloof, Faye Judith .... '56 '89 C.741 B.A. L.1003 J.D. 2115 Ontario St.
Wolk, Alan M., (AV) .... '32 '55 C.251 B.B.A. L.608 J.D. [A Monroe&Z.]
Wolk, Terry J. ...... '56 '82 C.363 B.S. L.1003 J.D. Asst. Dist. Coun., Dept. of Vet. Affairs
Wolters, Daniel C. .... '— '03 C.602 B.A. L.124 J.D. 1300 East Ninth Street, 14th Floor
Womer, George S., (BV) .... '27 '51 C&L.608 B.A., J.D. 601 Rockwell, Suite 411
Wong, Margaret W., (AV) .... '50 '77 C.927 B.S. L.107 J.D. [M.W.Wong&Assoc.] ⊙

Wong, Margaret W., & Associates Co., LPA, (AV) BB
3150 Chester Avenue, 44114 ⊙
Telephone: 216-566-9908 Fax: 216-566-1125 URL: http://www.lawyers.com/wonglaw
Email: wong@imwong.com URL: http://www.imwong.com
Margaret W. Wong.
Languages: Chinese, Filipino, French, Mandarin, Russian, Slovak, Spanish, Taiwanese, Ukrainian.
Immigration and Naturalization Law, H-1B, Work Visas, Labor Certifications, L-1A, L-1B, O-1, F-1, R-1, Criminal Aliens, Criminal Law, Removal Defense, Student, Business, Visa, Asylum, Amnesty, 245(i), Green Card, Family-based Immigration.
Reference: National City Bank.
Columbus, Ohio Office: 470 Olde Worthington Road, Suite 200, (Westerville, Ohio) 43082. Telephone: 614-221-8892.
Detroit, Michigan Office: 11201 Conner Avenue, 48213. Telephone: 313-527-9989.
See Professional Biographies, CLEVELAND, OHIO

Wood, Michael F. '54 '83 C.112 B.A. L.128 J.D.
(adm. in DC; not adm. in OH) U.S. Dept. of Jus.
Wood, Robert A. .... '39 '69 C.477 B.A. L.251 J.D. 2842 Lee Rd.
Wood, Thomas C., Jr. .... '43 '74 C&L.851 B.A., J.D. [© Stege&M.]
Wood, Timothy D., (AV) .... '42 '72 C.532 B.A. L.1003 J.D. [Brouse M.]
Wooley, James R., (AV) .... '57 '83 C.150 B.F.A. L.930 J.D. [Baker&H.]
Wopershall, Moira A. .... '74 '00 C.610 B.A. L.989 J.D. [A Wilsman&S.] (Pat.)
Worgull, Jason A. .... '73 '99 C.363 B.S. L.201 J.D. [A Renner,O.B.&S.] (See Pat. Sect.)
Workum, Denise B. .... '62 '87 C.524 B.A. L.1002 J.D. Nationwide Insurance
Worth, Monroe M. .... '09 '52 C.930 B.B.A. L.1003 J.D. 2920 Van Aken Blvd.‡
Woyt, Elia O. .... '— '01 C.116 B.A. L.178 J.D. [A Vorys,S.S.&P.]
Wright, Alan D., (AV) .... '29 '59 C.385 A.B. L.1003 J.D. [Porter W.M.&A.]
Wright, Daniel K., II, (AV) .... '54 '79 C.317 B.L.S. L.930 J.D. [Taft,S.&H.]
Wright, Elizabeth B., (AV) .... '59 '84 C.945 B.A. L.228 J.D. [Thompson H.]
Wright, Robert P. ..... '24 '55 C.679 B.S.Ch.E. L.1003 LL.B. 1100 Superior Ave. E. (Pat.)‡
Wright, Thomas W., (AV) .... '— '84 C.610 A.B. L.930 J.D. [Davis&Y.]
Wukovich, George N. .... '58 '85 C.473 B.A. L.930 J.D. 20312 Lorain Road, Suite 309
Wuliger, William T. .... '44 '69 C.473 B.A. L.930 J.D. [© Wuliger,F.&B.]

Wuliger, Fadel & Beyer, (AV) BB
The Brownell Building, 1340 Sumner Court, 44115
Telephone: 216-781-7777 Fax: 216-781-0621
Email: WFBLaw@wfblaw.com
Members of Firm: William I. Fadel; William D. Beyer; Joan E. Pettinelli. Of Counsel: William T. Wuliger; Matthew D. Greenwell; Richard G. Ross.
General Civil, Labor and Criminal Trial Appellate Practice in all State and Federal Courts. General Corporate, Partnership and Business Law, Domestic Relations Law, Personal Injury and Probate.
Reference: National City Bank.
See Professional Biographies, CLEVELAND, OHIO

Wurzman, Robert M., (AV) .... '15 '39 C&L.930 B.A., J.D. 23351 Chagrin Blvd.
Wyatt, Thomas R., (BV) .... '— '86 C.608 L.8 J.D. [A Ross,B.&S.]
Wymer, Martin T., (BV) .... '57 '84 C.150 B.S. L.608 J.D. [Baker&H.]
Wymor, Larry L., (AV) .... '36 '61 C&L.930 B.B.A., LL.B. 3162 Lander Road
Wyner, Jeffrey G., (AV) .... '46 '71 C.659 B.S. L.477 J.D. [Karberg,K.W.&T.]
Wynne, Thomas More, (AV) .... '68 '94 C.1044 B.S. L.851 J.D. [Ray,R.C.&D.]
Yaksic, Barbara Friedman, (AV) .... '56 '81 C.347 B.S. L.608 J.D. [McGlinchey S.]
Yallech, Robert Scott .... '— '02 [A Reminger&R.]
Yanchar, Georgia E. .... '74 '99 C.665 B.S. L.990 J.D. [A Calfee,H.&G.]
Yanchar, Jake P. '74 '01 C.645 B.S. L.1194 J.D.
(adm. in NY; not adm. in OH) [A Ulmer&B.]
Yanowitz, Alan E. .... '57 '85 C.588 B.S. L.930 J.D. Cleveland Financial Grp.
Yanowitz, Bennett, (AV) .... '23 '49 C.477 A.B. L.930 LL.B. [© Kahn K.]
Yarab, Donald S. '64 '90 C.20 A.B. L.930 J.D.
Off. for Civil Rights, U.S. Dept. of Educ.
Yarger, Jonathon M., (AV) .... '56 '81 C.610 B.A. L.37 J.D. [Chernett W.Y.&P.]
Yaro, John M. .... '55 '87 C&L.161 B.A., J.D. Atty., The Sherwin-Williams Co.
Yeagley, David D., (AV) .... '63 '89 C&L.607 B.S.B.A., J.D. [Ulmer&B.]
Yedid, Isaac A. .... '48 '74 C.976 B.A. L.309 J.D. Pres., Heritage Steel Corp.
Yelsky, Jeffrey M., (BV) .... '62 '91 C.381 B.G.S. L.1003 J.D. 75 Public Sq., Ste. 800
Yelsky, Leonard W., (BV) .... '31 '59 C.431 L.608 LL.B. [Yelsky&L.]
Yelsky & Lonardo Co., LPA, (BV) .... 75 Public Sq., Ste. 800
Yerrace, Lisa M. .... '77 '02 C.124 B.A. L.608 J.D. [A Calfee,H.&G.]
Yingling, Ronald C. .... '68 '96 C.201 B.S. L.1003 J.D. [A Nicola,G.&C.]
Yirga, John A. .... '69 '03 C.345 B.S. L.1003 J.D. [A Watts H.] (See Pat. Sect.)
Yoakum, Grant M. .... '69 '94 C.201 B.A. L.1003 J.D. [Buckingham,D.&B.]
Yoo, Steven R. .... '63 '90 C.608 B.A. L.1003 J.D. [A Frantz W.]
York, Nicholas C. .... '68 '93 C.610 B.A. L.117 J.D. [Tucker E.&W.]
Yormick, Jon P., (BV) .... '65 '90 C.116 B.A. L.930 J.D. [Yormick&Assoc.]

Yormick & Associates Co., L.P.A., (BV)
Key Tower — 52nd Floor, 127 Public Square, 44114
Telephone: 216-928-3474 Facsimile: 216-566-0857
URL: http://www.yormicklaw.com
Shareholder: Jon P. Yormick.
Languages: Spanish, Indonesian and Polish.
Agency and Distributorship Law, Arbitration, Business and Corporate Law, Business and Commercial Litigation, Commercial Collections, Cross-border Business, Customs Law, European Union Law, Export Law, Immigration, International Arbitration and Litigation, International Trade, NAFTA Law, Transportation Law.
See Professional Biographies, CLEVELAND, OHIO

Yost, Agnes J. .... '— '94 C.876 B.A. L.1003 J.D. 5194 Loxley Dr.‡
Young, Andrew R. .... '74 '99 C.611 B.A. L.124 J.D. [A Nurenberg,P.H.&M.]
Young, Charles M., (AV) .... '47 '74 C.271 B.A. L.1003 J.D. [Young,G.&S.]
Young, Daniel T. .... '67 '92 C.659 B.S. L.1068 J.D. [Thompson H.]
Young, David A. .... '70 '95 C.472 B.A. L.1003 J.D. [D.A.Young]
Young, Derek William ...... '56 '87 C.8 B.S.B.A. L.1003 J.D. Pres., Young Pat. Serv. Co.
Young, E. Mark .... '— '01 C.896 B.A. L.851 J.D. [A Roetzel&A.]
Young, Elin B. .... '73 '98 C.659 B.S.E. L.477 J.D. [A Ulmer&B.]
Young, J. Talbot, Jr., (AV) .... '48 '75 C&L.602 B.A., J.D. [Spieth,B.M.&N.]

Young, James E., (AV) .... '— '72 C.610 B.B.A. L.608 J.D. [Jones D.]
Young, Leonard D. .... '43 '75 C.473 B.S. L.1003 J.D. [Ulmer&B.]
Young, Matthew M. .... '76 '02 C.610 B.A. L.608 J.D. [Ⓐ Weltman,W.&R.]
Young, Sheldon M., (AV) .... '26 '51 C&L.608 B.A., J.D. [Ⓒ Walter&H.]
Young, Thomas E., (AV) '48 '75
C.608 B.S.E.E. L.930 J.D. [Ⓒ Fay,S.F.M.&M.] (See Pat. Sect.)

Young, David A., LLC, The Law Offices of
700 W. St. Clair Avenue Suite 316, 44113
Telephone: 216-621-5100 Fax: 216-621-7810
Email: dyoung@davidyounglaw.com URL: http://www.davidyounglaw.com
David A. Young.
Employment, Sexual Harassment, Sexual Discrimination, Age Discrimination, Racial Discrimination, Disability, Wrongful Termination.
See Professional Biographies, CLEVELAND, OHIO

Young, Guidubaldi & Sucher, P.L.L., (AV)
55 Public Square, Suite 1020, 44113
Telephone: 216-623-1123 Fax: 216-623-1124
Email: cmy1ooo@aol.com URL: http://www.sygslaw.com
Members of Firm: Charles M. Young; David J. Guidubaldi; Daniel M. Sucher; James P. Boyle; Anthony N. Palombo.
Personal Injury, Medical Malpractice, Auto Accidents, Products Liability, Legal Malpractice, Commercial Litigation.
See Professional Biographies, CLEVELAND, OHIO

Youngstrom, Karen D., (AV) .... '50 '76 C.976 B.A. L.309 J.D. [Thompson H.]
Yue, Deborah W. .... '— '94 C.119 B.S. L.1003 J.D. [Ⓐ Gallagher S.]
Yulish, Stanley, (BV) .... '29 '53 C.260 B.S. L.930 J.D. [Yulish,T.&Assoc.]
Yulish, Twohig & Associates, (BV) .... 1419 W. 9th St.
Yurechko, Amanda .... '75 '00 C.473 B.A. L.8 J.D. [Ⓐ Weltman,W.&R.]
Yurich, Robert R. .... '38 '64 C.124 B.S.M.E. L.8 LL.B. 6674 Pearl Rd. (Pat.)
Zaber, Brian Michael .... '— '02 [Ⓐ Reminger&R.]
Zaccagnini, Bruce A. .... '60 '86 C.608 B.S.B.A. L.1003 J.D. [Armstrong,M.D.&Z.]
Zachary, A. Dolores .... '— '83 C.930 B.A. L.1003 J.D. [Ⓒ Kramer&Assoc.]
Zaffiro, William Thomas, (BV) .... '45 '73 C.363 A.B. L.1003 J.D. 5555 Mayfield Rd.
Zagore, David A. .... '63 '88 C&L.608 B.A., J.D. [Squire,S.&D.]
Zahn, Jeffrey N. ...... '62 '04 C.161 B.S. L.1003 J.D. [Ⓐ Fay,S.F.M.&M.] (See Pat. Sect.)
Zaino, Thomas M., (AV) '64 '89 C.150 B.B.A. L.608 J.D.
[McDonald H.] (ⓒColumbus)
Zajac, John F. .... '18 '61 C.930 B.B.A L.1003 J.D. 2175 Professor St.
Zalenski, Thaddeus A., (AV) '36 '66 C.645 B.S. L.276 J.D.
(adm. in PA; not adm. in OH; See Pat. Sect.) [Ⓒ Pearne&G.]
Zalevsky, Marina V. '61 '04 C.999 B.S. L.1003 J.D.
[Ⓐ Fay,S.F.M.&M.] (See Pat. Sect.)
Zalic, John, Law Offices of .... '62 '91 C.62 B.A. L.179 J.D. 7515 Pearl Rd., Ste. 204
Zalud, Eric L. .... '60 '85 C.473 A.B. L.880 J.D. [Benesch,F.C.&A.]
Zambie, Allan J. .... '35 '60 C.207 B.A. L.930 LL.B. The John P. Murphy Foundation‡
Zamore, Joseph D., (AV) .... '44 '69 C.103 A.B. L.178 J.D. 20600 Chagrin Blvd.
Zangerle, Willis J. .... '13 '37 C&L.930 B.A., LL.B. 326 Northcliff Dr.‡
Zanghi, John S. .... '65 '95 C.161 B.E.E. L.8 J.D. [Ⓐ Fay,S.F.M.&M.] (See Pat. Sect.)
Zapka, Dennis P., (AV) .... '49 '75 C.980 A.B. L.276 J.D. [McLaughlin&M.]
Zaransky, Stephen P., (BV) .... '51 '80 C.29 B.S. L.1003 J.D. 614 Superior Ave., NW
Zaremsky, Michael L. .... '52 '78 C.150 B.A. L.851 J.D. 3659 Green Rd.
Zaretsky, Erwin V. ..... '36 '63 C.46 B.S. L.1003 J.D. 614 Superior Avenue, NW, Suite 911
Zarlenga, Audra J. .... '70 '96 C.150 B.A. L.1003 J.D. [Ⓐ Thompson H.]
Zarlingo, Pamela .... '50 '89 C.935 B.A. L.930 J.D. [Ⓐ Thompson H.]
Zashin, Andrew A., (AV) .... '68 '93 C.103 A.B. L.930 J.D. [Zashin&R.]
Zashin, Robert I., (AV) .... '40 '68 C.705 A.B. L.1003 J.D. [Zashin&R.]
Zashin, Stephen S. .... '69 '95 C.659 B.S. L.930 J.D. [Zashin&R.]

Zashin & Rich Co., L.P.A., (AV) BB
55 Public Square, 4th Floor, 44113-1901 ⊙
Telephone: 216-696-4441 Fax: 216-696-1618
Email: email@zrlaw.com URL: http://www.zrlaw.com
Robert I. Zashin; Andrew A. Zashin (Certified Specialist in Family Relations Law, Ohio State Bar Association); Stephen S. Zashin (Certified Specialist in Labor and Employment Law, Ohio State Bar Association); Jonathan A. Rich. Of Counsel: Lawrence J. Rich;—Deanna Lynn Di Petta; Lois A. Gruhin; Robert M. Fertel; Jennifer Sue Svec; Michele L. Jakubs; Helena J. Oroz; Robert W. Hartman; Ryan L. Long.
Domestic Relations, Labor and Employment, Corporate Law, Real Estate, Civil Litigation.
Columbus, Ohio Office: Fifth Third Center, Suite 1900, 21 East State Street, 43215. Telephone: 614-224-4411. Fax: 614-224-4433.
See Professional Biographies, CLEVELAND, OHIO

Zavarella, Gino .... '67 '95 C&L.128 Ph.B., J.D. 28749 Chagrin Boulevard, Suite 200
Zaverton, Michael D. .... '53 '87 C.165 A.B. L.930 J.D. [Ⓒ Benesch,F.C.&A.]
Zavesky, Robert J., (BV) .... '53 '83 C.62 B.A. L.1003 J.D. [Berger&Z.]
Zeiger, Richard G., (AV) .... '55 '82 C.608 B.S. L.161 J.D. V.P. & Sr. Coun., KeyCorp
Zeiser, Daniel G., (AV) .... '59 '84 C.385 A.B. L.930 J.D. P.O. Box 43280
Zeisler, Kenneth A., (AV) .... '36 '61 C&L.608 B.S., LL.B. [Zeisler&M.]
Zeisler, Lynne D. '63 '88 C.197 B.A. L.145 J.D.
(adm. in IL; not adm. in OH) 22550 Westchester Rd.
Zeisler & Morgan, (AV) .... 30000 Chagrin Blvd.
Zelasko, Bradford D., (AV) .... '53 '78 C.602 B.B.A. L.930 J.D. [Jeffries,K.F.&M.]
Zeller, Robert S., (AV) .... '52 '85 C&L.161 B.A., J.D. [Ⓐ Nurenberg,P.H.&M.]
Zellers, Carl A. '29 '58 C.610 B.Sc. L.161 LL.B.
Pres., Printing Industry Assn. of Northern Ohio
Zellmer, Ann E., (AV) ...... '52 '79 C.161 B.A. L.1003 J.D. The Cleveland Clinic Found.
Zellmer, Charles B., (AV) .... '47 '72 C.299 B.A. L.930 J.D. [McDonald H.]
Zepp, Charles W. .... '72 '97 C.973 B.S. L.608 J.D. [Ⓐ Porter W.M.&A.]
Zetzer, Paul Marc ..... '51 '83 C.930 B.A. L.1003 J.D. 614 W. Superior Avenue, Suite 804
Zgela, Ana M. .... '— '01 C.25 B.A. L.930 J.D. 1300 East Ninth Street, 14th Floor
Ziccarelli, Mark A., (BV) .... '54 '79 C.611 B.A. L.608 J.D. [Gibson,B.Z.&M.]
Zidar, Matthew A., (AV) .... '28 '54 C.610 B.S. L.930 LL.B. 1280 W. 3rd St., 1st Fl.
Zidek, Susan M. .... '67 '92 C.967 B.A. L.608 J.D. [Walter&H.]
Ziegler, Ann C. .... '77 '03 C.363 B.A. L.989 J.D. [Ⓐ Hahn L.&P.]
Ziegler, Elaine K. .... '— '01 C.97 B.A. L.150 J.D. 1300 East Ninth Street, 14th Floor
Ziegler, Paul W., (AV) .... '46 '71 C&L.276 A.B., J.D. [McNeal,S.A.&B.]
Ziegler, William L., (AV) .... '27 '55 C.197 A.B. L.930 J.D. 925 Euclid Avenue

Ziegler, Metzger & Miller LLP, (AV)
2020 Huntington Building, 925 Euclid Avenue, 44115-1441 ⊙
Telephone: 216-781-5470 Fax: 216-781-0714; Toll Free: 800-528-3300
Harold O. Ziegler (1899-1980); Roger L. Metzger (1908-1981). Members of Firm: Robert L. Metzger; William L. Spring; Stephen M. Darlington (Board Certified - Creditors' Rights Law - American Board of Certification); Richard T. Spotz, Jr.; Paul S. Klug; Stephen M. Bales; John E. Redeker; Joseph W. Kampman. Associates: Howard E. Hendershott, Jr. (Resident, Pepper Pike Office); Jeffrey L. Koberg; Christopher E. Soukup; Glen H. Garrett; Lisa J. Roth; Scott A. Norcross; Lori Kilpeck; Kathleen A. McLaughlan. Of Counsel: John J. Reidy, Jr.
General Civil Practice. Trials and Appeals in all Courts. Commercial, Personal Injury and General Litigation. Corporation, Estate Planning, Real Estate, Probate, Taxation, International and Insurance Law.

(This Listing Continued)

Ziegler, Metzger & Miller LLP (Continued)
Painesville, Ohio Office: 152 Main Street, 44077. Telephone: 440-352-3003. Fax: 440-354-3299.
Pepper Pike, Ohio Office: 29525 Chagrin Boulevard, Suite 310. Telephone: 216-360-9000. Fax: 216-360-0303.
See Professional Biographies, CLEVELAND, OHIO

Ziehm, Ronald J., (BV) .... '— '91 C.97 B.S. L.1003 J.D. [Ⓐ Davis&Y.]
Zielinski, Deborah D. .... '— '00 C.97 B.S.B.A. L.1003 J.D. [Ⓐ Buckley K.]
Zimmerman, David Mathew .... '55 '87 C.381 B.S. L.1003 J.D. Asst. Co. Pros.
Zimmerman, K. Ann, (AV) '66 '92
C.473 B.A. L.930 J.D. Gen. Coun., Cleveland Bar Assoc.
Zimmerman, Philip, (BV) .... '24 '50 2568 Brentwood Rd.
Zimmerman, Robert A., (BV) .... '66 '91 C&L.608 B.A., J.D. [Kahn K.]
Zimmerman, Caticchio, Eisenberg & Modica, (AV) .... 5001 Mayfield Rd., Ste. 105
Zimon, Jeffrey D. .... '63 '92 C.1036 A.B. L.930 J.D. [Benesch,F.C.&A.]
Zingale, Sam A. .... '42 '66 C&L.608 B.A., J.D. [Ⓒ Forbes,F.&Assoc.]
Zingales, J. Darryl, (BV) .... '51 '76 C.363 B.S.B.A. L.930 J.D. 6009 Landerhaven Dr.
Zink, Jeffrey E. .... '48 '73 C.381 B.A. L.608 J.D. Entire Supply Inc.
Zink, Marisa J. .... '75 '01 C.124 B.A. L.8 J.D. [Ⓐ Renner,O.B.&S.] (See Pat. Sect.)

Zipkin Whiting Co., L.P.A.
(See Beachwood)

Zirm, Kenneth A., (AV) .... '57 '84 C.81 B.A. L.1003 J.D. [Walter&H.]
Zitelli, William E. '41 '86 C.1494 B.S.E. L.228 J.D.
(adm. in PA; not adm. in OH; See Pat. Sect.) [Ⓐ Calfee,H.&G.]
Zix, Timothy L., (BV) .... '65 '91 C.201 B.S. L.1003 J.D. [Taft,S.&H.]
Zobec, Frank T., (BV) .... '55 '81 C.161 B.A. L.1003 J.D. 1370 Ontario St., Ste. 1616
Zocolo, Lori A. .... '59 '98 C.610 B.A. L.930 J.D. [Abel&Z.]
Zoeller, David L., (AVⓉ) '49 '74 C.802 B.A. L.345 J.D.
Sr. V.P., Gen. Coun. & Secy., Natl. City Corp.
Zoller, Elizabeth Marie .... '69 '01 C.608 B.A. L.989 J.D. [Ⓐ Kahn K.]
Zoller, Nancy A. .... '60 '87 C.436 B.A. L.607 J.D. [Ⓐ Gurney,M.&M.]
Zontini, J. Michael .... '52 '84 C.392 B.S.B.A. L.1003 J.D. Atty., East Ohio Gas Co.
Zucco, George C., (AV) .... '38 '64 C&L.930 B.A., J.D. [Monroe&Z.]
Zucco, Jeff T., (BV) .... '43 '71 C.381 B.S.Ed. L.1003 J.D. 1370 Ontario St.
Zujkowski, Melissa L. .... '78 '04 C.597 B.A. L.608 J.D. [Ⓐ Ulmer&B.]
Zukerman, Larry William, (AV) ...... '60 '85 C.901 A.B. L.930 J.D. [Zukerman,D.&L.]

Zukerman, Daiker & Lear, Co., L.P.A., (AV) BB
2000 East Ninth Street, Suite 700, 44115
Telephone: 216-696-0900 Fax: 216-696-8800
Email: lwz@duiohio.com URL: http://www.duiohio.com
Larry William Zukerman; Paul B. Daiker; S. Michael Lear.
White Collar Criminal Defense, Attorney Discipline, Personal Injury, Domestic Relations, Internet Law, Computer Crime, Drug Law Violations, DUI.
See Professional Biographies, CLEVELAND, OHIO

Zulandt, Robert E., III .... '73 '99 C.25 B.A. L.989 J.D. [Ⓐ Ulmer&B.]
Zullig, Olga Y. .... '72 '99 C&L.930 B.A., J.D. 1370 Ontario St., Ste. 1100
Zwick, Coleman D. .... '23 '64 C.608 B.S.B.A. L.1003 J.D. 1792 Beaconwood Avenue
Zwick, Gary A., (AV) .... '54 '80 C.381 B.B.A. L.1003 J.D. [Walter&H.]
Zych, Thomas F., (AV) .... '58 '83 C.473 B.A. L.228 J.D. [Thompson H.]

CLEVELAND HEIGHTS, 49,958, *Cuyahoga Co.*

Alexander, James, Jr., (BV) .... '45 '71 C.178 B.A. L.930 J.D. 2940 Noble Rd.
Balester, Vivian S. .... '31 '75 C.880 B.A. L.930 J.D. 2460 Edgehill‡
Barkoot, Michael G. .... '21 '49 C&L.851 J.D. 3481 St. Albans Rd.‡
Bell, Ellen F. .... '50 '78 C.1123 B.A. L.930 J.D. 3311 Clarendon‡
Berkeley, Jerome S. .... '33 '60 C.608 B.A. L.930 LL.B. 3229 Fairmount Blvd.
Berryman, Jerome W., II '37 '70 C.378 B.A. L.862 J.D.
(adm. in OK; not adm. in OH) Lillian Ratner Montessori School
Bielek, Robt. E. .... '19 '48 C&L.930 B.S., LL.B. 3298 Rumson Rd. (Pat.)
Buss, William D., II, (AV) .... '42 '70 C.976 B.A. L.930 J.D. 2214 Delamere Drive
Chudakoff, Reneé F. .... '61 '87 C.608 B.A. L.930 J.D. Asst. Dir. of Law
Cull, William J. .... '21 '54 C.363 A.B. L.161 LL.B. 3029 Meadowbrook Blvd.
David, Audrey D. .... '— '79 C.184 B.A. L.161 J.D. 3076 Fairmount Blvd.
DeBoer, Kathleen S. .... '45 '72 C.1044 A.B. L.930 J.D. 12675 Cedar Rd.‡
DeVito, Ronald A., (CV) .... '46 '75 C.980 B.A. L.117 J.D. 3180 Chelsea Dr.
Downey, Carolyn M. .... '57 '95 C.999 b.s. L.1003 J.D. Asst. City Law Dir.
Eloff, Kathryn Gonser .... '44 '81 C.477 B.A. L.930 J.D. 3820 Monticello Blvd.
Fahey, Melanie S. .... '68 '93 C.201 B.A. L.309 J.D. P.O. Box 181463

Fishman, Mark S., Law Offices of
(See Cleveland)

Gamble, Ranelle A. .... '41 '72 C.569 B.A. L.1003 J.D. 3370 Seaton Road
Garrison, David F. '43 '70 C.31 B.A. L.273 J.D.
(adm. in DC; not adm. in OH) 3100 Fairmount Blvd.‡
Guerra, John B. .... '27 '57 C.1028 B.S. L.1003 J.D. 3104 Coleridge Rd.‡
Gutfeld, Norman E., (AV) .... '11 '35 C&L.930 B.A., LL.B. 3189 Monmouth Rd.‡
Hahn, Richard H. .... '36 '64 C&L.309 A.B., LL.B. 12425 Fairhill Rd.
Hunter, Sara R. .... '31 '57 C&L.608 LL.B. Mun. J.
Knopf, Christopher D., (BV) ...... '62 '89 C.276 B.S.F.S. L.893 J.D. 1623 Compton Road
Lally, Marlene N. .... '48 '89 C.610 B.S. L.1003 J.D. 2351 N. Park Blvd.
Lee, John M., Jr. .... '23 '49 C.674 B.A. L.178 LL.B. 2468 Euclid Heights Blvd.‡
Mahar, Raymond J. .... '08 '35 C.659 B.S. L.982 LL.B. 2528 Lee Rd.‡
Mastandrea, Joseph M. .... '59 '87 C&L.161 B.A., J.D. 2520 Lee Rd.
Mastandrea, Rod R. .... '12 '41 C.251 B.A. L.930 LL.B. 2520 Lee Rd.
McCarthy, Charles J. .... '19 '50 C.363 Ph.B. L.1003 LL.B. 3945 Bluestone Rd.‡
Michel, Anthony R., (AV) .... '37 '64 C.976 B.A. L.477 J.D. 17485 Shelburne Rd.
Millett, Diane E. .... '48 '87 C.550 B.A. L.1003 J.D. [D.E.Millett]
Millett, Diane E., Co., L.P.A. .... 2504 Newbury Dr.
Oldenburg, Robt. L. .... '25 '56 C.930 B.A. L.1003 LL.B. 17430 Shelburne Rd.‡
Payne, Francis M., (AV) .... '16 '42 C.602 Ph.B. L.930 J.D. 2102 Lamberton Rd.‡
Prugh, David C., (AV) .... '21 '49 C.473 A.B. L.309 LL.B. 2176 N. St. James Pkwy.‡
Schade, Nancy VanSwol .... '57 '87 C&L.436 B.A., J.D. 2891 Meadowbrook Blvd.
Schreck, Richard A. .... '30 '53 C&L.608 B.S., J.D. 3616 Berkeley Rd.‡
Segebarth, Kim T. .... '48 '73 C.25 B.A. L.930 J.D. Asst. Law Dir.
Sierck, Carsten W. '66 '92 C.178 B.A. L.893 J.D.
(adm. in NY; not adm. in OH) 2229 Woodmere Dr.
Simon, Nathan R., (AV) .... '07 '29 L.989 J.D. 23511 Chagrin Blvd.‡
Sims, Mary Jane C. .... '18 '80 C.751 L.262 LL.B. 2874 Corydon Rd.
Small, Edward, (AV) .... '58 '83 C.112 A.B. L.930 J.D. 2831 Edgehill Road
Sterling, Howard T. .... '44 '75 C.25 B.A. L.930 J.D. 2940 Noble Road, Suite 202
Szczepanik, Carol Ann .... '53 '81 C.392 B.S. L.161 J.D. I.R.S.
Tyler, Frederick C., Jr. .... '22 '50 C&L.930 A.B., LL.B. 3802 Glenwood Rd.
Walker, Owen F., (AV) .... '11 '37 C.103 A.B. L.051 B.A. 17477 Shelburne Rd.‡
Woda, Elizabeth M. .... '47 '77 C.705 B.A. L.1003 J.D. [E.M.Woda&Assoc.]
Woda, Elizabeth M., A Legal Professional Association
3008 Monticello Boulevard Suite 225

Wrenick, Frank E. ... '39 '65 C.597 B.S. L.1119 LL.B. 2628 Queenston‡

CLEVES, 2,790, *Hamilton Co.*

Henz, Donald J. ... '37 '69 C.150 M.E. L.1340 J.D. Pres., Trillium Technologies, Inc.
Mohan, Patrick M. ... '65 '99 C.1044 B.S. L.1340 J.D. 3922 Von Rissen Ct.

CLINTON, 1,337, *Summit Co.*

Packan, John ... '13 '50 C.8 B.S. L.7 LL.B. 243 Yager Rd.
Scott Witner, Kristine ... '65 '94 C&L.8 B.A., J.D. 5th Dist. Ct. of Appl.
Witner, David A. ... '59 '94 C.608 B.S. L.8 J.D. 6456 Southview Drive

CLYDE, 6,064, *Sandusky Co.*

Bennett, Frank H., (BV) ... '24 '56 C.851 B.B.A. L.948 LL.B. 107 W. Buckeye St.
Dewey, John P., (BV) ... '47 '72 C.532 B.A. L.608 J.D. Co. J. [Dewey&D.]
Dewey, Thomas F., Jr., (BV) ... '45 '70 C.604 A.B. L.608 J.D. [Dewey&D.]
Dewey & Dewey, (BV) ... P.O. Box 28
Knight, Christopher, (BV) '52 '78
C.313 B.A. L.851 J.D. 422 East McPherson Highway, Suite #C

COLDWATER, 4,482, *Mercer Co.*

Bruns, David William ... '47 '75 C.97 B.S. L.607 J.D. [D.W.Bruns]
Bruns, David W. ... 123 W. Main St.
Howell, Paul E., (BV) ... '60 '85 C.1208 B.A. L.607 J.D. [P.E.Howell]
Howell, Paul E., & Co., L.P.A., (BV) ... 420 South First Street
Koesters, Judy A., (BV) ... '59 '86 C&L.201 B.S., J.D. [Koesters]
Koesters Law Office, (BV) ... 201 E. Vine St.

COLUMBIANA, 5,635, *Columbiana & Mahoning Cos.*

Fox, C. Richard ... '29 '52 C&L.607 B.A., J.D. 33 Pittsburgh St.
Frost, Mark A., (BV) ... '47 '74 C&L.608 B.A., J.D. Co. J.
Hum, Robert W., II, (CV) '52 '86 C.980 B.A. L.607 J.D.
117 Columbiana Shopping Plz.
Hutson, Mark A., (BV) ... '57 '83 C.608 B.A. L.117 J.D. [Stacey,H.S.&P.]
Kuhlman, Jack D. ... '20 '53 C.309 S.B. L.980 J.D. 44295 Columbiana Waterford Rd.‡
Mook, Robert W. ... '51 '84 C.980 B.S. L.7 J.D. 14179 New Buffalo Rd.
Powers, David P., (BV) ... '55 '84 C.980 B.S. L.7 J.D. [Stacey,H.S.&P.]

Roth, Blair, Roberts, Strasfeld & Lodge, L.P.A.
(See Youngstown)

Stacey, Lawrence W., (AV) ... '33 '59 C.607 L.608 J.D. [Stacey,H.S.&P.]
Stacey, Lawrence W., II, (CV) ... '61 '91 C.266 B.S. L.117 J.D. [Stacey,H.S.&P.]
Stacey, Hutson, Stacey & Powers, A Legal Professional Association, (AV)
20 South Main Street
Wright, James R., (BV) ... '30 '60 C&L.980 B.S., J.D. 11 S. Main St.

COLUMBIA STATION, —, *Lorain Co.*

Fetchet, Frank ... '22 '54 C.381 B.S. L.930 LL.B. 26091 Royalton Rd.
Haas, John M., (BV) '42 '67 C.215 A.B. L.930 J.D.
24545 Sprugue Rd. (⊙North Olmsted)

COLUMBUS, 711,470, *Delaware, Fairfield & Franklin Cos.*

Abdella, G. Michael '41 '68 C.759 B.S. L.851 J.D.
(adm. in WV; not adm. in OH) Pub. Serv. Librarian
Abel, Mark R. ... '44 '69 C.610 A.B. L.608 J.D. U.S. Mag. J.
Abraham, Daniel N., (BV) ... '56 '82 C.920 B.S. L.117 J.D. [Colley S.&A.]
Abraham, Rick Joseph, (BV) ... '58 '87 C.608 B.S. L.117 J.D. [Abraham]
Abraham, William J., (BV) ... '28 '57 C.610 B.Sc. L.608 J.D. [Abraham]
Abraham Law Offices, (BV) ... 24 North High Street
Abrams, James D., (BV) ... '45 '03 C.766 B.A. L.117 J.D. [[A] Chester,W.&S.]
Abramson, Lawrence D., (AV) ... '52 '78 C.94 B.A. L.150 J.D. [Abramson&O.]

Abramson & O'Connell, LLC, (AV)
695 Bryden Road, 43205
Telephone: 614-461-6066 Fax: 614-461-4524
URL: http://www.lawyers.com/abramson&oconnell
Lawrence D. Abramson; Thomas J. O'Connell.
Personal Injury, Wrongful Death, Medical Malpractice, Hospital Negligence, Professional Negligence, Premises Liability, Automobile Accidents.
See Professional Biographies, COLUMBUS, OHIO

Abromowitz, David M. ... '— '90 C.901 B.A. L.201 J.D. [Buckingham,D.&B.]
Abroms, Hillard M., (BV) ... '45 '72 C.49 B.A. L.117 J.D. 555 City Pk. Ave.

Acker, Alan S., (AV) '53 '77 C.339 B.S. L.146 J.D.
145 East Rich Street, Fourth Floor, 43215
Telephone: 614-220-8877 Facsimile: 614-220-8876
Email: alansacker@aol.com URL: http://www.lawyers.com/alanacker
Estate Planning, Family Wealth Transfer, Estate Administration, Gift and Estate Taxation, Charitable Giving, and Income Taxation of Trusts and Estates.
See Professional Biographies, COLUMBUS, OHIO

Acomb, James R. ... '46 '73 C.383 B.S. L.117 J.D. Asst. Atty. Gen.
Acton, John F., (BV) ... '46 '75 C.610 B.B.A. L.117 J.D. Nationwide Mut. Ins. Co.
Adams, Andrew S., (AV) ... '46 '75 C.610 B.S.Ed. L.117 J.D. [Earl,W.A.&D.]
Adams, Carly Dye ... '77 '05 C.97 B.A. L.608 J.D. 3442 Riverside Drive
Adams, Mark A., (BV) ... '53 '78 C.473 B.A. L.608 J.D. [Blumenstiel,H.&A.]
Adams, William A., (AV) ... '60 '85 C.473 B.A. L.117 J.D. [Bailey C.]
Addesa, Thomas J. ... '59 '85 C.754 B.S. L.117 J.D. [[A] Artz&D.]
Addison, Colborn M., (AV) ... '32 '60 C.197 A.B. L.477 LL.B. [[A] Vorys,S.S.&P.]
Adel, Mitchell Jordan ... '75 '01 C.354 B.S. L.117 J.D. Pub. Def.
Adler, Allen P. ... '43 '71 C.610 B.A. L.1003 J.D. Asst. Atty. Gen.
Adusei-Poku, Marilyn A. Specht '59 '87
C.321 A.B. L.128 J.D. Sr. Atty., Columbia Gas Distribution Cos.
Agee Clymer Mitchell & Laret, (AV) ... 89 East Nationwide Boulevard, Suite 200
Agler, Alfred P. ... '50 '74 C.608 B.A. L.117 J.D. Pub. Util Comm.
Agranoff, Jay Steven ... '62 '88 C.1349 B.A. L.608 J.D. Atty. Examiner, Pub. Util. Comm.
Airey, W. Jonathan, (AV) ... '44 '73 C.1163 B.A. L.1068 J.D. [Vorys,S.S.&P.]
Akamine, Nathan S. ... '70 '95 C.770 B.S. L.608 J.D. [McCord&A.]
Akers, Laing P. ... '71 '00 C.967 B.A. L.179 J.D. [[A] Squire,S.&D.]
Akers, Leslie Ann ... '55 '86 C.608 B.A. L.117 J.D. Ohio Dept. of Taxation
Alatis, Andrew J. ... '60 '89 C.118 B.A. L.930 J.D. Asst. Atty. Gen.
Alban, J. Calvin, (BV) ... '28 '52 C&L.608 B.S., LL.B. 686 Chaffin Ridge

Alber Crafton, PSC
501 W. Schrock Road, Suite 104 (Westerville), 43081 ⊙
Telephone: 614-890-5632 Fax: 614-890-5638
URL: http://www.albercrafton.com
Lee M. Brewer;—Douglas M. Beard.
Fidelity Surety Law, Construction Law, Directors & Officers and Errors & Omissions Litigation, Insurance Defense and Policy Litigation, Workers Compensation, Transportation Litigation, Commercial Litigation, Mediation, Arbitration.

(This Listing Continued)

Alber Crafton, PSC (Continued)

Troy, Michigan Office: 2301 West Big Beaver Road, Suite 300, 48054. Telephone: 248-822-6190. Fax: 248-822-6191.
Louisville, Kentucky Office: Hurstbourne Place, Suite 1300, 9300 Shelbyville Road, 40222. Telephone: 502-815-5000. Fax: 502-815-5005.
See Professional Biographies, COLUMBUS, OHIO

Albers, James B., (AV) ... '26 '50 C.276 L.150 LL.B. [Albers&A.]
Albers, James S., (AV) ... '52 '77 C.473 B.A. L.150 J.D. [Albers&A.]
Albers, John B., (AV) ... '57 '82 C.896 B.A. L.608 J.D. [Albers&A.]
Albers, Rebecca J. ... '52 '92 C&L.608 B.A., J.D. Asst. Atty. Gen.
Albers & Albers, (AV) ... 88 N. Fifth St.
Albert, John C., (AV) ... '55 '81 C.608 B.S. L.117 J.D. [Crabbe,B.&J.]
Albrecht, Benjamin Scott ... '75 '00 C.145 B.A. L.608 J.D. [[A] Downes,H.&F.]
Albrecht, Geoffrey E., (BV) ... '47 '75 C.608 B.A. L.117 J.D. [G.E.Albrecht]
Albrecht, Geoffrey E., Co., LPA, (BV) ... 673 Mohawk St.
Albright, Robert E., (AV) ... '21 '50 C&L.477 A.B., LL.B. [Lucas,P.A.G.&N.]
Alcalde, Luis M., (AV) ... '54 '80 C&L.608 B.A., J.D. [Crabbe,B.&J.]

Alden, John L., Law Offices of, (AV) '41 '72 C.610 B.B.A. L.608 J.D.
One East Livingston Avenue, 43215-5700
Telephone: 614-221-1306 614-221-3551 Email: JAlden@AldenLaw.net
Email: BEdwards@AldenLaw.net URL: http://www.aldenlaw.net
Associate: R.D. Benjamin Edwards. Of Counsel: John E. Breen; David L. McClure.
Transportation Law, Motor Carrier and Interstate Commerce Law, Traffic Law, Litigation, Business and Corporate Law, Public Utilities Law, Warehousing Law, Real Estate, Environmental Law, Mergers and Acquisitions and Employment Law.
See Professional Biographies, COLUMBUS, OHIO

Aldrich, Misty H., (AV) ... '57 '85 C.608 B.A. L.117 J.D. [Campbell,H.C.&V.]
Alexander, Arlene K. '60 '87
C.608 B.S. L.117 J.D. Assoc. Coun., White Castle Management Co.
Alexander, David W., (AV) ... '52 '78 C.967 B.A. L.608 J.D. [Squire,S.&D.]
Alexander, Nicholas Z., (AV) '36 '64 C.608 B.A. L.1003 J.D.
Deputy Director, Ohio Department of Insurance
Alleman, Brenda B., (BV) ... '43 '81 C.608 B.A. L.117 J.D. 4819 Sharon Ave.
Allen, Daniel J. ... '62 '89 C.608 B.S.B.A. L.851 J.D. 338 S. High Street
Allen, Eric Jonathan ... '71 '01 C.20 B.A. L.607 J.D. [E.J.Allen]
Allen, Jeffrey R., (AV) ... '47 '72 C.611 B.A. L.608 J.D. Chf. Coun., Pros. Off.
Allen, Jerry O., (AV) ... '53 '84 C&L.117 B.A., J.D. [Bricker&E.]
Allen, John R., (AV) ... '48 '73 C.49 B.A. L.608 J.D. [Mitchell,A.C.&B.]
Allen, Philip Lon, (BV) ... '— '86 C.473 B.A. L.608 J.D. 600 S. High Street, Suite 201
Allen, Thomas R., (AV) ... '56 '81 C.473 B.S. L.608 J.D. [Allen,K.&S.]
Allen, Eric J., Ltd., The Law Office of ... 713 S. Front

Allen, Kuehnle & Stovall LLP, (AV)
21 West Broad Street, Suite 400, 43215
Telephone: 614-221-8500 Fax: 614-221-5988
URL: http://www.akslaw.net
Members of the Firm: Thomas R. Allen; Kenton L. Kuehnle; Richard K. Stovall;—J. Matthew Fisher. Of Counsel: Lisa L. Norris.
Bankruptcy, Debtor and Creditor Rights, Insolvency and Workouts, Commercial Law, Real Estate, Condominium Law, Commercial Leasing, Litigation, Alternative Dispute Resolution.
See Professional Biographies, COLUMBUS, OHIO

Allerding, Michael, (BV) ... '46 '75 C.608 B.S. L.117 J.D. 895 S. High St.
Allison, Adrian Edward ... '72 '98 C.62 B.A. L.930 J.D. Dir., Dept. of Educ.
Allison, James H., (AV) ... '41 '68 C.608 B.A. L.851 J.D. 7737 Olentangy River Road
Allison, Linda Kay ... '64 '00 C.608 B.A. L.117 J.D. CASA of Franklin Co.
Alluis, Louise J. ... '46 '82 C.940 B.A. L.117 J.D. 657 Beautyview Ct.
Alo, Noure ... '78 '04 C.851 B.A. L.608 J.D. [[A] Shihab&Assoc.]
Alter, Mitchell J., (BV) ... '55 '81 C.604 B.A. L.608 J.D. [Vickery,R.&A.]
Altman, Marylou G. ... '64 '91 C.679 B.A. L.117 J.D. 373 South High Street, 12th Floor
Alton, Jack R., (AV) ... '25 '50 C&L.608 B.A., J.D. [Lane,A.&H.]
Alton, John M., (AV) ... '52 '77 C.228 B.A. L.802 J.D. [J.M.Alton]

Alton, John M., Co., L.P.A., (AV)
175 South Third Street, Suite 360, 43215
Telephone: 614-221-6751 Fax: 614-221-6788
Email: jalton@johnalton.com URL: http://www.johnalton.com
John M. Alton.
Medical Malpractice, Personal Injury, Wrongful Death, Automobile Accidents.
See Professional Biographies, COLUMBUS, OHIO

Amann, Paula S. ... '68 '96 C.1208 B.A. L.200 J.D. Franklin Co. Pub. Def.
Ambro, George R. ... '47 '74 C.608 B.A. L.607 J.D. 264 S. Washington Ave.
Ambrosio, Lawrence J., (AV) ... '51 '76 C.381 B.A. L.150 J.D. [Fullerton]
Amerine, Amy C. Cress ... '56 '81 C&L.150 B.A., J.D. Ohio Department of Insurance
Amerine, Marjorie F. ... '79 '04 C.315 B.A. L.910 J.D. [[A] Vorys,S.S.&P.]
Anderson, B. Douglas ... '42 '75 C.94 A.B. L.150 J.D. Asst. Atty. Gen.
Anderson, Daniel M. ... '68 '93 C.477 A.B. L.1066 J.D. [Schottenstein,Z.&D.]
Anderson, Douglas L. ... '64 '91 C.477 B.A. L.608 J.D. Atty.
Anderson, Douglas Robert ... '50 '93 C.608 D.D.S. L.117 J.D. [Anderson,D.R.]
Anderson, Jon M., (AV) ... '37 '61 C.610 A.B. L.309 J.D. [Porter W.M.&A.]
Anderson, Mark Shelton ... '45 '70 C.473 B.A. L.608 J.D. Liquor Control Commission
Anderson, Marty, (Ms.), (AV) ... '50 '77 C.473 B.S.Ed. L.150 J.D. [Sowald,S.&C.]
Anderson, Norman Q., (AV) ... '50 '77 C.57 B.A. L.117 J.D. Co. Pub. Def.
Anderson, Raymond D., (AV) ... '47 '79 C.434 B.A. L.608 J.D. [Vorys,S.S.&P.]
Anderson, Rodney W. '51 '85
C.923 B.S. L.117 J.D. Sr. Atty., Columbia Gas Distribution Cos.
Anderson, Sandra J., (AV) ... '51 '76 C.610 B.S.C. L.597 J.D. [Vorys,S.S.&P.]
Anderson, Scyld D. ... '63 '95 C&L.608 B.S.E.P., J.D. [[A] Isaac,B.L.&T.]
Anderson, Thomas R. '44 '69 C.602 A.B. L.608 J.D.
Exec. Dir., School Employees Retirement Sys.
Anderson, Douglas R. ... 141 S. 6th Street
Andorka, Gary D. ... '61 '86 C.851 B.A. L.608 J.D. [[A] Maguire&S.]
Andrew, Craig D., (AV) ... '54 '80 C.608 B.A. L.117 J.D. [Andrew]
Andrew Law Offices, LLC, (AV) ... Suite 200 454 East Main Street
Andrews, Alexander M., (BV) ... '56 '81 C.94 B.A. L.930 J.D. [Ulmer&B.]
Andrews, Charles F., (AV) ... '46 '74 C.611 B.A. L.608 J.D. Sr. Coun., Bank One Corp.
Andrews, Charles Roger, (AV) ... '31 '58 C.976 B.A. L.145 J.D. 380 S. 5th St.
Andrews, Donald Scott ... '71 '98 C.851 B.B.A. L.117 J.D. [[A] Maguire&S.]
Andrews, Scott R. ... '67 '02 C.608 B.A. L.117 J.D. 250 Civic Center Dr., Ste. 400
Andrioff, James J., (BV) ... '59 '85 C.608 B.S.B.A. L.117 J.D. [J.J.Andrioff]
Andrioff, James J., Co., L.P.A., (BV) ... 22 E. Gay St., Ste. 400
Anelli, Dianna Marie ... '55 '94 C.62 B.A. L.930 J.D. [D.M.Anelli]
Anelli, Dianna M., Attorney at Law ... 500 S. Front St., Ste. 102
Angel, Michael Wade ... '49 '78 C.161 B.A. L.117 J.D. Mag.
Angell, Lauren C. ... '61 '89 C.966 B.A. L.1003 J.D. Asst. Atty. Gen.
Angus, G. Peter ... '46 '78 C.446 B.A. L.930 J.D. Dept. of Taxation
Aninao, Joseph G. ... '58 '84 C.473 B.A. L.150 J.D. Legis. Serv. Comm.

Ankney, George W., Jr., (BV) .... '31 '59 C&L.608 B.A., J.D. 380 S. Fifth St.
Anspaugh, Donald L., (AV) .... '55 '80 C.97 B.A. L.608 J.D. [Isaac,B.L.&T.]
Anstaett, Elizabeth L. .... '— '91 C&L.608 B.A., J.D. [Ⓒ Dreher L.&T.]
Anstaett, Robt. E. '22 '49 C.207 B.A. L.477 J.D.
Pres., Town and Village Insurance Service, Inc.‡
Anthony, Carl A., (BV) .... '62 '91 C.136 B.A. L.608 J.D. [Freund,F.&A.]
Anthony, Laura Greenberg .... '70 '95 C&L.608 B.A., J.D. [Bricker&E.]
Anthony, Marcell Rose, LLC, Law Offices of '48 '72
C.737 B.A. L.608 J.D. [M.R.Anthony]
Anthony, Michael J. .... '70 '96 C.130 B.A. L.117 J.D. [Anthony]

Anthony Law Offices, LLC
555 South Front Street Suite 320, 43215-5668
Telephone: 614-340-0011 Fax: 614-228-3102 URL: http://www.mjanthonylaw.com
Email: mja@mjanthonylaw.com URL: http://www.lawyers.com/anthonylawoffices
Michael J. Anthony.
Business and commercial law, real estate, business organization, commercial transactions, contracts, commercial leasing, limited liability company law (LLCs), joint ventures, partnership law; corporate law; liability protection law; business succession, construction, mechanic's lien law, evictions and foreclosures.
See Professional Biographies, COLUMBUS, OHIO

Anthony, Marcell Rose, LLC, Law Offices of .... 3688 Bushmill Falls Dr.
Antolino, Ralph, Jr. .... '55 '80 C.608 B.S. L.117 J.D. V.P., Antolino & Assoc., Inc.
Antrim, Donald A., (AV) .... '47 '74 C.645 B.A. L.117 J.D. [Buckingham,D.&B.]
Apseloff, Stanford '58 '86 C.659 B.S.B.A L.608 J.D.
Pres. & C.E.O., Ohio Distinctive Sofware, Inc.

Armengau, Javier H. '62 '98 C.1019 B.A. L.117 J.D.
857 S. High Street, 43206
Telephone: 614-443-0516
URL: http://www.armengaulaw.com
Criminal Litigation in all Federal and State Courts.
See Professional Biographies, COLUMBUS, OHIO

Armstrong, Dale E. ...... '27 '56 C.347 B.S. L.1119 LL.B. Chmn., Armstrong Mtge. Co.‡
Armstrong, Maria J. .... '62 '87 C&L.608 B.A., J.D. [Ⓐ Bricker&E.]
Arndt, Randall S., (AV) ....'56 '81 C.597 B.A. L.273 J.D. [Schottenstein,Z.&D.]
Arnebeck, Clifford O., Jr., (BV) .... '45 '70 C.918 B.A. L.309 J.D. [Arnebeck]

Arnebeck Law Office, (BV)
341 S. 3rd Street, Suite 10, 43215
Telephone: 614-224-8771 Fax: 614-224-8082
Email: arnebeck@aol.com URL: http://www.lawyers.com/arnebecklaw
Member of Firm: Clifford O. Arnebeck, Jr. Of Counsel: Robert Fitrakis.
Civil and Federal Civil Litigation, Election Law, Fraud Litigation and Personal Injury Law.
See Professional Biographies, COLUMBUS, OHIO

Arnett, Henry A., (AV) .... '51 '76 C.97 B.L.S. L.608 J.D. [Livorno&A.]
Arnold, Bradford P. '62 '88 C.608 B.A. L.117 J.D.
Atty. Exam., State Bd. of Tax Appls.
Arnold, George J., (BV) ...... '42 '70 C.608 B.S. L.117 J.D. Dir., Dept. Trade & Develop.
Arnold, James E., (AV) .... '56 '87 C.608 B.S. L.117 J.D. [Clark,P.A.&S.C.]
Art, Andrew J., (AV) ....'62 '90 C.92 B.A. L.117 J.D. [Chester,W.&S.]
Arthur, Geoffrey W., Law Offices of '64 '91 C.880 B.A. L.608 J.D.
37 West Broad Street
Arthur, William E., (AV) .... '29 '53 C&L.608 B.S., J.D. [Ⓒ Porter W.M.&A.]
Artz, Brian S., (BV) .... '55 '80 C.608 B.A. L.200 J.D. [Artz&D.]
Artz & Dewhirst, LLP, (AV) .... 560 E. Town Street
Arville, Alan J. ....'— '03 C.201 B.A. L.276 J.D. [Ⓐ Schottenstein,Z.&D.]
Ary, Richard Earl .... '48 '87 C.608 B.S. L.117 J.D. Ary, Earman & Roepcke
Aschenbrand, Tara .... '77 '02 C&L.608 B.S.B.A., J.D. [Ⓐ Squire,S.&D.]
Asensio, M.J., III, (BV) ....'61 '85 C.477 B.A. L.1119 J.D. [Baker&H.]
Ashbourne, Anica DeNeen .... '59 '89 C.901 B.A. L.117 J.D. Ohio Dept. of Taxation
Ashton, Rick L. .... '76 '04 C.920 B.S. L.608 J.D. 1 Easton Oval, Ste. 550
Atchison, Julie L. ....'72 '98 C.608 B.A. L.597 J.D. [Ⓐ Porter W.M.&A.]
Atriano, Vincent ....'63 '88 C.608 B.A. L.477 J.D. [Squire,S.&D.]
Attridge, Ellen Martin ....'54 '79 C.385 B.A. L.117 J.D. Staff Hearing Ofc.
Aubrey, Joanne E., (BV) .... '38 '81 C.587 B.A. L.117 J.D. 209 E. State St.
Auch, Stephen E., (AV) ....'30 '54 C&L.608 B.S., J.D. 2201 Cambridge Blvd.
AuCoin, Paul M., (BV) .... '50 '76 C&L.608 B.A., J.D. [AuCoin,D.H.&Y.]
AuCoin, Du Pont, Hetterscheidt & Younkin LLC, (BV)
495 South High Street, Suite 250
Auge, Craig R. ....'65 '97 C.97 B.A. L.276 J.D. [Vorys,S.S.&P.]
Aukland, Duncan D., (BV) .... '54 '82 C.886 B.A. L.117 J.D. Adjutant Gen. Dept.
Aultman, Mark H., (BV) ...... '42 '68 C.276 A.B. L.893 LL.B. 150 E. Wilson Bridge Rd.
Austin, Russell P. '60 '86 C.136 B.S. L.851 J.D.
Assoc. Gen. Coun., Corp. Legal Servs., Battelle Memorial Institute
Auten, Anthony R., (AV) ....'47 '72 C.97 B.S.B.A. L.945 J.D. [Ⓐ Grossman]
Avellano, Andrew Paul ....'67 '94 C.473 B.A. L.117 J.D. [A.P.Avellano]
Avellano, Andrew Paul, LLC ....4181 East Main Street
Aveni, Carl A., II ....'69 '96 C.30 B.A. L.94 J.D. [Ⓐ Porter W.M.&A.]
Axelrod, David F. ....'53 '78 C.150 B.A. L.904 J.D. [Vorys,S.S.&P.]
Axtell, Amanda Marie '72 '99 C.8 B.A. L.124 J.D.
Consumer Fin. Coun., OH Div. of Fin. Instits.
Ayers, Gregory L., (AV) .... '47 '72 C.516 A.B. L.608 J.D. Ohio Pub. Def. Comm.
Ayers, James C., (AV) .... '34 '77 C.575 B.S.B.A. L.608 J.D. 165 N. High St.
Ayers, Steven B., (AV) ....'48 '75 C&L.575 B.S., J.D. [Crabbe,B.&J.]
Babbitt, Gerald J., (AV) .... '54 '79 C.473 B.S. L.608 J.D. [Babbitt&W.]

Babbitt & Weis LLP, (AV) BR
The Worly Building, 503 South Front Street Suite 200, 43215-5666
Telephone: 614-228-4200 Fax: 614-228-4224 URL: http://www.bwfamilylaw.com
Email: BW@BWFamilyLaw.com URL: http://www.babbittwellbaum.com
Gerald J. Babbitt (Certified Specialist in Family Relations Law, Ohio State Bar Association); Amy J. Weis (Certified Specialist in Family Relations Law, Ohio State Bar Association);—C. Gustav Dahlberg; Jennifer Brockmeyer.
Family and Matrimonial Law, Divorce, Dissolutions, Legal Separation, Spousal Support, Property Division, Child Custody, Child Support, Pre-Marital Agreements, Divorce Arbitration.
See Professional Biographies, COLUMBUS, OHIO

Bacha, James R. '54 '79 C.385 A.B. L.608 J.D.
Asst. Gen. Coun.-Regulatory Servs., Amer. Elec. Power Serv. Corp.
Bachmann, Gregg H. .... '58 '87 C.473 B.A. L.900 J.D. Coun., Nationwide Insurance
Bacon, Brian M. '58 '84 C.1122 B.A. L.201 J.D.
Asst. Gen. Coun., Nationwide Insurance
Bahlmann, Jerome R., (AV) '41 '67 C.1118 B.A. L.1340 J.D.
Sr. V.P., Gen. Coun. & Secy., Battelle Memorial Institute
Bahls, Steven C. '54 '79 C.352 B.B.A. L.597 J.D.
(adm. in WI; not adm. in OH) Dean & Prof. of Law, Capital Univ.
Bailey, Bruce E., (AV) ....'52 '78 C.967 B.A. L.117 J.D. 33 E. Schrock Rd.
Bailey, Dan A., (AV) ....'53 '78 C.97 B.S. L.608 J.D. [Bailey C.]

Bailey, Francis S., (AV) ....'21 '50 C.631 B.A. L.266 J.D. 33 E. Schrock Rd.‡

Bailey Cavalieri LLC, (AV) BR
Suite 2100, One Columbus, 10 West Broad Street, 43215-3422 ⊙
Telephone: 614-221-3155 Fax: 614-221-0479
URL: http://www.baileycavalieri.com
Members of Firm: William A. Adams; Dan A. Bailey; Gary S. Batke; Katharine B. Bowman; Richard D. Brooks, Jr.; D. David Carroll; Nick V. Cavalieri; Yvette A. Cox; Dan L. Cvetanovich; Donald A. Davies; Robert R. Dunn; Robert L. Eblin; Michael R. Goodstein (Not admitted in OH); Dennis D. Grant; James M. Groner; Daniel R. Hackett; Mary Jo Hudson; Darius N. Kandawalla; R. Stacy Lane; Michael P. Mahoney; Nancy J. Manougian; Donald G. Paynter; W. Evan Price, II; James G. Ryan; Dane Stinson. Of Counsel: John J. Dilenschneider; Jules L. Garel; Thomas E. Geyer; R. Clifton Gibbs; Sarah E. Lynn; Timothy A. Riedel; Anthony J. Sugar. Associates: Adam J. Biehl; Matthew J. Burkhart; Harlan S. Louis (Certified Specialist in Estate Planning, Trust and Probate Law, Ohio State Bar Association); Timothy B. McGranor; Tiffany C. Miller; David A. Muller; Amanda Music; Rita A. Perez; Todd J. Samples; Matthew T. Schaeffer; Jameel S. Turner; Jon C. Walden.
General Civil and Trial Practice. Director and Officer Liability, Antitrust, Banking, Bankruptcy and Commercial Transactions, Corporate, Corporate Financing, Creditors Remedies, Environmental, Employee Benefits and ERISA, Estate Planning, Trust, Probate, Intellectual Property, Internet and E-Commerce, Labor and Employment, Products Liability, Public Utility, Real Estate, Finance, Securities and Taxation Law. Appellate, Communications, Energy Deregulation, Health Care, Insurance, Mergers and Acquisitions, Professional Liability, Retail and Catalog Law, Technology and Science.
Dayton, Ohio Office: Kettering Tower, Suite 2310, 40 North Main Street, 45423-0001. Telephone: 937-223-4701. Fax: 937-223-0170.
See Professional Biographies, COLUMBUS, OHIO

Bain, Irwin A., (AV) '53 '78 C.347 B.S. L.345 J.D.
(adm. in IN; not adm. in OH) V.P. & Gen. Coun., Schottenstein Stores Corp.
Bain, John H. ....'40 '66 C.532 A.B. L.608 J.D. CEO, Homewood Corp.
Bair, Jodi J. ....'63 '93 C.880 B.A. L.1158 J.D. Asst. Atty. Gen.
Baird, John R. ....'47 '72 C&L.608 B.A., J.D. 2588 Woodstock Rd.
Baird-Veley, Catherine J. ....'72 '04 C.608 B.A. L.117 J.D. [Ⓐ Bricker&E.]
Baker, Amanda C. ....'75 '00 C.473 B.S. L.117 J.D. [Ⓐ Crabbe,B.&J.]
Baker, Bradley K. ....'50 '91 C.174 B.A. L.117 J.D. [Ⓐ Porter W.M.&A.]
Baker, David G., (AV) ....'47 '72 C.967 B.S. L.477 J.D. [Bricker&E.]
Baker, Frederick L. '56 '82 C.631 B.S. Ed. L.117 J.D.
Columbus State Community Coll.
Baker, Geoffrey L. ....'57 '95 C.33 B.A. L.201 J.D. 640 Brust St.
Baker, Gregory S. ....'71 '98 C.966 B.S. L.608 J.D. [Ⓐ Schottenstein,Z.&D.]
Baker, Michael R. ....'61 '88 C.97 B.S. L.117 J.D. Dept. of Taxation
Baker, Robert T. ....'30 '64 C.608 B.A. L.266 J.D. 42 E. Gay St.‡
Baker, Samuel M. ....'48 '72 C.608 B.A. L.145 J.D. 99 N. Cassingham
Baker, Shelagh F. '47 '79 C.1046 B.A. L.608 J.D.
H.H.S. Div. Chf., Legis. Serv. Comm.
Baker, Thomas S., Jr. .... '42 '68 C.607 B.S.M.E. L.930 J.D. [Ⓒ Gamble H.J.] (Pat.)

Baker & Hostetler LLP, (AV) BR
Capitol Square, Suite 2100, 65 East State Street, 43215-4260 ⊙
Telephone: 614-228-1541 Telecopier: 614-462-2616 To contact an attorney on the Internet use first initial and surname followed by @bakerlaw.com
URL: http://www.bakerlaw.com
Executive Partners: Alec Wightman; R. Steven Kestner (Resident at Cleveland Office). Office Managing Partner: George W. Hairston. Partners: M.J. Asensio, III; Otto Beatty, III; Edward J. Bernert; Jack A. Bjerke; Joseph P. Boeckman; Michael D. Bridges; John H. Burtch; Joseph C. Devine; Michael D. Dortch; R. Christopher Doyle; Sandra Parks Faulkner; Andrew M. Ferris; Christopher D. Fidler; Ellen J. Garling; Jeanne A. Griffin; Mary C. Pelini Grillo; Daniel J. Gunsett; Daniel J. Guttman; Elizabeth L. Hendershot; Charles H. Hire; Mark A. Johnson; Robert M. Kincaid, Jr.; Sherri Blank Lazear; David C. Levine; Ronald G. Linville; Thomas L. Long; Elizabeth A. McNellie; Michael E. Minister; Henry P. Montgomery; Georgeann G. Peters; Ben L. Pfefferle, III; Harlan W. Robins; Barry R. Robinson; Robert K. Rupp; Mark D. Senff; William B. Shearer; Amy M. Shepherd; Richard W. Siehl (Board Certified Health Law Lawyer, Florida Bar Board of Legal Specialization and Education); J. Stephen Van Heyde; Gary A. Wadman; David A. Whitcomb; Jeffrey T. Williams; Barry H. Wolinetz. Associates: Eric R. Barnett; Kirsten L. Bartholomew; Letitia S. Bryant; Rodger L. Eckelberry; Tara M. Ferrell; Sean P. Flynn; John J. Frost; Matthew W. Hoyt; Janine Hancock Jones; Richard Eugene Kozlowski; Marcella L. Lape; Susan Nolan Lubow; Frank C. Miller; Deborah A. Pickrel; William R. Post; Sommer L. Sheely; Lisa R. Stark; Stacy E. Wilhite; Leigh Ann Wilson; Julie M. Woolley; Rosanne T. Yang. Staff Attorneys: David R. Funk; M. Elizabeth Gill; Mary Arens Hale; Karen E. Sheffer.
General Practice.
In Cleveland, Ohio: 3200 National City Center, 1900 East Ninth Street. Telephone: 216-621-0200.
In Cincinnati, Ohio: 312 Walnut Street, Suite 3200. Telephone: 513-929-3400.
In Costa Mesa, California: 600 Anton Boulevard, Suite 900. Telephone: 714-754-6600.
In Denver, Colorado: 303 East 17th Avenue, Suite 1100. Telephone: 303-861-0600.
In Houston, Texas: 1000 Louisiana, Suite 2000. Telephone: 713-751-1600.
In Los Angeles, California: 333 South Grand Avenue, Suite 1800. Telephone: 213-975-1600.
In Orlando, Florida: SunTrust Center, Suite 2300, 200 South Orange Avenue. Telephone: 407-649-4000.
In Washington, D. C.: Washington Square, Suite 1100, 1050 Connecticut Avenue, N.W. Telephone: 202-861-1500.
In New York, N.Y.: 666 Fifth Avenue. Telephone: 212-589-4200.
See Professional Biographies, COLUMBUS, OHIO

Balcerzak, Thomas J., (BV) .... '63 '89 C.347 B.S. L.117 J.D. [Balcerzak]
Balcerzak Law Offices Co., L.P.A., (BV) .... 4656 Executive Dr.
Balch, John Randolph ....'52 '84 C.967 B.A. L.608 J.D. [Balch]
Balch Law Firm ....1335 Dublin Rd., Ste. 200A
Baldwin, Elizabeth J. ....'— '88 C.597 B.A. L.494 J.D. State Dept. of Youth Servs.
Baldwin, Melissa Waller .... '— '96 C.473 B.A. L.607 J.D. 4656 Burbank Dr.
Baldwin, R. Thomas .... '43 '68 C.608 B.S. L.623 J.D. Pomminx Co.
Ball, James M., (AV) ....'49 '74 C.473 B.A. L.145 J.D. [Vorys,S.S.&P.]
Ball, Steven L., (AV) ....'46 '74 C.608 B.Sc.Ed. L.851 J.D. [Ball&T.]

Ball & Tanoury, (AV)
700 Ackerman Road, Suite 450, 43202
Telephone: 614-447-8550 Fax: 614-447-1673
Members of Firm: Steven L. Ball; John L. Tanoury.
Civil Trial and Appellate Practice, Construction Contract Law, Business and Commercial Litigation, Liquor, State Boards and Agencies, Business Organizations and Planning, Real Estate Law, ERISA, Zoning and Land Development, Probate.
See Professional Biographies, COLUMBUS, OHIO

Ballard, Catherine M., (AV) ....'52 '85 C.421 B.A. L.608 J.D. [Bricker&E.]
Ballenger, Kathleen A., (AV) ....'47 '79 C.608 B.S. L.117 J.D. [Kessler&B.]
Balshone-Jacobs, Lynn ....'42 '86 C.788 B.A. L.851 J.D. Asst. Atty. Gen.
Baltes, Kathryn S. '77 '02 C&L.608 B.A., J.D.
(adm. in OR; not adm. in OH) [Ⓐ Porter W.M.&A.]
Balthaser, James H., (AV) ....'54 '78 C&L.608 B.A., J.D. [Thompson H.]
Banchefsky, Mitchell H., (BV) ......'53 '83 C.608 B.A. L.117 J.D. [Schottenstein,Z.&D.]
Banchefsky, Susan Hannon, (BV) ....'54 '79 C.608 B.A. L.117 J.D. Asst. Atty. Gen.
Bank, H. Randy ....'56 '84 C.385 B.A. L.608 J.D. [Bricker&E.]
Bankovich, Candace A. ....'— '96 C.419 B.A. L.345 J.D. [Ⓐ Jones D.]
Banvard, Kris .... '57 '03 C.629 B.A. L.179 J.D. [Ⓐ Zeiger,T.&L.]

Baran, Piper, Tarkowsky, Fitzgerald & Theis Co., L.P.A., (AV)
6877 North High Street, Suite 105, 43085 ⊙
Telephone: 614-436-0539 Fax: 614-436-1713
URL: http://www.baranlaw.com

(This Listing Continued)

Baran, Piper, Tarkowsky, Fitzgerald & Theis Co., L.P.A. (Continued)
John Tarkowsky.
General Civil Practice. Trials in all Courts. Insurance Defense, Corporate, Family Law, Estate Planning, Personal Injury, Products Liability and Construction Law. Commercial Litigation. Suretyship. Environmental and Governmental Liability. Professional Liability, Worker's Compensation.
See Professional Biographies, COLUMBUS, OHIO

Baranowski, Edwin M., (AV) '47 '72 C.299 B.A. L.893 J.D. [Porter W.M.&A.] (See Pat. Sect.)
Barath, William J., (AV) '60 '87 C.347 B.A. L.879 J.D. [Schottenstein,Z.&D.]
Barb, Donald E. '47 '74 C&L.608 B.A., J.D. Grange Mut. Cas. Co.

Barbanel, Roberta J. '58 '85 C.1036 B.A. L.421 J.D.
1799 W. 5th Avenue, Suite 143, 43212
Telephone: 614-221-5824 Fax: 614-621-9109
Commercial Real Estate, Commercial Leasing, Corporate Law, LLC, Contracts, Business Litigation, Contract Disputes, Real Estate, Buying and Selling a House, Residential Real Estate Closings.
See Professional Biographies, COLUMBUS, OHIO

Barber, Barbara L. '62 '97 C.973 B.S.B.A. L.1340 J.D. Asst. Atty. Gen.
Barbin, Bradley D., (AV) '57 '83 C.682 B.A. L.8 J.D. [Maguire&S.]
Barclay, Craig D., (AV) '48 '73 C&L.608 B.S., J.D. [Wolske&B.]
Bardash, James T. '69 '97 C.610 B.A. L.117 J.D. John Hancock Fin. Servs., Sig. Fin Netwk.
Barkan, Irving, (BV) '22 '57 C.309 A.B. L.608 J.D. [Barkan&B.]
Barkan, Irwin W. '16 '48 C.608 B.A. L.309 LL.B. 743 South Front Street‡
Barkan, Neal J., (BV) '53 '78 C.910 A.B. L.273 J.D. [Barkan&B.]
Barkan & Barkan Co., L.P.A., (BV) 150 East State Street
Barkan & Neff, A Legal Professional Association, (AV) 360 S. Grant Ave. (⊙New Orleans, LA)
Barker, Larry D., (BV) '48 '74 C.608 B.S. L.117 J.D. [Innis&B.]
Barley, Christopher E. '62 '93 C.150 B.A. L.117 J.D. Hearing Offr., Dept. of Human Servs.
Barley-McBride, Mary, (BV) '61 '86 C.608 B.A. L.851 J.D. [Lane,A.&H.]
Barnes, Belinda S., (AV) '63 '87 C&L.608 B.S., J.D. [Lane,A.&H.]
Barnes, James A., (BV) '59 '85 C.381 B.A. L.161 J.D. Atty. Gen.
Barnes, Jenny C. '63 '94 C.473 B.S. L.607 J.D. Sr. Coun.-Trans., Amer. Elect. Power Serv. Corp.
Barnes, Thomas E., (BV) '54 '78 C&L.608 B.A., J.D. Assoc. V.P., Assoc. Gen. Coun. & Asst. Secy., Nationwide Insurance
Barnes, Wallace R. '28 '58 C.228 A.B. L.309 LL.B. 200 Civic Ctr. Dr.
Barnett, Eric R. '— '99 C.597 B.S. L.813 J.D. [🄰 Baker&H.]
Barnett, Robert B., Jr., (AV) '49 '75 C&L.608 B.S., J.D. [Carlile P.&M.]
Barnett, Valerie T. '— '99 C.112 B.A. L.188 J.D. [🄰 Schottenstein,Z.&D.]
Barnhart, David B., (AV) '56 '81 C.935 B.A. L.117 J.D. [🄰 P.J.Fulton]
Barnhart, Richard A., (AV) '53 '79 C.980 B.S.B.A. L.608 J.D. [Schottenstein,Z.&D.]
Barno, John C. '68 '94 C.313 B.A. L.608 J.D. [Lane,A.&H.]
Barnum, Carol Lee '51 '77 C&L.608 B.A., J.D. State Div. of Securities
Barone, Joseph J., (AV) '49 '75 C.528 B.S.B.A. L.117 J.D. [Magnuson&B.]
Barone, Juliane Elizabeth '74 '01 C.201 B.A. L.608 J.D. OH Atty. Gen.'s Off.

Barren & Merry Co., L.P.A.
(See Westerville)

Barrett, Mark J. '49 '82 C.640 B.A. L.117 J.D. Chief Dep., Co. Sheriff's Dept.
Barrett, Phillip H., (AV) '43 '68 C&L.608 B.S., J.D. [Porter W.M.&A.]
Barron, John W. '— '01 C&L.608 B.A., J.D. Governor's Office
Barrows, Ted, (BV) '47 '76 C.67 B.A. L.608 J.D. Asst. Atty. Gen.
Barrymore, T. Jay, (AVⓉ) '56 '83 C&L.477 B.G.S., J.D. Coun., Columbia Energy Group Serv. Corp.
Barsotti, Stephen C. '76 '02 C.896 B.S. L.608 J.D. [🄰 Kegler,B.H.&R.]
Barstow, Todd W. '62 '91 C.902 B.A. L.117 J.D. 4185 E. Main St.
Bartemes, Amy Straker '68 '93 C.679 B.A. L.880 J.D. [🄰 Bricker&E.]
Bartholomew, Kirsten L. '— '04 C.608 B.A. L.117 J.D. [🄰 Baker&H.]
Bartholomew, Milton S. '29 '54 C&L.608 B.S., J.D. 1424 Clubview Blvd., S.‡
Bartlett, Keith T., (BV) '49 '81 C&L.608 B.A., J.D. Asst. Adm. Dir., Supm. Ct.
Bartley, John P. '54 '87 C.754 B.S. L.608 J.D. Asst. Atty. Gen.
Barwell, Gregory P. '70 '99 L.607 J.D. [🄱 Rich,C.&D.]
Basil, Brian A. '69 '95 C&L.608 B.S., J.D. [Murray M.M.&B.]
Basnett, Jeffrey M. '56 '91 C.329 B.A. L.608 J.D. 282 Woodland Ave.
Bass, Leon D. '72 '98 C.475 B.A. L.608 J.D. [🄱 Rich,C.&D.]
Bates, John H. '62 '93 C&L.117 B.A., J.D. 495 S. High St., Ste. 400
Bathija, Priya J. '— '04 C&L.608 B.S.B.A., J.D. [🄰 Buckingham,D.&B.]
Batke, Gary S., (AV) '59 '85 C.238 B.S. L.1119 J.D. [Bailey C.]
Batross, Martin Earl '40 '77 C.608 B.S. L.117 J.D. 201 S. Grant Avenue
Battisti, Eugene F., Jr. '61 '87 C.665 B.A. L.117 J.D. 987 S. High Street
Battisti, Linda Maria '53 '79 C.699 B.A. L.161 J.D. Atty. Gen.'s Off.

Bauernschmidt, Karen H., Co., LPA
(See Cleveland)

Baughman, Scott E. '67 '92 C.608 B.A. L.851 J.D. [Porter W.M.&A.]
Baum, James L. '49 '89 C.376 B.S. L.117 J.D. [🄰 Karr&S.]
Baumann, Mary Elisabeth (Lisa) '72 '99 C.741 B.A. L.608 J.D. [🄰 Purcell&S.]
Baumgarten, Marc T. '61 '86 C.477 B.A. L.608 J.D. Dep. Legal Coun., Dept. of Mental Health Legal Servs. Off.
Baumwell, Howard E. '56 '85 C.608 B.S.Ed L.607 J.D. 211 E. Livingston Avenue
Baxter, Martha Post, (BV) '50 '82 C.608 B.S. L.692 J.D. [Bricker&E.]
Baxter, Thomas E., (AV) '47 '74 C.608 B.A. L.117 J.D. 150 W. Wilson Bdge. Rd., Ste. 101
Bay, John A. '51 '80 C.608 B.S. L.117 J.D. 3012 Spruceview Ct.,N.
Beachler, Jinx Statler '53 '79 C.473 B.A. L.607 J.D. [Bidwell&B.]
Beagle, Peter F. J., (BV) '49 '78 C.867 B.A. L.117 J.D. 412 S. Yearling Rd.
Beal, Thomas D., (AV) '50 '75 C&L.117 B.A., J.D. 755 South High Street
Beale, Jennifer E. '— '01 C.608 B.S.B.A. L.117 J.D. [🄰 Porter W.M.&A.]
Beale, Victoria F. '72 '04 C.999 b.a. L.179 J.D. Training Academy Prog. Dir.
Beals, David A., (BV) '43 '87 C.273 B.A. L.117 J.D. [Lamkin,V.T.B.&D.]
Beard, Douglas M. '74 '01 C.610 B.S.J. L.608 J.D. [🄰 Alber C.]
Beatley, James R., Jr., (AV) '41 '65 C&L.608 B.A., J.D. [Vorys,S.S.&P.]
Beattey, Robert A. '74 '03 C.178 B.A. L.608 J.D. [🄰 McTigue L.]
Beatty, Laurel A. '74 '99 C.811 B.A. L.880 J.D. 233 S. High St., Ste. 300
Beatty, Otto, III '69 '94 C.511 B.A. L.477 J.D. [Baker&H.]
Beatty, Patrick William '66 '92 C.424 B.A. L.150 J.D. 30 E. Broad St., 31st Fl.
Beauchamp, Sarah Hubard '53 '86 C&L.608 B.A., J.D. 118 E. Main St.
Beausay, T. Jeffery, (BV) '— '87 C.608 B.A. L.851 J.D. [🄰 Twyford&D.]
Beaver, W. Ronald, (BV) '41 '73 C.603 B.A. L.117 J.D. 1620 Penworth Dr.
Beavers, John P., (AV) '47 '72 C&L.608 B.A., J.D. [Bricker&E.]
Bechtold, Timothy J. '50 '78 C.973 B.S. L.608 J.D. [🄰 Vorys,S.S.&P.]
Beck, Bethany A. '48 '77 C.608 B.A. L.117 J.D. Sr. V.P. & Gen. Coun., Pharmacia Inc.
Beck, David A. '— '00 C.385 B.A. L.893 J.D. [🄰 Jones D.]
Beck, Jonathan P., (BV) '56 '81 C.354 B.S. L.201 J.D. [🄱 Vorys,S.S.&P.]
Beck, Robert James, Jr. '73 '98 C.610 B.S.C. L.7 J.D. Atty. Franklin Co. Pub. Def. Off.
Beck, Stacey L., Attorney at Law '70 '00 C&L.608 B.A., J.D. 600 S. High St., Ste. 203
Becker, Michael R., (AV) '45 '71 C.610 B.S. L.575 J.D. [Becker&L.]
Becker, William C., (AV) '56 '81 C.477 B.G.S. L.201 J.D. Asst. Atty. Gen.
Becker & Lilly, (AV) 100 E. Broad St., Ste. 2320
Beckett, Donald L., (AV) '31 '57 C.313 A.B. L.608 J.D. [🄱 Porter W.M.&A.] (⊙Columbus)
Beckett, Donald L., (AV) '31 '57 C.313 A.B. L.608 J.D. [Robins,P.B.H.&S.] (⊙Columbus)
Bedell, Melissa Hand '71 '96 C.967 B.A. L.201 J.D. Co. Pub. Def.
Beebe, David K. '45 '75 C.608 B.A. L.117 J.D. V.P. & Mgr., Estate Planning Dept., Natl. City Corp.
Beekhuizen, Michael N. '69 '95 C.604 B.A. L.608 J.D. [🄱 Carpenter&L.]
Beeler, Jill Elizabeth '72 '98 C.608 B.A. L.179 J.D. Pub. Def. Comm.
Beeler, John C., (AV) '51 '76 C.197 A.B. L.228 J.D. [Porter W.M.&A.]
Beery, Eric W. '63 '96 C.879 B.S. L.1187 J.D. [Beery&S.]

Beery & Spurlock Co., L.P.A., (AV) 🄱🄱
275 East State Street, 43215
Telephone: 614-228-8575 FAX: 614-228-1408
Email: law@beeryspurlock.com URL: http://www.beeryspurlock.com
Paul F. Beery (1931-2002); Michael Spurlock; Eric W. Beery.
Transportation Law, Administrative Law, Litigation, Business Law, Corporate Law, Antitrust and Trade Regulation, Labor and Employment, Taxation, Workers Compensation, Environmental Law, Business Litigation.
Reference: Bank One of Columbus, N.A.
See Professional Biographies, COLUMBUS, OHIO

Beggs, Robert J. '47 '76 C.645 B.A. L.228 J.D. Pres., Fleetwood Management
Behal, Robert J., (AV) '53 '77 C&L.608 B.A., J.D. [Connor B.]
Beldy, Michael D. '47 '97 C.415 B.A. L.8 J.D. Coun., Nationwide Insurance
Belenker, Rachel Lisa '57 '81 C.446 B.A. L.607 J.D. OH Dept. of Health
Belinky, David A., (AV) '50 '77 C.610 B.S. L.607 J.D. 326 South High Street Suite 300
Belinky, Debra Manson '52 '78 C.608 B.S.E. L.117 J.D. Dept. of Mental Health
Bell, Albert J., (AV) '60 '85 C.608 B.A. L.117 J.D. Exec. V.P., Gen. Coun. & Secy., Consolidated Stores Corp.
Bell, Anker M., (AV) '53 '82 C.608 B.A. L.477 J.D. [Vorys,S.S.&P.]
Bell, Jessica '76 '02 C.967 B.A. L.608 J.D. [🄰 Perez&M.]
Bell, Langdon D., (AV) '39 '63 C.473 B.A. L.608 J.D. [Bell,R.&S.]
Bell, Robert A., (AV) '25 '56 C.608 B.S. L.266 J.D. 5757 Bastille Pl.‡
Bell, Robert A., Jr. '— '00 C.473 B.S. L.201 J.D. [🄰 Vorys,S.S.&P.]
Bell, Sandra F. '53 '86 C.999 B.A. L.8 J.D. Dist. Hearing Offr., Indus. Comm.

Bell, Royer & Sanders Co., L.P.A., (AV)
33 South Grant Avenue, 43215-3900
Telephone: 614-228-0704 FAX: 614-228-0201
Langdon D. Bell; Barth E. Royer; Judith B. Sanders.
General Civil Trial and Appellate Practice. Utilities, Taxation, Telecommunications, Municipal, Corporation, Motor Carrier, Environmental, Labor and Administrative Law.
Reference: The Huntington National Bank.
See Professional Biographies, COLUMBUS, OHIO

Belli, Dennis C., (AV) '54 '79 C.363 B.S. L.117 J.D. 844 S. Front St. (Pat.)
Bellman, Daniel A. '55 '80 C.201 B.A. L.150 J.D. 320 North Pearl Street
Belo, Vladimir P. '71 '97 C.112 B.A. L.1065 J.D. [🄰 Bricker&E.]
Belskis, Lawrence A. '46 '75 C.436 B.S. L.117 J.D. 373 S. High St., 22nd Fl.

Belton, John T., (AV) '47 '77 C.608 B.A. L.607 J.D.
2066 W. Henderson Road, Suite 102, 43220
Telephone: 614-457-2034 Fax: 614-457-0311
Email: Beltonlaw@aol.com
Civil Practice, Trial Practice, Criminal Law, Federal Criminal Law, Criminal Defense, Personal Injury, Driving While Intoxicated, Domestic Relations, Real Estate, Construction Litigation.
See Professional Biographies, COLUMBUS, OHIO

Belville, Barbara A., (BV) '57 '80 C.611 B.A. L.608 J.D. Asst Gen. Coun.-Litig., Amer. Elec. Power Serv. Corp.
Benbow, Brian W. '74 '99 C.1265 B.B.A. L.179 J.D. Jud. Staff Atty.
Bender, John F. '46 '71 C&L.608 B.A., J.D. Com. Pleas J.
Bendig, Charles H., (BV) '50 '75 C.608 B.S. L.228 J.D. [Wilcox,S.&B.]
Benedict, Spencer R. '48 '76 C.608 B.A. L.150 J.D. 400 S. Fifth St.

Benesch, Friedlander, Coplan & Aronoff LLP, (AV)
88 East Broad Street Suite 900, 43215-3506 ⊙
Telephone: 614-223-9300 Facsimile: 614-223-9330
URL: http://www.bfca.com
Members of Firm: Marc S. Blubaugh; Frank W. Carsonie; Orla Ellis Collier, III; Janet K. Feldkamp; N. Victor Goodman; C. David Paragas; Roger L. Schantz; John F. Stock; Mark D. Tucker; Thomas C. Washbush. Associates: Lyle B. Brown; J. Allen Jones, III; Donald M. Keller; Benjamen E. Kern; Jennifer M. Turk; Gary G. Yashko. Of Counsel: James F. DeLeone; Ronald L. House; Frank J. Reed, Jr.; Martha J. Sweterlitsch.
Bankruptcy, Bankruptcy Reorganization, Banks and Banking, Business Law, Casino and Gambling, Class Actions, Collections, Commercial Law, Commercial Real Estate, Complex and Multi-District Litigation, Construction Law, Consumer Law, Contracts, Copyrights, Corporate Law, Debtor and Creditor, Election Campaign and Political Law, Electronic Commerce, Employee Benefits, Environmental Law, Finance, Health Care, Immigration Law, Intellectual Property, Internet and Technology, Labor and Employment, Leases and Leasing, Mergers, Acquisitions, Divestitures, Mortgages, Patent, Probate, Product Liability, Real Estate, Resort and Leisure, Securities, Taxation, Trademarks, Transportation, Trusts and Estates, Wills, Workers Compensation, Zoning, Planning and Land Use.
Cleveland, Ohio Office: 2300 BP Tower, 200 Public Square, 44114-2378. Telephone: 216-363-4500. Facsimile: 216-363-4588.
See Professional Biographies, COLUMBUS, OHIO

Benis, Stuart A. '33 '71 C.608 B.S. L.117 J.D. 326 E. High St.
Benjamin, Robert V. '24 '51 C.434 A.B. L.930 LL.B. 200 Civic Ctr. Dr.‡
Bennett, Brad E. '73 '03 C.610 B.S. L.117 J.D. [🄰 Kennedy R.&K.]
Bennington, Jeffrey Roger '68 '00 City Atty.'s Off.

Benson, Michael E. '69 '97 C.8 B.A. L.117 J.D.
109 Town Street, 43230
Telephone: 614-418-4740 Fax: 614-418-5045
Email: mb007@columbus.rr.com URL: http://www.michaelbensonlaw.com
Bankruptcy Law, Foreclosures, Debtor and Creditor, Real Estate, Landlord and Tenant, Buying and Selling, Wills, Living Wills, Healthcare, Powers of Attorney.
See Professional Biographies, COLUMBUS, OHIO

Benson, William B., (AV) '65 '90 C.473 B.A. L.117 J.D. [Wiles,B.B.&B.]
Bentine, John W., (AV) '47 '75 C.437 B.B.A. L.608 J.D. [Chester,W.&S.]
Benton, Frederick D., Jr., (BV) '54 '80 C.728 B.A. L.117 J.D. [F.D.Benton,Jr.]
Benton, Shannon K. '75 '00 C&L.608 B.A., J.D. [🄰 Brenner,B.G.&M.]
Benton, Frederick D., Jr., LPA, (BV) 786 South Front Street
Benyo, Steven J. '64 '89 C.608 B.A. L.1003 J.D. Off. of Atty. Gen.
Berendsen, James R. '42 '71 C.610 B.B.A. L.117 J.D. [🄰 Bricker&E.]
Berg, John R. '44 '92 C.967 B.A. L.117 J.D. Claims Atty., Grange Mut. Cas. Co.

Berger, Lisa J. '70 '98 C.674 A.B. L.608 J.D. [Ⓐ Kayne]
Berger, Robert Ray, Jr. '64 '95 C.608 B.S. L.179 J.D. Co. CSEA
Bergman, Andrew S., (BV) '57 '86 C.293 B.A. L.494 J.D. [Ⓒ Porter W.M.&A.]
Bergman, Robert D., (BV) '44 '70 C.608 B.A. L.117 J.D. [Bergman&Y.]
Bergman & Yiangou, (BV) 3099 Sullivant Avenue
Bergmann, David Cleveland '49 '75 C.475 B.A. L.477 J.D. OH Consumers Coun.
Berkemer, Frederick L., (BV) '48 '77 C.608 B.A. L.117 J.D. [F.L.Berkemer]
Berkemer, Frederick L., & Co., LPA, (BV) 79 North Wilson Boulevard
Berkemeyer, Thomas G. '61 '86 C.880 B.A. L.150 J.D.
Assoc. Gen. Coun.-Fin. & Compl., Amer. Elec. Power Serv. Corp.
Berliner, Alan F., (AV) '51 '76 C.930 B.A. L.608 J.D. [Thompson H.]
Bernard, Robert M., (BV) '53 '79 C&L.608 B.A., J.D. Asst. Pub. Def.
Berndt, Ellen German, (BV) '53 '84
C.207 B.S. L.117 J.D. Borden, Inc. (Legal Department)
Berner, Michael G. '78 '03 C.732 B.A. L.823 J.D. [Ⓐ Vorys,S.S.&P.]
Bernert, Edward J., (AV) '52 '77 C.607 B.A. L.608 J.D. [Baker&H.]
Bernhard, George K., Jr. '24 '63 C.976 B.A. L.266 LL.B. 1251 Nantucket Ave.‡
Berridge, Thomas E. '46 '72
C.608 B.S. L.117 J.D. Asst. Gen. Coun., Nationwide Insurance
Berry, Carole C. '43 '70 C.475 B.S. L.608 J.D. Prof. of Law, Capital Univ.
Bersani, James L. '58 '85 C&L.823 B.S., J.D.
(adm. in NY; not adm. in OH) V.P., The Limited Inc.
Bertram, William Charles '50 '82 C.923 B.S. L.922 J.D. Sr. V.P., AON Consulting
Besser, Kenneth R. '59 '90 C.484 B.S. L.836 J.D. 4850 E. Main St.
Bessey, John P. '37 '66 C.608 B.S. L.266 J.D. Com. Pleas J.
Bethel, Blythe M., (BV) '57 '84 C.197 B.A. L.117 J.D. 400 S. 5th St.
Betsacon, Nicholas J. '49 '80 C.608 B.A. L.117 J.D. Asst. Atty. Gen.
Bettendorf, Margaret C. '70 '97 C.436 B.A. L.608 J.D. [Ⓐ Littler M.]
Bettis, J. Warren '24 '52 C.151 B.S.C. L.1340 LL.B. ODC
Beytagh, Francis X., Jr. '35 '64 C.602 B.A. L.477 J.D. Prof. of Law, Ohio State Univ.
Bhalla, Nivita '74 '00 C.608 B.B.A. L.365 J.D. [Ⓐ Maguire&S.]
Bhatt, Sanjay K. '66 '94 C.608 B.A.B.S. L.117 J.D. 300 S. 2nd St., 2nd Fl.
Bialczak, Stanley T., (BV) '59 '84 C.608 B.A. L.150 J.D. Atty. Supr., Dept. of Taxation
Bibart, Richard L., (AV) '42 '67 C&L.309 B.A., J.D. [Ⓒ Carlile P.&M.]
Bibbo, Jeffrey R., (BV) '64 '91 C.608 B.S.B.A. L.117 J.D. [Lyons&B.]
Bidwell, David, (BV) '53 '80 C.608 B.S. L.188 J.D. [Bidwell&B.]
Bidwell & Beachler Co., L.P.A., (BV) 865 Bryden Rd.
Biehl, Adam J. '69 '95 C.611 B.A. L.608 J.D. [Ⓐ Bailey C.]
Bielby, Jeanine Loehr '62 '87 C.715 B.A. L.228 J.D. V.P., Natl. City Corp.
Billings, James Russell '66 '93 C.431 B.A. L.607 J.D. [Zacks]
Bills, Joshua R. '73 '99 C.473 B.A. L.851 J.D. [Lane,A.&H.]
Binau, Dan J., (AV) '50 '76 C.608 B.S. L.117 J.D. [Harris,M.B.&C.]
Binkovitz, David J. '53 '78 C.473 B.A. L.851 J.D.
Litigation Mgr., State Industrial Comm.
Binning, J. Boyd, (AV) '44 '75 C.1112 B.S. L.607 J.D. 592 South Third Street
Birath, John F., Jr., (AV) '46 '71 C.473 B.A. L.910 J.D. [Bricker&E.]
Birden, Paul B., Jr. '49 '82 C.659 A.B. L.178 J.D.
(adm. in PA; not adm. in OH) 2720 Airport Drive, Suite 100
Birkhimer, William R., (AV) '24 '53 C&L.266 B.S., J.D. 1590 Noe-Bixby Rd.‡
Birrer, Scott B. '67 '94 C.608 B.A. L.221 J.D. [Swedlow,B.L.M.&D.]
Bissell, Barry S. '47 '74 C.339 B.S. L.93 J.D.
(adm. in NY; not adm. in OH; Pat.) Asst. Intell. Prop. Coun., Battelle Memorial Institute
Bittner, Paul L., (AV) '68 '93 C.117 B.A. L.608 J.D. [Schottenstein,Z.&D.]
Bivens, Gina S. '74 '99 C.967 B.A. L.608 J.D.
Coun.-Trans., Amer. Electric Power Serv. Corp.
Bjerke, Jack A., (AV) '45 '70 C.967 B.S. L.930 J.D. [Baker&H.]
Black, Christopher G. '— '97 C&L.117 B.A., J.D. [Ⓐ Maguire&S.]
Black, David Richard '75 '01 C.631 B.S. L.608 J.D. Legal Aid Society of Columbus
Black, Lori Anne, (BV) '65 '90 C.473 B.A. L.608 J.D. 172 E. State Street
Black, Robert N., Jr. '50 '75 C.477 B.A. L.608 J.D. 361 Indian Mound Rd.
Blackburn, John David '49 '74 C.346 B.S. L.150 J.D. 220 Winthrop Rd.
Blackburn, Thomas I., (AV) '— '79 C&L.608 B.S., J.D. [Buckley K.]
Blackman, Gordon A. '47 '75 C.932 B.A. L.117 J.D.
Staff Atty., Litig. Coun., American Commerce Insurance Company
Blackmore, Margaret L., (AV) '51 '81 C.608 B.S. L.117 J.D. [Tyack,B.&L.]
Blaine, William E., Jr. '24 '52 C.95 B.A. L.608 LL.B. 2929 Kenny Rd.
Blair, Adrianne May '36 '78 C.4 B.A. L.724 J.D. Asst. Atty. Gen.
Blair, Roger Sobel '43 '68 C.604 B.A. L.851 J.D. First Community Bank
Blake, Curtis Richard '63 '89 C.473 B.A. L.117 J.D. 2130 Arlington Ave.
Blake, Richard H. '60 '88 C.999 B.B.A. L.724 J.D.
(adm. in CT; not adm. in OH) U.S. Dept. of Jus.
Blakemore, Trina L. '71 '96 C.97 B.S. L.608 J.D. E.P.A.
Blanda, John J. '34 '70 C.999 B.S. L.117 J.D. Coun., Battelle Memorial Institute‡
Blaser, Jennifer R., (CV) '73 '99 C.610 B.A. L.608 J.D. [Ⓐ Peck,S.&W.]
Blaugrund, Herbert & Martin, Incorporated
(See Dublin)
Blocher, Janet George '58 '85 C.607 B.A. L.117 J.D. Capital Univ. Law School
Bloom, Theodore S., (BV) '55 '80 C.94 B.A. L.608 J.D. Baker Rental Co.
Bloomfield, David S., (AV) '44 '69 C&L.608 B.S., J.D. 199 S. 5th St.
Bloomfield, David S., Jr. '72 '97 C.311 B.A. L.608 J.D. [Ⓐ Porter W.M.&A.]
Bloomfield, Sally W., (AV) '43 '69 C.734 B.A. L.608 J.D. [Bricker&E.]
Blubaugh, Marc S. '71 '97 C.930 B.A. L.608 J.D. [Benesch,F.C.&A.]
Blue, Douglas J., (BV) '66 '92 C.967 B.A. L.1194 J.D. [Blue,W.&B.]
Blue, Jason A., (AV) '39 '64 C&L.608 B.S., J.D. [Blue,W.&B.]
Blue, Warren G. '26 '55 C&L.608 B.S., LL.B. Coun., R.E. Harrington

Blue, Wilson & Blue, L.L.C., (AV)
471 East Broad Street, Suite 1100, 43215
Telephone: 614-224-6969 Toll Free: 1-877-543-BLUE (2583) Fax: 614-224-6999 URL: http://www.bluewilsonbluelaw.com
Email: mailbox@bluewilsonbluelaw.com URL: http://www.lawyers.com/bwblaw
Jason A. Blue; Mark R. Wilson; Douglas J. Blue.
Medical and Dental Malpractice, Personal Injury and Products Liability Law, Wrongful Death, Automobile Accidents, Industrial Accidents, Airplane Crash Litigation, Nursing Home Litigation, Automobile Insurance. Civil and Appellate Practice in State and Federal Courts.
Reference: Bank One of Columbus, N.A.
See Professional Biographies, COLUMBUS, OHIO

Blum, Charles J., (BV) '37 '66 C.608 B.A. L.266 J.D. 52 W. Whittier St.
Blum, Laurel D. '56 '82 C.930 B.A. L.851 J.D. Asst. Atty. Gen.
Blumenstiel, James B., (AV) '42 '67 C.473 B.S. L.608 J.D. [Blumenstiel,H.&A.]
Blumenstiel, Huhn & Adams, LLC, (AV) 261 West Johnstown Road
Blumenthal, Kenneth S., (AV) '51 '83 C.434 B.A. L.117 J.D. [Rourke&B.]
Bluth, William H. '45 '69 C.563 B.A. L.93 J.D. Prof. of Law, Capital Univ.
Boatright, Douglas Craig, (BV) '57 '89 C&L.8 B.S.B.A., J.D. [Isaac,B.L.&T.]
Bobbitt, L. Christopher '65 '93 C.80 B.A. L.608 J.D. [Ⓐ Sanborn,B.D.&B.]
Boda, Daniel K., (AV) '49 '75 C.49 B.A. L.608 J.D. [Mitchell,A.C.&B.]
Bodiker, David H., (AV) '34 '63 C.309 B.A. L.608 J.D. Pub. Def.
Bodine, J. Joseph, Jr. '63 '89 C.569 B.F.A. L.117 J.D. 8 E. Long St.
Boeckman, Joseph P. '59 '87 C.150 B.B.A. L.608 J.D. [Baker&H.]
Boggs, Kelly A. '70 '98 C.608 B.A. L.209 J.D. [Ⓢ Vorys,S.S.&P.]
Boggs, Kenneth R. '55 '80 C.610 B.A. L.608 J.D. 1170 Old Henderson Road
Boggs, Patrick H., (AV) '— '85 C.602 B.B.A. L.117 J.D. [Onda,L.&R.]
Boggs, Theodore A., (AV) '55 '86 C.97 B.S. L.117 J.D. [Ⓒ Vorys,S.S.&P.]
Bojko, Andrew M. '70 '98 C.674 A.B. L.602 J.D. [Ⓐ Porter W.M.&A.]
Bolognone, Angela M. '67 '97 C.117 B.A. L.608 J.D. Off. of Co. Pros.
Bolon, Gordon K., (AV) '27 '53 C&L.608 B.A., J.D. 175 S. 3rd St.
Bolon, Thomas M., (AV) '33 '64 C.390 B.A. L.608 J.D. [Ⓒ Carlile P.&M.]
Bolon, Thomas M., Jr., (BV) '61 '91 C&L.608 B.A., J.D. 2513 E. Main St.
Bolon, William Thomas '47 '88 C.608 B.A. L.179 J.D. Def. Dept.
Bolyard, Beth C. '74 '01 C.607 B.A. L.117 J.D. [Ⓐ Squire,S.&D.]
Bonasera, Michael D. '75 '03 C.610 B.S. L.179 J.D. [Ⓐ Buckingham,D.&B.]
Bonasera, Thomas J., (AV) '48 '75 C.608 B.S. L.117 J.D. [Buckingham,D.&B.]
Bonaventura, Mark G., (BV) '52 '79 C.608 B.S. L.117 J.D. Asst. Atty. Gen.
Bondy, Melissa C. '71 '96 C.608 B.A. L.602 J.D. [Ⓐ Scott,S.&W.]
Booker, James D. '33 '61 C&L.608 J.D. Admin. Law J., Soc. Sec. Admn.
Boone, Timothy J., (AV) '47 '76 C.608 B.S. L.117 J.D. [Boone,S.&Assoc.]
Boone, Smith & Associates, LLC, (AV) 1349 East Broad Street, 2nd Floor
Booth, Sandra E., (BV) '51 '79 C.608 B.A. L.117 J.D. 3620 N. High St.
Born, Michael E., (BV) '63 '88 C.1265 B.S. L.477 J.D. [Shumaker,L.&K.]
Bornstein, Michael D. '63 '89 C.608 B.S. L.910 J.D. [Bornstein]
Bornstein Law Offices 580 South High Street, 3rd Floor
Borowicz, Stacey Garber '70 '03 C.608 B.S. L.117 J.D. [Ⓐ Porter W.M.&A.]
Borromeo, Alvin A. '66 '96 C.477 B.S. L.117 J.D. [Ⓐ Mallory&T.] (Pat.)
Bosley, David Joseph, (BV) '53 '78 C.610 B.B.A. L.117 J.D. Asst. U.S. Atty.
Bostos, Stephanie R. '65 '93 C.49 B.S.B.A. L.117 J.D. 500 S. Front St., Ste. 1200
Bott, April R. '72 '96 C.980 B.A. L.608 J.D. [Chester,W.&S.]
Botti, James P., (AV) '56 '82 C&L.608 B.A., J.D. [Porter W.M.&A.]
Bourne, Philip J. '22 '50 C&L.930 B.B.A., J.D. Sr. Claims Coun., PIE Mut. Ins. Co.
Bour-Stokes, Joann M., (BV) '61 '86 C.608 B.A. L.8 J.D. Asst. State Pub. Def.
Bowen, John W.E., IV '54 '80 C.802 B.B.A. L.178 J.D.
(adm. in NY; not adm. in OH) 2720 Airport Drive, Suite 100
Bower, Amelia, (AV) '54 '84 C.473 B.A. L.1003 J.D. [Plunkett&C.]
Bower, Eileen R. '65 '95 C&L.999 B.A., J.D. [Ⓐ Crabbe,B.&J.]
Bowers, Brenda K., (BV) '64 '90 C.607 B.A. L.608 J.D. [Ⓢ Vorys,S.S.&P.]
Bowers, John S., (BV) '22 '58 C.608 B.A. L.266 J.D. 720 S. High St.
Bowman, J. Scott '70 '98 C&L.608 B.S., J.D. [Ⓐ Plymale]
Bowman, Katharine B., (AV) '58 '83 C.608 B.A. L.477 J.D. [Bailey C.]
Bownas, James H., (AV) '47 '71 C.973 B.S. L.309 J.D. [Gamble H.J.]
Bowshier, Denis Jay '53 '90 C&L.608 B.A., J.D. 145 S. Front St.
Boyd, Alan B. '46 '74 C&L.608 B.A. I.R.S.
Boyd, James W., Sr. '28 '73 C.935 B.A. L.1003 J.D. 6090 Ashtree Pl.‡
Boyd, Jeffrey D., (AV) '57 '82 C.381 B.A. L.608 J.D. [Boyd]
Boyd, Robert E., III, (AV) '51 '79 C.610 B.G.S. L.251 J.D. [Ⓐ Onda,L.&R.]
Boyd, Robert E., Jr., (AV) '26 '52 C&L.608 B.A., J.D. [Boyd&B.]
Boyd, Sally W. '39 '81 C.207 B.A. L.117 J.D. Mag., Co. Dom. Ct., Juv. Div.
Boyd, Tracie Malinda '69 '98 C.1302 B.S. L.8 J.D. Asst. Pros. Atty.
Boyd & Boyd Co., L.P.A., (AV) 673 Mohawk Street
The Boyd Law Firm, (AV) 7792 Olentangy River Rd., Ste. K
Boyer, John N. '74 '00 C.188 B.S. L.1565 J.D. [Ⓐ Vorys,S.S.&P.]
Boyer, Mary Devitt '66 '91 C&L.608 B.S.N., J.D. Law Clk., Com. Pleas J.
Boyle, Kerry T. '73 '00 C.610 B.S. L.179 J.D. [Ⓐ Wiles,B.B.&B.]

Boyle, Sean O. '61 '88 C.608 B.A. L.117 J.D.
580 South High Street Suite 200, 43215-5644
Telephone: 614-457-7219 Fax: 614-538-2905
Email: sboyle@macb-law.com URL: http://www.lawyers.com/seanboyle
State and Federal Criminal Defense, Felonies and Misdemeanors, Juvenile Law.
See Professional Biographies, COLUMBUS, OHIO

Boyle, Thomas E., (AV) '47 '72 C&L.608 B.S., J.D. [Wiles,B.B.&B.]
Boyuk, Walter C., (BV) '43 '68 C.381 B.A. L.608 J.D. 34 W. Whittier St.
Bradigan, Brian J., (AV) '51 '81 C.294 B.A. L.117 J.D. [B.J.Bradigan]
Bradigan, Brian J., LLC, (AV) 3948 Townsfair Way, Suite 230
Bradley, Philip R., (BV) '24 '50 C&L.608 LL.B. 1620 E. Broad St.
Brady, John E., (AV) '45 '70 C.608 B.S. L.150 J.D. [Porter W.M.&A.]
Brady, Philip L. '45 '72 C&L.150 B.B.A., J.D.
Reg. Litig. Coun., Defense Logistics Agcy.
Brahm, Richard C., (AV) '45 '70 C&L.150 B.S., J.D. [Plank&B.] (Pat.)
Brainard, Thomas D. '54 '85 C.477 B.S. L.912 J.D.
(adm. in MI; not adm. in OH; Pat.) Sr. Coun., Abbott Labs.
Brandt, Adam K. '70 '96 C.951 B.A. L.608 J.D. [Vorys,S.S.&P.]
Brannock, Keith W., (AV) '25 '57 C.608 B.S. L.266 J.D. [K.W.Brannock]
Brannock, Keith W. Co., L.P.A., (AV) 1550 Old W. Henderson Rd.
Brant, Charles E., (AV) '30 '59 C.201 B.A. L.608 J.D. [Isaac,B.L.&T.]
Brant, Marjorie H. '47 '83 C.651 B.A. L.608 J.D.
Gen. Mgr., Shared Legal Svcs., Columbia Gas Distribution Cos.
Brantner, Jeffrey W., (BV) '46 '74 C.608 B.S.B.A. L.117 J.D. [Rance,P.B.K.&E.]
Brault, Eva Marie '72 '98 C.207 B.A. L.201 J.D. Atty. Gen. Off.
Braun, Jeffrey S. '75 '02 C.20 B.A. L.608 J.D. [Ⓐ Roetzel&A.]
Braun, Lawrence H., (BV) '34 '65 C.610 B.S.C. L.608 J.D.
Res. Legal Coun., Columbus City School Dist.
Braun, Robt. E. '21 '52 C&L.266 B.A., J.D. 4012 E. Mound St.
Braun, Tonya Blosser '— '02 C.228 B.A. L.608 J.D. [Ⓐ Jones D.]
Braunstein, Michael '47 '93 C.420 B.A. L.861 J.D.
[Ⓒ Crabbe,B.&J.] & [Goldman&B.] (⊙Columbus)
Braunstein, Michael '47 '93 C.420 B.A. L.861 J.D.
[Goldman&B.] & [Ⓒ Crabbe,B.&J.] (⊙Columbus)
Braverman, Loren L., (BV) '52 '77 C&L.608 B.A., J.D. 270 E. State St.
Bravo, Eric S. '65 '90 C.597 B.A. L.608 J.D. [Ⓐ Roetzel&A.]
Breen, John E., (BV) '56 '82 C.473 B.A. L.607 J.D. [Ⓒ J.L.Alden]
Brehm, Eric W. '— '01 C.608 B.A. L.117 J.D. 264 E. Breechwold Bvld.
Brehmer, Marcia L. '49 '76 C.473 B.A. L.94 J.D. Exec. Dir., Legal Aid Soc.
Breitfeller, Ralph E., (AV) '53 '78 C.676 B.A. L.276 J.D. [McGrath&B.]
Breitstadt, Charles P. '41 '74 C.222 B.A. L.117 J.D. 1 Nationwide Plaza
Brennan, Maureen R. '58 '83 C.201 B.S. L.117 J.D. Off. of Consumers' Coun.
Brenner, Todd Austin '65 '91 C&L.117 B.A., J.D. [Brenner,B.G.&M.]

Brenner, Brown, Golian & McCaffrey Co., L.P.A., (AV) BB
2109 Stella Court, 43215
Telephone: 614-258-6000 Telecopier: 614-258-6006
Email: pbrown@rrcol.com URL: http://www.lawyers.com/bbgm
Philip F. Brown; Joseph J. Golian; Todd Austin Brenner; Patrick McCaffrey, Jr. (Board Certified, Personal Injury Trial Law, Texas Board of Legal Specialization);—Michael E. Heffernan; Audrey E. Varwig; Jeffery S. Maynard; Shannon K. Benton; Melissa M. Prendergast.
(This Listing Continued)

Brenner, Brown, Golian & McCaffrey Co., L.P.A. (Continued)

ERISA, Life, Health and Disability Defense, Liability Defense and Insurance Coverage. Business and Corporate Law, General Civil Litigation, Motor Carrier Law.

See Professional Biographies, COLUMBUS, OHIO

Brenning, Mary F. ....'71 '96 C.967 B.S. L.117 J.D. [Ⓐ Kegler,B.H.&R.]
Bressman, David Allan ....'65 '90 C.201 B.A. L.608 J.D. [D.A.Bressman]
Bressman, David A., Law Offices of .... 3011 Bethel Rd.
Brewer, Larry W. '49 '76 C.930 B.A. L.851 J.D.
Asst. Gen. Coun.-Regul. Servs., Amer. Elect. Power Co.
Brewer, Lee M. ....'54 '89 C.838 B.S. L.117 J.D. [Alber C.]
Brey, Donald C., (AV) ....'55 '81 C.611 B.A. L.976 J.D. [Chester,W.&S.]
Bricker, Douglas M., (AV) ....'42 '69 C.235 B.A. L.383 J.D. [Bricker&M.]
Bricker, Timothy R. ....'65 '93 C.8 B.S. L.608 J.D. [Carpenter&L.]

Bricker & Eckler LLP, (AV)
100 South Third Street, 43215-4291
Telephone: 614-227-2300 Fax: 614-227-2390
Email: info@bricker.com URL: http://www.bricker.com
Partners: John W. Bricker (1893-1986); John Eckler (1913-1994); Edward A. Matto; Michael F. Sullivan; Sally W. Bloomfield; Nicholas A. Pittner; Richard F. Kane; John F. Birath, Jr.; Michael S. Holman; Richard C. Simpson (Managing Partner); John P. Beavers; David G. Baker; Jerry E. Nathan; Marshall L. Lerner; Randolph C. Wiseman; Donald R. Keller; Karen Mueller Moore; Steven R. Kerber; Charles H. Walker; Gordon W. Johnston; David A. Rogers; Charles H. Waterman III; Michael K. Gire; James A. Rutledge; David C. Spialter; Randall Edwin Moore; John W. Cook, III; Charles H. McCreary, III; James P. Burnes; Elisabeth A. Squeglia; Kenneth C. Johnson; Michael E. Flowers; Mark A. Engel; David K. Conrad; Richard S. Lovering; Rebecca Coleman Princehorn; Diane M. Signoracci; Luther L. Liggett, Jr.; Martha Post Baxter; Gretchen A. McBeath; Craig A. Haddox; Susan Beale Greenberger; William T. Conard, II; Robert C. Rafferty; Jerry O. Allen; H. Randy Bank; Anne Marie Sferra Vorys; Catherine M. Ballard; Gordon F. Litt; Sue Wyskiver Yount; James J. Hughes, III; Frank L. Merrill; Kurtis A. Tunnell; Betsy A. Swift; Jack R. Rosati, Jr.; Susan E. Geary; Sylvia Lynn Gillis; James F. Flynn; Price D. Finley; Harry Wright, IV; Drew H. Campbell; Stephen C. Gray; Karen D. Smith; James G. Petrie; Stephen Intihar; T. Earl LeVere; Bobbie S. Sprader; Kimberly J. Brown; Faith M. Williams; Christine M. Poth; Laura Greenberg Anthony; Nelson M. Reid. Senior Attorneys: Warren I. Grody; Amy Straker Bartemes; Susan L. Oppenheimer; Katherine Spies Giumenti; Maureen P. Taylor;—C. Allen Shaffer; Gregory T. Parks; Maria J. Armstrong; Emmett M. Kelly; Alexander M. Brown; Matthew L. Stout; Allen R. Killworth; Vladimir P. Belo; James S. Gray; John F. Furniss III; James P. Schuck; Miranda Creviston Motter; Mark E. Evans, P.E.; Terrence O'Donnell; James R. Berendsen; Theodore J. Gallagher; Alan D. Duffy; Christopher N. Swank; Elizabeth C. Stock; Natalie C. Trishman; Sean M. McGlone; Justin W. Ristau; Robert B. Holodnak; Phillip H. Lee (Not admitted in OH); Becky L. Ramseyer; Maggie F. Weber; Hope M. Sharett; John A. Ensign; Kevin M. Kinross; Stephanie T. Greene (Not admitted in OH); Sean A. Mentel; Karl J. Silverberg; Jennifer M. Nelson Carney; Doug L. Shevelow; Christopher N. Slagle; Scott W. Davis; Matthew A. Rich; Chuan Sun; Christopher L. McCloskey; Cavett R. Kreps; Jennifer Ann Flint; Dane A. Gaschen; Catherine J. Baird-Veley; Sarah E. Hurst. Of Counsel: James J. Hughes; Thomas R. Sant; Robert H. Katz; Kimball H. Carey; Thomas J. O'Brien; G. Samuel Wampler. Retired: Bruce G. Lynn; Richard C. Pickett; William H. Leighner; James S. Monahan; Elbert J. Kram.
Antitrust and Competitive Business Practices, Banking, Bankruptcy, Commercial, Construction, Corporate Governance, Corporation and Partnership, Cyberlaw, Creditor-Debtor, Education, Emerging Business, Employment Relations, Entertainment/Sports, Environmental, Federal Taxation, Governmental Agencies and Legislative Law, Health Care, Insurance, Intellectual Property, International Transactions, Litigation, Mental Retardation and Developmental Disabilities, Mergers and Acquisitions; Mortgage Lending, Pension and Employee Benefits, Public Finance, Public Utilities, OSHA, Real Estate, Securities, State and Local Taxation, Trusts and Estates, Workers' Compensation.
Cleveland, Ohio Office: 1375 East Ninth Street, Suite 1500, 44114-1718. Telephone: 216-523-5405. Fax: 216-523-7071.

See Professional Biographies, COLUMBUS, OHIO

Bricker & Maxfield, L.L.C., (AV)
Easton Town Center, 4100 Regent Street, Suite T, 43219
Telephone: 614-269-4900 Fax: 614-269-4901
URL: http://www.brickermaxfield.com
Members of Firm: Douglas M. Bricker; Michael L. Maxfield. Associate: Shane M. Dawson.
Labor and Employment, Workers Compensation Defense, OSHA, Products Liability, Intentional Torts.

See Professional Biographies, COLUMBUS, OHIO

Bridges, Michael D., (BV) ....'65 '93 C.473 B.A. L.117 J.D. [Baker&H.]
Bridgman, G. Ross, (AV) ....'47 '73 C.976 B.A. L.597 J.D. [Vorys,S.S.&P.]
Brigner, Julie E. ....'70 '96 C.597 B.A. L.608 J.D. [Ⓐ Hahn L.&P.]
Brigner, Nancy A. ....'67 '92 C.597 B.A. L.477 J.D. [Ⓒ Schottenstein,Z.&D.]
Brill, Lauren S. ....'78 '03 C.611 B.A. L.117 J.D. [Ⓐ Wiles,B.B.&B.]
Brill, William L. ....'55 '80 C.610 A.B. L.597 J.D. 30 W. Spring St., 7th Fl.
Bringardner, Daniel E., (AV) ....'53 '78 C.49 B.S. L.117 J.D. [Wiles,B.B.&B.]
Bringardner, Richard D., (BV) ....'53 '78 C.49 B.S. L.117 J.D. [Wiles,B.B.&B.]
Brininger, Tod A. ....'71 '98 C.1112 B.A. L.117 J.D. 2130 Arlington Ave.
Brinkman, Dale T., (AV) '52 '77
C.602 B.A. L.608 J.D. Gen. Coun., Worthington Industries, Inc.
Briscoe, Colleen H., (BV) ....'52 '77 C.473 A.B. L.117 J.D. [Briscoe&W.]
Briscoe, Emily Kaye, (BVⓉ) '69 '95 C.473 B.A. L.150 J.D.
Coun. to Clk., OH Supm. Ct.

Briscoe & Webber, (BV)
500 South Front Street, Suite 125, 43215
Telephone: 614-224-4149 Fax: 614-224-0738
URL: http://www.briscoelaw.com
Colleen H. Briscoe; Marci L. Webber.
Family Law, Divorce, Child Custody, Child Support, Child Support Mediation, Visitation Rights, Premarital Agreements.

See Professional Biographies, COLUMBUS, OHIO

Britt, James C., Jr., (BV) ....'47 '73 C.608 B.S. L.117 J.D. [Britt,C.N.&S.]
Britt, Campbell, Nagel & Sproat, (AV) .... 490 City Park Avenue
Britton, Glen H. ....'20 '52 C&L.608 B.S., LL.B. 740 Thomas Lane
Britton, John B. ....'65 '90 C&L.608 B.S., J.D. The Columbus Foundation
Brockmeyer, Jennifer ....'— '04 [Ⓐ Babbitt&W.]
Brodnik, Martyn T., (BV) ....'51 '80 C.161 B.S. L.1003 J.D. [Ⓒ Ulmer&B.]
Brody, John P., (AV) ....'53 '79 C.608 B.A. L.930 J.D. [Kegler,B.H.&R.]
Bronner, Howard C. ....'15 '56 C.608 L.266 J.D. 2574 Sonata Drive
Brooks, Paula L., (BV) ....'53 '83 C.980 A.B. L.117 J.D. [Brooks&W.]
Brooks, Richard D., Jr., (AV) ....'44 '72 C.434 B.A. L.930 J.D. [Bailey C.]
Brooks, Stephanie Bisca ....'59 '86 C&L.608 B.S.S.W., J.D. Mag., Ct. of App.
Brooks & Wilburn Co., L.P.A., (BV) .... 4921 Dierker Road
Brosius, Donald F., (AV) ....'54 '80 C.372 B.S. L.117 J.D. [Loveland&B.]
Brown, Alexander M. ....'74 '99 C.1375 B.A. L.893 J.D. [Ⓐ Bricker&E.]
Brown, Daniel A., (AV) ....'44 '71 C.210 A.B. L.477 J.D. Asst. U.S. Atty.
Brown, Donald A. ....'38 '77 C.651 B.S.Ed. L.851 J.D. [Ⓢ Vorys,S.S.&P.]
Brown, Eric L. ....'45 '80 C.178 B.A. L.1009 J.D. P.O. Box 9770
Brown, Gary E. ....'48 '73 C.932 B.A. L.1119 J.D. Asst. Atty. Gen.
Brown, Herbert R. ....'31 '56 C.207 A.B. L.477 J.D. 145 N. High St., 11th Fl.
Brown, J. Douglas '52 '91 C.610 B.M.E. L.623 J.D.
Claims Atty., Grange Mut. Cas. Co.
Brown, Jeffrey L., (AV) ....'54 '79 C.893 B.A. L.117 J.D. [Smith&H.]
Brown, Jeffrey M., (AV) ....'53 '79 C.967 B.A. L.608 J.D. [Crabbe,B.&J.]

Brown, Kenneth A. ....'51 '84 C.608 B.A. L.117 J.D. 1700 Lake Shore Drive
Brown, Kevin W., (BV) ....'58 '82 C&L.602 B.A., J.D. 3140 E. Broad St.
Brown, Kimberly J. ....'69 '95 C.631 B.A. L.117 J.D. [Bricker&E.]
Brown, Kristen J. ....'63 '90 C.608 B.A. L.117 J.D. [Ⓐ Squire,S.&D.]
Brown, Lori J. ....'66 '88 C.473 B.S. L.851 J.D. Disciplinary Coun., Supm. Ct.
Brown, Lyle B. ....'70 '98 C.311 B.A. L.608 J.D. [Ⓐ Benesch,F.C.&A.]
Brown, Matthew S. ....'72 '04 C.97 B.S. L.851 J.D. [Lane,A.&H.]
Brown, Nancy G., (AV) '41 '74 C.145 B.A. L.608 J.D.
Vice President, Secretary & General Counsel, Borden Foods Corporation
Brown, Paul W., (AV) ....'15 '39 C&L.608 A.B., J.D. 100 E. Broad St.
Brown, Philip A., (AV) ....'49 '74 C.276 B.A. L.477 J.D. [Vorys,S.S.&P.]
Brown, Philip F., (AV) ....'55 '85 C.608 B.A. L.117 J.D. [Brenner,B.G.&M.]
Brown, Ray G., (AV) ....'35 '61 C.976 A.B. L.608 J.D. 1971 Mackenzie Dr.
Brown, Richard D., (AV) ....'— '81 C.150 B.A. L.608 J.D. [Buckley K.]
Brown, Rowland C. W. '23 '51 C&L.309 A.B., LL.B.
(adm. in DC; not adm. in OH) 2711 Edington Rd.
Brown, Steven M., (BV) ....'59 '84 C&L.608 B.A., J.D. 2204 Ridgeview Road
Brown, Susan E., (AV) ....'46 '71 C&L.608 B.A., J.D. [Vorys,S.S.&P.]
Brown, William W., (BV) ....'33 '60 C.611 B.A. L.266 J.D. 2999 E. Dublin Granville Rd.
Brown, Wm. F., (BV) ....'29 '56 C&L.608 B.S., J.D. 3140 E. Broad St.
Brown, Yvette Mcgee ....'60 '85 C.610 B.S. L.608 J.D. Com. Pleas. J.
Browne, Kim Alana Lyons '66 '93
C.150 B.A. L.608 J.D. Com. Pleas J., Dom. Rel. & Juv. Ct. Div.

Brownfield, C. William, & Associates, (AV) '41 '71 C.473 B.A. L.273 J.D.
2661Charing Road, 43221
Telephone: 614-464-2201 Fax: 614-486-6492 Email: brownfieldlaw@msn.com
Email: brownfieldlaw@usa.net URL: http://www.brownfieldlawfirm.com
Business Litigation, Securities Litigation and Arbitration, Corporate Law, International Business Law.

See Professional Biographies, COLUMBUS, OHIO

Browning, Jon M., (BV) ....'58 '86 C.608 B.A.B.S. L.851 J.D. [Browning&C.]
Browning, Pamela Broer ....'54 '83 C.473 B.A. L.851 J.D. Mag., Com. Pleas Ct.
Browning, Stephen D., (BV) ....'66 '93 C.951 B.A. L.93 J.D. [Vorys,S.S.&P.]
Browning, William J., (AV) ....'57 '83 C&L.117 B.A., J.D. [Browning&M.]
Browning & Cooke, (BV) .... 243 North Fifth Street, 3rd Floor

Browning & Meyer Co., LPA, (AV)
8101 North High Street, Suite 370, 43235
Telephone: 614-471-0085 Fax: 614-430-8132 URL: http://www.elderlaw.us
URL: http://www.lawyers.com/bmslaw
William J. Browning; Richard F. Meyer (Certified Specialist in Estate Planning, Trust and Probate Law, Ohio State Bar Association).
Elder Law, Estate Planning, Administration and Litigation, Trusts and Estates, Wills and Probate, Medicare and Medicaid, Medicaid Hearings, Guardianship and Conservatorship, Asset Protection, Charitable Giving, Estate and Gift Taxation, Family Business Succession Planning, Small Business Planning, Taxation.

See Professional Biographies, COLUMBUS, OHIO

Brown-Schwart, Mary Anne ....'55 '92 C&L.608 B.A., J.D. [Schwart]
Broz, Alycia N. ....'71 '98 C.436 B.S. L.597 J.D. [Ⓐ Vorys,S.S.&P.]
Brubaker, Robert L., (AV) ....'47 '72 C.231 B.A. L.145 J.D. [Porter W.M.&A.]
Brudny, James J., Jr., (BV) ....'58 '83 C.529 B.A. L.117 J.D. [Ⓐ Reminger&R.]
Brunetto, Joseph A., (AV) ....'51 '80 C.150 B.A. L.117 J.D. [Vorys,S.S.&P.]
Brunner, Jennifer L., (BV) ....'57 '83 C.473 B.A. L.117 J.D. J. Co. Ct. of Comm. Pleas
Brunner, Rick L., (BV) ....'54 '80 C.528 B.A. L.117 J.D. 545 E. Town Street
Brunner, Stephen C. ....'43 '69 C&L.608 B.S., J.D. 717 City Park Ave.‡
Bruno, John ....'57 '83 C&L.608 B.S., J.D. 211 Bradenton Ave.
Brunton, Gregory D. ....'68 '93 C.8 B.A. L.608 J.D. [Ⓐ Reminger&R.]
Bryan, Jonathan M. ....'70 '95 C.980 B.A. L.608 J.D. [McNamara&M.]
Bryant, Letitia S. ....'— '04 C.473 B.A. L.608 J.D. [Ⓐ Baker&H.]
Bryant, Peggy Lynn ....'51 '76 C.473 B.A. L.608 J.D. 373 South High Street, 24th Floor
Buchbinder, Robert C., (BV) ....'58 '88 C.81 B.A. L.117 J.D. [Crabbe,B.&J.]
Buchenroth, Stephen R., (AV) ....'48 '74 C.967 A.B. L.145 J.D. [Vorys,S.S.&P.]
Buck, Elaine Sayers ....'56 '81 C.103 B.A. L.608 J.D. 1560 Fishinger Rd.

Buckingham, Doolittle & Burroughs, LLP, (AV)
191 West Nationwide Boulevard, 43215-3506
Telephone: 614-221-8448; Toll Free: 1-888-686-2825 Fax: 614-221-8590
Email: bdb@bdblaw.com URL: http://www.bdblaw.com
Managing Partner: Donald B. Leach, Jr. Shareholders: Donald A. Antrim; Thomas J. Bonasera; Jan E. Hensel; Richard A. Hernandez; Thomas W. Hess; Brett L. Miller (Certified Specialist in Workers' Compensation Law, Ohio State Bar Association); Andrew W. Owen; Brent D. Rosenthal (Certified Specialist in Business, Commercial and Industrial Real Property Law, Ohio State Bar Association); Thomas J. Sigmund; Charles E. Ticknor, III; Michael L. Williams. Partners: David M. Abromowitz; Michael F. Copley; Robert C. Preston; Susan G. Sheridan. Of Counsel: Kenneth A. Fisher, Jr.; Michael A. Renne. Associates: Priya J. Bathija; Michael D. Bonasera; Janice E. Casanova; Kimberly Cocroft; Joseph E. Ezzie; Peter W. Hahn; Kerry McConaghy Mackin; Frank Schuckmann.
Appellate, Closely Held Companies, Commercial Law and Litigation, Computer and Technology, Construction Law, Copyrights, Corporate and Business, Creditors Rights/Bankruptcy, Criminal Law, Employment Law, Environmental, Estate Planning, Family Law, Finance and Public Law, Franchise, Health Care, Immigration Law, Insurance Defense, Intellectual Property, Labor and Employment, Land Use and Zoning, Medical Malpractice Defense, Mergers and Acquisitions, Patents, Probate, Publicly Held Companies, Real Estate, School Law, Securities, Succession Planning, Taxation and Employee Benefits, Toxic Tort/Complex Litigation, Trademarks/Service Marks, Trade Secrets, Trial, Trusts and Estates, Venture Capital/Emerging Companies, Workers' Compensation.
Akron, Ohio Office: 50 South Main Street, P.O. Box 1500, 44309-1500. Telephone: 330-376-5300. Toll Free: 800-686-2825. Fax: 330-258-6559.
Canton, Ohio Office: 4518 Fulton Drive Northwest, P.O. Box 35548, 44735-5548. Telephone: 330-492-8717. Toll Free: 800-811-2825. Fax: 330-492-9625.
Cleveland, Ohio Office: 1375 East Ninth Street, Suite 1700, 44114. Telephone: 216-621-5300. Toll Free: 888-843-2825. Fax: 216-621-5440.
Boca Raton, Florida Office: 2500 North Military Trail, Suite 480, 33431. Telephone: 561-241-0414. Toll Free: 800-682-2825. Fax: 561-241-9766.

See Professional Biographies, COLUMBUS, OHIO

Buckles, Andre M., (BV) ....'42 '69 C.207 A.B. L.930 J.D. 65 S. 5th St.
Buckley, Shalu Tandon '66 '95 C&L.608 B.A., J.D.
Atty., Columbia Gas Distribution Cos.

Buckley King, A Legal Professional Association, (AV)
One Columbus, 10 West Broad Street, Suite 1300, 43215-3419
Telephone: 614-461-5600 Toll Free: 877-266-6625
Email: bkb-columbus.com URL: http://www.buckleyking.com
Thomas I. Blackburn; Richard D. Brown; Gary A. Gillett; Donell R. Grubbs; James E. Melle; Robert J. Walter;—Philip L. Judy.
Corporate, Litigation, Commercial, Estate Planning, Banking, Real Estate, Merger and Acquisition, Appellate, Bankruptcy, Professional and Executive (Directors and Officers) Liability, Insurance Law, Products Liability, Health Care, Hospital Law, Medical Malpractice Defense, Immigration/Naturalization, Toxic and Hazardous Materials, ERISA, Taxation, Environmental, Labor, Public Employment Relations, Employee Benefits. Workers Compensation and NLRB Matters, Patent and Trademark.
Cleveland, Ohio Office: 1400 Fifth Third Center. Telephone: 216-363-1400. Telecopier: 216-579-1020.
Cincinnati, Ohio Office: 1420 PNC Center, 201 East Fifth Street. Telephone: 513-412-5400. Telecopier: 513-412-5401.

(This Listing Continued)

Buckley King, A Legal Professional Association (Continued)

Atlanta, Georgia Office: Suite 1220 Lennox Building, 3399 Peachtree Road. Telephone: 404-816-7791. Telecopier: 404-816-9786.

See Professional Biographies, COLUMBUS, OHIO

Buda, David M., (BV) .... '46 '74 C.381 B.A. L.608 J.D. 35 E. Livingston Ave.
Bulgrin, Richard M. .... '56 '87 C&L.8 B.S.B.A., J.D. Hyatt Legal Servs.
Bull, Joseph O. ....'58 '86 C&L.608 B.S., J.D. 2400 Olentangy River Road
Bull, Julianna Farr ....'49 '84 309 S. 4th Street, Suite 222
Bull, Mary "Maggie" .....'66 '95 C.610 B.A. L.117 J.D. Sr. Coun., Nationwide Insurance
Bullock, Elizabeth S. ....'54 '80 C.608 B.A. L.117 J.D. Coun., Nationwide Insurance
Bullock, Howard N., (AV) .... '17 '43 C&L.608 B.S., J.D. 3349 Mansion Way
Bulson, Douglas W., Jr., (BV) .... '47 '73 C.610 B.B.A. L.608 J.D. 3099 Sullivant Ave.
Bumbico, James Franklin ....'63 '99 C&L.117 B.A., J.D. 30 East Broad St.
Bumgarner, Christopher D. ....'74 '04 C.1208 B.A. L.117 J.D. [C.Bumgarner]
Bumgarner, Christopher ....929 Harrison Ave., Ste. 302
Burke, Diane E. ....'73 '98 C&L.896 B.S., J.D. [🄰 Mueller&S.] (See Pat. Sect.)
Burke, Jennifer M. ....'70 '01 C.363 B.A. L.93 J.D. [🄰 Vorys,S.S.&P.]
Burkett, Elizabeth Schorpp, (BV) '60 '86 C&L.608 B.S., J.D.
[Volkema,T.M.B.S.&M.]
Burkhart, Matthew J. .... '71 '97 C.967 B.A. L.893 J.D. [🄰 Bailey C.]
Burkholder, Bruce H., (AV) ....'55 '80 C.97 B.S. L.117 J.D. [Wiles,B.B.&B.]
Burley, John D., (BV) .... '58 '83 C.597 B.A. L.608 J.D. VP, Red Capital Group
Burman, Robert N., (BV) ....'48 '73 C.97 B.S. L.117 J.D. [Burman&R.]

Burman & Robinson, (BV)
601 South High Street, 43215-5695
Telephone: 614-221-8900 Fax: 614-221-8912
Members of Firm: Robert N. Burman; Randal D. Robinson.
Commercial and Business Litigation, Creditors Rights, Collections, Corporate Law, Matrimonial Law.

See Professional Biographies, COLUMBUS, OHIO

Burnell, Brigette A. ....'— '02 C.453 B.S. L.608 J.D. [🄰 Jones D.]
Burnes, James P., (AV) ....'51 '78 C.611 B.A. L.117 J.D. [Bricker&E.]
Burns, Darla J. '— '85 C&L.608 B.S.S.W., J.D.
Gen. Coun., Ohio Rehabilitation Services Committee
Burns, Michael ....'49 '74 C.347 A.B. L.1119 J.D. Legis. Comm.
Burns, Michael J., (BV) ....'51 '79 C.608 B.A. L.117 J.D. U.S. Atty. Off.
Burns, Robert E. '53 '78 C.434 B.A. L.608 J.D.
Sr. Resch. Atty., Nat'l Regulatory Resch. Inst., The
Burns, Robert H. ....'26 '56 C.97 A.B. L.608 J.D. 1222 Lincoln Rd.‡
Burns, William Michael ....'49 '76 C.347 A.B. L.1119 J.D. Legisl. Srv. Comm.
Burnside-Kelly, Joseph A., (BV) ....'61 '91 C.205 B.A. L.117 J.D. 118 E. Main St.
Burpee, Robert L. ....'62 '95 C.309 A.B. L.818 J.D. Law Clk., Supm. Ct.
Burress, Stephanie D. '70 '96 C.610 B.S.J. L.117 J.D.
Dep. Chief Legal Coun., State Dept. of Transportation
Burrier, Brian C. ....'66 '92 C.608 B.S. L.117 J.D. [Gerrity&B.]
Burrington, Lori A. ....'65 '90 C.477 B.A. L.608 J.D. Online Computer Libr. Ctr., Inc.
Burtch, James M., III, (BV) ....'47 '73 C.641 B.A. L.802 J.D. Spec. Asst. Co. Pros.
Burtch, John H., (AV) ....'48 '74 C.207 B.A. L.608 J.D. [Baker&H.]
Burton, Robert E., Jr., (AV) ....'42 '67 C.197 A.B. L.228 LL.B. 5131 Post Road
Bush, Kevin R., (BV) ....'60 '85 C.607 B.A. L.117 J.D. [Keener D.C.&P.]
Butauski, Joseph A. ....'62 '87 C&L.608 B.A., J.D. 765 S. High St.
Butler, David J. ....'72 '97 C&L.602 B.B.A., J.D. [Chester,W.&S.]
Butler, E. William, (BV) ....'45 '75 C&L.608 B.A., J.D. 278 S. Ardmore Rd.
Butler, Eugene R., (BV) ...'54 '86 C.608 B.A. L.117 J.D. 326 South High Street Suite 400
Butler, Eugene W., (AV) ....'11 '40 C.266 B.B.S. L.117 J.D. 278 S. Ardmore Rd.‡
Butler, Jack C., (AV) ....'47 '72 C.473 A.B. L.150 J.D. [Swedlow,B.L.M.&D.]
Butler, James R. ....'19 '48 C.309 S.B. L.608 J.D. 5345C Yorkshire Terr. Dr.‡
Butler, Jolynn Barry ....'51 '76 C&L.608 B.S., J.D. Comr., State Pub. Util. Comm
Butler, Cincione & DiCuccio, (AV) .... 50 West Broad Street
Buzby, Brian L., (AV) ....'49 '74 C&L.608 B.A., J.D. [Porter W.M.&A.]
Byard, Robert Reed ....'64 '89 C.37 B.S. L.117 J.D. Jud. Clk. Supm. Ct.
Byers, Michael A., (BV) ....'53 '78 C.608 B.A. L.7 J.D. [Taft,S.&H.]
Byers, Renee L. ....'68 '99 C.737 B.A. L.608 J.D. Pub. Safety Dept.
Byrne, Robert J., (BV) ....'52 '88 C.763 B.A. L.608 J.D. Asst. Atty. Gen.
Byrne, Sean P. ....'— '97 C.692 B.A. L.477 J.D. [🄰 Jones D.]
Byrom, Robert G. ....'52 '77 C.608 B.S. L.851 J.D. Legal Aid Soc. of Columbus
Caborn, David A., (BV) ....'57 '86 C.608 B.A. L.117 J.D. 765 S. High St.
Cabot, Jeffery Alan .... '47 '87 L.117 J.D. 60 E. Broad St.
Cadwallader, John I., (AV) ....'52 '78 C.207 B.A. L.608 J.D. [Frost B.T.]
Cadwallader, John Rayburn '58 '83
C.659 B.A. L.150 J.D. Asst. Gen. Coun., Nationwide Insurance
Cahill, Timothy J. ....'72 '03 C.608 B.S. L.150 J.D. [🄰 Porter W.M.&A.]
Cain, David Edwin ....'43 '73 C.610 B.S. L.117 J.D. Ct. of Com. Pleas, Franklin Co.
Cain, Kenneth Richard, Jr. ....'69 '96 C.608 B.A. L.117 J.D. Bureau of Workers' Comp.
Cain, Lacey L. ....'75 '00 C.611 B.A. L.179 J.D. [🄰 Scott,S.&W.]
Calcaterra, Craig A. ....'73 '98 C.608 B.A. L.273 J.D. [🄰 Thompson H.]

Calfee, Halter & Griswold LLP, (AV) BR
1100 Fifth Third Center, 21 East State Street, 43215-4228 ⊙
Telephone: 614-621-1500 Telecopier: 614-621-0010
URL: http://www.calfee.com
Partners: P. Michael DeAngelo; Steven C. Karzmer; Albert J. Lucas; Douglas S. Morgan; Thomas E. O'Connor, Jr.; Leah Pappas; Kristopher Wahlers. Senior Attorneys: Christopher Jones; Erin E. Karzmer. Associates: Joan N. Drew; Mark A. Losey; William J. Michael; Courtney J. Miller; Sean C. Myers-Payne (Not admitted in OH); Daniel A. Reinhard; Peter A. Rosato; Christopher M. Ward; Stephen C. Wiley. Staff Attorneys: Lori Hannan; Anne E. Will. Senior Counsel: Stanley J. Dobrowski. Of Counsel: Richard H. Finan; J. Troy Terakedis.
General Practice and Litigation.
Cleveland, Ohio Office: 1400 McDonald Investment Center, 800 Superior Avenue. Telephone: 216-622-8200. Telecopier: 216-241-0816.

See Professional Biographies, COLUMBUS, OHIO

Calhoun, Donald E., Jr. ....'26 '51 C&L.608 B.A., J.D. Bkrptcy. J.‡
Calhoun, Jason Harris .....'56 '82 C.976 B.A. L.608 J.D. Ohio Bureau of Worker' Comp.s
Calig, Samuel L., (BV) ....'46 '74 C.608 B.A. L.607 J.D. [Calig&H.]

Calig & Handelman, LPA, (BV)
854 East Broad Street, 43205 ⊙
Telephone: 614-252-4885; 1-800-633-5000
URL: http://www.chohiolawyers.com
Samuel L. Calig; Robert B. Handelman; Terry V. Hummel; Kenneth P. Karlock; Lee A. Thompson.
Bankruptcy, Personal Injury, Probate, Real Estate, Social Security, Social Security Disability, Medical Malpractice, Wrongful Death, Civil Litigation, Domestic Relations Law.
Newark, Ohio Office: 29 S. Park Place, 43055. Telephone: 740-349-8581. Fax: 740-345-4101.
Lancaster, Ohio Office: 204 N. Columbus Street, 43130. Telephone: 740-653-4400. Fax: 740-653-0037.
Marion, Ohio Office: 274 S. Main Street, 43302. Telephone: 740-375-5051.

See Professional Biographies, COLUMBUS, OHIO

Caligiuri, Joseph M. '68 '95 C.1529 B.A.B.A. L.1202 J.D.
Asst. Disciplinary Coun., Disciplinary Counsel
Calloway, Sue Dill ....'54 '83 C&L.117 B.A., J.D. State Hosp. Assn.
Cameron, Bruce L., (BV) ....'42 '69 C.608 B.A. L.117 J.D. 1161 Bethel Rd.
Camillus, John C. ....'— '04 C.611 B.A. L.976 J.D. [🄰 Jones D.]
Campbell, Bruce A., (AV) .....'40 '65 C.679 B.S. L.608 J.D. Coun., Columbus Bar Assn.
Campbell, Drew H. ....'58 '90 C.94 B.F.A. L.608 J.D. [Bricker&E.]
Campbell, Fred M., (AV) ....'30 '54 C&L.608 B.S., J.D. [Campbell,H.C.&V.]
Campbell, Joel R., (AV) ....'46 '72 C.608 B.S.B.A. L.8 J.D. [Britt,C.N.&S.]
Campbell, Scott A. ....'62 '95 C.309 A.B. L.608 J.D. [Thompson H.]
Campbell, Scott Michael ....'74 '99 C.608 B.S. L.7 J.D. Atty. Gen.'s Off.
Campbell, Hornbeck, Chilcoat & Veatch LLC, (AV) ....7650 Rivers Edge Drive
Canestraro, C. Russell, (BV) ....'65 '93 C.608 B.A. L.607 J.D. [Agee C.M.&L.]
Canning, Susan M. '69 '97 C.363 B.S.E. L.215 J.D.
(adm. in MI; not adm. in OH) Sr. Coun., Bank One Corp.
Canowitz, Robin L. '67 '92 C.477 B.A. L.150 J.D.
Legal Services, Children's Hospital Inc.
Canter, Michael J., (AV) ....'47 '72 C.610 B.B.A. L.597 J.D. [Vorys,S.S.&P.]
Caplan, Robert L. ....'67 '94 C.608 B.A. L.117 J.D. 90 N. Nelson Rd.
Cardwell, John G., Jr. ....'25 '64 C.608 B.M.E. L.1003 J.D. 4473 White Leaf Way
Cardwell, Richard A., (BV) ....'63 '91 C.608 B.A. L.117 J.D. [Peck,S.&W.]
Carey, Kimball H. ....'52 '79 C.967 B.A. L.608 J.D. [🄲 Bricker&E.]
Carey, Laura M. ....'65 '98 C&L.1360 B.S., J.D. [🄰 Mallory&T.]

Carlile Patchen & Murphy LLP, (AV)
366 East Broad Street, 43215
Telephone: 614-228-6135 Fax: 614-221-0216
Email: CPM@cpmlaw.com URL: http://www.cpmlaw.com
Members of Firm: Huntington Carlile (1924-1990); Richard V. Patchen; Craig M. Stewart; James R. Moats; Dennis J. Concilla; Carol A. Sheehan; Michael H. Igoe; Robert B. Barnett, Jr.; Bryan K. Hogue; Michael A. Smith; John P. Wilkerson, Jr.; Joseph M. Patchen; Scott R. Mergenthaler; Marie-Joëlle C. Khouzam; Anthony Delligatti, Jr.; H. Ritchey Hollenbaugh; William Richard Yost; David A. Onega. Of Counsel: Andrew J. Federico; Thomas M. Bolon; Leon Friedberg; Stephen D. Enz; Richard L. Bibart; Daniel G. Rohletter. Associates: David S. Jackson; Thomas H. Wallace; Jane A. Higgins Marx; Douglas R. Jennings; Necol D. Russell-Washington; Stephanie D. Champ; Christopher A. Rinehart; Christopher J. Dusseau; Joseph M. Gillotti; Mary G. Menkedick; Brian T. Johnson; John Lewis Einstein, IV; Emily A. Smith.
Business Law; Corporate; Commercial; Banking; Civil Trial; Appellate Practice; Legislative and Administrative; Real Estate; Zoning, Planning and Land Use; Probate and Estate Planning; Securities; Mergers, Acquisitions and Divestitures; Municipal Bonds and Tax-Exempt Financing; Financial Services Regulations; Taxation; Partnership Law; Insurance; Contracts; Construction; Creditor's Rights; Collections; Family Law; Wills; Labor and Employment; Employment Relations; Trademarks; Bankruptcy; Franchising; Intellectual Property; Public Law; International Law; Transportation Regulations; Telecommunications; and Public Utility Regulations.
Representative Client: Novar Electronics Corp.

See Professional Biographies, COLUMBUS, OHIO

Carlin, David P. ....'38 '63 C.674 A.B. L.608 J.D. Mng. Dir., William M. Mercer, Inc.
Carlino, Steven G. ....'76 '01 C.610 B.S. L.117 J.D. [🄰 Keener D.C.&P.]

Carlisle, McNellie, Rini, Kramer & Ulrich Co., L.P.A., (AV)
Suite 200, 155 West Main Street, 43215 ⊙
Telephone: 614-464-2704
—Richard A. Utz.
General Civil Practice. Real Estate, Mortgage, Corporation, Probate, Bankruptcy and Family Law. Trials.
References: FirstMerit Bank, N.A.
Cleveland, Ohio Office: 24755 Chagrin Boulevard, Suite 200, 44122-5690. Telephone: 216-360-7200. Fax: 216-360-7210.

See Professional Biographies, CLEVELAND, OHIO

Carlson, Christopher T. ....'66 '91 C.602 B.A. L.117 J.S. Dep. Dir.
Carlson, Craig R., (AV) ....'66 '91 C.228 A.B. L.117 J.D. [Porter W.M.&A.]
Carlson, Leonard A., Attorney at Law, (BV) '48 '78
C.610 B.A. L.117 J.D. 2700 E. Main St., Ste. 111
Carlson, Melinda S. '55 '88 C.611 B.A. L.117 J.D.
Co. Child Support Enforcement Agcy.
Carman, Corrine S. ....'67 '92 C.923 B.A. L.117 J.D. [🅂 Vorys,S.S.&P.]
Carnahan, John A., (AV) .... '30 '55 C&L.228 B.A., J.D. 767 South 5th Street‡
Carney, John Patrick .... '76 '01 C&L.608 B.A., J.D. [🄰 Porter W.M.&A.]
Carney, Stephen P. ....'69 '94 C.973 B.A. L.150 J.D. Atty. Gen. Jim Petro
Carpenter, Elwood L. ....'14 '38 C&L.608 B.A., LL.B. 5300 E. Main St.
Carpenter, Errett L. ....'19 '54 C.421 A.B. L.1340 LL.B. 5300 E. Main St.
Carpenter, James C., (AV) ....'49 '75 C.610 B.A. L.608 J.D. [Lane,A.&H.]
Carpenter, Michael H., (AV) ....'53 '77 C&L.608 B.A., J.D. [Carpenter&L.]

Carpenter & Lipps LLP, (AV) BR
280 Plaza, Suite 1300, 280 North High Street, 43215
Telephone: 614-365-4100 Facsimile: 614-365-9145
URL: http://www.carpenterlipps.com
Members of Firm: Michael H. Carpenter; Jeffrey A. Lipps; David A. Wallace; Timothy R. Bricker; Daniel R. Mordarski; Angela M. Paul. Associates: Shannon M. Shoaff; Monique A. Hall; Katheryn M. Lloyd; Shana O. See; Daniel M. Massey; Joel E. Sechler; Caroline D. Imhoff. Of Counsel: Michael N. Beekhuizen.
General Civil Trial, Appellate and Federal Practice. Banking. Business. Commercial, Franchise Law, Employment, Media, First Amendment, Health Care, Libel, Communications Law, Products Liability, Professional Liability, Sports Law, Complex, Class Action and Multi-District Litigation.

See Professional Biographies, COLUMBUS, OHIO

Carr, James A. ....'51 '80 C.112 B.A. L.117 J.D. 30 E. Broad St., 25th Fl.
Carr, Velda K. Hofacker ....'— '88 C.8 B.A. L.273 J.D. Asst. Atty. Gen.
Carroll, D. David, (BV) .... '64 '90 C.608 B.A. L.117 J.D. [Bailey C.]
Carroll, James M., (BV) ....'50 '76 C.150 B.A. L.1340 J.D. Asst. Atty. Gen.
Carroll, Roger F., (BV) ....'54 '79 C.188 B.A. L.893 J.D. Asst. Atty. Gen.
Carruthers, David F., (BV) ....'55 '79 C.608 B.A. L.851 J.D. 1500 W. 3rd Ave.
Carson, Cynthia Butler '64 '94 C&L.608 B.A., J.D.
Sr. Coun.-Trans., Amer. Elect. Power Service Corp.
Carsonie, Frank W., (AV) ....'65 '92 C.967 B.A. L.117 J.D. [Benesch,F.C.&A.]
Carter, Danielle Marie ....'73 '99 C.473 B.A. L.117 J.D. [🄰 Isaac,B.L.&T.]
Carter, James M. '27 '56 L.893 LL.B.
(adm. in VA; not adm. in OH) [Mahota&C.]
Carter, Theresa L. ....'59 '85 C.436 B.S. L.608 J.D. Asst. City Atty.
Carter, Wanda L., (AV) ....'48 '82 C.97 B.S. L.608 J.D. [Moots,C.&W.]
Cary, Nelson D. ....'68 '94 C.20 B.A. L.902 J.D. [🄰 Vorys,S.S.&P.]
Casanova, Janice E. ....'73 '02 C.896 B.S. L.608 J.D. [🄰 Buckingham,D.&B.]
Case, Larry D., (BV) '57 '82
C.473 A.B. L.945 J.D. V.P., Sr. Coun., The Huntington Natl. Bk.
Case, William R., (AV) ....'48 '73 C.8 B.A. L.607 J.D. [Thompson H.]
Casey, John F., (AV) ....'39 '65 C&L.608 B.S., J.D. 600 South High Street
Casey, Karen S., (BV) .... '48 '91 C.737 B.A. L.608 J.D. 369 S. High St.
Cason-Adams, Sharon ....'— '97 C.266 B.S. L.117 J.D. [🄰 Roetzel&A.]
Casto, Jamie Ruff '70 '96
C.96 B.S.B.A. L.117 J.D. Corp. Coun., Compliance Nationwide Ins.

Casto, Jennifer B. .... '69 '05 C.631 B.A. L.117 J.D. [Ⓐ Wiles,B.B.&B.]
Catalano, William A., (AV) .... '49 '74 C.49 B.S. L.117 J.D. [Mitchell,A.C.&B.]
Cataldi, Donald A. .... '45 '83 C.209 B.A. L.117 J.D. Hearing Offr., Ohio Parole Bd.
Cavalaris, Nicholas C., (BV) .... '66 '93 C.473 B.S. L.424 J.D. [Ⓐ Smith&H.]
Cavalieri, Nick V., (AV) .... '47 '73 C&L.608 B.S.B.A., J.D. [Bailey C.]
Cavezza, Edward, (AV) .... '57 '82 C.754 B.S. L.602 J.D. [Peck,S.&W.]
Cecil, Andrew W., (BV) .... '60 '86 C.235 B.A.B.S. L.421 J.D. [Plymale]
Cecil, Cynthia A. .... '47 '79 C.1150 B.A. L.383 J.D. Appl. Ct. J.
Cennamo, Louis W., (CV) .... '50 '77 C.608 B.A. L.117 J.D. [L.Cennamo]
Cennamo, Louis, (CV) .... 5 E. Long St., Ste. 605
Chamblin and Snyder, (AV) .... 5600 Morse Road
Champ, Stephanie D. .... '68 '02 C&L.608 B.A., J.D. [Ⓐ Carlile P.&M.]
Chance, Sharlene I. .... '72 '99 C&L.117 B.A., J.D. [Ⓐ Maguire&S.]
Chapin, Lance .... '69 '98 C&L.608 B.A., J.D. [Stein,C.]
Chapman, Shirley Elaine .... '42 '93 C.1208 B.S. L.117 J.D. Atty. Gen., State of Ohio
Chappano, Perry M., (AV) .... '61 '86 C&L.608 B.A., J.D. [Chappano W.]
Chappano Wood, PLL, (AV) .... 8 E. Long St., 9th Fl.
Chappelear, Stephen E., (AV) .... '52 '77 C&L.608 B.A., J.D. [Hahn L.&P.]
Charney, Deborah J. .... '63 '92 C.705 B.A. L.117 J.D. Ind. Comm. of OH
Charvat, Marie, (BV) .... '51 '78 C.385 B.A. L.1003 J.D. Asst. Atty.Gen.

Chasser, Timothy G., (BV) '49 '76 C.201 B.A. L.161 J.D.
2109 West Fifth Avenue, Suite A, 43212-1976
Telephone: 614-777-7610 Fax: 614-777-7620 URL: http://www.chasserlawoffice.com
URL: http://www.lawyers.com/chasserlaw
Civil Practice. Personal Injury, Workers Compensation and Social Security Disability Law.
See Professional Biographies, COLUMBUS, OHIO

Chastang, Charles J., (AV) .... '06 '37 C.150 65 E. State St.‡
Cheap, Richard A. '51 '77 C.363 B.A. L.597 J.D.
Exec. V.P., Gen. Coun. & Secy., The Huntington Natl. Bk.
Cheek, Emerson, III, (AV) .... '44 '70 C&L.607 B.A., J.D. [Cheek&Z.]

Cheek & Zeehandelar, LLP, (AV) BB
471 East Broad Street, 12th Floor, P.O. Box 15069, 43215-3872
Telephone: 614-229-3888; 1-800-689-6677 Fax: 614-241-5865
Email: czlaw@czlaw.com
Members of Firm: Emerson Cheek, III; Steven J. Zeehandelar. Associates: Alessandro Sabatino; James C. Zury; Matthew Warner; Jon S. Doyle; Krishna K. Velayudhan.
Collections, Subrogation, and Creditors Rights.
See Professional Biographies, COLUMBUS, OHIO

Chesley, Dianna L. '61 '86
C.608 B.S. L.150 J.D. Asst. Disciplinary Coun., Supr. Ct.of Ohio
Chesley-Lahm, Diane .... '42 '76 C.856 A.B. L.117 J.D. Secy., State Supm. Ct.
Chester, Casey Edwin .... '60 '92 C.610 B.A. L.117 J.D. Chemical Abstracts Service
Chester, James J., (AV) .... '62 '87 C.31 B.A. L.930 J.D. [Chester,W.&S.]
Chester, John J., (AV) .... '20 '48 C.31 B.A. L.976 J.D. [Chester,W.&S.]
Chester, John J., Jr., (BV) .... '60 '89 C.608 B.A. L.117 J.D. [Chester,W.&S.]

Chester, Willcox & Saxbe LLP, (AV) BB
65 East State Street, Suite 1000, 43215-3413
Telephone: 614-221-4000 Fax: 614-221-4012
URL: http://www.cwslaw.com
Partners: Andrew J. Art; John W. Bentine; April R. Bott; Donald C. Brey; David J. Butler; James J. Chester; John J. Chester; John J. Chester, Jr.; J. Richard Emens; Stephen C. Fitch; Gary B. Gitlitz; Guy R. Humphrey; J. Anthony Kington; Eugene B. Lewis (Certified Specialist in Family Relations Law, Ohio State Bar Association); James V. Maniace; Sarah D. Morrison; Craig B. Paynter; Charles R. Saxbe; Elizabeth M. Stanton (Certified Specialist in Labor and Employment Law, Ohio State Bar Association); Elizabeth J. Watters; Roderick H. Willcox; Beatrice E. Wolper. Associates: James D. Abrams; W. Travis Garrison; Gerhardt A. Gosnell II; Timothy S. Horton; Lark T. Mallory; Joseph C. Pickens; Todd M. Rodgers; Jessica A. Shankle; Bobby Singh; Todd A. Weber. Of Counsel: William B. Saxbe.
Administrative, Bankruptcy, Business, Corporation, Education Law, Employment Law, Estate Planning, Family Law, General Practice, Intellectual Property Law, International Law, Legislative, Municipal, Oil and Gas, Probate, Public Utilities, Real Estate, Taxation, Trial and Appeals.
See Professional Biographies, COLUMBUS, OHIO

Cheugh, Robert W., II .... '54 '79 C&L.117 B.A., J.D. 2066 W. Henderson Road
Chicoine, Julie E., (BV①) .... '58 '93 C.1341 B.S. L.326 J.D. The OH State Univ.
Chilcoat, David L., (AV) .... '47 '84 C.665 B.A. L.117 J.D. [Campbell,H.C.&V.]
Chilcoat, Jeffrey R. .... '70 '98 C.608 B.A. L.117 J.D. [Campbell,H.C.&V.]
Chimbidis, Peter E. .... '67 '97 C.117 B.A. L.608 J.D. Pub. Def.
Chin, Pearl .... '— '05 C.976 B.A. L.339 J.D. [Ⓐ Vorys,S.S.&P.]
Cholar, Richard Thomas, Jr. '67 '92
C.757 B.S. L.117 J.D. State of OH, OH Dept. of Youth Servs.
Chretien, Alfred Michael .... '39 '92 C.454 B.A. L.117 J.D. Intellinetics, Inc.
Chrisley, Gail Darlene .... '— '99 C.888 B.S. L.117 J.D. Atty., Nationwide Trust Co.
Christensen, Jon A., (AV) .... '40 '81 C&L.608 B.A., J.D. [Christensen C.&D.]
Christensen, Mary W., (BV) .... '47 '83 C.945 B.A. L.608 J.D. [Christensen C.&D.]
Christensen, Michael Dean .... '61 '99 C.350 B.S. L.117 J.D. 1625 Bethel Road, Suite 102
Christensen, William J., (AV) .... '40 '68 C.210 A.B. L.608 J.D. 765 South High Street
Christensen Christensen & DeVillers, (AV) .... 401 North Front Street, Suite 350
Christie, Chester C. .... '56 '83 C.102 B.A. L.608 J.D. Dept. of Youth Servs.
Chubb, Kathryn A. .... '48 '91 C.999 B.S. L.161 J.D. [Ⓒ Garvin&H.]
Chuparkoff, Mark .... '73 '00 C.473 B.A. L.851 J.D. [Earl,W.A.&D.]
Cimperman, Anthony J. .... '61 '89 C.363 B.A. L.1003 J.D. 3130 N. High St.
Cincione, Alphonse P., (AV) .... '34 '61 C.973 B.S. L.608 J.D. [Butler,C.&D.]
Cincione, Karen A. .... '63 '89 C.473 B.A. L.575 J.D. [Ⓐ Vorys,S.S.&P.]
Cincione, Matthew P., (BV) .... '60 '85 C.608 B.A. L.117 J.D. [Ⓐ Butler,C.&D.]
Ciriaco, Anthony C., (AV) .... '58 '83 C.893 B.S. L.575 J.D. [Vorys,S.S.&P.]
Claggett, Edward R. '49 '74 C&L.608 B.S.B.A., J.D.
(adm. in MA; not adm. in OH) V.P., Taxes, The Scotts Co.
Clapp, Richard A. .... '26 '52 C&L.930 B.B.A., LL.B. State Bur. of Workers' Comp.
Clark, Alison "Tex" .... '73 '99 C.33 B.A. L.588 J.D. Pub. Def.
Clark, Allison A. .... '79 '04 C&L.201 B.A., J.D. [Ⓐ P.J.Fulton]
Clark, D. Lewis, Jr., (AV) .... '65 '90 C.8 B.A. L.608 J.D. [Squire,S.&D.]
Clark, Daniel J. .... '77 '02 C.967 B.A. L.608 J.D. [Ⓐ Vorys,S.S.&P.]
Clark, Jeffery W., (BV) .... '56 '81 C.207 B.A. L.608 J.D. Asst. Chief Atty. Gen.
Clark, Lynne M. .... '60 '85 C.932 B.B.A. L.150 J.D. 3 Limited Pkwy.
Clark, R. Michael .... '67 '92 C.94 B.A. L.276 J.D. [Clark&H.]
Clark, Shelli Turner .... '74 '00 C.967 B.A. L.608 J.D. [Ⓐ Taft,S.&H.]
Clark, Toki Michelle, (BV) .... '61 '89 C.381 B.A. L.608 J.D. [Clark]
Clark, William A., (BV) .... '51 '81 C.608 B.A. L.117 J.D. 600 S. High St.
Clark, William L., (AV) .... '33 '60 C.674 B.S.E. L.608 J.D. 1167 Millcreek Lane
Clark, William T. .... '25 '49 L.245 LL.B. 1 Nationwide Plaza

Clark & Hedien
2000 Bethel Road, 43220-5610
Telephone: 614-538-5381; 538-5382 Fax: 614-538-5380
Members of the Firm: R. Michael Clark; Mark J. Hedien.
Civil Litigation, Corporate, Securities, Immigration.
See Professional Biographies, COLUMBUS, OHIO

Clark Law Office, (BV) .... 233 South High Street

Clark, Perdue, Arnold & Scott Co, LPA, (AV)
471 East Broad Street Suite 1400, 43215-3853
Telephone: 614-469-1400 Fax: 614-469-0900 URL: http://www.cpaslaw.com
URL: http://www.lawyers.com/cpas
Dale K. Perdue; Paul O. Scott; James E. Arnold; D. Andrew List; David E. Kauffman; Glen R. Pritchard; Brandi Laser Seskes; Scott J. Stitt.
Personal Injury, Products Liability, Wrongful Death, Medical Malpractice, Insurance Law, Aviation Law, Railroad Law, Professional Negligence, Traumatic Brain Injury, Nursing Home Torts, Intentional Torts, Complex Civil and Commercial Litigation, Probate Litigation, Probate Administration, Estate Planning and Trusts.
See Professional Biographies, COLUMBUS, OHIO

Clarke, Elizabeth Ann '51 '85 C.518 A.B. L.339 J.D.
(adm. in MO; not adm. in OH) Ohio Judicial College
Clarke, Tricia L. .... '77 '04 C.608 B.A. L.117 J.D. [Ⓐ Maguire&S.]
Clary, Lori A. .... '67 '96 C.610 B.S. L.608 J.D. [Ⓐ Porter W.M.&A.]
Clary, Wendy .... '— '04 C&L.608 B.A., J.D. [Ⓐ Littler M.]

Cleary, Lora H., (BV) '66 '91 C&L.117 B.A., J.D.
1500 West Third Avenue, Suite 127, 43212
Telephone: 614-487-8210 Fax: 614-487-8212
Email: lcleary@aol.com URL: http://www.lawyers.com/lcleary
Family Law, Litigation, Mediation, Collaborative Law.
See Professional Biographies, COLUMBUS, OHIO

Cleary, Michael P., Attorney at Law, (BV) '51 '77
C.608 B.A. L.117 J.D. 2740 E. Main St.
Clifford, Dawn Colleen .... '60 '85 C.97 B.A. L.607 J.D. Nationwide Life Ins. Co.
Cline, Michael A., (AV) .... '54 '79 C&L.851 B.A., J.D. [Vorys,S.S.&P.]
Cline, Richard A., (AV) .... '55 '81 C.381 B.A.B.S. L.608 J.D. [R.A.Cline]

Cline, Richard A., & Co., LLC, (AV)
580 S. High Street, Suite 200, 43215
Telephone: 614-224-4114 Fax: 614-224-3804
Email: rcline@attorneycline.com URL: http://www.lawyers.com/richardcline
Member: Richard A. Cline.
Criminal Law, DUI, Traffic Tickets, Appellate, Misdemeanor Defense, Professional, License Defense, Medical and Legal License Defense.
See Professional Biographies, COLUMBUS, OHIO

Clinkscale, Debra Lynnette .... '58 '87 C.1208 B.A. L.201 J.D. E.P.A.
Clodfelder, Wiley H., (BV) .... '38 '83 C.608 B.F.A. L.117 J.D. 2555 Stafford Pl.
Cloppert, Frederick G., Jr., (AV) .... '43 '72 C.424 A.B. L.276 J.D. 225 E. Broad Street
Close, Michael L., (AV) .... '44 '75 C.608 B.S. L.117 J.D. [Wiles,B.B.&B.]
Cloud, Clifford R., (BV) .... '35 '61 C.611 B.A. L.608 J.D. [Cloud&O.]
Cloud, Linda Crawford, (BV) '43 '79
C.313 B.A. L.117 J.D. Admr., City Human Servs. Dept.
Cloud & Owen, (AV) .... 5354 N. High Street, Suite 3D
Clouse, Gerard J., (BV) .... '52 '84 C.608 B.S. L.117 J.D. [Sowald,S.&C.]
Clouse, Karen L., (BV) .... '61 '86 C.117 B.A. L.608 J.D. 5248 Parkcrest Lane
Clovis, Albert L., (AV) '35 '62 C.976 B.A. L.309 LL.B.
Prof. Emeritus, Ohio State Univ. College of Law
Clyde, Robert M., Jr., (CV) '41 '72
C.980 B.A. L.930 J.D. Exec. Dir., Ohio Legal Assistance Found.
Clymer, James G., (AV) .... '47 '74 C.608 B.A. L.851 J.D. [Agee C.M.&L.]
Clymer, Tony Allen .... '66 '91 C.610 B.A. L.117 J.D. [Clymer,T.A.]
Clymer, Tony A. .... 1420 Matthias Drive
Coady, Michael F. .... '57 '82 C&L.608 B.S., J.D. Pres., Coady Construction, Inc.
Coady, Thomas C., (AV) .... '38 '64 C&L.608 B.I.E., J.D. [Porter W.M.&A.]
Cobb, Tiffany Strelow .... '68 '94 C.675 B.A. L.910 J.D. [Ⓐ Vorys,S.S.&P.]
Cochran, Philip B. .... '52 '81 C.608 B.A. L.1187 J.D. [Ⓐ Thompson H.]
Cochran, Robert J. .... '66 '91 C.473 B.A. L.608 J.D. [Ⓒ Schottenstein,Z.&D.]
Cochran, Shirley A., (BV) .... '53 '79 C.8 B.A. L.7 J.D. Asst. Atty. Gen.
Coco, Mark S., (BV) .... '52 '77 C&L.608 B.A., J.D. [Harris,M.B.&C.]
Cocroft, Kimberly .... '73 '00 C&L.608 B.A., J.D. [Ⓐ Buckingham,D.&B.]
Cody, Robert M. .... '53 '82 C.608 B.A. L.117 J.D. Master Comr., Supm. Ct.
Coffee, Thomas P. .... '60 '87 C.381 B.A. L.7 J.D. 50 S. Main St., Ste. 502
Coffey, Mark S. .... '60 '85 C.81 B.A. L.117 J.D. John E. Sestina & Co.
Coffman, J. Gary, (AV) .... '43 '75 C.608 B.S. L.117 J.D. [Coffman&C.]
Coffman & Crowley, (AV) .... 150 West Wilson Bridge Road Suite 101
Cogan, J. Kevin, (AV) .... '— '78 C.210 B.A. L.930 J.D. [Jones D.]
Coglianese, Richard N. .... '67 '96 C.602 B.A. L.117 J.D. Atty. Gen. Off.
Cohan, Sanford Jerome .... '49 '74 P.O. Box 29027
Cohen, Bernard, (BV) .... '28 '52 C&L.608 B.A., J.D. 16 E. Broad St.
Cohen, David M. '47 '72 C&L.608 B.S.B.A., J.D.
Sr. Coun.-Credit, Fuel & Transp., Amer. Elect. Power Serv. Corp.
Cohen, Marshall Dean .... '59 '90 C.608 B.A. L.930 J.D. [M.D.Cohen]
Cohen, Mitchel D. .... '19 '47 C.608 B.S. L.266 J.D. 1141 S. High St.
Cohen, Richard .... '53 '80 C.08 B.S. L.07 J.D. 215 N. Front St.
Cohen, Robert Garrett, (AV) .... '63 '89 C.477 B.A. L.608 J.D. [Kegler,B.H.&R.]
Cohen, Robert H., (AV) .... '51 '76 C.473 B.A. L.150 J.D. [Porter W.M.&A.]
Cohen, Sheila Deselich '67 '92 C.201 B.S. L.608 J.D.
Associate General Counsel, Health Plan Services, Inc.
Cohen, Susan A., (BV) .... '62 '87 C.901 B.A. L.665 J.D. [Vorys,S.S.&P.]
Cohen, Marshall D., LLC .... 1299 Olentangy River Rd., Unit 2B
Cohn, Robert G. '56 '91 C.385 B.A. L.117 J.D.
Sr. Coun.-Human Resources, Amer. Elect. Power Serv. Corp.
Colasurd, Donald M., (AV) '30 '60
C.610 B.S.C. L.1003 J.D. Chm., The Indus. Comm. of Ohio
Colasurd, Michael D., (BV) .... '54 '84 C.608 B.S. L.117 J.D. [Kennedy&C.]
Colburn, Joseph L., Jr. .... '48 '78 C&L.608 B.A., J.D. 854 E. Broad St.

Colby, Richard D., (BV) '49 '74 C.608 B.A. L.117 J.D.
169 East Livingston Avenue, 43215
Telephone: 614-461-1516 Fax: 614-461-1520
Email: colbylaw@aol.com URL: http://www.lawyers.com/richardcolbylaw
Civil and Criminal Trials, Family Law, Divorce, Child Custody, Child Support, Visitation Rights, Securities Litigation, Securities Fraud, Small Business Law, Real Estate and Corporate Law.
See Professional Biographies, COLUMBUS, OHIO

Cole, Philip Earl '55 '82 C.97 B.A. L.851 J.D.
Ohio Assoc. of Community Action Agcys.
Cole, Stuart A. .... '52 '77 C.367 B.A. L.93 J.D. Asst. Atty. Gen., OH Atty. Gen. Off.
Cole, William J. .... '67 '97 C.207 B.A. L.1187 J.D. Asst. Atty. Gen.
Coleman, Alicia Regina .... '61 '94 C.918 B.A. L.93 J.D. [A.R.Coleman]
Coleman, Cynthia .... '64 '89 C.477 B.A. L.608 J.D. Spec. Asst. Pros. Atty.
Coleman, David G., (AV) .... '38 '63 C.674 A.B. L.309 LL.B. Harmony Ball Co.
Coleman, LaVawn D. '63 '89 C&L.608 B.A., J.D.
Asst. V.P., Asst. Secy., Asst. Gen. Coun., Grange Mutual Cas. Co.
Coleman, Michael A., (BV) .... '60 '86 C.216 B.A. L.117 J.D. [Harris,M.B.&C.]

Coleman, Paul H., (BV) . . . '43 '68 C&L.608 B.A., J.D. Dir., Gov. Off. of Recovery Servs.
Coleman, Alicia R., Law Office of . . . . P.O. Box 07938
Colley, David A., (BV) . . . . '53 '78 C.608 B.A. L.201 J.D. 1820 Northwest Blvd.
Colley, Michael F., (AV) . . . . '36 '61 C&L.608 B.A., J.D. [Colley S.&A.]

Colley Shroyer & Abraham Co., L.P.A., (AV) [BR]
Hoster and High Building, 536 South High Street, 43215-5674
Telephone: 614-228-6453 Fax: 614-228-7122
Email: csa@ee.net URL: http://www.colleyshroyerabraham.com
Michael F. Colley; David I. Shroyer; Daniel N. Abraham;—Roger Garcia.
Civil Trial Practice. Personal Injury, Medical Malpractice, Automobile Accidents, Wrongful Death, Railroad Accidents, Slip and Fall, Negligence, Product Liability and Toxic Torts.
Reference: Bank One of Columbus, NA.
See Professional Biographies, COLUMBUS, OHIO

Collier, Orla Ellis, III, (AV) . . . . . . '49 '75 C.608 B.A. L.607 J.D. [Benesch,F.C.&A.]
Collins, Brian F. '56 '82 C.209 B.A. L.424 J.D.
(adm. in IL; not adm. in OH) Bank One, Columbus, NA
Collins, Donald M., (BV) . . . . '50 '87 C.790 B.A. L.117 J.D. OH Indus. Comm.
Collins, Mark C. . . . . '65 '93 C.188 B.S. L.117 J.D. 225 E. Broad Street
Collins, Michael J. . . . . '69 '94 C.27 B.A. L.608 J.D. [🄰 J.C.Nemeth&Assoc.]
Collins, Philip M. . . . . '47 '73 [P.M.Collins&Assoc.]
Collins, Philip M., and Associates . . . . 21 E. State Street, Suite 930
Collis, Elizabeth Y. . . . . '63 '90 C.385 A.B. L.930 J.D. [Collis&C.]
Collis, Todd W., (BV) . . . . '65 '91 C.207 B.A. L.930 J.D. [Collis&C.]
Collis & Collis, LLC, (BV) . . . . 1650 Lake Shore Dr.
Colner, James D., (AV) . . . . '53 '79 C.608 B.A. L.117 J.D. [Smith&C.]
Colombo, J. Corey . . . . '75 '00 C.473 B.A. L.117 J.D. [🄰 Schottenstein,Z.&D.]
Colvin, Terra L. . . . . '73 '99 C.473 B.A. L.117 J.D. [D.G.Reinhard]
Comek, Laura MacGregor . . . . '71 '99 C.980 B.S.B.A. L.117 J.D. [Crabbe,B.&J.]
Comeras, Leonard A. . . . . . . '50 '75 C&L.608 B.A., J.D. Pres. & COO, Easton Shoes, Inc.
Compson, Geo. A. . . . . '25 '54 C.608 B.A. L.266 J.D. State Dept. of Health

Compton, Jeffrey P.
(See Grove City)

Conard, William T., II, (AV) . . . . '58 '83 C.631 B.A. L.608 J.D. [Bricker&E.]
Concilla, Dennis J., (BV) . . . . '51 '79 C.665 B.A. L.117 J.D. [Carlile P.&M.]
Conger-Cox, Pamela Alice . . . . '58 '86 C.30 B.S. L.851 J.D. Pub. Def.
Conklin, Mara E. '71 '96
C.1021 B.S. L.608 J.D. Staff Atty., Ct. Appointed Spec. Advoc. Off.
Conley, Donald W., (BV) . . . . '47 '73 C.608 B.A. L.930 J.D. 2695 Schaaf Dr.
Conley, Robert W. . . . . '79 '04 C.477 B.M. L.665 J.D. [🄰 Vorys,S.S.&P.]
Connelly, Chris L. . . . . '75 '04 C.608 B.S. L.201 J.D. [🄰 Vorys,S.S.&P.]
Conners, Kevin R., (BV) . . . . '59 '89 C.112 B.A. L.608 J.D. [🄲 Vorys,S.S.&P.]
Connor, Daniel D., (AV) . . . . '39 '68 C&L.608 B.S., J.D. [Connor B.]
Connor, John A. . . . . '40 '66 C.524 B.S. L.608 J.D. Com. Pleas J.
Connor, Thomas W., (AV) . . . . '19 '49 C&L.608 B.S., J.D. [T.W.Connor&Assoc.]

Connor Behal, LLP, (AV)
501 South High Street, 43215
Telephone: 614-464-2025 Fax: 614-224-8708 URL: http://www.connorbehal.com
URL: http://www.lawyers.com/ddconnorlaw
Daniel D. Connor; Robert J. Behal;—Dennis P. Evans; Kenneth S. Hafenstein (Certified Specialist in Workers Compensation Law, Ohio State Bar Association); Daniel Joseph Fusco; John P. Johnson; Gary P. Martin.
Civil and Criminal Litigation, Driving While Intoxicated, Criminal Defense, DUI, White Collar Crimes, Professional Licenses, Workers Compensation, Business Law, Tax Planning, Family Law, Divorce, Probate and Estate Planning, Personal Injury, Automobile Accidents, Negligence, Social Security, Disability.
Reference: Key Bank National Association.
See Professional Biographies, COLUMBUS, OHIO

Connor, Thomas W., & Assocs., (AV) . . . . 150 E. Mound St.
Connors, James P., (BV) . . . . '58 '86 C.473 B.A. L.608 J.D. 221 South High Street
Conrad, David K., (AV) . . . . '56 '80 C.385 A.B. L.608 J.D. [Bricker&E.]
Conroy, John T., (AV) . . . . '37 '62 C.610 B.S. L.607 J.D. 3363 Tremont Rd.
Conway, Daniel R., (AV) . . . . '55 '80 C.472 B.S. L.477 J.D. [Porter W.M.&A.]
Cook, A. Brant . . . . '75 '03 C.608 B.A. L.893 J.D. [🄰 Saia&P.]
Cook, Brian Charles '57 '87
C.608 B.A. L.117 J.D. Atty. Gen. Off., Charitable Organization
Cook, Christopher Shane . . . . '56 '91 C.610 B.S. L.117 J.D. Atty. Gen.'s Off.
Cook, Dale D., (BV) . . . . '56 '82 C.855 B.A. L.228 J.D. [🄰 Wiles,B.B.&B.]
Cook, David W., (BV) . . . . '62 '88 C.101 B.A. L.911 J.D. [Vorys,S.S.&P.]
Cook, Frank Hupp . . . . . '45 '96 C.280 A.B.J. L.861 J.D. City of Columbus, City Atty. Off.
Cook, Gwendolyn Alicia . . . . '48 '83 C.608 B.S. L.117 J.D. 1 Nationwide Plaza
Cook, John W., (AV) . . . . '52 '77 C.473 B.S. L.608 J.D. [Johrendt,C.&E.]
Cook, John W., III, (AV) . . . . '52 '78 C.118 B.A. L.608 J.D. [Bricker&E.]
Cook, Joseph R., (AV) '— '71
C.207 B.A. L.607 J.D. Sr. Assoc. Gen. Coun., Bank One Corp.
Cook, Laura Folkerth . . . . '69 '99 C.608 B.S. L.477 J.D. [🄰 Hammond,S.&W.]
Cook, Mona Lisa . . . . '64 '90 C.569 B.A. L.608 J.D. Child Supp. Enforcement
Cook, S. Ronald, Jr., (AV) . . . . '45 '70 C&L.608 B.A., J.D. [Porter W.M.&A.]
Cook, Todd A., (BV) . . . . '66 '91 C.851 B.A. L.607 J.D. [Plunkett&C.]
Cooke, Andrew P., (BV) . . . . '63 '88 C.477 B.A. L.930 J.D. [Browning&C.]
Cooke, Elizabeth Ilgen . . . . '69 '94 C.473 B.A. L.608 J.D. Supervising Atty.
Cooke, Reggie . . . . '55 '94 C.608 B.A. L.117 J.D. 336-338 S. High St.
Cookson, Eloise Gries, (BV) '50 '76 C&L.851 B.A., J.D.
Sr. Coun., Bank One Corporation
Cookson, Kenneth R., (AV) . . . . '51 '77 C.373 B.A. L.851 J.D. [Kegler,B.H.&R.]
Cooper, Charles H., Jr., (BV) . . . . '60 '86 C.893 B.A. L.1209 J.D. 2175 Riverside Dr.
Cooper, Christopher M. . . . . '55 '84 C.608 B.A. L.117 J.D. 3055 Cleveland Ave.
Cooper, Curt D. . . . . '60 '86 C.49 B.S. L.608 J.D. One Riverside Plaza‡
Cooper, Cynthia A. . . . . '69 '95 C.608 B.S. L.117 J.D. Asst. Atty. Gen.
Cope, Monette W. . . . . '— '88 C&L.608 B.A., J.D. [🄰 Weltman,W.&R.]
Copening, Frank L., Jr. '05 '30 L.878 J.D.
(adm. in UT; not adm. in OH) 4445 Castleton Rd. W‡
Copley, Michael F., (BV) . . . . '60 '86 C.15 B.S. L.179 J.D. [Buckingham,D.&B.]
Copp, Matthew R. . . . . '68 '94 C.473 B.A. L.608 J.D. 2291 Scioto Harper Dr.
Coppel, Paul S., (AV) '58 '84 C&L.608 B.A., J.D.
Pres., Land Oper., M/I Schottenstein Homes, Inc.
Corbin, Trisha M. . . . . '76 '01 C.318 B.A. L.150 J.D. [🄰 Vorys,S.S.&P.]
Corcoran, Elizabeth Ann . . . . '61 '89 C.880 B.S. L.472 J.D. 360 S. Grant Ave.
Corcoran, Matthew C. . . . . '— '04 C.477 B.A. L.608 J.D. [🄰 Jones D.]
Cordray, Margaret Meriwether '61 '90 C.169 B.A. L.1066 J.D.
Prof. of Law, Capital Univ.
Coriell, Angela . . . . '76 '03 C.608 B.A. L.179 J.D. [🄰 Weltman,W.&R.]
Corl, Christina L., (AV) . . . . '69 '95 C.932 B.S. L.1187 J.D. [Crabbe,B.&J.]
Cormany, Carl E. . . . . '54 '80 C.473 A.B. L.477 J.D. [🄰 Mazanec,R.&R.]
Cornelius, Patrick D. . . . . '70 '97 C.602 B.A. L.893 J.D. [🄰 Squire,S.&D.]

Corner, Barbara S. '52 '79 C.696 B.A. L.982 J.D.
(adm. in NY; not adm. in OH) 1917 Lytham Rd.‡
Cornett, Jack . . . . '53 '78 C.473 B.A. L.1003 J.D. Asst. Atty. Gen.
Cornwell, Virginia C., Law Offices of '69 '99 C.17 B.A L.608 J.D.
533 South Third Street
Corsi, Q. Albert . . . . '33 '62 C.608 B.S. L.1003 J.D. Asst. Atty. Gen.
Cosgrove, Timothy J., (AV) . . . '61 '87 C&L.161 B.A., J.D. [Squire,S.&D.] (☉Cleveland)
Costello, Daniel W., (BV) . . . . '52 '80 C.974 A.B. L.608 J.D. [Porter W.M.&A.]
Cottone, Carl N., Law Office of '46 '03 C.1097 B.S. L.117 J.D.
400 S. Fifth St., Ste. 102
Coughlan, Jonathan E., (AV) . . . . '53 '78 C.319 B.A. L.930 J.D. Disciplinary Counsel
Counts, Thomas Scott, (BV) . . . . '60 '85 C.607 B.A. L.608 J.D. State Teachers Retire. Sys.
Coval, Paul J., (BV) . . . . '49 '79 C.737 B.A. L.117 J.D. [Vorys,S.S.&P.]
Cowans, Timothy E., (BV) . . . . '63 '88 C.737 B.A. L.608 J.D. [Scott,S.&W.]
Cox, David G. . . . . '58 '89 C.608 B.A. L.117 J.D. [Lane,A.&H.]
Cox, Donald A. . . . . '54 '79 C.999 B.S. L.608 J.D. Judicial Alternatives of Ohio, Inc.
Cox, Edward J., Jr., (BV) . . . . '47 '72 C.97 B.A. L.477 J.D. [Cox,S.&P.]
Cox, Garth G., (BV) . . . . '56 '81 C.608 B.A. L.117 J.D. [Harris,M.B.&C.]
Cox, Matthew R. '73 '00 C.363 B.A. L.989 J.D.
Asst. Chf. Legal Coun., Auditor of State of Ohio
Cox, Paul L., (AV) . . . . '46 '75 C.367 B.A. L.1003 J.D. 222 E. Town St.
Cox, Yvette A., (AV) . . . . '48 '79 C.608 B.A. L.117 J.D. [Bailey C.]
Cox, Stein & Pettigrew Co., L.P.A., (AV) . . . . 115 W. Main St., Ste. 400

Crabbe, Brown & James LLP, (AV) [BR]
500 South Front Street, Suite 1200, 43215 ⊙
Telephone: 614-228-5511 Fax: 614-229-4559
Email: info@cbjLawyers.com URL: http://www.cbjLawyers.com
Vincent J. Lodico; Steven B. Ayers; Jeffrey M. Brown; Larry H. James; Richard D. Wetzel, Jr.; Luis M. Alcalde; John C. Albert; George R. McCue, III; Michael R. Henry; Robert C. Buchbinder; Steven A. Davis (Resident, Lancaster Office); John P. Kennedy; Michael T. Shannon; Christina L. Corl; Daniel J. Hurley; Laura MacGregor Comek. Associates: Steven E. Miller; Phillip A. Templeton; James L. Ervin, Jr.; Amanda C. Baker; Matthew R. Planey; Jeffrey D. Houser; Eileen R. Bower; Stephen D. Brown (Resident, Lancaster Office). Of Counsel: William A. Goldman; Michael Braunstein; Andy Douglas; Mark E. Kerns (Resident, Urbana Office); Brian R. McGraw (Resident, Cleveland Office).
General Insurance Defense, Product Liability, Professional Malpractice, Premises Liability, Environmental and Toxic Tort Claims, Employment and Labor Law, Tax Matters, General Business and Corporate Law and Litigation, Banking and Securities, Real Estate, Probate and Estate Planning, Criminal Law, Administrative, Regulatory and Governmental Law, Workers Compensation, Intellectual Property, Fire, Arson and Fraud, Fidelity and Surety Life, Accident and Health, Insurance Coverage Law, Construction Claims, Health and Hospital Law, Oil, Gas and Energy Law, Transportation Law, Automobile Dealer Law, Zoning, International Practice and Domestic Law, Land Use Planning, and Eminent Domain.
Cincinnati, Ohio Office: 30 Garfield Place, Suite 740, 45202. Telephone: 513-784-1525. Fax: 513-784-1250.
Cleveland, Ohio Office: 1280 W. Third Street. Telephone: 216-574-9312.
Lancaster, Ohio Office: 111 South Broad Street, Suite 209, 43130. Telephone: 740-689-1743. Fax: 740-689-1746.
Urbana, Ohio Office: 118 Scioto Street. Telephone: 937-652-4000.
See Professional Biographies, COLUMBUS, OHIO

Crabtree, Molly S. . . . . '75 '01 C.608 B.S. L.124 J.D. [🄰 Porter W.M.&A.]
Craig, Roger A. '62 '89 C.952 A.B. L.201 J.D.
Assoc. V.P. & Assoc. Gen. Coun., Nationwide Insurance
Craine, Kevin A., (AV) . . . . '56 '82 C.607 B.A. L.117 J.D. [Kincaid,R.&C.]
Crane, Michael S., (AV) . . . . '53 '78 C.309 B.A. L.608 J.D. Crane Plastics Co.
Crawford, Dale A. . . . . '43 '68 C&L.608 B.S., J.D. Com. Pleas J.
Crawford, Linda S. . . . . '58 '84 C.737 B.A. L.117 J.D. Leg. Serv. Comm.
Crawford, Timothy D. . . . . '69 '97 C.608 B.A. L.117 J.D. One Nationwide Plz.
Creed, Sheryl . . . . '59 '84 C.97 B.S. L.851 J.D. Asst. Atty. Gen.
Crespo, John C. '68 '94 C.228 B.S.E. L.276 J.D.
(adm. in NY; not adm. in OH)
Sr. Coun.-Credit, Fuel & Transp., Amer. Elect. Power Serv. Corp.
Crim, Connie A., (BV) . . . . '53 '89 C.528 B.A. L.608 J.D. 30 E. Broad St., 3rd Fl.
Criss, Michael Scott . . . . '69 '97 C.608 B.A. L.117 J.D. Atty. Gen.
Crist, Tyson A. . . . . '73 '99 C.970 B.A. L.608 J.D. [🄰 Schottenstein,Z.&D.]
Critchett, Eugene R. . . . . '75 '01 C.354 B.A. L.608 J.D. [🄰 Plymale]
Crites, D. Michael, (AV) . . . . '48 '78 C.871 B.S. L.607 J.D. [Rich,C.&D.]
Crognale, Corey V., (BV) . . . . '54 '80 C.434 B.A. L.117 J.D. [Schottenstein,Z.&D.]
Cromley, Robert E., Jr. . . . . '57 '82 C.117 B.A. L.150 J.D. State Indust. Comm.
Cronheim, George K. . . . . '61 '98 C&L.608 B.S., J.D. State Bur. of Wkrs. Comp.
Crosby, Eva Mae . . . . '11 '37 C.604 B.A. L.608 J.D. 2323 E. 5th St.
Cross, Jeffrey D. '56 '82 C&L.150 B.A., J.D.
Dep. Gen. Coun.- Corp., Amer. Elect. Power Serv. Corp.
Crossett, Kevin S. '60 '89 C.999 B.S. L.884 J.D.
V.P. & Assoc. Gen. Coun., Nationwide Insurance
Crow, Scot C. . . . . '72 '97 C.999 B.S. L.117 J.D. [🄰 Roetzel&A.]
Crowley, Timothy G., (BV) . . . . '48 '75 C.276 B.S.F.S. L.117 J.D. [Coffman&C.]
Culbreath, Stanlee E. . . . . '47 '75 C.608 B.A. L.117 [Culbreath&Assoc.]
Culbreath & Associates . . . . 90 N. Nelson Rd.
Culley, Christopher M., (AV) '54 '82
C.608 B.A. L.201 J.D. Dep. Gen. Coun., Ohio State University, The
Culshaw, Kelly L. . . . . '70 '96 C&L.608 B.A., J.D. Pub. Def. Off.
Cunningham, Catherine A., (BV) . . . . . . '58 '83 C.25 B.A. L.608 J.D. [🄰 Plank&B.] (Pat.)
Cunningham, Guy H. '41 '68 C.24 B.A. L.276 J.D.
Assoc. Gen. Coun., Battelle Memorial Institute
Cunningham, R. P., (AV) . . . . '24 '50 C&L.608 B.A., J.D. 10 W. Broad St.
Cupps, David S., (AV) . . . . '36 '66 C.309 A.B. L.608 J.D. [Vorys,S.S.&P.]
Cupps, Stewart H. . . . . '70 '99 C.608 B.S. L.201 J.D. [🄰 Kegler,B.H.&R.]
Curley, W. Charles, (AV) . . . . '53 '78 C&L.608 B.A., J.D. [Keener D.C.&P.]
Curp, John P. . . . . '70 '95 C.473 B.S. L.347 J.D. [Taft,S.&H.]
Curphey, James D., (AV) . . . . '58 '83 C.608 B.S. L.930 J.D. [Porter W.M.&A.]
Curran, Douglas A. . . . . '69 '95 C.107 B.A. L.608 J.D. Asst. Atty. Gen.
Currence, Kysha L. . . . . '— '02 C.608 B.S.B.A. L.273 J.D. [🄰 Porter W.M.&A.]
Currie, Michael W., (AV) . . . . '57 '83 C&L.608 B.S., J.D. [Thompson H.]
Curry, Bruce A., (BV) . . . . '65 '91 C&L.150 B.A., J.D. [Curry,R.S.&M.]
Curry, Roby, Schoenling & Mulvey Co., LLC, (BV) . . . . 8000 Ravine's Edge
Curtin, James B. . . . . '56 '85 C.473 B.S. L.117 J.D. [Jackson&C.]
Curtin, Kenneth C., (BV) . . . . '43 '69 C.884 A.B. L.188 J.D. 4949 Olentangy Blvd.
Curtin, Richard A., (BV) '48 '76 C.802 B.A. L.117 J.D.
Pres., American Alliance of Creditor Attorneys, Inc. (Legal Department)
Cusack, William W. . . . . '52 '85 C.184 B.A. L.117 J.D. 1874 Bluff Ave.
Custer, Kelly T. . . . . '70 '05 C.473 B.S. L.228 J.D. [🄰 Squire,S.&D.]
Cutter, James M., (BV) . . . . '51 '77 C.608 B.A. L.117 J.D. 85 E. Gay St.
Cvetanovich, Dan L., (AV) . . . . '52 '77 C.920 B.A. L.309 J.D. [Bailey C.]
Czerwonka, Kevin M. . . . . '65 '90 C&L.966 B.A., J.D. [Vorys,S.S.&P.]
Dachner, David A., (AV) . . . . '47 '72 C&L.608 B.A., J.D. 2369 E. Main St.
Dahlberg, C. Gustav . . . . '75 '01 C.610 B.A. L.608 J.D. [🄰 Babbitt&W.]

Dahmer, Douglas M. . . . . '52 '86 C.589 B.S. L.146 J.D. [Ⓐ Weltman,W.&R.]
Daicoff Baskin, Susan D. '62 '84 C&L.260 B.A., J.D.
(adm. in FL; not adm. in OH) Prof. of Law, Capital Univ.
Dailey, Gerald E. . . . . '55 '82 C.608 B.A. L.117 J.D. Coun., Nationwide Insurance
D'Alessandro, Mark T., (BV) . . . . '53 '79 C.93 A.B. L.117 J.D. Asst. Atty. Gen.
Daley, Richard C., (AV) '52 '78
C.117 B.A. L.608 J.D. Exec. V.P. & Gen. Coun., Pizzuti Inc.
D'Allura, Noelle D. . . . . '69 '94 C&L.201 B.S., J.D. Asst. Atty. Gen.
Damante, Mark A. . . . . '64 '90 C.473 B.A. L.930 J.D. 150 E. Broad Street
Damschroder, William R. . . . . '62 '88 C.610 B.B.A. L.608 J.D. Dept. of Commerce
Damsel, William Ray, II '56 '86 C.870 B.S. L.608 J.D.
OH Pub. Employees Retire. Sys.
Dana, Randall M., (AV) . . . . '45 '74 C.608 B.A. L.117 J.D. [Dana&P.]
Dana & Pariser Co., L.P.A., (AV) . . . . 800 E. Broad Street
Danchak, Michael G., (BV) . . . . '53 '78 C.385 A.B. L.659 J.D. [Frost&D.]
Dane, Philomena M., (AV) . . . . '55 '90 C.746 B.A. L.932 J.D. [Squire,S.&D.]
Dangel, Ruth Bope '52 '87
C&L.608 B.S.N., J.D. Staff Atty. Bd. of Comr. on Griev. & Disc.
Daniels, Gregory R. . . . . '76 '01 C.608 B.A. L.477 J.D. [Ⓐ Squire,S.&D.]
Daniels, Isiah, III . . . . '51 '76 C.8 B.A. L.7 J.D. Atty. Gen. Off.
Dankovic, Rae Ann . . . . '67 '93 C.477 B.A. L.215 J.D. Sr. Coun., Nationwide Insurance
Dansa, Jaime Allison . . . . '76 '02 C.607 B.S.B.A. L.117 J.D. [Ⓐ Porter W.M.&A.]
Darr, Elaine . . . . '75 '01 C.608 B.S.B.A. L.117 J.D. [Ⓐ Schottenstein,Z.&D.]
Dauber, Eric L. '59 '84 C.150 B.A. L.259 J.D.
(adm. in FL; not adm. in OH) Managing Trial Attorney, Nationwide Trial Division
Daugherty, Greg M. . . . . '79 '04 C.473 B.S. L.608 J.D. [Ⓐ Porter W.M.&A.]
Daulton, Stephen W., (AV) . . . . '49 '74 C&L.7 B.A., J.D. [S.W.Daulton&Assoc.]
Daulton, Stephen W., & Associates Co., L.P.A., (AV) . . . . 336 South High Street
Daum, Rebecca Lynn . . . . . '64 '90 C.608 B.A. L.117 J.D. 30 East Broad Street, 23rd Floor
D'Aurora, Jack, (AV) . . . . '55 '87 C.602 B.A. L.276 J.D. [Ⓒ Luper,N.&L.]
D'Aurora, John King . . . . '55 '91 50 W Broad St Ste 1200
Davidson, Alan J. . . . . '38 '64 C.645 B.A. L.309 LL.B. Exec. V.P., Natl. City Corp.
Davidson, James E., (AV) . . . . '56 '80 C.597 B.A. L.608 J.D. [Schottenstein,Z.&D.]
Davidson, Patricia A. . . . . . . '52 '85 C.973 A.B. L.150 J.D. Tenth District Court of Appeals
Davies, Donald A., (AV) . . . . '37 '62 C.197 A.B. L.608 J.D. [Bailey C.]
Davies, John L., (AV) . . . . '09 '32 C&L.608 B.A., J.D. 2741 Leeds Rd.‡
Davin, Elizabeth A. '64 '89
C.602 B.A. L.659 J.D. Asst. Gen. Coun., Nationwide Insurance
Davis, Claudia L., (BVⓉ) . . . . '56 '82 C.112 B.A. L.809 J.D. [Lane,A.&H.]
Davis, Gary E., (AV) . . . . '47 '76 C.197 A.B. L.477 J.D. [Vorys,S.S.&P.]
Davis, J. Todd, (CV) . . . . '63 '92 C.970 B.A. L.117 J.D. 115 W. Main St.
Davis, Jacquelin F. . . . . '54 '81 C&L.608 B.A., J.D. V. Chm., Ohio Employ. Relations Bd.
Davis, Kathleen V. . . . . '77 '03 C.473 B.A. L.608 J.D. [Ⓐ Scott,S.&W.]
Davis, Ronald E., (AV) . . . . '37 '62 C&L.608 B.S., LL.B. 341 S. Third St., Ste. 200
Davis, Scott W. . . . . '76 '04 C.150 B.S. L.608 J.D. [Ⓐ Bricker&E.]
Davis, Thomas Edward . . . . '65 '94 C.608 B.S. L.179 J.D. [T.E.Davis]
Davis, Thomas L., (AV) . . . . '56 '82 C.608 B.A. L.117 J.D. [Earl,W.A.&D.]
Davis, William A., (AV) . . . . '48 '74 C.210 B.A. L.930 J.D. [Ⓒ Butler,C.&D.]
Davis, William E. . . . . '65 '91 C.1260 B.A. L.117 J.D. [Ⓐ Wallace&W.]
Davis, Thomas E. . . . . 299 Taylor Ave.
Davisson, E. Rod . . . . '70 '02 C.266 B.S.B.A. L.117 J.D. [Ⓐ Kegler,B.H.&R.]
Dawicke, Jason . . . . '75 '02 C.608 B.A. L.117 J.D. [Ⓐ Granger]
Dawley, Kris M., (AV) . . . . '60 '85 C.967 B.A. L.117 J.D. [Schottenstein,Z.&D.]
Dawsey, David J. . . . . '— '02 C.1208 B.S. L.117 J.D. [Gallagher&D.]
Dawson, C. William, Jr., (BV) . . . . '38 '64 C.610 A.B. L.228 LL.B. [C.W.Dawson]
Dawson, Cynthia L. . . . . '67 '98 C.347 B.S. L.608 J.D. [Ⓐ R.A.Kelm]
Dawson, Shane M. . . . . '70 '96 C.608 B.S. L.117 J.D. [Ⓐ Bricker&M.]
Dawson, C. William Co., L.P.A., (BV) . . . . 1350 W. 5th Ave.
Day, Alison M. . . . . '72 '97 C.347 B.S. L.608 J.D. [Ⓐ Littler M.]
Day, Cynthia Page . . . . '57 '91 C.631 B.A. L.1048 J.D. State Indus. Comm.
Day, David L., (AV) . . . . '32 '67 C.992 B.A. L.608 J.D. [D.L.Day]
Day, Dennis G., (BV) . . . . '48 '82 C&L.608 B.A., J.D. 330 S. High St.
Day, Roger F., (AV) . . . . '29 '57 C.631 A.B. L.608 J.D. 1900 Huntington Ctr.‡
Day, David L., A Legal Professional Association, (AV) . . . 38 C South Fifth Street, Suite 3
Deal, John C., (AV) . . . . '47 '74 C&L.608 B.S., J.D. [Kisor&W.]
Deal, Roger F. . . . . '44 '88 C.266 B.S. L.117 J.D. 30 East Broad Street
Dean, Nannette B. . . . . '68 '95 C.94 B.A. L.117 J.D. 88 W. Mound St.
DeAngelo, P. Michael, (BV) . . . . '44 '69 C.363 B.A. L.930 J.D. [Calfee,H.&G.]
Deas, Brian T. . . . . '66 '93 C.473 B.S. L.608 J.D. [Manley D.K.]
Deavers, Maribeth, (AV) . . . . '59 '91 C.473 B.A. L.117 J.D. [Isaac,B.L.&T.] (Pat.)
Debolt, Sallie J. . . . . '48 '87 C&L.608 B.S., J.D. Asst. Atty. Gen.
Decile, Jeffrey Mark . . . . '51 '77 C.97 B.A. L.608 J.D. 165 N. High St., 2nd Fl.
Decker, Jack W., (BV) . . . . '49 '78 C.434 B.A. L.117 J.D. Asst. Atty. Gen.
Decker, Mark, (AV) . . . . '48 '73 C.737 B.A. L.608 J.D. [Decker,V.S.L.&V.]
Decker, Vonau, Seguin, Lackey & Viets Co., L.P.A., (AV) . . . . 620 E. Broad St.
Deeds, Gary W., (BV) . . . . '47 '77 C.608 B.S. L.1340 J.D. 3901 E. Livingston Ave.
Deep, Colleen A. . . . . '— '93 C.16 B.S. L.608 J.D. [Jones D.]
Deerwester, Steven J. . . . . . . '45 '75 C.973 B.S. L.930 J.D. Atty.,The Pub. Utilities Comm.
Deeter, Leann R. . . . . '58 '83 C.8 B.S. L.607 J.D. 854 E. Broad St.
DeFilippo, Richard M., Jr '64 '96
C.1323 B.S. L.117 J.D. Tax Consultant, Ernst & Young, L.L.P.
Defossez, Mark E., (BV) . . . . '57 '85 C.597 B.S. L.93 J.D. [Twyford&D.]
DeFrank, Stephen Edward, Jr. . . . . '64 '90 C.260 B.S.B.A. L.989 J.D. Atty. Gen.
DeGennaro, Nicholas C. . . . . . '69 '00 C.470 B.A. L.989 J.D. 445 Hutchinson Ave., Ste. 800
DeGenova, Jacqueline F. . . . . '65 '92 C.473 B.A. L.117 J.D. Jud. Law Clerk
Deisner, Vicki L. . . . . '55 '92 C.608 B.S. L.1340 J.D. Asst. Atty. Gen.
Dejelo, P. Jason . . . . '77 '03 C.659 B.A. L.608 J.D. [Ⓐ Vorys,S.S.&P.]
Deken, Christine E. . . . . '59 '84 C.608 B.A. L.117 J.D. 5220 Rockport Street
Delaney, Patricia A. . . . . '64 '90 C&L.851 B.A., J.D. City Atty.
deLanglade-Spriggs, Elise M. '71 '97 C.967 B.A. L.117 J.D.
Dir, Legis. Affairs, Ohio Home Builders Assn.
DelaRosa, Regina M. . . . . '56 '88 C.363 B.S. L.117 J.D. Def. Logistics Agcy.
De Leo, Robin Ronquillo '— '90 C.475 B.A. L.861 J.D.
(adm. in LA; not adm. in OH) [Ⓒ Dreher L.&T.]
DeLeone, James F., (AV) . . . . '26 '51 C&L.608 B.S.B.A., J.D. [Ⓒ Benesch,F.C.&A.]
deLevie, Raymond M. . . . . '48 '77 C.645 B.S. L.273 J.D. 81 S. 4th St., Ste. 300
Deley-Shimer, Julie A. . . . . '60 '91 C.473 B.S. L.117 J.D. Sr. Coun., Nationwide Insurance
Delligatti, Anthony, Jr., (AV) . . . . '43 '72 C.608 B.A. L.117 J.D. [Carlile P.&M.]
Delligatti, Michael J., (BV) '60 '88 C.923 B.S.B.Ad. L.117 J.D.
500 S. Front St., Ste. 250
Delos Santos, Luis Darlucio . . . . '72 '00 C&L.201 B.A., J.D. Pub. Def. Comm.
de Luca, Daniel J. '68 '94 C.659 B.A. L.831 J.D.
(adm. in PA; not adm. in OH) [Nelson L.d.&H.] ⊙
DeMartin, Joan . . . . '58 '84 C.608 B.A. L.117 J.D. Staff Atty., E.P.A.

Demers, David J., (CV) . . . . '65 '91 C.528 B.S. L.851 J.D. [Roetzel&A.]
Demian, Mark J.A. . . . . '— '94 C.164 B.A. L.930 J.D. [Javitch,B.&R.]
DeMonte, Jessica E. . . . . '75 '00 C&L.608 B.A., J.D. [Ⓐ Squire,S.&D.]
Denbow-Hubbard, Stefania A. . . . . '47 '84 C.610 B.A. L.117 J.D. 4388 Scenic Dr.
Dendis, Lorree L. . . . . '74 '00 C.999 B.A. L.608 J.D. [Ⓐ Williams&P.]
Dengler, A. Brian, (AV) . . . . '53 '85 C.381 B.A. L.117 J.D. [Ⓒ Vorys,S.S.&P.]
Denmead, Craig, (AV) . . . . '47 '72 C&L.608 B.S., J.D. [Denmead]

Denmead Law Office, (AV) BB
37 West Broad Street, Suite 1100-B, 43215
Telephone: 614-228-5271 Fax: 614-228-7624
Email: cdenmead@sbcglobal.net URL: http://www.denmeadlaw.com
Craig Denmead.
Civil Trial and Appellate Practice and Personal Injury, Traumatic Brain Injury (TBI), Professional Negligence and Complex Litigation including Class Actions, Patents, Civil Rights, Civil Litigation, RICO, Employment and Political Subdivision Liability issues.
See Professional Biographies, COLUMBUS, OHIO

Denney, Patti L., (BV) . . . . '36 '85 C.112 Ed.D. L.117 J.D. 1387 Portage Dr.
Dennie, Dale L. . . . . '51 '88 C.114 B.A. L.608 J.D. Ohio Legal Rights Serv.
Dennis, John R. . . . . '32 '57 C&L.608 B.S., J.D. 4330 Clime Rd., N.‡
Dennis, Keith A. . . . . '59 '84 C.473 B.S. L.802 J.D. Pres., CarCorp, Inc.
Dennis, Michael William . . . . '64 '95 C.608 Ph.D. L.117 J.D. Chem. Abstracts Serv.
Dennison, Sallynda Rothchild . . . . 500 S. Front St., Ste. 102
DePascale, Diane Kappeler, (BV) . . . . '57 '81 C&L.201 B.A., J.D. 786 Northwest Blvd.
DePascale, Paul A., (BV) . . . . '60 '87 C.608 B.S. L.117 J.D. Title First Agency, Inc.
De Pascale, Vincent, (BV) . . . . '41 '67 C.201 B.A. L.607 J.D. 786 Northwest Blvd.
DePew, Lloyd G., Jr., (AV) . . . . '52 '81 C.608 B.S.B.A. L.117 J.D. [Porter W.M.&A.]
DeRose, Robert Eugene, II . . . . '66 '91 C.901 B.A. L.200 J.D. 360 South Grant Avenue
DeRousie, Charles S., (AV) . . . . '47 '73 C.1154 B.A. L.477 J.D. [Vorys,S.S.&P.]
Dersom, Charles R., (BV) . . . . '35 '65 C.608 B.S. L.266 J.D. 3311 Cross Keys Road
De Shetler, Kenneth E. . . . . '28 '58 C.851 B.B.A. L.608 J.D. 1840 Zollinger Rd.
Deshler, Dana A. . . . . '37 '66 C.608 B.A. L.117 LL.B. 373 S. High St., 24th Fl.‡
DeTemple, Matthew J., (AV) '56 '82 C.608 B.A. L.30 J.D.
Chf. Coun., OH Dept. of Educ.
Detrick, Joanne Weber, (BV) . . . . '57 '89 C.608 B.A. L.851 J.D. [Ⓐ R.A.Kelm]
DeVennish, Joseph Briggs, (BV) . . . . '17 '46 C&L.608 B.A., J.D. 949 King Ave.
DeVictor, Audra Osmena '68 '96 C.473 B.A. L.608 J.D.
Asst. Chf. Legal Coun., Auditor of State of Ohio
DeVillers, Sean P. '67 '96 C.737 B.A. L.117 J.D. [Christensen C.&D.]
Devine, Joseph C. . . . . '66 '91 C.724 B.A. L.273 J.D. [Baker&H.]
Devine, Patrick A., (AV) . . . . '55 '80 C.967 B.A. L.117 J.D. [Schottenstein,Z.&D.]
Dewey, Addison E. '21 '46 C.117 B.A. L.608 J.D.
Prof. of Law, Capital Univ. Law Sch.
Dewhirst, Scot E., (AV) . . . . '52 '78 C.608 B.A. L.117 J.D. [Artz&D.]
DeWitt, Michael W. . . . . '58 '96 C.610 A.B. L.117 J.D. 77 E. Nationwide Blvd.
DeYoung, Kathleen A. . . . . '60 '99 C&L.215 B.A., J.D. [Ⓐ Maguire&S.]
Dice, Daniel S. . . . . '72 '98 C.473 B.A. L.201 J.D. [D.S.Dice]
Dice, Daniel S., Co., LPA . . . . 338 South High Street
Dicker, Gary H. . . . . '48 '87 C.352 B.A. L.117 J.D. 555 S. 3rd Street
Dickerson, Brian E. . . . . '71 '97 C.430 B.S. L.117 J.D. [Maguire&S.]
Dickinson, Richard J. '45 '70 C.477 B.A. L.228 J.D.
Gen. Coun., Ohio School Bds. Assn.
DiCuccio, N. Gerald, (AV) . . . . '41 '66 C.602 B.A. L.608 J.D. [Butler,C.&D.]
Dicuccio, Nicole . . . . '70 '99 C.608 B.A. L.117 J.D. [Ⓐ Butler,C.&D.]
Diehm, Paul C. . . . . '44 '69 C.497 L.607 J.D. OH Indus. Comm.
Dieker, Lawrence L. '38 '68
C.378 B.S. L.502 J.D. V.P. & Gen. Coun., Borden Chemical, Inc.
Dieterich, Eric R. . . . . '56 '82 C&L.851 B.E., J.D. 941 Chatham Ln.
Dietrich, Thomas W., (BV) '48 '76
C.5 B.A. L.117 J.D. V.P. & Assoc. Coun., Nationwide Insurance
DiFranco, Brian C. . . . . '73 '03 C.608 B.A. L.8 J.D. 199 South Fifth St., Suite 302
Dile, Madelyn M. '51 '84 C.608 B.A. L.117 J.D.
State Dept. of Health, Div. of Health Facilities Reg.
Dilenschneider, John J., (AV) . . . . '31 '59 C.602 A.B. L.597 J.D. [Ⓒ Bailey C.]
Dill, Ralph E., (BV) . . . . '50 '75 C.117 B.A. L.608 J.D. [Harris,M.B.&C.]
Dilling, Thomas A. . . . . '62 '87 C.734 A.B. L.608 J.D. The State Medical Bd.
Dillon, Cynthia L. . . . . '54 '89 C.150 B.A. L.608 J.D. Coun., Nationwide Insurance
Dillon, Richd. E. '30 '58 C.602 B.S. L.608 J.D. 4718 Widner Ct.‡
Dillon, Thomas A., (AV) . . . . '45 '74 C.827 B.S. L.608 J.D. [Roetzel&A.]
DiMasi, Brian M., (CVⓉ) '— '95 C.645 B.S. L.117 J.D.
(adm. in PA; not adm. in OH) Corp. Coun., Safelite Group, Inc.
DiMickele, Susan M. . . . . '70 '95 C.473 B.A. L.608 J.D. [Squire,S.&D.]
Dimond, Richard Lee, (BV) . . . . '33 '57 C&L.608 B.A., J.D. 601 S. High Street
Dingledy, Jay R., (AV) . . . . '47 '72 C&L.608 B.B.A., J.D. [Schottenstein,Z.&D.]

Dingus, M. Shawn '72 '98 C.510 B.A. L.7 J.D.
1141 S. High Street, 43206
Telephone: 614-542-0220 Fax: 614-542-0230
Email: sdingus@dinguslaw.com URL: http://www.dinguslaw.com
Personal Injury, Wrongful Death, Civil Litigation, Criminal Law, Juvenile Law and Family Law.
See Professional Biographies, COLUMBUS, OHIO

Dinsmore & Shohl LLP, (AV) BB
10th Floor, 175 South Third Street, 43215-5134 ⊙
Telephone: 614-628-6880 FAX: 614-628-6890
Email: info@dinslaw.com URL: http://www.dinslaw.com
—Rick A. Lavinsky; Wayne A. Jenkins; Michael L. Squillace (Certified Specialist in Workers Compensation Law, Ohio State Bar Association); Marilena R. Walters; William M. Mattes; Kirk M. Wall. Associates: John D. Jolley; Michael J. King; Kelly L. Kauffman.
Appellate Practice; Bankruptcy; Banks and Banking; Business Law; Commercial Real Estate; Construction Law; Contracts; Corporate Law; Education Law; Environmental Law; General Practice; Labor & Employment; Leases and Leasing; Litigation; Medical Malpractice; Mortgages; Probate; Real Estate; Taxation; Trusts & Estates; Wills; Workers' Compensation; Zoning, Planning and Land Use.
Cincinnati, Ohio Office: 255 East Fifth Street, Suite 1900, 45202-4700. Telephone: 513-977-8200. FAX: 513-977-8141.
Dayton, Ohio Office: One Dayton Centre, One South Main Street, Suite 1300, 45402. Telephone: 937-449-6400. FAX: 937-449-6405.
Lexington, Kentucky Office: Lexington Financial Center, 250 West Main Street, Suite 1400, 40507. Telephone: 859-425-1000. FAX: 859-425-1099.
Louisville, Kentucky Office: 1400 PNC Plaza, 500 West Jefferson Street, 40202. Telephone: 502-540-2300. FAX: 502-585-2207.
Pittsburgh, Pennsylvania Office: The Grant Building, 330 Grant Street, Suite 2415, 15219. Telephone: 412-281-5000. FAX: 412-281-5055.
Charleston, West Virginia Office: 900 Lee Street, Huntington Square, Suite 600, 25301. Mailing Address: P.O. Box 11887, 25339. Telephone: 304-357-0900. FAX: 304-357-0919.
See Professional Biographies, COLUMBUS, OHIO

Di Pietro, Dario E. . . . . '18 '56 C.608 B.S. L.266 J.D. 5653 Fraley Ct.‡
Dirina, John G. . . . . '54 '95 C.608 B.S. L.117 J.D. 3828 Norbrook Dr. (Pat.)
Diroll, David J. . . . . '51 '77 C.980 A.B. L.608 J.D. Dir., Crim. Sentencing Comm.

DiRosario, Lewis J., (BV) .... '30 '57 C&L.608 B.S., J.D. 150 E. Mound St Ste 104
DiRosario, Robert P., (BV) .... '34 '58 C&L.608 B.S., J.D. 150 E. Mound St.
Disantis, Paul V. .... '70 '96 C.97 B.S. L.117 J.D. [Ⓐ G.E.Webster]
Dismukes, Edward P. .... '56 '89 C.846 B.S. L.424 J.D. Sr. Coun., Bank One Corp.
Dittmer, Jeffrey A., (CV) .... '62 '89 C.608 B.A. L.117 J.D. [Rich,C.&D.]
Ditullio, Jessica K., (CV) .... '62 '87 C.607 B.A. L.608 J.D. Sr. Coun., Bank One Corp.
Ditullio, Mark, (AV) .... '60 '85 C.705 B.A. L.607 J.D. 169 E. Livingston Avenue
Dix, Mary Ann .... '49 '83 C.1118 B.A. L.1340 J.D. Chf. Dep. Clk., Supm. Ct.
Dixon, J. Michael .... '56 '86 C.608 B.S.Phar. L.117 J.D. Patent Coun., Accott Labs
Dixon, Matthew R. .... '— '02 C.611 B.A. L.117 J.D. [Ⓐ Luper,N.&L.]
Dixon, Thomas A., (AV) .... '57 '82 C.608 B.S. L.851 J.D. [Eastman&S.] (⊙Toledo)
Dixon, William B., (BV) .... '42 '69 C.207 B.A. L.117 J.D. 3174 Plymouth Pl.
Dlott, Steven P. .... '60 '85 C.569 B.A. L.930 J.D. Asst. Atty. Gen.
Dobres, Jacob .... '72 '99 C&L.608 B.A., J.D. [Ⓐ P.J.Fulton]
Dobrowski, Stanley J., (BV) .... '51 '76 C.602 B.A. L.608 J.D. [Ⓒ Calfee,H.&G.]
Dobyns, Timothy J. .... '71 '96 C.473 B.A. L.608 J.D. [Vorys,S.S.&P.]
Dodd, Stephen H., (BV) .... '59 '85 C&L.608 B.S., J.D. [Harris,M.B.&C.]
Dodgion, Jeremy .... '72 '97 C.610 B.B.A. L.117 J.D. 844 South Front Street
Doehrel, Andrew E. .... '52 '77 C.651 B.A. L.117 J.D. Dept. of Indus. Rel.
Dolchin, Marla R. .... '64 '89 C.831 B.A. L.117 J.D. Co. Pub. Def.
Dominguez, Salvador Antonio .... '59 '85 C.894 B.A. L.1119 J.D. U.S. Atty.'s Off.
Domis, Christian Brian .... '70 '98 C.473 B.S. L.117 J.D. Pros. Off.
Donahey, Richard S., (BV) .... '41 '68 C&L.608 B.C.E., J.D. [Twyford&D.] ⊙
Donahue, William C. .... '43 '70 C.207 B.A. L.608 J.D. [Ⓐ Maguire&S.]
Donato, Lisa M. .... '68 '98 C.631 B.A. L.7 J.D. Asst. Atty. Gen.
Doney, Timothy J., (BV) '59 '85 C.477 B.S. L.602 J.D.
Corporate Counsel, Worthington Industries, Inc.
Donnelly, Sarah E. .... '72 '98 C.602 B.A. L.608 J.D. State Bur. of Wkrs. Comp.
Donofrio, Susan Schneider '47 '79
C.523 A.B. L.276 J.D. Mng. Atty., Legal Aid Soc. of Columbus
Donovan, Richard J. .... '55 '80 C.350 B.A. L.477 J.D. [R.J.Donovan&Assoc.]
Donovan, Richard J., & Associates Co., L.P.A.
200 East Campus View Boulevard, Suite 200
Donovsky, Nicole M. .... '73 '00 C&L.117 B.A., J.D. [Ⓐ Means,B.B.&B.]
Dooley, Susan Warner, (CV) ... '58 '85 C.608 B.A. L.150 J.D. 4600 International Gateway
Doran, Perry W., II .... '68 '94 C&L.260 B.S., J.D. [Ⓐ Vorys,S.S.&P.]
Doran, Scott M., (AV) .... '57 '86 C.473 B.A. L.150 J.D. [Vorys,S.S.&P.]
Dorgan, Brandi L. .... '77 '03 C.475 B.A. L.608 J.D. [Ⓐ Isaac,B.L.&T.]
Dorgan, J.Quinn .... '74 '03 C.477 B.A. L.608 J.D. Atty Gen. Off., Employ. Law Sect.
Dorner, Nancy L. .... '69 '93 C&L.608 B.S.N., J.D. [Portman,F.&F.]
Dorrian, Julia L. .... '65 '97 C.602 B.A. L.608 J.D. Mun. Ct. J.
Dorris, Tomi L. .... '57 '89 C&L.608 B.A., J.D. Asst. Pros. Atty.
Dortch, Michael D., (BV) .... '58 '90 C.608 B.A. L.117 J.D. [Baker&H.]
Dotson, Wendi Lynn .... '74 '99 C.610 B.S. L.608 J.D. Pub. Def.
Doucet, Elizabeth H., (BV) .... '42 '71 C.831 B.S. L.425 J.D. [E.H.Doucet&Assoc.]
Doucet, Elizabeth H., & Associates, Co., L.P.A., (BV) .... 895 South High Street
Doucher, Kimberley A. .... '66 '96 C&L.608 B.A., J.D. [Ⓒ Keener D.C.&P.]
Doucher, Paul M., (BV) .... '48 '80 C.608 B.A. L.607 J.D. [Keener D.C.&P.]
Dougherty, Douglas B., (AV) .... '55 '80 C.608 B.A. L.607 J.D. 3010 Hayden Rd.
Dougherty, Gina M. .... '57 '82 C.608 B.A. L.117 J.D. 336 S. High St.
Dougherty, Kathy A. .... '55 '92 C&L.608 B.S., J.D. [Lamkin,V.T.B.&D.]
Doughty, H. Cort, Jr., (AV) .... '39 '65 C.973 B.A. L.923 LL.B. [Ⓒ Squire,S.&D.]
Doughty, Tara Lynn ...... '71 '01 C.608 B.A. L.117 J.D. Staff Atty., Ct of Common Pleas
Douglas, Andy .... '32 '60 L.851 J.D. [Ⓒ Crabbe,B.&J.]
Dove, Richard Allan .... '58 '83 C.967 B.A. L.117 J.D. Assoc. Dir., State Supm. Ct.
Downes, Jonathan J., (AV) .... '54 '79 C.886 B.S.B.A. L.930 J.D. [Downes,H.&F.]
Downes, Hurst & Fishel, (AV) .... 400 S. Fifth St., Ste. 200
Downey, Brian James .... '— '96 C.112 B.A. L.1209 J.D. [Ⓐ Jones D.]
Downey, Daniel T., (BV) .... '68 '94 C.980 B.A. L.608 J.D. [Isaac,B.L.&T.]
Downey, Philip F., (AV) .... '63 '88 C.705 B.A. L.608 J.D. [Vorys,S.S.&P.]
Doyle, Jon S. .... '67 '03 C.608 B.A. L.179 J.D [Ⓐ Cheek&Z.]
Doyle, Meghan E. .... '— '01 C&L.608 B.S.B.A., J.D. [Ⓐ Jones D.]
Doyle, Michael F. .... '42 '67 C.276 A.B. L.893 LL.B. Sr. Coun., Nationwide Insurance
Doyle, R. Christopher, (AV) .... '54 '79 C.737 B.A. L.608 J.D. [Baker&H.]
Dozer, Jodi L. .... '72 '97 C.266 B.S. L.117 J.D. [Ⓐ Maguire&S.]
Drake, Carol Nolan .... '60 '85 C.611 B.A. L.607 J.D. Chairman
Drake, Daniel W., (AV) .... '44 '70 C.473 B.A. L.150 J.D. First Asst. City Atty.
Drake, Donald M. .... '41 '72 C&L.608 B.M.E., J.D. Mag., Prob. Ct.
Drake, Laura L. .... '70 '97 C.347 B.A. L.494 J.D. [Manley D.K.]
Dreher, Darrell L., (AV) .... '— '74 C.608 B.A. L.273 J.D. [Dreher L.&T.]

Dreher Langer & Tomkies L.L.P., (AV)
2250 Huntington Center, 41 South High Street, 43215
Telephone: 614-628-8000 Facsimile: 614-628-1600
Email: ddreher@dltlaw.com URL: http://www.dltlaw.com
Members of Firm: Darrell L. Dreher; Jeffrey I. Langer; Michael C. Tomkies; Judith M. Scheiderer; Margaret M. Stolar. Senior Counsel: Elizabeth L. Anstaett. Associates: Charles Victor Gall; Vanessa A. Nelson. Of Counsel: Robin Ronquillo De Leo (Not admitted in OH); Robert J. Kapitan.
Banking and Consumer Financial Services. Regulation of Banks and Other Financial Institutions, Credit Cards, Mortgages and Other Consumer Finance Products, Debt Collection, Bankruptcy, Insurance, Reinsurance, Privacy and E-Commerce.
Representative Clients: Alliance Data Systems Corporation; American Express Company; BankAmerica Corp.; Capital One Financial Corporation; ChevronTexaco Corporation; Citigroup, Inc.; Deutsche Bank AG; General Electric Capital Corporation; J.P. Morgan Chase & Co.; Morgan Stanley Dean Witter & Co.
See Professional Biographies, COLUMBUS, OHIO

Dreifke, Stuart L. .... '48 '74 C.477 B.A. L.930 J.D. Stuart L. Dreifke Co., L.P.A.
Dreitler, Joseph R., (AV) .... '— '79 C.150 B.S. L.1340 J.D. [Jones D.]
Drew, Joan N. .... '79 '01 C.505 B.S. L.201 J.D. [Ⓐ Calfee,H.&G.] (Pat.)
Drew, Michael A. .... '46 '74 C.381 B.B.A. L.8 J.D. Yankee Exploration
Drexel, Ray P., (AV) .... '49 '74 C.608 B.S. L.117 J.D. [Gamble H.J.]
Dritz, Stanley B., (AV) ..... '46 '73 C&L.608 B.A., J.D. 50 West Broad Street, Suite 2200

Druen, William Sidney, (AV) '42 '68 C.301 A.B. L.893 LL.B.
85 East Deshler Avenue, 43230
Telephone: 614-444-7655 Fax: 614-444-7655
Email: druens@gmail.com URL: http://www.williamsidneydruen.com
Corporation Law, Real Estate, Securities Law, Finance Law.
See Professional Biographies, COLUMBUS, OHIO

Dryer, Aaron A. .... '71 '98 C.608 B.S.B.A. L.930 J.D. [Ⓐ Porter W.M.&A.]
Duckworth, William F. .... '16 '61 C.608 B.S. L.266 LL.B. 34 S. Napoleon‡
Dudley, Michelle R. .... '69 '99 C&L.608 B.A., J.D. [Ⓐ Shayne&G.]
Duffey, Mary S., (BV) .... '57 '87 C.477 B.A. L.608 J.D. [Peck,S.&W.]
Duffy, Alan D. .... '76 '02 C.385 B.A. L.608 J.D. [Ⓐ Bricker&E.]
Duffy, Drew M. .... '51 '86 C.97 B.A. L.607 J.D. 150 E. Gay St., 17th Fl.
Duffy, Kevin F., (BV) '46 '72 C.608 B.A. L.161 J.D.
Asst. Gen. Coun.-Regul. Servs., Amer. Elec. Power Serv. Corp.
Duffy, Paul J. .... '46 '74 C.608 B.A. L.117 J.D. Leg. Dir., Pub. Util. Comm.
Dugan, Patrick J., (AV) ...... '57 '82 C.97 B.S. L.608 J.D. [Squire,S.&D.] (⊙Cleveland)

Dugan, Vincent A., Jr. '55 '83 C.229 B.A. L.117 J.D.
500 South Fourth Street, 43206
Telephone: 614-222-8200 Fax: 614-222-8100
Email: vadmrlaw@sbcglobal.net
(Certified Specialist in Family Relations Law, Ohio State Bar Association).
Family Law, Divorce, Child Custody, Child Support, Adoption Law, Visitation Rights, Real Estate, Small Business Law, Traffic Violations.
See Professional Biographies, COLUMBUS, OHIO

Dugger, Glen A., (AV) .... '59 '84 C.610 B.B.A. L.608 J.D. [Smith&H.]
Dull, Patrick M. .... '66 '95 C&L.608 B.S., J.D. Asst. Atty. Gen.
Duncan, Robert M., (AV) .... '27 '52 C&L.608 B.Sc., J.D. 55 W. 12th Ave.‡
Dunkel, John A., (AV) .... '30 '56 C&L.608 B.S., J.D. 41 S. High St.
Dunlap, Byrle William .... '41 '66 C&L.608 B.A., LL.B. American Red Cross
Dunlap, William E., Jr. '47 '68 C.967 B.A. L.608 J.D.
Chf. Coun., State Bd. of Tax App.
Dunlay, Catherine T., (AV) .... '58 '84 C.150 B.A. L.608 J.D. [Schottenstein,Z.&D.]
Dunn, Gregory J., (AV) .... '53 '78 C.198 B.A. L.117 J.D. [Schottenstein,Z.&D.]
Dunn, Harvey, (AV) .... '38 '66 C.150 B.B.A. L.1340 J.D. [Schottenstein,Z.&D.]
Dunn, Marcus D. .... '67 '94 C.732 B.A. L.607 J.D. [Zacks]
Dunn, Robert R., (AV) .... '66 '91 C.383 B.A. L.880 J.D. [Bailey C.]
Dunn, William M. S. .... '31 '58 C.97 A.B. L.608 LL.B. Anderson Concrete Corp.
Dunson, Philip M. .... '21 '48 C&L.608 B.E.E., J.D. 1325 Kingsgate Rd. (Pat.)
Du Pont, Gregory S., (BV) .... '65 '92 C.608 B.S. L.117 J.D. [AuCoin,D.H.&Y.]
Duprey, Mary Ellen, (BV) .... '56 '85 C.608 B.A. L.117 J.D. The Limited, Inc.
Duran, Ysidro Edward, (CV) .... '60 '86 C.851 B.A. L.602 J.D. [Ⓐ Maguire&S.]
Durban, Lee, Law Office of, (BV) '53 '78
C.608 B.S. L.117 J.D. 1335 Dublin Road, Suite 200A
Durbin, Matthew W. '74 '02 C.191 B.A. L.607 J.D.
(adm. in IL; not adm. in OH) Enforce. Offr.
Durea, Ann M., (BV) .... '32 '58 C.608 B.A. L.477 LL.B. 4807 Bellann Rd.
Durfey, Miles C. .... '30 '70 C&L.608 B.I.E., J.D. Clk., Ct. of Claims
Durkin, Kevin Patrick, (AV) .... '55 '80 C.980 A.B. L.608 J.D. [Durkin,K.]

Durkin, Kevin, (AV)
471 East Broad Street, Suite 1100, 43215
Telephone: 614-884-1551 Fax: 614-884-1550
Email: info@atd-law.com URL: http://www.lawyers.com/atd-law
Kevin Patrick Durkin.
Civil and Criminal Trial and Appellate Practice in State and Federal Courts. Administrative Law, Business Litigation, Criminal Defense, Taxation.
See Professional Biographies, COLUMBUS, OHIO

Durst, Alan T., (BV) .... '40 '65 C.381 B.A. L.608 J.D. 1395 E. Dublin Granville Rd. #406
Dusseau, Christopher J. .... '76 '03 C.602 B.A. L.629 J.D. [Ⓐ Carlile P.&M.]
Dutton, F. Mitchell '55 '82 C.967 B.A. L.851 J.D.
Asst. Gen. Coun.-, Amer. Elec. Power Serv. Corp.
Dutton, Thomas E., (AV) .... '— '83 C.902 B.A. L.597 J.D. [Jones D.]
Duvall, James, (AV) .... '38 '63 C.610 A.B. L.117 J.D. [Sanborn,B.D.&B.]
Dyas, Charles R., Jr. .... '56 '86 C.610 B.A. L.117 J.D. [Ⓒ Kegler,B.H.&R.]
Dye, David A., (BV) .... '60 '85 C&L.608 B.S., J.D. [Swedlow,B.L.M.&D.]
Dykes, Robert G., (AV) .... '50 '79 C.216 B.A. L.893 J.D. [Vorys,S.S.&P.]
Eagleson, Freeman T., (BV) .... '19 '50 C.976 B.A. L.477 LL.B. 93 S. Murray Hill Rd.
Eakins, Alan Dale .... '54 '86 C.827 B.A. L.117 J.D. [Ⓐ S.Jaffy&Assoc.]
Earl, Ted, (AV) .... '34 '60 C.473 B.A. L.608 LL.B. [Earl,W.A.&D.]

Earl, Warburton, Adams & Davis, A Legal Professional Association, (AV)
136 West Mound Street, 43215
Telephone: 614-464-2392 Telecopier: 614-464-0754
Ted Earl; Dick M. Warburton, Jr.; Andrew S. Adams; Thomas L. Davis; Steven A. Hatten; Grier D. Schaffer; Bruce L. Hirsch; Christopher R. Walsh; Mark Chuparkoff.
General Trial and Appellate Practice. Insurance, Negligence, Products Liability, Medical and Professional Malpractice, Premises Liability, Workers Compensation, Corporate, Toxic Torts, Real Estate, Aviation and Probate Law.
Reference: BancOhio National Bank.
See Professional Biographies, COLUMBUS, OHIO

Eastham, Ryan G. .... '67 '97 C.610 B.B.A. L.608 J.D. [Ⓐ Squire,S.&D.]

Eastman & Smith Ltd., (AV)
100 East Broad Street, Suite 1300, 43215 ⊙
Telephone: 614-280-1770 Fax: 614-280-1777
URL: http://www.eastmansmith.com
Members of Firm: Richard T. Sargeant; Thomas A. Dixon; Thomas J. Gibney; Joseph A. Gregg; Dirk P. Plessner; David W. Nunn; Mark A. Shaw.
General Civil Practice: Corporate, Business, Banking, Taxation, Real Estate, Securities, Antitrust, Environmental, Public, Labor and Employment, Civil Rights, Employee Benefits, Insurance, Hospital and Health Care, Estate Planning, Pension and Estate Planning, Probate, Workers Compensation, Commercial Litigation, Litigation, Immigration and Naturalization.
Toledo, Ohio, Office: One Seagate, Twenty-Fourth Floor, P.O. Box 10032, 43699-0032. Telephone: 419-241-6000. Fax: 419-247-1777.
Findlay, Ohio Office: 725 South Main Street, 45840. Telephone: 419-424-5487. Fax: 419-424-9860.
See Professional Biographies, COLUMBUS, OHIO

Eaton, Douglas Wade .... '65 '92 C.608 B.A. L.117 J.D. Staff Atty., Ct of Appeals
Eaton, Rita Bash ..... '50 '83 C.608 B.A. L.117 J.D. Mag., Com. Pleas Ct. of Franklin Co.
Eberhart, Robert L., (AV) .... '39 '64 C&L.608 B.A., J.D. [Johrendt,C.&E.]
Eblin, Robert L., (AV) .... '63 '93 C.309 A.B. L.608 J.D. [Bailey C.]
Ebner, Cynthia Lynn .... '65 '93 C.608 B.S.B.A. L.117 J.D. [Ebner]
Ebner Law Offices .... 3455 E. Broad Street
Eck, Franklin E., Jr., (BV) .... '64 '89 C.363 B.A. L.602 J.D. [Ⓐ Plank&B.] (Pat.)
Eckelberry, Rodger L. .... '69 '99 C.1044 B.S. L.150 J.D. [Ⓐ Baker&H.]
Ecker, Deborah P., (AV) .... '54 '80 C.597 B.A. L.608 J.D. [Ⓐ Luper,N.&L.]
Eckhart, Anne E. .... '67 '93 C.473 B.A. L.608 J.D. Sr. Coun., Bank One Corp.
Eckhart, Henry W., (BV) .... '32 '58 C.608 B.S. L.477 J.D. 50 W. Broad St.
Economus, Basil G. .... '72 '99 C.608 B.A. L.117 J.D. [Ⓐ Havens W.]
Edana, Essa .... '63 '90 C.1044 B.A. L.276 J.D. Coun., Nationwide Insurance
Edelman, Joyce D., (AV) .... '57 '82 C.347 B.A. L.923 J.D. [Porter W.M.&A.]
Edelstein, Kimberly .... '— '02 C&L.253 B.A., J.D. [Ⓐ Robol]
Edmund, Robert W. .... '73 '98 C.608 B.A. L.309 J.D. [Ⓐ Porter W.M.&A.]
Edwards, Daniel F. .... '67 '92 C.473 B.S. L.276 J.D. [Ⓐ Thompson H.]
Edwards, Delena .... '57 '86 C.610 B.S. L.352 J.D. [D.Edwards]
Edwards, Kimberly Renee .... '69 '94 C&L.117 B.A., J.D. U.S. Dist. Ct.
Edwards, R.D. Benjamin .... '73 '00 C&L.608 B.A., J.D. [Ⓐ J.L.Alden]
Edwards, Delena, Co., LPA .... 2021 E. Dublin-Granville Road, Suite 173
Efta, Thomas J. .... '60 '87 C&L.608 B.A., J.D. Pub. Def. Off.
Eggenschwiler, James E., Jr. '58 '84 C.1288 B.A. L.999 J.D.
Dir., Asst. Gen. Coun. & Asst. Secy., Consolidated Stores Corporation
Eggspuehler, Jay B. .... '57 '86 C.608 B.S.B.A. L.607 J.D. [Wiles,B.B.&B.]
Ehler, Anthony L. .... '62 '87 C.602 B.A. L.896 J.D. [Vorys,S.S.&P.]

Ehrie, Dennis Broderick, Jr. '45 '76 C.608 B.S. L.179 J.D. 1492 E. Broad St.
Ehrle, Kathryn Collins '51 '93
C.1337 B.S.N. L.608 J.D. State of Ohio, Dept. of Rehab. and Corrs.
Eidelberg, David L., (BV) '63 '88 C.604 B.A. L.930 J.D. [Ulmer&B.]
Einstein, John Lewis, IV '68 '96 C.244 B.A. L.201 J.D. [Carlile P.&M.]
Eisen, Hermine G., (BV) '39 '81 C.930 B.A. L.1003 J.D. [Eisen&W.] ⊙
Eisen & Westfall, LLP, (BV) 1021 South High Street (⊙Akron, Cleveland)

Eisenman, Susan Garner, (BV) '50 '74 C&L.608 B.A., J.D.
336 South High Street, 43215
Telephone: 614-222-0540 Fax: 614-222-0543
Email: ADOPTOHIO@aol.com URL: http://www.adoptohiolaw.com
Adoption Law (Private, Interstate, International and Stepparent).
See Professional Biographies, COLUMBUS, OHIO

Eisnaugle, R. William, (AV) '35 '60 C.611 B.A. L.930 J.D. [Eisnaugle&G.]
Eisnaugle & Graham Co., L.P.A., (AV) 2001 Cambridge Boulevard
Elam, John W. '56 '82 C.231 B.A. L.477 J.D. Exec. Asst. to Pres., Ohio State Univ.
El-Amin, Taheerah K. '— '02 C.197 A.B. L.339 J.D. [Porter W.M.&A.]
Eldridge, Matthew X. '47 '84 C.181 B.A. L.1338 J.D. 233 S. High St.
Eley, James R., (BV) '52 '90 C.610 B.B.A. L.117 J.D. [Eley] (Pat.)
Eley Law Firm Co., (BV) 7870 Olentangy River Rd., Ste. 311 (Pat.)
Eliot, Adam S. '66 '94 C.188 B.A. L.608 J.D. 400 S. Fifth Street, Suite 102
Elk, Arthur M. '47 '73 C.930 B.B.A. L.161 J.D. [Elk&E.] ⊙
Elk, David J., (BV) '39 '65 C&L.930 B.B.A., J.D. [Elk&E.] ⊙

Elk & Elk Co., L.P.A., (BV)
Fifth Third Center Capital Square, 21 East State Street, Suite 320, 43215 ⊙
Telephone: 1-888-ELK-OHIO
Email: kthompson@elkandelk.com URL: http://www.elkandelklaw.com
David J. Elk; Arthur M. Elk.
Automobile Accidents, Product Defects, Nursing Home Neglect, Medical Malpractice, Personal Injury.
Cleveland, Ohio Office: Landerhaven Corporation Center, 6100 Parkland Boulevard, 44124-4187. Telephone: 888-355-6446.
See Professional Biographies, COLUMBUS, OHIO

Elkin, Joel K. '57 '84 C.645 B.S. L.117 J.D. 6119 E. Main St.
Ellcessor, Steven J. '52 '77 C.473 A.B. L.1565 J.D. [Frost B.T.]
Elleman, James R. '28 '65 C.608 B.Sc. L.266 J.D. [Elleman&N.]
Elleman & Newcome, (BV) 2904 W. Broad St.
Ellinger, Eve M. '76 '01 C.608 B.S. L.179 J.D. [Kegler,B.H.&R.]
Elliott, Cynthia L. '— '95 C.608 B.A. L.117 J.D. Sr. Corp. Coun., Safelite Group, Inc.
Elliott, Joseph F., (BV) '56 '82 C.93 B.A. L.893 J.D. [Porter W.M.&A.]
Elliott, Rex H., (AV) '62 '88 C.207 B.A. L.823 J.D. 2175 Riverside Dr.
Elliott, Steven P., (AV) '53 '79 C.473 B.A. L.608 J.D. [Wiles,B.B.&B.]
Ellis, George M., (BV) '46 '74 Chf. Coun., Franklin Co. Pros. Atty.
Ellis, Madry L. '69 '97 C.381 B.A. L.801 J.D. 233 South High Street, Suite 300
Ellman, Stephen B. '58 '84 C.1036 B.A. L.608 Pres., Host Industries
Elvers, Jason C. '— '00 C.608 B.A. L.880 J.D. [Vorys,S.S.&P.]
Ely, Donald E., (BV) '— '68 C&L.608 B.S., J.D. [Rance,P.B.K.&E.]
Embrey, Elizabeth A. '78 '04 C.608 B.A. L.117 J.D. 175 S. Third St., Ste. 360
Emens, J. Richard, (AV) '34 '59 C.210 A.B. L.477 LL.B. [Chester,W.&S.]
Emerson, Andrew C. '71 '99 C.209 B.A. L.608 J.D. [Porter W.M.&A.]
Enders, Warren M., (AV) '51 '76 C.567 B.A. L.1003 J.D. [Reminger&R.]
Engel, Mark A., (AV) '53 '79 C.477 B.A. L.117 J.D. [Bricker&E.]

Engle, John H., Attorney and Counselor at Law
(See Cincinnati)

Enns, Terri Lynn '58 '96 The Ohio State Univ., College of Law
Enright, Keith P. '74 '00 C.454 B.A. L.273 J.D.
Dir. Cust. Info. Management, LimitedBrands, Inc.
Ensign, John A. '72 '03 C.473 B.S. L.117 J.D. [Bricker&E.]
Ensminger, Rodman R., (BV) '37 '69 C.97 B.A. L.608 J.D. Com. Pleas Ct.
Enz, Stephen D., (AV) '42 '67 C&L.608 B.A., J.D. [Carlile P.&M.]
Epps, Richard M., (BV) '47 '76 C.611 B.A. L.117 J.D. 4170 Mumford Ct.
Epstein, Barry W., (BV) '42 '77 C.608 B.S. L.607 J.D.
580 South High Street, Suite 130
Erfurt, Edward W., III, (BV) '48 '77 C&L.607 B.A., J.D. 85 E. Gay St.
Ericsson, John M. '66 '94 C.608 B.A. L.150 J.D. Law Clk. to Chief Jus., Supm. Ct.
Erlenbach, Thomas S., (BV) '35 '60 C.611 B.A. L.607 LL.B. [Maguire&S.]
Erlichman, Sheryl, (BV) '60 '85 C.150 B.A. L.201 J.D. Asst. Atty. Gen.
Erney, Robert D., (AV) '53 '84 C.737 B.A. L.150 J.D. [R.D.Erney&Assoc.]
Erney, Robert D., & Associates Co., L.P.A., (AV) 1654 East Broad Street
Ernsberger, Todd A. '— '04 C.608 B.A. L.117 J.D. [Onda,L.&R.]
Ervin, Amy J. '71 '96 C.967 B.A. L.117 J.D. [Lane,A.&H.]
Ervin, James L., Jr., (AV) '70 '96 C.37 B.A. L.117 J.D. [Crabbe,B.&J.]
Erwin, Joseph V. '64 '91 C.608 B.A. L.117 J.D. 380 S. 5th St., Ste. 3
Esarove, Elizabeth A. '68 '94 C.97 B.S.B.A. L.608 J.D. 88 E. Broad St.
Esber, Mary Ann '64 '91 C.1260 B.A. L.8 J.D. OH State Univ., The
Eschleman, Lisa L., (BV) '59 '87 C.347 B.S.P.A. L.117 J.D. [Porter W.M.&A.]
Eshman, Patricia S. '55 '85 C.608 B.A. L.851 J.D. Asst. Atty. Gen.
Espinoza, David J. '56 '83 C.338 B.S. L.150 J.D. Asst. Atty. Gen.
Espy, Ben E., (BV) '43 '69 C.608 B.A. L.329 J.D. Sen.
Essey, Norman A., (BV) '61 '86 C.665 B.A. L.117 J.D.
SVP-Coml. Services/Midwest Reg., LandAmerica Financial Group
Etter, Terry '51 '89 C.610 B.S.C. L.128 J.D.
Asst. Consumers Coun., Ohio Consumers Counsel
Evans, Dennis P., (BV) '53 '85 C.608 B.S. L.117 J.D. [Connor B.]
Evans, Gordon D., II '— '01 C.384 B.A. L.179 J.D. [Twyford&D.]
Evans, J. Michael, (AV) '42 '67 C&L.608 B.A., J.D. 261 W. Johnstown Rd.
Evans, James M. '54 '81 C.81 B.A. L.117 J.D. Asst. Atty. Gen.,
Evans, Mark E., P.E. '70 '01 C.608 B.S.C.E. L.179 J.D. [Bricker&E.]
Evans, Mason, IV, (AV) '52 '77 C.473 B.A. L.273 J.D. [Porter W.M.&A.]
Evans, Matthew Craig '68 '00 C.473 B.S. L.117 J.D Huntington Bancshares, Inc.
Evans, R. Leland, (AV) '57 '83 C.608 B.S. L.930 J.D. [Porter W.M.&A.]
Evans, Ronda L. '— '89 C.610 B.S. L.117 J.D. Sr. Coun., Nationwide Insurance
Evans, William R. '46 '85 C&L.608 B.A., J.D. Ohio Bur.of Employ. Servs.
Everett, John K., (BV) '42 '71 C.313 B.A. L.117 J.D. 1005 S. High St.
Everly, Barry E. '45 '73 C.608 B.S. L.117 J.D. Asst. Atty. Gen.
Eyerly, Gloria Ann, (BV) '51 '76 C&L.608 B.A., J.D. Chf. Coun., Pub. Def. Comm.
Ezell, Larry Alan '68 '98 C.608 B.A. L.117 J.D. [L.A.Ezell]
Ezell, Larry A., Law Office of 500 S. Front St.
Ezzie, Joseph E. '77 '02 C.473 B.S. L.608 J.D. [Buckingham,D.&B.]
Fabro, Kathleen M. '67 '94 C.608 B.A. L.117 J.D. 171 E. Livingston Ave.
Faehnle, Matthew Carl, Law Office of '73 '00 C.608 B.S. L.179 J.D. [M.C.Faehnle]
Faehnle, Matthew C., Law Office of 2280 W. Henderson Rd., Ste. 202
Fagin, Marc K., (BV) '59 '85 C&L.161 B.B.S., J.D. [M.Fagin]
Fagin, Norman, (BV) '27 '55 C.174 B.A. L.608 J.D. 3120 E. Main St.
Fagin, Marc, (BV) 2388 E. Main St.
Fahey, Richard P., (AV) '44 '71 C.766 B.A. L.597 J.D. [Vorys,S.S.&P.]
Fahnenbruck, K. Clarke, (BV) '52 '78 C&L.930 B.A., J.D. [K.C.Fahnenbruck]
Fahnenbruck, K. Clarke, Co., L.P.A., (BV) 50 West Broad Street
Fairfield, Mary Ellen, (AV) '49 '73 C.679 B.A. L.608 J.D. [Vorys,S.S.&P.]
Fairman, Christopher M. '60 '94 C&L.846 B.A., J.D.
(adm. in TX; not adm. in OH) 2615 Camden Road
Fais, David W. '43 '70 C.631 B.S. L.607 J.D. Com. Pleas J.
Faller, Bryan R. '74 '00 C.610 B.S. L.608 J.D. [Porter W.M.&A.]
Falleur, Michael, (BV) '52 '77 C.473 B.A. L.117 J.D. 1625 Bethel Rd.
Fallon, Ann E. '61 '88 C.381 B.S. L.608 J.D. 366 E. Broad St.

Farlow & Associates LLC
(See Dublin)

Farmer, James B. '49 '76 C.188 B.A. L.608 J.D. [Taft,S.&H.]
Farnbacher, Barbara A., (BV) '61 '86 C&L.608 B.S.Ed., J.D. Asst. Pub. Def.
Farrar, Elizabeth Turrell, (AV) '57 '82 C.788 B.A. L.893 J.D. [Vorys,S.S.&P.]
Farrell, Clifford M., (AV) '56 '82 C.509 B.A. L.117 J.D. [Manring&F.]
Farrin, Richard C. '47 '72 C.473 B.A. L.608 J.D. [McDonald H.]
Fate, Jennifer L. '— '97 C.473 B.S. L.608 J.D. [Jones D.]
Fauber, Sue Ann '56 '82 C.150 B.A. L.930 J.D. [S.Jaffy&Assoc.]
Faulkner, Sandra Parks '69 '93 C.259 B.S. L.608 J.D. [Baker&H.]
Faure, David C. '69 '96 C&L.608 B.A., B.A. [Porter W.M.&A.]
Fay, Terrence M., (AV) '53 '78 C.62 B.S. L.608 J.D. [Frost B.T.]
Federico, Andrew J., (AV) '50 '78 C.611 B.A. L.117 J.D. [Carlile P.&M.]
Federle, Katherine Hunt '58 '83
C.668 B.A. L.678 J.D. Ohio State University College of Law
Feheley, Lawrence F., (AV) '46 '73 C&L.188 A.B., J.D. [Kegler,B.H.&R.]
Fein, William S., (AV) '47 '71 C.910 A.B. L.477 J.D. [Thompson H.]
Feldkamp, Janet K. '56 '90 C.502 B.S.N. L.734 J.D. [Benesch,F.C.&A.]
Fenlon, John Martin '63 '89 C.608 B.A. L.117 J.D. 8 E. Long St.
Fenlon, Mary Ryan '61 '88 C.608 B.A. L.117 J.D. 150 E. Gay Street
Fenner, David T. '56 '82 C.136 B.S. L.117 J.D. Thomas-Fenner-Woods Agcy.
Fenner, Paula Martin '56 '81 C.893 B.A. L.117 J.D. Capital Univ. Law School
Fennessey, Dennis J. '41 '76 C.229 B.S.B.A. L.117 J.D. 4878 Fairway oaks Dr.
Fenton, Scott A. '67 '97 C.97 B.A. L.117 J.D. [Lane,A.&H.]
Ferber, James M. L., (AV) '47 '71 C.645 B.A. L.831 J.D. [Littler M.]
Fergus, John C., II '52 '79 C.207 B.A. L.608 J.D. Multicon Develop. Co.
Fergus, Kevin B. '29 '61 C.363 B.S. L.1003 J.D. U.S. Trotting Assn.
Fergus, Ronda Hartman '55 '80 C&L.608 B.S., J.D. Pub. Utilities Comm.
Ferguson, Gerald P., (AV) '51 '79 C.1046 B.A. L.117 J.D. [Vorys,S.S.&P.]
Ferguson, Melissa M. '73 '98 C.347 B.S. L.117 J.D. [Lane,A.&H.]
Ferguson, Richard '52 '88 C.980 B.S. L.117 J.D. 3990 East Broad Street
Ferguson, Stephen E. '66 '96 C.1099 B.A. L.705 J.D.
(adm. in NJ; not adm. in OH) Coun., Nationwide Insurance
Ferguson, Victor J. '71 '98 C.967 B.A. L.8 J.D. [Vorys,S.S.&P.]
Fernald, Willard T. '51 '96 C&L.608 B.A., J.D.
V.P., Pers. Trust Mgr., Fifth Third Bank
Ferrell, Bradley T. '74 '99 C.610 B.A. L.608 J.D. [Zeiger,T.&L.]
Ferrell, Tara M. '— '03 C.610 B.S. L.608 J.D. [Baker&H.]
Ferriell, Jeffrey Thomas '53 '78 C.608 B.S. L.770 J.D.
(adm. in CA; not adm. in OH) Prof. of Law, Capital Univ.
Ferriman, David B. '47 '84 C.608 B.A. L.117 J.D. Metropolitan Human Servs.
Ferris, Andrew M. '68 '95 C.473 B.S. L.150 J.D. [Baker&H.]
Ferris, Boyd B., (AV) '42 '67 C&L.608 B.S., J.D. [Ferris&F.]
Ferris, David A. '67 '92 C.473 B.A. L.117 J.D. [Ferris&F.]
Ferris, Jacqueline A. '— '04 C.608 B.A. L.117 J.D. [Onda,L.&R.]
Ferris & Ferris, L.L.P., (AV) 2733 West Dublin-Granville Road
Ferron, John W. '56 '82 C.966 B.S. L.209 J.D. [Ferron&Assoc.]
Ferron & Associates, A Legal Professional Association 580 N. 4th St.
Fewell, Jennifer L. '— '03 C.610 B.S. L.608 J.D. [Schottenstein,Z.&D.]
Fey, Carol Ann, (BV) '54 '85 C.473 B.A. L.608 J.D. 454 E. Main St., Ste. 218
Fidler, Christopher D. '64 '92 C.608 B.A. L.117 J.D. [Baker&H.]
Field, Hal W. '29 '65 C.309 B.A. L.117 J.D. P.O. Box 26136‡
Fifner, W. Frederick, (AV) '48 '73 C.258 A.B. L.251 J.D. [Freund,F.&A.]
Figetakis, Frances L., (AV) '58 '87 C.8 B.A. L.7 J.D.
V.P. & Gen. Coun., JPMorgan Chase & Co., Gen. Coun. Off.
Finan, Richard H., (AV) '34 '59 C.201 B.S. L.150 J.D. [Calfee,H.&G.]
Findley, Stephen C., (AV) '49 '80 C.150 B.B.A. L.1340 J.D. [Freund,F.&A.]
Finegold, Jordan, (BV) '59 '86 C.951 B.A. L.588 J.D. Asst. Atty. Gen.
Finfrock, Teri Jo, (BV) '62 '87 C.901 B.A. L.851 J.D. Asst. Atty. Gen.
Fink, Howard P., (AV) '33 '58 C.188 B.S. L.976 LL.B. [Porter W.M.&A.]
Finley, Price D. '63 '90 C.117 B.A. L.608 J.D. [Bricker&E.]
Finn, Michael L., (BV) '43 '67 C&L.608 B.A., J.D. 2120 Cheshire Rd.
Finneran, M. Theresa '51 '89 C.608 B.A. L.117 J.D. [Porter W.M.&A.]
Finneran, Russell D. '30 '54 C&L.608 B.A., J.D. 5314 Woodglen Rd.
Finneran, Séan Paul '60 '87 C.894 A.B. L.608 J.D. 335 Southwood Avenue
Finneran, Thomas John '25 '54 C.608 B.A. One East Livingston Ave.
Finneran, Todd G., (BV) '49 '81 C.610 B.A. L.117 J.D. 380 South Fifth Street, Suite 4
Finnerty, Beth A. '66 '91 C.967 B.A. L.608 J.D. Asst. Atty. Gen.
Fireman, Steven H. '65 '92 C.1365 B.A. L.117 J.D.
General Counsel, Ennovations Unlimited/Ohio Energy
Firstenberger, Aaron C. '— '00 C.631 B.A. L.117 JD. [Strip,H.L.M.&T.]
Fischbein, William T. '67 '94 C&L.608 B.A., J.D. Ohio EPA
Fischberg, Jenna S. '73 '97 C.610 B.S. L.117 J.D. 500 S. 4th St.
Fischer, Hans H. '35 '81 C.383 M.A. L.8 J.D. Borden Foods Corporation
Fish, Jeffrey D. '65 '91 C.608 B.S.B.A. L.117 J.D. [White&F.]
Fishel, Joan Irwin '59 '87 C&L.608 B.S., J.D. Atty. Hearing Exam., State Medical Bd.
Fishel, Marc A., (BV) '62 '87 C.161 B.A. L.608 J.D. [Downes,H.&F.]
Fisher, David W., (AV) '53 '81 C.631 B.A. L.1340 J.D. [Kephart&F.]
Fisher, Donald Paul '56 '96 C.608 B.S. L.117 J.D. USDA
Fisher, George V., (AV) '26 '53 C&L.608 B.S., LL.B. 400 East Town Street, Suite 210
Fisher, J. Matthew '69 '96 C.967 B.A. L.607 J.D. [Allen,K.&S.]
Fisher, Judith M., (AV) '60 '86 C.381 B.A. L.608 J.D. Sr. Coun., Bank One Corp.
Fisher, Kenneth A., Jr. '66 '95 C.608 B.S. L.117 J.D. [Buckingham,D.&B.]
Fisher, Lloyd E., Jr., (AV) '23 '50 C&L.608 B.Sc., J.D. [Porter W.M.&A.]
Fisher, Mary B. Kelleher '63 '89 C.608 B.S.Ed. L.117 J.D. [M.B.K.Fisher]
Fisher, Roberta L., (AV) '52 '76 C.608 B.A. L.1565 J.D. [Squire,S.&D.]
Fisher, Theodore G., (AV) '44 '69 C.608 B.A. L.560 J.D. [Porter W.M.&A.]
Fisher, Windell F., (BV) '36 '61 C&L.608 B.A., J.D. Suite 1904, 50 W. Broad St.
Fisher, Mary Beth Kelleher 1500 W. 3rd Ave.
Fist, Leah Rebecca '63 '88 C.659 B.A. L.930 J.D. Asst. Atty. Gen.
Fitch, John K., (BV) '52 '79 C.608 B.S. L.201 J.D. 929 Harrison Avenue, Suite 303
Fitch, Stephen C., (AV) '48 '73 C&L.608 B.A., J.D. [Chester,W.&S.]
Fitrakis, Robert '— '03 C&L.608 J.D. [Arnebeck]

FitzGerald, Benjamin .... '— '89 C&L.150 B.A., J.D. Coun., Pure Title
Fitzsimmons, Susan '69 '94 C.352 B.A. L.221 J.D.
(adm. in IA; not adm. in OH) Coun., Nationwide Insurance
Flahive, Carolyn S. .... '— '00 C.608 B.A. L.117 J.D. [[A] Thompson H.]
Flahive, Shawn M. .... '59 '84 C.602 B.A. L.276 J.D. [Vorys,S.S.&P.]
Flanagan, F. Patrick, (BV) .... '49 '80 C.717 B.A. L.117 J.D. 478 Blenheim Rd.
Flax, Michael, (BV) .... '46 '74 C.608 B.A. L.117 J.D. Asst. Atty. Gen.
Fleischauer, Marc L. .... '65 '91 C.970 B.A. L.259 J.D. [Porter W.M.&A.]
Fletcher, Daniel J. .... '59 '85 C.930 B.A. L.117 J.D. 761 S. Front St.
Fletcher, Robert E. .... '51 '76 C.97 B.A. L.608 J.D. 200 E. Town St.
Flint, Christopher A. .... '69 '95 C.608 B.A. L.117 J.D. [Portman,F.&F.]
Flint, Jennifer Ann .... '65 '92 C.608 B.A. L.117 J.D. [[A] Bricker&E.]
Flowers, Michael E., (AV) .... '53 '79 C.105 B.S. L.608 J.D. [Bricker&E.]
Flynn, James F. .... '64 '90 C&L.602 B.A., J.D. [Bricker&E.]
Flynn, John J. '48 '78 C.656 B.A. L.1017 J.D.
(adm. in PA; not adm. in OH)
Director - Trial Division, Nationwide Mutual Insurance Company
Flynn, Nicole .... '76 '01 C.932 B.A. L.608 J.D. [[C] Mason]
Flynn, Sean P. .... '— '01 C.970 B.A. L.608 J.D. [[A] Baker&H.]
Foley, F. James, (AV) .... '52 '77 C&L.602 B.A., J.D. [Vorys,S.S.&P.]
Foley, K. Michael ... '39 '64 C.473 B.S. L.477 J.D. Admin. Law J., Social Security Admn.
Foley, Kevin P. .... '67 '92 C.608 B.A. L.1003 J.D. [[A] Reminger&R.]
Foley, Mark A., (BV) .... '44 '69 C.973 B.S. L.608 J.D. [Portman,F.&F.]
Foliano, Gregory B., (BV) .... '62 '90 C.473 B.A. L.1003 J.D. [Porter W.M.&A.]
Folk, Philip K. .... '27 '52 C&L.608 B.A., J.D. 2617 Swansea Rd.‡
Folkert, Douglas R. .... '56 '82 C.381 B.A. L.930 J.D. Asst. Atty. Gen.
Folkerth, Jeffrey T., (BV) '47 '72
C&L.608 B.A., J.D. Adm. Servs. Dir., Ohio Legal Rights Serv.
Foody, Thomas J. .... '42 '81 C.602 B.S.C.E. L.117 J.D. State Dept. of Transp.
Forbes, Brian C. .... '72 '99 C.608 B.A. L.117 J.D. [[A] Saia&P.]
Forbes, Nicole S. .... '67 '92 C&L.608 B.S.B.A., J.D. 3649 W. Broad St.
Forché, Alison B. .... '68 '95 C.608 B.A. L.117 J.D. 2733 West Dublin-Granville Road
Ford, Gail C., (AV) .... '46 '86 C&L.608 B.S., J.D. [Vorys,S.S.&P.]
Ford, Jacklyn J., (BV) .... '61 '91 C.604 A.B. L.930 J.D. [Vorys,S.S.&P.]
Ford, Winston M., (CV) .... '66 '91 C.103 B.A. L.930 J.D. Sec. Chief
Foreman, Ivery D., (AV) .... '51 '78 C.860 B.A. L.597 J.D. [Vorys,S.S.&P.]
Fornia, Luftman & Heck, LLP .... 495 S. High Street, Suite 220
Fornshell, Matthew L. .... '67 '93 C.610 B.B.A. L.879 J.D. [Schottenstein,Z.&D.]
Forry, Steven D. .... '75 '02 C.473 B.A. L.1119 J.D. [[A] Schottenstein,Z.&D.]
Forsythe, Frank E. .... '40 '65 C.967 A.B. L.145 J.D. Chicago Title Ins. Co.
Fortman, Judith Wilcox .... '48 '72 C.477 B.A. L.309 J.D. Asst. Atty. Gen.
Fossee, Christa S. '— '03 C.188 B.S. L.1541 J.D.
(adm. in PA; not adm. in OH) [[A] Littler M.]
Foster, Lorie S. .... '73 '98 C&L.608 B.A., J.D. Coun., Abbott Labs.
Foster, Robert H., (BV) .... '41 '73 C.608 B.S. L.117 J.D. 6094 Endicott Rd.
Fotta, Joan T. .... '68 '94 C.8 B.A. L.608 J.D. Ct. of Com. Pleas
Foust, Hollie K. .... '— '00 C&L.608 B.A., J.D. Coun., Abbott Labs.
Fox, Clenzo B., (BV) .... '28 '53 C.266 B.A. L.117 J.D. 209 S. High St.
Fox, Edward Alexander .... '29 '77 C.951 B.A. L.117 J.D. 8400 Nothatch Way‡
Fox, Elizabeth A. .... '66 '02 C&L.851 B.A., J.D. [[A] Vorys,S.S.&P.]
Fox, Timothy M., (BV) .... '62 '87 C.385 B.A. L.930 J.D. [Ulmer&B.]
Francis, Caryn A. Y. .... '64 '89 C.586 B.A. L.846 J.D. 77 S. High St.
Francis, John L., (BV) .... '24 '50 C&L.608 LL.B. Pub. Utilities Com.
Frank, David K., (BV) .... '48 '74 C&L.608 B.A., J.D. [Mazanec,R.&R.]
Frank, Marlene P., (AV) .... '— '82 C&L.608 B.A., J.D. [Jones D.]
Frank, Melinda Jeanne '54 '79
C.608 B.A. L.117 J.D. City of Columbus, Div. of Income Tax
Frankart, Robert J. '53 '78
C.207 B.A. L.880 J.D. Dept. Legal Coun., Dept. of Human Servs.
Franke, Janice R. .... '55 '83 C.788 A.B. L.608 J.D. Asst. Prof., Ohio State Univ.
Franklin, Charles E. .... '52 '77 C.97 B.S. L.117 J.D. 50 W. Broad St., Ste. 2100
Franzmann, Christopher J., (BV) .... '65 '91 C&L.347 B.S., J.D. [Squire,S.&D.]

Frasch, Joseph F., Jr., (BV) '48 '74 C&L.117 B.A., J.D.
1550 Old Henderson Road Suite N-130, P.O. Box 20387, 43220
Telephone: 614-326-5544 Fax: 614-457-4151
Email: jfrasch@ix.netcom.com URL: http://www.lawyers.com/frasch
Trusts and Estates, Wills, Probate, Estate Planning, Taxation, Estate and Gift Taxation, Income Tax, Real Estate.

See Professional Biographies, COLUMBUS, OHIO

Frasch, William E., Jr. .... '29 '58 C&L.608 B.S., LL.B. 936 Montrose Avenue
Frasier, Ralph K. .... '38 '65 C&L.574 B.Sc., J.D. [[C] Porter W.M.&A.]
Frazier, Jean M., (BV) .... '62 '87 C.347 B.S. L.1119 J.D. [Habash,R.&F.]
Freed, Robert P. .... '57 '03 C.608 B.B.A. L.117 J.D. [[C] Maguire&S.]
Freed, Ruth .... '— '58 C.994 B.S. L.178 LL.B. 464 E. Main St.
Freedom, John G. '25 '51
C.381 A.B. L.930 LL.B. Ohio Bureau of Workers' Compensation
Freel, David E. .... '51 '77 C.608 B.A. L.117 J.D. Exec. Dir., Ethics Comm.
Freeman, Chester T., (BV) .... '31 '57 C&L.608 B.Sc., LL.B. [C.T.Freeman]
Freeman, David L. .... '30 '57 C.62 A.B. L.930 LL.B. 41 S. High St.‡
Freeman, Sheryl Drake .... '71 '96 C.257 B.S. L.607 J.D. Pros. Off.
Freeman, Tamara ...... '71 '96 C.608 B.A. L.851 J.D. Claims Attty, Grange Mut. Cas. Co.
Freeman, Chester T., Co., L.P.A., (BV) .... 50 W. Broad St., Ste. 2100
Frees, Karen E. .... '51 '96 C.585 B.A. L.608 J.D. Columbus Foundation, The
Freiburger, Charles F., IV, (AV) .... '— '70 C.473 B.S. L.608 J.D. [Thompson H.]
French, Diane W., (CV) ...... '64 '87 C.846 B.S. L.607 J.D. Gen. Coun., DLZ Corporation
French, Mark A. .... '72 '97 C.473 B.A. L.608 J.D. 130 Buttles Ave.
Frenzer, Peter F. '34 '61 C.190 B.S.C. L.1035 LL.B.
(adm. in MN; not adm. in OH) 1 Nationwide Plaza
Fresco, Ronald A. .... '66 '92 C.608 B.A. L.117 J.D. [[A] Reminger&R.]

Freund, Freeze & Arnold, A Legal Professional Association, (AV)
Capitol Square Building, 65 East State Street Suite 800, 43215 ⊙
Telephone: 614-827-7300 Telecopier: 614-827-7303
Email: ffalawco@ffalaw.com URL: http://www.ffalaw.com
Stephen C. Findley; Mark L. Schumacher; Carl A. Anthony; W. Frederick Fifner;—Jennifer L. Hill; Sandra R. McIntosh; Kevin E. Hess.
Civil Litigation including Commercial Litigation, Employment Defense, Professional Malpractice Defense, Employer Intentional Torts, Construction Litigation, Civil Rights Defense, Local Government Defense, Nursing Home Defense, Environmental Litigation and Insurance Defense.
Local Counsel for: Auto-Owners Insurance Co.; CNA Insurance Co.; Crum and Foster Underwriters; Employers Reinsurance Corp.; Farmers Insurance Group; Lloyds of London; Medical Protective; Midwestern Group; State Farm Mutual Automobile Insurance Co.
Special Trial Counsel for: City of Dayton.
Dayton, Ohio Office: One Dayton Centre, One South Main Street, Suite 1800, 45402-2017. Telephone: 937-222-2424. Telecopier: 937-222-5369. Email: ffalawda@ffalaw.com.
Cincinnati, Ohio Office: Fourth and Walnut Centre, 105 East Fourth Street, Suite 1400, 45202-4006. Telephone: 513-665-3500. Telecopier: 513-665-3503. Email: ffalawci@ffalaw.com.

(This Listing Continued)

Freund, Freeze & Arnold, A Legal Professional Association (Continued)
Covington, Kentucky Office Suite: RiverCenter, 50 East RiverCenter Boulevard, Suite 408, 41011. Telephone: 859-292-2088. Telecopier: 859-292-2514. Email: ffalawky@ffalaw.com

See Professional Biographies, COLUMBUS, OHIO

Freytag, Daniel R., (AV) .... '49 '75 C.967 B.A. L.608 J.D. [[C] Zeiger,T.&L.]
Frick, Bradley N., and Associates, (AV) .... '48 '78 C.608 B.A. L.602 J.D. 1265 Neil Ave.
Frick, Jas. B., (BV) .... '23 '53 C.608 L.266 J.D. 261 S. Front St.
Fried, Samuel P., (AV) '51 '74 C.910 A.B. L.94 J.D.
Sr. V.P., Gen. Coun. & Sec., Limited Brands, Inc.
Friedberg, Leon, (AV) .... '47 '79 C.210 B.M. L.117 J.D. 366 East Broad Street
Friedman, Jerome E., (BV) '49 '77 C&L.608 B.A., J.D.
Asst. V.P. for Health Policy & Govt. Rel., The Ohio State University Med. Ctr., Off of Health Sciences
Friedman, Marc R. '48 '74 C&L.608 B.A., J.D.
Inheritance Tax Supvs., State Dept. of Taxation
Friedman, Scott N. .... '71 '98 C.473 B.A. L.117 J.D. [Friedman&M.]

Friedman, Thomas E., (BV) '46 '74 C.473 B.A. L.608 J.D.
502 South Third Street, 43215
Telephone: 614-221-0090 Fax: 614-221-7745
Email: tefriedman@thomasefriedman.com URL: http://www.thomasefriedman.com
(Certified Specialist in Family Relations Law, Ohio State Bar Association).
Family Law, Domestic Relations Law, Divorce, Child Custody, Child Support, Visitation Rights, Premarital Agreements, Juvenile Law, Professional and Commercial Collections.
Reference: National City Bank.

See Professional Biographies, COLUMBUS, OHIO

Friedman, Tod H., (AV) '62 '89 C.608 B.A. L.823 J.D.
V.P. & Asst. Gen. Coun., Schottenstein Stores Corporation
Friedman, William S., (AV) .... '41 '66 C.201 B.S. L.150 J.D. [Friedman&M.]

Friedman & Mirman Co., L.P.A., (AV) [BB]
The Worly Building, 503 South Front Street Suite 250, 43215-5666
Telephone: 614-221-0090 Fax: 614-221-7213 URL: http://www.friedmanmirman.com
URL: http://www.lawyers.com/friedmanmirman
William S. Friedman (Certified Specialist in Family Relations Law, Ohio State Bar Association); Denise M. Mirman (Certified Specialist in Family Relations Law, Ohio State Bar Association); Scott N. Friedman;—Kenneth R. Kline; Heather R. Gall.
Family Relations Law, Divorce.

See Professional Biographies, COLUMBUS, OHIO

Friend, Daniel K., (BV) .... '46 '73 C&L.608 B.A., J.D. [[C] C.J.Hudak]
Friscoe, Lou, (BV) .... '41 '72 C.608 B.A. L.117 J.D. 520 N. Park St.
Froehle, Thomas L. .... '— '93 C.737 B.A. L.117 J.D. [[C] McNees W.&N.]
Froling, David A. .... '66 '95 C.608 B.S.B.A. L.117 J.D. [[A] Vorys,S.S.&P.]
Froling, Lynne M. .... '71 '97 C.932 B.B.A. L.215 J.D. [[A] Vorys,S.S.&P.]
Fromm, Barry H. .... '50 '80 C.108 B.S. L.7 J.D. 919 Old Henderson Rd.
Fromson, Jeffrey E., (AV) .... '44 '69 C.473 B.A. L.608 J.D. [Roetzel&A.]
Frost, Earle R., Jr., (AV) .... '39 '69 C.473 B.S. L.608 J.D. [Frost&D.]
Frost, Gregory L. .... '49 '74 C.967 B.A. L.607 J.D. Com. Pleas J.
Frost, John J. .... '— '03 C.932 B.A. L.477 J.D. [[A] Baker&H.]
Frost, Robert E., (BV) .... '39 '64 C.201 B.A. L.602 LL.B. [Frost&M.]

Frost Brown Todd LLC, (AV)
One Columbus, 10 West Broad Street, 43215-3467 ⊙
Telephone: 614-464-1211 Telecopier: 614-464-1737
Email: info@fbtlaw.com URL: http://www.frostbrowntodd.com
Members: John I. Cadwallader; Steven J. Ellcessor; Terrence M. Fay; Jeffrey N. Lindemann; Thomas V. Williams; Michael K. Yarbrough. Senior Associate: Noel C. Shepard. Associates: William M. Harter; Christine L. Robek; Jeffrey G. Rupert; Kevin T. Shook.
Alternative Dispute Resolution, Bankruptcy and Reorganization, Business Acquisitions, Business and Corporate, Commercial Finance, Commercial Litigation, Commercial/Real Estate, Construction, Copyright, Corporate Responsibility and Defense, Employee Benefits, Energy and Natural Resources, Entrepreneurial, Environmental, Equine, Estate Planning and Administration, Financial Institutions, Fire and Explosion, Health Care, Immigration, International, Intellectual Property, International Business, Internet and Electronic Commerce, Labor and Employment Law, Litigation, Media, Mold and Water Intrusion, Multi-District Litigation, Patent Litigation, Personal Planning and Family Business, Privacy and Information Security, Product Liability, Public Finance, Securities, Tax, Tort & Insurance Law, Trademark, Venture Capital, General Trial Practice in all State and Federal Courts.
Cincinnati, Ohio Office: 2200 PNC Center, 201 East Fifth Street, 45202-4182. Telephone: 513-651-6800. Telecopier: 513-651-6981.
Middletown, Ohio Office: 300 North Main Street, Suite 200, 45042-1919. Telephone: 513-422-2001. Telecopier: 513-422-3010.
Lexington, Kentucky Office: 250 West Main Street, Suite 2700, 40507-1742. Telephone: 859-231-0000. Telecopier: 859-231-0011.
Louisville, Kentucky Office: 400 West Market Street, 32nd Floor, 40202-3363. Telephone: 502-589-5400. Telecopier: 502-581-1087.
Nashville, Tennessee Office: 424 Church Street, Suite 1600, 37219-2308. Telephone: 615-251-5550. Telecopier: 615-251-5551.
New Albany, Indiana Office: 120 West Spring Street, Suite 400, 47150-3655. Telephone: 812-948-2800. Telecopier: 812-948-7994.

See Professional Biographies, COLUMBUS, OHIO

Frost & Danchak, LLP, (AV)
50 West Broad Street, Suite 1810, 43215-5909
Telephone: 614-221-6424 Telecopier: 614-221-7122
Members of Firm: Earle R. Frost, Jr.; Michael G. Danchak.
General Practice. Corporate, Securities, Oil and Gas, Real Estate, Taxation, Administrative, Probate, Litigation in all State and Federal Courts and Agencies.
Reference: National City Bank.

Frost & Jacobs LLP
(See Frost Brown Todd LLC)

Frost & Maddox Co., L.P.A., (BV) .... 400 South Fifth Street Suite 301
Fry, Carl B., (BV) .... '46 '74 C&L.608 B.A., J.D. [Fry,W.&M.]
Fry, Waller & McCann Co., L.P.A., (AV) .... 35 East Livingston Avenue
Frye, Richard A. .... '48 '73 C.967 B.A. L.608 J.D. Com. Pleas J.
Fuhrer, Loriann E. .... '66 '97 C.528 B.A. L.851 J.D. [[A] Kegler,B.H.&R.]
Fulcher, Laura Phillips .... '47 '91 C.454 B.A. L.201 J.D. Ohio Civil Rights Comm.
Fulkert, Marc .... '— '03 C.434 B.A. L.150 J.D. [[A] Jones D.]
Fullen, Katina M. .... '72 '99 C&L.117 B.A., J.D. United Way of Franklin Co.
Fullerton, Dwight L., (AV) .... '26 '53 C.976 A.B. L.608 J.D. [Fullerton]
Fullerton, William D., (BV) .... '59 '86 C.976 B.A. L.608 J.D. [Fullerton]
Fullerton Law Offices, (AV) .... 975 S. High St.
Fullin, Daniel E. .... '57 '82 C.737 B.A. L.117 J.D. Legal Dept., Pub. Utilites Comm.
Fullin, Francis X. .... '60 '85 C.608 B.A. L.117 J.D. Express Title Serv(s). of OH
Fullin, James Lawrence, (AV) .... '23 '48 C.363 A.B. L.608 LL.B. 200 Civic Ctr. Dr.‡
Fulmer Stevenson, Amy M. '70 '97
C.608 B.S. L.117 J.D. 163 North Sandusky St., Ste. 103

Fulton, Philip J., Law Office, (AV) '55 '80 C.608 B.A. L.117 J.D. [BB]
89 East Nationwide Boulevard, Suite 300, 43215-2554
Telephone: 614-224-3838 Fax: 614-224-3933 URL: http://www.ohiocompensationlawyer.com
Email: phil@fultonlaw.com URL: http://www.philipfultonlaw.com

(This Listing Continued)

Fulton, Philip J., Law Office (Continued)

—William A. Thorman III; Lori Burns Painter; David B. Barnhart (Certified Specialist in Workers Compensation Law, Ohio State Bar Association); Jacob Dobres; Allison A. Clark.
Workers Compensation, Social Security Disability, Administrative Law, Civil Litigation, Legislative and Appellate Practice.

See Professional Biographies, COLUMBUS, OHIO

Fultz, Palmer '23 '51 C&L.608 B.A.E., LL.B. 4386 Stinson Dr. (Pat.)
Funk, David R. '74 '98 C.631 B.A. L.117 J.D. [Ⓢ Baker&H.]
Funk, John W. '37 '62 C&L.477 B.B.A., J.D. Pres., Pressware Intl., Inc.
Funkhouser, Douglas A. '69 '95 C.608 B.A. L.117 J.D. 729 South Third Street
Furniss, John F., III '75 '00 C.385 A.B. L.893 J.D. [Ⓐ Bricker&E.]
Fusco, Daniel Joseph '69 '99 C.49 B.S. L.179 J.D. [Ⓐ Connor B.]
Fusonie, Thomas H. '— '01 C.299 B.A. L.880 J.D. [Ⓐ Vorys,S.S.&P.]
Gaba, Elizabeth '55 '94 C.012 B.A. L.117 J.D. 1231 E. Broad St.
Gainey, Scott A. '67 '99 C&L.8 B.S., J.D. Coun., Nationwide Insurance
Galbreath, Gerald H., Jr. '16 '40 C&L.623 A.B., LL.B.
(adm. in OK; not adm. in OH) Galbreath Bros.
Galbreath, Michael D. '47 '72 C.610 B.A. L.117 J.D. 1977 Collingswood Rd.
Gale, Erick D. '— '02 C.970 B.A. L.608 J.D. [Ⓐ Jones D.]
Gall, Charles Victor '— '99 C&L.608 B.A., J.D. [Ⓐ Dreher L.&T.]
Gall, Heather R. '74 '99 C&L.608 B.A., J.D. [Ⓐ Friedman&M.]
Gall, John R., (AV) '45 '71 C.473 B.A. L.608 J.D. [Squire,S.&D.]
Gall, Maryann Baker, (AV) '— '70 C&L.608 B.A., J.D. [Jones D.]
Gallagher, James R., (AV) '56 '81 C.473 B.S. L.608 J.D. [Gallagher,G.P.T.&L.]
Gallagher, Mary L., (AV) '66 '92 C&L.608 B.A., J.D.
V.P. & Gen. Coun., Ohio Hospital Association
Gallagher, Michael James '51 '01 C.477 B.A. L.608 J.D. [Gallagher&D.]
Gallagher, Terence L., (BV) '58 '83 C.604 B.A. L.608 J.D. [Gallagher&K.]
Gallagher, Theodore J. '62 '91 C.025 B.A. L.851 J.D. [Ⓐ Bricker&E.]
Gallagher, Thomas J., (BV) '51 '85 C.473 B.A. L.336 J.D. [Ⓐ Maguire&S.]
Gallagher & Dawsey, LPA 533 S. Fifth St.
Gallagher, Gams, Pryor, Tallan & Littrell, L.L.P., (AV)
471 East Broad Street, 19th Floor
Gallagher & Kavinsky, A Legal Professional Association, (BV)
400 South Fifth Street Suite 304
Gallo, Bruce Steven '52 '82 C.563 B.A. L.7 J.D. 17 South High Street, Suite 1220
Gallon, Eric Benjamin '75 '99 C.608 B.A. L.145 J.D. [Ⓐ Porter W.M.&A.]
Gamble, Eric B. '75 '02 C.631 B.A. L.117 J.D. [Gamble H.J.]
Gamble, Kenneth A., (AV) '42 '72 C.610 B.B.A. L.608 J.D. [Gamble H.J.]
Gamble Hartshorn Johnson, LLC, (AV) One East Livingston Avenue (Pat.)
Gambs, Charles R., Jr. '23 '49 C&L.608 LL.B. 1789 Bedford Rd.‡
Gams, Mark H., (AV) '59 '84 C.608 B.A. L.117 J.D. [Gallagher,G.P.T.&L.]
Gantz, Curtis F., (AV) '43 '68 C.313 B.A. L.608 J.D. [Lane,A.&H.]
Garber, Kenneth E., (BV) '34 '67 C.608 B.S. L.266 J.D. [Garber&W.]
Garber & Wilcox, (BV) 3303 Sullivant Ave.
Garceau, Mary L. '72 '97 C.550 B.A. L.880 J.D. [Vorys,S.S.&P.]
Garcia, Daren S. '76 '02 C.608 B.A. L.1365 J.D. [Ⓐ Vorys,S.S.&P.]
Garcia, Roger '— '96 C.610 D.O. L.117 J.D. [Ⓐ Colley S.&A.]
Gardier, Robert W., Jr. '52 '77 C.945 A.B. L.608 J.D. 2520 Lane Rd.
Gardiner, Michael B. '67 '92 C.597 B.A. L.608 J.D. [Ⓒ Squire,S.&D.]
Gardner, Robert F., (BV) '30 '58 C.150 B.A. L.1340 LL.B. 601 S. High St.
Gardner, William A., (BV) '47 '79 C.608 B.S. L.607 J.D. P.O. Box 20352
Garel, Jules L., (AV) '30 '55 C.309 B.A. L.94 J.D. [Ⓒ Bailey C.]
Garling, Ellen J. '59 '89 C.608 B.A. L.117 J.D. [Baker&H.]
Garrett, William A. '62 '87 C.597 B.A. L.94 J.D. Sr. Coun., Bank One Corp.
Garrison, W. Travis '70 '03 C.651 B.S. L.608 J.D. [Ⓐ Chester,W.&S.]
Gartland, Sheila Nolan, (BV) '61 '86 C.201 B.S. L.851 J.D. [Vorys,S.S.&P.]
Garvin, Preston J., (AV) '49 '74 C.205 B.A. L.8 J.D. [Garvin&H.]

Garvin & Hickey, LLC, (AV)
181 East Livingston Avenue, 43215
Telephone: 614-225-9000 Fax: 614-225-9080
Email: wclaw@garvin-hickey.com URL: http://www.garvinhickey.com
Members of Firm: Preston J. Garvin; Michael J. Hickey;—Daniel M. Hall; Paul Joseph Hess, Jr. Of Counsel: Kathryn A. Chubb; Sandee E. Riem.
Labor and Employment, Workers Compensation Defense and Intentional Torts.

See Professional Biographies, COLUMBUS, OHIO

Garvine, Brian M. '— '97 C.608 B.A. L.851 J.D. [Ⓐ Onda,L.&R.]
Gaschen, Dane A., (BV) '57 '94 C.893 B.A. L.608 J.D. [Ⓐ Bricker&E.]
Gaskill, Charles R., II '51 '76 C&L.117 B.A., J.D. Motorists Mut. Ins. Co.
Gates, Timothy L. '70 '97 C.645 B.A. L.608 J.D. [Ⓐ Wallace&W.]
Gatterdam, Kort W. '62 '88 C.610 A.B. L.260 J.D. Asst. Pub. Def.
Gavin, Robert P. '58 '83 C.339 B.S. L.146 J.D. Gen. Coun., NBBJ East Limited
Gayton, Charles W., (BV) '37 '72 C.608 B.S. L.117 J.D. 3620 N. High Street
Geary, Susan E., (BV) '56 '89 C.651 B.S. L.117 J.D. [Bricker&E.]

Geary, William L., (AV) '52 '78 C.608 B.A. L.607 J.D.
Suite 101 Waterford Tower, 155 West Main Street, 43215-5000
Telephone: 614-228-1968 Fax: 614-228-7630
Email: gearylawoffices@aol.com URL: http://columbusfamilylawyer.com
Family Law, Divorce, Separation Agreements, Child Custody, Child Support, Visitation Rights, Alimony.

See Professional Biographies, COLUMBUS, OHIO

Geer, Christopher J., (BV) '48 '78 C.608 B.A. L.117 J.D. [Matan,G.&W.]
Gegenheimer, C. Michael '54 '85 C.119 B.S. L.608 J.D.
Asst. Intell. Prop. Coun., Battelle Memorial Institute (Pat.)
Gehring, Michelle Denise '68 '98 C.608 B.A. L.117 J.D. [Ⓐ Perez&M.]
Geiger, Franz A. '66 '91 C.477 B.A. L.608 J.D. Np Ltd. Ptnrshp.
Geiger, Heather L. '— '93 C&L.608 B.S., J.D.
Sr. Coun.-Trans., Amer. Elect. Power Serv. Corp.
Geiser, Michael Keith, (BV) '64 '91 C.608 B.A. L.117 J.D. [Plymale]
Gellman, Susan B., (AV) '57 '86 C.1036 B.A. L.608 J.D. [Ⓒ Wolman&Assoc.]
Genshaft, Nelson E., (AV) '— '73 C.659 B.S. L.930 J.D. [Strip,H.L.M.&T.]
Gentile, Mitchell L. '55 '81 C.608 B.A. L.1003 J.D. Prin. Atty., Atty. Gen. Off.
George, Fredk. C., (BV) '20 '52 C&L.608 B.S., LL.B. [George&M.]
George, Jason L. '72 '98 C.210 B.A. L.347 J.D. [Ⓐ Peck,S.&W.]
George, Lewis C. '64 '89 C.608 B.S. L.117 J.D. Dept. of Youth Servs.
George & Meyer Co., L.P.A., (BV) 4303 Cleveland Ave.
Gerber, Louis E., (AV) '30 '57 C.381 A.B. L.608 J.D. 10 W. Broad St.‡
Gerber, Richard S. '54 '84 C.608 B.S. L.117 J.D. [Ⓐ Maguire&S.]
Gerhardstein, Walter J., (BV) '47 '73 C.973 B.A. L.150 J.D. 225 E. Broad St.
Gerling, Joseph A., (AV) '52 '77 C.602 B.S. L.608 J.D. [Lane,A.&H.]
Gerrity, Timothy D., (AV) '44 '70 C.473 A.B. L.608 J.D. [Gerrity&B.]
Gerrity and Burrier, Ltd., (AV) 400 South Fifth Street, Suite 302
Gertmenian, Russell M., (AV) '47 '72 C.705 A.B. L.178 J.D. [Vorys,S.S.&P.]
Gertner, Michael H., (AV) '41 '66 C&L.608 B.A., J.D. [Gertner&G.]

Gertner & Gertner, (AV)
199 South Fifth Street, Suite 302, 43215
Telephone: 614-463-9393 Fax: 614-463-9669
Email: gertnerlaw@aol.com URL: http://www.michaelgertner.com
Members of Firm: Abraham Gertner (1909-1996); Michael H. Gertner.
Trials, Appeals, Personal Injury, Automobile Accidents and Injuries, Construction Site Accidents, Wrongful Death, Nursing Home Negligence, Premises Liability, Insurance Law, Medical Negligence, Criminal Law, White Collar Crimes, Business Litigation, Breach of Contract, Lawsuits, Securities Arbitration, Securities Fraud, Stockbroker Disputes, Investments, Police Misconduct, Employment Law, Sexual Assault/Rape Victims, Civil Litigation, Probate Litigation, Contested Wills, Contested Guardianships.

See Professional Biographies, COLUMBUS, OHIO

Geswein, Mary Frances '69 '94 C.602 B.A. L.608 J.D. [Ⓒ Schottenstein,Z.&D.]
Geyer, Catherine Cordial '65 '90 C.207 B.A. L.608 J.D. Motorists Mut. Ins. Co.
Geyer, Thomas E. '64 '90 C.602 B.B.A. L.608 J.D. [Ⓒ Bailey C.]
Ghidotti, Paul G. '64 '90 C.473 B.A. L.880 J.D. Daimler Grp., Inc.
Giampapa, Joseph A., (AV) '57 '83 C&L.608 B.S., J.D. Sr. Coun., Bank One Corp.
Gibbs, Jack Gilbert, Jr., (AV) '53 '82 C.475 B.A. L.117 J.D. 233 S. High St., Ste. 208
Gibbs, Lawrence A. '19 '54 C.608 B.S. L.150 LL.B. 2578 Fairwood Ave.
Gibbs, R. Cliffton, (AV) '35 '59 C&L.608 B.S., J.D. [Ⓒ Bailey C.]
Gibney, Thomas J., (BV) '60 '85 C&L.477 B.A., J.D. [Eastman&S.] (⊙Toledo)
Gibson, J. Miles, (AV) '53 '78 C.608 B.A. L.117 J.D. 673 Mohawk St., 4th Fl.
Gibson, Janet D., (BV) '52 '81
C&L.608 B.A.,B.S., J.D. Corp. Atty., The W.W. Williams Co.
Gibson, Rick J. '— '96 C.424 B.B.A. L.665 J.D. [Ⓐ Jones D.]
Gibson, Stephanie L. '71 '97 C.150 B.A. L.117 J.D. 500 S. 4th St.
Gideon, John J., (BV) '50 '78 C&L.608 B.A., J.D. 250 E. Stanton Ave.
Giffin, Robert E. '39 '73 C.920 B.S. L.117 J.D. [R.E.Giffin]
Giffin, Robert E., Co., L.P.A. 4924B Reed Rd.
Gifford, Brian L. '— '97 C.207 B.A. L.608 J.D. [Ⓐ Jones D.]
Gilbert, Coit H. '28 '61 C.610 B.S. L.266 J.D. [Gilbert&S.]
Gilbert, James D., (BV) '53 '81 C.967 B.A. L.117 J.D. 4025 Riverview Drive
Gilbert & Startzman 319 Canyon Dr. S.
Gilchrist, John, (BV) '43 '72 C.676 B.A. L.128 J.D. 341 S. 3rd St.
Gilcrest, Roger A., (AV) '55 '85 C.970 B.A. L.1049 J.D. [Schottenstein,Z.&D.] (Pat.)
Gildehaus, Ralph F. '60 '90 C.31 B.A. L.273 J.D. [Porter W.M.&A.]
Gill, Joseph S., (AV) '17 '41 C.610 A.B. L.309 LL.B. 100 S. 3rd St.
Gill, M. Elizabeth, (BV) '62 '88 C.150 B.A. L.608 J.D. [Ⓢ Baker&H.]
Gill, Sterling E., II '— '79 C&L.608 B.A., J.D.
Dist. Hearing Off., Ohio Industrial Comm.
Gilles, Susan M. '60 '85 C.999 LL.B. L.309 LL.M. Prof. of Law, Capital Univ.
Gillett, Gary A., (BV) '— '85 C.880 B.A. L.608 J.D. [Buckley K.]
Gillie, William Trescott '15 '41 C.930 A.B. L.161 J.D. Ret. Com. Pleas J.
Gilligan, John P., (AV) '49 '77 C.197 B.A. L.1066 J.D. [Schottenstein,Z.&D.]
Gillis, Mark H. '66 '96 C.610 B.B.A. L.1148 J.D. [Ⓐ Rich,C.&D.]
Gillis, Sylvia Lynn '54 '89 C.35 B.A. L.608 J.D. [Bricker&E.]
Gillotti, Joseph M. '66 '96 C.608 B.S. L.117 J.D. [Ⓐ Carlile P.&M.]
Ginther, Jeffrey D. '47 '73 C.318 B.A. L.208 J.D. 1199 Highland Street
Giorgianni, Paul '65 '95 C.602 B.A. L.608 J.D. [Ⓐ Thompson H.]
Giorgione, Edmund Emil, (BV) '47 '83 C.266 B.S.B.A. L.117 J.D.
Franklin Co. Common Pleas Ct., Appellate Div. [E.E.Giorgione]
Giorgione, Edmund E., (BV) 373 South High Street, Floor 22
Giovanetti, Richard J. '33 '62 C.608 B.A. L.117 J.D. 1777 Ardleigh Rd.‡
Gipe, Larry C. '35 '61 C&L.352 B.S.C., J.D.
(adm. in IA; not adm. in OH) 5500 Renner Rd.‡
Gire, Michael K., (AV) '47 '77 C.608 B.S. L.30 J.D. [Bricker&E.]
Gitlitz, Gary B. '51 '76 C.37 B.A. L.851 J.D. [Chester,W.&S.]
Gittes, Frederick M., (AV) '47 '75 L.608 J.D. [Gittes&S.]
Gittes & Schulte, (AV) 723 Oak St.
Giuliani, Anthony J. '62 '88 C&L.608 B.A., J.D. [Vorys,S.S.&P.]
Giumenti, Katherine Spies, (AV) '64 '89 C&L.608 B.A., J.D. [Ⓐ Bricker&E.]
Gjostein, Thomas Arthur '62 '88 C.477 B.A. L.117 J.D. Franklin Co. Pub. Def.
Gladman, Michael R. '— '92 C&L.608 B.S., J.D. [Ⓐ Jones D.]
Glaeden, Carrie E. '63 '89
C.966 B.A. L.608 J.D. Dep. Chief Legal Coun., Governor's Off.
Glaros, Christopher M. '— '03 C.178 B.A. L.813 J.D. [Ⓐ Jones D.]
Glas, Milton G. '20 '53 C.608 B.S. L.266 J.D. 923 East Broad Street
Glascor, H. Alfred '14 '39 C&L.608 B.A., J.D. 5755 Sunbury Rd.‡
Glasgow, Jeffrey L., (BV) '46 '75 C.313 B.A. L.608 J.D.
1st Asst., Co. Pros. Atty., Civil
Glasgow, Marcus Jeremey '70 '98 C.611 B.A. L.179 J.D. Atty. Gen. Off.
Glass, Greg C. '53 '78 C.253 B.S. L.851 J.D. Asst. Gen. Coun., State Dept. of Health
Glazer, Craig A. '55 '79 C.659 B.A. L.880 J.D. 180 E Broad St
Gleaves, Mark M., (BV) '53 '78 C.631 B.A. L.117 J.D. Atty. Gen.
Gleespen, Michael W., (AV) '58 '84 C.150 B.A. L.608 J.D. Asst. Atty. Gen.
Gluck, Myriam Waksman '65 '91 C.910 B.A. L.150 J.D.
400 East Town Street, Suite 210
Godby, Herbert R., (AV) '46 '73 C.610 B.B.A. L.477 J.D. [Schottenstein,Z.&D.]
Goddard, Gabriel L. '72 '98 C.347 B.A. L.608 J.D.
Staff Coun., Cincinnati Insurance Co.
Gold, David M. '50 '78 C.1349 B.A. L.608 J.D. Ohio Legis. Serv. Commission
Goldberg, Dale Ann, (BV) '51 '80 C.771 B.A. L.1065 J.D. Asst. U.S. Atty.
Goldberg, Ken '— '92 C.945 B.A. L.117 J.D. [Strip,H.L.M.&T.]
Goldberg, Richard, (BV) '58 '83 C.705 B.A. L.608 J.D. [Scott,S.&W.]
Goldberger, David A. '41 '68 C&L.145 B.A., J.D.
Isadore & Ida Topper Prof. of Law, Ohio State Univ., Coll. of Law
Golden, Keith E., (BV) '52 '84 C.608 B.S. L.117 J.D. [Krupman,G.M.M.&W.]
Golden, Sidney H. '25 '57 C.608 B.A. L.266 J.D. Ret. Mun. J.‡
Goldhand, Joanne I., (BV) '64 '88
C.674 A.B. L.569 J.D. V.P. & Gen. Couns., Skilken Properties
Goldin, Larry M. '55 '79 C.477 A.B. L.145 J.D. 85 E. Gay St., Ste. 612
Goldman, Dennis J., (BV) '42 '68 C.608 B.A. L.229 J.D. 800 Frebis Ave.
Goldman, Jerome S., (BV) '48 '73 C.1019 B.A. L.117 J.D. [Goldman&R.]
Goldman, Jessica D. '77 '03 C.385 B.A. L.880 J.D. [Ⓐ Squire,S.&D.]
Goldman, William A., (BV) '40 '66 C&L.608 B.S., J.D.
[Ⓒ Crabbe,B.&J.] & [Goldman&B.] (⊙Columbus)
Goldman, William A., (BV) '40 '66 C&L.608 B.S., J.D.
[Goldman&B.] & [Ⓒ Crabbe,B.&J.] (⊙Columbus)
Goldman & Braunstein, LLP, (BV) 454 East Main Street Suite 227

Goldman & Rosenthal, (BV)
5350 East Main Street, 43213
Telephone: 614-864-4359 Fax: 614-864-2818
URL: http://www.goldmanrosenthal.com
Jerome S. Goldman; Lee S. Rosenthal.

(This Listing Continued)

Goldman & Rosenthal (Continued)

Personal Injury, Family Law, Real Estate, Commercial Leasing, Construction and Mechanics Lien Law, Collections, Estate Planning and Probate, Corporate, Juvenile Law, Criminal. Civil and Criminal Trials in all Courts.

See Professional Biographies, COLUMBUS, OHIO

Goldson, Jennifer C. .... '70 '96 C&L.608 B.A., J.D. 1265 Neil Avenue
Goldstein, Amy R., (AV) .... '52 '82 C.930 B.A. L.161 J.D. 720 City Park
Goldstein, David A., (AV) .... '68 '95 C.608 B.A. L.117 J.D. [D.A.Goldstein]
Goldstein, Harry S. .... '13 '35 C&L.608 B.A., J.D. 77 S. Stanwood Rd.‡

Goldstein, David A., Co., L.P.A., (AV)
529 S. Third Street, 43215
Telephone: 614-222-1889 Fax: 614-222-1899
Email: dgoldstein@dgoldsteinlaw.com URL: http://www.davidagoldstein.com
David A. Goldstein;—Seth Kleinman.
Insurance Law, Insurance Coverage, Professional Liability, Legal Malpractice, Personal Injury, Products Liability, Wrongful Death, Automobile Accidents.

See Professional Biographies, COLUMBUS, OHIO

Golian, Joseph J., (AV) .... '60 '85 C.901 B.A. L.117 J.D. [Brenner,B.G.&M.]
Golonka, Kenneth A., Jr., (AV) .... '61 '86 C.602 B.A. L.608 J.D. [Vorys,S.S.&P.]
Gooden, R. Russell '51 '77 C&L.117 B.S., J.D.
Pub. Util. Comm., Sect. Chief, Gas & Electric Div.
Goodin, Eileen S., (AV) .... '55 '80 C.381 B.A. L.608 J.D. [Barkan&N.]
Goodman, J. David .... '67 '92 C.473 B.A. L.930 J.D. OH Senate
Goodman, Jonathan Howard .... '74 '99 C&L.608 B.A., J.D. 5900 Roche Dr., Ste. 502
Goodman, N. Victor, (AV) .... '36 '61 C.976 B.A. L.309 J.D. [Benesch,F.C.&A.]
Goodstein, Michael R., (AVⓉ) '64 '89 C.1036 B.A. L.904 J.D.
(adm. in MD; not adm. in OH) [Bailey C.]
Goodwin, Wilfred '23 '50 C&L.608 B.S., J.D.
Exec. Dir., Ohio Peace Officer Training Council
Gordon, Charles E. .... '58 '83 C.608 B.S. L.117 J.D. 584 City Park Ave.
Gordon, Clarence T., II, (BV) .... '50 '75 C.L.838 B.S., J.D. 394 W. Second Ave.
Gordon, James H., (BV) .... '42 '74 C.970 B.A. L.608 J.D. [Gordon]
Gordon, Nathan, (BV) .... '45 '72 C.150 B.A. L.608 J.D. 2485 East Broad Street
Gordon, Pamela Jean .... '60 '85 C&L.608 B.S., J.D. City Atty. Off.
Gordon, Thomas Steven .... '68 '00 C.1290 B.A. L.117 J.D. Co. Pros. Off.

Gordon Law Firm Co., LPA, (BV)
Fifth Third Center, 21 East State Street, Suite 1700, 43215
Telephone: 614-228-0888 Fax: 614-228-0850
Email: jgordon@rrcol.com URL: http://www.jameshgordon.com
James H. Gordon.
General Civil Trial and Appellate Practice, Real Estate, Small Business, Buying and Selling of Businesses, Business Formation, Partnerships, Limited Liability Company Law, Business Litigation, Contract Law, Collections, Corporate, Construction Litigation, Probate.
Reference: Bank One of Columbus, N.A.

See Professional Biographies, COLUMBUS, OHIO

Gormley, David M., (AV) '65 '90 C.477 B.A. L.309 J.D.
Dir., Legal Resources, Supreme Court of Ohio
Gorno, Lorri A. ..... '65 '91 C.97 B.S. L.851 J.D. Grant/Riverside Meth. Hosp. Ohiohealth
Gorospe, Gregory A. .... '— '93 C&L.608 B.S., J.D. [Jones D.]
Gorry, James R. .... '47 '72 C.473 B.A. L.477 J.D. [[C] Rich,C.&D.]
Goshay, Pamela Maria .... '72 '00 C.207 B.A. L.608 J.D. Ohio Legislative Serv. Comm.
Gosnell, Gerhardt A., II .... '67 '95 C.117 B.A. L.608 J.D. [[A] Chester,W.&S.]
Goss, Dianne, (AV) .... '57 '82 C.207 B.A. L.7 J.D. 632 N. High St.
Gosselin, Heather Lynn .... '74 '00 C.608 B.A. L.200 J.D. OH Atty. Gen. Off.
Gottfried, Gary J., (BV) .... '48 '73 C.434 B.A. L.117 J.D. [G.J.Gottfried]
Gottfried, Gary J., Co., L.P.A., (BV) .... 1265 Neil Avenue
Gottschall, Matthew D. .... '— '97 C.473 B.A. L.150 J.D. [[A] Vorys,S.S.&P.]
Gould, Craigg E. .... '68 '93 C.610 B.B.A. L.607 J.D. [[A] Saia&P.]
Goussetis, Harry A. '54 '79 C.4 B.A. L.851 J.D.
Asst. Gen. Coun., Worthington Industries, Inc.
Govern, Jodi A. '64 '89 C&L.608 B.A., J.D.
Asst. Coun. to Dir., Dept. of Liquor Control
Grabovac, Greg R. '67 '94
C&L.608 B.S.B.A., J.D. V.P. & Gen. Coun., The Fishel Company
Grady, Terrence A., (AV) .... '54 '82 C&L.117 B.A., J.D. [T.A.Grady&Assoc.]
Grady, Timothy E., (AV) .... '50 '79 C.98 B.A. L.339 J.D. [Porter W.M.&A.]

Grady, Terrence A., & Associates Co., L.P.A., (AV)
100 East Broad Street, Suite 2310, 43215
Telephone: 614-849-0378 Fax: 614-849-0379
Email: tgrady@tgradylaw.com URL: http://www.tgradylaw.com
Terrence A. Grady.
Civil and Criminal Tax Litigation in State and Federal Courts. Federal Criminal Tax and Federal White Collar Crime Defense, Tax Controversies, Substantive Federal Tax Planning; Complex IRS Collection Matters; Corporate and Small Business Services, Estate and Asset Protection Planning.

See Professional Biographies, COLUMBUS, OHIO

Graf, Ann B. '44 '84 C.876 B.A. L.1003 J.D.
Sr. Coun.-Fin. & Compl., Amer. Elec. Power Serv. Corp.
Graf, Brenda J. .... '57 '96 C.610 B.Admin. L.117 J.D. Carrington Health Sys.
Graf, Jack R., Jr. '47 '73 C.608 B.A. L.117 J.D.
Pres., Graf & Sons Overhead Doors, Inc.‡
Graf-Caswell, Mary Lynn .... '71 '96 C.473 B.A. L.608 J.D. Asst. City Pros. Atty.
Graff, Alison M. .... '51 '80 C.608 B.A. L.117 J.D. 1054 Highland Dr.
Graff, Douglas E., (BV) .... '53 '85 C.117 B.A. L.608 J.D. [Graff&Assoc.]
Graff & Associates, L.P.A., (BV) .... 604 East Rich Street
Graham, David T. .... '73 '98 C.97 B.S.B.A. L.608 J.D. [[A] Kegler,B.H.&R.]
Graham, James L. .... '39 '62 C&L.608 B.A., J.D. Sr. J.
Graham, Kathleen Elizabeth .... '52 '82 C.608 B.S. L.117 J.D. Admin. Ref., Mun. Ct.
Graham, Richard C., (AV) .... '42 '68 C.528 B.S. L.930 J.D. [Gamble H.J.]
Gramann, Margaret L., (BV) .... '— '85 C.320 B.A. L.893 J.D. [[C] Jones D.]
Grande, Monica .... '79 '04 C&L.608 B.S.B.A., J.D. [[A] Vorys,S.S.&P.]
Grandon, Pamela .... '53 '81 C&L.608 B.S., J.D. Atty. Examiner, Dept. of Commerce
Granger, Aaron L. .... '70 '97 C.611 B.A. L.608 J.D. [[A] Schottenstein,Z.&D.]
Granger, Mark .... '56 '97 C.631 B.A. L.117 J.D. [Granger]
Granger Co., LPA .... 132 Northwoods Boulevard
Grant, Dennis D., (AV) .... '40 '65 C.532 B.A. L.477 J.D. [Bailey C.]
Grassbaugh, Stephen P., (AV) .... '51 '84 C.608 B.S.B.A. L.930 J.D. [Peck,S.&W.]
Grauel, Dawn-Rae .... '72 '01 C.980 B.A. L.608 J.D. [[A] Hahn L.&P.]
Grauer, David W., (AV) .... '54 '85 C.378 B.S. L.117 J.D. [Squire,S.&D.]
Grauer, Myron C. .... '48 '75 C.882 B.A. L.665 J.D. Prof. of Law, Capital Univ.
Graver, Julia M. .... '65 '91 C.999 B.A. L.117 J.D. Asst. Atty Gen.
Graves, Arthur C., (BV) ...... '39 '64 C.385 A.B. L.608 J.D. 2929 Kenny Road (⊙Canton)
Gray, James S. .... '73 '00 C&L.608 B.A., J.D. [[A] Bricker&E.]
Gray, Stephen C., (BV) .... '65 '91 C.966 B.S. L.608 J.D. [Bricker&E.]
Grayem, Jeremy .... '74 '00 C.473 B.A. L.608 J.D. [[A] Schottenstein,Z.&D.]
Graziano, Robert B., (AV) .... '64 '91 C.229 B.A. L.930 J.D. [Roetzel&A.]
Greaney, Constance M., (BV) .... '63 '92 C.518 B.A. L.930 J.D. [Porter W.M.&A.]
Green, David M. .... '45 '70 C.473 B.A. L.1340 J.D. 300 East Broad Street, Suite 300‡
Green, James E., (BV) .... '57 '85 C.8 B.A. L.608 J.D. 375 S. High St.
Green, Kerry Renker .... '— '02 C.608 B.S. L.8 J.D. [[A] Jones D.]
Green, Matthew T. .... '77 '02 C&L.608 B.S.B.A., J.D. [[A] Schottenstein,Z.&D.]
Greenbaum, Arthur F. '51 '76 C.976 B.A. L.893 J.D.
(adm. in VA; not adm. in OH) Prof. of Law, Ohio State Univ.
Greenberger, Susan Beale .... '52 '79 C.1375 A.B. L.966 J.D. [Bricker&E.]
Greene, Stephanie T. '78 '04 C.1365 B.A. L.569 J.D.
(adm. in NY; not adm. in OH) [[A] Bricker&E.]
Greenfield, Gerald, (AVⓉ) '39 '64 C.867 B.A. L.982 J.D.
V.P. & Asst. Gen. Coun., Schottenstein Stores Corp.
Greentree, Hugh A., Law Offices of .... '59 '85 C&L.608 B.A., B.A. 3111 E. Broad St.
Greenwald, Gary D., (AV) .... '46 '71 C.473 B.A. L.608 J.D. [Shayne&G.]
Greer, David K. .... '61 '89 C.608 B.A. L.851 J.D. 1150 Morse Road, Suite 106
Gregg, Heather D. .... '— '01 C.608 B.A. L.117 J.D. [[A] Thompson H.]
Gregg, Joseph A., (BV) .... '56 '81 C.473 A.B. L.150 J.D. [Eastman&S.] (⊙Toledo)
Gregori, Terri B., (BV) .... '64 '93 C.679 B.A. L.608 J.D. 1598 Blackstone Drive
Gregory, Donald W., (AV) .... '57 '82 C.473 B.A. L.608 J.D. [Kegler,B.H.&R.]
Greim, David M. .... '58 '87 C.1073 B.A. L.911 J.D. 30 W. Spring St.
Gresko, Janice L. .... '— '96 C.318 B.A. L.607 J.D. [[A] Jones D.]
Greuel, Tracy M. .... '75 '01 C&L.608 B.A., J.D. Asst. Atty. Gen.
Gridley, Wendy H. .... '55 '84 C.886 B.S. L.608 J.D. Asst. Atty. Gen.
Grier, Jill S. .... '67 '93 C.473 B.S. L.608 J.D. Coun., Nationwide Insurance
Grieser, C. Richard, (AV) .... '20 '49 C.608 B.S. L.309 J.D. [[C] Blumenstiel,H.&A.]
Griesheimer, Jeffrey Arthur .... '49 '81 C.608 B.A. L.851 J.D. Admin. Law J.
Griesmer, Kelley M. .... '— '93 C.347 B.A. L.608 J.D. [Jones D.]
Griffaton, Michael C. .... '68 '93 C.611 B.A. L.930 J.D. [[A] Vorys,S.S.&P.]
Griffin, Jeanne A. .... '55 '84 C.906 B.A. L.494 J.D. [Baker&H.]
Griffin, Robert H., Jr. .... '60 '85 C.473 A.B. L.117 J.D. [[A] Maguire&S.]
Griffin, Robert L. .... '— '86 C.608 B.A. L.117 J.D. Asst. Atty. Gen.
Griffin, Vanessa Marie .... '73 '98 C.532 B.A. L.117 J.D. Co. Ct. of Com. Pleas
Griffith, Kevin E., (AV) .... '60 '86 C&L.602 B.A., J.D. [Porter W.M.&A.]
Griffiths, George K., (BV) .... '53 '78 C.1115 B.A. L.607 J.D. 613 Glenridge Place
Griggs, Peter N. .... '72 '01 C.608 B.A. L.8 J.D. [[A] Loveland&B.]
Grodhaus, D. Michael, (AV) .... '58 '84 C.473 A.B. L.930 J.D. First Asst. Atty. Gen.
Grody, Warren I. .... '60 '93 C.1208 B.A. L.117 J.D. [[A] Bricker&E.]
Groeber, Anthony A., (BV) '40 '72
C.973 M.B.A. L.117 J.D. 6877 N. High Street, Suite 300
Groner, James M., (AV) .... '65 '91 C.473 B.S. L.150 J.D. [Bailey C.]
Gross, Geo. W., (AV) .... '26 '54 C.608 B.S. L.266 J.D. 2800 Chateau Circle‡
Gross, James H., (AV) .... '41 '66 C.608 B.A. L.309 LL.B. [Vorys,S.S.&P.]
Gross, William F. .... '56 '81 C.216 B.A. L.117 J.D. Asst. Admr., OH Dept. of Taxation
Grossman, Andrew Scott .... '70 '96 C.378 B.A. L.117 J.D. [[A] Grossman]
Grossman, Jeffrey A., (AV) .... '46 '72 C.610 B.S.J. L.117 J.D. [Grossman]
Grossman, Lillian Yvonne .... '56 '84 C.608 B.S. L.117 J.D. Dept. of Youth Servs.

Grossman Law Offices, (AV)
32 West Hoster Street, 43215
Telephone: 614-221-7711 Fax: 614-221-7145
Email: lawyers@grossman-law.com URL: http://www.grossmanlawoffices.com
Jeffrey A. Grossman (Certified Specialist in Family Relations Law, Ohio State Bar Association);—Thomas J. Jedinak (Certified Specialist in Family Relations Law, Ohio State Bar Association); Anthony R. Auten (Certified Specialist in Family Relations Law, Ohio State Bar Association); Andrew Scott Grossman (Certified Specialist in Family Relations Law, Ohio State Bar Association); Alyson B. Miller; Julia L. Leveridge.
Family Law, Matrimonial Law, Child Custody, Divorce, Domestic Violence, Premarital Agreements, Child Support, Visitation Rights, Trial and Appellate Practice.

See Professional Biographies, COLUMBUS, OHIO

Grove, Raymond F. .... '39 '71 C.608 B.S. L.117 J.D. 25 Greenlawn Avenue
Grubb, Janet A., (BV) .... '50 '76 C.434 B.A. L.117 J.D. 375 S. High St., 13th Fl. - C
Grubbs, Donell R., (BV) .... '— '86 C.607 B.A. L.608 J.D. [Buckley K.]
Gruber, M. Ellen .... '47 '80 C.608 B.S. L.117 J.D. 37 N. High Street
Grubler, Gary L., Law Offices of, (BV) '60 '85
C.967 B.A. L.608 J.D. One Nationwide Plaza
Gruhin, Lois A. .... '47 '71 C.705 B.A. L.421 J.D. [[A] Zashin&R.] ⊙
Guiher, Virgil Leon .... '31 '56 C&L.608 B.S., LL.B. [Guiher,V.L.]
Guiher, Virgil L. .... 4060 Morse Rd., Suite 10
Guittar, Donald J., (BV) .... '32 '60 C.381 B.A. L.930 LL.B. Asst. Atty. Gen.
Guldin, John R. .... '40 '67 C.313 A.B. L.8 J.D. Legal Coun., Bur. of Motor Vehicles
Gumbinner, Fredric R. '59 '85 C.165 B.A. L.477 J.D.
Asst. Gen. Coun., Columbia Energy Group Serv. Corp.
Gunasekera, Eva U. .... '— '04 C.610 B.A. L.276 J.D. [[A] Jones D.]
Gunn, Jeannette E. .... '63 '94 C.999 B.S. L.117 J.D. Admin. Law J.
Gunner, Michael T., (BV) '48 '73
C&L.851 B.A., J.D. 3535 Fishinger Boulevard, Suite 220
Gunsett, Daniel J., (AV) .... '48 '74 C.477 B.S. L.575 J.D. [Baker&H.]
Gurian, Jonathan, (BV) '56 '85 C.608 B.S. L.117 J.D.
Claims Atty., Grange Mut. Cas. Co.
Gurile, Melissa A. .... '74 '04 C.454 B.A. L.201 J.D. [Lane,A.&H.]
Gusty, James .... '40 '84 C.608 B.S. L.201 J.D. 1147 Wyandotte Rd.
Guthrie, Jim .... '43 '71 C.608 B.A. L.117 J.D. Off. of the Atty. Gen.
Guttman, Daniel J. .... '72 '97 C.651 B.A. L.608 J.D. [Baker&H.]
Guzman, Becky .... '74 '01 C&L.608 B.A., J.D. Co. Pub. Def.
Gwinn, Susan L. .... '54 '79 C.610 A.B. L.851 J.D. Asst. Atty. Gen.
Haak, William H. '68 '94 C.8 B.S. L.930 J.D.
Sr. EH&S Coun., Hexion Specialty Chemicals, Inc.
Habash, Stephen J., (AV) .... '51 '78 C&L.608 B.A., J.D. [Habash,R.&F.]

Habash, Reasoner & Frazier LLP, (AV)
471 East Broad Street, Suite 800, 43215-3844
Telephone: 614-221-9400 Fax: 614-221-1214
URL: http://www.lawyers.com/hrf-law
Stephen J. Habash; W. Irl Reasoner, III; Jean M. Frazier; Tracy L. Turner. Of Counsel: Jean M. Luczkowski.
Employment Law, Labor Relations and Workers' Compensation.

See Professional Biographies, COLUMBUS, OHIO

Haberman, Mark A. ..... '53 '81 C.1024 B.A. L.117 J.D. Asst. Exec. Dir., OH Bldg. Auth.
Hacker, Cheryl R. .... '59 '88 C.91 B.A. L.117 J.D. Asst. Atty. Gen.
Hackett, Andrew M. '70 '95
C&L.602 B.B.A., J.D. Asst. Gen. Coun., Crane Plastics Company
Hackett, Daniel R., (AV) .... '61 '88 C.602 B.B.A. L.608 J.D. [Bailey C.]
Hackett, Lawrence J. .... '53 '65 C.980 B.S. L.1003 J.D. U.S. of Trustee Off.
Hackett, Patricia A. .... '64 '93 C.608 B.A. L.851 J.D. Glimcher Realty Tr.
Hadden, E. Bruce, (AV) .... '35 '60 C&L.608 B.S., J.D. [Hadden]
Hadden, James B., (AV) .... '67 '92 C.472 B.A. L.608 J.D. [Porter W.M.&A.]

Hadden Co., L.P.A., (AV) .... 132 Northwoods Boulevard
Haddow, Howard J., (AV) .... '36 '61 C&L.608 B.S., LL.B. 250 Civic Center Drive
Haddox, Craig A., (AV) .... '57 '82 C.228 B.A. L.477 J.D. [Bricker&E.]
Haddox, Jerome B. .... '33 '60 C&L.608 B.S., J.D. 3744 Romnay Rd.
Hafenstein, Kenneth S. .... '69 '94 C.967 B.A. L.608 J.D. [Ⓐ Connor B.]
Hagen, Theresa L. .... '— '90 C.679 B.S. L.1119 J.D. 4440 Haverford Ct.
Hahn, J. Victor .... '47 '75 C.207 B.A. L.273 J.D. Coun., Capital Univ.
Hahn, Peter W. .... '73 '98 C.970 B.A. L.910 J.D. [Ⓐ Buckingham,D.&B.]
Hahn, Susie L. .... '73 '98 C.575 B.S. L.910 J.D. [Ⓐ Leeseberg&V.]

Hahn Loeser & Parks LLP, (AV)
65 East State Street, Suite 1400, 43215 ⊙
Telephone: 614-221-0240 FAX: 614-221-5909/1-877-HAHNLAW
URL: http://www.hahnlaw.com
Resident Members: Stephen E. Chappelear; Marc J. Kessler; Thomas J. Riley; Arland T. Stein; Jeffrey W. Stiltner. Resident Associates: Julie E. Brigner; Dawn-Rae Grauel; Anthony J. Miller; Erica K. Williams; Jeffrey A. Yeager.
Business, Corporate and Securities, Litigation, Taxation and Employee Benefits, Estate Planning, Probate, Real Estate, Labor, Creditors Rights, Reorganization and Bankruptcy, Intellectual Property and Technology, Environmental, Patent, Trademark and Copyright Law, Telecommunications Law, Government Relations, Public Utility and Regulatory Law, Health Care, Construction Law.
References: County Savings Bank; The Fifth Third Bank of Columbus.
Cleveland, Ohio Office: 3300 BP Tower, 200 Public Square, 44114-2301. Telephone: 216-621-0150. Fax: 216-241-2824.
Akron, Ohio Office: One Gojo Plaza, Suite 300, 44311-1076. Telephone: 330-864-5550. Fax: 330-864-7986.
Naples, Florida Office: 3301 Bonita Beach Road, Suite 308, Bonita Springs, 34134. Telephone: 239-949-6989. Fax: 239-949-6687.
See Professional Biographies, COLUMBUS, OHIO

Haines, Kimberley K. '58 '90
C.266 B.S. L.608 J.D. Atty., State Teachers Retirement System
Haire, Theresa Gale .... '57 '82 C.893 B.A. L.608 J.D. Pub. Def. Off.
Hairston, George W., (AV) .... '42 '68 C.802 B.B.A. L.608 J.D. [Baker&H.]
Hale, Ben W., Jr., (AV) .... '44 '70 C.437 B.B.A. L.608 J.D. [Smith&H.]
Hale, Harland Hanna, (BV) .... '55 '79 C.631 B.A. L.851 J.D. Co. Pros. Atty.
Hale, Mary Arens .... '71 '96 C.602 B.A. L.608 J.D. [Ⓢ Baker&H.]
Hall, Andrew C. .... '— '96 C.631 B.A. L.117 J.D. [Ⓐ Strip,H.L.M.&T.]
Hall, Brian D., (AV) .... '60 '85 C.1044 B.S. L.575 J.D. [Porter W.M.&A.]
Hall, Daniel M. .... '66 '93 C.610 B.Sc. L.117 J.D. [Ⓐ Garvin&H.]
Hall, Monique A. .... '77 '02 C&L.608 B.A., J.D. [Ⓐ Carpenter&L.]
Hall, Stephen K. .... '71 '97 C&L.608 B.A., J.D. [Ⓐ McDonald H.] (⊙Cleveland)
Haller, John E., (BV) .... '54 '80 C.999 B.A. L.345 J.D. [Shumaker,L.&K.]
Haller, Kathryn .... '50 '75 C.473 B.A. L.608 J.D. 410 West 10th Avenue, Suite 5101
Halliburton-Cohen, Kim M. .... '57 '82 C.207 B.A. L.608 J.D. [Halliburton-Cohen]

Halliburton-Cohen Law Office
1776 West Lane Avenue, Suite B, 43221-3363
Telephone: 614-486-2600 Fax: 614-486-2609
Email: kmh-c@halliburton-cohen.com URL: http://www.halliburton-cohen.com
Kim M. Halliburton-Cohen.
Family Law, Divorce, Child Custody, Child Support, Visitation Rights, Adoptions.
See Professional Biographies, COLUMBUS, OHIO

Halpern, Sheldon W. '35 '59 C&L.188 B.A., LL.B.
(adm. in NY; not adm. in OH) 100 S. 3rd St.
Hamalian, Derek Spraker '49 '88
C.610 B.S. L.608 J.D. Staff Coun., OH Legal Rights Serv.
Hamilton, A. Patrick, (AV) .... '53 '79 C.432 B.S. L.117 J.D. 400 S. 5th St.
Hamilton, Elizabeth A. .... '69 '94 C.434 B.A. L.896 J.D. 120-A Northwoods Blvd.
Hamilton, Karen E. .... '62 '95 C.266 B.S. L.1003 J.D. [K.E.Hamilton]
Hamilton, Michael A. .... '70 '96 C.207 B.A. L.276 J.D. 3 Limited Pkwy., Ste. 1600
Hamilton, Nathan C. .... '63 '89 C.611 B.A. L.880 J.D. [Ⓒ Vorys,S.S.&P.]
Hamilton, Robert W., (AV) .... '— '87 C.597 B.S. L.309 J.D. [Jones D.]

Hamilton, Karen E., Attorney At Law Inc.
31 E. Whittier Street, 43206
Telephone: 614-443-7920; 1-800-774-8544 Fax: 614-443-7922
Email: khamiltonlaw@sbcglobal.net URL: http://www.khamiltonlaw.com
Karen E. Hamilton.
Bankruptcy Law, Debtor and Creditor Law, Estate Planning, Revocable Trusts, Living Trusts, Charitable Giving, Elder Law, Medicaid Planning.
See Professional Biographies, COLUMBUS, OHIO

Hamilton-McGranor, AshLee M. .... '— '00 C.63 B.S. L.608 J.D. [Ⓢ Jones D.]
Hammerstein, Anne L. .... '57 '82 C.608 B.A. L.117 J.D. Asst. Atty. Gen.
Hammond, Gary W., (AV) .... '51 '80 C.473 B.A. L.117 J.D. [Hammond,S.&W.]
Hammond, Karen K. .... '67 '94 C.608 B.S.B.A. L.117 J.D. [Ⓐ Porter W.M.&A.]

Hammond, Sewards & Williams, (AV)
556 East Town Street, 43215
Telephone: 614-228-6061 Fax: 614-228-5883
Members of the Firm: Gary W. Hammond; Frederick A. Sewards; Scott E. Williams. Associates: James M. McGovern; Laura Folkerth Cook.
Medical Malpractice Defense, Nursing Home Defense, Insurance, Personal Injury, Litigation.
See Professional Biographies, COLUMBUS, OHIO

Hampl, Lisa S. .... '64 '96 C.266 B.S. L.117 J.D. 411 Garden Rd.
Han, Kyu Chang .... '66 '04 C.1451 B.A. L.608 J.D. [Ⓐ Squire,S.&D.]
Han, Lisa Ge Shang .... '62 '93 C.999 LL.B. L.608 J.D. [Schottenstein,Z.&D.]
Handa, Brent, (CV) .... '59 '85 C.610 B.B.A. L.117 J.D. [B.Handa]
Handa, Brent, Co., L.P.A., (CV) .... 338 S. High St.
Handelman, Robert B., (BV) .... '51 '76 C.264 B.A. L.1003 J.D. [Calig&H.] (⊙Newark)
Handelman, Robert K., (BV) .... '41 '72 [Handelman&K.]
Handelman & Kilroy, (BV) .... 360 S. Grant Ave.
Handlan, Allen L., (AV) .... '47 '72 C.610 B.A. L.893 J.D. [Kegler,B.H.&R.]
Haney, Michael H. .... '42 '72 C&L.608 B.S., J.D. Dir., Reg. Affs., Ross Labs.
Hanke, Paul A., (AV) .... '36 '61 C.970 B.A. L.477 J.D. [Porter W.M.&A.]
Hankerson, Cheryl R. .... '72 '97 C.276 A.B. L.893 J.D. [Ⓐ Littler M.]
Hanks, John Conrad .... '69 '95 C.477 B.A. L.608 J.D. Gen. Cnsl., Homewood Corp.
Hanley, Kathleen A., (BV) .. '50 '81 C.608 B.S. L.117 J.D. 120-A Northwoods Boulevard
Hannan, Lori .... '71 '98 C.608 B.S. L.213 J.D. [Ⓢ Calfee,H.&G.]
Hanneman, James A. .... '67 '95 C.260 B.S.B.A. L.117 J.D. 3010 Hayden Road
Hans-Kaiser, Jo .... '49 '00 C.610 B.S. L.179 J.D. 155 W. Main St., Ste. 101
Hanson, David F. .... '65 '92 C.385 B.A. L.608 J.D. [Ⓐ Manley D.K.]
Hanson, Denise L. .... '69 '94 C&L.608 B.A., J.D. 41 South high Street
Hanson, James R. .... '27 '57 C.604 B.A. L.477 LL.B. 2247 Arlington Ave.‡

Harbold, R. Chris, and Associates, (AV) '48 '75 C.610 B.B.A. L.117 J.D. ⒷⒷ
500 S. Front Street, Suite 1140, 43215
Telephone: 614-255-1140 Fax: 614-255-1141
Email: lawyers@harboldlaw.com URL: http://www.lawyers.com/rcharboldlaw
(Certified Specialist in Family Relations Law, Ohio State Bar Association).
Associates: Amy M. McKinlay; Chad Kristian Hemminger.

(This Listing Continued)

Harbold, R. Chris, and Associates (Continued)
Family and Matrimonial Law including Divorce, Dissolution, Legal Separation, Annulment, Allocation of Parental Rights and Responsibilities (including child support and parenting time), Spousal Support, Antenuptial Agreements, Step-Parent Adoption, Civil Domestic Violence, Post-Decree Enforcement and Modification.
Reference: Bank One.
See Professional Biographies, COLUMBUS, OHIO

Hardesty, Michael J. .... '41 '66 C.309 A.B. L.150 J.D. Gen. Coun.
Hardin, Jennifer Anne .... '61 '89 C.150 B.A. L.608 J.D. OH Ethics Comm.
Hardwick, Stephen P. .... '67 '94 C.293 B.A. L.477 J.D. OH Pub. Def. Off.
Hardymon, David W., (AV) .... '49 '76 C.97 B.A. L.117 J.D. [Vorys,S.S.&P.]
Harildstad, Timothy N. .... '53 '91 C.579 B.A. L.608 J.D. 88 East Broad Street
Harkness, Diana K. .... '56 '88 C&L.608 B.A., J.D. Eagleland Title Agency, Inc.
Harley, Sean P. .... '58 '84 C&L.851 B.A., J.D. Stewart Title Guaranty Co.
Harmon, John T. '66 '94 C.324 B.A. L.117 J.D.
Asst. Gen. Coun., Nationwide Insurance
Harrell, Eric C. '73 '99 C.475 B.S. L.607 J.D.
Asst. Chf. Legal Coun., Auditor of State of Ohio
Harris, Felice Lisette .... '69 '95 C.207 B.A. L.179 J.D. Pub. Def. Off.
Harris, James B., (AV) .... '50 '76 C.1028 B.A. L.117 J.D. [Harris,M.B.&C.]
Harris, James Jeffrey '61 '89 C.81 B.A. L.117 J.D.
Assoc. Gen. Coun., Consolidated Stores Corp.
Harris, Kenneth E., (AV) .... '48 '75 C.608 B.S. L.117 J.D. [Harris&M.]
Harris, Marcia Jane .... '52 '79 C.446 B.S. L.201 J.D. 280 N. High Street, 4th Fl.
Harris, Polly J., (AV) .... '60 '85 C.473 B.A. L.608 J.D. [Porter W.M.&A.]
Harris, Robert A., (BV) .... '65 '92 C.385 B.A. L.608 J.D. [Vorys,S.S.&P.]
Harris, Sean .... '74 '00 C.611 B.A. L.608 J.D. [Ⓐ Kitrick&L.]
Harris, Steven M. .... '57 '85 C.473 B.A. L.851 J.D. [Musser,L.&H.]
Harris, Stuart W. .... '62 '92 C.473 B.A. L.365 J.D. [Ⓐ Kegler,B.H.&R.]
Harris, Urlin G., Jr. '36 '73 C.611 B.A. L.266 J.D.
Exec. V.P., CFO & Treas., State Auto. Mut. Ins. Co.
Harris & Mazza, (AV) .... 941 Chatham Lane Suite 201

Harris, McClellan, Binau & Cox, P.L.L., (AV)
Ninth Floor, Huntington Plaza, 37 West Broad Street, 43215
Telephone: 614-464-2572 Fax: 614-464-2245
URL: http://www.hmbc.com
Members of Firm: Curtis H. Porter (1920-1993); John H. Kozich; Dan J. Binau; James B. Harris; Scott R. Mote; Garth G. Cox; Ralph E. Dill; Mark S. Coco; Stephen H. Dodd; Michael A. Coleman. Of Counsel: John D. Hvizdos; Edward T. McClellan.
General Civil Practice. Corporation, Taxation, Securities, Creditors' Rights; Bankruptcy, Banking Law, Real Estate, Zoning, Shopping Center Law, Administrative, Civil Litigation, Criminal, Immigration, International Law, Family Law. Construction Law, Insurance Defense, Estate Planning and Probate. Trials in all Courts.
See Professional Biographies, COLUMBUS, OHIO

Harrison, Kimberly E. .... '77 '03 C.879 B.S. L.608 J.D. [Ⓐ Shihab&Assoc.]
Harrison, Lemuel E., Jr. .... '56 '90 C.640 Sc.B. L.200 J.D. Ohio Dept. of Human Servs.
Harrison, Rebecca J. .... '— '97 C.610 B.B.A. L.150 J.D. [Ⓐ Jones D.]
Harrison, Wade E. .... '65 '93 C.999 B.A. L.117 J.D. 1570 Fishinger Road
Hart, Robert M., (BV) .... '54 '82 C.38 B.A. L.608 J.D. Asst. Atty. Gen.
Harter, William M. .... '75 '99 C&L.608 B.A., J.D. [Ⓐ Frost B.T.]
Hartman, Elizabeth A. .... '77 '04 C.608 B.A. L.602 J.D. [Ⓐ Porter W.M.&A.]
Hartman, Mark E. .... '56 '93 C.1028 B.S. L.117 J.D. Sr. Coun., Nationwide Insurance
Hartmann, Philip K., (AV) .... '66 '92 C.117 B.A. L.608 J.D. [Schottenstein,Z.&D.]
Hartmann, Robert G. .... '63 '88 C&L.608 B.A., J.D. V.P. & Coun., Natl. City Corp.
Hartranft, Jay .... '69 '00 C.20 B.A. L.117 J.D. [Ⓐ Porter W.M.&A.]
Hartranft, Jeffrey B. .... '71 '97 C.309 B.A. L.608 J.D. [Lane,A.&H.]
Hartranft, John C., Sr., (AV) .... '42 '67 C.309 A.B. L.477 J.D. [Porter W.M.&A.]
Hartshorn, Michael W., (AV) .... '47 '72 C.973 B.S. L.608 J.D. [Gamble H.J.]
Hartsough, Tisha M. .... '69 '96 C.608 B.A. L.117 J.D. State Law Enforce.
Harty, Susan Barrett .... '55 '97 C&L.201 B.A., J.D. [Vorys,S.S.&P.]
Harvey, William C. .... '45 '72 C&L.309 B.A., J.D. 49 E Sycamore St
Hass, Cheri B. .... '66 '95 C.608 B.A. L.851 J.D. [Ⓐ Downes,H.&F.]
Hassay, Wayne .... '67 '91 C.980 B.A. L.8 J.D. [Maguire&S.]
Hatch, H. James, III '47 '76 C.659 B.A. L.260 J.D.
(adm. in FL; not adm. in OH) Dir., Ohio CLE Institute
Hatcher, Steven J., (BV) .... '45 '73 C&L.607 B.S.Ed., J.D. [S.J.Hatcher]
Hatcher, Steven J., Co., LPA, (BV) .... 50 W. Broad St., Ste. 1800
Hatfield, Heather Lu .... '61 '84 C&L.117 B.A., J.D. Deloitte, Haskins & Sells
Hatler, Patricia R., (AVⓉ) .... '54 '80 C.228 B.S. L.893 J.D. Gen. Coun., Nationwide Ins.
Hatten, Steven A., (AV) .... '53 '78 C.608 B.S. L.117 J.D. [Earl,W.A.&D.]
Haubiel, Charles W., II, (BV) '65 '92 C.679 B.S. L.608 J.D.
V.P., Gen. Coun. & Corp. Secy., Big Lots, Inc.
Haupt, Erika L., (AV) .... '68 '94 C.473 B.S.B. L.608 J.D. [Roetzel&A.]
Hauswirth, George M., (AV) .... '37 '68 C&L.608 B.S., J.D. Supr. Ct.
Hauswirth, Michael J. '71 '00 C.597 B.A. L.1565 J.D.
(adm. in IL; not adm. in OH) [Ⓐ Vorys,S.S.&P.]
Havener, John Lawrence '57 '83 C.318 B.A. L.179 J.D.
Indus. Comm. for the State of OH
Havens, James R., (BV) .... '56 '81 C&L.117 B.A., J.D. [Havens W.]
Havens, Jolie N. .... '— '00 C.611 B.A. L.608 J.D. [Ⓐ Vorys,S.S.&P.]
Havens Willis LLC, (BV) .... 141 East Town Street, Suite 200
Haverkamp, Robert J. .... '46 '71 C&L.608 B.A., J.D. OH State Univ.
Hawk, Kristina L. .... '70 '96 C.610 B.A. L.150 J.D. Staff Atty., Supm. Ct.
Hawkins, Laney .... '60 '97 C.608 B.S. L.117 J.D. Asst. State Pub. Def.
Hawley, Kevin '58 '83 C.823 B.A. L.228 J.D.
(adm. in DC; not adm. in OH) [Ⓒ Porter W.M.&A.]
Hawley, Robert B., II .... '63 '96 C.608 B.A. L.117 J.D. [Sowald,S.&C.]
Hay, David S. .... '48 '74 C.228 A.B. L.608 J.D. Sr. Coun., Bank One Corp.‡
Hayden, William Mayne .... '33 '61 C&L.436 A.B., J.D. 35 E. Livingston Avenue
Hayes, Jeffrey T., (BV) .... '48 '79 C.871 B.S. L.339 J.D. [Porter W.M.&A.]
Hayes, Steven B. .... '45 '70 C&L.608 B.A., J.D. Mun. J.
Hayes, Thomas F. .... '68 '93 C.308 B.A. L.117 J.D. Pub. Def. Off.
Haynes, Douglas James .... '56 '82 C.329 B.A. L.117 J.D. [Haynes&H.]
Haynes, Eleanor E. Beavers, (BV) .... '57 '84 C.608 B.A. L.117 LL.M. [Haynes&H.]
Haynes & Haynes, (BV) .... 399 E. Main St.
Hays, Mark Eric .... '50 '76 C.473 B.A. L.117 J.D. OH Atty. Gen.
Hazelton, Peter M. .... '66 '92 C.31 B.A. L.846 J.D. [Ⓐ Mallory&T.]
Head, Suzanne .... '45 '89 C.608 B.A. L.117 J.D. Ohio Dept. of Human Servs.
Headen, Raymond C. '60 '87 C.951 B.A. L.659 J.D.
[Schottenstein,Z.&D.] (⊙Cleveland)
Heaphy, William J., III .... '50 '75 C.321 A.B. L.818 J.D. State Leg. Serv. Comm.
Heath, John A. .... '23 '49 C&L.608 B.A., J.D. 3796 Patricia Dr.‡
Hebert, L. Camille .... '59 '82 C.375 B.A. L.378 J.D. Prof. of Law, Ohio State Univ.
Heckert, Chris E. .... '72 '00 C.16 B.A. L.117 J.D. [Heckert&H.]

Heckert & Hockensmith Co., L.P.A.
495 South High Street, Suite 220, 43215
Telephone: 614-224-7700 Fax: 614-224-7766
Email: info@heckerthockensmith.com URL: http://www.heckerthockensmith.com
Chris E. Heckert; Mark L. Hockensmith;—Jennifer M. Riley.
General Civil and Criminal Litigation in all Courts. Personal Injury, Automobile Accidents, Criminal Defense, Felonies, Misdemeanors, Drug Crimes, Sexual Assault, Parole and Probation, Driving While Intoxicated, Traffic Violations, Juvenile Law, Family Law, Divorce, Child Custody, Child Support, Visitation Rights, Spousal Support, Domestic Violence, Wills and Probate.
See Professional Biographies, COLUMBUS, OHIO

Heckman, C. Luther, (BV) ....'43 '69 C&L.608 B.A., J.D. 37 W. Broad St., 11th Flr.
Hedden, Herbert A., (AV) ....'56 '90 C.575 B.S. L.273 J.D. [Vorys,S.S.&P.]
Hedden, James H., (AV) ....'45 '71 C.918 B.A. L.145 J.D. 52 E. Gay St.‡
Hedden, Margaret M. ....'45 '70 C.25 B.A. L.145 J.D. 409 S. Parkview Ave.‡
Hedien, Mark J. ....'66 '92 C.813 B.A. L.276 J.D. [Clark&H.]
Hedrick, Billy R. ....'64 '96 C.679 B.A. L.608 J.D. Columbus City Prosecutor's Off.
Heer, Holly H. ....'67 '93 C.914 B.A. L.893 J.D. [Squire,S.&D.]
Heffernan, Michael E. ....'71 '98 C.276 B.S. L.608 J.D. [Ⓐ Brenner,B.G.&M.]
Heffernan, Terrence R., (AV) .....'51 '82 C.608 B.S.S.W. L.117 J.D. [Weltman,W.&R.]
Heffner, Jann Kathryn ....'48 '75 C.911 B.A. L.117 J.D. Co. Mental Health Bd.
Heid, Brigid E., (BV) ....'65 '90 C&L.608 B.A., J.D. [Luper,N.&L.]
Heier, David S., (BV) ....'53 '79 C&L.201 B.A., J.D. [Heier]
Heier, Patricia E. Wilkin ....'54 '79 C.502 B.J. L.201 J.D. Asst. Pros. Atty.
Heier Law Offices, (BV) .... 2303 Vicente Court, Suite 312
Heinlein, David J., (BV) ....'60 '88 C.608 B.A. L.117 J.D. 140 E. Town St.
Heintz, Michael E. ....'77 '03 C.679 B.S. L.347 J.D. [Ⓐ Porter W.M.&A.]
Helfrich, Kurt P. ....'67 '97 C.893 B.A. L.608 J.D. [Thompson H.]
Hellerstein, Cara S. '71 '96 C.608 B.A. L.1202 J.D.
(adm. in MA; not adm. in OH) The James Cancer Hosp.
Helling, Henry E., III ....'42 '67 C.62 B.A. L.607 J.D. Exec. Asst. Atty. Gen.
Helmreich, Richard J., (AV) ....'64 '89 C.97 B.S. L.608 J.D. [Porter W.M.&A.]
Hemminger, Chad Kristian .....'77 '04 C.608 B.A. L.989 J.D. [Ⓐ R.C.Harbold&Assoc.]
Hemphill, John C., (BV) ....'46 '73 C.221 B.A. L.608 J.D. 370 S. 5th St.
Hendershot, Elizabeth L. ....'70 '95 C.611 B.A. L.608 J.D. [Baker&H.]
Henderson, Jennifer L. ....'64 '94 C.473 B.A. L.117 J.D. Sr. Jud. Law Clk., U.S. Dist. Ct.
Henderson, Maurice Martin, III ....'71 '00 C.608 B.S. L.851 J.D. 336 S. High St.
Henke, Bruce R., (AV) ....'50 '79 C.473 B.A. L.276 J.D. [Vorys,S.S.&P.]
Henkener, Ann E. ....'48 '74 C.608 B.A. L.117 J.D. Asst. Atty. Gen.
Hennessey, Molly Ann ....'— '88 C.676 B.A. L.117 J.D. Legal Aid of Columbus
Hennessey, Thomas M. '53 '79 C.696 B.A. L.273 J.D.
(adm. in DC; not adm. in OH) Sr. Coun., Bank One Corp.
Henning, Harry L., (AV) '— '71
C&L.602 B.B.A., J.D. [Porter W.M.&A.] (⊙Naples, FL)
Henry, James E. ....'33 '57 C&L.607 B.A., LL.B. Ohio State Council of Retail Mchts.
Henry, Janet J. '— '84 C.475 B.A. L.608 J.D.
Assoc. Gen. Coun.-Envir. Health & Safety, Amer. Electric Power Serv. Corp.
Henry, Michael R., (AV) ....'57 '85 C.473 B.S. L.117 J.D. [Crabbe,B.&J.]
Henry, William Droxler ....'29 '53 C&L.608 B.S.B.A., J.D. 1850 Waltham Rd.‡
Hensel, Jan E., (AV) ....'61 '88 C&L.608 B.A., J.D. [Buckingham,D.&B.]
Hensley, Kimberly ....'67 '94 C.608 B.A. L.117 J.D. Coun., Nationwide Insurance
Henson, James J. '53 '79
C.967 B.A. L.201 J.D. General Counsel, Stonehenge Holdings, Inc.
Herald, James M., (BV) ....'46 '72 C&L.608 B.A., J.D. 867 Neil Avenue
Herath, Kirk Matthew ....'61 '94 C.150 B.A. L.117 J.D. Nationwide Insurance Co.
Herbe, Diana J. '46 '82 C.1216 B.A. L.1340 J.D.
Labor Rels. Consultant, Ohio Education Assn.
Herbert, Sarah L. ....'— '04 C.608 B.S.B.A. L.188 J.D. [Ⓐ Vorys,S.S.&P.]
Herd, David A., (AV) ....'67 '92 C.945 B.A. L.608 J.D. [Ⓐ J.C.Nemeth&Assoc.]
Herder, Mark Albert ....'66 '93 C.608 M.A. L.117 J.D. 901 S. High St.
Herlihy, Kimberly Weber ....'71 '97 C.93 B.A. L.276 J.D. [Vorys,S.S.&P.]
Herman, Lawrence '29 '53 C&L.150 A.B., LL.B.
Prof. of Law, Emeritus, Ohio State Univ.
Herman, Richard A. ....'62 '90 C.608 B.S./B.A. L.117 J.D. R.J. Solove & Associates
Hernandez, Richard A., (BV) ....'61 '86 C.608 B.A. L.117 J.D. [Buckingham,D.&B.]
Hersch, Thomas J. ....'— '01 C.608 B.A. L.893 J.D. [Ⓐ Jones D.]
Hersh, Jeffrey M. '51 '75 C.610 B.A. L.665 J.D.
Ohio Bureau of Employ. Servs. Bd. of Review
Hersha, Peter J. '56 '82 C.1122 B.A. L.823 J.D.
(adm. in NY; not adm. in OH) Nationwide Mutual Ins. Co.
Hershberger, Eric B., (CV) ....'65 '91 C.473 B.A. L.608 J.D. [Ⓐ G.E.Webster]
Hertel, Kari B. ....'68 '96 C.63 B.S. L.347 J.D. Senior Deputy Atty. Gen., Spec. Coun.
Hertenstein, Edward C., (AV) ....'51 '76 C&L.802 B.B.A., J.D. [Roetzel&A.]
Hess, Kevin E. ....'79 '04 C.1053 B.A. L.201 J.D. [Ⓐ Freund,F.&A.]
Hess, Paul Joseph, Jr., (BV) ....'56 '81 C.602 B.A. L.608 J.D. [Ⓐ Garvin&H.]
Hess, Paul R., (BV) ....'60 '86 C&L.477 A.B., J.D. [Kegler,B.H.&R.]
Hess, Rebecca J. ....'56 '84 C.477 B.M. L.930 J.D. Staff Atty., Ohio Legal Rights Serv.
Hess, Stephanie Elliott '72 '01
C&L.117 B.A., J.D. Dir. of HR, Franklin Co. Ct. of Com. Pleas
Hess, Thomas W. ....'51 '76 C.610 B.S. L.117 J.D. [Buckingham,D.&B.]
Hetterscheidt, Robert C., (BV) ....'45 '76 C.737 B.A. L.117 J.D. [AuCoin,D.H.&Y.]
Heyman, Ian A. '— '98 C.608 B.A. L.117 J.D.
Exec. Dir. & Coun., House of Tradition Charities
Hickey, Michael J., (AV) ....'42 '68 C&L.608 B.A., J.D. [Garvin&H.]
Higgins, Jenny L. ....'58 '91 C.608 B.A. L.117 J.D. Atty., Columbia Gas Distribution Cos.
Higgins, William J. ....'36 '67 C&L.117 B.A., J.D. V.P., Grange Mut. Cas. Co.
Higgins Marx, Jane A. ....'75 '00 C.207 B.A. L.608 J.D. [Ⓐ Carlile P.&M.]
Hilburn, Regina L. ....'65 '91 C&L.608 B.A., J.D. 118 East Main Street
Hildebrant, Kristin E. '63 '89 C.1208 B.S. L.608 J.D.
Staff Atty., Ohio Legal Rights Serv.
Hill, Alan D. ....'55 '81 C.631 B.A. L.150 J.D. 1435 Aberdeen Ave.
Hill, Jennifer L., (CV) ....'74 '99 C&L.201 B.S./B.A., J.D. [Ⓐ Freund,F.&A.]
Hill, Kathleen Blickenstaff ....'50 '98 C.608 B.S.N. L.117 J.D. [Ⓐ Porter W.M.&A.]
Hill, Richard C. ....'39 '66 C&L.608 B.S., J.D. Assoc. Dir., Rsch. Found., O.S.U.
Hill, Thomas W., (AV) ....'45 '70 C.293 A.B. L.188 J.D. [Kegler,B.H.&R.]
Hiller, David P., (AV) ....'41 '69 C.8 A.B. L.477 J.D. [Millisor&N.] (⊙Cleveland)
Hiller, Jeffrey S. '72 '99 C.477 B.A. L.608 J.D.
(adm. in NC; not adm. in OH) [Ⓐ Littler M.]
Hilsheimer, Lawrence A. '57 '83 C.608 B.S.B.A. L.117 J.D.
Mngr. Partner, Ohio Valley Off., Deloitte & Touche
Hilson, Daniel G., (BV) ....'59 '86 C.363 B.A. L.117 J.D. [Roetzel&A.]
Hilvert, Kevin M. ....'74 '02 C.967 B.A. L.608 J.D. [Ⓐ Schottenstein,Z.&D.]
Hines, Richard S. ....'53 '83 C.150 B.S. L.607 J.D. Asst. Pub. Def.
Hinshaw, Steven A. ....'51 '77 C.608 B.S.B.A. L.117 J.D. Huntington Bancshares Inc.
Hire, Charles H., (AV) ....'41 '66 C.207 A.B. L.608 J.D. [Baker&H.]
Hirsch, Bruce L., (BV) ....'51 '79 C.97 B.A. L.607 J.D. [Earl,W.A.&D.]
Hirsch, Burton M., (BV) ....'48 '74 C.665 B.A. L.1003 J.D. State Indus. Comm.
Hirsch, Dennis D. '62 '94 C.176 B.A. L.976 J.D.
(adm. in NY; not adm. in OH) Ass't Prof. of Law, Capital Univ.
Hissong, Anthony L. ....'67 '92 C.608 B.S. L.117 J.D. Prosecutor
Histed, Bradley J. ....'54 '81 C.528 B.A. L.117 J.D. Claims Atty., Grange Mut. Cas. Co.
Hite, Jennifer Page ....'70 '96 C.608 B.A. L.8 J.D. Cap. Post Convictor
Hix, John H., (CV) ....'45 '70 C.145 B.A. L.339 J.D. [Ⓐ Maguire&S.]
Hobson, Gordon, (BV) ....'52 '80 C.610 B.G.S. L.117 J.D. 76 E. Dunedin Rd.
Hockensmith, Mark L. ....'72 '97 C.473 B.A. L.201 J.D. [Heckert&H.]
Hockstad, Karen S., (AV) '65 '92 C.477 B.A. L.213 J.D.
[Hockstad] (⊙Richmond, VA)

Hockstad Law Office, Ltd., (AV)
471 E. Broad Street, Suite 800, 43215
Telephone: 614-224-1727 Fax: 614-463-1296
Email: khockstad@hockstadlaw.com URL: http://www.hockstadlaw.com
Karen S. Hockstad.
Business Law, Business Formation, Joint Ventures, Strategic Alliances, Limited Liability Companies, Partnerships, Family Business Law, Closely Held Businesses, Small Business Law, Business Planning, Franchise Law, Commercial Leasing, Business Litigation, Mergers and Acquisitions, Taxation, Tax Planning, Labor and Employment, Employment Contracts, Personnel Policies, Human Resources.
See Professional Biographies, COLUMBUS, OHIO

Hodge, David L. ....'— '02 C.383 B.A. L.117 J.D. [Ⓐ Smith&H.]
Hoeffel, Melissa R. ....'— '03 C.970 B.A. L.179 J.D. [Ⓐ Roetzel&A.]
Hoeffel, Sue E. '66 '92 C.901 B.A. L.608 J.D.
Staff Atty., The Homeless Families Found.
Hoffman, Deborah F., (BV) ....'54 '81 C.207 B.A. L.117 J.D. Asst. City Atty.
Hoffman, Eric J., & Associates ......'59 '84 C.608 B.A. L.179 J.D. 338 South High Street
Hoffman, F. Herbert, Jr., (AV) ....'18 '44 C.674 A.B. L.477 J.D. 17 S. High St.
Hoffman, George M., (BV) ....'54 '79 C.611 B.A. L.117 J.D. 261 W. Johnstown Rd.
Hoffman, John E., Jr. ....'59 '83 C.1115 B.A. L.608 J.D. U.S. Bkrptcy. Ct. J.
Hoffman, Judith Ann ....'52 '77 C.385 A.B. L.93 J.D. Chf. Elections Coun.
Hoffman, Richard Feindel '69 '99 C.610 B.A. L.117 J.D.
30 East Broad Street, 17th Floor
Hoffman, Robert M., (BV) ....'48 '73 C.610 B.S.C. L.117 J.D. 578 S. 5th St.
Hofheimer, Harry, (AV) ....'14 '35 C&L.893 LL.B. 6049 Cranberry Ct.‡
Hogan, Christopher E. ....'68 '98 C&L.608 B.A., J.D. [Moots,C.&H.]
Hogan, Dennis A., (AV) '50 '75
C.608 B.A. L.607 J.D. Chief Coun., Juv. Div., Co. Pros. Off.
Hogan, Mark ....'— '03 C.608 B.A. L.179 J.D. [Ⓐ Gerrity&B.]
Hogue, Bryan K., (AV) ....'59 '85 C.967 B.A. L.117 J.D. [Carlile P.&M.]
Hohl, Ruth Ann, (BV) ....'61 '86 C.973 B.A. L.608 J.D. 124 S. Washington Ave.
Holaday, Rodney A. ....'71 '97 C.473 B.S. L.608 J.D. [Ⓐ Vorys,S.S.&P.]
Holben, Marla R. ....'63 '89 C.1033 B.A. L.117 J.D. Pub. Def.
Holbrook, Michael J., (BV) ....'58 '83 C.608 B.A. L.117 J.D. 601 South High Street
Holder, Robert L., (BV) ....'46 '71 C&L.608 B.S., J.D. 370 West 9th Avenue
Holderman, Mark V. ....'51 '80 C.385 B.S. L.851 J.D. 77 South High Street
Holfinger, Jonathan ....'77 '02 C.473 B.S. L.608 J.D. [Ⓐ AuCoin,D.H.&Y.]
Holko, Mark E. ....'50 '80 C.97 B.S. L.7 J.D. Ind. Comm. of OH
Hollenbaugh, H. Ritchey, (AV) ....'47 '73 C.381 B.A. L.117 J.D. [Carlile P.&M.]
Hollern, Edwin J., (AV) ....'55 '88 C.608 B.A. L.117 J.D. [E.J.Hollern]

Hollern, Edwin J., Co., LPA, (AV)
77 North State Street, 43081
Telephone: 614-839-5700 Fax: 614-839-4200
Email: ehollern@ejhlaw.com URL: http://www.ejhlaw.com
Edwin J. Hollern;—Kevin J. Zimmerman; Romina P. Newsome.
Product Liability, Professional Liability, Insurance Coverage, Insurance Defense, Civil Litigation.
See Professional Biographies, COLUMBUS, OHIO

Hollins, Eugene L., (BV) ....'62 '88 C.880 B.A. L.608 J.D. [Wiles,B.B.&B.]
Hollon, Steven C. ....'54 '81 C.532 B.A. L.607 J.D. 30 E. Broad Street, 3rd fl.
Holloway, J. Eric ....'68 '94 C.945 B.A. L.8 J.D. [Ⓐ Isaac,B.L.&T.]
Holman, Michael S., (AV) ....'42 '72 C.871 B.S. L.608 J.D. [Bricker&E.]
Holmes, Douglas Jeffry ....'52 '79 C.608 B.A. L.851 J.D. OH Dept. of Job & Fam. Servs.
Holmes, Leanne M. ....'75 '03 C.608 B.A. L.117 J.D. [L.Holmes]

Holmes, Leanne
338 South High Street, 43215
Telephone: 614-679-9618 Fax: 614-481-8048
URL: http://www.leannecollaw.com
Leanne M. Holmes.
Bankruptcy, Domestic Relations, Child Custody, Child Support, Family Law, Juvenile Law.
See Professional Biographies, COLUMBUS, OHIO

Holmquist, Paul R. '43 '72
C.966 B.S. L.793 J.D. Gen. Coun., Motorists Mutual Insurance Co.
Holodnak, Robert B. ....'61 '89 C.608 B.A. L.117 J.D. [Ⓐ Bricker&E.]
Holschuh, John D. ....'26 '51 C.473 B.A. L.150 J.D. U.S. Dist. J.
Holthus, Douglas P., (BV) ....'60 '86 C.967 B.A. L.117 J.D. [Ⓐ Reminger&R.]
Holz, Richard W., (AV) ....'60 '85 C.607 B.S. L.608 J.D. [Schottenstein,Z.&D.]
Holzhall, Vincent I. ....'65 '94 C.602 B.A. L.339 J.D. [Lane,A.&H.]
Hombach, Stephen C. ....'45 '88 C.853 A.B. L.345 J.D. Ohio Department of Insurance
Hood, William S., Jr. '37 '70 C.679 B.S.C.E. L.169 J.D.
(adm. in CA; not adm. in OH) 2405 Onandaga Dr.
Hoover, Luann L. ....'67 '93 C.477 B.B.A. L.930 J.D. Atty., State E.P.A.
Hopper, William A., Jr. ....'50 '75 C.611 B.A. L.608 J.D. Atty. Gen. Off.
Hoppers, John Wm., (AV) ....'39 '68 C.920 B.A. L.608 J.D. [Strip,H.L.M.&T.]
Hopple, E. James, (AV) ....'36 '63 C.97 B.A. L.608 LL.B. [Schottenstein,Z.&D.]
Hopple, Roy E., Jr. ....'28 '53 C&L.608 B.A., J.D. 13 West State Street
Hornbeck, David B., (BV) ....'39 '70 C.611 B.A. L.608 J.D. [Campbell,H.C.&V.]
Horowitz, Abe '13 '37 L.142 LL.B.
(adm. in TN; not adm. in OH) 1848 Parsons Ave.‡
Horst, Robert T., (BVⓉ) '66 '91 C.645 B.S. L.884 J.D.
(adm. in PA; not adm. in OH) [Nelson L.d.&H.] ⊙
Horton, Timothy S. ....'70 '96 C.94 B.A. L.608 J.D. [Ⓐ Chester,W.&S.]
Horvath, Dennis E. ....'— '01 C.347 B.S. L.117 J.D. [Ⓐ Joseph&J.]
Horvath, Thomas L., (BV) ....'47 '73 C&L.608 B.A., J.D. 90 N. Nelson Rd.
Hosang, Michael T. ....'66 '92 C.976 B.A. L.117 J.D. 665 South High Street★
Hoskins, Cheryl D. ....'59 '85 C.610 B.S.E.D. L.117 J.D. Asst. Atty. Gen.
Hosterman, O. Charles ....'37 '65 C&L.608 B.S., J.D. Off. of Atty. Gen.
Hottensmith, Mark H. ....'57 '89 C.381 B.S. L.8 J.D. Asst. Co. Pros.
House, David C. '67 '92 C&L.608 B.S., J.D.
Sr. Coun.-Fin. & Compl., Amer. Elect. Power Serv. Corp.
House, Ronald L., (AV) ....'58 '86 C.473 B.S. L.608 J.D. [Ⓒ Benesch,F.C.&A.]
Houser, Jeffrey D. ....'78 '03 C.473 B.A. L.608 J.D. [Ⓐ Crabbe,B.&J.]
Howard, Lowell B. ....'25 '50 C.97 A.B. L.608 J.D. Ret. Com. Pleas J.
Howard, Stephen M. ....'51 '76 C&L.117 B.A., J.D. [Ⓒ Vorys,S.S.&P.]
Howarth, Robert F., (AV) ....'44 '70 C.207 B.A. L.608 J.D. [Shoemaker,H.&T.]

Howell, Georgena ... '21 '60 C.608 L.266 J.D. 5709 Saranac Dr
Howenstein, C. Bradley ... '67 '91 C.339 B.A. L.608 J.D. [Ⓐ Scott,S.&W.]
Hoy, Suzanne H. ... '50 '88 C.434 B.A. L.851 J.D. Atty., Franklin Co.
Hoylman, Barbara Nestor '65 '90
C.607 B.A. L.117 J.D. Dist. Hearing Offr., State Indus. Comm.‡
Hoyt, Matthew W. ... '74 '00 C.475 B.A. L.602 J.D. [Ⓐ Baker&H.]
Hrach, James A. ... '49 '91 C.608 B.S. L.117 J.D. [Ⓐ Barkan&B.]
Hubbard, Barton A. ... '56 '81 C.645 B.S. L.665 J.D. Asst. Atty. Gen.
Hubbard, Edward G. ... '66 '97 C.472 B.A. L.930 J.D. [Lane,A.&H.]
Hubler, Lloyd E., III '56 '85 C.1208 B.S. L.608 J.D.
V.P. of Admn., Cantlon Assoc. Inc.
Huckaby, Kristen J. ... '69 '95 C.427 B.A. L.179 J.D. Consultant, Nationwide Svces. Co.
Hudak, Clara J., (BV) ... '49 '74 C.734 A.B. L.608 J.D. [C.J.Hudak]
Hudak, Clara J., Co., L.P.A., (BV) ... 118 E. Main St.
Huddle, Wm. Gehrett '55 '81
C.674 A.B. L.608 J.D. V.P., The Fifth Third Bk. of Columbus
Huddleston, C. Lawrence, (BV) ... '50 '77 C.532 B.A. L.117 J.D. [Huddleston]
Huddleston Law Offices, (BV) ... 3650 Olentangy River Road
Hudok, Timothy D. ... '77 '02 C.97 B.A. L.608 J.D. [Ⓐ Vorys,S.S.&P.]
Hudson, Mary Jo ... '63 '89 C.473 B.A. L.150 J.D. [Bailey C.]
Huebert, J.H. ... '79 '04 C.294 B.A. L.145 J.D. [Ⓐ Porter W.M.&A.]
Huffman, Fordham E., (AV) ... '— '80 C&L.608 B.A., J.D. [Jones D.]
Huggins, Wm. G. ... '20 '55 C.966 B.A. L.1340 J.D. 1000 Urlin Ave.‡
Hughes, Anne M. ... '76 '01 C.92 B.A. L.117 J.D. [Ⓐ Porter W.M.&A.]
Hughes, D. Timothy ... '55 '84 C.381 B.B.A. L.1003 J.D. [Ⓐ Maguire&S.]
Hughes, Donald A., Jr. '52 '81 C.299 A.B. L.184 J.D.
(adm. in ND; not adm. in OH) Dir. Law Libr., Assoc. Prof. of Law, Capital Univ.
Hughes, Donald W. ... '60 '97 C.97 B.S. L.607 J.D. [Squire,S.&D.]
Hughes, James E., (AV) ... '46 '72 C.309 B.A. L.608 J.D. 4021 Longhill Rd.
Hughes, James J., (AV) ... '36 '62 C.602 A.B. L.276 J.D. [Ⓒ Bricker&E.]
Hughes, James J., III, (AV) ... '58 '86 C.867 B.A. L.117 J.D. [Bricker&E.]
Hughes, James M. ... '64 '94 C.608 B.S.B.A. L.117 J.D. [Ⓐ Wiles,B.B.&B.]
Hughes, Lawrence Bradfield ... '72 '99 C.385 B.A. L.201 J.D. [Ⓐ Porter W.M.&A.]
Hughes, Michael Thomas ... '74 '01 C.737 B.A. L.117 J.D. Pros. Off.
Hughes, Steven R. ... '52 '83 [Ⓐ Maguire&S.]
Huhn, Richard M., (BV) ... '44 '69 C.610 A.B. L.608 J.D. [Blumenstiel,H.&A.]
Hull, Karen B. ... '— '81 C.350 Ph.D. L.117 J.D. Asst. Disciplinary Coun., Supm. Ct.
Hull, Melissa Lynn ... '68 '98 C.150 B.A. L.179 J.D. Atty. Gen. Off., HHS Sect.
Human, Randy E. ... '65 '94 C.607 B.S.B.A. L.608 J.D. Legal Aid Soc. of Columbus
Hummel, Bradley, (AV) ... '34 '60 C&L.608 B.Sc., LL.B. Asst. City Atty.
Hummel, Gretchen J. ... '47 '79 C.610 A.B. L.117 J.D. [Ⓒ McNees W.&N.]
Hummel, Terry V., (BV) ... '55 '82 C&L.117 B.A., J.D. [Calig&H.] (⊙Marion)
Hummer, Mark A. ... '58 '86 C.608 B.A. L.117 J.D. Bailiff, Co. Mun. Ct. J.
Humphrey, Guy R., (AV) ... '60 '84 C.381 B.S. L.608 J.D. [Chester,W.&S.]
Hunker, Frederick '55 '81
C&L.608 B.S.I.D., J.D. V.P., Claims, Ohio Bar Liability Ins. Co.
Hunkins, Blaine B., (AV) ... '23 '52 C&L.608 B.A., J.D. 580 S. High St.
Hunsinger, Paul O. ... '20 '48 C&L.608 B.A., J.D. 74 Glencoe Rd.‡
Hunt, Herman E. ... '37 '70 C&L.607 B.S.Ph., J.D. Bur. of Workers' Comp.
Hunt, James F., Jr. '47 '76 C.27 B.A. L.608 J.D.
State Office Tower II, 77 South High Street-22nd Flr.
Hunter, Michael J., (AV) ... '47 '85 C.610 B.A. L.117 J.D. 3360 Tremont Rd., 2nd Fl.
Hunter, Thomas D., (AV) ... '48 '72 C.894 B.A. L.352 J.D. [Ⓐ Reminger&R.]
Huntley, Jeffrey L. ... '57 '83 C&L.608 B.A., J.D. 25 South Front Street, Mail Stop 707
Huntley, John E., (BV) ... '32 '69 C.608 B.S. L.117 J.D. 3280 Riverside Dr.
Huprich, Joseph J. '69 '98 C.800 B.A. L.1049 J.D.
(adm. in CA; not adm. in OH) [Ⓐ Thompson H.]
Hurd, Dwight I., (AV) ... '32 '59 C&L.608 B.B.A., J.D. [D.I.Hurd]

Hurd, Dwight I., Co., LPA, (AV)
4235 Westleton Court, 43221-4930
Telephone: 614-876-0480 Fax: 614-876-0565
Email: hurdlaw@columbus.rr.com URL: http://www.hurdlawoffice.com
Dwight I. Hurd.
Elder Law, General Business and Corporate Law, Estate Administration, Trusts and Estates, Business Succession and Small Business.
Representative Clients: Available Upon Request.
See Professional Biographies, COLUMBUS, OHIO

Hurley, Daniel J., (AV) ... '61 '86 C.973 B.A. L.1003 J.D. [Crabbe,B.&J.]
Hurst, Rufus B., (BV) ... '48 '87 C.207 B.A. L.117 J.D. [Downes,H.&F.]
Hurst, Sarah E. ... '73 '02 C.385 B.A. L.608 J.D. [Ⓐ Bricker&E.]
Husted, Gerald E. '36 '75 C.1208 B.S. L.117 J.D.
Dept. of Agriculture, Off. of Gen. Coun.
Huston, Catherine E. ... '51 '83 C.999 B.A. L.608 J.D. Asst. Atty. Gen.
Hutchins, W. James '46 '71
C.597 B.A. L.608 J.D. General Counsel, R.J. Solove & Associates
Hutson, Jeffrey W., (AV) ... '41 '66 C&L.477 A.B., LL.B. [Lane,A.&H.]
Hvizdos, Cynthia E. ... '46 '78 C.347 A.B. L.117 J.D. State Teachers Retire. Sys.
Hvizdos, John D., (AV) ... '47 '75 C&L.608 B.A., J.D. [Ⓒ Harris,M.B.&C.]
Hykes, John E. ... '43 '75 C.608 B.S. L.161 J.D. 1865 Torch Wood Dr.
Hysell, Jennifer L. ... '71 '97 C.608 B.A. L.117 J.D. Ct. Clms.
Iannotta, Mark William, (BV) ... '58 '88 C.207 B.A. L.117 J.D. 575 S. 3rd St.
Iannotta, Melissa J., (BV) '61 '87 C.205 B.S.A.S. L.117 J.D.
Dep. Chf. Legal Coun., Auditor of State of Ohio (Legal Department)
Ice, Matthew E. ... '70 '96 C&L.608 B.A., J.D. [Ⓐ J.C.Nemeth&Assoc.]
Idinopulos, Lea Spector ... '43 '83 C.999 B.Sc L.150 J.D. State Employ. Rel. Bd.
Ifeduba, Stephen E. ... '72 '97 C.970 B.A. L.608 J.D. Coun., Nationwide Insurance
Igo, C. Merle, (AV) ... '09 '33 C&L.608 LL.B. 2113 Mackenzie Dr.‡
Igo, Richard B., (BV) ... '45 '70 C.608 B.A. L.150 J.D. 3300 Indianola Ave.
Igoe, Daniel J., (BV) ... '43 '68 C.602 B.B.A. L.608 J.D. 60 E. Broad St.
Igoe, Michael H., (AV) ... '50 '75 C.602 B.B.A. L.851 J.D. [Carlile P.&M.]
Imhoff, Caroline D. ... '79 '04 C.8 B.A. L.896 J.D. [Ⓐ Carpenter&L.]
Imwalle, Randall J., (BV) ... '62 '88 C.201 B.A. L.608 J.D. Sr. Coun., Bank One Corp.
Ingram, Bruce L., (AV) ... '53 '78 C.608 B.A. L.477 J.D. [Vorys,S.S.&P.]
Ingram, Kasey T. ... '— '02 C.871 B.S. L.150 J.D. [Ⓐ Jones D.]
Ingram, Kathleen M. ... '59 '84 C.321 B.A. L.608 J.D. Asst. Atty. Gen.
Innis, Richard L., (BV) ... '44 '70 C.608 B.A. L.117 J.D. [Innis&B.]
Innis & Barker Co., L.P.A., (BV) ... 8415 Pulsar Pl.
Insley, David W., (BV) ... '45 '81 C.266 B.S.B.A. L.117 J.D. Asst. City Atty.
Intihar, Stephen ... '66 '93 C.103 Sc.B. L.608 J.D. [Bricker&E.]
Ireton, C. Andrew, Jr., (AV) ... '48 '73 C.602 B.B.A. L.608 J.D. [Porter W.M.&A.]
Irvine, Joseph R., (AV) '57 '86 C.381 B.B.A. L.228 J.D.
Tax Coun. & Assoc. Legal Counsel, Ohio State University, The
Isaac, Frederick M., (AV) ... '41 '66 C.976 B.A. L.880 LL.B. [Isaac,B.L.&T.]

Isaac, Brant, Ledman & Teetor LLP, (AV) BR
The Midland Building, 250 East Broad Street, 43215-3742
Telephone: 614-221-2121 Fax: 614-365-9516
Email: mail@isaacbrant.com URL: http://www.isaacbrant.com
Sol Morton Isaac (1911-1995); David H. Meade (1957-1994). Members of Firm: Charles E. Brant; James H. Ledman; Frederick M. Isaac; Dennis R. Newman; J. Stephen Teetor; Steve M. Soltis; Randy S. Kurek; Donald L. Anspaugh; Mark Landes; Steven G. LaForge; Timothy E. Miller; James M. Roper; Douglas J. Suter; David G. Jennings; Douglas Craig Boatright; Paul A. MacKenzie; Joanne S. Peters; Patrick M. Pickett; Daniel T. Downey; Maribeth Deavers. Associates: Danielle Marie Carter; John E. Vincent, Jr.; Jeffrey A. Stankunas; Michael V. Passella; J. Eric Holloway; Scyld D. Anderson; Jessica K. Walls; Jeffery J. Sniderman; Mark H. Troutman; Jerry L. Kaltenbach; Brandi L. Dorgan. Of Counsel: Mark R. Weaver.
Civil Trial and Appellate Practice in all State and Federal Courts, Medical Malpractice, General Business, Corporate, Intellectual Property, Taxation, Estate Planning, Probate, Guardianship, Real Estate, Political Subdivisions, Employment, Family, Negligence, Personal Injury, Civil Arson, Insurance Defense, Insurance, Professional Malpractice, Premises Liability, Products Liability, Carrier Liability and Motor Sports Law, Commercial, including Banking, OSHA and Securities Litigation, Mediation, Arbitration.
See Professional Biographies, COLUMBUS, OHIO

Ison, Richard G., (AV) ... '27 '53 C.611 A.B. L.608 J.D. [Ⓒ Vorys,S.S.&P.]
Ita, Amy Ruth ... '76 '02 C.273 B.A. L.608 J.D. [Ⓐ Squire,S.&D.]
Iten, Jonathan D., (AV) ... '57 '81 C.97 B.A. L.813 J.D. [Vorys,S.S.&P.]
Ivan, Paulette M. ... '67 '94 C.608 B.A. L.117 J.D. [Ⓐ Reminger&R.]
Izzo, John Albert ... '68 '93 C.339 B.A. L.8 J.D. Atty. Gen.'s Off.
Jabe, Daniel N. ... '— '01 C.477 A.B. L.309 J.D. [Ⓐ Jones D.]
Jack, Arnold L., (BV) ... '38 '64 C.381 B.S.B.A. L.608 J.D. [A.L.Jack]
Jack, Arnold L., Co., L.P.A., (BV) ... 572 E. Rich St.
Jackson, David S. ... '66 '98 C.280 B.A. L.117 J.D. [Ⓐ Carlile P.&M.]
Jackson, Douglas R. ... '50 '85 C.610 B.A. L.117 J.D. [Jackson&C.]
Jackson, Michael P. ... '43 '79 C.766 B.A. L.608 J.D. 1249 Linwood Ave.
Jackson, Patrick Ian ... '70 '02 C.309 B.A. L.966 J.D. [Ⓐ Porter W.M.&A.]
Jackson, Reginald W., (AV) ... '55 '80 C.188 B.A. L.659 J.D. [Vorys,S.S.&P.]
Jackson & Curtin, Co., LPA ... 171 E. Livingston Avenue
Jackson-Forbes, Johnlander ... '65 '93 C.999 B.S. L.608 J.D. Atty. Gen.
Jacobs, Bobbi Lynn ... '65 '92 C.94 B.A. L.989 J.D. Atty. Gen. Off.
Jacobs, Holly Anne ... '63 '91 C.980 B.A. L.608 J.D. Ohio Department of Insurance
Jacobs, Rebecca B. ... '73 '97 C.1169 B.A. L.880 J.D. [Ⓐ Ulmer&B.]
Jacobson, Michael T. ... '52 '80 C.30 B.S.B.A. L.1194 J.D. 546 Indian Mound Road
Jacobson, Paul H. '46 '75 C.446 B.A. L.1035 J.D.
Associate General Counsel/V.P. Trial Counsel, Nationwide Mutual Insurance Company
Jacoby, William U. ... '25 '53 C&L.665 A.B., J.D. 200 Civic Ctr. Dr.‡
Jacques, Laurie N. ... '58 '90 C.25 B.S. L.608 J.D. [Porter W.M.&A.] (See Pat. Sect.)
Jadwin, Jay E. '62 '87 C.117 B.A. L.608 J.D.
Sr. Coun., Real Estate, Amer. Elect. Power Corp.
Jaffe, Brett, (AV) ... '51 '78 C.393 B.A. L.117 J.D. 844 S. Front St.
Jaffe, Dan L., (AV) ... '59 '85 C.188 A.B. L.813 J.D. [Vorys,S.S.&P.]
Jaffe, Ky B., (Mrs.) '58 '84 C.1090 B.A. L.813 J.D.
(adm. in NJ; not adm. in OH) 2209 Fernleaf Ln.‡
Jaffy, Lynn Sharon ... '72 '97 C.477 B.A. L.537 J.D. 306 E. Gay Street
Jaffy, Marc J., (BV) ... '65 '90 C&L.597 B.A., J.D. [Ⓐ S.Jaffy&Assoc.]
Jaffy, Stewart R., (AV) ... '30 '59 C.610 A.B. L.608 J.D. [S.Jaffy&Assoc.]
Jaffy, Stewart, & Associates Co., L.P.A., (BV) ... 306 E. Gay St.
Jaite, Maura O'Neill ... '65 '92 C.610 B.S. L.989 J.D. Atty. Gen. Off.
Jakubow, Michael Roderick ... '60 '89 C&L.831 B.A., J.D. Co. Pros. Atty. Off.
Jakubowski, Stacey L. ... '69 '95 C.665 B.A. L.201 J.D. Atty. Gen. Off
James, Larry H., (AV) ... '51 '77 C.967 B.A. L.161 J.D. [Crabbe,B.&J.]
Jamieson, J. Scott, (AV) ... '53 '79 C.473 B.S. L.608 J.D. [Vorys,S.S.&P.]
Janes, Charles L. ... '23 '51 L.608 J.D. 1414 Lake Shore Dr.‡
Janes, Charles R. (Bob), (AV) ... '52 '77 C&L.608 B.A., J.D. [Ⓐ Ulmer&B.]
Janes, Ronald B., (BV) ... '44 '69 C.363 B.A. L.607 J.D. 326 S. High St.

Javitch, Block & Rathbone L.L.P., (AV)
33 North Third Street, Suite 300, 43215 ⊙
Telephone: 614-228-9550 Fax: 614-228-2818
URL: http://www.JBandR.com
Mark J.A. Demian.
Bankruptcy, Commercial, Corporate, Collection, General Civil Practice, Landlord-Tenant, Real Estate, Insurance Subrogation, Trials and Appeals.
Cleveland Office: 1300 East Ninth Street, 14th Floor, 44114-1503. Telephone: 216-623-0000. Fax: 216-623-0190.
Cincinnati Office: 602 Main Street, Suite 500, 45202. Telephone: 513-774-9600. Fax: 513-744-9602.
See Professional Biographies, CLEVELAND, OHIO

Jean, Martine ... '76 '03 C&L.608 B.A., J.D. OH Atty. Gen. Exec. Agencies
Jedinak, Thomas J., (AV) ... '47 '74 C.473 B.S. L.117 J.D. [Ⓐ Grossman]
Jeffries, Bryan L., (BV) ... '62 '87 C.473 B.A. L.117 J.D. [Jeffries]
Jeffries, Gretchen ... '75 '03 C.608 B.A. L.846 J.D. [Ⓐ Vorys,S.S.&P.]
Jeffries Company, The, (BV) ... 79 South State Street, Suite D-6 SW
Jelen, Scott ... '61 '86 C.381 B.A. L.608 J.D. Asst. Pub. Def.
Jelkin, Elizabeth A. ... '63 '88 C.610 B.A. L.608 J.D. Ohio Sch. Boards Assn.
Jenkins, Bruce ... '28 '52 C&L.608 B.S., J.D. Mun. J.
Jenkins, George L., (AV) ... '40 '66 C.381 A.B. L.477 J.D. [Vorys,S.S.&P.]
Jenkins, John A., (AV) ... '26 '54 C&L.608 B.E.E., J.D. 10 W. Broad St.
Jenkins, Mary Kathleen ... '57 '81 C.8 B.A. L.7 J.D. Asst. Atty. Gen.
Jenkins, Vicki L. ... '60 '85 C&L.608 B.A., J.D. Asst. Pros. Atty.
Jenkins, Wayne A., (AV) ... '53 '78 C.207 B.A. L.608 J.D. [Dinsmore&S.]
Jennings, David G. ... '58 '88 C.967 B.A. L.608 J.D. [Isaac,B.L.&T.]
Jennings, Douglas R. ... '62 '89 C&L.608 B.A., J.D. [Ⓐ Carlile P.&M.]
Jennings, L. Douglas '55 '85
C.608 B.A. L.150 J.D. Atty. Exam., State Pub. Utilities Comm.
Jennings, Sharon Ann, (BV) ... '62 '91 C&L.608 B.S.B.A., J.D. Atty. Gen.
Jernejcic, Junxia T. ... '— '02 C.999 B.M. L.124 J.D. [Ⓐ Jones D.]
Jewett, Bruce E. ... '52 '78 C.630 B.A. L.150 J.D. Ohio Dept. Human Servs
Jewett, James M., (BV) ... '48 '74 C.608 B.Sc. L.117 J.D. 2577 N. High St.
Jinkens, Jeffrey R., (AV) ... '53 '78 C&L.608 B.S., J.D. [Luper,N.&L.]
Johan, Andrea H., (BV) ... '50 '85 C.610 B.S.Ed. L.117 J.D. Asst. Pros. Atty.
Johns, Alan L. ... '46 '73 C.347 A.B. L.1119 J.D. 1 Nationwide Plz.
Johnson, Annrita S. ... '50 '76 C.381 B.B.A. L.7 J.D. 3001 Bethel Rd.
Johnson, Brian T. ... '67 '95 C.937 B.A. L.602 J.D. [Ⓐ Carlile P.&M.]
Johnson, Bryan B., (AV) ... '57 '83 C.207 B.A. L.117 J.D. [Gamble H.J.]
Johnson, C. Howard ... '26 '51 C.207 A.B. L.930 LL.B. 1501 Firwood Drive
Johnson, Calvin T., Jr. ... '69 '95 C.437 B.A. L.117 J.D. [Loveland&B.]
Johnson, Cleve M. ... '52 '79 C.608 B.A. L.117 J.D. 495 South High Street, Suite 400
Johnson, David L. ... '33 '79 C.627 B.G.E. L.608 J.D. Com. Pleas J.
Johnson, David L., (AV) ... '46 '71 C.611 B.A. L.1565 J.D. [Taft,S.&H.]
Johnson, Doreen C., (BV) ... '52 '79 C.608 B.S. L.7 J.D. Asst. Atty. Gen.
Johnson, Eric A. ... '61 '95 C.152 B.A. L.8 J.D. [Sabath&J.]
Johnson, Jack L., (AV) ... '28 '61 C.207 B.A. L.117 LL.B. 769 Marburn Dr.
Johnson, John P. ... '64 '93 C.611 B.A. L.117 J.D. [Ⓐ Connor B.]

Johnson, Katryna L. .... '61 '99 C.608 B.A. L.117 J.D. [K.Johnson]
Johnson, Kenneth C., (AV) .... '53 '79 C.207 B.A. L.893 J.D. [Bricker&E.]
Johnson, Leslie S. .... '70 '97 C.608 B.A. L.117 J.D. [Lane,A.&H.]
Johnson, Margaret N. .... '48 '74 C.881 B.A. L.930 J.D. 620 City Park Ave.
Johnson, Mark A., (AV) .... '60 '85 C.631 B.A. L.608 J.D. [Baker&H.]
Johnson, Martha D. '41 '88 C.610 B.S. L.117 J.D.
Asst. Dir., Legal Servs., Columbus Children's Hosp.
Johnson, Russel J. .... '77 '04 C.473 B.S. L.117 J.D. Internal Revenue Service
Johnson, Stephen H. ....'58 '84 C.383 B.A. L.608 J.D. 88 E. Broad St., Suite 1980
Johnson, Wayne E. .... '19 '50 L.607 J.D. 4590 Knightsbridge Blvd.‡
Johnson, William Charlie, Jr. .... '55 '91 C.999 B.A. L.608 J.D. Ct. of Common Pleas
Johnson, William E. '67 '95 C&L.276 B.S.F.S., J.D.
Sr. Coun.-Fin. & Compl., Amer. Elec. Power Serv. Corp.

Johnson, Katryna, LLC, Law Offices of
2525 Tiller Lane, Suite 104, 43231
Telephone: 614-895-1722 Fax: 614-895-1322
Email: katryna@katrynalaw.com URL: http://www.katrynalaw.com
Katryna L. Johnson.
Family Law, Divorce, Consumer Law, Internet Law, Estate Planning, Wills, Probate, Trusts and Estates.
See Professional Biographies, COLUMBUS, OHIO

Johnston, Craig E. .... '57 '83 C.446 B.A. L.608 J.D. Coun., Legent Corp.
Johnston, Gordon W., (AV) .... '51 '76 C.967 A.B. L.477 J.D. [Bricker&E.]
Johnston, LeRoy, III '54 '81 C&L.378 B.S., J.D.
Assoc. V.P and Assoc. Gen. Coun., Nationwide Insurance
Johnston, Philip C., (AV) .... '43 '68 C.165 A.B. L.309 LL.B. [© Vorys,S.S.&P.]
Johnston, William J. ....'33 '69 C.608 B.A. L.117 J.D. Ohio Industrial Comm.
Johnston, William W., (AV) .... '45 '70 C&L.608 B.A., J.D. 94 Northwoods Blvd.
Johrendt, Michael J., (AV) .... '53 '77 C&L.608 B.A., J.D. [Johrendt,C.&E.]

Johrendt, Cook & Eberhart, A Legal Professional Association, (AV)
471 East Broad Street, Suite 800, 43215
Telephone: 614-464-0082 Fax: 614-463-1296
Michael J. Johrendt; John W. Cook; Robert L. Eberhart.
Tax, Business, Estate Planning and Probate, Corporate, Partnership, Business Acquisitions, ERISA, Real Estate, Business, Tax and Securities Litigation.
References: The Huntington National Bank; Key Bank.
See Professional Biographies, COLUMBUS, OHIO

Jolley, John D. .... '67 '96 C.608 B.A. L.215 J.D. [Ⓐ Dinsmore&S.]
Jolstad, Joann Marie ....'61 '86 C.608 B.A. L.8 J.D. The Legal Aid Soc. of Columbus
Jones, Bernard .... '79 '04 C.802 B.A. L.602 J.D. [Ⓐ Porter W.M.&A.]
Jones, Charles Palmer, Jr. '52 '79
C.967 B.A. L.117 J.D. Franklin Co. Domestic Relations/Juvenile Ct.
Jones, Christopher, (AV) .... '57 '90 C.611 B.A. L.276 J.D. [Ⓐ Calfee,H.&G.]
Jones, David A. ....'43 '78 C.608 B.A. L.117 J.D. Asst. V.P., The Huntington Tr. Co.
Jones, Gary L., (AV) .... '38 '66 C.608 B.S. L.266 J.D. [G.L.Jones]
Jones, Glenn T. ....'66 '97 C.608 B.A. L.117 J.D. [Ⓐ Granger]
Jones, Grey W., (BV) ....'50 '78 C.608 B.Sc. L.300 J.D. 280 N High St Ste 920
Jones, J. Allen, III .... '73 '00 C.938 B.A. L.117 J.D. [Ⓐ Benesch,F.C.&A.]
Jones, Janine Hancock ....'— '01 C.811 B.A. L.329 J.D. [Ⓐ Baker&H.]
Jones, Jeffrey J., (AV) ....'— '85 C.383 B.B.A. L.309 J.D. [Jones D.]
Jones, John Holland ....'63 '91 C.125 B.A. L.607 J.D. Atty. Gen. Off.
Jones, Richard M. .... '57 '92 C.608 B.A. L.117 J.D. [Ⓐ Karr&S.]
Jones, Robyn R. .... '51 '89 C.610 B.S. L.117 J.D. [G.L.Jones]
Jones, Stacia M. ....'— '00 C&L.608 B.A., J.D. [Ⓐ Vorys,S.S.&P.]
Jones, Stephen D., (AV) .... '53 '81 C.631 B.A. L.117 J.D. [Roetzel&A.]
Jones, Verna M. .... '61 '92 C&L.608 B.A., J.D. Asst. Atty. Gen.
Jones, William E. .... '42 '75 C.608 B.S. L.117 J.D. 505 King Ave.

Jones Day, (AV)
325 John H. McConnell Boulevard Suite 600, 43215 ⊙
Telephone: 614-469-3939 Telecopier: 614-461-4198
Email: counsel@jonesday.com URL: http://www.jonesday.com
Members of Firm in Columbus: J. Kevin Cogan; Colleen A. Deep; Joseph R. Dreitler; Thomas E. Dutton; Marlene P. Frank; Maryann Baker Gall; Gregory A. Gorospe; Kelley M. Griesmer; Robert W. Hamilton; Fordham E. Huffman; Jeffrey J. Jones; Matthew A. Kairis; Jeffrey L. Kapp; Elizabeth P. Kessler; G. Roger King; James R. King; Matthew W. Lampe; Kevin D. Lyles; Douglas M. Mansfield; William E. Nakasian; Charles M. Oellermann; Michael K. Ording; Shawn J. Organ; Gayle E. Parkhill-Krein; Todd L. Sarver; Brian G. Selden; Todd Shawn Swatsler; Randall M. Walters. Counsel: Margaret L. Gramann; Helen L. Liebman; Joseph M. Witalec. Associates: Candace A. Bankovich; David A. Beck; Tonya Blosser Braun; Brigette A. Burnell; Sean P. Byrne; John C. Camillus; Matthew C. Corcoran; Brian James Downey; Meghan E. Doyle; Jennifer L. Fate; Marc Fulkert; Erick D. Gale; Rick J. Gibson; Brian L. Gifford; Michael R. Gladman; Christopher M. Glaros; Kerry Renker Green; Janice L. Gresko; Eva U. Gunasekera; Rebecca J. Harrison; Thomas J. Hersch; Kasey T. Ingram; Daniel N. Jabe; Junxia T. Jernejcic; J. Todd Kennard; Laura A. Kulwicki; Rodd B. Lape; Ronald E. Laymon; Justin C. Letts; Jeffrey D. Litle; Robert H. Miller; Chad A. Readler; E. Michael Rossman; Holly H. Saigo; Andrea L. Seidt; Matthew R. Shurte; Kerstin Sjoberg-Witt; Denise L. Skingle; Roger A. Stalnaker; Kelli Jones Stiles; Jonathan K. Stock; Mary E. Tait; Tracy C. Tate; Mary R. True; Shawn M. Turner; Seth J. Turoff; Jonathan M. Vaas; Scott C. Walker; Mark A. Whitt; Matthew R. Wilson; Jeffrey D. Winchester; Isaac S. Wofford; Mary Beth Young. Staff Attorneys: AshLee M. Hamilton-McGranor; Phyllis J. Shambaugh.
Languages: Chinese (Mandarin), French, Japanese, and Spanish.
Full-Service Civil Practice, Antitrust and Competition Law, Business Restructuring and Reorganization, Capital Markets, Complex Commercial and Multrijurisdictional Litigation, Corporate Criminal Investigations, Employee Benefits and Executive Compensation, Energy Delivery and Power, Government Regulation, Health Care, Intellectual Property and Technology, International Litigation and Arbitration, Issues and Appeals, Labor and Employment, Lending/Structured Finance and Derivatives, Life Sciences, Mergers and Acquisitions, Oil and Gas, Private Equity, Products Liability, Personal Injury Torts and Health Litigation, Real Estate and Environment, Securities and Shareholder Litigation, Tax.
In Cleveland, Ohio: North Point, 901 Lakeside Avenue. Telephone: 216-586-3939. Telecopier: 216-579-0212.
In Atlanta, Georgia: 1420 Peachtree Street, N.E., Suite 800. Telephone: 404-521-3939. Telecopier: 404-581-8330.
In Beijing, China: 3201 China World Tower 1, No. 1 Jianguomenwai Avenue. Telephone: 86-10-5866-1111. Telecopier: 86-10-5866-1122.
In Brussels, Belgium: Boulevard Brand Whitlocklaan 165, 1200 Brussels. Telephone: 32-2-645-14-11. Telecopier: 32-2-645-14-45.
In Chicago, Illinois: 77 West Wacker. Telephone: 312-782-3939. Telecopier: 312-782-8585.
In Dallas, Texas: 2727 North Harwood Street. Telephone: 214-220-3939. Telecopier: 214-969-5100.
In Frankfurt, Germany: Hochhaus am Park, Grüneburgweg 102, 60323 Frankfurt am Main. Telephone: 49-69-9726-3939. Telecopier: 49-69-9726-3993.
In Hong Kong, China: 31st Floor, Edinburgh Tower, The Landmark, 15 Queen's Road, Central. Telephone: 852-2526-6895. Telecopier: 852-2868-5871.
In Houston, Texas: 717 Texas, Suite 3300. Telephone: 832-239-3939. Telecopier: 832-239-3600.
In Irvine, California: 3 Park Plaza, Suite 1100. Telephone: 949-851-3939. Telecopier: 949-553-7539.
In London, England: 21 Tudor Street. Telephone: 44-20-7039-5959. Telecopier: 44-20-7039-5999.
In Los Angeles, California: 555 South Flower Street, Fiftieth Floor. Telephone: 213-489-3939. Telecopier: 213-243-2539.
In Madrid, Spain: Velázquez 51, 4th Floor. Telephone: 34-91-520-39-39. Telecopier: 34-91-520-39-38.
In Menlo Park, California: 2882 Sand Hill Road, Suite 240. Telephone: 650-739-3939. Telecopier: 650-739-3900.
In Milan, Italy: Via Turati, 16/18. Telephone: 39-02-7645-4001. Telecopier: 39-02-7645-4400.

(This Listing Continued)

Jones Day (Continued)

In Moscow, Russia: Smolenskaya Square 3, 9th Floor, 121099 Moscow. Telephone: 7-095-980-6769. Telecopier: 7-095-980-6765.
In Munich, Germany: Prinzregentenstr. 11, 80538 Munich. Telephone: 089-20 60 42-200. Telecopier: 089-20 60 42-293.
In New York, New York: 222 East 41st Street. Telephone: 212-326-3939. Telecopier: 212-755-7306.
In Paris, France: 120, rue du Faubourg Saint-Honoré. Telephone: 33-1-56-59-39-39. Telecopier: 33-1-56-59-39-38.
In Pittsburgh, Pennsylvania: 500 Grant Street, One Mellon Bank Center, 31st Floor. Telephone: 412-391-3939. Telecopier: 412-394-7959.
In San Diego, California: 12750 High Bluff Drive, Suite 300. Telephone: 858-314-1200. Telecopier: 858-314-1150.
In San Francisco, California: 555 California Street, 26th Floor. Telephone: 415-626-3939. Telecopier: 415-875-5700.
In Shanghai, China: 30th Floor, Shanghai Kerry Centre, 1515 Nanjing Road West. Telephone: 86-21-2201-8000. Telecopier: 86-21-5298-6569.
In Singapore, Singapore: 30 Cecil Street, #29-01 Prudential Tower. Telephone: 65 6 538 3939. Telecopier: 65 6 536 3939.
In Sydney, Australia: Australia Square, Level 38, 264-278 George Street. Telephone: 61-2-8272-0500. Telecopier: 61-2-8272-0599.
In Taipei, Taiwan: 6th Floor, 2 Tun Hwa South Road, Section 2. Telephone: (886-2) 2704-6808 or (886-2) 7712-3399. Telecopier: (886-2) 2704-6791.
In Tokyo, Japan: Shiroyama MT Building, 6th Floor, 1-17 Toranomon 4-chome, Minato-ku, Tokyo 105-0001. Telephone: 81-3-3433-3939. Telecopier: 81-3-5401-2725.
In Washington, D.C.: 51 Louisiana Avenue, N.W. Telephone: 202-879-3939. Telecopier: 202-626-1700.
See Professional Biographies, COLUMBUS, OHIO

Jones, Gary L., Co., L.P.A., (AV) BB
175 South Third Street, Suite 800, 43215
Telephone: 614-221-2300 Fax: 614-221-8428 URL: http://www.garyljonescolpa.com
URL: http://www.joneslaw-firms.com
Gary L. Jones; Robyn R. Jones.
General Civil Practice. Administrative, Alcoholic Beverages, Liquor and Licensing Law, Real Estate Taxation and Appeals.
See Professional Biographies, COLUMBUS, OHIO

Jones, John S.
(See Worthington)

Jones, Troyan, Pappas & Perkins, A Legal Professional Association, (AV)
1472 Manning Parkway, 43065
Telephone: 614-888-8500 Fax: 614-888-2560
URL: http://www.jonestroyan.com
James P. Jones (1927-1991); Gary M. Troyan; Robert T. Pappas; John R. Perkins, Jr.
Business Organization, Planning and Transactions; Estate Planning; Retirement Plans; Real Estate; Employment Law; Probate; Federal Income, Estate and Gift Taxation.
Reference: National City Bank, Columbus, Ohio.
See Professional Biographies, COLUMBUS, OHIO

Jordan, Donald W., (AV) .... '47 '76 C&L.339 B.A., J.D. [Porter W.M.&A.]
Jordan, Jeffrey H., (BV) .... '63 '90 C&L.608 B.A., J.D. [© Rich,C.&D.]
Jordan, Jerry D., (AV) .... '34 '63 C.207 B.S. L.477 J.D. CEO, Clinton Oil Co.
Jordan, Michael S. ....'71 '97 C.910 B.A. L.117 J.D. [Schottenstein,Z.&D.]
Jorgensen, Cheryl F. .... '58 '89 C&L.851 B.S., J.D. Dept. of Rehab. & Corrections
Jorgensen, Hanne Merete .... '51 '85 C.540 B.A. L.117 J.D. Juv. Ct. Mag.
Josenhans, Paul J. .... '36 '63 C.749 B.A. L.178 LL.B. 1280 Marlyn Drive‡
Joseph, Jennifer J. ....'53 '91 C.424 B.A. L.608 J.D. [Joseph&J.]
Joseph, John J., (AV) .... '53 '81 C&L.608 B.S., J.D. [Joseph&J.]

Joseph & Joseph, (AV) BB
931 South Front Street, 43206
Telephone: 614-449-8282 FAX: 614-449-8287 URL: http://www.josephandjosephlaw.com
Email: johnjoseph@josephandjoseph.com URL: http://www.josephandjoseph.com
Members of Firm: John J. Joseph; Jennifer J. Joseph. Associates: Dennis E. Horvath; Deborah L. McNinch.
Languages: Spanish and French.
General Civil Trial Practice. Real Estate, Corporate, Domestic and Family Law, Employment, Banking and Commercial Law.
See Professional Biographies, COLUMBUS, OHIO

Jost, Timothy S. .... '48 '75 C.112 B.A. L.145 J.D. Ohio State Univ.
Joyce, Deborah L. Dye ....'59 '85 C.473 B.A. L.607 J.D. Gen. Coun., State Dept. of Com.
Judge, Corie Marty .... '72 '98 C.207 B.A. L.608 J.D. [Ⓐ Squire,S.&D.]
Judy, Philip L. .... '— '97 C.608 B.F.A. L.117 J.D. [Ⓐ Buckley K.]
Julian, Christine S. ....'66 '92 C.207 B.A. L.608 J.D. Asst. Pros. Atty.
Jump, David S., (BV) .... '56 '81 C&L.608 B.A., J.D. Mag.
Jump, W. Mark, (BV) .... '67 '94 C.473 B.A. L.117 J.D. [Koffel&J.]
Jung, Jennifer L. .... '74 '00 C.610 B.S. L.117 J.D. [Ⓐ Porter W.M.&A.]
Junga, Christopher Thomas .... '74 '00 C&L.851 B.A., J.D. 373 S High St.
Jurca, Jeffrey J., (AV) .... '54 '79 C.385 A.B. L.608 J.D. [Lane,A.&H.]
Jurca, Melanie Campbell .... '59 '84 C.473 B.A. L.608 J.D. Dept. of Admn. Serv.
Jurus, Stanley R. .... '30 '54 1375 Dublin Rd.
Justice, Stewart, III .... '73 '01 C.922 B.S L.179 J.D. [Ⓐ T.E.Morgan&Assoc.]
Kacic, Glenn D. .... '59 '84 C.472 B.A. L.608 J.D. Retirement Study Comm.
Kaczmarek, Lili C. ....'65 '90 C.8 B.A. L.1003 J.D. Exec. Dir., Ohio State Dental Board
Kadela, David A., (BV) .... '56 '82 C.477 A.B. L.215 J.D. [Littler M.]
Kahn, Benita A., (AV) .... '49 '82 C.8 B.A. L.608 J.D. [Vorys,S.S.&P.]
Kaikis, Darla E. ....'63 '92 C.608 B.S. L.117 J.D. [Larrimer&L.]
Kairis, Matthew A. .... '— '91 C.602 B.A. L.309 J.D. [Jones D.]
Kaiser, R. Lamont, (AV) ...... '44 '69 C&L.608 B.A., J.D. [© Rich,C.&D.] (⊙Delaware)
Kalgreen, Andrew J. ....'53 '79 C.381 B.A. L.145 J.D. Sr. Coun., Bank One Corp.
Kaltenbach, Jerry L. .... '77 '02 C.610 B.A. L.179 J.D. [Ⓐ Isaac,B.L.&T.]
Kamb, William T. .... '76 '03 C.610 B.A. L.117 J.D. [Ⓐ Butler,C.&D.]
Kamer, Marc .... '72 '98 C&L.608 B.A., J.D. [Ⓐ Peck,S.&W.]
Kandawalla, Darius N. ....'71 '96 C.97 B.A. L.608 J.D. [Bailey C.]
Kane, Richard F., (AV) .... '43 '71 C.563 B.E. L.117 J.D. [Bricker&E.]
Kang, Catherine, Law Office of ..... '69 '95 C.800 B.A. L.608 J.D. 601 South High Street
Kanter, Bernard E., Law Office of, (BV) '33 '57
C&L.608 B.S., J.D. 601 South High Street
Kanter, Samuel I. .... '37 '63 C.608 B.A. L.607 J.D. 2584 Fair Ave.
Kantner, John M., (BV) .... '61 '87 C.207 B.A. L.608 J.D. 3776 South High Street
Kapitan, Robert J. ....'— '64 C.363 B.S.S. L.1003 J.D. [© Dreher L.&T.]
Kaplan, Aimee L. ....'— '03 C.322 B.A. L.608 J.D. [Kaplan,A.]
Kaplan, Aimee .... 1734 Ashland Ave.
Kaplin, Thomas L., Jr. .... '28 '59 C.608 B.S. L.266 J.D. 600 Cassady‡
Kapp, Jeffrey L. ....'— '93 C.473 B.A. L.608 J.D. [Jones D.]
Kaps, Charles T., (AV) .... '18 '48 C.363 B.S. L.930 J.D. 199 S. Fifth St.
Kapustin, Vladimir '61 '89
C.1260 B.A. L.8 J.D. Assoc. Gen. Coun., Nationwide Insurance
Karam, Joseph D. '28 '57 C&L.608 B.A., J.D.
Chm. of the Bd., CEO, Cedar Enterprises, Inc.
Karl, Robert J. .... '59 '84 C.1208 B.A. L.1194 J.D. [Ulmer&B.]
Karlock, Kenneth P. .... '68 '93 C.608 B.A. L.930 J.D. [Calig&H.]
Karr, David M., (AV) .... '66 '94 C.93 B.S. L.117 J.D. Nationwide Insurance

Karr, Douglas B. ...'53 '80 C.610 B.G.S. L.117 J.D. 690 Shore Dr.‡
Karr, Glennon J., (AV) ...'47 '74 C.896 B.A. L.117 J.D. [G.J.Karr]
Karr, Heather Eileen '71 '99 C.608 B.A. L.117 J.D.
Police Legal Advsr., Columbus City Atty.'s Off.
Karr, Keith M., (BV) ...'56 '83 C.473 B.A. L.117 J.D. [Karr&S.]

Karr, Glennon J., LLC, (AV)
1328 Oakview Drive, 43235
Telephone: 614-848-3100 Fax: 614-848-3160
Email: gkarr@karrlaw.com URL: http://www.lawyers.com/karrlaw
Glennon J. Karr.
Health Care and Insurance Regulation Law, Employment Law, Employee Benefits, Business and Corporate Law.
See Professional Biographies, COLUMBUS, OHIO

Karr & Sherman Co., L.P.A., (BV) ...1 Easton Oval
Karzmer, Erin E. ...'63 '90 C.602 B.S. L.569 J.D. [A Calfee,H.&G.]
Karzmer, Steven C. ...'63 '89 C.608 B.A. L.569 J.D. [Calfee,H.&G.]
Kasai, Jerry K., (BV) ...'59 '84 C.472 B.A. L.608 J.D. Asst. Atty. Gen.
Kass, Frederic R., Law Office, (BV) ...'45 '72 C.737 B.A. L.851 J.D. 761 S. Front St.
Kasson, D. Patrick, (BV) ...'67 '91 C.1118 B.A. L.201 J.D. [A Reminger&R.]
Kastner, Elizabeth ...'75 '01 C.347 B.A. L.608 J.D. [A Schottenstein,Z.&D.]
Katko, David P. ...'56 '90 C.608 B.S. L.117 J.D. State Medical Board of Ohio
Katz, Deborah Ann, (BV) ...'62 '89 C.659 B.A. L.608 J.D. P.O. Box 16562
Katz, Janyce, (BV) ...'49 '89 C.94 B.A. L.150 J.D. Asst. Atty. Gen.
Katz, Robert H., (BV) ...'45 '75 C.980 B.S.B.A. L.608 J.D. [© Bricker&E.]
Kauffman, David E. ...'68 '95 C.117 B.A. L.608 J.D. [Clark,P.A.&S.C.]
Kauffman, Kelly L. ...'71 '99 C.340 B.A. L.339 J.D. [A Dinsmore&S.]
Kaufman, David J. ...'78 '04 C.276 B.A. L.1365 J.D. [A Vorys,S.S.&P.]
Kaufman, Jeffrey Robert ...'72 '97 3106 Griggsview Ct.
Kaufman, Philip B., (BV) '51 '78 C.994 B.A. L.607 J.D.
341 South Third Street, Suite 300
Kaurich, Frank J. ...'26 '52 C.473 B.S. L.150 LL.B. 1680 Drew Ave.‡
Kavinsky, Keith A., (BV) ...'66 '92 C.967 B.A. L.117 J.D. [Gallagher&K.]
Kaylor, Jamie Z. Scott ...'64 '89 C.528 B.A. L.851 J.D. Asst. Pros. Atty.
Kayne, Daniel J., (AV) ...'51 '76 C.659 B.A. L.150 J.D. [Kayne] ⊙

Kayne Law Group, Co., P.A., (AV)
2461 East Main Street, 43209 ⊙
Telephone: 614-236-9900 Fax: 614-559-6768
Email: dkayne@kaynelaw.com URL: http://www.kaynelaw.com
Daniel J. Kayne;—Lisa J. Berger.
Commercial Real Estate, Real Estate Development, Retail Acquisition and Leasing, Finance, Commercial Leasing, Environmental Issues, Zoning and Land Use, Business Law, Closely Held Companies, Business Formation, Business Planning, Wills, Trusts and Estate Planning.
Charlotte, North Carolina Office: 521 E. Morehead Street, Suite 100, 28202. Telephone: 704-370-0031. Fax: 614-559-6768.
See Professional Biographies, COLUMBUS, OHIO

Keane, Aimee Pirone ...'— '04 C&L.608 B.A., J.D. [A Zeiger,T.&L.]
Keane, John B. '46 '72 C.103 A.B. L.309 J.D.
Sr. V.P., Gen. Coun. & Sec., Am. Elec. Power Serv. Corp.
Kearns, Greta M. ...'71 '97 C.378 B.A. L.352 J.D. [A Squire,S.&D.]
Keating, William H. ...'43 '72 C&L.608 B.A., J.D. 1289 Inglis Ave.
Keeling, John W., (AV) ...'49 '75 C&L.608 B.S., J.D. Pub. Def. Off.
Keenan, David C. '64 '94
C.695 B.A. L.923 J.D. Sr. Atty., Columbia Gas Distribution Cos.
Keener, Thomas J., (AV) ...'48 '75 C&L.608 B.A., J.D. [Keener D.C.&P.]
Keener Doucher Curley & Patterson, A Legal Professional Association, (AV)
88 East Broad Street, Suite 1750
Kegler, Charles J., (AV) ...'42 '68 C&L.608 B.S.B.A., J.D. [Kegler,B.H.&R.]
Kegler, Todd M. ...'68 '94 C.210 B.A. L.880 J.D. [Kegler,B.H.&R.]

Kegler, Brown, Hill & Ritter, (AV)
Capitol Square Suite 1800, 65 East State Street, 43215-4294 ⊙
Telephone: 614-462-5400 Telecopier: 614-464-2634 Cable Address: "Law KBHR" Telex: 246671
Email: info@keglerbrown.com URL: http://www.keglerbrown.com
John P. Brody; Robert Garrett Cohen; Kenneth R. Cookson; Lawrence F. Feheley; Donald W. Gregory; Allen L. Handlan; Paul R. Hess; Thomas W. Hill; Charles J. Kegler; Todd M. Kegler; R. Kevin Kerns; Helen Mac Murray; David M. McCarty; Larry J. McClatchey; Paul D. Ritter, Jr.; Richard W. Schuermann, Jr.; Robert G. Schuler; S. Martijn Steger; Geoffrey Stern; Roger P. Sugarman; Kevin L. Sykes; John R. Thomas; Timothy T. Tullis; Christopher J. Weber; Melvin D. Weinstein; Michael E. Zatezalo. Counsel: Charles R. Dyas, Jr.; Thomas D. Kitch; Robert D. Marotta; Ted M. McKinniss (Resident, Marion Office); Randall W. Mikes; S. Michael Miller; Michele Ann Shuster; Patsy A. Thomas. Associates: Stephen C. Barsotti; Mary F. Brenning; Stewart H. Cupps; E. Rod Davisson; Eve M. Ellinger; Loriann E. Fuhrer; David T. Graham; Stuart W. Harris; Rasheeda Z. Khan; Jennifer L. Mackanos; Traci A. McGuire; Vinita Mehra; Camille A. Miller; Jayme P. Moore; Angela Gugle Parsons; Jeffrey D. Porter; Anne D. Pouget; Rebecca Roderer Price; Mark R. Reitz; Eric B. Travers; Stephanie P. Union; Nicholas E. Wilkes; Michele Selig Worobiec (Resident, Marion Office).
Administrative Law/Governmental Relations; Banking; Bankruptcy and Creditor's Rights; Business, Corporations and Partnerships; Commercial; Construction; Energy; Estate Planning; Franchise; Gaming Law; Health Care; International; Labor and Employee Relations; Litigation; Mergers and Acquisitions; Oil and Gas; Patent, Trademark and Copyright Law; Probate; Professional Responsibility; Public Utilities; Real Estate; Securities; Tax.
Representative Clients: Columbus Metropolitan Housing Authority; Farmers Insurance Group; National City Bank; The Ohio State University Hospital.
Marion, Ohio Office: 250 Executive Drive, Suite B, P.O. Box 919. Telephone: 740-387-1120. Facsimile: 740-387-3630.
See Professional Biographies, COLUMBUS, OHIO

Keglewitsch, Josef ...'71 '96 C.373 B.A. L.930 J.D. [Schottenstein,Z.&D.]
Keglewitsch, Rebecca Alison '70 '96
C.502 A.B. L.124 J.D. V.P. Leasing & Develop., Skilken Properties
Keister, David L. ...'51 '80 C.610 B.S.Ed. L.608 J.D. 1010 Old Henderson Road
Keith, J. Russell ...'55 '79 C.473 B.S. L.117 J.D. Gen. Coun., Employ. Rel. Bd.
Kelbick, Matt ...'65 '02 C.1381 B.S. L.117 J.D. JP Morgan Asset Mgmt.‡
Kelbley, Jeffrey P. ...'50 '77 C.610 B.S.Ed. L.608 J.D. Grange Mut. Cas. Co.
Kelch, Donald F., Jr., (BV) ...'43 '68 C.610 B.S. L.608 J.D. 1631 NW Prof. Plz.
Kelleher, Duane J., (AV) ...'27 '53 C&L.608 B.A., J.D. Ret. U.S. Bkrptcy. J.
Kelleher, W. Sean, (BV) '48 '74
C.608 B.A. L.117 J.D. 1170 old Henderson Rd., Suite 109
Keller, Donald M. ...'74 '04 C.608 B.S. L.117 J.D. [A Benesch,F.C.&A.]
Keller, Donald R., (AV) ...'49 '74 C.313 B.A. L.608 J.D. [Bricker&E.]
Keller, John K., (AV) ...'50 '75 C.347 A.B. L.228 J.D. [Vorys,S.S.&P.]
Keller, Mark D. ...'42 '68 C&L.608 B.A., J.D. [Rance,P.B.K.&E.]
Keller, Steven R., (AV) ...'48 '84 C.737 B.A. L.117 J.D. Fed. Pub. Def.
Keller, Stuart A. ...'68 '96 C.787 B.A. L.117 J.D. 3649 W. Broad St.
Kelley, Kevin Winters ...'61 '89 C.97 B.S. L.179 J.D. U.S. Atty. Off.
Kelley, Michael J., (BV) ...'56 '81 C.610 B.B.A. L.608 J.D. [Keener D.C.&P.]
Kelley, Timothy M., (AV) ...'57 '83 C.602 B.A. L.608 J.D. 250 E. Broad St.
Kelly, Elizabeth M. ...'64 '94 C.608 B.A. L.117 J.D. [A Onda,L.&R.]
Kelly, Emmett M. ...'67 '99 C.319 B.A. L.179 J.D. [A Bricker&E.]
Kelly, John T., (BV) ...'61 '87 C.901 B.A. L.117 J.D. [A Keener D.C.&P.]
Kelly, Jon F. ...'52 '76 C.30 B.A. L.117 J.D. Coun., Ameritech
Kelly, William J., Jr., (AV) ...'51 '76 C&L.608 B.A., J.D. [Porter W.M.&A.]

Kelm, Russell A., (AV) '46 '71 C.1044 B.A. L.851 J.D.
Suite 860, 37 West Broad Street, 43215
Telephone: 614-246-1000 Fax: 614-246-8110
Email: kelm@kelmlawfirm.com
—Joanne Weber Detrick; Cynthia L. Dawson.
Litigation in the areas of Corporate, Securities, Commercial, Employment, Construction and Computer Law.
See Professional Biographies, COLUMBUS, OHIO

Kelsey, Mark G., (BV) ...'55 '82 C.93 B.A. L.117 J.D. Dept. of Transp.
Kelso, Daniel J. ...'49 '76 C.610 B.B.A. L.851 J.D. 172 E. State St., 2nd. Fl.
Kemp, Harold R., (AV) ...'50 '74 C.631 B.A. L.117 J.D. [Kemp,S.R.&L.]
Kemp, Jacqueline L. ...'70 '96 C.608 B.S.B.A. L.117 J.D. 88 W. Mound St.
Kemp, Terence P. ...'53 '77 C.103 A.B. L.893 J.D. U.S. Mag.
Kemp, Schaeffer, Rowe & Lardiere Co., L.P.A., (AV) ...88 W. Mound St.
Kempf, Christopher J. ...'59 '84 C.608 B.A. L.117 J.D. 199 S. 5th St.
Kendall, Darin G., (BV) ...'52 '79 C.608 B.S. L.878 J.D. 77 E. Nationwide Blvd.
Kennard, J. Todd ...'— '97 C.870 B.S. L.309 J.D. [A Jones D.]
Kennedy, Douglas M., (AV) ...'54 '80 C.611 B.A. L.851 J.D. [Roetzel&A.]
Kennedy, James P., (AV) ...'32 '60 C.910 A.B. L.477 J.D. [© Vorys,S.S.&P.]
Kennedy, Janice, (BV) ...'44 '81 C.150 M.Ed. L.117 J.D. [Kennedy&C.]
Kennedy, John P., (BV) ...'53 '78 C.1029 B.S. L.607 J.D. [Crabbe,B.&J.]
Kennedy, John W., (BV) ...'63 '89 C&L.608 B.A., J.D. 1570 Fishinger Road
Kennedy, Nicholas Edward ...'73 '99 C.97 B.S. L.607 J.D. [Kennedy R.&K.]
Kennedy & Colasurd, (BV) ...30 Spruce Street, 3rd Floor

Kennedy Reeve & Knoll
98 Hamilton Park, 43203 ⊙
Telephone: 614-228-2050 Facsimile: 614-228-3320
URL: http://www.krkattorneys.com/
Members of Firm: Laren Elizabeth Knoll; Gary A. Reeve; Nicholas Edward Kennedy. Associates: Brad E. Bennett; Patrick M. Watts (Resident, Cleveland Office).
Sexual Harassment, Americans with Disability Act, Age Discrimination in Employment Act, Title VII Race and Gender Discrimination, Family Medical Leave Act, National Origin Discrimination, Civil Service, State and Federal Civil Rights Litigation, Religion Discrimination, Representation to the Equal Employment Opportunity Commission and Ohio Civil Rights Commission, Administrative Law, Unemployment, Worker's Compensation Retaliation, Whistleblower Statute, Intentional Tort, Equal Protection and Due Process Violations, Employee Benefits, Wrongful Termination, Public Policy, Severance Package Review and Negotiation, Contract Review, Negotiation and Litigation, Small Business Start-Up and Consulting.
Cleveland, Ohio Office: 75 Public Square, Suite 1300, 44113. Telephone: 216-771-5511. Facsimile: 216-771-5511.
See Professional Biographies, COLUMBUS, OHIO

Kenney, Shawn F. ...'51 '76 C.313 B.S. L.1003 J.D. 30 E. Broad Street, Floor 17

Kenney-Pfalzer, Susan '71 '03 C&L.608 B.F.A., J.D.
P.O. Box 30466, 43230
Telephone: 614-337-2722 Fax: 614-418-0528
Email: skplaw@sbcglobal.net URL: http://www.skpfamilylaw.com
Family Law, Divorce, Dissolution, Child Custody, Spousal and Child Support, Visitation Rights, Adoptions, Paternity, Juvenile Law, Collaborative Law, Restraining Orders.
See Professional Biographies, COLUMBUS, OHIO

Kent, Joel Scott ...'49 '87 C.611 B.A. L.117 J.D. Exec. Dir., OHIONET
Kent, Megan V. ...'45 '91 C.347 B.S. L.790 J.D. Asst. V.P., Bank One Corp.
Kephart, Roger E., (AV) ...'44 '69 C&L.608 B.A., J.D. [Kephart&F.]
Kephart & Fisher, (AV) ...207 North Fourth Street
Kerber, Jack C. ...'44 '75 C.608 B.S. L.117 J.D. Exec. V.P., COO, Ohio Bankers League
Kerber, Steven R., (AV) ...'51 '76 C.97 B.S. L.608 J.D. [Bricker&E.]
Kern, Benjamen E. ...'— '03 C.207 B.S. L.117 J.D. [A Benesch,F.C.&A.]
Kern, Timothy J. ...'53 '86 C.973 B.S. L.1003 J.D. Asst. Atty. Gen.
Kerns, Keith Richard ...'74 '00 C.610 B.A. L.117 J.D. The Ohio Dental Assoc.
Kerns, R. Kevin, (AV) ...'52 '83 C.448 B.A. L.117 J.D. [Kegler,B.H.&R.]
Kerpsack, Robert W., (AV) ...'61 '89 C.608 B.S. L.117 J.D. [R.W.Kerpsack]

Kerpsack, Robert W., Co., L.P.A., (AV)
Fifth Third Center, 21 East State Street, Suite 300, 43215
Telephone: 614-242-1000 Fax: 614-242-4180 URL: http://www.rwklaw.com
Email: info@rwklaw.com URL: http://www.lawyers.com/kerpsacklaw
Robert W. Kerpsack.
Personal Injury, Wrongful Death, Professional Malpractice, Products Liability, Consumer Class Action.
See Professional Biographies, COLUMBUS, OHIO

Kessler, Elizabeth P., (CV) ...'— '93 C.477 B.S. L.608 J.D. [Jones D.]
Kessler, Marc J., (AV) ...'66 '92 C.216 B.A. L.117 J.D. [Hahn L.&P.]
Kessler, Russell W., (AV) ...'54 '79 C.473 B.S. L.117 J.D. [Kessler&B.]

Kessler & Ballenger Co., L.P.A., (AV)
7650 Rivers Edge Drive, 43235
Telephone: 614-888-3185 Fax: 614-433-0964 Email: kballenger@kb-law.net
Email: rkessler@kb-law.net URL: http://www.lawyers.com/kessler
Russell W. Kessler (Certified Specialist in Federal Tax and Estate Planning, Trust and Probate Law, Ohio State Bar Association); Kathleen A. Ballenger (Certified Specialist in Federal Tax Law and Estate Planning, Trust and Probate Law, Ohio State Bar Association).
Estate Planning and Probate. General Business and Corporate Law. Federal, State and Local Taxes, Real Estate, Taxation, Trusts and Estates, Wills and Probate, Contracts, Elder Law, Professional Liability, Business Law, Employee Benefits.
See Professional Biographies, COLUMBUS, OHIO

Ketcham, Richard S., (AV) ...'48 '74 C.97 B.S. L.117 J.D. [Ketcham&K.]

Ketcham & Ketcham, (AV)
755 South High Street, 43206
Telephone: 614-444-3900 Fax: 614-444-9086
Email: rsketch@msn.com
Members of Firm: Victor A. Ketcham (1913-2003); Richard S. Ketcham.
Criminal Trial and Appellate Practice.
Reference: Key Bank.
See Professional Biographies, COLUMBUS, OHIO

Keyser, Donald Gary ...'50 '79 C.608 B.A. L.150 J.D. Asst. Atty. Gen.
Keyser, Raymond C. ...'73 '02 C.999 B.A. L.608 J.D. [A Squire,S.&D.]
Keysor, Debora Gustin ...'63 '88 C.473 B.S. L.117 J.D. Ct. of Claims
Khan, Rasheeda Z. ...'68 '02 C&L.608 B.S., J.D. [A Kegler,B.H.&R.]
Khorrami, Mina N., (BV) ...'60 '85 C.502 B.S. L.879 J.D. [© Cox,S.&P.]
Khoury, Paul Thomas ...'64 '96 C.608 B.A. L.902 J.D. City Atty
Khouzam, Marie-Joëlle C., (AV) ...'63 '91 C.97 B.A. L.851 J.D. [Carlile P.&M.]
Kibbey, Thomas F. ...'64 '02 C.1111 B.A. L.608 J.D. [A Squire,S.&D.]
Kidd, Melissa L. ...'71 '99 C.477 B.A. L.930 J.D. [A Thompson H.]
Kiefer, Daran P. ...'69 '94 C.138 B.A. L.930 J.D. [Kreiner&P.] (⊙Cleveland)
Kielkopf, Andrew John, (BV) ...'64 '93 C.608 B.S.B.A. L.117 J.D. [Gallagher,G.P.T.&L.]
Kiger, Robert C., (AV) ...'33 '60 C.473 A.B. L.608 J.D. [Porter W.M.&A.]

Kilbride, Randall J. .... '71 '96 C.967 B.A. L.823 J.D. 360 S. Grant Ave.
Kilgore, Terry L., (BV) .... '48 '73 C.967 B.A. L.608 J.D. 3031 Birch Hollow Way
Killworth, Allen R. ....'72 '97 C.880 B.A. L.608 J.D. [🄰 Bricker&E.]
Killworth, Linda Klimas ...... '72 '97 C.475 B.A. L.608 J.D. Coun., Nationwide Insurance
Killworth, Melinda B. ......'69 '94 C.608 B.A. L.117 J.D. 789 South Front Street Suite 201

Killworth, Gottman, Hagan & Schaeff, L.L.P.
(See Dinsmore & Shohl LLP)

Kilroy, Mary Jo, (BV) ....'— '81 C.161 B.A. L.608 J.D. [Handelman&K.]
Kim, Edward S. ....'67 '94 C.473 B.A. L.8 J.D. [🄰 Downes,H.&F.]
Kimball, Dennis R. ....'53 '82 C.608 B.A. L.117 J.D. Mun. Ct. Mag.
Kimm, Lori-Lou, (BV) ....'62 '90 C.967 B.A. L.117 J.D. [Porter W.M.&A.]
Kincaid, Jennifer Dutton ....'72 '97 C&L.608 B.S. in B.A., J.D. Pros. Atty. Off.
Kincaid, Robert M., Jr., (AV) ....'52 '77 C.602 B.A. L.734 J.D. [Baker&H.]

Kincaid, Randall & Craine, (AV)
2201 Riverside Drive, 43221
Telephone: 614-224-7193 Fax: 614-586-4051
URL: http://www.lawyers.com/kincaidrandallcraine-law
Samuel B. Randall; Kevin A. Craine; S. Brewster Randall, II.
Probate Law, Estate Planning, Wills and Trusts, Estate Administration, Will or Trust Contests, Probate Litigation, Special Needs or Medicaid Payback Trusts, Living Wills, Power of Attorneys, Estate Planning for Parents of Disabled Children, Guardianship, Conservatorship, Elder Law, Business Law, Business Formation, Business Incorporation and General Practice.
See Professional Biographies, COLUMBUS, OHIO

Kindle, Kurt A. .... '23 '58 C.532 B.A. L.266 J.D. 1141 S. High‡
Kindred, Michael '38 '63 C&L.145 A.B., J.D.
(adm. in IA; not adm. in OH) Prof. of Law, Ohio State Univ.
King, Eugene R. .... '52 '83 C.610 B.G.S. L.608 J.D. Ohio State Legal Servs. Assn.
King, G. Roger, (AV) ....'— '71 C.473 B.S. L.188 J.D. [Jones D.]
King, Hamlin C., Jr., (BV) .... '41 '67 C&L.608 B.A., J.D. [🄰 Sanborn,B.D.&B.]
King, James A., (AV) ....'62 '88 C.477 B.A. L.608 J.D. [Porter W.M.&A.]
King, James A., Jr. '34 '61 C&L.93 B.S., J.D.
Vice President & General Counsel, Borden Services Company
King, James R., (AV) .... '— '74 C.473 B.A. L.608 J.D. [Jones D.]
King, Keith '35 '66 C.608 B.B.A. L.117 J.D.
Labor & Litig. Coun., Resource Partner, Inc.
King, Michael J. ....'71 '00 C&L.608 B.A., J.D. [🄰 Dinsmore&S.]
King, Nancy Barrett ....'52 '80 C.454 B.A. L.1003 J.D. Off. of Pub. Def.
King, Norah McCann ....'49 '75 C.700 B.A. L.608 J.D. U.S. Mag. J.
King, Philip Adrian ....'72 '00 C.329 B.A. L.150 J.D. Atty. Gen.'s Off.
King, Rebecca A. ....'70 '96 C.502 B.A. L.930 J.D. Consolidated Stores
King, Timothy A. '52 '84 C.608 B.S.B.A. L.117 J.D.
Asst. Gen. Coun.-Tax, Amer. Elec. Power Serv. Corp.
King, Tunney Lee, (AV) ....'49 '74 C&L.608 B.A., J.D. 380 S. 5th St.
Kingery, Jeanne W. '56 '81
C.1349 B.A. L.659 J.D. Atty. Examiner, Public Utilities Commission
Kington, J. Anthony, (AV) ....'53 '80 C&L.608 B.A., J.D. [Chester,W.&S.]
Kinnan, Brent E. .. '51 '76 C.473 B.S. L.7 J.D. Assoc. Gen. Coun., Borden Chemical, Inc.
Kinnan, Jimmie L. '51 '79 C.473 B.A. L.7 J.D.
Gen. Coun. & Dir., Legal & Legis., School Employees Retirement Sys.
Kinneary, Jos. P. ....'05 '35 C.602 B.A. L.150 J.D. U.S. Sr. Dist J.
Kinross, Kevin M. ....'74 '00 C.347 B.S. L.117 J.D. [🄰 Bricker&E.]
Kinsler, Stephanie D. ....'70 '00 C.631 B.A. L.117 J.D. Coun., Nationwide Insurance
Kinworthy, Christine '60 '89
C.608 B.A. L.117 J.D. Legal Coun., State Dept. of Adm. Servs.
Kinzer, Allen S., (AV) ....'63 '88 C.880 B.A. L.575 J.D. [Vorys,S.S.&P.]
Kiracofe, Bruce H. '49 '81 C.385 B.A. L.1162 J.D.
Exec. Dir., Columbus Housing Law Project, Inc.
Kirby, Edwin L., Jr. ....'49 '74 C.528 B.A. L.608 J.D. Appeals Ct.
Kirby, William J. ....'55 '80 C.385 B.A. L.608 J.D. Mag., Juv. Ct.
Kirchner, Steven ....'77 '02 C.1115 B.S. L.117 J.D. [🄰 Agee C.M.&L.]
Kirila, Jill S. ....'72 '97 C.608 B.A. L.276 J.D. [🄰 Squire,S.&D.] (☉Cincinnati)
Kirk, Jas. R. ....'25 '57 C.608 B.S. L.266 LL.B. 1200 Woodbrook Ln., Apt. D‡
Kirkman, Michael ......'51 '80 C.608 B.A. L.201 J.D. Legal Dir., Ohio Legal Rights Serv.
Kirsh, Andrea M. '55 '85 C.831 B.S. L.117 J.D.
Sr. Coun., American Electric Power Service Corp.
Kirsner, John M. ....'66 '92 C.477 B.A. L.608 J.D. [Squire,S.&D.]
Kirstein, Gregory W., (AV) '54 '82
C.608 B.A. L.229 J.D. Gen. Coun., Columbus Blue Jackets
Kirtley, John F., II ....'77 '04 C.1161 B.A. L.117 J.D. [🄰 Means,B.B.&B.]
Kirwin, Edw. J. ....'10 '35 C.602 L.608 LL.B. 3536 Race St.‡
Kisor, Geoffrey T. ....'57 '90 C.610 A.B. L.117 J.D. [Kisor&W.]

Kisor & Winkler, LLC, (AV)
555 City Park Avenue, 43215
Telephone: 614-559-3841 Fax: 614-559-3846
URL: http://www.columbuscounsel.com
John F. Winkler; John C. Deal; Geoffrey T. Kisor.
Languages: Italian and French.
Complex and Commercial Litigation, Appeals, Corporate Law, Admiralty, Business Law Negotiation, Banking and Securities Law.
See Professional Biographies, COLUMBUS, OHIO

Kissos, Dean George ....'56 '85 2 Miranova Place, Suite 800
Kitrick, Mark M., (AV) ....'55 '81 C.150 B.A. L.201 J.D. [Kitrick&L.]
Kitrick and Lewis Co., L.P.A., (AV) ....515 East Main Street, Suite 515
Kizer, Tanya Johnston ....'74 '01 C.851 B.A. L.608 J.D. 336 S. High Street
Klaben, Amy D., (BV) '57 '86 C.117 B.A. L.597 J.D.
Columbus Housing Partnership; General Counsel
Kladder, Ronald A. ....'47 '74 C.1154 B.A. L.477 J.D. [🄲 Vorys,S.S.&P.]
Klatt, William A., (AV) ...... '56 '81 C.473 A.B. L.602 J.D. Chief Coun. to the Governor
Klausman, C. William .... '68 '94 C.303 B.A. L.117 J.D. [Wiles,B.B.&B.]
Klayman, Elliot I. '45 '69
C&L.150 B.B.A., J.D. Assoc. Prof. of Bus. Law, Ohio State Univ.
Klein, John C., III, (BV) ....'46 '79 C.871 B.S. L.608 J.D. Asst. City Atty.
Klein, Michael A. '55 '80 C&L.150 B.B.A., J.D.
V.P., Tax Services, BISYS Fund Services
Kleinman, Seth ....'73 '02 C&L.608 B.A., J.D. [🄰 D.A.Goldstein]
Kleinman, Stephen R., (AV) ....'69 '95 C.188 B.S. L.608 J.D. [Schottenstein,Z.&D.]
Kline, Kenneth R. ....'75 '01 C.347 B.S. L.1119 J.D. [🄰 Friedman&M.]
Klitch, Jenny L. '— '94 C.608 B.A. L.477 J.D.
Pres. & Corp. Coun., Elite Recruiting, Inc.
Klodell, Alan H., (BV) ....'60 '86 C.980 B.A. L.851 J.D. Assoc. Asst. Atty. Gen.
Kloss, William D., (AV) ....'31 '58 C&L.608 B.S.B.A., J.D. [🄲 Vorys,S.S.&P.]
Kloss, William D., Jr., (AV) ....'63 '88 C.473 B.S. L.150 J.D. [Vorys,S.S.&P.]
Knapp, Ernestine M. ....'38 '91 C.608 B.A. L.117 J.D. [🄰 Barkan&B.]
Knapp, Kyle A. ....'73 '98 C.608 B.A. L.117 J.D. [🄰 Porter W.M.&A.]

Kneafsey, Brian M., Jr., (BV) .... '58 '83 C.383 B.B.A. L.923 J.D. [🄰 Reminger&R.]
Knecht, R. Stuart .... '50 '76 C.935 B.A. L.8 J.D. Sr. Coun., Nationwide Insurance
Knepper, William E., (AV) ....'09 '33 C&L.608 B.A. 10 West Broad St.‡
Knight, Barbara M. .... '47 '77 C.610 B.S. L.117 J.D. Sr. Coun., Bank One Corp.
Knisley, Daniel S., (BV) ....'52 '86 C.303 B.A. L.607 J.D. [Knisley L.]
Knisley, David L., (BV) ....'54 '89 C.608 B.A. L.607 J.D. [Knisley L.]
Knisley, Dean A., (BV) ....'59 '86 C.610 B.A. L.607 J.D. [Knisley L.] ☉
Knisley, Douglas C., (AV) ....'56 '82 C.473 B.A. L.117 J.D. [Knisley L.]
Knisley, Scott M., (AV) ....'27 '53 C.473 B.S. L.608 J.D. [Knisley L.]
Knisley Law, (AV) .... 1390 Dublin Road (☉Lima)
Knoll, Laren Elizabeth .... '68 '99 C.244 B.A. L.607 J.D. [Kennedy R.&K.]
Knopp, Melissa Ann ....'70 '95 C.967 B.A. L.1048 J.D. The Supm. Ct. of OH
Knueve, Mark A. ....'70 '96 C&L.893 B.S., J.D. [Vorys,S.S.&P.]
Knueve, Meredith K. ....'73 '99 C&L.608 B.S., J.D. [🄰 Vorys,S.S.&P.]
Knutti, Randall W., (AV) ....'59 '84 C.665 B.S. L.893 J.D. Asst. Atty. Gen.
Kobalka, Walter S. ....'48 '76 C.103 B.A. L.1003 J.D. Supm. Ct.

Koblentz, Robert A., (AV) '46 '70 C&L.608 B.A., J.D.
35 East Livingston Avenue, 43215
Telephone: 614-461-6666 Fax: 614-461-4666
Email: rk@rkoblaw.com URL: http://www.lawyers.com/koblentzlaw
(Certified Specialist in Family Relations Law, Ohio State Bar Association).
Family and Matrimonial Law, Divorce, Child Custody, Child Support, Spousal Support, Property Law, Premarital Agreements. Trials and Appellate Practice. Family Law Arbitration. Collaborative Law.
See Professional Biographies, COLUMBUS, OHIO

Koch, Ronald J. '64 '03 C.608 B.S.E.E. L.117 J.D.
4200 Regent Street, Suite 200, 43219
Telephone: 614-288-4740 Fax: 866-255-6793
Email: ronaldkoch@earthlink.net URL: http://www.kochattorneys.com
Litigation, Copyrights, Trademarks, Patents, Intellectual Property, Contracts, Forensic Science, Engineering, Juvenile, Criminal, Patent Law.
See Professional Biographies, COLUMBUS, OHIO

Kochalski, Edward M., (BV) ....'50 '75 C.107 B.A. L.851 J.D. [Manley D.K.]
Kocher, Walter W. ....'34 '60 C.262 B.S. L.477 J.D. 2470 Lane Rd.
Kocsis, Alexander S. ....'41 '77 C&L.608 B.A., J.D. Indus. Comm. of Ohio
Koeck, Roger McClelland ....'61 '92 C.25 B.A. L.608 J.D. [🄰 Merullo,R.&S.]
Koehler, Mark W. ....'59 '93 C.266 B.S. L.117 J.D. [🄲 Maguire&S.]
Koenig, Robert, Jr. .... '— '91 C.473 B.S. L.608 J.D. 30 East Broad Street, Floor 23
Koerner, Nancy L. ....'52 '84 C.63 B.S. L.117 J.D. Columbus Foundation, The
Koffel, Bradley Paul, (BV) .... '68 '93 C.608 B.S. L.117 J.D. [Koffel&J.]
Koffel & Jump, (BV) ....2130 Arlington Avenue
Kohler, Charles W. ....'50 '75 C.608 B.S.B.A. L.228 J.D. [C.Kohler]
Kohler, Charles, Law Office of ....100 E. Campus View Boulevard, Suite 250
Kohn, Richard L., (BV) ....'30 '54 C&L.608 B.A., J.D. 24 E. Frankfort St.
Kokensparger, Steven J. ....'69 '94 C.610 B.A. L.608 J.D. [Kokensparger]

Kokensparger Law Office, The
471 E. Broad Street, Suite 2001, 43215
Telephone: 614-232-0424 Fax: 614-280-9675
Email: steve@kokensparger.com URL: http://www.kokensparger-law.com
Steven J. Kokensparger (Certified Specialist in Family Relations Law, Ohio State Bar Association).
Domestic Relations, Divorce, Dissolution, Legal Separation, Child Custody, Paternity, Family Law.
See Professional Biographies, COLUMBUS, OHIO

Kolman, Marya C., (BV) '54 '78 C.645 B.A. L.976 J.D.
Supvr., Mediation Servs., OH Dom. Rel. & Juv. Ct., Franklin Co.
Koltak, Ronald J., (AV) ....'49 '77 C.381 B.A. L.608 J.D. 5 E. Long St.
Komasara, Tiffany L. ....'71 '01 C&L.117 B.Mus., J.D. [🄰 Squire,S.&D.]
Koncelik, Amy L. ...'70 '95 C.381 B.A. L.608 J.D. Atty., Columbia Gas Distribution Cos.
Koogler, Mark B., (AV) ....'54 '80 C.608 B.S. L.201 J.D. [Porter W.M.&A.]
Kooperman, Brian T. ....'78 '04 C.36 B.A. L.117 J.D. [🄰 Portman,F.&F.]
Koorn, Amy Beth ....'76 '01 C.210 B.S. L.117 J.D. Com. Pleas Atty.
Kopf, John B., III ....'75 '02 C.608 B.A. L.117 J.D. [🄰 Thompson H.]
Koprucki, Jane, Attorney at Law, (BV) '49 '81
C.339 B.S. L.150 J.D. 3965 Poplar Bend Drive
Korey, Vincent P. ....'34 '60 C.381 B.A. L.608 J.D. Asst. Atty. Gen.
Korn, David G., (BV) ....'51 '76 C.473 B.A. L.150 J.D. [🄰 Maguire&S.]
Korte, Nancy J. ....'52 '78 C&L.150 B.A., J.D. Asst. Atty. Gen.
Kossoudji, Scott A. ....'64 '00 C&L.608 B.A., J.D. [🄰 Vorys,S.S.&P.]
Kostreva, David K. ....'77 '03 [🄰 Curry,R.S.&M.]
Kosydar, Robert J., (AV) ....'31 '56 C.602 B.S. L.608 J.D. Twenty E. Broad St.
Kotte, Fred S., Jr. ....'09 '33 C&L.150 B.A., J.D. 348 Walnut Cliff Dr.‡
Kouns, Mark E. ....'50 '76 C.437 B.A. L.117 J.D. Sr. Exec. Legal Asst. to Governor
Kowalczyk, John William ....'40 '71 C.695 B.A. L.838 J.D. State Auto. Mut. Ins. Co.
Kozelek, James G. ....'67 '01 C.608 B.A. L.117 J.D. [🄰 Weltman,W.&R.]
Kozich, John H., (BV) ....'49 '75 C.381 B.A. L.608 J.D. [Harris,M.B.&C.]
Kozlowski, Richard Eugene ....'67 '98 C.676 B.A. L.880 J.D. [🄰 Baker&H.]
Kozlowski, Susan Hayest, (AV) ....'55 '80 C&L.608 B.A., J.D. 225 E. Broad St.
Kozyris, P. John .... '32 '61 L.188 J.D. Prof. of Law, Ohio State Univ.
Kram, Elbert J., (AV) ....'41 '66 C.347 B.S. L.145 J.D. [Bricker&E.] ‡
Kramer, Randall J. '64 '89 C.132 B.A. L.352 J.D.
(adm. in IA; not adm. in OH) Sr. Coun., Nationwide Insurance
Kranstuber, Charles W., (BV) ....'54 '79 C.608 B.A. L.1049 J.D. [Livorno&A.]
Kranyak, John T. .... '69 '97 C.282 B.A. L.179 J.D. Develop. Coun., Limited Brands, Inc.
Krauskopf, Joan M., (Mrs.) '32 '58
C.610 A.B. L.608 J.D. Prof., Ohio State Univ. Coll. of Law
Kravitz, Janet E., (AV) ....'52 '87 C.608 B.S. L.117 J.D. [Kravitz,G.&B.]
Kravitz, Max, (AV) ....'46 '73 C.608 B.A. L.117 J.D. [Kravitz,G.&B.]

Kravitz, Gatterdam & Brown, LLC, (AV)
145 East Rich Street, 43215
Telephone: 614-464-2000 Fax: 614-464-2002
Email: mkravitz@kgbllc.com URL: http://www.kgbllc.com
Max Kravitz; Janet E. Kravitz.
Federal and State Criminal Defense, Criminal Appeals, Post-Conviction and Federal Habeas, Criminal and Civil Asset Forfeiture, Equine and Administrative Law, International Criminal Law.
See Professional Biographies, COLUMBUS, OHIO

Kreiner, Fred J., (BV) ....'37 '64 C.424 B.S. L.1003 J.D. [Kreiner&P.] (☉Cleveland)
Kreiner & Peters Co., L.P.A., (BV)
6047 Frantz Road Suite 203 (☉Cincinnati, Cleveland)
Kreiter, Robert D. ....'54 '87 C.532 B.A. L.117 J.D. Staff Atty., Claims Ct.
Krejci, Matthew C. ....'77 '02 C.473 B.S. L.117 J.D. [🄰 Ulmer&B.]

Kremblas, Foster, Phillips & Pollick
(See Reynoldsburg)

Kreps, Cavett R. ....'77 '03 C.473 B.A. L.608 J.D. [🄰 Bricker&E.]
Krimm, John J., Jr., (AV) ....'60 '87 C.602 B.A. L.861 J.D. [Schottenstein,Z.&D.]
Krivda, Pamela Straughan ....'54 '88 C.608 B.A. L.117 J.D. Owens & Krivda Co., LPA

Kromer, Thomas R. . . . . '56 '82 C.363 B.S.B.A. L.930 J.D. Tax Partner, Deloitte & Touche
Krone, Gilbert L., (BV) . . . . . '36 '68 C.920 B.A. L.607 J.D. 2000 W. Henderson Rd.
Krum, Jean A. . . . . '58 '90 C.910 B.A. L.117 J.D. Atty., Workers' Comp. Bur.
Krumlauf, Martin . . . . . '15 '43 C&L.266 J.D. 3317 Colchester Rd.
Krumm, Nancy Marakas . . . . . '51 '80 C.910 B.A. L.201 J.D. Coun., Nationwide Insurance
Krummen, Robert J. . . . . . '79 '03 C.608 B.A. L.309 J.D. [🄰 Porter W.M.&A.]
Krupman, Victor S., (AV) . . . . . '34 '59 C.31 B.A. L.477 J.D. [Krupman,G.M.M.&W.]

Krupman, Golden, Meizlish, Marks & Wittenberg, LLP, (AV)
923 East Broad Street, 43205-1101
Telephone: 614-258-1983 Fax: 614-253-5071
URL: http://www.kgmmw.com
Victor S. Krupman; Keith E. Golden; Jodie Kay Meizlish; Irving B. (Buddy) Marks; Eric J. Wittenberg.
Business and Corporate Law, Business Planning, Buying or Selling a Business, Computers and Software, Entertainment and Publishing Law, Franchise Law, Commercial Law, Federal Civil and Criminal Practice, Construction Law, Limited Liability Companies, Collections, Estate Planning, Wills, Probate, Guardianships, Trusts, Family Law, Divorce, Child Custody, Visitation Rights, Personal Injury, Automobile Accidents, Insurance Coverage, Dental Malpractice, Commercial and Residential Real Estate.
See Professional Biographies, COLUMBUS, OHIO

Kubli, David F. . . . . '49 '75 C.980 B.A. L.8 J.D. Unemp. Comp. Bd. of Review
Kuehnle, Kenton L., (AV) . . . . . '45 '70 C.57 B.A. L.228 J.D. [Allen,K.&S.]
Kuhns, Keven J. . . . . '63 '89 C.645 B.S. L.200 J.D. Dept. of Taxation
Kulesa, Amy H. . . . . '67 '95 C.381 B.B.A. L.7 J.D. Asst. Pros. Atty.
Kulewicz, John J., (AV) . . . . . '54 '81 C.608 B.A. L.976 J.D. [Vorys,S.S.&P.]
Kullman, Jack R., Jr. . . . . '52 '77 C.473 B.S. L.117 J.D. Ct. Admr., 10th Dist. Ct. of App.
Kulwicki, Laura A. . . . . . '— '87 C&L.608 B.A., J.D. [🄰 Jones D.]
Kundtz, Alan J. . . . . '46 '81 C.608 B.C.E. L.117 J.D. S.E.A.,Inc.
Kurek, Randy S., (AV) . . . . . '54 '79 C.210 B.A. L.608 J.D. [Isaac,B.L.&T.]
Kurtz, Charles J., III, (AV) . . . . . '40 '65 C.951 B.A. L.608 J.D. [⊙ Porter W.M.&A.]
Kutell, Russell J., (AV) . . . . . '67 '92 C.659 B.A. L.276 J.D. [Schottenstein,Z.&D.]
Kuykendall, Laura G., (AV) . . . . . '53 '78 C&L.893 B.A., J.D. [Vorys,S.S.&P.]
La Bue, Anne Marie, (AV) . . . . . '66 '91 C&L.94 B.A., J.D. [🄰 Shayne&G.]
LaBuhn, Matthew A. . . . . . '70 '96 C.117 B.A. L.608 J.D. [Onda,L.&R.]
Lacey, Denise Platfoot '73 '01
C.201 B.A. L.989 J.D. Supm. Ct. of OH Comm. on Professionalism
Lackey, David L., (BV) . . . . . '65 '91 C.473 B.A. L.117 J.D. [Decker,V.S.L.&V.]
La Fayette, Paul-Michael . . . . . '69 '96 C.924 B.A. L.117 J.D. [🄰 Reminger&R.]
LaForge, Steven G., (AV) . . . . . '59 '86 C.339 B.A. L.608 J.D. [Isaac,B.L.&T.]
Lagana, Beth Broidy . . . . . '49 '80 C&L.608 B.S., J.D. P.O. Box 3990
Lahm, Gunther K., (AV) . . . . . '48 '87 C.967 B.A. L.117 J.D. [G.K.Lahm]

Lahm, Gunther K., LLC, Law Office of, (AV)
Suite 101, Waterford Tower, 155 West Main Street, 43215-5063
Telephone: 614-222-0963 Fax: 614-228-7630
Email: guntherlahm@aol.com URL: http://www.lawyers.com/guntherlahm
Gunther K. Lahm.
Professional Negligence, Insurance Bad Faith, Personal Injury, Automobile Accidents, Wrongful Death.
See Professional Biographies, COLUMBUS, OHIO

Laing, David A., (AV) '56 '81 C.930 B.A. L.608 J.D.
Sr. Coun.-Envir., Health & Safety, Amer. Elect. Power Serv. Corp.
Laliberte, Brian J. . . . . . '74 '99 C.477 B.A. L.124 J.D. [🄰 Vorys,S.S.&P.]
Lally, Mark S. . . . . '46 '75 C&L.608 B.A., J.D. 72 Garden Rd.
Lambert, Douglas W. . . . . '56 '81 C.945 B.A. L.608 J.D. 4581 Cleveland Ave.
Lambert, Marnie C. . . . . . '67 '93 C.473 B.A. L.990 J.D. [🄰 D.P.Meyer]
Lamkin, William W., (AV) . . . . . '34 '65 C.608 B.A. L.500 J.D. [Lamkin,V.T.B.&D.]

Lamkin, Van Eman, Trimble, Beals & Dougherty, LLC, (AV) BR
500 South Front Street, Suite 200, 43215-5671
Telephone: 614-224-8187 Fax: 614-224-4943 URL: http://www.lvtbd.com
URL: http://www.lawyers.com/lvtbd
Members of Firm: William W. Lamkin; Timothy L. Van Eman; Thomas W. Trimble; David A. Beals; Kathy A. Dougherty; Keri N. Yeager.
Personal Injury, Medical Malpractice, Products Liability, Negligence, Insurance Coverage, Stockbroker Malpractice & Fraud. Litigation and Trial Practice.
Reference: Huntington National Bank.
See Professional Biographies, COLUMBUS, OHIO

Lamm, Russell E. . . . . '36 '63 C.608 B.A. L.150 LL.B. 3368 Olentangy River Road
Lampe, Matthew W. . . . . . '— '89 C.385 B.A. L.188 J.D. [Jones D.]
Lampke, Matthew J. . . . . '72 '97 C.201 B.A. L.8 J.D. Asst. Atty. Gen.
Lampke, Monique B. . . . . . '71 '97 C.813 B.A. L.608 J.D. [🄰 Porter W.M.&A.]
Lampkin-Crafter, Odella . . . . . '63 '89 C.8 B.A. L.851 J.D. Child Support Mag.
Lancaster, George H., Jr. . . . . '62 '87 C.381 B.A. L.7 J.D. Pub. Def. Comm.
Lancione, David, (BV) . . . . . '52 '77 C.150 B.A. L.300 J.D. [D.Lancione&Assoc.]
Lancione, Robert M., (AV) . . . . . '51 '76 C.610 B.A. L.117 J.D. [Lancione]
Lancione, David, & Associates, LLC, (BV) . . . . . 1041 Summit Street
Lancione Law Office, LLC., (AV) . . . . . 875 Mount Vernon Ave.
Landes, Mark, (AV) . . . . . '56 '82 C.367 B.A. L.608 J.D. [Isaac,B.L.&T.]
Landolfi, John L., (AV) . . . . . '63 '89 C.935 B.A. L.608 J.D. [Vorys,S.S.&P.]
Landrum, Jaime Taryn . . . . . '77 '03 C.608 B.S. L.117 J.D. [🄰 Porter W.M.&A.]
Lane, R. Stacy . . . . . '58 '89 C.608 B.S. L.117 J.D. [Bailey C.]
Lane, Robert L. . . . . '55 '81 C.608 B.A. L.117 J.D. Chief Appl. Coun., Pub. Def. Comm.
Lane, William M., (AV) . . . . . '35 '60 C.31 B.A. L.477 J.D. [Lane,A.&H.]

Lane, Alton & Horst LLC, (AV)
175 South Third Street, 43215-5100
Telephone: 614-228-6885 Fax: 614-228-0146
Email: Lane@lah4law.com URL: http://www.lah4law.com
Members of Firm: Jack R. Alton; Mary Barley-McBride; Belinda S. Barnes; John C. Barno; Joshua R. Bills; Matthew S. Brown; James C. Carpenter; David G. Cox; Claudia L. Davis; Amy J. Ervin; Scott A. Fenton; Melissa M. Ferguson; Curtis F. Gantz; Joseph A. Gerling; Melissa A. Gurile; Jeffrey B. Hartranft; Vincent I. Holzhall; Edward G. Hubbard; Jeffrey W. Hutson; Leslie S. Johnson; Jeffrey J. Jurca; William M. Lane; Beth Anne Lashuk; William Scott Lavelle; Barbara K. Letcher; James W. Lewis; Rick E. Marsh; Alvin E. Mathews, Jr.; Theodore M. Munsell; D. Wesley Newhouse; Christopher T. O'Shaughnessy; Jeffery M. Poth; William H. Prophater, Jr.; Gregory D. Rankin; James K. Reuss; Karen Krisher Rosenberg; Corinne N. Ryan; Kimberly M. Schellhaas; Douglas J. Schockman; Thomas E. Switzer; Monica L. Waller; Richard O. Wuerth; Stephen B. Yurik.
Business Litigation, Construction Law, Employment Law, Family and Juvenile Law, Immigration Law, Legal and Judicial, Medical and Products Liability Law.
Representative Clients: American International Group; Auto Owners Insurance Co.; Chubb Group of Insurance Cos.; Cincinnati Insurance Co.; CNA Insurance; GRE Insurance Group; Home Insurance; Royal Insurance.
See Professional Biographies, COLUMBUS, OHIO

Lang, Robert K. . . . . '59 '89 C.608 B.A. L.117 J.D. 77 South High Street, 22nd Floor
Lange, Richard M. '49 '75 C.608 B.A. L.117 J.D.
Admin. Hearing Offr., Unemployment Comp. Rev. Comm.
Langer, Jeffrey I., (AV) . . . . . '— '80 C.339 A.B. L.597 J.D. [Dreher L.&T.]
Langlois, Jennifer L. . . . . '72 '97 C.999 B.A. L.607 J.D. 1625 Bethel Rd.
Lanier, Lorelei M. . . . . '55 '81 C.608 B.A. L.117 J.D. 1515 W. Lane Ave., Ste. 3

Lanker, Lois L. . . . . '28 '57 C&L.608 B.A., J.D. 97 S. Broadleigh Rd.
Lantz, Duane F., (BV) . . . . . '28 '60 C.967 B.A. L.608 J.D. 155 W. Main St.
Lantz, Susan M. . . . . '58 '83 C&L.117 B.A., J.D. 150 E. Mound St.
Lanzinger, Judith Ann . . . . . '46 '78 C&L.851 B.Ed., J.D. Supm. Ct. J.
Lape, Marcella L. . . . . . '— '04 C.607 B.S. L.608 J.D. [🄰 Baker&H.]
Lape, Rodd B. . . . . . '— '96 C&L.608 B.A., J.D. [🄰 Jones D.]
Lardiere, Christopher L., (BV) . . . . . '55 '83 L.117 J.D. [Kemp,S.R.&L.]
Laret, Joffre Scott, (BV) . . . . . '58 '84 C.980 B.A. L.607 J.D. [Agee C.M.&L.]
Larkin, Janet L. . . . . . '66 '01 C.608 B.S. L.117 J.D. [🄰 Volkema,T.M.B.S.&M.]
Larrimer, Courtney Ann . . . . . '71 '96 C.473 B.S.B. L.117 J.D. [Larrimer&L.]
Larrimer, Craig E. . . . . . '69 '97 C.228 B.A. L.608 J.D. [Larrimer&L.]
Larrimer, Gavin R., (AV) . . . . . '36 '61 C&L.608 B.S., J.D. [Larrimer&L.]
Larrimer, John H. . . . . . '68 '97 C.390 B.A. L.1003 J.D. [Larrimer&L.]
Larrimer, Kevin J. . . . . . '69 '97 C.477 B.A. L.117 J.D. [Larrimer&L.]
Larrimer, Terrence W., (AV) . . . . . '47 '72 C.674 B.A. L.477 LL.B. [Larrimer&L.]
Larrimer, Thomas G. . . . . '31 '61 C.608 B.A. L.266 J.D. 165 N. High St.

Larrimer & Larrimer, (AV)
165 N. High Street, 43215-2486
Telephone: 614-221-7548 Fax: 614-221-8659
URL: http://www.larrimer.com
Terrence W. Larrimer; Gavin R. Larrimer; Joseph F. Navin; Darla E. Kaikis; Courtney Ann Larrimer; John H. Larrimer; Kevin J. Larrimer; Craig E. Larrimer.
Employment Law and Workers Compensation.
See Professional Biographies, COLUMBUS, OHIO

La Salle, Lawrence . . . . . '51 '82 C.262 B.A. L.1003 J.D. Bd. of Tax App.
Laser Seskes, Brandi R. . . . . '75 '04 C.8 B.A. L.117 J.D. 471 E. Broad St., Ste. 1400
Lash, Lester S., (AV) . . . . . '31 '61 C.611 B.A. L.608 J.D. [⊙ Vorys,S.S.&P.]
Lashuk, Beth Anne . . . . . '65 '94 C.207 B.A. L.117 J.D. [Lane,A.&H.]
Lashutka, Gregory S., (AV) . . . . . '44 '74 C.608 B.S. L.117 J.D. Mayor
Lasley, Aneca E. . . . . . '75 '00 C.607 B.A. L.608 J.D. [🄰 Squire,S.&D.]
Latanick, David G., (AV) . . . . . '46 '74 C.97 B.A. L.608 J.D. 225 E. Broad Street
Latin, Oscar B. . . . . '23 '51 C&L.966 B.S., J.D. Asst. Atty. Gen.
LaTour, Randall D., (AV) . . . . . '54 '87 C&L.608 B.A., J.D. [Vorys,S.S.&P.]
Latsko, John M. . . . . . '46 '73 C.475 B.A. L.665 J.D. [Schottenstein,Z.&D.]
Lau, Edward H. . . . . '54 '88 C.477 B.A. L.607 J.D. Ohio Dept. of Taxation
Laughlin, Stanley K., Jr. '— '61 C.473 B.A. L.608 J.D.
Prof. of Law, Ohio State Univ. College of Law
Laughlin-Schopis, Susan K., (BV) '57 '82
C&L.608 B.A., J.D. Staff Atty. Franklin Co. Pub. Def. Off.
Lavelle, William Scott, (BV) . . . . . '55 '80 C.610 B.S. L.608 J.D. [Lane,A.&H.]
Lavinsky, Rick A., (AV) . . . . . '44 '69 C.319 B.A. L.597 J.D. [Dinsmore&S.]
Law, Sam S. . . . . '48 '99 C.608 B.E.E. L.117 J.D. 171 E. Livingston Avenue
Lawrence, James J. . . . . '48 '78 C.608 B.A. L.851 J.D. Ohio Dept. of Taxation
Lawrence, Linda Juergens . . . . . '65 '90 C&L.150 B.A., J.D. [Lawrence]
Lawrence, Rodd S., (BV) . . . . . '62 '88 C&L.880 B.A., J.D. 496 S. 3rd St.
Lawrence, Wayman C., III, (AV) . . . . '31 '59 C.674 A.B. L.608 J.D. [⊙ Porter W.M.&A.]
Lawrence Law Office . . . . . 496 S. 3rd St.
Laymon, Ronald E. . . . . . '— '97 C.102 B.A. L.145 J.D. [🄰 Jones D.]
Lazaroff, Risa Dinitz . . . . . '61 '88 C.477 B.A. L.608 J.D. 303 E. Broad St.
Lazarow, William S., (BV) . . . . . '46 '72 C.597 B.A. L.608 J.D. Asst. Pub. Def.
Lazear, Sherri Blank, (AV) . . . . . '58 '85 C&L.608 B.A., J.D. [Baker&H.]
Lazorishak, Karen L., (BV) . . . . . '59 '85 C.25 B.A. L.930 J.D. Asst. Atty. Gen.
Leach, Donald B., (BV) . . . . . '15 '42 C.273 A.B. L.178 LL.B. 2654 Dorset Road
Leach, Donald B., Jr., (AV) . . . . . '54 '82 C.865 B.A. L.608 J.D. [Buckingham,D.&B.]
Leach, Ellen C. . . . . '65 '92 C.608 B.A. L.851 J.D. 2615 Charing Rd., Apt. D
Leach, George W., Jr., Law Office of . . . . . '59 '01 C.8 B.A. L.1187 J.D. 112 E. Main St.
Leach, Russell . . . . . '22 '49 C&L.608 B.A., J.D. Ret. J., Ct. of Claims‡
Leahy, Walter R. '45 '71 C.363 B.A. L.607 J.D.
Asst. Gen. Coun., Nationwide Insurance
Lease, Charles H., (BV) . . . . . '59 '85 C.608 B.A. L.851 J.D. [🄰 Ricketts]
Lease, Diane M., (BV) . . . '61 '86 C.63 B.S. L.851 J.D. Ohio Police and Fire Pension Fund
Lecklider, Timothy A. . . . . '56 '83 C.97 B.A. L.1003 J.D. Employ. Rel. Bd.
Ledman, James H., (AV) . . . . . '40 '65 C.228 B.A. L.608 J.D. [Isaac,B.L.&T.]
Lee, Denise C. . . . . '— '94 C.608 B.A. L.150 J.D. State fo Ohio Gov.'s Off.
Lee, Kyu Steve . . . . . '73 '98 C.477 B.A. L.608 J.D. Claims Ct.
Lee, M. David . . . . . '68 '93 C&L.608 B.A., J.D. 100 E. Broad St.
Lee, Paul W., (BV) . . . . . '48 '78 C.608 B.S. L.117 J.D. 705 E. Livingston Ave.
Lee, Philip W. . . . . '59 '93 C.608 B.S. L.117 J.D. Coun., Nationwide Insurance
Lee, Phillip H. '71 '00 C.197 B.A. L.477 J.D.
(adm. in CA; not adm. in OH) [🄰 Bricker&E.]
Leeseberg, Gerald S., (AV) . . . . . '53 '79 C.97 B.L.S. L.608 J.D. [Leeseberg&V.]
Leeseberg & Valentine, (AV) . . . . . 175 South Third Street
Lefton, David E., (BV) . . . . . '60 '85 C.150 B.A. L.608 J.D. Asst. Atty. Gen.
Lehv, Michael S. . . . . '42 '94 C.696 A.B. L.117 J.D. [M.S.Lehv]
Lehv, Michael S., Co., L.P.A. . . . . 78 Park Dr.
Leibold, John W., (AV) . . . . . '31 '57 C&L.607 B.A., J.D. 3006 North High Street
Leickly, James R., (BV) . . . . . '58 '86 C&L.608 B.A., J.D. 114 Misty Oak Place
Leidner, Ellen Beth . . . . . '58 '83 C.347 B.S. L.608 J.D. Asst. Atty. Gen.
Leier, Rachel A. . . . . . '71 '99 C&L.608 B.A., J.D. [🄰 Manley D.K.]
Leighner, William H., (AV) . . . . . '29 '58 C.597 B.S. L.477 J.D. [Bricker&E.] ‡
Leinbach, O. Charles, Jr. . . . . '— '77 C.610 B.F.A. L.851 J.D. Asst. Atty. Gen.
Leist, Darrin C. . . . . '67 '99 C.207 B.A. L.608 J.D. 400 S. 5th St., Ste. 202
Leister, Craig D., (AV) . . . . . '49 '74 C.97 B.S.B.A. L.228 J.D. [Means,B.B.&B.]
Leithart, Paul W., (BV) . . . . . '55 '81 C.317 B.A. L.117 J.D. [Strip,H.L.M.&T.]
Leizman-Moses, Karen . . . . . '57 '84 C.477 B.A. L.989 J.D. Asst. Atty. Gen.
Lelli, Craig T., (BV) . . . . . '56 '81 C&L.607 B.A., J.D. 51 N. High St., Ste. 781
Le Master, Mark D. '69 '97 C.608 B.S. L.117 J.D.
[🄰 Nelson L.d.&H.] (⊙Blue Bell, PA)
Lentz, Frederick C. . . . . '21 '51 C.569 L.608 LL.B. 1094 E. Dunedin‡
Lentz, John C. . . . . '58 '98 C.610 B.S. L.851 J.D. 1094 E. Dunedin Rd.
Leonatti, Adam Henry . . . . . '69 '97 C.381 B.S. L.608 J.D. [Thompson,M.&D.]
Lerner, Marshall L., (AV) . . . . . '47 '73 C.475 B.A. L.309 J.D. [Bricker&E.]
Lerner, Michael J. . . . . '78 '03 C.610 B.A. L.608 J.D. [🄰 E.J.Hoffman&Assoc.]
Leshner, Jay Harris . . . . . '60 '85 C.608 B.A. L.117 J.D. 338 S. High Street
Leshy, Albert, (BV) . . . . . '22 '49 C&L.608 B.S., LL.B. 85 E. Gay St.
Leshy, George V., (BV) . . . . . '46 '73 C.608 B.S. L.607 J.D. 1390 Dublin Rd.
Leslie, Mark A., (AV) . . . . . '53 '78 C.473 B.A. L.608 J.D. 76 S. Powell Ave.
Lesser, Frances Shaiman . . . . . '54 '79 C.665 B.A. L.117 J.D. Off. of the Treas.
Lesser, Steven D. . . . . '52 '78 180 East Broad Street, 5th Floor
Letcher, Barbara K. . . . . . '57 '90 C&L.608 B.S., J.D. [Lane,A.&H.]
Letizia, Donald L., (BV Ⓣ) '62 '87
C.347 B.A. L.200 J.D. Sr. Atty., Battelle Memorial Institute
Letts, Justin C. . . . . . '— '05 C.511 B.A. L.228 J.D. [🄰 Jones D.]
Letts, Richard Dennis . . . . . '44 '74 C.475 B.A. L.607 J.D. Admin. Law J., Soc. Sec. Admn.

Leuby, William A. '57 '83 C.473 B.S. L.608 J.D.
V.P., Chief Operating Officer & General Counsel, Hamilton Capital Management, Inc.
Leuchtag, Emery J. . . . . '44 '83 C.8 B.A. L.7 J.D. [Ⓐ Maguire&S.]
Leutz, John R. . . . . '54 '79 C&L.117 B.A., J.D. 37 west Broad Street
LeVere, T. Earl, (AV) . . . . '69 '94 C.117 B.A. L.608 J.D. [Bricker&E.]
Leveridge, Julia L. . . . . '74 '00 C.383 B.A. L.117 J.D. [Ⓐ Grossman]
Levering, Robert Bruce . . . . '53 '80 C.608 B.S. L.117 J.D. City Atty.
Levey, Jack S., (AV) . . . . '50 '78 C.966 B.A. L.494 J.D. [Plunkett&C.]
Levine, Amy Michelle . . . . '— '01 C.437 B.A. L.117 J.D. [A.M.Levine]
Levine, David C., (BV) . . . . '52 '89 C.1154 B.A. L.608 J.D. [Baker&H.]
Levine, Judith D., (AV) . . . . '50 '75 C.999 B.A. L.208 J.D. [Roetzel&A.]
Levine, Kenneth T., (AVⓉ) '64 '90 C.273 B.S. L.831 J.D.
(adm. in PA; not adm. in OH) [Nelson L.d.&H.] ⊙
Levine, Richard L., (AV) . . . . '58 '84 C.347 B.A. L.245 J.D. [R.L.Levine]
Levine, Amy M., Attorney at Law, LLC . . . . 85 E. Gray Street, Suite 1006

Levine, Richard L., Co., L.P.A., (AV)
460 East Main Street, 43215-5344
Telephone: 614-227-0300 Fax: 614-227-6060
Email: richard@levinepa.com URL: http://www.richardllevine.com
Richard L. Levine.
Commercial Real Estate, Real Estate Development, Real Estate Finance, Commercial Leasing, Construction Law, Commercial Law, Mechanics Liens, Entity Formation, Corporate Law, Partnerships, Limited Liability Companies.
See Professional Biographies, COLUMBUS, OHIO

Levinson, Lawrence L. . . . . '68 '94 C.699 B.A. L.117 J.D. 511 S. High St.
Levy, Barbara R. . . . . '— '89 C.102 B.A. L.608 J.D. 235 South Drexel Ave.
Levy, Sarah Salter . . . . '56 '82 C.188 B.A. L.93 J.D. Asst. Atty. Gen.
Levy, Stefan C., (BV) . . . . '36 '60 C&L.608 B.A., J.D. 261 S. Front St.

Levy, Yale R. '70 '95 C.347 B.S. L.608 J.D.
903 Eastwind Drive, 43081
Telephone: 614-898-5200 Fax: 614-898-5230
Email: ylevy@popelevy.com
Collections, Creditor Representation, Bankruptcy, Corporate Law, Estate Planning, Structured Settlement Transfers.
See Professional Biographies, COLUMBUS, OHIO

Lewis, Eugene B., (BV) . . . . '57 '82 C.967 B.A. L.150 J.D. [Chester,W.&S.]

Lewis, Gregg R., (BV) '63 '89 C.608 B.S. L.117 J.D.
Formerly Harry Lewis Co., L.P.A.
625 City Park Avenue, 43206-1003
Telephone: 614-221-3938 Fax: 614-221-3713
Email: glewislaw@aol.com URL: http://www.gregglewislaw.com
Harry Lewis (1925-1995);—Eric E. Willison.
Family Law, Matrimonial Law and Civil Litigation.
See Professional Biographies, COLUMBUS, OHIO

Lewis, Jacqueline, (BV) . . . . '51 '80 C.389 B.A. L.117 J.D. 2735 Scottwood Rd.
Lewis, James W., (AV) . . . . '47 '75 C.608 B.A. L.117 J.D. [Lane,A.&H.]
Lewis, Jeffrey M., (AV) . . . . '56 '81 C.473 A.B. L.608 J.D. [Swedlow,B.L.M.&D.]
Lewis, Mark D. . . . . '68 '94 C.608 B.A. L.117 J.D. [Ⓐ Kitrick&L.]
Lewis, W. Blair . . . . '60 '98 C.608 B.S.C.E. L.117 J.D. [Ⓐ Thompson H.]
Li, Christine D. . . . . '— '04 C.608 B.S. L.893 J.D. [Ⓐ Porter W.M.&A.]
Lias, Katherine Ann Salvatore . . . . '41 '77 C.205 B.A. L.117 J.D. 373 South High Street
Liebersbach, John W., (AV) '49 '76 C.473 A.B. L.117 J.D.
Sr. V.P. & Mng. Coun., The Huntington Natl. Bk.
Liebman, Helen L. . . . . '— '74 C.66 B.A. L.93 J.D. [Ⓒ Jones D.]
Liggett, Luther L., Jr., (AV) . . . . '56 '81 C&L.273 B.A., J.D. [Bricker&E.]
Lilly, Phillip G., (AV) . . . . '58 '87 C.779 B.S. L.117 J.D. [Becker&L.]
Lim, Edwin Y. . . . . '50 '77 C.980 B.E. L.608 J.D. State E.P.A.
Lim, Lawrence S. . . . . '— '92 C.130 B.A. L.608 J.D. Com. Pleas Ct.

Liming, Roxi A. '52 '98 C.608 B.A. L.179 J.D.
1989 West Fifth Avenue, 43212
Telephone: 614-488-2053 Fax: 614-488-2069
Email: roxil@roxiliming.com URL: http://www.roxiliming.com
Immigration Law, Visas, Naturalization, H1-B Visas, Green Cards, Financé Visas, Investor Visas, Investor Green Cards, Labor and Employment, Wage and Hour Violations, Wrongful Discharge, Employment Discrimination, Americans with Disabilities Act, Sexual Harassment, Family and Medical Leave Act, Employment Contracts, Severance Package Negotiation, Personnel Policies.
See Professional Biographies, COLUMBUS, OHIO

Lin, Albert G. . . . . '73 '02 C.608 B.A. L.813 J.D. [Ⓐ Vorys,S.S.&P.]
Lindemann, Jeffrey N., (BV) . . . . '66 '91 C&L.477 A.B., J.D. [Frost B.T.]
Lindgren, Thomas G., (BV) . . . . '61 '87 C&L.607 B.A., J.D. Asst. Atty. Gen.
Lindley, Edgar L. . . . . '21 '53 C.608 L.117 J.D. 100 S. 3rd St.‡
Lindquist, Randall C. . . . . '53 '80 C.427 B.A. L.117 J.D. Two Miranova Place- Suite 310
Lindsay, G. Bruce '48 '75 C.473 B.A. L.365 J.D.
Sr. Hearings Offr., State Unemp. Comp. Bd. of Review
Lindsey, Heather B.Robinson . . . . '71 '96 C.475 B.A. L.608 J.D. Asst. City Pros.
Lindsey, Scott T. . . . . '71 '96 C.679 B.S. L.608 J.D. 1880 MacKenzie Dr.
Lindsey, Thomas H., (BV) . . . . '40 '65 C.679 B.Sc. L.608 J.D. 1880 Mackenzie Dr.
Lindsmith, Quintin F., (AV) . . . . '59 '84 C&L.608 B.A., J.D. 100 S. Third Street
Linhart, Brian E. . . . . '71 '99 C&L.608 B.B.A., J.D. [Ⓐ Havens W.]
Linnen, Stephen P. . . . . '70 '99 C.473 B.A. L.7 J.D. Leg. Coun. for Tax and Education
Linville, Ronald G., (AV) . . . . '54 '80 C.967 B.A. L.117 J.D. [Baker&H.]
Linville, Vicki W. . . . . '56 '82 C.967 B.A. L.117 J.D. 2371 Sandover Road‡
Lipchak, Melissa R. . . . . '66 '91 C.901 B.A. L.608 J.D. [Ⓐ S.B.Dritz]
Lipovsek, Kimberly M. . . . . '68 '93 C.138 B.A. L.608 J.D. Sr. Coun., Bank One Corp.
Lippe, Christine Bobbey '52 '86 C.97 B.S. L.117 J.D.
Asst. Prosecuting Atty., Franklin Co. Prosecuting Atty's Off.
Lippe, Jerry L., (Co., L.P.A.), (BV) . . . . '42 '67 C.473 A.B. L.608 J.D. 592 S. 3rd St.
Lipps, Jeffrey A., (AV) . . . . '56 '81 C&L.150 B.A., J.D. [Carpenter&L.]
Lira, Jan Rasmussen '70 '96 C.378 B.S. L.900 J.D.
(adm. in KS; not adm. in OH) KPMG LLP
Lisle, Shawn G. . . . . '— '93 C.934 B.A. L.7 J.D. [Ⓐ Porter W.M.&A.]
List, D. Andrew, (AV) . . . . '65 '91 C.896 B.A. L.608 J.D. [Clark,P.A.&S.C.]
Liston, Dennis D., (BV) . . . . '44 '74 C.352 B.A. L.608 J.D. [McNamara&M.]
Liston, Jefferson E., (AV) . . . . '54 '78 C.631 B.A. L.930 J.D. [Tyack,B.&L.]
Litle, Jeffrey D. . . . . '— '99 C.473 B.S. L.228 J.D. [Ⓐ Jones D.]
Litle, T. Bennett . . . . '75 '02 C.473 B.A. L.228 J.D. [Ⓐ Squire,S.&D.]
Litt, Gordon F., (AV) . . . . '57 '85 C.532 B.A. L.608 J.D. [Bricker&E.]
Little, Marion H., Jr., (AV) . . . . '64 '89 C&L.608 B.A., J.D. [Zeiger,T.&L.]

Littler Mendelson, A Professional Corporation, (AV)
Fifth Third Center, 21 East State Street Suite 1600, 43215 ⊙
Telephone: 614-463-4201 Fax: 614-221-3301
Email: info@littler.com URL: http://www.littler.com
James M. L. Ferber; David A. Kadela; Robert C. Long (Not admitted in OH; Also at Chicago, Ohio); Thomas M. L. Metzger; Daniel W. Srsic;—Margaret C. Bettendorf; Wendy Clary; Alison M. Day; Christa S. Fossee (Not admitted in OH); Cheryl R. Hankerson; Jeffrey S. Hiller (Not admitted in OH); Tracy Stott Pyles.

(This Listing Continued)

Littler Mendelson, A Professional Corporation (Continued)

Employment and Labor Law; Affirmative Action; Age Discrimination in Employment Civil Service; Collective Bargaining; Confidentiality Agreements; Covenants Not To Compete; Employee Drug Testing; Employee Privacy; Employer Liability; Employment Arbitration; Employment Breach of Contract; Employment Civil Rights; Employment Class Actions; Employment Discrimination; Employment Litigation; Equal Employment Opportunity Law; Fair Labor Standards; Family and Medical Leave Act; Harassment; Labor Relations; Labor Strikes; National Labor Relations Act; Noncompete Litigation; Noncompetition and Non-Solicitation Agreements; Personnel Policies; Prevailing Wage Litigation; Reductions in Force; Restrictive Covenants; Sexual Harassment; Title VII Discrimination; Unfair Labor Practices; Union Contract Negotiations; Union Elections; Union Organization; Wage and Hour Law; WARN Act; Whistleblower Litigation; Workplace Violence; Wrongful Termination; Wrongful Termination Defense.
Offices located in: Phoenix, Arizona; California — Fresno, Los Angeles, Sacramento, San Diego, San Francisco, San Jose, Santa Maria, Stockton and Walnut Creek; Denver, Colorado; Washington, D.C.; Miami, Florida; Atlanta, Georgia; Chicago, Illinois; Boston, Massachusetts; Minneapolis, Minnesota; Reno and Las Vegas, Nevada; Newark, New Jersey; New York, New York; Charlotte, North Carolina; Philadelphia and Pittsburgh, Pennsylvania; Dallas and Houston, Texas; Seattle, Washington.
See Professional Biographies, COLUMBUS, OHIO

Littrell, Barry W., (AV) . . . . '56 '83 C.967 B.A. L.608 J.D. [Gallagher,G.P.T.&L.]
Littrell, Rex A., (BV) . . . . '64 '89 C.363 B.A. L.608 J.D. [Ulmer&B.]
Livorno, John F., (BV) . . . . '46 '72 C&L.608 B.S., J.D. [Livorno&A.]

Livorno & Arnett Co., LPA, (AV)
280 N. High Street Suite 1410, 43215
Telephone: 614-224-7771 Fax: 614-224-7775
Email: livorno@megapathdsl.net URL: http://www.livornoarnett.com
John F. Livorno; Henry A. Arnett; Charles W. Kranstuber.
Workers Compensation, Labor and Employment, Discrimination, Americans with Disabilities Act, Sexual Harassment, Employment Contracts, Wrongful Termination, Civil Service, Government Agency Practice, Union Labor Law, Bankruptcy.
Reference: Bank One of Columbus.
See Professional Biographies, COLUMBUS, OHIO

Lloyd, Katheryn M. . . . . '76 '02 C.608 B.A. L.228 J.D. [Ⓐ Carpenter&L.]
Lloyd, Melissa C. . . . . '73 '99 C.37 B.A. L.608 J.D. [Ⓐ Schottenstein,Z.&D.]
Lodge, Connie M. . . . . '— '87 C&L.851 B.A., J.D. Ohio Department of Insurance
Lodge, Thomas E., (AV) . . . . '56 '81 C.610 B.A. L.930 J.D. [Thompson H.]
Lodico, Vincent J., (BV) . . . . '48 '73 C&L.262 B.A., J.D. [Crabbe,B.&J.]
Loewengart, Steven M., (BV) . . . . '53 '87 C.597 B.M. L.150 J.D. [Squire,S.&D.]
Logan, J. Anthony, (AV) '51 '78
C.608 B.A. L.1003 J.D. 5025 Arlington Centre Blvd, Ste 350
Logan, William B., Jr., (AV) . . . . '46 '74 C.674 B.A. L.608 J.D. [Luper,N.&L.]
Lohmann, Virginia E., (BV) . . . . '62 '87 C.207 B.S. L.608 J.D. 41 S. High Street
Long, James M. . . . . '51 '76 C.611 B.A. L.608 J.D. 4330 Mountview Road
Long, Kelly Ann . . . . '72 '01 C.1208 B.A. L.201 J.D. Title First Agency, Inc.
Long, Michael G., (AV) . . . . '44 '69 C.611 B.A. L.608 J.D. [Vorys,S.S.&P.]
Long, Richard S., (BV) . . . . '51 '76 C&L.8 B.A., J.D. [Musser,L.&H.]
Long, Robert C., (AVⓉ) '53 '79 C.388 B.A. L.309 J.D.
(adm. in IL; not adm. in OH) [Littler M.] (⊙Chgo., IL)
Long, Rodney C. . . . . '46 '71 C.280 B.B.A. L.608 J.D. 1806 North High Street
Long, Thomas L., (AV) . . . . '51 '76 C.602 B.A. L.608 J.D. [Baker&H.]
Lonsinger, Linda L. . . . . '55 '87 C.608 B.S.N. L.117 J.D. 4000 East Main Street
Looper-Friedman, Susan E. '55 '81 C.966 B.A. L.770 J.D.
(adm. in CA; not adm. in OH) Prof. of Law, Capital Univ.
Lopez, A. Ruben . . . . '55 '92 C.107 B.A. L.851 J.D. Asst. State Pub. Def.
Lopez, Christopher A. . . . . '63 '88 C.97 B.A. L.851 J.D. Gen. Coun., Ohio Education Assn.
Lopez, Robert Clayton . . . . '74 '99 C.923 B.A. L.117 J.D. Pros. Atty.
Lord, Christopher J. '59 '87
C.685 B.A. L.188 J.D. Coun., Columbia Energy Group Serv. Corp.
Lorenzo, Paul S. . . . . '67 '94 C.608 B.A. L.117 J.D. Asst. Pub. Def.
Losey, Mark A. . . . . '68 '94 C.473 B.A. L.930 J.D. [Ⓐ Calfee,H.&G.]
Lossing, Roger A. . . . . '55 '83 C.679 B.A. L.117 J.D. Banc One Investment Advisors
Loughry, Michael S. . . . . '69 '01 C.846 B.A. L.179 J.D. [Ⓐ Mazanec,R.&R.]
Louis, Harlan S., (AV) . . . . '66 '94 C.473 B.S. L.200 J.D. [Ⓐ Bailey C.]
Loveland, Curtis A., (AV) . . . . '46 '73 C.610 B.B.A. L.608 J.D. [Porter W.M.&A.]
Loveland, Richard L., (AV) . . . . '30 '57 C.473 B.S. L.608 J.D. [Loveland&B.]
Loveland, William L., (BV) . . . . '55 '82 C.207 B.A. L.608 J.D. [Loveland&B.]

Loveland & Brosius, (AV)
50 West Broad Street, Suite 3300, 43215
Telephone: 614-464-3563 Fax: Available Upon Request
Email: admin@lblaw.net
Richard L. Loveland; Donald F. Brosius; William L. Loveland; Calvin T. Johnson, Jr. Associates: Helen M. Quenemoen; Peter N. Griggs.
General Practice. Business, Real Estate, Condominium, Local Government, Land Use, Construction and Business Litigation, Estate Planning.
See Professional Biographies, COLUMBUS, OHIO

Lovering, Richard S., (AV) . . . . '54 '80 C.855 B.A. L.893 J.D. [Bricker&E.]
Lowe, A. James . . . . '41 '74 C.267 B.A. L.1003 J.D. Ref., Bur. of Employ. Servs.
Lowe, David C. . . . . '41 '71 C.846 B.A. L.796 J.D. Motorists Mutual Ins. Co.
Lowe, Gregory A. . . . . '59 '93 C.608 B.S. L.179 J.D. [Ⓒ Ulmer&B.]
Lowenstein, Roy . . . . '51 '76 C.604 B.A. L.608 J.D. 88 E. Broad St.
Lowther, John R. '50 '76 C.608 B.A. L.117 J.D.
V.P., Secy & Gen. Coun., State Automobile Mutual Insurance Company
Lubow, Barry L., (AV) . . . . '58 '83 C.30 B.A. L.608 J.D. DLZ Corporation
Lubow, Lauren . . . . '58 '83 C.608 B.A. L.117 J.D. State Medical Bd. of Ohio
Lubow, Susan Nolan . . . . '68 '95 C.604 B.A./B.M. L.309 J.D. [Ⓐ Baker&H.]
Lucas, Albert J., (BV) . . . . '59 '84 C.363 B.S.B.A. L.930 J.D. [Calfee,H.&G.]
Lucas, John C., (BV) . . . . '51 '76 C.473 B.S. L.930 J.D. [Lucas,P.A.G.&N.]

Lucas, Prendergast, Albright, Gibson & Newman, (AV)
600 South High Street, 43215
Telephone: 614-228-5711 Telecopier: 614-228-0982
URL: http://www.lpagnlaw.com
Members of Firm: Ralph M. Lucas (1880-1967); R. Rush Warren (1917-1967); John A. Brown (1926-1980); Arthur J. Prendergast, Jr. (1923-1987); Ralph W. Lucas (1920-1993); Robert E. Albright; William F. Newman; John C. Lucas;—Tonda L. Moore; Stacey L. Wideman.
General Civil Practice. Corporation, Wills, Probate, Taxation, Real Estate, Zoning, Public Utilities, Labor and Health Law. Estate Planning. Trials and Appeals.
Representative Clients: American Aggregates Corporation; Columbus Apartment Owners Association; County Commissioners' Association of Ohio; National Church Residences; Pontifical College Josephinum; Snyder Development Co.
See Professional Biographies, COLUMBUS, OHIO

Luchsinger, Ann L. '42 '85 C.62 B.A. L.608 J.D.
Admn. Coun., Co. Child Support Enforce. Agcy.
Luck, Rebecca Rofsky . . . . '52 '79 C.473 A.B. L.7 J.D. 28 S. Roosevelt Ave.‡
Luckett, Ermel Ray, Jr. . . . . '62 '89 C.473 B.A. L.124 J.D. [E.R.Luckett,Jr.]
Luckett, Ermel R., Jr. . . . . 24 N. High St.
Luczkowski, Jean M. . . . . '51 '78 C.363 A.B. L.608 J.D. [Ⓒ Habash,R.&F.]
Ludgin, John Richard . . . . '49 '87 C.273 M.D. L.930 J.D. V.P., PIE Mut. Ins. Co.
Lumpe, J. Richard, (AV) . . . . '34 '63 C.608 B.S. L.117 J.D. 37 W. Broad St., Ste. 730

Lunn, Anita Pope .... '36 '82 C.33 B.A. L.608 J.D. Asst. Pub. Def.
Luper, Frederick M., (AV) .... '40 '65 C.188 A.B. L.608 J.D. [Luper,N.&L.]
Luper, Neidenthal & Logan, (AV) .... 50 W. Broad Street
Lusenhop, Peter A. .... '65 '98 [Ⓐ Vorys,S.S.&P.]
Luther, Richard A. .... '49 '83 C.318 B.S. L.608 J.D. 2002 Mackenzie Dr.
Lyles, Kevin D., (AV) .... '— '86 C&L.608 B.S., J.D. [Jones D.]
Lyman, Chester T., Jr., (BV) .... '54 '82 C.309 A.B. L.893 J.D. [Lyman]
Lyman, Webster S., (BV) .... '22 '50 C&L.608 B.S., J.D. [Lyman]
Lyman Law Offices, (BV) .... 1313 E. Broad Street
Lynn, Arthur D., Jr. .... '21 '48 C&L.608 B.A., J.D. Prof. Emeritus, The Ohio State Univ.
Lynn, Bruce G., (AV) .... '16 '41 C.608 B.A. L.309 J.D. [Bricker&E.] ‡
Lynn, James M. .... '56 '98 C.473 B.S. L.117 J.D. State Pub. Util. Comm.
Lynn, Robt. John .... '20 '48 C&L.608 B.S., J.D. Prof. of Law, Emeritus, Ohio State Univ.
Lynn, Sarah E., (BV) .... '59 '87 C.347 B.A. L.273 J.D. [Ⓑ Bailey C.]
Lynskey, Sandra L. .... '54 '97 C.999 B.S. L.117 J.D. Asst. Atty. Gen.
Lyon, Tanisha L. .... '72 '97 C.659 B.A. L.608 J.D. Asst. Atty. Gen.
Lyons, Christina M. .... '— '04 C.608 B.S.N. L.117 J.D. [Ⓐ Vorys,S.S.&P.]
Lyons, Gary W., (BV) .... '39 '64 C&L.608 B.M., J.D. [Lyons&B.]
Lyons, George Alpheus .... '58 '84 C.967 B.A. L.608 J.D. Berlon & Timmel
Lyons and Bibbo, (BV) .... 336-338 S. High St.
Maas, Brandy M. .... '74 '01 C.1012 B.S. L.1292 J.D. [Ⓐ Rich,C.&D.]
MacAuley, James D., (AV) .... '32 '60 C&L.608 B.Sc., J.D. 1413 King Ave.‡
Macbeth, William H., III '69 '95
C.608 B.S.B.A. L.607 J.D. Sr. Coun., Big Lots Stores, Inc.
MacDonald, Alex E. '07 '37 L.128 LL.B.
(adm. in DC; not adm. in OH) 349 S. Chase Ave.‡
MacDonald, Carl J. .... '28 '51 C&L.607 LL.B. 1 Nationwide Plaza
Machle, Kathi J. .... '55 '81 L.477 J.D. 200 East Campus View Blvd.
Macias, Lisa A. .... '69 '96 C.1323 B.A. L.117 J.D. Law Clk., U.S. Dist. Ct.
Mack, Kevin D. '54 '80 C.276 B.A. L.229 J.D.
Sr. Coun.-Envir., Health & Safety, Amer. Elec. Power Serv. Corp.
Mackanos, Jennifer L. .... '64 '02 C.602 B.A. L.117 J.D. [Ⓐ Kegler,B.H.&R.]
Mackay, Hyrum J. .... '56 '90 C.878 B.S. L.930 J.D. Asst. State Pub. Def.
Macke, Frank, (BV) .... '49 '75 C.608 B.A. L.607 J.D. 400 S. 5th Street
Macke, Kenneth Wayne '47 '75
C.249 B.A. L.1119 J.D. Ct. of Appeals, 10th Appellate Dist.
MacKenzie, Paul A. .... '66 '92 C.473 B.A. L.608 J.D. [Isaac,B.L.&T.]
Mackin, Kerry McConaghy .... '— '02 C.746 B.A. L.117 J.D. [Ⓐ Buckingham,D.&B.]
MacKinnon, John J., (BV) .... '56 '83 C.201 B.A. L.117 J.D. 501 S. High St.
Macklin, George K. '50 '79
C.608 B.A. L.117 J.D. Assoc. Gen. Coun., Nationwide Insurance
MacLaughlin, Lewis H., III .... '44 '73 C.976 B.A. L.347 J.D. 107 E. Dunedin Rd.
Mac Murray, Helen, (BV) .... '60 '87 C.1214 B.A. L.851 J.D. [Kegler,B.H.&R.]
Macon-Bruce, Marcia Jo .... '63 '90 Atty. Gen. Off., Crime Victims Sect.
Madden, Kathleen Joy Crites .... '75 '01 C.631 B.S. L.117 J.D. 400 S. Fifth, Ste. 200
Maddox, Mark S., (BV) .... '59 '84 C.608 B.A. L.7 J.D. [Frost&M.]
Madriguera, Christina Marie .... '69 '00 C.802 B.A.Mus. L.608 J.D. The Ohio Senate
Magelaner, Thomas L. .... '56 '90 C.207 B.A. L.213 J.D. [Pope,M.&Assoc.]
Maggied, Pamela N., (AV) .... '52 '79 C.610 B.A. L.608 J.D. [P.N.Maggied]
Maggied, Pamela N., Co., L.P.A., (AV) .... 50 W. Broad Street, Suite 2250
Magnuson, James A., (AV) .... '47 '76 C.1030 B.A. L.117 J.D. [Magnuson&B.]
Magnuson & Barone, (AV) .... 1720 Zollinger Rd.
Maguire, Patrick D., (AV) .... '51 '76 C.967 B.A. L.607 J.D. [Maguire&S.]

Maguire & Schneider LLP, (AV)
250 Civic Center Drive, Suite 500, 43215 ⊙
Telephone: 614-224-1222 Fax: 614-224-1236
URL: http://www.maguire-schneider.com
Partners of Firm: Patrick D. Maguire; Karl H. Schneider; Keith W. Schneider; Brian E. Dickerson; Wayne Hassay; Bradley D. Barbin. Associates: Gary D. Andorka; Donald Scott Andrews; Nivita Bhalla; Christopher G. Black; Sharlene I. Chance; Tricia L. Clarke; Kathleen A. DeYoung; William C. Donahue; Jodi L. Dozer; Ysidro Edward Duran; Thomas S. Erlenbach; Thomas J. Gallagher; Richard S. Gerber; Robert H. Griffin, Jr.; John H. Hix; D. Timothy Hughes; Steven R. Hughes; David G. Korn; Emery J. Leuchtag; Andrea E. Martin; Matthew F.G. Martin; Ted P. McClatchey; Patricia L. Moore; Brice O. Recker; Manbir S. Sandhu; Jonathan R. Secrest; Tricia A. Sprankle; James G. Vargo; Phillip Lawrence Wright, Jr. Of Counsel: Robert Carl Schuler; Mark W. Koehler; Robert P. Freed.
Business Litigation, Labor and Employment, Insurance Defense, Directors Liability Errors and Omissions Defense, Real Estate Malpractice Claims, Real Estate, Corporate, Commercial Litigation, Health Care Law, Health Care Fraud and Abuse, Banking Law, Probate and Estate Planning, Family Law, Adoptions, Mediation, White Collar Crime, Criminal Defense, Consumer Law, Administrative Law, Creditor's Rights Law, Financial Institution Law, Intellectual Property, Internet Law, Lemon Law, Product Liability, and Worker's Compensation.
Cleveland, Ohio Office: 1370 Ontario Street, Suite 1700, 44113. Telephone: 800-600-1222. Fax: 216-274-9808.
See Professional Biographies, COLUMBUS, OHIO

Mahaffey, Carol, (BV) .... '50 '83 C.608 B.A. L.117 J.D. [Ⓐ Vorys,S.S.&P.]
Mahaffey, John P., (BV) .... '51 '80 C.473 A.B. L.608 J.D. 91 Glenmont Ave.
Maher, Daniel M., (AV) .... '45 '72 C.1027 B.S. L.893 J.D. [Squire,S.&D.]
Mahoney, Michael P., (AV) .... '45 '72 C&L.608 B.S., J.D. [Bailey C.]
Mahood, Margaret Wharton .... '49 '84 C.446 B.A. L.1035 J.D. Hearings & Appeals Off.
Mahota, John M., (AV) .... '38 '63 C.734 B.S. L.597 J.D. [Mahota&C.]
Mahota & Carter, (AV) .... 341 South Third Street, Suite 300
Maier, Robert C. .... '56 '90 C.732 B.A. L.608 J.D. Atty. Gen.
Malek, Andrew M. .... '61 '86 C.1349 B.S. L.608 J.D. Law Clk., U.S. Bkrptcy. J.
Malek, Edwin LeRoy .... '39 '69 L.117 J.D. [Malek&M.]
Malek, James Edwin .... '65 '95 L.161 J.D. [Malek&M.]

Malek & Malek
1227 South High Street, 43206
Telephone: 614-444-7440 Fax: 614-444-8836
URL: http://www.maleklawoffice.com
Edwin LeRoy Malek; James Edwin Malek.
Workers Compensation, Personal Injury, Railroad Accidents and Injuries, Automobile Accidents and Injuries, Wrongful Death, Dog Bites.
See Professional Biographies, COLUMBUS, OHIO

Malkoff, Daniel Allen .... '59 '85 C.473 B.A. L.851 J.D. Sr. Dep. Atty. Gen.
Mallett, Jacqueline S. .... '64 '92 C.608 B.S. L.930 J.D. Asst. Atty. Gen.
Mallett, Jeanne M. .... '— '80 C.608 B.A. L.276 J.D. Supvg, Atty., State E.P.A.
Mallory, Lark T. .... '69 '98 C&L.608 B.S.B.A., J.D. [Ⓐ Chester,W.&S.]
Mallory, Thomas H., Jr. .... '68 '95 C.347 B.A. L.117 J.D. [Mallory&T.]
Mallory & Tsibouris Co., LPA .... 88 East Broad Street, Suite 1560 (Pat.)
Malloy, Marie A., (BV) .... '66 '91 C&L.608 B.A., J.D. [Schottenstein,Z.&D.]
Malone, Margaret A. .... '50 '75 C.706 B.A. L.930 J.D. Asst. Atty. Gen.
Maloney, Kevin M., Law Office of, (AV) '58 '85
C.608 B.S. L.1003 J.D. 22 East Gay Street, Suite 401
Maloon, Jeffrey L., (AV) .... '58 '83 C.63 B.S. L.117 J.D. [Volkema,T.M.B.S.&M.]
Malrick, Russell A. .... '08 '30 C&L.851 457 Eastmoor Blvd.
Manchak, John F. .... '48 '74 C.930 B.A. L.1003 J.D. Asst. Ct. Rep., Ohio Supm. Ct.
Mancini, Joseph M. .... '34 '66 C&L.930 A.B., J.D. Atty. Gen.'s Off.
Maney, Thomas P., Jr. .... '56 '83 C&L.117 B.A., J.D. 92 Northwoods Blvd., Ste. B
Mangan, Patrick F. .... '53 '79 C.608 B.A. L.851 J.D. 2999 E. Dublin Granville Rd.
Mango, Dominic L. .... '68 '99 C&L.608 B.S., J.D. [Ⓐ Saia&P.]
Mangum, Mildred M. .... '21 '55 C.104 A.B. L.608 J.D. 57 Riverview Pk. Dr.‡
Maniace, James V., (AV) .... '56 '81 C.602 B.A. L.228 J.D. [Chester,W.&S.]
Manigault, Arthur L. .... '63 '89 C.207 B.A. L.150 J.D. Asst. Atty. Gen.
Manley, Theodore K. .... '64 '92 C.385 A.B. L.608 J.D. [Manley D.K.]

Manley • Deas • Kochalski LLC, (BV)
495 South High Street, Suite 300, 43215
Telephone: 614-220-5611 Fax: 614-220-5613
URL: http://www.mdk-llc.com
Members of the Firm: Theodore K. Manley; Brian T. Deas; Edward M. Kochalski; Laura L. Drake;—Holly N. Wolf; Rachel A. Leier; Kevin Lane Williams; David F. Hanson.
Real Estate, Mortgages, Foreclosures, Loss Mitigation, Creditors Rights, Bankruptcy, Evictions, Landlord and Tenant Law, Title Service, Mortgage Servicing, Real Estate Development Closings.
See Professional Biographies, COLUMBUS, OHIO

Mann, Frederick Martin, (BV) .... '42 '68 C&L.608 B.A., J.D. Asst. Co. Pros.
Mann, Joseph B. '70 '97 C.930 B.S. L.178 J.D.
(adm. in NY; not adm. in OH) [Ⓐ Vorys,S.S.&P.]
Mann, Richard L., (BV) .... '46 '72 C&L.608 B.S., J.D. 555 S. Front St.
Mann, Richard S. .... '37 '62 C.207 B.A. L.608 J.D. 5688 Bastille Place
Mann, Robert J. '63 '88
C.473 B.A. L.608 J.D. [Ⓑ G.M.Shihab] (⊙Wash., DC; Cleve., OH)
Mann, William, (AV) .... '53 '79 C.930 B.A. L.201 J.D. [Mitchell,A.C.&B.]
Mannion, Brian L. .... '69 '97 C.473 B.S. L.117 J.D. Coun., Nationwide Insurance
Mannion, Laurel E. .... '69 '94 C.472 B.A. L.930 J.D. OH Legis. Comm.
Manougian, Nancy J., (AV) .... '48 '85 C.504 B.A. L.117 J.D. [Bailey C.]
Manring, Daniel L., (BV) .... '51 '76 C&L.608 B.A., J.D. [Manring&F.]
Manring & Farrell, (AV) .... 167 N. High Street
Mansfield, Douglas M. .... '— '94 C.813 B.A. L.150 J.D. [Jones D.]
Manson, Marcie A. .... '56 '89 C.608 B.S.N. L.117 J.D. 155 East Broad Street, 13th Floor
Manuel, James C., Jr. '58 '83
C.608 B.S. L.7 J.D. Asst. Gen. Coun., Battelle Memorial Institute
Maquire, John K. .... '55 '83 C.607 B.A. L.851 J.D. Asst. Atty. Gen.
Marbley, Algenon L., (BV) .... '54 '80 C.575 B.A. L.597 J.D. U.S. Dist. J.
Marbley, Janet Green '54 '79 C.150 B.S. L.117 J.D.
Admr., Supm. Ct. Clients Sec. Fund
Marcellino, Samuel E., Jr. .... '38 '80 C.454 B.A. L.93 J.D. P.O. Box 91081
Marchese, Joseph A. .... '29 '54 C&L.608 A.B., J.D. 973 Birchmont Rd.‡
Marchese, Thomas J. .... '60 '85 C&L.608 B.S., J.D. 1017 Dublin Rd.
Margard, Werner, III .... '57 '82 C.945 A.B. L.608 J.D. Asst. Atty. Gen., Pub. Utility Sec.
Margiotta, William T., Jr. '37 '62 C.1030 B.S.S. L.184 LL.B.
(adm. in CT; not adm. in OH) 341 S. 3rd St.
Margulies, Pamela Lee .... '50 '76 C.475 B.A. L.150 J.D. Ohio Education Assn.
Marhevka, Donna M. .... '59 '84 C&L.608 B.S., J.D. Coun., Atty. Gen. Office, Educ. Sec.
Marks, Irving B. (Buddy), (BV) '45 '71 C.608 B.S. L.161 J.D.
[Krupman,G.M.M.&W.]
Marks, Janine M., (AV) '63 '88 C.266 B.P.A. L.117 J.D.
General Counsel, Unizan Bank
Markworth, Thomas, (AV) '42 '68 C.688 B.S. L.608 J.D.
900 Michigan Avenue, Suite B
Marlier, Haimavathi Varadan .... '79 '04 C.645 B.A. L.93 J.D. [Ⓐ Porter W.M.&A.]
Marlin, James J., Jr., Law Office of '39 '68
C.8 B.S.C.E. L.608 J.D. 2066 W. Henderson, Ste. 102
Marlin, Michael S., (BV) .... '46 '73 C.679 B.S. L.608 J.D. 5150 E. Main St.
Marotta, Robert D., (AV) .... '46 '75 C.602 A.B. L.46 J.D. [Ⓑ Kegler,B.H.&R.]
Marous, James M. .... '53 '79 C.611 B.A. L.930 J.D. Asst. Atty. Gen.

Marquardt & White Co., LPA
(See Dublin)

Marsh, John F., (AV) .... '63 '90 C.363 B.A. L.880 J.D. [Porter W.M.&A.]
Marsh, Judith L. .... '— '00 C.20 B.A. L.608 J.D. [Ⓐ Vorys,S.S.&P.]
Marsh, Rick E., (AV) .... '36 '60 C&L.608 B.A., J.D. [Lane,A.&H.]
Marshall, Colleen L. .... '56 '04 C.1564 B.A. L.117 J.D. [Ⓐ Porter W.M.&A.]
Marshall, John S., (AV) .... '57 '83 C.207 B.A. L.608 J.D. 111 W. Rich St.
Marshall, Jonathan W. '44 '70 C.608 B.A. L.117 J.D.
Secy., Bd. of Comrs. on Grievances & Discipline
Marshall, Rebecca J. .... '61 '99 C.266 B.S. L.117 J.D. State Med. Bd. of OH
Martello, Suzanne Elswick .... '— '90 C.608 B.A. L.117 J.D. [Martello&M.]
Martello, Thomas F., Jr. .... '— '92 C.976 B.A. L.117 J.D. [Martello&M.]
Martello & Martello .... 3079 W. Broad Street
Martens, Franklin A. '42 '67 C.97 B.A. L.608 J.D.
Chf. Hearing Examiner, Ohio Civil Rights Comm.
Marti, Todd R., (AV) .... '58 '83 C.610 B.S. L.117 J.D. Attorney General
Martin, Andrea E. .... '56 '82 C.608 B.A. L.117 J.D. [Ⓐ Maguire&S.] ‡
Martin, David A. '63 '89 C&L.602 B.A., J.D.
Transactions Atty., Battelle Memorial Institute
Martin, Gary P. .... '70 '96 C&L.608 B.A., J.D. [Ⓐ Connor B.]
Martin, J. Steven, (AV) .... '49 '83 C&L.117 B.A., J.D. [Artz&D.]
Martin, James D. .... '60 '96 C.610 B.M. L.8 J.D. Claims Coun., Nationwide Ins. Co.
Martin, Julie C. .... '65 '91 C.608 B.S. L.309 J.D. [Scott,S.&W.]
Martin, Jutta Elisabeth .... '52 '87 C.610 B.A. L.117 J.D. Asst. Atty. Gen.
Martin, Matthew F.G. .... '63 '91 C.608 B.A. L.930 J.D. [Ⓐ Maguire&S.]
Martin, Paige A., (BV) .... '51 '78 C.914 A.B. L.930 J.D. [P.A.Martin]
Martin, Suzanne C. .... '45 '83 C.737 B.A. L.117 J.D. V.P., Mount Carmel Med. Ctr.
Martin, Paige A. Co., L.P.A., (BV) .... 77 Outerbelt St.
Martin-Jones, Melanie '55 '99
C.608 B.S. L.179 J.D. [Ⓐ Porter W.M.&A.] (See Pat. Sect.)
Martz, Michael D., (BV) .... '63 '91 C.546 B.S. L.966 J.D. [Vorys,S.S.&P.]
Marziale, Arthur J., Jr., (AV) .... '57 '85 C.25 B.A. L.117 J.D. Atty. Gen. Off.
Masek, Richard E. .... '43 '80 C.597 A.B. L.117 J.D. Assoc. Dir., Ohio Leg. Serv. Comm.
Maser, Henry, (AV) .... '30 '56 C&L.608 B.Sc., J.D. 4740 Dierker Rd.‡
Maskas, George P. .... '23 '57 C.608 B.S. L.904 LL.B. 3361 Stonehenge Ct. (Pat.)‡
Maskovyak, Joseph V. .... '54 '85 C.97 B.A. L.608 J.D. Legal Aid Soc. of Columbus
Mason, Donald L. .... '56 '89 C.532 B.A. L.117 J.D. 180 East Broad Street
Mason, Doris Deniese .... '55 '86 C.610 B.A. L.150 J.D. [D.D.Mason]
Mason, James W., (BV) .... '48 '78 C.734 B.S. L.607 J.D. State Rep.
Mason, Jennifer K. .... '71 '96 C.597 B.A. L.608 J.D. [Ⓐ Schottenstein,Z.&D.]
Mason, Jonathan A., (AV) .... '47 '73 C&L.150 B.A., J.D. [Mason,S.&M.] ⊙
Mason, Ronald L., (AV) .... '51 '78 C.737 B.A. L.201 J.D. [Mason]
Mason, Doris D., Attorney at Law .... 209 S. High St., Ste. 512-G

Mason Law Firm Co., L.P.A., (AV)
425 Metro Place North, Suite 620, 43017
Telephone: 614-734-9450 Fax: 614-734-9451
Email: rmason@maslawfirm.com URL: http://www.maslawfirm.com
Ronald L. Mason. Of Counsel: David S. Timms; Nicole Flynn.
Representing and Advising Management in Labor and Employment Law, including Wrongful Termination, Employment Discrimination, Sexual Harassment, Americans with Disabilities Act, Family and Medical Leave Act, Wage and Hour Law, NLRB cases and Collective Bargaining, Unemployment Benefits, Employee Privacy Rights, OSHA, Railroad Law.

See Professional Biographies, COLUMBUS, OHIO

Mason, Schilling & Mason Co., L.P.A., (AV)
460 East Main Street, 43215-5398 ⊙
Telephone: 513-489-0829 1-800-840-3514 Fax: 513-489-0834
Email: msm@mason-law.com URL: http://www.mason-law.com
Jonathan A. Mason.
Commercial, Creditors Rights, Bankruptcy, Collection, Banking and Financial Institution Law, Civil Litigation, Federal Consumer Law Litigation, Foreclosures, Automobile Deficiencies, Credit Cards, Medical Debts, Bad Checks, Business Loans/Commercial Debt, Vehicle and Property Repossessions, Landlord Representation/Evictions/Lease Litigation, Equipment Leasing.
Covington, Kentucky Office: Heritage International, Suite 203, P.O. Box 2158. Telephone: 513-489-0829. Fax: 513-489-0834.
Cincinnati Office: 11340 Montgomery Road, Suite 210. Telephone: 513-489-0829, 800-840-3514. Fax: 513-489-0834.
Dayton Office: 319 Liberty Tower. Telephone: 513-489-0829. Fax: 513-489-0834.
Lima Office: P.O. Box 937. Telephone: 513-489-0829. Fax: 513-489-0834.
Madison, Indiana Office: 201 East Main Street. Telephone: 513-489-0829. Fax: 513-489-0834.

See Professional Biographies, COLUMBUS, OHIO

Massey, Daniel J., (BV) . . . '43 '70 C&L.117 B.A., J.D. [Porter W.M.&A.]
Massey, Daniel M. . . . '76 '03 C.93 B.A. L.896 J.D. [Ⓐ Carpenter&L.]
Massey, Lori A. . . . '63 '90 C.604 B.A. L.607 J.D. Asst. Atty. Gen.
Massucci, Leeann M. . . . '60 '03 C.16 B.S. L.117 J.D. 560 E. Town Street
Mastrangelo, Joseph C., (BV) . . . '53 '79 C.823 B.A. L.607 J.D. Atty. Gen.
Matan, Eugene L., (AV) . . . '31 '58 C&L.608 B.A., J.D. [Matan,G.&W.]

Matan, Geer & Wright, (AV)
261 South Front Street, 43215
Telephone: 614-228-2678 Fax: 614-228-6122 URL: http://www.mgwlawoffice.com
URL: http://www.mgwlawfirm.com
Members of Firm: Eugene L. Matan; Christopher J. Geer; Scott E. Wright; Robert Dean Noble.
General Trial and Appellate Practice. Commercial, Negligence, Personal Injury, Automobile Accidents, Products Liability, Medical Malpractice, Wrongful Death, Corporation, Family, Divorce, Child Custody, Child Support, Premarital Agreements, Insurance, Wills and Probate, Criminal Defense, Driving While Intoxicated and Employment Discrimination.

See Professional Biographies, COLUMBUS, OHIO

Mathews, Alvin E., Jr., (BV) . . . '62 '87 C.473 A.B. L.607 J.D. [Lane,A.&H.]
Mathews, Denise Rena . . . '67 '93 C.4 B.A. L.201 J.D. Franklin Co. Mun. Ct.
Mathless, Steven, (BV) . . . '58 '83 C&L.608 B.A., J.D. 800 E. Broad St.
Matisziw, Kristin E. . . . '75 '04 C.502 B.A. L.117 J.D. [Ⓐ Porter W.M.&A.]
Matsa, Aristotle R. . . . '— '84 C&L.608 B.S., J.D. P.O. Box 65
Mattes, William M. . . . '63 '88 C.1102 B.S. L.607 J.D. [Dinsmore&S.]
Matthews, Christina . . . '62 '87 C.473 B.A. L.117 J.D. Indus. Comm. of OH
Matthews, Dale E., Jr. . . . '52 '78 C&L.117 B.A., J.D. OH Dept. of Rehab. & Corr.‡
Matthews, Douglas R., (BV) . . . '62 '87 C.893 B.A. L.608 J.D. [Vorys,S.S.&P.]
Mattimoe, James M. . . . '63 '89 C.893 B.S. L.608 J.D. [Porter W.M.&A.]
Mattis, Theodore P., (BV) . . . '66 '91 C&L.608 B.A., J.D. [Vorys,S.S.&P.]
Matto, Edward A., (AV) . . . '41 '66 C&L.608 B.S., J.D. [Bricker&E.]
Matuska, Michael C., (BV) . . . '46 '72 C.201 B.A. L.607 J.D. Asst. City Atty.
Mauger, Jud R. . . . '56 '94 C.608 B.S. L.117 J.D. [Moore&Y.]
Maurer, James, (BV) . . . '34 '64 C.610 B.A. L.608 J.D. 199 S. Fifth St.
Maurer, John W. . . . '41 '79 C.8 B.S.Acctg. L.7 J.D. 2744 Kensington Pl.
Mauro, James C. . . . '47 '83 C.608 B.A. L.117 J.D. 3095 Scioto Trace
Maxfield, Jane Uhlman, (BV) . . . '51 '76 C.97 B.A. L.117 J.D. 825 S. Front St.
Maxfield, Michael L. . . . '59 '84 C.608 B.S. L.851 J.D. [Bricker&M.]
Maxfield, Sheryl L., (AV) . . . '59 '84 C.97 B.S. L.851 J.D. Asst. Atty. Gen.
Maxton, Bonnie L., (BV) . . . '53 '85 C.967 B.A. L.608 J.D. Asst. Pros. Atty.
Maxwell, James, Jr. . . . '25 '51 C.980 L.607 LL.B. 2101 S. Hamilton Rd.
Maxwell, Mark D. . . . '70 '96 C.608 B.A. L.880 J.D. Coun., Nationwide Insurance
May, Randall W. . . . '64 '90 C.207 B.A. L.880 J.D. Sr. Coun., Nationwide Insurance
Mayer, Donna C. . . . '— '80 C.1142 B.A. L.117 J.D. Legal Aid Soc. of Columbus
Mayle, Virginia K. . . . '42 '86 C.610 B.S.Ed. L.608 J.D. [Ⓐ Barkan&B.]
Maynard, Jeffery S. . . . '68 '01 C.608 B.S. L.117 J.D. [Ⓐ Brenner,B.G.&M.]
Maynard, William Dwayne . . . '58 '86 C.103 B.A. L.608 J.D. 375 South High Street
Mayton, Keith A., (AV) '58 '87
C.608 B.F.A. L.117 J.D. U.S. Courthouse, 85 Marconi Building

Mazanec, Raskin & Ryder Co., L.P.A., (AV)
Suite 400, 250 Civic Center Drive, 43215 ⊙
Telephone: 614-228-5931 Fax: 614-228-5934
Email: mrrlaw.com URL: http://www.mrrlaw.com
Robert H. Stoffers; David K. Frank;—Carl E. Cormany; Michael S. Loughry.
Civil Litigation, Insurance Defense, Construction Law, Negligence, Professional Negligence, Municipal Law, Civil Rights, Real Estate, Business Law, Probate, Estate Planning.
Cleveland, Ohio Office: 100 Franklin's Row, 34305 Solon Road 44139. Telephone: 440-248-7906. Fax: 440-248-8861.

See Professional Biographies, COLUMBUS, OHIO

Mazza, John P., (BV) . . . '52 '77 C&L.602 B.A., J.D. [Harris&M.]
Mazzei, Gina E., (BVⓉ) '66 '92 C&L.923 B.S., J.D.
(adm. in WV; not adm. in OH) Coun.-Litigation, Amer. Elec. Power Service Corp.
McAdams, Robert W., Jr., (BV) . . . '54 '87 C.201 B.S. L.1065 J.D. [Taft,S.&H.]
McAfee, Melinda R. . . . '70 '95 C.611 B.A. L.276 J.D. [Vorys,S.S.&P.]
McAlister, Lisa G. '— '02 C.240 B.A. L.608 J.D.
[Ⓐ McNees W.&N.] (⊙Harrisburg, PA)
McAndrew, Robert '54 '79 C.93 B.A. L.818 J.D.
(adm. in MA; not adm. in OH) The Limited, Inc.
Mc Anespie, Molly Jo . . . '73 '99 C.610 B.A. L.117 J.D. OH Pub. Def.
McBeath, Gretchen A., (AV) . . . '44 '82 C.608 B.A. L.117 J.D. [Bricker&E.]
McCaffrey, Patrick, Jr. . . . '60 '85 C.901 B.A. L.846 J.D. [Brenner,B.G.&M.]
McCandlish, Joseph M. . . . '71 '01 C.608 B.S. L.117 J.D. [Ⓐ Weltman,W.&R.]
McCane, Lisa A. . . . '69 '99 C.608 B.A. L.117 J.D. Chase Manhattan Mtge. Corp.
McCann, Dennis J., (BV) '54 '81
C.1115 B.S. L.608 J.D. Sr. Atty., Battelle Memorial Institute
McCann, George R., (AV) . . . '48 '73 C&L.608 B.A., J.D. [Fry,W.&M.]
McCann, Jack Maynard . . . '20 '48 C.473 A.B. L.150 LL.B. Asst. Atty. Gen.

McCarroll, John J.
(See Cleveland)

McCart, Linda Fay '51 '88 L.615 J.D.
(adm. in OK; not adm. in OH) Off. of Gov.
McCarthy, Deborah Beckerich '66 '93
C.608 B.A. L.930 J.D. Pub. Employees Retirement System of Ohio
McCarthy, Timothy P. . . . '47 '73 C&L.117 B.A., J.D. 369 S. High St.
McCarty, David M., (BV) . . . '63 '92 C.178 B.A. L.608 J.D. [Kegler,B.H.&R.]
McClaren, Robert J. . . . '64 '90 C.631 B.A. L.608 J.D. Pros. Atty.
McClatchey, Larry J., (AV) . . . '51 '75 C.347 B.A. L.1119 J.D. [Kegler,B.H.&R.]
McClatchey, Ted P. . . . '52 '94 C.608 B.S. L.117 J.D. [Ⓐ Maguire&S.]
McClellan, Edward T., (AV) . . . '47 '75 C.611 B.A. L.608 J.D. [Ⓒ Harris,M.B.&C.]
McClintock, Steven D. . . . '60 '87 C&L.893 B.A., J.D. 580 Bradley St.
McCloskey, Christopher L. . . . '72 '00 C.608 B.S.L.E. L.179 J.D. [Ⓐ Bricker&E.]
McCloud, Bradley Lawrence '61 '88 C.608 B.A. L.117 J.D.
Ohio Off. of Crim. Jus. Servs.
McClure, Anthony R. . . . '73 '03 C.473 B.S. L.146 J.D. [Ⓐ Porter W.M.&A.]
McClure, David L. . . . '39 '64 C&L.608 B.S., J.D. [Ⓒ J.L.Alden]
McClure, Lisa M. . . . '70 '01 C.611 B.A. L.117 J.D. [Ⓐ Means,B.B.&B.]
McCollum, James E. '47 '87
C.980 B.S.Ed. L.8 J.D. Exec. Dir., Inter-University Coucil of OH
McConnaughey, George C., (AV) . . . '25 '51 C.207 A.B. L.608 J.D. 10 W. Broad St.‡
McCord, Touré . . . '71 '96 C&L.851 B.A., J.D. [McCord&A.]
McCord & Akamine, L.L.P. . . . 844 South Front Street
McCormick, Jack E., (BV) . . . '43 '69 C.8 B.A. L.7 J.D. 500 City Park Ave.
McCormick, Tristan A. . . . '70 '95 C.608 B.A. L.117 J.D. [Gamble H.J.]
McCoy, Steven J., (AV) . . . '48 '73 C.608 B.A. L.1066 J.D. 1225 Dublin Rd.
McCoy, Watson A. . . . '22 '49 C&L.923 B.S., LL.B. 753 Euclaire Avenue
McCreary, Charles H., III, (AV) . . . '53 '78 C.228 A.B. L.880 J.D. [Bricker&E.]
McCreary, David M. . . . '25 '58 C&L.980 J.D. 5293 Butternut Ct., W.
McCue, George R., III, (AV) . . . '56 '81 C&L.608 B.S.B.A., J.D. [Crabbe,B.&J.]
McCutchan, Gordon E., (AV) '35 '59 C&L.188 A.B., LL.B.
Executive VP-Law & Corporate Services, Nationwide Insurance Enterprise
McCutchan, R. Lindsey . . . '65 '97 C.207 B.A. L.117 J.D. Coun., Nationwide Insurance
McDaniel, Jennifer M. . . . '77 '02 C.117 B.A. L.608 J.D. [Ⓐ Schottenstein,Z.&D.]
McDermott, Kevin R., (AV) . . . '52 '77 C.473 A.B. L.608 J.D. [Schottenstein,Z.&D.]
McDonald, John C., (AV) . . . '36 '61 C.207 A.B. L.608 J.D. [Schottenstein,Z.&D.]
McDonald, William, (BV) . . . '47 '75 C.494 B.A. L.851 J.D. Asst. Atty. Gen.

McDonald Hopkins Co., LPA, (AV)
41 South High Street, Suite 3650, 43215 ⊙
Telephone: 614-458-0025 Fax: 614-458-0028
Email: info@mcdonaldhopkins.com URL: http://www.mcdonaldhopkins.com
Richard C. Farrin; Thomas M. Zaino;—Stephen K. Hall; Vincent J. Nardone.
General Civil Trial and Appellate Practice. Corporate, Taxation, Pension and Profit Sharing, Professional Corporations, Insurance, Securities, Estate Planning, Probate, Real Estate, Family Law, Banking, Partnership, Employment and Labor Relations, Equipment Leasing, Bankruptcy, Communications, Computer Law, Health and Hospital Law.
West Palm Beach, Florida Office: McDonald Hopkins Co., PA, One Clearlake Centre, 250 Australian Avenue S., Suite 700, 33401-5007. Telephone: 561-472-7510. Fax: 561-472-2975.
Dennis, Massachusetts Office: 956 Main Street, 02638. Telephone: 508-385-5227. Fax: 508-385-4355.
Cleveland, Ohio Office: 600 Superior Avenue, E., Suite 2100, 44114-2653. Telephone: 216-348-5400. Telecopier: 216-348-5474.

See Professional Biographies, COLUMBUS, OHIO

McDonough, Kenneth E. '52 '78 C.679 B.S. L.347 J.D.
Asst. Gen. Coun.-Real Estate, Amer. Elec. Power Serv. Corp.
McElwee, Donald L. '50 '75 C.608 B.A. L.659 J.D.
Ref., Ohio Unployment Comp. Bd. of Review
McFadden, Mary Jane, (AV) . . . '50 '74 C.608 B.A. L.893 J.D. [McFadden W.&S.]

McFadden Winner and Savage, (AV)
175 South Third Street, Suite 210, 43215-5134
Telephone: 614-221-8868 Telecopier: 614-221-3985
Members of Firm: Mary Jane McFadden; Joseph C. Winner; James S. Savage, III. Associate: Douglas Jay Segerman.
Business and Commercial Litigation, Bankruptcy, Employment, Discrimination, Tax and White Collar Criminal Defense, Appellate Advocacy, Complex Personal Injury.
Representative Clients: Accel International, Inc. (insurance holding company); Cummins Engine Company; Cryobiology, Inc.; John Deere Company; Deere Credit Services, Inc.; Dick Masheter Ford, Inc.; DMF of Ohio, Inc.; The Ohio Dental Hygienist Association, Inc.; McDaniel's Construction Corp.; McGinnis & Associates, Inc.

See Professional Biographies, COLUMBUS, OHIO

McGaffick, Timothy D. . . . '46 '88 C.266 B.S. L.608 J.D. 85 Bywood Lane
McGarry, Kathleen A. . . . '56 '87 C.183 B.A. L.608 J.D. Asst. State Pub. Def.
McGee, Jonathon L. . . . '64 '89 C.607 B.A. L.608 J.D. 30 West Spring Street, 30th Floor
McGinley, J. Michael . . . '40 '71 C.608 B.S. L.117 J.D. 755 S. High St.
McGinn, Barbara A. . . . '62 '97 C.645 B.A. L.188 J.D. Asst. Atty. Gen.
McGinnis, Lori A. . . . '62 '92 C.49 B.S. L.607 J.D. 8 E. Long Street, 11th Floor
McGinty, Jas. L. . . . '21 '53 C.608 B.S. L.266 J.D. 4747 Widner Ct.
McGlone, Sean M. . . . '74 '02 C.967 B.A. L.608 J.D. [Ⓐ Bricker&E.]
McGoldrick, Joanne . . . '61 '86 C.705 N.J. L.1292 J.D. Nationwide Mutual Ins. Co.
McGough, John T. . . . '54 '81 C.381 B.B.A. L.190 J.D. McGough & Assocs., Inc.
McGovern, James M. . . . '66 '93 C.473 B.A. L.608 J.D. [Ⓐ Hammond,S.&W.]
McGranor, Timothy B. . . . '75 '00 C&L.608 B.A., J.D. [Ⓐ Bailey C.]
McGrath, Barbara Gates . . . '51 '79 C.608 B.S. L.117 J.D. Exec. Dir., Civil Serv. Comm.
McGrath, Keith, (BV) . . . '66 '92 C.437 B.A. L.608 J.D. Asst. City Pros.
McGrath, Michelle Davis . . . '73 '99 C.851 B.B.A. L.608 J.D. 30 Spruce Street, 3rd Floor
McGrath, Patrick M. . . . '42 '68 C&L.608 B.A., J.D. Com. Pleas J.
McGrath, Thomas R., (AV) . . . '43 '74 C.608 B.A. L.117 J.D. [McGrath&B.]
McGrath, Timothy J., (AV) . . . '43 '69 C&L.608 B.S., J.D. [Strip,H.L.M.&T.]

McGrath & Breitfeller, LLP, (AV)
140 East Town Street, Suite 1070, 43215
Telephone: 614-464-1201 Facsimile: 614-464-0572
Email: trmcgrath@attymail.com
Thomas R. McGrath; Ralph E. Breitfeller.
Real Estate Title Insurance, Real Estate Litigation, Federal State and Local Taxation, Tort Liability, Business Litigation, Corporate Litigation, Health Care Law, Pharmacy Law, Antitrust, Contract Litigation, Employment Law, Creditors Rights, Probate Administration and Estate Planning. Civil Litigation and Civil Appeals. General Practice in State and Federal Courts.

See Professional Biographies, COLUMBUS, OHIO

McGraw, Christopher E. . . . '65 '93 C.611 B.A. L.117 J.D. Bank One Invest. Advsrs. Corp.
McGuire, James W., (AV) '34 '60
C.611 B.A. L.608 J.D. 110 Northwood Blvd., Worthington
McGuire, Therese A. . . . '72 '99 C.473 B.A. L.608 J.D. 65 E. State St., Capitol Sq.
McGuire, Traci A. . . . '72 '99 C.473 B.A. L.608 J.D. [Ⓐ Kegler,B.H.&R.]
McHenry, Jerry L. . . . '52 '76 C.608 B.A. L.117 J.D. 8 East Long Street, 11th Floor
McIntosh, Sandra R. . . . '78 '04 C.473 B.S. L.117 J.D. [Ⓐ Freund,F.&A.]
McInturff, Judith M., (AV) '52 '80
C.473 B.S.Ed. L.117 J.D. 50 W. Broad Street, Suite 2600
McIntyre, Teresa C. '61 '87 C.473 B.A. L.150 J.D.
Sr. Coun.-Litig., Amer. Elect. Power Serv. Corp.
McIver, Kevin M. . . . '55 '80 C.973 A.B. L.734 J.D. Asst. Atty. Gen.

McKee, Susan Ellen .... '55 '84 C&L.201 B.S., J.D. Reg. Coun., Def. Logistics Agcy.
McKenna, Alvin J., (AV) .... '43 '66 C&L.116 A.B., J.D. [Porter W.M.&A.]
McKenzie, Myra L. .... '77 '02 C.811 B.A. L.602 J.D. [A Porter W.M.&A.]
McKenzie, W. Locke, Jr., (BV) ..... '50 '75 C.674 A.B. L.608 J.D. 380 South Fifth Street
McKinlay, Amy M. .... '71 '96 C.631 B.A. L.117 J.D. [A R.C.Harbold&Assoc.]
McKinley, Leroy T. .... '24 '54 C.608 B.S. L.266 J.D. 1505 Noe Bixby Rd.

McKinney, Charles A., Law Offices of, (BV) '55 '80 C.943 B.A. L.602 J.D.
141 East Town Street, Suite 102, 43215 ⊙
Telephone: 614-460-9000 Fax: 614-460-9001
Email: camlaw@woh.rr.com
Corporate Law, Business Planning, Contracts, Insurance, Lawsuits, Labor (Management) Law, Personal Injury Law, Automobile Accidents, Dog Bites, Sexual Abuse, Slip and Fall, Trusts and Estates, Estate Planning Law, Guardianship, Wills and Probate, Wrongful Death, Civil Litigation, Buying or Selling a Business, Formation, Closely Held Business, Limited Liability Companies, Partnerships, Small Business, Employment Law, Disability Accommodations, Discrimination, Sexual Harassment, Wrongful Termination.
Dayton, Ohio Office: 20 West Monument Avenue, 45402. Telephone: 937-461-9000. Fax: 937-461-9640.
See Professional Biographies, COLUMBUS, OHIO

McKirahan, Jay, (BV) .... '47 '72 C.532 B.A. L.477 J.D. 366 E. Broad St.
McLane, Michael J., (BV) ...... '62 '87 C.608 B.S. L.117 J.D. 140 E. Town St., Ste. 1015
McLaughlin, Kenneth C. .... '32 '66 C.363 B.S.S. L.1003 J.D. Atty. Gen.
McLaughlin, Kenneth L. .... '51 '78 C&L.608 B.S., J.D. Asst. Atty. Gen.
McLaughlin, Patricia A. '73 '99 C.473 B.S. L.851 J.D.
Coun.-Trans., American Elect. Power Serv. Corp.
McLaughlin, Peter F. '63 '93 C.178 B.A. L.276 J.D.
(adm. in NY; not adm. in OH) [A Mallory&T.]
McLaughlin, Tara L. .....'75 '00 C.473 B.A. L.851 J.D. 373 South High Street, 12th Floor
McLaughlin, Tracy A. '72 '97 C.473 B.S. L.117 J.D.
Credit Risk Management, American Electric Power
McLennan, Bruce A. .... '46 '73 C&L.209 B.S., J.D. 30 East Broad St., 24th Floor
McLeod, Mark A., (BV) .... '59 '87 C.610 B.A. L.117 J.D. [McLeod]
McLeod Law Office, (BV) .... 471 East Broad Street, 19th Floor

McLeskey, Waymon B., II, (BV) '53 '81 C.976 B.A. L.607 J.D.
Five East Long Street, Suite 405, 43215
Telephone: 614-232-9132 Fax: 614-232-9135
Email: mcleskeylaw@aol.com URL: http://www.mcleskeylaw.com
Creditor Bankruptcy, Foreclosures, Workouts, Collections, Replevins, Creditor Rights, Commercial Litigation.
See Professional Biographies, COLUMBUS, OHIO

McLoughlin, William J., (AV) .... '61 '86 C.631 B.A. L.851 J.D. 33 E. Schrock Rd.
McManus, John K., (BV) .... '59 '86 C.930 B.A. L.161 J.D. Asst. Atty. Gen.
McManus, Pamela Harrison .... '52 '77 C.1260 B.A. L.309 J.D. 1213 Glenn Ave.‡
Mcnair, Darren .... '76 '02 C.473 B.S. L.117 J.D. 88 W. Mound St.
McNally, John A. '69 '96 C.276 B.S.F.S. L.1003 J.D.
State Off. of Collective Bargaining
McNamara, Dennis W., (AV) ...... '50 '76 C&L.608 B.A., J.D. 88 E. Broad St., Ste. 1350
McNamara, Donald S., (AV) .... '11 '34 C.473 L.608 LL.B. 88 E. Broad St.‡
McNamara, Keith, (AV) .... '28 '53 C.31 B.A. L.608 J.D. [C McNamara&M.]

McNamara and McNamara, L.L.P., (AV) BB
Suite 1250, 88 East Broad Street, 43215-3558
Telephone: 614-228-6131 FAX: 614-228-6126
Email: mcnamaralaw@mcnamaralaw.us
Members of Firm: J. Paul McNamara (1908-1994); William H. Woods; Dennis D. Liston; Jonathan M. Bryan. Of Counsel: Keith McNamara; John L. Miller; Scott F. Sturges; Michael R. Szolosi, Sr. General Civil and Trial Practice. Fidelity and Surety, Insurance, Negligence, Products Liability, Construction, Administrative, Appellate Practice, Business Law, Probate and Real Estate Law.
See Professional Biographies, COLUMBUS, OHIO

McNamee, Thomas .... '55 '79 C&L.608 B.A., J.D. Asst. Atty. Gen.
McNeal, Earl Darren .... '60 '92 C.45 B.S.B.A. L.608 J.D. 330 S. High St.
McNeal, Kathleen Keller ....'48 '82 C.608 M.A. L.117 J.D. 1127 Cloverknoll Ct.
McNealey, J. Jeffrey, (AV) .... '44 '69 C.188 B.A. L.608 J.D. [Porter W.M.&A.]

McNees Wallace & Nurick LLC, (AV) BB
Fifth Third Center, 17th Floor, 21 East State Street, 43215-4228 ⊙
Telephone: 614-469-8000 Fax: 614-469-4653
Email: info@mwn.com URL: http://www.mwn.com
Member of the Firm: Samuel C. Randazzo (Resident). Resident Of Counsel: Thomas L. Froehle; Gretchen J. Hummel. Associates: Lisa G. McAlister; Daniel J. Neilsen (Resident).
Energy Law, Communications Law, Utility Law, Government Relations.
Harrisburg, Pennsylvania Office: 100 Pine Street, P.O. Box 1166, 17108. Telephone: 717-232-8000. Fax: 717-237-5300.
Washington, D.C. Office: Suite 401, 777 North Capitol, N.E., 20002. Telephone: 202-898-5700. Fax: 202-898-0688.
Hazleton, Pennsylvania Office: 1 South Church Street, Suite 302, 18201. Telephone: 570-455-8300. Fax: 570-455-8390.
State College, Pennsylvania Office: 1600 University Drive, 16801. Telephone: 814-867-8500. Fax: 814-867-6200.
Lancaster, Pennsylvania Office: 180 Good Drive, 17603. Telephone: 717-291-1177. Fax: 717-291-2186.
See Professional Biographies, COLUMBUS, OHIO

McNeil, Barbara A. .... '48 '80 C.608 B.S.S.W. L.117 J.D. [A Taft,S.&H.]
McNellie, Elizabeth A., (BV) .... '64 '90 C.473 Ph.B. L.178 J.D. [Baker&H.]
McNinch, Deborah L. .... '66 '91 C&L.608 B.A., J.D. [A Joseph&J.]
McNitt, Robert M., (BV) .... '57 '82 C.813 B.A. L.608 J.D. 492 City Park Avenue
McPhillips, Michael Cannon .... '60 '95 C.823 B.S. L.179 J.D. Mag.
McQuade, Shannon Leigh .... '71 '96 C.62 B.A. L.851 J.D. Dept. of Agric.
McQuain, Jill Marie Snitcher '70 '99
C.608 B.S. L.179 J.D. Asst. Bar Coun., Columbus Bar Association
McQuown, Richard C., (AV) .... '58 '86 C.608 B.A. L.117 J.D. [Porter W.M.&A.]
McTigue, Donald J., (AV) .... '54 '79 C.980 B.A. L.930 J.D. [McTigue L.]
McTigue Law, (AV) .... 3886 N. High St.
Meagher, Stephen W. ....'52 '82 C&L.608 B.A., J.D. Chief Coun., State Dept. of Nat.Res.
Means, Johnston H., (AV) .... '28 '58 C&L.608 B.S.B.A., J.D. 42 E. Gay St.‡

Means, Bichimer, Burkholder & Baker Co., L.P.A., (AV)
2006 Kenny Road, 43221-3502
Telephone: 614-485-2010 Fax: 614-485-2019
Email: mail@mbbblaw.com
Robert G. Stafford; Craig D. Leister; Robert M. Morrow; Richard W. Ross; Dennis J. Morrison;—Nicole M. Donovsky; Lisa M. McClure; Elizabeth L. Miller; John F. Kirtley II.
Antitrust, Estate Planning, Probate, Trust, Pension and Profit Sharing, Taxation, Corporate, Creditor's Rights, Insurance, Real Estate, Construction Litigation, Labor, Employment, Civil Rights, and School Law.
See Professional Biographies, COLUMBUS, OHIO

Mechling, William C. '56 '83 C.608 B.A. L.117 J.D.
Sr. V.P. & Corp. Secy., Central Benefits Mut. Ins. Co.
Meckler, Marcia Lipson .... '41 '75 C.608 B.A. L.117 J.D. 2369 East Main Street
Meeks, James E. '38 '63
C.604 A.B. L.178 LL.B. Prof. of Law, Ohio State Univ., Col. of Law

Meeks, R. William, (AV) '47 '75 C.150 B.S. L.117 J.D.
511 South High Street, 43215
Telephone: 614-228-4141 Fax: 614-228-0899
Criminal Trial and Appellate Practice in all State and Federal Courts.
Reference: Bank One of Columbus, Ohio.
See Professional Biographies, COLUMBUS, OHIO

Meena, James W. .... '55 '81 C&L.608 B.S., J.D. 2310 Indianola Ave.
Mehra, Vinita .... '76 '95 L.999 L.L.B. [A Kegler,B.H.&R.]
Meier, Harold C., (AV) .... '28 '56 C&L.608 B.A., J.D. [Thompson,M.&D.]
Meier, William A., (BV) .... '46 '78 C.608 B.A. L.117 J.D. [Thompson,M.&D.]

Meister, Frederick, (AV) '46 '80 C&L.608 B.S., J.D.
150 East Mound Street, Suite 200, 43215-5429
Telephone: 614-221-1644 Fax: 614-221-1696
Email: fmeister2@aol.com URL: http://www.lawyers.com/meisterlaw
(Certified Specialist, Family Relations Law, Ohio State Bar Association).
Family Law, Divorce, Dissolution, Legal Separation, Child Custody, Child Support, Visitation, Family Mediation, Matrimonial Arbitration, Premarital Agreements.
See Professional Biographies, COLUMBUS, OHIO

Meizlish, Jodie Kay, (BV) .... '55 '87 C.381 B.A. L.608 J.D. [Krupman,G.M.M.&W.]
Meizlish, Sanford A., (BV) .... '54 '79 C.502 B.J. L.117 J.D. [Barkan&N.]
Meldrum, Terri W. .... '68 '94 Asst. Gen. Coun., Ohio Health Corp.
Melko, Mark C. .... '72 '98 C.473 B.A. L.117 J.D. [A Wiles,B.B.&B.]
Melle, James E., (BV) .... '— '71 C.363 B.S.B.A. L.1003 J.D. [Buckley K.]
Melliere, Michael J. .... '67 '91 C.697 B.S. L.477 J.D. [Peck,S.&W.]
Mellon, Howard J. .... '52 '77 C.1040 B.B.A. L.608 J.D. 4823 Wynwood Court
Meloy, Thomas C. '40 '70 C.381 B.A. L.930 J.D.
Chief Claims Coun., Nationwide Insurance Co.
Melton, Katherine J. .... '56 '86 C&L.150 B.A., J.D. Ohio Department of Insurance
Melvin, John B. '50 '75 C.216 B.A. L.117 J.D.
V.P., Dir. of Claims, State Auto. Mut. Ins. Co.
Melvin, S. Noel, (AV) .... '28 '51 C.951 A.B. L.477 J.D. 65 East State Street‡
Melvin, William J., (AV) .... '24 '58 C.608 B.S. L.266 LL.B. 199 S. Fifth St.
Mendel, Linda R. .... '56 '81 C.381 B.B.A. L.608 J.D. [C Vorys,S.S.&P.]
Menkedick, Mary G. .... '71 '99 C&L.608 B.S., J.D. [A Carlile P.&M.]
Mentel, Sean A. .... '73 '04 C.475 B.A. L.117 J.D. [A Bricker&E.]
Mergenthaler, Scott R., (BV) .... '56 '81 C.8 B.A. L.1003 J.D. [Carlile P.&M.]
Merkel, Richard Lee .... '47 '73 C&L.608 B.S., J.D. 77 South High St., Riffe Ctr.
Merkle, H. Tim, (AV) .... '52 '79 C.323 B.A. L.117 J.D. [Winters&M.]
Merkle, Mark K., Jr., (AV) .... '44 '70 C.884 B.A. L.608 J.D. [Porter W.M.&A.]
Merrill, Frank L., (BV) .... '58 '87 C.197 B.A. L.150 J.D. [Bricker&E.]
Merrill, Tracy L. .... '75 '01 C.1365 B.A. L.276 J.D. [A Porter W.M.&A.]
Merry, Tony C., (AV) .... '51 '89 C.785 B.A. L.309 J.D. [Volkema,T.M.B.S.&M.]
Mertz, Mary C. .... '65 '02 C.30 B.A. L.608 J.D. [A Squire,S.&D.]
Merullo, Victor Davis, (AV) .... '42 '73 C.608 B.S. L.117 J.D. [Merullo,R.&S.]
Merullo, Reister & Swinford Co., L.P.A., (AV) .... 772 S. Front St.
Merwin, Earl N., (AV) .... '23 '51 C.532 B.A. L.608 J.D. 1085 Fishinger Rd.
Mescher, Richard M. '60 '93
C.608 B.S.M.E. L.201 J.D. [Porter W.M.&A.] (See Pat. Sect.)
Messenger, Walter W., Jr. ...... '72 '01 C.737 B.A. L.117 J.D. 100 S. Fourth St., Ste. 300
Metcalf, J. Seth .... '79 '04 C.608 B.A. L.188 J.D. [A Squire,S.&D.] (⊙Cleveland)
Metz, Douglas O., (BV) .... '58 '84 C.473 B.A. L.117 J.D. Motorists Mutual
Metz, John H. '47 '81 C.1030 A.B. L.1137 J.D.
(adm. in IN; not adm. in OH) [Valleau&M.]
Metz, Roy E., (AV) .... '22 '48 C.631 B.A. L.608 J.D. 33 E. Schrock Rd.‡
Metzger, Thomas M. L., (AV) .... '66 '92 C.910 B.A. L.665 J.D. [Littler M.]
Metzler, Jonathan Lewis .... '68 '94 C.473 B.A. L.851 J.D. Atty. Gen. Off.
Meyer, Carl J., (BV) .... '50 '78 C.608 B.A. L.201 J.D. [C.J.Meyer]
Meyer, David P., (AV) .... '70 '95 C.610 B.B.A. L.117 J.D. [D.P.Meyer]
Meyer, H. Theodore, (AV) .... '35 '62 C.976 B.E. L.188 J.D. 1900 Huntington Ctr.
Meyer, Martha Payne .... '54 '79 C&L.150 B.A., J.D. Coun., State Auditor
Meyer, Richard F., (AV) .... '55 '80 C.434 B.A. L.117 J.D. [Browning&M.]
Meyer, Robert A., Jr., (AV) .... '53 '78 C.347 B.S. L.608 J.D. [Porter W.M.&A.]
Meyer, Carl J., Company, LPA, (BV) .... 1243 South High St.

Meyer, David P., Co., L.P.A., (AV)
401 North Front Street, Suite 350, 43215
Telephone: 614-224-6000 Toll Free: 866-827-6537 Fax: 614-224-6066
Email: dmeyer@dmlaws.com URL: http://www.dmlaws.com
David P. Meyer;—Patrick G. Warner; Marnie C. Lambert.
Securities Consumer Arbitration, Securities Arbitration, Stockbroker Fraud and Misconduct, Securities Class Actions, Business Torts, Consumer Class Action.
See Professional Biographies, COLUMBUS, OHIO

Michael, Barbara J. .... '36 '91 C.477 B.S. L.179 J.D. [C Robins,P.B.H.&S.]
Michael, Jay E., Attorney at Law, (AV) .... '58 '85 C.920 B.S. L.117 J.D. 729 S. Front St.
Michael, William J. .... '73 '99 C&L.608 B.A., J.D. [A Calfee,H.&G.]
Miele, Philip R., (CV) .... '57 '84 C.97 B.A. L.607 J.D. [A Schottenstein,Z.&D.]
Mifsud, Charles Anthony, II .... '73 '99 C&L.608 B.S.B.A., J.D. [Mifsud,C.]
Mifsud, Charles, LLC, Law Offices of .... 326 S. High St. Annex, Ste. 201C
Mihaly, Peter H. .... '65 '92 C.381 B.S. L.608 J.D. 30 W. Spring St.
Mikes, Randall W., (BV) .... '63 '90 C.385 B.A. L.608 J.D. [C Kegler,B.H.&R.]
Miko, Matthew David .... '71 '97 C&L.608 B.A., J.D. Chf. Legal Coun.
Milenkovski, Katerina Eftimoff .... '67 '94 C.608 B.S. L.117 J.D. [Porter W.M.&A.]
Miles, James R. .... '37 '61 C&L.608 B.A., J.D. Mas. Comr., Supm. Ct.
Millard, William L. .... '31 '58 C.31 B.A. L.893 J.D. 1556 Trentwood Rd.
Miller, Allan L. '32 '56 C.197 A.B. L.309 LL.B.
(adm. in MA; not adm. in OH) 180 E. Broad St.‡
Miller, Alyson B. .... '— '04 C.473 B.A. L.446 J.D. [A Grossman]
Miller, Andrew D. M. .... '75 '02 C.610 B.B.A. L.608 J.D. [A Squire,S.&D.]
Miller, Anthony J. .... '71 '00 C.608 B.S. L.117 J.D. [A Hahn L.&P.]
Miller, Bonnie Weaver .... '59 '84 C&L.608 B.A., J.D. 1309 Carron Dr
Miller, Brett L., (AV) .... '56 '81 C.473 A.B. L.608 J.D. [Buckingham,D.&B.]
Miller, Brian G. .... '69 '94 C&L.608 B.S., J.D. [B.G.Miller]
Miller, C. William, II .... '63 '93 C.608 B.A. L.117 J.D. 199 S. 5th St.
Miller, Camille A. .... '79 '04 C.788 B.A. L.608 J.D. [A Kegler,B.H.&R.]
Miller, Carolyn S. .... '59 '88 C.631 B.A. L.117 J.D. Dept. of Taxation
Miller, Charles Michael .... '64 '89 C.347 B.S. L.608 J.D. Asst. Atty. Gen.
Miller, Christopher L. .... '67 '94 C.473 B.A. L.117 J.D. [Schottenstein,Z.&D.]
Miller, Courtney J. .... '66 '99 C.970 B.A. L.179 J.D. [A Calfee,H.&G.]
Miller, D. Michael, (AV) '47 '75 C.610 B.A. L.608 J.D.
Dep. Gen. Coun.-Litig. & Reg., Amer. Elec. Power Serv. Corp.
Miller, Darrell A. H. .... '— '03 C.992 B.A. L.309 J.D. [A Vorys,S.S.&P.]
Miller, Dixon F., (AV) '48 '76 C.918 B.A. L.930 J.D.
[Porter W.M.&A.] (⊙Naples, FL)

Miller, Donald R. . . . . '46 '71 C.216 A.B. L.184 J.D. Nationwide Ins.
Miller, Elizabeth L. . . . . '75 '01 C.294 B.A. L.1017 J.D [Ⓐ Means,B.B.&B.]
Miller, Frank C. . . . . '74 '99 C.473 B.A. L.930 J.D. [Ⓐ Baker&H.]
Miller, James William, Jr. . . . . . '52 '78 C.651 B.A. L.179 J.D. 1980 W. Broad St.
Miller, Jane L. '47 '76 C.608 B.S. L.117 J.D.
Exec. Dir., Higher Educ. Council of Columbus
Miller, Jeffrey Allen . . . .'— '00 C&L.608 B.S., J.D. [Ⓐ Vorys,S.S.&P.]
Miller, Jeffrey D. '68 '96 C.473 B.S. L.117 J.D.
Office of Gen. Counsel, Nationwide Insurance
Miller, John L., (AV) . . . .'34 '63 C.309 A.B. L.608 J.D. [Ⓒ McNamara&M.]
Miller, Joseph R. . . . .'72 '97 C.608 B.A. L.309 J.D. [Vorys,S.S.&P.]
Miller, Linda J., (BV) . . . .'50 '86 C.610 B.S. L.608 J.D. 35 E. Livingston Ave.
Miller, Mark J. . . . .'78 '03 C.532 B.A. L.117 J.D. 555 City Park Ave.
Miller, Mark S., (BV) . . . .'55 '81 C.347 B.S. L.608 J.D. 800 E. Broad St.
Miller, Martha Gaumer '51 '81 C.608 B.S. L.117 J.D.
V.P., Invest. & Tr. Planning, Natl. City Corp.
Miller, Mary J. . . . .'60 '86 C&L.117 B.A., J.D. 4590 East Broad Street
Miller, Matthew J. . . . .'78 '03 C.49 B.A. L.179 J.D. [Ⓐ Squire,S.&D.]
Miller, Maurice A. . . . .'05 '30 C&L.266 J.D. 1801 Riverside Dr.‡
Miller, Michael Lee . . . .'53 '79 C.1064 B.A. L.608 J.D. 373 S. High St., 22nd Fl.
Miller, Michael S., (AV) . . . . . .'58 '84 C.150 B.A. L.608 J.D. [Volkema,T.M.B.S.&M.]
Miller, Nodine . . . . '38 '76 C.473 B.A. L.117 J.D. Com. Pleas J.
Miller, Paul William . . . .'32 '70 C.608 B.S. L.117 J.D. 906 E. Broad St.‡
Miller, Richard L., (AV) . . . . . .'21 '46 C.608 A.B. L.966 LL.B. 65 S. Columbia Ave.‡
Miller, Richard T. . . . .'53 '91 C.174 B.A. L.208 J.D. [Ⓐ Vorys,S.S.&P.]
Miller, Robert H. . . . . '— '03 C.880 B.A. L.309 J.D. [Ⓐ Jones D.]
Miller, Robert P. . . . .'74 '00 C.967 B.A. L.645 J.D. [Ⓐ Rourke&B.]
Miller, S. Michael, (AV) . . . .'38 '63 C&L.608 B.S., J.D. [Ⓒ Kegler,B.H.&R.]
Miller, Steven E. . . . .'70 '96 C.737 B.A. L.117 J.D. [Ⓐ Crabbe,B.&J.]
Miller, Susan E. . . . . '55 '84 C&L.201 B.S., J.D. Asst. Atty. Gen.
Miller, Terrance M., (AV) . . . . . . '47 '72 C.319 B.A. L.893 LL.B. [Porter W.M.&A.]
Miller, Terry M., (AV) . . . .'47 '75 C&L.608 B.S., J.D. [Vorys,S.S.&P.]
Miller, Thos. O. . . . . '16 '43 C.473 A.B. L.608 LL.B. 684 City Park Ave.‡
Miller, Tiffany C. . . . .'73 '00 C&L.608 B.A., J.D. [Ⓐ Bailey C.]
Miller, Timothy E., (AV) . . . .'61 '86 C.679 B.S. L.117 J.D. [Isaac,B.L.&T.]
Miller, Timothy T. '58 '87 C.339 B.S. L.424 J.D.
(adm. in IL; not adm. in OH) General Counsel, Crane Plastics Company
Miller, William J. . . . . '46 '73 C.347 B.A. L.309 J.D. Ohio Environmental Protection Agcy.

Miller, Brian G., Co., L.P.A.
326 South High Street, Suite 500, 43215
Telephone: 614-221-4035 Fax: 614-222-1899
Email: bgm@bgmillerlaw.com URL: http://www.bgmillerlaw.com
Brian G. Miller.
Personal Injury, Employer Intentional Tort, Workplace Injuries, Premises Liability, Slip and Fall, Wrongful Death, Automobile Accidents, Motorcycle Accidents, Third Party Negligence, Torts, Civil Litigation.
See Professional Biographies, COLUMBUS, OHIO

Milless, Charles K., (AV) '46 '75 C.608 B.A. L.117 J.D.
400 South Fifth Street, Suite 303

Millisor & Nobil, A Legal Professional Association, (AV)
300 East Broad Street, Suite 190, 43215 ⊙
Telephone: 614-221-2234; 800-800-8807 Fax: 614-221-1278
Email: laborlaw@millisor.com URL: http://www.millisor.com
David P. Hiller.
Employment Law including Labor Relations, Equal Employment Opportunity, Public Sector, OSHA, Arbitration Law, Litigation, Workers Compensation Law, Human Resources Consulting and Employee Benefit Law.
Cleveland, Ohio Office: 9150 South Hills Boulevard, Suite 300, 44147-3599. Telephone: 440-838-8800. Telefax: 440-838-8805.
Canton, Ohio Office: 4117 Whipple Avenue NW, 44718. Telephone: 330-493-8525; 888-867-6869. Telefax: 330-493-8606.
See Professional Biographies, COLUMBUS, OHIO

Mills, Frederick E., (BV) . . . . '47 '73 C.608 B.S. L.117 J.D. [Ⓒ Vorys,S.S.&P.]
Mills, Jennifer T., (AV) . . . .'50 '83 C.611 B.A. L.608 J.D. [Porter W.M.&A.]
Mills, Melanie, The Law Offices of . . . '56 '93 C.36 B.S. L.117 J.D. 48 West Starr Avenue
Milne, Susan . . . . '53 '94 C.562 B.S. L.608 J.D. State Bd. of Nursing
Ming, Mary Egan . . . . '61 '88 C.97 B.A. L.201 J.D. Ohio CLE Institute
Minister, Michael E., (AV) . . . . '44 '74 C.608 B.S. L.117 J.D. [Baker&H.]
Minnillo, Christopher J., (BV) . . . . . . '54 '79 C&L.608 B.A., J.D. 1500 W. 3rd Ave.
Minor, Anne E. . . . . '52 '97 C.381 B.A. L.607 J.D. Asst. Gen. Coun., Nationwide Insurance
Minor, Robert A., (AV) . . . .'48 '75 C.228 A.B. L.608 J.D. [Vorys,S.S.&P.]
Minton, Harvey S., (AV) . . . .'33 '62 C&L.608 B.S., J.D. 6641 North High Street
Mirman, Denise M., (AV) . . . . '58 '82 C&L.608 B.A., J.D. [Friedman&M.]
Mirman, Joel H., (AV) . . . .'41 '66 C.610 B.B.A. L.608 J.D. [Gamble H.J.]
Miseta, Frank . . . .'22 '50 C&L.608 B.A., J.D. 3357 Leighton Rd.‡
Mitchell, A. Alan, (BV) '49 '75 C.967 A.B. L.117 J.D.
V.P. & Sr. Atty., Natl. City Corp.
Mitchell, Gregory R. . . . .'69 '93 C&L.851 B.B.A., J.D. [Agee C.M.&L.]
Mitchell, John S. . . . . '14 '37 C.611 A.B. L.608 J.D. [Mitchell,A.C.&B.] ‡
Mitchell, Keesha Redman . . . '66 '91 C.518 B.A. L.608 J.D. Atty. Gen., Health Care Fraud
Mitchell, Melissa J. . . . .'56 '83 C.207 B.A. L.930 J.D. [Ⓐ Vorys,S.S.&P.]
Mitchell, Robert C. . . . .'55 '81 C.207 B.A. L.150 J.D. [Ⓒ Vorys,S.S.&P.]
Mitchell, Timothy B., (BV) . . . . '56 '82 C.608 B.A. L.117 J.D. [Taft,S.&H.]
Mitchell, Allen, Catalano & Boda, Co., L.P.A., (AV) . . . . . . 580 S. High St., Ste. 200
Mittman, Lee C., (AV) . . . . '31 '58 C.381 A.B. L.608 J.D. [Ⓒ S.A.Mittman]
Mittman, Scott A., (BV) . . . .'64 '92 C.608 B.A. L.117 J.D. 502 South Third Street
Mix, Carol Pierce, (BV) . . . . . . '47 '90 C.381 B.S. L.117 J.D. 37 East Deshler Avenue
Moats, James R., (BV) . . . . '44 '69 C.207 B.A. L.608 J.D. [Carlile P.&M.]
Moats, Raymond F. . . . .'63 '93 C.112 B.A. L.284 J.D. [Ⓐ Weltman,W.&R.]
Mobley, Laura J. . . . . '67 '93 C&L.608 B.A., J.D. Co. Child Support Enforcement Agency
Moehring, Boyd K. . . . . '62 '89 C.117 B.A. L.608 J.D. [Thompson H.]
Mokhtari, Al A. . . . . '74 '00 C.608 B.A. L.930 J.D. [Ⓐ Reminger&R.]
Moloney, Monica A. . . . . '50 '78 C&L.607 B.A., J.D. Sr. Dep. Atty. Gen.
Monahan, James S., (AV) . . . . '33 '62 C.8 B.A. L.930 J.D. [Bricker&E.] ‡
Mone, Maria L., (BV) . . . . .'62 '88 C.602 B.A. L.608 J.D. Dept. of Health & Human Servs.
Mone, Robert P., (AV) . . . .'34 '59 C.201 B.A. L.602 J.D. [Thompson H.]
Monroe, Andromeda . . . . . . '55 '80 C.575 B.A. L.228 J.D. Dep. Dir., State Dept. of Ins.
Monteiro, Catherine A. . . . . '62 '86 C.201 B.A. L.607 J.D. Ofc. of the Pub. Def.
Montgomery, Betty D., (AV) . . . . '48 '76 C.97 B.A. L.851 J.D. Atty. Gen.
Montgomery, Henry P., (AV) . . . . . . '54 '79 C.97 B.S. L.608 J.D. [Baker&H.]
Moore, Elizabeth Berner '61 '86
C.347 B.S. L.608 J.D. V.P. & Sr. Coun., The Huntington Natl. Bk.
Moore, Jason Andrew . . . . '71 '96 C.607 B.A. L.608 J.D. Pros. Atty. Off.
Moore, Jayme P. . . . .'76 '03 C.602 B.S. L.608 J.D. [Ⓐ Kegler,B.H.&R.]
Moore, Karen Mueller, (AV) . . . .'50 '75 C.610 A.B. L.608 J.D. [Bricker&E.]

Moore, Michael Garth, Law Offices of . . . . .'48 '79 C&L.608 B.A., J.D. 1301 S. High St.
Moore, Nancy D. . . . . '61 '89 C&L.608 B.S., J.D. Asst. Co. Pros.
Moore, Patricia L. . . . . '57 '91 C.608 B.S.L.H.R. L.117 J.D. [Ⓐ Maguire&S.]
Moore, Randall Edwin, (AV) . . . . '49 '78 C.453 B.S. L.608 J.D. [Bricker&E.]
Moore, Thomas A. '55 '87 C.999 B.M. L.978 J.D.
Admin. Hearing Offr., Child Support Enfor. Agcy.
Moore, Tonda L. . . . .'68 '95 C.826 B.A. L.1003 J.D. [Ⓐ Lucas,P.A.G.&N.]
Moore, William Jeffrey, (BV) . . . . '55 '82 C.732 B.A. L.117 J.D. [Moore&Y.]
Moore & Yaklevich, (BV) . . . . 326 S. High St., Ste. 300
Moots, Philip R., (AV) . . . . '40 '65 C.608 B.S. L.309 J.D. [Moots,C.&H.]

Moots, Carter & Hogan, (AV)
A Legal Professional Association
3600 Olentangy River Road, 43214-3913
Telephone: 614-459-4140 FAX: 614-459-4503
Philip R. Moots; Wanda L. Carter; Christopher E. Hogan.
Private and Public Sector Labor and Employment Law. College and University Law, Township and Annexation Law, Non-Profit, Mediation, Administrative, Civil Trial and Appellate Practice.
See Professional Biographies, COLUMBUS, OHIO

Moran, Michael R. . . . . '67 '94 C.434 B.A. L.117 J.D. [M.R.Moran]

Moran, Michael R., Co., L.P.A.
181 Granville Street, P.O. Box 307437, 43230-7437
Telephone: 614-476-6453 Fax: 614-476-4157
Email: MRMoran@MRMoran.com URL: http://www.MRMoran.com
Michael R. Moran.
Administrative Law, Occupational and Professional Licensing, Health Law, Personal Injury, Municipal Law, Privacy and Freedom of Information, Government Law, White Collar Crime, Fraud, Corporate Compliance and Legislation, Trial Practice and Appeals, Firearm and 2nd Amendment Law.
See Professional Biographies, COLUMBUS, OHIO

Mordarski, Daniel R. . . . .'68 '94 C.97 B.A. L.1003 J.D. [Carpenter&L.]
Morgan, Dennis R. . . . .'42 '67 C.902 B.A. L.893 J.D. Asst. Atty. Gen.
Morgan, Douglas S., (AV) . . . .'56 '82 C.309 B.A. L.608 J.D. [Calfee,H.&G.]
Morgan, Edward W., (AV) . . . .'45 '72 C.207 B.A. L.608 J.D. Franklin Co. Pros. Atty.
Morgan, Frederick M., Jr., (AV) '56 '83
C.207 B.A. L.150 J.D. [Volkema,T.M.B.S.&M.] ⊙
Morgan, Kelly M., (BV) . . . . '51 '77 C.602 B.B.A. L.117 J.D. [Morgan&P.]
Morgan, Michael E. . . . .'68 '99 C&L.608 B.A., J.D. 169 East Livingston Avenue
Morgan, Richard A. . . . . . . '65 '01 C.608 B.S. L.117 J.D. Coun., Nationwide Insurance
Morgan, Robert James . . . .'75 '01 C.383 B.A. L.608 J.D. [Ⓐ Porter W.M.&A.]
Morgan, Thomas Evan, (AV) . . . . '49 '75 C.610 B.B.A. L.607 J.D. [T.E.Morgan&Assoc.]
Morgan & Petrucci, (AV) . . . . 380 South Fifth Street

Morgan, Thomas Evan, & Associates, A Legal Prof. Assoc., (AV)
906 East Broad Street, 43205
Telephone: 614-258-1133; Toll Free: 800-948-6200 Fax: 614-258-3344
Email: info@thomasevanmorgan.com
Thomas Evan Morgan. Associate: Stewart Justice, III.
Workers' Compensation and Social Security Disability Law.
See Professional Biographies, COLUMBUS, OHIO

Moriarty, Erin F. . . . . '52 '77 C&L.608 B.A., J.D. 2700 Vassar Pl.‡
Morje, Robert J., (AV) . . . . '50 '75 C.823 A.B. L.608 J.D. [Ⓒ Decker,V.S.L.&V.]
Morley, Sylvan H., III '72 '99 C.674 A.B. L.101 J.D.
(adm. in UT; not adm. in OH) HotDocs Prof. Svs., Lexis Nexis
Morris, Frank R., Jr., (AV) . . . . . .'29 '58 C.976 B.A. L.477 J.D. [Ⓒ Porter W.M.&A.]
Morrison, Dennis J., (AV) . . . .'54 '83 C.1044 B.S. L.117 J.D. [Means,B.B.&B.]
Morrison, George W., (BV) '22 '48
C&L.930 B.B.A., LL.B. V.P. & Gen. Coun., Landmark, Inc.
Morrison, Michael P. . . . .'51 '88 C.532 B.A. L.117 J.D. 137 E. State. St.
Morrison, Nancy E., (BV) '52 '82
C.608 B.S. L.117 J.D. 1170 Old Henderson Rd., Ste. 109
Morrison, Philip Daniel . . . . . . '66 '96 C.608 B.A. L.1148 J.D. U.S. Small Bus. Adm.
Morrison, Sarah D., (AV) . . . . '70 '97 C.608 B.A. L.179 J.D. [Chester,W.&S.]
Morrissey, Michael J., (BV) . . . . . . '44 '72 C.973 B.A. L.117 J.D. 34 W. Whittier St.
Morrow, Robert M., (AV) . . . . '57 '83 C.608 B.S. L.117 J.D. [Means,B.B.&B.]
Morsa, Barbara J. . . . . '66 '92 C.222 B.A. L.201 J.D. 150 East State St.

Morse, William A., A Legal Professional Association
(See Worthington)

Mortland, Jean A. . . . .'31 '64 C.608 B.S. L.266 J.D. Prof. of Law, Capital Univ. Law Sch.
Morton, Daniel W., (AV) '51 '77
C.1195 B.A. L.910 J.D. V.P. & Sr. Coun., The Huntington Natl. Bk.
Morton, Robert J. G., (BV) . . . .'10 '38 C.951 A.B. L.930 LL.B. [Robins,P.B.H.&S.]
Moses, Ambrose, III . . . .'64 '91 C&L.608 B.A., J.D. OCSEA-AFSCME, Local 11
Moses, Michael A., (BV) . . . . '52 '77 C.569 B.A. L.117 J.D. 330 South High Street
Mosholder, Richard S. . . . .'50 '80 C.608 B.A. L.117 J.D. Express Personnel Servs.
Moss, Linda A. . . . . '53 '80 C.518 B.A. L.117 J.D. State Bd. of Tax App.
Moss, Nicole S. . . . .'67 '92 C.611 B.A. L.1044 J.D. [E.H.Doucet&Assoc.]
Mote, Gretchen Koehler, (BV) '53 '78
C&L.117 B.A., J.D. Dir., Loss Prev., Ohio Bar Liability Ins. Co.
Mote, Scott R., (AV) . . . . '50 '77 C.1208 B.A. L.117 J.D. [Harris,M.B.&C.]
Motter, Miranda Creviston . . . .'74 '01 C.992 B.A. L.179 J.D. [Ⓐ Bricker&E.]
Moul, Geoffrey J., (AV) . . . .'68 '94 C.260 B.A. L.608 J.D. [Murray M.M.&B.]
Moul, William C., (AV) . . . .'40 '64 C.473 B.A. L.608 J.D. [Thompson H.]
Mount, Steven F., (BV) . . . . '53 '79 C.532 B.A. L.309 J.D. [Squire,S.&D.]

Mowery & Youell, Ltd.
(See Dublin)

Mowoe, Isaac J. . . . .'49 '82 C.610 B.S. L.117 J.D. Ohio State Univ.
Mowry, Sherry L. . . . . '76 '01 C.453 B.S. L.608 J.D. [Ⓐ Ulmer&B.]
Moyer, Stephen A., Law Office of, (BV) . . . . '56 '81 C.97 B.S. L.117 J.D. 9 E. Kossuth St.
Moyer, Thomas J. . . . . '39 '64 C&L.608 B.A., J.D. Chf. Jus., Supm. Ct.
Mozenter, Karen B., (AV) . . . .'58 '84 C.597 B.S. L.228 J.D. Ohio State Univ.
Muchnicki, E. Dennis . . . . '49 '74 C.30 B.A. L.276 J.D. 5650 Blazer Parkway
Mueller, Jerry K., Jr., (AV) '48 '73
C.124 B.S.Ch.E. L.608 J.D. [Mueller&S.] (See Pat. Sect.)
Mueller, Kevin M. . . . . '73 '02 C&L.608 B.S., J.D. [Ⓐ Schottenstein,Z.&D.]

Mueller and Smith, A Legal Professional Association, (AV)
Mueller-Smith Building, 7700 Rivers Edge Drive, 43235-1355
Telephone: 614-436-0600 Telecopier: 614-436-0057
Email: patents@muellersmith.com URL: http://www.lawyers.com/muellerandsmith
Jerry K. Mueller, Jr.; Gerald L. Smith;—Diane E. Burke; John J. Okuley.
Intellectual Property Law including Patents, Trademarks, Copyrights, Licensing, Computer Law, Unfair Competition and International Patent Law. Trial and Appellate Practice in all Courts.
Representative Clients: Ashland Chemical Co.; Damon's International; General Electric Superabrasives; Liebert Corp.; OCLC Online Computer Library Center, Inc.; The Edward Orton, Jr. Ceramic Foundation.
See Professional Biographies, COLUMBUS, OHIO

Muenz, Donald Paul . . . . '49 '74 C&L.608 B.S.B.A., J.D. 132 W. Rathbone Rd.

Muetzel, Andrew T. ... '72 '99 C.973 B.A. L.179 J.D. [Ⓐ Decker,V.S.L.&V.]
Mularski, Raymond J., (BV) '59 '84 C&L.608 B.S.B.A., J.D.
107 West Johnstown Road
Mulchaey, Rachel Ary ... '— '01 C.610 B.A. L.117 J.D. [Ⓐ Luper,N.&L.]
Muldoon, Damon P. ... '71 '98 C.383 B.A. L.117 J.D. Fifth Third Bk.
Muldrow-Harris, Joy D., (CV) ... '58 '86 C.914 B.A. L.569 J.D. Asst. Atty. Gen.
Muller, David A. ... '74 '00 C&L.608 B.A., J.D. [Ⓐ Bailey C.]
Mulligan, Richard S., (BV) ... '51 '79 C.385 A.B. L.117 J.D. [Roetzel&A.]
Mullin, Philip A. ... '48 '74 C.973 A.B. L.608 J.D. Leg. Serv. Comm.
Mullinax, Robert L. '46 '73 C&L.575 B.S., J.D.
Chf. Leg. Coun., Dept. of Human Servs.
Mulvey, Thomas J. ... '60 '85 C.207 B.A. L.117 J.D. [Curry,R.S.&M.]
Munsell, Theodore M., (AV) ... '54 '79 C.611 B.A. L.930 J.D. [Lane,A.&H.]
Murch, Kevin L. ... '69 '96 C.608 B.A. L.117 J.D. [Schottenstein,Z.&D.]
Murphey, David P. ... '52 '78 C.97 B.S. L.117 J.D. Cantlon Assoc.
Murphey, Richard R., Jr., (AV) ... '25 '50 C.910 A.B. L.309 LL.B. [Ⓒ Squire,S.&D.]
Murphy, Beth W. ... '73 '98 C&L.16 B.A., J.D. Grange Mut. Cas. Co.
Murphy, Brian K., (AV) ... '67 '94 C.999 B.A. L.608 J.D. [Murray M.M.&B.]
Murphy, Earl J. '28 '52 C.108 A.B. L.347 J.D.
(adm. in IN; not adm. in OH) 55 W. 12th Ave.
Murphy, Jenifer J. ... '74 '99 C.607 B.A. L.117 J.D. [Ⓐ Keener D.C.&P.]
Murphy, Joanne W. '34 '58 C.473 A.B. L.608 J.D.
Adjunct Prof. of Law, Ohio State Univ.
Murphy, Joseph J. ... '21 '53 C.608 B.S. L.150 J.D. 1295 Baskerville Drive
Murphy, Maureen, (BV) ... '52 '83 C.741 B.A. L.930 J.D. Asst. U.S. Atty.
Murphy, Sharon Werner ... '— '92 L.201 J.D. Atty. Hearing Exam., State Med. Bd. of OH
Murray, Anne M. ... '65 '91 C.976 B.A. L.477 J.D. Asst. City Atty.
Murray, Joseph F., (AV) ... '69 '94 C.800 B.S. L.608 J.D. [Murray M.M.&B.]
Murray Murphy Moul + Basil LLP, (AV) ... 1533 Lake Shore Dr.
Music, Amanda ... '77 '03 C&L.851 B.A., J.D. [Ⓐ Bailey C.]
Musilli, Stephen Craig, (BVⓉ) ... '68 '94 C.301 B.A. L.923 J.D. [Ⓑ Vorys,S.S.&P.]
Musser, Philip S., (BV) ... '44 '75 C.608 B.M.E. L.117 J.D. [Musser,L.&H.]
Musser, Long & Harris, (BV) ... 3404 Riverside Dr.
Myers, Bradley Allan ... '54 '80 C&L.608 B.S., J.D. 1800 Cannon Dr.
Myers, Craig S. ... '61 '89 C.604 B.A. L.608 J.D. Asst. Atty. Gen.
Myers, Eric C. ... '76 '02 C.602 B.B.A. L.608 J.D. [Ⓐ Porter W.M.&A.]
Myers, Robert W. ... '61 '88 C.608 B.A. L.1003 J.D. [Ⓐ Thompson H.]
Myers, Stanley L., (BV) ... '42 '67 C&L.608 B.S., J.D. 221 S. High St.
Myers, William Scott ... '57 '88 C.210 B.A. L.117 J.D. Sect. Chf., Atty. Gen.
Myers-Payne, Sean C. '67 '01 C.611 B.A. L.1209 J.D.
(adm. in VA; not adm. in OH; Pat.) [Ⓐ Calfee,H.&G.]
Nagel, Susan Kay ... '62 '90 C.1228 B.A. L.575 J.D. Ohio Admin. Servs.
Nagel, Tom H., (BV) ... '46 '71 C&L.608 B.A., J.D. [Britt,C.N.&S.]
Nagy, Timothy P., (AV) ... '49 '74 C.608 B.A. L.117 J.D. [Taft,S.&H.]
Nakasian, William E. ... '— '90 C.930 B.S. L.608 J.D. [Jones D.]
Naperstick, William ... '20 '50 C&L.851 B.B.A., LL.B. Asst. Atty. Gen.
Nardone, Vincent J., (BV) '70 '96 C.229 B.S. L.179 J.D.
[Ⓐ McDonald H.] (⊙Cleveland)
Nathan, Jerry E., (AV) ... '48 '73 C.608 B.S. L.976 J.D. [Bricker&E.]
Nationwide Realty Investors, LTD ... 375 N. Front St., Ste. 200
Nauman, Robert D. ... '71 '02 C.608 B.A. L.117 J.D. [Ⓐ Squire,S.&D.]
Naumoff, Jennifer ... '71 '01 C.473 B.S. L.608 J.D. [Ⓐ Vorys,S.S.&P.]
Naumoff, Mitchell A., Jr. ... '76 '04 C.124 B.S. L.273 J.D. [Ⓐ Porter W.M.&A.]
Navin, Joseph F. ... '60 '88 C.608 B.A. L.117 J.D. [Larrimer&L.]
Neal, John G., (BV) ... '46 '77 C.608 B.A. L.117 J.D. 399 E. Main St., Ste. 110
Neal, Marianne ... '54 '88 C&L.608 B.A., J.D. 10th Dist. Ct. of App.
Neale, William R. ... '42 '67 C&L.150 B.A., J.D. 180 E. Broad St., 27th Fl.
Nealy, Darren L. ... '76 '01 C.201 B.A. L.893 J.D. [Ⓐ Zeiger,T.&L.]
Nearhood, Constance A. ... '57 '82 C.967 B.A. L.930 J.D. Asst. Atty. Gen.
Nederveld, Allen G. ... '69 '97 C.114 B.A. L.608 J.D. Columbus Airport Auth.
Needleman, Scott R. ... '56 '91 C.608 B.A. L.117 J.D. [Nobile,N.&T.] ⊙
Neely, Demetries J. ... '57 '84 C.369 B.A. L.608 J.D. 1 Nationwide Plaza
Neely, Sandra L., (AV) '57 '83 C.8 B.A. L.150 J.D.
Assoc. V.P. & Assoc. Gen. Coun., Nationwide Insurance
Neff, Frank J., (AV) ... '34 '60 C.381 B.A. L.608 J.D. [Barkan&N.]
Neidenthal, K. Wallace, (AV) ... '46 '71 C&L.608 B.A., J.D. [Luper,N.&L.]
Neidenthal, Randall C., (AV) ... '51 '79 C.608 B.A. L.809 J.D. Sr. Coun., Bank One Corp.
Neilsen, Daniel J. ... '— '03 C.446 B.S. L.608 J.D. [Ⓐ McNees W.&N.]
Nekritz, Felicia B. ... '71 '96 C.608 B.A. L.117 J.D. Asst. State Pub. Def.
Nelson, Hugh W. ... '28 '59 C&L.608 B.A., LL.B. Lancaster Colony Corp.
Nelson, Janice A. ... '37 '92 C.608 B.A. L.117 J.D. [Ⓐ Porter W.M.&A.]
Nelson, Jas. A., (BV) ... '24 '53 C.608 B.A. L.1003 LL.B. 4495 E. Broad St.
Nelson, Michael R., (AVⓉ) '57 '92 C.999 B.S. L.831 J.D.
(adm. in PA; not adm. in OH) [Nelson L.d.&H.] ⊙
Nelson, Vanessa A. ... '— '00 C.674 A.B. L.124 J.D. [Ⓐ Dreher L.&T.]
Nelson, William M. ... '47 '79 C.932 B.S.I.E. L.117 J.D. Brooks Beverage Mgmt., Inc.
Nelson Carney, Jennifer M. ... '75 '04 C&L.608 B.A., J.D. [Ⓐ Bricker&E.]

Nelson Levine de Luca & Horst, LLC, (AVⓉ)
280 North High Street, Suite 920, 43215 ⊙
Telephone: 614-228-1398 Fax: 614-221-7529
URL: http://www.nldhlaw.com
Michael R. Nelson (Not admitted in OH); Kenneth T. Levine (Not admitted in OH); Daniel J. de Luca (Not admitted in OH); Robert T. Horst (Not admitted in OH). Associate: Mark D. Le Master.
Antitrust Litigation, Appellate Practice, Bad Faith Consulting and Litigation, Class Action Litigation, Construction Law, Insurance Regulatory, Consulting and Litigation, Large Loss Property and Workers' Compensation Subrogation.
Blue Bell, Pennsylvania Office: 4 Sentry Parkway, Suite 300, 19422. Telephone: 610-862-6500. Fax: 614-862-6501.
Princeton, New Jersey Office: 212 Carnegie Center, Suite 206, 08540. Telephone: 609-919-6320. Fax: 609-520-1863.

See Professional Biographies, COLUMBUS, OHIO

Nemecek, Julie C. ... '76 '04 C&L.608 B.A., J.D. [Ⓐ Slowik&R.]
Nemeth, John C., (AV) ... '45 '71 C.381 B.A. L.608 J.D. [J.C.Nemeth&Assoc.]
Nemeth, Julius J. ... '38 '64 C.980 A.B. L.276 J.D. Ref., Mun. Ct.

Nemeth, John C., and Associates, (AV)
21 East Frankfort Street, 43206-1069
Telephone: 614-443-4866 Fax: 614-443-4860 URL: http://www.nemethlaw.com
Email: nemeth@nemethlaw.com URL: http://www.lawyers.com/nemeth
John C. Nemeth (Certified as a Civil Trial Specialist by the National Board of Trial Advocacy).
Associates: David A. Herd; Michael J. Collins; Matthew E. Ice.
General Negligence Trials. Trials and Appeals. Insurance Defense, Medical/Legal Malpractice, Toxic Torts, Products Liability, Asbestos Litigation, Aviation, Complex and Multi-District Litigation, Arson, Premises Liability, Fraud Defense and Insurance Law.

See Professional Biographies, COLUMBUS, OHIO

Nesser, J. Michael '55 '83 C.117 B.A. L.608 J.D.
Mng. Dir., GBQ/Nesser Consulting Grp.
Nester, Elbert R., (AV) ... '43 '68 C.381 B.S. L.608 J.D. [E.R.Nester]
Nester, Elbert R., Associates & Co., L.P.A., (AV) ... 4621 Reed Rd.
Nestor, Lorraine M. ... '61 '87 C.980 B.A. L.8 J.D. Asst. Atty. Gen.
Neubauer, David M., (BV) ... '50 '75 C.608 B.A. L.94 J.D. 334 W. Third Ave.
Neuman, Todd H., (BV) ... '67 '92 C.608 B.A. L.923 J.D. 2739 W. Dublin-Granville Rd.,
Newcomb, Angelique Paul ... '69 '97 C.178 B.A. L.608 J.D. [Schottenstein,Z.&D.]
Newcomb, William S., Jr., (AV) ... '44 '69 C&L.608 B.S., J.D. [Vorys,S.S.&P.]
Newcome, Ron E., (BV) ... '53 '82 C.610 B.A. L.117 J.D. [Elleman&N.]
Newcomer, James D. ... '38 '64 C.473 B.S. L.608 J.D. Dept. of Taxation
Newhouse, D. Wesley, (AV) ... '58 '83 C.607 B.A. L.608 J.D. [Lane,A.&H.]
Newman, Dennis R., (AV) ... '43 '68 C.611 B.A. L.608 J.D. [Isaac,B.L.&T.]
Newman, William A. '47 '86
C.102 B.A. L.117 J.D. Asst. Law Libr., Capital Univ. Law Sch.
Newman, William F., (AV) ... '29 '55 C.610 B.S. L.608 J.D. [Lucas,P.A.G.&N.]
Newsom, Fred L., Jr. ... '19 '51 C.608 B.A. L.266 J.D. 806 Bulen Ave.
Newsome, Romina P. ... '78 '03 C&L.117 B.A., J.D. [Ⓐ E.J.Hollern]
Neyerlin, Amy L. ... '62 '88 C.1044 B.S. L.117 J.D. 373 South High Street, 12th Floor
Neymotin, Ita M. '72 '01 C.608 B.A. L.117 J.D.
(adm. in NJ; not adm. in OH) 246 S. Cassady Road
Nichelson, Lauren R. ... '76 '00 C.608 B.A. L.179 J.D. OH Pub. Employees Retire. Sys.
Nichols, Philip R. ... '70 '96 C.294 B.A. L.902 J.D. [Ⓐ Shayne&G.]
Nichols, Robert H., (AV) ... '60 '88 C.608 B.S.B.A. L.846 J.D. [Schottenstein,Z.&D.]
Nick, Paul Michael ... '65 '90 C.339 A.B. L.608 J.D. OH Ethics Comm.
Nickell-Thomas, Jennifer A. '64 '91
C.473 B.A. L.117 J.D. Sr. Coun., Nationwide Insurance
Nickerson, George R., (BV) ... '53 '76 C&L.608 B.A., J.D. 21 W. Broad St., 11th Fl.
Niehoff, David O., (AV) ... '41 '66 C.611 B.A. L.608 J.D. 501 South High Street
Nissl, Colleen K., (AV) '50 '75 C.611 B.A. L.851 J.D.
V.P. & Asst. Gen. Coun., Borden, Inc. (Legal Department)
Nobile, James E. ... '65 '92 C.608 B.A. L.117 J.D. [Nobile,N.&T.] ⊙

Nobile, Needleman & Thompson, LLC
5300 E. Main Street, Suite 109, 43213 ⊙
Telephone: 614-575-1188 Fax: 614-575-1186
Email: jenobile@n-n-t.com URL: http://www.n-n-t.com
Members of Firm: James E. Nobile; Scott R. Needleman; Matthew J. Thompson.
Bankruptcy Chapter 7, Bankruptcy Chapter 13, Bankruptcy Chapter 11, Bankruptcy Litigation, Bankruptcy Reorganization, Consumer Bankruptcy, Creditor Bankruptcy, Debtor Bankruptcy, Foreclosures, Insolvency, Liquidations, Personal Bankruptcy, Criminal Law, Juvenile Criminal Law, Assault and Battery, Burglary, Criminal Defense, Drivers License Suspensions, Driving While Intoxicated, Drug Crimes, Felonies, Misdemeanors, Traffic Violations, Consumer Law, Consumer Litigation, Consumer Rights, Fair Credit Reporting Act, Debtor Rights, Lemon Law, Wills, Estate Planning, Real Estate.
West Office: 4511 Cemetery Road, Suite B, Hilliard, Ohio 43026. Telephone: 614-529-8600. Fax: 614-529-8656.

See Professional Biographies, COLUMBUS, OHIO

Noble, Michele L. ... '— '00 C.608 B.A. L.179 J.D. [Ⓐ Thompson H.]
Noble, Peggy Lynnae ... '63 '00 C.1044 B.S. L.117 J.D. 4000 E. Main Street
Noble, Robert Dean, (BV) ... '63 '88 C.608 B.A. L.851 J.D. [Matan,G.&W.]
Nodes, Dwight D. ... '56 '86 C.608 B.A. L.117 J.D. Pub. Utilities Comm. of Ohio
Noel, Gerald T., Jr. ... '63 '94 C.629 B.S. L.150 J.D. State Legis. Serv. Comm.
Noel, Joseph M. '26 '60 C.645 B.A. L.229 LL.B.
(adm. in PA; not adm. in OH) 2191 Yorkshire Rd.‡
Noel, Mark A. ... '78 '03 C&L.383 B.A., J.D. [Ⓐ Thompson H.]
Noga, Ronald B., (AV) ... '46 '74 C&L.608 B.S., J.D. [Ⓐ Weltman,W.&R.]
Nolan, Laura Evans ... '69 '94 C.62 B.S. L.117 J.D. Com. Pleas. Ct.
Nolan, William A. ... '62 '89 C.188 B.A. L.309 J.D. [Squire,S.&D.]
Nolder, Steven Scott, (BV) ... '61 '87 C.608 B.A. L.117 J.D. 10 W. Broad St.
Nordstrom, Robert J., (AV) ... '24 '49 C.932 A.B. L.477 J.D. [Ⓒ Porter W.M.&A.]
Norman, A. Scott, (BV) ... '64 '89 C.967 B.A. L.117 J.D. [Frost&M.]
Norman, Craig A. ... '58 '83 C.967 B.A. L.608 J.D. 4181 E. Main St.
Norman, Jonathan M., (AV) ... '51 '76 C.610 A.B. L.608 J.D. [Vorys,S.S.&P.]
Norris, Lisa L. ... '66 '93 C.381 B.B.A. L.608 J.D. [Ⓒ Allen,K.&S.]
North, Chris J., (AV) ... '49 '80 C.150 B.S.M.E. L.608 J.D. [Vorys,S.S.&P.]
North, Scott E., (AV) ... '58 '83 C.477 A.B. L.893 J.D. [Porter W.M.&A.]
Northrop, David E., (AV) ... '48 '73 C.25 B.A. L.608 J.D. [Ⓒ Porter W.M.&A.]
Northrup, Judith A., (AV) ... '59 '84 C.862 B.A. L.608 J.D. 365 W. 5th Ave.
Noure, Alo ... '— '04 C.851 B.A. L.608 J.D. 65 E. State St.
Nourse, Steven T. ... '65 '90 C.97 B.S. L.117 J.D. Asst. Atty. Gen.
Nowak, Joseph Patrick ... '66 '92 C.477 B.A. L.608 J.D. Sr. Coun., Nationwide Insurance
Nuber, Anna Kathreen ... '79 '04 C.607 B.S.B.A. L.608 J.D. [Ⓐ Vorys,S.S.&P.]
Nunn, David W., (AV) ... '58 '91 C.97 B.S. L.851 J.D. [Eastman&S.] (⊙Toledo)
Nusken, Ralph E. ... '32 '70 C.608 B.Sc. L.117 J.D. 601 S. High St.
Nyce, Kinsley F., Attorney at Law, (BV) '52 '82
C.313 B.A. L.117 J.D. 1601 W. 5th Ave., Ste. 112
Oberle, John H. ... '70 '01 C.611 B.S. L.179 J.D. [Ⓐ Schottenstein,Z.&D.]
Obetz, Robin R., (AV) ... '38 '64 C.608 A.B. L.607 J.D. [Ⓒ Vorys,S.S.&P.]
O'Brien, Michael F. ... '57 '93 C.321 B.A. L.1003 J.D. [Ⓐ Vorys,S.S.&P.]
O'Brien, Robert Terence, (AV) ... '28 '59 C.473 A.B. L.266 J.D. 80 East Fulton Street
O'Brien, Ronald J., (AV) ... '48 '74 C.737 B.A. L.608 J.D. Co. Pros. Atty.
O'Brien, Thomas J. ... '60 '96 C.210 B.A. L.801 J.D. [Ⓒ Bricker&E.]
O'Bryan, Daniel W. '54 '79 C.532 B.A. L.608 J.D.
Asst. Gen. Coun., Mergers & Acquisitions, Battelle Memorial Institute
O'Callaghan, Michael J. ... '63 '90 C.477 A.B. L.215 J.D. [Shumaker,L.&K.]
O'Connell, Thomas J., (BV) ... '59 '85 C.608 B.S. L.201 J.D. [Abramson&O.]
O'Conner, Adele E., (AV) ... '51 '76 C.150 B.A. L.608 J.D. [Porter W.M.&A.]
O'Connor, Robert F. ... '53 '79 C.1044 B.A. L.608 J.D. 2414 Berwick Blvd.
O'Connor, Thomas E., Jr., (AV) ... '41 '67 C.602 B.S. L.477 J.D. [Calfee,H.&G.] (Pat.)
Odita, Florence C. Uwandu '— '85
C.347 B.S. L.117 J.D. Chief, Bur. of Reseach & Prog. Evaluation
O'Donnell, Terrence ... '76 '01 C.473 B.A. L.602 J.D. [Ⓐ Bricker&E.]
Oellermann, Charles M. ... '— '91 C.546 B.S. L.309 J.D. [Jones D.]
Oesterling, Peter J. '56 '83 C.657 B.A. L.678 J.D.
(adm. in PA; not adm. in OH) Asst. Gen. Coun., Nationside Insurance
Ogg, Benjamin W. ... '— '03 C.117 B.A. L.608 J.D. [Ⓐ Onda,L.&R.]
Oglesbee, Carla E. ... '67 '99 C.932 B.B.A. L.608 J.D. 4591 Indianola Ave.

Ogne, Alberts & Stuart, P.C.
(See Troy, Michigan)

O'Grady, James J. ... '36 '67 C.262 B.S. L.117 J.D. Com. Pleas J.
O'Keefe, Bobbie Corley ... '56 '92 C.473 B.A. L.117 J.D. [Ⓐ E.F.Whipps&Assoc.]
O'Keeffe, Siobhan Rose ... '73 '98 C.608 B.A. L.124 J.D. Pub. Def. Off.
Oklok, Kathi A. ... '58 '86 C&L.608 B.S., J.D. Asst. Atty. Gen.
Okuley, John J. ... '62 '03 C&L.608 B.S., J.D. [Ⓐ Mueller&S.]
Oliphant, James S., (AV) ... '45 '71 C.597 B.A. L.608 J.D. [Porter W.M.&A.]
Oliver, Jami S., (AV) ... '68 '93 C.607 B.A. L.608 J.D. [Oliver]

Oliver Law Office, (AV)
471 E. Broad Street, Suite 1303, 43215
Telephone: 614-220-9100 Fax: 614-242-3948
Email: joliver@jamioliver.com URL: http://www.jamioliver.com
Jami S. Oliver.
Products Liability, Personal Injury, Wrongful Death, Latex Allergy Litigation, Medical Malpractice, Vioxx Litigation, Automobile Accidents, Insurance Law, Employment Discrimination.
See Professional Biographies, COLUMBUS, OHIO

Olson, Kathy A. '52 '77 C.207 B.A. L.117 J.D. Asst. Gen. Coun., Legal, Battelle Memorial Institute
O'Malley, William J., (BV) .... '64 '91 C.293 B.A. L.608 J.D. 4591 Indianola Ave.
Oman, Richard Heer, (AV) .... '26 '51 C&L.608 B.A., J.D. [© Vorys,S.S.&P.]
Onda, Robert J., (AV) .... '57 '83 C.602 B.B.A. L.902 J.D. [Onda,L.&R.]

Onda, LaBuhn & Rankin Co., LPA, (AV)
266 North Fourth Street, Suite 100, 43215-2511
Telephone: 614-716-0500 Fax: 614-716-0511
URL: http://www.olr-law.com
Robert J. Onda; Matthew A. LaBuhn; Timothy S. Rankin; Patrick H. Boggs;—Robert E. Boyd, III; Todd A. Ernsberger; Benjamin W. Ogg; Brian M. Garvine; Elizabeth M. Kelly; Jacqueline A. Ferris.
Business Formation, Buying and Selling of Businesses, Business Law, Federal Tax Controversies, Commercial and General Litigation, Real Estate, Zoning, Land Use, Tax Deferred Exchanges, Estate and Gift Taxation, Estate Planning, Wills and Probate, Tax Planning, Mechanic's Lien Law, Construction Law, Criminal Defense, Banking Law, Finance, Lender and Borrower Representation, Employment, Representing Professionals in Administrative Proceedings.
See Professional Biographies, COLUMBUS, OHIO

Onega, David A. .... '69 '98 C.610 B.B.A. L.117 J.D. [Carlile P.&M.]
O'Neil, C. Richard .... '29 '53 C&L.608 B.S., J.D. 4201 Glenmawr Ave.‡
O'Neill, C. William, (AV) .... '46 '71 C.674 A.B. L.477 J.D. [Vorys,S.S.&P.]
O'Neill, Michael J. .... '64 '89 C.973 B.A. L.150 J.D. OH Legis. Serv. Comm.
O'Neill, Shari Winget .... '61 '89 C&L.150 B.A., J.D. Jud. Clk. to Ct. of App.
Onesto, John L., (BV) .... '45 '72 C.473 B.S. L.608 J.D. 887 S. High St.
Oppenheimer, Susan L. .... '62 '87 C.951 B.A. L.145 J.D. [Ⓐ Bricker&E.]
Ording, Michael K., (AVⓉ) .... '— '80 C&L.608 B.A., J.D. [Jones D.]
O'Reilly, Kelly C. .... '71 '96 C.608 B.A. L.117 J.D. Law Clk., U.S. Dist. Ct.
Orensten, David Kevin .... '76 '02 C.1119 B.S. L.608 J.D. [Ⓐ Porter W.M.&A.]
Organ, Shawn J., (AV) .... '— '89 C.473 B.S. L.150 J.D. [Jones D.]
Orlando, Jacqueline M. .... '55 '88 C.980 B.A. L.608 J.D. Capital Univ. Law School
Ormond, Regina R. .... '70 '97 C.602 B.A. L.150 J.D. Coun., Nationwide Insurance
Orosz, Nathaniel S. .... '— '04 Atty. Gen. Off.
Orr, Randall L. '54 '80 C.608 B.S. L.607 J.D. Assistant General Counsel, Nationwide Mut. Ins. Co.
Osborn, Larissa D. .... '73 '01 C.610 B.B.A. L.117 J.D. [L.Osborn]

Osborn, Larissa
454 East Main Street, 43215
Telephone: 614-538-9202 Fax: 614-267-8092
Email: larissaoh1@yahoo.com URL: http://www.larissaohlaw.com
Larissa D. Osborn.
Litigation, Products Liability, Aviation Law, Business Litigation.
See Professional Biographies, COLUMBUS, OHIO

Osborne-Pikelny, Julia L. .... '50 '78 C&L.608 B.A., J.D. Columbus Dispatch
Oser, Michael N., (BV) .... '53 '78 C.381 B.A. L.930 J.D. 35 E. Livingston Ave.
O'Shaughnessy, Christopher T. .... '71 '98 C.608 B.A. L.117 J.D. [Lane,A.&H.]
O'Shaughnessy, Maggie .... '— '97 C.602 B.A. L.608 J.D. [Ⓐ Vorys,S.S.&P.]
Oshima, June M. .... '55 '89 C.309 A.B. L.178 J.D. [Ⓐ Thompson H.]
Oster, Jody Michelle '63 '89 C.665 B.A. L.117 J.D. V.P. & Sr. Coun., The Huntington Natl. Bk.
Osterkamp, Kevin J., (AV) .... '49 '74 C.352 B.A. L.608 J.D. [Roetzel&A.]
Ostrowski, Edward L., Jr. .... '58 '95 C.608 B.S. L.117 J.D. [Ⓐ Scott,S.&W.]
Ouellette, Robert R., (AV) .... '65 '91 C&L.477 A.B., J.D. [Schottenstein,Z.&D.]
Owen, Allison MacLeod .... '70 '95 C.473 B.A.B.S. L.201 J.D. [Ⓐ Gallagher&K.]
Owen, Andrew W., (BV) .... '67 '92 C.893 B.A. L.273 J.D. [Buckingham,D.&B.]
Owen, James D., (AV) .... '54 '79 C.611 B.A. L.117 J.D. [Cloud&O.]
Owens, David Lynn .... '46 '78 C.347 B.S. L.851 J.D. Dept. of Labor
Ozier, J. Michael, (AV) ...... '47 '84 C.234 B.S. L.1119 J.D. 3021 Bethel Road, Suite 104
Pace, Richard W. .... '49 '82 C&L.608 B.S.S.W., J.D. 77 South High Street, 15th Floor
Pack-Adler, Ruth L. .... '67 '97 C.260 B.S. L.472 J.D. 35 E. Livingston Ave.
Paddock, Harold D., III .... '48 '73 C&L.608 B.S., J.D. [H.Paddock]
Paddock, Harold, Co., LPA .... 2600 Corporate Exchange Dr., Ste. 112
Paige, Bruce P. .... '76 '02 C.610 B.A. L.608 J.D. [Ⓐ Vorys,S.S.&P.]
Painter, Lori Burns, (BV) .... '63 '92 C.174 B.S. L.117 J.D. [Ⓐ P.J.Fulton]
Paley, Eileen Y., (BV) .... '63 '88 C.608 B.A. L.117 J.D. [Peden,P.&Assoc.]
Palmer, Eleanor J. ... '73 '98 C.999 B.S. L.608 J.D. Tax Consultant, Ernst & Young LLP
Palmer, John W. ... '33 '62 C.604 B.A. L.477 J.D. Prof. of Law, Capital Univ. Law Center
Palmer, Karen L. .... '72 '97 C.923 B.A. L.930 J.D. Legis. Aide., State House of Reps.
Palmer, Mark J., (AV) .... '57 '82 C.607 B.A. L.705 J.D. 1780 E. Broad St.‡
Palmer, Richard D., (BV) .... '47 '73 C.608 B.S.B.A. L.117 J.D. [R.D.Palmer]
Palmer, Robert G., (AV) .... '45 '70 C.210 B.A. L.910 J.D. [R.G.Palmer]
Palmer, Stephen E., (AV) .... '70 '95 C.970 B.A. L.117 J.D. [Yavitch&P.]
Palmer, Thomas W. .... '69 '01 C&L.608 B.A., J.D. [Ⓐ Thompson H.]
Palmer, Richard D., Co., LPA, (BV) .... 2550 Corporate Exchange Dr., Ste. 24

Palmer, Robert Gray, Co., LPA, (AV)
140 East Town Street, Suite 1200, 43215
Telephone: 614-484-1200 Fax: 614-484-1201
Email: bob@rgpalmerlaw.com URL: http://www.rgpalmerlaw.com
Robert G. Palmer.
Bad Faith Insurance, Personal Injury, Wrongful Death, Malpractice.
See Professional Biographies, COLUMBUS, OHIO

Palof, Marcia Elaine .... '48 '80 C.935 B.A. L.608 J.D. Legal Aid Soc. of Columbus
Pampush, Thomas A., (BV) .... '68 '93 C&L.608 B.S., J.D. [Schottenstein,Z.&D.]
Pandora, Frank T., II .... '47 '72 C.1062 B.A. L.665 J.D. Coun., OhioHealth
Pandora, Gary J., (BV) .... '53 '78 C.381 B.A. L.1003 J.D. 77 E. Nationwide Blvd.
Pannett, Thomas P. .... '68 '99 C.608 B.S. L.117 J.D. Asst. Legal Coun.
Paoletti, Paula Luna .... '66 '94 C.608 B.S. L.117 J.D. OH Atty. Gen. Off.
Papa, Nicole J. .... '70 '97 C.893 B.A. L.64 J.D. [Ⓐ Vorys,S.S.&P.]
Papp, Dennis M. .... '51 '76 C.967 A.B. L.608 J.D. Staff Atty., Ohio Leg. Serv. Comm.
Pappas, Leah, (BV) .... '66 '93 C.473 B.A. L.117 J.D. [Calfee,H.&G.]
Pappas, Robert T., (AV) .... '59 '84 C.118 B.A. L.608 J.D. [Jones,T.P.&P.]
Pappas, Thomas P., (AV) .... '60 '87 C.607 B.A. L.117 J.D. 66 E. Lynn Street
Paragas, C. David, (AV) .... '61 '90 C.611 B.A. L.117 J.D. [Benesch,F.C.&A.]
Parcher, Frederic C. .... '10 '33 C&L.608 B.S.B.A., J.D. 202 W. Schreyer Pl.‡
Pardi, James J., II .... '66 '92 C.608 B.A. L.117 J.D. 500 Southfront Street
Parello, Raymond S. .... '60 '96 C.323 B.A. L.117 J.D. 3363 Tremont Rd.
Pariser, David B., (BV) .... '49 '74 C.608 B.A. L.117 J.D. [Dana&P.]
Parisi, Donna J. .... '52 '01 C.266 B.S. L.117 J.D. 1111 Polaris Parkway
Parisi, Vincent A. .... '68 '01 C.608 B.A. L.117 J.D. Interstate Gas Supply
Park, Chan Wol .... '69 '00 C&L.608 B.A., J.D. Sheet Metal Contractors Association
Park, Howard C., (AV) .... '08 '31 C&L.608 LL.B. 4930 Reed Rd.‡
Parker, Darryl Odie .... '61 '99 C&L.117 B.A., J.D. [D.O.Parker]
Parker, Jennifer A. ...... '62 '87 C.473 B.A. L.608 J.D. Staff Atty., State Leg. Serv. Comm.
Parker, Darryl O., Co., L.P.A. .... 786 S. Front Street
Parkhill-Krein, Gayle E., (AV) .... '— '83 C.473 B.A. L.608 J.D. [Jones D.]
Parks, Edward Y. A., (BV) .... '51 '80 C.631 B.A. L.329 J.D. P.O. Box 1991
Parks, Gregory T. .... '65 '95 C.608 B.S. L.179 J.D. [Ⓐ Bricker&E.]
Parsell, Stuart G. .... '69 '94 C.1288 B.A. L.602 J.D. [Zeiger,T.&L.]
Parsons, Angela Gugle .... '72 '97 C.602 B.B.A. L.608 J.D. [Ⓐ Kegler,B.H.&R.]
Parsons, Benjamin J. .... '78 '03 C.473 B.A. L.608 J.D. [Ⓐ Taft,S.&H.]
Pask, Lisa M. .... '70 '99 C.150 B.A. L.117 J.D. [Ⓐ Pope,M.&Assoc.]
Passella, Michael V. .... '74 '00 C.608 B.A. L.117 J.D. [Ⓐ Isaac,B.L.&T.]
Patchen, Joseph M., (BV) .... '61 '87 C.93 A.B. L.608 J.D. [Carlile P.&M.]
Patchen, Richard V., (AV) .... '35 '59 C.1323 B.A. L.608 J.D. [Carlile P.&M.]
Patchen, Robert W. .... '59 '84 C.602 B.B.A. L.851 J.D. Asst. Atty. Gen.
Pate, Christina A. .... '77 '04 C.434 B.A. L.276 J.D. [Ⓐ Porter W.M.&A.]
Patel, Akhil .... '— '00 C.608 B.A. L.150 J.D. [Ⓐ Thompson H.]
Patrick, Gail Denise .... '54 '79 C.914 A.B. L.117 J.D. Legal Aid Soc. of Columbus
Patter, Jeffrey J., (BV) .... '56 '81 C.528 B.A. L.117 J.D. [Campbell,H.C.&V.]
Patterson, David C., (AV) .... '46 '75 C.309 A.B. L.477 J.D. [Readey&P.]
Patterson, David T., (AV) .... '51 '77 C.880 B.A. L.117 J.D. [Keener D.C.&P.]
Patterson, Gregory L., (AV) .... '53 '79 C.97 B.S. L.851 J.D. 43 Hamilton Pk.
Paul, Angela M. .... '72 '97 C.145 B.A. L.846 J.D. [Carpenter&L.]
Paulino, Harry R., (BV) .... '30 '59 C.604 A.B. L.608 J.D. 130 E. Wilson Bridge Rd.

Pausch, Carma R. '64 '94 C.608 B.A. L.117 J.D.
7100 N. High Street, Suite 307, 43085-2361
Telephone: 614-880-2303
URL: http://www.lawyers.com/carmarpausch
State and Federal Criminal Defense, Appellate Practice, Civil Litigation.
See Professional Biographies, COLUMBUS, OHIO

Pavarini, Peter A., (AV) .... '52 '77 C.1044 B.A. L.93 J.D. [Schottenstein,Z.&D.]
Pavlic, Paul V., (BV) .... '45 '70 C&L.608 B.A., J.D. 326 S. High St., Annex
Paxton, Robert C., II, (BV) .... '47 '72 C&L.608 B.A., J.D. [R.C.Paxton,II&Assoc.]
Paxton, Robert C., II & Associates, (BV) .... 10 W. Broad St., Ste. 1580
Payne, Timothy R. .... '59 '85 C.608 B.A. L.128 J.D. 5362 Gillette Ave.
Paynter, Craig B., (AV) .... '57 '82 C.207 B.A. L.8 J.D. [Chester,W.&S.]
Paynter, Donald G., (AV) .... '46 '71 C.473 B.S. L.608 J.D. [Bailey C.]
Payton, G. Michael, (BV) .... '53 '84 C.608 B.A. L.276 J.D. Admr., Off. of Real Estate
Pearlman, Kenneth T. '42 '68 C.659 A.B. L.178 J.D. (adm. in NY; not adm. in OH) 190 W. 17th Ave.
Pearsol-Christie, Erika .... '73 '98 C.381 B.A. L.608 J.D. 225 E. Broad St.
Peck, Richard Andrew '54 '96 C.1082 B.A. L.608 J.D. 369 S High Street, Courtroom 8A

Peck, Shaffer & Williams LLP, (AV)
175 South Third Street, Suite 600, 43215 ⊙
Telephone: 614-224-5205; 888-900-5205 Telecopier: 614-224-0069
Email: lawinfo@peck-shaffer.com URL: http://www.peck-shaffer.com
Members of Firm: Richard A. Cardwell; Edward Cavezza; Mary S. Duffey; Stephen P. Grassbaugh; Michael J. Melliere; Glendon B. Pratt; Dennis G. Schwallie; Thomas A. Wilson. Associates: Jennifer R. Blaser; Jason L. George; Marc Kamer; Nicole Stallworth (Not admitted in OH); Charles H. Waterman, IV.
Public Finance, Municipal Bonds, Municipal Bond Taxation, Municipal Securities. Tax Exempt Bonds, Housing and Urban Development, Health Care Finance, Tax Increment Finance, Municipal Leasing, Public Finance Taxation, Securities Finance, Blue Sky Law, Low Income Housing, Industrial Development Bonds, Municipal Bankruptcy, Public Construction Law.
Atlanta, Georgia Office: Peck, Shaffer & Williams LLP, Atlanta Financial Center, Suite M20, 3353 Peachtree Road, N.E. Telephone: 404-995-3850. Fax: 404-995-3851.
Chicago, Illinois Office: Peck, Shaffer & Williams LLP, 11 South LaSalle Street, Suite 2100. Telephones: 312-372-6060; 877-372-6060. Fax: 312-372-6085.
Cincinnati, Ohio Office: Peck, Shaffer & Williams LLP, 201 E. 5th Street, Suite 900. Telephones: 513-621-3394; 800-927-2663. Telecopier: 513-621-3813.
Covington, Kentucky Office: Peck, Shaffer & Williams LLP, 118 West 5th Street. Telephones: 859-431-7000; 888-431-7511. Telecopier: 859-431-0673.
Denver, Colorado Office: Peck, Shaffer & Williams LLP, 555 17th Street, Suite 845 South, 80202. Telephone: 303-296-3996; 877-296-0333. Fax: 303-296-0344.
Louisville, Kentucky Office: Peck, Shaffer & Williams LLP, 239 S. Fifth Street, Suite 1603. Telephone: 502-561-0054. Telecopier: 502-561-0058.
See Professional Biographies, COLUMBUS, OHIO

Peden, John, (BV) .... '56 '83 [Peden,P.&Assoc.]
Peden, Paley & Associates Co., L.P.A., (BV) .... 5969 E. Livingston Ave., Ste. 200
Peeples, Andrea Cheryl .... '69 '94 C.473 B.A. L.608 J.D. Asst. City Atty.
Peer, Jerry E., Jr. .... '— '02 C.737 B.A. L.117 J.D. [Ⓐ Strip,H.L.M.&T.]
Pelini Grillo, Mary C. .... '59 '94 C.910 B.S. L.608 J.D. [Baker&H.]
Pelteson, Edward F. .... '29 '60 C.608 B.S. L.1003 J.D. [E.F.Pelteson]
Pelteson, Edward F., Co., L.P.A. .... 85 E. Gay Street, Suite 404
Pencheff, Peter M., (Co., L.P.A.), (AV) .... '26 '52 C&L.608 B.A., J.D. 131 N. High St.
Peppers, Samuel Asa, III .... '56 '93 C.437 B.S. L.117 J.D. 373 S. High St., 22nd Fl.
Perdue, Dale K., (AV) .... '50 '80 C.607 B.A. L.608 J.D. [Clark,P.A.&S.C.]
Perez, John Xavier .... '69 '04 C.674 B.S.E. L.608 J.D. [J.X.Perez]
Pérez, Juan José G., (BV) .... '55 '85 C.999 B.A. L.851 J.D. [Perez&M.]
Perez, Rita A. .... '79 '04 C.117 B.A. L.8 J.D. [Ⓐ Bailey C.]
Perez, John Xavier, LLC, Law Office of .... 1505 Bethel Road, Suite 302
Perez & Morris, LLC, (BV) .... 8000 Ravines Edge Ct.
Perin, Charles H., Jr. .... '54 '80 C.976 A.B. L.150 J.D. Coun., Nationwide Insurance
Perkins, Catherine C., (BV) .... '58 '84 C.523 B.A. L.1003 J.D. Legal Coun. Coord.
Perkins, John R., Jr., (AV) .... '59 '84 C.473 B.A. L.150 J.D. [Jones,T.P.&P.]
Permar, David B. '46 '75 C.103 B.A. L.602 J.D. Chf. Legal Coun., Def. Logistics Agency, DCSC-G
Pernell, LeRoy .... '49 '74 C.264 B.A. L.608 J.D. Ohio State Univ., College of Law
Perrini, John J., (Co., L.P.A.), (BV) .... '32 '58 C&L.608 B.S., J.D. 155 W. Main St.
Perry, Carlyle V. .... '50 '79 C.36 B.S. L.208 J.D. 370 S. 5th St.‡
Perry, Jane P. .... '49 '85 C.437 B.A. L.851 J.D. Law Clk., U.S. Supm. Ct. J.
Perry, Paul E., (AV) .... '51 '76 C&L.608 B.A., J.D. [Ⓐ Plunkett&C.]
Perry, Robert J., & Associates, (AV) ...... '32 '62 C&L.608 B.A., J.D. 941 Chatham Lane
Pestello-Sharf, Stephanie, (BV) '54 '79 C.436 B.A. L.150 J.D. OH Atty. Gen. Off., Ct. of Claims Def. Sec.
Peterman, Laura M. .... '61 '86 C.473 B.A. L.607 J.D. 336 S. High Street
Peters, Dana Martin .... '53 '86 C.208 B.A. L.117 J.D. U.S. Atty.'s Off.
Peters, Geoffrey J. .... '69 '94 C.381 B.B.A. L.930 J.D. [Ⓐ Weltman,W.&R.]
Peters, Georgeann G., (AV) .... '52 '83 C.207 B.S. L.117 J.D. [Baker&H.]
Peters, James M., (BV) ... '50 '76 C.363 B.S.B.A. L.1003 J.D. [Kreiner&P.] (⊙Cincinnati)
Peters, Joanne S. .... '68 '94 C.966 B.B.A. L.608 J.D. [Isaac,B.L.&T.]
Peters, Megan Jones, (AV) .... '54 '80 C.473 B.S.Ed. L.117 J.D. 1390 Dublin Rd.
Peterson, Mark A., (BV) .... '62 '89 C.608 B.S.B.A. L.930 J.D. [Plank&B.]
Petitjean, David L., (BV) .... '55 '88 C.625 B.A. L.117 J.D. [© Chappano W.]
Petrecca, Michael A. .... '60 '85 C.1260 B.A. L.1003 J.D. 100 E. Broad St., Ste. 2100

Petree, Charles R. .... '33 '60 C&L.608 B.A., LL.B. Ct. of App. J.
Petrel, David B., (BV) .... '59 '84 C.81 B.A. L.117 J.D. 352 Bailey Place
Petrella, Barbara Jo .... '50 '89 C.381 B.A. L.851 J.D. Asst. Atty. Gen.
Petricoff, M. Howard, (AV) .... '49 '74 C.30 B.S. L.150 J.D. [Vorys,S.S.&P.]
Petrie, James G. .... '65 '92 C.473 B.A. L.608 J.D. [Bricker&E.]
Petro, James M., (AV) ....'48 '73 C.207 B.A. L.930 J.D. 1 Riverside Plaza
Petro, James M. '60 '99 C.446 B.S. L.1170 J.D.
(adm. in NH; not adm. in OH) Sr. Coun.-Nuclear, Amer. Elec. Power Serv. Corp.
Petro, John J., (AV) .... '37 '62 C&L.608 B.A., J.D. [Williams&P.]
Petro, John P., (BV) .... '67 '92 C.473 B.A. L.608 J.D. [Williams&P.]
Petro, Susan S.R. .... '64 '90 C.608 B.A. L.575 J.D. [Williams&P.]
Petrucci, Gretchen L. '65 '90
C.216 B.A. L.117 J.D. Atty. Examiner, Public Utilities Comm.
Petrucci, Mark C., (AV) .... '61 '90 C.608 B.A. L.117 J.D. [Morgan&P.]
Petrucci, Michael J., (AV) .... '30 '57 C.980 A.B. L.608 J.D. 380 S. 5th St.
Pettigrew, Grady L., Jr., (AV) .... '43 '71 C&L.608 B.A., J.D. [Cox,S.&P.]
Pettit, Chris R. .... '67 '98 C.610 B.S.E.D. L.608 J.D. [Shayne&G.]
Pettit, Ronald M. .... '44 '79 C.608 B.Sc. L.930 J.D. Defense Logistics Agency
Pettit, Susan .... '57 '97 C.266 B.S. L.117 J.D. 577 S. High St.
Pettys, Jeffrey C. .... '63 '93 C.608 B.S.B.A. L.117 J.D. 2720 Airport Drive
Petuchowski, Jonathan M. '59 '88 C.273 B.B.A. L.178 J.D.
(adm. in NY; not adm. in OH) 160 S. Dawson Ave.‡
Pfau, Edward L. .... '63 '91 C.150 B.A. L.117 J.D. 987 S. High St.
Pfefferle, Ben L., III, (AV) .... '54 '79 C.473 B.S.B.A. L.117 J.D. [Baker&H.]
Pfeifer, Paul E., (AV) .... '42 '67 C&L.608 B.A., J.D. Supm. Ct.
Pfeiffer, Barbara J. .... '60 '85 C&L.608 B.A., J.D. 375 S. High St., 7th Fl.‡
Pfeiffer, Beverly Y. .... '57 '83 C.608 B.S.Ed. L.607 J.D. Com. Pleas J.
Pfeiffer, Richard C., Jr. .... '44 '72 C.604 A.B. L.608 J.D. City Atty.
Pfeuffer, Alan John .... '55 '00 C.174 B.A. L.117 J.D. Fed. Pub. Def. Off.
Philbrick, Jon R., (BV) .... '52 '77 C.161 B.A. L.608 J.D. 326 S. High St., Annex
Phillips, Christopher G. .... '76 '01 C.851 B.A. L.1370 J.D. [Wiles,B.B.&B.]
Phillips, James E., (AV) .... '49 '75 C.94 B.A. L.930 J.D. [Vorys,S.S.&P.]
Phillips, Janet L. .... '56 '97 C.326 B.A. L.930 J.D. [Smith,P.&Assoc.]
Phillips, John D., (BV) .... '22 '49 C.97 A.B. L.608 J.D. 3100 Tremont Rd.
Phillips, Mark E., (BV) .... '54 '84 C.608 B.S.B.A. L.117 J.D. [Rich,C.&D.]
Phillips, Robert W., (BV) .... '23 '51 C&L.608 B.A., J.D. 3079 W. Broad St.‡
Phillips, Sherry M. .... '59 '87 C.473 B.F.A. L.608 J.D. Asst. Atty. Gen.
Phillips-Tate, Vivian A. .... '— '81 C.97 B.S. L.912 J.D. 5455 N High St
Piatt, Richard A. L. .... '68 '93 C.610 B.A. L.117 J.D. [Saia&P.]
Pickens, Joseph C. .... '— '03 C.228 B.A. L.608 J.D. [Chester,W.&S.]
Pickett, Patrick M. .... '63 '89 C.97 B.S. L.607 J.D. [Isaac,B.L.&T.]
Pickett, Richard C., (AV) .... '26 '55 C&L.608 B.S., J.D. [Bricker&E.] ‡
Pickrel, Deborah A. .... '— '04 C.884 B.A. L.608 J.D. [Baker&H.]

Pickrel, Schaeffer & Ebeling
(See Dayton)

Pierce, Eugene H., Jr. ...'54 '85 C.309 B.A. L.117 J.D. Pres., Pierce Communications, Inc.
Pierce, Janica A. .... '77 '02 C.838 B.A. L.608 J.D. [F.A.Ray]
Pierre, Darrell M., Jr. ..... '71 '96 C.217 B.A. L.608 J.D. 30 East Broad Street, 17th Floor
Pigman, Jack R., (AV) .... '44 '69 C.602 B.A. L.608 J.D. [Porter W.M.&A.]
Pilcher, Emily J. .... '79 '04 C.532 B.A. L.851 J.D. Asst. Chf.
Pinkerton, Sandra Elizabeth '61 '93
C.665 B.S. L.117 J.D. Assoc., First Allmerica Financial
Piper, Brian S., (BV) .... '50 '76 C.117 B.S. L.608 J.D. [B.S.Piper]
Piper, Brian S., Co., L.P.A., (BV) .... 555 West Schrock Road, Suite E
Pipino, Samuel M., (BV) .... '68 '93 C.604 B.A. L.608 J.D. [Wiles,B.B.&B.]
Pirik, Christine M. T. ... '60 '85 C.631 B.A. L.117 J.D. Atty. Exam., Pub. Utilities Comm.
Pirtle, Timothy A. .... '59 '88 C.608 B.S. L.117 J.D. P.O. Box 20221
Pittner, Nicholas A., (AV) .... '42 '70 C.608 B.A. L.117 J.D. [Bricker&E.]
Planey, Matthew R., (BV) .... '67 '96 C.980 B.A. L.851 J.D. [Crabbe,B.&J.]
Plank, Donald T., (AV) .... '52 '79 C.608 B.S. L.117 J.D. [Plank&B.]

Plank & Brahm, A Legal Professional Association, (AV)
145 East Rich Street Suite 400, 43215-5240
Telephone: 614-228-4546 Fax: 614-228-1472
Email: email@plankbrahm.com
Donald T. Plank; Richard C. Brahm; Mark A. Peterson;—Michael F. Ryan; Franklin E. Eck, Jr.; Catherine A. Cunningham; David Watkins; Jill Stemen Tangeman.
Civil Litigation, Trial Practice and Civil Appeals. Real Estate Development and Zoning Law. Construction Law, Corporate and General Business Law. Banking and Securities Law. Municipal Law. Land Annexation, Eminent Domain, Personal Injury and Negligence Law.
See Professional Biographies, COLUMBUS, OHIO

Plate, Norman Edward .... '61 '88 C.602 B.A. L.338 J.D. Atty. Gen.'s Off.
Platte, Walter R. .... '28 '64 C.124 B.S. L.266 J.D. 5597 Worcester Dr.‡
Platzer, Kathleen S. '62 '87 C.107 B.A. L.1187 J.D.
(adm. in NY; not adm. in OH) The Limited, Inc.
Plessner, Dirk P., (AV) ....'52 '87 C&L.851 B.B.A., J.D. [Eastman&S.] (Toledo)
Plinke, Eric J. .... '66 '92 C.303 B.A. L.851 J.D. [Porter W.M.&A.]

Plunkett & Cooney, P.C., (AV)
300 East Broad Street, Suite 590, 43215
Telephone: 614-629-3000 Fax: 614-629-3019
Email: plunkettinfo@plunkettcooney.com URL: http://www.plunkettcooney.com
Amelia Bower; Todd A. Cook; Jack S. Levey. Senior Associate: Paul E. Perry. Associate: David L. Van Slyke.
Alternative Dispute Resolution, Banking Law and Commercial Loans, Bankruptcy, Business Law, Construction Law, Corporate Law, Criminal Law, Debtor's Rights and Creditor's Rights, Environmental Law, Estate Planning, Food Service and Hospitality Law, Franchise Law, General Business and Civil Practice, Government Law, Health Care, Insurance, Intellectual Property Law, Labor and Employment Law, Legal Malpractice, Medical Malpractice, Municipal Law, Products Liability, Professional Liability, Real Estate Law, Securities, Taxation, Telecommunications Law, Trials in all Federal and State Courts and Worker's Compensation.
Offices also at: Detroit, Bloomfield Hills, Flint, Grand Rapids, Kalamazoo, East Lansing, Marquette, Mount Clemens and Petoskey, Mi.
See Professional Biographies, COLUMBUS, OHIO

Plymale, Ronald E., (BV) .... '41 '68 C&L.608 B.A., J.D. [Plymale]
Plymale, Stephen D., (BV) .... '50 '82 C&L.608 B.S., J.D. Atty. Gen. Off.

Plymale Partnership LLP, The, (BV)
495 South High Street, Suite 400, 43215
Telephone: 614-221-1166; 614-LAW-8000; 800-221-6675 Fax: 614-221-6633 URL: http://www.lawyers.com/protectingohio
Email: help@plymalelaw.com URL: http://www.protectingohio.com
Members of Firm: Andrew W. Cecil; Michael Keith Geiser. Associates: J. Scott Bowman; Eugene R. Critchett; C. Michael Wise; Sydney D. Stein. Of Counsel: Ronald E. Plymale.
Personal Injury, Products Liability, Wrongful Death, Medical Malpractice, Professional Negligence, Traumatic Brain Injury, Automobile Accidents, Nursing Home Torts, Civil Litigation.
See Professional Biographies, COLUMBUS, OHIO

Pocorus, Barbara Kirk .... '52 '84 C.999 B.S. L.229 J.D. Bank One, NA

Poe, Michael A., (AV) .... '53 '78 C&L.500 B.A., J.D. [Roetzel&A.]
Pohler, Susan Jean .... '55 '85 C.608 B.S. L.117 J.D. Ohio State Emply. Rela. Brd.
Pohlman, William J., (AV) .... '60 '88 C.604 B.A. L.608 J.D. [Vorys,S.S.&P.]
Polhamus, William R., (AV) .... '48 '73 C.475 B.A. L.608 J.D. [C.T.Freeman]
Pollack, Daniel .... '52 '84 C.604 B.A. L.161 J.D. Off. of the Gov.
Pollak, Lawrence Scott .... '56 '82 C.608 B.A. L.851 J.D. 336 South High Street
Pomeroy, Mark C., (AV) .... '56 '87 C.215 B.A. L.477 J.D. Sr. Coun., Bank One Corp.

Pomeroy, Rosemary Ebner, (AV) '55 '88 C.475 B.A. L.213 J.D.
120A Northwoods Boulevard, 43235
Telephone: 614-885-2101 Fax: 614-885-1783
Email: ebnerpom@netwalk.com URL: http://www.lawyers.com/rosemaryebnerpomeroylaw
Adoption, Estate Planning and Administration, Guardianships, Elder Law, Real Estate.
See Professional Biographies, COLUMBUS, OHIO

Pon, Christopher Elworth .... '59 '92 C.1044 B.S. L.608 J.D. Suprm. ct. of Ohio
Pontius, Donald H. .... '34 '58 C&L.608 B.A., J.D. Legal Dir., U.S. Trotting Assn.
Poole, Mark Randall .... '61 '01 C.610 B.B.A. L.117 J.D. Ohio Atty. Gen.
Pope, Julie A. .... '58 '84 C.81 B.A. L.607 J.D. [Pope,M.&Assoc.]
Pope, Robert A., (BV) .... '31 '58 C.608 B.A. L.607 J.D. 52 W. Whittier St.
Pope, Magelaner & Associates .... 31 E. Whittier St.
Popelsky, Steven Paul .... '57 '81 C.1271 B.A. L.150 J.D. Motorists Insurance Group
Popham, Kevin W. .... '62 '96 C.266 B.S. L.117 J.D. Asst. Atty. Gen.
Porembski, Chester P. .... '57 '84 C.608 B.Sc. L.117 J.D. 1087 Dennison Avenue‡
Porte, Stephen A. .... '61 '97 C.150 B.A. L.608 J.D. 192 Orchard Ln.
Porter, Anne Hoffman, (BV) '56 '84
C.915 B.A. L.117 J.D. Prof. of Law, Emeritus, Ohio State Univ.
Porter, Elise W. .... '52 '91 C.604 B.A. L.608 J.D. Asst. Atty. Gen.
Porter, Jeffrey D. .... '70 '96 C.532 B.A. L.117 J.D. [Kegler,B.H.&R.]
Porter, John T. '48 '86 C.1024 B.S. L.608 J.D.
Asst. Dir., Arbitration, OCSEA-AFSCME, Local 11
Porter, R. Gregory '54 '86
C.608 B.S. L.117 J.D. Chf. Atty. Hearing Exam., State Med. Bd.
Porter, Randall L. .... '51 '77 C.207 B.A. L.608 J.D. Asst. State Pub. Def.
Porter, Samuel H., (AV) .... '27 '53 C.31 A.B. L.608 J.D. [Porter W.M.&A.]
Porter, Susan, (AV) .... '61 '86 C.477 A.B. L.94 J.D. [Schottenstein,Z.&D.]
Porter, William G., II, (AV) .... '56 '84 C.31 B.A. L.930 J.D. [Vorys,S.S.&P.]

Porter Wright Morris & Arthur LLP, (AV)
41 South High Street, 43215-6194
Telephone: 614-227-2000; (800-533-2794) Fax: 614-227-2100
Email: columbus@porterwright.com URL: http://www.porterwright.com
Partners Columbus, Ohio Office: Jon M. Anderson; Edwin M. Baranowski; Phillip H. Barrett; Scott E. Baughman; John C. Beeler; James P. Botti; John E. Brady; Robert L. Brubaker; Brian L. Buzby; Craig R. Carlson; Thomas C. Coady; Robert H. Cohen; Daniel R. Conway; S. Ronald Cook, Jr.; Daniel W. Costello; James D. Curphey; Lloyd G. DePew, Jr.; Joyce D. Edelman; Joseph F. Elliott; Mason Evans, IV; R. Leland Evans; Lloyd E. Fisher, Jr.; Theodore G. Fisher; Marc L. Fleischauer; Gregory B. Foliano; Ralph F. Gildehaus; Timothy E. Grady; Constance M. Greaney; Kevin E. Griffith; James B. Hadden; Brian D. Hall; Paul A. Hanke; Polly J. Harris; John C. Hartranft, Sr.; Jeffrey T. Hayes; Richard J. Helmreich; Harry L. Henning; C. Andrew Ireton, Jr.; Laurie N. Jacques; Donald W. Jordan; William J. Kelly, Jr.; Robert C. Kiger; Lori-Lou Kimm; James A. King; Mark B. Koogler; Curtis A. Loveland; John F. Marsh; Daniel J. Massey; James M. Mattimoe; Alvin J. McKenna; J. Jeffrey McNealey; Richard C. McQuown; Mark K. Merkle, Jr.; Richard M. Mescher; Robert A. Meyer, Jr.; Katerina Eftimoff Milenkovski; Dixon F. Miller; Terrance M. Miller; Jennifer T. Mills; Scott E. North; Adele E. O'Conner; James S. Oliphant; Jack R. Pigman; Eric J. Plinke; Samuel H. Porter; Fred G. Pressley, Jr.; James H. Prior; W. John Pritchard; Diane C. Reichwein; John B. Rohyans; Donna M. Ruscitti; Christopher C. Russell; Joseph W. Ryan, Jr.; Christopher R. Schraff; Edward M. Segelken; Martin S. Seltzer; Darrell R. Shepard; David P. Shouvlin; Bradd N. Siegel; Erin F. Siegfried; Mark S. Stemm; John M. Stephen; H. Grant Stephenson; Karl J. Sutter; Robert J. Tannous; Richard G. Terapak; Jean Yingling Teteris; Kathleen McManus Trafford; Robert W. Trafford; David A. Tumen; Michael J. Underwood; Charles C. Warner; Franck G. Wobst; Nancy B. Young; Thomas A. Young. Associates Columbus, Ohio Office: Julie L. Atchison; Carl A. Aveni II; Bradley K. Baker; Kathryn S. Baltes (Not admitted in OH); Jennifer E. Beale; David S. Bloomfield, Jr.; Andrew M. Bojko; Stacey Garber Borowicz; Timothy J. Cahill; John Patrick Carney; Lori A. Clary; Molly S. Crabtree; Kysha L. Currence; Jaime Allison Dansa; Greg M. Daugherty; Aaron A. Dryer; Robert W. Edmund; Taheerah K. El-Amin; Andrew C. Emerson; Bryan R. Faller; David C. Faure; M. Theresa Finneran; Eric Benjamin Gallon; Karen K. Hammond; Elizabeth A. Hartman; Jay Hartranft; Michael E. Heintz; Kathleen Blickenstaff Hill; J.H. Huebert; Anne M. Hughes; Lawrence Bradfield Hughes; Patrick Ian Jackson; Bernard Jones; Jennifer L. Jung; Akihiko Kitaguchi (Not admitted in the United States); Kyle A. Knapp; Robert J. Krummen; Monique B. Lampke; Jaime Taryn Landrum; Christine D. Li; Shawn G. Lisle; Haimavathi Varadan Marlier; Colleen L. Marshall; Melanie Martin-Jones; Kristin E. Matisziw; Anthony R. McClure; Myra L. McKenzie; Tracy L. Merrill; Robert James Morgan; Eric C. Myers; Mitchell A. Naumoff, Jr.; Janice A. Nelson; David Kevin Orensten; Christina A. Pate; Andrew R. Post; Nicole S. Randall; Tracie Ransom; Paul G. Rozelle; Robert J. Schmidt; Lindsay M. Sestile; Aaron M. Shank; Kyle T. Shaw; Ryan Patrick Sherman; Jeremy David Siegfried; Mark A. Snider; Jenny T. Swinerton; Heather N. Taylor; M. Todd Taylor; John Kenneth Thien; Terry L. Thomson; Brett P. Thornton; Aaron T. Tulencik; Darin L. Van Vlerah; Kendall S. Verrett; Jay A. Yurkiw. Of Counsel Columbus, Ohio Office: William E. Arthur; Donald L. Beckett (Also Member of Robins, Beckett, Hammond & Sewards); Andrew S. Bergman; Howard P. Fink; Ralph K. Frasier; Kevin Hawley (Not admitted in OH); Charles J. Kurtz, III; Wayman C. Lawrence, III; Frank R. Morris, Jr.; Robert J. Nordstrom; David E. Northrop; Patrick J. Smith; George E. Zola. Counsel to the Firm: Lisa L. Eschleman.
Alternative Dispute Resolution, Agricultural Law, Antitrust and Trade Regulation, Business and Corporate, Complex Litigation, Construction, Employee Benefits, Energy and Utilities, Environment, Federal Administrative Law, Federal Contracting and Procurement, Financial Institutions, General Practice, Governmental Affairs, Health Care, Insurance, Intellectual Property, International Business, Labor and Employment, Litigation, Public Law, Public Finance, Real Estate, Securities, Taxation, Technology, Trusts and Estates.
Cincinnati, Ohio Office: 250 E. Fifth Street, Suite 2200, 45202-5117. Telephones: 513-381-4700; (800-582-5813). Fax: 513-421-0991. Internet: cincinnati@porterwright.com.
Cleveland, Ohio Office: 925 Euclid Avenue, Suite 1700, 44115-1483. Telephones: 216-443-9000; (800-824-1980). Fax: 216-443-9011. Internet: cleveland@porterwright.com.
Dayton, Ohio Office: One Dayton Centre, One South Main Street, Suite 1600, 45402-2028. Telephones: 937-449-6810; (800-533-4434). Fax: 937-449-6820. Internet: dayton@porterwright.com.
Naples, Florida Office: 5801 Pelican Bay Boulevard, Suite 300, 34108-2709. Telephones: 239-593-2900; (800-876-7962). Fax: 239-593-2990. Internet: naples@porterwright.com.
Washington, D.C. Office: 1919 Pennsylvania Avenue, N.W., Suite 500, 20006-3434. Telephones: 202-778-3000; (800-456-7962). Fax: 202-778-3063. Internet: washington@porterwright.com.
See Professional Biographies, COLUMBUS, OHIO

Portman, Frederic A., (AV) .... '47 '73 C&L.608 B.S.Ed., J.D. [Portman,F.&F.]
Portman, Foley & Flint LLP, (AV) .... 471 East Broad Street Suite 1820
Portugal, Gerald, (BV) .... '35 '70 C.339 B.S. L.117 J.D. Mag., Prob. Ct.
Post, Andrew R. .... '78 '03 C.210 B.A. L.117 J.D. [Porter W.M.&A.]
Post, G. Roger, (AV) '43 '71 C.532 B.A. L.608 J.D.
VP Sec. & Gen. Coun., White Castle Management Co.
Post, Roger C., (BV) .... '30 '66 C.474 B.S. L.117 J.D. 2657 Woodstock Rd.
Post, Sharon L. .... '49 '85 C&L.8 B.A., J.D. Assoc. Gen. Coun., Borden Chemical, Inc.
Post, William R. .... '— '00 C.473 A.B. L.124 J.D. [Baker&H.]

Postlewaite, Charles C., (AV) '55 '82 C.951 B.A. L.607 J.D.
3040 Riverside Drive, Suite 122, 43221
Telephone: 614-486-2111 Fax: 614-486-8943
Email: ccpostlaw@aol.com URL: http://www.lawyers.com/p&jlaw
Business, Corporation and Commercial Law, Family/Domestic Law, Collections, Construction Law, Mechanics Liens, Real Estate, Probate and Estate Planning, Personal Injury, Civil and Criminal Litigation in all State and Federal Courts.
See Professional Biographies, COLUMBUS, OHIO

Postlewaite, David M., (AV) ......'12 '37 C.951 A.B. L.608 LL.B. 370 N Columbia Ave.‡
Postlewaite, William N., Sr., (AV) .... '18 '47 C.951 B.A. L.608 J.D. 3040 Riverside Dr.‡
Poth, Christine M. ....'69 '95 C.150 B.A. L.608 J.D. [Bricker&E.]
Poth, Jeffery M., (BV) ....'68 '93 C.473 B.S. L.608 J.D. [Lane,A.&H.]
Pouget, Anne D. ....'75 '03 C.276 B.S. L.608 J.D. [🄰 Kegler,B.H.&R.]
Pouliot, John A. ....'48 '78 C&L.569 B.A., J.D. Ohio Department of Insurance
Powell, D. Scott ....'66 '92 C.608 B.A. L.597 J.D. [Vorys,S.S.&P.]
Powers, Victoria E., (AV) .... '59 '87 C.518 B.A. L.1065 J.D. [Schottenstein,Z.&D.]
Pratt, Glendon B., (AV) ....'57 '82 C.473 B.A. L.477 J.D. [Peck,S.&W.]
Pratt, Jennifer L., (BV) ....'61 '87 C.303 B.A. L.1119 J.D. Asst. Atty. Gen.
Pratt, Lawrence D., (BV) ....'48 '73 C.473 B.A. L.608 J.D. Asst. Atty. Gen.
Precario, Peter A., Law Offices of, (BV) ......'43 '70 C&L.608 B.A., J.D. 326 S. High St.
Preisse, Dana Suzanne, (BV) '60 '85
C.608 B.A. L.117 J.D. Com. Pleas Dom. Rel. & Juv. Div. J.
Prendergast, Melissa M. ....'75 '02 C.473 B.Phil. L.608 J.D. [🄰 Brenner,B.G.&M.]
Press, Katherine J., (BV) ....'57 '82 C.477 B.G.S. L.608 J.D. Asst. Pros. Atty.
Pressler, Timothy A. '47 '76 C.473 B.A. L.608 J.D.
Sr. Dir. Claims Oprts., Amer. Commerce Ins. Co.
Pressley, Fred G., Jr., (AV) ....'53 '78 C.999 B.A. L.597 J.D. [Porter W.M.&A.]
Preston, C. Kathryn, (AV) '57 '82
C&L.362 B.A., J.D. V.P., Sr. Coun., The Huntington Natl. Bk.
Preston, Charles A. ....'71 '97 C.999 B.A. L.117 J.D. 1265 Neil Ave.
Preston, Elizabeth A. '64 '94 C.608 B.A. L.117 J.D.
U.S. Dist. Ct., Southern Dist. of OH
Preston, Robert C., (AV) ....'34 '58 C&L.608 B.S., J.D. [Buckingham,D.&B.]
Price, Gary Paul, (BV) ....'48 '73 C.631 B.A. L.851 J.D. 555 City Park Ave.
Price, Rebecca Roderer ....'76 '01 C&L.608 B.S., J.D. [🄰 Kegler,B.H.&R.]
Price, Thelma Thomas ....'52 '76 C.1177 B.A. L.608 J.D. Asst. Atty. Gen.
Price, W. Evan, II ....'64 '91 C.197 B.A. L.260 J.D. [Bailey C.]
Princehorn, Rebecca Coleman, (AV) ....'57 '81 C.631 B.A. L.378 J.D. [Bricker&E.]
Prior, James H. ....'59 '85 C.645 B.A. L.893 J.D. [Porter W.M.&A.]
Prisley, Amy Wolfe ....'76 '01 C.610 B.A. L.117 J.D. Pub. Def. Off.
Pritchard, Glen R., (AV) ....'62 '88 C.207 B.A. L.608 J.D. [Clark,P.A.&S.C.]
Pritchard, W. John, (BV) ....'47 '72 C&L.966 B.B.A., J.D. [Porter W.M.&A.]
Pritchett, Clark P., Jr., (AV) ....'43 '68 C&L.608 B.A., J.D. [Rance,P.B.K.&E.]
Proctor, Penelope A., (AV) '55 '80 C.317 B.A. L.477 J.D.
V.P. & Asst. Gen. Coun., Riverside Methodist Hosp.
Proels, Sebastian E. ....'67 '99 C.145 B.A. L.124 J.D. [🄰 Vorys,S.S.&P.]
Prophater, Manderley Rush ..... '68 '94 C.967 B.A. L.201 J.D. Coun., BISYS Fund Servs.
Prophater, William H., Jr. ....'68 '98 C.676 B.S. L.201 J.D. [Lane,A.&H.]
Prosek, Bryan K. ....'66 '91 C&L.608 B.A., J.D. [Schottenstein,Z.&D.]
Prunte, Thomas J. '57 '82
C.608 B.A. L.117 J.D. Assoc. Gen. Coun., Nationwide Insurance
Pryce, Deborah D. ....'51 '76 C.608 B.A. L.117 J.D. (M.C.)
Pryor, David W., (AV) ....'56 '84 C.473 B.A. L.117 J.D. [Gallagher,G.P.T.&L.]
Puckett, Frederick D. ....'27 '51 C&L.608 B.S., J.D. Chf. Coun., State Legis. Serv. Comm.
Puckett, Milton A., (AV) ....'40 '70 C.610 A.B. L.608 J.D. 155 W. Main St.
Purcell, Cary W., (BV) ....'59 '84 C.339 B.S. L.221 J.D. [Purcell&S.]
Purcell & Scott, Co., L.P.A., (BV) .... 6035 Memorial Drive
Pursglove, Joseph, II, (BV) ....'51 '75 C.473 A.B. L.117 J.D. 1295 S. High Street
Pusateri, Paul D. ....'52 '77 C.611 B.A. L.117 J.D. 28 W. Henderson Road
Putnam, David H. ....'24 '49 C&L.608 B.S., J.D. 100 E. Broad St.
Pyles, Clement W. ....'— '75 C&L.608 B.A., J.D. 1405 Fahlander Drive N.
Pyles, Tracy Stott ....'73 '01 C.97 B.A. L.608 J.D. [🄰 Littler M.]
Quayle, Jeffrey D., (AV) '54 '78
C.473 B.S. L.608 J.D. OH Bkrs. League Trust & Investment D
Quenemoen, Helen M., (BV) ....'41 '85 C.118 B.A. L.608 J.D. [🄰 Loveland&B.]
Quinn, David Michael ....'51 '78 C.611 B.A. L.117 J.D. Div. of Securities
Radnor, Alan T., (AV) ....'46 '72 C.385 A.B. L.608 J.D. [Vorys,S.S.&P.]
Rafferty, Robert C., (AV) ....'53 '84 C.294 B.A. L.117 J.D. [Bricker&E.]
Rakestraw, W. Vincent ....'40 '68 C.610 B.S. L.117 J.D. 4930 Reed Rd.
Rall, Caroline E. ....'70 '96 C.210 B.A. L.117 J.D. Bureau of Workers Comp.
Ralph, Amauda S. ...'50 '83 C.446 B.S. L.273 J.D. Legal Dept., Ohio Envir. Prot. Agency
Ralph, H. Lowell '29 '58 C.101 L.878 J.D.
(adm. in UT; not adm. in OH) 4300 E. Fifth Ave.‡
Ralston, J. Christopher, (BV) ....'47 '72 C.362 B.A. L.117 J.D. 519 S. 4th St.
Ramseyer, Becky L. ....'77 '03 C.610 B.S. L.150 J.D. [🄰 Bricker&E.]
Rance, William E., (AV) ....'24 '51 C.885 B.A. L.608 J.D. [🄱 Rance,P.B.K.&E.]
Rance, Pritchett, Brantner, Keller & Ely Co., L.P.A., (AV) ....1720 Zollinger Rd.
Randall, Nicole S. ....'73 '00 C&L.608 B.A., J.D. [🄰 Porter W.M.&A.]
Randall, S. Brewster, II ....'68 '93 C.207 B.A. L.117 J.D. [Kincaid,R.&C.]
Randall, Samuel B., (AV) ....'26 '51 C&L.608 B.A., J.D. [Kincaid,R.&C.]
Randazzo, Samuel C., (AV) ....'49 '75 C.8 B.S. L.117 J.D. [McNees W.&N.]
Rankin, Gregory D., (AV) ....'52 '77 C.20 B.A. L.608 J.D. [Lane,A.&H.]
Rankin, Michael R., (AV) ....'53 '79 C.608 B.A. L.851 J.D. [Rankin]
Rankin, Timothy S. ....'65 '92 C&L.608 B.A., J.D. [Onda,L.&R.]
Rankin Law Offices, (AV) .... 545 E. Town Street
Ransier, Frederick L., III, (AV) ....'49 '74 C.1023 B.A. L.608 J.D. [Vorys,S.S.&P.]
Ransier, Kathleen H., (AV) ....'47 '74 C.926 B.A. L.608 J.D. [Vorys,S.S.&P.]
Ransom, Lenora Serlista ....'69 '99 C.610 B.B.A. L.117 J.D. Ct. of App.
Ransom, Tracie ....'79 '04 C.16 B.S. L.339 J.D. [🄰 Porter W.M.&A.]
Ranum, Darrell B. ....'52 '86 C.1257 B.A. L.117 J.D. V.P., OHIC Ins. Co.
Rastetter, Richard C., Jr. ....'46 '72 C.597 B.S.B.A. L.221 J.D. 5343 Castle Pines‡
Ratchford, Robert L., Jr. .... '44 '75 C.967 A.B. L.117 J.D. Pres., Dealers Alliance Corp.
Rathbun, Donald H., (BV) ....'15 '52 C.214 B.A. L.266 J.D. 416 Eastmoor Blvd.
Rattan, James E., (BV) ....'34 '62 C.608 B.A. L.178 LL.B. Asst. U.S. Atty.
Rau, John E. ....'56 '97 C.793 B.S. L.608 J.D. Legislative Serv. Comm.
Rawski, John ....'55 '88 C.648 B.S.Ed. L.117 J.D. Staff Atty., Ohio Ethics Comm.
Ray, Carol Lynn ... '62 '87 C.610 B.B.A. L.8 J.D. Off. of Gen. Coun., OH Dept. of Health
Ray, Frank A., (AV) ....'49 '73 C&L.608 B.A., J.D. [F.A.Ray]
Ray, Frank D. ....'40 '67 C&L.608 B.S.Ed., J.D. Dist. Dir., Small Bus. Adm.

Ray, Frank A., Co., L.P.A., (AV)
Suite 1000, 65 East State Street, 43215
Telephone: 614-221-7791 Fax: 614-221-4012
Email: far@raylaw.com
Frank A. Ray;—Janica A. Pierce. Of Counsel to: Chester, Willcox & Saxbe LLP.
Civil Trial and Appellate Practice in Personal Injury and Wrongful Death. Automobile Accidents, Negligence, Products Liability, Employer Intentional Tort, Business Litigation and Sports Law.
See Professional Biographies, COLUMBUS, OHIO

Raybuck, David W., (BV) ...... '60 '85 C.473 B.S. L.608 J.D. Sr. Coun., Bank One Corp.
Read, Robert O., (BV) ....'15 '39 C&L.608 B.S., J.D. 580 S. High St.
Readey, James A., (AV) ....'44 '70 C.210 B.A. L.608 J.D. [Readey&P.]
Readey & Patterson, (AV) ....37 W. Broad St., Ste. 420
Readler, Chad A. ....'— '97 C&L.477 B.A., J.D. [🄰 Jones D.]
Readler, Jennifer Dutey ....'71 '97 C.437 B.B.A. L.608 J.D. [Schottenstein,Z.&D.]
Real, Barbara M. ....'47 '77 C.97 B.S. L.1003 J.D. 194 W. Royal Forest Blvd.
Reasoner, W. Irl, III, (AV) ....'51 '78 C.347 B.A. L.790 J.D. [Habash,R.&F.]
Recchie, Joseph J., Jr., (BV) ....'54 '82 C.473 A.B. L.608 J.D. 1349 E. Broad St.
Rechner, Carl J. ....'49 '83 1966 Chatfield Road
Recker, Brice O. ....'48 '90 C.91 B.A. L.607 J.D. [🄰 Maguire&S.]
Reckless, Walter W., (AV) ....'36 '69 C&L.608 B.S., J.D. 33 North High Street
Rector, Susan D., (AV) ....'59 '84 C.896 B.A. L.575 J.D. [Schottenstein,Z.&D.]
Redick, Glenn B., (AV) ....'42 '70 C.608 B.A. L.117 J.D. City Atty's Off.
Redman, Timothy D. ....'49 '89 C.608 B.S. L.117 J.D. 1265 Neil Avenue
Redmon, Ronald L., Law Office, (BV) '39 '74
C.608 B.A. L.117 J.D. 520 S. High Street, Suite 200
Redmond, Charles D., (BV) ....'14 '54 C.608 B.S. L.117 J.D. 50 W. Broad St.
Reece, Guy Lester, II ....'43 '81 C.627 B.G.S. L.608 J.D. Com. Pleas J.‡
Reed, Frank J., Jr. ....'65 '91 C.608 B.A. L.117 J.D. [🄱 Benesch,F.C.&A.]
Reed, Joseph D. ....'52 '83 C.608 B.A. L.930 LL.B. 713 S. Front Street
Reed, Kristen S. ....'62 '89 C.97 B.S. L.117 J.D. Asst. Atty. Gen.
Reed, Michael R. ....'62 '94 C.25 B.A. L.608 J.D. [Squire,S.&D.]
Reed, Robt. R., (BV) ....'24 '52 C&L.608 B.S., J.D. 52 W. Whittier St.
Reed, Steven G., (BV) ....'47 '75 C.610 A.B. L.117 J.D. 200 N. High St.
Reedus, Benita Darlene Ford ....'61 '86 C.93 B.A. L.276 J.D. [B.D.Reedus]
Reedus, Benita D., Co., LPA ....2021 E. Dublin Granville Road, Suite 171
Reedy, Hollie F. ....'69 '95 C.381 B.A. L.608 J.D. Staff Atty., Ohio School Bds. Assn.
Rees, William Joseph ....'55 '81 C&L.117 B.A., J.D. 1332 Inglis Avenue
Reeve, Gary A. ....'56 '95 C&L.608 B.S.E.D., J.D. [Kennedy R.&K.]
Reeve, Simon Arthur ....'74 '00 C.608 B.A. L.117 J.D. Coun., Natl. Ins.
Reeves, James L., (AV) '47 '79 C.608 B.A. L.117 J.D.
Asst. Gen. Coun.-Litig., Amer. Elec. Power Serv. Corp.
Reibel, L. Leah ....'59 '91 C.608 B.A. L.1364 J.D. [🄱 Robol]
Reichel, Jeffrey L. ....'50 '89 C.608 B.S.B.A L.117 J.D. Asst. Pros.
Reichenbach, Seth T. ....'48 '93 C.266 B.S. L.117 J.D. 35 E. Livingston Ave.
Reichley, John P. ....'61 '90 C.532 B.A. L.117 J.D. Asst. Atty. Gen.
Reichley, Kevin R. ....'52 '79 C.930 B.A. L.608 J.D. Data Analysis Servs. Co.
Reichwein, Diane C., (AV) ....'52 '83 C.665 B.A. L.608 J.D. [Porter W.M.&A.]
Reid, Nelson M. ....'72 '97 C.197 B.A. L.228 J.D. [Bricker&E.]
Reidy, Joseph M., (AV) ....'55 '85 C.150 B.S. L.117 J.D. [Schottenstein,Z.&D.]
Reiff, Richard Theodore ....'47 '91 C.352 B.S. L.117 J.D. Dept. of Trans.
Reilly, Archer E. ....'18 '53 C.608 B.S. L.117 J.D. Ret. Ct. of Appl. J.
Reilly, Arlene Lynch ....'51 '78 C.741 B.A. L.117 J.D. Nationwide Life Ins. Co.
Reilly, John J. '64 '89 C.363 B.A. L.608 J.D.
Assoc. Legal Coun., Ohio State University, The
Reilly, Stephen A., (BV) ....'47 '75 C.608 B.A. L.117 J.D. Atty. Gen. Off.
Reinhard, Ann K. ....'42 '78 C.608 B.S. L.117 J.D. Pub. Utilities Comm. of Ohio
Reinhard, Daniel A. ....'74 '02 C.608 B.S. L.179 J.D. [🄰 Calfee,H.&G.]
Reinhard, Dean G., (BV) ....'40 '65 C&L.608 B.S., J.D. [D.G.Reinhard]
Reinhard, Dean G., Co., L.P.A., (BV) .... 501 S. High Street
Reinoehl, Erika M. ....'75 '00 C.608 B.A. L.117 J.D. Atty. Gen.'s Off.
Reis, Allen J., (AV) ....'51 '76 C&L.608 B.A., J.D. [Weltman,W.&R.]
Reis, Kevin J., (BV) ....'52 '77 C&L.608 B.A., J.D. 215 S. Kellner Road
Reissland, Gaibrelle Marie ....'61 '89 C&L.117 B.S.N., J.D. 410 W. 10th Ave.
Reister, Frederick T., (BV) ....'44 '72 C.973 B.S. L.1340 J.D. [Merullo,R.&S.]
Reisz, Lisa Pierce ....'67 '92 C.309 B.A. L.608 J.D. [Vorys,S.S.&P.]
Reitler, Angela K. ....'72 '01 C.150 B.S. L.607 J.D. [🄰 Vorys,S.S.&P.]
Reitz, Mark R. ....'67 '96 C.266 B.S. L.117 J.D. [🄰 Kegler,B.H.&R.]
Reminger & Reminger Co., L.P.A., (AV)
65 E. State St., 4th Fl. (⊙Covington, KY; Akron, Cin., Cleve., Sandusky, Toledo, Youngstown, OH)
Renick, Anderson Minor, III ....'61 '97 C.886 B.A. L.179 J.D. Ct. of Claims of Ohio
Renne, Michael A., (AV) ....'62 '87 C.385 B.A. L.930 J.D. [🄱 Buckingham,D.&B.]
Rennick, Kyme W. ....'53 '82 C.138 B.A. L.117 J.D. Dep. Dir., Dept. of Nat. Res.
Rentas-Pilutti, Rachael Teresa ....'67 '92 C.980 B.A. L.608 J.D. State Indus. Comm.
Resnick, Alice Robie ....'39 '64 C.999 Ph.B. L.215 J.D. Supm. Ct. Jus.
Resnik, Marvin I., (AV) '48 '73 C.610 B.B.A. L.608 J.D.
Asst. Gen. Coun.-Regul. Servs., Amer. Elec. Power Serv. Corp.
Reulbach, Sue Ann, (BV) ....'48 '85 C&L.608 B.J., J.D. 369 S. High St., 5th Fl.
Reuss, James K., (AV) ....'52 '79 C.473 B.A. L.608 J.D. [Lane,A.&H.]
Reves, Randal M. ....'59 '86 C.608 B.S.B.A. L.1209 J.D. 3207 N. High St.
Revta, George, Jr. ....'55 '87 C.381 B.S. L.1003 J.D. Asst. Atty. Gen.
Reynard, Jeffrey D. ....'72 '99 C&L.608 B.A., J.D. 35 E. Livingston Avenue
Reynolds, Chadwick P. '73 '99 C.346 B.A. L.117 J.D.
Asst. Gen. Coun & Asst. Corp. Secy., Big Lots, Inc.
Reynolds, Diane D. ....'59 '85 C.608 B.A. L.117 J.D. [🄱 Taft,S.&H.]
Reynolds, Jackson B., III, (CV) ....'58 '93 C.473 B.A. L.117 J.D. [Smith&H.]
Reynolds, Tyla Lynn .....'67 '93 C.231 B.A. L.1119 J.D. Sr. Coun., Nationwide Insurance
Rhea, Mark Lloyd ....'73 '99 C.610 B.A. L.851 J.D. Atty.
Rhee, Hansel H. ....'70 '95 C.967 B.A. L.823 J.D. [🄰 Schottenstein,Z.&D.]
Rhiel, Susan L., (BV) ....'59 '86 C.452 B.M. L.608 J.D. [Rhiel&Assoc.]
Rhiel & Associates Co., (BV) ....124 S. Washington Ave.
Rhodebeck, Larry ....'49 '80 C.381 B.A. L.608 J.D. Bur. of Workers Comp.
Rhodehamel, David R. '65 '90
C&L.608 B.A., J.D. V.P., Asset Mgmt., Wears Kahn McMenamy
Rhodes, Keely J. ....'77 '03 C.674 A.B. L.477 J.D. [🄰 Squire,S.&D.]
Rich, Jeffrey A., (AV) ....'45 '70 C.608 B.A. L.1003 J.D. [Rich,C.&D.]
Rich, Matthew A. ....'78 '04 C.1150 B.A. L.1556 J.D. [🄰 Bricker&E.]
Rich, Sandra L. ....'60 '86 C.8 B.S. L.608 J.D. [🄱 Nationwide R.I.]

Rich, Crites & Dittmer, LLC, (AV)
300 East Broad Street, Suite 300, 43215-3452 ⊙
Telephone: 614-228-5822 Telecopier: 614-540-7476
URL: http://www.RichCrites.com
Members of Firm: Jeffrey A. Rich; D. Michael Crites; Jeffrey A. Dittmer. Associates: Mark H. Gillis; Brandy M. Maas; Joseph E. Schmansky. Of Counsel: E. Joel Wesp; Rosemary Sova; James R. Gorry; R. Lamont Kaiser (Resident, Delaware Office); Leon D. Bass; Mark E. Phillips; Kenneth J. Molnar (Resident, Galena Office; Also practicing individually); Gregory P. Barwell; Jeffrey H. Jordan.
Corporate, Commercial, Real Estate, Zoning and Land Use, Family, Creditors Rights, Entertainment Law, Franchise, Tax, Bankruptcy, Administrative Law, General Civil Practice, Estate Planning, Administrative, Complex Litigation, Aviation Law, Personal Injury, Medical Malpractice, Automobile Accidents, Products Liability, Aviation Law, School and Municipal Law, White Collar Crime, Health Care Fraud, Government Law and Governmental Relations.
References: Huntington National Bank, N.A.; Key Bank.
Delaware, Ohio Office: 25 West Central Avenue, 43015-8340. Telephone: 740-363-1931; 800-619-5780. Fax: 740-363-4594.
Galena, Ohio Office: 21 Middle Street, P.O. Box 248, 43021-0248. Telephone: 740-965-3900. Fax: 740-965-2718.
See Professional Biographies, COLUMBUS, OHIO

Richards, J. Randall ....'61 '93 C.611 B.A. L.117 J.D. [🄰 G.E.Webster]
Richards, Kenneth M., (BV) ....'62 '88 C.645 B.A. L.608 J.D. [Luper,N.&L.]

Richards, Suzanne K., (AV) '47 '74 C.741 B.A. L.608 J.D. [Vorys,S.S.&P.]
Richards, William B. '43 '99 C.477 B.S.Ch.E. L.851 J.D.
Intell. Prop. Staff Atty., Battelle Memorial Institute (Pat.)
Richardson, Matthew J. '68 '03 C.813 A.B. L.608 J.D. [🄰 Vorys,S.S.&P.]
Richie, Crystal Renee '68 '95 C&L.117 B.A., J.D. [Gallagher,G.P.T.&L.]
Richner, Kristin E. '75 '00 C.207 B.A. L.112 J.D. [🄰 Squire,S.&D.]
Richter, Philip Clements '58 '95 C.473 B.A. L.117 J.D. Ohio Elections Comm.
Richter, Scott E., (AVⓉ) '56 '82
C&L.813 A.B., J.D. Sr. Assoc. Gen. Coun., Bank One Corp.
Rickard, Erik J. '72 '97 C.207 B.A. L.228 J.D. [🄰 Squire,S.&D.]
Rickards, Dorothy M. '— '94 C.608 B.A. L.117 J.D. Nationwide Life Ins. Col
Rickert, Benjamin J. '77 '03 C.49 B.A. L.966 J.D. [🄰 Vorys,S.S.&P.]
Ricketts, Richard T., (AV) '59 '86 C.608 B.S. L.117 J.D. [Ricketts]
Ricketts Co., L.P.A., (AV) 580 South High Street, 3rd Floor
Riddell, Peter H., (BV) '48 '74 C&L.607 B.A., J.D. [Riddell]
Riddell Law Office, (BV) 194 W. Johnstown Rd.
Ridgley, Thomas B., (AV) '40 '65 C.674 A.B. L.477 J.D. [Vorys,S.S.&P.]
Rieck, Kim A., (BV) '52 '77 C.930 B.A. L.608 J.D. [🄲 Squire,S.&D.]
Riedel, Timothy A. '60 '87 C.381 B.A. L.608 J.D. [🄲 Bailey C.]
Riedl, Daniel J. '78 '03 C.602 B.A. L.608 J.D. Asst. Prosecuting Atty.
Riehl, Lawrence A., (AV) '54 '79 C&L.608 B.S.B.A., J.D. [Vickery,R.&A.]
Riem, Sandee E. '71 '98 C.201 B.S. L.276 J.D. [🄲 Garvin&H.]
Riepenhoff, David A. '77 '02 C.631 B.A. L.117 J.D. [🄰 Downes,H.&F.]
Rigelman, Bruce D. '47 '84 C.494 B.A. L.893 J.D. Sr. Coun., Bank One Corp.
Rigg, Brian J., Attorney at Law, (BV) '59 '87 C.608 B.S.S.W. L.117 J.D.
755 S. High St.

Riggins, Melissa K., Attorney at Law '63 '88 C.97 B.A. L.8 J.D.
118 E. Main Street, 43215
Telephone: 614-228-6625 Fax: 614-228-6640
URL: http://www.rigginscriminallaw.com
Criminal Law, Felonies, Misdemeanors, Traffic Violations, Drug Crimes, Driving While Intoxicated, Domestic Violence and Drivers License Law.
See Professional Biographies, COLUMBUS, OHIO

Riggs, Warren G. '19 '53 C&L.266 B.S., J.D. 150 E. Mound St.‡
Rii, Ethan E. '74 '02 C.477 B.A. L.494 J.D.
(adm. in MI; not adm. in OH) [🄰 Squire,S.&D.]
Riley, Jennifer M. '76 '02 C.473 B.S. L.117 J.D. [🄰 Heckert&H.]
Riley, Thomas J., (AV) '44 '69 C&L.608 B.A., J.D. [Hahn L.&P.]
Rilley, Michael D. '64 '90 C.8 B.A. L.7 J.D. 55 East State Street
Rimelspach, Rene Lee '76 '01 C.602 B.A. L.608 J.D. Atty. Gen.'s Off.
Rinehart, Christopher A. '71 '99 C.967 B.S. L.608 J.D. [🄰 Carlile P.&M.]
Riseling, Jerry L., (AV) '37 '62 C&L.608 B.S., J.D. 165 N. High Street
Rishel, James R., (AV) '47 '72 C.610 A.B. L.608 J.D. 395 E. Broad St., Ste. 190
Ristau, Justin W. '77 '02 C.319 B.A. L.150 J.D. [🄰 Bricker&E.]
Ritchie, Brandy Ann '75 '99 C.610 B.A. L.608 J.D. Law Clk.
Ritter, Paul D., Jr., (AV) '30 '56 C.674 A.B. L.608 J.D. [Kegler,B.H.&R.]
Rivera, Rhonda R., (AV) '38 '68 C.705 B.A. L.912 J.D. Ohio State University
Roach, John R. '48 '74 C.602 B.A. L.608 J.D. [🄰 C.J.Hudak]
Roark, David T., (BV) '52 '80 C.611 B.A. L.117 J.D. Grange Mutual Cas. Co.
Roark, Sue Dovel '54 '80 C.893 B.A. L.117 J.D. 1970 Cardigan Rd.
Robbins, Pamela S., Law Office of '71 '97 C&L.608 B.A., J.D.
175 S. Third St., Suite 175
Robbins, Robt. L. '18 '46 C.188 A.B. L.266 J.D. Legal Advisor, Ohio Indus. Comm.
Robbins-Penniman, Gus E., (AV) '53 '78 C.894 B.A. L.117 J.D.
673 Mohawk St., 4th Fl.
Robek, Christine L. '78 '04 C.980 B.A. L.608 J.D. [🄰 Frost B.T.]
Robenalt, Robert M., (AV) '59 '89 C.473 B.A. L.1003 J.D. [Schottenstein,Z.&D.]
Roberts, Debra L. '59 '90 C&L.608 B.S., B.A., J.D. Dept. of Health
Roberts, Douglas S., (AV) '51 '76 C.610 B.A. L.608 J.D. 471 E. Broad St., Ste. 1400
Roberts, Janie D. '57 '85 C.610 B.G.S. L.117 J.D. Asst. Atty. Gen.
Roberts, Jeffrey D. '73 '01 C.473 B.S. L.893 J.D. [🄰 Vorys,S.S.&P.]
Roberts, Mary Agnes '61 '86 C.741 B.A. L.602 J.D. Ohio Dept. of Comm.
Roberts, Scott R., (AV) '51 '79 C.610 B.G. L.608 J.D. [S.R.Roberts&Assoc.]
Roberts, Stewart E. '48 '75 C.339 B.S. L.608 J.D. P.O. Box 298152
Roberts, Scott R., & Associates, Co., LPA, (AV) 1625 Bethel Road, Suite 102
Robertson, Jan E. '61 '91 C.339 A.B. L.273 J.D. Staff Atty. to Com. Pleas J.
Robinett, John D., (BV) '56 '82 C.532 B.A. L.930 J.D. [Schottenstein,Z.&D.]
Robins, Harlan W., (AV) '63 '88 C.477 B.A. L.245 J.D. [Baker&H.]
Robins, Ronald A., Jr., (AV) '63 '90 C.228 B.A. L.309 J.D. [Vorys,S.S.&P.]
Robins, Preston, Beckett, Hammond & Sewards, (AV) 556 E. Town St.
Robinson, Barry R., (AV) '46 '72 C.674 A.B. L.608 J.D. [Baker&H.]
Robinson, David J., (AV) '66 '92 C.97 B.A. L.608 J.D. [Schottenstein,Z.&D.]
Robinson, Janet Y. '64 '99 C.266 B.S. L.117 J.D. Supr. Ct. of OH
Robinson, Kenneth J. '72 '98 C.473 B.A. L.608 J.D. [Slowik&R.]
Robinson, Randal D., (BV) '49 '75 C.207 B.A. L.117 J.D. [Burman&R.]
Robinson, Tim J. '62 '90 C.608 B.S. L.588 J.D. [🄲 Squire,S.&D.]
Robison, Gary T., (BV) '35 '60 C&L.608 B.S., J.D. 3561 Kingsway Drive
Robison, Jennifer F. '71 '96 C.473 L.608 J.D. Coun., Abbott Labs.
Robol, Richard T., (AVⓉ) '52 '79 C.893 B.A. L.309 J.D. [Robol]

Robol Law Office LPA, (AVⓉ)
555 City Park Avenue, 43215
Telephone: 614-737-3739 Toll Free: 877-580-6859 Fax: 614-737-3756
Email: rrobol@robollaw.com URL: http://www.robollaw.com
Richard T. Robol. Of Counsel: Lori E. Shaw; L. Leah Reibel. Associate: Kimberly Edelstein.
Languages: Italian and French.
Civil Litigation, Trials and Appeals, Business Organizations, International, Admiralty and Maritime.
See Professional Biographies, COLUMBUS, OHIO

Robson-Higgins, Yanna Michelle '71 '98 C.575 B.A. L.1003 J.D. OH Asst. Atty. Gen.
Roby, Robert S. '70 '96 [Curry,R.S.&M.]
Rocco, Gerald A. '57 '86 C.381 B.S. L.607 J.D. Asst. Atty. Gen.
Rocco, Thomas J. '66 '92 C.608 B.A. L.365 J.D. Asst. Atty. Gen.
Rodgers, Todd M. '68 '93 C.473 B.A. L.150 J.D. [🄰 Chester,W.&S.]
Rodier, Ian Howard '64 '89 C.012 B.A. L.117 J.D. [Rodier]
Rodier Law Offices 221 South High Street
Roehrenbeck, Gabe J. '79 '04 C.840 B.A. L.117 J.D. [🄰 Thompson H.]
Roelle, Robert H., (BV) '28 '57 C.608 B.S. L.117 J.D. 100 W. Como Ave.‡

Roetzel & Andress, A Legal Professional Association, (AV) BR
National City Center, 155 East Broad Street, 12th Floor, 43215 ⊙
Telephone: 614-463-9770 Telecopier: 614-463-9792
Email: inquiries@ralaw.com URL: http://www.ralaw.com
Partners: David J. Demers; Thomas A. Dillon; Jeffrey E. Fromson; Robert B. Graziano; Erika L. Haupt; Edward C. Hertenstein (Certified Specialist in Federal Tax Law, Ohio State Bar Association); Daniel G. Hilson; Stephen D. Jones; Douglas M. Kennedy; Judith D. Levine; Richard S. Mulligan; Kevin J. Osterkamp; Michael A. Poe; Thomas L. Rosenberg; Charles D. Smith; Bradley L. Snyder;

(This Listing Continued)

Roetzel & Andress, A Legal Professional Association (Continued)
Michael S. Yashko;—Jeffrey S. Braun; Eric S. Bravo; Sharon Cason-Adams; Scot C. Crow; Melissa R. Hoeffel; Jamison S. Speidel; Vincent J. Squillace, III; Brian A. Tarian.
General Corporate and Business Law, Banking and Finance, Mergers, Acquisitions and Divestitures, Securities Law, Real Estate Law, Real Estate Development/Syndication/Condominium Law, Tax Law, Intellectual Property Law, Computer Law, Hospital and Health Care Law, Public Law and Finance, Governmental Relations, School Law, Commercial/Bankruptcy Law, Employment Law, Pension, Employee Benefits, Workers' Compensation, OSHA, Business and Commercial Litigation, Complex and Multidistrict Litigation, Antitrust Law, RICO, Federal Court Practice, Product Liability, Environmental Law/Toxic Torts, Insurance Law, Information Technology Law, Medical Malpractice Defense, Asbestos Litigation, Construction Law, 1st Amendment/Media Law, White Collar Criminal Defense, Railroad and FELA, Trucking and Transportation Law, Probate and Estate Planning, Utility Law, International Law, Trial and Appellate Practice.
Representative Clients: Akron City Hospital; Bank One, Akron, N.A.; Beacon Journal Publishing Co.; Capital University; Chessie Systems Railroads; General Motors Corp.; Pentair, Inc.; Seaman Corp.; State of Ohio; United States Fidelity & Guaranty Co.
Akron, Ohio Office: 222 South Main Street. Telephone: 330-376-2700. Telecopier: 330-376-4577.
Naples, Florida Office: 850 Park Shore Drive, Trianon Centre, 3rd Floor. Telephones: 239-649-6200; 800-535-7239. Telecopier: 239-261-3659.
Cleveland, Ohio Office: One Cleveland Center, 1375 East Ninth Street, 9th Floor. Telephone: 216-623-0150. Telecopier: 216-623-0134.
Cincinnati, Ohio Office: 250 East Fifth Street, 310 Chiquita Center. Telephone: 513-361-0200. Telecopier: 513-361-0335.
Fort Myers, Florida Office: 2320 First Street, Suite 1000. Telephone: 239-337-3850. Telecopier: 239-337-0970.
Toledo, Ohio Office: One SeaGate, 9th Floor. Telephone: 419-242-7985. Facsimile: 419-242-0316.
Tallahassee, Florida Office: 225 South Adams Street, Suite 250, P.O. Box 10369. Telephone: 850-222-7718. Telecopier: 850-222-8222.
Washington, D.C. Office: 1025 Connecticut Avenue, NW, Suite 220. Telephone: 202-625-0600. Telecopier: 202-338-6340.
See Professional Biographies, COLUMBUS, OHIO

Rogers, Barbara A. '67 '97 C.608 B.A. L.117 J.D. State Dept. of Educ.
Rogers, David A., (AV) '52 '76 C.608 B.S. L.309 J.D. [Bricker&E.]
Rogers, Donna M. '— '87 C.381 B.A. L.117 J.D. Atty. Gen.
Rogers, Douglas L., (AV) '46 '71 C.188 B.A. L.976 J.D. [Vorys,S.S.&P.]
Rogers, James Tullis, (BV) '42 '68 C.207 B.A. L.477 J.D. 1606 Lancaster Ave.
Rogers, Jeffrey Charles '60 '98 C.608 B.S. L.117 J.D. Franklin Co. Pros. Off.
Rogers, Nancy Hardin '48 '72 C.378 B.A. L.976 J.D.
Vice Provost & Pratt Prof. of Law, Ohio State Univ.
Rohletter, Daniel G., (AV) '59 '86 C&L.117 B.A., J.D. [🄲 Carlile P.&M.]
Rohyans, John B., (AV) '44 '69 C.473 B.S. L.608 J.D. [Porter W.M.&A.]
Romanello, George Michael '44 '74 [🄰 Reminger&R.]
Romanello, Michael, (AV) '44 '74 C.1044 B.A. L.117 J.D. 505 S. High St.
Romanoff, Marvin S. '40 '66 C&L.976 A.B., LL.B. Mun. J.
Rooney, Lisa Ann '59 '85 C.608 B.A. L.117 J.D. 30 E. Broad Street, Suite 1240
Root, Emily E. '76 '03 C&L.608 B.A., J.D. [🄰 Squire,S.&D.]
Roper, James M., (AV) '59 '87 C.528 B.S. L.117 J.D. [Isaac,B.L.&T.]
Rosati, Jack R., Jr. '58 '89 C&L.608 B.S.Phar., J.D. [Bricker&E.]
Rosato, Peter A. '70 '97 C.1103 B.A. L.608 J.D. [🄰 Calfee,H.&G.]
Roscoe, David A. '66 '01 C.1062 B.S. L.117 J.D. [🄰 Wolske&B.]
Rose, Daniel A. '62 '88 C.434 B.A. L.228 J.D. Two Limited Parkway
Rose, James V., (BV) '30 '58 C&L.608 B.Sc., J.D. 50 W. Broad St.
Rose, Michael D., (AV) '37 '63
C.611 B.A. L.930 J.D. Prof. of Law Emeritus, Ohio State Univ.
Roseboro, Anthony M. '60 '86 C.967 B.A. L.608 J.D. 109 N. Front Street
Roseman, D. Richard, Law Office '55 '95
C.980 B.S.B.A. L.179 J.D. 6016 Cleveland Avenue
Rosenberg, Eric John '65 '98 C.97 B.S. L.30 J.D. [Swedlow,B.L.M.&D.]
Rosenberg, Karen Krisher, (AV) '59 '84 C.967 B.A. L.608 J.D. [Lane,A.&H.]
Rosenberg, Neil, (BV) '54 '84 C.347 B.A. L.117 J.D. [N.W.Rosenberg]
Rosenberg, Thomas L., (AV) '55 '83 C.611 B.A. L.117 J.D. [Roetzel&A.]
Rosenberg, Neil W., (BV) 400 S. 5th St., Ste. 102
Rosenfeld, Aaron P., (AV) '51 '76 C.352 B.B.A. L.608 J.D. [Vorys,S.S.&P.]
Rosenthal, Brent D., (AV) '55 '84 C&L.608 B.A., J.D. [Buckingham,D.&B.]
Rosenthal, Janis B., (AV) '53 '81 C.347 B.A. L.150 J.D. [Thompson H.]
Rosenthal, Joseph Norbert '56 '84 C.25 B.A. L.117 J.D. Atty. Gen. Off.
Rosenthal, Lee S. '57 '82 C&L.608 B.A., J.D. [Goldman&R.]
Rosenthal, Martin S., (AV) '61 '85 C.150 B.A. L.608 J.D.
Sr. Coun.-Employ. Benef., Amer. Elect. Power Serv. Corp.
Rosenthal, Russell H. '69 '95 C.228 A.B. L.276 J.D. 317 S. Virginialee Rd.
Rosler, Russell R., (AV) '62 '87 C.902 B.A. L.188 J.D. [Vorys,S.S.&P.]
Ross, M. Andrew, (AV) '43 '67 C&L.608 B.A., J.D. 1660 Henderson Rd.‡
Ross, Marcus A. '67 '97 C.302 B.S. L.117 J.D. 375 S. High St.
Ross, Richard W., (BV) '53 '78 C.608 B.A. L.276 J.D. [Means,B.B.&B.]
Ross, Ruth Forte '35 '77 C.999 B.S. L.117 J.D. [R.F.Ross]
Ross, Stanley D., (AV) '40 '65 C.608 B.A. L.477 J.D. 1660 Old Henderson Rd.
Ross, William H. '51 '80 C.864 B.S. L.803 J.D. Supm. Atty.
Ross, R.F., Legal Service 2710 North Cassady Avenue
Rossman, E. Michael '— '98 C&L.477 B.S., J.D. [🄰 Jones D.]
Rossman, Jerry '33 '87 C&L.117 B.A., J.D. 3592 Corporate Dr., Ste. 105
Rossman, Kevin D. '61 '86 C.659 B.A. L.472 J.D. 3592 Corporate Drive
Roth, Allan E., (AV) '42 '72 C&L.608 B.A., J.D. P.O. Box 117
Rothchild-Dennison, Sallynda Pauline '61 '97 C.608 B.S.B.A. L.117 JD.
[S.R.Dennison]
Rothman, Robert A. '41 '66 C&L.608 B.S.B.A., J.D. Amusement Investment Co.
Rotondo, Eric P. '50 '75 C.301 B.A. L.607 J.D. 1276 Neil Ave.
Rourke, Michael J., (AV) '55 '81 C.608 B.A. L.309 J.D. [Rourke&B.]

Rourke & Blumenthal, LLP, (AV) BR
495 South High Street, Suite 450, 43215
Telephone: 614-220-9200 Toll Free: 866-257-9200 Fax: 614-220-7900 URL: http://www.randbllp.com
URL: http://www.rourkeblumenthal.com
Michael J. Rourke; Kenneth S. Blumenthal;—Robert P. Miller.
Personal Injury, Negligence, Products Liability, Medical Malpractice, Nursing Home Litigation, Wrongful Death, Intentional Tort, Insurance Disputes, Automobile Accidents, Civil Trial Practice, Aviation, Professional Liability.
See Professional Biographies, COLUMBUS, OHIO

Rowan, Charles Gregory '64 '89 C.201 B.A. L.608 J.D.
Ohio Dept. of Natural Resources
Rowe, Steven D., (BV) '49 '74 C.473 B.A. L.608 J.D. [Kemp,S.R.&L.]
Rowland, Jill Maureen '68 '93 C.8 B.A. L.608 J.D. Ohio Legis. Serv. Comm.
Rowland, Ronald L., (AV) '47 '72 C.967 B.A. L.608 J.D. [Vorys,S.S.&P.]
Royer, Barth E., (AV) '47 '72 C.309 A.B. L.477 J.D. [Bell,R.&S.]
Rozelle, Paul G. '72 '99 C.659 B.A. L.228 J.D. [🄰 Porter W.M.&A.]
Rozelle, Susan D. '73 '99 C.1175 B.A. L.228 J.D.
(adm. in MA; not adm. in OH) Asst. Prof., Capital Univ. Law Sch.

Rubadue, David W. '51 '84
C.608 B.S. L.117 J.D. Sr. Atty., Columbia Gas Distribution Cos.
Ruben, Don, (AV) .... '39 '64 C.478 A.B. L.150 J.D. 165 E. Livingston Ave.
Rubenstein, Richard W., (AV) .... '44 '69 C.31 B.A. L.569 J.D. [Squire,S.&D.]

Rubin, Daniel R., (BV) '57 '84 C.347 B.A. L.117 J.D.
4930 Reed Road, 43220
Telephone: 614-457-7700 Fax: 614-457-7878
Email: sandz10@yahoo.com URL: http://www.danielrubinlaw.com
Breach of Contract, Enforcement of Judgments, Business Formation and Termination, Business Start-Ups, Small Business Law, Creditors Rights, Commercial Law, Civil Litigation, Contracts.
See Professional Biographies, COLUMBUS, OHIO

Rubino, Joseph D. .... '60 '88 C.610 B.S. L.117 J.D. Asst. Atty. Gen.
Ruby, Thomas O., (AV) .... '57 '82 C.198 A.B. L.309 J.D. [Vorys,S.S.&P.]
Rucker, Retanio Anthony Joseph .... '59 '88 C.611 B.A. L.989 J.D. [R.A.Rucker]
Rucker, Retanio AJ, The, L.P.A. ....786 S. Front Street
Rudolph, Timothy J. .... '71 '99 C.608 B.A. L.201 J.D. 800 E. Broad St.
Rupert, David E. ..... '59 '99 C.608 B.S.B.A. L.117 J.D. Rupert Consolidated Enterprises
Rupert, Jeffrey G. ....'69 '95 C.597 B.A. L.608 J.D. [Ⓐ Frost B.T.]
Rupp, Daniel R. ...'44 '69 C.228 B.A. L.608 J.D. Asst. Gen. Coun., Nationwide Insurance
Rupp, Robert K., (BV) ....'57 '82 C.1260 B.A. L.608 J.D. [Baker&H.]
Ruscitti, Donna M., (AV) ....'52 '86 C.970 B.A. L.117 J.D. [Porter W.M.&A.]
Rusie, Jennifer S. ....'77 '03 C.880 B.A. L.569 J.D. [Ⓐ Vorys,S.S.&P.]
Rusie, Michael J. ....'77 '03 C.210 B.A. L.910 J.D. [Ⓐ Vorys,S.S.&P.]
Russell, Christopher C., (AV) ....'63 '88 C.385 B.A. L.608 J.D. [Porter W.M.&A.]
Russell, Gregory D. ....'49 '74 C.528 B.A. L.8 J.D. 52 E. Gay St.
Russell, Gregory D. ....'66 '92 C.902 B.A. L.309 J.D. [Vorys,S.S.&P.]
Russell, Paul A. '68 '93 C.293 B.A. L.117 J.D.
Asst. Chf. Legal Coun., Auditor of State of Ohio
Russell, Susan Leonard Fenderson '63 '88
C.970 B.A. L.608 J.D. School Employees Retirement System
Russell-Washington, Necol D. ....'66 '01 C.266 B.S. L.608 J.D. [Ⓐ Carlile P.&M.]
Russo, Gina R. ....'77 '02 C.97 B.A. L.896 J.D. [Ⓐ Vorys,S.S.&P.]
Rutledge, James A., (AV) ....'53 '78 C.201 B.A. L.608 J.D. [Bricker&E.]
Rutledge, John F., (BV) ....'49 '79 C.201 B.S. L.851 J.D. 854 E. Broad St.
Rutz, Allen L. ....'61 '98 C.150 B.S. L.117 J.D. [Ⓐ Vorys,S.S.&P.] (Pat.)
Ruzicho, Andrew J. .... '69 '94 C.477 B.A. L.902 J.D. 611 E. Weber Rd., Ste. 102
Ryan, Cheryl Lynn ....'72 '97 555 City Park Ave.
Ryan, Corinne N. ....'70 '96 C.363 B.A. L.117 J.D. [Lane,A.&H.]
Ryan, Daniel F., (AV) ....'48 '80 C.363 B.A. L.117 J.D. [Campbell,H.C.&V.]
Ryan, James G., (AV) .... '60 '85 C.201 B.A. L.608 J.D. [Bailey C.]
Ryan, Joseph E., Jr., (BV) ....'36 '64 C.602 B.S.C. L.215 J.D. [Ryan&R.]
Ryan, Joseph W., Jr., (AV) ....'48 '78 C.728 A.B. L.893 J.D. [Porter W.M.&A.]
Ryan, Laurence K. ....'64 '90 C.902 B.A. L.846 J.D. Banc One Investment Mgmt. Grp.
Ryan, Michael F. ....'45 '88 C.737 B.A. L.117 J.D. [Ⓐ Plank&B.]
Ryan, Randy G., (BVⓉ) '57 '82 C.234 B.A. L.862 J.D.
Asst. Gen. Coun.-Trans., Amer. Elect. Power Serv. Corp.
Ryan, Terise Fusco ....'67 '92 C.884 B.A. L.117 J.D. Indus. Comm. of Ohio
Ryan, Timothy J., (BV) ....'60 '91 C.473 L.608 J.D. [Gallagher,G.P.T.&L.]
Ryan & Ryan, (BV)
1890 Northwest Blvd. (⊙Honolulu, HI; Kalamazoo, MI; Williamson, WV; North Sydney, NS)
Saad, James A., (BV) ....'45 '77 C.737 B.A. L.117 J.D. [J.A.Saad]
Saad, Michael D., (AV) ....'41 '66 C&L.608 B.S., J.D. [Squire,S.&D.]
Saad, James A., LLC, (BV) ....2000 W. Henderson Road, Suite 400
Saalman, Gary J. ....'62 '89 C.473 B.S. L.602 J.D. [Vorys,S.S.&P.]
Sabath, Mark K. ....'66 '92 C.573 B.A. L.117 J.D. [Sabath&J.]
Sabath & Johnson Co., L.P.A. ....338 South High Street
Sabatino, Alessandro ....'68 '93 C.262 B.A. L.201 J.D. [Ⓐ Cheek&Z.]
Sabo, Roger L., (AV) ....'43 '68 C.608 B.A. L.276 J.D. [Schottenstein,Z.&D.]
Sabol, Garry Albert, (CV) ....'54 '82 C.650 B.A. L.117 J.D. 1526 DeMorest Rd.

Sabol, Suzanne Kay, (BV) '53 '83 C.650 B.S. L.117 J.D.
820 South High Street, 43206
Telephone: 614-445-0793 Fax: 614-445-7948
Email: s.sabol@gte.net URL: http://www.suzannekaysabol.com
Family Law and Domestic Relations.
See Professional Biographies, COLUMBUS, OHIO

Sadler, Lisa L. ....'57 '84 C.608 B.S.S.W. L.117 J.D. Com. Pleas J.
Sagartz, Andrew P. .... '67 '98 C.1433 B.S. L.608 J.D. [Ⓖ Slowik&R.] (⊙Gurnee, IL)
Sagone, Matthew L. ....'68 '94 C.608 B.A. L.117 J.D. [Ⓐ Squire,S.&D.]
Sagun, Stanley J., Jr. .... '63 '92 C.381 B.B.A. L.117 J.D. Columbia Gas Distribution Cos.
Saia, Jon J. ....'62 '87 C.1113 B.A. L.117 J.D. [Saia&P.]
Saia & Piatt, P.L.L. ....713 South Front Street (⊙Delaware)
Saigo, Holly H. .... '— '01 C.260 B.A. L.276 J.D. [Ⓐ Jones D.]
St. Clair, Clifford M., (BV) ....'22 '57 C.645 A.B. L.228 J.D. 1275 Kingsgate Rd.‡

St. Clair, Robert B., (AV) '48 '77 C&L.607 B.A., J.D.
580 South High Street, Suite 200, 43215-5644
Telephone: 614-224-4114 Fax: 614-224-3804
Email: rstclair@macb-law.com URL: http://www.stclairlaw.com
Trusts and Estates, Wills, Probate, Elder Law, Estate Planning, Estate Administration.
See Professional Biographies, COLUMBUS, OHIO

St. Pierre, Thomas G. '64 '89 C.473 A.B. L.608 J.D.
Sr. Coun.-Real Estate, Amer. Elec. Power Serv. Corp.
Saker, Theodore R. ....'22 '47 C.363 A.B. L.276 J.D. 2634 Clairmont Ct.
Saker, Theodore R., Jr. ....'60 '84 C.608 B.A. L.117 J.D. 1374 King Ave.
Salerno, Amelia Angela ....'56 '82 C.980 B.A. L.608 J.D. 295 W. 4th Ave.
Salimbene, John M., (AV) ....'44 '69 C&L.608 B.A., J.D. Asst. Pros. Atty.
Salzler, Mark J. ....'51 '76 C.363 B.A. L.607 J.D. 10 W. Broad St.
Samansky, Allan J. '45 '74 C.309 B.A. L.659 J.D.
(adm. in PA; not adm. in OH) Ohio State Univ.
Samples, Todd J. ....'75 '01 C.608 B.A. L.117 J.D. [Ⓐ Bailey C.]
Sams, Jeffrey B., (BV) ....'61 '87 C.610 A.B. L.608 J.D. [Luper,N.&L.]
Samsel, Edward C. ....'47 '83 C&L.608 B.S., J.D. Legal Coun., Dept. of Taxation
Samuel, Marcy B. ....'48 '83 C.831 B.A. L.117 J.D. 1331 Edgehill Rd.

Samuels, Harvey M., (AV) '49 '74 C.823 B.A. L.383 J.D. BR
500 South Front Street, Suite 1150, 43215
Telephone: 614-221-2580 Fax: 614-221-2575
Family Law, Divorce, Domestic Relations, Subrogation.
See Professional Biographies, COLUMBUS, OHIO

Samuels, Margaret Ann ... '34 '74 C.1101 A.B. L.608 J.D. Ohio Off. of Consumers Coun.
Samuels, Stephen P., (AV) ....'48 '75 C.477 B.A. L.588 J.D. [Schottenstein,Z.&D.]
Sanborn, Brandon, Duvall & Bobbitt Co., L.P.A., (AV) ....2515 W. Granville Road
Sandberg, Elisabet K. '73 '98 C.385 B.A. L.851 J.D.
Staff Atty., OH Legis. Serv. Comm.
Sander, Neil C. ....'78 '04 C.608 B.S. L.117 J.D. [Ⓐ Wiles,B.B.&B.]
Sanders, Deborah F. .... '54 '89 C.266 B.S. L.608 J.D. U.S. Atty. Off.
Sanders, Howard M. .... '50 '75 C.150 B.B.A. L.161 J.D. Asst. Chief Atty. Gen.
Sanders, Judith B., (AV) ....'52 '77 C.967 B.A. L.608 J.D. [Bell,R.&S.]
Sandhu, Manbir S. ....'— '00 C.8 B.A. L.1187 J.D. [Ⓐ Maguire&S.] ⊙
Sanford, Jay H. ....'46 '72 C&L.608 B.S., J.D. Mag.
Sant, Thomas R., (AV) ....'43 '73 C.385 A.B. L.607 J.D. [Ⓖ Bricker&E.]
Santangelo, Stephen A., (AV) ....'53 '78 C.970 B.A. L.930 J.D. [Weltman,W.&R.]
Santilli, Paul T. ....'29 '60 C.608 M.S.ChE. L.266 J.D. 1289 Fountaine Dr.‡
Sargeant, Richard T., (AV) ......'47 '75 C.117 B.S. L.608 J.D. [Eastman&S.] (⊙Toledo)
Sargus, Edmund A., Jr. ....'53 '78 C.103 A.B. L.930 J.D. U.S. Dist. J.
Sarrey, Michael P. '50 '77 C.608 B.S. L.245 J.D.
(adm. in GA; not adm. in OH) 2592 Canterbury Rd.‡
Sarver, Todd L. ....'— '93 C.607 B.S.B.A L.608 J.D. [Jones D.]
Sauer, Rena Guarnieri ....'69 '95 C.741 B.A. L.608 J.D. [Ⓐ Purcell&S.]
Saunders, Charles, Jr. .... '— '72 C&L.608 B.S., J.D. [Ⓖ Schottenstein,Z.&D.]
Saunders, Chas., (BV) ....'21 '47 C&L.608 B.S., J.D. 209 S. High St.
Saunders, O'Neal '66 '93
C&L.608 B.S.B.A., J.D. Fiduciary Coun., Auditor of State of Ohio
Sauter, John L. ....'40 '68 C.608 B.S.B.A. L.117 J.D. Sr. V.P., Natl. City Corp.
Sauter, Robert W., (AV) ....'47 '77 C.999 B.A. L.117 J.D. 225 E. Broad St.
Savage, James S., III, (AV) ....'56 '81 C.228 A.B. L.910 J.D. [McFadden W.&S.]
Savino, Angela M. Alexander ....'62 '88 C.150 B.S.N. L.117 J.D. [Ⓐ Perez&M.]
Saxbe, Charles R., (AV) ....'46 '75 C.802 B.A. L.608 J.D. [Chester,W.&S.]
Saxbe, William B. ....'16 '48 C&L.608 B.A., LL.B. [Ⓖ Chester,W.&S.]
Saxe, Charlene Anne ....'57 '89 C.818 B.S. L.117 J.D. State Med. Bd.
Saxon, Anne D. '64 '89 C.901 B.A. L.229 J.D.
Assoc. Gen. Coun., Nationwide Insurance
Saylor, Lyle R. '46 '74 C.473 B.A. L.608 J.D.
Mgr. Legal Analysis, Grange Mut. Cas. Co.
Scarsella, Paul Luke ....'70 '97 C.980 B.A. L.117 J.D. Co. Pros. Attorney's Off.
Schadek, Michael A., Law Offices of '68 '93 C.602 B.A. L.1003 J.D.
1537 Guilford Rd.
Schaefer, Carol S. ....'54 '87 C.610 B.A. L.608 J.D. Ohio Department of Insurance
Schaefer, Philip S. ....'44 '72 C.952 B.A. L.608 J.D. 2685 Haverford Rd.
Schaefer, Theresa Rittinger, (CV) '58 '85 C.532 B.A. L.608 J.D.
Assoc. Gen. Coun.-Offr., Nationwide Insurance
Schaeffer, Matthew T. ....'70 '96 C.608 B.A. L.117 J.D. [Ⓐ Bailey C.]
Schaeffer, Michael N., (AV) ....'49 '75 C&L.608 B.S.B.A., J.D. [Kemp,S.R.&L.]
Schafer, Dale C., (AV) ....'15 '49 C.381 L.948 J.D. 261 W. Johnstown Rd.
Schaffer, Grier D., (AV) ....'61 '88 C.397 B.A. L.117 J.D. [Earl,W.A.&D.]
Schaffner, Jeffery O. '59 '84
C.607 B.A. L.851 J.D. State Unemploy. Comp. Bd. of Review
Schantz, Roger L. .... '66 '91 C.607 B.S.B.A. L.608 J.D. [Benesch,F.C.&A.]
Scheaf, O. Judson, III, (AV) ....'58 '88 C.266 B.P.A. L.117 J.D. [Thompson H.]
Schear, Kathi L. ....'52 '78 C.322 B.A. L.8 J.D. 40 W. Gay St.
Scheiderer, Judith M. ....'— '91 C&L.608 B.A., J.D. [Dreher L.&T.]
Schellhaas, Kimberly M., (BV) ....'68 '93 C.475 B.A. L.117 J.D. [Lane,A.&H.]
Scherner, Hans, (AV) ....'42 '79 C.309 A.B. L.607 J.D. [Scherner,H.&C.] (⊙Delaware)

Scherner, Hanson & Cornwell, LLC, (AV) BR
130 Northwoods Boulevard, 43235-4725 ⊙
Telephone: 614-431-7200 Fax: 614-431-7262
Hans Scherner.
Civil Trial and Appellate Litigation in State and Federal Courts. Medical Malpractice and other Professional Liability, Personal Injury, Product Liability, Commercial, Corporate, Fraud and other Civil Litigation.
Delaware, Ohio Office: 5300 David Road. Telephone: 740-595-3366.
Lima, Ohio Office: 714 West North Street. Telephone: 419-222-1155. Fax: 419-227-3131.
See Professional Biographies, COLUMBUS, OHIO

Scherrer, Terrence M. .... '24 '58 C.608 L.266 J.D. 2860 Valleyview Dr.
Schiff, Michael S. '60 '86
C.150 B.F.A. L.910 J.D. Sr. Vice Pres., Schottenstein Invest. Corp.
Schimmer, Alexandra T. ....'— '02 C.674 A.B. L.976 J.D. [Ⓐ Vorys,S.S.&P.]
Schindler, Jerome R. ....'42 '68 C&L.608 B.S., J.D. 395 S. Chesterfield Road
Schira, D. Michael, (AV) ....'56 '90 C.608 B.S.C.E. L.840 J.D. [Vorys,S.S.&P.]
Schleppi, W. Joseph, (BV) '54 '79
C&L.117 B.A., J.D. Asst. Gen. Coun., Nationwide Insurance
Schlonsky, Michael A., (BV) '66 '91
C.597 B.A. L.608 J.D. Staff Coun., Consolidated Stores Corp.
Schlosser, Jacob A. ....'37 '62 C&L.608 B.S.B.A, J.D. [Wilcox,S.&B.]
Schmalz, Kurt Joseph ....'51 '89 C.473 B.S. L.117 J.D. 3316 North High Street
Schmansky, Joseph E. ....'67 '00 C.608 B.A. L.117 J.D. [Ⓐ Rich,C.&D.]
Schmidt, Robert J. ....'67 '93 C&L.893 B.A., J.D. [Ⓐ Porter W.M.&A.]
Schmidt, Sarah D. ....'51 '78 C.976 A.B. L.880 J.D. 800 Fairway Blvd.
Schmidt, William J. '55 '81 C.8 B.S. L.608 J.D.
Asst. to Dir., State Medical Bd. of Ohio
Schmitz, Patrick J. '65 '91 C.970 B.A. L.608 J.D.
Dep. Dir. of Legal Servs., Ohio School Bds. Assn.
Schneider, Karl H., (AV) ....'57 '82 C.207 B.A. L.117 J.D. [Maguire&S.]
Schneider, Keith W., (BV) ....'62 '89 C.473 B.A. L.117 J.D. [Maguire&S.]
Schneider, Mary Fairand, (BV) '61 '89 C.207 L.117 J.D.
Assoc. Legal Coun., Ohio State University, The
Schneider, William H., (AV) .... '25 '53 C&L.608 B.E.E., J.D. 2156 Portlow Dr.‡
Schoch, Frederick Carter ....'55 '80 C.597 B.A. L.608 J.D. Asst. Atty. Gen.
Schockling, Scott David ....'61 '89 C.608 B.S. L.851 J.D. 5073 Bixby Rd.
Schockman, Douglas J. ....'69 '94 C.851 B.S. L.117 J.D. [Lane,A.&H.]
Schoedinger, Daniel H., (AV) ....'44 '69 C.401 B.S. L.208 J.D. [Vorys,S.S.&P.]
Schoenberger, Josh L. ....'78 '04 C.253 B.A. L.608 J.D. [Ⓐ Williams&P.]
Schoenling, Lynne K., (BV) ....'61 '91 C&L.150 B.A., J.D. [Curry,R.S.&M.]
Scholl, Joseph M. ....'52 '79 C.608 B.A. L.117 J.D. 1 Nationwide Plaza
Scholl, Marcie M. '55 '80 C.608 B.S. L.117 J.D.
Admin. Law J., State Pers. Bd. of Review
Schooh, Frederick C. ....'55 '80 C.597 B.A. L.608 J.D. Asst. Atty. Gen.
Schottenstein, Edwin E., (AV) ....'40 '65 C.608 B.A. L.421 J.D. [Schottenstein]
Schottenstein, James M., (BV) ....'47 '72 C.966 B.B.A. L.608 J.D. [Schottenstein]

Schottenstein Law Offices, (AV) BR
Bank One Building Suite 1400, 100 East Broad Street, 43215
Telephone: 614-462-2266; 1-800-437-3757 Telecopier: 614-462-2406
Email: schott100@sbcglobal.net
Edwin E. Schottenstein.
Personal Injury Law, Automobile Accidents, Workers Compensation, Wrongful Death, Medical Malpractice.
See Professional Biographies, COLUMBUS, OHIO

Schottenstein Legal Services, (BV)
341 South Third Street, Suite 300, 43215-5444
Telephone: 614-464-1880 Fax: 614-464-3004 URL: http://www.schottensteinlaw.com
Email: jim@schottensteinlaw.com URL: http://www.lawyers.com/schottensteinlaw
James M. Schottenstein;—Radha Subramaniam.
Business Litigation, Business Law, Limited Liability Companies, Buying and Selling of Businesses, Business Formation, Corporate Law, Partnership Law, Commercial Real Estate, Commercial Leasing, Taxation, Trusts and Estates, Wills, Estate Planning, Employment Discrimination, Sexual Harassment.
See Professional Biographies, COLUMBUS, OHIO

Schottenstein Zox & Dunn Co., LPA, (AV) BB
250 West Street, 43215-2538 ⊙
Mailing Address: P.O. Box 165020, Columbus, OH 43216
Telephone: 614-462-2700 Telecopier: 614-462-5135 Telex: 650 24 444 365
Email: info@szd.com URL: http://www.szd.com
Daniel M. Anderson; Randall S. Arndt; Mitchell H. Banchefsky; William J. Barath; Richard A. Barnhart; Paul L. Bittner; Corey V. Crognale; James E. Davidson; Kris M. Dawley; Patrick A. Devine; Jay R. Dingledy; Catherine T. Dunlay; Gregory J. Dunn; Harvey Dunn; Matthew L. Fornshell; M. Colette Gibbons (Resident, Cleveland Office); Roger A. Gilcrest; John P. Gilligan; Herbert R. Godby; Lisa Ge Shang Han; Philip K. Hartmann; Raymond C. Headen; Richard W. Holz; E. James Hopple; Michael S. Jordan; Josef Keglewitsch; Stephen R. Kleinman; John J. Krimm, Jr.; Russell J. Kutell; John M. Latsko; Marie A. Malloy; Kevin R. McDermott; John C. McDonald; Christopher L. Miller; Kevin L. Murch; Marcia J. Myers (Resident, Cincinnati Office); Angelique Paul Newcomb; Robert H. Nichols; Robert R. Ouellette; Thomas A. Pampush; Peter A. Pavarini; Susan Porter; Victoria E. Powers; Bryan K. Prosek; Jennifer Dutey Readler; Susan D. Rector; Joseph M. Reidy; Robert M. Robenalt; John D. Robinett; David J. Robinson; H. Alan Rothenbuecher (Resident, Cleveland Office); Roger L. Sabo; Stephen P. Samuels; Melvin L. Schottenstein (1932-1993); Anthony D. Shaffer; Stephen J. Smith; Alan G. Starkoff; Robert M. Stefancin (Resident, Cleveland Office); Matthew J. Stockslager (Resident, Cleveland Office); Daniel R. Swetnam; Michael D. Tarullo; John Terakedis, Jr.; Felix C. Wade; Robert D. Weisman;—Alan J. Arville; Gregory S. Baker; Valerie T. Barnett; J. Corey Colombo; Tyson A. Crist; Elaine Darr; Jennifer L. Fewell; Steven D. Forry; Linda S. Gemind (Resident, Cleveland Office); Aaron L. Granger; Jeremy Grayem; Matthew T. Green; Kevin M. Hilvert; Elizabeth Kastner; Jay E. Krasovec (Resident, Cleveland Office); Melissa C. Lloyd; Meghan D. Majernik (Resident, Cleveland Office); Katherine G. Manghillis (Resident, Cleveland Office); Jennifer K. Mason; Jennifer M. McDaniel; Philip R. Miele; Kevin M. Mueller; John H. Oberle; Hansel H. Rhee; Michael T. Short; Denise R. Slazyk; Adam L. Smith; Stephen Jennings Smith; Joshua N. Stine; Eric M. Stoller; Catherine L. Strauss; Malinda L. Susalla; Evan R. Weidenhamer; Amanda L. Wickline; Stephen Withee; Aimee A. Zaleski; Brian M. Zets. Of Counsel: Nancy A. Brigner; Robert J. Cochran; Mary Frances Geswein; Jeffrey A. Perlmuter (Resident Cleveland Office); Charles Saunders, Jr.; Elizabeth E. Tulman; Benjamin L. Zox; Melissa L. Zox.
Business (Corporate, Banking and Lending, Real Estate/Land Use, General Tax, State and Local Tax, Employee Benefits, Estate Planning, White Collar Crime, E-Commerce, Intellectual Property/Technology Protection, International); Labor and Employment Law, Litigation, Health Law, Construction Law, Bankruptcy Law, Environmental Law, Debtor/Creditor Rights, Workers' Compensation, Municipal Law, Government Affairs.
Cincinnati, Ohio Office: Bank One Towers, 8044 Montgomery Road, Suite 630, 45236-2926. Telephone: 513-792-0792. Fax: 513-792-0803.
Cleveland, Ohio Office: USBank Centre, 1350 Euclid Avenue, Suite 1400, 44115. Telephone: 216-621-6501. Fax: 216-621-6502.
See Professional Biographies, COLUMBUS, OHIO

Schrader, Matthew L. .... '76 '01 C.973 B.A. L.201 J.D. [A Reminger&R.]
Schraff, Christopher R., (AV) .... '47 '72 C.363 A.B. L.602 J.D. [Porter W.M.&A.]
Schrag, Edward A., Jr., (AV) .... '32 '61 C.659 B.S. L.309 J.D. [C Vorys,S.S.&P.]
Schreibeis, G. Dennis .... '73 '98 C.477 B.A. L.117 J.D. [A Mallory&T.]
Schreibman, Jack Louis .... '74 '00 C&L.608 B.A., J.D. Atty. Gen.
Schroeder, Anthony D. .... '55 '91 C.608 B.A. L.851 J.D. Jud. Law Clk., Supm. Ct.
Schubert, James J. .... '60 '85 C&L.201 B.A., J.D. Asst. Atty. Gen.
Schubert, Paul R. '55 '87 C.1070 B.S. L.770 J.D.
(adm. in NY; not adm. in OH) Bk. One
Schuck, James P. .... '75 '00 C.97 B.A. L.179 J.D. [A Bricker&E.]
Schuckmann, Frank .... '— '97 C&L.8 B.S., J.D. [A Buckingham,D.&B.]
Schuermann, Richard W., Jr., (AV) ...... '57 '83 C&L.201 B.A., J.D. [Kegler,B.H.&R.]
Schuler, Robert Carl, (BV) .... '63 '90 C.473 B.A. L.117 J.D. [C Maguire&S.]
Schuler, Robert G., (AV) .... '61 '87 C.201 B.A. L.339 J.D. [Kegler,B.H.&R.]
Schulte, Kathaleen B., (AV) .... '51 '82 C&L.608 B.A., J.D. [Gittes&S.]
Schumacher, Donald C., (AV) .... '46 '74 C.608 B.S.B.A. L.117 J.D. 755 S. High St.
Schumacher, Mark L., (BV) .... '53 '81 C&L.851 B.A., J.D. [Freund,F.&A.]
Schupp, H. Herbert .... '39 '68 C.531 B.S. L.266 J.D. 100 E. Broad St.‡
Schuster, Elizabeth Luper .... '72 '97 C&L.608 B.A., J.D. Atty. Gen.'s Off.
Schuster, Richard D., (AV) .... '54 '81 C.473 B.A. L.608 J.D. [Vorys,S.S.&P.]
Schuster, Saundra D. .... '— '97 C.473 B.S. L.608 J.D. Asst. Atty. Gen.
Schwab, Gregory B. .... '57 '92 C&L.610 B.A., J.D. Staff Atty., State Legis. Serv. Comm.
Schwade, Joseph A. .... '72 '98 C.608 B.A. L.117 J.D. Asst. Atty. Gen.
Schwallie, Dennis G., (AV) .... '53 '78 C.150 B.B.A. L.608 J.D. [Peck,S.&W.]
Schwart, C. Jay, (CV) .... '53 '82 C.150 B.S. L.117 J.D. [Schwart]
Schwart Law Offices, (CV) .... 1620 W. 1st. Ave. (Grandview Heights)
Schwartz, Heidi Sue .... '67 '99 C.477 B.A. L.117 J.D. Saga Communications
Schwartz, Joel L. .... '58 '83 C.473 B.A. L.117 J.D. 2388 E. Main St., Ste. 103
Schwartz, Robert S., (AV) .... '47 '76 C.145 B.A. L.608 J.D. 268 N. Parkview Avenue
Schwarzmann, Valorie G. '59 '85 C.611 B.A. L.1202 J.D.
Tr. Offr. & Asst. V.P., Huntington Tr. Co., N.A.
Schwenker, Charles V., (AV) .... '14 '40 C&L.608 B.A., J.D. 2631 Berwyn Rd.‡
Schwenker, John D., (AV) ...... '20 '49 C&L.608 B.S. in B.A., LL.B. 2744 Abington Rd.‡
Schwepe, Alan P., (BV) .... '55 '81 C.608 B.S. L.607 J.D. Asst. Atty. Gen.
Schwolsky, Peter M. '46 '73 C.659 B.A. L.477 J.D.
Columbia Energy Group Serv. Corp.
Scopetti, Nina P. .... '54 '80 C.737 B.A. L.117 J.D. 155 West Main Street, Ste. 100
Scott, Craig P., (AV) .... '61 '89 C.608 B.A. L.117 J.D. [Volkema,T.M.B.S.&M.]
Scott, David A. .... '56 '88 C&L.608 B.A., J.D. Columbus Legal Aid Soc., Inc.
Scott, David M. .... '72 '97 C&L.608 B.A., J.D. [A Luper,N.&L.]
Scott, Gregory B., (AV) .... '51 '76 C&L.339 B.A., J.D. [Scott,S.&W.]

Scott, John '64 '98 C.421 B.S. L.150 J.D.
4719 Reed Street, Suite 146, 43220
Telephone: 614-267-5354 Fax: 614-267-8092
Email: backinthesaddle9@yahoo.com URL: http://www.johnscottlawfirm.com
Criminal Law, Driving While Intoxicated, Drug Crimes, Felonies, Assault, Misdemeanor, Traffic Violations, White Collar Crimes, Forgery.
See Professional Biographies, COLUMBUS, OHIO

Scott, Joseph E. .... '43 '93 C.878 B.A L.117 J.D. [J.E.Scott]
Scott, Keith A. .... '61 '97 C.331 B.A. L.117 J.D. Consolidated Stores Corporation
Scott, Paul, (AV) .... '31 '57 C&L.608 B.S., J.D. [P.Scott]
Scott, Paul, Jr., (AV) .... '62 '92 C.266 B.P.A. L.117 J.D. [P.Scott]
Scott, Paul O., (AV) .... '48 '74 C.607 B.A. L.117 J.D. [Clark,P.A.&S.C.]
Scott, Peggy A., (BV) .... '64 '91 C.1111 B.S. L.117 J.D. [Purcell&S.]
Scott, Ryan M. .... '71 '97 C.608 B.S.B.A. L.117 J.D. [C Cox,S.&P.]
Scott, Joseph E., Co. LPA .... 35 East Livingston Avenue
Scott, Paul, Co., L.P.A., (AV) .... 536 South High Street

Scott, Scriven & Wahoff LLP, (AV) BB
2600 LeVeque Tower, 50 West Broad Street (Franklin County), 43215
Telephone: 614-222-8686 Fax: 614-222-8688
URL: http://www.lawyers.com/scottscriven&wahoff
Members of Firm: Gregory B. Scott; Donald C. Scriven; William J. Wahoff; James K. Stucko, Jr.; Timothy E. Cowans; Richard Goldberg; Julie C. Martin. Associates: Edward L. Ostrowski, Jr.; Karla S. Soards; Jodie M. Taylor (Certified Specialist in Worker's Compensation Law, Ohio State Bar Association); Melissa C. Bondy; Lacey L. Cain; Kathleen V. Davis; C. Bradley Howenstein.
Representation of Public and Private Sector Employers in Labor and Employment Law Matters. Collective Bargaining, Arbitration, Employment Discrimination, Workers' Compensation, OSHA, ADA, Intentional Tort Defense and Education Law.
See Professional Biographies, COLUMBUS, OHIO

Scriven, Donald C., (AV) .... '48 '74 C.243 B.A. L.861 J.D. [Scott,S.&W.]
Scrutton, Suzanne J. .... '63 '90 C.20 B.A. L.117 J.D. [Vorys,S.S.&P.]
Scull, John M. '48 '75 C.532 B.A. L.117 J.D.
Hearing Offr., Unemployment Comp. Review Comm.
Seabrook, Eric Maurice .... '61 '98 C.608 B.A. L.117 J.D. Ohio Secy. of State
Seamon, Aaron A. .... '73 '99 C.967 B.A. L.201 J.D. [A Squire,S.&D.]
Sechler, Joel E. .... '77 '03 C.820 B.A. L.608 J.D. [A Carpenter&L.]
Seckerson, Cynthia L. ...... '59 '95 C.608 B.A. L.117 J.D. 375 South High Street, 7th Floor
Secrest, Jonathan R. .... '76 '02 C.210 B.A. L.179 J.D. [A Maguire&S.]
See, P. Brian .... '75 '00 C.976 B.A. L.228 J.D. [A Squire,S.&D.]
See, Shana O. .... '76 '02 C.385 B.A. L.228 J.D. [A Carpenter&L.]
Sefcovic, Paul F., (AV) .... '46 '71 C.201 B.S. L.477 J.D. [Squire,S.&D.]
Segal, David M. '51 '76
C.381 B.B.A. L.608 J.D. Corp. Coun., Lancaster Colony Corporation
Segel, Benjamin B., (BV) .... '54 '79 C.385 A.B. L.608 J.D. 445 Hutchinson Ave.
Segelken, Edward M., (AV) .... '58 '84 C.894 A.B. L.477 J.D. [Porter W.M.&A.]
Segerman, Douglas Jay .... '70 '95 C&L.150 B.B.A, J.D [A McFadden W.&S.]
Seguin, James P., (AV) .... '59 '84 C.851 B.B.A. L.608 J.D. [Decker,V.S.L.&V.]
Seidensticker, John W. '64 '90 C.602 B.A. L.608 J.D.
Sr. Coun.-Trans., Amer. Elec. Power Serv. Corp.
Seidt, Andrea L. .... '— '98 C&L.608 B.A., J.D. [A Jones D.]
Seiple, Stephen B. '56 '81
C.473 B.A. L.608 J.D. Sr. Atty., Columbia Gas Distribution Cos.
Selden, Brian G. .... '— '95 C.674 A.B. L.477 J.D. [Jones D.]
Seliovski, Liouhuv .... '— '03 L.179 J.D. [A Shihab&Assoc.]
Sellers, Barbara J. .... '40 '79 C.608 B.A. L.117 J.D. U.S. Bkrptcy. J.
Sellman, Jerry B., (AV) ... '50 '75 C.631 B.A. L.117 J.D. 88 East Broad Street, Suite 1220
Seltzer, Martin S., (AV) .... '37 '77 C.569 B.S.E. L.608 J.D. [Porter W.M.&A.]
Selvaggio, Nick A. .... '66 '91 C.473 B.A. L.161 J.D. 88 E. Broad St., Suite 1980
Semons, Tad Anthony .... '66 '98 C.608 B.A. L.179 J.D. 33 N. High St., Ste. 900
Senff, Mark D., (AV) .... '45 '71 C&L.608 B.S.Phar., J.D. [Baker&H.]
Sentz, Barbara A., (AV) .... '53 '83 C.97 B.A. L.608 J.D. 5 E. Long St., Suite 100
Serio, Joseph Philip .... '58 '86 C.607 B.A. L.117 J.D. Assoc. Consumer's Coun.
Serio, Kimberly K. Starr .... '60 '86 C.383 B.A. L.117 J.D. Jud. Clk., Ct. of App.
Serrott, Mark A., (AV) .... '54 '79 C&L.608 B.A., J.D. [M.A.Serrott]
Serrott, Mark A., Co., L.P.A., (AV) .... 502 S. Third St.
Serve, Barbara A., (BV) .... '44 '80 C.851 B.A. L.117 J.D. Asst. Atty. Gen.
Seskes, Brandi Laser .... '75 '04 C.8 B.A. L.117 J.D. [Clark,P.A.&S.C.]
Sestile, Lindsay M. .... '77 '02 C.20 B.A. L.602 J.D. [A Porter W.M.&A.]
Settineri, Michael J. .... '67 '01 C.477 B.S.C.E. L.117 J.D. [A Vorys,S.S.&P.]
Severance, Gregory S. .... '54 '81 C.150 B.A. L.117 J.D. Asst. Atty. Gen.
Severns, William C. .... '50 '75 C&L.608 B.A., J.D. Dir., Quality Assurance, State Auditor
Sewalk, Karen M. .... '58 '94 C.608 B.S. L.117 J.D. 221 S. High St.
Sewards, Frederick A., (AV) .... '65 '90 C&L.608 B.A., J.D. [Hammond,S.&W.]
Sexton, Robert E., (AV) .... '33 '61 C.608 B.S. L.117 J.D. [Sexton]
Sexton, Thomas P. .... '64 '91 C.385 B.A. L.117 J.D. [Sexton]
Sexton Law Offices, (AV) .... 580 South High Street, Suite 130
Sferrella, Nino A. .... '36 '64 C.608 B.A. L.607 J.D. Admin. Law J., Soc. Sec. Admn.
Sgalla, Cynthia Jo '73 '01
C.608 B.S. L.179 J.D. Staff Atty., Franklin Co. Ct. of Com. Pleas
Shady, John Michael Doyle .... '46 '73 C.347 B.S. L.117 J.D. [J.M.D.Shady]
Shady, John M. D. .... 132 Northwoods Blvd.
Shaeffer, Walter E. .... '28 '53 C&L.608 B.A., J.D. 8 E. Broad St.
Shaffer, Anthony D. .... '63 '95 C.610 B.A. L.117 J.D. [Schottenstein,Z.&D.]
Shaffer, C. Allen .... '56 '04 L.608 J.D. [A Bricker&E.]
Shaffer, Jody Gilkey .... '78 '04 C.607 B.S.B.A. L.608 J.D. [A Vorys,S.S.&P.]
Shailer, John L. '45 '81 C.608 B.Ch.E. L.117 J.D.
Admin. Law Judge, Public Utilities Commission of Ohio (Pat.)
Shamansky, Samuel H., (AV) .... '60 '85 C.608 B.A. L.117 J.D. [S.H.Shamansky]

Shamansky, Samuel H., Co., LPA, (AV)
511 South High Street, 43215
Telephone: 614-228-4141 Fax: 614-228-0899
Email: sshamansky@hotmail.com
Samuel H. Shamansky.
Criminal Trial and Appellate Practice in State and Federal Courts.
See Professional Biographies, COLUMBUS, OHIO

Shambaugh, Phyllis J. .... '54 '93 C.266 B.S. L.117 J.D. [C Jones D.]
Shaner, Nellie Jane, (BV) .... '42 '81 C.437 A.B. L.117 J.D. Sr. Asst. Co. Pros.
Shank, Aaron M. .... '71 '98 C.967 B.A. L.608 J.D. [A Porter W.M.&A.]
Shankle, Jessica A. .... '74 '01 C.97 B.S. L.117 J.D. [A Chester,W.&S.]
Shannon, Ann M. .... '67 '92 C.608 B.A. L.94 J.D. Asst. Law Dir., Bur. of Wkrs. Comp.
Shannon, Desiree T. .... '60 '89 C.631 B.A. L.117 J.D. Enforce. Atty., State Dept. of Com.
Shannon, Michael T., (AV) .... '57 '83 C.737 B.A. L.117 J.D. [Crabbe,B.&J.]
Shantz, Arthur W., Jr. '42 '71
C.363 A.B. L.930 J.D. Staff Hearing Offr., State Indus. Comm.
Shapiro, Rick J. '69 '94 C.473 B.S. L.608 J.D.
Sr. Coun.-Tax, Amer. Elect. Power Serv. Corp.
Shapiro, Robert M. .... '43 '68 C.645 B.A. L.608 J.D. State Legis. Serv. Comm.
Sharett, Hope M. .... '77 '03 C.880 B.A. L.608 J.D. [A Bricker&E.]
Sharma, Constance L., (AV) .... '48 '78 C&L.608 B.A., J.D. [Sharma]

Sharma Law Offices, LLC, (AV) BB
853 Pipestone Drive, 43235
Telephone: 614-436-1240 614-436-3874 Fax: 614-436-0220
Email: csharma@sharmalawoffices.com URL: http://www.sharmalawoffices.com
Constance L. Sharma.
Languages: Hindi, Czech, German.
Trusts and Estates, Wills, Probate, Guardianship and Conservatorship, Probate litigation, Estate Planning for Parents of Handicapped Children, Estate Planning for the Elderly, Special Needs Trusts, Taxation, Business Law, Business Formation, Limited Liability Companies, Business Immigration, Tax-Exempt Organization Law.
See Professional Biographies, COLUMBUS, OHIO

Sharpe, Thomas E. '63 '89 C.631 B.A. L.273 J.D.
Trans. Atty., Battelle Memorial Institute
Shaw, Douglas W., (BV) .... '49 '76 C.608 B.A. L.117 J.D. 555 City Park Ave.

Shaw, E. Scott, (BV) .... '49 '76 C.608 B.A. L.117 J.D. 500 S. Front St., Ste. 130
Shaw, Kyle T. .... '75 '03 C.477 B.A. L.966 J.D. [A Porter W.M.&A.]
Shaw, Lori E. .... '61 '87 C&L.201 B.S., J.D. [C Robol]
Shaw, Mark A. .... '66 '92 C.473 B.S. L.851 J.D. [Eastman&S.]

Shaw, Melissa J.
(See Gahanna)

Shay, Matthew R. '62 '87 C.967 B.A. L.608 J.D.
Asst. Gen. Coun., Ohio Council of Retail Merchants
Shay, W. Michael, (BV) .... '48 '75 C.930 A.B. L.608 J.D. 854 E. Broad St.
Shayne, Stanley H., (AV) .... '43 '69 C.473 B.S. L.273 J.D. [Shayne&G.]
Shayne & Greenwald Co., L.P.A., (AV) .... 221 South High Street
Shea, Frank P., Jr., (BV) .... '42 '68 C&L.608 B.S., J.D. 5699 Blinnton Place
Shea, John M. .... '17 '51 C&L.608 B.Sc., J.D. 1360 Dublin Rd.
Shearer, William B. .... '64 '94 C.160 B.A. L.575 J.D. [Baker&H.]
Sheehan, Carol A., (AV) .... '53 '78 C.477 B.A. L.608 J.D. [Carlile P.&M.]
Sheely, Sommer L. .... '77 '02 C.611 B.A. L.608 J.D. [A Baker&H.]
Sheeran, Patrick E. .... '50 '76 C.201 B.A. L.215 J.D. Mag.
Sheffer, Karen E. .... '53 '79 C.607 B.A. L.150 J.D. [S Baker&H.]
Sheffield, Douglas M. '51 '76
C.611 B.A. L.608 J.D. V.P., Professional Planning Consultants, Inc.
Shenk, Alyssa H. .... '76 '02 C.966 B.A. L.608 J.D. [A Wolman&Assoc.]
Shepard, Darrell R., (AV) .... '41 '81 C.546 B.A. L.1119 J.D. [Porter W.M.&A.]
Shepard, Noel C. .... '70 '96 C.528 B.A. L.117 J.D. [A Frost B.T.]
Shepherd, Amy M. .... '64 '89 C&L.608 B.A., J.D. [Baker&H.]
Sheppard, Alan Wayne, (AV) .... '44 '70 C&L.608 B.S., J.D. 1900 Crown Park Court
Sheridan, James W. .... '64 '89 C&L.608 B.A., J.D. 30 E. Broad St., 3rd Fl.
Sheridan, Susan G. .... '64 '89 C&L.608 B.A., J.D. [Buckingham,D.&B.]
Sheriff, Mark J., (AV) .... '45 '70 C.608 B.A. L.150 J.D. [Wiles,B.B.&B.]
Sherman, Kendra S. .... '70 '97 C.813 B.A. L.608 J.D. [A Squire,S.&D.]
Sherman, Robert P., (BV) .... '50 '76 C&L.150 B.A., J.D. [Karr&S.]
Sherman, Ryan Patrick .... '76 '02 C&L.608 B.A., J.D. [A Porter W.M.&A.]

Sherman, Terry K., (AV) '46 '71 C.610 B.A. L.608 J.D.
52 West Whittier Street, 43206-2503
Telephone: 614-444-8800 Fax: 614-445-9487
Email: ofc43206@aol.com URL: http://www.terrysherman-law.com
Practice Limited to Criminal Defense in both State and Federal Courts.
See Professional Biographies, COLUMBUS, OHIO

Sherman, Thomas L. .... '53 '79 C.610 B.A. L.608 J.D. Dep. Dir., Dept. of Revenue
Shevelow, Doug L. .... '66 '04 C.608 B.S.C.E. L.117 J.D. [A Bricker&E.]
Sheward, Richard S. .... '44 '74 C.610 B.B.A. L.117 J.D. Com. Pleas J.

Shihab, Gus M., (BV) '61 '93 C.608 B.S.C.E. L.117 J.D.
65 E. State Street, Suite 1550, 43215 ⊙
Telephone: 614-224-2428 Fax: 614-224-5080
Email: info@shihab.net URL: http://www.lawyers.com/eminentdomainohio
(Also partner, Shihab & Associates, Columbus & Cleveland and Washington, D.C.).
Of Counsel: Robert J. Mann.
Eminent Domain, Zoning, Planning and Land Use.
See Professional Biographies, COLUMBUS, OHIO

Shihab, Sam M., (BV) .... '62 '94 C.608 B.S.C.E. L.117 J.D. [Shihab&Assoc.] ⊙

Shihab & Associates, (BV)
65 East State Street, Suite 1550, 43215 ⊙
Telephone: 614-224-2428 Fax: 614-224-5080
Email: info@shihab.net URL: http://www.shihab.net
Gus M. Shihab; Sam M. Shihab. Associates: Kimberly E. Harrison; Noure Alo; Liouhuv Seliovski.
Languages: Arabic, Spanish, Portuguese, Hindi.
Immigration and Nationality Law, Business Immigration, Citizenship, Deportation, Employment Immigration, Family Immigration Law, Investor Visas, Labor Certification, Political Asylum, Eminent Domain, Zoning Planning and Land Use, Real Estate, Construction Law, Litigation.
Cleveland, Ohio Office: 600 Superior Avenue East, Suite 1300, 44114. Telephone: 216-479-7670. Fax: 216-479-7671.
Washington, DC Office: 1725 I Street NW, Suite 300, 2006. Telephone: 202-373-1535. Fax: 800-878-9405.
See Professional Biographies, COLUMBUS, OHIO

Shimberg, Jessica K. .... '65 '91 C.1036 B.A. L.608 J.D. 366 E. Broad St.
Shimeall, Kent M., (AV) ...... '51 '82 C.970 B.A. L.851 J.D. Prin. Atty., Atty. Gen. Off.
Shinn, Brian E. .... '71 '96 C.923 B.A. L.608 J.D. Asst. Disciplinary Coun.
Shipman, Lynn K., (AVⓉ) '50 '77 C.1044 B.A. L.724 J.D.
(adm. in NJ; not adm. in OH) Sr. Coun., Bank One Corp.
Shipman, Morgan E. ... '33 '58 C&L.846 B.B.A., LL.B. Osu Coll of Law, 1659 N High St
Shirey, Van R. .... '51 '76 C.25 B.A. L.607 J.D. 77 E. Nationwide Blvd.
Shoaff, Shannon M. .... '76 '01 C&L.851 B.A., J.D. [A Carpenter&L.]
Shoemaker, Brenda S. .... '55 '89 C.150 B.A. L.117 J.D. U.S. Dept. of Jus.
Shoemaker, Douglas L., (BV) ...... '60 '85 C&L.608 J.D. 373 South High Street, 5th Floor
Shoemaker, John W. .... '28 '55 C.999 A.B. L.608 J.D. Chf. Ohio Adult Parole Auth.
Shoemaker, Kevin L., (AV) .... '53 '79 C&L.150 B.A., J.D. [Shoemaker,H.&T.]

Shoemaker, Howarth & Taylor, LLP, (AV)
471 E. Broad Street, Suite 2001, 43215
Telephone: 614-469-0100 Telecopy: 614-280-9675
URL: http://www.midohiolaw.com
Kevin L. Shoemaker; Robert F. Howarth; Robert H. Taylor. Of Counsel: David A. Turano.
Business Litigation, Corporate Law, Legislative Practice and Government Relations, Real Estate, Probate Litigation and Civil Litigation, Trial and Appellate Practice.
See Professional Biographies, COLUMBUS, OHIO

Shook, Kevin T. .... '72 '01 C.207 B.A. L.608 J.D. [A Frost B.T.]
Short, Jennifer E. .... '72 '98 C.911 B.A. L.1358 J.D. [A Thompson H.]
Short, Michael T. .... '73 '98 C.473 B.S. L.608 J.D. [A Schottenstein,Z.&D.]
Shortridge, Amy M. '71 '97
C.197 A.B. L.902 J.D. Coun.-Litig., Amer. Elect. Power Serv. Corp.
Shouvlin, David P., (AV) .... '52 '79 C&L.896 B.A., J.D. [Porter W.M.&A.]
Shroyer, David I., (AV) .... '55 '80 C.608 B.S. L.117 J.D. [Colley S.&A.]
Shubitowski, John K., (AV) .... '56 '80 C.215 A.B. L.477 J.D. The Limited, Inc.
Shuler, Gordon P., (AV) .... '47 '73 C.608 B.S. L.477 J.D. [Shuler]
Shuler Law Firm LLC, (AV) .... 221 S. High Street, 3rd Floor
Shumaker, Gale C. .... '61 '87 C.97 B.A. L.607 J.D. 581 E. Town St.

Shumaker, Loop & Kendrick, LLP, (AV) BB
Huntington Center, 41 South High Street, Suite 2400, 43215 ⊙
Telephone: 614-463-9441 Fax: 614-463-1108
Resident Partners: Michael E. Born; John E. Haller; Michael J. O'Callaghan; Louis E. Tosi (Resident, Toledo, Ohio Office). Resident Associates: Michael A. Snyder; Katie L. Tournoux. Of Counsel: Walter W. Reckless.
Administrative Law; Advertising and Marketing; Agency and Distributorships; Agricultural Law; Alternative Dispute Resolution; Antitrust and Trade Regulation; Appellate Practice; Bankruptcy; Banks and Banking; Business Law; Business Crimes; Business Torts; Civil Rights; Commercial Law; Commercial Litigation; Commercial Real Estate; Communications and Media; Complex and Multi-District Litigation; Computers and Software; Construction Law; Contracts; Copyrights; Corporate

(This Listing Continued)

Shumaker, Loop & Kendrick, LLP (Continued)
Law; Federal Criminal Law; Debtor and Creditor; Domestic Relations; Education Law; Employee Benefits; Entertainment Law; Environmental Law; Fidelity and Surety; Finance; Franchises and Franchising; Health Care; Hospital Law; Immigration and Naturalization; Intellectual Property; International Law; Labor and Employment; Leases and Leasing; Litigation; Media Law; Medicare and Medicaid; Mergers, Acquisitions and Divestitures; Nonprofit and Charitable Organizations; Patent Litigation; Personal Injury; Probate; Products Liability; Professional Liability; Public Finance; Real Estate; Securities; Sports Law; Taxation; Torts; Trade Secrets; Trademarks; Trusts and Estates; Unfair Competition; Wills; Zoning, Planning and Land Use.
Representative Clients: AVAILABLE UPON REQUEST.
Toledo, Ohio Office: North Courthouse Square, 1000 Jackson, 43624-1573. Telephone: 419-241-9000. Fax: 419-241-6894.
Tampa, Florida Office: 101 East Kennedy Boulevard, Suite 2800, 33602-5151. Telephone: 813-229-7600. Fax: 813-229-1660.
Charlotte, North Carolina Office: 128 South Tryon Street, Suite 1800, 28202. Telephone: 704-375-0057. Fax: 704-332-1197.
See Professional Biographies, COLUMBUS, OHIO

Shumate, Alex, (AV) .... '50 '75 C.611 B.A. L.8 J.D. [Squire,S.&D.]
Shumate, Keith, (BV) .... '66 '91 C.08 B.A. L.608 J.D. [Squire,S.&D.]
Shumate, Kimberly C. '66 '92 C.597 B.A. L.608 J.D.
Assoc. Legal Coun., The Ohio State University
Shurte, Matthew R. .... '— '98 C.608 B.S.B.A. L.861 J.D. [A Jones D.]
Shuster, Michele Ann, (BV) .... '67 '93 C.150 B.B.A. L.284 J.D. [C Kegler,B.H.&R.]
Shwartz, Myron, (BV) .... '21 '67 C.33 B.A. L.608 J.D. 501 S. High St.
Sibbring, Donald A. .... '30 '55 C&L.607 J.D. Pres., Data Analysis Servs. Co.
Sico, Thomas .... '48 '78 C.453 S.B. L.608 J.D. Bur. of Wkrs. Comp.
Siculan, Nick, (AV) .... '20 '52 C&L.608 B.S., J.D. 2063 Farleigh Rd.
Sicuro, Robert A., (BV) .... '38 '72 C.381 B.A. L.117 J.D. Dept. of Taxation
Sidman, Robert J., (AV) .... '43 '68 C.711 B.A. L.602 J.D. [Vorys,S.S.&P.]
Sieck, William A. .... '— '00 C.145 B.A. L.659 J.D. [A Vorys,S.S.&P.]
Siegel, Bradd N., (AV) .... '52 '77 C.188 A.B. L.273 J.D. [Porter W.M.&A.]
Siegfried, Erin F. .... '71 '96 C.228 A.B. L.608 J.D. [Porter W.M.&A.]
Siegfried, Jeremy David .... '74 '99 C.575 A.B. L.608 J.D. [A Porter W.M.&A.]
Siehl, Richard W., (AV) .... '52 '77 C.473 B.A. L.339 J.D. [Baker&H.]
Siemer, Elizabeth M. .... '71 '97 C.401 B.S. L.117 J.D. Desco Corp.
Sies, Gary L. .... '50 '94 C.608 B.S.S.W. L.117 J.D. Ohio Dept. of Hlth.
Sigal, Marc Alan .... '52 '84 C.124 B.A. L.989 J.D. OH Atty. Gen.
Sigmund, Thomas J., (AV) .... '54 '78 C&L.608 B.A., J.D. [Buckingham,D.&B.]
Signet, Bradford R. '55 '81 C.97 B.S. L.7 J.D.
Assoc. Gen. Coun.-Trans., Amer. Elect. Power Serv. Corp.
Signoracci, Diane M. .... '50 '81 C.266 B.S. L.608 J.D. [Bricker&E.]
Silberman, Earl J., (BV) .... '23 '65 C.529 A.B. L.266 J.D. 234 E. Columbus St.
Silcott, Lori L. .... '69 '94 C&L.117 B.A., J.D. 876 Kenwick Rd.‡
Silk, Richard J., JR. .... '61 '01 C&L.608 B.A., J.D. [A Remingér&R.]
Sillins, Wm. M. .... '18 '48 C&L.608 B.A., J.D. 5049 Bridgeport Rd.‡
Silverberg, Karl J. .... '69 '03 C.688 B.S. L.724 J.D. [A Bricker&E.]
Silvian, Sidney J. .... '25 '50 C&L.150 J.D. Ohio Div. of Securities
Simaitis, David E. .... '58 '89 C.1031 B.S. L.823 J.D. Sr. Coun., Nationwide Insurance
Simakovsky, Inna '71 '98 C.150 B.A. L.608 J.D.
(adm. in WA; not adm. in OH) [A Slowik&R.]
Simcic, Peter M., Jr .... '70 '96 C.608 B.A. L.117 J.D. Law Clk., Supm. Ct.
Simmons, Gerald G., (AV) .... '37 '71 C.97 B.A. L.1003 J.D. 330 S. High St.
Simmons, Kent N. '60 '85 C.528 B.A. L.117 J.D.
Asst. Gen. Coun., Nationwide Insurance
Simmons, Sheryl, (AVⓉ) '61 '86 C.810 B.S. L.326 J.D.
(adm. in TX; not adm. in OH) P.O. Box 24696
Simms, Susan L., (BV) .... '51 '82 C.967 B.A. L.608 J.D. 1 Riverside Plz.
Simon, William Scott .... '64 '91 C&L.117 B.A., J.D. 37 W. Broad St., Ste. 710
Simpson, Richard C., (AV) .... '47 '72 C.475 B.A. L.477 J.D. [Bricker&E.]
Sims, Margaret Bowen '58 '88 C.117 B.A. L.930 J.D.
(adm. in CT; not adm. in OH) 2720 Airport Drive, Suite 100
Simunic, Nancy H. .... '52 '76 C.980 B.A. L.117 J.D. Sr. Atty.
Singer, Lawrence A., (BV) .... '42 '70 C.608 B.S. L.117 J.D. 4265 Camborne Road
Singh, Bobby .... '69 '00 C.645 B.S. L.179 J.D. [A Chester,W.&S.]
Sinnott, Bradley K., (AV) .... '61 '86 C.608 B.A. L.117 J.D. [Vorys,S.S.&P.]
Sisto, James E. P., (BV) .... '59 '84 C.611 B.A. L.117 J.D. [C Squire,S.&D.]
Sites, Richard L. .... '48 '73 C.970 B.A. L.208 J.D. Gen. Coun., Ohio Hospital Association
Sjoberg-Witt, Kerstin .... '— '03 C&L.608 B.A., J.D. [A Jones D.]
Skaggs, Kimberly Marcinko, (AV) '58 '93
C.923 B.A. L.608 J.D. Equal Justice Foundation
Skaggs, Robert C., Jr. '54 '79 C.198 B.A. L.923 J.D.
(adm. in WV; not adm. in OH) Pres. & CEO, Columbia Gas of Ohio, Inc.; Columbia Gas of Kentucky, Inc.; Bay State Gas Co.
Skeeles, Rebecca Laura .... '72 '99 C.608 L.117 Skeeles Mfg. Inc.
Skeens, Edwin L. .... '62 '87 C.437 B.A. L.893 J.D. Franklin Co. Common Pleas Ct.
Skestos, George A. .... '28 '52 C&L.477 B.A., J.D. Homewood Corp.‡
Skidmore, James Robert '45 '84 C.339 B.Mus. L.608 J.D.
Ohio Dept. of Job & Fam. Srvcs., Off. of Legal Srvcs.
Skingle, Denise L. .... '— '96 C&L.608 B.A., J.D. [A Jones D.]
Skrobot, David A., (AV) .... '46 '77 C.117 B.A. L.608 J.D. 400 E. Town St., Ste. 210
Sladoje, Douglas, Attorney at Law, (AV) '62 '88
C&L.608 B.S., J.D. 921 Chatham Lane, Suite 300 (⊙Chillicothe)
Slagle, Christopher N. .... '71 '04 C.473 B.A. L.117 J.D. [A Bricker&E.]
Slazyk, Denise R. .... '69 '98 C&L.024 B.Com., LL.B. [A Schottenstein,Z.&D.]
Slotnick, Marcia Katz '49 '82
C.347 B.A. L.608 J.D. Dept. of Job & Fam. Servs. Legal Off.
Slowik, Donald C., (BV) .... '52 '80 C.228 B.A. L.608 J.D. [Slowik&R.]

Slowik & Robinson, LLC, (BV)
250 E. Broad Street, Suite 250, 43215
Telephone: 614-884-4800 Facsimile: 614-884-4801
URL: http://www.s-r-law.com/
Members of Firm: Donald C. Slowik; Kenneth J. Robinson. Associates: Inna Simakovsky (Not admitted in OH); Julie C. Nemecek. Of Counsel: Andrew P. Sagartz.
Labor and Employment Law, Immigration Law, Small Business Law, Alternative Dispute Resolution, Business Formations.
See Professional Biographies, COLUMBUS, OHIO

Smallwood, Carl D., (AV) .... '56 '80 C&L.608 B.S., J.D. [Vorys,S.S.&P.]
Smallwood, Howard .... '34 '73 C.608 B.S. L.117 J.D. 209 S. Hight St.
Smalz, Michael Robert ... '51 '89 C.477 B.A. L.494 J.D. Ohio State Legal Services Assoc.
Smith, Adam L. .... '70 '99 C&L.608 B.S., J.D. [A Schottenstein,Z.&D.]
Smith, Andrew C., (AV) .... '58 '84 C.970 B.A. L.665 J.D. [Vorys,S.S.&P.]
Smith, Andrew O. '62 '89 C.659 B.S.Econ. L.145 J.D.
(adm. in NY; not adm. in OH) Yenkin-Majestic Paint Corp.
Smith, Bradley A. .... '58 '90 C.373 B.A. L.1565 J.D. [C Vorys,S.S.&P.]
Smith, Charles D., (AV) .... '58 '83 C.611 B.A. L.117 J.D. [Roetzel&A.]
Smith, Craig A., (AV) .... '59 '84 C&L.608 B.A., J.D. [Gamble H.J.]

Smith, Donald L., Jr. '48 '86 C.631 B.S. L.117 J.D.
Defense Logistics Agency - DCSC-G
Smith, Elizabeth Hanning .... '76 '03 C.518 B.A. L.608 J.D. [Ⓢ Vorys,S.S.&P.]
Smith, Elizabeth T., (AV) .... '59 '84 C.313 B.A. L.608 J.D. [Vorys,S.S.&P.]
Smith, Emily A. .... '76 '02 C.473 B.A. L.608 J.D. [Ⓐ Carlile P.&M.]
Smith, Fredric L., (AV) .... '38 '63 C.475 B.A. L.477 J.D. [Squire,S.&D.]
Smith, G. Frederick '55 '84 C.802 B.B.S. L.846 J.D.
(adm. in TX; not adm. in OH) Instantwhip Foods
Smith, G. Rand, (BV) .... '45 '74 C.15 B.S. L.117 J.D. [Boone,S.&Assoc.]
Smith, George C. .... '35 '59 C&L.608 B.A., J.D. U.S. Dist. J.
Smith, Gerald L., (AV) ...... '34 '64 C.608 B.S. L.446 J.D. [Mueller&S.] (See Pat. Sect.)
Smith, Harrison W., Jr., (AV) .... '26 '50 C.674 L.608 J.D. [Smith&H.]
Smith, J. Gregory .... '67 '93 C.597 B.A. L.608 J.D. [Ⓐ Ulmer&B.]
Smith, J. Theodore .... '70 '98 C.679 B.S. L.339 J.D. [Ⓐ Vorys,S.S.&P.]
Smith, Jeffery E., (AV) .... '53 '79 C&L.851 B.A., J.D. [Thompson H.]
Smith, Jeffrey E. .....'41 '69 C.473 B.S. L.1340 J.D. Coun., Bank One Corp. (Law Dept.)
Smith, Julie B. .... '79 '04 C.97 B.A. L.597 J.D. [Ⓐ Squire,S.&D.]
Smith, Karen D. .... '52 '91 C.610 B.S.N. L.150 J.D. [Bricker&E.]
Smith, Kristin Sacco .... '67 '94 C.229 B.S. L.8 J.D. Ohio Atty. Gen.
Smith, Lee, & Associates, (AV) '52 '78
C.610 B.G.S. L.201 J.D. 929 Harrison Ave., Ste. 300
Smith, Marc D. .... '71 '98 C.473 B.S. L.851 J.D. 7650 Rivers Edge Dr.
Smith, Mary Kathryn '63 '91
C.266 B.S. L.117 J.D. Sr. Tax Atty., Battelle Memorial Institute
Smith, Mary Kay .... '57 '81 C&L.8 B.A., J.D. Asst. Atty. Gen.
Smith, Michael A., (BV) .... '57 '82 C.385 A.B. L.608 J.D. [Carlile P.&M.]
Smith, Patricia A. .....'53 '79 C&L.150 B.B.A., J.D. Asst. Law Dir., Bur. of Wkrs. Comp.
Smith, Patrick F., Law Office of, (AV) '54 '79
C.602 A.B. L.150 J.D. 5025 Arlington Centre Blvd., Ste. 250
Smith, Patrick J., (AV) .... '39 '65 C.97 B.Sc. L.608 J.D. [Ⓒ Porter W.M.&A.]
Smith, R. Michael ...... '— '85 C.150 B.A. L.608 J.D. Sr. Staff Atty., Ohio Ct. of Claims
Smith, Ralph G., (AV) .... '10 '33 C&L.608 B.S., J.D. 354 Oakland Park Ave.‡
Smith, Rebecca Ann .... '66 '96 C&L.117 B.A., J.D. 122 E. Main Street
Smith, Robert F., (AV) .... '54 '78 C&L.608 B.A., J.D. Off. of Atty. Gen.
Smith, Robert H. .... '17 '40 C&L.421 87 S. Chesterfield Rd.‡
Smith, Robin Christopher '69 '96
C.923 B.A. L.608 J.D. Legal Coun., Ohio House Minority Caucus
Smith, Ronald Lee ......'48 '83 C.385 A.B. L.608 J.D. Sr. Coun., Ohio Legal Rights Serv.
Smith, Scott Elliot, (BV) .... '56 '82 C.383 B.A. L.607 J.D. [Smith,P.&Assoc.]
Smith, Stephen J., (AV) .... '46 '71 C.851 B.A. L.608 J.D. [Schottenstein,Z.&D.]
Smith, Stephen Jennings .... '73 '99 C.473 B.A. L.117 J.D. [Ⓐ Schottenstein,Z.&D.]
Smith, Steven Lee, (AV) .... '46 '73 C.63 B.S. L.608 J.D. [Smith&C.]
Smith, Warren J. .... '32 '59 C&L.608 B.A., J.D. 306 E. Gay St.

Smith & Colner, (AV)
261 South Front Street, 43215
Telephone: 614-228-6040 Fax: 614-228-6099
Email: SmithandColner@aol.com
Members of Firm: Steven Lee Smith; James D. Colner.
General Trial and Appellate Practice. Commercial, Negligence, Products Liability, Corporation and Insurance Law.
See Professional Biographies, COLUMBUS, OHIO

Smith & Hale, (AV) .... 37 West Broad Street
Smith, Phillips & Associates Co., L.P.A., (BV) ....6660 North High Street, Suite 3F
Smolik, Mark A. '62 '87 C.363 B.A. L.161 J.D.
Sr. VP, Gen Coun. & Secy., Safelite Group, Inc.
Snedaker, Robert H., III, (BV) .... '56 '81 C.608 B.B.A. L.117 J.D. 3010 Hayden Road
Snider, Blake A. .... '74 '99 C.608 B.S. L.309 J.D. [Ⓐ Vorys,S.S.&P.]
Snider, Mark A. .... '79 '04 C.207 B.S. L.902 J.D. [Ⓐ Porter W.M.&A.]
Sniderman, Jeffery J. .... '69 '95 C.696 B.A. L.7 J.D. [Ⓐ Isaac,B.L.&T.]
Snyder, Bradley L., (AV) .... '56 '81 C.608 B.S. L.117 J.D. [Roetzel&A.]
Snyder, Christopher A. '— '01 C.610 B.A. L.608 J.D.
(adm. in FL; not adm. in OH) [Ⓐ Vorys,S.S.&P.]
Snyder, Larry H., (AV) .... '25 '52 C.823 B.S. L.477 J.D. [Chamblin&S.]
Snyder, Michael A. .... '73 '98 C.610 B.A. L.117 J.D. [Ⓐ Shumaker,L.&K.]
Snyder, Patricia E. '47 '78 C.665 B.A. L.7 J.D.
Asst. Chf. Legal Coun., Auditor of State of Ohio
Snyder, Ronald H. .... '53 '80 C.980 B.A. L.608 J.D. 225 E. Broad St.
Soards, Karla S. .... '69 '98 C.610 B.A. L.179 J.D. [Ⓐ Scott,S.&W.]
Sobecki, Mark S. .... '— '86 C.276 B.S.B.A L.597 J.D. 625 Cleveland Avenue
Soden, Glenn W. '50 '76 C.935 B.A. L.8 J.D.
Assoc. V.P. & Asst. Secy., Nationwide Mutual Ins. Co.
Soll, Bruce A. '57 '82 C.154 B.A. L.800 J.D.
(adm. in CA; not adm. in OH) Limited, Inc., The
Solomon, Robert L., (BV) .... '62 '88 C.1064 B.A. L.608 J.D. U.S. Atty. Off.
Solove, Deborah A., (AV) .... '50 '81 C.923 A.B. L.117 J.D. Asst. U.S. Atty.
Solove, Larry M. .... '47 '72 C&L.608 B.S.B.A., J.D. Ron E. Roark Co.
Solove, M'liss K. .... '57 '83 C.737 B.A. L.117 J.D. 4444 Ravine Dr.
Solove, Ronald L., (AV) .... '45 '70 C&L.608 B.S., J.D. 79 Thurman Ave.
Soltis, Steve M., (BV) .... '40 '67 C&L.923 B.S., J.D. [Isaac,B.L.&T.]
Sommer, Joseph C. ...... '55 '83 C.610 B.B.A. L.851 J.D. Ohio Bureau of Workers Comp.
Somos, Tom .... '70 '99 C.025 B.A. L.117 J.D. [Ⓐ R.D.Erney&Assoc.]
Sonderman, Andrew J., (AV) ......'51 '76 C.381 B.A. L.608 J.D. 60 E. Broad St., Ste. 400
Sonnen, Craig A. ... '50 '75 C&L.117 B.A., J.D. Ref., Ohio Unemp. Comp. Bd. of Review
Soter, William J. .... '35 '61 C.608 B.A. L.607 J.D. 2 Sessions Dr.‡
Sours-Morehart, Cynthia Ann .... '53 '92 C.608 B.A. L.179 J.D. Pros. Off.
Sova, Rosemary, (BV) .... '50 '84 C.608 B.S. L.117 J.D. [Ⓒ Rich,C.&D.]
Sowald, Beatrice K., (AV) .... '27 '66 C&L.608 B.A., J.D. [Sowald,S.&C.]
Sowald, Heather G., (AV) .... '54 '79 C.930 B.A. L.117 J.D. [Sowald,S.&C.]
Sowald, Sowald & Clouse, (AV) .... 400 South Fifth Street
Spainhoward, Rebecca A. '— '89
C.608 B.S. L.851 J.D. Corp. Coun., CBC Companies, Inc.
Spalding, Jennifer McGowan .... '72 '97 C.138 B.A. L.117 J.D. Coun., Abbott Labs.
Spalding, Sloan T. .... '69 '97 C.878 B.S. L.117 J.D. [Ⓐ Ferron&Assoc.]
Spangler, Melissa D. .... '72 '97 C.313 B.A. L.117 J.D. Banc One Investment Mgmt.
Sparks, Danielle R. .... '66 '91 C.49 B.A. L.7 J.D. Pub. Def.
Spater, Alexander M., (AV) .... '43 '73 C.399 B.A. L.608 J.D. [Spater]
Spater Law Office, (AV) .... 565 E. Town Street
Speakman, Claudia J. ... '44 '76 C.273 B.B.A. L.117 J.D. Exec. Asst., State Dept. of Educ.
Speaks, George E. .... '65 '92 C.607 B.A. L.608 J.D. Franklin Co. Bd. of Comr.
Spector, David N., (CV) .... '52 '79 C.347 B.A. L.910 J.D. Wooster Iron & Metal Co.
Speidel, Jamison S. .... '70 '01 C.608 B.S.B.A. L.201 J.D. [Ⓐ Roetzel&A.]
Spencer, Gilda L. .... '62 '90 C.608 B.A. L.1049 J.D. Sr. Coun., Nationwide Insurance
Spencer, William W. .... '61 '86 C.117 B.S. L.608 J.D. 8178 Fairway Drive
Sperl, Kenneth J. .... '— '77 C.475 B.S. L.1187 J.D. [Ⓒ Mallory&T.]

Spialter, David C., (AV) .... '52 '78 C.309 A.B. L.178 J.D. [Bricker&E.]
Spiert, Ken .... '53 '87 C.91 B.A. L.608 J.D. 85 E. Gay St., Ste. 509
Spina, Anthony .... '71 '98 C.8 B.S. L.179 J.D. [Ⓐ Vorys,S.S.&P.]
Spirito, Maryellen C., (BV) '47 '83 C.787 B.S.R.N. L.608 J.D.
2075 Marble Cliff Off Park

Sponseller, Nancy L., Law Offices of
(See Dublin)

Sprader, Bobbie S. .... '69 '94 C.97 B.S.B.A. L.608 J.D. [Bricker&E.]
Sprague, James R. '57 '89 C.205 B.A. L.117 J.D.
Exec. Dir. & Chf. Adm. Law J., Pers. Bd. of Review
Sprankle, Tricia A. .... '69 '99 C.967 B.A. L.117 J.D. [Ⓐ Maguire&S.]
Spratley, William A. .... '47 '73 C.970 B.A. L.608 J.D. Consumers Counsel
Springer, Jennifer L. ...... '73 '01 C.383 B.A. L.989 J.D. The Legal Aid Soc. of Columbus
Sproat, John W., (BV) .... '46 '87 C.608 B.A. L.117 J.D. [Britt,C.N.&S.]
Spurlock, Michael, (AV) .... '49 '74 C&L.608 B.S., J.D. [Beery&S.]
Squeglia, Elisabeth A., (AV) .... '49 '79 C&L.608 B.A., J.D. [Bricker&E.]
Squillace, Michael L., (AV) .... '55 '80 C.602 B.A. L.851 J.D. [Dinsmore&S.]
Squillace, Vincent J., III .... '75 '02 C.602 B.A. L.117 J.D. [Ⓐ Roetzel&A.]
Squire, Tamara A., (CV) .... '58 '83 C.608 B.S. L.851 J.D. Off. of Atty. Gen.

Squire, Sanders & Dempsey L.L.P., (AV) BB
1300 Huntington Center, 41 South High Street, 43215-6197 ⊙
Telephone: 614-365-2700 Fax: 614-365-2499
URL: http://www.ssd.com
Partners: Columbus Office: David W. Alexander; Vincent Atriano; D. Lewis Clark, Jr.; Timothy J. Cosgrove; Philomena M. Dane; Susan M. DiMickele; Patrick J. Dugan; Christopher J. Franzmann; John R. Gall; David W. Grauer; Holly H. Heer; Donald W. Hughes; John M. Kirsner; Steven M. Loewengart; Daniel M. Maher; Steven F. Mount; William A. Nolan; Michael R. Reed; Richard W. Rubenstein; Michael D. Saad; Paul F. Sefcovic; Alex Shumate; Keith Shumate; Fredric L. Smith; Gregory W. Stype; William M. Todd; Bryan J. Venesy; Lee A. Wendel; Karen A. Winters; C. Craig Woods. Counsel: Columbus Office: Roberta L. Fisher; Richard R. Murphey Jr.; Fred A. Summer. Of Counsel: Columbus Office: H. Cort Doughty, Jr.; Michael B. Gardiner; Kim A. Rieck; Tim J. Robinson; James E. P. Sisto. Senior Counsel: Columbus Office: David J. Young. Senior Attorney: Columbus Office: Craig A. Sturtz. Associates: Columbus Office: Laing P. Akers; Tara Aschenbrand; Beth C. Bolyard; Kristen J. Brown; Patrick D. Cornelius; Kelly T. Custer; Gregory R. Daniels; Jessica E. DeMonte; Ryan G. Eastham; Jessica D. Goldman; Kyu Chang Han; Amy Ruth Ita; Corie Marty Judge; Greta M. Kearns; Raymond C. Keyser; Thomas F. Kibbey; Jill S. Kirila; Tiffany L. Komasara; Aneca E. Lasley; T. Bennett Litle; Mary C. Mertz; J. Seth Metcalf; Andrew D. M. Miller; Matthew J. Miller; Robert D. Nauman; Keely J. Rhodes; Kristin E. Richner; Erik J. Rickard; Ethan E. Rii (Not admitted in OH); Emily E. Root; Matthew L. Sagone; Aaron A. Seamon; P. Brian See; Kendra S. Sherman; Julie B. Smith; Heather L. Stutz; Johnathan E. Sullivan; Pamela Hackes Thurston; Jeffrey R. Wahl; Greg R. Wehrer; Philip R. Westerman; Lori Maiorca Zancourides.
Bankruptcy and Reorganization, Chemicals, Communications, Construction and Engineering, Corporate Transactions and Securities Regulation, E-Commerce, Economic Regulation, Education, Energy, Environmental, Health and Safety, Financial Institutions and Services, Financial Services, Gaming and Casinos, Government and Administrative Agencies, Health Care and Hospitals, Health Sciences, Hospitality and Recreation, Insurance, Intellectual Property, International Dispute Resolution, Labor and Employment, Life Sciences, Litigation, Manufacturing, Media and Entertainment, Private Equity, Project Finance, Public Finance, Real Estate, Real Estate and Hospitality, Sports, Steel, Taxation, Technology, Transportation and Utilities.
The Americas Offices: Cincinnati, Cleveland, Houston, Los Angeles, Miami, New York, Palo Alto, Phoenix, San Francisco, Tallahassee, Tampa, Tysons Corner, Washington DC, West Palm Beach, Caracas, Santo Domingo, Rio de Janeiro.
European Offices: Bratislava, Brussels, Budapest, London, Madrid, Milan, Moscow, Prague, Warsaw.
Asia Offices: Beijing, Hong Kong, Shanghai, Tokyo.
Associated Offices: Bucharest, Dublin, Kyiv, Buenos Aires, Santiago.
Revisor of the Ohio and Texas Law Digests for this Directory
See Professional Biographies, COLUMBUS, OHIO

Srsic, Daniel W. .... '70 '94 C.651 B.A. L.659 J.D. [Littler M.]
Staats, Larry E., (BV) .... '33 '57 C&L.608 B.A., J.D. Case Trustee in Bkrptcy.
Stafford, Robert G., (AV) .... '38 '68 C.608 B.E.E. L.117 J.D. [Means,B.B.&B.]
Staggers, L. Rahmond '75 '01 C.1243 B.B.A. L.1463 J.D.
(adm. in PA; not adm. in OH) American Electric Power Service Corp.
Stallworth, Nicolle '74 '04 C.302 B.S. L.262 J.D.
(adm. in NY; not adm. in OH) [Ⓐ Peck,S.&W.] (⊙Cincinnati)
Stalnaker, Roger A. .... '— '04 C.437 B.B.A. L.893 J.D. [Ⓐ Jones D.]
Stamp, Matthew E. .... '73 '98 C.528 B.A. L.117 J.D. Mgr., Deloitte & Touche
Stankunas, Jeffrey A. .... '— '00 C.97 B.A. L.608 J.D. [Ⓐ Isaac,B.L.&T.]
Stanley, Edward D. .... '30 '57 C.610 A.B. L.608 LL.B. 35 East Gay Street
Stanton, Elizabeth M., (AV) .... '47 '79 C.223 B.S. L.326 J.D. [Chester,W.&S.]
Stark, Leo P. .... '23 '50 C.930 L.608 LL.B. Ret. Mun. J.
Stark, Lisa R. .... '— '02 C.613 B.A. L.608 J.D. [Ⓐ Baker&H.]
Starkoff, Alan G., (AV) .... '50 '75 C.608 B.S. L.161 J.D. [Schottenstein,Z.&D.]
Startzman, Thos. L. .... '29 '54 C.97 B.A. L.608 J.D. [Gilbert&S.]
Stasiewicz, Suzanne, (BV) '60 '88
C.610 B.A. L.608 J.D. 5969 East Livingston Avenue, Suite 200
Stauffer, Timothy D. .... '56 '82 C.385 B.A. L.851 J.D. Dept. of Taxation

Stebelton, Aranda & Snider, A Legal Professional Association
(See Lancaster)

Stebenne, David L. '60 '86 C.976 B.A. L.178 J.D.
(adm. in MD; not adm. in OH) Ohio State Univ.
Steele, Athornia, (Mr.) .... '51 '77 C&L.117 B.A., J.D. Prof. of Law, Capital Univ.
Steele, Dathard V. .... '53 '77 C.945 B.B.A. L.117 J.D. 1800 Moler Road
Steele, William J., (BV) .... '58 '83 C.234 B.A. L.608 J.D. 225 E. Broad St.
Stefanelli, Luisa Vingenza '47 '79
C.608 B.S. L.179 J.D. 3099 Sullivant Avenue, 2nd Floor
Steffee, Laura J. .... '62 '88 C.25 B.A. L.1003 J.D. Asst. Atty. Gen.
Steger, S. Martijn, (AV) .... '56 '83 C.473 B.Ph. L.608 J.D. [Kegler,B.H.&R.]
Stehura, Paul .... '56 '82 C.381 B.A. L.608 J.D. [Ⓒ Cox,S.&P.]
Stein, Arland T., (AVⓉ) .... '38 '65 C.679 B.S. L.893 J.D. [Hahn L.&P.] (See Pat. Sect.)
Stein, David K. .... '64 '89 C.608 B.A. L.117 J.D. [Stein,C.]

Stein, Stanley R., (AV) '45 '71 C.610 B.B.A. L.1003 J.D.
280 North High Street Suite 220, 43215
Telephone: 614-224-7077 Fax: 614-224-5519
Email: stanstein@ssatty.ldmi.net URL: http://www.stansteinlaw.com
Workers Compensation (Defense/Claimant), Social Security Disability, Civil Litigation.
See Professional Biographies, COLUMBUS, OHIO

Stein, Sydney D. .... '78 '03 C.608 B.A. L.117 J.D. [Ⓐ Plymale]
Stein, Chapin, & Associates LLC .... 32 W. Hoster St., Ste. 200
Stelling, Andrea Mote .... '42 '79 C.788 B.A. L.966 J.D. Dept. of Human Servs.
Stelzer, Lawrence J., Jr. ...... '64 '91 C&L.260 B.S., J.D. State Coun. of Retail Merchants
Stemm, Mark S., (AV) .... '59 '84 C.475 B.S. L.608 J.D. [Porter W.M.&A.]
Stempien, James H., Jr. '58 '87
C.611 B.A. L.117 J.D. 6100 Channingway Boulevard, Suite 306
Stepanic, Mary J. .... '61 '87 C.97 B.S. L.851 J.D. Asst. Atty. Gen.
Stephen, John M., (AV) .... '54 '79 C.210 B.A. L.608 J.D. [Porter W.M.&A.]
Stephens, Eric B. .... '68 '94 C.980 B.A. L.608 J.D. Ohio Consumers' Counsel

Stephens, Jay '55 '90 C.1147 B.S. L.146 J.D.
(adm. in IL; not adm. in OH) P.O. Box 711065
Stephenson, H. Grant, (AV) ....'49 '79 C.610 B.A. L.608 J.D. [Porter W.M.&A.]
Stepter, Rayl L. ....'62 '90 C.477 B.A. L.309 J.D. [Stepter]
Stepter Law Office ....111 W. Rich St., Ste. 430
Stern, Ernest ....'23 '54 C.608 B.S. L.266 J.D. 150 E. Broad St.‡
Stern, Geoffrey, (AV) ....'42 '68 C&L.608 B.A., J.D. [Kegler,B.H.&R.]
Stern, Herbert G. ....'26 '53 C.705 B.S. L.569 LL.B. 111 N. Edgevale Rd.
Stevenson, Judith M., (AV) ....'42 '74 C.262 B.A. L.117 J.D. Co. Pub. Def.
Stevenson, Mary Denning ....'49 '75 C&L.574 B.A., J.D. Ohio Indus. Comm.
Stewart, Carter M. '69 '98 C.813 B.A. L.1565 J.D.
(adm. in CA; not adm. in OH) [Ⓐ Vorys,S.S.&P.]
Stewart, Craig M., (AV) ....'43 '67 C&L.608 B.S., J.D. [Carlile P.&M.]
Stewart, Jackie Lee, (BV) ....'51 '80 C&L.608 B.A., J.D. [Luper,N.&L.]
Stewart, Janet Blair ....'51 '76 C.373 B.A. L.339 J.D. Asst. Atty. Gen.
Stewart, Joseph R., (BV) ....'48 '73 C.813 B.A. L.976 J.D. Atty., Sprint Corp.
Stichter, Philip W., (AV) ....'39 '66 C.597 B.A. L.309 J.D. 8135 Blind Brook Court
Stickrath, Thomas J. '54 '79
C&L.608 B.S.B.A., J.D. Asst. Dir., Dept. of Rehab. & Corrections
Stiles, Kelli Jones ....'— '03 C&L.608 B.A, J.D. [Ⓐ Jones D.]
Still, Nan M. ....'46 '87 C&L.608 B.S.Ed., J.D. Ohio Farm Bureau Fed.
Stiltner, Jeffrey W. ....'70 '95 C.363 B.A. L.117 J.D. [Hahn L.&P.]
Stine, Joshua N. ....'— '03 C.347 B.A. L.608 J.D. [Ⓐ Schottenstein,Z.&D.]
Stinson, Dane ....'56 '81 C.698 B.A. L.608 J.D. [Bailey C.]
Stir, Theresa Lynn ....'57 '93 C.523 B.S.N. L.179 J.D. Ohio Board of Nursing
Stith, Robin S., Law Offices of, (BV) '56 '80 C.597 B.A. L.276 J.D.
13 E. Kossuth Street
Stitt, Scott J. ....'72 '01 C.94 B.A. L.608 J.D. [Clark,P.A.&S.C.]
Stock, Christopher D. ...'75 '02 C&L.608 B.A, J.D. Dep. Atty. Gen., Ohio Atty. Gen. Off.
Stock, Elizabeth C. ....'76 '02 C.473 B.A. L.608 J.D. [Ⓐ Bricker&E.]
Stock, John F., (AV) ....'56 '81 C&L.608 B.A., J.D. [Benesch,F.C.&A.]
Stock, Jonathan K. ....'— '95 C.197 B.A. L.309 J.D. [Ⓐ Jones D.]
Stoffers, Robert H., (BV) ....'57 '82 C.631 B.A. L.851 J.D. [Mazanec,R.&R.]
Stokes, Angela ....'53 '84 C.446 B.A. L.329 J.D. Asst. Atty. Gen.
Stolar, Margaret M. ....'— '90 C.25 B.S. L.665 J.D. [Dreher L.&T.]
Stoll, Sheryl Clark, (BVⓉ) ....'48 '81 C.187 B.A. L.352 J.D. [Ⓒ Vorys,S.S.&P.]
Stoll, William F., Jr. ...'48 '73 C.276 B.S. L.930 J.D. Sr. V.P. & Gen. Coun., Borden, Inc.
Stoller, Eric M. ....'74 '99 C.610 B.B.A. L.608 J.D. [Ⓐ Schottenstein,Z.&D.]
Stone, Jill Eileen ....'52 '79 C.161 B.A. L.608 J.D. Pub. Def. Off.
Stone, Thomas A. ....'60 '85 C&L.608 B.S.B.A., J.D. Mag., Prob. Ct.
Stonecipher, Sheryl C. ....'51 '75 C&L.608 B.A., J.D. I.R.S. Atty.-Estate Tax
Stoneking, Janet K. '50 '96 C&L.117 B.A., J.D.
Atty. Examiner, Pub. Ut. Comm. of OH
Stopa, John R. '53 '78 C.971 B.S. L.94 J.D.
V.P. & Sr. Coun., The Huntington Natl. Bk.
Stout, Charles J. ....'51 '80 C.473 B.S. L.117 J.D. General Reins. Corp.
Stout, Matthew L. ....'71 '99 C.477 B.B.A. L.608 J.D. [Ⓐ Bricker&E.]
Stout, Thomas A., Jr. ....'50 '75 C.367 B.A. L.446 J.D. 1050 Freeway Drive North
Stovall, Richard K., (AV) ....'60 '85 C.97 B.A. L.851 J.D. [Allen,K.&S.]
Stover, Stephan W. ....'46 '75 C.608 B.S. L.910 J.D. OH State Bar Assn.
Strait, Anne Berry, (BV) ....'56 '83 C.373 B.A. L.608 J.D. Asst. Atty. Gen.
Stratton, Evelyn Lundberg ....'53 '79 C.8 B.A. L.608 J.D. Supm. Ct. Jus.
Strausbaugh, Dean ....'18 '48 C.228 A.B. L.477 J.D. Ret. Appl. Ct. J.
Strause, Edgar A., (AV) ....'27 '53 C.352 B.A. L.477 J.D. [Ⓒ Vorys,S.S.&P.]
Strauss, Catherine L. ....'75 '00 C.608 B.a. L.273 J.D. [Ⓐ Schottenstein,Z.&D.]
Strautz, Elizabeth M. ....'62 '97 C&L.608 B.F.A., J.D. [Ⓐ Barkan&B.]
Strayer, Susan L. ....'58 '96 C.607 B.A. L.117 J.D. [Britt,C.N.&S.]
Streb, Joseph S., (BV) ....'52 '84 C.608 B.S. L.117 J.D. [J.S.Streb]
Streb, Joseph S., Co., L.P.A., (BV) .... 736 Neil Avenue
Strelou, Karen Lee ....'50 '84 C.967 B.A. L.117 J.D. State Dept. of Taxation
Strip, A. C., (AV) ....'36 '60 C&L.608 B.A., J.D. [Strip,H.L.M.&T.]

Strip, Hoppers, Leithart, McGrath & Terlecky Co., LPA, (AV)
575 S. 3rd Street, 43215
Telephone: 614-228-6345 Fax: 614-228-6369 URL: http://www.columbuslawyer.net
Email: jwh@columbuslawyer.net URL: http://www.lawyers.com/shlmtlpa
A. C. Strip; John Wm. Hoppers; Paul W. Leithart; Timothy J. McGrath; Myron N. Terlecky; Nelson E. Genshaft; Ken Goldberg;—Aaron C. Firstenberger; Andrew C. Hall; Jerry E. Peer, Jr.
Business Matters, Corporations, Limited Liability Companies, Insolvency, Receivership, Bankruptcy, Construction, Probate, Personal Injury, Estate Planning, Professional Associations, Ethics Representation, Civil Litigation, Family Law, Real Estate, Trusts and Wills, Elder Law, Zoning and Acquisition, Tax Planning, Discrimination.
See Professional Biographies, COLUMBUS, OHIO

Stroup, Catherine Anne ....'52 '89 C.787 B.A. L.117 J.D. Historic Preservation Off.
Stucko, James K., Jr., (BV) ....'63 '88 C.207 B.A. L.602 J.D. [Scott,S.&W.]
Studer, Raymond J., (BV) ....'51 '76 C&L.608 B.S.W., J.D. Asst. Atty. Gen.

Stumler, Rebecca J. '61 '90 C.421 B.A. L.117 J.D.
1500 W. 3rd Avenue, Suite 127, 43212
Telephone: 614-487-8210 Fax: 614-487-8212
Email: rjstumler@aol.com URL: http://www.stumlerlaw.com
Family Law, Divorce, Child Custody, Child Support, Visitation Rights, Adoption Law, Paternity, Domestic Violence, Bankruptcy Law, Civil Litigation.
See Professional Biographies, COLUMBUS, OHIO

Sturges, Scott F. ....'51 '82 C.611 B.A. L.608 J.D. [Ⓒ McNamara&M.]
Sturm, Laurel I. ....'50 '86 C.473 B.S. L.608 J.D. Gen. Coun., Escape Enterprises
Sturtz, Craig A., (BV) ....'67 '92 C.347 B.S. L.117 J.D. [Ⓐ Squire,S.&D.]
Stutz, Heather L. ....'80 '04 C&L.607 B.A., J.D. [Ⓐ Squire,S.&D.]
Styduhar, Robert J., (AV) ....'49 '77 C&L.930 B.S.C.E., J.D. [Vorys,S.S.&P.]
Stype, Gregory W., (AV) ....'55 '82 C.970 B.A. L.608 J.D. [Squire,S.&D.]
Subramaniam, Radha ....'66 '01 C&L.608 B.A., J.D. [Ⓐ Schottenstein]
Suchta, Arthur M. ....'48 '73 C.150 B.A. L.607 J.D. Admn. Coun., Ohio Dept. of Tax.
Suffron, Benjamin F., III '52 '78
C.473 B.S.B.A. L.117 J.D. Mag., Franklin Co., OH Probate Ct.
Sugar, Anthony J., (BV) ....'63 '91 C&L.659 B.A., J.D. [Ⓒ Bailey C.]
Sugar, David B. ...'67 '94 C.608 B.A. L.117 J.D. Tr. Offr., The Huntington Tr. Co., N.A.
Sugarman, Roger P., (AV) ....'50 '75 C.880 B.A. L.851 J.D. [Kegler,B.H.&R.]
Suhr, Robert W., (BV) ....'42 '70 C.608 B.S. L.117 J.D. 755 S. High St.
Sullivan, Angela M. '76 '02 C.201 B.A. L.608 J.D.
Staff Atty, Franklin Co. Ct. of Common Pleas
Sullivan, Christine A. '52 '79
C.802 B.A. L.851 J.D. Staff Hearing Offr., Indus. Comm. of Ohio
Sullivan, John E. ....'22 '52 C.363 B.S. L.930 LL.B. 246 S. Davison Ave.‡
Sullivan, Johnathan E. ....'73 '00 C&L.608 B.A., J.D. [Ⓐ Squire,S.&D.]
Sullivan, Michael F., (AV) ....'42 '67 C.976 B.A. L.145 J.D. [Bricker&E.]
Sullivan, Roseanne ...'48 '83 C&L.608 B.A., J.D. Claims Atty., Nationwide Mut. Ins. Co.
Sullivan, Susan M., (BV) .....'— '77 C.970 B.A. L.150 J.D. Princ. Atty., State Atty. Gen.

Sully, Ira B., (BV) '47 '74 C&L.608 B.A., J.D.
844 South Front Street, 43206
Telephone: 614-443-3930 Fax: 614-443-7463
URL: http://www.lawyers.com/irasullylaw
Real Estate, Business and Commercial Law. Commercial Collections, Contracts, Small Business Law, Wills and Probate, Trusts and Estate Planning.
Representative Clients: Borden, Inc.; Caravan Trailer Park, Inc.; Thomas Fortin Realtors; Star Time Video; Badurina Construction Co., Inc.; Barnes Stucco, Inc.
Approved Agent For: Ohio Bar Title Insurance Co.; First American Title Insurance Co.
Local Counsel For: Central Ohio Chapter, Video Software Dealers Assn.
See Professional Biographies, COLUMBUS, OHIO

Sumi, Christopher E. ....'77 '02 C&L.608 B.A., J.D. [Ⓐ Vorys,S.S.&P.]
Summer, Fred A., (AV) ....'46 '74 C.309 A.B. L.477 J.D. [Ⓒ Squire,S.&D.]
Sumner, John H. ....'51 '80 C.611 B.A. L.117 J.D. 2099 Haverford Rd.
Sun, Chuan ....'73 '04 C.999 B.A. L.597 J.D. [Ⓐ Bricker&E.]
Sunbury, Gerald T., (AV) ....'46 '74 C.608 B.S. L.117 J.D. [Sunbury&Y.]
Sunbury & Young, (AV) ....495 South High Street, Suite 400
Sunderland, John T., (AV) ....'54 '83 C.385 A.B. L.117 J.D. [Thompson H.]
Susalla, Malinda L. ....'— '95 C.475 B.S. L.273 J.D. [Ⓐ Schottenstein,Z.&D.]
Suter, Douglas J., (AV) ....'62 '88 C.920 B.S.B.A. L.117 J.D. [Isaac,B.L.&T.]
Sutker, Dory A., (AV) ....'52 '78 C.930 B.A. L.221 J.D. [Ⓐ Barkan&B.]
Sutter, Andrew I., (AV) ....'52 '83 C.994 B.A. L.608 J.D. Sr. Coun., Bank One Corp.
Sutter, Karl J., (AV) ....'57 '82 C.610 B.S. L.851 J.D. [Porter W.M.&A.]
Sutter, Michelle T. ....'53 '81 C.1260 B.A. L.7 J.D. 30 E. Broad St.
Sutton, Gregory E., (BV) ....'67 '92 C.696 B.A. L.117 J.D. Sr. Coun., Bank One Corp.
Sutton, Joseph Raymond ....'70 '95 C.611 B.A. L.608 J.D. 1375 Dublin Road
Sutton, Maximillian C. ....'72 '98 C.602 B.A. L.608 J.D. Off. of Co. Pub. Def.
Swaim, Stephen ....'53 '78 C.473 B.A. L.902 J.D. 118 East Main Street
Swaneck, Anthony J. '57 '96 C.150 B.S.M.E. L.117 J.D.
Sr. Coun.-Trans., Amer. Elec. Power Serv. Corp.
Swank, Christopher N. ....'76 '02 C.473 B.A. L.608 J.D. [Ⓐ Bricker&E.]
Swanson, Daniel T., (AV) ....'49 '74 C.207 B.A. L.880 J.D. 2757 Elginfield Rd.
Swanson, Judith Ann ....'45 '76 C.475 B.A. L.608 J.D. 759 South 6th St.
Swart, Gregory W., (AV) '51 '80
C.930 B.A. L.117 J.D. Dept. of Mental Retard. and Developmental
Swary, Wendy M. '72 '01 C.228 B.A. L.608 J.D.
(adm. in NY; not adm. in OH) [Ⓐ Vorys,S.S.&P.]
Swatsler, Todd Shawn, (AV) ....'— '81 C&L.608 B.A., J.D. [Jones D.]
Swedlow, Gerald H., (AV) ....'36 '61 C&L.608 B.S., J.D. [Swedlow,B.L.M.&D.]
Swedlow, Butler, Lewis, Madison & Dye Co., L.P.A., (AV)
10 West Broad Street, Suite 2400
Sweebe, Richard D., (AV) ......'51 '79 C.381 B.A. L.7 J.D. 88 E. Broad St. (ⓒCleveland)
Sweeney, Asher W. ....'20 '49 C.980 L.228 LL.B. Supm. Ct. Jus.
Sweeney, Thomas L. ...'36 '74 C.124 B.S. L.117 J.D. Assoc. V.P., Ohio State Univ. (Pat.)
Swepston, Donald S. ....'32 '57 C&L.608 B.A., J.D. Admr., State Dept. of Taxation
Sweterlitsch, Martha J., (AV) ....'45 '83 C&L.608 B.A., J.D. [Ⓒ Benesch,F.C.&A.]
Swetnam, Daniel R., (AV) ....'57 '82 C.608 B.A. L.150 J.D. [Schottenstein,Z.&D.]
Swift, Betsy A., (AV) ....'54 '88 C.473 B.S. L.608 J.D. [Bricker&E.]
Swift, David A., (AV) ....'52 '78 C.473 A.B. L.608 J.D. [Vorys,S.S.&P.]
Swinerton, Jenny T. ....'76 '04 C.851 B.A. L.117 J.D. [Ⓐ Porter W.M.&A.]
Swinford, Leslie B., Jr., (AV) '45 '75
C.608 B.A. L.117 J.D. Asst. Atty. Gen. [Merullo,R.&S.]
Swisher, Thomas R. ....'31 '60 C&L.150 B.A., LL.B. Ohio State Bar Foundation
Switzer, Thomas E. ....'70 '97 C.117 B.A. L.607 J.D. [Lane,A.&H.]
Sykes, Kevin L., (AV) ....'48 '79 C.72 B.A. L.608 J.D. [Kegler,B.H.&R.]
Szilagyi, Richard A. ....'28 '69 C.381 B.S. L.1003 J.D. Sr. Asst. Atty. Gen.
Szolosi, Michael R., Sr., (AV) ....'44 '69 C.851 B.A. L.608 J.D. [Ⓒ McNamara&M.]
Szykowny, Thomas E., (AV) ....'57 '82 C.207 B.A. L.608 J.D. [Vorys,S.S.&P.]
Tabb, Kimberly B. ....'— '00 C.811 B.A. L.494 J.D. Coun., Nationwide Insurance
Tackett, Brian ....'70 '01 C&L.608 B.A., J.D. [Ⓐ Keener D.C.&P.]
Taft, Robert A., II, (AV) ....'42 '76 C.976 B.A. L.150 J.D. Governor‡

Taft, Stettinius & Hollister LLP, (AV) BB
Twelfth Floor 21 East State Street, 43215-4221 ⊙
Telephone: 614-221-2838 Facsimile: 614-221-2007
URL: http://www.taftlaw.com
Members of Firm: David L. Johnson; Lawrence D. Walker; Timothy P. Nagy; Michael A. Byers; Robert W. McAdams, Jr.; Timothy B. Mitchell; John P. Curp; James B. Farmer. Of Counsel: Frank A. Titus; Diane D. Reynolds. Resident Associates: Shelli Turner Clark; Benjamin J. Parsons; Barbara A. McNeil.
Antitrust, Bankruptcy and Debtor/Creditor Rights, Business and Finance, E-Business (Internet and E-Commerce), Employee Benefits/ERISA and Tax-Planning, Environmental Law, Family Law, Family Business Planning, Franchise, General Litigation, Health Care, Immigration, Institutional Finance, Intellectual Property and Technology Group, International, Japanese Practice, Labor and Employment, Mergers and Acquisitions, Nonprofit and Tax-Exempt Organizations, Product Liability and Personal Injury, Public Finance, Real Property, Securities, Tax, Probate and Estate Planning, Workers' Compensation.
Cincinnati, Ohio Office: 425 Walnut Street, Suite 1800. Telephone: 513-381-2838
Covington, Kentucky Office: 1717 Dixie Highway, Suite 340. Telephone: 859-331-2838; 513-381-2838.
Cleveland, Ohio Office: 3500 BP Tower, 200 Public Square. Telephone: 216-241-2838.
Dayton, Ohio Office: 110 North Main Street, Suite 900. Telephone: 937-228-2838.
See Professional Biographies, COLUMBUS, OHIO

Taggart, Brent C., (AV) ....'61 '88 C.188 A.B. L.477 J.D. [Vorys,S.S.&P.]
Taggart, Thomas M., (AV) ....'37 '65 C.197 B.A. L.309 LL.B. [Ⓒ Vorys,S.S.&P.]
Tait, Amy C. ....'72 '98 C.475 B.A. L.608 J.D. Ohio Atty. Gen.
Tait, Mary E. ....'— '99 C.546 B.A. L.597 J.D. [Ⓐ Jones D.]
Tait, Robert E., (AV) ....'46 '73 C.385 B.A. L.477 J.D. [Vorys,S.S.&P.]
Talbott, Harold B. ....'18 '52 C.610 B.S.C. L.607 J.D. 1180 S. High Street
Tallan, Mitchell M., (BV) ....'59 '84 C&L.608 B.A., J.D. [Gallagher,G.P.T.&L.]
Tammaro, Bradford L. ....'54 '85 C.1038 B.S. L.201 J.D. [Ⓒ Thompson H.]
Taneff, Thomas N., (BV) '61 '88 C.608 B.S. L.117 J.D.
600 South High Street, Suite 201
Tangeman, Jill Stemen ....'71 '96 C.207 B.A. L.608 J.D. [Ⓐ Plank&B.]
Tanner, Philip G. ....'54 '79 C.608 B.A. L.117 J.D. 2019 Andover Rd.
Tanner, Robert E., Jr. '57 '89
C.608 B.A. L.117 J.D. Gen. Coun. & Dir., Columbus Airport Auth.
Tannous, Marlo B., (BV) '62 '88 C.97 B.A. L.608 J.D.
Chief Legal Coun., State Dept. of Development
Tannous, Robert J., (AV) ....'62 '87 C&L.608 B.S., J.D. [Porter W.M.&A.]
Tanoury, John L., (AV) ....'51 '77 C.608 B.S. L.117 J.D. [Ball&T.]
Tantra, Dina A. ....'69 '94 C.668 B.A. L.608 J.D. Nationwide Ins.
Taps, Richard T., (AV) ....'47 '78 C.207 B.A. L.608 J.D. 713 S. Front Street
Tarian, Brian A. ....'55 '82 C.276 B.A. L.8 J.D. [Ⓐ Roetzel&A.]
Tarkowsky, John, (BV) '54 '78 C.62 B.A. L.607 J.D.
[Baran,P.T.F.&T.] (ⓒMansfield, Worthington)
Tarpy, Thomas M., (AV) ....'45 '69 C.363 A.B. L.608 J.D. [Vorys,S.S.&P.]
Tarullo, Michael D., (AV) ....'49 '89 C.421 B.S. L.117 J.D. [Schottenstein,Z.&D.]
Tassie, James George ....'70 '95 C.188 B.A. L.608 J.D. State's Atty. Gen., Edu. Sect.

Tate, Tracy C. .... '— '03 C.136 B.S. L.477 J.D. [Ⓐ Jones D.]
Taylor, Anne .... '51 '79 C.608 B.S. L.117 J.D. Mun. J.
Taylor, Heather N. .... '77 '03 C.303 B.A. L.1119 J.D. [Ⓐ Porter W.M.&A.]
Taylor, Joan Gibb .... '54 '80 C&L.608 B.A., J.D. U.S. Small Bus. Admn.
Taylor, Jodie M. .... '69 '95 C.473 B.A. L.7 J.D. [Ⓐ Scott,S.&W.]
Taylor, Joel Sanford, (AV) '42 '69
C.821 B.A. L.178 LL.B. 90 West Broad Street, 4th Floor‡
Taylor, Josefina B. .... '— '00 C.347 B.A. L.117 J.D. [Ⓐ Mallory&T.]
Taylor, M. Todd .... '73 '00 C.105 B.A. L.188 J.D. [Ⓐ Porter W.M.&A.]
Taylor, Mary Ten Eyck, (BV) .... '53 '85 C.703 B.A. L.117 J.D. [Ⓐ Wiles,B.B.&B.]
Taylor, Maureen P., (BV) .... '42 '89 C&L.477 A.B., J.D. [Ⓐ Bricker&E.]
Taylor, Robert H., (AV) .... '44 '74 C.363 A.B. L.608 J.D. [Shoemaker,H.&T.]
Teaford, Hamilton J., (AV) .... '40 '66 C.918 B.A. L.309 J.D. 91 E. Deshler Ave.
Teaford, Murray R. .... '50 '89 C.868 B.A. L.117 J.D. 302 Chatham Road
Teague, Rodney B., (BV) ..... '45 '74 C.608 B.A. L.607 J.D. Co. Child Supp. Enforcement
Teetor, J. Stephen, (AV) .... '51 '77 C.608 B.S. L.117 J.D. [Isaac,B.L.&T.]
Templeton, Phillip A., (BV) .... '66 '92 C.434 B.A. L.117 J.D. [Ⓐ Crabbe,B.&J.]
Tenenbaum, Lee J. .... '37 '78 C.575 B.S. L.201 J.D. 325 South Dawson Avenue
Tenuta, Luigia, (BV) .... '54 '81 C.473 A.B. L.117 J.D. 6400 Riverside Dr.
Terakedis, J. Troy .... '69 '96 C.385 B.A. L.930 J.D. [Ⓒ Calfee,H.&G.]
Terakedis, John, Jr., (AV) .... '45 '70 C.62 B.S. L.309 J.D. [Schottenstein,Z.&D.]
Terapak, Richard G., (AV) .... '46 '72 C&L.608 B.A., J.D. [Porter W.M.&A.]
Terbeek, Jeffrey L., (BV) ..... '48 '73 C.610 B.B.A. L.161 J.D. 1010 Old Henderson Road
Terlecky, Myron N., (AV) .... '59 '84 C.363 B.A. L.117 J.D. [Strip,H.L.M.&T.]
Terveer, Thomas B. '58 '83
C.608 B.S.B.A. L.117 J.D. Assoc. Gen. Coun., Nationwide Insurance
Terwilleger, Kenneth B. '56 '84 C&L.902 B.A., J.D.
(adm. in DC; not adm. in OH) Sr. Coun., Bank One Corp.
Terzian, Barbara A., (AV) .... '50 '75 [Ⓒ Gittes&S.]
Teteris, Jean Yingling, (AV) .... '— '75 C&L.608 B.A., J.D. [Porter W.M.&A.]
Thaxton, Forrest F. .... '34 '61 C&L.608 B.A., J.D. 4211 E. Broad St.
Theiss, Douglas J. .... '54 '81 C&L.117 B.A., J.D. P.O. Box 1559
Theller, Robert Thomas .... '63 '98 C.1044 L.117 Treas. of the State of Ohio, Invests.
Thernes, Linda Jane '52 '89 C&L.8 B.A.S.W., J.D.
State Dept. Mental Health, Legal & Labor Sect.
Thien, John Kenneth .... '57 '99 C.130 B.A. L.893 J.D. [Ⓐ Porter W.M.&A.]
Thomas, Alexander G. .... '26 '74 C.381 B.S. L.8 J.D. Atty. Gen.
Thomas, Amy S. '69 '98 C.602 B.A. L.878 J.D.
(adm. in UT; not adm. in OH) [Ⓐ Reminger&R.]
Thomas, Bethany R. .... '78 '02 C.473 B.A. L.608 J.D. [Ⓐ Vorys,S.S.&P.]
Thomas, Collin N. .... '70 '95 C&L.117 B.A., J.D. 341 South Third Street Suite 300
Thomas, David H. .... '74 '99 C.967 B.A. L.608 J.D. 511 South High Street
Thomas, Duke W., (AV) .... '37 '64 C&L.608 B.S., J.D. [Ⓒ Vorys,S.S.&P.]
Thomas, Ernest V., III, (BV) .... '58 '82 C.1118 B.A. L.150 J.D. [Thomas&T.] ⊙
Thomas, Fred, Jr., (BV) .... '31 '77 C&L.608 B.A., J.D. 875 Mt. Vernon Ave.

Thomas, J. Patrick, (BV) '51 '77 C&L.608 B.A., J.D.
211 East Livingston Avenue, 43215
Telephone: 614-221-2331 Fax: 614-221-4125
Email: pat@jpthomaslawfirm.com URL: http://www.jpthomaslawfirm.com
Collections, Credit Union Law, Hospital Collections, Creditors Rights, Mechanics Liens, Construction Law, Real Estate, Contracts, Probate; Probate Law, Creditors Bankruptcy, Commercial and Consumer Collections, Secured Collections, Replevin, Leases and Leasing.
See Professional Biographies, COLUMBUS, OHIO

Thomas, James D. .... '62 '88 C&L.201 B.A., J.D. 2563 Berwyn Rd.
Thomas, John R., (AV) .... '42 '68 C&L.608 B.A., J.D. [Kegler,B.H.&R.]
Thomas, Kathryn A. .... '59 '84 C&L.608 B.S., J.D. Asst. State Pub. Def.
Thomas, Michael R., (AV) .... '51 '76 C&L.477 B.A., J.D. [Ⓐ Vorys,S.S.&P.]
Thomas, Patsy A. .... '60 '94 C.266 B.A. L.117 J.D. [Ⓒ Kegler,B.H.&R.]
Thomas, Peter Mathews .... '62 '88 C.347 B.A. L.790 J.D. Atty. Gen.
Thomas, Warner M., Jr., (AV) ... '49 '79 C.85 B.S. L.607 J.D. [Volkema,T.M.B.S.&M.]

Thomas Law Group
(See Dublin)

Thomas & Thomas, (BV)
#24 Huber Village Boulevard (⊙Newport, KY; Cin., Cleve., OH)
Thompson, Bruce R. .... '56 '82 C.347 B.S. L.608 J.D. One Nationwide Plz.
Thompson, H. Lee, (BV) .... '45 '75 C.1023 B.S. L.184 J.D. [Thompson]
Thompson, Helen A. .... '70 '96 C.381 B.A. L.229 J.D. [Kreiner&P.] (⊙Cleveland)
Thompson, Jeffrey G. .... '62 '94 C.776 B.A. L.608 J.D. 601 S. High St.
Thompson, Lance E. .... '56 '84 C.608 B.A. L.117 J.D. Asst. Atty. Gen.
Thompson, Lee A., (BV) .... '52 '83 C.381 B.S. L.7 J.D. [Calig&H.] (⊙Lancaster)
Thompson, Lisa Fields '71 '97 C.604 B.A. L.608 J.D.
Traffic Pros., Off. of the City Pros.
Thompson, Matthew J. .... '63 '88 C&L.608 B.A., J.D. [Nobile,N.&T.] ⊙
Thompson, Myron Abner .... '69 '94 C.1349 B.A. L.608 J.D. Hall of Jus.
Thompson, Paul L. .... '19 '54 C.608 L.266 J.D. 1910 Knoll Ridge Ct.
Thompson, Thomas D., (BV) .... '45 '71 C.473 B.A. L.150 J.D. [Thompson,M.&D.]
Thompson, Tommy L. .... '34 '61 C&L.608 B.A., J.D. Com. Pleas J.

Thompson Hine LLP, (AV)
10 West Broad Street, Suite 700, 43215-3435 ⊙
Telephone: 614-469-3200 Fax: 614-469-3361
Email: info@ThompsonHine.com URL: http://www.ThompsonHine.com
Amos Burt Thompson (1871-1965); Charles P. Hine (1877-1942); Walter L. Flory (1880-1951); Michael L. Hardy (Partner-in-Charge, Cleveland); Patricia Mann Smitson (Partner-in-Charge, Cincinnati); Anthony C. White (Partner-in-Charge, Columbus); Robert M. Curry (Partner-in Charge, Dayton Office); Nicholas J. DiMichael (Partner-in-Charge, Washington, D.C.); George J. Walsh III (Partner-in-Charge, New York City); Ludo Deklerck (Not admitted in OH; Partner-in-Charge, Brussels); Walt A. Linscott (Partner-in-Charge, Atlanta). Partners: James H. Balthaser; Alan F. Berliner; Scott A. Campbell; William R. Case; Michael W. Currie; William S. Fein; Charles F. Freiburger, IV; Kurt P. Helfrich; Thomas E. Lodge; Boyd K. Moehring; Robert P. Mone; William C. Moul (Group Leader, Labor and Employment); Janis B. Rosenthal; O. Judson Scheaf III; Jeffery E. Smith; John T. Sunderland; Jerry Vande Werken; Peter D. Welin; Anthony C. White (Partner-in-Charge); William C. Wilkinson. Of Counsel: Bradford L. Tammaro; Michael V. Wible. Associates: Craig A. Calcaterra; Daniel F. Edwards; Carolyn S. Flahive; Paul Giorgianni; Heather D. Gregg; Joseph J. Huprich (Not admitted in OH); Melissa L. Kidd; John B. Kopf, III; W. Blair Lewis; Robert W. Myers; Michele L. Noble; Mark A. Noel; June M. Oshima; Thomas W. Palmer; Akhil Patel; Gabe J. Roehrenbeck; Jennifer E. Short; Martha S. Van Hoy; Glen A. Varchetti. Senior Attorney: Philip B. Cochran.
Administrative Law, Admiralty and Maritime Law, Agency and Distributorships, Antitrust and Trade Regulation, Aviation and Aerospace, Bankruptcy, Banks and Banking, Biotechnology, Business Law, *Business Litigation, Business Regulation, Business Transactions,* Closely Held Business Law, Joint Ventures, Class Actions, Commercial Law, Commercial Real Estate, Communications and Media, FCC Regulation, Computers and Software, Construction Law, Contracts, Copyrights, Corporate Law, Corporate Finance, Corporate Litigation, Corporate Tax Controversies, Debtor and Creditor, Employee Benefits, ERISA, Energy, Energy Regulation, Environmental Law, Finance, Commercial Finance, Franchises and Franchising, General Practice, Government, False Claims Act, Qui Tam Litigation, Government Contracts, Health Care, Insurance Coverage, Insurance Regulation, Intellectual Property, International Law, International Trade, Internet Law, Labor and Employment, Life Sciences, Litigation, Complex Litigation, Medicare Fraud and Abuse, Mergers, Acquisitions and

(This Listing Continued)

Thompson Hine LLP (Continued)

Divestitures, Natural Resources, Nonprofit and Charitable Organizations, Occupational Safety and Health, OSHA, Partnership Law, Patents, Probate, Products Liability, Product Safety, Professional Liability, Public Finance, Railroad Law, Real Estate, Regulatory Law, Drug and Medical Device Regulation, Food and Drug Regulation, International Regulatory Law, Regulated Industries, Securities, Initial Public Offerings, Public Offerings, Taxation, Tax Controversies, Toxic Torts, Trade Secrets, Trademarks, Transportation, Trusts and Estates, Unfair Competition, Utility Law, White Collar Crime, Zoning, Planning and Land Use.
Cleveland, Ohio Office: 3900 Key Center, 127 Public Square, 44114-1291. Telephone: 216-566-5500. Fax: 216-566-5800. Email: info@ThompsonHine.com.
Cincinnati, Ohio Office: 312 Walnut Street, 14th Floor, 45202-4089. Telephone: 513-352-6700. Fax: 513-241-4771. Email: info@ThompsonHine.com.
Dayton, Ohio Office: 2000 Courthouse Plaza, N.E., P.O. Box 8801, 45401-8801. Telephone: 937-443-6600. Fax: 937-443-6637, 937-443-6635. Email: info@ThompsonHine.com.
Washington, D.C. Office: 1920 N Street, N.W., Suite 800, 20036-1600. Telephone: 202-331-8800. Fax: 202-331-8330. Email: info@ThompsonHine.com.
New York, N.Y. Office: One Chase Manhattan Plaza, 58th Floor, 10005-1401. Telephone: 212-344-5680. Fax: 212-809-6890. Email: info@ThompsonHine.com.
Brussels, Belgium Office: Avenue Louise 375 - b8, 1050 Brussels, Belgium, Telephone: 011 (32-2) 626-3280. Fax: 011 (32-2) 626-3299. Email: info@ThompsonHine.com.
Atlanta, Georgia Office: Proscenium Center, Suite 1200, 1170 Peachtree Street, 30309-7673. Telephone: 404-541-2900. Fax: 404-541-2905. Email: info@ThompsonHine.com.
See Professional Biographies, COLUMBUS, OHIO

Thompson Law Firm, The, (BV) .... 85 East Gay Street, Suite 810
Thompson, Meier & Dersom, (AV) .... 929 Harrison Ave., Ste. 205
Thomson, Terry L. .... '65 '03 C.999 B.A. L.1119 J.D. [Ⓐ Porter W.M.&A.]
Thorman, William A., III, (BV) .... '62 '88 C.399 B.A. L.608 J.D. [Ⓐ P.J.Fulton]
Thornton, Brett P. .... '75 '01 C.608 B.S. L.273 J.D. [Ⓐ Porter W.M.&A.]
Thornton, Gregg B. .... '63 '91 C.329 B.A. L.930 J.D. Asst. Atty. Gen.
Thraen, Melanie Rae .... '74 '99 C&L.608 B.A., J.D. City Atty. Off.
Thurston, F. Timothy .... '50 '79 C.691 B.A. L.276 J.D. 1944 Arlington Avenue
Thurston, Pamela Hackes, (AV) .... '53 '78 C.914 B.A. L.276 J.D. [Ⓐ Squire,S.&D.]
Tibbles, Lance .... '38 '64 C&L.629 B.S., J.D. Cap. Univ. Law School
Ticknor, Charles E., III, (BV) .... '63 '89 C&L.608 B.A., J.D. [Buckingham,D.&B.]
Tierney, Eugene F. '30 '56 C&L.184 B.A., LL.B.
(adm. in CT; not adm. in OH) 1 Nationwide Plaza‡
Tigges, Steven W., (AV) .... '52 '81 C&L.608 B.S., J.D. [Zeiger,T.&L.]
Tilton, Richard J. .... '49 '85 C.608 B.S. L.117 J.D. Admn.
Timms, David S. .... '— '99 C.8 B.A. L.276 J.D. [Ⓒ Mason]
Timms, Lisa Hyre '73 '99 C&L.608 B.A., J.D.
Asst. Chf. Legal Coun., Ohio Treasurer of State
Tingley, John B., (AV) .... '29 '54 C.207 A.B. L.608 J.D. 65 E. State St.‡
Tinianow, Jerome C. .... '55 '80 C&L.273 B.A., J.D. Exec. Dir., Audubon Ohio
Tippins, Adria Michele .... '76 '02 C.217 B.A. L.608 J.D. [A.M.Tippins]
Tippins, Adria M., Law Office of .... P.O. Box 13049
Titus, Frank A. .... '46 '79 C.608 B.A. L.117 J.D. [Ⓒ Taft,S.&H.]
Tobin, John M. .... '28 '53 C.381 B.A. L.608 J.D. 5238 Lola Way‡
Tobin, Susan G. .... '56 '81 C.385 B.A. L.608 J.D. Ohio Legal Rights Serv.
Todaro, Frank E., (AV) .... '57 '87 C.1044 B.A. L.117 J.D. [Todaro&W.]
Todaro, Gerald J., (AVⓉ) .... '46 '74 C.838 B.S. L.117 J.D. [G.J.Todaro]
Todaro, Gerald J., Co., L.P.A., (AVⓉ) .... 115 W. Main St.

Todaro & Wagoner, (AV)
471 East Broad Street, Suite 1303, 43215
Telephone: 614-242-4333; 1-800-510-4680 Telecopier: 614-242-3948 Email: bob@todarolaw.com
Email: frank@todarolaw.com URL: http://www.lawyers.com/todaro-law
Members of Firm: Frank E. Todaro (Board Certified as a Civil Trial Advocate by the National Board of Trial Advocacy); Robert J. Wagoner.
Civil Trial and Appellate Practice in Medical and Legal Malpractice, Personal Injury, Wrongful Death. Negligence, Products Liability, Business and Insurance Law.
See Professional Biographies, COLUMBUS, OHIO

Todd, William M., (AV) .... '52 '76 C.602 B.A. L.608 J.D. [Squire,S.&D.]
Toler, William A., (BV) .... '19 '48 C.999 B.S. L.608 J.D. 875 Mt. Vernon Ave.

Tome, Lisa M. '72 '01 C.25 B.A. L.665 J.D.
511 South High Street, 43215
Telephone: 614-228-4141 Fax: 614-228-0899
URL: http://www.lawyers.com/lisatome
Criminal Defense, Driving While Intoxicated, Traffic Violations, Juvenile Law, Appellate Practice.
See Professional Biographies, COLUMBUS, OHIO

Tomkies, Michael C. .... '— '86 C.301 B.A. L.309 J.D. [Dreher L.&T.]
Tongren, Robert S., (BV) .... '47 '72 C.210 B.A. L.7 J.D. Consumers' Coun.
Tonks, Paul H. .... '69 '96 C.101 B.A. L.117 J.D. Staff Atty., Ct. of App.
Tonti, A. Patk. .... '29 '54 C.602 B.S. L.608 LL.B. 34 N. High St.
Tootle, Heather W., Law Offices of ...... '70 '96 C.967 B.A. L.117 J.D. 3010 Hayden Rd.
Tootle, Thomas, (BV) .... '68 '93 C.608 B.A. L.8 J.D. 85 E. Gay St., Ste. 900

Topper, Richard D., (AV) '54 '79 C.473 B.S. L.851 J.D.
1500 West Third Avenue, Suite 400, 43212
Telephone: 614-486-4805 Fax: 614-481-7905
Email: rictopper@aol.com URL: http://www.lawyers.com/topperlaw
Plaintiff's Medical Malpractice, Personal Injury, Automobile Accidents and Injuries, Wrongful Death, Insurance Law, Products Liability and Negligence.
See Professional Biographies, COLUMBUS, OHIO

Tormey, Edmund J. .... '64 '90 C&L.352 B.A., J.D. Supervising Atty., State E.P.A.
Torriero, Dolores F. .... '57 '95 C.1385 B.A. L.8 J.D. [Ⓐ Downes,H.&F.]
Tosca, Gary L. '51 '85 C.347 B.A. L.796 J.D.
(adm. in TX; not adm. in OH) 221 S. High Street
Totten, Mark S. .... '57 '82 C.117 B.A. L.608 J.D. [Ⓐ Purcell&S.]
Tour, Jeffrey H., (BV) .... '57 '82 C.823 B.A. L.273 J.D. [Ⓒ Vorys,S.S.&P.]
Tournoux, Katie L. .... '— '02 C.993 B.A. L.608 J.D. [Ⓐ Shumaker,L.&K.]
Tower, Jessie M. .... '60 '95 C.161 B.B.A. L.117 J.D. 3100 Pittston Ct.
Townsend, Timi J. .... '51 '80 C&L.608 B.A., J.D. Asst. State Pub. Def.
Trafford, Kathleen McManus, (AV) ... '49 '79 C.540 B.A. L.117 J.D. [Porter W.M.&A.]
Trafford, Robert W., (AV) .... '51 '77 C&L.608 B.A., J.D. [Porter W.M.&A.]
Trail, Douglas R. .... '28 '54 C&L.608 B.S., J.D. Ohi Building Authority‡
Travalio, Gregory M. .... '47 '85 C&L.665 B.A., J.D. OH State Univ.
Travers, Eric B. .... '72 '98 C.393 B.A. L.273 J.D. [Ⓐ Kegler,B.H.&R.]
Travis, Alan C. .... '40 '65 C.532 A.B. L.608 J.D. Com. Pleas J.
Travis, Paul .... '46 '73 C.608 B.A. L.117 J.D. 2929 Kenny Rd.
Treasure, Anne J. .... '61 '86 C.81 B.A. L.880 J.D. Tax Mgr., Ernst & Young
Treneff, Craig P., (AV) '52 '81
C.608 B.A. L.117 J.D. [C.P.Treneff] & [Ⓒ Flanagan B.B.]

Treneff, Craig P., Law Office, (AV)
555 South Front Street, Suite 320, 43215-5668
Telephone: 614-228-3715 Fax: 614-228-3102 URL: http://www.treneff.com
Email: ctreneff@treneff.com URL: http://www.lawyers.com/trenefflaw
Craig P. Treneff (Certified Specialist in Family Relations Law, Ohio State Bar Association).

(This Listing Continued)

Treneff, Craig P., Law Office (Continued)

Family Law, Divorce, Dissolution, Child Custody, Child Support, Premarital Agreements, Real Estate Taxation.

See Professional Biographies, COLUMBUS, OHIO

Trethewey, Virginia M., (AV) ... '45 '77 C.911 B.A. L.608 J.D. 4285 Randmore Road
Trianfo, Dominic A., (BV) ... '18 '56 C.608 B.S. L.117 J.D. 1876 Fairhaven Rd.
Trimble, Thomas W., (AV) ... '54 '83 C.97 B.S. L.117 J.D. [Lamkin,V.T.B.&D.]
Trishman, Natalie C. ... '78 '02 C.608 B.A. L.117 J.D. [A Bricker&E.]
Trout, Gregory C. '51 '78
C.967 A.B. L.117 J.D. State Dept. of Rehabilitation & Correction
Troutman, Mark H. ... '78 '03 C&L.608 B.A., J.D. [A Isaac,B.L.&T.]
Troyan, Gary M., (AV) ... '53 '78 C.81 B.A. L.608 J.D. [Jones,T.P.&P.]
Truax, William H., (BV) ... '50 '76 C&L.608 B.A., J.D. 171 E. Livingston Ave.
True, Mary R. ... '— '90 C&L.150 B.M., J.D. [A Jones D.]
Tsevdos, Noelle T. ... '62 '89 C.30 B.S. L.930 J.D. Asst. Atty. Gen.
Tsibouris, Dino ... '68 '94 C.130 B.A. L.179 J.D. [Mallory&T.]
Tsiliacos, Olga ... '23 '53 C.608 B.A. L.1003 J.D. 2323 Indianola Avenue
Tuch, Robert L. '51 '78 C.259 B.A. L.1206 J.D.
(adm. in FL; not adm. in OH) Sr. Coun., Nationwide Insurance
Tuch, Socrates H. ... '66 '95 C.1077 B.A. L.117 J.D. OH Dept. of Health
Tucker, Debra James ... '53 '78 C.207 B.A. L.477 J.D. Civil Rights Comm.
Tucker, Mark D., (AV) ... '60 '86 C&L.608 B.A., J.D. [Benesch,F.C.&A.]
Tucker, Michael L. ... '54 '86 C.800 A.B. L.424 J.D. Sr. Coun., Bank One Corp.
Tulencik, Aaron T. ... '— '00 C.999 B.A. L.615 J.D. [A Porter W.M.&A.]
Tullis, Timothy T. ... '63 '89 C.970 B.S. L.608 J.D. [Kegler,B.H.&R.]
Tulman, Elizabeth E., (BV) ... '— '82 C.1365 B.A. L.150 J.D. [C Schottenstein,Z.&D.]
Tumen, David A., (BV) ... '55 '81 C.902 B.A. L.150 J.D. [Porter W.M.&A.]
Tunnell, Kurtis A., (AV) ... '60 '87 C.310 B.A. L.608 J.D. [Bricker&E.]
Turadian, Allan R. ... '52 '82 C.282 B.A. L.64 J.D. Sr. Coun., Nationwide Insurance
Turano, David A., (AV) ... '46 '71 C.381 B.S. L.608 J.D. [C Shoemaker,H.&T.]
Turk, Jennifer M. ... '71 '01 C.436 B.A. L.608 J.D. [A Benesch,F.C.&A.]
Turner, Jameel S. ... '77 '04 C.851 B.A. L.608 J.D. [A Bailey C.]
Turner, Shawn M. ... '— '04 C.303 B.A. L.124 J.D. [A Jones D.]
Turner, Tracy L. ... '72 '98 C.473 B.A. L.608 J.D. [Habash,R.&F.]
Turoff, Seth J. ... '— '04 C.49 B.A. L.893 J.D. [A Jones D.]
Tuttle, Cheryl L. ... '59 '86 C.610 B.B.A. L.1003 J.D. Jud. Law Clk., Supm. Ct.
Tuttle, John R. ... '56 '91 C.473 B.S. L.117 J.D. 7370 Minuteman Way
Twyford, George W. ... '27 '58 Dom. Rel. J.
Twyford, Thomas L., (BV) ... '35 '65 C&L.608 B.S., J.D. [Twyford&D.]

Twyford & Donahey, P.L.L., (BV)
Brewery District, 495 South High Street, 43215-5058 ⊙
Telephone: Toll Free: 1-800-686-1699 Fax: 614-849-0475
Email: help@twyforddonahey.com URL: http://www.twyforddonahey.com
Senior Partners: Thomas L. Twyford; Richard S. Donahey; Mark E. Defossez. Associates: T. Jeffery Beausay; Gordon D. Evans, II; Rebekah G. Weiss.
Personal Injury Litigation, Wrongful Death, Medical Malpractice, Products Liability, Automobile Accidents, Trucking Accidents, Head and Spinal Injuries, Motorcycle Accidents and Injuries, Uninsured Motorists, Insurance Law, Airplane Crash Litigation, Railroad Accidents, Slip and Fall, Dog Bites, Work Related Injuries, Birth Injuries, Nursing Home Abuse and Neglect.
References: The Huntington National Bank; Bank One of Columbus; BancOhio National Bank.
Circleville, Ohio Office: 214 South Court Street, 43113. Telephone: Toll Free: 1-800-686-1699. Email: help@twyforddonahey.com.
Delaware, Ohio Office: 163 N. Sandusky Street, Suite 103, 43015. Telephone: Toll Free: 1-800-686-1699. Email: help@twyforddonahey.com.
Lancaster, Ohio Office: 3794 Old Columbus Road, N.W., 43130. Telephone: Toll Free: 1-800-686-1699. Email: help@twyforddonahey.com.
Newark, Ohio Office: 137 West Main Street, Suite C, 43025. Telephone: Toll Free: 1-800-686-1699. Email: help@twyforddonahey.com.
London, Ohio Office: 25 West Fifth Street, 43140. Telephone: Toll Free: 1-800-686-1699. Email: help@twyforddonahey.com.

See Professional Biographies, COLUMBUS, OHIO

Twynham, Theodore T., (BV) ... '22 '52 C&L.08 A.B., J.D. 165 N.High St.
Tyack, David Bruce ... '54 '82 C.608 B.A. L.117 J.D. [D.B.Tyack]
Tyack, James P. ... '75 '00 C.207 B.A. L.608 J.D. [Tyack,B.&L.]
Tyack, Jonathan T. ... '71 '96 C.207 B.A. L.608 J.D. [Tyack,B.&L.]
Tyack, Thomas M., (AV) ... '40 '65 C&L.608 B.A., J.D. [Tyack,B.&L.]

Tyack, Blackmore & Liston Co., L.P.A., (AV)
536 South High Street, 43215
Telephone: 614-221-1341 Fax: 614-228-0253 URL: http://www.tblattorneys.com
URL: http://www.lawyers.com/tyackblackmore&liston
Thomas M. Tyack; Margaret L. Blackmore; Jefferson E. Liston; Jonathan T. Tyack; James P. Tyack.
General Criminal, Civil Trial and Appellate Practice in all State and Federal Courts. Negligence, Medical Malpractice, Personal Injury, Automobile Accidents, Family Law, Divorce, Child Custody, Adoption Law, Juvenile Law.
References: US Bank, NA; Bank One of Columbus, NA.

See Professional Biographies, COLUMBUS, OHIO

Tyack, David B. ... 820 South High Street
Tyner, Michaele ... '— '76 C.477 B.S. L.7 J.D. Asst. Atty. Gen.
Tyson, Renny J., (BV) ... '55 '81 C.976 B.A. L.930 J.D. [R.J.Tyson]
Tyson, Renny J., Co., L.P.A., (BV) ... 1465 East Broad St.
Uhlmann, Beth A. ... '72 '97 C.477 B.A. L.904 J.D. Coun., Nationwide Insurance

Ulmer & Berne LLP, (AV)
88 East Broad Street, Suite 1600, 43215 ⊙
Telephone: 614-229-0000 FAX: 614-229-0001
Email: infocolumbus@ulmer.com URL: http://www.ulmer.com/
Partners: Alexander M. Andrews (Partner-in-Charge); Timothy M. Fox; Robert J. Karl; Rex A. Littrell. Of Counsel: Martyn T. Brodnik; Gregory A. Lowe. Senior Attorneys: Charles R. (Bob) Janes; J. Gregory Smith. Associates: David L. Eidelberg; Rebecca B. Jacobs; Matthew C. Krejci; Sherry L. Mowry; Christine E. Watchorn.
Antitrust; Banking and Commercial Lending; Broker/Dealer and Securities Litigation; Business Law; Business Litigation; Business Restructuring; Class Action Defense; Construction Law; Corporate Finance; Corporate Restructuring and Creditors' Rights; Corporate Succession Planning; Emerging Businesses; Employee Benefits; Employment and Labor; Environmental; Fair Housing; Financial Institution Compliance; General Counsel Services; Health Care; Income Tax; Insurance Coverage; Intellectual Property and Technology; Joint Ventures; Liability Defense; Mass Torts; Mergers, Acquisitions and Divestitures; Nonprofit; OSHA; Pharmaceutical; Product Liability; Public Law; Real Estate; Securities; Securities Regulatory Compliance; Subrogation; Tax; Technology Transactions; Toxic Tort Defense; Trade Secrets/Unfair Competition; Trusts and Estates; Venture Capital; Workers' Compensation; Trial and Appellate Practice in All Courts.
Cleveland, Ohio Office: Skylight Office Tower, 1660 West 2nd Street, Suite 1100. Telephone: 216-583-7000. FAX: 216-583-7001.
Cincinnati, Ohio Office: 600 Vine Street, Suite 2800. Telephone: 513-698-5000. FAX: 513-698-5001.
Chicago, Illinois Office: One North Franklin Street, Suite 1825. Telephone: 312-324-8000. FAX: 312-324-8001.

See Professional Biographies, COLUMBUS, OHIO

Umpleby, John I., (BV) ... '49 '74 C.611 B.A. L.117 J.D. 2444 Ottawa Dr.
Underhill, Aaron Lee ... '74 '00 C.970 B.A. L.117 J.D. Law Clk., OH Supm. Ct.
Underwood, Charles D., (BV) ... '46 '80 C.611 B.A. L.117 J.D. 412 S. Yearling Rd.
Underwood, Michael J., (AV) ... '54 '80 C&L.665 B.A., J.D. [Porter W.M.&A.]
Union, Stephanie P. ... '74 '99 C.473 B.S. L.150 J.D. [A Kegler,B.H.&R.]
Unver, Douglas R., (CV) ... '65 '91 C.608 B.A. L.117 J.D. Asst. Atty. Gen.
Uprichard, James E., Jr. ... '42 '70 C.717 B.A. L.128 J.D. Asst. Atty. Gen.
Utz, Richard A., (AV) ... '52 '77 C&L.608 B.A., J.D. [A Carlisle,M.R.K.&U.]
Vaas, Jonathan M. ... '— '04 C.608 B.A. L.1565 J.D. [A Jones D.]
Valentine, Anne M., (AV) ... '55 '82 C.608 B.S. L.117 J.D. [Leeseberg&V.]
Valleau, Norma Kathryn Sass '43 '81 C&L.1137 B.S.L., J.D.
(adm. in IN; not adm. in OH) [Valleau&M.]
Valleau & Metz ... 2677 Quarry Valley Rd.
Valot, Dennis A. ... '46 '71 C.363 B.A. L.608 J.D. Dept. of Taxation
Vamos, Stephen J., III ... '56 '81 C.602 B.A. L.851 J.D. 2100 Stella Court
Vande Werken, Jerry, (AV) ... '50 '74 C.323 B.A. L.608 J.D. [Thompson H.]
Van De Mark, Julie Ann, (BV) ... '57 '82 C.473 B.A. L.608 J.D. 492 City Park Avenue
Van Dervoort, John W., (AV) ... '31 '54 C&L.608 B.A., J.D. 5150 Reed Rd.
Van Deusen, Edwin H. ... '30 '63 C.645 B.A. L.831 J.D. 1044 Parkleigh Rd.‡
Van Doorn, Paul K. ... '55 '80 C.604 B.A. L.930 J.D. [VanDoorn]
Van Doorn & Co., LPA ... 60 E. Broad St.
Van Dyke, Omia Nadine ... '47 '83 C.608 B.A. L.117 J.D. Ct. of Domestic Rel., Juv. Div.
Van Eman, Timothy L., (AV) ... '55 '81 C.737 B.A. L.117 J.D. [Lamkin,V.T.B.&D.]
Van Fossen, Larry J., (AV) ... '37 '63 C.150 B.B.A. L.608 J.D. 2531 Tiller Lane
Van Heyde, G. James ... '44 '76 C.608 B.S.B.A. L.117 J.D. Asst. Atty. Gen.
Van Heyde, J. Stephen, (AV) ... '43 '68 C.602 B.B.A. L.608 J.D. [Baker&H.]
Van Hoy, Martha S. ... '77 '04 C.276 B.A. L.893 J.D. [A Thompson H.]
Van Kley, Jack A., (AV) ... '54 '79 C.879 B.A. L.273 J.D. [VanKley&W.]

Van Kley & Walker, LLC, (AV)
132 Northwoods Boulevard, Suite C-1, 43235 ⊙
Telephone: 614-431-8900 Fax: 614-431-8905
Email: jvankley@vankleywalker.com URL: http://www.vankleywalker.com
Jack A. Van Kley.
Air Pollution, Brownfields Redevelopment, Environmental Administrative Law, Environmental Auditing, Environmental Cost Recovery, Environmental Cleanup, Environmental Due Diligence, Environmental Legislative Practice, Environmental Permitting, Hazardous Waste, Nuclear Waste, Sick Building Syndrome, Solid Waste, Superfund, Underground Storage Tanks, Water Pollution, Wetlands Regulation.
Dayton Office: 137 North Main Street, Suite 316, 45402. Telephone: 937-226-9000. Fax: 937-226-9002.

See Professional Biographies, COLUMBUS, OHIO

Vannatta, Julie Dunwell, (AV) '62 '87 C.473 B.A. L.608 J.D.
Assoc. Legal Coun., Ohio State University, The
Vannatta, Mark E., (AV) ... '62 '87 C.97 B.S. L.608 J.D. [Vorys,S.S.&P.]
VanSickler, Kimberly T. ... '63 '91 C.473 B.S. L.117 J.D. Asst. City Pros.
Van Slyke, David L. ... '78 '04 C.62 B.A. L.161 J.D. [A Plunkett&C.]
Vanterpool, Donald L. ... '45 '87 C.415 B.A. L.608 J.D. Ohio Environ. Prot. Agency
Van Vlerah, Darin L. ... '73 '03 C.608 B.S. L.94 J.D. [A Porter W.M.&A.]
Varanese, John R., The Law Offices of '57 '90
C.608 B.A. L.365 J.D. 85 E. Gay St., Ste. 1000
Varchetti, Glen A. ... '— '99 C.475 B.A. L.608 J.D. [A Thompson H.]
Vargo, James G. ... '69 '97 C.980 B.S. L.7 J.D. [A Maguire&S.]
Vargo, Thomas W., (AV) ... '44 '72 C.608 B.A. L.117 J.D. 299 East Livingston Avenue
Varhus, Alan P., (BV) ... '45 '74 C.446 B.S. L.117 J.D. Asst. City Atty.
Varveris, Nicholas M. ... '65 '91 C.980 B.A. L.608 J.D. Jud. Law Clk.
Varwig, Audrey E. ... '71 '01 C.97 B.S.B.A. L.608 J.D. [A Brenner,B.G.&M.]
Vascura, Chelsey M. ... '78 '03 C.81 B.A. L.608 J.D. [A Vorys,S.S.&P.]
Vaughn, Jonathan R., (AV) ... '57 '82 C.228 B.S. L.880 J.D. [Vorys,S.S.&P.]
Vaughn, Robert ... '70 '98 C.608 B.A. L.117 J.D. Staff Atty., Ct. of Claims
Vawter, Jana R. ... '63 '90 C&L.608 B.S., J.D. 77 S. High St., 9th Fl.
Veatch, Alan K., (AV) ... '57 '82 C.608 B.A. L.117 J.D. [Campbell,H.C.&V.]
Velayudhan, Krishna K. ... '75 '02 C.970 B.A. L.117 J.D. [A Cheek&Z.]
Velie, Garwin P., (BV) ... '50 '80 C.608 B.A. L.117 J.D. 132 Northwoods Blvd.
Venesy, Bryan J., (BV) ... '63 '88 C.611 B.A. L.150 J.D. [Squire,S.&D.] (⊙Cincinnati)
Veri, Joan D. ... '62 '88 C.473 B.A. L.608 J.D. [C Jeffries]
Verkamp, Jennifer M. ... '70 '96 C.973 B.S. L.276 J.D. [Volkema,T.M.B.S.&M.] ⊙
Verrett, Kendall S. ... '78 '03 C.207 B.A. L.150 J.D. [A Porter W.M.&A.]
Vickers, Richard J. ... '49 '86 C.434 B.A. L.117 J.D. Asst. State Pub. Def.
Vickery, Byron, (AV) ... '37 '65 C&L.608 B.A., LL.B. [Vickery,R.&A.]
Vickery, Riehl & Alter, (AV) ... 500 S. Front St.
Vidmar, John M. ... '76 '03 C.266 B.S. L.117 J.D. 2035 Innis Road
Viergutz, Mary E. '61 '92 C&L.436 M.S.N., J.D.
(adm. in WI; not adm. in OH) Loss Prev. Coord., Ohio Hospital Insurance Company
Vierow, Frederick A., (BV) ... '34 '60 C.930 B.A. L.608 LL.B. 21 W. Broad St.
Vieth, James M. ... '11 '68 C.629 B.S. L.765 J.D. 3950 N. High St.
Viets, James D., (BV) ... '58 '83 C.473 B.A. L.201 J.D. [Decker,V.S.L.&V.]
Vince, Charles A. ... '43 '69 C&L.608 B.A., J.D. Nationwide Develop. Co.
Vincent, John E., Jr. ... '71 '99 C.932 B.B.A. L.117 J.D. [A Isaac,B.L.&T.]
Visco, Louis Gerald '60 '93 C.354 B.A. L.1209 J.D.
(adm. in NY; not adm. in OH) Asst. Gen. Coun., Glimcher Realty Tr.
Vitale, Anne P. '— '78 C&L.055
(adm. in Paris; not adm. in OH) 1324 W. 6th Ave., Apt. B
Vizy, Nick J. ... '64 '89 C.363 B.A. L.608 J.D. Law Clk. to Bk. J.
Voelker, Dirken T., (AV) ... '32 '56 C.902 A.B. L.608 J.D. [Voelker&V.]
Voelker, Dow T., (BV) ... '62 '87 C.608 B.S.B.A. L.117 J.D. [Voelker&V.]

Voelker & Voelker, (AV)
1635 West First Avenue, 43212
Telephone: 614-481-6500 Fax: 614-481-6505
Members of Firm: Harold H. Voelker (1902-1977); Dirken T. Voelker; Dow T. Voelker.
General Civil Practice. Real Estate and Probate Law.
Agents for: Old Republic Title Insurance Company.

Voinovich, George V. '36 '61 C.610 A.B. L.608 J.D.
Riffe Building, 30th Floor, 77 South High Street
Volkema, Daniel R., (AV) ... '53 '79 C.907 B.A. L.607 J.D. [Volkema,T.M.B.S.&M.]

Volkema, Thomas, Miller, Burkett, Scott & Merry, A Legal Professional Association, (AV) BB
140 East Town Street, Suite 1100, 43215 ⊙
Telephone: 614-221-4400 Telecopier: 614-221-6010 URL: http://www.volkemathomas.com
Email: attorneys@vt-law.com URL: http://www.vt-law.com
Elizabeth Schorpp Burkett; Jeffrey L. Maloon; Tony C. Merry; Michael S. Miller; Frederick M. Morgan, Jr.; Craig P. Scott; Warner M. Thomas, Jr.; Jennifer M. Verkamp; Daniel R. Volkema;—Janet L. Larkin.
Civil State and Federal Trial and Appellate Practice. Personal Injury. Malpractice, Nursing Home Negligence, HMO Liability, Class Actions, Wrongful Death, Automobile Accidents, Product Liability, Employee Benefits, Insurance Bad Faith, Aviation and Tort Law, ERISA, Qui Tam (Whistleblower), False Claims Act.
Reference: Huntington National Bank.
Cincinnati, Ohio Office: 700 Walnut Street, Suite 400. 45202-2015. Telephone: 513-651-4400. Fax: 513-651-4405.

See Professional Biographies, COLUMBUS, OHIO

Vollmer, Sara R. '64 '88 C.25 B.A. L.117 J.D.
Chief Coun., Dept. of Alcohol & Drug Addiction Servs.
Voltolini, Bruno E., (AV) .... '29 '57 C.8 B.A. L.608 J.D. [Voltolini&V.]
Voltolini, John .... '60 '86 C.608 B.A. L.117 J.D. [Voltolini&V.]
Voltolini, Mathew J. .... '62 '88 C&L.608 B.A., J.D. [Voltolini&V.]
Voltolini & Voltolini, (AV) ....1350 W. 5th Ave.
Vonau, James M., (BV) .... '56 '81 C.608 B.A. L.150 J.D. [Decker,V.S.L.&V.]
Vorys, Anne Marie Sferra, (AV) .... '60 '85 C.97 B.S. L.608 J.D. [Bricker&E.]
Vorys, Jeanny M. .... '60 '89 C.951 B.A. L.352 J.D. Asst. Atty. Gen.
Vorys, John C., (AV) .... '53 '80 C.951 B.A. L.117 J.D. [Vorys,S.S.&P.]
Vorys, Webb I., (AV) .... '58 '85 C.197 B.A. L.608 J.D. [Vorys,S.S.&P.]
Vorys, Yolanda V., (BV) '52 '81 C.951 B.A. L.608 J.D.
Asst. Dir., Ohio Consumers Coun.

Vorys, Sater, Seymour and Pease LLP, (AV) BR
52 East Gay Street, P.O. Box 1008, 43216-1008 ⊙
Telephone: 614-464-6400 Facsimile: 614-464-6350
URL: http://www.vssp.com
Arthur I. Vorys (1856-1933); Lowry F. Sater (1867-1935); Augustus T. Seymour (1873-1926); Edward L. Pease (1873-1924). Partners: James R. Beatley, Jr.; Thomas B. Ridgley; Robert W. Werth (Managing Partner); David S. Cupps; James H. Gross; George L. Jenkins; Robert J. Sidman; Michael G. Long; William S. Newcomb, Jr.; Daniel H. Schoedinger; Thomas M. Tarpy; Susan E. Brown; Richard P. Fahey; C. William O'Neill; Douglas L. Rogers; Michael J. Canter; Russell M. Gertmenian; Joseph D. Lonardo (Resident, Washington, D.C. Office); Alan T. Radnor; Ronald L. Rowland; W. Jonathan Airey; G. Ross Bridgman; Charles S. DeRousie; Mary Ellen Fairfield; Robert E. Tait; James M. Ball; Philip A. Brown; Stephen R. Buchenroth; M. Howard Petricoff; Suzanne K. Richards; Frederick L. Ransier, III; Kathleen H. Ransier; John K. Keller; Terry M. Miller; Robert A. Minor; James E. Phillips; Sandra J. Anderson; Gary E. Davis; David W. Hardymon; Jonathan M. Norman; Aaron P. Rosenfeld; F. James Foley; Robert J. Styduhar; James A. Yano; David F. Axelrod; Ivery D. Foreman; Bruce L. Ingram; Laura G. Kuykendall; David A. Swift; Raymond D. Anderson; Michael A. Cline; Robert G. Dykes; Gerald P. Ferguson; Bruce R. Henke; J. Scott Jamieson; Paul J. Coval; Roger E. Lautzenhiser (Resident, Cincinnati Office); John P. Wellner; Joseph A. Brunetto; Reginald W. Jackson; Chris J. North; Carl D. Smallwood; John C. Vorys; Jonathan D. Iten; John J. Kulewicz; Richard D. Schuster; Anker M. Bell; Benita A. Kahn; Elizabeth Turrell Farrar; Thomas O. Ruby; Thomas E. Szykowny; Jonathan R. Vaughn; Anthony C. Ciriaco; Shawn M. Flahive; William G. Porter II; Andrew C. Smith; Elizabeth T. Smith; Thomas R. Winters; Dan L. Jaffe; Webb I. Vorys; Robert N. Webner; John B. Weimer; James A. Wilson; Scott M. Doran; Gail C. Ford; Sheila Nolan Gartland; Kenneth A. Golonka, Jr.; Bradley K. Sinnott; Susan A. Cohen; Anthony L. Ehler; Randall D. LaTour; Douglas R. Matthews; Russell R. Rosler; Mark E. Vannatta; David W. Cook; Philip F. Downey; Anthony J. Giuliani; Allen S. Kinzer; William D. Kloss, Jr.; William J. Pohlman; Brent C. Taggart; John L. Landolfi; Kristin L. Watt; Gary J. Saalman; Kevin M. Czerwonka; Herbert A. Hedden; Ronald A. Robins, Jr.; Travis J. Wahl; D. Michael Schira; Suzanne J. Scrutton; Jacklyn J. Ford; Michael D. Martz; Theodore P. Mattis; Robert A. Harris; D. Scott Powell; Lisa Pierce Reisz; Gregory D. Russell; Nina I. Webb-Lawton; Stephen D. Browning; Melinda R. McAfee; Adam K. Brandt; Timothy J. Dobyns; Mark A. Knueve; Craig R. Auge; Mary L. Garceau; Susan Barrett Harty; Kimberly Weber Herlihy; Joseph R. Miller; Scott J. Ziance. Senior Attorneys: Timothy J. Bechtold; Carol Mahaffey; Karen A. Cincione; Richard T. Miller; Anthony Spina. Associates: Melissa J. Mitchell; Michael C. Griffaton; Michael F. O'Brien; Kyong W. Nahm Wahl; Nelson D. Cary; Tiffany Strelow Cobb; Perry W. Doran II; David A. Froling; Kelly Jennings Yeoman; Lynne M. Froling; Matthew D. Gottschall; Rodney A. Holaday; Joseph B. Mann (Not admitted in OH); Maggie O'Shaughnessy; Nicole J. Papa; Alycia N. Broz; Victor J. Ferguson; Peter A. Lusenhop; Allen L. Rutz; J. Theodore Smith; Carter M. Stewart (Not admitted in OH); Meredith K. Knueve; Brian J. Laliberte; Sebastian E. Proels; Blake A. Snider; Anthony D. Weis; Heidi L. Yurkiw; Robert A. Bell, Jr.; John N. Boyer; Jason C. Elvers; Michael J. Hauswirth (Not admitted in OH); Jolie N. Havens; Stacia M. Jones; Scott A. Kossoudji; Judith L. Marsh; Jeffrey Allen Miller; William A. Sieck; Jennifer M. Burke; Trisha M. Corbin; Thomas H. Fusonie; Jennifer Naumoff; Angela K. Reitler; Jeffrey D. Roberts; Michael J. Settineri; Christopher A. Snyder (Not admitted in OH); Wendy M. Swary (Not admitted in OH); Daniel J. Clark; Elizabeth A. Fox; Daren S. Garcia; Timothy D. Hudok; Albert G. Lin; Bruce P. Paige; Gina R. Russo; Alexandra T. Schimmer; Christopher E. Sumi; Bethany R. Thomas; Tamara J. Watts; Michael G. Berner; P. Jason Dejelo; Gretchen Jeffries; Darrell A. H. Miller; Matthew J. Richardson; Benjamin J. Rickert; Jennifer S. Rusie; Michael J. Rusie; Chelsey M. Vascura; Nathan J. Wautier; Marjorie F. Amerine; Robert W. Conley; Chris L. Connelly; Monica Grande; Sarah L. Herbert; David J. Kaufman; Christina M. Lyons; Anna Kathreen Nuber; Jody Gilkey Shaffer; Todd A. Walter; Robin G. Wyckoff; Pearl Chin. Of Counsel: Richard Heer Oman; Norton R. Webster; Richard G. Ison; Edgar A. Strause; William D. Kloss; Colborn M. Addison; Lester S. Lash; Edward A. Schrag, Jr.; Robin R. Obetz; Duke W. Thomas; Thomas M. Taggart; Philip C. Johnston; Frederick E. Mills; Ronald A. Kladder; Stephen M. Howard; Michael R. Thomas; Linda R. Mendel; Robert C. Mitchell; Sheryl Clark Stoll; Jeffrey H. Tour; A. Brian Dengler; Theodore A. Boggs; Kevin R. Conners; Nathan C. Hamilton; Bradley A. Smith; James P. Kennedy. Staff Attorneys: Donald A. Brown; Jonathan P. Beck; Gregory J. Zelasko; Brenda K. Bowers; Corrine S. Carman; Stephen Craig Musilli; Kelly A. Boggs; Elizabeth Hanning Smith.
Alternative Dispute Resolution, Antitrust, Trade Regulation, Customs, Banks and Banking, Finance, Bankruptcy, Biotechnology, Business Law, Civil Rights, Debtors and Creditors Rights, Computers and Software, Congressional Investigations, Construction Law, Contracts, Copyrights, Disabilities, Election, Campaign and Political Law, Employee Benefits, Environmental Law, Probate, Guardianship and Conservatorship, General Practice, Health Care, Labor, Employment, Occupational Safety and Health, Workers Compensation, Corporate Law, Securities, Energy, Natural Resources, Franchises and Franchising, Government Contracts, Hospital Law, Immigration and Naturalization, Insurance, Intellectual Property, International Law, International Trade, Legal Ethics and Professional Responsibility, Litigation, Media Law, Medicare and Medicaid, Mergers, Acquisitions and Divestitures, Municipal Law, Telecommunications, Personal Injury, Products Liability, Railroad Law, Real Estate, RICO, Sports Law, Taxation, Technology and Science, Torts, Toxic Torts, Trade Secrets, Transportation, Trusts and Estates, Unfair Competition, Utility Law, White Collar Defense, Wills, Zoning, Planning and Land Use.
Representative Client: Honda of America Mfg., Inc.
Local Counsel: Abbott Laboratories; Anheuser-Busch, Inc.; Anthem Insurance Compnies, Inc.; Bob Evans Farms, Inc.; Borden, Inc.; Connecticut General Life Insurance Co.; Coopers & Lybrand; Eaton Corporation; General Motors Corp.
Washington, D.C. Office: 1828 L Street, N.W., 20036-5109. Telephone: 202-467-8800. Facsimile: 202-467-8900.
Cleveland, Ohio Office: 2100 One Cleveland Center, 1375 East Ninth Street, 44114-1724. Telephone: 216-479-6100. Facsimile: 216-479-6060.
Cincinnati, Ohio Office: Atrium Two, Suite 2000, 221 East Fourth Street, P.O. Box 0236, 45201-0236. Telephone: 513-723-4000. Facsimile: 513-723-4056.
Alexandria, Virginia Office: 277 South Washington Street, Suite 310, 22314. Telephone: 703-837-6999. Facsimile: 703-549-4492.
Akron, Ohio Office: First National Tower, 106 South Main Street, Suite 1100, 44308. Telephone: 330-208-1000. Facsimile: 330-208-1001.
See Professional Biographies, COLUMBUS, OHIO

Wachtman, Kristen .... '68 '93 C.776 B.A. L.117 J.D. The Limited, Inc.
Waddy, John W., Jr., (BV) .... '54 '79 C.967 B.A. L.117 J.D. 111 Hamilton Park
Wade, Ethel Roberta .... '51 '91 C&L.608 B.A., J.D. [Wade]
Wade, Felix C., (AV) .... '49 '77 C.347 B.A. L.1340 J.D. [Schottenstein,Z.&D.]
Wade, Robert J., Jr. .... '38 '65 C.347 B.S. L.477 J.D. Capital Univ. Law Sch.
Wade Law Office, L.L.C. .... 673 Mohawk Street
Wadkowski, Gerald P., (BV) '38 '64 C.229 B.A. L.1003 LL.B.
2400 Water's Edge Blvd.
Wadman, Gary A., (AV) .... '57 '85 C.63 B.S. L.1119 J.D. [Baker&H.]
Wagenbach, Adam J. '48 '73
C.610 B.A. L.608 J.D. Senior Attorney, Battelle Memorial Institute
Wagoner, Robert J. .... '72 '98 C.363 B.S. L.117 J.D. [Todaro&W.]
Wahl, Jeffrey R. .... '76 '02 C&L.607 B.A., J.D. [A Squire,S.&D.]
Wahl, Kyong W. Nahm .... '— '93 C.013 B.A.Sc. L.035 LL.B. [A Vorys,S.S.&P.]
Wahl, Travis J. .... '63 '90 C.839 B.B.A. L.326 J.D. [Vorys,S.S.&P.]
Wahlers, Kristopher .... '63 '91 C.280 A.B. L.477 J.D. [Calfee,H.&G.]
Wahoff, William J., (AV) .... '56 '82 C.473 A.B. L.608 J.D. [Scott,S.&W.]

Waid, Elizabeth O. '60 '85 C.935 B.A. L.608 J.D.
Dir. - Legal Svcs. & Asst. Gen. Coun., Ohio Education Assn.
Walden, Jon C. .... '68 '94 C.477 B.G.S. L.608 J.D. [A Bailey C.]
Walker, Brian A. .... '59 '89 C.266 B.S. L.608 J.D. Coopers & Lybrand
Walker, Charles H., (AV) .... '51 '76 C.860 B.A. L.1365 J.D. [Bricker&E.]
Walker, Kris H. .... '44 '90 C.610 B.F.A. L.179 J.D. P.O. Box 21834
Walker, Lawrence D., (AV) .... '48 '73 C.262 B.A. L.597 J.D. [Taft,S.&H.]
Walker, Richard L., (BV) .... '40 '66 C.434 B.A. L.608 J.D. 162 Webster Park Avenue
Walker, Scott C. .... '— '94 C.381 B.A. L.1003 J.D. [A Jones D.]★
Walker, Susan C., (BV) .... '56 '90 C.381 B.A. L.8 J.D. Princ. Asst. Atty. Gen.
Wall, Kirk M. .... '67 '93 C.608 B.A. L.117 J.D. [Dinsmore&S.]
Wallace, David A. .... '59 '85 C.696 B.A. L.273 J.D. [Carpenter&L.]
Wallace, Paul L., (BV) .... '48 '80 C.608 B.A. L.117 J.D. [Wallace&W.]
Wallace, Thomas H. .... '64 '90 C.96 B.S. L.117 J.D. [A Carlile P.&M.]
Wallace & Warner, Co., L.P.A., (BV) .... 171 E. Livingston Ave.
Waller, Barry A., (BV) .... '49 '74 C&L.608 B.A., J.D. [Fry,W.&M.]
Waller, Monica L. .... '74 '99 C&L.608 B.A., J.D. [Lane,A.&H.]
Walls, Jessica K. .... '78 '03 C.473 B.S. L.608 J.D [A Isaac,B.L.&T.]
Walsh, Christopher R. .... '58 '95 C.608 B.A. L.200 J.D. [Earl,W.A.&D.]
Walter, Robert J., (AV) .... '— '72 C.473 B.A. L.608 J.D. [Buckley K.]
Walter, Todd A. .... '77 '04 C.473 B.S. L.276 J.D. [A Vorys,S.S.&P.]
Walters, Ben R. '47 '88 C.421 B.A. L.117 J.D.
Staff Atty., Child Support Enforce. Agcy.
Walters, Marilena R. .... '54 '84 C&L.610 B.S., J.D. [Dinsmore&S.]
Walters, Randall M., (AV) .... '— '78 C&L.608 B.S., J.D. [Jones D.]
Walters, Sally Ann, (BV) .... '53 '80 C&L.608 B.A., J.D. State Atty. Gen.
Wampler, Elizabeth C. .... '47 '02 C&L.608 B.S., J.D. Asst. Atty. Gen.
Wampler, G. Samuel, (BV Ⓣ) .... '47 '78 C.1137 B.S.L. L.608 J.D. [C Bricker&E.]
Warburton, Dick M., Jr., (BV) .... '35 '61 C.381 B.A. L.608 LL.B. [Earl,W.A.&D.]
Ward, Christopher M. .... '78 '03 C.201 B.A. L.608 J.D. [A Calfee,H.&G.]
Ward, Paul F., (AV) .... '15 '39 L.608 J.D. 580 S. High St.
Ware, John Patrick '68 '93 C.475 B.A. L.608 J.D.
OH State Bd. of Career Coll. & Schools
Warheit, Melissa A., (AV) '55 '79
C.260 B.A. L.608 J.D. Sect. Chief/Opinions, Atty. Gen.'s Off.
Warner, Charles C., (AV) .... '42 '70 C.976 B.A. L.608 J.D. [Porter W.M.&A.]
Warner, Matthew .... '76 '02 C.1457 B.A. L.117 J.D. [A Cheek&Z.]
Warner, Patrick G. .... '66 '95 C.608 B.S. L.117 J.D. [A D.P.Meyer]
Warner, Roger, (AV) .... '55 '81 C.162 B.A. L.117 J.D. [R.Warner]
Warner, Roger, Co. LPA, (AV) .... 171 E. Livingston Ave.
Washburn, Robert L., Jr., (AV) .... '49 '77 C.473 B.A. L.117 J.D. 225 E. Broad St.
Washbush, Thomas C. .... '57 '91 C&L.117 B.A., J.D. [Benesch,F.C.&A.]
Wasson, Christopher E. .... '67 '97 C.385 B.A. L.608 J.D. Off. of Atty. Gen.
Watchorn, Christine E. .... '72 '03 C.611 B.A. L.117 J.D. [A Ulmer&B.]
Waterman, A. Joseph .... '28 '59 C&L.608 B.S.B.A., LL.B. P.O. Box 20425
Waterman, Charles H., III, (AV) .... '51 '77 C&L.608 B.S., J.D. [Bricker&E.]
Waterman, Charles H., IV .... '74 '01 C.37 B.A. L.608 J.D. [A Peck,S.&W.]
Waterman, Gerald H., (AV) .... '48 '74 C.347 B.S. L.7 J.D. Asst. Atty. Gen.
Watkins, David, (BV) .... '55 '92 C.72 B.A. L.117 J.D. [A Plank&B.]
Watkins, W. Hale .... '36 '60 C&L.923 A.B., LL.B. 200 Civic Ctr. Dr.‡
Watson, Alfred N. .... '10 '55 C.608 A.B. L.262 J.D. 1000 Urlin Ave.‡
Watson, Michael H. .... '56 '88 C.608 B.A. L.117 J.D. U.S. Dist. J.
Watson, Robert Terence .... '54 '87 C.608 B.S. L.117 J.D. Robert Weiler Co.
Watt, Kristin L., (BV) .... '63 '89 C&L.608 B.S.B.A., J.D. [Vorys,S.S.&P.]
Watters, Elizabeth J., (AV) .... '65 '90 C&L.608 B.A., J.D. [Chester,W.&S.]
Watters, Mark M. .... '57 '82 C.473 B.A. L.607 J.D. 180 E. Broad St., 27th Fl.
Watters, W. Robinson .... '27 '52 C.611 B.A. L.608 J.D. Admin. Law J.
Watts, Elizabeth H. .... '56 '82 C.980 B.A. L.8 J.D. Dept. Coun.
Watts, Tamara J. .... '76 '02 C.203 B.S. L.608 J.D. [A Vorys,S.S.&P.]
Wautier, Nathan J. .... '74 '03 C.145 B.A. L.957 J.D. [A Vorys,S.S.&P.]
Weaver, Diane M., (AV) .... '49 '77 C.999 B.A. L.201 J.D. Asst. Atty. Gen.
Weaver, Mark R., (AV) .... '61 '89 C.652 B.S. L.1338 J.D. [C Isaac,B.L.&T.]
Webber, Marci L. .... '70 '97 C.608 B.S.B.A. L.117 J.D. [A Briscoe&W.]
Webb-Lawton, Nina I. .... '65 '92 C.604 B.A. L.1066 J.D. [Vorys,S.S.&P.]
Weber, Christopher J., (BV) .... '66 '92 C.363 B.A. L.851 J.D. [Kegler,B.H.&R.]
Weber, Maggie F. .... '76 '03 C.967 B.A. L.904 J.D. [A Bricker&E.]
Weber, Todd A. .... '71 '96 C.896 B.S. L.117 J.D. [A Chester,W.&S.]
Webner, Robert N., (AV) .... '57 '85 C.608 B.A. L.276 J.D. [Vorys,S.S.&P.]

Webster, Geoffrey E., (AV) '48 '75 C.608 B.S. L.117 J.D. BR
Suite 310, Two Miranova Place, 43215-3413
Telephone: 614-461-1156 Fax: 614-461-7168
Email: gewebster@gewebster.com URL: http://www.lawyers.com/gewlaw
Associates: J. Randall Richards; Eric B. Hershberger; Paul V. Disantis.
Health Care Administration, Facility Licensing, Facility Regulation, Contracts and Finance, Long Term Care, Nursing Home Regulation, Patients Rights and Pharmacy Law. Health Care Mergers and Acquisitions Regulation and Reimbursement, and Civil Litigation.
Representative Clients: Strategic Nursing Systems, Inc.; Lancia Nursing Homes, Inc.; St. Rita's Home for the Aged, Inc.; Carington Health Systems; Marketing Services by Vectra, Inc.; The Ohio Academy of Nursing Homes, Inc.; Beacon Skilled Care Pharmacy.
See Professional Biographies, COLUMBUS, OHIO

Webster, Norton R., (AV) .... '28 '52 C&L.608 B.A., LL.B. [C Vorys,S.S.&P.]
Webster, Victoria G. .... '51 '77 C&L.608 B.A., J.D. Ohio Dept. of Taxation
Wecker, Andrew P. '67 '96 C.610 B.S. L.608 J.D.
Counsel, Commercial Division, Title First Agency, Inc.
Weeks, Thomas W., (AV) .... '49 '75 C.604 B.A. L.477 J.D. 555 Buttles Ave.
Weeks, Winnifred Norah '48 '87
C.162 B.A. L.608 J.D. Sr. Staff Atty., Ohio Legal Rights Service

Wegman, Hessler & Vanderburg, A Legal Professional Association
(See Cleveland)

Wehr, Howard F. .... '16 '49 C&L.608 A.B., LL.B. 652 Olde Towne Ave.
Wehrer, Greg R. .... '72 '97 C.97 B.A. L.880 J.D. [A Squire,S.&D.]
Weidenhamer, Evan R. .... '73 '99 C.49 B.S. L.608 J.D. [A Schottenstein,Z.&D.]
Weiland, Kurt H., (AV) .... '46 '76 C.381 B.A. L.608 J.D. [K.Weiland]
Weiland, Kurt, (AV) .... 471 S. Drexel Ave.
Weiler, Robert J. .... '35 '83 C.37 B.S. L.117 LL.B. 41 S. High St.‡
Weimer, John B. .... '59 '85 C.473 B.A. L.802 J.D. [Vorys,S.S.&P.]
Weinberg, Denice, (BV) .... '65 '92 C.207 B.A. L.608 J.D. City Atty. Off.
Weiner, Jerry, (BV) .... '27 '52 C.608 L.117 J.D. 19 W. Beck St.
Weiner, Samuel, (AV) .... '43 '73 C.608 B.A. L.117 J.D. [S.B.Weiner]

Weiner, Samuel B., Co., L.P.A., (AV) BR
743 South Front Street, 43206
Telephone: 614-443-6581 Fax: 614-443-9978
Email: sbwesq@ameritech.net URL: http://www.samuelbweinerlawcolpa.com
Samuel Weiner.

(This Listing Continued)

Weiner, Samuel B., Co., L.P.A. (Continued)

Criminal Trial and Appellate Practice, Felonies and Misdemeanors in all State and Federal Courts. White Collar Crime, Arson.

See Professional Biographies, COLUMBUS, OHIO

Weinstein, Melvin D., (AV) .... '47 '73 C.608 B.A. L.150 J.D. [Kegler,B.H.&R.]
Weis, Amy J. .... '69 '96 C.608 B.A. L.117 J.D. [Babbitt&W.]
Weis, Anthony D. .... '74 '99 C.97 B.S.B.A. L.608 J.D. [A Vorys,S.S.&P.]
Weisenberg, William K., (AV) '44 '69
C.823 B.A. L.564 J.D. Dir., Govt. Affrs., Ohio State Bar Assn.
Weiser, Joan C. .... '53 '79 C.8 B.A. L.7 J.D. Asst. Atty. Gen.
Weislogel, Stacy '39 '80
C.608 B.A.E. L.117 J.D. Assoc. Dean, Ohio State Univ. Coll. of Engr.
Weisman, J. Scott, (AV) ..... '65 '90 C&L.608 B.S., J.D. Staff Atty., Off. of Co. Pub. Def.
Weisman, Robert D., (AV) .... '48 '75 C.930 B.A. L.1003 J.D. [Schottenstein,Z.&D.]
Weiss, Carol A. .... '50 '77 C.741 B.A. L.1003 J.D. Ohio Dept. of Commerce
Weiss, Daniel K. .. '60 '85 C.607 B.S. L.608 J.D. Chf. Fin. Offr., Hwy. Patrol Retire. Sys.
Weiss, Eugene P., (BV) .... '45 '72 C.608 B.A. L.117 J.D. 536 South Third Street
Weiss, Rebekah G. .... '78 '04 C.608 B.A. L.117 J.D. [A Twyford&D.]
Weiss, Stephen M., (BV) .... '42 '68 C.679 B.S. L.1119 J.D. 601 South High Street
Welch, Derek W. .... '71 '01 C.608 B.A. L.150 J.D. UBS Financial Services
Welch, John R. .... '19 '55 C.608 B.S. L.117 J.D. 1030 Birchmont Rd.‡
Welch, Mark A. .... '52 '77 C.473 B.A. L.608 J.D. One Riverside Plaza
Welcome, Kristen Jane .... '74 '99 C.473 B.A. L.150 J.D. [Zacks]
Weldon, Thomas P. .... '68 '94 C.473 B.A. L.117 J.D. Asst. Pros. Atty.
Welin, Peter D., (AV) .... '56 '88 C.350 B.S.C.E. L.608 J.D. [Thompson H.]
Wellner, John P., (AV) .... '51 '79 C.651 B.S. L.608 J.D. [Vorys,S.S.&P.]
Wells, N. Douglas '52 '81 C.511 B.A. L.838 J.D.
(adm. in MO; not adm. in OH) Assoc. Prof., Capital Univ. Law School
Welsh, G. Duane .... '44 '72 C.611 B.A. L.117 J.D. Dep. Atty. Gen.

Weltman, Weinberg & Reis Co., L.P.A., (AV)
175 South 3rd Street, Suite 900, 43215 ⊙
Telephone: 614-228-7272 Fax: 614-222-2193
Email: wwr@weltman.com URL: http://www.weltman.com
Allen J. Reis; Stephen A. Santangelo; Terrence R. Heffernan;—Monette W. Cope; Angela Coriell; Douglas M. Dahmer; James G. Kozelek; Joseph M. McCandlish; Raymond F. Moats; Ronald B. Noga; Geoffrey J. Peters; Brian D. Wood.
Burlington, New Jersey Office: Telephone: 609-914-0437.
Chicago, Illinois Office: Telephone: 312-786-9676.
Cincinnati, Ohio Office: Telephone: 513-723-2200.
Cleveland, Ohio Office: Telephone: 216-685-1000.
Deerfield, Illinois Office: Telephone: 847-940-9812.
Philadelphia, Pennsylvania Office: Telephone: 215-599-1500.
Pittsburgh, Pennsylvania Office: Telephone: 412-434-7955.
Troy, Michigan Office: Telephone: 248-362-6100.

See Professional Biographies, COLUMBUS, OHIO

Wendel, Lee A., (AV) .... '62 '87 C.611 B.A. L.477 J.D. [Squire,S.&D.]
Wendt, Tracy Q. .... '67 '96 C.97 B.S. L.117 J.D. 555 City Park Ave.
Werth, Robert W., (AV) .... '40 '65 C&L.608 B.A., J.D. [Vorys,S.S.&P.]
Wesner, Arthur G., (BV) .... '32 '58 C.937 B.A. L.608 J.D. 999 South High Street
Wesp, E. Joel, (AV) .... '46 '70 C.894 B.A. L.930 J.D. [C Rich,C.&D.]
West, Charles E. ...... '48 '74 C&L.608 B.A., J.D. Jr. Claims Atty., Grange Mut. Cas. Co.
West, Patrick A. T. .... '41 '74 C.999 A.B. L.117 J.D. 39 Clinton Hgts. Ave.‡
West, Scott B., (AV) '56 '82
C.473 B.S. L.608 J.D. V.P. & Assoc. Gen. Coun., Pizzuti Inc.
Westbrook, Gayle R. '47 '80 C.208 B.A. L.893 J.D.
Gen. Coun., Advanced Drainage Systems, Inc.
Westerburg, Cheri L. .... '63 '88 C.970 B.A. L.930 J.D. Asst. Atty. Gen.
Westerman, Philip R. .... '67 '96 C.894 B.A. L.608 J.D. [A Squire,S.&D.]
Westfall, James W. .... '51 '77 C.150 B.A. L.930 J.D. [Eisen&W.] ⊙
Westfall, Lee W. .... '67 '96 C.608 B.S. L.117 J.D. 941 Chatham Lane, Ste. 201
Weston, Bruce J. .... '55 '80 C.150 B.B.A. L.608 J.D. 169 West Hubbard Avenue
Wettlaufer, Karl F. '36 '61 C.165 A.B. L.477 LL.B.
Two Nationwide Plaza, 280 N. High Street 12th Floor
Wetzel, Jonathan H. .... '49 '74 C.347 A.B. L.8 J.D. Nationwide Mut. Ins. Co.
Wetzel, Richard D., Jr., (AV) .... '57 '82 C.610 B.A. L.1017 J.D. [Crabbe,B.&J.]
Wetzel, Sandra K. .... '52 '77 C&L.8 B.A., J.D. Nationwide Ins. Co.
Whaley, Douglas J., (AV) '43 '68 C.446 B.A. L.846 J.D.
Ohio State Univ. College of Law
Wharton, Garry L., (AV) .... '36 '61 C.610 A.B. L.608 J.D. 417 E. Broad St.‡
Wheat, Ralph D. .... '29 '56 C&L.608 B.S., J.D. 3789 Olentangy Blvd.‡
Wheatley, John C., (BV) .... '22 '52 C.611 A.B. L.266 J.D. 150 E. Mound St.
Wheeler, James W., (AV) .... '43 '68 C&L.608 B.A., J.D. [Wiles,B.B.&B.]
Wheeler, Pelton W. .... '29 '88 C.608 D.D.S. L.117 J.D. P.O. Box 21170
Wheeler, Terrence T. .... '60 '85 C&L.608 B.A., J.D. 560 E. Town St.
Whetzel, Eugene P. .... '48 '74 C.645 B.A. L.608 J.D. Ohio Mfrs. Assn.

Whipps, Edward F., & Associates, (AV) '36 '61 C.611 B.A. L.608 J.D.
500 South Front Street, Suite 860, 43215 ⊙
Telephone: 614-461-6006 Fax: 614-461-6010 URL: http://www.efwhipps.com
Email: efwhipps@efwhipps.com URL: http://www.lawyers.com/efwhipps
Associate: Bobbie Corley O'Keefe.
Family, Matrimonial and Domestic Relations Law, Divorce Taxation, Child Custody, Visitation Rights, Premarital Agreements.
Dublin, Ohio Office: 555 Metro Place North, Suite 100, 43017. Telephone: 614-461-6007. Fax: 614-461-6010.

See Professional Biographies, COLUMBUS, OHIO

Whitaker, Roger T., (AV) .... '51 '76 C.477 A.B. L.608 J.D. [Luper,N.&L.]
Whitcomb, David A. .... '66 '91 C.608 B.A. L.477 J.D. [Baker&H.]
White, Anthony C., (BV) .... '— '93 C.608 B.S. L.597 J.D. [Thompson H.]
White, Arnold S., (AV) .... '44 '69 C.608 B.A. L.30 J.D. [White&F.]
White, David L., (AV) '53 '81
C.608 B.S. L.201 J.D. Asst. Gen. Coun., Nationwide Insurance
White, Duane M. .... '47 '76 C.970 B.A. L.910 J.D. Asst. Atty. Gen., Atty. Gen. Off.
White, Janice G. .... '— '78 C.930 B.A. L.117 J.D. Capital Univ.
White, Joseph L. .... '34 '59 C&L.608 B.A., LL.B. Ohio Dept. of Ins.

White & Fish, L.P.A., Inc., (AV) BB
1335 Dublin Road Suite 201 (C), 43215
Telephone: 614-485-9300 Fax: 614-485-9462 URL: http://www.whiteandfish.com
Email: wflpa@centralohioattorneys.com URL: http://www.centralohioattorneys.com
Arnold S. White; Jeffrey D. Fish (Certified Specialist in Family Relations Law, Ohio State Bar Association).
Civil Litigation, Bankruptcy, Workouts, Chapter 11, Collections, Corporate Law, Small Business Law, Commercial, Family Law, Divorce, Personal Injury, Real Estate, Estate Litigation, Employment Contracts, Wrongful Termination.

See Professional Biographies, COLUMBUS, OHIO

Whitehouse, Richard A. .... '57 '87 C.980 B.A. L.8 J.D. Off. of Inspec. Gen.
Whiteside, Alba L., (AV) ..... '28 '54 C&L.608 B.A., J.D. 2770 East Main Street, Suite 28
Whitt, Mark A. .... '— '97 C&L.8 B.S., J.D. [A Jones D.]
Whittaker, David M., (AV) .... '52 '79 C.1208 B.A. L.608 J.D. [Luper,N.&L.]
Whittaker, Maria C. .... '58 '83 C.309 A.B. L.145 J.D. Jewish Community Ctr.
Whitworth, Jill Ann .... '58 '88 C.475 B.A. L.228 J.D. 65 E. State St., Suite 1800
Wible, Michael V. .... '62 '87 C.473 B.A. L.904 J.D. [C Thompson H.]
Wickham, Henry P., Jr., (BV) .... '50 '79 C.385 A.B. L.201 J.D. [Luper,N.&L.]
Wickline, Amanda L. .... '— '03 C.207 B.A. L.896 J.D. [A Schottenstein,Z.&D.]
Wideman, Clark W., (BV) .... '47 '75 C.608 B.S. L.117 J.D. 4737 Nugent Dr.
Wideman, Stacey L. .... '77 '03 C.150 B.S. L.117 J.D. [A Lucas,P.A.G.&N.]
Widmaier, James L. .... '35 '65 C.631 B.S. L.266 J.D. 901 S. High St.
Wiesmann, Klaus H. '43 '79 C.150 B.S.E.E. L.608 J.D.
Sr. Intell. Prop. Atty., Battelle Memorial Institute (Pat.)
Wiest, Christopher D. .... '77 '04 C&L.150 B.B.A., J.D. Asst. Atty. Gen.
Wightman, Alec, (AV) .... '51 '75 C.228 A.B. L.608 J.D. [Baker&H.]
Wigton, Charles E., III, (AV) '50 '76
C.967 B.A. L.117 J.D. V.P. & Tr. Coun., Natl. City Corp.
Wilburn, Melissa L. .... '63 '89 C.643 B.A. L.665 J.D. 30 E. Broad St., Fl. 25
Wilcox, Ronald L., (BV) .... '36 '61 C&L.608 B.A., J.D. [Garber&W.]
Wilcox, Schlosser & Bendig Co., L.P.A., (BV) .... 4937 W. Broad St.
Wile, John .... '24 '50 C&L.608 B.A., J.D. 2759 Minerval Lake Rd.
Wiles, Daniel G., (AV) .... '41 '66 C.608 B.S. L.607 J.D. [Wiles,B.B.&B.]
Wiles, James M., (AV) .... '45 '70 C.973 B.S. L.607 J.D. [Wiles,B.B.&B.]

Wiles, Boyle, Burkholder & Bringardner Co., L.P.A., (AV) BB
300 Spruce Street, Floor 1, 43215
Telephone: 614-221-5216 Fax: 614-221-5692; 221-0624
Email: mail@wileslaw.com URL: http://www.wileslaw.com
Daniel G. Wiles; James W. Wheeler; James M. Wiles; Mark J. Sheriff; Thomas E. Boyle; Michael L. Close; Richard D. Bringardner; Daniel E. Bringardner; Steven P. Elliott; Bruce H. Burkholder; Dale D. Cook; Mary Ten Eyck Taylor; Jay B. Eggspuehler; Eugene L. Hollins; William B. Benson; Samuel M. Pipino; C. William Klausman; James M. Hughes; Mark C. Melko; Kerry T. Boyle; Christopher G. Phillips; Lauren S. Brill; Neil C. Sander; Jennifer B. Casto.
General Practice, Insurance Defense, Medical Legal, Products Liability, Aviation, Motor Carrier, Business, Corporate, Municipal, Construction, Real Estate, Commercial Leasing, Hospitality and Restaurant, Estate Planning Law, Trusts, Wills and Probate, Taxation, Trial, and Appellate Practice, Bankruptcy, Foreclosure and Debtor-Creditor Law.
Representative Insurance Clients: Aetna Life & Casualty Co.; All-state Insurance Co.; Associated Aviation Underwriters, Inc.; Physician's Insurance Company of America; United States Aviation Underwriters, Inc.; Zurich-American Insurance Co.; Carolina Casualty Ins. Co.; Travel Air Ins. Co.; Underwriters at Lloyd's of London.

See Professional Biographies, COLUMBUS, OHIO

Wiley, Stephen C. .... '60 '97 C.631 B.A. L.179 J.D. [A Calfee,H.&G.]
Wilhelm, Anne M. ..... '59 '84 C.473 B.A. L.930 J.D. V.P., Legal Affs., Ohio Mfrs. Assn.
Wilhelm, James E., (AV) .... '39 '64 C&L.608 B.A., J.D. 1390 Dublin Road
Wilhelm, Joseph Edmond .... '57 '91 C.610 B.S. L.150 J.D. Pub. Def.
Wilhite, Stacy E. .... '— '98 C.473 B.S. L.201 J.D. [A Baker&H.]
Wilkens, James B. '30 '72 C.188 Ph.D. L.161 J.D.
Pat. Admr., The Ohio State Univ. Resch. Foundation (Pat.)
Wilkerson, John P., Jr., (AV) .... '54 '81 C.608 B.S. L.117 J.D. [Carlile P.&M.]
Wilkes, Nicholas E. .... '70 '95 C.610 B.A. L.608 J.D. [A Kegler,B.H.&R.]
Wilkins, Linda A. .... '48 '96 C.608 B.A. L.117 J.D. 2680 Southridge Dr.
Wilkinson, William C., (AV) .... '47 '76 C.8 B.A. L.7 J.D. [Thompson H.]
Will, Anne E. .... '77 '03 C&L.608 B.A., J.D. [B Calfee,H.&G.]
Willcox, Roderick H., (AV) .... '34 '58 C.951 B.A. L.477 LL.B. [Chester,W.&S.]
Wille, Charles L. ...... '53 '79 C.651 B.A. L.989 J.D. OH Atty. Gen. Capitol Crimes Sect.

Willi Law Offices
(See Westerville)

Williams, April M. .... '69 '94 C.473 B.A. L.851 J.D. Maj. Legal Coun., State Senate
Williams, Charles T., (BV) .... '46 '74 C.867 B.A. L.93 J.D. Remax First Ltd.
Williams, Dale, Jr. .... '53 '79 C.967 B.A. L.608 J.D. Asst. U.S. Atty.
Williams, Douglas L., (AV) .... '53 '80 C.1070 B.S. L.608 J.D. Limited, Inc.
Williams, Erica K. .... '70 '96 C.262 B.A. L.930 J.D. [A Hahn L.&P.]
Williams, Faith M., (BV) .... '58 '93 C.30 B.S. L.276 J.D. [Bricker&E.]
Williams, Jeffrey T., (AV) .... '59 '88 C&L.878 B.S., J.D. [Baker&H.]
Williams, John T. .... '50 '78 C.8 B.A. L.150 J.D. Asst. Atty. Gen.
Williams, Kevin Lane .... '61 '93 C.385 A.B. L.608 J.D. [A Manley D.K.]
Williams, Lewis E., (AV) .... '48 '74 C.608 B.S. L.117 J.D. [L.E.Williams]
Williams, Mark D. .... '69 '95 C.172 B.A. L.208 J.D. Schuler Manufacturing
Williams, Megan J. F. .... '66 '92 C.117 B.A. L.608 J.D. Law Clk., Ct. of App.
Williams, Michael L., (BV) .... '67 '92 C.117 B.A. L.608 J.D. [Buckingham,D.&B.]
Williams, Othello '47 '75 C.910 B.S. L.734 J.D.
Assist. Gen. Coun., Nationwide Insurance
Williams, Richard A., (BV) .... '57 '82 C.473 B.S. L.851 J.D. [Williams&P.]
Williams, Sandra K. '— '83 C.97 B.A. L.117 J.D.
Sr. Coun.-Regul., Amer. Electric Power Serv. Corp.
Williams, Scott E., (BV) .... '56 '92 C.608 B.S. L.117 J.D. [Hammond,S.&W.]
Williams, Thomas H. .... '32 '59 L.608 J.D. 786 Chaffin Ridge St.
Williams, Thomas V., (AV) .... '51 '77 C.150 B.B.A. L.851 J.D. [Frost B.T.]
Williams, Lewis E., Co., L.P.A., (AV) .... 330 South High Street

Williams & Petro Co., L.L.C., (BV)
338 South High Street, 2nd Floor, 43215-4546
Telephone: 614-224-0531 Fax: 614-224-0553 URL: http://www.williamspetro.com
Email: generalcounsel@wplaw.org URL: http://www.wplaw.org
Richard A. Williams; John P. Petro;—Lorree L. Dendis; Susan S.R. Petro; Josh L. Schoenberger. Of Counsel: John J. Petro.
Insurance Defense, Personal Injury, Automobile Accidents, Wrongful Death, Municipal Law, Construction Law, Employment Law, Business Representation, Estate Planning and Administration, Probate Administration, Advisory/Coverage Opinions, Family Law.

See Professional Biographies, COLUMBUS, OHIO

Willis, Mary Ann '47 '87 C.967 B.A. L.150 J.D.
Dir., Career Services, Capital Univ. Law Sch.
Willis, William L., Jr., (BV) .... '62 '87 C.207 B.A. L.117 J.D. [Havens W.]
Willison, Eric E. .... '66 '96 C.608 B.A. L.117 J.D. [A G.R.Lewis]
Wills, G. Benjamin '53 '85
C.1135 B.A. L.1292 J.D. Staff Atty., OH Assn. of Pub. School Empls.
Wilson, Charles E., (AV) '52 '77
C.378 B.S. L.569 J.D. Assoc. Prof. of Law, Ohio State Univ.
Wilson, Howard F. .... '14 '53 C.608 B.Sc. L.117 J.D. 89 Powhatan Ave.
Wilson, James A., (AV) .... '60 '85 C.473 A.B. L.178 J.D. [Vorys,S.S.&P.]
Wilson, Karin E. .... '65 '90 C.705 B.A. L.8 J.D. Asst. Atty. Gen.
Wilson, Leigh Ann .... '59 '99 C.528 B.A. L.117 J.D. [A Baker&H.]
Wilson, Mark R., (BV) .... '57 '82 C.1208 B.A. L.608 J.D. [Blue,W.&B.]
Wilson, Matthew R. .... '— '00 C.207 B.A. L.893 J.D. [A Jones D.]
Wilson, Nicholas B., (BV) .... '35 '74 C.870 B.S. L.608 J.D. 720 S. High St.
Wilson, Thomas A., (AV) .... '60 '85 C.20 A.B. L.276 J.D. [Peck,S.&W.]
Winchester, Jeffrey D. .... '— '97 C.37 B.A. L.188 J.D. [A Jones D.]

Winkler, Dirken D. ....'— '97 C.920 B.S. L.117 J.D. [D.D.Winkler]
Winkler, John F., (AV) ....'46 '83 C.976 B.A. L.608 J.D. [Kisor&W.]
Winkler, Dirken D., Attorney at Law LLC .... 169 E. Livingston Avenue
Winner, Joseph C., (AV) ....'49 '76 C.679 B.S.Ch.E. L.608 J.D. [McFadden W.&S.]
Winningham, R. C. ....'25 '55 C&L.608 B.S., J.D. 8 E. Broad St.‡
Wintering, Michael R., (BV) '52 '78 C.608 B.A. L.117 J.D.
1103 Schrock Road, Suite 209
Winters, Chas. W., (BV) ....'27 '53 C.608 L.266 J.D. 150 E. Mound St.
Winters, David C., (AV) ....'44 '75 C&L.608 B.A., J.D. [Winters&M.]
Winters, Karen A., (AV) ....'56 '81 C.97 B.A. L.7 J.D. [Squire,S.&D.]
Winters, Leslie Ann ....'56 '80 C.608 B.S. L.117 J.D. Rickenbacker Port Auth.
Winters, Susan J. ....'48 '82 C.611 B.A. L.117 J.D. 333 Arden Road
Winters, Thomas R., (AV) ....'50 '84 C.737 A.B. L.117 J.D. [Vorys,S.S.&P.]

Winters & Merkle, (AV)
500 South Front Street, Suite 900, 43215
Telephone: 614-228-0068 FAX: 614-228-1660
URL: http://www.wintersmerkle.com
David C. Winters; H. Tim Merkle.
Civil and Criminal Trial and Appellate Practice in all State and Federal Courts, Business and White Collar Crimes, Environmental Crimes, Health Care Fraud, Grand Jury Investigations, Personal Injury. Business and Commercial Litigation. Insurance Coverage and Bad Faith Litigation.
Reference: National City Bank.
See Professional Biographies, COLUMBUS, OHIO

Wirt, Laurie Blossom ....'63 '92 C.608 B.A. L.1209 J.D. 7752 Northwind Ct.
Wirth, David S. ....'75 '01 C&L.150 B.A., J.D. [D.Wirth]

Wirth, David
829 Bethel Road, 43214
Telephone: 614-267-5354 Fax: 614-875-6606
Email: wirthman@hotmail.com
David S. Wirth.
Insurance Law, Negligence, Legal Malpractice, Subrogation, Personal Injury, Probate.
See Professional Biographies, COLUMBUS, OHIO

Wise, C. Michael ....'59 '88 C&L.608 B.A., J.D. [Ⓐ Plymale]
Wise, Dean W. ....'22 '49 C&L.608 B.Sc., J.D. 2458 Johnston Rd.‡
Wise, Katherine J. '72 '97 C.473 B.A. L.608 J.D.
Dir., Student Housing Legal Clinic, Ohio St. Univ. Coll. of Law‡
Wiseman, Randolph C., (AV) ....'46 '74 C.835 B.S. L.117 J.D. [Bricker&E.]
Wiseman, Thomas L. ....'44 '69 C.117 B.S. L.930 J.D. F.B.I.
Wisner, Edwin A. ....'40 '66 C&L.607 B.A., J.D. Coun., Republic Franklin Ins. Co.
Witalec, Joseph M. ....'— '94 C.608 B.S.B.A. L.309 J.D. [Ⓒ Jones D.]
Withee, Stephen ....'69 '95 C.473 A.B. L.902 J.D. [Ⓐ Schottenstein,Z.&D.]
Witherspoon, Lewis S. ....'22 '50 C&L.608 B.A., J.D. 1414 Westminster Dr.
Wittenberg, Eric J., (BV) ....'61 '87 C.216 B.A. L.665 J.D. [Krupman,G.M.M.&W.]
Wiviott, Sheryl D. ....'60 '85 C.150 B.A. L.201 J.D. Asst. Atty. Gen.
Wobst, Franck G., (AV) ....'58 '83 C.856 B.A. L.902 J.D. [Porter W.M.&A.]
Woelfel, Bradford B. ....'49 '83 C.604 B.A. L.117 J.D. 3356 Lindstrom Drive
Wofford, Isaac S. ....'— '02 C&L.339 B.A., J.D. [Ⓐ Jones D.]
Wolery, Don E., (BV) ....'51 '79 C.608 B.S. L.117 J.D. 3620 N. High St.
Wolf, Holly N. ....'71 '97 C.201 B.A. L.608 J.D. [Ⓐ Manley D.K.]
Wolfe, Gerald P., II ....'49 '81 C.608 B.S. L.117 J.D. 3280 Riverside Dr.
Wolfe, Grant A. ....'56 '81 C&L.117 B.A., J.D. P.O. Box 1505
Wolfram, Jill A. ....'66 '96 C.608 B.A. L.117 J.D. Grange Mut. Cas. Co.
Wolinetz, Barry H., (AV) ....'44 '71 C&L.608 B.A., J.D. [Baker&H.]
Wolken, Susan Ackerman ....'50 '81 C.608 B.S. L.117 J.D. 1 Nationwide Plaza
Wolman, Benson A., (AV) ....'36 '88 C.597 B.A. L.117 J.D. [Wolman&Assoc.]
Wolman & Associates, (AV) .... 341 South Third Street, Suite 301
Wolper, Beatrice E., (AV) ....'45 '78 C.150 B.S. L.1340 J.D. [Chester,W.&S.]
Wolske, Walter J., Jr., (AV) ....'32 '56 C&L.608 B.S., J.D. [Wolske&B.] ⊙

Wolske & Barclay, A Legal Professional Association, (AV) [BB]
580 South High Street, 43215-5672 ⊙
Telephone: 614-221-6969 800-862-6969 Fax: 614-228-4367 URL: http://www.wolskeandbarclay.com
Email: Firm@wolskeandbarclay.com URL: http://www.lawyers.com/wolskeandbarclay
Walter J. Wolske, Jr.; Craig D. Barclay;—David A. Roscoe; Sarah J. Wolske-Donaldson; Jason K. Wright.
Civil and Appellate Practice in State and Federal Courts. Medical and Dental Malpractice, Nursing Home Negligence, Personal Injury and Products Liability Law, Worker's Compensation and Industrial Accidents, Automobile Accidents, Airplane Crash Litigation.
Reference: Bank One of Columbus, N.A.
See Professional Biographies, COLUMBUS, OHIO

Wolske-Donaldson, Sarah J. ....'68 '01 C.771 B.A. L.117 J.D. [Ⓐ Wolske&B.]
Womer Benjamin, Ann H., (AV) '53 '78
C.880 B.A. L.930 J.D. Ohio Department of Insurance
Wong, Margaret W., (AV) ....'50 '77 C.927 B.S. L.107 J.D. [M.W.Wong&Assoc.] ⊙
Wong, Margaret W., & Associates Co., LPA, (AV)
470 Olde Worthington Road, Suite 200 (⊙Detroit, MI; Cleve., OH)
Wonnell, Harold E., (AV) ....'23 '53 C&L.608 B.S.C., J.D. 330 S. High St.
Wonnell, Nancy K., (BV) ....'40 '87 C&L.608 B.A., J.D. 330 S. High Street
Wood, Brian D. ....'76 '02 C.608 B.A. L.179 J.D. [Ⓐ Weltman,W.&R.]
Wood, Lee M., (BV) ....'55 '86 C.473 A.B. L.608 J.D. [Chappano W.]

Wood, Herron & Evans, L.L.P.
(See Cincinnati)

Woodbeck, Charles A. '38 '91 C.723 B.S. L.117 J.D.
Compl. Grp. Enforce. Coord., State Medical Bd.
Woods, C. Craig, (AV) ....'56 '81 C.197 B.A. L.893 J.D. [Squire,S.&D.]
Woods, William H., (AV) ....'46 '73 C&L.608 B.S., J.D. [McNamara&M.]
Woodward, Lisa M. ....'61 '99 C.136 B.S. L.117 J.D. 85 Marconi Blvd.
Woodward, Robert J., Jr. ....'41 '71 C&L.117 B.S., J.D. 1 Nationwide Plaza
Wooldridge, Gregory D. ....'62 '88 C.347 B.S. L.1119 J.D. 600 S. Pearl St.
Woolley, Julie M. ....'77 '03 C.901 B.A. L.608 J.D. [Ⓐ Baker&H.]
Wooten, Marchelle E. ....'73 '98 C&L.608 B.A., J.D. Ohio State Univ., College of Law
Workman, John R., (AV) ....'46 '74 C.608 B.A. L.117 J.D. 1375 Dublin Rd.
Worley, G. Thomas ....'54 '83 C.608 B.A. L.117 J.D. Adm., Bureau of Mediation
Wrachford, Jason S. '73 '97
C.999 B.S. L.117 J.D. Coun., Columbus-America Discovery Grp.
Wright, Beth A. ....'69 '95 C.608 B.A. L.117 J.D. P.O. Box 21299
Wright, Harry, III, (AV) ....'25 '51 C.383 B.S. L.309 LL.B. 41 S. High St.‡
Wright, Harry, IV, (AV) ....'58 '90 C.902 B.A. L.1365 J.D. [Bricker&E.]
Wright, J. Craig R. ....'29 '54 C.383 B.A. L.976 LL.B. 65 East State Street, Suite 1000‡
Wright, Jason K. ....'70 '01 C.610 B.A. L.117 J.D. [Ⓐ Wolske&B.]
Wright, Phillip Lawrence, Jr. ....'69 '00 C.1494 B.A. L.117 J.D. [Ⓐ Maguire&S.]
Wright, Richard E. ....'25 '58 C.381 A.B. L.266 J.D. 13 W. State St.‡
Wright, Rosa P. ....'56 '91 C.608 B.A. L.117 J.D. Asst. Atty. Gen.
Wright, Scott E., (AV) ....'62 '89 C.608 B.S. L.117 J.D. [Matan,G.&W.]
Wrightsel, Bradley Benedict, (BV) .....'65 '93 C.207 B.A. L.607 J.D. 3300 Riverside Dr.
Wrightsel, R. Douglas, (AV) '40 '65 C.207 B.A. L.880 J.D.
3300 Riverside Dr., Ste. 100
Wuerth, Richard O., (AV) ....'46 '73 C.967 B.A. L.910 J.D. [Lane,A.&H.]
Wyckoff, Robin G. ....'— '04 C&L.608 B.A., J.D. [Ⓐ Vorys,S.S.&P.]
Yaeger, Keri N. ....'74 '01 C.381 B.B.A. L.608 J.D. [Lamkin,V.T.B.&D.]
Yaffe, Robert J. '49 '75 C.546 B.A. L.190 J.D.
(adm. in NE; not adm. in OH) The Jewish Ctr.
Yagoda, Andrea Renee, (BV) ....'53 '77 C.107 B.A. L.117 J.D. 897 S. Front Street
Yaklevich, John A., (BV) ....'54 '78 C.597 B.A. L.608 J.D. [Moore&Y.]
Yale, Beverly S. ....'57 '83 C.150 B.S. L.607 J.D. Asst. Atty. Gen.
Yang, Rosanne T. ....'— '99 C&L.608 B.A., J.D. [Ⓐ Baker&H.]
Yano, James A., (AV) ....'51 '77 C.645 B.S. L.893 J.D. [Vorys,S.S.&P.]
Yarbrough, Heather Ann ....'69 '96 C.610 B.B.A. L.851 J.D. Nationwide Mutual Ins. Co.
Yarbrough, Michael K., (AV) ....'48 '76 C.602 B.A. L.597 J.D. [Frost B.T.]
Yashko, Gary G. ....'— '97 C&L.608 B.A., J.D. [Ⓐ Benesch,F.C.&A.]
Yashko, Michael S., (AV) '61 '87
C.608 B.S.B.A. L.597 J.D. [Roetzel&A.] (⊙Fort Myers, FL)
Yates, Christopher Robert ....'68 '95 C.608 B.A. L.930 J.D. U.S. Atty's. Off.
Yavitch, Bernard Z., (BV) ....'43 '71 C.608 B.S. L.117 J.D. 592 South Third Street
Yavitch, Eric J., (AV) ....'69 '95 C.62 B.A. L.117 J.D. [Yavitch&P.]

Yavitch & Palmer Co., L.P.A., (AV)
511 South High Street, 43215
Telephone: 614-224-6142 Facsimile: 614-228-6078
Email: spalmer@yp-lawyers.com URL: http://www.yp-lawyers.com
Eric J. Yavitch; Stephen E. Palmer.
Criminal Defense, Appellate Practice, Post-Conviction Remedies, and Trial Practice in All State and Federal Courts.
See Professional Biographies, COLUMBUS, OHIO

Yeager, Jeffrey A. ....'70 '97 C.97 B.S. L.608 J.D. [Ⓐ Hahn L.&P.]
Yearling, Joseph H., Jr., (AV) ....'31 '56 C.597 B.S. L.608 J.D. 3220 Riverside Dr.

Yeazel, Keith A., (AV) '56 '89 C.608 B.A. L.117 J.D.
Attorney at Law
65 South Fifth Street, 43215
Telephone: 614-228-7005 Fax: 614-224-2347
Email: yeazel@netwalk.com
Federal and White Collar Criminal Defense, U.S. Guideline Sentencing Litigation.
See Professional Biographies, COLUMBUS, OHIO

Yeoman, Kelly Jennings ....'71 '96 C.207 B.A. L.273 J.D. [Ⓐ Vorys,S.S.&P.]
Yiangou, Andrew ....'61 '91 C.967 B.A. L.608 J.D. [Bergman&Y.]
Yontz, Randall E., (BV) ....'51 '77 C.967 B.A. L.607 J.D. Asst. U.S. Atty.
Yost, Cynthia A., (BV) ....'52 '89 C.608 B.S. L.117 J.D. Asst. U.S. Pub. Def.
Yost, William Richard, (AV) ....'46 '72 C.608 B.S. L.117 J.D. [Carlile P.&M.]
Young, Betty Kay ....'55 '00 C.608 B.B.A. L.117 J.D. Franklin University
Young, Carrie Carnahan ....'61 '86 C.97 B.A.C. L.608 J.D. Ohio Bd. of Tax App.
Young, David C., (BV) ....'61 '86 C.473 B.S. L.910 J.D. [Sunbury&Y.]
Young, David J., (AV) ....'32 '55 C.201 L.608 J.D. [Ⓒ Squire,S.&D.]
Young, Gregory S. ....'61 '86 C.347 B.A. L.930 J.D. [G.S.Young]
Young, John C. ....'27 '54 C.381 B.S. L.608 J.D. Ct. of App. J.
Young, Mary Beth ....'01 C.383 B.S. L.145 J.D. [Ⓐ Jones D.]
Young, Nancy B., (AV) ....'52 '77 C.97 B.A. L.608 J.D. [Porter W.M.&A.]
Young, Stephen A. ....'55 '84 C.97 B.A. L.1003 J.D. Dept. of Rehab. and Correction
Young, Thomas A., (AV) ....'47 '73 C.608 B.S. L.117 J.D. [Porter W.M.&A.]
Young, Gregory S., Company L.P.A. .... 30 E. Broad Street, 15th Floor
Younger, Mary Ann, (BV) ....'49 '84 C.608 B.A. L.117 J.D. Off. of Pub. Def.
Younkin, Tracy A., (BV) ....'64 '94 C.608 B.S. L.117 J.D. [AuCoin,D.H.&Y.]
Yount, Sue Wyskiver, (BV) ....'60 '86 C.610 B.B.A. L.608 J.D. [Bricker&E.]
Yurik, Stephen B. ....'58 '85 C.475 B.A. L.912 J.D. [Lane,A.&H.]
Yurkiw, Heidi L. ....'74 '99 C.610 B.S. L.608 J.D. [Ⓐ Vorys,S.S.&P.]
Yurkiw, Jay A. ....'72 '97 C.602 B.A. L.608 J.D. [Ⓐ Porter W.M.&A.]
Yurovich, Dale R., (BV) ....'58 '84 C&L.608 B.A., J.D. 5 E. Long St.
Zaccaria, Joseph J. ....'59 '92 C.945 B.A. L.477 J.D. Asst. Atty. Gen.
Zacks, Arnold O., (AV) ....'34 '58 C&L.608 B.S., J.D. 1251 E. Broad St.
Zacks, Benjamin S., (BV) ....'60 '88 C.608 B.A. L.117 J.D. [Zacks]
Zacks Law Group, (BV) ....33 South James Road, 3rd Floor
Zadnik, Rudolph S. ....'27 '51 C&L.930 A.B., LL.B. Exec. V.P., Armstrong Mtge. Co.
Zafris, James ....'55 '89 C.197 A.B. L.309 J.D. 85 Marconi Blvd.
Zaino, Thomas M., (AV) '64 '89 C.150 B.B.A. L.608 J.D.
[McDonald H.] (⊙Cleveland)
Zaleski, Aimee A. ....'— '98 C.1028 B.A. L.608 J.D. [Ⓐ Schottenstein,Z.&D.]
Zalimeni, Gail M. ....'63 '90 C.610 B.B.A. L.608 J.D. [Ⓐ Butler,C.&D.]
Zamora, Charles ....'65 '91 C.1273 B.A. L.8 J.D. [C.Zamora]
Zamora, Charles, LLC ....85 East Gay Street Suite 200
Zancourides, Lori Maiorca ....'78 '03 C.117 B.A. L.608 J.D. [Ⓐ Squire,S.&D.]
Zapp, William A. ....'47 '72 C.608 B.A. L.117 J.D. Mas. Comr., Supr. Ct.
Zaremski, Laura M. ....'74 '00 C.473 B.S. L.117 J.D. [Ⓐ Luper,N.&L.]
Zashin & Rich Co., L.P.A., (AV) ....2242 S. Hamilton Road, Suite 101 (⊙Cleveland)
Zatezalo, Michael E., (AV) ....'49 '75 C.923 B.S.A.E. L.608 J.D. [Kegler,B.H.&R.]
Zeehandelar, Steven J., (BV) ....'54 '82 C.150 B.A. L.608 J.D. [Cheek&Z.]
Zeiger, John W., (AV) ....'47 '72 C&L.608 B.S., J.D. [Zeiger,T.&L.]
Zeiger, Matthew S. ....'76 '02 C.806 B.A. L.724 J.D. [Ⓐ Zeiger,T.&L.]

Zeiger & Carpenter
(See Carpenter & Lipps, LLP)

Zeiger, Tigges & Little LLP, (AV)
3500 Huntington Center, 41 South High Street, 43215
Telephone: 614-365-9900 Fax: 614-365-7900
Email: zeiger@lithohio.com URL: http://www.litohio.com
John W. Zeiger; Steven W. Tigges; Marion H. Little, Jr.; Stuart G. Parsell;—Bradley T. Ferrell; Matthew S. Zeiger; Kris Banvard; Darren L. Nealy; Aimee Pirone Keane. Of Counsel: Daniel R. Freytag.
See Professional Biographies, COLUMBUS, OHIO

Zelasko, Gregory J., (BV) ....'56 '81 C.528 B.S. L.117 J.D. [Ⓢ Vorys,S.S.&P.]
Zelizer, Carol, (AV) ....'50 '77 C&L.608 B.S.S.W., J.D. 2374 Bexley Park Road
Zemba, Mark J. ....'57 '86 C.363 B.A. L.117 J.D. Asst. Atty. Gen.
Zets, Brian M. ....'71 '96 C.608 B.S. L.851 J.D. [Ⓐ Schottenstein,Z.&D.]
Ziance, Scott J. ....'70 '97 C.97 B.A. L.309 J.D. [Vorys,S.S.&P.]
Zibners, Amanda Kay ....'76 '01 C.294 B.A. L.608 J.D. [Ⓐ Stein,C.]
Zieg, Robert L. '33 '62 C.1229 B.I.E. L.273 LL.B.
(adm. in IL; not adm. in OH; Pat.) Asst. Gen. Coun., Battelle Memorial Institute
Ziegler, Jon A. ....'38 '63 C.861 B.B.A. L.608 J.D. 225 E. Broad St.‡
Ziegler, Michael Sheldon ......'64 '89 C.967 B.A. L.117 J.D. State's Atty. Gen.'s Off.
Ziewacz, Elizabeth K. ....'72 '97 C.477 B.A. L.608 J.D. Asst. Atty. Gen.
Zimmer, Dale A. ....'53 '78 C.861 B.A. L.7 J.D. State Employees Relations Board
Zimmerman, Kevin J. ....'71 '99 C.97 B.S. L.117 J.D. [Ⓐ E.J.Hollern]
Zimmers, Neal F., Jr., (BV) ....'42 '67 C.207 B.A. L.273 LL.B. 37 W Broad St., Ste 1050

Zisser, Steven L. '53 '79 C.696 B.A. L.982 J.D.
Assist. Gen. Coun., Nationwide Insurance
Zola, George E. . . . . . '54 '85 C.608 B.S. L.117 J.D. [© Porter W.M.&A.]
Zox, Benjamin L., (AV) . . . . '37 '62 C.951 B.A. L.608 J.D. [© Schottenstein,Z.&D.]
Zox, Melissa L., (BV) . . . . '64 '90 C.597 B.S. L.608 J.D. [© Schottenstein,Z.&D.]
Zox, William P. . . . . '67 '92 C.951 B.A. L.608 J.D. 375 North Front Street
Zuber, Joan E. . . . . '— '57 C&L.608 B.A., J.D. 4710 Scenic Dr.‡
Zuber, Thomas J., (BV) . . . . '28 '58 C.424 B.A. L.608 J.D. 1487 W. 5th Avenue
Zuk, Nicholas W., (AV) '52 '78 C.910 B.S.B.A. L.117 J.D.
Asst. Sec. Corp. Coun., White Castle Management Co.
Zury, James C. . . . . . '68 '95 C.8 B.S. L.117 J.D. [Ⓐ Cheek&Z.]
Zwyer, David Alan . . . . '47 '77 C.97 B.A. L.608 J.D. Ohio Develop. Disabilities Council

COLUMBUS GROVE, 2,231, *Putnam Co.*

Balyeat, William B., (BV) . . . . '33 '57 C&L.608 B.S., J.D. P.O. Box 147 (⊙Lima)
Everett, Bonnie E., (BV) . . . . '51 '86 C.216 B.A. L.607 J.D. 666 Olt Rd.
Huffman, Med Z. . . . . '18 '48 C.607 A.B. L.851 J.D. 21012 Rd. 14‡
Kendall, William G., (BV) . . . . '45 '73 C&L.607 B.A., J.D. 107 N. High (⊙Lima)
Lehman, Scott C. . . . . '66 '93 C.273 B.A. L.893 J.D. United Bancshares, Inc.

CONCORD, —, *Lake Co.*

Andrews, Richard Craig . . . . '37 '69 C.930 B.A. L.1003 J.D. 7474 Auburn Road
Chesnik, Richard A. . . . . '50 '77 C.901 B.A. L.665 J.D. 7291 Players Club Dr.
Cornell, John W. '55 '81 C.999 B.A. L.665 J.D.
(adm. in PA; not adm. in OH; Pat.) 7590 Auburn Road, Suite 16J
Dalheim, Theodore J., (BV) . . . . '35 '70 C.161 B.B.A. L.1003 J.D. 10255 Cherry Hill Dr.
Dalheim, Theodore J., Jr., (BV) '62 '90 C.473 B.S.B.A. L.1003 J.D.
10255 Cherry Hill Dr.
Demeter, Richard V., (CV) '53 '84 C.318 B.A. L.607 J.D.
9944 Johnnycake Ridge Road

Gornik, David J. '54 '90 C.161 B.A. L.1003 J.D.
7103 Brightwood Drive, 44077
Telephone: 440-392-9580 Fax: 440-392-9155
Email: david@davidgornik.com URL: http://www.davidgornik.com
Corporate Law, Real Estate Law, International Business Law, Business Law, Intellectual Property Licensing, Commercial Litigation, Employment Law, Mergers and Acquisitions, Employment Contracts, Business Planning, Joint Ventures, Limited Liability Companies, Partnerships, Energy Law, Landlord Tenant, Strategic Alliances, Commercial Leasing, Consumer Law, Contracts, Buying and Selling Business.
See Professional Biographies, CONCORD, OHIO

Higgins, Charles N., Jr., (AV) '40 '68 C.103 A.B. L.893 J.D.
9930 Johnnycake Ridge Rd.
Pleska, Kenneth W., Attorney at Law . . . '55 '81 C.970 B.A. L.930 J.D. 8348 Browning Ct.
Starkey, Laurence E., (BV) . . . . '17 '46 C.930 A.B. L.161 LL.B. 7300 Hunters Trail
Sweeney, Maureen A., (BV) . . . . '61 '86 C.207 B.A. L.608 J.D. 11805 Girdled Rd.
Whitaker, William S. . . . . '56 '84 C.385 B.A. L.923 J.D. 10301 Barchester Drive

CONNEAUT, 12,485, *Ashtabula Co.*

Coxon, Gary L., (BV) . . . . '45 '71 C.203 B.S. L.608 J.D. 180 Washington St.
Fox, Vincent L., (AV) . . . . '21 '49 C.381 B.S. L.608 J.D. 25-B Drive‡
Gallagher, Luke P., (CV) . . . . '64 '90 C.313 B.A. L.851 J.D. 365 Main St.
Harris, Thomas E. . . . . '57 '82 C.8 B.S. L.7 J.D. Mun. J.
Iarocci, Nicholas A., (CV) . . . . '63 '89 C.473 B.S. L.851 J.D. [Iarocci]
Iarocci Law Firm, The, Ltd., (CV) . . . . 213 Washington St.
Lafferty, Charles N., (BV) . . . . '50 '77 C.62 B.A. L.607 J.D. 365 Main St.
Lamer, Lori Beth, (BV) . . . . '57 '83 C.381 B.S. L.607 J.D. [L.B.Lamer]
Lamer, Lori B., (BV) . . . . 119 S. Ridge Road E.
Naylor, Robert E., (BV) . . . . '47 '72 C&L.930 B.A., J.D. P.O. Box 203
Thayer, Walter E., (BV) . . . . '25 '50 L.607 J.D. 171 Broad Street

CONOVER, 1,078, *Miami Co.*

Lomason, Philip E., (BVⓉ) '41 '68 C.475 B.S. L.213 J.D.
(adm. in MI; not adm. in OH) 7890 N. Bollinger Rd.

COPLEY, 14,735, *Summit Co.*

Cooper, Angela T. . . . . '54 '78 C.930 B.A. L.831 J.D. 2523 Lawnshire Drive
Gillis, Eugene T. . . . . '38 '79 C.85 B.A. L.1206 J.D. 190 Montrose West Ave., Ste. 100
Green, Frederick J. . . . . '45 '90 C&L.8 B.S., J.D. 1627 Sunnyacres Rd.
Loucas, George E., (AV) . . . . '59 '85 C.923 B.S.Phar. L.1003 J.D. 1973 Katherine's Lane
McGown, Daniel J., Sr., (BV) . . . . '46 '77 C.8 B.A. L.7 J.D. P.O. Box 4375
Sandel, Kevin S. . . . . '69 '95 C.473 B.A. L.8 J.D. Progressive Ins. Co.
Schwartz, Brenda S. . . . . '68 '94 C.608 B.A. L.8 J.D. 4690 Remington Avenue
Shama, Cynthia . . . . '53 '89 C&L.8 B.S., J.D. 2414 Frashure Dr.

CORTLAND, 6,830, *Trumbull Co.*

Campbell, Thomas A., (BV) . . . . '59 '89 C.381 B.A. L.7 J.D. Co. Ct.
Duff, Leo W. . . . . '10 '49 C&L.980 J.D. 537 Sycamore Trail
Gessner, George E., (BV) . . . . '45 '69 C.318 B.A. L.8 J.D. [Gessner&P.] ⊙
Gessner, John F., (AV) . . . . '19 '54 C.318 B.A. L.980 J.D. [Gessner&P.] ⊙
Gessner & Platt Co., L.P.A., (AV) . . . . 212 W. Main St. (⊙Warren)
Grundy, John C., (BV) . . . . '59 '87 C.935 B.A. L.7 J.D. [J.C.Grundy]
Grundy, John C., Co., LPA, (BV) . . . . P.O. Box 591
Platt, Robert M., Jr., (BV) . . . . '47 '74 C.631 B.A. L.7 J.D. [Gessner&P.] ⊙
Platt, Robert M., Sr., (BV) . . . . '24 '54 C&L.980 J.D. [Gessner&P.] ⊙
Polak, Jenna Gessner . . . . '73 '98 C.610 B.A. L.7 J.D. [Gessner&P.]
Rouzzo, David Thomas . . . . '67 '01 C.980 B.A. L.8 J.D. [D.T.Rouzzo]
Rouzzo, David T., Co., LPA . . . . 3333 Niles Cortland Rd. N.E.
Zimmer, Fred C., (AV) . . . . '29 '59 C&L.608 B.Sc., J.D. 306 Tournament Trail‡

COSHOCTON, * 11,682, *Coshocton Co.*

Battista, Anthony A., III . . . . '72 '99 C.62 B.A. L.989 J.D. Asst. Pros. Atty.
Baxter, Terrence J. . . . . '55 '91 C.927 B.A. L.200 J.D. 239 N. 4th St.
Blanchard, Van, (AV) . . . . '26 '53 C.610 A.B. L.477 J.D. 402 Main St.
Burns, David W., (AV) . . . . '43 '68 C.602 A.B. L.150 J.D. [Pomerene,B.&S.]
Carrick, Eleanor S. . . . . '11 '40 C.611 A.B. L.989 LL.B. 445 N. Whitewoman St.‡
Coffman, Robert W. . . . . '39 '64 C.611 A.B. L.608 J.D. 75 Kensington Rd.‡
Evans, Richard I. . . . . '46 '71 C&L.608 B.A., J.D. Com. Pleas J.
Finney, Jas. W. . . . . '24 '53 C&L.608 B.S., J.D. 409 1/2 Main St.‡
Foster, Susan Metz . . . . '57 '84 C.610 B.A. L.930 J.D. Mag. J.
France, Timothy L., (BV) . . . . '55 '81 C.607 B.A. L.608 J.D. 442 Chestnut St.

Frase, Weir, Baker & McCullough Co., L.P.A., (AV)
305 Main Street, 43812-1582
Telephone: 740-622-6464 Fax: 740-622-8107
Email: law@fwbm.com URL: http://www.fwbm.com
Milan E. Frase (1919-1983); Eugene R. Weir (1930-1997); Robert Quincy Baker, III (1944-2002); Michael P. McCullough; Robert E. Weir.

(This Listing Continued)

Frase, Weir, Baker & McCullough Co., L.P.A. (Continued)
Personal Injury, Negligence, Civil Litigation, Criminal Defense, Probate, Estate Planning, Business Law, Business Planning, Corporate Law, Real Estate Law, Family and Taxation.
Representative Clients: Pretty Products, Inc. (Div. of Lancaster Colony Corp.); Clow Water Systems Corporation, Div. of McWane, Inc.; The Beach Company; Coshocton County Agricultural Society, Inc.; Primary Vision Care, Inc.; Baker's Management, Inc.; Apache Aggregate & Paving Co.; Hathaway, Inc.
Approved Attorneys for: The Ohio Bar Title Insurance Co.
Reference: Bank One, Coshocton.

Hostetler, David L. . . . . '49 '76 C.381 B.G.S. L.7 J.D. Mun. J.
Johnson, Antonia K. . . . . '40 '84 C.383 A.B.J. L.8 J.D. Mag.
Leech, Thomas B., (AV) . . . . '18 '46 C.473 A.B. L.309 LL.B. [Leech,S.&P.]
Leech, Scherbel & Peddicord, (AV) . . . . 240 S. 4th St.
Lyons, Christie M. . . . . '74 '99 C&L.608 B.A., J.D. 309 Main St.
Manning, Michael D., (BV) . . . . '49 '75 C.381 B.A. L.607 J.D. [Owens&M.]
Mathay, Charles E. . . . . '35 '72 C.999 B.M.E. L.1003 J.D. [C.E.Mathay]
Mathay, Charles E., Co., L.P.A. . . . . 1687 Evergreen Park Dr.
McCoy, Carl, Attorney at Law
(See Newark)
McCullough, Michael P., (AV) . . . . '46 '74 C.918 B.A. L.188 J.D. [Frase,W.B.&M.]
Nelson, Christie M. L. . . . . '74 '99 C&L.608 B.A., J.D. [Ⓐ Pomerene,B.&S.]
Owens, William M., (BV) . . . . '47 '72 C&L.608 B.A., J.D. [Owens&M.]
Owens & Manning, (BV) . . . . 413 Main Street, 2nd Floor
Parkhill, Don R. . . . . '58 '84 C.608 B.S. L.851 J.D. P.O. Box 1030‡
Peddicord, Randall H., (BV) . . . . '53 '82 C.49 B.A. L.201 J.D. [Leech,S.&P.]
Pierce, C. Fenning . . . . '47 '73 C.611 B.A. L.880 J.D. Com. Pleas J.
Pomerene, Burns & Skelton, (AV) . . . . 309 Main Street
Rodgers, Michael A. . . . . '59 '85 C.608 B.A. L.150 J.D. 1322 South 6th★
Scherbel, Paul R., (AV) . . . . '48 '73 C&L.117 B.S., J.D. [Leech,S.&P.]
Skelton, James R., (BV) . . . . '66 '92 C&L.201 B.S., J.D. [Pomerene,B.&S.]
Skelton, Joseph R., (AV) . . . . '49 '74 C.602 B.A. L.8 J.D. [Pomerene,B.&S.]
Skelton, Robert A., (BV) . . . . '64 '90 C&L.201 B.A., J.D. [Pomerene,B.&S.]
Weir, Robert E., (AV) . . . . '58 '83 C.970 B.A. L.930 J.D. [Frase,W.B.&M.]
Wirth, David
(See Columbus)

COVINGTON, 2,603, *Miami Co.*

O'Donnell, James Roger . . . . '34 '66 C.967 B.A. L.607 J.D. 9 North High Street
Sicking, Albert G., Jr. . . . . '35 '60 C.201 B.S. L.150 J.D. I.R.S.

CRESTLINE, 5,088, *Crawford Co.*

Berger, J. Sebastian . . . . '78 '03 C.610 B.A. L.8 J.D. [Ⓐ Garner&B.]
Berger, John W., (BV) . . . . '40 '66 C.610 A.B. L.607 J.D. [Garner&B.]
Garner, Nelson, (AV) . . . . '28 '56 C.97 B.A. L.608 J.D. [Garner&B.]
Garner & Berger, (AV) . . . . 211 N. Seltzer St.

CUMBERLAND, 318, *Guernsey Co.*

Howard, Patrick J. . . . . '48 '89 C.980 B.A. L.8 J.D. [Howard]
Howard Law Office, The . . . . 425 Carl St.

CURTICE, —, *Lucas & Ottawa Cos.*

Cottrell, Ernest E. . . . . '26 '53 C&L.851 B.A., LL.B. Ref. Dom. Rel.

CUYAHOGA FALLS, 49,374, *Summit Co.*

Barrett, Gerald Van . . . . '36 '85 L.8 J.D. 1772 State Road
Baum, Richard M. . . . . '28 '63 C.631 B.A. L.7 LL.B. 2282 Parkview Drive
Berkowitz, Richard E. . . . . '71 '96 C.273 B.A. L.7 J.D. [Berkowitz-Folk]
Berkowitz-Folk . . . . 113 Portage Trail
Bierce, James M. . . . . '31 '65 C.8 L.7 LL.B. Mun. J.
Bowen, Lisa R. '68 '93 C.177 B.A. L.190 J.D.
(adm. in IA; not adm. in OH) Proto Circuit, Inc.
Brouse, Karen H. . . . . '58 '02 C.980 B.A. L.7 J.D. [Brouse]
Brouse Law Office . . . . 1013 Portage Trail, Suite 7
Cacioppo, Mary . . . . '22 '45 C.381 L.7 LL.B. Ct. of App. J.
Campbell, David A., Jr. . . . . '48 '74 C&L.8 B.S., J.D. Gen. Coun., Alside Inc.
Cole, Leza A. . . . . '— '02 C.528 B.A. L.7 J.D. [Ⓐ M.H.Kreiner]
Dean, Lisa Carey . . . . '70 '99 C.381 B.A. L.989 J.D. [Gibson&L.]
DeMarco, J. Christopher . . . . '54 '92 C.381 B.Mus. L.8 J.D. 431 Stow St.
Durr, Susan T., (BV) . . . . '58 '83 C.8 B.A. L.7 J.D. 2674 N. Haven Blvd.
Endress, Ned R., (BV) . . . . '18 '54 C.8 B.S. L.7 J.D. 2251 Front St.‡
Eshelman, C. Richard, (BV) . . . . '37 '68 C.656 B.S. L.7 J.D. [Eshelman] ⊙
Eshelman Legal Group, (BV)
263 Portage Trail, Ext. W. (⊙Canton, Cleveland, Youngstown)
Evans, Diane K. . . . . '54 '97 C.8 B.S.B.A. L.7 J.D. 2253 Hoch Dr.
Falcone, Vincent J., (BV) . . . . '55 '80 C.8 B.A. L.7 J.D. 2233 4th St.
Farine, Cheryl . . . . '51 '88 C.923 B.S. L.161 J.D. 2020 Front St. (Pat.)
Finan, Christine D., (BV) . . . . '58 '91 C.8 B.A. L.7 J.D. 2674 N. Haven Blvd.
Folk, Alexander R. . . . . '66 '96 C.381 B.A. L.7 J.D. [Berkowitz-Folk]
Frisby, John D., Jr., (BV) . . . . '48 '80 C.8 B.A. L.7 J.D. P.O. Box 374
Froble, Ronald F., (BV) . . . . '41 '78 C.381 B.A. L.8 J.D. Ref. Mun. Ct.
Gibson, Kenneth L., (BV) . . . . '53 '79 C.675 B.A. L.178 J.D. [Gibson&L.]
Gibson & Lowry, (AV) . . . . 234 Portage Trail
Ginther, Sharyl W., (BV) . . . . '50 '91 C.473 B.S.Ed. L.8 J.D. [Gibson&L.]
Graham, Kent M. . . . . '49 '82 C.8 B.A. L.7 J.D. Mag., Com. Pleas Ct. J.
Haring, Brian J., (BV) . . . . '71 '99 C.473 B.A. L.8 J.D. [Ⓐ Hoover,H.&H.]
Herrnstein, John M., (BV) . . . . '57 '83 C&L.608 B.S., J.D. [Hoover,H.&H.]
Heydorn, Robert W., (BV) . . . . '46 '75 C.8 B.A. L.7 J.D. [Hoover,H.&H.]
Hoover, Kim R., (BV) . . . . '54 '79 C.446 B.A. L.7 J.D. Mun. J.
Hoover, Orval R., (AV) . . . . '30 '59 C.8 B.A. L.930 J.D. [Hoover,H.&H.]
Hoover, Heydorn & Herrnstein Co., L.P.A., (AV) . . . . 527 Portage Trail
Hosey, Richard A. . . . . '51 '77 C.8 B.A. L.7 J.D. 2875 12th St.
Jones, Dwayne K., (BV) . . . . '61 '87 C.610 B.A. L.7 J.D. City Law Dept.
Jones, John F. . . . . '22 '56 C.585 B.S. L.7 J.D. 2724 Cedar Hill Rd. (Pat.)
Kaess, Warren V. . . . . '10 '55 C.8 A.B. L.7 LL.B. 1845 12th St.‡
Kaufman, Craig I. . . . . '56 '81 C.477 B.B.A. L.472 J.D. 3773 State Rd
Kaufman, Donald L. . . . . '31 '55 C&L.608 B.S., LL.B. Pres. & CEO, Alside, Inc.
Keith, George G., (BV) . . . . '54 '83 C.381 B.A. L.1003 J.D. 135 Portage Trail
Kennedy, Geoffrey W. . . . '52 '80 C.399 B.A. L.7 J.D. Dir. of Law, City of Cuyahoga Falls
Kisling, Gary W., (BV) . . . . '51 '77 C.352 B.A. L.8 J.D. [Eshelman]
Kreiner, Margaret H. . . . . '44 '85 C.381 B.S. L.8 J.D. [M.H.Kreiner]
Kreiner, Margaret H., The Law Office of . . . . 2020 Front St., Ste. 202
LaPorte, Mary Clare Cullen . . . . '50 '85 C.876 B.A. L.7 J.D. 2754 Front Street, Suite 114
Larko, John, (BV) . . . . '45 '73 C.665 B.S.E.E. L.8 J.D. 234 Portage Trail
Learner, Edward C., (CV) . . . . '55 '84 C&L.8 B.A., J.D. 1200 Portage Trail, W.
Leipply, Gerald R., (BV) . . . . '34 '59 C.313 A.B. L.477 J.D. [Leipply]
Leipply Law Office, (BV) . . . . 2101 Front St.

Lowry, Randal A., (AV) .... '51 '76 C.472 B.B.A. L.7 J.D. [Gibson&L.]
Malyuk, Michael A., (BV) .... '46 '75 C&L.8 B.S., J.D. 2020 Front St., Ste. 207
McDowall, Robert H., (AV) .... '30 '62 C.381 B.S. L.7 J.D. 130 Portage Trail
Montalto, Gayle M. .... '56 '90 C.207 B.A. L.8 J.D. 1708 8th Street
Moore, Robert S., (BV) .... '30 '61 C.381 L.7 LL.B. 111 Stow Ave.
Moore, William T., (AV) .... '24 '52 C.381 L.7 LL.B. 3084 E. Edgerton Rd.‡
Moran, Michael J., (AV) .... '52 '78 C.645 B.A. L.7 J.D. [Gibson&L.]
Nehrer, John A., (Co., L.P.A.), (BV) .... '26 '66 C.381 B.S. L.7 J.D. 111 Stow Ave.
Nestico, Alberto R. .... '— '99 C.035 B.A. L.1325 J.D. [A Eshelman]
Oldham, Robert L. .... '45 '71 C.8 B.S. L.7 J.D. 126 Portage Tr.
Pagel, Thomas R. .... '51 '79 C.8 B.A. L.7 J.D. Dir. of Mktg., Dodson-Stilson, Inc.
Pike, William B. .... '28 '58 C.381 B.S. L.1003 J.D. Mun. J.
Redick, Robert W. .... '63 '99 C.473 B.A. L.8 J.D. [Eshelman]
Reidy, Jerome G., (BV) .... '48 '74 C.8 B.A. L.7 J.D. [Gibson&L.]
Rogachefsky, Barbara J. .... '69 '97 C.823 B.A. L.7 J.D. [© Berkowitz-Folk]
Schwartz, Steven J., (AV) .... '45 '73 C&L.8 B.A., J.D. Mag., Mun. Ct.

Shryock & Morrison
(See Wickliffe)

Shunk, Laura Funk .... '57 '83 2020 Front Street, Suite 307
Snoderly, John, (BV) .... '29 '59 C.8 B.A. L.7 J.D. 1037 Curtis Ave.
Terilla, J. Anthony, (BV) .... '45 '74 C.705 B.A. L.7 J.D. [Gibson&L.]
Thomason, Jacqueline, (CV) .... '54 '89 C.824 B.A. L.8 J.D. 2525 State Rd.
Varga, Michael J. .... '69 '95 C.381 B.S. L.7 J.D. 132 Ravenshollow Drive
Vasvari, Thomas M., (BV) .... '64 '90 C.980 B.A. L.930 J.D. [A Eshelman]
Weick, David C., (BV) .... '58 '84 C.930 B.A. L.7 J.D. [Gibson&L.]
Weick, Paul A., (AV) .... '30 '54 C.976 B.A. L.930 LL.B. 234 Portage Trail
Weinberger, Mark S., (BV) .... '60 '84 C&L.8 B.A., J.D. P.O. Box 535
Weinberger, Michael A., (BV) .... '46 '72 C&L.8 B.S., J.D. 234 Portage Trail
Williams, Glen A. .... '31 '61 C.679 B.S. L.7 J.D. 1031 Curtis Ave.‡
Wittbrod, Harry J. C. .... '61 '96 C.97 B.S.B.A. L.8 J.D. 234 Portage Trail
Woodside, Robert N., (BV) .... '43 '72 C.62 B.A. L.124 J.D. Cuyahoga Falls Mun. Ct.
Zerrusen, Sandra Kelly .... '74 '99 C.363 B.S. L.8 J.D. [A Gibson&L.]

DALTON, 1,605, *Wayne Co.*

Kauffman, Roland B., (CV) .... '54 '82 C.288 B.A. L.607 J.D. 40 W. Main Street

DAMASCUS, —, *Columbiana & Mahoning Cos.*

Bandy, Kenneth L., (CV) .... '48 '74 C&L.608 B.A., J.D. 28787 Salem-Alliance Rd.

DANVILLE, 1,104, *Knox Co.*

Busenburg, J. Robt. .... '27 '52 C.385 A.B. L.309 LL.B. 29079 Walhonding Rd.‡

DAYTON, * 166,179, *Montgomery Co.*

Abramson & O'Connell, LLC
(See Columbus)

Ackermann, John R., Jr. .... '57 '82 C.201 B.A. L.477 J.D. Law V. P., NCR Corp.
Adams, Jay Allen .... '73 '00 C.265 B.A. L.201 J.D. 424 Patterson Rd.
Adams, Karen R., (BV) .... '59 '91 C.108 B.S. L.201 M.B.A. [Chernesky,H.&K.]
Adkins, Dennis J., (BV) .... '55 '86 C.201 B.S. L.1340 J.D. [Altick&C.]
Adkinson, Patrick K., (BV) .... '55 '80 C.611 B.A. L.851 J.D. [Adkinson&Assoc.]
Adkinson & Associates, L.L.C., (BV) .... 4244 Indian Ripple Rd.
Adler, Deborah J., (BV) .... '56 '82 C.201 B.S. L.200 J.D. [Altick&C.]
Ahearn, Todd Matthew, (BV) .... '73 '98 C.250 B.S. L.201 J.D. Pros. Off.
Albert, Jeffrey P. .... '46 '71 C.608 B.S. L.930 J.D. 4403 N. Main St.
Allbery, Charles F., III, (AV) .... '51 '78 C.608 B.A. L.201 J.D. [Allbery C.F.]

Allbery Cross Fogarty, (AV)
137 North Main Street, Suite 500, 45402-1770
Telephone: 937-228-5912 Fax: 937-228-0671
Email: allbery@allberycrossfogarty.com
Charles F. Allbery, III; James E. Cross (1935-2003); Canice J. (C.J.) Fogarty. Associate: Gregory M. Gantt.
General Civil Practice, Environmental Law, Zoning, Planning and Land Use, Real Estate, Condominium, Probate, Estate Planning, Elder Law, Corporation Law, Personal Injury, Foreclosure Law, Bankruptcy Law, Commercial, Family and Criminal Law. Trials and Appeals in all Courts.

Altick & Corwin Co., L.P.A., (AV) BR
1700 One Dayton Centre, One South Main Street, 45402
Telephone: 937-223-1201 Fax: 937-223-5100
Email: info@altickcorwin.com URL: http://www.altickcorwin.com
Hugh H. Altick (1905-1990); Robert K. Corwin (1913-1998); Robert N. Farquhar; Marshall D. Ruchman; Dennis J. Adkins; Philip B. Herron; Deborah J. Adler; Stephen M. McHugh; Scott A. Liberman; Donald K. Scott; Dalma C. Grandjean; Peter R. Certo; Jonathan B. Freeman; Matthew D. Stokely;—David E. Larson; Brent A. Crane; Julie Cope Hammond; Lynne M. Fleming. Of Counsel: David L. Hall; Adele M. Riley.
General Practice. Administrative, Bankruptcy, Business, Collections, Condominium, Creditors' Rights, Criminal, Commercial Law, Decedent's Estates, Employee Benefits, Elder Law, Employment, Estate Planning, Family Law, Immigration and Naturalization, Insurance Defense, Labor Relations, Local Government, Military Law, Municipal, Personal Injury, Probate, Products Liability, Real Estate, Social Security, Taxation, Workers' Compensation, Zoning.
Representative Clients: City of Centerville; City of Beavercreek; City of Oxford; The Miami Conservancy District; Miami Valley Cable Council; Woodland Cemetery Assn.; City of Trotwood; City of Riverside; City of Oakwood.

See Professional Biographies, DAYTON, OHIO

Ambrose, James T., Law Offices of, (BV) '48 '75 C.201 B.A. L.607 J.D.
130 W. 2nd St.
Ames, Arthur A., (BV) .... '44 '69 C.608 B.A. L.607 J.D. [Ames&A.]
Ames & Armstrong, (BV) .... 1311 Talbott Tower
Amos, John Coleman, (CV) .... '72 '00 C.63 B.S. L.923 J.D. Co. Pros. Off.
Andary, Fred J., Law Offices of, (BV) '25 '50 C.201 L.150 LL.B.
1616 First National Plz.
Anderson, Bradley D. .... '65 '93 C.970 B.A. L.477 J.D. [A Faruki I.&C.]
Andreozzi, Louis J., (AV) '59 '84 C.705 B.A. L.776 J.D.
(adm. in NJ; not adm. in OH)
President and CEO, N. Amer. Legal Markets, Lexis-Nexis Grp.
Angelo, Thomas, III, (BV) .... '58 '83 C&L.201 B.S., J.D. [© Flanagan,L.H.&S.]
Anglin, Richard D., II, (BV) .... '59 '86 C.1208 B.S. L.201 J.D. 1516 Stanley Ave.
Anspach, Douglas C. .... '— '01 C.602 B.A. L.945 J.D. [A Coolidge,W.W.&L.]
Apocotos, T. Gregory .... '50 '81 C.549 B.A. L.464 J.D. 2000 Courthouse Plz., N.E.
Arkenberg, Kenneth J. .... '26 '53 C.201 B.S. L.150 J.D. 4133 N. Dixie Dr.
Armanini, Debra Bonifas, (BV) .... '56 '82 C&L.201 B.S., J.D. 301 W. 3rd St.
Armanini, Joseph S., (BV) '55 '82 C.608 B.S. L.201 J.D.
V.P. & Gen. Coun., BellSouth Corp./L.M. Berry & Co.
Armstrong, James S., (BV) .... '52 '78 C.980 B.S. L.161 J.D. [Ames&A.]
Arnold, Gordon D., (AV) .... '50 '75 C.473 B.A. L.7 J.D. [Freund,F.&A.]
Arnold, Michael F. .... '68 '03 C.446 B.S. L.724 J.D. [A Surdyk,D.&T.]
Arnovitz, Theodore M., (BV) .... '32 '60 C.608 B.S. L.607 J.D. 2324 Stanley Ave.
Arntz, Matthew Ryan, (BV) .... '55 '82 C.388 B.A. L.201 J.D. P.O. Box 4235
Arquilla, Thomas J., (BV) .... '59 '84 C&L.201 B.S., J.D. 1 Wyoming Street
Arthur, Richard Paul .... '59 '86 C&L.607 B.S., J.D. [R.Arthur]
Arthur, Richard, Law Office of .... 1634 S. Smithville Road
Ary, William R., (BVⓉ) .... '39 '64 C&L.861 LL.B. Fifth Third Ctr.
Attkisson, Kevin W. .... '64 '97 C.1111 B.A. L.200 J.D. [A Dyer,G.M.&S.]
Auman, Gary W., (BV) .... '47 '76 C.421 B.E.E. L.608 J.D. [Dunlevey,M.&F.]
Austin, Matthew D. .... '— '03 C.608 B.A. L.201 J.D. [A Coolidge,W.W.&L.]
Axtell, Stephen J. .... '63 '88 C.712 B.S. L.1044 J.D. [Thompson H.]
Bach, Michelle D., (CV) .... '— '95 C.473 B.A. L.665 J.D. [A Coolidge,W.W.&L.]
Bacon, Steven E., (BV) .... '68 '92 C.937 B.A. L.150 J.D. [Breidenbach,O.&B.]
Badonsky, Deborah K. '48 '73 C.879 B.A. L.851 J.D.
Prof., Sinclair Community College
Baggott, Horace W., (AV) .... '06 '29 C&L.608 J.D. 600 Schenck Ave.‡

Baggott, Thomas M., (AV) '43 '71 C.608 B.A. L.607 J.D.
130 West Second Street, Suite 2103, 45402
Telephone: 937-461-8800 Fax: 937-461-8818
Email: tom@baggottlaw.com URL: http://www.baggottlaw.com
Wills, Probate, Trusts and Estates, Estate Planning, Guardianship, Adoption Law, Conservatorship, Small Business Corporations Law.

See Professional Biographies, DAYTON, OHIO

Bailey, Dennis L., (BV) .... '47 '82 C.473 B.A. L.201 J.D. 14 West Fourth Street
Bailey, Kenneth L., (AV) .... '34 '60 C&L.608 B.S., J.D. [K.L.Bailey]

Bailey Cavalieri LLC, (AV)
Kettering Tower, Suite 2310, 40 North Main Street, 45423-0001 ⊙
Telephone: 937-223-4701 Fax: 937-223-0170
URL: http://www.baileycavalieri.com
Principal of Firm: Robert B. Berner.
General Civil and Trial Practice. Director and Officer Liability, Antitrust, Banking, Bankruptcy and Commercial Transactions, Corporate, Corporate Financing, Creditors Remedies, Environmental, Employee Benefits and ERISA, Estate Planning, Trust, Probate, Intellectual Property, Internet and E-Commerce, Labor and Employment, Products Liability, Public Utility, Real Estate, Finance, Securities and Taxation Law. Appellate, Communications, Energy Deregulation, Health Care, Insurance, Mergers and Acquisitions, Professional Liability, Retail and Catalog Law, Technology and Science.
Columbus, Ohio Office: Suite 2100, One Columbus, 10 West Broad Street. 43215-3422. Telephone: 614-221-3155. Fax: 614-221-0479.

See Professional Biographies, DAYTON, OHIO

Bailey, Kenneth L., Co., LPA, (AV) .... 226 Talbott Tower
Bair, Erin A. .... '78 '04 C&L.608 B.S., J.D. [A Faruki I.&C.]
Baker, Theresa A., (BV) .... '55 '92 C.201 B.S. L.117 J.D. 120 W. 2nd St., Ste. 1700
Baldwin, Bradley S., (CV) .... '70 '98 C.823 B.S. L.200 J.D. [Copley V.&B.]
Ballard, Tracey L. .... '70 '98 C.788 B.A. L.608 J.D. Asst. Co. Prosecutor
Ballato, Lynnette Pisone, (BV) .... '70 '95 C.25 B.A. L.607 J.D. [Subashi,W.&B.]
Baller, Wayne D. .... '51 '77 C.276 B.S. L.472 J.D. 425 Kramer Rd
Balmer, Joseph E., III, (BV) ...... '63 '89 C.1365 B.A. L.608 J.D. [Holzfaster,C.M.&M.]
Barbato, Matthew J. .... '75 '03 C.973 B.A. L.201 J.D. [A Rion,R.&R.]
Barnes, Kevin R. .... '67 '94 C.329 B.A. L.150 J.D. Mag.
Barney, William H., III, (BV) .... '51 '77 C.855 B.A. L.201 J.D. [Dunlevey,M.&F.]
Bart, David R. .... '45 '71 C.201 B.A. L.150 J.D. 6776 Loop Rd.
Bartlett, Robert P., Jr., (AV) .... '38 '64 C.207 B.A. L.608 J.D. [© Faruki I.&C.]
Bates, Betty Bartels .... '25 '81 C.608 B.A. L.201 J.D. 1140 Ridgeway Road‡
Baxley, Gregory A. .... '62 '93 C.734 B.S. L.602 J.D. 2373 Edgewater Drive
Bazelak, Leonard J., (BV) .... '66 '94 C.197 A.B. L.201 J.D. [Freund,F.&A.]
Beasley, Jesse B. .... '54 '85 C.893 B.A. L.245 J.D. 303 Hacker Road
Beasley, John H., (BV) '47 '76
C.870 B.S. L.818 J.D. Environ. Coun., MeadWestvaco Corp.
Beck, Jonathon L. .... '76 '02 C.436 B.A. L.201 J.D. [A Young&A.]
Becker, Mabel L. .... '35 '80 C.201 B.S. L.200 J.D. 303 West Second Avenue‡
Beckmann, Richard J., (AV) .... '48 '74 C.150 B.B.A. L.273 J.D. [Dinsmore&S.]
Behnke, Stephen D. .... '75 '00 C.932 B.A. L.201 J.D. [A Botros&S.]
Beiting, Mary Ann .... '64 '91 C.973 B.S.B.A. L.150 J.D. LEXIS-NEXIS
Bell, Robin Olinger .... '64 '89 C&L.150 B.A., J.D. 2000 Courthouse Plaza, N.E.
Bennett, John F. .... '72 '02 C.755 B.A. L.150 J.D. [A Porter W.M.&A.]
Bennington, C. Christopher .... '79 '04 C.532 B.A. L.608 J.D. [A Young&A.]
Bennington, Christopher .... '51 '76 C.1208 B.A. L.117 J.D. [Spalla&S.]
Benton, Julia McNeil .... '63 '89 C.329 B.B.A. L.608 J.D. City Atty.
Bergen, Van '47 '72 C.390 A.B. L.262 J.D.
(adm. in NJ; not adm. in OH) Proj. Mgr., LEXIS-NEXIS
Berger, Robert N., (BV) .... '38 '70 C.201 B.S. L.1340 J.D. 111 W. First St.
Berman, Neil M. .... '70 '95 C.473 B.A. L.851 J.D. 120 West Third Street
Bernal-Olson, Patricia '64 '98 C.752 B.A. L.200 J.D.
Staff Atty., University of Dayton (Legal Department)
Berner, Robert B., (BV) .... '59 '84 C.347 B.S. L.117 J.D. [Bailey C.]
Bernstein, Elaine S., (BV) .... '45 '89 C.999 B.Sc. L.201 J.D. 130 W. 2nd St., Ste. 1818

Berry, Thomas D., (BV) '50 '78 C&L.608 B.Sc., J.D.
1839 East Stroop Road, 45429
Telephone: 937-294-7398 Fax: 937-294-6812
Email: 110968@msn.com URL: http://www.daytonbankruptcylawyer.com
Probate, Wills, Bankruptcy, Consumer Bankruptcy, Chapter 7 and Chapter 13.

See Professional Biographies, DAYTON, OHIO

Beyer, James E. .... '67 '95 C.150 B.S. L.30 J.D. [Dinsmore&S.] (Pat.)
Beyer, Martin A., (BV) .... '66 '92 C.317 B.A. L.201 J.D. [Sebaly,S.&D.]
Beyoglides, Harry G., Jr., (BV) .... '50 '78 C.608 B.S. L.200 J.D. [Johnson,D.B.&L.]
Bhat, Aniruddha D. .... '— '01 C.477 B.A. L.124 J.D. [A Coolidge,W.W.&L.]
Biegel, Alan A., (BV) .... '41 '67 C.201 B.A. L.1340 J.D. [A.A.Biegel]
Biegel, Alan A., Co., L.P.A., (BV) .... 5975 Kentshire Dr.
Bieser, Irvin G., Jr., (AV) .... '41 '66 C&L.309 A.B., LL.B. [Bieser,G.&L.]

Bieser, Greer & Landis, LLP, (AV) BR
400 National City Center, 6 North Main Street, 45402-1908
Telephone: 937-223-3277 Fax: 937-223-6339
Email: biesergreer.com URL: http://www.biesergreer.com
Members of Firm: Irvin G. Bieser (1902-1989); Rowan A. Greer, Jr. (1907-1967); Robert K. Landis (1915-1991); Charles D. Shook; Edward L. Shank; David C. Greer; Irvin G. Bieser, Jr.; Leo F. Krebs; Howard Penn Krisher, II; Michael W. Krumholtz; John F. Haviland, Jr.; David P. Williamson; James H. Greer; Charles F. Shane; Joseph C. Oehlers; Carla J. Morman; James P. Fleisher; Karen T. Dunlevey (Certified Specialist in Labor and Employment Law, Ohio State Bar Association). Associates: Joseph L. Feller; Gretchen M. Treherne; Jennifer L. Stueve; John D. Bodin.
General Civil Practice, Trial Practice, Business Litigation, Professional Liability Defense, Personal Injury Defense, Products Liability Defense, Corporate Law, Employment Law, Commercial Law, Probate, Tax Law, White Collar Criminal Defense, Arbitration, Mediation.
Representative Clients: Dayton Power & Light Co.; Miami Valley Regional Transit Authority; Kettering Medical Center; The Dayton Foundation; Greater Dayton Public Television, Inc.; Medical Protective Co.; St. Paul Insurance Co.; Continental Loss Adjusting Services; Motorists Insurance Co.; National City Bank.

See Professional Biographies, DAYTON, OHIO

Bilott, Raymond L., (BV) .... '35 '83 C.570 B.S.M.E. L.200 J.D. 3910 Pepper Tree Ct.
Birt, James E., (BV) .... '36 '63 C&L.608 B.S., LL.B. 111 W 1st St.
Bissonnette, Brett R. .... '— '03 C.1430 B.B.A. L.607 J.D. [A Hochman&P.]

Blackburn, R. Scott, (AV) .... '— '77 C.610 B.B.A. L.851 J.D. [Coolidge,W.W.&L.]
Blackwell, Karen J., (AV) .... '47 '76 C&L.608 B.A., J.D. 9443 Springboro Pike
Blair, Amy R. .... '75 '01 C.473 B.A. L.608 J.D. [A Rogers&G.]
Blake, Jonathan I. '72 '01 C.608 B.A. L.179 J.D.
Opers. Coun., Bellsouth Corp./L.M. Berry & Co.
Blaschak, Thomas R. .... '67 '92 C.665 B.A. L.200 J.D. [Blaschak]
Blaschak Law Office .... 1692 Woodman Dr.
Blasik-Miller, Susan, (AV) .... '59 '84 C&L.201 B.A., J.D. [Freund,F.&A.]
Blatt, Shawn M., (BV) .... '64 '91 C.10 B.S. L.201 J.D. [Freund,F.&A.]
Blattner, J. Wray, (AV) .... '55 '80 C.207 B.A. L.276 J.D. [Thompson H.]
Block, Barry M., (AV) .... '49 '75 C.674 A.B. L.477 J.D. [Thompson H.]

Bloomfield, Roger E., (AV) '45 '74 C.967 B.S.B.A. L.930 J.D.
P.O. Box 9218, 45409-9218
Telephone: 937-438-5310
Email: bloomfield_law@att.net
Business Law, Nonprofit and Charitable Organizations, Taxation, Trusts and Estates, Wills and Probate, Real Estate.
Reference: Fifth Third Bank.
See Professional Biographies, DAYTON, OHIO

Blucher, Jonathan P. '49 '74 C&L.94 B.A., J.D.
(adm. in NY; not adm. in OH) 3916 Shagbark Ln.‡
Blumenthal, Gary M., (AV) .... '49 '74 C.473 B.S. L.608 J.D. [Horenstein,N.&B.]
Bly, L. Michael, (BV) .... '63 '89 C.646 B.S. L.201 J.D. [Pickrel,S.&E.]
Bodin, John D. .... '78 '03 C.967 B.A. L.851 J.D. [A Bieser,G.&L.]
Boesch, Charles H. .... '11 '34 C&L.201 A.B., LL.B. 531 Belmonte Park N.‡
Bogin, Asher, (AV) .... '27 '50 [Bogin P.E.S.&S.] ‡

Bogin Patterson Ellis Slaton & Stump LLP, (AV) BR
1200 Talbott Tower, 131 North Ludlow Street, 45402-1135
Telephone: 937-226-1200 FAX: 937-226-1625
Email: bp@bpess.com
Members of Firm: Dennis L. Patterson; James C. Ellis; Curtis F. Slaton; Randall L. Stump; Asher Bogin (Retired).
Secured Creditors, Bankruptcy and Reorganization (Creditors), General Litigation, Arbitration, Real Estate Law, General Business Law, Non-Profit Corporation Law, Computer Law, Construction Law.
See Professional Biographies, DAYTON, OHIO

Booher, Michael R. .... '56 '81 C.473 B.A. L.608 J.D. 3640 Colonel Glenn Highway
Booth, Michael A., (BV) .... '67 '95 C.473 B.S. L.150 J.D. [Sebaly,S.&D.]
Bostick, Robert A., (BV) .... '31 '58 C.97 B.A. L.930 LL.B. P.O. Box 60745
Bothmann, Randall N. .... '45 '70 C.610 A.B. L.150 J.D. 2550 S. Patterson Blvd.‡
Botros, Michael R. .... '70 '96 C.150 B.B.A. L.124 J.D. [Botros&S.]
Botros & Schulte, LLC, (BV) .... 5785 Far Hills Avenue
Bottoms, James M. .... '70 '01 C.150 B.A. L.201 J.D. [A Young&A.]
Boucher, Richard A., (BV) .... '60 '87 C.610 B.S. L.117 J.D. [Boucher&B.]
Boucher & Boucher Co., L.P.A., (BV) .... 12 W. Monument Ave., Ste. 200
Bower, Glenn L., (AV) .... '— '77 C.645 B.A. L.309 J.D. [Coolidge,W.W.&L.]
Bowers, Gwendolyn Ruth, (BV) .... '— '78 C.608 B.S.B.A. L.201 J.D. 1712 W. 3rd St.
Bradley, Gina A. .... '73 '98 C.49 B.S. L.201 J.D. Asst. Pros. Atty.

Bradley, Karen Denise, (BV) '64 '96 C.262 B.A. L.201 J.D.
130 West 2nd Street, Suite 1818, 45402
Telephone: 937-226-1212 Fax: 937-226-1224
Email: bradlw@main-net.com URL: http://www.karenlawfirm.com
Immigration Law.
See Professional Biographies, DAYTON, OHIO

Braig, Kevin P. .... '67 '93 C.610 B.S. L.150 J.D. [A Dinsmore&S.]
Brannon, Dwight D., (AV) .... '48 '74 C.201 B.S. L.1340 J.D. [Brannon&Assoc.]

Brannon & Associates, (AV)
130 West Second Street, Suite 900, 45402-1590
Telephone: 937-228-2306 Fax: 937-228-8475
Email: dbrannon@branlaw.com URL: http://www.branlaw.com
Dwight D. Brannon.
Personal Injury, Complex Litigation, Commercial Litigation, Medical Malpractice, Criminal Litigation and Appellate Practice Law, Matrimonial Law.
See Professional Biographies, DAYTON, OHIO

Brasier, Susan M., (BV) .... '59 '86 C.473 B.Phil. L.201 J.D. [Falke&D.]
Braud, John O. '53 '79 C.1099 B.A. L.425 J.D.
(adm. in LA; not adm. in OH) F.B.I.
Breidenbach, Heidi S., (BV) .... '69 '95 C.210 B.A. L.201 J.D. [Breidenbach,O.&B.]
Breidenbach, John E., (AV) .... '42 '68 C&L.608 B.S., J.D. [Breidenbach,O.&B.]
Breidenbach, O'Neal & Bacon, (AV) .... 131 North Ludlow Street
Breidenbaugh, J. Christopher '54 '81 C.607 B.A. L.851 J.D.
(adm. in TX; not adm. in OH) 761 W. Spring Valley Rd.‡
Brennan, James M., (AV) .... '31 '57 C&L.608 B.A., J.D. [Young&A.]
Brenner, Joan B., (BV) .... '54 '81 C.473 B.S.Ed. L.608 J.D. [E.S.Gallon&Assoc.]
Brenner, Susan W. '47 '81 C.622 B.A. L.1119 J.D.
(adm. in IN; not adm. in OH) Prof. of Law, Univ. of Dayton
Bricker, Charles E. '38 '72 C.630 B.S. L.986 J.D.
(adm. in KS; not adm. in OH; Pat.) Pat. Atty., Dept. of Air Force
Brinkman, Daniel E., (BV) .... '54 '82 C.1208 B.S. L.201 J.D. [Izenson,F.&B.]
Brinkman, Justin D. .... '— '03 C.477 B.A. L.339 J.D. [A Coolidge,W.W.&L.]
Brinsfield, Gary T., (BV) .... '42 '68 C.473 B.S. L.607 J.D. [Dunlevey,M.&F.]
Brogan, James A. .... '39 '64 C.602 A.B. L.276 J.D. Dist. Ct. of Apps. J.
Broock, Richard A., (AV) .... '46 '72 C&L.477 A.B., J.D. [Chernesky,H.&K.]
Brooks, Adrienne D. .... '79 '04 C.201 B.A. L.861 J.D. [A L.P.Mulligan&Assoc.]
Brooks, Richard C. .... '42 '68 C.608 B.A. L.607 J.D. Mag., Probate Ct.
Brossart, Joseph A. '65 '99 C.473 B.A. L.602 J.D.
Law Clerk, U.S. Dist. Ct., Southern Dist. of Ohio
Brown, Alan I. .... '54 '79 C.347 B.A. L.608 J.D. [G Myers&F.]
Brown, Christopher M. .... '— '03 C.130 B.A. L.201 J.D. [A Chernesky,H.&K.]
Brown, Diana S. .... '62 '96 C.97 B.S. L.477 J.D. [A Logothetis,P.&D.]
Brown, Jacqueline V. .... '79 '04 C.210 B.A. L.1119 J.D. [A Faruki I.&C.]
Brown, Robert J., (AV) .... '42 '68 C.608 B.A. L.607 J.D. [Thompson H.]
Brown, Robert M. .... '25 '51 C&L.608 B.A., J.D. Com. Pleas J.
Brown, William J., (BV) .... '47 '73 C.201 B.A. L.838 J.D. [G Gottschlich&P.]
Brubaker, James Duane .... '49 '77 C.631 B.A. L.608 J.D. Atty.
Bruder, Matthew D., (BV) .... '73 '98 C.5 B.A L.8 J.D. [A Dyer,G.M.&S.]
Brumbaugh, Suzanne P. .... '77 '02 C.651 B.S. L.201 J.D. [A Pickrel,S.&E.]
Bruns, Julie A., (BV) .... '71 '96 C.473 B.S. L.201 J.D. Asst. Pros.
Bruzzese, Anthony E. .... '— '03 C.473 B.S. L.201 J.D. [A Chernesky,H.&K.]
Bryant, Todd E. .... '74 '00 C.999 B.A. L.201 J.D. [A Chernesky,H.&K.]
Buchanan, Joseph P., (AV) .... '29 '56 C.473 B.S. L.608 LL.B. [Crew&B.]

Buechner, Haffer, O'Connell, Meyers, Healey & Koenig Co., L.P.A.
(See Cincinnati)
Buenning, Charles Anthony, Jr. '50 '75
C&L.608 B.S., J.D. Chf., Labor Law, U.S. Air Force
Burdge, Michael J., (BV) .... '50 '78 C.231 A.B. L.201 J.D. [Young,P.L.&J.]
Burdge, Ronald L., (BV) .... '48 '78 C.763 B.A. L.201 J.D. [Burdge]

Burdge Law Office Co., LPA, (BV)
2299 Miamisburg-Centerville Road, 45459-3817
Telephone: 937-432-9500 Fax: 937-432-9503 Toll Free: 888-331-6422 URL: http://www.ohioconsumerlaw.com
Email: Ron@OhioLemonLaw.com URL: http://www.OhioLemonLaw.com
Ronald L. Burdge;—Amy L. Wells; Elizabeth A. Wells.
Consumer Law, Lemon Law, Class Actions, Consumer Fraud, Consumer Protection, Warranty Law, Ohio Consumer Sales Practices Act, Fair Credit Reporting.
See Professional Biographies, DAYTON, OHIO

Burick, Lawrence T., (AV) .... '43 '68 C.473 A.B. L.597 J.D. [Thompson H.]
Burke, Robert A. .... '52 '79 C.754 B.S. L.201 J.D. [A Dyer,G.M.&S.]
Burnette, Erica Littlejohn .... '72 '97 C.329 B.A. L.309 J.D. 1253 Hook Estate Dr.
Burns, Belinda A. .... '53 '79 C&L.607 B.A., J.D. Tax Mgr., Coopers & Lybrand
Burton, Chad E. .... '79 '04 C.473 B.A. L.124 J.D. [A Faruki I.&C.]
Burton, Donald E., (BV) .... '63 '88 C.851 B.A. L.608 J.D. [A Faruki I.&C.]
Burton, Melinda K. .... '68 '95 C.880 B.A. L.472 J.D. [A Faruki I.&C.]
Busch, Betty L. .... '29 '60 C.128 L.607 J.D. Law Libr., Dayton Law Library Assn.
Butler, Mariah D. .... '78 '03 C.890 B.S. L.201 J.D. [A Rogers&G.]
Butler, Timothy R., (BV) .... '58 '83 C.235 B.B.A. L.477 J.D. Asst. Law V.P., NCR Corp.
Byrd, James E., (BV) '58 '84 C.201 B.S. L.200 J.D.
Sr. Dir. & Assoc. Gen. Coun., Content Acquisition, LEXIS-NEXIS
Byrnes, John J. '— '82 C.276 B.S.B.A. L.608 J.D.
Dir., Tax Coun. & Planning, Corp. Taxes, NCR Corporation
Cajacob, Jennifer Goeke .... '74 '00 C.472 B.A. L.851 J.D. 40 West 4th Street
Campbell, Noelle D., (BV) .... '69 '94 C&L.201 B.S., J.D. Atty., NCR Corp.
Cannon, James F. '51 '76 C.475 B.A. L.188 J.D.
(adm. in MN; not adm. in OH) 335 W. 3rd St.‡
Cannon, James F. .... '31 '78 C.1208 B.A. L.201 J.D. Mun. J.
Capelle, Louis C. .... '16 '40 L.150 LL.B. 200 Haver Rd.
Capizzi, Anthony, (BV) '54 '79
C.712 B.A. L.201 J.D. 2103 First National Plz., 130 W. 2nd St.
Caras, Sam G. .... '55 '80 C.1208 B.A. L.201 J.D. [S.G.Caras]
Caras, Sam G., Co., LPA .... 130 W. 2nd St., Ste. 310
Carlile, Richard F., (AV) .... '41 '69 C.610 B.B.A. L.477 J.D. [Thompson H.]
Carlisle, Arbutus Likens .... '— '94 C.905 B.A. L.146 J.D. [A Coolidge,W.W.&L.]
Carr, Richard L., Jr., (BV) .... '59 '84 C.475 B.A. L.93 J.D. [Dunlevey,M.&F.]
Carr, William L., (BV) .... '43 '68 C&L.477 B.B.A., J.D. 3864 North Dixie
Carrigg, Christopher W., (BV) .... '53 '83 C.999 B.A. L.201 J.D. [Freund,F.&A.]
Carson, L. Turner .... '24 '49 C.610 L.150 J.D. 7825 N. Dixie Dr.‡
Carson, Lloyd Christopher '62 '89 C.347 B.S. L.477 J.D.
Pres., Metropolitan Builders & Developers Inc.
Carter, Gary J. .... '57 '83 C.1208 B.S. L.201 J.D. Hyatt Legal Servs.
Carter, R. Douglas, (BV) .... '31 '54 C.201 L.150 LL.B. 4428 North Dixie Drive
Carter, Russell L. .... '19 '47 C.608 B.S. L.309 J.D. 1504 Hulman Bldg.
Carver, Todd B., (BV) .... '58 '91 C.1208 B.A. L.201 J.D. Sr. Atty., NCR Corp.
Cary, Dina M. .... '— '97 C.608 B.A. L.201 J.D. [A Coolidge,W.W.&L.]
Case, John Arthur .... '54 '83 C.528 B.A L.851 J.D. US Air Force, AFMCLO/JAF
Caspar, Frederick J., (AV) .... '55 '81 C.1208 B.S. L.608 J.D. [Chernesky,H.&K.]
Casper, E. Jeffrey, (BV) ...... '47 '72 C&L.150 B.A., J.D. [Casper&C.] (⊙Middletown)

Casper and Casper, (AV)
First National Plaza Building, 130 West Second Street, Suite 1950, 45402 ⊙
Telephone: 937-224-1122
E. Jeffrey Casper.
Personal Injury, Workers Compensation and Social Security Disability Law. Products Liability Litigation. Trials.
Middletown, Ohio Office: Gas and Electric Building, One North Main Street, P.O. Box: 510, 45042. Telephone: 513-424-2401.
Cincinnati, Ohio Office: 119 East Court Street, Fourth Floor, Suite 410, 45202. Telephone: 513-381-7096.
Hamilton Office: 2 South 3rd Street, Suite 360, 45011. Telephone: 513-892-2560.
See Professional Biographies, DAYTON, OHIO

Cass, William O., Jr., (BV) .... '56 '86 C.150 B.S. L.607 J.D. [Schneble,C.&Assoc.]
Caudill, Mary Beth, (BV) .. '55 '83 C.381 B.A. L.201 J.D. 306 South Patterson Boulevard
Cavanaugh, William D. .... '50 '86 C.63 B.S. L.200 J.D. 1557 Glenbeck Ave.★
Cecil, Thomas C., (AV) ...... '27 '52 C.611 B.A. L.477 LL.B. 1105 Wilmington Avenue‡
Certo, Peter R., (BV) .... '52 '79 C&L.201 B.A., J.D. [Altick&C.]
Cervay, John A., (AV) .... '43 '68 C.201 B.A. L.608 J.D. [A Hochman&P.]
Chambers, John C., (AV) .... '— '85 C.610 B.A. L.201 J.D. [Coolidge,W.W.&L.]
Chan, Michael .... '55 '88 C.930 B.S.E.E. L.1003 J.D. Sr. Atty., NCR Corp. (Pat.)
Chema, Susan R., (BV) .... '56 '82 C.201 B.A. L.608 J.D. Sr. Atty., NCR Corp.
Chernesky, Richard J., (AV) .... '39 '66 C&L.608 B.A., J.D. [Chernesky,H.&K.]

Chernesky, Heyman & Kress P.L.L., (AV)
10 Courthouse Plaza, SW, Suite 1100, 45402
Mailing Address: P.O. Box 3808, Dayton, OH 45401-3808
Telephone: 937-449-2800 Facsimile: 937-449-2821
URL: http://www.chklaw.com
Partners of Firm: Karen R. Adams; Richard A. Broock; Frederick J. Caspar; Richard J. Chernesky; Andrew K. Cherney; Thomas L. Czechowski; Bradley W. Evers; Mark S. Feuer; Ralph E. Heyman; Edward M. Kress; William J. Leibold; Lisa S. Pierce; Donna S. Tweel; Steven R. Watts; Thomas P. Whelley II; David R. Wickham; Philip A. Zukowsky;—Christopher M. Brown; Anthony E. Bruzzese; Todd E. Bryant; Carrie E. Herman; Rachael L. Rodman; Kevin V. Simon; Susan D. Solle. Of Counsel: L. Douglas Kneisly; James David Ruffner, II; Gail H. Littlejohn; James R. Mitchell.
Languages: Hebrew, Japanese.
General Business, General Litigation, Taxation, Corporate and Real Estate Practice. Partnerships, Mergers and Acquisitions, Syndications, Antitrust, Zoning, Banking, Securities Regulation, Estate Planning, Probate, Trust and Charitable Organization, Employment, Products Liability and Health Care Law.
See Professional Biographies, DAYTON, OHIO

Cherney, Andrew K., (AV) .... '47 '73 C.797 B.A. L.608 J.D. [Chernesky,H.&K.]
Chilson, Mark R., (AV) .... '56 '81 C.965 B.B.A. L.201 J.D. [Young&A.]
Chinault, Jeffrey .... '78 '03 C.886 B.S. L.201 J.D. [A Dyer,G.M.&S.]
Ciambrone, Richard A., (BV) .... '53 '80 C.602 B.A. L.200 J.D. [A Thompson H.]
Cicero, Anthony R., (BV) '70 '95
C.966 B.S. L.201 J.D. [Cicero&K.] (⊙Bloomington, IL)

Cicero & Kollin PLL, (BV)
500 East 5th Street, 45402
Telephone: 937-424-5390 Fax: 937-424-5393 URL: http://www.cicerokollinfirm.com
Email: cicero@woh.rr.com URL: http://www.cicero-kollin.com
Anthony R. Cicero; Thomas M. Kollin.
Criminal Defense, Personal Injury, Family Law.
See Professional Biographies, DAYTON, OHIO

Clark, William A. ... '28 '52 C&L.477 A.B., J.D. U.S. Bkrptcy. J.
Clawson, Carissa E. ... '77 '03 C.1208 B.A. L.608 J.D. [Ⓐ Sebaly,S.&D.]
Clayman, Raymond, (AV) ... '34 '59 C&L.608 B.S.C., J.D. 11 W. Monument Ave.
Claypoole, Erin Leigh, (CV) ... '72 '97 C.665 B.S. L.608 J.D. Asst. Pros. Atty.
Claypoole, Howard F., (AV) ... '35 '61 C&L.608 B.A., J.D. Suite 1760
Cloud, John M., (BV) ... '51 '76 C.973 B.A. L.150 J.D. [Rogers&G.]
Clough, John E., (CV) ... '66 '94 C.1021 B.A. L.201 J.D. [Ⓒ Thompson H.]
Cochran, Rebecca A., (BV) '52 '84 C.170 B.A. L.365 J.D.
Prof. of Law, Univ. of Dayton
Cohen, Stanley J., (AV) ... '34 '58 C&L.966 B.S., LL.B. Ste. 200, 1 1st. Natl. Plza.
Cole, James D., (AV) ... '53 '80 C.1208 B.A. L.201 J.D. Co. Pros. Off.
Coleman, Danyelle S.T. ... '71 '00 C.188 B.A. L.608 J.D. [Ⓐ Sebaly,S.&D.]
Collins, Lori J. ... '56 '87 C.107 B.S. L.1044 J.D. Sr. Atty., NCR Corp.
Compton, Brooks A., (BV) ... '54 '79 C&L.607 B.A., J.D. 401 E. Sroop Road
Comunale, Anthony Francis, (BV) ... '66 '93 C.94 B.A. L.201 J.D. 130 W. 2nd St.
Conard, Christopher R., (BV) ... '— '88 C&L.201 B.A., J.D. [Ⓐ Coolidge,W.W.&L.]
Conley, Andrew P. ... '76 '03 C.347 B.S. L.124 J.D. [Ⓐ Hall&M.]
Connell, James M., (BV) ... '44 '69 C.201 B.A. L.602 J.D. 342 Wonderly Ave.
Connell, Kevin C., (BV) ... '69 '94 C.473 B.A. L.923 J.D. [Freund,F.&A.]
Connelly, Jos. F. ... '23 '49 C.201 L.150 LL.B. 546 Garden Rd.‡
Constable, Edward T. '30 '52 C.712 B.A. L.724 LL.B.
(adm. in NY; not adm. in OH) Dayton Aerospace, Inc.
Conway, Mark A., (AV) ... '57 '83 C.207 B.A. L.61 J.D. [Thompson H.]
Cook, C. Brant ... '68 '93 C.473 B.A. L.608 J.D. 2000 Courthouse Pz. NE (Pat.)

Coolidge, Wall, Womsley & Lombard, A Legal Professional Association, (AV)
Suite 600, 33 West First Street, 45402-1289
Telephone: 937-223-8177 Fax: 937-223-6705
URL: http://www.coollaw.com
John C. Lombard; Ronald S. Pretekin; Jonas J. Gruenberg; Merle F. Wilberding; Glenn L. Bower; J. Stephen Herbert; Fred A. Ungerman, Jr.; R. Scott Blackburn; Richard A. Schwartz; Sam Warwar; Terence L. Fague; Timothy D. Hoffman; John C. Chambers; Janice M. Paulus; Jeffrey A. Mullins; Richard A. Talda; David N. Reed; R. Brent Gambill; M. Shannon Martin; Lance A. Gildner (Certified Specialist in Federal Tax Law, Ohio State Bar Association); Nicholas E. Davis, Jr.; Kristin A. Finch; David P. Pierce; Lowell T. Woods, Jr.;—C. Mark Kingseed; David C. Korte (Certified Specialist in Workers Compensation Law, Ohio State Bar Association); John L. Green; Mary L. Wiseman; David M. Rickert; Edie England Crump; Dina M. Cary; Shannon L. Costello; Christopher R. Conard; Arbutus Likens Carlisle; Gregory M. Ewers; Jill A. May; Allison D. Michael; Sylvie J. Derrien; Michelle D. Bach (Certified Specialist in Workers Compensation Law, Ohio State Bar Association); Douglas C. Anspach; Chad D. Hansen; Steven M. Wachstein; Lisa K. Wiseman; Aniruddha D. Bhat; Justin D. Brinkman; My'chael D. Jefferson; Peter L. Jenkins; Matthew D. Austin; Brian M. Wakefield; Joshua R. Lounsbury.
Corporate, Partnerships, Securities, International Transactions, Antitrust, Tax, Labor, Employment, Employment Immigration, Employee Benefits, Banking, Real Estate, Municipal, Zoning, Environmental, Commercial Transactions, Bankruptcy, Health Care, Civil and Criminal Trials and Appeals, Commercial Litigation, Personal Injury, Products Liability, Workers Compensation, Insurance Defense, Estate and Financial Planning, Probate and Trust Law.
References provided on request.
See Professional Biographies, DAYTON, OHIO

Cooper, Charles D. ... '70 '96 C.938 B.A. L.602 J.D. [Ⓐ Thompson H.]
Cooper, Janet K., (AV) ... '46 '78 C.942 B.A. L.862 J.D. [Cooper&G.]

Cooper & Gentile Co., A Legal Professional Association, (AV) BR
Talbott Tower, Suite 850, 118 West First Street, 45402
Telephone: 937-224-5300 Fax: 937-224-5301
Email: dlgentile@cooperandgentile.com URL: http://www.lawyers.com/cooperandgentile
Janet K. Cooper; Diane L. Gentile.
General Practice.
See Professional Biographies, DAYTON, OHIO

Copley, C. Douglas, (BV) ... '49 '96 C.640 B.S. L.117 J.D. [Copley V.&B.]
Copley Valley & Baldwin, LLC, (BV) ... 854 E Franklin Street
Costello, Shannon L. ... '— '98 C.608 B.A. L.150 J.D. [Ⓐ Coolidge,W.W.&L.]
Coughlin, Robert B., (BV) ... '53 '78 C&L.150 B.A., J.D. [Young,P.L.&J.]
Cousineau, Richard L., (BV) '32 '59
C.896 B.A. L.602 LL.B. 120 W. 2nd St., Liberty Tower
Cowan, Christopher F., (AV) ... '50 '81 C.608 B.A. L.201 J.D. [Cowan&H.]
Cowan & Hilgeman, (AV) ... 12 W. Monument Avenue

Cowden, Pfarrer, Crew & Becker
(See Crew & Buchanan)

Cowdrey, Robert F., (AV) ... '49 '75 C&L.150 B.A., J.D. [Ⓒ Statman,H.S.&E.]
Cox, Bobby Joe, (BV) ... '40 '73 C.201 B.S. L.1340 J.D. 130 W. 2nd St.
Cox, Jeffrey T., (BV) ... '60 '91 C.473 B.A. L.201 J.D. [Faruki I.&C.]
Cox, Jennifer Dehner, (BV) ... '59 '88 C.741 B.A. L.273 J.D. 5017 Rolling Woods Trl.
Cox, Ray A., (AV) ... '34 '68 C.347 B.S. L.345 J.D. [Cox&G.]
Cox, Steven M., (BV) ... '49 '75 C.378 B.A. L.608 J.D. [Ⓒ Ames&A.]
Cox & Ginger, (AV) ... 267 Regency Ridge Dr.
Cramer, Carl A., (BV) ... '47 '73 C.201 B.A. L.150 J.D. 2323 W. Schantz
Crane, Brent A. ... '— '95 C.1208 B.A. L.117 J.D. [Ⓐ Altick&C.]
Creech, Dale E., Jr., (AV) '54 '78 C.243 B.A. L.1003 J.D.
Sr. V.P. & Chief Legal Officer, Med Amer. Health Systems Corp.
Creech, Herbert, Jr. ... '47 '73 C&L.383 A.B., J.D. [H.Creech]
Creech, Herbert ... 200 Jamestown Cir., Apt. F
Crew, Robert B., (AV) ... '12 '36 C&L.597 B.S., J.D. [Crew&B.]

Crew & Buchanan, (AV)
Formerly Cowden, Pfarrer, Crew & Becker
2580 Kettering Tower, 45423-2580
Telephone: 937-223-6211 Facsimile: 937-223-7631
Email: office@crewbuchanan.com
Members of Firm: Charles A. Craighead (1857-1926); Robert E. Cowden (1886-1954); Robert E. Cowden, Jr. (1910-1968); Charles P. Pfarrer (1905-1984); Philip Rohrer Becker (1905-1989); Robert B. Crew; Joseph P. Buchanan; Jeffrey A. Swillinger; Robert J. Davidek. Associate: Jennifer Hann Harrison.
General Civil Practice. Corporate, Employment, Employment Intentional Tort, Labor, Personal Injury, Probate, Real Estate, Tax and Workers' Compensation Defense Law. Trials.
Representative Clients: Daimler Chrysler; Diamond Tool & Die Co.; General Motors Corp.; Grandview/Southview Hospitals; James River Corp.; Mays-Shedd Sales, Inc.; Rodgers Pontiac Company; Serra Chevrolet; US Gaming Exporters, Inc.
See Professional Biographies, DAYTON, OHIO

Crim, Gary W., (BV) ... '47 '73 C.1208 M.B.A. L.608 J.D. 943 Manhattan Ave.
Crist, Maria P. ... '56 '81 C.597 B.A. L.477 J.D. Univ. of Dayton Sch. of Law
Cromer, William M., (AV) ... '18 '49 C.97 A.B. L.608 J.D. [Cromer&F.]
Cromer & Faber, (AV) ... 345 W. 2nd St.
Crossman, F. Ann ... '52 '89 C.610 B.A. L.201 J.D. [Winwood C.&Assoc.]
Crump, Edie England ... '— '91 C.502 B.S. L.421 J.D. [Ⓐ Coolidge,W.W.&L.]
Cumming, John A., (AV) ... '48 '73 C.97 B.S. L.608 J.D. Montgomery Co. Pros. Off.
Cumming, John E., (AV) ... '23 '49 C&L.608 LL.B. Legal Dept., Prob. Ct.
Cummiskey, John P. ... '56 '87 C.1208 B.A. L.201 J.D. P.O. Box 751793
Cunningham, Elizabeth A. McGee '54 '81 C.832 B.S. L.383 J.D.
(adm. in KY; not adm. in OH) 1518 Benson Dr.‡

Curry, Robert M., (AV) ... '53 '78 C.473 A.B. L.608 J.D. [Thompson H.]
Czechowski, Thomas L. ... '— '74 C.682 B.A. L.861 J.D. [Chernesky,H.&K.]
Dahms, Kenneth C. ... '45 '73 C.612 B.A. L.309 J.D. Co. Health Dist.
Daly, Denis G., (AV) '42 '69 C.1118 A.B. L.1340 J.D.
V.P., Gen. Coun. & Secy., Amcast Indus. Corp.
Daly, William T., (CV) ... '64 '88 C.1044 B.A. L.201 J.D. 120 W. 2nd St.
Dankof, Steven K., (AV) ... '51 '76 C.608 B.B.A. L.846 J.D. [Weisbrod&D.]
Davidek, Robert J., (AV) ... '56 '81 C.608 B.A. L.851 J.D. [Crew&B.]
Davido, Scott J. '61 '87 C&L.930 B.S., J.D.
Sr. V.P. & Gen. Coun., The Elder-Beerman Stores Corp.
Davies, Scott S. ... '75 '03 C.30 B.S.B.A. L.201 J.D. [Ⓐ Sebaly,S.&D.]
Davis, G. Jack, Jr., (BV) ... '43 '68 C.97 B.S. L.608 J.D. 41 N. Perry St.
Davis, Nicholas E., Jr. ... '— '90 C.381 B.A. L.201 J.D. [Coolidge,W.W.&L.]
Davis, Peter W., (BV) ... '56 '81 C.894 A.B. L.178 J.D. Sr. Atty., NCR Corp.
Davis, Steven J., (BV) ... '61 '87 C.604 B.A. L.228 J.D. [Ⓐ Thompson H.]
Dawson, Wayne H., (AV) ... '42 '67 C.967 B.A. L.150 J.D. [Dinsmore&S.]
Dean, Steven O., (BV) ... '58 '83 C&L.607 B.A., J.D. [Young&A.]
Deas, William G., (AV) ... '47 '72 C.608 B.S. L.150 J.D. [Porter W.M.&A.]
DeBrosse, Thomas E., (AV) ... '50 '80 C&L.608 B.S.B.A., J.D. [Thompson H.]
Deddens, Robert L., (AV) ... '40 '67 C&L.150 Ch.E., J.D. 55 Park Ave.
DeLuca, Thomas J. ... '45 '70 C.201 B.S. L.602 J.D. 1700 Courthouwe Plaza, N.E.‡
Dendwick-Gordon, Laurie A. ... '73 '02 C.585 B.A. L.201 J.D. [Ⓐ Dunlevey,M.&F.]
Deneke, Albert J., Jr. ... '39 '64 C.201 B.A. L.607 J.D. Juv. Ct. Ref.

Denmead Law Office
(See Columbus)

Dennis, James D., (BV) ... '51 '76 C.532 B.A. L.930 J.D. 130 W. 2nd St.
Denny, Larry J., (AV) ... '47 '74 C.138 B.A. L.1340 J.D. 371 West First Street
Depoorter, Kent J., (BV) ... '62 '92 C.707 B.A. L.201 J.D. 7501 Paragon Rd.
Deptula, David M. ... '58 '84 C.1208 B.S. L.851 J.D. 1700 Courthouse Plaza, N.E.
Derrien, Sylvie J. ... '— '00 C&L.150 B.A., J.D. [Ⓐ Coolidge,W.W.&L.]
DeSio, Laura C. ... '72 '99 C.97 B.A. L.608 J.D. [Ⓐ Rogers&G.]
Dettmer, Anne R., (BV) ... '67 '93 C.914 B.A. L.893 J.D. Off. of Co. Pros. Atty.
Deuser, Charles W., II, (BV) '46 '71
C.951 B.A. L.94 J.D. Rel. Mgr., Bank One Tr. Co., N.A.
Deutsch, David M., (AV) ... '43 '69 C.608 B.S. L.192 J.D. [D.M.Deutsch]

Deutsch, David M., Co., L.P.A., (AV) BR
The Pollack House, 208 West Monument Avenue, 45402
Telephone: 937-223-7170 Facsimile: 937-223-7180
Email: groundcrew@deutsatlaw.com URL: http://www.deutschlawoffice.com
David M. Deutsch.
Personal Injury, Product Liability, Wrongful Death, Medical Malpractice.
See Professional Biographies, DAYTON, OHIO

DeVeny, Dain N., (BV) ... '48 '74 [Thompson&D.]
DeVita, Stephen Lawrence, (CV) ... '56 '83 C.608 B.A. L.851 J.D. Dayton Bd. of Educ.
Dewar, Glen Hudson, (BV) ... '57 '89 C&L.201 B.A., J.D. Dir.
DiCicco, Matthew D. ... '75 '00 C.1062 B.A. L.201 J.D. [Ⓐ Freund,F.&A.]
Dickens, Norma M. ... '63 '91 C.724 B.S. L.94 J.D. 101 W. 3rd St.
Dieterle Judge, Dianne ... '55 '93 C.679 B.S. L.200 J.D. Miami Valley Hosp.

Dinsmore & Shohl LLP, (AV) BR
One Dayton Centre, One South Main Street, Suite 1300, 45402 ⊙
Telephone: 937-449-6400 FAX: 937-449-6405
Email: info@dinslaw.com URL: http://www.dinslaw.com
New address effective April 1, 2004: One Dayton Centre, One South Main Street, Suite 1300, 45402.
Members of Firm: Richard J. Beckmann; Laura Goehring Harrelson; Merideth A. Trott; Nicholas C. Hollenkamp; Ames Gardner, Jr.; Wayne H. Dawson; James E. Beyer; Kimberly Gambrel; James F. Gottman; Timothy W. Hagan; Richard A. Killworth; B. Joseph Schaeff. Associates: Theresa M. Muhic (Certified Specialist in Workers' Compensation Law, Ohio State Bar Association); Michael G. Frey; William A. Jividen; John D. Reed; Kristina E. Swanson; Paul M. Ulrich; Gregory M. Kaskey; Matthew A. Molloy; Kevin P. Braig. Of Counsel: Patricia L. Prior; David A. Shough.
General Practice.
Cincinnati, Ohio Office: 255 East Fifth Street, Suite 1900, 45202-4700. Telephone: 513-977-8200. FAX: 513-977-8141.
Columbus, Ohio Office: 10th Floor, 175 South Third Street, 43215-5134. Telephone: 614-628-6880. FAX: 614-628-6890.
Lexington, Kentucky Office: Lexington Financial Center, 250 West Main Street, Suite 1400, 40507. Telephone: 859-425-1000. FAX: 859-425-1099.
Louisville, Kentucky Office: 1400 PNC Plaza, 500 West Jefferson Street, 40202. Telephone: 502-540-2300. FAX: 502-585-2207.
Pittsburgh, Pennsylvania Office: The Grant Building, 330 Grant Street, Suite 2415, 15219. Telephone: 412-281-5000. FAX: 412-281-5055.
Charleston, West Virginia Office: 900 Lee Street, Huntington Square, Suite 600, 25301. Mailing Address: P.O. Box 11887, 25339. Telephone: 304-357-0900. FAX: 304-357-0919.
See Professional Biographies, DAYTON, OHIO

Divine, Richard W., (BV) ... '47 '75 C.429 B.A. L.221 J.D. 301 W. 3rd St.
Dockins, Dennis S. '60 '86 C.338 B.S. L.597 J.D.
General Counsel & Secretary, DT Industries, Inc.
Dodd, Lynda Ashbery '72 '97
C.294 B.A. L.201 J.D. Asst. Pros. Atty., Montgomery Co. Pros. Off.
Dodge, Richard S. ... '41 '69 C&L.800 A.B., J.D. Com. Pleas J.
Doll, John R., (BV) ... '51 '78 C.608 B.S. L.201 J.D. [Logothetis,P.&D.]
Donahue, Peter J., (AV) '28 '55 C&L.602 B.A., LL.B.
1406 Liberty Tower, 120 W. Second Street (⊙Annapolis, MD)
Donaldson, Lynn Robert ... '53 '89 L.608 J.D. Asst. City Atty., City of Dayton, OH
Donoff, Marilyn R., (BV) ... '52 '81 C.1208 B.A. L.150 J.D. 131 N. Ludlow
Donovan, Mary Elizabeth, (AV) ... '50 '77 C.150 B.A. L.201 J.D. 41 N. Perry St.
Dorsten, John E. ... '43 '73 C.97 B.A. L.1340 J.D. Mag., Co. Juv. Ct.
Douple, Daryl R., (BV) ... '53 '79 C.610 B.B.A. L.608 J.D. [Johnson,D.B.&L.]
Dowd, Edward J., (AV) ... '57 '83 C.602 B.A. L.201 J.D. [Surdyk,D.&T.]
Dowling, Jon C. ... '60 '86 C.121 B.A. L.575 J.D. 2000 Courthouse Plaza, N.E.
Dressel, Frederick W., (BV) ... '56 '81 C.610 B.A. L.608 J.D. [Ruffolo,S.&D.]
Ducker, John T., (AV) ... '31 '58 C.301 A.B. L.923 LL.B. [Talbot&D.] ‡
Dues, Gavin C. ... '72 '98 C.473 B.A. L.1003 J.D. 6 North Main Street, Suite 550
Duff, Trisha M. ... '66 '91 C.608 B.S. L.201 J.D. 424 Patterson Road
Duncan, Richard L., (BV) ... '47 '73 C.679 B.S. L.150 J.D. 7501 Paragon Rd.
Duncan, Robert K. ... '19 '57 C.679 B.S.E.E. L.1340 J.D. 4390 Baker Rd.‡
Duncombe, Barbara A. ... '52 '80 C.30 B.A. L.273 J.D. [Ⓒ Sebaly,S.&D.]
Dundes, Raymond J., (BV) ... '56 '89 C.150 B.S. L.201 J.D. Asst. Co. Pros.

Dungan & LeFevre, A Legal Professional Association
(See Troy)

Dunlevey, Karen T., (BV) ... '70 '96 C.648 B.S. L.201 J.D. [Bieser,G.&L.]
Dunlevey, Robert T., Jr., (AV) ... '47 '73 C.608 B.A. L.150 J.D. [Dunlevey,M.&F.]

Dunlevey, Mahan & Furry, A Legal Professional Association, (AV)
110 North Main Street, Suite 1000, 45402-1738
Telephone: 937-223-6003 Fax: 937-223-8550
URL: http://www.dmfdayton.com

(This Listing Continued)

Dunlevey, Mahan & Furry, A Legal Professional Association (Continued)

Robert T. Dunlevey, Jr.; Charles W. Mahan; Stephen A. Watring; Gary W. Auman; Gary T. Brinsfield; William H. Barney, III; Richard L. Carr, Jr.;—Donald B. Rineer; Amy C. Mitchell; Laurie A. Dendwick-Gordon. Of Counsel: Richard L. Furry.
Business Law, Labor and Employment Law, Workers' Compensation, OSHA, Government Contracts, Securities, Mergers and Acquisitions, Real Estate and Construction Law, Environmental, Litigation and Appeals, Estate Planning and Administration.
See Professional Biographies, DAYTON, OHIO

Dunphy, Patrick K., (BV) ... '57 '82 C.745 B.A. L.150 J.D. [Falke&D.]
Dunsky, Gregory P., (AV) ... '50 '77 C.201 B.A. L.477 J.D. Asst. U.S. Atty.
Duren, Mark W. ... '55 '83 C.1044 B.A. L.982 J.D. NCR Corporation - Gasper Division
Durham, James Geoffrey '51 '76 C.112 A.B. L.1067 J.D. (adm. in CA; not adm. in OH) Prof., Univ. of Dayton School of Law
Durham, Joan Drake '48 '76 C.813 A.B. L.1067 J.D. VP, Gen. Coun., Moto Franchise Corp.
Duvall, Nancy L. ... '58 '85 C.210 B.S. L.201 J.D. LEXIS-NEXIS
Dybvig, Roger S., (AV) ... '33 '59 C.260 B.S. L.273 J.D. [Dybvig&D.] (Pat.)
Dybvig & Dybvig, (AV) ... 22 Green Street (Pat.)
Dyer, James A., (AV) ... '56 '80 C&L.228 B.A., J.D. [Sebaly,S.&D.]
Dyer, Michael E., (BV) '53 '80 C.269 B.A. L.201 J.D. [Dyer,G.M.&S.] (⊙Troy, Xenia)

Dyer, Garofalo, Mann & Schultz, A Legal Professional Association, (AV)
Talbott Tower, 131 North Ludlow Street Suite 1400, 45402 ⊙
Telephone: 937-223-8888 Fax: 937-223-0127 URL: http://www.dgmslaw.com
URL: http://www.lawyers.com/dgmslaw
Michael E. Dyer; Carmine M. Garofalo; Douglas A. Mann; Ronald E. Schultz; John A. Smalley; Kenneth J. Ignozzi;—Diane E. Hanson; Henry Hyde, III; David W. Marquis; Matthew D. Bruder; Kevin W. Attkisson; F. Mark Maier; Edward C. Yim; Robert A. Burke; Douglas Ray Miley; Jason Saldanha; Jeffrey Chinault; J. Pierre Tismo.
Plaintiffs Personal Injury, Medical Malpractice, Products Liability.
Springfield, Ohio Office: 1714 Valley Loop Road, 45504. Telephone: 937-324-1440. Fax: 937-327-0488.
Middletown, Ohio Office: 1420 South Breiel Boulevard, 45044. Telephone: 513-727-3580. Fax: 513-727-3584.
Piqua, Ohio Office: 308 Looney Road, Suite E, 45356. Telephone: 937-778-9966. Fax: 937-778-2380.
Huber Heights, Ohio Office: 4420 Taylorsville Road, 45424. Telephone: 937-235-1229. Fax: 937-727-3584.
Lima, Ohio Office: 2727 Harding Highway, P.O. Box 1569, 45802. Telephone: 419-224-8564. Fax: 419-224-0287.
Bellefontaine, Ohio Office: 1709 South Main Street, 43311. Telephone: 937-599-1300. Fax: 937-599-1306.
Wilmington, Ohio Office: 712 South Street, 45177. Telephone: 937-283-9300. Fax: 937-283-9303.
Richmond, Indiana Office: 3733 National Road East, 47374. Telephone: 765-983-3500.
Troy, Ohio Office: 1850 W. main Street, 45373. Telephone: 937-440-9414.
Xenia, Ohio Office: 547 W. Second Street, 45385. Telephone: 937-223-8888.
See Professional Biographies, DAYTON, OHIO

Earhart, Scott William ... '69 '95 C.210 B.A. L.117 J.D. 580 Lincoln Park Blvd.
Early, Katherine L. ... '76 '02 C.273 B.A. L.608 J.D. [Ⓐ Sebaly,S.&D.]
Ebenger, Joseph R., (BV) ... '50 '77 C.712 B.A. L.200 J.D. [E.S.Gallon&Assoc.]
Eckhart, Michael R., (BV) '46 '73 C.1208 B.A. L.150 J.D. 580 Lincoln Park Blvd., Ste. 244
Edsall, Richard L. '46 '82 C.1208 B.A. L.1340 J.D. Air Force Materiel Command Law Off.★
Eichelberger, Jack W. ... '31 '56 C.197 B.S. L.94 LL.B. 1510 Kettering Tower
Eichelman, Nate ... '75 '03 C.1208 B.S. L.201 J.D. [Ⓐ Fox&Assoc.]
Eichner, Roland F., (AV) ... '30 '58 C.973 B.S.B.A. L.150 J.D. [Ⓒ Porter W.M.&A.]
Eilerman, Robert J., (AV) ... '33 '57 C.201 L.608 LL.B. [Ensley&E.]
Elleman, Jennifer N. ... '72 '98 C.473 B.A. L.608 J.D. Sr. Corp. Coun., LexisNexis (Pat.)
Elleman, Steven J. ... '70 '96 C&L.608 B.S.A.A.E., J.D. [Thompson H.] (See Pat. Sect.)
Ellerbrock, Michael J., (BV) ... '48 '79 C.97 B.S. L.851 J.D. 4403 N. Main St., 2nd Fl.
Elliott, Steven E., (BV) ... '55 '89 C.1208 B.A. L.201 J.D. [Ⓒ Hollencamp&H.]
Ellis, James C., (BV) ... '56 '81 C.201 B.A. L.608 J.D. [Bogin P.E.S.&S.]
Ellison, Kathy L., (BV) ... '46 '79 C.788 A.B. L.201 J.D. 208 Talbott Tower
Emrick, Nicholas R. ... '55 '82 C.1229 B.M.E. L.608 J.D. P.O. Box 933
Engel, Scott H. ... '61 '92 C.150 B.A. L.201 J.D. Staff Atty., Dist. Ct. of App.
Engler, Gregory T., (BV) ... '63 '88 C.967 B.A. L.150 J.D. P.O. Box 49717
Engling, Mark, (CV) ... '74 '99 C.201 B.A. L.1003 J.D. [Ⓐ Jenks,P.&O.]
Ensley, Theodore M., (AV) ... '28 '57 C.201 L.607 J.D. [Ensley&E.]
Ensley & Eilerman, (AV) ... 1406 Hulman Bldg.
Epling, Joshua '77 '02 C.437 B.A. L.200 J.D. (adm. in KY; not adm. in OH) [Ⓐ Subashi,W.&B.]
Erickson, Douglas E. '43 '74 C.453 B.S.A.E. L.629 J.D. [Ⓐ Thompson H.] (See Pat. Sect.)
Ernst, Herbert, Jr., (BV) ... '34 '60 C.207 B.A. L.597 J.D. 120 W. 3rd St.
Esala, Philip J. '49 '75 C.879 B.A. L.259 J.D. (adm. in IL; not adm. in OH) Emmanuel Lutheran Church
Esler, C. Marshall, Jr., (AV) ... '60 '87 C.473 B.S. L.607 J.D. [Scudder&E.]
Eubank, David L., (BV) ... '50 '89 C.150 B.U.P. L.201 J.D. 3430 S. Dixie Dr.
Evans, Robert G. '64 '89 C.679 B.A. L.880 J.D. (adm. in IN; not adm. in OH) Sr. Atty., NCR Corp.
Evers, Bradley W., (AV) ... '55 '80 C.1369 B.S. L.945 J.D. [Chernesky,H.&K.]
Ewers, Gregory M. ... '— '96 C.473 B.S. L.365 J.D. [Ⓐ Coolidge,W.W.&L.]
Faber, Richard V., (BV) ... '30 '54 C&L.607 J.D. [Cromer&F.]
Fague, Terence L., (BV) ... '— '78 C.952 A.B. L.608 J.D. [Coolidge,W.W.&L.]
Fain, Mike ... '46 '73 C.976 B.A. L.659 J.D. Ct. App. J.
Falke, Lee C., (AV) ... '30 '55 C&L.608 B.S., J.D. [Falke&D.]

Falke & Dunphy, LLC, (AV)
30 Wyoming Street, 45409
Telephone: 937-222-3000; 800-322-1410 Fax: 937-222-1414
URL: http://www.ohiolawyers.cc
Lee C. Falke; Patrick K. Dunphy. Members: Gregory P. Spears; Susan M. Brasier; Thomas J. Intili;—Robert J. Howard.
Personal Injury, Complex Litigation, Divorce, Probate Law, Will Contests, Estate Planning, Living Trusts, Real Estate and Corporation. General, Civil and Trial Practice.
See Professional Biographies, DAYTON, OHIO

Falknor, William L. ... '28 '52 C.347 B.S. L.1119 J.D. 8710 Sugarcreek Pt.‡
Fallang, Dennis J. ... '47 '77 C.608 B.A. L.851 J.D. 301 W. 3rd St.
Farley, Keri E. ... '78 '03 C.201 B.A. L.200 J.D. [Ⓐ Rion,R.&R.]
Farquhar, Harold R. ... '49 '75 C.97 B.A. L.607 J.D. 3723 Wilmington Pike
Farquhar, Robert N., (AV) ... '36 '61 C.385 A.B. L.188 J.D. [Altick&C.]
Faruki, Charles J., (AV) ... '49 '74 C.150 B.A. L.608 J.D. [Faruki I.&C.]

Faruki Ireland & Cox P.L.L., (AV)
500 Courthouse Plaza, S.W., 10 North Ludlow Street, 45402
Telephone: 937-227-3700 Fax: 937-227-3717
Email: admin@ficlaw.com URL: http://www.ficlaw.com
Members of Firm: Charles J. Faruki; D. Jeffrey Ireland; Paul L. Horstman; Jeffrey T. Cox; Thomas R. Kraemer; Laura A. Sanom; Ronald I. Raether, Jr.; Jeffrey S. Sharkey. Counsel: Robert P. Bartlett, Jr.;—Bradley D. Anderson; Erin A. Bair; Jacqueline V. Brown; Chad E. Burton; Donald E. Burton;

(This Listing Continued)

Faruki Ireland & Cox P.L.L. (Continued)

Melinda K. Burton; John A. Fischer; Martin A. Foos; R. Holtzman Hedrick; Robert W. Kiefaber; Andrew D. LeMar; Michele A. Murphy; Timothy G. Pepper; K. Lynn Preston; Andrew J. Reitz; Angela M. Sinkovits; Nicholas M. Smith; Erin E. Stefanec; Ian A. Taronji; Eric P. Voigt; Katrina L. Wahl; Brian D. Wright; Julie E. Zink.
Civil and Criminal Trial and Appellate Practice in all Courts. Business and Commercial Litigation, Environmental Litigation, White Collar Criminal Defense, Governmental Investigations, Intellectual Property Litigation, Products Liability Defense, Bankruptcy Litigation.
See Professional Biographies, DAYTON, OHIO

Feller, Joseph L., (BV) ... '72 '98 C.602 B.B.A. L.201 J.D. [Ⓐ Bieser,G.&L.]
Felman, H. Marvin, (BV) ... '25 '75 C.608 B.S. L.1340 J.D. 100 N. Jefferson St.
Ferguson, Douglas K. ... '30 '55 C.504 B.A. L.309 LL.B. Admin. Law Judge‡
Ferrante, Francesco A., (AV) ... '55 '81 C.724 B.A. L.823 J.D. [Thompson H.]
Feuer, Mark S., (AV) ... '52 '78 C.976 B.A. L.201 J.D. [Chernesky,H.&K.]
Finch, Kristin A. ... '— '95 C.1208 B.S. L.150 J.D. [Coolidge,W.W.&L.]
Finefrock, James L., (BV) ... '45 '75 C&L.608 B.M.E., J.D. [J.L.Finefrock&Assoc.]
Finefrock, James L., and Associates Co., L.P.A., (BV) .. 5335 Far Hills Avenue, Suite 318
Finke, R. Peter, (AV) ... '37 '68 C.602 B.S. L.1340 J.D. [Nolan,S.S.&F.]
Finley, Gale S., (AV) ... '52 '81 C.608 B.A. L.201 J.D. [Sebaly,S.&D.]
Finn-DeLuca, Valerie M. ... '67 '94 C.215 B.A. L.150 J.D. Staff Atty., Ct. of App.
Fischer, John A., (CV) ... '68 '97 C.1208 B.A. L.608 J.D. [Ⓐ Faruki I.&C.]
Fisher, Arthur O. ... '20 '50 C.201 A.B. L.150 LL.B. Com. Pleas J.
Flagel, Gerald P. ... '36 '61 C.597 B.S. L.608 J.D. 300 Talbott Tower‡
Flanagan, Patrick A., (BV) ... '38 '67 C.201 B.S. L.1340 J.D. [Flanagan,L.H.&S.]
Flanagan, Lieberman, Hoffman & Swaim, (AV) ... 318 W. 4th St.
Fleisher, James P., (BV) ... '66 '92 C.602 B.A. L.150 J.D. [Bieser,G.&L.]
Fleming, Kyra M., (BV) '66 '92 C&L.608 B.A., J.D. Atty., The Dayton Power & Light Co.
Fleming, Lynne M. ... '70 '97 C.1116 B.A. L.644 J.D. [Ⓐ Altick&C.]
Fogarty, Canice J. (C.J.), (BV) ... '58 '83 C&L.608 B.S., J.D. [Allbery C.F.]
Foley, Patrick J. ... '32 '56 C&L.602 B.Sc., J.D. Com. Pleas J.
Folfas, Paul A., (AV) ... '44 '72 C.923 B.A. L.608 S.J.D. Asst. Co. Pros.
Folkerth, John R., Jr., (BV) ... '55 '83 C.1216 B.A. L.201 J.D. 120 W 2nd St
Folkerth, Karen S. ... '61 '86 C.475 B.A. L.201 J.D. 1812 Kettering Tower
Foos, Martin A., (BV) ... '70 '95 C&L.602 B.A., J.D. [Ⓐ Faruki I.&C.]
Foote, Douglas S. ... '50 '82 C.446 B.S.E.E. L.1294 J.D. Law V.P., NCR Corp. (Pat.)
Ford, Julie C., (AV) ... '59 '88 C.608 B.A. L.273 J.D. [Logothetis,P.&D.]
Forster, Peter H. ... '42 '73 C.966 B.S.E.E. L.1009 J.D. Courthouse Plaza S.W.
Foster, Brett L., (CV) '64 '94 C.952 B.A. L.117 J.D. Sr. V.P. & Gen. Coun., Liberty Capital Inc.
Foster, Mark S., (BV) ... '53 '80 C.62 B.S. L.117 J.D. [Knostman&F.]
Fowler, Susan Stansfield '54 '86 C.802 B.S.,B.A.S. L.201 J.D. Dir., Planned Giving, Univ. of Dayton
Fox, Charles B. ... '31 '58 C&L.608 B.S.B.A., J.D. [Fox&Assoc.]
Fox, Chas. B., (BV) ... '31 '54 C&L.608 B.S., J.D. 1340 Woodman Dr.

Fox & Associates Co., L.P.A.
1344 Woodman Drive Suite F, 45432
Telephone: 937-258-3668 Fax: 937-258-3098
Email: cfoxlaw@aol.com URL: http://www.foxassociatescolapa.com
Charles B. Fox;—Nate Eichelman; William S. Russell.
Bankruptcy, Chapter 7, Chapter 13, Foreclosures, Divorce, Adoptions, Child Custody, Visitation Rights, Estate Planning, Wills and Trusts, Driving While Intoxicated and Traffic Violations.
See Professional Biographies, DAYTON, OHIO

Franceschelli, David M., (BV) ... '53 '79 C.1122 B.A. L.201 J.D. 120 W. 2nd St. S
Frapwell, William H., (AV) '52 '78 C.276 B.S.B.A. L.201 J.D. Coun., Chicago Title Ins. Co.
Frayne, Anne M., (BV) ... '54 '79 C&L.608 B.S., J.D. [Myers&F.]
Freeman, Jonathan B., (BV) ... '68 '97 C.901 B.A. L.201 J.D. [Altick&C.]
Freeze, Stephen V., (AV) ... '48 '74 C.1024 B.S. L.930 J.D. [Freund,F.&A.]
Freudiger, Ray C., (CV) ... '60 '91 C&L.150 B.B.A., J.D. [Freund,F.&A.]
Freund, Neil F., (AV) ... '45 '70 C.201 B.A. L.607 J.D. [Freund,F.&A.]

Freund, Freeze & Arnold, A Legal Professional Association, (AV)
One Dayton Centre, Suite 1800, One South Main Street, 45402-2017 ⊙
Telephone: 937-222-2424 Telecopier: 937-222-5369
Email: ffalawda@ffalaw.com URL: http://www.ffalaw.com
Neil F. Freund; Stephen V. Freeze; Gordon D. Arnold; Patrick J. Janis; Robert N. Snyder; Christopher W. Carrigg; Susan Blasik-Miller; Wayne E. Waite; Christopher F. Johnson; Shawn M. Blatt; Ray C. Freudiger; Kevin C. Connell; T. Andrew Vollmar; Robert W. Young; Leonard J. Bazelak;—John G. Witherspoon, Jr.; Lisa A. Hesse; Cinamon S. Houston; Michele L. King; Nicole A. Mitchell; Matthew D. DiCicco; Heather M. Loridas; Jason E. Treherne; Vaseem S. Hadi; Jamey T. Pregon; Bryan J. Mahoney; Kimberly S. Kislig; Michael N. Rhinehart; Julia A. Turner; Justin D. Harris; Lindsay M. Johnson; Jesse R. Lipcius; Thomas P. Sullivan; Jennifer M. White; Rory E. Garrity.
Civil Litigation including Commercial Litigation, Employment Defense, Professional Malpractice Defense, Employer Intentional Torts, Construction Litigation, Civil Rights Defense, Local Government Defense, Nursing Home Defense, Environmental Litigation and Insurance Defense.
Local Counsel for: Auto-Owners Insurance Co.; CNA Insurance Co.; Crum and Foster Underwriters; Employers Reinsurance Corp.; Farmers Insurance Group; Lloyds of London; Medical Protective; Midwestern Group; State Farm Mutual Automobile Insurance Co.
Special Trial Counsel for: City of Dayton.
Cincinnati, Ohio Office: Fourth and Walnut Centre, 105 East Fourth Street, Suite 1400, 45202-4006. Telephone: 513-665-3500. Telecopier: 513-665-3503. Email: ffalawci@ffalaw.com.
Columbus, Ohio Office: Capitol Square Office Building, 65 East State Street, Suite 800, 43215. Telephone: 614-827-7300. Telecopier: 614-827-7303. Email: ffalawco@ffalaw.com.
Covington, Kentucky Office Suite: RiverCenter, 50 East RiverCenter Boulevard, Suite 408, 41011. Telephone: 859-292-2088. Telecopier: 859-292-2514. Email: ffalawky@ffalaw.com
See Professional Biographies, DAYTON, OHIO

Frey, Michael G. ... '70 '98 C.523 B.A. L.150 J.D. [Ⓐ Dinsmore&S.] (Pat.)
Frick, Dawn M. ... '68 '98 C&L.608 B.S., J.D. [Ⓐ Surdyk,D.&T.]
Fries, Joseph C. ... '64 '91 C&L.150 B.S., J.D. Refer. Atty., LEXIS-NEXIS
Friesinger, Patricia Jean ... '75 '00 C&L.851 B.A., J.D. [Ⓐ Rieser&Assoc.]
Froelich, Gary L., (AV) ... '43 '68 C.473 B.A. L.608 J.D. [Froelich]
Froelich, Jeffrey E. ... '46 '72 C.473 B.A. L.477 J.D. Com. Pleas J.

Froelich Law Office LPA, (AV)
1812 Kettering Tower, 40 N. Main Street, 45423-1812
Telephone: 937-226-1776 Fax: 937-226-1945
Email: froelich4law@aol.com URL: http://www.lawyers.com/froelichlaw
Gary L. Froelich.
General Business Practice. Trials. Probate, Trust, Estate Planning, Corporation, Negligence, Business Litigation, Real Estate, Employment, Administrative Law.
Reference: Key Bank, N.A. of Dayton, Ohio.
See Professional Biographies, DAYTON, OHIO

Frumer, Marc J. ... '63 '88 C.012 B.A. L.930 J.D. 2000 Courthouse Plz. N.E.
Frydman, Joel M. ... '54 '79 C.597 B.A. L.273 J.D. V.P., Midwest Iron & Metal Co.
Fuchsman, David H., (BV) ... '58 '83 C.886 B.A. L.201 J.D. [Izenson,F.&B.]
Fulero, Solomon M., PHD JD Associates, (BV) '50 '80 C.446 B.A. L.629 J.D. 2705 Far Hills Ave., Ste. 4

Fullenkamp, James J., Law Offices, (BV) '59 '84
C&L.201 B.S.B.A., J.D. 131 N. Ludlow St., Ste. 1315
Furry, Richard L., (AV) .... '— '50 C&L.145 Ph.B., J.D. [Ⓒ Dunlevey,M.&F.]
Gabel, Alan D., (BV) .... '49 '84 C.150 B.A. L.201 J.D. 411 East 5th Street
Galen, Barry S., & Associates, (BV) ....'59 '89 C.200 B.S. L.1325 J.D. 111 W. 1st St.
Gallagher, Edward R. '53 '85 C.793 A.B. L.976 J.D.
(adm. in MA; not adm. in OH) Sr. Atty., NCR Corp.
Gallagher, Joseph S. ....'52 '77 C.608 B.A. L.8 J.D. Co. Probate Ct.
Gallagher, Julie D. ....'48 '84 C.45 B.S.E. L.976 J.D. Sr. Atty., NCR Corp.

Gallon, E. S., & Associates, (AV) BB
40 West Fourth Centre Suite 2200, 45402
Telephone: 937-586-3100; 800-998-4374 Fax: 937-586-3200
URL: http://www.esgallon.com
Members of Firm: David A. Saphire (Certified Specialist in Workers' Compensation Law, Ohio State Bar Association).; Joseph R. Ebenger (Certified Specialist in Workers' Compensation Law, Ohio State Bar Association).; Joan B. Brenner (Certified Specialist in Workers' Compensation Law, Ohio State Bar Association).; James R. Piercy; Richard M. Malone (Certified Specialist in Workers' Compensation Law, Ohio State Bar Association). Associates: David R. Salyer; Martin L. Malloy.
Personal Injury, Defective Product Liability, Workers' Compensation, Social Security Disability, Trials and Appeals, General Practice, Divorce, DWI, DUI, Traffic Violations, Family Law, Adoptions, Child Custody, Automobile Accidents, Slip and Fall, Child Support, Premarital Agreements, Nursing Home Litigation.
See Professional Biographies, DAYTON, OHIO

Gambill, R. Brent ....'— '79 C.210 B.A. L.347 J.D. [Coolidge,W.W.&L.]
Gambrel, Kimberly, (AV) ....'60 '88 C.473 B.A. L.150 J.D. [Dinsmore&S.] (Pat.)
Gammell, Jeffrey W., (BV) ....'63 '91 C.610 B.B.A. L.1340 J.D. [Gammell,H.K.&R.]
Gammell, Hoshor, Kendo & Ross, LLP, (BV) ....7925 Paragon Rd.
Gantt, Gregory M., (BV) ....'66 '95 C.201 B.A. L.1187 J.D. [Ⓐ Allbery C.F.]
Gapinski, Frank A. ....'31 '59 C.381 A.B. L.1009 LL.B. 5049 Sweetleaf Dr.
Gardner, Ames, Jr., (AV) ....'40 '65 C.674 B.A. L.893 LL.B. [Dinsmore&S.]
Garman, Richard Kent ....'33 '57 C&L.608 LL.B., J.D. 7501 Paragon Road
Garofalo, Carmine M., (BV) ....'48 '74 C.610 B.B.A. L.608 J.D. [Dyer,G.M.&S.]
Garrity, Rory E. ....'79 '04 C.1165 B.A. L.201 J.D. [Ⓐ Freund,F.&A.]
Gehres, Daniel G., (BV) ....'53 '78 C.432 B.S. L.201 J.D. Mun. J.
Geidner, Charles F., (BV) ....'48 '73 C.150 B.A. L.608 J.D. [Flanagan,L.H.&S.]
Gentile, Diane L., (BV) ....'56 '86 C&L.201 B.A., J.D. [Cooper&G.]
Gentry, Boyd W. ....'74 '99 C.117 B.A. L.851 J.D. [Ⓐ Surdyk,D.&T.]
Gentry, Caroline H., (BV) ....'70 '96 C.373 B.A. L.976 J.D. [Porter W.M.&A.]
Gerren, Nicholas L., Jr. ....'47 '73 C.378 B.A. L.851 J.D. 120 W. 2nd St.
Gerson, Barry L. ....'50 '77 C.201 B.A. L.607 J.D. 250 Folsom Dr.
Getty, Jennifer S. ....'75 '01 C&L.201 B.A., J.D. [Ⓐ Ruffolo,S.&D.]
Gianuglou, C. Dino, (AV) ....'35 '60 C&L.150 B.A., J.D. [Gianuglou,S.&R.]
Gianuglou, Skilken & Replogle, LLP, (AV) ....One First National Plaza, Suite 2110
Gibson, Gregory C., (AV) ....'47 '77 C.282 B.A. L.201 J.D. [G.C.Gibson]

Gibson, Gregory C., Co., L.P.A., (AV)
40 North Main Street Suite 2810, 45423
Telephone: 937-643-0600 Fax: 937-586-9495
Email: ggibson@gibsoncolpa.com URL: http://www.ggibsoncolpa.com
Gregory C. Gibson;—Stephen P. O'Keefe; Camille Louise Harlan.
Medical Malpractice, Serious Personal Injury, Wrongful Death.
See Professional Biographies, DAYTON, OHIO

Gilbert, Paul D., (BV) ....'36 '62 C.145 L.266 J.D. 120 W. 2nd Street, Suite 503
Gildner, Lance A., (AV) ....'— '91 C.347 B.A. L.201 J.D. [Coolidge,W.W.&L.]
Gilene, Salvatore A. ....'77 '02 C.602 B.A. L.201 J.D. [Ⓐ Pickrel,S.&E.]
Ginger, David S., (AV) ....'43 '70 C.473 B.S. L.150 J.D. [Cox&G.]
Glankler, John R. ....'57 '88 C.228 B.A. L.150 J.D. [Sebaly,S.&D.]
Glasper, Thomas, (CV) ....'— '81 C.943 B.A. L.1162 J.D. Mid City Station
Goelz, Robert D., (BV) ....'51 '78 C&L.201 B.A., J.D. [Flanagan,L.H.&S.]
Goerz, Deborah Ann Giddings ....'57 '86 C.33 B.A. L.201 J.D. Lexis-Nexis
Goldman, Rubin & Shapiro, (AV) ....1340 Woodman Drive
Goodall, L. Sharon ....'57 '92 C.967 B.A. L.201 J.D. Mag., Montgomery Co. Juv. Ct.
Goodwin, Charles S., (AV) ....'49 '74 C.475 B.A. L.831 J.D. 3500 Plantation Place
Goraleski, Carl George, (BV) ....'49 '83 C.201 B.S. L.1340 J.D. Co. Pub. Def.
Gorman, Barbara Pugliese ....'48 '77 C.436 B.A. L.201 J.D. Com. Pleas J.
Gottman, Andrew J., (BV) ....'74 '99 C.893 B.A. L.902 J.D. [Ⓐ Porter W.M.&A.]
Gottman, James F., (AV) ....'46 '74 C.150 B.S.E.E. L.276 J.D. [Dinsmore&S.] (Pat.)
Gottschlich, Gary W., (AV) ....'46 '71 C.201 B.S. L.602 J.D. [Gottschlich&P.]

Gottschlich & Portune, LLP, (AV)
The Historic Armory, 201 E. Sixth Street, 45402-2836
Telephone: 937-913-0200 Fax: 937-824-2818 URL: http://www.gplawdayton.com
Email: dsmith@gplawdayton.com URL: http://www.gplawoffices.com
Members of Firm: Gary W. Gottschlich; Robert E. "Buzz" Portune; John R. Mohr; Mary E. Lentz. Associates: Jeffrey R. Myers; Benjamin K. McComas. Of Counsel: William J. Brown.
Administrative Law, Business Planning, Business Transactions, Commercial Law, Construction Law, Franchise Law, Labor and Employment, Media Law, First Amendment Law, Mergers and Acquisitions, Municipal Law, Real Estate and Leasing, Zoning, Commercial, Fiduciary, Professional Malpractice and Personal Injury Litigation.
See Professional Biographies, DAYTON, OHIO

Gould, James R., (AV) ....'32 '58 C.210 B.A. L.309 LL.B. 3600 Shroyer Rd.
Gounaris, George J. ....'28 '60 C.201 L.1340 LL.B. Prob. J.
Gounaris, Nicholas G., (BV) '67 '95
C.473 B.A. L.201 J.D. 130 West 2nd Street, Suite 450
Gowdown, David A. ....'48 '72 C.610 B.B.A. L.608 J.D. Com. Pleas J.
Gower, John W. ....'16 '49 C.119 B.S. L.150 LL.B. 1431 Wilmington Ave.‡
Grandjean, Dalma C., (BV) ....'— '77 C&L.201 B.A., J.D. [Altick&C.]
Granzow, Paul H., (AV) ....'27 '50 C.201 L.150 LL.B. 50 E. 3rd St.‡
Greaney, Dennis J. ....'45 '79 C&L.201 B.A., J.D. Mag., Mun. Ct.
Green, John L., (AV) ....'— '82 C.27 A.B. L.607 J.D. [Ⓢ Coolidge,W.W.&L.]
Green, Thomas M. ....'— '75 C.385 A.B. L.608 J.D. [Green&G.]
Green & Green, Lawyers, (AV) ....109 North Main Street
Greene, James R., III, & Associates, (BV) '59 '86
C.1208 B.A. L.608 J.D. 120 West 2nd Street, Suite 900
Greene, Nelson F. ....'63 '88 C&L.880 B.A., J.D. Law V.P., NCR Corp.
Greer, David C., (AV) ....'37 '62 C&L.976 B.A., LL.B. [Bieser,G.&L.]
Greer, James H., (BV) ....'64 '90 C.347 B.A. L.201 J.D. [Bieser,G.&L.]
Gregg, Scott A. '63 '88 C.1150 B.A. L.421 J.D.
(adm. in KY; not adm. in OH) Assoc. Tax Coun., NCR Corp.
Grieshop, David B., (BV) ....'45 '71 C.608 B.S. L.607 J.D. [Flanagan,L.H.&S.]
Gruenberg, Jonas J., (AV) ....'— '70 C.659 B.S. L.880 J.D. [Coolidge,W.W.&L.]
Guay, Ronald O. '— '99 C&L.431 B.A., J.D.
(adm. in ME; not adm. in OH) Energy Coun., MeadWestvaco Corp.
Gudorf, Theodore G., (BV) ....'55 '86 C.1208 B.A. L.201 J.D. [Gudorf]
Gudorf Law Offices, (BV) ....318 W. 4th St.
Gulas, John S. ....'58 '83 C.980 B.A. L.851 J.D. 34 North Main Street
Gump, Dennis E., (BV) ....'44 '69 C.610 B.B.A. L.607 J.D. [Gump]

Gump Law Office, (BV)
2541 Shiloh Springs Road, 45426-2197
Telephone: 937-854-4900 Fax: 937-854-0320
Email: gump@gumplaw.com URL: http://www.lawyers.com/gumplawoffice
Dennis E. Gump.
Family Law, Adoption Law, Divorce, Child Custody, Child Support, Wills and Probate, Trusts and Estates, Personal Injury, Automobile Accidents, Criminal Defense, Traffic Violations, Social Security, Workers Compensation.
See Professional Biographies, DAYTON, OHIO

Gunnoe, Gerald E., (BV) ....'48 '73 C.610 B.S. L.150 J.D. 2525 St. Route 725
Haaker, Christine M., (BV) ....'69 '94 C.201 B.S. L.608 J.D. [Thompson H.]
Hackert, Timothy J., (AV) ....'53 '80 C.309 B.A. L.569 J.D. [Thompson H.]
Hadi, Vaseem S. ....'75 '02 C.1208 B.A. L.201 J.D. [Ⓐ Freund,F.&A.]
Hadley, Robert J., (AV) ....'38 '63 C.608 B.A. L.309 LL.B. [Thompson H.]
Hagan, Timothy W., (AV) ....'49 '76 C.188 B.S. L.276 J.D. [Dinsmore&S.] (Pat.)
Hahn, Douglas C., (BV) ....'52 '76 C.303 B.A. L.851 J.D. [Hunt&W.]
Hale, Tarin Stuart ....'66 '92 C.381 B.G.S. L.150 J.D. [Ⓐ S.G.Caras]
Hall, David L., (BV) ....'40 '68 C.952 A.B. L.930 J.D. [Ⓒ Altick&C.] (⊙Wilmington)
Hall, Dennis L., (AV) ....'44 '69 C&L.150 B.A., J.D. [Hall&M.] ⊙
Hall, Keith Richard, (BV) ....'47 '73 C&L.607 B.A., J.D. First National Plaza, Suite 2103
Hall, W. Leland ....'25 '53 C&L.608 J.D. 2591 Old Whipp Ct.‡

Hall & Mueller, A Legal Professional Association, (AV) BB
51 Irongate Park Drive, 45459 ⊙
Telephone: 937-912-8910 Facsimile: 937-912-8920
URL: http://www.hallmuellerlaw.com
Dennis L. Hall; Carolyn L. Mueller;—Andrew P. Conley. Of Counsel: Steven C. Katchman.
General Business Practice. Corporation, Labor and Employment Law, Banking, Commercial Collections, Taxation, Probate, Estate Planning, Real Estate Law. Trials and Appeals.
Fairborn, Ohio Office: 3040 Presidential Drive, Suite 222, 45324. Telephone: 937-912-8910. Facsimile: 937-912-6920.
See Professional Biographies, DAYTON, OHIO

Hallinan, Paul G., (AV) ....'53 '80 C.602 A.B. L.200 J.D. [Porter W.M.&A.]

Hamilton, Karen E., Attorney At Law Inc.
(See Columbus)

Hammond, Julie Cope ....'73 '00 C.303 B.A. L.201 J.D. [Ⓐ Altick&C.] (Pat.)
Hamrick, Winn C., (AV) ....'23 '50 L.150 LL.M. 1241 Brooklands Rd.
Hanaghan, Dennis M., (BV) ....'39 '66 C.347 B.A. L.1119 LL.B. 34 N. Main St.
Hancock, George L., Jr. ....'53 '79 C.383 B.A. L.851 J.D. 7235 New Carlisle Rd.★
Hanseman, Robert G., (BV) ....'69 '95 C.608 B.A. L.273 J.D. [Ⓐ Sebaly,S.&D.]
Hansen, Chad D. ....'— '97 C.877 B.A. L.336 J.D. [Ⓐ Coolidge,W.W.&L.]
Hansen, Thomas A., Law Offices of, (BV) '40 '65
C.607 A.B. L.608 J.D. 130 W. 2nd St., Ste. 1900
Hanson, Diane E., (CV) ....'53 '93 C.150 B.A. L.201 J.D. [Ⓐ Dyer,G.M.&S.]
Haper, Cori R. ....'76 '04 C.865 B.S. L.201 J.D. [Ⓐ Thompson H.]
Harker, Donald F., III, (AV) ....'44 '75 C.1208 B.A. L.607 J.D. 130 W. Second St.
Harlamert, Irvin H., Jr. ....'30 '55 C.207 A.B. L.608 J.D. 330 Southview Road
Harlan, Camille Louise ....'57 '94 C.1208 B.A. L.201 J.D. [Ⓐ G.C.Gibson]
Harmon, Sean H. ....'70 '97 C.602 B.A. L.201 J.D. [Jablinski,F.R.&M.]
Harr, Josie Olsvig ....'57 '88 C.1208 B.A. L.1019 J.D. Co. Pros. Atty. Off.
Harrelson, Laura Goehring, (BV) ....'57 '83 C.608 B.A. L.117 J.D. [Dinsmore&S.]
Harrington, Thomas J., (AV) ....'35 '60 C&L.150 B.B.A., J.D. [Ⓒ Pickrel,S.&E.]
Harris, Justin D. ....'79 '04 C.97 B.S. L.608 J.D. [Ⓐ Freund,F.&A.]
Harrison, Jennifer Hann, (BV) ....'69 '96 C.658 B.A. L.1017 J.D. [Ⓐ Crew&B.]
Harrison, John Clayton ....'33 '66 C.385 B.A. L.999 J.D. [J.Harrison]
Harrison, Jack ....130 W. 2nd Street, Suite 604
Harson, Linn S., (BV) ....'65 '96 C.608 B.S. L.201 J.D. [Thompson H.]
Hart, John E., (BV) ....'59 '86 C.130 B.A. L.201 J.D. Gen. Coun., Univ. of Dayton
Hart, Tami L. ....'79 '04 C.150 B.S. L.201 J.D. [Ⓐ Porter W.M.&A.]
Hart, Terry Ray ....'50 '97 C.1112 L.201 J.D. Law Off. of the Pub. Def.
Hartwig, Gordon E. '43 '70 C&L.546 B.S., J.D.
(adm. in NE; not adm. in OH) 17 S. Patterson Blvd.‡

Harvey, Anne Catherine, (BV) '61 '85 C&L.201 B.S., J.D.
5335 Far Hills Avenue, Suite 313, 45429 ⊙
Telephone: 937-439-5708 Fax: 937-439-5710
Email: lawyeranneharvey@yahoo.com URL: http://www.lawfirmanneharvey.com
Languages: Sign Language.
Trials, Appeals, Federal, State and Municipal Criminal Defense, Divorce, Dissolution, Child Custody, Military Domestic Relations Law.
Cincinnati Office: Tri-State Building, 432 Walnut Street, Suite 1001, 45202. Telephone: 513-721-2960. Fax: 513-621-3017.
See Professional Biographies, DAYTON, OHIO

Hatton, Frederick B. ....'72 '00 C.1208 B.S. L.201 J.D. [Ⓐ Myers&F.]
Hatton, Nicole Kristen ....'75 '00 C&L.201 B.A., J.D. 2nd Dist. Ct. of Appeals
Havemann, William L., (BV) ....'45 '70 C.597 B.A. L.930 J.D. 2049 Brandy Mill Ln.
Havener, Charles R. ....'57 '83 C.608 B.S. L.201 J.D. LEXIS-NEXIS
Haviland, John F., Jr., (AV) ....'59 '85 C&L.201 B.S., J.D. [Bieser,G.&L.]
Hawk, Wilbert, Jr. '28 '55 C.97 B.S. L.608 J.D.
Asst. Gen. Coun. & Chf. Coun., Intell. Prop. Law, NCR Corp. (Pat.)
Hawkins, H. Donald ....'28 '53 C&L.477 A.B., J.D. 435 Hulman Bldg. (⊙Centerville)
Hebert, William F. '28 '52 C.1021 B.A. L.1009 LL.B.
(adm. in NY; not adm. in OH) 4155 Meadowsweet Dr.‡
Heck, Cynthia M., (BV) ....'53 '79 C&L.201 B.A., J.D. 120 W. 2nd. St., Rm. 1510
Heck, Mathias H., Jr., (AV) ....'47 '72 C.436 B.S. L.276 J.D. Pros. Atty.
Hedrick, James E., (AV) ....'54 '78 C.243 B.A. L.477 J.D. [Hedrick&J.]
Hedrick, R. Holtzman ....'79 '04 C.347 B.A. L.1119 J.D. [Ⓐ Faruki I.&C.]

Hedrick & Jordan Co., A Legal Professional Association, (AV)
Suite 300 124 East Third Street, 45402
Telephone: 937-228-3889 Fax: 937-223-3848
James E. Hedrick; April Ann Jordan; John G. Jansing.
Real Estate Development, Leasing, Financing, Business Formation and Collections.
See Professional Biographies, DAYTON, OHIO

Helms, Jeffrey R. ....'76 '02 C.973 B.A. L.201 J.D. [Ⓐ Jablinski,F.R.&M.]
Hemenway, James K., (BV) ....'57 '88 C.347 B.S. L.201 J.D. [Young&A.]
Hemmert, William F., (BV) ....'41 '73 C.608 B.S. L.1340 J.D. 6326 Far Hills Avenue
Hempfling, Richard, (BV) ....'54 '85 C&L.201 B.S., J.D. [Ⓐ Flanagan,L.H.&S.]
Henderson, Toby K. ....'70 '99 C.63 B.S. L.201 J.D. [Ⓐ Sebaly,S.&D.]
Henke, Lawrence W., III, (BV) ....'43 '70 C.201 B.A. L.1340 J.D. [Henke]
Henke Law Offices, (BV) ....371 W. First St.
Henrici, Kelly A. '62 '94
C.339 B.A. L.201 J.D. Gen. Coun. & Sec., The Relizon Company
Henry, R. Mark, (BV) ....'54 '93 C&L.201 B.A., J.D. 130 W. 2nd Street, Suite 1818
Henschen, Deborah Jean '— '80
C.216 B.A. L.1017 J.D. Coun., Nationwide Mutual Ins. Co.
Herbert, J. Stephen, (AV) ....'— '78 C.976 B.A. L.893 J.D. [Coolidge,W.W.&L.]

Herdman, G. Douglas, (BV) '52 '83 C.1163 B.A. L.200 J.D.
Magistrate Montgomery County Juvenile Court
Herman, Carrie E. .... '73 '99 C.608 B.S.B.S.B.A. L.94 J.D. [Ⓐ Chernesky,H.&K.]
Heron, John J., (AV) .... '40 '65 C&L.608 B.S.B.A., J.D. [Porter W.M.&A.]
Herr, J. Michael, (AV) ....'43 '68 C.602 A.B. L.608 J.D. [Thompson H.]
Herron, Philip B., (BV) ....'39 '66 C.611 B.A. L.608 J.D. [Altick&C.]
Hesse, Lisa A., (BV) .... '64 '89 C.910 B.A. L.201 J.D. [Ⓐ Freund,F.&A.]
Heyman, Ralph E., (AV) .... '31 '56 C.197 A.B. L.309 LL.B. [Chernesky,H.&K.]
Hickey, Robert E., Jr., (AV) ....'49 '74 C&L.608 B.S., J.D. 2000 Courthouse Plz.
Hilgeman, John P., (BV) ....'57 '83 C.150 B.A. L.201 J.D. [Cowan&H.]
Hilker, Samuel R. ....'44 '76 C.610 B.B.A. L.1003 J.D. Dep. Dir., AFMC Law Center
Hill, James M., (BV) ....'59 '85 C.1208 B.S. L.880 J.D. [J.M.Hill]
Hill, Patricia L. .... '74 '00 C&L.201 B.C.E., J.D. [Ⓐ Statman,H.S.&E.]
Hill, James M., Co., L.P.A., (BV) ....2365 Lakeview Dr., Ste. A
Hinds, Joseph J. '47 '74 C.383 B.A. L.69 J.D.
(adm. in TX; not adm. in OH) 9770 Rose Arbor Dr.‡

Hines, Dean Edward, (BV) '62 '94 C.476 B.B.A. L.150 J.D.
5335 Far Hills Avenue, Suite 313, 45429
Telephone: 937-439-5708 Fax: 937-439-5710
Email: hineslpa@ameritech.net
Taxation, Business Taxation, Estate and Gift Taxation, Property Tax Appeals, IRS Audits, Domestic Relations, Family Law, Divorce, Child Custody, Domestic Violence, Child Custody, Visitation Rights, Adoption Law, Alimony.
See Professional Biographies, DAYTON, OHIO

Hitter, Joseph I. '44 '70 C.415 B.S. L.724 J.D.
(adm. in NY; not adm. in OH) Vice Pres., The Mead Corp.
Hix, Ernest T. ....'22 '52 C&L.273 B.M.E., LL.B. 53 E. Thurston Blvd. (Pat.)‡
Hoak, Jonathan S., (AV) '49 '77 C.174 B.A. L.221 J.D.
(adm. in IA; not adm. in OH) Sr. V.P. & Gen. Coun., NCR Corp.
Hobson, Sandra K., (BV) ....'53 '78 C.597 B.A. L.608 J.D. Asst. Co. Pros. Atty.
Hochman, James B., (BV) .... '41 '66 C&L.608 B.S., J.D. [Hochman&P.]

Hochman & Plunkett, (BV)
Suite 650 Talbott Tower, 45402
Telephone: 937-228-2666 Fax: 937-228-0508
URL: http://www.hochmanplunkett.com
James B. Hochman; Gary D. Plunkett (Certified Specialist in Workers' Compensation Law, Ohio State Bar Association);—Jeffrey D. Snyder (Certified Specialist in Workers' Compensation Law, Ohio State Bar Association); Carla J. Lauer; Todd T. Miller (Certified Specialist in Workers' Compensation Law, Ohio State Bar Association); John A. Cervay; Brett R. Bissonnette.
Personal Injury, Automobile Accidents, Workers' Compensation and Social Security Disability Law. General Civil and Criminal Practice in all Courts.
Reference: Society Bank, N.A.
See Professional Biographies, DAYTON, OHIO

Hodapp, Ruey F., Jr., (BV) .... '28 '58 C&L.150 B.B.A., LL.B. 3490 S. Dixie Ave.

Hodge, Victor A., (BV) '47 '81 C.1150 B.A. L.201 J.D.
130 West Second Street, Suite 810, 45402
Telephone: 937-461-0009; 898-4632 Fax: 937-461-1639
Email: attyhodge@sbcglobal.net URL: http://www.lawyers.com/hodgelaw
Criminal Defense, Family Law, Personal Injury, Probate, Divorce, Custody, Support, Paternity, Felonies, Misdemeanors, Driving While Intoxicated. Civil Appeals, Trial and Appellate Practice.
See Professional Biographies, DAYTON, OHIO

Hoefflin, Reynold C., (BV) .... '35 '60 C.631 B.A. L.607 J.D. 144 Thruston Blvd. E.
Hoffman, Craig A. ....'77 '02 C&L.150 B.A., J.D. [Ⓐ Porter W.M.&A.]
Hoffman, Louis I., (AV) ....'36 '61 C&L.608 B.A., J.D. [Flanagan,L.H.&S.]
Hoffman, Timothy D., (AV) ....'— '81 C&L.117 B.A., J.D. [Coolidge,W.W.&L.]
Hollencamp, Arthur R., (AV) ....'51 '80 C.734 B.A. L.201 J.D. [Hollencamp&H.]
Hollencamp, Robt. A. ....'24 '50 C&L.602 B.S., B.L. 5136 Tabitian Pl.‡
Hollencamp & Hollencamp, (AV)
130 W. Second Street, Suite 2107, First National Plaza
Hollenkamp, Nicholas C., (AV) ....'37 '64 C.973 B.S. L.150 J.D. [Dinsmore&S.]
Hollingsworth, Jonathan, (AV) ....'57 '83 C.309 B.A. L.477 J.D. [J.Hollingsworth]
Hollingsworth, J., LLC, (AV) ....137 N. Main St., Ste. 1002
Hollins, Gerald B. '32 '70
C.421 B.S.E.E. L.1340 J.D. Patent Atty., Dept. of the Air Force (Pat.)
Holm, Carol J., (CV) '38 '82 C.352 B.A. L.201 J.D.
130 West Second Street, Suite 1010
Holmes, Nathan E. ....'70 '01 C&L.150 B.A., J.D. [Ⓐ Thompson H.]
Holt, Jon D. ....'70 '96 C.473 B.A. L.201 J.D. Corp. Coun., LexisNexis
Holton, Thomas A., (AV) ....'41 '67 C.608 B.S. L.215 J.D. [Porter W.M.&A.]
Holz, Michael H., (BV) ...... '42 '68 C.967 A.B. L.150 J.D. 507 Wilmington Ave., Ste. 1
Holzer, Richard J. ....'40 '75 C.282 B.A. L.1340 J.D. 2251 Charleston Way
Holzfaster, Byron E., (AV) ....'15 '40 C.610 L.150 1105 Wilmington Avenue‡

Holzfaster, Cecil, McKnight & Mues, A Legal Professional Association, (AV)
1105 Wilmington Avenue, 45420-4108
Telephone: 937-293-2141 FAX: 937-293-0914
Email: hcmm@hcmmlaw.com URL: http://www.hcmmlaw.com
Members of the Firm: Robert L. Mues; Joseph E. Balmer, III; R. Anne Shale. Associate: Tammy C. Nortman.
General Civil Practice. Corporate, Wills and Probate, Trusts & Estates, Asset Protection, Charitable Giving, Estate Litigation, Estate Planning, Guardianship and Conservatorship, Personal Injury Law, Motor Vehicle Accidents and Injuries, Dog Bites, Slip and Fall, Medical Malpractice, Domestic Relations, Divorce and Custody, Adoptions, Child Support, Domestic Violence, Premarital Agreements, Spousal Support, Insurance and Real Estate, Buying and Selling of Businesses, Family Business Law, Limited Liability Company Law, Partnership Law, Small Business Law, Driving While Intoxicated, Juvenile Law, Misdemeanors, Education Law, School Law, Elder Law.
Representative Clients: Cumis Insurance Society Inc.; Cuna Mutual Insurance Society.
Reference: KeyBank, N.A.
See Professional Biographies, DAYTON, OHIO

Hong, Thomas S. ....'— '01 C.1494 B.A. L.112 J.D. 6077 Far Hills Ave.
Horan, Kevin R., (BV) ....'64 '91 C.823 A.B. L.201 J.D. Pros. Atty.
Horenstein, Steven B., (AV) ....'46 '71 C.454 B.A. L.597 J.D. [Horenstein,N.&B.]
Horenstein, Nicholson & Blumenthal, (AV) ....124 E. 3rd. St.
Horstman, Paul L., (BV) ....'42 '67 C.201 B.A. L.150 J.D. [Faruki I.&C.]
Horwitz, Jonathan A., (BV) ....'72 '97 C.347 B.A. L.150 J.D. Asst. Pros. Atty.
Horwitz, Jonathan A., (BV) ....'44 '75 C.201 B.A. L.221 J.D. [J.A.Horwitz]
Horwitz, Jonathan A., Co., L.P.A., (BV) ....6927 N. Main St., Ste. 202
Hoshor, Peter B. ....'63 '92 C.610 B.S. L.117 J.D. [Gammell,H.K.&R.]
Hoskins, Joseph C. '66 '93 C.851 B.B.A. L.607 J.D.
Asst. Gen. Coun., Liberty Capital Inc.
Houliston, Deborah Battle ....'54 '88 C.1161 B.A. L.1340 J.D. Lexis-Nexis
Houston, Cinamon S., (BV) ....'69 '97 C.339 B.S. L.201 J.D. [Ⓐ Freund,F.&A.]
Howard, Robert J. ....'73 '02 C.1208 B.S. L.201 J.D. [Ⓐ Falke&D.]
Howarth, Cooley R., Jr. '49 '76
C.475 B.A. L.208 J.D. Assoc. Prof., Univ. of Dayton, Sch. of Law
Hruska, Gary M., (BV) ....'53 '80 C.932 B.B.A. L.201 J.D. [Ⓐ Flanagan,L.H.&S.]
Huber, Matthew Barton ....'70 '96 C.150 B.B.A. L.200 J.D. NCR

Hungerford, Eric S. '39 '67 C.201 B.A. L.150 J.D.
Sr. V.P., Secy. & Legal Coun., The Beerman Realty Co.
Hunt, Deborah D., (BV) ....'51 '88 C.923 B.A. L.201 J.D. [Sebaly,S.&D.]
Hunt, Gary L. .... '48 '73 C&L.923 B.S., J.D. 2000 West Dorothy Lane
Hunt, Kevin Michael ....'67 '01 C&L.201 B.A., J.D. Richard M. Hunt Co.
Hunt, Nathan C. ....'74 '01 C.1208 B.A. L.851 J.D. [Ⓐ Thompson H.]
Hunt, Richard M., (AV) ....'38 '66 C.201 B.A. L.1340 J.D. [Hunt&W.]
Hunt & Wehner, (AV) ....One 1st National Plaza
Hunter, Stephen C., (BV) ....'48 '74 C&L.608 B.S., J.D. Talbott Twr., Ste. 226
Hustad, John C. F. '31 '63 C.912 L.213 LL.B.
(adm. in MI; not adm. in OH) 1500 Heritage St.‡
Huston, Steven C. '54 '80 C.337 B.A. L.365 J.D.
(adm. in IL; not adm. in OH) Dayton Superior Corp. (⊙Des Plaines, IL)
Hutzel, Rachel A. ....'56 '91 C.1149 B.A. L.201 J.D. 2000 Courthouse Plz., N.E.
Hyde, Henry, III, (CV) ....'67 '94 C.884 B.A. L.201 J.D. [Ⓐ Dyer,G.M.&S.]
Ignozzi, Kenneth J., (BV) ....'67 '91 C.25 B.S. L.201 J.D. [Dyer,G.M.&S.]
Imperato, Ralph E., (BV) ....'70 '96 C.676 B.S. L.201 J.D. Asst. Pros. Atty.
Intili, Thomas J., (BV) ....'59 '86 C.651 B.A. L.930 J.D. [Falke&D.]
Ireland, D. Jeffrey, (AV) ....'54 '80 C.207 B.A. L.201 J.D. [Faruki I.&C.]
Izenson, Fred M., (AV) ....'34 '59 C.472 B.B.A. L.608 J.D. [Izenson,F.&B.]
Izenson, Fuchsman & Brinkman, (AV) ....120 W. Second St.
Jablinski, David S., (BV) ....'59 '85 C&L.201 B.S., J.D. [Jablinski,F.R.&M.]
Jablinski, Eugene A., (AV) ....'29 '56 C.201 B.A. L.150 J.D. [Ⓒ Jablinski,F.R.&M.] ‡

Jablinski, Folino, Roberts & Martin, A Legal Professional Association, (AV)
Historic Huffman House, 214 W. Monument Avenue, P.O. Box 10068, 45402-7068
Telephone: 937-461-5980 Fax: 937-461-4139
Email: sean@jfrmlaw.com URL: http://www.jfrmlaw.com
Thomas P. Martin; Brian M. Roberts; David S. Jablinski; John H. Stachler; Sean H. Harmon;—Jeffrey R. Helms. Of Counsel: Eugene A. Jablinski (Retired); Shearl J. Roberts (Retired); Thomas F. Folino (1928-2002).
Personal Injury, Probate, Estate Planning, Corporation, Real Estate, Family, Commercial and Bankruptcy Law. Trials and Appeals. General Civil Practice.
See Professional Biographies, DAYTON, OHIO

Jacklitch, Thomas R., Jr. .... '42 '67 C&L.930 B.A., J.D. [Ⓐ Gammell,H.K.&R.]
Jacobs, Ellis ....'53 '81 C.999 B.S. L.201 J.D. Legal Aid Society of Dayton
Jacobs, Richard E., (AV) '53 '80 C&L.608 B.S.B.A., J.D.
V.P., Law & Dep. Gen. Coun., LEXISNEXIS
Jacobson, James L., (AV) ....'52 '78 C.477 B.S. L.608 J.D. [Pickrel,S.&E.]
Jacox, William R., (AV) '19 '50 C.791 B.S.E.E. L.1340 J.D.
2310 Far Hills Ave. (Pat.)‡

Jacox, Meckstroth & Jenkins, (AV)
Far Hills Building, 2310 Far Hills Avenue, 45419 ⊙
Telephone: 937-298-2811 Fax: 800-298-7418
Email: law@jmj.biz
Members of Firm: Alan F. Meckstroth; Matthew R. Jenkins.
Intellectual Property, Patent, Trademark and Copyright Law. Domestic and International.
Bradenton, Florida Office: 1205 Mantee Avenue West. 34205. Telephone: 941-747-0339. Fax: 800-298-7418.
Sarasota, Florida Office: 6320 Venture Drive, Suite 104, 34202. Telephone: 941-388-9532. Fax: 800-298-7418.

Jacques, Robert F. ....'74 '02 C.894 A.B. L.608 J.D. [Ⓐ Hollencamp&H.]
Jaeger, Charles E. ....'46 '71 C&L.851 B.B.A., J.D. Product Mgr., NexTech, Inc.‡
Janes, Robert J., (BV) ....'51 '85 C.608 B.A. L.117 J.D. 130 W. 2nd St., Ste. 1850
Janis, Patrick J., (AV) ....'57 '82 C.967 B.A. L.608 J.D. [Freund,F.&A.]
Jankowski, Joseph J., Jr., (BV) '47 '74
C.363 B.A. L.851 J.D. Corp. Coun., C.H. Dean & Assocs., Inc.
Jansen, Susan D., (AV) ....'62 '87 C&L.201 B.A., J.D. [Logothetis,P.&D.]
Jansing, John G., (BV) ....'63 '88 C.150 B.A. L.201 J.D. [Hedrick&J.]
Jefferis, Robert F., Sr., (BV) ....'23 '50 C.473 B.S. L.597 J.D. 2533 Far Hills Ave.
Jefferson, My'chael D. ....'— '03 C.692 B.A. L.201 J.D. [Ⓐ Coolidge,W.W.&L.]
Jenkins, Matthew R., (AV) ....'56 '82 C.608 B.S. L.201 J.D. [Jacox,M.&J.] (Pat.) ⊙
Jenkins, Peter L. ....'— '03 C.207 B.A. L.150 J.D. [Ⓐ Coolidge,W.W.&L.]
Jenks, Thomas E., (AV) ....'29 '53 C.473 L.608 J.D. [Jenks,P.&O.]

Jenks, Pyper & Oxley Co., L.P.A., (AV)
Courthouse Plaza SW, Suite 901, 10 N. Ludlow Street, 45402
Telephone: 937-223-3001 Fax: 937-223-3103
Email: lawyers@jpolawyers.com URL: http://www.jpolawyers.net
Thomas E. Jenks; Thomas H. Pyper; Scott G. Oxley;—P. Christian Nordstrom; Mark Engling; Chad M. Kohler.
General Liability, Property, Workers Compensation, Bad Faith, First Party Coverage, Third Party Coverage, Construction Defect, Environmental, Toxic Tort, Employment Practices, SUI, PIP/Med Pay, Inland Marine, Intellectual Property, Sexual Harassment, Subrogation, Professional Liability, including Accountants, Real Estate, Architects & Engineers, D&O and Agents E&O, Professional Malpractice, including Dental, Attorney and Medical.
See Professional Biographies, DAYTON, OHIO

Jerardi, Peter J., Jr., (AV) ....'40 '65 C.610 B.Sc. L.608 J.D. [Young,P.L.&J.]
Jewson, Matthew T. ....'— '94 C.610 B.B.A. L.608 J.D. [Ⓐ Pickrel,S.&E.]
Jividen, William A. ....'67 '99 C.871 B.S. L.1170 J.D. [Ⓐ Dinsmore&S.] (Pat.)
Jocha-Ervin, Joanne, (BV) '47 '91
C.608 B.S. L.201 J.D. 135 West Dorothy Lane, Suite 101
Johnsen, Kirk D. ....'61 '87 C.813 B.A. L.659 J.D. Asst. Law V.P., NCR Corp.
Johnson, C. Terry, (AV) ....'37 '64 C.855 B.A. L.178 J.D. [Porter W.M.&A.]
Johnson, Charles A., (BV) ....'40 '72 C.608 B.Sc. L.1340 J.D. [Johnson,D.B.&L.]
Johnson, Christopher F., (AV) ....'53 '80 C.970 B.A. L.7 J.D. [Freund,F.&A.]
Johnson, Debbie Watts, (BV) .....'56 '91 C.150 B.S.E.E. L.608 J.D. Sr. Atty., NCR Corp.
Johnson, Lindsay M. ....'78 '04 C.201 B.A. L.608 J.D. [Ⓐ Freund,F.&A.]
Johnson, Douple, Beyoglides & Leve, (BV) .... 130 W. 2nd St., Ste. 1900
Jones, Helen L., (BV) '51 '86
C.473 B.S.Ed. L.201 J.D. Exec. Dir., Montgomery Co. Children Servs.
Jones, Robert Wesley ....'57 '84 C.97 B.S. L.607 J.D. 12 W. Monument Ave.
Jones, Scott K., (BV) ....'72 '98 C.473 B.S.B.A. L.201 J.D. [Ⓐ Porter W.M.&A.]
Jones, Taylor, Jr., (BV) ....'40 '76 C.231 B.S. L.1340 LL.B. 1308 Talbott Tower
Jones, Teresa D., (AV) ....'48 '88 C.502 B.A. L.201 J.D. [Thompson H.]
Jordan, April Ann, (AV) ....'61 '87 C.346 B.S. L.201 J.D. [Hedrick&J.]
Justice, J. Steven ....'58 '94 C.992 B.A L.150 J.D [Taft,S.&H.]
Justice, Tabitha ....'76 '02 C.610 B.A. L.201 J.D. [Ⓐ Subashi,W.&B.]
Kagan, Rebecca Appenzeller, (BV) '52 '89 C.812 B.A. L.1003 J.D.
1900 Kettering Tower
Kanak, Joseph R. ....'47 '74 C.201 B.A. L.150 J.D. 1301 Lamar St.
Kane, John F. ....'60 '98 C.1208 B.S. L.201 J.D. [Ⓐ Thompson H.] (See Pat. Sect.)
Kantosky, William H. ....'48 '77 C.49 B.A. L.7 J.D. V.P., Chicago Title Ins. Co.
Kapp, Marshall B. '49 '74 C.367 B.A. L.273 J.D.
(adm. in FL; not adm. in OH) Prof., Wright State Univ.
Kaskey, Gregory M. ....'75 '01 C.610 B.B.A. L.200 J.D. [Ⓐ Dinsmore&S.]
Katchman, Steven C., (CV) ....'60 '89 C.150 B.A. L.201 J.D. [Ⓒ Hall&M.]
Katchmer, George A. ....'48 '81 C.655 B.A. L.201 J.D. [Ⓒ L.P.Mulligan&Assoc.]

Kearney, Keith R., (AV) ....'56 '84 C.651 B.A. L.201 J.D. [Rogers&G.]
Kearney, Philip F., Jr. ....'46 '75 C.608 B.S. L.117 J.D. 1158 Jeanette Dr.
Keck, Emerson R., (BV) ....'46 '75 C.210 B.A. L.608 J.D. [A Flanagan,L.H.&S.]
Keelor, Robert K. '33 '64
C.631 B.A. L.1340 J.D. Pres., International Display Systems, Inc.
Keeton, Anne P. ....'78 '03 C.893 B.A. L.383 J.D. [A Subashi,W.&B.]
Kegerreis, Melissa A. ....'56 '81 C.608 B.S.B.A. L.273 J.D. 642 Orlando Ter.
Keish, Rodney D. ....'45 '72 C.999 B.S. L.1340 J.D. 4428 N. Dixie Dr.
Kelleher, James W., (AV) ....'50 '79 C.201 B.A. L.200 J.D. [Pickrel,S.&E.]
Kellner, Jeffrey M. ....'53 '85 C.608 B.S. L.117 J.D. 131 N. Ludlow St.
Kemper, Richd. J. ....'30 '57 C.151 B.S. L.1340 LL.B. 120 W. 2nd St.
Kendo, Thomas W., Jr., (BV) ....'66 '92 C.901 B.A. L.201 J.D. [Gammell,H.K.&R.]
Kern, Lillian M. ....'31 '64 C.472 A.B. L.150 J.D. Ret. Pleas J.
Kessler, John W. ....'42 '68 C.473 B.A. L.851 J.D. Com. Pleas J.
Kessler, Philip E. ....'70 '99 C.851 B.A. L.201 J.D. [A Porter W.M.&A.]
Kidwell, Charles Y., Jr., (AV) ....'58 '85 C.473 B.S. L.201 J.D. [Porter W.M.&A.]
Kiefaber, Robert W. ....'76 '02 C.385 B.S. L.436 J.D. [A Faruki I.&C.]
Killworth, Richard A., (AV) ....'43 '70 C.679 B.S. L.273 J.D. [Dinsmore&S.] (Pat.)

Killworth, Gottman, Hagan & Schaeff, L.L.P.
(See Dinsmore & Shohl LLP)

King, Addie Jane ....'76 '01 C.607 B.A. L.201 J.D. City of Dayton, Pros. Off.
King, Judith Ann ....'46 '77 301 W. Third Street, 2nd Floor
King, Michele L. ....'63 '91 C.94 B.L.S. L.818 J.D. [A Freund,F.&A.]
King, Scott A., (AV) ....'61 '86 C&L.608 B.A., J.D. [Thompson H.]
Kingseed, C. Mark, (AV) ....'— '79 C.473 A.B. L.276 J.D. [A Coolidge,W.W.&L.]
Kinlin, Donald J., (AV) ....'38 '76 C.823 B.S. L.546 J.D. [Thompson H.]
Kinney, Winfield E., III, (Co., L.P.A.) '34 '61
C.150 B.A. L.266 J.D. 120 W. 2nd St., 20th Fl.
Kirkland, James R., (AV) ....'44 '69 C.611 B.A. L.608 J.D. [J.R.Kirkland&Assoc.]

Kirkland, James R., & Associates, Co., L.P.A., (AV)
One Eleven West First Street Suite 518, 45402-1131
Telephone: 937-223-0697 Fax: 937-223-5318
Email: kirkland@sbcglobal.net URL: http://www.lawyers.com/kirklandlaw
James R. Kirkland (Certified Specialist, Family Relations Law, Ohio State Bar Association).
Family, Custody, Divorce and Juvenile Law. Civil Trials. Probate.
See Professional Biographies, DAYTON, OHIO

Kislig, Kimberly S. ....'63 '03 C.1049 B.B.A. L.607 J.D. [A Freund,F.&A.]
Kissinger, Scott V. '58 '85 C.478 B.A. L.597 J.D.
(adm. in IN; not adm. in OH; Pat.)
VP, Law and Dep. Gen Coun., Cust. & Coml. Trans., LexisNexis
Kloppenberg, Lisa A. ....'62 '87 C&L.800 B.A., J.D. Univ. of Dayton Sch. of Law
Knapp, William G., III, (BV) ....'50 '81 C.201 B.A. L.200 J.D. 8881 Susan Dr.
Kneisly, L. Douglas ....'36 '62 C&L.150 B.B.A., LL.B. [C Chernesky,H.&K.]
Knight, Randal S., (BV) ....'59 '92 C.381 B.A. L.201 J.D. 427 Telford Ave.
Knostman, Richard G., (BV) ....'47 '72 C.201 B.A. L.851 J.D. [Knostman&F.]
Knostman & Foster, (BV) .... 4428 North Dixie Drive
Knoth, Thomas A., (AV) ....'59 '84 C.201 B.S. L.945 J.D. [Thompson H.]
Koenig, Joseph A., (BV) ....'49 '75 C.999 B.A. L.607 J.D. 419 Lewiston Rd.
Kohler, Chad M. ....'76 '01 C.201 B.A. L.124 J.D. [A Jenks,P.&O.]
Kolberg, John F., (BV) ....'57 '83 C&L.201 B.A., J.D. 3131 S. Dixie Dr.
Kollin, Thomas M. ....'68 '96 C.610 B.S. L.201 J.D. [Cicero&K.]
Kolotkin, Beth Ann ....'54 '80 C.1505 B.A. L.201 J.D. P.O. Box 138
Kordik, James G., (AV) ....'57 '83 C.1208 B.S. L.201 J.D. [Rogers&G.]
Korte, David C., (BV) ....'— '80 C.473 A.B. L.150 J.D. [A Coolidge,W.W.&L.]
Kosanovich, Daniel N., (AV) ....'51 '77 C.901 B.A. L.201 J.D. 28 E. Rahn Road
Koverman, John R., Jr., (AV) ....'32 '59 C.201 B.A. L.608 J.D. [Koverman&S.]

Koverman & Smith, (AV) BB
1300 Liberty Tower, 45402
Telephone: 937-222-6926 Fax: 937-222-6901
Robert J. Stoecklein (1917-1990); John R. Koverman, Jr.; Patrick K. Smith.
General Civil Practice. Business, Probate, Domestic Relations, Personal Injury, Estate Planning, Real Estate, Zoning Law, and Litigation.
See Professional Biographies, DAYTON, OHIO

Kovich, Don E., (BV) ....'53 '78 C&L.201 B.A., J.D. [A Johnson,D.B.&L.]
Kozar, Ronald J., (BV) ....'64 '89 C.679 B.A. L.228 J.D. 40 North Main Street
Koziar, Stephen F., Jr. '44 '71 C.201 B.S. L.1340 J.D.
Pres. & CEO, The Dayton Power & Light Co.
Kraemer, Thomas R., (BV) ....'61 '90 C.893 B.A. L.665 J.D. [Faruki I.&C.]
Krall, Michael Francis ....'54 '81 C&L.201 B.A., J.D. Hobart Corp.
Kramer, Scott A. ....'62 '00 C.766 B.A. L.201 J.D. [S.A.Kramer]

Kramer, Scott A., LLC, Law Office of
130 W. Second Street, Suite 924, 45402
Telephone: 937-222-1700 Fax: 937-224-0420
Email: scottakramer@sbcglobal.net
Scott A. Kramer.
See Professional Biographies, DAYTON, OHIO

Krebs, Leo F., (AV) ....'37 '66 C.201 B.A. L.276 J.D. [Bieser,G.&L.]
Kreiss, Robert A. '42 '78 C.685 B.A. L.813 J.D.
Prof. & Dir., Prog. Law & Tech., Univ. of Dayton Law Sch.
Kremer, Debra Staggs ....'56 '91 C.1056 B.A. L.208 J.D. 34 N. Main St.
Kress, Edward M., (AV) ....'49 '74 C.473 B.S. L.608 J.D. [Chernesky,H.&K.]
Krisher, Howard Penn, II, (AV) ....'47 '75 C.674 A.B. L.608 J.D. [Bieser,G.&L.]
Krumholtz, Michael W., (AV) ....'53 '79 C.207 B.A. L.150 J.D. [Bieser,G.&L.]
Krygowski, Walter J., (BV) ....'70 '96 C.1154 B.A. L.201 J.D. Asst. City Atty.
Kuczak, Konrad ....'43 '69 C.201 B.A. L.1340 J.D. 130 W. 2nd St.
Kuhns, M. Edward, (AV) ....'26 '51 C.659 A.B. L.150 LL.B. 134 Balmoral Dr.‡
Kundert, Thomas L. '46 '74
C.215 B.E.E. L.128 J.D. Pat. Atty., Dept. of the Air Force (Pat.)
Kuntz, Henry N., Jr., (BV) ....'43 '74 C.201 B.S. L.851 J.D. Com. Pleas J., Juv. Div.
Lachey, Robert E. ....'45 '73 C.1208 B.A. L.1340 J.D. [A Flanagan,L.H.&S.]
Lacouture, Paul E., (AV) ....'20 '48 C&L.976 B.A., LL.B. 2000 Courthouse Plaza, N.E.‡
Lafferty, Sheila Gay, (BV) ....'64 '89 C.608 B.S. L.201 J.D. Asst. U.S. Atty.
LaForge, Eric '45 '74 C.169 A.B. L.284 J.D.
(adm. in CA; not adm. in OH) Dir., Tax Audits & Assoc. Tax Coun., NCR Corporation
LaForte, Rene M. ....'68 '93 C.645 B.A. L.201 J.D. [C Thompson H.]
Lafuente, Cynthia B. '63 '88 C.228 B.A. L.146 J.D.
(adm. in IL; not adm. in OH) 1700 S. Patterson Blvd.
Lambert, Richard A. '58 '88 C.679 B.S.E. L.150 J.D.
(adm. in KY; not adm. in OH; Pat.) Pat. Atty., Dept. of the Air Force

Lamkin, Van Eman, Trimble, Beals & Dougherty, LLC
(See Columbus)

Lamme, Kathryn A., (AV) '46 '80 C.188 A.B. L.201 J.D.
Gen. Coun. & Sec., Standard Register Company, The
Lang, Wilbur S., (AV) ....'33 '58 C&L.608 B.S., J.D. [C Breidenbach,O.&B.]
Lantz, Kevin A. ....'57 '94 C.362 B.S. L.201 J.D. [A Surdyk,D.&T.]
Larson, David E., (BV) ....'45 '79 C.967 B.A. L.608 J.D. [A Altick&C.]
Lasky, Laurence Alan ....'52 '77 [Lasky&S.]
Lasky & Scharrer .... 130 W. Second St.
Lauer, Carla J., (BV) ....'51 '88 C.935 B.A. L.770 J.D. [A Hochman&P.]
Lavin, Richard W. '25 '54
C.215 B.Ae.E. L.1003 J.D. Sr. Intell. Prop. Atty., NCR Corp. (Pat.)
Lee, Roger A. ....'48 '76 C&L.150 B.A., J.D. 40 W. Fourth St. Ctr., Ste. 2200
Lees, Thomas E. ....'68 '98 C.608 B.S.E.E. L.117 J.D. [Stevens&S.] (Pat.)
Leffak, Ellen S., (BV) '49 '85 C.331 B.A. L.201 J.D.
Assoc. Coun., The Dayton Power & Light Co.
Lehman, Robert F. '42 '70 C&L.347 A.B., J.D.
(adm. in IN; not adm. in OH) V.P. & Gen. Coun., Charles F. Kettering Found.
Leibold, William J., (AV) ....'57 '82 C.201 B.A. L.608 J.D. [Chernesky,H.&K.]
LeMar, Andrew D. ....'77 '03 C&L.347 B.A., J.D. [A Faruki I.&C.]
Lenehan, John F. ....'40 '67 C.363 B.S.S. L.1003 J.D. Staff Atty., Dayton Bd. of Educ.
Lennen, Kevin L. ....'— '87 C.97 B.L.S. L.1003 J.D. [Rion,R.&R.]
Lentz, Mary E., (CV) ....'61 '90 C.608 B.S. L.117 J.D. [Gottschlich&P.]
Leppla, Gary J., (AV) ....'53 '78 C&L.608 B.A., J.D. [Leppla]

Leppla Associates, (AV) BB
2100 S. Patterson Boulevard, 45409
Telephone: 937-294-5959 Fax: 937-294-4411
Email: gjleppla@LepLaw.com URL: http://www.LepLaw.com
Members of Firm: Gary J. Leppla; Eric S. Thompson. Of Counsel: Jay M. Simpson; Valerie Stocklin.
Civil Litigation, Personal Injury, Medical Malpractice, Insurance, Zoning Law, Land Use, Wills and Probate, Legal Malpractice and Ethics.
See Professional Biographies, DAYTON, OHIO

Leve, Stephen J., (BV) ....'40 '66 C.16 B.A. L.851 J.D. [Johnson,D.B.&L.]
Levine, Jeffrey L. ....'51 '76 C.473 B.S. L.117 J.D. Pres., Larry Stein Realty Co.
Levinson, James R., (AV) '42 '73
C.1036 B.A. L.150 J.D. Chief, Crim. Div., Co. Pros. Off.
Levy, Mark P., (AV) ....'51 '77 C.602 B.S. L.273 J.D. [Thompson H.] (See Pat. Sect.)
Lewis, Michael V., (BV) ....'56 '81 C.607 B.A. L.201 J.D. 117 S. Main Street
Lewis, Terry L., (BV) ....'48 '79 C.1208 M.S. L.201 J.D. [T.L.Lewis]
Lewis, Vincent Anthony ....'65 '99 C.587 B.S. L.201 J.D. [A S.D.Miles]
Lewis, W. Walker, Jr., (AV) ....'15 '40 C.197 A.B. L.309 J.D. 2000 Courthouse Plz. N.E.
Lewis, Terry L., Co., L.P.A., (BV) .... 111 W. 1st Street, Room 1000
Liberman, Scott A., (BV) ....'66 '92 C.347 B.S. L.201 J.D. [Altick&C.]
Lieberman, Dennis A., (AV) ....'52 '78 C.473 B.A. L.201 J.D. [Flanagan,L.H.&S.]
Lienesch, Theodore D., (AV) '51 '76
C.477 B.S.M.E. L.150 J.D. [Thompson H.] (See Pat. Sect.)
Lincoln, William T. '43 '70 C.477 A.B. L.912 J.D.
(adm. in MI; not adm. in OH) Pres., Berry Invests., Inc.
Lind, Harry S. ....'69 '94 C.973 B.S.B.A. L.145 J.D. 2000 Courthouse Plz. N.E.
Lindsay, Karen Ruth Lavy ....'71 '98 C.367 B.A. L.201 J.D. U.S. Dist. Ct.
Lipcius, Jesse R. ....'77 '04 C.1356 B.S. L.201 J.D. [A Freund,F.&A.]
Lipowicz, Richard A.F., (BV) '55 '80 C.867 B.A. L.1048 J.D.
130 W. 2nd St., Ste. 1900
Little, Don, (BV) ....'41 '66 7501 Paragon Rd.
Littlejohn, Bill C., (BV) ....'44 '73 C.1023 B.S. L.607 J.D. 323 Salem Ave.
Littlejohn, Gail H. ....'— '83 C.607 B.A. L.201 J.D. [C Chernesky,H.&K.]
Litvin, Joseph ....'35 '73 C.477 B.S.E. L.608 J.D. 6460 Noranda Drive‡
Lockhart, Gregory Gordon ....'46 '76 C.1208 B.S. L.608 J.D. Asst. U.S. Atty.
Logan, Ronald G., (BV) ....'31 '58 C.473 A.B. L.608 J.D. 1336 Woodman Dr.
Logothetis, Sorrell, (AV) ....'36 '66 C.381 B.S. L.276 LL.B. [Logothetis,P.&D.]
Logothetis, Pence & Doll, (AV) ....Suite 1100, 111 West First Street
Lombard, John C., (AV) ....'— '59 C.309 A.B. L.93 LL.B. [Coolidge,W.W.&L.]
Long, Michael J. ....'31 '59 C.201 A.B. L.150 LL.B. 1401 W. Dorothy Ln.
Lopez, Alvin J., (BV) ....'55 '86 C&L.201 B.A., J.D. 438 Patterson Road

Lopez, Severt & Pratt Co., L.P.A.
(See Troy)

Loridas, Heather M. ....'76 '01 C&L.201 B.A., J.D. [A Freund,F.&A.]
Lounsbury, Joshua R. ....'— '04 C.475 B.A. L.846 J.D. [A Coolidge,W.W.&L.]
Lowe, Charles D., (AV) ....'39 '64 C.210 B.A. L.893 LL.B. 130 West Second Street
Lowery, Kermit F., (BV) '54 '84
C.1208 B.A. L.201 J.D. Asst. Gen. Coun., LEXIS-NEXIS
Lowman, Charles A., III ....'42 '72 C.610 B.S. L.607 J.D. Judge
Lowry, Bruce R., (AV) ....'52 '77 C&L.608 B.A., J.D. 2000 Courthouse Plz., N.E.
Lucas, Joseph C. '78 '04 C.309 A.B. L.659 J.D.
(adm. in PA; not adm. in OH) Assoc.
Lush, L. Anthony, (BV) ....'60 '90 C.679 B.S. L.201 J.D. [Rogers&G.]
Lutz, Frederick B., (BV) ....'25 '50 C.473 B.S. L.150 LL.B. [A Flanagan,L.H.&S.]
Lux, Carl A. ....'— '04 C.608 B.A. L.94 J.D. [A Thompson H.]
Lynch, Chanda L. ....'75 '00 C.1208 B.A. L.602 J.D. [A Sebaly,S.&D.]
Lynch, Jane M., (AV) ....'— '82 C.1208 B.A. L.201 J.D. [Green&G.]
Lynch, Teresa J. '65 '96 C.1175 B.S. L.362 J.D.
(adm. in FL; not adm. in OH) Tax Atty., NCR Corp.
Lynn, James T., Jr., (AV) ....'20 '49 C&L.608 B.A., J.D. [Young,P.L.&J.]
Lynn, Karyn June ....'68 '95 C.473 B.A. L.930 J.D. Co. Pros. Off.
Maciorowski, Michelle M. '70 '97 C.201 B.S. L.930 J.D.
Magistrate, Montgomery Co. Ohio Juvenile Ct.
Macklin, Crofford J., Jr., (AV) ....'47 '77 C&L.608 B.A., J.D. [Thompson H.]
MacMillan, William W., Jr. ....'27 '53 C&L.602 Ph.B., LL.B. Ret. Com. Pleas J.‡
Maffett, Jennifer L. ....'76 '02 C.201 B.A. L.200 J.D. [A Thompson H.]
Mahan, Charles W., (BV) ....'45 '71 C.339 B.S. L.608 J.D. [Dunlevey,M.&F.]
Mahoney, Bryan J. ....'74 '99 C.201 B.A. L.724 J.D. [A Freund,F.&A.]
Mahoney, Joan A. ....'62 '95 C.676 B.A. L.201 J.D. 9797 Springboro Pike
Maier, F. Mark ....'49 '81 C.608 B.A. L.851 J.D. [A Dyer,G.M.&S.]
Makley, Roger J., (AV) ....'35 '60 C&L.276 B.S., J.D. 12 W. Monument St., Ste. 200
Malhotra, Rajshree ....'64 '93 C&L.201 B.A., J.D. Asst. Pros.
Malloy, Martin L., (BV) ....'49 '77 C&L.201 B.A., J.D. [A E.S.Gallon&Assoc.]
Malocu, Frank A., (BV) ....'66 '91 C.754 B.S. L.201 J.D. 130 W. 2nd St., Ste. 2100
Malone, Richard M., (BV) ....'51 '77 C.608 B.A. L.117 J.D. [E.S.Gallon&Assoc.]
Mancz, Barry W., (BV) ....'52 '77 C.1208 B.S. L.174 J.D. [Rogers&G.]
Mann, Douglas A., (BV) ....'59 '84 C.97 B.S. L.851 J.D. [Dyer,G.M.&S.]
Manning, Gractia Sharpenberg ....'70 '98 C.81 B.A. L.201 J.D. 848C E. Franklin Street
Manuszak, Ronald J. ....'36 '68 C&L.851 B.B.A., J.D. 3rd Natl. Bk. & Tr. Co.
Marquis, David W., (BV) ....'63 '91 C.1376 B.S. L.200 J.D. [A Dyer,G.M.&S.]
Marsh-Cook, Stephanie Lynne, (BV) ....'67 '96 C.21 B.A. L.200 J.D. City Pros. Off.

Martin, K. Duane ...... '77 '04 C.354 B.A. L.201 J.D. Staff Atty., Premier Health Partners
Martin, Laura J. .... '72 '03 C.350 B.S. L.150 J.D. [🄰 Botros&S.]
Martin, M. Shannon, (AV) .... '— '93 C.363 B.A. L.1003 J.D. [Coolidge,W.W.&L.]
Martin, Paul W. .... '56 '89 C.871 B.S.E.E. L.608 J.D. Sr. Atty., NCR Corp.
Martin, Thomas P., (AV) .... '49 '75 C.201 B.S. L.607 J.D. [Jablinski,F.R.&M.]
Martin-Cross, Denise L. .... '53 '79 C.943 B.A. L.8 J.D. Mag., Co. Juv. Ct.
Martinson, Charles L. .... '46 '76 C.436 A.B. L.597 J.D. 6385 Jason Ln.
Marx, Dianne F., (AV) .... '56 '82 C.473 A.B. L.602 J.D. [🄲 Sebaly,S.&D.]
Mason, Jonathan A., (AV) .... '47 '73 C&L.150 B.A., J.D. [Mason,S.&M.] ⊙

Mason, Schilling & Mason Co., L.P.A., (AV)
319 Liberty Tower, 120 West Second Street, 45402 ⊙
Telephone: 513-489-0829 800-840-3514 Fax: 513-489-0834
Email: msm@mason-law.com URL: http://www.mason-law.com
Jonathan A. Mason.
Commercial, Creditors Rights, Bankruptcy, Collection, Banking and Financial Institution Law, Civil Litigation, Federal Consumer Law Litigation, Foreclosures, Automobile Deficiencies, Credit Cards, Medical Debts, Bad Checks, Business Loans/Commercial Debt, Vehicle and Property Repossessions, Landlord Representation/Evictions/Lease Litigation, Equipment Leasing.
Covington, Kentucky Office: Heritage International, Suite 203, P.O. Box 2158. Telephone: 513-489-0829. Fax: 513-489-0834.
Columbus Office: 460 E. Main Street. Telephone: 513-489-0829. Fax: 513-489-0834.
Cincinnati Office: 11340 Montgomery Road, Suite 210. Telephone: 513-489-0829. Fax: 513-489-0834.
Lima Office: P.O. Box 937. Telephone: 513-489-0829. Fax: 513-489-0834
Madison, Indiana Office: 201 East Main Street. Telephone: 513-489-0829. Fax: 513-489-0834.

See Professional Biographies, DAYTON, OHIO

Mattison, Gwen M. Banachowski '54 '84
C&L.851 B.A., J.D. 3640 Colonel Glenn Highway
Matusoff, Robert B., (AV) .... '30 '55 C.477 A.B. L.309 J.D. 3033 Kettering Blvd.

Maurer Law Offices, LLC
(See Centerville)

May, Jill A. .... '— '00 C.5 B.A. L.851 J.D. [🄰 Coolidge,W.W.&L.]
May, Kenneth F. .... '49 '78 C&L.201 B.S., J.D. P.O. Box 9416‡
Mayerson, Lynn .... '53 '86 C.347 B.S. L.201 J.D. 563 Heather Dr.
Mayhew, Kimberly Hite .... '58 '91 C&L.608 B.A., J.D. Natl. City Bk.
McBride, Robert L. .... '10 '34 C&L.201 A.B., J.D. Ret. App. Ct. J.‡
McCann, Gregory L., (AV) '57 '82 C.602 B.A. L.608 J.D.
Exec. V.P., Gen. Coun. & Secy., The Danis Cos.
McCann, John M. .... '— '00 C.188 B.A. L.893 J.D. [🄰 Thompson H.]
McClain, Martin J. '54 '80 C.326 B.S. L.972 J.D.
(adm. in WY; not adm. in OH) Univ. of Dayton School of Law
McCollum, Alice O. .... '47 '72 C.577 B.A. L.150 J.D. Mun. Ct. J.
McComas, Benjamin K. .... '78 '04 C.130 B.A. L.477 J.D. [🄰 Gottschlich&P.]
McCray, Alfred L., (BV) .... '40 '66 C.197 B.A. L.477 LL.B. [McCray&M.]
McCray, Risa C. .... '49 '74 C.313 B.A. L.851 J.D. 827 W. Grand Ave.
McCray, Samuel A., (AV) .... '13 '38 C.197 A.B. L.477 LL.B. [McCray&M.]
McCray and McCray, (AV) .... 418 Grants Trl.
McCulley, Melanie G. '67 '95 C.160 B.A. L.790 J.D.
(adm. in VA; not adm. in OH) 214 Adams St.

McCulloch, Felger, Fite & Gutmann Co., L.P.A.
(See Piqua)

McDermott, Jo E. .... '— '82 C.623 B.A. L.276 J.D. LEXIS-NEXIS
McDonald, Gerald Louis .... '62 '93 C.475 B.A. L.362 J.D. [🄰 Pickrel,S.&E.]
McGee, James H. .... '18 '49 C.943 B.S. L.608 J.D. 1518 Benson Dr.‡
McGinnis, Carlo C., (BV) .... '51 '77 C&L.770 B.A., J.D. [Young,P.L.&J.]
McGuinn, Wm. Patrick, (BV) .... '27 '57 C.130 L.1340 LL.B. City Legal Dept.
McGuire, James C. .... '41 '80 C.446 B.S.E.E. L.201 J.D. F-15 Intl. Progs. Chf.
McHugh, Stephen M., (BV) .... '53 '79 C&L.607 B.A., J.D. [Altick&C.]

McKinney, Charles A., Law Offices of, (BV) '55 '80 C.943 B.A. L.602 J.D.
20 West Monument Avenue, 45402 ⊙
Telephone: 937-461-9000 Fax: 937-461-9640
Email: camlaw@woh.rr.com URL: http://www.charlesamckinney.com
Corporate Law, Business Planning, Contracts, Insurance, Lawsuits, Labor (Management) Law, Personal Injury Law, Automobile Accidents, Dog Bites, Sexual Abuse, Slip and Fall, Trusts and Estates, Estate Planning Law, Guardianship, Wills and Probate, Wrongful Death, Civil Litigation, Buying or Selling a Business, Formation, Closely Held Business, Limited Liability Companies, Partnerships, Small Business, Employment Law, Disability Accommodations, Discrimination, Sexual Harassment, Wrongful Termination.
Columbus, Ohio Office: 141 East Town Street, Suite 102, 43215. Telephone: 614-460-9000. Fax: 614-460-9001.

See Professional Biographies, DAYTON, OHIO

McKnight, Daniel H. .... '51 '77 C.347 B.A. L.201 J.D. 1105 Wilmington Avenue‡
McLeran, William T., Jr. .... '18 '49 C&L.930 B.B.A., LL.B. 255 N. Main St.‡
McMurry, Donna M., (BV) '63 '88 C.473 B.S. L.150 J.D.
Gen. Coun., LEXIS-NEXIS Special Services Inc.
Mcnew, Michael A. .... '74 '99 C.25 B.A. L.201 J.D. [🄰 Logothetis,P.&D.]
McPeek, Anna Lee .... '59 '85 C.473 B.A. L.200 J.D. Lexis-Nexis
McQuiston, Jeffrey R., (AV) ..... '51 '76 C.210 B.A. L.436 J.D. 130 W. 2nd St., Ste. 1818
McSherry, Shauna K., (BV) .... '51 '79 C.97 B.S. L.201 J.D. 4169 Sugar Leaf Drive
McSwiney, C. Ronald, (AV) '43 '68 C.385 A.B. L.150 J.D.
Senior VP, General Counsel & Secretary, Danis Companies
McTigue, Terrence P., Jr., (BV) ...... '67 '93 C.150 B.A. L.201 J.D. [🄰 Flanagan,L.H.&S.]
Meadows, Jerry A., (BV) .... '50 '75 C.532 B.A. L.607 J.D. 580 Lincoln Park Blvd.
Meadows, Mary E. .... '72 '98 C.610 B.A. L.200 J.D. Off. of Prosecutor
Meagher, John M. .... '42 '66 C.201 B.A. L.150 J.D. 2501 Adirondack Trail
Meckstroth, Alan F., (AV) '35 '60 C.679 B.S.M.E. L.477 LL.B.
[Jacox,M.&J.] (Pat.) ⊙
Meehling, John C., The Law Offices of '60 '04 C.47 B.A. L.201 J.D.
4625 Far Hills Ave.
Meily, William D., (BV) .... '49 '78 C.150 B.A. L.201 J.D. 22 Clay Street
Merz, Michael R. .... '45 '70 C&L.309 A.B., J.D. U.S. Mag.
Metzcar, Jeffrey C. .... '75 '00 C.201 B.M.E. L.930 J.D. [🄰 Thompson H.]
Meyer, Arthur G. '50 '82 C.967 B.A. L.117 J.D.
V.P., Legal and Corp. Affairs, The Dayton Power & Light Co.
Meyer, Beverly A. .... '69 '94 C.608 B.M.E. L.201 J.D. [🄰 Logothetis,P.&D.]
Michael, Allison D. .... '— '99 C.1208 B.A. L.201 J.D. [🄰 Coolidge,W.W.&L.]
Michelsen, Gregory .... '75 '00 C.1044 B.A. L.823 J.D. Asst. Staff Judge Advocate★
Milanick, Russel S. .... '17 '50 C.529 Ph.B. L.831 LL.B. 831 Patterson Rd.‡
Miles, Stephen D., (BV) .... '51 '77 C.967 B.A. L.945 J.D. 18 W. Monument Avenue
Miley, Douglas Ray, (BV) .... '68 '93 C.446 B.A. L.201 J.D. [🄰 Dyer,G.M.&S.]
Militello, Colleen R., (BV) .... '71 '96 C.347 B.A. L.201 J.D. Fed. Bkrptcy. Ct.
Miller, Todd T., (BV) .... '68 '94 C.473 B.S. L.851 J.D [🄰 Hochman&P.]
Miller, William R. .... '73 '97 C.383 B.A. L.201 J.D. [🄰 Botros&S.]

Miller & Luring
(See Troy)

Millonig, Arthur F., Jr., (AV) .... '44 '69 C.201 B.A. L.150 J.D. [A.F.Millonig,Jr.]
Millonig, Michael J., (BV) '56 '81 C.383 B.S. L.608 J.D.
7601 Paragon Road, Suite 103
Millonig, Arthur F., Jr., Co., L.P.A., (AV) .... 6776 Loop Rd.
Mills, Paul W., (BV) .... '63 '89 C.1257 B.A. L.201 J.D. 1313 Talbot Tower
Minella, Shirley C., (BV) .... '51 '92 C&L.201 B.A., J.D. 131 N Ludlow St.
Mischler, Frederick Focke .... '62 '94 C.150 B.B.A. L.201 J.D. P.O. Box 10068
Mitchell, Amy C. .... '73 '98 C.201 B.A. L.150 J.D. [🄰 Dunlevey,M.&F.]
Mitchell, James R. .... '— '03 C.838 B.A. L.150 J.D. [🄲 Chernesky,H.&K.]
Mitchell, Nicole A. .... '72 '97 C.473 B.A. L.150 J.D. [🄰 Freund,F.&A.]
Mohr, John R., (AV) .... '47 '72 C&L.608 B.S.B.A., J.D. [Gottschlich&P.]
Molloy, Matthew A. .... '77 '04 C.659 B.S. L.201 J.D. [🄰 Dinsmore&S.] (Pat.)
Moloney, Michael P., (AV) .... '52 '80 C.473 B.A. L.608 J.D. [Sebaly,S.&D.]
Monday, Franklin T. .... '32 '61 C.5 A.B. L.469 LL.B. 4604 Airway Rd.
Mondock, Joseph J. .... '75 '02 C.97 B.A. L.201 J.D. [🄰 Thorson,S.W.&S.]
Monroe, William J., (BV) .... '44 '75 C.97 B.S.B.A. L.851 J.D. Co. Pub. Def.
Monta, Michael L., (BV) .... '43 '73 C&L.607 B.A., J.D. [Monta&M.]
Monta, Vasso K., (BV) .... '47 '77 C.1044 B.A. L.201 J.D. [Monta&M.]
Monta & Monta, (BV) .... 3625 Old Salem Rd.
Montgomery, David H., (BV) .... '72 '98 C.473 B.A. L.201 J.D. [🄰 Pickrel,S.&E.]
Moore, Erin B., (BV) .... '— '93 C.1119 B.A. L.608 J.D. [Green&G.]
Moorman, Colette E., (BV) .... '65 '91 C&L.201 C.R.J., J.D. Asst. Pros.
Morman, Carla J., (BV) .... '70 '96 C.645 B.A. L.201 J.D. [Bieser,G.&L.]
Morris, Jeffrey W., (AV) .... '52 '77 C.676 B.A. L.902 J.D. [🄲 Porter W.M.&A.]
Moser, Stephen V., (AV) '55 '80 C&L.477 A.B., J.D.
(adm. in CO; not adm. in OH)
Assoc. Gen. Coun. & Chf. Envir. Coun., MeadWestvaco Corp.
Mount, Ronald E., (BV) .... '49 '80 C.473 B.A. L.201 J.D. Ct. Admin., Ct. App.
Muckenthaler, George J. '24 '63 C.375 B.S.E.E. L.862 LL.B.
(adm. in OK; not adm. in OH; Pat.) Sr. Intell. Prop. Atty., NCR Corp.
Mueller, Carolyn L., (BV) .... '46 '95 C.994 B.A. L.201 J.D. [Hall&M.] ⊙
Mues, Robert L., (AV) .... '54 '78 C.967 B.A. L.201 J.D. [Holzfaster,C.M.&M.]
Muhic, Theresa M., (BV) .... '63 '88 C&L.201 B.A., J.D. [🄰 Dinsmore&S.]
Mulligan, James J., (AV) .... '21 '49 C.433 B.B.A. L.178 J.D. 812 Timberlake Court
Mulligan, L. Patrick .... '59 '84 C.1113 B.A. L.150 J.D. [L.P.Mulligan&Assoc.]

Mulligan, L. Patrick, & Associates L.P.A. Co., Law Offices of
28 N. Wilkinson Street, 45402
Telephone: 937-228-9790 Fax: 937-228-9788
Email: acquit1@woh.rr.com URL: http://www.daytoncriminallaw.com
L. Patrick Mulligan. Associate: Adrienne D. Brooks. Of Counsel: George A. Katchmer.
Criminal Defense, Family Law.

See Professional Biographies, DAYTON, OHIO

Mullins, Jeffrey A., (AV) .... '— '90 C&L.201 B.A., J.D. [Coolidge,W.W.&L.]
Murphy, Michele A. .... '55 '85 C.276 B.S. L.150 J.D. [🄰 Faruki I.&C.]
Murphy, Tricia S. .... '57 '86 C.880 B.A. L.201 J.D. Jud. Clk., Ct. of App.
Murphy, W. Elisa .... '64 '94 C.679 B.S. L.7 J.D. LEXIS/NEXIS
Murry, Michael K., (BV) .... '52 '83 C.1208 B.S.Ed. L.210 J.D. 130 W. 2nd St.
Musto, John C., (CV) .... '74 '99 C.679 B.S. L.1119 J.D. Asst. City Atty.
Muth, Alison Haley ...... '64 '90 C.473 B.A. L.851 J.D. Dir., Prof. Servs., Sheridan Safety
Myers, Jacob A., (AV) .... '35 '59 C&L.608 B.S., J.D. [Myers&F.]
Myers, Jeffrey R. .... '72 '99 C.231 B.A. L.201 J.D. [🄰 Gottschlich&P.]

Myers & Frayne Co., L.P.A., (AV)
18 West First Street, Suite 200, 45402
Telephone: 937-224-0076 Fax: 937-224-5782
Email: annefrayne@myersandfrayne.com URL: http://www.myersandfraynelaw.com
Jacob A. Myers; Anne M. Frayne;—Sue Seeberger; Frederick B. Hatton. Of Counsel: Alan I. Brown.
Business, Corporations, Real Estate, Creditors Rights, Commercial Planning, Estate Planning, Probate, Chapter 11 Reorganizations, and Litigation.

See Professional Biographies, DAYTON, OHIO

Nagle, Daniel A., (BV) .... '33 '59 C.201 B.A. L.150 LL.B. 1401 W. Dorothy Ln.
Nash, Nancy A. '56 '82 C&L.201 B.A., J.D.
V.P., Law & Dep. Gen. Coun., Litig., LEXIS-NEXIS
Nauman, Joseph G., (AV) .... '28 '53 C.602 B.S. L.276 J.D. 696 Renolda Woods Court
Neidhold, Terri Wethern '55 '94
C.280 B.A. L.1161 J.D. SS Admin., Off of Hearings & Appeals
Neltner, Michael M. .... '59 '94 C.215 B.A. L.150 J.D. [🄰 Green&G.]
Neuhardt, David A., (AV) .... '54 '79 C.473 B.A. L.608 J.D. [Thompson H.]
Neuhardt, Sharen Swartz, (AV) .... '51 '76 C.597 B.A. L.276 J.D. [Thompson H.]
Neuherz, Rebekah .... '73 '99 C.1047 B.A. L.124 J.D. [🄰 Surdyk,D.&T.]
Neuman, Edward B. .... '39 '66 C.381 A.B. L.608 J.D. 101 W. 3rd St.
Nicholson, Bruce I., (AV) .... '48 '77 C.608 B.A. L.201 J.D. [Horenstein,N.&B.]
Nicholson, Mark W., (BV) '60 '85
C.276 B.S.F.S. L.930 J.D. Assoc. Gen. Coun., LEXIS-NEXIS
Nilles, Victoria L. .... '— '98 C.870 B.S. L.900 J.D. [🄰 Thompson H.]
Nolan, Bobbe S. .... '42 '85 C.1208 B.S.N. L.201 J.D. Senior Citizens Ctr.

Nolan, Sprowl, Smith & Finke, (AV)
1812 Kettering Tower, 40 North Main Street, 45423
Telephone: 937-228-7104 Fax: 937-226-1945
Members of Firm: Nicholas F. Nolan (1946-1982); Milton L. Sprowl (Retired); R. Peter Finke; Edward M. Smith (Certified Specialist in Estate Planning, Trust and Probate Law, Ohio State Bar Association).
General Civil Practice. Bankruptcy, Creditors Rights, Commercial, Collections, Real Estate, Taxation, Estate Planning, Probate, Corporation, Business Law, Family Practice.
References: Key Bank, N.A.; Bank One, N.A.

See Professional Biographies, DAYTON, OHIO

Noland, Thomas R., (AV) .... '45 '70 C.611 B.A. L.150 J.D. [Statman,H.S.&E.]
Nordstrom, P. Christian, (BV) .... '70 '95 C.228 B.S. L.910 J.D. [🄰 Jenks,P.&O.]
Norris, Allen R., (AV) .... '58 '83 C.473 B.A. L.150 J.D. [Thompson H.]
Norris, Patricia C., (AV) '62 '87 C.323 B.A. L.150 J.D.
Assoc. Gen. Coun. & Sr. Corp. Coun., MeadWestvaco Corp.
Nortman, Tammy C. .... '74 '01 C.473 B.A. L.424 J.D. [🄰 Holzfaster,C.M.&M.]
Nugent, Robert L. ...... '47 '72 C.472 B.S. L.339 J.D. V.P., Bank One Ohio Tr. Co., N.A.
Nypaver, Edward W. '30 '62 C.665 B.S. L.273 LL.B.
(adm. in DC; not adm. in OH; Pat.) Pat. Atty., Dept. of the Air Force
Nyquist, Laura K. '53 '80 C.182 B.A. L.494 J.D.
(adm. in MN; not adm. in OH) V.P. Law & Secy., NCR Corp.
Nystrom, Richard A., (CV) '35 '88
C.860 B.S. L.1003 J.D. 120 West 2nd Street, Suite 1502
Oberle, Cheryl B. .... '64 '88 C.763 B.A. L.851 J.D. LEXIS-NEXIS
O'Brien, Daniel J., (BV) ..... '36 '61 C.201 A.B. L.215 LL.B. Ste 1210, 131 N Ludlow St
O'Brien, Mychael Patrick .... '54 '95 C.608 B.A. L.117 J.D. 110 N Main St.
O'Connell, Timothy N. .... '55 '80 C.201 B.A. L.200 J.D. Mag., Com. Pleas Ct.
Oehlers, Joseph C., (AV) .... '65 '95 C.309 B.A. L.201 J.D. [Bieser,G.&L.]
O'Keefe, Stephen P. .... '69 '95 C.473 B.A. L.1003 J.D. [🄰 G.C.Gibson]
Olive, Ben E. .... '35 '61 C&L.477 A.B., LL.B. 900 Cedar Creek Circle‡
O'Malley, Jeffrey S. .... '68 '94 C.473 B.S. L.201 J.D. Univ. of Dayton

O'Neal, Robert M., (BV) ....'57 '84 C&L.347 A.B., J.D. [Breidenbach,O.&B.]
Otto, Craig W. .... '51 '78 C.339 B.S. L.201 J.D. 6900 Normancrest Court
Overholser, James N., (BV) '46 '72
C.608 B.S.B.A. L.150 J.D. 1 First National Pl., 130 W. 2nd St.
Ovington, Sharon L., (AV) .... '56 '81 C.150 B.A. L.201 J.D. 200 W. Second St.
Owen, W. James, (BV) ....'46 '73 C.294 A.B. L.607 J.D. 580 Lincoln Park Boulevard
Owens, Alvarene N., (BV) ....'47 '77 C.623 B.A. L.150 J.D. [A.N.Owens]
Owens, Mark E., (CV) ....'56 '81 C.1208 B.A. L.201 J.D. Ct. Clk., Mun. Ct.
Owens, Alvarene N., Co., L.P.A., (BV) ....1101 Salem Avenue
Oxley, Scott G., (BV) ....'62 '87 C.473 B.A. L.150 J.D. [Jenks,P.&O.]
Packard, Dwight A. .... '46 '77 C.97 B.A. L.1340 J.D. 9319 Cincinnati-Columbus Rd.
Page, Gregory S., (BV) ....'69 '95 C.150 B.A. L.851 J.D. [Ⓐ Pickrel,S.&E.]
Pappayliou, George S., (AV) '54 '79
C.228 B.S. L.1292 J.D. Gen. Coun., Tomkins Industries, Inc.
Parisi, Georgianna I., (CV) ....'53 '82 C&L.201 B.A., J.D. 3430 S. Dixie Dr.
Patricoff, George B., (AV) ....'49 '79 C.201 B.S.S. L.607 J.D. Asst. Pros. Atty.
Patterson, Dennis L., (AV) ....'39 '64 C&L.930 B.B.A., J.D. [Bogin P.E.S.&S.]
Patterson, Lisa L. ....'68 '96 C.025 B.A. L.117 J.D. [Ⓐ Taft,S.&H.] (⊙Cincinnati)
Paulus, Janice M., (AV) .... '— '85 C.608 B.A. L.201 J.D. [Coolidge,W.W.&L.]
Payson, Frank M. ....'43 '91 C.923 B.S.A.E. L.200 J.D. [F.M.Payson]
Payson, Frank M., P.C. ....120 W. 2nd St.
Pensyl, Michelle L. .... '62 '88 C.970 B.A. L.150 J.D. Chicago Title Ins. Co.
Pepper, Timothy G., (BV) ....'69 '99 C&L.608 B.A., J.D. [Ⓐ Faruki I.&C.]

Peterson & Peterson
(See Xenia)

Petzold, John P., (BV) .... '38 '62 C.431 B.A. L.902 LL.B. Com. Pleas J.
Pfarrer, David A. ....'65 '90 C&L.608 B.A., J.D. Staff Atty., Second Dist. Ct. of App.

Pfarrer, Stephen M., (AV) '41 '67 C.399 B.A. L.930 J.D. BR
Suite 2100, First National Plaza, 130 West Second Street, 45402-1502
Telephone: 937-228-0894 Fax: 937-461-2923
Email: pfarrer@smpfarrerlawyer.com URL: http://www.lawyers.com/stephanmpfarrer
Civil Litigation, Corporate Law, Construction, Health Care, Employment Law, Commercial Law.

See Professional Biographies, DAYTON, OHIO

Phillips, Stanley S., (AV) .... '36 '60 C&L.608 B.S., J.D. 4699 Salem Ave.
Pickrel, John S. ....'45 '70 C.201 B.A. L.608 J.D. Mun. J.

Pickrel, Schaeffer & Ebeling, (AV)
2700 Kettering Tower, 45423-2700
Telephone: 937-223-1130 Facsimile: 937-223-0339
URL: http://www.pselaw.com
William G. Pickrel (1931-1966); Virgil Schaeffer (1932-1958); Philip C. Ebeling (1931-1963); Bradley J. Schaeffer (1935-1992); Paul J. Winterhalter; Paul E. Zimmer; Alan B. Schaeffer; Andrew C. Storar; Jon M. Rosemeyer; James W. Kelleher; James L. Jacobson (Certified Specialist in Estate Planning, Trust and Probate Law, Ohio State Bar Association); Jeffrey S. Senney; L. Michael Bly; Michael W. Sandner;—Gregory S. Page; David H. Montgomery; R. Joseph Wessendarp; Gerald Louis McDonald; Matthew T. Jewson; Salvatore A. Gilene; Suzanne P. Brumbaugh. Of Counsel: Donald G. Schweller; Thomas J. Harrington; Ira H. Thomsen.
Banking, Civil, Corporate, General Business, Commercial Lending, Mergers and Acquisitions, Insurance, Labor and Employment, Healthcare, Municipal and Zoning, Personal Injury and Products Liability, Probate, Trust and Estate Planning, Construction, Computer, Real Estate, Environmental, Workers' Compensation Defense, Immigration, Bankruptcy and Tax Law. Trials and Appeals, School Law and Title Insurance.
Representative Clients: STC Broadcasting (WDTN-TV2); Allstate Insurance Co.; American Mutual Liability Co.; Miami Valley Cardiologists; American Aggregates; Sinclair Community College; Bridgestone/Firestone.

See Professional Biographies, DAYTON, OHIO

Pierce, David P., (BV) ....'— '93 C.880 B.A. L.150 J.D. [Coolidge,W.W.&L.]
Pierce, Lisa S., (BV) ....'68 '95 C.385 B.A. L.150 J.D. [Chernesky,H.&K.]
Piercy, James R., (AV) .... '48 '73 C.645 B.A. L.930 J.D. [E.S.Gallon&Assoc.]
Pierson, Steven T., (BV) ....'— '84 C.610 B.S. L.150 J.D. [Rion,R.&R.]
Piper, Angela F. .... '67 '96 C.640 B.S. L.200 J.D. Systech Envir. Corp.
Plunkett, Gary D., (BV) ....'64 '90 C.1021 B.S. L.201 J.D. [Hochman&P.]
Poley, John D., (BV) ....'47 '78 C.999 B.A. L.201 J.D. 46 Rogge Street
Popp, Vincent P., (BV) .... '52 '77 C.573 B.S. L.201 J.D. [Popp&T.]
Popp & Tuss, (BV) ....137 N. Main St., Ste. 712
Poppenhouse, Thomas O. ....'53 '79 C.8 B.S. L.7 J.D. Tax Refund Consultants, Inc.
Porter, Brian K. .... '47 '77 C.1208 B.S. L.477 J.D. LEXIS-NEXIS

Porter Wright Morris & Arthur LLP, (AV)
One Dayton Centre, One South Main Street, Suite 1600, 45402-2028 ⊙
Telephone: 937-449-6810; (800-533-4434) Fax: 937-449-6820
Email: dayton@porterwright.com URL: http://www.porterwright.com
Resident Partners: William G. Deas; Caroline H. Gentry; Paul G. Hallinan; John J. Heron; Thomas A. Holton; C. Terry Johnson (Certified Specialist in Estate Planning, Trust and Probate Law, Ohio State Bar Association); Charles Y. Kidwell, Jr.; Walter Reynolds; R. Bruce Snyder. Resident Associates: John F. Bennett; Andrew J. Gottman; Tami L. Hart; Craig A. Hoffman; Scott K. Jones; Philip E. Kessler; H. John Proud; Robin D. Ryan. Of Counsel: Roland F. Eichner; Jeffrey W. Morris.
Alternative Dispute Resolution, Agricultural Law, Antitrust and Trade Regulation, Business and Corporate, Complex Litigation, Construction, Employee Benefits, Energy and Utilities, Environment, Federal Administrative Law, Federal Contracting and Procurement, Financial Institutions, General Practice, Governmental Affairs, Health Care, Insurance, Intellectual Property, International Business, Labor and Employment, Litigation, Public Law, Public Finance, Real Estate, Securities, Taxation, Technology, Trusts and Estates.
Columbus, Ohio Office: 41 South High Street, 43215-6194. Telephones: 614-227-2000; (800-533-2794). Fax: 614-227-2100. Internet: columbus@porterwright.com.
Cincinnati, Ohio Office: 250 E. Fifth Street, Suite 2200, 45202-5117. Telephones: 513-381-4700; (800-582-5813); Fax: 513-421-0991. Internet: cincinnati@porterwright.com.
Cleveland, Ohio Office: 925 Euclid Avenue, Suite 1700, 44115-1483. Telephones: 216-443-9000; (800-824-1980). Fax: 216-443-9011. Internet: cleveland@porterwright.com.
Washington, D.C. Office: 1919 Pennsylvania Avenue, N.W., Suite 500, 20006-3434. Telephones: 202-778-3000; (800-456-7962). Fax: 202-778-3063. Internet: washington@porterwright.com.
Naples, Florida Office: 5801 Pelican Bay Boulevard, Suite 300, 34108-2709. Telephones: 239-593-2900; (800-876-7962). Fax: 239-593-2990. Internet: naples@porterwright.com.

See Professional Biographies, DAYTON, OHIO

Portune, Robert E. "Buzz", (AV) ....'48 '73 C.473 B.A. L.228 J.D. [Gottschlich&P.]
Posey, Terry Wayne, (BV) ....'50 '88 C.201 B.S. L.117 J.D. 7460 Brandt Pike
Poulton, Thomas M., (BV) ....'47 '79 C.602 B.B.A. L.201 J.D. P.O. Box 744
Pregon, Jamey T. ....'73 '99 C.352 B.A. L.221 J.D. [Ⓐ Freund,F.&A.]
Preston, K. Lynn .... '79 '04 C.893 B.A. L.201 J.D. [Ⓐ Faruki I.&C.]
Pretekin, Ronald S., (AV) ....'— '66 C.623 A.B. L.477 LL.B. [Coolidge,W.W.&L.]
Prior, Patricia L. .... '59 '86 C.602 B.S. L.608 J.D. [Ⓒ Dinsmore&S.] (Pat.)
Proud, H. John ....'48 '04 C&L.201 B.A., J.D. [Ⓐ Porter W.M.&A.]
Pyper, Thomas H., (AV) ....'56 '81 C.610 B.A. L.150 J.D. [Jenks,P.&O.]
Radabaugh, Tom B., (BV) ....'33 '60 C.951 B.A. L.178 LL.B. Interstate Mtge. Co.
Raether, Ronald I., Jr., (BV) ....'69 '97 C.608 B.A. L.201 J.D. [Faruki I.&C.]
Raines, David A. ....'54 '90 C.1208 B.A. L.976 J.D. Wright State Univ. Sch. of Med.
Randall, Vernellia R. '48 '87 C.846 B.S. L.596 J.D.
(adm. in OR; not adm. in OH) Asst. Prof. of Law, Univ. of Dayton‡
Randolph, Thomas P., (BV) '31 '60
C&L.608 B.A., J.D. 100 N. Jefferson Street, Room 702

Rapp, Donald J. ....'33 '59 C.631 B.A. L.608 LL.B. Prob. Ct. Ref.
Rauch, Thomas G., (BV) ....'46 '75 C.201 B.S. L.1161 J.D. Asst. Pros. Atty.
Readey, Mary Lynn, (AV) ....'53 '87 C.798 B.A. L.201 J.D. 1900 Kettering Tower
Redder, Edward C., (CV) ....'72 '98 C.532 B.A. L.608 J.D. [Ⓐ Thompson H.]
Redmond, David A. '42 '75 C.265 A.B. L.345 J.D.
(adm. in IN; not adm. in OH) Admin. Law J., Soc. Sec. Admin.
Reed, David N., (BV) ....'— '91 C.197 B.A. L.602 J.D. [Coolidge,W.W.&L.]
Reed, John D. ....'59 '97 C.150 B.S. L.1340 J.D. [Ⓐ Dinsmore&S.] (Pat.)
Reed, Linda F., (BV) ....'— '91 C.802 B.B.A. L.602 J.D. Asst. Pros. Atty.
Reed, Shelley A., (BV) ....'55 '80 C.207 B.A. L.851 J.D. Sr. Atty., NCR Corp.
Reid, Lorine M. ....'32 '73 C.912 B.A. L.851 J.D. Asst. Pros.
Reid Saba, Delia ....'70 '98 C.201 B.A. L.200 J.D. Corp. Coun., LexisNexis
Reitz, Andrew J. ....'78 '03 C.894 A.B. L.1119 J.D. [Ⓐ Faruki I.&C.]
Reno, Barbara E., (BV) ....'60 '86 C&L.201 B.S., J.D. 22 Brown Street
Replogle, Thomas J., (BV) ....'55 '89 C.885 B.A. L.201 J.D. [Gianuglou,S.&R.]
Reynolds, Lynn M., (AV) '69 '95 C.1113 B.A. L.201 J.D.
Sr. Dir. & Assoc.Gen. Coun., LEXIS-NEXIS Group (Legal Department)
Reynolds, Walter, (AV) ....'53 '79 C.943 B.A. L.201 J.D. [Porter W.M.&A.]
Rhinehart, Michael N. .... '78 '03 C.421 B.A. L.200 J.D. [Ⓐ Freund,F.&A.]
Rice, Richard F. ....'33 '60 C.970 B.A. L.608 J.D. 3461 Office Park Dr.
Rice, Ted W., (BV) ....'40 '67 C.381 B.S. L.608 J.D. Asst. Pub. Def.
Rice, Timothy G., (AV) '54 '79
C&L.607 B.A., J.D. Sr. Coun., The Dayton Power & Light Co.
Rice, Walter Herbert ....'37 '63 C.597 B.A. L.178 J.D. 200 West Second Street‡
Rickert, David M., (AV) .... '— '78 C.589 B.A. L.145 J.D. [Ⓐ Coolidge,W.W.&L.]
Rickert, Mark W. .... '51 '76 C.5 B.S. L.851 J.D. LEXIS-NEXIS
Rieder, John P. '68 '99 C.999 B.S. L.1338 J.D.
(adm. in WI; not adm. in OH) Asst. Staff J. Advocate, U.S. Air Force★
Rieser, John Paul, (AV) ....'56 '81 C.597 B.A. L.309 J.D. [Rieser&Assoc.] ⊙

Rieser & Associates LLC, (AV) BR
1520 First National Bank Plaza, 130 West Second Street, 45402-1519 ⊙
Telephone: 937-224-4128 Fax: 937-224-3090
Managing Member: John Paul Rieser. Associates: Patricia Jean Friesinger.
General Civil Practice. Litigation, Corporate, Commercial and Complex Litigation, Business Planning and Transactions, Bankruptcy, Workouts and Reorganization, Estate Planning. Trust/Estate Litigation. Trials and Appeals in all Courts.
West Palm Beach, Florida Office: Phillips Point, 777 S. Flagler Drive, Suite 800-West Tower, 33401-6161. Telephone: 561-515-6019. Fax: 561-515-6119.

See Professional Biographies, DAYTON, OHIO

Rigot, Joseph M., (AV) ....'43 '73 C.201 B.A. L.910 J.D. [Thompson H.]
Riley, Adele M., (BV) ....'47 '82 C.94 B.S. L.200 J.D. [Ⓒ Altick&C.]
Rineer, Donald B. ....'74 '99 C.150 B.A. L.201 J.D. [Ⓐ Dunlevey,M.&F.]
Ring, Steven J., (BV) .... '49 '82 C.260 B.A. L.1340 J.D. Asst. Pros. Atty.
Rion, James P. ....'41 '69 C.608 B.A. L.851 J.D. 333 W. 1st. St.
Rion, John H., (AV) .... '43 '70 C.608 B.A. L.851 J.D. [Rion,R.&R.]
Rion, Jon Paul, (BV) .... '— '96 C.273 L.200 J.D. [Rion,R.&R.]

Rion, Rion & Rion, L.P.A. Inc., (AV) BR
Suite 2150, One First National Plaza, 130 West Second Street, P.O. Box 10126, 45402
Telephone: 937-223-9133 Fax: 937-223-7540
Email: info@rionlaw.com URL: http://www.lawyers.com/rionlaw
John H. Rion; Jon Paul Rion; Kevin L. Lennen; Steven T. Pierson;—Keri E. Farley; Matthew J. Barbato. Of Counsel: Matthew H. Wilson.
Criminal Law. Felonies, Misdemeanors, Drug Crimes, DUI, Murder, Manslaughter, Death Penalty. Family Law, Divorce, Child Custody.

See Professional Biographies, DAYTON, OHIO

Rizer, Edward N., (BV) '57 '83 C.201 B.A. L.150 J.D.
Assoc. Coun., The Dayton Power & Light Co.
Robenson, Todd E. .... '74 '00 C.347 B.S. L.904 J.D. [Ⓐ Sebaly,S.&D.]
Roberson, Nancy A., (BV) .... '49 '82 C.347 A.B. L.201 J.D. [N.A.Roberson]
Roberson, Nancy A., Co., LPA, (BV) ....2390 S. Dixie Highway
Roberts, Brian M., (BV) ....'57 '82 C.473 B.S. L.201 J.D. [Jablinski,F.R.&M.]
Roberts, Shearl J., (AV) ....'30 '58 C.201 B.A. L.150 J.D. [Ⓒ Jablinski,F.R.&M.] ‡
Robinson, Eugene, (BV) ....'34 '67 C.1016 B.S.C. L.146 J.D. 333 W. 1st St.
Rock, W. Randall, (BV) ....'53 '84 C.610 B.G.S. L.201 J.D. 34 N Main St., Ste. 911
Roddy, Joan H., (AV) ....'53 '81 C.1208 B.A. L.200 J.D. [Thompson H.]
Roderer, Paul B., (AV) ....'42 '67 C.201 B.A. L.150 J.D. [Roderer]
Roderer, Paul Bernard, Jr., (BV) .... '67 '94 C.1208 B.S. L.201 J.D. [Roderer]
Roderer Law Offices, (AV) ....4 East Schantz Avenue
Rodman, Rachael L. .... '76 '01 C&L.150 B.A., J.D. [Ⓐ Chernesky,H.&K.]
Roedersheimer, Charles J. ....'42 '67 C.1115 B.S. L.150 J.D. [Thompson&D.]
Rogers, Richard H. ....'39 '64 C.473 B.S. L.228 J.D. 7333 Paragon Rd.
Rogers, William A., Jr., (AV) .... '34 '60 C&L.309 B.A., LL.B. [Rogers&G.]

Rogers & Greenberg, L.L.P., (AV) BR
2160 Kettering Tower, 45423
Telephone: 937-223-8171 Fax: 937-223-1649
URL: http://www.rogersgreenberg.com
Members of Firm: William A. Rogers, Jr.; Stanley Z. Greenberg (1939-2003); John M. Cloud (Certified Specialist in Estate Planning, Trust and Probate Law, Ohio State Bar Association); Barry W. Mancz; Keith R. Kearney; James G. Kordik; L. Anthony Lush; Michelle S. Vollmar;—Amy R. Blair; Laura C. DeSio; Mariah D. Butler.
General Practice. Corporation, Tax, Labor, Estate Planning and Probate Law, Family Law, Employee Benefits/ERISA. Trials.
General Counsel for: Heartland Federal Credit Union; National Management Association; Moraine Materials Co.; Washington Township Park District; Daniel S. German Enterprises; New Carlisle Chrysler-Dodge; Victory Wholesale Grocers; Precision Machining, Inc.; Harvest Info, Inc.; Dayton Aerospace Associates, Inc.

See Professional Biographies, DAYTON, OHIO

Roll, Patricia H. '30 '78 C.450 B.A. L.201 J.D.
Assoc. Dean, Univ. of Dayton Sch. of Law
Rose, Mary Jo ....'46 '82 C&L.201 B.S., J.D. Coun., Mall 2000, Inc.
Rose, Thomas M. .... '48 '74 C.610 B.S. L.150 J.D. Com. Pleas J.
Rosemeyer, Jon M., (AV) ....'54 '84 C.339 B.A. L.201 J.D. [Pickrel,S.&E.]
Ross, Anne E., (BV) ....'69 '95 C.174 B.S. L.150 J.D. [Ⓐ Gammell,H.K.&R.]
Ross, Robert D., (BV) ....'68 '94 C.473 B.S. L.201 J.D. [Gammell,H.K.&R.]
Rubin, Ira, (AV) ....'31 '54 C.415 L.1009 LL.B. [Goldman,R.&S.]
Ruchman, Marshall D., (AV) ....'34 '64 C.347 B.S. L.1119 J.D. [Altick&C.]
Rudwall, David F., (BV) ....'53 '82 C.272 B.S. L.608 J.D. 500 E. 3rd St., Apt. 239
Rueth, Joseph E. ....'54 '80 C.1208 B.S. L.607 J.D. 9330 Springboro Pike
Ruffner, James David, II, (BV) .... '58 '94 C.1208 B.S. L.201 J.D. [Ⓒ Chernesky,H.&K.]
Ruffolo, John M., (AV) ....'57 '82 C&L.201 B.A., J.D. [Ruffolo,S.&D.]
Ruffolo, Stone & Dressel, (AV) ....7501 Paragon Rd.
Russell, Michael, (BV) ....'45 '71 C.201 B.A. L.607 J.D. Asst. Pros. Atty.
Russell, William S. ....'80 '04 C.973 B.S. L.200 J.D. [Ⓐ Fox&Assoc.]
Rutledge, Marybeth W., (BV) ....'45 '82 C.530 B.A. L.201 J.D. [Winwood C.&Assoc.]
Ryan, Edwin L., Jr. .... '30 '57 C.602 B.S.M.E. L.209 J.D. 1974 Woodson Ct.‡

Ryan, Robin D. . . . . . '73 '01 C.610 B.A. L.201 J.D. [Ⓐ Porter W.M.&A.]
Sager, Barbara L., (BV) . . . . . '56 '86 C.150 B.A. L.309 J.D. [B.L.Sager]

Sager, Barbara L., Co., LPA, (BV)
120 West 2nd Street, Suite 1111, 45402
Telephone: 937-443-0295 Fax: 937-443-0457
Email: bsager@bsager.com URL: http://www.bsager.com
Barbara L. Sager.
Mergers and Acquisitions, Securities Regulations, Venture Capital, Corporate Law.
See Professional Biographies, DAYTON, OHIO

Saldanha, Jason . . . . . '78 '03 C&L.608 B.A., J.D. [Ⓐ Dyer,G.M.&S.]
Salyer, David R., (BV) . . . . . '59 '91 C.946 B.A. L.201 J.D. [Ⓐ E.S.Gallon&Assoc.]
Salyers, Lance Steven . . . . . '74 '00 C.613 B.A. L.902 J.D. Pros. Off.
Samonas, Michael . . . . . '59 '86 C.980 B.S. L.201 J.D. 103 Frank St.
Samson, Paul M. '59 '85 C.893 B.A. L.245 J.D.
(adm. in CA; not adm. in OH) Sr. Atty., NCR Corp.
Samuels, Ellen J. . . . . . '55 '86 C&L.150 B.A., J.D. Asst. Law V.P., NCR Corp.
Sandner, Lisa A., (BV) . . . . . '68 '94 C.262 B.A. L.201 J.D. Staff Atty., Univ. of Dayton
Sandner, Michael W., (BV) . . . . . '69 '94 C.183 B.A. L.201 J.D. [Pickrel,S.&E.]
Sanom, Laura A. . . . . . '62 '87 C.373 B.A. L.273 J.D. [Faruki I.&C.]
Santez, David L., (AV) '54 '79
C.1208 B.S. L.201 J.D. Assoc. Gen. Coun., MeadWestvaco Corp.
Saphire, David A., (AV) . . . . . '44 '70 C&L.608 B.A., J.D. [E.S.Gallon&Assoc.]
Saul, Irving I., (AV) . . . . . '29 '52 C.901 B.A. L.665 LL.B. 113 Bethpolamy Court
Sawyer, J. Anthony . . . . . '40 '70 Chief, City Law Dept.
Saxton, Kathleen E. . . . . . '62 '89 C&L.201 B.A., J.D. Law Clk., Ohio Ct. of Appeals
Scaccia, John J., (CV) . . . . . '54 '83 C.754 B.S. L.201 J.D. 130 West 2nd Street
Scanlon, Erin E. . . . . . '68 '94 C.967 B.A. L.665 J.D. Ct. of Appeals
Scearce, Bobby D. . . . . . '38 '72 C.124 B.S. L.1340 J.D. Pat. Atty., Dept. of the Air Force
Schaeff, B. Joseph, (AV) . . . . . '50 '75 C.201 B.A. L.608 J.D. [Dinsmore&S.] (Pat.)
Schaeffer, Alan B., (AV) . . . . . '46 '74 C.317 B.A. L.608 J.D. [Pickrel,S.&E.]
Schaeffer, Beth W., (AV) . . . . . '48 '75 C.317 A.B. L.117 J.D. 134 Patterson Rd.
Schaengold, Gary C., (BV) . . . . . '56 '82 C.473 B.A. L.201 J.D. [G.Schaengold]
Schaengold, Gary, The Law Office of, (BV) . . . . . 120 W. 2nd St., Ste. 1406
Schaltenbrand, Rebecca K. . . . . . '70 '95 C.611 B.A. L.117 J.D. Asst. City Atty.
Scharff, Martin, (BV) . . . . . '30 '59 C.201 B.S. L.150 LL.B. 4 S. Main Street, Suite 615
Scharrer, Richard C., (BV) . . . . . '24 '51 C.197 B.A. L.150 LL.B. [Ⓖ Lasky&S.]
Schmidt, David R., (BV) '49 '84 C.260 B.A. L.201 J.D.
1200 E. Dorothy Ln. (⊙Kettering)
Schmitt, Robert F. . . . . . '34 '63 C.494 B.A. L.1035 LL.B. 1644 Chartwell Dr.‡
Schneble, Alfred Wm., III, (BV) . . . . '56 '81 C.436 B.S. L.607 J.D. [Schneble,C.&Assoc.]

Schneble, Cass & Assoc. Co., L.P.A., (BV)
11 West Monument Avenue, Suite 402, 45402
Telephone: 937-222-1232 Fax: 937-222-5622
Email: Schneble-Cass-and-Assoc.com URL: http://www.awslawoffice.com
Alfred Wm. Schneble III; William O. Cass, Jr.
Civil Litigation, Corporate Law, Contract Litigation, Medical and Legal Malpractice, Personal Injury, Liquor Licensing, Tax Appeals and Court, Bankruptcy Reorganizations, Bankruptcy Litigation, Real Estate, Domestic Relations, Probate and Criminal Law.
See Professional Biographies, DAYTON, OHIO

Schram, Deborah C., (BV) '50 '78
C&L.201 B.A., J.D. Suite 408, 11 West Monument Building
Schulte, Richard W., (BV) . . . . . '68 '96 C.1082 B.A. Science L.879 J.D. [Botros&S.]
Schultz, Ronald E., (AV) '42 '67 C.610 B.S. L.608 J.D.
[Dyer,G.M.&S.] (⊙Bellefontaine, Huber Heights, Lima, Middletown, Piqua, Springfield)
Schwartz, Richard A., (AV) . . . . . '— '78 C.851 B.A. L.608 J.D. [Coolidge,W.W.&L.]
Schweller, Donald G., (AV) . . . . . '30 '57 C.201 B.A. L.150 J.D. [Ⓖ Pickrel,S.&E.]
Scott, Donald K., (BV) . . . . . '51 '86 C.1208 B.A. L.1340 J.D. [Altick&C.]
Scott, Gregory T. . . . . . '52 '84 C.1208 B.A. L.201 J.D. Mag., Juv. Ct.
Scudder, Steven C., (AV) . . . . . '54 '81 C.697 B.A. L.910 J.D. [Scudder&E.]
Scudder & Esler Co., L.P.A., (AV) . . . . . 2912 Springboro West, Suite 105
Sealy, Albert H., (AV) . . . . . '17 '42 C.608 A.B. L.309 LL.B. 2000 Courthouse Plaza, N.E.
Searcy, E. Dale '37 '63
C.1229 B.Mech.E. L.347 J.D. Prof. of Law, Univ. of Dayton Law Sch.
Sebaly, Jon M., (AV) . . . . . '36 '65 C&L.477 B.A., LL.B. [Sebaly,S.&D.]

Sebaly, Shillito & Dyer, A Legal Professional Association, (AV)
1900 Kettering Tower, 45423
Telephone: 937-222-2500 Telefax: 937-222-6554; 222-8279
URL: http://www.ssdlaw.com
Martin A. Beyer; Michael A. Booth; James A. Dyer; Gale S. Finley; John R. Glankler; Deborah D. Hunt; Michael P. Moloney; Jon M. Sebaly; Beverly F. Shillito; Jeffrey B. Shulman; Karl R. Ulrich. Of Counsel: Barbara A. Duncombe; Dianne F. Marx;—Carissa E. Clawson; Danyelle S.T. Coleman; Scott S. Davies; Katherine L. Early; Robert G. Hanseman; Toby K. Henderson; Chanda L. Lynch; Todd E. Robenson; Suzanne Sumner (Not admitted in OH); Heather Duffey Welbaum.
Business, Business Litigation, Government Contracts Law, Health Care, Labor and Employment, Workers Compensation, Commercial and Creditor Rights, Antitrust, Real Estate, Securities, Technology, Products Liability, Construction Law, Probate, Trust and Estate Planning, Insurance and ERISA.
See Professional Biographies, DAYTON, OHIO

Sebree, Ronald H. . . . . . '57 '94 C.1161 B.A. L.201 J.D. 6118 Alter Rd.
Seeberger, Sue, (BV) . . . . . '56 '92 C.1208 B.A. L.201 J.D. [Ⓐ Myers&F.]
Segreti, A. Mark, Jr., Attorney at Law, (BV) '45 '70
C.967 A.B. L.608 J.D. 1405 Streamside Dr.
Seligman, William Scott . . . . . '68 '93 C.184 B.A. L.1003 J.D. [W.S.Seligman]
Seligman, William S. . . . . . 4227 Linchmere Drive
Senney, Jeffrey S., (AV) . . . . . '54 '86 C.97 B.S.B.A. L.201 J.D. [Pickrel,S.&E.]
Serr, Willis O., II, (AV) '51 '75 C&L.608 B.A., J.D.
Pres. & CEO, Lutheran Social Services of Mid-America
Shale, R. Anne, (BV) . . . . . '46 '88 C.923 B.S.N. L.201 J.D. [Holzfaster,C.M.&M.]
Shaman, Wm. I. . . . . . '25 '52 C.608 B.A. L.607 J.D. 4 E. Schantz Ave.‡
Shane, Charles F., (AV) . . . . . '67 '93 C.473 B.S. L.201 J.D. [Bieser,G.&L.]
Shaneyfelt, Paul H., (CV) . . . . . '68 '95 C.178 B.A. L.930 J.D. [Ⓐ Statman,H.S.&E.]
Shank, Anne, (BV) . . . . . '61 '88 C.597 B.A. L.608 J.D. LEXIS-NEXIS
Shank, Edward L., (AV) . . . . . '29 '56 C.473 B.S. L.477 J.D. [Bieser,G.&L.]
Shanks, John T., (BV) . . . . . '22 '49 C&L.608 B.S., J.D. P.O. Box 20190
Shapiro, Joel S., (AV) . . . . . '42 '67 C&L.260 B.S.B.A., J.D. [Goldman,R.&S.]
Sharkey, Jeffrey S., (BV) . . . . . '67 '97 C.201 B.S. L.608 J.D. [Faruki I.&C.]
Shearer, Robert Bruce . . . . . '28 '52 C&L.383 LL.B. 5585 Brandt Pk.
Sheils, Melodee H. . . . . . '53 '79 C.150 B.A. L.273 J.D. Legacy Mort. Co.
Sherk, Arik A., (AV) . . . . . '59 '84 C.477 B.A. L.273 J.D. [Thompson H.]

Sherrets Law Offices, LLC
(See Kettering)

Shia, Johnna M. . . . . . '71 '97 C.1115 B.A. L.201 J.D. Co. Pros.
Shillito, Beverly F., (AV) . . . . . '53 '78 C.150 B.A. L.813 J.D. [Sebaly,S.&D.]

Shipman, Dixon & Livingston Co., L.P.A.
(See Troy)

Shira, William A., III . . . . . '42 '67 C.385 A.B. L.930 J.D. 432 Silvercrest Ter.
Shook, Charles D., (AV) . . . . . '27 '52 C.145 A.B. L.608 LL.B. [Bieser,G.&L.]
Short, Frank C., (BV) . . . . . '26 '52 C.319 B.A. L.607 J.D. Asst. Pros. Atty.
Shough, David A., (BV) . . . . . '54 '85 C.477 B.M. L.930 J.D. [Ⓖ Dinsmore&S.] (Pat.)
Showalter, Robert L. '60 '89
C.383 B.S. L.904 J.D. [Stevens&S.] (Pat.) (⊙Lexington, KY)
Shulman, Jeffrey B., (AV) . . . . . '38 '63 C.951 B.A. L.477 J.D. [Sebaly,S.&D.]
Shulman, Louis T., (AV) . . . . . '05 '29 L.608 LL.B. 3401 Southdale Dr.‡
Signom, Robert E., II, (BV) . . . . . '45 '70 C.473 B.S. L.608 J.D. 420 S. Ludlow St.
Silberstein, Susan Stewart . . . . . '50 '77 C.970 B.A. L.989 J.D. Dayton Civil Serv. Bd.

Silverstein, Jeffrey M., and Associates, (AV) '55 '80 C.94 B.A. L.201 J.D.
627 S. Edwin C. Moses Boulevard Suite 2-C, 45408
Telephone: 937-228-3731 Fax: 937-228-2252
Email: jeff@silversteinlaw.com URL: http://www.lawyers.com/silversteinlaw
(Certified Specialist in Labor & Employment Law, Ohio State Bar Association).
Employment and Labor Law.
See Professional Biographies, DAYTON, OHIO

Simon, Kevin V. . . . . . '69 '94 C.201 B.A. L.880 J.D. [Ⓐ Chernesky,H.&K.]
Simpson, Jay M., (BV) . . . . . '52 '81 C.1208 B.A. L.201 J.D. [Ⓖ Leppla]
Sinder, Fredric L. . . . . . '49 '75 C.124 B.S. L.477 J.D. Pat. Atty., Dept. of Air Force (Pat.)
Singer, Gregory F., (AV) . . . . . '51 '79 C.150 B.A. L.201 J.D. [Tucker,F.&S.]
Sinkovits, Angela M. . . . . . '68 '03 C.1175 B.A. L.893 J.D. [Ⓐ Faruki I.&C.]
Skelton, Richard S., (BV) . . . . . '53 '88 C.1208 B.A. L.201 J.D. 130 W. Second St.
Skilken, Ralph A., Jr., (BV) . . . . . '41 '68 C.679 B.A. L.607 J.D. [R.A.Skilken,Jr.]
Skilken, Thomas E., (BV) . . . . . '51 '78 C.604 B.A. L.607 J.D. 130 W. Second St., Ste. 310
Skilken, Ralph A., Jr., Co. LPA, (BV) . . . . . 580 Lincoln Park Blvd., Ste. 222
Skinner, Robert A., (BV) . . . . . '32 '59 C&L.608 B.S.C., J.D. Asst. Pros. Atty.
Slaton, Curtis F., (BV) . . . . . '60 '86 C.1208 B.A. L.201 J.D. [Bogin P.E.S.&S.]
Slavens, John M., (BV) . . . . . '45 '70 C.473 B.S. L.607 J.D. [Ⓐ Hollencamp&H.]
Slicer, Charles W., III, (BV) . . . . . '66 '92 C.316 B.A. L.607 J.D. [Slicer]
Slicer, Charles W., Jr., (BV) . . . . . '41 '66 C.610 A.B. L.607 J.D. 111 W. 1st St., # 401
Slicer Law Office, (BV) . . . . . 111 W. First St., Ste. 401
Slonaker, William M., Sr. '46 '72
C.201 B.S. L.608 J.D. Assoc. Prof., Bus. Law, Wright State Univ.‡
Slone-Stiven, Ruth A., (BV) . . . . . '50 '85 C&L.201 B.S.B.A., J.D. P.O. Box 3340

Slowik & Robinson, LLC
(See Columbus)

Smalley, John A., (AV) . . . . . '59 '85 C.383 B.A. L.201 J.D. [Dyer,G.M.&S.]
Smith, Andrew T. '50 '75 C.951 B.A. L.902 J.D.
(adm. in FL; not adm. in OH) Sr. V.P., Lion Apparel, Inc.
Smith, Bradley C., (BV) . . . . . '53 '78 C.608 B.A. L.201 J.D. [Flanagan,L.H.&S.]
Smith, Edward M., (BV) . . . . . '48 '73 C&L.602 A.B., J.D. [Nolan,S.S.&F.]
Smith, Larry A., (BV) . . . . . '41 '67 C&L.150 B.B.A., J.D. [Young,P.L.&J.]
Smith, Nicholas M. . . . . . '78 '03 C.610 B.S. L.608 J.D. [Ⓐ Faruki I.&C.]
Smith, Patrick K., (BV) . . . . . '52 '78 C.138 B.A. L.201 J.D. [Koverman&S.] (⊙L.A., CA)
Smith, R. Todd . . . . . '59 '87 C.473 B.S. L.201 J.D. [Ⓖ Flanagan,L.H.&S.]
Smith, William Michael . . . . . '59 '85 C&L.378 B.A., J.D. 2121 Mershon Avenue
Snead, Jeffrey W., (BV) . . . . . '68 '94 C.347 B.A. L.851 J.D. [Thorson,S.W.&S.]

Snell, Richard G., (AV) '28 '56 C&L.608 A.B., J.D.
Suite 506 Liberty Tower, 120 West Second Street, 45402
Telephone: 937-224-5297 Fax: 937-224-3325
Email: snellaw@aol.com URL: http://www.ohioaviationlawyer.com
Aviation, Personal Injury, Probate, and Probate Litigation.
Representative Clients: Aero Tech Projects, Inc; Commander-Aero, Inc.; Coppersmith, Inc. (Dubai, U.A.E.); Sachs Marketing Group.
References: National City Bank; KeyBank.

Snow, Edwin C., Sr. . . . . . '15 '46 C.28 L.93 J.D. 405 Marley Rd.‡
Snyder, Gary A., (BV) . . . . . '34 '60 C.231 A.B. L.150 J.D. 11 West Monument Building
Snyder, Jeffrey D., (BV) . . . . . '68 '94 C.967 B.A. L.150 J.D. [Ⓐ Hochman&P.]
Snyder, Larry R. . . . . . '57 '84 C.201 B.A. L.607 J.D. 5575 Hummock Rd.
Snyder, Monte K., (CV) . . . . . '50 '85 C.510 B.A. L.201 J.D. [Ⓐ L.S.Stukey&Assoc.]
Snyder, R. Bruce, (AV) . . . . . '45 '73 C.976 B.A. L.608 J.D. [Porter W.M.&A.]
Snyder, Robert N., (AV) . . . . . '55 '85 C.608 B.A. L.201 J.D. [Freund,F.&A.]
Soifer, Stacey M. (Rubens) . . . . . '58 '88 C.477 B.G.S. L.424 J.D. [Soifer,S.M.]
Soifer, Stacey M. . . . . . P.O. Box 751704
Solle, Susan D. . . . . . '68 '99 C.606 B.A. L.201 J.D. [Ⓐ Chernesky,H.&K.]
Sommer, Louis F., III . . . . . '72 '99 C.608 B.S.B.A. L.607 J.D. [Ⓐ Horenstein,N.&B.]
Sommers, Brian A. . . . . . '67 '00 C.346 B.S. L.201 J.D. [Ⓐ Botros&S.]
Sorey, Roger L. . . . . . '48 '86 C.103 A.B. L.117 J.D. Lawyers Title Insurance Corp.
Sorrell, Janet R., (BV) . . . . . '51 '81 C.473 B.A. L.201 J.D. Montgomery Co. Pub. Def.
Soter, Mary K. C., (BV) . . . . . '40 '75 C.1208 B.A. L.150 J.D. 5518 N. Main St.
Southern, Heidi L., (BV) . . . . . '72 '98 C.473 B.A. L.201 J.D. 111 W. First St., Suite 519
Souvé, Todd W., (BV) '61 '86 C.1044 B.A. L.201 J.D.
Mng. Atty., Advocates for Basic Legal Equality
Sowar, Gerard D., (AV) '58 '87 C.201 B S.C.E. L.851 J.D.
V.P. & Sr. Coun., The Standard Register Company
Spaeth, Edward J. '61 '89
C.150 B.A. L.1340 J.D. Sr. Dir. & Assoc. Corp. Coun., LexisNexis
Spaeth, Paul H., (BV) . . . . . '57 '83 C.473 B.A. L.608 J.D. [P.H.Spaeth]

Spaeth, Paul H., Co., L.P.A., (BV)
130 West 2nd Street, Suite 450, 45402
Telephone: 937-223-1655 Fax: 937-223-1656
Email: pspaeth@phslaw.com URL: http://www.phslaw.com
Paul H. Spaeth.
Bankruptcy (Chapters 7, 11, 13, Business Reorganizations), Collections, Debtor and Creditor Rights, Business Law, Business Formations, Bankruptcy Litigation.
See Professional Biographies, DAYTON, OHIO

Spalla, A. J. Jim, (AVⓉ) '45 '70 C.610 B.A. L.259 J.D.
(adm. in FL; not adm. in OH) [Ⓖ Spalla&S.] (⊙Tallahassee, FL)
Spalla & Spalla . . . . . 7229 Taylorsville Road
Spanel, Claudette M. . . . . . '59 '84 C.201 B.A. L.608 J.D. Univ. of Dayton Resch. Instit.
Spayd, Robert V., (AV) . . . . . '26 '53 C.674 A.B. L.309 LL.B. 386 Rue Marseille‡
Spears, Gregory P., (BV) . . . . . '56 '82 C.97 B.L.S. L.851 J.D. [Falke&D.]
Spidel, George J. . . . . . '35 '64 C.967 B.S. L.607 J.D. Admin. Law J., Soc. Sec. Admin.
Sprowl, Milton L. . . . . . '21 '50 C&L.150 A.B., LL.B. [Nolan,S.S.&F.] ‡
Stachler, John H., (BV) . . . . . '67 '94 C.973 B.S.B.A. L.201 J.D. [Jablinski,F.R.&M.]
Staley, Jack E., (BV) . . . . . '27 '52 C.201 L.150 LL.B. 238 Towerview
Stamper, Maxwell H., Jr., (AV) . . . . . '22 '49 C.362 A.B. L.309 LL.B. 175 Lookout Dr.
Stamps, Eric Alan, (CV) . . . . . '73 '99 C.1208 B.S. L.201 J.D. 3814 Little York Rd.

Standley Law Group LLP
(See Dublin)

Stanley, Lu Ann, (BV) . . . . . '55 '85 C.473 B.S. L.851 J.D. [Ⓐ Flanagan,L.H.&S.]

Statman, Harris, Siegel & Eyrich, LLC, (AV)
Fifth Third Street, 110 North Main Street, Suite 1520, 45402 ⊙
Telephone: 937-222-1090 Fax: 937-222-1046
Member of Firm: Thomas R. Noland. Associates: Paul H. Shaneyfelt; Tina F. Woods; Patricia L. Hill. Of Counsel: Robert F. Cowdrey.
General Civil Trial and Appellate Practice in Federal and State Courts. Commercial Litigation, Bankruptcy, Banking, Personal Injury and Family Law. Corporate Acquisitions, Dispositions, Spin-Offs, Corporate Formation, Financings, Real Estate, Banking and Commercial Law, Reorganizations, Restructurings, Bankruptcy, Civil Litigation, General Business, Intellectual Property, Taxation, Estate Planning.
Cincinnati, Ohio Office: 2900 Chemed Center, 255 East Fifth Street, 45202-2912. Telephone: 513-621-2666. Telecopier: 513-621-4896.
Chicago, Illinois Office: 333 West Wacker Drive, Suite 1710, 60606. Telephone: 312-263-1070. Fax: 312-263-1201.
See Professional Biographies, DAYTON, OHIO

Staton, James C. ....'71 '97 C.473 B.A. L.201 J.D. 5613 Brandt Pike
Stefanec, Erin E. .... '— '04 C.473 B.A. L.201 J.D. [Ⓐ Faruki I.&C.]
Steigerwald, Jean M., (BV) ....'54 '86 C.1208 B.A. L.201 J.D. 423 Kling Dr.
Stein, S. Larry '30 '54 C.477 B.A. L.986 J.D.
(adm. in MO; not adm. in OH) Chmn., Larry Stein Realty Co.
Stephan, Wayne P., (BV) .... '49 '74 C.201 B.S. L.607 J.D. [Flanagan,L.H.&S.]
Stevens, Richard C., (AV) '45 '77
C.608 B.E.E. L.146 J.D. [Stevens&S.] (Pat.) (⊙Lexington, KY)

Stevens & Showalter, L.L.P., (AV)
7019 Corporate Way, 45459-4238
Telephone: 937-438-6848 Fax: 937-438-2124
Email: ssllp@speakeasy.net
Richard C. Stevens; Robert L. Showalter; Thomas E. Lees. Of Counsel: Michael D. Folkerts; Charlene L.H. Stukenborg.
Intellectual Property, Patents, Trademarks, Copyright and Unfair Competition.
See Professional Biographies, DAYTON, OHIO

Stewart, Jeff C. ....'73 '00 C.234 B.S. L.339 J.D. [Ⓐ Thompson H.]
Stiakakis, Nicole Christina ....'72 '97 C.473 B.A. L.117 J.D. Pros. Off.
Stirling, Scott T. .... '62 '93 C.150 B.M. L.477 J.D. [Ⓐ Thompson H.]
Stock, Otto F., Jr. .... '35 '61 C.197 A.B. L.477 LL.B. 7171 Mohawk Trail Road
Stocklin, Valerie, (BV) ....'45 '81 C.851 B.A. L.201 J.D. [© Leppla]
Stoermer, Elaine, (BV) .... '53 '81 C.473 B.A. L.201 J.D. 716 Bowen St.
Stokely, Matthew D., (BV) .... '60 '86 C.1030 B.A. L.1029 J.D. [Altick&C.]
Stone, J. V., (BV) ....'23 '55 C.611 B.A. L.665 J.D. [Ruffolo,S.&D.]
Stone, Mark Edward, (BV) .... '55 '82 C.97 B.S. L.201 J.D. [M.Stone]
Stone, Scot A., (BV) ....'55 '82 C.611 B.A. L.201 J.D. [Ruffolo,S.&D.]
Stone, Mark, Co., LPA, (BV) .... 42 Woodcroft Trl.
Storar, Andrew C., (AV) ....'52 '81 C.1208 B.A. L.200 J.D. [Pickrel,S.&E.]
Stout, Scott Gerard .... '57 '82 C&L.607 B.A., J.D. 131 N. Ludlow Street
Stover, James ....'57 '88 C.1344 B.S.E.E. L.213 J.D. Sr. Atty., NCR Corp.
Strahorn, Derrick A., Law Offices of, (CV) '60 '86 C.813 B.A. L.846 J.D.
2 Redlands St.
Straus, Thomas J. ....'51 '78 C.150 B.B.A. L.1340 J.D. Citizens Fed. Bk., F.S.B.
Stroh, David L. .... '49 '75 C.473 B.S. L.607 J.D. 5045 N. Main St.
Stueve, Jennifer L. .... '77 '02 C.473 B.S. L.201 J.D. [Ⓐ Bieser,G.&L.]
Stukenborg, Charlene L.H., (BV) '66 '95
C.608 B.S.E.E. L.201 J.D. [© Stevens&S.] (Pat.)
Stukey, Linda S., & Associates, (CV) '45 '78
C.1023 B.S. L.201 J.D. 333 W. 1st St., Ste. 200
Stump, Randall L., (BV) ....'59 '84 C&L.201 B.A., J.D. [Bogin P.E.S.&S.]
Suarez, Luis Javier .... '57 '94 C.150 B.A. L.607 J.D. Analyst, Lexis Nexis
Subashi, Nicholas E., (AV) ....'54 '80 C.205 A.B. L.1017 J.D. [Subashi,W.&B.]

Subashi, Wildermuth & Ballato, (AV)
The Oakwood Building, 2305 Far Hills Avenue, 45419
Telephone: 937-534-0500 Fax: 937-534-0505
Email: lawoffices@swbohiolaw.com URL: http://www.swbohiolaw.com
Nicholas E. Subashi; Brian L. Wildermuth; Lynnette Pisone Ballato;—Tabitha Justice; Joshua Epling (Not admitted in OH); Heather R. Zilka; Anne P. Keeton.
Insurance Defense, Insurance Coverage, Professional Liability, School Law, Governmental Immunities, Civil Rights, Employment Law, Civil Litigation, Medical Malpractice.
See Professional Biographies, DAYTON, OHIO

Sullivan, Thomas P. ....'69 '04 C.17 B.A. L.851 J.D. [Ⓐ Freund,F.&A.]
Sumner, Suzanne '68 '93 C.549 B.A. L.1410 J.D.
(adm. in CO; not adm. in OH) [Ⓐ Sebaly,S.&D.]
Surdyk, Robert J., (AV) .... '47 '72 C.602 B.A. L.150 J.D. [Surdyk,D.&T.]

Surdyk, Dowd & Turner, Co., L.P.A., Law Offices of, (AV)
Kettering Tower 1610, 40 North Main Street, 45423
Telephone: 937-222-2333 Fax: 937-222-1970
Robert J. Surdyk; Edward J. Dowd; Jeffrey C. Turner;—Boyd W. Gentry; Rebekah Neuherz; Dawn M. Frick; Kevin A. Lantz; Michael F. Arnold.
See Professional Biographies, DAYTON, OHIO

Svoboda, Frank J., Jr. .... '08 '43 C.602 A.B. L.161 J.D. 526 Willowhurst St.‡
Swaim, James E., (BV) ....'46 '71 C.473 B.S. L.150 J.D. [Flanagan,L.H.&S.]
Swanson, Kristina E. .... '68 '02 C.477 B.S. L.665 J.D. [Ⓐ Dinsmore&S.] (Pat.)
Swillinger, Jeffrey A., (AV) .... '52 '79 C.94 B.A. L.1218 J.D. [Crew&B.]
Switala, Gilbert B., Jr., (BV) .... '64 '91 C.665 B.A. L.201 J.D. [Thorson,S.W.&S.]
Sylvain, Nicholas Peter '68 '93
C.201 B.Ch.E. L.945 J.D. Montgomery Co. Common Pleas Court

Taft, Stettinius & Hollister LLP, (AV)
110 North Main Street, Suite 900, 45402-1786 ⊙
Telephone: 937-228-2838 Facsimile: 937-228-2816
URL: http://www.taftlaw.com
Resident Members: J. Steven Justice; Hugh E. Wall, III. Associates: Lisa L. Patterson; Matthew J. Wiles; Gregory Turner.
Antitrust, Bankruptcy and Debtor/Creditor Rights, Business and Finance, E-Business (Internet and E-Commerce), Employee Benefits/ERISA and Tax-Planning, Environmental Law, Family Law, Family Business Planning, Franchise, General Litigation, Health Care, Immigration, Institutional Finance, Intellectual Property and Technology Group, International, Japanese Practice, Labor and Employment, Mergers and Acquisitions, Nonprofit and Tax-Exempt Organizations, Product Liability and Personal Injury, Public Finance, Real Property, Securities, Tax, Probate and Estate Planning, Workers' Compensation.
Columbus, Ohio Office: Twelfth Floor, 21 East State Street. Telephone: 614-221-2838.
Covington, Kentucky Office: 1717 Dixie Highway, Suite 340. Telephone: 859-331-2838; 513-381-2838.
Cleveland, Ohio Office: 3500 BP Tower, 200 Public Square. Telephone: 216-241-2838.
Cincinnati, Ohio Office: 425 Walnut Street, Suite 1800. Telephone: 513-381-2838
See Professional Biographies, DAYTON, OHIO

Talbot, Thomas B., Jr., (AV) .... '49 '74 C.138 B.A. L.150 J.D. [Talbot&D.]

Talbot & Ducker, (AV)
903 Key Bank Building, 45402
Mailing Address: P.O. Box 384, Wright Bros. Station, Dayton, OH 45409
Telephone: 937-224-1006 Fax: 937-224-1009
Email: Ttalbotjr@aol.com

(This Listing Continued)

Talbot & Ducker (Continued)
Members of Firm: Thomas B. Talbot, Jr.; John T. Ducker.
General Civil Practice. Commercial Collections, Commercial Law, Bankruptcy, Liens, Corporation, Probate Law and Mechanics' Liens. Trials.
Reference: Fifth Third Bank.
See Professional Biographies, DAYTON, OHIO

Talda, Richard A., (AV) .... '— '82 C.967 B.A. L.851 J.D. [Coolidge,W.W.&L.]
Talmage, William H. ....'30 '53 C.381 A.B. L.930 LL.B. Legal Dept., NCR Corp.
Taronji, Ian A. .... '71 '00 C.477 B.A. L.912 J.D. [Ⓐ Faruki I.&C.]
Tassone, Joseph V. '30 '62 C.923 B.S. L.1340 J.D.
V.P. & Gen. Coun., DAYCO Products, Inc. (Pat.)
Taylor, Edward M., Jr., (BV) .... '28 '51 L.607 J.D. Mag. [Taylor&T.]
Taylor, Jeffrey, (BV) .... '42 '84 C.117 B.A. L.201 J.D. 115 W. Monument Ave., Apt. 904
Taylor, Mary J., (BV) .... '26 '51 C.266 L.607 J.D. [Taylor&T.]
Taylor & Taylor, (BV) .... 7417 N. Main St.
Thiele, Howard N., Jr., (AV) .... '30 '55 C.473 A.B. L.477 J.D. 2000 Courthouse Plz. N.E.
Thomas, Maxine S. '48 '73 C&L.911 B.A., J.D.
(adm. in WA; not adm. in OH)
Secretary, General Counsel & Program Officer, Kettering Foundation
Thompson, Eric S. ....'74 '99 C.608 B.A. L.124 J.D. [Leppla]
Thompson, Kenneth R., II, (BV) '60 '85 C.117 B.A. L.150 J.D.
V.P. & Actg. Gen. Coun., LEXIS-NEXIS Group
Thompson, Lester R., (BV) ....'49 '74 C.97 B.S.B.A. L.607 J.D. [Thompson&D.]
Thompson, Michael Cash ....'61 '89 C.420 B.A. L.861 J.D. 5 N. Williams St.

Thompson and DeVeny Co., L.P.A., (BV)
1340 Woodman Drive, 45432
Telephone: 937-252-2030 Fax: 937-252-9425
Email: info@thompsonanddeveny.com
Lester R. Thompson; Dain N. DeVeny; Charles J. Roedersheimer.
Bankruptcy Law, Divorce, Child Custody, Child Support.
See Professional Biographies, DAYTON, OHIO

Thompson Hine LLP, (AV)
2000 Courthouse Plaza, N.E., P.O. Box 8801, 45401-8801 ⊙
Telephone: 937-443-6600 Fax: 937-443-6635
Email: info@ThompsonHine.com URL: http://www.ThompsonHine.com
Amos Burt Thompson (1871-1965); Charles P. Hine (1877-1942); Walter L. Flory (1880-1951); Michael L. Hardy (Partner-in-Charge, Cleveland); Patricia Mann Smitson (Partner-in-Charge, Cincinnati); Anthony C. White (Partner-in-Charge, Columbus); Robert M. Curry (Partner-in Charge, Dayton); Nicholas J. DiMichael (Partner-in-Charge, Washington, DC); George J. Walsh III (Partner-in-Charge, New York City); Ludo Deklerck (Partner-in-Charge, Brussels); Walt A. Linscott (Partner-in-Charge, Atlanta). Partners: Stephen J. Axtell; J. Wray Blattner; Barry M. Block; Robert J. Brown; Lawrence T. Burick; Richard F. Carlile; Mark A. Conway; Robert M. Curry (Partner-in-Charge); Thomas E. DeBrosse; Steven J. Elleman; Francesco A. Ferrante; Christine M. Haaker; Timothy J. Hackert; Robert J. Hadley; Linn S. Harson; J. Michael Herr; Teresa D. Jones; Scott A. King; Donald J. Kinlin; Thomas A. Knoth; Mark P. Levy (Group Leader, Intellectual Property); Theodore D. Lienesch; Crofford J. Macklin, Jr. (Group Leader, Personal and Succession Planning); David A. Neuhardt; Sharen Swartz Neuhardt; Allen R. Norris; Joseph M. Rigot; Joan H. Roddy; Arik A. Sherk; Jeremy L. Trahan. Associates: Charles D. Cooper; Cori R. Haper; Nathan E. Holmes; Nathan C. Hunt; John F. Kane; Carl A. Lux; Jennifer L. Maffett; John M. McCann; Jeffrey C. Metzcar; Victoria L. Nilles; Edward C. Redder; Jeff C. Stewart; Scott T. Stirling; Victor J. Wasylyna; David O. Zimmer. Senior Attorneys: Richard A. Ciambrone; Steven J. Davis; Douglas E. Erickson. Of Counsel: John E. Clough; Rene M. LaForte.
Administrative Law, Admiralty and Maritime Law, Agency and Distributorships, Antitrust and Trade Regulation, Aviation and Aerospace, Bankruptcy, Banks and Banking, Biotechnology, Business Law, Business Litigation, Business Regulation, Business Transactions, Closely Held Business Law, Joint Ventures, Class Actions, Commercial Law, Commercial Real Estate, Communications and Media, FCC Regulation, Computers and Software, Construction Law, Contracts, Copyrights, Corporate Law, Corporate Finance, Corporate Litigation, Corporate Tax Controversies, Debtor and Creditor, Employee Benefits, ERISA, Energy, Energy Regulation, Environmental Law, Finance, Commercial Finance, Franchises and Franchising, General Practice, Government, False Claims Act, Qui Tam Litigation, Government Contracts, Health Care, Insurance Coverage, Insurance Regulation, Intellectual Property, International Law, International Trade, Internet Law, Labor and Employment, Life Sciences, Litigation, Complex Litigation, Medicare Fraud and Abuse, Mergers, Acquisitions and Divestitures, Natural Resources, Nonprofit and Charitable Organizations, Occupational Safety and Health, OSHA, Partnership Law, Patents, Probate, Products Liability, Product Safety, Professional Liability, Public Finance, Railroad Law, Real Estate, Regulatory Law, Drug and Medical Device Regulation, Food and Drug Regulation, International Regulatory Law, Regulated Industries, Securities, Initial Public Offerings, Public Offerings, Taxation, Tax Controversies, Toxic Torts, Trade Secrets, Trademarks, Transportation, Trusts and Estates, Unfair Competition, Utility Law, White Collar Crime, Zoning, Planning and Land Use.
Cleveland, Ohio Office: 3900 Key Center, 127 Public Square, 44114-1291. Telephone: 216-566-5500. Fax: 216-566-5800. Email: info@ThompsonHine.com.
Cincinnati, Ohio Office: 312 Walnut Street, 14th Floor, 45202-4089. Telephone: 513-352-6700. Fax: 513-241-4771. Email: info@ThompsonHine.com.
Columbus, Ohio Office: 10 West Broad Street, Suite 700, 43215-3435. Telephone: 614-469-3200. Fax: 614-469-3361. Email: info@ThompsonHine.com.
Washington, D.C. Office: 1920 N Street, N.W., Suite 800, 20036-1600. Telephone: 202-331-8800. Fax: 202-331-8330. Email: info@ThompsonHine.com.
New York, N.Y. Office: One Chase Manhattan Plaza, 58th Floor, 10005-1401. Telephone: 212-344-5680. Fax: 212-809-6890. Email: info@ThompsonHine.com.
Brussels, Belgium Office: Avenue Louise 375 - b8, 1050 Brussels, Belgium, Telephone: 011 (32-2) 626-3280. Fax: 011 (32-2) 626-3299. Email: info@ThompsonHine.com.
Atlanta, Georgia Office: Proscenium Center, Suite 1200, 1170 Peachtree Street, 30309-7673. Telephone: 404-541-2900. Fax: 404-541-2905. Email: info@ThompsonHine.com.
See Professional Biographies, DAYTON, OHIO

Thomsen, Ira H., (AV) '54 '79 C.188 B.A. L.221 J.D.
[© Pickrel,S.&E.] (⊙Springboro)
Thorson, James M., Jr., (BV) .... '64 '90 C.608 B.S. L.201 J.D [Thorson,S.W.&S.]

Thorson, Switala, Wilkins & Snead, LLP, (BV)
First National Plaza, 130 West Second Street, Suite 1508, 45402
Telephone: 937-228-9000 Fax: 937-228-3550
URL: http://www.tswslaw.com
James M. Thorson, Jr.; Gilbert B. Switala Jr.; Lawrence A. Wilkins; Jeffrey W. Snead;—Joseph J. Mondock.
Medical Malpractice, Nursing Errors, Wrongful Death Claims, Nursing Home Negligence, Automobile Collisions, Motorcycle and Bicycle Injuries, Dog Bite Injuries, Other accidents involving serious injury or loss of life.
See Professional Biographies, DAYTON, OHIO

Thurman, Brett L., (BV) '60 '85 C.894 A.B. L.228 J.D.
General Counsel & Human Resources Manager, Dayton Newspapers, Inc.
Thyer, James W. ....'43 '63 C.610 B.B.A. L.608 J.D. Touche Ross & Co.
Tismo, J. Pierre, (BV⊤) .... '66 '91 C&L.201 B.A., J.D. [Ⓐ Dyer,G.M.&S.]
Todd, Harlan H. '29 '53 C&L.930 B.A., LL.B.
Pres., Dayton Forging & Heat Treating Co.

Tomb Law
(See Troy)

Trahan, Jeremy L. .... '69 '96 C.808 B.S. L.602 J.D. [Thompson H.]
Treese, David M. '64 '91 C.645 B.S. L.273 J.D.
(adm. in VA; not adm. in OH) Corp. Coun., Bonbright Distributors, Inc.
Treese, Margaret Anderson .... '66 '91 C.893 B.A. L.273 J.D. Sr. Atty., NCR Corp.
Treherne, Gretchen M. .... '76 '01 C.812 B.A. L.201 J.D. [Ⓐ Bieser,G.&L.]

Treherne, Jason E. .... '76 '01 C.608 B.A. L.201 J.D. [Ⓐ Freund,F.&A.]
Trissell, Stanley L., Jr., (CV) ....'46 '92 C&L.201 B.C.E., J.D. 7535 Turtle Creek Dr.
Trott, Merideth A., (AV) ....'49 '75 C.243 B.A. L.800 J.D. [Dinsmore&S.]
Tucker, Michael L., (AV) ....'55 '80 C.1208 B.A. L.201 J.D. [Tucker,F.&S.]
Tucker and Singer, (AV) .... 131 N. Ludlow St.
Turner, Dennis J., (BV) .... '45 '70 C&L.276 B.A., J.D. Prof. of Law, Univ. of Dayton
Turner, Gregory ....'64 '01 C&L.201 B.S., J.D. [Ⓐ Taft,S.&H.]
Turner, J. David, Law Office, (BV) ..... '54 '84 C.1208 B.A. L.200 J.D. 2443 S. Dixie Dr.
Turner, Jeffrey C., (BV) ....'61 '94 C.973 B.S. L.201 J.D. [Surdyk,D.&T.]
Turner, Jonathan Clay .... '67 '95 C.1208 B.A. L.494 J.D. City of Dayton Dept. of Law
Turner, Julia A. ....'— '03 C.150 B.S.N. L.117 J.D. [Ⓐ Freund,F.&A.]
Turner, Michael R., (BV) ....'60 '85 C.607 B.A. L.930 J.D. 33 W. 1st St., 2nd Fl.
Tuss, Mark A., (BV) ....'52 '81 C.201 B.A. L.608 J.D. [Popp&T.]
Tweel, Donna S., (BV) ....'60 '90 C.437 B.A. L.200 J.D. [Chernesky,H.&K.]
Tye, Timothy N., (AV) ....'53 '78 C.473 B.A. L.608 J.D. [Tye&T.]

Tye and Tye, (AV)
A Legal Professional Association
5975 Kentshire Drive, 45440
Telephone: 937-291-8646 Telecopier: 937-291-8650
URL: http://www.lawyers.com/tye&tye
Member of Firm: Timothy N. Tye.
Business Law, Closely Held Business Law, Residential and Commercial Real Estate, Probate, Trusts and Estates, Family Law, Funeral Directors Liability.
References: National City Bank; Bank One, Dayton N.A.
See Professional Biographies, DAYTON, OHIO

Ulrich, Karl R., (BV) ....'61 '86 C.999 B.A. L.602 J.D. [Sebaly,S.&D.]
Ulrich, Laura G. ....'— '94 C.201 B.A. L.546 J.D. Asst. Pros. Atty.
Ulrich, Paul M. ....'67 '99 C.150 B.S.M.E. L.201 J.D. [Ⓐ Dinsmore&S.] (Pat.)
Ungerman, Fred A., Jr., (AV) ...... '— '80 C.294 A.B. L.228 J.D. [Coolidge,W.W.&L.]
Utacht, Edward C., II .... '46 '74 C.201 B.S. L.607 J.D. 335 W. 3rd St.
Valley, Theodore D. ....'72 '99 C&L.201 B.S., J.D. [Copley V.&B.]
Vallone, Sean J., (CV) ....'69 '94 C.610 B.S. L.201 J.D. 4612 Salem Ave.
Vanderburgh, Ann Marie S. '— '69 C.1078 B.A. L.201 J.D.
(adm. in IL; not adm. in OH) 337 Peach Orchard Ave.‡
Vanderschaaff, Bertis J., IV, (BV) ....'67 '96 C.800 B.A. L.200 J.D. [Scudder&E.]
Van Ho, Adam Michael ....'75 '01 C.25 B.A. L.989 J.D. Pros. Atty. Off.

Van Kley & Walker, LLC, (AV)
137 North Main Street, Suite 316, 45402 ⊙
Telephone: 937-226-9000 Fax: 937-226-9002
Email: cwalker@vankleywalker.com URL: http://www.vankleywalker.com
Christopher A. Walker.
Air Pollution, Brownfields Redevelopment, Chemical Regulation, Conservation Easements, Environmental Auditing, Environmental Compliance, Due Diligence and Permitting, Environmental Dispute Resolution, Groundwater Contamination, Hazardous Materials and Substances, Hazardous Waste, National Environmental Policy Act (NEPA), Oil Pollution, Pesticide Regulation, Property Remediation, Permitting, Solid Waste, Underground Storage Tanks, Water Pollution, Wetlands Regulation.
Columbus Office: 132 Northwoods Boulevard, Suite C-1, 43235. Telephone: 614-431-8900. Fax: 614-431-8905.
See Professional Biographies, DAYTON, OHIO

VanNoy, Anthony S., (BV) ....'71 '96 C.63 B.S. L.201 J.D. [Wright&V.]
VanSchaik, Chris R. V., (AV) ....'41 '70 C.201 B.A. L.150 J.D. Asst. Pros.
Vaughn, Navay M., (CV) ....'63 '89 C&L.201 B.A., J.D. 5 N. Williams St.
Vaughn, Noel W., (BV) ......'37 '79 C.210 B.A. L.201 J.D. 131 N. Ludlow St., Ste. 1205
Vinolus, Athan A. .... '61 '88 C.565 B.S. L.851 J.D. Coun., Tomkins Industries, Inc.
Vogt, Kenneth J. ....'14 '37 C&L.546 B.Sc., J.D. 2801 Far Hills Ave.
Voigt, Eric P. ....'78 '03 C.575 B.A. L.1119 J.D. [Ⓐ Faruki I.&C.]
Vollmar, Michelle S., (BV) ....'70 '95 C.473 B.S. L.201 J.D. [Rogers&G.]
Vollmar, T. Andrew, (BV) ....'69 '94 C.973 B.A. L.201 J.D. [Freund,F.&A.]
von Meister, Peter F., (BV) ....'— '72 C.388 B.A. L.150 J.D. [Green&G.]
Vradelis, Anthony J., (AV) .... '27 '52 C.385 L.150 LL.B. 2000 Courthouse Plz. N.E.
Vradelis, Theodore J., (AV) .... '26 '51 C.385 L.150 LL.B. 2000 Courthouse Plz. N.E.
Wachstein, Steven M. ....'— '01 C.473 B.A. L.150 J.D. [Ⓐ Coolidge,W.W.&L.]
Wagner, Bruce F., (BV) ....'48 '73 C.610 B.B.A. L.608 J.D. Asst. Pub. Def.
Wahl, Katrina L. ....'76 '03 C.210 B.A. L.602 J.D. [Ⓐ Faruki I.&C.]
Waite, Wayne E., (BV) ....'57 '82 C.999 B.A. L.201 J.D. [Freund,F.&A.]

Waite, Schneider, Bayless & Chesley Co., L.P.A.
(See Cincinnati)

Wakefield, Brian M. ....'— '04 C.1333 B.S. L.607 J.D. [Ⓐ Coolidge,W.W.&L.]
Wald, Kathryn S., (BV) ....'28 '80 C.739 B.A. L.201 J.D. 4533 Wing View Lane
Waldron, Thomas F. ....'42 '67 C.973 B.S. L.150 J.D. Chief U.S. Bkruptcy. J.
Walker, Christopher A., (AV) ....'63 '88 C.201 B.A. L.880 J.D. [VanKley&W.]
Walker, Geoffrey P., (AV) '59 '86
C.130 B.A. L.201 J.D. Corp. Coun., Miami Valley Hosp.
Walker, Joseph W., (BV) ....'48 '78 C.1116 B.A. L.201 J.D. [J.W.Walker]
Walker, Tom J. E. ....'14 '39 C.124 B.S. L.930 LL.B. 6936 Polk Blvd. (Pat.)
Walker, Joseph W., Company, L.P.A., (BV) ....2233 Miamisburg Centerville Road
Wall, Hugh E., III, (AV) ....'46 '72 C.755 B.A. L.150 J.D. [Taft,S.&H.]
Walsh, J. Joseph, (BV) ....'37 '63 C.201 B.S. L.608 LL.B. 111 W. 1st Street
Waltensperger, George R. '06 '34 C.477 A.B. L.213 J.D.
(adm. in MI; not adm. in OH) 3073 Morningview Dr.‡
Walter, Lawrence S. ....'50 '86 C.378 B.A. L.150 J.D. Bkrptcy. J.
Wampler, E. James (Jim), (BV) '39 '65
C.604 A.B. L.608 J.D. 120 W. 2nd St. (⊙New Lebanon)
Wampler, Sherry, (BV) '43 '77 C.362 B.A. L.1340 J.D.
120 W. 2nd St. (⊙New Lebanon)
Ward, Daryl '57 '85 C.970 B.A. L.276 J.D.
Pres. & Chf. Oper. Offr., United Theological Seminary
Ward, Steven H. .... '54 '79 C.1118 A.B. L.201 J.D. Indus. Comm., State of Ohio
Ware, Mark F. '25 '50 C.201 B.S. L.150 LL.B.
(adm. in NY; not adm. in OH) P.O. Box 2306
Wargo, Elmer '28 '61 C.705 B.S. L.228 LL.B.
(adm. in DC; not adm. in OH; Pat.) Legal Dept., NCR Corp.
Warwar, Sam, (AV) ....'— '81 C.608 B.A. L.200 J.D. [Coolidge,W.W.&L.]
Washington, Dwight A. ....'49 '77 C.610 B.S. L.383 J.D. 4 S. Main St., Ste. 1200
Wasylyna, Victor J. ...'78 '03 C.608 B.S. L.930 J.D. [Ⓐ Thompson H.] (See Pat. Sect.)
Watring, Stephen A., (AV) ....'54 '81 C.1208 B.A. L.201 J.D. [Dunlevey,M.&F.]
Watson, P. Kimberly, (CVⓣ) ...... '65 '90 C.853 B.A. L.383 J.D. Staff Atty., Ct. of App.
Watts, Steven R., (AV) ....'55 '81 C.608 B.A. L.200 J.D. [Chernesky,H.&K.]
Wawrose, Susan C. ....'58 '90 C.914 B.A. L.588 J.D. Univ. of Dayton Sch. of Law
Weaver, Brian D., (BV) ....'44 '69 C.610 B.A. L.607 J.D. Asst. Pub. Def.
Wehner, D.K. Rudy, (BV) ....'52 '76 C.201 B.A. L.150 J.D. [Hunt&W.]
Weiner, Dan D. ....'32 '56 C.986 L.910 J.D. 4848 Marshall Rd.
Weisbrod, Alfred J., (AV) ....'42 '69 C.608 B.S. L.150 J.D. [Weisbrod&D.]
Weisbrod & Dankof, (AV) ....580 Lincoln Park Boulevard Suite 222

Welbaum, Heather Duffey ....'74 '99 C&L.201 B.A., J.D. [Ⓐ Sebaly,S.&D.]
Wells, Amy L. ....'73 '04 C&L.201 M.B.A., J.D. [Ⓐ Burdge]
Wells, Elizabeth A. ....'77 '04 C.160 B.A. L.851 J.D. [Ⓐ Burdge]
Weltner, Robert B. '55 '81 C&L.201 B.S., J.D.
Sr. Atty. & Chf. Coun. for Global Procurement, NCR Corp.
Wenzke, James F. ....'43 '69 C.201 B.A. L.607 J.D. Pub. Def. Off.
Wessendarp, R. Joseph ....'54 '80 C.150 B.A. L.215 J.D. [Ⓐ Pickrel,S.&E.]

Whalen & Compton, A Legal Professional Association
(See Akron)

Whelley, Thomas P., II, (AV) ....'49 '77 C.524 B.A. L.201 J.D. [Chernesky,H.&K.]
Whisman, Victor T., (BV) ....'50 '82 C.1208 B.A. L.201 J.D. Asst. Co. Pros.
White, Jennifer M. ....'79 '04 C.269 B.A. L.201 J.D. [Ⓐ Freund,F.&A.]
White, Richard J. '54 '82 C.755 B.A. L.494 J.D.
(adm. in MN; not adm. in OH) 101 W. Schantz Ave.
Wickham, David R., (AV) ....'58 '83 C&L.608 B.A., J.D. [Chernesky,H.&K.]
Wiechel, David R. .... '48 '75 C.611 B.A. L.228 J.D. 1839 Tennyson Ave.‡
Wilberding, Merle F., (AV) .... '— '69 C.742 B.A. L.602 J.D. [Coolidge,W.W.&L.]
Wilcoxson, Clinton Ralph, II '64 '93
C.608 B.S. L.742 J.D. Se. Mag., Montgomery Co. Juv. Ct.
Wilder, Lucas Wayne .... '76 '01 C.999 B.A. L.201 J.D. [L.W.Wilder]
Wilder, Lucas W., Law Office of, P.C. .... 120 W. Second St., Ste. 400
Wildermuth, Brian L. ....'70 '96 C.473 B.A. L.851 J.D. [Subashi,W.&B.]
Wildfeuer, Steven R. '69 '96
C.347 B.S. L.209 J.D. Sr. Dir. & Assoc. Gen. Coun., LexisNexis
Wiles, Matthew J. ....'77 '02 C.97 B.S. L.200 J.D. [Ⓐ Taft,S.&H.]
Wilhelm, Jenifer L., (BV) ....'65 '90 C&L.201 B.A., J.D. Asst. Pros. Atty.
Wilkins, Lawrence A. ....'68 '95 C.313 B.S. L.161 J.D. [Thorson,S.W.&S.]
Williams, Frank B., III '46 '77 C.880 B.A. L.1340 J.D.
Tr. Dept., Natl. City Bk., Dayton
Williams, Karen S. ....'43 '69 C&L.878 B.A., J.D. [Williams]
Williams, Roy A. '55 '81 C.309 A.B. L.276 J.D.
(adm. in UT; not adm. in OH) Dir. of Aviation
Williams Law Office ....133 Lake Forest Dr.
Williamson, David P., (AV) ....'53 '78 C.610 B.A. L.608 J.D. [Bieser,G.&L.]
Wilson, Matthew H. ....'52 '84 C.473 B.A. L.201 J.D. [Ⓒ Rion,R.&R.]
Winterhalter, Paul J., (AV) ....'41 '66 C.201 B.A. L.150 J.D. [Pickrel,S.&E.]
Winwood, Jeffrey A., (AV) ....'45 '71 C.165 B.S. L.347 J.D. [Winwood C.&Assoc.]
Winwood Crossman & Associates, (AV) ....3077 Kettering Boulevard, Suite 210

Wirth, David
(See Columbus)

Wiseman, Lisa K. ....'— '01 C.1208 B.A. L.201 J.D. [Ⓐ Coolidge,W.W.&L.]
Wiseman, Mary L., (AV) ....'— '88 C.63 B.S. L.1243 J.D. [Ⓐ Coolidge,W.W.&L.]
Wiseman, Wm., (BV) ....'20 '53 C.976 A.B. L.851 J.D. 934 Soc. Bk. Bldg.
Wissinger, Norman R., (BV) ....'27 '51 C.679 B.S. L.345 LL.B. 3103 Winding Way (Pat.)
Witherspoon, John G., Jr., (AV) .... '52 '83 C.878 B.A. L.893 J.D. [Ⓐ Freund,F.&A.]
Wolf, Rebecca J. ....'51 '83 C.473 B.S. L.201 J.D. Ref. in Juv. Ct.
Wolff, William H., Jr. ....'42 '68 C&L.276 A.B., J.D. Ct. of App. J.
Wolk, Reuben ....'16 '50 C.446 B.S. L.273 LL.B. 3849 Seiber Ave. (Pat.)‡
Womsley, Robert B., (AV) ....'33 '58 C.103 A.B. L.150 LL.B. 33 West First Street‡

Wood, Herron & Evans, L.L.P.
(See Cincinnati)

Woods, Lowell T., Jr. ....'— '94 C&L.347 B.A., J.D. [Coolidge,W.W.&L.]
Woods, Tina F. ....'68 '94 C.576 B.A. L.345 J.D. [Ⓐ Statman,H.S.&E.]
Woryk, Mildred P., (BV) '59 '84
C.610 B.S. L.150 J.D. Asst. Gen. Coun., Tomkins Industries, Inc.
Wright, Brian D. ....'77 '02 C.62 B.A. L.124 J.D. [Ⓐ Faruki I.&C.]
Wright, Michael L., (CV) ....'68 '97 C&L.150 B.S.M.E., J.D. [Wright&V.]
Wright & Vannoy, LPA, Inc., (BV) ....32 N. Main St., Ste. 801
Wuebben, Kristi A. ....'70 '00 C.1208 B.A. L.201 J.D. [Ⓐ Flanagan,L.H.&S.]
Yates, Teresa L. ....'62 '89 C&L.201 B.A., J.D. LEXIS-NEXIS
Yenovkian, Donald M. ....'68 '95 C.454 B.A. L.329 J.D. Sr. Trial Atty.
Yim, Edward C. ....'71 '96 C.1494 B.A. L.201 J.D. [Ⓐ Dyer,G.M.&S.] (⊙Richmond, IN)
Yoder, Susan M. ....'47 '77 C.303 B.A. L.150 J.D. LEXIS-NEXIS
Young, Frederick N. ....'32 '57 C.918 A.B. L.309 J.D. Dist. Ct. App. J.
Young, Fredric L., (BV) ....'64 '92 C.610 B.A. L.8 J.D. 130 W. 2nd St.
Young, Margaret R., (BV) ....'56 '84 C.518 A.B. L.597 J.D. [Young&A.]
Young, Robert W., (BV) ....'68 '95 C.608 B.A. L.117 J.D. [Freund,F.&A.]
Young, Timothy, (BV) ....'65 '92 C&L.201 B.A., J.D. Asst. Pub. Def.

Young & Alexander Co., L.P.A., (AV) BB
130 West Second Street, Suite 2000, 45402-7670 ⊙
Telephone: 937-224-9291 Fax: 937-224-9679; 224-8977
URL: http://www.youngandalexander.com
Robert F. Young (1905-1978); Robert C. Alexander (1912-1982); James M. Brennan; Mark R. Chilson; Steven O. Dean; Thomas P. Erven (Resident, Cincinnati Office); James K. Hemenway; Margaret R. Young;—James M. Bottoms; Jonathon L. Beck; C. Christopher Bennington.
Business Law, Health Care, Insurance Law, Labor and Employment, Nonprofit and Charitable Organizations, Personal Injury, Products Liability, Real Estate, Toxic Torts, Trusts and Estates, Wills and Probate, Commercial Litigation.
Counsel for: The Children's Medical Center, Dayton, Ohio; The Colonial Stair & Woodwork Co.; The Greater Dayton Area Hospital Assn.; Moorman Pontiac, Inc.; Metropolitan Life Insurance Co.; General Electric Insurance Co.
Local Counsel for: Colonial Penn Insurance Co.; John Hancock Mutual Life Insurance Co.; Hertz Corp.; State Farm Insurance Co.
Cincinnati, Ohio Office: 110 Boggs Lane, Suite 242. Telephone: 513-326-5555. FAX: 513-326-5550.
See Professional Biographies, DAYTON, OHIO

Young, Pryor, Lynn & Jerardi, (AV)
800 First National Plaza, 130 West Second Street, 45402
Telephone: 937-224-1981 Fax: 937-224-5649
Charles F. Young (1921-1993); Richard E. Pryor (1913-2005). Members of Firm: Michael J. Burdge; Robert B. Coughlin; Peter J. Jerardi, Jr.; Carlo C. McGinnis; Larry A. Smith. Retired: James T. Lynn, Jr.
General Civil Practice. Corporation, Commercial, Tax, Insurance, Personal Injury, Probate and Real Estate Law. School, Hospital and Medical Law. Trials. Environmental Law.
General Counsel for: Brookville National Bank.

Yuhas, Steven E., (BV) ....'59 '86 C&L.201 B.S., J.D. [Ⓐ Flanagan,L.H.&S.]
Yung, Gerald E. ....'43 '75 C.383 B.A. L.999 J.D. V.P., Govt., LEXIS-NEXIS
Zetzer, Carla Irene ....'61 '89 C.150 B.A. LEXIS-NEXIS
Ziegler, Edward H. '48 '75 C.602 A.B. L.383 J.D.
(adm. in KY; not adm. in OH) Prof. of Law, Univ. of Dayton
Zilka, Heather R. ....'73 '99 C.901 B.A. L.117 J.D. [Ⓐ Subashi,W.&B.]
Zimmer, David O. ....'— '95 C.608 B.A. L.201 J.D. [Ⓐ Thompson H.]
Zimmer, Patricia Ann .... '47 '84 C.139 B.S. L.201 J.D. Career Law Clk., U.S. Cts.
Zimmer, Paul E., (AV) ....'48 '73 C.602 B.A. L.228 J.D. [Pickrel,S.&E.]
Zimmerman, Jane A. '54 '83 C.959 B.S. L.966 J.D.
(adm. in WI; not adm. in OH) 143 Spirea Dr.‡

Zink, Julie E. .... '73 '99 C.1208 B.A. L.201 J.D. [Ⓐ Faruki I.&C.]
Zipperstein, Irvin J., (AV) ....'25 '49 C&L.150 LL.B. Talbott Tower
Zukowsky, Philip A., (AV) .... '55 '80 C&L.424 A.B., J.D. [Chernesky,H.&K.]

DEFIANCE, * 16,465, *Defiance Co.*

Aplin, Christa Marie .... '75 '00 C.999 B.A. L.607 J.D. UAW Legal Serv. Plan
Aplin, Robert Douglas .... '73 '00 C.381 B.A. L.607 J.D. [Ⓐ Weaner,Z.B.Y.&H.]
Archer, Stephen R., (CV) ....'52 '78 C.1178 B.A. L.930 J.D. 106 Clinton St.
Arthur, Rodney M., (AV) .... '41 '69 C&L.607 B.A., J.D. [Arthur,O.M.&B.]
Arthur, O'Neil, Mertz & Bates Co., L.P.A., (AV) .... 901 Ralston Avenue
Bates, E. Charles, (BV) ....'61 '86 C.679 B.A. L.150 J.D. [Arthur,O.M.&B.]
Borland, James S., (BV) ....'44 '69 C.608 B.S. L.607 J.D. 110 Clinton St.
Brewster, Jody Moser ....'47 '83 C.203 B.A. L.1137 J.D. 428 Franklin St.
Calvert, William L. .... '43 '69 C&L.607 B.S., J.D. Defiance Hosp.

Clemens, Korhn, Liming & Warncke, Ltd., (AV)
Block Six Business Center, 419 Fifth Street, Suite 2000, P.O. Box 787, 43512 ⊙
Telephone: 419-782-6055 Telecopier: 419-782-3227
Tellis T. Shaw (1868-1951); David W. Williams (1917-1987); Erwin L. Clemens (1910-1999); Stephen F. Korhn; John M. Liming; Marc F. Warncke;—Troy A. Essex.
General Practice. Real Estate, Banking Law, Title Examination and Insurance, Personal Injury and Wrongful Death, Probate and Estate Planning, Insurance Defense, Corporate, Family/Domestic Relations and Municipal Law. Trials and Appeals.
Representative Clients: B & O Railroad Co. (Chessie System); First Federal Bank of Midwest; Defiance Hospital, Inc.; Allstate Insurance Co.; State Farm Insurance; Cincinnati Insurance; Central Mutual Ins.
Hicksville, Ohio Office: First Federal Savings & Loan Building, 201 E. High Street. Telephone: 419-542-7705.
See Professional Biographies, DEFIANCE, OHIO

Cooper, Robert, III ....'68 '94 C.209 B.S. L.823 J.D. 13537 Fruit Ridge Dr.‡
Essex, Troy A. .... '75 '00 C.607 B.A. L.851 J.D. [Ⓐ Clemens,K.L.&W.]
Goldenetz, John P., (BV) ....'42 '69 C.607 B.A. L.879 J.D. 515 5th St.
Herman, Russell R., (CV) .... '— '97 C.107 B.A. L.8 J.D. Asst. Co. Pros.
Hubbard, Stephen F., (CV) ....'59 '84 C.608 B.S. L.851 J.D. [Weaner,Z.B.Y.&H.]
Korhn, Stephen F., (AV) .... '47 '72 C.608 B.S. L.851 J.D. [Clemens,K.L.&W.] ⊙
Liming, John M., (BV) ....'56 '81 C.293 B.A. L.477 J.D. [Clemens,K.L.&W.] ⊙
Mertz, Eric A., (BV) ....'54 '79 C.608 B.A. L.851 J.D. [Arthur,O.M.&B.]
Michel, Daniel R., (CV) .... '69 '96 C.999 B.S. L.851 J.D. [Ⓐ Arthur,O.M.&B.]
O'Neil, Joseph W., (BV) ....'51 '77 C.608 B.A. L.117 J.D. [Arthur,O.M.&B.]
Reighter, Tiffany Elizabeth ....'70 '99 C&L.851 B.A., J.D. 110 Clinton St.
Renollet, Tamara S., (CV) .... '64 '90 C.203 B.S. L.851 J.D. 1261 Hilton Head Ct.
Rohrs, John T., III ....'55 '82 C.608 B.A. L.607 J.D. Mun. J.
Ruyle, Stephen W. .... '47 '77 C.607 B.S.Ed. L.851 J.D. Com. Pleas J.
Schmenk, Joseph N. .... '56 '80 C.851 B.A. L.602 J.D. Com. Pleas J.
Seibel, Peter R., (BV) ....'46 '71 C.385 B.A. L.228 J.D. 621 W. 2nd St.
Smith, Donald B., Jr. '46 '74 C.282 B.A. L.1017 J.D.
Cty. Dept. of Job and Family Svcs.
Snavely, Stephen K., (BV) .... '47 '73 C&L.607 B.A., J.D. [S.K.Snavely]

Snavely, Stephen K., Co., L.P.A., (BV)
505 Fourth Street, P.O. Box 759, 43512
Telephone: 419-782-8846 Fax: 419-784-5285
Email: snavely@adelphia.net URL: http://www.snavelylaw.com
Stephen K. Snavely.
General Civil Practice. Personal Injury, Wrongful Death, Automobile Accidents, Probate, Wills, Trusts, Estate Planning, Family Law, Domestic Relations, Divorce, and Real Estate Law. Trials and Appeals.
Approved Attorney For: The Ohio Bar Title Insurance Co.
Representative Clients: Strait Realty, Inc.; Arps Dairy, Inc.; Fort Defiance Servicemaster, Inc.
References: The State Bank and Trust Co.; First National Bank of North-Western Ohio.
See Professional Biographies, DEFIANCE, OHIO

Sondergaard, Steven J., (CV) '57 '91
C.1318 B.A. L.201 J.D. 101 Clinton Street, Suite 1500
Steinhauser, Rebecca J. .... '68 '96 C.107 B.A. L.201 J.D. 201 E. 2nd St.
Strausbaugh, Jeffrey A., (BV) .... '56 '86 C.203 B.S. L.851 J.D. Co. Pros. Atty.
Stupka, Renee A. ....'61 '97 C&L.851 B.S., J.D. 230 Ruth Ann Drive
Warncke, Marc F., (BV) ......'64 '89 C.608 B.S.B.A. L.602 J.D. [Clemens,K.L.&W.] ⊙
Weaner, James K., (CV) ....'65 '96 C.608 B.S. L.851 J.D. [Weaner,Z.B.Y.&H.]
Weaner, John W., (BV) ....'35 '64 C.473 B.S. L.608 J.D. [Weaner,Z.B.Y.&H.]
Weaner, Zimmerman, Bacon Yoder & Hubbard, Ltd., (AV)
401 Wayne Avenue (⊙Hicksville)
Williams, David H., (BV) .... '51 '76 C.608 B.A. L.851 J.D. City Atty.
Wilson, Latanya Raquel ....'— '95 C.515 B.A. L.608 J.D. 1500 Baltimore Road
Yoder, Stanley J., (BV) .... '53 '80 C.1124 B.S. L.851 J.D. [Weaner,Z.B.Y.&H.] ⊙
Zimmerman, John E., (AV) ....'24 '51 C.851 A.B. L.608 J.D. [Weaner,Z.B.Y.&H.] ⊙

DEGRAFF, 1,212, *Logan Co.*

Minnich, Michael G., (CV) ....'59 '87 C.967 B.A. L.608 J.D. P.O. Box 400

DELAWARE, * 25,243, *Delaware Co.*

Abrams, Robert A., (BV) '68 '93 C.611 B.A. L.608 J.D.
House Coun., Celina Insurance Group, Litigation Group
Ash, Charles Wayne .... '61 '93 C&L.608 B.S.C.I.S., J.D. [C.W.Ash]
Ash, Charles W. .... P.O. Box 1401

Babbitt & Weis LLP
(See Columbus)

Bennington, Daniel B., (BV) .... '46 '73 C.611 B.A. L.930 J.D. 1 S. Sandusky St.

Benson, Michael E.
(See Columbus)

Birch, David H., (CV) ....'51 '85 C.608 B.A. L.117 J.D. 2 W. Winter St.
Blair, James W., (AV) ....'08 '33 C.611 B.A. L.608 J.D. 25 W. Central Ave.‡

Blaugrund, Herbert & Martin, Incorporated
(See Dublin)

Boger, Keith A., (BV) '55 '81 C&L.273 B.A., J.D.
61 North Sandusky Street, 43015
Telephone: 740-363-9412; 548-6533 Fax: 740-548-6533
Email: keithboger@yahoo.com URL: http://www.lawyers.com/bogerlaw
General Civil and Criminal Practice. Personal Injury, Products Liability, Family/Domestic Relations, Real Estate, Probate and Estate Planning, Criminal and Traffic Law, Driving While Intoxicated, Commercial Collections.
See Professional Biographies, DELAWARE, OHIO

Boyle, Sean O.
(See Columbus)

Calig & Handelman, LPA
(See Columbus)

Chester, Willcox & Saxbe LLP
(See Columbus)

Clark, Thomas C., (AV) .... '36 '60 C&L.608 B.S., LL.B. [Clark,T.C.]
Clark, Thomas C., II, (BV) ....'66 '91 C.150 B.A. L.608 J.D. [Clark,T.C.]
Clark, Thomas C., (AV) .... 61 N. Sandusky St.
Coldren, Robert H., (AV) .... '33 '59 C&L.608 B.S., LL.B. 30 Troy Rd.
Cole, April B. .... '70 '98 C.473 B.S. L.117 J.D. 41 N. Sandusky St.
Darr, Frank P., (BV) ....'57 '82 C.8 B.A. L.608 J.D. Asst. Pros.
Dietz, James M., (BV) .... '60 '85 C.117 B.A. L.608 J.D. [Manos,M.P.&D.]
Donahey, Richard S., (BV) .... '41 '68 C&L.608 B.C.E., J.D. [Twyford&D.] ⊙

Dugan, Vincent A., Jr.
(See Columbus)

Farlow & Associates LLC
(See Dublin)

Featherstone, James E., (BV) ....'54 '96 C.1271 B.A. L.7 J.D. 1501 Braumiller Rd.
Firestone, Richard L., (AV) .... '13 '39 C.611 B.A. L.1340 J.D. [Firestone&B.] ‡
Firestone & Brehm, (AV) ....15-17 West Winter Street
Flahive, Edward A. ....'23 '52 C.611 L.266 J.D. 312 Co. Bk. Bldg.‡
Flahive, Edward F., Attorney at Law, (BV) '52 '77
C.477 B.A. L.607 J.D. 312 Delaware Co. Bag Bldg.
Flahive, Terrence P., (BV) .... '55 '84 C.608 B.S. L.1187 J.D. 312 Delaware Co. Bk. Bldg.
Flahive, Timothy I., (BV) .... '57 '83 C.602 B.A. L.607 J.D. 41 N. Sandusky St.

Friedman & Mirman Co., L.P.A.
(See Columbus)

Fuller, Randall Dean, (BV) .... '69 '95 C.608 B.S. L.851 J.D. 43 East Central Avenue
Gabel, E. Marianne, (BV) ....'48 '77 C.813 B.A. L.659 J.D. 103 N. Union St.

Geary, William L.
(See Columbus)

Goldman & Rosenthal
(See Columbus)

Goldstein, David A., Co., L.P.A.
(See Columbus)

Gordin, Robert H., (BV) ....'53 '80 C.611 B.A. L.117 J.D. [Ⓐ Heald&L.]
Gordon, David J., (BV) .... '44 '69 C&L.607 B.S., J.D. 40 N. Sandusky St., Ste. 300
Gray, Thayne D., (BV) .... '55 '80 C.210 B.A. L.608 J.D. [Ⓐ Manos,M.P.&D.]
Haines, Quentin R., (BV) ....'52 '77 C.97 B.S. L.280 J.D. 15 N. Franklin St.
Heald, Anthony M., (AV) .... '48 '74 C.611 A.B. L.608 J.D. [Heald&L.]
Heald, Chad A. ....'76 '02 C.119 B.A. L.608 J.D. [Ⓐ Heald&L.]
Heald & Long, (AV) .... 125 N. Sandusky St.
Hedlund, Lowell A. .... '56 '81 C.967 B.A. L.608 J.D. [⊡ Manos,M.P.&D.]
Heimlich, Michael M. ....'58 '84 C.608 B.S. L.607 J.D. 103 N. Union Street, Suite E
Herzog, Louis Henry .... '62 '98 C.207 B.A. L.117 J.D. 43 E. Central Ave.
Hutchins, Shelby V., (BV) .... '32 '61 C.473 B.S. L.608 J.D. 3491 Olentangy River Rd.
Jones, Nicholas W., (BV) ....'45 '75 C.893 B.A. L.851 J.D. 2 Winter Street

Joseph & Joseph
(See Columbus)

Kaiser, R. Lamont, (AV) ...... '44 '69 C&L.608 B.A., J.D. [⊡ Rich,C.&W.] (⊙Columbus)

Kenney-Pfalzer, Susan
(See Columbus)

Krueger, Everett H. .... '50 '75 C.303 B.A. L.117 J.D. Com. Pleas J.
Krueger, Nancy K. .... '56 '95 C.788 A.B. L.117 J.D. 4908 Dublin Rd.

Lamkin, Van Eman, Trimble, Beals & Dougherty, LLC
(See Columbus)

Lewis, Clyde E., (AV) .... '16 '46 C.611 A.B. L.930 LL.B. 31 W. Winter St.‡
Lewis, Jonathan C., (BV) .... '49 '74 C.207 B.A. L.8 J.D. 31 W. Winter St.

Lewis, Gregg R.
(See Columbus)

Long, O. Ross, (AV) ....'48 '73 C.611 B.A. L.150 J.D. [Heald&L.]
Lord, George E. ....'41 '67 C.611 B.A. L.607 J.D. Asst. Pros. Atty.
Louden, Thomas E. .... '42 '68 C&L.607 B.S., J.D. Prob. J.

Lucas, Prendergast, Albright, Gibson & Newman
(See Columbus)

Mango, Dominic L. .... '68 '99 C&L.608 B.S., J.D. [Ⓐ Saia&P.]

Manos, Martin, Pergram & Dietz Co., LPA, (AV) BB
50 North Sandusky Street, 43015-1926
Telephone: 740-363-1313 Telecopier: 740-363-1314 URL: http://www.mmpdlaw.com
Email: mail@mmpdlaw.com URL: http://www.lawyers.com/mmpdlaw
Peter J. Manos (1922-2004);—Stephen D. Martin; Dennis L. Pergram; James M. Dietz;—Thayne D. Gray. Of Counsel: Lowell A. Hedlund.
Administrative, Appellate Practice, Litigation, Business, Contracts, Corporate, Zoning, Planning and Land Use, Real Estate, Labor and Employment, Trusts and Estates, and Wills and Probate.
See Professional Biographies, DELAWARE, OHIO

Martin, Stephen D., (AV) .... '47 '74 C.705 B.A. L.117 J.D. [Manos,M.P.&D.]
Martz, Gary R., (AV) ....'58 '82 C.851 B.A. L.608 J.D. Greif Bros. Corp.
Mast, Daniel D. .... '20 '50 C.679 B.S. L.7 J.D. 320 Crackler Rd.‡
Maxwell, Judith Rebecca, (BV) ..... '60 '85 C.970 B.A. L.117 J.D. 39 West Winter Street
Merrell, John R. ....'56 '81 C.347 B.A. L.117 J.D. V.P., The Ohio Co.
Miller, Gary Scott ....'57 '84 C.608 B.S. L.117 J.D. [G.S.Miller]
Miller, G. Scott ....103 N. Union Street
Musgrave, Megan L. ....'65 '90 C.914 B.A. L.608 J.D. 22 Yorkshire Dr.
Nelson, April, (BV) .... '56 '81 C.1051 B.A. L.596 J.D. 98 N. Union St.
Osborne, Wesley William .... '75 '00 C.347 B.S. L.1339 J.D. [Ⓐ Shade&S.]
Owen, William J., (AV) ....'48 '86 C.608 B.A. L.117 J.D. 140 No. Sandusky St.
Owens, Robert M. ....'73 '98 C.611 B.A. L.117 J.D. [Owens]
Owens Law Office ....46 N. Sandusky St., Ste. 202
Pergram, Dennis L., (AV) ....'47 '77 C.610 B.S. L.851 J.D. [Manos,M.P.&D.]
Preston, Ralph W., (AV) .... '45 '76 C.608 B.S. L.976 J.D. 1900 Timberlake Dr.
Rich, Crites & Wesp, LLC, (AV) ....25 West Central Avenue (⊙Columbus, Galena)

Riggins, Melissa K., Attorney at Law
(See Columbus)

Rourke & Blumenthal, LLP
(See Columbus)

Ruffing, Peter Bingham ....'55 '82 C.363 B.S. L.608 J.D. City Pros. Off.
Saia & Piatt, P.L.L. ....46 North Sandusky Street, Suite 204 (⊙Columbus)
Sanchez, Mario .... '— '91 145 West Lincoln Ave.
Scherner, Hans, (AV) ..... '42 '79 C.309 A.B. L.607 J.D. [Scherner,H.&C.] (⊙Columbus)
Scherner, Hanson & Cornwell, LLC, (AV) .... 5300 David Rd. (⊙Columbus, Lima)

Schulze, Howard & Cox
(See Marysville)

Shade, David C., (BV) .... '47 '73 C.610 B.S. L.608 J.D. [Shade&S.]

Shade, Michael R., (BV) .... '48 '80 C.737 B.A. L.117 J.D. [Shade&S.]
Shade & Shade, (BV) ....41 N. Sandusky
Shaw, Henry E., Jr. .... '38 '65 C.757 B.A. L.607 J.D. Com. Pleas J.

Stumler, Rebecca J.
(See Columbus)

Thomas, William R. .... '65 '91 C.567 B.S. L.201 J.D. [Thomas]
Thomas & Company, L.P.A. ....163 N. Sandusky St., Ste. 103

Thomas Law Group
(See Dublin)

Twyford & Donahey, P.L.L., (BV)
163 N. Sandusky Street, Suite 103, 43015 ⊙
Telephone: Toll Free: 1-800-686-1699 Fax: 614-849-0475
Email: help@twyforddonahey.com URL: http://www.twyforddonahey.com
Richard S. Donahey.
Personal Injury Litigation, Wrongful Death, Medical Malpractice, Products Liability, Automobile Accidents, Trucking Accidents, Head and Spinal Injuries, Motorcycle Accidents and Injuries, Uninsured Motorists, Insurance Law, Airplane Crash Litigation, Railroad Accidents, Slip and Fall, Dog Bites, Work Related Injuries, Birth Injuries, Nursing Home Abuse and Neglect.
References: The Huntington National Bank; Bank One of Columbus; BancOhio National Bank.
Columbus, Ohio Office: 495 South High Street, 43215-5058. Telephone: Toll Free: 1-800-686-1699. Email: help@twyforddonahey.com.
Circleville, Ohio Office: 214 South Court Street, 43113. Telephone: Toll Free: 1-800-686-1699. Email: help@twyforddonahey.com.
Lancaster, Ohio Office: 3794 Old Columbus, N.W., 43130. Telephone: Toll Free: 1-800-686-1699. Email: help@twyforddonahey.com.
Newark, Ohio Office: 137 West Main Street, Suite C., 43025. Telephone: Toll Free: 1-800-686-1699. Email: help@twyforddonahey.com.
London, Ohio Office: 25 West Fifth Street, 43140. Telephone: Toll Free: 1-800-686-1699. Email: help@twyforddonahey.com.
See Professional Biographies, DELAWARE, OHIO

Vatsures, Peter T., (BV) .... '27 '54 C&L.608 B.S., J.D. 15 Central Ave.
Warnock, Douglas W., (AV) .... '53 '78 C.611 B.A. L.608 J.D. [D.W.Warnock]
Warnock, Douglas W., Co., L.P.A., Law Office of, (AV) .... 20 East Central Avenue
Whitney, Thomas R., (AV) .... '48 '73 C.967 B.A. L.851 J.D. P.O. Box 70

Wirth, David
(See Columbus)

Wolf, Scott A., (BV) .... '58 '84 C.208 A.B. L.201 J.D. 98 Union St.

Wolske & Barclay, A Legal Professional Association
(See Columbus)

Worly, Donald Glenn '51 '89
C.608 B.A. L.117 J.D. Pres., Worly Steel & Supply Company, Inc.
Young, Don J., III .... '72 '98 C.611 B.A. L.602 J.D. [Firestone&B.]

DELPHOS, 6,944, *Allen & Van Wert Cos.*

Clark, Edward F., (BV) .... '21 '53 C&L.607 B.S., J.D. 214 W. 2nd St.
Clark, James H., (BV) .... '22 '49 C&L.602 LL.B. 1609 Fort Jennings Rd.
Clark, Nicholas J., (BV) .... '63 '89 C.97 B.S.Ed L.607 J.D. 214 W. 2nd St.
Marsh, Minzing and Metzner, (BV) ....302 West First Street
Metzner, John A., Jr., (BV) .... '30 '57 C.1024 B.S. L.607 J.D. [Marsh,M.&M.]
Minzing, Paula, (BV) .... '24 '49 C.441 B.A. L.128 J.D. [Marsh,M.&M.]
Moening, Ronald S., (AV) .... '48 '73 C.973 A.B. L.851 J.D. Lakeview Farms
Osting, Clayton P., (CV) .... '48 '84 C.610 B.A. L.851 J.D. 1101 Krzept St
Shenk, John A., (AV) .... '06 '39 C.930 A.B. 226 N. Pierce St.‡
Waldick, Juergen Arthur .... '58 '85 C.30 B.S. L.607 J.D. P.O. Box 304

DELTA, 2,849, *Fulton Co.*

Barber, Kaper, Stamm & Robinson, (AV)
206 Main Street, 43515 ⊙
Telephone: 419-822-3211 Fax: 419-822-4593
URL: http://www.lawyers.com/bksr
Terry J. Kaper (Resident).
General Civil and Criminal Practice. Personal Injury, Insurance, Probate, Real Estate, Title Examination, Collections, Commercial, Municipal and Banking Law. Trials and Appeals in all Courts.
Reference: Farmers and Merchants State Bank.
Wauseon, Ohio Office: 124 N. Fulton Street. Telephone: 419-337-5065. FAX: 419-337-1136.
See Professional Biographies, WAUSEON, OHIO

Kaper, Terry J., (AV) .... '38 '68 C.27 B.S. L.607 J.D. [Barber,K.S.&R.]
Meister, Joan B., (BV) .... '30 '61 C.930 B.S.N. L.851 LL.B. [Meister&M.]
Meister, Sheldon C., (BV) .... '28 '52 C.610 B.A. L.608 J.D. [Meister&M.]
Meister & Meister, (BV) .... 321 Main St.
VanGunten, Gregory L., (BV) .... '49 '76 C.699 B.A. L.851 J.D. 106 Main St.

DESHLER, 1,876, *Henry Co.*

Collier, John S., (BV) .... '53 '79 C.967 B.A. L.851 J.D. Mun. Ct. J.
Gribbell, Justin J. .... '16 '39 C&L.608 LL.B. [Gribbell&S.] ‡
Gribbell & Sunderman, (BV) ....114 E. Main St.
Rode, James D. .... '71 '99 C.432 B.A.Sc. L.851 J.D. 114 E. Main St.
Sunderman, John D., (BV) ....'47 '80 C.97 B.S. L.851 J.D. [Gribbell&S.]

DIAMOND, 200, *Portage Co.*

Henry, Cynthia Lynn .... '57 '85 C.8 B.S. L.7 J.D. 3856 Jones Rd.

DILLONVALE, 3,716, *Jefferson Co.*

Boothe, Lawrence I., (CV) .... '54 '79 C.49 B.S.Ed. L.1003 J.D. P.O. Box 684

DOVER, 12,210, *Tuscarawas Co.*

Bauer, Erick L., (BV) ....'64 '91 C.608 B.A. L.607 J.D. [Black M.H.D.&B.&Assoc.]

Black McCuskey Hanhart Deeds & Bauer, A Legal Professional Association, (AV)
130 W. Third Street, 44622 ⊙
Telephone: 330-364-6553 Fax: 330-364-2739
URL: http://www.bmsa.com
Resident Members: David M. Hanhart; C. Jason Deeds; Erick L. Bauer. Of Counsel: Richard M. Hanhart.
General Civil Practice in all State and Federal Courts. Administrative, Antitrust, Banking, Bankruptcy, Commercial, Construction, Corporate, Environmental, Estate Planning and Probate, Family Law, Franchising, Government, Healthcare Law, Labor, Litigation, Oil and Gas, Personal Injury, Real Estate, Securities, Taxation Law, Wrongful Death and Zoning.
Representative Clients: The Hoover Co.; Diebold, Inc.; Travelers Insurance Co.
Canton, Ohio Office: 220 Market Avenue South, Suite 1000, 44702. Telephone: 330-456-8341; 877-656-8341. Telecopier: 330-456-5756; 877-456-5746.
See Professional Biographies, DOVER, OHIO

Bohse, Frederick H., (BV) .... '42 '68 C.631 A.B. L.607 J.D. [Woodard&B.]
Border, Jeffrey C. ....'57 '83 C.473 B.S. L.7 J.D. Pres., TV Specialties Co., Inc.
Boynton, John R. .... '41 '69 C.970 B.A. L.7 J.D. Pres., A. J. Weigand, Inc.
Buckley, Sharon, (CV) .... '61 '84 C.49 B.A. L.1003 J.D. 303 E. Iron
Burch, Robert L. .... '49 '75 C.381 B.A. L.276 J.D. State Sen. [ⓒ Space&S.]
Corsi, Mario D., (AV) ....'26 '51 C&L.930 B.A., LL.B. 117 East Third Street
Deeds, C. Jason, (BV) ....'62 '89 C.207 B.A. L.607 J.D. [Black M.H.D.&B.&Assoc.]
Fox, Thomas W., (BV) ....'46 '73 C.610 B.S.Ed. L.273 J.D. [Traver,W.&F.]
Gordon, Paul N., (BV) ....'50 '77 C.8 B.S. L.7 J.D. 1900 N. Walnut St.
Hanhart, David M., (BV) .....'55 '80 C.207 B.A. L.930 J.D. [Black M.H.D.&B.&Assoc.]
Hanhart, Richard M., (AV) '26 '51
C.207 A.B. L.930 LL.B. [ⓒ Black M.H.D.&B.&Assoc.]

Hisrich, Thomas H., (BV) '41 '66 C.381 B.S.B.A. L.608 J.D.
121 West Fourth Street, 44622-2961
Telephone: 330-343-8834 Fax: 330-343-0709
General Civil Practice. Corporation, Federal State and Local Taxation, Real Estate, Eminent Domain, Wills Probate, Estate Planning, Agriculture and Negligence Law. Personal Injury, Automobile Accidents, Medical Malpractice, Mineral and Mining Law.
References: Huntington National Bank, Dover, Ohio; Bank One of Dover, N.A.
See Professional Biographies, DOVER, OHIO

Markworth, Lawrence '46 '72
C.608 B.S. L.607 J.D. V.P., The Huntington Nat'l Bank, N. Amer.
Ostapuck, John A., (BV) .... '46 '72 C.201 B.S. L.150 J.D. P.O. Box 2237
Pietro, Frank W., II, (CV) .... '51 '78 C.610 A.B. L.285 J.D. P.O. Box 337
Renner, Richard ....'58 '81 C.453 B.S. L.569 J.D. 505 N. Wooster Ave.
Space, Socrates J. .... '30 '59 C&L.608 B.A., J.D. [Space&S.]
Space, Zachary T., (BV) .... '61 '86 C.385 B.A. L.608 J.D. [Space&S.]
Space & Space, (BV) ....714 N. Wooster Avenue
Spies, Harlan R. .... '25 '55 C.473 B.S. L.948 LL.B. Ret. Com. Pleas J.

Stephenson, Stephenson & Carrothers
(See New Philadelphia)

Traver, Dennis D., (BV) .... '48 '73 C&L.8 B.A., J.D. [Traver,W.&F.]
Traver, Worth & Fox, (BV) ....232 West Third St.
Woodard, John L. ....'16 '40 C&L.608 B.S., J.D. [Woodard&B.]
Woodard and Bohse, (BV) ....121 W. Third St.
Worth, David W., (BV) .... '52 '77 C.528 B.A. L.608 J.D. [Traver,W.&F.]

DOYLESTOWN, 2,799, *Wayne Co.*

Beaumont, Lynn A., (BV) .... '46 '72 C.608 B.A. L.851 J.D. 29 N. Portage Street
Brent, Theodore W., Jr. .... '47 '75 C&L.8 B.S.B.A., J.D. 13036 Mark Path
Haney, John D. ....'26 '52 C.46 B.S.ME L.8 J.D. 13939 Doylestown Rd.‡
Hollis, Cheryl A. .... '58 '92 C.610 B.S. L.1522 J.D. P.O. Box 201

DUBLIN, 31,392, *Delaware, Franklin & Union Cos.*

Adams, Bret A., (AV) ....'59 '84 C.610 B.A. L.117 J.D. [Ⓐ Blaugrund,H.&M.]
Aebker, Jill Emily .... '71 '97 C&L.608 B.A., J.D. Wendy's International, Inc.
Alig, Wesly A. .... '77 '02 C.49 B.S. L.201 J.D. [Ⓐ Standley] (See Pat. Sect.)
Allen, Andrew B. '31 '65 C&L.862 B.S., J.D.
(adm. in OK; not adm. in OH) Sr. Litig. Coun., Corp. Law Dept., Ashland Chem. Co.
Arenstein, G. Gregory, (CV) '69 '94 C.861 B.A. L.117 J.D.
5775 Perimeter Dr., Ste. 275
Atkins, Lisa Ann ....'61 '96 C.608 B.S. L.117 J.D. Nationwide Ins.
Babner, David W. ....'— '93 C.454 B.A. L.117 J.D. [Ⓐ Blaugrund,H.&M.]
Baker, Raymond W., (BV) '44 '71 C.375 B.A. L.900 J.D.
(adm. in KS; not adm. in OH) V.P. & Asst. Gen. Coun.-Intl., Wendy's Intl., Inc.
Banks, James H. .... '45 '80 P.O. Box 40
Bare, Glen E. ....'30 '60 C.313 B.A. L.902 LL.B. 9159 Muirkirk Drive
Barrett, David C., Jr., (AV) .... '56 '81 C.608 B.S. L.851 J.D. [Barrett,E.C.&E.]

Barrett, Easterday, Cunningham & Eselgroth LLP, (AV) BR
7269 Sawmill Road, 43016
Telephone: 614-210-1840 Facsimile: 614-210-1841 URL: http://www.ohiocounsel.com
Email: info@ohiocounsel.com URL: http://www.lawyers.com/dbarrett
Partners: David C. Barrett, Jr.; Jeffrey A. Easterday; Russell N. Cunningham (Certified Specialist in Estate Planning, Trust and Probate Law, Ohio State Bar Association); Carolyn D. Eselgroth. Of Counsel: Larry E. Hoover. Associate: Troy A. Callicoat.
Agricultural Law, Agribusiness, Business Arbitration, Alternative Dispute Resolution, Commodities, Debtor and Creditor, Corporate Law, Commercial Law, Commercial Transactions, Antitrust, Trade Association Law, Environmental Law, Federal Civil Litigation, Commercial Litigation, Civil Litigation, Estate Planning, Estate Administration, Probate, Taxation, Real Estate Exchanges, Estate and Gift Taxation, Like Kind Exchanges, Trusts and Estates Taxation, Bankruptcy, Environmental Law.
See Professional Biographies, DUBLIN, OHIO

Bellinger, Scott P., (BV) ....'64 '92 C.608 B.A. L.117 J.D. 6065 Frantz Rd.
Bennett, Stephen A., (AVⓉ) .... '53 '83 C.602 B.A. L.378 J.D. [S.A.Bennett]
Bennett, Stephen Alan, (AVⓉ) ....7000 Cardinal Place
Berky, Robert R. ....'53 '88 C.665 B.A. L.117 J.D. 5900 Sawmill Road
Billman, Donald Lynn .... '40 '72 C.967 B.S. L.851 J.D. 6956 Mesquite Ct.
Birch, Elizabeth J. ....'63 '89 C.381 B.S. L.124 J.D. [Ⓐ Mowery&Y.]
Blackford, Wm. H. ....'10 '37 C.473 L.607 J.D. NA-H 8609 Craigston Ct.‡
Blaugrund, David S., (AV) ....'53 '77 C.473 A.B. L.608 J.D. [Blaugrund,H.&M.]

Blaugrund, Herbert & Martin, Incorporated, (AV)
5455 Rings Road, Suite 500, 43017-7517
Telephone: 614-764-0681 Fax: 614-764-0774
Email: bhm@bhmlaw.com URL: http://www.bhmlaw.com
David S. Blaugrund; John W. Herbert; David S. Kessler; Steven A. Martin; Sharon L. R. Miller; Marc E. Myers; Stephen P. Postalakis; Teri G. Rasmussen;—Bret A. Adams; David W. Babner; Christopher T. Cline; Maryellen Corna; Jonathan M. Gabel; Fazeel S. Khan; Geoff P. Scott; Bobbie J. Stonerock; Carole D. Weiss. Of Counsel: Francis A. Kovacs, Jr.
Administrative Law, Bankruptcy, Civil Rights Litigation, Civil Service, Commercial Collections, Corporate Law, Debtor-Creditor Law, Disability Law, Employment Discrimination, Employment Law, Estate Administration, Estate Planning, General Civil Practice, Labor Relations, Limited Liability Companies, Limited Liability Partnerships, Liquor Law, Litigation, Motor Vehicle Law, Non-profit Corporation Law, Probate, Real Estate and Construction Law, State and Local Government Law, Trade Association Law, UCC, Workers Compensation, Zoning, Planning and Land Use, Alternative Dispute Resolution, Appellate Practice and Administrative Appeals.
See Professional Biographies, DUBLIN, OHIO

Boland, James A., Jr. ....'54 '02 C.269 B.A. L.608 J.D. [Ⓐ Farlow&Assoc.]
Borror, David S., (AV) ... '57 '82 C&L.608 B.A., J.D. Exec. V.P., Dominion Homes, Inc.‡
Brown, James R. ... '62 '92 C.112 B.A. L.284 J.D. Staff Coun., Progressive Insurance Co.
Buckham, William C. '45 '70 C.608 B.A. L.150 J.D.
V.P. & Asst. Gen. Coun., CheckFree Corporation
Burda, Robert T. .... '52 '80 C.201 B.S. L.608 J.D. 4288 West Dublin Granville Rd.
Burleigh, Barbra .... '77 '03 C&L.117 B.A., J.D. [Ⓐ Farlow&Assoc.]
Buzash, George E. '65 '90
C.207 B.A. L.597 J.D. Sr. Atty., Online Computer Library Ctr., Inc.
Byrne, Laura D. ....'59 '84 C.608 B.S. L.117 J.D. [Byrne&B.]
Byrne, Thomas J., (AV) ....'55 '88 C.608 B.A. L.117 J.D. [Byrne&B.]
Byrne & Byrne, (AV) ....5695 Avery Road, Suite C
Callicoat, Troy A. ....'77 '03 C.608 B.S. L.117 J.D. [Ⓐ Barrett,E.C.&E.]
Calloway, George H. ....'55 '83 C.597 B.A. L.124 J.D. [Linebarger G.B.&S.]
Cameron, Philip D., (BV) .... '42 '69 C.608 B.S. L.215 J.D. 8382 Kirkaldy Ct.
Carroll, William A., (AV) .... '21 '43 C&L.262 LL.B. Comr., Ct. of Claims

Castrodale, Gloria Pascale, (BV) ....'61 '88 C.980 B.S. L.989 J.D. 5170 Reddington Drive
Catri, Jeffrey Alan .... '56 '84 C.97 B.S. L.7 J.D. 4618 Stockport Circle
Chapin, Don H. .... '49 '89 C.188 B.S.M.E. L.031 J.D. [Chapin]
Chapin Law Offices .... 5960 Wilcox Pl., Ste. B
Chieffo, Dominic J., (BV) .... '42 '66 C.610 B.B.A. L.608 J.D. 15 Grandview Dr.
Choi, Monica H. .... '69 '96 C.339 B.S.E.E. L.309 J.D. 4243 Hertford La. (Pat.)
Clancey, Michael T. '55 '81
C.276 A.B. L.1017 J.D. Gen. Coun. & Secy., HBD Industries, Inc.
Cline, Christopher T., (BV) ....'50 '75 C.608 B.A. L.117 J.D. [Ⓐ Blaugrund,H.&M.]
Coburn, Patricia A. '44 '78 C.150 B.S. L.851 J.D.
(adm. in MO; not adm. in OH; Pat.) V.P. & Gen. Coun., Neoprobe Corp.
Coles, Carl E. ....'62 '91 C&L.608 B.S.B.A., J.D. 6735 Ballantrae Pl.
Connaughton, Martin '50 '93 C.476 B.S. L.851 J.D.
Pat., Trademark & Copyright Coun., Ashland Chem. Co. (Pat.)
Corna, Maryellen, (BV) ....'57 '92 C&L.608 B.A., J.D. [Ⓐ Blaugrund,H.&M.]
Cummings, Cynthia C. ....'53 '78 C.674 A.B. L.608 J.D. 2136 Surrywood Dr.
Cunningham, Russell N. ....'63 '89 C.608 B.S. L.930 J.D. [Barrett,E.C.&E.]
Cutler, Kimberly M. ....'78 '02 C.610 B.B.A. L.117 J.D. [Ⓐ WrightCo]
Danis, Laurie W. ....'56 '82 C.150 B.S. L.608 J.D. 4886 Chatelaine Dr.
Danis, Peter A. ....'56 '81 C.201 B.S. L.608 J.D. 4886 Chatelaine Dr
Danison, Nanci L., (AV) ....'50 '77 C.516 B.S. L.608 J.D. [N.L.Danison]
Danison, Nanci L., LPA, Law Office of, (AV) .... 4757 Aberdeen Avenue #B
Davis, Natasha Nadeen ....'74 '01 C.692 B.A. L.150 J.D. City of Dublin
Davis, Thomas F. '50 '75 C.602 B.A. L.421 J.D.
(adm. in KY; not adm. in OH)
Admin. V.P. & Gen. Coun., Corp. Law Dept., Ashland Chem. Co.
DeMatteo, Lucia ....'72 '00 C.97 B.S. L.608 J.D. Sterling Commerce
DeVore, Cheryl H. ....'56 '91 C.608 B.S. L.117 J.D. [Ⓒ Thomas]
Donahue, Kerry Michael .... '62 '91 C.608 B.S. in B.A. L.179 J.D. 6065 Frantz Road
Dreitler, Beth L. '57 '93 C.473 B.A. L.1161 J.D.
Asst. Gen. Coun.-R.E., Wendy's International, Inc.
Dunning, Edward ....'26 '78 C.323 B.A. L.117 J.D. 5777 Frantz Rd. (Pat.)‡
Dunsizer, Jennifer B. '68 '93
C.696 B.A. L.608 J.D. Sr. Corp. Coun., Wendy's International, Inc.
Duren, David L., (AV) ....'51 '80 C.967 B.A. L.117 J.D. [Metcalf,D.M.S.&W.]
Easterday, Jeffrey A. ....'54 '83 C.608 B.S. L.117 J.D. [Barrett,E.C.&E.]
Eichenberger, Jerry A., (BV) ....'47 '75 C.608 B.S. L.117 J.D. [Eichenberger&Assoc.]
Eichenberger & Associates, LPA, (BV) ....6099 Frantz Road
Eidelberg, Ilana S. ....'69 '94 C.477 B.A. L.608 J.D. Checkfree
Einstein, Dianne D. ....'69 '96 C.381 B.S. L.200 J.D. [Ⓐ Mowery&Y.]
Eselgroth, Carolyn D. ....'58 '92 C&L.608 B.S., J.D. [Barrett,E.C.&E.]
Falk, Stephen T. '65 '94 C.608 B.S. L.477 J.D.
Assistant General Counsel-Mergers & Acquisitions, Cardinal Health, Inc.
Faoro, Therese Marie, (BV) ....'56 '88 C.610 B.S. L.117 J.D. [T.M.Faoro]
Faoro, Therese M., Attorney at Law, (BV) ....5900 Sawmill Rd., Ste. 220
Fardal, Patrick M. .... '47 '92 C.959 B.S. L.117 J.D. 365 Stonewall Ct.‡
Farlow, Beverly J., (BV) ....'45 '85 C.967 B.A. L.608 J.D. [Farlow&Assoc.]

Farlow & Associates LLC, (BV)
270 Bradenton Avenue, 43017
Telephone: 614-734-1270 Fax: 614-923-1031
Email: bjf@farlowlaw.com URL: http://www.lawyers.com/farlowassoc
Beverly J. Farlow (Certified Specialist in Family Relations Law, Ohio State Bar Association);—James A. Boland, Jr.; Barbra Burleigh; Vicki K. Johnston; Ross A. Gillespie; Michelle R. Sayers.
Family Law, Divorce, Child Custody, Child Support, Premarital Agreements, Post-Decree Enforcements, Employment Law, School Law, Personal Injury.
See Professional Biographies, DUBLIN, OHIO

Fitzgerald, Scott M. .....'69 '95 C.347 B.A. L.365 J.D. Asst. Dir., Bur. of Workers Comp.
Fogle, Shawn Clark .... '64 '90 C&L.851 B.B.A., J.D. [S.C.Fogle]
Fogle, Shawn C. .... 6035 Memorial Dr.
Ford, Brendan A. ....'58 '86 C.473 B.S. L.608 J.D. Cardinal Distribution, Inc.
Forth, David R. '46 '79 C.937 B.S. L.623 J.D.
(adm. in OK; not adm. in OH) 4900 Blazer Pkwy.‡
French, Joseph A. '52 '88 C&L.421 B.A., J.D.
(adm. in KY; not adm. in OH) Sr. Envir. Atty., Ashland Inc.
Frey, Ann Luerssen ....'61 '86 C.473 B.A. L.1119 J.D. 9201 Lerwick Drive
Fulmer, Amy M. ....'70 '97 C.608 B.A. L.117 J.D. [Fulmer]
Fulmer & Company LPA, LLC .... 5910 Venture Dr.
Gabel, Jonathan M. ....'60 '85 C.608 B.A. L.150 J.D. [Ⓐ Blaugrund,H.&M.]
Galeano, Judith E., (BV) ....'65 '90 C.851 B.A. L.608 J.D. [Mowery&Y.]
Gardner, Dirk R. '66 '98 C.101 B.A. L.910 J.D.
(adm. in MO; not adm. in OH) Corp. Coun., Wendy's Int'l. Inc.
Gayan, Eric M. ....'66 '98 C.980 B.S.M.E. L.117 J.D. [Ⓐ Standley] (See Pat. Sect.)
Gentry, Steven G., (BV) .... '52 '82 C.813 B.S. L.597 J.D. [S.G.Gentry]
Gentry, Steven G., Ltd., (BV) ....220 W. Bridge Street, Suite 200
Giacalone, Robert P. '59 '89 C.339 B.S. L.209 J.D.
V.P., Regulatory Affairs, Cardinal Health, Inc.
Giller, Victoria H. '72 '97 C.880 B.A. L.608 J.D.
Corp. Coun., BMW Financial Services NA, LLC
Gillespie, Ross A. ....'— '03 C.608 B.A. L.7 J.D. [Ⓐ Farlow&Assoc.]
Goldberg, Scott D. ....'65 '90 C.477 B.B.A. L.608 J.D. Golden Title Agency, Inc.
Goodman, Heather E., (BV) '68 '93
C.966 B.A. L.930 J.D. Senior Counsel, Cardinal Health, Inc.
Grant, Stephen L., (BV) '53 '88 C.608 B.S.Ch.E. L.8 J.D.
[Ⓐ Standley] (See Pat. Sect.)
Gray, Cynthia D. '54 '85 C.882 B.A. L.1029 J.D.
(adm. in CT; not adm. in OH) Gen. Mng., BMW Financial Servs. NA, LLC
Greely, Randy L. .... '54 '82 C.923 B.S.B.A. L.229 J.D. 5200 Upper Metro Place
Hadley, Greg A. '63 '88
C.97 B.S. L.150 J.D. Sr. Corp. Coun., Wendy's International, Inc.
Halleran, James H. ....'46 '78 C.610 B.G.S. L.117 J.D. Cardinal Health Inc.
Hays, Michelle L. .... '67 '93 C.608 B.S. L.117 J.D. Coun., Nationwide Insurance
Hedden, David L. '46 '74 C.930 A.B. L.861 J.D.
Div. Pat., Trademark & Copyright Coun., Ashland Chem. Co. (Pat.)
Heflinger, James D. '54 '79 C.97 B.A. L.150 J.D.
V.P. & Gen. Coun., Litel Communications Inc.
Herbert, John W., (BV) ....'50 '75 C&L.608 B.S., J.D. [Blaugrund,H.&M.]
Hess, Charley, Attorney at Law, (BV) '49 '81
C&L.117 B.A., J.D. 7211 Sawmill Rd., Ste. 200
Hessler, Robert J., (BV) '54 '79
C.477 B.B.A. L.608 J.D. Dir. of Franchise Dev., Wendy's Intl., Inc.
Hickman, Gregory A., (BV) '59 '88
C.347 B.A. L.608 J.D. Sr. Corp. Coun., Wendy's International, Inc.
Hiestand, Kristen Davidson '68 '93
C&L.608 B.A., J.D. Staff Coun., Ohio Automobile Dealers Assn.
Himmelrick, Matthew Todd .... '73 '99 C.437 B.A. L.608 J.D. 7215 Sowmill Road

Hoag, Wesley F., (BV) ....'57 '84 C.976 B.A. L.117 J.D. 6000 Memorial Dr.
Hoffman, Cynthia Jo .....'62 '91 C.97 B.S. L.273 J.D. Dir. Tax Coun., Wendy's Int'l. Inc.
Hoover, Albert K., (AV) '60 '86 C.597 B.A. L.309 J.D.
Senior VIce President & General Counsel, Sterling Commerce, Inc.
Hoover, Larry E. ....'66 '96 C.608 B.S. L.150 J.D. [Ⓒ Barrett,E.C.&E.]
Houfek, James T., (BV) '45 '69 C.602 B.B.A. L.608 J.D.
V.P. and Gen. Coun., OCLC Online Computer Libr. Ctr., Inc.
Howard, Charles C. '65 '94
C.608 B.A. L.117 J.D. Staff Coun., Ohio Automobile Dealers Assn.
Hunter, Jason Christopher ....'71 '01 C.610 B.E. L.117 J.D 6047 Frantz Rd., Ste. 203
Inzetta, Mark S. '56 '80 C.150 B.B.A. L.7 J.D.
V.P. & Asst. Gen. Coun., Gen. Corp. & Canadian, Wendy's Intl., Inc.
Jacobs, Francine I., (AV) ....'38 '80 C.608 B.A.B.S. L.117 J.D. 5050 Thornhill Lane
Jankowski, Daniel R. ....'74 '01 C.611 B.A. L.608 J.D. Stanley Steemer International, Inc.
Johnston, Vicki K. ....'70 '04 C.608 B.S.S.W. L.972 J.D. [Ⓐ Farlow&Assoc.]
Jordan, Joan B. ....'59 '99 C.523 B.A. L.117 J.D. 4970 Chaddington Dr.
Kalson, Lisa S. ....'57 '95 C.1494 B.A. L.608 J.D. 5911 Newbridge Dr.
Kammerer, William ....'16 '56 C.150 Ch.E. L.1009 LL.B. 8839 Bigham Ct. N.‡
Karasarides, Shawn Harrold '64 '93 C.381 B.S. L.7 J.D.
Mng. Corp. Coun., Wendy's International, Inc.
Karpowicz, Joseph R., (BV) '56 '81 C.602 B.B.A. L.608 J.D.
V. P. Asst. Gen. Coun. Lit., Wendy's Intl., Inc.

Kenney-Pfalzer, Susan
(See Columbus)

Kessler, David S., (BV) ....'64 '89 C.8 B.S. L.117 J.D. [Blaugrund,H.&M.]
Kevern, Thomas R. ....'29 '58 C.930 A.B. L.1003 LL.B. 2683 Cedarlake Dr.
Khan, Fazeel S. ....'72 '05 C.043 B.A. L.031 LL.B. [Ⓐ Blaugrund,H.&M.]
Klein, Dana W., (AV) '53 '79 C&L.117 B.A., J.D.
V.P., Asst. Gen. Coun & Asst. Secy., Wendy's Intl., Inc.
Koch, Kenneth H., (AV) '55 '79
C.659 B.A. L.608 J.D. V.P., Gen. Coun. & Secy., Insilco Corp.
Kovacs, Francis A., Jr., (BV) ....'53 '80 C.608 B.A. L.117 J.D. [Ⓒ Blaugrund,H.&M.]
Kramer, Ronald A. ....'46 '71 C&L.608 B.S., J.D. 8420 Kilbirnie Court
Kwak, James L. .... '69 '96 C.679 B.S.E.E. L.608 J.D. [Standley] (See Pat. Sect.)
Lacksonen, Todd Andrew '63 '92
C&L.851 B.A., J.D. Mng. Govt. Rel., Tap Pharmaceuticals
Lampkin-Isabel, Robin, (BV) '63 '90
C&L.608 B.A., J.D. Sr. Litig. Coun., Ashland Chem. Co.
Lee, Dorothy L. ....'55 '90 C.608 B.S. L.273 J.D. 7728 Windwood Drive
Leermakers, Stephen W. '43 '68 C.918 B.A. L.228 J.D.
(adm. in VT; not adm. in OH) 5200 Blazer Pkwy.‡
Lenzotti, Dean M. ....'66 '90 C.8 B.S.B.A. L.608 J.D. Information Dimensions
Leonard, James K., (BV) ....'48 '78 C.674 A.B. L.208 J.D. [WrightCo]
Letizia, Frances R. ....'62 '87 C.999 B.S. L.200 J.D. 7609 Bellepointe Pl.‡
Lewis, Emily J., Law Offices of, (BV) '55 '84
C.1265 B.S. L.213 J.D. 5650 Blazer Pkwy., Ste. 100
Lillard, Samuel N., (BV) ....'63 '88 C.201 B.A. L.150 J.D. [Mowery&Y.]
Linebarger Goggan Blair & Sampson, LLP, (AV)
5080 Tuttle Crossing Blvd. (ⓒPhoenix, AZ; L.A., CA; Jacksnvl., Miami, FL; Chgo., IL; New Orleans, LA; Harrisburg, Phila., PA; Memphis, TN; Austin, Beaumont, Brownsville, Conroe, Corpus Christi, Corsicana, Dallas, Edinburg, El Paso, Fort Worth, Greenville, Hous., Jacksboro, Longview, Lufkin, Odessa, Orange, Pampa, Richmond, San Angelo, San Antonio, Sherman, Texas City, The Woodlands, Tyler, Victoria, Waco, TX; Richmond, VA)
Lipari, Gretchen Marie Ratcliff ....'66 '93 C&L.608 B.S., J.D. 5500 Frantz Road
Lucas, Mark J. .... '55 '81 C.5 B.A. L.608 J.D. 5100 Park Center Avenue, Suite 120
Maloon, Jerry L., (AV) ....'38 '75 C.608 B.S. L.117 J.D. 9155 Moors Place, North
Marquardt, Richard F. ....'— '00 C.16 B.S. L.851 J.D. [Marquardt&W.]

Marquardt & White Co., LPA
5455 Rings Road, Suite 100, 43017
Telephone: 614-789-1622 Fax: 614-789-1623
Richard F. Marquardt.
Personal Injury, Automobile Accidents, Negligence, Wrongful Death, Motorcyle Accidents, Dog Bites, Slip and Fall, Medical Malpractice, Wills and Trusts.
See Professional Biographies, DUBLIN, OHIO

Marsalka, Joseph P. ....'28 '58 C.610 B.Sc. L.1003 J.D. Pres., Startec Inc.
Martin, Steven A., (AV) ....'53 '88 C.174 B.S.B.A. L.608 J.D. [Blaugrund,H.&M.]
Mason Law Firm Co., L.P.A.
(See Columbus)

McAdow, Sam J. .... '38 '64 C.597 B.S. L.608 J.D. 6194 Memorial Dr.‡
McCarthy, James W. .... '47 '72 C&L.608 B.S., J.D. King Thompson Realtors
McCash, Thomas M., (BV) ....'61 '92 C.608 B.S. L.117 J.D. P.O. Box 3101
McCorkle, Leon M., Jr., (AV) '41 '72 C.309 A.B. L.608 J.D.
Exec. V.P., Gen. Coun. & Secy., Wendy's International, Inc.
McCormick, Michael D., (AVⓣ) '48 '80 C.228 B.A. L.345 J.D.
Exec. V.P., Gen. Coun. & Secy., Bindley Western Industries
McCune, Diana R., (BV) .... '47 '88 C.266 B.S. L.117 J.D. Sr. Atty., Ashland Chem. Co.
McCurdy, Gay Lynn ....'48 '88 C.608 B.S.Ed. L.117 J.D. 5148 Reserve Dr.
Metcalf, Richard B., (AV) ....'24 '51 C.608 L.266 J.D. [Metcalf,D.M.S.&W.] ‡
Metcalf, Duren, Morris, Starkey & Waid, L.L.C., (AV) .... 665 South Metro Place
Michael, Thomas P., (BV) ....'43 '68 C&L.608 B.S., J.D. 7652 Sawmill Rd., Ste. 229
Miller, Sharon L. R., (AV) .... '52 '79 C.381 B.S. L.607 J.D. [Blaugrund,H.&M.]
Mohamed, Aneezal H. '— '97 C.445 B.S. L.1187 J.D.
Senior Attorney, Securities & Corporate Goverance, Cardinal Health, Inc.
Morris, Robert V., II, (AV) ....'53 '79 C.608 B.A. L.117 J.D. [Metcalf,D.M.S.&W.]
Morrison, Melinda '71 '97 C.473 B.A. L.884 J.D.
OCLC Online Computer Libr. Ctr., Inc.
Mowery, James S., Jr., (AV) ....'48 '73 C.611 B.A. L.117 J.D. [Mowery&Y.]

Mowery & Youell, Ltd., (AV)
425 Metro Place North Suite 420, 43017
Telephone: 614-764-1444 Fax: 614-760-8654 URL: http://www.mowery-youell.com
URL: http://www.lawyers.com/mowery&youell
Members of Firm: James S. Mowery, Jr.; Spencer M. Youell; Samuel N. Lillard (Certified Specialist in Labor and Employment Law, Ohio State Bar Association); Judith E. Galeano. Associates: Karen L. Poling; Elizabeth J. Birch; Dianne D. Einstein (Resident); Merl H. Wayman (Certified Specialist in Labor & Employment Law and Workers' Compensation Law, Ohio State Bar Association).
General Trial including Federal Practice, Labor, Employment Discrimination, Sexual Harassment, Americans With Disabilities Act, Family and Medical Leave Act, Corporate, Business, Real Estate and Family Law.
References: The Huntington National Bank; BancOne of Columbus, N.A.
See Professional Biographies, DUBLIN, OHIO

Muchnicki, Edward Dennis ....'49 '74 C.30 B.S. L.273 J.D. [Muchnicki]
Muchnicki Law Office ....5650 Blazer Parkway
Myers, Marc E., (AV) ....'51 '76 C.610 B.A. L.607 J.D. [Blaugrund,H.&M.]

Najjar, Nina Marie . . . . . . '58 '82 C.363 B.A. L.608 J.D. P.O. Box 40
Nelson, Larry N., (AV) '51 '76 C.705 B.A. L.665 J.D.
(adm. in PA; not adm. in OH)
Sr. V.P. & Assoc. Gen. Coun., Develop., Wendy's Intl., Inc.
Nesdore, Bruce G. . . . . . . '62 '89 C.25 B.S. L.117 J.D. 9115 Tartan Fields Dr.
Nevada, Eugene P., (BV) . . . '50 '76 C.434 B.A. L.608 J.D. Clemans Nelson & Assoc., Inc.
Norris, Jeffrey C. . . . . . . '69 '96 C.679 B.S.E.E. L.201 J.D. [A Standley] (See Pat. Sect.)
O'Kane, Michael G., (BV) '56 '81
C.608 B.A. L.851 J.D. Mng. Corp. Coun., Wendy's Intl., Inc.
Opelt, Vivian L., (BV) '54 '85 C&L.608 B.S., J.D.
Mng. Corp. Coun., Wendy's Intl., Inc.
Patterson, Matthew T. '56 '82
C.383 B.S. L.607 J.D. Sr. Tax Atty., Intl., Tax Dept., Ashland Inc.
Pennington, David S. . . . . . . '52 '83 C.911 B.A. L.608 J.D. [A WrightCo]
Petras, David J. '62 '96 C&L.930 B.A., J.D.
545 Metro Place South Suite 100, PMB No. 19
Phillips, Thomas M. . . . . . . '42 '72 C&L.608 B.S., J.D. P.O. Box 53
Phipps, Kathryn B. . . . . . . '69 '94 C.608 B.A. L.117 J.D. Asst. Corp. Corp.
Picken, Mary E. . . . . . . '37 '80 C.604 A.B. L.608 J.D. 5200 Blazer Pkwy. (Pat.)‡
Pittaluga, Cindy Hide '56 '84 L.326 J.D.
(adm. in TX; not adm. in OH) Pres., Penelope Price, Inc.
Poling, Karen L. . . . . . . '69 '98 C.276 B.S.B.A. L.608 J.D. [A Mowery&Y.]
Postalakis, Stephen P. . . . . . . '68 '94 C.473 B.A. L.608 J.D. [Blaugrund,H.&M.]
Rasmussen, Teri G., (BV) . . . . . . '59 '84 C.352 B.A. L.477 J.D. [Blaugrund,H.&M.]
Reall, Christopher S. '69 '96
C.266 B.S. L.117 J.D. Chicago Title Agency of Columbus, OH
Reed, Frederick R., (AV) '48 '73 C.309 A.B. L.608 J.D.
COO, General Counsel, Development Specialists, Inc.
Resch, Frederick David, (BV) . . . . '44 '78 C.980 A.B. L.117 J.D. 5060 Bradenton Avenue
Reynolds, Mark A., (CV) '63 '89 C.631 B.A. L.201 J.D.
Mgr. Corp. Coun., Wendy's International, Inc.
Richards, R. L. . . . . . . '48 '75 C.967 B.A. L.608 J.D. 5131 Post Rd.
Rinehart, Laurie A. . . . . . . '64 '94 C&L.608 B.S., J.D. 4353D Tuller Rd.
Roberts, James E., (BV) '64 '92
C.608 B.S. L.117 J.D. Corp. Coun., Wendy's International, Inc.
Robinson, Kerry L. . . . . . . '63 '88 C.610 B.A. L.362 J.D. Sr. Coun., Nationwide Ins.
Roeger, Deborah L. . . . . . . '53 '89 C.266 B.S.B.A. L.117 J.D. Sr. Coun., AirTouch Comm.
Rogers, Brent A. . . . . '71 '97 C.608 B.A. L.117 J.D. Sr. Contract Specialist, Sterling Com.
Rolletta, Sandra Marie . . . '57 '83 C.473 B.A. L.851 J.D. Hearing Offr., Indus. Com. of OH
Root, William K., (AV) . . . . . . '48 '78 C.608 B.A. L.117 J.D. 5060 Bradenton Avenue
Rose, Clayton W. . . . . . . '27 '52 C&L.608 B.S., J.D. 5075 Thornhill Ln.‡
Rose, David E. . . . . . . '44 '78 C.608 B.S. L.117 J.D. 2125 Olde Sawmill Blvd.
Rose, Donald G., (BV) . . . . . . '38 '66 C&L.608 B.S., J.D. 195 Stonefence Ln.
Rothgeb, Karlton, (BV) . . . . . . '38 '63 C.937 B.A. L.608 J.D. 220 W. Bridge St.

Roubanes, Barbara A. '69 '97 C.631 B.A. L.117 J.D.
555 Metro Place North, Suite 575, 43017
Telephone: 614-793-8113 Fax: 614-793-8957
Email: bar@roubaneslaw.com URL: http://www.roubaneslaw.com
Personal Injury, Automobile Accidents, Products Liability, Wrongful Death.
See Professional Biographies, DUBLIN, OHIO

Rozycki, Andrew G. '65 '97 C.945 B.S. L.300 J.D.
(adm. in MN; not adm. in OH; Pat.) Sr. Pat. Coun., Cardinal Health, Inc.
Ryser, Philip P., (AV) '52 '78 C.930 B.A. L.608 J.D.
Executive Vice President & General Counsel, Stanley Steemer International, Inc.
Sayers, Michelle R. . . . . . . '— '04 C.608 B.S.B.A. L.117 J.D. [A Farlow&Assoc.]
Schoenmarklin, Susan L. . . . . . '59 '84 C.378 B.S. L.352 J.D. Amer. Cancer Soc., Inc.
Schuerman, Robert E., (AV) '52 '76
C.150 B.A. L.228 J.D. Mg. Corp. Coun., Wendy's Intl

Schulze, Howard & Cox
(See Marysville)

Scoliere, Michael E., (BV) '61 '86
C.831 B.A. L.665 J.D. [Linebarger G.B.&S.] (⊙Harrisburg, PA)
Scotney, Cheryl S. . . . . . . '54 '98 C.63 B.S. L.117 J.D. [A Standley] (See Pat. Sect.)
Scott, Geoff P. . . . . . . '68 '97 C.608 B.S. L.179 J.D. [A Blaugrund,H.&M.]
Sechler, Kenneth R., (BV) . . . . . . '48 '74 C.610 A.B. L.597 J.D. 425 Metro Pl. N.
Senecal, Theodore F. . . . . . . '44 '72 C.201 B.A. L.607 J.D. 7384 Christie Chapel Rd.
Sharkey, Beverly Jane . . . . . . '47 '89 C.608 B.S. L.117 J.D. Aerosafe, Inc.
Sherrer, Kendell F. . . . . . . '63 '90 C.621 B.S. L.623 J.D. 7000 Cardinal Place
Sickles, Blaine T. . . . . . . '25 '55 C.473 B.S. L.472 J.D. 7997 Clark Ave.‡
Smith, Ruth Ann Hunter '49 '77 C&L.608 B.S., J.D.
Scherer Companies-National Realty
Sovern, Julie D. '65 '94 C.882 B.S. L.178 J.D.
(adm. in NY; not adm. in OH) Corp. Coun., BMW Financial Services NA, LLC
Speed, F. Michael, Jr. . . . . . . '65 '95 C.839 B.S. L.608 J.D. [A Standley]

Sponseller, Nancy L., Law Offices of, (AV) '51 '77 C&L.608 B.A., J.D.
425 Metro Place North, Suite 640, 43017
Telephone: 614-764-0423 Fax: 614-764-2486 URL: http://www.nancysponseller.com
Email: nsponseller@netwalk.com URL: http://www.lawyers.com/nancysponseller
Franchise Law, Small Business Law, Divorce Dissolutions, Pre-Marital Agreements, Child Custody, Child Support, Family Law, Estate Planning, Wills and Probate.
See Professional Biographies, DUBLIN, OHIO

Stach, Mark A. '61 '87 C.383 B.A. L.923 J.D.
(adm. in WV; not adm. in OH) Senior Attorney, Ashland Inc.
Standley, Jeffrey S., (AV) '61 '89 C.608 B.S.M.E. L.117 J.D.
[Standley] (See Pat. Sect.)

Standley Law Group LLP, (AV)
495 Metro Place South, Suite 210, 43017-5319
Telephone: 614-792-5555 Telecopier: 614-792-5536
Email: lawyers@standleyllp.com URL: http://www.standleyllp.com
Partners of Firm: Jeffrey S. Standley; Carol G. Stovsky; James L. Kwak;—Jeffrey C. Norris; Eric M. Gayan; Cheryl S. Scotney; F. Michael Speed, Jr.; Stephen L. Grant; Michael R. Stonebrook; Wesly A. Alig. Of Counsel: Michael R. Szolosi, Jr.
Domestic and Foreign Intellectual Property Law, including Patent, Trademark, Copyright, Unfair Competition and Trade Secret Law and related Litigation, Licensing, International Trade Matters, related Antitrust, Computer and other Technology Law.
See Professional Biographies, DUBLIN, OHIO

Starkey, David H., (AV) . . . . . . '52 '77 C&L.608 B.S.I.E., J.D. [Metcalf,D.M.S.&W.]
Steffensmeier, Michael D. '64 '92
C.352 B.S.E.E. L.846 J.D. Asst. Gen. Coun., Cardinal Health Inc. (Pat.)
Stonebrook, Michael R. . . . . . . '72 '02 C.8 B.S. L.117 J.D. [A Standley] (See Pat. Sect.)
Stonerock, Bobbie J. . . . . . . '64 '93 C.610 B.A. L.608 J.D. [A Blaugrund,H.&M.]
Stovsky, Carol G. . . . . . . '60 '94 C.477 B.S. L.608 J.D. [Standley] (See Pat. Sect.)
Strehl, Christine E. . . . . . . '72 '04 C.610 B.A. L.608 J.D. [A Thomas]
Szolosi, Michael R., Jr. '69 '95 C.1229 B.S.M.E. L.201 J.D.
[C Standley] (See Pat. Sect.)
Teets, Scott D. '57 '97 C.108 B.S. L.345 J.D.
Sr. Coun. & Asst. Secy., Bindley Western Industries
Thomas, Terry L. . . . . . . '47 '85 C.150 B.S. L.117 J.D. [Thomas]

Thomas Law Group
5148 Blazer Parkway, Suite A, 43017
Telephone: 614-761-7701 Fax: 614-761-7703
Email: cstrehl@thomaslawgroup.com URL: http://www.thomas-lawgroup.com
Member of Firm: Terry L. Thomas. Associate: Christine E. Strehl. Of Counsel: Cheryl H. DeVore. Family Law, Divorce, Child Custody, Child Support, Visitation Rights, Business Litigation, Corporate, Small Business Law, Business Formation, Partnerships, Limited Liability Companies, Buying and Selling of Businesses, Contracts, Personal Injury, Automobile Accidents, Wrongful Death, Medical Malpractice, Estate Planning, Wills and Probate, Trusts and Estates, Estate Administration.
See Professional Biographies, DUBLIN, OHIO

Tilton, Jerry E., (BV) . . . . . . '35 '75 C.608 B.S. L.117 J.D. 5998 Kiakwall Court, W.
Troxell, Elizabeth M. . . . . . . '65 '90 C.473 B.A. L.597 J.D. Atty., AirTouch Comm.
Troxell, Richard H. . . . . . . '65 '96 C.801 B.S. L.608 J.D. [R.Troxell]
Troxell, Richard, Law Office of . . . . . . 5640 Frantz Rd.
Venne, Vernon F. '46 '74 C.611 B.A. L.851 J.D.
(adm. in DC; not adm. in OH; Pat.)
Assoc. Div. Coun., Pat. & Trademark Dept., Ashland Chem. Co.
Vidra, Kirk A. '74 '99 C.383 B.S. L.734 J.D.
(adm. in MO; not adm. in OH) Corp. Coun., Wendy's Intl., Inc.
Wagner, John C., (AV) . . . . . . '22 '50 C.117 B.A. L.608 J.D. 9110 Moors Place N.‡
Waid, Phillip A., (BV) . . . . . . '46 '73 C.679 B.S. L.117 J.D. [Metcalf,D.M.S.&W.]
Walkup, Christine M. '75 '03 C.608 B.A. L.117 J.D.
Corp. Coun., Nationwide Insurance
Wang, Thomas L. . . . . . . '52 '77 C&L.608 B.A., J.D. 10812 Winchcombe Dr.
Ward, T.A., II . . . . . . '65 '96 C.608 B.S. L.117 J.D. Real Estate Coun., Dominion Homes
Warren, Jeffrey Scott . . . . . . '67 '99 C.787 B.A. L.117 J.D. 5134 Blazer Pkwy
Warren, Kenneth J., (AV) . . . . . . '43 '66 C.610 B.A. L.1009 LL.B. 5134 Blazer Pkwy.
Wayman, Merl H., (AV) . . . . . . '52 '83 C.610 B.A. L.1003 J.D. [A Mowery&Y.]
Weiss, Carole D., (BV) . . . . . . '62 '86 C.608 B.A. L.575 J.D. [A Blaugrund,H.&M.]
Welch, Porter R. . . . . . . '73 '99 C.119 L.608 7215 Sawmill Rd.
Whann, Keith E., (BV) . . . . . . '59 '84 C.318 B.A. L.1003 J.D. 6300 Frantz Rd.
Whipps, Edward F., & Associates, (AV) '36 '61
C.611 B.A. L.608 J.D. 555 Metro Place N. (⊙Columbus)
Williams, Paul S., (AV) '59 '84 C.309 A.B. L.976 J.D.
Vice President & Assistant General Counsel, Cardinal Health, Inc.
Wires, Eileen Marie . . . . . . '57 '86 C&L.607 B.A., J.D. Sterling Commerce, Inc.
Wirt, W. Stephen . . . . . . '53 '78 C.339 A.B. L.608 J.D. 4288 W. Dublin Granville Rd.
Woods, Kristina M. '56 '84 C.174 B.A. L.208 J.D.
(adm. in CO; not adm. in OH) Sr. Envir. Atty., Corp. Law Dept., Ashland Chem. Co.
Wright, H. LeArthur, II, (AV) '49 '81
C.999 B.S. L.923 J.D. Sr. Corp. Coun., Wendy's Intl., Inc.
Wright, Paul L., (AV) . . . . . . '38 '78 C.608 B.S. L.851 J.D. [WrightCo]

Wright Law Co. LPA, (AV)
Brickstone Commons, 4266 Tuller Road, Suite 101, 43017-5027
Telephone: 614-791-9112 Fax: 614-791-9116 URL: http://www.lawyers.com/wright-lawco
Email: law@wright-law.net URL: http://www.wright-law.net
Paul L. Wright; James K. Leonard;—Kimberly M. Cutler; David S. Pennington.
Agricultural Law, Business Planning, Estate Administration, Estate Planning, Real Estate, Tax, Litigation.
See Professional Biographies, DUBLIN, OHIO

Wynn, James F., (BVⓉ) '53 '81 C.645 B.S. L.1187 J.D.
(adm. in MI; not adm. in OH) CEO & Gen. Coun., National Wholesale Drug Co.
Youell, Spencer M., (AV) . . . . . . '39 '66 C&L.326 B.B.A., J.D. [Mowery&Y.]
Young, Ivor H. . . . . . . '33 '59 C&L.608 B.S., J.D. 5697 Strathmore Ln.
Young, Ronald G. . . . . . . '47 '96 C&L.117 B.A., J.D. 5430 Briardale Ln.
Zaino, Michael J., (AV) . . . . . . '57 '83 C&L.201 B.A., J.D. [Zaino&H.]
Zaino & Humphrey, LPA, (AV) . . . . . . 5775 Perimeter Dr.
Zawaly, Peter P., II., (AV) . . . . . . '45 '73 C.1044 B.A. L.161 J.D. 6238 Inverurie Dr., W.
Zitesman, James A. . . . . . . '60 '93 5701 Springburn Drives

EAST CANTON, 1,629, *Stark Co.*

Weisend, Wm. E., (BV) . . . . . . '25 '54 C.381 L.948 LL.B. 456 N. Wood St.

EAST CLEVELAND, 33,096, *Cuyahoga Co.*

(See Cleveland)

EASTLAKE, 20,255, *Lake Co.*

Andrews, Charles M., (CV) . . . . . . '51 '78 C.161 B.B.A. L.930 J.D. 35110 Euclid Ave.
Barner, Donald, (BV) . . . . . . '50 '86 C.392 B.S. L.1003 J.D. 36515 Starboard Dr.
Dame, Stacy E. . . . . . . '— '02 C.608 B.A. L.124 J.D. [Wiles&R.]
Germano, Michael P., (BV) . . . . . . '60 '88 C.161 B.A. L.607 J.D. [Wiles&R.]
Lucas, Michael C., (BV) . . . . . . '54 '80 C.161 B.A. L.1003 J.D. [Wiles&R.]
Myers, Neil . . . . . . '32 '65 C.381 B.S. L.1003 J.D. 35350 Curtis Blvd.‡
Richards, Daniel F., (AV) . . . . . . '36 '65 C.363 B.S. L.1003 J.D. [Wiles&R.]
Rosenthal, Gary H., (CV) . . . . . . '49 '74 C.319 B.A. L.989 J.D. 35350 Curtis Boulevard
Simpson, Robert A. . . . . . . '70 '97 C.651 B.A. L.117 J.D. [Wiles&R.]
Spangler, Mathew E. . . . . . . '— '02 C.999 B.A. L.7 J.D. [Wiles&R.]
Tekavec, James W. . . . . . . '45 '72 C.363 A.B. L.1003 J.D. 35350 Curtis Blvd
Weaver, Geoffrey W., (CV) . . . . . . '64 '91 C.210 B.A. L.569 J.D. [Wiles&R.]
Wiles, John W., (AV) . . . . . . '31 '59 C.923 B.S. L.1003 J.D. [Wiles&R.]
Wiles and Richards, (AV) . . . . . . 35350 Curtis Boulevard, Suite 530
Zele, Ronald, (BV) . . . . . . '42 '71 C.930 B.A. L.1003 J.D. [Zele&Z.]
Zele, Scott J. . . . . . . '72 '98 C.161 B.A. L.1003 J.D. [Zele&Z.]
Zele & Zele, Co., L.P.A., (BV) . . . . . . 35350 Curtis Boulevard, Suite 330

EAST LIVERPOOL, 13,089, *Columbiana Co.*

Aronson, George A. . . . . . . '11 '35 C.608 L.266 [Aronson,F.&D.]
Aronson, Fineman and Davis, Co., L.P.A., (AV) . . . . . . 124 E. 5th Street
Barnett, Troy David . . . . . . '70 '00 C.980 B.A. L.8 J.D. 124 East Fifth St.
Berman, Ben H. . . . . . . '13 '38 C.608 A.B. L.309 LL.B. 114 W. 6th St.‡
Brookes, Timothy R., (BV) . . . . . . '54 '79 C.381 B.A. L.608 J.D. 517 Broadway
Buzzard, J. David, (BV) . . . . . . '41 '69 C.207 B.A. L.930 J.D. 517 Broadway
Byers-Emmerling, Melissa, (BV) . . . . . . '56 '84 C.473 B.A. L.7 J.D. J., Mun. Ct.
Ciccarelli, Mark A. '61 '87
C.645 B.A. L.229 J.D. Dir. Legal Assisting Tech., Kent State Univ.
Cooper, Joseph W. C., (BV) . . . . . . '17 '41 C.935 L.150 J.D. 517 Bway.
Davidson, Marian D. . . . . . . '69 '96 C.980 B.S.B.A. L.607 J.D. 420 Market St
Davis, William J., (AV) . . . . . . '48 '73 C&L.608 B.A., J.D. [Aronson,F.&D.]
Emmerling, Frederick C., (BV) . . . . . . '53 '78 C.381 B.A. L.7 J.D. 114 W. 6th St.

Fannin, Thomas N., (BV) .... '43 '68 C.611 B.A. L.930 J.D. P.O. Box 2226
Fineman, Bernard, (AV) .... '34 '58 C.923 L.608 LL.B. [Aronson,F.&D.]
Gbur, George A. ....'61 '89 C.575 B.A. L.884 J.D. Social Sec. Admn.
Kapp, J. Michael, (BV) .... '41 '67 C.165 A.B. L.477 J.D. [Kapp]
Kapp Law Office, (BV) ....P.O. Box 115
Kater, H. Janet ... '46 '84 C.999 B.S. L.608 J.D. Gen. Coun., East Liverpool City Hospital
Kelly, Kyde L. .... '78 '02 C.920 B.S. L.989 J.D. 128 West Fifth Street
Kontnier, Kellie S., (CV) .... '66 '91 C.528 B.A. L.608 J.D. 124 E. 5th St.
Lang, Mary Sue, (BV) ....'36 '74 C.611 B.F.A. L.161 J.D. 517 Broadway Street
Payne, Charles L. ....'57 '82 C.1323 B.A. L.229 J.D. 617 St. Clair Ave.
Smith, Lawrence W., (AV) ....'13 '41 C.602 B.A. L.229 LL.B. 124 W. Fifth St.‡
Vodrey, Jackman Stroud, (BV) '35 '63 C.674 A.B. L.477 J.D.
517 Broadway - Third Floor

EAST PALESTINE, 4,917, *Columbiana Co.*

Allison, J. Bradley, (AV) ....'60 '85 C.451 B.A. L.838 J.D. 139 N. Merket St.
Blasdell, Daniel A., (BV) ....'44 '73 C.532 A.B. L.607 J.D. 139 N. Market St.
Dickey, Larry Morgan, (BV) ....'39 '70 C.980 B.A. L.1003 J.D. Hartford & Dickey
Hill, Stephen A., (CV) ....'54 '79 C&L.607 B.A., J.D. 284 N. Market St.
King, Douglas, (CV) ....'65 '91 C.980 B.A. L.8 J.D. Off. of the Co. Prosecutor
Rockenberger, Dorothy H. .... '20 '49 C.699 L.980 J.D. 210 E. Martin St.‡

EATON, * 8,133, *Preble Co.*

Abruzzo, David N. .... '48 '73 C.475 B.S. L.608 J.D. Com. Pleas J.
Amiott, Laura M. '59 '95 C.973 B.S.B.A. L.1340 J.D.
Corporate Counsel, Henny Penny Corporation
Bennett, Gray W., (BV) ....'60 '91 C.228 A.B. L.8 J.D. [Bennett&B.]
Bennett & Bennett, (BV) .... 200 West Main Street

Bieser, Greer & Landis, LLP
(See Dayton)

Bruns, Stephen R., (BV) ....'58 '83 C.150 B.A. L.608 J.D. 123 W. Main St.
Clark, Karen M., (CV) ....'58 '90 C.473 B.S. L.201 J.D. 101 N. Barron St.
Clayton, Robert B. ....'46 '71 C&L.608 B.A., J.D. 136 Deer Trail Dr.★
Dues, Wilfrid G. .... '50 '75 C.602 B.A. L.607 J.D. Com. Pleas J.
Dye, John V. .... '29 '57 C.145 L.608 J.D. Ret. Prob. & Juv. J.
Earley, Dirk ....'— '00 C.473 B.A. L.201 J.D. [Earley&E.]
Earley, George J., (AV) ....'38 '64 C.303 B.A. L.607 J.D. [Earley&E.]
Earley & Earley, (AV) .... 112 North Barron Street
Ferguson, Rebecca J., (BV) .... '50 '75 C.608 B.A. L.896 J.D. Courthouse
Fieselmann, Benj. W. ....'13 '37 C.226 A.B. L.273 LL.B. 824 N. Maple St.‡
Henry, Paul D. ....'48 '81 C.473 B.S. L.201 J.D. Mun. J.
Holtzmuller, Paul E., (BV) ....'44 '68 C&L.945 A.B., J.D. 115 W. Main St.
Hubler, Charles D., (BV) ....'43 '69 C.610 B.S. L.607 J.D. [C.D.Hubler]
Hubler, Charles D., L.P.A., (BV) .... 201 S. Barron St.
Kalil, Edmund H., (BV) ....'63 '89 C.573 B.A. L.201 J.D. P.O. Box 655
Lane, Donald L., (BV) ....'29 '57 C.473 B.A. L.608 J.D. 115 W. Main St.
Lindstrom, Carol Perritt, (BV) ....'49 '80 C.956 B.A. L.608 J.D. 121 E. Main Street
Line, Eric E., (CV) ....'62 '94 C.473 B.A. L.201 J.D. 232 S. Barron St.
Peltier, Paul E. ....'52 '77 C.97 B.A. L.806 J.D. ENB Trust
Petry, John L., (BV) ....'43 '69 C.231 A.B. L.910 J.D. 132 North Barron Street
Sambol, Mary Lee Gill, (BV) ....'38 '81 C.473 B.A.M.A. L.201 J.D. P.O. Box 366
Thomas, James W., (BV) ....'49 '74 C.201 B.S. L.607 J.D. [Thomas]
Thomas, James W., Jr. ....'76 '01 C.201 B.A. L.607 J.D. [Thomas]

Thomas Law Office, The, (BV)
112 North Barron Street, 45320
Telephone: 937-456-4103 Fax: 937-456-2960
Email: jthomaslaw@yahoo.com URL: http://www.jthomaslaw.com
James W. Thomas; James W. Thomas, Jr.
General Trial and Appellate Practice, Real Estate, Criminal Law including D.U.I. and Defense of Drug Cases, Domestic Relations, Personal Injury, Wrongful Death, Probate, Estate Planning, Construction Defects, Mechanics Liens, Breach of Contract, Corporate Law, Creditors Rights, Family Law, Automobile Insurance, Automobile Accidents, Wills.
See Professional Biographies, EATON, OHIO

Votel, Martin P. ....'68 '97 C.973 B.S. L.596 J.D. Asst. Pros. Atty.

EDON, 880, *Williams Co.*

Blue, Steven J. .... '61 '89 C.5 B.A. L.851 J.D. V.P. & Gen. Coun., Edon State Bk.

ELMORE, 1,334, *Ottawa Co.*

Weis, Kenton P., (BV) ....'50 '75 C.317 B.A. L.607 J.D. 340 Rice Street
Yeasting, Maynard C., (AV) '11 '48
C.679 M.S.E. L.851 J.D. 17967 W. Portage River S. Rd.‡

ELYRIA, * 55,953, *Lorain Co.*

Anderson, Charlita Delayne ......'61 '88 C.591 B.S. L.1003 J.D. Lorain Co. Dom. Rel. Ct.
Anderson, Kurt D., (CV) ....'65 '90 C.130 B.A. L.930 J.D. [Fauver,K.&D.L.&Assoc.]
Anglewicz, Gregory A. '77 '04 C.161 B.A. L.150 J.D.
LandAmerica Financial Group / Lawyers Title
Arredondo, Michele Silva '51 '81 C.473 B.A. L.989 J.D.
Mag., Lorain Co. Dom. Rel. Ct.
Augustine, Sheila M. R. ....'52 '88 C.201 B.S. L.1003 J.D. 138 Woodridge Drive‡
Baggett, Jessica Ann ....'66 '94 C.608 B.A. L.607 J.D. Co. Juv. Ct.

Baker, Jason T.
(See Cleveland)

Balena, William J., (CV) ....'53 '78 C.645 B.A. L.1003 J.D. [Balena]
Balena Law Firm, (CV) .... 320 Broad St.
Basinski, David A. ....'37 '66 C.363 A.B. L.930 J.D. Com. Pleas J.
Belcher, Billie Jo ....'74 '00 C.161 B.A. L.851 J.D. Pros. Off.
Bennett, Gary C., (BV) ....'52 '77 C.967 B.A. L.602 J.D. [C St.Marie]
Berki, Jenifer .... '79 '04 C.608 B.A. L.117 J.D. 124 Middle Ave., Ste. 800
Betleski, Mark A., (BV) ....'58 '86 C.608 B.A. L.851 J.D. Com. Pleas J.
Bilancini, Darrel A., (BV) ....'53 '78 C.363 B.A. L.1003 J.D. 595 W. Broad St.
Blevins, Paul E. ....'65 '92 C.197 A.B. L.1068 J.D. [McCray,M.S.&M.]
Bond, Anthony R. '55 '93
C.980 B.S. L.1003 J.D. Admr., Co. Child Support Enforce. Agcy.
Boyson, Frank A., (BV) ....'47 '74 C&L.607 B.A., J.D. 802 Elyria Svgs. & Tr. Bldg.
Breunig, Kurt A., (BV) ....'54 '79 C.161 B.A. L.930 J.D. 409 East Avenue, Suite B
Brill, Douglas M., (AV) ....'52 '78 C.608 B.A. L.851 J.D. [Spike&M.]
Butler, Harry F., (BV) ....'22 '52 C.62 B.A. L.1003 J.D. 475 Middle Ave.
Butler, Linda Marie ....'63 '88 C&L.8 B.A., J.D. 225 Court St., 6th Fl.
Carroll, Timothy Sheridan ....'43 '76 347 Midway Boulevard, Suite 312
Charles, Adelbert K. '40 '67 C&L.976 B.A., LL.B.
(adm. in NY; not adm. in OH) Del Lumber Co.
Chavez, Stephen P. ....'64 '95 C.381 B.B.A. L.7 J.D. [Fauver,K.&D.L.&Assoc.]

Couch, James R., (BV) ....'47 '75 C.201 B.S. L.161 J.D. [Spike&M.]
Deery, James A., (BV) .... '49 '77 C.608 B.A. L.1003 J.D. 300 Fourth St.
Donovan, Kevin Wm., (AV) .....'48 '73 C.454 B.A. L.94 J.D. [Fauver,K.&D.L.&Assoc.]
Doyle, Michael D., (BV) ....'66 '91 C.107 B.S. L.1003 J.D. 134 Middle Ave.
Edleman, Jeffrey G. ....'69 '94 C&L.8 B.A., J.D. 401 Broad Street, Suite 203
Farren, John Edward .... '70 '99 C.602 B.B.A. L.8 J.D. [Farren,J.E.]
Farren, John E. ....105 Court Street
Fauver, Worth A., Jr., (BV) ...'35 '63 C.31 A.B. L.930 LL.B. [Fauver,K.&D.L.&Assoc.]

Fauver, Keyse-Walker & Donovan, A Legal Professional Association, (AV)
5333 Meadow Lane Court, 44035-1469
Telephone: 440-934-3700 Telefax: 440-934-3708
URL: http://www.fkwdlaw.com
Retired Partner: Worth A. Fauver, Jr. Members of Firm: John L. Keyse-Walker; Kevin Wm. Donovan; Kurt D. Anderson; Stephen P. Chavez. Associates: Brett D. Wieber; Howard T. Lane; Kristina M. King; Robert C. White.
General Civil Practice. Trials and Appeals, Business Organizations, Acquisitions, Education, Probate and Estate Planning, Insurance, Taxation, Real Estate, Commercial, Employment Relations.
General Counsel for: Oberlin College.
See Professional Biographies, ELYRIA, OHIO

Ferguson, George H. ....'30 '56 C.602 A.B. L.608 J.D. Mun. J.
Flanagan, Martin R., (BV) '59 '84 C.161 B.A. L.1003 J.D.
Lorain Co. Administration Bldg, 226 Middle Avenue, 3rd Floor
Fritz, Joel D., (BV) ....'61 '91 C.610 B.S. L.851 J.D. [Rothgery&Assoc.]
Gammons, Ann C. ....'— '97 C.161 B.S. L.1003 J.D. Asst. Co. Pros.

Gardner, Mark, Attorney and Counselor at Law
(See Cleveland)

George, David C., (BV) .... '29 '56 C.970 B.A. L.930 LL.B. 715 Elyria Svgs. & Tr. Bldg.
Giamboi, Frank Charles, II ....'56 '86 C.381 B.A. L.1003 J.D. [A Spike&M.]
Glavas, Kosma J. .... '30 '59 C.62 B.A. L.602 J.D. Com. Pleas J.
Godles, Michael J., (CV) ....'62 '89 C.608 B.S.B.A. L.8 J.D. 371 Broad Street
Gurchik, Stephen J., (BV) ....'40 '65 C.602 B.A. L.276 J.D. 1026 Gulf Road
Hamister, Kenneth C. ....'25 '51 C.385 A.B. L.477 J.D. 295 Overbrook Rd.‡
Harkacz, Myron .... '49 '79 C.610 B.S. L.851 J.D. Mag., Lorain Co. Prob. Ct.
Haynes, John S., (BV) ....'42 '68 C.610 B.A. L.608 J.D. 134 Middle Ave.
Hendershot, Margaret A. ....'73 '98 C.607 B.A. L.930 J.D. [A St.Marie]
Henderson, J. P. .... '21 '49 C&L.608 B.A., J.D. Ref./Mag., Mun. Ct.
Horvath, Frank J., (BV) ....'36 '61 C.610 B.S. L.602 LL.B. Prob. J.
Howard, John A. ....'23 '49 C.257 B.A. L.117 J.D. Mun. J.
Hubbard, Neal '41 '69 C.62 B.A. L.1003 J.D.
Pres. & CEO, The Northern Svgs. & Loan Co.
Hume, Ernest E., Jr., (BV) ....'29 '71 C.62 B.A. L.1003 J.D. [Hume&P.]
Hume & Pulito, Co., L.P.A., (BV) .... 230 Third St., 2nd Fl.
Hyman, Charles M. ....'30 '55 C&L.477 B.B.A., LL.B. 614 Elyria Svgs. Tr. Bldg.‡
Ignatz-Hoover, Gail M., (BV) '57 '81
C.608 B.S.S.W. L.930 J.D. Lorain Cty. Common Pleas Court
Illner, Michael D., (BV) ....'48 '85 C.97 B.S. L.7 J.D. [Spike&M.]
Innes, Gerald A., (AV) ....'50 '75 C&L.607 B.A., J.D. 105 Court St.
Janas, Thomas W., (AV) ....'51 '76 C.62 B.A. L.851 J.D. Com. Pleas J.
Keys, John Robert ....'51 '86 C.610 B.S.J. L.161 J.D. Lorain Co. Ct. of Com. Pleas
Keys, Michael B. ....'48 '78 C.610 B.S.J. L.7 J.D. 328 Broad Street
Keyse-Walker, John L., (AV) '56 '81 C.970 B.A. L.228 J.D.
[Fauver,K.&D.L.&Assoc.]
Kile, Carol A. ....'46 '91 C.967 B.A. L.1003 J.D. Staff Atty., Legal Aid Soc.
Kilfoyle, William E. ....'28 '56 C.363 L.1003 J.D. 1004 Garford Avenue
King, Kristina M. ....'75 '01 C.608 L.989 J.D. [A Fauver,K.&D.L.&Assoc.]

Knevel & Associates Co. LPA
(See Cleveland)

Kocsis, Paul M. ....'73 '99 C.94 B.A. L.989 J.D. 300 4th St.
Kovacs, John J., (BV) ....'47 '77 C.999 B.A. L.1003 J.D. 105 Court Street, Room 522
Kryszak, Andrea C. ....'70 '03 C.107 B.S. L.989 J.D. [A R.E.Lessing,Jr.&Assoc.]
Kuhn, Paula A. ....'59 '99 C.608 B.S.B.A. L.989 J.D. [A McCray,M.S.&M.]
Lane, Howard T. ....'67 '93 C.611 B.A. L.989 J.D. [A Fauver,K.&D.L.&Assoc.]
LaPlaca, Anthony C., (AV) '58 '84 C.659 B.S. L.94 J.D.
V.P. & Gen. Coun., Bendix Commercial Vehicle Systems LLC

Laubenthal, Marilu '44 '82 C.62 B.A. L.1003 J.D.
Lawyers' Loft, 633 W. Broad Street, Suite 200, 44035
Telephone: 440-322-5505 Fax: 440-322-5509
Email: mlaubenthalesq@yahoo.com
Criminal Law, Estate Planning, Real Estate, Mediation.
See Professional Biographies, ELYRIA, OHIO

Leitch, David B. ....'62 '94 C.999 B.S. L.1003 J.D. 300 4th Street
Lessing, Robert E., Jr., (BV) ....'44 '69 C.117 B.A. L.879 J.D. [R.E.Lessing,Jr.&Assoc.]

Lessing, Robert E., Jr., A Legal Prof. Association, Law Offices of, (BV)
374 Broad Street, Suite 1, 44035
Telephone: 440-322-5441 Fax: 440-323-5393
Email: lesslaw@less-law.com URL: http://www.lawyers.com/less-law
Robert E. Lessing, Jr. Associate: Andrea C. Kryszak.
Languages: Spanish.
Estate Planning, Asset Protection, Tax Planning, Guardianship, Trusts and Estates, Estate and Trust Administration, Wills and Probate, Elder Law, Small Business, Closely Held Business, LLC or Limited Liability Companies; Real Estate, Buying or Selling Home or Business; Partnerships, Business Start-Ups, Immigration.
Grafton, Ohio Office: 943 Main Street, 44044. Telephone: 440-926-3818
See Professional Biographies, ELYRIA, OHIO

Long, David C., (BV) ....'47 '75 C.161 B.E.E. L.1003 J.D. [Rothgery&Assoc.]
Mangan, Thomas M., (BV) ....'48 '81 C.973 B.A. L.1003 J.D. Asst. Co. Pros.
Massung, Howard G. '40 '74 C.602 B.S.E.E. L.229 J.D.
(adm. in PA; not adm. in OH; Pat.) 901 Cleveland St.
McClain, James M., (BV) ....'48 '75 C.967 B.A. L.989 J.D. 105 Court St.
McConnell, Lucinda Coleman ....'73 '00 C.608 B.A. L.989 J.D. Pros. Off.
McCray, J. William, (AV) ....'25 '50 C.611 B.A. L.477 J.D. [C McCray,M.S.&M.]

McCray, Muzilla, Smith & Meyers Co., L.P.A., (AV)
260 Burns Road, Suite 150, 44035
Telephone: 440-366-9930 Fax: 440-366-1910
Thomas J. Smith; Kim R. Meyers; Thomas A. Muzilla; Paul E. Blevins;—Paula A. Kuhn; Lisa Jane McGuire. Of Counsel: J. William McCray; Raymond A. Muzilla.
General Civil Practice, Corporate, Personal Injury, Medical Malpractice, Probate and Estate Planning, Labor and Employment, Government, Real Estate, Insurance Defense, Health, Tax, Civil Litigation, Product Liability, Communications and Copyright Issues and Environment. Trial and Appellate Practice in all Courts.
Local Counsel for: Nordson Corp.
See Professional Biographies, ELYRIA, OHIO

McGuire, Lisa Jane ....'68 '01 C.161 B.A. L.7 J.D. [A McCray,M.S.&M.]
McGuire, Thomas J., Attorney at Law ... '75 '01 C.1529 B.A. L.989 J.D. 134 Miami Ave.

Meckler, Stephen G., (AV) .... '40 '65 C&L.608 B.S., J.D. [Spike&M.]
Merrell, Bruce R. '48 '74 C.95 A.B. L.588 J.D.
Exec. Dir., Legal Aid Soc. of Lorain Co.
Merrill, Douglas Wilson .... '74 '00 C.49 B.A. L.989 J.D. [Rothgery&Assoc.]
Meyers, Kim R., (AV) ....'56 '84 C.36 B.A. L.201 J.D. [McCray,M.S.&M.]
Miklich, Thomas R. ....'47 '74 C&L.1003 B.B.A., J.D. 899 Cleveland Street
Morrisson, John G., (BV) .... '41 '77 C.207 B.A. L.930 J.D. 105 Court St. (⊙Lorain)
Murray, Garrett J., (BV) ....'33 '59 C.363 B.S.S. L.930 J.D. [G.J.Murray] (⊙Lagrange)
Murray, Garrett J., Co., L.P.A., (BV) .... 1030 Gulf Rd.
Muzilla, Raymond A., (AV) .....'32 '58 C.97 B.S.B.A. L.309 J.D. [ⓒ McCray,M.S.&M.]
Muzilla, Thomas A., (AV) ....'60 '86 C.608 B.S. L.930 J.D. [McCray,M.S.&M.]

Myers, David A., (BV) '48 '73 C.363 A.B. L.128 J.D.
374 Broad Street, Suite 2, 44035-5504
Telephone: 440-323-1111 Fax: 440-323-4284
Email: myers@aginglaw.com URL: http://www.aginglaw.com
Elder Law.

See Professional Biographies, ELYRIA, OHIO

Nagy, Stephen R. .... '26 '50 C.967 L.150 LL.B. Ret. Mun. J.

Naticchia, A. Dale
(See Cleveland)

Nelson, Jill Elaine ...... '52 '00 C.62 B.A. L.930 J.D. EMH Regional Health Care System
Noll, Carl F., (BV) .... '46 '74 C.608 B.Sc. L.1003 J.D. 511 Broad St.

Pagano, Wilson, Thomarios, Gillissie & Lenahan LLC
(See Cleveland)

Piazza, Robert A. ....'44 '69 C&L.608 B.Sc., J.D. 1270 N. Abbe Rd.
Pulito, Gino, (BV) ....'57 '87 C.161 B.B.A. L.1003 J.D. [Hume&P.]
Ramage, Barbara K., (BV) '55 '80
C.608 B.A. L.930 J.D. Legal Aid Society of Lorain Co., Inc.
Riedthaler, Jennifer Margaret ....'76 '01 C.62 B.A. L.124 J.D. Asst. Pros. Atty.
Robinson, Jeanette M., Attorney at Law, (CV) '66 '92
C.940 B.A. L.61 J.D. 401 Broad St., Ste. 311
Robison, Deanne Linsley ....'64 '93 347 Midway Boulevard, Suite 312
Rothgery, Kenneth P., (BV) ....'35 '69 C.251 A.B. L.1003 J.D. [Rothgery&Assoc.]
Rothgery & Associates, (BV) ....230 Third St.
Russell, Anson H. ....'26 '56 C.124 B.S. L.1003 J.D. P.O. Box 509
Saddler, H. McConnell, (CV) ....'26 '56 C.62 A.B. L.930 LL.B. 1059 Gulf Rd.
St. Marie, Paul R., (BV) .... '55 '81 C.97 B.A. L.1003 J.D. [St.Marie]
St. Marie, Thomas A., (AV) .... '46 '75 C.363 B.A. L.1003 J.D. [St.Marie]

St. Marie Law Firm Co., L.P.A., (AV)
409 East Avenue, Suite A, 44035
Telephone: 440-323-1808 FAX: 440-323-6135
Thomas A. St. Marie; Paul R. St. Marie; Margaret A. Hendershot. Associate Counsel: Gary C. Bennett.
General Civil and Criminal Practice. Insurance, Corporate, Foreclosure, Collections, Probate and Estate Planning, Banking Law, Real Estate, Personal Injury Law, Family/Domestic Relations. Trials and Appeals.
Representative Clients: Alco Manufacturing Corp.; PremierBank & Trust; American General Finance Inc.; Cascade Management Inc.; Tri-City Medical Services, Inc.; Plastic Components, Inc.
Approved Attorneys for: Farmers Home Administration; Ohio Bar Title Company.
Reference: PremierBank & Trust.

See Professional Biographies, ELYRIA, OHIO

Sanders, Bryan H. .... '60 '85 C.999 B.S. L.1288 J.D. V.P., Logos Develop. Corp.
Savoy, Jerome J., (BV) ....'45 '73 C.253 B.S. L.1003 J.D. 595 W. Broad St.
Schwartz, Richard Kenneth .... '56 '85 C&L.608 B.A., J.D. Mun. Ct. Mag.
Shilling, Terry S., (BV) ....'41 '68 C.610 A.B. L.608 J.D. 230 3rd St.
Silver, Michael D. ...... '54 '88 C.161 B.A. L.597 J.D. 347 Midway Boulevard, Suite 312
Smith, Stourton Scott ....'69 '95 C.610 B.A. L.879 J.D. [S.S.Smith] ⊙
Smith, Thomas J., (BV) ....'41 '66 C.610 B.S.C. L.608 J.D. [McCray,M.S.&M.]

Smith, Stourton Scott, Co., LPA
633 West Broad Street, Suite 200, 44035 ⊙
Telephone: 440-284-0101 Fax: 440-322-5509
Email: stourtonsmith@sbcglobal.net URL: http://www.aggressivelegalrep.com
Stourton Scott Smith.
Criminal Law, DWI, Bankruptcy, Personal Injury, Divorce, Family Law.
Cleveland, Ohio Office: 75 Public Square, Suite 800, 44113. Telephone: 216-344-9338. Fax: 216-344-9337.

See Professional Biographies, ELYRIA, OHIO

Spenzer, Sherry Newman, (BV) ....'53 '78 C.608 B.A. L.352 J.D. Asst. Pros. Atty.
Spike, Allen S., (AV) ....'39 '64 C.608 B.S. L.930 J.D. [Spike&M.]
Spike, Neil H. ....'69 '97 C.608 B.A. L.851 J.D. [Ⓐ Spike&M.]

Spike & Meckler Law Firm, The, LLP, (AV)
1551 West River Road North, 44035
Telephone: 440-324-5353 Fax: 440-324-5363
URL: http://www.spikemeckler.com
Members of Firm: Allen S. Spike; Stephen G. Meckler; Douglas M. Brill (Certified Specialist in Family Relations Law, Ohio State Bar Association); Michael D. Illner; James R. Couch. Associates: Neil H. Spike; Frank Charles Giamboi, II.
General Civil Trial Practice. Personal Injury, Medical Malpractice, Family and Domestic Relations, Real Estate, Probate.

See Professional Biographies, ELYRIA, OHIO

Springfield, Freddie M.W., (BV) .... '43 '81 C.62 B.A. L.1003 J.D. 114 Middle Ave.
Strait, Gerald E. ....'48 '78 C.610 B.A. L.161 J.D. Ref., Dom. Rel. Ct.
Swansinger, Laura Ann E. ....'67 '92 C.608 B.A. L.930 J.D. Co. Pros. Off.
Szekely, Michael, (BV) ....'49 '74 C.473 B.A. L.1003 J.D. 230 Third Street, Suite 200
Tassie, James G., (BV) ....'29 '55 C.62 A.B. L.930 LL.B. 300 4th Street
Taylor, James N., (BV) ....'56 '81 C.610 B.S. L.1003 J.D. [J.N.Taylor]
Taylor, William D., (BV) .... '50 '79 C.610 B.A. L.161 J.D. Exec. Dir., Legal Aid Soc.
Taylor, James N., Co., LPA, (BV) .... 409-B East Avenue
Tonry, Eugene A., (BV) .... '28 '57 C.62 B.A. L.1003 J.D. 105 Court St.
Ward, Susan Lee, (CV) ....'54 '92 C.798 B.S. L.1003 J.D. Ct., Admr., Dom. Rel.
West, Harold A., (BV) .... '29 '54 C&L.608 B.A., J.D. 212 Middle Ave.
White, Gregory A., (AV) ....'49 '77 C.381 B.A. L.161 J.D. Pros. Atty.
White, Robert C., (BV) .... '59 '91 C.161 B.A. L.1003 J.D. [Ⓐ Fauver,K.&D.L.&Assoc.]

Wickens, Herzer, Panza, Cook & Batista, A Legal Professional Association
(See Avon)

Wieber, Brett D. ....'75 '01 C.97 B.A. L.7 J.D. [Ⓐ Fauver,K.&D.L.&Assoc.]
Yanick, Michael Eli ....'57 '82 C.49 B.S. in B.A. L.989 J.D. First Merit Bank
Zafarana, Renee ....'56 '86 C.161 B.A. L.124 J.D. Domestic Relations Court
Zerbini, Elio P., (Co., L.P.A.), (BV) ...'34 '65 C.930 B.B.A. L.1003 J.D. 315 Middle Ave.
Zieba, Joseph C. .... '24 '51 C.610 B.A. L.930 LL.B. Dom. Ct. J.

ENGLEWOOD, 12,235, *Montgomery Co.*

Bloom, Jerome P. .... '19 '52 C.912 B.S.M. L.273 LL.B. 4460 Valley Brook Dr. (Pat.)
Crowell, Larry G., (BV) .... '41 '75 C.1229 B.M.E. L.151 J.D. [L.G.Crowell]
Crowell, Larry G., Co., L.P.A., (BV) ....207 S. Main St.
Geisenfeld, James R., (BV) ....'34 '58 C&L.966 B.S., LL.B. 440 South Main Street
Latessa, Anthony V. ....'71 '96 C&L.201 B.A., J.D. 5121 Seville Drive
Ledford, George W., (AV) ....'38 '74 C.999 B.S.I.E. L.1340 J.D. 23 N. Main St.
Titus, Gary L., (BV) .... '54 '84 C.608 B.A. L.201 J.D. 3754 Phillipsburg Union Rd.
Treherne, James E., (BV) ....'45 '73 C&L.607 B.A., J.D. 633 W. National Rd.

ENON, 2,605, *Clark Co.*

Berry, Timothy J., (BVⓉ) '57 '86 C.839 B.S. L.383 J.D.
(adm. in KY; not adm. in OH) Speedway SuperAmerica LLC
Cook, William R. .... '70 '98 C.97 B.A. L.150 J.D. Speedway SuperAmerica LLC
De La Cruz, Jaime J. .... '73 '00 C.450 B.A. L.607 J.D. Speedway SuperAmerica LLC
Dimitry, Edward S. .... '56 '84 C&L.201 B.S., J.D. Atty., Emro Marketing Company
Franz, Bernard E. '23 '51 C.679 B.S. L.602 LL.B.
(adm. in IN; not adm. in OH) 180 Davis Ave.‡
González, José Luis, Jr. '51 '84 C.502 B.J. L.851 J.D.
(adm. in IL; not adm. in OH) Atty., Speedway SuperAmerica LLC
Hollingsworth, David M., (BV) ....'53 '77 C.1208 B.A. L.851 J.D. 7602 Dayton Rd.
Williams, Ralph B. '45 '77
C.477 B.S. L.930 J.D. Sr. Coun., Speedway SuperAmerica LLC

EUCLID, 52,717, *Cuyahoga Co.*

Biggins, Mary Janice ....'51 '89 C.161 B.A. L.1003 J.D. [M.J.Biggins]
Biggins, Mary J. ....22551 Hadden Rd.
Brdar, Robert Allan ....'52 '84 C.161 B.B.A. L.1003 J.D. P.O. Box 32177
Cook, Schuyler Mouser ....'59 '88 [S.M.Cook]
Cook, Schuyler M., Esq. ....801 E. 232nd St.
Davies, William B., (BV) ....'55 '83 C.139 B.A. L.1003 J.D. [W.B.Davies]
Davies, William B., Co., L.P.A., (BV) ....21801 Lakeshore Blvd.
Deyo, Kenneth D., (BV) .... '37 '63 C.823 A.B. L.930 J.D. 27801 Euclid
Foti, Anthony L. ....'63 '88 C&L.608 B.S., J.D. 1233 East 222nd Street
Frye, Thomas E., Law Offices of '41 '72 C.608 B.A. L.1003 J.D.
22034 Lakeshore Blvd.
Gonakis, Spiros E., (AV) ....'50 '75 C.608 B.A. L.930 J.D. [S.E.Gonakis]
Gonakis, Spiros E., Company, L.P.A., (AV) .... 20050 Lakeshore Boulevard
Hribar, Joyce Ann ....'57 '89 C.161 B.A. L.1003 J.D. 27801 Euclid Ave., Ste. 500
Hribar, Paul J., (AV) ....'13 '41 C.363 Ph.B. L.161 J.D. 27801 Euclid Ave.
Johnson, Almeta A., (BV) ....'47 '71 C.369 A.B. L.608 J.D. 489 East 260th Street
Joyce, Margaret H. ....'58 '85 C.599 B.A. L.161 J.D. 19200 Newton Ave.
Kirn, John J., Jr., (AV) ....'41 '71 C.930 A.B. L.1003 J.D. 2004 S. Belvoir‡
Kordic, Gregory L. ....'48 '83 C.851 B.Ed. L.161 J.D. 1422 Euclid Avenue
Lavigna, Michael P., (BV) .... '47 '74 C.608 B.A. L.607 J.D. 27801 Euclid Ave.
LeBarron, Deborah Ann ....'59 '84 C.712 B.B.A. L.124 J.D. 555 East 222nd Street
Lynch, David M., (BV) ....'57 '82 C.363 B.A. L.276 J.D. 585 E. 222 Street

Mamrack, E. Daniel, (BV) '54 '79 C.318 B.A. L.1003 J.D.
27801 Euclid Avenue, Suite 500, 44132-3547
Telephone: 216-261-0200 Ext. 213 Fax: 216-261-7334
Email: edmatty@amenitech.net
Collections, Creditors Rights, Real Estate and Probate Law.

See Professional Biographies, EUCLID, OHIO

Molnar, Bruce F., (CV) .... '43 '74 C.610 B.B.A. L.1003 J.D. 25000 Euclid Ave.
Murphy, Gerald J. ....'25 '54 C.97 A.B. L.1003 LL.B. 573 E. 260th St.
Niccum, Robert F. ....'25 '57 C.608 B.A. L.1003 J.D. Mun. J.
Oyaski, Paul F. ....'52 '77 C.161 B.A. L.608 J.D. City Dir. of Law
Ozan, Gerald M., (BV) .... '31 '60 C.608 B.B.A. L.1003 J.D. [G.M.Ozan]
Ozan, Gerald M., Co., L.P.A., (BV) ....27691 Euclid Ave.
Pearl, Robert M. ....'37 '62 C.951 B.A. L.145 J.D. 26241 Lakeshore Boulevard
Perme, Michael R., (BV) .... '44 '74 C.363 A.B. L.1003 J.D. 27801 Euclid Ave.
Pigman, Edwin P. ....'50 '82 C.473 B.A. L.1003 J.D. 25000 Euclid Ave., Ste. 102
Polke, Dennis J. ....'53 '81 C.161 B.A. L.1003 J.D. 394 Walworth Ave.
Powall, Constance A. ....'64 '91 C.97 B.A.C. L.1003 J.D. 27801 Euclid Ave.
Quinn, Patrick D., (BV) ....'51 '76 C.477 B.A. L.1003 J.D. 2180 Lakeshore Blvd.
Roesmann, Matej ....'20 '55 L.930 LL.B. 22051 Hadden Road

Rosman, Barbara Goldberg
(See South Euclid)

Toma, Timothy N., (BV) ....'59 '87 C.201 B.S. L.930 J.D. 27801 Euclid Ave. Ste. 500
Vento, Phyllis Lucia .... '— '93 C.381 B.F.A. L.989 J.D. City of Euclid, Law Dept.

EVENDALE, 3,175, *Hamilton Co.*

Fletcher, Robert S. ....'70 '96 C.608 B.A. L.93 J.D. Coun., GE Aviation Services, Inc.

FAIRBORN, 32,052, *Greene Co.*

Barber, Catherine M. ....'47 '79 C.610 B.A. L.201 J.D. Mun. J.
Brezine, Donald F., (CV) ....'35 '84 C.424 A.B. L.215 J.D. [Carretta,C.B.]
Brown, Richard T., (CV) .... '50 '77 C.589 B.S. L.46 J.D. 2190 Gateway Dr.
Carretta, Cornish, Brezine & Co., L.P.A., (BV) .... 188 W. Hebble Ave.
Coates, Joseph A., (CV) .... '63 '88 C.385 B.S. L.201 J.D. P.O. Box 2185
Cornish, David R., (BV) .... '50 '76 C.608 B.A. L.607 J.D. [Carretta,C.B.]
Cusack, David J. ....'68 '94 C.1208 B.A. L.8 J.D. 510 West Main Street
Hall, Dennis L., (AV) ....'44 '69 C&L.150 B.A., J.D. [Hall&M.] ⊙
Hall & Mueller, A Legal Professional Association, (AV)
3040 Presidential Drive, Suite 222 (⊙Dayton)
Hess, Loren H. ....'47 '76 C.494 B.A. L.489 J.D. Mgr., Grumman Data Systems
Houston, Douglas G., Attorney at Law '62 '95
C.608 B.S.B.A. L.201 J.D. 1158 Kauffman Ave.
Johnson, Giselle S. ....'61 '86 C.477 B.A. L.607 J.D. 188 W. Hebble Ave.‡
Katchman, Steven C., (CV) ....'60 '89 C.150 B.A. L.201 J.D. [ⓒ Hall&M.]
Kramer, Thomas G., (BV) '57 '83
C.610 B.B.A. L.150 J.D. 640 E. Dayton Yellow Springs Rd.
Martin, John O., (AV) ....'37 '61 C.742 B.S. L.930 LL.B. [Martin,M.R.&W.]
Martin, McCarty, Richman & Wright Co., L.P.A., (AV) ....26 N. Wright Ave.
Mayer, Michael A., (BV) ....'65 '94 C.473 B.S. L.851 J.D. [G.E.Schlafman]
McCarty, William R., (AV) ....'33 '58 C.473 A.B. L.477 LL.B. [Martin,M.R.&W.]
Miles, David R., (BV) .....'55 '81 C.967 B.A. L.851 J.D. 125 West Main Street, Suite 201
Morse, David Robert ....'47 '00 C.734 A.B. L.1187 J.D. 188 W. Hebble Ave.
Mueller, Carolyn L., (BV) .... '46 '95 C.994 B.A. L.201 J.D. [Hall&M.] ⊙
Perry, Monique Marie ....'68 '94 75 Loretta Avenue
Richman, S. Richard, (AV) .... '24 '50 C.994 B.A. L.128 J.D. [Martin,M.R.&W.]
Root, Beth Wilhelm ....'66 '92 C.473 B.A. L.608 J.D. Mag.
Schlafman, Gerald E., (AV) ...... '30 '54 C&L.608 B.A., J.D. City Solr. [G.E.Schlafman]
Schlafman, Gerald E., Co., L.P.A., (AV) ....510 W. Main St.
Vaughn, Robert A., (AV) ....'30 '59 C.473 A.B. L.477 J.D. 2628 Colonel Glenn Hwy.
Welch, William H. '17 '42 C&L.16 LL.B.
(adm. in AL; not adm. in OH) 1 1/2 S. Central Ave.‡

Wilson, Y. Nicole ....'78 '03 C.952 B.A. L.851 J.D. 26 N. Wright Avenue
Wolaver, Stephen A., (BV) ....'50 '75 C.473 B.S. L.879 J.D. Chf. Trial Coun.
Wright, Gary E., (AV) ....'52 '78 C.473 B.S. L.608 J.D. [Martin,M.R.&W.]

FAIRFIELD, 42,097, *Butler Co.*

Atwell, Kevin H. ....'60 '85 C.473 B.S. L.150 J.D. 5670 Dixie Highway
Balzano, David J. '61 '93 C.150 B.B.A. L.1340 J.D.
Staff Coun., Cincinnati Insurance Co.
Berlon, Henry G., Jr. ....'33 '65 C.363 B.S. L.1003 J.D. 6200 S. Gilmore Rd.
Bruewer, Henry J. ....'23 '49 C.973 L.150 J.D. 521 Vinnedge Court
Campbell, Joyce Ann ....'58 '88 C&L.930 B.A., J.D. 4951 Dixie Highway
Carter, Bruce, Law Office of ....'56 '91 C.437 B.A. L.8 J.D. 5458 Yosemite Dr.
Clemmons, John H., (BV) ....'51 '76 C.473 B.S. L.150 J.D. [Millikin&F.]
Conliff, Charles Michael, (CV) ....'61 '92 C.473 B.S. L.150 J.D. 6660 Dixie Hwy.
Cracas, Teresa C. ....'65 '98 C.608 B.S. L.1340 J.D. Assoc. Coun., Cincinnati Ins. Co.
Crane, Debra K. '57 '96 C.150 B.B.A. L.1161 J.D.
Sr. Vice President & Corporate counsel, Ohio Casualty Insurance Company
DeCresce, Michele Ann ....'56 '91 C.381 B.S.Ed. L.7 J.D. [M.A.DeCresce]
DeCresce, Michele A. ....5458 Yosemite Dr.
Eichhold, Paul R., Sr. ....'28 '60 C.150 B.B.A. L.1340 J.D. 1512 Evalie Dr.‡
Felerski, Heather ....'67 '91 C.347 B.A. L.150 J.D. P.O. Box 181342
Fox, Jonathan N., (BV) ....'54 '88 C.117 B.A. L.150 J.D. 1251 Nilles Road, Suite 10
Gelfand, Eugene M. ....'45 '71 C.607 B.A. L.1003 J.D. Coun., Cincinnati Ins. Co.
Gordon, Abram S. ....'63 '87 C&L.94 B.A., J.D. The Kroll-O'Gara Co.
Gressel, Michele M., (BV) ....'52 '78 C.347 B.A. L.201 J.D. [Millikin&F.]
Grove, Jack F., (BV) ....'53 '79 C.608 B.S. L.201 J.D. 1251 Nilles Rd.
Kyrios, Helen ....'71 '98 C.473 B.A. L.1340 J.D. Staff Coun., Cincinnati Ins. Co.
Lewis, G. Gregory '53 '79
C.150 B.A. L.117 J.D. Coun. & Dep. Gen. Mgr., Cincinnati Ins. Co.
Lierman, Dale O., (BV) ....'42 '77 C&L.150 A.B., J.D. [D.O.Lierman]
Lierman, Dale O., L.P.A., Company, (BV) .... 1244 Nilles Road, Suite 9
Love, Lisa A. '59 '91 C.838 B.S. L.1340 J.D.
Assoc. Coun. & Mgr., Insur. Op. Div., Cincinnati Ins. Co.
McMackin, Thomas K. ... '55 '80 C.430 B.A. L.150 J.D. Assoc. Coun., Cincinnati Ins. Co.
Meyer, Barry A. ....'50 '76 C.150 B.A. L.1340 J.D. Assoc. Coun., Cincinnati Ins. Co.
Miller, Kimberly Vashon '68 '95 C.608 B.A. L.201 J.D.
Cincinnati Financial Corporation

Millikin & Fitton Law Firm, A Legal Professional Association, (AV)
530 Wessel Drive, Suite 2A, 45014 ⊙
Telephone: 513-829-6700 Fax: 513-829-0258
John H. Clemmons; Michele M. Gressel; Stephen J. Wolterman.
General Practice. Real Estate, Probate, Estate Planning, Corporation, Taxation, Family Law and Litigation.
Hamilton, Ohio Office: 6 S 2nd Street, 6th Floor, 45011. Telephone: 513-863-6700. Fax: 513-863-0031.
Oxford, Ohio Office: 5020 B College Corner Pike, 45056. Telephone: 513-523-3700. Fax: 513-523-0463.
Mason, Ohio Office: 6900 Tylersvile Road, Suite B, 45040. Telephone: 513-336-6363. Fax: 513-336-9411.

Moser, Donald K., (BV) ....'58 '86 C.880 B.A. L.945 J.D. [Moser]
Moser Law Firm LLC, (BV) .... 1040 Symmes Rd.
Packer, Dennis Michael ....'59 '92 C.477 B.S. L.150 J.D. 100 Commercial Drive
Piper, Robert N., III, (BV) ....'53 '82 C.473 B.A. L.200 J.D. [Piper]
Piper Law Offices, (BV) ....890 Abbot Drive
Pustinger, David Alan '62 '97
C.999 B.S.B.A. L.150 J.D. Ast. V.P. Mkgt., Ohio Casualty Ins. Co., The
Schnell, James M., (BV) ....'43 '73 C&L.150 B.A., J.D. 1251 Nilles Road
Semple, Kathleen M. ....'57 '83 C.1260 B.A. L.150 J.D. 5494 Boehm Drive
Skinner, Matthew R. ....'65 '91 C.150 B.S. L.201 J.D. Staff Coun., Cincinnati Ins. Co.
Spaeth, Keith M. ....'61 '86 C.679 B.S. L.201 J.D. Mun. J.
Stofel, Steven F. '56 '01
C.767 B.S. L.1340 J.D. Staff Coun., Cincinnati Insurance Company
Thompson, Grace H., (CV) ....'35 '86 C&L.150 B.A., J.D. 1116B Hicks Blvd.
Wear, Maxwell N., (BV) ....'35 '67 C.150 B.S. L.1340 J.D. P.O. Box 218
Wolterman, Stephen J. ....'69 '94 C.607 B.S.B.A. L.150 J.D. [Millikin&F.]

FAIRLAWN, 7,307, *Summit Co.*

Beatty, Kenneth M. ....'53 '79 C.8 B.S. L.7 J.D. 175 Ghent Rd.
Bonsky, Jack A. ....'38 '64 C.610 A.B. L.608 J.D. 175 Ghent Rd.‡
Cochran, Charles J., Jr., (CV) ....'57 '90 C&L.8 B.A., J.D. 41 Merz Blvd.
DeCamp, Clifford L., (BV) .....'58 '85 C.980 B.A. L.8 J.D. 3250 W. Market St., Ste. 203
DeCamp Roth & Devany, (BV) .... 3250 West Market Street
Devany, David M., (BV) ....'60 '85 C.381 B.B.A. L.7 J.D. [DeCamp R.&D.]
Ennis, Charles R. ....'32 '58 C.197 A.B. L.178 J.D. 175 Ghent Rd.‡
Fairfax, Terry ....'64 '97 C.8 B.A. L.7 J.D. 55 South Miller Road
Garson, Harold M. ....'16 '40 C.608 L.7 LL.B. 286 N. Cleveland Massillon Rd.
Graves, James R., (Co. L.P.A.), (BV) '29 '57
C.8 A.B. L.7 J.D. Dir. of Law, City of Fairlawn
Groner, Betty, The Law Office of, (BV) .....'48 '85 C.966 B.S. L.8 J.D. P.O. Box 13514
Haueisen, Anthony J. '45 '72 C.728 B.S. L.500 J.D.
V.P. & Gen. Coun., RJF Intl. Corp.
Humphrey, Michael B. ....'54 '85 C&L.8 B.S., J.D. P.O. Box 13326
Kalavity, Louis, (CV) ....'32 '65 C.145 B.A. L.8 J.D. 3161 Morewood Rd.
Kostoff, Thomas W., (BV) ....'54 '80 C.8 B.A. L.7 J.D. 41 Merz Blvd.
Kroeger, Tia M. ....'60 '94 C.93 B.A. L.117 J.D. 334 Fieldcrest Drive
LeMay, James C. '56 '82 C.97 B.S. L.608 J.D.
Sr. V.P., Bus. Devel. & Gen. Coun., OMNOVA Solutions, Inc.
Lowry, David M., Attorney at Law, (BV) '54 '82
C.608 B.S. L.7 J.D. 66 S. Miller Rd., Ste. 100
Mack, Michael R., (BV) ....'45 '73 C&L.8 B.S.I.M., J.D. [M.R.Mack]
Mack, Michael R., Co., L.P.A., (BV) ....34 Merz Blvd., Ste. B
Nace, R. Bryan, (BV) ....'59 '85 C.8 B.A. L.7 J.D. 3250 W. Market St., Ste. 203
Nagucki, Robert E., (BV) '67 '93 C.385 B.A. L.851 J.D.
Assist. Gen. Coun, OMNOVA Solutions, Inc.
Robbins, Howard S. ....'51 '77 C.608 B.S.E.E. L.8 J.D. 2521 Durand Rd. (Pat.)
Roth, William J., Jr., (BV) ....'58 '83 C.1044 B.A. L.7 J.D. [DeCamp R.&D.]
Roush, George W. ....'18 '47 C&L.477 A.B., LL.B. 341 Edmore Rd.‡
Syrvalin, Kristine C. '68 '93 C.473 B.A. L.930 J.D.
Corp Sec. and Assist. Gen. Coun., OMNOVA Solutions, Inc.

Yashnik, Steven L., (BV) ....'60 '85 C.8 B.S. L.7 J.D. 3250 W. Market Street, Suite 14

FAIRPORT HARBOR, 3,180, *Lake Co.*

Brigham, Anne T. ....'50 '99 C.8 B.S. L.989 J.D. 679 2nd St., Unit 11

FAIRVIEW PARK, 17,572, *Cuyahoga Co.*

Bennett, Robert T., (AV) ....'39 '67 C.608 B.S. L.1003 J.D. 4800 Valley Pkwy.
Bryan, Bradric T. ....'65 '90 C.951 B.A. L.930 J.D. 22050 Mastick Road
Carlin, Hugh A., Attorney at Law, (AV) '52 '83 C.161 B.A. L.7 J.D.
21270 Lorain Road
Companey, Roy T. ....'30 '59 C&L.930 B.B.A., LL.B. 4090 West 226th
Despins, Martin P., (CV) ......'36 '72 C.976 B.A. L.1003 J.D. 19510 Lorain Rd., Ste. 303
Dever, Veronica M., (BV) ....'40 '70 C.876 A.B. L.1003 J.D. Asst. Co. Pros.
Esber, Kevin James ....'78 '04 C.97 L.989 J.D. 22050 Mastick Road
Fox, Thomas Charles, Jr. ....'57 '92 C.381 B.S. L.989 J.D. 21300 Lorain Road
Griswold, Desmond Richard ....'65 '93 19443 Lorain Rd.
Hildebrand, John Patrick, Jr. ....'70 '97 C.608 B.S.B.A. L.161 J.D. 22050 Mastick Rd.
Kowalski, Theodore R. ....'35 '67 C.251 B.B.A. L.1003 J.D. 20777 Lorain Rd
Kreps, Robert C., (BV) ....'48 '75 C.62 B.A. L.1003 J.D. 21400 Lorain Rd.
Krupansky, Blanche E. ....'25 '49 C&L.930 A.B., J.D. Ret. Ct. App. J.
Markus, Richard M., (AV) ......'30 '54 C.597 B.S. L.309 J.D. Private Judicial Serv., Inc.‡
Mazanec, Rosaleen K. ....'55 '80 C.860 B.A. L.930 J.D. 21867 N. Park Dr.
McCrone, Kathleen A. ....'— '89 C.201 B.A. L.1003 J.D. 22649 Lorain Rd.
McGowan, Thomas B., III '45 '69
C.321 A.B. L.477 J.D. Pres., McGowan & Company, Inc.
McGowan, Thomas B., IV ......'70 '96 C.1030 B.A. L.734 J.D. McGowan & Company Inc.
Mills, Richard B. ....'27 '58 C.610 L.1003 LL.B. 3722 Addington Court
Murphy, Eugene D. ....'27 '51 C.62 B.A. L.930 J.D. 18879 Timber Ln.
Nanowsky, Gail A. ....'57 '91 C.980 B.A. L.161 J.D. 21020 Seabury Ave.
Penfield, George R., (BV) ....'44 '70 C.381 A.B. L.1003 J.D. 19443 Lorain Rd.
Rini, Charles A., Jr. ....'64 '92 C.363 B.A. L.1003 J.D. V.P., Rini Realty Co.
Smith, Victoria Nagy, Law Office of ...'70 '95 C.97 B.A. L.989 J.D. 22050 Mastick Road
Streeter, David Allen, JR. ....'75 '01 C.321 B.A. L.124 J.D. 22050 Mastick Road
Wagoner, Byron Richmond, Jr. '41 '70
C.967 B.S. L.851 J.D. 22021 Brookpark Road, Suite 100

FAYETTE, 1,248, *Fulton Co.*

Molitierno, Thomas, (CV) ....'47 '82 C.203 B.A. L.851 J.D. 104 E. Main St.

FAYETTEVILLE, 372, *Brown Co.*

Tissandier, Stephen J., (CV) ....'64 '90 C.973 B.A. L.150 J.D. 73 E. Pike St.

FELICITY, 856, *Clermont Co.*

Motta, Alan C. ....'60 '86 C.608 B.S. L.150 J.D. [A.C.Motta]
Motta, Alan Curtiss .... 2783 Bert Reed Road

FINDLAY, * 38,967, *Hancock Co.*

Alge, William S., Jr., (BV) ....'46 '73 C&L.607 B.A., J.D. [Snyder&A.]
Alt, Damon D. ....'77 '04 C.476 B.B.A. L.851 J.D. [D.D.Alt]

Alt, Damon D., Attorney at Law, L.L.C.
612 S. Main Street, Suite 105, 45840
Telephone: 419-425-0455 Fax: 419-425-0045
URL: http://www.altlawfirm.com
Damon D. Alt.
General Practice. Business Law, Taxation, Estate Planning and Probate Law.
See Professional Biographies, FINDLAY, OHIO

Andes, Ronald L. '44 '88
C.645 Fuel Sci. L.229 J.D. Sr. Atty., Marathon Ashland Petroleum LLC
Armstrong, Mark F. '47 '81 C.1108 B.S. L.776 J.D.
V.P., Cooper Tire & Rubber Company
Barto, Vincent A. ....'57 '85 C&L.150 B.Ch.E., J.D. Marathon Ashland Petroleum LLC
Bauer, Bernard K., (AV) ....'47 '72 C.203 A.B. L.607 J.D. [B.K.Bauer]

Bauer, Bernard K., Co., L.P.A., (AV) BR
410 West Sandusky Street, Suite One, 45840
Telephone: 419-423-2673 FAX: 419-423-2127
Email: bauertrial@turbosurf.net
Bernard K. Bauer.
Civil Litigation and Appellate Practice. Personal Injury, Products Liability and Medical and Legal Malpractice.
See Professional Biographies, FINDLAY, OHIO

Baumgartner-Novak, Patti, (CV) '66 '91
C.313 B.S. L.851 J.D. 612 S. Main Street, Suite 105
Behrendt, Elizabeth A. Putnam ....'69 '94 C.473 B.S. L.124 J.D. [A Betts,M.&R.]
Bennett, Sandra L. '55 '82 C&L.602 B.B.A., J.D.
(adm. in NY; not adm. in OH) 401 Mona Lane★
Benson, Jeffrey L. '50 '76 C&L.608 B.A., J.D.
Sr. Grp. Coun., Marathon Ashland Petroleum LLC
Betts, Christopher D. ....'71 '97 C.317 B.A. L.607 J.D. Asst. Pros. Atty.
Betts, Stephen C., (AV) ....'47 '73 C.610 B.B.A. L.607 J.D. [Betts,M.&R.]

Betts, Miller & Russo, (AV)
101 West Sandusky Street, 45840
Telephone: 419-422-5565 Fax: 419-423-1868
Email: mail@bmrattorneys.com
John E. Betts (1863-1935); Richard A. Betts (1911-1996); Jackson E. Betts (1904-1993). Members of Firm: Stephen C. Betts; Roger L. Miller; Ralph D. Russo. Associate: Elizabeth A. Putnam Behrendt.
General Civil Practice. Probate and Estate Planning, Corporations, Real Estate, Insurance Defense, Personal Injury, Medical Malpractice, Family/Domestic Relations, Commercial, and Insurance Law. Trials and Appeals in all Courts.
Representative Clients: The Arlington Natural Gas Co., Van Buren, Ohio; Findlay Pub. Co.; Nationwide Insurance Co.; Bank One, NA; The Ohio Bank; Physicians Insurance Co. of Ohio.
See Professional Biographies, FINDLAY, OHIO

Beutler, Robert A., Jr., (BV) ....'44 '71 C.608 B.S. L.117 J.D. [Hackenberg,B.&R.]
Breidenbach, David Carl '51 '77 C.610 B.S. L.608 J.D.
Marathon Ashland Petroleum LLC
Brimley, J. Bruce, (BV) ....'49 '78 C.97 B.L.S. L.1048 J.D. [Brimley]
Brimley Law Firm, L.L.C., (BV) ....337 S. Main St., Ste. 300
Brown, Garth W., (CV) ....'68 '93 C.424 B.A. L.221 J.D. [Drake,P.K.&C.]
Brucklacher, James F. ....'23 '50 C.207 A.B. L.930 LL.B. 560 Deer Lake Dr.‡
Callahan-Brown, Linda J. '65 '93
C&L.851 B.A., J.D. Atty., Marathon Ashland Petroleum LLC
Campbell, Dow L. ....'61 '90 C.473 B.A. L.326 J.D. Marathon Oil Company
Candler, Elizabeth, (BV) ....'44 '80 C.643 B.A. L.607 J.D. 131 Hancock St.
Carson, Loretta A., (CV) ....'52 '82 C.97 B.S. L.1003 J.D. Dom. Rel. Mas.
Cervenka, Albert W. '30 '57 C.714 A.B. L.326 LL.B.
(adm. in TX; not adm. in OH) 601 Orchardl Ln.‡

Christopher, Steven D., (BV) '58 '84
C&L.607 B.S.B.A., J.D. 330 South Main Street (⊙Kenton)
Clark, Kristi L. .... '— '96 C.631 B.A. L.608 J.D. 539 S. Main St.
Clark, William E., (AV) .... '43 '68 C.253 B.A. L.607 J.D. [Drake,P.K.&C.]
Coleman, Kenneth E. '47 '73 C&L.923 B.A., J.D.
(adm. in WV; not adm. in OH) Senior Attorney, Marathon Ashland Petroleum LLC
Collette, Anni W. '52 '79 C.383 B.A. L.1206 J.D.
(adm. in FL; not adm. in OH) 1128 S. Main St.
Collette, Daniel K.C. '46 '71 C&L.607 B.A., J.D.
Asst. Co. Pros., Hancock Co. Pros. Off.
Combs, James J. '41 '67
(adm. in NY; not adm. in OH) Inter. Coun., Cooper Tire & Rubber Co.
Compson, John E. .... '27 '52 C&L.608 B.A., J.D. 858 Washington Ave.‡

Contrada & Associates
(See Toledo)

Crow, Robroy Lee, (CV) .... '56 '86 C.608 B.A. L.911 J.D. [Crow]
Crow Law Offices, Ltd., (CV) .... 124 W. Front St., Ste. 204
Culp Claypool, Patricia "Beth" '63 '88
C.437 B.S. L.1015 J.D. Marathon Ashland Petroleum LLC
Davenport, Julie A. .... '53 '79 C.97 B.S. L.851 J.D. [Ⓐ Oxley,M.H.O.&W.]
Davis, Allan H. .... '43 '68 C.97 B.S. L.607 J.D. Prob. J.
Downing, Robert B. .... '24 '56 C.207 B.A. L.802 LL.B. 139 Woodley Ave.‡
Drake, Robert W., (AV) .... '17 '48 C.253 B.A. L.607 J.D. [Drake,P.K.&C.]
Drake, Thomas D., (AV) .... '52 '77 C.602 B.A. L.607 J.D. [Drake,P.K.&C.]

Drake, Phillips, Kuenzli & Clark, (AV)
Suite 3, 301 South Main Street, 45840
Telephone: 419-423-0242 Telecopier: 419-423-0186
URL: http://www.findlaylaw.com
Members of Firm: Lloyd D. Phillips (1928-1994); Robert W. Drake; David P. Kuenzli; William E. Clark; Thomas D. Drake; John D. Oman; Philip L. Rooney; Garth W. Brown;—Christie L. Ranzau. Of Counsel: William E. Ruse.
General Civil and Criminal Practice. Corporation, Probate and Estate Planning, Family and Domestic Relations, Real Estate, Municipal and Creditor's Rights. Trials and Appeals.
See Professional Biographies, FINDLAY, OHIO

Eastman & Smith Ltd., (AV)
725 South Main Street, 45840 ⊙
Telephone: 419-424-5847 Fax: 419-424-9860
URL: http://www.eastmansmith.com
Member of Firm: John H. Koehler.
General Civil Practice: Corporate, Business, Banking, Taxation, Real Estate, Securities, Antitrust, Environmental, Public, Labor and Employment, Civil Rights, Employee Benefits, Insurance, Hospital and Health Care, Estate Planning, Pension and Estate Planning, Probate, Workers Compensation, Commercial Litigation, Litigation, Immigration and Naturalization.
Toledo, Ohio, Office: One Seagate, Twenty-Fourth Floor, P.O. Box 10032, 43699-0032. Telephone: 419-241-6000. Fax: 419-247-1777.
Columbus, Ohio, Office: 100 East Broad Street, Suite 1300, 43215. Telephone: 614-280-1770. Fax: 614-280-1777.
See Professional Biographies, FINDLAY, OHIO

Ellerbe, James M., Law Office of, (BVⓣ) '57 '84 C.170 B.A. L.972 J.D.
(adm. in WY; not adm. in OH) 330 Greenlawn Ave.

Elliott, Howard A., (BV) '57 '86 C&L.607 B.A., J.D.
330 South Main Street, 45840
Telephone: 419-422-7178 Fax: 419-424-8882
Email: theboyes@aol.com
Civil Litigation, Family, Divorce, Criminal, Real Estate, Wills and Probate, Trusts and Estates, Estate Planning, Debtor and Creditor Bankruptcy.
See Professional Biographies, FINDLAY, OHIO

Evans, Thomas D. '55 '80
C.207 B.A. L.851 J.D. Sr. Atty., Marathon Ashland Petroleum LLC
Everett, Robert W., (BVⓣ) '53 '88
C.608 B.S.C.E. L.117 J.D. Marathon Ashland Petroleum LLC
Farmer, C. Eugene, Jr. '61 '86
C.92 B.S. L.607 J.D. Atty., Marathon Ashland Petroleum LLC
Feighner, Robert E., Jr. .... '73 '99 C.97 B.S.B.A. L.607 J.D. [Ⓐ Hackenberg,B.&R.]

Firmin, Sprague & Huffman Co., L.P.A., (AV)
220 West Sandusky Street, P.O. Box 963, 45839
Telephone: 419-423-4321 Fax: 419-423-8484
Email: fshlaw@fshlaw.net
John C. Firmin (1917-2005); Robert F. Sprague; Douglas W. Huffman; Thomas P. Kemp; Stephen A. Roepke. Associate: Matthew L. Klein.
General Civil Practice. Probate and Estate Planning, Corporation, Computer, Commercial, Taxation and Real Estate Law. Trials.
Representative Clients: National Lime & Stone Co.; The Hercules Tire & Rubber Co.; TLB, Inc. (Solomon Software).
Approved Attorneys for: Chicago Title Insurance Co.; The Mutual Benefit Life Insurance Co.
See Professional Biographies, FINDLAY, OHIO

Fitzgerald, Dennis M., (AV) .... '51 '76 C.602 B.A. L.608 J.D. [Fitzgerald]

Fitzgerald Law Firm LLC, (AV)
400 South Main Street, 45840
Telephone: 419-420-9312 Fax: 419-420-9314
Email: fitzgerald@findlayfitzlaw.com
Members: Dennis M. Fitzgerald; Bret A. Spaeth. Associate: Drew J. Mihalik.
Personal Injury, Products Liability, Insurance, Trusts and Estates, Wills and Probate.
See Professional Biographies, FINDLAY, OHIO

Flannery, Matthew C. '67 '94 C.659 B.A. L.831 J.D.
(adm. in PA; not adm. in OH) Sr. Litig. Coun., Cooper Tire & Rubber Co.
Flowers, Richard W., (CV) .... '50 '96 C.885 B.S. L.607 J.D. 219 S. Main St.
Foster, William C., (AV) .... '14 '41 C.97 L.607 J.D. 100 E. Main Cross
Furr, Christine R. .... '65 '98 L.117 J.D. Dir., Reg. Planning Comm.
Gaberman, Robert N., (CV) .... '32 '56 C&L.912 B.A., J.D. 1995 Tiffin Ave.
Gagle, Suzanne ... '65 '92 C&L.851 B.B.A., J.D. Atty., Marathon Ashland Petroleum LLC
Galiber, Rochelle B. ..... '56 '86 C.222 B.A. L.705 J.D. Marathon Ashland Petroleum LLC
Galose, Michael Carmen .... '57 '90 C.980 B.S. L.7 J.D. Co. Pub. Def.'s Off.
Gearheart, James W. '62 '88 C&L.383 B.S., J.D.
(adm. in TX; not adm. in OH) Marathon Ashland Petroleum LLC
Gompf, Clayton N., Jr. '46 '72 C.269 B.A. L.790 J.D.
(adm. in SC; not adm. in OH) Sr. Litig. Coun., Cooper Tire & Rubber Co.
Griffin, Daniel Alexander '71 '96
C.363 B.A. L.607 J.D. Marathon Ashland Petroleum LLC
Hackenberg, Alan D., (CV) .... '69 '94 C.150 B.B.A. L.607 J.D. [Hackenberg,B.&R.]
Hackenberg, David A., (BV) '39 '68 C.313 B.A. L.607 J.D.
Law Dir. [Hackenberg,B.&R.]
Hackenberg, Beutler & Rasmussen, (BV) .... 314 W. Crawford, Mezzanine Level
Haffenden, Philip E. '59 '84 C.477 B.A. L.117 J.D.
Sr. Group Coun., Marathon Ashland Petroleum LLC

Hales, Steven C.
(See Toledo)

Hampton, Kent B., (AV) .... '20 '49 C.293 A.B. L.477 J.D. 605 Sutton Pl.‡
Hancock, Paul D. '53 '78 C.980 A.B. L.851 J.D.
Grp. Coun., Envir., Marathon Ashland Petroleum LLC
Hawkins, Jeffrey V., (CV) .... '61 '87 103 E. Sandusky St.
Higgins, Patterson William .... '44 '72 C&L.851 B.B.A., J.D. [P.Higgins]
Higgins, Patterson .... 1175 Main St.
Hollister, Robert B., (AV) .... '40 '77 C.793 B.S. L.607 J.D. [Oxley,M.H.O.&W.]
Horstman, Richard L. .... '53 '78 C.1024 B.A. L.607 J.D. Marathon Oil Co.
Huffman, Douglas W., (AV) .... '51 '76 C.679 B.S. L.477 J.D. [Firmin,S.&H.]
Hunziker, Robin Morris '63 '92
C.879 B.S.E.E. L.851 J.D. Atty., Marathon Ashland Petroleum LLC
Jetton, Girard R., Jr. .... '24 '51 C.273 B.S. L.309 LL.B. 170 Orchard Lane‡
Johnson, Kristen Kaiser '65 '93
C.1213 B.S. L.851 J.D. Hancock County Assistant Prosecutor
Jordan, Michael F. '48 '76 C.1019 B.A. L.1009 J.D.
(adm. in NY; not adm. in OH) Sr. Atty., Marathon Ashland Petroleum LLC
Kaiman, Stan C., (BV) '38 '65
C.546 B.S.M.E. L.273 LL.B. Secy., Cooper Tire & Rubber Co. (Pat.)
Kemp, Thomas P., (BV) .... '53 '78 C&L.602 B.A., J.D. [Firmin,S.&H.]
Kissh, John A., Jr., (BV) '40 '76 C.608 B.Sc. L.851 J.D.
Co. Child Support Enforce. Agcy.
Klein, Matthew L. .... '71 '01 C.97 B.S. in B.A. L.602 J.D. [Ⓐ Firmin,S.&H.]
Kline, James E. '41 '66 C.363 B.S. L.608 J.D.
V.P., Gen. Coun. & Secy., Cooper Tire & Rubber Co.
Koehler, John H., (BV) .... '50 '79 C.253 B.S. L.851 J.D. [Eastman&S.] (⊙Toledo)
Kose, William Henrik .... '46 '86 C.608 M.D. L.607 J.D. 200 W. Pearl St.‡

Kostyo, John F. '55 '81 C.363 B.A. L.930 J.D.
1100 E. Main Cross Street, Suite 200, 45840
Telephone: 419-422-7700 Fax: 419-425-0042
Email: jfk@kostyolaw.com URL: http://www.kostyolaw.com
Banks and Banking, Creditor Bankruptcy, Commercial Law, Civil Litigation, Contractor/Construction Law, Family Law.
See Professional Biographies, FINDLAY, OHIO

Kuenzli, David P., (AV) .... '36 '64 C.610 A.B. L.608 J.D. [Drake,P.K.&C.]
Land, Lucinda M., (CV) '63 '89
C&L.607 B.A., J.D. Asst. Co. Pros., Hancock Co. Pros. Off.
Larick, Barbara Doane, (BV) .... '40 '85 C.97 B.F.A. L.607 J.D. 219 S. Main Street
Lather, Kenneth L., (BV) .... '52 '78 C.473 B.S. L.607 J.D. 725 S. Main St.
Lay, Lisa A., (BV) '69 '94 C&L.150 B.A., J.D.
Atty., Marathon Ashland Petroleum LLC
Lichtinger, Michele M. '65 '90 C.1367 B.A. L.851 J.D.
(adm. in MI; not adm. in OH)
Corp. Coun., American Family Debt Counseling Ctrs., Inc.

Liming, Roxi A.
(See Columbus)

Maekask, Paul Vladimir .... '70 '97 C.679 B.A. L.607 J.D. Pub. Def.
Magee, Timothy A., Law Office of .... '63 '96 C.1044 B.A. L.150 J.D. 130 Sherman Drive
Maguire, John K. .... '55 '83 C.607 B.A. L.851 J.D. Marathon Ashland Petroleum LLC
Malone, Michael J., (AV) .... '47 '73 C.1024 B.S. L.607 J.D. [Oxley,M.H.O.&W.]
Marks, R. Edward .... '58 '88 C.575 B.A. L.352 J.D. ABLE, Inc.
McCracken, Jack J. '63 '90 C.645 B.S. L.607 J.D.
Assist. Sec., Cooper Tire & Rubber Co. (Pat.)
McMath, Tracy L. .... '62 '88 C.473 B.S. L.150 J.D. 11085 County Rd. 40
Melin, Douglas R. '54 '78
C.62 B.A. L.1003 J.D. Sr. Atty., Marathon Ashland Petroleum LLC
Meyers, Gregory E., (BV) '52 '77 C.473 B.A. L.607 J.D.
Assist Gen. Coun., Cooper Tire & Rubber Company
Mihalik, Drew J. .... '78 '04 C.253 B.A. L.851 J.D. [Ⓐ Fitzgerald]
Miller, Roger L., (AV) .... '45 '73 C.473 B.A. L.966 J.D. [Betts,M.&R.]
Needles, J. Stanley, (BV) .... '42 '69 C.611 B.A. L.607 J.D. 219 S. Main St.
Niemeyer, Joseph H. .... '49 '75 C.973 B.A. L.607 J.D. Com. Pleas J.
Noble, John D. .... '36 '61 C.203 B.A. L.607 J.D. 230 Crystal Ave.
Noggle, Michael C., (BV) .... '61 '86 C.97 B.A. L.851 J.D. [Noggle]

Noggle Law Office, LLC, (BV)
101 West Sandusky Street, Suite 200 C, 45840
Telephone: 419-422-1887 Fax: 419-422-1830
Email: attynoggle@ameritech.net URL: http://www.nogglelawoffice.com
Michael C. Noggle.
Trusts and Estates, Real Estate, Business Law, Elder Law, Estate Planning.
See Professional Biographies, FINDLAY, OHIO

O'Malley, Michael E., (BV) '42 '68 C.276 A.B. L.930 J.D.
[Oxley,M.H.O.&W.] & [M.E.O'Malley] (⊙Ottawa)
Oman, John D., (BV) .... '57 '82 C.607 B.A. L.608 J.D. [Drake,P.K.&C.]

Oxley, Malone, Hollister, O'Malley & Warren, P.L.L., (AV) BR
301 East Main Cross Street, P.O. Box 1086, 45840
Telephone: 419-422-8713 Fax: 419-422-6495
Email: oxleylaw@oxleylaw.com
Members of Firm: Garver Oxley (1919-1997); Michael J. Malone; Robert B. Hollister; Michael E. O'Malley; Bradley S. Warren. Of Counsel: Julie A. Davenport.
General Civil and Trial Practice. Probate and Estate Planning, Insurance Defense Personal Injury, Family and Domestic Relations, Bankruptcy, Real Estate, Medical Malpractice Defense, Products Liability Law and Appellate Practice.
Representative Clients: CNA Insurance Co.; Hancock-Wood Electric Cooperative, Inc.; Buckeye State Mutual Insurance Co.; American States Insurance Co.; Auto-Owners Insurance Co.; Western Reserve Group; Buckeye State Mutual Insurance Co.; Lima Memorial Hospital; Blanchard Valley Regional Health Center.
See Professional Biographies, FINDLAY, OHIO

Patterson, John T. .... '30 '66 C.608 B.A. L.607 J.D. Presid. J., Com. Pleas Ct.
Pfeiffer, Ronald C. '48 '73
C.967 B.A. L.930 J.D. 1st V.P., McDonald & Co. Securities, Inc.
Powell, Steven Michael, (CV) .... '56 '93 C.253 B.A. L.851 J.D. [S.M.Powell]
Powell, Steven M., Co., LPA, (CV) .... 108 E. Main Cross St.
Power, Jan Geiselman '49 '74 C&L.846 B.S., J.D.
(adm. in TX; not adm. in OH) Environmental Treatment & Technologies Corp.
Preston, Vernon L., (BV) .... '50 '80 C.253 B.S. L.851 J.D. Mun. J.
Pry, C. Nicholas .... '41 '68 C.611 B.A. L.608 J.D. 551 Lake Cascades Parkway‡
Putnam Behrendt, Elizabeth A., (CV) .... '69 '94 C.473 B.S. L.930 J.D. Co. Staff Atty.
Rader, Roger L., (BV) .... '53 '78 C&L.607 B.A., J.D. 330 S. Main Street
Rakestraw, Gregory A., (BV) .... '49 '74 C.967 B.A. L.608 J.D. [Rakestraw&R.]
Rakestraw, Russell E., (AV) .... '25 '51 C.967 L.188 LL.B. [Rakestraw&R.]
Rakestraw & Rakestraw, (AV) .... 119 East Crawford Street
Ranzau, Christie L. .... '77 '02 C.347 B.A. L.607 J.D. [Ⓐ Drake,P.K.&C.]

Rasmussen, Donald J., (BV) .... '59 '84 C&L.607 B.S.B.A., J.D. [Hackenberg,B.&R.]
Reinhardt, J. Alec '42 '68
C.150 B.S.E.E. L.608 J.D. Exec. V.P., Cooper Tire & Rubber Company
Ricketts, Anne E. ....'— '93 C.97 B.S. L.117 J.D. 15470 Lakeview Pkwy.
Rinebolt, Richard J. ....'22 '48 C.597 L.607 J.D. Ret. Com. Pleas J.‡

Ritter, Robinson, McCready & James
(See Toledo)

Robinson, Clifford O., (AV) ....'31 '59 C.608 B.S. L.188 J.D. 6540 Willowick Drive
Roepke, Stephen A., (BV) ....'57 '81 C.97 B.A. L.228 J.D. [Firmin,S.&H.]
Rogers, Michelle M. ...... '59 '84 C&L.339 B.A., J.D. Marathon Ashland Petroleum LLC
Roman, Bridgette C., (AV) '62 '88
C.608 B.A. L.229 J.D. Sr. Lit. Coun., Cooper Tire & Rubber Co.
Rooney, Philip L., (CV) ....'65 '92 C.608 B.S. L.607 J.D. [Drake,P.K.&C.]
Roszman, Valerie Mers, (CV) ....'62 '89 C.203 B.S. L.851 J.D. 410 W. Sandusky St.
Routson, Reginald J. ....'53 '81 L.851 J.D. Com. Pleas Ct. J.
Rubin, Elizabeth F. '68 '94 C&L.150 B.S., J.D.
Atty., Marathon Ashland Petroleum LLC
Ruse, William E. ....'34 '72 C.607 B.Sc. L.851 J.D. [Drake,P.K.&C.] ‡
Russo, Ralph D., (BV) ....'51 '78 C.893 B.A. L.607 J.D. [Betts,M.&R.]
Sackmann, William A. ....'19 '47 C.174 B.S. L.208 LL.B. Ret. Mun. Ct. Mag.‡
Sausser, John C. '11 '61 C.253 A.B. L.607 J.D.
Chmn. of the Bd., John Sausser Steel Co., Inc.
Schroeder, Jerome B. '52 '78
C.1024 B.S. L.607 J.D. V.P. & Secy., Knueven, Schroeder & Co.
Schroeder, Kimberly B. '67 '92
C.294 B.A. L.608 J.D. Atty., Marathon Ashland Petroleum LLC
Schuck, Robert D. ....'17 '46 C&L.608 A.B., J.D. 200 W. Sandusky St.‡
Schuck, Robert E., (CV) .... '57 '83 C.473 B.Phil. L.1288 J.D. 200 W. Sandusky Street
Shaw, Patricia Woodson ....'— '82 C.302 B.A. L.734 J.D. Cir. Ct. Juv. Div.
Simmons, Joe A., (BV) '55 '80 C.607 B.A. L.851 J.D.
Senior Group Counsel, Marathon Ashland Petroleum LLC
Smith, Kevin C., (BV) ....'54 '83 C.869 B.S. L.1003 J.D. Mun. Ct. J.
Snyder, Daniel M., (BV) ....'35 '59 C&L.608 B.A., J.D. [Snyder&A.]
Snyder & Alge, (BV) ....410 W. Sandusky St.
Spaeth, Bret A. ....'70 '97 C.473 B.A. L.851 J.D. [Fitzgerald]

Spitler, Huffman, Yoon & Newlove, LLP
(See Bowling Green)

Sprague, Robert F., (AV) ....'43 '68 C.97 B.A. L.608 J.D. [Firmin,S.&H.]
Standley, Thomas R. ......'51 '81 C.475 B.A. L.851 J.D. Sr. Atty., Marathon Oil Company
Swope, William L., (BV) ....'56 '85 C.97 B.A. L.851 J.D. 221 S. Main St.
Taylor, J. Morton ....'21 '45 C&L.846 B.A., LL.B. L. 610 Bittersweet Dr.‡
Van Horn, Andrew Joseph ......'65 '97 C.999 B.A. L.607 J.D. 108 East Main Cross Street
Walker, Robert D. ....'25 '51 C.253 B.S. L.607 J.D. Ret. Com. Pleas J.
Walter, Douglas M., (CV) ....'58 '84 C.97 B.S.B.A. L.851 J.D. 101 W. Sandusky St.
Warren, Bradley S., (CV) ....'70 '95 C.611 B.A. L.607 J.D. [Oxley,M.H.O.&W.]
Welch, Carol Runnels, (BVⓣ) '51 '79 C.43 B.S. L.420 J.D.
(adm. in LA; not adm. in OH) [C.R.Welch]
Welch, Scott E. .... '72 '99 C.611 B.A. L.117 J.D. 108 E. Main Cross
Welch, Carol R., Law Office of, (BVⓣ) ....8379 Lakeside Drive
Wenner, Cheryl Garrett, (CV) .....'— '89 C.260 B.A. L.851 J.D. Charles Associates, Inc.‡
Whiteleather, Larry W., (AV) '52 '79
C.97 B.A. L.851 J.D. Grp. Coun., Marathon Oil Company
Whitman, Jeffrey J. ....'52 '77 C&L.607 B.S., J.D. 101 W. Sandusky St.
Wilder, J. Michael, (AV) '52 '78 C&L.383 B.A., J.D.
General Counsel, Marathon Ashland Petroleum LLC.
Winkeljohn, J. Theodore '47 '72 C.201 B.S. L.851 J.D.
V.P., Ohio Automotive Supply Co.
Wolph, Alexandra K., (CV) ....'47 '87 C.97 B.S. L.851 J.D. 314 W. Crawford Street
Wortman, Drew Alexander .... '75 '00 C.610 B.A. L.851 J.D. Hancock Co. Pros. Off.
Young, Elizabeth S. '63 '88
C.839 B.S. L.326 J.D. Atty., Marathon Ashland Petroleum LLC

FORT LORAMIE, 1,344, *Shelby Co.*

Faulkner, Harry N., (AV) ....'41 '66 C.611 B.A. L.607 J.D. [Faulkner,G.K.&S.] ⊙
Faulkner, Garmhausen Keister & Shenk, A Legal Professional Association, (AV)
31 South Main Street (⊙Sidney)

FOSTORIA, 13,931, *Hancock, Seneca & Wood Cos.*

Bennett, Donald S., (BV) ....'57 '89 C.1154 B.A. L.851 J.D. 125 S. Main St.
Burger, Robert M., (BV) ....'26 '54 L.215 LL.B. 131 W. North St.
Dauterman, William D., (BV) ....'34 '59 C.97 B.S. L.607 J.D. 307 N. Main St.
Dibble, Barbara A., (CV) ....'64 '94 C.253 B.A. L.607 J.D. Asst. Pros.
Echelbarger, Fred R., (AV) ....'23 '50 C.97 B.A. L.607 J.D. P.O. Box 310‡
Guernsey & Guernsey, (BV) .... 142 W. Tiffin St.
Gutknecht, John W., (AV) ....'09 '32 C&L.607 J.D. 118 W. Tiffin St.
Hadacek, John D. .... '49 '75 C.608 B.A. L.607 J.D. Mun. J., Fostoria Mun. Ct.
Hammonds, Samuel Free, (BV) ....'25 '57 C&L.851 B.B.A., J.D. 111 W. Center Street
Kinn, Frank J. ....'30 '60 C.659 B.S. L.477 J.D. 1602 N. Union St.‡
Marley, Barbara L., (BV) ....'47 '73 C.741 B.A. L.851 J.D. [Marley&M.]
Marley, Francis M., Jr., (BV) ....'42 '71 C.602 A.B. L.607 J.D. [Marley&M.]
Marley & Marley, (BV) .... 100 N. Poplar St.
McKay, Alicia Wolph ....'67 '92 C.608 B.A. L.851 J.D. City Law Dir.
Mennel, Donald M., (BV) ....'18 '86 C.976 A.B. L.607 J.D. 1192 Pelton Road
Reffner, Carol L., (BV) ....'49 '87 C.477 B.A.Ed. L.851 J.D. [Guernsey&G.]
Stotzer, Jonathan G., (BV) ....'57 '82 C.473 B.A. L.546 J.D. 111 W. Center Street

FRANKLIN, 11,396, *Warren Co.*

Bronson, Barbara J., (BV) ....'49 '73 C.392 B.A. L.150 J.D. [Ruppert,B.&R.]
Burns, Joshua Grant ....'76 '01 C.473 B.A. L.896 J.D. [Ⓐ Ruppert,B.&R.]
Chicarelli, David A., (BV) ....'50 '75 C.473 A.B. L.150 J.D. [D.A.Chicarelli]
Chicarelli, David A., Co. L.P.A., (BV) ....1200 E. 2nd St., Ste. C

Eagle, Thomas G., Co., L.P.A.
(See Lebanon)

Lahmann, Barbara A., (CV) ....'60 '87 C.597 B.A. L.150 J.D. [Ⓐ D.A.Chicarelli]
Long, Patrick D., (BV) ....'51 '77 C.929 B.A. L.201 J.D. P.O. Box 8233
Runge, Steven M., (BV) ....'49 '75 C.679 B.S. L.607 J.D. Pros. Atty.
Ruppert, James D., (AV) ....'36 '66 C.870 B.S. L.150 J.D. [Ruppert,B.&R.]
Ruppert, Jeffrey A. ....'70 '99 C.473 B.A. L.150 J.D. [Ⓐ Ruppert,B.&R.]
Ruppert, Ronald W., (BV) ....'63 '88 C.150 B.A. L.629 J.D. [Ruppert,B.&R.]
Ruppert, Rupert E., (BV) ....'43 '76 C.608 B.A. L.117 J.D. [Ruppert,B.&R.]
Ruppert, Bronson & Ruppert, L.P.A., (AV)............................1063 East Second Street

FREDERICKTOWN, 2,443, *Knox Co.*

Bringman, William Paul ....'44 '70 C.608 B.S. L.607 J.D. [W.P.Bringman]
Bringman, William P., Co., L.P.A. ....13 East College Street
Connett, Kimberly M. ....'70 '96 C.608 B.A. L.117 J.D. Kokosing Construction Co.

FREMONT, * 17,375, *Sandusky Co.*

Adams, Herbert E., (BV) ....'41 '72 C.339 B.S. L.1340 J.D. 714 Court St.
Albrechta, Joseph F., (BV) .... '57 '84 C.473 B.Ph. L.851 J.D. [Albrechta&C.] (⊙Toledo)
Albrechta and Coble, (AV) .... 2255 Christy Road (⊙Perrysburg, Toledo)
Ansted, Barbara J., (BV) ....'49 '78 C.967 B.A. L.990 J.D. 201 N. Park Ave.
Bowlus, Thomas M., (CV) ....'69 '94 C&L.608 B.S., J.D. [Bowlus&B.]
Bowlus, William R., (AV) ....'37 '62 C.610 B.S. L.608 J.D. [Bowlus&B.]

Bowlus & Bowlus, Ltd., (AV)
207 North Park Avenue, 43420
Telephone: 419-332-8260 Fax: 419-332-4387
Email: contact@bowluslaw.com
William R. Bowlus; Thomas M. Bowlus.
General Civil Practice, Real Estate, Probate, Estate Planning, Personal Injury, Corporations, LLCs, and Business Entities, Environmental, Brownfield Redevelopment.
Representative Clients: The Croghen Colonial Bank; Sky Bank; Memorial Hospital, Inc.; Appleby Lumber Supply; Zimmerman Paint Contractors; Park Avenue Title Agency, Inc; Steinle Oldsmobile Cadillac Pontiac; Beck Suppliers, Inc.; GW Contractors, Inc.
Approved Attorney and Agent for: Lawyers Title Insurance Corp.

Bristley, C. Wesley, (BV) ....'26 '51 C.610 L.150 LL.B. 323 High St.
Brudzinski, Daniel L., (BV) ....'65 '91 C.201 B.S. L.851 J.D. 501 W. State St.
Burkett, Michael L. ....'48 '75 C.97 B.S. L.851 J.D. Mun. J.
Chambers, John L. ....'25 '50 C.97 L.607 LL.B. Com. Pleas J.
Coble, John A., (AV) ....'56 '84 C.473 B.Ph. L.851 J.D. [Albrechta&C.] (⊙Toledo)
Cooper, Alfred J., (AV) ....'32 '60 C&L.608 B.S., J.D. 714 Court St.
Culbert, R. Bradford '57 '83 C.970 B.A. L.851 J.D.
Com. Pleas Co. Ct., Prob. & Juv. Div.
Culbert, Roger A., (BV) ....'47 '73 C.608 B.A. L.851 J.D. [Culbert&C.]
Culbert & Culbert, (BV) ....200 South Arch Street
Dorobek, David A., (BV) ....'58 '85 C.610 B.S.J. L.851 J.D. 201 N. Park Avenue
Elder, Benjamin Robert ....'62 '98 C.235 B.S. L.851 J.D. Pros. Off.
Feiszli, William John '49 '87 C.62 B.M.E. L.851 J.D.
Gen. Mgr. & Gen. Coun., Bowlus Trucking Co., Inc.
Fiegl, Christopher P., (CV) ....'64 '92 C.588 B.S. L.161 J.D. [Fiegl]
Fiegl Law Office, (CV) .... 113 S. Clover St.
Geiger, Michael R. ......'41 '72 C&L.607 B.A., J.D. Ct. Admr. & Mag., Prob. & Juv. Ct.
Hafford, Roger W., (BV) ....'47 '77 C.608 B.A. L.851 J.D. 621 Croghan St.
Hall, John F., (BV) ....'43 '70 C&L.851 B.A., J.D. 707 Napoleon St.
Heid, Robert C., (AV) ....'30 '64 C.608 B.S. L.266 J.D. 915 Croghan St.
Heid, Sally Ann Reardon ....'30 '54 C&L.608 B.A., J.D. 915 Croghan Street
Hobbs, Veronica, (BV) ....'64 '91 C.588 B.S. L.1066 J.D. 121 N. Arch St.
Ickes, L. Scott, (BV) ....'50 '75 C&L.607 B.A., J.D. 2323 Countryside Dr.
Kane, Jeffrey A., (CV) ....'61 '87 C&L.851 B.A., J.D. 203 N. Park Ave.
Kridler, William W., (BV) .... '18 '48 C.970 B.A. L.930 LL.B. 1917 Glen Springs Dr.
Lease, Daniel H. .....'26 '51 C&L.608 B.S., J.D. Chmn. of the Bd., Wahl Refractories Inc.
Lockshin, Andrew C. ....'76 '02 C.97 B.A. L.608 J.D. 802 Court Street
Mayle, Andrew R. .... '77 '02 C.363 B.A. L.602 J.D. [Mayle]
Mayle, Ronald J., (BV) ....'46 '74 C.215 B.E.E. L.8 J.D. 210 S. Front
Mayle Law Firm ....210 South Front Street
Newell, Beverly S. .... '60 '96 C.610 B.S. L.851 J.D. 2511 Country Side Drive
Quigley, Richard W., Jr., (BV) ....'48 '73 C.851 B.A. L.608 J.D. 1101 Birchard Ave.
Sargeant, Harry A., Jr. ....'33 '58 C.970 B.A. L.608 J.D. Com. Pleas J.
Scranton, Nancy M., (BV) ....'46 '73 C.879 B.A. L.494 J.D. 204 Justice Street
Semer, Jerry, (BV) ....'49 '74 C&L.930 B.A., J.D. 617 Croghan
Snyder, Lisa M., Law Offices of ....'67 '98 C&L.851 B.S., J.D. 714 Court St.
Solze, Norman P., (BV) ....'44 '70 C.608 B. Sc. L.607 J.D. 617 Croghan St.
Stout, Thomas C., (AV) ....'17 '48 C.473 A.B. L.930 J.D. 55 River Run Dr.‡
Weaver, Margaret K. ....'30 '73 C.451 B.A. L.851 J.D. Com. Pleas J.
Wingard, William A., (BV) ....'48 '73 C.473 B.A. L.150 J.D. 410 Croghan St.

Zinkand, John L., (AV) '43 '68 C.62 A.B. L.608 J.D.
The Gusdorf Building, 211 South Park Avenue, 43420
Telephone: 419-332-5579 Fax: 419-332-5570
Email: zinkandlaw@aol.com
General Civil Practice. Probate, Trust and Estates, Estate Planning, Real Property, Personal Injury, Corporate, Commercial, Trials.
See Professional Biographies, FREMONT, OHIO

GAHANNA, 32,636, *Franklin Co.*

Angell, Robert C., (BV) ....'51 '93 C.608 B.Mus. L.117 J.D. 346 Halsbury Circle
Baker, Adam J. '60 '88 C.339 B.S. L.424 J.D.
Staff Atty., World Fin. Network Natl. Bnk.

Benson, Michael E.
(See Columbus)

Bicking, Carol D. ....'49 '94 C.1111 B.S. L.117 J.D. 664 Bugle Court
Blake, Jeffrey A., (BV) .... '62 '88 C&L.608 B.A., J.D. 172 Granville St.
Bonham, William T., (BV) .....'57 '88 C.608 B.S.B.A. L.117 J.D. 107 W. Johnstown Rd.
Burnside-Kelly, Susan ....'58 '91 C.608 B.F.A. L.117 J.D. Staff Atty., Com. Pleas J.
Cohen, Linda M. ....'54 '90 C.62 B.A. L.161 J.D. Mag.
Cohen, Robert D., (BV) ....'47 '76 C.831 B.A. L.7 J.D. 146 Granville St.
Creed, Lawrence Clark ....'62 '97 C.980 B.E. L.117 J.D. 170 Mill St.
Daneman, Sara Jane, (BV) ....'49 '79 C.502 B.S. L.589 J.D. 62 Mill St.
Faist, Julia Grooms, (BV) ....'55 '78 C.333 B.A. L.117 J.D. [J.Faist]
Faist, Julia, (BV) .... 142 Granville St.
Galeano, Michael J., (AV) '63 '89
C.363 B.S.B.A. L.851 J.D. Dir. & Assoc. Coun., Alliance Data Systems
Hall, Hazel A. ....'58 '83 C.20 B.A. L.851 J.D. World Financial Network Natl. Bk.

Kenney-Pfalzer, Susan
(See Columbus)

King, Ray J., Attorney at Law, (BV) '45 '74
C.473 B.A. L.117 J.D. 107 W. Johnstown Rd., Ste. D
Knauber, Deborah L. ....'60 '89 C.607 B.S.B.A. L.117 J.D. 292 Amfield Ct.
Krippel, Darrolyn C., (BV) ....'54 '80 C&L.608 B.A., J.D. 4062 Fortress Place
Lucente, James M. ....'54 '85 C.980 B.S. L.1003 J.D. 171 Greenbank Rd.
Mancuso, Anthony O., (BV) ....'61 '86 C.201 B.A. L.608 J.D. [Mancuso]
Mancuso Law Office, (BV) .... 135 North Hamilton Road
Martin, Lance S. '66 '91 C.37 B.A. L.602 J.D.
(adm. in IL; not adm. in OH) Dir. & Assoc. Coun., Alliance Data Systems

Moran, Michael R., Co., L.P.A.
(See Columbus)

Morauski, Karen A., (BV) '61 '87 C.959 B.S. L.190 J.D.
(adm. in NE; not adm. in OH) V.P. & Coun., Alliance Data Systems
Mosbacher, Linda F. '49 '89 C.631 B.A. L.608 J.D. 6381 Clark State Rd.
Murray, Bernard M., (BV) '42 '69 C.117 B.S. L.608 J.D. 66 Mill St.
Schmidt, Thomas Franklin '49 '83 C.645 B.S. L.117 J.D. [T.F.Schmidt]
Schmidt, Thomas Franklin, Co., L.P.A. 172 Granville St.

Shaw, Melissa J. '66 '97 C.235 B.A. L.117 J.D.
107 West Johnstown Road, 43230
Telephone: 614-472-2529 Fax: 614-471-4581
Email: ms@shaw4law.com URL: http://www.shaw4lawfirm.com
Business Law, Business Planning and Formation, Contracts, Corporate, Partnership, Family Business, Wills, Trusts and Estates, Contested Wills, Estate and Gift Taxation, Estate Planning, Living Wills, Powers of Attorney, Probate, Elder Law, Guardianship, Medicaid Eligibility.
See Professional Biographies, GAHANNA, OHIO

Stehle, William L., (BV) '38 '64 C.602 B.B.A. L.608 J.D.
136 N. Hamilton Rd., Suite 137
Taylor, James R. '68 '00 C&L.608 B.S.B.A., J.D.
Position 7 Dir., ADS Alliance Data System, Inc., State & Local Tax
Tripp, Thomas N. '42 '67 C.475 B.A. L.273 J.D. 5420 Clark State Rd.
Wood, David W., (AV) '51 '81 C&L.966 B.B.A., J.D. 750 Gulfstream Court

GALENA, 361, *Delaware Co.*

Butts, Diana Fay '65 '89 C&L.608 B.S., J.D. 10333 Hoover Woods
Hartman, Ronald F., (BV) '31 '67 C.339 B.S. L.117 J.D. 11720 Gorsuch Rd.
McCaughan, Lorie L. '— '96 C.631 B.S. L.117 J.D. 5492 Red Bank Road

Molnar, Kenneth J., (BV) '46 '74 C.201 B.A. L.117 J.D.
21 Middle Street, P.O. Box 248, 43021-0248
Telephone: 740-965-3900 Fax: 740-965-2718 URL: http://www.KMolnar@columbus.rr.com
URL: http://www.molnarlaw.com
(Also Of Counsel, Rich, Crites & Wesp, LLC).
Civil Trial Practice. Municipal and Zoning, Family Law, Divorce, Child Custody, Child Support, Visitation Rights, Real Estate, Wills and Probate, Trusts and Estates, Estate Planning, Collections.
Approved Attorney for: Ohio Bar Title Insurance Co.
See Professional Biographies, GALENA, OHIO

Paisley, Marian, (CV) '19 '58 C.608 B.Sc. L.266 J.D. 1955 S. Galena Rd.
Rich, Crites & Wesp, LLC, (AV) 21 Middle Street (⊙Columbus, Delaware)
Spicer, Kenneth J., (AV) '42 '72 C&L.608 B.A., J.D. 1720 S. Galena Rd.

GALION, 11,341, *Crawford Co.*

Erlsten, Steven J., (BV) '40 '68 C.879 B.S.C.E. L.1003 J.D. 135 Harding Way W.
Garverick, Debra A., (BV) '58 '83 C&L.607 B.A., J.D. 112 W. Church
Garverick, Lowell B., (AV) '32 '59 C&L.608 B.S., J.D. [Hottenroth,G.T.&G.]
Hardy, C. Thomas, (CV) '41 '84 C.434 B.A. L.607 J.D. 315 Evans Dr.
Hesby, Philip S. '24 '50 C.475 B.A. L.188 J.D. 342 Harding Way W.‡
Hottenroth, E. Richard, (AV) '36 '62 C.117 A.B. L.608 J.D. [Hottenroth,G.T.&G.]
Hottenroth, Garverick, Tilson & Garverick Co., L.P.A., (AV) 126 S. Market St.
Jones, Edward H. '16 '49 C.611 A.B. L.930 LL.B. 545 Park Ave.‡
Keller, David Wm., (BV) '57 '82 C.97 B.A. L.608 J.D. City Pros. [Keller,Z.&M.]
Keller, Zeisler & Murphy, (BV) 659 Harding Way West
Laughbaum, Rolland E. '23 '56 C&L.607 B.A., LL.B. 451 Harding Way, W
Murphy, Clifford Joseph, (CV) '68 '94 C.1214 B.S. L.851 J.D. [Keller,Z.&M.]
Palmer, Thomas N., Law Office of, (CV) '58 '92
C.878 B.A. L.608 J.D. 140 W. Church St.
Ricksecker, Robert S., (AV) '20 '48 C.970 B.A. L.930 LL.B. 118 Harding Way W.
Ryan, C. E. '10 '34 L.608 LL.B. 674 Park Ave.‡
Tilson, Stephen F., (AV) '49 '74 C.611 B.A. L.608 J.D. [Hottenroth,G.T.&G.]
Wagner, Jay D., (BV) '59 '84 C&L.607 B.S.B.A., J.D. [Wagner]
Wagner, John L., (BV) '28 '55 C.97 B.A. L.608 J.D. [Wagner]
Wagner Law Firm, P.L.L., (BV) 118 Harding Way W.
Zeisler, Jeffrey D., (CV) '59 '93 C.608 B.S. L.117 J.D. [Keller,Z.&M.]

GALLIPOLIS, * 4,180, *Gallia Co.*

Adkins, Charles J., (BV) '60 '86 C&L.608 B.A., J.D. Asst. Pros. Atty.
Cain, Joseph L. '45 '71 C&L.608 B.S., J.D. Comm. Pleas J.
Calhoun, Ronald R. '31 '58 C&L.608 B.S., J.D. 444 Second Ave.
Cherrington, Moulton & Evans, (CV) 463 Second Avenue
Conley, William D., (CV) '43 '72 C.608 B.S. L.607 J.D. 537 2nd Ave.
Cowles, Douglas M., (BV) '47 '75 C.473 B.A. L.1065 J.D. 435 2nd St.
Eachus, William N. '45 '74 C.608 B.S. L.117 J.D. 417 2nd Ave.
Evans, D. Dean '45 '72 C.437 B.B.A. L.117 J.D. Com. Pleas J.
Evans, David Cherrington '74 '01 C&L.150 B.A., J.D. [Cherrington,M.&E.]
Finley, Jeffery L. '68 '98 C.150 B.A. L.8 J.D. 417 Second Ave.
Halliday, Sheets & Saunders, (AV) 19 Locust St.
Jenkins, R. William '37 '61 C.880 B.A. L.608 J.D. P.O. Box 445‡
Lentes, John R., (BV) '55 '85 C.473 B.A. L.1003 J.D. 537 1/2 2nd Ave.

Lewis, Richard M.
(See Jackson)

Medley, William S. '49 '80 C.8 B.S.B.A. L.7 J.D. Mun. J.
Moulton, Thomas S. '32 '60 C&L.608 B.S., J.D. Prob. & Juv. J.
Moulton, Thomas S., Jr., (CV) '71 '97 C.473 B.S. L.607 J.D. [Cherrington,M.&E.]
Nelson, William R. '28 '51 C&L.608 B.S., J.D. 616 4th Ave.‡

Offutt, Fisher & Nord
(See Huntington, West Virginia)

Roderick, Richard, (BV) '42 '67 C.999 B.A. L.838 J.D. 21 Locust St.
Saunders, Brent A., (BV) '58 '83 C.437 B.B.A. L.117 J.D. [Halliday,S.&S.]
Sheets, Mark E., (BV) '61 '87 C&L.608 B.A., J.D. [Halliday,S.&S.]
Sheets, Warren F., (AV) '24 '50 C.999 L.607 J.D. [Halliday,S.&S.]

GALLOWAY, —, *Franklin Co.*

Fink, Joan Kathleen '52 '79 C.608 B.S. L.117 J.D. [J.K.Fink]
Fink, Joan K., Law Offices of P.O. Box 492
Gander, Van A. '62 '87 C.117 B.A. L.608 J.D. [Gander]
Gander Law Office 994 Galloway Road
Kurilchick, Dianne M., (BV) '60 '84 C.980 B.S. L.8 J.D. 706 Aldengate Dr.
Srail, Donald J. '54 '79 C.117 B.A. L.608 J.D. 6375 Tamara Ave.

GAMBIER, 1,871, *Knox Co.*

Lapeza, David H. '50 '82 C&L.477 A.B., J.D.
(adm. in CT; not adm. in OH) Kenyon College
Leech, Charles R., Jr., (AV) '30 '55 C.385 A.B. L.608 J.D. 20285 Zion Rd.‡
Ryerson, John T., Jr., (CV) '50 '91 C.385 B.A. L.608 J.D. P.O. Box 323

Sheffield, Ellen E. '54 '81 C.930 B.S. L.608 J.D. [Sheffield&S.]
Sheffield, Ricci S., (BV) '54 '79 C&L.930 B.A., J.D. [Sheffield&S.]
Sheffield & Sheffield, (BV) P.O. Box 73

GARFIELD HEIGHTS, 30,734, *Cuyahoga Co.*

Bednar, Michael A., (BV) '56 '83 C.363 B.A. L.1003 J.D. 4824 E. 86th St.
Briggs, Beverly Marie, Law Offices of '48 '72
C.161 B.B.A. L.1003 J.D. 10629 Elmwood Ave.
Crimaldi, Lisa M. '72 '98 C.381 B.A. L.1003 J.D. 5706 Turney Road
Grau, Paul A., (AV) '51 '76 C.999 B.A. L.161 J.D. 5306 Transportation Blvd.
Holtz, Theodore S., (BV) '24 '52 C.930 L.1003 LL.D. 5706 Turney Rd.
Klonowski, Stephen M., (AV) '46 '74 C.97 B.S. L.851 J.D. 5306 Transportation Blvd.
Pietras, J. Scott '58 '95 C.712 B.S,M.T. L.1003 J.S. Marymount Hospital‡
Price, James M. '54 '01 C.1271 B.A. L.989 J.D. 5407 Turney Rd.
Schentur, Raymond E. '25 '56 C.608 B.S., B.A. L.1003 LL.B. 5001 Turney Rd.
Slivka, Andrew P. '21 '54 C.251 B.S. L.1003 J.D. Mun. J.
Snider, Richard J. '25 '51 C.363 B.B.A. L.128 LL.B.
(adm. in DC; not adm. in OH) 10608 Elmwood Ave.‡
Stralka, Kenneth R. '31 '54 C&L.607 J.D. Mun. J.
Weiler, Jennifer Pechman '51 '79 C.610 B.A. L.251 J.D. Mun. Ct. J.

GARRETTSVILLE, 2,262, *Portage Co.*

Kohli, S. Kim, (CV) '57 '94 C.318 B.S. L.1003 J.D. 8134 Main Street
Manlove, Mark L., (BV) '49 '74 C.401 B.A. L.161 J.D. [M.L.Manlove]
Manlove, Mark L., Co., L.P.A., (BV) 8052 State St.
Mishler, Robert E. '29 '60 C.381 B.S.B.A. L.8 LL.B. 8121 Main St.‡

GATES MILLS, 2,508, *Cuyahoga Co.*

Artz, Mauri A. '60 '85 C.861 B.A. L.930 J.D. P.O. Box 700
Bissell, Robert K., (AV) '27 '52 C.821 A.B. L.309 LL.B. 1540 Chagrin River Rd.
Bogomolny, Richard J. '35 '61 C.930 A.B. L.1003 J.D. 17000 Rockside Rd.
Bozza, Guido V. '30 '59 C.363 L.1003 LL.B. 34000 Dorchester Rd.
Britton, Joseph A. '18 '50 C&L.930 A.B., LL.B. 6703 Walnut Dr.‡
Doran, Joseph S. '44 '90 C.161 B.A. L.1003 J.D. P.O. Box 221
Dunn, Steven J. '53 '81 C.354 B.A. L.818 J.D.
(adm. in MA; not adm. in OH) 7400 Daisy's Wood Lane
Frutig, Patricia R., (CV) '45 '84 C.183 B.A. L.1003 J.D. P.O. Box 173
Frutig, Thomas R., (BV) '43 '69 C.608 B.A. L.930 J.D. P.O. Box 173
Goldstein, Ronald '47 '74 C.205 B.A. L.362 J.D.
(adm. in FL; not adm. in OH) P.O. Box 421
Johnson, A. Robert '25 '51 C&L.930 A.B., LL.B. 381 Timberidge Trail
Kalberer, Jean C. '33 '81 C&L.930 B.A., J.D. 1259 W. Hill Dr.‡
Lawley, Patricia M. '59 '85 C.161 B.A. L.1003 J.D. 797 Hanover Rd.
Mekedis, Alex P. '19 '50 C.610 A.B. L.1003 J.D. 6959 Gates Rd.‡
Mulligan, Thomas P., (AV) '16 '41 C.602 B.A. L.309 J.D. 1279 West Hill Dr.‡
Pike, Nelson E. '13 '47 C&L.930 A.B., LL.B. 758 Oakwood Dr.‡
Puette, Thomas J., Esq. '43 '69 C.930 B.B.A. L.1003 J.D. 675 Echo Drive
Terrell, Seymour A., (AV) '15 '36 C&L.608 J.D. P.O. Box 236‡

GENEVA, 6,597, *Ashtabula Co.*

Curry, Robert F., (AV) '29 '54 C.610 L.1003 LL.B. [Curry&P.]
Curry & Pasqualone, (AV) 302 S. Bway.
DiFabio, Louis A., (BV) '35 '68 C.1212 B.S. L.1003 J.D. 299 S. Broadway, Suite 203
Epstein, Sherry J. '60 '85
C.881 A.B. L.665 J.D. Gen. Coun., ATC Lighting & Plastics, Inc.
Gerken, Philip D., (BV) '54 '79 C.97 B.A. L.851 J.D. 743 N. Nearing Cir.
Mayle, Timothy L. '65 '99 C.250 B.S. L.989 J.D. 645 W. Main St.
Pasqualone, Gary L., (BV) '48 '74 C.473 A.B. L.838 J.D. [Curry&P.]
Piper, Kenneth L., (BV) '48 '75 C.30 B.A. L.930 J.D. 185 Water St.
Schwegler, Benedict R. '13 '48 C&L.930 B.A., J.D. Pres., Audubon Lakes Resort, Inc.‡
Stevens, Richard L. '47 '77 C&L.607 B.A., J.D. 27 W. Main St.
Warner, Edwin M., (CV) '13 '41 C&L.309 A.B., LL.B. P.O. Box 327
Webb, Robert D. '18 '49 C.473 B.S. L.208 Ret. Co. J.

GENOA, 2,262, *Ottawa Co.*

Bowland, Geo., (AV) '17 '49 C&L.851 LL.B. 629 Main St.
Cottrell, Ernest E., Jr., (BV) '61 '85 C.851 B.A. L.608 J.D. 21980 State Rte. 51 W.
Cottrell, Stephen E., (BV) '47 '73 C&L.851 B.A., J.D. 634 Main St.

GEORGETOWN, * 3,627, *Brown Co.*

Clark, Margaret Ann, (BV) '49 '77 C.999 B.A. L.150 J.D. Co. J.
Corbin, Robert A., (BV) '47 '73 C&L.150 B.A., J.D. Pros. Atty.
Cutrell, Jay D., (BV) '51 '76 C&L.608 B.A., J.D. [McConn&C.]
Dvorachek, Ronald S. '40 '71 C.966 B.S.Ch.E. L.1340 J.D. Prob. & Juv. J.
Grennan, Thomas Forbes, (BV) '46 '75
C.201 B.S. L.1009 J.D. Pros. Atty., Brown Co. Pros. Off.

Hennekes, Jason
(See Cincinnati)

McConn & Cutrell, (BV)
118 South Main Street, 45121
Telephone: 937-378-6165; 378-3256 1-800-378-6167 Fax: 937-378-6567
Email: mail@mcconn-cutrell.com
Members of Firm: Philip K. McConn (1922-1998); Jay D. Cutrell; Julie A. McConn-Pirman.
General Civil Trial Practice in all Courts. Real Estate, Probate, Corporation, Banking, Family Law and Municipal Law.
Representative Clients: National Bank & Trust Co., Georgetown, Ohio; Villages of Georgetown, Ripley and Aberdeen, Ohio; First Safety Bank; Waynoka Property Owners Association, Inc.
Approved Attorneys for: Ohio Bar Title Insurance Co.; Farm Credit Services of Mid America ACA; USDA Rural Economics & Community Development Services.
Reference: National Bank & Trust Co.

McConn-Pirman, Julie A., (BV) '54 '79 C&L.150 B.A., J.D. [McConn&C.]
McMullen, Mary Gloeckner, (CV) '71 '96 C.523 B.A. L.150 J.D. Co. Pros. Off.
Purdy, Stanley K., (BV) '37 '65 C&L.608 B.S., J.D. [Purdy&R.]

Purdy & Ring, (BV)
318 West State Street, 45121
Telephone: 937-378-4119; 937-378-3077 Fax: 937-378-3077
Email: purdyring@siscom.net URL: http://www.purdyandring.com
Members of Firm: Stanley K. Purdy; C. Nicholas Ring.
Criminal Law, DUI, Family Law, Divorce, Dissolution of Marriage, Personal Injury, Estates, Wills, Probate, Business Law, Real Estate, Appellate Practice.
Approved Attorneys for: Lawyers Title Insurance Co. (Agent); The Ohio Bar Title Insurance Co. (Agent); Farmers Home Administration; Fifth Third Bank, Ohio Valley; Brown County Title Agency.
See Professional Biographies, GEORGETOWN, OHIO

Reifin, Melvin H., (BV) '36 '62 C&L.150 B.A., LL.B. 200 East Cherry Street
Ring, C. Nicholas, (BV) '67 '93 C&L.383 B.A., J.D. [Purdy&R.]
Stapleton, William B. '33 '64 C.258 B.S. L.1340 J.D. Com. Pleas J.
Worley, Joseph M., (BV) '55 '83 C.383 B.A. L.1340 J.D. 932 Mount Orab Pike

GERMANTOWN, 4,916, *Montgomery Co.*

Izor, David E., (BV) .... '47 '74 C.473 B.A. L.1340 J.D. 52 N. Main St.
Kelley, Lynn Meade, (BV) .... '38 '63 C.894 A.B. L.150 J.D. 141 W. Market Street

Leppla Associates
(See Dayton)

Mead, Sean M., (CVⓉ) '66 '96 C&L.347 B.A., J.D.
(adm. in IN; not adm. in OH) 16 Hoover Place
Rosario, Kay M. .... '57 '84 C&L.201 B.S., J.D. Pub. Def.
Steele, Harriet M. W. .... '25 '55 C.608 B.S. L.1340 LL.B. 26 N. Main St.

GIBSONBURG, 2,579, *Sandusky Co.*

Beck, Ladd W., (BV) .... '53 '80 C.473 B.S. L.851 J.D. 4590 St. Rte. 600
Bronson, John W. .... '20 '44 C.97 A.B. L.228 J.D. 419 W. Madison St.‡

GIRARD, 10,902, *Trumbull Co.*

Angelo, Barbara J., (CV) .... '39 '85 C.980 B.S. L.7 J.D. 103 Crumlin Ave.
Bernard, Michael A. .... '54 '80 C.8 B.A. L.607 J.D. Mun. Ct. J.
Cervello, Mark C., (CV) .... '59 '91 C.980 B.S. L.1003 J.D. 52 Townsend Ave.
Denney, James A., (CV) .... '49 '77 C.980 A.B. L.117 J.D. 1631 S. State Street
Flevares, William M. .... '66 '92 C.145 A.B. L.800 J.D. [🄰 J.W.Thomas]
Griffith, Robt. I. .... '15 '52 C.967 A.B. L.1003 LL.B. Griffith Agcy., Inc.
Masternick, John, (CV) .... '25 '55 C.424 L.980 J.D. 20 E. Liberty St. (⊙Youngstown)
Masternick, John J. .... '64 '91 C.604 B.A. L.260 J.D. Pres., Windsor House, Inc.
Paronish, Terry Lee .... '56 '92 C.980 B.S.N. L.7 J.D. 2873 W. Liberty St. S.E.
Snyder, Emmor F., (BV) .... '27 '70 C.273 B.S. L.7 J.D. 3 N. State Street
Thomas, James W., (AV) .... '36 '60 C.608 B.A. L.607 J.D. [J.W.Thomas]
Thomas, James W., (Co., L.P.A.), (AV) .... 42 E. Wilson Ave.
Tyler, John F. .... '22 '50 C.197 A.B. L.893 LL.B. 2381 Tibbetts-Wick Rd.‡
Zauderer, Philip Q. .... '35 '64 C.608 B.A. L.266 J.D. 6345 Sodom Hutchings Rd.

GLENDALE, 2,188, *Hamilton Co.*

Slap, Albert J., (AVⓉ) .... '49 '74 C.659 B.A. L.884 J.D. 20 Erie Avenue

GNADENHUTTEN, 1,226, *Tuscarawas Co.*

Cochran, Michael A., (BV) .... '50 '75 C.381 B.A. L.7 J.D. Asst. Co. Pros.

GRAFTON, 2,302, *Lorain Co.*

Borling, David C. .... '48 '74 C.437 B.S. L.607 J.D. 13001 Indian Hollow Rd.
Giuffre, Susan G. .... '47 '83 C.363 B.A. L.1003 J.D. 13001 Indian Hollow Rd.
Spitzer, Charles E. .... '27 '73 C.608 B.S., Pharm. L.1003 J.D. 12335 Grafton Rd.

GRAND RAPIDS, 955, *Wood Co.*

Lipski, Clarence A. .... '27 '52 C&L.851 B.A., LL.B. 24165 Front St.
Marsh, C. Richard, (AV) .... '— '55 C.97 B.S. L.150 J.D. [Marsh&M.] ⊙
Marsh & Marsh, (AV) .... Front St. (⊙Bowling Green)
Rosa, Bruno A. .... '40 '72 C&L.851 B.S.M.E., J.D. P.O. Box 292

GRANDVIEW HEIGHTS, 6,695, *Franklin Co.*

Ballam, William Frederick .... '46 '80 C&L.608 B.A., J.D. 1358 W. 1st Avenue

GRANVILLE, 3,167, *Licking Co.*

Adams, Russell J., (CV) .... '51 '76 C.477 B.A. L.608 J.D. 111 N. Prospect Street
Barns, Stephen W. '66 '95 C.608 B.S. L.30 J.D.
Sr. Intellectual Prop. Corp., Owens Corning (Pat.)
Binkovitz, Jean Gatwood '59 '89 C.117 B.A. L.494 J.D.
(adm. in MN; not adm. in OH) 258 Carmarthen Way‡
Cassell, John J. '27 '56 C&L.923 LL.B.
(adm. in WV; not adm. in OH) 216 E. College St.‡
Diewald, Jodi S. .... '73 '99 C.608 B.S.B.A. L.117 J.D. Paramount Financial Grp., Inc.
Dottavio, James J. '63 '95 C.1229 B.S.M.E. L.912 J.D.
(adm. in MI; not adm. in OH) Sr. Coun., Owens Corning
Eckert, Inger Hansen '66 '94
C.645 B.S.E.E. L.201 J.D. Dir. Intellectual Prop., Owens Corning (Pat.)
Helser, Gregory C. .... '60 '90 C.610 B.B.A. L.117 J.D. [Helser]
Helser Law Office .... 527 Newark-Granville Road, Suite 4
Hill, Terrie Lee .... '49 '76 C.679 B.S. L.607 J.D. 500 Millrace Rd.
Jump, James R. .... '39 '73 C.608 B.A. L.117 J.D. 143 Thresher St.‡

Kenney-Pfalzer, Susan
(See Columbus)

Klark, E. Louis, (CV) .... '53 '84 C.608 B.S. L.117 J.D. 1911 Loudon Street
Kolb, Henry G. '50 '81 C.494 B.S. L.851 J.D.
Assoc. Dir., Owens-Corning Fiberglas Corporation
Little, Anne C. .... '59 '84 C.967 B.A. L.310 J.D. Dir. Litg., Owens Corning
Mc Farland, J. Drew .... '61 '87 C.81 B.A. L.607 J.D. [McFarland]
Mc Farland Law Office .... 120 E. Broadway, Ste. 200
Mershon, Steven W., (AV) .... '— '81 C.999 B.A. L.608 J.D. 128 S. Main St., Ste. 100
Minklei, Lisa A. .... '60 '87 C.821 B.A. L.446 J.D. Denison Univ.
Morris, Linda L. .... '57 '83 C.967 B.A. L.117 J.D. 68 Stone Hedge Dr.
Sadauskas, Renée M. .... '66 '94 C&L.851 B.A., J.D. 4585 Columbus Rd.
Senn, John E. .... '18 '50 C.608 B.Sc. L.266 J.D. 3940 Hankinson Rd.‡
Sharkey, Gregory J. .... '62 '87 C.207 B.A. L.884 J.D. Sr. Develop. Offr., Denison Univ.
Stritzke, Jerry Dale, (BVⓉ) '60 '85 C.612 B.S. L.623 J.D.
(adm. in OK; not adm. in OH) 244 Pinehurst Dr.
Todd, Sara L., (BV) '56 '81 C.608 B.A. L.597 J.D.
Assoc. Gen. Coun., Paramount Financial Group, Inc.
Wernet, William R. .... '— '81 C.207 B.S. L.608 J.D. 134 S. Mulberry St.
Wince, Philip D., (BV) .... '48 '76 C.207 B.A. L.150 J.D. 2350 Broadway W.

GREENFIELD, 4,906, *Highland Co.*

Curren, Conrad A. .... '34 '59 C&L.150 B.A., LL.B. 330 Jefferson St.
Hayes, Larry D., (BV) .... '50 '76 C.473 B.S. L.150 J.D. [Judkins&H.]
Judkins, Robert J., (BV) .... '50 '75 C.611 B.A. L.150 J.D. Co. Ct. J. [Judkins&H.]
Judkins & Hayes, (BV) .... 303 W. Jefferson St.
Quance, Peter D., (CV) .... '55 '84 C.228 A.B. L.025 LL.B. 344 Jefferson St

GREENVILLE, * 13,294, *Darke Co.*

Amick, Jeffrey L., (BV) .... '51 '77 C.473 B.A. L.201 J.D. [Amick&B.]
Amick & Breaden, (BV) .... 414 Walnut Street
Aslinger, Jason R., (CV) .... '71 '96 C.97 B.S. L.851 J.D. [🄰 Amick&B.]
Benkert, William J., Jr. .... '17 '53 C.610 B.S. L.7 LL.B. Equitable Life of N.Y.

Bieser, Greer & Landis, LLP
(See Dayton)

Bradley, Karen Denise
(See Dayton)

Brand, Eric H., (BV) .... '52 '78 C.608 B.A. L.150 J.D. [Goubeaux&B.]
Breaden, Randall E., (BV) .... '54 '79 C&L.607 B.A., J.D. [Amick&B.]
Brown, Gary L., (BV) .... '44 '72 C.1229 B.I.E. L.851 J.D. [Marchal&B.]
Brumbaugh, Anne Jenkins .... '49 '78 C.207 B.A. L.607 J.D. Ct. Ref., Com. Pleas
Cooper, William H., (BV) .... '49 '77 C.97 B.S. L.607 J.D. [Hanes,S.H.M.C.&G.]
Detling, James S., (CV) .... '61 '89 C.608 B.S. L.851 J.D. [Hanes,S.H.M.C.&G.]
Donadio, Raymond M., Jr. .... '55 '80 C&L.607 B.A., J.D. 1400 North Broadway
Durham, Darrell Todd '71 '96
C.210 B.A. L.117 J.D. Tr. Offr., Second National Bank Tr. Servs.
Felton, Mary K. .... '59 '99 C.150 B.A. L.201 J.D. P.O. Box 215
Finnarn, Theodore O., (CV) .... '49 '76 C.473 B.S.Ed. L.851 J.D. 201 E. 5th St.
Flinn, Gary L., (BV) .... '48 '78 C.608 Ph.D. L.8 J.D. [Flinn&M.] ⊙
Flinn and Muntean Co., L.P.A., (BV) .... 429 Memorial Dr. (⊙Sidney)
Foley, Kandy Heavilin, (CV) '64 '89
C.381 B.B.A. L.150 J.D. Darke Co. Job & Family Servs.

Freund, Freeze & Arnold, A Legal Professional Association
(See Dayton)

Fry, Lee E., (BV) .... '43 '72 C&L.607 B.A., J.D. P.O. Box 294
Goubeaux, James J., (AV) .... '36 '61 C.894 A.B. L.309 J.D. [Goubeaux&B.]

Goubeaux & Brand, (AV) BB
100 Washington Avenue, P.O. Box 158, 45331
Telephone: 937-548-2211 Fax: Available Upon Request
Members of Firm: Edward A. Goubeaux, Jr. (1906-1964); Jerome H. Goubeaux (1908-1978); Robert L. Morris (1928-2003); James J. Goubeaux; Eric H. Brand; Mark E. Heggie.
General Civil Practice. Trials. Probate and Estate Planning, Banking, Finance, Corporation and Real Estate Law.
Representative Clients: Fifth Third Bank; Osgood State Bank; Second National Bank; United Telephone Company of Ohio.
Local Counsel for: Penn Central Co.; Corning Glass Works; The St. Henry Bank, St. Henry, Ohio; New Amsterdam Casualty Co.
See Professional Biographies, GREENVILLE, OHIO

Graber, Thomas H., II, (BV) .... '53 '79 C.473 B.S. L.607 J.D. [Hanes,S.H.M.C.&G.]
Green, Jesse J., (CV) .... '62 '88 C.63 B.S. L.200 J.D. Darke County Courthouse, Floor 3
Guillozet, Thomas L., (CV) .... '59 '85 C.434 B.A. L.201 J.D. [Hanes,S.H.M.C.&G.] ⊙
Hanes, Thomas C., (Co., L.P.A.), (AV) .... '30 '59 C&L.607 J.D. [Hanes,S.H.M.C.&G.]
Hanes, Schipfer, Hurley, McClurg, Cooper & Graber, Ltd., (AV)
507 South Broadway (⊙Versailles)
Hanson, Lewis Kenneth, III .... '70 '95 C.434 B.A. L.608 J.D. [Marchal&B.]
Hayes, Margaret B., (CV) .... '64 '89 C.473 B.A. L.150 J.D. 127 W. Fifth St.
Heggie, Mark E., (BV) .... '49 '74 C.473 B.A. L.607 J.D. [Goubeaux&B.]
Hein, Jonathan P. .... '56 '81 C.473 A.B. L.851 J.D. Common Pleas J.
Hole, Richard E., II .... '37 '66 C&L.607 B.A., J.D. Prob. J.
Hoover, Phillip D., (CV) .... '58 '86 C.959 B.A. L.607 J.D. 504 S. Broadway
Howell, Richard M., (BV) .... '53 '78 C.608 B.A. L.607 J.D. Darke Co. Pros. Atty.
Hurley, Roger L., (Co., L.P.A.), (AV) '48 '74 C.8 B.S.E.E. L.7 J.D.
[Hanes,S.H.M.C.&G.]
Marchal, John F. .... '70 '96 C.602 B.A. L.608 J.D. [Marchal&B.]
Marchal, John F., (AV) .... '33 '58 C&L.602 A.B., LL.B. [Marchal&B.]
Marchal & Brown, (AV) .... 116 West Fourth Street
McClurg, Michael D., (BV) .... '46 '76 C.1208 B.S. L.607 J.D. [Hanes,S.H.M.C.&G.] ⊙

Miller & Luring
(See Troy)

Monnin, Julie L., Co., LPA .... '71 '96 C.1208 B.S. L.200 J.D. [J.L.Monnin]
Monnin, Julie L., Co., LPA .... 771 Martin Street
Muntean, Susan M., (CV) .... '52 '78 C.881 A.B. L.7 J.D. [Flinn&M.]
Ross, Dean Edward .... '68 '01 C.608 B.S. L.117 J.D. [🄰 S.D.Rudnick]
Rudnick, Scott D., (BV) .... '55 '79 C.21 B.A. L.607 J.D. [S.D.Rudnick]
Rudnick, Scott D., LTD, Law Offices of, (BV) .... 121 West Third Street
Schipfer, Daniel C., Jr., (BV) .... '42 '70 C.611 B.A. L.607 J.D. [Hanes,S.H.M.C.&G.]
Stollings, Jerry C. .... '70 '00 C.992 B.A. L.851 J.D. [🄰 S.D.Rudnick]

GROVE CITY, 27,075, *Franklin Co.*

Anderson, Jeffrey Scot .... '53 '78 C.608 B.A. L.976 J.D. 3083 Columbus Street
Beck, Mary Joseph .... '57 '82 C.276 A.B. L.150 J.D. Hoover Road
Bennett, John I. .... '48 '73 C.608 B.A. L.117 J.D. 3350 Bigrun South Rd
Bowshier, Stephen J., (BV) .... '57 '81 C&L.608 B.A., J.D. 4030 Broadway St.
Brandt, Michael T., (BV) .... '42 '68 C.532 B.A. L.608 J.D. [Brandt&H.]
Brandt & Hull, (AV) .... 3793 Bway.
Breckenridge, Donald O., (BV) .... '55 '85 C.608 B.S. L.117 J.D. 3009 Columbus St.
Buskirk, Jeffrey Eugene, (CV) .... '57 '84 C.610 B.A. L.117 J.D. [J.E.Buskirk]
Buskirk, Jeffrey E., (CV) .... 4178 Broadway
Carnes, Conrad Dew .... '36 '66 C&L.608 B.A., J.D. 1843 Stoneview Court
Cellura, Frank A. .... '50 '78 C.930 B.A. L.1003 J.D. 5450 Hoover Rd
Clark, Thomas R., (BV) .... '50 '75 C.473 B.S. L.117 J.D. Law Dir.

Compton, Jeffrey P. '63 '89 C.610 B.A. L.117 J.D.
4178 Broadway, 43123-3024
Telephone: 614-875-7233 Fax: 614-875-0480
Email: jcompton@jeffreypcompton.com URL: http://www.jeffreypcompton.com
Personal Injury, Automobile Accidents, Insurance, Medical Malpractice, Wrongful Death, Slip and Fall, Family Law, Divorce, Child Custody, Child Support, Visitation Rights, Real Estate, Buying or Selling, Business Formation, Buying and Selling of Businesses, Small Business Law, Partnerships, Limited Liability Companies, Corporate, Contracts, Bankruptcy, Wills and Probate, Estate Administration, Powers of Attorney and Health Care documents, Consumer Law, IRS Negotiations.
See Professional Biographies, GROVE CITY, OHIO

Edwards, Steve J., (BV) .... '54 '79 C&L.608 B.S., J.D. 4030 Bway.
Elliott, Bryan Keith .... '69 '95 C.608 B.A. L.117 J.D. 3793 Broadway
Fulton, Christopher L. .... '49 '74 C.967 B.A. L.607 J.D. 4541 Bent Creek Place
Galasso, John G. .... '58 '96 C.640 B.A. L.117 J.D. [J.Galasso]
Galasso, John .... 2229 Blue Bell Lane
Hamilton, Raymond Kelly .... '68 '96 C&L.117 J.D. P.O. Box 824
Hilt, John F., (BV) .... '47 '75 C.608 B.S. L.117 J.D. 3793 Broadway
Hudson, Thomas L. .... '47 '87 C.608 B.A. L.117 J.D. 4501 Hoover Road
Hull, Joseph W., (AV) .... '50 '76 C.608 B.A. L.930 J.D. [Brandt&H.]
Knisely, Anne M. .... '— '62 C.705 B.S. L.608 J.D. 4117 Georgesville-Wrightsville Rd.
Lett, Jack, (BV) .... '26 '51 C&L.608 B.A., LL.B. [J.Lett]
Lett, Jack, Co., LPA, (BV) .... 3031 Columbus St.
Lewis, John H., (BV) .... '14 '45 L.608 J.D. 4030 Bway. St. (⊙Westerville)
Ozmun, Kent F., (BV) .... '29 '56 C.62 A.B. L.608 J.D. 2167 Hills Wood Dr.
Saros, John .... '43 '74 C&L.8 B.A., J.D. 1951 Gantz Road
Smith, Stanley S., (BV) .... '39 '64 C&L.608 B.S., LL.B. 3697 Bway.
Walsh, Eugene J. .... '21 '59 C.862 B.S.P.E. L.266 J.D. 3515 Rolling Hills Lane‡
Wilcox, James L. .... '38 '62 C&L.608 B.A., J.D. 3980 Broadway
Zorn, James Edgar, Sr. '53 '88 C.1175 B.A. L.608 J.D.
Franklin County Children Services

GROVEPORT, 3,865, *Franklin Co.*

Froehlich, Mark S., (AV) . . . . '53 '80 C.608 B.A. L.117 J.D. 576Main St.
Mashburn, John B., (BV) . . . . '49 '74 C.999 B.A. L.608 J.D. 518 Main St.
McCarty, Kevin R. . . . . '66 '92 C.201 L.117 [K.R.McCarty]
McCarty, Kevin R., Co. L.P.A. . . . . 495 Main Street
Stewart, Lynne Louise . . . . '55 '84 C.161 B.A. L.1003 J.D. Franklin Co. Childrens Svs.

GUYSVILLE, 250, *Athens Co.*

Wirtshafter, Donald M., Jr. . . . . '51 '85 C.610 B.G.S. L.930 J.D. Pres., Ohio Hempery, Inc.

HAMILTON, * 60,690, *Butler Co.*

Adams, Dennis . . . . '71 '97 C.611 B.A. L.607 J.D. [Davidson,A.&C.]
Allen, James M., (BV) . . . . '40 '68 C.150 B.B.A. L.1340 J.D. 240A Park Ave.

Arnold, James S., & Associates
(See Cincinnati)

Baden & Jones Co., L.P.A., (BV) . . . . 246 High Street
Bartels, Robert L. . . . . '22 '49 C.473 B.S. L.150 LL.B. 301 South Front Street
Battcher, Donald S. '57 '83 C&L.421 B.S.C., J.D.
(adm. in KY; not adm. in OH) Exec. V.P. & Gen. Mgr., Cincinnati Auto Auction, Inc.
Beane, Gregory S., (BV) . . . . '55 '80 C.97 B.S. L.150 J.D. 350 N. 2nd Street
Beimford, Louis A., (AV) . . . . '24 '50 C.473 B.S. L.273 LL.B. 607 1st Natl. Bk. Bldg.

Bieser, Greer & Landis, LLP
(See Dayton)

Borst, Samuel D. . . . . '57 '89 C.610 B.S. L.150 J.D. Asst. Co. Pros. Atty.

Bossin, Phyllis G., Co., L.P.A.
(See Cincinnati)

Brandenburger, Mark, (BV) . . . . '49 '74 C.473 B.S. L.150 J.D. Dep. City Mgr.
Braun, Michael P., (BV) . . . . '55 '81 C.473 B.S. L.201 J.D. Ref. Juv. Ct.
Bressler, H. J. . . . . '39 '68 C.473 B.A. L.1340 J.D. J., Comm. Pleas Ct.
Bruck, Edw. G., (BV) . . . . '21 '47 C.473 A.B. L.608 J.D. 110 N. 3rd St.
Bruck Law Office . . . . 110 N. 3rd St.

Buechner, Haffer, O'Connell, Meyers, Healey & Koenig Co., L.P.A.
(See Cincinnati)

Burress, Brad Alexander . . . . '75 '00 C.150 L.201 J.D. Asst. Pros. Atty., Pros. Off.
Cade, Daniel S. '55 '82 C.318 B.A. L.607 J.D.
Dir., Butler Co. Child Support Enforcement Agcy.
Carlson, Timothy W. . . . . '60 '86 C.385 B.A. L.607 J.D. 301 High Street
Casper, Arthur Brandeis, (AV) '40 '67
C.473 A.B. L.607 J.D. [Casper&C.] (⊙Middletown)

Casper and Casper, (AV)
2 South 3rd Street, Suite 360, 45011 ⊙
Telephone: 513-424-2401-Middletown; 937-224-1122-Dayton 513-381-7096-Cincinnati 513-892-2560-Hamilton 513-892-2560; Toll Free: 1-800-784-2889 Fax: 513-424-0622
URL: http://www.casperlaw.com
Arthur Brandeis Casper.
Personal Injury, Workers Compensation and Social Security Disability Law. Products Liability Litigation. Trials.
Middletown, Ohio Office: Gas and Electric Building, One North Main Street, P.O. Box: 510, 45042. Telephone: 513-424-2401.
Dayton, Ohio Office: First National Plaza Building, 130 West Second Street, Suite 1950, 45402. Telephone: 937-224-1122.
Cincinnati, Ohio Office: 119 East Court Street, Fourth Floor, Suite 410, 45202. Telephone: 513-381-7096.
See Professional Biographies, HAMILTON, OHIO

Cohen, Jack Edward . . . . '50 '75 C.861 B.A. L.276 J.D. Daniel Cohen Enterprises, Inc.
Condo, Gilbert E., (BV) . . . . '10 '32 C.473 A.B. L.150 LL.B. 301 S. Front St.
Conese, Mark . . . . '57 '83 C.473 B.A. L.150 J.D. [Conese]

Conese Law Office
21 Ludlow Street, 45011
Telephone: 513-737-7044 Fax: 513-894-1141 URL: http://www.coneselawoffice.com
Email: info@coneselawoffice.com URL: http://www.lawyers.com/coneselawoffice
Mark Conese.
Adoption Law, Bankruptcy, Child Support, Criminal Law, Child Custody, Visitation Rights, Driving While Intoxicated, Divorce, Family Law, Probate, Estate Administration, Wills.
See Professional Biographies, HAMILTON, OHIO

Connaughton, John B. (J.B.) . . . . '38 '64 C.973 B.S.B.A. L.150 J.D. 2332 Morman Road
Cooney, James E., (BV) . . . . '46 '75 C.610 B.S. L.1340 J.D. 723 Dayton St.
Cornett, Jackie Lane . . . . '53 '78 C.473 B.A. L.161 J.D. [J.Cornett]
Cornett, Jack . . . . 1400 Eaton Ave.
Craft, Ronald R., (BV) . . . . '49 '74 C.608 B.A. L.117 J.D. 115 Pondrun Circle
Creach, Larry H., Jr. . . . . '74 '99 C.473 B.S. L.1340 J.D. [Davidson,A.&C.]
Crehan, Matthew J. . . . . '36 '71 C.433 B.B.A. L.1340 J.D. Com. Pleas J.

Daiker, Victoria, (BV) '42 '77 C.706 B.A. L.150 J.D.
Fifth Third Bank Building, 301 High Street, 45011
Telephone: 513-868-3911 FAX: 513-868-3988
General Civil and Trial Practice. Commercial Collections, Wrongful Death, Personal Injury, Probate and Estate Planning, Wills and Trusts, Juvenile Law, Domestic Relations, Spousal Support, Premarital Agreements, Domestic Violence, Adoptions, Child Custody and Support, Divorce and Dissolution, Alternative Dispute Resolution, Mediation, Collaborative Law.
Representative Clients: Cincinnati Gas & Electric; Cincinnati Bell Preble County Credit Bureau; Somerville National Bank; State of Ohio (Special Counsel to Ohio Attorney General).
References: First Financial Bank; Great Lakes Bancorp.
See Professional Biographies, HAMILTON, OHIO

Daly, Gerald Robert . . . . '46 '72 C.973 B.A. L.1340 J.D. 10 Journal Square, 3rd Floor
Davidson, David T., (BV) . . . . '60 '86 C.967 B.A. L.851 J.D. [Davidson,A.&C.]
Davidson, Adams & Creach L.P.A., (BV) . . . . 127 North 2nd Street
Dierling, Thomas A. . . . . '74 '01 C.473 B.A. L.1340 J.D. [Ⓐ Millikin&F.]
Doellman, Norbert M., Jr., Attorney at Law, (BV) '49 '76
C.602 B.A. L.608 J.D. P.O. Box 475
Duckett, Douglas E. '57 '82
C&L.608 B.A., J.D. Personnel Dir. & Labor Coun., Co. Comr.
Eberwein, Thomas C. . . . . '48 '73 C.473 B.A. L.150 J.D. Pers. Dir., Children Servs. Bd.
Eichel, Daniel G., (AV) . . . . '51 '76 C.473 A.B. L.150 J.D. 1st Asst. Pros. Atty.
Elliott, George H. . . . . '26 '50 C.473 L.150 J.D. Com. Pleas J.

Ellis, Paris K.
(See Middletown)

Evans, Catherine L. . . . . '71 '96 C.150 B.A. L.201 J.D. [Millikin&F.]
Evans, Jeremy Jean . . . . '74 '04 C.347 B.A. L.30 J.D. [J.J.Evans]
Evans, Timothy R., (AV) . . . . '49 '74 C&L.150 B.A., J.D. [Holbrock&J.]
Evans, Jeremy J., Attorney at Law . . . . 29 N. "D" St.
Ferris, Carl D., (CV) . . . . '55 '80 C.276 B.A. L.1003 J.D. [Ferris]
Ferris, Donald L., (BV) . . . . '24 '52 C.473 B.S. L.608 LL.B. [Ferris]
Ferris Law Office, (BV) . . . . 225 Court Street
Fette, Glenn P. . . . . '63 '92 C.973 B.S. L.1340 J.D. 345 High Street
Fiehrer, Lawrence P., (BV) . . . . '47 '74 C.201 B.S. L.1340 J.D. 10 Journal Sq., Ste. 400
Fischer, Daniel B., (CV) . . . . '34 '64 C.201 B.A. L.1340 J.D. 308 N. 2nd St.
Foley, J. Patrick, III . . . . '48 '76 C.609 B.A. L.150 J.D. Ohio Bureau of Workers' Comp.
Franke, Paul G. . . . . '62 '89 C.973 B.S. L.1340 J.D. [Millikin&F.]

Freund, Freeze & Arnold, A Legal Professional Association
(See Dayton)

Froelke, Frank J., (BV) . . . . '41 '66 C.602 L.150 J.D. Pres., Midland Title Sec., Inc.
Froelke, Gerald G., (BV) . . . . '38 '63 C.602 B.B.A. L.150 J.D. Ste. 315
Fryman, Robert E., (AV) . . . . '28 '53 C.473 B.S. L.150 J.D. [Parrish,F.&M.] ‡
Fulton, Michael A., (BV) . . . . '42 '70 C&L.150 B.B.A., J.D. [Millikin&F.]
Garretson, John A., (AV) . . . . '49 '77 C.674 B.A. L.1340 J.D. [J.A.Garretson]
Garretson, Patrick W., (BV) . . . . '54 '84 C.999 B.S. L.1340 J.D. 924 Laurel Avenue
Garretson, John A., Co. L.P.A., (AV) . . . . 616 Dayton Street
Gates, Roger S., (BV) . . . . '53 '79 C.473 B.A. L.150 J.D. [Morgenstern&M.]
Gattermeyer, Daniel John, (BV) . . . . '58 '83 C.610 B.A. L.930 J.D. 301 High St.
Gedling, James L., (BV) . . . . '47 '80 C.275 B.A. L.1340 J.D. [Holbrock&J.]
Gehlmann, Gregory A. '61 '88 C.201 B.A. L.608 J.D.
Gen. Coun., First Financial Bancorp
Gmoser, Michael T., (AV) . . . . '45 '73 C.473 B.A. L.1340 J.D. Second and High Streets
Gmoser, Olga Faye, (BV) . . . . '39 '92 C.473 B.A. L.201 J.D. [Ⓐ M.T.Gmoser]
Hanchin, Lori Lynn . . . . '73 '98 C.602 B.A. L.902 J.D. Com. Pleas J.
Harris, Karl R., (CV) . . . . '64 '91 C.473 B.A. L.201 J.D. Asst. Co. Prosecutor
Hayslip, Michael W. . . . . '62 '94 C.150 B.S. L.201 J.D. Lithko Contracting, Inc.
Hedric, Craig D., (CV) . . . . '61 '86 C.473 B.A. L.851 J.D. 4510 Hamilton Mason Road
Henderson, Ralph A., (BV) . . . . '29 '53 C&L.608 B.Sc., J.D. 120 N. 2nd St.
Hirka, Sara C. . . . . '72 '97 C.967 B.A. L.608 J.D. [Parrish,F.&M.]
Hofstadter, Louis J., (AV) . . . . '20 '49 C&L.150 J.D. 6 S. 2nd St‡
Holbrock, Hugh D. . . . . '26 '53 C.473 L.1340 LL.B. 315 South Monument Avenue‡
Holbrock & Jonson, (AV) . . . . 315 South Monument Avenue
Holcomb, Jeffrey G., (CV) . . . . '71 '98 C.973 B.A. L.851 J.D. [Ⓐ J.A.Garretson]
Holcomb, John F., (AV) . . . . '37 '62 C.976 A.B. L.150 J.D. 311 Society Bk. Bldg.
Holcomb, John M., (BV) . . . . '65 '91 C.473 B.A. L.150 J.D. [Holcomb&H.]
Holcomb & Hyde LLP, (BV) . . . . 311 Key Bank Building
Holden, Kathryn L. . . . . '58 '86 C.608 B.A. L.117 J.D. 3561 Dawn Drive
Horwitz, Barbara L. . . . . '47 '94 C.108 B.S. L.150 J.D. [Ⓐ M.A.Wolf]
Howard, John Gregory, (BV) . . . . '60 '87 C.383 B.B.A. L.1340 J.D. [J.G.Howard]
Howard, J. Gregory, (BV) . . . . 723 Dayton Street
Hull, Gregory E., (BV) . . . . '58 '83 C.602 B.A. L.851 J.D. [Millikin&F.]
Humbach, Thomas E., (CV) . . . . '48 '77 C.473 A.B. L.678 J.D. 723 Dayton Street
Hurchanik, Richard L., (CV) . . . . '44 '82 C.610 B.S.C.E. L.150 J.D. 110 N. 3rd St.
Hyde, Richard A., (BV) . . . . '64 '89 C.473 B.A. L.851 J.D. [Holcomb&H.]
Imfeld, Bert C., (BV) . . . . '29 '55 L.1340 J.D. 214 High St.
Jacobs, Michael E. . . . . '69 '96 C.150 B.A. L.800 J.D. [McGowan&J.]
Jones, Charles H., (BV) . . . . '18 '48 C.608 B.S. L.150 J.D. [Ⓒ Baden&J.]
Jones, Wanda J. . . . . '73 '98 C.974 B.S. L.150 J.D. Pros. Off.
Jonson, George N., (BV) . . . . '34 '58 C.608 B.A. L.150 LL.B. [Holbrock&J.]
Jusick, Jill A. . . . . '73 '99 C.741 B.A. L.201 J.D. [Ⓐ Davidson,A.&C.]
Keck, William C., (BV) . . . . '44 '70 C.973 B.S. L.602 J.D. [Millikin&F.]
Kennedy, Sharon L., (CV) . . . . '62 '91 C&L.150 B.S.W., J.D. Rutler Co. D.R. Ct.
Kidd, Thomas W., Jr. . . . . '69 '96 C.473 B.A. L.608 J.D. Asst. Pros. Atty.
Kiesey, Cassandra E., (CV) . . . . '63 '90 C.269 B.A. L.201 J.D. Asst. Pros. Atty.
Kindley, Zane Edward . . . . '63 '87 C.607 B.A. L.608 J.D. Child Supp. Enfrcmnt. Agency
Koehler, Lester W. . . . . '23 '49 C.473 L.150 LL.B. 24 Piccadilly Dr.‡
Koehler, Richard N., II, (CV) . . . . '52 '78 C.473 B.A. L.1340 J.D. 5 S. Second St.
Kusel, Mary Lou, (CV) . . . . '47 '80 C.473 B.S. L.1340 J.D. 118 South Second Street
Landis, David H., (BV) . . . . '52 '79 C.473 A.B. L.117 J.D. 246 High Street
LeRoy, Donald C., (BV) . . . . '48 '77 C.608 B.S. L.1340 J.D. 304 N. 2nd St.
Lewis, Heather Sanderson . . . . '66 '91 C.945 B.A. L.893 J.D. [Millikin&F.]
Linsenmann, William M. . . . . '19 '50 C.381 A.B. L.1003 J.D. 628 Sanders Dr.
Litzelfelner, Donald L. . . . . '25 '56 C.473 A.B. L.1340 J.D. P.O. Box 477‡

Lopez, Hodes, Restaino, Milman & Skikos, A Law Corporation
(See Cincinnati)

Manley Burke, A Legal Professional Association
(See Cincinnati)

Marcum, Stephen S., (BV) . . . . '57 '83 C.880 B.A. L.201 J.D. [Parrish,F.&M.]
Masana, Henry A., (BV) . . . . '21 '57 C.973 B.S. L.1340 LL.B. 220 S. Monument Ave.
Masana, Michael P., (BV) . . . . '46 '74 C.473 B.A. L.607 J.D. 220 S. Monument
McCauley-Myers, Janie P. '62 '94
C.432 B.A. L.347 J.D. Legal Offr., First Financial Bancorp
McCracken, John James . . . . '64 '89 C.249 B.S. L.851 2 South 3rd. St.
McGowan, Jack C., (AV) . . . . '47 '74 C.150 B.S.M.E. L.273 J.D. [McGowan&J.]

McGowan & Jacobs, LLC, (AV)
246 High Street, 45011
Telephone: 513-844-2000 Fax: 513-868-1190
Jack C. McGowan; Michael E. Jacobs.
General Civil Practice, Insurance and Personal Injury Law, Trials and Appeals in all Courts, Products Liability, Architects, Engineers, Medical, Dental, and Legal Malpractice, Patent, Trademark and Copyright Law, Political Subdivision Liability, Land Use, Zoning and Eminent Domain Law, Fraud Investigations.
Local Counsel for: Medical Protective Co.; The Travelers Insurance Co.; State Auto Mutual Insurance Co.; Nationwide Insurance Co.; Grange Mutual Casualty Co.; Liberty Mutual Insurance Co.; Metropolitan Property & Liability Insurance Co.; Prudential Casualty Insurance Co.; Ohio Bar Liability Insurance Co.
See Professional Biographies, HAMILTON, OHIO

McKenzie, Kyle B. . . . . '68 '94 C.473 B.S. L.150 J.D. [McKenzie]
McKenzie Law Offices . . . . 315 Maple Ave.
Meyers, Pamela Sue . . . . '51 '77 C.188 A.B. L.309 J.D. 8509 Berk Blvd.
Miller, Fred S., (BV) . . . . '53 '79 C.861 B.A. L.607 J.D. [F.S.Miller]
Miller, Fred S., Co., L.P.A., (BV) . . . . 246 High St.
Millikin, Thomas J., (AV) . . . . '32 '57 C.473 L.150 J.D. 6 S Second St.‡

Millikin & Fitton Law Firm, A Legal Professional Association, (AV)
6 S 2nd Street, 6th Floor, 45011 ⊙
Telephone: 513-863-6700 Fax: 513-863-0031
Stanley D. Rullman; William C. Keck; James E. Michael (Resident, Oxford Office); John H. Clemmons (Resident, Fairfield Office); Michael A. Fulton; John J. Reister; Michele M. Gressel (Resident, Fairfield Office); Jeffrey L. Rulon; Gregory E. Hull; Paul G. Franke; Stephen J. Wolterman (Resident, Fairfield Office); Catherine L. Evans; Heather Sanderson Lewis; Jon P. Whalen;—Thomas A. Dierling; Steven A. Tooman. Of Counsel: Louis E. Wynn.
General Practice. Real Estate, Probate, Estate Planning, Corporation, Taxation, Personal Injury and Litigation.
Representative Clients: City of Fairfield, Ohio; Union Federal Savings Bank; Fort Hamilton Hospital; Miami University, Oxford, Ohio; Key Bank; Waterfield Mortgage Co., Inc.

(This Listing Continued)

Millikin & Fitton Law Firm, A Legal Professional Association (Continued)

Fairfield, Ohio Office: 530 Wessel Drive, Suite 2A, 45014. Telephone: 513-829-6700. Fax: 513-829-0258.
Oxford, Ohio Office: 5020 B College Corner Pike, 45056. Telephone: 513-523-3700. Fax: 513-523-0463.
Mason, Ohio Office: 6900 Tylersville Road, Suite B, 45040. Telephone: 513-336-6363. Fax: 513-336-9411.

Moeller, Patrick G., (CV) ....'58 '84 C.608 B.S. L.1340 J.D. Asst. Pros. Atty.
Moreland, Vickie G., (BV) ....'52 '77 C.610 B.S. L.851 J.D. 955 Ridgefield Road
Morgan, Ronald C. ....'41 '66 C.231 B.A. L.1340 J.D. 118 South Second St.
Morgenstern, Barbara L., (BV) ....'52 '86 C.35 B.A. L.150 J.D. [Morgenstern&M.]
Morgenstern, Carl, (AV) '21 '49 C.930 L.309 LL.B. [Morgenstern&M.] (⊙Rockville, MD)
Morgenstern & Morgenstern Co., L.P.A., (AV) ....300 High Street, Suite 604
Moser, John R. ....'27 '53 C.473 A.B. L.150 LL.B. 515 Northwood Terrace
Muench-McElfresh, Jennifer R. ....'71 '97 C&L.150 B.A., J.D. 315 High Street, 11th fl.
Nardiello, Mary Anne, (CV) ....'62 '89 C.473 A.B. L.201 J.D. Asst. Pros. Atty.
Nastoff, Daniel A. (Andy) ....'66 '91 C.980 B.A. L.150 J.D. [Ⓐ M.A.Wolf]
Nerenberg, Jonathon O., (BV) ....'50 '77 C.608 B.S., B.A. L.1340 J.D. [Baden&J.]
Niehaus, David J. ....'44 '71 C.608 B.Sc. L.1340 J.D. Juv. Ct. J.
Oney, Patricia S., (CV) ....'42 '75 C&L.150 B.S., J.D. Common Pleas Court
Parker, Deborah L. ....'53 '87 C.156 B.A. L.705 J.D. Mag., Ct. of Com. Pleas
Parks, Brenda Bruck ....'50 '91 C.473 B.M. L.150 J.D. [Bruck]
Parrish, Lee H., (AV) ....'43 '68 C.608 B.A. L.150 J.D. [Parrish,F.&M.] ⊙

Parrish, Fryman & Marcum Co., L.P.A., (AV)
First Financial Bank Building, 300 High Street, Suite 704, P.O. Box 747, 45012-0747 ⊙
Telephone: 513-863-8270 Telecopier: 513-863-9999
Email: contact@parrishattys.com URL: http://www.parrishattys.com
Huntington V. Parrish (1906-1973); Cyrus J. Fitton (1889-1978); Francis S. Beeler (1908-1990); Lee H. Parrish; Stephen S. Marcum; Sara C. Hirka; Cynamon T. Trokhan. Retired: Neil B. Smith; Robert E. Fryman.
Business, Real Estate, General Practice, Probate, Estate Planning, Banking Law and Creditor Rights.
Counsel for: First National Bank of Southwestern Ohio; Firstar Bank, N.A. (Butler County); Home Federal Savings & Loan Assn.; Ohio Casualty Corp.
Oxford, Ohio Office: 5995 Fairfield Road, Unit One, 45056. Telephone: 513-863-8270.
See Professional Biographies, HAMILTON, OHIO

Pater, Charles Lloyd ....'50 '93 C.999 B.A. L.1340 J.D. Com. Pleas J.
Pater, Clem, III, (BV) ....'42 '69 C.973 A.B. L.150 J.D. [Pater,P.&P.]
Pater, Gerald L., (BV) ....'43 '68 C.973 A.B. L.150 J.D. [Pater,P.&P.]
Pater, Pater & Pater Co., L.P.A., (BV) ....315 S. Front St.
Persson, E. Hjalmar ....'10 '37 C.473 B.A. L.150 J.D. 6 S Second St‡

Peterson & Peterson
(See Xenia)

Phillabaum, Jason Richard ....'74 '00 C.383 B.A. L.1187 J.D. Pros. Off.
Pierce, John A., (AV) ....'27 '51 C.473 L.150 LL.B. P.O. Box 476
Piper, Robert N. ....'23 '50 C.434 L.150 LL.B. 300 High St.
Reilly-Shefcik, Patricia A. '62 '87 C.967 B.A. L.150 J.D. Assoc. Coun., Ohio Life Insurance Company
Reister, John J., (BV) ....'49 '78 C.207 B.A. L.1003 J.D. [Millikin&F.]
Reyes, Roger O. ....'57 '96 C.101 B.S. L.879 J.D. 246 High Street
Rogers, Randy T. ....'51 '76 C.659 B.S. L.150 J.D. Prob. J.
Rullman, Stanley D., (AV) ....'39 '67 C.853 A.B. L.150 J.D. [Millikin&F.] (⊙Mason)
Rulon, Jeffrey L., (BV) ....'58 '83 C.473 B.A. L.201 J.D. [Millikin&F.]
Sage, Michael J. ....'49 '79 C.473 A.B. L.201 J.D. State J.
Schiavone, Frank Joseph, (BV) ....'47 '78 C.473 B.S. L.201 J.D. 520 Rentschler Bldg.
Schul, David D. ....'44 '79 C.117 B.A. L.1340 J.D. 1st Fin. Bk., N.A.
Seel, Thomas R., (CVⓉ) '62 '89 C.973 H.A.B. L.150 J.D. Staff Atty., Legal Aid Soc. of Greater Cincinnati
Shanahan, Megan Elizabeth ....'73 '00 C.381 B.A. L.150 J.D. Butler Co. Pros. Off.
Shanks, Michael D., (BV) ....'46 '76 C.473 B.A. L.150 J.D. [Holbrock&J.]
Sheets, Gary L., (CV) ....'55 '80 C.437 B.A. L.851 J.D. 315 High Street, 6th Floor
Smith, Glenda A. ....'61 '92 C&L.347 B.S., J.D. P.O. Box 1084
Smith, Neil B. ....'34 '60 C.473 B.S. L.1340 J.D. [Parrish,F.&M.] ‡
Snyder, Christopher John ....'62 '88 C.136 B.S. L.608 J.D. 315 Maple Ave.
Songer, Diana L. ....'68 '93 C.473 B.A. L.150 J.D. 29 North D Street
Sphar, Kristen Lynn ....'73 '98 C.150 B.S. L.201 J.D. Butler Co. Pros. Off.
Spillane, Leslie C. ....'43 '74 C.473 B.A. L.1340 J.D. Dom. Rel. J.
Stephens, Gregory Scott ....'70 '95 C.473 B.S. L.200 J.D. Chf. Asst. Prosecutor, Juv. Div.
Stephenson, Nicole M. ....'72 '98 C.63 B.S. L.201 J.D. 30 North D Street
Stubbs, Thomas H., Jr. ....'42 '69 C.228 B.A. L.150 J.D. Com. Pleas Ct.
Temin, Andrew M. ....'55 '79 C.659 B.A. L.569 J.D. 301 High Street
Thomas, John W., (CV) ....'25 '50 C.473 L.150 J.D. 404 First National Bk. Bldg.
Tooman, Steven A. ....'70 '96 C.967 B.A. L.201 J.D. [Ⓐ Millikin&F.]
Trokhan, Cynamon T. ....'71 '96 C&L.124 B.A., J.D. [Parrish,F.&M.] (Pat.)
Tumblison, Joan Mary ....'52 '99 C.952 B.A. L.1340 J.D. 4110 Hamilton Middletown Rd.
Uhl, John W., (BV) ....'44 '70 C.321 B.A. L.477 J.D. 301 High St.
Ulreich, Jacqueline Michelle ....'76 '01 C.473 B.A. L.201 J.D. Pros. Off.

Waite, Schneider, Bayless & Chesley Co., L.P.A.
(See Cincinnati)

Walsh, H. Vincent, (BV) ....'44 '72 C.150 B.A. L.1340 J.D. 301 S. Front St.
Weil, Rick Lee ....'73 '98 C.150 B.S. L.201 J.D. Pros. Off.
Weisbrod, Michael P., (BV) ....'55 '85 C&L.150 B.B.A., J.D. 304 N. Second Street
Wessel, Richard J., (AV) ....'25 '52 C.473 L.1340 J.D. [Wessel&W.]
Wessel, Robert F., (BV) ....'22 '51 C.473 L.1340 J.D. [Wessel&W.]
Wessel & Wessel, (AV) ....S. Second St.
Whalen, Jon P. ....'71 '97 C.383 B.A. L.201 J.D. [Millikin&F.]
Wilks, Harry T. ....'25 '50 C.473 L.150 LL.B. 220 High St.‡
Willard, John T., (CV) ....'40 '66 C.973 A.B. L.150 J.D. 6 S. 2nd Street, Suite 206
Wolf, Myron A., (AV) ....'46 '75 C.473 B.A. L.150 J.D. [M.A.Wolf]

Wolf, Myron A., The Law Offices of, (AV)
120 North Second Street, P.O. Box 741, 45012
Telephone: 513-863-0664 Fax: 513-868-1800
Email: mawolf@fuse.net URL: http://www.mwolflaw.com
Myron A. Wolf. Associates: Barbara L. Horwitz; Daniel A. (Andy) Nastoff.
Family Law, Divorce and Custody, Insurance Defense and Criminal Law.
Representative Client: State Farm Insurance.
See Professional Biographies, HAMILTON, OHIO

Wolfgang, Rex A., The Law Office of, (BV) '59 '88 C.973 B.S. L.150 J.D.
246 High Street, 45011
Telephone: 513-868-2731 Fax: 513-868-1190
Email: rawolfgan@aol.com URL: http://www.rexwolfgang.com
Civil Practice, Environmental Law, Product Liability, Personal Injury, Real Estate, Construction Law, Community Association Law.
See Professional Biographies, HAMILTON, OHIO

Wynn, Louis E., (BV) ....'28 '55 C.150 L.1340 LL.B. [Ⓒ Millikin&F.]

Young & Alexander Co., L.P.A.
(See Dayton)

Youngs, Eugene W. ....'12 '39 C.966 B.A. L.309 LL.B. 2101 Millville Shandon Rd.‡

Zegarski & Ice Co., L.P.A.
(See Cincinnati)

Zettler, Jack A., (BV) ....'51 '77 C.473 B.S. L.1340 J.D. [J.A.Zettler]
Zettler, Jack A., Co., L.P.A., (BV) ....15 N. 3rd Street
Zornow, Harry B., (BV) '59 '84 C.231 A.B. L.930 J.D. 860 N.W. Washington Blvd., Ste. J

HARRISON, 7,518, *Hamilton Co.*

Charls, Jerome J., (BV) ....'56 '82 C.610 B.A. L.607 J.D. 10150 Harrison Ave.
Ennis, William J., (AV) ....'35 '66 C.973 B.S. L.1340 J.D. [Ennis,R.&F.] ⊙
Ennis, Roberts and Fischer, (AV) ....114 S. Walnut Street (⊙Cincinnati)
Haft, James E., (BV) ....'46 '72 C&L.150 B.B.A., J.D. 115 N. Walnut St.
Kilgo, David M. ....'50 '78 C.150 B.A. L.1340 J.D. Tr. Offr., Southern Ohio Bk.
McKenery, Deborah Lee ....'52 '85 C.651 B.A. L.117 J.D. 106 Harrison Avenue
Peters, Craig M. ....'57 '90 C.150 B.B.A. L.1340 J.D. 10150 Harrison Ave.

HARTVILLE, 2,174, *Stark Co.*

Gaynor, Norman J., III ....'46 '74 C.301 B.A. L.902 J.D. P.O. Box 696
Goldthorpe, Christopher J., (BV) ....'45 '72 C.434 B.A. L.930 J.D. [Lundgren,G.&Z.] ⊙
Hite, C. E., (BV) ....'44 '69 C.610 B.B.A. L.851 J.D. 140 Sunnyside St.
Lundgren, David J., (BV) ....'47 '76 C.967 B.A. L.930 J.D. [Lundgren,G.&Z.] ⊙
Lundgren, Goldthorpe & Zumbar, (BV) ....849 West Maple (⊙Alliance)
McPherson, J. W., Jr. ....'20 '49 C.381 L.273 LL.B. 81 W. Dr.‡
Moe, Paul G. '24 '53 C.178 L.564 LL.B. (adm. in NY; not adm. in OH) Pres., King Electronics Co.
Zumbar, Andrew L., (BV) ....'67 '92 C.528 B.A. L.930 J.D. [Lundgren,G.&Z.] ⊙

HEATH, 8,527, *Licking Co.*

Bindley, Richard S., (BV) ....'51 '78 C.608 B.S. L.117 J.D. [Morrison&B.]
Morrison, David C., (BV) ....'49 '75 C.610 B.B.A. L.7 J.D. [Morrison&B.]
Morrison and Bindley, (BV) ....987 Prof. Pkwy., Unit B
Payne, Walter R. J., Jr. ....'51 '78 C&L.117 B.A., J.D. 672 Alpine Circle

HEBRON, 2,076, *Licking Co.*

Kane, Ira O. ....'46 '72 C.1019 B.A. L.1003 J.D. Pres., MPW Industrial Serv., Inc.
Peck, Jimmy R. '78 '04 C.610 B.B.A. L.608 J.D. In-house Coun., MPW Industrial Services
Tosi, James G., (BV) ....'45 '71 C.608 B.A. L.150 J.D. P.O. Box 658

HICKSVILLE, 3,664, *Defiance Co.*

Clemens, Korhn, Liming & Warncke, Ltd., (AV) ....201 East High Street (⊙Defiance)
Korhn, Stephen F., (AV) ....'47 '72 C.608 B.S. L.851 J.D. [Clemens,K.L.&W.] ⊙
Liming, John M., (BV) ....'56 '81 C.293 B.A. L.477 J.D. [Clemens,K.L.&W.] ⊙
Pelton, Robert D. ....'54 '83 C&L.607 B.A., J.D. 620 N. Main St.
Warncke, Marc F., (BV) ....'64 '89 C.608 B.S.B.A. L.602 J.D. [Clemens,K.L.&W.] ⊙
Weaner, Zimmerman, Bacon, Yoder & Hubbard, Ltd., (AV) 105 E. High St. (⊙Defiance)
Yoder, Stanley J., (BV) ....'53 '80 C.1124 B.S. L.851 J.D. [Weaner,Z.B.Y.&H.] ⊙
Zimmerman, John E., (AV) ....'24 '51 C.851 A.B. L.608 J.D. [Weaner,Z.B.Y.&H.] ⊙

HIGHLAND HEIGHTS, 8,082, *Cuyahoga Co.*

Bernard & Haffey Co., L.P.A.
(See Cleveland)

Catalano, Cynthia A. ....'47 '73 C.739 B.A. L.930 J.D. 5612 Wilson Mills
Cull, William J., Sr. '45 '72 C.363 B.A. L.1003 J.D. V.P. & Gen. Coun., Marconi Medical Systems, Inc.
Gamin, Mark A., (BV) ....'52 '83 C.33 B.A. L.930 J.D. Progressive Cas. Ins. Co.
Jackson, Jennifer S. ....'69 '93 C.221 B.A. L.930 J.D. Progressive Ins. Co.
Legree, Ernest W. ....'21 '53 C.012 B.E.E. L.1003 LL.B. 925 Eastlawn Dr.‡
Norgard, David W. ....'48 '86 C.377 B.S. L.161 J.D. Picker Intl., Inc.
Redmond, James N. '46 '89 C.124 B.S. L.1003 J.D. Corp. Coun., Marconi Medical Systems, Inc.

HIGHLAND HILLS, 1,618, *Cuyahoga Co.*

Slezak, David G. '60 '85 C.62 B.A. L.930 J.D. Senior Vice President & General Counsel, Metropolitan Bank and Trust Company

HILLIARD, 24,230, *Franklin Co.*

Bahnsen, Deborah Nay ....'58 '84 C&L.608 B.S., J.D. 3401 Mill Run Dr.
Bell, Irene Dvoraczky ....'60 '89 C.473 B.Phil. L.201 J.D. 4143 Main Street
Bodycombe, Paul A., (BV) ....'50 '80 C.108 B.A. L.117 J.D. 3535 Fishinger Blvd.
Bostic, Amy L., (BV) ....'62 '88 C.608 B.S. L.117 J.D. [Ⓐ Nobile,N.&T.]

Boyle, Sean O.
(See Columbus)

Cooper, Almeta Elise ....'50 '84 C.915 B.A. L.597 J.D. Ohio State Medical Association
Craig, Steve A., (BV) ....'52 '76 C&L.608 B.A., J.D. 5251 Norwich St.
Crowley, James W. ....'55 '85 C.381 B.A. L.117 J.D. 4149 Maystar Way
Fischer, Thomas M. ....'52 '89 C&L.117 B.A., J.D. 4676 Huntwicke Dr.
Gallant, Howard J., (BV) ....'29 '56 C&L.608 B.S., J.D. 3750 Rutledge Dr.
Gillette, Nancy Pekkanen '57 '92 C.967 B.A. L.608 J.D. Staff Coun., Ohio State Medical Association
Haney, John L., Jr., (BV) ....'49 '76 C.608 B.A. L.117 J.D. 3544 Main St.
Hyslop, Bruce A., (BV) ....'39 '66 C.937 B.A. L.608 J.D. 3955 Brown Park Drive, Ste. B
Hyslop, Jean Forquer, (BV) ....'49 '91 C.737 B.A. L.608 J.D. 3955 Brown Park Dr.
Keith, Charles L. '52 '80 C.610 B.S.C.E. L.117 J.D. Chairman & CEO, Hi-Way Paving, Inc.
Mallory, Diane, (BV) ....'45 '80 C&L.608 B.A., J.D. 4834 Sarasota Dr.
Mills, Steven R. ....'48 '85 C.610 B.A. L.117 J.D. Chicago Title Ins. Co.
Mulgrew, Donald Brent ....'50 '75 C.81 B.A. L.608 J.D. 3401 Mill Run Drive
Needleman, Scott R. ....'56 '91 C.608 B.A. L.117 J.D. [Nobile,N.&T.] ⊙
Nobile, James E. ....'65 '92 C.608 B.A. L.117 J.D. [Nobile,N.&T.] ⊙
Nobile, Martin C. ....'67 '94 C.473 B.S. L.117 J.D. 4511 Cemetery Rd., Ste. B
Nobile, Needleman & Thompson, LLC ....4911 Cemetery Road (⊙Columbus)
Paparodis, Chris O. ....'53 '82 C.381 B.S. L.7 J.D. 5275 Norwich St.
Sarver, Eden R. ....'70 '02 C.266 B.S. L.117 J.D. [Ⓐ Nobile,N.&T.]
Simmons, Robert M. ....'59 '91 C.608 B.S.B.A. L.851 J.D. [Simmons]
Simmons & Company, LPA ....3468 Fairway Commons
Thompson, Matthew J. ....'63 '88 C&L.608 B.A., J.D. [Nobile,N.&T.] ⊙
White, Daniel J., (BV) ....'53 '80 C.150 B.S. L.1003 J.D. 5999 Heritage Lakes
Yannon, Albert A., (BV) ....'31 '57 C&L.608 B.A., J.D. 3380 Ridgewood Dr.

HILLSBORO, * 6,368, *Highland Co.*

Armintrout, G. William, (BV) .... '55 '84 C.473 B.S. L.1187 J.D. 120 Gov. Trimble Pl.
Beery, Forrest F., (BV) .... '21 '50 C.174 B.A. L.150 J.D. [Beery&B.]
Beery, Fred Jerome, (BV) .... '55 '82 C.608 B.Ch.E. L.117 J.D. City Sol. [Beery&B.]
Beery & Beery, (BV) .... 125 N. High St.
Coss, Rocky A., (AV) .... '51 '76 C&L.608 B.A., J.D. 149 E. Main St.
Davis, Richard L. .... '24 '48 C&L.608 B.S., J.D. Ret. Prob. & Juv. J.‡
Davis, Susan L., (BV) .... '55 '80 C.473 B.S. L.607 J.D. 107 Governor Foraker Pl.
DeGallery, Lisa M. '— '96 C.631 B.A. L.454 J.D.
(adm. in MA; not adm. in OH) 9450 State Rte. 73
de Milliano, Maryanne, (BVⓉ) '43 '82 C.424 B.S.N. L.1137 J.D.
(adm. in CA; not adm. in OH) 235 W. South St.
Gamble, Kathy L., (BV) .... '48 '73 C&L.150 B.A., J.D. Rural Legal Aid
Greer, Kevin L., (BV) .... '55 '80 C.1118 B.A. L.851 J.D. Asst. Pros. Atty.
Hapner, James D., (AV) .... '28 '51 C&L.608 B.A., J.D. [Hapner&H.] ‡
Hapner, Jon C., (BV) .... '34 '58 C&L.608 B.A., J.D. [Hapner&H.]
Hapner, Kathryn .... '65 '96 C.1142 B.A. L.69 J.D. [Hapner&H.]
Hapner and Hapner, (AV) .... 127 N. High St.
Hoskins, Jeffrey J., (BV) .... '48 '75 C.610 B.B.A. L.602 J.D. 105 N. High St.
Koogler, Lee David .... '74 '01 C.150 B.A. L.201 J.D. 112 N. High Street

Lyle, Jeffrey Jon, (BV) '57 '83 C.1024 B.S. L.930 J.D.
139 East Beech Street, 45133
Telephone: 937-393-4731 Fax: 937-840-9579
Criminal and Juvenile Law.

McGuire-Haines, Kimberly J. .... '69 '96 C.1154 B.A. L.912 J.D. P.O. Box 793
McKenna, David H., (BV) .... '52 '85 C.575 A.B. L.421 J.D. 149 E. Main St.
McKinney, Carroll V., (AV) .... '27 '60 C.608 B.S. L.266 J.D. 131 E. Beech St.
McMullen, Robert B., Jr. .... '28 '57 C.631 B.A. L.607 LL.B. Com. Pleas J.‡
Ondre, Schaunette Marie .... '70 '98 C.65 B.A. L.999 J.D. Legal Servs. Assn.
Pence, David W., (BV) .... '44 '73 C.275 B.A. L.117 J.D. 120 Governors Trimble Pl.
Pyle, Eugene A. .... '20 '48 C.381 B.S. L.930 J.D. 1848 S.R. 73‡
Swonger, Ronald L., (AV) .... '22 '60 C.952 B.S. L.151 J.D. 120 S. West St.
Trueblood, Brooks G. .... '21 '50 C&L.607 LL.B. 7260 Woodland Trail‡
Turner, Lynn W., (CV) .... '52 '92 C.967 B.A. L.201 J.D. Asst. Pros. Atty.
Van Zant, Gregory F., (CV) .... '62 '88 C.952 A.B. L.902 J.D. 110 N. High Street
Wagoner, Jacob Douglas .... '— '01 C.610 B.S. L.117 J.D. 212 N. High Street
Winner, James Michael '72 '99 C.1070 B.S. L.1522 J.D.
(adm. in CA; not adm. in OH) Air Force JAG

HINCKLEY, —, *Medina Co.*

Abboud, Ruth Sharon .... '57 '82 C.970 B.A. L.1003 J.D. 470 Boston Rd.
Lutz, Timothy R. .... '56 '89 C&L.8 B.S., J.D. 489 Eastwood Rd.
Mahlay, Oleh .... '69 '95 C.124 B.A. L.608 J.D. 705 Stony Hill Road
McCormack, Thomas A., (AV) .... '50 '79 C.161 B.A. L.930 J.D. [McCormack&W.]
McCormack & Wolgamuth Company, L.P.A, (AV) .... 1450 Hinckley Hills Road
Petras, Frank B. .... '65 '91 C.62 B.A. L.930 J.D. [Petras&Assoc.]
Petras & Associates Co., L.P.A. .... 2488 Canyon Creek Drive
Rausch, Edward W., Jr. .... '48 '74 C.714 B.A. L.607 J.D. 153 Brookside Blvd
Wolgamuth, Keith R., (BV) .... '55 '82 C.1044 B.A. L.930 J.D. [McCormack&W.]
Zore, Ernest F. .... '51 '78 C.161 B.S. L.1003 J.D. 645 McKee Trl.

HIRAM, 1,242, *Portage Co.*

Weber, Kirk D. .... '56 '82 C.475 B.A. L.930 J.D. P.O. Box 161

HOLLAND, 1,210, *Lucas Co.*

Atkinson, James R., Law Offices of, (BV) '43 '80
C.608 B.S.Ed. L.851 J.D. 6904 Spring Valley Dr., Ste. 303
Ayers, Andrew J., (BV) .... '53 '79 C.317 B.A. L.851 J.D. [Ⓐ Bahret&Assoc.]
Bahret, Robert J., (AV) .... '53 '80 C.150 B.A. L.851 J.D. [Bahret&Assoc.]

Bahret & Associates Co., L.P.A., (AV) ⒷⒻ
Attorneys at Law
7050 Spring Meadows West, 43528
Telephone: 419-861-7800 Fax: 419-861-7808
Robert J. Bahret. Associates: Andrew J. Ayers; David W. Doerner; Kevin A. Pituch; Jeffrey B. Charles; Mandy M. Gerken; Keith J. Watkins. Of Counsel: Marc J. Meister.
Civil Litigation and Insurance Defense Law.
Representative Clients: American Modern Homes Insurance Company; Auto-Owners Insurance Co.; Central Mutual Insurance Co.; Century Surety Co.; Cincinnati Insurance Company; Dairyland Insurance Group; General Casualty Insurance Co.; German Mutual Insurance Company; Harco National Insurance Co.

See Professional Biographies, HOLLAND, OHIO

Bair, C. William, (BV) .... '48 '83 C.105 B.S. L.851 J.D. [Wagoner&S.]
Bender, Anthony J. .... '49 '83 C&L.851 B.S., J.D. 7456 Annin St.
Bialecki, Korleen M., (BV) .... '61 '89 C&L.851 B.A., J.D. [Wagoner&S.]
Brandt, Stephen D. '46 '76 C.97 B.A. L.608 J.D.
V.P., Schindler Haughton Elevator Corp.
Charles, Jeffrey B., (BV) .... '57 '95 C.97 B.A. L.94 J.D. [Ⓐ Bahret&Assoc.]
Craig, Brian D. .... '54 '80 C.97 B.A. L.117 J.D. 6904 Spring Valley Dr., Suite 303
Doerner, David W. .... '50 '76 C.97 B.S. L.930 J.D. [Ⓐ Bahret&Assoc.]
Fadell, Frederick J., (BV) .... '24 '59 C&L.851 B.B.A., J.D. 8021 N. Shoreline Dr.‡
Friedmar, Richard S., (BV) .... '38 '76 C.477 B.A. L.851 J.D. [Ⓒ Wagoner&S.]
Gerken, Mandy M. .... '79 '04 C.473 B.A. L.607 J.D. [Ⓐ Bahret&Assoc.]
Kestner, Tara J., (BV) .... '66 '96 C&L.851 B.A., J.D. [Ⓐ Wagoner&S.]
Kohli, Leslie Ann, (CV) .... '70 '00 C.333 B.A. L.851 J.D. [L.A.Kohli]
Kohli, Leslie A., Law Offices of, (CV) .... 1236 Clark Street, Suite B
Kovach, Susan A., (AVⓉ) '60 '85 C.967 B.A. L.608 J.D.
(adm. in MI; not adm. in OH) 8935 Oak Valley Rd.
Kuhnle, Carl A., (BV) .... '39 '71 C&L.851 B.S.M.E., J.D. [Ⓐ Wagoner&S.]
Meister, Marc J., (BV) .... '54 '79 C.31 B.A. L.851 J.D. [Ⓒ Bahret&Assoc.]
Morgan, James E., (BV) .... '51 '76 C&L.851 B.A., J.D. 6912 Springvalley Drive
Oathout, James M., (AV) '44 '69 C.197 A.B. L.94 J.D.
(adm. in MA; not adm. in OH) 8850 Royal Oak Dr.‡
Overley, Thomas G., (BV) .... '52 '84 C.347 B.A. L.851 J.D. [Wagoner&S.]
Pituch, Kevin A., (BV) .... '56 '88 C.1293 B.A. L.851 J.D. [Ⓐ Bahret&Assoc.]
Sanders, Richard L., (BV) .... '51 '81 C.97 B.S. L.851 J.D. P.O. Box 221
Smith, Kevin Xavier '52 '77
C.973 B.S.B.A. L.851 J.D. Mgr. Real Estate Dev., Bostleman Corp.
Snavely, David A. ...... '46 '74 C.477 B.A. L.608 J.D. Partner, Trust Company of Toledo
Snyder, Edward L., (BV) ..... '56 '83 C&L.851 B.A., J.D. 6910 Airport Highway, Suite 11
Steinberg, Harold M., (BV) .... '40 '66 C.477 B.A. L.851 J.D. [Ⓐ Wagoner&S.]
Teague, Jan K., (BVⓉ) .... '37 '69 C&L.851 B.A., J.D. 18 Wolf Ridge Drive
Wagoner, Helen Bish .... '46 '80 C.648 B.S. L.851 J.D. [Ⓒ Wagoner&S.]
Wagoner, John E., (AV) .... '39 '65 C&L.851 B.B.A., J.D. [Wagoner&S.]
Wagoner, Mark D., (BV) .... '43 '68 C&L.607 B.S., J.D. [Wagoner&S.]
Wagoner & Steinberg, Ltd., (AV) .... 7445 Airport Highway

Watkins, Keith J., (BV) .... '— '81 C.150 B.A. L.851 J.D. [Ⓐ Bahret&Assoc.]
Yoder, Thomas Alan, (BV) .... '51 '77 C.607 B.A. L.851 J.D. P.O. Box 818
Zhang, Fan .... '67 '98 C.999 B.A. L.1059 J.D. [Ⓐ Wagoner&S.]

HOPEDALE, 984, *Harrison Co.*

Stickles, Steven A. .... '70 '03 C.659 B.A. L.923 J.D. 85147 Blackburn Road

HOWARD, —, *Knox Co.*

Cea, Anthony E. .... '58 '86 C.608 B.S.E.E. L.117 J.D. 157 Green Valley Dr.‡
Jones, Gene A., (BV) .... '17 '48 C.610 B.S.E. L.608 J.D. 4001 Apple Valley Way
Lee, William Johnson .... '24 '48 C.8 L.608 J.D. 704 Country Club Drive
Ragan, William A., Jr. .... '62 '94 C.608 B.S.B.A. L.851 J.D. 521 Lakeview Dr. Hts.

HUBBARD, 8,248, *Trumbull Co.*

Adler, Jeffrey D., (BV) ...... '63 '90 C.980 B.A. L.607 J.D. 973 W. Liberty Street, Suite C
Blackwell, Joseph W. .... '23 '51 L.608 J.D. 418 Parkview Rd.‡
Daugherty, Teresa Rice, Law Office of, (BV) '53 '78
C.980 B.S. L.7 J.D. 48 W. Liberty St.
Duda, Donald A., Jr., (CV) .... '65 '94 C.980 B.S.B.A. L.8 J.D. 48 W. Liberty St.
LaCivita, Richard J., (BV) ..... '48 '75 C.980 B.S.B.A. L.7 J.D. 973 W. Liberty St., Ste. B
Love, Cynthia M., (CV) .... '69 '94 C.980 B.S. L.851 J.D. 48 W. Liberty St.
Marks, Ronald A., (BV) .... '42 '72 C.980 B.A. L.607 J.D. 4765 Topper Hill Drive
Mimna, Roy A., (BV) .... '44 '75 C.608 B.A. L.1017 J.D. 520 Meadowland Dr.
Moran, John J. .... '21 '53 C.363 B.B.A. L.980 J.D. 140 Belle Vista Dr.‡
Rice, Cynthia Westcott, (BV) .... '57 '85 C.679 B.S. L.8 J.D. 48 W. Liberty St.
Rice, Ronald J., (BV) .... '56 '85 C.980 B.A. L.8 J.D. [R.J.Rice]
Rice, Ronald J., Co., LPA, (BV) .... 48 W. Liberty Street

HUBER HEIGHTS, 38,212, *Montgomery Co.*

Caspar, Robert Lee, Jr., (BV) .... '50 '88 C.1208 B.S. L.117 J.D. 7460 Brandt Pike
Conboy, Patrick J., (CV) .... '72 '98 C.107 B.S. L.201 J.D. 5613 Brandt Pike
Dyer, Garofalo, Mann & Schultz, (AV)
4420 Taylorsville Road (ⓒRichmond, IN; Bellefontaine, Dayton, Lima, Middletown, Piqua, Springfield, Troy, Wilmington, Xenia, OH)
Fricker, Keith A., (BV) .... '60 '86 C.1208 B.A. L.851 J.D. 7460 Brandt Pike
Penn, Ralph W., (BV) .... '48 '74 C.999 B.S. L.607 J.D. [R.W.Penn]
Penn, Ralph W., Co. L.P.A., (BV) .... 7049 Taylorsville Rd.
Renshaw, Jeffrey A. '60 '85 C.420 B.A. L.425 J.D.
(adm. in LA; not adm. in OH) Law Clk., Dist. Ct. J.
Schultz, Ronald E., (AV) '42 '67 C.610 B.S. L.608 J.D.
[Dyer,G.M.&S.] (ⓒBellefontaine, Dayton, Lima, Middletown, Piqua, Springfield)
Tomlinson, Jon S., Attorney at Law '55 '99 C.117 B.A. L.179 J.D.
5689 Troy Villa Blvd.

HUDSON, 22,439, *Summit Co.*

Bayer, Frank J. .... '28 '54 C.381 B.A. L.930 LL.B. Ret. Com. Pleas J.
Billick, Timothy R., (BV) .... '52 '77 C.363 B.A. L.851 J.D. 5601 Hudson Dr., Ste. 400
Bockanic, William N. .... '48 '73 C.363 A.B. L.1003 J.D. 7536 Warren Point Lane‡
Carter, Katharine S. .... '28 '83 C.604 B.A. L.1003 J.D. 140 Aurora St.‡
Carter, Van P. .... '46 '73 C&L.802 B.F.A., J.D. 2117 Edgeview Dr.
Chudyk, Peter .... '53 '80 C.363 B.S.B.A. L.1003 J.D. 2580 Brunswick Ln.
Clunk, John D. .... '57 '82 C.611 B.A. L.930 J.D. 5601 Hudson Drive
Cox, Anthony A., (BV) .... '40 '65 C.602 B.A. L.597 J.D. 118 W. Streetsboro St. #95
Crane, Robert L., Jr., (BV) .... '48 '73 C.473 B.S. L.608 J.D. 10 W. Statesboro St.
Curtin, Cynthia K. .... '61 '89 C.347 B.S. L.1003 J.D. 119 North Hayden Pkwy.
Davidson, Ronald H. .... '14 '50 C.381 B.S. L.7 LL.B. 5500 Sullivan Road‡
Diskin, David W. '44 '68 C&L.477 B.A., J.D.
(adm. in NY; not adm. in OH) 7178 Huntington Rd.
Dye, Edward R. .... '41 '73 C.251 B.B.A. L.1003 J.D. 6021 Willow Lake Drive
Ealy, Stephen T. .... '54 '90 C.381 B.B.A. L.8 J.D. 25 Mildford Dr.
Elliott, Frances C., (BV) .... '50 '83 C.608 B.S. L.7 J.D. 83 Sussex Rd.
Ewald, Michael J. '70 '96 C.363 B.S. L.930 J.D.
Team Member Relations Spec., Jo-Ann Stores, Inc.
Gasper, Carol L. .... '63 '88 C.381 B.A. L.150 J.D. 10 W. Streetsboro St., Ste. 301
Gold, Robert H. .... '33 '76 C.473 B.A. L.1003 J.D. 80 Trumbull Dr.
Gray, Neil S. .... '29 '52 C&L.209 J.D. 135 S. Hayden Pkwy.‡
Green, Cynthia Lee Carte .... '61 '87 C.97 B.A. L.1003 J.D. Allstate
Guzzo, Diane R., (BV) .... '61 '89 C&L.8 B.A., J.D. [Weisman&G.]
Hoose, Robert A. .... '74 '01 C.8 B.A. L.989 J.D. 5601 Hudson Dr., Ste. 400
Humbert, Ted A. .... '57 '81 C.381 B.A. L.7 J.D. 5601 Hudson Dr., Ste. 400
Jacobstein, Pamela G. .... '53 '82 C.381 B.A. L.1003 J.D. 6404 Canterbury Dr.
Jahn, Frederick J. .... '50 '92 C.97 B.S. L.8 J.D. Commerce Title
Jordan, David Edward, (AV) .... '38 '67 C.25 B.A. L.659 LL.B. 2881 Blaikley Dr.
Keating, Diana Marie .... '55 '89 C.381 B.S.N. L.8 J.D. 6124 Stone Rd.
Klingshirn, Nancy A. .... '61 '86 C.363 B.S. L.608 J.D. 5785 Williamsburg Circle
Kordel, Douglas A. .... '70 '97 C.851 B.B.A. L.201 J.D. 6098 Eastham Way
Kuhn, David A. .... '29 '54 C.385 A.B. L.930 LL.B. 704 Cutler Ln.‡
Lawko, Susan Marie .... '59 '84 C.385 B.A. L.851 J.D. 56 Milford Dr., Ste. 404
LeFaiver, William A., (Co. L.P.A.) .... '44 '69 C.436 B.S. L.8 J.D. 8010 McGhee Ln.
Lehman, David W. .... '56 '96 C&L.930 B.A., J.D. 1998 E. Haines Hill Rd.
Maher, Robert V. .... '20 '49 C.8 B.A. L.7 LL.B. 15 Baldwin Street
Mastrangelo, Ellen Lee '63 '89
C.385 B.A. L.150 J.D. Gen. Coun., Clarke Automotive Group
Michaels, Lisa M. .... '68 '96 C.645 B.S. L.1003 J.D. 5601 Hudson Drive
Miller, Charles D. .... '15 '40 C.25 A.B. L.976 LL.B. 64 Aurora St.‡
Mosteller, Brenda L. .... '63 '87 C.013 B.A. L.7 J.D. 5821 Fortrose Circle
Norman, Sarah Goss .... '66 '91 C.289 A.B. L.930 J.D. 2212 Edgeview Drive
Nye, J. Randall .... '63 '89 C.1111 B.A. L.8 J.D. [J.R.Nye]
Nye, J. Randall, Co., L.P.A., Law Offices of .... 7941 Ravenna Road
Paisley, Andrew A. .... '62 '89 C.882 B.A. L.930 J.D. 5601 Hudson Drive
Piccirillo, Francis C. '49 '76 C.1062 B.S.I.M. L.1003 J.D.
V.P. & Treas., Fabri-Centers of America, Inc.
Polzin, Mark F. '45 '70 C.959 B.S. L.436 J.D.
(adm. in WI; not adm. in OH) 7481 Hudson Park Dr.
Randazzo, Mary E. .... '70 '98 C.363 B.S.B.A. L.1003 J.D. 522 Meadowridge Way
Rosskamm, Alan D. .... '50 '75 C.821 B.A. L.145 J.D. 5555 Darrow Road
Rothenberg, Marc .... '56 '83 C.473 A.B. L.930 J.D. 5555 Darrow Road
Sahr, R. Lawrence .... '42 '75 C&L.229 B.S., J.D. 1707 Edgar Dr. (Pat.)
Santa, Kevin J., (AV) .... '54 '86 C&L.161 B.B.A., J.D. 1654 Carriage Hill
Smart, John F. '66 '91 C.966 B.A. L.215 J.D.
(adm. in MI; not adm. in OH) 2204 Olde Farm Ln.

Steuer, Escovar, Berk & Brown Co., L.P.A.
(See Cleveland)

Swift, David .... '36 '66 C.63 B.S. L.1340 J.D. 7553 Greenthorn Dr.

Umbaugh, David G., (BV) '49 '74 C.473 A.B. L.597 J.D.
110 W. Streetsboro Street, Suite 3A, 44236
Telephone: 330-650-6608 Fax: 330-655-7617 URL: http://www.davidumbaugh.com
Email: umbaugh@alltel.net URL: http://www.davidumbaugh.net
Estate Planning, Probate, Business Law, Business Law with Exit Planning, Elder Care, Trusts and Estates, Wills, Civil Practice.
See Professional Biographies, HUDSON, OHIO

Warburton, Phillip L. '42 '70 C.318 B.A. L.8 J.D. 2680 Deer Holw
Weisman, Mark B., (BV) '56 '87 C.381 B.S. L.7 J.D. [Weisman&G.]
Weisman & Guzzo, (BV) 230 N. Main St.
White, Daniel S. '57 '83 C.607 B.A. L.124 J.D. 34 Parmelee Dr.
Whitlatch, Walter G. '08 '33 C&L.930 A.B., LL.B. 200 Laurel Lake Dr.‡
Young, Peter F. '37 '62 C&L.930 B.B.A., J.D. 7679 Sugarbush Trail

HUNTSVILLE, 454, *Logan Co.*

Bennett, Charles A. '49 '81 C.473 B.S. L.607 J.D. 6986 Road 39‡
Graham, Joseph V. '47 '90 C.473 B.S. L.117 J.D. 9450 S.R. 368

HURON, 7,958, *Erie Co.*

DeLamatre, Richard D., (BV) '30 '58 C.528 B.A. L.608 J.D. [DeLamatre&D.]
Delamatre, Robert Charles, (BV) '62 '87 C.607 B.S.B.A. L.851 J.D. [DeLamatre&D.]
DeLamatre & DeLamatre, (BV) 74 Mill St.
Johnson, Lawrence P. '37 '80 C.1229 B.M.E. L.851 J.D. 401 Winona Ave.‡
Pickering, Harry E. '19 '44 C&L.477 A.B., J.D. 411 Leisure Dr.‡
Pisano, Ralph C., (AV) '24 '51 C.608 L.215 LL.B. [Pisano&P.]
Pisano, Ralph C., Jr., (BV) '50 '90 C.97 B.S. L.161 J.D. [Pisano&P.]
Pisano & Pisano, (AV) 202 Cleveland Rd., W.

INDEPENDENCE, 7,109, *Cuyahoga Co.*

Alkire, Richard C., (AV) '55 '80 C.321 A.B. L.1003 J.D. [R.C.Alkire]
Alkire, Richard C., Co. L.P.A., (AV) 6060 Rockside Woods Blvd.
Asseff, Carl F. '41 '84 C.608 B.A. L.161 J.D. 6638 Kings Cote Park
Bakula, Charles A. '64 '92 C.161 B.A. L.989 J.D. [⊡ O'Rourke&Assoc.]

Bernard Law Firm, The
(See Cleveland)

Bernstein, Stephen C. '65 '91
C.597 B.A. L.1065 J.D. Acct. Exec/Claims Coun., FEDELI Grp., The
Birmingham, Fletcher A. '56 '88 C.801 B.S. L.7 J.D. V.P., Work in N.E. OH Council
Brokaw, Glenn J. '42 '67 C.705 B.A. L.862 J.D. 4890 Hickory Nut Ln.
Brown, Peter T. '49 '74 C&L.930 A.B., J.D. V.P., Kamalt Corp.
Clevenger, Sherman Gary '38 '70 C.930 B.A. L.1003 J.D. I.R.S.
Connors, Maureen '76 '01 C.599 B.A. L.989 J.D. 5005 Rockside Rd., Ste. 100
Courtney, Mary Llamas '51 '78 C.876 B.A. L.1003 J.D. Estate Tax Atty., I.R.S.
Daprile, Joseph R., (AV) '56 '84 C.980 B.B.A. L.326 J.D. Premier Farnell Corp.
Deegan, Jon Francis '57 '86 C.201 B.A. L.1003 J.D. Realty One
Deller, Danielle S. '70 '96 C.124 B.S. L.1009 J.D AGA Gas, Inc. (Legal Department)
Duffy, Matthew M. '70 '99 C.381 B.A. L.8 J.D. Staff Coun.
Eder, James Robert '62 '89 C.532 B.A. L.930 J.D. 7100 E. Pleasant Valley Rd.
Ellis, Brian R. '45 '73 C.608 B.S.B.A L.910 J.D. I.R.S.
Gaiduk, Louis R. '10 '43 C.251 B.B.A. L.161 J.D. 7893 Dalebrook Rd.‡
Gallas, George S. '28 '59 C.381 B.S.B.A. L.1003 J.D. 6982 Carol Dr.
Gordon, Eric S. '71 '98
C.608 B.S.B.A. L.1003 J.D. Assoc. Gen. Coun., Bristol West Insur. Grp.
Grabow, Raymond J., (BV) '32 '58 C.381 B.S.B.A. L.930 LL.B. Mayor
Greene, Joan E. '68 '94 C.8 B.A. L.608 J.D. AGA Gas, Inc. (Legal Department)
Greenslade, Victor F., Jr. '27 '53 C&L.608 B.S., LL.B. 6200 Oak Tree Blvd.
Gruber, Lynn Frances Ondrey '55 '82 C.165 B.A. L.124 J.D. Cigna Healthcare
Hehr, Albert G., III '68 '99 C.161 B.A. L.989 J.D. [Hehr&M.]
Hehr, Albert G., Jr. '36 '74 C.610 B.S.M.E. L.1003 J.D. [⊡ Hehr&M.]
Hehr & Myers, Co., L.P.A. 4401 Rockside Road
Hice, Brooke M. '75 '00 C.198 B.A. L.124 J.D.
Gen. Coun., Heidelberg Distributing Co.
Hopkins, Kathleen Carrabine '63 '89 C.208 B.A. L.930 J.D. Kamalt Corp.
Kozelka, Frank J., (BV) '45 '70 C.363 A.B. L.161 J.D. P.O. Box 31401
Lissauer, Charles William '38 '64 C.473 B.S. L.930 LL.B. 5990 W. Creek Road
Maybaum, Scott D. '51 '78 C.347 B.S. L.930 J.D. 6000 Freedom Square Dr., Ste. 380
McCarroll, Elaine '52 '77 C.207 B.A. L.161 J.D. I.R.S.
Melnick, Mark G. '73 '00 C.607 B.A. L.989 J.D. Corp. Coun., AGA Gas, Inc.
Morris, Daniel G. '62 '88 C.276 B.A. L.930 J.D. 7809 Old Rockside Road
Moss, Debbie L. '53 '78 C.477 B.S. L.930 J.D. The Dalad Grp.
Myers, Richard A., Jr. '60 '88 C.161 B.A. L.989 J.D. [Hehr&M.]
Nieding, Dean C., (AV) '55 '83 C.930 B.A. L.1003 J.D. [⊠ R.C.Alkire]
Novak, Geoffrey R. '70 '98 C.363 B.A. L.989 J.D. [G.Novak]
Novak, Geoffrey 6611 Rockside Rd., Ste. 110
O'Rourke, R. Russell, (BV) '55 '84 C.882 B.A. L.1003 J.D. [O'Rourke&Assoc.]

O'Rourke & Associates Co., L.P.A., (AV)
2 Summit Park Drive, Suite 650, 44131
Telephone: 216-447-9500 Fax: 216-447-9501
URL: http://www.orourke-law.com
R. Russell O'Rourke; Michael J. Warrell. Of Counsel: Charles A. Bakula.
All aspects of Construction Law including Contracts, Change Orders, Mechanic's Liens, Bond Claims, Litigation, Arbitration and Mediation.
See Professional Biographies, INDEPENDENCE, OHIO

Ricchetti, Eugene T. '39 '66 C.610 B.S.I.T. L.1003 J.D. 5005 Rockside Rd., Ste. 500
Sabo, Aberdeen H. '42 '67 C.207 B.A. L.930 J.D. Atty., I.R.S.
Schmid, Gordon '43 '76 C&L.161 B.B.A., J.D. 6000 Freedom Square Dr., Ste. 380
Severyn, Myra Staresina '62 '87 C.161 B.A. L.930 J.D. Asst. Prosecutor
Simmons, Milton L. '22 '59 C.502 B.S. L.1003 J.D. P.O. Box 31637 (Pat.)
Visconsi, Thomas A., Jr. '42 '75
C.276 B.S.B.A. L.930 J.D. Sr. V.P. & Gen. Coun., FEDELI Grp., The
Wachs, William Powell '71 '00 C.477 B.A. L.851 J.D. RWK Services
Walsh, Terrence Raymond '72 '98 C.259 B.A. L.989 J.D. IRS
Warrell, Michael J., (AV) '54 '80 C.821 B.A. L.608 J.D. [O'Rourke&Assoc.]
Weller, Mark D., (AV) '56 '82 C.645 B.A. L.1003 J.D.
Sr. V.P., Gen. Coun. & Secy., AGA Gas, Inc.

IRONTON, * 11,211, *Lawrence Co.*

Anderson, Robert C., (BV) '52 '78 C.437 A.B. L.607 J.D. [Anderson&A.]
Anderson, W. Mack, (BV) '47 '77 C.610 B.S. L.607 J.D. [Anderson&A.]
Anderson & Anderson, (BV) 408 Park Avenue
Ater, Kenneth B. '23 '59 C&L.607 B.A., J.D. Ret. Com. Pleas J.
Bentley, Richard F., (BV) '53 '78 C.608 B.S. L.851 J.D. [Wolfe&B.]
Burwell, Karen E., (CV) '53 '79 C.610 B.B.A. L.607 J.D. 328 Chestnut St
Burwell, Lloyd W. '25 '53 C.610 B.S.C. L.607 J.D. 2410 South 11th Street
Collins, O. Clark, Jr. '47 '73 C.610 B.A. L.608 J.D. Mun. J.
Cooper, Charles, (BV) '47 '73 C.608 B.A. L.117 J.D. [Cooper&V.]
Cooper, William Charles '47 '73 C.608 B.A. L.179 J.D. [C.Cooper]
Cooper, Charles, Co. LPA 407 Center Street
Cooper & VanAntwerp, (AV) 407 Center St.
Destocki, Paul E. '42 '74 C.886 B.S.C.E. L.1340 J.D. 336 Center St.
Dillon, David Reid, (CV) '48 '80 C.437 A.B. L.608 J.D. 311 South Third Street
Edwards, Carl D., Jr., (AVⓉ) '51 '76
C&L.383 B.B.A., J.D. [Cooper&V.] (⊙Ashland, KY)
Jenkins, Christopher D. '71 '97 C.473 B.A. L.902 J.D.
(adm. in WV; not adm. in OH) 1388 Carl Dr.‡
Kehoe, John E. '43 '71 C.610 B.S. L.608 J.D. Com. Pleas Mun. Ct. Ref.
Kennedy, Richard D. '63 '88 C&L.608 B.A., J.D. 419 Center St.
Kennedy, William D., (CV) '27 '57 C.608 B.A. L.930 LL.B. 409 Center St.
Klein, Thomas L., (BV) '56 '81 C.150 B.B.A. L.851 J.D. 211 Center St
Lambert, Randall L., (BV) '54 '79 C.610 B.B.A. L.117 J.D. 4th & Vernon

Marsteller Law Offices
(See Huntington, West Virginia)

McCann, Kimberly Scott, (BV) '61 '86
C.235 B.S. L.383 J.D. [Cooper&V.] (⊙Ashland, KY)
McCown, David H., (BV) '33 '60 C.473 B.S. L.477 J.D. 311 Park Ave.
McCown, Frank J., (BV) '40 '65 C.473 B.S. L.608 J.D. Com. Pleas J.
McCown, Mark K., (CV) '71 '97 C.473 B.A. L.276 J.D. 311 Park Ave.
McWhorter, Donald Lee, II, (BV) '60 '87 C.235 B.S. L.200 J.D. 215 S. 4th St.

Offutt, Fisher & Nord
(See Huntington, West Virginia)

Payne, David '57 '86 C.383 B.S. L.117 J.D. Prob. J.
Riley, James C., (AV) '17 '41 C.437 B.A. L.608 LL.B. 122 S. 4th St.‡
Smith, Jason P. '74 '99 C.610 B.A. L.608 J.D. P.O. Box 297
Smith, Jeffrey M., (BV) '56 '84 C.477 B.G.S. L.117 J.D. 411 Center Street
Spears, David R., (AV) '50 '78 C.117 B.S. L.1187 J.D.
[Spears&S.] & [Spears&Assoc.]
Spears, Harold D., (AV) '19 '48 C.437 A.B. L.228 J.D.
[Spears&S.] & [Spears&Assoc.]
Spears & Associates Co., L.P.A. 122 S. Fourth St.

Spears & Spears, (AV)
122 South Fourth Street, 45638-1520
Telephone: 740-532-5815; 740-532-6913 Fax: 740-532-5816
Email: spearslawoff@hotmail.com
Harold D. Spears; David R. Spears.
General Civil Practice. Personal Injury, Workers Compensation, Social Security, Probate, Wills, Estates, Guardianships, Real Estate Law.
See Professional Biographies, IRONTON, OHIO

VanAntwerp, Howard, III, (AV) '27 '51 C.138 A.B. L.477 J.D.
(adm. in KY; not adm. in OH) [Cooper&V.] (⊙Ashland, KY)
Waldo, James M., (CV) '49 '78 C.510 A.B. L.1187 J.D. 413 Center St.
Waldo, Jas. E., (CV) '19 '50 C&L.608 B.A., J.D. 413 Center St.
Waldo, Kevin J., (BV) '55 '80 C&L.607 B.A. [Waldo]
Waldo Law Office, (BV) 413 Center St.
Walton, W. Richard '38 '66 C&L.608 B.S., J.D. Com. Pleas J.
Wolfe, John, (BV) '39 '69 C.610 B.S.C. L.608 J.D. [Wolfe&B.]
Wolfe & Bentley, (BV) 425 Center Street

JACKSON, * 6,144, *Jackson Co.*

Benjamin, Dana E., (CV) '65 '96 C.381 B.S.M.A. L.608 J.D. Dept. of Human Servs.
Blanton, Jonathan David '73 '98 C.610 B.A. L.383 J.D. Pros. Atty.
Cole, William S., (BV) '52 '77 C.610 A.B. L.1003 J.D. 227 East Main Street
DeLay, Thomas S. '23 '53 C.611 B.A. L.150 J.D. Ret. Com. Pleas J.‡
Detty, John L. '55 '81 C&L.607 B.A., J.D. 266 East Main Street
Douthett, Marshall B. '32 '62 C.611 B.A. L.608 J.D. Mun. J.
Forshey, Timothy Erwin, (CV) '55 '87 C.999 B.S. L.607 J.D. 212 Pearl
Holzapfel, Leonard F. '52 '78 C.610 B.B.A. L.117 J.D. Com. Pleas J.
Hunter, Richard S., (BV) '27 '50 C&L.608 B.A., J.D. 212 Pearl Street
Kunze, Mary Bone, (BV) '25 '50 C.610 A.B. L.930 LL.B. 235 Pearl Street

Lewis, Richard M., (AV) '57 '82 C.608 B.A. L.117 J.D.
295 Pearl Street, P.O. Box 664, 45640
Telephone: 740-286-0071 Telefax: 740-286-2988 URL: http://www.richardmlewis.com
Email: richard@richardmlewis.com URL: http://www.lawyers.com/richardlewis
Associate: Jill H. Shriver.
General Trial and Appellate Practice, Tort Law, Insurance Law, Medical Negligence, Employment Law, Personal Injury, Commercial Litigation, Domestic Relations, Corporation, Real Estate, Probate and Banking Law, Debtor-Creditor and Criminal Law.
See Professional Biographies, JACKSON, OHIO

Moore, Christopher M. '71 '99 C.952 B.A. L.179 J.D. 287 Pearl St.
Musick, Mark T., (CV) '56 '86 C.610 B.B.A. L.117 J.D. [M.T.Musick]
Musick, Mark T., L.P.A., (CV) 287 Pearl St.
Shriver, Jill H. '78 '03 C.610 B.B.A. L.179 J.D. [⊠ R.M.Lewis]
Smith, Barry L., (BV) '56 '81 C.608 B.A. L.607 J.D. 233 East Main Street

JEFFERSON, * 3,572, *Ashtabula Co.*

Geary, Michael P. '54 '80 C.276 A.B. L.744 J.D. [McNair&G.]
Hague, Charles G. '42 '69 C.318 B.A. L.930 J.D. Com. Pleas J.
Hutchins, Calvin W. '21 '49 C.473 L.150 LL.B. Ret. Prob. & Juv. J.
Jacques, Charles J., Jr., (BVⓉ) '40 '65 C.645 B.S. L.665 J.D. P.O. Box 478
Lemire, Jerome A., (BV) '47 '76 C&L.608 B.S., J.D. 838 State Rte. 46 N.
Loha, Joseph '17 '48 C&L.608 B.A., LL.B. 634 Public Rd.
Mackey, Alfred W. '41 '67 C.318 B.A. L.930 J.D. Com. Pleas J.
Mahoney, Joseph E. '23 '49 C&L.602 B.S., LL.B. Ct. App. J.
Mallone, Joseph P. '15 '50 C&L.607 B.S., J.D. Ret. Com. Pleas J.
McNair, Robert M., (BV) '43 '70 C&L.608 B.S., J.D. [McNair&G.]
McNair & Geary, Co., L.P.A., (BV) 35 W. Jefferson St.
Miller, Virginia Kay '59 '89 C.161 B.A. L.1003 J.D. 36 W. Jefferson St.
Miller, Virginia Kay '59 '89 C.161 B.A. L.989 J.D. 36 West Jefferson St.
Painter, Kevin Richard '63 '94 C.381 B.B.A. L.8 J.D. Co. Legal Aid
Ptaszek, Edward G. '24 '53 C.318 A.B. L.930 LL.B. Ref. Dom. & Juv. Ct.
Reese, Anne M., (BV) '58 '85 C.392 B.A. L.1003 J.D. 121 E. Walnut
Sezon, Marianne '71 '98 C.363 B.A. L.7 J.D. Law Clk., Com. Pleas Ct.
Smith, Kyle B., (BV) '53 '80 C.112 B.A. L.950 J.D. 36 West Jefferson
Vettel, Ronald W. '41 '66 C&L.602 A.B., J.D. Com. Pleas J.

Warren and Young PLL
(See Ashtabula)

Wetherholt, Tamara A. '72 '98 C.381 B.A. L.1003 J.D. Asst. Pros.
Winton, Jeffrey D. '53 '79 C.607 B.A. L.1003 J.D. Ashtabula Co. Joint Vocational Sch.

Wynn, Robert S., (BV) .... '49 '73 C.608 B.A. L.7 J.D. 7 Lawyers Row

JOHNSTOWN, 3,440, *Licking Co.*

Doughten, Robert E., (CV) .... '10 '36 C.473 L.607 J.D. P.O. Box 603
Nicks, John Michael .... '69 '01 C.152 B.A. L.179 J.D. P.O. Box 356
Shafer, Larry F., (BV) .... '49 '80 C&L.117 B.M.E., J.D. 795 W. Coshocton Street

JUNCTION CITY, 770, *Perry Co.*

Vigue, Ronald R. .... '58 '84 C.473 B.A. L.201 J.D. [R.R.Vigue]
Vigue, Ronald R., Attorney, Inc. .... P.O. Box 296

KENT, 27,906, *Portage Co.*

Antognoli, Benito C. R., (BV) .... '54 '79 C&L.8 B.A., J.D. [Williams,W.&K.]
Arthur, Frank, (CV) .... '43 '74 C.381 B.A. L.1003 J.D. 1325 S. Water St.
Averill, Sue N. '52 '95 C.608 B.A. L.8 J.D.
Exec. Dir., Amer. Assn. of Univ. Professors, Kent State Chapter‡
Beck, Robert P., (BV) ...... '44 '74 C.970 B.A. L.902 J.D. Univ. Coun., Kent State Univ.
Can, Errol Anthony, (CV) .... '64 '92 C.20 B.S. L.1187 J.D. [Williams,W.&K.]
Clegg, C. Bailey, (BV) .... '48 '76 C.97 B.A. L.161 J.D. 131 Columbus St.
Conner, Marjorie L. '57 '94
C.381 B.S. L.8 J.D. In-house Coun., The Davey Tree Expert Co.
Coogan, Alan Hall .... '29 '77 C.1375 B.A. L.7 J.D. P.O. Box 3052
Delbene, Louis J. .... '64 '91 C&L.8 B.A., J.D. 1001 S. Water St.
Dubetz, Shirley Arlene .... '27 '54 L.948 LL.B. 1511 River Edge Drive
Dyer, James David, (CV) .... '46 '76 C.381 B.A. L.7 J.D. 123 North Water Street
Giffen, Daniel H. .... '38 '75 C.945 A.B. L.930 J.D. Prof. Emeritus, Kent State Univ.‡
Grim, Nancy E., (BV) .... '55 '84 C.381 B.A. L.8 J.D. 237 E. Main Street
Hamilton, Reid H. '56 '81 C.934 B.A. L.880 J.D.
(adm. in MO; not adm. in OH) 302 Wilson Ave.
Hart, Timothy, (CV) .... '54 '80 C.604 A.B. L.7 J.D. 136 N. Water St.
Hirt, David S., (CV) .... '65 '94 C.381 B.S. L.347 J.D. [Hirt&H.]
Hirt, Lisa J., (CV) .... '65 '93 C&L.347 B.A., J.D. [Hirt&H.]
Hirt & Hirt, (CV) .... P.O. Box 219
Ickes, James E.J. .... '75 '00 C.610 B.B.A. L.608 J.D. [Ⓐ Williams,W.&K.]
Jackman, Titus, (BV) .... '29 '54 C.381 B.A. L.608 J.D. 136 N. Water St., Suite 211
Kratcoski, Peter C., (BV) .... '63 '88 C&L.608 B.A., J.D. [Williams,W.&K.]
Martell, Donald H., (BV) .... '45 '71 C&L.8 B.S., J.D. 1646 Morris Rd.

Naticchia, A. Dale
(See Cleveland)

Nome, William A., (BV) .... '51 '76 C.8 B.A. L.1003 J.D. 1325 S. Water St.
Oates, Ralph L., (BV) .... '38 '70 C.381 B.S. L.7 J.D. 217 E. Main St.
Ochmann, David Leonard '60 '92
C.381 B.S. L.7 J.D. Kent State Univ., Off. of Univ. Coun.
Rissland, Karl R., (CV) .... '46 '90 C.381 B.A.,B.S. L.1003 J.D. 506 Brentwood Ave.
Schultz, William J. .... '54 '79 C.381 B.A. L.930 J.D. Councilman
Scuba, Audrey A. .... '44 '79 C.381 B.S. L.7 J.D. 1188 Munroe Falls Rd.

Slater, Zurz & Gilbert
(See Akron)

Smith, Stephen J., (BV) .... '63 '91 C.381 B.B.A. L.851 J.D. 132 S. Water St.
Smith, Timothy D. .... '43 '77 C.608 B.A. L.7 J.D. 119 Taylor Hall

Stephens & Rosenberg
(See Ravenna)

Vitone, Patrick Michael .... '50 '82 C.381 B.G.S. L.8 J.D. 1750 Campus Center Dr.
Watson, James R. .... '54 '83 C.381 B.A. L.7 J.D. Kent Univ.

Weber, Edward C.
(See Akron)

Welser, Howard T., Jr., (BV) .... '43 '69 C.473 B.A. L.608 J.D. [Williams,W.&K.]
Williams, David E., (BV) .... '49 '76 C.20 B.A. L.117 J.D. [Williams,W.&K.]

Williams, Welser & Kratcoski, (BV)
Eleven South River Street, P.O. Box 396, 44240
Telephone: 330-673-3444 Tele-Fax: 330-673-6460
URL: http://www.wwklaw.com
Members of Firm: Howard T. Welser, Jr.; David E. Williams; Peter C. Kratcoski; Errol Anthony Can; Benito C. R. Antognoli. Associate: James E.J. Ickes.
Business Law, Corporate Law (Formation, Operation, Acquisition and Sale of Corporations, Partnerships, and Limited Liability Companies); Commercial and Residential Real Estate Law (Purchase, Sale, and Development including Condominiums, Subdivisions, and Zoning); Commercial and Residential Construction Law (including Mechanics Liens); Commercial and Residential Landlord Tenant Law; Domestic Relations Law (Divorce, Dissolution, Child Support and Custody); Estate Planning and Probate (Wills, Trusts, and Estate Administration); Traffic Law (Personal Injury, Automobile Accidents, Traffic Violations, and DUI); Criminal Law (Misdemeanors and Felonies); and Litigation Capability in all Practice Areas.
Counsel For: Huntington National Bank; Portage County Automobile Dealers Assn.; Hall-Green Agency, Inc.; Ted Bare Enterprises, Inc.; J.B. Mfg., Inc.; Havre Motor Corp.; Kent Credit Union; Century Management; Twin Lakes Association; Wright Heating and Air Conditioning.
See Professional Biographies, KENT, OHIO

Wilson, Richard A., (BV) .... '46 '74 C.381 B.A. L.8 J.D. 1221 S. Water St.

KENTON, * 8,356, *Hardin Co.*

Ansley, James G. .... '54 '79 C.235 B.A. L.607 J.D. 202 E. Pattison Ave.‡
Bailey, Bradford W., (BV) .... '53 '79 C.608 B.S.B.A. L.607 J.D. 28 N. Main St.
Barrett, Scott N., (BV) .... '51 '76 C&L.607 B.A., J.D. 218 W. Columbus St.
Christopher, Steven D., (BV) '58 '84 C&L.607 B.S.B.A., J.D.
22 N. Main St. (⊙Findlay)
Crates, James L., (BV) .... '40 '65 C&L.607 B.S., J.D. [McKinley&C.]
Crates, Randy L. .... '54 '86 C.1111 B.A. L.607 J.D. 618 W. Kohler St.
Dowd, Thos. M. .... '15 '51 C&L.607 J.D. Ret. Com. Pleas J.
Faulkner, David C. .... '39 '64 C.318 A.B. L.608 J.D. Com. Pleas J.
Fischmann, Garron R. .... '64 '97 C.1111 B.A. L.607 J.D. [G.Fischmann]
Fischmann, Garron, Law Office .... 102 W. Columbus St., Ste. E
Hanna, Mark E., (AV) .... '37 '61 C&L.608 B.A., J.D. 211 W. Franklin St.
Hart, William D., (CV) .... '49 '80 C.608 B.S. L.607 J.D. 111 West Franklin Street
Hord, Terry L. .... '53 '82 C.608 B.S. L.607 J.D. 102 W. Columbus St.
Lange, Keith A., (CV) ...... '56 '81 C.97 B.S. L.607 J.D. 15 N. Detroit Street, Suite 1000
Markley, Frederick E., (BV) .... '37 '61 C&L.608 B.A., LL.B. 109 E. Franklin St.
McKinley, Paul N., Jr., (BV) '50 '75 C.608 B.S.Ed. L.607 J.D.
Law Dir. [McKinley&C.]
McKinley & Crates, (BV) .... 936 E. Franklin St.
Mounts, Kelly L. .... '66 '94 C.901 B.A. L.607 J.D. Asst. Pros. Atty.

Oliver Law Office
(See Columbus)

Rapp, James S. .... '51 '76 C.97 B.A. L.607 J.D. Prob. & Juv. Ct. J.
Roof, Thomas A., (BV) .... '51 '79 C.610 B.B.A. L.607 J.D. 218 W. Columbus St.
Schwemer, David J., (BV) .... '45 '70 C.97 B.A. L.607 J.D. 109 E. Franklin St.
Schwemer, Mark B. .... '75 '02 C.854 B.S.B.A. L.213 J.D. 109 E. Franklin St.
Sinn-Bailey, Holly Ann, (CV) .... '54 '79 C.475 B.A. L.607 J.D. [Sinn-Bailey]
Sinn-Bailey Law Office, (CV) .... 28 N. Main St.
Smith, Burke E. .... '25 '54 C.473 B.S. L.607 LL.B. Prob. & Juv. J.
Tudor, John M., (BV) .... '37 '62 C.608 B.A. L.228 J.D. 22 N. Main St.
Watkins, Elizabeth M. .... '61 '87 C&L.608 B.S., J.D. 9800 T.R. 179
Woods, Melanie J. Caw .... '61 '86 C.607 B.A. L.880 J.D. Asst. Pros.

KETTERING, 57,502, *Montgomery Co.*

Adams, John J., (BV) .... '32 '60 C&L.851 B.A., J.D. 5600 Kentshire Drive
Beach, Jane E., (BVⓉ) .... '56 '85 C.473 B.A. L.36 J.D. 401 E. Stroop Rd.

Berry, Thomas D.
(See Dayton)

Blake, John F. .... '37 '70 C.201 B.A. L.607 J.D. City Pros.
Coen, William R., (BV) .... '27 '53 C&L.608 B.S., J.D. [W.R.Coen]
Coen, William R., L.P.A., (BV) .... 2185 S. Dixie Ave.
Demos, John .... '31 '58 C&L.339 B.A., LL.B. 3233 Newark Dr.
Durbin, Fithian L. .... '14 '42 C.138 L.383 LL.B. 921 Cottonwood Rd.‡
Eitreim, Anthony C. '48 '73 C.118 A.B. L.228 J.D.
(adm. in NC; not adm. in OH) Chf. Coun., U.S. Dept. of Energy

Falke & Dunphy, LLC
(See Dayton)

Glaser, Carol J. .... '— '84 C&L.201 B.S., J.D. 1160 Waving Willow Dr.
Gordon, Edwin J. '33 '59 C.563 B.B.A. L.178 LL.B.
(adm. in NY; not adm. in OH) 1208 Brooklands
Grass, Joseph J. '33 '61 C.339 B.S.M.E. L.146 J.D.
Monarch Marking Systems, Inc. (Pat.)
Greenberg, Marc N. .... '77 '04 C&L.201 B.S., J.D. [Ⓐ Sherrets]
Hanaghan, Ralph J. .... '07 '30 L.201 LL.B. 4525 Troon Trail‡
Hanna, Thomas M. .... '47 '81 C&L.201 B.S., J.D. Mun. Ct. J.

Harvey, Anne Catherine
(See Dayton)

Hawkey, Philip A. .... '46 '76 C.62 B.A. L.1003 J.D. City Manager
Hochwalt, Michael A., (BV) .... '53 '84 C.150 B.A. L.201 J.D. [Hochwalt&S.]
Hochwalt & Schiff, LLC, (BV) .... 500 Lincoln Park Boulevard, Suite 216
Horn, Charles F., (AV) .... '24 '54 C.679 B.S.E.E. L.161 J.D. [Horn&R.]
Horn, Charles J., (AV) .... '57 '83 C.150 B.A. L.999 J.D. 2185 S. Dixie Ave.
Horn & Rife, (AV) .... 2323 W Schantz Ave
Kaylor, Teresa Dorow .... '58 '83 C.201 B.A. L.608 J.D. 4949 Concordia Circle
Long, James Francis .... '59 '84 C.607 B.A. L.608 J.D. 3600 Shroyer Road‡
Mescher, Carl J. .... '33 '56 C.201 L.608 LL.B. 4249 Schrubb Dr.‡
Moore, Larry W. .... '44 '69 C.610 B.B.A. L.383 J.D. Ret. Mun. J.‡
Moore, Robert L. .... '45 '72 C.201 B.A. L.607 J.D. Mun. J.
Morrow, Edwin P., III '68 '98 C.362 B.A. L.596 J.D.
Keybank/McDonald Financial Group
Newberry, Forde J., (BV) .... '47 '73 C.610 B.S. L.1003 J.D. Pros. Atty.
Newlin, John R. .... '20 '49 C.967 A.B. L.477 LL.B. 420 Stoneybrook Dr.‡
Porter, Walter A. .... '24 '49 C&L.150 B.S., LL.B. 872 Timberlake Ct.
Reuther, Albert H. '29 '53
C.201 B.E.E. L.150 LL.B. 2185 S. Dixie Avenue, Room 213 (Pat.)
Rife, Harry P., (AV) .... '37 '62 C&L.608 B.A., J.D. [Horn&R.]
Schiff, Thomas R., (BV) .... '59 '88 C.623 B.A. L.201 J.D. [Hochwalt&S.]
Schmidt, David R., (BV) '49 '84 C.260 B.A. L.201 J.D.
1200 E. Dorothy Ln. (⊙Dayton)
Sessler, Albert L., Jr. '25 '54 C.350 B.S.M.E. L.273 J.D.
(adm. in DC; not adm. in OH) 533 Enid Ave.‡
Sherrets, Carl D., (AV) .... '60 '88 C.381 B.B.A. L.150 J.D. [Sherrets]

Sherrets Law Offices, LLC, (AV) BB
580 Lincoln Park Boulevard, Suite 399, 45429
Telephone: 937-299-9607 Fax: 937-299-9618
Email: carlsherrets@dayton-attorneys.com URL: http://www.dayton-attorneys.com
Carl D. Sherrets. Associate: Marc N. Greenberg.
Probate, Estate Planning, Personal Injury, Business Law, Business Planning, Real Estate, Litigation, Collections, Automobile Accidents, Guardianship, Conservatorship, Wills, Trusts and Estates, Bankruptcy, Family Law, Divorce, Domestic Relations, Child Support, Child Custody, Spousal Support.
See Professional Biographies, KETTERING, OHIO

Wurts, John W. .... '36 '64 C.201 A.B. L.150 J.D. Mun. J.
Zimmerman, George E. .... '24 '55 C.201 B.A. L.150 LL.B. 736 W. Stroup Rd.‡

KIDRON, —, *Wayne Co.*

Pedrozo, Raul A. .... '55 '84 C.235 B.S. L.608 J.D. 1377 Emerson Rd.★

KINGSTON, 1,032, *Ross Co.*

Delong, Richard W., (AV) .... '47 '74 C.608 B.S. L.117 J.D. One N. Main Street

KINGSVILLE, 1,129, *Ashtabula Co.*

Madden, Daniel L., (BV) .... '48 '75 C.608 B.S. L.117 J.D. Village Solr.
Rose, Richard C. .... '20 '47 C&L.930 B.B.A., LL.B. 5993 Lake St.‡

KINSMAN, —, *Trumbull Co.*

Herman, Robert L. .... '64 '90 C.97 B.A. L.1048 J.D. P.O. Box 21
Jones, C. Richard .... '30 '62 C.607 B.S.Ed. L.1003 J.D. 8349 State Rd.‡
Wilde, Kandis D., (CV) .... '66 '94 C.608 B.S. L.8 J.D. P.O. Box 126

KIRTLAND, 6,670, *Lake Co.*

Barnard, Laura C. '56 '83 C.518 A.B. L.608 J.D.
Dir. of Paralegal Studies, Lakeland Community Coll.
Knox, D. J. .... '25 '75 C.930 B.A. L.1003 J.D. 10965 Crestwood Dr.‡
Mitchell, Kenneth L. .... '54 '82 C&L.161 B.M.E., J.D. 9213 Chillicothe Road (Pat.)
Podgurski, John A. .... '49 '84 C.381 B.B.A. L.7 J.D. 9155 Chilicoths Road
Rust, Charles R., (AV) ..... '27 '56 C.251 B.Ch.E. L.1003 LL.B. [Woodling,K.&R.] (Pat.)
Swetland, Donald J., (BV) .... '24 '55 C.930 L.1003 LL.B. 10488 Grandview Dr.
Tawil, Linda E. .... '48 '86 C.608 B.S. L.930 J.D. 7700 Clock Tower Drive
Woodling, Krost & Rust, (AV) .... 9213 Chillicothe Road (Pat.)

LAGRANGE, 1,815, *Lorain Co.*

Murray, Garrett J., (BV) .... '33 '59 C.363 B.S.S. L.930 J.D. P.O. Box 521 (⊙Elyria)

LAKE MILTON, —, *Mahoning Co.*

Kelley, L. Patrick, Jr., (CV) .... '47 '73 C.973 B.S. L.1003 J.D. 17019 Headland

LAKEMORE, 2,561, *Summit Co.*

Hewitt, Bradley J. .... '75 '01 C.970 B.A. L.8 J.D. StarPro Sports Management, LLC

LAKESIDE, —, *Ottawa Co.*

Hagemeyer, J. Lyndal .... '26 '52 C.207 B.A. L.893 LL.B. 606 Wesleyan Dr.‡
Mazur, James Andrew .... '41 '68 C.851 B.B.A. L.1003 J.D. 7597 E. Harbor Road
Witten, Sally Sue .... '24 '48 C.611 B.A. L.150 LL.B. 9400 N. Shore Blvd.‡

LAKEVIEW, 1,056, *Logan Co.*

Cheney, Richard E. .... '22 '50 C&L.607 J.D. 9607 Cottage Grove Ave.‡
Schrader, Chris A., (BV) .... '50 '76 C.97 B.S. L.607 [Shirk&S.]
Shirk, William E., (BV) .... '28 '57 C.207 B.S. L.608 LL.B. [Shirk&S.]
Shirk & Schrader, (BV) .... 500 Main St.

LAKEWOOD, 56,646, *Cuyahoga Co.*

Adrain-Piccorelli, Suzanne H. .... '56 '86 C.930 B.A. L.1003 J.D. 1054 Summit Ave.‡
Bartos, David S. .... '71 '99 C.201 L.989 J.D. [Bartos]
Bartos & Company, LPA .... 13363 Madison Avenue
Blank, David M. .... '48 '78 C.528 B.S. L.161 J.D. 15303 Lake Ave.‡
Burda, Joan M. .... '52 '82 C.97 B.L.S. L.990 J.D. 2035 Elmwood Ave.
Campbell, Paul B., (AV) .... '30 '55 C&L.477 B.B.A., J.D. 12700 Lake Ave.‡
Canary, Nancy H., (AV) .... '41 '68 C.930 B.A. L.1003 J.D. [N.H.Canary] ⊙

Canary, Nancy H., PC, (AV)
12500 Edgewater Drive, Unit 1806, 44107 ⊙
Telephone: 216-226-7466 Fax: 216-266-7426
Email: nacanary@cs.com
Nancy H. Canary.
Estate Planning Law, Probate Law, Personal Planning, Successions.
Palm Beach, Florida Office: 125 Worth Avenue, Suite 117, 33480. Telephone: 561-833-5900. Fax: 561-833-5951.
See Professional Biographies, LAKEWOOD, OHIO

Chandrasekar, Ashvin .... '66 '93 C&L.999 B.A., J.D. 156 Madison Ave.
Clevenger, Daniel E., II, (CV) .... '73 '98 C&L.8 B.A., J.D. 14650 Detroit Ave.
Costanzo, Raymond J., (BV) .... '53 '78 C.602 B.A. L.1003 J.D. [Costanzo&L.]
Costanzo & Lazzaro, (BV) .... 13317 Madison Ave.
Curran, John J. .... '27 '57 C.602 B.A. L.1003 J.D. 13363 Madison Ave.‡
Davies-Watson, Melissa J. ....'67 '96 C.788 B.A. L.1003 J.D. 2142 Wyandotte Ave.
DeJohn, Stephen E. '44 '72
C.999 B.A. L.1003 J.D. Chf. Legal Coun., Ohio Lottery Comm.
Desimone, John P. ....'59 '93 C.381 B.B.A. L.1003 J.D. 1335 Cove Ave., #10
Dowling, John L. ...... '48 '77 C.161 A.B. L.1003 J.D. 14900 Detroit Avenue, Room 211
Elliott, Daniel R., III .... '62 '89 C.477 A.B. L.608 J.D. United Transportation Union
Ellison, Wildon V. ....'65 '93 C.1529 B.A. L.161 J.D. 12020 Lake Ave.
Essi, Brian J., (BV) ....'59 '84 C.1155 B.S. L.1003 J.D. 15306 Edgewater
Essi, David, Jr. .... '31 '59 C&L.930 B.B.A., LL.B. 1246 Manor Park
Fagnilli, Sara J., (AV) ....'60 '85 C.318 B.A. L.1003 J.D. 12650 Detroit Ave.
Fedor, George E., (AV) ....'09 '40 C.930 A.B. L.161 J.D. 12500 EdgewaterDr.‡
Fegen, David A. ....'42 '73 C.363 B.A. L.1003 J.D. 14701 Detroit Ave.
Gallagher, John W. ....'44 '70 Juv. Ct. J.
Gallo, Thea Lucy ....'57 '84 C.161 B.A. L.1003 J.D. 1239 Donald Ave.
Garrity, Robert J. ....'59 '99 C.966 B.S. L.1003 J.D. 1196 Summit Ave.
Gauntner, Timothy J., (BV) .... '41 '70 C.363 B.S.S. L.161 J.D. [T.J.Gauntner]
Gauntner, Timothy J., Co., LPA, (BV) ....14701 Detroit Avenue
Gelfand, Martin David ....'60 '97 C.722 B.A. L.930 J.D. 14400 Detroit Ave.
Glassman, Alan B., (BV) ....'52 '78 C.150 B.B.A. L.117 J.D. Liberty Mut. Ins. Co.
Gordon, Chester E., (AV) .... '31 '55 C.309 A.B. L.930 LL.B. 1100 Wilbert Road
Gruss, Raymond S. .... '57 '91 C.470 B.A. L.1003 J.D. [A Murman&Assoc.]
Guion, Harry E. .... '40 '72 C.930 B.A. L.1003 J.D. 14701 Detroit Ave., Ste. 540
Haas, Ralph R. ....'17 '48 L.1003 LL.B. 1086 Forest Cliff‡
Harris, Russell W., (BV) ....'47 '75 C.207 B.A. L.1003 J.D. 13215 Detroit Ave.

Hunt & Cook LLC
(See Westlake)

Jacobs, Joseph J. .... '67 '96 C.97 B.Ed. L.989 J.D. [Jacobs]
Jacobs Legal Group .... 15614 Detroit Ave.
Jankite, Susan K. ....'50 '99 C.1219 B.A. L.1003 J.D. 1253 Arlington Road
Jones, David W. ....'44 '87 C.112 B.A. L.1003 J.D. 14701 Detroit Ave., Ste. 575
Joseph, George Wm., Jr., (BV) ....'35 '62 C.930 L.1003 LL.B. 12211 Madison Ave.
Kagels, Edward G., (AV) ....'— '63 C.97 B.S.B.A. L.608 J.D. 14701 Detroit Avenue
Kerber, Anthony W., (BV) ....'42 '73 C.62 B.A. L.1003 J.D. [A.W.Kerber]
Kerber, Anthony W., Co., L.P.A., (BV) .... 14701 Detroit Ave.
Kohler, John E., (AV) .... '36 '69 C.251 B.A. L.1003 J.D. 11740 Clifton Blvd.
Konchan, James E., (BV) ....'47 '73 C.932 B.B.A. L.1003 J.D. 15203 Detroit Ave.
Lanton, Joseph L. '— '00 C.161 B.A. L.930 J.D.
Dir., Legal Affairs, The Eliza Jennings Group
Lazzaro, S. Robert E., (BV) .... '53 '78 C.473 B.A. L.201 J.D. [Costanzo&L.]
McHugh, Terrence P. '60 '85 C.473 B.B.S. L.851 J.D.
14600 Detroit Avenue, Suite 1378
McLaughlin, Ronald L. ....'57 '86 C.363 B.A. L.1003 J.D. [R.L.McLaughlin]
McLaughlin, Ronald L., Co., L.P.A. ....14701 Detroit Avenue, Suite 747
Miller, Clinton J., III .... '47 '75 C.477 A.B. L.608 J.D. United Transportation Union
Murman, Michael E., (AV) ....'46 '75 C.201 B.A. L.161 J.D. [Murman&Assoc.]

Murman & Associates, (AV)
14701 Detroit Avenue, Suite 555, 44107
Telephone: 216-228-6996 Fax: 216-226-9011
Email: MURMANLAW@AOL.COM URL: http://www.lawyers.com/murman&associates
Member of Firm: Michael E. Murman. Associate: Raymond S. Gruss.
Municipal Law, Probate and Estate, Professional Responsibility Legal Ethics and Criminal Law in regards to Professional Licensing.
See Professional Biographies, LAKEWOOD, OHIO

Neumann, Arthur W. .... '25 '53 C.251 B.S.Ch.E. L.1003 J.D. 11800 Edgewater Dr.
Patsouras, Peter L. .... '43 '75 C&L.1003 B.A., J.D. V.P., United Transportation Union
Patta, John D. ....'63 '88 C.980 B.S.B.A. L.1003 J.D. 13317 Madison Ave.
Pierson, Ira C. '29 '54 C.674 A.B. L.309 J.D.
(adm. in IL; not adm. in OH) 7 Edgewater Sq.‡
Polatsek, William ....'21 '47 C.188 A.B. L.930 LL.B. 2291 Niagara Dr.‡
Randall, Kerry L. ....'59 '84 C.608 B.A. L.1003 J.D. Liberty Mut. Ins. Co.
Rasmussen, John V., (BV) .....'53 '78 C.363 B.A. L.213 J.D. Coun., Liberty Mut. Ins. Co.
Ray, Jared S. ....'73 '98 C.1288 B.A. L.930 J.D. [A C.L.Sumpter&Assoc.]
Roberts, Neil E., (BV) .... '48 '73 C&L.930 B.A., J.D. 1615 Rosewood
Robinson, Andrew Stairs, JR. '75 '01 C.25 B.A. L.989 J.D.
City Pros. Atty., Law Dept. City of Lakewood
Rupert, John E. .... '27 '51 C&L.188 A.B., LL.B. 18129 W. Clifton Rd.‡
Sagan, Nicholas R. ....'27 '58 C&L.930 A.B., LL.B. 16621 Madison
Salisbury, Elizabeth W., (AV) ....'57 '84 C.228 B.A. L.790 J.D. 15700 West Shore Ct.
Saurman, Jan A., (AV) '53 '78 C.150 B.B.A. L.851 J.D.
Res. Atty., Liberty Mut. Ins. Co.
Schillawski, Philip C., Attorney at Law '55 '87
C.930 B.S.Ch.E. L.477 J.D. 2366 Woodward Ave.
Scott, Curtis, Jr., (BV) ....'47 '79 C.254 B.A. L.1340 J.D. Liberty Mut. Ins. Co.
Shaw, Christopher J., (BV) ....'57 '85 C.276 A.B. L.1003 J.D. 15203 Detroit Ave.
Shinn, Maria L. ....'68 '97 C.532 B.A. L.1003 J.D. 2164 Glenbury Avenue
Shively, Jeffrey A., (BV) ....'51 '77 C.608 B.A. L.1003 J.D. 14701 Detroit Avenue
Sinagra, Anthony C., (AV) .... '40 '67 C.363 B.S. L.1003 J.D. [A.C.Sinagra&Assoc.]
Sinagra, A. C., & Associates, (AV) .... 14701 Detroit Avenue Suite 757
Smith, Richard F., Jr. ....'59 '85 C.610 B.A. L.124 J.D. P.O. Box 771280
Souris, Theodore G. ....'28 '57 C.930 B.A. L.1003 J.D. 1245 W. Clifton Blvd.‡
Splain, Jeanne T. ....'28 '59 C&L.930 B.S., LL.B. 2301 Niagara Dr.
Sroka, Marianne Dennstedt ....'54 '85 C.161 B.S. L.989 J.D. 1284 Manor Park
Stanford, Teresa G., (BV) ....'51 '85 C.97 B.S. L.161 J.D. Liberty Mut. Ins. Co.
Strachan, Shannon Cooper ....'62 '89 C.473 B.S.B. L.124 J.D. [S.C.Strachan]
Strachan, Shannon C. ....16712 Edgewater Drive
Struger, Marlene S. ....'— '80 L.1003 J.D. 15203 Detroit Ave.
Sumpter, Chester L., (AV) ....'58 '85 C.275 B.A. L.893 J.D. [C.L.Sumpter&Assoc.]
Sumpter, Chester L., & Associates, LLC, (AV) .... 16927 Detroit Ave., Ste. 4
Tibbetts, Roger D., (BV) ....'43 '69 C.608 B.A. L.1003 J.D. 14701 Detroit Ave.
Toner, John J. ....'15 '50 C.363 Ph.B. L.1003 J.D. 12550 Lake Ave., Apt. 105‡
Utrata, Carl I. ....'40 '72 C.276 B.S.F.S. L.930 J.D. 1506 Arthur Avenue
Waag, Christian F., Jr., (BV) .... '28 '57 C.347 B.S. L.1003 J.D. 14701 Detroit Ave.
Wehr, Karen R. ....'64 '90 C&L.107 B.A., J.D. [A T.P.McHugh]
Wypasek, Michael A. ....'56 '83 C.201 B.S. L.1003 J.D. 1466 Orchard Grove Ave.

LANCASTER, * 35,335, *Fairfield Co.*

Aiman, Scott A. ....'44 '69 C.930 B.A. L.309 J.D. P.O. Box 2571
Aranda, James C., (BV) .... '46 '71 C.973 A.B. L.602 J.D. [Stebelton,A.&S.]

Babbitt & Weis LLP
(See Columbus)

Barnes, Kenneth M., (AV) .... '30 '57 C.610 B.S. L.608 J.D. [Miller,B.&C.]
Beery, Edward T., (BV) .... '44 '70 C.608 B.S. L.851 J.D. [E.T.Beery]
Beery, Edward Thomas, (BV) ....371 Baldwin Dr.

Benson, Michael E.
(See Columbus)

Berens, Randall S., (BV) .... '53 '78 C.610 B.G.S. L.851 J.D. [Berens&B.]
Berens, Richard E., (BV) ....'57 '85 C.473 B.A. L.117 J.D. [Berens&B.]
Berens & Berens, (BV) ....126 E. Main St.
Bibler, R. Mark, (BV) .... '56 '81 C&L.608 B.S., J.D. [Dagger,J.M.O.&H.]
Boltz, G. Brian, (AV) .... '36 '59 C&L.607 B.A., J.D. 3265 Wheeling Rd. N.E.
Boone, Mary Ann, (CV) ....'59 '87 C.229 B.A. L.1003 J.D. 260 Scott Dr.
Bornstein, Meredith L. '71 '00 C.473 B.A. L.117 J.D.
123 South Broad Street, Suite 214
Brown, Stephen D. ....'63 '98 C.610 B.B.A. L.117 J.D. [A Crabbe,B.&J.]

Calig & Handelman, LPA, (BV)
204 N. Columbus Street, 43130 ⊙
Telephone: 740-653-4400 Fax: 740-653-0037
URL: http://www.chohiolawyers.com
Lee A. Thompson.
Bankruptcy, Personal Injury, Probate, Real Estate, Social Security, Social Security Disability, Medical Malpractice, Wrongful Death, Civil Litigation, Domestic Relations Law.
Columbus, Ohio Office: 854 East Broad Street, 43205. Telephone: 614-252-4885; 1-800-633-5000.
Newark, Ohio Office: 29 S. Park Place, 43055. Telephone: 740-349-8581. Fax: 740-345-4101.
Marion, Ohio Office: 274 S. Main Street, 43302. Telephone: 740-375-5051.
See Professional Biographies, LANCASTER, OHIO

Christian, T. Michael, (BV) .... '47 '72 C.610 A.B. L.608 J.D. [Miller,B.&C.]
Clark, Jonathan C. ....'69 '02 C.317 B.A. L.117 J.D. [A Dagger,J.M.O.&H.]
Clark, Joseph T. .... '41 '66 C&L.607 B.A., J.D. Com. Pleas J.

Colley Shroyer & Abraham Co., L.P.A.
(See Columbus)

Conrad, Aaron R. .... '74 '02 C.150 B.S. L.117 J.D. [A Dagger,J.M.O.&H.]
Corbin, Thomas J., and Associates, (BV) '53 '78
C.610 A.B. L.117 J.D. 842 N. Columbus St.
Courtright, Thurman T. ....'11 '35 C&L.604 J.D. 2126 Sunnyhill Dr.‡

Crabbe, Brown & James LLP, (AV)
111 South Broad Street, Suite 209, 43130 ⊙
Telephone: 740-689-1743 Fax: 740-689-1746
Email: info@cbjLawyers.com URL: http://www.cbjLawyers.com
Steven A. Davis. Associate: Stephen D. Brown.
General Insurance Defense, Product Liability, Professional Malpractice, Premises Liability, Environmental and Toxic Tort Claims, Employment and Labor Law, Tax Matters, General Business and Corporate Law and Litigation, Banking and Securities, Real Estate, Probate and Estate Planning, Criminal Law, Administrative, Regulatory and Governmental Law, Workers Compensation, Intellectual Property, Fire, Arson and Fraud, Fidelity and Surety Life, Accident and Health, Insurance Coverage Law, Construction Claims, Health and Hospital Law, Oil, Gas and Energy Law, Transportation Law, Automobile Dealer Law, Zoning, International Practice and Domestic Law, Land Use Planning, and Eminent Domain.
Columbus, Ohio Office: 500 South Front Street, Suite 1200, 43215. Telephone: 614-228-5511. Fax: 614-229-4559.
Cincinnati, Ohio Office: 30 Garfield Place, Suite 740, 45202. Telephone: 513-784-1525. Fax: 513-784-1250.
Cleveland, Ohio Office: 1280 W. Third Street. Telephone: 216-574-9312.
Urbana, Ohio Office: 118 Scioto Street. Telephone: 937-652-4000.
See Professional Biographies, LANCASTER, OHIO

Dagger, Johnston, Miller, Ogilvie & Hampson, LLP, (AV)
144 East Main Street, P.O. Box 667, 43130 ⊙
Telephone: 740-653-6464; Columbus Direct Line: 614-837-1545; For 614/740 Area Code Only: 800-339-4618 Telecopier: 740-653-8522
URL: http://www.daggerlaw.com
Members of Firm: Robert E. Johnston; Norman J. Ogilvie, Jr. (Certified Specialist in Family Relations Law, Ohio State Bar Association); Mark R. Riegel; Raymond R. Michalski; R. Mark Bibler; Randy L. Happeney (Certified Specialist in Family Law, Ohio State Bar Association); Brian D. Shonk; D. Joe Griffith; Scott P. Wood;—Aaron R. Conrad; Jonathan C. Clark; Carrie S. Snoke; Jeff J. Spangler. Of Counsel: James W. Miller.
General Trial Practice. Business, Commercial, Tax, Estate Planning, Elder Law, Probate, Labor, Real Estate, Corporation, Family Law, Insurance, Personal Injury, Wrongful Death, Oil and Gas Law, Employment, Criminal Law, OMVI Law, Traffic Defense, Juvenile Law.
Thornville, Ohio Office: East Columbus Street, P.O. Box 272. Telephone: 740-246-6337.
Portsmouth, Ohio Office: 801 John Street. Telephone: 740-355-6644.
See Professional Biographies, LANCASTER, OHIO

Davis, Sandra W., (BV) ....'51 '91 C.960 B.S. L.117 J.D. 109 North Broad Street
Davis, Steven A., (BV) .... '63 '91 C.37 B.A. L.846 J.D. [Crabbe,B.&J.]
Donahey, Richard S., (BV) .... '41 '68 C&L.608 B.C.E., J.D. [Twyford&D.] ⊙

Dugan, Vincent A., Jr.
(See Columbus)

Edwards, James A., (BV) ....'47 '75 C.611 B.A. L.477 J.D. [Edwards&E.]

Edwards, Judith L., (BV) ....'50 '78 C.611 B.A. L.608 J.D. [Edwards&E.]
Edwards & Edwards, (BV) .... 136 E. Main St. (⊙Valdosta, GA)
Finnen, George R. ....'30 '65 C.610 B.S. L.607 J.D. 212 Marvel Dr.‡

Friedman & Mirman Co., L.P.A.
(See Columbus)

Fruth, Daniel J. ....'77 '02 C.313 B.S. L.117 J.D. 109 North Broad Street
Gibbs, David R. ....'45 '78 C.645 A.S.M.E. L.7 J.D. Diamond Power Intl., Inc.

Goldman & Rosenthal
(See Columbus)

Green, Frank W., (CV) .... '41 '69 C.381 B.S. L.8 J.D. 123 S. Broad Street, Suite 230
Griffith, D. Joe, (BV) ....'64 '91 C.434 B.A. L.851 J.D. [Dagger,J.M.O.&H.]
Happeney, Randy L., (BV) ....'58 '85 C.473 B.A. L.608 J.D. [Dagger,J.M.O.&H.]
Harker, John D., (BV) ....'47 '74 C.608 B.A. L.117 J.D. 123 S. Broad Street, Suite 230
Harris, Patrick Noll ... '63 '91 C.97 B.S. L.608 J.D. Co. Admr., Fairfield Co. Comr.'s Off.
Haselberger, Christina E. ....'76 '03 C.611 B.A. L.608 J.D. Spec. Asst. Pros. Atty.
Hensley, Paul R. ....'70 '97 C.381 B.S.B.A. L.608 J.D. 109 North Broad Street
Jackson, S. Farrell ....'32 '55 C&L.608 B.S., J.D. Com. Pleas J.
Jarvis, Timothy P., Attorney at Law '69 '02
C.610 B.B.A. L.1340 J.D. 123 S. Broad St., Ste. 234
Johnson, Matthew E. ....'73 '99 C.347 B.A. L.179 J.D. 109 North Broad Street
Johnson, Rodger K. '26 '55 C&L.597 B.S., J.D.
(adm. in IL; not adm. in OH) 370 Timber Lane‡
Johnston, Robert E., (AV) ....'29 '54 C.611 B.A. L.150 J.D. [Dagger,J.M.O.&H.] ⊙
Kellner, George K., Jr., (BV) ....'41 '69 C.924 B.S. L.607 J.D. 419 E. Main Street

Kenney-Pfalzer, Susan
(See Columbus)

Kistler, Judson C., (BV) ....'12 '37 C&L.608 B.A., J.D. 1400 E. Main St.
Kolehmainen, Kay A. ....'55 '80 C.313 B.A. L.851 J.D. Ref. Comm. Pleas Ct.
Landefeld, David L., (BV) ....'51 '76 C.385 A.B. L.608 J.D. Pros. Atty.
Lantz, James A., (AV) ....'21 '47 C.207 B.A. L.608 J.D. [Lantz,L.&L.]
Lantz, Lantz & Lipp Co., L.P.A., (AV) ....129 W. Chestnut St.
Lentz, E. R., (BV) ....'23 '52 C.97 B.A. L.608 J.D. 746 Orchard Dr.

Lewis, Gregg R.
(See Columbus)

Libert, Donald J., (AV) ....'28 '56 C&L.276 B.S., J.D. 127 W. Wheeling St.‡
Linehan, James M., (CV) ....'63 '88 C.473 B.S. L.904 J.D. 120 1/2E. Main
Luse, James W. ....'42 '68 C.381 B.S. L.608 J.D. Mun. J.
Maley, Larry M., (BV) ....'49 '91 C.823 B.A. L.117 J.D. 1381 Pinecrest Dr., N.E.
Marx, Carol Seubert, (BV) ....'54 '79 C.851 B.A. L.608 J.D. 106 Starret St., Ste. 210
Marx, Gregg, (BV) ....'55 '79 C&L.608 B.A., J.D. [C.S.Marx]

McCoy, Carl, Attorney at Law
(See Newark)

Michalski, Raymond R., (BV) ....'51 '76 C.608 B.A. L.607 J.D. [Dagger,J.M.O.&H.]
Miller, James W., (AV) ....'28 '55 C&L.608 B.S., J.D. [Dagger,J.M.O.&H.]
Miller, Barnes and Christian, (AV) ....420 East Main Street
Nelson, Stephanie Ann Graubner ....'70 '01 C&L.117 B.A., J.D. Lancaster City Pros. Off.
Northness, Robert C., (CV) '57 '87
C.878 B.S. L.608 J.D. 201 South Broad Street, Floor Four
Ogilvie, Norman J., Jr., (BV) ....'43 '68 C.597 B.A. L.608 J.D. [Dagger,J.M.O.&H.]
Pechar, Todd D. ....'72 '98 C.967 B.A. L.117 J.D. 109 North Broad Street
Pieplow, Richard A. ....'42 '82 C.266 B.S. L.117 J.D. 357 Betz Rd., N.W.

Plymale Partnership LLP, The
(See Columbus)

Price, Jason A. ....'69 '94 C.831 B.A. L.117 J.D. 126 E. Chestnut St.
Ralston, Joseph R. ....'21 '52 C&L.266 J.D. Ret. Mun. J.
Reed, Charles E., (AV) ....'27 '51 C.608 L.879 J.D. 450 Mound St.‡
Riegel, Mark R., (BV) ....'51 '77 C.967 B.A. L.608 J.D. [Dagger,J.M.O.&H.]
Rose, Martha A., (BV) ....'54 '79 C.150 B.A. L.608 J.D. 229 E. Main

Rourke & Blumenthal, LLP
(See Columbus)

Sabol, Suzanne Kay
(See Columbus)

Seeley, Robert H., (AV) ....'22 '47 C.611 A.B. L.930 J.D. 123 S. Broad St.
Shonk, Brian D., (BV) ....'61 '86 C.930 B.A. L.93 J.D. [Dagger,J.M.O.&H.]
Sitterley, William J., (BV) ....'47 '73 C.20 B.A. L.608 LL.B. [Sitterley&V.]
Sitterley & Vandervoort, Ltd., (BV) .... 123 S. Broad St., Ste. 211
Smith, Laura B. ....'69 '94 C.117 B.A. L.608 J.D. 224 Main Street
Snider, John M., (BV) ....'57 '82 C&L.117 B.A., J.D. 109 North Broad Street
Snider, Rick L., (BV) ....'54 '79 C&L.608 B.A., J.D. [Stebelton,A.&S.]
Snoke, Carrie S. ....'— '02 C.610 B.A. L.117 J.D. [Dagger,J.M.O.&H.]
Spangler, Jeff J. ....'79 '04 C.500 B.B.A. L.608 J.D. [Dagger,J.M.O.&H.]
Spires, Jeremiah J. ....'37 '65 C.229 B.A. L.608 LL.B. 735 Franklin Avenue
Stebelton, Gerald L., (AV) ....'39 '70 C.608 B.S.Engr. L.117 J.D. [Stebelton,A.&S.]

Stebelton, Aranda & Snider, A Legal Professional Association, (AV)
109 North Broad Street, 43130
Telephone: 740-654-4141 Fax: 740-654-2521
Email: saslaw@sas-lawfirm.com URL: http://www.sas-lawfirm.com
Gerald L. Stebelton; James C. Aranda; Rick L. Snider.
Personal Injury, Automobile Accidents and Injuries, Wrongful Death, Medical Malpractice, Civil Litigation, Business and Tax Planning and Corporations, Family Law, Divorce, Child Custody, Child Support and Adoptions, Residential and Commercial Real Estate, Probate, Elder Law, Estate Planning and Employment Law.
See Professional Biographies, LANCASTER, OHIO

Stoughton, Ronald C., Sr., (CV) ....'45 '79 C.610 B.S. L.117 J.D. [R.C.Stoughton,Sr.]
Stoughton, R. C., Sr., (CV) ....121 N. High St.

Stumler, Rebecca J.
(See Columbus)

Supman, Jack ....'20 '47 C.437 B.A. L.608 J.D. 285 Timber Lane‡
Thompson, Lee A., (BV) ....'52 '83 C.381 B.S. L.7 J.D. [Calig&H.] (⊙Columbus)

Twyford & Donahey, P.L.L., (BV)
3794 Old Columbus Road, N.W., 43130 ⊙
Telephone: Toll Free: 1-800-686-1699 Fax: 614-849-0475
Email: help@twyforddonahey.com URL: http://www.twyforddonahey.com
Richard S. Donahey.
Personal Injury Litigation, Wrongful Death, Medical Malpractice, Products Liability, Automobile Accidents, Trucking Accidents, Head and Spinal Injuries, Motorcycle Accidents and Injuries, Uninsured Motorists, Insurance Law, Airplane Crash Litigation, Railroad Accidents, Slip and Fall, Dog Bites, Work Related Injuries, Birth Injuries, Nursing Home Abuse and Neglect.
References: The Huntington National Bank; Bank One of Columbus; BancOhio National Bank.
Columbus, Ohio Office: 495 South High Street, 43215-5058. Telephone: Toll Free: 1-800-686-1699. Email: help@twyforddonahey.com

(This Listing Continued)

Twyford & Donahey, P.L.L. (Continued)
Circleville, Ohio Office: 214 South Court Street, 43113. Telephone: Toll Free: 1-800-686-1699. Email: help@twyforddonahey.com.
Delaware, Ohio Office: 163 N. Sandusky, Suite 103, 43015. Telephone: Toll Free: 1-800-686-1699. Email: help@twyforddonahey.com.
Newark, Ohio Office: 137 West Main Street, Suite C., 43025. Telephone: Toll Free: 1-800-686-1699. Email: help@twyforddonahey.com.
London, Ohio Office: 25 West Fifth Street, 43140. Telephone: Toll Free: 1-800-686-1699. Email: help@twyforddonahey.com.
See Professional Biographies, LANCASTER, OHIO

Vandervoort, Craig M., (BV) ....'67 '92 C.473 B.S. L.608 J.D. [Sitterley&V.]
Vandervoort, Jeffrey K., (CV) ....'70 '95 C.347 B.S.B. L.851 J.D. [Sitterley&V.]
Vandervoort, Peter M., (BV) ....'36 '63 C.477 B.A. L.607 J.D. [Sitterley&V.]
Venie, Todd M. ....'73 '98 C.347 B.A. L.608 J.D. Asst. Pros. Atty.
Voss, Jack D. ....'21 '49 L.309 J.D. 212 S. Broad St.
Wentz, Gregory C., (BV) ....'54 '81 C&L.117 B.A., J.D. P.O. Box 1028
Wilson, William B., Jr. ....'21 '45 C.608 B.A. L.930 LL.B. P.O. Box 1068

Wirth, David
(See Columbus)

Wolske & Barclay, A Legal Professional Association
(See Columbus)

Wood, Scott P., (BV) ....'68 '94 C.610 B.A. L.608 J.D. [Dagger,J.M.O.&H.]
Zigan, Steven E. ....'72 '99 C.117 B.A. L.608 J.D. Atty. & Jud. Clk., Com. Pleas Ct.
Zimpfer, George F., (BV) ....'15 '41 C.608 L.607 LL.B. 109 E. Main St.

LEBANON, * 16,962, *Warren Co.*

Allen, Mitchell Wade, (CV) ....'65 '91 C&L.608 B.A., J.D. [Allen&C.]
Allen & Crossley, (CV) ....52 East Mulberry Street
Anderson, Keith W., (BV) ....'57 '83 C.679 B.S. L.150 J.D. Asst. Pros.
Anthony, Mark A. ....'59 '91 C.999 B.A. L.201 J.D. 20 Desales Ave., Suite A
Bednarczuk, Robert ....'24 '62 C.608 B.S. L.1340 J.D. 2283 Bone Rd. Rt. 4
Bennett, Charles Kirby ....'47 '73 C.970 B.A. L.608 J.D. 801 Wildwood Court

Bieser, Greer & Landis, LLP
(See Dayton)

Bogen, Mark R., (BV) ....'48 '73 C.967 A.B. L.150 J.D. 41 N. Broadway

Bossin, Phyllis G., Co., L.P.A.
(See Cincinnati)

Bronson, Neal B. ....'48 '72 C.94 B.S. L.150 J.D. Com. Pleas J.

Buechner, Haffer, O'Connell, Meyers, Healey & Koenig Co., L.P.A.
(See Cincinnati)

Casper and Casper
(See Middletown)

Chalfie & Farley, Co., L.P.A.
(See Cincinnati)

Cole, Thomas T., (BV) ....'48 '83 C.608 B.A. L.1340 J.D. 12 W. South Street
Courtney, Darren L. ..... '64 '91 C.473 B.S. L.902 J.D. Corp. Coun., Fujitec America, Inc.
Crist, Renee L. ....'71 '01 C.383 B.A. L.201 J.D. [Rittgers&R.]
Crossley, Paige Anne, (CV) ....'67 '92 C&L.608 B.A., J.D. [Allen&C.]
Dearie, James A. ....'68 '93 C.602 B.A. L.280 J.D. [Rittgers&R.]
Demos, Gregory John, (BV) ....'66 '94 C.608 B.A. L.1187 J.D. [Diehl&D.]
Diehl, Thomas J., (BV) ....'63 '88 C.473 B.S. L.150 J.D. [Diehl&D.]
Diehl & Demos, LLP, (BV) ....304 East Warren Street
Duning, J. William, (AV) ....'43 '68 C&L.150 B.A., J.D. [Gray&D.]
Duvelius, Carolyn A., (BV) ....'61 '88 C&L.201 B.S., J.D. 500 Justice Dr.
Eagle, Thomas G., (BV) ....'61 '86 C.235 B.A. L.383 J.D. [T.G.Eagle]

Eagle, Thomas G., Co., L.P.A., (BV)
3386 N. State Route 123, 45036
Telephone: 937-743-2545
Email: eaglelawoffice@cs.com URL: http://www.lawyers.com/eagle
Thomas G. Eagle.
General Civil and Criminal Trial and Appellate Practice in State and Federal Courts, in Ohio and Kentucky, including Personal Injury, Wrongful Death, Criminal Law, Civil Rights, Consumer Law, Commercial and Business Litigation, Bankruptcy, Real Estate, Family Law and others.
See Professional Biographies, LEBANON, OHIO

Faulkner, Derek Brandon ....'73 '99 C.347 B.A. L.201 J.D. Pros. Off.
Fedders, P. Daniel ....'37 '61 C.602 L.150 LL.B. Com. Pleas J.
Flannery, James L. ....'49 '74 C.97 B.S. L.150 J.D. Com. Pleas J.
Florence, Mark T., (BV) ....'53 '80 C.473 B.A. L.1340 J.D. [Kaufman&F.]
Fowler, William G., (BV) ....'47 '73 C.610 B.A. L.150 J.D. 12 W. South Street
Gelbert, Pamela P. ....'61 '86 C.705 B.A. L.150 J.D. Fujitec America, Inc.
Gray, Jon F. ....'57 '86 C.930 B.S.E.E. L.1003 J.D. 75 Rough Way, Unit C

Gray & Duning, (AV)
130 East Mulberry, 45036
Telephone: 513-932-2871 Cincinnati: 513-398-7388 Fax: 513-932-5532 TDD: 513-932-2871
Email: duning@grayandduning.com URL: http://www.grayandduning.com
Members of Firm: Meryl B. Gray (1907-1989); J. William Duning; Donald E. Oda, II.
Civil Trial Practice. Probate, Estate Planning, Family, Real Estate, Personal Injury, Juvenile, Criminal, Annexation, Zoning and Municipal Law. Trials.
See Professional Biographies, LEBANON, OHIO

Hash, Joanne V., (CV) ....'32 '79 C.603 A.B. L.150 J.D. Asst. Pros. Atty.
Hasselbach, W. Andrew, (BV) ....'58 '91 C&L.150 B.A., J.D. 500 Justice Drive
Hedges, Jackson C., (BV) ....'38 '63 C.207 B.A. L.477 J.D. 24 N. Broadway
Herdman, Paul N., (AV) ....'27 '51 C.952 A.B. L.150 LL.B. 730 E. Main St.‡
Herriott, Scott H. ....'45 '75 C.532 B.S. L.117 J.D. Gen. Coun., Fujitec America, Inc.
Howard, Anne K., Attorney at Law ..... '66 '01 C.012 B.A. L.150 J.D. 785 Lake Bluff Ct.
Hubbell, Martin E. ....'73 '01 C.846 B.S. L.201 J.D. [Diehl&D.]
Iversen, Yvonne A., (BV) ....'63 '92 C&L.201 B.A., J.D. Mag.
Jarnicki, Harold, (BV) ....'49 '74 C.150 B.A. L.607 J.D. 576 Mound Ct., Ste. B

Jenks, Pyper & Oxley Co., L.P.A.
(See Dayton)

Jones, Fred E., (AV) ....'26 '51 C.473 L.1340 LL.B. Ret. Ct. of App. J.
Kaminsky, Brenda Stacie ....'76 '00 C.30 B.A. L.989 J.D. Pros. Off.
Kaufman, William H., (AV) ....'43 '71 C.473 B.S. L.1340 J.D. [Kaufman&F.]
Kaufman, Wm. Robert, (BV) ....'72 '01 C.473 B.A. L.150 J.D. [Kaufman&F.]

Kaufman & Florence, (AV)
144 East Mulberry Street, P.O. Box 280, 45036
Telephone: 513-932-1515; 423-1363 Fax: 513-932-9172
Email: wkaufman@go-concepts.com
Members of Firm: William H. Kaufman; Mark T. Florence. Associate: Wm. Robert Kaufman.
General Practice. Corporation, Probate, Insurance, Criminal, Real Estate, Family, Equine and Negligence Law, Trials, Mediation, Arbitration.

(This Listing Continued)

Kaufman & Florence (Continued)

Representative Clients: Farm Credit Services; Lebanon Raceway; Lebanon Citizens National Bank. Local Counsel for: Cincinnati Gas & Electric Co.; Celina Mutual Insurance Co.; Western Water Company.
Approved Agents and Attorneys for: Old Republic National Title Insurance Co.; Farmers Home Administration.

See Professional Biographies, LEBANON, OHIO

Kearin, Kathy H., (BV) ....'51 '76 C&L.607 B.A., J.D. 730 E. Main Street

Krehbiel, Anne Einspanier, (BV) '55 '80 C.383 B.S. L.150 J.D.
42 East Mulberry Street, Suite B, 45036
Telephone: 513-934-3200 Fax: 513-934-3223
Email: AEKLAW@go-concepts.com
Probate, Estate Planning and Administration, Elder Law, Wills and Trusts, and Guardianship.

See Professional Biographies, LEBANON, OHIO

Lopez, Hodes, Restaino, Milman & Skikos, A Law Corporation
(See Cincinnati)

Loxley, Gary A. .... '61 '87 C.473 B.A. L.607 J.D. Asst. Pros.★

Manley Burke, A Legal Professional Association
(See Cincinnati)

McKay, Leroy F. .....'51 '83 C.827 B.A. L.150 J.D. Tr. Offr., Lebanon Citizens Natl. Bk.

Mengle, John S., The Law Offices of, (BV) '52 '78 C.473 A.B. L.1340 J.D.
Clark Building, 42 East Silver Street, 45036
Telephone: 513-932-2047 Fax: 513-932-3269
Email: mengle@go-concepts.com URL: http://www.menglelaw.com
Associate: Jane A. Short.
General Civil and Criminal Trial Practice, Business Law, Negligence, Family Law, Adoptions, Child Custody, Divorce, Premarital Agreement, Wills and Probate, Trusts and Estates, Estate Planning, Equine Law, Municipal Law, Bankruptcy, Real Estate Law, Mental Health Law, Personal Injury, Dog Bites, Auto Accidents, Slip and Fall, Wrongful Death, Collaborative Law, Collections.

See Professional Biographies, LEBANON, OHIO

Nixon, C. Keith, Jr. ....'72 '99 C.608 B.A. L.117 J.D. Warren Co. Pros. Off.
Oda, Donald E., II, (CV) ....'69 '95 C.608 B.A. L.151 J.D. [Gray&D.]
Oliver, Lois A., (BV) .... '49 '76 C.473 B.A. L.150 J.D. 324 E. Warren Street
Oliver, Timothy A., (BV) .... '50 '74 C&L.608 B.S.B.A., J.D. Pros. Atty.
Peters, Erik A., (BV) ....'47 '74 C.659 B.A. L.150 J.D. 570 Justice Drive

Pickrel, Schaeffer & Ebeling
(See Dayton)

Powers, Dallas Paul ....'34 '68 C.201 B.S. L.1340 J.D. Co. Ct. J.
Revelson, Jay D., (BV) ....'50 '76 C.861 B.A. L.607 J.D. P.O. Box 175
Rittgers, Charles H., (AV) ....'51 '78 C.473 B.A. L.150 J.D. [Rittgers&R.]
Rittgers, Ellen B., (BV) ....'53 '79 C.473 B.A. L.150 J.D. [Rittgers&R.]

Rittgers & Rittgers, (AV) 🅱🅱
12 East Warren Street, 45036
Telephone: 513-932-2115; 513-459-0355 Facsimile: 513-934-2201
Email: silfvenk@rittgers.com URL: http://www.lawyers.com/rittgers&rittgers
Members of Firm: Charles H. Rittgers; Ellen B. Rittgers; Jason A. Showen; James A. Dearie; Renee L. Crist.
Criminal Law, Family Law, Personal Injury, Civil Litigation, Insurance Law.

See Professional Biographies, LEBANON, OHIO

Rosen, Matthew, (CV) '54 '81 C.787 B.A. L.1340 J.D.
Gen. Coun., Fujitec America, Inc.
Rupp, Margaret A. ....'72 '98 C.610 B.A. L.607 J.D. Lexis Nexis
Secrest, Elizabeth A., (CV) .... '68 '94 C.473 B.Ph. L.201 J.D. Asst. Co. Pros.
Shilleh, Laila J. ....'66 '90 C.1161 B.A. L.1340 J.D. Fujitec America, Inc.
Short, Jane A. ....'72 '00 C.473 B.Phil. L.201 J.D. [Ⓐ J.S.Mengle]
Showen, Jason A. ....'64 '00 C.260 B.S. L.1410 J.D. [Rittgers&R.]
Sievers, Andrew L. ....'63 '94 C&L.201 B.S., J.D. Asst. Pros.
Simendinger, Mark, (CV) ....'52 '80 C.608 B.A. L.1340 J.D. 225 Kirby Rd.
Staton, Roger D. ....'50 '75 C.473 B.S. L.608 J.D. 355 Summit St., 101 Dave Ave. E.
Summers, Jillora H., (BV) ....'59 '83 C.607 B.S. L.999 J.D. P.O. Box 781
Tamashasky, Anne L. ....'52 '95 C.973 B.A. L.201 J.D. Asst. Pros. Atty.
Tepe, Timothy N., (BV) ....'59 '84 C&L.201 B.S., J.D. P.O. Box 148

Thompson and DeVeny Co., L.P.A.
(See Dayton)

Tippett, C. Lewis '58 '86 C.1063 B.A. L.280 J.D.
(adm. in GA; not adm. in OH) LEXIS-NEXIS

Waite, Schneider, Bayless & Chesley Co., L.P.A.
(See Cincinnati)

Watkins, Christopher A., (BV) .... '58 '83 C.473 B.A. L.150 J.D. Pros. Atty

Wirth, David
(See Columbus)

Wright, Bernard H., Jr. '48 '75
C.970 B.A. L.861 J.D. V.P. & Tr. Offr., The Lebanon Natl. Bk.
Young, Marvin E., (AV) ....'15 '40 C.473 L.1340 LL.B. 484 Creekside Dr
Young, Warren C., (AV) .... '10 '33 C.201 L.999 Lebanon Bank Bldg., Ste. 300
Yurick, Mark Stephen ....'62 '87 C.8 B.S. L.150 J.D. City of Lebanon

LEETONIA, 2,070, *Columbiana Co.*

Shelar, Richard C., (BV) ....'39 '69 C.980 B.A. L.7 J.D. 710 Columbia St.
Zarnick, Jacklynn M. ....'39 '89 C.980 B.A. L.8 J.D. 446 Sleepy Hollow Drive

LEIPSIC, 2,203, *Putnam Co.*

Weaver, Robert B., (AV) .... '32 '57 C&L.477 B.B.A., J.D. 214 S. Belmore St.‡

LEWISBURG, 1,798, *Preble Co.*

Anzman, Mark C., (CV) .... '62 '92 C.172 B.S. L.201 J.D. P.O. Box 221
Ditmer, Mary A., Attorney at Law ....'66 '96 107 N. Commerce St.
Faber, Richard V., Jr., (BV) ....'54 '78 C&L.607 B.A., J.D. 200 N. Commerce St.
Hobbs, H. Steven, (BV) ....'58 '83 C&L.201 B.S., J.D. P.O. Box 489 (ⓞMiamisburg)

LEWIS CENTER, —, *Delaware Co.*

Blue, Allan Marshall ....'41 '66 C.608 B.S.B.A. L.260 J.D. 5542 Columbus Pike
Master, John E. ....'55 '83 C.608 B.A. L.851 J.D. 3817 Nicoya Ct.
Pemberton, David L., (AV) ....'40 '66 C&L.608 B.A., J.D. 2626 Lewis Center Rd.
Slayton, Thomas F. ....'42 '75 C&L.851 B.B.A., J.D. P.O. Box 211
Smith, Eric M. ....'— '96 L.117 J.D. 3306 Arctic Avenue
Welch, Rosemarie Ann ....'72 '99 C.434 B.A. L.117 J.D. [R.A.Welch]
Welch, Rosemarie A., Co. LPA .....................................P.O. Box 322

LEXINGTON, 4,124, *Richland Co.*

Brown, R. Joshua, (BV) ....'58 '84 C.967 B.A. L.117 J.D. 32 Lutz Ave.
Hire, John S., (AV) .... '56 '82 C.608 B.A. L.117 J.D. Red Diamond Limited

LIMA, * 40,081, *Allen Co.*

Anderson, Michael P., (BV) ....'61 '87 C.363 B.A. L.117 J.D. [Cory,M.W.R.&C.]
Baldwin, Charles E. ....'22 '49 C.97 B.S. L.477 J.D. Box 660, 201 North Elizabeth
Balyeat, Clay W., (BV) ....'59 '85 C.235 B.S. L.607 J.D. [Daley,B.&L.]
Balyeat, Robert L., (AV) ....'28 '52 C.473 A.B. L.608 LL.B. 1728 Allentown Road‡
Balyeat, William B., (BV) '33 '57 C&L.608 B.S., J.D.
[Daley,B.&L.] (ⓞColumbus Grove)
Banks, Farley K. .... '57 '95 C.446 B.A. L.607 J.D. 311 Market St., Ste. 201

Baran, Piper, Tarkowsky, Fitzgerald & Theis Co., L.P.A., (AV)
121 West High Street, Suite 905, P.O. Box 568, 45802 ⓞ
Telephone: 419-227-5858 Fax: 419-227-4569
URL: http://www.baranlaw.com
Robert B. Fitzgerald; Mark A. Van Dyne; Richard T. Reese;—Angela M. Elliott; Kenneth J. Heisele.
General Civil Practice. Trials in all Courts. Insurance Defense, Corporate, Family Law, Estate Planning, Personal Injury, Products Liability and Construction Law. Commercial Litigation. Suretyship. Environmental and Governmental Liability. Professional Liability, Worker's Compensation.

See Professional Biographies, LIMA, OHIO

Bartels, N. Shannon, (CV) ....'69 '94 C.16 B.A. L.930 J.D. [Ⓐ Siferd&M.]
Batté, Leslie K. ....'— '92 C.966 B.A. L.602 J.D. [Mihlbaugh]
Baumeister, Michelle L. ....'47 '94 C.607 B.A. [Baumeister]
Baumeister Law Office ....3495 Woodhaven Lane
Becker, Stephen L., (BV) .... '49 '75 C.215 A.B. L.607 J.D. [Huffman,K.B.&B.]
Bennett, Richard C., (CV) ....'19 '49 C.108 A.B. L.607 J.D. 3235 Allentown Road
Berry, M. Daniel, (BV) ....'44 '72 C.288 B.A. L.607 J.D. [M.D.Berry]
Berry, M. Daniel, L.P.A., (BV) ....212 N. Elizabeth Street
Blair, James F., & Associates, (BV) '47 '74
C&L.607 B.A., J.D. 212 N. Elizabeth St., 1st Fl.
Bowers, Anthony J. ....'15 '39 C&L.607 J.D. 212 N. Elizabeth St.‡
Bowers, David E., (BV) ....'43 '70 C.203 B.S. L.607 J.D. Pros. Atty.
Brock, T. Blain, II, (BV) .... '68 '93 C.851 B.B.A. L.607 J.D. [Huffman,K.B.&B.]
Brown, Christi L. ....'63 '94 C.967 B.A. L.117 J.D. [C.Brown]
Brown, Christi ....850 Bellefontaine Ave.
Bryant, Thomas F. ....'32 '66 C.97 B.A. L.607 J.D. Ct. of App. J.
Buckley, Michael Edward ....'70 '98 C.679 B.S. L.179 J.D. Jud. Clk.
Butler, Bruce B. ....'26 '58 C.688 B.M.E. L.851 J.D. Standard Oil Chem. Co.
Cannon, Terri Lynn .... '75 '01 C.851 B.S. L.607 J.D. 3rd Dist. Ct. of Appeals of Ohio
Chamberlain, F. Stephen, (BV) .... '62 '88 C&L.607 B.A., J.D. 400 W. North St.
Cheney, David A., (AV) .... '48 '74 C.608 B.S.B.A. L.607 J.D. [Cory,M.W.R.&C.]
Cornwell, Ted E., (BV) ....'51 '76 C.97 B.S.B.A. L.607 J.D. [Scherner,H.&C.]
Cory, Frank B., (AV) ....'30 '55 C.197 B.A. L.477 LL.B. [Cory,M.W.R.&C.]

Cory, Meredith, Witter, Rumer & Cheney, A Legal Professional Association, (AV)
101 N. Elizabeth Street Suite 607, P.O. Box 1217, 45802-1217
Telephone: 419-228-6365 Fax: 419-228-5319
Frank B. Cory; Donald J. Witter; Michael A. Rumer; Sumner E. Walters; David A. Cheney; Michael P. Anderson; Robert J. Meredith; Victoria U. Maisch; J. Alan Smith.
General Civil Practice. Corporation, Commercial, Banking, Utilities, Negligence, Family and Domestic Relations Law, Taxation and Insurance Laws, Probate and Estate Planning, Real Property, Labor and Employment Law, Trials and Appeals in all Courts.
General Counsel For: Univ. of Northwestern Ohio.
Local Counsel for: Diminion East Ohio Gas Company; Premcor; Motorist Insurance Co.; Grange Insurance Co.; Auto Owners Insurance Co.; Cincinnati Insurance.

See Professional Biographies, LIMA, OHIO

Crawford, Leslie L. .....'70 '00 C.97 B.S. L.607 J.D. Gen. Coun., Investor Life Servs., Inc.
Cunningham, Mariah M. ....'77 '03 C.97 B.A. L.607 J.D. [Scherner,H.&C.]
Cupp, Robert R., (BV) ....'50 '76 C&L.607 B.A., J.D. 3003 W. Hume Rd.
Daley, Charles W., (AV) .... '25 '49 C.607 A.B. L.150 J.D. [Daley,B.&L.]
Daley, Douglas A., (BV) ....'55 '80 C.602 B.S. L.608 J.D. [Daley,B.&L.]
Daley, Balyeat & Leahy, LLC, (AV) ....1728 Allentown Road
Da Pore, Joseph C., (AV) ....'30 '54 C&L.607 A.B., LL.B. [J.C.DaPore&Assoc.]
DaPore, Joseph C., & Associates Co., L.P.A., (AV) .... 130 W. North St.
Davis, Mark E. G. ....'— '99 C.966 B.A. L.862 J.D. [Ⓐ Hunt&J.]

Denmead Law Office
(See Columbus)

Derryberry, Glenn H., (CV) ....'51 '77 C.97 B.S. L.607 J.D. Chf. Mag., Juv. Ct.
De Stephens, William P., (CV) ....'23 '62 C.532 B.A. L.607 J.D. 232 N. Main St.
Dickason, Oren E., (AV) ....'13 '38 C&L.607 J.D. 2260 W. High St.‡
Donohue, Gregory W., (CV) '54 '80 C.381 B.B.A. L.607 J.D.
311 E. Market St., Ste. 306
Drexler, Deborah L., (BV) ....'57 '83 C&L.607 B.A., J.D. Mag.
Dugan, Michael E., (BV) ....'47 '74 C.711 B.S. L.607 J.D. [M.Dugan]
Dugan, Michael, (BV) ....138 W. High St.
Dyer, Garofalo, Mann & Schultz, A Legal Professional Association, (AV)
2727 Harding Highway (ⓞRichmond, IN; Bellefontaine, Dayton, Huber Heights, Middletown, Piqua, Springfield, Troy, Wilmington, Xenia, OH)
Edwards, Joe S., Jr., (CV) ....'42 '68 C.611 B.A. L.802 J.D. 2626 Shoreline Drive
Elliott, Angela M. ....'78 '04 C.97 B.A. L.124 J.D. [Ⓐ Baran,P.T.F.&T.]
Emerick, Jana E., (CV) ....'65 '92 C&L.607 B.A., J.D. Asst. Co. Pros.
Emerick, William Clayton ....'75 '00 C.851 L.607 J.D. 212 N. Elizabeth St.
Evans, John R. .... '28 '52 C.473 B.S. L.607 J.D. Ret. Ct. Appls. J.
Fisher, James P., (AV) ....'38 '63 C.967 B.A. L.607 J.D. [Fisher&V.]
Fisher & Vandemark, (AV) ....303 E. High St.
Fitzgerald, Robert B., (AV) ....'57 '82 C&L.607 B.A., J.D. [Baran,P.T.F.&T.]
Geiger, Anthony L., (BV) '57 '83 C&L.201 B.S.B.A., J.D.
209 N. Main Street, 6th Floor
Good, Danielle Adele ....'71 '97 C.967 B.A. L.1187 J.D. 417 North West Street
Gottschalk, Craig A., (CV) .... '71 '97 C.231 B.A. L.607 J.D. [Huffman,K.B.&B.]
Guernsey, J. Thomas ....'17 '40 C&L.477 B.A., J.D. Ret. App. Ct. J.
Haddad, Tina R. ....'61 '89 C.161 B.A. L.607 J.D. Asst. Pros. Atty.
Hadley, Ronald E. .... '36 '64 C&L.607 A.B., J.D. Appl. Ct. J.
Hamman, Timothy C., (CV) .... '48 '73 C.91 B.A. L.607 J.D. Admin. Co. Prob. Ct.
Hawk, Janet Corey ....'60 '85 C.602 B.A. L.851 J.D. 4733 Kitamat Trail‡
Heeter, Richard D. ....'23 '59 C.967 A.B. L.607 J.D. 811 Canyon Dr.‡
Heisele, Kenneth J. ....'78 '05 C.1292 B.A. L.607 J.D. [Ⓐ Baran,P.T.F.&T.]
Hermon, Gary R., (AV) .... '41 '66 C.885 B.A. L.607 J.D. [Ⓒ Hunt&J.]
Hill, Janet R. ....'59 '91 C.383 B.B.A. L.421 J.D. Law Clk., Ct. of App.
Honigford, Robert Joseph .... '53 '91 C.91 B.A. L.851 J.D. 234 North Main Street
Huffman, John C., (BV) ....'63 '89 C.97 B.A. L.851 J.D. [Huffman,K.B.&B.]
Huffman, Lawrence A., (BV) ....'53 '81 C&L.607 B.A., J.D. [Huffman,K.B.&B.]
Huffman, Lawrence S., (AV) ....'30 '58 C&L.607 J.D. [Huffman,K.B.&B.]
Huffman, Matthew C., (AV) ....'60 '85 C.602 B.A. L.150 J.D. [Huffman,K.B.&B.]

Huffman, Kelley, Becker & Brock, LLC, (AV)
127-129 North Pierce Street, P.O. Box 546, 45802
Telephone: 419-227-3423 Fax: 419-228-1937
Email: info@hkbblaw.com URL: http://www.hkbblaw.com

(This Listing Continued)

Huffman, Kelley, Becker & Brock, LLC (Continued)

Fred Wemmer Gooding (1914-1972); John R. Evans (1928-2000); Lawrence S. Huffman; C. Bradford Kelley; Lawrence A. Huffman; Stephen L. Becker; Matthew C. Huffman; John C. Huffman; T. Blain Brock, II; Craig A. Gottschalk.
Civil Practice. Plaintiff's Personal Injury, Negligence Law, Medical Malpractice Defense, Trials and Appeals in all Courts, Family/Domestic Relations, Real Estate, Corporations, Construction Law, Probate and Estate Planning.
Representative Clients: The Medical Protective Co.; Physicians Insurance Company of Ohio; Hamilton Mutual Insurance Co.; Bank One, Lima, Ohio; Superior Metal Products; Urology Assoc. of Ohio, Inc.; Spartech Corp.

See Professional Biographies, LIMA, OHIO

Hunt, James I., (AV) .... '14 '48 L.607 J.D. [Hunt&J.]

Hunt & Johnson, (AV)
400 West North Street, 45801-4298
Telephone: 419-222-1040 Fax: 419-227-1826 URL: http://www.hjelawoffice.com
URL: http://www.hjelaw.com
Members of Firm: James I. Hunt; Jerry M. Johnson. Associate: Mark E. G. Davis. Of Counsel: Gary R. Hermon.
Family Law, Adoptions, Child Custody, Child Support, Divorce, Domestic Violence, Premarital Agreements, Spousal Support, Corporate Law, Breach of Contract, Mechanics Liens, Collections, Real Estate, Commercial Real Estate, Condominium Law, Landlord and Tenant Law, Mortgages, Taxation, Estate and Gift Taxation, Income Tax, Property Tax, Trusts and Estates, Asset Protection, Charitable Giving, Estate Litigation, Estate Planning, Guardianship and Conservatorship, Wills and Probate.

See Professional Biographies, LIMA, OHIO

Hursh, Tammie K. .... '65 '92 C.97 B.S. L.851 J.D. 1000 Wardhill Ave.
Huston-Kinworthy, Carlene .... '51 '92 C.253 B.A. L.607 J.D. [Huston-Kinworthy]
Huston-Kinworthy Law Office .... 211-215 N. Elizabeth St.
Jacobs, Ann Elizabeth .... '— '77 C.273 B.A. L.128 J.D. [A.E.Jacobs]
Jacobs, Ann E., Attorney at Law .... 558 W. Spring St.
Jenson, Margaret I., (CV) .... '56 '84 C.878 B.S. L.607 J.D. Lima Tech. Coll.
Johnson, Jerry M., (AV) .... '48 '75 C&L.607 B.S., J.D. [Hunt&J.]
Kelley, C. Bradford, (BV) .... '52 '79 C.611 B.A. L.607 J.D. [Huffman,K.B.&B.]
Kendall, William G., (BV) '45 '73
C&L.607 B.A., J.D. Asst. Co. Pros. (⊙Columbus Grove)
Kill, James L., (AV) .... '38 '65 C.610 B.S.C. L.607 J.D. 1800 Allentown Rd.
King, James C., (BV) .... '40 '67 C&L.607 B.S., J.D. 212 N. Elizabeth St.
Kinworthy, David R. .... '35 '65 C&L.607 B.A., J.D. Com. Pleas J., Juv. & Prob. Div.
Kluge, William F., (AV) .... '50 '76 C.23 B.A. L.607 J.D. 124 S. Metcalf St.
Knisley, Dean A., (BV) .... '59 '86 C.610 B.A. L.607 J.D. [Knisley L.] ⊙
Knisley Law, (AV) .... 2100 Harding Highway (⊙Columbus)

Kuhn, Thomas R., (BV) '45 '70 C.602 B.A. L.607 J.D.
973 West North Street, 45805
Telephone: 419-228-2122 Fax: 419-999-6298; URL: http://www.kuhnlawoffice.com
Email: trkuhnatty@wcoil.com URL: http://www.kunhlawoffice.com
Personal Injury, Wrongful Death, Criminal Law, Traffic Law, Probate, Family Law, Adoption, Wills, Domestic Relations.

See Professional Biographies, LIMA, OHIO

LaSovage, Michael E. '44 '69 C.477 B.A. L.912 J.D.
(adm. in MI; not adm. in OH) V.P. & Treas., The LaSovage Behrendt Co.
Lauber, William G. .... '50 '75 C.932 B.S. L.607 J.D. Mun. J.
Lawson, Walter M., III, (BV) .... '44 '69 C.608 B.A. L.607 J.D. [Ⓐ W.M.Lawson,Jr.]
Lawson, Walter M., Jr., Law Office of, (AV) '19 '48
C&L.608 B.A., J.D. 119 North West Street
Leahy, John M., (AV) .... '39 '66 C.363 B.S. L.608 J.D. [Daley,B.&L.]
Leahy, John Michael, (BV) .... '72 '98 C.473 B.A. L.851 J.D. [Daley,B.&L.]
Leonard, Paul R. '43 '69 C.610 B.S. L.1340 J.D.
Pres. & Dir., West Central Ohio Reg. Develop. Bd.
Leonard, Robert K., (AV) .... '44 '69 C.118 B.A. L.608 J.D. [R.K.Leonard]
Leonard, Robert K., LLC, Law Offices, (AV) .... 119 N. West St., Ste. 101
Light, Robt. M. .... '17 '47 C&L.608 B.A., LL.B. Ret. Com. Pleas J.
Lortie, Daniel John .... '52 '94 C.608 B.S.N. L.851 J.D. Dist. Hearing Offr.
Macke, Jason A. .... '71 '98 C.610 B.A. L.608 J.D. Law Clk., Ct. App.
Maisch, Victoria U., (BV) .... '54 '94 C.607 B.A. L.201 J.D. [Cory,M.W.R.&C.]
Martin, Dan .... '44 '85 C.608 B.S. L.607 J.D. 2727 Harding Hwy.
Mason, Jonathan A., (AV) .... '47 '73 C&L.150 B.A., J.D. [Mason,S.&M.] ⊙

Mason, Schilling & Mason Co., L.P.A., (AV)
P.O. Box 937, 45802 ⊙
Telephone: 800-840-3514 Fax: 513-489-0834
Email: msm@mason-law.com URL: http://www.mason-law.com
Jonathan A. Mason.
Commercial, Creditors Rights, Bankruptcy, Collection, Banking and Financial Institution Law, Civil Litigation, Federal Consumer Law Litigation, Foreclosures, Automobile Deficiencies, Credit Cards, Medical Debts, Bad Checks, Business Loans/Commercial Debt, Vehicle and Property Repossessions, Landlord Representation/Evictions/Lease Litigation, Equipment Leasing.
Cincinnati Office: 11340 Montgomery Road, Suite 210. Telephone: 513-489-0829; 800-840-3514. Fax: 513-489-0834.
Covington, Kentucky Office: Heritage International, Suite 203, P.O. Box 2158. Telephone: 513-489-0829. Fax: 513-489-0834.
Columbus Office: 460 E. Main Street. Telephone: 513-489-0829. Fax: 513-489-0834.
Dayton Office: 319 Liberty Tower. Telephone: 513-489-0829. Fax: 513-489-0834.
Madison, Indiana Office: 201 East Main Street. Telephone: 513-489-0829. Fax: 513-489-0834.

See Professional Biographies, LIMA, OHIO

McCluskey, Holly Lee, (BV) .... '53 '93 C.999 R.N. L.607 J.D. [Siferd&M.]
Meredith, Robert J., (BV) .... '61 '88 C.608 B.S. L.117 J.D. [Cory,M.W.R.&C.]
Mihlbaugh, Michael P. .... '67 '93 C.145 A.B. L.602 J.D. P.O. Box 1141
Mihlbaugh, Robert H. .... '32 '57 C&L.602 A.B., J.D. P.O. Box 1141

Mihlbaugh Law Firm, The, LLP
The Mihlbaugh Law Building, P.O. Box 1141, 45802-1141
Telephone: 419-229-5886 Fax: 419-227-6445
Email: mihlbaughlawfirm@earthlink.net
Leslie K. Batté.
Civil Litigation, General Corporate, Intellectual Property, Trademarks, Copyrights.

See Professional Biographies, LIMA, OHIO

Miller, Gregory B. .... '65 '91 C.608 B.A. L.117 J.D. Admin. Coun., Ct. of App.
Miller, Richard William, III .... '70 '96 C&L.851 B.A., J.D. [Daley,B.&L.]
Minnard, Lawrence R., (AV) .... '43 '68 C&L.607 B.S., J.D. [Rizor,M.&R.]
Minnich, Sheila E., (CV) .... '60 '87 C&L.607 B.S.B.A., J.D. 714 W. North St.
Moritz, Larry G. .... '42 '68 C&L.607 B.S., J.D. 400 W. North St.‡
Novak, Gregory M., Law Office of, (BV) '46 '72 C.476 B.S. L.607 J.D.
128 W. High St.
Nyers, Athena J. .... '67 '92 C&L.607 B.S., J.D. 119 N. West Street, Suite 102
Patrick, James P., (CV) .... '44 '72 C.91 B.S. L.607 J.D. 1037 W. Market St.
Pedlow, Edward B., IV, (BV) .... '59 '85 C.317 B.A. L.607 J.D. 119 N. West St., Ste. 101
Pedlow, Edward B., Jr. .... '29 '55 C.97 B.S. L.607 LL.B. 119 Northwest St.‡
Pitts, Jerry Owen, Law Office of, (CV) '51 '87 C.388 B.A. L.734 J.D.
124 S. Metcalf St.
Prueter, Susan M. '62 '92
C.473 B.A. L.201 J.D. Admin. Coun., Ct. of App., 3rd Appl. Dist.
Quatman, George B., III, (BV) .... '46 '72 C.436 E.E. L.607 J.D. 327 N. Elizabeth St.
Quatman, Janice Ann .... '50 '91 C.608 B.S. L.607 J.D. [J.Quatman]
Quatman, Joseph B., (AV) .... '16 '41 C.201 B.A. L.930 J.D. 327 N. Elizabeth St.
Quatman, Janice .... 317 N. Elizabeth St.
Rakestraw, Adam Edwin .... '75 '01 C.97 B.S.B.A. L.607 J.D. Ct. of Appeals
Reed, Jeffrey Lee .... '58 '83 C.608 B.A. L.607 J.D. Com. Pleas J.
Reese, Richard T., (BV) .... '56 '81 C&L.607 B.A., J.D. [Baran,P.T.F.&T.]
Reeves, Randy L., (BV) .... '53 '80 L.607 J.D. [R.L.Reeves]
Reeves, Randy L., Co., L.P.A., (BV) .... 973 W. North St.
Reinicke, Daniel E. .... '48 '75 C.49 B.A. L.607 J.D. 880 Algonkin Trail
Rexford, Kenneth J. .... '68 '95 C.47 B.A. L.276 J.D. [K.J.Rexford]
Rexford, Kenneth J., & Co., L.L.C. .... 112 N. West St.
Rizor, Barbara D. .... '24 '47 C.20 B.A. L.607 LL.B. 1570 Putters Lane‡
Rizor, Paul D., (BV) .... '51 '76 C&L.607 B.A., J.D. [Rizor,M.&R.]
Rizor, Minnard & Rizor, L.P.A., (AV) .... 1045 Mackenzie Dr.
Robenalt, John A., (AV) .... '22 '48 C.473 B.A. L.608 J.D. [Robenalt&R.] ⊙
Robenalt, John F., (AVⓉ) .... '52 '79 C&L.607 B.A., J.D. [Robenalt&R.] ⊙
Robenalt & Robenalt, (AV) .... 211 North Elizabeth Street (⊙Sarasota, FL)
Roberts, Raymond M., (BV) .... '22 '53 C.610 B.A. L.607 J.D. 119 W. North St.
Rodabaugh, David A., (BV) .... '52 '77 C.967 B.A. L.607 J.D. [D.A.Rodabaugh]
Rodabaugh, David A., Law Office, (BV) .... 234 N. Main St.
Roeder, James A. .... '77 '03 C&L.607 B.A., J.D. [Ⓐ W.M.Lawson,Jr.]
Romey, Steven A., (BV) .... '54 '79 C.882 B.A. L.607 J.D. [Romey&V.]
Romey and Vandemark, (AV) .... 330 N. Main St. (⊙Bluffton)
Roush, Brad C., (AV) '53 '79 C&L.607 B.A., J.D.
Sr. V.P., Secy. & Gen. Coun., Cora Health Services, Inc.
Roush, W. Thomas, (BV) .... '47 '73 C.91 B.A. L.851 J.D. 317 W. Elizabeth Street
Rumer, Michael A., (BV) .... '44 '70 C.97 B.S. L.607 J.D. [Cory,M.W.R.&C.]
Sabol, John A., (BV) .... '42 '72 C.610 B.S. L.607 J.D. 128 W. High St.

Scherner, Hanson & Cornwell, LLC, (AV)
714 West North Street, 45801-3923 ⊙
Telephone: 419-222-1155 Fax: 419-227-3131
Ted E. Cornwell; Mariah M. Cunningham.
Civil Trial and Appellate Litigation in State and Federal Courts. Medical Malpractice and other Professional Liability, Personal Injury, Product Liability, Commercial, Corporate, Fraud and other Civil Litigation, Domestic Relations, Family Law.
Columbus, Ohio Office: 130 Northwoods Boulevard. Telephone: 614-431-7200. Fax: 614-431-7262.
Delaware, Ohio Office: 5300 David Road. Telephone: 740-595-3366.

See Professional Biographies, LIMA, OHIO

Schramski, Nancy Susan .... '45 '87 C.347 B.G.S. L.607 J.D. 119 N. West Street, Suite 102
Schultz, Ronald E., (AV) '42 '67 C.610 B.S. L.608 J.D.
[Dyer,G.M.&S.] (⊙Bellefontaine, Dayton, Huber Heights, Middletown, Piqua, Springfield)
Shaw, Stephen R. .... '49 '75 C.231 B.A. L.607 J.D. Ct. of App. J.
Siferd, Richard E., (AV) .... '44 '73 C.608 B.A. L.930 J.D. [Siferd&M.]

Siferd & McCluskey, LPA, (AV) BB
212 N. Elizabeth Street, Suite 310, 45801-4338
Telephone: 419-222-5045 Fax: 419-222-0473
Willis S. Siferd (1909-2003); Richard E. Siferd; Holly Lee McCluskey. Associate: N. Shannon Bartels.
Personal Injury (Plaintiffs Counsel), Workmen's Compensation, Family Law and Other Civil Litigation Matters.

Smith, J. Alan, (BV) .... '63 '89 C&L.930 B.S., J.D. [Cory,M.W.R.&C.]
Staley, Matt C. .... '54 '79 C.608 B.A. L.607 J.D. Com. Pleas J.
Vandemark, Dale M., (BV) .... '55 '84 C&L.607 B.A., J.D. [Romey&V.]
Vandemark, William C., (AV) .... '35 '62 C.91 L.607 J.D. [Fisher&V.]
Van Dyne, Mark A., (BV) .... '64 '90 C.610 B.B.A. L.607 J.D. [Baran,P.T.F.&T.]
Villarreal, Teresa .... '59 '89 C.233 B.S. L.608 J.D. Jud. Law Clk., Dist. Ct. of App.
Votava, Andrew R. .... '67 '94 C.473 B.A. L.851 J.D. Asst. Pros. Atty.
Walters, Sumner E. .... '49 '74 C&L.607 B.A., J.D. [Cory,M.W.R.&C.]
Warren, Richard K. .... '41 '66 C.313 B.A. L.607 J.D. Com. Pleas J.
Weick, James K., Jr. .... '64 '94 C.363 B.A. L.607 J.D. Asst. City Pros.
Weir, Joseph H., II .... '47 '78 C.608 B.S. L.607 J.D. Mag., Mun. Ct.
White, Walter L., (BV) .... '19 '48 C&L.607 A.B., J.D. 1004 Bank One Tower
White, William H., (CV) .... '42 '70 C&L.607 B.A., J.D. 311 N. Elizabeth St.
Whitlatch, Robert E. .... '51 '82 C.608 B.A. L.607 J.D. Mag., Co. Juv. Ct.
Willamowski, John R., (CV) .... '60 '85 C.602 B.A. L.607 J.D. [Willamowski&W.]
Willamowski, Mona L., (CV) .... '58 '87 C.922 B.S. L.607 J.D. [Willamowski&W.]
Willamowski & Willamowski, Co., L.P.A., (CV) .... 730 West North Street
Williams, Jeffrey G., (CV) .... '57 '83 C.608 B.A. L.607 J.D. 2244 Baton Rouge
Wiseman, Lesley J. .... '74 '01 C.385 B.A. L.607 J.D. 3rd Dist. Ct. of Appeals
Witter, Donald J., (AV) .... '37 '62 C.631 B.A. L.477 LL.B. [Cory,M.W.R.&C.]
Workman, RicKard A. .... '47 '84 C.1112 B.S. L.607 J.D. Mun. J.
Younkman, Derek Alan .... '66 '93 C.473 B.A. L.117 J.D. 212 N. Elizabeth St.

LISBON, * 2,788, *Columbiana Co.*

Baronzzi, Joseph J., (BV) .... '33 '59 C.381 B.S. L.608 J.D. 120 S. Market St.
Calhoun, Melody Mabel Elma .... '48 '84 C.294 A.B. L.8 J.D. [M.Calhoun]
Calhoun, Melody .... 37 1/2 North Park Ave.
Dailey, Coleen Hall .... '55 '81 C.980 A.B. L.150 J.D. Mag., Com. Pleas Ct.
Hanley, Cynthia A., (BV) .... '58 '85 C.473 B.A. L.930 J.D. 105 South Market Street
Herron, Robert L., (BV) .... '52 '77 C.608 B.A. L.117 J.D. Co. Pros. Atty.
Horvath, Peter, (CV) .... '55 '81 C.318 B.A. L.201 J.D. [P.Horvath]
Horvath, Peter, LPA, (CV) .... 38294 Industrial Park Rd.
Jenkins, Douglas C. .... '46 '74 C.363 A.B. L.1003 J.D. Com. Pleas J.
Kennedy, Richard D. .... '21 '51 C&L.608 B.S., J.D. Ret. Com. Pleas J.
Liebschner, Sherill L. .... '66 '96 C.473 B.S. L.7 J.D. Asst. Co. Pros.
McNicol, Timothy J., (CV) .... '65 '91 C.608 B.A. L.117 J.D. Asst. Pros. Atty.

Nadler Nadler & Burdman Co., L.P.A.
(See Youngstown)

Pike, C. Ashley .... '50 '75 C.970 B.S. L.7 J.D. Com. Pleas J.
Reisch, Steven A. .... '63 '97 C.528 B.A. L.8 J.D. Asst. Pros.
Thorne, John C., Jr., (CV) .... '42 '67 C.608 B.A. L.607 J.D. Asst. Atty. Gen.
Tobin, David .... '49 '75 C.608 B.A. L.607 J.D. Com. Pleas J.
Ward, Jerry J., Law Office of, (BV) .... '48 '74 C.381 B.A. L.8 J.D. 115 N. Beaver Street
Ward, John Paul .... '48 '74 C.381 B.A. L.7 J.D. 115 N. Beaver Street

LODI, 3,042, *Medina Co.*

Bowers, Neal E., (BV) .... '25 '54 C.49 A.B. L.930 LL.B. [Ⓐ Laribee,H.&K.]
Laribee, Hertrick & Kray, (BV) .... 218 Baker Street (⊙Brunswick, Medina)

LOGAN, * 6,725, *Hocking Co.*

Beal, Larry E., (BV) .... '54 '78 C.937 B.A. L.1003 J.D. Co. Pros.
Dillon, Neal, (AV) .... '25 '52 C.610 A.B. L.608 J.D. [N.Dillon]
Dillon, Neal, Co., L.P.A., (AV) .... 340 W. Main St.
Galbraith, Randall Larry, (CV) .... '73 '98 C.679 B.A. L.801 J.D. 4 E. Main St.
Gerken, Charles A., (BV) .... '51 '77 C&L.117 A.B., J.D. Pros. Atty.
Gerken, Thomas H. .... '53 '78 C.608 B.A. L.1051 J.D. Com. Pleas J.
Henderson, William W., (BV) .... '53 '79 C.607 B.A. L.201 J.D. 30 W. Hunter Street
Henniger, Louis Jackson, II, (BV) .... '43 '73 L.117 J.D. [L.J.Henniger&Assoc.]
Henniger, L. Jackson, & Associates, (BV) .... 4 E. Main St., Ste. 200
Johnson, Leslie G. .... '17 '48 C.585 B.S. L.608 J.D. 324 Midland Place‡
Johnston, Edwin C. .... '29 '56 C.610 B.S.C. L.608 J.D. 119 E. Hunter St.
Kernen, Will, (BV) .... '51 '77 C.455 B.A. L.608 J.D. 158 East Main Street
Lewis, James C., III .... '54 '79 C.945 A.B. L.930 J.D. Citizens Bk.
Lilley, Robert L., (AV) .... '44 '72 C.610 B.A. L.608 J.D. [R.L.Lilley]
Lilley, Robert L., Co., L.P.A., (AV) .... 9 East Second Street
Mong, Frederick .... '37 '75 C.294 B.A. L.117 J.D. Prob. & Juv. J.
Nangle, Patricia, (CV) .... '— '73 L.117 30 W. Main St.
Rolston, G. Drew, (BV) .... '47 '72 C.923 A.B. L.608 J.D. 61 N. Market St., Rear
Soddy, Susan J. .... '50 '96 C.911 B.A. L.117 J.D. Asst. Pros. Atty.
Stohs, Daniel J., (BV) .... '50 '77 C&L.608 B.A., J.D. 450 Gallagher

Twyford & Donahey, P.L.L.
(See Columbus)

Veidt, Christopher E., (AV) .... '43 '68 C.610 B.A. L.608 J.D. 37 E. Hunter St.
Wallace, John T., (CV) .... '55 '86 C.790 B.A. L.1003 J.D. 38 1/2 N. Market Street
Wallar, Richard M. .... '53 '81 C.610 B.A. L.608 J.D. Mun. J.

LONDON, * 8,771, *Madison Co.*

Ailes, Aleita J., (BV) .... '47 '72 C.607 B.A. L.608 J.D. [A.Ailes]

Ailes, Aleita, Attorney at Law, LLC, (BV)
P.O. Box 588, 43140
Telephone: 740-845-0300 Fax: 740-845-0500
Email: aailes@columbus.rr.com URL: http://www.aileslawfirm.com
Aleita J. Ailes.
Divorce, Dissolution, Separation, Child Custody, Visitation Rights, Paternity, Adoption, Real Estate, Contracts, Leases, Wills and Trusts, Business, Litigation, General Practice.
See Professional Biographies, LONDON, OHIO

Beathard, Maurice E., (BV) .... '26 '50 C&L.608 J.D. [Beathard&B.]
Beathard, Steven P., (BV) .... '52 '78 C.608 B.S. L.851 J.D. [Beathard&B.]
Beathard & Beathard, (BV) .... 63 N. Main St.

Benson, Michael E.
(See Columbus)

Calig & Handelman, LPA
(See Columbus)

Carter, David W. .... '70 '98 C.851 B.S. L.1187 J.D. Asst. Pros.
Donahey, Richard S., (BV) .... '41 '68 C&L.608 B.C.E., J.D. [Twyford&D.] ⊙
Flax, Richard E., (BV) .... '48 '74 C.473 B.S. L.608 J.D. [Nichols,S.&F.]
Freeman, Robin R., (AV) .... '34 '59 C&L.608 LL.B. [Wildman S.]
Hamilton, Glenn S. .... '47 '77 C.607 B.A. L.201 J.D. Prob. J.

Hansgen, Shirley C., (BV) '51 '79 C.610 B.S. L.608 J.D.
26 South Main Street, 43140-1211
Telephone: 740-852-1576 Fax: 740-852-2760
Email: schansgen@sbcglobal.com URL: http://www.lawyers.com/hansgenlaw
Associate: Renae E. Zabloudil.
General Practice. Real Estate, Estate Planning, Probate, Personal Injury, Corporate and Family Law. Trials and Appeals, Criminal Law and Traffic Violations.
References: Huntington National Bank of London; Citizens Loan & Savings Co.
See Professional Biographies, LONDON, OHIO

Hume, Stephen L., (CV) .... '53 '87 C.97 B.S. L.851 J.D. 113 N. Main Street
Jackman, David H., (BV) .... '39 '64 C.532 B.A. L.150 J.D. 60 S. Main St.
Londergan, Gary W., (BV) .... '45 '76 C.266 B.S. L.117 J.D. 27 E. 4th St.
Nichols, Robert D. .... '42 '67 C.528 B.A. L.608 J.D. Com. Pleas J.
Nichols, Stonecipher & Flax, (BV) .... 117 W. High St., Ste. 105
Payer, Charissa Diane '66 '95 C.980 B.A. L.989 J.D.
Sr. Asst. Atty. Gen., OH Atty. Gen.'s Off.-BCI
Picken, R. David, (BV) .... '45 '74 C.25 B.A. L.930 J.D. Pros. Atty.
Pitstick, Mark J. .... '56 '92 C.967 B.A. L.851 J.D. P.O. Box 189
Pronai, Stephen, (BV) .... '55 '84 C.1208 B.A. L.607 J.D. Madison Cnty. Pros.
Richmond, Charles D., (AV) .... '22 '50 C.575 B.S. L.472 J.D. 207 E. High St.‡
Robinson-Bond, Alice L., (BV) .... '59 '84 C&L.607 B.A., J.D. Co. Pros. Off.
Rolfes, James W., Sr., (CV) .... '42 '75 C.150 B.S. L.1161 J.D. 17 S. Main St.

Rourke & Blumenthal, LLP
(See Columbus)

Schooley, Eric M. .... '71 '97 C.473 B.A. L.851 J.D. [Wildman S.]
Starr, Wendy J. .... '49 '96 C.130 B.A. L.117 J.D. 15 South Main, 2nd Fl-F
Stonecipher, Timothy R., (BV) .... '46 '75 C.188 B.S. L.608 J.D. [Nichols,S.&F.]
Theodotou, Pamela I. .... '64 '89 C.207 B.S. L.930 J.D. 2108 Palouse Dr. N.W.

Twyford & Donahey, P.L.L., (BV)
25 West Fifth Street, 43140 ⊙
Telephone: Toll Free: 1-800-686-1699 Fax: 614-849-0475
Email: help@twyforddonahey.com URL: http://www.twyforddonahey.com
Richard S. Donahey.
Personal Injury Litigation, Wrongful Death, Medical Malpractice, Products Liability, Automobile Accidents, Trucking Accidents, Head and Spinal Injuries, Motorcycle Accidents and Injuries, Uninsured Motorists, Insurance Law, Airplane Crash Litigation, Railroad Accidents, Slip and Fall, Dog Bites, Work Related Injuries, Birth Injuries, Nursing Home Abuse and Neglect.
References: The Huntington National Bank; Bank One of Columbus; BancOhio National Bank.
Columbus, Ohio Office: 495 South High Street, 43215-5058. Telephone: Toll Free: 1-800-686-1699. Email: help@twyforddonahey.com.
Circleville, Ohio Office: 214 South Court Street, 43113. Telephone: Toll Free: 1-800-686-1699. Email: help@twyforddonahey.com
Delaware, Ohio Office: 163 N. Sandusky Street, Suite 103, 43015. Telephone: Toll Free: 1-800-686-1699. Email: help@twyforddonahey.com
Lancaster, Ohio Office: 3794 Old Columbus, N.W., 43130. Telephone: Toll Free: 1-800-686-1699. Email: help@twyforddonahey.com
Newark, Ohio Office: 137 West Main Street, Suite C., 43025. Telephone: Toll Free: 1-800-686-1699. Email: help@twyforddonahey.com
See Professional Biographies, LONDON, OHIO

Wheat, Sandra Jean .... '— '88 C.266 B.S. L.117 J.D. State Rt. 56
White, Monte C. .... '32 '70 C.612 B.S.E.E. L.117 J.D. 102 1/2 South Main Street, Suite G
Wildman, Austin P., (AV) .... '44 '71 C.381 B.A. L.607 J.D. [Wildman S.]
Wildman Schooley LLC, (AV) .... 26 East Fourth Street
Woods, Corey Robert .... '69 '00 C.130 B.A. L.117 J.D. [Woods]
Woods, Robert Dean, (BV) .... '43 '69 C&L.607 B.A., J.D. 66 W. High St.
Woods Law Office .... 66 W. High Street
Zabloudil, Renae E. .... '76 '01 C.631 B.S L.608 J.D. [A S.C.Hansgen]

LORAIN, 68,652, *Lorain Co.*

Angel, Stephen B., (CV) .... '44 '72 C.231 B.A. L.94 J.D. 750 Broadway, Ste. 205
Arroyo, Angel L., (CV) .... '51 '77 C.161 B.B.A. L.1003 J.D. [A.Arroyo]
Arroyo, Angel, (CV) .... 4223 Edgewood Dr.
Baker, Edward J. .... '52 '89 C.980 B.S. L.7 J.D. V.P., Lorain National Bank
Balunek, Adelbert A., (BV) .... '33 '66 C.473 A.B. L.1003 J.D. Ref. Dom. Rel. Ct.
Barkus, Michael M., Law Firm, (CV) .... '45 '79 C.959 B.A. L.161 J.D. P.O. Box 1236
Barrett, Benjamin F., Jr., (BV) .... '— '87 C.30 B.A. L.930 J.D. [Miraldi&B.]
Barrett, Benjamin F., Sr., (AV) .... '— '66 C.363 B.A. L.1003 J.D. [Miraldi&B.]
Barrett, Matthew H., (BV) .... '— '96 C.1333 B.S. L.1003 J.D. [Miraldi&B.]
Betleski, Adrian F. .... '17 '50 C&L.608 B.A., J.D. 1723 E. Erie Ave.‡
Blake, Stephen K. .... '61 '00 C.161 B.A. L.989 J.D. 215 Eighth St.
Bodnar, Rebecca J. .... '69 '99 C.318 B.A. L.930 J.D. Atty., Emerson Network Power
Bradley, Jack W., (BV) .... '49 '77 C.930 B.A. L.1003 J.D. [Bradley&G.]
Bradley & Giardini, (BV) .... 520 Broadway Ave.
Brosky, Michael E., (CV) .... '67 '92 C.473 B.A. L.7 J.D. 4463 Oberlin Ave.
Burge, James M., (AV) .... '47 '75 C.381 B.A. L.1003 J.D. [J.M.Burge]
Burge, James M., Co., L.P.A., (AV) .... 600 Broadway
Camera, Michael J. .... '54 '80 C.608 B.A. L.1003 J.D. 520 Broadway, Suite 200
Chattman, Gerald B., (AV) '42 '67 C.477 B.A. L.930 J.D.
[Chattman,G.&S.] (⊙Cleveland)
Chattman, Gaines & Stern, (AV) .... 5300 Baumbart Rd. (⊙Cleveland)
Colella, Richard, (AV) .... '35 '60 C&L.930 A.B., J.D. [Colella&W.]
Colella, Richard J., (BV) .... '62 '87 C.604 B.A. L.896 J.D. [Colella&W.]

Colella & Weir, P.L.L., (AV) BR
6055 Park Square Drive Oak Point Professional Park, 44053
Telephone: 440-988-9000 Telecopier: 440-988-9002
Email: rjcolella@cnwlaw.com URL: http://www.cnwlaw.com
Richard Colella; Richard J. Colella; Jeffrey H. Weir II;—Joshua Lamb.
Corporate, Business, Real Estate, Business and Commercial Litigation, Construction Law, Industrial Law, International Business, Corporate Financing, Business Acquisitions, Bankruptcy, Federal and State Administrative Law, Probate, Estate Planning, Licensing, Technology Law.
References: FirstMerit Bank, N.A.; FirstMerit Corp.
See Professional Biographies, LORAIN, OHIO

Conger, Neal A. .... '41 '69 C.318 A.B. L.1003 J.D. 457 Broadway
Cook, D. Chris, The Law Office of .... '64 '93 C.477 B.G.S. L.851 J.D. 209 W. 6th St.
Curci, Nicholas R., (BV) '39 '65 C.610 A.B. L.607 J.D.
1700 Cooper Foster Park Rd., W.
Dlugosz, Robert W., (CV) .... '52 '85 C.381 B.B.A. L.989 J.D. 219 Root Rd.
Downie, Thomas A., (BV) .... '53 '78 C.645 B.A. L.1003 J.D. [Gary,N.&T.]
Duff, Michael J. .... '54 '80 C.49 B.S. L.1003 J.D. 715 Bway.
Elwell, Thomas J., Jr., (BV) .... '53 '78 C.215 A.B. L.1003 J.D. 4463 Oberlin Ave.
Ewers, Robt. A. .... '28 '54 C.62 A.B. L.930 LL.B. Mun. Ct. J.

Felber, Mark B.
(See Cleveland)

Fetterman, Robert J., (AV) .... '20 '51 C.930 B.B.A. L.800 L.L.B. 502 Broadway‡
Francis, J. Bruce .... '48 '77 C.973 B.S.B.A. L.215 J.D. [Martinek&F.]
Gargasz, Robert J., (CV) .... '59 '83 C.851 B.A. L.607 J.D. 1670-C Cooper Foster Rd.
Gary, Robert D., (BV) .... '41 '66 C&L.930 B.A., J.D. [Gary,N.&T.]

Gary, Naegele & Theado, LLC, (AV)
446 Broadway, 44052
Telephone: 440-244-4809 Fax: 440-244-3462
Email: office@gntlaw.com URL: http://www.gntlaw.com
Members of Firm: Robert D. Gary; Jori Bloom Naegele; Thomas R. Theado; Thomas A. Downie.
Class Actions, Pension Litigation, Consumer Fraud, Employee Rights, Complex Civil Litigation, Substantial Personal Injury.
See Professional Biographies, LORAIN, OHIO

Gehlmann, Donald E. .... '30 '60 C.363 B.S. L.276 J.D. 1860 E. 34th Street
Giardini, Anthony B., (BV) .... '51 '76 C.473 B.A. L.930 J.D. [Bradley&G.]
Goldberg, Hyman S. .... '21 '54 C.608 L.1003 J.D. 444 Broadway‡
Gordon, Ronald H., (BV) .... '37 '63 C.976 B.A. L.930 J.D. [R.H.Gordon]
Gordon, Ronald H., Co., LPA, (BV) .... 5315 Oberlin Avenue
Griffin, Paul A. '66 '94 C.1051 B.A. L.188 J.D.
(adm. in WA; and limited adm. in OH) [P.Griffin]
Griffin, Paul, Law Offices of .... 600 Broadway
Grunda, Jay B., (BV) .... '60 '86 C.831 B.A. L.607 J.D. 522 Bway
Grunda, Joseph C., (BV) .... '51 '79 C.970 B.A. L.607 J.D. [Grunda&G.]
Grunda, Joseph R., (BV) .... '33 '58 C.97 L.1003 LL.B. [Grunda&G.]
Grunda & Grunda, (BV) .... 522 Bway.

Henretta Law Offices
(See Akron)

Januzzi, Thomas A., (BV) .... '56 '82 C.49 B.S. L.1003 J.D. 5750 Cooper Foster Park Rd.
Jesensky, Alex, Jr., (BV) .... '36 '71 C.608 B.S. L.128 LL.B. Mag.
Jones, Frederick C. .... '17 '46 C.318 A.B. L.930 LL.B. 4642 Oberlin Ave.‡
Kessler, Robert S. .... '26 '61 C.823 B.S. L.1003 J.D. 2483 E. Erie Ave.
Kinlin, Michael J. .... '70 '98 C.610 B.C.J. L.1003 J.D. City Atty.
Koury, E. G. "Leo", (Co., L.P.A.), (BV) '28 '53
C.610 B.S.C. L.150 LL.B. 520 Broadway "The Commons", 2nd Fl.
Koury, George I., Jr., (BV) .... '50 '75 C.610 B.G.S. L.607 J.D. [Riley,K.&R.]
Kuzela, Dennis M., (CV) .... '44 '72 C.381 B.S. L.1003 J.D. 6645 Lemonwood Ct.
Lamb, Joshua .... '78 '03 C.96 B.A. L.851 J.D. [A Colella&W.]
Lasco, Robt J. .... '26 '55 C.608 B.A. L.1003 J.D. 4260 Shore Dr.‡
Mahon, Richard J., Jr. '55 '92
C.610 B.B.A. L.1003 J.D. Mgr., Labor Rel., USS/Kobe Steel Co.
Martinek, Steven, (CV) .... '50 '75 C&L.602 A.B., J.D. [Martinek&F.]
Martinek & Francis Co., L.P.A., (CV) .... 700 Bway.
Mason, Emma N. '37 '79 C.470 A.B. L.930 J.D.
Sr. Tr. Offr. & Sr. V.P., Lorain National Bank
Mihok, Mark J., (BV) .... '53 '82 C.608 B.A. L.930 J.D. 520 Broadway
Miraldi, David P., (AV) .... '— '78 C.970 B.A. L.608 J.D. [Miraldi&B.]
Miraldi, James L., (AV) .... '— '77 C.970 B.A. L.228 J.D. [Miraldi&B.]
Miraldi & Barrett Co., L.P.A., (AV) .... 6061 S. Broadway
Morgan, Brian D. '60 '86
C.161 B.B.A. L.1003 J.D. V.P. & Tr. Offr., Lorain National Bank
Morrisson, John G., (BV) .... '41 '77 C.207 B.A. L.930 J.D. 209 W. 6th St. (⊙Elyria)
Motsch, Barry B., (CV) .... '49 '76 C.363 B.A. L.930 J.D. Lorain City Pros. Off.
Naegele, Jori Bloom, (BV) .... '53 '80 C.150 B.A. L.930 J.D. [Gary,N.&T.]
Nocjar, David E. '48 '73 C.973 B.S.B.A. L.602 J.D.
V.P. & Tr. Offr., Bank One Ohio Tr. Co., N.A.
Nolan, Quentin J., (BV) .... '48 '74 C.381 B.S. L.1003 J.D. [Q.J.Nolan]

Nolan, Quentin J., Co., LPA, (BV) .... 1700 Cooper Foster Park Road
Nunez, Gustalo .... '34 '67 C.610 B.S.E.E. L.8 J.D. Mun. J.

Obral & Mays & Associates
(See Cleveland)

Ortner, Kenneth N. ..... '52 '98 C.610 B.S. L.1003 J.D. 520 Broadway Avenue, 3rd Floor
Otero, John B., Jr., (BV) .... '48 '74 C.967 B.A. L.607 J.D. [Otero&O.]
Otero & Otero Co., L.P.A., (BV) .... 2100 Reid Ave.
Parobek, James S., (CV) .... '29 '52 C.610 B.A. L.608 J.D. 763 Broadway
Provenza, Kenneth J., (BV) .... '39 '67 C.610 A.B. L.930 J.D. 218 8th Street
Provenza, Michael K., (BV) .... '67 '92 C.608 B.A. L.851 J.D. 218 8th St.
Provenza, Russell D., (BV) .... '36 '64 C.608 B.A. L.1003 J.D. [K.J.Provenza]
Quinn, A. James .... '32 '72 C.999 L.1003 J.D. Catholic Diocese of Cleve.
Rader, Joseph .... '23 '52 C.8 L.7 LL.B. 2916 McKinley St.‡
Resar, Kenneth R., (BV) .... '54 '79 [Riley,K.&R.]
Riley, Patrick D., (BV) .... '52 '79 C.473 B.A. L.1003 J.D. [Riley,K.&R.]
Riley, Koury & Resar, (BV) .... 520 Broadway
Ruskan, Ronald Jan, (CV) .... '51 '77 C.970 B.A. L.273 J.D. 1623 Broadway
Scherach, Michael J., (BV) .... '45 '71 C.97 B.A. L.608 J.D. Asst. Co. Pros.
Simonetti, Carol G. '45 '82 C.608 B.A. L.1003 J.D.
Exec. Dir., The Community Found. of Greater Lorain Co.
Simonoff, Zachary Barnett .... '65 '98 C.273 B.A. L.161 J.D. 4463 Oberlin Ave.

Smith, Stourton Scott, Co., LPA
(See Cleveland)

Stephenson, Mark E., (BV) '55 '80
C.97 B.A. L.1003 J.D. 5750 Cooper Foster Park Rd., Ste. 101
Stone, Russell B. .... '49 '83 C.602 A.B. L.1003 J.D. 814 Reid Avenue
Swenski, Lisa Irene .... '63 '99 C&L.851 B.A., J.D. 4463 Oberlin Ave.
Szabo, Jeffrey S., (CV) ..... '53 '78 C.930 B.A. L.161 J.D. 1700 Cooper Foster Pk. Rd. W.
Taylor, Phillip P. .... '29 '62 C.381 B.S. L.1003 J.D. 3530 Oberlin Ave.
Theado, Thomas R., (AV) .... '50 '79 C.604 B.A. L.930 J.D. [Gary,N.&T.]
Timko, V. Paul .... '27 '67 C.381 B.S.B.A. L.1003 J.D. Mun. J.
Trigilio, Timothy S., (BV) ...... '55 '80 C&L.608 B.A., J.D. 5750 Cooper Foster Park Rd.
Tully, Michael D., (BV) .... '54 '80 C.1024 B.A. L.1003 J.D. [M.D.Tully]
Tully, Michael D., Co., L.P.A., (BV) .... 600 Broadway
Walther, James Thomas, (BV) ... '59 '87 C.161 B.B.A. L.1003 J.D. 4324 Hickoy Hill Ave.
Weir, Jeffrey H., II, (CV) .... '62 '87 C.604 B.A. L.477 J.D. [Colella&W.]
Zaleski, Donald M., (BV) .... '59 '84 C.8 B.S. L.1003 J.D. 4463 Oberlin Ave.
Zaleski, Edward M., (BV) .... '39 '68 C.610 B.S.C. L.930 J.D. Com. Pleas Ct. J.

LOUDONVILLE, 2,915, *Ashland & Holmes Cos.*

Hunter, David M., (CV) .... '69 '96 C.49 B.A. L.851 J.D. 244 West Main Street
Hyde, Andrew G., (BV) .... '65 '94 C.608 B.S. L.596 J.D. 144 N. Water Street
Kick, Erin Roberta .... '72 '98 C.62 B.A. L.7 J.D. [E.R.Kick]
Kick, Erin R. .... 15694 Holmes County Rd. 385

LOUISVILLE, 8,904, *Stark Co.*

Bishop, Paul R. .... '43 '72 C.608 B.S. L.7 J.D. Pres., H-P Products, Inc.
McCue, Thomas P., (BV) .... '51 '76 C.201 B.A. L.93 J.D. 824 W. Main St.
Shockling, Robt. J. .... '22 '49 C&L.608 LL.B. 920 S. Mill St.‡

LOVELAND, 11,677, *Clermont, Hamilton & Warren Cos.*

Balogh, Merlin J. .... '52 '79 C.97 B.A. L.150 J.D. 253 Sinclair
Barnett, Richard S. '66 '92 C.659 B.A. L.608 J.D.
Sr. Coun.-Intellectual Prop., International Paper Co.
Bauer, Robert C., (BV) .... '53 '78 C&L.150 B.A., J.D. 501 W. Loveland Avenue
Becker, Dennis A., (AV) .... '51 '77 C.150 B.A. L.851 J.D. 526 Wards Corner Rd. A
Brehm, John E., Jr., (BV) .... '58 '82 C.973 A.B. L.734 J.D. 8977 Columbia Road
Brueggeman, Edward P. .... '47 '72 C.973 B.S. L.150 J.D. 10507 Butterworth Rd.
Cadwallader, Brian J. '59 '85 C.932 B.B.A. L.734 J.D.
Gen. Coun.-xpedx Div., International Paper Co.

Chalfie & Farley, Co., L.P.A.
(See Cincinnati)

Ewald, Brian Alexander .... '73 '98 C.645 B.S. L.150 J.D. 550 Wards Corner Rd., Ste.102
Fletcher, Melvin D. '61 '95 C.436 B.S.M.E. L.1119 J.D.
(adm. in MI; not adm. in OH; Pat.) Coun., Intellectual Property, International Paper
Frank, Armin, (BV) .... '33 '74 C.103 A.B. L.150 J.D. 1632 Woodville Pike
Frank, Erich .... '58 '84 C.103 A.B. L.150 J.D. 1632 Woodville Pike
Gordon, Bruce W. '35 '67 C.597 B.S. L.209 J.D.
(adm. in FL; not adm. in OH) 826 Oak Canyon‡
Hearth & Associates, (BV) .... 8977 Columbia Rd.
Heath, James V., (BV) .... '34 '66 C.150 B.S. L.1340 J.D. [Hearth&Assoc.]
Hopkins, Curt Y. '30 '56 C&L.793 B.S., LL.B.
(adm. in SD; not adm. in OH) 9539 Old Village Dr.‡
Jemail, John M. '62 '91 C.103 A.B. L.1202 J.D.
(adm. in PA; not adm. in OH) 729 Windfield Dr.
Kothman, David M., (BV) .... '58 '83 C.201 B.A. L.602 J.D. 1641 Lindenhall Dr.
Lobb, Christopher Montez ...... '62 '91 C.624 B.A. L.201 J.D. Nutter Consulting Services
Pedicone, Alfred J. .... '60 '97 C&L.1161 B.S., J.D. Webster Packaging Corp.
Ranz, Albert D. .... '53 '85 C&L.150 B.S., J.D. 6574 Branch Hill-Miamiville Rd
Schaffner, Jefferson N. .... '48 '74 C.25 B.A. L.117 J.D. 711 Arrowhead Trl.★
Stall, Mark G. ..... '62 '88 C.473 B.S. L.150 J.D. Sr. Coun.-xpedx, International Paper Co.
Stelter, Daniel C. '68 '96 C.961 B.S.M.E. L.201 J.D.
Sr. Coun.-Intell. Prop., International Paper Co. (Pat.)
Stewart, Richard C., II '46 '76 C.925 B.S. L.188 J.D.
(adm. in NY; not adm. in OH; Pat.) Chief Coun., Intell. Prop., International Paper Co.
Stiver, Vernon, (BV) .... '25 '51 C.383 L.1340 LL.B. 501 W. Loveland Ave.
Street, Gary D. .... '43 '69 C&L.546 B.S., J.D. 244 Shadow Wood Ct. (Pat.)
Thompson, Brenda V., (AV) '55 '93 C.59 B.A. L.150 J.D.
Employ.& Labor Coun., xpedx Div., International Paper Co,
Todaro, Thomas G. '53 '97 C.433 B.S. L.724 J.D.
(adm. in NY; not adm. in OH) 9672 Waterford Pl.
Voyles, David R. .... '38 '85 C.346 B.S. L.1340 J.D. 6669 Quailrun Ct.

LUCAS, 620, *Richland Co.*

Turner, James D., (BV) .... '39 '72 C&L.851 B.B.A., J.D. Pros. Atty.

LUCASVILLE, 1,588, *Scioto Co.*

Reno, Ottie W. .... '29 '53 C&L.266 B.S., J.D. Ret. Com. Pleas J.‡

LYNDHURST, 15,279, *Cuyahoga Co.*

Apple, Sheldon A. .... '35 '63 C.381 B.S. L.1003 J.D. 5171 Mayfield Rd.
Dolan, John F., (AV) .... '25 '50 C.309 A.B. L.930 LL.B. 1424 Richmond Rd.
Ginsberg, Amy J. .... '59 '94 C.260 B.A. L.930 J.D. 2102 Cottingham Dr.‡
Grano, Robert H., Jr., (AV) .... '57 '84 C.313 B.A. L.851 J.D. Asst. Co. Pros.
Grogan, Robert J. .... '25 '51 C.951 B.A. L.930 LL.B. Mun. J.
Holeski, Walter L. .... '48 '77 C.161 B.A. L.1003 J.D. 5001 Mayfield Rd.

Kingsbury, Dorothea J., (AV) '52 '81 C.876 A.B. L.1003 J.D.
5031 Mayfield Road, Suite 230, 44124
Telephone: 216-382-5454
Email: dkingsbury@kingsburylaw.com URL: http://www.kingsburylaw.com
Probate, Estate Planning and Corporate Law.
See Professional Biographies, LYNDHURST, OHIO

Leanza, Anthony V. .... '21 '49 C&L.930 B.A., LL.B. 5811 Alberta Dr.‡
Marks, Bruce W. .... '48 '79 C.608 B.S.B.A. L.1003 J.D. 5410 Harleston Dr
Naylor, James B. .... '24 '49 C.608 B.A. L.1003 LL.B. 5001 Mayfield Road, Suite 203
Pasiadis, Christopher F. .... '54 '86 C.161 B.A. L.1003 J.D. P.O. Box 241005
Rubenstein, Ken .... '59 '91 C.930 B.S. L.989 J.D. 2112 Acacia Park Drive
Schick, Brian S. .... '61 '90 C.881 A.B. L.146 J.D. 1516 Sunview Road
Van Pelt, George W. .... '18 '51 C.930 L.1003 J.D. 1691 Lyndhurst Rd.‡
Weiss, Joseph H., Sr. .... '11 '38 C.363 B.A. L.1003 J.D. 4855 N. Sedgewick Rd.
White, Mark Christopher .... '53 '83 C.161 B.S. L.1003 J.D. 5035 Mayfield Rd.

MACEDONIA, 9,224, *Summit Co.*

Beres, Steven A. .... '52 '79 C.385 B.A. L.7 J.D. UAW Legal Servs. Plan
Caldwell, Diana M. .... '59 '89 C&L.8 B.A., J.D. UAW Legal Servs. Plan
Colavecchio, Paul V. .... '56 '81 C.381 B.A. L.1003 J.D. 8536 Crow Drive, Suite 110
Freimuth, Sharon Sager .... '46 '92 C.494 B.A. L.930 J.D. Century Products Co.
Giller, Lee S. .... '57 '82 C.381 B.A. L.7 J.D. 1380 Highland Road
Norwillo, Vincent T. .... '65 '90 C.1113 B.S.B.A. L.273 J.D. Tradesmen International
One, Joan '— '87 C.930 B.S. L.1137 J.D.
(adm. in IN; not adm. in OH) P.O. Box 123
Sciortino, Steven D. .... '61 '90 C.161 B.A. L.1003 J.D. 8536 Crow Drive, Suite 215

MADISON, 2,921, *Lake Co.*

Archinal, David D. .... '67 '92 C.648 B.S.B.A. L.124 J.D. 5726 Heritage Ave.
Avellone, Ross D. .... '26 '60 C.62 B.A. L.1003 J.D. Ret. Com. Pleas J.
Dean, J. Thomas, (BV) .... '33 '59 C.611 A.B. L.930 LL.B. 56 Liberty St.
Feller, Katherine Christine .... '09 '44 C.930 B.A. L.989 J.D. 6079 Middle Ridge Rd.‡
Fiederer, Pamela Rish .... '52 '85 C.610 B.S. L.989 J.D. 6908 Lake Rd. E.
Lalka, Colman R., (CV) .... '44 '81 C.161 B.A. L.1003 J.D. [C.R.Lalka]
Lalka, Colman R., Co., L.P.A., (CV) .... P.O. Box 813
Schafer, Scott Patrick .... '70 '95 C.318 B.A. L.1003 J.D. 1954 Hubbard Road
Vince, George A., Jr., (BV) .... '52 '84 C.161 B.B.A. L.930 J.D. 13 W. Main St.
Vogelgesang, Janette P. .... '13 '36 C&L.930 A.B., LL.B. P.O. Box 335‡
Wagner, James L., (BV) .... '40 '75 C.36 B.A. L.607 J.D. 5626 Trask Road

MAGNOLIA, 937, *Carroll & Stark Cos.*

Holler, Edward J. .... '24 '54 C.645 B.S. L.948 LL.B. R.R. 2 Hilltop Dr. (Pat.)

MAINEVILLE, 885, *Warren Co.*

Beaton, James D., Jr., (BV) .... '48 '73 C.886 B.S. L.607 J.D. 2263 W. US 22-3
Bernard, Christopher J. .... '66 '91 C.610 B.A. L.851 J.D. 513 Weeping Willow Ln.
Heath, James J., (BV) .... '62 '88 C.473 B.A. L.1340 J.D. P.O. 4770
Reiss, Anthony E. .... '57 '83 C.1349 B.S. L.823 J.D. 8445 Kelso Dr.

MALVERN, 1,218, *Carroll Co.*

Pettie, B. Paul, Jr. '39 '65 C.1126 A.B. L.575 LL.B.
(adm. in FL; not adm. in OH) P.O. Box 845‡

MANSFIELD, * 49,346, *Richland Co.*

Allen, John Wesley, (BV) .... '48 '74 C.62 B.A. L.1003 J.D. [Allen&Assoc.]
Allen & Associate, (BV) .... 24 W. 3rd, Ste. 200
Anderson, Will, O'Donnell & Kitzler, LLP, (BV) .... 703 Richland Trust Bldg.
Arbaugh, David R. .... '20 '48 C.105 L.607 J.D. Ret. Dom. Rel. J.
Ardis, Frank, Jr., (BV) .... '49 '74 C.608 B.S. L.8 J.D. [Bayer,J.&A.]
Badnell, Kelly L., (CV) .... '66 '94 C.901 B.A. L.607 J.D. [Baran,P.T.F.&T.]
Baran, Edward C., (AV) .... '42 '67 C&L.930 B.A., J.D. [Baran,P.T.F.&T.]
Baran, Gregory G., (AV) .... '45 '70 C.967 A.B. L.608 J.D. [Baran,P.T.F.&T.]

Baran, Piper, Tarkowsky, Fitzgerald & Theis Co., L.P.A., (AV)
3 N. Main Street, Suite 500, 44902-1725 ⊙
Telephone: 419-524-6682 Fax: 419-525-4571
URL: http://www.baranlaw.com
Edward C. Baran; Gregory G. Baran; John Tarkowsky; Gary A. Piper; Robert B. Fitzgerald (Resident, Lima Office); John P. Calandra; Donald E. Theis (Resident, Toledo Office); Mark A. Van Dyne (Resident, Lima Office); Rose A. Patti (Resident, Brecksville Office); Janet L. Miggins (Resident, Brecksville Office); Richard T. Reese (Resident, Lima, OH Office); Kelly L. Badnell; Michael L. Jones (Resident, Portsmouth Office);—Stephen D. Long (Resident, Toledo Office); Chad P. Hanke; Angela M. Elliott (Resident, Lima Office); Kenneth J. Heisele (Resident, Lima Office).
General Civil Practice. Trials in all Courts. Insurance Defense, Corporate Law, Family Law, Trusts and Estates, Personal Injury, Products Liability and Construction Law. Commercial, Fidelity and Surety. Environmental Law, Governmental, Professional Liability and Worker's Compensation.
General Counsel for: Roger J. Au and Son, Inc. (Heavy Construction and Marine Contracting); Mansfield Flooring (Industrial and Road Contracting); Automatic Welding & Manufacturing Co., Inc. (Acoustics).
Lima, Ohio Office: 121 W. High Street, #905, P.O. Box 568, 45802. Telephone: 419-227-5858. Fax: 419-227-4569.
Columbus, Ohio Office: 6877 North High Street, Suite 105, 43085. Telephone: 614-436-0539. Fax: 614-436-1713.
Toledo, Ohio Office: 608 Madison Avenue, Suite 1620, 43604. Telephone: 419-241-2900. Fax: 419-241-3002.
Brecksville, Ohio Office: 8748 Brecksville Road, Suite 200, 44141. Telephone: 440-746-1177. Fax: 440-746-9637.
Portsmouth Office: 633 Seventh Street, Suite A, 45662. Telephone: 740-353-4700. Fax: 740-353-4747.
See Professional Biographies, MANSFIELD, OHIO

Bayer, Jerger and Ardis Co., L.P.A., (BV) .... 362 Lexington Avenue
Beddow, Kenneth R., (AV) .... '56 '81 C.97 B.S. L.851 J.D. [Sauter H.&B.]
Bemiller, F. Loyal, (AV) .... '33 '58 C.610 A.B. L.477 J.D. [Brown,B.M.M.V.&H.]
Blunt, James L., II, (CV) .... '63 '94 C.398 B.S. L.1003 J.D. [J.Blunt]
Blunt, James, (CV) .... 105 Sturges Ave.
Bourdeau, Julia M. .... '62 '99 C.999 B.S. L.989 J.D. [Calhoun,K.H.&C.]
Bove, Ralph R., (BV) .... '53 '78 C.754 B.S. L.607 J.D. 16 W. 2nd Street
Brown, Charles M., (AV) .... '43 '72 C.201 B.A. L.607 J.D. [Weldon,H.&K.]
Brown, John T., (AV) .... '31 '58 C.313 L.608 J.D. [Brown,B.M.M.V.&H.]

Brown, Bemiller, Murray, McIntyre, Vetter & Heck, L.L.P., (AV)
70 Park Avenue West, 44902
Telephone: 419-525-1611 FAX: 419-525-3810
URL: http://www.brownbemiller.com
Of Counsel: John T. Brown; F. Loyal Bemiller. Members of Firm: D. Kim Murray; William T. McIntyre; Jeffrey Molyet (1951-2003); Adam (Bud) Vetter, Jr.; J. Jeffrey Heck; Jason B. Murray; David N. Haring.
General Civil Practice, Corporate Law, Banking, Business, Casualty and Life Insurance, Trusts and Estates, Wills and Probate, Estate Planning, Real Estate Law, Labor, Employment, Personal Injury, Medical Malpractice, Legal Malpractice. Trials and Appeals, Arbitration and Mediation.

(This Listing Continued)

Brown, Bemiller, Murray, McIntyre, Vetter & Heck, L.L.P. (Continued)

Local Counsel for: Royal & Sun Alliance; Westfield Companies; Ohio Edison Co.; Grange Mutual Casualty Co.; Buckeye Union Insurance Co.; Shelby Insurance; Montgomery Ward & Co.; Artesian Industries, Inc.; CNA; Auto-Owners Ins. Co.

See Professional Biographies, MANSFIELD, OHIO

Burton, Jon K., (BV) .... '49 '74 C.608 B.A. L.8 J.D. [Renwick,W.&B.]
Busler, David E., (CV) .... '52 '77 C.273 B.A. L.893 J.D. 3 N. Main St.
Calhoun, William A., (AV) .... '15 '39 C.381 L.608 J.D. 616 Cline Ave.‡
Calhoun, Kademenos, Heichel & Childress Co., L.P.A., (AV)
6 West Third Street, Suite 200 (⊙Sandusky)
Cannon, Karen L. .... '— '92 Asst. Law Dir., Mansfield City Law Dir.'s Off., Crim. Div.
Carto, David D., (BV) .... '56 '81 C.611 B.A. L.930 J.D. [Weldon,H.&K.]
Cerni, Michele G., (CV) .... '46 '92 C.150 B.A. L.8 J.D. 3 N. Main St., Ste. 500
Childress, Elizabeth A.H. '55 '86 C.600 A.B. L.383 J.D.
(adm. in KY; not adm. in OH) 2441 Kenwood Circle
Childress, James L., (CV) .... '55 '85 C.871 B.S. L.383 J.D. [Calhoun,K.H.&C.] ⊙
Chisnell, Brian J., (CV) .... '50 '80 C.970 B.A. L.7 J.D. UAW-GM Legal Servs. Plan
Christiansen, Richd. M. .... '28 '51 C&L.608 B.A., J.D. Prob. J.
Clark, Christopher S. .... '57 '91 C&L.851 B.A., J.D. [Ⓐ Calhoun,K.H.&C.]
Cockley, Heather M. .... '66 '91 C.367 B.A. L.608 J.D. 16 West Second Street
Cockley, Stephen, (CV) .... '51 '76 C.434 B.S. L.607 J.D. 13 Park Ave. W.
Cole, Thomas L., (AV) .... '37 '61 C&L.607 B.A., J.D. [Ⓒ Weldon,H.&K.]
Copp, Dianna Bessemer .... '57 '85 C.385 B.A. L.201 J.D. City Law Director's Off.
Corley, Jas. R., (CV) .... '26 '52 C.645 B.A. L.608 LL.B. 3 N. Main St.
Davis, Bernard R., (BV) .... '46 '72 C.473 B.S. L.608 J.D. 3 N. Main St.
Davis, Harold H. .... '36 '68 C.434 B.S. L.608 J.D. V.P. & Tr. Offr., Microdyne Company
Dees, Jodie D., (CV) .... '57 '86 C.49 B.A. L.608 J.D. 3 N. Main St.
DeWeese, James .... '46 '79 C.473 B.S. L.201 J.D. Com. Pleas J.
Donaldson, John D., (BV) .... '61 '87 C.973 B.S. L.201 J.D. 233 Marion Avenue
Dorner, T. Michael, (BV) .... '48 '74 C&L.607 B.A., J.D. [Knell,D.&G.]
Emmens, David P. '48 '74 C.385 A.B. L.608 J.D.
Corporate Counsel and Secretary, The Gorman-Rupp Co.
Enderle, John R., (BV) .... '46 '74 C.473 B.S. L.150 J.D. [Inscore,R.W.&E.]
Fesmier, Raymond G., (BV) .... '46 '85 C.203 B.S. L.851 J.D. [R.Fesmier]
Fesmier, Raymond, Attorney At Law, (BV) .... 28 Park Ave. W., Ste. 501
Fithian, William C., III, (CV) .... '56 '81 C.645 B.A. L.608 J.D. [W.C.Fithian]
Fithian, William C., Co., L.P.A., (CV) .... 111 N. Main St.
Flippin, Wilbur H., Jr. .... '29 '57 C.943 B.A. L.161 J.D. [W.H.Flippin,Jr.]
Flippin, Wilbur Henry, Jr. .... 30 S. Park
Fowler, Richard R., (BV) .... '28 '53 C&L.608 B.S., J.D. [Ⓒ Weldon,H.&K.]
Frecka, John A. '29 '67 C.437 B.A. L.912 J.D.
(adm. in MI; not adm. in OH) Exec. Coun., Ultra Tech Plastics
Freda, Michael M., (BV) .... '47 '72 C&L.608 B.S., J.D. UAW-GM Legal Servs. Plan
Fry, Randall E., (BV) .... '53 '78 C.8 B.A. L.607 J.D. 10 West Newlon Ave.
Gandert, William F. '26 '50 C&L.608 B.A., J.D.
Exec. Dir. & Gen. Coun., City Housing Auth.
Gerhardt, Dan E., (BV) .... '46 '87 C.473 B.S. L.8 J.D. [Knell,D.&G.]
Gibson, Harold E., Jr. .... '27 '56 C&L.228 A.B., LL.B. 55 S. Franklin Ave.
Goldberger, Robert .... '49 '76 C.477 B.A. L.588 J.D. 13 Park Ave. W., Ste. 605
Goldman, Catherine D. .... '56 '81 C.882 B.A. L.608 J.D. [Ⓐ Weldon,H.&K.]
Hall, George, (AV) .... '24 '52 C.665 A.B. L.930 LL.B. [Ⓒ Weldon,H.&K.]
Hanke, Chad P. .... '77 '03 C.967 B.A. L.608 J.D. [Ⓐ Baran,P.T.F.&T.]
Haring, David N., (CV) .... '69 '94 C.473 B.A. L.851 J.D. [Brown,B.M.M.V.&H.]
Harper, Roeliff E., (CV) .... '59 '91 C.610 B.A. L.851 J.D. 13 Park Ave., W.
Heck, J. Jeffrey, (BV) .... '59 '85 C.608 B.S. L.260 J.D. [Brown,B.M.M.V.&H.]
Heichel, William D., (AV) .... '44 '72 C.381 B.A. L.7 J.D. [Calhoun,K.H.&C.] ⊙
Hendricks, Richard E., (CV) .... '36 '69 C.282 B.A. L.1003 J.D. 3 N. Main St.
Henson, James D. .... '42 '69 C&L.608 B.A., J.D. Com. Pleas J.
Hines, Adrienne Marie .... '71 '96 C.610 B.A. L.851 J.D. [Ⓐ Calhoun,K.H.&C.] ⊙
Hitchman, Terry D., (CV) .... '57 '88 C.528 B.A. L.1003 J.D. 3 N. Main St., Ste. 701
Hoerig, Joseph P., (CV) .... '67 '95 C.980 B.A. L.8 J.D. [Ⓐ Sauter H.&B.]
Hohenberger, Wayne P., (AV) .... '46 '73 C.97 B.A. L.608 J.D. [Sauter H.&B.]
Holmes, John Allen, (BV) .... '53 '84 C.275 B.A. L.383 J.D. [Weldon,H.&K.]
Hoover, Donald E., (CV) .... '54 '80 C.49 B.S.B.A. L.8 J.D. [Weldon,H.&K.]
Inscore, Larry L., (AV) .... '32 '59 C&L.608 B.S., J.D. [Inscore,R.W.&E.]
Inscore, Michael L., (BV) .... '58 '84 C&L.608 B.S., J.D. [Inscore,R.W.&E.]
Inscore, Rinehardt, Whitney & Enderle Co., L.P.A., (AV) .... 13 Park Avenue West
Jacobs, Thomas L., (CV) .... '47 '86 C.475 B.A. L.8 J.D. [Ⓐ Knell,D.&G.]
Jerger, Joseph L., (CV) .... '65 '90 C&L.607 B.S.B.A., J.D. [Bayer,J.&A.]
Jones, Kenneth D., Jr., (CV) '44 '96 C.608 D.D.S. L.117 J.D.
13 Park Ave. W., Ste. 300
Kademenos, Victor P., (BV) .... '45 '71 C.610 B.A. L.608 J.D. [Calhoun,K.H.&C.] ⊙
Keith, Arthur Lee '50 '95 C.434 B.S. L.213 J.D.
(adm. in FL; not adm. in OH) Mansfield Correctional Inst.
Keller, Jennifer D. .... '76 '01 Staff. Atty., Community Legal Aid Services, Inc.

Keyser, George R., (BV) '47 '73 C.258 B.A. L.362 J.D.
44 Park Avenue West Suite 202, 44902-1610
Telephone: 419-526-2301 Fax: 419-526-2826
Email: keysergeorge@earthlink.net URL: http://www.keyserlaw.com
Civic and Criminal Litigation in all Courts. Personal Injury, Automobile Accidents, Slip and Fall, Products Liability, Wrongful Death, Family Law, Divorce, Child Custody, Child Support, Visitation Rights, Adoption Law, Juvenile Law, Criminal Defense, Driving While Intoxicated, Drug Crimes, Felonies, Misdemeanors.

See Professional Biographies, MANSFIELD, OHIO

Kitzler, Benjamin D. .... '75 '00 C.967 B.A.B.S. L.7 J.D. [Ⓐ Anderson,W.O.&K.]
Kitzler, David L., (BV) .... '51 '76 C.97 B.A. L.276 J.D. [Anderson,W.O.&K.]
Kitzler, Patricia O'Donnell, (BV) .... '51 '88 C.97 B.S. L.7 J.D. [Anderson,W.O.&K.]
Knell, George H., (BV) .... '30 '58 C&L.608 B.S., J.D. [Knell,D.&G.]
Knell, Dorner & Gerhardt Co., L.P.A., (BV) .... 3 N. Main St.
Kramer, Jeffrey N., (BV) ... '52 '82 C.871 B.S. L.260 J.D. 24 West Third Street, Suite 300

Lamkin, Van Eman, Trimble, Beals & Dougherty, LLC
(See Columbus)

Liming, Roxi A.
(See Columbus)

Linsker, Jeffrey A., (BV) .... '51 '76 C.473 B.S. L.117 J.D. Mag., Com. Pleas Ct.
Lynch, Charles D. .... '50 '75 C.970 B.A. L.607 J.D. [Ⓐ Calhoun,K.H.&C.]
Mabee, Robert E., (BV) .... '23 '50 C&L.607 A.B., J.D. [Mabee&M.]
Mabee & Mills, (BV) .... 24 W. Third St.
Mack, Deborah L. .... '63 '96 C.62 B.A. L.1003 J.D. 34 S. Park Bldg.
Massie, Nancy Helen, (CV) .... '61 '88 C.381 B.S. L.607 J.D. Asst. Co. Pros.
Matthews, A. Robert .... '25 '51 C.970 A.B. L.309 LL.B. 171 S. Brookwood Way‡
Mayer, James, Jr., (BV) .... '49 '77 C.608 B.S. L.607 J.D. 38 South Park Street
Mayer, Philip Alan B., Law Offices of, (CV) '50 '77
C.608 B.S. L.607 J.D. 564 Park Avenue West
McDonald, John A. '32 '58
C&L.352 B.S.C., J.D. Sr. V.P., McDonald & Co. Securities, Inc.
McIntyre, William T., (AV) .... '50 '75 C.97 B.S. L.608 J.D. [Brown,B.M.M.V.&H.]
Miller, Eric S., (BV) .... '50 '76 C.207 B.A. L.608 J.D. 13 Park Avenue West, Suite 608
Mills, Reese F., (BV) .... '46 '75 C.207 B.A. L.477 J.D. [Mabee&M.]
Morrison, Jeffrey Stephen .... '54 '94 C.1023 B.A. L.989 J.D. OH Edison Co.
Morton, Norman R. .... '35 '64 C.97 B.A. L.607 J.D. 55 S. Diamond St.
Murray, D. Kim, (AV) .... '45 '73 C.608 B.A. L.7 J.D. [Brown,B.M.M.V.&H.]
Murray, G. J. .... '23 '50 C.970 A.B. L.930 J.D. 714 Cloverleaf Ct.‡
Murray, Jason B., (BV) .... '70 '95 C.611 B.A. L.608 J.D. [Brown,B.M.M.V.&H.]
Musilli, Dale M., (CV) .... '55 '87 C.608 B.S. L.930 J.D. 105 Sturges Avenue
Naylor, Robert S. .... '63 '91 C.608 B.A. L.228 J.D. [Ⓐ Calhoun,K.H.&C.]
Negin, Arthur W. .... '13 '37 C.608 L.989 J.D. 3100 Park Ave. West Rd.‡
O'Donnell, James J., (BV) .... '29 '54 C.602 A.B. L.262 J.D. [Ⓒ Anderson,W.O.&K.] ‡
O'Donnell, John C., III, (CV) '53 '80
C.97 B.A. L.851 J.D. 13 Park Avenue, West, Suite 605
Olecki, Joseph T. .... '61 '94 C.918 B.A. L.893 J.D. [Ⓐ Weldon,H.&K.]

Oliver Law Office
(See Columbus)

Otto, Richard H., (BV) .... '54 '81 C.951 B.A. L.94 J.D. [Weldon,H.&K.]
Perry, Kathleen Elaine .... '55 '83 C.608 B.S. L.607 J.D. UAW-GM Legal Servs. Plan
Piper, Gary A., (AV) .... '49 '75 C.97 B.S. L.851 J.D. [Baran,P.T.F.&T.]
Pitzer, N. Jeanne .... '60 '97 C.49 B.A. L.1003 J.D. Asst. Co. Pros., Co. Pros. Off.

Plymale Partnership LLP, The
(See Columbus)

Poland, Depler and Shepherd Co., L.P.A.
(See Shelby)

Remy, David L., (BV) .... '49 '75 C&L.607 B.A., J.D. 228 Fairlawn Ave.
Renwick, J. Roger .... '39 '66 C&L.607 B.A., J.D. [Renwick,W.&B.] ‡
Renwick, Welsh & Burton, (AV) .... 9 N. Mulberry St.
Rinehardt, John J., (BV) .... '32 '56 C.473 L.608 LL.B. [Inscore,R.W.&E.]
Rinehardt, John K., (BV) .... '60 '86 C&L.608 B.A., J.D. [J.K.Rinehardt]
Rinehardt, John K., Law Firm, Llc., (BV) .... 2404 Park Avenue West
Robinson, Brent N., (CV) .... '69 '94 C.631 B.A. L.117 J.D. Asst. Pros. Atty.
Robinson, Charles T., (BV) .... '41 '66 C.62 B.A. L.607 J.D. 3 N. Main
Roby, John S. .... '42 '68 C.608 B.S. L.930 J.D. Pres., Roby Foster Miller Earick Inc.
Rotell, Ava Marie, (BV) .... '67 '92 Asst. Pros.

Rourke & Blumenthal, LLP
(See Columbus)

Ryan, H. Eugene, (AV) .... '12 '37 C.502 B.A. L.309 LL.B. 730 Glendale Blvd.‡
Sauter, George V., (AV) .... '19 '46 C.679 B.S. L.930 J.D. [Sauter H.&B.] ‡
Sauter, Jean U., (Mrs.) .... '22 '46 C.788 B.A. L.930 LL.B. 520 Edgewood Rd.‡

Sauter Hohenberger & Beddow, (AV)
24 West Third Street, Suite 306, 44902
Telephone: 419-522-6242 Fax: 419-525-0258
URL: http://www.shbfirm.com
Members of Firm: George V. Sauter (Retired); Wayne P. Hohenberger; Kenneth R. Beddow. Associate: Joseph P. Hoerig.
Insurance, Probate and Estate Planning, Negligence and Products Liability Law. Trials and Appeals.
Representative Clients: State Farm Insurance Cos.; Celina Insurance Group; Auto Owners (Mutual) Insurance Co.; Transamerica Group; St. Paul Insurance Group; Cincinnati Insurance Cos.

See Professional Biographies, MANSFIELD, OHIO

Scherner, Hanson & Cornwell, LLC
(See Columbus)

Schulz, Alicia A. '48 '80 C.352 B.A. L.597 J.D.
Pres. & Corp. Atty., Microdyne Company
Siegenthaler, John H., (AV) .... '39 '64 C.207 A.B. L.608 J.D. [Ⓒ Weldon,H.&K.]
Spon, Ronald D. .... '47 '73 C.608 B.A. L.607 J.D. Com. Pleas J.

Standley Law Group LLP
(See Dublin)

Stewart, John (Jack) P., (CV) .... '63 '91 C.201 B.S. L.1003 J.D. 6 W. 3rd St.
Sturgill, Judith Lynn Messner .... '47 '85 C.381 B.S. L.8 J.D. North Central State Coll.
Sukys, Paul A. .... '48 '80 C.363 B.A. L.161 J.D. Prof., N. Central Technical College
Tarkowsky, John, (BV) '54 '78 C.62 B.A. L.607 J.D.
[Baran,P.T.F.&T.] (⊙Columbus, Worthington)
Taylor, Curtis Stanley .... '25 '50 C&L.608 B.A., J.D. 741 Yale Ave., Lot 38‡
Teffner, Donald R., (BV) .... '49 '77 C.608 B.S. L.7 J.D. Com. Pleas Ct. Mag.
Tenison, Dennis C., (CV) '50 '79 C.429 B.A. L.930 J.D.
Mng. Atty., Community Legal Aid Services, Inc.
Them, Jerod M. .... '78 '04 C.608 B.S. L.117 J.D. [Ⓐ Weldon,H.&K.]
Thomas, Rebecca M., (CV) .... '50 '92 C.999 B.S. L.8 J.D. 2294 Park Ave. W.
Thompson, C. Richard, (BV) .... '51 '76 C&L.607 B.A., J.D. [C.R.Thompson]
Thompson, Dale A. .... '50 '75 C.347 B.S. L.608 J.D. 649 Westview Blvd.
Thompson, C. Richard Co., L.P.A., (BV) .... 13 Park Ave., W.
Thrush, Douglas L., (BV) .... '50 '75 C&L.607 B.A., J.D. 13 Park Ave. W.

Twyford & Donahey, P.L.L.
(See Columbus)

TyRee, James A., (CV) .... '47 '83 C.36 B.S. L.607 J.D. 13 Park Ave. W.
Underwood, Jeffrey A., (CV) .... '71 '96 C.91 B.A. L.1003 J.D. [Bayer,J.&A.]
Vecchio, Robert J., (BV) .... '55 '82 C.260 B.A. L.1188 J.D. [R.J.Vecchio] ⊙
Vecchio, Robert J., Co., L.P.A., (BV) .... 44 Park Avenue West (⊙Cleveland)
Vetter, Adam (Bud), Jr., (BV) .... '60 '85 C.97 B.S. L.1003 J.D. [Brown,B.M.M.V.&H.]
Wagner, James K., Attorney at Law, (BV) '50 '76
C.150 B.A. L.851 J.D. 3 N. Main St., Ste. 808
Wagner, Leslie K. .... '10 '38 C.608 B.S. L.150 J.D. 13 Park Ave. W.‡
Wagner, Leslie K., Jr., (BV) .... '42 '67 C&L.608 B.S., J.D. 3 N. Main St.
Weiler, Samuel P. .... '77 '04 C.610 B.B.A. L.608 J.D. 13 Park Ave. W., 4th Fl.

Weldon, Huston & Keyser, L.L.P., (BV)
Bank One Building, 28 Park Ave W, 44902-1692
Telephone: 419-524-9811 Fax: 419-522-5758
William McE. Weldon (1868-1952); C. H. Huston (1871-1957); Henry P. Huston (1903-1984); George H. Keyser (1917-1998). Members of Firm: David D. Carto; Richard H. Otto; John Allen Holmes; Donald E. Hoover. Associates: Joseph T. Olecki; Catherine D. Goldman; Jerod M. Them. Of Counsel: George Hall; Richard R. Fowler; John H. Siegenthaler; Thomas L. Cole; Charles M. Brown.
General Civil and Criminal Practice. Probate and Estate Planning. Business Law, Labor and Employment Law, Insurance Law, Personal Injury, Real Estate, Family/Domestic Relations, Divorce.
Representative Clients: Mechanics Savings Bank; The Richland Trust Company (Richland Bank); MedCentral Health System; Motorists Insurance Co.; General Motors Acceptance Corp.; Reeder Lumber Co.; Whitey's Auto Mall; North Central State College Foundation; Ohio Ski Slopes, Inc.

See Professional Biographies, MANSFIELD, OHIO

Welsh, Harry M., (AV) ... '41 '66 C&L.851 B.A., J.D. [Renwick,W.&B.]
Wendling, Anne Channon ... '48 '89 3 N. Main St.
Werstiuk, Allen D. ... '55 '82 C.608 B.S. L.117 J.D. 600 Park Ave. W.
White, E. A. ... '24 '50 C.253 A.B. L.607 J.D. 306 Willodell Dr.
Whitney, M. Lore', (CV) ... '61 '92 C.313 B.S. L.607 J.D. [Inscore,R.W.&E.]
Whitney, R. Rolf, (BV) ... '57 '82 C.207 B.A. L.201 J.D. [Inscore,R.W.&E.]
Whitney, Robert H., (AV) ... '35 '62 C&L.607 A.B., J.D. [Inscore,R.W.&E.]

Wiles, Boyle, Burkholder & Bringardner Co., L.P.A.
(See Columbus)

Wolf, Marcus A. ... '46 '80 C.1080 B.A. L.607 J.D. [M.A.Wolf]
Wolf, Marcus A., Co., LPA ... 13 Park Avenue West, Suite 300
Zaller, Mark T., (BV) ... '59 '85 C.363 B.A. L.201 J.D. 13 Park Avenue W, Suite 605

MANTUA, 1,046, *Portage Co.*

Schickler, Ronald S. ... '58 '91 C.381 B.B.A. L.1003 J.D. 18510 May Ct.

MAPLE HEIGHTS, 26,156, *Cuyahoga Co.*

Augustine, Susan M. ... '52 '89 C.930 B.B. L.1003 J.D. 17388 Broadway Ave.
Bocci, Lawrence Michael '69 '98
C.381 B.B.A. L.989 J.D. 20676 Southgate Park Boulevard
Broski, Gerald F. ... '43 '68 C.363 B.S. L.1003 J.D. Maple Hts. Bd. of Educ.
Canestraro, Donald C., (BV) ... '37 '66 C.1115 B.A. L.1003 J.D. [D.C.Canestraro]
Canestraro, Donald C., Co., L.P.A., (BV) ... 15950 Libby Rd.
Caron, Brian L. ... '69 '95 C&L.124 B.A., J.D. [Crombie] (⊙University Heights)
Crombie Law Firm, The ... 5334 Northfield Road (⊙North Olmsted, University Heights)
Pells, Richard R. ... '35 '61 C.611 B.A. L.930 LL.B. Hertz Claim Mgmt.
Shipan, James V., (BV) ... '22 '50 C.207 A.B. L.1003 LL.B. 5251 Lee Rd.

MARENGO, 393, *Morrow Co.*

Bennett, Earl W. ... '45 '70 C.631 B.A. L.477 J.D. 20 West Walnut St.
Minadeo, Joseph M. ... '69 '96 C.602 B.A. L.1194 J.D. 1071 County Road 24
Vaile, George Q. B. ... '42 '68 C&L.608 B.A., J.D. 776 Worthington New Haven Rd.

MARIEMONT, 3,408, *Hamilton Co.*

Parker, E. Allen, (BV) ... '21 '51 C.150 L.1340 J.D. 6614 Elm St.

MARIETTA, * 14,515, *Washington Co.*

Addison, James R., (Co., L.P.A.), (AV) ... '29 '53 C&L.608 B.S., J.D. [Addison&F.]
Addison & Funk, (AV) ... 202 Wes Banco Building
Atkinson, Thomas R., (BV) ... '41 '69 C.207 B.S. L.607 J.D. [Atkinson&B.]
Atkinson & Burton, (BV) ... 312 Putnam St.
Bertram, Paul G., Jr. ... '37 '62 C.608 B.A. L.150 LL.B. 412 3rd St.
Boyer, Susan E. ... '48 '73 C.381 B.A. L.7 J.D. Com. Pleas J.
Bozian, Robin A., (BV) '52 '77 C.150 B.A. L.124 J.D.
Mng. Atty., Southeastern Ohio Legal Services
Brock, Jerry A., (AV) ... '38 '63 C.610 B.S.C. L.150 J.D. [Theisen B.]
Brum, Nancy Edwards, (BV) ... '56 '82 C.473 B.A. L.608 J.D. [Atkinson&B.]
Buell, Michael D., (BV) ... '52 '78 C.434 B.A. L.851 J.D. [Buell&S.]

Buell & Sipe Co. L.P.A., (BV)
322 3rd Street, 45750
Telephone: 740-373-3219 Fax: 740-373-2892
Email: attorneys@buellsipe.com URL: http://www.lawyers.com/buell&sipe
Michael D. Buell; Dennis L. Sipe.
Personal Injury, Automobile Accidents, Wrongful Death, Civil Litigation, Estate Planning, Wills and Probate, Trusts and Estates, Employment Discrimination, Sexual Harassment, Family Law, Divorce, Child Custody, Child Support, Adoptions, Criminal Defense, Driving While Intoxicated, Traffic Violations, Appellate Law including Habeas Corpus.
See Professional Biographies, MARIETTA, OHIO

Burnworth, Randall G., (CV) ... '51 '76 C.976 B.A. L.930 J.D. 429 2nd St.
Burton, William L., (BV) ... '46 '74 C.434 B.A. L.362 J.D. [Atkinson&B.]
Carlisle, Matthew C. ... '71 '98 C.610 B.B.A. L.608 J.D. [Theisen B.]
Cauthorn, Alison L., (BV) ... '64 '89 C.611 B.A. L.608 J.D. Asst. Co. Pros.
Cook, Colleen E., (BV) ... '57 '83 C&L.608 B.A., J.D. [Theisen B.]

Cosenza & Merriman, PLLC
(See Parkersburg, West Virginia)

Davidson, Heckler, Riggs & Fouss, (BV)
311 Fourth Street, P.O. Box 567, 45750
Telephone: 740-373-7572 Fax: 740-373-7081
Email: dhrf@sbcglobal.net
Members of Firm: Roland W. Riggs, III; Daniel A. Fouss.
General Practice in State and Federal Courts. Corporation, Small Business Law, Business Formation, Buying and Selling of Businesses, Real Estate, Probate, Trusts and Estates. Trials.
Representative Clients: The Marietta Savings Bank; Citizens Bank Co., Beverly, Ohio.
See Professional Biographies, MARIETTA, OHIO

Dehmlow, Jonathan C. ... '65 '92 C.938 B.A. L.69 J.D. [A W.A.Fields]

Denmead Law Office
(See Columbus)

Dobbins-Bucklad, Mary, (CV) ... '60 '86 C.607 B.A. L.851 J.D. 301 Putnam Street
Dotsenko, Juliana C. ... '60 '88 C.437 B.S. L.117 J.D. Mun. Ct. Mag.
Ellis, Robert, (CV) ... '47 '77 C.454 B.S. L.1048 J.D. [Ellis&E.]
Ellis & Ellis, A Legal Professional Association, (CV) ... 328 Fourth St.
Emrick, Gregg M., (BV) ... '52 '77 C.838 B.S. L.608 J.D. [McCauley,W.&E.] ⊙
Erb, John E., (AV) ... '44 '69 C&L.608 B.S.B.A., J.D. [Theisen B.]
Evans, Robert E. ... '40 '67 C.607 B.S. L.117 J.D. Pres. & CEO, Peoples Bancorp Inc.
Fields, William A., (AV) ... '39 '64 C.608 B.S. L.309 J.D. 125 Putnam Street
Fogle & Frazier, (BV) ... 330 Fourth St.
Folwell, Norman L., Law Offices ... '65 '91 C.923 B.A. L.607 J.D. 407 2nd St.
Fouss, Daniel A., (BV) ... '52 '80 C.610 B.A. L.851 J.D. [Davidson,H.R.&F.]
Frazier, Janet F., (BV) ... '47 '77 C.434 B.A. L.7 J.D. [Fogle&F.]
Frye, Gary F., (BV) ... '42 '68 C&L.608 B.A., J.D. [Theisen B.]
Funk, Rustin J., (BV) ... '53 '77 C.473 A.B. L.608 J.D. [Addison&F.]
Garrison, Jennifer D., (CV) ... '62 '87 C.973 B.S. L.128 J.D. 115 2nd. Street, 2nd Floor
Hallock, Walter E., Jr. ... '30 '56 C&L.930 B.B.A., J.D. 201 Lee Ave.‡
Harrington, Dennis, (CV) ... '54 '86 C.150 B.A. L.930 J.D. 427 Second Street
Heckler, Charles K. ... '18 '49 C.434 B.A. L.150 LL.B. 214 Putnam Ave.‡
Hirschi, Helen ... '59 '91 C.1335 B.A. L.763 J.D. 703 Colgate Dr.
Huggins, James S., (AV) ... '56 '81 C&L.608 B.A., J.D. [Theisen B.]
Hunsaker, Charles R., (BV) '45 '72
C.475 B.A. L.851 J.D. Gen. Coun., Peoples Bancorp Inc.
Jones, Donald L., (CV) ... '35 '63 C.473 B.S. L.564 LL.B. 421 2nd St.
Keegan, Anne E. ... '55 '80 C.97 B.S. L.930 J.D. 130 Seneca Dr.‡
Kerenyi, Mark, (BV) ... '66 '96 C.657 B.A. L.1003 J.D. Asst. Pros. Atty.
Lane, N. Edward, Jr. ... '50 '77 C&L.117 B.A., J.D. Com. Pleas J.
Leeper, M. Dale, (AV) ... '48 '74 C.970 B.A. L.608 J.D. [Theisen B.]
McCauley, James H., (BV) ... '45 '69 C&L.923 B.S.J., J.D. [McCauley,W.&E.] ⊙
McCauley, Webster & Emrick, (BV) ... 225 Putnam Street (⊙Belpre)
Montera, Susan A., (CV) ... '55 '93 C.150 B.A. L.229 J.D. [Newhart&M.]
Newhart, Anita Lynne, (CV) ... '56 '83 C.434 B.A. L.150 J.D. [Newhart&M.]
Newhart & Montera, (CV) ... 227 Third Street
Nichols, Curtis B., (BV) ... '49 '80 C.610 B.B.A. L.7 J.D. 324 4th St., Ste. 100
Nuzum, W. Milton, III ... '51 '81 C.608 B.S.Phar. L.1119 J.D. Mun. J.
Rawson, Robert G. ... '25 '55 C&L.608 B.E., J.D. Ret. Com. Pleas. J.
Reynolds, Catherine Ingram ... '67 '92 C.473 B.A. L.150 J.D. Asst. City Law Dir.
Richardson, Lynn McMains, (CV) ... '46 '77 C.1176 B.A. L.1048 J.D. [Ellis&E.]
Riggs, Roland W., III, (BV) ... '47 '72 C.276 B.S. L.930 J.D. [Davidson,H.R.&F.]
Ritter, Khadine L. ... '75 '00 C.221 B.A. L.124 J.D. [Theisen B.]
Sauer, George D. ... '14 '42 C.473 B.S. L.607 J.D. 322 3rd St.‡
Sellers, Abe, (CV) ... '72 '97 C.610 B.S. L.608 J.D. [Theisen B.]
Sipe, Dennis L., (BV) ... '48 '73 C.475 B.S. L.608 J.D. [Buell&S.]
Smith, Harry L. '35 '77 C.476 B.A. L.213 J.D.
(adm. in MI; not adm. in OH) 508 Foster Lane‡
Spahr, Michael G., (BV) ... '43 '74 C.610 B.A. L.607 J.D. Pros. Atty.
Taylor, John K. ... '35 '64 C.608 B.S. L.150 J.D. 100 Meadow Ln.
Theisen, Paul T., (AV) ... '31 '57 C&L.150 A.B., LL.B. [C Theisen B.]

Theisen Brock, A Legal Professional Association, (AV)
424 Second Street, P.O. Box 739, 45750
Telephone: 740-373-5455 Fax: 740-373-4409
Email: theisenbrock@theisenbrock.com URL: http://www.theisenbrock.com
Of Counsel: Paul T. Theisen. Members of Firm: Jerry A. Brock (Certified Specialist in Estate Planning, Trust and Probate Law, Ohio State Bar Association); Gary F. Frye; John E. Erb; M. Dale Leeper; James S. Huggins; Colleen E. Cook (Certified Specialist in Labor & Employment Law, Ohio State Bar Association); John E. Triplett, Jr.; Abe Sellers; Khadine L. Ritter; Matthew C. Carlisle;—Ethan T. Vessels.
General Practice, Trials, Personal Injury, Insurance Law and Insurance Defense, Corporation, Partnership and Business Law, Labor and Employment Law, Probate and Estate Planning, Bankruptcy Law, Real Estate and Oil and Gas Law, Health Care Law, Export Law.
Counsel for: Peoples Bank and Trust Co.; Broughton Foods Co.; Marietta College; Marietta Memorial Hospital; Forma Scientific Inc. (Laboratory Equipment).
Local Counsel for: Monongahela Power Co.; Nationwide Mutual Insurance Co.; State Farm Insurance Cos.; Cincinnati Insurance Co.; Erie Insurance.
See Professional Biographies, MARIETTA, OHIO

Thomas, Christina M. '56 '86 C.434 B.S. L.796 J.D.
(adm. in TX; not adm. in OH) 304 Wooster St.
Thomas, Richard J. ... '26 '51 C&L.608 B.A., J.D. 200 Putnam St.
Triplett, John E., Jr., (BV) ... '59 '84 C.880 B.A. L.607 J.D. [Theisen B.]
Vessels, Ethan T. ... '73 '03 C.870 B.S. L.608 J.D. [A Theisen B.]
Webster, Thomas P., (BV) ... '50 '75 C.381 B.S. L.608 J.D. [McCauley,W.&E.] ⊙
Welch, Janet Dyar, (BV) ... '54 '80 C.434 B.A. L.608 J.D. 311 Scammel St.
Wesel, Marilyn S., (CV) ... '62 '93 C.608 B.S. L.150 J.D. Mag. J.
Westbrock, Paul G. ... '68 '93 L.201 J.D. Legal Affs. Dir., Marietta Health System
Willard, Michele Hilden, (BV) '42 '84 C.242 B.A. L.608 J.D.
100 Front Street, Suite 302
Williams, Timothy A. ... '58 '84 C&L.607 B.A., J.D. Prob. Ct. J.
Wyant, Daniel M. ... '67 '95 C.611 B.A. L.117 J.D. East Ohio Land Title Agency, Inc.

MARION, * 35,318, *Marion Co.*

Alspach, Deborah A. ... '52 '88 C.608 B.S. L.607 J.D. Com. Pleas J.

Armengau, Javier H.
(See Columbus)

Arter, John C. A., Jr. ... '27 '52 C.608 L.607 340 Mt. Vernon Ave.
Babich, Lawrence H., (BV) ... '50 '75 C.608 B.A. L.228 J.D. Asst. Co. Pros.
Babich, Ted B. ... '49 '74 C.608 B.A. L.276 J.D. [T.Babich]
Babich, Ted, The Law Office of ... 399 E. Church St.
Bacon, Forrest H., (AV) ... '24 '51 C&L.608 LL.B. [Roth B.Y.] ⊙
Baker, Holley F., (CV) ... '23 '52 C.607 L.879 LL.B. 120 S. Main St.
Ballinger, Teresa L. ... '57 '94 C.737 B.A. L.117 J.D. 391 S. Main St.
Bartram, John C., (AV) ... '46 '73 C.611 B.A. L.597 J.D. [Bartram&B.]
Bartram & Bartram, (AV) ... 146 E. Center Street
Bruder, Susan M., (BV) ... '57 '83 C.473 A.B. L.608 J.D. 232 S. Prospect St.
Burt, Jasper N., (BV) ... '40 '66 C.532 B.A. L.607 J.D. 284 S. State St., Ste. 531

Calig & Handelman, LPA, (BV)
274 S. Main Street, 43302 ⊙
Telephone: 740-375-5051
URL: http://www.chohiolawyers.com
Terry V. Hummel; Kenneth P. Karlock.
Bankruptcy, Personal Injury, Probate, Real Estate, Social Security, Social Security Disability, Medical Malpractice, Wrongful Death, Civil Litigation, Domestic Relations Law.
Columbus, Ohio Office: 854 East Broad Street, 43205. Telephone: 614-252-4885; 1-800-633-5000.
Newark, Ohio Office: 29 S. Park Place, 43055. Telephone: 740-349-8581. Fax: 740-345-4101.
Lancaster, Ohio Office: 204 N. Columbus Street, 43130. Telephone: 740-653-4400. Fax: 740-653-0037.
See Professional Biographies, MARION, OHIO

Chaffin, Steven E., (CV) ... '54 '81 C.1042 B.A. L.1049 J.D. Asst. Law Dir.‡
Collins, Kevin P., (BV) ... '60 '85 C.607 B.A. L.608 J.D. [Collins&L.]
Collins & Lowther, A Legal Professional Association, (BV) ... 125 South Main Street
Conkle, Louis B., (AV) ... '20 '43 C&L.608 B.A., J.D. 408 Uhler Ave.‡
Coulter, Ted I., Attorney at Law, (BV) ... '55 '81 C.117 B.A. L.930 J.D. 391 S. Main St.
Cramer, Ronald D., (AV) ... '48 '75 C.608 B.S. L.7 J.D. [Michel,D.&C.]
Croskey, Jennifer S.M. ... '74 '00 C.851 B.A. L.608 J.D. Asst. Pros. Atty.
Crowder, Mary Kay, (CV) ... '67 '92 C.999 B.A. L.990 J.D. 334 E. Center St.
Davidson, Robert Stephen, (BV) ... '53 '78 C.201 B.A. L.607 J.D. J., Com. Pleas Ct.

Dingus, M. Shawn
(See Columbus)

Dowler, Harry L., Jr., (AV) ... '32 '61 C.611 B.A. L.608 J.D. 131 S. Prospect St.
Ebert, Douglas E., (BV) ... '49 '76 C&L.608 B.A., J.D. [Harris&E.]
Fetter, Thomas C. ... '18 '46 L.607 J.D. Ret. Com. Pleas J.
Finnegan, William R. ... '54 '79 C.201 B.A. L.608 J.D. Mun. J.
Firstenberger, John P., (AV) ... '34 '59 C&L.607 B.A., J.D. 127 E. Center St.
Fragale, Robert D., (BV) ... '56 '82 C.657 B.S. L.117 J.D. [Nemo&F.]
Frericks, Theodore P., (BV) ... '17 '43 C&L.602 A.B., J.D. [Frericks&H.]
Frericks, Theodore P., IV ... '44 '70 C.602 B.A. L.608 J.D. [Frericks&H.]
Frericks, Thomas A., (AV) ... '45 '71 C.602 A.B. L.608 J.D. [Frericks&H.]
Frericks, Timothy M., (CV) ... '49 '74 C.602 B.A. L.607 J.D. [Frericks&H.]
Frericks and Howard, A Legal Professional Association, (AV) ... 152 East Center Street
Goodman, Malcolm L., (BV) ... '48 '74 C.610 B.A. L.7 J.D. 131 S. Prospect St.
Hall, F. Riley, (AV) ... '22 '51 C.532 L.607 LL.B. [Hall&H.] ‡
Hall, Kevin R., (BV) ... '58 '87 C.381 B.S. L.117 J.D. [Hall&H.]
Hall & Hall, (AV) ... 355 East Center Street
Harraman, Brent M., (BV) ... '52 '77 C.97 B.S. L.7 J.D. 399 E. Church Street
Harris, James Alan, (AV) ... '39 '68 C&L.607 B.A., J.D. [Harris&E.]
Harris & Ebert, (AV) ... 136 S. Main St.

Hummel, Terry V., (BV) .... '55 '82 C&L.117 B.A., J.D. [Calig&H.] (⊙Columbus)
Hypes, Maria L., (BV) .... '55 '91 C.608 B.S. L.607 J.D. 232 South Prospect Street
Jacob, Dean L., (BV) .... '61 '86 C.602 B.A. L.608 J.D. 1138 Brook Park Rd.
Jenkins, Stephen L. .... '40 '65 C.611 B.A. L.597 J.D. 896 Christopher Dr.‡
Jenkins, Thomas K. .... '37 '62 C.611 B.A. L.607 J.D. Prob. J.
Karlock, Kenneth P. .... '68 '93 C.608 B.A. L.930 J.D. [Calig&H.]

Kegler, Brown, Hill & Ritter, (AV)
250 Executive Drive, Suite B, P.O. Box 919, 43302 ⊙
Telephone: 740-387-1120 Facsimile: 740-387-3630
Email: info@keglerbrown.com URL: http://www.keglerbrown.com
Counsel: Ted M. McKinniss;—Michele Selig Worobiec.
Administrative Law/Governmental Relations; Banking; Bankruptcy and Creditor's Rights; Business, Corporations and Partnerships; Commercial; Construction; Energy; Estate Planning; Franchise; Gaming Law; Health Care; International; Labor and Employee Relations; Litigation; Mergers and Acquisitions; Oil and Gas; Patent, Trademark and Copyright Law; Probate; Professional Responsibility; Public Utilities; Real Estate; Securities; Tax.
Columbus, Ohio Office: Capitol Square, Suite 1800, 65 East State Street. Telephone: 614-462-5400. Telecopier: 614-464-2634. Cable Address: "Law KBHR". Telex: 246671. Email: info@kbhr.com.
See Professional Biographies, MARION, OHIO

Kenney-Pfalzer, Susan
(See Columbus)

Kochheiser, Keith A., (BV) .... '50 '78 C.49 B.S. L.607 J.D. [Wilson&K.]

Lamkin, Van Eman, Trimble, Beals & Dougherty, LLC
(See Columbus)

Libster, Mitchell A., (BV) '50 '76
C.608 B.S. L.117 J.D. Mng. Atty., Legal Aid Soc. of Columbus

Liming, Roxi A.
(See Columbus)

Logsdon-Babich, Sara Elizabeth .... '57 '84 C.607 B.A. L.201 J.D. Asst. Co. Pros.
Lowther, David H. .... '69 '96 C.610 B.S. L.607 J.D. [Collins&L.]
Luton, James P., (BV) .... '47 '76 C.608 B.A. L.117 J.D. 740 Laura Dr.
Mathews, Thomas A., (BV) .... '52 '77 C.253 B.S. L.7 J.D. 127 E. Center St.
McKinniss, Ted M., (AV) .... '50 '76 C.473 A.B. L.607 J.D. [⊠ Kegler,B.H.&R.]
Michel, Davis & Cramer, (AV) .... 116 South Main Street
Mitchell, Edwin L., (AV) .... '12 '37 C&L.608 A.B., J.D. 800 Cambridge Ave.‡
Moore, Gerald A. .... '54 '86 C&L.608 B.A., J.D. Asst. Co. Pros.‡
Moore, Walter D., (AV) .... '11 '35 C&L.607 LL.B. 899 Barks Ave.‡
Nemo, Robert C., (BV) .... '54 '79 C.347 B.A. L.150 J.D. [Nemo&F.]

Nemo & Fragale Co., L.P.A., (BV)
495 South State Street, P.O. Box 1176, 43301-1176
Telephone: 740-387-7438 Fax: 740-387-6367
Email: nemo-fragale@verizon.net
Robert C. Nemo; Robert D. Fragale.
Insurance Defense, Personal Injury, Environmental, Adoption, Bankruptcy, Corporate, Criminal, Estate Planning, Family, Probate, Trials and Appeals.
See Professional Biographies, MARION, OHIO

Oliver Law Office
(See Columbus)

Phillips, Frank W. .... '15 '48 C&L.608 B.S. in B.A., J.D. 146 S. Main St.‡
Piacentino, C. Michael, (BV) .... '48 '73 C.602 B.S. L.608 J.D. [Piacentino&P.]
Piacentino & Piacentino, (BV) .... 198 East Center Street

Plymale Partnership LLP, The
(See Columbus)

Reber, Frank K., (BV) .... '46 '73 C.117 B.A. L.930 J.D. 198 E. Center St.
Reed, David T. .... '68 '94 C.608 B.A. L.117 J.D. The Legal Aid Soc.
Rogers, J. W., (BV) .... '38 '62 C&L.607 J.D. 334 E. Center St.
Rogers, Richard M. .... '44 '72 C&L.607 B.A., J.D. Com. Pleas J.
Roth Bacon Young, (AV) .... 605 East Center Street (⊙Sycamore, Upper Sandusky)
Rowland, Brent A., (BV) .... '55 '80 C.97 B.S. L.608 J.D. 148 E. Center Street
Russell, Mark D. .... '65 '90 C.610 B.B.A. L.607 J.D. City Law Dir.
Scharer, Ronald J. .... '48 '73 C.631 B.A. L.608 J.D. 444 E. Center Street

Scherner, Hanson & Cornwell, LLC
(See Columbus)

Slagle, Jim, (BV) .... '55 '80 C&L.608 B.S., J.D. Co. Pros. Atty.
Thomas, Staci Kathleen .... '75 '00 C.608 B.A. L.117 J.D. Legal Aid Society of Columbus

Twyford & Donahey, P.L.L.
(See Columbus)

Wiedemann, William .... '28 '52 C.97 L.607 J.D. Com. Pleas J.
Williamson, David E., (BV) .... '45 '72 C.608 B.A. L.260 J.D. [Williamson&W.]
Williamson, Jonathan, (BV) '49 '76 C.207 B.A. L.607 J.D.
355 E. Center Street, Suite 101
Williamson & Williamson, (BV) .... 196 1/2 West Center Street
Wilson, Robert E., (AV) .... '42 '68 C.967 A.B. L.896 J.D. [Wilson&K.]
Wilson & Kochheiser Co., L.P.A., (AV) .... 132 S. Main St.

Wirth, David
(See Columbus)

Worobiec, Michele Selig .... '66 '96 C&L.608 B.S., J.D. [⊠ Kegler,B.H.&R.]
Zeigler, S. Frederick, (BV) .... '44 '69 C.150 B.A. L.607 J.D. 144 E. Center St.

MARTINS FERRY, 7,226, *Belmont Co.*

Berhalter, Christopher M. .... '70 '96 C&L.608 B.A., J.D. [Sommer,L.&B.]
Frazier, John P. .... '25 '50 C.611 L.150 J.D. 10 N. 5th St.‡
Liberati, David K., (BV) .... '56 '82 C.103 A.B. L.608 J.D. [Sommer,L.&B.]
Sommer, Karl W., Jr., (BV) .... '35 '63 C.608 B.S. L.117 J.D. 10 N. 5th Street
Sommer, Keith A., (AV) .... '41 '66 C.97 B.S. L.608 J.D. [Sommer,L.&B.]
Sommer, Liberati & Berhalter Co., L.P.A., (AV) .... 409 Walnut Street
Thomas, William L. .... '48 '75 C.610 B.A. L.607 J.D. 16 S. 4th St.

MARYSVILLE, * 15,942, *Union Co.*

Allen, David F., (AV) .... '37 '61 C&L.608 B.A., J.D. [Allen,Y.&M.]

Allen, Yurasek & Merklin, (AV) ⊞
233 West Fifth Street, P.O. Box 391, 43040-0391
Telephone: 937-642-4070 Telecopier: 937-644-4390
Email: aymucta@imetweb.net
Members of Firm: Gwynn Sanders (1906-1989); David F. Allen; Stephen J. Yurasek; Jeffrey A. Merklin. Associate: Tina Owens-Ruff.
General Civil Practice. Corporate, Probate and Estate Planning, Real Estate, and Banking Law. Trials and Appeals in all Courts.
General Counsel for: Ohio Grain Co.; Conklin Dairy Farms, Inc.; Richwood Banking Co.; Community Foundation of Union County; Tuffco Sand & Gravel Co.; Franke's Wood Products, Inc.; Picklesimer Trucking, Inc.

(This Listing Continued)

Allen, Yurasek & Merklin (Continued)
Local Counsel for: John Hancock Mutual Life Insurance Co.; Honda Federal Credit Union; Metropolitan Life Insurance Co.
See Professional Biographies, MARYSVILLE, OHIO

Behrens, Daniel E. .... '43 '68 C.473 A.B. L.608 J.D. Mag., Mun. Ct.
Bridges, Robert L., (AV) .... '53 '79 C.967 B.A. L.117 J.D. [Cannizzaro,F.B.&J.]
Brockman, Vincent C. '63 '88 C.473 B.A. L.608 J.D.
V.P., Asst. Gen. Coun. & Chf. Ethics & Compl. Offr, The Scotts Co.

Calig & Handelman, LPA
(See Columbus)

Cannizzaro, John F., (BV) .... '53 '80 C.696 B.A. L.117 J.D. [Cannizzaro,F.B.&J.]
Cannizzaro, Fraser, Bridges & Jillisky, (AV) .... 302 S. Main Street
Coleman, Stephen G., (BV) .... '49 '77 C.611 B.A. L.607 J.D. [Coleman&E.]
Coleman & Eufinger, (BV) .... 110 S. Court St.

Colley Shroyer & Abraham Co., L.P.A.
(See Columbus)

Cox, Faye Danielle .... '76 '01 C.97 B.A. L.608 J.D. [Schulze,H.&C.]
Dailey, Jeanne L. .... '31 '55 C&L.608 B.Sc., J.D. 259 W. 5th St.
Dailey, John W., Jr., (BV) .... '31 '55 C&L.608 B.S., J.D. 259 W. 5th St.
De Lorenzo, Peter V. .... '53 '90 C.184 B.A. L.117 J.D. 14100 Hinton Mill Road
Dennison, Judith L. '64 '93 C.347 B.A. L.608 J.D.
(adm. in IL; not adm. in OH) Honda of Amer. Mfg., Inc.
DuBoise, Nancy F. '60 '88 C.188 B.S. L.1009 J.D.
(adm. in NY; not adm. in OH) 24000 Honda Parkway
Eufinger, Charlotte Coleman, (BV) .... '47 '72 C.473 A.B. L.608 J.D. [Coleman&E.]
Eufinger, John M., (BV) .... '46 '72 C.611 B.A. L.608 J.D. [Coleman&E.]

Farlow & Associates LLC
(See Dublin)

Francis, Stephen S. .... '58 '84 C.511 B.A. L.608 J.D. Honda of Amer. Mfg., Inc.
Fraser, Don W., (BV) .... '52 '79 C.608 B.S. L.117 J.D. [Cannizzaro,F.B.&J.]
Goldfarb, Lewis H. .... '58 '88 C&L.608 B.S.B.A., J.D. Honda of America Mfg., Inc.
Grigsby, Joseph B. .... '19 '48 C.608 B.A. L.477 J.D. Ret. Com. Pleas J.
Grigsby, Michael J., (CV) .... '50 '80 C.723 B.A. L.300 J.D. 125 S. Main St.
Hamilton, Robert O., (BV) .... '27 '53 C.473 A.B. L.477 J.D. 116 South Court Street
Howard, Frank, (BV) .... '50 '75 C.381 B.S. L.607 J.D. [Schulze,H.&C.]
Howard, Lowell B., Jr. .... '59 '87 C.473 B.A. L.608 J.D. Honda of America Mfg., Inc.
Hust, Robert L. '58 '86 C&L.608 B.A., J.D.
Coun. & Manager, Honda of America Mfg., Inc.
Jillisky, Donald R., (BV) .... '47 '79 C.1266 B.A. L.744 J.D. [Cannizzaro,F.B.&J.]
Jillisky, Nancy L., (BV) .... '59 '95 C.1083 B.S. L.117 J.D. [Cannizzaro,F.B.&J.]
Johnson, Frederick B., (BV) .... '51 '77 C.97 B.A. L.201 J.D. 214 S. Court St.

Kenney-Pfalzer, Susan
(See Columbus)

Konstantacos, T. William .... '61 '86 C.610 A.B. L.608 J.D. 24000 Honda Pkwy.
Korleski, Christopher .... '58 '87 C&L.608 B.S., J.D. Honda of America Mfg., Inc.
LaFleur, Joseph F. .... '60 '86 C.610 B.B.A. L.150 J.D. Honda of America Mfg., Inc.

Lamkin, Van Eman, Trimble, Beals & Dougherty, LLC
(See Columbus)

Lewis, Gregg R.
(See Columbus)

Liggett-Pelanda Co., L.P.A., (BV) .... 122 E. 5th St.
McDonald, Alan T. .... '49 '74 C.705 B.S. L.326 J.D. Honda of America Mfg., Inc. (Pat.)
McKinley, Gary F. .... '40 '66 C.631 B.A. L.607 J.D. Prob. & Juv. Ct. J.
Merklin, Jeffrey A., (BV) .... '60 '85 C.532 B.A. L.608 J.D. [Allen,Y.&M.]
Mickley, Richard S. .... '39 '71 C.970 B.A. L.608 J.D. 112 E. 5th St.
Music, Lisa Walczak .... '70 '98 C.608 B.A. L.851 J.D. 111 W. 6th St.

Oliver Law Office
(See Columbus)

Owens-Ruff, Tina .... '69 '99 C.608 B.A. L.607 J.D. [⊠ Allen,Y.&M.]
Parrish, Jack M. .... '10 '36 C&L.608 LL.B. 20485 SR 4
Parrott, Robert W., (BV) .... '59 '85 C&L.607 B.S., J.D. 127 W. 6th St.
Parsons, Perry R. .... '68 '95 C&L.608 B.A., J.D. 111 W. 6th Street
Pelanda, Dorothy Liggett, (BV) .... '56 '82 C.473 A.B. L.7 J.D. [Liggett-P.]
Pelanda, Kevin, (BV) .... '56 '81 C.381 L.7 J.D. [Liggett-P.]
Schmenk, Christiane W., (AV) '59 '84
C.607 B.A. L.608 J.D. Director, Legal Affairs, Scotts Company
Schneider, R. Larry, (BV) .... '41 '69 C.698 A.B. L.502 J.D. 111 West Sixth St.
Schostek, Rick '56 '86 C.1229 B.I.A. L.161 J.D.
V.P., Secy. & Gen. Coun., Honda of American Mfg., Inc.
Schulze, Dennis A., (BV) .... '43 '68 C.528 B.A. L.608 J.D. [Schulze,H.&C.]

Schulze, Howard & Cox, (BV)
110 S. Main Street, 43040-1552
Telephone: 937-644-3849 Fax: 937-644-1426
URL: http://www.shc-lawfirm.net
Dennis A. Schulze; Frank Howard; Faye Danielle Cox.
Civil Trial Practice, Personal Injury, Corporate, Commercial, Probate and Trust, Real Estate Law, Estate Planning, Contract Law, Business Law, Consumer Law.
See Professional Biographies, MARYSVILLE, OHIO

Streng, Michael John .... '75 '00 C&L.117 B.A., J.D. [⊠ Cannizzaro,F.B.&J.]

Twyford & Donahey, P.L.L.
(See Columbus)

Watson, Yvonne M. '63 '01 C.920 B.S. L.608 J.D.
Union County Asst. Prosecutor, Union County Prosecutor's Office

Wiles, Boyle, Burkholder & Bringardner Co., L.P.A.
(See Columbus)

Wolske & Barclay, A Legal Professional Association
(See Columbus)

Yurasek, Stephen J., (AV) .... '48 '79 C&L.608 B.S., J.D. [Allen,Y.&M.]

MASON, 22,016, *Warren Co.*

Batsche, D. Andrew, (CV) .... '71 '96 C.473 B.A. L.1161 J.D. [Batsche&B.]
Batsche, David K., (BV) .... '41 '66 C.473 B.S. L.150 J.D. [Batsche&B.]
Batsche & Batsche, (BV) .... 300 W. Main Street
Beck, Carter A. .... '61 '88 C&L.150 B.M., J.D. Dir. & Coun., Anthem Ins. Cos., Inc.
Beck, Patrick E. .... '60 '92 C.973 B.S. L.201 J.D. Anthem Ins. Cos., Inc.
Beebe, Stephen Douglas .... '66 '93 C.5 B.A. L.823 J.D. Coun., Anthem Ins. Cos., Inc.
Benintendi, Laurie .... '63 '91 C.117 B.S.N. L.245 J.D. Coun., Anthem Ins. Cos., Inc.

Borders, Keith L. '64 '89 C.623 B.A. L.966 J.D.
(adm. in WI; not adm. in OH) Sr. Atty. & Sr. Dir. Assoc. Relations, Luxotica Retail
Bott, Cynthia Marie .... '65 '99 C.475 B.S. L.150 J.D. Procter & Gamble
Brown, Allen, (AV) .... '19 '47 C&L.150 B.A., J.D. 6266 Lakeshore‡

Bueckman, Lynn A., The Law Offices of
(See Cincinnati)

Chalfie & Farley, Co., L.P.A.
(See Cincinnati)

Claypool, Cynthia Lee '69 '02 C.383 B.S. L.1340 J.D.
Corp. Coun., Procter & Gamble Co., IP Div. (Pat.)
Coil, Nicole Tipton .... '71 '96 C.896 B.A. L.150 J.D. 6589 Charleston Park Drive
Curtis, Mildred Adams, (BV) '56 '81
C.643 B.A. L.150 J.D. Sr. V.P. - Legal & H.R., Luxottica Retail
Davis, Michael J., (CV) ... '65 '90 C.473 B.A. L.201 J.D. 8093 Columbia Road, Suite 103
Donnelly, Karen S. .... '60 '90 C&L.150 B.S.N., J.D. [Peeler,M.&Z.]
Evans, Marlene M. .... '52 '91 C.913 B.S. L.477 J.D. Coun., Anthem Ins. Cos., Inc.
Farrish, Craig L. '61 '96 C.473 B.S. L.1161 J.D.
Staff Atty., American Family Insurance
Fetters-Berner, Melissa A. '63 '90
C.383 B.S. L.245 J.D. Anthem Blue Cross & Blue Shield
Fischer, Robert S. .... '70 '96 C.443 B.S. L.245 J.D. [Sams,F.&S.]
Franks, Steven L. .... '64 '94 C.471 B.A. L.851 J.D. Federated Dept. Stores‡
Goldman, Elmer M. .... '26 '50 C&L.150 B.S., LL.B. 6659 Villager Pl.‡
Graber, Matthew J. .... '72 '98 C.107 B.A. L.201 J.D. [A Peeler,M.&Z.]
Hasse, Donald E. .... '53 '78 C.602 B.S. L.790 J.D. [Hasse&N.] (Pat.)
Hasse & Nesbitt, LLC .... 7577 Central Park Blvd., Ste. 316 (Pat.)
Helbling, John J. .... '64 '90 C.973 B.A. L.930 J.D. 105 E. Main St., Ste. 202

Hennekes, Jason
(See Cincinnati)

Hicks, Andrea N., (CV) .... '69 '95 C.473 B.A. L.150 J.D. 226 Reading Rd.
Hieatt, Steven W. .... '71 '96 C.473 B.S. L.602 J.D. Sr. Corp. Coun., Clopay Corp.
Holley, Cathy E., (BV) .... '63 '88 C.929 B.A. L.880 J.D. Sr. Atty. II, Luxottica Retail
Hoskins, Steven A. '49 '78 C.101 B.A. L.336 J.D.
(adm. in ID; not adm. in OH) 5300 Kings Island Dr.
Hoyt, Bradley R. .... '45 '82 C.201 M.B.A. L.999 J.D. Cedar Village Drive
Kellerman, James C. .... '67 '97 C.150 B.S. L.1218 J.D. Coun., The Procter & Gamble Co.
Lampley, Paula D. ...... '64 '92 C.943 B.A. L.150 J.D. Corp. Coun., Anthem Ins. Cos., Inc.
Lazarus, Doris E. .... '14 '38 L.608 LL.B. 4705 Governors Pt.
Lopez, David B., (AV) '38 '63
C.604 B.A. L.309 LL.B. Sr. V.P., Gen. Coun. & Secy., Clopay Corp.
Lovejoy, Wallace W. '50 '77
C.802 B.A. L.846 J.D. V.P., Professional Relations, Luxottica Retail
McGary, Bruce Alan, (BV) .... '63 '91 C.531 B.S. L.1340 J.D. [Peeler,M.&Z.]
McMahon, Mary P. '59 '92 C.518 A.B. L.1202 J.D.
Assoc. Dir. Pharmaceutical IP, The Procter & Gamble Co. (Pat.)

Millikin & Fitton Law Firm, A Legal Professional Association, (AV)
6900 Tylersvile Road, Suite B, 45040 ⊙
Telephone: 513-336-6363 Fax: 513-336-9411
Stanley D. Rullman.
General Practice. Real Estate, Probate, Estate Planning, Corporation, Taxation, Personal Injury and Litigation.
Representative Clients: City of Fairfield, Ohio; Union Federal Savings Bank; Fort Hamilton Hospital; Miami University, Oxford, Ohio; Key Bank; Waterfield Mortgage Co., Inc.
Hamilton, Ohio Office: 6 S 2nd Street, 6th Floor, 45011. Telephone: 513-863-6700. Fax: 513-863-0031.
Fairfield, Ohio Office: 530 Wessel Drive, Suite 2A, 45014. Telephone: 513-829-6700. Fax: 513-829-0258.
Oxford, Ohio Office: 5020 B College Corner Pike, 45056. Telephone: 513-523-3700. Fax: 513-523-0463.

Nesbitt, Daniel F. .... '55 '87 C.665 B.S.Ch.E. L.1161 J.D. [Hasse&N.] (Pat.)
Neville, Joseph B. '54 '81 C&L.802 B.S., J.D.
(adm. in TX; not adm. in OH) Assoc. V.P., Regulatory Svcs., Luxottica Retail
Peeler, Robert W., (BV) .... '52 '82 C.531 B.S. L.1340 J.D. [Peeler,M.&Z.]
Peeler, McGary & Zopff Co., L.P.A., (BV) .... 423 Reading Road
Reuss, Michael J. '67 '93
C.608 B.S.B.A. L.201 J.D. Staff Atty., American Family Insurance
Rice, Paul D., (AV) .... '41 '75 C.865 B.A. L.1340 J.D. 5412 Courseview Dr.
Robbins, Fredric J., (AV) .... '49 '74 C.473 B.S. L.150 J.D. [Robbins,K.P.&T.] ⊙
Robbins, Kelly, Patterson & Tucker, A Legal Professional Association, (AV)
315 West Main Street (⊙Cincinnati)
Rudd, Myron S. .... '22 '49 C&L.150 B.A., LL.B. 3764 Sandtrap Circle‡
Rullman, Stanley D., (AV) .... '39 '67 C.853 A.B. L.150 J.D. [Millikin&F.] (⊙Hamilton)
Sams, Jonathan D., (CV) .... '67 '96 C.1044 B.A. L.245 J.D. [Sams,F.&S.]
Sams, Fischer & Schuessler, (BV) .... 209 Reading Road
Sansbury, Amy Zeldin '53 '81
C.150 B.S. L.1340 J.D. V.P. & Coun., Anthem Ins. Cos., Inc.
Schaller, Stephen J. .... '67 '92 C.337 B.S. L.339 J.D. CNG Financial Corp.
Scholl, Amy M. .... '74 '00 C.473 B.A. L.150 J.D. Luxottica Retail
Schuessler, Delores C., (BV) .... '— '89 C.473 B.A. L.150 J.D. [Sams,F.&S.]
Shackleford, Thomas D., (BV) .... '43 '68 C.473 B.A. L.608 J.D. 224 Reading Road
Shade, Jerry H. .... '70 '01 C.532 B.A. L.150 J.D. [Whitaker]
Simon, Steven E., (BV) '46 '75
C.228 B.A. L.851 J.D. 7577 Central Park Boulevard, Suite 130
Spitz, Mark A., (BV) .... '59 '89 C.309 B.A. L.93 J.D. Sr. Atty., Luxottica Retail
Squier, Moira J., (BV) .... '65 '92 C.347 B.A. L.1119 J.D. Gen. Coun., MedPlus, Inc.
Stone, Angela Marie .... '69 '99 C.608 B.S. L.1340 J.D. Proctor & Gamble Co.
Thomas, Brian J. .... '65 '90 C&L.150 B.A., J.D. Coun., Anthem, Inc.
Tobin, Seth E. .... '73 '00 C.347 B.S. L.150 J.D. Investment Analyst, Summer Hill, Inc.
Troller, David E., (BV) '58 '84 C.893 B.A. L.945 J.D.
Senior Corporate Counsel, Clopay Corporation
Upite, David Viesturs .... '— '00 C.97 B.S. L.201 J.D. The Proctor & Gamble Co.
Vago, James C. '66 '95
C.150 B.S. L.1340 J.D. Sr. Coun., Pat., Procter & Gamble Co. (Pat.)
Whitaker, James A., (BV) .... '47 '72 C.610 B.B.A. L.150 J.D. [Whitaker]
Whitaker Law Offices, (BV) .... 226 Reading Road
Wilson, Robin R. .... '— '93 C.257 B.S. L.150 J.D. Sr. Staff Atty., LensCrafters, Inc.
Wireman, Daniel R. .... '67 '95 C&L.150 B.S.C.M., J.D. Cleveland Construction, Inc.
Wood, Elizabeth H. .... '64 '89 C&L.150 B.A., J.D. Lenscrafters, Inc.
Zopff, John S., (AV) .... '28 '53 C&L.150 A.B., LL.B. 423 Reading Rd.‡

MASSILLON, 31,325, *Stark Co.*

Breyfogle, Edwin H., (BV) ..... '49 '76 C&L.608 B.A., J.D. 11 Lincoln Way, W, Suite 2B
Brown, Paul E., (AV) .... '09 '42 C.381 B.S. L.948 LL.B. [⊙ Brown&P.]
Brown and Percival Co., L.P.A., (BV) .... 1231 Lincoln Way East
Carter, Allen G., Sr., (CV) .... '50 '86 C.49 B.S. L.8 J.D. [A.G.Carter,Sr.]
Carter, Allen G., Sr. Co., L.P.A., (CV) .... 4155 Georgia Street, N.W.
Centrone, C. Roland, (BV) .... '45 '80 C.201 B.S. L.7 J.D. 2 James Duncan Plz.
Chapanar, Lawrence E., (BV) .... '41 '84 C.608 B.Sc. L.7 J.D. 1312 Beechtree Cir. NE
Chapis, Richard M. .... '43 '75 C.705 B.A. L.7 J.D. P.O. Box 179
Christhilf, George H. .... '67 '95 C.8 B.S. L.693 J.D. 2956 Bridgton St. N.W.
Christoff, William Z., (CV) .... '51 '76 C.528 B.A. L.861 J.D. 26 S. Erie St.
Conley, James M. .... '44 '77 C.602 B.B.A. L.7 J.D. Pres., J.A. Conley Co.
Connelly, Alan M. .... '30 '57 C.473 A.B. L.976 LL.B. [A.M.Connelly]
Connelly, Alan M., Co., L.P.A. .... 2830 Connecticut Ave., S.W.
DeLong, James C., (CV) .... '23 '57 C.475 B.A. L.948 LL.B. 31 City Hall St., S.E.
Demsky, William E., (CV) .... '51 '76 C.528 B.A. L.117 J.D. 54 Federal Ave., N.E.
Egbert, Margaret Ann '51 '84 C.518 A.B. L.312 J.D.
(adm. in HI; not adm. in OH) 9066 Ontario St., N.W.
Elum, Edward J. .... '52 '77 C.602 B.A. L.607 J.D. Mun. J.
Fairless, Robert J. .... '32 '57 C.381 A.B. L.608 J.D. Central States Can Co.
Fellmeth, Scott E., (BV) .... '55 '80 C.610 B.A. L.607 J.D. 46 Federal Ave. NW
Ferrero, John D., Jr., (BV) .... '56 '81 C.201 B.S. L.607 J.D. 46 Fed. Ave., N.W.
Fichter, Joel C., Attorney At Law, (BV) '59 '84 C.97 B.A. L.7 J.D.
46 Federal Ave., N.W.
Frieg, John Henry .... '47 '82 C.381 L.8 J.D. [J.H.Frieg]
Frieg, John H. .... 108 3rd Street, N.E.
Geis, Raymond M. .... '72 '04 C.1260 B.A. L.8 J.D. P.O. Box 564
Hutsell, Randall A. .... '54 '84 C&L.8 B.S., J.D. Electra Cord Inc.
Jarvis, Keith L., (BV(T)) .... '44 '69 C.631 B.A. L.930 J.D. 46 Federal Avenue, N.W.
Jollay, R. Dean, Jr., (AV) .... '45 '74 C.207 B.A. L.117 J.D. CorrChoice, Inc.

Jones, Douglas D., Co., LPA
(See Canton)

Kelly, Harold V. '31 '56 C.682 B.A. L.692 J.D.
(adm. in VA; not adm. in OH) V.P. & Gen. Coun., Republic Engineered Steels, Inc.
Kettler, Richard T., (BV) .... '44 '74 C.381 B.A. L.608 J.D. Mun. J.
Kimmins, Thomas W., (BV) .... '35 '63 C.970 B.S. L.7 J.D. 11 Lincoln Way E.
Kincaid, Dale B., (BV) .... '41 '67 C.124 B.S. L.930 J.D. 2137 Wales Ave. N.W., Ste. 2
Kurtzman, John L., (BV) .... '40 '66 C.608 B.S. L.607 J.D. [Stergios&K.]
LaPenna, Anthony .... '58 '83 C.608 B.S. L.8 J.D. Pros. Atty.
Leffler, William G., (CV) '53 '92 C.294 B.S. L.8 J.D.
2300 Wales Ave. N.W., Suite 205
Maier, Erich J. .... '71 '96 C.473 B.A. L.851 J.D. 2200 Wales Road, N.W.
Maier, Richard F., (BV) .... '25 '51 C.976 B.A. L.477 J.D. 2200 Wales Road, N.W.
Matecheck, Vincent G., (BV) .... '44 '71 C.473 B.S. L.7 J.D. 46 Federal Ave., N.W.
Milliken, Paul E. .... '28 '63 C.608 B.S. L.8 LL.B. 9061 Wall St., N.W. (Pat.)
Netzly, Dwight H., (BV) ...... '19 '52 C.381 B.S.B.A. L.948 LL.B. 1237 Lincoln Way E.
Oberlin, Robert J. .... '31 '61 C.381 A.B. L.8 LL.B. Fleming Foods of Ohio, Inc.
Paulson, Paul .... '22 '51 C.381 B.S. L.608 J.D. 1604 Lincoln Way E.‡
Percival, Mark R., (BV) .... '52 '77 C.20 A.B. L.213 J.D. [Brown&P.]
Pfendler, Christopher C., (BV) .... '54 '79 C.381 B.A. L.7 J.D. 8455 Acadia St. N.W.
Reale, Frank C. .... '57 '94 C.607 B.S.Ph. L.8 J.D. 602 Ropxbury Ave., N.W.
Rosenblithe & Slagle, (BV) .... 2200 Wales Road, N.W.
Schwartz, John L. .... '39 '65 C.967 B.S.B.A. L.923 J.D. Pres., Capital Plastics Inc.
Simpson, John H., (BV) .... '59 '85 C.1260 B.A. L.8 J.D. Chf. City Pros.
Sirak, Norman L. .... '47 '72 C.473 B.S. L.30 J.D. 4035 Cinwood St.
Slagle, Larry V., (BV) .... '51 '77 C&L.930 B.A., J.D. [Rosenblithe&S.]
Snively, James D., (BV) .... '41 '66 C.967 A.B. L.930 J.D. 11 Lincoln Way E.
Stergios, J. Fred, (BV) .... '44 '69 C.528 B.A. L.608 J.D. [Stergios&K.]
Stergios, Paul J., (AV) .... '31 '61 C&L.608 B.S., J.D. [Stergios&K.]
Stergios, Pericles G., (BV) '61 '86
C.97 B.S.B.A. L.607 J.D. 2859 Aaronwood Avenue, N.E., Suite 101

Stergios & Kurtzman Co., L.P.A., (AV)
Suite 101, 2859 Aaronwood Avenue, N.E., 44646-2371
Telephone: 330-832-9878 Telecopier: 330-832-2963
Email: jfs@sklegal.com
Paul J. Stergios; John L. Kurtzman; J. Fred Stergios.
General Civil Trial and Appellate Practice. Hospital and Health, Personal Injury, Corporate, Family, Real Estate, Probate, Workers' Compensation, Estate Planning, Criminal and Traffic.
Representative Clients: Aaronwood Title Agency, Inc.; Aultman Health Foundation; Austin-Bailey Health and Wellness Foundation; City of Massillon, Ohio; Doctors Hospital, Inc. of Stark County; FirstMerit Bank, N.A.; Midwestern Industries, Inc.; R.W. Screw Products, Inc.
Approved Attorneys for: Ohio Bar Title Insurance Company.
References: Bank One, N.A.; FirstMerit Bank, N.A.

Warstler, Keith Allen, Jr. .... '71 '00 C.381 B.A. L.8 J.D. 2 James Duncan Plaza
Yost, Stephen T., (BV) .... '45 '72 C.930 B.S. L.1003 J.D. 1718 10th St. NE

MASURY, 2,618, *Trumbull Co.*

Smith, Eugene R. .... '22 '56 C&L.980 B.S., J.D. 7880 Elm St. (⊙North Lima)

MAUMEE, 15,237, *Lucas Co.*

Alvarez, Tatiana .... '71 '02 L.472 J.D. [A Boss&V.]
Amon, Kathy J., (BV) .... '61 '96 C&L.851 B.S.I.S., J.D. [K.J.Amon]
Amon, Kathy J., LLC, The Law Office of, (BV) .... 1745 Indian Wood Cir.
Asbury, Karen E. .... '63 '88 C&L.851 B.A., J.D. [K.E.Asbury]
Asbury, Karen E., LLC .... 415 Conant St., Ste. L7
Baker, Chad R., (BV) .... '73 '99 C.610 B.S.B.A. L.851 J.D. [Weber&S.]
Barkan, William I., (AV) .... '30 '55 C.477 B.B.A. L.851 LL.B. [Barkan&R.]
Barkan and Robon Ltd., (AV) .... 1701 Woodlands Drive
Battin, Robert C. .... '60 '88 C.97 B.S.B.A. L.851 J.D. 99 Conant Street
Bayer, Papay & Steiner, Co., L.P.A., (BV) .... 1925 Indian Wood Circle
Behrendt, Harry M., (BV) '40 '67 C&L.851 B.A., J.D.
Pres., The LaSovage Behrendt Co.
Bennett, Robert G. '37 '64 C&L.472 B.B.A., J.D.
(adm. in FL; not adm. in OH) CEO, Bennett Mgmt. Corp.
Boss, Charles M., (BV) .... '52 '81 C.97 B.S. L.851 J.D. [Boss&V.]
Boss & Vitou, (BV) .... 111 W. Dudley St.
Brennan, William J., (BV) '51 '80 C&L.851 B.A., J.D.
Exec. V.P., Home Builders Assn. of Greater Toledo
Brogan, Allan J., (AV) .... '29 '58 C.610 B.S.C. L.851 J.D. [Marsh M.]
Byers, Gary L., (AV) .... '55 '81 C.318 B.A. L.851 J.D. 410 Conant Street
Chamberlain, Richard M. .... '67 '92 C.861 B.A. L.259 J.D. [Bayer,P.&S.]
Coe, Helen M., (BV) .... '42 '73 C.679 B.S. L.851 J.D. 302 Conant St.
Damicone, Jason S. .... '74 '03 C.608 B.A. L.7 J.D. [A Barkan&R.]
Davis, R. Ethan .... '74 '01 C.607 B.A. L.851 J.D. [A Barkan&R.]
Elder, Gregory R., (BV) .... '60 '86 C.970 B.A. L.851 J.D. [Barkan&R.]
Fallat, Dale W., (AV) .... '44 '70 C.1024 B.A. L.851 J.D. The Andersons
Farrar, Richard G., Law Offices of, (BV) '35 '66
C.610 A.B. L.851 J.D. 1605 Indian Wood Circle
Galbraith, John A., (BV) .... '23 '49 C&L.477 A.B., LL.B. 602 Pierce
Hall, Elizabeth J., (AV) .... '51 '80 C.473 A.B. L.851 J.D. Coun., The Andersons, Inc.
Hankison, J. E. .... '16 '41 C.608 L.851 J.D. 2902 River Rd.‡

Jarvela, Dennis L. '44 '69 C.118 B.A. L.145 J.D.
Vice President, Corporate Law & Asst. Secretary, Owens Corning World Headquarters
Jensen, Julie A. '65 '98 C&L.851 B.S.N., J.D. St. Luke's Hospital
Katz, Michael S., (BV) '59 '84 C.608 B.S. L.851 J.D. 1930 Indianwood Circle
Keller, Stephen S. '73 '99 C.383 B.S. L.851 J.D. [Weber&S.]
Kuns, Gary F., (BV) '43 '68 C.97 B.A. L.851 J.D. 99 Conant St.
Madrzykowski, Jeffrey Jon, (BV) '65 '92
C&L.851 B.B.A., J.D. 1789 Indian Wood Cir., Ste. 140
Marsh, Benjamin F., (AV) '27 '55 C.611 A.B. L.273 J.D. [Marsh M.]
Marsh McAdams Ltd., (AV) 204 W. Wayne St.
Mays, Richard D., (BV) '47 '78 C&L.851 B.B.A., J.D. 7511 Valhalla Dr.
McAdams, Sheilah H., (BV) '51 '78 C.610 B.G.S. L.851 J.D. City Solr. [Marsh M.]
McBride, Beverly J., (AV) '41 '66 C.967 B.A. L.851 J.D.
V.P., Gen. Coun. & Secy., The Andersons, Inc.
Moore, Everett Daniel '51 '77 C.381 B.S.Ed. L.851 J.D. 5714 Monclova Rd.
Norton, Suzanne Belot, (BV) '57 '83 C.608 B.S. L.229 J.D. 204 West Wayne Street
Papay, Debbie J., (BV) '56 '85 C.1367 B.A. L.851 J.D. [Bayer,P.&S.]
Parker, Marilyn Loch '55 '82 C&L.851 B.A., J.D. Co. Child. Servs. Bd.
Radon, Paul A., (BV) '56 '81 C&L.851 B.A., J.D. [Barkan&R.]
Raitz, Glenn N., (AV) '31 '63 C&L.851 B.B.A., LL.B. [Ⓒ Bayer,P.&S.]
Restivo, Francis C. '21 '49 C&L.851 P.H.B., J.D. Ret. Com. Pleas J.
Robon, Marvin A., (AV) '41 '66 C.97 B.S.B.A. L.851 J.D. [Barkan&R.]
Runner, George F., (BV) '46 '75 C.608 B.A. L.851 J.D. [Runner&R.]
Runner, Raymond A., (BV) '50 '76 C&L.851 B.A., J.D. Asst. Solr. [Runner&R.]
Runner & Runner, (BV) 1018 River Rd.
Schaefer, Stephen A., (BV) '45 '73 C&L.851 B.A., J.D. [Marsh M.]
Spinazze, Dominic J., (BV) '66 '92 C&L.851 B.B.A., J.D. 1438 Arrowhead Drive
Springborn, Harvey E. '21 '65 C.610 B.S. L.1003 J.D. 1224 Shaker Dr.‡
Steiner, Chris E., (BV) '52 '78 C&L.851 B.Ed., J.D. [Bayer,P.&S.]
Sterling, Robert V., (AV) '44 '71 C&L.851 B.S., J.D. [Weber&S.]
Straub, John C., (AV) '41 '66
C.851 B.B.A. L.477 J.D. Chmn. of the Bd. & CEO, Therma-Tru Corp.
Szozda, Veronica L., (BV) '46 '88 C.319 B.A. L.851 J.D. [Marsh M.]
Tesznar, Cynthia Godbey, (BV) '53 '84 C.880 B.A. L.851 J.D. [Ⓐ Barkan&R.]
Torda, Joseph R., (BV) '63 '90 C.97 B.A. L.851 J.D. [Ⓐ Barkan&R.]
Tuschman, James M., (AV) '41 '66 C.473 B.S. L.608 J.D. [Ⓒ Barkan&R.]
Vitou, Mark F., (BV) '52 '79 C.97 B.A. L.851 J.D. [Boss&V.]

Weber & Sterling, LLC, (AV)
1721 Indian Wood Circle, Suite 1, 43537-4065
Telephone: 419-893-3360 Fax: 419-893-7146
Email: attorneys@webersterlinglaw.com URL: http://www.weberandsterling.com
Members: Robert V. Sterling; Dennis P. Williams (Certified Specialist in Estate Planning, Trust and Probate Law, Ohio State Bar Association); Stephen S. Keller; Chad R. Baker.
Probate and Estate Planning, Trusts, Wills, Business Succession.
Representative Clients: Toledo Community Foundation; Toledo Museum of Art; Key Trust Company of Ohio, N.A.
References: The Fifth Third Bank of Northwestern Ohio, N.A.; National City Bank; Key Trust Company of Ohio, N.A.
See Professional Biographies, MAUMEE, OHIO

Willey, David S.
(See Toledo)

Williams, Dennis P., (AV) '52 '90 C.96 B.B.A. L.851 J.D. [Weber&S.]
Zouhary, Kathleen Maher, (AV) '51 '76
C.473 B.A. L.602 J.D. V.P. & Gen. Coun., St. Luke's Hospital

MAYFIELD, 3,462, *Cuyahoga Co.*

Bernard & Haffey Co., L.P.A.
(See Cleveland)

Crane, Roderick J. '50 '83 C.381 B.A. L.7 J.D. Progressive Cas. Ins. Co.

MAYFIELD HEIGHTS, 19,386, *Cuyahoga Co.*

Aley, Charles R. '56 '81 C.271 B.A. L.665 J.D.
VP, Gen. Coun. & Sec. Tax Coun., Alcan Corp.
Balistreri, Karen A., (AVⓉ) '— '85 C&L.966 B.A., J.D. Rockwell Automation ⊙
Ballesteros, Gary W. '62 '88 C.339 B.S. L.477 J.D. Rockwell Automation ⊙
Becker, Gordon P. '50 '78 C.24 B.S. L.8 J.D. Pat. Coun., Alcan Corp. (Pat.)
Bittenbender, Charles A., (AV) '49 '80 C.154 B.A. L.161 J.D.
V.P., Gen. Coun. & Secy., NACCO Industries, Inc.
Byrnes, Michael T. '69 '95 C&L.966 B.A., J.D. Rockwell Automation ⊙
Calise, William J., Jr., (AVⓉ) '38 '63 C.105 A.B. L.178 J.D. Rockwell Automation ⊙
Carr, L. Bryan '70 '97 C.800 B.S. L.1003 J.D. [L.B.Carr]
Carr, Leonard F., (AV) '46 '74 C&L.161 B.B.A., J.D. [Carr,F.&C.]
Carr, Feneli & Carbone, Co., L.P.A., (AV) 1392 S.O.M. Center Rd.
Carr, L. Bryan, Co., L.P.A. 1392 Som Center Road
Coppins, Kent G. '53 '78 C.97 B.S. L.851 J.D. Rockwell Automation ⊙
Craig, André A. '57 '82 C.97 B.A. L.930 J.D. Reg. Lit. Atty., Progressive Cas. Ins. Co.
Cronin, Julie Thomas '62 '89 C.66 B.A. L.273 J.D.
(adm. in MA; not adm. in OH) Assistant General Counsel, Rockwell Automation
Deckman, William L. '14 '48 C.363 Ph.B. L.930 LL.B. 1540 Algiers Rd.‡
DiMarco, Richard P. '48 '75 C&L.930 B.A., J.D. Urology Servs. Inc.

Dinn, Hochman & Potter, LLC
(See Cleveland)

Dyson, Schmidlin & Foulds, Co., L.P.A., (AV) 5843 Mayfield Rd.
Foulds, Robert J., (BV) '56 '81 C&L.930 B.A., J.D. [Dyson,S.&F.]
Gallagher, Hugh R. '07 '39 L.180 LL.B.
(adm. in DC; not adm. in OH) 250 Chatham Way‡
Henderson, David B. '64 '92 C.201 B.S. L.1003 J.D. [Ⓐ Dyson,S.&F.]
Intili, Ann Marie '65 '90 C.651 B.S. L.930 J.D.
Sr. Claims Atty., Progressive Casualty Ins. Co.
Kartman, Marc G. '54 '79 C.228 B.A. L.813 J.D. Rockwell Automation ⊙
Kerwin, Timothy L. '65 '91
C.62 B.A. L.1003 J.D. Corp. Claims Atty., Progressive Insurance
Kuszewski, Alexander R. '71 '96 C&L.436 B.S.E.E., J.D. Rockwell Automation (Pat.)
Margolis, Jeffrey H. '61 '86 C.477 B.A. L.124 J.D. Sirva Relocation LLC
Meola, Sylvester J., Jr. '24 '56 C.318 B.A. L.1003 J.D. 6617 Kingswood Dr.‡
Miller, Pamela S. '63 '88 C.980 A.B. L.930 J.D. CoreComm
O'Shaughnessy, James P. '47 '77 C.688 B.S. L.276 J.D. Rockwell Automation (Pat.) ⊙
Ours, John Winthrop, (AV) '46 '72
C.967 B.A. L.893 J.D. Corporate Claims Atty, Progressive Ins. Co.
Peterman, Michael J., (AV) '47 '73 C.659 B.S. L.930 J.D.
Exec. V.P. & Gen. Coun., North Pointe Realty, Inc.
Rassin, Julius '22 '59 C.161 B.S. L.1003 LL.B. 6030 Mayfield Rd.‡
Rivera-Sanchez, Kim M. '68 '94
C.228 B.A. L.309 J.D. VP, Law Dept., Rockwell Automation
Rolla, Dudley B. '28 '57 C.610 B.A. L.1003 LL.B. 31915 Cedar Rd.‡
Roth, Henry A. '40 '66 C.475 B.A. L.989 J.D. 6070 Parkland Boulevard
Salibra, Lawrence A., II, (AV) '46 '74 C.918 B.A. L.966 J.D.
(adm. in WI; and limited adm. in OH) Sr. Coun., Alcan Corp.
Schenk, Jeffrey A. '64 '91 C.62 B.A. L.1003 J.D. 6055 Parkland Boulevard
Schmidlin, Raymond J. '35 '65 C.201 L.1003 J.D. [Dyson,S.&F.]
Schmidlin, Raymond J., Jr., (AV) '64 '89 C.201 B.a. L.930 J.D. [Dyson,S.&F.]
Smith, Ward G. '30 '55
C.309 A.B. L.107 J.D. Chmn. of the Bd., NACCO Industries, Inc.‡
Speroff, R. Scott '60 '92 C.150 B.S.E.E.T. L.201 J.D. Rockwell Automation (Pat.) ⊙
Sweeney, David M., (AV) '48 '75 C.97 B.B.A. L.851 J.D.
Corp. Gen. Coun., NESCO, Inc.
Taormina, Robert A. '58 '89 C.851 B.S. L.608 J.D.
Assoc. Gen. Coun., Pioneer Standard Electronics, Inc.
Thomas, Julie '— '89 C.178 B.A. L.273 J.D.
(adm. in MA; not adm. in OH) Asst. Gen. Coun., Rockwell International
Thomas, Rita A. '66 '91 C.8 B.A. L.608 J.D.
Assoc. Gen. Coun., Pioneer Standard Electronics
Tillman, John C. '61 '89 C.161 B.A. L.1003 J.D. Assoc. Coun., Alcan Corp.
Tsipis, Constantine E. '58 '91 C.930 B.A. L.161 J.D.
Asst. Gen. Coun. & Asst. Secy., NACCO Industries, Inc.
Vanderwist, Kathryn Kariotis, (AV) '59 '84 C.665 B.A. L.309 J.D.
V.P. & Gen. Coun., Pioneer Standard Electronics
Van Ness, Charles J. '64 '90 C.97 B.S. L.347 J.D. [C.J.Van Ness&Assoc.]
Van Ness, Charles J., & Associates 6181 Mayfield Rd.
Vetter, William '45 '72 C.918 B.A. L.813 J.D. Rockwell Automation ⊙
Wagner, Mark R. '53 '80 C.973 H.A.B. L.608 J.D. 1392 Som Center Rd.
Walbrun, William R. '66 '93 C.959 B.S. L.365 J.D. Rockwell Automation (Pat.) ⊙
Wells, Natasha A. '71 '96 C.610 B.A. L.851 J.D. 6110 Parkland Blvd.
Whitley, David N. '52 '77 Rockwell Automation ⊙
Yokaitis-Skutnik, Judith A. '57 '86 C.754 B.S. L.124 J.D. 5920 Landerbrook Drive
Zoeckler, John P. '72 '99 C.1115 B.A. L.362 J.D. Progressive Corp. Claims Legal

MAYFIELD VILLAGE, 3,435, *Cuyahoga Co.*

Albert, Peter J., (AV) '63 '88
C.97 B.S. L.608 J.D. Asst. Gen. Coun., Progressive Cas. Ins. Co.
Aveni, James V., (AV) '66 '93 C.967 B.A. L.692 J.D. 6685 Beta Dr.
Bloomfield, Louis J. '36 '65 C.197 A.B. L.1003 J.D.
Dir., Real Estate, Progressive Casualty Insurance Company
Brown, Ronald Boyd, (BV) '40 '68 C.473 B.S. L.1003 J.D. Lancer Ins.
Corwin, Patricia M. '55 '87 C.893 B.A. L.930 J.D. 300 North Commons Boulevard
D'Amico, Louis Anthony, (BV) '56 '88 C.363 B.S. L.1003 J.D. 6449 Wilson Mills Rd.
Degnan, Martin J., (BV) '46 '74 C&L.851 B.A., J.D. 6690 Beta Drive
Dobscha, Stephen F., (BV) '62 '87
C.363 B.A. L.930 J.D. Corp Claims Atty., Progressive Ins.
Domeck, John W. '62 '88 C.597 B.A. L.228 J.D. Corp. Coun., Progressive Cas. Ins. Co.
Dunn, Paul Lee '66 '91 C.161 B.A. L.607 J.D. 6685 Beta Drive
Duvin, Deborah Capps '64 '90 C.207 B.A. L.273 J.D.
Senior Claims Attorney, Progressive Insurance
Fitts, John T. '49 '77 C.62 B.A. L.1003 J.D. Dep. Gen. Coun., Progressive Cas. Ins. Co.
Garfunkel, Steven B., (BV) '48 '72
C.401 B.S. L.930 J.D. Asst. Gen. Coun., Progressive Cas. Ins. Co.
Greene, Christopher B. '63 '95 C.9 B.S. L.87 J.D.
Corporate Attorney, Progressive Insurance Company
Hauptman, Vida I. '59 '85 C.999 B.S. L.1003 J.D. 589 Timberline Trail
Heberle, Tracy L. '71 '96 C.973 B.S.B.A. L.201 J.D. Progressive Ins.
Herubin, John F. '62 '87 C.980 A.B. L.1003 J.D. Skoda, Minotti, Reeves & Company
Iwler, Jerome '52 '77 C&L.665 B.A., J.D.
(adm. in PA; not adm. in OH) Progressive Casualty Ins. Co.
Jarrett, Charles E., (AV) '57 '84
C.197 B.A. L.477 J.D. Chf. Legal Offr., The Progressive Corp.
Jiannetti, Michael A., (AV) '54 '82 C.363 B.A. L.1003 J.D. 6449 Wilson Mills Road
Kerner, William J., Jr '65 '91 C.363 B.A. L.150 J.D. Progressive
Lamb, David C. '63 '90 C.62 B.A. L.930 J.D.
Corp. Atty., Progressive Casualty Insurance Co.
Lardakis, Moira Gambrill '51 '81 C.161 B.A. L.1003 J.D. The Progressive Corp.
Ling, Raymond S. '61 '90 C.97 B.S. L.477 J.D. 300 N. Commons
Major, Lynn N. '65 '90 C.105 B.A. L.1003 J.D. Corp. Atty., Progressive Cas. Ins. Co.
Marsteller, Marcia E. '70 '95 C.381 B.A. L.309 J.D. Progressive Ins.
Ranallo, Robert A., (AV) '55 '80
C.602 B.B.A. L.608 J.D. Skoda, Minotti, Reeves & Company
Sablack, Michael A. '67 '96 C.313 B.S. L.1003 J.D.
Corp. Atty., Progressive Cas. Ins. Co.
Schneider, David M., (AV) '37 '62
C.976 A.B. L.309 LL.B. Chf. Legal Offr., Progressive Cas. Ins. Co.‡
Schwartz, Gregory '66 '94 C.608 B.S. L.1003 J.D.
Corp. Atty., Progressive Cas. Ins. Co.
Shaw, Karen '72 '97 C.381 B.A. L.930 J.D. Corp. Atty., Progressive Cas. Ins. Co.
Shrallow, Dane A., (AV) '46 '71
C.902 B.S. L.188 J.D. Assoc. Gen. Coun., Progressive Cas. Ins. Co.
Silver, Terry L. '52 '77 C.473 B.S. L.1003 J.D. Skoda, Minotti, Reeves & Company
Uth, Michael R. '53 '79 C.473 B.A. L.245 J.D.
Asst. Gen. Coun., Progressive Cas. Ins. Co.
Vierkorn, Katherine A. '66 '92
C.323 B.A. L.608 J.D. Compl. Atty., Progressive Cas. Ins. Co.
West, Jennifer Nicole '75 '00 C.381 B.A. L.1003 J.D. Progressive Cas. Ins. Co.

McARTHUR, * 1,912, *Vinton Co.*

Curran, Chas. '12 '51 C.151 Ret. Com. Pleas J.
Gleeson, Timothy P., (BV) '65 '90 C.973 B.S. L.150 J.D. Pros. Atty.
Griffith, Jeffrey Randolph '61 '01 C.610 B.A. L.117 J.D. 114 West Main Street
Grillo, N. Robert, (BV) '56 '83 C.608 B.S.B.A. L.851 J.D. [Grillo,N.R.&J.P.S.]
Grillo, N. Robert and James P. Salyer, (BV) 114 West Main Street
Kessler, David '30 '54 C&L.608 LL.B. Vinton County Courthouse
Kieckhefer, Frederick B., JR., (CV) '46 '87
C.472 B.B.A. L.383 J.D. Corp. Legal Coun., Benedict, Inc.
Kimes-Brown, Trecia, The Law Office of, (CV) '73 '98
C.1115 B.A. L.8 J.D. 103 South Market Street

Lewis, Richard M.
(See Jackson)

Lotz, Warren J. '26 '73 C.339 B.S. L.851 J.D. Com. Pleas J.
Rose, Philip H. '46 '74 C.610 A.B. L.150 J.D. Prob. Juv. J., Div. of Comm. Pls.
Salyer, James Patrick, (CV) '69 '94 C.608 B.A. L.201 J.D. [Grillo,N.R.&J.P.S.]
Simmons, Jeffrey L. '54 '79 C.610 B.B.A. L.608 J.D. Co. J.

McCONNELSVILLE, * 1,676, *Morgan Co.*

Christie, Robert J., (BV) ....'47 '74 C.477 B.A. L.228 J.D. [Christie,C.&W.]
Christie, Christie & Wells, (BV) ....36 W. Main St.
Dye, Ralph D., Jr. ....'31 '58 C.608 B.S. L.980 J.D. P.O. Box 178
Favreau, Dan W. ....'45 '74 C.923 B.S. L.117 J.D. Com. Pleas J., Morgan Co.
Ross, Richard L., (CV) ....'51 '76 C.138 B.A. L.117 J.D. Pros. Atty.
Wells, John A., (CV) ....'68 '94 C&L.608 B.A., J.D. [Christie,C.&W.]

McDERMOTT, 3,566, *Scioto Co.*

Sesser, Stephen Kemmer ....'73 '01 C&L.117 B.A., J.D. 18253 State Route 73

MECHANICSBURG, 1,803, *Champaign Co.*

Dever, Jonathan T. ....'— '02 C.150 B.A. L.117 J.D. [J.T.Dever]
Dever, Jonathan T., L.L.C. ....16 South Main Street

MEDINA, * 25,139, *Medina Co.*

Amodio, James A., (BV) ....'52 '78 C.1019 B.A. L.477 J.D. [Brown&A.]
Arnold, Alanna S., (P.C.) ....'51 '91 C.381 B.A. L.425 J.D. 200 Glenshire Lane
Bailey, Steve C., (CV) ....'55 '89 C&L.8 B.A., J.D. [Marco,M.&B.]
Ballard, John S. ....'22 '48 C.8 A.B. L.477 LL.B. 171 Granger Rd.‡
Batchelder, William G., Jr., (AV) ....'14 '39 C.611 A.B. L.150 J.D. [Williams&B.]
Berry, Ralph A., Jr., (BV) ....'42 '73 C.607 B.A. L.1003 J.D. [Largent,B.P.&J.] ⊙
Berry, Robert C., (BV) ....'66 '91 C&L.608 B.S., J.D. [Critchfield,C.&J.]

Bhakuni, Pravin S., Attorney At Law '69 '02 C&L.8 B.S., J.D.
474 South Medina Line Road, 44321
Telephone: 330-607-5871 Fax: 330-668-9479
Email: bhakuni@adelphia.net
Tax, Small Business, Estate Planning, Domestic Relations, Probate.
See Professional Biographies, MEDINA, OHIO

Bougher, Frederick C., (BV) ....'52 '82 C&L.8 B.S., J.D. 326 North Court Street
Bowers, Edmond F., (CV) ....'42 '86 C.8 B.A. L.607 J.D. 6440 Ryan Road
Bramley, Jeffrey L., (BV) ....'56 '81 C.473 B.S. L.7 J.D. [Williams&B.]
Brandel, Lawrence S., (BV) ....'42 '75 C.819 B.S. L.7 J.D. 122 Public Sq.
Brandon, Amy Y. ....'64 '90 C.610 B.A. L.8 J.D. 5184 Glenmoore Wy.
Brown, Christopher T., (BV) ....'48 '77 C.318 B.A. L.7 J.D. 978 Lancaster Dr.
Brown, David N., (AV) ....'44 '72 C.608 B.A. L.309 J.D. [Brown&A.]
Brown, James N., III ....'42 '66 C.385 A.B. L.930 J.D. 325 N. Broadway‡
Brown, Stephen J., (AV) ....'41 '70 C.930 B.B.A. L.1003 J.D. 326 N. Court St.‡

Brown and Amodio, A Legal Professional Association, (AV)
109 West Liberty Street, 44256
Telephone: 330-725-8816 Fax: 330-723-5448
Email: brownlaw@zoominternet.net
David N. Brown; James A. Amodio;—Gerald L. Jeppe; Maryann C. Chandler.
Civil Trial and Appellate Practice. Negligence, Banking, Construction, Commercial, Real Estate, Business and Corporate Law, Employment, Land Use, Zoning, Bankruptcy and Probate and Estate Planning.
Representative Clients: FirstMerit Bank, N.A.
See Professional Biographies, MEDINA, OHIO

Bux, Robert J., (AV) ....'49 '78 C.608 B.S.M.E. L.150 J.D. [Williams&B.]
Cameron, John Brooks, & Associates ....'60 '91 C.8 B.S. L.608 J.D. 247 E. Smith Road
Cameron, Pedro B. ....'69 '01 C.101 B.S. L.989 J.D. 215 W. Washington
Campbell, Kevin R. ....'56 '82 C.8 B.A. L.7 J.D. 4065 Fairway Dr.
Campbell, Robert B., (CV) ....'67 '92 C.970 B.A. L.930 J.D. 52 Public Sq.
Carey, Chris D., (CV) ....'64 '94 C.161 B.A. L.608 J.D. [A Laribee&H.]
Chandler, Maryann C. ....'73 '04 C.161 B.A. L.989 J.D. [A Brown&A.]
Chase, Dale H. ....'50 '75 C.30 B.A. L.128 J.D. Mun. J.
Collier, Christopher J., (BV) ....'54 '79 C.1260 B.A. L.161 J.D. Medina Co. Com. Pleas
Cooper, Clark R., (AV) ....'18 '48 C.532 A.B. L.477 LL.B. 325 N. Broadway St.‡
Courtney, Lawrence J. ....'47 '73 C.201 B.A. L.1003 J.D. Asst. City Pros.‡

Critchfield, Critchfield & Johnston, Ltd., (AV)
3985 Medina Road, Suite 100, 44256 ⊙
Telephone: 330-723-6404 Telecopier: 330-721-7644
URL: http://www.ccj.com
Robert C. Berry; Amy L. Demlow.
General Practice in all Courts. Business, Corporate Law, Insurance, Estate Planning, Wills and Probate, Labor and Employment, ERISA, Health Care, Environmental Law, Workers Compensation, Banking, Taxation, Antitrust and Trade Regulation, Oil and Gas Law, Litigation, Debtor and Creditor, Municipal Law, School Law, Real Estate, Commercial Law, Construction Law.
Representative Clients: Rubbermaid Inc.; Wooster Brush Co.; The College of Wooster; Bank One of Akron, N.A.; First Federal Savings & Loan Association of Wooster; Sandy Supply Co.; Buehler Food Markets, Inc.; Wayne Dalton Corp.; Ohio Packaging Corporation.
Wooster, Ohio: 225 North Market Street, P.O. Box 599, 44691-0599. Telephone: 330-264-4444.
Millersburg, Ohio: 138 E. Jackson Street, 44654. Telephone: 330-674-3055.
Mt. Vernon, Ohio: 10 South Gay Street, 43050-3546. Telephone: 740-397-4040.
See Professional Biographies, MEDINA, OHIO

Cross, Judith A. ....'45 '78 C.381 B.A. L.8 J.D. Com. Pleas J.
Demlow, Amy L. ....'69 '94 C&L.08 B.S., J.D. [Critchfield,C.&J.]
Dequinze, Robert M. ....'45 '81 C.665 B.A. L.7 J.D. Veteran's Admn.
Dick, Bernard E. ....'35 '76 C.973 A.B. L.607 LL.B. 4284 Huffman Rd.‡
Dillon, Amanda Michelle Gashel ....'73 '98 C.934 B.A. L.124 J.D. [Walker&J.]
Dornshuld, Carl L., (CV) ....'55 '83 C.980 A.B. L.7 J.D. Ref., Juv. Ct.
Dunn, Kevin W., (BV) ....'64 '91 C.473 B.A. L.8 J.D. [K.W.Dunn]
Dunn, Kevin W., Co., L.P.A., Inc., (BV) ....600 East Smith Road
Edmonds, Marie Mirro, (BV) ....'47 '79 C.741 B.A. L.930 J.D. [M.M.Edmonds]
Edmonds, Marie Mirro, Co., L.P.A., (BV) ....807 East Washington, Suite 200
Einbund, Lewis, (AV) ....'30 '53 C&L.930 B.A., J.D. 247 East Smith Road
Fini, Rosalina M., (CV) ....'69 '94 C.363 B.A. L.1003 J.D. Asst. Pros.
Funk, Susan L., (CV) ....'55 '88 C.8 B.S. L.7 J.D. [Jones,D.&F.]

Gedrock, David V. '54 '80 C.363 B.A. L.607 J.D.
209 South Broadway, 44256
Telephone: 330-723-4947 Fax: 330-764-9739
Email: dgedrock@aol.com URL: http://www.davidvgedrock.com
Appeals, Criminal Law, Felony, Misdemeanors, Domestic, Family Law, Child Custody, Divorce, Visitation, Support, Post Decree, Spousal Support, Debt Relief Agency, Traffic Violations, Driving Under Influence, Wills, Deeds, Civil Litigation, Personal Injury and Probate.
See Professional Biographies, MEDINA, OHIO

Granzier, Paul A., (AV) ....'27 '59 C.363 B.B.A. L.1003 LL.B. 2628 Pearl Rd.‡
Griesinger, Charles Clark, (Co., L.P.A.) '25 '51
C.385 A.B. L.930 LL.B. 696 E. Washington St.‡
Haberman, Ian S., (BV) ....'45 '82 C.103 A.B. L.930 J.D. 225 E. Liberty Street
Hall, Bruce, (BV) ....'48 '74 C.112 B.A. L.1065 J.D. [B.Hall]
Hall, Bruce, Co., L.P.A., (BV) ....227 W. Liberty
Hanwell, Robert M., (CV) ....'54 '85 C.8 B.A. L.7 J.D. 52 Public Square
Happ, Gregory W., (CV) ....'47 '72 C.839 B.A. L.326 J.D. 238 W. Liberty St.
Hathcock, Alicia M. ....'78 '04 C.62 B.A. L.161 J.D. [A Oberholtzer,F.&L.]
Hecht, Julien A., (AV Ⓣ) '52 '78 C.976 B.A. L.446 J.D.
(adm. in MD; not adm. in OH) V.P. & Gen. Coun. & Asst. Secy., RPM, Inc.
Heck, Jill R. ....'52 '81 C.473 B.S.Ed. L.7 J.D. Prob. J.
Henry, Phillip J. ....'73 '99 C.851 B.A. L.7 J.D. 232 North Court Street
Hensal, Jennifer L., (BV) ....'67 '93 C.8 B.A. L.851 J.D. [Oberholtzer,F.&L.]
Hertrick, Paul W., (BV) ....'49 '75 C.97 B.A. L.1003 J.D. [Laribee&H.]
Hiteman, Carl G., (CV) ....'50 '83 C.363 B.A. L.851 J.D. 226 North Broadway
Hitsman, David Vincent ....'74 '00 C.608 B.S. L.1003 J.D. Medina Co. Pros. Off.
Holman, Dean ....'50 '80 C.8 B.A. L.7 J.D. Medina Co. Pros. Atty.
Horvath, George, (CV) ....'57 '85 C.8 B.S. L.7 J.D. 200 Countryside Drive
Huber, Gregory A., (BV) ....'58 '84 C&L.8 B.A., J.D. [Williams&B.]
Ingraham, Arnold A. ....'41 '67 C.472 B.A. L.930 J.D. 3060 Pearl Rd.‡
Ingraham, Roger R. ....'37 '63 C&L.930 A.B., LL.B. Mag., Juv. Ct.
Jackson, A. Michelle ....'67 '02 C.49 B.A. L.7 J.D. [A Oberholtzer,F.&L.]
Jeandrevin, John T., (BV) ....'32 '59 C.970 A.B. L.477 J.D. 600 E. Smith Rd.
Jeppe, Gerald L., (BV) ....'44 '69 C.25 A.B. L.930 J.D. [A Brown&A.]
Jocke, Ralph E. ....'53 '81 C.161 B.M.E. L.1003 J.D. [Walker&J.] (Pat.)
Johnson, C. Nevada, Jr., (AV) ....'38 '63 C.385 A.B. L.607 J.D. [Williams&B.]
Jones, Glenn R., (BV) ....'45 '74 C.608 B.S. L.1003 J.D. [Jones,D.&F.]
Jones, L. Ray ....'48 '74 C.608 B.A. L.1003 J.D. 215 W. Washington St.
Jones, Davies & Funk, A Legal Professional Association, (BV) ....3995 Medina Road
Kimbler, James L. ....'49 '74 C.610 B.A. L.930 J.D. Comm. Pleas Ct.
Kinney, Jack M., (AV) ....'31 '58 C.610 B.S. L.608 J.D. [J.M.Kinney]
Kinney, Jack M., Co. L.P.A., (AV) ....4134 E. Normandy Park Dr.
Kleckner, Janet L., (CV) ....'50 '81 C.965 B.S.Ed. L.188 J.D. Com. Pleas Mag.
Korduba, Andrew M. ....'73 '98 C.851 B.A. L.989 J.D. 319 South Court Street
Kovach, Mary Ann M., (BV) ....'48 '75 C.161 B.A. L.7 J.D. Chf. Asst. Pros. Atty.
Kovack, Mary Rose ....'63 '89 C.970 B.A. L.124 J.D. Medina Co. Ct. of Com. Pleas
Kramer, Patricia Susan ....'52 '97 C.602 B.A. L.124 J.D. [Walker&J.]
Kraushaar, Vern T. ....'32 '56 C.210 B.A. L.930 LL.B. 4931 Nettleton Rd.‡
Kray, Paul J., (CV) ....'65 '91 C.97 B.S.B.A. L.930 J.D. [Laribee&H.] (⊙Brunswick)
Lanier, J. Matthew ....'71 '98 C.611 B.A. L.472 J.D. 600 East Smith Road
Lapp, Deborah A. ....'49 '85 C.8 B.A. L.7 J.D. 3629 Trails End Dr.
Largent, Berry, Preston & Jamison Co., L.P.A., (AV) ....232 North Court Street (⊙Berea)
Laribee, Gillian Agnes ....'75 '01 C.999 B.A. L.7 J.D. [A Laribee&H.]
Laribee, Michael Lee, (CV) ....'69 '96 C.611 B.A. L.1003 J.D. [A Laribee&H.]
Laribee, Ray E., (BV) ....'42 '68 C.611 B.A. L.930 J.D. [Laribee&H.]
Laribee & Hertrick, (BV) ....325 N. Broadway (⊙Brunswick, Lodi)
Latchney, John D., (CV) ....'63 '90 C.201 B.A. L.1003 J.D. [Tomino&L.]
Lawrie, Charles T. ....'51 '86 C.1323 B.A. L.1003 J.D. Mun. Ct. Mag.
Layton, David A., (CV) ....'69 '96 C.235 B.A. L.383 J.D. [A Marco,M.&B.]
Leaver, James R. ....'56 '90 C.8 B.S. L.7 J.D. Com. Pleas J., Dom. Rel. Div.
Lesiak, Theodore J., (BV) ....'64 '89 C.610 B.A. L.8 J.D. [Oberholtzer,F.&L.]
Lohn, John J., (BV) ....'57 '83 C.602 B.B.A. City Pros.
Loyer, Richard A., (CV) ....'21 '78 C.363 B.S.B.A. L.1003 J.D. 445 E. Washington
Lyons, Michael K., (BV) ....'54 '85 C.161 B.A. L.930 J.D. Asst. Pros.
Maag, Robert Edward, Jr. ....'51 '83 L.1003 J.D. 855 Andrews Road
Mahon, Brian P., Law Office of ....'60 '93 C.967 B.A. L.1003 J.D. 250 Halifax Lane
Marco, Kenneth J., (CV) ....'63 '91 C.8 B.A. L.1003 J.D. [A Marco,M.&B.]
Marco, Richard J., Jr., (BV) ....'57 '81 C.607 B.A. L.1003 J.D. [C Marco,M.&B.]
Marco, Richard J., Sr., (AV) ....'32 '57 C.62 L.1003 J.D. [C Marco,M.&B.]
Marco, Marco & Bailey, (CV) ....52 Public Square
Maynard, Patricia Francis ....'53 '89 C.381 M.B.A. L.1003 J.D. 246 W. Liberty Street
Michelson, Allan M., (BV) ....'49 '77 C.532 B.A. L.930 J.D. Vil. Solr.
Moran, John D. '58 '84
C.161 B.B.A. L.1003 J.D. General Counsel, Corrpro Companies, Inc.
Morgan, Dwight D. ....'56 '82 C.381 B.J. L.7 J.D. 3693 Foskett Rd.
Oberholtzer, John C., (BV) ....'42 '67 C.970 B.A. L.930 J.D. [Oberholtzer,F.&L.]

Oberholtzer, Filous & Lesiak, A Legal Professional Association, (BV)
39 Public Square, Suite 201, P.O. Box 220, 44258-0220
Telephone: 330-725-4929 Fax: 330-723-4929 URL: http://www.lawyers.com/medinalaw
Email: counsel@medinalaw.com URL: http://www.medinalaw.com
Clayton J. Oberholtzer (1913-1986); Thomas J. Filous (1948-1995); John C. Oberholtzer; Theodore J. Lesiak; Jennifer L. Hensal. Associates: Michelle L. Slimak; Alicia M. Hathcock; A. Michelle Jackson.
Civil and Criminal Trial and Appellate Practice, Banking, Business and Corporate, Negligence, Personal Injury, Commercial, Family/Domestic Relations, Real Estate, Probate and Estate Planning, Oil and Gas Law, Communications, Construction Law, Municipal and Government Law, Bankruptcy Law, Social Security Disability.
Representative Clients: Mack Industries; Horner Jones, Inc.
References: National City Bank; First Merit Bank; Sky Bank, Medina, Ohio.
See Professional Biographies, MEDINA, OHIO

Obral & Mays & Associates
(See Cleveland)

Olson, Conrad G. ....'55 '95 C.645 B.S. L.8 J.D. [A J.B.Cameron&Assoc.]
Owen, Jackie L. ....'48 '88 C.528 B.A. L.8 J.D. Com. Pleas Ct. Mag.
Palmquist, James B., III, (BV) ....'51 '76 C.62 B.A. L.421 J.D. [J.B.Palmquist,III]
Palmquist, James B., III, Co., L.P.A., (BV) ....5 Public Sq.
Parish, Bruce D., (BV) ....'39 '70 C.381 B.S. L.161 J.D. 211 S. Court St.
Parker, Andrew M. ....'76 '03 C.363 B.A. L.851 J.D. 600 East Smith Road
Parmelee, Christopher L. ....'68 '98 C.930 B.S. L.1003 J.D. [Walker&J.] (Pat.)

Paul, Dennis E., (AV) '49 '75 C.610 B.S. L.607 J.D.
211 South Court Street, 44256
Telephone: 330-725-6082 Fax: 330-722-2534
URL: http://www.medinadivorcelaw.com
Personal Injury, Divorce, Adoption Advocate.
See Professional Biographies, MEDINA, OHIO

Pedro, Cameron B. ....'69 '01 C.101 B.S. L.989 J.D. 246 East Washington
Piszczek, Gerald D., (BV) ....'53 '77 C.161 B.A. L.608 [G.D.Piszczek]
Piszczek, Gerald D., Company, L.P.A., (BV) ....412 N. Court St.
Porzio, Barbara B., (BV) ....'54 '79 C.184 B.A. L.107 J.D. 93 Public Square
Proia, Michelle M. ....'70 '95 C.696 B.A. L.665 J.D. Assoc. Gen. Coun, RPM Intl. Inc.
Rabe, Herman E., (AV) ....'09 '35 C.8 A.B. L.930 LL.B. 5192 Lake Rd.‡
Razavi, Matthew K. ....'71 '96 C.473 B.A. L.124 J.D. 5201 Morning Song Dr.
Reeves, Nancy L. ....'56 '98 C.604 A.B. L.7 J.D. [Walker&J.]
Reineke, Juliana Webber ....'69 '98 C.20 B.A. L.989 J.D. 4004 Fox Meadow Dr.
Renswick, Julien C., (AV) ....'23 '48 C.107 A.B. L.309 LL.B. 326 N. Court St.

Richard Law Office, LLC
(See Wooster)

Riehl, David S.
(See Brunswick)

Russo, Dorcas A. ....'56 '81 C.881 A.B. L.930 J.D. Mag., Ct. of Com. Pleas
Sankoe, Shayne M. ....'— '01 C&L.8 B.A., J.D. [A L.T.Skidmore]
Schaffrath, Kurt A. ....'39 '73 C.999 B.A. L.145 J.D. 3202 Rustic Valley Drive

Scheetz, Stanley D., (BV) ... '46 '74 C&L.607 B.A., J.D. [S.D.Scheetz]
Scheetz, Stanley D., Co., L.P.A., (BV) ... 225 East Liberty Street
Sharratt, Thomas W., (BV) ... '21 '52 C&L.930 B.A., LL.B. 860 Lindenwood Lane
Sheldon, David ... '61 '88 C.473 B.A. L.989 J.D. [🄰 J.B.Cameron&Assoc.]
Shirer, Albert D., (CV) ... '50 '94 C.381 B.A. L.1003 J.D. P.O. Box 713
Shockley, Carol, (BV) '47 '87 C.363 A.B. L.161 J.D.
Asst. Pros. Atty., Civil Div., Medina Co. Pros. Off.
Skidmore, Claudia M. ... '70 '96 C.999 B.A. L.1003 J.D. [🄰 L.T.Skidmore]
Skidmore, L. Thomas '32 '59
C.236 A.B. L.930 LL.B. Com. Pleas J., Prob. Div. (Juv. Jurisdiction)

Skidmore, Lee Thomas, (BV) '58 '85 C.999 B.A. L.7 J.D.
748 North Court Street, 44256
Telephone: 330-725-5936; Cleveland: 330-273-2943 Fax: 330-725-3145
Email: LeeSkid@mctainc.com URL: http://www.skidmoreandhall.com
Associates: Claudia M. Skidmore; Robert C. Skidmore; Shayne M. Sankoe.
Commercial and Residential Real Estate, Title Examinations, Condominium Law. Real Estate Development, Zoning, Criminal Trial Practice, Family Law, Collections, Estate Planning, Probate, Personal Injury.

Skidmore, Robert C. ... '70 '01 C.999 B.A. L.8 J.D. [🄰 L.T.Skidmore]
Slimak, Michelle L. ... '72 '99 C.610 B.A. L.7 J.D. [🄰 Oberholtzer,F.&L.]
Spears, Ronald S. ... '69 '98 C.235 B.A. L.383 J.D. [🄰 Marco,M.&B.]
Spink, Prudence C., Attorney at Law, (BV) '50 '81 C.477 A.B. L.8 J.D.
316 W. Liberty St.
Sprenger, Michael T. ... '73 '98 C.528 B.A. L.608 J.D. Legal Coun., RPM Intl. Inc.
Stanley, Ronald R. ... '47 '74 C.98 B.S.E.E. L.1003 J.D. P.O. Box 571 (Pat.)
Steingass, Jonathan M., (CV) ... '45 '87 C.313 A.B. L.7 J.D. [🄰 Williams&B.]
Thorne, William L., (BV) .. '47 '73 C.381 B.A. L.608 J.D. 60 Public Sq., Bank One Bldg.
Tomino, Nick C., (BV) ... '53 '78 C.363 B.A. L.1003 J.D. [Tomino&L.]
Tomino & Latchney, LLC, (BV) ... 803 East Washington Street
Tompkins, P. Kelly, (AV) '56 '81
C.470 B.A. L.1003 J.D. Sr. V.P., Gen. Coun. & Secy., RPM,Inc.
Truman, Vance P. ... '55 '93 C.1089 B.S. L.201 J.D. 319 South Court Street
Walker, Patricia A. ... '53 '81 C.294 A.B. L.1003 J.D. [Walker&J.]
Walker & Jocke, L.P.A. ... 231 South Broadway (Pat.)
Weiner, William H., (BV) ... '47 '72 C.8 B.S.B.A. L.930 J.D. 171 Granger Rd.
Weingart, Denise Herron ... '62 '91 C.8 B.S.N. L.1003 J.D. Pros. Off.
Widder, Karen E. '67 '92 C&L.608 B.A., J.D.
Mng. Atty., Community Legal Aid Services, Inc.

Williams and Batchelder, LLP, (AV)
105 West Liberty Street, P.O. Box 394, 44258-0394
Telephone: 330-725-6666; Cleveland Direct Line: 330-225-1300 Fax: 330-723-4227
Email: wmsbatchattys@zoominternet.net
Members of Firm: William G. Batchelder, Jr.; C. Nevada Johnson, Jr.; Robert J. Bux; Jeffrey L. Bramley; William B. Young; Gregory A. Huber. Associate: Jonathan M. Steingass.
General Civil Practice in all Courts. Corporate, Banking, Probate and Estate Planning, Real Estate, Zoning and Insurance Law. Trials and Appeals.
Representative Clients: Westfield Cos. (Ohio Farmers Insurance Co.); Old Phoenix Bank, Aetna Casualty and Surety Co.; Motorists Mutual Insurance Co.; Nationwide Insurance Co.; Medina General Hospital.
See Professional Biographies, MEDINA, OHIO

Wright, Barbara ... '61 '87 C.381 B.S. L.608 J.D. 5675 Arlyne Lane
Yoder, Lois Jean ... '55 '80 C.8 B.S. L.7 J.D. Assoc. Prof., Kent State Univ.
Young, William B., (BV) ... '53 '78 C.432 B.A. L.150 J.D. [Williams&B.]
Zanath, Debra Ann R. '60 '91
C.876 B.S. L.161 J.D. V.P. Legal Affairs, Medina General Hospital

MENTOR, 50,278, *Lake Co.*

Aliberti, Louis S. ... '— '99 C.381 L.161 J.D. 9255 Jordan Dr.
Axelrod, Jon D. ... '71 '05 C.251 B.B.A. L.989 J.D. 6966A Heisley Rd.
Balin, Paulette F., (BV) '55 '78
C.930 B.A. L.910 J.D. 7372 Lakeshore Boulevard (⊙Cleveland)
Bencin, Patricia DiRosa, (CV) ... '35 '81 C.161 B.A. L.1003 J.D. 5800 Andrews Rd.
Biales, Robert Craig ... '60 '93 L.1187 J.D. [R.C.Biales]
Biales, Robert C., & Co. ... 6966A Heisley Rd.
Brahms, William A. ... '29 '54 C&L.930 B.A., LL.B. 7306 Mentor Ave.
Brennan, Jane Brewster ... '63 '96 C.608 B.A. L.989 J.D. 7575 Tyler Blvd. C-4
Bush, Mary Elizabeth ... '64 '90 C.161 B.A. L.8 J.D. [M.E.Bush]
Bush, Mary E. ... 9373 Kings Hollow Ct.
Callender, Jamie, Jr. ... '65 '92 C.161 B.A. L.1003 J.D. [McNamara,H.C.&L.]
Canala, John Steven ... '54 '89 C.923 B.S. L.1003 J.D. 9240 Kathleen Dr.

Cannon, Stern, Aveni and Loiacono Co., L.P.A.
(See Painesville)

Clancy, Timothy G., (BVⓉ) '63 '88
C.473 B.A. L.930 J.D. Sr. Corp. Coun., STERIS Corp.
Clapp, R. Jack, & Assoc. Co., L.P.A., (BV)
7784 Reynolds Rd. (⊙Wash., DC; Cleve., OH)
Coffey, Michael D. ... '28 '60 C.354 B.S. L.1003 J.D. [Coffey,G.&D.]
Coffey, Gambol & DiPalma, (BV) ... 9853 Johnnycake Ridge Rd.
Collins, Leo R., (BV) ... '34 '62 C.363 B.S.B.A. L.1003 J.D. 7333 Center St.
Collins, Peter H. B. ... '58 '84 C.500 B.B.A. L.836 J.D. 7323 Center St.★
Conway, Neil J. ... '25 '51 C.363 B.S. L.930 LL.B. 9397 Canterbury Lane‡
Cooper, William F. ... '20 '52 C.97 A.B. L.174 LL.B. 7147 Erie Dr.‡

Cooper & Forbes
(See Painesville)

Davis, Roy ... '20 '59 C.150 Ch.E. L.1340 J.D. P.O. Box 8000 (Pat.)
Denman, Alfred, (BV) ... '37 '70 C.381 B.A. L.1003 J.D. [Denman&L.]
Denman & Lerner, Co., LPA, (BV) ... 8039 Broadmoor Road
DiCello, Mark Andrew ... '69 '94 C.201 B.A. L.161 J.D. [R.J.DiCello]
DiCello, Robert F. ... '68 '00 C.201 B.A. L.989 J.D. [🄰 R.J.DiCello]
DiCello, Robert J., (AV) ... '45 '71 C.363 A.B. L.1003 J.D. [R.J.DiCello]
DiCello, Robert J., Co., L.P.A., (AV) ... 7556 Mentor Avenue
DiPalma, William J., (BV) ... '50 '77 C.930 B.A. L.201 J.D. [Coffey,G.&D.]
Everett, P. David, II ... '60 '85 C.363 B.A. L.1003 J.D. [Everett&Assoc.]
Everett & Associates Co. LPA ... 8451 Mentor Ave.
Farone, Nicole L. ... '— '98 C.363 B.S. L.1003 J.D. 7550 Adams Ct.
Field, Harry E., (BV) ... '45 '71 C.608 B.A. L.930 J.D. 6988 Spinach Dr.
Fitzgerald, Janette M. ... '56 '84 C.161 B.A. L.7 J.D. 8720 Pleasant Run Ln.
Flora, James H. ... '50 '78 C.930 B.S. L.1003 J.D. 7235 Taft Street‡
Freeman, Amy Marie ... '72 '97 C.970 B.A. L.1119 J.D. [🄰 McNamara,H.C.&L.]
Frost, Merrie M., (CV) ... '59 '92 C.810 B.B.A. L.1003 J.D. [🄰 R.J.Clapp&Assoc.]
Gallovic, John G., (CV) ... '42 '75 C.251 B.B.A. L.161 J.D. 8518 Mentor Ave., Ste. A
Gambol, Robert A., (BV) ... '47 '73 C.93 A.B. L.228 J.D. [Coffey,G.&D.]
Goff, Robert E., (BV) ... '41 '68 C.363 B.S.S. L.1003 J.D. 7821 Hidden Hollow
Gorjanc, Henry A. ... '26 '55 C.821 B.S.E.E. L.1003 LL.B. 8260 Deepwood Blvd.‡
Graham, Ron, (BV) ... '58 '87 C.980 B.A. L.1003 J.D. City Pros. Atty.
Hanahan, Geoffrey C., (BV) ... '53 '79 C.808 B.A. L.425 J.D. 8383 Mentor Ave., Ste. 101
Hanrahan, Patrick R., (BV) ... '49 '74 C.339 B.A. L.1003 J.D. [McNamara,H.C.&L.]
Hartory, Timothy P., and Associates '45 '72 C.251 B.B.A. L.1003 J.D.
8320 Mentor Ave.
Irvin, James D. ... '46 '74 C.610 B.A. L.161 J.D. 8512 Mentor Ave.
Jelenic, Barbara A. ... '63 '96 C.599 B.A. L.1003 J.D. 7501 Brenel Dr.
King, Woods, Jr. ... '28 '53 C.976 B.A. L.893 LL.B. 10025 Little Mountain Road‡
Klammer, Lisa Maria ... '74 '99 C.473 B.Phil. L.989 J.D. [Klammer]
Klammer, Theodore R., (BV) ... '46 '70 C.97 B.S. L.1003 J.D. 6990 Lindsay Dr.
Klammer Law Office, The, Ltd. ... 6990 Lindsay Dr., Ste. 7
Kleiman, Michael M., (CV) ... '50 '79 C.161 B.A. L.1003 J.D. P.O. Box 1668
Kline, William S., III ... '59 '99 L.1003 J.D. 9168 Lakeshore Blvd.
Kovacs, Joseph ... '22 '66 C.251 B.B.A. L.1003 J.D. 7444 Case Rd.‡

Kravitz, Lee R.
(See Cleveland)

Kuhel, Anthony E., Jr. ... '75 '00 C.273 B.A. L.124 J.D. Corp. Coun., STERIS Corp.
Lerner, Michael J., (CV) ... '66 '92 C.880 B.A. L.930 J.D. [Denman&L.]
Lombardo, Catherine M. ... '— '79 C.363 A.B. L.851 J.D. 9074 Richards Dr.
Loxterman, Kirk F., (BV) ... '49 '85 C.967 A.B. L.930 J.D. [McNamara,H.C.&L.]
Manning, Francis Patrick ... '59 '90 C.161 B.B.A. L.989 J.D. 7556 Mentor Avenue
Manning, Joseph J., Jr. ... '48 '77 C.124 B.S. L.1003 J.D. 7310 Brownell Ave.
Manning, Karen T. ... '62 '95 C.93 B.A. L.1003 J.D. FirstMerit Bk., N.A.
McCarter, William K., (BV) '36 '67 C.363 B.S. L.1003 J.D.
9720 Johnnycake Ridge Road
McGinley, Mark D. '56 '82
C.363 B.S.B.A. L.989 J.D. V.P., Gen. Coun. & Sec., STERIS Corp.
McNamara, Walter J., III, (BV) ... '45 '69 C.930 A.B. L.228 J.D. [McNamara,H.C.&L.]
McNamara, Hanrahan, Callender & Loxterman, (BV) ... 8440 Station Street
Misseldine, Russell W., Law Office of ... '54 '96 C.161 B.A. L.989 J.D. 6184 Lake Street
Mocilnikar, Frank C., Jr. ... '50 '76 C.97 B.S. L.1003 J.D. 6442 Carter Blvd.
Negin, Morton S. ... '28 '54 C.381 L.1003 LL.B. 9205 Idlewood Dr.
Niebes, Roger S., (CV) ... '38 '73 C.381 B.S. L.1003 J.D. 8080 Meadowdale Dr.
Nozik, Albert C. ... '12 '35 C.473 L.608 J.D. 7833 Lake Shore Blvd.
O'Leary, James R. ... '55 '88 C.961 B.A. L.1202 J.D. 6988 Spinach Drive
Osborn, David C. ... '20 '60 C.401 B.S. L.930 LL.B. 8674 Mentor Ave.‡
Picardini, Joseph B. ... '42 '71 C.251 B.B.A. L.1003 J.D. 8815 East Avenue
Rose, Ronald, (CV) ... '46 '91 C.161 B.B.A. L.1003 J.D. 5636 Primavera Dr.
Ryan, Patrick T., (BV) ... '51 '78 C.363 B.S.B.A. L.7 J.D. 8000 Plaza Blvd.
Sacerich, Thomas J., (BV) ... '54 '80 C.363 B.A. L.8 J.D. 6988 Spinach Dr.
Shovlin, Gerald Lee ... '43 '82 C.201 B.A. L.1003 J.D. 8611 Forestview Ave.
Sikora, Michael J., III ... '73 '98 C.608 B.S.B.A. L.117 J.D. [Sikora]
Sikora Law LLC ... 7340 Center St.
Sirvaitis, Algis, (BV) ... '39 '66 C.363 B.S.S. L.1003 J.D. 7662 Tyler Blvd. (⊙Cleveland)
Stefl, Scott Richard, (CV) ... '56 '82 C.901 B.A. L.930 J.D. 7844 Lakeshore Boulevard
Sternberg, David J., (BV) ... '48 '73 C.473 B.S. L.608 J.D. [Sternberg&Z.]

Sternberg & Zeid Co., L.P.A., (BV)
7547 Mentor Avenue, Suite 301, 44060
Telephone: 440-942-6267 Fax: 440-942-6504 URL: http://www.sternbergzeidlaw.com
URL: http://www.sternbergandzeid.com
David J. Sternberg; Gary D. Zeid.
Personal Injury, Automobile Accidents, Wrongful Death, Workers Compensation, Municipal Law, Zoning Law, Bankruptcy, Domestic Relations, Family Law, Divorce, Child Custody, Guardianship, Real Estate, Probate, Estate Planning, Trusts and Wills, Business, Corporate, Contract Law, General Civil Trial Practice in State and Federal Courts.
See Professional Biographies, MENTOR, OHIO

Strader, Clancy ... '25 '54 C.381 B.A. L.1003 J.D. 6122 Cabot Ct.‡
Studen, Greg E. ... '45 '73 C&L.309 B.A., J.D. Pres., Donray Co.
Swain, Richard A. ... '34 '63 C.611 A.B. L.266 J.D. Mun. J.
Taylor, David B. ... '57 '83 C.161 B.A. L.1003 J.D. 7548 Monterey Bay Dr.
Todoroff, James G., (BV) ... '40 '73 C.851 B.E. L.1003 J.D. 9853 Johnnycake Ridge Rd.
Valentino, Nicholas Donald ... '57 '84 C.930 B.A. L.851 J.D. 6820 Rockport Ln.
Vazzana, James Leigh ... '50 '87 C.930 B.S. L.1003 J.D. P.O. Box 792
West, Kathleen D., (BV) ... '40 '79 C.679 B.S. L.930 J.D. 8957 Perkins Dr.
Wiegand, Richard A. ... '52 '78 C.608 B.S. L.851 J.D. 7602 Andrea Dr.★
Zangerle, J. Adam, (BV) '66 '91 C.732 B.A. L.930 J.D.
Asso. Gen. Coun., STERIS Corp.
Zeid, Gary D., (BV) ... '48 '75 C.161 B.B.A. L.1003 J.D. [Sternberg&Z.]

METAMORA, 543, *Fulton Co.*

Hunt, Charles N., (BV) ... '31 '58 C&L.608 B.S., LL.B. 119 W. Main St. (⊙Sylvania)

MIAMISBURG, 19,489, *Montgomery Co.*

Anderson, Christopher Jude ... '66 '95 C.30 B.A. L.1187 J.D. 9443 Springboro Pike
August, James E. ... '69 '97 C&L.201 B.A., J.D. 9393 Springboro Pike
Baver & Bookwalter, Co., L.P.A., (BV) ... 202 E. Central Ave.
Bookwalter, Thomas E., (BV) ... '46 '70 C.201 B.A. L.150 J.D. [Baver&B.]
Bragg, Holly J. ... '59 '83 C&L.607 B.A., J.D. V.P., Natl. City Corp.
Buckler, Warren A., Jr. '51 '76 C.932 B.A. L.146 J.D.
(adm. in MI; not adm. in OH) 1309 Belvo Rd.
Burk, Christine Louise, (BV) ... '63 '90 C.967 B.A. L.201 J.D. Pros. Atty.
Casteel, Douglas, (BV) ... '41 '75 C.77 B.A. L.1340 J.D. 101 N. 1st St.
Croskey, Thomas P. ... '51 '80 C.473 B.A. L.851 J.D. [Croskey]
Croskey Law Office ... 126 S. 7th St.
Cummings, Brian K. ... '70 '95 C.610 B.B.A. L.608 J.D. 3445 Newmark Drive
Cummings, Carrie Watkins ... '58 '93 C.22 B.A. L.851 J.D. Prod. Consult., LexisNexis
Dalton, David M. ... '51 '78 C.97 A.B. L.201 J.D. 1543 Casilla Court
Daniels, Deana M. ... '69 '94 C.473 B.A. L.201 J.D. LEXIS-NEXIS
Denny, Richard G., (BV) ... '43 '73 C.201 B.S. L.1340 J.D. 110 E. Central
De Serna, Alexander C. ... '59 '89 C.973 A.B. L.150 J.D. Lexis-Nexis
Doles, Paul W., II ... '69 '96 C&L.201 B.A., J.D. LexisNexis
Edington, Robert L. ... '57 '83 C.607 B.A. L.245 J.D. Lexis-Nexis
Ellis, Robert C. '54 '79 C.294 B.A. L.930 J.D.
Sr. V.P. & Asst. Gen. Coun., Natl. City Corp.
Enneking, Patrick J. ... '68 '93 C&L.150 B.A., J.D. LEXIS-NEXIS
Euvrard, LeRoy E., Jr. ... '43 '73 C.178 A.B. L.94 J.D. Roy F. Weston, Inc.
Fening, M. Brady ... '69 '94 C.473 B.A. L.851 J.D. 9443 Springboro Pike
Fobes, Ronald L., (BV) ... '38 '66 C.201 B.A. L.378 J.D. Pros. Atty.
Gaffin, Dana L. ... '69 '99 C.473 B.A. L.8 J.D. 9443 Springboro Pike
Garry, Rita M. ... '61 '86 C.363 B.A. L.608 J.D. LEXIS-NEXIS
Geva, Liora, Law Offices of ... '51 '01 C.1530 B.A. L.999 LL.B. 8838 Motter Ln.
Goedde, Thomas J. ... '58 '83 C.602 B.A. L.608 J.D. LEXIS-NEXIS
Gressly, Brian K. ... '65 '90 C.992 B.A. L.150 J.D. LEXIS-NEXIS
Hartnett, Caroline M. ... '65 '91 C.518 A.B. L.150 J.D. LEXIS-NEXIS
Hauck, Daniel Alan ... '69 '94 C.472 B.A. L.150 J.D. Ref. Atty., Lexis-Nexis

Hearn, Robert L. ... '48 '74 C&L.150 B.S.E.E., J.d. LEXIS-NEXIS
Hensley, Michael Robert ... '58 '84 9443 Springboro Pike
Hobbs, H. Steven, (BV) ... '58 '83 C&L.201 B.S., J.D. [Ruschau,L.&H.] (⊙Lewisburg)
Hopkins, Susan E. '— '93
(adm. in MA; not adm. in OH) LexisNexis
Irizarry, Francisco A. ... '62 '88 C&L.201 B.A., J.D. LEXIS-NEXIS
Jones, John Alan ... '53 '81 C&L.64 B.A., J.D. Gen. Coun., Babcock & Wilcox of Ohio
Koehler, Alan W. ... '60 '86 C.8 B.A. L.607 J.D. 10 Prestige Pl.
Kurtz, Christy L. Ebbeson ... '60 '89 C.231 B.A. L.8 J.D. 9443 Springboro Pike
Lachman, Marshall G. '64 '88 C.339 B.S. L.608 J.D.
(adm. in IL; not adm. in OH) Lexis-Nexis
Larrier, Damon E. ... '70 '00 C.28 B.A. L.201 J.D. Lexis-Nexis
Lasky, Lynn M. ... '53 '86 C.347 B.S. L.201 J.D. LEXIS-NEXIS
Lehman, Joseph A., (BV) ... '49 '77 C&L.201 B.S., J.D. [Ruschau,L.&H.]
Lenski, Kathleen Swiger, (CV) ... '72 '98 C.275 B.A. L.201 J.D. [Ⓐ Baver&B.]
Logsdon, Robert G. ... '45 '81 C.473 B.S. L.201 J.D. LEXIS-NEXIS
Ludlow, Vicki L. ... '52 '89 C.210 A.B. L.347 J.D. Lexis-Nexis
Mantel, Kaila Ann ... '67 '93 LexisNexis
Massa, Susan ... '68 '93 C.610 B.B.A. L.200 J.D. Reed Elsevier Tech.
Messham, Robert E., Jr. ... '46 '72 C&L.608 B.A., J.D. 10 North 1st Street
Meyer, Tricia L. '75 '99 C.63 B.A. L.1119 J.D.
(adm. in IN; not adm. in OH) Quality Auditor, LexisNexis
Michaud, Nancy Heckard, (AV) '46 '80
C.741 B.A. L.201 J.D. V.P., Gen. Coun. & Secy., Huffy Corp.
Murray, Erin ... '60 '87 C.608 B.A. L.425 J.D. Lexis-Nexis
Noble, Greg R. ... '61 '86 C.610 B.A. L.201 J.D. LEXIS-NEXIS
Olsen, Tracey '65 '90 C.339 B.A. L.770 J.D.
(adm. in IL; not adm. in OH) Sr. Quality Editor, LexisNexis
Puncer, William O. ... '55 '80 C.724 B.A. L.201 J.D. LEXIS-NEXIS
Rath, Pamela K. ... '62 '94 C.150 B.A. L.201 J.D. LEXIS-NEXIS
Relles, George '48 '72 C&L.966 B.A., J.D.
(adm. in WI; not adm. in OH) Sr. Dir., LEXIS-NEXIS
Ruschau, Steve J., (BV) ... '52 '77 C&L.201 B.A., J.D. [Ruschau,L.&H.]
Ruschau, Lehman & Hobbs, (BV) ... 610 Evans Avenue
Schmitt, John J. ... '74 '01 C.973 B.S.B.A. L.851 J.D. Application Consultant, LexisNexis
Sempeles, Leigh Anne ... '57 '83 C.1208 B.A. L.200 J.D. 9443 Springboro Pike
Silver, Harry R. ... '48 '88 C.659 B.A. L.477 J.D. 9555 Springboro Pike
Smith, Wm. Michael '59 '85 C&L.378 B.A., J.D.
(adm. in KS; not adm. in OH) LEXIS-NEXIS
Sprowl, John O. ... '65 '93 C&L.201 B.S., J.D. 10 Prestige Plaza Drive
Talk, John Gordon, IV '64 '90
(adm. in TX; not adm. in OH) 705 E. Linden Ave.
Teeters, Bruce A., (AV) ... '65 '91 C.607 B.A. L.150 J.D. Assoc. Gen. Coun., Huffy Corp.
Thackery, Hope Ann ... '58 '81 C.347 B.A. L.200 J.D. Lexis-Nexis
Thomas, Michael D. ... '58 '83 C.860 B.A. L.201 J.D. Partner, Knauper & Thomas Co.
Uzelac, Lauren L. ... '73 '98 C.645 B.S. L.607 J.D. 1965 Amelia Ct.
Vanden Bosch, Virginia C., (BV) ... '49 '85 C&L.201 B.S., J.D. Res. Atty., Lexix-Nexis
Wells, Cheryl A. ... '57 '83 C.25 B.A. L.201 J.D. Lexis-Nexis
Wenz, George L., III ... '64 '92 C.573 B.A. L.201 J.D. LexisNexis
Wilkinson, Charles Joseph '66 '94 C&L.201 B.S., J.D.
(adm. in MD; not adm. in OH) LEXIS-NEXIS
Williams, Angela M. ... '— '88 C.901 B.A. L.665 J.D. LEXIS-NEXIS
Wilson, Vernon ... '26 '52 C.473 L.150 LL.B. [Ruschau,L.&H.] ‡
Wirth, Gerald R., (BV) ... '33 '73 C.631 B.S. L.1340 J.D. 110 E. Central Ave.
Zehring, Robert H., Jr., (BV) ... '21 '54 C.610 L.607 LL.B. 126 S. 7th St.

MIDDLEBURG HEIGHTS, 15,542, *Cuyahoga Co.*

Amsdell, Robert J., (AV) '40 '65
C.935 B.A. L.930 J.D. Pres. and Gen. Coun., The Amsdell Cos.‡
Carlisle, Gerald K., (AV) '34 '60
C.970 B.A. L.1003 LL.B. [Ⓒ Carlisle-Kesling&M.] (⊙Cleveland)
Carlisle-Kesling, Kathryn J. ... '73 '99 C.150 B.A. L.851 J.D. [Carlisle-Kesling&M.]
Carlisle-Kesling & Morgan ... 7083 Pearl Road
Caster, Cynthia M. '58 '90 C.363 B.S. L.1003 J.D.
Claim Team Mng., State Farm Insurance Companies
Doslak, William R., (AV) '52 '81
C.97 B.S.Ed. L.1003 J.D. Mng. Atty., SAFECO Prop. & Cas. Ins. Co.
Harpst, Ronald J. ... '32 '63 C.1062 B.A. L.1003 J.D. 14881 Cherokee Trail
Hilliard, Carol Rogers, (BV) '43 '84 C.739 B.S. L.1003 J.D.
7550 Lucerne Drive Suite 401
Hull, C. D. '35 '61 C&L.862 B.S., LL.B.
(adm. in OK; not adm. in OH) 7474 James Dr.‡
Jones, Jonathan E., (BVⓉ) ... '56 '81 C.119 B.S. L.665 J.D. 6981 Fry Rd.
Kramer, Monica E. ... '77 '02 C.363 B.A. L.7 J.D. [Carlisle-Kesling&M.]
Madachik, Joseph M. ... '57 '96 C.161 B.B.A. L.1003 J.D. 7530 Lucerne Drive, Suite 200
Mille, Dennis G., (BV) ... '47 '72 C&L.117 B.A., J.D. [Phillips,M.&C.]
Morgan, Michael D. ... '71 '99 C.610 B.S. L.851 J.D. [Carlisle-Kesling&M.]
Phillips, Nicholas E., (BV) ... '47 '73 C.381 B.A. L.7 J.D. [Phillips,M.&C.]
Phillips, Mille & Costabile Co. L.P.A., (BV) ... 7530 Lucerne Dr., Ste. 200
Proe, Stephen J. ... '— '96 7123 Pearl Rd., Ste. 304
Ramsey, Lloyd J., (BV) ... '46 '74 C.381 B.A. L.7 J.D. 7530 Lucerne Drive, Suite 200
Reardon, Michael Edward ... '65 '93 C.150 B.A. L.989 J.D. [M.E.Reardon]
Reardon, Michael E., Co., LPA ... 7050 Engle Road, Suite 100
Stampfel, J. Raymond ... '31 '61 7330 Brookside Pkwy.
Tetlak, Edw. J. ... '18 '52 C.608 B.S. L.1003 J.D. 7454 Briarcliff Pkwy.
Tomsik, Donald M. ... '34 '59 C&L.930 B.B.A., J.D. 14961 Cherokee Trail
Wilson, Stewart S. ... '49 '79 C.610 B.G.S. L.1003 J.D. 7530 Lucerne Dr. (⊙Cleveland)
Worthing, Donald E., (BV) '45 '77 C.381 B.B.A. L.1003 J.D.
In House Coun., SAFECO
Zomparelli, Gino, (AV) '62 '89
C.363 B.S.B.A. L.1003 J.D. Gen. Coun., Ohio Tpke. Comm.

MIDDLETOWN, 51,605, *Butler & Warren Cos.*

Allare, John P. ... '50 '77 C.602 A.B. L.608 J.D. Gen. Coun., NN Admin., Inc.
Allen, Patrick W., (AV) ... '39 '65 C.201 B.A. L.607 J.D. [Casper&C.]
Allen, Thomas B., (BV) ... '64 '94 C.473 B.S. L.150 J.D. [Frost B.T.]
Allen, William P. ... '69 '94 C.853 B.A. L.201 J.D. [Casper&C.]
Atkins, Christopher G., (BV) '51 '84
C.1208 B.A. L.201 J.D. 1081 N. University Blvd., Ste. B
Barr, Eric James, (CV) ... '50 '81 C.473 B.A. L.1340 J.D. 1523 1st Avenue
Batliner, Jennifer, (CV) ... '51 '82 C.608 B.S. L.150 J.D. 1440 South Breiel Boulevard
Becker, Paul A., (CV) ... '46 '78 C.970 B.A. L.8 J.D. 1701 S. Breiel Blvd.
Beeken, Scott H. ... '50 '75 C.473 B.S. L.245 J.D. Corp. Dir., Tax, Armco, Inc.
Bolinger, Bradley Drew, (CV) ... '62 '88 C.150 B.A. L.201 J.D. 305 Lylburn Road
Bowen, William L., (BV) ... '49 '78 C.608 B.S. L.201 J.D. 1 N. Main St.
Boyd, Clinton D. ... '25 '52 C.473 B.A. L.608 J.D. 4726 Manchester Rd.‡
Bryant, Jerry M., (BV) ... '44 '72 C.150 B.S. L.117 J.D. [Bryant&S.]
Bryant & Sanzone, (BV) ... 1600 First Ave.
Buchert, Thomas R. ... '46 '75 C.611 B.A. L.150 J.D. 56 S. Main St.‡
Caneris, Thomas A., (BV) ... '62 '87 C&L.150 B.A., J.D. AK Steel Corp.
Casper, Arthur Brandeis, (AV) '40 '67 C.473 A.B. L.607 J.D.
[Casper&C.] (⊙Hamilton)
Casper, Douglas W., (AV) ... '49 '75 C.150 B.B.A. L.1340 J.D. [Casper&C.]
Casper, E. Jeffrey, (BV) ... '47 '72 C&L.150 B.A., J.D. [Casper&C.] (⊙Dayton)
Casper, Sanford I., (BV) ... '52 '81 C.473 B.A. L.200 J.D. [Casper&C.]

Casper and Casper, (AV) BR
Cinergy Building, 1 North Main Street 5th and 6th Floors, P.O. Box 510, 45042 ⊙
Telephone: 513-424-2401-Middletown; 937-224-1122-Dayton 513-381-7096-Cincinnati 513-892-2560-Hamilton Toll Free: 1-800-784-2889 Fax: 513-424-0622
URL: http://www.casperlaw.com
I. A. Casper (1910-1981); Jack A. Casper (1912-1996); Arthur Brandeis Casper; E. Jeffrey Casper; Douglas W. Casper; Sanford I. Casper; Ronald M. Kabakoff; Rebecca L. Wilkinson; Patrick W. Allen; Barbara L. Strady; Margaret Halnon McCollum; Mark A. Summers; Megan Richards; William P. Allen; Michael J. Hallee; Stephen R. Fogle; Robin R. Partin.
Personal Injury, Workers Compensation and Social Security Disability Law. Products Liability Litigation. Trials.
Dayton, Ohio Office: First National Plaza Building, 130 West Second Street, Suite 1950, 45402. Telephone: 937-224-1122.
Cincinnati, Ohio Office: 119 East Court Street, Fourth Floor, Suite 410, 45202. Telephone: 513-381-7096.
Hamilton Office: 2 South 3rd Street, Suite 360, 45011. Telephone: 513-892-2560.
See Professional Biographies, MIDDLETOWN, OHIO

Clark, Gregory Michael ... '59 '86 C.97 B.S. L.201 J.D. 12th Dist. Ct. of Appeals
Combs, C. Edward, (BV) ... '44 '73 C.383 B.S. L.421 J.D. [Combs&S.]
Combs & Schaefer, (BV) ... 1081 N. University Blvd.
Crain, Donald L., (AV) ... '48 '73 C.473 B.S. L.150 J.D. [Frost B.T.]
Curp, John H., (AV) ... '47 '74 C.999 B.S. L.607 J.D. 8110 Thomas Rd.
DeClark, Candice R., (BV) ... '52 '83 C.150 B.B.A. L.1340 J.D. 160 N. Breiel Blvd.
Dumes, Robert M., (BV) ... '50 '77 C.347 B.A. L.1340 J.D. 1058 N. University Blvd.
Dyer, Garofalo, Mann & Schultz, A Legal Professional Association, (AV)
1420 South Breiel Boulevard (⊙Richmond, IN; Bellefontaine, Dayton, Huber Heights, Lima, Piqua, Springfield, Troy, Wilmington, Xenia, OH)

Eagle, Thomas G., Co., L.P.A.
(See Lebanon)

Ellis, Paris K., (BV) '44 '80 C.473 B.S. L.1340 J.D.
1501 South Breiel Boulevard, 45044
Telephone: 513-423-0194 Fax: 513-423-0863
Email: pkeut@aol.com URL: http://www.lawyers.com/parisellis
Criminal Law, Drug Crimes, Driving While Intoxicated, Alcoholic Beverages, Family Law, Divorce, Wrongful Death, Wills and Probate, Federal Criminal, White Collar Crimes, Embezzlement, Parole Violations, Sex Crimes, Rape, Murders, Juvenile Crimes, Custody, Domestic Violence, Support.
See Professional Biographies, MIDDLETOWN, OHIO

Fogle, Stephen R. ... '63 '93 C&L.117 B.A., J.D. [Ⓐ Casper&C.]

Frost Brown Todd LLC, (AV)
300 North Main Street, Suite 200, 45042-1919 ⊙
Telephone: 513-422-2001 Telecopier: 513-422-3010
Email: info@fbtlaw.com URL: http://www.frostbrowntodd.com
Members: Thomas B. Allen; Donald L. Crain; Thomas A. Swope. Associates: W. Joseph Scholler.
Alternative Dispute Resolution, Bankruptcy and Reorganization, Business Acquisitions, Business and Corporate, Commercial Finance, Commercial Litigation, Commercial/Real Estate, Construction, Copyright, Corporate Responsibility and Defense, Employee Benefits, Energy and Natural Resources, Entrepreneurial, Environmental, Equine, Estate Planning and Administration, Financial Institutions, Fire and Explosion, Health Care, Immigration, International, Intellectual Property, International Business, Internet and Electronic Commerce, Labor and Employment Law, Litigation, Media, Mold and Water Intrusion, Multi-District Litigation, Patent Litigation, Personal Planning and Family Business, Privacy and Information Security, Product Liability, Public Finance, Securities, Tax, Tort & Insurance Law, Trademark, Venture Capital, General Trial Practice in all State and Federal Courts.
Cincinnati, Ohio Office: 2200 PNC Center, 201 East Fifth Street, 45202-4182. Telephone: 513-651-6800. Telecopier: 513-651-6981.
Columbus, Ohio Office: One Columbus, 10 West Broad Street, 43215-3467. Telephone: 614-464-1211. Telecopier: 614-464-1737.
Lexington, Kentucky Office: 250 West Main Street, Suite 2700, 40507-1742. Telephone: 859-231-0000. Telecopier: 859-231-0011.
Louisville, Kentucky Office: 400 West Market Street, 32nd Floor, 40202-3363. Telephone: 502-589-5400. Telecopier: 502-581-1087.
Nashville, Tennessee Office: 424 Church Street, Suite 1600, 37219-2308. Telephone: 615-251-5550. Telecopier: 615-251-5551.
New Albany, Indiana Office: 120 West Spring Street, Suite 400, 47150-3655. Telephone: 812-948-2800. Telecopier: 812-948-7994.
See Professional Biographies, MIDDLETOWN, OHIO

Frost & Jacobs LLP
(See Frost Brown Todd LLC)

Gose, Donald M. ... '21 '52 C.473 A.B. L.150 J.D. 507 Eastline Dr.‡
Hagen, Melissa L. '64 '90 C.383 B.S. L.608 J.D.
(adm. in GA; not adm. in OH) 31 Crawford St.★
Hallee, Michael J. ... '69 '02 C.1248 B.S. L.201 J.D. [Ⓐ Casper&C.]
Haugen, Halver H. ... '31 '68 C.208 B.S.B.A. L.1340 J.D. 613 Regent Dr.‡
Herr, John W., (BV) ... '41 '66 C.201 B.A. L.150 J.D. 2 N. Main St.
Hicks, Lawrence W. ... '40 '72 C.336 B.S.M.E. L.276 J.D. Armco, Inc.
Hildreth, Gary R. ... '38 '63 C.347 B.S. L.1119 J.D. Armco, Inc.
Hoyt, Lawrence K. ... '57 '86 C.178 B.S. L.208 J.D. A K Steel Corp
Hritz, John G. ... '54 '85 C.980 B.S. L.7 J.D. Asst. Gen. Coun., AK Steel Corp.

Imhoff, Don, Jr., (BV) '47 '72 C&L.150 B.A., J.D.
2 North Main Street, Suite 603, 45042-1975
Telephone: 513-423-3462 Fax: 513-422-5141
Wills and Probate, Estate Planning, Real Estate, Corporation Law, Business Law, Bankruptcy, Creditor and Debtor Rights and Collections, Real Estate Foreclosures, Evictions.
Co-Counsel For: American Savings & Loan Assn.
Representative Clients: Commercial Realty Co.; City of Middletown; Beneficial Finance.
Agents For: Chicago Title Insurance Co.; Ohio Bar Title Insurance Co.
Approved Attorneys For: Lawyers Title Insurance Corp.; Ohio Bar Title Insurance Corp.
See Professional Biographies, MIDDLETOWN, OHIO

Ingram, Robert Alan, (CV) ... '55 '79 C.473 B.A. L.608 J.D. 2211 Central Avenue
Kabakoff, Ronald M., (BV) ... '51 '77 C.150 B.A. L.1340 J.D. [Casper&C.]
Kash, Kevin, (CV) ... '56 '82 C.473 B.S. L.201 J.D. 1440 S. Breiel Boulevard, Suite A
Kaup, Gary H., (BV) ... '43 '67 C.973 B.S. L.602 LL.B. 2 N. Main St., Ste. 703
Kipp, Frank S. '45 '75 C.477 B.A. L.1294 J.D.
(adm. in MI; not adm. in OH) V.P., Aeronca Inc.
Kowalski, Susan Michele ... '67 '98 C.381 B.S. L.1340 J.D. Dist. Ct. of Appeals
Landen, Leslie S., (BV) ... '52 '79 C.473 B.S. L.200 J.D. City Law Dir.

Lazarow, Jeffrey W. '52 '77 C&L.861 B.A., J.D. Pres. & CEO, Rogers Ltd., Inc.
Lord, Mary C., (BV) '23 '51 C.631 B.A. L.608 J.D. 2120 Central Avenue
Martinez, Lisa Ann '55 '91
C.523 B.S. L.150 J.D. Middletown Reg. Hosp. & Healthcare Sys.
Matejkovic, Joseph R., (BV) '65 '91
C&L.608 B.A., J.D. First Natl. Bnk. Bldg., 2 N. Main St.
McCausland, Patrick Edward '72 '98 C.97 B.S. L.150 J.D. [Ⓐ Pratt,S.&T.]
McCollum, Margaret Halnon, (BV) '51 '92 C.473 B.A. L.608 J.D. [Casper&C.]
Milbauer, Jeffrey K., (CV) '55 '81 C.138 B.A. L.608 J.D. 2907 Orlando Avenue
Moody, LoVeen J. '46 '84 C.959 B.A. L.477 J.D.
(adm. in MI; not adm. in OH) Armco, Inc.
Newlin, Joseph E. '43 '68 C.967 A.B. L.930 J.D. 1701 S. Breiel Blvd.
O'Connor, John P. '63 '90 C.473 B.S. L.150 J.D. Labor Coun., AK Steel Corporation
Partin, Robin R. '69 '95 C.967 B.A. L.608 J.D. [Ⓐ Casper&C.]

Pickrel, Schaeffer & Ebeling
(See Dayton)

Powell, Stephen Walter '55 '81 C.313 B.A. L.200 J.D. Ct. of Appeals
Pratt, Gregory K., (BV) '52 '77 C.607 B.A. L.608 J.D. [Pratt,S.&T.]
Pratt, Singer & Thomas Co., L.P.A., (BV) 301 N. Breiel Blvd.
Preheim, Randall F. '46 '74 C.791 B.S. L.378 J.D.
(adm. in KS; not adm. in OH) V.P., Gen. Coun. & Secy., AK Steel Corp.
Rathman, William E., (AV) '27 '52 C.385 L.608 1081 N. University Blvd.‡
Repper, Theodore, Jr., (BV) '27 '55 C.473 A.B. L.930 LL.B. 201 S. Main St.
Richards, Megan, (BV) '57 '83 C.608 B.A. L.150 J.D. [Casper&C.]
Robertson, Charles S. '34 '95 C.032 B.S. L.201 J.D. P.O. Box 948
Ross, Fred, (BV) '26 '51 C.665 B.A. L.150 J.D. Suite 505
Sanzone, Vincent A., (BV) '48 '75 C.608 B.S. L.150 J.D. [Bryant&S.]
Schaefer, Edward B. '72 '01 C&L.1208 B.A., J.D. [Ⓐ Combs&S.]
Schaefer, Gene E., (BV) '39 '64 C.608 B.S. L.150 J.D. [Combs&S.]
Scholler, W. Joseph '75 '00 C.473 B.A. L.201 J.D. [Ⓐ Frost B.T.]
Schultz, Ronald E., (AV) '42 '67 C.610 B.S. L.608 J.D.
[Dyer,G.M.&S.] (⊙Bellefontaine, Dayton, Huber Heights, Lima, Piqua, Springfield)
Schwartz, Peter J. '50 '76 C.861 B.A. L.472 J.D. Gen. Coun., The Rogers Jewelry Co.
Sherron, James E., (BV) '60 '86 C.473 B.A. L.201 J.D. 2226 Central Ave.
Shew, J. C., (BV) '44 '69 C.970 B.A. L.8 J.D. 16 N. Main St.
Singer, Andrew N., (BV) '46 '74 C.473 B.S. L.1340 J.D. 301 N. Breiel Blvd.
Sisson, Vincent A. '20 '48 C.62 A.B. L.150 LL.B. 1301 Reynolds St.‡
Smith, James C., (CV) '58 '84 C.150 B.S.B.A. L.607 J.D. 4000 Roosevelt Boulevard
Strady, Barbara L., (BV) '65 '91 C.20 B.A. L.201 J.D. [Casper&C.]
Strand, Sheldon A., (BV) '32 '75 C.494 B.A. L.1340 J.D. 1 City Centre Plaza
Summers, Mark A., (BV) '56 '85 C.545 B.A. L.150 J.D. [Casper&C.]
Swope, Thomas A., (BV) '48 '73 C.363 A.B. L.767 J.D. [Frost B.T.]
Terhune, Charles P., Jr. '48 '78 C.1111 B.S. L.809 J.D. 2906 Rusmar Ct.
Thomas, Bruce M. '24 '52 C.188 B.M.E. L.904 J.D.
(adm. in DC; not adm. in OH) 4201 Fisher Ave.‡
Thurman, Thomas D. '46 '75 C.1042 B.S. L.851 J.D. Armco, Inc.
Valen, Anthony '32 '60 C.902 B.A. L.150 J.D. Ct. of App. J.

Waite, Schneider, Bayless & Chesley Co., L.P.A.
(See Cincinnati)

Wall, Mark W., (BV) '46 '73 C.473 B.A. L.150 J.D. Mun. J.
Walsh, James E. '33 '66 C.999 B.S. L.1340 J.D. Mun. Judge
Washienko, Theodore, Jr. '64 '90 C&L.347 B.S., J.D. Law Clk. to Ct. App. J.
Weinrich, Lancer R., Jr., (BV) '45 '72 C.473 B.A. L.607 J.D.
2 N. Main Street, Suite 304
Whittington, John A., (BV) '51 '77 C.608 B.A. L.851 J.D. 2 N. Main St.
Wilkinson, Rebecca L. '58 '83 C.249 B.S. L.347 J.D. [Casper&C.] (⊙Cincinnati)
Wilmer, Richard A., (AV) '17 '47 C.188 A.B. L.150 J.D. 200 Fifth Third Office Bldg.
Winans, Stacy Anne '74 '00
C.210 B.A. L.200 J.D. 1 North Main Street, 5th and 6th Floors
Winiger, Tammy Goebel '69 '94 C.383 B.B.A. L.1340 J.D. Jud. Law Clk., Ct. of App.
Young, William W. '37 '61 C.473 L.1340 J.D. Ct. of App. J.

MILAN, 1,445, *Erie & Huron Cos.*

Huber, Richard R. '27 '55 C.608 B.A. L.188 J.D. 11 W. Church Street
Ruffing, Vickie B., (BV) '55 '81 C.207 B.A. L.851 J.D. 16 W. Church St.
Strickler, Randal L., (BV) '60 '86 C.473 B.A. L.1003 J.D. [R.L.Strickler]
Strickler, Randal L., Co., L.P.A., (BV) 16 West Church Street
Vitaz, Heather Trueman '72 '97 C.8 B.A. L.851 J.D. [H.T.Vitaz]
Vitaz, Heather Trueman, Co., LPA 16 W. Church Street

MILFORD, 6,284, *Clermont Co.*

Anderson, Isaac L., III '62 '88 C.150 B.A. L.190 J.D. 1157 State Route 131
Boller, W. Steven '42 '68 C.610 A.B. L.1340 LL.B. 405 Mill St.‡
Buschbacher, Michael, (BV) '45 '73 C.150 B.A. L.1340 J.D. 1019 Main St.
Calderhead, David C., (AV) '61 '87 C.827 B.A. L.1003 J.D.
[Calderhead] & [TrionaC.&L.] (⊙Cincinnati, Milford)
Calderhead, David C., (AV) '61 '87
C.827 B.A. L.1003 J.D. [Triona C.&L.] (⊙Cincinnati, Milford)
Calderhead Law Office, LLC, (AV) 200 TechneCenter Drive, Suite 100
Cassidy, Michael W., (CV) '53 '84 C.150 B.A. L.117 J.D. 19 Water St.
Cloud, Robert L., (BV) '43 '76 C.424 B.A. L.1340 J.D. 2646 Blackhoof Trl.
Condit, Thomas W., (BV) '56 '89 C.929 B.A. L.150 J.D. P.O. Box 275
Conradi, Lesley M. '60 '86 C.150 B.B.A. L.902 J.D. 727 Alpine Dr.
Crowe, Stephen C., (BV) '50 '76 C.150 B.A. L.1340 J.D. [Crowe&W.]
Crowe & Welch, (BV) 1019 Main St.
Dooley, Lloyd D., (BV) '38 '66 C.952 B.S. L.1340 J.D. 1120 State Route 131, Ste. C
Douglas, Flach, (BV) '31 '57 C&L.150 A.B., LL.B. [F.Douglas] (⊙Cincinnati)
Douglas, Flach, & Co., LPA, (BV) 114 Main Street
Eckerson, Mark D., (BV) '51 '77 C.150 B.A. L.1340 J.D. One Crestview Dr.
Hall, Suzy T. '55 '80 C.385 A.B. L.945 J.D.
(adm. in VA; not adm. in OH) 773 Twin Fox Dr.‡
Hercl, Daniel P. '64 '97 C.801 B.A. L.608 J.D. Coun., Advanced Distribution Sys.
Hoseus, Edwin L., Jr., (CV) '47 '74 C.973 B.S. L.1340 J.D. 741 Milford Hills Dr.
Kichler, David Alton '65 '90 C.231 B.A. L.851 J.D. [D.A.Kichler]
Kichler, David A. 714 Beechwood Ln.
Marcin, Edward W. '71 '97 C.1494 B.A. L.201 J.D. [Marcin&M.]
Marcin, Melissa A. '72 '98 C.611 B.A. L.201 J.D. [Marcin&M.]
Marcin & Marcin 931 State Route 28, Ste. 309
Marler, K. A., (CV) '42 '82 C&L.150 B.A., J.D. 1201 Sorrel Lane
Martin, C. Richard '62 '96 C.150 B.S. L.1161 J.D. [Ⓢ F.Douglas]
Mason, Ronald A., (CV) '57 '85 C.510 B.A. L.150 J.D. 110 Main St.
Masterson, Michael E., (CV) '65 '93 C&L.201 B.S., J.D. 1019 Main St.
McCune, David S., (BV) '53 '79 C.138 B.A. L.851 J.D. 626 Main St.
Minniear, Michael, Law Office, (BV) '48 '73 C.473 A.B. L.150 J.D. 626 Main St.
Nelson, Barry E., Law Offices of '57 '84 C.1161 B.S. L.880 J.D. 575 Chamber Drive
Plank, Kevin D., (BV) '54 '79 C.49 B.S.B.A. L.607 J.D. 741 Milford Hills Dr.
Reynolds, William J., Law Offices of '54 '93
C.150 B.S. L.1340 J.D. 5772 Observation Court
Riley, Michael J., Law Office of '48 '83 C.608 B.A. L.201 J.D. 5854 Cinema Dr.
Rosenwald, Sharon B. '52 '82 C.150 B.S. L.1340 J.D. 1 Crestview Dr.
Schilling, William H. '49 '75 C.150 B.S. L.1340 J.D. 5714 Signal Hill St.
Schmieg, Michael M., (BV) '47 '78 C&L.150 B.A., J.D. 110 Main St.
Schneebeck, Robert W. '33 '58 C.473 B.S. L.150 LL.B. 1700 Edison Dr.‡
Staley, James A., (BV) '47 '76 C.1334 B.A. L.851 J.D. [J.A.Staley]
Staley, James A., Co., L.P.A., (BV) One Crestview Drive
Thaxton, James E. '63 '88 C.201 B.A. L.150 J.D.
Vice President, Business Affairs & Counsel, Gibson Greetings, Inc.
Thomson, Douglas W., (BV) '53 '78
C.880 B.A. L.607 J.D. 400 Technecenter Dr., Ste. 400
Triona Calderhead & Lockemeyer, (AV)
200 TechneCenter Drive, Suite 100 (⊙Cincinnati)
Van Pelt, Jeanne A. '49 '97 C&L.150 B.A., J.D. [VanPelt]
Van Pelt Law Offices P.O. Box 773
Van Pelt-Kurtz, Marcia L. '56 '81 C&L.150 B.A., J.D. 5648 Willnean Dr.★
Vollman, Norman E. '49 '75 C.973 A.B. L.1340 J.D. 5829 Jeb Stuart Dr.
Ward, Marcia A., (BV) '46 '78 C.608 B.A. L.1340 J.D. 741 Milford Hills Dr., Ste. C
Welch, Robert H., Jr., (BV) '49 '76 C.693 B.S. L.1340 J.D. [Crowe&W.]
Zimmerman, Elizabeth W. '68 '92 C&L.930 B.A., J.D. 400 Technecenter Drive

MILFORD CENTER, 651, *Union Co.*

Shanklin, Charles E., (AV) '29 '53 C.97 B.A. L.608 J.D. 1091 N. McMahill Rd.‡

MILLERSBURG, * 3,326, *Holmes Co.*

Baserman, Mark W., Sr., (BV) '53 '78 C.117 B.A. L.1003 J.D. [Baserman]
Baserman Law Office, (BV) 45 South Monroe Street
Bower, Blair A., (CV) '52 '89 C.608 B.S. L.1339 J.D. 111 S. Washington St.
Corcoran, Maureen A. '57 '86 C.385 B.A. L.608 J.D. 138A E. Jackson St.

Critchfield, Critchfield & Johnston, Ltd., (AV)
138 E. Jackson Street, 44654 ⊙
Telephone: 330-674-3055 Telecopier: 330-674-4469
URL: http://www.ccj.com
John R. Waltman; Daniel L. Mathie; Steven J. Shrock; Garrett M. Roach; Mark E. Leininger;—Sean M. Warner.
General Practice in all Courts. Business, Corporate Law, Insurance, Estate Planning, Wills and Probate, Labor and Employment, ERISA, Health Care, Environmental Law, Workers Compensation, Banking, Taxation, Antitrust and Trade Regulation, Oil and Gas Law, Litigation, Debtor and Creditor, Municipal Law, School Law, Real Estate, Commercial Law, Construction Law.
General Counsel for: The Commercial & Savings Bank; Shreiner Sole Co., Inc.; Holmes-Wayne Rural Electric Co-op.
Local Counsel for: Nationwide Insurance Co.; State Automobile Mutual Insurance Co.
Wooster, Ohio: 225 North Market Street, P.O. Box 599, 44691-0599. Telephone: 330-264-4444.
Mt. Vernon, Ohio: 10 South Gay Street, 43050-3546. Telephone: 740-397-4040.
Medina, Ohio: 3985 Medina Road, Suite 100, 44256. Telephone: 330-723-6404.
See Professional Biographies, MILLERSBURG, OHIO

Dailey, Stephen Paul '52 '80 C&L.608 B.A., J.D. 225 E. Jackson St.
Douglas, Thomas C., (CV) '46 '74 C.610 B.S. L.347 J.D. 5820 State Route 241
Gindlesberger, Thomas D., (BV) '26 '55 C.608 B.S. L.266 LL.B. 127 E. Adams St.
Hines, Robert B., (CV) '51 '76 C.602 B.A. L.851 J.D. 19 W. Jackson St.
Holtzmann, Cassandra Ann '64 '99
C.161 B.A. L.7 J.D. Holmes Co. Dept. of Job & Family Srvcs.
Irving, Jane Ellen, (BV) '47 '72 C.97 B.S. L.608 J.D. Co. J.
Knowling, Stephen D., (BV) '49 '75 C.966 B.S. L.930 J.D.
Asst. Co. Pros. [Rinfret&K.]
Lang, Kimberly A. '69 '98 C.608 B.A. L.117 J.D. [Ⓐ Miller&M.]
Leininger, Mark E., (CV) '69 '95 C.49 B.S. L.1003 J.D. [Critchfield,C.&J.]

Logee, Hostetler, Stutzman & Lehman, LLC
(See Wooster)

Mason, Grant A., (CV) '65 '94 C.970 B.A. L.117 J.D. [Ⓐ Miller&M.]
Mast, Diane Stromme, (BV) '52 '81 C.970 B.A. L.7 J.D. [Miller&M.]
Mathie, Daniel L., (BV) '58 '83 C&L.607 B.S., J.D. [Critchfield,C.&J.]
Miller, Max A., (BV) '56 '81 C.49 B.A. L.228 J.D. [Miller&M.]
Miller, Paul A., (CV) '42 '72 C.999 B.A. L.8 J.D. 5797 Township Road
Miller & Mast, Ltd., (BV) 88 South Monroe Street
Rinfret, Robert D., (BV) '46 '72 C.81 B.A. L.608 J.D. Co. Pros. Atty. [Rinfret&K.]
Rinfret & Knowling, (BV) 184 E. Jackson St.
Roach, Garrett M., (BV) '67 '92 C.610 B.S. L.1003 J.D. [Critchfield,C.&J.]
Schmid, Laurel J., (BV) '52 '76 C.882 B.A. L.851 J.D. P.O. Box 268
Schuler, John W. '18 '50 C&L.608 B.S., J.D. 138 E. Jackson St.‡
Shrock, Steven J., (BV) '68 '92 C.970 B.A. L.494 J.D. [Critchfield,C.&J.]
Steimel, Samuel M., (BV) '57 '83 C.970 B.A. L.851 J.D. [Steimel]

Steimel Law Office, (BV)
111 South Clay Street, 44654-1307
Telephone: 330-674-0001 Fax: 330-674-3985
Email: smslaw@valkyrie.net URL: http://www.lawyers.com/steimellawoffice
Samuel M. Steimel.
General Civil Practice in all State and Federal Courts. Commercial, Corporate, Oil and Gas, Real Estate, Probate and Estate Planning, Banking Law.
Representative Clients: Rustic Realty, Inc.; SMS Leasing; Tall Timber Industries; Hill Drilling, Inc.; Charm Center Corp.; Holmes Cheese Co.
Approved Attorney for: Farm Credit Services.
See Professional Biographies, MILLERSBURG, OHIO

Waltman, John R., (AV) '42 '70 C.532 B.A. L.607 J.D. [Critchfield,C.&J.]
Warner, Sean M. '76 '02 C&L.608 B.A., J.D. [Ⓐ Critchfield,C.&J.]
White, Thomas D., (BV) '55 '81 C&L.608 B.A., J.D. Com. Pleas J.

MILLERSPORT, 1,010, *Fairfield Co.*

Roland, Christian D., (CV) '63 '90 C.107 B.A. L.117 J.D. 4431 N. Bank Rd.

MINERAL CITY, 841, *Tuscarawas Co.*

Johnston, Jos W. '21 '49 C&L.930 B.S., J.D. 3543 Anchor Lane, N.E.‡

MINERAL RIDGE, 3,900, *Mahoning & Trumbull Cos.*

Hudzik, John C., (CV) '56 '83 C.980 B.S.B.A. L.7 J.D. 1752 Salt Springs Rd.
Polanski, Stanley J., (BV) '21 '48 C.610 A.B. L.150 LL.B. 3742 Niles-carner Rd.

MINERVA, 3,934, *Carroll, Columbiana & Stark Cos.*

Baker, Marjorie H. '47 '80 C.1260 B.A. L.7 J.D. 1437 Bellflower Rd. N.E.
Battista, Clark E., (BV) '57 '83 C.473 B.S. L.608 J.D. [Battista&B.]

Battista, Rudolph E., (BV) ....'24 '51 C.381 B.S. L.608 J.D. [Battista&B.]
Battista & Battista, Co., L.P.A., (BV) ....211 N. Market St.
Chaddock, Susan Clark ....'71 '97 C.528 B.A. L.117 J.D. 201 N. Market St.
Clark, Luther J., Jr., (BV) ....'27 '56 C.532 B.A. L.948 LL.B. 201 N. Market St.
Clark, Robert A., (CV) ....'65 '91 C.532 B.A. L.117 J.D. 201 N. Market St.
Martin, Jack E., (BV) ....'54 '80 C.528 B.A. L.7 J.D. 200 N. Main
Martin, Robert D. ....'37 '69 C.610 B.A. L.7 J.D. 850 McDaniel Ave.
Oberholtzer, Kim R., (BV) ....'55 '87 C.381 B.G.S. L.7 J.D. 1055 Bellflower, N.W.

MINFORD, —, *Scioto Co.*

Wrage, Eric Andrew ....'69 '99 C.610 B.A. L.862 J.D. [E.A.Wrage]
Wrage, Eric A. ....564 Bull Run Road

MINSTER, 2,794, *Auglaize Co.*

Bernhold, James A., Attorney At Law, (BV) '46 '72
C&L.215 B.S., J.D. 12 Eagle Dr., Ste. B
Henkener, Roger J. ....'22 '49 C&L.608 B.A., J.D. 14 S. Hanover St.‡
Jauert, Douglas S., (BV) ....'45 '72 C&L.608 B.A., J.D. [Weger J.&H.] ⊙
Weger, James E., (AV) ....'24 '51 C&L.608 J.D. [Weger J.&H.]
Weger Jauert & Herman LLP, (AV) ....112 W. 4th St. (⊙Wapakoneta)

MOGADORE, 3,893, *Portage & Summit Cos.*

Bronstrup, Charles Lewis, II ....'31 '88 C.930 Ph.D. L.7 J.D. 1186 Shenk Rd.
Brooks, Richard R. ....'57 '86 C.608 B.A. L.8 J.D. [R.Brooks]
Brooks, Richard ....3808 Mogadore Rd.
Pry, Russell M., (BV) ....'58 '84 C.381 B.A. L.7 J.D. 86 S. Cleveland Ave.
Ziga, Timothy P., Sr., (BV) ....'50 '83 C.8 B.A. L.7 J.D. ASW Services Inc.

MONCLOVA, 4,285, *Lucas Co.*

Ochu, Ann M. ....'48 '83 C.97 B.S.E. L.851 J.D. 4349 S. Eber Rd.
Webb, Thomas I., (AV) ....'27 '51 C.951 L.608 J.D. 7720 Monclova Rd.
Zoltanski, Edward F., (BV) ....'26 '58 C.688 B.S.E.E. L.851 LL.B. P.O. Box 84

MONROE, 7,133, *Butler Co.*

Altiere, James N., III, (CV) '63 '90 C.608 B.S.B.A. L.851 J.D.
Corp. Coun., Professional Corps. Mgmt. Co., Inc.
Baron & Budd, A Professional Corporation, (AV⊤)
43B New Garver Road (⊙Glen Carbon, IL; Baton Rouge, LA; Cleve., OH; Dallas, TX)
Hendrickson, Robert Allen, (BV) ....'59 '84 C.150 B.A. L.117 J.D. 110 Old St.
Hendrickson, Wm. R. ....'26 '52 C.201 B.A. L.150 J.D. Ret. Ct. of App. J.
Nelson, Theresa Lynn ....'75 '00 C.610 B.A. L.150 J.D. [Baron&B.]

MONROEVILLE, 1,433, *Huron Co.*

Rathbun, Timothy J. '63 '89 C.97 B.S.B.A. L.930 J.D.
Vice President - Administrative & Legal Affairs, Venture Packaging, Inc.

MONTGOMERY, 10,163, *Hamilton Co.*

Immerman, Harvey A., (BV) ....'25 '50 C&L.150 LL.B. 10823 Montgomery Rd.
Johns, James S. ....'33 '59 C.388 B.A. L.861 LL.B. [J.Johns]
Johns, James ....9400 Main St.
McCarthy, Dennis Kevin ....'41 '73 C.150 B.A. L.1340 J.D. [D.K.McCarthy]
McCarthy, Dennis K. ....7800 Cooper Rd., Ste. 201
Payne, Thomas F. ....'47 '91 C.602 A.B. L.880 J.D. 9726 Delray Dr.
Rozic, Stanley W. ....'24 '54 C.473 B.S. L.1340 LL.B. 9423 Montgomery Rd.
Schulzinger, Edward, (BV) ....'17 '47 C&L.150 B.A., LL.B. 10823 Montgomery Rd.

MONTPELIER, 4,299, *Williams Co.*

Bechtol, Denver G., (BV) ....'52 '77 C.317 A.B. L.851 J.D. P.O. Box 313
Newcomer, Shaffer & Spangler, (AV) ....104 Empire St. (⊙Bryan)
Spangler, Michael W., (BV) ....'59 '86 C.395 B.A. L.790 J.D. [Newcomer,S.&S.] ⊙

MORELAND HILLS, 3,354, *Cuyahoga Co.*

Bell, Helen M. ....'56 '89 C.161 B.A. L.930 J.D. 31870 Hiram Trail
Burns, Stephen J., (AV) ....'29 '57 C&L.262 B.S., LL.B. 55 Windrush
Cooley, Peter W. '59 '84 C.188 B.S. L.362 J.D.
(adm. in PA; not adm. in OH) 135 Meadowhill Lane
Groetzinger, Jon, Jr., Law Offices of, (AV) '49 '74
C.478 A.B. L.188 J.D. 37455 Miles Road
Kinchen, Gilbert H., (AV) '27 '55 C.930 A.B. L.1003 LL.B.
35250 South Woodland Road
Lang, Charles Victor, (AV) ....'62 '88 C.659 B.A. L.178 J.D. [Langs]
Langs, (AV) ....3800 Chagrin River Road
Rowlinson, David W., (AV) ....'27 '52 C.20 A.B. L.477 J.D. 70 Greentree Rd.‡
Trimble, David L. ....'56 '90 C.929 B.S. L.1003 J.D. 150 Hunting Trail
Wolstein, Bertram L., (BV) ....'27 '53 C.930 L.161 J.D. 34555 Chagrin Blvd.
Wuliger, Timothy F., (AV) ....'51 '76 C.1365 B.A. L.276 J.D. 20 Basswood Lane

MORRAL, 373, *Marion Co.*

Washburn, Dean R., (CV) ....'46 '75 C.97 B.S. L.117 J.D. P.O. Box 92

MT. GILEAD, * 3,290, *Morrow Co.*

Brown, Bemiller, Murray, McIntyre, Vetter & Heck, L.L.P.
(See Mansfield)

Calig & Handelman, LPA
(See Columbus)

Curl, Dean E. ....'37 '64 C.207 B.A. L.150 J.D. Ret. Com. Pleas J.‡
Elkin, Tom C., (BV) ....'58 '83 C.608 B.S. L.150 J.D. [T.C.Elkin]
Elkin, Tom C., Company, LPA, (BV) ....19 E. High St.
Hildebrand, Dale, (BV) ....'26 '52 C&L.607 J.D. [Hildebrand&W.]
Hildebrand & Wick, (BV) ....23 E. High St.
Howland, Charles S., (CV) .....'53 '83 C.528 B.A. L.117 J.D. The Morrow Co. Pros. Off.
Howland, Hollis, (CV) ....'55 '85 C.528 B.A. L.608 J.D. [Howland]
Howland Law Firm, (CV) ....58 N. Main St.
McClelland, Lee W., (BV) ....'47 '74 C.97 B.A. L.930 J.D. Co. J.
McClelland, Shawn Robert ....'75 '01 C.282 B.A. L.930 J.D. [McClelland]
McClelland Law Offices ....15 South Main Street

Oliver Law Office
(See Columbus)

Perry, Gregory Alan ....'70 '95 C.97 B.S. L.200 J.D. Pros. Atty, Morrow Co.
Smith, James R., II ....'63 '90 C.437 B.B.A. L.117 J.D. Asst. Pros. Atty.
Steiger, Amy ....'73 '00 C.347 B.A. L.179 J.D. Asst. Pros.
Wick, Donald K., (BV) ....'57 '83 C&L.607 B.A., J.D. [Hildebrand&W.]

MT. HEALTHY, 7,149, *Hamilton Co.*

Cossaboom, Ewing O., (AV) ....'17 '41 C.853 A.B. L.150 J.D. 1622 Kemper Ave.

MT. HOPE, —, *Holmes Co.*

Wolf, Donald D., (CV) ... '50 '77 C.970 B.A. L.607 J.D. Legal Mgr., Wayne-Dalton Corp.

MT. ORAB, 2,307, *Brown Co.*

Houser, John B. (Ben), (BV) ....'41 '71 C.473 B.S.Ed. L.150 J.D. 221 S. High St.
Kelly, Michael P., (AV) ....'43 '73 C.745 B.A. L.1340 J.D. 108 S High St
Kelly, Timothy J., (BV) ....'51 '91 C.184 B.A. L.1340 J.D. P.O. Box 3740
Lewis, Val Eugene ....'72 '99 C.150 B.A. L.1161 J.D. 108 S. High St.
Potts, Cecelia J., (BV) ....'49 '86 C.150 B.A. L.1340 J.D. P.O. Box 474
Wallace, Bruce Sanford, (BV) ....'58 '83 C&L.150 B.B.A., J.D. 108 S. High St.

MT. STERLING, 1,865, *Madison Co.*

Baynes, Gerald T., (AV) '36 '64 C.575 B.S. L.608 J.D.
16 North Market Street, P.O. Box 147, 43143-0147
Telephone: 740-869-2393; Columbus Direct Line: 614-877-9191 Fax: 740-869-2960
General Civil Practice. Probate, Real Estate, Taxation, Family and Corporate Law. Trials.
Representative Clients: First National Bank of New Holland; Ohio Willow Wood Co.

Brooks, L. Steven ....'55 '87 C.878 B.S. L.101 J.D. 23 East Columbus Street

MT. VERNON, * 14,375, *Knox Co.*

Aebi, John W., (AV⊤) ....'52 '78 C.589 B.S. L.61 J.D. [Aebi]

Aebi Law Firm, (AV⊤)
111 South Mulberry, 43050
Telephone: 740-397-8875 Fax: 740-393-0781
John W. Aebi.
Personal Injury, Civil Litigation, Criminal Law, Estate Planning, Probate, Social Security Disability.
See Professional Biographies, MT. VERNON, OHIO

Alden, Noel B. ....'68 '96 C.188 B.S. L.608 J.D. [Zelkowitz,B.&C.]
Ayers, Charles W. ....'22 '50 C.385 A.B. L.930 LL.B. Ret. Com. Pleas J.
Baker, John W., (BV) ....'56 '81 C.207 B.A. L.117 J.D. Pros. Atty.

Calesaric, Robert E., Attorney at Law
(See Newark)

Calig & Handelman, LPA
(See Columbus)

Colley Shroyer & Abraham Co., L.P.A.
(See Columbus)

Critchfield, Critchfield & Johnston, Ltd., (AV)
10 South Gay Street, 43050-3546 ⊙
Telephone: 740-397-4040 Telecopier: 740-397-6775
URL: http://www.ccj.com
Kim M. Rose; Laura A. Wakefield;—James R. Norris; Kathy L. Swihart; Adam B. Landon. Of Counsel: Richard F. Ritter.
General Practice in all Courts. Business, Corporate Law, Insurance, Estate Planning, Wills and Probate, Labor and Employment, ERISA, Health Care, Environmental Law, Workers Compensation, Banking, Taxation, Antitrust and Trade Regulation, Oil and Gas Law, Litigation, Debtor and Creditor, Municipal Law, School Law, Real Estate, Commercial Law, Construction Law.
Representative Clients: Rubbermaid Inc.; Wooster Brush Co.; The College of Wooster; Bank One of Akron, N.A.; First Federal Savings & Loan Association of Wooster; Sandy Supply Co.; Buehler Food Markets, Inc.; Wayne Dalton Corp.; Ohio Packaging Corporation.
Wooster, Ohio: 225 North Market Street, P.O. Box 599, 44691-0599. Telephone: 330-264-4444.
Millersburg, Ohio: 138 E. Jackson Street, 44654. Telephone: 330-674-3055.
Medina, Ohio: 3985 Medina Road, Suite 100, 44256. Telephone: 330-723-6404.
See Professional Biographies, MT. VERNON, OHIO

Cullers, James J., (AV) ....'30 '59 C.610 B.S.C. L.608 J.D. [Zelkowitz,B.&C.]
Eyster, Otho ....'43 '75 C&L.608 B.F.A., J.D. Com. Pleas J.

Farlow & Associates LLC
(See Dublin)

Febus, Charles Elwood ....'61 '94 C.608 B.A. L.179 J.D. 120 1/2 East High Street
Folland, Robert F., (CV) ....'37 '66 C.473 B.S. L.607 J.D. 112 N. Main Street
Fowler, Wendi M. ....'72 '01 C.231 B.A. L.124 J.D. [⊠ Zelkowitz,B.&C.]
Giles, James A., (BV) ....'56 '81 C.385 B.A. L.608 J.D. 109 E. High Street
Grindle, Larry J., (AV) ....'61 '86 C.49 B.S.B.A. L.930 J.D. [Zelkowitz,B.&C.]
Johnson, Jonathan J., (BV) ....'64 '92 C.970 B.A. L.117 J.D. [⊠ McDevitt,M.&M.]
Kahrl, Clyde C., (CV) ....'55 '80 C.188 B.A. L.608 J.D. 236 S. Main Street
Kepko, William J. ....'45 '86 C.980 B.A. L.7 J.D. One E. Vine St.
Landon, Adam B. ....'75 '01 C.608 B.A. L.851 J.D. [⊠ Critchfield,C.&J.]
Lane, Kenneth E., (BV) ....'48 '78 C.608 B.A. L.117 J.D. P.O. Box 888
Lee, Robert D., (BV) ....'53 '79 C.608 B.A. L.117 J.D. 136 S. Main Street, Suite 200
Lehmkuhl, Phillip D., (AV) ....'51 '77 C.608 B.A. L.201 J.D. 100 North Main Street
Levering, Eileen B. '17 '41 C.494 A.B. L.174 LL.B.
(adm. in ND; not adm. in OH) 406 N. Main St.‡
Maiorino, Patricia Warren ....'50 '82 C.303 B.A. L.383 J.D. 5 N. Gay Street
Malek, Bruce J., (BV) ....'52 '77 C.49 B.A. L.851 J.D. [McDevitt,M.&M.]
Mayhew, Elaine ....'20 '43 C.607 L.608 J.D. 501 B E. Gambier St.‡
Mayhew, Fred E., (BV) ....'44 '70 C.381 B.A. L.607 J.D. [McDevitt,M.&M.]
McDevitt, Mayhew & Malek, L.P.A., (BV) ....1 Public Sq.
Murray, Richard B., (BV) ....'36 '77 C.608 B.A. L.117 J.D. 305 E. High St.
Norris, James R., (BV) ....'50 '76 C.608 B.S. L.117 J.D. [⊠ Critchfield,C.&J.]

Oliver Law Office
(See Columbus)

Plymale Partnership LLP, The
(See Columbus)

Pullins, Scott A. ....'68 '03 C.608 B.A. L.117 J.D. [S.A.Pullins]

Pullins, Scott A., Ltd., LPA
110 East Gambier Street Suite 5, P.O. Box 1186, 43050
Telephone: 740-392-3505
Email: scott@pullinslaw.com URL: http://www.pullinslaw.com
Scott A. Pullins.
Election and Campaign Finance Law, Non-Profit Law, Business Organizations, Civil Rights, Constitutional Law, Municipal Law and Local Government Law, General Practice, Zoning, Administrative Law, Asset Protection, Business Law, Collections, Computers and Software, Consumer Law, Contracts, Copyrights, Corporate Law, Libel, Slander and Defamation, Litigation, Probate, Trusts and Estates.
See Professional Biographies, MT. VERNON, OHIO

Railsback, David E., (AV) ....'42 '70 C.303 A.B. L.608 J.D. [Zelkowitz,B.&C.]
Ressing, T. Garrett ....'41 '66 C.532 B.A. L.607 J.D. 10 E. Vine St.
Ritter, Richard F., (BV) ....'41 '69 C.62 B.A. L.608 J.D. [⊡ Critchfield,C.&J.]
Ronk, James M. ....'46 '72 C.207 B.A. L.608 J.D. Prob. Juv. J.
Rose, Kim M., (BV) ....'56 '81 C.610 B.B.A. L.117 J.D. [Critchfield,C.&J.]
Rutherford, Leland R. ....'12 '35 C&L.608 LL.B. Ret. Ct. of App. J.
Schlemmer, Michael David, (BV) ....'49 '74 C.385 B.A. L.7 J.D. Staff Atty.
Smith, William D., (BV) ....'50 '75 C.967 B.A. L.607 J.D. City Law Dir.
Spurgeon, Paul E., Jr. ....'48 '76 C.608 B.S. L.117 J.D. Mun. Ct. J.

Stebbins, Carol G., (BV) .... '54 '81 C.813 B.A. L.893 J.D. [C.G.Stebbins]
Stebbins, Carol G., L.P.A., (BV) .... 118 East Gambier Street

Stumler, Rebecca J.
(See Columbus)

Swihart, Kathy L. .... '68 '96 C.999 B.A. L.179 J.D. [Ⓐ Critchfield,C.&J.]
Turner, Harry E., (BV) .... '27 '54 C.62 B.A. L.607 J.D. 118 E. High Street

Twyford & Donahey, P.L.L.
(See Columbus)

Wakefield, Laura A. .... '71 '97 C.201 B.A. L.930 J.D. [Critchfield,C.&J.]
Weston, Robert B., (BV) .... '46 '71 C.631 B.A. L.607 J.D. [Zelkowitz,B.&C.]
Williams, Jeffrey Clark, (CV) .... '52 '87 C.313 B.A. L.117 J.D. Mag.
Zanghi, Mark A. .... '54 '04 C.999 B.S. L.607 J.D. 1 Public Sq.

Zelkowitz, Barry & Cullers, Ltd., (AV)
121 East High Street, 43050
Telephone: 740-397-5262 Fax: 740-397-2682
URL: http://www.ZBCLaw.com
Members of Firm: James J. Cullers; David E. Railsback; Robert B. Weston; Larry J. Grindle; Noel B. Alden. Associate: Wendi M. Fowler.
General Civil Practice in all Courts. Corporation, Probate and Estate Planning, Real Estate, Commercial and Banking, Insurance and Oil and Gas Law. Trials and Appeals.
Representative Clients: The First-Knox National Bank of Mount Vernon; The Ohio Power Co.; Knox Community Hospital; Kenyon College; Cooper Industries; Columbia Gas of Ohio, Inc.; Weyerhaeusser Co.; Ariel Corp.; Wenco, Inc.
Approved Agents for: Ohio Bar Title Insurance Co.
See Professional Biographies, MT. VERNON, OHIO

MUNROE FALLS, 5,359, *Summit Co.*

Damicone, Mary T., (CV) .... '40 '92 C&L.8 B.A., J.D. 100 Ridge Side Ct.
McLeland, Joseph C., (BV) .... '27 '64 C&L.8 LL.B. 576 Willow Grove Dr.‡

NAPOLEON, * 9,318, *Henry Co.*

Altman, Richard L., (BV) .... '57 '83 C&L.851 B.S., J.D. P.O. Box 70
DelFavero, Christopher D. .... '69 '95 C.608 B.A. L.179 J.D. 614 N. Perry Street
Donovan, James, (AV) .... '27 '53 C&L.477 A.B., J.D. 609 N. Perry St.‡
Donovan, John, (BV) .... '57 '83 C.477 A.B. L.930 J.D. 609 N. Perry St.
Fisher, Richard A., (BV) .... '49 '74 C.97 B.S.B.A. L.608 J.D. [Hoeffel,F.H.&F.]
Gerken, Brent C. .... '55 '81 C.608 B.S. L.851 J.D. V.P., Gerken Paving, Inc.
Grahn, David M. .... '55 '90 C.203 B.S.C.J. L.851 J.D. City Law Dir.
Hanna, John H., (AV) .... '46 '72 C.608 B.A. L.851 J.D. [Hoeffel,F.H.&F.]
Hoeffel, Funkhouser, Hanna & Fisher, (AV) .... Corner Perry & Shelby St.
Lammy, James E. .... '33 '78 C.475 B.S. L.851 J.D. 1025 W. Clairmont‡
Lankenau, Jeffrey R., (BV) .... '60 '86 C.473 B.S. L.608 J.D. 105 W. Main St.
Lankenau, Ronald P., (AV) .... '33 '59 C.475 L.608 J.D. 105 W. Main St.‡
Laver, Gerald D., (BV) .... '56 '83 C.494 B.S. L.851 J.D. [Ⓐ Hoeffel,F.H.&F.]
Manahan, David A. .... '60 '87 C.97 B.S.B.A. L.608 J.D. P.O. Box 531
McColley, Denise Herman, (BV) ...... '53 '81 C.97 B.S. L.608 J.D. Mag., Com. Pleas Ct.
Meekison, David, (AV) .... '13 '36 C.309 L.608 LL.B. [Meekison]
Meekison, David F., (AV) .... '47 '72 C&L.602 A.B., J.D. [Meekison]

Meekison Law Firm, (AV)
123 West Washington Street, 43545-1739
Telephone: 419-592-6801 Fax: 419-592-6944
Members of Firm: David Meekison; David F. Meekison.
Divorce, Family Law, Personal Injury, Probate, Estate Planning, Wills and Real Estate.
See Professional Biographies, NAPOLEON, OHIO

Muehlfeld, Keith P. .... '51 '76 C.608 B.S. L.851 J.D. Com. Pleas J., Henry Co. Ct.
Peper, Edmund G., (AV) .... '29 '57 C.879 B.A. L.608 J.D. [Peper]
Peper Law Firm, (AV) .... 555 Monroe St.
Rogers, George C. .... '46 '74 C.610 B.S. L.608 J.D. 6884 State Route 110
Schnitkey, Mark D., (CV) .... '54 '84 C.608 B.S. L.851 J.D. 118 W. Washington

Snavely, Stephen K., Co., L.P.A.
(See Defiance)

Wesche, Michael J., (BV) .... '47 '73 C.207 B.A. L.930 J.D. 105 W. Main Street
Witt, A. Marlowe, (BV) .... '17 '46 C.97 L.607 J.D. 324 W. Washington St.
Witt, Barbara A. .... '20 '44 C.473 A.B. L.150 J.D. 324 W. Washington St.‡

NAVARRE, 1,440, *Stark Co.*

Bentzel, Todd H., (BV) .... '57 '83 C.381 B.A. L.7 J.D. 105 N. Main St.
Shedlarz, Robert J., (BV) .... '45 '73 C.569 B.A. L.602 J.D. 4 Wooster Street, N.E.

NELSONVILLE, 5,230, *Athens Co.*

Grey, Lawrence .... '40 '69 C.610 B.A. L.1003 J.D. Ret. Ct. of App. J.‡
Nolan, Michael, (BV) .... '43 '69 C.610 B.S.J. L.607 J.D. [M.Nolan]
Nolan, Michael, Co., LPA, (BV) .... 55 W. Washington Street

NEW ALBANY, 3,711, *Franklin Co.*

Blaugrund, Herbert & Martin, Incorporated
(See Dublin)

Bluestone, Charles L., Law Office of, (BV) '60 '87
C&L.705 B.A., J.D. 6530 W. Campus Oval, Ste. 300
Cohen, Lawrence H., (CV) .... '68 '97 C&L.608 B.S.B.A., J.D. [Demers&C.]
Cohen, Richard, (AVⓉ) '55 '80
C.107 B.S. L.7 J.D. Sr. V.P. & Mng. Dir., GCG, Legal Servs.
Demers & Cohen, LLC, (CV) .... 3 North High Street
Grimm, Patricia L. .... '49 '82 C.608 B.A. L.117 J.D. 6245 Evans Road
Jeffers, Kevin .... '58 '88 C.150 B.S. L.117 J.D. 220 Market St # 201

Kenney-Pfalzer, Susan
(See Columbus)

Mazzitti, M. Linda .... '— '82 C.929 B.A. L.7 J.D. V.P., The Garden City Group
Reed, Barry S. '— '81 C.911 B.A. L.128 J.D.
(adm. in PA; not adm. in OH) [Ⓒ Swartz]
Reusser, Carl A. .... '44 '91 C.645 B.S. L.989 J.D. P.O. Box 165
Roggenkamp, Richard D. '57 '82 C.473 B.S. L.608 J.D.
Asst. V.P., First Intercontinental Realty Corp.
Romick, Ina S. H. .... '44 '76 C.326 B.S. L.117 J.D. 3954 Baughman Grant

Shaw, Melissa J.
(See Gahanna)

Soska, Christine Vernard .... '69 '97 C.49 B.S. Ed. L.117 J.D. P.O. Box 398
Swartz, Dean E., (AVⓉ) .... '— '74 C.813 A.B. L.851 J.D. [Swartz]

Swartz Law Firm, The, (AVⓉ)
220 Market Street, Suite 208, 43054
Telephone: 614-775-5000 Fax: 614-775-1104

(This Listing Continued)

Swartz Law Firm, The (Continued)
Member of Firm: Dean E. Swartz. Of Counsel: Barry S. Reed (Not admitted in OH).
Personal Injury, Product Liability and Medical Negligence Litigation.
See Professional Biographies, NEW ALBANY, OHIO

NEWARK, * 46,279, *Licking Co.*

Albright, Mary M. .... '52 '97 C.201 B.A. L.117 J.D. [Reese,P.D.&M.]
Altmaier, Martin D., (AV) .... '— '67 C.228 A.B. L.608 J.D. [Morrow,G.&B.]
Anderson, Eric L. .... '63 '97 C.1273 B.A. L.117 J.D. Asst. Pros. Atty.
Baldwin, Craig R., (BV) .... '63 '92 C.610 B.S. L.117 J.D. [Jones,N.M.&H.]
Barrett, Thomas H., II, (BV) .... '60 '86 C.1154 B.A. L.477 J.D. P.O. Box 920
Beck, R. Stewart, (CV) .... '34 '63 C.473 A.B. L.266 J.D. 50 North Fourth Street
Becker, Robert L., (BV) .... '45 '74 C.610 A.B. L.117 J.D. 20 W. 2nd St., 4th Fl.

Benson, Michael E.
(See Columbus)

Berryhill, John C., (BV) .... '43 '70 C&L.608 B.S., J.D. P.O. Box 121
Branstool, W. David, (BV) .... '66 '94 C.608 B.A. L.117 J.D. [Jones,N.M.&H.]
Bunning, Karen J., (CV) .... '50 '77 C.970 B.A. L.608 J.D. 275 Upson Downs Rd.
Burkett, J. Kristin, (BV) .... '58 '90 C.608 B.A. L.117 J.D. [K.Burkett]
Burkett, Kristin, Law Offices of, (BV) .... 21 W. Church St., Ste. 21

Calesaric, Robert E., Attorney at Law, (CV) '66 '94 C.608 B.A. L.117 J.D.
35 S. Park Place Suite 201, 43055
Telephone: 740-345-6454 Fax: 740-345-0031 URL: http://www.Calesariclaw.com
Email: rcalesaric@Alltel.net URL: http://www.calesariclawfirm.com
Personal Injury, Wrongful Death, D.U.I., O.V.I., O.M.V.I. and Criminal Defense.
See Professional Biographies, NEWARK, OHIO

Calig & Handelman, LPA, (BV)
29 S. Park Place, 43055 ⊙
Telephone: 740-349-8581 Fax: 740-345-4101
URL: http://www.chohiolawyers.com
Robert B. Handelman.
Bankruptcy, Personal Injury, Probate, Real Estate, Social Security, Social Security Disability, Medical Malpractice, Wrongful Death, Civil Litigation, Domestic Relations Law.
Columbus, Ohio Office: 854 East Broad Street, 43205. Telephone: 614-252-4885; 1-800-633-5000.
Lancaster, Ohio Office: 204 N. Columbus Street, 43130. Telephone: 740-653-4400. Fax: 740-653-0037.
Marion, Ohio Office: 274 S. Main Street, 43302. Telephone: 740-375-5051.
See Professional Biographies, NEWARK, OHIO

Campbell, Thomas K., (BV) .... '46 '74 C.608 B.A. L.117 J.D. [Schaller,C.&U.]
Carnes, Carolyn J. .... '— '96 C&L.117 B.A., J.D. [Morrow,G.&B.]
Carter, Gregory Erwin, (CV) .... '60 '87 C.150 B.A. L.1003 J.D. 21 W. Church St.
Castner, Joseph F., (BV) .... '47 '80 C.610 B.B.A. L.117 J.D. 1 S. Park Pl.
Christiansen, Vicky M., (BV) .... '54 '79 C&L.117 B.A., J.D. [Christiansen&W.]
Christiansen and Wentworth, Co., L.P.A., (BV) .... 172 Hudson Avenue
Clovis, Siobhan R. .... '73 '98 C.608 B.A. L.124 J.D. [Ⓐ Reese,P.D.&M.]
Cooper, James R., (AV) .... '— '72 C.602 B.B.A. L.608 J.D. [Morrow,G.&B.]
Cooper, Timothy M. .... '— '98 C.602 B.A. L.851 J.D. [Morrow,G.&B.]
Crawford, J. Andrew, (BV) .... '56 '81 C.491 B.A. L.347 J.D. [Reese,P.D.&M.]
Donahey, Richard S., (BV) .... '41 '68 C&L.608 B.C.E., J.D. [Twyford&D.] ⊙
Dove, Dennis E., (BV) .... '59 '91 C.608 B.S. L.117 J.D. 20 South Second Street
Drake, Robert N., (AV) .... '47 '72 C.970 B.A. L.477 J.D. [Reese,P.D.&M.]
Ellsworth, Mary Ellen .... '54 '01 C.49 B.S.B.A. L.607 J.D. Newark City Law Dir. Off.
Ennen, Bruce A., (CV) .... '54 '79 C.473 B.A. L.930 J.D. P.O. Box 4461
Erhard, Robert T., (BV) .... '50 '77 C.207 B.A. L.117 J.D. [Morrow&E.]
Fleming, Mary '— '78 C.20 B.A. L.999 J.D.
(adm. in MI; not adm. in OH) 754 Robinhood‡

Friedman & Mirman Co., L.P.A.
(See Columbus)

Fullem, Brett E. .... '75 '00 C.901 B.A. L.117 J.D. [Ⓐ Swank&Assoc.]
Gard, John S. .... '54 '81 C.49 B.A. L.607 J.D. 50 N. 3rd Street
Gardner, Mark Douglas, (CV) '56 '82
C.317 B.A. L.851 J.D. Asst. Dir. of Law [M.D.Gardner]
Gardner, Mark D., (CV) .... 30 W. Locust Street

Goldman & Rosenthal
(See Columbus)

Gordon, L. James, (AV) .... '27 '53 C.207 B.A. L.976 LL.B. [Ⓒ Morrow,G.&B.]
Gramza, Michelle L. .... '66 '91 C.124 B.A. L.150 J.D. [Ⓐ Schaller,C.&U.]
Green, Robin Lyn, (BV) .... '48 '73 C.608 B.A. L.117 J.D. 33 W. Main Street
Greene, Steven T., (AV) .... '— '73 C.103 A.B. L.608 J.D. [Morrow,G.&B.]
Hand, James R., (BV) .... '47 '72 C&L.608 B.A., J.D. [Ⓐ J.B.Mantonya]
Handelman, Robert B., (BV) '51 '76 C.264 B.A. L.1003 J.D.
[Calig&H.] (⊙Columbus)
Harmon, Paul D., Attorney at Law '53 '79
C.608 B.A. L.201 J.D. 964 North 21st Street, Suite A
Higgins, Michael F., (BV) .... '48 '77 C.650 B.S. L.117 J.D. Admin. Judge
Hite, David L., (BV) .... '16 '46 C.381 B.S. L.117 J.D. 964 N. 21st St.
Hoover, Robert H. '48 '75 C.532 B.A. L.608 J.D.
Ct. of Comm. Pleas J., Prob. & Juv. Div.
Hostetter, James W., (BV) .... '48 '76 C.967 B.A. L.117 J.D. 40 W. Main St., 4th Fl.
Howarth, Rodney L., (BV) .... '33 '61 C.473 A.B. L.608 J.D. [Jones,N.M.&H.]
Hubbuch, Carol Ann. '51 '99 C.608 B.S. L.117 J.D.
V.P., Corp. Compliance, Licking Memorial Health Systems
Jones, Norpell, Miller & Howarth, (BV) .... 2 N. 1st St.
Judge, Geoffrey Graham, (BV) .... '52 '79 C.473 B.A. L.607 J.D. [G.G.Judge]
Judge, Geoffrey G., (BV) .... 964 N. 21st St., Ste. A
Kennedy, Ann Munro, (BV) .... '43 '81 C.309 J.D. L.608 J.D. [Reese,P.D.&M.]

Kenney-Pfalzer, Susan
(See Columbus)

Kincaid, Taylor & Geyer
(See Zanesville)

King, J. Michael, (BV) .... '53 '79 C.608 B.A. L.201 J.D. [Jones,N.M.&H.]
Kirchner, Mary G. .... '49 '81 C.706 B.A. L.608 J.D. Central Ohio Legal Aid Society, Inc.
Koehler, C. Herbert, Jr., (BV) .... '38 '63 C&L.597 B.A., J.D. [Jones,N.M.&H.]

Lamkin, Van Eman, Trimble, Beals & Dougherty, LLC
(See Columbus)

Laughlin, Neil M. .... '24 '52 C.528 L.607 LL.B. Ret. Com. Pleas J.
LeGendre, Edward M. .... '11 '38 C.476 A.B. L.608 1490 Pleasant Valley Rd.

Lewis, Gregg R.
(See Columbus)

Liming, Roxi A.
(See Columbus)

Lowe, Wm. Douglas, (BV) .... '59 '85 C.610 B.A. L.608 J.D. [Reese,P.D.&M.]

Luther, Raymond P., (CV) .... '31 '69 C.608 B.A. L.117 J.D. P.O. Box 4010
Mantonya, John B., (AV) .... '22 '49 C.901 A.B. L.608 J.D. [J.B.Mantonya]
Mantonya, John B., A Legal Professional Association, (AV) .... 3 N. Third
Marcelain, Thomas M. .... '57 '83 C.49 B.A. L.831 J.D. Mun. Ct. J.
Martin, David L. .... '49 '73 C.318 B.A. L.607 J.D. 27 N. 4th St.

McCoy, Carl, Attorney at Law, (CV) '55 '82 C.610 B.G.S. L.117 J.D.
195 Union Street, 43055
Telephone: 740-345-4545 Fax: 740-345-3644
Email: cemccoy@alltel.net
Criminal Law, Divorce, Family Law, Medical Malpractice, Personal Injury, Automobile Accidents, Child Custody, Child Support, General Practice, Trusts and Estates, Wills and Probate Law, Driving While Intoxicated, Drug Crimes, Elder Law, Estate Planning, Insurance, Slip and Fall, Traffic Violations, Wrongful Death, Dog Bites, Domestic Violence, Parole and Probation, Visitation Rights, White Collar Crime, Automobile Insurance, Automotive Products Liability, Felonies, Misdemeanors, Premarital Agreements, Sexual Assault, Spousal Support and Motorcycle Accidents.
See Professional Biographies, NEWARK, OHIO

McGonagle, Patrick J. '54 '80 C&L.117 B.A., J.D.
V.P. & Gen. Coun., National Gas & Oil Corp.
McGraw, Scott .... '72 '01 46 N. Fourth St., Ste. 204
Meyer, Christopher R., (AV) .... '52 '77 C&L.608 B.A., J.D. [Reese,P.D.&M.]
Miller, Elizabeth Gaglione .... '56 '81 C.207 B.A. L.904 J.D. Licking Co. Ins. Off.
Miller, Jack, (AV) .... '32 '60 C&L.608 B.S., J.D. 887 N. Village Dr.‡
Moore, Robert J. .... '36 '62 C&L.608 B.S. in B.A., J.D. Ret. Prob. J.‡
Morris, Robert L. .... '— '85 C.608 B.S. L.117 J.D. 51 N. 3rd St., Ste. 505
Morrow, C. Arthur, (AV) .... '41 '71 C.207 B.A. L.208 J.D. [Morrow&E.]
Morrow, E. Clark, (AV) .... '08 '33 C.207 A.B. L.930 LL.B. [Morrow,G.&B.]

Morrow & Erhard Co., L.P.A., (AV)
10 West Locust Street, P.O. Box 487, 43058-0487
Telephone: 740-349-7262 Fax: 740-345-0490
URL: http://www.morrow-erhard.com
C. Arthur Morrow; Robert T. Erhard;—W. Prentice Snow.
General Practice, Corporations, Oil and Gas, Taxation, Real Estate, Probate and Estate Planning, and Insurance.
Reference: The Park National Bank.
See Professional Biographies, NEWARK, OHIO

Morrow, Gordon & Byrd, Ltd., (AV)
33 West Main Street, P.O. Box 4190, 43058-4190
Telephone: 740-345-9611 Columbus: 614-221-4810 Fax: 740-349-9816
Email: mgblaw@nextek.net URL: http://www.mgbohiolaw.com/
Martin D. Altmaier; Glenn A. White; A. Terrance Treneff; Steven T. Greene; James R. Cooper; Adam K. Vernau; Carolyn J. Carnes; Timothy M. Cooper. Of Counsel: E. Clark Morrow; L. James Gordon.
Personal Injury, Probate, Real Estate, Corporate, Eminent Domain, Taxation, Insurance and Oil and Gas Law. Trials in all Courts.
General Counsel for: Denison University; Weakley Apartments, Inc.; Licking Memorial Hospital; Dunacraft Golf Products, Inc.
Local Counsel for: Motorists Mutual Insurance Co.; Grange Mutual Casualty Co.; The Park National Bank, Granville, Ohio; Cincinnati Insurance Co.
See Professional Biographies, NEWARK, OHIO

Nelson, Rodney A., (BV) .... '55 '92 C.375 B.S. L.117 J.D. [Reese,P.D.&M.]
Norpell, Thomas E., (AV) .... '20 '48 C.255 M.A. L.477 J.D. [Jones,N.M.&H.]
Oswalt, Kenneth W., (BV) .... '60 '86 C.966 B.A. L.930 J.D. Asst. Pros. Atty.
Price, T. David .... '36 '70 C.608 B.S. L.117 J.D. 964 N. 21st St.‡
Pyle, James W., (AV) .... '44 '71 C.188 B.A. L.477 J.D. [Reese,P.D.&M.] ‡
Reed, Brian C. .... '74 '00 C.967 B.A. L.607 J.D. [Reese,P.D.&M.]
Reese, J. Gilbert, (AV) .... '25 '52 C&L.608 B.A., J.D. [Reese,P.D.&M.]

Reese, Pyle, Drake & Meyer, P.L.L., (AV)
36 North Second Street, P.O. Box 919, 43058-0919
Telephone: 740-345-3431 Fax: 740-345-7302
Email: rpdm@rpdm.com URL: http://www.rpdm.com
Members of Firm: Robert H. Flory (1910-1962); William F. Fitzgibbon (1902-1975); James W. Pyle (Retired); J. Gilbert Reese; Robert N. Drake; Christopher R. Meyer; I. Russell Suskind; Ann Munro Kennedy; David W. Wenger; J. Andrew Crawford; Wm. Douglas Lowe; Rodney A. Nelson; Mary M. Albright; Michael H. Whitehead;—Brian C. Reed; Siobhan R. Clovis.
General Civil Practice in all Courts, State and Federal. Corporation, Banking, Insurance, Taxation, Probate and Estate Planning, Real Estate Law and Employment Law. Trials and Appeals.
General Counsel for: The Park National Bank; First Federal Savings and Loan Assn.; United Carriers Corp.; Central Ohio Technical College; Newark City Schools.
Local Counsel for: Licking Memorial Hospital; Alltel Ohio, Inc.; State Farm Insurance Co.; St. Paul Fire & Marine Insurance Co.; American Electric Power.
See Professional Biographies, NEWARK, OHIO

Reidy, Thomas A., (AV) .... '52 '78 C.401 B.A. L.893 J.D. Longaberger Co.
Rickrich, C. William, II, (BV) .... '52 '79 C.608 B.A. L.851 J.D. [Rickrich,C.W.]
Rickrich, C. William, (BV) .... Licking Co. Courthouse
Rieser, Jack D. .... '54 '85 C.117 B.A. L.608 J.D. Asst. Law Dir., City of Newark
Ripko, Cindy, (BV) .... '52 '82 C.608 B.A. L.117 J.D. 35 S. Park Pl.
Robison, Frank A., (AV) .... '16 '41 C&L.608 B.A., J.D. 843 E. Village Dr.‡
Robison, Joseph A., (BV) .... '48 '75 C.930 N.D. L.1003 J.D. [Jones,N.M.&H.]
Romaker, Robert Ronald '65 '90 C.608 B.A. L.851 J.D.
Southeastern Ohio Legal Services

Rourke & Blumenthal, LLP
(See Columbus)

Schaller, James M. .... '24 '51 C&L.608 B.S., J.D. [Schaller,C.&U.] ‡
Schaller, Stephen E., (AV) .... '47 '73 C.611 B.A. L.150 J.D. [Schaller,C.&U.]
Schaller, Campbell & Untied, (AV) .... 32 N. Park Pl.
Schumaker, Kenneth B., (CV) .... '41 '68 C.532 B.A. L.1003 J.D. 41 S. Park Place
Seeds, Melinda Gayle .... '67 '94 C.473 B.S. L.150 J.D. Chief, Juv. Div., Co. Pros. Off.
Shapiro, Harvey H., (BV) .... '43 '71 C.610 A.B. L.30 J.D. 30 W. Locust St.
Shenk, Brent W. .... '41 '76 C.608 B.S. L.117 J.D. 20 South Second Street
Simms, Brian E. .... '62 '94 C.608 B.A. L.117 J.D. Asst. Pros.
Snow, W. Prentice, (CV) .... '56 '81 C.608 B.A. L.117 J.D. [Morrow&E.]
Spahr, Jon R. .... '39 '64 C.473 B.S. L.608 J.D. Com. Pleas J.
Steiner, Russell A. .... '35 '72 C.201 B.Ch.E. L.117 J.D. Com. Pleas J.
Stokes, David B. .... '43 '79 C.608 B.S.B.A. L.117 J.D. 21 W. Church St., Ste. 206
Stone, George E. .... '27 '52 C&L.923 A.B., LL.B. 2600 Dayton Rd., NE‡

Stumler, Rebecca J.
(See Columbus)

Suskind, I. Russell, (BV) .... '43 '71 C.98 B.S. L.477 J.D. [Reese,P.D.&M.]
Swank, J. Gerard, (BV) .... '48 '74 C.608 B.S. L.607 J.D. [Swank&Assoc.]
Swank & Associates, (BV) .... 68 West Church Street, Suite 205
Taylor, Tyra L., The Law Office of '67 '94 C.610 B.S. L.117 J.D.
964 North 21st, Suite A
Treneff, A. Terrance, (BV) .... '— '72 C.608 B.S. L.117 J.D. [Morrow,G.&B.]
Tuhy, Elena V. .... '68 '95 C.999 B.A. L.1003 J.D. Asst. Dir. of Law

Twyford & Donahey, P.L.L., (BV)
137 West Main Street, Suite C, 43025 ⊙
Telephone: Toll Free: 1-800-686-1699 Fax: 614-849-0475
Email: help@twyforddonahey.com URL: http://www.twyforddonahey.com

(This Listing Continued)

Twyford & Donahey, P.L.L. (Continued)
Richard S. Donahey.
Personal Injury Litigation, Wrongful Death, Medical Malpractice, Products Liability, Automobile Accidents, Trucking Accidents, Head and Spinal Injuries, Motorcycle Accidents and Injuries, Uninsured Motorists, Insurance Law, Airplane Crash Litigation, Railroad Accidents, Slip and Fall, Dog Bites, Work Related Injuries, Birth Injuries, Nursing Home Abuse and Neglect.
References: The Huntington National Bank; Bank One of Columbus; BancOhio National Bank.
Columbus, Ohio Office: 495 South High Street, 43215-5058. Telephone: Toll Free: 1-800-686-1699. Email: help@twyforddonahey.com.
Circleville, Ohio Office: 214 South Court Street, 43113. Telephone: Toll Free: 1-800-686-1699. Email: help@twyforddonahey.com.
Delaware, Ohio Office: 163 N. Sandusky Street, Suite 103, 43015. Telephone: Toll Free: 1-800-686-1699. Email: help@twyforddonahey.com.
Lancaster, Ohio Office: 3794 Old Columbus, N.W., 43130. Telephone: Toll Free: 1-800-686-1699. Email: help@twyforddonahey.com.
London, Ohio Office: 25 West Fifth Street, 43140. Telephone: Toll Free: 1-800-686-1699. Email: help@twyforddonahey.com.
See Professional Biographies, NEWARK, OHIO

Untied, Wesley K., (BV) .... '59 '85 C.608 B.S. L.117 J.D. [Schaller,C.&U.]
Van Winkle, Richard M., (BV) .... '42 '75 C.610 B.S. L.117 J.D. [Van Winkle&Assoc.]
Van Winkle & Associates Co., L.P.A., (BV) .... 8 Arcade Place, Suite 200
Vernau, Adam K., (BV) .... '— '89 C.923 B.S. L.117 J.D. [Morrow,G.&B.]

Volkema, Thomas, Miller, Burkett, Scott & Merry, A Legal Professional Association
(See Columbus)

Wenger, David W., (AV) .... '54 '79 C.970 B.A. L.608 J.D. [Reese,P.D.&M.]
Wentworth, Karen A. .... '60 '87 C&L.347 B.A., J.D. [Christiansen&W.]
White, Glenn A., (AV) .... '— '69 C.210 B.A. L.273 J.D. [Morrow,G.&B.]
Whitehead, Michael H. .... '72 '00 C.473 B.A. L.608 J.D. [Reese,P.D.&M.]
Wigginton, David Q., (BV) .... '60 '85 C&L.608 B.A., J.D. [Schaller,C.&U.]
Wilson, Christina Ritchey .... '68 '93 C.608 B.A. L.851 J.D. P.O. Box 722
Wilson, Stephen B., Attorney at Law, (BV) '55 '88
C.640 B.S. L.117 J.D. 35 South Park Place Suite 201

Wolske & Barclay, A Legal Professional Association
(See Columbus)

Young, Philip R. .... '48 '73 C&L.276 B.S.F.S., J.D. 3 N. Third‡

NEW BOSTON, 2,340, *Scioto Co.*

Canter, Richard L. .... '18 '50 C.235 B.S. L.608 J.D. 4265 Oak St.‡

NEW BREMEN, 2,909, *Auglaize Co.*

Edwards, Wesley F. '49 '82 C.45 B.A. L.502 J.D.
(adm. in CA; not adm. in OH) Assoc. Gen. Coun., Crown Equip. Co.
Hinders, Rodney J. '52 '85
C.150 B.G.S. L.201 J.D. Assoc. Gen. Coun., Crown Equip. Corp.
Maxa, John G. '50 '75 C.97 B.L.S. L.608 J.D.
V.P. & Gen. Coun., Crown Equip. Corp.
Montgomery, Ogden K. '47 '78
C.532 B.A. L.201 J.D. Assoc. Gen. Coun., Crown Equip. Corp.
Smith, Stephen L., (BV) .... '47 '72 C&L.608 B.A., J.D. [S.L.Smith]
Smith, Stephen L., Co., L.P.A., (BV) .... 209 E. Monroe St.
Tate, John E. '55 '80 C.901 B.A. L.276 J.D.
Vice Pres-European Oper., Crown Equip. Corp.
This, Jason E., (BV) .... '66 '92 C.1208 B.A L.607 J.D. P.O. Box 42

NEWBURGH HEIGHTS, 2,310, *Cuyahoga Co.*

Ferrin, Mark A. '50 '76 C.878 B.S. L.101 J.D.
Gen. Coun., Thiokol Propulsion Div., Cordant Technologies Inc.
Lindblad, Lisa M.J. ..... '59 '84 C&L.878 B.S., J.D. Sr. Coun., Cordant Technologies Inc.
Lyons, Ronald L. '35 '70 C.835 B.S.Chem. L.838 J.D.
Dir., Intell. Prop. & Lic., Cordant Technologies Inc. (Pat.)
North, Edwin M. '45 '74 C.535 B.S. L.607 J.D.
V.P. & Corp. Secy., Cordant Technologies Inc.

NEWBURY, —, *Geauga Co.*

Frimel, Michael P. .... '53 '96 C.392 B.S.B.A. L.1003 J.D. 14392 Ravenna Rd.
Slusarz, G. Vincent, (BV) '56 '81 C.97 B.A. L.930 J.D.
Vice President, General Counsel & Secretary, Kinetico Incorporated
Smidansky, Kurt J., (AV) .... '59 '84 C&L.930 B.A., J.D. [K.J.Smidansky]
Smidansky, Kurt J., Co., LPA, (AV) .... 11691 Pekin Road
Yaksic, Michael, (BV) ..... '56 '81 C.381 B.A. L.608 J.D. General Counsel, Kinetico Inc.

NEW CARLISLE, 5,735, *Clark Co.*

Brichacek, John I., (BV) .... '44 '75 C&L.623 B.S.Ed., J.D. 101 S. Main St.
Craig, Edward L., Jr. .... '58 '84 C.607 B.A. L.838 J.D. 401 Kennison Ave.
Daniel, Theodore D., (BV) .... '48 '73 C.235 B.A. L.383 J.D. 133 S. Main St.
Glew, James Paul .... '67 '98 C.608 L.117 101 S. Main St.
Janning, Charles W. .... '36 '67 C.309 A.B. L.930 LL.B. 5255 S. Westland
Simpson, Charles J., (BV) .... '32 '60 C.201 A.B. L.1066 LL.B. 157 Lammes Ln.
Wingert, Howard E. .... '56 '85 C.608 B.S. L.201 J.D. Corp. Coun., Concrete Sealants, Inc.

NEW CONCORD, 2,651, *Muskingum Co.*

Tabachnick, David E. '55 '88 C.299 B.A. L.966 J.D.
(adm. in WI; not adm. in OH) 188 Comin St., Apt. 1

NEW HOLLAND, 841, *Fayette & Pickaway Cos.*

Esselburne, Peter C. .... '44 '75 C.734 B.S. L.117 J.D. 27735 Egypt Pk.

NEW LEBANON, 4,323, *Montgomery Co.*

Keener, Ronald D., (BV) .... '44 '69 C&L.608 B.Sc., J.D. 129 W. Main Street
Manning, James L. .... '46 '74 C.201 B.A. L.851 J.D. 195 S. Clayton Road
Turrell, Claudia J., (BV) .... '53 '83 C.577 B.A. L.326 J.D. 129 W. Main Street
Wampler, E. James (Jim), (BV) '39 '65
C.604 A.B. L.608 J.D. 116 W. Main St. (⊙Dayton)
Wampler, Sherry, (BV) .... '43 '77 C.362 B.A. L.1340 J.D. 116 W. Main St. (⊙Dayton)

NEW LEXINGTON, * 4,689, *Perry Co.*

Allen, Joseph M., (BV) .... '36 '62 C.201 B.S. L.150 J.D. P.O. Box 61
Boyer, Tina M., (CV) ..... '69 '94 C.610 B.A. L.117 J.D. Co. Ct. of Common Pleas; Mag.
Collins, Clyde H., (BV) .... '28 '53 C&L.607 LL.B. 108 S. Main St.
Cooperrider, Luann .... '55 '83 C.608 B.S. L.117 J.D., Prob.-Juv. Ct.
Dodd, Robert J., Jr., (BV) ..... '40 '65 C.363 B.S.S. L.608 LL.B. Peoples Nat. Bank Bldg.
Flautt, Joseph A., (BV) .... '54 '80 C.473 B.S. L.117 J.D. [Flautt,J.A.]
Flautt, Joseph A., Ltd., L.P.A., (BV) .... 111 North High Street
Howdyshell, Walter J., (Co. L.P.A.), (BV) '26 '51 L.607 J.D.
Peoples National Bank Bldg.
Lewis, Linton D., Jr. .... '52 '79 C.608 B.S. L.201 J.D. Com. Pleas J.

Lewis, Thomas A., (BV) .... '48 '77 C.235 B.B.A. L.607 J.D. [T.A.Lewis]
Lewis, Thomas A., Co., LPA, (BV) .... 121 S. Main Street
O'Neil, Cindy Marie .... '59 '99 C.610 B.B.A. L.117 J.D. P.O. Box 508
Schnittke, Steven P., (CV) .... '50 '75 C&L.607 B.A., J.D. [Schnittke&S.]
Schnittke & Smith, (CV) .... 114 S. High St.
Smith, Linda L., (CV) .... '50 '76 C&L.117 B.A., J.D. [Schnittke&S.]
Tague, Robert G. .... '15 '40 C&L.608 B.A., J.D. Ret. Com. Pleas J.
Wilson, Dean L., (BV) .... '53 '83 C.610 B.A. L.117 J.D. 105 N. Main Street

NEW LONDON, 2,642, *Huron Co.*

Bennett, Stephen, (CV) .... '37 '65 C.608 B.S. L.64 LL.B. 136 W. Main St.

NEW MIDDLETOWN, 1,682, *Mahoning Co.*

Taylor, Douglas B., (BV) '55 '90
C.1175 B.A. L.117 J.D. 11490 1/2 Youngstown-Pittsburgh Rd.

NEW PHILADELPHIA, * 17,056, *Tuscarawas Co.*

Anderson, Steven A., (CV) .... '70 '96 C.608 B.A. L.117 J.D. [Fitzpatrick,Z.&R.]

Baker, Dublikar, Beck, Wiley & Mathews
(See North Canton)

Barnhouse, Jas. R., (BV) .... '25 '51 C.611 L.608 LL.B. 120 N. Bway.
Barrow, James J. .... '62 '87 C.5 B.A. L.851 J.D. E. Ohio Land Title Agcy., Inc.
Berry, Traci Ann .... '— '94 Tuscarawas Co., CSEA

Black McCuskey Souers & Arbaugh, A Legal Professional Association
(See Canton, Ohio)

Blackwell, David L. .... '52 '94 C.473 B.S. L.7 J.D. Mag.
Bond, Douglas C., (BV) .... '64 '89 C.608 B.S.B.A. L.117 J.D. [🄰 Hardin&S.]
Bornhorst, Amanda Spies, (BV) .... '63 '89 C.608 B.A. L.7 J.D. Pros. Atty.
Brown-Tolloti, Lisa M. '64 '96
C.532 B.A. L.989 J.D. Staff Atty., Tuscarawas Co. Com. Pleas Ct.
Buehler, Trevor K., (BV) .... '48 '73 C.967 A.B. L.608 J.D. 1136 Hilltop Rd. N.W.
Carrothers, James M., (BV) .... '46 '73 C.8 B.S. L.7 J.D. [Stephenson,S.&C.]
Contini, James F., II, (BV) '67 '92 C.8 B.S. L.930 J.D.
[Krugliak,W.G.&D.] (⊙Canton)
Cunningham, Arthur B., (AV) .... '38 '63 C.679 B.S. L.608 J.D. [🄰 Hardin&S.]
Deedrick, R. Scott, (CV) .... '66 '92 C.607 B.A. L.608 J.D. 300 E High Ave
De GarmoVon Allman, Nanette, (BV) ... '57 '84 C.381 B.F.A. L.8 J.D. 134 2nd St., N.W.
Demis, George J. .... '28 '56 C.532 B.A. L.948 LL.B. Com. Pleas J.
Durmann, Glenn G., (BV) .... '47 '72 C.967 A.B. L.608 J.D. [Miller&K.]
Dzigiel, Judith E. .... '60 '99 C.999 B.A. L.8 J.D. Southeastern Ohio Legal Servs.
Erdman, Deborah Lynn '67 '95 C&L.851 B.B.A., J.D.
Tuscarawas Co. Child Support Enforce. Agcy.
Ernest, Michael J. .... '— '96 C.381 B.S. L.1003 J.D. [🄰 Johnson U.&R.]
Finzel, Kristen Ann .... '75 '01 C.935 B.A. L.945 J.D. Southeastern Ohio Legal Servs.
Fitzpatrick, Francis G., (AV) ...... '24 '51 C.602 A.B. L.930 LL.B. [Fitzpatrick,Z.&R.] ‡

Fitzpatrick, Zimmerman & Rose Co., L.P.A., (AV)
140 Fair Avenue, N.W., P.O. Box 1014, 44663-1014
Telephone: 330-364-1614 FAX: 330-343-3077
URL: http://www.fzrlaw.com
Donald W. Zimmerman; Frank J. Rose, Jr.; D. Brad Zimmerman; Eugene H. Nemitz, Jr.; J. Greg Miller; Steven A. Anderson; Francis G. Fitzpatrick (Retired).
General Civil Practice. Creditors Bankruptcy, Foreclosures and Collections; Corporate-Business Planning and Litigation; Banking and Thrifts; Real Estate Conveyancing and Development; Mineral Resources Law; Estate Probating and Planning; Personal Injury, Accident and Wrongful Death Litigation in State and Federal Courts, Criminal Law.
See Professional Biographies, NEW PHILADELPHIA, OHIO

Goforth, Richd. E., (BV) .... '20 '47 C&L.607 A.B., J.D. [R.E.Goforth]
Goforth, Richd. E., Co., L.P.A., (BV) .... 219 W. High Ave.
Greene, William C., (CV) .... '56 '92 C&L.150 B.S.C.H., J.D. 123 W. High Ave.
Greenham, Deborah E., (CV) .... '53 '88 C.199 B.S. L.923 J.D. 134 4th Street, N.W.

Grisi & Riegler
(See Akron)

Hardin, Thomas W., (BV) .... '56 '81 C&L.607 B.A., J.D. [Hardin&S.]
Hardin & Schaffner, LPA, (BV) .... 132 Fair Avenue N.W.
Haverfield, David William, (CV) '70 '95
C.97 B.A. L.930 J.D. Tuscarawas Co. Dept. of Human Servs.
Hinig, Richard W., (BV) .... '49 '79 C.8 B.S.M.E. L.117 J.D. 217 N. Broadway
Hipp, David C. .... '50 '76 C.608 B.A. L.117 J.D. 108 E. High Ave.
Hoopingarner, John M., (BV) '54 '79 C.532 B.A. L.607 J.D.
Gen. Mgr. & Secy., Muskingum Watershed Conservancy District
Johnson, Danny D. .... '— '50 C&L.608 LL.B. [Johnson U.&R.] ‡
Johnson, Michael C., (BV) .... '— '73 C.608 B.A. L.7 J.D. [Johnson U.&R.]
Johnson Urban & Range Co., LPA, (BV) .... 117 S. Broadway

Krugliak, Wilkins, Griffiths & Dougherty Co., L.P.A., (AV)
158 N. Broadway Street, 44663 ⊙
Telephone: 330-364-3472 Fax: 330-602-3187
Email: legal@kwgd.com URL: http://www.kwgd.com
James F. Contini II (Certified Specialist in Estate Planning, Trust and Probate Law, Ohio State Bar Association).
Corporate Law, Mergers and Acquisitions, Labor and Employment (Private and Public Sector), Employee Benefits, Real Estate, Taxation, Complex Litigation, Contracts, Insurance Defense, Estates and Trusts, Probate, Elder Law, Commercial Litigation, Oil and Gas, Occupational Safety and Health, Environmental Law, Health Care Law, Hospital Law, Bankruptcy, Banks and Banking, Securities, Construction Law, Family Law, Education Law, Workers Compensation, Personal Injury Litigation, Collections, Debtor and Creditor, Government, Media Law and Electronic Commerce.
Canton, Ohio Office: 4775 Munson Street, N.W. Telephone: 330-497-0700. Fax: 330-497-4020.
Alliance, Ohio Office: KeyBank Building, 960 West State Street. Telephone: 330-823-9262.
See Professional Biographies, NEW PHILADELPHIA, OHIO

Kyler, William A., (AV) .... '38 '64 C.611 B.A. L.228 LL.B. [Miller&K.]
Lehigh, Daniel T. .... '26 '57 C.8 L.608 J.D. 158 N. Broadway
Lile, Roger G. .... '40 '70 C&L.930 B.A., J.D. Ret. Com. Pleas J.‡
Lorenz, Charles E., (CV) .... '50 '84 C.381 B.A. L.7 J.D. 114 East High Street
Lundholm, J. Kevin, (BV) .... '59 '85 C.1101 B.A. L.851 J.D. [Miller&K.]
Maxwell, John P., (CV) .... '68 '94 C.602 B.A. L.608 J.D. [🄰 Hardin&S.]
McGonegal, Terrance J., (BV) ..... '— '77 C.363 A.B. L.327 J.D. 120 N. Broadway Street
McLane, William G., (CV) .... '44 '69 C.271 B.A. L.607 J.D. 138 2nd St. N.W.
Miller, J. Greg, (CV) .... '53 '90 C.473 B.A. L.8 J.D. [Fitzpatrick,Z.&R.]

Miller & Kyler, L.P.A., (AV)
405 Chauncey Avenue N.W., P.O. Box 668, 44663
Telephone: 330-343-5585 Fax: 330-343-7977
URL: http://www.millerkyler.com
William A. Kyler; James J. Pringle; Glenn G. Durmann; J. Kevin Lundholm;—Brent L. Moore; Harry C.E. Tolhurst, III.
General Civil Practice, Corporation, Intellectual Property, Probate, Real Estate, Political Subdivisions, Personal Injury and Insurance Law. Trials and Appeals.

(This Listing Continued)

Miller & Kyler, L.P.A. (Continued)
Chief Counsel: Muskingum Watershed Conservancy District.
Counsel: National City Bank; First Federal Savings Bank of Dover.
See Professional Biographies, NEW PHILADELPHIA, OHIO

Moore, Brent L. .... '71 '99 C.8 B.S. L.7 J.D. [🄰 Miller&K.]
Nemitz, Eugene H., Jr., (BV) .... '48 '73 C.967 B.A. L.608 J.D. [Fitzpatrick,Z.&R.]
O'Farrell, Edward E. .... '46 '75 C.812 B.S. L.602 J.D. Com. Pleas J.
Ong, James J., (CV) .... '71 '97 C.318 B.A. L.8 J.D. [Stephenson,S.&C.]
Patrick, James S., (BV) .... '28 '54 C.674 A.B. L.477 LL.B. [J.S.Patrick]
Patrick, James S., Co., L.P.A., (BV) .... 204 2nd St. N.E.
Pringle, James J., (BV) .... '52 '79 C&L.150 B.S.B.A., J.D. [Miller&K.]
Range, James A., (BV) .... '— '80 C.610 B.S. L.851 J.D. [Johnson U.&R.]
Reed, Joy E., (BV) .... '51 '77 C.608 B.S. L.607 J.D. Mag., Co. Prob. & Juv. Ct.
Rose, Frank J., Jr., (AV) .... '49 '74 C.363 A.B. L.930 J.D. [Fitzpatrick,Z.&R.]
Schaffner, David K., (BV) .... '63 '88 C.475 B.A. L.851 J.D. [Hardin&S.]
Stephan, Nicole R., Attorney at Law ...... '75 '02 C.434 B.A. L.117 J.D. 138 2nd St. N.W.
Stephenson, Elizabeth W., (BV) .... '64 '89 C.608 B.A. L.150 J.D. Common Pl.
Stephenson, Richard L., (AV) .... '33 '58 C.532 B.A. L.608 J.D. [Stephenson,S.&C.]
Stephenson, Robert R., II, (BV) .... '59 '86 C.608 B.S. L.7 J.D. [Stephenson,S.&C.]

Stephenson, Stephenson & Carrothers, (AV)
P.O. Box 992, 44663-0992
Telephone: 330-339-6444 Fax: 330-339-6228
Email: lawyerssc@adelphia.net
Members of Firm: James F. Stephenson (1863-1938); Robert R. Stephenson (1897-1968); James R. Stephenson (1927-2003); Richard L. Stephenson; James M. Carrothers; Robert R. Stephenson II; James J. Ong.
General Civil Practice. Litigation, Appellate Practice, Business Law, Corporate Law, Hospital Law, Wills, Probate, Aged and Aging, Collections, Commercial Law, Construction Law, Consumer Law, Contacts, Eminent Domain, Environmental Law, Guardianship and Conservatorship, Insurance, Labor and Employment, Medicare and Medicaid, Nonprofit and Charitable Organizations, Personal Injury, Railroad Law, Zoning, Planning and Land Use, Mediation, Health Care, Trusts and Estate, Real Estate, Family Law.
Agents for: Guardian Title Insurance Co.; Ohio Bar Title Insurance Company.
See Professional Biographies, NEW PHILADELPHIA, OHIO

Thomakos, Elizabeth L. .... '63 '87 C.1322 B.A. L.8 J.D. Com. Pleas J., Tuscarawas Co.
Tolhurst, Harry C.E., III .... '74 '00 C.999 B.A. L.150 J.D. [🄰 Miller&K.]
Tripodi, Joseph I., (Co., L.P.A.), (BV) '40 '67 C.1323 B.A. L.607 J.D.
114 E. High Ave.
Urban, Robert C., Jr., (BV) .... '59 '85 C.610 B.A. L.7 J.D. [Johnson U.&R.]
Vodrey, William F.B., (CV) '64 '92
C.604 B.A. L.930 J.D. Staff Atty., S.E. Ohio Legal Servs.
Von Allman, Nanette DeGarmo, (CV) .... '57 '84 C.381 B.F.A. L.8 J.D. [N.D.VonAllman]
Von Allman, Nanette DeGarmo, Co., LPA, (CV) .... 134 Second Street, N.W.
Wallick, Tina Galigher, (CV) .... '61 '86 C.473 B.S. L.608 J.D. 114 East High Avenue
Wright, Edd K., (BV) .... '39 '68 C.973 B.S. L.1065 J.D. 134 4th St., N.W.
Zimmerman, D. Brad, (BV) .... '53 '78 C.611 B.A. L.930 J.D. [Fitzpatrick,Z.&R.]
Zimmerman, Donald W., (AV) .... '25 '51 C.611 A.B. L.930 J.D. [Fitzpatrick,Z.&R.]

NEW RICHMOND, 2,219, *Clermont Co.*

Clendenin, Charles E. .... '44 '72 C.923 B.S.B.A. L.607 J.D. 797 Greenmound Rd.
Davis, Robert H., (AV) .... '36 '67 C.150 B.A. L.1340 J.D. 1225 Fagin Run Rd.
Hollister, Lisa Harris .... '56 '87 C.787 B.A. L.117 J.D. 849 10 Mile Rd.
McCachran, Marshall T., (AV) .... '48 '77 C.967 B.A. L.880 J.D. [M.McCachran]
McCachran, Marshall, (AV) .... 1769 Cedar Trl.
Zayas-Davis, Marilyn '64 '97 C.563 B.S. L.150 J.D.
(adm. in CO; not adm. in OH) 2810 Sugartree Dr.‡

NEW STRAITSVILLE, 865, *Perry Co.*

Weed, Charles B. .... '45 '71 C&L.608 B.A., J.D. 6340 Monday Creek

NEWTON FALLS, 5,002, *Trumbull Co.*

Luca, Nicholas J., (CV) .... '40 '69 C.532 B.A. L.607 J.D. 30 E. Broad St.
Old, Thomas L. .... '46 '73 C.528 B.A. L.150 J.D. Mun. J., Newton Falls Mun. Ct.
Palmer, Thomas H., (AV) .... '44 '69 C.967 B.A. L.608 J.D. 41 W. Broad Street
Walrath, Terry J., Sr. .... '45 '70 C.381 B.A. L.608 J.D. The Cadle Co.
Ziegler, Charles A., (BV) .... '55 '80 C&L.608 B.A., J.D. 127 N. Canal

NEW VIENNA, 1,294, *Clinton Co.*

Uible, Harold Hiestand, (BV) .... '25 '50 C&L.930 B.B.A., LL.B. 280 W. Main Street

NEW WATERFORD, 1,391, *Columbiana Co.*

Robb, Carol Ann, (BV) .... '52 '83 C.980 B.S. L.7 J.D. 46033 Hatcher Rd.

NILES, 20,932, *Trumbull Co.*

Bogen, Curt P., (CV) .... '64 '89 C.381 B.B.A. L.910 J.D. 42 S. Main St.
Boker, David E., (BV) .... '49 '75 C&L.608 B.A., J.D. 724 Youngstown Warren Rd.
Clayman, Joel A., (CV) .... '57 '81 C.604 B.A. L.117 J.D. P.O. Box 166
De Matteis, Martin D., (BV) .... '54 '80 C.980 B.S. L.117 J.D. [Witten&D.]
DeVicchio, Matthew Louis, (CV) .... '72 '99 C.980 B.A. L.161 J.D. [M.L.DeVicchio]
DeVicchio, Matthew L., Co., LPA, (CV) .... 720 Youngstown Warren Rd., Ste. B
Dragelevich, J. Walter, (BV) ...... '41 '67 C.610 B.A. L.823 J.D. 1170 Niles Cortland Rd.
Dull, Joseph T., (BV) .... '51 '76 C.645 B.A. L.8 J.D. [Dull,J.T.]
Dull, J. Terrence, (BV) .... 52 E. Park Ave.
Goodman, Richard L. '47 '74
C.608 B.S.I.E. L.117 J.D. 720 Youngstown-Warren Rd., Ste E
Hickton, Dawne S. '57 '83 C.696 B.A. L.665 J.D.
(adm. in PA; not adm. in OH) VP & Gen. Coun., RTI International Metal Inc.
Joseph, John Eric .... '75 '01 C.757 B.S. L.8 J.D. 5704 Youngstown-Warren Road
Joseph, Michael Dennis .... '44 '73 C.980 B.A. L.7 J.D. [M.D.Joseph]
Joseph, Michael D. .... 815 Robbins Avenue
Latell, Kurt David .... '67 '93 C.8 B.S.I.M. L.117 J.D. Blair & Latell Co., L.P.A.
Lorenzetti, Jack C., Jr., (CV) '57 '82
C.150 B.B.A. L.602 J.D. American Land Title Agency, Inc.
MacQueen, James R., (AV) .... '17 '42 C.473 A.B. L.930 J.D. 919 John St.
Neuman, Douglas J., (BV) .... '52 '77 C.880 B.A. L.930 J.D. [Neuman&P.]
Neuman & Parry, (BV) .... 761 N. Cedar St.
Parry, Patrick E., (CV) .... '69 '94 C.980 B.S. L.117 J.D. [Neuman&P.]
Pentz, Matthew A., (CV) .... '57 '84 C.363 B.S. L.930 J.D. 150 N. Crandon Ave.
Rogers, Clement Hall, (CV) .... '56 '84 C.980 B.S. L.607 J.D. 363 Robbins Ave.
Shaker, Christopher J., (BV) .... '58 '83 C.608 B.S. L.117 J.D. [Shaker&S.]
Shaker, Robert I., (BV) .... '62 '87 C.381 B.A. L.8 J.D. [Shaker&S.]
Shaker & Shaker, (BV) .... National City Bank Building Suite 502
Townley, Thomas W. .... '50 '75 C.318 B.A. L.607 J.D. Mun. J.
Virgalitte, Sherri A. .... '68 '94 C.473 B.S. L.8 J.D. Hyatt Legal Servs.
Witten, Debora K., (CV) .... '55 '80 C.608 B.A. L.117 J.D. [Witten&D.]
Witten & DeMatteis, (BV) .... 465 Robbins Ave.

Zubyk, Charles B. .... '25 '60 C&L.980 B.A., J.D. Mun. J.
Zuzolo, Ralph A. .... '42 '68 C.644 B.A. L.851 J.D. 700 Youngstown Warren Road

NORTH BALTIMORE, 3,361, *Wood Co.*

Bechtel, Allen H., (AV) .... '24 '51 C&L.608 A.B., J.D. [Bechtel&T.]
Bechtel & Thompson, (AV) .... 119 E. Broadway
Brown, Daniel H. .... '55 '81 C.97 B.S.B.A. L.150 J.D. Pres., The D.S. Brown Co.
Parsons, Glenn C. .... '27 '52 C.97 A.B. L.607 J.D. 211 S. Main St.‡
Thompson, George G., (BV) .... '51 '76 C.608 B.A. L.607 J.D. [Bechtel&T.]

NORTH BEND, 541, *Hamilton Co.*

Carman, Dorothy N. .... '51 '80 C.473 A.B. L.157 J.D. 7834 Bridgetown Rd.
DuMond, John W., (BVⓉ) '50 '75 C.347 B.A. L.345 J.D.
(adm. in IN; not adm. in OH) 53 Muirfield Drive
James, Daniel J., (BV) .... '52 '77 C.973 B.A. L.734 J.D. P.O. Box 157
James, Diane M. Busch, (BV) .... '62 '88 C&L.150 B.A., J.D. P.O. Box 157

NORTH CANTON, 16,369, *Stark Co.*

Anderson, James W. .... '13 '40 C.607 L.948 LL.B. 700 Lindy Lane, S.W.‡
Baker, Jack R., (AV) .... '44 '69 C.97 B.A. L.150 J.D. [Baker,D.B.W.&M.]

Baker, Dublikar, Beck, Wiley & Mathews, (AV) BR
400 South Main Street, 44720
Telephone: 330-499-6000 Telecopier: 330-499-6423
URL: http://www.bakerfirm.com
Members of Firm: Jack R. Baker; Ralph F. Dublikar; Gregory A. Beck; Donald P. Wiley; James F. Mathews; Mel L. Lute, Jr.; Daniel J. Funk; John B. Lindamood; James P. Hanratty; Kimberly Kay Wyss;—Anthony E. Brown; Jude B. Streb; Andrea Kaye Ziarko; Niki Domenick Di Cola; Justin A. Dublikar.
General Civil Trial and Appellate Practice in all Courts. Insurance, Products Liability, Environmental, Malpractice, Political Subdivision, Real Estate, Corporate, Commercial and Family Law.
See Professional Biographies, NORTH CANTON, OHIO

Beck, Gregory A., (AV) .... '56 '81 C.885 B.A. L.7 J.D. [Baker,D.B.W.&M.]
Bing, Jason Nicholas .... '74 '00 C.1369 B.A. L.124 J.D. 6370 Mt. Pleasant St. N.W.
Brian, Richard F., (BV) .... '55 '82 C.931 B.A. L.7 J.D. [Brian&B.]
Brian, Steven J., (BV) .... '61 '88 C.381 B.A. L.7 J.D. [Brian&B.]
Brian & Brian, (BV) .... 5770 Dressler Rd., N.W.
Brown, Anthony E. .... '70 '98 C.1260 B.A. L.200 J.D. [A] Baker,D.B.W.&M.]
Corrigan, Michael James '64 '96
C.608 B.S. L.8 J.D. Sr. Patent Atty., The Hoover Company (Pat.)
Cox, Kevin C. .... '75 '01 C.528 B.A. L.124 J.D. 1401 S. Main St., Ste. 202
Dettinger, Warren W., (AV) '54 '80
C&L.851 B.S., J.D. V.P., Gen. Coun. & Secy., Diebold, Inc.
Di Cola, Niki Domenick .... '66 '03 C.648 B.A. L.8 J.D. [A] Baker,D.B.W.&M.]
Dublikar, Justin A. .... '77 '04 C.436 B.A. L.150 J.D. [A] Baker,D.B.W.&M.]
Dublikar, Ralph F., (AV) .... '49 '74 C.973 A.B. L.150 J.D. [Baker,D.B.W.&M.]
Freeman, Christopher, (CV) .... '66 '91 C.8 B.S. L.608 J.D. P.O. Box 2985
Funk, Daniel J., (BV) .... '65 '94 C.597 B.A. L.8 J.D. [Baker,D.B.W.&M.]
Gatien, J. Michael, (CV) .... '51 '84 C.381 B.A. L.7 J.D. [J.M.Gatien]
Gatien, John Michael, (CV) .... 2371 Chestnut Hill Street, N.W.
Gibbs, Richard P., & Associates, (AV) '54 '79
C.97 B.A. L.607 J.D. 1001 South Main Street
Gruber, Michael S., (AV) .... '51 '77 C&L.150 B.A., J.D. P.O. Box 2985
Hanratty, James P., (BV) .... '64 '89 C.1260 B.A. L.7 J.D. [Baker,D.B.W.&M.]
Harbert, Robert P., II .... '67 '95 C.25 B.A. L.7 J.D. 149 Wilbur Drive, N.E.
Hesse, Chad F. '72 '00 C.97 B.S.B.A. L.989 J.D.
Corp. Coun. & Asst. Secy., Diebold Inc.
Hoffman, John R., Sr. .... '20 '53 C.381 L.948 LL.B. Ret. Dist. Ct. App. J.
Howard, Michael L. .... '51 '79 C.611 B.A. L.7 J.D. Mag., Ct. of Com. Pleas‡
Howes, Shirley E. .... '28 '96 C.381 B.S.B.A. L.7 J.D. 210 Summit St Sw
Kandel, Harry N. .... '24 '52 C.473 B.S. L.948 LL.B. 1394 Butler Circle, S.E.
Kingsbury, Thomas R. '67 '97 C.201 B.E.E. L.8 J.D.
Sr. Patent & Trademark Atty., Maytag Corporation
Lensman, Todd A., (BV) .... '64 '92 C&L.8 B.S.B.A., J.D. [Lensman&Assoc.]
Lensman & Associates, (BV) .... 6273 Frank Ave. N.W.
Lindamood, John B., (AV) .... '41 '66 C.210 A.B. L.930 J.D. [Baker,D.B.W.&M.]
Lindroos, Michael E. .... '52 '83 C.8 B.A. L.7 J.D. Sr. Corp. Coun., Diebold, Inc.
Lowe, A. Burgess '46 '75 C.383 B.S.E.E. L.8 J.D.
Assoc. Gen. Coun., Intell. Prop., Maytag Corporation (Pat.)
Lute, Mel L., Jr., (BV) .... '65 '90 C.473 B.A. L.150 J.D. [Baker,D.B.W.&M.]
Marsh, Joseph H. .... '40 '83 C.8 B.S.B.A. L.7 J.D. 5201 Limerick, NW
Martin, Curtis C. .... '14 '37 L.608 J.D. 723 E. Bachtel‡
Mathews, James F., (BV) .... '63 '88 C.528 B.A. L.930 J.D. [Baker,D.B.W.&M.]
McCune, Richard E., (CV) .... '46 '72 C.381 B.A. L.8 J.D. 4526 Massillon Rd.
McNulty, Gregory F., Jr. ..... '19 '57 C.381 L.948 LL.B. 7300 Beverly Ave. N.E., Apt 15
Milhoan, Douglas Alan .... '66 '92 C&L.608 B.S.B.A., J.D. [Milhoan,D.A.]
Milhoan, Douglas A. .... 601 S. Manin St.
Milligan, John R. .... '28 '52 C.970 A.B. L.477 J.D. Ct. App. J.‡
Minkler, Patricia P., (BV) .... '52 '79 C.608 B.A. L.161 J.D. P.O. Box 2985
Pousoulides, Dimitrios S. .... '65 '90 C.967 B.A. L.608 J.D. [Pousoulides]
Pousoulides Law Offices Inc. .... 931 N. Main St.
Ranges, Dawn E. .... '63 '96 C.693 B.S. L.8 J.D. National MD
Richards, Homer R., (BV) .... '52 '77 C.385 A.B. L.930 J.D. [H.R.Richards]
Richards, Homer R., Co., LPA, (BV) .... 2632 Fordham Cir. N.W.
Ritchie, James E., (AV) .... '24 '51 C.528 B.A. L.930 J.D. 705 Deerfield Dr. S.W.
Russell, Michael S., (CV) .... '52 '77 C.967 B.A. L.607 J.D. [Russell]
Russell Law Offices, (CV) .... 601 South Main Street
Sekula, J. Wm., (BV) ...... '48 '73 C.381 B.A. L.930 J.D. Sr. Corp. Coun., Diebold, Inc.
Serra, Rosemary C., (BV) ..... '52 '84 C.1260 B.A. L.8 J.D. 2624 Cottington Circle, N.W.
Soles, Robert E., Jr., (BV) .... '65 '90 C.980 B.A. L.362 J.D. [R.E.Soles,Jr.]
Soles, Robert E., Jr., Co., LPA, Law Offices of, (BV) .... 1401 S. Main St., Ste. 202
Sommer, Joseph J. .... '27 '52 C.381 A.B. L.930 LL.B. 102 N. Circle Dr. S.W.‡
Stelea, Barbara J., (BV) .... '53 '89 C.381 B.A. L.8 J.D. 1030 N. Main St., #8
Streb, Jude B. .... '73 '99 C.602 B.B.A. L.124 J.D. [A] Baker,D.B.W.&M.]
Swift, Dean A., (BV) .... '52 '78 C.797 B.A. L.893 J.D. 2522 Sheffield St Nw
Swope, Raymond A., Jr. .... '44 '71 C.532 A.B. L.930 J.D. P.O. Box 2548
Thomas, Christopher J., (CV) ...... '65 '91 C&L.608 B.S., J.D. 2381 Macnaughten St. N.W.
Tolbert, Valerie L. .... '71 '97 C.8 B.S. L.117 J.D. 6370 Mt. Pleasant St., N.W.
Turgeon, Lisa P. .... '58 '83 C.473 B.A. L.117 J.D. 1215 Coral Ave., N.W.‡
Vitale, Joseph M., (AV) .... '41 '67 C.363 B.S. L.930 J.D. 46 La Salle Court
Wendell, William D., (AV) .... '41 '67 C.381 B.A. L.930 J.D. 6608 Mt. Pleasant, N.W.
Wiley, Donald P., (AV) .... '59 '84 C.294 B.A. L.7 J.D. [Baker,D.B.W.&M.]
Winkhart, Thomas W., (BV) .... '64 '89 C.851 B.A. L.8 J.D. 801 South Main Street
Wyss, Kimberly Kay, (BV) .... '67 '93 C.8 B.A. L.607 J.D. [Baker,D.B.W.&M.]
Zackaroff, Peter T., (BV) .... '55 '80 C.1046 B.A. L.7 J.D. 5399 Lauby Road Ste.230
Ziarko, Andrea Kaye .... '76 '01 C.347 B.S. L.608 J.D. [A] Baker,D.B.W.&M.]
Zielasko, Gus W. .... '15 '50 C.970 B.A. L.948 LL.B. 1105 Shalimar Circle, N.W.‡

Zollinger, Fred H., Jr., (AV) .... '47 '73 C.401 B.S.C.E. L.608 J.D. P.O. Box 2985

NORTHFIELD, 3,827, *Summit Co.*

Ania, Anthony Leo .... '65 '91 C.473 B.A. L.161 J.D. 10360 Northfield Road
Bevan, Keith D., (BV) .... '35 '72 C.381 B.S. L.1003 J.D. 10360 Northfield Rd.
Bevan, Thomas William .... '66 '91 C.473 B.A. L.7 J.D. [Bevan&Assoc.]
Bevan & Associates, L.P.A. .... 10360 Northfield Road
Bieman, Richard W. .... '48 '86 C.701 B.S. L.1003 J.D. P.O. Box 372
Dick, William M. .... '52 '78 C.8 B.A. L.7 J.D. 8194 Crystal Creek Rd.★
Fletcher, Peter F. .... '41 '75 C.607 B.A. L.94 J.D. 115 W. Aurora Road
Grisanti, Robtert C. .... '18 '43 C.602 Ph.B. L.930 J.D. 9393 Olde Eight Rd.‡
Halberg, William S. .... '36 '70 C.608 B.S. L.161 J.D. [Halberg&Assoc.]
Halberg & Associates Co., L.P.A. .... 198 E. Aurora Rd.
Lepri, A. J. .... '36 '65 C.363 B.S. L.8 LL.B. 8775 Olde Eight Rd.
Marsh, Linda Sue .... '46 '89 C.352 B.S.N. L.1003 J.D. 1756 Sagamore Rd.‡
Neubert, Eleanore S. .... '30 '54 C&L.930 B.A., LL.B. 9555 Olde Eight Rd.
Pearl, James R., Jr. .... '71 '96 C.608 B.S. L.150 J.D. 9391 Olde Eight Rd.
Rudder, Verner R., Jr., (BV) .... '57 '83 C.607 B.A. L.930 J.D. 181 W. Aurora Rd.
Skelton, James R. .... '63 '97 C.97 B.S. L.1187 J.D. 8758 Eaton Dr.
Weiss, Leslie Ann .... '62 '90 C.970 B.A. L.161 J.D. [A] Halberg&Assoc.]

NORTHFIELD CENTER, 2,570, *Summit Co.*

Burney, Stephanie Beaupain .... '75 '00 C.473 B.A. L.200 J.D. 588 Azalea Circle

NORTH JACKSON, —, *Mahoning Co.*

Hess, Thomas, (CV) .... '27 '59 C.980 B.A. L.1003 J.D. 14009 Mahoning Ave.
Kisan, Peter J., (BV) .... '55 '85 L.734 J.D. 1130 N. Duck Creek Rd.
Kravitz, Solomon J. .... '57 '82 C.608 B.A. L.930 J.D. Kravitz Bagels, Inc.

NORTH KINGSVILLE, 2,672, *Ashtabula Co.*

Irons, David R., (CV) .... '45 '80 C.381 B.G.S. L.1003 J.D. Bridge Colonial Plaza

NORTH LIMA, —, *Mahoning Co.*

Smith, Eugene R. .... '22 '56 C&L.980 B.S., J.D. 11695 Market St. (⊙Masury)

NORTH OLMSTED, 34,204, *Cuyahoga Co.*

Albenze, Donald P., (BV) .... '30 '59 C.665 L.1003 J.D. Pros.
Alston, Richard N. .... '51 '79 C.930 B.S. L.1003 J.D. 3963 Tennyson Ln.
Baranowski, Stanley J. .... '25 '49 C.251 B.B.A. L.930 LL.B. 3752 Columbia Rd.‡
Bates, Mickey Charles .... '57 '89 C.62 B.A. L.989 J.D. [M. C.B.]
Bourne, Alfia M. .... '20 '56 L.1003 J.D. P.O. Box 839‡
Caron, Brian L. .... '69 '95 C&L.124 B.A., J.D. [Crombie]
Crombie Law Firm, The
4615 Great Northern Boulevard (⊙Maple Heights, University Heights)
Davies, Daniel R., (BV) ..... '58 '85 C.473 B.A. L.930 J.D. Staff Atty., Hyatt Legal Servs.
Dobbins, Lloyd R. .... '19 '57 C.930 L.1003 LL.B. 23242 Alexander Rd.‡
Dorchak, Thomas J., (BV) .... '40 '66 C.973 A.B. L.93 J.D. [A] Crombie]
Douglass, Thomas E. '26 '51 C&L.862 LL.B.
(adm. in OK; not adm. in OH) 4097 Shelley Dr.
Dubelko, James M., (AV) .... '50 '79 C.138 B.A. L.1003 J.D. 6051 Sandpiper Lane
Duffy, John J., (BV) .... '43 '78 C.363 A.B. L.1003 J.D. 23823 Lorain Rd.
Eddy, Theron F. .... '15 '54 C.363 A.B. L.1003 J.D. 5140 Douglas Dr.
Fehribach, Michael Ray .... '57 '92 C.62 B.A. L.1003 J.D. 4367 Georgette Ave.
Gareau, David M. .... '71 '96 C.608 B.A. L.1003 J.D. 23823 Lorain Rd.
Gareau, Michael R., (AV) .... '40 '67 C.381 B.A. L.1003 J.D. [A] M.Gareau&Assoc.]
Gareau, Michael R., Jr. .... '71 '96 C.608 B.A. L.1003 J.D. [M.Gareau&Assoc.]
Gareau, Michael, and Associates .... 23823 Lorain Rd., Ste. 200
Haas, John M., (BV) '42 '67
C.215 A.B. L.930 J.D. 26130 Lorain Rd. (⊙Columbia Station)
Hawrylak, Thomas E. .... '49 '79 C.161 B.B.A. L.1003 J.D. 6079 Christman Dr.
Hayes, Catherine Kisil .... '51 '94 C.599 B.A. L.1003 J.D. P.O. Box 238
Hussey, Robert R., II, (AV) .... '42 '71 C.124 B.S.M.E. L.1003 J.D. [R.R.Hussey] (Pat.)
Hussey, Robert R., Co., L.P.A., (AV) .... 801 Citizens Building (Pat.)
James, Teresa, (CV) .... '44 '81 C.604 B.A. L.930 J.D. 23556 Marion Road
Johnson, Robert C. .... '49 '76 C.201 B.S. L.1003 J.D. 24783 Arlington Ln.
Kasler, Carolyn, (BV) .... '50 '89 C.97 L.1003 J.D. 3946 Shelley Dr.
Kilbane, James Patrick .... '23 '52 C.363 B.S. L.930 J.D. Ret. Com. Pleas J.
Kozel, Thomas .... '65 '90 C&L.851 B.A.B.A., J.D. P.O. Box 534
Lavelle, Gregory J. .... '— '75 C.381 B.B.A. L.930 J.D. 27346 Edgepark Dr.
Liedtke, Will .... '44 '71 C.363 A.B. L.1003 J.D. Corp. Coun., All Crane Rental
McCarthy, Donald G. .... '35 '60 C.321 B.S. L.930 LL.B. 25111 Country Club Blvd.
McCormick, Keith L. '47 '76 C.734 B.S. in A.E. L.64 J.D.
(adm. in IA; not adm. in OH) 26760 Hyannis Port Drive‡
M. Charles Bates .... 4596 Porter Road
Meredith, Colleen .... '52 '87 C.161 B.S.N. L.1003 J.D. 6429 Stafford
O'Malley, Bryan P., (BV) .... '62 '88 C.610 B.S. L.1003 J.D. 5477 Jacqueline Ln.
Patton, Richard F., (BV) .... '27 '54 C.930 B.A. L.1003 J.D. 23203 Lorain Rd.
Pelka, Karen M. .... '64 '94 C.161 B.A. L.1003 J.D. 6784 Cypress Dr.
Ratesic, Judith I. .... '59 '91 C.970 B.A. L.1003 J.D. Staff Atty., Hyatt Legal Servs.
Rudy, Donald M. .... '37 '68 C.97 B.S. L.1003 J.D. 23201 Lorain Rd.
Shook, Ann L. .... '25 '56 C.967 A.B. L.948 LL.B. [Shook&S.]
Shook, Gene E., Sr. .... '26 '56 C.608 B.M.E. L.948 LL.B. [Shook&S.]
Shook & Shook .... 5130 Devon Dr.
Ursu, Daniel John .... '56 '86 C.201 B.C.E. L.930 J.D. URS Dalton Inc.
Vernon, Eileen B. '35 '92 L.1003 J.D.
V.P., American Arbitration Assn., Cleveland Reg. Off.

NORTH RIDGEVILLE, 22,338, *Lorain Co.*

Andolsen, Robert R. .... '40 '94 C.363 B.A. L.1003 J.D. Asst. Law Dir.
Bryer, Terry A. .... '59 '85 C.999 B.S. L.1003 J.D. 37 Cadet Dr.
Corcoran, Kevin '68 '98 C.754 B.S. L.1003 J.D.
V.P., Gen. Coun. & Secy., Bob Schmitt Homes, Inc.
Feeley, James D. .... '21 '69 C.21 B.S. L.1003 J.D. 4906 Charles Rd.
Gray, Robert W. .... '39 '65 C.930 B.A. L.607 J.D. 35945 Center Ridge Rd.
Grimm, Josephine Victoria .... '60 '85 C.313 B.A. L.1003 J.D. 37 Cadet Dr.
Guerini, David W. .... '63 '89 C.473 B.S. L.1119 J.D. V.P., Plastic Components, Inc.
Laska, Walter J. .... '34 '62 C.645 B.A. L.161 LL.B. 33932 Sunflower Lane‡
McDonough, William F. .... '46 '74 C.381 B.Ed. L.1003 J.D. [McDonough S.]
McDonough Sfiscko & Co., (AV) .... 35888 Center Ridge Road, Unit 3
Miller, Stanley R., (AV) .... '37 '65 C.375 B.S.M.E. L.273 J.D. 6835 Case Rd. (Pat.)
Morgan, Toni Lou .... '50 '96 C.561 B.S. L.989 J.D. City of N. Ridgeville
Musson, John R., (AV) .... '50 '75 C&L.8 B.A., J.D. 7064 Avon Belden Rd.
Ryan, Kevin M. .... '72 '98 C.970 B.A. L.989 J.D. [K.M.Ryan&Assoc.]
Ryan, Kevin M., & Associates Co., LPA .... 7064 Avon Belden Road
Sfiscko, Johanna M., (AV) .... '48 '74 C.717 B.A. L.851 J.D. [McDonough S.]

Smith, Stourton Scott, Co., LPA
(See Cleveland)

Spike & Meckler Law Firm, The, LLP
(See Elyria)

Yount, J. Herman, (AV) ....'25 '51 C.604 A.B. L.273 J.D. 4869 N Barton Rd. (Pat.)

NORTH ROYALTON, 28,648, *Cuyahoga Co.*

Boldt, David R., (BV) .... '60 '86 C.161 B.A. L.1003 J.D. [Kirner&B.]
Broz, Glenn A., (BV) ....'47 '74 C.930 B.A. L.1003 J.D. 6060 Royalton Road
Cieslak, James L. .... '44 '78 C.381 B.B.A. L.1003 J.D. 8261 Montridge Ct.
Drescher, Cathy S., (BV) .... '57 '83 C.381 B.A. L.7 J.D. 3560 Valley Pkwy.
Evenchik, Aaron S. ....'76 '01 C&L.608 B.S.C.E., J.D. Gross Builders
Holcomb, Kent Martin .... '48 '76 4490 Sir Richard Ave.
Kirner, Paul T., (BV) ....'47 '72 C.436 B.S. L.1003 J.D. [Kirner&B.]
Kirner & Boldt, Co., L.P.A., (BV) ....8025 Corporate Circle
Lotenero, Dale J. ....'49 '75 C.97 B.S. L.1003 J.D. 11903 Royalton Rd.
Osterland, Charles E., (BV) ....'41 '69 C.610 B.S. L.1003 J.D. 6060 Royalton Rd.
Pechnik, Thomas M. ....'45 '82 C.161 B.E.E. L.1003 J.D. 9451 State Rd.‡
Shanks, Thomas A. ....'55 '80 C.631 B.A. L.930 J.D. 17359 Waterbridge Dr.
Shumate, C. Keith .... '30 '66 C.251 B.E.E. L.1003 J.D. 11651 York Rd.‡
Stano, Susan L. ....'61 '96 C.62 B.S. L.1003 J.D. 4882 Princeton Dr.
Thomas, Phillip E., (BV) .... '47 '81 C.608 B.S. L.1003 J.D. 12800 York Rd.
Vozar, Donna M. ....'56 '92 C.62 B.A. L.1003 J.D. P.O. Box 33724
Weltman, S. Randall, (AV) '55 '85
C.846 B.A. L.7 J.D. Ohio Patrolmen's Benevolent Assn.

NORTHWOOD, 5,506, *Wood Co.*

Ballenger, Brian J., (BV) ....'59 '85 C.97 B.A. L.851 J.D. [Ballenger&M.] ⊙
Ballenger & Moore Co., L.P.A., (BV) .... 3401 Woodville Rd. (⊙Toledo)
Moore, Troy L., (BV) ....'60 '85 C.347 B.S. L.851 J.D. [Ballenger&M.] ⊙
Wasch, Tida K. ....'67 '96 C&L.851 B.S., J.D. 3484 Zepplin Ct.

NORTON, 11,477, *Summit Co.*

Connolly, Lisa Ann, (BV) ....'63 '89 C.679 B.A. L.8 J.D. 4290 Suttle Drive
Headley, David L., (BV) .... '27 '58 C.8 B.A. L.7 J.D. P.O. Box 1438
Judge, Christopher P. .... '77 '03 C.607 B.A. L.989 J.D. 4071 S. Cleve-Mass Rd.
Judge, John D. ....'36 '62 C.8 B.S.B.A. L.608 J.D. 3610 Wooddale Drive
Kennedy, David R. ....'56 '86 C.473 B.S.B.A. L.8 J.D. [Walkley&K.]
Tonies, Theresa Mary ....'62 '95 C.8 B.S.N. L.117 J.D. 2005 Connect Rd.
Walkley, Thomas L., (BV) ....'58 '86 C.130 B.A. L.8 J.D. [Walkley&K.]
Walkley & Kennedy, (BV) ....4071 S. Cleveland Masland Road

NORWALK, * 16,238, *Huron Co.*

Allton, John D., (BV) .... '47 '72 C.97 B.A. L.228 J.D. [Hiltz,W.A.&K.]
Baird, John D. ....'47 '75 C&L.862 B.S., J.D. 85 Benedict Avenue
Brown, Clifford F. .... '16 '38 C&L.602 B.A., LL.B. Ret. Supm. Ct. Jus.‡
Derby, Charles P., (CV) ....'53 '91 C.97 B.S.B.A. L.1003 J.D. Asst. Pros.
Fegen, Michael R., Law Offices, (BV) .... '41 '66 C.363 A.B. L.477 J.D. P.O. Box 465
Ford, George Cook, III, (CV) .... '46 '77 C.854 B.A. L.201 J.D. Co. Pub. Def. [G.C.Ford]
Ford, George Cook, (CV) ....9 Whittlesey Ave.
Freeman, Harold J., (BV) ....'46 '73 C.231 A.B. L.607 J.D. [Freeman&F.]
Freeman, Ronald H., (BV) ....'38 '66 C.30 B.A. L.150 J.D. 54 East Main Street
Freeman, Thomas H., (CV) .... '47 '75 C.49 B.S. L.607 J.D. [Freeman&F.]
Freeman and Freeman, (BV) .... 12 Whittlesey Ave.
Gentzel, Robert W., (BV) .... '53 '78 C.610 A.B. L.851 J.D. [R.W.Gentzel]
Gentzel, Robert W., Co., LPA, (BV) .... 32 Benedict Ave.
Gilbert, Danita A. .. '62 '88 C&L.608 B.S., J.D. Mag., Com. Pleas Ct., Juv. & Prob. Divs.
Harwood, David B., (BV) ....'48 '73 C.610 A.B. L.608 J.D. [Thornton,T.&H.] ⊙
Heydinger, Thomas E. ....'40 '67 C.201 B.A. L.607 J.D. Prob. & Juv. Ct. J.
Hiltz, Wiedemann, Allton & Koch Co., LPA, (AV) ....49 Benedict Ave
Kalfs, William D. ....'49 '83 C.608 B.A. L.117 J.D. Tucker Abstract & Title Co., Inc.
Kasper, Daivia S., The Law Office of ....'60 '95 C.679 B.S. L.930 J.D. 12 E. Main Street
Koch, Curtis J., (BV) .... '60 '85 [Hiltz,W.A.&K.]
Laycock, Jeffrey P., (BV) .... '44 '68 C.608 B.A. L.930 J.D. 54 E. Main St.
Leffler, Russell V., (BV) ....'52 '77 C.309 A.B. L.930 J.D. Shuron Co. Pros. Off
Longo, David J., (CV) .... '60 '86 C.532 B.A. L.607 J.D. Co. Pub. Def.
Lux, Paul G., (AV) ....'57 '81 C.8 B.S.I.M. L.1003 J.D. 3 Stower Lane, Unit 6
Lynch, Richard Standish, (BV) ....'48 '74 C.49 B.A. L.161 J.D. [Lynch&W.]
Lynch & White, (BV) ....51 E. Main St., Ste. B
McDaniel, H. Francis, Jr., (AV) .... '46 '72 C.611 B.A. L.477 J.D. 54 E. Main St.
Owens, William W., (BV) .... '43 '69 C.124 B.S.E.E. L.1003 J.D. 2 Oak St.
Paffenbarger, Thomas L., (AV) .... '25 '51 C&L.608 B.S., J.D. 3 Stower Lane, Suite 1‡
Palmer, Steven .... '62 '92 C.97 B.A. L.851 J.D. City of Norwalk, Law Dir.
Ridge, John, (BV) .... '54 '79 C.97 B.S. L.608 J.D. Norwalk Mun. Ct.
Ruggles, Warren W., Law Office, (BV) '38 '65 C.97 B.A. L.608 J.D.
10 1/2 Benedict Ave.
Ruggles, West M., Attorney at Law '76 '02 C.317 B.A. L.602 J.D.
10 1/2 Benedict Ave.
Schoren, James A. ....'59 '84 C&L.161 B.A., J.D. Asst. Pub. Def.
Swanson, Laura Perkovic ....'73 '00 C.150 B.F.A. L.851 J.D. 54 E Main St
Thornton, K. Alec, (BV) .... '60 '85 C.967 B.A. L.851 J.D. [Thornton,T.&H.]
Thornton, M. Kenneth, (AV) .... '22 '51 C&L.930 A.B., LL.B. [Thornton,T.&H.] ⊙
Thornton, Robert F., (AV) ....'32 '58 C&L.608 B.Sc., LL.B. [Thornton,T.&H.] ⊙
Thornton, Thornton & Harwood, (AV) ....50 N. Linwood Avenue (⊙Willard)
Waugh, Frederick F., (AV) .... '30 '63 C.97 B.S. L.1003 J.D. 12 E. Main Street
Weisenburger, Eric R., (BV) .... '64 '90 C.81 B.A. L.117 J.D. [Ⓐ Thornton,T.&H.]
White, Beverly M. Barr, (BV) .... '31 '60 C.97 B.S. L.607 J.D. [Lynch&W.]
White, Phillip M., Jr., (BV) .... '30 '60 C.97 A.B. L.607 J.D. Com. Pleas J.
Wiedemann, Robert A., (AV) ....'26 '52 C.645 B.S.C.E. L.365 J.D. [Hiltz,W.A.&K.]
Wineman, Reese M., (BV) ....'48 '76 C&L.851 B.A., J.D. 38 Whittlesey Avenue

NORWOOD, 21,675, *Hamilton Co.*

Shea, Joseph W., Jr., (BV) .... '18 '43 C.973 B.A. L.1340 LL.B. 4000 Montgomery Rd.
Strasser, Elmer ....'12 '37 C&L.150 LL.B. Secy. & Treas., Knowlton Mfg. Co.
Wall, Stacy M. ....'73 '98 C&L.607 B.A., J.D. Asst. City Law Dir.

NOVELTY, —, *Geauga Co.*

Bash, Gary M., (BV) .... '54 '81 C.477 B.A. L.161 J.D. 23780 Shaker Blvd.
Bialosky, Alan Mayer ....'32 '82 C.197 A.B. L.1003 J.D. 7489 Fairmont Road
Boyer, Elizabeth M. ....'— '47 C.97 B.S. L.1003 J.D. 7657 Dines Rd.
Curtis, Robert M. .... '43 '69 C.319 B.A. L.178 LL.B. 9261 Pecan Rd.‡
Evans, Janice S. .... '45 '78 C.161 B.S.Ed. L.1003 J.D. Mag.
Gordon, Murray B. ....'20 '52 C.102 B.A. L.1003 LL.B. 14669 Russell Lane‡
McGinty, Mary Jane ....'52 '83 C.339 B.S.N. L.1003 J.D. 9399 Pekin Road
Olds, Harry B., Jr. .... '23 '48 C&L.930 A.B., LL.B. 8626 Music St.‡

Shane, Barry, (BV) .... '44 '71 14094 Sweetbriar Ln.
Wiseley, Paul J. .... '21 '50 C.608 B.S. L.161 J.D. 13645 Fox Den E.

OAK HARBOR, 2,841, *Ottawa Co.*

Christie, Michelle Lynn .... '68 '93 C&L.608 B.A., J.D. [Graves,K.&C.]
Croy, Lorrain Rae .... '67 '95 C.835 B.S. L.1187 J.D. 218 E. Main St.
Graves, Gene W., (AV) .... '31 '60 C.970 B.A. L.851 LL.B. [Graves,K.&C.]
Graves, Kohli & Christie, (AV) .... 142 West Water Street
Kohli, Gary A., (AV) ....'46 '71 C.608 B.S. L.851 J.D. [Graves,K.&C.]
Krasniewski, Walter J. .... '29 '55 C.973 B.S. L.851 J.D. U.S. Bkrptcy. J.
McKean, Pamela A., (BV) .... '57 '85 C.97 B.S. L.851 J.D. 159 W. Water St.
Robertson, Jerry D., (BV) .... '48 '74 C.97 B.S. L.851 J.D. 132 West Water Street

OAKWOOD, 9,215, *Montgomery Co.*

Hickey, James P., (BV) ....'40 '68 C.201 B.A. L.1340 J.D. 4 E. Schantz Ave.
Holman, Robert B. .... '75 '00 C.347 B.A. L.7 J.D. 24262 Broadway Ave.

OBERLIN, 8,191, *Lorain Co.*

Baxter, Norman T., Jr. ....'42 '69 C.251 B.B.A. L.1003 J.D. Green Circle Growers, Inc.
Birmingham, John T. .... '42 '85 C.321 B.A. L.1003 J.D. 141 S. Professor St.‡
Brittingham, Smith R., III, (AV) .... '38 '79 C.604 A.B. L.930 J.D. 151 Forest Street
Dougan, Thomas J., (BV) .... '43 '73 C.161 B.A. L.1003 J.D. 5 W. College St.
Eckstein, Barry S., (BV) ....'45 '71 C.473 B.S. L.161 J.D. 5 W. College St.
Fauver, Robert N., (AV) ....'10 '35 C.31 B.A. L.477 J.D. 5 W. College St.
Harris, Nancy E. ....'53 '83 C.62 B.A. L.161 J.D. 46785 W. Hamilton St.
Heberling, Martin M., Co. (L.P.A.), (BV) ....'32 '65 C&L.608 B.S., J.D. P.O. Box 179
Jonesco, Jane R. .... '49 '80 C.611 B.A. L.209 J.D. Oberlin Coll.‡
Palmer, Robert A., (CV) .... '34 '76 C.381 B.A. L.7 J.D. 281 N. Prospect St.
Piraino, Thomas A. ....'21 '48 C.604 A.B. L.930 LL.B. 32 Kendal Dr.‡
Ressler, Jon H. .... '63 '97 C.8 B.A. L.930 J.D. [Roose&R.L.&Assoc.]
Roose, Kirk B., (BV) .... '46 '72 C.821 B.A. L.659 J.D. [Roose&R.L.&Assoc.]
Roose & Ressler, A Legal Professional Association, (BV)
5 South Main Street, Suite 301
Runyan, Wm. A. ....'16 '39 C&L.145 A.B., J.D. 101 Kendal Dr.‡
Sarringhaus, Kurt G., (BV) ....'51 '76 C.610 A.B. L.608 J.D. 5 S. Main St., Ste. 310
Severs, Eric R., (BV) ....'48 '75 C.207 B.A. L.161 J.D. [E.R.Severs]
Severs, Eric R., Co., L.P.A., (BV) ....5 S. Main St.
Willey, Loretta J., (BV) .... '62 '96 C.97 B.S. L.851 J.D. [Ⓐ Roose&R.L.&Assoc.]

OHIO CITY, 784, *Van Wert Co.*

Walters, Sumner J. ....'16 '40 C&L.607 J.D. Ret. Mun. J.

OLMSTED FALLS, 7,962, *Cuyahoga Co.*

Carpenter, Paul Philip .... '59 '84 C.381 B.A. L.8 J.D. 8 Cherry Ln.
Druhot, Raymond M. ....'27 '51 C.611 B.A. L.930 LL.B. 24699 Nobottom Rd.‡
Stuhr, Fredk. .... '18 '42 C&L.930 A.B., LL.B. 84 Florentine Way‡

ORANGE VILLAGE, 3,236, *Cuyahoga Co.*

Rudy, Herbert E. ....'17 '44 C.608 L.161 LL.B. 3791-4 Lander Road‡

OREGON, 19,355, *Lucas Co.*

Bihn, Jane F. .... '59 '83 C.1260 B.A. L.851 J.D. 860 Ansonia St., Ste. 11
Breier, Gary A., (BV) ....'51 '78 C&L.851 B.A., J.D. [Schlageter,B.&B.] ⊙
Davies, James L. '54 '97 C&L.851 J.D.
Sen. Coun., Sunoco Inc. (R&M) Toledo Refinery
Garand, John D., (BV) ....'43 '71 C.97 B.A. L.851 J.D. 860 Ansonia St.
Garand, Richard C., (BV) .... '38 '64 C.97 B.A. L.851 J.D. 860 Ansonia Street, Suite 113
Garand, Richard E., The Law Officse of '65 '00 C&L.851 B.A., J.D.
860 Ansonia Street
Hohenberger, Christopher E., (BV) .... '60 '88 C&L.851 B.Ed., J.D. 461 Bridgewater Dr.
Koehn, Richard W., (BV) '48 '79
C.610 B.B.A. L.851 J.D. 3015 Navarre Avenue, Suite 214
Mikesell, William H. ....'23 '50 C&L.851 B.B.A., J.D. 43 Ponderosa Dr.‡
Petroff, Donald Z. ....'38 '67 C&L.851 B.B.A., J.D. Mun. J.
Schlageter, Thomas G., (BV) ....'50 '75 C.321 B.A. L.851 J.D. [Schlageter,B.&B.] ⊙
Schlageter, Breier & Bryce, Co., L.P.A., (BV) ....715 S. Coy Rd. (⊙Toledo)
Winckowski, Scott A., (BV) .... '64 '89 C.476 B.S. L.851 J.D. 715 S. Coy Road

ORRVILLE, 8,551, *Wayne Co.*

Ekonomon, Adam M., (BV) '64 '89 C.980 B.S. L.7 J.D.
Asst. Gen. Coun., The J.M. Smucker Company
Forrer, Carl E., (CV) .... '47 '72 C.381 B.A. L.117 J.D. 136 E. Market St.
Harlan, M. Ann, (BV) .... '59 '85 C.787 B.A. L.930 J.D. The J.M. Smucker Company
Helmuth, R. J., (BV) .... '49 '79 C.381 B.S. L.7 J.D. [Johnson&H.]
Hohenberger, Raymond W., (BV) ....'46 '74 C&L.608 B.A., J.D. [Kropf,W.H.&L.]
Jackwood, Renee J. ....'60 '95 C.8 B.S. L.7 J.D. [Ⓐ Johnson&H.]
Johnson, John E., (BV) .... '37 '75 C.313 B.A. L.7 J.D. [Johnson&H.]
Johnson, John E., Jr., (BV) .... '61 '87 C.608 B.S. L.8 J.D. [Johnson&H.]
Johnson & Helmuth, (BV) ....343 S. Crownhill Rd.
Kirkbride, Cheryl Marie ....'69 '01 C.363 B.A. L.7 J.D. [Ⓐ Kropf,W.H.&L.]
Knudsen, Jeannette L. .... '69 '98 C&L.08 B.S., J.D. The J.M. Smucker Company
Kropf, John W., (BV) .... '43 '68 C.62 B.A. L.608 J.D. Law Dir. [Kropf,W.H.&L.]
Kropf, Wagner, Hohenberger & Lutz, L.L.P., (AV) ....100 N. Vine St.
Lutz, Daniel Robert, (BV) ....'62 '87 C.25 B.A. L.608 J.D. [Kropf,W.H.&L.]
Shinaberry, Shannon L. '69 '96 C.608 B.S.B.A. L.930 J.D.
Corp. Coun., The J.M. Smucker Company, Employ., Labor & Litig.
Vansickle, Timothy Ray .... '73 '98 C.8 B.S. L.7 J.D. [Ⓐ Kropf,W.H.&L.]
Wagner, Richard S., (AV) ....'34 '58 C&L.608 B.S., LL.B. [Kropf,W.H.&L.]
Waltman, P. Dean, (BV) .... '40 '65 C.608 B.S. L.607 J.D. 144 N Main St

OTTAWA, * 4,367, *Putnam Co.*

Basinger, Randall .... '52 '77 C.97 B.A. L.930 J.D. Com. Pleas J.
Blankemeyer, Anna Mae, (BV) .... '55 '81 C.1024 B.S. L.930 J.D. [Ⓐ Schroeder,S.&O.]
Bohrer, Bruce B., (CV) .... '51 '83 C.91 B.A. L.607 J.D. P.O. Box 85
Cunningham, Ann Recker, (BV) ....'38 '68 C.608 B.A. L.607 J.D. [Cunningham&C.]
Cunningham, Margaret Ann ....'38 '68 C.608 B.A. L.607 J.D. 749 N. Perry St.
Cunningham, Matthew A. .... '72 '99 C.201 B.S. L.851 J.D. [Cunningham&C.]
Cunningham, Paul H., (BV) .... '39 '65 C.608 B.S. L.1119 LL.B. [Cunningham&C.]
Cunningham & Cunningham, (BV) .... 749 N. Perry St. (⊙West Palm Beach, FL)
Gerschutz, Daniel R., (BV) .... '47 '75 C.97 B.S. L.851 J.D. Co. Pros. Atty.
Huntsman, Clair L. .... '31 '54 C&L.607 J.D. Prob. J.
Lammers, Gary L., (CV) .... '64 '89 C.608 B.A. L.607 J.D. 125 W. Main St.
Leopold, Jill Susann ....'74 '99 C&L.117 B.A., J.D. 321 E. Main Street
Leopold, Larry E., (BV) .... '47 '74 C&L.607 B.A., J.D. 321 E. Main St.
O'Malley, Michael E., (BV) '42 '68 C.276 A.B. L.930 J.D.
[M.E.O'Malley] & [Oxley,M.H.O.&W.] (⊙Findlay)

O'Malley, Michael E., LLC, (BV) ....P.O. Box 368
Sahloff, Kurt W., (BV) ....'68 '94 C&L.851 B.A., J.D. 321 E. Main St.
Schroeder, Clyde A., (BV) ....'38 '70 C.97 B.A. L.117 J.D. [Schroeder,S.&O.]
Schroeder, Joseph C., (CV) ....'65 '91 C.97 B.A. L.608 J.D. [Schroeder,S.&O.]
Schroeder, Schroeder & O'Malley, (BV) ....315 East Main Street
Shartzer, D. Jean, (CV) ....'48 '86 C&L.607 B.P.S., J.D. 145 Court St.
Unverferth, Thomas A. ....'29 '60 C.309 A.B. L.930 J.D. Prob. J.

OTTAWA HILLS, 4,564, *Lucas Co.*

Walter, James E. ....'42 '67 C.473 A.B. L.477 J.D. 2125 Hawthorne Rd.

OXFORD, 21,943, *Butler Co.*

Armogida, Harry ....'15 '72 C.608 B.A. L.1340 J.D. 11 Patrick Dr.
Bennett, Jay C. ....'49 '74 C.473 B.S. L.8 J.D. 5995 Fairfield Rd.
Bolin, L. Robert ....'67 '93 C.201 B.S. L.150 J.D. 29 N. Beech St.
Brinck, Melinda S. ....'74 '99 C.712 L.326 J.D. U.S. JAG Corps, Army
Deters, Dennis P. ....'75 '00 C.602 B.A. L.150 J.D. 121 W. High St.
Goldner, Arthur P., (BV) ....'23 '59 C.473 B.S. L.1340 J.D. 5995 Fairfield St.
Goodell, George S. '21 '49 C.145 M.B.A. L.436 LL.B.
(adm. in WI; not adm. in OH) 124 Country Club Dr.‡
Gump, W. Robert ....'28 '52 C.207 B.A. L.477 J.D. Miami University
Herron, Daniel J. '53 '78 C.473 A.B. L.930 J.D.
Assoc. Prof. of Bus. Legal Studies, Miami University
Huss, Dan E., (BV) ....'40 '65 C.473 B.S. L.1340 J.D. 29 N. Beech Street
Lawton, Anne '56 '87 C&L.477 A.B., J.D.
(adm. in MI; not adm. in OH) Asst. Prof., Miami Univ.
Lipnickey, Susan Cross, (CV) ....'53 '91 C.657 B.S. L.1340 J.D. [Robinson&L.]
Lospinoso, Nicholas A. '44 '79 C.201 B.A. L.150 J.D.
(adm. in MA; not adm. in OH) 25 Brigid Circle‡
Michael, James E., (BV) ....'48 '73 C.31 B.A. L.608 J.D. [Millikin&F.]

Millikin & Fitton Law Firm, A Legal Professional Association, (AV)
5020 B College Corner Pike, 45056 ⊙
Telephone: 513-523-3700 Fax: 513-523-0463
James E. Michael.
General PraCtice, Real Estate, Probate, Estate Planning, Corporation, Taxation, Personal Injury and Litigation.
Hamilton, Ohio Office: 6 S 2nd Street, 6th Floor, 45011. Telephone: 513-863-6700. Fax: 513-863-0031.
Fairfield, Ohio Office: 530 Wessel Drive, Suite 2A, 45014. Telephone: 513-829-6700. Fax: 513-829-0258.
Mason, Ohio Office: 6900 Tylersvile Road, Suite B, 45040. Telephone: 513-336-6363. Fax: 513-336-9411.

Parker, Robin L., (BV) ....'56 '82 C.608 B.S. L.838 J.D. Gen. Coun., Miami University
Parrish, Lee H., (AV) ....'43 '68 C.608 B.A. L.150 J.D. [Parrish,F.&M.] ⊙

Parrish, Fryman & Marcum Co., L.P.A., (AV)
5995 Fairfield Road, Unit One, 45056 ⊙
Telephone: 513-863-8270
URL: http://www.parrishattys.com
Lee H. Parrish.
Business, Real Estate, General Practice, Probate, Estate Planning and Banking Law.
Hamilton, Ohio Office: First National Bank Building, 300 High Street, Suite 704, P.O. Box 747, 45012-0747. Telephone: 513-863-8270. Telecopier: 513-863-9999.
See Professional Biographies, OXFORD, OHIO

Reardon, Rebecca Sue ....'55 '80 C.473 B.A. L.150 J.D. Miami Univ.
Robinson, James G., (BV) ....'46 '74 C.363 A.B. L.424 J.D. 14 W. Park Pl., Ste. D
Robinson & Lipnickey Co., L.P.A., (CV) ....Park Place West
Schoonover, Paul Edwin ....'47 '88 C.473 B.S. L.150 J.D. 115 W. High Street
Spohn, Monica L., (CV) ....'63 '96 C.473 B.A. L.1161 J.D. [M.L.Spohn]
Spohn, Monica L., Co., L.P.A., (CV) ....15 North Beech Street
Staton, Wayne, (CV) ....'47 '76 C.473 B.S. L.7 J.D. [W.Staton]
Staton, Wayne, Co., L.P.A., (CV) ....110 N. Beech St.
Thomas, Randi Malcolm ....'64 '93 C.473 B.A. L.880 J.D. Miami Univ.

PAINESVILLE, * 17,503, *Lake Co.*

Amery, Eric J., (CV) '57 '83
C.381 B.S. L.930 J.D. Legal Aid Society of Lake/Geauea Cos.
Anderson, George F. ....'54 '81 C.97 B.S.B.A. L.8 J.D. 1610 Mentor Ave., Ste. 2
Armstrong, John Andrew ....'70 '98 C.608 B.A. L.161 J.D. Staff Atty., Ct. of Com. Pleas
Aveni, Anthony J., (AV) ....'38 '66 C.602 B.S. L.1003 J.D. [Cannon,S.A.&L.]
Aveni, Benjamin L. ....'67 '92 C.802 B.A. L.1003 J.D. [Cannon,S.A.&L.]
Baetzel, Robert C. ....'54 '96 C.894 B.A. L.179 J.D. Fiscal Off., City of Painesville
Baker and Hackenberg Co., L.P.A., (AV) ....77 North St. Clair St.
Bartolotta, Mark J., (BV) ....'62 '92 C.8 B.S. L.1003 J.D. Asst. Pros. Atty.
Bell, Janette M., (BV) ....'65 '90 C.473 B.A. L.1003 J.D. Asst. Pros. Atty.
Berezin, Alec, (AV) ....'47 '74 C.473 B.A. L.930 J.D. [Dworken&B.]
Bernstein, Harry S. '62 '88 C.861 B.A. L.1003 J.D.
Owner, Gil Schwartz Distributors LLC
Bernstein, Howard W., (AV) ....'31 '55 C.610 A.B. L.608 J.D. [Dworken&B.]
Bevack, Gina M. ....'78 '03 C.363 B.A. L.1003 J.D. [Cannon,S.A.&L.]
Black, Jeffrey H., (BV) ....'57 '92 C.608 B.A. L.1003 J.D. [J.H.Black]
Black, Jeffrey H., Co. L.P.A., (BV) ....1501 Madison Avenue
Brown, Dale F., (BV) ....'37 '68 C.363 B.S. L.1003 J.D. 152 Main St.
Bruening, Francine M. ....'42 '71 C.999 B.A. L.1003 J.D. Com. Pleas J.
Bryan, Edward G., (BV) ....'66 '91 C.250 B.S. L.1003 J.D. Chief Asst. Pub. Def.
Cahill, Kenneth Jude, (CV) ....'64 '91 C.363 B.A. L.1003 J.D. 1959 Mentor Ave.
Campbell, Margaret S., (BV) ....'69 '95 C.473 B.S. L.607 J.D. Asst. Pub. Def.
Cannon, Charles E., (AV) ....'28 '54 C.201 L.1003 J.D. [Cannon,S.A.&L.] ‡
Cannon, Timothy P., (BV) ....'55 '80 C.363 B.A. L.1003 J.D. [Cannon,S.A.&L.]

Cannon, Stern, Aveni and Loiacono Co., L.P.A., (AV)
Milburn Building, 41 East Erie Street, 44077-3983
Telephone: 440-357-5537; Cleveland Direct Line: 440-942-5232 Telefax: 440-357-9234 URL: http://www.csalawgroup.com
Email: csal@csalawgroup.com URL: http://www.csallaw.com
Wayne R. Milburn (1910-1976); Charles E. Cannon (Retired); Anthony J. Aveni; James V. Loiacono; Timothy P. Cannon; Nicholas A. D'Angelo; Paul R. Malchesky;—Benjamin L. Aveni; Gina M. Bevack.
General Civil and Criminal Practice. Corporation, Small Business, Municipal, Family, Divorce, Probate, Trust and Estate Planning, Personal Injury, Environmental Law, Real Estate Law, Litigation and Medical Malpractice.
Counsel for: Hamann Construction Co.
See Professional Biographies, PAINESVILLE, OHIO

Cave, Gilbert T. ....'32 '60 C.363 B.S.S. L.1003 J.D. 7834 Brakeman Rd.‡
Chemnitz, Gregory R. '57 '84
C.692 B.A. L.276 J.D. Grp. Coun., RMWW, Avery Dennison Corp.
Cicconetti, Michael A. ....'51 '80 C.1290 B.A. L.1003 J.D. Mun. J.
Conway, Neil J., (BV) ....'50 '83 C.363 B.S.B.A. L.1162 J.D. 162 Main Street
Cooper, Linda D., (BV) ....'— '78 C.235 B.S. L.1003 J.D. [Cooper&F.]

Cooper & Forbes, (BV)
Main Street Law Building, 166 Main Street, 44077
Telephone: 440-357-6211 Cleveland Direct: 942-9027 Fax: 440-357-1634
Email: cooperandforbes@prodigy.net URL: http://www.cooperandforbes.lawoffice.com
Glenn E. Forbes; Linda D. Cooper (Certified Specialist in Family Relations Law, Ohio State Bar Association). Associate: Paul Eugene Miller.
Commercial and Retail Collections, Commercial Law, Bankruptcy, Domestic Relations, Chapter 11, Debtors Rights, General Civil Trial Practice, Creditors Rights. Trials and Appeals in all Courts.
See Professional Biographies, PAINESVILLE, OHIO

Corrigan, Victoria Marie ....'59 '99 C.251 B.B.A. L.989 J.D. Jud. Staff Atty.
Cort, Kenneth M., (BV) ....'34 '71 C.477 B.B.A. L.1003 J.D. 1111 Mentor Ave.
Coulson, Charles E., (AV) ....'44 '74 C.381 B.A. L.8 J.D. Co. Pros.
Crouse, Gregory A. '53 '84 C.970 B.A. L.365 J.D.
(adm. in IL; not adm. in OH) 1195 Madison Ave.‡
Cruikshank, David E., (AV) ....'45 '73 C.210 B.A. L.930 J.D. 8 N. State St.
Culotta, Vincent A. ....'65 '90 C.97 B.S., B.A. L.608 J.D. Com. Pleas J.
Dana, Richard L., Jr. ....'69 '95 C.608 B.S. L.930 J.D. [Talikka&I.]
D'Angelo, Nicholas A., (BV) ....'62 '87 C.363 B.A. L.7 J.D. [Cannon,S.A.&L.]
Delong, Hallryn Sue ....'75 '00 C.473 B.A. L.124 J.D. Pub Def.
DiFranco, Carl L., Esquire '71 '98 C.679 B.A. L.645 J.D.
2603 Riverside Drive, Suite 100
Dukowski, Darryl J. ....'47 '87 C.62 B.A. L.7 J.D. I.R.S.
Dworken, David M. ....'32 '56 C&L.608 B.A., LL.B. 60 South Park Place‡
Dworken, Marvin P., (AV) ....'35 '59 C&L.608 B.S.C., J.D. [Dworken&B.]
Dworken & Bernstein Co., L.P.A., (AV) ....60 South Park Place
Eiger, Marley F., (BV) ....'49 '74 C.599 B.A. L.1003 J.D. Legal Aid Soc.
Falkowski, Colleen A. ....'53 '79 C.876 B.A. L.1003 J.D. Judge
Farren, David E., (BV) ....'54 '83 C.434 B.A. L.150 J.D. Co. Pub. Def.
Forbes, Glenn E., (BV) ....'53 '79 C.970 B.A. L.930 J.D. [Cooper&F.]
Fram, Jeffrey W., (CV) ....'52 '77 C.318 B.A. L.607 J.D. Mag., Dom. Rel. Ct.

Gardner, Mark, Attorney and Counselor at Law
(See Cleveland)

Gilson, Gregory M., (CV) ....'47 '72 C.97 B.S. L.1003 J.D. 6949 Morley Road
Gurley, Joanne G., (CV) ....'47 '81 C.97 B.S. L.1003 J.D. 270 E. Main St.
Gurley, Joseph M., (BV) ....'47 '75 C.97 B.S. L.420 J.D. Law Dir.
Hackenberg, I. James, (AV) ....'38 '64 C.62 B.A. L.930 J.D. [Baker&H.]
Haskell, George B. P., (BV) ....'44 '75 C.976 B.A. L.930 J.D. 8 N. State St.
Hennig, Richard A., (BV) ....'55 '83 C.473 B.A. L.1003 J.D. [Baker&H.]
Hurley, John J., Jr., (AV) ....'43 '68 C.363 A.B. L.930 J.D. [Nelson,S.&H.]
Hurley, Michael P., (BV) ....'46 '74 C.363 B.S.B.A. L.1003 J.D. [Nelson,S.&H.]
Ischie, Wilbur N., (BV) ....'49 '75 C.967 B.S. L.930 J.D. [Talikka&I.]
Jackson, James W. ....'34 '63 C.473 B.S. L.150 J.D. Com. Pleas J.
Kaiser, Mark Alan ....'55 '85 C.510 B.A. L.989 J.D. [M.A.Kaiser]
Kaiser, Mark A. ....P.O. Box 632
Kidd, Patricia Ann ....'63 '99 C.392 B.S. L.989 J.D. 54 S. State Street
Kilpeck, Lori ....'75 '02 C.161 B.A. L.989 J.D. [Ziegler,M.&M.] (⊙Cleveland)

Klein & Carney Co., L.P.A.
(See Cleveland)

Klucher, Gregory W. ....'61 '86 C.8 B.A. L.161 J.D. Chf. Dep. Clk. to Mag.

Knevel & Associates Co. LPA
(See Cleveland)

Koerner, David E., (BV) ....'58 '85 C&L.201 B.A., J.D. 11770 Painesville Warren Road
Koerner, James P., (BV) ....'50 '75 C.210 B.A. L.607 J.D. 270 E. Main St.
Kondas, Dale R., (BV) ....'51 '79 C.161 B.A. L.1003 J.D. Chf. Asst. Pros. Atty.
Kraus, Keith R., (BV) ....'59 '84 C.1365 B.A. L.930 J.D. [Dworken&B.]
Kubyn, R. Russell, (CV) ....'58 '84 C.930 B.A. L.161 J.D. 100 S. Park Pl.
LaForce, Robert W. ....'51 '81 C.610 B.S. L.1003 J.D. 10870 Tanglewood Trail
Lawson, Karen D., (BV) ....'56 '82 C.129 B.A. L.1003 J.D. 402 Bank Street
Linden, Taylir K. ....'69 '94 C.81 B.A. L.117 J.D. Co. Pros. Off.
Lister, Kevin S. ....'58 '86 C.604 B.A. L.930 J.D. 7 N. Park Pl., Apt. 21
Loiacono, James V., (BV) ....'53 '78 C.999 B.A. L.607 J.D. [Cannon,S.A.&L.]
Lucci, Eugene A., (BV) ....'54 '80 C.930 B.A. L.1003 J.D. Common Pleas J.
Madden, Richd. A., L.P.A., (CV) ....'32 '57 C.930 L.608 LL.B. 1 New Market Pl.
Malchesky, Paul R. ....'72 '97 C.161 B.A. L.1003 J.D. [Cannon,S.A.&L.]

Mann, Theodore M., Jr., Law Firm
(See Cleveland)

McGuinness, Clare Ignatia ....'35 '85 C.363 B.A. L.989 J.D. 8 North State Street
Miller, Paul Eugene ....'65 '97 C.381 B.A. L.989 J.D. [Cooper&F.]
Mitrovich, Paul H. ....'34 '66 C.608 B.S. L.851 J.D. Com. Pleas J.
Moseman, Heather L. ....'70 '03 C.1342 B.A. L.8 J.D. [H.L.Moseman]

Moseman, Heather L., Esq., L.L.C.
P.O. Box 730, 44077
Telephone: 440-350-4779 Fax: 440-350-4613
Email: mosemanlaw@yahoo.com URL: http://www.lawyers.com/mosemanlaw
Heather L. Moseman.
Estate Planning, Probate, Civil Litigation, General Practice, Bankruptcy.
See Professional Biographies, PAINESVILLE, OHIO

Murphy, Patrick T., (BV) ....'61 '86 C.381 B.A. L.1003 J.D. [Dworken&B.]
Murray, Michael Doran, (BV) ....'61 '88 C.610 B.A. L.1003 J.D. [Redmond W.&M.]
Myers, Robert H., Jr., (BV) ....'50 '91 C.392 B.S. L.1003 J.D. [R.H.Myers,Jr.]
Myers, Robert H., Jr., Co., PA, (BV) ....56 Liberty St., Ste. 201
Nelson, Sweet & Hurley, (AV) ....8 North State Street, Suite 201
Nocero, Patricia A., (BV) ....'51 '80 C.392 A.B. L.930 J.D. 55 Mentor Avenue
Okin, Gary S., (BV) ....'52 '77 C.902 B.A. L.1003 J.D. [Dworken&B.]
Orosz, Richard T., (BV) ....'42 '71 C.392 B.S. L.1003 J.D. 56 Liberty St.
Parks, Martin O. ....'42 '68 C.363 B.S. L.930 J.D. Com. Pleas J.
Perotti, Patrick J., (BV) ....'56 '82 C.161 B.A. L.1003 J.D. [Dworken&B.]
Peters, Jennifer L. ....'70 '99 C.150 B.A. L.989 J.D. Lake Co. Ct. of Common Pleas
Plassard, Brett J., (CV) ....'59 '85 C.392 B.S. L.607 J.D. 1875 W. Jackson St.
Ponce de Leon, Agustin ....'66 '97 C.677 B.A. L.930 J.D. Asst. Co. Pub. Def.

Potash, Lester S., Law Offices of
(See Cleveland)

Prokop, Joseph M., (CV) ....'20 '52 C.602 B.S. L.1003 LL.B. Juv. Ct. Ref.
Rabb, Howard S., (BV) ....'60 '86 C.608 B.S.B.A. L.1003 J.D. [Dworken&B.]
Raj, Manav H. ....'70 '96 C.608 B.A. L.1003 J.D. [Dworken&B.]
Redmond, Edward C., (BV) ....'21 '57 C.966 B.B.A. L.1003 J.D. [Redmond W.&M.]
Redmond Walker & Murray, (BV) ....174 North St. Clair Street
Resnick, Melvyn E., (BV) ....'41 '66 C.610 B.S. L.930 J.D. [Dworken&B.]
Rice, Michael W. '66 '90 C.97 B.A. L.608 J.D.
(adm. in WV; not adm. in OH) [Rice&Assoc.]
Rice & Associates, L.C. ....1520 Clipper Cv.

Richards, David J., Jr., (AV) ... '47 '71 C.473 B.A. L.161 J.D. [Dworken&B.]
Richer, Donald A., Law Offices of, (BV) '49 '75
C.381 B.A. L.930 J.D. 270 Main Street, Suite 160
Rizzo, Rudolph V., (CV) ... '26 '52 C.381 L.1003 J.D. 77 N. St. Clair St.
Roll, Kenneth R. ... '54 '80 C.161 B.A. L.1003 J.D. Mag.
Rosner, Irving, (BV) ... '53 '79 C.608 B.S. L.1003 J.D. [Dworken&B.]
Schulz, Martin C. ... '63 '92 C.188 B.A. L.273 J.D. Asst. Pros. Atty.
Selby, Richard N., II, (CV) ... '66 '92 C&L.930 B.S., J.D. [🄰 Dworken&B.]
Sherlock, Kristen M. ... '75 '01 C.97 B.S. L.989 J.D. [🄰 Dworken&B.]

Shryock & Morrison
(See Wickliffe)

Silakoski, Linda G. ... '52 '97 C.528 B.M.Ed. L.1003 J.D. 8 N. State St., Ste. 400
Skok, Fred V. ... '30 '56 C.674 A.B. L.930 J.D. Prob. J.
Sommers, JoAnne V., (CV) ... '31 '73 C.97 B.S. L.1003 J.D. 53 E. Erie Street
Spink, Myra Jane A. ... '16 '41 C&L.930 B.A., LL.B. 311 S. St. Clair St.‡
Spink, Roland B. ... '13 '42 C&L.930 A.B., LL.B. 311 S. St. Clair St.‡
Stender, Jonathan T. ... '65 '99 C.911 B.A. L.930 J.D. [🄰 Dworken&B.]

Sternberg & Zeid Co., L.P.A.
(See Mentor)

Svete, McGee & Carrabine Co., L.P.A.
(See Chardon)

Sweeney, John J. ... '18 '48 C.363 A.B. L.1003 LL.B. 69 Stratford Rd.‡
Szmagala, Taras G., Jr. '66 '91 C&L.893 B.A., J.D
Grp. Coun., Converted Prod. Grp., Avery Dennison Corp.
Talikka, Leo J., (BV) ... '39 '68 C.318 B.A. L.607 J.D. [Talikka&I.]
Talikka and Ischie, (BV) ... 2603 Riverside Dr.
Tinkler, Timothy E. '38 '73
C.392 B.S.Ch. L.1003 J.D. Secy. & Gen. Coun., Ricerca, Inc. (Pat.)
Tomaszewski, Jodi Littman ... '72 '99 C&L.124 B.A., J.D. [🄰 Dworken&B.]
Trimble, Kathy D. '63 '88 C.294 B.A. L.665 J.D.
(adm. in WV; not adm. in OH) [🄲 Rice&Assoc.]
Turoff, Geoffrey H. ... '— '88 C.608 B.S. L.1003 J.D. [🄰 Dworken&B.]
Ulrich, Joseph R., (BV) ... '44 '69 C.363 B.A. L.930 J.D. 1959 Mentor Ave.
Unterweiser, Carl H. '58 '84 C.97 B.A. L.150 J.D.
Gen. Coun., Lake Hospital System Inc.
Walker, Gerald R., (BV) ... '48 '73 C.611 B.A. L.930 J.D. [Redmond W.&M.]
Warmeling, Jonathan R., (CV) ... '63 '93 C.161 B.A. L.1003 J.D. P.O. Box 1011
Weaver, William W. ... '36 '67 C.363 B.S. L.1003 J.D. Juv. Ct. J.
Weiss, Francis P. ... '56 '82 C.602 B.A. L.930 J.D. Mag. Juv. Ct.
Wilson, Neil R., (BV) ... '43 '73 C.381 B.A. L.930 J.D. 56 Liberty Street, Suite 205
Ziegler, Metzger & Miller LLP, (AV) ... 152 Main Street (⊙Cleveland, Pepper Pike)

PANDORA, 1,188, *Putnam Co.*

Diller, Jon N., (BV) ... '48 '75 C.97 B.A. L.607 J.D. 208 E. Main Street
Steingass, Bruce D. ... '57 '85 C.97 B.L.S. L.607 J.D. 3381 Rd. Q

PARMA, 85,655, *Cuyahoga Co.*

Asad, Samuel C. ... '16 '42 C.363 L.161 LL.B. 11401 West Pleasant Valley
Bazarko, Volodymyr O., (BV) ... '40 '70 C.672 B.S. L.1003 J.D. 5566 Pearl Rd.
Belovich, Robert F., (BV) ... '20 '52 C.363 L.1003 LL.B. 5638 Ridge Rd.
Belovich, Robert S., (BV) ... '51 '77 C.930 B.A. L.1003 J.D. 5638 Ridge Rd.
Boyko, Timothy A., (AV) ... '61 '89 C.161 B.A. L.1003 J.D. [Boyko&D.]
Boyko & DoBeck, (AV) ... 6741 Ridge Rd.
Bubna, Walter P., (BV) ... '54 '80 C.161 B.B.A. L.1003 J.D. 5700 Pearl Rd, Ste 304
Chimples, Constantine G. ... '48 '73 C.611 B.A. L.94 J.D. Pres., Amac Enterprises, Inc.
Cichocki, Bruce M., (BV) ... '50 '75 C.97 B.S.Ed. L.930 J.D. 2525 Brookpark Rd.
Courey, Bruce Michael, (BV) ... '64 '89 C.602 B.A. L.930 J.D. Asst. Pros. Atty.
Dobeck, Timothy G., (AV) ... '61 '86 C.161 B.A. L.1003 J.D. [Boyko&D.]
Dorocak, John R. ... '52 '77 C.973 A.B. L.930 J.D. 5954 Broadview Rd.
Dugan, Thomas A., (AV) ... '31 '58 C.363 A.B. L.930 LL.B. 7520 Dogwood Lane‡
Dunning, Mary Louise ... '37 '86 C.62 B.A. L.365 J.D. Mun. J.
Dyck, John D. ... '46 '75 C.97 B.A. L.477 J.D. 6502 Renwood
Falconi, Ronald E., Law Office of ... '69 '95 C.363 B.A. L.8 J.D. 5509 Ridge Road
Fink, Edward J., (AV) ... '51 '76 C.62 B.A. L.851 J.D. Ref. Mag.
Finnerty, David J., (BV) ... '64 '92 C.161 B.A. L.1003 J.D. 5700 Pearl Road, Suite 202
Fletcher, Robert ... '20 '48 C.610 B.F.A. L.930 LL.B. 5801 Hollywood Dr.‡
Gatz, Joseph W. ... '20 '55 C.930 L.1003 J.D. 5566 Pearl Rd.
Graves, Harold D., (BV) ... '34 '61 C.381 B.S. L.1003 J.D. 5788 Ridge Rd.
Hamann, Thos. J. ... '25 '56 C.363 B.S.S. L.1003 J.D. 2911 Standish Ave.
Koscianski, Raymond Anthony ... '27 '58 C.363 B.S.S. L.989 J.D. 5700 Pearl Road
Leary, Lynn Walter, (AV) ... '32 '63 C.201 B.A. L.1003 J.D. [L.Leary]
Leary, Lynn, Co., L.P.A., (AV) ... 5700 Pearl Road
McCauley, Christopher J., (BV) ... '60 '86 C.608 B.S.B.A. L.1003 J.D. 5454 State Rd.
Myers, William E. ... '23 '48 C&L.150 LL.B. 8208 Valley Lane
Nebesh, Eugene ... '34 '71 C&L.1003 B.S., J.D. 1949 W. Pleasant Valley Rd.
Oryshkewych, George R., (BV) ... '65 '92 C&L.930 B.A., J.D. [🄰 G.V.Oryshkewych]
Oryshkewych, George V., (BV) ... '38 '71 C.363 B.S. L.1003 J.D. 5566 Pearl Rd.
Papcke, Mary Elizabeth ... '55 '84 C.8 B.S. L.161 J.D. [M.E.Papcke]
Papcke, Mary E. ... 12936 Huffman Rd.
Petrenko, George P. ... '52 '77 C.930 B.A. L.1003 J.D. 1823 Brookview Blvd.‡
Russo, Basil M., (BV) ... '47 '72 C.363 B.A. L.1003 J.D. [B.Russo]
Russo, Basil, & Company, L.P.A., (BV) ... 6656 Ridge Road
Savage, Walter A. ... '25 '51 C&L.930 B.A., J.D. Ret. Mun. J.
Schutz, Otto W., (AV) ... '10 '36 C&L.930 B.A., J.D. 8322 Fernhill Ave.‡
Tischer, Michelle Julia Galaska ... '60 '87 C.161 B.A. L.1003 J.D. 6502 Charles Ave.
Tryk, Julia Osborne '49 '78 C&L.560 B.U.S., J.D.
(adm. in NM; not adm. in OH) Assoc. Prof., Cuyahoga Community College
Walick, Joseph A. ... '24 '63 C.251 B.E.E. L.1003 J.D. 5225 Thoreau Dr.
Weaver, Jeannette Marie ... '61 '88 [🄲 Boyko&D.]
Weisenborn, Denise ... '54 '80 C.161 B.A. L.1003 J.D. 6905 Ridge Rd. #3D
Zampedro, Anthony John ... '64 '91 C&L.851 B.S., J.D. 6611 Ridge Road

PARMA HEIGHTS, 21,659, *Cuyahoga Co.*

Adamczyk, Beverly A., (BV) ... '52 '90 C.62 B.A. L.1003 J.D. 6929 W. 130th St.
Chizmar, Gregory A., (BV) ... '52 '77 C.228 B.A. L.1003 J.D. City Pros.
Feola, Dennis L., (BV) ... '42 '74 C.381 B.S. L.1003 J.D. 6684 Fernhurst Ave.
Fitzgerald, Arthur R., (BV) ... '32 '62 C.321 B.S. L.1003 J.D. 11410 Holliston Lane
Gartman, Thomas N., (BV) ... '49 '76 6358 Pearl Road
Gulyassy, Victor J., (BV) ... '20 '50 C&L.602 A.B., LL.B. 6461 Pearl Rd.‡
Kamps, Eugene A. ... '23 '62 L.1003 J.D. 6500 Pearl Rd.‡
Kulig, John J., (BV) ... '31 '60 C.930 A.B. L.608 J.D. 6325 York Road
Mize, Timothy J. ... '54 '84 C.161 B.A. L.999 J.D. 5868 Lotusdale Dr.
Pojman, Paul J. ... '17 '42 C.363 Ph.B. L.930 J.D. 5851 Pearl Rd.
Schad, Mildred K., (BV) ... '39 '68 C.610 B.S. L.1003 J.D. 6325 York Rd.

Spanagel, George W. ... '24 '50 C&L.930 B.B.A., LL.B. 5871 Wickfield Dr.‡
Travis, Gary Nicholas, (BV) ... '56 '82 C.161 B.A. L.1003 J.D. 10983 Lafayette Dr.
Wilbur, Thomas Blair, (BV) ... '42 '68 C.381 B.S. L.1003 J.D. 6325 York Road, Suite 305

PATASKALA, 10,249, *Licking Co.*

Benson, Michael E.
(See Columbus)

Brush, C. Bernard, (BV) ... '49 '75 C.951 B.A. L.117 J.D. 5530 Columbia Rd., S.W.

Colley Shroyer & Abraham Co., L.P.A.
(See Columbus)

Corban, William V. ... '43 '71 C&L.608 B.S., J.D. P.O. Box 34
Floyd, Dixie K. ... '57 '88 C.608 B.S. L.117 J.D. 3390 Watkins Road
Handley, Bobby J. ... '69 '98 C.608 B.A. L.117 J.D. 464 Broadview Ct.
Hayes, W. Scott ... '68 '93 C.473 B.S. L.608 J.D. [Hayes]
Hayes, William C., (BV) ... '44 '78 C&L.117 B.S., J.D. [Hayes]
Hayes Law Office, (BV) ... 195 E. Broad St.

Kenney-Pfalzer, Susan
(See Columbus)

Peters, John I., (CV) ... '40 '75 C.608 B.Sc. L.117 J.D. [J.I.Peters]
Peters, John I., Co., L.P.A., (CV) ... 26 1/2 E. Front St.
Philabaum, Laura Blanchard ... '57 '89 C.610 B.B.A. L.8 J.D. 61 Thomas Christopher Ln.
Shackelford, Margaret O'Connor '43 '87 C.737 B.A. L.608 J.D.
Exec. V.P. & Gen. Coun., Allen Refractories Co.
Sims, August C. ... '48 '84 C.640 B.A. L.117 J.D. 7010 Gale Rd. S.W.

PAULDING, * 3,595, *Paulding Co.*

Burkard, Joseph R., (CV) ... '60 '92 C.253 B.A. L.851 J.D. [Cook,T.&B.]
Cook, Norman E., (AV) ... '41 '68 C.608 A.B. L.607 J.D. [Cook,T.&B.]
Cook, Troth & Burkard, Ltd., (AV) ... 112 North Water Street
DeMuth, John A. ... '53 '79 C.608 B.A. L.117 J.D. Prob. & Juv. Ct. J.
Gorrell, Brian S. ... '76 '02 C&L.851 B.B.A., J.D. [🄰 Cook,T.&B.]
Hyman, Harvey E. ... '17 '40 C.610 L.607 LL.B. 123 N. Main St.
Jones, Michael C., (BV) ... '52 '79 C&L.117 B.A., J.D. 308 North Main Street
McMaster, Russell J. ... '35 '66 C.203 A.B. L.477 J.D. 115 N. Williams St., 2nd Fl.‡
Pieper, Timothy R., (BV) ... '58 '86 C.992 B.A. L.851 J.D. P.O. Box 296

Sponseller, James M., (BV) '49 '74 C&L.607 B.S.Ed., J.D.
200 North Williams Street, 45879-1252
Telephone: 419-399-2217 Fax: 419-399-2535
Real Estate and Probate and Estate Planning. General Civil Practice. Commercial, Corporation, Municipal Corporations.
Representative Clients: A list will be furnished upon request.
Agent for: The Ohio Bar Title Insurance Co.
References: Sky Bank, Paulding, Ohio; State Bank & Trust Co., Paulding, Ohio.

Spriggs, James P., (BV) ... '45 '73 C.203 B.S. L.607 J.D. 308 North Main Street
Troth, Glenn Hancock, (BV) ... '51 '82 C.611 B.F.A. L.607 J.D. [Cook,T.&B.]
Webb, J. David ... '46 '71 C.215 A.B. L.607 J.D. Com. Pleas J.
Young, Patrick H., (BV) ... '38 '66 C.97 B.S. L.215 J.D. [P.H.Young]
Young, Patrick H., Co., L.P.A., (BV) ... 106 1/2 E. Jackson Street, Suite A

PEMBERVILLE, 1,279, *Wood Co.*

Davies, R. Nigel, (AV) ... '49 '76 C.051 L.851 J.D. [Davies&R.] ⊙

Davies & Ruck, PLL, (AV)
427 W. College Avenue, P.O. Box 412, 43404 ⊙
Telephone: 419-287-3233 Fax: 419-287-3215
Email: ndaviesruck@aol.com
Members of Firm: R. Nigel Davies; J. Douglas Ruck.
General Civil Trial Litigation in all Local Courts, Estate and Tax Planning, Probate, Trusts, Real Estate Law and Development, Business Law, Corporations and Partnerships, Family Law, Personal Injury, Criminal Law and Traffic Violations.
Bowling Green, Ohio Office: 441 Frazee Avenue, Suite C, 43402. Telephone: 419-287-3233. Fax: 419-287-3215.
Woodville, Ohio Office: 109 W. Main Street, 43469. Telephone: 419-849-2583. Fax: 419-849-3211.

Kuhlman, Robert A., (BV) ... '55 '79 C&L.851 B.S., J.D. 221 E. Front St.
Ruck, J. Douglas ... '67 '97 C.97 B.S. L.851 J.D. [Davies&R.] (⊙Bowling Green)

PEPPER PIKE, 6,040, *Cuyahoga Co.*

Aggers, Joseph & Cheverine Co., L.P.A.
(See Cleveland)

Berman, Nora Krasney ... '52 '78 C.477 A.B. L.884 J.D. 2645 Hickory Lane‡
Brouman, Alvin ... '30 '55 L.1003 J.D. Pres., Gen. Coun., Brouman's Inc.
Brown, Harvey A. ... '39 '65 C.930 B.A. L.1003 29525 Chargin Blvd., Suite 312
Byrne, Neil J. ... '28 '53 C.930 A.B. L.1003 J.D. 29915 Bolingbrook Rd.‡
Caplan, Leah M. ... '60 '86 C.597 B.A. L.309 J.D. [🄰 Margulies&L.]
Carpenter, William H. ... '29 '54 C.674 A.B. L.477 LL.B. 3137 Fox Hollow Dr.‡
Elder, Judith L. '51 '75 C.910 B.A. L.623 J.D.
(adm. in OK; not adm. in OH) 29600 Bryce Rd.‡
Engel, James J. ... '34 '63 C.973 B.S.B.A. L.1340 J.D. 32149 S. Woodland Rd.

Gold, Rosemary Grdina, (AV) '48 '82 C.599 B.A. L.161 J.D.
33000 Pine Tree Road, 44124
Telephone: 216-593-0001 Fax: 216-591-1514
Email: rggoldlaw@adelphia.net
Family Law, Civil Litigation, Divorce, and Appellate Practice.
Downtown Cleveland Office: 1140 Leader Building, 526 Superior Ave. E., Cleveland, OH 44114. Telephone: 216-696-6122.

See Professional Biographies, PEPPER PIKE, OHIO

Greenfield, Mark R. '55 '81 C.273 B.A. L.1003 J.D.
Corp. Coun., Robert L. Stark Enterprises, Inc.
Hendershott, Howard E., Jr., (AV) ... '26 '53 C.453 B.S. L.930 J.D. [🄰 Ziegler,M.&M.]

Karberg, Kurant, Wachter & Turner Co., L.P.A.
(See Cleveland)

Khoury, Alisa K. ... '71 '99 C&L.124 B.A., J.D. [🄰 Margulies&L.]
Kozak, Henry ... '12 '42 C.124 B.S. L.989 J.D. 30779 Shaker Blvd.‡
Krenzler, Alvin I. ... '21 '48 C&L.930 A.B., LL.B. 28099 North Woodland Road
Levinson, Jeffrey M., (AV) ... '60 '90 C.597 B.S.E.E. L.930 J.D. [Margulies&L.]
Margulies, James W. ... '64 '94 C.608 B.S. L.705 J.D. [Margulies&L.]

Margulies & Levinson LLP, (AV)
30100 Chagrin Boulevard Suite 250, 44124
Telephone: 216-514-5997 Fax: 216-514-5996
URL: http://www.ml-legal.com
James W. Margulies; Jeffrey M. Levinson;—Leah M. Caplan; Alisa K. Khoury.
Business Reorganization, Creditors' Rights, Public and Private Securities, Mergers and Acquisitions, E-Commerce, Computer Licensing, Technology Agreements, Business Law, Emerging Growth Companies.

See Professional Biographies, PEPPER PIKE, OHIO

Matas, Vytas R. ....'40 '71 C.363 B.S. L.1003 J.D. 2412 Cedarwood (Pat.)
McKown, Michael O. ....'53 '77 C&L.8 B.A., J.D. Amer. Coal Co.
Montello, John J. ....'59 '87 C.381 B.B.A. L.1003 J.D. 30550 S Woodland Rd
Parisi, Stephen T., (AV) .... '40 '66 C.973 B.S. L.930 J.D. 30800 Brookwood Drive
Sadler, Richard T. .... '26 '54 C.966 B.S. L.1003 LL.B. 2726 S.O.M. Center Road
Singer, Melvin J., (Co., L.P.A.), (BV) ...'34 '60 C&L.930 B.B.A., LL.B. 3463 Lander Rd.
Soukup, Christopher E. '48 '75 C.608 B.A. L.930 J.D.
[Ziegler,M.&M.] (Cleveland)
Tognetti, Edward J. '51 '77
C.902 B.A. L.365 J.D. Sr. V.P. & Chf. Fid. Offr., Sky Trust, N.A.
Vivarronda, Steven James ....'59 '00 C.363 B.A. L.989 J.D. 30195 Chargin Boulevard
Whitehill, Joan B. ....'45 '81 L.161 J.D. 28101 Cambridge Lane
Wortzman, William A. ....'43 '74 C&L.1003 B.B.A., J.D. Pres., The Wortzman Company
Ziegler, Metzger & Miller, (AV)
29525 Chagrin Boulevard, Suite 310 (Cleveland, Painesville)

PERRY, 1,195, *Lake Co.*

Goldstein, Noreen Koppelman '— '90
C.930 B.S. L.1019 J.D. Pres. & Corp. Atty., Midwest Materials
Robbins, Brian D. '69 '94 C.477 B.A. L.569 J.D.
(adm. in CT; not adm. in OH) Mid-West Materials, Inc.
Wadding, Edward Arthur ....'71 '01 C.827 B.A. L.124 J.D. 3537 North Ridge Rd.

PERRYSBURG, 16,945, *Wood Co.*

Albrechta and Coble, (AV) .... 138 East Third Street (Fremont, Toledo)
Amato, Christopher J. ....'51 '78 C.602 B.A. L.851 J.D. 909 Bexton Drive
Aubry, P. Martin, (BV) ....'44 '82 C.313 B.A. L.851 J.D. 110 W. 2nd. St.
Aufderstrasse, David L., (AV) '33 '62 C.97 B.A. L.597 J.D.
(adm. in IL; not adm. in OH) 11085 Riverbend East Court
Barefoot, Charles R., Jr., (AV) ......'20 '50 C&L.851 A.B., LL.B. 29625 Shelbourne Rd.‡
Beier, Gayle K. ....'75 '00 C.97 B.A. L.851 J.D. [S.A.Skiver]
Brown, Timothy J. ....'54 '84 C&L.851 B.A., J.D. 27457 Holiday Ln.
Buchanan, J. Matthew '69 '00 C.608 B.S. L.851 J.D.
(adm. in MI; not adm. in OH; Pat.) [Fraser M.B.M.]
Celley, Walter J., (BV) ....'52 '87 C.97 B.L.S. L.851 J.D. 27457 Holiday Ln.
Christman, Judith H. ....'51 '76 C&L.477 B.A., J.D. 29263 Belmont Lake Rd.‡
Clark, Mary C., (CV) ....'55 '93 C.1216 B.A. L.851 J.D. 27457 Holiday Ln.
Coble, Richard A., (BV) ....'31 '69 C.313 B.S. L.851 J.D. [Albrechta&C.]
Cordova, Carlos A., (CV) ....'22 '50 C.96 L.851 J.D. 146 E. 2nd St.
Croy, Paul E., (BV) ....'64 '89 C&L.851 B.A., J.D. 801 W. South Boundary, Ste. C
Dombey, Philip L., (AV) ....'48 '73 C.317 A.B. L.608 J.D. [Leatherman,W.D.H.N.H.&S.]
Donahue, John P., (BV) ....'46 '83 119 W. 2nd St.
Doner, Gary W. ...... '51 '90 C.1208 B.S. L.851 J.D. Tax Dir., Cooper Tire & Rubber Co.

Eastman & Smith Ltd.
(See Toledo)

Eckel, Cory P. ....'64 '91 C.101 B.A. L.608 J.D. Gen. Coun., Eckel Personnel, Inc.
Eckel, Paul Cornell ....'64 '91 C.1335 B.A. L.608 J.D. Adecco Employment Svcs.
Foster, Stephen V. ....'39 '71 C.976 B.S. L.851 J.D. 25001 W. River Rd.‡
Fraser, Donald R., (AV) ....'27 '57 C.851 B.S. L.273 J.D. [Fraser M.B.M.] (Pat.)

Fraser Martin Buchanan Miller LLC, (AV)
132 West Second Street, 43551-1401
Telephone: 419-874-1100 Fax: 419-874-1130
Email: firm@fmbmlaw.com
Donald R. Fraser; Richard G. Martin; J. Matthew Buchanan (Not admitted in OH); James D. Miller.
Patent Prosecution, Intellectual Property Transactions, Intellectual Property Litigation, Trademarks.
See Professional Biographies, PERRYSBURG, OHIO

Gwyn, Peter D., (BV) ....'43 '68 C.434 B.A. L.851 J.D. 110 W. 2nd. St.
Handwork, B. Thomas, Jr., (AV) ....'43 '68 C.597 B.A. L.893 J.D. [Handwork S.&K.]
Handwork Sanderson & Kerscher, LLP, (AV) ....900 W. South Boundary, Ste. B
Hart, James H., (BV) ....'49 '74 C.477 B.A. L.851 J.D. [Leatherman,W.D.H.N.H.&S.]
Hendel, Sharon S. ....'47 '94 C.97 B.S. L.851 J.D. 9915 Sheffield Rd
Hovland, Valerie Bruce ....'62 '93 C.645 B.A. L.851 J.D. 27457 Holiday Ln.
Howard, Kay L., (BV) ......'57 '92 C&L.851 B.B.A., J.D. [Leatherman,W.D.H.N.H.&S.]
Howard, Susan E., (CV) '58 '84
C.611 B.A. L.851 J.D. 900 W. South Boundary St., Ste. 10
Johnson, Jack L. '44 '69
C.432 B.A. L.851 J.D. Mgr., Benefits & Risk, Consol. Biscuit Co.
Keller, Dennis F., (AV) ....'45 '75 C&L.851 B.A., J.D. 842 W. South Boundary
Keller, Marvin E., (BV) ....'47 '75 C&L.851 B.B.A., J.D. 27457 Holiday Ln.
Kerscher, Jeffrey Maynard ....'59 '93 C&L.851 B.A., J.D. [Handwork S.&K.]
Kienzle, David W., (BV) ....'51 '80 C.967 B.A. L.851 J.D. 28321 W. River Rd.
Klapp, Austin F. ....'71 '98 C&L.851 B.A., J.D. [Spore&Assoc.]
Knight, Milton F., (BV) ....'48 '80 C.97 B.S. L.851 J.D. Peak Transp.
Kobil, Gerald M., (AV) ....'46 '75 C&L.851 B.B.A., J.D. 118 W. South Boundry
Kurt, Thomas P., (BV) ....'57 '82 C&L.851 B.A., J.D. 410 Lousiana Avenue
Landwehr, John F. ....'18 '48 C&L.851 Ph.B., J.D. 28600 Stonecroft Dr.‡
Leatherman, Wayne M., (AV) '21 '50 C.97 B.S. L.608 J.D.
[Leatherman,W.D.H.N.H.&S.]
Leatherman, Witzler, Dombey, Hart, Noll, Howard & Skaff, (AV) .... 353 Elm Street
Martin, Richard G. ....'50 '81 C.429 B.A. L.1035 J.D. [Fraser M.B.M.]
Miller, Gerald W. ....'38 '73 C&L.851 B.B.A., J.D. 10160 Ford Rd.
Miller, James D. ....'64 '00 C&L.851 B.S.M.E., J.D. [Fraser M.B.M.] (Pat.)
Miller, John H. '37 '71 C.502 B.S. L.273 J.D.
(adm. in VA; not adm. in OH) Pres., Technology Services Company
Miller, Robert T., Jr. ....'57 '83 C.477 B.B.A. L.851 J.D. 402 Arrowhead Dr.
Noll, T. Hamilton, (BV) ... '55 '82 C.610 B.G.S. L.851 J.D. [Leatherman,W.D.H.N.H.&S.]
Osterud, S. Dwight ....'44 '74 C&L.851 B.Ed., J.D. Mun. J.
Person, Allen S. '31 '58 C&L.145 B.A., J.D.
(adm. in NY; not adm. in OH) 29755 E. River Rd.
Pheils, David R. ....'34 '74 C&L.851 B.E., J.D. 410 Louisana Ave.
Pummill, Brian S. ....'61 '89 C.473 B.A. L.602 J.D. 2062 Lexington Dr.
Reams, Frazier, Jr. '29 '55
C.902 A.B. L.477 J.D. Pres. & Gen. Coun., Reams Bdcstg. Corp.
Siegel, Gregory B. ....'52 '84 C&L.851 B.S., J.D. 632 Holbrook Ct.
Simmons, Donald D. ....'34 '58 C.97 B.A. L.608 J.D. P.O. Box 5
Skaff, Paul Allan ....'69 '98 C.150 B.B.A. L.851 J.D. [Leatherman,W.D.H.N.H.&S.]
Skiver, Stephen A., The Law Offices of, (AV) '49 '89
C.610 B.S. L.851 J.D. 30025 East River Road
Smith, Cynthia B., (BV) ....'60 '88 C.608 B.A. L.851 J.D. 110 West Second Street
Spore, John S., (CV) ....'55 '86 C.610 B.A. L.851 J.D. [Spore&Assoc.]
Spore, Judson P., Jr. ....'29 '62 C.210 A.B. L.851 J.D. Ret. Mun. J.‡
Spore & Associates, (CV) ....115 West Front Street
Sturgill, Russell I. ....'27 '53 C&L.851 LL.B. Gen. Coun., Bennett Enterprises
Weiss, Dan M., (BV) ....'64 '96 C.801 B.S. L.851 J.D. P.O. Box 1012
Wetmore, Kenneth H. '47 '75 C.930 B.S. L.851 J.D.
V.P., Gen. Coun. & Secy., Glasstech, Inc. (Pat.)
Wilson, David H., Jr., (AV) .... '25 '51 C.188 B.S.E.E. L.569 LL.B. 424 E. Front St. (Pat.)
Wisniewski, Marshall D. ....'51 '81 C&L.851 B.A., J.D. 410 Louisiana Ave.

PERRYSVILLE, 816, *Ashland Co.*

Sexton, Andrea J. '64 '93 C.475 B.A. L.1187 J.D.
In-House Coun., Mansfield Plumbing Products, LLC
Wood, Kenneth ....'47 '74 C.161 B.A. L.1003 J.D. 1065 Ashland Co. Rd. 3275

PETERSBURG, 800, *Mahoning Co.*

Dickson, David B. ....'23 '54 C.930 B.A. L.980 J.D. 51298 Dickson Rd.

PICKERINGTON, 9,792, *Fairfield & Franklin Cos.*

Betzel, Daniel Martin ....'60 '93 C.130 B.A. L.608 J.D. 11299 Stonecreek Dr.
Burt, Loann Quinn '69 '95 C&L.378 B.A., J.D.
(adm. in KS; not adm. in OH) 462 Bleheim Ct.‡
Capella, Robert A. ....'34 '66 C&L.923 B.S., J.D. Ref., Ohio Bd. of Review, OBES
Daniel, Frederick T., (BV) ....'42 '75 C.608 B.S. L.117 J.D. [F.T.Daniel]
Daniel, Frederick T., (BV) ....49 Hill Rd. N.
Edwards, John B. ....'53 '00 C.161 B.B.A. L.989 J.D. 990 Gray Drive
Elwing, Thomas Richard ....'61 '98 C.8 B.S. L.179 J.D. [Elwing,T.R.]
Elwing, Thomas R. .... 60 W. Columbus St.
Faulkner, John W. '43 '76 C.475 B.A. L.213 J.D.
(adm. in MI; not adm. in OH) 13022 Heatherstone Cir.‡
Feyko, Jeffrey, (BV) ....'58 '85 C.608 B.A. L.117 J.D. 115 N. Center St.
Fields, Orval E., II, (BV) ....'47 '75 C.610 B.S.J. L.117 J.D. 660 Hill Rd., N.
Mahler, Eric A. ....'60 '95 C.1142 B.A. L.8 J.D. 3260 Long Cove Ct.
Mapes, Robert Edgar ....'46 '74 C.611 B.A. L.608 J.D. City Law Dir.
Mazel, Joel M., Law Offices of '64 '90 C.1083 B.A. L.201 J.D.
60 West Columbus Street
Ort, Mark Philip ....'57 '82 C.608 B.S. L.117 J.D. 12931 Edgewood Ct.★
Poston, David W., (BV) ....'57 '82 C.608 B.A. L.150 J.D. 49 Hill Rd., N.
Rose, Sara L., (BV) ....'69 '95 C.446 B.A. L.117 J.D. [S.L.Rose]
Rose, Sara L., LLC, (BV) ....P.O. Box 188
Schwarz, Jerrold W., (BV) ....'46 '90 C.973 B.S. L.117 J.D. P.O. Box 482
Shaver, David B., (BV) ....'55 '86 C.207 B.A. L.117 J.D. 512 Chatham Ct.
Thompson, Paul C. ....'68 '02 C.610 B.S. L.1161 J.D. 60 West Columbus Street
Vanderhoff, Anna M. ....'66 '99 C.659 B.A. L.117 J.D. 12161 Twin Creek Road
Willette, Philip B. ....'47 '76 C&L.64 B.S., J.D. [P.B.Willette]
Willette, Philip B., Co., LPA .... 27 W. Columbus St.
Zuravsky, Marvin A., D.D.S. '35 '91
C.608 D.D.S. L.117 J.D. 1255 Hill Road, N., Suite 102

PIKETON, 1,907, *Pike Co.*

Rittenour, John T., (AV) ....'18 '49 C.608 B.S. L.607 J.D. 553 S. West St.‡
Uhlinger, James R. '35 '66 C.188 B.S. L.776 LL.B.
(adm. in NJ; not adm. in OH) Lockheed Martin Utility Services, Inc.
Walker, Willis, (BV) '51 '81 C&L.8 B.A., J.D.
Chf. Coun., Lockheed Martin Energy Systems, Inc.

PIQUA, 20,738, *Miami Co.*

Buecker, Thomas J., (BV) ....'44 '69 C.347 B.S. L.150 J.D. [T.J.Buecker]
Buecker, Thomas J., Co., L.P.A., (BV) ....306 W. High St.
Davis, Dale G., (BV) ....'51 '76 C.228 B.A. L.276 J.D. [McCulloch,F.F.&G.]
DePriest, Roy H. ....'30 '59 C&L.608 B.A., LL.B. 429 N. Main St.‡
DeWeese, J. H., (AV) ....'11 '33 C.763 L.150 LL.B. 600 N. Wayne St.‡

Dungan & LeFevre, A Legal Professional Association, (AV)
111 West Ash Street, P.O. Box 1529, 45356
Telephone: 937-773-8054 Fax: 937-773-3379
Email: mail@dungan-lefevre.com URL: http://www.dungan-lefevre.com
John E. Hemm (Resident);—J. Andrew Wannemacher, Jr. (Resident).
General Civil and Criminal Trial Practice, including Personal Injury, Wrongful Death, Medical Malpractice, Products Liability, Insurance Defense, Wrongful Discharge Defense, Business Law and Commercial Litigation in all Courts, Real Estate, Condominium, Banking, Insurance, Corporate and Business, Wills and Probate, Trusts and Estates, Estate Planning, Family and Domestic Relations, Driving While Intoxicated, Tax, Bankruptcy, Municipal, Zoning and Planning and Collection Law. Appeals in all Courts.
Troy, Ohio Office: 210 West Main Street. Telephone: 937-339-0511. Fax: 937-335-5802.
See Professional Biographies, PIQUA, OHIO

Dyer, Garofalo, Mann & Schultz, A Legal Professional Association, (AV)
308 Looney Road, Suite E (Richmond, IN; Bellefontaine, Dayton, Huber Heights, Lima, Middletown, Springfield, Troy, Wilmington, Xenia, OH)
Freed, Frederick D., (AV) ....'35 '62 C.145 A.B. L.477 LL.B. [Freed]
Freed Law Firm, (AV) .... 409 N. Main St.
Gutmann, Elizabeth Simms ....'57 '84 C.1208 B.A. L.150 J.D. Mun. J.
Gutmann, Michael E., (BV) ....'59 '84 C.473 B.S. L.150 J.D. [McCulloch,F.F.&G.]
Gutmann, Paul P., (AV) ....'32 '57 C.757 B.A. L.608 J.D. [McCulloch,F.F.&G.] ‡
Hemm, John E., (BV) ....'57 '82 C.473 B.S. L.201 J.D. [Dungan&L.]
Hiser, Benjamin E. ....'30 '80 C&L.201 B.A., J.D. 1607 Margene Drive‡
Hornish-Schlosser, Laura ....'74 '00 C.5 B.A. L.851 J.D. [McCulloch,F.F.&G.]
Kindell, Louie R., (BV) ....'52 '83 C.150 B.A. L.201 J.D. 419 N. Wayne St.

McCulloch, Felger, Fite & Gutmann Co., L.P.A., (AV)
Fifth Third Bank Building, 123 Market Street, Second Floor, P.O. Drawer 910, 45356
Telephone: 937-773-3212 Fax: 937-773-9672; 937-773-4022
Email: mffg@wesnet.com
William M. McCulloch (1901-1980); Carl B. Felger (1900-1984); Robert P. Fite (1920-2000); Paul P. Gutmann (Retired); William B. McNeil (Certified Specialist in Estate Planning, Trust and Probate Law, Ohio State Bar Association); Jack L. Neuenschwander; Dale G. Davis; Michael E. Gutmann; Daniel E. Ramer; Frank J. Patrizio;—Laura Hornish-Schlosser.
General Civil Practice. Corporation, Insurance, Taxation, Labor and Employment, Trust and Estate Administration, Estate Planning, Commercial, Real Estate, Pension and Profit Sharing, Family and Domestic Relations, Personal Injury Law, Litigation and Civil Trials.
General Counsel for: Pioneer Rural Electric Co-op; Hartzell Industries, Inc.; French Oil Mill Machinery Co.; Midwest Plastic Systems, Inc.; Piāua Concrete Co.; Little Printing Co.; Dan Hemm Auto Group.
Attorneys for: Fifth Third Bank Western, Ohio; Unity National Bank; Hartzell Propeller, Inc.
See Professional Biographies, PIQUA, OHIO

McNeil, William B., (AV) ....'40 '64 C.645 B.S. L.309 J.D. [McCulloch,F.F.&G.]

Miller & Luring
(See Troy)

Neuenschwander, Jack L., (AV) ....'42 '67 C.309 A.B. L.477 J.D. [McCulloch,F.F.&G.]
Nicholas, Dimitri P. ....'14 '40 C&L.569 B.A., LL.B. 10789 North Hardin Road
Patrizio, Frank J., (CV) ....'66 '91 C.201 B.S. L.608 J.D. [McCulloch,F.F.&G.]

Phillips, Brian W. '42 '69 C.97 B.A. L.251 J.D.
Sr. Trust Officer, Fifth Third Bk. of Western Ohio
Pratt, Robert A., (AV) ....'35 '61 C.610 A.B. L.150 LL.B. [Robert A.P.]
Ramer, Daniel E., (BV) ....'53 '78 C.472 B.A. L.608 J.D. [McCulloch,F.F.&G.]
Robert A. Pratt Co., L.P.A., (AV) ....312 North Wayne Street
Schultz, Ronald E., (AV) '42 '67 C.610 B.S. L.608 J.D.
[Dyer,G.M.&S.] (⊙Bellefontaine, Dayton, Huber Heights, Lima, Middletown, Springfield)
Tinkler, Cornelia E., (CV) ....'40 '96 C.608 B.S. L.201 J.D. 45 Orchard Rd.
Wannemacher, J. Andrew, Jr., (CV) ......'66 '93 C.473 B.A. L.851 J.D. [Ⓐ Dungan&L.]
Wilson, R. K. ....'22 '51 C.967 B.A. L.608 J.D. 1308 Park Ave.‡

PLAIN CITY, 2,832, *Madison & Union Cos.*

Chuha, Edward F., (BV) ....'43 '68 C.363 A.B. L.608 J.D. 10856 Tioga Springs Cricle
Houchard, John Emil ....'34 '62 C&L.608 B.S., J.D. 128 West Main Street
Janetzke, Ronald H. ....'32 '59 C.57 B.A. L.597 J.D. 8189 State Route 736
Smith, Frank S., (BV) ....'47 '76 C&L.608 B.A., J.D. 128 W. Main St.‡
Swisher, Sara J. ....'71 '99 C.96 B.S. L.117 J.D. 7844 Cook Road
Valentine, Clifton G., Jr. ....'56 '82 C.62 B.A. L.117 J.D. 128 W. Main Street

PLEASANTVILLE, 877, *Fairfield Co.*

Turpin, William W., (BV) ....'17 '53 C&L.608 B.M.E., J.D. 207 S. Main St.

POLAND, 2,886, *Mahoning Co.*

Andrews, James H. ....'57 '82 C.105 B.A. L.893 J.D. 7227 Yellow Creek Dr.‡
Brooks, Donald R. ....'22 '49 C.608 B.S. L.930 LL.B. 6107 Celesta Rd.‡
Cocco, James M. '45 '88 C.112 B.S. L.284 J.D.
(adm. in CA; not adm. in OH) 7558 Elmland Ave.
DeSanto, Donald J., (BV) ....'53 '81 C.965 B.S. L.7 J.D. [DeSanto&D.]
DeSanto, Jeanne Bitonte, (CV) ....'60 '87 C.980 B.A. L.8 J.D. 807 Southwestern Run
DeSanto, Joseph D., (BV) ....'26 '68 C.980 B.S. L.8 J.D. [DeSanto&D.]
DeSanto & DeSanto, (BV) ....607 Southwestern Run
Katz, Louis E. ....'48 '75 C.381 B.A. L.161 J.D. 70 W. McKinley Way
Meloy, William Stephen, (AV) ....'36 '61 C.674 A.B. L.477 J.D. [Meloy]
Meloy Law Offices, (AV) ....211 S. Main St.
Montgomery, Richard Kent ....'43 '74 C.980 B.S.B.A. L.8 J.D. 7335 Cobblers Run
Powers, John Weed, (AV) ....'20 '49 C.918 A.B. L.477 J.D. 409 S. Main St.‡
Roberts, B. Edward ....'37 '63 C.865 A.B. L.607 LL.B. 335 W. McKinley Way‡
Rucci, Sebastian ....'60 '95 C.980 B.S.B.A. L.1137 J.D. 3058 Chardonnay Lane
Smith, Shirley J. ....'66 '97 C.1260 B.S. L.8 J.D. 7651 Mulberry Walk
Wright, C. Robert ....'23 '58 C.604 A.B. L.980 LL.B. 427 Pamela Ct.

POMEROY, * 1,966, *Meigs Co.*

Buck, Robert E. ....'46 '72 C.610 B.B.A. L.608 J.D. Prob. J.
Crow, Fred W., III ....'45 '70 C.610 B.B.A. L.608 J.D. Com. Pleas J.
Crow, I. Carson, (AV) ....'48 '75 C.610 B.S.J. L.607 J.D. [Crow&C.]
Crow and Crow, (AV) ....110 West Second Street
Fultz, Bernard V., (AV) ....'28 '56 C.607 B.S. L.608 J.D. 1111/2 W. 2nd St.
Knight, Charles H., (BV) ....'48 '74 C.610 B.A. L.608 J.D. 109 W. 2nd Street

Lewis, Richard M.
(See Jackson)

Little, Douglas W., (BV) ....'54 '79 C&L.608 B.S., J.D. [Little,S.&W.]
Little, Sheets & Warner, (BV) ....211-213 E. 2nd St.
O'Brien, James B., (CV) ....'16 '41 C.608 A.B. L.607 LL.B. [O'Brien&O.]
O'Brien, Patrick H., (BV) ....'52 '77 C.611 B.A. L.607 J.D. [O'Brien&O.]
O'Brien & O'Brien, (BV) ....102 1/2 W. Main St. (⊙Holyoke, MA)
Powell, Larry S. ....'— '94 C.610 B.B.A. L.215 J.D. 114 Mulberry Ave.
Sheets, Jennifer L., (BV) ....'45 '82 C.608 B.S. L.117 J.D. [Little,S.&W.]
Story, Steven L., (BV) ....'54 '79 C.608 B.A. L.607 J.D. 236 West 2nd Street
Warner, Linda R., (BV) ....'62 '88 C.610 B.S. L.117 J.D. [Little,S.&W.]

PORT CLINTON, * 6,391, *Ottawa Co.*

Barney, James C., (BV) ....'62 '94 C.843 B.B.A. L.851 J.D. [Kocher&G.]
Coppeler, John A., (AV) ....'47 '75 C&L.608 B.A., J.D. [Flynn,P.&K.] ⊙
Corogin, Thomas L., (AV) ....'27 '53 C&L.608 B.S., J.D. 132 Madison St.‡

Flynn, Py & Kruse, A Legal Professional Association, (AV)
115 West Perry Street, 43452 ⊙
Telephone: 419-734-3174 Fax: 419-734-3175
John A. Coppeler.
General Civil Practice. Corporation, Banking, Antitrust, Labor and Employment, Taxation, Insurance, Personal Injury, Workers Compensation, Environmental Law, Probate and Estate Planning, Commercial Litigation, Pension and Profit Sharing, Employee Benefits, Real Estate. Trials and Appeals in State and Federal Courts.
Sandusky, Ohio Office: 165 East Washington Row. Telephone: 419-625-8324. Fax: 419-625-9007.

See Professional Biographies, PORT CLINTON, OHIO

Frederick, Mark Allen ....'62 '87 C.97 B.A. L.851 J.D. 125 Jefferson St.
Gillum, Richard R., III ....'72 '98 C.610 B.A. L.608 J.D. [Kocher&G.]
Gulas, Ruth M., (BV) ....'37 '87 C.97 B.S. L.851 J.D. [Kline&C.]
Heigel, Catherine Edwards ....'70 '96 C.790 B.A. L.608 J.D. [Kocher&G.]
Johannsen, Kyle J., (CV) ....'57 '90 C.607 B.A. L.851 J.D. 217 Madison St.
Kennedy, Shelly L. ....'63 '89 C.937 B.A. L.117 J.D. 318 Madison Street
Kline, Dale A., (BV) ....'30 '64 C&L.851 B.S., J.D. [Kline&C.]
Kline & Corogin, Co., L.P.A., (BV) ....132 Madison St.
Kocher, John A., (AV) ....'42 '74 C.679 B.S.C.E. L.879 J.D. [Kocher&G.]

Kocher & Gillum, (AV)
101 1/2 Madison Street, 43452
Telephone: 419-732-3135 Fax: 419-734-5644
Email: catherine@kochergillum.com URL: http://www.kochergillum.com
Members of Firm: John A. Kocher; Richard R. Gillum, III; Catherine Edwards Heigel; James C. Barney.
Real Estate, Business Transactions, General Civil Litigation, Probate, Estate Planning, Construction Law.

See Professional Biographies, PORT CLINTON, OHIO

Kroeger, Linda L. ....'48 '93 C&L.851 B.A., J.D. [Kline&C.]
Loeffler, D. Bowen, (BV) ....'57 '85 C.970 B.A. L.851 J.D. 122 Adams St.
Manahan, Pietrykowski, Bamman & DeLaney, (AV) ....125 Jefferson Street (⊙Toledo)
Melena, Donald R., (AV) ....'31 '57 C.97 B.S. L.930 LL.B. 201 Madison St.
Menucci, William R. ....'48 '78 C.959 B.A. L.117 J.D. P.O. Box 528256‡
Moon, Paul C. ....'37 '62 C.363 B.S.S. L.276 J.D. Com. Pleas J.
Mulligan, Mark E., (BV) ....'52 '77 C&L.851 B.B.A., J.D. Co. Pros.
Nation, Sarah Ann ....'74 '00 C&L.851 B.A., J.D. Ottawa Co. Com. Pleas. Ct.
Noblitt, Larry, (BV) ....'43 '68 C.610 B.B.A. L.608 J.D. 318 Madison St.
Patterson, Michael P. '60 '90 C.97 B.S. L.851 J.D.
Co. Child Support Enforcement Agcy.
Petersen, Barbara B. H., (BV) ....'48 '73 C.339 B.A. L.145 J.D. Asst. Pros. Atty.
Petersen, Lowell S., (AV) ....'27 '52 C&L.608 B.A., J.D. 122 W. Second St.
Pietrykowski, William F., (BV) ......'58 '83 C.602 B.B.A. L.607 J.D. [Manahan,P.B.&D.]
Reinheimer, Frank W., (BV) ....'38 '65 C.97 B.S. L.607 J.D. [Reinheimer&R.]
Reinheimer, James L. ....'66 '92 C.607 B.S.B.A. L.851 J.D. [Reinheimer&R.]
Reinheimer & Reinheimer, (BV) ....208 Madison St.
Rudes, Terrence R., (BV) ....'48 '77 C&L.851 B.A., J.D. 216 Adams St.
Sandwisch, Michael W., (BV) ....'57 '82 C.608 B.S. L.851 J.D. 240 Jefferson St
Thierry, James E. ....'22 '49 C.381 B.A. L.608 J.D. Ret. Com. Pleas J.
Wagner, Glen W. ....'20 '48 C.475 B.A. L.477 LL.B. 3858 N. Cliff Rd.‡
Wargo, Louis P., III, (BV) ....'55 '81 C.188 B.A. L.851 J.D. 122 Adams St.
Wilber, Adair C., (AV) ....'17 '48 C&L.608 A.B., J.D. 2850 Cleveland Rd.‡
Wilber, George C., (BV) ....'51 '77 C.97 B.A. L.117 J.D. City Law Dir.
Winters, Bruce, (CV) ....'57 '88 C&L.851 B.S., J.D. Asst. Pros. Atty.
Woodson, R. Donald ....'31 '84 C.378 B.A. L.851 J.D. 4445-E Marin Pines
Zeitzheim, David A. ....'38 '68 C.363 B.S.S. L.1003 J.D. Prob. & Juv. Ct. J.

PORTSMOUTH, * 20,909, *Scioto Co.*

Aalyson, Mark Ettor ....'52 '90 711 Findlay Street

Bannon, Howland & Dever Co., L.P.A., A Legal Professional Association, (AV)
602 Chillicothe Street, Suite 325, P.O. Box 1384, 45662-1384
Telephone: 740-353-1157 Fax: 740-353-6237
Email: bhad@bhadlaw.com
Henry T. Bannon (1867-1950); Louis D. Bannon (1899-1991); William Lee Howland (1916-2000); Robert E. Dever; Robert R. Dever; Steven M. Willard; Sherry D. Davis.
Insurance Defense, Medical Malpractice, Personal Injury, Probate, Estate Planning, Real Estate, Hospital Law, Banking, Worker's Compensation.

See Professional Biographies, PORTSMOUTH, OHIO

Baran, Piper, Tarkowsky, Fitzgerald & Theis Co., L.P.A., (AV)
633 Seventh Street, Suite A, 45662 ⊙
Telephone: 740-353-4700 Fax: 740-353-4747
URL: http://www.baranlaw.com
Michael L. Jones.
General Civil Practice, Trials in all Courts, Insurance Defense, Corporate, Family Law, Personal Injury, Worker's Compensation.
General Counsel for: Roger J. Au and Son, Inc. (Heavy Construction and Marine Contracting); Mansfield Flooring (Industrial and Road Contracting); Automatic Welding & Manufacturing Co., Inc. (Acoustics).

See Professional Biographies, PORTSMOUTH, OHIO

Beck, David B., (CV) ....'70 '97 C.999 B.A. L.117 J.D. [Ⓒ Kimble&C.]
Bender, Stanley C., Law Offices of, (AV) '51 '76 C.608 B.A. L.930 J.D.
707 Sixth Street
Berry, John F., (AV) ....'49 '76 C.610 B.B.A. L.608 J.D. 707 Sixth Street
Book, Thomas Todd, (CV) ....'68 '94 C.932 B.A. L.945 J.D. 800 Gallia St. #800
Brown, Charles Asa ....'12 '38 C.885 B.A. L.930 J.D. Hillview, Rm. 320‡
Brown, J. Rick, (BV) ....'51 '76 C&L.608 B.S., J.D. 625 7th St.
Buckler, Jerry L., (CV) ....'65 '96 C.999 L.117 J.D. [Buckler]
Buckler, Ruth A. ....'60 '01 C.999 B.A. L.117 J.D. [Buckler,T.&S.]
Buckler Law Office, (CV) ....531 Sixth St.
Buckler, Tieman & Sayre, (CV) ....531 Sixth St.
Campbell, Richard W., (CV) ....'57 '83 C.608 B.S.B.A. L.607 J.D. 1024 Kinney's Lane
Clark, Roger L., (BV) ....'40 '68 C.610 B.S. L.607 J.D. [Kimble&C.]

Colley Shroyer & Abraham Co., L.P.A.
(See Columbus)

Davis, Anna ....'64 '00 C.610 B.S.Ed. L.117 J.D. [Ⓐ Ruggiero&H.]
Davis, George L., III, (BV) ....'54 '80 C.207 B.A. L.607 J.D. 602 Chillicothe St., Ste. 802
Davis, Sherry D., (CV) ....'72 '97 C.607 B.A. L.117 J.D. [Bannon,H.&D.]

Denmead Law Office
(See Columbus)

Dever, Robert E., (AV) ....'31 '56 C.610 L.569 J.D. [Bannon,H.&D.]
Dever, Robert R., (BV) ....'55 '80 C.207 B.A. L.117 J.D. [Bannon,H.&D.]
Donohue, Stephen P. ....'46 '77 C.870 B.S. L.362 J.D. Shawnee State Univ.★
Edwards, Wallace Edward, Jr. ....'54 '82 C.611 B.S. L.179 J.D. 538 Sixth Street
Eisnaugle, Richard L., (AV) '23 '50
C.473 B.S. L.150 J.D. Dom. Rel. Ref., Com. Pleas. Ct.
Enriquez, Rick J. ....'60 '87 C.768 B.A. L.930 J.D. [R.Enriquez]
Enriquez, Rick ....721 5th Street
Fitch, James C., (BV) ....'30 '55 C.477 B.A. L.608 J.D. [Miller,S.&F.]
Fitch, Lee O., (AV) ....'15 '50 C.477 L.608 J.D. [Miller,S.&F.]
Garaczkowski, Joan M., (CV) ....'65 '92 C.1044 B.S. L.117 J.D. [J.Garaczkowski]
Garaczkowski, Joan, (CV) ....602 Chillicothe St.
Gerard, Christopher Charles ....'73 '00 C.999 B.A. L.851 J.D. [C.Gerard]
Gerard, Chris, Attorney at Law ....602 Chillicothe St.
Gerlach, Cynthia Koehler, (CV) ....'36 '85 C.150 B.S. L.117 J.D. [Gerlach&G.]
Gerlach, Franklin T., (BV) .....'35 '61 C&L.150 B.B.A., J.D. Mayor [Gerlach&G.]
Gerlach, Valarie K., (CV) ....'62 '87 C.150 B.A. L.117 J.D. [Ⓐ Gerlach&G.]
Gerlach & Gerlach, (BV) ....814 7th St.
Haas, John R., (BV) ....'65 '90 C.608 B.A. L.117 J.D. [Ruggiero&H.]
Hale, Joseph L., (CV) ....'58 '83 C.610 B.A. L.607 J.D. 547 6th St.
Hamm, G.R. ....'69 '02 C.510 B.A. L.8 J.D. 721 Fifth Street
Harcha, Howard H., III ....'57 '82 C.608 B.S. L.607 J.D. Com. Pleas J.
Harcha, Howard H., Jr., (AV) ....'27 '52 C&L.608 J.D. National City Bk. Bldg.
Harsha, William H. ....'21 '47 C.385 B.A. L.930 LL.B. 3210 Brookwood Dr.‡
Haven, Aaron Alan, (CV) ....'66 '92 C.608 B.A. L.1003 J.D. Asst. Co. Pros.
Herdman, Harry T. ....'25 '51 C.610 L.383 LL.B. M-115 Masonic Bldg.‡
Hoover, Marie Moraleja, (CV) ....'69 '94 C.473 B.A. L.608 J.D. [Hoover]
Hoover, R. Tracy ....'63 '88 C.610 B.A. L.117 J.D. [Hoover]
Hoover Law Group, The, (CV) ....621 7th Street
Horr, Chas. C. ....'17 '42 C.611 A.B. L.150 LL.B. Vandervort Supply Co.
Horr, William H., (AV) ....'14 '39 C.611 A.B. L.150 J.D. 602 Chillicothe St.‡
Howard, Joshua D. ....'79 '04 C.999 B.S. L.117 J.D. [Ⓐ Johnson&O.]
Huddleston, David M., (CV) '52 '77 C.207 B.A. L.608 J.D.
Scioto Co. Children Servs. Bd.
Johnson, C. Clayton, (AV) ....'44 '70 C.611 B.A. L.477 J.D. [Johnson&O.]

Johnson & Oliver, A Legal Professional Association, (AV) [BR]
701 Sixth Street, P.O. Box 1505, 45662
Telephone: 740-354-4200 Telecopier: 740-353-2413 Email: cjohnson@johnsonoliverlaw.com
Email: soliver@johnsonoliverlaw.com
C. Clayton Johnson; Stephen L. Oliver;—Joshua D. Howard.
General Civil Practice. Corporations, Business, Estate Planning, Real Estate, Banking, Finance and Probate Law.
Representative Clients: OSCO Industries, Inc.; Citizens Deposit Bank and Trust; Home Federal Savings and Loan; Oak Hill Banks; McNational, Inc.; Mitchellace, Inc.
Approved Attorney for: Lawyers Title Insurance Co.

See Professional Biographies, PORTSMOUTH, OHIO

Jones, Michael L. ....'69 '94 C&L.117 B.A., J.D. [Baran,P.T.F.&T.]★

Kegley, Russell D., (CV) ....'54 '82 C.607 B.A. L.117 J.D. Mag.

Kimble & Clark, (BV)
622 Sixth Street, 45662
Telephone: 740-354-3214 Fax: 740-353-6910
Email: kimbleandclark@hotmail.com URL: http://www.kimbleandclarklaw.com
Roger L. Clark. Of Counsel: David B. Beck; Jack D. Young.
Real Estate, Medical Malpractice, Automobile Accidents and Injuries, Wrongful Death, Slip and Fall, Criminal Defense, Driving While Intoxicated, Drug Crimes, Felonies, White Collar Crimes, Juvenile Criminal Law, Traffic Violations, Embezzlement, Fraud.
See Professional Biographies, PORTSMOUTH, OHIO

Kirsch, James W. ....'45 '71 C&L.608 B.A., J.D. Com. Pleas, Prob. & Juv. J.
Kleemann, Carl Lawrence, (CV) '48 '73
C.475 B.A. L.477 J.D. Staff Atty., Southeastern Ohio Legal Servs.
Kleha, Jeffrey A., Attorney at Law ....'65 '03 C.645 B.A. L.7 J.D. 721 Fifth St.
Kuhn, David W., (BV) ....'43 '69 C&L.150 B.S.Ch.E., J.D. City Solr.
Lemons, R. Alan, (BV) ....'60 '85 C.608 B.S. L.7 J.D. [Miller,S.&F.]
Lytten, Walter C. ....'45 '72 C.610 B.B.A. L.117 J.D. Com. Pleas J.
Marshall, J. B., Jr., (BV) ....'53 '79 C.383 B.A. L.150 J.D. 717 Wasington Street
Marshall, John B. ....'22 '49 C.611 B.A. L.150 J.D. Judge‡
Marshall, William T., (CV) ....'56 '83 C&L.150 B.A., J.D. 728 2nd St.
McFarland, Matthew W. ....'67 '92 C&L.117 B.A., J.D. Ct. App. J.
McKenzie, Ronald E., (AV) ....'49 '73 C.501 B.S. L.500 J.D. 703 National City Bank
Mearan, Michael H., (BV) ....'46 '71 C&L.608 B.S., J.D. [M.H.Mearan]
Mearan, Michael H., L.P.A. Co., Inc., (BV) .... 812 Sixth Street
Miller, Margaret Apel, (BV) ....'64 '89 C.610 B.A. L.608 J.D. [Miller&R.]

Miller & Rodeheffer, (AV) BR
630 6th Street, 45662
Telephone: 740-354-1300 Fax: 740-354-1301
Email: srodeheffer@sciotowireless.net URL: http://www.rodehefferlaw.com
Margaret Apel Miller; Stephen C. Rodeheffer.
General Practice.
See Professional Biographies, PORTSMOUTH, OHIO

Miller, Searl & Fitch, A Legal Professional Association, (AV)
806 Sixth Street, Suite 200

Offutt, Fisher & Nord
(See Huntington, West Virginia)

Oliver, Stephen L., (BV) ....'56 '81 C.473 A.B. L.608 J.D. [Johnson&O.]
Parker, Danielle M. ....'78 '03 C.610 B.C.J. L.607 J.D. [Ⓐ Hoover]
Pekar, Patricia R., (CV) ....'57 '92 C.161 B.A. L.8 J.D. 710 Court St.
Rodeheffer, Stephen C., (AV) ....'51 '76 C.608 B.A. L.607 J.D. [Miller&R.]

Rourke & Blumenthal, LLP
(See Columbus)

Ruggiero, Daniel P., (AV) ....'47 '73 C.473 B.A. L.851 J.D. [Ruggiero&H.]

Ruggiero & Haas, (AV)
600 National City Bank, 800 Gallia Street, P.O. Box 150, 45662
Telephone: 740-353-9805 Telecopier: 740-353-9808
Email: info@rhlawfirm.net URL: http://www.rhlawfirm.net
Daniel P. Ruggiero; John R. Haas. Associate: Anna Davis.
General Civil Trial Practice. Insurance Defense and Medical Malpractice Law, Personal Injury Litigation.
See Professional Biographies, PORTSMOUTH, OHIO

Rumble, Robert R., Jr., (CV) ....'50 '75 C.827 A.B. L.150 J.D. Asst. Pros. Atty.
Sayre, Chadwick Kyle, (CV) ....'72 '99 C.607 B.A. L.179 J.D. [Buckler,T.&S.]
Schisler, Richard T. ....'39 '67 C.473 A.B. L.150 J.D. Mun. J.
Scott, Christine M. ....'69 '00 C.608 B.S. L.1228 J.D. 842 Gallia St.
Shaw, William K., Jr., (CV) ....'49 '76 C.610 B.A. L.161 J.D. City Solr.
Shedroff, Marcia I., (CV) ....'57 '87 C&L.150 B.A., J.D. Southeastern Ohio Legal Servs.
Smith, James Scott, (BV) ....'55 '79 C.608 B.S.B.A. L.607 J.D. 538 6th Street
Spears, David E. ....'44 '72 C.510 B.B.A. L.150 J.D. Com. Pleas J.
Stephenson, Marilee, (CV) ....'— '91 C.383 L.1340 J.D. [Stephenson]

Stephenson Law Office, LLC, (CV)
530 Sixth Street, 45662
Telephone: 740-354-3761 Fax: 740-353-8654
Email: majdrew@bright.net URL: http://www.marileestephenson.com
Marilee Stephenson.
Decedents Estates, Business Law, Probate Administration, Trust Planning, Real Estate, Contracts, Asset Protection.
See Professional Biographies, PORTSMOUTH, OHIO

Thatcher, John W., (BV) ....'38 '64 C.473 B.S.B.A. L.477 J.D. 309 Washington St.
Tieman, Shane A. ....'72 '98 C.608 B.A. L.607 J.D. [Buckler,T.&S.]
Tracy, Larry A. ....'50 '82 C.610 B.B.A. L.117 J.D. 1632 Fourth St.★
Triplett, Aaron R., (CV) ....'57 '83 C.150 B.A. L.607 J.D. 4705 Old Scioto Tr.

Twyford & Donahey, P.L.L.
(See Columbus)

Volkema, Thomas, Miller, Burkett, Scott & Merry, A Legal Professional Association
(See Columbus)

Widdig, Rebecca L., (CV) ....'69 '95 C.150 B.A. L.1340 J.D. 500 Chillicothe St.
Willard, Steven M., (BV) ....'62 '87 C.150 B.B.A. L.117 J.D. [Bannon,H.&D.]
Willis, Jay Shannon ....'70 '97 C&L.117 B.A., J.D. Scioto Co. Dom. Rel. Ct. Mag.
Young, Jack D., (BV) ....'30 '61 C.610 B.S.C. L.1340 LL.B. [Ⓒ Kimble&C.]

POWELL, 6,247, *Delaware Co.*

Clark, William J., (AV) ....'48 '77 C.608 B.S. L.117 J.D. 78 E. Scioto Dr.
Coleman-Irwin, C., (BV) ....'47 '81 C.679 B.S. L.117 J.D. 339 Bear Woods Dr.
Egan, D. Shane ....'47 '87 C&L.608 B.A., J.D. 1985 Plains Blvd.
Faires, Wayne A. ....'49 '77 C.610 B.A. L.8 J.D. 453 Highmeadows Village Dr.‡
Gulker, O. Allan, (AV) ....'30 '54 C&L.608 B.A., J.D. 460 Charlescarn Drive‡
Holmes, Robert E. ....'22 '49 C.610 A.B. L.608 LL.B. Ret. Supr. Ct. Jus.
Hutchinson, Darrell A. ....'33 '65 C.608 B.S. L.1065 LL.B. CEO, GFS Chemicals, Inc.
Ison, David A., (BV) ....'59 '83 C.608 B.S. L.117 J.D. 10 Village Pointe Drive
Jeffers, Michael D., (BV) ....'63 '91 C.597 B.S. L.608 J.D. 732 Weston Park Dr.

Jones, Troyan, Pappas & Perkins, A Legal Professional Association
(See Columbus)

Kauffman, Ronald P., (BV) ....'36 '61 C&L.608 B.S., J.D. 10233 Southfork Lane
Kelley, Brendan W. ....'63 '88 C.473 B.A. L.851 J.D. 161 Beech Ridge Dr.
Klein, John William ....'67 '97 101 Heather Ln.

Manos, Martin, Pergram & Dietz Co., LPA
(See Delaware)

McCarthy, Michael J. ....'54 '80 C.203 B.S. L.851 J.D. 15 N. Liberty Street
Mess, Michael A., (AV) ....'51 '76 C.679 B.A. L.273 J.D. 5139 Preston Ct.
Messmer, Gail Elizabeth ....'50 '83 C.201 B.S.S. L.117 J.D. 440 Highmeadows Vil. Dr.
Myers, Charlton ....'10 '35 C.473 A.B. L.607 J.D. 505 Retreat Ln.‡
Myers, Wendy L. '57 '89 C.1044 B.S. L.982 J.D.
(adm. in NY; not adm. in OH) 7525 Cook Rd.
Nims, Ronald K. ....'52 '82 C.608 B.S. L.117 J.D. 10172 Windsor Way
Pfister, Jeanne N. ....'33 '84 C&L.608 B.S., J.D. 1325 Wren Ln.
Reed, Jane Williams '49 '76 C.914 B.A. L.966 J.D.
(adm. in WI; not adm. in OH) 10870 Weymouth Ave
Richardson, Herbert M., III ....'60 '86 C.313 B.A. L.608 J.D. [Richardson&Assoc.]
Richardson & Associates .... 3809 Wedgewood Place Drive
Roberts, Mary Ann ....'55 '81 C.741 B.A. L.117 J.D. 4808 Seven Lakes Pl.
Sturtz, Laurence E., (AV) ....'42 '67 C&L.608 B.A., J.D. 8474 Stonewoods Lane
Tenwick, David Anders ....'37 '63 C&L.150 B.B.A., J.D. 8503 Misty Woods Circle
Trott, Kara J. ....'61 '91 C.611 B.A. L.608 J.D. 445 Retreat Ln. W.
Whitaker, Philip W., (AV) ....'44 '69 C&L.608 B.A., J.D. 8131 Hillingdon Drive

PROCTORVILLE, 620, *Lawrence Co.*

Capper, Donald R., Law Office of, (BV) '55 '81
C.437 B.S. L.851 J.D. 135 State St., Ste. 619
Pierce, James A. ....'51 '92 C.610 B.B.A. L.117 J.D. P.O. Box 995
Stillpass, Marty J., (CV) ....'47 '83 C.437 B.B.A. L.607 J.D. 116 State St.

PROSPECT, 1,191, *Marion Co.*

Shifflet, Daniel E. ....'42 '81 4947 Prospect Upper Sandusky Rd.

PUT-IN-BAY, 141, *Ottawa Co.*

Lunt, Thomas C. ....'18 '52 C.608 L.1003 J.D. Stonehenge St.‡

RAVENNA, * 11,771, *Portage Co.*

Aylward, James J., (BV) ....'49 '81 C.8 B.S.L.E. L.7 J.D. Chf. Mag.
Badger, Richard J., Co., L.P.A., (BV) ....'43 '73 C.645 B.S.Ch.E L.7 J.D. 224 W. Main St.
Berger, Robert W., (BV) ....'50 '77 C.381 B.S. L.64 J.D. [Giulitto&B.]
Bertrand, Louis R., (BV) ....'42 '68 C.107 B.A. L.851 J.D. 409 South Prospect Street
Brode, David M., (BV) ....'— '90 C.381 B.B.A. L.8 J.D. 8000 Infirmary Rd.
Carnes, Thomas ....'46 '73 C.611 B.A. L.930 J.D. Com. Pleas J.

Cimino, Frank J., (BV) '47 '72 C.318 B.A. L.7 J.D.
250 S. Chestnut, #18, 44266
Telephone: 330-297-5788 Fax: 330-297-7578
Email: officeF3@aol.com
Trial Practice, Appellate Practice. Personal Injury, Automobile Accidents, Corporate, Business Law, Family, Divorce, Municipal, Zoning and Land Use, Collection, Real Estate, Probate Law, Bankruptcy.
Representative Clients: S & S Aggregate; Country Estates Mobile Home Park; Courtesy Auto World; Courtesy Chrysler, Plymouth, Dodge; Beck Sand and Gravel; Quality Aggregates, Inc.
References: Portage Community Bank; Bank One.
See Professional Biographies, RAVENNA, OHIO

Codrea, John E. '47 '75 C.318 B.A. L.930 J.D.
Mng. Atty., Community Legal Aid Services, Inc.
Colecchi, Stephen, (BV) '54 '79
C.381 B.B.A. L.8 J.D. Pres. & CEO, Robinson Memorial Hospital
Cox, Thomas A., (BV) ....'46 '75 C.381 B.A. L.7 J.D. P.O. Box 1098
Davis, Anita L., (CV) ....'56 '83 C.381 B.A. L.8 J.D. 466 S. Chestnut St.
Dickinson, Perry G. ....'26 '60 C.381 B.S.B.A. L.8 J.D. Mun. Ct. J.‡
Dodson, Davida J. '53 '90 C.62 B.A. L.930 J.D.
Staff Atty., Western Reserve Legal Servs.
Enlow, John A. ....'45 '72 C.610 A.B. L.8 J.D. Com. Pleas J.
Ford, Seabury H., (AV) ....'02 '25 C&L.930 A.B., J.D. 200 W. Main St.
Giulitto, Joseph, (AV) ....'35 '61 C.381 B.A. L.930 LL.B. [Giulitto&B.]
Giulitto, Michael A., (CV) ....'62 '88 C.473 B.S. L.8 J.D. [Ⓐ Giulitto&B.]
Giulitto, Paula C., (BV) ....'67 '92 C.473 B.S. L.7 J.D. [Ⓐ Giulitto&B.]
Giulitto & Berger, (AV) ....222 W. Main St.
Graham, Gerald B., (BV) ....'40 '70 C.381 B.A. L.7 J.D. 204 S. Meridian St.
Grueschow, Michael E. ....'50 '77 C.597 B.A. L.930 J.D. 101 E. Main Street
Hayes, Jerry L. ....'34 '71 C.381 B.A. L.8 J.D. Com. Pleas J., Dom. Div.
Heisa, Mark H., (CV) ....'49 '78 C.381 B.A. L.8 J.D. 215 S. Chestnut St.
Hogle, Law Offices of, (BV) ....202 S. Prospect St.
Hogle, James E., Jr., (BV) ....'36 '65 C.381 B.S. L.8 J.D. [Hogle]
Jalbert, Michael J., (BV) ....'51 '83 C.690 B.S. L.7 J.D. 2398 Fox Circle
Jennings, Jonathan P. '73 '99 C.999 B.A. L.124 J.D.
Staff Atty., Community Legal Aid Services, Inc.
Kainrad, Joseph R. ....'33 '58 C.381 A.B. L.608 LL.B. Com. Pleas J.
Kane, Ronald J., (CV) ....'35 '62 C.62 L.1003 J.D. [Kane&K.]
Kane, Terry G. P., (BV) ....'51 '77 C.228 B.A. L.930 J.D. [Kane&K.]
Kane & Kane, (BV) ....101 East Main Street
Kent, Robt. L. ....'20 '47 C&L.930 A.B., LL.B. Ret. Com. Pleas J.
Lager, Dennis Day, (BV) ....'46 '76 C.347 A.B. L.1003 J.D. 449 S. Meridan Street
Lawson, Stephen C., (CV) ....'50 '90 C.381 B.A. L.8 J.D. 250 S. Chestnut Street, Suite 17
Lentz, William D., (BV) ....'52 '76 C.653 B.A. L.7 J.D. [Sandvoss&L.]
Lombardi, Richard C., (BV) ....'45 '71 C.8 B.A. L.608 J.D. 240 S. Chestnut Street
Masi, James, (BV) ....'63 '89 C.229 B.A. L.8 J.D. [Wilson&M.]
Myers, Jeffrey David ....'60 '96 C.381 B.A. L.8 J.D. 409 S. Prospect St.
Myers, Louis R., (BV) ....'42 '72 C.381 B.A. L.1003 J.D. [Myers&P.]
Myers & Plough, (BV) ....229 1/2 S. Chestnut
Nolfi, Edward A. ....'58 '83 C.103 A.B. L.7 J.D. 4965 State Route 14
O'Neill, John P., (BV) ....'41 '71 C.363 B.S. L.1340 J.D. Mag., Mun. Ct.
Perk, Kelli Kay ....'63 '97 C.8 B.A. L.61 J.D. Mag., Portage Co. Com. Pleas Ct.
Plough, John J., (BV) ....'47 '72 C.381 B.A. L.94 J.D. [Myers&P.]

Poland, Kevin T., Law Offices of, (BV) '61 '86 C.381 B.B.A. L.7 J.D.
240 S. Chestnut Street, 44266
Telephone: 330-296-9122
General Practice, Personal Injury, Criminal Law, Traffic Violations, Automobile Accidents and Injuries, Driving While Intoxicated, Probate, Family Law, Divorce, Child Custody.
See Professional Biographies, RAVENNA, OHIO

Ricciardi, Francis M., (BV) ....'48 '77 C.381 B.S.Ed. L.7 J.D. 240 S. Chestnut St.
Rosenberg, Robert E. ....'62 '89 C.161 B.B.A. L.1003 J.D. [Stephens&R.]
Roubic, Melissa R. ....'63 '96 C.381 B.B.A. L.8 J.D. [M.Roubic]
Roubic, Melissa .... 222 W. Main St., 2nd Fl.
Sandvoss, Norman W., (AV) ....'42 '68 C.608 B.S. L.607 J.D. [Sandvoss&L.]
Sandvoss & Lentz, (AV) ....228 W. Main St.
Scavdis, Antonios C., (BV) ....'47 '74 C.381 B.A. L.7 J.D. 261 W. Spruce
Scavdis, Antonios Constantinos, Jr. ....'76 '01 C.473 B.S. L.124 J.D. 261 W. Spruce Ave.
Schneider, O. J. ....'26 '51 C.381 B.S. L.930 J.D. 231 S. Chestnut St.‡
Sed, David A., (BV) ....'52 '77 C.1062 B.A. L.7 J.D. 269 W. Main Street
Sendry, Douglas J., (BV) ....'46 '74 C.381 B.A. L.7 J.D. Mag., Dom. Rel. Ct.
Sicuro, Thomas J., (BV) ....'42 '68 C.381 B.A. L.7 J.D. [Sicuro&S.]
Sicuro & Simon, An Association of Attorneys, (AV) .... 213 South Chestnut

Simon, William G., (AV) ... '42 '72 C.608 B.A. L.7 J.D. [Sicuro&S.]

Slater, Zurz & Gilbert
(See Akron)

Steinle, Richard J. ... '45 '81 C.602 B.A. L.7 J.D. Mediator, Ct. Com. Pleas
Stephens, Craig M., (BV) ... '44 '74 C.381 B.A. L.7 J.D. [Stephens&R.]

Stephens & Rosenberg, (BV)
206 South Meridian Street, Suite A, P.O. Box 229, 44266-0229
Telephone: 330-296-3434 FAX: 330-296-3435
Email: cmslaw@neo.rr.com
Members of Firm: Craig M. Stephens; Robert E. Rosenberg.
General Civil and Criminal Trial Practice. Personal Injury, Family, Corporate, Real Estate, Municipal, Juvenile and Probate Law.
Reference: Bank One of Ravenna, N.A.
See Professional Biographies, RAVENNA, OHIO

Thomas, Timothy R., (BV) ... '51 '77 C.610 B.A. L.851 J.D. 206 S. Meridian St.
Toepfer, David M. ... '72 '97 C.980 B.S.B.A. L.8 J.D. Asst. Pros.
Vannelli, Gail L., (CV) ... '51 '86 C.117 B.A. L.800 J.D. Asst. Co. Pros.
Vari, Frank G. ... '40 '85 C.318 B.A. L.8 J.D. Portage Co. Bd. od MRDD
Vigluicci, Victor V., (BV) ... '52 '77 C.1260 B.A. L.7 J.D. Co. Pros.
Watson, Barbara R. ... '36 '80 C.610 A.B. L.7 J.D. Mun. J.

Weber, Edward C.
(See Akron)

Weisenburger, Dan J., (BV) ... '53 '81 C.381 B.A. L.1003 J.D. [D.Weisenburger]
Weisenburger, Dan, (BV) ... 121 E. Main Street

Williams, Welser & Kratcoski
(See Kent)

Wilson, Stephen M., (BV) ... '54 '79 C.611 B.A. L.608 J.D. [Wilson&M.]
Wilson & Masi, (BV) ... 250 S. Prospect St.
Zavinski, Dennis M., (BV) ... '42 '74 C.381 B.A. L.7 J.D. [D.Zavinski]
Zavinski, Dennis, (BV) ... 409 S. Prospect St.
Zawadski, Thaddeus Francis '49 '75
C.602 B.A. L.8 J.D. Gen. Coun., Robinson Memorial Hospital

RAYMOND, 350, *Union Co.*

Millard, Christen M. ... '69 '97 C.691 L.1356 21001 State Route 739 (Pat.)

READING, 11,292, *Hamilton Co.*

Gertz, Anthony J., (BV) ... '45 '72 C.1118 B.A. L.1340 J.D. [Gertz]
Gertz Law Firm, (BV) ... 401 Pike St.

REEDSVILLE, —, *Meigs Co.*

Lavelle, Francis (Frank) A., (BV) ... '55 '82 C.610 B.A. L.179 J.D. [Lavelle] ⊙
Lavelle Law Offices, L.P.A., (BV) ... 66717 State Route 124 (⊙Athens)

REYNOLDSBURG, 32,069, *Fairfield, Franklin & Licking Cos.*

Akin, Dain C. '52 '78 C.473 B.S. L.607 J.D.
Act. Gen. Coun. & V.P., Cardinal Realty Servs., Inc.
Arbuckle, Charles Hoover ... '52 '90 C.608 B.S. L.117 J.D. Corporate Counsel, Dynalab
Baer, Christopher J. ... '57 '82 C&L.608 J.D. 777 Waggoner Rd. S.
Bally, James P., (AV) ... '36 '61 C&L.608 B.A., J.D. 6606 Tussing Rd.

Benson, Michael E.
(See Columbus)

Berlin, Lawrence A., (BV) ... '44 '70 C.608 B.A. L.150 J.D. 6422 E. Main St.
Biswas, Naren, (BV) ... '31 '59 C.207 A.B. L.608 LL.B. 6504 E. Main St.
Brant, John W., (BV) ... '43 '77 C.443 B.S. L.117 J.D. State Dept. Comm.
Brusk, Norman, (BV) ... '41 '92 C.912 B.S. L.117 J.D. [Brusk&B.]
Brusk, Susan Pam ... '44 '92 C.801 B.A. L.117 J.D. [Brusk&B.]
Brusk & Brusk, (BV) ... 7100 East Livingston Avenue
Coriell, Karen Bond ... '56 '94 C.434 B.A. L.608 J.D. 2152 Wayfaring Dr.
Curtis, Harry A. ... '25 '53 C.97 L.1003 J.D. 7148 E. Main St.
Damaser, Hilary R. ... '64 '92 C.821 B.A. L.608 J.D. Asst. Atty. Gen.
D'Amico, Jodelle M., (BV) ... '58 '83 C.473 B.A. L.117 J.D. 7110 E. Livingston Ave.
Danco, Ernest J. ... '28 '54 C&L.608 B.A., J.D. 7109 Ellen Ct.‡
Foster, Frank H., (AV) '40 '66 C&L.608 B.E.E., J.D.
[Kremblas,F.P.&P.] (See Pat. Sect.)
Foster, Jason H. ... '68 '95 C.608 B.S.M.E. L.117 J.D. [Kremblas,F.P.&P.]
Friedman, Alan P., (BV) ... '51 '76 C.608 B.A. L.117 J.D. 7110 E. Livington Ave.
Fuerman, Ross D. '53 '82
C.150 B.A. L.273 J.D. Asst. Gen. Coun., Cardinal Industries, Inc.
Gallutia, Christopher Andrew ... '60 '85 C.608 B.A. L.117 J.D. 7668 Slate Ridge Road
Hardgrove, James A., (AV) ... '45 '78 C.610 B.B.A. L.117 J.D. 7600 Slate Ridge Blvd.
Haynes, S. Scott ... '62 '92 C.130 B.A. L.117 J.D. 6445 E. Livingston Ave.
Herkins, Robert C., (BV) ... '14 '37 C.201 L.608 c/o Belinda Herkins, 1775 Kaiser Drive
Hiland, Tammy L. ... '70 '97 C.266 B.P.A. L.117 J.D. Asst. City Pros.
Humphrey, David L., (AV) ... '59 '86 C.266 B.S. L.117 J.D. 7658 Slate Ridge Blvd.
Kremblas, Frank T., (AV) '37 '64
C&L.608 B.Ch.E., J.D. [Kremblas,F.P.&P.] (See Pat. Sect.)

Kremblas, Foster, Phillips & Pollick, (AV)
7632 Slate Ridge Boulevard, 43068-8159
Telephone: 614-575-2100 Fax: 614-575-2149
Email: info@ohiopatent.com URL: http://www.ohiopatent.com
Members of Firm: Frank T. Kremblas; Frank H. Foster; Patrick P. Phillips; Philip J. Pollick (Co., L.P.A.); Jason H. Foster.
Patent, Trademark, Copyright and Intellectual Property Law. Foreign Patent and Trademarks Law. Litigation. Licensing.
See Professional Biographies, REYNOLDSBURG, OHIO

Mosier, James F. '48 '73 C.608 B.A. L.575 J.D.
Gen. Coun. & Corp. Secy., Physicians Ins. Co. of Ohio
Newbold, Garold L., (BV) ... '57 '83 C&L.608 B.A., J.D. 1535 Stouder Dr.
Pachuta, Paul A., (BV) ... '29 '59 C&L.608 B.Sc., J.D. 7400 E. Main St.
Phillips, Patrick P., (BV) ... '55 '80 C.692 B.A. L.117 J.D. [Kremblas,F.P.&P.]
Plank, Rhett A., (AV) ... '56 '82 C.608 B.S. L.117 J.D. 7600 Slate Ridge Blvd.
Pollick, Philip J., (Co., L.P.A.) '42 '87
C.608 Ph.D. L.117 J.D. [Kremblas,F.P.&P.] (See Pat. Sect.)
Pursley, Gerald Lee '45 '78 C.381 B.A. L.7 J.D.
Ohio Dept. of Commerce, Div. of State Fire Marshall
Roth, Kelleen Ann ... '67 '95 C.97 B.A. L.117 J.D. City Pros.
Rovito, Joel Robert ... '69 '94 [J.R.Rovito]
Rovito, Joel R. ... 7538 Slate Ridge Blvd.
Sain, George R. ... '39 '98 C.999 B.S.E. L.117 J.D. 6906 Starfire Drive
Sanders, Robert M., (BV) ... '44 '68 C.8 B.S.B.A. L.608 J.D. Jab Properties
Schaefer, Robert Bruce ... '55 '87 C&L.608 M.B.A., J.D. Lexford Properties, Inc.
Schermer, Amy K. ... '72 '97 C.97 B.S. L.608 J.D. 8372 Firstgate Drive
Shultz, Eugene R. ... '48 '77 C&L.608 B.A., J.D. 1266 Glenveiw St.
Sigall, Leonard S., (AV) ... '35 '59 C.381 B.S. L.608 J.D. 6470 E. Main St.
Southern, James Edward ... '56 '93 7538 Slate Ridge Boulevard
Stewart, J. Douglas, (BV) ... '53 '79 C.207 B.A. L.117 J.D. 7518 Slate Ridge Blvd.
Stone, Steven Donald ... '69 '96 C.1505 B.A. L.1206 J.D. 6470 E Main Street
Strawser, Eric Jason ... '74 '00 C.999 B.A. L.608 J.D. 1654 Brice Road
Swope, Kristy, (BV) ... '58 '86 C.473 B.Ph. L.117 J.D. [Swope&S.]
Swope, Richard F., (AV) ... '28 '56 C&L.608 B.S., J.D. [Swope&S.]
Swope and Swope, (AV) ... 6504 East Main Street
Thompson, James C., (BV) ... '38 '61 C.610 A.B. L.608 J.D. 7509 E. Main St.
Thompson, Timothy Charles '68 '93 C&L.608 B.A., J.D.
Dept. of Commerce, Div. of State Fire Marshall
Underwood, William F., (BV) '41 '74
C.560 B.S.M.E. L.117 J.D. 7610 Slate Ridge Boulevard
Wristen, Ellen L., Law Offices, (BV) '47 '74 C&L.117 B.A., LL.B.
7347 East Main Street

RICHFIELD, 3,286, *Summit Co.*

Anderson, David P. '68 '93 C.625 B.A. L.608 J.D.
(adm. in PA; not adm. in OH) Sr. Cnsl., Risk International Services, Inc.
Elsmore, Venetia M. ... '65 '95 C.318 B.A. L.1003 J.D. 4150 Kinross Lakes Parkway
Hernandez, Carlos M. '54 '79
C.679 B.S.C.E. L.472 J.D. Gen. Coun. & Secy., Mittal Steel USA
Holden, James T., Jr. ... '26 '55 C.423 L.64 J.D. 2597 Motor Rd.
Mayland, Gail B. '54 '78 C&L.659 B.A., J.D.
V.P., & Sr. Corp. Coun., Charles Schwab & Co., Inc., Corp. Coun. Off.
Musacchia, Jacqueline A. '63 '88 C.970 B.A. L.930 J.D.
V.P. & Gen. Coun., ProQuest Business Solutions, Inc.
Rudolph, Jennifer L. ... '70 '98 C.602 B.S. L.1003 J.D. Corp. Atty., Charles Schwab
Siwik, Lori L. ... '61 '87 C.381 B.A. L.150 J.D. V.P. & Coun., Risk Intl. Srvcs. Inc.
Siwik, Mark, (AV) '64 '88 C.8 B.A. L.150 J.D.
Sr. Cnsl., Risk International Services, Inc.
Thomas-Boehnlein, Karen M., Law Office of, (BV) '64 '91
C.161 B.A. L.8 J.D. P.O. Box 366

RICHMOND HEIGHTS, 10,944, *Cuyahoga Co.*

Dawson, James G. ... '45 '79 C.161 B.B.A. L.1003 J.D. 4881 Foxlain Traic
Fishman, Martin A. '41 '68 C.608 B.S. L.930 J.D.
Gen. Coun., V.P. & Secy., Assoc. Estates Realty Corp.
Kornbluth, David A. ... '69 '96 C.012 B.A. L.930 J.D. 5025 Swetland Ct.‡
Kronenberg, Janet L., (AV) ... '48 '79 C.569 B.A. L.1003 J.D. 339 Claymore
Macauda, Vincent, (BV) ... '60 '91 C.363 B.S. L.1003 J.D. [V.Macauda]
Macauda, Vincent, Co., LPA, (BV) ... 26301 Curtiss Wright Parkway, Suite 210
Svec, Matthew James ... '74 '00 C.1260 B.A. L.989 J.D. 691 Richmond Road
Weiss, Lita L. ... '32 '78 C.930 B.A. L.161 J.D. Assoc. Estates Realty Corp.
Wertheim, Walter Reinold ... '25 '50 C.1353 L.1009 LL.M 486 Donald Ave.‡

RICHWOOD, 2,186, *Union Co.*

Evans, Jeffrey Lee, (AV) ... '56 '81 C&L.607 B.A., J.D. [Evans,E.&H.]

Evans, Evans & Hoffman L.L.P., (AV)
15 West Ottawa Street, 43344-1138
Telephone: 740-943-2325 Fax: 740-943-2326
Jeffrey Lee Evans; Scott L. Hoffman.
Banking and Lending, Business Law, Corporation Law, Estate Planning, Finance Law, Guardianships, International Law, Probate, Project Finance, Real Estate.
See Professional Biographies, RICHWOOD, OHIO

Hoffman, Scott L., (AV⊤) ... '57 '83 C.607 B.A. L.823 J.D. [Evans,E.&H.]

RIPLEY, 1,816, *Brown Co.*

Pfeffer, Michael S., (BV) ... '47 '73 C.608 B.S. L.150 J.D. 112 Main St.
Zachman, Thomas F., (BV) ... '45 '71 C.611 B.A. L.228 J.D. 134 N. Front Street

RISING SUN, 698, *Wood Co.*

Buchanan, J. Vincent ... '51 '76 C.97 B.A. L.851 J.D. 8500 U.S. 23 N.

RITTMAN, 6,314, *Medina & Wayne Cos.*

Bower, Kevin George, (BV) ... '51 '76 C.611 B.A. L.607 J.D. [Bower]
Bower Law Offices, (BV) ... 19 N. Main St., Ste. B
Cain, Julia A. ... '64 '89 C.8 B.A. L.608 J.D. 34 South Main
Clark, Mark C., (BV) ... '49 '74 C.608 B.A. L.7 J.D. [Flynn&C.]
Flynn, Thomas T., (BV) ... '44 '69 C.528 B.A. L.930 J.D. [Flynn&C.]
Flynn & Clark, (BV) ... 99 E. Ohio Ave.
Kindsvatter, Leo R. ... '13 '46 C.273 A.B. L.276 J.D. Ret. Prob. J.
Landers, William D., (BV) ... '63 '91 C.381 B.S. L.8 J.D. 20 W. Ohio Ave.
Winchell, V. Lee, (CV) ... '52 '77 C.49 A.B. L.7 J.D. 34 S. Main Street

ROCKBRIDGE, —, *Hocking Co.*

Moses, Robert P., (BV) ... '41 '70 L.608 J.D. 20040 Carroll Rd.
Stilwell, James E. ... '22 '53 C&L.608 B.S., J.D. 13975 State Rte. 374‡

ROCKY RIVER, 20,735, *Cuyahoga Co.*

Allen, Thomas E., (AV) ... '27 '54 C.610 B.S.C. L.472 LL.B. 21010 Center Ridge Rd.
Annandale, Melinda J. ... '48 '91 C.161 B.A. L.1003 J.D. 20033 Detroit Rd.
Arabian, Anjanette Chris '73 '01 C.893 B.A. L.989 J.D.
20575 Center Ridge Rd., Ste. 314
Batal, Susan E. ... '43 '84 C.161 B.A. L.1003 J.D. [Shalala&B.]
Battle, Colleen P., (AV) ... '45 '86 C.1109 B.A. L.1003 J.D. [Battle&M.]

Battle & Miller P.L.L., (AV)
1340 Depot Street, Suite 100, 44116-1741
Telephone: 440-895-9700 Fax: 440-895-1442
Email: miller@battlemillerlaw.com URL: http://www.lawyers.com/battle&miller
Colleen P. Battle; Sharon L. Miller. Associates: James W. Ellis; Steven C. Polly.
Labor Law, Employment Law, Workers Compensation, OSHA.
See Professional Biographies, ROCKY RIVER, OHIO

Beebe, Linda G., (BV) ... '42 '82 C.381 B.A. L.1003 J.D. 19111 Detroit Road, Suite 205
Blair, Leslie H. ... '20 '58 C.934 A.B. L.851 LL.B. 21111 W. Wager Circle (Pat.)
Boutton, Mary L. ... '54 '79 C.473 B.A. L.273 J.D. 2801 Kingsbury Dr.
Burney, Jon R. ... '42 '68 C.207 B.A. L.608 J.D. [Burney&H.]
Burney & Herthneck Co., L.P.A., (BV) ... 20220 Center Ridge Road
Byrne, J. Vaughan ... '12 '51 C.363 A.B. L.161 J.D. 18741 Inglewood Dr.‡
Cachat, Joseph A. ... '26 '52 C.280 L.1003 J.D. 19702 Center Ridge Rd.‡
Campbell, Robert W. ... '13 '38 C&L.930 A.B., LL.B. 20325 Center Ridge Rd.‡
Christensen, George A. ... '15 '58 C.62 B.A. L.1003 LL.B. Old Detroit Rd.
Ciocco, Mary Beth ... '69 '94 C.201 B.A. L.851 J.D. 22255 Center Ridge Rd., Ste. 106
Cleary, Edward Francis ... '59 '88 C.573 B.A. L.1003 J.D. [Edward F.C.]

Corso, Joseph John, (BV) .... '34 '61 C.363 B.S. L.1003 LL.B. 20220 Center Ridge Road
Cummings, David A. ....'55 '91 C.161 B.B.A. L.1003 J.D. [D.A.Cummings]
Cummings, David A., Co., L.P.A. .... 20800 Center Ridge Rd., Ste. 200
Devito, Maureen M. .... '64 '99 C.602 B.A. L.161 J.D. DeVito Consulting
Distin, John H. .... '45 '90 C.869 B.S. L.477 J.D. 3492 Middlepost Lane
Donahue, Joseph F., (AV) .... '22 '50 C.602 A.B. L.161 LL.B. 840 Orchard Park Dr.‡
Dorfmeyer, Robt. E. ....'16 '44 C.97 B.S. L.1003 J.D. 3595 Eldorado Dr.
Drain, Joseph A. ....'55 '82 C&L.930 B.A., J.D. [A Grady&Assoc.]
Dunsmore, Robert B. .... '22 '62 C.645 B.A. L.1003 J.D. 20146 Beachcliff Blvd.‡
Edward F. Cleary .... 20800 Center Ridge Road
Ellis, James W. .... '71 '00 C.97 B.A. L.1003 J.D. [A Battle&M.]
Farah, Benjamin F. .... '56 '81 C.273 B.B.A. L.930 J.D. 1154 Linda Street
Fausnaugh, Hal A. .... '25 '52 C.611 B.A. L.1003 LL.B. 20126 Westhaven Lane‡
Fitzsimmons, Donna Congeni ....'51 '76 C.93 A.B. L.273 J.D. Mun. J.
Gorski, Pamela L., (BV) .... '44 '92 C.930 B.S. L.1003 J.D. 19111 Detroit Road, Suite 205
Grady, Francis X., (AV) .... '57 '84 C.276 B.S.F.S. L.608 J.D. [Grady&Assoc.]

Grady & Associates, (AV)
20950 Center Ridge Road Suite 100, 44116-4307
Telephone: 440-356-7255 Fax: 440-356-7254
URL: http://www.gradyassociates.com
Francis X. Grady;—Joseph A. Drain; Scott M. Puglise.
Banking and Securities Law.
See Professional Biographies, ROCKY RIVER, OHIO

Gray, Susan M.
(See Cleveland)

Hayman, Edward A. .... '23 '63 C.363 L.1003 J.D. 2725 Lakeview Ave.‡
Herthneck, Richard E., (BV) ....'45 '72 C.473 B.A. L.161 J.D. [Burney&H.]
Higgins, Ralph P., (AV) ......'29 '60 C.251 B.B.A. L.1003 LL.B. 21010 Center Ridge Rd.
Holmes, Milton D. ....'27 '50 C.610 A.B. L.930 LL.B. Mun. J.
Jones, Vickie Lynne, Law Office of .... '63 '99 C.216 B.A. L.989 J.D. 20575 Center Road
Kelley, John J., III ....'63 '93 C.363 B.A. L.1003 J.D. [J.J.Kelley]
Kelley, John J., Co., L.P.A. .... 19525 Hilliard Blvd.
Kilbane, James V. .... '30 '67 C.608 B.S. L.1003 J.D. 2680 Struhar Dr.‡
Klima, Gregory K. ....'61 '86 C.967 B.A. L.309 J.D. 20006 Detroit Road
Klima, Ronald Edward .... '39 '76 C.610 B.B.A. L.989 J.D. [R.E.Klima]
Klima, Ronald E. ....40 Pond Drive
Lampus, Robert William .... '47 '73 C.608 B.S. L.161 J.D. Dawson Insurance
Lindon, Elizabeth Ann .... '71 '99 C.363 B.A. L.607 J.D. [Lindon&L.]
Lindon, James ....'— '97 C.37 B.S.Ph. L.607 J.D. [Lindon&L.] (Pat.)

Lindon & Lindon, LLC
1250 Linda Street, 44116
Telephone: 440-333-0011 Fax: 419-710-4925
Email: Patent@2-INVENT.COM URL: http://www.2-INVENT.COM
Dr. James Lindon; Elizabeth Ann Lindon.
All areas of Intellectual Property including Patent, Trademark, Copyright, Trade Dress, Trade Secret, and Litigation as well as Pharmacy Law.
See Professional Biographies, ROCKY RIVER, OHIO

Louth, Richard P., (BV) .... '37 '73 C.930 B.A. L.1003 J.D. 21580 Hilliard Boulevard
Markstrom, Paul F., (BV) .... '44 '72 C.363 A.B. L.161 J.D. 22255 Center Ridge Rd.
McCullough, George V., (BV) .... '28 '51 C.150 L.607 J.D. 22255 Center Ridge Rd.
McDermott, John M., (BV) ....'46 '71 C.973 B.S. L.608 J.D. [McDermott&M.]
McDermott & McDermott Co., L.P.A., (BV) .... 21851 Center Ridge Rd.
McDonough, Brian M. .... '74 '00 C.602 B.S. L.989 J.D. P.O. Box 16252
McDowell, James M. ....'30 '58 C.178 B.A. L.446 J.D. P.O. Box 161034
McNally, Frank J. .... '25 '55 C.363 B.S.S. L.1003 LL.B. 19800 Center Ridge Rd.
McQuillan, Jean M., (AV) ....'55 '80 C.602 B.A. L.930 J.D. 21612 Kenwood Avenue
Meckler, Theodore E., (BV) '49 '75
C.705 A.B. L.1003 J.D. 20525 Center Ridge Rd., Ste. 700

Milano Weiser, Attys. & Counselors at Law, A Legal Prof. Assoc.
(See Cleveland)

Miller, Sharon L., (AV) ....'62 '91 C.97 B.S. L.1003 J.D. [Battle&M.]
Mills, Charles E., (BV) .... '54 '80 C.5 B.A. L.851 J.D. 22255 Center Ridge Road
Mills, Ronald H., (BV) '46 '72 C.62 B.A. L.1003 J.D.
22255 Center Ridge Rd., Ste. 106
Monjot, James A., (BV) ....'47 '72 C.608 B.S. L.1003 J.D. 21851 Center Ridge Rd.
Murphy, Michael H. ....'69 '94 C.999 B.A. L.989 J.D. 20325 Center Ridge Rd.
Nicklawsky, Frank T., (AV) ....'11 '50 C.585 B.S. L.1003 J.D. 1762 Lakeview Ave.
O'Donnell, Terrence ....'46 '71 C.381 B.A. L.1003 J.D. 3400 Delmar Drive‡
Patronite, Sal J. ....'23 '52 C&L.930 B.B.A., LL.B. 1148 Elmwood Rd.‡
Percio, Joseph M. ....'50 '75 C.930 B.S. L.1003 J.D. 19111 Detroit Road
Polly, Steven C. ....'68 '99 C.932 B.S. L.607 J.D. [A Battle&M.]
Portmann, Richard W., (AV) '25 '50
C&L.930 B.A., LL.B. 20220 Center Ridge Rd., Plaza W. Bldg.
Puglise, Scott M. ....'70 '00 C.1208 B.S. L.161 J.D. [A Grady&Assoc.]

Purcell, Kevin, Co., L.P.A.
(See Cleveland)

Putka, Andrew C. ....'26 '52 C&L.930 B.A., J.D. 28 Pond Dr.
Rhein, Clyde K., (AV) ....'23 '49 C.385 B.A. L.930 LL.B. 20545 Center Ridge Rd.
Riordan, Timothy P. ....'59 '87 C.161 B.A. L.1003 J.D. 11 Aberdeen Court
Ryan, John D., (AV) .... '38 '66 C.970 B.A. L.1003 J.D. 20800 Center Ridge Rd.
St. Leger, Robert E. .... '28 '58 C.251 B.B.A. L.1003 J.D. 2762 Gasser Blvd.‡
Seelie, John F., (AV) ....'42 '68 C.973 B.S.B.A. L.383 J.D. 19111 Detroit Road
Shalala, Edna C., (BV) .... '11 '52 C.608 B.S. L.1003 LL.B. [Shalala&B.]
Shalala & Batal, (BV) .... 2600 Wooster Rd.
Shiffra, Robert, (AV) ....'32 '66 C.251 B.B.A. L.1003 J.D. 1058 Creek Ln.‡
Simon, Charles T., (BV) .... '46 '77 C.363 B.S.B.A. L.1003 J.D. [C.T.Simon]
Simon, Charles T., Co., LPA, (BV) ....21220 Center Ridge, Suite 250
Skonce, Ralph T., Jr., (AV) '54 '79 C.161 B.A. L.1003 J.D.
1154 Linda Street, Suite 175
Smith, Catherine Kurela '69 '96 C.97 B.S. L.989 J.D.
Delta Theta Phi Law Fraternit, Int'l.
Strnisha, Herman J. ....'28 '63 C.124 B.S. L.1003 J.D. 17 Pond Dr.‡
Sweeney, Matthew J. .... '59 '85 C.473 A.B. L.365 J.D. 2055 Lakeview Ave.★
Taft, Homer S., (BV) ....'45 '70 C.381 B.A. L.930 J.D. P.O. Box 16216
Taylor, Timothy A. '42 '70 C.473 A.B. L.1003 J.D.
20800 Center Ridge Road, Suite 220
Tenwick, Thomas J., (BV) ....'42 '71 C.692 B.S. L.989 J.D. 3511 Wooster Road
Thomas, James E. ....'38 '67 C.610 B.S.C. L.1003 J.D. 19488 Beachcliff Blvd.
Thomas, Michael A., (BV) ... '47 '75 C.97 B.A. L.1003 J.D. 1154 Linda Street, Suite 250
Thompson, Rebecca A. .... '74 '99 C.610 B.B.A. L.989 J.D. 19120 Detroit Road
Tjotjos, Sophia Papandreas, (BV) ....'59 '84 C.608 B.A. L.930 J.D. 231 Yacht Club Dr.
Valponi, Barbara Dawn ...... '54 '79 C.610 B.A. L.989 J.D. Mag., Rocky River Mun. Ct.
Wall, Philip J. .... '27 '56 C.385 B.A. L.1003 LL.B. 20800 Center Ridge
Wilcox, Darlene A. .... '49 '98 C.1102 B.A. L.1003 J.D. 1154 Linda Street
Wojton, Francine J. ....'51 '94 C.381 B.S.N. L.1003 J.D. 3640 Bradfords Gate
Zak, Edward A., (BV) .... '41 '68 C.363 A.B. L.1003 J.D. 3780 River Lane

ROME, 99, *Ashtabula Co.*

Winer, Jonathan W., Attorney at Law, (BV) '52 '87
C.161 B.A. L.1003 J.D. 5276 Rome-Rock Creek Rd.

ROOTSTOWN, 6,585, *Portage Co.*

Murdock, Chad E. ....'54 '91 C.381 B.S. L.8 J.D. P.O. Box 334
Sabarese, Sharon Ann, (CV) .... '56 '89 C.318 B.A. L.8 J.D. P.O. Box 964
Schimer, Maria R., (CV) ....'51 '84 C.1044 B.A.B.S.N. L.7 J.D. Asst. Atty. Gen.

ROSS, 1,971, *Butler Co.*

Zea, Betty J. ..... '— '91 C&L.150 B.S., J.D. Pat. Atty., The Procter & Gamble Co. (Pat.)
Zerby, Kim William ..... '56 '84 Associate General Counsel, Procter & Gamble Company

ROSSFORD, 6,406, *Wood Co.*

Huffman, Rex H., (BV) .... '53 '79 C.473 B.S. L.851 J.D. [Spitler,H.Y.&N.] ⊙
Paterson, David Grant, (CV) ....'54 '82 C.273 B.B.A. L.851 J.D. 1016 Dixie Hwy.
Spitler, Huffman, Yoon & Newlove, LLP, (AV) ....932 Dixie Hwy. (⊙Bowling Green)

RUSSELLS POINT, 1,619, *Logan Co.*

Brooks, Harriet L. '55 '82 C.788 A.B. L.930 J.D.
(adm. in MO; not adm. in OH) 14879 Trappers Trail‡
Snyder, Cheryl Wright, (CV) '45 '81 C.1322 B.A. L.201 J.D.
7310 Road 94 (Lewistown)

SABINA, 2,780, *Clinton Co.*

Buckley, Miller & Wright, (AV) ....34 N. Howard St. (⊙Wilmington)
Campbell, Michael T. .... '73 '98 C.973 B.S. L.851 J.D. [A Rose&D.] (⊙Blanchester)
Rose, Gordon L., (BV) ....'51 '80 C.952 B.A. L.117 J.D. [Rose&D.] (⊙Blanchester)
Rose & Dobyns Co., L.P.A., (BV)
411 East Washington Street (⊙Blanchester, Wilmington)
Wright, Jeffrey L., (BV) .... '49 '74 C&L.608 B.Sc., J.D. [Buckley,M.&W.] ⊙

SAGAMORE HILLS, —, *Summit Co.*

Furber, Philip C., (AV) ....'43 '75 C.347 B.S. L.1003 J.D. 839 Woodbridge Trail
Giordano, Deena M. .... '74 '01 C.381 B.A. L.124 J.D. 7926 Chaffee Rd.
Larkin, Brent W. ....'47 '87 C.608 B.S.S. L.1003 J.D. 874 Hemlock Lane
Tuzi, Louis A. .... '24 '56 C.665 B.S. L.1003 J.D. 761 Stoney Brook Rd.‡
Utley, Sue Ellen ....'45 '70 C.518 A.B. L.228 J.D. 8509 Waterside Dr.‡

ST. CLAIRSVILLE, * 5,057, *Belmont Co.*

Banker, Alan, (AV) ....'32 '57 C&L.608 B.A., J.D. [Banker&W.] ⊙
Banker & White, (AV) ....151 W. Main St. (⊙Bellaire)
Barnes, David L., (BV) ....'31 '58 C.610 A.B. L.602 J.D. Masonic Temple Bldg.
Bean, Charles H., (AV) ....'47 '72 C.610 A.B. L.608 J.D. [Thornburg,B.&G.]
Bench, Rebbeca L. ....'73 '02 C.498 B.S. L.607 J.D. [A Hanlon,D.E.&M.]
Burech, Stanley G., (AV) ....'44 '69 C.604 A.B. L.477 J.D. [Burech&C.]
Burech & Crow, (AV) .... 121 Newell Avenue
Cassidy, Myers, Cogan, Voegelin & Tennant, L.C., (BV)
126 E. Main St. (⊙Wheeling, WV)
Costine, Eric, (BV) ....'57 '86 C.999 B.A. L.607 J.D. [Costine]
Costine, J. Mark, (BV) ....'54 '79 C.896 B.A. L.607 J.D. Com. Pleas J.
Costine, John O., (BV) ....'24 '51 C.81 A.B. L.607 LL.B. [Costine]
Costine Law Firm The, (BV) ....136 W. Main St.
Crow, Donna L., (CV) ....'63 '89 C&L.923 B.S.B.A., J.D. [Burech&C.]
Dolan, Richard E. ....'33 '60 C.229 B.A. L.884 LL.B. 67810 Brokaw Dr.‡
Duff, Gerald P., (AV) ....'47 '71 C.1057 B.A. L.602 J.D. [Hanlon,D.E.&M.]
Estadt, John R., (BV) ....'50 '83 C.381 B.A. L.930 J.D. [Hanlon,D.E.&M.]
Glick, Elizabeth L., (BV) ....'62 '87 C.954 B.A. L.923 J.D. [Thornburg,B.&G.]
Hanlon, Lodge L., (BV) ....'31 '58 C.831 B.S.B.A. L.608 J.D. [C Hanlon,D.E.&M.]

Hanlon, Duff, Estadt & McCormick Co., LPA, (AV) BR
46457 National Road West, 43950-9721
Telephone: 740-695-1444 Fax: 740-695-1563
Email: hdem@localnet.com
Gerald P. Duff; John R. Estadt; Michael P. McCormick; Erik Alan Schramm;—Rebbeca L. Bench.
Of Counsel: Lodge L. Hanlon.
General Civil Trial and Appellate Practice in all Courts. Corporate, Labor, Insurance, Taxation, Personal Injury, Probate, Real Estate Law. Estate Planning, Workers Compensation, Occupational Disease, Medical Malpractice Defense.
Reference: Belmont National Bank, St. Clairsville, Ohio.
See Professional Biographies, ST. CLAIRSVILLE, OHIO

Harper, Marlin J., (BV) ....'49 '75 C.610 B.A. L.608 J.D. [Harper&H.]
Harper & Hazlett, (BV) .... 185 W. Main St. (⊙Wheeling, WV)
Hazlett, Thomas Mck., (BV) .... '52 '77 C.385 A.B. L.923 J.D. [Harper&H.] ⊙
Henry, C. Kenneth ....'23 '51 C.81 A.B. L.930 J.D. Ret. Prob. J.
Kigerl, Jack J., (BV) ....'49 '74 C.608 B.A. L.117 J.D. 1320W. Main Street
Kinder, Duncan C., (CV) ....'55 '83 C.674 B.A. L.608 J.D. 68761 Hammond Rd.
Kinder, Gordon T., (AV) ....'19 '49 C.674 A.B. L.893 LL.B. 185 W. Main St.
Kinder, John C., (AV) ....'23 '50 C.674 B.A. L.893 LL.B. 185 W. Main St.
Knapp, Charles F. ....'23 '50 C&L.608 B.S., J.D. Com. Pleas J.
Kota, Robert C. '46 '75 C.920 B.S. L.923 J.D.
Gen. Coun., Health Plan of Upper Ohio Valley, Inc.

Lancione & Lloyd Law Office, Co., L.P.A.
(See Bellaire)

Malik, John J., Jr. ....'28 '54 C.363 L.602 J.D. Prob. J.
McCormick, Michael P., (BV) ....'59 '89 C.999 B.A. L.607 J.D. [Hanlon,D.E.&M.]
McDermott & Bonenberger, P.L.L.C., (BV) ............P.O. Box 163 (⊙Wheeling, WV)
Mellor, Adam K. ....'74 '99 C.970 B.A. L.608 J.D. [A Harper&H.]
Myers, Thomas M., (BV) .... '54 '80 C.608 B.S. L.201 J.D. [Cassidy,M.C.V.&T.]
Paleudis, John George, (BV) .... '44 '73 C.608 B.A.B.S. L.1003 J.D. 100 West Main Street
Quirk, Robert W., (BV) ....'50 '75 C.696 B.A. L.851 J.D. Co. Pros. Off.
Saines, W. Gus, (BV) ....'59 '85 C.339 B.A. L.1003 J.D. [McDermott&B.] ⊙
Sargus, Jennifer L. ....'53 '79 C&L.880 B.S., J.D. Com. Pleas J.
Schramm, Erik Alan ....'61 '98 C.81 B.S. L.923 J.D. [Hanlon,D.E.&M.]
Shaheen, Michael J. ....'64 '89 C.229 B.A. L.417 J.D. Asst. Pros. Atty.
Skorich, Elaine L. .... '68 '98 C.381 B.A. L.1003 J.D. 227 East Main Street
Solovan, John M., II ....'47 '71 C.973 B.S. L.93 J.D. Com. Pleas J.
Thomas, Mark A., (BV) .... '60 '87 C.381 B.B.A. L.607 J.D. 118 W. Main St.

Thornburg, Bean & Glick, (AV) BR
113 West Main Street, P.O. Box 96, 43950
Telephone: 740-695-0532 Telefax: 740-695-8039
Email: tbean@1st.net

(This Listing Continued)

Thornburg, Bean & Glick (Continued)

Carter Thornburg (1908-1979); Charles H. Bean; Elizabeth L. Glick.
General Civil Practice. Corporate, Personal Injury, Probate, Insurance and Real Estate Law. Title Examinations. Trials in all Courts. Mining Law.
Local Counsel for: North American Coal Corp.; State Automobile Insurance Co.; Ohio Bell Telephone Co.; Ohio Edison Co.; Marietta Coal Co.; Quarto Mining Co.; Grange Mutual Casualty Co.; Ohio Casualty Insurance Co.

See Professional Biographies, ST. CLAIRSVILLE, OHIO

Tomlan, John R., (BV) .... '59 '83 C.188 B.A. L.608 J.D. 108 E. Main St.

Tribbie, Scott, Plummer and Padden
(See Cambridge)

Trouten, David S., Jr., (CV) .... '66 '93 C&L.608 B.A., J.D. 103 Martha Drive
Vavra, John Andrew, (BV) .... '52 '83 C.920 B.A. L.7 J.D. [J.Vavra]
Vavra, John, Law Office, (BV) .... 132 W. Main St.
White, Harry W., (AV) .... '47 '73 C.610 A.B. L.608 J.D. [Banker&W.] ⊙
Yonak, Helen .... '55 '95 C.1115 B.A. L.179 J.D. 147 A W. Main St.

ST. MARYS, 8,441, *Auglaize Co.*

Herzing, Philip H. .... '26 '59 C.976 B.A. L.608 J.D. 305 South Main Street
Hitchen, Kenneth E., Attorney at Law, (BV) '43 '71 C&L.607 B.A., J.D. 510 W. South St.
Huber, William E., (BV) .... '43 '68 C&L.607 B.S., J.D. Co. Bd. of Elections
Kemp, Barrett G. .... '32 '59 C.610 B.S. L.607 J.D. E. Spring St.‡
Kuffner, John F., (BV) .... '28 '55 C.610 A.B. L.228 LL.B. [Kuffner&P.]
Kuffner and Pierce, Law Office, (BV) .... 201 W. North St.
Moul, Chas. E. .... '05 '29 L.608 LL.B. 11300 Circle Dr.‡
Pendleton-Dominguez, Dianna .... '61 '87 C&L.201 B.S., J.D. 401 N. Main St.
Pierce, Edwin A., (BV) .... '55 '80 C.150 B.A. L.607 J.D. [Kuffner&P.]
Wilson, Gregory D., (BV) .... '42 '69 C.608 B.Sc. L.607 J.D. 101 N. Front St.

SALEM, 12,233, *Columbiana Co.*

Apple, K. Bret, (BV) .... '61 '87 C.318 B.A. L.8 J.D. [Williams&A.]
Baronzzi, Christopher '78 '04 C.363 B.S.E. L.7 J.D. [Ⓐ Harrington,H.&M.] (⊙Youngstown)
Barry, Timothy A., (BV) .... '52 '87 C.901 B.A. L.930 J.D. [Fitch,K.C.R.&B.]
Cecil, Larry G., (BV) .... '47 '72 C&L.608 B.A., J.D. [Fitch,K.C.R.&B.]
Christian, Shirley J., (AV) '54 '86 C.650 B.S. L.607 J.D. [Harrington,H.&M.] (⊙Youngstown)
Coe, Thomas H. .... '29 '59 C&L.608 B.A., J.D. 294 Brooklyn Ave.‡
Conn, Harry R., (AV) .... '41 '73 C.610 A.B. L.7 J.D. [Harrington,H.&M.]
DeFazio, J. Diane, (CV) .... '45 '80 C.980 B.A. L.7 J.D. 601 N. Ellsworth Ave.
Duff, David W. .... '49 '74 C.935 B.A. L.930 J.D. 601 N. Ellsworth Ave.
Erb, Shawna L., (CV) '70 '96 C.528 B.A. L.608 J.D. [Harrington,H.&M.] (⊙Youngstown)

Fitch, Kendall, Cecil, Robinson & Barry Co., L.P.A., (BV)
600 East State Street, P.O. Box 590, 44460-0590
Telephone: 330-337-8761 Fax: 330-337-9453
Email: FitchKendall@Compuserve.com
Alfred L. Fitch (1913-1992); Bryce W. Kendall (1923-1995); Larry G. Cecil; Ian Robinson; Timothy A. Barry. Of Counsel: Whitman Robinson.
General Civil Trial Practice in federal and state courts and administrative agencies. Probate, Real Estate, Personal Injury, Family, Products Liability, Estate Planning, Insurance, Corporate, Taxation, Labor and Employment Law.
Representative Clients: Eljer Mfg. Div. of Eljer Industries; Worthington Industries, Inc. and Worthington Custom Plastics, Inc.; Firestone Electric Co.; The Ohio Pump Co.; Home Savings & Loan Co. of Youngstown; Farm Credit Services of Mid-America, ACA.
Agents for: Ohio Bar Title Insurance Co.; ACS Title and Closing Services.

See Professional Biographies, SALEM, OHIO

Goll, Geoffrey S., (BV) .... '44 '73 C.207 B.A. L.608 J.D. [G.S.Goll]
Goll, Geoffrey S., Co., LPA, (BV) .... 200 E. Pershing Street
Gorby, Jennifer Ann .... '75 '01 C.528 B.A. L.8 J.D. 585 E. State Street

Harrington, Hoppe & Mitchell, Ltd., (AV)
2235 E. Pershing Street, Suite A, 44460 ⊙
Telephone: 330-337-6586 Telefax: 330-337-6662
Email: info@hhmlaw.com URL: http://www.hhmlaw.com
Harry R. Conn; Shawna L. Erb; Alan D. Wenger; Shirley J. Christian; Neil H. Maxwell; Lance A. Morrison;—Christopher Baronzzi.
General Civil Trial and Equity Practice in all State and Federal Courts. Corporation, Banking, Creditors Rights and Bankruptcy, Labor, Probate, Estate Planning, Hospital and Health, Insurance Law, Real Estate Law, Commercial Law, Business Transactions.
Youngstown, Ohio Office: 26 Market Street, Suite 1200, 44503-1508. Telephone: 330-744-1111. Telecopier: 330-744-2029.
Warren, Ohio Office: 108 Main Avenue, S.W., Suite 500, 44481. Telephone: 330-392-1541. Telecopier: 330-394-6890.

See Professional Biographies, SALEM, OHIO

Horning, Richard A., (BV) .... '43 '73 C.8 B.S. L.7 J.D. 245 North Ellsworth Avenue
Humphrey, Don W., Jr., (CV) .... '52 '77 C&L.607 B.A., J.D. 52 E. State Street
Kirkland, Samuel L., (BV) .... '51 '85 C.980 A.B. L.7 J.D. 585 E. State St.
Macala, Brian J., (CV) .... '67 '92 C.980 B.A. L.1003 J.D. 192 South Lincoln Avenue
Maxwell, Neil H., (BV) '59 '84 C.528 B.S. L.8 J.D. [Harrington,H.&M.] (⊙Youngstown)
Miller, Earl R., (BV) .... '26 '52 C.980 B.A. L.608 J.D. 300 East State Street
Miller, John F. .... '65 '91 C.980 B.S.A.S. L.851 J.D. 1113 E. 3rd St.★
Morrison, Lance A., (CV) '66 '92 C&L.608 B.A., J.D. [Harrington,H.&M.] (⊙Youngstown)

Naragon, Frederic E., (BV) '45 '71 C.294 B.S. L.930 J.D.
248 East State Street, P.O. Box 317, 44460-0317
Telephone: 330-337-9578 Fax: 330-337-1223
Email: frednaragon@neo.rr.com
General Civil and Criminal Practice in all Courts. Family, Corporate and Business, Commercial and Retail Collections, Negligence, Real Estate, Taxation and Probate Law, Estate Planning, Trials, Patent, Trademark and Copyright and Banking Law, Oil and Gas and Mining Law.
Representative Client: Keybank.
References: Keybank; Bank One of Northeastern Ohio, N.A.

See Professional Biographies, SALEM, OHIO

Plummer, Barbara J., (BV) .... '38 '85 C.381 G.S. L.7 J.D. [B.Plummer]
Plummer, Barbara, (BV) .... 1265 E. State St.
Rice-Bartlett, Kathleen .... '68 '94 C.473 B.A. L.1003 J.D. 585 E. State St.
Roberts, Robert C., (BV) .... '52 '77 C.967 B.A. L.150 J.D. 585 E. State St.
Robinson, Ian, (BV) .... '48 '79 C.381 B.G.S. L.608 J.D. [Fitch,K.C.R.&B.]
Robinson, Whitman .... '74 '03 C.608 B.S. L.117 J.D. [Ⓒ Fitch,K.C.R.&B.]
Scharf, Shawn D. .... '71 '98 C.980 B.A. L.7 J.D., Atty., Ct. of App.
Schiller, Royal A. .... '30 '73 C.251 B.M.E. L.8 J.D. 861 S. Lincoln Ave.
Schory, Earl A., II, (BV) .... '50 '75 C.967 B.A. L.607 J.D. 288 E. State St.

Taus, James P., (BV) .... '46 '74 C.150 B.S.M.E. L.7 J.D. 220 N. Lundy Street
Wenger, Alan D., (BV) '52 '77 C.1124 B.A. L.930 J.D. [Harrington,H.&M.] (⊙Youngstown)
Williams, C. Bruce, (BV) .... '56 '83 C.980 B.A. L.8 J.D. [Williams&A.]

Williams & Apple, A Legal Professional Corporation, (BV)
Highland Corner, 1376 East State Street, 44460-2327
Telephone: 330-337-3253; 330-337-6624 Fax: 330-337-0424
Email: epu237a@williamsandapple.com URL: http://www.williamsandapple.com
C. Bruce Williams; K. Bret Apple.
General Civil Trial Practice. Personal Injury, Domestic Relations, Contracts, Probate, Estates, Business Law, Corporate Law. Collections. Insurance, Civil Litigation, Real Estate.
Representative Clients: MVP Video Productions; Digital Interface Systems, Inc.; RK Campf Transport; Quality Water Systems; Salem Oil, Inc.; Four Seasons, Inc.; Hollender House.
References: Sky Bank; Farmers Bank.

SANDUSKY, * 27,844, *Erie Co.*

Bacon, John O. .... '50 '75 C.228 B.A. L.608 J.D. Pres., Mack Iron Works Co., The
Bailey, K. Ronald, (BV) .... '47 '83 C.97 B.L.S. L.1003 J.D. [K.R.Bailey&Assoc.]
Bailey, K. Ronald, & Associates Co. LPA, (BV) .... 220 West Market Street
Ball, John R., (BV) .... '61 '88 C.851 B.A. L.117 J.D. [Buckingham,L.M.&Z.]
Bartle, William H., (BV) .... '49 '75 C.299 A.B. L.930 J.D. [Murray&M.]
Baxter, Kevin J., (BV) .... '57 '82 C.610 B.A. L.607 J.D. Co. Pros.
Bechtel, Steven C., (BV) .... '58 '83 C.610 B.A. L.608 J.D. [Ⓐ Murray&M.]
Begam, J. Arthur, (AV) .... '25 '52 C.930 A.B. L.1003 J.D. 158 E. Market St.
Birkett, Mary S. .... '49 '77 C.788 A.B. L.94 J.D. 111 East Shoreline Drive
Bogden, Kenneth E., (BV) .... '52 '78 C.942 B.A. L.851 J.D. [Reno,B.&F.]

Buckingham, Lucal, McGookey & Zeiher Co., L.P.A., (AV) BB
414 Wayne Street, P.O. Box 929, 44870 ⊙
Telephone: 800-410-0414; 419-627-0414 Fax: 419-627-0009
Email: attorneys@buckinghamlaw.com URL: http://www.buckinghamlaw.com
Maurice L. McDermond, Jr.; John D. Frankel; Kevin J. Zeiher; W. Zack Dolyk†; Daniel L. McGookey; Duffield E. Milkie; Troy Wisehart; John R. Ball;—David J. Claus†. Of Counsel: Frederick D. Waldock; Lawrence H. Schell (Retired); Dean S. Lucal (Retired); Richard D. Holzapfel (Retired); Arthur W. Zeiher (1920-2003); Thomas S. Buckingham (1926-2002).
Trials in all State and Federal Courts. Wrongful Death, Personal Injury, Product Liability, Domestic Relations, Family Law, Corporate Law, Business Law, Banking, Real Estate Law, Employment Law, Probate, Estate Planning, Commercial, Workers Compensation, Bankruptcy Law, Criminal Defense (Felonies and Misdemeanors), Medicaid Planning.
Local Counsel: Citizens BankingCo.
General Counsel: Sandusky Newspapers, Inc.; Firelands Regional Medical Center.
Vermilion, Ohio Office: 1513 State Route 60, 44089. Telephone: 440-967-6136. Fax: 440-967-8541.
†Sandusky and Vermilion, Ohio Offices

See Professional Biographies, SANDUSKY, OHIO

Calhoun, Kademenos, Heichel & Childress Co., L.P.A., (AV) 502 West Washington Street (⊙Mansfield)
Catri & Kellam Co., L.P.A., (BV) .... 165 E. Washington Row
Chapman, Benjamin M., (BV) .... '52 '79 C.532 B.A. L.607 J.D. [Sipe&C.]
Childress, James L., (CV) .... '55 '85 C.871 B.S. L.383 J.D. [Calhoun,K.H.&C.] ⊙
Claus, David J. .... '72 '99 C.97 B.A. L.7 J.D. [Ⓐ Buckingham,L.M.&Z.]
Conway, James William .... '63 '88 C.851 B.A. L.608 J.D. Asst. Pros.
Coppeler, John A., (AV) .... '47 '75 C&L.608 B.A., J.D. [Flynn,P.&K.] ⊙
Demmitt, Denise M. .... '68 '00 C.161 B.A. L.1003 J.D. P.O. Box 1417
Dempsey, Timothy Hunt .... '55 '81 C.161 B.A. L.201 J.D. [T.H.Dempsey]
Dempsey, Timothy H., Co., L.P.A. .... 158 E. Market Street
Didelius, William E., (AV) .... '08 '33 C&L.608 B.S., J.D. 414 Wayne St.‡
Dolyk, W. Zack, (BV) .... '53 '78 C.607 B.A. L.608 J.D. [Buckingham,L.M.&Z.] ⊙
Dusza, Thomas M., (BV) .... '65 '90 C&L.851 B.A., J.D. [Ⓐ Reno,B.&F.]
Egger, Robert C., (BV) .... '43 '70 C.124 B.S. L.1003 J.D. 189 E. Market St.
Evans, Donna Jean A. .... '53 '00 C.1216 B.A. L.1003 J.D. [Ⓐ Murray&M.]
Ferber, Gary S., (BV) .... '52 '77 C.532 B.A. L.930 J.D. [Reno,B.&F.]

Flynn, Py & Kruse, A Legal Professional Association, (AV) BB
165 East Washington Row, 44870 ⊙
Telephone: 419-625-8324 Fax: 419-625-9007
James F. Flynn (1887-1963); John R. Py (1908-1969); Richard R. Kruse (1910-1997); Melvyn J. Stauffer; George M. Muehlhauser, III; John A. Coppeler; John E. Rosino; James W. Hart; Mary Jane S. Hill; Christopher M. Marinko;—Eric M. Muehlhauser; Wm. R.S. Steuk.
General Civil Practice. Corporation, Banking, Antitrust, Labor and Employment, Taxation, Insurance, Personal Injury, Workers Compensation, Environmental Law, Probate and Estate Planning, Commercial Litigation, Pension and Profit Sharing, Employee Benefits, Real Estate. Trials and Appeals in State and Federal Courts.
Representative Clients: First National Bank of Bellevue; Norfolk and Southern Corp.; First Energy Corp.; Dorn Foundation; Lutheran Memorial Home; J.H. Routh Packing Co.; Firelands Regional Medical Center.
Port Clinton, Ohio Office: 115 West Perry Street. Telephone: 419-734-3174. Fax: 419-734-3175.

See Professional Biographies, SANDUSKY, OHIO

Frankel, John D., (AV) .... '49 '75 C.210 B.A. L.117 J.D. [Buckingham,L.M.&Z.]
Galloway, Duane L., (BV) .... '42 '77 C.313 B.S. L.851 J.D. [Pfefferle&G.]
Giesler, E. Ann S., (BV) .... '30 '77 C.97 B.S.Ed. L.851 J.D. 8 Harbour Pkwy.
Griffith, Terry R., (CV) .... '41 '88 C.215 B.S. L.851 J.D. Asst. Pros. Atty.
Gross, Gerhard R., (CV) .... '56 '86 C.608 B.A. L.326 J.D. [Gross&G.]
Gross, Mark R., (BV) .... '67 '95 C.97 B.A. L.851 J.D. [Gross&G.]
Gross & Gross, (BV) .... 231 West Washington Row
Grubbe, Richard E., (BV) .... '38 '65 C.1027 B.S. L.930 J.D. [Tone,G.M.&V.]
Hart, James W., (AV) .... '51 '80 C.611 B.A. L.744 J.D. [Flynn,P.&K.]
Heebsh, Philip S. .... '— '03 [Ⓐ Reminger&R.]
Heichel, William D., (AV) .... '44 '72 C.381 B.A. L.7 J.D. [Calhoun,K.H.&C.] ⊙
Hersch, Marvin H. .... '26 '54 C.930 B.B.A. L.1003 J.D. 158 E. Market St.‡
Hill, Mary Jane S., (BV) .... '59 '84 C.207 B.A. L.930 J.D. [Flynn,P.&K.]
Hines, Adrienne Marie .... '71 '96 C.610 B.A. L.851 J.D. [Ⓐ Calhoun,K.H.&C.] ⊙
Holzapfel, Richard D., (AV) '19 '45 C.31 B.A. L.309 LL.B. [Ⓒ Buckingham,L.M.&Z.] ‡
Icsman, Donald C., (BV) .... '48 '81 C.608 B.S. L.851 J.D. 422 E. Monroe
Kademenos, Victor P., (BV) .... '45 '71 C.610 B.A. L.608 J.D. [Calhoun,K.H.&C.] ⊙
Kaufman, Michael D. .... '71 '98 C&L.851 B.S.C.J., J.D. [Kaufman,K.&Assoc.]
Kaufman, Ronald G., (BV) .... '40 '66 C&L.851 B.E., J.D. [Kaufman,K.&Assoc.]
Kaufman, Kaufman & Associates, Co., L.P.A., (BV) .... 422 East Monroe Street
Kellam, James R., (BV) .... '39 '68 C.473 B.S. L.1003 J.D. [Catri&K.]
Kelsey, Robert T., Attorney at Law, (BV) '56 '82 C.363 B.A. L.117 J.D. 326 E. Market St.
Kirwan, John F., (BV) .... '44 '71 C.116 B.S. L.1003 J.D. 189 E. Market St.
Koch, Richard D. .... '55 '80 C&L.117 B.A., J.D. Koch Aluminum Co.
Lawson, Michael J. .... '54 '87 C.650 B.A. L.851 J.D. 158 E. Market Street
Lehrer, John W., (AV) .... '16 '40 C.385 B.A. L.608 J.D. [Smith&L.]
Lickfelt, Gary A., (BV) .... '44 '73 C.97 B.S. L.608 J.D. Asst. Co. Pros.
Lucal, Dean S., (AV) .... '37 '62 C&L.608 B.A., J.D. [Ⓒ Buckingham,L.M.&Z.] ‡
Lucal, Jane B. .... '38 '62 C.999 B.A. L.608 J.D. Com. Pleas J.
Lucas, Thomas Russell .... '71 '00 C.1391 B.A. L.851 J.D. 421 Jackson Street
Maddrell, Donald B. .... '20 '48 C&L.930 B.A., LL.B. 2215 Westwind Dr.‡

Marinko, Christopher M., (BV) ... '63 '88 C&L.608 B.A., J.D. [Flynn,P.&K.]
Maschari, Ann B. ... '52 '78 C.97 B.S. L.851 J.D. Com. Pleas J.
McDermond, Maurice L., Jr., (BV) '45 '71 C.210 B.A. L.1119 J.D. [Buckingham,L.M.&Z.]
McGookey, Daniel L., (BV) ... '53 '79 C.602 B.B.A. L.851 J.D. [Buckingham,L.M.&Z.]
McGookey, James E., (BV) '50 '75 C.602 B.B.A. L.851 J.D. Sr. V.P. & Gen. Coun., First Citizens Banc Corp.
McGory, Gregory S., (CV) ... '59 '96 C.870 B.S. L.8 J.D. [Tone,G.M.&V.]
McGory, Peter J., (BV) ... '48 '73 C.473 B.A. L.150 J.D. [Tone,G.M.&V.]
Miles, Gaye Harris ... '59 '86 C.483 B.A. L.851 J.D. 121 W. Water Street
Milkie, Duffield E., (BV) ... '65 '91 C&L.851 B.A., J.D. [Buckingham,L.M.&Z.]
Moir, Linda Tucker, (BV) ... '58 '87 C&L.851 B.A., J.D. [Tone,G.M.&V.]
Moracz, Donald J. ... '66 '91 C.363 B.A. L.930 J.D. [A Reminger&R.]
Moreland, Garnetta P. ... '53 '02 C.510 B.A. L.607 J.D. [A Murray&M.]
Muehlhauser, Eric M. ... '62 '93 C.97 B.S. L.117 J.D. [A Flynn,P.&K.]
Muehlhauser, George M., III, (AV) ... '30 '55 C.477 A.B. L.608 J.D. [Flynn,P.&K.]
Mullin, Jeanne Marie ... '73 '99 [A Reminger&R.]
Murphy, Michael P. ... '67 '96 C.363 B.A. L.1187 J.D. [A Reminger&R.]
Murphy, Troy A. ... '75 '03 C.97 B.S.B.A. L.851 J.D. [A K.R.Bailey&Assoc.]
Murray, Charles M., (BV) ... '65 '91 C.973 B.A. L.201 J.D. [Murray&M.]
Murray, Dennis E., Jr., (AV) ... '62 '87 C&L.976 B.A., J.D. [Murray&M.]
Murray, Dennis E., Sr., (AV) ... '39 '63 C.321 B.S. L.477 J.D. [Murray&M.]
Murray, James L. ... '72 '97 C.93 B.A. L.124 J.D. [Murray&M.]
Murray, James T., (AV) ... '39 '65 C.93 B.S. L.930 J.D. [Murray&M.]
Murray, Jerry B. '40 '66 C.363 B.S. L.93 J.D. C/O Michael Murray, 111 East Shoreline Drive
Murray, John T., (AV) ... '53 '79 C.201 B.S. L.607 J.D. [Murray&M.]
Murray, Margaret M. ... '70 '96 C.321 B.A. L.930 J.D. [Murray&M.]
Murray, Michael T., (BV) ... '44 '70 C.363 B.S. L.251 J.D. [Murray&M.]
Murray, Thomas J., (AV) ... '37 '65 C.93 B.A. L.893 J.D. [Murray&M.]
Murray, W. Patrick, (AV) ... '40 '65 C.201 B.A. L.607 LL.B. [Murray&M.]

Murray & Murray Co., L.P.A., (AV)
Murray Building, 111 East Shoreline Drive, P.O. Box 19, 44871-0019
Telephone: 419-624-3000 Fax: 419-624-0707
Email: firm@murrayandmurray.com URL: http://www.murrayandmurray.com
Emmett Murray (1903-1980); Thomas J. Murray (1907-1974); Kirk J. Delli Bovi (1952-1996); Dennis E. Murray, Sr.; Thomas J. Murray; W. Patrick Murray; James T. Murray; Michael T. Murray; John T. Murray; Dennis E. Murray, Jr.; Charles M. Murray; Margaret M. Murray; James L. Murray; William H. Bartle;—Steven C. Bechtel; Molly O'Neill; Donna Jean A. Evans; James S. Timmerberg; Garnetta P. Moreland.
General Civil and Trial Practice in all State and Federal Courts. Commercial Class Actions, Personal Injury, Products Liability, Toxic Torts and Security Litigation. Limited to Plaintiff's Trial Practice.
See Professional Biographies, SANDUSKY, OHIO

Nath, Michael J. ... '48 '76 C.197 B.A. L.1003 J.D. 5000 Heywood Rd.
Ogden-Dellisanti, Nancy L. ... '51 '89 C.851 B.A. L.608 J.D. Common Pleas Ct.
O'Hara, G. Stuart, Jr., (BV) ... '54 '79 C.645 B.A. L.930 J.D. Asst. Co. Pros.
O'Neill, Molly ... '49 '77 C.788 A.B. L.94 J.D. [A Murray&M.]
Pfefferle, John A., (BV) ... '36 '66 C.602 B.S. L.161 J.D. [Pfefferle&G.]
Pfefferle & Galloway, (BV) ... 538 Huron Ave.
Ramsey, Donald L. ... '47 '75 C.608 B.A. L.607 J.D. 247 Columbus Ave.
Reminger & Reminger Co., L.P.A., (AV) 237 W. Washington Row, 2nd Fl. (⊙Covington, KY; Akron, Cin., Cleve., Columbus, Toledo, Youngstown, OH)
Rengel, D. Jeffery ... '57 '82 C.97 B.A. L.1003 J.D. 421 Jackson St.
Reno, Robert M., (BV) ... '51 '76 C.207 B.A. L.851 J.D. [Reno,B.&F.]
Reno, Bogden & Ferber, Co., L.P.A., (BV) ... 725 Sycamore Line
Rhode, Edward W. ... '18 '41 C&L.607 J.D. 231 E. Adams St.‡
Rhode, Edward W., III, (BV) ... '50 '80 C.608 B.S. L.117 J.D. 231 E. Adams St.
Rice, Pamela Dawn '72 '97 C.97 B.A. L.1017 J.D. Staff Atty., UAW-GM Legal Services Plan
Roeder, Mary Alice '43 '89 C.523 B.S.N. L.851 J.D. Dir., Providence Hosp. School of Nursing
Rosino, John E., (AV) ... '51 '77 C.611 B.A. L.309 J.D. [Flynn,P.&K.]
Saferstein, Melvin A. ... '39 '66 C&L.378 B.A., J.D. [A Smith&L.]
Sammon, James P., (AV) ... '69 '94 C.473 B.A. L.1003 J.D. [A Reminger&R.]
Schell, Lawrence H. ... '32 '64 C.321 B.S. L.1003 J.D. [C Buckingham,L.M.&Z.] ‡
See, Daniel ... '49 '81 C.313 B.A. L.851 J.D. Staff Atty., UAW-GM Legal Services Plan
Sharp, Barbara M. ... '63 '91 C.999 B.S. L.851 J.D. 5014 W. Bogart Rd.
Sipe, David L., (BV) ... '47 '73 C&L.607 B.A., J.D. [Sipe&C.]
Sipe & Chapman, (BV) ... 602 Jackson St.
Smith, C. Ross, III, (BV) '50 '78 C.381 B.A. L.1003 J.D. Mng. Atty., UAW-GM Legal Services Plan
Smith, William H., Jr., (BV) ... '41 '69 C.363 B.A. L.1003 J.D. [Smith&L.]
Smith & Lehrer Co., L.P.A., (AV) ... 308 W. Adams St.
Sprunk, Thomas R., (CV) ... '41 '97 C.97 B.S.Ed. L.851 J.D. 326 E. Market St.
Stacey, Jas. A. ... '25 '52 C.611 L.1003 Ret. Mun. J.‡
Stauffer, Melvyn J., (AV) ... '26 '51 C.608 A.B. L.477 LL.B. [Flynn,P.&K.]
Steuk, Wm. R.S., (AV) ... '71 '96 C.477 B.A. L.607 J.D. [A Flynn,P.&K.]
Stuckey, Mark A., (CV) ... '57 '85 C.97 B.S. L.607 J.D. 607 Bimini Drive
Timmerberg, James S. ... '65 '97 C.231 B.A. L.930 J.D. [A Murray&M.]
Tone, Tygh M., (BV) ... '61 '89 C&L.851 B.A., J.D. Asst. Pros. [Tone,G.M.&V.]
Tone, Grubbe, McGory, & Vermeeren, LTD, (BV) ... 1401 Cleveland Road
Tucker, Edward W. ... '41 '67 C.602 A.B. L.309 J.D. 308 W. Adams St.
Vermeeren, Barry W., (BV) ... '49 '75 C.207 B.A. L.851 J.D. [Tone,G.M.&V.]
W. Wagner & G. Wagner, Co., L.P.A., (BV) ... P.O. Box 376
Wagner, Gregg M., (CV) '58 '83 C.473 B.A. L.851 J.D. Housing Ct. Ref. [W.Wagner&G.W.]
Wagner, Walter R., (BV) ... '32 '61 C.97 B.S. L.1003 J.D. [W.Wagner&G.W.]
Waldock, Frederick D., (BV) '30 '54 C&L.608 B.Sc., J.D. [C Buckingham,L.M.&Z.] ‡
Wisehart, Troy, (BV) ... '63 '91 C.475 B.A. L.851 J.D. [Buckingham,L.M.&Z.]
Wood, Deborah Lynn ... '51 '88 C.97 B.S. L.851 J.D. [D.L.Wood]
Wood, Deborah L., The Law Office of ... 330 E. Madison Street
Zeiher, Bernhardt G. ... '09 '40 C.119 B.S. L.1003 J.D. 1122 Meadowlawn Dr.‡
Zeiher, Kevin J., (AV) ... '51 '77 C.473 B.A. L.201 J.D. [Buckingham,L.M.&Z.]
Zelvy, Robert, & Associates, (BV) ... '38 '69 C.610 B.S.C. L.1003 J.D. 158 E. Market St.

SEBRING, 4,848, *Mahoning Co.*

Brennan, Frederick, Vouros & Yarwood, Ltd.
(See Youngstown)

Cardinal, Kenneth J., (BV) ... '48 '74 C.528 B.A. L.607 J.D. [Cardinal]
Cardinal Law Office, (BV) ... 758 North Fifteenth Street
May, Joyce A., (BV) ... '49 '78 C.381 B.A. L.930 J.D. [Turner,M.&S.] ⊙
Shepherd, David A., (BV) ... '56 '81 C.980 B.A. L.7 J.D. [Turner,M.&S.] ⊙
Turner, Lawrence S., (BV) ... '40 '66 C.8 B.S. L.930 J.D. [Turner,M.&S.] ⊙
Turner, May & Shepherd, (BV) ... 256 N. 15th St. (⊙Warren)

SEVEN HILLS, 12,080, *Cuyahoga Co.*

Askin, William P. ... '63 '91 C.390 B.A. L.564 J.D. Smythe Cramer Co.
Carolin, Thomas M. ... '52 '77 C.161 B.A. L.1003 J.D. 7183 Rustic Oval
Ciavarella, Nick E. ... '68 '97 C.1229 B.S.M.E. L.1003 J.D. 921 Justo Lane
Curtis, Scott David ... '67 '93 C.8 B.S. L.989 J.D. [S.D.Curtis]
Curtis, Scott D., Attorney at Law ... 4141 Rockside Rd., Ste. 230
DiChiro, Patrick, Attorney at Law '63 '89 C.363 B.A. L.1003 J.D. 4141 Rockside Rd., Ste. 230
Handlovics, Steve J. ... '19 '51 C.930 L.1003 LL.B. 1052 E. Dantmoor Ave.‡
Koloda, Richard J. ... '51 '98 C.161 B.A. L.1003 J.D. 365 E. Pleasant Valley
Loreta, Daniel R. ... '57 '89 C.8 B.S. L.1003 J.D. 3610 Sparrow Flight Dr.
Miller, Bernice G. ... '17 '51 C.251 L.1003 LL.B. 7543 Broadview Rd.
Miller, Stephen C. '49 '74 (adm. in VA; not adm. in OH) 3360 Forest Overlook
Naticchia, A. Dale, & Associates, (BV) '52 '86 C.363 B.A. L.1003 J.D. 4141 Rockside Rd., Ste. 230
Riczo, John Joseph, Jr. ... '50 '75 C.930 B.A. L.1003 J.D. 6751 Broadview Rd.
Snitzky, Lawrence S. ... '28 '65 C.363 B.B.A. L.1003 J.D. 2033 Hillside Rd.‡
Tobin, Christine M. ... '58 '82 C.569 B.A. L.1003 J.D. 4141 Rockside Rd., Ste. 230

SEVILLE, 2,160, *Medina Co.*

Doty, Joseph E., (BV) '69 '98 C.532 B.A. L.8 J.D.
23 West Main Street, P.O. Box 73, 44273
Telephone: 330-769-4544 Fax: 330-769-4543
Email: JEDLAW69@msn.com URL: http://www.josephdotyesq.com
Estate Planning, Probate, Guardianship, Medicaid Planning, Elder Law.
See Professional Biographies, SEVILLE, OHIO

Firestone, Arden E. ... '08 '32 C.8 A.B. L.477 J.D. 3433 Blake Rd‡
Noderer, Eric W. ... '53 '94 C.608 B.A. L.8 J.D. 179 Center St.‡

SHADYSIDE, 3,675, *Belmont Co.*

Melanko, Richard E., (BV) ... '49 '74 C.610 B.B.A. L.608 J.D. 3892 Central Avenue
Ryncarz, Thomas M. ... '70 '95 C.532 B.A. L.117 J.D. 3814 Central Avenue

SHAKER HEIGHTS, 29,405, *Cuyahoga Co.*

Adrine, Herbert A. ... '15 '52 C.943 B.S. L.1003 J.D. 18308 Chagrin Blvd.‡
Adrine, Russell T., (BV) ... '17 '55 C.943 B.S. L.1003 J.D. 3156 Ludlow Rd.
Arrington, Joan K. '64 '91 C.318 B.A. L.930 J.D. (adm. in IN; not adm. in OH) 15925 Van Aken Blvd.‡
Arsham, James M. ... '42 '68 C.473 B.S. L.1003 J.D. 2767 Landon Rd.
Auster, Douglas '47 '71 C.1041 B.A. L.705 J.D. (adm. in NY; not adm. in OH) 23489 Lyman Blvd.
Bain, Jeffrey M., (BV) ... '51 '76 C.696 B.A. L.472 J.D. 2562 Coventry Rd.
Belkin, Keith E., (BV) ... '51 '76 C.477 B.A. L.161 J.D. 20600 Chagrin Boulevard
Berman, Paul B. ... '53 '80 C.610 B.A. L.1003 J.D. 24105 Duffield Rd.
Booth, Geo. E., Jr. ... '17 '49 C.473 A.B. L.930 LL.B. 3268 Braemar Rd.‡
Breese, Betsy A. ... '59 '85 C.473 B.A. L.930 J.D. 3114 Warrington Road
Breidenbach, Paul ... '26 '49 C&L.930 A.B., LL.B. 3310 Dorchester Rd.‡
Brennan, Terrence L. ... '53 '78 C.62 B.A. L.161 J.D. Asst. Law Dir. & Chief Coun.
Bright, Mary S. ... '51 '76 C.706 A.B. L.276 J.D. 2857 Courtland Blvd.
Bulloff, Frances W., (BV) ... '49 '78 C.477 B.A. L.1003 J.D. 2684 Claythorne Rd.
Byrne, Cornelia, (BV) '51 '75 C.741 B.A. L.1003 J.D. Clk. of Ct., Shaker Heights Mun. Ct.
Caterino, Bartholomew M., (BV) '34 '60 C.363 B.S. L.276 J.D. 3550 Warrensville Center Rd.
Cochran, Edward W., (BV) ... '49 '75 C.309 A.B. L.178 J.D. 20030 Marchmont Rd.
Comella, Ignatius A. ... '26 '51 C&L.930 A.B., J.D. 2624 Courtland Oval‡
Cone, Sanford A. ... '20 '61 C.930 B.B.A. L.1003 J.D. 3028 Woodbury Road
Floyd, Dea L. Character ... '57 '89 C.329 B.S. L.1003 J.D. 3055 Ludlow Road
Foote, Richard C., (BV) ... '51 '76 C.309 B.A. L.930 J.D. 20133 Farnsleigh Rd.
Forman, Thomas M. ... '45 '73 C&L.477 B.S., J.D. Forman Venture Capital, Inc.
Franchot, Douglas W. ... '22 '50 C&L.976 B.A., J.D. 2560 N. Moreland Blvd.‡
Friedman, Sydney S., (AV) ... '24 '50 C.930 A.B. L.477 J.D. 15520 Aldersyde Dr.‡
Gerhart, Ann Tarbutton, (BV) ... '47 '72 C.611 B.A. L.150 J.D. 14400 Shaker Boulevard
Gleisser, Brian S. ... '56 '88 C.597 B.A. L.161 J.D. Pres., Boswell Group Ltd., The
Gobel, John H., (AV) ... '26 '51 C&L.209 B.A., J.D. 23911 Duffield Rd.‡
Gries, Donald S. ... '61 '92 C.976 B.A. L.930 J.D. 3329 Dorchester Rd.
Gross, Robert E., (BV) ... '52 '79 C.156 A.B. L.930 J.D. 20133 Farnsleigh Rd.
Harkins, Jas. L., Jr. ... '29 '54 C&L.930 B.S., LL.B. 18590 Parkland Dr.‡
Herrick, Mary T. ... '39 '64 C.788 B.A. L.597 J.D. 21150 Brantley Rd.‡
Horvath, Theodore J., (AV) ... '28 '52 C.608 A.B. L.309 J.D. 2843 Southington Rd.‡
Jackson, Gary Beggs ... '50 '79 C.1375 B.A. L.112 J.D. 22001 Fairmount Boulevard
Jackson, Gerald M., (BV) ... '43 '72 C.381 B.A. L.124 J.D. [Jackson]
Jackson Law Company, The, (BV) ... 3673 Lee Road
Kahn, Lawrence M., (BV) ... '41 '66 C.976 B.A. L.930 J.D. 24200 Chagrin Blvd.
Kane, Francis E. ... '15 '51 C.627 L.1003 J.D. 20600 Chagrin Blvd.‡
Kral, Donald J. ... '54 '88 C.473 B.A. L.309 J.D. 3317 Ingleside Rd.
Landefeld, Anne M. ... '26 '52 C.788 B.A. L.930 LL.B. 2881 Southington Rd.
Landever, Arthur R. ... '36 '61 C&L.569 A.B., LL.B. Prof. of Law, Cleveland State Univ.
Lederman, Barbara W. ... '38 '90 C.477 B.A. L.1003 J.D. 2731 Shelley Rd.
Levin, Ann R. ... '51 '80 C.831 B.A. L.1003 J.D. 2666 Rocklyn Rd.
Lincoln, Emma S. ... '22 '50 C&L.930 A.B., LL.B. 19715 N. Park Blvd.‡
Lind, Rosalind Cardone '48 '77 C.604 B.A. L.930 J.D. (adm. in IL; not adm. in OH) 2996 Kingsley Rd.‡
Lombardo, John J. ... '44 '71 C.119 B.S. L.1003 J.D. Assoc. Coun., Shaker Svgs. Assn.
Lurie, Elana Turoff ... '68 '92 C.112 B.A. L.1003 J.D. 20320 Farnsleigh Rd.
Melamed, Alan L., (BV) ... '45 '76 C.608 B.S. L.930 J.D. 24249 Lyman Boulevard
Miller, Peter D. ... '44 '79 C.309 B.A. L.1003 J.D. 22131 Byron Road
Mitchell, Robert A. ... '53 '84 C.611 B.A. L.608 J.D. 2676 Rochester Road
Montgomery, K. J. ... '53 '77 C.313 B.M. L.1003 J.D. Mun. J.
Nagle, Theresa A. ... '72 '97 C.473 B.A. L.930 J.D. Sr. Busin. Analyst, OfficeMax.com
Newton, Mark, (BV) ... '57 '85 C.932 B.B.A. L.851 J.D. 3325 Norwood Rd.
O'Connell, Martin James ... '53 '03 C.150 B.A. L.989 J.D. 22626 Rye Road (⊙Cleveland)
Paley, Rochelle L. ... '63 '89 C.381 B.A. L.161 J.D. 19606 Scottsdale Blvd
Petler, Gary S. ... '46 '73 C.851 B.B.A. L.477 J.D. 23999 Lyman Blvd.
Polster, Dorothea M., (AV) '59 '88 C.363 B.S.B.A. L.1003 J.D. 2711 Landon Road (Beachwood)
Pryatel, Robert L. ... '30 '59 C.628 B.S. L.150 LL.B. 20600 Chagrin Blvd.
Rawson, Judith Harris, (AV) ... '48 '76 C.518 B.A. L.930 J.D. 21300 Brantley Rd.‡
Resnick, Lois S. ... '43 '82 C.665 A.B. L.930 J.D. Ref. Mag., Mun. Ct.
Rosendale, J. King, (AV) ... '17 '48 C.976 A.B. L.930 LL.B. 3035 Huntington Rd.‡
Rosett, Wendy S., Attorney At Law '56 '91 C.318 B.A. L.930 J.D. 16781 Chagrin Blvd.
Thalman, John ... '46 '73 C.165 A.B. L.930 J.D. 2919 Huntington Rd.

Thompson, Siobhan ....'59 '87 C.741 B.A. L.245 J.D. 2986 Glengary Road
Troha, Jane C. .... '48 '80 C.930 B.A. L.1003 J.D. 2893 Southington Rd.‡
Udisky, Warren L., (AV) ....'39 '65 C&L.608 B.S., J.D. 2738 Sulgrave Road
Weinberg, Annette Ballou ....'60 '93 C&L.802 B.A.B.S., J.D. 3188 Somerset Drive
Weinberg, Kenneth G., (AV) ....'20 '48 C.473 B.B.S. L.309 J.D. 3015 Huntington Rd.‡
Woodling, George V., Jr. ....'40 '66 C.679 B.S. L.607 J.D. 22250 McCauley‡
Yen, Dominic F. ....'56 '81 C.976 B.A. L.930 J.D. 2757 Landon Rd.

SHARON CENTER, 400, *Medina Co.*

Brannon, Ellis B., (AV) ....'20 '51 C.8 L.37 J.D. [E.B.Brannon]
Brannon, Ellis B., Co., L.P.A., (AV) .... 6294 Ridge Road
Hail, Gregory Lee ....'66 '92 C.970 B.A L.8 J.D. [Holland&M.]
Holland, J. Jeffrey ....'61 '87 C.207 B.A. L.1218 J.D. [Holland&M.] ⊙
Holland & Muirden .... 1343 Sharon-Copley Road (⊙Akron)
Johnson, Eric W. ....'68 '94 C.475 B.S. L.7 J.D. [Holland&M.]
Mantkowski, Gary T., (BV) ....'56 '82 C.608 B.S.M.E. L.7 J.D. [Ⓐ E.B.Brannon]
Muirden, Marjorie Anne ....'61 '88 C.938 B.A. L.1218 J.D. [Holland&M.] ⊙
Simmons, Franklin Bruce, III ....'52 '87 C.150 Ph.D. L.8 J.D. 7444 Beach Rd

SHARONVILLE, 13,804, *Butler & Hamilton Cos.*

Hanket, Mark J. ....'43 '68 C.363 A.B. L.608 J.D. Asst. Gen. Coun., Diversey Lever, Inc.
Rubenstein, Jeffrey Barnet, (BV) ....'58 '83 C.602 B.A. L.1119 J.D. 9672 Tamarack Ter.
Saksefski, Louis M. ....'49 '76 C.960 B.B.A. L.1340 J.D. U.S. Treasury Dept.

SHEFFIELD LAKE, 9,371, *Lorain Co.*

Jancura, Diana Delmar ....'66 '98 C.161 B.A. L.1003 J.D. [D.Jancura&Assoc.]
Jancura, D., & Associates, L.L.C. .... 689 Sunset Avenue
Kaderbek, M.L. ....'50 '96 L.161 J.D. 4171 E. Lake Rd., Ste. D
Levin, Arnold S. ....'09 '34 C&L.608 J.D. 5555 Lake Road
Levin, Harriet J. ....'14 '40 C.597 B.S. L.145 J.D. 5555 Lake Rd.‡
Mosier, Margaret M. ....'49 '82 C.1044 B.A. L.1003 J.D. 480 Irving Park Blvd.‡

SHEFFIELD VILLAGE, 2,949, *Lorain Co.*

Alderman, Larry D., (BV) ....'50 '75 C.611 B.A. L.930 J.D. [Baumgartner&O.]
Baumgartner, Charles E., (BV) ....'45 '72 C.532 B.A. L.930 J.D. [Baumgartner&O.]
Baumgartner & O'Toole, (AV) .... 5455 Detroit Road (⊙Wellington)
Bond, Stephen P., (AV) ....'51 '76 C.161 B.A. L.1003 J.D. [Baumgartner&O.]
Carlson, Frank S., (BV) ....'49 '74 C.604 B.A. L.930 J.D. [Baumgartner&O.]
Clark, Jon D. ....'58 '93 C.604 B.A. L.989 J.D. [Baumgartner&O.]
Coey, Larry E., (BV) ....'46 '73 C.610 A.B. L.1003 J.D. [Ⓒ Baumgartner&O.]
Keller, Stanley S., (AV) ....'33 '58 C.381 A.B. L.930 LL.B. [S.S.Keller&Assoc.] ⊙

Keller, Stanley S., & Associates Co., LPA, (AV)
5455 Detroit Road, 44054 ⊙
Telephone: 440-930-4039 Fax: 440-934-7205
Email: keller@en.com
Stanley S. Keller.
Cleveland, Ohio Office: Suite 330 The Hanna Building, 1422 Euclid Avenue, 44115-1901. Telephone: 216-566-7100. Fax: 216-566-5430.

See Professional Biographies, SHEFFIELD VILLAGE, OHIO

Lieberman, Abraham, (AV) ....'50 '76 C.930 B.S. L.477 J.D. [Baumgartner&O.]
Loughman, Michael J., (AV) ....'47 '73 C.608 B.A. L.930 J.D. [Baumgartner&O.]
Mason, Daniel D., (BV) ....'61 '91 C.610 B.A. L.117 J.D. [Baumgartner&O.]
McGlamery, Heidi K. ....'75 '98 C.62 B.A. L.608 J.D. [Baumgartner&O.]
McLaughlin, Russell T., (AV) ....'50 '74 C.161 B.B.A. L.1003 J.D. [Baumgartner&O.]
Nedwick, Michelle D. ....'68 '93 C&L.608 B.S., J.D. [Baumgartner&O.]
O'Bryon, Margaret Ann ....'59 '93 C.97 L.930 J.D. 5455 Detroit Road
O'Toole, Dennis M., (BV) ....'48 '74 C.686 A.B. L.117 J.D. [Baumgartner&O.]
Pecora, Anthony R. ....'72 '98 C.851 B.Ed. L.989 J.D. [Baumgartner&O.]
Serazin, Scott F., (BV) ....'52 '77 C.201 B.A. L.930 J.D. [Baumgartner&O.]
Stumphauzer, Kenneth S., (BV) ....'45 '76 C.610 B.B.A. L.7 J.D. [Baumgartner&O.]
Warhola, Andrew J., (AV) ....'26 '51 C&L.477 A.B., J.D. [Ⓒ Baumgartner&O.]

SHELBY, 9,821, *Richland Co.*

Benham, Frank L., III, (BV) ....'54 '79 C.880 B.A. L.117 J.D. [F.L.Benham]
Benham, Frank L., Co., L.P.A., (BV) .... 150 Mansfield Ave.
Brooks, Robert D. '42 '70
(adm. in GA; not adm. in OH) 175 Mansfield Ave.
Depler, Thomas A., (BV) ....'49 '75 C.97 B.S.B.A. L.607 J.D. [Poland,D.&S.]
Eyster, Gordon Matthew ....'76 '01 C.49 B.A. L.607 J.D. 10 Mansfield Ave.
McKown, Neil A., (BV) ....'53 '78 C&L.607 B.A., J.D. [McKown&M.]
McKown, Robt. A., (CV) ....'26 '52 C.608 L.607 J.D. [McKown&M.]
McKown & Mckown, (BV) .... 10 Mansfield Ave.
Phelan, Vincent R. ....'25 '51 C.867 A.B. L.276 J.D. Ret. Mun. J.
Poland, F. Herbert, (BV) ....'26 '52 C&L.608 B.S., J.D. [Poland,D.&S.]

Poland, Depler and Shepherd Co., L.P.A., (BV)
6 Water Street, 44875-1297
Telephone: 419-347-7421 FAX: 419-342-5116
Email: office@pds-law.com
G. William Depler (1912-1978); F. Herbert Poland (Retired); Thomas A. Depler; R. Lee Shepherd.
General Civil Practice in all Courts. Real Estate, Probate and Estate Planning, Corporate, Banking, Family, Domestic Relations and Commercial Law. Trials.

See Professional Biographies, SHELBY, OHIO

Ream, Jeffrey S., (BV) ....'61 '90 C.608 B.A. L.117 J.D. [Ⓐ McKown&M.]
Schaefer, Jon P. ....'48 '74 C.84 B.S. L.836 J.D. Mun. J.
Shepherd, R. Lee, (BV) ....'51 '77 C.608 B.S.Ed. L.1003 J.D. [Poland,D.&S.]
Wagner, Richard K. ....'16 '42 C&L.930 A.B., J.D. 87 Parkwood Dr.‡

SHERRODSVILLE, 284, *Carroll Co.*

Burkhart, Sandra Edwards ....'42 '75 C.1119 B.A. L.228 J.D. 1225 Taft Street S.W.

SHREVE, 1,584, *Wayne Co.*

Hitchcock, Harold K., (BV) ....'22 '50 C.970 A.B. L.930 J.D. 250 Park Drive

SIDNEY, * 20,211, *Shelby Co.*

Bauer, Ralph A., (CV) ....'63 '88 C.967 B.A. L.150 J.D. [R.A.Bauer]
Bauer, Ralph A., Co., LPA, (CV) .... 108 East Poplar Street
Beigel, Jeffrey J., (CV) ....'60 '86 C.473 B.P. L.608 J.D. 868 Crescent Dr.
Bensman, Daniel A., (CV) ....'65 '94 C.201 B.S. L.893 J.D. [Faulkner,G.K.&S.]
Berghausen, Andrew A., (CV) ....'66 '93 C.835 B.A. L.150 J.D. Asst. Pros. Atty.
Blake, Rodney R., (AV) ....'15 '39 C&L.607 J.D. 132 W. Poplar St.‡
Blake, Rodney R., Jr., (BV) ....'40 '66 C.608 B.S. L.607 J.D. 124 W. Poplar St.
Boller, Michael F., (BV) '39 '64 C&L.150 A.B., J.D.
Asst. Pros. Atty. [Kerrigan,B.S.&G.]
Chrisman, James J., (BV) ....'48 '79 C&L.608 B.S.B.A., J.D. 223 1/2 N. Main Ave.
Christman, Harold E., (AV) ....'24 '50 C&L.608 B.A., LL.B. 223 1/2 N. Main Ave.‡
Deeds, John M. ....'77 '03 C.532 B.S. L.608 J.D. [Faulkner,G.K.&S.]
Elsass, Eugene P., (AV) ....'30 '57 C.608 B.S. L.607 J.D. [Elsass,W.E.S.]
Elsass, Wallace, Evans, Schnelle & Co., L.P.A., (AV) .... 100 South Main Street Suite 102
Evans, Stanley R., (AV) ....'55 '82 C.321 A.B. L.851 J.D. [Elsass,W.E.S.]
Faulkner, Harry N., (AV) ....'41 '66 C.611 B.A. L.607 J.D. [Faulkner,G.K.&S.] ⊙

Faulkner, Garmhausen Keister & Shenk, A Legal Professional Association, (AV)
Courtview Center, Suite 300, 100 South Main Avenue, 45365-2727 ⊙
Telephone: 937-492-1271 Telecopier: 937-498-1306
URL: http://www.fgks-law.com
Harry N. Faulkner; John M. Garmhausen; Ralph F. Keister; James R. Shenk; Michael A. Staudt; James L. Thieman; Thomas J. Potts; Daniel A. Bensman; David B. Shuffelton; Bryan A. Niemeyer; John M. Deeds; Joshua A. Koltak.
General Civil and Trial Practice, Corporations, Real Estate and Development, Banking, Probate and Estate Planning, Florida Probate, Trust, Taxation, Employment and Employee Benefits, Bankruptcy and Creditor's Rights, Business Litigation, and Insurance Defense.
Minster, Ohio Office: 96 West Fourth Street. Telephone: 419-628-3677.
Fort Loramie, Ohio Office: 31 South Main Street, P.O. Box 320, 45845-0320. Telephone 937-295-2983. Telecopier: 937-295-3633.

See Professional Biographies, SIDNEY, OHIO

Flinn, Gary L., (BV) ....'48 '78 C.608 Ph.D. L.8 J.D. [Flinn&M.] ⊙
Flinn and Muntean Co., L.P.A., (BV) .... 113 N. Ohio Ave. (⊙Greenville)
Garmhausen, John M., (AV) ....'48 '73 C.611 B.A. L.608 J.D. [Faulkner,G.K.&S.]
Geise, Steven J., (CV) ....'61 '94 C.608 B.S. L.117 J.D. [Ⓐ Elsass,W.E.S.]
Goettemoeller, Duane A., (CV) '54 '82
C.1024 B.A. L.150 J.D. Asst. Pros. Atty. [Kerrigan,B.S.&G.]
Guillozet, Melanie Ellis ....'58 '93 C.1208 B.A. L.607 J.D. Co. Juv. Ct.
Gusching, Gregory J. ....'60 '86 C.201 B.A. L.851 J.D. 555 Doorley Rd.
Hax, Priscilla L., (BV) ....'49 '77 C.1208 B.S. L.7 J.D. 108 W. Poplar Street
Hegemann, Heath H. ....'68 '93 C.313 B.A. L.851 J.D. 126 N. Main Ave.
Keister, Ralph F., (BV) ....'42 '67 C&L.608 B.A., J.D. [Faulkner,G.K.&S.]
Kerrigan, Thomas W., II, (CV) '55 '84
C.473 B.A. L.607 J.D. Asst. Pros. Atty. [Kerrigan,B.S.&G.]
Kerrigan, Thomas W., Sr. ....'28 '59 C.602 A.B. L.1340 LL.B. 582 E. Russell Rd.‡
Kerrigan, Boller, Stevenson & Goettemoeller Co., L.P.A., (BV) .... 126 N. Main Ave.
Koltak, Joshua A. ....'78 '04 C.473 B.A. L.608 J.D. [Faulkner,G.K.&S.]
Luce, Donald G. ....'48 '76 C.97 B.S. L.818 J.D. Mun. Ct. J.
Mazurowski, Suellen (Miller), (CV) ....'42 '83 C.665 B.S. L.851 J.D. 120 N. Main Ave.

McCulloch, Felger, Fite & Gutmann Co., L.P.A.
(See Piqua)

Metzer, Robert W., (BV) '47 '76
C.21 B.A. L.607 J.D. Corp. Coun., Monarch Machine Tool Co.

Miller & Luring
(See Troy)

Niemeyer, Bryan A. ....'71 '97 C.608 B.A. L.174 J.D. [Faulkner,G.K.&S.]
Potts, Thomas J., (BV) ....'63 '88 C.473 B.S.B.A. L.608 J.D. [Faulkner,G.K.&S.]
Pulfer, Anthony R., (BV) ....'62 '88 C&L.201 B.S., J.D. [Ⓐ Elsass,W.E.S.]
Richard, Jonathan M. ....'67 '97 C.499 B.S.B.A. L.201 J.D. [J.M.Richard]
Richard, Jonathan M., Co. LPA .... 108 E. Poplar Street
Schmitt, John D. ....'44 '70 C.973 B.S. L.607 J.D. Com. Pleas J.
Schnelle, Keith M., (BV) ....'55 '81 C.608 B.S. L.884 J.D. [Elsass,W.E.S.]
Sell, Timothy S., (BV) ....'57 '83 C.434 B.A. L.608 J.D. 108 E. Poplar Street
Shannon, Michael K. '50 '78 C.679 B.S. L.424 J.D.
(adm. in IL; not adm. in OH) Gen. Coun., Copeland Corp.
Shenk, James R., (AV) ....'49 '75 C.473 B.A. L.608 J.D. [Faulkner,G.K.&S.]

Shipman, Dixon & Livingston Co., L.P.A.
(See Troy)

Shuffelton, David B., (BV) ....'44 '69 C.473 A.B. L.607 J.D. [Faulkner,G.K.&S.]
Smith, Michael L., (Co., L.P.A.), (BV) ....'46 '73 C.611 B.A. L.607 J.D. City Law Dir.
Snavley, James T. ....'65 '91 C&L.608 B.S., J.D. 7543 Baker Road
Staudt, Michael A., (BV) ....'57 '84 C.8 B.A. L.608 J.D. [Faulkner,G.K.&S.]
Stevenson, James F., (BV) ....'50 '75 C.608 B.A. L.150 J.D. Co. Pros. [Kerrigan,B.S.&G.]
Swinger, W. Lynn, (BV) ....'37 '60 C.502 L.608 J.D. 111 East Court Street
Thieman, James L., (AV) ....'55 '80 C.608 B.S. L.851 J.D. [Faulkner,G.K.&S.]
Thompson, Daniel K. ....'54 '79 C&L.607 B.A., J.D. Monnier & Co.

Tomb Law
(See Troy)

Wallace, Richard H., (AV) ....'47 '75 C.117 B.S. L.607 J.D. [Elsass,W.E.S.]
Zimmerman, William R., (BV) ....'53 '79 C&L.607 B.A., J.D. [W.R.Zimmerman]
Zimmerman, William R., Co., L.P.A., (BV) .... 108 E. Poplar Street

SILVER LAKE, 3,052, *Summit Co.*

Ryan, John S. ....'63 '04 C.381 B.S. L.7 J.D. 3139 Harriett Rd.

SOLON, 21,802, *Cuyahoga Co.*

Arnson, Gerald I., (AV) ....'27 '65 C.608 B.S. L.1003 J.D. [G.I.Arnson]
Arnson, Gerald I., Co. L.P.A., (AV) .... 37177 Cherrybank Dr.
Basil, Deborah A. ....'54 '80 C.967 B.A. L.930 J.D. Corp. Litig. Coun., Weston Inc.
Bencivengo, Mary L. ....'54 '80 C.161 B.A. L.1003 J.D. 5953 Richmond Rd.
Besman, Douglas ....'56 '81 C.260 B.A. L.1017 J.D. Nestle USA, Inc.
Casey, Patrick J. J. ....'42 '70 C.177 B.A. L.1003 J.D. Health Action Council
Church, J. Jeffrey ....'50 '79 C&L.930 B.A., J.D. 32915 Aurora Rd.
Condon, Eric ....'61 '88 C.472 B.S.C.E. L.1003 J.D. 5980 Hansom Dr
Condon, Frederick J. ....'35 '70 C.645 B.S. L.1003 J.D. P.O. Box 39663
Condon, Patrick J. ....'72 '99 C.473 B.S. L.989 J.D. P.O. Box 39663
Corrigan, Daniel P., (BV) ....'60 '87 C.363 B.A. L.1003 J.D. 35291 Solon Rd.

Emery, Marlene P., (AV) '50 '79 C.597 B.A. L.7 J.D.
Solon Centre Building, 6370 SOM Center Road, Suite 200, 44139
Telephone: 440-498-0070 Fax: 440-498-1779
Domestic Relations, Family Law, Divorce, Probate and Estate, Business Law, Taxation and Personal Injury.

Erdelack, Wayne F., (AV) '46 '73
C.696 A.B. L.930 J.D. V.P. & Dep. Gen. Coun., Nestle USA, Inc.

Fouts, Douglas R., (BV) '50 '75 C.532 A.B. L.1003 J.D.
30575 Bainbridge Road, Suite 160, 44139
Telephone: 440-248-6700 Fax: 440-248-7511
Email: dfoutslaw@sbcglobal.net URL: http://www.lawyers.com/dfoutslaw
Probate, Estate Planning, Estate and Gift Taxation, Elder Law (including Medicaid), Trust Law, Wills, Employer/Employee, Administrative Law, Guardianship, Real Estate, Small Business Law, Corporate Law, Contract Litigation, Income & Estate Taxation, Divorce, Family Law, Domestic Relations, Personal Injury and Mold Litigation.

See Professional Biographies, SOLON, OHIO

Glanz, David S. '62 '92 C.880 B.S. L.312 J.D.
(adm. in HI; not adm. in OH) 34150 Ada Drive

Goldberg, J. Michael, (BV) ... ’60 ’90 C.610 B.B.A. L.1003 J.D. [Ⓐ Goldberg,S.M.]
Goldberg, Steven M., (BV) ... ’62 ’89 C.36 B.A. L.117 J.D. [Goldberg,S.M.] ⊙

Goldberg, Steven M., Co., L.P.A., (BV)
34055 Solon Road, 44139 ⊙
Telephone: 440-519-9900 Fax: 877-464-4652
URL: http://attorneys@goldberglaw.net
Steven M. Goldberg;—J. Michael Goldberg.
Personal Injury and Wrongful Death arising out of Medical, Hospital and Nursing Home Negligence; General Civil Trial and Appellate Practice arising out of Auto/Motorcycle/Pedestrian/Railroad Negligence; Pharmaceutical Litigation; Criminal Trial and Appellate Practice.
Canfield, Ohio Office: 6600 Summit Drive, 44406. Telephone: 330-533-8302.

Hakes, James E. ’41 ’67 C&L.602 B.A., LL.B.
(adm. in MO; and limited adm. in OH) Sr. Coun., Nestle USA, Inc.

Jacob, Harry J., III, (BV) ’56 ’81 C.381 B.S. L.930 J.D.
30405 Solon Road, Unit 14, 44139
Telephone: 440-349-3301 Fax: 440-349-3382
Email: jacoblaw@apk.net
General Civil and Business Law, Litigation, Domestic Relations, Negligence and Personal Injury, Real Estate, Probate and Commercial Law.

See Professional Biographies, SOLON, OHIO

Karberg, Kurant, Wachter & Turner Co., L.P.A.
(See Cleveland)

Kehr, Edward C. ... ’25 ’54 C.381 L.1003 LL.B. 30003 Bainbridge Rd.
Kenen & Snider Co., L.P.A, (AV) ... 33595 Bainbridge Rd.
Kolt, Jeffrey A., Attorney at Law, (BV) ’44 ’70
C.608 B.S. L.1003 J.D. 33840 Aurora Road, Suite 200
Kraus, Bonnie G. ... ’62 ’88 C.608 B.S. L.161 J.D. 32685 Stony Brook Ln.
Lichtman, Douglas Gary ... ’70 ’97 32957 Sringside Lane

Mann, Theodore M., Jr., Law Firm
(See Cleveland)

Manning, Charles H. ... ’49 ’75 C.207 B.A. L.880 J.D. 30505 Bainbridge Rd.
McAndrews, James Patrick, (AV) ’29 ’53 C.754 B.S. L.262 LL.B.
6638 Duneden Avenue
McMahon, John J. ... ’09 ’37 C.363 A.B. L.930 LL.B. Ret. Com. Pleas J.
Meinwald, Harlan Mark ... ’52 ’84 C.188 B.S. L.1003 J.D. Stouffer Foods
Pelsozy, Dale F., (BV) ... ’52 ’78 C.363 B.A. L.607 J.D. 34535 Appleview Way
Pilla, Mary Lee, (AV) ’53 ’81
C.876 B.A. L.1003 J.D. V.P. & Dep. Gen. Coun., Nestle USA, Inc.
Podor, Kenneth C., (BV) ... ’52 ’78 C.608 B.A. L.1003 J.D. [Podor&Assoc.]

Podor & Associates, (BV)
33565 Solon Road, 44139
Telephone: 440-914-LAWS (5297) Fax: 440-914-0377
URL: http://www.podorlaw.com
Kenneth C. Podor.
Family Law, Adoption Law, Child Support, Child Custody, Visitation Rights, Divorce, Business Law, Commercial Law, Civil Rights, Criminal Law, DUI/DWI, Discrimination, Employment Law, Insurance Law, Legal Malpractice, Pediatric Malpractice, Medical Malpractice, Motor Vehicle Accidents, Nursing Home Litigation, Plaintiffs Personal Injury, Products Liability Law, Professional Malpractice Law, Sexual Harassment, Toxic Torts, Traffic Violations, White Collar Crimes, Workers Compensation.

See Professional Biographies, SOLON, OHIO

Pryatel, August ... ’13 ’42 C.318 B.A. L.161 J.D. 5880 Glasgow Lane‡
Roj, William H., (AV) ... ’49 ’75 C.928 B.A. L.893 J.D. Pres., Ereco International Corp.
Rosenfeld, Robert C. ... ’49 ’74 C.381 B.S. L.1003 J.D. [R.C.Rosenfeld]
Rosenfeld, Robert Charles ... 32545 Stony Brook Ln.
Singerman, Donna D. ... ’64 ’90 C.876 B.S.N. L.161 J.D. 6900 Waterpepper Circle
Snider, Harvey A., (AV) ... ’36 ’61 C.608 B.A. L.930 J.D. [Kenen&S.]

Steuer, Escovar, Berk & Brown Co., L.P.A.
(See Cleveland)

Strobel, Ben E. ... ’17 ’49 C.317 B.S. L.161 J.D. V.P., Smythe-Cramer Co.
Vacik, Paul J. ... ’63 ’89 C.381 B.A. L.150 J.D. 5155 Harper Rd.
Varcho, Raymond A. ’56 ’84 C.381 B.B.A. L.161 J.D.
V.P., Gen. Coun. & Secy., Natl. Auto Credit, Inc.
Wyatt, Jack D. ... ’45 ’74 C.608 B.S. L.851 J.D. Sr. Coun., Nestle USA, Inc.
Zingales, Joseph A. ... ’24 ’52 C.363 B.S. L.1003 J.D. Ret. Mun. J.

SOMERSET, 1,549, *Perry Co.*

Derr, Vicki B., (BV) ... ’51 ’79 C&L.608 B.S., J.D. 5380 Township Road 143 NE

SOUTH EUCLID, 23,537, *Cuyahoga Co.*

Christie, Edward C. ... ’42 ’70 C.363 B.S. L.1003 J.D. 4320 Elmwood Rd.
Ginsberg, Melvin R. ... ’42 ’75 C.381 B.A. L.1003 J.D. [M.R.Ginsberg]
Ginsberg, Melvin R., Co., LPA ... 2000 Warrensville Center Rd., Ste. 9
Husock, Bernard ... ’25 ’86 C.223 B.S.E.E. L.161 J.D. P.O. Box 21042
Ivins, John E. ... ’26 ’59 C.251 B.B.A. L.1003 J.D. 1030 Avondale Road
Keller, Paul V. ... ’62 ’97 C.367 B.S. L.930 J.D. [P.V.Keller] (Pat.)
Keller, Paul V., LLC ... 4585 Liberty Rd. (Pat.)
Kleri, Patricia S. ... ’38 ’76 C.1042 B.A. L.1003 J.D. Mun. Ct. J.
Kohn, Vilma Lavetti ... ’27 ’71 C.107 B.A. L.930 J.D. 2060 S. Belvoir Blvd.‡
Lefkowitz, Kathleen Kelly ... ’54 ’78 C&L.607 B.A., J.D. 4021 Wilmington
Lucey, Richard G. ... ’28 ’62 1367 Winston Road
Markman, Max L. ... ’18 ’57 C.930 L.1003 J.D. 4105 Harwood Rd.‡
Patsch, Glenn F. ... ’28 ’73 C.644 B.S.I.E. L.1003 J.D. 1144 Dorsh Rd.
Schorr, Brian D. ... ’61 ’86 C.381 B.A. L.1003 J.D. 1579 S. Belvoir Blvd.
Schwartz, Fred Phillip ... ’53 ’78 C.696 B.A. L.813 J.D. [Schwartz]
Schwartz Law Firm ... 13967 Cedar Rd., Ste 200
Smith, Thomas Edward ... ’47 ’72 C.215 A.B. L.608 J.D. U.S. Dept. of Vet. Affairs
Wieder, Michael D. ... ’44 ’69 C.930 B.B.A. L.1003 J.D. 4625 Birchwold Rd.

SOUTH POINT, 3,742, *Lawrence Co.*

Greiner, Cathy L., (CVⓉ) ’64 ’91 C.437 B.A. L.923 J.D.
(adm. in WV; not adm. in OH) 4081 County Road 15
Zolman, Courtney Lynn ... ’74 ’99 L.117 J.D. 294 Township Road 1076

SOUTH WEBSTER, 764, *Scioto Co.*

McHenry, John K., (CV) ... ’44 ’87 C.610 M.S. L.117 J.D. P.O. Box 93

SPENCERVILLE, 2,288, *Allen Co.*

Pohlman, James D., (BV) ... ’47 ’79 C.91 B.A. L.607 J.D. [J.D.Pohlman]
Pohlman, James D., Law Office, (BV) ... 105 N. Broadway St.

SPRINGBORO, 12,380, *Montgomery & Warren Cos.*

Anderson, Randal A., Jr. ... ’21 ’51 C&L.150 LL.B. 1215 W. St. Rte. 73‡
Brandenburg, Cynthia L., (CV) ... ’60 ’86 C.1208 B.A. L.200 J.D. [Ⓐ Kirby&K.]
Cavender, J. T. ... ’24 ’56 C.383 B.S.E.E. L.1340 J.D. 185 Elinor Dr. (Pat.)
Cornyn, Christopher J., (BV) ... ’54 ’79 C.1208 B.S. L.150 J.D. [C.J.Cornyn]
Cornyn, Christopher J., Co., L.P.A., (BV) ... 10 Fairway Drive
Czechowski, Donna K., (BV) ... ’51 ’89 C.960 B.S.N. L.201 J.D. [J.D.Smith]
Hughes, Kevin Dale ... ’70 ’95 C.383 B.A. L.201 J.D. [C.J.Cornyn]
Kirby, Jeffrey T., (BV) ... ’60 ’88 C.473 B.A. L.201 J.D. [Kirby&K.]
Kirby, Joseph W., (CV) ... ’64 ’95 C.473 B.S. L.1340 J.D. [Kirby&K.]
Kirby, Thomas B., Jr., (BV) ... ’35 ’68 C.201 B.A. L.1340 J.D. [Kirby&K.]
Kirby & Kirby, L.P.A., (BV) ... 4 Sycamore Creek Drive
Kolb, Stanley E. ... ’31 ’59 C.97 B.A. L.608 LL.B. P.O. Box 142
Laurito, Jeffrey V., (AV) ... ’45 ’73 C.793 A.B. L.61 J.D. 35 Commercial Way
Lawson, Edward, (BV) ... ’41 ’66 C.383 B.A. L.150 J.D. [Ⓐ Kirby&K.]
Marrocco, Michael A., (BV) ... ’67 ’94 C.266 B.S. L.201 J.D. [J.D.Smith]
Messer, Steven Lawrence ... ’55 ’80 C.339 B.S. L.150 J.D. 400 Victory Drive
Office, James R., (AV) ’55 ’80 C.347 B.S. L.201 J.D.
V.P. & Gen. Coun., Victory Wholesale Grocers

Pickrel, Schaeffer & Ebeling
(See Dayton)

Reiling, Richard B., (BV) ... ’70 ’95 C.676 B.A. L.94 J.D. 66 Remick Blvd.
Sharts, John E., III, (BV) ... ’48 ’74 C.150 B.A. L.1340 J.D. [J.E.Sharts]
Sharts, John E., Attorney at Law, (BV) ... 310 W. Central Ave.
Smith, John D., (AV) ... ’54 ’80 C.602 B.A. L.201 J.D. [J.D.Smith]
Smith, Rebecca Barthelemy ... ’55 ’80 C&L.201 B.A., J.D. 185 Teakwood Ln.
Smith, John D., Co., L.P.A., (AV) ... 130 N. Main St.
Sooy, Jennifer E. ’58 ’84 C.683 B.A. L.201 J.D.
Sooy & Sooy Assocs., Govt. Affs. Consultant
Stull, Tracy L. ... ’71 ’98 C.932 B.A. L.607 J.D. 125 Cambridge Dr.
Thomsen, Ira H., (AV) ’54 ’79 C.188 B.A. L.221 J.D.
515 South Main Street (⊙Dayton)
West, Richard E., (CV) ... ’58 ’86 C.728 B.S. L.831 J.D. 195 E. Central Ave.

SPRINGFIELD, * 65,358, *Clark Co.*

Ailes, Aleita, Attorney at Law, LLC
(See London)

Altick & Corwin Co., L.P.A.
(See Dayton)

Anderson, Gerald Lee, (CV) ... ’41 ’77 C.879 B.A. L.117 J.D. 1640 Woodrow Dr.
Anderson, Susan Collins ... ’43 ’82 C.608 B.A. L.201 J.D. Co. Mun. J.
Andreoff, Alexander, (BV) ... ’37 ’62 C.610 L.608 LL.B. 31 E. High St., Suite 222
Angle, Tammi J., (BV) ... ’58 ’94 C.967 B.M. L.201 J.D. [Cole A.H.D.]
Bailey, Edward G., (BV) ... ’46 ’70 C.37 B.A. L.597 J.D. [Bailey&B.]
Bailey and Bailey, (BV) ... 4 W. Main St.
Barnett, Cynthia Singleton, (BV) ... ’61 ’94 C.150 B.B.A. L.201 J.D. [Cole A.H.D.]
Barnett, Hugh, (AV) ... ’35 ’62 C.674 A.B. L.477 LL.B. [Martin,B.H.&H.]
Bennett, LaMar J. ... ’46 ’75 C.608 B.S. L.117 J.D. 3311 Tamarack Avenue‡
Berry, James A., (AV) ... ’30 ’53 C.967 L.607 LL.B. 10 W. Columbia St.

Bieser, Greer & Landis, LLP
(See Dayton)

Boblitt, Ronald R. ... ’47 ’86 C.1112 B.S. L.117 J.D. 1 S. Limestone Street, Suite 777
Bonar, Byron Keith ... ’50 ’79 C.510 B.A. L.989 J.D. Legal Aid of Western OH
Borley, Robert L., (BV) ... ’49 ’75 C.970 B.A. L.1003 J.D. 4 W. Main St., Suite 720
Bosca, D’orsi ’52 ’81 C.967 B.A. L.1187 J.D.
(adm. in MI; not adm. in OH) V.P., Hugo Bosca Co.

Bradley, Karen Denise
(See Dayton)

Brown, Matthew M. ... ’13 ’40 C&L.276 B.S., J.D. 1201 W. Main St.
Brucker, Joseph C., (AV) ... ’24 ’52 C.967 A.B. L.150 LL.B. 28 N. Fountain Ave.
Buchanan, Leslie Stobbs ... ’56 ’80 C.608 B.A. L.117 J.D. 2257 North Fountain Blvd.
Busch, Thomas H., (BV) ... ’34 ’58 C.143 A.B. L.150 LL.B. 216 Brighton Rd.
Butz, John R., (AV) ... ’44 ’69 C&L.608 B.A., J.D. [Cole A.H.D.]
Calaway, Todd E. ’71 ’99
C.1208 B.A. L.150 J.D. St. Atty. Clark County Public Defender Off.
Carey, Daniel D., (CV) ... ’63 ’91 C.473 B.A. L.607 J.D. 4 W. Main St., Ste. 404
Carey, Norman C. ... ’18 ’48 C.967 A.B. L.477 J.D. 1601 N. Fountain Blvd.‡
Carey, Richard P., (BV) ... ’58 ’83 C.602 B.A. L.607 J.D. Mun. J.
Carter, Darnell E., (BV) ... ’53 ’79 C.182 B.A. L.221 J.D. Asst. Pros. Atty.
Catanzariti, Frank Paul ’60 ’85
C.201 B.A. L.117 J.D. Rural Legal Aid Soc. of W. Central Ohio
Catanzaro, Michael A., (BV) ... ’49 ’77 C.201 B.S. L.117 J.D. [Pavlatos,C.&L.]
Cole, Richard T. ... ’20 ’49 C&L.608 B.S. in B.A., LL.B. Com. Pleas J.

Cole Acton Harmon Dunn, A Legal Professional Association, (AV)
Riverbend Condominiums, 333 North Limestone Street, P.O. Box 1687, 45501
Telephone: 937-322-0891 Fax: 937-322-9931
John M. Cole (1879-1960); Abe Gardner (1903-1964); Fred M. Cole (1909-1975); George W. Cole (1914-1982); Robert C. Acton (1924-1987); James A. Harmon (Retired); Edward W. Dunn; Barry P. Reich; William C. Hicks; John R. Butz; Joseph A. Dunn; Tammi J. Angle; Cynthia Singleton Barnett; Paul J. Kavanagh. Of Counsel: Phyllis S. Nedelman; Elizabeth Jucius Dunn.
General Civil Practice. Business and Corporate, Insurance, Taxation, Real Estate, Probate, Criminal Law, Family Law, Banking, Labor and Employment Law, Personal Injury Law. Litigation.
Representative Clients: Key Bank; Huntington National Bank; Navistar International; Springfield Newspapers, Inc.; Chakeres Theatres, Inc.; Springfield Metropolitan Housing Authority; Clark State Community College; Community Mercy Health Partners; Laughlin & Scanlan Construction Co., Inc.

See Professional Biographies, SPRINGFIELD, OHIO

Collier, Glenn W., (BV) ... ’40 ’66 C.611 B.A. L.188 LL.B. [Martin,B.H.&H.]
Collins, Alan Elhannon, (CV) ’64 ’90
C.608 B.S.B.A. L.1202 J.D. 20 South Limestone Street, Suite 390
Comer, Randall M. ... ’70 ’00 C.140 B.S. L.150 J.D. [Ⓐ Martin,B.H.&H.]
Dean, Clarence J., Jr. ... ’23 ’50 C&L.910 J.D. 1918 Devon Dr.‡
Doughty, Jon A., (BV) ... ’53 ’78 C.1208 B.A. L.608 J.D. [Doughty&D.]
Doughty & Doughty, (BV) ... 39 N. Fountain Ave.
Dressel, Quinton R., (BV) ... ’57 ’83 C.608 B.A. L.150 J.D. 50 E. Columbia St.
Dunn, Edward W., (AV) ... ’30 ’55 C.967 A.B. L.276 J.D. [Cole A.H.D.]
Dunn, Elizabeth Jucius ... ’51 ’76 C.170 B.A. L.37 J.D. [Ⓒ Cole A.H.D.]
Dunn, Joseph A., (BV) ... ’55 ’80 C.96 B.A. L.602 J.D. [Cole A.H.D.]
Dyer, Garofalo, Mann & Schultz, A Legal Professional Association, (AV)
1714 Valley Loop Road (⊙Richmond, IN; Bellefontaine, Dayton, Huber Heights, Lima, Middletown, Piqua, Troy, Wilmington, Xenia, OH)
Eckels, Howard R. ... ’17 ’42 C.347 B.S. L.477 J.D. 306 Northfield Blvd.‡
Elder, Andrew H., (BV) ... ’58 ’85 C.108 B.A. L.150 J.D. [Elder,R.&E.]
Elder, John M., (BV) ... ’43 ’68 C.231 B.A. L.608 J.D. [Elder,R.&E.]
Elder, Kenneth M., (BV) ... ’53 ’78 C.303 B.A. L.150 J.D. [Elder,R.&E.]
Elder, Roberts & Elder, (BV) ... 2233 N. Limestone St.
Emerich, John D., (AV) ... ’39 ’64 C.610 B.S. L.930 J.D. [Emerich&P.]

Emerich & Peifer, (AV)
Suite 300 The Edison Center, 20 South Limestone Street, P.O. Box 1087, 45501
Telephone: 937-325-7365 Fax: 937-325-9584
John D. Emerich; James F. Peifer.
General Civil Practice. Corporation, Wills and Probate, Municipal, Health and Hospital, Labor Relations, Real Estate, Zoning and Annexation, Insurance and Negligence Law. Trials, Civil.
General Counsel for: Taylor Mfg. Co.; Community Hospital of Springfield and Clark County; Monte Zinn Chevrolet Co.
Local Counsel for: State Farm Mutual Ins. Cos.; Ohio Casualty Co.
Approved Attorneys for: The Ohio Bar Title Insurance Co.
See Professional Biographies, SPRINGFIELD, OHIO

Filhart, Eddie L. . . . . . '41 '66 C&L.607 B.A., J.D. Mun. Ct. Mag.
Fisher, Terry L. . . . . . '52 '85 C.201 B.S. L.117 J.D. City Police Div.
Flack, Sanford H., (BV) . . . . . '43 '70 C.381 B.A. L.1003 J.D. 101 N. Fountain Ave.
Foley, Margaret L. . . . . . '59 '91 C.150 B.S. L.893 J.D. Security Nat. Bd. & Tr. Co.

Fox & Associates Co., L.P.A.
(See Dayton)

Freund, Freeze & Arnold, A Legal Professional Association
(See Dayton)

Gorman, Veskauf, Henson & Wineberg, (AV) . . . . . 4 W. Main St., Suite 723
Gould, John E. . . . . . '34 '60 C.999 B.A. L.150 LL.B. [J.E.Gould]
Gould, John E., Co., L.P.A. . . . . . 649 E. High Street
Grady, Thomas J. . . . . . '41 '68 C.161 B.A. L.383 J.D. Ct. App. J.
Griffin, James N., (BV) . . . . . '47 '76 C&L.607 B.A., J.D. 4 West Main Street, Suite 526
Grinvalds, Edwin Arthur, (CV) . . . . . '55 '83 C.1208 B.S. L.150 J.D. 12 W. Main St.
Groves, William R., (BV) . . . . . '54 '79 C.610 B.S. L.608 J.D. [Martin,B.H.&H.]
Hamer, Robert M. '50 '75 C.992 B.A. L.150 J.D.
(adm. in IA; not adm. in OH) 1701 Calais Dr.★
Hampel, Elizabeth M., (CV) '54 '80
C.1118 A.B. L.201 J.D. Rural Legal Aid Soc. of W. Central Ohio

Harkins, Daniel C., (BV) '60 '85 C.970 B.A. L.930 J.D.
333 North Limestone Street Suite 203, 45501-1125
Telephone: 937-324-8482 Fax: 937-324-8011
Email: dch@dharkins.com
General Practice, Corporate, Taxation, Estate Planning, Probate and Health Care.
See Professional Biographies, SPRINGFIELD, OHIO

Harley, Robert E., (AV) . . . . . '31 '57 C&L.608 B.S., LL.B. [Martin,B.H.&H.]
Harmon, James A., (AV) . . . . . '27 '52 C&L.477 A.B., LL.B. [🄲 Cole A.H.D.]
Harper, John O., (AV) . . . . . '17 '48 C.610 B.S.Ed. L.608 J.D. [Martin,B.H.&H.] ‡
Hasselbach, Kurt S., (BV) . . . . . '46 '75 C&L.851 B.B.A., J.D. [Schmenk,S.&H.]
Heath, James E., (BV) . . . . . '49 '74 C.608 B.A. L.500 J.D. [Ronemus&H.]
Heil, Richard F., Jr., (BV) . . . . . '52 '86 C.967 B.A. L.1003 J.D. [Martin,B.H.&H.]
Henderson, John W. . . . . . '28 '52 C&L.608 B.S., J.D. Ret. Com. Pleas J.
Henson, Douglas A., (BV) . . . . . '47 '72 C.201 B.A. L.150 J.D. [Gorman,V.H.&W.]
Herier, David Douglas . . . . . '71 '98 C.1208 B.A. L.200 J.D. 4 W. Main Street, Suite 723
Hicks, William C., (BV) . . . . . '43 '74 C.197 A.B. L.608 J.D. [Cole A.H.D.]
Hobson, David L. '36 '65 C.611 B.A. L.608 J.D.
(adm. in KY; not adm. in OH) U.S. Congressman, 7th Ohio Dist.

Hochman & Plunkett
(See Dayton)

Hofbauer, Lawrence J., (CV) . . . . . '49 '96 C.608 B.A. L.851 J.D. [Hofbauer&M.]
Hofbauer & Marshall, (BV) . . . . . 4 West Main Street, Second Floor
Hoffman, William D., (CV) . . . . . '65 '90 C.473 B.S. L.608 J.D. Asst. Co. Pros.
Husted, Stanley N., II, (CV) . . . . . '44 '72 C.967 A.B. L.607 J.D. 1009 Moorefield Rd.
Jewett, Reed P. . . . . . '32 '60 C.999 L.607 J.D. 1345 W. 1st St.‡
Juergens, Carl E., (BV) . . . . . '30 '54 C.967 A.B. L.608 J.D. [Juergens&J.]
Juergens, John C.A., (CV) . . . . . '62 '86 C.967 B.A. L.607 J.D. [Juergens&J.]
Juergens, Joseph M., (BV) . . . . . '45 '72 C.967 B.S. L.117 J.D. 39 N. Fountain Ave.
Juergens, U. Timothy, (AV) . . . . . '33 '58 C.967 A.B. L.608 LL.B. [Juergens&W.]
Juergens & Juergens, (BV) . . . . . 1504 N. Limestone St.
Juergens & Wilt, (AV) . . . . . 200 N. Fountain Ave.
Kavanagh, Paul J. . . . . . '69 '95 C.960 B.S. L.607 J.D. [Cole A.H.D.]
King, Courtney Dawn . . . '74 '99 C&L.201 B.A., J.D. Staff Atty., The Community Hospital
Kinsler, Christopher Lee . . . . . '73 '01 C.473 B.A. L.608 J.D. [🄰 Schmenk,S.&H.]
Kohler, Anthony E., (CV) . . . '58 '84 C&L.607 B.A., J.D. Owner, Kohler Legal Svs., LLC
Lagos, James H., (BV) . . . . . '51 '73 C.967 B.A. L.608 J.D. [Lagos&L.]
Lagos, Thomas H., (BV) . . . . . '49 '72 C.967 B.A. L.608 J.D. [Lagos&L.]
Lagos & Lagos, (BV) . . . . . 1 S. Limestone St.
Lambacher, William G. . . . . . '26 '52 C.62 A.B. L.1003 J.D. 1 S. Fountain Ave.‡

Lamkin, Van Eman, Trimble, Beals & Dougherty, LLC
(See Columbus)

Lancaster, Robert N., Jr., (BV) . . . . . '61 '87 C.967 B.A. L.201 J.D. [Pavlatos,C.&L.]
Latham, W. D. Shane, (BV) . . . . . '61 '88 L.999 LL.B. [Gorman,V.H.&W.]
Lehmkuhl, Allen M., (CV) . . . . . '45 '74 C.967 B.S. L.117 J.D. [A.M.Lehmkuhl]
Lehmkuhl, Allen M., Co., L.P.A., (CV) . . . . . 111 E. Cecil Street
Lorig, Gerald F. . . . . . '35 '60 C.475 B.A. L.608 J.D. Com. Pleas J.
Malina, Paul D., (AV) . . . . . '34 '62 C.608 B.S. L.1003 LL.B. [🄲 P.D.Malina] ‡
Malina, Paul D., Co., L.P.A., (BV) . . . . . 6 W. High St.
Marshall, James D., (BV) . . . . . '56 '83 C&L.607 B.S., J.D. [Hofbauer&M.]
Martin, David M., (BV) . . . . . '44 '75 C.674 A.B. L.208 J.D. [D.M.Martin]

Martin, Browne, Hull & Harper, P.L.L., (AV) ▦
One South Limestone Street Suite 800, P.O. Box 1488, 45501-1488
Telephone: 937-324-5541 Fax: 937-325-5432 1-800-324-5562
Email: mbhhlaw@martinbrowne.com URL: http://www.martinbrowne.com
Members of the Firm: Oscar T. Martin (1848-1913); Paul C. Martin (1876-1939); Homer C. Corry (1887-1955); John C. Durfey (1902-1960); Anson E. Hull (1915-1983); Oscar T. Martin (1908-1995); Bitner Browne (1914-2003); Hugh Barnett; Robert E. Harley; Glenn W. Collier; Walter A. Wildman; David A. Weaver; William R. Groves; Steven J. McCready; Richard F. Heil, Jr.; Lauren M. Ross; R. Michael Osborn. Retired Partner: John O. Harper;—Wayne E. Southward; Randall M. Comer. Of Counsel: Karen W. Osborn.
General Civil Practice. Corporate, Commercial, Insurance, Insurance Defense, Litigation, Environmental, Business, Contracts, Banking, Estate Planning, Probate, Real Estate, Taxation, Education, Labor and Employment. Trials and Appeals in State and Federal Courts.
See Professional Biographies, SPRINGFIELD, OHIO

Martin, David M., Co., L.P.A., (BV)
4 West Main Street, Suite 707, 45502-1316
Telephone: 937-324-5000 Telecopier: 937-322-7572
Email: davidmartin@erinet.com URL: http://www.lawyers.com/davidmartin
David M. Martin.
General Civil and Criminal Practice. Bankruptcy, Business Law, Corporation, Collection, Debtor and Creditor, Criminal Law, Driving While Intoxicated, Family Law, Dissolution, Guardianship, Conservatorship, Children, Real Estate, Probate, Wills, Trusts and Estates.
Representative Clients: National City Bank; H.S. Stevenson & Sons, Inc.; Ear, Nose & Throat of Springfield, Inc.
Reference: National City Bank, Springfield, Ohio.
See Professional Biographies, SPRINGFIELD, OHIO

Mattes, David D. . . . . . '37 '62 C.967 B.A. L.608 LL.B. Com. Pleas J.
Matthies, Roland C. . . . . . '10 '34 C.210 A.B. L.145 J.D. 1500 Villa Rd.‡
Mayhall, Richard E., (BV) . . . . . '57 '82 C.473 B.A. L.608 J.D. 777 Benjamin Drive
McCready, Steven J., (BV) . . . . . '57 '83 C.473 A.B. L.608 J.D. [Martin,B.H.&H.]
McDonough, John P., (BV) . . . . . '29 '54 C.967 A.B. L.608 J.D. 2100 E. High St., Ste. 108
Mlicki, Teresa C., (CV) . . . . . '48 '80 C&L.608 B.A., J.D. [🄰 P.D.Malina]
Monnin, Joseph N., (BV) . . . . . '55 '80 C.1024 B.S. L.884 J.D. 101 E. Columbia St.
Morris, Gregory Michael, (BV) . . . . . '60 '89 C.1111 B.A. L.117 J.D. Asst. Pros. Atty.

Myers & Frayne Co., L.P.A.
(See Dayton)

Nedelman, Phyllis S., (BV) . . . . . '36 '82 C.150 B.S. L.608 J.D. [🄲 Cole A.H.D.]
Nevius, Eugene S. . . . . . '47 '72 C.973 B.S. L.607 J.D. Mun. J.
O'Keefe, Daniel M. '44 '69 C.201 B.A. L.608 J.D.
V.P. & Tr. Offr., Security National Bank and Trust Company
O'Neill, Richard J. . . . . . '49 '76 C.973 A.B. L.734 J.D. Com. Pleas J.
Osborn, Karen W. . . . . . '71 '94 C&L.383 B.S., J.D. [🄲 Martin,B.H.&H.]
Osborn, R. Michael . . . . . '68 '95 C.473 B.A. L.383 J.D. [Martin,B.H.&H.]
Pappas, Pete F., (BV) . . . . . '42 '67 C&L.608 B.S., J.D. 28 N. Fountain Ave.
Parks, Kimberly Sue '64 '96 C.967 B.A. L.117 J.D.
The Community Hospital of Springfield and Clark County
Parmley, Terri L., (BV) . . . . . '58 '88 C.235 B.S. L.201 J.D. [P.D.Malina]
Pavlatos, Robt. B., (BV) . . . . . '21 '49 C.967 L.608 J.D. [Pavlatos,C.&L.]
Pavlatos, Stacey R., (BV) . . . . . '51 '77 C.967 B.A. L.201 J.D. [Pavlatos,C.&L.]
Pavlatos, Catanzaro & Lancaster Co., L.P.A., (BV) . . . . . 700 E. High St.
Pedraza, Miguel A., Jr., (CV) . . . . . '60 '85 C.602 B.A. L.150 J.D. [Strozdas&P.]
Peifer, James F., (BV) . . . . . '46 '72 C.967 B.A. L.339 J.D. [Emerich&P.]
Pennington, Anthony B., (CV) '53 '77 C.1208 B.A. L.1049 J.D.
1107 Upper Valley Pike

Peterson & Peterson
(See Xenia)

Petroff, Samuel J., (BV) . . . . . '55 '80 C.303 B.A. L.608 J.D. [🄰 Lagos&L.]
Pickering, Andrew Parker . . . . . '69 '97 C.608 B.A. L.101 J.D. Clark Co. Pros.

Plymale Partnership LLP, The
(See Columbus)

Potter, Wilfred L. . . . . . '44 '78 C.1023 B.S. L.607 J.D. 234 N. Limestone St.
Powers, Paula M., (BV) . . . . . '47 '75 C.856 A.B. L.273 J.D. 4 W. Main St., Ste. 630
Rastatter, Douglas M., (CV) . . . . . '69 '94 C.659 B.A. L.150 J.D. Asst. Pros. Atty.
Reckley, Kathryn A., (BV) . . . . . '51 '86 C.477 B.A. L.851 J.D. Pros. Off.
Reich, Barry P., (AV) . . . . . '45 '70 C.631 B.A. L.276 J.D. [Cole A.H.D.]
Reynard, Jack P., Jr., (CV) . . . . . '39 '64 C.967 B.A. L.607 J.D. 6 W. High Street
Ricketts, Charles N., (BV) . . . . . '43 '68 C&L.608 B.S., J.D. 302 N. Plum Street
Roberts, Mark F., (BV) . . . . . '54 '79 C.608 B.S. L.117 J.D. [Elder,R.&E.] ‡
Ronemus, Thor G., (BV) . . . . . '30 '55 C&L.608 B.S., J.D. [Ronemus&H.]
Ronemus & Heath Co., L.P.A., (BV) . . . . . 5 E. Columbia St.
Ross, Lauren M., (BV) . . . . . '59 '84 C.478 B.A. L.930 J.D. [Martin,B.H.&H.]
Rush, Kenneth G., (AV) . . . . . '30 '57 C.966 B.S. L.309 LL.B. 4 W. Main St.
Schmenk, Gerald E., (AV) . . . . . '41 '66 C.201 B.A. L.608 J.D. [Schmenk,S.&H.]
Schmenk, Spencer & Hasselbach, (AV) . . . . . 20 North Limestone Street
Schultz, Ronald E., (AV) '42 '67 C.610 B.S. L.608 J.D.
[Dyer,G.M.&S.] (©Bellefontaine, Dayton, Huber Heights, Lima, Middletown, Piqua)
Schumaker, Stephen A., (BV) . . . . . '53 '78 C.967 B.A. L.608 J.D. Pros. Atty.
Schutte, Stephen E., (CV) . . . . . '48 '73 C.610 A.B. L.150 J.D. 31 E. High
Shipley, Robert M., II, (CV) . . . . . '48 '84 C.967 B.A. L.201 J.D. 2105 Miracle Mile
Skogstrom, James W., (BV) . . . . . '55 '80 C.608 B.A. L.564 J.D. 39 N. Fountain Ave.
Smith, David E., (BV) . . . '49 '75 C.608 B.S. L.607 J.D. 50 E. Columbia Street, 4th Floor
Smith, Elbert G., (BV) . . . . . '32 '58 C.967 A.B. L.608 J.D. [Smith&W.]
Smith & West, (BV) . . . . . 200 N. Fountain Ave.
Snead, Cozette, (CV) . . . . . '52 '95 C.4 B.S.W. L.1357 J.D. 101 E. Columbia St.
Sommer, Eric Michael . . . . . '70 '96 C&L.608 B.A., J.D. 200 N. Fountain Ave.
Southward, Wayne E., (BV) . . . . . '58 '83 C.967 B.A. L.94 J.D. [🄰 Martin,B.H.&H.]
Spencer, John M., (BV) . . . . . '57 '83 C.631 B.A. L.117 J.D. 30 Warder St., Ste. 250
Spencer, Richard A., (BV) . . . . . '46 '72 C&L.608 B.S., J.D. [Schmenk,S.&H.]

Standley Law Group LLP
(See Dublin)

Stegner, Dennis E., (BV) . . . . . '47 '72 C.967 B.A. L.608 J.D. 111 E. Cecil St.
Stewart, Albert, Jr., (BV) . . . . . '46 '73 C.943 B.S. L.930 J.D. Traffic Mag.
Stockstill, Lowell E. . . . . . '47 '83 C.473 B.S. L.851 J.D. Wittenberg Univ.
Stoll, Wm. J., (BV) . . . . . '21 '50 C.174 B.A. L.150 LL.B. 22 S. Limestone St.
Strozdas, Jerome M., (BV) . . . . . '53 '80 C.150 B.A. L.201 J.D. [Strozdas&P.]
Strozdas & Pedraza LLP, (BV) . . . . . 20 South Limestone Street, Suite 330
Swaney, Charles D., (BV) . . . . . '47 '76 C&L.608 B.S., J.D. 515 Fountain Ave.
Taylor, Shawn M. . . . . . '65 '96 C.150 B.A. L.117 J.D. 777 Benjamin Drive
Tehan, John N., (BV) . . . . . '19 '48 C.385 A.B. L.607 J.D. 22 S. Limestone St.
Thomas, Shawn Allen, (CV) . . . . . '63 '88 C.1062 B.A. L.117 J.D. Asst. Pub. Def.
Thoresen, Alice D., (CV) . . . . . '46 '92 C.713 B.A. L.300 J.D. 28 N. Fountain Ave.

Thorson, Switala, Wilkins & Snead, LLP
(See Dayton)

Trempe, Thomas E., (BV) . . . . . '55 '80 C.607 B.A. L.608 J.D. Mun. J.

Twyford & Donahey, P.L.L.
(See Columbus)

Valente, Paul R., (BV) . . . . . '41 '67 C.399 B.A. L.608 J.D. 10 S. Spring St.
Veskauf, Thomas J., (AV) . . . . . '31 '55 C.707 L.150 LL.B. [Gorman,V.H.&W.]
Ward, Roger Allen . . . . . '66 '95 C.611 B.A. L.200 J.D. Clark Co. Pros. Atty.'s Off.
Warren, James R., (BV) . . . . . '32 '59 C.473 A.B. L.477 LL.B. 934 National City Bank
Weaver, David A., (AV) . . . . . '46 '72 C.610 B.B.A. L.575 J.D. [Martin,B.H.&H.]
West, William D., (BV) . . . . . '39 '65 C&L.607 B.A., J.D. [Smith&W.]
Wildman, Walter A., (BV) . . . . . '41 '68 C.608 B.A. L.150 J.D. [Martin,B.H.&H.]
Wilson, Thomas W., (BV) . . . . . '53 '79 C.385 A.B. L.201 J.D. 466 N. Plum St.
Wilt, Valerie R., (BV) . . . . . '63 '88 C.473 B.A. L.201 J.D. [Juergens&W.]
Wineberg, Robert A., (CV) . . . . . '52 '80 C.97 B.S. L.851 J.D. [Gorman,V.H.&W.]
Winks, Paul William, (AV) . . . . . '43 '71 C.608 B.S. L.851 J.D. [W.Winks]

Winks, William, Attorney At Law, (AV)
Suite 102, 2525 North Limestone Street, 45503-7100
Telephone: 937-399-7580 Fax: 937-399-7591
Email: wwinks@williamwinks.com URL: http://www.williamwinks.com
Mr. Paul William Winks.
Insurance, Civil Litigation, Civil Practice, Probate, Negligence.
State Farm Insurance Companies.
See Professional Biographies, SPRINGFIELD, OHIO

Winwood, George M., (AV) . . . . . '17 '42 C.604 A.B. L.477 J.D. [🄲 Gorman,V.H.&W.]

Wise, Eric W. '40 '65 C.197 A.B. L.477 J.D.
Pres., Duplex Mill & Manufacturing Company
Zimmer, Osias D. '62 '88 C&L.117 B.A., J.D. Asst. Pros. Atty.
Zimmerman, Charles B., Jr., (AV) '31 '58 L.150 J.D. 10 S. Spring St.

STEUBENVILLE, * 19,015, *Jefferson Co.*

Abrams, James T., (BV) '47 '73 C.610 B.B.A. L.607 J.D. 401 Market Street
Adulewicz, Casimir T., (AV) '36 '63 C.608 B.S. L.607 J.D. 339 Market St.
Agresta, Emanuela, (BV) '58 '90 L.229 J.D. [Ⓐ Hayes,C.C.&P.]
Allen, Craig Joseph '— '90 Asst. Pros.
Almeida, Joseph A. '59 '88 C.1532 B.A. L.884 J.D. 1705 Oregon Ave.
Becker, Christopher, (BV) '62 '90 C.8 B.S. L.851 J.D. Chief Dep. Pros. Atty.
Bednar, Michael C., (BV) '58 '84 C.381 B.G.S. L.8 J.D. Co. Ct. J.
Blake, Shawn Michael '71 '99 C.608 B.S. L.8 J.D. 4110 Sunset Boulevard
Blake, William F., Jr., (BV) '44 '74 C.999 B.S. L.7 J.D. [Blake,W.F.]
Blake, William F., Jr., Company, L.P.A., (BV) 4110 Sunset Blvd.
Blischak, Michael '24 '52 C.659 B.S. L.608 J.D. P.O. Box 1492
Brondou, Derek M. '— '02 C.116 B.A. L.8 J.D. [Ⓐ Dickie,M.&C.] (⊙Pitts., PA)
Brown, Jeffrey O., (BV) '53 '79 C.901 B.A. L.607 J.D. [Fisher,B.&S.]
Bruzzese, Frank J., (AV) '49 '74 C.367 B.S. L.607 J.D. [Bruzzese,M.S.&S.]
Bruzzese, Joseph J., Jr., (BV) '51 '76 C&L.607 B.S., J.D. [Bruzzese,M.S.&S.]
Bruzzese, Joseph J., Sr., (AV) '18 '47 C&L.607 J.D. [Bruzzese,M.S.&S.] ‡
Bruzzese, Moreland, Straus & Spahn, (AV) 300 Sinclair Bldg.
Calabria, Michael J., (AV) '52 '77 C.81 B.A. L.608 J.D. [Hayes,C.C.&P.]
Campbell, William D., (AV) '25 '49 C.436 B.N.S. L.608 J.D. [Hayes,C.C.&P.]
Carpino, Joseph Simon '35 '63 C.610 A.B. L.607 LL.B. 227 North Fifth Street
Chalfant, R. Peterson, (AV) '40 '65
C.659 B.A. L.608 J.D. Ohio Valley Towers Mezzanine Suite 3
Christof, Joseph S. D., II, (AVⓉ) '— '74 C.321 B.A. L.880 J.D.
[Dickie,M.&C.] (⊙Pitts., PA; Wheeling, WV)
Corabi, Joseph M., (BV) '52 '77 C.1323 B.S. L.607 J.D. [Corabi&C.]
Corabi, Mary F., (CV) '59 '88 C.1323 B.A. L.607 J.D. [Corabi&C.]
Corabi & Corabi, (BV) 424 Market St.
Cottrell, Cerryn Renee '75 '01 C.207 B.A. L.117 J.D. Pros. Off.
Cozza, Piero P. '— '00 C.381 B.S. L.179 J.D. [Ⓐ Dickie,M.&C.]
D'Anniballe, Robert J., Jr., (BVⓉ) '56 '81 C.1323 B.S. L.8 J.D. [Pietragallo B.&G.]

Dickie, McCamey & Chilcote, A Professional Corporation, (AVⓉ)
401 Market Street , Suite 401, 43952-2846 ⊙
Telephone: 740-284-1682 Fax: 740-284-1692
Email: info@dmclaw.com URL: http://www.dmclaw.com
Shareholders: Richard C. Polley; Melvin F. O'Brien; Joseph S. D. Christof, II; David M. Neuhart; Stephen M. Houghton (Also at Pittsburgh, Pa. and Wheeling, W. Va. Offices); John T. Pion. Associates: Derek M. Brondou; Piero P. Cozza; Keith R. Huntzinger; Brant T. Miller.
General Practice including Alternative Dispute Resolution; Appellate Advocacy; Antitrust; Asbestos; Bad Faith; Bankruptcy; Business Law; Business Torts; Civil Litigation; Class Actions; Commercial Agreements; Commercial Litigation; Commercial Transactions; Compliance Programs; Construction Law; Contract Disputes; Contract Drafting; Corporate Compliance; Computer Law; Corporate Finance; Corporate Governance; Corporate Law; Corporate Services; Creditors' Rights; Education Law; Employment Law; Environmental Law; Estate Planning and Administration; Estates and Trusts; Family Law; First Amendment/Defamation; Finance Law and Financial Institutions; Food and Beverage; General Liability; Health Law Business; Insurance Defense; Insurance Law and Litigation; Insurance and Risk Management; Intellectual Property; Labor Law; Lender Liability; Licenses; Litigation; Medical Malpractice Defense; Mergers and Acquisitions; Product Liability; Professional Liability; Real Estate Transactions; Securities; Silica; Surety; Technology Law; Technology Transfer; Telecommunications; Toxic Tort; Transportation Law; White Collar Crime; Workers' Compensation.
Pittsburgh, Pennsylvania Office: Dickie, McCamey & Chilcote, P.C., Two PPG Place, Suite 400, 15222-5402. Telephone: 412-281-7272. Fax: 412-392-5367.
Camp Hill, Pennsylvania Office: Dickie, McCamey & Chilcote, P.C., 1200 Camp Hill Bypass, Suite 205, 17011-3700. Telephone: 717-731-4800. Fax: 717-731-4803.
Philadelphia, Pennsylvania Office: Dickie, McCamey & Chilcote, P.C., Public Ledger Building, Suite 901, 150 South Independence Mall, West, 19106-3409. Telephone: 215-925-2289. Fax: 215-925-0307.
Washington, D.C. Office: Dickie, McCamey & Chilcote, P.C., 1301 Pennsylvania Avenue, N.W., Suite 1000, 20004-1707. Telephone: 1-888-434-5566.
Haddonfield, New Jersey Office: Dickie, McCamey & Chilcote, P.C., 30 N. Haddon Avenue, Suite 100, 08033-2429. Telephone: 856-354-0192. Fax: 856-354-8164.
Charlotte, North Carolina Office: Dickie, McCamey & Chilcote, P.C.: 212 South Tryon Street, Suite 465, 28281-0007 Telephone: 704-334-1108. Fax: 704-334-1163.
Wheeling, West Virginia Office: Dickie, McCamey & Chilcote, L.C., 1233 Main Street, Suite 2002, 26003-2839. Telephone: 304-233-1022. Fax: 304-233-1026.
See Professional Biographies, STEUBENVILLE, OHIO

Dittmar, David N., (AV) '48 '78 C.134 B.S. L.229 J.D. 606 Sinclair Building
Evans, Augustus H., Jr., (BV) '26 '51 C.97 L.607 J.D. 325 N. 4th St.
Felmet, Bryan H. '51 '77 C&L.608 B.A., J.D. Pros. Off.
Fisher, William M., (BV) '42 '69 C.415 B.A. L.150 J.D. [Fisher,B.&S.]
Fisher, Brown & Swartz, (BV) 2017 Sunset Boulevard
Glasgow, Deborah J. '72 '97 C.381 B.A. L.608 J.D. Southeastern Ohio Legal Servs.
Gorman, Michelle L., (CVⓉ) '72 '96 C.920 B.S. L.117 J.D. [Ⓐ Pietragallo B.&G.]
Hallock, Gary M. '47 '77 C.1323 B.A. L.607 J.D. 4017A Sunset Boulevard
Hargrave, Robert C., (AV) '45 '70 C.532 B.A. L.608 J.D. [Hargrave,S.&J.]
Hargrave, Scurti & Jack, (AV) 200 Sinclair Building
Hayes, Cooper, Campbell & Prest, (AV) P.O. Box 1506
Hayman, Milton A., Law Offices of '26 '60 C.608 B.S. L.989 J.D. 401 Market St.
Heasley, Phillip L. '58 '90 C.645 B.A. L.930 J.D. Southeastern Ohio Legal Servs.
Henderson, David E., (BV) '47 '73 C.277 B.S.I.E. L.469 J.D. 301 Market St.

Hershey, Adrian V., (BV) '48 '75 C.920 B.A. L.7 J.D.
4110 Sunset Boulevard, 43952
Telephone: 740-264-1651 Fax: 740-264-6720
Email: ehershey@clover.net
General Corporate Practice, Estate Planning Law, Criminal Law, Domestic Relations, Divorce Law, Personal Injury Litigation, Personal Injury Law, Probate and Estates, and Collections.
See Professional Biographies, STEUBENVILLE, OHIO

Houghton, Stephen M., (AVⓉ) '— '78 C&L.477 B.A., J.D.
[Dickie,M.&C.] (⊙Pitts., PA; Wheeling, WV)
Huntzinger, Keith R., (CVⓉ) '— '95
C.920 B.A. L.923 J.D. [Ⓐ Dickie,M.&C.] (⊙Wheeling, WV)
Isla, Roger A., (BV) '66 '92 C.999 B.S. L.229 J.D. 4017 Sunset Boulevard, Suite A
Jack, Otto A., Jr., (BV) '46 '74 C.1323 B.S.B.A. L.150 J.D. [Hargrave,S.&J.]
Keenan, Jane Margaret '69 '01 C.608 B.S. L.229 J.D. Ste 300
Kerr, Samuel W. '40 '66 C.901 B.A. L.608 J.D. Com. Pleas J.
Krason, Stephen M. '54 '80 C.397 B.A. L.107 J.D.
(adm. in MA; not adm. in OH) Prof. of Pol. Sci., Franciscan Univ. of Steubenville
LaRue, David A., (BV) '60 '87 C.608 B.A. L.229 J.D. [Scarpone,L.&Assoc.]
Leist, Robert C. '56 '83 C.999 B.A. L.607 J.D. 2610 Devonshire Rd.‡
Leonard, A. G., (BV) '09 '33 C.276 L.150 J.D. [Palumbo,L.P.&V.]
Mansmann, Peter J., (AVⓉ) '36 '61 C&L.229 B.S., J.D.
(adm. in PA; not adm. in OH) [Mansmann&M.] ⊙
Mansmann & Moore, (AVⓉ) 153 North 4th Street (⊙Pitts., PA)
Marker, Rita Lorraine '40 '98 C.988 B.A. L.999 J.D. 1233 Maryland Avenue
Marshall, Michael J. '51 '95 C.1323 B.S. L.229 J.D. 339 Market Street
Mascio, John J., (BV) '65 '92 C.97 B.A. L.607 J.D. 329 N. 4th St., Ste. 2
Mascio, John J. '40 '65 C.1323 B.A. L.607 J.D. Com. Pleas J.
Mastros, Costa Damian '69 '95 C.901 B.A. L.8 J.D. Bank One Building, Suite 1210
McKenna, James R., (CV) '27 '57 C.610 B.S.C. L.607 LL.B. 325 N. 4th St.
Miller, Andrew W. '25 '51 L.608 LL.B. 200 Lovers Ln.
Miller, Brant T. '— '98 C.901 B.A. L.665 J.D. [Ⓐ Dickie,M.&C.] (⊙Pitts., PA)
Moore, Francis M., Jr. '65 '90 C.901 B.A. L.665 J.D. [Mansmann&M.] ⊙
Moreland, Carl C., (AV) '37 '62 C.385 B.A. L.607 J.D. [Bruzzese,M.S.&S.]
Neuhart, David M., (AVⓉ) '— '76 C&L.665 B.A., J.D. [Dickie,M.&C.] (⊙Pitts., PA)
Noble, Frank W., Jr. '68 '95 2017 Sunset Blvd.
O'Brien, Melvin F., (CVⓉ) '— '94
C.97 B.S.B.A. L.1003 J.D. [Dickie,M.&C.] (⊙Wheeling, WV)
Olivito, Dominick E. '21 '49 C.923 A.B. L.1003 J.D. Com. Pleas J.
Olivito, Peter S., (AV) '37 '62 C.923 B.S. L.607 J.D. 606-612 Sinclair Bldg.
Palumbo, Robt. J., (BV) '30 '55 C.1323 B.A. L.608 J.D. [Palumbo,L.P.&V.]
Palumbo, Leonard, Powell & Vukelic, (BV) World Savings Twrs.
Pate, Samuel A., (BV) '50 '80 C.610 B.A. L.607 J.D. Sinclair Bldg., Ste. 700
Pietragallo Bosick & Gordon LLP, (BVⓉ)
100 North Fourth Street (⊙Pitts., PA; Weirton, WV)
Pion, John T., (AVⓉ) '— '85 C.665 B.A. L.229 J.D. [Dickie,M.&C.] (⊙Pitts., PA)
Polley, Richard C., (BVⓉ) '— '81 C.25 B.S. L.665 J.D.
[Dickie,M.&C.] (⊙Pitts., PA; Wheeling, WV)
Powell, Judith A., (CV) '49 '75 C.97 B.A. L.851 J.D. [Palumbo,L.P.&V.]
Powell, Richard L. '28 '53 C.610 B.S. L.607 J.D. Mun. J.
Prest, Joseph G., (AV) '39 '64 C.679 B.S. L.607 J.D. [Hayes,C.C.&P.]
Repella, S. Gary, (CV) '52 '79 C.608 B.A. L.607 J.D. City Law Dir.
Ryland, Raymond O. '21 '75 C.663 A.B. L.1049 J.D. 900 Granard Pkwy.
Savinell, Alvin J. '22 '52 C.1323 L.602 LL.B. 325 N. 4th St.
Scarpone, David John, (BV) '62 '87 C.608 B.S. L.607 J.D. [Scarpone,L.&Assoc.]
Scarpone, LaRue & Associates, (BV) 2021 Sunset Boulevard

Schrader Byrd & Companion, PLLC
(See Wheeling, West Virginia)

Scurti, Adam E., (AV) '39 '66 C.610 B.A. L.880 J.D. [Hargrave,S.&J.]
Shaffer, John R., (CV) '42 '81 C.136 B.S. L.229 J.D. 316 N. Fourth St.
Shaw, Byron Keith '69 '00 C.608 B.A. L.1137 J.D. Jefferson Co. Pros. Off.
Snyder, Charles L., Jr. '19 '49 C&L.608 B.A., LL.B. 586 Braybarton Blvd.‡
Spahn, G. Daniel, (BV) '49 '82 C.105 B.A. L.665 J.D. [Bruzzese,M.S.&S.]
Stern, Gary M., (BV) '45 '78 C.659 B.A. L.117 J.D. [Stern,S.&S.]
Stern, James A., (BV) '50 '77 C.150 B.A. L.117 J.D. 102 N. 3rd St.
Stern, Nathan, (BV) '13 '38 C&L.608 B.A., J.D. Stern Law Bldg.
Stern, Stephen M., (BV) '46 '73 C.472 B.Ed. L.117 J.D. Pros. Atty.
Stern, Stern & Stern Co., L.P.A., (BV) 502 Bank One Building
Stewart, Susan P., (CV) '52 '77 C.97 B.A. L.607 J.D. 4130 Sunset Blvd.
Straus, Thomas R., (BV) '52 '78 C.94 B.A. L.607 J.D. [Bruzzese,M.S.&S.]
Swartz, Heather Fisher '70 '96 C.473 B.S.Ed. L.8 J.D. [Fisher,B.&S.]
Taylor, William W. '70 '95 C.1349 B.A. L.607 J.D. 140 E. Carlton Rd.
Vukelic, David A., (BV) '52 '77 C&L.607 B.A., J.D. [Palumbo,L.P.&V.]
Wilson, Thomas S., (BV) '50 '76 C.1323 B.A. L.607 J.D. 4017 Sunset Blvd.

STOW, 32,139, *Summit Co.*

Abell, Jack R. '47 '73 C.475 B.S. L.893 J.D.
(adm. in VA; not adm. in OH) 2907 Heatherwood Ct.‡
Banks, Christopher P., (CVⓉ) '58 '84 C.184 B.A. L.201 J.D.
(adm. in CT; not adm. in OH) 4401 Foresthill Road
Bosko, Daniel P. '42 '75 C&L.8 B.S.I.M., J.D. Ohio Bell Tel. Co.
Conn, ClydeL., (CV) '22 '49 C.381 A.B. L.930 J.D. 4466 Darrow Rd.
Crawford, Joseph Arden '38 '87 C.124 B.S. L.8 J.D. 4161 Bridgewater Parkway
Falconer, Ralph C. '26 '61 C.966 B.S.E.E. L.8 J.D. Pres., Falconer Grp.‡
Feltner, David L., (AV) '46 '76 C.249 B.S.M.E. L.7 J.D.
Sr. Project Atty., FirstEnergy Corp. (Legal Department)
Greif, Carl '56 '96 L.8 J.D. P.O. Box 1554
Haas, Richard H. '21 '49 C.453 B.S. L.309 J.D. 1101 Aberdeen Cir. (Pat.)
Haefner, Joseph P. '63 '96 C.188 B.S. L.124 J.D. City of Stow Law Dept.
Hoffman, Harry A. '17 '42 C&L.607 LL.B. 1934 Hawthorne‡
Landi, Albert J. '20 '54 C.229 B.S. L.7 LL.B. 3672 Oak Rd.‡
Loepp, Thomas C., (CV) '63 '90 C.347 B.A. L.8 J.D. 3580 Darrow Rd.
Maistros, Georgia '63 '90 C.8 B.S. L.7 J.D. 3580 Darrow Rd.
Martin, Richard P., (BV) '48 '77 C.8 B.A. L.7 J.D. [R.P.Martin]
Martin, Richard P. Co., L.P.A., (BV) 3603 Darrow Road
Nemer, Robert J. '67 '95 C&L.08 B.S., J.D. 3916 Clark Pointe Trl., Ste. 101
Pickut, Sandra J., (BV) '48 '76 C.323 B.A. L.7 J.D. V.P. & Gen. Coun., Max-Trac Tire
Raffath, Bernard A., Jr. '28 '59 C.8 B.S. L.7 LL.B. 3876 Leewood Dr.
Schrier, Lynn E. '28 '76 C.679 Ch.E. L.7 J.D. 3892 Kenwood Drive
Teleis, Kenneth R., Attorney at Law '67 '93 C.1062 B.A. L.8 J.D. 5187 Camden Dr.
Ward, Eileen K. Kelly '25 '45 C.930 B.B.A. L.1003 J.D. 1743 Lafayette Cir.
Ziobert, Felix J. '44 '68 C.381 B.A. L.930 J.D. P.O. Box 1338

STRASBURG, 2,310, *Tuscarawas Co.*

Fox, Richard L., (BV) '48 '76 C.631 B.A. L.7 J.D. 122 S. Wooster Ave.

STREETSBORO, 12,311, *Portage Co.*

Lanier, Lance A., Attorney at Law '70 '98 C&L.8 B.A., J.D.
775 Bridgeport Ave., Ste. 106
Wood, Rick, Attorney at Law '57 '83 C.434 B.S. L.607 J.D. 9294 State Rt. 43

STRONGSVILLE, 43,858, *Cuyahoga Co.*

Binns, Cynthia A. '53 '95 C.62 B.A. L.1003 J.D.
Assoc. Gen. Coun. & Asst. Secy., Glidden Company, The d/b/a/ ICI Paints
Blech, Kenneth A., (BV) '46 '79 C.679 B.S. L.161 J.D. [K.A.Blech]

Blech, Kenneth A., Company, L.P.A., (BV)
10850 Pearl Road, Suite D-3, 44136
Telephone: 440-238-7887 Fax: 440-238-9532 URL: http://www.blechlaw.com
Email: kenblech@ameritech.com URL: http://www.kenblech.com
Kenneth A. Blech. Associate: Lauren E. Davidson.
Taxation Law, Probate Law, Bankruptcy Law, Real Estate, Personal Injury, Small Business Law.
See Professional Biographies, STRONGSVILLE, OHIO

Davidson, Lauren E. '74 '03 C.475 B.A. L.607 J.D. [Ⓐ K.A.Blech]
Ellis, James D. '— '98 C.161 B.B.A. L.1003 J.D. 13977 Trenton Oval
Esper, Thomas L., (BV) '40 '71 C.608 B.S. L.161 J.D. 19749 Stoughton Dr.
Foth, Arthur, Jr., (BV) '41 '74 C.363 A.B. L.1003 J.D. [Foth,K.&U.]
Foth, Kelly & Urban Co., L.P.A., (BV) 11221 Pearl Rd.
Goldsmith, Harvey S. '39 '66 C.608 B.S.B.A. L.1003 J.D. P.O. Box 360556‡
Grieselhuber, Pierre A., (BV) '38 '69 C.150 B.B.A. L.1003 J.D. 17030 Greenbrier Dr.

Hanna, John T., (BV) '63 '90
C.161 B.B.A. L.1003 J.D. Assoc. Gen. Coun., Litig., ICI Paints
Homolak, Diane I. '57 '89
C.610 B.B.A. L.1003 J.D. Contracts Negotiator, Hewlett-Packard Co.‡
Julian, Andrea M. .... '74 '99 C.62 B.S. L.989 J.D. 11221 Pearl Rd.
Jusek, Frank R. .... '12 '36 C.477 L.608 LL.B. 19246 Pearl Rd.‡
Kelly, Thomas A., III, (BV) .... '48 '74 C.363 A.B. L.1003 J.D. [Foth,K.&U.]
Kraus, Kenneth A., (AV) ....'47 '72 C&L.477 B.A., J.D. Law Dir., City of Strongsville
Li, Peter B., Law Office of .... '58 '96 C.999 B.S. L.1003 J.D. 16394 Falmouth Drive
Lick, Fred, Jr. .... '31 '61 C.473 A.B. L.1003 J.D. 17800 Royalton Rd.
Maugans, Todd D. .... '61 '96 C.473 B.S. L.1003 J.D. 22061 Woodfield Trail
Minni, Dennis E., Law Office of .... '43 '73 C.107 B.A. L.64 J.D. 14761 Pearl Rd.
Papandreas, Joyce M., (BV) .... '64 '91 C.602 B.A. L.930 J.D. 14193 Basswood Cir.
Pasz, David J., (BV) .... '53 '82 C.473 B.S. L.1003 J.D. 12001 Prospect Road
Paulett, H. Kenneth .... '51 '82 C.161 B.A. L.1003 J.D. Cleveland Metroparks
Ramsey, Kenneth E. .... '30 '63 C.62 B.A. L.161 J.D. 13451 Pearl Rd.‡
Ramsey-Caputo, Donna Jean, (BV) .... '59 '84 C.8 B.S. L.161 J.D. 13451 Pearl Road

Riehl, David S.
(See Brunswick)

Rossen, Joel M. .... '47 '73 C.150 B.A. L.851 J.D. 20523 Wildwood Ln.
Russo, Christine A., Law Offices of ... '64 '89 C.610 B.A. L.851 J.D. 11005 Pearl Road
Sabrey, James F. .... '65 '00 C.62 B.A. L.989 J.D. 17732 Ash Drive
Schoening, Mary D., (BV) '55 '80 C&L.383 B.A., J.D.
(adm. in KY; not adm. in OH)
Asst. Gen. Coun., Cons./Dlr. Div., Glidden Company, The d/b/a/ ICI Paints
Sedory, Allen R. .... '34 '61 C.930 A.B. L.276 J.D. 17178 Woodleaf Rd.‡
Sheehe, Lawrence G., Jr., (BV) '53 '83
C.973 B.S. L.1003 J.D. 11925 Pearl Road, Suite 402-A
Smith, Gary D. .... '47 '72 C.235 B.B.A. L.607 J.D. 11005 Pearl Rd.
Smith, Gary D., Law Offices of .... '54 '79 C.97 L.607 J.D. 11005 Pearl Road
Stachel, Kenneth J. '48 '75 C&L.229 B.S., J.D.
(adm. in PA; not adm. in OH; Pat.) Assoc. Gen. Coun., Intell. Prop., ICI Paints
Todia, William C. .... '33 '57 C.973 B.S. L.477 J.D. 17311 Falling Water‡
Tymcio, Deborah .... '52 '00 C.1077 B.A. L.989 J.D. P.O. Box 360413
Urban, John J., (BV) .... '49 '75 C.363 A.B. L.1003 J.D. [Foth,K.&U.]
Westerhaus, Michael Frank .... '49 '74 C.97 B.A. L.930 J.D. 14255 Peppercreek Dr.

STRUTHERS, 11,756, *Mahoning Co.*

Almasy, John P., (BV) .... '30 '55 C.980 L.610 LL.B. Home Svgs. & Loan Bldg.
Clemente, Michael C., (BV) .... '27 '53 C.473 A.B. L.477 J.D. [Clemente&W.]
Clemente & Wagner Co., L.P.A., (BV) .... 700 Fifth Street
Munn, Robert S., (BV) .... '12 '38 C&L.930 B.A., LL.B. 524 Youngstown-Poland Rd.
Wagner, Carol Clemente, (BV) .... '58 '88 C.980 B.S.B.A. L.7 J.D. [Clemente&W.]

STRYKER, 1,468, *Williams Co.*

Brenner, William J., (BV) .... '52 '77 C&L.851 B.A., J.D. 112 N. Defiance Street

SUGARCREEK, 2,174, *Tuscarawas Co.*

Frautschy, Douglas Doyle ....'64 '99 C.999 B.A. L.7 J.D. 747 E. Steinebrey Ridge Rd.
Miller, Thomas E., (BV) .... '25 '55 C.631 B.S. L.174 LL.B. 232 N. Factory St.

SUNBURY, 2,630, *Delaware Co.*

Adams, W. Mark, (CV) .... '62 '87 C.610 B.B.A. L.608 J.D. 241 Greenbriar Road
Connelly, John Mark, II .... '55 '80 C&L.117 B.A., J.D. 15326 Hartford Rd.

Manos, Martin, Pergram & Dietz Co., LPA
(See Delaware)

Miller, Marvin C., (BV) .... '39 '64 C.851 B.A. L.608 J.D. 50 East Granville Street
Morris, David R. .... '51 '76 C.207 B.A. L.117 J.D. Pres., Whitney Ins. Agcy., Inc.
Schilder, Joseph W., (BV) .... '36 '64 C.608 A.B. L.266 J.D. 50 E. Granville St.

SWANTON, 3,307, *Fulton Co.*

Borrillo, Donato J. .... '64 '96 C.116 B.A. L.930 J.D. [D.Borrillo]
Borrillo, Donato, MD .... 11100 Airport Hwy.
Hallett, Terrence E., (BV) .... '27 '53 C&L.851 J.D. [T.E.Hallett]
Hallett, Terrence E., Law Offices, LPA, (BV) .... 115 W. Airport Highway
Keiser, J. Alan, (BV) .... '49 '78 C.608 B.S. L.851 J.D. 110 W. Airport Hwy.
Kimmelman, William C., (BV) .... '58 '87 C&L.851 B.B.A., J.D. 113 W. Airport Hwy.
Lehenbauer, Alan J., (BV) '59 '84 C&L.851 B.B.A., J.D.
[⊠ McQuades] (⊙Whitehouse)
Marshall, Bruce L. .... '55 '82 C.679 B.S. L.213 J.D. 11777 W. Airport Service Road
McQuade, Colin J., (BV) ....'55 '80 C.5 B.A. L.851 J.D. [McQuades] (⊙Whitehouse)
McQuade, Daniel P., (AV) .... '42 '67 C.424 B.S. L.608 J.D. [McQuades] ⊙
McQuade, Richard B., Jr. .... '40 '65 C&L.851 B.A., J.D. 2036 Country Rd. F

McQuades Co., The, L.P.A., (AV)
Lincoln at Broadway, P.O. Box 237, 43558 ⊙
Telephone: 419-826-0055 Fax: 419-825-3871
Email: mcquadelaw@earthlink.net URL: http://www.mcquadelaw.com
Richard B. McQuade, Sr. (1912-1996); Daniel P. McQuade; Colin J. McQuade;—Alan J. Lehenbauer.
General Civil Practice. Personal Injury, Wrongful Death, Products Liability, Medical Malpractice, Real Estate, Corporate and Business Law. Probate and Estate Planning, Collections, Municipal and Zoning Law. Family Law, Criminal Law. Trials and Appellate Practice in all Courts.
Archbold, Ohio Office: 200 N. Defiance Street. Telephone: 419-445-3755.
Whitehouse, Ohio Office: 6632 Providence Street. Telephone: 419-877-0746.
See Professional Biographies, SWANTON, OHIO

Saxer, Robert H. .... '36 '70 C.97 B.S. L.851 J.D. 207 W. Garfield Ave.
Sheperak, Thomas J., (BV) .... '41 '66 C&L.851 B.A., J.D. 114 St. Richards Court
Smith, Gary L., (CV) .... '49 '89 C&L.150 B.M., J.D. 138 N. Main Street

SYCAMORE, 919, *Wyandot Co.*

Bacon, Forrest H., (AV) .... '24 '51 C&L.608 LL.B. [Roth B.Y.] ⊙
Fox, Mary E., (BV) .... '56 '81 C&L.607 B.A., J.D. [Osborn&F.]
Osborn, Thomas E., (BV) .... '46 '75 C.62 B.A. L.607 J.D. Mun. J. [Osborn&F.]
Osborn & Fox, L.P.A., (BV) .... 130 S. Sycamore Ave.
Roth Bacon Young, (AV) .... S. Sycamore Ave. (⊙Marion, Upper Sandusky)

SYLVANIA, 18,670, *Lucas Co.*

Abood, Charles D. .... '44 '70 C.477 B.A. L.851 J.D. Dispute Resolution Servs.
Abramson, Mark C., (AV) .... '56 '81 C.150 B.A. L.904 J.D. [Udell&A.]
Barton, Jery E. .... '47 '72 C.309 A.B. L.94 J.D. [⊠ Kenney&N.]
Bauman, Robert F., (BV) .... '23 '58 C&L.851 B.Ed., J.D. 6905 Brint Rd.
Beightol, Sharon Stine .... '50 '80 C&L.851 B.S., J.D. 4917 Alexis Rd.
Bocik, Edward J. .... '50 '74 C.602 B.A. L.608 J.D. V.P., Labor Rel., Honeywell
Burke, Steven M., (BV) ....'54 '82 C.608 B.A. L.1187 J.D. 4930 Holland-Sylvania Rd.
Clair, Mark D. .... '61 '97 C.1359 B.B.A. L.851 J.D. 7135 Sylvania Ave.
Douglas, Thomas S., (BV) ... '44 '75 C&L.851 B.B.A., J.D. 4930 N. Holland Sylvania Rd.
Drescher, Wolfgang, (AV) .... '44 '69 C.477 B.S.E. L.851 J.D. 6611 Maplewood Ave.
Dymarkowski, Douglas A., (CV) '65 '94
C.851 B.B.A. L.930 J.D. 4930 Holland-Sylvania Road
Erb, William W. .... '22 '58 C.935 B.B.A. L.851 LL.B. Mun. J.
Fisher, Timothy Hugh '60 '87 C.317 B.A. L.1187 J.D.
(adm. in MI; not adm. in OH) 4811 Wickford Green Rd.
Gersz, Theodore, (BV) .... '46 '73 C.107 B.S. L.851 J.D. 5800 Monroe St.
Gold, Kalman .... '33 '72 C.912 B.A. L.851 J.D. 5831 Monroe St.‡
Grega, Richard John .... '66 '92 C.608 B.S.B.A. L.8 J.D. P.O. Box 513
Hensien, Christopher J. .... '52 '03 C.608 B.S. L.851 J.D. [⊠ Kenney&N.]
Hunt, Charles N., (BV) .... '31 '58 C&L.608 B.S., LL.B. [Hunt,M.&O.] (⊙Metamora)
Hunt, Walter F. .... '21 '50 C&L.607 J.D. 4626 Gaines Mill Dr.‡
Hunt, Millican & O'Brien, (BV) .... P.O. Box 370
Hyrne, Clarence F., Jr. .... '18 '48 C.260 A.B. L.150 LL.B. 6002 Grandville Dr.‡
Jones, Brian D. .... '50 '77 C.165 B.A. L.851 J.D. [B.Jones]
Jones, Brian .... 5658 Main St.
Joyce, Kevin E., (BV) .... '57 '82 C.930 B.A. L.851 J.D. P.O. Box 788
Judge, Michael E. .... '28 '56 C.602 B.S. L.851 LL.B. 7031 Apple Creek Rd.‡
Justen, Frank A., (BV) .... '40 '70 C&L.851 B.B.A., J.D. 4930 Holland-Sylvania Rd.
Kenney, Kevin J., (BV) .... '55 '81 C.602 B.A. L.851 J.D. [Kenney&N.]

Kenney & Niehaus, Ltd., (BV)
5470 Main Street, Suite 300, 43560
Telephone: 419-517-7000 Fax: 419-517-7001
Email: lastname@kenneyniehauslaw.com URL: http://www.lawyers.com/kenneyniehauslaw
Kevin J. Kenney; Charles D. Niehaus. Associates: Laurie A. Schoonmaker; Christopher J. Hensien; Jery E. Barton.
Corporate, Business, Securities, Banking, Estate Planning, Probate, Real Estate, Litigation.
See Professional Biographies, SYLVANIA, OHIO

Killam, Catherine H., (AV) .... '53 '79 C&L.851 B.E., J.D. [⊠ Udell&A.]
Kitchen, Margaret Applegate, (BV) .... '22 '53 C.477 A.B. L.851 J.D. 7209 Grenlock
Klar, Marilyn F. .... '53 '78 C.477 B.A. L.1003 J.D. 4545 Weldwood Ln.‡
Kujawa, Kenneth T. .... '47 '71 C&L.851 B.A., J.D. 7749 Westbourne Ct.
Lynn, Michael '62 '00 C.831 B.B.A. L.215 J.D.
(adm. in MI; not adm. in OH) 8768 Big Cypress Cir
Manning, Pamela .... '56 '99 C&L.851 B.A., J.D. 5800 Monroe Street
Millican, Patrick R., (BV) .... '58 '87 C.477 B.A. L.851 J.D. [Hunt,M.&O.]
Moan, James E., (AV) .... '46 '72 C&L.851 B.A., J.D. 4930 Holland-Sylvania Rd.
Niehaus, Charles D., (BV) .... '59 '86 C.1217 B.S. L.851 J.D. [Kenney&N.]
Nolan, John T. '24 '50 C.645 B.A. L.188 J.D.
(adm. in IA; not adm. in OH) 7121 Pine Birr Lane‡
O'Brien, Isobel T., (BV) .... '64 '89 C.602 B.A. L.851 J.D. [Hunt,M.&O.]
Pfeiffer, James J. .... '31 '57 C.602 Ph.B. L.851 LL.B. 5504 Bent Oak
Pheasant, Merle E., Jr. ... '45 '72 C&L.8 B.A., J.D. Gen. Coun., Continental Capital Corp.
Ramey, M. Scott .... '48 '73 C.210 B.A. L.228 J.D. Mun. J.
Rauh, Sue N. .... '25 '58 C&L.851 J.D. Secy. & Treas., Std Delivery Service, Inc.
Rimelspach, Ron L., (AV) .... '47 '73 C.97 B.A. L.851 J.D. 5800 Monroe St.
Rosenthal, James A. '59 '84
C.597 B.A. L.800 J.D. V.P. & Gen. Coun., Rosenthal Foods Corp.
Schoonmaker, Laurie A., (CV) .... '65 '99 C&L.851 B.B.A., J.D. [⊠ Kenney&N.]
Schroeder, Charles F. .... '18 '51 C.46 B.S. L.209 J.D. 7344 Country Commons Ln. (Pat.)

Simko, David
(See Toledo)

Snow, Raymond P., Jr. .... '21 '48 C.473 B.S. L.930 LL.B. 5749 Foxpointe Dr.‡
Stack, Francis J. .... '23 '59 C.475 A.B. L.851 J.D. 4058 New Castle
Strong, Dennis P., Law Offices of, (BV) '49 '80
C.723 B.A. L.851 J.D. 5600 Monroe Street
Sullivan, Daniel J. .... '49 '02 C.184 B.S. L.851 J.D. [D.J.Sullivan]
Sullivan, Daniel J., Esq., L.L.C. .... 5660 Monroe St., Ste. 3
Summers, Ann H. .... '32 '58 C&L.851 B.A., LL.B. 5922 Whiteford Rd.‡
Turner, Jeffrey Alan .... '66 '95 C&L.851 B.A., J.D. Capital Bank N.A.
Udell, Louis, (AV) .... '58 '83 C.473 B.S. L.608 J.D. [Udell&A.]

Udell & Abramson, Ltd., (AV)
5738 Main Street, 43560
Telephone: 419-724-2600 Fax: 419-724-2601
Email: LU@ualegal.com
Louis Udell; Mark C. Abramson. Of Counsel: Catherine H. Killam.
Business Law, Corporate and Succession Planning, Mergers and Acquisitions, ERISA, Pension and Profit Sharing Plans, Real Estate, Taxation, Tax Litigation, Nonprofit Corporations, Estate Planning and Probate, Family Law, Employment, Litigation.
See Professional Biographies, SYLVANIA, OHIO

Wilson, C. Gary, (BV) .... '51 '77 C.473 A.B. L.851 J.D. 4930 Holland-Sylvania Rd.
Yarbrough, Stephen A. .... '46 '74 C&L.851 B.B.A., J.D. Ret. J.‡
Zraik, T. Joseph .... '41 '77 C.97 B.S. L.851 J.D. 5579 Monroe Street
Zraik, Thomas G., (BV) .... '37 '64 C.851 L.608 J.D. 5579 Monroe St

TALLMADGE, 16,390, *Portage & Summit Cos.*

Alfera, Vincent J., (BV) .... '50 '75 C.207 B.A. L.1003 J.D. P.O. Box 515
Bowser, Sharyn Shaw '63 '88 C.651 B.A. L.1017 J.D.
(adm. in PA; not adm. in OH) 554 Vandalia Dr.‡
Ferguson-Rich, Mary Ann, (BV) .... '57 '83 C.741 B.A. L.8 J.D. 1166 Broadview Rd.
Jenkins, Craig N. '53 '83 C&L.8 B.S.B.A., J.D.
(adm. in NC; not adm. in OH) P.O. Box 317★
Kamlowsky, Lisa Marie '67 '93
C&L.8 B.A., J.D. Summit County Board of Mental Retardation
Lawrence, Fred W., (BV) .... '28 '53 C&L.608 B.A., LL.B. [Lawrence&L.]
Lawrence, Walter R., (AV) .... '55 '85 C.8 B.S. L.7 J.D. [Lawrence&L.]
Lawrence & Lawrence, Co., LPA, (AV) .... 101 Northeast Ave.
Maguire, Robert D., (BV) .... '46 '75 C.1131 B.A. L.8 J.D. 190 East Avenue
Merrow, Donald L. .... '24 '52 C&L.607 LL.B. 278 Smith Dr.
Mihiylov, Robert L. .... '46 '75 C.8 B.S.E.E. L.7 J.D. 12 Southwest Ave.
Miller, George M., (BV) .... '43 '68 C.874 B.A. L.930 J.D. 143 Northwest Ave.
Moreland, Gary A. .... '54 '79 C.8 B.S. L.1003 J.D. 355 Kent Dr.
Mumper, John E. .... '51 '82 C&L.8 B.A., J.D. Mag., Juvenile Ct.
Schunk, Richard A., (BV) .... '45 '74 C.901 B.A. L.8 J.D. City Law Dir.
Sherrod, H. John P. .... '77 '04 C.25 B.A. L.8 J.D. 190 E. Ave.
Smolk, Edward C. .... '33 '58 C&L.930 B.B.A., LL.B. 388 East Avenue

TERRACE PARK, 2,273, *Hamilton Co.*

Davis, Hayden D., Jr. .... '21 '60 C.608 B.S. L.1340 LL.B. 300 Wanoka Woods‡
Longano, Thomas P., (AV) .... '46 '74 C.150 B.S. L.1340 J.D. Chf. Asst. Pros.
Naylor, Paul D., (AV) .... '25 '48 C&L.150 J.D. 304 Amherst Ave.
Thoman, Henry N., (BV) .... '57 '82 C.228 B.A. L.145 J.D. P.O. Box 51‡

THORNVILLE, 758, *Perry Co.*

Dagger, Johnston, Miller, Ogilvie & Hampson, LLP, (AV)
E. Columbus St. (⊙Lancaster)

Johnston, Robert E., (AV) ... '29 '54 C.611 B.A. L.150 J.D. [Dagger,J.M.O.&H.] ⊙
Walser, Thomas E. ... '57 '83 C.608 B.S. L.117 J.D. 39 14878 S.R. 13

TIFFIN, * 18,135, *Seneca Co.*

Barga, John T., (BV) ... '46 '76 C.608 B.A. L.851 J.D. 120 Jefferson St.
Barga, Rita Bobowick ... '46 '77 C.102 B.A. L.851 J.D. 120 Jefferson St.‡
Behm, Karen Streacker ... '63 '89 C&L.608 B.S., J.D. [Lange&B.]
Bendure, Randall S., Law Offices of, (BV) ... '48 '73 C&L.607 B.A., J.D. 31 Court St.
Burtis, Paul F. ... '62 '90 C.597 B.S. L.347 J.D. [Dell,B.&A.]

Contrada & Associates
(See Toledo)

Curtin, John Vinton ... '52 '88 C&L.851 B.A., J.D. 2578 W. Township Rd.
Daniel, Frederick R. ... '53 '78 C&L.602 B.A., J.D. Mun. Ct. J.

Davis, B. Mark, (AV) '55 '80 C.97 B.A. L.608 J.D.
100 East Perry Street, 44883-2346
Telephone: 419-448-8000 Fax: 419-448-1584
Email: bmdavis@tiffinohio.com
Trial and Appellate Practice in all Courts. Litigation, Criminal Defense, Personal Injury, Family Law.
References: Fifth Third Bank.

Dell, Jane C., (BV) ... '64 '90 C.276 B.S. L.347 J.D. [Dell,B.&A.]
Dell, Burtis & Anspach LLP, (AV) ... 60 Sycamore Street (⊙Buffalo, NY; Toledo, OH)
DeVine, Derek W., (BV) ... '67 '93 C.249 B.S. L.607 J.D. [Supance&H.]
Dore, Frank T., (AV) ... '12 '38 C.313 L.608 LL.B. 126 Hampden Park‡
Eberly, Dennis J., (BV) ... '61 '85 C.607 B.A. L.851 J.D. [Eberly&E.]
Eberly, Thomas J., (AV) ... '39 '65 C.313 A.B. L.930 J.D. [Eberly&E.]
Eberly & Eberly, (AV) ... 180 S. Washington Street
Egbert, Kenneth H., Jr., (CV) ... '64 '89 C.608 B.A. L.851 J.D. Pros. Atty.
Forrest, Clair M. ... '23 '50 C.97 B.S. L.880 LL.B. 400 Melmore St.‡
Forrest, Clair M., Jr., (CV) ... '51 '85 C&L.608 B.S., J.D. 140 Riverside Dr.
Forrest, George L. ... '27 '54 C.97 L.607 J.D. Ret. Prob. J.
Fruth, James W. ... '70 '95 C.313 B.A. L.117 J.D. [Ⓐ Dell,B.&A.]
Gillmor, Paul E., (BV) ... '39 '65 C.611 B.A. L.477 J.D. State Sen.
Gordon, Richard H., (AV) ... '17 '40 C&L.607 J.D. 3 Linda Ln.‡
Gordon, Thomas J., (AV) ... '43 '68 C.231 B.A. L.608 J.D. 23 Court Street
Graham, Arthur F., (AV) '31 '60
C.313 B.A. L.608 LL.B. Mag., Com. Pleas Ct. [A.F.Graham]
Graham, Arthur Frances, (AV) ... Westgate Shopping Center
Gucker, James R., (BV) ... '62 '88 C.97 B.A. L.851 J.D. 106 E. Market St.
Harrison-Kahler, Jennifer Lynn, (CV) ... '69 '96 C.136 B.S. L.1187 J.D. [Kahler&K.]
Henry, Dean, (BV) ... '63 '89 C.610 B.S. L.851 J.D. [Lange&B.]
Howard, Brent T., (BV) ... '61 '87 C.339 A.B. L.608 J.D. [Supance&H.]
Howard, Susan Hering ... '62 '88 C.207 B.A. L.608 J.D. [Supance&H.]
Huth, Lester C., (AV) ... '24 '51 C&L.602 J.D. 80 Northwood Dr.
Jones, Susan M., (CV) ... '64 '90 C.207 B.S. L.851 J.D. P.O. Box 400
Kahler, John M., II ... '68 '96 C.473 B.A. L.1187 J.D. [Kahler&K.]
Kahler, Richard A. ... '40 '66 C.381 A.B. L.608 J.D. [Kahler&K.]
Kahler and Kahler, (CV) ... 210-216 S. Washington St.
Kelbley, Michael P. '51 '76
C.363 A.B. L.930 J.D. Com. Pleas J., Seneca Co. Com. Place Ct.
Knutson, Elaine J., (BV) ... '39 '76 C.378 B.A. L.851 J.D. [Patino&K.]
Koop, Martin D. ... '64 '98 C&L.851 B.A., J.D. [Supance&H.]
Kutscher, Paul F., Jr. ... '54 '78 C&L.607 B.A., J.D. Com. Pleas J.
Lange, Anne Margaret ... '64 '00 C&L.851 B.B.A., J.D. [Lange]
Lange, Michael B., (AV) ... '35 '61 C&L.215 Ph.B., LL.B. [Lange&B.]
Lange & Behm, (AV) ... 187 S. Washington St.
Lange Law Offices, LLC ... 174 S. Washington Street
McKinney, Samuel R., (BV) ... '12 '37 C&L.930 A.B., LL.B. [McKinney&M.]
McKinney, Samuel R., Jr., (BV) ... '48 '75 C.49 A.B. L.607 J.D. [McKinney&M.]
McKinney & McKinney, (BV) ... 1945 S. Winfield Dr. (⊙Fairfield, TX)
Meyer, Gerald D. ... '44 '68 C&L.607 B.S., J.D. 106 S. Market
Nord, Kent D., (CV) ... '68 '93 C.967 B.A. L.851 J.D. P.O. Box 340
Nordholt, James S., Jr., (AV) ... '44 '74 C&L.608 B.S., J.D. [Ⓒ Supance&H.]
Patino, Leticia G. ... '53 '82 C.999 B.S.E. L.128 J.D. [Patino&K.]

Patino & Knutson, (BV)
159 S. Washington Street, 94883
Telephone: 419-455-9508 Fax: 419-455-9509
Members of Firm: (Ms) Leticia G. Patino; (Ms) Elaine J. Knutson.
Legislative Law, Administrative Law, Bankruptcy, Domestic Relations, Juvenile Law, Education, Criminal Law, Mediation, Drainage and Levee, Probate.

See Professional Biographies, TIFFIN, OHIO

Shuff, Steve C. ... '53 '78 C.313 B.A. L.896 J.D. Com. Pleas J.
Spellerberg, Thomas R. ... '25 '51 C&L.608 B.A., J.D. Com. Pleas J.
Supance, James D., (AV) ... '47 '72 C&L.477 B.A., J.D. [Supance&H.]
Supance & Howard, (AV) ... 84-88 South Washington Street
Williams, Carl A. ... '19 '53 C&L.851 B.B.A., J.D. 103 E. Perry St.‡

TILTONSVILLE, 1,329, *Jefferson Co.*

Piergallini, Lawrence T., (BV) ... '55 '80 C&L.608 B.S., J.D. 131 3rd St.

TIPP CITY, 9,221, *Miami Co.*

Andersen, Nicholas I. ... '79 '04 C.608 B.S. L.117 J.D. [Ⓐ Dysinger,S.&D.]
Cochran, Thomas Reeves ... '53 '88 C.610 B.A. L.117 J.D. [T.R.Cochran]
Cochran, Thomas R., Co., LPA ... 17 West Main Street
Downing, Joseph A., (CV) ... '69 '96 C.201 B.A. L.608 J.D. [Dysinger,S.&D.]
Dysinger, Thomas E., (BV) ... '53 '77 C&L.608 B.S., J.D. [Dysinger,S.&D.]

Dysinger, Stewart & Downing, LLC, Attorneys at Law, (BV)
249 South Garber Drive, 45371-1183
Telephone: 937-667-4481 Facsimile: 937-667-5393
Email: info@dsdlawyers.com URL: http://www.dsdlawyers.com
Thomas E. Dysinger; Bryan K. Stewart; Joseph A. Downing; Andrew B. Stewart. Associate: Nicholas I. Andersen.
Business Law, Business Litigation, Mergers and Acquisitions, Civil Litigation, Commercial Real Estate, Corporate Law, Criminal Law, Estate Planning, Family Law, Guardianship, Litigation, Personal Injury, Probate, Real Estate, Trusts & Estates, Wills, Business Planning, Collections, Divorce, Dissolutions, Wrongful Death, Tax Planning, Medicaid Planning, Elder Law.
Representative Clients: Monroe Federal Savings & Loan Assn.; SK Mold & Tool Co.; Ishmael Precision Tool Corp.; Unidev Corp.; Vital Connections Inc.; Black River Development, Inc.; Dayton Paper Products, Inc.

See Professional Biographies, TIPP CITY, OHIO

Hunt, Carroll E. ... '26 '51 C&L.608 B.A., J.D. 825 Charrington Way
Johnston, Terry J. ... '62 '87 C.607 B.A. L.608 J.D. 249 S. Garber Dr.
Lovett, George H., (BV) ... '62 '88 C.473 B.A. L.608 J.D. 1420 W. Main St.
Lovett, Roselyn G., (BV) ... '52 '89 C.1376 B.A. L.117 J.D. 1420 W. Main St.
Pearson, John D., (CV) ... '45 '70 C.473 B.A. L.150 J.D. 23 W. Main St.
Schneder, Theresa A. ... '50 '89 C.107 B.A. L.982 J.D. 8945 W. State Rte. 202

Stewart, Andrew B. ... '66 '99 C.269 B.A. L.665 J.D. [Dysinger,S.&D.]
Stewart, Bryan K., (BV) ... '57 '89 C.1208 B.A. L.608 J.D. [Dysinger,S.&D.]
Wist, E. John, (AV) ... '43 '68 C.201 B.A. L.607 J.D. 8 S. 3rd St.

TOLEDO, * 313,619, *Lucas Co.*

Abercrombie, Gene R., (BV) ... '69 '96 C&L.851 B.B.A., J.D. [Ⓐ Eastman&S.]
Accettola, Paul E., (AV) ... '47 '75 C.222 B.A. L.851 J.D. [Herschel,A.B.&M.]
Adams, Mark W. ... '61 '90 C.610 B.A. L.1003 J.D. 3922 Lagrange Street
Ahern, Stephen F., (BV) ... '49 '76 C.602 A.B. L.8 J.D. [Manahan,P.B.&D.]
Albrechta, Joseph F., (BV) ... '57 '84 C.473 B.Ph. L.851 J.D. [Albrechta&C.] (⊙Fremont)
Albrechta and Coble, (AV) ... 3230 Central Park West, Suite 200 (⊙Fremont, Perrysburg)
Albright, Alfred, Jr., (BV) '50 '79
C.173 B.A. L.150 J.D. Mng. Atty., UAW Legal Servs. Plan
Alexander, Gregory G., (AV) ... '29 '54 C.976 A.B. L.309 J.D. [Ⓒ Shumaker,L.&K.]
Allotta, Joseph J., (AV) ... '47 '72 C.30 B.A. L.930 J.D. [Allotta&F.]
Allotta & Farley Co., L.P.A., (AV) ... 2222 Centennial Rd.
Allsop, D. Meredith ... '30 '78 C&L.851 B.A., J.D. 5142 Grosse Pointe Parkway‡

Alt, Damon D., Attorney at Law, L.L.C.
(See Findlay)

Altenburger, Scott R. ... '60 '85 C&L.851 B.Ed., J.D. Lucas Co. Dom. Rel. Ref.
Amend, Lisa A. ... '68 '94 C.473 B.A. L.150 J.D. Legal Coun., Dana Corporation
Anderson, Andrew E., (AV) ... '20 '48 C&L.477 A.B., J.D. [Ⓒ Spengler N.]
Anderson, Charles R., II '51 '78
C&L.851 B.B.A., J.D. Dist. Hearing Offr., Indus. Com. of OH
Anderson, J. Chris, (AV) ... '54 '80 C.967 B.A. L.851 J.D. Asst. Pros. Atty.
Anderson, James C., (AV) ... '53 '79 C.851 B.A. L.607 J.D. [Spengler N.]
Andres, Van P., (BV) ... '63 '89 C.608 B.A. L.851 J.D. [Ⓐ Ritter,R.M.&J.]
Anspach, Robert M., (AV) '48 '73 C&L.188 B.A., J.D.
[Anspach M.E.] (⊙Buffalo, NY)

Anspach Meeks Ellenberger LLP, (AV) BR
300 Madison Avenue, Suite 1600, 43604-2633 ⊙
Telephone: 419-246-5757 Fax: 419-321-6979
URL: http://www.anspachlaw.com
Robert M. Anspach; Mark D. Meeks; Richard F. Ellenberger; Paul F. Burtis (Resident, Tiffin, Ohio Office); Jane C. Dell (Resident, Tiffin, Ohio Office); Kent D. Riesen; John J. Jablonski (Resident, Buffalo, New York Office); Garrick O. White; James R. Carnes; Marjan Neceski (Not admitted in OH);—Daria A. Carr (Resident, Buffalo, New York Office); James W. Fruth (Resident, Tiffin, Ohio Office); Gregory H. Wagoner; J. Christine Chiriboga (Resident, Buffalo, New York Office); Steven E. Carr (Resident, Buffalo, New York Office); Kevin J. Kruppa (Not admitted in OH; Resident, Buffalo, New York Office); Jessica W. Straub; J. Randall Engwert; Nathan R. Boyd; Michael W. Jackson; Joohong Park (Not admitted in OH; Resident, Buffalo, New York Office); Cheryl L. Hitzel (Resident, Buffalo, New York Office). Of Counsel: John R. Wanick.
Insurance Defense and Corporate Litigation, Railroad Defense, Employers Intentional Tort Defense, Unemployment Compensation, Environmental Law, Employment Law, Products Liability Law, Risk Management and Medical Malpractice Defense. Trials and Appeals. Probate Law, Trust Law, Real Estate Law, Banking Law.
Tiffin, Ohio Office: Dell, Burtis & Anspach, L.L.P., 60 Sycamore Street, 44883. Telephone: 419-447-6181. Fax: 419-447-6332.
Buffalo, New York Office: Main Place Tower, Suite 2400, 14202-3724. Telephone: 716-856-5012. Fax: 716-852-2485.

See Professional Biographies, TOLEDO, OHIO

Antonini, Michael J., (BV) ... '58 '83 C.602 B.A. L.851 J.D. 520 Madison Ave.
Antonini, Thomas J., (AV) ... '63 '88 C&L.602 B.A., J.D. [Robison,C.&O.]
Arce, Roman, (BV) ... '67 '92 C.602 B.A. L.477 J.D. [Marshall&M.]
Armacost, James Stephen, (BV) ... '47 '76 C.347 B.S. L.851 J.D. Lucas Co. CSEA
Armbruster, Clare Cass, (BV) ... '61 '86 C.105 B.S.B.A. L.608 J.D. [Ⓒ Wise&D.]
Armstrong, Vernelis Kinsey ... '35 '61 C&L.912 B.A., J.D. U.S. Cts.
Arnold, Gregory L., Law Offices of, (AV) '53 '80
C&L.851 B.B.A., J.D. 608 Madison Avenue, Suite 1400
Arnold, W. David, (AV) ... '49 '74 C&L.477 B.A., J.D. [Arnold,C.G.&B.]

Arnold, Caruso, Green & Belazis, Ltd., (AV)
1822 Cherry Street, 43608-2801
Telephone: 419-241-2200 Telecopier: 419-255-7623
URL: http://www.arnoldandcaruso.com
Members of Firm: W. David Arnold; Paul T. Belazis; James D. Caruso; Merritt W. Green, III. Of Counsel: R. Michael Frank; Merritt W. Green, II; James H. Ellis, III.
Business, Bankruptcy, Creditors Rights, Constitutional Law, Contract Law, Commercial Litigation, Federal Practice, Civil Litigation, Personal Injury, Wrongful Death, Admiralty Maritime, F.E.L.A., Municipal, Civil Rights, Employment Law, Civil Trial Practice in State and Federal Courts, Products Liability, Medical Malpractice, Professional Attorney Discipline.
Reference: Fifth Third Bank of Toledo.

See Professional Biographies, TOLEDO, OHIO

Arquette, James A. ... '— '90 C&L.851 B.B.A., J.D. Art Iron Inc.
Ashley, William ... '71 '98 C.243 B.A. L.851 J.D. 416 N. Erie Street, Suite 200
Atkin, Jean E. ... '54 '79 C.97 B.S. L.608 J.D. Admr., Com. Pleas Ct.
Atkins, Maureen O., (BV) ... '64 '94 C.97 B.S. L.851 J.D. 7140 Finchley Ct
Aubry, Jude T., (AV) ... '40 '66 C.608 B.A. L.851 J.D. 608 Madison Avenue
Aubry, M. Scott, (BV) ... '69 '95 C.602 B.A. L.608 J.D. [Shumaker,L.&K.]
Ault, Tim Allen, (BV) ... '59 '86 C.97 B.S. L.851 J.D. [Malone,A.&F.]
Austin, Douglas V. ... '37 '78 C.611 B.A. L.851 J.D. 3450 W. Central Ave.
Avery, Laurie J. ... '70 '98 C.696 B.A. L.930 J.D. [Ⓐ Reminger&R.]
Avila, Janine T., (BV) ... '50 '91 C.473 B.A. L.851 J.D. [Connelly,J.&C.]
Baehren, James W., (AV) '50 '78 C.608 B.S. L.851 J.D.
Sr. V.P., Gen. Coun. and Secy., Owens-Illinois, Inc.
Baer, Elizabeth E., (BV) ... '67 '95 C.475 B.A. L.851 J.D. [Marshall&M.]
Bainbridge, David R., (AV) ... '58 '83 C.473 B.S. L.851 J.D. [Fuller&H.]
Baither, C. Philip, III, (BV) ... '53 '80 C.976 B.A. L.851 J.D. [Robison,C.&O.] ⊙
Baker, Gerald A., (CV) ... '50 '89 C.608 B.S. L.857 J.D. 3539 Turret Green Dr.
Baker, Kenneth C., (AV) ... '52 '77 C.473 A.B. L.608 J.D. [Eastman&S.]
Baker, Kimberly S. ... '69 '00 C.1283 B.S. L.607 J.D. [Ⓐ Eastman&S.]
Baker, Richard S., (AV) ... '29 '57 C.309 A.B. L.477 J.D. 2819 Falmouth Rd.
Baldwin, Raymond D. ... '02 '40 C&L.851 LL.B. 3033 March Dr.‡
Balk, Hess and Miller, LLP, (BV) ... 5744 Southwyck Boulevard
Ballenger, Brian J., (BV) ... '59 '85 C.97 B.A. L.851 J.D. [Ballenger&M.] ⊙
Ballenger & Moore Co., L.P.A., (BV) ... 405 Madison Ave., Ste. 2020 (⊙Northwood)
Balyeat, Thomas M., (BV) ... '51 '76 C.363 B.S. L.851 J.D. [Cline,C.&W.]
Bamman, H. William, (AV) ... '34 '63 C&L.851 B.A., LL.B. [Ⓒ Manahan,P.B.&D.]
Banks, Gerald William ... '38 '73 C&L.851 B.B.A., J.D. 709 Madison Avenue, Suite 314

Baran, Piper, Tarkowsky, Fitzgerald & Theis Co., L.P.A., (AV)
608 Madison Avenue, Suite 1620, 43604 ⊙
Telephone: 419-241-2900 Fax: 419-241-3002
URL: http://www.baranlaw.com
Donald E. Theis;—Stephen D. Long.
General Civil Practice. Trials in all Courts. Insurance Defense, Corporate, Family Law, Estate Planning, Personal Injury, Products Liability and Construction Law. Commercial Litigation. Suretyship. Environmental and Governmental Liability, Professional Liability, Worker's Compensation.

See Professional Biographies, TOLEDO, OHIO

Barber, Kaper, Stamm & Robinson
(See Wauseon)

Barciz, Rosemarie Ann '55 '83 C.607 B.A. L.851 J.D.
Sr. Atty., Advocates for Basic Legal Equality, Inc.
Barger, Brian P., (BV) . . . . '54 '84 C.608 B.A. L.851 J.D. [Brady,C.&S.]
Barkenquast, David L., (BV) . . . . '39 '67 C&L.851 B.A., J.D. 1 Seagate
Barnes, Mark S., (BV) . . . . '64 '95 C.893 B.A. L.446 J.D. [Bugbee&C.]
Barnett, Michael R. . . . . '76 '02 C.607 B.S. L.150 J.D. [Eastman&S.]
Baronas, Ann M., (CV) . . . . '68 '93 C&L.851 B.B.A., J.D. 413 N. Michigan Street
Barone, Guy T., (AV) '46 '73 C.201 B.S. L.851 J.D.
320 North Michigan Street, 4th Floor
Barone, John J. . . . . '13 '36 C.473 L.608 LL.D. 2841 Westchester‡
Barrett, John Adams, Jr. '62 '88 C.31 B.A. L.309 J.D.
(adm. in CO; not adm. in OH) Univ. of Toledo Coll. of Law
Barron, John C., (AV) . . . . '51 '78 C.477 B.A. L.813 J.D. [Shumaker,L.&K.]
Barrow, Craig S. . . . . '51 '80 C&L.851 B.B.A., J.D. 4972 Damascus Dr.
Barry, Gordon R., (BV) . . . . '48 '76 C.851 B.B.A. L.285 J.D. [Barry&F.]
Barry & Feit, (BV) . . . . 520 Madison Ave.
Bates, James D. . . . . '47 '72 C.354 B.A. L.851 J.D. Com. Pleas J.
Bates, Julia R., (AV) . . . . '50 '77 C.967 B.A. L.851 J.D. Asst. Co. Pros.
Bates, William F., (AV) . . . . '44 '69 C.97 B.A. L.851 J.D. [Watkins,B.&C.]
Battani, Joseph A., JR., (BV) '55 '86
C.1121 B.S. L.851 J.D. 4032 N. Holland Sylvania Rd.
Bauer, Albin, II, (BV) . . . . '62 '90 C.1229 B.S. L.851 J.D. [Eastman&S.]
Bauer, David O., (AV) . . . . '46 '76 C.473 B.S. L.851 J.D. Mng. Asst. U.S. Atty.
Baum, Rick . . . . '64 '91 C.477 B.A. L.851 J.D. Asst. Pros., Lucas Co. Pros. Off.
Bayer, Richard W. . . . . '28 '59 C&L.851 J.D. 4540 Heatherdowns‡
Bayford, Anthony, (BV) . . . . '44 '74 C.97 B.S.B.A. L.851 J.D. 3126 W. Sylvania Ave.
Beach, William V., (BV) . . . . '62 '88 C.665 B.A. L.851 J.D. [Robison,C.&O.]
Beck, Margaret G., (AV) . . . . '67 '92 C.475 B.A. L.477 J.D. 4052 Holland-Sylvania Rd.
Beebe, Raymond L., (BV) . . . . '54 '81 C&L.851 B.A., J.D. [R.L.Beebe]
Beebe, Raymond L., Co., LPA, (BV) . . . . 1107 Adams St.
Belazis, Paul T., (BV) . . . . '54 '79 C.207 B.A. L.851 J.D. [Arnold,C.G.&B.]
Bella, Johna M., (BV) . . . . '61 '86 C.602 B.A. L.851 J.D. [Goranson,P.&B.]
Bellman, Alan N. . . . . '48 '73 C.477 B.S.E. L.608 J.D. Pres., Bell Binders Co.
Belt, Jenifer A., (AV) . . . . '71 '95 C.473 B.A. L.851 J.D. [Shumaker,L.&K.]
Bennett, Marshall A., Jr., (AV) . . . . '55 '80 C.851 B.A. L.608 J.D. [Marshall&M.]
Bennett, Yvonne D., (BV) . . . . '62 '89 C.393 B.A. L.477 J.D. [Bunda S.&D.]
Benziger, Julia E. . . . . '72 '02 C.607 B.S. L.851 J.D. [Robison,C.&O.]
Berebitsky, Michael J., (AV) . . . . '48 '73 C.347 B.S. L.1119 J.D. 500 Madison Ave.
Berry, Richard L., Jr., (AV) '58 '83
C.679 B.S. L.851 J.D. Sr. Div. Coun., Opers., Owens Corning
Best, Eileen M. . . . . '60 '93 C&L.851 B.B.A., J.D. [Shumaker,L.&K.]
Best, Libbey W. Call, (BV) . . . . '72 '97 C.94 B.A. L.851 J.D. [Cooper&W.] ⊙
Bhalla, Roma '75 '00 C.477 B.A. L.494 J.D.
(adm. in KY; not adm. in OH) Assoc. Coun., ProMedica Health System
Biesiada, Shawn Thomas . . . . '74 '00 C&L.851 J.D. [S.T.Biesiada]
Biesiada, Shawn T., Esq. . . . . 500 Madison Ave., Ste. 555
Bingle, William J., (AV) . . . . '46 '71 C.602 B.A. L.851 J.D. 520 Madison Ave., Ste. 524
Birchall, David R. . . . . '27 '60 C.645 B.S. L.8 LL.B. 3700 Heatherdowns Blvd. (Pat.)
Bires, Steven A. . . . . '55 '99 C&L.851 B.S., J.D. 3450 W. Central
Birmingham, John D., Sr., (CV) . . . . '64 '90 C.253 B.A. L.851 J.D. 4522 Lewis Ave.
Bishop, Daniel A., (AV) . . . . '52 '78 C.150 B.A. L.851 J.D. 608 Madison Ave., Ste. 1400
Bishop, J. James, II . . . . '53 '79 C&L.851 B.A., J.D. [Chase,G.&B.]
Bixler, R. Jeffrey, (AV) '45 '72 C.201 B.S. L.851 J.D.
V.P., Gen. Coun., & Secy., HCR Manor Care
Blachman, Marci J., (BV) '69 '94 C.910 B.A. L.365 J.D.
420 Madison Avenue, Suite 1100
Blake, Scott A., (BV) . . . . '66 '95 C&L.851 B.S.M.E., J.D. [MacMillan,S.&T.] (Pat.)
Blandin, Bradley L. . . . . '75 '04 C.333 B.S. L.851 J.D. [Robison,C.&O.]
Blank, Thomas C., (AV) . . . . '56 '81 C.473 A.B. L.930 J.D. [Shumaker,L.&K.]
Blaufuss, John A., Law Office of, (BV) '65 '91
C.851 B.A. L.608 J.D. 709 Madison Ave., Ste. 218
Bloom, Charles E., (BV) . . . . '46 '70 C.347 A.B. L.1119 J.D. [Herschel,A.B.&M.]
Bluhm, Graham A., (BV) . . . . '69 '95 C.49 B.S.B.A. L.851 J.D. [Eastman&S.]
Bobowick, Morton, (AV) . . . . '42 '66 C.102 B.A. L.309 J.D. [Eastman&S.]
Bodie, John F., Jr., (BV) . . . . '66 '91 C.679 B.A. L.851 J.D. [Marshall&M.]
Boesel, Milton C., Jr., (AV) . . . . '28 '53 C.976 A.B. L.309 J.D. [Ritter,R.M.&J.]
Boggs, Howard W., (AV) . . . . '13 '39 C.207 A.B. L.477 J.D. 5916 Cresthaven Lane‡
Boggs, John H., (AV) . . . . '46 '72 C.967 B.A. L.477 J.D. [Eastman&S.]
Bohl, Steven C. . . . . '53 '80 C.477 B.S.E. L.851 J.D. 534 Laskey Rd.
Bohmer, Robert W., (BV) . . . . '69 '94 C.97 B.S.Ed. L.851 J.D. [Watkins,B.&C.]
Boissoneault, Kevin J., (BV) . . . . '62 '88 C&L.851 B.A., J.D. [Gallon&T.]
Boldt, Daniel James . . . . '59 '86 C&L.851 B.A., J.D. 4912 N. Summit
Boldt, Richd. W., (BV) . . . . '19 '51 C&L.851 B.B.A., J.D. 920 Spitzer Bldg.
Bolotin, Samuel G., (BV) . . . . '45 '75 C.188 B.S. L.851 J.D. [Bolotin]
Bolotin, Sandra Campo, (BV) . . . . '45 '79 C&L.851 B.A., J.D. 5241 Southwyck Blvd.
Bolotin Co., LPA, (BV) . . . . 4349 Talmadge Road
Boney, Jacqueline M., (AV) . . . . '50 '76 C.477 B.A. L.851 J.D. [Cooper&W.]
Bonfiglio, Michael A., (AV) . . . . '55 '85 C.97 B.S. L.851 J.D. [Connelly,J.&C.]
Bonfiglio, Paul R., (AV) . . . . '57 '89 C.381 B.S. L.851 J.D. [Vassar,D.D.&B.]
Bonini, Aleta M., (AV) . . . . '54 '79 C.976 A.B. L.575 J.D. [Shumaker,L.&K.]
Borell, John A., (BV) . . . . '47 '81 C.1044 B.A. L.851 J.D. Asst. Co. Pros. Atty.
Borell, John A., Jr., (BV) . . . . '69 '97 C&L.851 B.B.A., J.D. [Marshall&M.]
Borgess, Pamela A., (BV) . . . . '74 '00 C.97 B.A. L.851 J.D. [Zoll&K.]
Borgstahl, Gene T., (BV) . . . . '56 '84 C.226 B.S. L.851 J.D. [Borgstahl&Z.]
Borgstahl & Zychowicz, Ltd., (BV) . . . . 6591 W. Central Avenue, Suite 201
Borman, Amy J., (BV) . . . . '54 '90 C.967 B.Mus. L.851 J.D. [Eastman&S.]
Boss, Mark H., (BV) . . . . '64 '97 C&L.851 B.B.A., J.D. [Eastman&S.]
Bostelman, Lisa L. . . . . '76 '01 C.473 B.A. L.851 J.D. [Fuller&H.]
Bottoni, Paris M., (BV) . . . . '— '85 C.1044 B.A. L.851 J.D. 606 Adams St.
Bourguignon, Henry '31 '71 C.424 M.A. L.477 J.D.
(adm. in MI; not adm. in OH) Prof. of Law, Univ. of Toledo, College of Law
Bowman, J. Ronald . . . . '30 '59 C&L.851 B.B.A., J.D. Com. Pleas J.
Bowman, Theodore A., (AV) . . . . '53 '79 C.231 B.A. L.608 J.D. [Gallon&T.]
Boxell, Charles K., (AV) . . . . '44 '74 C.477 B.B.A. L.851 J.D. [Shindler,N.H.S.&M.]
Boyd, Nathan R. . . . . '75 '04 C.610 B.A. L.851 J.D. [Anspach M.E.]
Boyer, Peter G., (BV) . . . . '63 '92 C&L.851 B.S., J.D. 316 N. Michigan St.
Boyk, Charles E., (BV) . . . . '58 '83 C.97 B.A. L.851 J.D. [C.E.Boyk]
Boyk, Fredric M., (BV) . . . . '53 '94 C&L.851 B.B.A., J.D. 520 Madison Ave.

Boyk, Charles E., Law Offices, LLC, (BV)
502 Madison Avenue, Suite 655, 43604
Telephone: 419-241-1395 Fax: 419-241-8731
Charles E. Boyk.

(This Listing Continued)

Boyk, Charles E., Law Offices, LLC (Continued)
Personal Injury, Criminal Law.
See Professional Biographies, TOLEDO, OHIO

Bracy, William H., (AV) . . . . '45 '72 C&L.851 B.B.A., J.D. [Bracy&K.]
Bracy & Kuhl, A Legal Professional Association, (AV) . . . . 4127 Monroe Street
Brady, Jack J., (BV) . . . . '58 '84 C&L.851 B.B.A., J.D. [Brady,C.&S.]
Brady, Coyle & Schmidt, LLP, (BV) . . . . 4052 Holland-Sylvania Rd.
Bragg, Michael W., (BV) . . . . '60 '85 C.970 B.A. L.930 J.D. [Spengler N.]
Bragg, Ralph, (AV) . . . . '34 '59 C.631 B.A. L.309 J.D. [Spengler N.]
Braun, Timothy Francis . . . . '59 '87 C.705 B.A. L.608 J.D. Pros. Off.
Brazeau, James E., (AV) . . . . '53 '78 C&L.851 B.A., J.D. [Robison,C.&O.]
Brebberman, James A., (BV) . . . . '55 '82 C&L.851 B.A., J.D. 1030 Spitzer Bldg.
Breese, Donald E. '30 '55 C.473 A.B. L.930 LL.B.
Sr. V.P., The Fifth Third Bk. of Northwestern Ohio, N.A.
Breier, Gary A., (BV) . . . . '51 '78 C&L.851 B.A., J.D. [Schlageter,B.&B.] ⊙
Breier, Gregory J., (BV) . . . . '53 '81 C.97 B.L.S. L.851 J.D. 4149 Holland-Sylvania Rd.
Briley, Michael M., (AV) . . . . '45 '69 C.473 A.B. L.608 J.D. [Shumaker,L.&K.]
Britton, Eric D., (AV) . . . . '60 '85 C.685 B.A. L.1066 J.D. [Shumaker,L.&K.]
Britz, Harland M., (AV) . . . . '31 '56 C&L.477 B.A., LL.B. 416 North Erie Street, Suite 100
Brockel, Kathleen C. '62 '96 C.1352 B.A. L.1059 J.D.
Staff Atty., Advocates for Basic Legal Equality, Inc.
Brossia, Anne M. . . . . '— '01 C.1434 B.S.N. L.851 J.D. [Kitch D.W.V.&S.]
Browarsky, Phillip . . . . '50 '78 C.228 B.A. L.851 J.D. [P.Browarsky]
Browarsky, Phillip, & Co., L.L.C. . . . . 43 S. Huron St.
Browning, Melvin Lyle . . . . '45 '88 C.97 B.S. L.801 J.D. Appeals Ct.
Brubaker, Marcus J., (BV) . . . . '54 '81 C.608 B.S.B.A. L.851 J.D. [Eastman&S.]
Bruno, Dominic M., (BV) . . . . '33 '64 C&L.851 B.A., J.D. 608 Madison Ave.
Bruss, Howard G., (AV) . . . . '38 '67 C.215 B.S.Ch.E. L.851 J.D. [Fuller&H.] (Pat.)
Bryan, David A., (BV) . . . . '47 '76 C.532 B.A. L.851 J.D. [Wasserman,B.L.&H.]
Buchanan, Maria Quinto . . . . '51 '76 C&L.851 B.A., J.D. UAW Legal Servs. Plan
Buckey, Warren E. . . . . '26 '51 C.62 B.B.A. L.930 J.D. 1000 Jackson
Buckley, Kevin Patrick . . . . '55 '82 C.215 B.A. L.851 J.D. Chief Mag., Co. Prob. Ct.

Bugbee & Conkle, (AV)
Suite 1300, National City Bank Building, 405 Madison Avenue, 43604
Telephone: 419-244-6788 Telefax: 419-244-7145
Email: attorneys@bugbee-conkle.com
Members of Firm: John F. Wetli; Gregory B. Denny; Tybo Alan Wilhelms; Robert L. Solt, III; Robert P. King; Mark S. Barnes. Associates: Harvey C. Miller, Jr.; Andrew J. Wilhelms; Janelle M. Troendle. Of Counsel: Harry S. Bugbee (1895-1982); Allan J. Conkle.
General Civil Practice in all Courts, Corporation, Insurance, Labor and Employment, Real Estate, Personal Injury, Workers Compensation, Probate and Estate Planning and Trust Law, Taxation, Trials and Appeals.
Representative Clients: Ford Motor Co.; General Motors Corp.; Cooper Tire & Rubber Co.; Johnson Controls; Whirlpool Corporation.
See Professional Biographies, TOLEDO, OHIO

Bula, Megan A. Fitzpatrick . . . . '66 '98 C.912 B.S. L.477 J.D. [Shumaker,L.&K.]
Bullock, Joan R. '59 '83 C.475 B.A. L.851 J.D.
(adm. in MI; not adm. in OH) [J.R.Bullock]
Bullock, Joan R., PC . . . . 2801 W. Bancroft
Bunda, Robert A., (AV) . . . . '51 '77 C.602 A.B. L.477 J.D. [Bunda S.&D.]

Bunda Stutz & DeWitt, PLL, (AV)
One SeaGate, Suite 650, 43604
Telephone: 419-241-2777 Telecopier: 419-241-4697
URL: http://www.bsd-law.com
Robert A. Bunda; Barbara J. Stutz; Theresa R. DeWitt; David L. Gray; Yvonne D. Bennett; Sue A. Sikkema; Rebecca C. Sechrist;—Douglas E. Stallings (Resident); Barbara E. Machin; David C. Shook.
General Civil Trial and Appellate Practice in all State and Federal Courts. Insurance Defense, Personal Injury, Toxic Torts, Product's Liability, Workman's Compensation, Corporate, Commercial and Labor Law.
See Professional Biographies, TOLEDO, OHIO

Burke, Michael J., (BV) . . . . '47 '73 C.608 B.B.S. L.851 J.D. [Scheer,G.&B.]
Burkhardt, James G., (BV) . . . . '51 '76 C.645 B.A. L.851 J.D. Sr. Atty.
Burkhart, John J., (AV) . . . . '20 '49 C.850 A.B. L.607 J.D. 1234 Eleanor Ave.‡
Burns, Craig P., (BV) . . . . '65 '90 C.473 B.A. L.893 J.D. [Marshall&M.]
Burson, John H., (AV) . . . . '43 '68 C.951 A.B. L.477 J.D. [Shumaker,L.&K.]
Butler, Amy L. . . . . '72 '02 C&L.851 B.A., J.D. [Roetzel&A.]

Byers, Fritz, (AV) '55 '83 C.228 B.A. L.309 J.D.
Suite 824, The Spitzer Building, 43604
Telephone: 419-241-8013 Telecopier: 419-241-4215
Email: fbyers@accesstoledo.com
Communication Law, Constitutional Law, Health Care, Civil Trial Practice and Appellate Litigation, Labor and Employment Law.
General Counsel for: Block Communications, Inc.; Toledo Blade Co.; Buckeye Cablevision, Inc.; Pittsburgh Post Gazette.
Reference: Fifth Third.
See Professional Biographies, TOLEDO, OHIO

Cabanski, Robert W., (AV) . . . . '54 '79 C.851 B.B.A. L.477 J.D. [Fuller&H.]
Calamunci, Anthony J., Sr., (BV) . . . . '68 '94 C.24 B.A. L.607 J.D. [Roetzel&A.]
Calcamuggio, Larry G., (BV) '51 '77
C&L.851 B.B.A., J.D. 4149 Holland-Sylvania Rd., Ste. 2
Callahan, John J., (AV) . . . . '22 '52 C.363 A.B. L.477 LL.B. [McHugh,D.&M.]
Callahan, Margaret W. . . . . '16 '53 C.523 A.B. L.851 J.D. 3658 Willow Ln. Dr.‡
Callender, C. Duane, (AV) . . . . '42 '67 C&L.608 B.A., J.D. Fiberglas Tower
Cameron, Donald H., (AV) . . . . '50 '80 C.608 B.S. L.851 J.D. 413 Mich. St.
Camick, Daniel G., (BV) . . . . '61 '87 C.607 B.A. L.851 J.D. [Camick&K.]
Camick & Keil, L.P.A., (BV) . . . . 3230 Central Park West, Suite 106
Campbell, Bruce A. '41 '74 C.210 B.A. L.477 J.D.
(adm. in MI; not adm. in OH) Prof. of Law, Univ. of Toledo
Candiello, Vedo R., (BV) . . . . '47 '73 C.973 B.S. L.851 J.D. [V.R.Candiello]
Candiello, V. Robert, Attorney at Law, (BV) . . . . 4859 W. Sylvania Ave., Ste. A
Canestraro, Eugene F., (BV) . . . . '59 '85 C.608 B.A. L.851 J.D. [Cline,C.&W.]
Carey, John M., (AV) . . . . '51 '78 C.951 B.A. L.851 J.D. [Watkins,B.&C.]
Carlisle, James Edward . . . . '44 '97 C.980 B.A. L.851 J.D. 110 Harmony Lane
Carnes, James R. . . . . '72 '98 C.476 B.S. L.851 J.D. [Anspach M.E.]
Carr, James G. . . . . '40 '66 C.385 B.A. L.309 LL.B. Chief U.S. Dist. J.
Carr, Richard H. . . . . '57 '83 C&L.851 B.A., J.D. [Balk,H.&M.]
Caruso, James D., (AV) . . . . '47 '78 C.608 B.A. L.851 J.D. [Arnold,C.G.&B.]
Casey, Julia K., (BV) . . . . '46 '73 C.911 B.A. L.851 J.D. [Casey&S.]
Casey, Peter R., III, (AV) . . . . '44 '74 C&L.851 B.A., J.D. [Eastman&S.]
Casey & Slaybod, (BV) . . . . 520 Madison St.
Cathey, Richard A., (CV) . . . . '54 '80 C.381 B.A. L.8 J.D. Nationwide Ins. Co.
Cavanaugh, Patrick B. . . . . '65 '00 C.1208 B.F.A. L.851 J.D. [Kitch D.W.V.&S.]
Cecil, Daniel O. . . . . '67 '04 C.1208 B.A. L.930 J.D. [Eastman&S.]

Chabler, Allan J., (BV) ....'35 '61 C&L.851 B.A., J.D. 6800 W. Central Ave.
Chang, Cynthia L., (BV) ....'54 '83 C.385 B.A. L.128 J.D. 4127 Monroe St.
Chapman, George L., (AV) '47 '76 C.188 A.B. L.145 J.D.
Pres., Health Care R.E.I.T., Inc.
Chappell, Erik Grant, (BV) ....'69 '94 C.477 B.A. L.851 J.D. [Lyden,L.&C.]
Chase, Richard A., (BV) ....'41 '67 C&L.851 B.A., J.D. [Chase,G.&B.]
Chase, Goff & Bishop, (BV) ....2650 North Reynolds Road Suite 3
Cherry, Jonathan B., (BV) ....'48 '75 C.97 B.A. L.851 J.D. 311 N. Superior St.
Choka, Byron S., (AV) ....'55 '80 C.611 B.A. L.851 J.D. [Spengler N.]
Christen, Frederick C. ......'29 '56 C.679 B.S. L.851 LL.B. The Fred Christen & Sons Co.
Christensen, A. Thomas, (AV) ....'52 '77 C.340 B.A. L.851 J.D. [Marshall&M.]
Christiansen, Robert G. ....'48 '73 C.97 B.A. L.851 J.D. Com. Pleas J.
Christy, John W. ....'58 '83 C.197 A.B. L.597 J.D. V. P. Transactions, Owens Corning
Chuparkoff, David F., (BV) ....'63 '88 C.980 B.A. L.161 J.D. [Ⓐ Manahan,P.B.&D.]
Cimerman, Adrian P., (AV) ....'53 '79 C.107 B.A. L.851 J.D. Spitzer Bldg.
Clark, Michael Leo '50 '89 C.260 B.A. L.213 J.D.
Staff Coun., Cincinnati Insurance Co.
Clark, Robert L., Jr., (BV) ....'46 '80 C.922 B.S. L.851 J.D. 1 Government Ctr.
Clark, Roger N. ....'37 '67 C.610 A.B. L.851 J.D. 2451 Cherry Hill Rd.
Cline, Cook & Weisenburger Co., L.P.A., (AV) .... 300 Madison Ave., Ste. 1100
Closius, Phillip J. '50 '75 C.602 B.A. L.178 J.D.
(adm. in NY; not adm. in OH) Law Prof.
Coble, John A., (AV) ....'56 '84 C.473 B.Ph. L.851 J.D. [Albrechta&C.] (⊙Fremont)
Cocoves, Spiros P., (BV) ....'53 '85 C.1154 B.A. L.851 J.D. 610 Adams St., 2nd Fl.
Cohen, Richard A., (AV) ....'43 '70 C&L.851 B.A., J.D. 626 Madison Ave.
Cole, David A., (BV) ....'60 '86 [Gressley,K.&P.]
Cole, Eddie M., (AV) ....'20 '51 C&L.851 A.B., J.D. [Cole,E.M.]
Cole, Eddie M., L.P.A., (AV) .... 1117 Mackow Dr.
Coleman, Pariss M., II ....'70 '96 C.473 B.A. L.608 J.D. [Ⓐ Cooper&W.]
Collier, Steven P., (AV) ....'55 '81 C.967 B.A. L.150 J.D. [Connelly,J.&C.]
Collins, M. Charles, (BV) ....'64 '95 C.203 B.S. L.851 J.D. [Eastman&S.]
Commons, Donald W. ......'51 '76 C.377 B.A. L.597 J.D. Legal Coun., Dana Corporation
Conkle, Allan J., (AV) ....'18 '48 C&L.608 B.S., J.D. [Ⓒ Bugbee&C.]
Conklin, George J., (BV) ....'51 '78 C&L.851 B.A., J.D. [Gressley,K.&P.]
Conn, Charles L., (BV) ....'50 '75 C.597 B.A. L.851 J.D. 608 Madison Ave.
Connelly, Kristen A., (BV) ....'72 '98 C.174 B.A. L.851 J.D. [Ⓐ Marshall&M.]
Connelly, William M., (AV) ....'39 '64 C.363 B.S.S. L.608 J.D. [Connelly,J.&C.]

Connelly, Jackson & Collier LLP, (AV)
405 Madison Avenue Suite 1600, 43604
Telephone: 419-243-2100 Fax: 419-243-7119
URL: http://www.cjc-law.com
Members of Firm: William M. Connelly; Reginald S. Jackson, Jr.; Steven R. Smith; Steven P. Collier; Michael A. Bonfiglio; Janine T. Avila; Anthony E. Turley. Associates: Jason A. Hill; Tammy Geiger Lavalette; Timothy P. Nackowicz.
Trial Practice.

See Professional Biographies, TOLEDO, OHIO

Connelly-Gilliland, Karen ....'74 '01 C.93 B.A. L.851 J.D. Lucas Co. Pros. Off.
Connors, Timothy D., (BV) ....'51 '84 C.607 B.A. L.851 J.D. 4303 Talmadge Road
Contrada, Carol A., (BV) ....'51 '79 C.207 B.A. L.851 J.D. [Contrada&Assoc.]
Contrada, Charles V., (AV) ....'51 '79 C.385 A.B. L.851 J.D. [Contrada&Assoc.]

Contrada & Associates, (AV) BR
6641 Sylvania Avenue, Suite 8, 43560-3921
Telephone: 419-841-4400 Fax: 419-841-4463
Carol A. Contrada; Charles V. Contrada.
Plaintiff Personal Injury, Wrongful Death, Products Liability, Asbestos Litigation, Medical Malpractice, Auto Accidents.

See Professional Biographies, TOLEDO, OHIO

Cook, Gary G., (BV) ....'61 '92 C&L.851 B.S., J.D. Asst. Co. Pros.
Cooper, Candace Cohen, (BV) ....'48 '73 C&L.273 B.A., J.D. Asst. Pros. Atty.
Cooper, Cary Rodman, (AV) ....'42 '69 C.610 B.S. L.851 J.D. [Cooper&W.] ⊙
Cooper, David F., (AV) ....'45 '73 C.154 B.A. L.273 J.D. [Eastman&S.]
Cooper, David Rodman, (AV) ....'70 '95 C.472 B.A. L.228 J.D. [Cooper&W.] ⊙
Cooper, Kevin J. ....'— '01 C.313 B.S. L.851 J.D. [Ⓐ Spitler&W.L.&Assoc.]

Cooper & Walinski, A Legal Professional Association, (AV)
900 Adams Street, 43624 ⊙
Telephone: 419-241-1200 Fax: 419-242-5675
Email: toledo@cooperwalinski.com URL: http://www.cooperwalinski.com
Cary Rodman Cooper; Richard S. Walinski; T. Scott Johnston; John Czarnecki; Jacqueline M. Boney; Joseph P. Thacker; John K. Nelson; Janis E. Susalla Foley; Margaret J. Lockhart; Wm. Miles McKee; Janet E. Hales; David P. Strup; Joel M. Shere (Resident, Ann Arbor, Michigan Office); Gerald R. Kowalski; Lucy M. Snyder (Resident, Ann Arbor, Michigan Office); David Rodman Cooper; Beth A. Wilson; Libbey W. Call Best;—Kimberly Todd-Terpinski; Meredith L. Mercurio; E. Sharon Clark (Resident, Ann Arbor, Michigan Office); Pariss M. Coleman II; Jodi D. Spencer; Marguerite E. Zinz; Brad Francis Hubbell; Susan M. Heywood (Miedler); Jennifer Steves; George C. Ward (Retired); Jennifer S. Mistry; Joseph V. McNamara; Janelle M. Romp; Suzi Zazycki; Dusty Renée Tinsley; Nicole K. Schwieterman.
Business Planning, Civil Rights, Commercial Litigation, Commercial Transactions, Criminal, Employee Benefits, ERISA, Health Care, Insurance Coverage, Labor and Employment, Public Law, Probate Litigation, Product Liability, Professional Negligence, Real Estate, School Law.
Ann Arbor, Michigan Office: 206 South Fifth Avenue, Suite 400. Telephone: 734-663-6535. Fax: 734-663-0996.

See Professional Biographies, TOLEDO, OHIO

Cooperman, Ronald M., (AV) ....'43 '73 C.473 B.S. L.851 J.D. [Stockwell&C.]
Cosme, Keila D. ....'68 '94 C.94 B.A. L.1003 J.D. 202 N. Erie St.
Cotter, Thomas A. ....'62 '88 C&L.477 B.A., J.D. [Shumaker,L.&K.]
Cottier, Geoffrey A., (BV) ....'47 '76 C.608 B.A. L.851 LL.B. 520 Madison Ave.
Cottrill-Bell, Marlene (Neema) M., (BV) '52 '87
C.97 B.A. L.851 J.D. [Shumaker,L.&K.]
Covrett, C. Craig, (BV) .....'48 '75 C&L.851 B.B.A., J.D. 2727 N. Holland-Sylvania Rd.
Cox, Beverly J. ....'65 '90 C.97 B.A. L.851 J.D. [Ⓐ Dixon&H.]
Coy, Edwin A., (AV) ....'49 '74 C.117 B.A. L.608 J.D. [Coy,K.&P.]

Coy, Konieczny & Peppel, LLC, (AV)
405 Madison Avenue, Suite 700, 43604
Telephone: 419-724-5252 Fax: 419-724-5255
Email: gpeppel@ckp-law.com URL: http://www.ckp-law.com
Edwin A. Coy; Timothy A. Konieczny; Gregg A. Peppel; Evy M. Jarrett.
Commercial Real Estate, Corporate and Finance, Estate Planning and Probate, Commercial Litigation, Insurance Coverage Litigation.

See Professional Biographies, TOLEDO, OHIO

Coyle, David J., (BV) ....'60 '87 C.63 B.S. L.608 J.D. [Shumaker,L.&K.]
Coyle, Lori A., (BV) ....'61 '98 C&L.851 B.S., J.D. [Ⓒ Rohrbachers L.C.&T.]
Cramer, Bruce A., (AV) ....'36 '68 C&L.851 B.B.A., J.D. 3146 W. Central Ave.
Cramer, Dorcas ....'60 '86 C.236 B.A. L.607 J.D. Dist. Ct. of Appls.
Creamer, Jeffrey S., (AV) ....'51 '79 C.201 B.A. L.930 J.D. [Shumaker,L.&K.]
Cron, Nicholas J., (BV) ....'48 '74 C.1024 B.S. L.851 J.D. [Rohrbachers L.C.&T.]
Croniser, Gretchen E., (CV) ....'57 '96 C&L.851 B.A., J.D. 5742 Cresthaven Lane

Crosgrove, Darrell Marion ....'62 '93 C&L.851 B.S., J.D. [D.M.Crosgrove]
Crosgrove, Darrell M., Law Offices of ....5660 Southwyck Blvd., Ste. 100
Crosser, Joan M. ....'— '93 C.97 B.S.B.A. L.851 J.D. [Ⓐ Allotta&F.]
Crotte, Alberto D. ....'67 '94 C&L.851 B.B.A., J.D. Toledo Legal Aid Soc.
Crouch, Victor R., (AV) '46 '78 C.97 B.A. L.851 J.D.
V.P. & Gen. Coun., Port Lawrence Title & Tr. Co.
Crozier, Ryan E. ....'74 '03 C.608 B.A. L.1370 J.D. [Ⓐ Kitch D.W.V.&S.]
Cubbon, Denise Navarre, (AV) ....'53 '81 C.30 B.A. L.851 J.D. Asst. Co. Pros.
Cubbon, Frank W., Jr., (AV) ....'— '53 C.25 A.B. L.851 J.D. [Cubbon&Assoc.]
Cubbon, Kyle Alison ....'54 '84 C&L.851 B.S., J.D. [Cubbon&Assoc.]
Cubbon, Stuart F., (AV) ....'57 '81 C.105 B.A. L.851 J.D. [Cubbon&Assoc.]
Cubbon and Associates Co., L.P.A., (AV) .... 405 North Huron Street
Culver, Jeffery A. ....'70 '02 C.124 B.A. L.851 J.D. [Ⓐ Eastman&S.]
Cuneo, Richard P. ....'65 '92 C.473 B.A. L.451 J.D. [Ⓐ Reminger&R.]
Curphey, John M., (AV) ....'26 '53 C&L.608 B.A., J.D. [Robison,C.&O.]
Czarnecki, John, (AV) ....'40 '72 C&L.851 B.B.A., J.D. [Cooper&W.]
Czerniakowski, Joseph L., (AV) ....'28 '54 C&L.276 A.B., J.D. 3626 S. Detroit‡
Dalrymple, Thomas L., (AV) ....'21 '47 C&L.477 A.B., J.D. 1 Seagate
Damrauer, Carol L., (BV) ....'— '82 C&L.851 B.A., J.D. 1018 Adams St.
D'Angelo, Joseph M., (BV) ....'65 '94 C.980 B.A. L.1003 J.D. 202 N. Erie St.
Dansack, Michael P., Jr., (BV) ....'60 '85 C&L.851 B.S.I.E., J.D. [Gallon&T.]
D'Arcangelo, Bradley M., (BV) ....'70 '97 C.473 B.S. L.851 J.D. [Ⓐ Kroncke,D.S.&F.]
D'Arcangelo, Joseph M., (BV) ....'59 '84 C.473 B.S. L.851 J.D. [Kroncke,D.S.&F.]
D'Arcangelo, Julie M., (BV) ....'65 '91 C.473 B.S. L.851 J.D. 2255 West Laskey Road
D'Arcangelo, Michael J., (AV) ....'32 '63 C&L.851 B.A., LL.B. [Kroncke,D.S.&F.]
Davis, Diane Vulich, (AV) ....'56 '83 C.97 B.L.S. L.930 J.D. [Shumaker,L.&K.]
Davis, Geoffrey H., (BV) ....'43 '73 C.967 B.A. L.850 J.D. 3501 Wesleyan Dr.
Davis, Guy-Michael B. ....'36 '66 C.95 B.A. L.851 J.D. Pres., Sam Davis Co., Inc.
Davis, Paul A. ....'51 '80 C.648 B.S. L.851 J.D. Rumpf Develpm't Corp.
Davis, Philip C., (BV) ....'49 '77 C.851 B.A. L.607 J.D. 626 Madison Ave.
Davis, Terrance K., (BV) ....'56 '89 C.1154 B.A. L.912 J.D. [Shumaker,L.&K.]
Dawson, Jennifer J., (AV) ....'56 '84 C.473 B.A. L.851 J.D. [Marshall&M.]
Dawson, Joseph P., (AV) ....'55 '81 C.608 B.A. L.851 J.D. [Vassar,D.D.&B.]
Day, Clarence A. ....'10 '36 C.851 L.608 LL.B. 5017 Macklyn Dr.
Day, Willis F., IV ......'55 '80 C.610 B.B.A. L.851 J.D. V.P., Willis Day Properties, Inc.
Dear, H. James ....'45 '77 [H.J.Dear]
Dear, H. James Law Office ....4817 Walker Avenue
De Backer, Michael L. '47 '73 C&L.900 B.A., J.D.
(adm. in KS; not adm. in OH) V.P., Gen. Coun. & Secy., Dana Corp.
Dech, Merle R., Jr., (BV) ....'61 '91 C.477 B.A. L.851 J.D. 915 Spitzer Bldg.
Decker, Lori W., (AV) ....'54 '78 C&L.37 B.A., J.D. [Marshall&M.]
Decker, Michael E. '55 '82 C.97 B.S. L.851 J.D.
V.P., Fifth Third Bk. of Northwestern Ohio, N.A.
DeClark, Peter O., (BV) ....'65 '90 C.352 B.B.A. L.1209 J.D. [Ⓐ Williams,J.L.G.&S.]
Degidio, Anthony J., Jr. ....'55 '98 C&L.851 B.A., J.D. 3738 Treelawn Dr.
Deitch, Michele Yve '61 '86 C.31 B.A. L.309 J.D.
(adm. in MA; not adm. in OH) Off. of Spec. Master
DeLaney, Cormac B., (AV) ....'49 '75 C.363 A.B. L.851 J.D. [Manahan,P.B.&D.]
Deller, Scott G., (BV) ....'64 '90 C.477 B.A. L.347 J.D. [Shumaker,L.&K.]
Deller, Stefanie E. ....'74 '99 C.477 B.A. L.880 J.D. [Ⓐ Shumaker,L.&K.]

Denmead Law Office
(See Columbus)

Denny, Gregory B., (AV) ....'48 '73 C.910 B.S.B.A. L.608 J.D. [Bugbee&C.]
DeNune, Ralph, III, (AV) ....'44 '75 C.610 B.F.A. L.851 J.D. [McHugh,D.&M.]
Desmond, Patrick J. ....'60 '97 C&L.851 B.A., J.D. 4626 Willys Pkwy.
Dettinger, James F., (BV) ......'43 '74 C.973 B.S.B.A. L.851 J.D. [Shindler,N.H.S.&M.]
Devaney, Kevin D., (AV) ....'63 '91 C.107 B.S. L.117 J.D. [Eastman&S.]
Devine, Andy ....'21 '48 C.999 L.436 LL.B. Juv. Ct. J.
Dewhirst, Peter A., (BV) ....'68 '94 C.477 A.B. L.851 J.D. [Shindler,N.H.S.&M.]
DeWitt, Theresa R., (BV) ....'53 '83 C.477 B.G.S. L.150 J.D. [Bunda S.&D.]
Diesing, Gary R., (AV) ....'48 '75 C&L.477 B.B.A., J.D. [Shumaker,L.&K.]
Diller, Steven L., (BV) ....'55 '80 C.432 B.S. L.851 J.D. 1107 Adams St.
Dillon, Thomas P., (BV) ....'65 '90 C.477 B.A. L.602 J.D. [Shumaker,L.&K.]
Dills, Alan B., (AV) ....'44 '73 C&L.851 B.B.A., J.D. [Vassar,D.D.&B.]
DiSalle, Anthony B., (AV) ....'39 '66 C&L.851 B.B.A., J.D. 316 N. Michigan St.
DiSalle, John D., (BV) ....'64 '91 C.347 B.S. L.851 J.D. One Seagate #999
Dixon, Blondell ....'48 '74 C.217 B.A. L.930 J.D. 316 N. Michigan, Suite 514

Dixon, Randall C., (AV) '53 '80 C&L.851 B.A., J.D.
3361 Executive Parkway, 43606 ⊙
Telephone: 419-536-8600 Fax: 419-534-5934
(Also Member, Dixon & Hayes, Ltd.).
Civil Litigation, Real Estate, Consumer Law.

See Professional Biographies, TOLEDO, OHIO

Dixon, Randall C., (AV) ....'53 '80 C&L.851 B.A., J.D. [Dixon&H.] (⊙Toledo)
Dixon, Robert B., (BV) ....'28 '53 C.851 B.A. L.477 J.D. [Ⓐ Dixon&H.]
Dixon, Thomas A., (AV) .....'57 '82 C.608 B.S. L.851 J.D. [Eastman&S.] (⊙Columbus)
Dixon & Hayes, Ltd., (AV) ....3361 Executive Pkwy., Ste. 100
Doherty, James H.O. ....'— '99 C.477 B.A. L.228 J.D. 1000 Jackson
Dolgorukov, D. Edward, (BVⓉ) '44 '72
C&L.912 B.S.I.E., J.D. [Marshall&M.] (See Pat. Sect.)
Doneghy, Charles J. ....'38 '65 C&L.851 B.B.A., J.D. Com. Pleas J.
Donovan, Kimberly A. ....'71 '02 C.97 B.S. L.851 J.D. [Ⓐ Kerger&Assoc.]
Dorf, Michael D., (BV) ....'41 '66 C&L.851 B.A., J.D. 2 Maritime Plz.
Dorner, Renisa A. ....'63 '88 C.203 B.S. L.150 J.D. [Wise&D.]
Douglas, Julie A. ....'74 '01 C&L.851 B.A., J.D. [Ⓐ Roetzel&A.]
Dover, Thomas E., (AV) ....'— '80 C&L.201 B.S., J.D. [Gallagher S.] ⊙
Dow, Martin P., (BV) ....'48 '73 C.1113 B.S. L.851 J.D. 1030 Spitzer Building
Downey, Patrick J. ....'54 '93 C.475 B.S. L.150 J.D. [Ⓐ Eastman&S.]
Doyle, Lewis & Warner, (AV) .... P.O. Box 2168
Drabik, Sandra Ann ....'47 '80 V.P. & Gen. Coun.
Driscoll, Perry F., (BV) ....'45 '72 C&L.851 B.A., J.D. Juv. Pros.
Drowatzky, John N. ....'36 '79 C.378 B.S. L.851 J.D. 3332 Brantford Rd.‡
Ducey, Ernest D., (BV) '58 '83 C.608 B.S. L.851 J.D.
5330 Heatherdowns Blvd., Ste. 105
Duffin, John P., (BV) '51 '77 C&L.851 B.A., J.D.
(adm. in MI; not adm. in OH) 608 Madison Avenue
Dugan, Thomas A., (BV) ....'47 '74 C&L.851 B.S., J.D. 2460 Navarre Avenue
Duggan, James F., (AV) ....'30 '60 C.276 B.S. L.273 LL.B. 1000 Jackson
Duhart, Myron C., (BV) ....'69 '97 C.971 B.A. L.851 J.D. 1024 Indiana Avenue
Dunn, Darlene Jeanne, (BV) ....'51 '77 C.1154 B.A. L.851 J.D. 2945 Riva Ridge Rd.
Dzienny, Michael A. ....'61 '86 C.97 B.B.A. L.851 J.D. [Dzienny&Assoc.]
Dzienny & Associates, LPA .... 500 Madison Ave., Ste 200
Easterwood, Cynthia A. '56 '89 C.1021 B.A. L.851 J.D.
V.P., Tr. Dept., National City Bank, Northwest

Eastman & Smith Ltd., (AV)
One Seagate, Twenty-Fourth Floor, P.O. Box 10032, 43699-0032 ⊙
Telephone: 419-241-6000 Fax: 419-247-1777
Email: firm@eastmansmith.com URL: http://www.eastmansmith.com
Members of Firm: Frank D. Jacobs; Patrick J. Johnson; James F. Nooney; Bruce L. Smith; Morton Bobowick; Henry N. Heuerman; John H. Boggs; John T. Landwehr; David L. Kuhl; Richard T. Sargeant; Kenneth C. Baker; Robert J. Gilmer, Jr.; Peter R. Casey, III; David F. Cooper; Rudolph A. Peckinpaugh, Jr.; Ronald J. Tice; Thomas A. Dixon; Gary M. Harden; Barry W. Fissel; Joseph A. Gregg; Roger Paul Klee; Stuart J. Goldberg; Thomas J. Gibney; Steven D. Reinbolt; Dirk P. Plessner; James L. Rogers; David W. Nunn; David C. Krock; Albin Bauer, II; Peggy Mattimoe Sturgeon; Lane D. Williamson; Michael W. Regnier; Kevin D. Devaney; Bennett H. Speyer; Amy J. Borman; Marcus J. Brubaker; Matthew D. Harper; M. Charles Collins; Graham A. Bluhm; Michael P. Henry; Bruce D. Lazar; James W. Millon; James B. Yates; Mark A. Shaw (Resident, Columbus Office); John H. Koehler. Associates: Mark H. Boss; Mary Jo Tarini; Scott D. Newsom; Gary L. Miller; Jeffrey M. Stopar; Jeffrey D. Snavely; Kimberly S. Baker; Fadi Victor Nahhas; Gene R. Abercrombie; Heidi N. Eischen; Carrie L. Sponseller; Michael R. Barnett; Lynn Vuketich Luther; Patrick J. Downey; Laurie A. Watson; Richard L. Johnson; Maria Limbert Markakis; Connie S. Swemba; Alexandra M. Stump; Anthony R. Modd; A. Brooke Phelps; Jeffery A. Culver; Roy V. Pitman; Shawn M. Tracey; Kimberly A. Starr; Denise A. Mueller; Daniel O. Cecil; Sarah E. Pawlicki; Andrea B. Smoktonowicz. Of Counsel: Howard M. Friedman.
General Civil Practice: Corporate, Business, Banking, Taxation, Real Estate, Securities, Antitrust, Environmental, Public, Labor and Employment, Civil Rights, Employee Benefits, Insurance, Hospital and Health Care, Estate Planning, Pension and Estate Planning, Probate, Workers Compensation, Commercial Litigation, Litigation, Immigration and Naturalization.
Counsel for: DaimlerChrysler Corp.; Envirosafe Service of Ohio, Inc.; Glasstech, Inc.; The Hartford; Huntington National Bank; Toledo-Lucas County Port Authority.
Columbus, Ohio, Office: 100 East Broad Street, Suite 1300, 43215. Telephone: 614-280-1770. Fax: 614-280-1777.
Findlay, Ohio Office: 725 South Main Street, 45840. Telephone: 419-424-5487. Fax: 419-424-9860.
See Professional Biographies, TOLEDO, OHIO

Edwards, Richard Walton '35 '59 C&L.188 B.A., J.D.
(adm. in NY; not adm. in OH) 3405 Darlington Road‡
Effler, Fanny P., (BV) ....'52 '79 C.276 B.A. L.851 J.D. 2830 Collingwood Boulevard
Eickholt, William C., (BV) .... '43 '68 C&L.851 B.A., J.D. [Cline,C.&W.]
Eischen, Heidi N. .... '75 '01 C&L.851 B.A., J.D. [Ⓐ Eastman&S.]
Eisler, Beth A. '46 '73 C&L.273 A.B., J.D.
(adm. in DC; not adm. in OH) Assoc. Dean, Univ. Toledo Col. of Law

Elk & Elk Co., L.P.A.
(See Cleveland)

Ellenberger, Richard F., (AV) .... '40 '65 C.611 B.A. L.608 LL.B. [Anspach M.E.]
Elliott, Thomas B. .... '64 '96 C&L.851 B.B.A., J.D. 4612 Luann Ave.
Ellis, Daniel T., (BV) .... '57 '87 C.116 B.A. L.851 J.D. [Fuller&H.]
Ellis, James H., III, (AVⓉ) .... '56 '81 C.950 B.S. L.1049 J.D. [Ⓒ Arnold,C.G.&B.]
Elrod, Bradley C., (BV) '56 '82 C.608 B.A. L.930 J.D.
608 Madison Avenue, Suite 1400
Emch, Gregg W., (AV) ....'59 '85 C.608 B.A. L.851 J.D. [MacMillan,S.&T.] (Pat.)

Emch, Schaffer, Schaub & Porcello Co., L.P.A., (AV)
One Seagate, Suite 1980, P.O. Box 916, 43697-0916
Telephone: 419-243-1294 Fax: 419-243-8502
URL: http://www.essp-law.com
Mark C. Schaffer; Charles R. Schaub; James F. Porcello, Jr.; Philip M. Rice; Patrick P. Pacella.
Patent, Trademark, Copyright, Licensing, Unfair Competition and Related Litigation.
See Professional Biographies, TOLEDO, OHIO

Emerson, Edwin G., (AV) ....'38 '66 C.207 B.A. L.477 J.D. [Shumaker,L.&K.]
Emery, Richard L., (BV) ....'64 '91 C.607 B.S.B.A. L.851 J.D. [Shindler,N.H.S.&M.]
Engel, Lauri Ann '70 '95 C.473 B.S. L.851 J.D.
Assoc. Coun., ProMedica Health Sys., Inc.
English, Ian Bradford ....'70 '01 C&L.851 B.A., J.D. Pros. Off., Lucas Co.
Engwert, J. Randall .... '73 '99 C.610 B.S. L.851 J.D. [Ⓐ Anspach M.E.]
Entenmann, Richard A., (AV) ....'27 '54 C&L.477 B.A., J.D. [Ⓒ Spengler N.]
Epstein, Robert, (BV) ....'52 '91 C&L.851 B.A., J.D. 5550 W. Central Ave.
Errington, Michael D., (AV) ....'42 '70 C&L.851 B.A., J.D. 3626 S. Detroit
Evans, Stephen P. .. '72 '98 C.608 B.S.A.A.E. L.851 J.D. [Marshall&M.] (See Pat. Sect.)
Evans, Denise Faith, (BV) ....1900 Monroe
Evans Klucas, Denise F., (BV) ....'58 '85 C.97 B.S. L.857 J.D. [D.F.Evans]
Failor, Gray L. ... '46 '75 C&L.851 B.A., J.D. Pres. & CEO, Toledo-Lucas Co. Port Auth.
Farell, Gregory C., (BV) ....'59 '84 C&L.851 B.B.A., J.D. [Malone,A.&F.]
Farley, Larry D., (BV) ....'51 '77 C.97 B.S. L.851 J.D. [Allotta&F.]
Farris, Ray A., (AV) ....'49 '75 C&L.608 B.A., J.D. [Fuller&H.]
Farthing, Dana M. ....'68 '99 C.777 B.A. L.851 J.D. Asst. Coun., Mid Am Bank
Fech, Matthew N. ....'74 '01 C.347 B.S. L.851 J.D. [Fech&F.]
Fech, Nicole Y. ....'— '01 C.827 B.S. L.851 J.D. [Fech&F.]

Fech & Fech, L.L.C.
Inns of Court Building, 405 North Huron Street, Suite 200, 43604
Telephone: 419-242-0461 Fax: 419-242-0463
Email: information@fech-law.com URL: http://www.fech-law.com
Members of Firm: Matthew N. Fech; Nicole Y. Fech.
Criminal Law, Juvenile Law, Delinquency, Misdemeanors, Felonies, Driving While Intoxicated, White Collar Crimes, Traffic Violations, Family Law, Divorce, Child Custody, Visitation Rights, Child Support, Dissolution.
See Professional Biographies, TOLEDO, OHIO

Feit, Elliot H., (BV) ....'51 '76 C.331 A.B. L.285 J.D. [Barry&F.]
Feldstein, Eden S., (BV) '42 '67 C.608 B.A. L.477 J.D.
316 N. Michigan Street, Suite 210
Feldstein, Jay E., (BV) ....'55 '79 C&L.851 B.A., J.D. [Kalniz,I.&F.]
Fell, George N., II, (BV) '41 '66
C.602 A.B. L.608 J.D. 3425 Executive Parkway, Suite 207
Ferguson, Kevin M., (BV) ....'55 '86 C&L.851 B.B.A., J.D. [Schnorf&F.]
Fernandes, Trevor Neil ....'68 '95 C&L.851 B.A., J.D. Probate Ct.
Fernandez-Bigras, Rita '54 '92 C.910 B.S. L.378 J.D.
Staff Atty., Advocates for Basic Legal Equality, Inc.
Fickel, David J. ....'53 '78 C.282 B.A. L.851 J.D. U.S. Bkrptcy. Ct.
Fiedler, Robert W., Jr. ....'67 '96 C.1122 B.A. L.851 J.D. [R.W.Fiedler,Jr.]
Fiedler, Robert W., Jr., LLC, Law Office of .... 202 N. Erie St.
Fink, Maara Adrianne '70 '96 C.156 B.A. L.851 J.D.
University of Toledo College of Law
Fischer, Edward J., (BV) ....'54 '84 C&L.851 B.Ed., J.D. 1900 Monroe
Fischer, Matthew J., (BV) ....'59 '91 C&L.851 B.B.A., J.D. [Marshall&M.]
Fischer, Raymond C., (BV) ....'47 '82 C.599 B.A. L.851 J.D. [Cline,C.&W.]
Fischer, William G., (AV) ....'48 '73 C.97 B.S.B.A. L.608 J.D. [Shumaker,L.&K.]
Fisher, Allan Scott, (BV) ....'42 '72 C.473 B.A.S. L.851 J.D. 4115 Overlook Blvd.
Fiske, Rex D. ....'46 '89 C.608 B.A. L.851 J.D. City of Toledo, Dept. of Law
Fissel, Barry W., (AV) ....'56 '81 C.608 B.A. L.150 J.D. [Eastman&S.]
Fister, Anna S. ....'— '03 C.318 B.A. L.201 J.D. [Ⓐ Gallagher S.] ⊙

FitzGerald, Sharon A., (BV) ....'44 '84 C.440 B.S. L.851 J.D. 2343 Old Stone Court
Fitzgerald, Timothy J., (AV) .... '— '89 C.436 B.S. L.1003 J.D. [Gallagher S.] ⊙
Fletcher, Pamela W., (BV) '45 '76 C.604 B.A. L.851 J.D.
Legal Coun., Dana Corporation
Flowers, Phyllis Denise ...'56 '01 C&L.851 B.S., J.D. Advocates for Basic Legal Equality
Foley, Elizabeth M., (CV) ....'73 '97 C.788 B.A. L.930 J.D. HCR Manor Care
Foley, Janis E. Susalla, (AV) ....'58 '86 C.932 B.A. L.831 J.D. [Cooper&W.] ⊙
Foley, Patrick J., (AV) .... '41 '66 C.602 A.B. L.851 J.D. Asst. U.S. Atty.
Folk, Vivian C., (BV) ....'51 '76 C.611 B.A. L.930 J.D. [Shumaker,L.&K.]
Forcht, Melan M. ....'71 '01 405 North Huron Street, Suite 200
Ford, Claudia Ann ....'52 C.97 B.S. L.851 J.D. 717 Madison Ave.
Fort, Jeffrey E., (AV) ....'52 '82 C.871 B.S. L.608 J.D. [Shumaker,L.&K.]
Fournier, Heather J. ....'76 '02 C.97 B.Agr. L.1148 J.D. [Ⓐ Shindler,N.H.S.&M.]
Fox, James H., (BV) ....'07 '32 C&L.851 J.D. 243 N. Huron St.
Frank, R. Michael, (AV) ....'40 '65 C.446 B.A. L.188 J.D. [Ⓒ Arnold,C.G.&B.]
Franklin, John D., (BV) '62 '91 C.8 B.S. & A.S. L.851 J.D.
420 Madison Ave., Ste. 1101
Franklin, Pauline ....'53 '00 C&L.851 B.A., J.D. [Franklin]
Franklin, Robert V., Jr. ....'26 '50 C.511 B.A. L.851 J.D. Ret. Com. Pleas J.‡
Franklin Law Office ....3601 W. Alexis Rd., Ste. 102, 1st Fl.
Franks, Ruth Ann ....'46 '75 C.412 B.A. L.851 J.D. Ct. of Common Pleas
Fraser, William H. ....'54 '78 C.103 A.B. L.588 J.D. 520 Madison Ave.
Frederickson, Craig F., (AV) ....'46 '73 C.475 B.A. L.597 J.D. [Frederickson,H.&K.]

Frederickson, Heintschel & King Co., L.P.A., (AV)
Suite 1212, 405 Madison Avenue, 43604-1207
Telephone: 419-242-5100 Fax: 419-242-5556
Craig F. Frederickson; Thomas W. Heintschel; Douglas W. King.
General Civil Practice. Trial and Appellate Practice. Creditor's Rights, Bankruptcy, Corporate, Real Estate, Business, Commercial, Probate and Estate Planning Law.
See Professional Biographies, TOLEDO, OHIO

Frey, Francis C., (BV) ....'49 '75 C.161 B.A. L.851 J.D. 608 Madison

Friedes, David E., & Associates, (BV) '58 '84 C.107 B.A. L.851 J.D.
6545 W. Central Avenue Suite 209, 43617-1034
Telephone: 419-842-9902 Fax: 419-842-0623
Email: daveatty@buckeye-express.com URL: http://www.toledodisabilitylaw.net
Bankruptcy, Consumer Bankruptcy, Juvenile Law, Family Law, Divorce, Personal Injury, Automobile Accidents, Dog Bites, Slip and Fall, Residential Real Estate Sales, Social Security, Social Security Disability, Workers Compensation.
See Professional Biographies, TOLEDO, OHIO

Friedman, Howard M., (AV) ....'41 '65 C.608 B.A. L.309 J.D. [Ⓒ Eastman&S.]
Friedman, Lawrence Michael, (BV) '54 '84
C.309 A.B. L.188 J.D. Pres., Toledo Building Servs. Co.
Fruth, Lynn L. ....'50 '76 C&L.851 B.A., J.D. V.P., The Danberry Co.
Fudacz, Paul M. '60 '91 C.339 B.S. L.365 J.D.
(adm. in IL; not adm. in OH) Legal Coun., Dana Corporation
Fugée, Patricia B., (AV) .... '65 '91 C.914 B.A. L.1292 J.D. [Roetzel&A.]
Fuhrman, Charles A. .... '33 '57 C&L.966 B.S., LL.B. Tamaron Country Club

Fuller & Henry Ltd, (AV)
One SeaGate Suite 1700, P.O. Box 2088, 43603-2088
Telephone: 419-247-2500 Telecopier: 419-247-2665
URL: http://www.FullerHenry.com
Members of Firm: Fred E. Fuller (1901-1981); Leslie Henry (1904-1976); James M. Morton, Jr.; Stephen J. Stanford; Ray A. Farris; Thomas M. George; Craig J. Van Horsten; Glenn L. Rambo; David R. Bainbridge; Dennis A. Lyle; Daniel T. Ellis; John E. Mauntler; Robert W. Cabanski; Scott T. Janson. Counsel: Fred J. Lange, Jr.; Howard G. Bruss. Associates: Melissa M. Oostmeyer; Lisa L. Bostelman.
General Civil Practice: Civil Litigation in all State and Federal Courts, Commercial, Labor and Employment, Workers' Compensation, Taxation, Estate Planning, Probate, Corporate Law, Real Estate, Health Care, Information Technology and Electronic Commerce.
See Professional Biographies, TOLEDO, OHIO

Fulop, Sharon M. ....'72 '97 C.851 B.A. L.608 J.D. [Shumaker,L.&K.]
Furey, Thomas R., (AV) .... '49 '75 C.973 B.S.B.A. L.851 J.D. [Kroncke,D.S.&F.]
Fynes, Jack G., (AV) ....'52 '77 C.980 B.A. L.851 J.D. [Shumaker,L.&K.]
Gabalac, Stephan M., (BV) ....'34 '61 C.604 B.A. L.608 J.D. 405 N. Huron St.
Gabriel, Gary E. .... '29 '56 C&L.851 B.A., J.D. Staff Atty.
Galernik, Gerald Eugene ....'45 '89 One Owens Corning Pkwy., 1E
Gall, Joanne Frances ....'49 '79 C.161 B.A. L.1003 J.D. [J.F.Gall]
Gall, Joanne F. ....2828 West Central Avenue, Suite 9
Gallagher, Thomas W., (AV) ...... '47 '75 C.973 B.S. L.1340 J.D. [Williams,J.L.G.&S.]

Gallagher Sharp, (AV)
(Formerly Hauxhurst, Sharp, Mollison & Gallagher)
420 Madison Avenue, Suite 1250, 43604 ⊙
Telephone: 419-241-4860 Telecopier: 419-241-4866
URL: http://www.gallaghersharp.com
Members of Firm: Thomas E. Dover; Timothy J. Fitzgerald;—Anna S. Fister; Thomas F. Naughton.
General Civil Practice. Insurance, Product Liability, Aviation, Railroad, Professional Negligence, Mass Tort, Construction, Environmental, Corporation, Securities, Probate Law, Workers' Compensation, Appellate.
Representative Clients Available Upon Request.
Cleveland, Ohio Office: Bulkley Building, Sixth Floor, 1501 Euclid Avenue, 44115. Telephone: 216-241-5310. Telecopier: 216-241-1608.
See Professional Biographies, TOLEDO, OHIO

Gallon, Jack E., (AV) ....'31 '55 C&L.477 B.A., J.D. [Gallon&T.]
Gallon & Takacs Co., L.P.A., (AV) ....3516 Granite Circle
Galvin, June R. ....'38 '64 C&L.851 B.A., J.D. Ret. Com. Pleas J.‡
Gamso, Jeffrey M., (AV) ....'49 '87 C.475 M.A. L.845 J.D. [Gamso H.&H.]
Gamso Helmick & Hoolahan, (AV) .... 1119 Adams St., 2nd Fl

Garrett, Stanley J., (BV) '60 '92 C.476 B.S. L.851 J.D.
5249 Secor Road, Suite 4, 43623
Telephone: 419-471-1488 Fax: 419-255-4513
Criminal Law, Traffic Violations, Misdemeanors, Felonies, Drivers License Suspension, Domestic Violence, Driving While Intoxicated, Trucking Law, Juvenile Criminal Law.
See Professional Biographies, TOLEDO, OHIO

Garwood, John A. ....'43 '69 C&L.851 B.B.A., J.D. Secy., Champion Spark Plug Co.
Gehring, Edwin F. ....'49 '78 C.679 B.A. L.851 J.D. 5360 Dubois St.
Geller, Paul L., (BV) ....'44 '71 C.331 B.A. L.851 J.D. Spitzer Building, Suite 450
George, Shannon Julienne, (BV) ....'70 '94 C.317 B.A. L.851 J.D. [Ⓐ Ritter,R.M.&J.]
George, Thomas M., (AV) ....'49 '75 C.951 B.A. L.930 J.D. [Fuller&H.]
Gerken, George E., (BV) ....'47 '97 C&L.851 B.S., J.D. 412 14th Street
Gernot, George, III, Law Office of, (AV) '48 '74
C.97 B.S. L.851 J.D. 520 Madison Avenue, Suite 545
Gertner, Marc, (AV) ....'32 '57 C.309 A.B. L.608 J.D. [Ⓒ Shumaker,L.&K.]
Gess, Thomas C., (BV) .... '47 '82 C&L.851 B.B.A., J.D. [Watkins,B.&C.]
Gessel, Barbara Faye ....'62 '87 C.610 B.B.A. L.851 J.D. The Blade
Geudtner, Mark C., (BV) ....'52 '79 C.97 B.S. L.851 J.D. 610 Adams Street, 2nd Floor

Gibb, James A. ....'62 '88 C.737 B.A. L.117 J.D. V.P. Litig., Owens Corning
Gibbons, Llewellyn J. '60 '92 C.999 B.A. L.588 J.D.
(adm. in NY; not adm. in OH) Univ. of Toledo, Coll. of Law
Gibney, Thomas J., (BV) ....'60 '85 C&L.477 B.A., J.D. [Eastman&S.] (☉Columbus)
Gibson, Lawrence, (BV) ....'46 '73 C&L.851 B.B.A., J.D. 5415 Monroe St.
Gibson, Thomas A., (AV) ....'56 '84 C&L.851 B.S.C.E., J.D. [Robison,C.&O.]
Gillespie, Ted C., (AV) ....'47 '75 C.477 B.S.E. L.851 J.D. [MacMillan,S.&T.] (Pat.)
Gilmer, Robert J., Jr., (AV) ....'50 '75 C.607 A.B. L.851 J.D. [Eastman&S.]
Glasser, George M. ....'28 '53 C&L.851 A.B., J.D. Ct. of App. J.
Goff, Martin E., (BV) ....'59 '85 C.97 B.A. L.851 J.D. [Chase,G.&B.]
Goldberg, Marcia R. ....'35 '64 C.608 B.A. L.851 J.D. Univ. of Toledo
Goldberg, Paul S., (BV) .....'47 '77 C.610 B.A. L.851 J.D. 6800 W. Central Ave., Ste. F3
Goldberg, Stuart J., (AV) ....'60 '85 C.31 B.A. L.94 J.D. [Eastman&S.]
Golden, Gary M. ....'51 '76 C.477 B.A. L.215 J.D. Legal Coun., Dana Corporation
Goldstein, Jeffrey I., (BV) ....'42 '68 C&L.851 B.A., J.D. [J.I.Goldstein]
Goldstein, Jeffrey Ira, (BV) .... 804 Spitzer Building
Gonzalez, Michael A., (CV) ....'72 '98 C.97 B.A. L.851 J.D. [Marshall&M.]
Goodwin, Thomas P. ....'61 '90 C.97 B.A. L.1003 J.D. Toledo Legal Aid Soc.
Goranson, James E., (AV) ....'52 '78 C.608 B.S. L.851 J.D. [Goranson,P.&B.]
Goranson, Roger W., (AV) ....'48 '76 C.5 B.A. L.851 J.D. [Goranson,P.&B.]

Goranson, Parker & Bella, The Law Offices of, (AV)
405 Madison Avenue Suite 2200, 43604
Telephone: 419-244-9500 Telecopier: 419-244-9510
URL: http://www.gplaw.com
Roger W. Goranson; Christopher F. Parker; Johna M. Bella; James E. Goranson. Associate: Gretchen F. Weston.
Real Estate, Bankruptcy, Insurance Defense, Negligence Law, Civil Litigation, Construction Law, Labor and Employment, Bank Law, Probate.
See Professional Biographies, TOLEDO, OHIO

Gorman, Francis X. ....'40 '67 C&L.851 B.A., J.D. Mun. J.
Gosline, Robert B., (AV) .... '13 '36 C.851 A.B. L.608 J.D. 5916 Cresthaven Ln.‡
Gosline, William H., (AV) ....'44 '70 C.207 B.A. L.608 J.D. [Shumaker,L.&K.]
Gottlieb, Arnold N., Law Office of, (BV) '52 '78
C.150 B.B.A. L.851 J.D. 608 Madison Avenue, Suite 1523
Gottlieb, Judith B., (CV) ....'36 '81 C.930 B.S. L.851 J.D. Lucas Co. Prob. Ct.
Gould, Kenneth D. ....'48 '75 C.608 B.S. L.117 J.D. Owens Corning
Goulding, Michael R., (BV) ....'66 '96 C.608 B.A. L.851 J.D. [Shindler,N.H.S.&M.]
Gouttiere, John P, (AV) ....'49 '74 C.97 B.A. L.607 J.D. [J.P.Gouttiere]

Gouttiere, John P, Co LPA, (AV)
520 Madison Avenue, Suite 1026, 43604-1341
Telephone: 419-242-9900 Fax: 419-244-8620 URL: http://www.lawyers.com/gouttiere
Email: johng@gouttierelaw.com URL: http://www.gouttierelaw.com
John P Gouttiere.
Business, Real Estate, Creditors Rights, Bankruptcy, Estate Planning, Elder Law, Probate, General Civil Practice in all State and Federal Courts.
Representative Clients: Banc One Corporation; National City Bank; Owens Illinois Inc.; Miles Homes Inc.; Lexington Insurance Co.; Medical Value Plan HMO; High Point Animal Hospitals, Inc.; Miller Ocular Prosthetics, Inc.
See Professional Biographies, TOLEDO, OHIO

Graham, Alan R., (BV) '57 '83 C.215 B.S. L.213 J.D.
(adm. in MI; not adm. in OH)
VP-Legal & Corp. Affairs, General Counsel & Secre., Pilkington North America, Inc.
Gray, David L. ....'52 '77 C.475 B.A. L.477 J.D. [Bunda S.&D.]
Green, Donald I., (BV) ....'41 '66 C.608 B.A. L.851 J.D. [Scheer,G.&B.]
Green, Merritt W., II ....'30 '55 C&L.447 B.A., LL.B. [▣ Arnold,C.G.&B.]
Green, Merritt W., III, (BV) ....'50 '76 C.385 B.A. L.851 J.D. [Arnold,C.G.&B.]
Greenberg, Nathan, (BV) ....'18 '42 C&L.851 Ph.B., LL.B. 3514 Orchard Trail
Greenfield, R. Kevin, (AV) ....'56 '81 C.97 B.A. L.851 J.D. 420 Madison Ave., Ste. 1101
Greenwood, Truman A., (AV) ....'49 '79 C.207 B.A. L.851 J.D. [Spengler N.]
Gregg, Joseph A., (BV) ......'56 '81 C.473 A.B. L.150 J.D. [Eastman&S.] (☉Columbus)

Gressley, Kaplin & Parker, LLP, (AV)
Suite 930, 608 Madison Avenue, 43604-1129 ☉
Telephone: 419-244-8336 Telecopy: 419-244-1914
Email: gkp@gkplaw.net URL: http://www.gkandp.com
Lynn H. Gressley (1913-2001); Julian M. Kaplin (1927-1995); Jerome R. Parker; Bruce S. Schoenberger; Rosalind Reiser (Resident, Monroe, Michigan Office); George J. Conklin; David A. Cole;—Todd J. Kuhn. Of Counsel: Howard B. Hershman.
General Civil Practice. Corporate, Tax, Real Estate, Banking, Land Use, Zoning, Business, Business Planning, Business Litigation, Contracts, Commercial, Bankruptcy, Wills and Probate, Trusts and Estates and Estate Planning Law. Trial and Appellate Practice, Commercial Collections, Retail Collections.
Representative Clients: Better Business Bureau Serving N.W. Ohio and S.E. Michigan, Inc.; Catawba Cleveland Development Corp.; Catawba Island Club; CBT Credit Services, Inc.; CBT Financial Services, Inc.; The Cavalear Corp.; Cavalear Realty Co.; Centel Cellular; The Credit Bureau of Toledo, Inc.; Faraday, Inc.
Monroe, Michigan Office: 324 Washington Street. 48161. Telephone: 734-384-1021. Fax: 734-384-1021.
See Professional Biographies, TOLEDO, OHIO

Griffin, Sharon L., (BV) ......'39 '83 C.477 B.A. L.851 J.D. 520 Madison Ave., Ste. 1039
Grigsby, Teresa L., (AV) ....'59 '85 C.97 B.S. L.851 J.D. [Spengler N.]
Groth, Stevin J., (CV) ....'62 '94 C.112 B.A. L.426 J.D. [S.J.Groth]
Groth, Stevin J., LLC, Law Offices of, (CV) .... 4032 Secor Road, Suite A
Grude, David G., (BV) ....'50 '79 C&L.851 B.E., J.D. 4253 Monroe St.
Guerin, Marshall W., (BV) '67 '92 C.231 B.A. L.851 J.D.
Trial Atty., Nationwide Mutual Insurance Co.
Gurecky, Marcia S., (BV) '56 '87 C&L.851 B.S., J.D.
Assoc. Coun., Fifth Third Bk. (Northwestern Ohio)
Gusses, George, (BV) ....'46 '73 C&L.851 B.Ed., J.D. [G.Gusses]
Gusses, George Co., L.P.A., (BV) .... 411 Michigan St.
Gustafson, John P., (BV) '59 '85 C.473 B.A. L.912 J.D.
316 N. Michigan Street, Suite 501
Gutchess, Allen D., Jr., (BV) ...'28 '60 C.477 B.S. L.851 LL.B. 1806 Madison Ave. (Pat.)
Gutowitz, Norton ....'24 '51 C&L.851 B.B.A., J.D. 4754 Whiteford Rd.
Guynes, Marlene, (CV) ....'52 '90 C.473 B.A. L.851 J.D. 4934 Rudgate Boulevard
Gwinn, Yolanda Denise ....'56 '84 C.382 B.S. L.607 J.D. Law Clk., U.S. Dist. Ct.
Hafner, Mark Alan ....'61 '87 C.999 B.A. L.851 J.D. 701 Jefferson Avenue
Halas, Daniel F. ....'22 '51 C&L.851 B.Sc., J.D. Spitzer Bldg.
Hales, Janet E., (BV) ....'57 '91 C.97 B.Ed. L.851 J.D. [Cooper&W.] ☉

Hales, Steven C. '60 '99 C.313 B.B.A. L.851 J.D.
5151 Monroe Street, Suite 105, 43623
Telephone: 419-346-7423 Fax: 419-841-0812
Email: shalesesq@myway.net URL: http://www.stevenhaleslaw.com
Family Law, Divorce, Child Custody, Child Support, Visitation Rights, Business Litigation, Business Formation, Corporations, Partnerships, Limited Liability Company Law, Mergers and Acquisitions, Business Planning, Small Business Law, Business Succession Planning, Family Business Law, Contracts, Licensing Agreements, Taxation, Real Estate, Commercial Leasing, Trusts and Estates.
See Professional Biographies, TOLEDO, OHIO

Hall, Nathan A. ....'78 '03 C.317 B.A. L.602 J.D. [▣ Shumaker,L.&K.]
Hamel, Gregory J. ....'57 '94 C&L.851 B.S.N., J.D. Coun., ProMedica Health Sys., Inc.
Hamilton, Ann D. ....'35 '77 C.915 B.A. L.851 J.D. Ref., Lucas Co. Domestic Rel. Ct.
Hamilton, Mary K., (AV) ....'26 '58 C.783 B.S. L.851 J.D. 606 Madison Ave.‡
Hamilton, Richard A., (BV) ....'32 '57 C&L.477 A.B., J.D. 520 Madison Ave.
Hamner, Jessica R. ....'78 '03 C.5 B.B.A. L.851 J.D. [▣ Watkins,B.&C.]
Hamner, Scott E. ....'53 '78 C.150 B.B.A. L.851 J.D. Findley, Davies & Co.
Handwork, Peter M. ....'41 '66 C.393 B.A. L.851 J.D. Ct. App. J.
Hanley, Harold T., Jr. ....'27 '55 C&L.851 A.B., J.D. 2465 Scottwood Ave.‡
Hanneman, Donna Pfouts ....'50 '90 C.97 B.A. L.851 J.D. Toledo Legal Aid Soc.
Hanson, Anastasia K. ....'56 '00 C&L.851 B.A., J.D. [Spengler N.]
Hanusz, Richard W. '37 '63
C.363 A.B. L.93 LL.B. Legal Coun., Co. Dept. of Human Servs.
Harden, Gary M., (AV) ....'55 '80 C.602 B.B.A. L.851 J.D. [Eastman&S.]
Hargreaves, Carol Jacobson ....'47 '78 C.97 B.A. L.851 J.D. Toledo Legal Aid Soc.
Harlett, William A. ....'40 '67 C&L.851 B.B.A., J.D. V.P., Louisville Title Agency
Harold, David Thomas ....'72 '00 C.97 B.A. L.851 J.D. Pros. Off.
Harper, Matthew D., (AV) ....'67 '92 C.49 B.A. L.851 J.D. [Eastman&S.]
Harris, Jay, (AV) ....'44 '69 C.532 B.S. L.851 J.D. [Harris R.T.]
Harris • Reny • Torzewski, LPA, (AV) .... 2 Maritime Plz., 3rd Fl.
Hartman, Stephen D. ....'71 '02 C&L.851 B.A, J.D. [▣ Kerger&Assoc.]
Harves, D. Scott ....'71 '96 C.473 B.A. L.851 J.D. Coun., Owens Corning
Hasbrook, Denise M., (AV) ....'60 '84 C&L.851 B.A., J.D. [Roetzel&A.]
Hasbrook, Richard C., (BV) ....'52 '77 C.610 B.S.C. L.851 J.D. 608 Madison Ave.
Haselman, Scott A., (BV) ....'69 '95 C&L.851 B.B.A., J.D. [Robison,C.&O.]
Hathaway, Lisa A. ....'60 '89 C&L.150 B.S., J.D. Health Care & Retire. Corp.
Hattner, Louis J., (AV) ....'27 '68 C&L.851 B.S., J.D. [▣ Spengler N.]
Hauptman, W. Reed ....'71 '98 C.473 B.S. L.880 J.D. [▣ Shumaker,L.&K.]
Hawes, Charles A. ....'50 '79 C.608 B.S. L.851 J.D. Stautzenberger Coll.
Hayes, Jill, (BV) ....'59 '90 C.608 B.S.S.W. L.851 J.D. [Dixon&H.]
Haynam, Douglas G., (AV) ....'54 '80 C.473 B.S. L.608 J.D. [Shumaker,L.&K.]
Hayward, John F., (AV) ....'37 '66 C.602 A.B. L.276 J.D. [▣ Shumaker,L.&K.]
Hayward, John P., (BV) ....'66 '95 C.602 B.A. L.851 J.D. [Spengler N.]
Haywood, Ryan H. '47 '79 C&L.477 B.A., J.D.
(adm. in MI; not adm. in OH) Asst. Gen. Coun., Owens-Illinois, Inc.
Hazard, Daniel G. ....'72 '01 C.608 B.A. L.851 J.D. [▣ Robison,C.&O.]
Heintschel, Thomas W., (AV) ....'52 '78 C.363 B.A. L.767 J.D. [Frederickson,H.&K.]
Helberg, Tom R., (BV) ....'59 '84 C.800 B.A. L.851 J.D. 5215 Monroe St., Ste. 4
Heller, Mark R. '51 '77 C.63 B.S. L.910 J.D.
Supvr. Atty., Migrant Div., Spec. Litig. Unit, Advocates for Basic Legal Equality, Inc.
Helmick, Jeffrey J., (AV) ....'60 '88 C.477 A.B. L.608 J.D. [Gamso H.&H.]
Helmick, Karen Henry ....'62 '89 C.183 B.A. L.608 J.D. Staff Atty., 6th Dist. Ct. of App.
Hendershott, Patrick David ....'66 '93 1900 Monroe St., Ste. 112
Henderson, David T., (BV) ....'71 '96 C.477 B.A. L.851 J.D. [▣ Kitch D.W.V.&S.]
Henderson, Karlene D. ....'64 '03 C&L.851 B.A., J.D. Asst. Co. Pros. Atty.
Henderson, Ronald R., Law Office of, (BV) '43 '73
C.871 B.S. L.608 J.D. 520 Madison Avenue, Suite 524
Henning, Fred E., (AV) ....'40 '66 C.851 B.A. L.608 J.D. 608 Madison Ave.
Henry, Michael P., (BV) ....'69 '94 C.436 B.A. L.146 J.D. [Eastman&S.]
Herbert, Edwin L. ....'50 '75 C.602 B.A. L.608 J.D. [Shumaker,L.&K.]
Herring, Barbara E., (BV) .....'45 '84 C&L.851 B.E., J.D. Dir. of Law, City Dept. of Law
Herschel, Henry B., (AV) ....'42 '67 C.693 B.S. L.851 J.D. [Herschel,A.B.&M.]
Herschel, Accettola, Bloom & Mills, (AV) ....615 Adams Street
Hershman, Howard B., (BV) ....'53 '78 C.851 B.A. L.608 J.D. [▣ Gressley,K.&P.]
Hess, H. Robert, (BV) ....'44 '70 C.610 B.B.A. L.851 J.D. [▣ Balk,H.&M.]
Heuerman, Henry N., (AV) ....'45 '70 C&L.608 B.A., J.D. [Eastman&S.]
Heyman, Joseph S., (AV) ....'13 '37 C&L.608 A.B., J.D. [▣ Spengler N.] ‡
Heywood, William H., III, (AV) ....'44 '69 C.207 B.A. L.208 J.D. [Shumaker,L.&K.]
Heywood (Miedler), Susan M. ....'76 '02 C.477 B.A. L.608 J.D. [▣ Cooper&W.]
Hickman, Gregg D., (BV) '52 '78 C.97 B.S.Ed. L.851 J.D.
3230 Central Park W., Ste. 106
Hicks-Hudson, Paula S. ....'51 '82 C.811 B.A. L.352 J.D. Lucas Co. Board of Elections
Higley, William E., II, (BV) ....'48 '76 C&L.851 B.A., J.D. 520 Madison Avenue
Hilbert, John W., II, (AV) ....'46 '71 C&L.608 B.A., J.D. [Shumaker,L.&K.]
Hill, Jason A. ....'74 '00 C.97 B.S. L.608 J.D. [▣ Connelly,J.&C.]
Hillebrand, Joseph R. ....'21 '58 C.602 A.B. L.851 J.D. 1010 Spitzer Bldg.
Hiller, Charles W., (AV) ....'54 '86 C.97 B.S. L.851 J.D. [Shumaker,L.&K.]
Hillmer, Felicity M. ....'64 '89 C.207 B.A. L.608 J.D. O.C.S. Management Corp.
Hirsch, Gordon H., (BV) '36 '72 C.610 B.S.C. L.851 J.D.
2727 N. Holland Sylvania Road
Hitaffer, Thedford I. ....'60 '97 C.890 B.A. L.1389 J.D. [▣ MacMillan,S.&T.] (Pat.)
Hixon, Mark A. ....'66 '92 C.150 B.S. L.607 J.D. [▣ Marshall&M.] (See Pat. Sect.)
Hoblet, Vaughn A., (AV) ....'46 '74 C.608 B.S. L.851 J.D. [Marshall&M.]
Hoch, Brian J., (BV) ....'56 '82 C.97 B.S. L.851 J.D. [Balk,H.&M.]
Hochberg, Sue Ann '56 '86
(adm. in FL; not adm. in OH) Center for Effective Govt.
Hoffer, Jeremiah Anthony, II, (BV) ....'46 '83 C&L.851 B.B.A., J.D. Dep. Co. Auditor
Hoffman, Edward L. ....'45 '73 C&L.851 B.A., J.D. 450 W. Delaware Ave., Rm. 3
Hollins, Sharon E. ....'61 '92 C&L.851 B.A., J.D. Legal Coun.
Holmes, Martin J., (AV) ....'45 '71 C.436 B.S. L.851 J.D. [Shindler,N.H.S.&M.]
Holmes, Martin J., Jr., (BV) ....'70 '95 C.309 B.A. L.851 J.D. [Shindler,N.H.S.&M.]
Holmes, Terry S., (CV) '65 '96 C&L.851 B.B.A., J.D.
Staff Atty., UAW Legal Servs. Plan
Honold, David L., (BV) ....'54 '79 C.967 B.A. L.851 J.D. [Wasserman,B.L.&H.]
Hoolahan, Catherine G., (AV) ....'46 '87 C.706 B.A. L.851 J.D. [Gamso H.&H.]
Horne, Timothy J., (BV) ......'49 '85 C.970 B.A. L.851 J.D. 4303 Talmadge Rd., Ste. 102
Horner, Patricia, (BV) ....'55 '88 C.942 B.A. L.900 J.D. 412 Fourteenth Street
Horvath, Jeffrey J. ....'75 '01 C&L.851 B.A., J.D. [▣ Wasserman,B.L.&H.]
House, Stephen E., (BV) ....'70 '98 C&L.851 B.B.A., J.D. [▣ Manahan,P.B.&D.]
Hubbell, Brad Francis ....'61 '02 C.475 B.A. L.1187 J.D. [▣ Cooper&W.]
Huffman, John L., (BV) ....'59 '88 C.608 B.S. L.851 J.D. 520 Madison Avenue, Suite 520
Hummer, Donal, Jr., (BV) ....'57 '83 C.477 B.G.S. L.851 J.D. [Spitzer&H.]
Hunter, John J., Jr., (BV) ....'61 '86 C&L.851 B.A., J.D. [Hunter&S.]

Hunter & Schank Co., L.P.A., (BV)
One Canton Square, 1700 Canton Avenue, 43624-1378
Telephone: 419-255-4300 Fax: 419-255-9121
Thomas J. Schank; John J. Hunter, Jr.;—Kurt J. Lindower.
Business Law, Bankruptcy, Bankruptcy Litigation, Creditor's Rights, Probate, Small Business Consulting and Real Estate Law. Civil Litigation in all Federal and State Courts.
References: Community First Bank; Farm Credit Services of Mid-America; ACA; Ag Credit, ACA.
See Professional Biographies, TOLEDO, OHIO

Hutcheson, William G. ....'48 '83 C.913 B.A. L.851 J.D. Mag., Comm. Pleas
Hyrne, Michael E., (AV) ....'53 '80 C&L.851 B.A., J.D. [Doyle,L.&W.]
Ingram, Arthur C., (BV) ....'53 '83 C&L.851 B.A., J.D. [Mollenkamp&I.]

Inks, Allen W., (BV) '54 '92 C.912 B.E.T. L.851 J.D. [MacMillan,S.&T.] (Pat.)
Irmen, James H., (BV) '59 '86 C&L.851 B.B.A., J.D. [Marshall&M.]
Jackson, Louise A., (AV) '48 '77 C.97 B.A. L.851 J.D. [Spengler N.]
Jackson, Michael W. '77 '03 C&L.608 B.S.B.A., J.D. [Ⓐ Anspach M.E.]
Jackson, Reginald S., Jr., (AV) '46 '71 C&L.608 B.A., J.D. [Connelly,J.&C.]
Jacobs, Frank D., (AV) '35 '59 C.851 B.B.A. L.477 J.D. [Eastman&S.]
Jacobs, Marvin K., (AV) '30 '53 C.851 B.A. L.477 J.D. 241 N. Superior Street
Jaffee, Thomas J. '58 '85 C&L.851 B.B.A., J.D.
Ptnr., Lublin, Sussman, Rosenberg & Damrauer CPA's
James, Mary M. '57 '99 C&L.851 B.A., J.D. [Steltenpohl,J.&M.]
James, Timothy C., (AV) '54 '80 C.473 B.A. L.608 J.D. [Ritter,R.M.&J.]
Janson, Scott T., (BV) '57 '91 C&L.851 B.B.A., J.D. [Fuller&H.]
Jarrett, Evy M., (BV) '66 '91 C.880 B.A. L.228 J.D. [Coy,K.&P.]
Jeffery, James R., (AV) '38 '65 C.608 B.A. L.851 J.D. [Spengler N.]
Jenks, William J. '48 '84 C&L.851 B.A., J.D. P.O. Box 351750
Jennings, Linda J., (BV) '49 '89 C&L.851 B.A., J.D. 413 N. Michigan St.
Jennings, William G. '47 '86 C&L.851 B.S., J.D. 413 North Michigan St.
Jensen, James D., (AV) '43 '70 C.967 B.A. L.851 J.D. 700 Adams St.
Jermann, Edmond L., Jr. '24 '56 C&L.851 J.D. 4222 W. Alexis Rd.
Jilek, Michael F., Sr., (AV) '41 '70 C.201 B.A. L.851 J.D. [Williams,J.L.G.&S.]
Joelson, Philip R., (BV) '34 '61 C.851 B.B.A. L.608 J.D. [Joelson&M.]
Joelson & Manore Co., L.P.A., (BV) 1776 Tremainsville Road
Johns, Jeanne Deimling '52 '82 C.608 B.A. L.851 J.D.
Litig. Dir., Advocates for Basic Legal Equality, Inc.
Johnson, D. Lee '63 '90 C.97 B.A.C. L.851 J.D. 3335 Meijer Dr.
Johnson, Justice G., Jr., (AV) '39 '64 C.473 B.A. L.477 LL.B. [Marshall&M.]
Johnson, Patrick J., (AV) '41 '67 C&L.851 B.S., J.D. [Eastman&S.]
Johnson, Richard L. '57 '94 C.999 B.S. L.851 J.D. [Ⓐ Eastman&S.]
Johnson, Willard A., (AV) '28 '54 C&L.851 LL.B. 4540 Heatherdowns Blvd.
Johnston, Jeffery B., (BV) '52 '81 C&L.851 B.A.B.Ed., J.D. 3645 Roberta Dr.
Johnston, T. Scott, (AV) '45 '70 C.210 B.A. L.851 J.D. [Cooper&W.] ⊙
Jones, Christopher F., (BV) '49 '78 C&L.502 A.B., J.D. [Jones&S.]
Jones, Ellen Garrison '48 '80 C.440 B.A. L.851 J.D.
Exec. Dir., Lucas Co. Children Servs.
Jones, Linda Ann, (BV) '51 '85 C&L.851 B.A., J.D. 520 Madison
Jones, Stewart W., (BV) '60 '89 C&L.851 B.A., J.D. Two Maritime Plaza, Third Floor

Jones & Scheich, (BV)
1600 Fifth Third Center, 608 Madison Avenue, 43604-1117
Telephone: 419-241-6450 Telecopier: 419-241-1540
Email: j-slaw@jonesscheich.com
Christopher F. Jones; Richard A. Scheich. Associate: Craig J. Wakefield.
Civil Litigation, Real Estate, Commercial Transactions, Corporate Law, Business Law, Contracts, Creditors Rights, Bankruptcy.
See Professional Biographies, TOLEDO, OHIO

Jordan, Joseph P., (AV) '37 '62 C.973 B.S. L.436 J.D.
4127 Monroe Street, 43606
Telephone: 419-473-1300 Fax: 419-473-0329
Email: joejordan355@aol.com URL: http://www.joejordanlaw.com
Civil and Criminal Litigation, DUI/DWI, Drug Crimes, Felonies, Juvenile Law, Misdemeanors, Parole and Probation, Traffic Violations, White Collar Crime, Zoning, Annexation, Municipal Law, Real Estate, Business Law, Personal Injury, Automobile Accidents, Dog Bites, Slip and Fall, Wrongful Death.
See Professional Biographies, TOLEDO, OHIO

Joseph, Regina M., (AV) '52 '79 C&L.608 B.A., J.D. [Shumaker,L.&K.]
Kaczala, Larry A., (BV) '56 '83 C&L.851 B.A., J.D. One Government Ctr.
Kalmbach, Frederick E. '68 '02 C&L.851 B.S., J.D. [Ⓐ McHugh,D.&M.]
Kalniz, Burton A., (BV) '39 '67 C.608 B.S. L.607 J.D. [Kalniz,I.&F.]
Kalniz, Steven M. '68 '03 C.1293 B.A. L.851 J.D. 2 Maritime Plz., 2nd Fl.
Kalniz, Iorio & Feldstein, (BV) 5550 W. Central Ave. (⊙Grand Rapids, MI)
Kanios, Peter N., (BV) '54 '82
C.608 B.S. L.851 J.D. Tr. Offr., Fifth Third Bk. N.W. Ohio
Kaplan, Robert Zachary, Law Office of '69 '02 C&L.851 B.A., J.D.
520 Madison Avenue
Kaplan, Robt. Z., (AV) '28 '55 C&L.608 B.A., LL.B. 830 Spitzer Bldg.
Katz, Arthur H. '25 '50 C.851 B.B.A. L.608 LL.B. 1101 Monroe St.
Katz, David A. '33 '57 C&L.608 B.S., J.D. 1716 Spielbusch Ave.‡
Katz, Randolph S., (BV) '54 '79 C.608 B.S. L.851 J.D. 1101 Monroe St.
Kean, John V., (BV) '44 '73
C.610 B.B.A. L.851 J.D. 3230 Central Park West Drive, Suite 116
Keeler, Dianne L. '48 '75 C.347 A.B. L.345 J.D. Staff Atty., Children's Servs.
Keener, Rex C. '30 '68 C.516 B.S. L.851 J.D.
Asst. V.P., The Fifth Third Bk. of Northwestern Ohio, N.A.
Keiffer, Lance M. '64 '89 C.276 B.A. L.477 J.D. Pros. Atty.'s Off.
Keil, Dennis M., (BV) '49 '84 C&L.851 B.Ed., J.D. [Camick&K.]
Keller, Jeffery Bruce, (BV) '59 '88 C&L.851 B.A., J.D. 416 N. Erie St., Ste. 200
Kelley, Thomas J., (BV) '57 '82 C.851 B.A. L.188 J.D. [Cline,C.&W.]
Kelly, Jill Bridgett '51 '82 C.477 B.A. L.851 J.D. Staff Atty., Ct. of App.
Kemnitz, Walter Robert, Jr. '57 '90
C.476 B.S. L.851 J.D. Law Clk., Lucas Co. Common Pleas Ct.
Kennedy, Wm. R. '19 '51 C&L.851 B.B.A., LL.B. 506 Spitzer Bldg.‡

Kenney & Niehaus, Ltd.
(See Sylvania)

Kerger, Richard M., (AV) '45 '74 C&L.608 B.A., J.D. [Kerger&Assoc.]

Kerger & Associates, (AV)
33 South Michigan Street, Suite 201, 43602
Telephone: 419-255-5990 Facsimile: 419-255-5997 URL: http://www.kergerkerger.com
Email: attorneys@kergerkerger.com URL: http://www.lawyers.com/kergerkerger
Richard M. Kerger. Associates: Stephen D. Hartman (Law Clerk); Kimberly A. Donovan.
Trial Practice, Appellate Practice, Criminal Law, Litigation.
See Professional Biographies, TOLEDO, OHIO

Killam, Thomas P., (AV) '46 '76 C&L.851 B.E., J.D. [Marshall&M.]
Kincade, Donald H. '50 '80 C.610 B.G.S. L.851 J.D. Pres. & CEO, First Merit Bank
King, Douglas W., (BV) '63 '91 C&L.851 B.A., J.D. [Frederickson,H.&K.]
King, Robert P., (BV) '57 '83 C.198 B.A. L.851 J.D. [Bugbee&C.]
King, Thos. R., (BV) '30 '55 C&L.602 A.B., LL.B. 300 Bell Bldg.
Kirby, Michael D. '55 '84 C.136 B.A. L.851 J.D. Mag., Luca Co. Dom. Rel. Ct.
Kirk, Hugh Adam, (AV) '16 '39 C.851 B.S. L.537 S.J.D. 4120 Tantara Dr. (Pat.)
Kirker, Judith A., (BV) '56 '81 C.216 B.A. L.851 J.D. Asst. Pros. Atty.
Kirkhope, Anne M., (BV) '66 '97 C.436 B.A. L.851 J.D. Asst. Pros. Atty.
Kirkpatrick, Joel J., Law Offices of '65 '00 C.49 B.S. L.215 J.D. 4895 Monroe Street
Kiroff, Carole R., (AV) '38 '83 C.97 B.S.Ed. L.851 J.D. 2770 Sandalwood Ave.
Kiroff, Donna Lee '48 '79 C.980 B.A. L.851 J.D. Ct. Admin.

Kitch Drutchas Wagner Valitutti & Sherbrook, (BV)
A Professional Corporation
Attorneys and Counselors
405 Madison Avenue Suite 1500, 43604-1235 ⊙
Telephone: 419-243-4006 Fax: 419-243-7333
URL: http://www.kitch.com
Principal: John Stephen Wasung (Principal). Associate Principal: Valerie A. Trudel. Senior Associates: Anne M. Brossia; Patrick B. Cavanaugh; David T. Henderson; Lori L. Perné. Associate: Ryan E. Crozier.
General Civil and Trial Practice in all State and Federal Courts. Appellate Practice. Medical, Legal, Products Liability, Food, Drug and Cosmetic, General Negligence, Insurance Coverage, Hospital, Environmental, Toxic Torts, Professional Liability, Employment Discrimination, Wrongful Discharge and Workers Compensation, Corporate Practice, Health Care, Commercial Litigation, Estate Planning and Securities, Federal and State Taxation.
Insurance Clients: CNA Insurance Co.; Crawford & Company; Hanover Insurance Company; Harco National Insurance Co.; Liberty Mutual Insurance Co.; Mackinaw Administrators, LLC; RLI/Mr. Hawley Insurance Co.; State Farm Insurance Co.; Vesta/Shelby Insurance Co.
Detroit, Michigan Office: One Woodward Avenue, Suite 2400, 48226-5485. Telephone: 313-965-7900. Fax: 313-965-7403.
Mount Clemens, Michigan Office: 10 South Main Street, Suite 307, 48043-7903. Telephone: 586-463-9770. Fax: 586-463-8994.
Okemos, Michigan Office: 2379 Woodlake Drive, 48864. Telephone: 517-381-4426. Fax: 517-381-4427.
Ann Arbor, Michigan Office: 303 Detroit Street, Suite 400, P.O. Box 8610, 48107-8610. Telephone: 734-994-7600. Fax: 734-994-7626.
Marquette, Michigan Office: Old City Hall, 220 West Washington, Suite 500, 49855-4344. Telephone: 906-228-0001. Fax: 906-228-0003.
See Professional Biographies, TOLEDO, OHIO

Kitchen, Margaret Ann '56 '83 C.643 B.A. L.851 J.D. [M.A.Kitchen]
Kitchen, Margaret A. 3230 Central Park West, Ste. 200
Klee, Roger Paul, (BV) '48 '74 C.475 B.A. L.477 J.D. [Eastman&S.]
Kleeberger, Patricia J. '69 '98 C&L.851 B.A., J.D. [Ⓐ Brady,C.&S.]
Klein, James Martin '44 '69 C.477 A.B. L.124 J.D. University of Toledo, Coll. of Law
Klumb, Marci L., (BV) '61 '87 C.477 B.S. L.273 J.D. [Ⓞ Lyden,L.&C.]
Knepp, James R., II, (AV) '64 '92 C.528 B.A. L.851 J.D. [Robison,C.&O.]
Knepp, Linda M. '66 '92 C.912 B.A. L.851 J.D.
Admin. Hearing Offr., Child Support Enforce. Agcy.
Knepper, Richard W. '47 '74 C&L.851 B.B.A., J.D. Ret. Ct. of App. J.
Koder, Stephen D., (BV) '51 '78
C.608 B.A. L.851 J.D. 3361 Executive Parkway, Suite 101
Koehler, John H., (BV) '50 '79 C.253 B.S. L.851 J.D. [Eastman&S.] (⊙Findlay)
Koenig, Robert A., (AV) '58 '83 C.930 B.A. L.564 J.D. [Shumaker,L.&K.]
Koester, Anne Y., (BV) '62 '88 C.97 B.S. L.851 J.D. One Seagate
Kolb, Matt, (AV) '17 '45 C&L.851 J.D. 405 Madison Avenue, Suite 2000‡
Kolb, Richard, (AV) '42 '67 C.210 B.A. L.608 J.D. [Kolb&Z.]

Kolb & Zigray, (AV)
National City Bank Building, 405 Madison Avenue, Suite 2000, 43604
Telephone: 419-244-3006 Fax: 419-246-4754
URL: http://www.kolbzigraylaw.com
Partners of Firm: Richard Kolb; Daniel F. Zigray.
Will Contests, Trust Contests, Will Constructions, Guardianship Disputes, Joint and Survivorship Disputes, Claims Against Estates, Claims Against Executors and other Fiduciaries, Power of Attorney Disputes, Probate Litigation, Trial and Appellate Practice.
See Professional Biographies, TOLEDO, OHIO

Kolodgy, Kathleen W., (BV) '58 '85 C.473 B.A. L.150 J.D.
520 Madison Ave., Suite 330
Kondalski, Kimberly S., (BV) '61 '87 C.97 B.A. L.851 J.D. [Watkins,B.&C.]
Konieczny, Timothy A., (AV) '57 '82 C.103 B.A. L.930 J.D. [Coy,K.&P.]
Konop, Alan S., (AV) '36 '63 C.477 B.A. L.851 LL.B. 413 Michigan St.
Kosydar, Walter J., (BV) '29 '73 L.851 J.D. 1020 Spitzer Bldg.
Kountouris, Louis E., (BV) '51 '82 C&L.851 B.E., J.D. Asst. Pros. Atty.
Kovacik, Leslie Ann '67 '98 C&L.851 B.A., J.D. City of Toledo, Dept. of Law
Kovacs, Patricia Ann '63 '93 C&L.851 J.D. 500 Madison Ave., Suite 525
Kowalski, Gerald R., (AV) '52 '80 C&L.851 B.S., J.D. [Cooper&W.]
Kranz, Michelle L., (BV) '67 '93 C.473 B.S. L.851 J.D. [Zoll&K.]
Kraus, Paul M., (AV) '32 '57 C&L.602 B.S.C., LL.B. [Ⓞ Marshall&M.]
Kreps, Gene A. '29 '57 C&L.851 B.B.A., LL.B. 4540 Vermaas Ave.‡
Kress, Kathleen A., (AV) '58 '84 C.201 B.A. L.178 J.D. [Shumaker,L.&K.]
Kreutz, William L., (AV) '23 '51 C.597 B.S. L.930 LL.B. 3904 W. Bancroft‡
Krick, Gene W. '28 '56 C&L.309 A.B., LL.B. 3450 W. Central Ave.
Krock, David C., (AV) '56 '82 C.97 B.S. L.851 J.D. [Eastman&S.]
Kroncke, William G., (AV) '34 '64 C&L.851 B.B.A., J.D. [Kroncke,D.S.&F.]
Kroncke, D'Arcangelo, Sutter & Furey, (AV) 2255 West Laskey Road
Krugh, Timothy D., (AV) '53 '78 C.528 B.A. L.851 J.D. [Robison,C.&O.]
Krull, Stephen K. '65 '90 C.234 B.S. L.146 J.D.
Sr. V.P. & Gen. Coun. & Secy., Owens Corning
Kruppa, Kevin J. '75 '03 C.1349 B.A. L.107 J.D.
(adm. in NY; not adm. in OH) [Ⓐ Anspach M.E.] (⊙Buffalo, NY)
Kuhl, David L., (AV) '50 '75 C.177 B.A. L.477 J.D. [Eastman&S.]
Kuhl, John R., (BV) '48 '77 C&L.851 B.A., J.D. [Bracy&K.]
Kuhlman, Timothy C., (BV) '66 '91 C.317 B.A. L.851 J.D. Mun. J.
Kuhn, Jeffrey C., (BV) '56 '82 C.97 B.A. L.1003 J.D. PorMedica Health System
Kuhn, Todd J. '76 '02 C.97 B.S. L.851 J.D. [Ⓐ Gressley,K.&P.]
Kurek, Kimberly Christine, (BV) '71 '98
C.97 B.A.C. L.851 J.D. 520 Madison Avenue, Suite 520
Kurt, Edward J., Jr., (BV) '51 '79
C&L.851 B.B.A., J.D. Legal Coun., Mercy & St. Charles Hospitals
Kurt, Patricia Hayden, (BV) '55 '82 C.475 B.A. L.851 J.D. [Spengler N.]
Lackey, Gerald B., (AV) '38 '62 C&L.608 B.A., J.D. [Ⓞ Harris R.T.]
Lackey, Jane L., (BV) '43 '79 C.608 B.Sci. L.851 J.D. 2107 Central Grv.
Lafferty, Jon A., (AV) '48 '73 C.97 B.S. L.607 J.D. [Williams,J.L.G.&S.]
Lah, Jack J. '79 '04 C.318 B.A. L.607 J.D. [Ⓐ Rohrbachers L.C.&T.]
Lambdin, Jennifer Marie '71 '98 C&L.851 B.A., J.D Staff Atty., Comm. Pleas. Ct.
Landry, Francis J., (AV) '51 '76 C.973 A.B. L.851 J.D. [Wasserman,B.L.&H.]
Landry, John A., (AV) '52 '77 C.973 A.B. L.851 J.D. [Wasserman,B.L.&H.]
Landwehr, John T., (AV) '44 '74 C.967 B.A. L.851 J.D. [Eastman&S.]
Lange, Fred J., Jr., (AV) '50 '75 C.97 B.S. L.608 J.D. [Ⓞ Fuller&H.]
LaRowe, William Clair '53 '86 C.854 B.S.E.E. L.851 J.D.
(adm. in VA; not adm. in OH) Sys. Integrator, Insite Digital Tech.‡
LaRue, Carl F., (AV) '29 '57 C.309 A.B. L.477 LL.B. 3553 Brookside Rd.‡
LaRue, Lawrence B., (CV) '44 '75 C&L.851 B.B.A., J.D. P.O. Box 23271
Latez, Glenn A. '48 '73 C&L.851 B.B.A., J.D. I.R.S.
Lauer, Steven K. '47 '77 C.823 A.B. L.1003 J.D. IRS
Lavalette, Peter N., (BV) '63 '94 C.869 B.S. L.851 J.D. [Robison,C.&O.]
Lavalette, Tammy Geiger, (BV) '69 '99 C.610 B.A. L.851 J.D. [Ⓐ Connelly,J.&C.]
LaValley, Daniel J., (AV) '60 '85 C&L.851 B.B.A., J.D. [LaValley,L.T.&S.]
LaValley, Richard G., (AV) '29 '53 C&L.851 B.B.A., J.D. [Ⓞ LaValley,L.T.&S.]
LaValley, Richard G., Jr., (AV) '58 '83 C&L.851 B.B.A., J.D. [LaValley,L.T.&S.]

LaValley, LaValley, Todak & Schaefer Co., L.P.A., (AV)
Building F, 5800 Monroe Street, P.O. Box 8726, 43623
Telephone: 419-882-0081 FAX: 419-882-4635
Email: office@lavalley-law.com URL: http://www.lavalley-law.com
Richard G. LaValley, Jr.; Daniel J. LaValley; Michael J. Todak; James E. Schaefer; Deidre A. Liedel; Timothy J. Semro. Of Counsel: Richard G. LaValley.
Taxation, Probate, Estate Planning, Trust, Corporate, Partnership, Entity Formation, Mergers & Acquisitions, Corporate Finance, Real Estate, Employee Benefits.
References: Capital Bank; Key Bank, Ohio.
See Professional Biographies, TOLEDO, OHIO

Lavender, Barbara Ann ....'51 '94 C&L.851 B.A., J.D. [B.Lavender]
Lavender, Barbara ....520 Madison Ave., Ste. 323
Lazar, Bruce D., (BV) ....'68 '95 C.363 B.S.B.A. L.851 J.D. [Eastman&S.]
Lebo, Louis S., (BV) ....'09 '44 C.608 B.A. L.851 J.D. 709 Madison Ave.
Lehman, Walter M., (AV) ....'14 '38 C.112 A.B. L.1066 LL.B. 840 Spitzer Bldg.
Leizerman, E. J., (AV) ....'46 '76 C&L.851 B.E., J.D. 717 Madison Ave.
Leizerman, Joseph-Jacques Sylvain, (BV) ... '57 '93 C&L.851 B.S., J.D. 7150 Granite Cir.
Lenavitt, David J., Attorney at Law, (BV) '68 '95
C.94 B.S. L.851 J.D. 4032 N. Holland-Sylvania Rd.
Lenga, Charles F., (BV) ....'22 '55 C&L.851 J.D. 620 Starr Ave.
Leonardi, Robert M. '48 '74 C&L.8 B.S.M.E., J.D.
Pat. & Trademark Coun., Dana Corporation (Pat.)
Leonhardt, Ronald F., (BV) ....'53 '92 C&L.851 B.A., J.D. 717 Madison Ave.
Leveton, Morton E., (BV) ....'29 '55 C&L.851 B.B.A., LL.B. 920 Spitzer Bldg.
Levin, Anita ....'50 '98 C.966 B.S.N. L.851 J.D. Co. Juv. Ct.
Levin, Marc S., (AV) ...... '54 '80 C.902 B.S. L.910 J.D. Legal Coun., Dana Corporation
Levine, Arleen R. ....'56 '82 C.608 B.S. L.851 J.D. 2026 Orchard Rd.
Levine, Joel A. ....'38 '63 C&L.477 B.A., J.D. [Ⓖ Spengler N.]
Levine, Marilyn Joy Brenner ....'56 '01 C.608 B.A. L.851 J.D. 3516 Granite Circle
Levy, Jeffrey D., (BV) ....'51 '77 C.608 B.S. L.851 J.D. 840 Spitzer Bldg.
Lewandowski, Paul S. .... '56 '91 C.477 B.S. L.276 J.D. Dir., Reg. Law, Owens Corning
Lewis, Debra Jean ....'54 '93 C.631 B.A. L.851 J.D. [D.J.Lewis]
Lewis, Ralph J., (BV) ....'40 '71 C&L.851 B.Ed., J.D. City Law Dept.
Lewis, Debra J. ....4841 Monroe Street, Suite 350
Liebenthal, Jon B., (AV) ....'60 '86 C.473 B.S. L.851 J.D. [Lyden,L.&C.]
Liedberg, Douglas H. '67 '92 C.697 B.A. L.602 J.D.
(adm. in IL; not adm. in OH) Sr. Coun., M&A, Dana Corp.
Liedel, Deidre A., (BV) ....'69 '98 C&L.851 B.B.A., J.D. [LaValley,L.T.&S.]
Light, C. Randolph, (AV) .... '40 '66 C.309 A.B. L.597 J.D. [Rohrbachers L.C.&T.]
Light, Neil H., (BV) ....'53 '79 C.150 B.A. L.851 J.D. 608 Madison Ave., Sre. 1400
Lindower, Kurt J. ....'63 '90 C.967 B.A. L.150 J.D. [Ⓐ Hunter&S.]
Lindsey, Robert K., (BV) ....'41 '70 C.97 B.A. L.851 J.D. [R.K.Lindsey]
Lindsey, Robert Kemp, (BV) ....615 Adams St.
Lingo, Jeffrey D., (BV) ....'57 '90 C&L.851 B.S., J.D. Off. Of Co. Pros.
Linker, Carol Wood ....'48 '79 C.476 B.B.A. L.851 J.D. Univ. of Toledo
Lipinski, Tracy A. ....'78 '03 C.62 B.A. L.8 J.D. 520 Madison Ave., Ste. 615
Lipton, Andrew S., (AV) ..... '52 '78 C.164 B.A. L.93 J.D. 316 N. Michigan St., Ste. 800
Lockhart, Margaret J., (AV) ....'60 '87 C.945 B.A. L.705 J.D. [Cooper&W.] ⊙
Lodge, Gregory T., (AV) ....'54 '82 C.851 B.A. L.602 J.D. [Shumaker,L.&K.]
Lodge, Terry Jonathan, (BV) ....'50 '79 C.880 B.A. L.851 J.D. 316 N. Michigan St.
Loisel, Michael J. ....'72 '98 C.473 B.A. L.851 J.D. Co. Prosecutor
Lombardo, Carla A. ....'62 '92 C.62 B.S. L.851 J.D. [Ⓐ Spitler&W.L.&Assoc.]
Long, Stephen D. ....'64 '94 C.607 B.A. L.851 J.D. [Ⓐ Baran,P.T.F.&T.]
Longthorne, William E., (BV) ...... '26 '51 C.851 A.B. L.477 J.D. 3425 Executive Pkwy.
Loukx, Adam Wade .... '64 '93 C.608 B.A. L.117 J.D. City of Toledo Dept. of Law
Lowenstein, J. Jeffrey, (BV) ....'48 '75 C.967 B.A. L.851 J.D. [Cline,C.&W.]
Ludd, Oksana M., (AV) ....'54 '80 C.823 B.A. L.851 J.D. [Shumaker,L.&K.]
Lupica, Thomas A., (BV) ....'64 '90 C&L.851 B.A., J.D. [Spengler N.]
Luther, Lynn Vuketich ....'75 '02 C.837 B.A. L.851 J.D. [Ⓐ Eastman&S.]
Luxon, Susan L., (CV) ....'60 '85 C.97 B.S. L.851 J.D. Asst. Pros.
Lyden, Patricia G., (BV) ....'56 '80 C.260 B.A. L.851 J.D. [Lyden,L.&C.]

Lyden, Liebenthal & Chappell, Ltd., (AV) BR
5565 Airport Highway, Suite 101, 43615
Telephone: 419-867-8900 Fax: 419-867-8909
Email: lydenlaw.com
Patricia G. Lyden; Jon B. Liebenthal; Erik Grant Chappell;—Brenda A. Ray. Of Counsel: Marci L. Klumb.
Business, Commercial, Corporate, Taxation, Probate and Estate Planning, Real Estate, Civil, Business and Commercial Litigation, Family Law, Labor and Employment Law
See Professional Biographies, TOLEDO, OHIO

Lydy, R. Jeffrey, (AV) '46 '72 C&L.851 B.S., J.D.
4930 Holland-Sylvania Road, 43560-2149
Telephone: 419-882-7100 Fax: 419-882-7201
Email: jefflydy@lydymoan.com URL: http://www.rjeffreylydy.com
Civil Trial and Appellate Practice, Insurance Defense, Personal Injury, Negligence, Products Liability, Wrongful Death, Legal and Medical Malpractice, Civil Rights, Litigation, Business Litigation.
See Professional Biographies, TOLEDO, OHIO

Lyle, Dennis A., (AV) ....'58 '84 C.97 B.B.S. L.851 J.D. [Fuller&H.]
Lynch, Patricia A., (AV) '50 '75
C.851 B.A. L.1292 J.D. Dir. Emply. & Govt. Rel., Owens Corning
MacHarg, James C., (BV) ....'46 '74 C.4 B.A. L.851 J.D. 411 Michigan St.
MacHarg, Suzan A. ....'54 '80 C&L.851 B.B.A., J.D. 2428 Bexford Place
Machin, Barbara E. ....'47 '78 C.378 B.S. L.851 J.D. [Ⓐ Bunda S.&D.]
Mack, David J. ....'70 '00 C&L.851 B.A., J.D. [Ⓐ Shumaker,L.&K.]
MacKay, John N., (AV) ....'46 '75 C.623 B.A. L.608 J.D. [Shumaker,L.&K.]
MacMillan, Richard S., (AV) '55 '80 C.679 B.S.E.E. L.608 J.D.
[MacMillan,S.&T.] (Pat.)
MacMillan, Sobanski & Todd, L.L.C., (AV) .... 720 Water Street (Pat.) (⊙Livonia, MI)
Madigan, John T., (BV) ....'47 '73 C.031 B.A. L.608 J.D. Gen. Coun., City Law Dept.
Maguire, E. Thomas, (AV) ....'37 '63 C.197 A.B. L.608 J.D. [Ⓖ Robison,C.&O.]
Majdalani, Brenda J., (CV) .... '60 '89 C&L.851 B.Ed., J.D. Lucas Co. Pros. Off.
Malkoski, Kathleen M., The Law Office of '54 '99 C&L.851 B.B.A., J.D.
2589 W. Village
Malone, Nicholas D. ....'79 '04 C.602 B.A. L.347 J.D. [Ⓐ Shumaker,L.&K.]
Malone, Richard R., (AV) ....'52 '77 C.602 B.A. L.851 J.D. [Malone,A.&F.]

Malone, Ault & Farell, (AV)
7654 West Bancroft Street, 43617-1604
Telephone: 419-843-1333 Fax: 419-843-3888
Email: maf@maf-law.com
Richard R. Malone; Tim Allen Ault; Gregory C. Farell. Associates: Bradley R. Waugh; Milton E. Pommeranz.
General Civil Practice in Corporate Law and Commercial Law. Real Estate, Taxation, Probate and Trusts and Estates, Civil Litigation in all State and Federal Courts.
Representative Clients: Surface Combustion, Inc.; Transtar Electric, Inc.; Schroeder Co.; Marleau-Hercules Fence Co.; Toledo Ticket Company; Image Integration Systems, Inc.; Art Kuhn Company; Willson Builders, Inc.

(This Listing Continued)

Malone, Ault & Farell (Continued)
Reference: Signature Bank.
See Professional Biographies, TOLEDO, OHIO

Manahan, Marsha A. '55 '80 C.880 B.A. L.851 J.D.
V.P., Fifth Third Bk. of Northwestern Ohio, N.A.
Manahan, Michael J., (AV) .... '53 '79 C.608 B.A. L.851 J.D. [Manahan,P.B.&D.]
Manahan, Pietrykowski, Bamman & DeLaney, (AV)
414 North Erie Street (⊙Port Clinton)
Mandell, Steven L., (BV) ....'44 '83 C.401 B.A. L.851 J.D. 2652 Falmouth Rd.
Mandross, Suzanne Cotner, (BV) .... '55 '80 C.97 B.A. L.851 J.D. P.O. Box 2534
Manore, John J., III, (BV) ....'57 '94 C&L.851 B.Ed., J.D. 615 Adams St.
Mansour, Linda N., (BV) .... '56 '81 C.851 B.A. L.1049 J.D. Pres., Legal Coun. and Litig.
Marcus, Steven E., (BV) '53 '78
C.473 A.B. L.851 J.D. 3425 Executive Parkway, Suite 207
Margelefsky, Michael P., (BV) .... '52 '77 C.107 B.A. L.851 J.D. [M.P.Margelefsky]
Margelefsky, Michael P., LLC, (BV) ....709 Madison Ave.
Markakis, Maria Limbert ....'75 '00 C&L.608 B.S., J.D. [Ⓐ Eastman&S.]
Markwood, Theodore, (AV) ....'19 '45 C.851 A.B. L.477 J.D. 405 Madison Ave.‡

Marshall & Melhorn, LLC, (AV)
Four SeaGate, Eighth Floor, 43604
Telephone: 419-249-7100 Facsimile: 419-249-7151 Cable Address: "Patlex Toledo"
Email: attorneys@marshall-melhorn.com URL: http://www.marshall-melhorn.com
Members of Firm: Edwin J. Marshall (1873-1946); Donald F. Melhorn (1889-1974); Justice G. Johnson, Jr.; Thomas W. Palmer; Kenneth J. White; Thomas P. Killam; Vaughn A. Hoblet; Michael S. Scalzo; Marshall A. Bennett, Jr.; Ruth A. Meacham; Lori W. Decker; A. Thomas Christensen; Nancy D. Moody; Gerardo Roy Rollison; David L. O'Connell; Jennifer J. Dawson; James H. Irmen; D. Edward Dolgorukov; Mark H. Rose; Donald A. Schurr; Kenneth J. Mauer; Amy M. Natyshak; John F. Bodie, Jr.; Roman Arce; Craig P. Burns; Matthew J. Fischer; Elizabeth E. Baer; Michael A. Gonzalez; Stephen P. Evans; Bridgett J. Root. Associates: Mark A. Hixon; Kristen A. Connelly; John A. Borell, Jr.; Stephen M. Sadowski. Counsel: Donald F. Melhorn, Jr.; Paul M. Kraus; Phillip S. Oberlin; Clare K. Smith.
General Civil Practice in Corporate and Commercial Law, Securities, Banking, Tax, Antitrust, Admiralty, Bankruptcy, Computer Law, Probate and Estate Planning and Administration, Real Estate, Health Services, Insurance Defense, Medical Malpractice Defense, Pension and Profit Sharing Law, Labor and Employment Law, Litigation, Patent, Trademark and Copyright Law.
Counsel for: Libbey-Owens-Ford Co.; Owens-Corning Fiberglas Corp.; DeVilbiss Company; The Lathrop Co.; General Mills, Inc.; Toledo Engineering Co.
See Professional Biographies, TOLEDO, OHIO

Martin, Edwin E. ....'22 '60 C&L.851 J.D. CEO, Louisville Title Agency
Martin, John W. .... '49 '76 C.174 B.A. L.851 J.D. Pres., Louisville Title Agency
Massé, Drew R., (BV) .... '55 '84 C.608 B.A. L.851 J.D. [Ⓐ Williams,J.L.G.&S.]
Mather, John G., (BV) ....'46 '83 C&L.851 Bus. Ed., J.D. 1018 Adams St.
Mattimoe, John G., Law Offices of, (AV) '30 '54
C&L.215 Ph.B., LL.B. 5947 Park Center Court
Mattimoe, John I., (BV) .... '62 '89 C.973 B.A. L.851 J.D. 5749 Park Center Ct.
Mauer, Kenneth J., (BV) ..... '49 '85 C&L.851 B.S., J.D. [Marshall&M.] (See Pat. Sect.)
Mauntler, John E., (BV) ....'62 '88 C.117 B.A. L.608 J.D. [Fuller&H.]
Mazziotti, Mary L. ....'26 '67 C&L.851 B.B.A., J.D. 2252 Georgetown Ave.
McAleenan, Donald F. '54 '81 C.276 B.S.F.S. L.569 J.D.
(adm. in NY; not adm. in OH) Deputy General Counsel, Fibreboard Corporation
McArdle, Thomas J., (BV) .... '52 '87 C.339 B.A. L.851 J.D. [Ⓐ Cubbon&Assoc.]
McBee, Clint M., (BV) '42 '79
C&L.851 B.S., J.D. 1100 Edison Plaza, 300 Madison Avenue
McBride, B. Gary, (AV) ....'39 '64 C&L.950 A.B., J.D. [Spengler N.]
McCarter, C. Thomas, Law Office of, (AV) '46 '71
C.608 B.A. L.896 J.D. 421 N. Michigan, Suite D
McCarthy, Timothy C., (AV) ....'54 '79 C&L.608 B.A., J.D. [Shumaker,L.&K.]
McCauley, Ann M. ....'74 '99 C.896 B.S. L.851 J.D. [Ⓐ Watkins,B.&C.]
McClay, Susan D., (AV) ....'50 '76 C.932 B.B.A. L.477 J.D. [Shumaker,L.&K.]
McConnell, C. Allen, (BV) ....'44 '73 C.999 B.S. L.851 J.D. [McConnell&T.]
McConnell, Karyn R., (CV) ....'72 '98 C.473 B.A. L.930 J.D. [McConnell&T.]
McConnell & Taylor, (BV) ....316 North Michigan Street Suite 700
McCormick, Daniel James ....'50 '83 C.97 B.S. L.851 J.D. [McCormick,D.J.]
McCormick, Edward J., Jr., (AV) ...... '21 '48 C.363 B.S. L.930 J.D. 3161 Haughton Dr.
McCormick, James E. ....'28 '64 C.97 B.S. L.851 J.D. 8340 W. Bancroft St.
McCormick, Daniel J. ....8340 West Bancroft
McCready, Jennifer C., (BV) ..... '72 '99 C.150 B.A. L.851 J.D. [Ⓐ Williams,J.L.G.&S.]
McCready, William S., (AV) ....'44 '69 C.608 B.A. L.851 J.D. [Ritter,R.M.&J.]
McCrory, Dorothy B., (BV) .... '38 '65 C&L.851 B.A., J.D. [McCrory&Assoc.]
McCrory, Paul A., Jr., (CV) ....'34 '65 C.717 B.S. L.851 J.D. 3601 W. Alexis Rd.
McCrory & Associates Co., L.P.A., (BV) .... 1709 Spielbusch Avenue
McCrury, L. Douglass '48 '76 C.112 B.A. L.94 J.D.
Staff Atty., UAW Legal Servs. Plan
McCulley, David C., (BV) .... '52 '83 C&L.851 B.Ed., J.D. [Ⓐ Balk,H.&M.]
McGowan, Michael S., (AV) ....'57 '82 C&L.851 B.B.A., J.D. [Shumaker,L.&K.]
McGowan, P. Chris, (BV) ....'59 '89 C&L.851 B.B.A., J.D. [Ⓐ Harris R.T.]
Mc Grail, Michael T. .... '62 '87 C.473 B.A. L.851 J.D. 519 Madison Ave., 3rd Fl.
McHugh, John J., III, (AV) .... '51 '76 C&L.602 A.B., J.D. [McHugh,D.&M.]

McHugh, DeNune & McCarthy, Ltd., (AV)
5580 Monroe Street, 43560
Telephone: 419-885-3597 Fax: 419-885-3861
John J. McHugh, III; Ralph DeNune, III; Stephen B. Mosier (Resident);—Karen J. Wensink; Frederick E. Kalmbach. Of Counsel: John J. Callahan.
Trial and Appellate Practice in Civil, Criminal and Domestic Relations Law, Employment Law, Probate and Estate Planning, Corporate and Commercial Law, Non-Profit Organizations and Real Estate.
See Professional Biographies, TOLEDO, OHIO

McKee, Wm. Miles ....'45 '79 C.659 B.S. L.213 J.D. [Cooper&W.] ⊙
McMahon, Brian N., (BV) ....'52 '78 C.608 B.A. L.117 J.D. [Shumaker,L.&K.]
McMahon, John W. .... '68 '94 C.473 B.A. L.851 J.D. 316 N. Michigan, Suite 600
McManus, Martin James ....'61 '87 C.602 B.A. L.851 J.D. 303 Bell Bldg.
McMurray, Michael W., Attorney at Law '72 '05
C.250 B.S. L.851 J.D. 520 Madison Ave., Ste. 405
McNamara, Joseph V. ....'— '03 C.477 B.A. L.569 J.D. [Ⓐ Cooper&W.]
McNulty, M. Sean, Law Office of, (BV) '68 '94
C.352 B.S. L.851 J.D. 316 N. Michigan St., Ste. 600

McQuades Co., The, L.P.A.
(See Swanton)

McWeeny, Philip, (AV) '39 '65 C.321 B.S. L.477 J.D.
V.P. & Gen. Coun.-Corp., Owens-Illinois, Inc.
McWilliam, John A. .... '30 '57 C.197 B.A. L.851 J.D. Toledo-Lucas Co. Port Auth.‡
McWilliam, John L. .... '56 '86 C.473 B.A. L.607 J.D. 333 North Summit Street, 5th Floor
Meacham, Ruth A., (AV) .... '39 '81 C&L.851 B.A., J.D. [Marshall&M.]
Meeks, Mark D., (BV) .... '63 '88 C.999 B.S. L.851 J.D. [Anspach M.E.]
Melhorn, Donald F., Jr., (AV) .... '35 '60 C.976 B.A. L.309 LL.B. [Ⓖ Marshall&M.]

Menacher, William R., (BV) .... '53 '84 C&L.851 B.A., J.D. [Spitler&W.L.&Assoc.]
Mercer, Mark E. .... '66 '02 C&L.851 B.A., J.D. [Shumaker,L.&K.]
Mercurio, Meredith L., (BV) .... '74 '99 C&L.851 B.A., J.D. [Cooper&W.]
Merlino, Thomas R. '44 '73 C.119 B.S. L.818 J.D.
Dir. Envir. Liabilities Resolution, Owens Corning
Merritt, Frank S. ....'43 '68 C.318 B.A. L.930 J.D. Prof., Univ. of Toledo Sch. of Law
Mesner, Susan Marie .... '59 '93 C.97 B.S. L.851 J.D. 416 N. Erie St.
Messenger, Michael S., (AV) .... '58 '83 C.276 B.S.B.A. L.608 J.D. [Robison,C.&O.]
Messinger, Steven J. .... '51 '75 C.264 A.B. L.245 J.D. Asst. Co. Pros.
Metz, Douglas E., (AV) .... '40 '65 C.117 B.A. L.608 J.D. [Robison,C.&O.]
Mewhort, Donald M., Jr., (AV) .... '40 '65 C&L.228 A.B., LL.B. [Shumaker,L.&K.]
Meyer, Brenda G. .... '61 '86 C.203 B.S. L.851 J.D. Adams and Erie St.
Meyer, Fred C., (AV) '48 '81 C&L.851 B.B.A., J.D.
Coun., Port Lawrence Title & Tr. Co.
Meyer, Larry P., (BV) ....'59 '85 C.97 B.S. L.851 J.D. [Manahan,P.B.&D.]
Meyer, Randy L. .... '59 '99 C.203 B.A. L.851 J.D. [Spengler N.]
Meyer, William G., (AV) '49 '77 C.640 B.A. L.851 J.D.
608 Madison Avenue, Suite 1400
Mezinko, Vincent Samuel .... '59 '85 C&L.851 B.S., J.D. 709 Madison Avenue, Suite 301
Michael, G. Gregory '37 '62 C.475 B.A. L.477 LL.B.
Chief Dep., Law Enforcement Div.
Michalak, Richd. F., (BV) .... '23 '51 C.363 B.S. L.215 J.D. 243 N. Huron St.
Michalski, Thomas R. ....'26 '63 C.494 B.B.A. L.851 J.D. 3141 Orchard Trail‡
Mickel, Kenneth L., (BV) .... '38 '65 C&L.851 B.A., J.D. 520 Seitzer Bldg.
Miesle, Gary E., (BV) ....'56 '81 C&L.851 B.B.A., J.D. [Dixon&H.]
Miller, Barbara Kaye .... '64 '90 C&L.352 B.A., J.D. Co. Pros. Off.
Miller, Gary L., (BV) .... '48 '99 C.651 B.S. L.851 J.D. [Eastman&S.]
Miller, Harvey C., Jr. .... '70 '99 C.493 B.A. L.607 J.D. [Bugbee&C.]
Miller, Jim, (BV) .... '48 '76 C.473 B.S. L.851 J.D. [Balk,H.&M.]
Miller, Nancy Alice ....'55 '88 C&L.851 B.A., J.D. Mag., Probate Ct.
Miller, Russell R., (AV) ....'49 '77 C.610 B.S.Ed. L.607 J.D. [Roetzel&A.]
Miller, William S. .... '17 '40 L.608 LL.B. 4644 Penridge Rd.‡
Miller Mickel, Marilyn D., (BV) .... '39 '82 C&L.851 B.Ed., J.D. 608 Madison, Suite 940
Millon, James W., (BV) .... '50 '76 C&L.851 B.A., J.D. [Eastman&S.]
Mills, Gerald L., (AV) .... '40 '68 C.473 B.B.A. L.608 J.D. [Herschel,A.B.&M.]
Millward, Richard L., (BV) .... '31 '58 C&L.851 B.A., J.D. 520 Madison Ave.g.
Mistry, Jennifer S. .... '74 '00 C.475 B.A. L.851 J.D. [Cooper&W.]
Mitchell, Keith L., Law Offices of, (BV) '50 '87
C.1077 B.A. L.851 J.D. 124 N. Summit St., Ste. 210
Mitchell, Mary Clare .... '69 '03 C.201 B.A. L.851 J.D. Ste 650, 1 Seagate
Mitchell, Mary J. .... '52 '01 C&L.851 B.A., J.D. [Borgstahl&Z.]
Mittelstaedt, David J., (AV) .... '57 '83 C&L.851 B.A., J.D. Spitzer Building
Mittelstaedt, Earl A. ....'12 '53 C.966 B.A. L.851 LL.B. 1231 Michele Dr.
Modd, Anthony R. .... '76 '02 C.607 B.A. L.608 J.D. [Eastman&S.]
Mohler, Edward T., (BV) .... '62 '89 C.363 B.A. L.851 J.D. 420 Madison Avenue
Mohler, Martin E., (AV) .... '48 '73 C.363 B.A. L.851 J.D. [Shindler,N.H.S.&M.]
Mohr, David M., (AV) .... '40 '66 C.610 B.S. L.851 J.D. 608 Madison Ave.
Mohr, Kathryn M., (BV) .... '62 '87 C.5 B.A. L.851 J.D. [Robison,C.&O.] ⊙
Molaro, Catherine Michelle .... '67 '93 C.532 B.A. L.851 J.D. 800 Jackson Street
Molaro, Salvatore C., Jr. .... '61 '87 C.5 B.A. L.851 J.D. 610 Adams Street, 2nd Floor
Mollenkamp, Alan L., (AV) .... '46 '74 C.851 B.A. L.426 J.D. [Mollenkamp&I.]
Mollenkamp & Ingram, LLC, (AV) .... 411 North Michigan Street, Suite 300
Molnar, John B. .... '41 '83 C&L.851 B.S., J.D. [MacMillan,S.&T.] (Pat.)
Mondville, Jeffrey John, (BV) .... '54 '95 C&L.851 B.S.A.S., J.D. 709 Madison Ave.
Moody, Nancy D., (BV) .... '46 '82 C.97 B.S.N. L.607 J.D. [Marshall&M.]
Moore, Bradene L. '— '85 C.475 B.A. L.851 J.D.
(adm. in MI; not adm. in OH) Law Clk., U.S. Bkrptcy. J.
Moore, Troy L., (BV) .... '60 '85 C.347 B.S. L.851 J.D. [Ballenger&M.] ⊙
Moran, James P., (BV) .... '41 '75 C&L.851 B.B.A., J.D. 2254 Townley Rd.
Moran, Mary Beth, (AV) .... '64 '89 C.317 B.A. L.851 J.D. [Moran&M.]
Moran, Peter L., (AV) .... '25 '53 C.477 L.851 J.D. [Moran&M.]
Moran & Moran, (AV) .... 626 Madison Avenue, Suite 300
Morano, Anthony A. '33 '61 C.31 B.A. L.262 LL.B.
(adm. in CT; not adm. in OH) Prof. of Law, Univ. of Toledo
Moreland, Ruth .... '61 '97 C.97 B.S. L.851 J.D. 6079 Secor Rd.
Morgan, Frieda Goldman .... '49 '75 C&L.851 B.A., J.D. 2625 Amara Dr.
Morris, Robert G., (AV) .... '27 '51 C&L.851 B.B.A., J.D. 2823 Manchester Blvd.‡
Morrison, Jennifer L., (BV) '59 '86 C.97 B.A. L.851 J.D.
Lit. & Claims Dir., The Port Lawrence Title & Tr. Co.
Morrissey, Martin B., (BV) '60 '92 C.118 B.A. L.851 J.D.
Gen. Coun., St. Vincent Mercy Medical Center
Morton, James M., Jr., (AV) .... '42 '67 C.1154 B.A. L.477 J.D. [Fuller&H.]
Mosier, Stephen B., (AV) .... '52 '77 C.97 B.A. L.597 J.D. [McHugh,D.&M.]
Mueller, Denise A. .... '72 '00 C&L.851 B.A., J.D. [Eastman&S.]
Murphree, R. Kent, (BV) .... '69 '95 C&L.851 B.A., J.D. [Watkins,B.&C.]
Murphy, Veronica M., (BV) ....'42 '84 C.731 B.A. L.851 J.D. 1055 Spitzer Building
Musachio, Rosalie N., (BV) ....'51 '77 C.710 B.A. L.285 J.D. 4334 W. Central Ave.
Muska, Susan Hartman .... '42 '77 C.33 B.A. L.851 J.D. 608 Madison Ave.
Mutchler, Alan D., (BV) ....'51 '76 C.1154 B.A. L.851 J.D. Toledo Legal Aid Soc.
Myers, Judith A. .... '68 '00 C&L.851 B.S., J.D. 316 N. Michigan St., Ste. 800
Nackowicz, Timothy P. .... '77 '03 C.473 B.A. L.608 J.D. [Connelly,J.&C.]
Nahhas, Fadi Victor .... '— '00 C.1161 B.S. L.150 J.D. [Eastman&S.]
Natyshak, Amy M., (BV) .... '65 '90 C.96 B.A. L.851 J.D. [Marshall&M.]
Naughton, Thomas F., (BV) .... '— '94 C.608 B.A. L.213 J.D. [Gallagher S.] ⊙
Neceski, Marjan '68 '96 C.033 B.A. L.851 J.D.
(adm. in NY; not adm. in OH) [Anspach M.E.]
Nedom, Francis Paul .... '56 '89 C&L.851 B.A., J.D. A.R.E.A. Title Agency, Inc.
Neff, Carter, (AV) .... '43 '68 C&L.608 B.F.A., J.D. [Shindler,N.H.S.&M.]
Neff, Theresa M. ....'79 '04 C.97 B.S.B.A. L.989 J.D. [Shindler,N.H.S.&M.]
Neisler, Alexandra D. .... '67 '95 C.210 B.A. L.851 J.D. 7110 W. Central Ave.‡
Nelson, John K., (AV) .... '54 '79 C.473 B.A. L.851 J.D. [Cooper&W.]
Nelson, Richard N. '40 '80 C.679 M.S.M.E. L.273 J.D.
(adm. in MI; not adm. in OH) Teledyne CAE
Nelson, Susan B., (BV) .... '53 '81 C.477 B.A. L.851 J.D. [Spengler N.]
Ness, Howard L. .... '20 '49 C&L.851 B.B.A., J.D. 2365 Goddard Rd.
Newnham, Gary C. ....'49 '79 C.97 B.A. L.851 J.D. Co. Child Support Enforce. Agcy.
Newsom, Scott D., (BV) .... '71 '96 C.385 B.A. L.851 J.D. [Eastman&S.]
Nicholson, Brent B., (BV) ....'54 '79 C.97 B.S. L.608 J.D. [Rohrbachers L.C.&T.]
Nitschke, Drew A. .... '75 '00 C.477 B.A. L.851 J.D. [Stockwell&C.]
Noble, Catherine H., (BV) .... '44 '78 C.602 B.A. L.851 J.D. [Shindler,N.H.S.&M.]
Nolte, Lynne .... '55 '83 C.851 B.A. L.477 J.D. Dist. Hearing Offr., Indus. Comm.
Nooney, James F., (AV) .... '41 '66 C.207 B.A. L.880 LL.B. [Eastman&S.]
Novak, Karen A., (BV) .... '58 '84 C.8 B.A. L.851 J.D. 316 N. Michigan St.
Nowak, James S., Law Offices of .... '51 '76 C&L.851 B.Ed., J.D. 4808 N. Summit Street
Nowland, Rodney A. '51 '76 C&L.477 B.S.E., J.D.
(adm. in IN; not adm. in OH) Dir. Corp. Law & Asst. Secy., Owens Corning
Nugent, Samuel J., (BV) .... '52 '78 C.831 B.A. L.851 J.D. 416 N. Erie St.
Nunn, David W., (AV) .... '58 '91 C.97 B.S. L.851 J.D. [Eastman&S.] (⊙Columbus)

Nunnari, Jeffrey P., (BV) '62 '92 C.1208 B.A. L.851 J.D.
3425 Executive Parkway, Suite 111, 43606
Telephone: 419-578-9246 Fax: 419-531-5675
Email: jp59691@yahoo.com
Civil Litigation, Criminal Law, Appellate Practice, Drug Crimes, Felonies, Homicide, Misdemeanors, Parole and Probation, Sexual Assault.
See Professional Biographies, TOLEDO, OHIO

Nusbaum, Melvin G., (AV) .... '33 '57 C&L.608 B.S.B.A., J.D. [Harris R.T.]
Oberlin, Phillip S. ....'33 '59 C.679 B.S. L.273 J.D. [Marshall&M.] (See Pat. Sect.)
O'Brien, Jean M., (AV) .... '50 '89 C.624 B.S. L.851 J.D. [Robison,C.&O.] ⊙
O'Connell, David L., (AV) .... '56 '84 C.951 B.A. L.930 J.D. [Marshall&M.]
O'Connell, Katherine Raup, (BV) ..... '57 '84 C.967 B.A. L.608 J.D. [Stockwell&C.]
O'Connell, Maurice D., (AV) .... '29 '56 C.951 B.A. L.188 LL.B. [Robison,C.&O.]
O'Doherty, James H., (CV) ....'73 '99 C.477 B.A. L.228 J.D. [Shumaker,L.&K.]

Ogne, Alberts & Stuart, P.C.
(See Troy, Michigan)

Olender, Lori L., (BV) .... '69 '97 C&L.851 B.A., J.D. Lucas Co. Pros. Off.
Olsaver, Michael R. '74 '99 C.475 B.A. L.209 J.D.
(adm. in MI; not adm. in OH) [Robison,C.&O.] ⊙
Oostmeyer, Melissa M. .... '— '99 C.999 B.A. L.215 J.D. [Fuller&H.]
Orlow, Gary M., (BV) '50 '78
C.97 B.L.S. L.851 J.D. In-House Coun., Bd. of Lucas Co. Comrs.
Osborne, Gary W., & Associates, (AV) '50 '75 C.608 B.A. L.851 J.D.
7150 Granite Circle
Osgood, Marla Ruth Feldstein ....'53 '78 C.959 B.A. L.851 J.D. Pros. Off.

Osnowitz, Samuel, (BV) '45 '71 C.851 B.B.A. L.273 J.D.
2727 N. Holland Sylvania Road, Suite K, 43615-1800
Telephone: 419-531-1021 FAX: 419-531-1026
Email: SamOsnowitz@buckeye-express.com URL: http://www.osnowitzlaw.com
Commercial Law, Condominium Law, Buying and Selling of Businesses, Starting a Business, Business Enterprises, Small Business, Limited Liability Company Law, Family Business, Wills and Probate, Real Estate Law.
Reference: Fifth Third Bank of Toledo, Ohio N.A.
See Professional Biographies, TOLEDO, OHIO

Osowik, Thomas John .... '55 '82 C&L.851 B.A., J.D. Mun. J.
Ozimek, Mark A. .... '79 '04 C.97 B.A. L.851 J.D. [Robison,C.&O.]
Pacella, Patrick P. ....'42 '68 C.608 B.S.E.D. L.602 J.D. [Emch,S.S.&P.] (See Pat. Sect.)
Palmer, Robert C. ....'44 '78 C.62 B.A. L.851 J.D. V.P., Maumee Valley Fabricators, Inc.
Palmer, Thomas W., (AV) .... '47 '72 C.611 B.A. L.477 J.D. [Marshall&M.]
Palm-Kuebler, Lisa .... '73 '03 C&L.851 B.A., J.D. [Roetzel&A.]
Pangle, Laurie J., (AV) .... '58 '83 C.477 B.A. L.879 J.D. [Spengler N.]
Papps, Thos. G. .... '31 '55 C.97 B.A. L.608 LL.B. 1258 Sylvania
Pardee, John Keith, III, (BV) '46 '74
C.475 B.A. L.851 J.D. 4334 W. Central Ave., Ste. 201
Parker, Christopher F., (AV) .... '58 '84 C.473 B.A. L.851 J.D. [Goranson,P.&B.]
Parker, Ericka S., (BV) .... '72 '97 C.97 B.A. L.851 J.D. [E.Parker]
Parker, Jerome R., (AV) .... '46 '73 C&L.851 B.A., J.D. [Gressley,K.&P.]
Parker, Ericka, Law Offices of, (BV) .... 1709 Spielbusch Ave., Ste. 100
Patberg, William L., (AV) .... '47 '78 C.390 B.A. L.494 J.D. [Shumaker,L.&K.]
Pavelko, Douglas V., (AV) '60 '90 C.980 B.S.M.E. L.851 J.D.
[MacMillan,S.&T.] (Pat.)
Pawlicki, Sarah E. .... '74 '03 C.473 B.A. L.851 J.D. [Eastman&S.]
Pazzo, Michael P. .... '73 '00 C.645 B.A. L.124 J.D. [Allotta&F.]
Pearson, Craig T., (BV) .... '52 '85 C.97 B.A. L.851 J.D. 2614 Westmar Ct.
Peckinpaugh, Rudolph A., Jr., (AV) ....'54 '80 C.611 B.A. L.851 J.D. [Eastman&S.]
Penn, Robt. W. .... '23 '53 C.864 B.S. L.930 LL.B. Mun. J.
Pennington, Stephen T., Law Office of, (BV) '57 '84
C&L.851 B.A., J.D. 5403 N. Summit St.
Peppel, Gregg A., (BV) .... '71 '99 C&L.851 B.A., J.D. [Coy,K.&P.]
Perkins, Jeffrey J., (AV) .... '53 '82 C.999 B.A. L.851 J.D. [Shindler,N.H.S.&M.]
Perlman, James M., (BV) ....'54 '80 C.608 B.A. L.851 J.D. 1776 Tremainsville Road
Perlmutter, Steven J. ... '45 '75 C.477 B.S. L.588 J.D. V.P. & Coun., People's Jewelry Co.
Perné, Lori L. .... '53 '01 C.1434 B.I.S. L.851 J.D. [Kitch D.W.V.&S.]
Pesin, Donna K. .... '59 '85 C.66 B.A. L.978 J.D. 2909 Secretariat Rd.
Peters, George T. '64 '89 C.912 B.A. L.477 J.D.
(adm. in MI; not adm. in OH) Sr. Coun., Opers., Owens Corning
Peterson, Walter W. .... '21 '55 C&L.851 B.B.A., LL.B. 2821 Meadowwood Dr.‡
Petlow, James J. .... '38 '67 C.477 A.B. L.608 J.D. 520 Madison Ave.
Pettiford, Nadine S. .... '60 '95 C&L.851 B.B.A., J.D. Toledo Legal Aid Soc.
Phelps, A. Brooke .... '77 '02 C&L.851 B.B.A., J.D. [Eastman&S.]
Phifor, B. Janelle Butler ....'49 '75 C&L.329 B.A., J.D. Toledo Legal Aid Soc.
Philipps, David S. .... '38 '66 C&L.851 B.A., J.D. 4554 River Rd.
Phillips, Jerome, (AV) .... '44 '69 C.851 B.B.A. L.608 J.D. 520 Madison Ave., Ste. 840
Pietrykowski, Mark L. '54 '79 C.602 B.A. L.607 J.D.
Ct. of App. J., 6th Dist. Ct. of App.
Pigott, Thomas D., (BV) .... '65 '94 C&L.851 B.A., J.D. 2828 West Central Avenue
Pilkington, Joseph H., (AV) .... '34 '59 C.851 B.A. L.477 J.D. [J.H.Pilkington]
Pilkington, Joseph H., & Co., L.P.A., (AV) .... One SeaGate, Suite 720
Pinkus, Fredric, (BV) .... '36 '83 C.608 B.S.C. L.851 J.D. 1241 Michele Dr.
Pioch, Susan M., (BV) .... '56 '81 C.207 B.S. L.851 J.D. 4303 Talmadge Rd., Ste. 201
Pisanelli, Mary Ellen, (AV) .... '52 '82 C.882 B.A. L.831 J.D. [Shumaker,L.&K.]
Pitman, Roy V. .... '75 '04 C.608 B.S. L.150 J.D. [Eastman&S.]
Pizza, Anthony G., (AV) .... '21 '50 C&L.851 Ph.B., LL.B. Pros. Atty.
Pizza, Lisa E., (BV) .... '54 '81 C.473 B.A. L.851 J.D. [Spengler N.]
Pizzimenti, Lee A. '55 '81 C.477 B.G.S. L.912 J.D.
(adm. in MI; not adm. in OH) Univ. of Toledo Law School
Platz, Sarah L. .... '59 '94 C.303 B.A. L.851 J.D. 3217 Escott
Plessner, Dirk P., (AV) .... '52 '87 C&L.851 B.B.A., J.D. [Eastman&S.] (⊙Columbus)
Pletz, Francis G. .... '17 '50 C.755 B.A. L.851 J.D. 3605 Orchard Trail Dr.‡
Pletz, Thomas G., (AV) .... '43 '71 C.602 B.A. L.851 J.D. [Shumaker,L.&K.]
Podolsky, Michael J. .... '69 '02 L.124 J.D. [Shumaker,L.&K.]
Pohl, Lisa M. .... '67 '96 C.999 B.B.A. L.1187 J.D. Ernst & Young, LLP
Polizzi, Arturo '72 '97 C.473 B.S. L.851 J.D.
Assoc. Gen. Coun., ProMedica Health Sys., Inc.
Pollex, Yvonne Tertel, (BV) .... '58 '84 C.260 B.S. L.851 J.D. Sr. Dep. Atty. Gen.
Pollock, Robert E., (BV) '43 '71
C.150 B.S. L.1340 J.D. Legal Coun., Dana Corporation (Pat.)

Polofka, John R., Law Office, (BV) '55 '80
C.473 B.A. L.851 J.D. 500 Madison Ave., Ste. 525
Pommeranz, Milton E. ....'77 '02 C&L.851 B.S., J.D. [🄰 Malone,A.&F.]
Popil, James J., (BV) .... '61 '86 C.97 B.S. L.851 J.D. 300 Madison Ave., Ste. 1406
Porcello, James F., Jr., (AV) '51 '77
C.679 B.S.E. L.117 J.D. [Emch,S.S.&P.] (See Pat. Sect.)
Porritt, Russell W., II, (AV) .... '54 '82 C.475 B.A. L.1187 J.D. [Ward,A.P.&B.] ⊙
Posner, Curtis E., (BV) .... '40 '67 C&L.851 B.A., J.D. Chf. Asst. Pros. Atty.
Potter, John W. .... '18 '47 C.851 Ph.B. L.477 J.D. Sr. U.S. Dist J.
Potter, Theodore Alan '57 '88 C.339 B.S., M.S. L.851 J.D.
Asst. Law Libr., Univ. of Toledo, Univ. of Toledo Coll. of Law Library

Potts, John F. '52 '78 C.293 B.A. L.851 J.D.
National City Bank Building, 405 Madison Avenue, Suite 1010, 43604-1211
Telephone: 419-255-2800 Fax: 419-255-1105 URL: http://www.jfplain.com
Email: jfplaw@ameritech.net URL: http://www.jfplaw.com
Criminal Defense, White Collar Criminal Defense, Criminal Forfeiture, Civil Forfeiture, Federal Criminal Law, Post-Conviction Remedies, Habeas Corpus, Business Litigation, Commercial Litigation, Civil Litigation, Trial Practice, Appellate Practice Federal Litigation.
See Professional Biographies, TOLEDO, OHIO

Poturalski, Steven J. ....'70 '97 C&L.851 B.B.A., J.D. [🄰 Stockwell&C.]
Powell, Max Courtney .... '19 '43 C&L.502 A.B., LL.B. 50 Canterbury Ct.‡

Powers, Mark L.
(See Wauseon)

Prephan, Michael, (CV) .... '34 '69 C&L.851 B.Ed., J.D. 3123 Lagrange St.
Price, Douglas R. .... '43 '75 1018 Adams St.
Priestap, Stephen T., (BV) .... '66 '92 C&L.851 B.S., J.D. 316 N. Michigan St.
Proctor, James W. .... '28 '56 C.851 B.B.A. L.608 J.D. 6537 Dorr St.
Puffenberger, Jack R. .... '51 '79 C.381 B.A. L.851 J.D. Prob. J.
Purcel, Jerry P. .... '— '80 C&L.851 B.A., J.D. [J.P.Purcel]
Purcel, Jerry P., L.P.A. .... 3425 Executive Parkway, Suite 206
Purdue, David C., (BV) .... '57 '83 C.477 B.S. L.851 J.D. [🄰 Purdue] (Pat.)
Purdue, John C., (AV) .... '21 '49 C.477 A.B. L.851 LL.B. [Purdue] (Pat.)
Purdue Law Offices, (AV) .... 2735 N. Holland-Sylvania Rd. (Pat.)
Racine, Charles E., (BV) '37 '67
C.210 A.B. L.851 J.D. 4149 Holland Sylvania Road, Suite 2
Raduege, Tammy J. .... '61 '89 C.965 B.A. L.1035 J.D. Staff Atty.
Rahal, Ronald L., (BV) .... '54 '87 C&L.851 M.Ed., J.D. [R.L.Rahal]
Rahal, Ron L., (BV) .... 4303 Talmadge Rd., Ste. 102
Raitt, Ronald D. '31 '59 C&L.546 B.S., LL.B.
(adm. in NE; not adm. in OH) Assoc. Prof. of Law, Univ. of Toledo
Raker, Arthur F., (BV) .... '36 '62 C&L.851 B.B.A., J.D. 4127 Monroe
Ralph, Walter S. .... '47 '80 C&L.851 B.B.A., L.L.B. 5949 Sweetwater Ct.
Rambo, Glenn L., (AV) .... '51 '80 C.610 B.B.A. L.608 J.D. [Fuller&H.]
Ramsey, Brian M. .... '57 '91 L.851 J.D. 500 Madison Ave., Ste. 520
Randall, Jane S., (BV) .... '42 '83 C.187 B.A. L.851 J.D. 608 Madison Ave., Ste. 1400
Rankin, Bonnie Rae, (BV) .... '65 '93 C.97 B.A. L.851 J.D. 1109 Adams St.
Ray, Brenda A. .... '69 '98 C.851 B.B.A. L.608 J.D. [🄰 Lyden,L.&C.]
Ray, James Alan .... '40 '76 C.747 B.A. L.851 J.D. Juv. Ct. J.
Rectenwald, David J., (BV) .... '61 '86 C.602 B.A. L.608 J.D. [Shumaker,L.&K.]
Regnier, Michael W., (BV) .... '67 '93 C.323 B.A. L.851 J.D. [Eastman&S.]
Reinbolt, Steven D., (AV) .... '59 '85 C.851 B.A. L.150 J.D. [Eastman&S.]
Reiser, George Kott, (BV) .... '62 '87 C.473 B.S. L.851 J.D. [Reiser&R.]
Reiser, George R., (AV) .... '29 '52 C&L.608 B.A., J.D. [Reiser&R.] ‡
Reiser and Reiser, (AV) .... P.O. Box 2952
Rejent, Ronald P. .... '16 '41 C.363 A.B. L.602 J.D. 3529 Secor Rd.‡
Relation, A. Joseph '58 '83 C.930 B.A. L.602 J.D.
Sr. Div. Coun., Opers., Owens Corning
Reminger & Reminger Co., L.P.A., (AV)
405 Madison Ave., 23rd Fl. (⊙Covington, KY; Akron, Cin., Cleve., Columbus, Sandusky, Youngstown, OH)
Renberg, Paul M. '64 '99 C.475 B.S. L.213 J.D.
(adm. in MI; not adm. in OH) Legal Counsel, Dana Corporation
Reny, D. Michael, (AV) .... '50 '77 C&L.851 B.B.A., J.D. [Harris R.T.]
Rerucha, Cynthia L., (AV) .... '59 '84 C.851 B.A. L.228 J.D. [Shumaker,L.&K.]
Resnick, Melvin L. .... '27 '52 C.851 L.608 J.D. Ct. of App. J.
Restivo, James B., (BV) .... '67 '95 C&L.851 B.A., J.D. [Brady,C.&S.]
Retske, Robert A., (BV) .... '45 '70 C&L.608 B.A., J.D. 5414 Monroe St.
Reynolds, Frank, (BV) .... '51 '83 C.967 B.A. L.851 J.D. 420 Madison Ave.
Reynolds, Timothy R., (BV) .... '49 '79 C.475 B.S. L.851 J.D. 1107 Adams Street
Rice, Kollin L., (CV) .... '70 '96 C&L.851 B.A., J.D. 3730 Upton Ave.
Rice, Philip M. .... '31 '62 C.477 B.S.E. L.851 LL.B. [Emch,S.S.&P.] (See Pat. Sect.)
Richman, William M. '49 '75 C.659 B.A. L.446 J.D.
(adm. in MD; not adm. in OH) Distinguished Univ. Prof., Univ. of Toledo Coll. of Law
Rideout, Joseph A., (AV) .... '51 '76 C.197 B.A. L.893 J.D. [Shumaker,L.&K.]
Rideout, Patricia L. '57 '81
C.597 B.A. L.813 J.D. Family Servs. Coord., Co. Children Servs.
Rider, J. Allen, III .... '65 '91 C.244 B.A. L.838 J.D. Counsel, Dana Corp.
Ries, Deborah Kay .... '56 '01 C.999 B.S. L.851 J.D. Pilkington North America, Inc.
Riesen, Kent D., (BV) .... '63 '88 C.607 B.A. L.851 J.D. [Anspach M.E.]
Rife, Joan Helen, (AV) .... '57 '82 C.5 B.A. L.851 J.D. [J.H.Rife]

Rife, Joan H., (AV)
Two Maritime Plaza, 43604
Telephone: 419-244-4000 Fax: 419-241-1900
Email: jrife4000@aol.com
Joan Helen Rife.
Workers Compensation, Transportation, Social Security Disability.
See Professional Biographies, TOLEDO, OHIO

Riley, Ted B., (BV) .... '62 '88 C.608 B.A. L.851 J.D. [Manahan,P.B.&D.]
Riley, Tyrone .... '56 '85 C.381 B.A. L.803 J.D. 416 N. Erie St., Ste. 200

Ritter, Robinson, McCready & James, (AV) BR
1850 National City Bank Building, 405 Madison Avenue, 43604
Telephone: 419-241-3213 FAX: 419-241-4925
URL: http://www.rrmjlaw.com
Members of Firm: George W. Ritter (1886-1979); Milton C. Boesel, Sr. (1893-1993); Ellis F. Robinson (Retired); Milton C. Boesel, Jr. (Retired); William S. McCready (Retired); Timothy C. James; Mark P. Seitzinger. Associates: Shannon Julienne George; Van P. Andres.
General Civil Practice. Insurance, Trials and Appeals, Municipal Law, Corporation, Probate, Estate Planning, Real Estate, Personal Injury, Product Liability, Labor and Employment. Federal Practice.
Counsel for: Chrysler Corp.; Rubini Motors, Inc.; Ohio Casualty Insurance Co.; National Mutual Insurance Co.; Celina Mutual Insurance Co.; Westfield Insurance Co.; Northwestern National Insurance Co.; Midwestern Insurance Co.; United Ohio Insurance Co.; Toledo Auto Electric Co.
See Professional Biographies, TOLEDO, OHIO

Roach, Stephen C., (BV) .... '57 '84 C.373 B.A. L.851 J.D. 300 Madison Avenue
Roberts, H. Buswell, Jr., (AV) .... '46 '75 C.1044 B.S. L.851 J.D. [Shumaker,L.&K.]
Roberts, Richard L., Sr., (BV) .... '49 '89 C&L.851 B.S., J.D. 1122 Adams St.
Robinette, Gregory W. .... '60 '00 C.679 B.S.I.M. L.851 J.D. [🄰 MacMillan,S.&T.]
Robinson, Ellis F., (AV) .... '24 '51 C.611 A.B. L.477 J.D. [Ritter,R.M.&J.] ‡
Robinson, Mark A., (BV) ..... '50 '79 C.381 B.S. L.851 J.D. 608 Madison Ave., Ste. 1400
Robison, Jerome .... '34 '61 C&L.608 B.A., J.D. Key Bank Natl. Assoc.

Robison, Curphey & O'Connell, Limited Liability Company, (AV)
Ninth Floor Four Seagate, 43604 ⊙
Telephone: 419-249-7900 Telecopier: 419-249-7911
Email: firm@rcolaw.com URL: http://www.rcolaw.com
Members of Firm: Douglas E. Metz; David W. Stuckey; Timothy D. Krugh; C. Philip Baither, III (Certified Specialist in Labor and Employment Law, Ohio State Bar Association); James E. Brazeau; Michael S. Messenger; Julia Smith Wiley; Thomas A. Gibson; Jean Ann S. Sieler; Kathryn M. Mohr; Thomas J. Antonini; William V. Beach; Jean M. O'Brien; D. Casey Talbott; James R. Knepp, II; Peter N. Lavalette; Scott A. Haselman. Associates: Michael R. Olsaver (Not admitted in OH); Daniel G. Hazard; Julia E. Benziger; Kimberly M. Thomas; Bradley L. Blandin; Mark A. Ozimek. Retired: John M. Curphey (Retired). Of Counsel: Maurice D. O'Connell; E. Thomas Maguire; James J. Robison (1922-1986).
Litigation, Appellate Practice, Business Law, Corporate Law, Commercial Law, Construction Law and Probate, Commercial Real Estate, Real Estate, Health Care, Hospital Law, Insurance, Insurance Defense, Personal Injury, Labor and Employment, Medical Malpractice Defense, Bankruptcy and Creditor's Rights, Environmental Law, Employee Benefits, Railroad Law, Trusts and Estates, Estate Planning, Arbitration and Mediation.
Counsel for: Nationwide Insurance Cos.; St. Paul Fire & Marine Insurance; Motorists Insurance Cos.; PICOM Insurance Co.
Adrian, Michigan Office: 123 E. Maumee Street. Telephone: 517-263-8811. Fax: 517-263-8733.
Findlay, Ohio Office: 330 South Main Street. Telephone: 419-429-7900. Fax: 419-429-7911.
See Professional Biographies, TOLEDO, OHIO

Roca, John M., (BV) .... '57 '86 C.677 B.S.A. L.851 J.D. [🄰 Gallon&T.]
Rodgers, Damian M.P., (BV) .... '68 '94 C.385 B.A. L.851 J.D. [🄰 Shumaker,L.&K.]
Roemer, Wellington F., III, (CV) '57 '89
C&L.608 B.A., J.D. Gen. Coun. & V.P., W.F. Roemer Ins. Inc.

Roetzel & Andress, A Legal Professional Association, (AV) BR
One SeaGate, 9th Floor, 43604 ⊙
Telephone: 419-242-7985 Facsimile: 419-242-0316
Email: inquiries@ralaw.com URL: http://www.ralaw.com
Partners: Anthony J. Calamunci, Sr.; Patricia B. Fugée; Denise M. Hasbrook; Russell R. Miller; Douglas E. Spiker (Certified Specialist in Workers' Compensation, Ohio State Bar Association); Thomas S. Zaremba;—Amy L. Butler; Julie A. Douglas; Lisa Palm-Kuebler.
General Corporate and Business Law, Banking and Finance, Mergers, Acquisitions and Divestitures, Securities Law, Real Estate Law, Real Estate Development/Syndication/Condominium Law, Tax Law, Intellectual Property Law, Computer Law, Hospital and Health Care Law, Public Law and Finance, Governmental Relations, School Law, Commercial/Bankruptcy Law, Employment Law, Pension, Employee Benefits, Workers' Compensation, OSHA, Business and Commercial Litigation, Complex and Multidistrict Litigation, Antitrust Law, RICO, Federal Court Practice, Product Liability, Environmental Law/Toxic Torts, Insurance Law, Information Technology Law, Medical Malpractice Defense, Asbestos Litigation, Construction Law, 1st Amendment/Media Law, White Collar Criminal Defense, Railroad and FELA, Trucking and Transportation Law, Probate and Estate Planning, Utility Law, International Law, Trial and Appellate Practice.
Akron, Ohio Office: 222 South Main Street. Telephone: 330-376-2700. Telecopier: 330-376-4577.
Cleveland, Ohio Office: One Cleveland Center, 1375 East Ninth Street, 9th Floor. Telephone: 216-623-0150. Telecopier: 216-623-0134.
Columbus, Ohio Office: National City Center, 155 E. Broad Street, 12th Floor. Telephone: 614-463-9770. Telecopier: 614-463-9792.
Naples, Florida Office: 850 Park Shore Drive, Trianon Centre, 3rd Floor. Telephones: 239-649-6200; 800-535-7239. Telecopier: 239-261-3659.
Cincinnati, Ohio Office: 250 East Fifth Street, 310 Chiquita Center. Telephone: 513-361-0200. Telecopier: 513-361-0335.
Fort Myers, Florida Office: 2320 First Street, Suite 1000. Telephone: 239-337-3850. Telecopier: 239-337-0970.
Tallahassee, Florida Office: 225 South Adams Street, Suite 250, P.O. Box 10369. Telephone: 850-222-7718. Telecopier: 850-222-8222.
Washington, D.C. Office: 1025 Connecticut Avenue, NW, Suite 220. Telephone: 202-625-0600. Telecopier: 202-338-6340.
See Professional Biographies, TOLEDO, OHIO

Rogers, James L., (AV) .... '61 '87 C.97 B.S. L.851 J.D. [Eastman&S.]
Rogers, Jon A., (CV) .... '56 '83 C.651 B.A. L.851 J.D. 1530 Lombard Ave.
Rogers, Robert J. .... '53 '83 C.347 B.S. L.851 J.D. Findley, Davies & Co.
Rohrbacher, David J., (BV) ...... '49 '75 C.432 B.A. L.851 J.D. [Rohrbachers L.C.&T.]
Rohrbacher, Matthew J., (BV) ... '53 '80 C.432 B.A. L.851 J.D. [Rohrbachers L.C.&T.]

Rohrbachers Light Cron & Trimble Co., L.P.A., (AV)
405 Madison Avenue, 43604-1243
Telephone: 419-248-2600 Fax: 419-248-2614 URL: http://www.rlct-law.com
URL: http://www.rlctlaw.com
Vernon E. Rohrbacher (1920-1978). Shareholders: David J. Rohrbacher; Matthew J. Rohrbacher; C. Randolph Light; Nicholas J. Cron; J. Mark Trimble; Todd M. Zimmerman;—Tracy B. Selis; Jack J. Lah. Of Counsel: Brent B. Nicholson; Lori A. Coyle.
General Civil Practice. Corporate and Business, Insurance Defense, Personal Injury, Tax, Products Liability, Real Estate, Probate and Estate Planning, Trials and Appeals, Environmental Law, Labor and Employment, Products Liability Defense, including Drug and Medical Device Defense.
See Professional Biographies, TOLEDO, OHIO

Rollison, Gerardo Roy, (BV) .... '54 '80 C.608 B.S. L.851 J.D. [Marshall&M.]
Roman, Laura J. .... '64 '97 C.161 B.S.E.E. L.1003 J.D. 2419 Cheshire Woods Road
Romanoff, Rollind W., (BV) .... '36 '61 C&L.608 B.S., J.D. 6591 W. Central Ave.
Romp, Janelle M. .... '— '03 C.97 B.A. L.150 J.D. [🄰 Cooper&W.]
Romstadt, Lori Anne ... '71 '99 C&L.851 B.S., J.D. Fifth Third Bk. (Northwestern Ohio)
Root, Bridgett J., (BV) .... '73 '98 C.607 B.S.B.A. L.851 J.D. [Marshall&M.]
Rorick, Horton C. .... '23 '77 C.976 L.851 J.D. 3900 Estateway Rd.‡
Rose, Mark H. .... '61 '87 C.347 B.S. L.276 J.D. [Marshall&M.]
Rosen, Sheldon M., (AV) .... '34 '63 C&L.851 B.B.A., J.D. Law Dir.
Rost, Peter G., (AV) .... '49 '77 C&L.851 B.Ed., J.D. 830 Spitzer Building
Roth, Thomas Joseph .... '43 '85 C.610 B.S. L.851 J.D. [T.J.Roth]
Roth, Thomas J. .... 2424 Copland Blvd.
Rothschild, James I., (BV) .... '64 '93 C.597 B.S. L.851 J.D. [Shumaker,L.&K.]
Rothschild, Stephen A., (AV) .... '63 '88 C&L.597 B.S., J.D. [Shumaker,L.&K.]
Rotman, Phillip A., II '66 '93
C.880 B.S. L.201 J.D. Legal Coun., Dana Corporation (Pat.)
Rowell, Charles S., Jr. .... '48 '74 C.323 B.A. L.851 J.D. 955 Spitzer Bldg.
Rowen, Theodore M., (AV) .... '45 '70 C.882 B.A. L.150 J.D. [Spengler N.]
Rozic, John W., (BV) .... '51 '78 C.930 B.S. L.851 J.D. [Shindler,N.H.S.&M.]
Rubin, Daryl K., (BV) .... '56 '82 C.608 B.A. L.851 J.D. [D.Rubin]
Rubin, Joanne, Law Office of, (BV) '51 '84
C.787 B.A. L.851 J.D. 520 Madison Avenue, Suite 610
Rubin, Sheldon J., (BV) .... '29 '53 C&L.851 B.A., LL.B. 2127 Monroe St.
Rubin, Daryl, Law Office, (BV) .... 2127 Monroe St.
Rubinoff, Norman J., (AV) .... '41 '66 C.608 B.A. L.930 J.D. [Spengler N.]
Rump, Deborah Kovac, (BV) .... '58 '84 C.651 B.A. L.770 J.D. Asst. U.S. Atty.
Rust, John G. .... '15 '40 C&L.893 A.B., LL.B. 4628 Lewis Avenue
Ruyle, J. Philip '49 '79 C.8 B.S. L.851 J.D.
Sr. V.P. & Tr. Offr., Mid American Natl. Bk. & Tr. Co.
Ryan, Terrance L., (AV) .... '47 '76 C&L.851 B.A., J.D. [Shanahan] ⊙
Sadowski, Stephen M., (BV) .... '70 '96 C.363 B.S. L.851 J.D. [🄰 Marshall&M.]
Saglioccolo, Gaetano .... '62 '92 C.563 B.S. L.851 J.D. 2215 Parkwood Ave.

St. Clair, Donald D., (BV) . . . . '32 '92 C.347 B.S. L.851 J.D. P.O. Box 23185
Salas, Jesus R. '— '90 C&L.629 B.A., J.D.
Supvr. Atty., Advocates for Basic Legal Equality, Inc.
Salem, Nadeem S., (CV) . . . . '59 '96 C&L.851 B.A., J.D. 4427 Talmadge Road
Salem, Robert S. '64 '90 C&L.851 B.A., J.D. Toledo Legal Aid Soc.
Sallah, Charles H., (BV) . . . . '53 '81 C&L.851 B.A., J.D. Asst. Pros.
Sanderson, Michael G., (BV) . . . . '55 '81 C.97 B.S. L.851 J.D. [Shumaker,L.&K.]
Santiago, Lourdes, (BV) . . . . '49 '79 C.677 B.A. L.851 J.D. City Law Dept.
Sargeant, Richard T., (AV) '47 '75 C.117 B.S. L.608 J.D.
[Eastman&S.] (⊙Columbus)
Sass, James C., (BV) . . . . '47 '73 C.5 B.A. L.851 J.D. 3230 Central Park W., Suite 200
Sass, Kenneth J., (BV) . . . . '68 '94 C&L.851 B.S., J.D. 1870 Atwood Road
Saum, Scott J., (BV) '46 '75 C.608 B.S. L.851 J.D.
320 North Michigan Street, 2nd Floor

Savage, Barry E. '40 '65 C&L.477 B.A., J.D.
500 Madison Avenue, Suite 315, 43604
Telephone: 419-255-3557; 1-800-944-4660 Fax: 419-255-4660
Email: barsav@aol.com URL: http://www.barsav.com
Commercial Litigation, Banking Law, Bankruptcy, Business Law, Contracts, Real Estate, Investments, Financial Services Law, Estate Planning, Trusts and Estates.
See Professional Biographies, TOLEDO, OHIO

Sawan, Dennis P., (BV) . . . . '51 '88 C.1293 B.M. L.1330 J.D. P.O. Box 352018
Scalzo, Joseph R., Jr., (BV) . . . . '46 '77 C&L.851 B.B.A., J.D. 520 Madison Ave.
Scalzo, Michael S., (BV) . . . . '53 '79 C&L.851 B.S.I.E., J.D. [Marshall&M.]
Schaefer, James E. . . . . '57 '82 C.363 B.S.B.A. L.851 J.D. [LaValley,L.T.&S.] ‡
Schaffer, Mark C., (AV) . . . . '42 '69 C&L.608 B.A., J.D. [Emch,S.S.&P.] (See Pat. Sect.)
Schall, Alan M., (BV) . . . . '43 '84 C.800 B.A. L.851 J.D. P.O. Box 23303
Schank, Laura J. . . . . '62 '93 C&L.851 B.A., J.D. Staff Hearing Off., Indus. Comm.
Schank, Thomas J., (BV) . . . . '50 '77 C&L.851 B.A., J.D. [Hunter&S.]
Schaub, Charles R., (AV) '47 '73
C&L.851 B.S.M.E., J.D. [Emch,S.S.&P.] (See Pat. Sect.)
Scheer, Harold, (AV) . . . . '20 '43 L.851 J.D. [Scheer,G.&B.]
Scheer, Green & Burke, Co., L.P.A., (AV) . . . . P.O. Box 1323
Scheich, Richard A., (BV) . . . . '54 '84 C.477 B.A. L.851 J.D. [Jones&S.]
Scheidel, Rolf H., (AV) . . . . '40 '65 C.124 B.S. L.930 J.D. [Shumaker,L.&K.]
Schlageter, John J., III, (BV) . . . . . . '72 '97 C.150 B.A. L.851 J.D. [Shindler,N.H.S.&M.]
Schlageter, John J., Jr., (AV) . . . . '48 '73 C&L.851 B.A., J.D. [Shindler,N.H.S.&M.]
Schlageter, Thomas G., (BV) . . . . '50 '75 C.321 B.A. L.851 J.D. [Schlageter,B.&B.] ⊙
Schlageter, Breier & Bryce, L.P.A., (BV) . . . . 3536 Glendale Avenue (⊙Oregon)
Schlatter, Donald A. . . . . '29 '56 C.453 S.B. L.851 LL.B. Chmn., Art Iron, Inc.
Schlaudecker, David G. . . . . '47 '75 C.973 B.S. L.1049 J.D. Leadership Toledo Inc.
Schmidt, Philip L., (BV) . . . . '48 '74 C&L.851 B.A., J.D. [Brady,C.&S.]
Schmollinger, Mark S. . . . . '56 '82 C.299 B.A. L.851 J.D. City of Toledo Law Dept.
Schnorf, Brandon G., Jr., (AV) . . . . '31 '58 C.197 B.A. L.608 J.D. [Schnorf&F.]
Schnorf, David M., (AV) . . . . '37 '64 C.608 B.A. L.851 J.D. [Schnorf&S.]
Schnorf & Ferguson, (AV) . . . . 5217 Monroe St
Schnorf & Schnorf Co., L.P.A., A Professional Corporation, (AV) . . . 405 Madison Avenue
Schoenberger, Bruce S., (BV) . . . . '57 '83 C.473 B.A. L.608 J.D. [Gressley,K.&P.]
Schrader, Charles D. '41 '67 C&L.215 A.B., J.D. 2917 Latonia Blvd.‡
Schroeder, Jeffery Alan . . . . '67 '94 C.610 B.S. L.851 J.D. [A Joelson&M.]
Schuchmann, John J. . . . . '27 '54 C.363 B.B.S. L.215 J.D. 520 Madison Ave.‡
Schuller, James L., (BV) . . . . . '51 '77 C&L.851 B.A., J.D. 3450 W. Central Ave., Ste. 242
Schurr, Donald A., (BV) . . . '63 '89 C.930 B.S. L.851 J.D. [Marshall&M.] (See Pat. Sect.)
Schwab, S. Scott, (AV) . . . . . '51 '78 C.861 B.A. L.851 J.D. 316 N. Michigan St., Suite 600
Schweikert, James D. . . . . '73 '03 C&L.851 B.A., J.D. [A MacMillan,S.&T.]
Schweikert, Staci E. . . . . '75 '02 C&L.851 B.S.C.E., J.D. [A MacMillan,S.&T.] (Pat.)
Schwieterman, Nicole K. . . . . '— '99 C.97 B.S. L.851 J.D. [A Cooper&W.]
Scott, Darrel J., (BVⓉ) . . . . '— '90 C.347 B.A. L.421 J.D. [C Shumaker,L.&K.]
Scott, John N. . . . . '59 '84 C&L.851 B.B.A., J.D. 1122 Adams St.‡
Scott, Robert B. . . . . '67 '01 C.608 B.A. L.851 J.D. 608 Madison, Ste. 1400
Scott, Robert M. '44 '69 C&L.846 B.B.A., J.D.
(adm. in TX; not adm. in OH) 416 N. Erie St.‡
Scott, Robert M., (AV) . . . . '59 '84 C.734 B.A. L.851 J.D. [Williams,J.L.G.&S.]
Scott, Robert W. . . . . '27 '59 C.608 B.S.B.A. L.851 J.D. [Ballenger&M.] ‡
Scott, Rose Mock . . . . '69 '99 C&L.851 B.A., J.D. Pros. Off.
Sczesny, Daniel J. . . . . '— '03 C&L.851 B.A., J.D. [A S.J.Groth]
Searfoss, Robert E., III . . . . '77 '05 C.97 B.S. L.851 J.D. [A Shumaker,L.&K.]
Sechrist, Rebecca C., (BV) . . . . '61 '86 C.970 B.A. L.851 J.D. [Bunda S.&D.]
Secor, Richard T., (AV) . . . . '24 '51 C.477 A.B. L.851 LL.B. 2102 Whitehall Rd.‡
Secor, Thomas O., (BV) . . . . '52 '77 C.631 B.A. L.851 J.D. Asst. U.S. Atty.
Seitzinger, Mark P., (BV) . . . . '63 '89 C.381 B.A. L.608 J.D. [Ritter,R.M.&J.]
Selis, Tracy B. . . . . '75 '01 C.97 B.A. L.851 J.D. [A Rohrbachers L.C.&T.]
Semro, Timothy J. . . . . '73 '99 C.475 B.A. L.851 J.D. [LaValley,L.T.&S.]
Shanahan, J. Kearney, (AV) . . . . '44 '72 C.674 A.B. L.276 J.D. [Shanahan] ⊙
Shanahan Law Firm, The, LLC, (AV)
6600 Sylvania Avenue, Suite 270 (⊙Wash., DC; Cleve., OH)
Sharfman, Mervin S., (AV) . . . . '42 '67 C.477 A.B. L.851 J.D. 626 Madison Ave.
Sheehy, Joseph P. . . . . '22 '49 C.851 L.421 LL.B. 421 N. Huron St.
Shemas, James F., (BV) . . . . '18 '47 C&L.851 B.A., LL.B. [A Balk,H.&M.] ‡
Sherman, Nina . . . . '27 '58 C.851 B.A. L.607 J.D. 5925 319th St.
Shinaberry, Richard A., (BV) . . . . '40 '73 C&L.851 B.B.A., J.D. 520 Madison Ave.
Shindler, James V., Jr., (AV) '39 '66 C.608 B.S.B.A. L.851 J.D.
[Shindler,N.H.S.&M.]

Shindler, Neff, Holmes, Schlageter & Mohler, L.L.P., (AV)
1200 Edison Plaza, 300 Madison Avenue, 43604-1537
Telephone: 419-243-6281 Fax: 419-243-0129
Partners: James V. Shindler, Jr.; Carter Neff; Martin J. Holmes; John J. Schlageter, Jr.; Martin E. Mohler; Charles K. Boxell; Daniel A. Worline; John W. Rozic; James F. Dettinger; Catherine H. Noble; Jeffrey J. Perkins; Mary E. Smith; James A. Sulewski; Louis J. Yoppolo; Richard L. Emery; Peter A. Dewhirst; Martin J. Holmes, Jr.; Michael R. Goulding; John J. Schlageter, III. Associates: Heather J. Fournier; Theresa M. Neff.
See Professional Biographies, TOLEDO, OHIO

Shook, David C., (BV) . . . . '63 '90 C&L.851 B.A., J.D. [A Bunda S.&D.]
Shope, Gregory J. . . . . '73 '01 C&L.608 B.A., J.D. [A Shumaker,L.&K.]
Shousher, Eileen Sullivan . . . . '64 '90 C.116 B.A. L.851 J.D. Prob. Ct.
Shousher, Mohamed . . . . '54 '80 C&L.851 B.A., J.D. [M.Y.Shousher&Assoc.]
Shousher, Mohamed Y., & Assocs. . . . . 618 Adams St.
Shull, Mark E. . . . . '66 '92 C.385 A.B. L.851 J.D. 2650 N. Reynolds Rd., Ste. 3
Shumaker, Gregory S., (AV) . . . . '48 '73 C.473 A.B. L.276 J.D. [Shumaker,L.&K.]

Shumaker, Loop & Kendrick, LLP, (AV) [BB]
North Courthouse Square, 1000 Jackson, 43624-1573 ⊙
Telephone: 419-241-9000 Fax: 419-241-6894
URL: http://www.slk-law.com
Partners of Firm: Erin Smith Aebel (Resident, Tampa, Florida Office); Peter C. Anderson (Resident, Charlotte, North Carolina Office); M. Scott Aubry; Jaime Austrich (Resident, Tampa, Florida Office);

(This Listing Continued)

Shumaker, Loop & Kendrick, LLP (Continued)

John C. Barron; Jenifer A. Belt; Kathleen M. Bickelhaupt (Resident, Tampa, Florida Office); Thomas C. Blank; Aleta M. Bonini; Michael E. Born (Resident, Columbus, Ohio Office); Michael M. Briley; Eric D. Britton; John H. Burson; C. Philip Campbell, Jr. (Resident, Tampa, Florida Office); C. Graham Carothers, Jr. (Resident, Tampa, Florida Office); Mark A. Catchur (Resident, Tampa, Florida Office); Philip S. Chubb (Resident, Charlotte, North Carolina Office); David Harris Conaway (Resident, Charlotte, North Carolina Office); Mark A. Connolly (Resident, Tampa, Florida Office); Thomas A. Cotter; Marlene (Neema) M. Cottrill-Bell; David J. Coyle; Jeffrey S. Creamer; Mary Li Creasy (Board Certified Labor and Employment Lawyer, Florida Bar Board of Legal Specialization and Education) (Resident, Tampa, Florida Office); Duane A. Daiker (Resident, Tampa, Florida Office); Diane Vulich Davis; Terrance K. Davis; Scott G. Deller; Gary R. Diesing; Thomas P. Dillon; Jonathan J. Ellis (Resident, Tampa, Florida Office); Edwin G. Emerson; Julio C. Esquivel (Resident, Tampa, Florida Office); William G. Fischer; Vivian C. Folk; Jeffrey E. Fort; Sharon M. Fulop; Jack G. Fynes; Bruce H. Gordon (Resident, Tampa, Florida Office); William H. Gosline; Kevin H. Graham (Resident, Tampa, Florida Office); David M. Grogan (Resident, Charlotte, North Carolina Office); John E. Haller (Resident, Columbus, Ohio Office); Daniel R. Hansen (Resident, Charlotte, North Carolina Office); Douglas G. Haynam; Edwin L. Herbert; William H. Heywood, III; John W. Hilbert, II; Charles W. Hiller; William Kent Ihrig (Resident, Tampa, Florida Office); John S. Inglis (Resident, Tampa, Florida Office); Regina M. Joseph; Robert A. Koenig; Kathleen A. Kress; Gregory T. Lodge; Oksana M. Ludd; Moses Luski (Resident, Charlotte, North Carolina Office); Paul R. Lynch (Resident, Tampa, Florida Office); John N. MacKay; Ernest J. Marquart (Resident, Tampa, Florida Office); Timothy C. McCarthy; Susan D. McClay; Owen P. McGill (Resident, Tampa, Florida Office); Michael S. McGowan; Brian N. McMahon; William H. McNair (Resident, Charlotte, North Carolina Office); Donald M. Mewhort, Jr.; Michael J. O'Callaghan (Resident, Columbus, Ohio Office); Barbara R. Pankau (Resident, Tampa, Florida Office); William L. Patberg; Mary Ellen Pisanelli; Thomas G. Pletz; David J. Rectenwald; Cynthia L. Rerucha; Edward J. Richardson (Resident, Tampa, Florida Office); Joseph A. Rideout; Michael H. Robbins (Resident, Tampa, Florida Office); H. Buswell Roberts, Jr.; James I. Rothschild; Stephen A. Rothschild; Michael G. Sanderson; Rolf H. Scheidel; Steven G. Schember (Resident, Tampa, Florida Office); Gregory S. Shumaker; John J. Siciliano; Peter R. Silverman; Joseph S. Simpson; Darrell C. Smith (Resident, Tampa, Florida Office); Lyman F. Spitzer; Angelina M. Stayton (Resident, Tampa, Florida Office); Scott M. Stevenson (Resident, Charlotte, North Carolina Office); Mark C. Stewart; John L. Straub; William H. Sturges (Resident, Charlotte, North Carolina Office); Theodore C. Taub (Not admitted in OH; Board Certified Real Estate Lawyer, Florida Bar Board of Legal Specialization and Education); W. Thompson Thorn, III (Resident, Tampa, Florida Office); Frederick M. Thurman, Jr. (Resident, Charlotte, North Carolina Office); J. Todd Timmerman (Resident, Tampa, Florida Office); Louis E. Tosi; Michael T. Trocke (Resident, Tampa, Florida Office); Barton L. Wagenman; Robert R. Warchola (Resident, Tampa, Florida Office); David F. Waterman; Thomas I. Webb, Jr.; Martin D. Werner; David W. Wicklund; Dennis P. Witherell; Thomas M. Wood (Resident, Tampa, Florida Office); Kathryn J. Woodward; Gregory C. Yadley (Resident, Tampa, Florida Office). Associates: Eileen M. Best; Rebecca A. Briggs (Resident, Tampa, Florida Office); Megan A. Fitzpatrick Bula; William C. Bunting, Jr. (Resident, Charlotte, North Carolina Office); Ryan M. Cardoso (Resident, Tampa, Florida Office); C. Christopher Clark (Resident, Charlotte, North Carolina Office); Edward J. Comey (Resident, Tampa, Florida Office); Stefanie E. Deller; Andrew P. Felix (Resident, Tampa, Florida Office); Matthew J. Ginsburg (Not admitted in OH; Resident, Charlotte, North Carolina Office); Nathan A. Hall; Gregory-Scott R. Haney (Resident, Tampa, Florida Office); W. Reed Hauptman; Robin L. Henderson (Resident, Tampa, Florida Office); John D. Kocher (Resident, Charlotte, North Carolina Office); Samuel R. Linsky (Resident, Tampa, Florida Office); Kathleen K. Lucchesi (Resident, Charlotte, North Carolina Office); David J. Mack; Patricia Wilson Magee (Resident, Charlotte, North Carolina Office); Nicholas D. Malone; Jason M. Manor (Resident, Tampa, Florida Office); David A. Matthews (Resident, Charlotte, North Carolina Office); Gregory E. Matton (Resident, Tampa, Florida Office); Steven A. Meckler (Resident, Charlotte, North Carolina Office); Mark E. Mercer; James H. O'Doherty; W. Jan Pietruszka (Resident, Tampa, Florida Office); Michael J. Podolsky; Maria C. Ramos (Resident, Tampa, Florida Office); Damian M.P. Rodgers; Joseph J. Santaniello (Resident, Charlotte, North Carolina Office); S. Alban Scott (Resident, Tampa, Florida Office); Robert E. Searfoss, III; Gregory J. Shope; Christopher M. Smith; Michael A. Snyder (Resident, Columbus, Ohio Office); John J. Staler; Cynthia L.K. Steele; Karen H. Stiles (Resident, Charlotte, North Carolina Office); Robert Ernest Sumner, IV (Resident, Charlotte, North Carolina Office); Katie L. Tournoux (Resident, Columbus, Ohio Office); Mark D. Wagoner, Jr.; S. Frederick Winiker, III (Resident, Charlotte, North Carolina Office); Mechelle Zarou. Of Counsel: Gregory G. Alexander; Marc Gertner; John F. Hayward; A. Edward McGinty (Resident, Tampa, Florida Office); Walter W. Reckless (Resident, Columbus, Ohio Office); Darrel J. Scott. Counsel: Alejandro J. Fernandez (Resident, Tampa, Florida Office); Tammy N. Giroux (Not admitted in OH; Resident, Tampa, Florida Office); James F. White, Jr.
Administrative Law; Advertising and Marketing; Agency and Distributorships; Agricultural Law; Alternative Dispute Resolution; Antitrust and Trade Regulation; Appellate Practice; Bankruptcy; Banks and Banking; Business Law; Business Crimes; Business Torts; Civil Rights; Commercial Law; Commercial Litigation; Commercial Real Estate; Communications and Media; Complex and Multi-District Litigation; Computers and Software; Construction Law; Contracts; Copyrights; Corporate Law; Federal Criminal Law; Debtor and Creditor; Domestic Relations; Education Law; Employee Benefits; Entertainment Law; Environmental Law; Fidelity and Surety; Finance; Franchises and Franchising; Health Care; Hospital Law; Immigration and Naturalization; Intellectual Property; International Law; Labor and Employment; Leases and Leasing; Litigation; Media Law; Medicare and Medicaid; Mergers, Acquisitions and Divestitures; Nonprofit and Charitable Organizations; Patent Litigation; Personal Injury; Probate; Products Liability; Professional Liability; Public Finance; Real Estate; Securities; Sports Law; Taxation; Torts; Trade Secrets; Trademarks; Trusts and Estates; Unfair Competition; Wills; Zoning, Planning and Land Use.
Representative Clients: AVAILABLE UPON REQUEST.
Tampa, Florida Office: 101 East Kennedy Boulevard, Suite 2800, 33602-5151. Telephone: 813-229-7600. Fax: 813-229-1660.
Charlotte, North Carolina Office: 128 South Tryon Street, Suite 1800, 28202. Telephone: 704-375-0057. Fax: 704-332-1197.
Columbus, Ohio Office: Huntington Center, 41 South High Street, Suite 2400, 43215. Telephone: 614-463-9441. Fax: 614-463-1108.
See Professional Biographies, TOLEDO, OHIO

Shuster, Myrna A. . . . . '62 '89 C.150 B.A. L.930 J.D. 5580 Monroe St., Suite 200
Siciliano, John J., (AV) . . . . '53 '78 C.477 B.B.A. L.215 J.D. [Shumaker,L.&K.]
Siegel, Joseph A. . . . . '14 '38 C.851 L.608 LL.B. 4102 Garden Estates Dr.‡
Sieler, Jean Ann S., (AV) . . . . '61 '87 C&L.851 B.S., J.D. [Robison,C.&O.] ⊙
Sikkema, Gary D., (AV) . . . . '47 '75 C&L.477 B.B.A., J.D. [Spengler N.]
Sikkema, Sue A., (BV) . . . . '48 '82 C&L.477 A.B., J.D. [Bunda S.&D.]
Silk, James P., Jr., (BV) . . . . '68 '93 C.228 B.A. L.477 J.D. [Spengler N.]
Silk, James P., Sr., (AV) . . . . '31 '62 C.602 A.B. L.851 LL.B. [C Spengler N.]
Silverman, Nathan L., (BV) . . . . '36 '61 C&L.851 B.B.A., J.D. Spitzer Bldg.
Silverman, Peter R., (AV) . . . . '55 '82 C.273 B.A. L.477 J.D. [Shumaker,L.&K.]

Simko, David, (AV) '49 '75 C.851 B.A. L.117 J.D.
6620 West Central Avenue, 43617
Telephone: 419-517-5555 Fax: 419-517-5556
URL: http://www.lawyers.com/davidsimko
Estate Planning, Real Estate, Small Business.
See Professional Biographies, TOLEDO, OHIO

Simpson, Joseph S., (BV) . . . . '62 '88 C.55 B.S. L.851 J.D. [Shumaker,L.&K.]
Singer, Arlene, (BV) . . . . '48 '76 C&L.851 B.A., J.D. 6th Dist. Ct. of App.
Skinner, Robert A., Law Offices of, (BV) '41 '69
C.294 B.A. L.851 J.D. 3601 W. Alexis Rd., Ste. 102
Skotynsky, Walter J., (CV) . . . . '46 '76 C.477 B.S.M.E. L.851 J.D. 1018 Adams Street
Skow, William J. . . . . '41 '67 C.309 A.B. L.477 J.D. Com. Pleas J.
Slater, James Alexander, Jr. . . . . '40 '66 C.385 A.B. L.309 LL.D. Dist. J.
Slaybod, Sheldon M., (BV) . . . . '50 '75 C.107 B.S. L.851 J.D. [Casey&S.]
Sloma, Anthony P. . . . . '68 '97 C&L.851 B.S.Ch.E., J.D. Perstorp Polyols Inc.

Slowik & Robinson, LLC
(See Columbus)

Smith, Arthur H., (AV) . . . . '35 '60 C.164 B.A. L.146 J.D. Libbey, Inc.
Smith, Bruce L., (AV) . . . . '41 '66 C&L.608 B.A., J.D. [Eastman&S.]
Smith, Christopher M. . . . . '72 '00 C.381 B.A. L.607 J.D. [A Shumaker,L.&K.]

Smith, Clare K., (BV) '68 '94 C.210 B.A. L.347 J.D. [🄲 Marshall&M.]
Smith, H. Terrence '56 '81 C.215 B.A. L.309 J.D.
(adm. in MI; not adm. in OH) Sr. V.P. & Gen. Coun., Mercy Health Partners
Smith, J. P., (CV) '51 '97 C&L.851 B.S., J.D. 412 Fourteenth Street
Smith, Jeffrey T. '68 '93 4149 Holland-Sylvania Rd., Ste. 7
Smith, Mary E., (BV) '43 '85 C.44 B.A. L.851 J.D. [Shindler,N.H.S.&M.]
Smith, Steven R., (AV) '53 '80 C.473 B.A. L.851 J.D. [Connelly,J.&C.]
Smith, Susan L. '55 '00 C&L.851 B.S., J.D. Atty., Owens-Illinois, Inc.
Smith, Victoria Lynn '57 '87 C.8 B.A. L.7 J.D. 3139 Evergreen Road
Smoktonowicz, Andrea B. '78 '04 C.608 B.A. L.607 J.D. [🄰 Eastman&S.]
Snavely, Jeffrey D., (BV) '69 '96 C&L.851 B.B.A., J.D. [🄰 Eastman&S.]
Snyder, Constance A., (BV) '56 '83 C&L.851 B.S., J.D. 405 Madison Ave., Ste. 2020
Sobanski, Mark J., (AV) '55 '82 C&L.851 B.S.E.E., J.D. [MacMillan,S.&T.] (Pat.)

Sobecki, Thomas A., (BV) '56 '81 C.851 B.A. L.597 J.D.
520 Madison Avenue, Suite 811, 43604 ⊙
Telephone: 419-242-9908 Fax: 419-242-9937
Email: tsobecki@tomsobecki.com URL: http://www.lawyers.com/tomsobecki
Civil Rights, Discrimination, Libel, Slander and Defamation, Contracts, Breach of Contract, Education Law, School Law, Labor and Employment, Americans with Disabilities Act, Family and Medical Leave Act, Sexual Harassment, Wrongful Termination, Law Enforcement, Police Misconduct, Military Law.

See Professional Biographies, TOLEDO, OHIO

Sodeman, William A., Jr. '36 '97 C.502 B.A. L.851 J.D. 2017 Shenandoah Rd.
Solt, Robert L., III, (AV) '59 '84 C.473 B.A. L.851 J.D. [Bugbee&C.]
Sommer, Gary O., (BV) '55 '84 C.473 B.A. L.851 J.D. [Watkins,B.&C.]
Souders, Kenneth M. '50 '78 C.610 B.S. L.851 J.D. 3236 Zone Ave.
Sparrow, Keithley B., (BV) '46 '79
C.611 B.A. L.851 J.D. 608 Madison Avenue Suite 1400
Speer, Richard L. '41 '66 C&L.607 B.S., J.D. U.S. Bkrptcy. J.
Spencer, Jodi D. '74 '01 C.97 B.A. L.851 J.D. [🄰 Cooper&W.]
Spencer, Scott E., (AV) '48 '79 C&L.851 B.A., J.D. Spitzer Building

Spengler Nathanson P.L.L., (AV)
608 Madison Avenue, Suite 1000, 43604-1169
Telephone: 419-241-2201 FAX: 419-241-8599
Email: jsilksr@spenglernathanson.com URL: http://www.spenglernathanson.com
Otto H. Spengler (1890-1970); John J. McCarthy (1909-1969); J.H. Nathanson (1906-1992); Frank T. Pizza (1925-2000); Benjamin B. Durfee (1919-2000). Members of Firm: Ralph Bragg; James R. Jeffery; Norman J. Rubinoff; B. Gary McBride; David G. Wise; Theodore M. Rowen; Gary D. Sikkema; Truman A. Greenwood; Cheryl F. Wolff; Louise A. Jackson; Richard E. Wolff; Byron S. Choka; James C. Anderson; Susan B. Nelson; Lisa E. Pizza; Joan C. Szuberla; Teresa L. Grigsby; Michael W. Bragg; James P. Silk, Jr.; Laurie J. Pangle; Patricia Hayden Kurt; Thomas A. Lupica; Anastasia K. Hanson; John P. Hayward. Associate: Randy L. Meyer. Of Counsel: Joel A. Levine; James P. Silk, Sr.; Joseph S. Heyman (Retired); Andrew E. Anderson; Richard A. Entenmann; Louis J. Hattner.
General Civil and Trial Practice in all State and Federal Courts. Federal and State Civil and Criminal Practice. Corporation, Taxation, Probate and Estate Planning, Real Estate, Education, Labor and Employment, Workers' Compensation, Commercial, Securities, Bankruptcy, Health Care, Employee Benefits, Public Sector Law and Environmental Law.
Counsel for: Fifth-Third Bank of Northwestern Ohio, N.A.; Huntington Bank of Toledo; Society Bank & Trust; Seaway Food Town, Inc.; The University of Toledo; AP Parts; Toledo Lucas County Port Authority; Toledo Board of Education.

See Professional Biographies, TOLEDO, OHIO

Speyer, Bennett H., (BV) '60 '85 C.472 B.A. L.851 J.D. [Eastman&S.]
Speyer, Sharon S., (BV) '59 '85
C.608 B.A. L.851 J.D. Sr. V.P. & Gen. Coun., Mid Am Bank
Spiker, Douglas E., (AV) '61 '86 C.528 B.A. L.607 J.D. [Roetzel&A.]
Spitler, Steven M., (BV) '54 '81 C.97 B.A. L.851 J.D. [Spitler&W.L.&Assoc.]

Spitler, Huffman, Yoon & Newlove, LLP
(See Bowling Green)

Spitler & Williams-Young , A Legal Professional Association, (BV)
1000 Adams Street, Suite 200
Spitzer, John B., (AV) '18 '47 C&L.976 B.A., LL.B. [Spitzer&H.]
Spitzer, Lyman F., (AV) '49 '76 C.951 B.A. L.477 J.D. [Shumaker,L.&K.]
Spitzer & Hummer Legal Services, (AV) 520 Madison Ave., Ste. 915
Spohler, Norman Gerhard '47 '81 C.97 B.L.S. L.851 J.D. 2551 Oak Grove Place
Sponseller, Carrie L. '76 '01 C.97 B.A. L.851 J.D. [🄰 Eastman&S.]
Squillante, David G., Law Office of, (BV) '58 '82
C.150 B.A. L.228 J.D. Suite 1523, 608 Madison Avenue
Staler, John J. '71 '99 C&L.851 B.A., J.D. [🄰 Shumaker,L.&K.]
Stallings, Douglas E. '65 '94 C.101 B.A. L.851 J.D. [🄰 Bunda S.&D.]
Stancati, Joseph A., (AV) '47 '72
C.1031 B.A. L.851 J.D. Dir. of Litig., Dana Corporation
Stanford, Stephen J., (AV) '49 '75 C&L.608 B.S., J.D. [Fuller&H.]
Starcher, John Marius, Jr. '70 '01
C.97 B.S.B.A. L.851 J.D. St. Vincent Mercy Medical Center
Starr, Kimberly A. '71 '99 C.8 B.S.B.A. L.851 J.D. [🄰 Eastman&S.]
Steele, Cynthia L.K. '63 '92 C.851 B.S.N. L.37 J.D. [🄰 Shumaker,L.&K.] ‡
Steen, Daniel K. '61 '87 C.890 B.A. L.893 J.D.
(adm. in VA; not adm. in OH) Dir., Govt. Affs., Owens-Illinois, Inc.
Steinbock, Daniel J. '46 '72
C&L.976 B.A., J.D. Prof. of Law, Univ. of Toledo Coll. of Law
Steltenpohl, Darrell David '52 '99 C&L.851 B.S., J.D. [Steltenpohl,J.&M.]

Steltenpohl, James & Menacher, Co., LPA, (BV)
421 N. Michigan Street, Suite A, 43624
Telephone: 419-243-6200 Fax: 419-243-6280
Email: toledolaw@mail.com
William L. Menacher (1924-2004); Darrell David Steltenpohl; Mary M. James.
Family Law, Divorce, Dissolution, Child Custody, Child Support, Visitation Rights, Adoption, Bankruptcy, Criminal Law, Juvenile Law, Traffic Violations, DWI, Misdemeanors, Felonies, Trusts and Estates, Wills and Probate, Corporate Law, Business Law, Business Litigation, Business Formation, Personal Injury, Slip and Fall, Automobile Accidents, Truck Accidents, Real Estate Law.

See Professional Biographies, TOLEDO, OHIO

Steves, Jennifer '59 '02 C.473 B.S. L.851 J.D. [🄰 Cooper&W.]
Stewart, Mark C. '47 '72 C.604 B.A. L.494 J.D. [Shumaker,L.&K.]
Stockwell, John P., (AV) '46 '73 C.608 B.S. L.851 J.D. [Stockwell&C.]

Stockwell & Cooperman, A Legal Professional Association, (AV)
Suite 1610, One SeaGate, 43604
Telephone: 419-247-1500 Telecopier: 419-247-1575
URL: http://www.stockwellandcooperman.com
John P. Stockwell; Ronald M. Cooperman;—Steven J. Poturalski; Drew A. Nitschke. Of Counsel: Katherine Raup O'Connell.
Taxation, Wills and Probate, Trusts and Estate, Elder Law, Estate Planning, Business Law, Corporate, Partnership, Mergers and Acquisitions, Corporate Finance, Real Estate, Buying and Selling of Business, Family Business, LLC Law, Partnership Law, Small Business, Contracts, Charitable Giving, Non Profit-Organizations.
Reference: Fifth Third Bank, Toledo, Ohio.

See Professional Biographies, TOLEDO, OHIO

Stoner, Amy Elizabeth '71 '00 C.201 B.A. L.851 J.D. [A.E.Stoner]
Stoner, Amy E. 520 Madison Ave., Ste. 545
Stopar, Jeffrey M. '70 '96 C.8 B.A. L.851 J.D. [🄰 Eastman&S.]
Straub, Jessica W. '76 '03 C.477 B.A. L.851 J.D. [🄰 Anspach M.E.]
Straub, John L., (AV) '45 '70 C.477 B.A. L.851 J.D. [Shumaker,L.&K.]
Strauss, Steven D. '65 '90 C.318 B.A. L.930 J.D.
(adm. in NY; not adm. in OH) 3156 Kylemore Rd.
Strup, David P., (AV) '60 '86 C.602 B.B.A. L.608 J.D. [Cooper&W.]
Stuckey, David W., (AV) '50 '75 C.117 B.A. L.608 J.D. [Robison,C.&O.]
Stump, Alexandra M. '74 '03 C.150 B.S. L.851 J.D. [🄰 Eastman&S.]
Sturgeon, Peggy Mattimoe, (AV) '64 '90 C.973 B.A. L.893 J.D. [Eastman&S.]
Stutz, Barbara J., (AV) '51 '83 C&L.851 B.Ed., J.D. [Bunda S.&D.]
Stutz, Paul F. '25 '56 C&L.851 B.S.Ch. Eng., J.D. 520 Madison Ave. (Pat.)
Sulewski, James A., (BV) '54 '87 C&L.851 B.B.A., J.D. [Shindler,N.H.S.&M.]
Sullivan, Michelle T. '72 '99 C.610 B.S.Ed. L.200 J.D. [🄰 Allotta&F.]
Sullivan, Richard J., (BV) '31 '58 C.363 B.S. L.851 J.D. 520 Madison Ave.
Sutter, Gary M. '55 '84 C.879 B.A. L.1119 J.D. [🄰 MacMillan,S.&T.] (Pat.)
Sutter, Jude F., (AV) '29 '59 C.215 L.851 J.D. [Kroncke,D.S.&F.]
Sweetnam, John W. '43 '72 C&L.851 B.Ed., J.D. 3 Exmoor
Swemba, Connie S. '55 '03 C&L.851 B.A., J.D. [🄰 Eastman&S.]
Syring, Paul F., (CV) '63 '90 C.608 B.S., B.A. L.851 J.D. City of Toledo, Dept. of Law
Syring, William J. '18 '42 C&L.602 A.B., LL.B. 316 N. Michigan St.
Szczepaniak, Richard J., (BV) '51 '77 C.608 B.Sc. L.851 J.D. P.O. Box 501
Szuberla, Joan C., (BV) '42 '83 C.999 B.A. L.851 J.D. [Spengler N.]
Szuch, David P. '52 '82 C&L.851 B.B.A., J.D. Atty., Bureau of Workers Comp.
Szyperski, Thomas J., (BV) '42 '70 C&L.851 B.B.S., J.D. 411 Michigan
Tafelski, Joseph Robert '46 '71 C.973 B.S. L.93 J.D. 520 Madison Ave., Ste. 740
Takacs, William E., (BV) '51 '76 C.381 B.G.S. L.851 J.D. [Gallon&T.]
Talbott, D. Casey, (BV) '64 '90 C&L.608 B.A., J.D. [Robison,C.&O.]
Tanner, Harold W. '22 '54 C&L.851 B.B.A., J.D. 4841 Monroe St.‡
Taoka, L. Mari, (BV) '51 '79
C.851 B.A. L.608 J.D. National City Bank N.W., 405 Madison Ave.
Tardy, Cassandra L. '67 '92
C.1044 B.A. L.107 J.D. Fin. Admr., NorthRiver Develop. Corp.
Tarini, Mary Jo, (BV) '47 '91 C.608 B.S. L.851 J.D. [🄰 Eastman&S.]
Tassie, Deborah S., (BV) '49 '79 C.174 B.A. L.851 J.D. 4853 Monroe St.
Taub, Theodore C., (AVⓉ) '— '60 C.228 B.A. L.260 J.D.
(adm. in FL; not adm. in OH) [Shumaker,L.&K.] (⊙Tampa, FL)
Taylor, David R., III '49 '76 C&L.851 B.A., J.D. [McConnell&T.]
Taylor, Gary R., (BV) '50 '88 C.608 B.A. L.851 J.D. Dept. of Law
Testa, Chas. R., (AV) '15 '42 C.999 Ph.B. L.851 J.D. 407 Raymer Blvd.
Thacker, Joseph P., (AV) '53 '78 C&L.851 B.A., J.D. [Cooper&W.]
Thakur, Nirakar C., (BV) '60 '95 C&L.851 M.B.A., J.D. 416 N. Erie St., Ste. 200
Theis, Donald E., (BV) '54 '79 C.973 A.B. L.477 J.D. [Baran,P.T.F.&T.]
Thomas, Kimberly M. '77 '03 C.608 B.S.N. L.607 J.D. [🄰 Robison,C.&O.]
Thomas, Wm. N., Sr., (BV) '12 '51 C&L.851 B.E., J.D. 1060 Lincoln Ave.
Thomson, Joseph M., (BV) '54 '80 C.373 B.A. L.851 J.D. [🄰 Balk,H.&M.]
Tice, Ronald J., (AV) '47 '73 C.882 B.A. L.851 J.D. [Eastman&S.]
Timonere, Steven, Law Offices of, (AV) '31 '55 C.610 B.S.C. L.608 J.D.
4355 River Road
Tinsley, Dusty Renée '— '00 C.696 B.S. L.851 J.D. [🄰 Cooper&W.]
Todak, Michael J., (AV) '57 '82 C&L.851 B.B.A., J.D. [LaValley,L.T.&S.]
Todd, Oliver E., Jr., (AV) '40 '67 C.477 B.S.E.E. L.273 J.D. [MacMillan,S.&T.] (Pat.)
Todd-Terpinski, Kimberly '— '98 C.97 B.S. L.851 J.D. [🄰 Cooper&W.]
Tomczak, Thomas N., (BV) '40 '68 C&L.851 B.E., J.D. 2673 Goddard Rd.
Torzewski, Joan, (AV) '52 '77 C&L.851 B.A., J.D. [Harris R.T.]
Tosi, Louis E., (AV) '49 '74 C&L.608 B.A., J.D. [Shumaker,L.&K.]
Toska, Anita S. '73 '03 C&L.851 B.S.I.E., J.D. [🄰 MacMillan,S.&T.]
Toska, David L., (BV) '53 '83 C&L.851 B.A., J.D. Asst. Pros. Atty.
Touschner, Anthony J. '44 '73 C.999 B.A. L.930 J.D.
Staff Atty., Advocates for Basic Legal Equality, Inc.

Traband, Charles M., Jr., (BV) '50 '78 C&L.851 B.A., J.D.
608 Madison Avenue, Suite 1400, 43604-1121
Telephone: 419-242-1400 Fax: 419-246-5764
Email: chuck@trabandlaw.com
Labor and Employment Relations (Management Only), Corporate, Real Estate, Civil Litigation.
Reference: Key Bank, Toledo.

See Professional Biographies, TOLEDO, OHIO

Tracey, Shawn M. '71 '01 C&L.851 B.B.A., J.D. [🄰 Eastman&S.]
Trachsel, Kenneth R. '49 '89
C.381 B.B.A. L.851 J.D. Assoc. Coun., ProMedica Health System
Trimble, J. Mark, (BV) '61 '90 C.97 B.S.B.A. L.851 J.D. [Rohrbachers L.C.&T.]
Trimboli, Mary G., (BV) '53 '78 C.116 B.A. L.851 J.D. Mun. J.
Troendle, Janelle M. '76 '03 C&L.851 B.E., J.D. [🄰 Bugbee&C.]
Trudel, Valerie A. '61 '97 C&L.851 B.S., J.D. [Kitch D.W.V.&S.]
Trusiak, Robert G. '60 '86 C.8 B.S. L.1003 J.D. 4 Seagate
Tucker, Robert P., (BV) '38 '64 C&L.273 B.A., LL.B. [🄰 Balk,H.&M.]
Tucker, Theodore B., III, (BV) '51 '76 C&L.851 B.Ed., J.D. 421 Michigan St., Ste. B
Turin, John C., (BV) '44 '70 C&L.851 B.A., J.D. 6545 W. Central Ave., Ste. 209
Turley, Anthony E., (BV) '63 '98 C&L.851 B.S., J.D. [Connelly,J.&C.]
Turner, James N., (BV) '52 '78 C.207 B.A. L.851 J.D. One Gov't. Ctr.
Tuschman, Chad M., (CV) '70 '95 C.347 B.S. L.851 J.D. [🄰 Williams,J.L.G.&S.]

Udell & Abramson, Ltd.
(See Sylvania)

Underwood, Jane Lindsay '54 '84 C.610 B.A. L.7 J.D. Libr., Co. Pub. Libr.
Vail, James E., Jr., (BV) '49 '76 C.5 B.A. L.851 J.D. Asst. Co. Pros.
Valtin, James D. '70 '03 C.97 B.A. L.851 J.D. [🄰 Balk,H.&M.]
Van Berkom, Trevor Paul, (BV) '66 '92 C&L.585 B.B.A., J.D. 500 Madison Ave.
Van Gunten, Edward A., (BV) '37 '62 C&L.851 B.S., LL.B. [E.VanGunten]
Van Gunten, Edward, & Co., L.P.A., (BV) 6545 W. Central Ave., Ste. 209
Van Horsten, Craig J., (AV) '51 '76 C.473 B.A. L.608 J.D. [Fuller&H.]
Varner, Philip W. '58 '92 C&L.851 B.A., J.D. 2510 Consaul St.
Vassar, J. Michael, (AV) '40 '68 C.608 B.A. L.851 J.D. [Vassar,D.D.&B.]
Vassar, Dills, Dawson & Bonfiglio, LLC, (AV) 420 Madison Ave., Ste. 1102
Vaughan, Deon '58 '90 C.705 B.A. L.851 J.D.
V.P. Enviro. Health & Safety, Owens Corning
Viren, Jack P., Jr. '45 '78 C.707 B.A. L.851 J.D. 1018 Adams Street
Voller, Cindy M., (BV) '61 '92 C&L.851 B.A., J.D. 101 Main St., 2nd Fl.
Wachowiak, Joseph Walter '50 '83 C&L.851 B.S., J.D. 2823 Kendale
Wagenman, Barton L., (AV) '42 '67 C.472 B.S. L.309 LL.B. [Shumaker,L.&K.]
Wagner, Peter J., (BV) '44 '72 C&L.851 B.B.A., J.D. 608 Madison Ave., 14th Fl.
Wagoner, Gregory H. '74 '01 C.477 B.A. L.851 J.D. [🄰 Anspach M.E.]
Wagoner, Mark D., Jr., (BV) '71 '97 C.276 B.A. L.608 J.D. [🄰 Shumaker,L.&K.]
Wakefield, Craig J. '79 '04 C.97 B.A. L.851 J.D. [🄰 Jones&S.]

Walinski, Richard S., (AV) .... '43 '69 C&L.851 B.A., J.D. [Cooper&W.]
Walinski, Thaddeus N. .... '12 '39 C.851 Ph.B. L.607 2619 Densmore Dr.‡
Walker, Jodi L. .... '70 '96 C.97 B.S.B.A. L.851 J.D. Ernst & Young LLP
Wallin, Janet L., (Mrs.) '33 '61 C.476 L.424 LL.B.
Law Libr., Acquis. Dept., Univ. of Toledo College of Law
Wanick, John R., (AV) .... '45 '70 C.473 B.A. L.851 J.D. [Anspach M.E.]
Ward, David A., (AV) .... '34 '58 C&L.608 B.A., J.D. 3356 Brookside Rd.
Ward, George C., (AV) .... '49 '76 C.103 B.A. L.851 J.D. [Cooper&W.]
Ward, Anderson, Porritt & Bila, (AV)
3230 Central Park W. Drive (Bloomfield Hills, MI)
Wasielewski, Glenn E., (BV) .... '56 '82 C.97 B.A. L.851 J.D. [Manahan,P.B.&D.]
Wasserman, John C., (BV) .... '39 '64 C.215 Ph.B. L.608 J.D. [Wasserman,B.L.&H.]
Wasserman, Bryan, Landry & Honold, LLP, (AV) .... 405 North Huron Street
Wasung, John Stephen, (BV) .... '58 '84 C.477 B.A. L.912 J.D. [Kitch D.W.V.&S.]
Waterman, David F., (AV) .... '49 '75 C.674 B.S.E. L.477 J.D. [Shumaker,L.&K.]

Watkins, Bates & Carey, LLP, (AV)
National City Bank Building, 405 Madison Avenue, Suite 1900, 43604-1207
Telephone: 419-241-2100 Telecopier: 419-241-1960
Email: postoffice@wbc-law.com URL: http://www.wbc-law.com
Members of Firm: Harley A. Watkins (1902-1979); William F. Bates; John M. Carey; Gary O. Sommer; Thomas C. Gess; Kimberly S. Kondalski; Robert W. Bohmer; R. Kent Murphree. Senior Attorney: Ann M. McCauley. Associate: Jessica R. Hamner.
General Civil Practice. Trials and Appeals. Trust, Probate and Estate Planning, Corporation, Health and Hospital, Non-Profit Organizations, Real Estate, Taxation, Bankruptcy Law, Workers Compensation, Labor Law and Employment Law.
Counsel for: Flower Hospital; Fostoria Community Hospital; National City Bank, Northwest; Heidtman Steel Products, Inc.; Nazar Rubber Co.
See Professional Biographies, TOLEDO, OHIO

Watson, Laurie A. .... '74 '02 C.97 B.S. L.851 J.D. [Eastman&S.]
Waugh, Bradley R. .... '71 '99 C&L.851 B.S., J.D. [Malone,A.&F.]
Wawrzyniak, Jeffery J., (BV) '67 '91 C&L.851 B.A., J.D.
Litigation Coun., Dana Corp.
Weaver, Donna M., Law Offices of, (BV) '45 '82 C.97 B.S. L.930 J.D.
1022 Shadow Lane
Webb, Linde Hurst, (BV) .... '48 '73 C.381 B.S. L.930 J.D. 2630 Edgehill Road
Webb, Thomas I., Jr., (AV) .... '48 '73 C.951 B.A. L.930 J.D. [Shumaker,L.&K.]

Weber & Sterling, LLC
(See Maumee)

Webster, John B. .... '33 '82 C.611 B.A. L.851 J.D. 4719 Springbrook‡
Wedding, Donald K. .... '34 '64 C.421 B.S.Ch.E. L.30 J.D. Univ. of Toledo
Weghorst, Richard Dietrich .... '66 '00 C.886 B.A. L.851 J.D. Off. of the Secy. of State
Weglian, John J., (BV) .... '43 '72 C&L.851 B.Ed., J.D. Chief, Spec. Units Div.
Weiher, Roger R. .... '26 '56 C.932 B.S. L.851 LL.B. Mun. J., Housing & Envir.
Weinberg, Mark D., (BV) .... '50 '75 C.473 A.B. L.851 J.D. 5414 Monroe St.
Weir, Francis Fauquier .... '50 '87 C.802 B.F.A. L.851 J.D. Toledo Legal Aid Soc.
Weisenburger, Margaret M., (BV) .... '52 '78 C&L.851 B.Ed., J.D. 617 Miami St.
Weisenburger, Thomas E., (AV) .... '36 '62 C.215 Ph.B. L.770 J.D. [Cline,C.&W.]
Weller, Lucinda J. .... '69 '97 L.851 J.D. 520 Madison Avenue, Suite 837
Wells, Michael H. .... '47 '87 C&L.851 B.S.C.E., J.D. 4912 N. Summit St.‡
Wensink, Karen J. .... '71 '02 C.608 B.A L.851 J.D. [McHugh,D.&M.]
Werner, Kim Whitmer .... '44 '71 C&L.930 B.A., J.D. [K.W.Werner]
Werner, Martin D., (AV) .... '56 '81 C.851 B.A. L.930 J.D. [Shumaker,L.&K.]
Werner, Kim W., LPA .... 3034 Barrington Drive
Westmeyer, Joseph W., III, (CV) ..... '73 '99 C.973 B.S.B.A. L.851 J.D. [Westmeyer]
Westmeyer, Joseph W., Jr. .... '41 '66 C.973 B.S.B.A. L.851 J.D. [Westmeyer]

Westmeyer Law Offices
421 North Michigan Street, Suite C, 43624-2394
Telephone: 419-244-7041 Fax: 419-244-1140
Email: joe@westmeyer.com URL: http://www.westmeyerlaw.com
Joseph W. Westmeyer, Jr. Associate: Joseph W. Westmeyer, III.
Trial Practice, Personal Injury, Automobile Accidents, Slip and Fall, Wrongful Death, Products Liability, Wills and Probate, Trusts and Estates, Estate Planning, Real Estate, Corporate Law, Business Law, Contracts, Criminal Defense, Felonies, Misdemeanors, Driving While Intoxicated, Juvenile Law, Traffic Violations, Bankruptcy, Domestic Relations, Family Law, Adoptions, Divorce, Child Custody, Child Support.
See Professional Biographies, TOLEDO, OHIO

Weston, Gretchen F. .... '72 '03 C.5 B.A. L.851 J.D. [Goranson,P.&B.]
Westrick, Timothy A. .... '72 '97 C&L.851 B.A., J.D. Co. Pros.
Wetli, John F., (AV) .... '44 '69 C.602 B.A. L.930 J.D. [Bugbee&C.]
Whipple, Mary Ann .... '56 '81 C.477 A.B. L.813 J.D. U.S. Bankruptcy J.
Whitcomb, Howard C., III, (BV) .... '54 '91 C.679 B.S. L.851 J.D. 405 Madison Ave.
White, David A. .... '53 '79 C.473 B.S. L.851 J.D. 1 SeaGate, 12th Fl.‡
White, Garrick O., (BV) .... '72 '98 C.20 B.A. L.851 J.D. [Anspach M.E.]
White, James F., Jr., (AV) '40 '65
C.674 A.B. L.608 J.D. [Shumaker,L.&K.] (Tampa, FL)
White, Kenneth I., Sr. '35 '61 C&L.851 B.A., J.D.
Chmn. & C.E.O., American 1st Title Agency, Inc.
White, Kenneth J., (AV) .... '48 '74 C.97 B.S. L.851 J.D. [Marshall&M.]
Wicklund, David W., (AV) .... '49 '74 C.951 B.A. L.851 J.D. [Shumaker,L.&K.]
Widman, Marilyn L., (AV) .... '67 '97 C.884 B.A. L.851 J.D. [Allotta&F.]
Wiley, David F., (BV) .... '35 '63 C&L.851 B.S., LL.B. 624 Main Street
Wiley, Julia Smith, (AV) .... '59 '84 C.201 B.A. L.608 J.D. [Robison,C.&O.]
Wilhelms, Andrew J. .... '69 '96 C.473 B.A. L.117 J.D. [Bugbee&C.]
Wilhelms, Tybo Alan, (AV) .... '49 '76 C.475 B.A. L.851 J.D. [Bugbee&C.]
Wilke, Jeffrey S. '65 '90 C.912 B.A. L.477 J.D.
V. P & Ast. Gen. Coun., Owens Corning
Wilkins, Douglas A., (BV) '56 '82
C.234 B.A. L.999 J.D. 1931 Scottwood Avenue, Suite 700
Wilkowski, Arthur R. .... '28 '59 C.97 B.S. L.851 J.D. Ct. of App. J.

Willey, David S. '54 '02 C.197 B.A. L.851 J.D.
366 Spitzer Building, 520 Madison Avenue, 43604
Telephone: 419-241-3310 Fax: 419-241-3312
Email: davidwilley@aol.com
Plaintiffs Personal Injury, Automobile Accidents, Dog Bites, Slip and Fall, Wrongful Death.
See Professional Biographies, TOLEDO, OHIO

Williams, Brian R., (BV) .... '52 '78 C.967 B.A. L.851 J.D. 420 Madison Ave
Williams, Martin W., (AV) .... '42 '69 C&L.851 B.A., J.D. [Williams,J.L.G.&S.]
Williams, Robert B. .... *'37 '67 C.410 A.B. L.851 J.D. Asst. Pros.*
Williams, Vernos J., (BV) .... '47 '76 C.967 B.A. L.607 J.D. [Gallon&T.]
Williams, Vesper C., II .... '45 '73 C.1112 B.S. L.851 J.D. [V.C.Williams]

Williams, Jilek, Lafferty, Gallagher & Scott Co., L.P.A., (AV)
500 Toledo Legal Building, 416 North Erie Street, 43624-1696
Telephone: 419-241-2122 Facsimile: 419-245-3849
Email: firm@wjlgs.com URL: http://www.WJLGS.com

(This Listing Continued)

Williams, Jilek, Lafferty, Gallagher & Scott Co., L.P.A. (Continued)
David R. Goldberg (1932-1982); Martin W. Williams; Michael F. Jilek, Sr.; Jon A. Lafferty; Thomas W. Gallagher; Robert M. Scott;—Drew R. Massé; Peter O. DeClark; Jennifer C. McCready; Chad M. Tuschman.
Trial and Appellate Practice. Negligence, Personal Injury, Wrongful Death, Products Liability, Legal and Medical Malpractice and Railroad.
See Professional Biographies, TOLEDO, OHIO

Williams, Vesper C. .... 4643 Sylvania Ave.
Williamson, Lane D., (BV) .... '62 '89 C.97 B.A. L.851 J.D. [Eastman&S.]
Williams-Young, Marc G., (BV) ... '54 '82 C.473 B.A. L.851 J.D. [Spitler&W.L.&Assoc.]
Willinger, Lavelle A. .... '13 '53 C&L.851 B.B.A., J.D. 3106 Radford Ave.‡
Wilson, Beth A., (BV) .... '71 '97 C&L.851 B.A., J.D. [Cooper&W.]
Wilson, Joseph R., (BV) .... '55 '81 C.97 B.L.S. L.851 J.D. 4 Seagate
Wineland, Erik J. .... '69 '00 C.253 B.S. L.851 J.D. [Spitzer&H.]
Wingart, R. Paul, (AV) .... '20 '50 L.851 J.D. [Bracy&K.]
Wingate, Ronnie L., (AV) .... '52 '79 C.955 B.A. L.851 J.D. 1119 Adams St.
Winkler, James R. .... '50 '88 C.30 B.A. L.851 J.D. Medical College of Ohio
Winterhalter, Keith J., (BV) .... '52 '85 C&L.851 B.Ed., J.D. [Vassar,D.D.&B.]
Winters, Steven B. .... '66 '96 C.608 B.A. L.851 J.D. [Cline,C.&W.]
Wise, David G., (AV) .... '42 '67 C.967 B.A. L.477 J.D. [Spengler N.]
Wise, Patricia A. .... '61 '85 C.97 B.A.C. L.851 J.D. [Wise&D.]
Wise & Dorner, Ltd. .... 151 North Michigan Street
Wisniewski, Jeffrey Thomas '74 '00 C&L.851 B.A., J.D.
ProMedica Health System, Inc.
Witcher, Jenelda E., Law Office of '53 '95
C&L.851 B.A., J.D. 1900 Monroe Street, Suite 111
Witherell, Dennis P., (AV) .... '51 '77 C.477 B.A. L.608 J.D. [Shumaker,L.&K.]
Witt, Robert E., (BV) .... '38 '66 C&L.851 B.S.Ch.E., J.D. 316 N. Mich. St. (Pat.)
Wittenberg, Charles S., (BV) .... '47 '73 C&L.851 B.A., J.D. 700 Adams St.
Wittenberg, Joseph L., (AV) .... '44 '72 C&L.851 B.B.A., J.D. [J.L.Wittenberg]
Wittenberg, Sheldon S. .... '44 '69 C.608 B.A. L.150 J.D. Spitzer Bldg.
Wittenberg, Joseph L., A Legal Professional Association, (AV)
2727 North Holland Sylvania Road
Wohl, Doris K., (BV) .... '29 '73 C.477 A.B. L.851 J.D. [Wohl&Assoc.]
Wohl & Assocs., (BV) .... 563 Spitzer Bldg.
Wojtas, Yvonne Ann .... '76 '04 [Y.A.Wojtas]
Wojtas, Yvonne A., Law Office of .... 405 N. Huron St., Ste. 200
Wolf, Philip H. .... '53 '78 C.611 B.A. L.608 J.D. Key Bank
Wolff, Cheryl F., (AV) .... '53 '79 C.473 B.S. L.608 J.D. [Spengler N.]
Wolff, Richard E., (BV) .... '55 '80 C.473 B.A. L.945 J.D. [Spengler N.]
Wood, Douglas M. .... '62 '87 C&L.851 B.A., J.D. 1431 Beecham St.
Wood, Karen E. .... '57 '89 C&L.851 B.A.B.S., J.D. Mun. Ct.
Woodley, Robert A. .... '47 '77 C&L.851 B.A., J.D. 1900 Monroe Street
Wood-Lively, Tamara L. '63 '94 C&L.608 B.A., J.D.
Advocates for Basic Legal Equality
Woodward, Kathryn J., (BV) .... '47 '87 C.631 B.A. L.851 J.D. [Shumaker,L.&K.]
Worline, Daniel A., (BV) .... '48 '74 C.97 B.S.B.A. L.851 J.D. [Shindler,N.H.S.&M.]
Worline, Robin Ann .... '75 '01 C.97 B.S.B.A. L.851 J.D. 33 South Huron Street
Wroblewski, Dennis E. .... '48 '79 C&L.851 B.B.A., J.D. 2639 Wimbledon Park Blvd.
Wurster, Lisa A., (BV) ..... '59 '85 C.97 B.S. L.851 J.D. Legal Coun., Dana Corporation
Wurster, Phillip D., (BV) .... '57 '83 C&L.851 B.A., J.D. Dept. of Pub. Utilities
Yates, James B., (BV) .... '65 '90 C.201 B.A. L.608 J.D. [Eastman&S.]
Yavorcik, James E., (AV) .... '54 '79 C.608 B.A. L.851 J.D. [Cubbon&Assoc.]
Yerman, John W., Jr., (BV) .... '45 '77 C.381 B.A. L.851 J.D. 3706 Treelawn Dr.
Yoppolo, Louis J., (BV) .... '51 '80 C&L.851 B.A., J.D. [Shindler,N.H.S.&M.]
Young, Jeremy Glenn .... '75 '01 C.921 B.A. L.851 J.D. 864 Spitzer Building
Young, Kurt M., (CV) .... '68 '93 C.8 B.A. L.930 J.D. [K.M.Young]
Young, Robert G., (BV) .... '45 '71 C.967 A.B. L.851 J.D. Sr. Atty.
Young, Thomas L., (AV) '44 '72 C.1258 B.A. L.602 J.D.
Dir. & Exec. V.P. and Chief Financial Offices, Owens-Illinois, Inc.

Young, Kurt M., LLC, Law Offices of, (CV)
709 Madison Avenue, Suite 307, 43624
Telephone: 419-244-7885 Fax: 419-244-7886 URL: http://www.kmylaw.com
Email: kmy@kmylaw.com URL: http://www.kurtyounglaw.com
Member of Firm: Kurt M. Young (Certified Specialist in Workers' Compensation Law, Ohio State Bar Association).
Workers Compensation.

Youssef-Coyle, Lami, (BV) .... '59 '84 C&L.851 B.A., J.D. [Brady,C.&S.]
Zalewski, Cynthia Marie '67 '94 C&L.851 B.A., J.D.
Sr. Legal Coun., HCR Manor Care
Zaner, Lorin J., (BV) .... '48 '76 C&L.851 B.S.Ch.E., J.D. Spitzer Bldg.
Zaremba, Thomas S., (AV) .... '51 '77 C.317 A.B. L.930 J.D. [Roetzel&A.]
Zarou, Mechelle .... '74 '00 C.477 B.A. L.228 J.D. [Shumaker,L.&K.]
Zazycki, Suzi .... '— '03 C.473 B.S. L.851 J.D. [Cooper&W.]
Zeisloft, Keith, (BV) .... '49 '82 C.23 B.A. L.851 J.D. Family Ct. Ctr.
Zemmelman, Norman G., (AV) '43 '69
C.415 B.A. L.851 J.D. 429 Michigan, Domestic Relations Ct.
Zigray, Daniel F., (BV) .... '62 '91 C&L.851 B.B.A., J.D. [Kolb&Z.]
Zilba, Jeffrey Charles .... '61 '87 124 N. Summit St., Ste. 210
Zima, John Paul .... '51 '87 C.813 B.S. L.930 J.D. 7014 Mourning Dove Court
Zimmerman, Roger King .... '45 '79 C.608 B.A. L.851 J.D. 2735 N. Holland Sylvania
Zimmerman, Todd M., (BV) .... '72 '97 C&L.608 B.S.B.A., J.D. [Rohrbachers L.C.&T.]
Zinz, Marguerite E. .... '76 '01 C.934 B.S. L.124 J.D. [Cooper&W.]
Zoll, David W., (BV) .... '52 '77 C.150 B.M. L.851 J.D. [Zoll&K.]
Zoll & Kranz, LLC, (BV) .... 6620 West Central Avenue, Suite 200
Zouhary, Jack .... '51 '76 C.197 B.A. L.851 J.D. Com. Pleas J.
Zugay, Anthony A., Jr. '44 '70 C.610 B.B.A. L.851 J.D.
V.P., Fifth Third Bk. of Northwestern Ohio, N.A.
Zychowicz, Michael J., (BV) .... '56 '85 C.473 B.A. L.851 J.D. [Borgstahl&Z.]
Zychowicz, Ralph C., (BV) .... '48 '79 C.870 B.S. L.851 J.D. Asst. Co. Pros.
Zyndorf, Sol, (BV) .... '49 '74 C.473 B.A. L.851 J.D. 320 N. Michigan St., 2nd Flr.

TORONTO, 5,676, *Jefferson Co.*

Haynes, William, Jr. .... '54 '80 C.81 B.A. L.117 J.D. 806 Franklin St.

TRENTON, 8,746, *Butler Co.*

Binns, Patrick A., (BV) .... '47 '80 C.608 B.A. L.1340 J.D. 102 E. State St.
Taylor, Evelyn .... '11 '60 C.608 B.S. L.1340 J.D. 4669 Jacksonburg Rd.‡
Yauch, Elizabeth Ann, (BV) .... '62 '88 C.473 B.A. L.383 J.D. 240 E. State St.

TROTWOOD, 27,420, *Montgomery Co.*

Flora, Bruce J. .... '54 '81 C&L.201 B.S., J.D. V.P., Trotwood Corp.

TROY, * 21,999, *Miami Co.*

Altier, Mark W., (CV) .... '48 '73 C.528 B.A. L.930 J.D. P.O. Box 633
Baer, Michael A., (AV) .... '46 '74 C&L.608 B.A., J.D. [Dungan&L.]

Becht, Janet R., (CV) .... '50 '83 C.201 B.S. L.607 J.D. 2040 North Country Road
Beitzel, David E., (BV) .... '51 '76 C.473 A.B. L.8 J.D. 22 N. Short St.
Bennett, James D., (BV) .... '56 '85 C.1208 B.S. L.201 J.D. Miami Co. Prosecutor's Off.
Berry, Richard C., (BV) '50 '77
C.473 B.A. L.201 J.D. Gen. Coun. & Secy., Hobart Bros. Co.

Bieser, Greer & Landis, LLP
(See Dayton)

Bradley, Karen Denise
(See Dayton)

Brookshire, James D., (BV) .... '58 '91 C.235 B.A. L.201 J.D. [A Dungan&L.]
Brosh, Leneé M. .... '76 '02 C.231 B.A. L.201 J.D. [Shipman,D.&L.] ⊙
Brumbaugh, Jeffrey .... '55 '01 C.1208 B.S. L.117 J.D. [Brumbaugh]
Brumbaugh Law Firm, L.P.A., Inc. .... 11 S. Market St.
Cargill, Michael L., (BV) .... '47 '79 C.473 B.S. L.201 J.D. [Dungan&L.]

Cicero & Kollin PLL
(See Dayton)

Clark, Christopher D., (CV) .... '69 '95 C.231 B.A. L.607 J.D. [Lopez,S.&P.]
Cotner, John M., (BV) .... '45 '70 C&L.607 B.A., J.D. 22 North Short Street
Dicks, James Randolph, Jr. .... '70 '96 C.1208 B.A. L.8 J.D. Asst. Pros. Atty.
Dixon, W. McGregor, Jr., (BV) ...... '49 '75 C.473 B.A. L.744 J.D. [Shipman,D.&L.] ⊙
Dixon, William M., (AV) .... '22 '49 C.473 A.B. L.150 J.D. [Shipman,D.&L.] ‡
Donnelly, Dennis M., (BV) .... '48 '76 C&L.607 B.A., J.D. 124 W. Main St.

Dungan & LeFevre, A Legal Professional Association, (AV)
210 West Main Street, 45373 ⊙
Telephone: 937-339-0511 Fax: 937-335-5802
Email: mail@dungan-lefevre.com URL: http://www.dungan-lefevre.com
J. Cameron Dungan (1903-1977); Richard H. LeFevre (1910-1980); William J. McGraw, III, Certified Specialist in Estate Planning, Trust and Probate Law, Ohio State Bar Association; Michael A. Baer; Alan M. Kappers; Michelle J. Gearhardt; Michael L. Cargill; John E. Hemm (Resident, Piqua, Ohio Office); David L. Mikel; J. Andrew Wannemacher, Jr. (Resident, Piqua Office); James D. Brookshire; Matthew C. Sorg. Of Counsel: Wendy Jean Goodenough.
General Civil and Criminal Trial Practice, including Medical Malpractice, Personal Injury, Wrongful Death, Products Liability, Insurance Defense, Wrongful Discharge Defense, Business Law and Commercial Litigation in all Courts, Real Estate, Condominium, Banking, Insurance, Corporate and Business, Wills and Probate, Trusts and Estates, Estate Planning, Family and Domestic Relations, Driving While Intoxicated, Tax, Bankruptcy, Municipal, Zoning and Planning and Collection Law. Appeals in all Courts.
References: U.S. Bank N.A., Troy; National City Bank.
Piqua, Ohio Office: 111 West Ash Street. P.O. Box 1529. Telephone: 937-773-8054. Fax: 937-773-3379.
See Professional Biographies, TROY, OHIO

Dyer, Michael E., (BV) '53 '80 C.269 B.A. L.201 J.D.
[Dyer,G.M.&S.] (⊙Dayton, Xenia)
Dyer, Garofalo, Mann & Schultz, A Legal Professional Association, (AV)
1850 W. Main Street (⊙Richmond, IN; Bellefontaine, Dayton, Huber Heights, Lima, Middletown, Piqua, Springfield, Wilmington, Xenia, OH)
Evans, Nika R. .... '74 '00 C.608 B.A. L.607 J.D. [A Miller&L.]
Farley, Jason R. .... '76 '02 C.631 B.A. L.201 J.D. [A Miller&L.]

Faust, Harrelson, Fulker, McCarthy & Schlemmer, (AV)
12 South Cherry Street, P.O. Box 8, 45373
Telephone: 937-335-8324 Fax: 937-339-7155
Email: 1fhfms@woh.rr.com
Members of Firm: Charles F. Faust (1875-1950); William M. Harrelson (1921-1985); J. Andrew Fulker (1953-1989); Leo H. Faust (1899-1996); John E. Fulker; Robert A. McCarthy; Robert N. Schlemmer; William J. Fulker; Robert M. Harrelson. Of Counsel: Richard J. Fraas.
General Civil and Criminal Trial Practice. Negligence, Insurance, Probate, Workers Compensation, Family, Commercial and Corporation Law. Estate Planning and Real Estate Law, Elder Law.
Counsel: Aetna Casualty & Surety Co.; Aetna Life Insurance Co.; Troy Lumber Co.; Fifth-Third Bank of Western Ohio; Westfield Insurance Companies; Firstar Bank, N.A.; Upper Valley Medical Center; ARC Abrasives, Inc.; Miami Mutual Insurance Co.; Summit Insurance Co.
See Professional Biographies, TROY, OHIO

Fraas, Richard J. .... '32 '59 C.473 B.S. L.608 J.D. [C Faust,H.F.M.&S.]

Freund, Freeze & Arnold, A Legal Professional Association
(See Dayton)

Fulker, John E., (AV) .... '29 '53 C.473 A.B. L.178 J.D. [Faust,H.F.M.&S.]
Fulker, William J., (BV) .... '57 '82 C.608 B.A. L.607 J.D. [Faust,H.F.M.&S.]
Gearhardt, Michelle J., (BV) .... '55 '80 C.608 B.A. L.851 J.D. [Dungan&L.]
Gee, Christopher M., (BV) .... '47 '78 C.150 B.A. L.201 J.D. Com. Pleas J.
Geisinger, Bruce .... '19 '49 C.473 L.472 LL.B. 1619 Monroe-Concord Rd.‡
Goater, Richard A. '21 '49 C.611 A.B. L.150 J.D.
(adm. in FL; not adm. in OH) Prob. & Juv. J.
Goodenough, Wendy Jean .... '70 '98 C&L.608 B.A., J.D. [C Dungan&L.]
Greenwald, Carol E., (CV) .... '52 '77 C.970 B.A. L.201 J.D. 22 N. Short St.
Harbor, William S. .... '53 '79 C.347 B.A. L.608 J.D. 2955 Hickorywood Dr.‡
Harrelson, Robert M., (BV) .... '57 '82 C.473 B.S. L.117 J.D. [Faust,H.F.M.&S.]
Harvey, Randal A., (BV) .... '59 '85 C.8 B.A. L.7 J.D. [R.A.Harvey]
Harvey, Randal A., Co., L.P.A., (BV) .... 9 West Water Street
Hemm, Michael W. .... '48 '74 C.973 A.B. L.1340 J.D. Mun. J.
Henson, JillAnn .... '64 '96 C.117 B.A. L.201 J.D. 1911 Fox Run
Herndon, John A. .... '67 '96 C.801 B.A. L.201 J.D. [Shipman,D.&L.]

Hochman & Plunkett
(See Dayton)

Huffman, Kathryn Maher, (BV) .... '67 '92 C&L.851 B.A., J.D. [Huffman,L.&W.]
Huffman, Mary Katherine, (BV) .... '61 '90 C.1208 B.A. L.201 J.D. [Huffman,L.&W.]
Huffman, Robert J., (AV) .... '31 '60 C&L.607 B.A., J.D. [Huffman,L.&W.]
Huffman, Robert J., Jr., (BV) .... '63 '88 C.473 B.A. L.201 J.D. [Huffman,L.&W.]
Huffman, Samuel L., (CV) .... '66 '95 C.97 B.A. L.607 J.D. [A Huffman,L.&W.]
Huffman, Landis & Weaks, Co., L.P.A., (AV) .... 80 S. Plum St.

Jenks, Pyper & Oxley Co., L.P.A.
(See Dayton)

Johnston, Robert C., (BV) .... '52 '78 C.228 B.A. L.930 J.D. [Shipman,D.&L.] ⊙
Jones, Phillip M. .... '45 '74 C.608 B.S. L.8 J.D. Tr. Admr., First Natl. Bk. & Tr. Co.
Kappers, Alan M., (BV) .... '52 '77 C&L.607 B.A., J.D. [Dungan&L.]
Katzenberger, George L. .... '44 '75 C.17 B.A. L.607 J.D. 333 S. Short St.
Kemmer, Mel, (BV) .... '48 '78 C.608 B.S. L.201 J.D. Miami Co. Mun. Court
Kerber, Grant D. .... '72 '97 C.201 B.A. L.150 J.D. [Shipman,D.&L.] ⊙
King, Stephen W. .... '42 '72 C.150 B.A. L.608 J.D. [Princi&K.]
Kremmel, Donn A. '50 '79 C&L.966 B.A., J.D.
Assoc. Gen. Coun., Hobart Corp. (Food Equipment Grp.)
Landis, Raymond L., (AV) .... '38 '67 C&L.607 B.A., J.D. [Huffman,L.&W.]
Lindeman, Robert J. .... '47 '73 C.150 B.A. L.851 J.D. Com. Pleas J.
Littleton, Charles D. .... '19 '51 C.253 B.A. L.607 J.D. 47 S. Dorset Street
Livingston, James R., (BV) .... '43 '69 C&L.608 B.S., J.D. [Shipman,D.&L.] ⊙
Lopez, Jose, (AV) .... '52 '79 C.608 B.A. L.201 J.D. [Lopez,S.&P.]

Lopez, Severt & Pratt Co., L.P.A., (AV) BB
18 East Water Street, 45373
Telephone: 937-335-5658 Facsimile: 937-339-6446
Email: lsplaw@lsplaw.org URL: http://www.lopezsevertpratt.com
Members of Firm: Jose Lopez; Todd D. Severt; Andrew R. Pratt; Christopher D. Clark; Jonathan S. Zweizig. Associate: Andrew D. Lucia.
Civil Litigation, Personal Injury, Automobile Accidents, Truck Accidents, Slip and Fall, Wrongful Death, Commercial Litigation, Criminal Law, Drug Crimes, DUI/DWI/ Juvenile Law, Traffic Violations, Family Law, Divorce, Adoptions, Child Custody, Child Support, Visitation Rights, Business Law, Business Contracts, Business Litigation, Business Enterprises, Business Formation, Buying and Selling a Business, Construction Law, Contracts, Medical Malpractice, Real Estate, Estate Planning, Trusts and Estates, Resorts and Leisure Law, Wills and Probate.
See Professional Biographies, TROY, OHIO

Lucia, Andrew D., (BV) .... '69 '96 C.446 B.S. L.201 J.D. [A Lopez,S.&P.]
Luring, Roger E., (AV) .... '— '75 C.473 A.B. L.150 J.D. [Miller&L.]
McCarthy, Robert A., (AV) .... '31 '55 C&L.608 B.A., J.D. [Faust,H.F.M.&S.]

McCulloch, Felger, Fite & Gutmann Co., L.P.A.
(See Piqua)

McGraw, William J., III, (AV) .... '48 '73 C.610 B.B.A. L.608 J.D. [Dungan&L.]
Mikel, David L., (CV) .... '64 '89 C.347 B.A. L.201 J.D. [Dungan&L.]

Miller & Luring, (AV) BB
314 West Main Street, 45373
Telephone: 937-339-2627 Fax: 937-339-5444
URL: http://www.milleruringlaw.com
Roger E. Luring;—Nika R. Evans; Jason R. Farley.
General and Trial Practice, Collections, Estate Planning, Bankruptcy, Personal Injury, Civil, Family/ Domestic Relations, Corporation, Negligence, Tax, Municipal, Probate and Real Estate.
References: U.S. Bank, N.A., Troy, Ohio; Peoples Bank, Troy, Ohio.
See Professional Biographies, TROY, OHIO

Nasal, Gary A., (BV) .... '58 '88 C.1208 B.A. L.201 J.D. Co. Pros.

Pickrel, Schaeffer & Ebeling
(See Dayton)

Pratt, Andrew R., (BV) .... '68 '94 C.610 B.S. L.1187 J.D. [Lopez,S.&P.]
Pratt, Jeannine N. .... '67 '94 C.264 B.A. L.1187 J.D. 201 W. Main St.
Princi, Paul R. F., (BV) .... '46 '72 C&L.150 B.A., J.D. [Princi&K.]
Princi & King Co., L.P.A., (BV) .... 221 S. Market St.
Roll, Jennifer J., (CV) .... '72 '96 C.201 B.A. L.8 J.D. [A Huffman,L.&W.]
Schlemmer, Robert N., (AV) .... '43 '69 C.967 B.A. L.930 J.D. [Faust,H.F.M.&S.]
Sell, Charles H., II, (BV) .... '47 '73 C.932 B.A. L.851 J.D. [Shipman,D.&L.] ⊙
Severt, Katherine Kemp, (BV) .... '65 '91 C.190 B.A. L.201 J.D. 18 East Water Street
Severt, Todd D., (BV) .... '64 '92 C.790 B.A. L.201 J.D. [Lopez,S.&P.]

Shipman, Dixon & Livingston Co., L.P.A., (AV)
215 West Water Street, P.O. Box 310, 45373 ⊙
Telephone: 937-339-1500 Fax: 937-339-1519
URL: http://www.sdl-law.com
Leonard H. Shipman (1874-1955); Frank Leonard Shipman (1906-1973); William M. Dixon (Retired); James R. Livingston; Charles H. Sell, II; W. McGregor Dixon, Jr.; Robert C. Johnston; Grant D. Kerber; Leneé M. Brosh; John A. Herndon.
Civil Trials in all Courts. Personal Injury, Environmental, Corporation, Real Estate, Insurance Defense Law, Probate and Estate Planning, Social Security, Municipal and Zoning. General Practice. Civil Rights Defense Law.
General Counsel for: Firstar, N.A., Troy; City of Troy; Troy Board of Education.
Local Counsel for: Celina Group; Commonwealth Insurance Co.; Companion Insurance Co.; Farmland Insurance Co.; Heritage Insurance Co.
West Milton, Ohio Office: 316 South Miami Street, P.O. Box 5. Telephone: 937-698-4164.
See Professional Biographies, TROY, OHIO

Smith, DeWayne .... '43 '72 C.980 B.E. L.607 J.D. 606 South Ridge Avenue
Sorg, Matthew C. .... '67 '94 C&L.201 B.A., J.D. [A Dungan&L.]
Swinehart, Susan Strayer .... '46 '85 C.608 B.A.Ed. L.201 J.D. 206 W. Main Street

Thompson and DeVeny Co., L.P.A.
(See Dayton)

Thornburgh, William H., (AV) .... '23 '51 C.150 L.1340 J.D. 223 W. Main St.
Tomb, Jeremy .... '68 '05 C.1208 B.A. L.851 J.D. [Tomb L.]

Tomb Law
124 West Main Street, 45373
Telephone: 937-689-3539
Email: jeremytomb@hotmail.com URL: http://www.tomblaw.com
Jeremy Tomb.
Real Estate, Business Law, Construction Law.
See Professional Biographies, TROY, OHIO

Utrecht, James D., (AV) .... '52 '77 C&L.150 B.B.A., J.D. 12 S. Plum St.
Wagner, Lynnita K. C. .... '43 '67 C&L.607 B.A., J.D. Juv. Ct. Mag.
Weaks, Gary L., (AV) .... '45 '70 C&L.607 B.A., J.D. [Huffman,L.&W.]
Weigl, William .... '26 '58 C.97 B.S. L.1003 J.D. 1805 Conwood Dr. (Pat.)‡
Welbaum, Jeffrey M. .... '52 '77 C.203 B.S. L.607 J.D. Com. Pleas J.
Zuhl, Gary E., (BV) .... '52 '76 C.201 B.A. L.150 J.D. Mun. Mag.
Zweizig, Jonathan S. .... '73 '98 C.967 B.S. L.607 J.D. [Lopez,S.&P.]

TWINSBURG, 17,006, *Summit Co.*

Brown, Kevin E., (BV) .... '51 '80 C.999 B.A. L.161 J.D. 8737 Darrow Rd.
Carr, Adam E., (BV) .... '68 '93 C.691 B.A. L.1003 J.D. [Williams,S.&S.]
Cichocki, Charles F., (BV) .... '54 '79 C.97 B.A. L.930 J.D. [C Williams,S.&S.]
Dandino, Patrick E. '57 '83 C.210 B.A. L.623 J.D.
(adm. in OK; not adm. in OH) Sr. Frnchs. Coun., Cole Nat'l Corp.
Doyle, Duane L. .... '42 '71 C.1062 B.A. L.930 J.D. 8415 Tower Park Dr.
Eyhusen, Edward A., (AV) .... '51 '77 C.967 B.A. L.976 J.D. 10349 Sandalwwood Dr.
Grigsby, Kelly N. .... '69 '96 C.970 B.A. L.124 J.D. [A Williams,S.&S.]
Hirsch, Susan Lee .... '48 '85 C.150 B.C.P. L.208 J.D. Assoc. Coun., Whitlatch & Co.
Hura, Mark S., (BV) .... '60 '85 C.679 B.S. L.930 J.D. [A Williams,S.&S.]
Katz, Richard S., (AV) .... '56 '84 C.608 B.A. L.930 J.D. 1959 Summit Commerce Pk.
Kosla, Phillip C. .... '69 '97 C&L.608 B.A., J.D. [A Williams,S.&S.]
Lah, Kristina Irene .... '68 '94 C.973 B.A. L.989 J.D. 2132 Case Parkway North
Levine, Bernard .... '29 '56 C&L.930 A.B., LL.B. 2889 Orin Way‡
Martin, Donald L. ... '40 '64 C.309 B.A. L.477 J.D. Secy. & Gen. Coun., Whitlatch & Co.
McCaughey, Maura A., (CVⓉ) .... '63 '88 C.81 B.A. L.30 J.D. 2305 E. Aurora St.
Moliterno, Louis R. .... '67 '95 C.381 B.A. L.1003 J.D. [Williams,S.&S.]
Neff, Owen C., (AV) .... '18 '48 C.611 B.A. L.477 J.D. 2610 E. Aurora Rd., Ste. 205
Nelson, Sidney Gene, Jr. .... '58 '90 C.645 B.S. L.37 J.D. Sorbent Technologies Corp.
Petsche, Jack A., III & Associates '54 '89
C.1086 B.A. L.1003 J.D. 2305 East Aurora Road, Unit A-9
Rader, Clarence B., III .... '63 '89 C.97 B.A. L.930 J.D. [C.B.R.III Llc]
Rader, Clarence B., III, LLC .... 2112 Chase Pkwy South, Suite 9
Randazzo, Joseph C. .... '70 '99 C.363 B.A. L.1003 J.D. 2212 Enterprise Parkway, East
Reimer, Dennis, (BV) .... '42 '68 C&L.607 A.B., J.D. 2450 Edison Boulevard
Richner, R. Andrew, (BV) .... '51 '76 C.8 B.S. L.930 J.D. [R.A.Richner]

Richner, R. Andrew, Co., L.P.A., (BV) .... 2305 East Aurora Road, Unit A1
Roehl, Carla Jean '— '81 C.492 B.S. L.494 J.D.
(adm. in MN; not adm. in OH) 10132 Luman Lane
Sah, Perrin I. .... '70 '95 C.97 B.A. L.1003 J.D. [Ⓐ Williams,S.&S.]
Sennett, James A., (AV) .... '52 '80 C.93 B.A. L.930 J.D. [Williams,S.&S.]
Shannon, Colleen M. .... '62 '89 C.741 B.A. L.893 J.D. (Cole Managed Vision, Inc.)
Sherriff, David J., (BV) '45 '70 C.608 B.A. L.1003 J.D.
V.P., Secy. & Gen. Coun., Cole Vision Corp. & Pearle Vision Corp.
Staph, Jack A. '45 '73 C.980 B.S.B.A. L.1003 J.D.
Sr. V.P., Secy. & Gen. Coun., Revco D.S., Inc.
Wantz, Joseph H., (BV) .... '56 '82 C.602 B.B.S. L.930 J.D. [Williams,S.&S.]
Williams, Roger H., (AV) .... '54 '79 C.319 B.A. L.930 J.D. [Williams,S.&S.]

Williams, Sennett & Scully Co., L.P.A., (AV) BB
2241 Pinnacle Parkway, 44087-2367 ⊙
Telephone: 330-405-5061 Fax: 330-405-5586
Email: attorneys@wsslaw.com URL: http://www.wsslaw.com
Roger H. Williams; James A. Sennett; William F. Scully, Jr.; Adam E. Carr; Louis R. Moliterno; Joseph H. Wantz;—Kelly N. Grigsby; Mark S. Hura; Perrin I. Sah; Phillip C. Kosla. Of Counsel: Charles F. Cichocki.
General Civil Trial and Appellate Practice in all Courts. Insurance, Casualty and Surety, Life, Accident and Health, Negligence Litigation, Medical-Legal, Products Liability, Labor and Employment Law, Commercial Litigation.
Representative Clients: Allstate Insurance Co.; Coregis Insurance Co.; Giant Eagle, Inc.; GMAC Insurance Co.; Goodyear Tire & Rubber Co.; Harleysville Insurance Co.; Leader National Insurance Co.; Nationwide Mutual Insurance Co.; Progressive Insurance Co.; Royal & Sun Alliance.
Cleveland, Ohio Office: 113 St. Clair Avenue N.E., Suite 430, 44114-1214. Telephone: 216-771-8660. Fax: 216-771-8831.
See Professional Biographies, TWINSBURG, OHIO

UHRICHSVILLE, 5,604, *Tuscarawas Co.*

Connolly, Hillyer & Welch, (BV) .... 201 N. Main St.
Gossett, Jay Matthew .... '61 '87 608 W. High St.
Hillyer, William Hudson ...... '28 '53 C&L.608 B.A., J.D. Co. Ct. J. [Connolly,H.&W.] ‡
Jackson, Jason L. .... '76 '01 C.473 B.A. L.37 J.D. [Ⓐ Connolly,H.&W.]
Reed, John P., (AV) .... '18 '48 C.610 A.B. L.930 J.D. 113 S. Water St.
Welch, Kenneth R., (BV) .... '50 '79 C.920 B.S. L.7 J.D. [Connolly,H.&W.]
Wheeler, John W., (BV) .... '23 '69 C.910 B.A. L.8 J.D. [Wheeler&W.]
Wheeler, Joseph A., (BV) .... '— '84 C.381 B.B.A. L.7 J.D. [Wheeler&W.]
Wheeler & Wheeler, (BV) .... 113 E. 3rd St.

UNIONTOWN, 2,802, *Stark Co.*

Barnoff, Michelle Stine, (BV) .... '62 '88 C.8 B.A. L.7 J.D. P.O. Box 816
Chambers, Walter R. '53 '79 C&L.229 B.A., J.D.
(adm. in PA; not adm. in OH) 9610 Brixton Ave. NW‡
Demczyk, Michael V., (BV) .... '46 '82 C.608 B.I.E. L.8 J.D. [Ⓐ McNamara&F.]
Donohew, Monty L., (BV) .... '61 '87 C.234 B.A. L.910 J.D. [M.L.Donohew&Assoc.]
Donohew, Monty L., & Associates, LPA, (BV) .... 3570 Executive Drive, Suite 106
Fortado, Matthew .... '53 '77 C.95 B.S. L.188 LL.B. [Ⓒ McNamara&F.]
Freeman, Sidney N., (BV) .... '52 '77 C.712 B.A. L.7 J.D. [Ⓐ McNamara&F.]
Gibson, Joseph W., (BV) .... '47 '72 C.657 B.S. L.7 J.D. 1550 Corporate Woods Pkwy.
Harris, G. Bernard, (BV) .... '21 '48 C.381 B.A. L.930 LL.B. 2099 Beechtree Lane
Lang, Paul A. .... '43 '77 C.851 B.S. in Phar. L.8 J.D. 1299 Sunset Cir. NW
May, Robert R. .... '26 '52 C.8 L.7 LL.B. 2571 Myersville Rd.‡
McNamara, Robert F. .... '51 '77 C.872 B.A. L.7 J.D. [McNamara&F.]
McNamara & Freeman Co., L.P.A. .... 12370 Cleveland Ave., N.W.
Muse, E. Spencer, (BV) .... '64 '89 C.294 B.A. L.7 J.D. 3570 Executive Dr., Ste. 203
Olson, Martin Luther .... '42 '73 C&L.8 B.A., J.D. [M.Olson]
Olson, Martin .... 13312 Cleveland Avenue, NW
Thayer, Wayne H. '50 '76 C.930 A.B. L.94 J.D.
(adm. in PA; not adm. in OH) 667 Southwood Dr.‡
Weimer, David P., (BV) .... '51 '85 C.207 B.A. L.7 J.D. [Weimer]
Weimer & Co., LLC, (BV) .... 1790 Town Park Boulevard
Youtz, Carol A. .... '53 '85 C&L.8 B.S., J.D. 3970C Royal Liverpool

UNIVERSITY HEIGHTS, 14,146, *Cuyahoga Co.*

Armon, Edward F. .... '42 '79 C.363 B.S. L.1003 J.D. 3886 Tyndall Rd.‡
Caron, Brian L. .... '69 '95 C&L.124 B.A., J.D. [Crombie] (⊙Maple Heights)
Crombie Law Firm, The .... 2177 South Taylor Road (⊙Maple Heights, North Olmsted)
Delsander, Dominic C., (BV) .... '28 '64 C.363 L.1003 J.D. 3809 Northwood Rd.
Dembe, Harold N. .... '21 '48 C&L.930 A.B., LL.B. 4066 Silsby Rd.
DeRocco, Gary D., (BV) .... '47 '74 C.363 B.A. L.1003 J.D. Asst. Co. Pros.
Etowski, Earl J., Jr. .... '42 '74 C.602 B.A. L.161 J.D. Sr. V.P., National City Bank
Gross, Joanne, (AV) .... '55 '86 C.876 B.A. L.161 J.D. 20700 N. Park Blvd.
Hill, Robert W. .... '32 '59 C.674 A.B. L.930 LL.B. 2509 Milford Rd.
Hils, David F. .... '39 '64 C.363 A.B. L.128 J.D. 2436 Saybrook Rd.
Jackson, Myron E. .... '27 '60 C.97 A.B. L.161 J.D. 2564 Dysart Road
Katz, Solomon .... '20 '59 C.563 B.B.A. L.1003 J.D. 14434 E. Carroll Blvd.‡
LoPresti, Carl L. .... '42 '76 C&L.161 B.B.A., J.D. 2402 Eardley Road
Luxenburg, Mitchel Erik .... '71 '99 C.381 B.B.A. L.7 J.D. 4454 Silsby Rd.
Marino, Lucien R., (BV) .... '45 '72 C.602 B.A. L.930 J.D. 2286 S. Belvoir Blvd.
Matts, Joseph Jay .... '— '92 C.610 B.S.C.E. L.930 J.D. V.P., HWH A.E.P., Inc.
Sills, Alan J., (AV) .... '57 '82 C.473 B.S. L.1003 J.D. 13882 Cedar Road
Sugerman, Martin A. .... '27 '58 C.608 B.S. L.930 LL.B. 2381 Charney Road
Swenson, Elizabeth von Fischer .... '41 '86 C.860 B.S. L.161 J.D. John Carroll Univ.

UPPER ARLINGTON, 33,686, *Franklin Co.*

Beacham, Andrea J., (CVⓣ) '57 '86 C.798 B.M.E. L.986 J.D.
(adm. in MO; not adm. in OH) 4001 Newall Rd.

Boyle, Sean O.
(See Columbus)

Huston, Daniel H., (BV) .... '64 '89 C&L.607 B.A., J.D. 1540 Berkshire Road
Irwin, Karl H. .... '25 '51 C&L.608 B.Sc., J.D. 3600 Tremont Rd.‡

Kincaid, Randall & Craine
(See Columbus)

Lindsey, Thomas K., (BV) .... '59 '86 C.473 B.S. L.802 J.D. Asst. City Atty.
O'Neill, Lynne Turel .... '58 '90 C.607 B.S. L.8 J.D. 1794 Harwich Rd
Rojas, Guillermo J. .... '72 '98 C&L.608 B.A., J.D. 2533 North Star Rd.★
Schooley, Ruth Koutras .... '58 '86 C&L.608 B.S., J.D. 2235 Picket Post Lane

UPPER SANDUSKY, * 6,533, *Wyandot Co.*

Aubry, Kathleen A., (BV) '52 '77 C&L.851 B.A., J.D.
Com. Pleas J., Com. Pleas Ct. in Wyandot Co.
Bacon, David F., (BV) .... '52 '77 C.207 B.A. L.117 J.D. [Roth B.Y.]
Bacon, Forrest H., (AV) .... '24 '51 C&L.608 LL.B. [Roth B.Y.] ⊙
Bartholomew, Charles L., (BV) .... '46 '72 C&L.607 B.A., J.D. [Bartholomew]
Bartholomew Law Office, (BV) .... 110 E. Wyandot Ave.
Beck, Bruce J. ...... '51 '81 C.608 B.S. L.851 J.D. Sr. V.P., The Commercial Savings Bank
Browne, David Joseph '62 '88
C.97 B.S. L.150 J.D. Staff Coun., Commercial Savings Bank
Ellis, Mark J., (BV) .... '52 '77 C.608 B.A. L.607 J.D. 110 S. Sandusky Ave.
Funk, James C. .... '50 '83 C.97 B.S.Ed. L.851 J.D. 18407 TH 103
Grafmiller, Richard A., Law Office, (BV) ...... '46 '73 C.97 B.A. L.117 J.D. 118 N. 5th St.
Hunter, John G. .... '39 '67 C&L.607 B.A., J.D. Juv., Prob. & Com. Pleas J.
Mason, David C., (BV) .... '35 '61 C.611 A.B. L.607 J.D. 110 S Sanddusky Ave.
Miller, Jonathan K., (BV) .... '57 '82 C.951 B.A. L.608 J.D. [Ⓐ Roth B.Y.]
Pfeifer, Agnes A., (BV) .... '59 '86 C.608 B.S. L.607 J.D. [Pfeifer&P.]
Pfeifer, Dennis E., (BV) .... '51 '79 C.1112 B.S. L.607 J.D. [Pfeifer&P.]
Pfeifer, E. Michael, (BV) .... '47 '73 C.610 B.S.Ed. L.607 J.D. 110 E. Wyandot Ave.
Pfeifer and Pfeifer Law Firm, (BV) .... 114 E. Wyandot Ave.
Roth, Jeffrey P., (BV) .... '47 '72 C.472 B.A. L.117 J.D. [Roth B.Y.]
Roth Bacon Young, (AV) .... 50 Court Street (⊙Marion, Sycamore)
Rowland, Douglas D. .... '75 '02 C.851 B.A., B.S. L.1187 J.D. [Ⓐ Pfeifer&P.]
Ruhlen, James M. .... '72 '98 C.97 B.A. L.607 J.D. 116 E. Wyandot Ave.
Scheck, Laurie A. .... '— '97 C.253 B.A. L.607 J.D. [Schoenberger&S.]
Schoenberger, Loren C., (BV) .... '20 '49 C&L.607 B.A., J.D. [Schoenberger&S.]
Schoenberger & Scheck, (BV) .... 106 East Wyandot Avenue
Young, Kenneth L., (BV) .... '65 '93 C.611 B.A. L.608 J.D. [Roth B.Y.]

URBANA, * 11,613, *Champaign Co.*

Cole Acton Harmon Dunn, A Legal Professional Association
(See Springfield)

Crabbe, Brown & James LLP, (AV)
118 Scioto Street, 43078 ⊙
Telephone: 937-652-4000
Email: info@cbjLawyers.com URL: http://www.cbjLawyers.com
Of Counsel: Mark E. Kerns.
General Insurance Defense, Product Liability, Professional Malpractice, Premises Liability, Environmental and Toxic Tort Claims, Employment and Labor Law, Tax Matters, General Business and Corporate Law and Litigation, Banking and Securities, Real Estate, Probate and Estate Planning, Criminal Law, Administrative, Regulatory and Governmental Law, Workers Compensation, Intellectual Property, Fire, Arson and Fraud, Fidelity and Surety Life, Accident and Health, Insurance Coverage Law, Construction Claims, Health and Hospital Law, Oil, Gas and Energy Law, Transportation Law, Automobile Dealer Law, Zoning, International Practice and Domestic Law, Land Use Planning, and Eminent Domain.
Columbus, Ohio Office: 500 South Front Street, Suite 1200. Telephone: 614-228-5511. Fax: 614-229-4559.
Cincinnati, Ohio Office: 30 Garfield Place, Suite 740, 45202. Telephone: 513-784-1525. Fax: 513-784-1250.
Cleveland, Ohio Office: 1280 W. Third Street. Telephone: 216-574-9312.
Lancaster, Ohio Office: 111 South Broad Street, Suite 209, 43130. Telephone: 740-689-1743. Fax: 740-689-1746.
See Professional Biographies, URBANA, OHIO

Davidson, Harley A., (BV) .... '51 '77 C.97 B.A. L.945 J.D. [Wagner,M.D.&G.]
Denkewalter, William F., (BV) .... '69 '95 C.967 B.A. L.851 J.D. [Houston,H.&D.]
Dodd, Donald L. .... '29 '54 C.381 A.B. L.608 LL.B. Ret. Com. Pleas J.‡
Gilbert, Brett A., (CV) .... '67 '92 C.952 B.A. L.851 J.D. [Wagner,M.D.&G.]
Harris, Richard O., (AV) .... '26 '58 C.608 B.A. L.266 J.D. [Houston,H.&D.]
Heckman, Darrell, (CV) .... '49 '75 C.608 B.A. L.851 J.D. 107 N. Main Street
Houston, Harris & Denkewalter, L.L.C., (AV) .... One Monument Sq., Ste. 200
Kerns, Jos. D. .... '22 '48 C.473 L.150 Ret. Ct. of App. J.
Kerns, Mark E., (BV) .... '55 '80 C.97 B.S. L.201 J.D. [Ⓒ Crabbe,B.&J.]

Martin, Browne, Hull & Harper, P.L.L.
(See Springfield)

Maurice, Allen R., (AV) .... '44 '70 C.473 A.B. L.607 J.D. [Wagner,M.D.&G.]
Nau, Richard E., (CV) .... '37 '85 C.197 A.B. L.608 J.D. 300 N. Main St.

Oliver Law Office
(See Columbus)

Paulig, Karl E., (AV) .... '29 '53 C&L.608 B.A., J.D. [Paulig&S.]

Paulig & Singer, (AV) BB
40 Monument Square Suite 300, 43078
Telephone: 937-653-5257 Facsimile: 937-653-3027
Karl E. Paulig; Brad C. Singer.
General Civil and Criminal Trial and Appellate Practice in all Courts. Negligence, Personal Injury, Probate and Estate Planning, Family and Domestic Relations and Insurance Law.
Representative Clients: Nationwide Mutual Insurance Co.; Ohio Casualty Insurance Co.; Republic Franklin Insurance Co.; Bodey & Sons, Inc. (Building Contractor); Georgia, Inc.; Cincinnati Insurance Co.; Akins Printing, Inc.; The Stephen L. Bodey Co. (Contracting); Urbana City Board of Education; Champaign County Preservation Alliance.
See Professional Biographies, URBANA, OHIO

Schneider, Philip S., (CV) .... '34 '68 C.967 B.A. L.607 J.D. 108 S. Main St.
Selvaggio, Nicola Antonio .... '66 '91 C.473 B.A. L.989 J.D. Co. Pros. Off.
Singer, Brad C., (CV) .... '61 '89 C.1208 B.A. L.596 J.D. [Paulig&S.]
Strapp, Robert M., (BV) .... '43 '76 C&L.608 B.A., J.D. 112 E. Court St.
Tompkins, William Clinton, (BV) ...... '25 '51 C.611 A.B. L.150 LL.B. 107 W. Court St.
Valore, Joseph P. .... '36 '62 C&L.607 B.A., J.D. 120 N. Main Street
Wagner, Clifford R., (AV) .... '13 '37 C.608 B.S. L.150 LL.B. 117 W. Court St.‡

Wagner, Maurice, Davidson & Gilbert Co., L.P.A., (AV)
117 West Court Street, 43078
Telephone: 937-653-7174 Fax: 937-653-7782
Allen R. Maurice; Harley A. Davidson; Brett A. Gilbert.
Corporation, Probate, Estate Planning and Real Estate Law. Banking Law, Family Law/Domestic Relations.
General Counsel for: Champaign National Bank; Peoples Savings Bank.
Counsel for: The Ohio Bar Title Insurance Co.; Tech II Inc. (Plastic injection Molding); Farm Credit Services; Hall Company; Champaign Landmark, Inc.

Waterman, Ronald L. .... '69 '01 C.608 B.S. L.117 J.D. 601 Scioto St.
Weithman, Cathy Jo, (CV) .... '53 '78 C.473 B.A. 201 W. Court St.
Weithman, Gil, (BV) .... '56 '83 C&L.607 B.A., J.D. P.O. Box 109
Whitesell, Jack W., Jr. .... '49 '89 C.675 B.A. L.608 J.D. Pros. Atty
Wilson, Roger B. .... '37 '61 C.207 A.B. L.608 J.D. Com. Pleas J.

UTICA, 2,130, *Licking Co.*

Gustafson, Alan P., (BV) .... '48 '73 C&L.608 B.A., J.D. P.O. Box 484
Heath, F. Richard, (BV) .... '42 '69 C.383 B.S.C. L.1340 J.D. 26 South Main St.
Light, Sara Grundish, (BV) .... '62 '87 C.385 B.A. L.608 J.D. 26 South Main St.
Rogers, Marilyn C. .... '72 '97 C.845 B.A. L.117 J.D. 26 South Main St.

VANDALIA, 14,603, *Montgomery Co.*

Baker, Jeffery P., (BV) .... '58 '84 C.201 B.A. L.200 J.D. 461 E. Alkaline
Bannister, Richard J., (BV) .... '34 '61 C&L.608 B.S., J.D. Mun. J.

Courtney, Paul M., (BV) .... '57 '82 C.436 B.A. L.201 J.D. 575 S. Dixie Dr.
De Marco, Alex V., (Co., L.P.A.), (BV) '35 '61 C.1046 L.607 LL.B.
212 W. National Rd.
Duffy, Edward J., Jr., (CV) .... '27 '51 C.201 L.602 LL.B. 32 N. Dixie Drive
Fischer, William E., (BV) .... '50 '77 C&L.201 B.A., J.D. 2033 Waterfall Lane
Gibson, Joseph E., (CV) .... '64 '90 C&L.201 B.A., J.D. 545 Helke Rd.
Gramza, Jeffrey Thomas .... '62 '91 C.473 B.A. L.150 J.D. 410 Corporate Center
Klein, Stephen E., (BV) .... '48 '75 C.025 B.A. L.851 J.D. 282 James Bohanan Drive
Lias, Elizabeth A. .... '62 '89 C.473 B.A. L.608 J.D. 410 Corp. Ctr. Dr.
Moore, Joseph P., (BV) .... '46 '74 C.679 B.A. L.421 J.D. [Moore&Assoc.]
Moore & Associates, (BV) .... 410 Corporate Center Dr.
Rice, Bonnie Beaman, (BV) .... '50 '79 C.347 B.S. L.201 J.D. Ct. Ref. & Mag.
Rollert, Joyce Adele, (BV) .... '46 '88 C.1208 B.A. L.201 J.D. 150 West National Road
Stamps, Dana A. .... '49 '77 C.1208 B.A. L.201 J.D. Montgomery Co. Auditor
Stipancich, John K. '68 '93 C.851 B.B.A. L.608 J.D.
V.P., Gen. Coun. & Corp. Secy., Evenflo Company, Inc.
Turner, Gerald L., (AV) .... '39 '66 C.973 B.S. L.1340 J.D. [Turner&Assoc.]
Turner & Associates, (AV) .... 150 Stonequarry Rd.

VAN WERT, * 10,690, *Van Wert Co.*

Bashore, Sandra K., (BV) '58 '84 C&L.607 B.A., J.D.
Mng. Atty., Allen Co.-Blackhoof Area Legal Servs. Assn.
Bradford, Kent M. .... '47 '73 C.952 B.A. L.150 J.D. Gen. Coun., Central Mut. Ins. Co.

Burchfield, Martin D., (BV) '61 '86 C&L.851 B.A., J.D.
124 North Washington Street, 45891
Telephone: 419-238-6553 FAX: 419-238-5056
Email: burchfieldlaw@hotmail.com URL: http://www.burchfieldlaw.com
Civil Trial Litigation in all Courts, Family/Domestic Relations, Juvenile Law, Municipal and Zoning Law.
See Professional Biographies, VAN WERT, OHIO

Cahoon, James P. .... '26 '51 C&L.150 J.D. 1023 Maplewood Dr.‡
Campbell, Phil W. .... '47 '76 C.97 B.S. L.608 J.D. 124 S. Market St.
Dwyer, Kenneth D. .... '60 '95 C&L.347 B.A., J.D. Sr. Claims Atty., Central Mut. Ins. Co.
Fortney, Rex D. .... '50 '75 C.91 B.A. L.607 J.D. Prob./Juv. J.
Gordon, Scott R., Law Office of ..... '59 '88 C.500 B.B.A. L.117 J.D. 116 W. Main Street
Harrington, Cathryn L. .... '17 '41 C.926 B.A. L.150 LL.B. 1027 Elm Street
Hatcher, W. Edward, (BV) .... '47 '74 C.347 A.B. L.607 J.D. [Hatcher]
Hatcher Law Offices, (BV) .... 124 E. Main
Johnson, Donald J., (BV) .... '38 '74 C.999 B.A. L.607 J.D. 113 N. Washington St.
Keister, Stephen E., (AV) '47 '74
C.1024 B.A. L.607 J.D. 1175 Westwood Drive, Suite 200
Kennedy, C. F., III, (BV) '48 '79 C.97 B.A. L.607 J.D.
Co. Pros. Atty. [C.F.Kennedy III]
Kennedy, C.F., III, Co., L.P.A., (BV) .... 101 E. Main St.
Kirkendall, Michael W., (CV) .... '55 '80 C.381 B.G.S. L.7 J.D. 303 S. Shannon St.
Koch, Charles F., (BV) .... '55 '80 C.608 B.S. L.607 J.D. [Koch]
Koch Law Offices, (BV) .... 106 W. Main St.
Putman, Shaun A. .... '77 '02 C.473 B.A. L.201 J.D. 111 E. Main St., Ste. 105
Quatman, Joseph E., Jr., (BV) .... '53 '79 C.884 B.S. L.607 J.D. Common Pleas J.
Rauch, Kelly Joanne, Law Offices of ...... '71 '98 C.381 B.A. L.8 J.D. 124 E. Main Street
Runser, C. Allan, (AV) .... '42 '67 C.597 B.S. L.607 J.D. 111 E. Main St.
Simpson, Todd E. ..... '70 '95 C&L.347 B.A., J.D. Sr. Claims Atty., Central Mut. Ins. Co.
Steele, Charles D., (AV) .... '47 '81 C.97 B.S. L.607 J.D. Common Pleas Ct. J.
Summers, Jeffrey A. '56 '82 C.607 B.A. L.477 J.D.
Sr. Claims Atty., Central Mut. Ins. Co.
Taylor, Kevin H., (BV) .... '51 '77 C.97 B.A. L.851 J.D. [Young,T.&Y.]
Unterbrink, Gregory W., (CV) .... '50 '81 C.343 B.A. L.851 J.D. 614 High Street
Yarger, Eva J., (BV) .... '64 '89 C.608 B.A. L.36 J.D. [Young,T.&Y.]
Young, Robert C., (BV) .... '37 '64 C.260 B.S. L.607 J.D. [Young,T.&Y.]
Young, Taylor & Yarger, (BV) .... 120 W. Main St.
Zeigler, David L., (BV) .... '30 '57 C.597 B.S. L.608 J.D. 1152 S. Walnut St.

VERMILION, 10,927, *Erie & Lorain Cos.*

Ashar, Michael Kenneth .... '47 '85 C.437 B.E.S. L.7 J.D. 13010 Darrow Rd.

Buckingham, Lucal, McGookey & Zeiher Co., L.P.A., (AV)
1513 State Route 60, 44089 ⊙
Telephone: 440-967-6136
Email: vermilion@buckinghamlaw.com URL: http://www.buckinghamlaw.com
W. Zack Dolyk.
Trials in all State and Federal Courts. Wrongful Death, Personal Injury, Product Liability, Cycling Injuries, Domestic Relations, Family Law, Corporate Law, Business Law, Banking, Real Estate Law, Tax Law. Employment Law, Probate, Estate Planning, Commercial, Workers Compensation, Bankruptcy Law, Criminal Defense (Felonies and Misdemeanors); Medicaid Planning.
References: The Western Security Bank; The Third National Bank; Trust Corp. Bank, Ohio.
Sandusky, Ohio Office: 414 Wayne Street, P.O. Box 929, 44870. Telephone: 419-627-0414; 800-410-0414. Fax: 419-627-0009.
See Professional Biographies, VERMILION, OHIO

Clark, Jonathan F. .... '54 '84 C.49 B.S.B.A. L.851 J.D. 5548 S. St.
Dolyk, W. Zack, (BV) .... '53 '78 C.607 B.A. L.608 J.D. [Buckingham,L.M.&Z.] ⊙
Downie, John F., (AV) .... '34 '59 C.363 B.B.S. L.215 LL.B. 5300 Park Dr.
Elden, John A., Jr., (AV) .... '32 '57 C.31 B.A. L.477 J.D. 15008 Holiday Dr.‡
Gammons, Patrick E. .... '44 '71 C.744 B.S. L.1003 J.D. 1610 Cooper Foster Park Rd.
Reeves, Gayle A. .... '55 '84 C.999 B.S. L.1003 J.D. 1605 State Rd.
Romp, Thomas L. .... '43 '68 C&L.228 A.B., J.D. Pres., Romp's Water Port, Inc.
Ryan, Joseph T., (BV) .... '28 '56 C.573 B.S. L.608 J.D. 656 Main St.
Schaffer, Gail M. .... '38 '77 C.930 B.S.N. L.161 J.D. P.O. Box 174
Schaffer, Michael V. .... '33 '65 C.973 B.S.B.A. L.1003 J.D. P.O. Box 174
Smith, Timothy T., (AV) .... '44 '69 C.1024 B.A. L.930 J.D. [Smith&S.] ⊙
Smith and Smith, (AV) .... 656 Main Street (⊙Avon Lake)
Wakefield, Elizabeth Petersen .... '49 '84 C.72 B.A. L.1003 J.D. 5626 Huron Street
Walsh, James L., (CV) .... '40 '81 C.120 A.B. L.930 J.D. Oberlin Coll.
Walsh, Katherine H., (CV) .... '44 '76 C.665 B.A. L.1003 J.D. State Rep.
Williams, Wm. H. .... '09 '35 C.610 A.B. 5571 Liberty Ave.

VERSAILLES, 2,589, *Darke Co.*

Guillozet, Thomas L., (CV) .... '59 '85 C.434 B.A. L.201 J.D. [Hanes,S.H.M.C.&G.] ⊙
Hanes, Schipfer, Hurley, McClurg, Cooper & Graber, A Prtnshp. incl. Prof. Corps., (AV)
207 E. Main St. (⊙Greenville)
Hoellrich, Gene R., (BV) .... '46 '71 C&L.608 B.A., J.D. 7947 Martz Rd.
McClurg, Michael D., (BV) .... '46 '76 C.1208 B.S. L.607 J.D. [Hanes,S.H.M.C.&G.] ⊙

VIENNA, 994, *Trumbull Co.*

Lutseck, John P., (CV) '56 '84
C.980 B.A. L.1003 J.D. 771 Youngstown-Kingsville Rd. NE
Shaffer, Emmett C. .... '25 '80 C.980 B.A. L.7 J.D. N. Warner Rd.‡

WADSWORTH, 18,437, *Medina Co.*

Allison, Howard M. .... '43 '69 C&L.8 B.A., J.D. 637 Messina Drive
Bowers, Harold F., Jr., (BV) .... '49 '78 C.8 B.A. L.7 J.D. 102 Main Street
Brague, Norman E., (BV) .... '46 '71 C.610 B.B.A. L.608 J.D. City Pros.
Callow, Michael J. .... '70 '95 C.97 B.S.B.A. L.8 J.D. One Park Centre Drive, Suite 100
Dickey, Richard D., (BV) .... '35 '63 C&L.608 B.A., J.D. 126 King Street
Foreman, Joseph E., (BV) .... '36 '65 C.611 B.A. L.608 J.D. 122 Broad St.
Gerstenschlager, Neal Jon .... '45 '76 C.473 B.S. in B.A. L.7 J.D. [Neal J.G.]
Gigiano, Daniel Frank .... '68 '93 C.339 B.A. L.424 J.D. [D.F.Gigiano]

Gigiano, Daniel F., Co., L.P.A.
111 Broad Street, Suite 206, 44281-1867
Telephone: 330-336-3330 Fax: 330-336-3331
Email: dgigiano@msn.com URL: http://www.dangigianolaw.com
Daniel Frank Gigiano.
Criminal Litigation, Bankruptcy, Family Law, Civil Litigation.
See Professional Biographies, WADSWORTH, OHIO

Hackenberg, Anthony W. .... '51 '80 C.8 B.S.E.D. L.7 J.D. N.A.S.A.
Hall, Jeffrey L. .... '61 '91 C.608 B.S. L.8 J.D. 537 Weatherstone Dr.
Hoffmann, Linda, (BV) .... '59 '84 C.201 B.A. L.150 J.D. [Palecek,M.H.&M.]
Jack, David C., (BV) .... '57 '83 C.8 B.S. L.7 J.D. 145 Arkon Road
Johnston, Charles F., Jr., (AV) .... '29 '54 C&L.608 B.S., J.D. 102 Main St.‡
Manning, Elizabeth B., (BV) .... '49 '81 C.477 B.A. L.8 J.D. Wadsworth-Ritman Hosp.
McIlvaine, Andrew S., (CV) .... '— '96 C.434 B.A. L.608 J.D. [A Palecek,M.H.&M.]
McIlvaine, James R., (AV) .... '44 '69 C.532 B.A. L.608 J.D. [Palecek,M.H.&M.]
McIlvaine, Stephen B. .... '53 '78 C.532 B.A. L.607 J.D. Mun. J.
Michaels, Andrew J., (AV) '26 '53 C.8 B.A. L.477 J.D.
840 South Medina Line Road (Akron-West/Montrose)
Morris, Thomas J. .... '73 '98 C.608 B.S. L.8 J.D. [A Palecek,M.H.&M.]
Morse, Mary Jo, (BV) .... '58 '83 C.741 B.B.A. L.8 J.D. [Palecek,M.H.&M.]
Neal J. Gerstenschlager .... 315 Eric Lane
Palecek, Thomas E., (BV) .... '38 '69 C.717 B.S. L.7 J.D. [Palecek,M.H.&M.]
Palecek, McIlvaine, Hoffmann & Morse Co., L.P.A., (AV) ... 200 Smokerise Dr., Ste. 200
Reiter, Carol Conrad, (CV) .... '53 '80 C.8 B.A. L.7 J.D. 252 Falk Ave.
Schrock, Page Cline, III '49 '78 C.8 B.A. L.7 J.D.
City of Wadsworth, Law Director's Off.

WAITE HILL, 529, *Lake Co.*

Griffith, Pamela Blodgette .... '52 '81 C.608 B.S. L.930 J.D. 7375 Reserve Dr.
Rorick, Alan G., (AV) .... '18 '48 C.870 B.S. L.930 LL.B. 7610 Eagle Road‡
Sowards, Buckley D. '29 '58 C.437 B.S. L.923 J.D.
(adm. in WV; not adm. in OH) 10078 Gardenside Dr.

WALBRIDGE, 2,546, *Wood Co.*

Welch, John E. .... '59 '88 C&L.851 B.A., J.D. 28562 E. Bway.

WALTON HILLS, 2,371, *Cuyahoga Co.*

Churchmack, Allan G., (BV) '62 '89
C.161 B.A. L.1003 J.D. Gen. Coun., Arhaus Furniture
Durback, Nick V., (BV) .... '27 '57 C.930 B.B.A. L.1003 J.D. 16605 Egbert Rd.
Megargel, Ralph C. .... '61 '92 C.381 B.A. L.930 J.D. 7140 Northfield Rd.
Polster, Scott H. .... '55 '82 C.264 B.A. L.851 J.D. 7500 Northfield Rd.
Sapir, George R. .... '42 '75 C.97 B.S. L.930 J.D. 7140 Northfield Road
Weis, Geri Lynn .... '54 '99 C.318 B.A. L.989 J.D. Transtar Industries, Inc.

WAPAKONETA, * 9,474, *Auglaize Co.*

Brunner, John D. .... '65 '93 C.347 B.S. L.201 J.D. Auglaize Co. Child Support
Burton, Courtney Wiesenmayer .... '69 '95 C&L.608 B.S., J.D. 15 Willipie Street
Derryberry, Quentin M., II .... '43 '70 C.611 B.A. L.607 J.D. P.O. Box 2056
Faller, Dennis P., (BV) .... '54 '79 C.473 B.S. L.150 J.D. 6 Perry St.
Herman, Gary W. .... '49 '74 C.826 B.A. L.607 J.D. Mun. J.

Hunt & Johnson
(See Lima)

Jauert, Douglas S., (BV) .... '45 '72 C&L.608 B.A., J.D. [Weger J.&H.] ⊙
Kehoe, Robert William .... '49 '89 C.1111 B.A. L.201 J.D. 201 East Auglaize Street
Miller, Ronald H., (BV) .... '43 '68 C&L.608 B.S., J.D. 5 Willipie St.
Pepple, Frederick D. .... '54 '78 C.97 B.S. L.607 J.D. Com. Pleas J.
Poppe, John A., (BV) .... '38 '72 C.608 B.S. L.607 J.D. 1100 W. Auglaize St.
Rone, Gerald J., Jr. .... '23 '55 C.631 B.S. L.607 J.D. Ret. Com. Pleas J.
Siesel, Gerald F., (BV) .... '47 '76 C.313 B.A. L.607 J.D. 119 W. Auglaize Street
Stroebel, Edward, (AV) .... '16 '42 C.967 B.A. L.607 J.D. 108 West Auglaize Street
Weger Jauert & Herman LLP, (AV) .... 10 W. Auglaize St., 2nd Floor (⊙Minster)

WARREN, * 46,832, *Trumbull Co.*

Alpern, Jack N., (BV) .... '45 '71 C&L.608 B.A., J.D. [J.N.Alpern]
Alpern, Jack N., Co., L.P.A., (BV) .... 103 W. Market St. Ste. 202
Ambrosy, Curtis J., (AV) .... '52 '77 C.207 B.A. L.880 J.D. [Ambrosy&F.]
Ambrosy and Fredericka, (AV) .... 144 N. Park Ave., Suite 200
Annos, James G., (BV) .... '32 '57 C.97 B.S. L.608 J.D. 200 Chestnut St., NE
Antonucci, Anthony L., (CV) .... '50 '80 C.980 B.A. L.607 J.D. 137 E. Market St.
Anzellotti, Sperling, Pazol & Small Co., L.P.A., (BV)
295 Harmon Avenue, N.W. (⊙Youngstown)
Arbie, Phillip S. .... '42 '73 C.980 B.A. L.7 J.D. 155 S. Park
Ashelman, Robert K., II .... '44 '75 C.318 B.A. L.7 J.D. Co. Law Librarian
Ask, Andrew C. .... '42 '70 C.350 B.S. L.8 J.D. 3179 Meadow Lane N.E.
Bailey, Kenneth Neil .... '44 '71 C.610 B.A. L.30 J.D. Pros. Off., Crim. Div.
Barber, Diane Lee .... '67 '98 C.97 B.A. L.7 J.D. Trumbull Co. Pros. Off.
Basile, Andrew R., (CV) .... '61 '86 C.97 B.A. L.201 J.D. 1129 Niles Cortland Rd., S.E.
Bauer, Roger R., (BV) .... '48 '73 C.980 B.A. L.7 J.D. 244 Seneca Avenue
Bauman, Richard G. '17 '41 C.16 L.608 LL.B.
Chmn. of the Bd., Bauman Land Title, Inc.
Bennett, Bruce W., (BV) .... '53 '86 C.980 B.S. L.8 J.D. [A Urban]
Bernard, Elizabeth A., (BV) .... '62 '88 C.980 B.A. L.7 J.D. [Harshman&B.] ⊙
Birrell, Bruce, (BV) .... '27 '53 C.976 B.A. L.930 J.D. Suite 712
Bluedorn, Samuel F. .... '64 '92 C.381 B.A. L.8 J.D. [Bluedorn&O.]
Bluedorn and Ohlin Co., L.P.A. .... 144 North Park Avenue, Suite 310
Bodor, C. Andrew .... '44 '72 C.363 A.B. L.161 J.D. [C.A.Bodor]
Bodor, Frank R., (BV) .... '31 '56 C.117 B.A. L.608 J.D. 157 Porter St., N.E.
Bodor, C. Andrew, Co., L.P.A. .... 280 N. Park Ave.
Bombeck, Scott C., (CV) .... '57 '84 C.980 B.A. L.117 J.D. [S.C.Bombeck]
Bombeck, S. C., (CV) .... 269 Seneca Ave. N.E.
Brainard, Todd L., (CV) .... '47 '91 C.381 B.A. L.7 J.D. 925 State Rd., N.W.
Brown, B. Lane, (BV) .... '13 '36 C.528 L.607 LL.B. 295 Harmon St., N.W.
Bumstead, Mark E., (BV) .... '53 '80 C.294 A.B. L.7 J.D. [Letson,G.W.L.&R.]
Burkey, Robert F., (BV) .... '41 '66 C.318 B.A. L.930 J.D. 200 Chestnut Ave., NE

Buzulencia, Michael D., Law Offices of, (BV) '58 '84
C.980 B.A. L.1003 J.D. 150 E. Market St., Ste. 300
Cantalamessa, Enzo C. '73 '03 C.363 B.A. L.1560 J.D. [Ⓐ Davis&Y.]
Carey, Thomas G., Jr., (AV) '48 '78 C.197 B.A. L.608 J.D. [Harrington,H.&M.]
Carpenter, Dennis L., (BV) '51 '77 C.980 B.A. L.616 J.D. 410 Mahoning Ave.
Carr, J. Craig, (BV) '48 '73 C.473 A.B. L.608 J.D. First Place Bank
Christine, Anthony P., (BV) '53 '84 C.980 B.S.A.S. L.7 J.D. [Ⓐ Urban]
Collins, Susan Porter, (CV) '60 '86
C.1265 B.B.A. L.1187 J.D. Atty., Co. Children Servs. Bd.
Cornicelli, Anthony M., (AV) '53 '79 C.150 B.A. L.7 J.D. Chief Mag./Ct. Admr.
Crisan, James John '57 '95 C.381 B.G.S. L.989 J.D. Martin F. White Co., L.P.A.
Daugherty, David D., (BV) '55 '80 C.967 B.A. L.7 J.D. 410 Mahoning Ave.

Davis & Young, (AV)
A Legal Professional Association
108 Main Street, SW Suite 1000, 44481 ⊙
Telephone: 330-373-1717 Fax: 330-395-0610
Email: atty@davisyoung.com URL: http://www.davisyoung.com
William Jack Meola. Associate: Enzo C. Cantalamessa.
General Trial and Appellate Practice, Products Liability, General Tort, Insurance Coverage, Personal Injury, Toxic Torts, Complex Mass Tort Claims, Legal and Medical Malpractice, Municipal Liability, Civil Rights, Employment Practices Liability, and Environmental and Commercial Liability.
Counsel for: Westfield Companies; Cincinnati Insurance Co.; University Hospitals of Cleveland; Central Mutual Insurance Co.; St. Paul Insurance Co.; State Farm Insurance Cos.; Progressive Insurance Cos.; Erie Insurance Group; Motorists Mutual Insurance Group; SYSCO Food Services of Cleveland, Inc.
Cleveland, Ohio Office: 1700 Midland Building, Suite 1700, 44115. Telephone: 216-348-1700. Fax: 216-621-0602.
Akron, Ohio Office: National City Center, One Cascade Plaza, Suite 800, 44308. Telephone: 330-376-1717. Fax: 330-376-1797.
Youngstown, Ohio Office: The Commerce Building, 201 East Commerce Street, Suite 100, 44503. Telephone: 330-743-1717.
See Professional Biographies, WARREN, OHIO

De Capito, Alberta '42 '66 C.472 B.A. L.930 J.D. 159 Kenilworth Ave., S.E.‡
Dimartino, Heaven Rose '70 '01 C&L.8 B.S., J.D. 11th Dist. Ct. of Appeals
Dixon, Rodger L., (BV) '51 '89 C.980 B.S.B.A. L.8 J.D. Asst. Pros. Atty.
Donlin, Patrick J., (CV) '44 '71 C.980 A.B. L.930 J.D. 308 Porter Street, N.E.
Downey, John H. '18 '51 C.980 A.B. L.948 LL.B. 295 Harmon St., N.W.
Dull, David A., Sr., (BV) '26 '56 C&L.980 J.D. 808 N. Park Ave.
Dull, David Austin, Jr., (BV) '61 '86 C.607 B.A. L.851 J.D. 808 N. Park Ave.
Elkins, Stanley A. '59 '85 C.203 B.S. L.7 J.D. Asst. City Law Dir.
Finamore, Mark S., (BV) '56 '82 C.980 B.A. L.7 J.D. 258 Seneca Ave. N.E.
Fodor, Jeffrey W., (BV) '48 '73 C.608 B.A. L.7 J.D. P.O. Box 1706
Ford, Donald R. '31 '57 C.81 A.B. L.477 J.D. Appl. J.
Fredericka, James A., (AV) '53 '78 C.602 A.B. L.930 J.D. [Ambrosy&F.]
Gessner, George E., (BV) '45 '69 C.318 B.A. L.8 J.D. [Gessner&P.] ⊙
Gessner, John F., (AV) '19 '54 C.318 B.A. L.980 J.D. [Gessner&P.] ⊙
Gessner & Platt Co., L.P.A., (AV) 808 N. Park Ave. (⊙Cortland)
Glaros King, Koula, (CV) 522 High St., N.E.
Glaros-King, Koula Elias, (CV) '58 '83 C.381 B.A. L.7 J.D. [K.GlarosKing]
Gold, Ned C., Jr., (BV) '41 '66 C&L.734 B.S., J.D. [Harrington,H.&M.]
Goodman, Jeffrey V., (CV) '63 '91 C.81 B.A. L.8 J.D. 252 Seneca Avenue, NE
Gray, James E., (CV) '46 '74 C.381 B.A. L.607 J.D. [J.E.Gray&Assoc.]
Gray, James E., & Associates, L.P.A., (CV) 8528 E. Market St.
Griffith, David M. '17 '43 C.473 L.150 Ret. Com. Pleas J.
Griffith, Lynn B., III, (BV) '56 '82 C.231 B.A. L.608 J.D. [Letson,G.W.L.&R.]
Grinstein, Jeffrey M. '60 '85
C.1365 B.A. L.608 J.D. Gen. Coun., American Waste Servs., Inc.
Grove, Michael E., (BV) '53 '78 C.473 B.A. L.608 J.D. [M.E.Grove]
Grove, Michael E., Co., L.P.A., (BV) 1125 Niles-Cortland Road, S.E.
Guarnieri, Donald L., (AV) '34 '60 C.318 A.B. L.1003 J.D. [D.L.Guarnieri]
Guarnieri, Fred R. '11 '34 C.128 A.B. L.930 LL.B. 3132 Crescent Dr., N.E.‡
Guarnieri, Donald L., Co., L.P.A., (AV) 431 East Market Street

Guarnieri and Secrest, (AV)
Guarnieri Block, 151 East Market Street, P.O. Box 4270, 44482-4270
Telephone: 330-393-1584 Fax: 330-395-3831
Email: ganslaw@netdotcom.com
Members of Firm: Lewis L. Guarnieri (1896-1976); George W. Secrest (1894-1959); Paul A. Guarnieri (1912-1992); Anthony G. Rossi; Randil J. Rudloff; Michael D. Rossi; Anthony G. Rossi, III. Associate: Deborah Smith.
General Civil Practice. Corporation, Banking and Finance, Insurance, Wills, Trusts and Probate, Condemnation, Family Law, Employment Relations, Personal Injury, Workers Compensation, Administrative Law and Civil Rights, Motor Vehicle Dealerships, Estate Planning, Trials and Appeals (State and Federal).
Local Counsel for: Fireman's Fund American Insurance Group; State Farm Mutual Insurance Co.
See Professional Biographies, WARREN, OHIO

Gysegem, Thomas P. '59 '84 C.935 B.A. L.8 J.D. Mun. Ct. J.
Harlan, Michael D. '68 '98 C.980 B.A. L.8 J.D.
[Ⓐ Harshman&B.] (⊙Boardman, OH; Sharon, PA)

Harrington, Hoppe & Mitchell, Ltd., (AV) BB
108 Main Avenue, S.W., Suite 500, 44481 ⊙
Telephone: 330-392-1541 Fax: 330-394-6890
Email: info@hhmlaw.com URL: http://www.hhmlaw.com
John L. Pogue; Ned C. Gold, Jr. (Certified Specialist in Labor & Employment Law, Ohio State Bar Association); Michael G. Marando; William L. Hawley; Thomas G. Carey, Jr.; Kevin P. Murphy; Patrick K. Wilson;—Michael J. McGee.
General Civil Trial and Equity Practice in all State and Federal Courts. Corporation, Banking, Creditors Rights and Bankruptcy, Labor, Probate, Estate Planning, Hospital and Health, Insurance Law, Real Estate, Commercial, Business Transactions.
Representative Clients: Forum Health Hospitals and Medical Centers; Aqua Ohio Water Company (Public Utility); SYGNET Communications, Inc.; The Public Library of Youngstown and Mahoning County; Simon-DeBartolo Group; Mahoning Valley Economic Development Corporation; National City Bank.
Youngstown, Ohio Office: 26 Market Street, Suite 1200, 44503-1508. Telephone: 330-744-1111. Telecopier: 330-744-2029.
Salem, Ohio Office: 2235 E. Pershing Street, Suite A, 44460. Telephone: 330-337-6586. Telecopier: 330-337-6662.
See Professional Biographies, WARREN, OHIO

Harshman, Michael S., (BV) '40 '66 C.608 B.A. L.846 J.D. [Harshman&B.] ⊙
Harshman & Bernard LLC, (BV)
103 W. Market Street (⊙Boardman, Youngstown, OH; Sharon, PA)
Hatchner, Jeffrey A. '46 '79 C.980 B.S.B.A. L.7 J.D.
V.P., Tr. Admin., Second Natl. Bk.
Hawley, William L., (BV) '54 '79 C.62 B.A. L.608 J.D. [Harrington,H.&M.]
Heller, Laurie E. '68 '94 C.597 B.A. L.930 J.D. Jud. Law Clk., Ct. of App. J.
Heltzel, Paul E., (BV) '45 '82 C.363 B.S. L.602 J.D. 155 Pine Ave., N.E.
Hicks, Gregory V. '50 '85 C.980 B.S. L.7 J.D. City Law Dir.
Hill, Donald W., (BV) '47 '74 C.608 B.A. L.7 J.D. 175 Franklin St., S.E.
Hlaudy, Richard '70 '01 C.999 B.A L.1541 J.D. [Ⓐ J.E.Gray&Assoc.]
Hollister, John A., (BVⓉ) '46 '79 C.33 B.A. L.818 J.D. 7546 Pegotty Dr., N.E.

Iannucci, Anthony A., Jr. '47 '73 C.363 B.S.B.A. L.1003 J.D. City Auditor
Ivanchak, Terry F., (BV) '53 '78 C.473 B.A. L.607 J.D. 173 W. Market St.
James, Richard L., (BV) '50 '81 C.318 B.A. L.7 J.D. Dom. Relations Ct. J.
Johnson, Robert L., (CV) '63 '89 C.980 B.A. L.8 J.D. Pub. Def. Off.
Kafantaris, George Nicholas '53 '81 C.980 B.S. L.851 J.D. 720 N. Park Avenue
Keating, Brendan J., Attorney at Law, (CV) '72 '98
C.97 B.A. L.851 J.D. 144 N. Park Ave., Ste. 315
Keating, Daniel G., (BV) '56 '82 C.09 B.A. L.851 J.D. [Keating,K.&K.]
Keating, W. Leo, (AV) '22 '50 C.602 B.A. L.436 LL.B. [Keating,K.&K.]

Keating, Keating & Kuzman, (AV)
170 Monroe Street, N.W., 44483
Telephone: 330-393-4611; 393-0121 Fax: 330-394-0101
Email: KEATINGLAW@EARTHLINK.NET URL: http://www.lawyers.com/keatingkeating&kuzman
W. Leo Keating; Daniel G. Keating. Of Counsel: John J. Kuzman (Jr.).
Litigation, Insurance Defense, Personal Injury, Automobile Accidents, Medical Malpractice, Criminal Law, Driving While Intoxicated, Hospital, Healthcare, Airport, Trust, Business, Probate and Estate Planning.
See Professional Biographies, WARREN, OHIO

King, John E., (AV) '24 '56 C.381 A.B. L.948 LL.B. [Phelps&K.]
Kmetz, Kimberlee J., (CV) '69 '94 C.980 B.A. L.8 J.D. [Ⓐ Harshman&B.] ⊙
Knepp, Patricia Ann '64 '93 C.980 B.A. L.7 J.D. [J.A.Leopardi]
Kontos, Peter James '54 '79 C.97 B.A. L.608 J.D. Common Pleas J.
Kovoor, Sarah Thomas '61 '98 C.696 B.A. L.8 J.D. Asst. Pros. Atty.
Kragalott, Samuel R., (BV) '57 '82 C.608 B.A. L.607 J.D. [Letson,G.W.L.&R.]
Kurtz, John W., (BV) '26 '50 C&L.150 J.D. 174 N. Park Ave.
Kuzman, John J., (Jr.), (BV) '52 '86 C.980 B.S.A.S. L.8 J.D. [Ⓒ Keating,K.&K.]
Lake, David G., (BV) '39 '84 C.980 A.B. L.7 J.D. 175 Franklin Street, S.E.
Lambert, Marc D., Law Office of '71 '98
C.550 B.A L.124 J.D. 144 N. Park Ave., Ste. 101
LaPolla, Thomas A., (AV) '37 '62 C&L.608 B.S., J.D. 155 Pine Ave., N.E.
Larmi, Allan R. '23 '51 C&L.608 B.A., LL.B. 3056 E. Market St.‡
Lavelle, Edward L., (BV) '47 '73 C.608 B.A. L.117 J.D. [Letson,G.W.L.&R.]
Legow, Christine Blair, (BV) '52 '79
C.318 B.A. L.930 J.D. Mng. Atty., Northern Ohio Legal Servs.
Leopardi, John A., (BV) '30 '57 C&L.608 B.A., J.D. [J.A.Leopardi]
Leopardi, John A., Co., L.P.A., (BV) 409 Harmon Ave., N.W.
Letson, Daniel B., (BV) '57 '86 C.294 B.A. L.7 J.D. [Letson,G.W.L.&R.]
Letson, Thomas B. J., (CV) '52 '88 C.381 B.A. L.7 J.D. [Letson,G.W.L.&R.]
Letson, William N., (AV) '30 '55 C&L.309 A.B., J.D. [Letson,G.W.L.&R.]
Letson, Griffith, Woodall, Lavelle & Rosenberg Co., L.P.A., (AV)
155 South Park Avenue, Suite 250
Lewis, James F., (BV) '46 '72 C.610 B.A. L.7 J.D. Pub. Def., OH Pub. Def. Comm.
Logan, Andrew D. '50 '79 C.608 B.A. L.117 J.D. Admin. J., Trumbull Co. Police Ct.
Maas, Paula D. '— '80 C.880 B.A. L.896 J.D. [Ⓐ C.L.Richards]
Makridis, Irene K. '56 '81 C.980 B.S. L.851 J.D. 183 W. Market Street, Suite 201
Marando, Michael G., (BV) '48 '74 C.610 B.B.A. L.884 J.D. [Harrington,H.&M.]
Marik, Deborah E., (CV) '50 '91 C.980 B.S. L.8 J.D. Co. Prob. Ct.
Marowitz, Albert W. '12 '42 C.318 B.A. L.980 J.D. 106 E. Market St.‡
Masek, Raymond J. '46 '77 C.161 B.B.A. L.1003 J.D. 183 W. Market St., Ste. 300
May, Joyce A., (BV) '49 '78 C.381 B.A. L.930 J.D. [Turner,M.&S.] ⊙
Maynard, Robert C., (AV) '36 '62 C.363 B.S.S. L.276 LL.M. [Ⓐ C.L.Richards]
McGee, Michael J. '69 '95 C.608 B.A. L.365 J.D. [Ⓐ Harrington,H.&M.]
McGuire, William Paul, (BV) '55 '80 C.473 B.S. L.607 J.D. [W.P.McGuire]
McGuire, William Paul, Co, LPA, (BV) 106 E. Market Street
McHenry, Aaron Michael '74 '99 C.610 B.A. L.8 J.D. Staff Atty.
McKay, W. Wyatt '47 '73 C.381 B.A. L.7 J.D. Com. Pleas J.
McLain, David F. '28 '53 C.674 A.B. L.309 J.D. Com. Pleas J.
McLain, David H., (CV) '63 '92 C.473 B.A. L.851 J.D. 144 N. Park Avenue, Suite 301
McLain, William P., (BV) '32 '58 C&L.602 B.S.C., LL.B. City Law Dir.
Meermans, Robert S., (AV) '21 '48 C.901 A.B. L.930 LL.B. 159 E. Market St.
Meola, William Jack, (BV) '59 '84 C.473 B.A. L.930 J.D. [Davis&Y.]
Morgione, Greg '73 '98 C.150 B.B.A. L.1003 J.D. 1129 Nile-Cortland Rd.
Moro, Joseph A., (BV) '59 '85 C.980 B.A. L.150 J.D. 8096 E. Market St., Ste. 2
Morrow, Charles LeRoy '60 '88 C.234 B.A. L.851 J.D. Co. Pros. Off.
Mucklow, David A. '59 '88 C.1069 B.A. L.365 J.D. Staff Atty., First Place Bank
Murphy, Kevin P., (BV) '60 '85 C.201 B.S. L.608 J.D. [Harrington,H.&M.]
Myers, Milfert W. '22 '55 C.421 A.B. L.192 J.D.
(adm. in FL; not adm. in OH) 2845 E. Market St.‡
Nader, Paul G., (AV) '25 '53 C.930 B.A. L.1003 LL.B. [Nader&N.]
Nader, Rachel E. '63 '90 C.980 B.S.A.S. L.8 J.D. Northeast Ohio Legal Servs.
Nader, Robert A. '28 '53 C&L.930 B.A., LL.B. Ct. of App. J.
Nader, Thomas C., (BV) '62 '87 C.608 B.S.B.A. L.930 J.D. [Nader&N.]

Nader and Nader, (AV)
155 South Park Avenue, 44481
Telephone: 330-395-7555; 330-395-9586 FAX: 330-392-5443
Email: lawfirm@naderandnader.com
Paul G. Nader; Thomas C. Nader.
General Civil Practice in all Courts. Municipal, Corporate, Domestic, Trials, Environmental Law, Public Utility Law, Ohio Administrative Agencies and Real Estate Law.
Agents for: Ohio Bar Title Insurance Co.
See Professional Biographies, WARREN, OHIO

Nadler Nadler & Burdman Co., L.P.A.
(See Youngstown)

Napolet, Mario Robert '68 '99 L.8 J.D. [M.R.Napolet]
Napolet, Mario Robert, Ltd., Law Offices of 269 Seneca Ave., N.E.
Natale, Anthony Maurice '44 '75 C.363 B.S.E. L.1000 J.D.
Mag. & Ct. Admin., Trumbull Co. Family Ct.
Neuman, Craig H. '42 '74 C.980 B.A. L.8 J.D. Dir., Trumbull Co. Children Servs. Bd.
Norton, Thomas F. '43 '69 C.757 B.A. L.930 J.D. Dom. Rel. J.
O'Day, Michael P. '57 '86 C.611 B.A. L.930 J.D. Staff Atty., 11th Dist. Ct. of App.
Ognibene, Michael A., (BV) '53 '81
C.381 B.A. L.7 J.D. 204 Monroe Street, N.W., Suite 2
Ohlin, Charles E. '63 '88 C.381 B.A. L.608 J.D. [Bluedorn&O.]
Paajanen, Reynold A., (BV) '28 '61 C.381 B.S.B.A. L.980 J.D. 108 N. Pk. Ave.
Pazol, James L., (BV) '37 '62 C&L.608 B.A., J.D. [Anzellotti,S.P.&S.] ⊙

Pfau, Pfau & Marando
(See Youngstown)

Phelps & King, (AV) 106 E. Market Street
Phillips, Clifford L., (CV) '44 '72 C.980 B.S.B.A. L.851 J.D. 1569 Woodland St., N.E.
Pico, John J. '57 '88 C.970 B.A. L.7 J.D. Mag.
Platt, Robert M., Jr., (BV) '47 '74 C.631 B.A. L.7 J.D. [Gessner&P.] ⊙
Platt, Robert M., Sr., (BV) '24 '54 C&L.980 J.D. [Gessner&P.] ⊙
Pogue, John L., (AV) '44 '69 C.210 B.A. L.347 J.D. [Harrington,H.&M.]

Pond, George .... '33 '63 C.611 A.B. L.309 J.D. 295 Harmon Avenue, N.W.
Rich, Gary R. ....'53 '81 C.608 B.A. L.7 J.D. 342 Mahoning Ave., N.W.

Richards, Charles L., Law Office of, (AV) '42 '69 C.602 B.B.A. L.7 J.D.
159 East Market Street, Suite 300, 44481-1122
Telephone: 330-373-1000 Fax: 330-394-5291
Email: CLRichards@onecom.com
Associates: Robert C. Maynard; Paula D. Maas; Jason M. Toth.
Products Liability, Civil Rights Defense, Insurance Defenses, Legal Malpractice, Medical Malpractice, Litigation, Professional Liability.
See Professional Biographies, WARREN, OHIO

Rieger, Gilbert L., (AV) .... '41 '70 C.610 A.B. L.851 J.D. 410 Mahoning Ave.
Ries, James R., (BV) ....'50 '75 C.381 B.A. L.7 J.D. 244 Seneca N.E.
Rintala, Pamela A. ....'50 '80 C.381 B.A. L.7 J.D. Family Ct. J.
Robinson, L. Steven, (BV) .... '25 '52 C.665 B.A. L.1003 J.D. 179 W. Market St.
Rose, Traci Timko .... '72 '98 C.608 B.A. L.124 J.D. Law Dept., City of Warren
Rosenberg, Michael W., (AV) .... '41 '66 C&L.477 A.B., J.D. [Letson,G.W.L.&R.]
Ross, Douglas W. ....'71 '97 C.473 B.S. L.930 J.D. 106 E. Market St.
Rossi, Anthony G., (AV) .... '35 '61 C.363 B.S. L.128 J.D. [Guarnieri&S.]
Rossi, Anthony G., III, (BV) ....'66 '91 C.473 B.A. L.607 J.D. [Guarnieri&S.]
Rossi, Michael D., (AV) ....'50 '75 C.602 B.A. L.128 J.D. [Guarnieri&S.]
Roux, William M., (CV) '56 '83 C.980 B.S.B.Ed. L.7 J.D.
106 E. Market Street, Suite 305
Rucker, Gilbert Robert, III ......'55 '86 C.363 B.S.B.A. L.1000 J.D. 135 Pine St., Ste. 203
Rudloff, Randil J., (AV) ....'48 '73 C.381 B.A. L.607 J.D. [Guarnieri&S.]
Saker, James T., (BV) .... '52 '83 C.381 B.A. L.117 J.D. 149 Washington St., N.E.
Savakis, Alexander J., (BV) ....'53 '78 C.980 B.A. L.930 J.D. Com. Pleas Mag.
Scala, Michael A., (CV) .... '51 '76 C.602 B.A. L.7 J.D. 244 Seneca Avenue, N.E.
Scheid, Katherine Ann .... '57 '87 C.161 B.S.C.E. L.7 J.D. Dep. Clk., Probate Ct.
Schubert, Thomas E. ....'41 '70 C.980 B.S. L.8 J.D. 269 Seneca Avenue, N.E.
Shaker, Mitchell F. .... '22 '48 C.363 A.B. L.930 J.D. Com. Pleas J.
Shaw, Kenneth N., (CV) .... '45 '80 C.381 B.A. L.8 J.D. 145 Niles-Cortland Road NE
Shepherd, David A., (BV) ....'56 '81 C.980 B.A. L.7 J.D. [Turner,M.&S.] ⊙
Sheth-Massacci, Shibani ....'71 '97 C.381 B.A. L.7 J.D. Staff Atty., Ct. of App.
Sieman, Nathan L. ....'06 '30 C&L.608 J.D. 777 Wildwood NE‡
Smith, Deborah, (CVⓉ) .... '70 '95 C.651 B.S. L.930 J.D. [Ⓐ Guarnieri&S.]
Stack, Dene M. ....'42 '00 C.980 B.A. L.7 J.D. [Letson,G.W.L.&R.]
Stanitz, Christopher .... '48 '74 C.734 B.S. L.930 J.D. 108 Main Avenue S.W.
Stuard, John M. ....'39 '65 C.848 A.B. L.383 J.D. Com. Pleas J.
Swader, David Scott .... '74 '02 C.980 B.A. L.8 J.D. [Ⓐ Letson,G.W.L.&R.]
Swartz, Albert F. .... '26 '54 L.980 J.D. 149 E. Market St.‡
Swartz, Charles I. .... '31 '68 C.665 B.B.A. L.930 J.D. [C.I.Swartz]
Swartz, Charles I., Co., L.P.A. ....746 Elm Road, N.E.
Swauger, Terry A., (CV) ....'69 '95 C.608 B.A. L.117 J.D. 106 E. Market St., Ste. 308
Swift, Thomas A. ....'42 '69 C.381 B.A. L.7 J.D. Prob. J.
Tackett, Dennis, The Law Offices of, (CV) '55 '91
C.381 B.G.S. L.8 J.D. 106 E. Market Street, Suite 308
Theisler, Charles ....'50 '93 C.980 B.A. L.7 J.D. [Ⓐ J.E.Gray&Assoc.]
Thomas, Daniel A., (BV) .... '65 '93 C.608 B.S.B.A. L.851 J.D. 155 Pine Ave., N.E.
Thomas, Daniel P., (BV) ....'41 '66 C&L.608 B.S., J.D. 155 Pine Ave., N.E.
Tisone, Raymond J. .... '47 '72 C&L.930 A.B., J.D. 4087 Youngstown-Warren Rd., S.E.

Toot, Douglas M.
(See Canfield)

Toth, Jason M. .... '75 '01 C.980 B.A. L.608 J.D. [Ⓐ C.L.Richards]
Turner, Lawrence S., (BV) .... '40 '66 C.8 B.S. L.930 J.D. [Turner,M.&S.] ⊙
Turner, May & Shepherd, (BV) .... 185 High St., N.E. (⊙Sebring)
Ujczo, Dennis E., Law Offices of, (CV) '51 '76
C.930 B.A. L.1003 J.D. 689 N. Park Avenue
Urban, William J., Jr., (BV) .... '44 '69 C.641 B.A. L.851 J.D. [Urban]
Urban Co., L.P.A., (BV) .... 434 High St., N.E.
Vazmina, Shelley C., (BV) '47 '89
C.25 B.S. L.7 J.D. V.P. & Corp. Compl. Offr., Forum Health
Vennitti, Louis J., (BV) .... '33 '57 C.363 B.S. L.276 J.D. 280 N. Park Ave.
Vigorito, Philip M., Law Office of, (BV) '57 '89
C.980 B.S.A.S. L.7 J.D. 552 N. Park Ave.
Walker, Keith M. ....'51 '76 C.475 B.A. L.608 J.D. P.O. Box 1294
Wallace, Lisa R. '60 '94
C.980 B.S.B.A. L.7 J.D. Asst. Gen. Coun., Avalon Holdings Corp.
Watkins, Dennis, (AV) ....'46 '73 C.980 A.B. L.930 J.D. Pros. Atty.
Wear, Cheryl A. ....'64 '92 C&L.8 B.A., J.D. Law Clk., 11th Dist. Ct. of App.
Weddell Harwood, Sandra Stabile '50 '91
C.381 B.A. L.7 J.D. State Rep., Ohio Gen. Assembly, 65th Dist.
Wern, Charles E., III .... '73 '99 C.363 B.A. L.117 J.D. [Ⓐ Wern]
Wern, Charles E., Jr., (AV) .... '32 '59 C.228 B.A. L.607 J.D. [Wern]

Wern Law Firm, The, LLC, (AV)
210 Scott Street, N.E., 44483
Telephone: 330-392-2533 Fax: 330-395-3403
Email: info@WernLegal.com
Charles E. Wern, Jr.;—Charles E. Wern III.
Corporate, Estate Planning, Probate, Real Estate.
See Professional Biographies, WARREN, OHIO

White, Martin F., (AV) .... '52 '77 C&L.608 B.A., J.D. [M.F.White]

White, Martin F., Co., L.P.A., (AV)
156 Park Avenue N.E., 44481
Telephone: 330-394-9692 Fax: 330-394-8589
Email: mfw850@aol.com
Martin F. White.
Litigation and Plaintiffs Practice. Wrongful Death, Medical Malpractice, Personal Injury.
See Professional Biographies, WARREN, OHIO

Williford, Robin J. ....'54 '80 C.161 B.A. L.1003 J.D. 999 Pine Ave, S.E.
Wilson, Patrick K., (BV) .... '63 '88 C.884 B.A. L.851 J.D. [Harrington,H.&M.]
Wolfe, David J., Jr., (BV) '67 '93 C.575 B.S.B.A. L.608 J.D.
Staff Coun., First Place Bank
Wood, Gabrielle M. ....'62 '88 C.381 B.A. L.930 J.D. Jud. Clk. to Ct. of App.
Woodall, W. Dallas, (AV) .... '37 '67 C.980 B.S.Ed. L.608 J.D. [Letson,G.W.L.&R.]
Woodward, Calvin J., (BV) ....'36 '68 C.980 B.S. L.8 J.D. 366 Mahoning, N.W.
Yakubek, Nancy E. ....'50 '83 C.980 B.A. L.7 J.D. 524 North Park Avenue
York, Robert L. ....'41 '67 C.381 B.S.B.A. L.608 J.D. 138 East Market St.
Young, Charles A. ....'21 '50 C&L.128 LL.B. 8560 Deer Creek Lane, NE

WARRENSVILLE HEIGHTS, 15,109, *Cuyahoga Co.*

Gassaway, Russell .... '25 '55 C.608 B.A. L.1003 LL.B. 20859 Ellacott Pkwy.‡
Shapiro, Alan J., (AV) ....'38 '62 C.477 B.A. L.930 J.D. 4469 Renaissance Parkway

WASHINGTON C. H., * 13,524, *Fayette Co.*

Barr, Michael L., (CV) .... '47 '75 C&L.383 B.A., J.D. 318 E. Court Street
Bender, David B., (CV) .... '61 '86 C&L.851 B.B.A., J.D. 251 E. Court St.

Benson, Michael E.
(See Columbus)

Bryan, John C., (BV) ....'33 '59 C.210 A.B. L.150 J.D. 306 Westwood Dr., S.W.
Butler, James L., (BV) .... '49 '74 C.201 B.A. L.150 J.D. 200 E. Market St.
Coffman, Evelyn W. .... '18 '43 C.150 L.1340 LL.B. 226 E. Market St.‡
Hammond, Nancy D. ....'42 '67 C.610 B.S. L.608 J.D. Prob. & Juv. Ct. J.
Hammond, Robert L., (BV) ....'43 '67 C&L.608 B.A., J.D. 129 North Hinde Street
Junk, William M., (AV) ....'17 '46 C.473 A.B. L.150 LL.B. [Junk&J.]
Junk, William Thomas, (BV) ....'53 '79 C.611 B.A. L.150 J.D. [Junk&J.]
Junk and Junk, (AV) .... 213 North Main Street
Kiger, David V. .... '66 '92 C.631 B.A. L.201 J.D. 132 S. Main St.
Kiger, James A., (BV) .... '30 '62 C.510 B.A. L.150 LL.B. 132 S. Main St.
Marchant, Rollo M. .... '25 '53 C&L.608 LL.B. Ret. Prob. Com. Pleas J.
Marshall, D. Brent .... '71 '97 C.228 B.A. L.383 J.D. 200 E. Market St.
Schwart, Omar A. ....'21 '50 C.178 L.150 LL.B. Sr. J., Ct. of Com. Pleas
Stout, Gary C. .... '45 '71 C&L.607 B.S., J.D. Mun. J.
Terhune-Olaker, Landis L. .... '74 '01 C&L.117 B.A., J.D. P.O. Box 895

Twyford & Donahey, P.L.L.
(See Columbus)

Wead, John H., (BV) ....'45 '76 C.207 B.A. L.150 J.D. 112 Central Pl.

WATERVILLE, 4,828, *Lucas Co.*

Frey, Lou Ann, (BV) ....'54 '84 C&L.851 J.D. 109 N. River Rd.
Kontak, James Robert, (BV) .... '41 '76 C.999 B.A. L.851 J.D. 6651 N. River Road
Waggoner, Geoffrey, (BV) .... '53 '80 C.608 B.A. L.851 J.D. 7527 Timbers Blvd.
Williams, George R., II, (BV) ....'26 '58 C.880 A.B. L.851 LL.B. 204 Farnsworth Rd.

WAUSEON, * 7,091, *Fulton Co.*

Barber, James E. .... '46 '73 C.597 B.A. L.851 J.D. Com. Pleas J.

Barber, Kaper, Stamm & Robinson, (AV)
124 N. Fulton Street, 43567 ⊙
Telephone: 419-337-5065 Fax: 419-337-1136
URL: http://www.lawyers.com/bksr
Members of Firm: John H. Barber (1921-1986); Terry J. Kaper; Jan H. Stamm; Jeffrey L. Robinson.
Associates: Stephen P. Buehrer; Carrie J. Nixon.
General Civil and Criminal Practice. Personal Injury, Insurance, Probate and Estate Planning, Real Estate, Title Examination, Collections, Commercial, Municipal and Banking Law. Trials and Appeals in all Courts.
Reference: Farmers and Merchants State Bank.
Delta, Ohio Office: 206 Main Street. Telephone: 419-822-3211.
See Professional Biographies, WAUSEON, OHIO

Buehrer, Stephen P., (CV) .... '67 '97 C.97 B.S. L.179 J.D. [Ⓐ Barber,K.S.&R.]
Bumb, Michael J. ....'53 '78 C.608 B.A. L.851 J.D. Prob. J.
Hallett, Lester S. ....'14 '39 C.851 L.150 J.D. 132 S. Fulton St.
Hallett, Timothy W., (BV) ....'47 '72 C.97 B.S. L.851 J.D. [Hallett,H.&N.]
Hallett, Hallett & Nagel, (BV) ....132 S. Fulton St.
Kaper, Terry J., (AV) .... '38 '68 C.27 B.S. L.607 J.D. [Barber,K.S.&R.]

McQuades Co., The, L.P.A.
(See Swanton)

McWatters, Thomas A., III .... '59 '86 C.827 B.S. L.851 J.D. 13847 County Rd., H
Nagel, Eric Kenn ....'75 '01 C.97 B.S. L.851 J.D. [Ⓐ Hallett,H.&N.]
Nagel, Roger D., (BV) .... '47 '73 C.97 B.A. L.851 J.D. [Hallett,H.&N.]
Nixon, Carrie J. ....'75 '00 C.63 B.A. L.124 J.D. [Ⓐ Barber,K.S.&R.]

Plassman, Rupp, Short & Hagans
(See Archbold)

Poorman, Gary L., (CV) .... '53 '84 C.851 B.Ed. L.1187 J.D. 8520 16th

Powers, Mark L., (BV) '55 '80 C&L.607 B.A., J.D.
142 North Fulton Street, P.O. Box 393, 43567-0393
Telephone: 419-335-3971 Fax: 419-335-5040
Email: mlpowers@powersupply.net URL: http://www.mlpowers.com
General Civil Trial Practice in all State Courts. Personal Injury, Wills and Probate, Trusts and Estates, Estate Planning, Real Estate, Bankruptcy, Creditors Rights, Family Law, Divorce, Adoptions, Child Custody, Child Support, Domestic Relations, Collections, Commercial.
Reference: Farmers & Merchants State Bank, Wauseon, Ohio.
See Professional Biographies, WAUSEON, OHIO

Robinson, Jeffrey L., (BV) .... '52 '77 C.473 B.S. L.851 J.D. [Barber,K.S.&R.]
Stamm, Jan H., (BV) ....'52 '78 C.288 B.A. L.930 J.D. [Barber,K.S.&R.]
Stuckey, Kurt A. .... '52 '87 C.97 B.A. L.851 J.D. 112 1/2 Washington
Swigart, William R., Law Office of, (BV) .... '48 '76 C.97 B.S. L.851 J.D. 15724 SH 2

WAVERLY, * 4,477, *Pike Co.*

Bevens, Gordon E. .... '45 '71 C.839 B.S. L.383 J.D. Com. Pleas J., Prob. & Juv. Div.
Bevens, William W., (BV) .... '47 '74 C.608 B.S.B.A. L.7 J.D. 112 N. Market St.
Bolt, Cassandra Shoemaker ....'49 '86 C.150 B.M. L.117 J.D. Com. Pleas J.
Catanzaro, Jerome D., (BV) .....'52 '77 C.150 B.A. L.608 J.D. Co. Ct. J. [Catanzaro&R.]
Catanzaro & Rosenberger, (BV) ....100 N. Market St.
Cole, Jesse, Jr. ....'26 '56 C&L.608 B.Sc., J.D. Prob. & Juv. Ct. J.
Dailey, Bruce R. '56 '96 C.15 B.S. L.796 J.D.
(adm. in TX; not adm. in OH) 229 E. North St.
Deering, Randy D., (BV) ....'49 '74 C&L.608 B.A., J.D. 109 Vine St.
Drennen, Jas. M. .... '18 '48 C&L.608 B.S.Ed., J.D. Ret. Com. Pleas J.
Fosson, John L., (AV) .... '49 '75 C.610 A.B. L.150 J.D. 211 E. Second St.

Lewis, Richard M.
(See Jackson)

Pachuta, George O. ....'21 '52 C&L.608 B.A., J.D. Ret. Prob. J.
Rhoads, Ed, (BV) ....'55 '82 C&L.608 B.A., J.D. 305 N. Market St.
Rosenberger, Robert N., (BV) .... '52 '81 C.610 B.A. L.607 J.D. Pros.Off. [Catanzaro&R.]

Rourke & Blumenthal, LLP
(See Columbus)

Seif, David D., (BV) ....'49 '74 C.608 B.S. L.607 J.D. 110 E. Emmitt Avenue

WAYNE, 803, *Wood Co.*

Mitchell, L. Snowden, (BV) ....'18 '48 C.851 L.472 LL.B. 6401 Bays Road
Stewart, Beryl W. ....'28 '64 C.851 B.S. L.1003 J.D. 103 W. Main St.

WAYNESFIELD, 831, *Auglaize Co.*

Dulebohn, Diana G., (CV) .... '50 '80 C.608 B.S. L.607 J.D. 215 W. Mulberry
Reed, Kristine H., (CV) .... '70 '96 C.473 B.A. L.607 J.D. [Yale] ⊙

Yale, Benjamin F., (BVⓉ) ....'51 '80 C.976 B.A. L.607 J.D. [Yale] ⊙
Yale Law Office, L.P., (BV) ....527 N. Westminster Street (⊙Wash., DC)

WAYNESVILLE, 2,558, *Warren Co.*

Dotson, Douglas C. ....'48 '74 C.243 B.A. L.607 J.D. 7791 Township Line Rd.
Foley, Michael E., (BV) ....'52 '77 C.610 A.B. L.851 J.D. 258 Miami St.
Opsahl, Yvonne ....'54 '93 4353 E. State, Rte. 73

WELLINGTON, 4,511, *Lorain Co.*

Ashbaugh, Frank E., (BV) ....'— '73 C.528 B.A. L.1003 J.D. [Baumgartner&O.]
Baumgartner & O'Toole, (AV) ....110 Herrick Avenue West (⊙Sheffield Village)
Brownsberger, Alecia J. ....'67 '93 C.608 B.A. L.117 J.D. [Baumgartner&O.]
Katz, Eugene J. ......'41 '73 C.608 B.A. L.1003 J.D. c/o Precision Fittings, 709 N Main St

WELLSTON, 6,049, *Jackson Co.*

Gilliland, Kyle R., (CV) ......'57 '83 C.608 B.A. L.150 J.D. City Law Dir. [Gilliland&G.]
Gilliland, Roy J., (BV) ....'27 '52 C&L.608 B.S., J.D. [Gilliland&G.]
Gilliland and Gilliland, (BV) ....23 E. Bway.
Heiser, Lawrence A., (BV) ....'48 '73 C.473 B.S. L.150 J.D. [Oths,H.&M.]
Johnston, Lorene G., (BV) '52 '82 C.473 B.S. L.201 J.D.
209 North Pennsylvania Avenue
Miller, Robert R., (CV) ....'58 '90 C.923 B.S. L.117 J.D. [Oths,H.&M.]
Oths, Joseph A., (AV) ....'34 '61 C.201 B.A. L.1340 LL.B. [Oths,H.&M.]
Oths, Heiser and Miller, (AV) ....Sixteen East Broadway
Robb, Jeffrey L. ....'58 '84 C.999 B.S. L.904 J.D. 215 East B St.★
Weber, Shannon Shane ....'75 '01 C.429 B.A. L.608 J.D. 16 E. Broadway

WELLSVILLE, 4,133, *Columbiana Co.*

Amato, Charles Christopher ....'63 '90 C.608 L.1187 J.D. [A N.T.Amato]
Amato, Nicholas T., (BV) ....'61 '89 C.608 B.A. L.607 J.D. 991 Main Street
Beech, Andrew A., (BV) ....'60 '85 C.532 B.A. L.117 J.D. 611 Main St.
Bush, William L., (BV) ....'25 '51 C.381 A.B. L.477 J.D. 431 Riverside Ave.
Telzrow, Wm. J., Jr., (BV) ....'34 '60 C.363 B.S. L.930 LL.B. Asst. Pub. Def.

WEST ALEXANDRIA, 1,460, *Preble Co.*

Fahrenholz, Everett, (BV) ....'16 '50 C.117 A.B. L.266 J.D. 61 Hope Ave.

WEST CARROLLTON, 13,818, *Montgomery Co.*

Carney, Patrick G., (BV) ....'33 '66 C.201 B.A. L.150 J.D. 534 E. Dixie Dr.
Galvas, Walter W., (BV) ....'62 '89 C&L.201 B.A., J.D. [A Tracy&T.]
Haddick, Reid J. '53 '84 C.970 B.A. L.201 J.D.
1129 Miamisburg Centerville Road, Suite 305
Tracy, Bridget A., (BV) ....'57 '84 C.608 B.S. L.201 J.D. [Tracy&T.]
Tracy, John P., (BV) ....'54 '84 C.150 B.B.A. L.201 J.D. [Tracy&T.]
Tracy, Louis E., (AV) ....'26 '52 C&L.602 Ph.B., J.D. [Tracy&T.]
Tracy and Tracy, (AV) ....31 East Central Avenue

WEST CHESTER, —, *Butler Co.*

Bernat, Stephen M. ....'71 '98 C.610 B.B.A. L.1161 J.D. [A McCaslin,I.&M.] ⊙
Campisi, Peter I. '31 '60 C.262 B.S. L.569 LL.B.
(adm. in NY; not adm. in OH) 8173 Long Meadow Dr.
Casper, S. Robert, (BV) ....'43 '72 C.608 B.A. L.607 J.D. 8469 Eagle Ridge Dr.
Caudill, Rhonda L. ....'68 '95 C.610 B.S. L.117 J.D. Procter & Gamble

Chalfie & Farley, Co., L.P.A.
(See Cincinnati)

Coley, William P., II, (AV) ....'60 '86 C.201 B.S. L.1003 J.D. [Coley&Assoc.]
Coley & Associates Co., LPA, (AV) ....9334 Union Centre Blvd.
Concannon, John P., (AV) ....'49 '76 C.973 B.S. L.1340 J.D. [S McCaslin,I.&M.] ⊙
Cussen, Michael P. ....'69 '95 C.973 B.A. L.1340 J.D. [A McCaslin,I.&M.] ⊙
Dinan, Terence D. ....'37 '62 C&L.608 B.A., LL.B. 8025 Fox Cub Ct.‡
Gaffield, Diane K., (BV) ....'49 '85 C.66 B.A. L.978 J.D. 8259 Paddington Ct.
Gruber, Joseph C., (BV) ....'61 '86 C.602 B.A. L.150 J.D. [McCaslin,I.&M.] ⊙
Gruber, Thomas J., (AV) ....'54 '79 C.973 B.A. L.150 J.D. [McCaslin,I.&M.] ⊙
Hicks, Bryan Scott .....'67 '95 C.1091 B.A. L.150 J.D. 7109 Hamilton Mason Rd., Unit C
Hurd, John K., (AV) ....'43 '74 C.473 B.S. L.1340 J.D. [McCaslin,I.&M.] ⊙
Kendrick, Helen M. ....'49 '79 C.183 B.A. L.851 J.D. 5658 McCarthy Ct.
Keys, James G., Jr., (BV) ....'49 '76 C.1023 B.S. L.150 J.D. [J.G.Keys]
Keys, J.G., Co., L.L.C., Law Offices of, (BV) ....7442 Great Waters Lane
Landis, Richard M., (BV) '44 '69 C.231 B.A. L.150 J.D.
7665 Monarch Court, Suite 106B
Lyons, Robert D. ....'33 '59 C&L.150 B.B.A., J.D. 6836 Tylersville Road
Marsick, Philip J. ....'41 '72 C.973 B.S. L.1340 J.D. [McCaslin,I.&M.] ⊙
McCaslin, Imbus & McCaslin, A Legal Professional Association, (AV)
7969 Cincinnati-Dayton Road (⊙Cincinnati)
Meadows, Jeffrey Charles ....'64 '97 8310 Princeton Glendale Rd., Ste. B
Miller, Stanton R. ....'48 '78 C.701 B.S.M.E. L.1340 J.D. 6788 Apache Way

Nesbitt, Patrick T., (BV) '56 '81 C.611 B.A. L.477 J.D.
8050 Beckett Center Drive Suite 113, 45069
Telephone: 513-755-2600 Fax: 513-874-5205
Email: pnesbitt@one.net URL: http://www.pnesbitt.com
Business Law; Small Business Law; Business Formation; Business Planning; Business Taxation; Business Transactions; Business Transfers; Buying and Selling of Businesses; Capitol Formation; Closely Held Business Planning; Closely Held Business Law; Emerging Business Law; Emerging Growth Companies; Entrepreneurial Business Law; Family Business Law; Family Business Successions; Limited Liability Company Law; Professional Practices; Sole proprietorships; Joint Ventures; Partnerships.
See Professional Biographies, WEST CHESTER, OHIO

Oldendick, Lee A., (BV) ....'50 '80 C.150 B.A. L.851 J.D. Asst. Pros. Atty.
Schumacher, Lynn Marie '58 '85
C.473 B.S. L.150 J.D. Schumacher Dugan Construction, Inc.
Slone, Thomas J. ....'29 '73 C.1161 B.S. L.1340 J.D. 6442 Ashley Oaks Ct. (Pat.)
Smith, Ian R. ....'71 '97 C.385 B.A. L.150 J.D. [A McCaslin,I.&M.] ⊙
Wharton, Bernard W., (BV) ....'67 '94 C.668 B.A. L.150 J.D. [A McCaslin,I.&M.] ⊙
Winters, R. Gary, (AV) ....'48 '76 C&L.150 B.A., J.D. [McCaslin,I.&M.] ⊙
Yonas, John J. ....'73 '00 C&L.608 B.S.B.A., J.D. 9100 Centre Pointe, Ste. 250

WESTERVILLE, 35,318, *Delaware & Franklin Cos.*

Akin, Sherrille D., (BV) ....'65 '89 C&L.362 B.A., J.D. [Akin G.]
Akin Guthrie LLC, (BV) ....100 Dorchester Square Lane, Suite 202
Auker, Jeffrey A., (BV) '58 '83 C.645 B.A. L.117 J.D.
Comm. Underwriting Coun., The Talon Group
Bale, David G., (BV) ....'52 '78 C.117 B.A. L.161 J.D. [Bale,B.&Assoc.]

Bale, Begin & Associates, Ltd., (BV)
140 Commerce Park Drive, 43082-7935
Telephone: 614-895-5600 Facsimile: 614-895-6899
Email: dgbale@aol.com URL: http://www.lawyers.com/bb&altd

(This Listing Continued)

Bale, Begin & Associates, Ltd. (Continued)
David G. Bale; James S. Begin.
Estate Planning, Administration and Litigation, Probate, Business Succession Planning, Nonprofit Organizations, Small Business Law, Business Formation, Limited Liability Company Law, Partnership Law, Corporate Law, Contracts, Personal Injury, Automobile Accidents, Civil Litigation.
See Professional Biographies, WESTERVILLE, OHIO

Ball, Theodore C., (AV) ....'31 '54 C&L.608 B.S., J.D. 8331 Cleveland Avenue, N.W.
Ballard, F. V. ....'31 '56 C.610 B.S.C. L.608 J.D. Ret. Prob. J.‡
Barren, Michael J. ....'58 '83 C.674 B.A. L.608 J.D. [Barren&M.]

Barren & Merry Co., L.P.A.
110 Polaris Parkway, Suite 302, 43082
Telephone: 614-776-1000 Fax: 614-865-3396
Email: mbarren@barrenmerrylaw.com URL: http://www.barrenandmerry.com
Michael J. Barren; Thomas R. Merry;—Beth M. Miller; Lawrence S. Helkowski.
Creditors Rights, Workouts, Bankruptcy Law, Banking and Finance, Commercial Law, Breach of Contracts, Business Litigation.
See Professional Biographies, WESTERVILLE, OHIO

Bates, Anna L. ....'64 '85 C.608 B.A. L.117 J.D. 168 South State Street
Begin, James S., (BV) ....'45 '73 C.477 A.B. L.608 J.D. [Bale,B.&Assoc.]
Bell, Albert L. ....'30 '59 C&L.608 B.A., J.D. 1104 Bryan Dr.‡
Blaine, Craig J. ....'46 '82 C.999 A.B. L.117 J.D. 1195 Hooverview Dr.
Bohan, Gerald F., Attorney & Counselor at Law, (BV) '52 '77
C.608 B.A. L.851 J.D. 1001 Eastwind Dr., Ste. 305
Brown, Ralph H. ....'19 '62 C.709 L.266 J.D. 4968 Wintersong Lane
Cassady, Carrie Marie ....'70 '97 C.679 B.A. L.179 J.D. 390 Worthington Road
DiAlbert, John E. ....'56 '85 C.549 B.S. L.607 J.D. 483 Dempsey Rd.
Easley, Sue A. ....'55 '88 C.970 B.A. L.117 J.D. 5961 Torrey Pines Ave.
Egbert, William M. ....'50 '78 C.608 B.S.Ed. L.201 J.D. 209 Mainsail Drive
Elliott, Jerry E., (BV) ....'50 '75 C.631 B.A.Econ. L.117 J.D. American Ceramic Soc.
Flagler, H. Glen, (BV) ....'53 '78 C.305 B.A. L.607 J.D. P.O. Box 1452
Flaherty, James G., (AV) '58 '84
C.473 B.S. L.201 J.D. 575 Charring Cross Drive, Suite 100
Foley, John Edward ....'51 '99 C.608 B.A. L.117 J.D. [J.E.Foley]
Foley, J. Edward, Attorney at Law ....299 S. State St.
Fusco, Michael J., (BV) ....'51 '79 C.178 B.A. L.608 J.D. [Fusco,M.M.&W.]
Fusco, Mackey, Mathews & Watkins, LLP, (BV) ....655 Cooper Road
Gannon, Patrick J., (AV) .....'49 '78 C.1115 B.S. L.1003 J.D. Indus. Comr. [P.J.Gannon]
Gannon, Patrick J., Co., L.P.A., (AV) ....15 Spring Creek Dr.
George, Michael F., (AV) ....'49 '73 C.886 B.S. L.608 J.D. [M.F.George]
George, Michael F., LPA, Company, (AV) ....575 Copeland Mill Road, Suite 1B
Girvin, Amy J. ....'62 '87 C.201 B.A. L.608 J.D. 1260 Stone Ridge Ct.‡
Gluntz, Paula S. ....'61 '98 C&L.608 B.S.I.S.E., J.D. [P.S.Gluntz]
Gluntz, Paula S., Esq., LLC ....1475 Worthington Park Boulevard
Goehring, Todd M. ....'67 '92 C.608 B.S. L.910 J.D. Gen. Coun., Tradecorp., Inc.
Gonzales, John M., (AV) ....'62 '87 C.437 B.A. L.117 J.D. [Gonzales&R.]
Gonzales & Rowland, LLP, (AV) ....140 Commerce Park Dr.
Graeff, David J., (AV) ....'43 '72 C.908 B.A. L.117 J.D. 4756 Crazy Horse Ln.
Guthrie, Graham D. ....'66 '93 C.608 B.S. L.117 J.D. [Guthrie]
Guthrie Law Office, LLC ....100 Dorchester Square Lane, Suite 202
Hane, Wilbur ....'59 '90 C.385 B.A. L.146 J.D. Sr. Staff Atty., Amer. Fam. Ins. Grp.
Hartlaub, Joseph V. ....'51 '77 C.8 B.Acct. L.7 J.D. 12 Westerville Square
Hasselback, David George ....'43 '85 C.901 B.A. L.117 J.D. 168 South State Street
Hatcher, Judi K., Law Offices of, (BV) '57 '83 C.607 B.A. L.117 J.D.
570 Polaris Pkwy
Helkowski, Lawrence S. ....'71 '97 C.665 B.A. L.607 J.D. [A Barren&M.]
Herron, Robert L. ....'24 '50 C.500 B.A. L.930 J.D. 6136 Charmar Dr.‡
Hertlein, Donald A., (BV) ....'30 '62 C.608 B.S. L.266 J.D. 476 S. Spring Rd.
Higgins, Thomas Peter ....'54 '87 C.472 B.A. L.851 J.D. Bk. One Ins. Servs. Corp.
Hindes, Thomas Joseph ...'53 '84 C.608 B.A. L.117 J.D. Admin. Assoc., Ohio State Univ.
Holmes, Christy M. '73 '98
C.608 B.A. L.851 J.D. Staff Atty., American Family Insurance
Hondros, John G., (BV) ....'43 '71 C.378 B.S. L.616 J.D. Hondros College
Hoover, Larry E., The Law Office of '66 '96
C.608 B.S. L.150 J.D. 130 Wetherby Ln. (⊙Dublin)
Hosking-Linch, Suzanne ....'50 '75 C&L.150 B.S., J.D. 5181 Sharps Ct.‡
Hudson, Edward L. '54 '79 C&L.150 B.A., J.D.
Mgr. of Real Estate and Capital, Kroger Company, The
Hulthen, Martin R., (BV) '63 '88 C.8 B.S. L.7 J.D.
Sr. Staff Atty., Amer. Fam. Ins. Grp.
Irwin, Michael T., (BV) ....'51 '80 C.97 B.L.S. L.117 J.D. 280 S. State St.
John, Sidney C., (AV) ....'39 '65 C.608 B.A. L.607 J.D. 6954 Lakeside Ct.
Jordan, James W., (BV) ....'41 '66 C.930 A.B. L.608 J.D. 80 Dorchester Sq.
Kitchen, Alison M. ....'54 '88 C.882 B.S. L.117 J.D. 980 Landing Loop S.
Kottman-Gregory, Janet ....'57 '82 C.473 B.A. L.608 J.D. Ohio School Boards Assoc.
Levine, Richard J. ....'50 '75 C.108 B.S. L.608 J.D. 101 Green Meadows Drive South
Lewis, John H., (BV) ....'14 '45 L.608 J.D. 204 Mockernut Lane (⊙Grove City)
Linch, Heather Lu ....'61 '84 C&L.117 B.A., J.D. Toukan & Company, CPA'S
Linch, M. Jebb, (BV) ....'48 '77 C.611 B.A. L.607 J.D. 483 Dempsey Rd.
Mackey, Jeffrey D., (BV) ....'56 '81 C&L.608 B.A., J.D. [Fusco,M.M.&W.]
Malech, Arnold M. ....'30 '53 C.102 A.B. L.1009 LL.B. 681 Maplerun Lane‡
Mathews, Gregory B., (BV) ....'60 '88 C.827 B.A. L.117 J.D. 655 Cooper Road
Matthews, Mark A. '50 '76 C.282 B.A. L.221 J.D.
(adm. in IA; not adm. in OH) 605 Big Rock Dr.‡
McKenna, Todd J. '55 '84 C.150 B.A. L.8 J.D.
Staff Atty., American Family Insurance
McNenny, James H., (BV) ....'34 '61 C.473 B.A. L.273 J.D. State Farm Fire Cas.
Merrell, Clyde Nelson '44 '74 C.572 B.A. L.790 J.D.
(adm. in SC; not adm. in OH) 7645 Lee Rd.
Merry, Thomas R. ....'63 '89 C.650 B.A. L.602 J.D. [Barren&M.]
Miller, Beth M. ....'72 '00 C&L.608 B.S., J.D. [A Barren&M.]
Milligan, Fred J., (AV) ....'42 '67 C&L.608 B.A., J.D. [F.J.Milligan,Jr.]
Milligan, Fred J., Jr., Co., L.P.A., (AV) ....483 Dempsey Rd.
Mills, Julie S. ....'68 '98 C.347 B.A. L.1119 J.D. 575 Charring Cross
Mount, Kathleen Draper '53 '81 C.019 B.A. L.012 J.D.
(adm. in VT; not adm. in OH) 8701 Robin Hood Circle‡
Paragas, Leonore Tavill '63 '89 C.363 B.S.B.A. L.1003 J.D.
Gen Coun. & Chief Compl. Off., Mt. Carmel Health Plan, Inc.
Price, Alise M. ....'70 '96 C.608 B.A. L.117 J.D. 6650 Springview Dr.
Reed, Todd Wellington '62 '92 C.923 B.S. L.117 J.D.
(adm. in WV; not adm. in OH) 5252 Parkmoor Dr.
Rowland, Robert R. ....'65 '99 C.8 B.S. L.117 J.D. [Gonzales&R.]
Ryba, Michael D. '47 '73 C.679 B.A. L.879 J.D.
(adm. in IL; not adm. in OH) 235 West Schrock Rd.‡
Sammons, Jeffery D., (BV) ....'57 '82 C.610 B.B.A. L.117 J.D. [Sammons&Assoc.]

Sammons & Associates, (BV) .... 635 Park Meadow Road Suite 101
Schumann, William M., (BV) .... '42 '67 C.528 B.A. L.150 J.D. 1001 Eastwind Dr.
Sheffer, Brent A. .... '57 '90 C.608 B.S.B.A. L.117 J.D. [Sheffer]
Sheffer Law Office .... 5663 Bashaw Dr.
Shoemaker, Fred J. .... '24 '51 C.631 B.A. L.608 LL.B. 5500 Ulry Rd.‡
Shumsky, Sabrina L. .... '71 '96 C.510 B.A. L.608 J.D. Ohio State Bar Foun.
Sidner, Mark C. .... '46 '74 C.363 A.B. L.930 J.D. 5413 Rockingham Ct.
Sidor, David S., (AV) .... '45 '72 C.823 B.A. L.1119 J.D. General Counsel, Excel, Inc.
Sinkhorn, Mark W. .... '49 '74 C&L.608 B.A., J.D. Mgr., Lawyers Title Ins. Corp.
Snyder, Douglas A. .... '51 '81 C&L.608 B.A., J.D. 1001 Eastwind Dr., Ste. 106

Snyder, Tamie I. '68 '99 C.608 B.S.W. L.117 J.D.
299 South State Street, 03081
Telephone: 614-895-8258 Fax: 614-436-0347
URL: http://www.tamiesnyderlaw.com
Bankruptcy, Bankruptcy Chapter 7, Bankruptcy Chapter 13, Child Support, Child Custody, Visitation Rights, Divorce, Dissolution, Post Decree Modification, Spousal Support, Family Law.
See Professional Biographies, WESTERVILLE, OHIO

Storey, Robert M., (CV) .... '54 '80 C&L.608 B.A., J.D. 737 Enterprise Dr.
Struble, Carla I., (BV) .... '50 '84 C.608 B.S. L.117 J.D. 855 S. Sunbury Road
Thompson, William A. .... '56 '81 C.608 B.A. L.117 J.D. 4140 Executive Parkway
Tressler, James A., (AV) .... '25 '52 C.631 A.B. L.608 J.D. 96 E. Walnut‡
Tsiliacos, Narcus J., (BV) .... '37 '64 C.608 B.A. L.266 J.D. 647 Park Meadow Rd.
Ullom-Morse, Norman Jay, (AV) '52 '79
C.608 B.A. L.117 J.D. 575 Copeland Mill Road, Suite 1B
Underwood, Kenneth L. .... '40 '73 C.608 B.S.I.E. L.117 J.D. 39 Collegeview Road
Watkins, Alison A. .... '68 '93 C.608 B.A. L.117 J.D. [Fusco,M.M.&W.]
Watson, Sue A. .... '68 '97 C.608 B.S.S.W. L.117 J.D. 470 Olde Worthington Road
Westervelt, C. E., Jr., (BV) .... '22 '48 C&L.608 B.A., J.D. 18 W. College Ave.
Wetterauer, Damon E., Jr., (BV) .... '44 '74 C.604 B.A. L.117 J.D. 425 W. Schrock Road
Willi, Kaye P. .... '55 '83 C.473 B.A. L.228 J.D. [Willi]

Willi Law Offices
Kaye P. Willi, Attorney at Law
79 S. State Street Suite D-4, 43081
Telephone: 614-888-7090 Fax: 614-888-7064
URL: http://www.willilaw.com
Kaye P. Willi (Certified Specialist in Estate Planning, Trust and Probate Law, Ohio State Bar Association).
Estate Planning, Business Succession Planning, Tax Planning, Small Business Law, Business Start-Ups, Real Estate, Trust Administration, Asset Protection, Charitable Giving, Guardianships, Premarital Agreements, Trusts and Estates, Probate.
See Professional Biographies, WESTERVILLE, OHIO

Wilt, David L. '41 '66 C.363 B.S.B.A. L.276 J.D.
(adm. in DC; not adm. in OH) David Wilt & Associates, Inc.
Wolery, John J. .... '29 '58 C.201 L.266 J.D. 4988 Wintersong Ln.

WESTFIELD CENTER, 1,054, *Medina Co.*

Batchelder, John T. H., (BV) '56 '82 C.385 A.B. L.608 J.D.
Corp. Coun., Westfield Group
Beach, C. G. .... '07 '39 C.62 B.A. L.161 J.D. 6707 McVay Dr.‡
Brockman, Phoebe M. .... '58 '83 C.473 B.A. L.117 JD. Westfield Group
Carrino, Frank Anthony .... '61 '87 C.8 B.S. L.7 J.D. Corp. Atty., Westfield Group
Cluse, Mark E. .... '68 '95 C.980 B.A. L.8 J.D. Staff Oper. Coun., Westfield Group
Hutson, William F. .... '61 '91 C.252 B.S.B.A. L.117 J.D. Asst. V.P., Westfield Group
Kahelin, William J. '47 '74
C.381 B.A. L.7 J.D. Mng. Bond Claim Coun., Westfield Group
Lytle, Edward L. .... '46 '71 C&L.608 B.A., J.D. Corp. Atty., Westfield Group
Perry, Alfred Campbell, Jr. .... '64 '99 C.999 B.S.B.A. L.7 J.D. Westfield Companies
Popelmayer, Richard A. ... '59 '86 C.161 B.B.A. L.1003 J.D. Corp. Atty., Westfield Group
Sterling, William Fisher '58 '83 C.385 B.A. L.608 J.D.
Reg. Asst. V.P., Westfield Group
Stith, Anne M., (AV) '47 '86 C&L.1209 B.I.S., J.D.
Bond Claim Coun., Westfield Group
Walker, James M. .... '57 '81 C.8 B.S. L.608 J.D. Bond Claim Coun., Westfield Group
Winkler, Daniel A. .... '69 '94 C&L.8 B.A., J.D. Corp. Atty., Westfield Group
Yogmour, Gus, Jr. .... '51 '85 C&L.8 B.E., J.D. Bond Claim Coun., Westfield Group

WEST JEFFERSON, 4,331, *Madison Co.*

Parsons, Ronald C., (BV) .... '42 '67 C.645 B.S. L.608 J.D. 8 E. Main St.
Sams, David A. .... '64 '91 C&L.608 B.A., J.D. P.O. Box 40

WESTLAKE, 31,719, *Cuyahoga Co.*

Aldrich, Kimberley A. .... '69 '95 C.888 B.A. L.607 J.D. [⊠ Kolick&K.]
Baden, Steven L. ...... '58 '84 C.608 B.A. L.1003 J.D. Sr. Corp. Coun., Scott Fetzer Co.
Brandt, Natasha E. .... '65 '90 C.347 B.A. L.930 J.D. V.P., WHM Mgmt. Svcs., Inc.
Brown, Richard T. .... '13 '38 C&L.930 B.A., J.D. 800 Brickmill Tun‡
Burns, James L. .... '58 '90 C.970 B.A. L.1003 J.D. 24441 Detroit Rd., Ste. 300
Cables, Thomas A. .... '31 '62 C.610 B.A. L.930 J.D. 25746 Yeoman Drive
Caito, Harry J., (BV) .... '46 '72 C.608 B.S. L.930 J.D. 2579 Shiloh Avenue

Carney, Joseph D., & Associates, L.L.C.
(See Cleveland)

Ciszczon, William J. '50 '83 C.161 B.B.A. L.1003 J.D.
V.P. & Controller, United Consumer Fin. Servs.
Claypool, Oliver H., Jr. .... '50 '74 C.610 B.A. L.161 J.D. 2500 Bradley Rd.
Coen, Beverly J. '46 '77 C.532 B.A. L.930 J.D.
Asst. Cntr - Dir. of Taxes, Benefit & Insurance, Nordson Corporation
Coltman, Thomas J. .... '33 '64 [⊠ Valore&C.]
Columbro, Elaine J. .... '35 '62 C.930 B.A. L.1003 LL.B. 1858 Settler's Reserve Way‡
Cook, Brian Anthony .... '66 '92 C.1030 B.A. L.989 J.D. [Hunt&C.]
Costa, Gregory James .... '51 '93 [D.K.Fifner]
Coury, Elias J. .... '62 '87 C.851 B.B.A. L.1003 J.D. 24340 Sperry Drive
Cruse, Brian C., (AV) .... '58 '89 C.611 B.A. L.1003 J.D. [Valore&C.]
Curry, Robert L. .... '30 '63 C.363 B.S. L.161 J.D. 1500 Queen Annes Gate
Daray, Stephen Edward ..... '72 '97 C.475 B.A. L.930 J.D. 24500 Center Ridge Rd., #175
DeGrandis, Fred M., (AV) '50 '78
C.477 B.S. L.1003 J.D. Pres., St. John West Shore Hospital
Dowling, Dawn M., Law Office of '65 '91
C.732 B.A. L.930 J.D. 25935 Detroit Road, Suite 162
DuVall, Michael Alan, (AV) .... '50 '75 C.473 B.S. L.150 J.D. P.O. Box 45038
Egert, Howard E., (AV) .... '17 '54 C.477 B.S. L.1003 J.D. [Egert,M.&H.]
Egert, Mayer & Hack, (AV) .... 1991 Crocker Rd.
Fifner, Douglas K., (AV) .... '53 '79 C.797 B.A. L.1003 J.D. [D.K.Fifner]
Fifner, Elaine, (AV) .... '54 '79 C.967 B.A. L.1003 J.D. [D.K.Fifner]
Fifner, Douglas K., Co., L.P.A., (AV) .... 24441 Detroit Road, Suite 300
Fitz, Robert Edward .... '46 '72 C.161 B.B.A. L.1003 J.D. [R.E.Fitz]
Fitz, Robert E. .... 1650 Crossings Pkwy., Ste. C
Giesser, Rosemary Ann .... '44 '81 C.532 B.A. L.989 J.D. [R.A.Giesser]
Giesser, William R., (BV) .... '43 '68 C.62 B.A. L.608 J.D. 28899 Center Ridge Rd.
Giesser, Rosemary A. .... 28899 Center Ridge Road
Gill, Michael L. .... '40 '67 C&L.8 B.S.M.E., J.D. 3145 Creekside Dr. (Pat.)
Gogul, Ronald J. .... '43 '70 C.930 B.A. L.161 J.D. 1991 Crocker Rd.
Grace, Charles H. ...... '26 '71 C.119 D.S.E.E. L.161 J.D. 30803 Breckenridge Trail (Pat.)‡
Hack, Edward G., (AV) .... '47 '79 C.363 B.S.B.A. L.1003 J.D. [Egert,M.&H.]
Hamilton, James L., Law Offices of, (BV) '43 '73
C.381 B.S. L.1003 J.D. 24441 Detroit Road, Suite 300
Hofelich, James A., (AV) .... '43 '69 C.967 B.S. L.930 J.D. [Hofelich&H.] ⊙
Hofelich & Hofelich, (AV) .... 29550 Detroit (⊙Cleveland)

Hom, Harold L., Co., LPA
(See Cleveland)

Hood, D. Russell .... '66 '92 C&L.930 B.A., J.D. Travel Centers of America
Huffman, Charles S., Jr., (AV) .... '22 '52 C.611 B.A. L.1003 J.D. 24441 Detroit Rd.
Huffman, William C., (AV) .... '55 '80 C.970 B.A. L.930 J.D. 24441 Detroit Rd.
Hunt, William Harry .... '47 '75 C.679 B.S. L.1003 J.D. [Hunt&C.]

Hunt & Cook LLC
Gemini Tower II, Suite 530, 2001 Crocker Road, 44145
Telephone: 440-892-0400 Fax: 440-892-1966
Email: attorneys@huntcooklaw.com URL: http://www.huntcooklaw.com
William Harry Hunt; Brian Anthony Cook.
Civil Litigation and Appeals, Business and Commercial Law, Commercial Collections, Criminal Law, Divorce and Family Law, Wills and Estates, Personal Injury.
See Professional Biographies, WESTLAKE, OHIO

Infosino, John M. '55 '91 C.1376 B.S. L.215 J.D.
(adm. in MI; not adm. in OH) Ford Motor Company
Isaac, Frank K., (AV) ... '21 '52 C.930 B.B.A. L.1003 J.D. 24441 Detroit Road-Suite #200
Janis, Edward M., (BV) .... '49 '76 C.602 B.B.A. L.150 J.D. [E.M.Janis]
Janis, Edward M., Co., L.P.A., (BV) .... 24461 Detroit Rd.
King, John F., (AV) .... '57 '83 C.657 B.S. L.161 J.D. [King&Assoc.]

King & Associates, (AV)
28871 Center Ridge Road Suite 102, 44145
Telephone: 440-899-3900 Fax: 440-892-3900
Email: jfking@kingandassociates.com URL: http://www.kingandassociates.com
John F. King.
Personal Injury, Medical Malpractice, Wrongful Death, Business Litigation, Aviation Law, Litigation.
See Professional Biographies, WESTLAKE, OHIO

Koepke, Robert J. .... '29 '59 C.610 B.S.C. L.1003 LL.B. 2269 Brigadoon Ct.‡
Kolick, Daniel J., (BV) .... '50 '75 C.321 B.A. L.930 J.D. [Kolick&K.]
Kolick & Kondzer, (BV) .... 24500 Center Ridge Rd.
Kondzer, Thomas A., (BV) .... '50 '75 C.363 B.S.B.A. L.930 J.D. [Kolick&K.]
Krause, Marcella A. ..... '38 '91 C.62 B.A. L.1003 J.D. COO, Far West Mental Health Ctr.
Kwarciany, Dale L. .... '51 '76 C.363 B.S. L.1003 J.D. [D.K.Fifner]
Lauber, Richard E. .... '55 '81 C.930 B.A. L.1003 J.D. Fidelity Nat'l. title Ins. Co.
Leaheey, J. Bradford, (AV) '46 '74 C.215 B.E.E. L.128 J.D.
(adm. in DC; not adm. in OH; Pat.) Asst. Gen. Coun., Intell. Prop., Nordson Corp.
Lee, Steven C., (AV) '63 '89 C.318 B.A. L.477 J.D.
V.P. & Gen. Coun., Travel Centers of America
Levenberg, Jessica A. .... '78 '04 C.914 B.A. L.124 J.D./MBA Corp. Coun., Plantrex
Levine, Lisa K. ... '68 '96 C.886 B.A. L.823 J.D. Corp. Coun., The Scott Fetzer Company
Liwosz, John C., Jr. .... '29 '64 C.363 B.S. L.1003 J.D. 27397 Detroit Rd.
Ljubi, Sharon Judith .... '55 '81 C.161 B.A. L.989 J.D. 25109 Detroit Road
Long, Clare Smith .... '58 '84 C.145 B.A. L.930 J.D. 2001 Crocker Rd., Ste. 400 (Pat.)
Malloy, Thomas E. .... '28 '58 C.363 B.S.S. L.1003 LL.B. 23286 E. Maybelle Dr.
Mayer, W. James, Jr., (BV) .... '44 '70 C.973 A.B. L.930 J.D. [Egert,M.&H.]
Mittendorf, William J., (AV) ..... '42 '72 C.573 A.B. L.161 J.D. 24803 Detroit Rd., Ste. 2
Musial, Mark N., (BV) .... '60 '85 C.473 B.S. L.117 J.D. [Musial&M.]
Musial, Norman T. .... '31 '61 C.851 B.S.M.E. L.1003 J.D. [Musial&M.]
Musial and Musial Co., L.P.A., (BV) .... 28885 Center Ridge Rd.
O'Neill, William J. .... '21 '53 C.309 A.B. L.1003 J.D. Ret. U.S., Bkrptcy. J.‡
Opsitnick, Timothy Michael '60 '85
C.611 B.A. L.124 J.D. Sr. Part. & Gen. Coun., JurlInnov Ltd.
Parchem, David F. .... '55 '80 C&L.602 B.A., J.D. Staff Atty., Ct. of App.
Parker, Stephen E. .... '30 '54 C.674 B.A. L.930 J.D. 1641 Allen Drive
Patton, Dennis P. .... '49 '77 C.1323 B.S. L.930 J.D. Hillow, Gornik & Co.
Poulos, John D. .... '62 '88 C.930 B.S. L.1003 J.D. 25849 Hidden Acres Dr.
Prendergast, Kevin P. .... '62 '87 C.97 B.S.J. L.1003 J.D. 27999 Clemens Rd.
Ruhe, Linda J., (CV) .... '49 '83 C.665 B.S. L.7 J.D. [L.J.Ruhe]
Ruhe, Linda J., Co., LPA, (CV) .... 31044 Pinehurst Drive
Salvagni, Brian C. '61 '88 C.705 B.A. L.201 J.D.
Gen. Coun., Level Propane Gases, Inc.
Sanda, Constance S. .... '24 '48 C&L.930 B.A., J.D. 25374 Howard Ave.
Sava, Michael Frank, (BV) .... '57 '82 C.161 B.A. L.1003 J.D. 2720 Horseshoe Boulevard
Scanlon, Patricia M., (AV) '59 '85
C&L.602 B.A., J.D. V.P. & Gen. Coun., The Scott Fetzer Co.
Schreiner, Thomas E. '53 '82
C.473 B.A. L.7 J.D. Mgr., Corp. Admn., The Scott Fetzer Co.
Sciangula, Francis A., (BV) '38 '63
C.381 B.S. L.999 J.D. 24500 Center Ridge Rd., Ste. 175
Sherman, David C. .... '46 '72 C.610 A.B. L.1003 J.D. [Sherman&Assoc.]
Sherman & Associates Law Offices .... 2396 Wingedfoot
Simiele, Thomas C. .... '43 '71 C.999 A.B. L.930 J.D. 30080 Persimmon Drive
Skulina, Thomas R., (AV) .... '33 '59 C.363 A.B. L.930 J.D. 24803 Detroit Road
Slattery, Raymond J., III, (BV) '55 '83
C.8 B.S.E.E. L.7 J.D. Sr. Pat. Atty., Nordson Corp. (Pat.)
Soucie, Paul M., (AV) .... '56 '82 C.363 B.S.B.A. L.1003 J.D. 28024 Stonegate Cir.
Spalding, Walter T., Jr., (BV) .... '29 '56 C.188 B.S. L.161 LL.B. 24500 Center Rdige Rd.

Steuer, Escovar, Berk & Brown Co., L.P.A.
(See Cleveland)

Thomas, Daniel J. .... '64 '89 C.473 B.S. L.608 J.D. [⊠ Kolick&K.]
Thomas, Joan Jacobs .... '56 '84 C.62 B.A. L.1003 J.D. 23850 Center Ridge Road
Thompson, Barbara A. .... '28 '54 C.608 B.A. L.1003 J.D. 31170 Hilliard Rd.
Thompson, Brian .... '39 '75 C.161 B.B.A. L.1003 J.D. 2156 Walter Rd.
Valore, Dean Michael .... '70 '00 C.473 B.S. L.989 J.D. 23550 Center Ridge
Valore, Joseph A., (BV) .... '37 '70 C.62 B.A. L.1003 J.D. [Valore&C.]
Valore & Cruse, Co., L.P.A., (AV) .... 23550 Center Ridge Rd
Veillette, Robert E. '52 '78 C.665 B.A. L.7 J.D.
Secy. & Asst. Gen. Coun., Nordson Corp.
Viscomi, William A., (AV) .... '44 '69 C.363 A.B. L.930 J.D. 29688 Hilliard Oak Dr.
Wasp, Edmund J. '53 '78 C.1074 B.S.I.E. L.1065 J.D.
Sr. Pat. Atty., Nordson Corp. (Pat.)

Weaver, Susan M., (BV) ......'48 '80 C.930 B.A. L.989 J.D. 24961 Detroit Road, Suite E
Weishar, Fred A. ....'19 '55 C.930 L.1003 J.D. 1814 Donna Dr.
Yantek, Kenneth R. ....'53 '86 C.93 B.S. L.1003 J.D. King James Grp.

WEST LIBERTY, 1,813, *Logan Co.*

Brandt, Phillip, (BV) ....'46 '82 C.608 B.A.B.S. L.607 J.D. 109 S. Detroit St.
Fansler, Steven R., (BV) ....'55 '80 C.999 B.S. L.150 J.D. 212 N. Detroit St.

WEST MILTON, 4,645, *Miami Co.*

Brosh, Leneé M. ....'76 '02 C.231 B.A. L.201 J.D. [Shipman,D.&L.] ⊙
Dixon, W. McGregor, Jr., (BV) ....'49 '75 C.473 B.A. L.744 J.D. [Shipman,D.&L.] ⊙
Johnston, Robert C., (BV) ....'52 '78 C.228 B.A. L.930 J.D. [Shipman,D.&L.] ⊙
Kerber, Grant D. ....'72 '97 C.201 B.A. L.150 J.D. [Shipman,D.&L.] ⊙
Livingston, James R., (BV) ....'43 '69 C&L.608 B.S., J.D. [Shipman,D.&L.] ⊙
Sell, Charles H., II, (BV) ....'47 '73 C.932 B.A. L.851 J.D. [Shipman,D.&L.] ⊙
Shipman, Dixon & Livingston Co., L.P.A., (AV) .... 316 S. Miami St. (⊙Troy)
Wagner, Allyn S., (CV) ....'44 '69 C&L.607 B.A., J.D. 102 S. Miami Street

WEST SALEM, 1,534, *Wayne Co.*

Williams, Barbara L., (CV) ....'41 '79 C.473 B.S. L.1003 J.D. P.O. Box 261

WEST UNION, * 2,903, *Adams Co.*

Armstrong, Kenneth L., Jr., (BV) '49 '77 C.608 B.A. L.972 J.D.
209 N. Cross St., Ste. 236
Blanton, Kristofer Daniel ....'77 '01 C&L.923 B.A., J.D. 225 N. Cross St.
Bubp, Danny R., Law Office of, (BV) ... '54 '84 C.150 B.S. L.607 J.D. 307 N. Market St.
Caldwell, John B., (BV) ....'47 '73 C.117 B.A. L.1340 J.D. [Young&C.]
Carroll, Gregory Alan ....'61 '88 C.952 B.A. L.607 J.D. 225 N. Cross St.
Castor, Robert D., (AV) ....'47 '76 C&L.608 B.A., J.D. 228 Market St.
Foster, Alan W., (BV) ....'50 '76 C.610 A.B. L.851 J.D. Co. J.
Gabbert, Roy E., Jr., (AV) ....'65 '89 C&L.608 B.A., J.D. 301 N. Market St.
Gabbert, Roy E., Sr. ....'25 '52 C&L.608 B.A., J.D. 10381 State Rte. 125‡
Grimes, David E., Law Office of ....'70 '96 C.608 B.S. L.851 J.D. 231 North Cross Street
Lawler, John H., (BV) ....'61 '87 C.150 B.B.A. L.923 J.D. [J.Lawler]
Lawler, John, Company LPA, (BV) .... 14088 State Route 41

Purdy & Ring
(See Georgetown)

Purtell, Steven W. ....'53 '78 C.902 B.A. L.879 J.D. 307 N. Market St.★
Schlueter, James W., (BV) ....'47 '74 C.150 B.A. L.1340 J.D. Mag., Com. Pleas Ct.
Spencer, Brett M., (BV) ....'59 '89 C.608 B.S. L.851 J.D. 231 N. Cross Street
Whalen, Dana Nichole ....'75 '00 C.999 B.S. L.1340 J.D. [Whalen]
Whalen Law Office LLC ....216 N. Market St.
Wilson, Charles H., Jr., (BV) ....'34 '59 C.318 A.B. L.150 LL.B. [Wilson,W.&W.]
Wilson, David D., (BV) ....'32 '60 C&L.607 A.B., J.D. Co. J. [Wilson,W.&W.]
Wilson, David D., Jr. '58 '89 C.491 B.S. L.1137 J.D.
(adm. in IN; not adm. in OH) [🄰 Wilson,W.&W.]
Wilson, Wilson & Wilson, (BV) .... Wilson Bldg.
Young, Vernon L. ....'19 '42 C&L.607 J.D. [Young&C.] ‡
Young & Caldwell, (BV) .... 225 N. Cross St.

WHEELERSBURG, 6,471, *Scioto Co.*

Blume, T. Kevin, (BV) ....'— '81 C.608 B.S. L.607 J.D. [Mowery&B.]
Faulkner, Rick L., (BV) ....'54 '79 C.608 B.S. L.896 J.D. 8055 Hayport Rd.
Mowery, Steven L., (AV) ....'53 '79 C.608 B.A. L.383 J.D. [Mowery&B.]
Mowery and Blume, (AV) .... 9050 Ohio River Road
Porter, Kenneth W., (BV) ....'54 '81 C.608 B.S. L.851 J.D. 8055 Hayport Rd.

WHITEHALL, 19,201, *Franklin Co.*

McGraw, Michael Scott ....'72 '01 C.181 B.S.B.A. L.8 J.D. 4517 East Main Street
Wood, Donald E. ....'52 '98 C.608 M.B.A. L.117 J.D. 4437 Wright Avenue

WHITEHOUSE, 2,733, *Lucas Co.*

Lehenbauer, Alan J., (BV) ....'59 '84 C&L.851 B.B.A., J.D. [McQuades] (⊙Swanton)
McQuade, Colin J., (BV) ....'55 '80 C.5 B.A. L.851 J.D. [McQuades] (⊙Swanton)
McQuade, Daniel P., (AV) ....'42 '67 C.424 B.S. L.608 J.D. [McQuades] ⊙
McQuades Co., The, L.P.A., (AV) ..................P.O. Box 2460 (⊙Archbold, Swanton)

WICKLIFFE, 13,484, *Lake Co.*

Adams, James W., Jr. '— '70 C.152 B.S. L.1003 LL.B.
Assoc. Gen. Coun., The Lubrizol Corp. (Pat.)‡
Adelman, Eugene M., (BV) ....'32 '56 C&L.930 B.A., LL.B. Mag. [E.M.Adelman]
Adelman, Eugene Merle, (BV) ....28833 Euclid Ave.
Bauer, Joseph W. ....'53 '81 C&L.851 B.A., J.D. V.P. & Gen. Coun., The Lubrizol Corp.
Bednar, Gerald ......'46 '74 C&L.602 A.B., J.D. Asst. Prof., St. Marys Seminary & Univ.
Cheverine, Carolyn E., (BV) ...'62 '90 C.659 B.S. L.893 J.D. Coun., The Lubrizol Corp.
Day, Suzanne F. ....'69 '93 C.893 B.A. L.930 J.D. Counsel, The Lubrizol Corp.
Denney, Jon E., (AV) ....'39 '64 C.611 B.A. L.477 J.D. Spec. Coun., The Lubrizol Corp.
DiCicco, Richard D. .....'38 '66 C.381 B.S. L.1003 J.D. 29435 Euclid Avenue, Room 100
Dougan, Arthur L., (AV) ....'11 '35 C.910 A.B. L.309 LL.B. The Lubrizol Corp.‡
Drake, Eric M. ....'58 '93 C.1044 B.A. L.1003 J.D. 30432 Euclid Avenue, Suite 204
Esposito, Michael F. '46 '73 C.1030 B.S. L.128 J.D.
(adm. in VA; not adm. in OH) Chf. Pat. Coun., Lubrizol Corp., The
Fokens, Jason Scott '73 '03 C.474 B.S. L.475 J.D.
(adm. in MI; not adm. in OH) Coun., Lubrizol Corp.
Gardiner, A. Theodore, III, (AV) ....'47 '75 C.611 B.A. L.608 J.D. 29400 Lakeland Blvd.
Gilbert, Teresan W. ....'54 '83 C.97 B.S. L.1003 J.D. Pat. Coun., Lubrizol Corp. (Pat.)
Gilcher, Robert H. ....'18 '59 C.608 B.S. L.1003 LL.B. 2218 Pine Ridge Dr.
Gregor, Robert J., (BV) ....'42 '67 C.363 B.S. L.930 J.D. 29944 Euclid Ave.
Grenell, David J. '— '87 C.607 B.A. L.8 J.D.
Senior Attorney, Americas & Asia, ABB Automation Inc.
Grunawalt, Karen Cockley ....'55 '80 C.385 A.B. L.930 J.D. 29400 Lakeland Blvd.
Hansell, Herbert J. ....'25 '49 C.453 B.S. L.976 LL.B. Lubrizol Corporation, The
Hoose, Richard A. ....'17 '51 C.381 L.161 J.D. Ret. Com. Pleas J.
Hsu, Roger Y. K. ....'27 '64 C.454 M.S. L.930 J.D. The Lubrizol Corp. (Pat.)
Kidder, Fred D., (AV) ....'22 '50 C.8 B.S. L.930 J.D. 29400 Lakeland Boulevard
Laferty, Samuel ......'56 '83 C.49 B.S. L.8 J.D. Patent Coun., Lubrizol Corp. The (Pat.)
Leach, Robert S., (BV) ....'52 '78 C.161 B.A. L.1003 J.D. 29339 Euclid Avenue
Manson, William D., (AV) .....'52 '85 C.97 B.A. L.886 J.D. Coun., The Lubrizol Corp.
Marlowe, Cecil, (AV) ....'62 '87 C.478 B.A. L.930 J.D. Counsel, The Lubrizol Corp.
Morrison, Richard P., (BV) ....'51 '80 C.608 B.A. L.117 J.D. [Shryock&M.]
Novosat-Gradert, Lisa, (BV) ....'61 '88 C.851 B.A. L.7 J.D. The Lubrizol Corp.
Pawlikowski, Beverly A. '64 '94 C.158 Ch.E. L.128 J.D.
(adm. in PA; not adm. in OH; Pat.) 29400 Lakeland Blvd.
Reynolds, Leslie M. '60 '88 C.347 B.S. L.339 J.D.
Corp. Secy. & Ethics Offr., The Lubrizol Corp.
Rickin, Michael M. '42 '74 C.563 B.E.E. L.1009 J.D.
(adm. in NJ; not adm. in OH; Pat.) Asst. Gen. Coun., Intell. Prop., ABB Inc.
Santo, Mark V. '56 '82 C&L.229 B.A., J.D.
Group Vice President & General Counsel, Elsag Bailey Process Automation
Shold, David M. '50 '91 C.937 B.S. L.1338 J.D.
(adm. in DE; not adm. in OH; Pat.) Pat. Coun., The Lubrizol Corp.
Shryock, John, (CV) ....'51 '79 C&L.607 B.A., J.D. [Shryock&M.]

Shryock & Morrison, (BV)
30601 Euclid Avenue, 44092
Telephone: 440-944-7020 Fax: 440-943-3096
URL: http://www.euclidavelaw.com
Members of Firm: John Shryock; Richard P. Morrison.
Family Law, Domestic Relations, Mediation, Juvenile Law, Criminal Law, Traffic Violations, Personal Injury.

See Professional Biographies, WICKLIFFE, OHIO

Silbiger, Mark Curtis ....'58 '88 C.930 B.B.A. L.989 J.D. The Lubrizol Corp.
Sussman, Jason R. ....'72 '99 C.608 B.S. L.1003 J.D. Coun., Lubrizol Corp.
Thiele, Terry V. '54 '79 C.674 B.A. L.569 J.D.
Envir. Policy & Reg. Affrs., The Lubrizol Corporation
Turi, Louis A., (BV) ....'23 '50 C.363 L.1003 J.D. 30432 Euclid Ave.
Webb, William J. ....'46 '73 C.500 B.S.Ch.E. L.734 J.D. Spec. Coun., Lubrizol Corp.

WILBERFORCE, 1,579, *Greene Co.*

Hughey, Andrew C. ....'58 '85 C.665 B.A. L.229 J.D. Gen. Coun., Central State Univ.

WILLARD, 6,806, *Huron Co.*

Brosteau, Clarence A. '06 '29 C&L.213 LL.B.
(adm. in MI; not adm. in OH) 91 Lake Holiday Ln.‡
Harwood, David B., (BV) ....'48 '73 C.610 A.B. L.608 J.D. [Thornton,T.&H.] ⊙
Hauser, Richard B., (BV) ....'47 '73 C.91 B.S. L.607 J.D. 110 1/2 Myrtle Avenue
Martin, James J., (BV) ....'48 '74 C.608 B.A. L.117 J.D. 1050 S. Main St.
Thornton, M. Kenneth, (AV) ....'22 '51 C&L.930 A.B., LL.B. [Thornton,T.&H.] ⊙
Thornton, Robert F., (AV) ....'32 '58 C&L.608 B.Sc., LL.B. [Thornton,T.&H.] ⊙
Thornton, Thornton & Harwood, (AV) .... 111 Myrtle Ave. (⊙Norwalk)

WILLIAMSBURG, 2,322, *Clermont Co.*

Burgess, T. David ....'45 '71 C.473 B.S. L.1340 J.D. [T.D.Burgess]
Burgess, T. David, Co., L.P.A. .... 110 N. Third St.
Littman, Donald F. ....'31 '65 C.973 M.A. L.1340 J.D. 5014 Burdsall Rd.‡

WILLOUGHBY, 22,621, *Lake Co.*

Allen, B. Lawrence ....'38 '72 C.381 B.A. L.161 J.D. Mun. J.
Behnke, Mark L. ....'56 '81 C.473 B.A. L.930 J.D. P.O. Box 1172
Bergen, Ann Stirling ....'66 '92 C.363 B.A. L.989 J.D. 24 Public Square
Birnbaum, Gary I. ....'52 '91 C.1044 B.S. L.1003 J.D. 35040 Chardon Rd.
Brancatelli, Frank R., (CV) ....'46 '73 C.161 B.M.E. L.1003 J.D. P.O. Box 790
Byron, Barry M., (AV) ....'31 '56 C.276 B.S. L.930 J.D. [Byron&B.]
Byron, Stephen L., (CV) ....'66 '91 C.385 B.A. L.930 J.D. [Byron&B.]
Byron & Byron, Co., L.P.A., (AV) ....4230 State Rt. 306
Campbell, Paul E. '52 '78 C.477 B.G.S. L.215 J.D.
(adm. in MI; not adm. in OH) 4420 Sherwin Rd.
Cantrell, Doreen M. ....'56 '88 C.381 B.A. L.7 J.D. 37223 Euclid Ave.
Clair, Mary Joseph, (BV) ....'52 '77 C.363 B.S. L.200 J.D. 4132 Erie St.
Courtright, Joy Zeiler ....'— '00 C.187 B.S.S. L.989 J.D. 37841 Euclid Ave., Ste. 2
Coyne, Wm. H. ....'21 '53 C.363 B.S.S. L.161 LL.B. 5953 Halle Farm Dr.
Crotser, Michele L. ....'57 '85 C.62 B.A. L.1003 J.D. P.O. Box 1091
Davies, David H., (BV) ....'46 '73 C.608 B.A. L.161 J.D. 38108 Third Street
Deeb, Charles G., (BV) '43 '76
C.150 B.S.Ch.E. L.161 J.D. 4230 State Route 306, Suite 240
Doganiero, John A., (BV) ....'53 '78 C.473 B.S.B.A. L.161 J.D. 35104 Euclid Avenue
Donner, Terry A., Esq. ....'62 '88 C.876 B.S.N. L.1003 J.D. P.O. Box 64
Freeburg, Antoinette E. ....'74 '99 C.161 L.1003 J.D. [🄰 C.P.Kasunic]
Fudale, William F., (CV) ....'31 '67 C.381 B.S. L.1003 J.D. [W.F.Fudale]
Fudale, William Frank, (CV) ....38052 Euclid Ave.
Futterer, Stephen J., (BV) ....'50 '75 C.161 B.A. L.1003 J.D. 38052 Euclid Ave., Ste. 105
Glinski, Mark A. ....'53 '79 C.381 B.A. L.1003 J.D. [M.Glinski]
Glinski, Mark ....35104 Euclid Ave., Ste. 304
Greene & Tulley Co., L.P.A., (AV) .... 38021 Euclid Avenue
Guroy, John R., Jr. ....'16 '49 C.124 B.S. L.161 LL.B. 38027 Euclid Ave.
Harthun, Luther A. '35 '61 C.879 B.A. L.145 J.D.
(adm. in CA; not adm. in OH) Sr. V.P. & Legal Secy., Figgie Intl. Inc.
Hegyes, Bryan F. ....'73 '02 C.610 B.A. L.930 J.D. [🄰 Jones&H.]
Hegyes, Dean K., (BV) ....'67 '92 C.473 B.S. L.930 J.D. [Jones&H.]
Hentemann, Paul H., (BV) ....'33 '62 C.363 B.A. L.1003 LL.B. 35000 Kaiser Ct.
Hill, Stephen A., (AV) ....'47 '74 C.453 B.S. L.930 J.D. [Rankin,H.P.&C.] (Pat.) ⊙
Hutton, Bruce A., (BV) ....'51 '76 C.25 B.A. L.823 J.D. 38052 Euclid Avenue, #101
Jones & Hegyes Co., L.P.A., (BV) ....38040 Euclid Ave.
Judy, Michael T., (CV) ....'68 '95 C.712 B.A L.117 J.D. 4230 State Rte. 306, #310
Kasunic, Carl P., (BV) ....'55 '86 C.161 B.A. L.1003 J.D. [C.P.Kasunic] ⊙
Kasunic, Carl P., Co., L.P.A., (BV) .... 38033 Euclid Avenue (⊙Cleveland)
King, David M., (BV) ....'59 '84 C.970 B.A. L.117 J.D. 4230 State Rte. 306, Ste. 310
Kotoch, Norman Anthony ....'63 '90 C.363 B.A. L.1003 J.D. Norcon Properties Ltd.
Krebs, Scott T. ....'58 '89 C.36 B.S. L.1003 J.D. 5463 Oak Ridge Dr.
Ledman, David E., (BV) .....'62 '87 C.473 B.A. L.608 J.D. 35000 Chardon Rd., Ste. 105
Lory, Roger W. ....'41 '87 C.81 B.S. L.607 J.D. 38621 Eagle Nest Drive
Lustri, Ralph Robert ....'61 '87 C.930 B.S. L.1003 J.D. 9446 Chillicothe Rd.
Mako, Emery R. ....'21 '48 C&L.930 B.S., LL.B. 989 Bellvue Dr.
Margolis, Ronald A. ....'57 '83 C.150 B.A. L.1003 J.D. Misny & Assoc.
Mastrangelo, E. W. ....'23 '52 C&L.608 B.S., J.D. 35100 Euclid Ave.
Misny, Timothy P. ....'55 '81 C.363 B.A. L.1003 J.D. P.O. Box 1356
Mramor, James P. ....'43 '03 C.980 B.S. L.989 J.D. 3070 Nantukcet Dr.
Nash, Jeffrey P. ....'58 '85 C.381 B.S. L.1003 J.D. 38210 Glenn Ave.
Nelson, Lisa V. ....'71 '99 C.1208 B.A. L.1003 J.D. P.O. Box 755
Patterson, David N. ....'39 '64 C.203 B.A. L.607 J.D. 33579 Euclid Ave.
Perez, Richard J., (BV) ....'47 '74 C.434 B.A. L.161 J.D. [Rosplock&P.]
Plasco, Marvin R., (BV) ....'43 '69 C.473 B.S. L.1003 J.D. 38040 Euclid Ave.
Polen, Albert B., (BV) ....'30 '60 C.477 B.B.A. L.1003 J.D. 38052 Euclid Ave.
Purola, Albert L., (AV) ....'43 '70 C.95 A.B. L.1003 J.D. 38108 3rd St.
Rankin, Hill, Porter & Clark LLP, (AV) ....4080 Erie Street (Pat.) (⊙Cleveland)
Rosplock, Robert S., (BV) ....'47 '73 C.97 B.A. L.161 J.D. [Rosplock&P.]
Rosplock & Perez, (BV) .... 4230 State Route 306
Rubin, Irl D., (BV) ....'50 '76 C.608 B.A. L.1003 J.D. 35401 Euclid Avenue
Schraff, Patricia Jane, (BV) '51 '80 C.363 B.A. L.1003 J.D.
4230 State Rte 306, No. 310
Slattery, Lisa J., (BV) ....'61 '86 C.473 A.B. L.1003 J.D. [L.J.Slattery]

Slattery, Lisa J., Co., L.P.A., (BV) .... 38033 Euclid Ave., Ste. 1
Teple, Edwin R., (AV) .... '13 '36 C.607 A.B. L.608 J.D. 36500 Euclid Ave.‡
Tulley, Joseph P., (AV) .... '22 '49 C.363 A.B. L.930 LL.B. [Greene&T.]
Walker, Sheldon R. .... '26 '57 C.477 B.B.A. L.1003 LL.B. 4187 Lyons Ave.
Weddleton, Terry C. .... '50 '84 C.705 B.A. L.838 J.D. 34750 Oaktree Dr.
Weston, William G. .... '45 '84 C.608 B.S. L.161 J.D. [W.Weston]
Weston, William .... 30841 Euclid Avenue
Wick, Douglas, (AV) '17 '47 C.976 B.S. L.930 J.D.
Chmn. of the Bd., Bob Krihwan Pontiac GMC Truck, Inc.
Wilson, Jane P., (AV) .... '55 '84 C.475 B.S. L.477 J.D. [J.P.Wilson&Assoc.]
Wilson, Jane P., & Associates Company, L.P.A., (AV) .... 8580 Eagle Rd.
Wilt, Daniel D., (BV) .... '44 '70 C&L.930 B.A., J.D. 35000 Chardon Road, Suite 125
Wright, Nina, (CV) .... '32 '78 C.930 B.A. L.1003 J.D. [N.Wright]
Wright, Nina, Co., L.P.A., (CV) .... 4230 State Route 306, Ste. 310
Zatyko, Donald R. .... '36 '75 C.197 B.A. L.1003 J.D. 38041 Lake Shore Blvd.

WILLOUGHBY HILLS, 8,595, *Lake Co.*

Driggs, Charles M., (AV) .... '24 '51 C&L.976 B.S., J.D. [Driggs,H.&F.]

Driggs, Hogg & Fry Co., LPA, (AV)
38500 Chardon Road, 44094
Telephone: 440-391-5100 Fax: 440-391-5101
URL: http://www.lawyers.com/driggslaw
Charles M. Driggs; William N. Hogg; John J. Fry.
Corporate Law, Trusts and Estate, Business Law, Real Estate, Intellectual Property, Patents, Copyrights, Trademarks, Trade Secrets, Unfair Competition.

See Professional Biographies, WILLOUGHBY HILLS, OHIO

Fry, John J. .... '61 '91 C.930 B.S.E.E. L.989 J.D. [Driggs,H.&F.] (Pat.)
Hogg, William N. .... '31 '59 C.679 B.M.M.E. L.930 LL.B. [Driggs,H.&F.] (Pat.)
Lang, Donna K. '54 '84 C.1322 B.F.A. L.846 J.D.
(adm. in TX; not adm. in OH) 37601 Eagle Rd.
LaRiche, Anthony A., Jr. '52 '77 C.880 B.A. L.61 J.D.
(adm. in AZ; not adm. in OH) The South East Chevrolet Co.
Matoh, James E. .... '56 '85 C.309 A.B. L.1003 J.D. Progressive Ins. Co.
McDevitt, John F. .... '26 '57 C.679 B.S. L.1003 LL.B. 2255 Par Lane (Pat.)‡
Ristity, Donald W. .... '38 '66 C&L.930 B.A., J.D. 27700 Bishop Park Drive, Suite 906
Speece, Robert L. .... '21 '64 C.920 B.A. L.1003 J.D. 36371 Maple Grove‡

WILLOWICK, 14,361, *Lake Co.*

Bosco, John W. .... '44 '72 C.381 B.A. L.161 J.D. [J.W.Bosco]
Bosco, John W., Co., L.P.A. .... 31805 Vine Street
Komarjanski, Stephen, (BV) .... '41 '71 C.930 B.S. L.161 J.D. 31809 Vine St.
Lobur, John Stephan .... '56 '01 C.767 B.A. L.124 J.D. 32212 Lake Shore Blvd.
Rozanc, Frank J., (CV) .... '64 '90 C.161 B.A. L.1003 J.D. 240 Shoregate Mall, Suite 218

WILMINGTON, * 11,921, *Clinton Co.*

Bradley, Geoffrey J., (BV) .... '69 '94 C&L.347 B.A., J.D. Asst. Pros. Atty.
Brake, Daniel J. .... '67 '93 C.473 B.S. L.597 J.D. Assoc. Gen. Coun., R & L Carriers, Inc.
Bryant, J. D., (AV) .... '47 '74 C.1302 B.S. L.347 J.D. [Bryant]
Bryant Law Offices, (AV) .... 21 North South Street
Buckley, Karen, (BV) .... '51 '76 C.945 B.A. L.893 J.D. [Buckley,M.&W.]
Buckley, Miller & Wright, (AV) .... 145 North South Street (⊙Sabina)
Carey, Chad L., (CV) .... '63 '88 C.952 B.A. L.117 J.D. Mun. Ct. J.
Carey, Ronald C., L.P.A., (BV) .... '38 '64 C.952 A.B. L.1340 J.D. [R.C.Carey]
Carey, Ronald C., L.P.A., (BV) .... 283 N. South St.
Caudill, David R., Jr., (CV) .... '63 '91 C.1161 B.A. L.150 J.D. [Ⓐ Peelle]
Cook, Charles T. .... '65 '00 C.952 B.S. L.117 J.D. [Ⓐ Peelle]
Daugherty, Michael T., (CV) .... '69 '94 C.952 B.A. L.201 J.D. [Peterson&D.]
Denier, C. Patrick .... '71 '03 C.150 B.S. L.200 J.D. [Ⓐ Peelle]
Dennis, Joseph H., (BV) .... '52 '86 C.902 B.A. L.201 J.D. [Dennis&W.]
Dennis and Williams Co., L.P.A., (BV) .... 245 North South Street
Dobyns, J. Michael, (BV) .... '49 '80 C.266 B.S. L.117 J.D. [Rose&D.]
Dyer, Garofalo, Mann & Schultz, A Legal Professional Association, (AV)
712 South Street (⊙Richmond, IN; Bellefontaine, Dayton, Huber Heights, Lima, Middletown, Piqua, Springfield, Troy, Xenia, OH)
Elder, Steven E. .... '54 '81 C.97 B.S. L.1003 J.D. 731 Fife Avenue
Federle, Richard L., (CV) .... '68 '93 C.952 B.A. L.607 J.D. [Rose&D.]
Fife, David M., (CV) .... '44 '75 C.608 B.S. L.383 J.D. [Fife&F.]
Fife, Elaine Harner, (CV) .... '50 '75 C.608 B.A. L.426 J.D. Pub. Def. [Fife&F.]
Fife & Fife, (CV) .... 27 N. South St.
Gano, G. Allen .... '50 '76 C.608 B.A. L.117 J.D. Prob. & Juv. J.
Gano, Judy A., (BV) .... '54 '78 C.43 B.A. L.45 J.D. [Gano]
Gano Law Office, (BV) .... 169 N. South St.
Hall, David L., (BV) .... '40 '68 C.952 A.B. L.930 J.D. [Ⓒ Peelle] (⊙Dayton)
McCracken, William B. .... '45 '72 C.473 A.B. L.150 J.D. Com. Pleas J.
McElwee, Mary Hellmann .... '52 '77 C.973 B.A. L.150 J.D. Ct. of Common Pleas
Miars, Mark J., (BV) .... '53 '78 C.945 B.A. L.150 J.D. [Ⓐ Bryant]
Miller, James P., (AV) .... '38 '63 C.610 B.S.C. L.608 J.D. [Buckley,M.&W.]
Moke, Paul .... '53 '82 C.952 B.A. L.608 J.D. Prof. of Law, Wilmington College‡
Payne, William Joseph .... '63 '92 C.150 B.B.A. L.201 J.D. Airborne Express
Peelle, Carol S., (CV) .... '54 '86 C.608 B.S.Ed. L.201 J.D. [Peelle]
Peelle, Robert C., (AV) .... '51 '76 C.608 B.S. L.607 J.D. [Peelle]
Peelle, William E., (AV) .... '49 '75 C.608 B.S.B.A. L.607 J.D. [Peelle]
Peelle Law Offices Co., L.P.A., (AV) .... 1929 Rombach Avenue
Peterson, Shaun D., (CV) .... '58 '91 C.1208 B.S. L.383 J.D. [Peterson&D.]
Peterson & Daugherty, (CV) .... 111 East Sugartree Street
Quigley, Deborah, (CV) .... '57 '91 C.473 B.S. L.201 J.D. Asst. Pros.
Rose & Dobyns Co., L.P.A., (BV) .... 97 N. South St. (⊙Blanchester, Sabina)
Rowlands, Helen L., (BV) .... '62 '97 C.971 B.S. L.117 J.D. 169 N. South St.
Rudduck, John W. .... '49 '76 C.473 B.A. L.608 J.D. Com. Pleas Ct. J.
Scheiner-Albl, Suzanne .... '66 '01 C.705 B.A. L.150 J.D. Asst. Coun., ABX Air, Inc.
Schutt, Walter E., (AV) .... '17 '48 C.473 A.B. L.150 J.D. 36 1/2 N. South St.‡
Williams, James H., (BV) .... '52 '79 C.608 B.S. L.851 J.D. [Dennis&W.]
Wright, Jeffrey L., (BV) .... '49 '74 C&L.608 B.Sc., J.D. [Buckley,M.&W.] ⊙

WINTERSVILLE, 4,102, *Jefferson Co.*

Hocking, Melanie E. '51 '86 C.434 B.S. L.229 J.D.
(adm. in PA; not adm. in OH) Indian Creek Local Sch. Dist.

WOODMERE, 834, *Cuyahoga Co.*

Davis, William T. .... '61 '86 C.896 B.A. L.930 J.D. Gen. Coun., Galt Enterprises, Inc.
Rubin, Steven K. '52 '78 C.94 B.A. L.809 J.D.
(adm. in CA; not adm. in OH) Gen. Coun., Robert Stark Enterprises, Inc.
Seders, Julianne M. '57 '97 C.363 B.S.B.A. L.930 J.D.
Finance Compliance Officer, Galt Enterprises, Inc.

WOODSFIELD, * 2,598, *Monroe Co.*

Burkhart, George F. .... '24 '51 C.608 L.607 J.D. Com. Pleas J.
Coury, Robert G. .... '36 '66 C.610 B.A. L.923 J.D. 316 S. Main St.
Morrison, Mark .... '49 '75 C.610 A.B. L.607 J.D. [Morrison]
Morrison Law Office .... 117 N. Main St.
Peters, James W., (BV) .... '54 '81 C.608 B.A. L.117 J.D. Co. J.
Riethmiller, L. Kent, Law Office, (BV) .... '51 '77 C&L.608 B.A., J.D. 110 N. Main Street
Selmon, Julie Richardson .... '74 '99 C&L.117 B.A., J.D. 316 S. Main Street
Sherry, Allan, (AV) .... '27 '54 C.381 L.948 LL.B. 116 N. Main St.
Starr, Walter R., (BV) .... '54 '79 C.8 B.A. L.607 J.D. Monroe Co. Probate/Juv. Ct.

Thornburg, Bean & Glick
(See St. Clairsville)

Yoss, Richard A., (AV) .... '43 '68 C&L.608 B.S., J.D. 122 N. Main Street

WOODVILLE, 1,953, *Sandusky Co.*

Davies, R. Nigel, (AV) .... '49 '76 C.051 L.851 J.D. [Davies&R.] ⊙
Davies & Ruck, PLL, (AV) .... 109 West Main Street (⊙Bowling Green, Pemberville)

WOOSTER, * 24,811, *Wayne Co.*

Bailey, K. William .... '46 '78 C.970 B.A. L.8 J.D. Com. Pleas J.
Baker, Susan Eileen, (BV) .... '54 '92 C.49 B.S.N. L.930 J.D. [Critchfield,C.&J.]

Baker, Dublikar, Beck, Wiley & Mathews
(See North Canton)

Barnard, G. Kenneth, (BV) '46 '71 C.970 B.A. L.608 J.D.
322 W. Liberty Street, Suite B
Barrington, John, (BV) .... '42 '68 C.970 B.A. L.608 J.D. P.O. Box 624
Bauders, Jerry A. .... '48 '74 C.383 B.S. L.7 J.D. Dom. Rel. J.
Behlke, William M. .... '61 '91 C.8 B.S.I.M. L.426 J.D. Coun., Newell Rubbermaid, Inc.
Benson, Richard R., Jr., (CV) .... '54 '82 C.62 B.A. L.1003 J.D. Law Dir.
Broehl, Margo E., (BV) .... '48 '77 C.970 B.A. L.8 J.D. 105 W. Pine St.
Brown, Robert J. .... '49 '80 C.608 B.A. L.851 J.D. Com. Pleas J.
Burridge, Robert George, Jr. .... '63 '91 C.608 B.S. L.8 J.D. Asst. Pros.
Buytendyk, Michael G., (BV) .... '53 '86 C.970 B.A. L.851 J.D. [Kennedy,C.K.&B.]
Cicconetti, Frank, (BV) .... '43 '69 C.970 B.A. L.7 J.D. [Kennedy,C.K.&B.]
Colclaser, H. Alberta .... '11 '36 C.970 A.B. L.930 J.D. 361 Holmes Blvd.‡
Coleman, Thomas J., (BV) .... '23 '51 C.8 L.150 LL.B. 420 McDonald St.
Cook, Stephen R., (CV) .... '45 '96 C.446 B.A. L.7 J.D. [Schmitt]
Cornelius, H. Lloyd .... '26 '74 C.970 B.A. L.8 J.D. 1906 Neal Dr.‡

Critchfield, Critchfield & Johnston, Ltd., (AV)
225 North Market Street, P.O. Box 599, 44691-0599 ⊙
Telephone: 330-264-4444 Telecopier: 330-263-9278
URL: http://www.ccj.com
John C. Johnston, III; Daniel H. Plumly; J. Douglas Drushal; Peggy J. Schmitz; Susan Eileen Baker (Certified Specialist in Workers' Compensation Law, Ohio State Bar Association); David J. Wigham; Robert C. Gorman; Roger D. Proper, Jr.; Timothy B. Pettorini;—Elizabeth Krieder Wright; John H. Schaeffer; Tricia L. Plant; Andrew P. Lycans; Kevin J. McAllister. Of Counsel: Lincoln P. Oviatt; Bonnie C. Drushal.
General Practice in all Courts. Business, Corporate Law, Insurance, Estate Planning, Wills and Probate, Labor and Employment, ERISA, Health Care, Environmental Law, Workers Compensation, Banking, Taxation, Antitrust and Trade Regulation, Oil and Gas Law, Litigation, Debtor and Creditor, Municipal Law, School Law, Real Estate, Commercial Law, Construction Law.
Representative Clients: Rubbermaid Inc.; Wooster Brush Co.; The College of Wooster; Bank One of Akron, N.A.; First Federal Savings & Loan Association of Wooster; Sandy Supply Co.; Buehler Food Markets, Inc.; Wayne Dalton Corp.; Ohio Packaging Corporation.
Millersburg, Ohio: 138 E. Jackson Street, 44654. Telephone: 330-674-3055.
Mt. Vernon, Ohio: 10 South Gay Street, 43050-3546. Telephone: 740-397-4040.
Medina, Ohio: 3985 Medina Road, Suite 100, 44256. Telephone: 330-723-6404.

See Professional Biographies, WOOSTER, OHIO

Cullis, David H., (BVⓉ) .... '53 '80 C.608 B.S. L.851 J.D. 1809 Sherck Blvd
Dark, Edward Allen '59 '89 C&L.8 B.A., J.D.
Claims Atty., Wayne Mutual Insurance Company
Dix, R. Victor .... '34 '62 C.210 B.A. L.8 J.D. Daily Record, The
Drushal, Bonnie C., (CV) .... '53 '82 C.339 B.A. L.8 J.D. [Ⓒ Critchfield,C.&J.]
Drushal, J. Douglas, (AV) .... '53 '77 C.597 B.A. L.608 J.D. [Critchfield,C.&J.]
Eberhart, Edward K., (BV) .... '33 '60 C.970 B.A. L.145 J.D. 517 North Market Street
Finney, Christopher N. .... '76 '03 C.607 B.S. L.8 J.D. [Ⓐ Logee,H.S.&L.]
Fleischner, Warren E. .... '20 '58 C.309 A.B. L.1003 J.D. 760 Fairview Circle‡
Frantz, Martin H., (BV) '52 '78 C&L.608 B.A., J.D.
Wayne Co. Pros., Wayne Co. Prosecuting Atty. Off.
Gluck, Robert N., (Co., L.P.A.), (BV) .... '44 '69 C.473 B.A. L.607 J.D. 231 Buckeye St.
Gorman, Robert C. .... '61 '95 C.602 B.A. L.7 J.D. [Critchfield,C.&J.]
Graven, Marion F., III, (CV) .... '36 '69 C.870 B.S. L.8 J.D. 133 E. Larwill St.

Grisi & Riegler
(See Akron)

Grosjean, Walter C. .... '29 '54 C.970 B.A. L.477 LL.B. 225 North Market Street‡
Hays, Frank M., (AV) .... '31 '60 C.970 B.A. L.608 J.D. [Ⓒ Taggart L.&Assoc.]
Hemphill, Joi E., (BV) .... '60 '87 C.318 B.A. L.8 J.D. Mag., Ct. Administrator
Holtman, Ronald E., (AV) .... '43 '67 C.207 B.S. L.930 J.D. [Logee,H.S.&L.]
Hostetler, Daniel J., (BV) .... '48 '73 C.967 B.A. L.228 J.D. [Logee,H.S.&L.]
Johnston, John C., III, (BV) .... '48 '75 C.970 B.A. L.597 J.D. [Critchfield,C.&J.]
Keating, John Thomas, (BV) .... '58 '83 C.970 B.A. L.608 J.D. [Keating]
Keating, Louise Walsh, (BV) .... '55 '80 C.970 B.A. L.7 J.D. [Keating]
Keating, Richard M., (BV) .... '26 '52 C.930 L.1003 J.D. [Keating]
Keating Law Offices, (BV) .... 141 E. Liberty
Kennedy, Charles A., (AV) .... '40 '69 C.510 A.B. L.7 J.D. [Kennedy,C.K.&B.]
Kennedy, Cicconetti, Knowlton & Buytendyk, L.P.A., (AV) .... 558 North Market Street
Kienzle, Roger W., Jr., (BV) .... '47 '74 C.999 B.A. L.608 J.D. Ref., Juv. Ct.
Knowlton, David C. .... '66 '92 C.970 B.A. L.1003 J.D. [Kennedy,C.K.&B.]
Lane, Joseph V., Jr. .... '10 '33 C&L.262 B.A., LL.B. 3572 Mechanicsburg Rd.‡
Lanham, James J. .... '57 '85 C.970 B.A. L.7 J.D. [Taggart L.&Assoc.]
Lehman, Ralph E., (AV) .... '47 '79 C.999 B.A. L.7 J.D. [Logee,H.S.&L.]
Leisy, Raymond Eugene .... '49 '83 C.313 B.A. L.851 J.D. J., Wayne Co. Juv./Prob. Ct.
Leonard, John J. .... '68 '96 C.381 B.A. L.851 J.D. Pub. Def. Off.

Logee, Hostetler, Stutzman & Lehman, LLC, (AV)
2171-B Eagle Pass, 44691
Telephone: 330-264-6115 FAX: 330-262-5729
Members of Firm: Daniel J. Hostetler; Morris Stutzman; Ralph E. Lehman; Jerry S. Packard; Ronald E. Holtman;—Christopher N. Finney.
General Practice. Insurance Law, Insurance Defense, Probate, Estate Planning, Real Estate, Corporate Law and Taxation. Trials.
Representative Clients: Western Reserve Mutual Casualty Co.; Wayne Mutual Insurance Co.
Approved Attorneys for: Commonwealth Land Title Insurance Co.

See Professional Biographies, WOOSTER, OHIO

Lycans, Andrew P. .... '76 '04 C.8 B.A. L.477 J.D. [Ⓐ Critchfield,C.&J.]

McAllister, Kevin J. ....'79 '04 C.970 B.A. L.608 J.D. [🄰 Critchfield,C.&J.]
Moore, Marie Loudette .... '63 '98 C.790 B.S. L.7 J.D. Pros. Off.
Morrison, Meredith Horton '71 '00 C.311 B.A. L.276 J.D.
Northeast Ohio Legal Services
Murphy, John P., Jr. .... '45 '73 C.970 B.A. L.7 J.D. Pres., Western Reserve Grp.
Musselman, Jeffrey D. ....'67 '97 C.970 B.A. L.8 J.D. [Taggart L.&Assoc.]
Oviatt, Lincoln P., (AV) ....'28 '56 C.611 L.608 LL.B. [🄲 Critchfield,C.&J.]
Owens, Clarke Wayne .... '51 '99 C.1060 B.A. L.8 J.D. [C.W.Owens]
Owens, Clarke W. .... 132 South Market Street, Suite 204
Packard, Jerry S., (BV) .... '50 '77 C.8 B.A. L.608 J.D. [Logee,H.S.&L.]

Pagano, Wilson, Thomarios, Gillissie & Lenahan LLC
(See Cleveland)

Pettorini, Timothy B. .... '72 '98 C.970 B.A. L.7 J.D [Critchfield,C.&J.]
Plant, Tricia L. ....'76 '02 C.207 B.A. L.608 J.D. [🄰 Critchfield,C.&J.]
Plumly, Daniel H., (AV) ....'53 '78 C.532 B.A. L.930 J.D. [Critchfield,C.&J.]
Proper, Roger D., Jr. ....'71 '97 C.473 B.S. L.851 J.D. [Critchfield,C.&J.]
Rauckhorst, Robert J. ....'73 '99 C.8 B.A. L.851 J.D. [🄰 Kennedy,C.K.&B.]
Rehm, Ronald L., (BV) ....'50 '79 C.188 A.B. L.930 J.D. 2922 Cleveland Road
Reynolds, Craig R., (BV) .... '61 '86 C.967 B.A. L.608 J.D. 441 W. Liberty St.
Reynolds, Don L., (AV) ....'32 '57 C.62 A.B. L.477 J.D. 441 West Liberty St.
Reynolds, Robert J., (BV) ....'57 '82 C.967 B.A. L.608 J.D. 441 West Liberty St.
Richard, James M., (BV) .... '47 '74 C.91 B.S. L.607 J.D. [Richard]

Richard Law Office, LLC, (BV)
127 East Liberty Street, Suite 100, 44691
Telephone: 330-262-0034 Fax: 330-262-0080
Email: james@richardlawoffice.com URL: http://www.richardlawoffice.com
James M. Richard.
Corporate, Business Law, Oil and Gas, Personal Injury, Wrongful Death, Estate Planning, Probate, Divorce, Dissolution, Real Estate, Litigation, Probate Avoidance.
See Professional Biographies, WOOSTER, OHIO

Rodgers, Patricia A., (BVⓉ) ....'— '78 C.651 B.A. L.851 J.D. [L.&P.A.R.Vinion]
Ross, Ford G., (AV) ....'10 '35 C.970 A.B. L.309 J.D. [Ross]
Ross, James H., (BV) ....'47 '81 C.532 B.A. L.851 J.D. [Ross]
Ross, William F., (BV) ....'49 '75 C.967 B.A. L.117 J.D. [Ross]

Ross Law Offices P.L.L., (AV)
406 North Market Street, 44691-3598
Telephone: 330-264-1213 Fax: 330-263-6054
URL: http://www.ross-law.net
W. Howard Ross (1879-1966); Ford G. Ross; William F. Ross (Certified Specialist in Estate Planning, Trust and Probate Law, Ohio State Bar Association); James H. Ross.
Estate Planning, Trusts and Estates, Probate, Elder Law, Guardianship, Real Estate, Taxation.
References: FirstMerit Bank, N.A. (Wooster Office); National City Bank (Wooster Office); Bank One, N.A. (Wooster Office).
See Professional Biographies, WOOSTER, OHIO

Schaeffer, John H., (BVⓉ) ....'64 '89 C.608 B.A. L.851 J.D. [🄰 Critchfield,C.&J.]
Schmitt, Christopher A. ....'69 '94 C.631 B.A. L.117 J.D. [Schmitt]
Schmitt Law Office, (CV) ....105 East Liberty Street
Schmitz, Peggy J., (BV) ....'52 '78 C.97 B.A. L.7 J.D. [Critchfield,C.&J.]
Schuler, John H. ....'36 '74 C.604 B.A. L.1003 J.D. 4346 Lattasburg Rd.‡
Shearer, Keith A. ....'31 '58 C.970 B.A. L.608 J.D. Pros. Atty.‡
Slabey, Vernon A. ....'20 '57 C.610 B.S. L.1003 J.D. 1551 Saunders Dr.‡
Spitler, Corey E., (BV) ....'55 '88 C.216 B.A. L.7 J.D. Mag.
Stefancin, Jocelyn, (CV) ....'65 '90 C.901 B.S. L.930 J.D. Asst. Pros. Atty.
Stone, M. Blake, (BV) ....'47 '73 C&L.608 B.S., J.D. [M.B.Stone]
Stone, M. Blake, L.P.A., (BV) .... 231 N. Buckeye Street
Stutzman, Morris, (BV) .... '49 '75 C.91 B.A. L.930 J.D. [Logee,H.S.&L.]
Taggart, James W., (BV) ....'33 '65 C.631 B.A. L.608 J.D. [🄲 Taggart L.&Assoc.]
Taggart Law Firm, A Legal Professional Association, (BV) .... 142 W. Liberty Street
Tschantz, David Edward '60 '89 C.381 B.A. L.8 J.D.
V.P., Claims, Wayne Mutual Insurance Company
Vest, Margaret E. .... '61 '89 C.1208 B.A. L.161 J.D. Wooster-Wayne Legal Aid Soc.
Vinion, Lon, (BV) ....'— '79 C.980 B.S. L.326 J.D. [L.&P.A.R.Vinion]

Vinion, Lon & Patricia A. Rodgers, Law Office of, (BV)
2206 Mechanicsburg Road, 44691
Telephone: 330-262-2510 Fax: 330-262-2524
Email: Vinionlaw@sssnet.com URL: http://www.vinionlaw.com
Lon Vinion (Certified Specialist in Family Relations Law, Ohio State Bar Association); Patricia A. Rodgers.
Practice limited to Matrimonial, Divorce and Family Law.
See Professional Biographies, WOOSTER, OHIO

Waldron, Suzanne M., (CV) .... '52 '89 C.923 B.S. L.8 J.D. 248 N. Walnut St
Weygandt, Thomas J. .... '55 '95 C.608 B.S. L.7 J.D. 3484 McAfee Rd.
Wiest, Karin Connolly, (CV) .... '64 '89 C.970 B.A. L.608 J.D. 2873 Happy Valley Rd.
Wiest, Mark K. ....'47 '72 C.434 B.A. L.150 J.D. Com. Pleas J.
Wigham, David J., (CV) .... '59 '92 C.970 B.A. L.1003 J.D. [Critchfield,C.&J.]
Wigham, John T., (AV) .... '29 '54 C.930 A.B. L.309 LL.B. 1 Salter Place
Wire, Beverly J., (BV) ....'52 '85 C.980 A.B. L.8 J.D. 113 W. Liberty St.
Wright, Elizabeth Krieder ....'71 '01 C.207 B.A. L.124 J.D. [🄰 Critchfield,C.&J.]
Zacour, Wayne A., (BV) ....'52 '79 C.970 B.A. L.608 J.D. [Taggart L.&Assoc.]
Zoller, Thomas M., (BV) .... '15 '74 C.313 A.B. L.607 J.D. 1615 Cleveland Rd.

WORTHINGTON, 14,125, *Franklin Co.*

Alban, David R., (BV) .... '32 '55 C&L.608 B.S., J.D. [Alban&C.]
Alban, Glenn F. .... '64 '92 C.608 B.S. L.117 J.D. [Alban&C.]
Alban & Carlson, LLP, (BV) ....7100 N. High St., Ste. 102
Albert, Robert H., Sr., (AV) .... '31 '60 C.608 B.S. L.117 J.D. [Kagay,A.D.&G.]
Amerine, Hal D. .... '58 '86 C.608 B.A. L.117 J.D. 6360 Fieste Dr.
Ashton, Richard Wallace '36 '77 C.1029 B.S. L.229 J.D.
(adm. in PA; not adm. in OH) 668 Sinsbury Dr.‡
Atzberger, Thomas William '45 '76 C.363 B.A. L.1003 J.D.
Mooney Financial Serv., Inc.
Avery, Barbara .... '37 '75 C.188 B.A. L.608 J.D. 488 Greenglade Ave.
Bailey, Richard W., (BV) ....'33 '57 C&L.608 B.A., J.D. [Bailey&S.]
Bailey and Slavin, (BV) .... 6877 N. High St.

Baran, Piper, Tarkowsky, Fitzgerald & Theis Co., L.P.A., (AV)
6877 N. High Street, Suite 105, 43085-2516 ⊙
Telephone: 614-436-0539 Fax: 614-436-1713
URL: http://www.baranlaw.com
John Tarkowsky.
General Civil Practice. Trials in all Courts. Insurance Defense, Corporate, Family Law, Estate Planning, Personal Injury, Products Liability and Construction Law. Commercial Litigation. Suretyship. Environmental and Governmental Liability. Professional Liability, Worker's Compensation.
See Professional Biographies, WORTHINGTON, OHIO

Blazek, James Nicholas .... '64 '93 C.477 B.A. L.910 J.D. 33 E. Norh St.
Bolen, Alan L. .... '54 '83 C.608 B.S. L.117 J.D. 190 W. Selby Blvd.
Boynton Acklin, Kristina L. .... '69 '96 C.967 B.A. L.200 J.D. [🄰 Kagay,A.D.&G.]
Bush, Hobert H. .... '07 '39 C.923 A.B. L.608 J.D. 6837 Olentangy River Rd.‡
Carlson, Valerie H., (BV) .... '64 '90 C.966 B.S. L.608 J.D. [Alban&C.]
Cesner, Robert E., Jr., (BV) .... '40 '68 C.610 B.S. L.117 J.D. 456 Haymore Ave., N.
Compton, John S., (BV) ....'43 '77 C.266 B.S. L.930 J.D. 6463 Proprietors Rd.
Cooper, David S., (BV) ....'49 '76 C.532 B.A. L.608 J.D. 91 Colburn Court
DeBoard, J. C. ....'48 '77 C.437 B.B.A. L.117 J.D. [DeBoard,J.C.]
DeBoard, J. C., & Co. .... 5878 N. High St.
Demaree, Karin E. .... '68 '98 C.473 B.S. L.179 J.D. P.O. Box 416
Diehl, William D., (AV) ....'32 '66 C.608 B.Sc. L.266 J.D. [Kagay,A.D.&G.]
Drumm, Cynthia J. ....'54 '79 C.967 B.A. L.734 J.D. 933 High St.
Duffey, John J., (AV) ....'26 '51 C&L.477 B.A., J.D. 451 Colonial Ave.‡
Durham, Joseph Ross .... '64 '91 C.970 B.A. L.596 J.D. 6641 N. High St., Ste. 209
Elliott, Richard K., (BV) .... '28 '57 C.207 B.A. L.477 LL.B. P.O. Box 351
Evans, Craig E., (BV) .... '48 '73 C&L.608 B.F.A., J.D. 6660 N. High St.
Friedlander, David E., (AV) ....'20 '49 C&L.608 B.S., J.D. 5785 Pioneers Ct.‡
Frix, Robert L., (BV) ....'26 '56 C.608 B.S. L.266 J.D. 5701 N. High St.
Fulkerson, Kimberly ....'75 '01 C.434 B.A. L.117 J.D. [🄰 Alban&C.]
Gilbert, Stacey A. ....'76 '01 C.201 B.A. L.608 J.D. [Gilbert]
Gilbert Law Office LLC .... 500 W. Wilson Bridge Road, Suite 110
Good, William A., Law Office, (AV) '54 '80 C.610 B.A. L.169 J.D.
870 High St., Ste. 17
Grayson, R. Sean '60 '85 C.608 B.A. L.851 J.D.
Gen. Coun., Ohio Council 8, AFSCME, AFL-CIO
Green, Rebecca Mills, (BV) .....'63 '88 C.303 B.A. L.608 J.D. 150 E. Wilson Bridge Rd.
Groeber, John Andrew ....'64 '90 C&L.608 B.S.B.A., J.D. [Kagay,A.D.&G.]
Hall, James, (BV) ....'46 '79 C.608 B.S. L.327 J.D. 47 East Wilson Bridge Road
Harmon, Phillip L., (BV) ....'54 '80 C.188 B.S. L.117 J.D. 6649 N. High Street, Suite 105
Hayes, Susan N. ....'67 '92 C.607 B.A. L.608 J.D. 5878 N. High St.
Hemmer, Paul K. .... '58 '83 C.602 B.A. L.608 J.D. 7100 N. High St., Ste. 301
Hill, John W. ....'25 '52 C.608 B.S.B.A. L.117 J.D. 7737 Olentangy River Rd.
Hill, John W., Jr., (AV) .....'57 '82 C.631 B.S.B.A. L.117 J.D. 7737 Olentangy River Rd.
Hobart, Keith K. ....'20 '49 C.387 L.477 J.D. 443 Hinsdale Ct.‡
Holmes, Robert D., (BV) ....'23 '49 C.273 B.A. L.309 LL.B. 7100 N. High St.
Holmes, Scott D. ....'53 '80 C.608 B.A. L.851 J.D. 7100 N. High St.
Hoover, Douglas E., (AV) ....'47 '73 C&L.608 B.S., J.D. 6660 N. High Street
Hrabcak, Michael, (BV) .... '64 '91 C.266 B.A. L.117 J.D. [Hrabcak]
Hrabcak & Co., L.P.A., (BV) .... 67 E. Wilson Bridge Rd.
Hubbard, James C. '12 '37 C&L.900 Ph.B., LL.B.
(adm. in KS; not adm. in OH) 108 E. Granville Rd.‡
Hughes, Martin J., III, (AV) '58 '83 C.473 B.A. L.276 J.D.
150 East Wilson Bridge Road

Jones, John S., (BV) '50 '76 C.207 B.A. L.608 J.D.
867 High Street, Suite C, 43085
Telephone: 614-885-8118 Fax: 614-885-5559
Email: jsj@jsjlaw.com URL: http://www.lawyers.com/jsjlaw
Estate Planning, Estate Administration, Wills, Trusts, Probate, Estates, Elder Law, Real Estate.
See Professional Biographies, WORTHINGTON, OHIO

Kagay, Albert, Diehl & Groeber, (AV) .... 6877 North High St.
Kettlewell, Charles J. ....'— '00 C.610 B.A. L.117 J.D. [Kettlewell&K.]

Kettlewell & Kettlewell, LLC, (AV)
870 High Street, Suite 102, 43085
Telephone: 614-436-2750 Fax: 614-436-2865 URL: http://www.kettlewells.com
URL: http://www.lawyers.com/charleskettlewelllaw
Charles W. Kettlewell (1941-2005); Charles J. Kettlewell.
Legal Ethics and Professional Responsibility, Attorney Discipline, Preventative Consultations and Advisory Opinions, Admissions, Expert Witness in Legal Malpractice, Conflicts and Fee Disputes and Risk Management Analysis.
See Professional Biographies, WORTHINGTON, OHIO

King, Gale R., III, (BV) .... '41 '72 C.608 B.A. L.117 J.D. 870 High St., Ste. 16
Kirk, Edward R., (BV) ....'47 '73 C.611 B.A. L.608 J.D. [E.R.Kirk]
Kirk, Edward Russell, (BV) .... 6660 N. High Street, Suite 3A
Kyle-Reno, Shelia A. '51 '83
C.1208 B.A. L.201 J.D. Reg. Dir., Ohio Council 8, AFSCME
Lazar, Theodore A. .... '20 '51 C.137 L.365 J.D. 270 Bryant Ave.‡
Lehman, David B., (BV) .... '48 '74 C.381 B.A. L.117 J.D. 142 Park Boulevard
Malley, Kingston E., Jr., (BV) ...'47 '72 C.119 B.S. L.608 J.D. 89 E. Wilson Bridge Road

Manos, Martin, Pergram & Dietz Co., LPA
(See Delaware)

Marshall, Dwight A. .... '31 '69 C.150 E.E. L.1340 J.D. 1159 Blind Brook Dr. (Pat.)
Massengill, Kimm A. '60 '92 C.150 B.B.A. L.608 J.D.
Assoc. Gen. Coun., Ohio Council 8, AFSCME, AFL-CIO
McElwee, L. A. ....'47 '91 C.608 B.A. L.117 J.D. 369 E. Clearview
McLinden, Peter M. '70 '97 L.7 J.D.
Asst. Gen. Coun., Ohio Council 8, AFSCME, AFL-CIO
McNeil, Christopher B., (AV) ....'55 '81 C&L.378 B.G.S., J.D. P.O. Box 595
Morris, William R. .... '14 '50 C.610 A.B. L.117 J.D. 8039 Golfview Ct.‡
Morse, William A., (AV) ....'44 '72 C.473 B.S. L.608 J.D. [W.A.Morse]

Morse, William A., A Legal Professional Association, (AV)
Suite 140, 933 High Street, 43085
Telephone: 614-436-8010 Fax: 614-436-8330
Email: wmorse@wamorselaw.com URL: http://www.lawyers.com/morsefirm
William A. Morse.
Estate Planning, Probate, Small Business and Non-Profit Corporations.
See Professional Biographies, WORTHINGTON, OHIO

Moss, Patricia A. '47 '81
C.610 B.A. L.1003 J.D. V.P., Ohio Council 8, AFSCME, AFL-CIO
Mulbarger, Matthew J. .... '70 '96 C.608 B.S. L.117 J.D. 7794 Willow Green Ct.★
Norman, Pamela Brady ....'58 '83 C&L.276 A.B., J.D. 275 Bristol Way‡
Patterson, James R., (AV) .... '58 '83 C.228 A.B. L.477 J.D. 65 E. Wilson Bridge Road
Pliskin, Lawrence E. '66 '91 C.659 B.A. L.94 J.D.
Dir. Compliance & Qual. Assurance, American Health Holding, Inc.
Roberts, Cynthia Bailey, (BV) ....'63 '91 C.608 B.S. L.117 J.D. [🄰 Bailey&S.]
Robinson, Stanley U., Jr. .... '16 '44 C&L.266 B.S., J.D. 312 E. South St.‡
Schermer, Marsha Rockey, (AV) '40 '80 C.33 B.A. L.608 J.D.
V.P.-Regulatory, Time Warner Communications
Schuster, Richard C., (AV) ....'54 '81 C.473 B.A. L.1340 J.D. 800 Oxford St.
Simon, Frederick J. .... '28 '59 C.117 B.A. L.266 J.D. 75 E. Wilson Bridge Rd.
Slavin, Richard C., (BV) ....'53 '79 C.473 B.A. L.421 J.D. [Bailey&S.]
Somers, Paul P. ....'11 '42 C.347 L.266 J.D. 178 West New England Avenue
Squeo, Robin L. ....'67 '96 C.266 B.S. L.117 J.D. Corp. Coun., Eage Land Title Agcy.

Stebens, Robert E., (AV) '32 '60 C.966 B.S.E.E. L.608 J.D. 6501 Strathaven Ct. N. (Pat.)
Strauss, Jay Richard '44 '73 C.1349 B.A. L.284 J.D. (adm. in CA; not adm. in OH) Team America, Inc.
Tarkowsky, John, (BV) '54 '78 C.62 B.A. L.607 J.D. [Baran,P.T.F.&T.] (⊙Columbus, Mansfield)
Thomas, Arthur Hudson, Jr. '39 '64 C.353 B.A. L.608 J.D. P.O. Box 766
Van Sickle, John A. '57 '83 C.608 B.S. L.117 J.D. [J.A.Van Sickle]
Van Sickle, John A., Co., L.P.A. 1000 High Street
Walczak, Lisa A. '70 '98 C.608 B.A. L.851 J.D. Coun., Morrison Title Servs.
Whitlock, Scott Nickerson, (AV) '42 '67 C.207 B.A. L.309 LL.B. [S.N.Whitlock]
Whitlock, Scott N., (AV) 6081 Olentangy River Road
Winkle, Cynthia L. '63 '88 C.207 B.A. L.117 J.D. 154 Northigh Drive

WYOMING, 8,261, *Hamilton Co.*

Burke, Kim Wilson, (AV) '58 '83 C&L.608 B.A., J.D. 1007 Mary St.
Gentry, Vanessa L. '55 '82 C.915 B.A. L.150 J.D. 726 Burns Ave.
Shear, Donald '27 '53 C&L.150 B.B.A., J.D. 537 Chisholm Trail
Stonehill, David N., (BV) '56 '80 C&L.150 B.A., J.D. [D.N.Stonehill]
Stonehill, David N., Co., LPA, (BV) 400 Oliver Rd.

XENIA, * 24,164, *Greene Co.*

Abel, Jeannette M. '53 '84 C.235 B.S. L.972 J.D. C.E.O., First Frontier, Inc.‡
Anderson, Alan G., (BV) '48 '73 C.1208 B.S. L.608 J.D. 53 West Main St.
Baker, R. Jeffrey, (BV) '49 '81 C.112 A.B. L.767 J.D. [Miller,F.M.&B.]
Beard, Phillip L., (BV) '47 '73 C.510 A.B. L.383 J.D. [Brandabur,C.F.J.W.&B.]

Bieser, Greer & Landis, LLP
(See Dayton)

Bogenschutz, Stephen A., (BV) '47 '73 C.575 A.B. L.608 J.D. [Bogenschutz]
Bogenschutz Law Office, (BV) 58 Hardacre Dr.
Brandabur, James F., (AV) '34 '59 C.973 A.B. L.150 LL.B. [Brandabur,C.F.J.W.&B.]
Brandabur, Campbell, Finlay, Johnson, Weckstein & Beard, (AV) 260 North Detroit Street
Buckwalter, Michael A., (AV) '57 '84 C.1208 B.S. L.201 J.D. [Buckwalter]
Buckwalter Law Office, (AV) P.O. Box 580
Campbell, J. Timothy, (AV) '40 '65 C.973 B.S. L.150 J.D. [Brandabur,C.F.J.W.&B.]
Carrera, Nicholas A. '38 '62 C.473 L.150 J.D. 115 N. Whiteman St.
Chappars, Timothy S., (BV) '52 '78 C.228 B.S. L.150 J.D. [Chappars]
Chappars Law Office, (BV) P.O. Box 280
Cox, David W., (BV) '51 '76 C.611 B.A. L.608 J.D. 85 W. Main St.
De Wine, R. Michael, (BV) '47 '72 C.473 B.S. L.607 J.D. (M.C.)
Dyer, Michael E., (BV) '53 '80 C.269 B.A. L.201 J.D. [Dyer,G.M.&S.] (⊙Dayton, Troy)
Dyer, Garofalo, Mann & Schultz, A Legal Professional Association, (AV) 547 W. Second Street (⊙Richmond, IN; Bellefontaine, Dayton, Huber Heights, Lima, Middletown, Piqua, Springfield, Troy, Wilmington, OH)
Ferguson, Lester L. '42 '69 C.608 B.A. L.1340 J.D. 3010 U.S. State Rte. 35 E
Finlay, John A., (BV) '41 '66 C.611 B.A. L.930 J.D. [Brandabur,C.F.J.W.&B.]
Finney, Charles R., (AV) '23 '49 C.504 B.S. L.150 J.D. [⊡ Miller,F.M.&B.]

Fox & Associates Co., L.P.A.
(See Dayton)

Goldie, Susan L., (BV) '50 '78 C.477 B.A. L.150 J.D. Mun. J.
Graf, Joseph C., (BV) '47 '71 C.107 B.A. L.900 J.D. Pub. Def.Off.
Hagler, Robert A. '40 '65 C.207 B.A. L.608 J.D. Prob. & Juv. J.
Haller, Stephen K., (AV) '50 '75 C.952 A.B. L.851 J.D. 330 North Detroit Street
Hendrix, Robert K., (BV) '61 '86 C.473 A.B. L.150 J.D. Co. Pros. Off.
Hieber, Raymond C. '26 '57 C.201 A.B. L.150 J.D. Mun. J.
Hurley, Steven L., (BV) '52 '77 C.235 B.A. L.201 J.D. 330 N. Detroit St.
Hutcheson, Robert W. '50 '75 C.228 B.A. L.802 J.D. Juv. J.
Johnson, Gary R., (AV) '43 '72 C.235 A.B. L.607 J.D. [Brandabur,C.F.J.W.&B.]
Keller, Ronald P., (BV) '58 '83 C.705 B.A. L.851 J.D. 85 W. Main St.
Lennon, Cynthia, (BV) '56 '81 C.201 B.A. L.347 J.D. Pros. Off.
Lewis, Ronald Chess '66 '93 C&L.607 B.S.B.A., J.D. City of Xenia
Massie, Marshall J., (BV) '21 '51 C.943 L.329 J.D. 119 E. 2nd St.
Mathewson, Thomas G. '56 '97 C.1044 B.A. L.201 J.D. 987 Old 35
Maurath, Iona C. '25 '47 C.25 A.B. L.930 LL.B. 2334 Lostwood Ct.
McKeown, Noel K., (BV) '46 '72 C.207 B.A. L.1017 J.D. [Miller,F.M.&B.]
Metzler, Kimberly I. '71 '96 C.741 B.A. L.200 J.D. Rural Legal Aid Soc. of W. Central Ohio
Miller, Finney, McKeown & Baker, (BV) 20 King Avenue
Millien, Jennifer C. '72 '97 C.1086 B.A. L.201 J.D. Asst. Pros. Atty.
Moran, Timothy J. '52 '94 C.508 B.A. L.117 J.D. 1653 Oakwood Trail
Murray, Christopher A., (BV) '66 '92 C.1208 B.S.B. L.608 J.D. Asst. Co. Pros.
Neal, Scott E. '69 '98 C.201 B.A. L.1194 J.D. [⊡ Brandabur,C.F.J.W.&B.]
Orlins, David A., (BV) '47 '75 C.823 A.B. L.608 J.D. [Silverberg,Z.&O.]
Pendry, David L., (AV) '53 '80 C.610 B.S. L.201 J.D. [Smith&P.]
Peterson, David S., (BV) '59 '84 C.1208 B.A. L.607 J.D. [Peterson&P.]
Peterson, Marshall E., (BV) '31 '55 C.532 L.607 LL.B. [Peterson&P.]
Peterson, Sigurd R., Jr., (CV) '61 '87 C.860 B.A. L.659 J.D. Pros. Off.

Peterson & Peterson, (BV)
87 S. Progress Drive, 45385
Telephone: 937-372-3584 Fax: 937-372-7218
Partners of Firm: Marshall E. Peterson; David S. Peterson.
Automobile and Motorcycle Accidents, Workers Compensation, Job-Related Injuries, Wrongful Death, Bus and Truck accidents, Negligence Claims, Insurance Claims, Probate, Estates, Wills, Living Trust, Guardianship, Power of Attorney, Real Estate, Contracts, Deeds, Evictions, Family Law, Divorce, Custody, Visitation, Domestic Violence, Criminal, Traffic Violations, Felonies, Misdemeanors, DUI, License Suspension, Juvenile, Bankruptcy.
See Professional Biographies, XENIA, OHIO

Phipps, David L., (BV) '50 '75 C.1023 B.S. L.930 J.D. 53 West Main St.

Pickrel, Schaeffer & Ebeling
(See Dayton)

Reid, M. David '41 '66 C.631 B.A. L.607 J.D. Com. Pleas J.
Root, J. Andrew, (BV) '66 '92 C.363 B.A. L.608 J.D. [Stephan&R.]
Schenck, William F., (BV) '46 '70 C.692 B.A. L.608 J.D. E. Main St.
Schmidt, James W., (BV) '46 '73 C.473 B.S. L.362 J.D. Co. Treas. [Schmidt&S.]
Schmidt, Suzanne McPeak, (BV) '54 '79 C.436 B.A. L.201 J.D. Asst. Pros. [Schmidt&S.]
Schmidt & Schmidt, (BV) 63 1/2 E. Main St. (⊙Laguna Niguel, CA; Phila., PA; Mason, TX; Wausau, WI)
Schornak, Donald G. '28 '56 C&L.608 B.A., J.D. 85 W. 2nd Street
Shattuck, Judson L., Jr. '38 '72 C.973 B.S.B.A. L.1340 J.D. Com. Pleas J.
Shaver, Mark A. '68 '98 C.150 B.G.S. L.608 J.D. 45 N. Detroit Street
Sheets, Kenneth R., Attorney at Law '59 '84 C&L.201 B.A., J.D. 46 S. Detroit St.
Short, Jack E. '33 '58 C.611 A.B. L.930 LL.B. Kelly-Creswell Co. Inc.
Sidell, Arthur L., III, (BV) '47 '73 C.1208 B.A. L.150 J.D. 330 N. Detroit St.
Silverberg, Eric, (AV) '44 '69 C.97 B.A. L.851 J.D. [Silverberg,Z.&O.]
Silverberg, Zaharieff & Orlins Co., L.P.A., (AV) 100 E. Market St.
Smith, Geo. R., (AV) '20 '47 C&L.607 J.D. [Smith&P.]
Smith & Pendry, (AV) 133 E. Market St.
Stafford, Thomas R., (BV) '52 '77 C.473 A.B. L.851 J.D. 968 Mound Ct.
Stephan, Peter D., (BV) '49 '74 C&L.117 B.S., J.D. [Stephan&R.]
Stephan and Root, (BV) 1354 N. Monroe Dr.
Stump, Kimberly Metzler '71 '96 C.741 B.A. L.201 J.D. Rural Legal Aid Soc. of W. Central Ohio
Theodor, Christ, (BV) '45 '77 C&L.201 B.T., J.D. 1721 Ireland Rd.
Vasquez, Jose L., (CV) '66 '91 C.473 B.A. L.930 J.D. Staff Atty., Rual Legal Aid Soc.
Wead, Richard A., (BV) '40 '67 C.97 B.S.B.A. L.608 J.D. 53 West Main St.
Weckstein, Donald, (AV) '38 '62 C&L.150 A.B., J.D. [Brandabur,C.F.J.W.&B.]
Zachritz, James D., (BV) '33 '65 C.210 A.B. L.1340 J.D. 67 W. Main St.
Zaharieff, Anthony J., (AV) '45 '70 C&L.150 B.A., J.D. [Silverberg,Z.&O.]

YELLOW SPRINGS, 3,761, *Greene Co.*

Hammond, John R. '54 '80 C.608 B.S. L.607 J.D. 721 E. Hyde Rd.
Kellogg, Scott '52 '91 C.339 B.S. L.734 J.D. 114 W. N. College★
Lang, Michael D. '44 '69 C.309 A.B. L.94 J.D. (adm. in MA; not adm. in OH) McGregor Sch. of Antioch Univ.

Martin, Browne, Hull & Harper, P.L.L.
(See Springfield)

YOUNGSTOWN, * 82,026, *Mahoning & Trumbull Cos.*

Abbarno, Kenneth P. '66 '92 C.116 B.A. L.161 J.D. [⊡ Reminger&R.] (⊙Cleveland)
Abrams, Karen Harless, (BV) '54 '81 C.385 B.A. L.930 J.D. Real Estate Coun., Phar-Mor, Inc.
Abrams, Richard A., (BV) '55 '80 C.165 A.B. L.930 J.D. [Green H.S.]
Aduma, Kenyetta T. '— '94 C.302 B.A. L.608 J.D. Northeast Ohio Legal Servs.
Akins, Kim F., (CV) '57 '90 C.207 B.A. L.8 J.D. 212 Outlook Avenue
Amendolara, Samuel G., (BV) '53 '79 C.980 B.S. L.1003 J.D. Spec. Coun., Off. of Atty. Gen.
Ames, C. Douglas '49 '92 C.381 B.S. L.8 J.D. [⊡ Heller,M.M.&M.]
Ams, John A. '73 '02 C&L.8 B.A., J.D. [⊡ Pfau,P.&M.]
Amstutz, C. John, (AV) '33 '58 C.604 A.B. L.145 J.D. [⊡ Friedman&R.] ‡
Anzellotti, Sperling, Pazol & Small Co., L.P.A., (BV) 21 North Wickliffe Circle (⊙Warren)
Atway, Neal G., (CV) '66 '92 C.124 B.S. L.1003 J.D. 19 East Front Street
Baker, Brent E., (CV) '63 '00 C.47 M.Div. L.7 J.D. [Newman,O.&K.]
Bannon, Chas. J. '28 '58 C&L.980 A.B., J.D. Com. Pleas J.
Barbee, David S., (BV) '62 '86 C.999 B.A. L.608 J.D. [Roth,B.R.S.&L.]
Baringer, Linette S., (CV) '65 '90 C.980 B.S. L.608 J.D. Chf. Civil Pros., Mahoning Co. Pros. Off.
Baronzzi, Christopher '78 '04 C.363 B.S.E. L.7 J.D. [⊡ Harrington,H.&M.] (⊙Salem)
Bateman, Melissa Faye '77 '01 C.381 B.A. L.8 J.D. Law Clk., Ct. of App.
Beard, Ralph A., (AV) '47 '75 C.980 B.A. L.608 J.D. [Harrington,H.&M.]
Beatrice, Mark A., (BV) '55 '81 C.5 B.A. L.228 J.D. [Manchester,B.P.&U.]
Beck, Mark J., (BV) '63 '89 C.150 B.B.A. L.260 J.D. Tax Coun., The Cafaro Co.
Belinky, Mark A., (BV) '52 '77 C.610 B.A. L.665 J.D. 600 Metropolitan Tower
Bennett, Franklin S., Jr., (AV) '54 '80 C.188 A.B. L.930 J.D. Gen. Coun. & CAO, Butler, Wick & Co., Inc.
Bernard, Anthony M. '18 '42 C&L.602 B.S., J.D. 107 Mill Run‡
Bernard, Elizabeth A., (BV) '62 '88 C.980 B.A. L.7 J.D. [Harshman&B.] ⊙
Bernard, Lynn M., (Miss) '20 '53 C.381 B.S. L.980 J.D. 4529 Green Glen Dr.‡

Billak, Damian Andrew, (CV) '70 '95 C.97 B.A. L.989 J.D.
103 East Boardman Street, 44503-1828
Telephone: 330-740-0200 Fax: 330-740-0201
Email: dbillak@aol.com URL: http://www.billakcriminaldefenselaw.com
Criminal Defense, Civil Rights, Personal Injury, Appellate Practice.
See Professional Biographies, YOUNGSTOWN, OHIO

Bishara, Joseph C., (CV) '71 '96 C.602 B.A. L.150 J.D. [Roth,B.R.S.&L.]
Blair, Richard B., (AV) '45 '70 C.264 B.A. L.607 J.D. [Roth,B.R.S.&L.]
Blomstrom, James L., (AV) '49 '74 C.659 B.A. L.145 J.D. [Harrington,H.&M.]
Boano, Michael L. '53 '80 C.381 B.A. L.851 J.D. 412 Boardman Canfield Rd.
Bodoh, William T. '38 '64 C.610 B.S.C. L.608 J.D. U.S. Bkrptcy. J.‡
Boetcher, Martin J., (BV) '61 '87 C.608 B.S.C.E. L.7 J.D. [Harrington,H.&M.]
Bolton, Stephen T., (AV) '46 '72 C&L.893 B.A., LL.B. [Manchester,B.P.&U.]
Bouffard, Robert S., (BV) '51 '79 C.602 B.B.A. L.1003 J.D. 721 Boardman-Poland Road
Boyd, John C., (BV) '40 '66 C.923 A.B. L.266 J.D. [Boyd,R.&C.]
Boyd, Rummell & Carach, (BV) 400 Mahoning Bk. Bldg.

Brennan, Frederick, Vouros & Yarwood, Ltd., (BV)
29 East Front Street, 2nd Floor, 44503-1439
Telephone: 330-743-4116 Fax: 330-743-2536
Email: bfvy@sbcglobal.net URL: http://www.bfvy.com
Harry Frederick; Joseph E. Vouros; Ronald D. Yarwood; Anne Frederick Crawford; Damian P. DeGenova.
General Trial Practice in all Courts. Corporation and Business Law. Criminal Defense, Negligence, Family and Probate Law. Estate Planning, Personal Injury.
Reference: The Mahoning National Bank.
See Professional Biographies, YOUNGSTOWN, OHIO

Briach, George G., (BV) '54 '83 C.980 A.B. L.7 J.D. 755 Boardman-Canfield Rd.
Bryan, Jerry M., (BV) '66 '91 C.980 B.A. L.608 J.D. [Henderson,C.M.N.&T.]
Bryan, Joseph R. '28 '51 C.980 L.607 J.D. Mag. Com. Pleas J.
Buck, Marshall D., (BV) '51 '81 C.610 B.S. L.607 J.D. [Comstock,S.&W.]
Budinsky, Robert, (BV) '52 '78 C.980 B.A. L.7 J.D. 3130 Hummingbird Hill Dr.
Burdman, B. Richard, (AV) '33 '56 C.980 B.A. L.228 J.D. [Nadler N.&B.] ‡
Burdman, Babette F., (BV) '38 '82 C.608 B.S. L.7 J.D. 20 Federal Plaza W., Ste. 600
Burdman, Bonnie Deutsch, (BV) '65 '91 C.188 B.S. L.30 J.D. 400 Natl. City Bank Bldg.
Burgess, Richard L. '41 '84 C.980 M.A. L.7 J.D. 1404 Thorn Hill Rd.‡
Bush, Joseph J., III, (BV) '55 '87 C.980 B.A. L.8 J.D. [Schiavoni,S.&B.]
Bush, Richard T., (BV) '58 '83 C.604 B.A. L.608 J.D. 400 Natl. City Bank Bldg.
Bush, Robert E., (CV) '47 '92 C.980 B.S. L.8 J.D. 26 S. Pelps St.
Bushey, Martha L., (BV) '48 '89 C.980 B.S.N. L.8 J.D. [Manchester,B.P.&U.]
Butler, Ernest W. '16 '81 C&L.980 B.A., J.D. 1168 Miami Ave.
Callen, James Bruce '45 '76 C.608 B.A. L.7 J.D. 11 Federal Plaza Central
Carach, Herman J., (BV) '51 '77 C.980 B.A. L.930 J.D. [Boyd,R.&C.]
Carlin, Clair M., (AV) '47 '73 C&L.608 B.S., J.D. [C.M.Carlin]

Carlin, Clair M., LLC, (AV)
62 South Main Street, 44514
Mailing Address: P.O. Box 5369, Poland, OH 44514-0369
Telephone: 330-707-0377 Fax: 330-707-0398
Email: cmc@carlin-law.com URL: http://www.carlin-law.com
Clair M. Carlin;—Amy L. Higgins.
Practice Limited to Civil Trial Practice, including Commercial Litigation, Medical Malpractice, Personal Injury, Product Liability, Insurance Coverage Issues and Professional Liability.
See Professional Biographies, YOUNGSTOWN, OHIO

Cartwright-Jones, Rhys B. ....'78 '04 C&L.161 B.A., J.D. Asst. Prosecutor & Appl. Coun.
Casey, Robert E., (CV) ....'40 '76 C.980 B.A. L.7 J.D. 8070 Paulin Dr.
Chagnot, Jeffrey L. '50 '86 C.980 B.S. L.8 J.D.
Dir., Economic Develop., City of Youngstown, Ohio
Cherrill, E. Donna ....'20 '44 L.980 J.D. City Hall
Christian, Robert J., (BV) ....'48 '77 C.911 B.S. L.607 J.D. 26 Market St., Ste. 904
Christian, Shirley J., (AV) '54 '86 C.650 B.S. L.607 J.D.
[Harrington,H.&M.] (Salem)
Chuparkoff, George A., (BV) ....'29 '55 C.980 B.A. L.930 J.D. 42 N. Phelps Street
Ciambotti, Anna Marie, (CV) ....'50 '87 C.650 B.S.Ed. L.8 J.D. [A.M.Ciambotti]
Ciambotti, Anna M., (CV) .... 755 Boardman Canfield Rd.
Cloonan, Terrence F. ....'56 '81 C.318 B.A. L.930 J.D. The Mahoning Natl. Bk.
Close, A. L., Jr. ....'21 '58 C.473 B.S. L.980 J.D. 4859 Oak Knoll Dr.‡
Codjoe, Carmen V. ....'79 '04 C.776 B.A. L.608 J.D. [Harrington,H.&M.]
Collins, William Martin ....'25 '58 4319 Market St.
Comstock, David C., (AV) ....'32 '59 C.611 B.A. L.930 LL.B. [Comstock,S.&W.]
Comstock, David C., Jr., (BV) ....'62 '88 C.970 B.A. L.608 J.D. [Comstock,S.&W.]

Comstock, Springer & Wilson Co., L.P.A., (AV)
100 Federal Plaza East, Suite 926, 44503-1811
Telephone: 330-746-5643 Fax: 330-746-4925
Lawrence R. Springer; Thomas J. Wilson; Marshall D. Buck; Wm. Scott Fowler; David C. Comstock, Jr.; Douglas J. Kress; Margo S. Meola;—Bobbie L. Flynt; Kenneth L. Golden. Of Counsel: David C. Comstock.
General Civil Practice in all State and Federal Courts. Insurance Defense and Coverage, Medical Malpractice and Products Liability Law. Trials.
Local Trial Counsel for: Ohio Bar Liability Insurance Co.; State Farm Auto Insurance Co.; Shelby Mutual Casualty Co.; Grange Mutual Casualty Co.
See Professional Biographies, YOUNGSTOWN, OHIO

Coombs, Frederick S., III, (AV) .....'50 '75 C.207 B.A. L.608 J.D. [Harrington,H.&M.]
Copperman, Samuel H., (AV) ....'13 '37 C.790 L.608 J.D. 831 Wick Ave.‡
Cornelius, Charles R. '42 '80 C.665 B.S.M.E. L.229 J.D.
(adm. in PA; not adm. in OH) 4001 Monticello Blvd.
Corroto, Thomas Leonard, Jr. ....'22 '48 C&L.608 B.S., LL.B. 101 Market St.
Corsell, Joseph D. '70 '96 C.980 B.S.B.A. L.851 J.D.
Leasing Coun./Leasing Agent, Cafaro Co., The
Crawford, Anne Frederick, (CV) ....'63 '91 C&L.607 B.A., J.D. [Brennan,F.V.&Y.]
Creatore, Ronald M. ......'64 '92 C.473 B.S. L.8 J.D. Pres., EnviBion Management Corp.
Cubbison, Theo. R., (BV) ....'22 '48 C.980 A.B. L.930 LL.B. 4317 Sheridan Rd.
Cunahan, Wm. E. ....'17 '49 C.970 B.A. L.607 LL.B. 1640 Canfield Rd.‡
Cunning, Patrick Paul, (BV) ....'52 '84 C.980 B.S.B.A. L.999 J.D. [Green H.S.]
Curry, Charles E., Sr., (CV) ....'54 '94 C.980 L.7 J.D. 203 Legal Center
Czopur, Edward C., (BV) ....'48 '73 C.980 B.A. L.608 J.D. 945 Windham Ct., Ste. 3
Czopur-Gaffney, Melanie Ann ......'76 '01 C.980 B.S.A.S. L.8 J.D. 7th Dist. Ct. of App.
Dann, Marc E., (CV) ....'62 '87 C.477 A.B. L.930 J.D. [Dann&F.]
Dann & Falgiani, LLC, (CV)
4531 Belmont Avenue, Suite C 2nd Level, Churchill Square Plaza
D'Apolito, David A., (CV) ....'64 '89 C.980 B.A. L.8 J.D. 4800 Market St.
D'Apolito, Lou A., (AV) ....'44 '73 C.980 B.S. L.8 J.D. 4800 Market St.
Darvanan, Avetis G., (BV) ....'24 '50 C.980 L.150 LL.B. 700 Wick Bldg.
Davies, Louis M., (AV) ....'29 '54 C.528 B.A. L.930 LL.B. 1200 Mahoning Bk.‡

Davis & Young, (AV)
A Legal Professional Association
The Commerce Building, 201 East Commerce Street, Suite 100, 44503
Telephone: 330-743-1717
Email: atty@dyoungstown.com URL: http://www.davisyoung.com
Larry D. Wilkes. Associates: Susan M. Weber; John Jeffrey Limbian.
General Trial and Appellate Practice, Products Liability, General Tort, Insurance Coverage, Personal Injury, Toxic Torts, Complex Mass Tort Claims, Legal and Medical Malpractice, Municipal Liability, Civil Rights, Employment Practices Liability, and Environmental and Commercial Liability.
Cleveland, Ohio Office: 1700 Midland Building, Suite 1700, 44115. Telephone: 216-348-1700. Fax: 216-621-0602.
Akron, Ohio Office: National City Center, One Cascade Plaza, Suite 800, 44308. Telephone 330-376-1717. Fax: 330-376-1797.
Warren, Ohio Office: 108 Main Street, SW, Suite 1000, 44481. Telephone: 330-373-1717. Fax: 330-395-0610.
See Professional Biographies, YOUNGSTOWN, OHIO

DeAngelo, Edward S., (BV) ......'45 '85 C.610 B.S. L.8 J.D. 1040 S. Commons PL #200
DeBonis, Scott R., (BV) ....'69 '95 C.608 B.S. L.607 J.D. [Roth,B.R.S.&L.]
DeGenaro, M. Mary ....'61 '86 C.980 B.A. L.989 J.D. Ct. of App. J.
DeGenova, Damian P., (CV) ....'67 '94 C.381 B.A. L.117 J.D. [Brennan,F.V.&Y.]
Dellick, F. Theresa ....'58 '84 C.980 B.S. L.851 J.D. Juv. Ct. J.
Dellick, John T., (BV) ....'56 '85 C.980 B.E. L.7 J.D. [Harrington,H.&M.]

Denmead Law Office
(See Columbus)

Detec, David A., (AV) ....'53 '80 C.980 A.B. L.7 J.D. [Manchester,B.P.&U.]
Dietz, James B., (BV) ....'64 '91 C.201 B.S. L.851 J.D. [Friedman&R.]
DiMartino, Dennis Armand ....'61 '87 C.980 B.A. L.989 J.D. [D.A.DiMartino]
DiMartino, Dennis A., Co., LPA .... 6004 Market St.
Dineen, Robert N., (AV) '32 '62
C.602 A.B. L.930 J.D. The Commerce Bldg., 201 E. Commerce St.
Dobran, James M., (BV) ......'57 '82 C.674 A.B. L.665 J.D. Chf. Coun., The Cafaro Co.
Dockry, Michael B., (CV) ....'56 '82 C.980 B.S. L.7 J.D. 296 N. Canfiels Niles Rd.
Donchess, Joseph S., (AV) ....'21 '54 C&L.980 J.D. 34 Federal Plz W.‡
Donofrio, Gene ....'53 '78 C.980 B.A. L.7 J.D. Ct. of App. J.
Donofrio, Jos. ....'25 '55 C&L.980 B.S., J.D. Ret. Ct. App. J.
Dougan, Patricia, (CV) ....'51 '94 C.980 A.B. L.8 J.D. 4907 Sheridan Rd.
Downey, J. Patrick '44 '68 C&L.851 B.A., J.D.
V.P, Human Res., Coml. Intertech Corp.
Draa, Charles M., (CV) '55 '81
C.97 B.A. L.851 J.D. 1315 Boardman Canfield Road, Suite 2
Dunn, James C., (CV) ....'50 '86 C.1260 B.A. L.8 J.D. 8255 South Ave.
Durkin, Dawn M., (CV) ....'73 '98 C.980 B.A. L.1003 J.D. Mahoning Co. Pros. Off.
Durkin, John M., (BV) ....'58 '83 C&L.201 B.A., J.D. 120 Market St.
Dutton, Paul M., (AV) ....'47 '72 C.980 B.A. L.930 J.D. [Harrington,H.&M.]
Economus, Peter C. ....'43 '71 C.980 B.A. L.8 J.D. U.S. Dist. J.

Elk & Elk Co., L.P.A.
(See Cleveland)

Engler, David L. ....'60 '85 C&L.930 B.A., J.D. 100 Debartolo Pl., Ste. 225
Eppstein, Stanley M. ....'12 '37 C.923 A.B. L.477 J.D. P.O. Box 2119‡
Epstein, Bruce R., (BV) ....'52 '77 C.597 B.A. L.607 J.D. 5500 Market St.
Erb, Shawna L., (CV) ......'70 '96 C.528 B.A. L.608 J.D. [Harrington,H.&M.] (Salem)
Eshelman, C. Richard, (BV) ....'37 '68 C.656 B.S. L.7 J.D. [Eshelman]
Eshelman Legal Group, (BV)
945 Windham Court, Suite 5 (Canton, Cleveland, Cuyahoga Falls)
Essad, Scott C., (CV) ....'69 '96 C.608 B.A. L.851 J.D. [Henderson,C.M.N.&T.]
Evans, James P., (BV) '52 '86 C.475 B.S. L.8 J.D.
Sr. V.P. & Gen. Coun., Forum Health
Falgiani, John D., Jr., (CV) ....'59 '85 C.602 B.A. L.823 J.D. [Dann&F.]
Fantauzzi, David A., (BV) .....'55 '80 C.930 B.A. L.365 J.D. Asst. Coun., The Cafaro Co.
Fehr, Eugene John '53 '78 C.610 B.B.A. L.276 J.D.
Mahoning County Common Pleas Ct.
Fekete, Matthew T., (BV) '57 '83
C.980 B.A. L.7 J.D. 725 Boardman Canfield Rd., Unit L-1
Fekett, S. Samuel ....'15 '48 C.980 L.607 J.D. 5332 Old Oxford Lane
Ferris, Ted A., (CV) ....'51 '79 C.161 B.A. L.607 J.D. 26 Market St., Ste. 610
Ficarro, John R., (BV) '52 '78 C&L.823 B.A., J.D.
(adm. in FL; not adm. in OH) Sr. V.P. & Gen. Coun., Phar-Mor, Inc.
Fine, Irvin ....'22 '51 C&L.980 B.A., LL.B. 4114 Monticello Blvd., Apt. #101
Fine, Raymond ....'13 '42 L.980 J.D. P.O. Box 735‡
Flavin, John E. '42 '68 C&L.424 B.B.A., J.D.
(adm. in IL; not adm. in OH) 3007 Canfield‡
Fleck, Jeffrey B., & Associates, (AV) '42 '67
C.472 B.B.A. L.1003 J.D. 845 Woodfield Court
Fleming, Alfred J., (BV) ....'47 '75 C.980 B.A. L.8 J.D. [A.J.Fleming]
Fleming, Alfred J., Co., L.P.A., (BV) .... 400 City Centre One
Floyd, James G., (BV) ....'38 '71 C.207 B.S.S. L.208 J.D. [Newman,O.&K.]
Flynt, Bobbie L., (BV) ....'67 '96 C.1208 B.S. L.201 J.D. [Comstock,S.&W.]
Foley, Robert J., Jr. ....'71 '98 C.980 B.A. L.8 J.D. [Heller,M.M.&M.]
Fowler, Wm. Scott, (BV) ....'58 '84 C.611 B.A. L.608 J.D. [Comstock,S.&W.]
Franken, Timothy E., (BV) ....'48 '79 C.980 B.A. L.7 J.D. P.O. Box 3506
Frederick, Harry, (BV) ....'26 '51 C&L.607 J.D. [Brennan,F.V.&Y.]

Friedman & Rummell Co., L.P.A., (AV)
City Centre One, Suite 300, 100 E. Federal Street, 44503-1810
Telephone: 330-744-4137 Fax: 330-744-9962
Email: fandrlaw@fandrlaw.com URL: http://www.fandrlaw.com
Joseph Friedman (1908-1957); Evan J. Rummell (1917-1964); Robert B. Weimer (1932-1964); Arthur N. K. Friedman (1939-2003); W. Terry Patrick; Carl D. Rafoth; Leonard D. Schiavone; James B. Dietz (Certified Specialist in Estate Planning, Trust and Probate Law, Ohio State Bar Association);—Robert M. Palma; Christopher J. Schiavone; Michele L. McBride. Of Counsel: C. John Amstutz (Retired); Norman A. Rheuban.
General Civil Practice in all Courts. Real Estate, Probate, Trust and Estate Planning, Taxation, Collections, Creditors Rights, Corporate, Commercial, Bankruptcy, Family Law, Business Law, Banking Law, Bankruptcy.
References: The Dollar Savings & Trust Co.; Metropolitan Savings Bank.
See Professional Biographies, YOUNGSTOWN, OHIO

Fulton, Robert S., (BV) ....'46 '72 C.980 B.S. L.930 J.D. [Newman,O.&K.]
Gacse, Thomas M., (BV) ......'55 '80 C.97 B.S.B.A. L.7 J.D. General Counsel, Sky Bank
Gaglione, Karen Markulin, (BV) '67 '92
C&L.8 B.A., J.D. Asst. Pros., Mahoning Co. Pros. Off.
Gains, Paul J., (BV) ....'51 '82 C.980 B.S. L.7 J.D. Pros.
Galip, Ronald G., (BV) ....'34 '57 C.980 B.A. L.608 J.D. 721 Boardman-Poland Road
Gallitto, Robyn R., (BV) ....'62 '89 C.473 B.A. L.117 J.D. [J.B.Fleck&Assoc.]
Gallo, Michael A., (AV) ....'42 '67 C.436 A.B. L.128 J.D. [Nadler N.&B.]
Garea, Stephen R. ....'52 '77 C.980 B.S. L.607 J.D. 8571 Foxwood Ct.
Gaughan, Patrick H. ....'62 '89 C.178 B.A. L.893 J.D. 241 Federal Plaza West
Gemma, Anthony N., (BV) ....'51 '76 C.608 B.S. L.117 J.D. [Gemma&G.]
Gemma, Wm. A., (CV) ....'22 '46 C.607 L.930 LL.B. [Gemma&G.]
Gemma & Gemma, (BV) ....1040 S. Commons PL #200
Gentile, James S., (BV) '50 '76 C.610 B.A. L.607 J.D.
44 Federal Plaza Central, Ste. 200A
Gerchak, Michael A., (BV) ....'31 '59 C&L.980 B.S., J.D. 120 Market St.
Gerson, Rebecca M. ....'67 '94 C.980 A.B. L.930 J.D. 600 Metropolitan‡
Gervelis, Mark S., (BV) ....'46 '76 C.980 B.A. L.1003 J.D. [Gervelis]

Gervelis Law Firm, (BV)
1045 Tiffany South, 44514
Telephone: 330-758-5899 Fax: 330-533-4822
URL: http://www.gervelislaw.com
Mark S. Gervelis.
Plaintiff Personal Injury Law, Wrongful Death Law, Products Liability Law.
See Professional Biographies, YOUNGSTOWN, OHIO

Giannini, Matthew C. ....'50 '78 C.980 B.S. L.201 J.D. 1040 S. Commons Place
Gilboy, M. Daniel, (BV) ....'48 '83 C.980 B.S.A.S. L.8 J.D. Asst. Co. Pros.
Gilliland, Robert C., (Co., L.P.A.) ....'24 '59 C.657 B.S. L.980 J.D. 799 Brookfield‡
Gilmartin, Vincent E., (BV) ....'28 '54 C.309 B.A. L.607 J.D. [V.E.Gilmartin]
Gilmartin, Vincent Edward, (BV) .... 219 W. Boardman St.
Golden, Kenneth L. ....'78 '04 C.608 B.A. L.124 J.D. [Comstock,S.&W.]
Goske, Stephen P., (CV) ....'52 '81 C.980 B.S. L.7 J.D. 120 Westchester Dr.
Gottfried, R. Mark ....'60 '87 C.802 B.A. L.124 J.D. [Stefanski&Assoc.]
Graora, David J., (CV) ....'52 '86 C.980 B.S. L.8 J.D. [Heller,M.M.&M.]
Greaves, Elaine B. .....'53 '80 C.262 B.A. L.569 LL.M. 34 Federal Plaza, West, Suite 810
Green, William, Jr. ....'23 '54 C&L.980 B.A., J.D. 34 Federal Plaza West, Suite 810
Green Haines Sgambati Co., L.P.A., (AV) .... 16 Wick Avenue, Suite 400 (Canton)
Grenga, Terry A., (CV) ....'66 '98 C.980 B.S.B.A. L.8 J.D. 7000 S. Ave., Ste. 4
Grinstein, Deborah L. '60 '85 C.1365 B.A. L.1325 J.D.
Endowment Dir., Youngstown Area Jewish Federation
Grinstein, Peter B., (BV) ....'36 '61 C&L.966 B.B.A., J.D. [Nadler N.&B.]
Gurbach, Matthew D. ....'77 '03 C.980 A.B. L.124 J.D. [Harrington,H.&M.]
Haas, William C. ....'44 '72 C.976 B.A. L.309 J.D. 7620 Market St.
Hackett, Timothy R., (BV) ....'55 '84 C.980 B.S.B.A. L.607 J.D. [Wellman,J.H.]
Haines, Dennis, (AV) ....'37 '62 C.610 B.S.C. L.273 LL.B. [Green H.S.]
Hall, Leonard D., (BV) ....'59 '85 C.980 B.S. L.161 J.D. Corp. Coun., Cafaro Co., The
Hammond, Robert M., (AV) ....'16 '41 C.477 A.B. L.150 J.D. 311 Mahoning Bk. Bldg.
Hanni, Don L. ....'25 '53 C&L.980 B.A., J.D. 219 Boardman St.
Haralambie, John P. ....'06 '37 C.608 Bs.Ed. L.477 LL.B. 901 Bank One Bldg.‡
Harlan, Michael D. ....'68 '98 C.980 B.A. L.8 J.D. [Harshman&B.]

Harrington, Hoppe & Mitchell, Ltd., (AV)
26 Market Street, Suite 1200, 44503-1508
Telephone: 330-744-1111 Telecopier: 330-744-2029
Email: info@hhmlaw.com URL: http://www.hhmlaw.com
Paul M. Dutton; James L. Blomstrom; Frederick S. Coombs, III; Ralph A. Beard; Alan D. Wenger; John T. Dellick; Kelly J. Morrison (Certified Specialist in Business, Commercial and Industrial Real

(This Listing Continued)

Harrington, Hoppe & Mitchell, Ltd. (Continued)

Property Law, Ohio State Bar Association); Shirley J. Christian; Neil H. Maxwell; Martin J. Boetcher; Neil D. Schor; Shawna L. Erb; Lance A. Morrison;—Matthew D. Gurbach; Christopher Baronzzi; Carmen V. Codjoe.
General Civil Trial and Equity Practice in all State and Federal Courts. Corporation, Banking, Creditors Rights and Bankruptcy, Labor, Probate, Estate Planning, Hospital and Health, Insurance Law, Real Estate, Commercial, Business Transactions.
Representative Clients: Forum Health Hospitals and Medical Centers; Aqua Ohio Water Company; Hill, Barth & King, CPAs; Youngstown Warren Regional Chamber of Commerce; Educational Credit Management Corporation; General Extrusions, Inc.; Nationwide Mutual Insurance Co.; V&V Real Estate Investments; Public Library of Youngstown and Mahoning County.
Warren, Ohio Office: 108 Main Avenue, S.W., Suite 500, 44481. Telephone: 330-392-1541. Telecopier: 330-394-6890.
Salem, Ohio Office: 2235 E. Pershing Street, Suite A, 44460. Telephone: 330-337-6586. Telecopier: 330-337-6662.

See Professional Biographies, YOUNGSTOWN, OHIO

Harshman, Michael S., (BV) ... '40 '66 C.608 B.A. L.846 J.D. [Harshman&B.] ⊙
Harshman & Bernard LLC, (BV)
105 East Boardman Street (⊙Boardman, Warren, OH; Sharon, PA)
Hartford, Robert S., Jr., (BV) ... '49 '74 C.381 B.B.A. L.8 J.D. [Nadler N.&B.]
Hartwig, Edward Joseph, (CV) ... '73 '98 C.363 B.S. L.8 J.D. [Wellman,J.H.]
Heino, John T., (CV) ... '71 '96 C.318 B.A. L.851 J.D. [[A] Henderson,C.M.N.&T.]
Heinrich, Julian ... '69 '02 C.980 B.A. L.8 J.D. Atty., The Cafaro Co.
Heintz, Jeffrey D., (BV) ... '59 '84 C.935 B.A. L.893 J.D. [Manchester,B.P.&U.]
Heller, Robert L., (BV) ... '53 '81 C.473 B.A. L.851 J.D. [Heller,M.M.&M.]
Heller, Maas, Moro and Magill Co., L.P.A., (BV) ... P.O. Box 4144

Henderson, Covington, Messenger, Newman & Thomas Co., L.P.A., (AV)
Suite 1300, 6 Federal Plaza Central, 44503-1473 ⊙
Telephone: 330-744-1148 Telefax: 330-744-3807
Andrew M. Henderson (1904-1950); C. A. Covington, Jr. (1917-1999); James L. Messenger; Christopher J. Newman; Richard J. Thomas; David K. Holmquist; Jerry M. Bryan;—George L. White, IV; Scott C. Essad; John T. Heino.
General Civil Trial and Appellate Practice in all Courts. Banking, Commercial, Bankruptcy, Corporate, Probate, Business, Family, Labor Relations, Public Employment Relations and School Law.
Representative Clients: Aerolite Extrusion Co.
Carnegie, Pennsylvania Office: 213 East Main Street, 15106. Telephone: 419-279-7025.

See Professional Biographies, YOUNGSTOWN, OHIO

Hendrickson, Jeffrey Eric ... '60 '00 C.970 B.A. L.7 J.D. 7th Dist. Ct. of App.
Hendrickson, Robt. ... '24 '55 C.604 A.B. L.980 J.D. 2324 5th Ave.‡
Hendryx, Bruce Douglas ... '61 '87 C&L.930 B.A., J.D. Mahoning Natl. Bk.
Henkin, Robert A., (BV) ... '44 '73 C.980 B.S. L.1003 J.D. 905 Bank One Bldg.

Henretta Law Offices
(See Akron)

Herberger, Robert J., Jr., (BV) ... '59 '90 C.980 B.E. L.8 J.D. [McLaughlin&M.] (Pat.)
Herriott, Donald P., (AV) ... '45 '74 C.528 B.S. L.831 J.D. [Newman,O.&K.]
Higgins, Amy L. ... '66 '02 C.980 B.A. L.7 J.D. [[A] C.M.Carlin]
Hill, Thomas A. '58 '84 C.318 B.A. L.273 J.D.
Secy. & Gen. Coun., Capitol Oil & Gas, Inc. (A Subsidiary of North Coast Energy, Inc.)
Holmquist, David K. ... '36 '61 C&L.608 B.S.B.A., J.D. [Henderson,C.M.N.&T.]
Horlick, Chester W., (BV) ... '35 '58 C&L.608 B.A., J.D. [Horlick&Assoc.]
Horlick & Associates, (BV) ... 5815 Market Street
Houser, Joseph M., (BV) ... '56 '81 C.980 B.A. L.150 J.D. [Manchester,B.P.&U.]
Houser, Mary Beth, (BV) ... '57 '82 C.980 B.A. L.608 J.D. [Newman,O.&K.]
Huberman, Mark A., (BV) ... '51 '76 C.665 B.A. L.607 J.D. Mag.
Hume, Martin S., (BV) ... '56 '81 C.918 B.A. L.608 J.D. [M.S.Hume]
Hume, Martin S., Co., L.P.A., (BV) ... 6 Federal Plz. Central, Ste. 905
Humphrey, Theodore '26 '56
C.276 B.S. L.980 J.D. Secy. & Treas., Wedgewood Plaza Inc.
Ingram, J. Gerald, (AV) ... '52 '78 C.97 B.A. L.161 J.D. 7330 Market St.
Ingram, Mark D. ... '55 '82 C.980 B.A. L.1003 J.D. 427 West Midlothian Blvd.
Jacob, Timothy J., (BV) ... '51 '77 C.602 A.B. L.228 J.D. [Manchester,B.P.&U.]
James, Carl G., (BV) ... '52 '77 C.611 B.A. L.300 J.D. 4450 Market Street
Jeren, John A., Jr., (AV) ... '46 '73 C.608 B.S. L.607 J.D. [Wellman,J.H.]
Joltin, Benjamin, (CV) ... '74 '00 C.980 B.A. L.989 J.D. [[A] Dann&F.]
Jones, Tammie Marie ... '61 '85 C&L.607 B.A., J.D. Northeast Ohio Legal Servs.
Juhasz, John B., Jr., (AV) ... '57 '83 C.980 B.A. L.8 J.D. [J.B.Juhasz]
Juhasz, John B., (AV) ... 7330 Market St.
Kalafut, Robert J. ... '29 '54 C.980 B.S. L.930 LL.B. 206 Legal Arts Centre
Kalasky, James F. ... '49 '75 C.608 B.A. L.472 2445 Belmont Avenue
Kannensohn, Fredric A., (AV) ... '39 '64 C.659 B.S. L.477 J.D. [Millstone&K.] ⊙
Katz, Susan Stanton, (BV) ... '51 '79 C.980 B.S. L.7 J.D. 1200 Mahoning Bk. Bldg.
Kicz, John Allen, (BV) ... '39 '64 C.980 B.S. L.477 J.D. 635 Ferndale Ave.
Kissinger, William, (CV) ... '67 '92 C.980 L.7 8255 South Ave.
Kivlighan, Michael O. ... '77 '03 C.610 B.A. L.989 J.D 219 West Boardman Street
Kmetz, Kimberlee J., (CV) ... '69 '94 C.980 B.A. L.8 J.D. [[A] Harshman&B.] ⊙
Knickerbocker, Ronald, (BV) '52 '82
C.980 B.S.A.S. L.7 J.D. 725 Boardman-Canfield Rd., Univt L-1
Kress, Douglas J., (BV) ... '69 '94 C.8 B.A. L.851 J.D. [Comstock,S.&W.]
Kretzer, Alan R., (AV) ... '43 '68 C.610 A.B. L.930 J.D. [A.R.Kretzer]
Kretzer, Alan R., Co., L.P.A., (AV) ... 107 S. Champion St.
Krichbaum, R. Scott, (AV) ... '52 '79 C.980 B.S. L.7 J.D. 120 Market Street
Kryzan, Frank X. ... '13 '39 C&L.980 A.B., J.D. Ret. Mun. J.
Kutlick, Paula S., (CV) ... '53 '94 C.980 L.8 755 Boardman-Canfield Road, Suite K-4
Lacich, Christopher P., (CV) ... '63 '92 C.980 B.A. L.793 J.D. [Roth,B.R.S.&L.]
Laczko, John P., (CV) ... '64 '91 C.980 B.A. L.8 J.D. 4800 Market Street
Laine, Barry, (AV) ... '48 '73 C.705 B.A. L.1003 J.D. [Green H.S.]
Lanz, C. Scott, (BV) ... '54 '80 C.420 B.A. L.608 J.D. [Manchester,B.P.&U.]
Lanzo, Angela M., (CV) ... '71 '96 C.980 A.B. L.8 J.D. The Cafaro Co.
Lanzo, James Edward, (CV) ... '71 '98 C.437 B.A. L.7 J.D. [[A]]
Lanzo, James R. ... '44 '72 C.437 B.S. L.7 J.D. 4126 Youngstown-Poland Road
Latas, Mark, (CV) ... '56 '81 C.473 B.A. L.607 J.D. 101 Market St., Ste. 203
Latas, Milan, (BV) ... '28 '58 C&L.980 A.B., LL.B. 101 Market St.
Legow, Elliot P., (BV) ... '51 '78 C&L.477 A.B., J.D. 998 Colonial Drive
Leone, Donald P., (BV) ... '49 '76 C.980 B.A. L.796 J.D. 24 W. Boardman St.
Leskovyansky, John J. ... '25 '53 C&L.980 J.D. Com. Pleas J.
Lev, Steven A., (CV) ... '48 '82 C.473 B.A. L.8 J.D. 1871 Selma Ave.
Levy, Louis K. ... '36 '65 C.197 B.A. L.1003 J.D. Mun. J.
Libby, Harold L. ... '25 '54 C&L.608 B.S., J.D. Stambaugh Bldg.
Limbert, George James ... '40 '65 C.367 B.A. L.930 J.D. U.S. Mag. Judge
Limbian, John Jeffrey, (CV) ... '59 '91 C.980 B.A. L.251 J.D. [[A] Davis&Y.]
Lipka, Thomas J., (CV) ... '69 '96 C.604 B.A. L.608 J.D. [Manchester,B.P.&U.]
Lisotto, Robert G. ... '46 '73 C.980 A.B. L.744 J.D. 120 Market St.
Lodge, Thomas J., (AV) ... '52 '77 C.363 B.A. L.607 J.D. [Roth,B.R.S.&L.]
Lucci, Joseph C., (BV) ... '53 '78 C.1175 B.A. L.259 J.D. [Nadler N.&B.]
Luckhart, Elton W. ... '10 '47 C.16 B.S. L.980 J.D. 309 Legal Arts Centre‡
Lynch, John J., Jr. ... '15 '40 C&L.608 A.B., J.D. Ret. Ct. of App. J.
Lynd, Alice ... '30 '85 C.1016 B.A. L.665 J.D. Northeast Ohio Legal Servs.
Lynd, Staughton, (BV) ... '29 '76 C.309 B.A. L.145 J.D. Sr. Atty., N.E. Ohio Legal Servs.
Maas, Steven D., (BV) ... '55 '80 C.49 B.S. L.896 J.D. [Heller,M.M.&M.]
MacDonald, Stewart D., (BV) ... '47 '72 C.935 B.A. L.1017 J.D. 3143 Mahoning Avenue
Macejko, Theodore T., (BV) ... '11 '37 C.980 A.B. L.607 LL.B. [Macejko&M.]
Macejko, Theodore T., Jr., (BV) ... '38 '63 C&L.607 B.A., J.D. [Macejko&M.]
Macejko & Macejko, (BV) ... 808 Wick Bldg.
Mackall, Robert L., III ... '71 '00 C&L.8 B.A., J.D. Asst. Coun., The Cafaro Co.
Magill, Richard L. "Pete", (BV) ... '61 '87 C.608 B.A. L.1003 J.D. [Heller,M.M.&M.]
Malkin, Michael L. ... '56 '81 C.276 A.B. L.930 J.D. Asst. Gen. Coun., Phar-Mor, Inc.
Malkoff, Solomon, (BV) ... '18 '42 C&L.608 B.A., J.D. [[C] Boyd,R.&C.]
Maloney, Timothy P. ... '49 '85 C.980 B.S. L.8 J.D. Prob. J.
Manchester, Gilbert M., (BV) '44 '69
C.390 A.B. L.930 J.D. V.P. & Gen. Coun., Coml. Intertech Corp.

Manchester, Bennett, Powers & Ullman, A Legal Professional Association, (AV) [BR]
Atrium Level Two The Commerce Building, 201 East Commerce Street, 44503-1641
Telephone: 330-743-1171 Fax: 330-743-1190
URL: http://www.mbpu.com
Curtis A. Manchester (1876-1951); James Eugene Bennett (1889-1964); Franklin B. Powers (1887-1960); Myron E. Ullman (1889-1974); Stephen T. Bolton; Timothy J. Jacob; C. Scott Lanz; Mark A. Beatrice; Joseph R. Young, Jr.; Joseph M. Houser; Jeffrey D. Heintz; Edwin Romero; Martha L. Bushey; David A. Detec; Thomas J. Lipka; Gina Agresta Richardson;—John T. Savage; Gregory S. Smith.
General Civil Practice in all State and Federal Courts. Antitrust and Unfair Trade Practices, Commercial, Construction, Corporation, Creditor-Debtor, Bankruptcy, Employer-Employee Relations, Environmental, Estate Planning and Administration, General Business, Health Care, Insurance, Labor Relations, Litigation, Pension and Employee Benefits, Probate, Real Estate, Public Finance, Securities, School Law, Taxation, Trials, Workers Compensation.
Local Counsel for: City of Youngstown; Farmers Insurance Group; The Vindicator Printing Company; WFMJ Television, Inc.; Youngstown State University.
General Counsel for: Butler Wick & Company; Home Savings and Loan Company.

See Professional Biographies, YOUNGSTOWN, OHIO

Mangie, Mark G., (BV) ... '50 '75 C.608 B.A. L.607 J.D. 945 Windham Ct.
Manley-Dutton, Maria ... '68 '00 C.469 B.B.A. L.8 J.D. Asst. Coun., The Cafaro Co.
Marando, Michael P., (AV) ... '50 '77 C.610 B.A. L.607 J.D. [Pfau,P.&M.]
Marshall, William M., Jr., (BV) ... '47 '74 C&L.930 B.A., J.D. 1110 Old Furnace Rd.
Masternick, John, (CV) ... '25 '55 C.424 L.980 J.D. 555 Catalina Ave. (⊙Girard)
Matavich, Alan J., (BV) ... '50 '76 C.980 B.A. L.608 J.D. 945 Windham Ct.
Matune, Frank J., (BV) ... '48 '79 C.750 B.A. L.1187 J.D. [Nadler N.&B.]
Matune, Timothy J., (BV) ... '59 '84 C.473 B.Ph. L.1292 J.D. Coun., The Cafaro Co.
Maxin, Joseph J., (BV) ... '62 '87 C.201 A.B. L.851 J.D. Asst. Co. Pros. [Maxin&M.]
Maxin, Joseph W., (BV) ... '27 '61 C&L.980 A.B., J.D. [Maxin&M.]
Maxin and Maxin, (BV) ... 945 Windham Ct.
Maxwell, Neil H., (BV) ... '59 '84 C.528 B.S. L.8 J.D. [Harrington,H.&M.] (⊙Salem)
McBride, Michele L. ... '02 C.599 B.A. L.1003 J.D. [[A] Friedman&R.]
McCollum, Donna J., (BV) ... '57 '85 C.980 B.S.A.S. L.7 J.D. 3332 Sunnybrook Dr.
McLaughlin, Richard P., (AV) ... '34 '62 C.980 B.A. L.276 LL.B. [McLaughlin&M.]
McLaughlin and McNally, (AV) ... 500 City Centre One (Pat.)
McNally, John A., III, (BV) ... '45 '71 C&L.276 B.S.F.S., J.D. [McLaughlin&M.]
Meola, Margo S., (BV) ... '69 '95 C.363 B.A. L.607 J.D. [Comstock,S.&W.]
Meranto, Anthony P., (CV) ... '61 '96 C.980 B.S.B.A. L.8 J.D. 4822 Market Street
Messenger, James L., (AV) '42 '67 C.610 B.B.A. L.823 LL.B.
[Henderson,C.M.N.&T.]
Miklandric, William J., Jr. ... '76 '01 C.970 B.A. L.8 J.D. Assoc. Coun., The Cafaro Co.
Mikulka, Angela J., (BV) ... '55 '84 C.980 B.A. L.8 J.D. [Anzellotti,S.P.&S.]
Mikulka, Thomas L. ... '54 '98 C.980 B.S. L.8 J.D. [[A] Anzellotti,S.P.&S.]
Milich, Robert P. ... '42 '78 C.980 B.S. L.7 J.D. Mun. Ct. J.

Millstone & Kannensohn, (AV)
15 Federal Plaza Central 2nd Floor, 44503 ⊙
Telephone: 330-743-5181 Fax: 330-743-9704
Email: milkann@hotmail.com
Member of Firm: Fredric A. Kannensohn.
General Civil Practice, Commercial Law and Collections.
Representative Clients: Bank One of Youngstown, N.A.; Norwest Financial Services; Credit Union One, Inc.; Ohio Bell Telephone Co.; Phar Mor; Sears Roebuck Co.; Kaufmann's (May Department Stores); Youngstown Business Journal; City of Youngstown.

See Professional Biographies, YOUNGSTOWN, OHIO

Mirkin, Ira J., (AV) ... '53 '79 C.608 B.A. L.851 J.D. [Green H.S.]
Modarelli, Nicholas E., (BV) '51 '83 C.980 B.S.A.S. L.7 J.D.
60 Westchester Drive, Ste. 1
Moore, David M., (CV) ... '66 '93 C.381 B.A. L.8 J.D. [[A] Roth,B.R.S.&L.]
Moore, Robert S. ... '47 '73 C.207 B.A. L.930 J.D. [Green H.S.]
Morgione, Vincent Joseph, (BV) ... '63 '89 C.980 B.S. L.1003 J.D. 3680 Starr Center Dr.
Morley, Michael, Law Office of, (BV) '56 '81
C.980 B.A. L.150 J.D. 721 Boardman-Poland Rd.
Morrison, Kelly J., (BV) ... '59 '85 C.980 B.A. L.990 J.D. [Harrington,H.&M.]
Morrison, Lance A., (CV) ... '66 '92 C&L.608 B.A., J.D. [Harrington,H.&M.] (⊙Salem)
Muldowney, Shawn R., (CV) ... '66 '92 C.381 B.A. L.117 J.D. [Schiavoni,S.&B.]
Mulligan, Joseph P. ... '62 '91 C.473 B.S. L.608 J.D. Asst. Coun., Cafaro Co., The
Murphy, Bobby Joe ... '50 '84 C.999 B.A. L.7 J.D. 104 cover Dr.
Myers, William Anthony ... '64 '93 C.980 B.A. L.8 J.D. 33 Melrose Avenue

Nader and Nader
(See Warren)

Nadler, Myron J., (AV) ... '23 '50 C.659 B.S. L.477 J.D. [Nadler N.&B.] ‡

Nadler Nadler & Burdman Co., L.P.A., (AV)
20 Federal Plaza West, Suite 600, 44503-1559
Telephone: 330-744-0247; 330-747-8621 Telecopier: 330-744-8690
Email: scpatton@nnblaw.com
Peter B. Grinstein; Michael A. Gallo; Jay M. Skolnick; Marc S. Stein; Joseph C. Lucci; Robert S. Hartford, Jr.; Donn D. Rosenblum; Edward F. Smith; Timothy M. Reardon; John F. Petrony; Frank J. Matune; Murray A. Nadler (1899-1986); Myron J. Nadler (Retired); B. Richard Burdman (Retired).
General Civil Practice in all State and Federal Courts. Commercial, Creditor Rights and Collections, Bankruptcy, Reorganization, Taxation, Employment and Labor Law, Corporation, Partnership, Venture Capital, Banking, Real Estate, Shopping Center, Franchising, Environmental, Pension and Profit Sharing, Estate Planning, Probate, and Trials and Appeals.

See Professional Biographies, YOUNGSTOWN, OHIO

Newman, Christopher J., (BV) '48 '73 C.207 B.A. L.930 J.D.
[Henderson,C.M.N.&T.]
Newman, John M., (AV) ... '15 '42 C.665 A.B. L.980 J.D. [Newman,O.&K.]

Newman, Olson & Kerr, A Legal Professional Corporation, (AV)
First National Tower, 11 Federal Plaza Central Suite 1200, 44503-1516
Telephone: 330-747-4404 Fax: 330-747-6056
John M. Newman; E. Carroll Thornton, Jr.; Donald P. Herriott; Robert S. Fulton; Mary Beth Houser; James G. Floyd; Leo J. Puhalla; Brent E. Baker. Of Counsel: Leonard A. Olson; Patrick A. Sebastiano.
General Civil and Trial Practice in all Courts. Corporation, Banking, Commercial, Bankruptcy, Labor, Estate Planning, Probate, Insurance, Health, Personal Injury, Real Estate, Church, Non-Profit, Construction.

(This Listing Continued)

Newman, Olson & Kerr, A Legal Professional Corporation (Continued)
General Counsel for: The East Fairfield Coal Co.; St. Elizabeth Hospital Medical Center. Finance Co.
See Professional Biographies, YOUNGSTOWN, OHIO

Nohra, Jude J. '68 '97 C.980 B.S.B.A. L.930 J.D.
V.P., Gen. Coun & Sec., The Home Savings and Loan Company
Nunziato, Carl A. '38 '71 C.980 B.A. L.930 J.D.
V.P., Tr. Develop., Natl. City Bk., N.E.
O'Halloran, Janice T., (BV) '50 '82 C.62 B.A. L.7 J.D. [Stefanski&Assoc.]
Ohanian, Eric J. '64 '90 C.724 B.A. L.8 J.D. [Stefanski&Assoc.]
O'Horo, Kristen L. '73 '98 C.980 B.S. L.8 J.D. Law Clk., Ct. App.
Olson, Leonard A., (AV) '27 '53 C&L.980 B.A., J.D. [Newman,O.&K.]
Orlando, Jacqueline A. '62 '98 C.608 B.A. L.7 J.D. Tax Assoc., The Cafaro Co.
Osborne, Clyde W. '17 '49 C.473 L.980 J.D. Ret. Com. Pleas J.
Palma, Robert M., (BV) '46 '75 C.980 A.B. L.7 J.D. [Friedman&R.]
Palombaro, Albert A., (BV) '53 '84 C.980 B.S. L.7 J.D. 1032 BoadmanCanfield
Palusak, Julie Dohar, (CV) '68 '94 C.980 B.A. L.1003 J.D. 625 Squirrel Hill Dr.
Patrick, W. Terry, (AV) '49 '77 C.980 A.B. L.7 J.D. [Friedman&R.]
Pazol, James L., (BV) '37 '62 C&L.608 B.A., J.D. [Anzellotti,S.P.&S.] ⊙
Perkins, John R. '27 '55 C.473 A.B. L.980 J.D. 906 Metropolitan Twr.‡
Perkins, Nancy L. '56 '84 C.607 B.A. L.980 J.D. Metropolitan Svgs. Bk.
Petraglia, Catherine T. '28 '80 C.452 A.B. L.7 J.D.
Co. Child Support Enforcement Agcy.
Petrony, John F., (BV) '68 '93 C.980 B.A. L.608 J.D. [Nadler N.&B.]
Petruzzi, Frank M., (BV) '56 '82 C.980 B.S.B.A. L.7 J.D. 1522 McCollom Road
Pfau, John C., (AV) '54 '80 C.385 B.A. L.607 J.D. [Pfau,P.&M.]
Pfau, William E., III, (AV) '51 '79 C.95 B.A. L.851 J.D. [Pfau,P.&M.]
Pfau, William E., Jr., (AV) '19 '47 C.31 A.B. L.477 J.D. [Pfau,P.&M.]

Pfau, Pfau & Marando, (AV)
P.O. Box 9070, 44513
Telephone: 330-702-9700 Fax: 330-702-9704
Email: ppm@ppmlegal.com
William E. Pfau, Sr. (1889-1963); William E. Pfau, Jr. (Retired). Members of Firm: William E. Pfau III; John C. Pfau; Michael P. Marando. Associate: John A. Ams.
General Civil Practice in all State and Federal Courts. Insurance, Malpractice and Products Liability and Personal Injury Law, Constitutional and Real Estate Law. Trials.
See Professional Biographies, YOUNGSTOWN, OHIO

Philibin, Gary J., (BV) '49 '87 C.980 B.S. L.8 J.D. 181 Ridgewood Dr.
Piatt, Timothy R., (BV) '52 '88 C.381 B.A. L.8 J.D. 400 Natl. City Bank Bldg.
Piccirillo, Michael R., (BV) '64 '91 C.980 A.B. L.8 J.D. 7301 West Blvd., Ste. C2
Pipino, James D. '60 '86 C.150 B.A. L.989 J.D. James S. Pipino Ins. Agcy.
Pochiro, Patrick R., (BV) '42 '67 C.980 B.A. L.602 LL.B. 2503 S. Schenley Ave.
Popio, Loren A. '54 '80 C.608 B.S. L.607 J.D. Mag. J.
Pridham, Herbert H. '29 '55 C.980 B.A. L.930 LL.B. [Roth,B.R.S.&L.]
Prislipsky, Thomas A. '67 '97 C.980 B.S. L.8 J.D. [Reminger&R.]
Puhalla, Leo J., (CV) '70 '96 C.980 B.A. L.8 J.D. [Newman,O.&K.]
Rafidi, Joseph F., The Law Office of '53 '00 C.980 A.B. L.1187 J.D.
3627 South Avenue
Rafoth, Carl D., (BV) '40 '68 C.150 B.S. L.608 J.D. [Friedman&R.]
Rafoth, James, (BV) '64 '89 C&L.930 B.S., J.D. 108 W. Western Reserve Rd.
Reardon, Timothy M., (BV) '67 '92 C.97 B.A. L.851 J.D. [Nadler N.&B.]
Reed, W. Brooks, (AV) '06 '33 C.935 B.A. L.659 LL.B. 1200 Mahoning Bk.‡
Regenstreich, Myron J., (BV) '19 '51 C.608 B.B.A. L.930 J.D. 1110 Wick Bldg.
Reich, Jerry '29 '55 C&L.608 B.A., J.D. 7120 Harrington Avenue
Reminger & Reminger Co., L.P.A., (AV)
11 Federal Plaza Central, Ste. 300 (⊙Covington, KY; Akron, Cin., Cleve., Columbus, Sandusky, Toledo, OH)

Renner, Kenner, Greive, Bobak, Taylor & Weber, A Legal Professional Association
(See Akron)

Rheuban, Norman A., (BV) '21 '48 C.608 B.A. L.659 LL.B. [Friedman&R.]
Richards, Lawrence H., (BV) '48 '76 C.980 B.S.B.A. L.7 J.D. [L.H.Richards]
Richards, Lawrence H., Co., LPA, (BV) 400 City Centre One
Richardson, Gina Agresta, (CV) '72 '99 C.602 B.A. L.7 J.D. [Manchester,B.P.&U.]
Ridder, Bryan M., (BV) '57 '83 C.604 B.A. L.8 J.D. [B.M.Ridder]
Ridder, Bryan M., Co., LPA, (BV) 107 S. Champion Street
Ridler, Gregory L. '46 '70 C.303 A.B. L.608 J.D.
Pres. & CEO, The Mahoning Natl. Bk.
Roberts, James E. "Ted", (AV) '46 '74 C.980 B.A. L.8 J.D. [Roth,B.R.S.&L.]
Rohde, R. Keller '48 '75 C.610 B.S. L.608 J.D.
Hearing Ofcr., Unemployment Comp. Bd. of Review
Romero, Edwin, (BV) '49 '78 C.150 A.B. L.608 J.D. [Manchester,B.P.&U.]
Rosenblum, Donn D., (BV) '54 '79 C.94 B.S.B.A. L.117 J.D. [Nadler N.&B.]
Rosenthal, Pat Booher '43 '81 C.980 B.A.Ms.Ed. L.1003 J.D.
Northeast Ohio Legal Servs.
Ross, Ronald J. '35 '65 C.381 B.S. L.8 J.D. The Cafaro Co.
Rossi, Daniel L., (AV) '27 '52 C.980 L.607 J.D. [Rossi&R.]
Rossi, E. Jeffrey '53 '78 C&L.128 B.A., J.D. E.J. Rossi & Co.
Rossi, Gregg A., (BV) '65 '90 C.602 B.A. L.930 J.D. [Rossi&R.]
Rossi & Rossi, (AV) 802-804 Mahoning Bk. Bldg.
Rotar, Daniel R. '57 '90 C.119 B.S. L.8 J.D. 1310 Barbie Dr.
Roth, Daniel B., (AV) '29 '56 C.473 B.S. L.930 J.D. [Roth,B.R.S.&L.]

Roth, Blair, Roberts, Strasfeld & Lodge, L.P.A., (AV)
100 Federal Plaza East, Suite 600, 44503-1508
Telephone: 330-744-5211 Fax: 330-744-3184
URL: http://www.roth-blair.com
Oscar A. Stephens (1888-1975); Benjamin F. Roth (1894-1978); Daniel B. Roth; Richard B. Blair; James E. "Ted" Roberts; Stuart A. Strasfeld; Thomas J. Lodge; David S. Barbee; Christopher P. Lacich; Scott R. DeBonis; Joseph C. Bishara;—David M. Moore; John Nicholas Zomoida, Jr. Of Counsel: Herbert H. Pridham; Glenn J. Schwartz (Co., L.P.A.).
General Civil Practice in all State and Federal Courts, Banking, Commercial, Corporate, Partnership, and General Business Law, Education Law, Employee Benefits and ESOP's, Estate Planning and Administration, Family Law, Employment Law, Management and Labor Relations, Insurance Defense, Mergers and Acquisitions, Pension, Profit Sharing and Retirement Plans, Personal Injury, Probate, Product Liability, Commercial, Industrial and Residential Real Estate, School Law, Securities, Trials, Venture Capital, Workers Compensation.
See Professional Biographies, YOUNGSTOWN, OHIO

Rummell, Randall W., (BV) '58 '83 C.381 B.S. L.608 J.D. [Boyd,R.&C.]
Sabine, J. David '42 '67 C.97 B.A. L.477 J.D. Sr. V.P. & Sr. Tr. Offr., Sky Trust N.A.
Sakmar, Michael A. '62 '92 C.980 B.A. L.989 J.D. 4410 Market Street
Sands, Morton H. '22 '59 C.205 A.B. L.980 LL.B. 1310 Fox Run‡
Savage, John T. '70 '01 C.980 B.A. L.8 J.D. [Manchester,B.P.&U.]
Schafer, Kenneth C., (AV) '07 '32 C.477 A.B. L.150 LL.B. 1200 Mahoning Bk.‡
Schiavone, Christopher J. '74 '01 C.980 B.S.A.S. L.607 J.D. [Friedman&R.]
Schiavone, Leonard D., (BV) '52 '77 C.679 B.S. L.150 J.D. [Friedman&R.]
Schiavoni, Joseph, (BV) '20 '46 C&L.608 B.A., J.D. [Schiavoni,S.&B.]
Schiavoni, Louis, (BV) '56 '83 C.608 B.A. L.1187 J.D. [Schiavoni,S.&B.]
Schiavoni, Schiavoni & Bush Co., L.P.A., (BV) 87 Westchester Dr.
Schiraldi, Richard J. '54 '81 C.980 B.A. L.7 J.D. Cohen & Co., CPA's
Schoenike, Jonathan K., (BV) '60 '91 C.958 B.S. L.8 J.D.
Gen. Coun., Amer. Architectural Products Corp.
Schor, Neil D., (BV) '63 '89 C.477 A.B. L.608 J.D. [Harrington,H.&M.]
Schwartz, Glenn J., (Co., L.P.A.), (BV) '49 '74
C.473 B.A. L.608 J.D. [Roth,B.R.S.&L.]
Schwartz, Richard N. '47 '72 C.608 B.A. L.61 J.D.
1570 S Canfield Niles Rd., Ste B101
Sebastiano, Patrick A., (BV) '57 '82 C.980 B.S.B.A. L.851 J.D. [Newman,O.&K.]
Seely, Donald R. '34 '65 C.980 A.B. L.8 LL.B. 8166 Market St.
Shagrin, Steven S., (CV) '56 '81 C.472 B.B.A. L.930 J.D. 4657 Logangate Road
Shells, Lori L., (BV) '63 '91 C.7 B.S. L.8 J.D. Asst. Co. Pros.
Shultz, John F., (BV) '51 '76 C.980 B.A. L.117 J.D. 4822 Market St., Ste. 220
Siciliano, Anthony, (CV) '64 '89 C.980 B.A. L.1003 J.D. [J.B.Fleck&Assoc.]
Sinclair, R. Allen, (BV) '63 '91 C.999 B.S. L.1187 J.D. 11 Overhill Rd.
Sisek, James H. '46 '74 C.930 A.B. L.1003 J.D. Butler Wick Trust Co.
Skolnick, Jay M., (AV) '41 '67 C.1365 A.B. L.150 J.D. [Nadler N.&B.]
Skoufatos, Nikitas, (BV) '55 '88 C.980 B.A. L.607 J.D. [Wellman,J.H.]
Slavens, Kathleen M., (CV) '64 '92
C.980 B.A. L.7 J.D. 755 Boardman Canfield Road, Suite P-4
Slipski, Ronald E., (BV) '53 '79 C.980 B.A. L.7 J.D. [Green H.S.]
Smith, Beth A., (BV) '56 '83 C.608 B.S. L.607 J.D. J., Div. of Domestic Rels.
Smith, Edward F., (BV) '62 '88 C.910 A.B. L.930 J.D. [Nadler N.&B.]
Smith, Gregory S. '78 '03 C.610 B.A. L.608 J.D. [Manchester,B.P.&U.]
Smith, Wade W., Jr., (BV) '51 '82 C.980 B.S. L.7 J.D. P.O. Box 3965
Sobnosky, Edward N. '23 '55 C&L.980 A.B., J.D. 34 Federal Plz., W.
Sowinski, Edward A., Jr. '33 '64 C.665 B.B.A. L.7 J.D. 950 Windham Ct.‡
Sperling, Adam L., (CV) '66 '92 C.473 B.A. L.228 J.D. [Anzellotti,S.P.&S.]
Sperling, Victor, (BV) '35 '60 C.980 B.A. L.930 J.D. [Anzellotti,S.P.&S.]
Springer, Lawrence R., (AV) '36 '61 C.970 B.A. L.477 J.D. [Comstock,S.&W.]
Stanos, Steve P. '26 '58 C.610 B.Sc. L.980 J.D. 20 W. Boardman St.‡
Stebelton, Richard A. '35 '59 C.980 B.A. L.608 LL.B.
Pres., Commonwealth Land Title Agency, Inc.
Steen, Jon R. '55 '82 C.980 B.A. L.1003 J.D. 5437 Mahoning Avenue, Suite 21
Stefanski, D. Kim, (BV) '54 '79 C&L.150 B.A., J.D. [Stefanski&Assoc.] ⊙

Stefanski & Associates LLC, (BV)
5437 Mahoning Avenue, Suite 22, 44515 ⊙
Telephone: 330-792-6220 Fax: 330-792-6250
Email: kstefanski@stefanski-law.com URL: http://www.stefanski-law.com
Member: D. Kim Stefanski. Associates: Eric J. Ohanian; R. Mark Gottfried; Janice T. O'Halloran.
Contract and Business Law, Insurance, Labor and Employment, Workers' Compensation, Civil Litigation, Trials and Appeals.
Cleveland, Ohio Office: 1144 Rockefeller Building. 613 West Superior Avenue. 44113. Telephone: 216-348-2800. Fax: 216-348-1557.
See Professional Biographies, YOUNGSTOWN, OHIO

Stein, Harold, (AV) '17 '39 C&L.608 J.D. 34 Federal Plaza W.‡
Stein, Marc S., (BV) '50 '75 C.597 B.A. L.930 J.D. [Nadler N.&B.]
Steiskal, A. Robert, (BV) '40 '70 C.980 A.B. L.607 J.D. 4431 Mahoning Ave.
Stephens, Jerry O., (AV) '28 '52 C.207 B.A. L.607 J.D. 1100 Bank 1 Bldg.‡
Stephens, Mary Jane, (BV) '41 '83 C.980 B.S. L.7 J.D. 7330 Market Street
Stevens, Paul E., (AV) '16 '41 C&L.608 J.D. [P.E.Stevens]
Stevens, Paul E., (Co., L.P.A.), (AV) 960 Boardman Canfield Rd., Ste. 6
Strasfeld, Stuart A., (AV) '52 '77 C.473 A.B. L.930 J.D. [Roth,B.R.S.&L.]
Sturgeon, Edward Francis '52 '79 C.980 B.S. L.607 J.D. 4822 Market Street
Suhar, Andrew W., (BV) '64 '92 C.381 B.A. L.8 J.D. P.O. Box 1497
Sweeney, John W. '31 '53 C.262 A.B. L.564 J.D. 810 Southwestern Run
Tarasuck, Raymond M., Jr., (CV) '65 '95 C.318 B.A. L.08 J.D. P.O. Box 3965
Tareshawty, Brian Julius, (CV) '63 '90 C.980 B.S. L.930 J.D. 4410 Market Street
Theofilos, Gus K. '50 '77 C.679 B.A. L.851 J.D. 910 Metropolitan Twr.
Thomas, Griffith V. '22 '57 C&L.980 B.A., J.D. 3897 Nottingham Ave.‡
Thomas, Richard J., (AV) '56 '85 C.980 B.S. L.665 J.D. [Henderson,C.M.N.&T.] ⊙
Thornton, E. Carroll, Jr., (AV) '46 '71 C.610 B.B.A. L.150 J.D. [Newman,O.&K.]
Tiberio, Michael A., (BV) '65 '93 C.276 B.S. L.8 J.D. [Wellman,J.H.]

Tipping Co., L.P.A. A Legal Professional Association
(See Akron)

Tomlinson, Kimberly A. '60 '94 C&L.8 B.A., J.D. Sky Trust, N.A.

Toot, Douglas M.
(See Canfield)

Tucker, Don E., (AV) '28 '56 C.58 A.B. L.976 LL.B. 1775 Logan Ave.
Tumbri, John A. '20 '54 C&L.980 B.A., J.D. 219 W. Boardman St.
Tzagournis, George '36 '60 C.608 B.S. L.607 J.D. 26 Market St., Ste. 508
Uhrain, Paul J. '24 '58 C.980 B.S. L.1003 LL.B. 2595 Spitler Rd.
Van Brocklin, Gary L. '47 '75 C.980 B.A. L.8 J.D. 44 Federal Plz. Central, Ste. 200A
Vaporis, John '31 '60 C.665 A.B. L.178 LL.B. 304 Legal Arts Center
Varner, Donald J. '31 '57 C.759 L.607 J.D. Home Svgs. & Loan Co.
Vitullo, James A. '56 '82 C.980 B.S. L.8 J.D. 5232 Nashua Dr.
Vouros, Joseph E., (BV) '— '50 C&L.980 B.S., J.D. [Brennan,F.V.&Y.]
Vukovich, Joseph J., (BV) '45 '73 C.980 B.A. L.7 J.D. Ct. of App. J.
Waite, Cheryl Lynne '59 '85 C.980 B.A. L.1003 J.D. Asst. Law Dir.
Walling, Michael I., (BV) '41 '65 C.207 B.A. L.477 LL.B. 2439 Jennifer Dr.
Weber, Susan M. '53 '89 C.446 B.S.N. L.1017 J.D. [Davis&Y.]
Weimer, William A., (BV) '46 '75 C.980 A.B. L.7 J.D. B.J. Alan Co.

Weiner, Keith D., & Associates Co., L.P.A.
(See Cleveland)

Wellman, Jeren, Hackett Co. LPA, (AV) 4990 Mahoning Ave.
Wenger, Alan D., (BV) '52 '77 C.1124 B.A. L.930 J.D. [Harrington,H.&M.] (⊙Salem)
Wexler, Ilan, (BV) '55 '80 C.608 B.S. L.910 J.D. [Anzellotti,S.P.&S.]
White, George L., IV, (BV) '67 '96 C.1071 B.S. L.336 J.D. [Henderson,C.M.N.&T.]
White, Richard N., (BV) '51 '76 C.97 B.A. L.607 J.D. 755 Boardman-Canfield Rd.

White, Martin F., Co., L.P.A.
(See Warren)

Wigley, Charles J., III '53 '78 C.980 A.B. L.7 J.D. 2451 Bainbridge St.
Wilkes, Larry D., (BV) '— '84 C.980 A.B. L.607 J.D. [Davis&Y.]

Williams, Sennett & Scully Co., L.P.A.
(See Twinsburg)

Wilson, Thomas J., (AV) '50 '76 C.884 A.B. L.851 J.D. [Comstock,S.&W.]
Wolfcale, Arthur D., Jr. '29 '54 C.980 A.B. L.930 LL.B.
Sr. V.P., & Gen. Coun., DeBartolo Property Group
Woodman, George B., (AV) '23 '47 C.970 B.A. L.477 LL.B. 1310 Fifth Avenue
Woods, Kay, (AV) '52 '81 C.97 B.S. L.608 J.D. U.S. Bkrptcy. J.

Yarwood, Ronald D., (BV) .... '68 '97 C.999 B.S. L.862 J.D. [Brennan,F.V.&Y.]
Young, Joseph R., Jr., (BV) .... '57 '82 C.597 B.A. L.228 J.D. [Manchester,B.P.&U.]
Young, Maurice A. .... '14 '36 C.930 L.608 J.D. Pres., Young Steel Products Co.
Yourstowsky, Ronald J. .... '65 '91 C.980 B.A. L.989 J.D. Asst. Coun., Cafaro Co., The
Yurchison, Michael .... '18 '56 C&L.980 B.A., J.D. 1460 Alissa Pl.
Zahar, Deborah A. '53 '87
C.363 B.A. L.597 J.D. Asst. Gen. Coun., DeBartolo Property Group
Zamary, Gary, (BV) .... '57 '83 C.980 B.S.B.A. L.7 J.D. P.O. Box 3965
Zena, Thomas E., (BV) '47 '72
C.980 B.A. L.930 J.D. 1032 Boardman-Canfield Road, Suite 101
Zlotnick, Julius A., (AV) .... '17 '48 C.608 L.607 J.D. 3941 Lockwood Blvd.‡
Zomoida, John Nicholas, Jr. .... '74 '00 C.980 B.A. L.989 J.D. [Ⓐ Roth,B.R.S.&L.]

ZANESVILLE, * 25,586, *Muskingum Co.*

Arnold, John J. .... '28 '75 C.705 A.B. L.117 J.D. Prof., Ohio Univ.‡
Baker, Herbert W., Jr., (CV) .... '51 '76 C.178 A.B. L.607 J.D. P.O. Box 400
Baldwin, Steven R., (BV) .... '58 '83 C.97 B.S. L.201 J.D. [Micheli,B.N.]
Beam, J. Robert, (AV) .... '36 '60 C&L.607 B.A., J.D. [Gottlieb,J.B.&D.P.]
Beam, Jeff Robert, (CV) .... '57 '82 C&L.607 B.A., J.D. [Gottlieb,J.B.&D.P.]
Bopeley, Thomas R., (AV) .... '33 '58 C.165 A.B. L.608 LL.B. [Ⓒ Micheli,B.N.]
Borowitz, Paul J., (BV) .... '37 '65 C&L.608 B.S., LL.B. 27 N. 5th St.
Brown, James P., (CV) .... '58 '84 C&L.607 B.A., J.D. [Cultice&B.]
Brown, Susan Cultice, (BV) .... '53 '83 C.473 B.A. L.607 J.D. [Cultice&B.]
Bryan, Michael Thomas .... '75 '01 C.608 B.S. L.117 J.D. [Ⓐ Stubbins,W.&E.]
Buck, Steven E., (CV) .... '51 '75 C&L.608 B.A., J.D. Mag., Juv. Ct.
Burkhart, Francis H. .... '21 '52 C.610 L.266 J.D. Ret. Com. Pleas, Prob. & Juv. Ct. J.

Calig & Handelman, LPA
(See Columbus)

Chess, Walter K., Jr., (BV) .... '50 '75 C.945 B.S. L.608 J.D. Asst. Pros. Atty.
Coffman, Ward D., III, (BV) .... '53 '78 C.97 B.A. L.607 J.D. [Coffman]

Coffman Law Offices, (BV)
604 Main Street, P.O. Box 159, 43702-0159
Telephone: 740-454-1010 Fax: 740-454-1181
Email: info@coffmanlaw.com URL: http://www.coffmanlaw.com
Ward D. Coffman, III.
Banking, Business, Business Formations, Estate Planning, Wills, Probate, Real Estate and Title Insurance Law.

See Professional Biographies, ZANESVILLE, OHIO

Cultice, Peter N., (BV) .... '58 '83 C.1365 B.A. L.607 J.D. [Cultice&B.]

Cultice & Brown, (BV)
121 North Fourth Street, P.O. Box 490, 43702-0490
Telephone: 740-453-0888 Telecopier: 740-453-0277
Email: cultice_brown@rrohio.com URL: http://www.culticebrown.com
C. Alfred Zinn (1903-1977); R. Donald Cultice (1922-1998); Susan Cultice Brown; Peter N. Cultice; James P. Brown.
Business, Business Formation, Partnerships, Limited Liability Companies, Banking, Bankruptcy, Creditors Rights, Health Care, Hospital, Elder Law, Estate Planning, Probate, Estate and Trust, Administration, Taxation, Employment and Labor, Real Estate, Title Insurance, Construction Law, Employee Benefits, Discrimination, Wrongful Termination, Natural Resources, Environmental, Oil & Gas, Matrimonial and Family Law, Divorce, Child Custody, Child Support, Personal Injury, Wrongful Death, Automobile Accidents, Insurance Defense and General Civil Litigation.

See Professional Biographies, ZANESVILLE, OHIO

Cultice-Brown, Susan Clawson .... '53 '83 C.473 B.A. L.607 J.D. 121 N. Fourth St.
Dal Ponte, Don A., (BV) .... '47 '73 C.973 B.S. L.602 J.D. [Gottlieb,J.B.&D.P.]

Denmead Law Office
(See Columbus)

Dick, Trafford, (CV) .... '57 '83 C.532 B.A. L.930 J.D. 205 E. Military Rd.
Dickman, James L. .... '33 '65 C&L.608 B.S., J.D. 604 Main Street
Eickelberger, Scott D., (BV) .... '66 '91 C.473 B.A. L.200 J.D. [Kincaid,T.&G.]
Erhard, Gerald A., Jr., (BV) .... '46 '79 C.446 B.A. L.117 J.D. [Stubbins,W.&E.]
Fitz, Todd B., (CV) .... '61 '96 C.528 B.A. L.117 J.D. 2429 Linden Ave.
Fleegle, Mark C., (BV) .... '53 '79 C.97 B.S. L.607 J.D. Com. Pleas Ct. J.
Fries, Miles D., (BV) .... '53 '78 C.102 B.A. L.607 J.D. [Gottlieb,J.B.&D.P.]
Gerstner, Cole J., (BV) .... '57 '82 C.607 B.A. L.851 J.D. [Gottlieb,J.B.&D.P.]
Geyer, R. William, (AV) .... '31 '55 C.532 B.A. L.607 J.D. [Kincaid,T.&G.]
Gormley, Joseph A. .... '40 '65 C&L.608 B.A., J.D. Prob. and Juv. Ct. J.

Gottlieb, Johnston, Beam & Dal Ponte, P.L.L., (AV)
320 Main Street, P.O. Box 190, 43702-0190
Telephone: 740-452-7555 Fax: 740-452-2257
Email: gjbd@zanesvillelaw.com URL: http://www.zanesvillelaw.com
Ross L. Johnston (Retired). Members of Firm: J. Robert Beam; Don A. Dal Ponte; Miles D. Fries; James R. Krischak; Jeff Robert Beam; Donald A. Wietmarschen; Philip S. Phillips; Cole J. Gerstner; Mark E. Kaido. Of Counsel: Wayne W. Phillips, II. Associates: Susan J. Montgomery McDonald; Aaron B. Phillips.
General Civil and Criminal Trial and Appellate Practice. Corporate, Taxation, Real Estate, Personal Injury, Family, Estate Planning, Probate, Insurance, Products Liability, Hospital and Bankruptcy Law.

See Professional Biographies, ZANESVILLE, OHIO

Graham, Clay P., (BV) .... '55 '80 C.207 B.A. L.608 J.D. 2900 West Dr. d.
Gullifer, Amy Elizabeth .... '76 '01 C.161 B.A. L.608 J.D. Southeastern Ohio Legal Servs.
Haddox, D. Michael, (CV) .... '57 '82 C.532 B.A. L.607 J.D. Pros. Atty.
Hillis, Scott T., (CV) .... '64 '89 C.62 B.A. L.124 J.D. [Hillis&S.]
Hillis & Small, (CV) .... 825 Adair Avenue
Hooper, Jeffrey A. .... '49 '74 C.473 A.B. L.902 J.D. Co. J.
Johnston, Ross L. .... '15 '43 C&L.608 B.A., J.D. [Gottlieb,J.B.&D.P.]

Joseph, William D. .... '44 '69 C.602 B.S. L.150 J.D. 1105 Maple Ave.
Kaido, Mark E., (CV) .... '61 '91 C.473 B.A. L.117 J.D. [Gottlieb,J.B.&D.P.]

Kincaid, Taylor & Geyer, (AV) BR
50 North Fourth Street, P.O. Box 1030, 43702-1030
Telephone: 740-454-2591 Telecopier: 740-454-6975
Email: ktglaw@kincaidlaw.com URL: http://www.kincaidlaw.com
J. Donald Kincaid (1908-2001). Members of Firm: R. William Geyer; William J. Taylor; Scott D. Eickelberger; David J. Tarbert. Associate: Gerald J. Tiberio, Jr.
Business, Banks and Banking, Health Care, Estate Planning, Estate Administration, Real Estate, Title Insurance, Environmental, Oil and Gas, Civil Litigation, Domestic Relations, Family Law, Construction, General Civil and Criminal Trial and Appellate Practice.
Attorneys for: American Electric Power Company; Century National Bank; Genesis Healthcare Company; Guernsey-Muskingum Electric Coop.; Haliburton Services; The Oxford Oil Co.; McDonalds of Zanesville; Muskingum College.
Reference: Century National Bank.

See Professional Biographies, ZANESVILLE, OHIO

Krischak, James R., (BV) .... '51 '77 C.608 B.Sc. L.117 J.D. [Gottlieb,J.B.&D.P.]
LaAsmar, Ronald G., (BV) .... '44 '69 C.610 B.A. L.608 J.D. 27 N. 5th Street
Levion, Leon L. .... '28 '52 C&L.145 B.A., J.D. 36 N. 4th Street, Suite 408
Magaziner, Blair L., (BV) .... '52 '77 C.674 A.B. L.472 J.D. 44 S. 6th St., Ste. 1
Marczewski, Mitchell Christopher .... '61 '01 C.610 B.S.S. L.117 J.D. [Marczewski]
Marczewski Law Offices .... 2994 Maple Avenue
Martin, Eric D. .... '69 '95 C.610 B.A. L.8 J.D. 27 N. Fifth St.
Massey, Jefferson H. .... '45 '75 C.608 B.S.,M.A. L.7 J.D. 30 S. 4th St.
McDonald, Susan J. Montgomery '73 '02 C.532 B.A. L.179 J.D.
[Ⓐ Gottlieb,J.B.&D.P.]
McLendon, Jeremy M. .... '77 '02 C&L.607 B.A., J.D. [Ⓐ Micheli,B.N.]
Micheli, Frank J., (AV) .... '29 '53 C.363 L.607 J.D. [Micheli,B.N.]
Micheli, Michael J., (AV) .... '55 '80 C.97 B.A. L.607 J.D. [Micheli,B.N.]

Micheli, Baldwin, Northrup, LLP, (AV) BR
3808 James Court, Suite 2, P.O. Box 788, 43702-0788
Telephone: 740-454-2545 Fax: 740-454-6372 URL: http://www.zanesvilleattorneys.com
URL: http://www.lawyers.com/mb&nc
Frank J. Micheli; Michael J. Micheli; James C. Micheli (1956-1992); Steven R. Baldwin; Michael A. Northrup;—Jeremy M. McLendon; David E. Mortimer. Of Counsel: Thomas R. Bopeley.
Civil Trial Practice in State and Federal Courts. Insurance Defense, Medical Malpractice, Family and Domestic Relations, Probate and Estate Planning, Railroad, Business Law, Oil and Gas, Corporation and Commercial Law. Appellate Practice. Accident Claims, Workers Compensation, Contracts, Real Estate, Title Insurance.
Representative Clients: Bank One Cambridge, N.A.; Consolidated Rail Corp.; Medical Protective Co.; Nationwide Insurance Cos.; Continental Insurance Cos.; Motorists Mutual Insurance Co.; Frontier Insurance Co.; S.E.O. Title Agency, Ltd.
Reference: Mutual Federal Savings Bank

See Professional Biographies, ZANESVILLE, OHIO

Miller, Ray G. .... '28 '54 C.347 B.S. L.1119 J.D. Ret. Com. Pleas J.‡
Mills, Thomas M. .... '49 '82 C.174 B.A. L.150 J.D. 1105 Maple Avenue
Moorehead, D. Anderson .... '48 '78 C.610 B.B.A. L.117 J.D. 58 North 5th Street
Mortimer, David E. .... '76 '02 C&L.607 B.A., J.D. [Ⓐ Micheli,B.N.]
Northrup, Michael A., (BV) .... '54 '79 C.608 B.A. L.117 J.D. [Micheli,B.N.]
Pattison, Jeff Arthur .... '73 '98 C&L.607 B.S.Ph., J.D. 45 N. 4th St.
Payne, Thomas, (BV) .... '28 '52 C.532 L.607 J.D. Co. J.
Pembroke, John '55 '82
C.604 B.A. L.608 J.D. South Eastern Ohio Legal Services Program
Phillips, Aaron B. .... '75 '00 C.1053 B.S.B.A. L.607 J.D. [Ⓐ Gottlieb,J.B.&D.P.]
Phillips, Philip S., (BV) .... '48 '75 C.482 A.B. L.608 J.D. [Gottlieb,J.B.&D.P.]
Phillips, Wayne W., II, (BV) .... '45 '72 C&L.607 B.A., J.D. [Ⓒ Gottlieb,J.B.&D.P.]

Plymale Partnership LLP, The
(See Columbus)

Randles, Steven G. .... '63 '89 C.532 B.A. L.930 J.D. Century Natl. Bk.
Ryan, Sherry L., (CV) .... '49 '74 C.967 B.A. L.607 J.D. 309 Main St.
Sanford, Larry Lee, Jr. .... '69 '00 C.608 B.A. L.117 J.D. Ohio Bureau of Workers Comp.
Small, Susan Ellen .... '48 '96 C.610 B.S.N. L.608 J.D. [Hillis&S.]

Standley Law Group LLP
(See Dublin)

Stubbins, Brent A., (AV) .... '52 '78 C.385 B.A. L.608 J.D. [Stubbins,W.&E.]
Stubbins, James B., (BV) .... '18 '43 C&L.608 B.Sc., J.D. [Ⓒ Stubbins,W.&E.]
Stubbins, Mark W., (BV) .... '57 '83 C.473 B.S. L.150 J.D. [Stubbins,W.&E.]
Stubbins, Watson & Erhard Co., (AV) .... 59 North 4th Street
Tabatowski, Thomas L. '50 '85 C.912 B.A. L.213 J.D.
(adm. in IN; not adm. in OH) 5175 Hampton Ct.‡
Tarbert, David J., (BV) .... '68 '93 C.532 B.S. L.608 J.D. [Kincaid,T.&G.]
Tarbert, Molly L., (BV) .... '68 '93 C.518 B.A. L.608 J.D. 45 N. 4th St.
Taylor, William J., (AV) .... '47 '73 C&L.608 B.A., J.D. [Kincaid,T.&G.]
Tiberio, Gerald J., Jr. .... '78 '04 C.201 B.S. L.8 J.D. [Ⓐ Kincaid,T.&G.]
Tompkins, Thomas J. .... '59 '85 C.607 B.A. L.608 J.D. Mag., Ct. of Common Pleas

Twyford & Donahey, P.L.L.
(See Columbus)

Van Horn, Kevin, (BV) .... '60 '85 C.532 B.S. L.117 J.D. 715 Adair Avenue
Vinsel, Jay F. .... '55 '83 C.532 B.S. L.117 J.D. Co. J., Miscanium Co. Ct.
Watson, Mark A., (BV) .... '58 '83 C.608 B.A. L.150 J.D. [Stubbins,W.&E.]
Wietmarschen, Donald A., (BV) ..... '54 '81 C.737 B.A. L.607 J.D. [Gottlieb,J.B.&D.P.]
Wolfe, W. Allen .... '42 '71 C.434 B.A. L.8 J.D. Com. Pleas J.‡
Workman, James E., Jr., (BV) .... '48 '78 C.610 B.B.A. L.608 J.D. P.O. Box 3462
Zellar, Crystal I., (CV) .... '61 '87 C.608 B.S. L.117 J.D. 720 Market St.
Zwelling, Howard S. .... '36 '62 C.532 B.A. L.607 J.D. Com. Pleas J.

[illegible]
Kahn, Mark [illegible]
[illegible]
Telephone [illegible]
[illegible]

Zanwood, Ronald B. [illegible]
Young, Joseph [illegible]
Young, [illegible]
[illegible]
Zinn, Deborah [illegible]
[illegible]

ZANESVILLE [illegible]

[illegible]

OKLAHOMA

CAPITAL: OKLAHOMA CITY

Oklahoma Bar Association
1901 N. Lincoln Boulevard
P.O. Box 53036
Oklahoma City, Oklahoma 73152-3036
Telephone: 405-416-7000
Fax: 405-416-7001

Index of Towns and Cities Listed by County

*Indicates County Seat

Adair County
Proctor
* Stilwell

Alfalfa County
* Cherokee

Atoka County
* Atoka

Beaver County
* Beaver

Beckham County
Elk City
Erick
* Sayre

Blaine County
Hydro
Okeene
* Watonga

Bryan County
Caddo
Calera
* Durant

Caddo County
* Anadarko
Carnegie
Hinton
Hydro

Canadian County
* El Reno
Mustang
Okarche
Oklahoma City
Piedmont
Yukon

Carter County
* Ardmore
Healdton

Cherokee County
Cookson
Moodys
* Tahlequah
Welling

Choctaw County
* Hugo

Cimarron County
* Boise City

Cleveland County
Moore
Noble
* Norman
Oklahoma City

Coal County
* Coalgate

Comanche County
Fort Sill
Indiahoma
* Lawton

Cotton County
* Walters

Craig County
Ketchum
* Vinita

Creek County
Bristow
Drumright
Mannford
* Sapulpa

Custer County
* Arapaho
Clinton
Thomas
Weatherford

Delaware County
Grove
* Jay

Dewey County
* Taloga

Ellis County
* Arnett
Shattuck

Garfield County
Drummond
* Enid

Garvin County
Lindsay
Maysville
* Pauls Valley
Stratford
Wynnewood

Grady County
Blanchard
* Chickasha
Minco
Rush Springs

Grant County
* Medford

Greer County
* Mangum

Harmon County
* Hollis

Harper County
* Buffalo
Laverne

Haskell County
* Stigler

Hughes County
* Holdenville

Jackson County
* Altus

Jefferson County
* Waurika

Johnston County
* Tishomingo

Kay County
Blackwell
* Newkirk
Ponca City
Tonkawa

Kingfisher County
Cashion
Hennessey
* Kingfisher
Okarche

Kiowa County
* Hobart
Mountain View
Snyder

Latimer County
* Wilburton

Le Flore County
Heavener
* Poteau
Spiro
Talihina

Lincoln County
* Chandler
Prague
Stroud
Wellston

Logan County
Cashion
Crescent
* Guthrie

Love County
Burneyville
* Marietta
Overbrook

Major County
* Fairview

Marshall County
Lebanon
* Madill

Mayes County
Langley
* Pryor
Salina

McClain County
Blanchard
Newcastle
* Purcell
Washington

McCurtain County
Broken Bow
* Idabel
Watson

McIntosh County
Checotah
* Eufaula

Murray County
Davis
* Sulphur

Muskogee County
Fort Gibson
* Muskogee

Noble County
* Perry

Nowata County
* Nowata

Okfuskee County
* Okemah
Weleetka

Oklahoma County
Arcadia
Bethany
Choctaw
Del City
Edmond
Harrah
Jones
Luther
Midwest City
Newalla
Nichols Hills
* Oklahoma City
Spencer
Warr Acres

Okmulgee County
Beggs
Henryetta
* Okmulgee

Osage County
Fairfax
* Pawhuska
Sand Springs
Skiatook
Tulsa

Ottawa County
Afton
* Miami

Pawnee County
Cleveland
Mannford
* Pawnee

Payne County
Cushing
Drumright
Glencoe
Perkins
* Stillwater
Yale

Pittsburg County
Haileyville
Hartshorne
* McAlester

Pontotoc County
* Ada

Pottawatomie County
Maud
McLoud
Oklahoma City
* Shawnee
Tecumseh

Pushmataha County
* Antlers

Roger Mills County
* Cheyenne

Rogers County
Catoosa
Chelsea
* Claremore
Inola

Seminole County
Seminole
* Wewoka

Sequoyah County
Gore
* Sallisaw
Vian

Stephens County
Comanche
* Duncan
Marlow

Texas County
* Guymon
Hooker

Tillman County
* Frederick

Tulsa County
Bixby
Broken Arrow
Collinsville
Jenks
Mannford
Owasso
Sand Springs
Skiatook
Sperry
* Tulsa

Wagoner County
Bixby
Catoosa
Coweta
* Wagoner

Washington County
* Bartlesville
Ochelata

Washita County
* Cordell
Dill City

Woods County
* Alva

Woodward County
Mooreland
* Woodward

*Indicates County Seat

ADA, * 15,691, *Pontotoc Co.*

Armstrong, James L. .... '21 '49 C&L.623 B.S., LL.B. P.O. Box 27‡

Atkins & Markoff
(See Oklahoma City)

Austin, H. Leo, (BV) .... '47 '74 C.619 B.A. L.623 J.D. 2021 Arlington Blvd.
Baulch, Terry Alvin .... '50 '95 C.621 B.A. L.623 J.D. 127 E. 6th

Bennett, Bob E., (AV) '30 '58 C.618 B.S. L.623 J.D.
402 American Building, P.O. Box 1631, 74821-1631
Telephone: 580-332-5311 Fax: 580-332-5351
General Civil Practice in all State and Federal Courts. Estate Planning, Trusts, Estates, Wills, Banking, Real Estates, Probate, Oil and Gas, Corporate, Health Law, Negligence, and Family Law.
References: First National Bank & Trust Co.; Oklahoma State Bank.
See Professional Biographies, ADA, OKLAHOMA

Braly, George W., (AV) .... '48 '74 C.103 B.A. L.623 J.D. [Braly&B.&C.]

Braly & Braly and Coyne, (AV)
A Partnership of Professional Corporations
201 West 14th Street, P.O. Box 2739, 74820
Telephone: 580-436-0871 Fax: 580-436-0889
George W. Braly; Dania Deschamps-Braly; H. Buckmaster Coyne, Jr.
General Civil Trial Practice in all State and Federal Courts. Personal Injury, Products Liability, Medical Malpractice, Plaintiff and Defense, Commercial, Banking, Oil and Gas, Securities, Water Rights Law, Commercial and Real Estate, Trusts and Estate Planning.
Reference: First National Bank of Coalgate, Oklahoma.
See Professional Biographies, ADA, OKLAHOMA

Burkhart, Barry G., (BV) ....'65 '91 C.618 B.S. L.623 J.D. 120 South Broadway
Cheadle, Robert Martin ....'46 '92 C.618 B.A. L.623 J.D. [Cheadle&G.]
Cheadle & Gustitus ....520 East Arlington
Cook, Wm. Bailey, III, (CV) .... '61 '89 C.618 B.S. L.612 J.D. 121 S. Broadway
Corbin, Laura J., (CV) '72 '96 C.618 B.S. L.616 J.D.
[Smith,S.S.C.&W.] (⊙Tishomingo)
Coyne, H. Buckmaster, Jr., (BV) .... '45 '74 C.198 B.A. L.575 J.D. [Braly&B.&C.]
Davison, Denver N., (AV) .... '43 '68 C&L.623 B.B.A., J.D. [Deaton,D.&K.]
Deaton, Austin R., Jr., (AV) .... '26 '51 C.618 L.623 LL.B. [Deaton,D.&K.]

Deaton, Davison & Kessinger, A Professional Corporation, (AV) [BB]
300 South Rennie, P.O. Box 1219, 74820
Telephone: 580-332-1752 Fax: 580-332-0827
Austin R. Deaton, Jr.; Denver N. Davison; C. Steven Kessinger.
General Civil Practice in all State and Federal Courts. Trials. Corporation, Insurance, Real Estate, Probate, Indian Affairs, Medical Legal, Oil and Gas Law and Domestic Relations.
See Professional Biographies, ADA, OKLAHOMA

Deschamps-Braly, Dania, (BV) .... '43 '79 C.472 B.A. L.623 J.D. [Braly&B.&C.]
Files, Alvin D., (BV) .... '51 '75 C&L.623 B.A., J.D. City Atty., City Atty. Off.
Gray, Robert W., Attorney at Law, (CV) ... '60 '89 C.618 B.A. L.616 J.D. 211 W. 13th St.
Green, Jesse D. .... '52 '77 C.618 B.A. L.623 J.D. 301 E. Main Street
Gustitus, Darlene J. '46 '80 C.352 B.S. L.1136 J.D.
(adm. in CA; not adm. in OK) [Cheadle&G.]
Hall, E. Harold, (BV) .... '27 '58 C.999 L.616 LL.B. 630 E. 17th
Hammond, Heather Lin ....'72 '00 C.618 B.S. L.615 J.D. [H.L.Hammond]
Hammond, Heather L., Attorney at Law ....1729 Wingedfoot Dr.
Herman, Charlotte A., (Mrs.) '— '53 C.298 L.861 J.D.
(adm. in LA; not adm. in OK) P.O. Box 2086‡
Huntsman, Kristine Franke .... '— '96 C.586 B.S. L.802 J.D. [Huntsman]
Huntsman, Mitch ....'69 '97 C.560 B.A. L.802 J.D. [Huntsman]
Huntsman Law Firm, P.L.L.C. .... P.O. Box 1968
Jaques, Frank H., (AV) .... '34 '58 C&L.623 B.A., LL.B. 118 S. Broadway
Jaques, Robert H., II, (CV) ....'62 '87 C&L.623 B.A., J.D. 2004 N. Broadway

Johnson, Kenneth R., (AV) '40 '65 C&L.623 B.B.A., J.D.
George B. Thompson Building, 331 South Rennie, P.O. Box 1690, 74820
Telephone: 580-332-2558 Fax: 580-332-2777
URL: http://www.lawyers.com/kennethrjohnson
Associate: Kirk E. Johnson.
General Civil Practice in all State and Federal Courts. Corporation, Insurance, Probate, Commercial, Indian Affairs, Family, Real Estate and Oil and Gas Law.
Reference: First National Bank and Trust Company of Ada, Ada, Oklahoma.
See Professional Biographies, ADA, OKLAHOMA

Johnson, Kirk E., (CV) ....'72 '98 C&L.623 B.B.A., J.D. [A K.R.Johnson]
Kemp, Jim ....'63 '88 C.618 B.S. L.616 J.D. Mun. Ct. J.
Kessinger, C. Steven, (BV) .... '64 '89 C.618 B.S. L.623 J.D. [Deaton,D.&K.]
Kilgore, Martha K. .... '54 '82 C.962 B.S. L.623 J.D. Assoc. Dist. J.
Loman, Lori Lynn, (BV) .... '61 '95 C.618 B.S. L.623 J.D. [L.L.Loman]
Loman, Lori L., P.C., (BV) ....108 East 12th Street
Lowry, Denzil F., Jr., (AV) ....'48 '79 C&L.623 B.S.E.E., J.D. 206 W. 12th St.
Mayhue, Charles D., (BV) .... '42 '70 C&L.623 B.S., J.D. 114 South Broadway
Mayhue, G. C., Jr., (AV) .... '21 '49 C&L.623 LL.B. 114 South Broadway
Mayhue, John Bruce ....'55 '83 C.1315 B.S. L.623 J.D. 600 W. 9th
Miller, John D. ....'53 '81 C.82 A.B. L.623 J.D. Spec. Dist. J.
Morris, Bryan W., (CV) ....'65 '92 C.612 B.A. L.623 J.D. [Taylor&M.]
Morris, David L. ....'53 '83 C.618 B.S. L.616 J.D. 8446 State Highway 19
Newmaster, T. Walter, (BV) '47 '73 C.707 B.A. L.623 J.D.
Suite 304 American Building
Peterson, Dean, (Ms.), (BV) '46 '78
C.623 B.A. L.616 J.D. Prof., E. Central OK State Univ.
Peterson, William N., (BV) ....'43 '75 C.623 B.B.A. L.616 J.D. Dist. Atty.
Remer, Kursten G. .... '59 '88 C.375 B.S. L.623 J.D. 222 E. 12th St.
Ross, Chris, (BV) .... '57 '82 C&L.623 B.B.A., J.D. Asst. Dist. Atty.
Saunders, Gregory E., (BV) .... '45 '75 C.618 B.A. L.616 J.D. 17th & Mississippi
Saunders, Kyle J. .... '61 '89 C.618 B.A. L.623 J.D. P.O. Box 1605
Scrivner, James R., (AV) .... '44 '70 C&L.623 B.B.A., J.D. [Smith,S.S.C.&W.]
Shew, D. Craig, (AV) .... '40 '84 C.303 B.A. L.623 J.D. [Smith,S.S.C.&W.]
Shew, Nancy M., (BV) ....'43 '81 C.45 M.A. L.623 J.D. 1st Asst. Dist. Atty.
Smith, Michael G., (AV) .... '42 '67 C.378 B.S. L.623 J.D. [Smith,S.S.C.&W.]
Smith, Shew, Scrivner, Corbin & Watts, P.C., (AV)
120 East 14th Street (⊙Oklahoma City, Tishomingo)

Speed, William Wayne, (CV) '67 '92 C.612 B.S. L.228 J.D.
314 South Broadway, Suite 211, 74820
Mailing Address: P.O. Box 878, Ada, OK 74821
Telephone: 580-436-9090 Fax: 580-436-9066
Email: wspeed@cableone.net URL: http://www.lawyers.com/speed
Insurance Defense, Personal Injury, Civil Litigation, Wills. Trusts and Estates, Family Law.
Representative Clients: EMC Insurance Companies; Oklahoma Farm Bureau Mutual Insurance Company; Quad J Acoustic & Drywell, Inc.; Joe Brown Company.
See Professional Biographies, ADA, OKLAHOMA

Stout, Frank, (BV) .... '63 '88 C.618 B.S. L.616 J.D. 115 N. Bway.
Taylor, Gregory S., (BV) ....'48 '74 C.859 B.A. L.623 J.D. [Taylor&M.]

Taylor and Morris, P.C., (BV)
117 South Broadway, P.O. Box 1737, 74821
Telephone: 580-332-7717 Fax: 580-332-7752
Email: tmlaw@cableone.net
Gregory S. Taylor; Bryan W. Morris.
Probate, Trusts and Estate Planning, Real Estate, Commercial, Corporate, Oil and Gas, Bankruptcy, Divorce, Workers' Compensation, Personal Injury and Civil Litigation in all State and Federal Courts.
See Professional Biographies, ADA, OKLAHOMA

Ward, W. B. (Barney), Jr., (BV) ....'27 '52 C.618 B.A. L.623 LL.B. Amer. Bldg.
Younger, Leslie B., (BV) ..... '20 '53 C.612 B.S.I.E. L.623 LL.B. 531 S Country Club Rd

AFTON, 1,118, *Ottawa Co.*

Cavin, John H. ....'31 '58 C&L.862 A.B., LL.B. Dep. Chf. Coun., Douglas Aircraft Co.
Crutchfield, David L., (BV) ....'48 '79 C.840 B.A. L.862 J.D. 56558 E. Hwy. 125

ALTUS, * 21,447, *Jackson Co.*

Atkins & Markoff
(See Oklahoma City)

Baker, Boyd .... '27 '59 C.612 B.S. L.623 J.D. 301 E. Commerce
Bellamy, Thomas P., (CV) ...... '44 '77 C.617 B.A. L.616 J.D. 3000 N. Main St., Ste. 500
Braddock, David B., (AV) ....'57 '82 C&L.623 B.A., J.D. [C Latham,N.&Assoc.]
Coke, Catherine J., (BV) .... '50 '75 C.616 B.A. L.623 J.D. City Atty.
Coke, Mark T., (AV) ....'50 '75 C.622 B.A. L.623 J.D. [M.T.Coke]

Coke, Mark T., (AV)
205 West Cypress, P.O. Box 652, 73522
Telephone: 580-482-5474 Fax: 580-482-8405
Email: mtcoke@swbell.net
Robert B. Harbison (1906-1983); Mark T. Coke.
General Civil Practice in all State and Federal Courts. Corporation, Insurance, Probate, Estate Planning, Oil and Gas, Real Property and Municipal Law.
Counsel for: National Bank of Commerce, Altus, Okla.; Farm Credit Bank of Wichita; Town of Olustee; Republic Gypsum Company.
See Professional Biographies, ALTUS, OKLAHOMA

Darby, Ken M., (BV) .... '52 '90 C.622 B.S. L.623 J.D. 115 N. Hudson
Darby, Richard B. .... '58 '84 C.622 B.A. L.623 J.D. Dist. J.
Deaver, Danny Ray, (BV) .... '44 '77 C.612 B.S. L.616 J.D. 1st Asst. Dist. Atty.
Dresback, Glen Lloyd ....'68 '96 C&L.623 B.A., J.D. Dist. Atty. Ofc.
Duffy, Michael K., (BV) ....'64 '89 C.612 B.S. L.623 J.D. [Duffy&W.]
Duffy & Wray, (BV) .... 501 North Hudson Street
Gunkel, Renee Walker, (BV) .... '62 '87 C.612 B.S. L.623 J.D. P.O. Box 1124
Hall, Rafe Robert, (BV) ....'68 '95 C.612 B.A. L.615 J.D. 115 N. Hudson St.
Haynie, Timothy C. .... '58 '83 C.623 B.B.A. L.616 J.D. 222 W. Cypress
Horton, Charles P. .... '49 '77 C.623 B.B.A. L.616 J.D. [Horton&Assoc.] ⊙

Horton & Associates
216 West Commerce Street, 73521 ⊙
Telephone: 580-482-3355 Facsimile: 580-482-0363 URL: http:www.//chorton@pacer.com
Email: chorton@pacer.com URL: http://www.lawyers.com/altuslaw
Charles P. Horton.
General Civil Practice, Trusts, Probate, Estate Planning, Personal Injury, Real Estate, Business, Divorce, Interstate Custody, Military, Municipal, Public Finance and Aviation Law.
Magnum Office: 122 North Oklahoma Ave., 73554. Telephone: 580-782-3348. Fax: 580-782-2836.
See Professional Biographies, ALTUS, OKLAHOMA

Huey, Clark E. .... '60 '85 C.622 B.S. L.326 J.D. Dist. J.
Kuhnell, Ludolf R., III '32 '64 C.586 B.A. L.802 L.L.B.
(adm. in TX; not adm. in OK) 2909 Shiloh Lane‡
Latham, Darrell E., (BV) ....'57 '85 C.622 B.A. L.623 J.D. [Latham,N.&Assoc.]
Latham, Nelson & Associates, PLLC, (BV) .... 1000 N. Main
Lederer, Robert D., (BV) '39 '75
C.225 B.S. L.616 J.D. Mgn. Atty., Legal Aid of Western Okla., Inc.
Leverett, Brad D., (BV) ....'59 '85 C.612 B.A. L.623 J.D. Asst. Dist. Atty.
McMahan, Daniel E., (BV) ....'57 '83 C.612 B.S. L.623 J.D. 501 MainSt.
McMahan, Robert Allen, (BV) ....'51 '91 C.612 B.S. L.623 J.D. [R.McMahan]
McMahan, Robert, Attorney at Law, (BV) ....217 W. Commerce St.
Mollison, C. Suzanne ....'43 '74 C&L.623 B.A., J.D. Spec. Dist. J.
Moore, James R., Jr., (BV) ...... '48 '73 C.622 B.S. L.623 J.D. 909 Falcon Rd. (⊙Hollis)
Nelson, Phillip L., (BV) .... '61 '86 C.612 B.S. L.623 J.D. [Latham,N.&Assoc.]
Oden, W. T. (Tal), Jr., (AV) ....'29 '52 C&L.623 B.A., J.D. [T.Oden]

Oden, Tal, Law Office, (AV)
209 North Hudson Street, P.O. Box 1130, 73522
Telephone: 580-482-3456 Facsimile: 580-482-2945 Toll Free: 1-800-503-2063
Email: taloden@swbell.net
T. M. Robinson (1875-1960); Waldo T. Oden (1895-1980); W. T. (Tal) Oden, Jr.
Real Estate, Business, Probate, Estate Planning, General Practice.

Olson, J. Phillip, (BV) .... '49 '86 C.623 B.B.A. L.616 J.D. [J.P.Olson]
Olson, John Phillip, (BV) .... 115 N. Hudson
Roberts, Kelly Tice, (BV) .... '56 '89 C.639 B.S. L.862 J.D. Asst. Dist. Atty.
Warren, Rena Jacobsma, (BV) .... '47 '87 C.1300 B.A. L.623 J.D. 1st Asst. Dist. Atty.
Widmann, Jonathan P. '69 '95 C.112 B.A. L.1049 J.D.
(adm. in CA; not adm. in OK) Air Force Leg. Servc. Agncy, Central Cir.
Wilcox, Ben H., (BV) ....'65 '93 C.612 B.S. L.615 J.D. 2801 N. Main
Wray, B. Christopher, III, (BV) .... '56 '89 C.623 B.B.A. L.616 J.D. [Duffy&W.]

ALVA, * 5,288, *Woods Co.*

Bays, Larry L., (BV) .... '43 '70 C.620 B.A. L.623 J.D. 522 Flynn Ave.
Benson, Donald L., (AV) ....'33 '61 C&L.623 B.B.A., J.D. [Benson]
Benson Law Firm, (AV) .... 615 Barnes Avenue
Bittle, Ronald W., (CV) ....'42 '86 C.663 B.A. L.623 J.D. 410 4th St.
Downer, Richard R., (AV) .... '25 '49 C&L.623 LL.B. 425 Myers Dr.‡
Hadwiger, Kyle B., (BV) .... '60 '86 C.612 B.S. L.862 J.D. [Hadwiger,J.&K.] ⊙
Hadwiger, Mickey J., (BV) .... '60 '86 C.612 B.S. L.900 J.D. 2016 S. 11th St.
Hadwiger, Jungman & Kline, P.L.L.C., (BV) ....521 Barnes Avenue (⊙Cherokee)
Hardaway, Roger D. '49 '79 C&L.836 B.S., J.D.
(adm. in NM; not adm. in OK) 1800 Oklahoma Blvd.‡
Jungman, Marcus A. .... '74 '01 C.620 B.A. L.623 J.D. [Hadwiger,J.&K.]
Kline, Jesse D. .... '76 '01 C.620 B.A. L.623 J.D. [Hadwiger,J.&K.]
Linder, Ray Dean ....'35 '60 C.622 B.A. L.623 LL.B. Chief Dist. J.
Mitchel, Michael W., (AV) '48 '73
C.620 B.S. L.623 J.D. [Mitchel,G.R.&R.] (⊙Woodward)
Mitchel, Gaston, Riffel & Riffel, P.L.L.C., (AV)
907 Oklahoma Blvd. (⊙Enid, Fairview, Woodward)
Prigmore, Nancy L., (BV) .... '47 '85 C&L.623 B.A., J.D. P.O. Box 491
Ritter, Westline Helen Mae .... '68 '96 C.972 B.S. L.623 J.D. [A E.E.Sutter&Assoc.]
Smith, Herbert D., (AV) ....'26 '58 C&L.623 B.S.Ch.E., LL.B. 411 Barnes Ave.
Sutter, Edward E., (BV) .... '50 '75 C.612 B.S. L.616 J.D. [E.E.Sutter&Assoc.]
Sutter, Edward E., & Associates, (BV) .... 401 College

ANADARKO, * 6,586, *Caddo Co.*

Atkins & Markoff
(See Oklahoma City)

Black, Amos Earl, III .... '43 '69 C.612 B.S. L.862 J.D. [A.E.Black,III]
Black, Amos E., III, Law Office .... 101 W. Broadway
Burns, Tony R., Law Office of, (BV) .... '45 '74 C&L.623 B.B.A., J.D. 129 W. Broadway
Buzbee, John P., (AV) .... '36 '60 C.613 B.A. L.623 LL.B. [Buzbee&U.] ⊙

Buzbee & Upchurch, (AV)
203 West Broadway, P.O. Box 765, 73005 ⊙
Telephone: 405-247-2568 Fax: 405-247-2569
Members of Firm: John P. Buzbee; Virgil L. Upchurch.
General Civil and Criminal Practice. Probate, Trusts. Real Estate, Oil and Gas, Insurance, Personal Injury, Negligence, Corporation Law and Trials.
Representative Clients: Anadarko Bank & Trust Co.; Cyril State Bank, Cyril, Oklahoma; Washita Valley Bank, Fort Cobb, Oklahoma; First Bank, Apache, Oklahoma; Board of Education of Binger, Oklahoma.
Approved Title Attorneys for: American First Title Insurance Co., Southwest Title & Trust Co., both of Oklahoma City.
Hinton, Oklahoma Office: Professional Building, Suite A, 116 West Main, Hinton, Oklahoma 73047. Telephone: 405-542-3990.

See Professional Biographies, ANADARKO, OKLAHOMA

Cagle, Damon Troy ....'69 '99 C.613 B.S.Ed. L.623 J.D. 112 W. Main
Davis, Oliver E. .... '15 '52 L.616 LL.B. P.O. Box 877
Frampton, James H. ....'44 '70 C&L.623 B.S., J.D. 629 Tottingham Rd.★
Gardner, Robert A. ....'56 '81 C&L.966 B.A., J.D. Spec. Dist. J.
Garland, John W., (AV) .... '42 '66 C&L.623 B.B.A., LL.B. [Pain&G.]
Herndon, John E., (BV) .... '54 '88 C.619 B.A. L.862 J.D. 1300 Oxford Way
Hill, Stacy Wyatt ....'65 '92 C.1300 B.B.A. L.615 J.D. Asst. Dist. Atty.
Jackson, Mary Alice G. .... '32 '78 C.914 B.A. L.421 J.D. 109 W. Bway.
Johnson, Patricia L. ....'38 '75 C.617 B.S. L.623 J.D. Bur. of Indian Affairs‡

Johnston & Associates
(See Chickasha)

Kirby, Richard Wayne, (BV) .... '62 '87 C&L.623 B.B.A., J.D. Asst. Dist. Atty.
McFadyen, F. M., (Mrs.) .... '11 '35 C&L.623 P.O. Box 999‡
Morgan, C.W. Bill, (BV) .... '42 '81 C.622 B.S. L.616 J.D. Asst. Dist. Atty.

Pain and Garland, (AV) BR
111 S.W. Second Street, P.O. Box 158, 73005
Telephone: 405-247-3365 Fax: 405-247-7177
Email: jgarland@caddoelectric.net
Members of Firm: Leslie Pain (1913-2005); John W. Garland. Associate: Richard A. Williams.
General Civil Practice, Real Estate, Probate, Trusts, Estate Planning and Trials.
Representative Clients: First State Bank, Anadarko, Okla.; Caddo Electric Cooperative, Binger, Okla.; Town of Cement, Okla.; Community Bank; Federal Land Bank of Wichita; City of Anadarko, Okla.

See Professional Biographies, ANADARKO, OKLAHOMA

Powell, David E. .... '44 '80 C.999 B.C.A. L.616 J.D. Assoc. Dist. J.
Reiss, Evelyn Ann, (BV) .... '48 '85 C.1300 B.S. L.616 J.D. [E.A.Reiss]
Reiss, Evelyn Ann, P.C., (BV) ....516 East Central
Stephens, David A. ....'55 '87 C.612 B.S. L.623 J.D. 110 West Main St.
Upchurch, Virgil L., (AV) ....'30 '59 C&L.623 B.A., LL.B. [Buzbee&U.] ⊙
Williams, Richard A., (BV) ....'46 '76 C.622 B.S. L.616 J.D. [A Pain&G.]
Zynda, Thomas R., (BV) ....'51 '76 C&L.623 B.B.A., J.D. 101 W. Broadway

ANTLERS, * 2,524, *Pushmataha Co.*

Blan, Kenneth R. .... '39 '78 C.612 B.S. L.356 J.D. Rt. 1, Box 9080‡
Branam, James T., (BV) ....'50 '75 C.618 B.A. L.623 J.D. [Dennis&B.]
Burgess, Lowell R., Jr. .... '47 '76 C.612 B.A. L.862 J.D. Assoc. Dist. J.
Dennis, Gerald C., (BV) .... '47 '75 C.621 B.S. L.616 J.D. [Dennis&B.]
Dennis & Branam, (BV) ....115 W. Main St.
Grant, Larry, (BV) ....'43 '78 C.618 B.A. L.623 J.D. Dist. Atty.
Huffman, Sean Kent .... '73 '99 C.612 B.S. L.623 J.D. [A Dennis&B.]
Perrin, Jackie Jo .... '64 '02 C.621 B.S. L.615 J.D. [Stamper&P.]

Reasor, Shannon, Law Offices of
(See Atoka)

Sniegiecki, Stephen P., (CV) .... '52 '86 C.455 B.A. L.862 J.D. 336 W. Main

Stamper & Perrin, PLLC
112 North High Street, P.O. Box 100, 74523
Telephone: 580-298-3153; 580-298-3332 Fax: 580-298-3263
Email: jackieperrin@sbcglobal.net URL: http://www.stamperperrin.com
Members of Firm: Joe Stamper (1914-2004); Jackie Jo Perrin.
General and Trial Practice, Personal Injury. Commercial. Probate and Real Estate Law. Banking. Family Law. Health Law, Labor, Employment and Civil Rights Law.
Representative Clients: Town of Antlers; U. S. F. & G. Co; Oasis Telecom; Indian Springs Water Company.

See Professional Biographies, ANTLERS, OKLAHOMA

ARAPAHO, * 802, *Custer Co.*

Duncan, Jacqueline Phelps ....'52 '78 C.620 B.A. L.623 J.D. Spec. Dist. J.
McPhearson, Ricky A., (BV) '63 '91
C.622 B.S. L.623 J.D. ADA Custer Co. Dist. Atty. Off.

Meacham & Meacham, A Professional Corporation
(See Clinton)

Smith, Dennis A., (BV) .... '54 '87 C.620 B.S. L.616 J.D. Asst. Dist. Atty.
Weedon, Jill Carpenter, (BV) .... '67 '92 C.170 B.A. L.623 J.D. P.O. Box 180

ARCADIA, 320, *Oklahoma Co.*

Cravens, Yvonne .... '30 '59 C.804 B.S. L.623 LL.B. 9601 E. Danforth
Croom, John A. ....'23 '49 C&L.623 J.D. P.O. Box 418‡
Howard, John C., (AV) .... '42 '69 C.623 B.A. L.616 J.D. [Howard&H.] ⊙
Howard, Scarlett A., (BV) ....'66 '91 C&L.623 B.A., J.D. [Howard&H.] ⊙
Howard & Howard, (AV) .... P.O. Box 299 (⊙El Reno)

ARDMORE, * 23,711, *Carter Co.*

Andrews, Joe Scott .... '64 '94 C.612 B.S. L.615 J.D. 1601 Red Oak Dr.

Atkins & Markoff
(See Oklahoma City)

Austin, Julie J. ....'77 '02 C.612 B.A. L.623 J.D. [A Fischl C.M.C.B.&L.]
Bachman, Tammy Jo, (CV) .... '68 '93 C.60 B.A. L.623 J.D. 20 B. St. SW, Ste. 202
Bahner, S. Brent, (AV) ....'57 '82 C.69 B.B.A. L.623 J.D. [Fischl C.M.C.B.&L.]
Baldwin, Thomas K., Law Office of, (BV) ....'62 '94 C&L.623 B.A., J.D. 405 W. Main
Bolles, R. Brad, (AV) .... '65 '90 C&L.623 B.A., J.D. [R.B.Bolles]

Bolles, R. Brad, P.C., (AV)
107 West Main, 73401
Telephone: 580-226-5700 Fax: 580-226-5774
Email: rbb_atty@sbcglobal.net URL: http://www.lawyers.com/rbradbolles

(This Listing Continued)

Bolles, R. Brad, P.C. (Continued)
R. Brad Bolles.
Plaintiff's Personal Injury Law and General Civil Trial Practice.

See Professional Biographies, ARDMORE, OKLAHOMA

Burns, Glen C., (AV) .... '45 '74 C.622 B.A. L.616 J.D. [Thompson,C.V.&B.]
Card, Lee ....'50 '75 C&L.623 B.A., J.D. Assoc. Dist. J.
Carlock, Thomas R. ....'45 '70 C.934 B.A. L.862 J.D. 215 Stanley‡
Cawley, Michael A., (AV) .... '47 '72 C&L.623 B.A., J.D. [◙ Thompson,C.V.&B.]
Chaffin, Donald J., (AV) ....'52 '77 C.612 B.A. L.623 J.D. [Fischl C.M.C.B.&L.]
Clark, Cheri, (CV) .... '47 '81 C.618 B.A. L.623 J.D. [J.A.Clark]
Clark, James A., (AV) .... '41 '67 C.623 B.B.A. L.616 J.D. [J.A.Clark]
Clark, James A., Law Offices, (AV) .... 130 B Street, S.W.
Colbert, John R., (CV) .... '65 '90 C&L.623 B.S., J.D. [Colbert&C.]
Colbert, Mark H., (BV) ....'57 '83 C.502 B.A. L.616 J.D. [Colbert&C.]

Colbert & Colbert, (BV)
200 Stanley, P.O. Box 2169, 73402
Telephone: 580-226-1911 Facsimile: 580-226-1907
Email: colbertlaw@aol.com URL: http://www.lawyers.com/colbertlaw
Mark H. Colbert; John R. Colbert.
General Practice, Civil Trial Practice, Personal Injury, Workers' Compensation.

See Professional Biographies, ARDMORE, OKLAHOMA

Collins, L. Fred, (BV) ....'52 '78 C.621 B.A. L.615 J.D. [L.F.Collins]
Collins, Lorenzo T., (BV) ....'57 '82 C&L.623 B.B.A., J.D. [Collins&C.]
Collins, T. Fred, (AV) ....'23 '48 C&L.623 B.S., J.D. [Collins&C.]

Collins & Collins, Inc., (AV)
Collins Building, 16 Stanley, P.O. Box 1781, 73402-1781
Telephone: 580-223-8350 Fax: 580-223-0810
Email: ltcollin@swbell.net
T. Fred Collins; Lorenzo T. Collins.
General Civil and Trial Practice in all State and Federal Courts, Real Estate, Commercial, Municipal, Probate, Trusts and Estate Planning, Bankruptcy, Corporation, Banking and Domestic Relations Law.

See Professional Biographies, ARDMORE, OKLAHOMA

Collins, L. Fred, P.C., (BV) .... 11 N. Washington
Cooper, Heather, Law Office of ....'74 '00 C.621 B.A. L.623 J.D. 29 B. Street S.W.
Dale, Frank Rodolf, (BV) '55 '80
C.170 B.A. L.862 J.D. Gen. Coun., Keith F. Walker Oil & Gas Co.
Dolman, James B., (AV) ....'38 '62 C&L.623 B.S., J.D. [Dolman]

Dolman Law Offices, (AV)
10 W. Main, 503 Colston Building, P.O. Box 1388, 73402-1388
Telephone: 580-223-3619 Fax: 580-223-6415
Email: southok@prodigy.net
Members of Firm: James L. Dolman (1905-1999); James B. Dolman.
General Civil Practice. Trust and Estates, Taxation, Real Estate, Farm, Ranch, Corporate, Oil and Gas and Banking Law.

See Professional Biographies, ARDMORE, OKLAHOMA

Dyer, Martin E., (AV) ....'28 '54 C&L.623 B.S., LL.B. 507 Colston Bldg.
English, James I., III, Law Office of, (CV) '55 '82
C.612 B.A. L.623 J.D. 5 S. Commerce, Ste. 6
Farabough, Gary W., (BV) ....'48 '74 C.623 B.B.A. L.500 J.D. [Pasley&F.]

Fischl Culp McMillin Chaffin Bahner & Long, LLP, (AV)
100 E Street, S.W., P.O. Box 1766, 73402
Telephone: 580-223-4321 FAX: 580-226-4795
Email: fcmcb@swbell.net
Members of Firm: Louis A. Fischl (1898-1973); Joseph M. Culp (1914-1997); F. Lovell McMillin (Retired); Donald J. Chaffin; S. Brent Bahner; Robert D. Long. Associate: Julie J. Austin.
General Civil Practice in all State and Federal Courts. Trials. Probate, Trusts and Estate Planning, Insurance Defense, Banking, Real Estate, Oil and Gas Law.
Representative Clients: First National Bank and Trust Co. of Ardmore; Allstate Insurance Co.; Chubb Group of Insurance Cos.; Employers Mutual Cos.; Chevron North America Exploration; Mercy Memorial Hospital; Winn-Dixie, Inc.; The Quintin Little Company; L.E. Jones Production Company;.

See Professional Biographies, ARDMORE, OKLAHOMA

Frock, Harry Edward ....'60 '85 C.502 B.A. L.862 J.D. [E.Frock]
Frock, Edward .... 10 W. Main, Ste. 403
Gallagher, W. Scott, (BV) ....'68 '95 C&L.623 B.S., J.D. [Little,L.L.W.C.O.&G.]
Gardner, Bill R. ....'31 '60 C.623 B.B.A. L.616 LL.B. 333 W. Main
George, Woodrow ....'13 '42 C.174 L.623 LL.B. Ret. Dist. J.
Goodin, Patricia Annette ...... '57 '90 C.939 B.A. L.623 J.D. Legal Aid of Western Okla.
Hester, Michael J., (BV) ....'46 '77 C.871 B.S. L.623 J.D. [M.J.Hester]

Hester, Michael J., Inc., (BV)
414 South Commerce, P.O. Box 2148, 73402
Telephone: 580-226-6060 Fax: 580-226-6061
Email: mhesterlaw@aol.com
Michael J. Hester.
General Civil Trial Practice. Corporate, Commercial, Farm, Ranch and Equine Law, Probate, Real Estate, Personal Injury, Wills, Trusts and Estate Planning.

See Professional Biographies, ARDMORE, OKLAHOMA

Hicks, T. Todd ....'68 '95 C.1315 B.S. L.623 J.D. 333 W. Main, Ste. 450

Hisey, D. Michael, (AV) '47 '72 C&L.623 B.A., J.D.
Suite 450 Neustadt Plaza, 333 West Main, P.O. Box 66, 73402
Telephone: 580-226-6270 Fax: 580-226-0571
Email: hiseylaw@cableone.net
Contracts, Adoption (In State and Inter-State), Probate, Real Estate, Trusts and Estates, Estate Planning, Guardianship, Corporate and Commercial.

See Professional Biographies, ARDMORE, OKLAHOMA

Johnson, Gregory L., (BV) ....'60 '85 C.1288 B.A. L.862 J.D. 18 South Washington
Jones, Eric R., (CV) ....'50 '78 C&L.861 B.A., J.D. Lincoln Ctr.
Little, Little, Little, Windel, Coppedge, Oliver & Gallagher, P.L.L.C., (AV)
One West Main (⊙Madill, Tishomingo)
Long, Robert D., (AV) ....'52 '78 C&L.623 B.S., J.D. [Fischl C.M.C.B.&L.]
McGuire, Derril W., (BV) ....'40 '64 C.621 B.S. L.623 LL.B. Colston Bldg.
McMillin, F. Lovell, (AV) .... '— '60 C&L.623 B.B.A., J.D. [Fischl C.M.C.B.&L.] ‡
Mordy, Burke, (AV) ....'30 '54 C&L.623 B.S., LL.B. [Mordy&M.]
Mordy, David G., (AV) ....'59 '85 C&L.623 B.B.A., J.D. [D.G.Mordy]
Mordy, Michael C., (AV) ....'55 '80 C.623 B.B.A. L.616 J.D. [Mordy&M.]

Mordy, David G., P.C., (AV)
333 West Main Street, Suite 450, P.O. Box 486, 73402
Telephone: 508-226-3311 Fax: 508-223-1168
Email: dgmlaw@sbcglobal.net
David G. Mordy.
Civil Litigation, Insurance Defense, Personal Injury, School Law, Municipal Law, Condemnation, Criminal Law.

See Professional Biographies, ARDMORE, OKLAHOMA

Mordy & Mordy, P.C., (AV)
110 West Main Street, P.O. Box 457, 73402
Telephone: 580-223-4384 Facsimile: 580-226-0823
Email: mordylaw@sbcglobal.net
Burke Mordy; Michael C. Mordy.
Civil State and Federal Practice, Corporate, Commercial Litigation, Oil and Gas, Real Estate, Ad Valorem Taxation, Probate and Employment Law.
See Professional Biographies, ARDMORE, OKLAHOMA

Morris, Dennis, (CV) ....'57 '90 C.59 B.A. L.623 J.D. 10 W. Main, Ste. 205
Oliver, Stephen E. ....'68 '99 C.276 B.S.F.S. L.69 J.D. [Little,L.L.W.C.O.&G.]
Otey, John Dubiel, (BV) ....'56 '91 C.623 B.S. L.862 J.D. [Otey]
Otey Law Offices, P.L.L.C., (BV) ....22 "D" SW
Pasley, Ted J., (BV) ....'40 '66 C&L.502 B.A., J.D. [Pasley&F.]
Pasley & Farabough, (BV) ....333 West Main Suite 325
Pitts, Paul E., (BV) ....'54 '81 C&L.623 B.A., J.D. [Ⓒ Thompson,C.V.&B.]
Roberts, Darryl F., (BV) ....'44 '74 C.621 B.S. L.623 J.D. P.O. Box 1568
Shilling, Thomas K., (AV) ....'54 '79 C&L.623 B.B.A., J.D. [Shilling&S.]
Shilling & Shilling, P.C., (AV) ....205 W. Main St.
Taylor, April Deann ....'59 '01 C.621 B.B.A. L.615 J.D. 107 W. Main St.
Thomas, Frank, (BV) ....'24 '50 C&L.623 J.D. 227 Stonewall Rd.

Thompson, Cawley, Veazey & Burns, A Professional Corporation, (AV)
422 Second Avenue N.W., P.O. Box 2460, 73402
Telephone: 580-223-3020 Fax: 580-223-1942
Email: tcvb@swbell.net
James E. Thompson (1915-1999); Samuel J. Veazey; Glen C. Burns. Of Counsel: Michael A. Cawley; Paul E. Pitts.
Oil and Gas, Corporation, Real Estate, Estate Planning, Probate and Banking Law.
Representative Clients: Noble Affiliates, Inc.; Samedan Oil Corp.
See Professional Biographies, ARDMORE, OKLAHOMA

Tipps, Michael D., (CV) '55 '82 C.623 B.S. L.616 J.D.
Member, Tourism & Recr. Comm.
Veazey, Samuel J., (AV) ....'46 '70 C&L.623 B.A., J.D. [Thompson,C.V.&B.]
Veith, Jimmy L., (CV) ....'55 '80 C.612 B.A. L.623 J.D. P.O. Box 607
Walker, Thomas S. ....'45 '74 C.663 B.A. L.623 J.D. Dist. J.
Williams, Charles F. '45 '74 C.623 B.B.A. L.273 J.D.
V.P. & Sr. Tr. Offr., Citizens Bank And Trust Co., Tr. Dept.
Williams, James W., (BV) ....'29 '58 C.446 B.S. L.276 J.D. P.O. Box 1587
Wilson, Robert J. '44 '73 C.846 B.A. L.845 J.D.
(adm. in TX; not adm. in OK) 25 B St., S.W.‡
Worsham, Diane L., Law Office of, (BV) '53 '85 C.621 B.S. L.623 J.D.
29 B Street SW
Worthen, Ronald E., (AV) ....'43 '68 C&L.45 B.S.B.A., J.D. [R.E.Worthen]

Worthen, Ronald E., P.C., (AV)
11 North Washington, P.O. Box 1991, 73402
Telephone: 580-223-3735 Fax: 580-226-2528
Email: ronworthen@yahoo.com
Ronald E. Worthen.
Civil Practice, Criminal Law, Family Law, Divorce, including Custody, Modificating, Personal Injury, Labor Law and Probate Litigation.
See Professional Biographies, ARDMORE, OKLAHOMA

ARNETT, * 547, *Ellis Co.*

Barton, Charley W. ....'32 '62 C.1147 B.A. L.616 LL.B. Assoc. Dist. J.
Brady, Danna Kay Archer, (BVⓉ) ....'48 '75 C.846 B.S. L.616 J.D. P.O. Box 178
Hays, Laurie E., (CV) ....'62 '87 C&L.862 B.S., J.D. P.O. Box 16
Jackson, Joe L. ....'42 '70 C.1012 B.S. L.862 J.D. Assoc. Dist. J.
Word, Marshall, (AV) ....'15 '40 C&L.623 A.B., J.D. 222 S. Jackson‡

ATOKA, * 2,988, *Atoka Co.*

Gabbard, J. Douglas, II ....'52 '78 C&L.623 B.S., J.D. Dist. J.
Matheson, Mark Darin ....'69 '96 C&L.862 B.S.B.A, J.D. [Ⓐ Moore M.&Y.]
Mayfield, Reid K. ....'37 '66 C.621 B.A. L.616 J.D. 516 N. Hickory Rd.
Mayfield, Richard E., (CV) ......'55 '80 C.612 B.S. L.623 D.J.P. 211 E. Court St., Ste. 15
Merriott, Neal, (AV) ....'39 '64 C.612 B.A. L.623 LL.B. 109 Redbud Ln.
Moore, Bill, (AV) ....'30 '56 C.621 B.S. L.623 J.D. [Ⓒ Moore M.&Y.]
Moore Mowdy & Youngblood, (BV) .... 109 South Pennsylvania (⊙Coalgate)
Mowdy, D. Clay, (BV) ....'58 '84 C.612 B.S. L.615 J.D. [Moore M.&Y.] ⊙

Reasor, Shannon, Law Offices of, (BV) '68 '93 C.621 B.A. L.623 J.D.
209 East Court, P.O. Box 393, 74525
Telephone: 580-889-3343 Fax: 580-889-9334
Email: sdreasor@yahoo.com URL: http://www.reasorlaw.com
General Practice, Real Estate, Probate, Estate Planning, Civil Litigation.
See Professional Biographies, ATOKA, OKLAHOMA

Wilson, Christopher J., (CV) ....'64 '89 C.1315 B.S. L.623 J.D. Asst. Dist. Atty.
Witcher, Harold L. ....'29 '54 C.999 L.616 LL.B. HC 80, Box 350
Youngblood, David, (BV) ....'55 '84 C.1143 B.S. L.616 J.D. [Moore M.&Y.]

BARTLESVILLE, * 34,748, *Washington Co.*

Akers, Johnny P., (CV) ....'59 '84 C&L.900 B.A., J.D. City Atty.
Akright, James R. ....'13 '37 C&L.623 A.B., LL.B. 2412 Circle Dr.‡
Ambler, Lewis B., (AV) ....'35 '59 C&L.910 A.B., J.D. [Ambler&C.]
Ambler & Conatser, (AV) ....415 S. Dewey
Anderson, Jeffrey R. ...... '63 '97 C.171 L.623 J.D. Sr. Coun., ConocoPhillips Co. (Pat.)

Atkins & Markoff
(See Oklahoma City)

Baldwin, Eberle A. ....'26 '55 C.763 A.B. L.900 J.D. 5717 S.E. Cornell Dr.‡

Barrow & Grimm, P.C.
(See Tulsa)

Beckert, Sherry Redding '63 '88
C&L.862 B.A., J.D. Staff Atty., Legal Servs. of Eastern Ok., Inc.
Bloomfield, Anne H. '66 '92 C&L.378 B.A., J.D.
(adm. in CO; not adm. in OK) 2107 S.E. Skyline Pl.★

Brewer, Worten, Robinett, (AV)
117 W. 5th Street 500 Professional Building, P.O. Box 1066, 74005-1066 ⊙
Telephone: 918-336-4132 Fax: 918-336-9009
Email: attorney@bwrlawoffice.com
Members of Firm: Chester A. Brewer (1901-2002); Jesse J. Worten (1920-1983); Bruce W. Robinett; Jesse J. Worten, III; David B. King; James M. Elias; P. Scott Buhlinger. Associate: Thomas J. Brown. Of Counsel: John M. Keefer.
General Civil Practice. State and Federal Litigation. Corporate, Banking, Real Estate, Oil and Gas, Probate, Trust and Estate Planning, Family and Employment Law, Personal Injury and Insurance Defense.
Representative Clients: Arvest Bank; First National Bank, Vinita; First National Bank, Bartlesville, Mullendore Cross Bell Ranch; Oklahoma Bar Association Professional Liability Insurance Company; Cylx Engineering and Construction Company; Overlees Woods Lumber Co.; Central States Business Forms; Blue Ribbon Ranch, Inc.; Malone Motors, Inc.; Mark Roberts Motors.

(This Listing Continued)

Brewer, Worten, Robinett (Continued)
Pawhuska, Oklahoma Office: 204 First National Bank Building, 74005. Telephone: 918-287-2200.
See Professional Biographies, BARTLESVILLE, OKLAHOMA

Brown, Thomas J. ....'69 '98 C.305 B.S. L.623 J.D. [Ⓐ Brewer,W.R.]
Buchanan, Kevin D., (BV) ....'59 '84 C.612 B.S. L.862 J.D. [Garrison,B.C.&B.]
Buhlinger, P. Scott, (BV) ....'63 '88 C.1120 B.A. L.378 J.D. [Brewer,W.R.]
Carlson, Alan R., (AV) ....'47 '73 C.612 B.S. L.862 J.D. [Garrison,B.C.&B.]
Clemens, Shelley K.G. ....'70 '96 C.35 B.G.S. L.623 J.D. Co. Dist. Atty. Off.
Conatser, James E., (CV) ....'27 '61 C&L.862 B.S., LL.B. 300 S. Shawnee Ave.
Conatser, Steve, (BV) ....'48 '74 C.862 B.A. L.45 J.D. [Ambler&C.]
Cone, Todd A., (CV) ....'65 '92 C&L.623 B.B.A., J.D. 611 Brookhollow Ct.
Connor, James W., (AV) ....'32 '59 C.711 B.S. L.623 LL.B. [Selby,C.M.&J.]
Cross, Ryan N. ....'— '90 C.612 B.S. L.623 J.D. Coun., ConocoPhillips Co. (Pat.)
Cubbage, T. L., II, (AV) ....'39 '64 C.602 B.B.A. L.623 LL.B. 2325 Windsor Way S.E.
Dalrymple, Elizabeth H. '39 '68 C&L.862 LL.B.
Sr. V.P. & Location Mgr., Arvest Asset Mgmt.
David, Kenneth D. '29 '68 C&L.900 B.B.A., J.D.
(adm. in KS; not adm. in OK) P.O. Box 1234‡
Davis, Glenn E. ....'38 '65 C.529 B.A. L.705 J.D. 117 W. 5th St.
Delapp, Curtis, (BV) ....'66 '91 C&L.623 B.A., J.D. Asst. Dist. Atty.
Dickey, Perry J. '29 '57 C&L.208 B.S.L., LL.B.
(adm. in CO; not adm. in OK) 4407 Bridle Rd.‡
Dollar, Beverly M. '61 '88 C.623 B.S. L.862 J.D.
Chf. Intell. Prop. Counsel, ConocoPhillips Co. (Pat.)
Dreiling, Janice P. ....'44 '80 C.375 B.A. L.862 J.D. Assoc. Dist. J.
Drummond, F. Ford ....'62 '90 C.813 B.A. L.893 J.D. 1200 S. Johnstone Ave.
Durham, Paul H. ....'32 '60 L.862 LL.B. 401 S. Dewey, Reda Bldg.
Elias, James M., (BV) ....'63 '89 C.612 B.S. L.623 J.D. [Brewer,W.R.]
Esser, Frederick Scott, (BV) '52 '77 C.862 B.A. L.623 J.D.
420 S. Johnstone, Room 222
Fish, John M., Jr. .... '37 '63 C&L.623 B.S.M.E., LL.B. 4620 Rolling Meadows Rd. (Pat.)
Fletcher, Bradley G. '64 '91 C&L.101 B.A., J.D.
(adm. in MO; not adm. in OK) 2145 Mountain Rd.‡
Froehlich, Marion R. ....'30 '59 C.691 B.A. L.326 J.D. 1217 Adams Bldg.‡

Garrison, Brown, Carlson & Buchanan, PLLC, (AV) BR
530 Southeast Delaware, P.O. Box 1217, 74003
Telephone: 918-336-2520 Fax: 918-336-7709
Email: gbcbblaw@aol.com URL: http://www.lawyers.com/gbcbb
Alan R. Carlson; Kevin D. Buchanan.
General Civil and Criminal Practice in all State and Federal Courts. Corporation, Taxation, Probate, Oil and Gas, Real Estate, Personal Injury, Products Liability, Negligence, Insurance, Family Law, Estate Planning, Commercial, Bankruptcy and Criminal Law. Trials.
Representative Clients: Phillips Petroleum Co.; Foster Petroleum Corp.; 66 Federal Credit Union; Midwest Pancake Houses, Inc.; Kaw Pancake Houses, Inc.; Major Enterprises, Inc.; Gorman, Inc.; Treco Sales, Inc.
See Professional Biographies, BARTLESVILLE, OKLAHOMA

Griffin, Charles R. ....'30 '54 C&L.336 B.A., LL.B. 1712 S.E. Skyline Dr.‡
Hall, George W., (BV) ....'39 '64 C&L.862 LL.B. P.O. Box 1464‡
Harris, E. Ray, (BV) ....'40 '68 C.619 B.S. L.862 J.D. 401 S.E. Dewey, Ste. 210
Heskett, Jack, (AV) ....'32 '60 C.612 B.S. L.862 J.D. [Heskett&H.]
Heskett, John Franklin, (BV) ....'61 '87 C.612 B.A. L.862 J.D. [Heskett&H.]

Heskett & Heskett, (AV)
501 South Johnstone Avenue, Suite 501, 74003-6610
Telephone: 918-336-1773 Fax: 918-336-3152
Email: hesklaw@cableone.net
Members of Firm: Bill Heskett (1933-1993); Jack Heskett; John Franklin Heskett.
General Civil Practice in all Courts, Estates, Corporate, Securities, Commercial, Municipal, Bonds, International Transactions and Real Estate.
Representative Clients: Osage Federal Bank; First National Bank in Hominy; City of Hominy; City of Barnsdall; City of Shidler; City of Kaw City; Town of Romona; Gabriel Technologies Corp.; Strike Axe Non-Profit Water Co.

Holden, John C., (BV) ....'49 '85 C.846 B.A. L.862 J.D. 403 East 6th Street
Huchteman, Ralph D. ....'46 '72 C.612 B.A. L.623 J.D. 217 S. Choctaw Ave.
Hughes, James H. ....'19 '60 C.623 B.S.M.E. L.273 J.D. 1707 S.E. Skyline Dr.‡
Hunt, D. Lynne ....'47 '85 C.619 B.A. L.623 J.D. P.O. Box 1403
Janer, Thomas, (BV) ....'59 '85 C.1111 B.A. L.623 J.D. [Selby,C.M.&J.]
Jolly, Lynda S. ....'— '86 C.970 B.A. L.862 J.D. Sr. Coun., ConocoPhillips Co.(Pat.)
Jones, Carl W. ....'16 '45 C&L.846 B.A., LL.B. 925 Briarwood Dr.‡
Kane, Mark, (BV) ....'53 '78 C&L.378 B.A., J.D. [Kane,K.K.&R.]
Kane, Richard, (AV) ....'17 '41 C.378 B.A. L.477 J.D. Osage & Adams‡
Kane, Robert M., (BV) ....'42 '67 C.378 B.A. L.623 J.D. [Kane,K.K.&R.]
Kane, Kane, Kane & Roark, (BV) ....Osage & Adams
Keefer, John M. ....'42 '67 C&L.862 B.A., J.D. [Ⓒ Brewer,W.R.]
King, David B., (AV) ....'55 '80 C.934 B.A. L.623 J.D. [Brewer,W.R.]
Kunzweiler, Stephen A. ....'62 '89 C.502 B.S.A. L.862 J.D. Asst. Dist. Atty.
Lacey, Frank M. ....'31 '58 C.025 B.A. L.477 J.D. 1115 S. Dewey‡
Lanning, John G. ....'43 '68 C.378 B.S. L.623 J.D. Dist. J.
Lansdown, Myrna ....'57 '81 C.350 B.A. L.862 J.D. Spec. Dist. J.
Laughlin, James H. ....'27 '53 C.613 L.623 LL.B. 210 S. Keeler‡
Maddux, Jerry M., (AV) ....'41 '66 C&L.623 B.B.A., J.D. [Selby,C.M.&J.]
McGinnis, James W. ....'43 '91 C.377 B.S.B.A. L.862 J.D. 501 S. Johnstone
Mitchell, Richard ....'— '90 L.803 J.D. P.O. Box 784
Musgrave, Chas. R., Jr. ....'17 '42 C&L.623 P.O. Box 519‡
Parker, Paul J. ....'08 '31 C&L.378 B.A., J.D. 1600 Shawnee St.‡
Patterson, Margaret J. ....'33 '74 C&L.972 B.S., J.D. 4812 Brookline Dr.‡
Privitt, Bill R. ....'31 '60 C&L.862 B.S., J.D. 4100 S.E. Adams Rd.
Reynolds, Leslie Reeve ....'46 '83 C.3 M.A. L.101 J.D. [L.R.Reynolds]
Reynolds, Leslie R. ....118 S. Choctaw
Roark, Patrick H., (BV) ....'41 '67 C&L.378 B.S., J.D. [Kane,K.K.&R.]
Robbins, Archie Lew ....'34 '66 C.804 A. B L.862 J.D. 2401 Oakdale (Pat.)
Robinett, Bruce W., (AV) ....'43 '67 C.612 B.S. L.623 LL.B. [Brewer,W.R.]
Roff, Alan L. ....'36 '67 C&L.378 B.A., J.D. 2247 Mountain Dr.
Rowland, Brent ....'63 '89 C&L.862 B.A., J.D. Legal Servs. of Eastern Okla.
Rowland, David P., (BV) ....'48 '74 C&L.802 B.A., J.D. [Rowland&R.]
Rowland, Lloyd A., (AV) ....'18 '41 C&L.477 A.B., J.D. P.O. Box 1436‡
Rowland & Rowland, (BV) ....P.O. Box 1436
Ryan, Dennis J. '53 '83 C.860 B.A. L.734 J.D.
(adm. in TX; not adm. in OK) Phillips Petro. Co.
Sanders, Kristi Kay, Law Office of '57 '96
C.99 B.A. L.615 J.D. 415 S. Dewey Ave., Ste. 302
Schmidt, Barbara ....'48 '82 C.622 B.Ed. L.862 J.D. P.O. Box 259‡
Selby, Charles W., (AV) ....'11 '37 C&L.623 LL.B. [Ⓒ Selby,C.M.&J.]

Selby, Connor, Maddux & Janer, P.L.P., (AV)
416 East Fifth Street, Drawer Z, 74005
Telephone: 918-336-8114 Fax: 918-336-6441
Email: scmj@sbcglobal.net
Of Counsel: Charles W. Selby. Members of Firm: James W. Connor; Jerry M. Maddux; Thomas Janer. Associate: Russell C. Vaclaw.
General Civil Practice, all State and Federal Courts. Probate, Insurance, Negligence, Real Estate, Taxation, Corporate, Estate Planning, Commercial and Oil and Gas Law. Trials, Family Law.
Representative Clients: City of Bartlesville; Plaza Medical Laboratory, Inc.; 66 Federal Credit Union; Superior Welding, Inc.; Bluestem Clinic; The Lyon Foundation; Oakley Pontiac-Buick; Farmland Industries, Inc.

See Professional Biographies, BARTLESVILLE, OKLAHOMA

Serran, Ruben J. ... '43 '81 C.1126 B.A. L.862 J.D. 4630 Barlow Pl.
Stilwell, Betty L. ... '48 '89 C&L.862 B.A., J.D. Sr. Coun., ConocoPhillips Co.
Stocker, Allan H., (AV) ... '26 '51 C.612 L.502 J.D. 715 S.E. Dewey
Vaclaw, Russell C. ... '73 '00 C&L.623 B.A., J.D. [Ⓐ Selby,C.M.&J.]
Welch, Scott H., (BV) ... '62 '89 C&L.101 B.A., J.D. Sr. Coun., ConocoPhillips Co.
Welvaert, Bronwyn ... '— '01 C.383 B.A. L.862 J.D. Coun., ConocoPhillips Co.
Williford, John L. ... '36 '60 C.623 B.A. L.846 J.D. 1500 Cherokee Hills Drive
Wilson, Shirley Carolyn ... '60 '94 C.187 B.A. L.37 J.D. 220 N.W. Virginia
Worten, Jesse J., III, (AV) ... '50 '76 C.612 B.S. L.616 J.D. [Brewer,W.R.] ⊙
Yost, Kenneth R. ... '49 '80 C&L.623 B.S., J.D. 2401 Terrace Drive
Zahn, F. Anthony, (AV) ... '40 '65 C.976 B.A. L.623 LL.M. 4702 Harned Ct.

BEAVER, * 1,570, *Beaver Co.*

Drum, Keith, (AV) ... '16 '40 C&L.623 B.A., LL.B. [Drum&V.] ‡

Drum & Venable, A Professional L.L.C., (AV)
45 West 2nd Street, P.O. Box 340, 73932-0340
Telephone: 580-625-4526 Fax: 580-625-4716
Email: jerryv@ptsi.net URL: http://www.lawyers.com/drumvenable
Keith Drum (Retired); Jerry L. Venable.
General Civil Practice, Probate and Estate Planning, Real Estate, Wills and Trusts; Oil and Gas, Family Law, Trials and Appeals, Commercial and Business Law.
Representative Clients: Ralph E. Barby Estate; H.G. Adams, III Ranch; The Bank of Beaver City; Nichols Water Service, Inc.; Hardberger & Smylie, Inc.; Colorado Interstate Gas Co.

See Professional Biographies, BEAVER, OKLAHOMA

Goetzinger, Robert, (BV) ... '34 '59 C&L.623 B.B.A., J.D. Asst. Dist. Atty.
Kee, Robert J., (AV) ... '49 '75 C&L.623 B.B.A., J.D. [Trippet&K.]
Loepp, Jim, (BV) ... '46 '71 C.612 B.A. L.623 J.D. [J.Loepp]
Loepp, Jim, P.C., Law Office, (BV) ... 409 Douglas
Reddick, Ryan D. ... '71 '97 C.921 B.S. L.623 J.D. Dist. J.
Riffe, Gerald H. ... '46 '76 C.612 B.S. L.862 J.D. Assoc. Dist. J.
Trippet, Richard P., (AV) ... '38 '62 C.16 L.862 LL.B. [Trippet&K.] ⊙
Trippet, Todd ... '64 '99 C.808 B.S. L.623 J.D. [Trippet&K.]
Trippet and Kee, (AV) ... P.O. Box 728 (⊙Hooker)
Venable, Jerry L., (AV) ... '45 '71 C&L.623 B.S., J.D. [Drum&V.]

BEGGS, 1,428, *Okmulgee Co.*

Culbert, Samuel S. ... '47 '84 C.618 B.S. L.623 J.D. 5185 Garfield Road

BETHANY, 20,307, *Oklahoma Co.*

Berry, James W. '47 '73 C&L.352 B.S., J.D.
(adm. in IA; not adm. in OK) 3 Wiley Post Airport‡
Brown, Patsy H. (Pat), (AV) ... '43 '92 C.82 B.A. L.615 J.D. 3810 N. Peniel
Dearman, Ryan Paul ... '75 '00 C.663 B.A. L.623 J.D. 7008 N.W. 63rd St., Ste. 100
Densmore, F. Trent, (BV) ... '43 '69 C.36 B.S. L.623 J.D. [Petty,S.&D.]
Dockum, Bobbye J. ... '45 '88 C.174 B.A. L.623 J.D. Michael L. Loyd & Assocs., Inc.
Dyer, Stephen E., (CV) ... '61 '87 C.621 B.S. L.623 J.D. [Dyer]
Dyer Law Center, P.C., (CV) ... 6632 N.W. 39th Expwy.
Gertson, Richard G. ... '52 '80 C.839 B.A. L.352 J.D. City Mgr.
Hedglon, Mead J., III ... '43 '67 C&L.823 A.B., J.D. [M.Hedglon]
Hedglon, Mead ... 7006 N.W. 63rd St.
Loyd, Michael L., (BV) ... '47 '73 C.82 B.S. L.845 J.D. 3810 N. Peniel
Lyon, Eldon D. ... '31 '65 C.612 B.S.M.E. L.615 J.D. Western Elec. Co.
Macrory, Harry B. ... '23 '50 C.82 A.B. L.616 LL.B. 4704 N. Peniel‡
Malson, Chas. E. ... '30 '56 C&L.623 B.B.A., LL.B. 7400 N.W. 19th St.
McCutchen, Royce C. ... '22 '50 C&L.623 LL.B. 6212 N.W. 31st Terr.‡
Mercer, Libby Anne, Law Office of ... '53 '87 C&L.623 B.A., J.D. P.O. Box 1029
Mills, Timothy Edward ... '63 '03 C.1085 B.S. L.615 J.D. [T.E.Mills]

Mills, Timothy E., P.C.
3910 N. College, Suite A, 73008
Telephone: 405-789-2225 Fax: 405-789-2369
Email: timmillslaw@sbcglobal.net URL: http://www.timmillslaw.com
Timothy Edward Mills.
Labor and Employment, Collections, Family Law, Estate Planning, Real Estate.

See Professional Biographies, BETHANY, OKLAHOMA

Petree, John A., (BV) ... '49 '76 C.612 B.A. L.616 J.D. 6814 N.W. 23rd
Petty, Jack H., (BV) ... '40 '66 C.82 B.S. L.616 J.D. [Petty,S.&D.]
Petty, Shaw and Densmore, (BV) ... 6666 N.W. 39th Expwy.
Pierce, Peter G., III, (AV) '49 '74 C.623 B.A. L.802 J.D.
Exec. V.P. & Gen. Coun., The First Natl. Bk. of Bethany
Porter, John H. ... '23 '59 C&L.616 A.B., LL.B. 7904 N.W., 28 Terrace‡
Posey, James N., (AV) ... '34 '57 C.82 A.B. L.623 J.D. 3807 N. Asbury
Schnorr, Jimmie J. ... '30 '66 C.467 B.S. L.616 J.D. [J.J.Schnorr] ‡
Schnorr, Jimmie J., P.C. ... P.O. Box 1535
Shaw, Larry D., (BV) ... '49 '76 C.82 B.S. L.616 J.D. [Petty,S.&D.]

BIXBY, 13,336, *Tulsa & Wagoner Cos.*

Carone, Kaaren '49 '78 C.1058 B.A. L.800 J.D.
(adm. in CA; not adm. in OK) 6623 E. 117th St.‡
Ferris, James H., (AV) ... '49 '75 C.623 B.A. L.862 J.D. [Moyers,M.S.I.&T.] ⊙
Lapan, Joseph ... '29 '59 C.612 B.S.C.E. L.862 J.D. 113 West Dawes
Mabrey, Scott Purves ... '72 '98 C&L.623 B.A., J.D. 9164 E. 117th Place S.
McDonald, Cary Jean Edwards ... '66 '90 C&L.623 B.A., J.D. 10221 E. 113th St. South

Moyers, Martin, Santee, Imel & Tetrick, L.L.P., (AV)
Formerly Moyers, Martin, Conway, Santee & Imel
113 West Dawes, Suite 100, 74008 ⊙
Telephone: 918-366-3935 Fax: 918-366-3936
Email: info@moyersmartin.com URL: http://www.moyersmartin.com
Jack H. Santee; Steven A. Stecher; James H. Ferris. Of Counsel: Charles B. Tetrick.
Civil Practice, Banks and Banking, Bankruptcy, Business Law, Commercial Law, Construction Law, Contracts, Corporate Law, Education Law, Employee Benefits, Energy, Federal Practice, Insurance, Labor and Employment, Leases and Leasing, Litigation, Mergers, Acquisitions and Divestitures, Natural Resources, Personal Injury, Probate, Real Estate, Taxation, Trusts and Estates.
Tulsa, Oklahoma Office: 1100 Mid-Continent Tower, 401 South Boston Avenue, 74103. Telephone: 918-582-5281.

See Professional Biographies, BIXBY, OKLAHOMA

Santee, Jack H., (AV) ... '31 '56 C&L.623 B.S., LL.B. [Moyers,M.S.I.&T.] ⊙
Shirley, Houston I. ... '46 '75 C.623 B.A. L.862 J.D. [H.Shirley]
Shirley, Houston ... 113 W. Dawes Ave.
Stecher, Steven A., (AV) ... '48 '73 C.623 B.B.A. L.846 J.D. [Moyers,M.S.I.&T.] ⊙
Tetrick, Charles B., (AV) ... '33 '65 C.623 B.B.A. L.862 J.D. [Ⓒ Moyers,M.S.I.&T.] ⊙

BLACKWELL, 7,668, *Kay Co.*

Boersma, Kirk R., (BV) '54 '79 C.612 B.A. L.862 J.D.
111 West Blackwell, P.O. Box 309, 74631
Telephone: 580-363-3323 888-726-4334 Fax: 580-363-3393 URL: http://www.boersmalaw.com
Email: kirk@boersmalaw.com URL: http://www.lawyers.com/boersmalaw
Probate, Real Estate, Trusts and Estates, Wills, Natural Resources, Mortgages, Banking Law, Corporate Law, Business Law, Leases and Leasing, Nonprofit and Charitable Organizations.

See Professional Biographies, BLACKWELL, OKLAHOMA

Denton, David O. ... '45 '72 C.621 B.A. L.862 J.D. 124 S. Main

Ihrig, Jonathan C., & Associates, (AV) '47 '74 C.612 B.S. L.616 J.D.
107 West Blackwell, P.O. Box 389, 74631
Telephone: 580-363-4300 Fax: 580-363-4308
Email: jcilaw@kskc.net URL: http://www.lawyers.com/ihriglaw
General Civil Practice, Trials. Real Estate, Personal Injury, Automobile Accidents, Probate and Estate Planning, Trusts, Public Utility, Banking, Business Litigation, Insurance and Negligence Law, Wrongful Termination, Employment.

See Professional Biographies, BLACKWELL, OKLAHOMA

McClung, Daniel C., (AV) ... '24 '66 C&L.623 B.S., J.D. 417 Bel Aire‡
Menzer, James L., (BV) ... '62 '87 C.612 B.S. L.623 J.D. [Menzer]
Menzer Law Office, (BV) ... 211 W. Blackwell

Rodgers, James R., (AV) '43 '68 C.623 A.B. L.802 J.D. BR
105 North Main, P.O. Box 514, 74631
Telephone: 580-363-3684 Fax: 580-363-2434
Email: attorney@cyber-rover.com URL: http://www.lawyers.com/rodgerslaw
William W. Rodgers (1907-1979).
General Civil Practice. Probate, Estate Planning, Real Estate, School Law, Education, Business Law, Personal Injury, Commercial and Oil and Gas Law. Trials.

See Professional Biographies, BLACKWELL, OKLAHOMA

Rogers, Max E. ... '20 '69 C&L.623 B.S., J.D. 116 N. East St.‡
Shuart, Scott Adam, (BVⓉ) ... '59 '92 C&L.612 B.S., J.D. 206 W. Blackwell
Wiseman, Brian O., (BV) ... '63 '88 C.999 B.S. L.862 J.D. 107 W. Blackwell

BLANCHARD, 2,816, *Grady & McClain Cos.*

Bruce, Richard A. ... '61 '96 C.623 B.A. L.616 J.D. 811 Pine Cir.
Dowers, Camille D., (CV) ... '57 '84 C&L.623 B.A., J.D. 7612 Lakeview Dr.
Melot, John Paul ... '68 '93 C.612 B.S. L.616 J.D. 1019 N. Council, Ste. 3
Richey, Anne W. ... '65 '92 C.612 B.S. L.616 J.D. [Richey]
Richey Law Firm, PLLC ... 219 N.E. 9th St.
Stallings, G. Thorne, Jr., (BV) ... '61 '86 C.608 B.S. L.610 J.D. 510 N. Main Blanchard

BOISE CITY, * 1,509, *Cimarron Co.*

Lathrop, Jerry ... '36 '68 C.612 B.S. L.615 J.D. Asst. Dist. Atty.
Manske, Stanley Ed, (AV) ... '47 '72 C.1270 B.A. L.623 J.D. [Manske]
Manske Law Office, P.C., (AV) ... 10 S.W. Square

BRISTOW, 4,325, *Creek Co.*

Barnett, Dana Jones, (AV) ... '53 '79 C.623 B.S. L.862 J.D. 119 W. 6th Ave., Ste. 200
Foster, Stephen H. '38 '62 C.612 B.S. L.623 LL.B.
Trial Atty., OK Indigent Def. System
Gibson, C.M., (BV) ... '52 '77 C.862 B.S. L.623 J.D. Gen. Coun., SpiritBank, N.A.
Hake, Kelvin (Kelly), (BV) ... '56 '84 C.352 B.A. L.862 J.D. [K.Hake]
Hake, Kelvin, (BV) ... 143 W. 7th St.
Ham, C. Keith, (AV) ... '54 '79 C&L.862 B.A., J.D. [Loeffler A.&H.] ⊙
Ihrig, Mark Andrew, (BV) ... '50 '97 C.612 B.S. L.862 J.D. 200 North Main Street
Jones, Walter Michael, (AV) ... '52 '77 C&L.623 B.B.A., J.D. [Jones]
Jones Law Office, (BV) ... 116 North Elm St.
Jones Law Office, (AV) ... 116 N. Elm St.
Loeffler, Michael S., (BV) ... '63 '88 C&L.623 B.B.A., J.D. [Loeffler A.&H.] ⊙
Loeffler Allen & Ham, (AV) ... 116 W. 6th St. (⊙Sapulpa)
Lyon, Danny Leon ... '49 '97 C.612 B.S. L.615 J.D. P.O. Box 31
McMillan, Harry M., (AV) ... '29 '53 C&L.623 B.S., LL.B. 143 W. 7th Ave.
Souter, M. Alan, (BV) ... '67 '93 C.612 B.S. L.986 J.D. [Jones]
Vassar, Joe Sam, (AV) ... '45 '70 C.337 B.A. L.623 J.D. P.O. Box 354

BROKEN ARROW, 74,859, *Tulsa Co.*

Anderson, Kurt Malcolm ... '62 '87 C&L.623 B.B.A., J.D. P.O. Box 2242
Braly, Mack Muratet, (AV) ... '39 '70 C.623 B.A. L.569 J.D. 4545 S. Midway Rd.‡

Bryant, James D.
(See Tulsa)

Cheek, Caroline Langley ... '39 '88 C.623 B.A. L.862 J.D. 12812 S. 121 E. Ave.
Cook, John Duane, Jr. ... '60 '01 C&L.862 B.S., J.D. [Cook P.]
Cook Law Office, PLLC ... 2220 W. Houston, Suite E
Cotter, David Alan, (BV) ... '48 '80 C.624 B.A. L.365 J.D. [D.A.Cotter]
Cotter, David A., (BV) ... 7832 S. Elm Pl.
Couch, Richard W., (BV) ... '53 '83 C.623 B.B.A. L.862 J.D. P.O. Box 2647
Dyer, Marion M., (Mr.), (BV) ... '33 '65 C.619 B.S. L.862 J.D. 848 W. Commercial St.
Dyer, Marshall K., (BV) ... '59 '89 C.1362 B.S. L.862 J.D. 319 W. Wash.

Edgar & Perigo, P.C.
(See Tulsa)

Eudey, Scott R. ... '73 '98 C.862 B.A. L.802 J.D. 106 N. Main St.
Folsom, James D. ... '44 '99 C.619 B.A. L.862 J.D. 614 S Aspen Ave.
Francy, J. Kenton, (AV) ... '50 '76 C&L.862 B.S., J.D. [Francy] ⊙
Francy Law Firm, (AV) ... 110 South Main Street (⊙Tulsa)
Frieze, H. Delbert, (AV) ... '43 '75 C.623 B.B.A. L.862 J.D. 107 W. Commercial‡
Glick, Yvonne Fisher ... '— '98 C&L.862 B.S.B.A., J.D. 3245
Graham, Scott L. '35 '63
C.273 B.A. L.623 J.D. Chmn. & CEO, The 1st Natl. Bk. & Tr. Co.
Guyton-Wilkening, Elizabeth Anne ... '68 '93 C&L.623 B.A., J.D. Asst. City Atty.
Harper, Franklin M., (BV) ... '53 '80 C.619 B.A. L.862 J.D. 4008 S. Elm Pl.
Hart, Amy K. ... '74 '99 C.862 B.A. L.623 J.D. [Hart]

Hart Law Office
8409 East Lansing Street, P.O. Box 140206, 74014
Telephone: 918-271-1487 Fax: 918-296-3761
Email: amykhart@yahoo.com URL: http://www.tulsaestatelaw.com
Member of Firm: Amy K. Hart.
Estate Planning, Wills, Trusts, Probate, Living and Contested Wills, Power of Attorney, Personal Injury, Automobile and Railroad Accidents, Medical Malpractice, Property Damage, Unsafe Products, Wrongful Death.

See Professional Biographies, BROKEN ARROW, OKLAHOMA

Hartzog, Steven L. '63 '89 C.263 B.A. L.208 J.D.
(adm. in CO; not adm. in OK) [S.Hartzog]
Hartzog, Steven .... 8629 Willow Springs Ct.
Hendren, Scott A., (BV) .... '60 '90 C.612 B.S. L.862 J.D. 11626 E. 64th St.
Mai, Christan P. .... '51 '77 C&L.972 B.A., J.D. 121 W. Commercial St.
Mook, Ronald H., (BV) .... '33 '68 C&L.862 B.S., J.D. 10524 S. 241st East Ave.
Moore, Theodore L., Jr., (BV) .... '43 '81 C.612 B.S. L.862 J.D. [T.L.Moore]
Moore, Ted L., (BV) .... 103 N. Main
Neeley, Pamela Marie, (CV) .... '64 '98 C.619 B.S. L.862 J.D. [Neeley]
Neeley Law Office P.C., (CV) .... 308 N. Aspen Ave., Ste. 108
O'Dell, Donald E. ..... '47 '95 C.1031 B.S. L.862 J.D. Owner, Petrmoax Acquisition Co.‡
Orchard, Susan L. .... '49 '82 C.69 B.A. L.862 J.D. 5816 W. Orlando Circle
Perkins, Vicki, (BV) .... '54 '92 C&L.862 B.S., J.D. P.O. Box 140218
Peterson, Russell D., (BV) .... '51 '77 C.612 B.S. L.846 J.D. 107 W. Commercial St.
Philcox, Carrie M. .... '67 '94 C.910 B.A. L.862 J.D. 2446 S. Umbrella Place
Phillips, George P., (BV) .... '42 '73 C.347 B.S. L.862 J.D. 12713 136th St. S.
Roberts, Jay Samuel .... '24 '57 C.986 L.862 J.D. 1209 S. Walnut Ave.
Ross, Jack W., (BV) .... '44 '69 C&L.623 B.A., J.D. 106 N. Main
Sagely, Dennis Allen .... '73 '99 C.188 B.S. L.623 J.D. 800 A S. 9th
Schmeltz, Andrew H., Jr. .... '43 '68 C.188 A.B. L.659 LL.B. 716 S. Main
Seeber, Vonna Marie .... '60 '97 C.56 B.A. L.602 J.D. 709 N. Dogwood Ave.

Spence Law Office
(See Tulsa)

Stewart, Murray B. .... '31 '55 C&L.623 B.A., J.D. 7308 S. Juniper Avenue
Straub, Bruce G., (BV) .... '54 '82 C.037 B.B.A. L.862 J.D. 614 S. Aspen Ave.
Thompson, Gary E. .... '51 '98 C.377 B.S. L.862 J.D. P.O. Box 550
Vogle, Ted G., (BV) .... '39 '88 C&L.862 B.A., J.D. 2300 W. Twin Oaks Street
Willis, J. R. .... '26 '64 C.623 B.S. L.862 LL.B. 3704 Mimosa Ave.‡
Wilson, Phillip B. '69 '94 C.57 B.A. L.477 J.D.
(adm. in IL; not adm. in OK) V.P. & Gen. Coun., LRI Mgmt. Servs., Inc.
Zeigler, April Y. '71 '97 C.228 A.B. L.260 J.D.
(adm. in FL; not adm. in OK) 1010 W. Kenosha St., Apt. 21

BROKEN BOW, 4,230, *McCurtain Co.*

Craytor, G. Gail .... '32 '73 C.174 B.S. L.208 J.D. 310 Clay St.‡
McClendon, Jim, (AV) .... '45 '70 C&L.623 B.B.A., J.D. [J.McClendon]
McClendon, Jim, - Lawyer, P.C., (AV) .... 117 N. Broadway
Nix, Terry Jay, (CV) .... '58 '88 C.1147 B.B.A. L.616 J.D. Route 1
Pratt, Justin R. .... '72 '97 C.612 B.S. L.623 J.D. [J.Pratt]
Pratt, Justin .... 2100 S. Park Drive
Walters, George, (AV) .... '41 '70 C.612 B.S. L.862 J.D. [G.Walters]
Walters, George, Inc., (AV) .... 700 S. Park
Webb, David A. .... '54 '80 C.383 B.A. L.623 J.D. Dist. Atty.

BUFFALO, * 1,200, *Harper Co.*

Harkins, Jim Neil, (BV) .... '43 '73 C.622 B.A. L.623 J.D. [Holcomb&H.] ⊙
Holcomb, M. Marcus, (AV) .... '32 '56 C.612 L.623 LL.B. [Holcomb&H.] ⊙
Holcomb & Harkins, (AV) .... Holcomb Building (⊙Laverne)

BURNEYVILLE, —, *Love Co.*

Armstrong, G. Timothy .... '42 '67 C.612 B.S. L.623 J.D. 201 Turner Cir
Sheehan, Daniel R., (BV) .... '28 '67 C.97 B.S. L.616 J.D. 26 Fifteenth Dr.‡

CADDO, 944, *Bryan Co.*

Reasor, Shannon, Law Offices of
(See Atoka)

CALERA, 1,739, *Bryan Co.*

Mattson, Carter Alan .... '— '97 C.621 B.A. L.623 J.D. 1672 Sterret Rd.

CARNEGIE, 1,593, *Caddo Co.*

Squires, Barry P., (BV) .... '66 '93 C.612 B.S. L.615 J.D. [B.Squires]
Squires, Barry, (BV) .... 109 W. Main St.

CASHION, 635, *Kingfisher & Logan Cos.*

Baker, Cindy L. .... '50 '84 C.623 B.A. L.616 J.D. R.R. 1
Waswo, Charles R. .... '— '91 C.622 B.S. L.616 J.D. RR 1, Box 157

CATOOSA, 5,449, *Rogers & Wagoner Cos.*

Benningfield, R. Allen, (BV) .... '42 '75 P.O. Box 490
Berry, Ronald, (BV) .... '42 '75 C.619 B.A. L.862 J.D. 426 S. Cherokee
Huffman, Robert A., Jr., (AV) '50 '77 C&L.623 B.B.A., J.D.
Gen. Coun., Cherokee Nation Enterprises, Inc.
McCarty, Naomi J. .... '— '82 C.377 B.A. L.862 J.D. 1000 N. Lynn Ln. Rd.
Torkelson, Nelda .... '27 '82 C.613 B.S. L.862 J.D. 18780 Woodbriar Ln.

CHANDLER, * 2,842, *Lincoln Co.*

Ashwood, Cynthia Ferrell, (BV) .... '60 '85 C&L.623 B.A., J.D. [C.F.Ashwood]

Ashwood, Cynthia Ferrell, P.C., (BV)
814 Manvel Avenue, P.O. Box 526, 74834
Telephone: 405-258-0097 Fax: 405-258-1412
Email: cfaatty@brightok.net
Cynthia Ferrell Ashwood.
General Civil Practice in all State and Federal Courts. Probate, Real Estate, Banking, Adoption, Commercial.
Representative Clients: Central Oklahoma Telephone Co., Inc.; First Bank of Chandler; First State Bank of Harrah, Okla.
See Professional Biographies, CHANDLER, OKLAHOMA

Atkins & Markoff
(See Oklahoma City)

Barnett, Barney K., (BV) .... '47 '86 C.612 B.A. L.623 J.D. Asst. Dist. Atty.

Butts & Lenora, (AV) BB
116 West Eighth Street, P.O. Box 337, 74834-0337
Telephone: 405-258-1334 Fax: 405-258-0249 Email: lenoralaw@sbcglobal.net
Email: lenora@brightok.net URL: http://www.lawyers.com/lenoralaw
Members of Firm: Benjamin E. Butts (1933-1997); Larry K. Lenora. Associate: Gregory A. Upton.
Criminal Law, Civil Litigation, Family Law, Probate, Real Estate, Wills, Trusts and Estates, Personal Injury, Oil and Gas and Title Examinations.
Representative Clients: The Abstract Guaranty Company of Lincoln County; First Bank of Chandler; City of Chandler, Oklahoma; Wellston Oklahoma Public Works Authority; National American Insurance Company; Realty Plus, Inc.; Lincoln County Sewer and Water Dist.; Triple W Oil Co.; Independent Industries.
Approved Title Examiners for: First American Title & Trust Co., Oklahoma City; Chicago Title & Trust Co.
See Professional Biographies, CHANDLER, OKLAHOMA

Craig, Milton C. .... '25 '52 C&L.623 B.A., LL.B. Ret. Dist. J.
Dargel, Michael E., (BV) '57 '82
C.436 B.A. L.37 J.D. Staff Coun., Nat. American Ins. Co.

Eagleton & Nicholson, P.C., (AV)
109 W. 9th, 74834 ⊙
Telephone: 405-258-5301 Fax: 405-258-5302
Email: pordos@brightok.net
Mark J. Pordos.
General Practice, Real Estate, Corporate Law, Commercial Law, Oil & Gas Law, Probate, Family Law, Bankruptcy, Estate Planning, Banking and Commercial Collections, Civil Litigation.
Oklahoma City Office: 3100 Bank One Center, 100 N. Broadway Avenue, 73102. Telephone: 405-236-0550. Fax: 405-236-0560. Email: eaglenk@coxinet.net
See Professional Biographies, CHANDLER, OKLAHOMA

Erwin, Dan A., (AV) '37 '63 C&L.623 B.B.A., LL.B.
118 West Eighth Street, 74834
Telephone: 405-258-1336 Fax: 405-258-0764
General Practice. Trials. Probate, Real Estate, Corporate, Negligence, Personal Injury, Real Property, Oil and Gas Law, Wills, Trusts and Estate Planning.
See Professional Biographies, CHANDLER, OKLAHOMA

Finley, Thomas C. .... '56 '85 C.1147 B.A. L.1288 J.D. National American Ins. Co.
Foster, Robert L. .... '25 '50 C&L.623 B.A., LL.B. Ret. Assoc. Dist. J.‡

Gilmore, R. Patrick, (AV) '51 '76 C.1147 B.A. L.623 J.D. BB
P.O. Box 9, 74834
Telephone: 405-258-4262 Fax: 405-258-4520
General Civil Trial Practice, State and Federal Courts.
See Professional Biographies, CHANDLER, OKLAHOMA

Hall, Rex M. .... '31 '67 C&L.623 B.A., J.D. Dept. of Labor
Key, Craig S. .... '65 '92 C&L.623 B.A., J.D. 808 Manvel
Kirk, Sheila Gatlin .... '61 '92 C.614 B.A. L.616 J.D. [S.G.Kirk]
Kirk, Sheila G. .... 814 Manuel
Lenora, Larry K., (AV) .... '51 '76 C.351 B.A. L.623 J.D. [Butts&L.]
Pordos, Mark J., (BV) .... '58 '85 C&L.623 B.A., J.D. [Eagleton&N.]
Swanson, Robert Lee, The Law Office of '— '70 C.966 B.S. L.879 J.D.
109 1/2 W. 9th St.
Upton, Gregory A., (CV) .... '71 '96 C&L.623 B.A., J.D. [Ⓐ Butts&L.]
Vassar, Paul M. .... '40 '64 C.934 L.623 J.D. Dist. J.
Welch, David .... '45 '77 L.623 J.D. Assoc. Dist. J.
Zimmerman, Miles C., (BV) .... '49 '77 C.986 B.A. L.45 J.D. 808 Manvel Avenue

CHECOTAH, 3,481, *McIntosh Co.*

Allen, Larry L. .... '38 '70 C.1147 B.A. L.616 J.D. City Atty.
Freeman, Regina Gay Slaton .... '64 '91 C&L.623 B.S., J.D. Fam. Ct. J.
LeMasters, Joseph M., Jr. .... '43 '72 C.619 B.S. L.862 J.D. 116 S. Broadway‡

CHELSEA, 2,136, *Rogers Co.*

Bates, Timothy J., (CV) .... '66 '92 C&L.862 B.A., J.D. 502 Pine

CHEROKEE, * 1,630, *Alfalfa Co.*

Angle, Loren E., (CV) .... '62 '88 C.612 B.S. L.623 J.D. P.O. Box 193
Cullen, David P. .... '31 '60 C.623 M.C.E. L.273 J.D. Assoc. Dist. J.
Hadwiger, Kyle B., (BV) .... '60 '86 C.612 B.S. L.862 J.D. [Hadwiger,J.&K.] ⊙
Hadwiger, Ronald R. .... '34 '63 C.612 B.A. L.623 LL.B. 120 South Grand‡
Hadwiger, Jungman & Kline, P.L.L.C., (BV) .... 120 South Grand (⊙Alva)
Jungman, Marcus A. .... '74 '01 C.620 B.A. L.623 J.D. [Hadwiger,J.&K.]
Kline, Jesse D. .... '76 '01 C.620 B.A. L.623 J.D. [Hadwiger,J.&K.]
Mitchell, Allan E., (CV) .... '44 '94 C.620 B.A. L.623 J.D. [Mitchell L.]
Mitchell Law, P.L.L.C., (CV) .... P.O. Box 63

CHEYENNE, * 778, *Roger Mills Co.*

Goodwin, Thomas B., (AV) '49 '78 C.639 B.S. L.623 J.D.
429 Broadway, P.O. Box 160, 73628
Telephone: 580-497-3378 Fax: 580-497-2297
Email: US544@aol.com
General Civil Trial Practice. Real Estate, Probate, Personal Injury, Negligence, Oil and Gas Law, Wills, Trusts.
See Professional Biographies, CHEYENNE, OKLAHOMA

Ivester, Ivester & Ivester
(See Sayre)

Smith, Gale F. .... '37 '71 C.622 B.A. L.623 J.D. Assoc. Dist. J.
Versteeg, F. Pat, (CV) .... '50 '79 C.804 B.A. L.616 J.D. Asst. Dist. Atty.
Vick, Leroy .... '10 '40 C.999 B.S. L.623 LL.B. P.O. Box 744

Wright, Newell E., Jr., (AV) '38 '70 C.621 B.A. L.623 J.D. BB
429 Broadway, P.O. Box 160, 73628
Telephone: 580-497-3378 Fax: 580-497-2297
Practice limited to Trials and Appeals in all State and Federal Courts.
See Professional Biographies, CHEYENNE, OKLAHOMA

CHICKASHA, * 15,850, *Grady Co.*

Alford, Oteka, (Mrs.) .... '48 '73 C&L.623 B.M., J.D. Assoc. Dist. J.‡
Allen, Richard L., (BV) .... '44 '70 C.612 B.A. L.616 J.D. [Allen,A.&T.]
Allen, Walt .... '11 '38 C.1023 L.273 LL.B. [Allen,A.&T.]
Allen, Allen & Tack, P.A., (BV) .... 210 W. Chickasha Ave.

Atkins & Markoff
(See Oklahoma City)

Avery, Richard I. .... '78 '03 C.1147 B.A. L.623 J.D. [Ⓐ Frailey,C.C.P.S.&M.]
Beal, Robert W., (BV) .... '49 '84 C&L.623 B.Pol.Sc. Asst. Dist. Atty.
Bingaman, Samuel Calvin, III, (CV) '56 '95 C.999 B.A. L.623 J.D.
411 Chickasha Avenue
Blodgett, John L. .... '72 '99 C.1300 B.A. L.623 J.D. [Ⓐ Frailey,C.C.P.S.&M.]
Brown, Jeromy E. .... '72 '98 C.80 B.A. L.616 J.D. [Ⓐ Frailey,C.C.P.S.&M.]
Caves, Jamie M. .... '75 '00 C.612 B.S. L.623 J.D. 1228 S. 8th St.
Caywood, Kerry W., (AV) .... '37 '63 C.612 B.S. L.623 LL.B. [Park,N.C.J.]
Chaffin, Michael R., (AV) .... '47 '72 C.622 B.S. L.623 J.D. [Frailey,C.C.P.S.&M.]
Chasteen, April D., (BV) .... '66 '92 C.614 B.A. L.615 J.D. [Ivy,R.&C.]
Cordell, F. Thomas, Jr., (AV) .... '54 '79 C.612 B.A. L.336 J.D. [Frailey,C.C.P.S.&M.]
Dickson, Patricia L. K., (BV) .... '52 '78 C.622 B.A. L.623 J.D. Mun. J.
Dugger, William D. .... '40 '66 C&L.616 B.S., J.D. 106 Morningside
Ewing, Catharine V. .... '— '01 C.691 B.A. L.623 J.D. [Ⓐ Frailey,C.C.P.S.&M.]
Ferguson, Donald P., (BV) '49 '74
C.623 B.S.Ed. L.846 J.D. 411 Chickasha Avenue, Suite 200
Ford, Michael P., (CV) .... '60 '86 C.623 B.B.A. L.862 J.D. 601 S. 7th St.
Frailey, Tom A., (AV) .... '51 '76 C.1147 B.B.A. L.623 J.D. [Frailey,C.C.P.S.&M.]
Frailey, Chaffin, Cordell, Perryman, Sterkel & McCalla, L.L.P., (AV)
201 North Fourth Street

Gordon, Phil W., (BV) .... '52 '78 C.612 B.S. L.623 J.D. [Hays&G.]
Graves, John H. .... '77 '03 C&L.623 B.A., J.D. [Ⓐ Johnston&Assoc.]
Harris, Michael L. .... '47 '90 C.612 B.S. L.616 J.D. P.O. Box 1117
Hays, Robert J., (AV) .... '39 '65 C&L.623 B.A., J.D. [Hays&G.]

Hays & Gordon, (AV)
Third Floor Mid-First Bank Building, 228 West Chickasha Avenue, 73018-2669
Telephone: 405-224-1950 405-224-7575 Fax: 405-222-1033
URL: http://www.haysgordon.com
Robert J. Hays; Phil W. Gordon.
General Civil Practice. Probate, Real Estate, Estate Planning, Commercial Law, Commercial Litigation, Health Law.
Representative Clients: Chickasha Bank & Trust Co.; Hermetic Switch, Inc.; Southern Plains Medical Center, P.C.; Bank of Union; Cement Bank.
Local Counsel: Farmers Home Administration; Ward Petroleum Corp.
See Professional Biographies, CHICKASHA, OKLAHOMA

Heck, Keith W., (BV) .... '49 '83 C.618 B.S.Ed. L.623 J.D. [K.W.Heck]
Heck, Keith W., P.C., (BV) .... 411 Chickasha Avenue, Suite 200
Horn, Donald H., (BV) .... '47 '73 C.612 B.S. L.623 J.D. [D.H.Horn]
Horn, Donald H., P.C., (BV) .... 411 Chickasha Ave.
Ivy, Red, (BV) .... '21 '49 L.623 LL.B. 308 Choctau Ave.
Ivy, Ratcliff & Chasteen, P.C., (BV) .... 308 W. Choctaw Ave.
Johnston, Kenneth R., (AV) .... '44 '74 C&L.623 B.S., J.D. [Johnston&Assoc.]
Johnston, Wes, (CV) .... '64 '89 C&L.623 B.A., J.D. [Johnston&Assoc.]

Johnston & Associates, (AV) BB
118 North Fourth Street, P.O. Box F, 73023
Telephone: 405-224-4000 Fax: 405-224-0003
Email: johnstonlawfirm@sbcglobal.net
Kenneth R. Johnston; Wes Johnston. Associate: John H. Graves.
General Practice, Environmental Law. including Land Use, Landowners Rights Wills and Probate.
See Professional Biographies, CHICKASHA, OKLAHOMA

Jones, Angela Caywood .... '71 '00 C.612 B.A. L.623 J.D. [Park,N.C.J.]
Maher, Clarence L., (BV) .... '30 '57 C&L.623 B.A., LL.B. 315 Choctaw
McCalla, Stephen R., (BV) .... '53 '90 C&L.623 B.S., J.D. [Frailey,C.C.P.S.&M.]
Moon, Deborah A., (BV) .... '53 '90 C.612 B.A. L.623 J.D. [Moon&M.]
Moon, W. R., Sr., (CV) .... '55 '85 C.623 B.B.A. L.616 J.D. [Moon&M.]
Moon and Moon, (BV) .... 721 Country Club Rd.
Moore, Rick .... '55 '87 C.309 L.623 410 Choctaw Ave.
Nelson, John M., (AV) .... '39 '63 C&L.623 B.A., LL.B. [Park,N.C.J.]
Park, Charles W., (BV) .... '51 '76 C&L.623 B.A., J.D. [Park,N.C.J.]
Park, Robert B., (AV) .... '24 '49 C&L.623 LL.B. [Park,N.C.J.] ‡

Park, Nelson, Caywood, Jones, (AV)
122 North Fourth Street, P.O. Box 968, 73023-0968
Telephone: 405-224-0386 Telecopier: 405-224-0907
URL: http://www.pncj.com
Members of Firm: Robert B. Park (Retired); John M. Nelson; Kerry W. Caywood; Charles W. Park; Angela Caywood Jones.
Civil Practice, Probate, Real Estate, Environmental Law, Commercial Law, Oil and Gas Law.
Representative Clients: The First National Bank & Trust Co., Chickasha; Badgett Steam Lubricator Corp.
Reference: The First National Bank & Trust Co., Chickasha.
See Professional Biographies, CHICKASHA, OKLAHOMA

Perryman, David L., (BV) .... '57 '83 C.612 B.S. L.623 J.D. [Frailey,C.C.P.S.&M.]
Ratcliff, David K., (BV) .... '64 '90 C.612 B.S. L.623 J.D. [Ivy,R.&C.]
Rivas, Ryland L., (BV) .... '49 '74 C&L.623 B.B.A., J.D. 628 Choctaw Ave.
Schlecht, James C. .... '59 '91 C.612 B.S. L.446 J.D. 3034 Lacey Dr.

Sisson, B. David
(See Norman)

Sterkel, Deborah A., (BV) .... '51 '85 C.999 B.A. L.623 J.D. [Frailey,C.C.P.S.&M.]
Stiger, Timothy Allen .... '56 '82 C&L.623 B.A., J.D. [T.Stiger]
Stiger, Tim .... 1727 S. 16th
Tack, Scott R., (BV) .... '56 '82 C.477 B.S. L.623 J.D. [Allen,A.&T.]
Thomas, John '— '93 C.276 B.S. L.312 J.D.
(adm. in HI; not adm. in OK) Astra International
Van Dyck, Richard G. .... '57 '88 C.617 B.S. L.616 J.D. District Judge
Welch, Debra J. '61 '90 C.623 B.A. L.744 J.D.
(adm. in CO; not adm. in OK) P.O. Box 1242‡
Young, Z. Joseph, III, (CV) .... '71 '97 C.623 B.A. L.615 J.D. 111 N. 5th St.

CHOCTAW, 9,377, *Oklahoma Co.*

Abbamondi, John G., (BV) .... '47 '97 C.397 B.A. L.623 J.D. P.O. Box 736
Gatewood, Harry D., II .... '54 '85 C.623 B.A. L.329 J.D. P.O. Box 853

CLAREMORE, * 15,873, *Rogers Co.*

Antinoro, Mark D., (CV) .... '69 '98 C.19 B.A. L.862 J.D. [Taylor,B.F.M.D.&R.]
Bassmann, G. Raymond, (AV) .... '09 '32 C&L.623 A.B., J.D. 214 S. Missouri
Benjamin, Walter M. '44 '78 C&L.174 B.S., J.D.
(adm. in PA; not adm. in OK; Pat.) 9965 E. Clover Creek Dr.
Bisceglia, Erinn Shaw .... '74 '99 C.36 B.A. L.616 J.D. 319 W 1st Street
Burrage, Carole Tillman, (CV) '69 '94 C&L.623 B.B.A., J.D.
1701 W. Will Rogers Blvd.
Burrage, Sean, (AV) .... '68 '93 C&L.623 B.B.A., J.D. [Taylor,B.F.M.D.&R.]
Carden, Edwin D. .... '31 '64 C&L.862 LL.B. Ret. Assoc. Dist. J.
Carle, John R., (AV) .... '29 '57 C&L.862 B.A., LL.B. [Carle,M.&F.]
Carle, Mosier & Farbro, (AV) .... 417 West First Street
Cary, John H., (AV) .... '49 '74 C.339 B.S. L.623 J.D. P.O. Box 2881
Cass, Robert G. ("Bob") .... '56 '89 C&L.546 B.S., J.D. Div. Coun., Centrilift
Chaves, Carl R., (BV) .... '52 '78 C.326 B.S. L.862 J.D. Asst. Dist. Atty.
Condren, Sheila A., (BV) .... '62 '87 C.375 B.A. L.862 J.D. Spec. Dist. Ct. J.
Danker, Brian R., (CV) .... '66 '95 C.612 B.S. L.862 J.D. 405 W. 1st St.
Downs, Darrell W., (BV) .... '62 '87 C&L.623 B.B.A., J.D. [Taylor,B.F.M.D.&R.]
Ely, James W., Jr., (BV) .... '49 '92 C&L.862 B.A., J.D. Asst. Dist. Atty.
Evans, Amy L. .... '68 '92 C&L.862 B.S.B.A., J.D. [Taylor,B.F.M.D.&R.]
Farbro, Barry A., (BV) .... '58 '87 C.612 B.S.B.A. L.862 J.D. [Carle,M.&F.]
Fathree, Wade L. .... '53 '90 C.618 B.A. L.862 J.D. 524 W. Will Rogers
Foster, Toney D., (BV) .... '50 '95 C.616 B.A. L.862 J.D. [Taylor,B.F.M.D.&R.]
Frizzell, Kent '29 '55 C.268 B.A. L.900 J.D.
(adm. in KS; not adm. in OK) Prof. of Law Emeritus, Univ. of Tulsa‡
Gordon, Jack E., Jr. .... '44 '69 P.O. Box 1167
Greever, F. Mack, (AV) .... '42 '70 C.376 B.S. L.862 J.D. 104 S. Missouri
Hasselman, Raymond L., (BV) .... '52 '79 C.1211 B.A. L.862 J.D. Asst. Dist. Atty.
Haynes, Ernest Eugene, Jr., (BV) .... '55 '80 C&L.623 B.A., J.D. Dist. Atty. Off.
Higgins, William R., (BV) .... '49 '74 C.45 B.A. L.616 J.D. 417 W. 1st St.
Jones, Samantha Rae .... '73 '99 C.1359 B.A. L.862 J.D. [Ⓐ Carle,M.&F.]
Kissinger, Leslie Ann Ellis, (BV) .... '56 '85 C.623 B.A. L.862 J.D. Mun. J.

Lepak, Linda Stoia, (BV) .... '56 '81 C&L.623 B.B.A., J.D. 3217 Heritage Dr.

Logan & Lowry, LLP
(See Vinita)

Mallett, Bradley H., (BV) .... '68 '93 C.623 B.B.A. L.309 J.D. [Taylor,B.F.M.D.&R.]
Marlar, Dale R., (BV) .... '49 '74 C&L.623 B.A., J.D. City Atty. [Williams&M.]
Mayberry, Jack K. .... '27 '54 C.612 L.623 J.D. Assoc. Dist. J.
Mosier, Richard D., (AV) .... '58 '83 C.612 B.S. L.862 J.D. [Carle,M.&F.]
Murray, A. G., Jr., (BV) .... '42 '68 C&L.623 B.A., J.D. 121 S. Muskogee
Parker, Janette L. .... '64 '92 C.612 B.S. L.623 J.D. 11925 E. Cedar Dr.
Post, Dynda .... '52 '80 C.613 B.A. L.623 J.D. 219 S. Missouri St.
Price, Jeffrey A., The Law Office of '71 '97 C&L.623 B.A., J.D.
403 W. 1st St., Ste. 300
Price, Robert E., (BV) .... '48 '73 C&L.623 B.A., J.D. 423 West Will Rogers Blvd.
Rahmeier, Larry E., (BV) .... '57 '83 C&L.378 B.S.C.E., J.D. [Scarth&R.]
Ramsey, Mark H., (BV) .... '58 '85 C.1147 B.A. L.623 J.D. [Taylor,B.F.M.D.&R.]
Russell, Clint .... '71 '01 C.645 B.A. L.615 J.D. [Taylor,B.F.M.D.&R.]
Scarth, Bill R., (AV) .... '33 '63 C&L.862 B.S., LL.B. [Scarth&R.]
Scarth & Rahmeier, (AV) .... 214 S. Missouri
Shallenburger, Brant E. .... '70 '03 C.619 B.S. L.862 J.D. [Shallenburger]
Shallenburger Law Firm, The, P.C. .... 319 West First Street
Steidley, J. Dwayne, (CV) .... '59 '85 C.612 B.A. L.862 J.D. Spec. Dist. J.
Summerlin, James W., (AV) .... '31 '58 C.619 B.A. L.623 LL.B. 501 W. 1st. St.
Tanner, James P., Law Offices, (BV) '46 '73
C&L.623 B.A., J.D. 302 E. Will Rogers Blvd.
Taylor, Stratton, (AV) .... '56 '83 C&L.862 B.S.E., J.D. [Taylor,B.F.M.D.&R.]

Taylor, Burrage, Foster, Mallett, Downs & Ramsey, P.C., (AV) BB
400 West Fourth Street, P.O. Box 309, 74018-0309
Telephone: 918-343-4100 Fax: 918-343-4900 URL: http://www.soonerlaw.com
URL: http://www.lawyers.com/soonerlaw
Members of Firm: Stratton Taylor; Sean Burrage; Toney D. Foster; Bradley H. Mallett; Darrell W. Downs; Mark H. Ramsey; Mark D. Antinoro; Clint Russell; Amy L. Evans.
Civil and Criminal Practice in all State and Federal Courts. Employment Law, Healthcare Law, Medical Malpractice, Professional Liability, Insurance Defense, Real Estate, Probate, Guardianships, Corporation, Commercial and Personal Injury Law.
See Professional Biographies, CLAREMORE, OKLAHOMA

Wantland, Melinda Dawn, (CV) '58 '97 C.1147 B.A. L.615 J.D.
104 S. Missouri, Ste. 102
Wantland, Timothy Doyal, (BV) '57 '91 C.1147 B.A. L.615 J.D.
104 S. Missouri, Ste. 102
Willhoite, J. Todd, (BV) .... '— '91 C.862 B.A. L.623 J.D. 415 W. Patti Page Blvd.
Williams, Thomas H., (AV) .... '40 '68 C.612 B.S. L.616 J.D. [Williams&M.]
Williams & Marlar, P.C., (AV) .... 501 W. 1st St.

CLEVELAND, 3,282, *Pawnee Co.*

Arney, Charles D., (BV) .... '35 '71 C&L.862 B.A., J.D. Route 3
Burt, Richard F., (AV) .... '21 '53 L.862 LL.B. 123 S. Broadway
Carter, Jon Michael .... '54 '98 C.1111 B.A. L.472 J.D. 211 S. Broadway
Goldsmith, Karl R. .... '18 '48 C.494 A.B. L.976 LL.B. 123 S. Broadway St.‡
Oakley, Jessie M. .... '53 '91 C.619 B.C.J. L.862 J.D. P.O. Box 345
Pickerill, Jerry L., (AV) .... '37 '70 C.377 B.S. L.900 J.D. [Pickerill]
Pickerill Law Office, P.C., (AV) .... 109 S. Broadway

CLINTON, 8,833, *Custer Co.*

Annett, Debra .... '57 '88 C.846 B.A. L.616 J.D. OK Indigent Def. Sys.
Cabaniss, Ellis, (AV) .... '47 '73 C.622 B.S.Ed. L.623 J.D. [Graft&C.]
Cornell, Patrick T., (AV) .... '48 '73 C&L.623 B.B.A., J.D. [P.T.Cornell]

Cornell, Patrick T., P.C., (AV)
117 N. 5th, P.O. Box 847, 73601
Telephone: 580-323-6133 Fax: 580-323-7074
Email: patrickcornell@sbcglobal.net URL: http://www.lawyers.com/cornell
Patrick T. Cornell.
General Practice in all State and Federal Courts. Probate, Personal Injury, Real Estate, Oil and Gas, Condemnation, Family, Corporation, Criminal and Banking Law.
See Professional Biographies, CLINTON, OKLAHOMA

Eeds, Avery A., Jr., (BV) .... '53 '79 C.622 B.A. L.623 J.D. P.O. Box 966
Foster, Roger W., (BV) .... '45 '89 C.620 B.S. L.616 J.D. [Rodolph&F.] ⊙
Goodwin, Charles L. .... '38 '62 C&L.623 LL.B. Dist. J.
Graft, C. B., (AV) .... '41 '66 C.622 B.A. L.623 J.D. [Graft&C.] ⊙
Graft & Cabaniss, (AV) .... P.O. Box 1269 (⊙Thomas)
Jones, Stephanie C. .... '72 '98 C&L.623 B.A., J.D. P.O. Box 1494
Kluver, Paul Franklin .... '56 '98 C.623 B.A. L.616 J.D. 800 W. Gary Blvd
Laughlin, Charles Timothy .... '67 '98 C&L.623 B.A., J.D. Def. Coun.
Maisch, Donald D., (CV) .... '61 '87 C.502 B.A. L.616 J.D. Legal Aid of Western Okla.
Meacham, Denver W., II, (AV) .... '39 '63 C&L.623 B.B.A., LL.B. [Meacham&M.]
Meacham, Randolph S., (AV) .... '47 '72 C&L.623 B.A., J.D. [R.S.Meacham]

Meacham & Meacham, A Professional Corporation, (AV)
801 Frisco, P.O. Box 996, 73601
Telephone: 580-323-6323 Fax: 580-323-1100
Email: dmeacham@itlnet.net
Denver W. Meacham, II.
General Civil Practice. Trials. Probate, Trusts and Estate Planning, Real Estate, Oil and Gas, Commercial Law.
General Counsel: Oklahoma Bank & Trust Co., Clinton; Custer County State Branch, Arapaho; First State Bank, Canute; First National Bank and Trust of Elk City, Elk City; Foss Reservoir Master Conservancy District.

Meacham, Randolph S., P.C., (AV)
525 South 30th Street, P.O. Box 1236, 73601
Telephone: 580-323-4370 Fax: 580-323-4968
Email: meachamr@itlnet.net
Randolph S. Meacham. Of Counsel: Michael G. Smith.
General Practice, Civil, Trial, Family Law, Criminal Law, Personal Injury, Bankruptcy, Agricultural Law, Commercial Litigation, Banking..
See Professional Biographies, CLINTON, OKLAHOMA

Mooneyham, Sonya C. .... '72 '97 C&L.623 B.A., J.D. Pub. Def.

Phillips, Richard J., (BV) '61 '86 C.622 B.S. L.623 J.D.
5th and Frisco Avenue, P.O. Box 1296, 73601
Telephone: 580-323-3044 Fax: 580-323-3059
Email: rjphill@swbell.net
General Civil and Criminal Practice. Probate, Real Estate, Taxation, Oil and Gas, Personal Injury, Bankruptcy and Family Law, Business Law, Wills and Estates.
Cheyenne, Oklahoma Office: Beavin Building, P.O. Box 43, 73628. Telephone: 580-497-2423.
See Professional Biographies, CLINTON, OKLAHOMA

Rodolph, Don, (AV) .... '43 '69 C.622 B.S. L.623 J.D. [Rodolph&F.]

Rodolph & Foster, (AV)
Not a partnership
123 South 6th Street, P.O. Box 277, 73601 ⊙
Telephone: 580-323-6090 Fax: 580-323-6102
Don Rodolph; Roger W. Foster.
General Civil and Criminal Practice in all State and Federal Courts. Probate, Real Estate, Oil and Gas, Personal Injury, Negligence, Banking Law, Family Law, Divorce, Custody, Wills.
Representative Clients: Town of Leedey; First National Bank of Leedey; Clinton Production Credit Assn.; Town of Foss; Farmrail System, Inc.; Farmrail Corporation; Grainbelt Corp.
Approved Examining Attorney For: American First Title & Trust.
Taloga, Oklahoma, Office: Collier Building . Telephone: 580-328-5494.

See Professional Biographies, CLINTON, OKLAHOMA

Smith, Michael G., (BVⓉ) ...'55 '92 C&L.623 B.A., J.D. [R.S.Meacham]
Stratton, David S., (BV) ...'39 '65 C.612 B.S. L.623 J.D. 801 Frisco
Tisdal, Mart, (AV) ...'48 '76 C&L.623 B.A., J.D. 814 Frisco
Tutwiler, Glea H. ...'17 '40 C&L.623 B.S., LL.B. 209 Regency Dr.‡

COALGATE, * 2,005, *Coal Co.*

Baird, Becky Dahms, (BV) ...'62 '88 C.862 B.S. L.623 J.D. Asst. Dist. Atty.
Branam, Richard E., (BV) ...'51 '80 C.618 B.A. L.616 J.D. 4 N. Main St.
Lawson, John T., (BV) ...'42 '70 C.614 B.S. L.616 J.D. Asst. Dist. Atty.
Moore Mowdy & Youngblood, (BV) ...24 North Main (⊙Atoka)
Mowdy, D. Clay, (BV) ...'58 '84 C.612 B.S. L.615 J.D. [Moore M.&Y.] ⊙
Mowdy, Robert F. ...'24 '50 C&L.623 LL.B. 33 N. Main

COLLINSVILLE, 4,077, *Tulsa Co.*

Flanagan, William S. ("Pat"), Jr. ...'47 '71 C.931 B.A. L.862 J.D. 1322 Walnut St.
Hackathorn, Bill, (CV) ...'52 '93 C.620 B.S./B.A. L.862 J.D. 12211 E. 81st Pl. N.
Mitchell, Joel K. ...'73 '00 C.1147 B.A. L.623 J.D. 116 N. 14th Street
Powell, Morgan K., Attorney at Law, (AV) '46 '71
C&L.623 B.A., J.D. 118 N. 11th St., Ste. 104
White, Joe L., (BV) ...'45 '83 C.942 B.A. L.862 J.D. [J.L.White]
White, Joe L., P.C., (BV) ...1718 W. Bway.

COMANCHE, 1,556, *Stephens Co.*

Martin, Max A. ...'42 '69 C.612 B.A. L.623 J.D. [Martin&M.]
Martin, Nancy ...'45 '70 C.614 B.A. L.623 J.D. [Martin&M.]
Martin & Martin ... 100 Oak Main (⊙Berkeley, CA; Hamilton, ON)

COOKSON, —, *Cherokee Co.*

Deason-Toyne, Denise '58 '83 C.134 B.S.B.A. L.986 J.D.
(adm. in MO; not adm. in OK) 36720 S. Oak Lane

CORDELL, * 3,261, *Washita Co.*

Emerson, Ralph W. ...'26 '70 C.921 B.S. L.623 J.D. Assoc. Dist. J.
Herren, Rex E., Attorney at Law ...'48 '74 C&L.623 B.A., J.D. P.O. Box 188
Jones, Ray L., Jr., (AV) ...'44 '69 C&L.623 B.A., J.D. 922 N. Temple St.
Mason, Walter Scott, III, (BV) ...'52 '92 C.612 B.S. L.616 J.D. 127 East Main
Wesner, Mark R., (BV) ...'54 '79 C&L.623 B.A., J.D. [Wesner&W.]
Wesner, Ronald L., (AV) ...'28 '53 C&L.623 B.A., J.D. [Wesner&W.]
Wesner & Wesner, (AV) ...121 East Main Street

COWETA, 7,139, *Wagoner Co.*

Smith, George W., (CV) ...'57 '82 C&L.862 B.S., J.D. 107 E. Chestnut St.

CRESCENT, 1,236, *Logan Co.*

Lorance, Steven R., (BV) ...'51 '76 C.810 B.S. L.623 J.D. Mun. J.

CUSHING, 8,371, *Payne Co.*

Ahrberg, William W., (BV) ...'55 '81 C.612 B.S. L.862 J.D. 118 W. Broadway
Anderson, B. Davis ...'55 '86 C&L.862 B.S., J.D. Big 4 Petro
Arthurs, J. Stewart, (AV) ...'40 '66 C.620 B.A. L.623 J.D. 317 W. Broadway
Branyan, Tyson E., (BV) ...'50 '91 C.139 B.A. L.846 J.D. 402 E. Moses
Cubbage, Stephen B., (BV) ...'41 '71 C.612 B.A. L.862 J.D. [Forsyth,C.&Assoc.]
Cubbage, William R., (BV) ...'44 '69 C.623 B.A. L.862 J.D. P.O. Box 550
Ellington, Billy Joe, (CV) '56 '83 C.612 B.S. L.616 J.D.
115 N. Harrison St. (⊙Pawnee)
Forsyth, John E., (AV) ...'54 '78 C.190 B.S.B.A. L.623 J.D. [Forsyth,C.&Assoc.]

Forsyth, Cubbage & Associates, P.C., (AV) BB
200 E. Oak Street, Suite 101, P.O. Box 7, 74023
Telephone: 918-225-7700 Fax: 918-225-7200
URL: http://www.fca-law.com
John E. Forsyth; Stephen B. Cubbage.
Mediation, Business Law, Estate Planning, Trusts, Probate, Real Estate, Commercial Law, Banking Law.

See Professional Biographies, CUSHING, OKLAHOMA

Shaw, Sidney Wade, (CV) ...'65 '91 C.612 B.S. L.623 J.D. P.O. Box 307
Szlichta & Ramsey
(See Stillwater)
Wilcoxon, Jimmie N. ...'20 '75 C.1362 B.A. L.616 J.D. 402 E. Walnut‡
Withiam, Sam ...'38 '61 C&L.623 —, — P.O. Box 1368

DAVIS, 2,543, *Murray Co.*

Chaffin, Bill M., (BV) ...'44 '77 C.613 B.A. L.616 J.D. 706 E. Main St.
Hurst, McNeil & Gordon, (AV) ...219 East Main (⊙Sulphur)
McNeil, Edd R., (AV) ...'45 '71 C&L.623 B.A., J.D. [Hurst,M.&G.] ⊙
Wilson, James Harmon Brown ...'56 '84 C&L.623 B.A., J.D. Dist. Atty. Off.

DEL CITY, 22,128, *Oklahoma Co.*

Chavez, N. Michael, (BV) ...'52 '78 C&L.623 B.A., J.D. [N.M.Chavez]
Chavez, N. Michael, P.C., (BV) ... P.O. Box 15792
Forrest, James T. ...'49 '77 C&L.623 B.A., J.D. 3213 Oakbrook Dr.★
Fried, Jack B., (BV) ...'44 '74 C&L.623 B.A., J.D. P.O. Box 15040
Hayden, Robert W., (AV) ...'45 '77 C.912 B.A. L.213 J.D. 2828 Linda Lane
Martin, Molly ...'68 '93 C.1315 B.A. L.623 J.D. Midwest Trophy Company
Pool, Garrett N., (BV) ...'69 '94 C&L.602 B.A., B.A. [Pool,B.V.&P.] ⊙
Pool, Ted N., (AV) ...'39 '64 C.612 B.S. L.623 J.D. [Pool,B.V.&P.] ⊙
Pool, Blankenship, Vincent & Pool, A Professional Association, (AV)
1919 South Sunny Lane, Suite 200 (⊙Oklahoma City)
Stewart, Boyd, (BV) ...'29 '64 L.616 1491 S. Sunnylane Rd.
Talley, Barry W., (CV) ...'56 '85 C.1147 L.616 J.D. 805 Scott St.
Vincent, Raymond A., (AV) ...'51 '86 C.101 B.S. L.616 J.D. [Pool,B.V.&P.] ⊙

DILL CITY, 526, *Washita Co.*

Turner, Jimmy D., (BV) ...'34 '71 C.622 B.S. L.208 J.D. P.O. Box 315

DRUMMOND, 408, *Garfield Co.*

Horrall, Curtis L. ...'30 '57 C.614 B.A. L.616 LL.B. Pres., Bank of Drummond

DRUMRIGHT, 2,905, *Creek & Payne Cos.*

Daniel, Charles E., (BV) ...'28 '53 C&L.623 B.A., LL.B. 128 E. Bdway.
Daniel, Timothy W., (CV) ...'56 '88 C.615 B.S. L.900 J.D. [Daniel L.]
Daniel Law, (CV) ... 128 E. Broadway
Watson, Charles D., Jr., (AV) ...'43 '67 C&L.623 B.A., LL.B. [C.D.Watson,Jr.]

Watson, Charles D., Jr., LLC, (AV)
141 East Broadway, P.O. Box 647, 74030
Telephone: 918-352-2567 Fax: 918-352-3871
Doyle Watson (1916-2003); Charles D. Watson, Jr.
General Civil Practice, all State and Federal Courts. Trials, Antitrust, Probate, Real Estate, Negligence, Oil and Gas Law, Commerical Litigation, Civil Rights Litigation, Class Actions.

Woodson, Charles Scott ...'29 '57 C.623 B.B.A. L.862 J.D. Active Retired District Judge‡

DUNCAN, * 22,505, *Stephens Co.*

Allen, Dan G. ...'65 '93 C.613 B.S.E. L.616 J.D. P.O. Box 1468
Archer, Jeffery, (CV) ...'65 '95 C.1300 B.B.A. L.623 J.D. [Kee]
Atkins & Markoff
(See Oklahoma City)
Bailey, Robert O. ...'33 '64 C.612 B.F.A. L.623 LL.B. Route 4
Benefield, Catherine Marie ...'55 '93 C&L.623 B.A., J.D. Mack Energy Co.
Benefield, David L., (BV) ...'53 '78 C.259 B.A. L.623 J.D. [Bonney C.]
Bonney, Henry C., (AV) ...'36 '61 C&L.623 B.S.E., LL.B. [Bonney C.]

Bonney Corley LLP, (AV)
Suite 300 BancFirst Building, 16 South 9th Street, 73533
Telephone: 580-255-5600 Fax: 580-255-5843
Email: bcbsc@texhoma.net URL: http://www.bonneycorley.com
Members of Firm: Henry C. Bonney; Ronald E. Corley; David L. Benefield; Scott W. Stone; John E. Campbell, Jr.; Carl O. LaMar.
General Civil Trial and Appellate Practice, State and Federal Courts. Corporation, School Law, Probate, Estate Planning, Oil and Gas, Banking, Real Property, Employment Law, Commercial Law, Domestic Relations and Personal Injury.
Representative Clients: AmQuest Bank, N.A.; Mack Oil Co.; Thomas Drilling Co.; M & M Supply Co.; Investors Trust Co.; AmQuest Financial Corp.; L. E. Jones Production Co.; Duncan Public Schools; Duncan Equipment Co.

See Professional Biographies, DUNCAN, OKLAHOMA

Branch, Malcolm Howell ...'43 '70 C.663 B.S. L.615 J.D. P.O. Box 1062
Buckholts, E. J., II, (BV) ...'52 '79 C.623 B.B.A. L.616 J.D. [Ellis,L.&B.]
Campbell, John E., Jr., (BV) ...'60 '85 C.623 B.B.A. L.616 J.D. [Bonney C.]
Carey, Edwin J., JR, (BV) ...'33 '90 C.659 B.S. L.623 J.D. Asst. Dist. Atty.
Christian, Robert E., (AV) ...'58 '83 C&L.623 B.B.A., J.D. Dist. Atty.
Cooper, Don ...'38 '71 C.613 B.S. L.616 J.D. 1015 Bois D'Arc‡
Cooper, John B., (AV) ...'28 '53 C&L.623 B.A., LL.B. 1113 Crescent Dr.‡
Corley, Ronald E., (AV) ...'42 '70 C.612 B.A. L.623 J.D. [Bonney C.]
DeBois, Sherrill and Reynolds, (AV) ... 15 North Ninth Street, Suite 205
Dixon, Richard E. ...'36 '64 C&L.623 B.A., LL.B. 16 S. 9th St.
DuFort, Douglas F., (CV) ...'54 '81 C.112 B.A. L.767 J.D. 1107 W. Walnut Ave.
Ellis, Thomas T., (AV) ...'50 '75 C&L.623 B.A., J.D. [Ellis,L.&B.]

Ellis, Leonard & Buckholts, (AV) BB
Patterson Building, 929 West Willow, 73533-4921
Telephone: 580-252-3240 Fax: 580-252-9596
Email: elb@texhoma.net URL: http://www.lawyers.com/duncanok
Thomas T. Ellis; Phillip H. Leonard (Retired); E. J. Buckholts, II.
General Civil Practice in all Courts. Banking, Commercial Law, Oil and Gas, Real Estate, Domestic Relations, Personal Injury, Probate, Estate Planning, Bankruptcy Law, Employment Law, Insurance Defense, Adoptions and Criminal Law.
References: BancFirst, Duncan, Oklahoma; First Bank & Trust Co., Duncan, Oklahoma; Arvest, Duncan, Oklahoma.

See Professional Biographies, DUNCAN, OKLAHOMA

Frieda, James M., (BV) ...'42 '81 C.1182 B.A. L.615 J.D. [Stuart,F.&H.]
Gaddis, Jan Preece, (BV) '46 '88 C.623 B.M.E. L.616 J.D.
1111 West Willow, Suite 203
Gardner, Gene M. ...'26 '54 C.861 L.623 LL.B. 1020 Main St.
Garvin, Harold T., (AV) ...'20 '43 C&L.623 B.A., LL.B. 16 South 9th Street, Ste. 300‡
Giddens, Devin J., (CV) ...'64 '91 C.612 B.S. L.615 J.D. 1111 W. Willow Ave.

Gossett, William A., (AV) '52 '78 C&L.623 B.B.A., J.D.
East Court Center, 122 South 11th, Suite 100, 73533-4704
Telephone: 580-255-3300 Fax: 580-255-3310
Email: wagatlaw@texhoma.net
General Civil Practice. Trials and Appeals in State and Federal Courts. Real Estate Law, Wills, Trusts and Estates, Corporations and Business Planning, Banking and Commercial Law, Debtor/Creditor and Bankruptcy, Insurance Claims and Disputes, Oil and Gas Law, Family Law, Personal Injury and Wrongful Death.

See Professional Biographies, DUNCAN, OKLAHOMA

Green, John R., (AV) '42 '67 C.612 B.A. L.623 LL.B. BB
1106 West Maple Avenue, P.O. Box 700, 73534-0700
Telephone: 580-255-7400 Facsimile: 580-255-0800
Email: johnrgreen@sbcglobal.net URL: http://www.lawyers.com/johngreenlaw
General Civil Practice, Real Estate, Probate, Commercial, Insurance, Corporation, Banking, Estate Planning, Oil and Gas Law. Trials. No Small Collections.

See Professional Biographies, DUNCAN, OKLAHOMA

Hammond, David W., (BV) ...'60 '87 C.623 B.B.A. L.45 J.D. [Stuart,F.&H.]
Hicks, Jason Matthew ...'69 '01 C.1300 B.S. L.623 J.D. Asst. Dist. Atty., Dist. Atty's Off.
Johnson, Lisa A. ...'60 '84 C&L.623 B.A.Accty., J.D. Coun. Co. Profit Sharing Plan
Jones, Jay D. ...'19 '47 L.623 LL.B. 1001 Ranchwood Pl.‡
Kee, James L., (AV) ...'35 '66 C.618 B.S. L.616 J.D. [Kee]

Kee Law Firm, (AV) BB
1102 Maple, P.O. Box 1646, 73534
Telephone: 580-252-2120 Telefax: 580-252-8647
Email: kanda@texhoma.net URL: http://www.lawyers.com/kee&archer
James L. Kee; Jeffery Archer.
Civil Litigation, Domestic Relations, Criminal Law, Environmental Law, International Law, Personal Injury.

See Professional Biographies, DUNCAN, OKLAHOMA

Kent, Robert A. ...'52 '77 C.612 B.S. L.623 J.D. Sr. Coun., Halliburton Co.
LaMar, Carl O., (CV) ...'61 '86 C.612 B.S. L.45 J.D. [Bonney C.]

Leach, Sullivan, Sullivan & Watkins, (AV) BB
921 Main Street, P.O. Box 160, 73534
Telephone: 580-255-1111 Telecopier: 580-255-5587
URL: http://www.leachsullivan.com
Members of Firm: William O. Leach (1919-1990); Paul D. Sullivan; Patrick D. Sullivan; Michael P. Sullivan; Kent P. Sullivan; Jay B. Watkins; Scott P. Sullivan.
General Civil Practice in all State and Federal Courts. Real Estate, Insurance, Probate, Commercial, Corporation, Banking, Estate Planning and Oil and Gas Law. Trials. No small collections.
Representative Clients: Citizens' Bank, Velma, Oklahoma; Leffler Construction Co.; Jackson Ranches, Inc.; Jackson Cattle Corp.; Legacy Bank; BancFirst of Marlow; L.A. Edwards Trust; John E. Jackson Trust; Interstate Petroleum Corp.; PaceCo Financial Services, Inc.

See Professional Biographies, DUNCAN, OKLAHOMA

Leonard, Phillip H., (BV) ... '39 '63 C&L.623 B.A., J.D. [Ellis,L.&B.]
Lindley, George W. ... '45 '70 C.623 B.A. L.846 J.D. Sr. Dist. J.‡
Lindley, Susan Shea ... '43 '70 C.276 B.S.F.S. L.846 J.D. 1202 W. Elder
Link, Antony C. (Tony), (AV) ... '47 '73 C&L.623 B.A., J.D. 1503 Brookwood Avenue
McCoy, William C., (AV) ... '30 '56 C.614 B.A. L.623 LL.B. 2514 Linwood Lane‡
McPhail, W. Rex, (AV) '59 '84
C&L.862 B.S., J.D. Gen. Coun., LeNorman Energy Corp. (Pat.)
Pennington, Hal H. ... '53 '89 C.1147 B.A. L.616 J.D. P.O. Box 1468
Renyer, Thomas Michael ... '47 '95 C.1300 B.A. L.623 107 S. 12th St.
Reynolds, Michael M., (BV) ... '47 '75 C.622 B.S. L.623 J.D. [DeBois,S.&R.]
Rice, Robt. E. ... '22 '49 C.197 A.B. L.477 LL.B. P.O. Box 1314‡
Roddy, Craig W. ... '65 '92 C.612 B.S. L.623 J.D. Sr. Coun., Halliburton Co.
Rodgers, Ricardo J. (Rick), (AV) ... '34 '65 C&L.623 B.B.A., J.D. [R.Rodgers]
Rodgers, Rick, Law Firm, (AV) ... 2206 Carolin Dr.
Russell, Gaylon Brent, (BV) ... '59 '85 C.612 B.S. L.623 J.D. Asst. Dist. Atty.
Ryan, Elizabeth E., (CV) ... '54 '81 C&L.623 B.A., J.D. Asst. Dist. Atty.
Sherrill, George D., Jr., (AV) ... '42 '70 C.612 B.S. L.623 J.D. [DeBois,S.&R.]
Steely, Ellen C. ... '39 '68 C&L.616 B.A., J.D. 1313 Ash
Stone, Scott W., (BV) ... '59 '84 C&L.623 B.A., J.D. [Bonney C.]
Stuart, John M., (AV) ... '49 '75 C.846 B.A. L.616 J.D. [Stuart,F.&H.]

Stuart, Frieda & Hammond, P.C., (AV)
Suite 100, Court Plaza Building, 1111 West Willow Avenue, 73533
Telephone: 580-252-9033 Facsimile: 580-252-6251
Email: sfhpc@texhoma.net
John M. Stuart; James M. Frieda; David W. Hammond;—Joe K. White.
Litigation, Civil & Criminal and Appellate Practice. Probate, Oil and Gas, Corporate, Domestic Relations, Bankruptcy, Real Estate, Personal Injury, Municipal and Workers' Compensation Law, Trusts and Estates, Clergy Sexual Misconduct, Death Penalty, Public Sector Law.
See Professional Biographies, DUNCAN, OKLAHOMA

Sullivan, Kent P., (AV) ... '55 '81 C&L.623 B.A., J.D. [Leach,S.S.&W.]
Sullivan, Michael P., (AV) ... '47 '72 C&L.623 B.A., J.D. [Leach,S.S.&W.]
Sullivan, Patrick D., (AV) ... '27 '51 C&L.623 B.A., LL.B. [Leach,S.S.&W.]
Sullivan, Paul D., (AV) ... '18 '47 C&L.623 A.B., LL.B. [Leach,S.S.&W.]
Sullivan, Scott P., (BV) ... '68 '93 C&L.623 B.B.A., J.D. [Leach,S.S.&W.]
Watkins, Jay B., (BV) ... '62 '87 C.1147 B.A. L.623 J.D. [Leach,S.S.&W.]
Weaver, Thomas R. ... '38 '68 C.560 B.S.Ch.E. L.846 J.D. 12 South 8th (Pat.)
White, Joe K. ... '73 '02 C.612 B.S. L.623 J.D. [Ⓐ Stuart,F.&H.]
Wustenberg, John W. ... '60 '92 C&L.623 B.S.E.E., J.D. Halliburton Co.

DURANT, * 13,549, *Bryan Co.*

Atkins & Markoff
(See Oklahoma City)

Bedwell, E. M. ... '37 '87 C.621 B.A.Ed. L.623 J.D. P.O. Box 1515
Boydston, M. Brent, (CV) ... '61 '88 C.623 B.A. L.615 J.D. [M.B.Boydston]
Boydston, M. Brent, P.C., (CV) ... P.O. Box 5113
Campbell, Mark R. ... '64 '92 C.623 B.A. L.615 J.D. Dist. Atty.
Cathey, G. Wendell, (BV) ... '38 '67 C&L.623 B.B.A., J.D. 113 N. 3rd
Criswell, Thomas Owen, IV '70 '96 C.802 B.A. L.623 J.D.
(adm. in NY; not adm. in OK) [Ⓒ Criswell&C.] & [Ⓐ LevineP.&M.] (⊙New York, NY)
Criswell, Tom, III, (AV) ... '37 '64 C.621 B.A. L.623 LL.B. [Criswell&C.]

Criswell & Criswell, Inc., (AV)
Criswell Building, 122 North Third Avenue, P.O. Box 541, 74702-0541
Telephone: 580-924-2119 Fax: 580-924-6468
Email: TCRISWEL@swbell.net
T. O. Criswell (1913-1969); Tom Criswell, III. Of Counsel: Thomas Owen Criswell, IV (Not admitted in OK).
Foreclosures, Guardianship, Wills, Probate, Property Law, Real Estate, Child Custody, Divorce, Family Law.

Faulkner, Mary, (BV) ... '48 '81 C.623 M.S. L.616 J.D. 119 N. 3rd Ave.
Haggerty, Don M., (BV) ... '44 '88 C.612 B.S. L.900 J.D. 121 N. Third
Haggerty, Don Michael, II ... '72 '96 C&L.623 B.A., J.D. 121 N. 3rd Ave.
Hatch, Farrell M. ... '35 '68 C.315 B.A. L.623 J.D. Dist. J.

Kelly, David W., (AV) '42 '68 C.621 B.S. L.623 J.D.
512 West Evergreen Street, P.O. Box 1047, 74702
Telephone: 580-924-1202 FAX: 580-924-4665
Email: kellydw57@yahoo.com
General Civil and Criminal Trial Practice. Personal Injury, Trusts, Probate, Real Estate, Family Law. No collections under $5000.
Representative Clients: Farm Credit Bank of Wichita.
References: First United Bank & Trust Co.; First Texoma National Bank in Durant.

Knight, Micah D., (BV) ... '58 '91 C.621 B.S. L.623 J.D. [M.D.Knight]
Knight, Micah D., P.C., (BV) ... 123 N. 7th Street
Long, Richard R. ... '55 '88 C&L.623 B.S.A., J.D. 3047 Quail Ridge Circle‡
Mawer, William T., II, (BVⓉ) '48 '73
C.851 B.S. L.607 J.D. Professor, Southeastern OK State Univ.
McGehee, Theresa Grego ... '54 '85 C.612 B.S. L.623 J.D. [McGehee&Assoc.]

McGehee & Associates
1319 W. Main Street, 74701-4903
Telephone: 580-920-0303 Fax: 580-920-9949
Email: trgmcgehee@aol.com
Member of Firm: Theresa Grego McGehee.
Criminal Defense, Personal Injury, Family Law.
See Professional Biographies, DURANT, OKLAHOMA

McPheron, Alan B., (AV) ... '14 '37 C.621 L.623 LL.B. 1504 Red Bud Ln.‡
Morrison, Mark A., (BV) ... '58 '86 C.621 B.S. L.623 J.D. 524 W. Evergreen
Nabors, Mary Kay, (BV) ... '50 '91 C.799 B.S. L.616 J.D. 118 North 3rd Street
Phelps, P.L. Pat, (AV) ... '39 '65 C.621 B.A. L.623 J.D. [P.L.P.Phelps]
Phelps, Rodney M. ... '43 '71 C.69 B.A. L.802 J.D. P.O. Box 882

Phelps, P.L. Pat, P.C., (AV)
325 West Evergreen, P.O. Box 882, 74702
Telephone: 580-924-1166 Fax: 580-924-1551
Email: plphelps@netcommander.com URL: http://www.lawyers.com/plphelps
P.L. Pat Phelps.
General Trial Practice. Probate, Real Estate, Family, Personal Injury.
Representative Clients: Furnished upon request.
References: First National Bank, Durant; First United Bank and Trust Co., Durant; Landmark Bank.
See Professional Biographies, DURANT, OKLAHOMA

Powers, Rocky L. ... '51 '76 C.621 B.A. L.862 J.D. Assoc. Dist. J.
Rainbolt, Kenneth D., (AV) ... '46 '75 C.612 B.S. L.623 J.D. P.O. Box 207
Tacheira, Russell M. ... '72 '01 C.618 B.A. L.623 J.D. State's Atty.
Taylor, Margaret P. Byers, (CV) ... '41 '78 C.621 B.A. L.623 J.D. P.O. Box 329

Taylor, Burrage, Foster, Mallett, Downs & Ramsey, P.C.
(See Claremore)

Wilhite, Byron L., (BV) ... '48 '75 C.623 B.B.A. L.616 J.D. Mun. J.

EDMOND, 68,315, *Oklahoma Co.*

Abney, Joe L. '41 '74 C.618 B.A. L.796 J.D.
(adm. in TX; not adm. in OK) [J.L.Abney] ‡
Abney, Joe L., P.C. ... 701 Bay Hill Pl.
Adams Charles "Andy", (BV) ... '58 '83 C.612 B.S. L.45 J.D. 2300 S. Broadway
Ainsworth-Southerland, Cheryal Kay, (BV) '50 '91 C.614 B.A. L.623 J.D.
Asst. City Atty.
Alizadeh-Fard, Melinda L. ... '62 '99 C.233 B.S. L.615 J.D. P.O. Box 5232
Allred, LLC ... P.O. Box 1838
Allred, Bradley Sterling ... '69 '94 C&L.623 B.S., J.D. [Allred]
Andersen, Darian Bruce ... '42 '70 L.878 J.D. [D.B.Andersen]
Andersen, Darian B., PC ... 3893 E. Memorial Rd.
Angel, Steven M., & Associates, (BV) '50 '76 C.446 B.S. L.615 J.D.
2313 Silverfield Ln.
Antkowiak, Michael D. ... '71 '97 C.612 B.A. L.623 J.D. 27 E. Ayers St.
Atkinson, Jack L., (BV) ... '48 '75 C.910 B.S. L.623 J.D. 12 Stoney Tr.
Austin Brent A. ... '64 '89 C.612 B.A. L.276 J.D. 1 S. Bway., Ste. 100
Austin, Jonathan B. ... '76 '03 C.612 B.S. L.623 J.D. [Ⓐ McAlister,M.M.&T.]
Avey, Bradley D., Law Office of, (BV) '59 '86
C.1315 B.S. L.623 J.D. 500 W. 15th St., Ste. 4
Bado, Barbara K. Arentz, (AV) ... '48 '78 C.623 B.A. L.30 J.D. [Bado&B.]
Bado, John Terry, (AV) ... '47 '71 C&L.69 B.A., J.D. [Bado&B.]
Bado and Bado, (AV) ... 1800 Canyon Park Circle
Baker, John R., Jr. ... '21 '52 C.623 B.S. L.616 LL.B. 1604 Sandpiper Drive, N.‡
Baker, Teresa E. ... '20 '52 L.616 LL.B. 1604 Sandpiper Drive, N.‡
Barnes, B. Don, (AV) ... '24 '49 C&L.623 LL.B 15700 N. Western‡
Barnes, Don ... '24 '49 L.623 LL.B. J.
Beech, Johnny G., (AV) ... '54 '80 C.622 B.S. L.45 J.D. [Ⓒ Lester,L.&D.]
Berkowitz, Lewis A., (BV) ... '57 '81 C.1044 B.A. L.862 J.D. [Berkowitz]
Berkowitz Law Firm, Inc., (BV) ... 15513 Himalaya Rdg.
Bizé, Susan Walters ... '— '84 C.691 B.A. L.846 J.D. [Ⓒ Lester,L.&D.]
Boehler, Orlie J. ... '38 '81 C.791 B.S. L.616 J.D. P.O. Box 5763
Booker, Steven R. ... '68 '94 C.845 B.A. L.615 J.D. [S.R.Booker]

Booker, Steven R., P.C., Law Office of
212 E. 2nd Street, 73034 ⊙
Telephone: 800-842-2212
Steven R. Booker.
Elder Law, Accidents, Slip and Fall, Products Defects, Dram Shop Cases, Railroad Accidents, Dog Bites, Automobile Negligence, Wrongful Death, Breach of Warranty, Nursing Home Negligence, Civil Litigation, Plaintiff Personal Injury, Probate Litigation, Contested Wills.
Wichita Falls, Texas Office: 705 8th Street, Suite 820, 76301. Telephone: 940-264-2108. Fax: 940-264-2106.
See Professional Biographies, EDMOND, OKLAHOMA

Bost, Janice Wilson ... '63 '95 C.612 B.S. L.623 J.D. P.O. Box 6934
Boyd, Kris M. ... '75 '03 C.45 B.A. L.616 J.D. [Ⓐ Zlotogura&Z.]
Brasher, Kimberly J. ... '— '93 C.101 B.S. L.623 J.D. 3893 E. Memorial Road
Bratcher, Monty L., (AV) ... '38 '62 C&L.623 A.B., LL.B. P.O. Box 1528
Brodt Charles E. ... '48 '83 C.613 B.A. L.615 J.D. 805 E. Covell Rd.
Bryan, Connie M., (BV) ... '42 '89 C.1147 B.S. L.616 J.D. 171 Stonebridge Blvd.

Burnett & Gelnar, PLLC
(See Oklahoma City)

Buxton, James H., (AV) ... '52 '77 C&L.616 B.A., J.D. Edmond Law Ctr.
Call, John A., (BV) ... '48 '80 C&L.378 B.A., J.D. 416 N. Crown Colony Dr.
Campo, Henry A. (Drew) ... '52 '79 C.623 B.B.A. L.615 J.D. 3409 Persimmon Creek Dr.

Carter, Craig D. '66 '94 C&L.623 B.B.A., J.D.
1300 E. 15th Street, Suite 190, 73013
Telephone: 405-340-5971 Fax: 405-348-7238
—Michelle Brown Robnett.
Corporate Law, Securities, Taxation, Estate Planning, Health Care, Commercial Law, Bankruptcy, Business and General Practice.
See Professional Biographies, EDMOND, OKLAHOMA

Casey, Jarold W. ... '42 '67 C.612 B.S. L.623 LL.B. Casey Ins. Co.
Casey, Patrick Jon, (AV) ... '43 '74 C.623 B.B.A. L.616 J.D. [McDivitt&C.]
Cathey, Kim F. ... '74 '00 C.1147 B.A. L.623 J.D. 3893 E. Memorial Rd.
Cherry, Cameron Davis ... '55 '93 C.623 B.A. L.615 J.D. P.O. Box 2807
Cohea, Sally Wright ... '54 '91 C.612 B.S. L.623 J.D. 2809 Sweetbriar
Collier, Freda M. Haack ... '40 '78 C.622 B.S. L.616 J.D. 8201 N.E. 140th St.
Combs, John Byron, (BV) '48 '76
C.1147 B.A. L.612 J.D. Gen. Coun., Sooner Invest. Cos.
Conner, Leslie L., Jr., (AV) ... '39 '63 C&L.623 B.A., LL.B. [L.L.Conner,Jr.]
Conner, Leslie L., Jr., P.C., (AV) ... P.O. Box 30426
Cook, David M. ... '18 '42 C&L.623 B.A., LL.B. Sr. Dist. J.‡
Cooke, Don, (AV) ... '49 '75 C.131 B.A. L.616 J.D. 1019 Waterwood Pkwy.
Cupp, Ann Agnew ... '44 '97 C.1369 B.A. L.790 J.D. 3301 Ridgewood Dr.
Daniel, Clifton D. ... '39 '78 C.627 B.G.S. L.623 J.D. 19417 Yearling Way★
Danley, Forrest J., (BV) ... '60 '86 C.618 B.S. L.623 J.D. [Danley]
Danley Law Firm, P.C., (BV) ... 3233 E. Memorial Rd.
Davies, Shannon F., (AV) ... '— '89 C.623 B.A. L.616 J.D. [Lester,L.&D.]
Davis, Stephen W. "Steve", (BV) ... '46 '74 C&L.623 B.A., J.D. P.O. Box 30010
Dixon, James B. '48 '76 C&L.616 B.A., J.D.
V.P. & Gen. Coun., Okla. City Abstract & Title Co.
Donaldson, LeAnn Bradley ... '56 '80 C.494 B.S. L.623 J.D. 1106 St. Andrews Dr.
Donaldson, Mark A., (BV) ... '54 '79 C&L.623 B.B.A., J.D. [Donaldson]
Donaldson Law Office, (BV) ... 609 S. Kelly Ave., Ste. C-2
Draelos, Kay Lynn ... '64 '94 C.613 B.A. L.1202 J.D. 808 Rock Hollow Rd.
Duncan, Kathleen M., (BV) ... '47 '80 C.999 B.S.E. L.623 J.D. 18616 Wolf Creek Dr.
Durocher, Daniel L., (AV) ... '48 '84 C.69 B.S. L.616 J.D. 5801 Whitetail Run
Durrell, Roderick W. ... '44 '76 C.882 B.S. L.623 J.D. P.O. Box 30453
Easter, David Norman, II, (AV) ... '56 '84 C.1315 B.S.E. L.623 J.D. [D.N.Easter,II]
Easter, D. Norman, II, Law Office of, (AV) ... 3500 South Blvd., Ste. 14B
Edwards, Eddie V. ... '30 '69 C&L.616 B.A., J.D. 2114 Mistletoe Lane‡

Fagin, Brown, Bush, Tinney & Kiser, A Professional Corporation
(See Oklahoma City)

Fenner, Jami J., (BV) ... '63 '89 C.425 B.B.A. L.861 J.D. [Ⓒ Lester,L.&D.]
Fernald, Paul F., (AV) ... '40 '66 C.612 B.S. L.623 J.D. 1603 S.E. 19th St., Ste. 204
Feuerhelm, Leonard Norman, Jr. ... '49 '94 C.612 B.S. L.615 J.D. 14309 Oxford Dr
Fine Mike W., (BV) ... '52 '78 C.619 B.S. L.616 J.D. 3509 French Park Dr.
Fisher, Jack D., (BV) ... '50 '76 C.622 B.S. L.616 J.D. 105 N. Hudson
Fitzpatrick, Brenda Regina ... '67 '00 C.623 B.A.S. L.615 J.D. 2008 Running Branch Rd.
Flaniken, Robert S. ... '44 '74 C.921 B.B.A. L.744 J.D. [R.S.Flaniken]
Flaniken, Robert S., P.C. ... 1705 Deason Drive
Foley, Hugh J. '15 '38 C&L.262 A.B., LL.B.
(adm. in NY; not adm. in OK) 2509 Brookdale St.‡

Franklin, Marvin L. ....'16 '55 C.619 B.A. L.616 LL.B. 609 N.W. 167‡
Freedman, George S. ....'— '93 C&L.502 B.A., J.D. [Ⓑ Lester,L.&D.]
Freeman, Jack L., (AV) ....'27 '53 C.619 L.623 LL.B. 2600 South Broadway
Gaidaroff, Walter R., (BV) ....'50 '81 C.1147 B.S. L.616 J.D. 1900 S. Bway.
Garic, John M., (BVⓉ) '54 '79 C.1099 B.A. L.425 J.D.
(adm. in LA; not adm. in OK) Univ. of Central Oklahoma
Gelczer, Rhonda F. ....'65 '91 C.612 B.S. L.615 J.D. 2724 Century Dr.
Gerrity, Patricia M. ....'53 '81 C.728 B.A. L.831 J.D. 2900 Ashe Brooke Pl.
Gile, John W., (AV) ....'53 '79 C&L.623 B.B.A., J.D. 320 N. Broadway, 2nd Fl.
Grammer, Jonathan R. ....'75 '03 C.845 B.A. L.616 J.D. 320 N. Broadway, Ste. 201

Hackett, Benjamin F., & Associates, (AV) '48 '76 C.612 B.S. L.623 J.D.
1301 South Broadway Suite 300, 73034
Telephone: 405-340-8854 Fax: 405-340-8299
Email: benhackett@sbcglobal.net
Oil and Gas Law, Oil and Gas Regulation, Oil and Gas Title Examination, Real Estate, Probate, Estate Planning; Administrative Law, Corporate Law and Partnership Law, General Practice.
See Professional Biographies, EDMOND, OKLAHOMA

Halliburton, Janet D., (BV) ....'52 '77 C.619 B.A. L.623 718 Hawthorne Place
Hammett, Bruce W., (BV) ....'44 '70 C.377 B.A. L.862 J.D. 815 Buckingham Way
Hammond, Gary D., (AV) ....'63 '90 C&L.623 B.B.A., J.D. [Hammond&Assoc.]

Hammond & Associates, (AV)
1320 E. 9th Street, #4, 73034
Telephone: 405-216-0007 Facsimile: 405-216-0671
Email: gary@hammondassociateslaw.com URL: http://www.hammondassociateslawfirm.com
Member of the Firm: Gary D. Hammond.
Contracts, Business Law, Commercial Litigation, Bankruptcy, Consumer Bankruptcy.
See Professional Biographies, EDMOND, OKLAHOMA

Hammons, Samuel G., (AV) ....'50 '77 C.613 B.A. L.623 J.D. P.O. Box 6894
Hanson, Ramona S., (BV) ....'53 '85 C.232 B.A. L.616 J.D. [R.S.Hanson]
Hanson, Ramona Shannon, P.C., (BV) ....301 S. Bryant Avenue
Harper, Chris, (BV) ....'58 '83 C.612 B.S. L.616 J.D. 1501 Renaissance Boulevard
Harris, Kelley Dee ....'67 '92 C.1310 B.S.B.A. L.615 J.D. 1620 Yosemite Pl.

Haupt Brooks Vandruff, PLLC
(See Oklahoma City)

High, Harriett B. ....'22 '45 C&L.623 A.B., LL.B. 2955 Village Cir.‡
Hitchcock, Mark L. ....'59 '84 C.612 B.S. L.616 J.D. 2005 Turtlecreek Rd.
Hoose, Mark L., (BV) ....'61 '91 C.1147 B.S. L.623 J.D. 17 E. 1st
Horn, Jesse J. ....'28 '62 C.612 L.615 LL.B. P.O. Box 5196
Irish, Jennifer E., (AV) ....'49 '85 C.259 B.A. L.623 J.D. [Irish]
Irish Law Firm, (AV) ....1441 N.W. 150th St.
Jacobson, J. David, (AV) ....'55 '88 C.999 B.S. L.616 J.D. [Jacobson&L.]

Jacobson & Laasch, (AV)
212 East Second Street, 73034
Telephone: 405-341-3303 Fax: 405-341-6686
Email: jdj8788@aol.com
J. David Jacobson; Jon W. Laasch.
General Civil Trial Practice, Bankruptcy, Commercial Law, Telecommunications, Telephone Utility Regulation, Electric Utility Law, Public Utility Law, Administrative Law, Business Law, Corporate Law, Litigation, Appellate Practice, Insurance Defense, Debtor and Creditor, Contracts, Negligence, Oil and Gas Law.
See Professional Biographies, EDMOND, OKLAHOMA

Johnson, Cloise E., Jr. ....'40 '92 C.1147 B.S. L.616 J.D. 237 Shortgrass Road
Jolley, Joseph Clark, (BV) '70 '95 C.613 B.A. L.623 J.D.
922 South Boulevard, Suite 300
Kamp, Randall W., (AV) ....'60 '87 C.612 B.S. L.623 J.D. [R.W.Kamp]
Kamp, Randall W., P.C., (AV) ....1900 E. 15th St.
Karam, Richard S. ....'32 '65 C.612 B.S. L.616 J.D. 2728 Blue Quail Pass
Kirksey, Jerry, (BV) ....'48 '85 C&L.623 B.A., J.D. 212 E. 2nd St.
Laasch, Jon W., (BV) ....'60 '85 C.623 B.A. L.862 J.D. [Jacobson&L.]
Larson, B. A. ....'20 '48 C&L.623 B.A., LL.B. P.O. Box 782
Lashley, Gary J. ....'64 '97 C.614 B.S. L.615 J.D. 428 Wild Wind Rd.
Lee, Edward O., (AV) ....'50 '78 C.612 B.A. L.616 J.D. [E.O.Lee]
Lee, Mary M., (AV) ....'51 '83 C.880 B.S.N. L.623 J.D. [M.M.Lee] (See Pat. Sect.)
Lee, Edward O., P.C., (AV) ....1300 E. 9th St., Ste. 3

Lee, Mary M., P.C., Law Office of, (AV)
1300 E. 9th Street, Suite 4, 73034-5760
Telephone: 405-285-4490 Fax: 405-285-4491
Email: mml@marymlee.com URL: http://www.marymlee.com
Mary M. Lee.
Patents, Trademarks, Copyrights, Trade Secrets, Unfair Competition and Related Licensing and Litigation.
See Professional Biographies, EDMOND, OKLAHOMA

Lester, Andrew W., (AV) ....'— '81 C.228 B.A. L.276 J.D. [Lester,L.&D.]

Lester, Loving & Davies, P.C., (AV)
1701 South Kelly Avenue, 73013
Telephone: 405-844-9900 Fax: 405-844-9958
Email: lld@lldlaw.com URL: http://www.lldlaw.com
Andrew W. Lester; Susan Brimer Loving; Shannon F. Davies; Scott Thompson; Courtney Davis Powell. Of Counsel: Susan Walters Bizé; George S. Freedman; Jami J. Fenner; Johnny G. Beech.
Civil Litigation in all State and Federal Courts. Civil Rights, Employment, Labor, Defamation, Personal Injury, Environmental, Energy, Estate Planning, Wills and Trusts, Local Government, Land Use, Corporate, Banking, Commercial, Sports, Administrative, Mediation, State Government, Equine, Non-Profit Association and Governance, Insurance, Criminal Law, Appellate Advocacy and Tax.
See Professional Biographies, EDMOND, OKLAHOMA

Lewis, Steven, (AV) ......'58 '84 C&L.623 B.A., J.D. 3233 E. Memorial Road, Suite 108
Lidia, D. Daryl, (BV) ....'63 '88 C.1315 B.S. L.623 J.D. [Lidia]
Lidia, Rebecca Nichols ....'64 '89 C.1315 B.A. L.623 J.D. [Lidia]
Lidia Law Firm, A Professional Corporation, (BV) ....1320 E. 9th St., Ste. 9
Linehan, James R., (AV) ....'56 '87 C.612 B.S. L.616 J.D. [J.R.Linehan]
Linehan, James R., PC, (AV) ....3126 S. Boulevard St., Ste. 286
Lisle, Kenneth E., Jr., (BV) ....'51 '76 C.623 B.A. L.616 J.D. P.O. Box 322
Listen, Gary Wayne ....'53 '91 C.1147 B.S. L.623 J.D. 617 Doe Trail
Loving, Susan Brimer, (AV) ....'— '80 C&L.623 B.A., J.D. [Lester,L.&D.]
Lynn, Thomas Neil, III, (BV) ....'56 '81 C&L.623 B.A., J.D. 2700 Julies Trail
Mace, Connie S., (AV) ....'52 '78 C&L.623 B.A., J.D. 2601 Persimmon Creek Dr.
Manning, Joe R., Jr. ....'46 '73 C.612 B.A. L.623 J.D. P.O. Box 2762
Massey, Jeffery W., (BV) ....'62 '91 C.45 B.S. L.623 J.D. 922 South Boulevard
Maxey, Joseph Willard, Jr. ....'41 '66 C.623 B.B.A. L.273 J.D. MAXCO Intl.
McAlister, Karla, (AV) ....'55 '80 C.612 B.S. L.846 J.D. [McAlister,M.M.&T.]
McAlister, Lloyd G., (AV) ....'55 '80 C.612 B.S. L.846 J.D. [McAlister,M.M.&T.]

McAlister, McAlister, McKinnis & Tuggle, P.C., (AV)
Kirkpatrick Bank Building, 15 East 15th Street, Suite 200 Post Office Box 1569, 73083-1569
Telephone: 405-359-0701 Fax: 405-359-0806
Email: mmmtlaw@mmmtlaw.com URL: http://www.mmmtlaw.com
Lloyd G. McAlister; Karla McAlister; Todd A. McKinnis; Judy A. Tuggle;—Jonathan B. Austin; Wendy L. McMahon.
Estate and Gift Taxation, Business Law, Contracts, Commercial Law, Corporate Law, Partnership Law, Commercial Transaction, Civil Litigation, Estate Litigation, Trust Litigation, Probate, Real Estate, Mergers, Acquisitions and Divestures, Taxation, Wills, Labor and Employment Law, Estate Planning, Elder Law, Guardianship and Conservatorship, Nonprofit and Charitable Organizations.
Reference: Kirkpatrick Bank, Edmnd, Okla.
See Professional Biographies, EDMOND, OKLAHOMA

McArdle, Scott A., (BV) ....'59 '92 C.546 B.A. L.615 J.D. 3500 S. Boulevard
McDivitt, Richard Frank, (AV) ....'24 '55 C&L.616 B.S., LL.B. [Ⓑ McDivitt&C.]
McDivitt & Casey, P.C., (AV) ....1900 East 15th, Building 900
McGregor, Frank H., III, Law Office of ...'50 '89 C&L.623 B.A., J.D. 1900 E. 15th Street
McKenzie, Gregory A., (AV) ....'47 '72 C.623 B.A. L.273 J.D. [G.A.McKenzie]
McKenzie, Gregory A., P.C., (AV) ....19100 Saddle River Drive
McKinney, Edith G. ....'16 '44 C.617 L.615 506 Timberdale Ter.
McKinnis, Todd A., (AV) ....'67 '94 C&L.623 B.A., J.D. [McAlister,M.M.&T.]
McLaughlin, Michael K., (BV) ......'50 '78 C&L.623 B.S., J.D. 2600 Glen Hollow Road
McMahon, Wendy L. ....'76 '04 C.612 B.S. L.623 J.D. [Ⓐ McAlister,M.M.&T.]
McNaught, Kelsey Lynne .....'57 '84 C&L.623 B.A., J.D. 301 S. Bryant Ave., Ste. C200
Meadows, William C. ....'25 '67 C&L.616 B.S., J.D. 5825 Chestnut Ct.‡
Metzer, Greg A., (AV) ....'60 '85 C&L.623 B.B.A., J.D. 1 S. Broadway, Ste. 100
Miley, David Allen, (BV) ....'59 '86 C&L.623 B.A.C., J.D. [D.Miley]
Miley, David, (BV) ....1019 Waterwood Parkway, Suite B
Mitzner, Miles L., (BV) ....'57 '87 C.623 B.A. L.616 J.D. [Mitzner&Assoc.]
Mitzner & Associates, Inc., (BV) ....171 Stonebridge Blvd.
Mogilka, Henry J. ....'60 '98 C.494 B.S. L.615 J.D. 3005 Hidden Valley Rd.
Montazzoli, John E., (BV) .....'47 '81 C.516 B.A. L.616 J.D. 3209 S. Broadway, Ste. 229
Morelli, Brad, (BV) ....'56 '80 C.1147 B.A. L.616 J.D. Univ. of Central Oklahoma
Mosca, Pasquale ....'17 '51 C.563 L.724 LL.B. Ret. U.S. Admin. Law J.
Murdock, Ben L., (AV) ....'04 '29 C&L.862 1312 Sims Ave.‡
Murdock, Stephen T., (AV) ....'57 '82 C.1147 B.A. L.623 J.D. City Atty.
Myers, H. Keith, (AV) ....'31 '64 C.136 B.S. L.862 J.D. 2705 E. Summit Dr.
Nelson, W. Dan, (BV) ....'43 '69 C&L.623 B.A., J.D. 2500 South Broadway
Niblett, Sandra Lee, (BV) ....'45 '85 C.1147 B.A. L.616 J.D. 2016 Glendale Dr.
Nunn, David L., (AV) ....'64 '91 C.618 B.A. L.616 J.D. [D.L.Nunn]

Nunn, David L., P.C., (AV)
17 East First Street, 73034
Telephone: 405-330-4053 Fax: 405-330-8470
URL: http://www.oklahomalegal.org
David L. Nunn.
Commercial Law, Corporate Law, Commercial Collections, Bankruptcy (Creditors only), Automotive Warranty and Finance Law, Consumer Finance, Creditors Rights, Contracts, Litigation.
See Professional Biographies, EDMOND, OKLAHOMA

Owens, Phillip P., II, (BV) ....'— '93 C&L.623 B.A., J.D. [Ⓐ C.Harper]
Paul, Homer ....'32 '59 C&L.623 B.A., LL.B. 2705 Windmill Road
Powell, Courtney Davis ....'— '02 C.45 B.A. L.615 J.D. [Lester,L.&D.]
Powers, Don Marvin ....'— '00 C.862 M.B.A. L.615 J.D. [Powers]
Powers, G. Kay ....'— '00 C.612 Ph.D. L.615 J.D. [Powers]
Powers at Law, LLC ....1420 Bond Street
Preston, John R., (AV) ....'45 '71 C.97 B.A. L.930 J.D. 2501 East Coffee Creek Road
Prince, Thomas Edward, (AV) ....'57 '82 C.1094 B.S. L.616 J.D. [Prince]
Prince Law Firm, (AV) ..............P.O. Box 2911
Putnam, Jerry W., (BV) ....'49 '78 C.927 B.A. L.616 J.D. 169 S.E. 32nd
Raney, Cara Jenkins ....'71 '97 C&L.616 B.S., J.D. 313 W. 7th
Ratcliffe, Giles K. ....'26 '58 C.623 L.616 LL.B. 5904 E. 15th‡
Reagan, John S. ....'44 '73 C.840 B.A. L.744 J.D. 1613 Tahlequah Dr.
Rice, Barry T., (AV) ....'53 '82 C.1147 B.B.A. L.616 J.D. [B.T.Rice]
Rice, Barry T., PC, (AV) ....17 E. 1st. St.
Robinson, J. Randall, (AV) ....'44 '69 C&L.623 B.A., J.D. [J.R.Robinson]
Robinson, J. Randall, P.C., (AV) ....212 E. Second St.
Robnett, Michelle Brown, (BVⓉ) ....'58 '92 C.378 B.S. L.623 J.D. [Ⓐ C.D.Carter]
Ross, Jacqueline Kay Stahly ....'56 '90 C.82 B.A. L.616 J.D. 509 N.W. 166th St.
Rubenstein, Michael A., (AV) ......'54 '81 C.025 B.A. L.623 J.D. 171 Stonebridge Blvd.
Rudkin, Bob, (AV) ....'30 '57 C.1147 B.S. L.616 J.D. 116 S. Broadway
Ryan, J. Dennis, (BV) ....'34 '61 C.602 B.A. L.623 LL.B. P.O. Box 2945
Schlinke, Bennett, (BV) ....'43 '71 C.1147 B.S. L.616 J.D. 17 E. First St.
Schooling, Roy L. ....'26 '56 C&L.616 B.S., LL.B. 1417 E. Sims Ave.‡
Shadid, Randel C., (BV) ....'47 '73 C&L.623 B.B.A., J.D. [R.Shadid]
Shadid, Randel, (BV) ....19 N. Broadway
Shirley, Michael R. '56 '81
C.612 B.A. L.623 J.D. Prof. of Law, Univ. of Central Oklahoma
Shoemaker, Robert G., (AV) ....'52 '79 C.623 B.B.A. L.616 J.D. P.O. Box 2138
Singer, Harry J. ....'48 '83 C.870 B.S. L.45 J.D. 1800 Canyon Park Circle
Smith, Donnie E. ....'50 '80 C.39 B.S. L.862 J.D. 1616 S. Air Depot Blvd.
Smith, Edw. W. ....'14 '40 C&L.623 B.S., LL.B. 2613 Little Timber‡
Snapp-Holloway, Nicole R. ....'70 '99 C.473 B.A. L.615 J.C. 325 Dean A. Mcgee
Sommer, Patricia, (AV) ....'56 '82 C.846 B.A. L.615 J.D. 11 Darwin Rd.
Sowders, Henry C., III ....'38 '69 C.862 B.S. L.616 J.D. 3305 Prairie St.‡
Speegle, C. Max, (AV) ....'45 '74 C.612 B.S. L.623 J.D. 19 N. Broadway
Stack, Michael D., (AV) ....'50 '75 C.623 B.B.A. L.616 J.D. [M.D.Stack]
Stack, Michael D., PC, (AV) ....3500 S. Blvd., Ste. 5D
Stout, Cynthia K. ....'57 '93 C.612 B.S. L.616 J.D. [Stout& S.]
Stout, Richard E., (AV) ....'57 '83 C.612 B.S. L.616 J.D. [Stout& S.]
Stout& Stout, (AV) ....3200 E. Memorial Rd.
Stratton, G. Robinson, III, (AV) ....'60 '91 C.1147 B.B.A. L.616 J.D. [G.R.Stratton,III]
Stratton, G. Robinson, III, P.C., (AV) ..............P.O. Box 7834
Streck, Paul ....'64 '89 C.663 B.S. L.623 J.D. [Streck&Assoc.]

Streck & Associates
2300 South Broadway, Suite 100, 73013
Telephone: 405-330-1303 Facsimile: 405-330-1903
URL: http://www.lawyers.com/streck&associates
Paul Streck.
Divorce, Family, Property Division, Alimony, Paternity, Child Support, Child Custody, Adoption, Guardianships, Probate, DUI.
See Professional Biographies, EDMOND, OKLAHOMA

Synar, Alan E., (AV) ....'55 '80 C&L.623 B.B.A., J.D. 1900 S. Bdwy.
Tawwater, Caroline Drummond ....'72 '01 C.612 B.S. L.623 J.D. 1509 Nw 149th St
Teague, R. Glenn, (AV) ....'49 '77 C.1315 B.A. L.616 J.D. [Teague]
Teague Law Office, (AV) ....3004 E. Memorial Rd., Ste. 4
Thompson, Scott ....'— '96 C.612 B.A. L.273 J.D. [Lester,L.&D.]

Tolson, Steven L., (AV) '54 '88 C.1147 B.B.A. L.616 J.D. [S.L.Tolson]
Tolson, Steven L., P.C., (AV) P.O. Box 5108
Tresler, Kendall W. '52 '76 C&L.623 B.A., J.D. 16904 Halbrooke Cir.
Tucker, Phillip James, (BV) '54 '83 C.1147 B.S. L.615 J.D. [Tucker]
Tucker Law Firm, The, (BV) P.O. Box 601
Tuggle, Judy A., (AV) '54 '92 C.1 B.S. L.623 J.D. [McAlister,M.M.&T.]
Vaughn, Raymond L., Jr., (AV) '48 '76 C.1315 B.A. L.616 J.D. Rep., OK House of Reps.
Vervinck, Robert N. '39 '66 C&L.912 B.S., J.D. (adm. in OH; not adm. in OK) 3109 Viewmont Court‡
Walke, Geary L. '51 '76 C.623 B.A. L.616 J.D. Dist. J.
Walling, David L., (AV) '54 '80 C.622 B.A. L.615 J.D. 14701 Collingwood Lane
Walters, John Paul, (AV) '21 '50 C&L.623 LL.B. 300 N. Broadway
Walters, John Paul, Jr. '50 '79 C.813 A.B. L.623 J.D. 15 E. 1st St.
Wavers, Nicholas A. '50 '76 C&L.623 B.B.A., J.D. [N.Wavers]
Wavers, Nick, Attorney at Law 1112 Alexanders Trail
Webb, W. Roger '41 '67 C.612 B.A. L.623 J.D. Pres., Univ. of Central Okla.
Webster, Kenneth R., (AV) '41 '65 C.602 B.A. L.623 J.D. 4220 Oakdale Forest Rd.
West, William O., (AV) '41 '66 C&L.623 B.S., J.D. [W.O.West]
West, William O., A Professional Corporation, (AV) P.O. Box 5126
Wiggins, Susan G., (BV) '57 '82 C.1147 B.S. L.623 J.D. Central Okla. Mediation Assn., L.L.C.
Willey, Benjamin T., Jr., (BV) '46 '76 C.1142 B.A. L.616 J.D. 2300 Rosewood Ln.
Williams, Charles V., Jr. '30 '61 C&L.862 B.A., LL.B. 19505 Sportsman Rd.‡
Williams, George H. '45 '74 C.823 B.S. L.616 J.D. 6013 Country Club Dr.
Willits, Phillip H., (AV) '50 '78 C.622 B.A. L.616 J.D. 1900 S. Broadway
Winton, Matthew Lon '73 '00 C.1315 B.A. L.623 J.D. 2801 E. Memorial Rd., Ste. 110
Wright, Alvin R., (AV) '52 '81 C.1147 B.A. L.616 J.D. 1800 Canyon Park Circle
Yadon, R. B., Jr. '16 '39 C&L.623 B.A., J.D. 906 N. Boulevard St.‡
Young, Carl W., (AV) '30 '74 C&L.616 B.S., J.D. [Young&Y.]
Young, Steven A. '64 '99 C.623 B.B.A. L.615 J.D. [Young&Y.]
Young & Young, A Prof. Corp., (AV) 515 S. Santa Fe
Zlotogura, Barry, (BV) '56 '87 C.252 B.S. L.616 J.D. [Zlotogura&Z.]
Zlotogura, Carol K., (BV) '56 '92 C.475 B.S. L.615 J.D. [Zlotogura&Z.]
Zlotogura and Zlotogura, (BV) 27 East Ayers Street

ELK CITY, 10,428, *Beckham Co.*

Albert, Mark W., (BV) '62 '88 C&L.623 B.A., J.D. [Albert&A.]
Albert, Paul Anthony, (AV) '53 '79 C.623 B.A. L.862 J.D. [Albert&A.]

Albert and Albert, (AV)
205 West Broadway, P.O. Box 1748, 73648
Telephone: 580-225-2010 Telefax: 580-225-2011
Email: markalbert@it/net.net
Paul Anthony Albert; Mark W. Albert.
General Civil Practice. Bankruptcy, Workers Compensation, Probate, Family, Real Estate, Banking, Commercial, Corporate, Insurance Bad Faith, All Personal Injury Claims, Accidental Death, Wrongful Death, Nursing home Neglect, Criminal Defense Law, Driving While Intoxicated, Drug Crimes, Felonies, Misdemeanors, Domestic Relations, Custody, Divorce. No Collections under $4,500.00.
Reference: Bank of Western Oklahoma.

See Professional Biographies, ELK CITY, OKLAHOMA

Atkins & Markoff
(See Oklahoma City)

Brown, James A., (BV) '44 '70 C&L.623 B.A., J.D. Mun. J.
Harrel, Celo, (BV) '62 '87 C.622 B.A. L.616 J.D. 119 S. Jefferson

Holloway, Steven L., (AV) '53 '78 C.622 B.S. L.623 J.D.
622 West Third Street, P.O. Box 932, 73648
Telephone: 580-225-0392 Fax: 580-243-5560
General and Civil Practice. Civil Litigation, Real Estate, Probate and Domestic Relations Law.

Ivester, John Ed T., (BV) '33 '65 C.623 B.A. L.616 J.D. [Ivester,I.&I.] ⊙

Ivester, Ivester & Ivester, (AV)
114 N. Adams, P.O. Box 1950, 73648-1950 ⊙
Telephone: 580-225-6525 Fax: 580-225-2806
Email: ivesterlaw@itlnet.net URL: http://www.ivesterlaw.com
John Ed T. Ivester.
Civil Litigation, Business Law, Commercial Law, Corporate Law, Partnership Law, Insurance, Real Estate, Family Law, Oil & Gas, Probate, Taxation, Trusts and Estates.
Sayre Office: P.O. Box 160, 73662-0160. Telephone: 580-928-2116. Fax: 580-928-5353.

See Professional Biographies, ELK CITY, OKLAHOMA

McComas, Edwin, (AV) '42 '67 C&L.623 B.A., J.D.
203 West Broadway, P.O. Box 849, 73648
Telephone: 580-225-0400 Fax: 580-225-0408
Email: mccomaslaw@itlnet.net
General Civil Practice, Probate, Trust and Real Estate Law.

McGinn, Gary P., (BV) '38 '66 C.623 B.B.A. L.616 J.D. 1607 W. Ave. "D"
Pixton, Thomas R., (BV) '43 '73 C.418 B.A. L.861 J.D. 211 W. 5th St.
Sorelle, Alicia Carrington, (BV) '64 '89 C.612 B.S. L.862 B.S. 119 South Jefferson

EL RENO, * 16,212, *Canadian Co.*

Bass, James C., (AV) '38 '66 C.623 B.B.A. L.616 J.D. [Bass]
Bass, John A., (AV) '49 '75 C.623 B.B.A. L.616 J.D. [Bass]
Bass Law Firm, A Professional Corporation, (AV) 104 North Rock Island Avenue
Boling, Tammy '59 '88 C.1147 B.B.A. L.616 J.D. 203 N. Bickford Ave., Ste. A
Cantrell, Mark Lea (Beau), (CV) '51 '77 C&L.623 B.A., J.D. 210 North Choctaw
Cunningham, Edward C. '49 '79 C&L.623 B.B.A., J.D. Dist. J.
Dickerson, Kenneth W. '39 '72 C.663 B.S. L.616 J.D. Spec. Dist. J.
Dominic, Kenneth Leslie '64 '98 C&L.623 B.A., J.D. Asst. Dist. Atty.
Flanagan, William Spencer '44 '72 C.840 B.B.A. L.862 J.D. Asst. Dist. Atty.
Fogg, Richard M., (AV) '41 '65 C&L.623 B.A., J.D. [Fogg,F.&H.]
Fogg, Fogg & Handley, (AV) 421 South Rock Island
Gahan, Michael S., (BV) '57 '82 C.205 B.A. L.623 J.D. Asst. Dist. Atty.
Haley, Timothy C., (BV) '60 '87 C.612 B.S. L.862 J.D. [Haley]
Haley Law Office, (BV) 219 North Bickford Street
Halley, David H., (CV) '63 '88 C.623 B.B.A. L.615 J.D. [D.H.Halley]
Halley, David H., Attorney at Law, PC, (CV) 200 N. Choctaw Ave., Ste. 100
Handley, Fletcher Dal, Jr., (AV) '48 '79 C&L.623 B.A., J.D. [Fogg,F.&H.]
Henricksen, Lanita, (BV) '48 '92 C.999 B.A. L.615 J.D. [Henricksen&H.] ⊙
Henricksen, Mark, (AV) '54 '78 C&L.623 B.A., J.D. [Henricksen&H.]

Henricksen & Henricksen Lawyers, Inc., (AV)
210 North Choctaw, 73036-2647 ⊙
Mailing Address: P.O. Box 1129, El Reno, OK 73036-1129
Telephone: 405-262-0983 Fax: 405-262-2049
Mark Henricksen; Lanita Henricksen.
General Civil and Criminal Trial Practice State and Federal Courts, Banking, Bankruptcy, Family, Probate and Personal Injury Law, Criminal Law, Constitutional Law.
Oklahoma City, Oklahoma Office: 6440 Avondale Drive, Suite 200, 73116. Telephone: 405-848-3977.

See Professional Biographies, EL RENO, OKLAHOMA

Hockett-King, Jennifer M., (CV) '70 '97 C.612 B.A. L.615 J.D. Asst. Dist. Atty.
Howard, John C., (AV) '42 '69 C.623 B.A. L.616 J.D. [Howard&H.] ⊙
Howard, Scarlett A., (BV) '66 '91 C&L.623 B.A., J.D. [Howard&H.] ⊙
Howard & Howard, (AV) 210 North Choctaw (⊙Arcadia)
Hughey, Bob W., (CV) '60 '85 C&L.623 B.B.A., J.D. [Hughey&P.]
Hughey and Parker, (CV) 100 N. Choctaw St.
Lewis, Richard T., (BV) '39 '73 C.112 B.A. L.616 J.D. 300 N. Choctaw
McCann, Scott Earle, (CV) '62 '97 C.612 B.S. L.615 J.D. [Haley]
McCurdy, Gary D., (BV) '52 '80 C.612 B.A. L.862 J.D. Spec. Dist. Ct. J.
Miller, Gary '46 '78 C.1147 B.A. L.616 J.D. Assoc. Dist. J.
Morrison, Robt. L., (BV) '24 '47 C&L.623 LL.B. 210 N. Choctaw
Parker, Gregory K., (CV) '49 '91 C.623 B.B.A. L.615 J.D. [Hughey&P.]

Ramey & Tharp
(See Yukon)

Rinehart, James Roger '61 '87 C.612 B.A. L.862 J.D. [Rinehart,R.&R.]
Rinehart, R. Dean, (AV) '31 '56 C.623 L.862 LL.B. [Rinehart,R.&R.]
Rinehart, Roger, (BV) '61 '87 C.612 B.A. L.862 J.D. [Rinehart,R.&R.]
Rinehart, William J., (CV) '48 '89 C.1147 B.A. L.616 J.D. 515 Matthews
Rinehart, Rinehart & Rinehart, P.C., (AV) 115 South Rock Island
Stevener, Arthur B., Jr., (AV) '42 '70 C.612 B.S. L.616 J.D. 200 N. Choctaw
Weaver, Joseph P., (CV) '56 '94 C&L.623 B.B.A., J.D. [Bass]
Wolking, John L. '52 '78 C&L.623 B.S.E.E., J.D. Spec. Dist. J.

ENID, * 47,045, *Garfield Co.*

Anderson, R. Patrick '69 '94 C.612 B.S. L.623 J.D. Asst. V.P. & Tr. Offr., Central Natl. Bank & Tr. Co. of Enid, OK‡

Atkins & Markoff
(See Oklahoma City)

Atkinson, Brendon S. '77 '02 C.612 B.S. L.623 J.D. [Gungoll,J.C.B.&D.]
Beam, Elizabeth Ward, (CV) '42 '97 C.37 B.S. L.425 J.D. 224 N. Independence, Ste. 800
Beebe, Timothy R., (BV) '63 '88 C&L.623 B.A., J.D. 323 W. Cherokee
Belcher, Page, Jr., (AV) '24 '49 C&L.623 LL.B. 205 W. Maple
Bigheart, Michael C., (AV) '50 '83 C.942 B.B.A. L.862 J.D. [Mitchell&D.]
Blakley, Terri K., (BV) '57 '90 C&L.623 B.A., J.D. 2901 Wildwood Dr.
Blakley, Thomas G., (BV) '47 '81 C.663 B.A. L.623 J.D. [Blakley]
Blakley Law Firm, (BV) P.O. Box 5676
Box, Craig L., (BV) '57 '83 C.620 B.S. L.862 J.D. [Gungoll,J.C.B.&D.]
Braley, Timothy Shawn, (BV) '70 '96 C.663 B.S. L.623 J.D. Asst. Dist. Atty.
Brown, G. L. (Gary), III, (AV) '— '80 C.623 B.B.A. L.862 J.D. [Brown&Assoc.]

Brown & Associates Attorneys & Counselors at Law, P.L.L.C., (AV)
201 North Grand, Suite 301, 73701
Telephone: 580-234-6600 Fax: 580-234-6606
Email: mail@brownlaw-ok.com URL: http://www.brownlaw-ok.com
G. L. (Gary) Brown, III. Associate: Sarah J. Lane.
Business Transactions, Estate Planning, Probate Administration, Business Association Law, Tax Law, Tax Controversies, Family Law.

See Professional Biographies, ENID, OKLAHOMA

Butler, David C., (AV) '45 '76 C&L.623 B.A., J.D. [Mitchell&D.]
Buvinger, Margaret S. '22 '48 C&L.150 A.B., LL.B. (adm. in OH; not adm. in OK) 1502 Ramona Dr.‡
Cameron, Stephen P. '67 '05 C.1147 B.A. L.623 J.D. 324 W. Maine
Camp, John G., (CV) '64 '90 C&L.623 B.A., J.D. [Camp&J.]
Camp & Jones, Law Firm, P.L.L.C, (BV) 109 North Grand
Collins, David M., (AV) '48 '78 C.663 B.A. L.623 J.D. [Gungoll,J.C.B.&D.]
Conrad, Frantz C., Jr., (BV) '22 '49 C&L.623 B.A., LL.B. 15th Fl. Continental Twr.
Cox, James R., (AV) '32 '65 C&L.623 B.S., J.D. [J.R.Cox]
Cox, James R., P.C., (AV) 302 North Independence
Crowley, Tim J., (AV) '40 '66 C.614 B.S. L.862 J.D. 300 W. Cherokee, Ste. 102
Crump, Richard S., (CV) '55 '95 C&L.623 B.A., J.D. 205 W. Maple, Ste. 107
Culver, Karig P., (BV) '58 '86 C.612 B.S. L.862 J.D. [Gungoll,J.C.B.&D.]
Cumpston, H. Max '28 '76 C.612 B.S. L.616 J.D. Chf. Environmentalist, Northrop-Grumman Corp.
Davenport, Bradley E. '73 '00 C.623 B.A. L.880 J.D. [Gungoll,J.C.B.&D.]
Davis, April McCurdy '72 '98 C.623 B.S. L.585 J.D. [Jones,O.D.N.&J.]
Davis, Chad N. '76 '03 C&L.623 B.S., J.D. [Gungoll,J.C.B.&D.]
Davis, Matthew Neill, (CV) '68 '95 C.187 B.S.M.S. L.623 J.D. 324 West Maine
DeClerck, Tim E., (BV) '56 '83 C&L.623 B.A., J.D. [Mitchell&D.]
DeVaughn, Forrest L. Pepper '74 '00 C.612 B.S. L.862 J.D. [Mitchell&D.]
Devoll, Glenn A., (AV) '52 '77 C.1147 B.S. L.623 J.D. [Gungoll,J.C.B.&D.]
Ediger, Roger L. '54 '02 C.999 B.A. L.623 J.D. [Mitchell&D.]
Edwards, Eric Nathan '68 '93 C.612 B.S. L.623 J.D. P.O. Box 5188
Elliott, Clifford L., Jr., (AV) '49 '76 C.623 B.A. L.616 J.D. [Elliott,E.N.&E.]
Elliott, Enabnit, Newby & Ezzell, A Professional Corporation, (AV) Broadway Twr., 114 E. Broadway, Ste. 500
Enabnit, Nancy L., (AV) '58 '83 C&L.623 B.A., J.D. [Elliott,E.N.&E.]
Evans, Elise D. '79 '05 C&L.623 B.B.A., J.D. [Traynor,L.W.&W.] ⊙
Ezzell, J. David, (AV) '54 '84 C.586 B.S. L.623 J.D. [Elliott,E.N.&E.]
Faulk, Robert R. '— '04 C.612 B.A. L.616 J.D. 109 N. Grand
Faulkner, Rex L. '62 '88 C.620 B.S. L.45 J.D. 118 E. Randolph
Field, David L., (AV) '16 '40 C&L.623 B.A., LL.B. [Field,T.L.&S.]
Field, Trojan, Long & Sedbrook, P.C., (AV) 106 W. Randolph St.
Fields, Michael J., (BV) '72 '97 C&L.623 B.A., J.D. Asst. Dist. Atty.
Fischbach, Donald P., Jr., (AV) '58 '87 C.473 B.A. L.616 J.D. Corp. Coun. & Secy., Continental Resources, Inc.

Ford, Jon R., (AV) '43 '69 C.612 B.S. L.623 J.D.
1625 W. Owen K. Garriott, Suite G, 73703-5653
Telephone: 580-234-0253 Fax: 580-234-0256
Email: jon@jfordlaw.com URL: http://www.jfordlaw.com
Family Law, Divorce, Custody, Civil Litigation, Probate, Personal Injury, Wills, Trusts, Estate Planning.

See Professional Biographies, ENID, OKLAHOMA

Franklin, Ronald G. '40 '66 C.612 B.S. L.623 J.D. Dist. J.
Fries, Robert J., (CV) '48 '89 C.623 B.B.A. L.862 J.D. 2902 Whippoorwill Ln.
Gideon, Jennifer J. '69 '98 C&L.623 B.A., J.D. [Jones,O.D.N.&J.]

Gill, Amber McLaughlin, (BV) '60 '86 C.760 B.S. L.845 J.D.
Continental Center, South Tower, 205 West Maple, Suite 806, P.O. Box 3802, 73702-3802
Telephone: 580-233-3797 Fax: 580-237-2766
Email: ambergill@coxinet.net
Criminal Law, Drugs and Narcotics, Family Law, Children, White Collar Crime.

See Professional Biographies, ENID, OKLAHOMA

Graham, Jill J. '79 '05 C.612 B.S. L.862 J.D. [Jones,O.D.N.&J.]

Gregory, Robert L., (BV) .... '27 '51 C&L.623 LL.B. 100 S. Washington
Grey, Norman L., (BV) .... '46 '72 C.862 B.A. L.846 J.D. [N.Grey]
Grey, Norman, (BV) ....902 Westwood Rd.
Gungoll, Bradley A., (AV) .... '53 '80 C.612 B.S. L.616 J.D. [Gungoll,J.C.B.&D.]
Gungoll, James H. ....'37 '74 C.612 B.A. L.623 J.D. Henry Gungoll Operating, Inc.

Gungoll, Jackson, Collins, Box & Devoll, P.C., (AV)
323 West Broadway, P.O. Box 1549, 73701
Telephone: 580-234-0436 Fax: 580-233-1284
Email: smith@enidlaw.com URL: http://www.enidlaw.com
Bradley A. Gungoll; Douglas L. Jackson; David M. Collins; Craig L. Box; Glenn A. Devoll; Julia Christina Rieman; Vance T. Nye;—Karig P. Culver; Bradley E. Davenport; Brendon S. Atkinson; Chad N. Davis. Of Counsel: Richard L. McKnight.
Civil Litigation, Commercial Transactions, Bankruptcy, Real Estate, Environmental Law, Family Law, Criminal Defense, Probate, Oil and Gas and Personal Injury Law, Appeals, Tax Law, Estate Planning, Products Liability.

See Professional Biographies, ENID, OKLAHOMA

Hall, Tina A., Law Offices, (CV) .... '— '90 C.612 B.S. L.616 J.D. 1705 S. Van Buren St.
Halstead, Bill G., (BV) ....'38 '67 C.612 B.S.E.E. L.623 J.D. Asst. City Atty.
Hamm, Sue Ann .... '56 '80 C&L.862 J.D. Continental Resources, Inc.
Harvey, J. Bruce ....'42 '72 C.620 B.A. L.616 J.D. Spec. Dist. J.
Henneke, David C., (AV) .... '55 '81 C.612 B.S. L.862 J.D. [D.Henneke]
Henneke, David, (AV) ....102 S. Van Buren

Hladik, Dennis W., (AV) '49 '75 C.612 B.S. L.623 J.D.
300 Continental Center North, 302 North Independence, 73701
Telephone: 580-234-6945 Fax: 580-234-6947
Email: dennishladik@coxinet.net URL: http://www.lawyers.com/enid-law
Divorce, Family Law, Child Custody, Debtor and Creditor, Creditors Rights, Trusts and Estates, Criminal Defense, Real Estate Law, Title Opinions, Title Examinations, Business Law, Bankruptcy, Oil & Gas, Commercial Collections, Commercial Litigation, Personal Injury, Automobile Accidents, Wrongful Death, Driving While Intoxicated, Wills, Probate, Civil Litigation.

See Professional Biographies, ENID, OKLAHOMA

Hodgden, P. John, (CV) ....'64 '91 C&L.623 B.A., J.D. [Ⓒ Mitchell&D.]
Holden, Edna Mae, Law Office of, (BV) '55 '83
C.622 B.S. L.623 J.D. 128 N. Independence
Hume, Edward C. ....'40 '65 C.663 A.B. L.276 J.D. P.O. Box 5175★
Ingraham, L. Lee, (CV) ....'34 '70 C.612 B.S. L.616 J.D. 2226 W. Great Lakes Rd.
Jackson, Douglas L., (AV) ....'51 '77 C.612 B.S. L.30 J.D. [Gungoll,J.C.B.&D.]
Johnston, Roger L., (AV) '34 '64 C.622 B.S. L.623 LL.B.
302 North Independence #300
Jones, Ron R., (BV) ....'57 '93 C.1147 B.S. L.616 J.D. [Camp&J.]
Jones, Stephen, (AV) ....'40 '66 C.846 L.623 LL.B. [Jones,O.D.N.&J.]

Jones, Otjen, Davis, Nixon & Juhl, A Professional Association of Attorneys, (AV)
Suite 1100 Broadway Tower, 114 East Broadway, P.O. Box 472, 73702
Telephone: 580-242-5500 Fax: 580-242-4556
URL: http://www.stephenjoneslaw.com
Stephen Jones; April McCurdy Davis; Rodney A. Nixon; Deanna Juhl. Associates: Jennifer J. Gideon; Jill J. Graham.
Litigation and related matters in State and Federal Courts including: Insurance Defense, Criminal Defense and Grand Jury Practice, White Collar Crime, Complex Civil and Commercial Litigation, Business/Corporate Law, Divorce and Child Custody, School Law, Employment Law, Contested Wills and Estates, Regulation of Professionals, Professional Malpractice, and Appeals of Civil and Criminal Matters, Aviation Law.
Representative Clients: Mesa Limited Partnership; Wells Fargo; City of Enid; Sears & Roebuck, Co.; St. Paul Property and Liability; International Oil, Chemical and Atomic Workers Union; Associated Aviation Underwriters; Independent Petroleum Association of America; Haliburton Industries; Tandy Corp.
Oklahoma City, Oklahoma Office: 311 North Harvey Avenue, Suite 103, 73102. Telephone: 405-604-5312. Fax: 405-604-5313.

See Professional Biographies, ENID, OKLAHOMA

Juhl, Deanna ....'76 '02 C.734 B.A. L.1048 J.D. [Jones,O.D.N.&J.]
Kennedy, Bryce S., Jr., (BV) ....'56 '79 C.831 B.A. L.623 J.D. [B.S.Kennedy]
Kennedy, Bryce S., P.C., (BV) ....P.O. Box 10605
Kocher, John J. ....'49 '82 C.846 B.A. L.623 J.D. 110 S. Collidge
Lahman, Carol Hambrick, (BV) .... '58 '85 C.880 B.A. L.623 J.D. City Atty.
Lahman, Larry D., (AV) ....'43 '73 C.620 B.S. L.623 J.D. [Mitchell&D.]
Lamb, Norman A., (BV) ....'35 '63 C&L.623 B.S., LL.B. 222 W. Bway.
Lamunyon, Justin L., (CV) ....'65 '94 C.612 B.S. L.623 J.D. [Lamunyon]
Lamunyon Law Firm, (CV) ....201 N. Grand, Ste. 500
Lane, Sarah J. ....'76 '02 C.862 B.S.B.A. L.692 J.D. [Ⓐ Brown&Assoc.]
Liggett, Jennifer Ann ....'77 '03 C.620 B.S. L.623 J.D. 118 E. Randolph Ave.
Long, James F., (AV) ....'48 '74 C.663 B.A. L.900 J.D. [Traynor,L.W.&W.] ⊙
Long, Randy J., (AV) ....'56 '82 C.612 B.S. L.623 J.D. [Field,T.L.&S.]
Lovell, Brian N., (BV) ....'65 '91 C.612 B.S. L.616 J.D. 300 W. Cherokee, Ste. 102
Martin, Michael R., (BV) ....'52 '79 C&L.862 B.S., J.D. 300 W. Cherokee, Ste. 102
Maxwell, William B., (CV) .... '48 '73 C.846 B.A. L.623 J.D. 205 W. Maple
McCubbins, Robert R. .... '19 '45 C.612 B.S. L.623 LL.B. 3119 W. Oklahoma Ave.‡

McKeever, Clark, (AV) '54 '79 C.840 B.B.A. L.623 J.D.
3rd Floor, Continental Tower, P.O. Box 1026, 73702
Telephone: 580-234-4133 Fax: 580-234-4137
H.G. McKeever (1872-1940); H. H. McKeever (1906-1975); Douglas C. McKeever (1918-1985).
Probate, Guardianship, Real Estate, Commercial Law, Estate Planning.

See Professional Biographies, ENID, OKLAHOMA

McKnight, Richard L., (AV) ...... '36 '63 C&L.623 A.B., LL.B. [Ⓒ Gungoll,J.C.B.&D.]
McPhail, John W., (BV) ....'57 '84 C.107 B.A. L.862 J.D. Asst. Dist. Atty.
McVay, Dalen D. ....'77 '05 C.1147 B.S. L.616 J.D. [Ⓐ Mitchel,G.R.&R.]
Michael, John W. .... '46 '72 C.612 B.A. L.623 J.D. Dist. J.
Mitchel, Gaston, Riffel & Riffel, P.L.L.C., (AV)
201 N. Grand, Fourth Floor (⊙Alva, Fairview, Woodward)

Mitchell & DeClerck, P.L.L.C., (AV)
202 West Broadway, 73701-4018
Telephone: 580-234-5144 Facsimile: 580-234-8890
P.C. Simons (1870-1962); E. B. Mitchell (1895-1976); Earl B. Mitchell, Jr. (1924-2003); Edward A. DeClerck (1916-2002); Larry D. Lahman; E. W. (Bill) Shaw; David C. Butler; Michael C. Bigheart; Tim E. DeClerck. Of Counsel: P. John Hodgden; Forrest L. Pepper DeVaughn; Roger L. Ediger.
General Civil Practice Litigation. Banking, Commercial, Corporate, Personal Injury, Insurance, Real Estate, Estate Planning, Collections (Professionals) Debtor Creditor, Probate, Bankruptcy, Trusts, Family Law, Wills, Estates.
Counsel for: Cleo State Bank; Bank of Drummond; First State Bank of Waynoka; National Bank of Commerce; First State Bank, Waukomis; Central National Bank & Trust Co. of Enid; Farm Credit of Enid, ACA; Farm Credit of Wichita; Pope Distributing; Spess Oil Company.

See Professional Biographies, ENID, OKLAHOMA

Newby, Tom L., (AV) .... '58 '83 C.620 B.S. L.623 J.D. [Elliott,E.N.&E.]
Nixon, Rodney A. ....'69 '03 C.612 B.B.A. L.862 J.D. [Jones,O.D.N.&J.]
Nye, Vance T., (BV) ....'68 '93 C.622 B.S. L.862 J.D. [Gungoll,J.C.B.&D.]
Outhier, Philip J. ....'62 '92 C.612 B.S. L.616 J.D. [Phillips&O.]
Overstreet, Ann Hurst, (BV) .... '41 '90 C.612 B.S. L.862 J.D. [Elliott,E.N.&E.]

Perry, Richard M. ....'46 '77 C&L.616 B.A., J.D. Assoc. Dist. J.
Phillips, Dale Peter ....'32 '99 C.57 B.A. L.623 J.D. [D.P.Phillips]
Phillips, Jill Patterson ....'70 '95 C.862 B.A. L.623 J.D. [Phillips&O.]
Phillips, Dale P. ....509 S. Garfield St.
Phillips & Outhier .... 205 W. Maple Ave., Ste. 906
Pickens, Linda McKnight, (BV) ....'45 '75 C.1264 B.A. L.862 J.D. Mun. J.
Pickens, Richard W. ....'29 '61 L.616 LL.B. Ret. Dist. J.
Proctor, John L., (BV) ....'40 '66 C.640 A.B. L.862 J.D. 1st Asst. Dist. Atty.
Retz, Lynn M. ....'66 '92 C.942 B.S. L.616 J.D. [Ⓐ Mitchel,G.R.&R.] (⊙Woodward)
Richter, Karl L., (BV) ....'39 '74 C.1147 B.A. L.616 J.D. 224 N. Independence St.
Rieman, Julia Christina, (BV) .... '62 '92 C.622 B.S. L.862 J.D. [Gungoll,J.C.B.&D.]
Riffel, Craig, (BV) '67 '95
C.612 B.S. L.616 J.D. [Mitchel,G.R.&R.] (⊙Fairview, Woodward)
Riffel, Katresa J., (CV) '67 '92 C.612 B.S. L.616 J.D.
[Mitchel,G.R.&R.] (⊙Woodward)
Roberts, Michael D., (BV) ...... '60 '89 C.612 B.S. L.623 J.D. 205 West Maple, Suite 806
Sawyer, Lowell T., (AV) .... '19 '50 C&L.623 B.S., LL.B. 100 S. Washington
Schaub, David H. '39 '75 C.502 B.A. L.273 J.D.
(adm. in VA; not adm. in OK) P.O. Box 632
Scott, John L., (BV) .... '46 '74 C.612 B.A. L.623 J.D. 205 W. Maple
Sedbrook, Matt J., (BV) ....'57 '83 C.612 B.S. L.623 J.D. [Field,T.L.&S.]
Shaw, E. W. (Bill), (AV) ....'42 '74 C.624 B.S. L.862 J.D. [Mitchell&D.]
Shirley, Shera D., (CV) ....'56 '82 C.663 B.S. L.221 J.D. 323 W. Cherokee Ave.
Singer, Steven D., (BV) ....'59 '84 C&L.623 B.A., J.D. 324 W. Maine St.
Slabotsky, Bryan D., (BV) '53 '93 C.1229 B.I.A. L.845 J.D.
Garfield Co. Dist. Atty. Off.
Stocker, Cathy Lee, (AV) .... '51 '75 C&L.623 B.A., J.D. Dist. Atty.
Strubhar, Khristan K., (BV) ....'64 '89 C.82 B.A. L.623 J.D. Dist. Atty. Off.
Thomas, John S., (CV) ....'42 '73 C&L.623 B.S., J.D. [J.S.Thomas]
Thomas, John S., P.C., (CV) .... P.O. Box 3906
Traynor, Timothy R., (AV) .... '43 '68 C&L.623 B.B.A., J.D. [Traynor,L.W.&W.] ⊙

Traynor, Long, Wynne & Woodward, P.C., A Professional Corporation, (AV)
1010 West Maple, P.O. Box 3247, 73702 ⊙
Telephone: 580-233-4455 Toll Free: 1-877-439-4455 Fax: 580-233-4502
Email: tlww@coxinet.net
Will T. Wright (1908-1986); Timothy R. Traynor; James F. Long; John H. Wynne; Paul K. Woodward;—Elise D. Evans.
General Civil and Criminal Practice in all State and Federal Courts, Personal Injury, Insurance Law, Family Law, Wills and Trusts, Probate and Estate Planning, Business Organizations, Sales, Mergers and Acquisitions, Reorganizations, Real Estate, Commercial, Business Law, Criminal, Municipal Law, Education Law.
References: Central National Bank & Trust Company of Enid; Security National Bank, Enid, Oklahoma.
Okeene, Oklahoma Office: 214 South Main Street. 73763. Telephone 580-822-4458. Fax: 580-822-4473.

See Professional Biographies, ENID, OKLAHOMA

Trojan, David G., (BV) ....'53 '78 C.612 B.S. L.623 J.D. [Field,T.L.&S.]
Wagner, Randolph L., (CV) ....'68 '92 C.620 B.A. L.623 J.D. [Wagner]
Wagner Law Firm, (CV) ....118 E. Randolph Ave.
Warren, Robert J., (CV) '69 '95 C.846 B.A. L.623 J.D.
Suite 1100 Broadway Tower, 114 East Broadway
Willis, Ronald W., (BV) .... '52 '88 C.623 B.A. L.616 J.D. 222 West Broadway
Wilson, George H., II, (BV) ....'44 '71 C.663 B.S. L.862 J.D. [Wilson&W.]
Wilson, Owen D., (AV) .... '37 '61 C&L.623 B.A., J.D. [Wilson&W.]
Wilson & Wilson, (AV)
114 E. Bdy. (⊙Redwood City, CA; Countryside, IL; Salt Lake City, UT)
Woodward, Paul K., (BV) ....'59 '85 C.1315 B.S. L.616 J.D. [Traynor,L.W.&W.] ⊙
Woolbright, Novy R., Jr. ....'56 '84 C.663 B.A. L.616 J.D. 723 W. Wabash Ave.
Wynne, John H., (AV) ....'49 '74 C.612 B.S. L.862 J.D. [Traynor,L.W.&W.] ⊙

EUFAULA, * 2,652, *McIntosh Co.*

Barris, Oliver R., III, (BV) ....'57 '82 C&L.623 B.A., J.D. Asst. Dist. Atty.
Burnham, W. R., (BV) ....'46 '74 C.619 B.S. L.623 J.D. 150 Foley Ave.
Dawson, Cindy M., (CV) ....'60 '97 C.1147 B.B.A. L.615 J.D. 112 Selmon Rd.
Mowery, Gene F. ....'38 '68 C.619 L.616 LL.B. Assoc. Dist. J.
Payne, Robert S., (AV) .... '51 '78 C.612 B.S. L.616 J.D. Rt. 1
Pratt, James R., (BV) ....'51 '77 C&L.623 B.B.A., J.D. P.O. Box 938
Pyle, Kirk B. ....'26 '78 C.623 B.S.E.E. L.1209 J.D. Spec. Dist. J.
Reheard, Deborah A., Law Office, (BV) '56 '87
C.619 B.A. L.862 J.D. 100 North Second Street
Wall, Laura Kay Robbins, (BV) .... '51 '77 C.622 B.A. L.623 J.D. City Atty.
Wendel, Fred P., (AV) .... '47 '73 C.612 B.S. L.623 J.D. 115 South Main

FAIRFAX, 1,555, *Osage Co.*

Grigg, Lockwood K. .... '28 '54 C.623 L.616 LL.B. 30 S. 5th St.‡
Young, Kelly Dee, Mr., (BV) .... '41 '64 C.334 L.862 LL.B. P.O. Box 544

FAIRVIEW, * 2,733, *Major Co.*

Bailey, Mary R. ....'29 '57 C.623 B.S. L.616 J.D. 125 North 12th‡
Bailey, Victor E. ....'29 '60 C.35 B.S. L.616 J.D. 102 West Broadway
Barefoot, N. Vinson ......'47 '79 C.1147 B.A. L.616 J.D. Dist. J., N. Vinson Barefoot Off.
Church, Wm. Scott, (CV) ....'69 '95 C.612 B.S. L.623 J.D. [Houk&C.]

Hallren, Mitchell A., (AV) '52 '78 C&L.623 B.A., J.D.
116 East Elm, P.O. Box 428, 73737
Telephone: 580-227-4449 Fax: 580-227-4448
Email: hallrenlaw@sbcglobal.net
Trial Practice, Probate, Real Property, Oil and Gas Law, Real Estate Title Law, Commercial and Family Law.

See Professional Biographies, FAIRVIEW, OKLAHOMA

Houk, Joe C., (AV) ....'28 '55 C&L.623 B.A., LL.B. [Houk&C.]
Houk & Church, (AV) .... 111 W. Broadway

McCue, John W., II, (AV) '43 '68 C.612 B.S. L.623 J.D.
118 East Broadway, P.O. Box 503, 73737
Telephone: 580-227-3939 Fax: 580-227-3607
Email: mccuelaw@io2online.com
General, Real Estate, Probate, Oil and Gas Law and Banking Law.

See Professional Biographies, FAIRVIEW, OKLAHOMA

Mitchel, Gaston, Riffel & Riffel, P.L.L.C., (AV)
124 E. Broadway, Suite 6 (⊙Alva, Enid, Woodward)
Morris, Dorinda K., (BV) ....'52 '77 C.1270 B.A. L.623 J.D. Dept. of Human Servs.
Riffel, Craig, (BV) '67 '95 C.612 B.S. L.616 J.D.
[Mitchel,G.R.&R.] (⊙Enid, Woodward)
Schoeppel, James, (AV) .... '52 '78 C.612 B.S. L.623 J.D. P.O. Box 190‡
Thorp, Hollis, (BV) ....'47 '74 C.620 B.A. L.616 J.D. Asst. Dist. Atty.
Wilkinson, James A. .... '30 '58 C.623 B.B.A. L.616 LL.B. Ret. Assoc. Dist. J.

FORT GIBSON, 4,054, *Muskogee Co.*

Carnagey, James B., (BV) .... '42 '84 C.619 B.S. L.862 J.D. 131 S. Lee Avenue

FORT SILL, 12,107, *Comanche Co.*

Bennett, Russell D. ....'45 '70 C.934 B.A. L.623 J.D. U.S. Army, Staff J. Advocate
Brooker, John W. .... '76 '03 C.896 B.A. L.575 J.D. Captain, U.S. Army, J.A.G.
Harwood, James Glenn '69 '01 C.690 B.S. L.945 J.D.
(adm. in VA; not adm. in OK) Off of the Staff J. Advocate
Jamison, Yolanda Y. ....'68 '98 C.10 B.A. L.259 J.D. Off. of the Staff J. Adv.★
Suarez, Flor M. ....'— '97 C.37 B.A. L.36 J.D. 1307 Upton Rd.★
Ward, Susan Bates ....'47 '84 C.614 B.A. L.623 J.D. 2593 Currie Rd.
Washburn, Marc B. '73 '99 C.589 B.A. L.823 J.D.
(adm. in MA; not adm. in OK) Trial Def. Coun., U.S. Army Trial Def. Ser.

FREDERICK, * 4,637, *Tillman Co.*

Amyx, Clyde H., II, (BV) .... '44 '70 C&L.623 B.B.A., J.D. 215 E. Josephine
Barnett, David A. ....'45 '76 C.612 B.S. L.623 J.D. Assoc. Dist. J.
Benson, Bradford L., (BV) .... '64 '92 C.623 B.B.A. L.802 J.D. [Benson&B.]
Benson, Loyd L., (AV) ....'40 '65 C&L.623 B.A., J.D. [Benson&B.]

Benson & Benson, Inc., A Professional Corporation, (AV)
124 North 9th Street, P.O. Box 486, 73542-0486
Telephone: 580-335-7541 Fax: 580-335-7543
Email: Bensonlawfirm@pldi.net URL: http://www.bensonlawfirm.net
Loyd L. Benson; Bradford L. Benson.
General Civil Practice. Banking, Corporation, Insurance, Oil and Gas, Probate and Real Estate Law. Civil Trials, Trusts and Estates, Estate Planning, Family Law, Criminal Law.
Representative Clients: First Southwest Bank, Frederick, Hobart Anadarko; Southwest Rural Electric Assn. Inc.; First State Bank of Davidson; First State Bank in Grandfield; Farmers Home Administration; Tillman Co. Industrial Trust Authority.
See Professional Biographies, FREDERICK, OKLAHOMA

Evans, Michael D., (AV) ....'46 '73 C.612 B.A. L.623 J.D. [Massad,E.&K.]
Johnson, Ty .... '75 '02 C&L.880 B.S., J.D. [⊡ Massad,E.&K.]
Kent, John P. (Pat), (AV) ....'50 '76 C.612 B.S. L.623 J.D. [Massad,E.&K.]
Lagerberg, Jon Oscar, (BV) '50 '83 C.1300 B.A. L.623 J.D.
Asst. Dist. Atty., OK Dist. 3
Massad, Anthony M., (AV) .... '28 '55 C&L.623 B.A., J.D. [Massad,E.&K.]

Massad, Evans & Kent, Inc., A Professional Corporation, (AV)
120 North Ninth Street, Drawer 606, 73542
Telephone: 580-335-5531 Fax: 508-335-5532
Email: meklaw@pldi.net URL: http://www.lawyers.com/meklaw
Anthony M. Massad; Michael D. Evans; John P. (Pat) Kent; John B. Wilson, Jr. (1912-1971);—Ty Johnson.
General Civil and Criminal Practice in Oklahoma state courts, Agricultural Law, Bank and Banking, Bankruptcy, Business Law, Children, Collections, Contracts, Education Law, Eminent Domain, Family Law, Guardianship and Conservatorship, Insurance, Legal Ethics and Professional Responsibility, Mortgages, Municipal Law, Personal Injury, Real Estate, Trusts and Estates, Wills.
See Professional Biographies, FREDERICK, OKLAHOMA

McBee, Benson & Benson
(See Benson & Benson)

GLENCOE, 583, *Payne Co.*

Padilla, Stefani A. ....'70 '97 C.612 B.S. L.615 J.D. P.O. Box 36

GORE, 850, *Sequoyah Co.*

Storts, M. Dean .... '22 '50 L.862 LL.B. P.O. Box 888‡

GROVE, 5,131, *Delaware Co.*

Black, Richard A., (BV) ....'44 '70 C&L.862 B.A., J.D. 26391 S. 615 Rd.
Curnutte, Mark W., (AV) .... '54 '79 C&L.623 B.B.A., J.D. [Logan&L.] ⊙
Gurley, Richard A. .... '48 '84 C&L.623 B.A., J.D. 520 S. Main St.
Hormel, Benjamin A., Law Offices of, (CVⓣ) '34 '79 C.1310 B.A. L.502 J.D.
(adm. in MO; not adm. in OK) P.O. Box 40315
Jenkins, Robert C., (BV) ....'45 '78 C.1147 B.S. L.616 J.D. P.O. Box 452079
Johnston, O. B., III, (AV) ....'41 '66 C.69 B.B.A. L.862 J.D. [Logan&L.] ⊙
Jones, David E., (BV) ....'65 '90 C&L.378 B.S., J.D. [Logan&L.] ⊙
Kardos, Ivan Frank ....'20 '49 C.563 L.569 J.D. 508 Summit Dr.
Lanway, Erin, Attorney at Law, (CV) .... '50 '78 C.477 B.A. L.862 J.D. 308 S. Main
Logan, J. Duke, (AV) ....'31 '55 C&L.623 B.A., LL.B. [Logan&L.] ⊙
Logan, Leonard M., IV, (AV) .... '57 '85 C.623 B.B.A. L.862 J.D. [Logan&L.] ⊙

Logan & Lowry, LLP, (AV)
19 East 3rd Street, P.O. Box 452469, 74345-2469 ⊙
Telephone: 918-786-7511 Fax: 918-786-5687
Email: loglow@galstar.com
Members of Firm: J. Duke Logan; Richard W. Lowry; O. B. Johnston, III; Thomas J. McGeady; Mark W. Curnutte; Leonard M. Logan, IV; Donna L. Smith; Robert Alan Rush; David E. Jones. Of Counsel: Charles E. West.
General Practice, Including Trials in all State and Federal Courts, Eminent Domain, Environmental and Coal, Banking, Commercial Transactions, Creditors' Rights and Bankruptcy, Corporation, Public Utility, Real Estate, Estate Planning and Probate, Criminal, Domestic Relations, Appellate Practice and Administrative Law.
General Counsel: First National Bank & Trust Company of Vinita; Northeast Oklahoma Electric Cooperative, Inc.
Representative Clients: Northeast Area Vo-Tech Schools; Afton Cooperative Assn.; C & L Supply, Inc.; Oklahoma Wildlife Federation; Craig General Hospital; Alternate Fuels, Inc.
Vinita, Oklahoma Office: 101 South Wilson Street. P.O. Box 558. 74301-0558. Telephone: 918-256-7511. Fax: 918-256-3187.
See Professional Biographies, GROVE, OKLAHOMA

Lowry, Richard W., (AV) .... '37 '63 C.623 B.A. L.862 LL.B. [Logan&L.] ⊙
McGeady, Thomas J., (AV) ....'51 '76 C.893 B.A. L.276 J.D. [Logan&L.] ⊙
Reppart, William C., Jr., (BV) .... '52 '94 C&L.900 B.B.A., J.D. P.O. Box 451780
Rowe, Dorothy Parker, (BV) .... '47 '89 C.1147 B.B.A. L.623 J.D. 25201 S. 627 Rd.
Rush, Robert Alan, (BV) .... '63 '88 C.543 B.S. L.378 J.D. [Logan&L.] ⊙
Sandell, David W., (AVⓣ) '40 '64 C&L.911 B.A., LL.B.
(adm. in WA; not adm. in OK) P.O. Box 450428
Smith, Donna L., (BV) .... '50 '88 C.377 B.S.Ed. L.862 J.D. [Logan&L.] ⊙
Strange, Bill D. '28 '53 C&L.900 B.A., LL.B.
(adm. in KS; not adm. in OK) P.O. Box 212‡
Strutton, Monte Lynn ....'57 '94 C.622 B.S. L.623 J.D. 227 Anchor Rd.
Wallace, James E., (BV) ....'48 '74 C&L.862 B.S., J.D. Mun. J.
West, Charles E., (AV) .... '47 '78 C.619 B.S. L.862 J.D. [⊡ Logan&L.] ⊙

GUTHRIE, * 9,925, *Logan Co.*

Atkins & Markoff
(See Oklahoma City)

Brooks, Larry R. ....'49 '76 C.612 B.S. L.623 J.D. Assoc. Dist. J.

Davis, Frank W., (AV) '36 '59 C.618 B.A. L.623 LL.B.
115 North Division, 73044
Telephone: 405-282-1420 Fax: 405-282-4423

(This Listing Continued)

Davis, Frank W. (Continued)
General Civil and Criminal Practice. Probate, Real Estate and Oil and Gas Law.
Representative Clients: Masonic Charity Foundation of Oklahoma; Guthrie Greenhouses, Inc.; Logan County Industrial Development Authority; Rural Water District #1, Logan County.
See Professional Biographies, GUTHRIE, OKLAHOMA

Green, Tim W., (AV) ....'52 '78 C.1147 B.B.A. L.616 J.D. [T.W.Green]
Green, Timothy Wayne, (BV) .... '57 '82 C&L.623 B.B.A., J.D. 213 E. Oklahoma Avenue

Green, Tim W., P.C., (AV)
213 East Oklahoma Avenue, 73044
Telephone: 405-282-1919 Fax: 405-282-1930
Email: greentiml@aol.com
Tim W. Green.
General Civil Practice, Oil and Gas, Real Property, Election Law, Wills, Trusts, Probate, Estate Planning, Corporate Law, Articles of Incorporation, Mineral Law, Oil and Gas Conservation Law, Farm and Ranch Law, Civil Litigation.
See Professional Biographies, GUTHRIE, OKLAHOMA

Hirzel, Jeff L., (AV) .... '45 '70 C&L.623 B.A., J.D. [J.L.Hirzel]
Hirzel, Jeff L., Inc., (AV) ....119 South Broad Street
Hood, Ralph T., Jr., (AV) ....'41 '65 C.612 B.S. L.623 J.D. 123 Broad St.
Hudson, Robert L., (BV) ....'57 '83 C.612 B.S. L.623 J.D. 213 E. Oklahoma Ave.
Jones, Sidney W. .... '62 '97 C.623 B.A. L.616 J.D. 2180 E. Charter Oak Road
Moore-Henson, Julie ....'68 '95 C.612 B.A. L.615 J.D. Asst. Dist. Atty.
Morgan, Bruce ....'45 '71 C&L.623 B.A., J.D. P.O. Box 1401
Patterson, Mildred L., (Miss) .... '12 '45 L.615 Ret. Assoc. Dist. J.
Smotherman, Richard, (CV) ...... '65 '91 C&L.615 B.S.A., J.D. Asst. Dist. Atty, Suite 300
Wheeler, William W. ....'46 '72 C.612 B.A. L.623 J.D. Spec. J.

GUYMON, * 10,472, *Texas Co.*

Board, John, (AV) .... '35 '62 C&L.623 B.A., LL.B. 220 North Main
Carter, Peggy L., (BV) ....'69 '94 C.612 B.A. L.615 J.D. [Wright,D.J.&C.]
Dale, Don ....'18 '56 C.502 B.J. L.623 LL.B. [⊡ Wright,D.J.&C.]
Dale, Douglas Don, (BV) ....'50 '77 C.623 B.B.A. L.862 J.D. [Wright,D.J.&C.]
Field, Larry L., (AV) ....'37 '64 C.612 B.S. L.623 J.D. [Field&H.]

Field & Hicks, P.C., (AV)
400 Northeast 12th Street, P.O. Box 1347, 73942
Telephone: 580-338-6503 Fax: 580-338-6505
Email: llfpc@ptsi.net URL: http://www.lawyers.com/larryfield-law
Larry L. Field; Cory Brandon Hicks.
Real Estate, Trusts and Estates, Business Law, Litigation, Commercial Law, Banking Law, Construction, Contracts, Wills and Probate, Government and Insurance.
See Professional Biographies, GUYMON, OKLAHOMA

Fletcher, James R., (AV) ....'46 '75 C.612 B.S. L.623 J.D. 218 W. 5th
Harbison, Ricky Wayne, (BV) .... '55 '94 C.36 B.S. L.615 J.D. [R.Harbison]
Harbison, Rick, P.L.L.C., (BV) ....108 NE 5th Street
Hicks, Cory Brandon ....'— '02 C.613 B.A. L.623 J.D. [Field&H.]
Hitch, Jason W. ....'70 '97 C.612 B.S. L.623 J.D. Hitch Enterprises, Inc.
Jett, A. Clark, (AV) ....'51 '77 C&L.623 B.B.A., J.D. [Wright,D.J.&C.]
Parsley, Jon K., (BV) ....'69 '94 C.1147 B.A. L.623 J.D. [J.K.Parsley]
Parsley, Jon K., PLLC, (BV) .... 112 N.E. 4th St.
Petty, David K., (AV) .... '39 '64 C.612 B.S. L.623 J.D. [D.K.Petty]

Petty, David K., A Professional Corporation, (AV) BB
301 West Fifth, P.O. Box 1187, 73942
Telephone: 580-338-5484 Fax: 580-338-0066
Email: pettyd@ptsi.net
David K. Petty.
General, Civil Trial Practice, Personal Injury, Probate, Real Estate, Oil and Gas, Municipal and Banking Law.
Attorney for: First National Bank, Texhoma, Oklahoma; Dorchester Minerals Operating LP; Town of Hardesty; City of Guymon; Town of Goodwell; CJ NutraCon, Inc.; Seaboard Corporation.
See Professional Biographies, GUYMON, OKLAHOMA

Wood, Don E., (BV) .... '35 '64 C.639 B.A. L.623 LL.B. Dist. Atty., 1st Jud. Dist.
Wright, Bryan L., (AV) .... '39 '66 C.612 B.S. L.900 J.D. [Wright,D.J.&C.]

Wright, Dale, Jett & Carter, (AV) BB
Dale Building, 114 East 4th Street, P.O. Box 591, 73942
Telephone: 580-338-6591 Fax: 580-338-8244
Email: blwlaw@ptsi.net
Members of Firm: F. Hiner Dale (1881-1969); Vincent Dale (1912-1977); Bryan L. Wright; Douglas Don Dale; A. Clark Jett; Peggy L. Carter. Of Counsel: Don Dale.
General Practice. Corporation, Real Estate, Oil and Gas, Estate Planning, Wills, Probate and Tax Law. Trials.
See Professional Biographies, GUYMON, OKLAHOMA

Zigler, Greg A. .... '56 '83 C.612 B.S. L.616 J.D. Dist. J.

HAILEYVILLE, 918, *Pittsburg Co.*

McRee, Ronald A. '49 '78 C&L.500 B.A., J.D.
(adm. in MS; not adm. in OK) P.O. Box 449‡

HARRAH, 4,719, *Oklahoma Co.*

Sparkman, John H. ....'17 '51 C&L.616 B.A., J.D. 5901 Dobbs Rd., N.

HARTSHORNE, 2,120, *Pittsburg Co.*

Lerblance, Richard C., (BV) .... '46 '79 C.1147 B.A. L.615 J.D. Drawer K

HEALDTON, 2,872, *Carter Co.*

LeVally, Earl E., (BV) ....'21 '48 C&L.623 B.A., LL.B. 445 W. Main
Pinkerton, Bobby L., (BV) ....'51 '78 C.621 B.S. L.623 J.D. [Pinkerton]
Pinkerton Law Offices, P.C., (BV) .... 11 N. 4th St.
Scott, Esther Elaine ....'46 '95 C&L.623 B.A., J.D. [E.Scott]
Scott, Elaine ....P.O. Box 815

HEAVENER, 3,201, *Le Flore Co.*

Hamilton, James E., (AV) ....'35 '60 C.612 L.623 J.D. Rt. 1; Box 1450‡

HENNESSEY, 2,058, *Kingfisher Co.*

Mesis, Vincent, Jr., (BV) ....'47 '73 C&L.623 B.A., J.D. [V.Mesis,Jr.]
Mesis, Vincent, Jr., PC, (BV) ....100 S. Main

Traynor, Long, Wynne & Woodward, P.C. A Professional Corporation
(See Enid)

HENRYETTA, 6,096, *Okmulgee Co.*

Dale, William J. ....'20 '61 C&L.862 B.S., LL.B. RR2 Box 475
Davis, Beryl Ray, (BV) .... '51 '80 C.612 B.S. L.623 J.D. Asst. Dist. Atty.
Gaither, Luke ....'72 '98 C.619 B.A. L.862 J.D [Inglish&G.] ⊙
Inglish & Gaither, Professional Corporation, (AV)
405 West Trudgeon Street (⊙Okmulgee)

Moudy, Lou Ann, (CV) … '64 '89 C.618 B.S. L.623 J.D. 506 W. Main St.
Smith, Stephen W. … '46 '71 C&L.623 B.A., J.D. [S.W.Smith]
Smith, Stephen W., P.C. … 115 N. Fifth St.
Woodliff, Duane A., (AV) … '41 '66 C&L.623 B.B.A., J.D. 405 W. Trudgeon St.

HINTON, 2,175, *Caddo Co.*

Buzbee, John P., (AV) … '36 '60 C.613 B.A. L.623 LL.B. [Buzbee&U.] ⊙
Buzbee & Upchurch, (AV) … 116 W. Main (⊙Anadarko)
Upchurch, Virgil L., (AV) … '30 '59 C&L.623 B.A., L.L.B. [Buzbee&U.] ⊙

HOBART, * 3,997, *Kiowa Co.*

Gentry, William E., (AV) … '45 '70 C.612 B.S. L.623 J.D. [Perry,G.P.&M.]
Marsh, Ricky A., (BV) … '59 '84 C.612 B.S. L.623 J.D. [Perry,G.P.&M.]
Metcalf, William Wendell … '25 '53 C.309 A.B. L.623 LL.B. 605 N. Lowe St.
Mitchell, Anthony G., (BV) … '45 '90 C.622 B.S. L.30 J.D. [🄰 Talley&T.]
Montgomery, John D., (AV) … '28 '55 C&L.623 B.S., LL.B. 325 S Main
Perry, Nellie, (AV) … '29 '82 C.612 B.S. L.623 J.D. [Perry,G.P.&M.] ‡
Perry, Gentry, Perry & Marsh, (AV) … Abstract Building
Pfenning, Marian Guest … '35 '83 C&L.623 B.S., J.D. 415 S. Park Rd.
Reeder, Lloyd R. … '18 '51 Retired Asso. Dist. J.
Russell, Norman L., (AV) … '50 '76 C&L.616 B.S., J.D. Kiowa Co. Cthse., 316 S. Main
Talley, Thomas W., (BV) … '51 '76 C&L.623 B.S., J.D. [Talley&T.]
Talley, William W. … '14 '39 C&L.623 B.A., LL.B. [Talley&T.]
Talley & Talley, (BV) … P.O. Box 841

HOLDENVILLE, * 4,792, *Hughes Co.*

Allen, B. Gordon, (BV) … '50 '76 C&L.623 B.A., J.D. 110 N. Broadway
Allford, Patricia A., (CV) … '48 '88 C.612 B.S. L.616 J.D. P.O. Box 767
Blockcolski, Christopher … '79 '04 C.619 B.B.A. L.623 J.D. [🄰 H.E.Heath]
Chesnutt, Ken, (BV) … '43 '68 C.623 B.A. L.846 LL.B. 101 East Main
Daugherty, J. C., (AV) … '25 '53 C.1300 B.A. L.623 LL.B. P.O. Box 72
Evans, Linda G., (AV) … '57 '83 C.619 B.A. L.623 J.D. Asst. Dist. Atty.
Heath, Harold E., (AV) … '47 '74 C.1147 B.A. L.623 J.D. [H.E.Heath]

Heath, Harold E., Law Offices, (AV)
103 West Main - P.O. Box 472, 74848
Telephone: 405-379-5445 Fax: 405-379-5446
Email: harold@heathlawoffice.com
Harold E. Heath. Associate: Christopher Blockcolski.
Banking, Real Estate, Bankruptcy, Probate, Oil and Gas and Corporation Law. General and Criminal Trial Practice.
Representative Clients: First United Bank & Trust Company, Holdenville, Ok.; Bank of Commerce, Wetumka, Ok.; The Bank, N.A., Holdenville, Ok.; First State Bank.
Approved Attorney for: Southwest Title & Trust Co.; First American Title & Trust Co.; Lawyers Title Insurance.
References: First United Bank & Trust Co., Holdenville, Ok.; The Bank, N.A., Holdenville, Ok.
See Professional Biographies, HOLDENVILLE, OKLAHOMA

Huser, Stanley, Jr., (AV) … '22 '48 C&L.623 LL.B. 104 North Broadway
Oliphant, George William … '09 '54 C.934 L.623 B.L. P.O. Box 849
Pettis, Clay B., (BV) … '54 '80 C.999 B.A. L.623 J.D. [C.B.Pettis]
Pettis, Clay B., PC, (BV) … 624 N. Hinckley
Rodgers, James W., Jr., (BV) … '17 '48 L.623 J.D. 110 N. Broadway
Smith, Greggory M. … '49 '75 C&L.616 B.S., J.D. Assoc. Dist. J.
Turner, David H. … '21 '48 C&L.623 A.B., LL.B. 401 E. 12th St.‡
Warren, Wm. H. … '11 '38 C.623 B.A. L.192 J.D. 308 Country Club Dr.‡
Wilbanks, Cran H., Jr. … '16 '41 C&L.623 LL.B. 700 N. Burgess‡

HOLLIS, * 2,264, *Harmon Co.*

Cummins, David L., (BV) … '47 '73 C&L.623 B.B.A., J.D. [Cummins]
Cummins Law Office, (BV) … 215 N. 2nd
Moore, James R., Jr., (BV) … '48 '73 C.622 B.S. L.623 J.D. [J.R.Moore] (⊙Altus)
Moore, James R., (BV) … P.O. Box 788
Warren, Mike, (BV) … '54 '81 C.802 B.B.A. L.862 J.D. Assoc. Dist. J.

HOOKER, 1,778, *Texas Co.*

Kurt, Shelley K. '58 '84 C.305 B.A. L.1243 J.D.
(adm. in AR; not adm. in OK) P.O. Box 1345‡
Trippet, Richard P., (AV) … '38 '62 C.16 L.862 LL.B. [Trippet&K.] ⊙
Trippet and Kee, (AV) … P.O. Box 640 (⊙Beaver)

HUGO, * 5,536, *Choctaw Co.*

Blakely, Maria Tasi … '56 '80 C.623 B.A. L.615 J.D. 702 E. Jackson St.
Bounds, John K., (BV) … '49 '75 C.612 B.A. L.862 J.D. 309 E. Duke St.
Cox, Ronald Douglas, (BV) … '41 '72 C.428 B.S. L.616 J.D. 216 E. Duke

Hadley, Thomas J., (BV) '51 '88 C.869 B.S. L.665 J.D.
115 S. Broadway, 74743
Telephone: 580-326-3108 Fax: 580-326-3182
General Practice, Trial Practice, Personal Injury, Labor and Employment.
See Professional Biographies, HUGO, OKLAHOMA

LeForce, Clark H., (BV) … '61 '87 C.623 B.A. L.862 J.D. Asst. Dist. Atty.
Muntz, John C., (BV) … '40 '68 C&L.623 B.S., J.D. 111 N. Third St.
Payne, Don Ed, (AV) … '38 '62 C&L.862 B.A., LL.B. J.
Rabon, Bob, (AV) … '39 '68 C.621 B.S. L.623 J.D. [Rabon,W.&R.]
Rabon, Robert L., (BV) … '61 '89 C.612 B.A. L.616 J.D. [Rabon,W.&R.]

Rabon, Wolf & Rabon, (AV)
402 East Jackson, P.O. Box 726, 74743
Telephone: 580-326-6427 Fax: 580-326-6032
Email: rawol@sbcglobal.net
Members of Firm: Bob Rabon; J. Frank Wolf, III; Robert L. Rabon.
General Civil Practice in all State and Federal Courts. Indian, Negligence, Insurance, Commercial, Real Estate and Probate Law. Trials. No Collections under $5000.00.
Representative Clients: Lone Star Gas Co.; General Accident Group.
General Counsel for: Security First National Bank, Hugo; Choctaw Nation; Chickasaw Nation; Housing Authority of Choctaw Nation of Oklahoma; Hugo Municipal Authority; Hugo Airport Authority; Hugo Industrial Authority; Red River Farmers Cooperative.
See Professional Biographies, HUGO, OKLAHOMA

Songer, Vester, (AV) … '23 '47 C&L.623 B.S., LL.B. 202 N. 2nd St.
Watkins, Joe R., (BV) … '58 '86 C.616 B.S.N. L.623 J.D. P.O. Box 189
Welch, Mandy, (AVⓉ) … '44 '76 C.623 B.A. L.862 J.D. 900 E. Jackson Street
Wolf, J. Frank, III, (BV) … '59 '85 C.618 B.S. L.862 J.D. [Rabon,W.&R.]
Wolfe, James R., (BV) … '44 '73 C.623 B.A. L.616 J.D. RR 2

HYDRO, 977, *Blaine & Caddo Cos.*

Retherford, Barry, (CVⓉ) … '59 '89 C.612 B.S. L.862 J.D. RR 3

IDABEL, * 6,957, *McCurtain Co.*

Benson, John A. … '48 '73 C.621 B.S. L.623 J.D. Assoc. Dist. J.‡
Brock, Gary L., (BV) … '43 '69 C.612 B.A. L.623 J.D. 1701 SE Avenue N.
Brown, Jon Ed, (AV) … '65 '94 C.623 B.S. L.477 J.D. [LeForce&M.]
DeBerry, Michael D., (BV) … '44 '69 C.612 B.S. L.623 J.D. [M.D.DeBerry]
DeBerry, Michael D., P.C., (BV) … 121 N. Central
De Witt, John W. … '48 '73 C.612 B.S. L.623 J.D. Spec. Dist. J.
Driesel, Willard L., Jr. … '53 '86 C&L.623 B.A., J.D. Dist. J.
Farley, Kenneth R., (BV) … '47 '81 C&L.623 B.A., J.D. [K.R.Farley]
Farley, Kenneth R., P.C., (BV) … 121 N. Central, Suite C
Hamilton, L. Walter, (BV) … '60 '88 C.1315 B.S.E. L.623 J.D. Dist. Atty. Off.
LeForce, Carl E., (BV) … '35 '63 C.170 B.A. L.623 LL.B. [LeForce&M.]
LeForce & McCombs, P.C., (AV) … 117 North Central Avenue
Leonard, Mitchell Kevin … '62 '90 C.612 B.S. L.862 J.D. 8 N.W. Martin Luther King
Longacre, J.P. … '73 '02 C.612 B.S. L.615 J.D. [🄰 LeForce&M.]
McCombs, Jerry L., (AV) … '43 '75 C.1147 B.A. L.616 J.D. [LeForce&M.]
Ragland, Tim T., (BV) … '67 '94 C.612 B.S. L.378 J.D. [🄰 LeForce&M.]
Sain, Kevin T. … '71 '98 C.619 B.S. L.615 J.D. [🄰 LeForce&M.]
Sanders, Virginia DeCarlo, (BV) … '63 '88 C&L.623 B.A., J.D. Asst. Dist. Atty.
Wooten, William B. … '77 '02 C.612 B.S. L.623 J.D. [🄰 LeForce&M.]

INDIAHOMA, 337, *Comanche Co.*

Perry, Kenneth D., (CV) … '53 '78 C.1300 B.S. L.623 J.D. Mun. J.

INOLA, 1,589, *Rogers Co.*

Striplin, Geo. P. … '16 '49 C&L.862 J.D. RR 02‡

JAY, * 2,482, *Delaware Co.*

Bales, Waldo F., (AV) … '22 '58 C.942 A.B. L.862 J.D. P.O. Box 1140
Cartwright and Associates … P.O. Box 1330

Davis & Thompson, (AV)
Davis-Thompson-Underwood Building, Drawer 487, 74346
Telephone: 918-253-4298 FAX: 918-253-8110
URL: http://www.lawyers.com/davisandthompson
Gene A. Davis (1930-1987); Phil K. Thompson; Bobby C. Ramsey; Tommy R. Dyer, Jr.; Brandon A. Johnson.
Residential and Commercial Real Estate, Family Law, Divorce, Criminal Law, Personal Injury, Banking Law.
Representative Clients: Available on Request.
See Professional Biographies, JAY, OKLAHOMA

Denney, Barry V., (BV) … '51 '85 C.612 B.S. L.862 J.D. 1st Asst. Dist. Atty.
Dyer, Tommy R., Jr., (BV) … '65 '90 C.612 B.S. L.862 J.D. [Davis&T.]
James, Richard D., (BV) '58 '82 C.610 A.B. L.862 J.D.
[Wallace,O.L.G.M.W.W.&J.] ⊙
Johnson, Brandon A., (BV) … '60 '88 C.623 B.B.A. L.615 J.D. [Davis&T.]

Logan & Lowry, LLP
(See Vinita)

Morton, Kathryn R. … '66 '93 C.619 B.A. L.623 J.D. Legal Servs. of Eastern Okla., Inc.
Pitts-Cartwright, Betty Ann … '53 '90 C.619 B.A.Ed. L.862 J.D. [Cartwright&Assoc.]
Ramsey, Bobby C., (BV) … '56 '83 C.48 B.A. L.862 J.D. [Davis&T.]

Taylor, Burrage, Foster, Mallett, Downs & Ramsey, P.C.
(See Claremore)

Thompson, Phil K., (AV) … '47 '72 C.804 B.S. L.862 J.D. [Davis&T.]
Tulk, David Lee … '60 '00 C&L.862 B.S., J.D. P.O. Box 1110
Wallace, Owens, Landers, Gee, Morrow, Wilson, Watson & James, A Professional Corporation, (AV)
5 Krause Street (⊙Miami)
Wright, Christianna L. … '68 '97 C.424 B.A. L.623 J.D. 518 Krause St.

JENKS, 9,557, *Tulsa Co.*

Busby, Wilson H. '48 '77 C&L.45 B.S.B.A., J.D.
(adm. in AR; not adm. in OK) 12310 S. Skyline Dr.‡
Farish, Margaret (Peggy) Cantrell, (BV) '51 '79
C.802 B.A. L.862 J.D. Assoc. Coun., State Dept. of Pub. Safety
Gerkin, John M., (BV) … '50 '75 C.862 B.A. L.623 J.D. [Gerkin&W.]
Gerkin & Williams, (BV) … 505 E. Main St.
Hammond, Malcom P. "Bundy", (BV) '41 '72
C.623 B.B.A. L.862 J.D. 951 W. Main St., Ste. 302
Hill, Laura C. … '77 '02 C.623 B.A. L.862 J.D. [🄰 Landreth P.]
Landreth, Lloyd W., (AV) … '59 '87 C.612 B.S. L.174 J.D. [Landreth P.]

Landreth Law Firm PLC, (AV)
801 E. B Street, 74037
Telephone: 918-296-0460 Fax: 918-296-0404
Email: llandreth@landrethlaw.com URL: http://www.landrethlaw.com
Lloyd W. Landreth;—Laura C. Hill.
Environmental Law, Natural Resources, Administrative Law.
See Professional Biographies, JENKS, OKLAHOMA

Mceachin, Scott William, (AV) '51 '76 C.112 B.A. L.623 J.D.
117 North Birch Street, 74037
Telephone: 918-296-0405 Facsimile: 918-296-3628
Email: scott@mceachinlaw.com
Oil and Gas Law, Corporate Law, Small Business Law, Business Law.
See Professional Biographies, JENKS, OKLAHOMA

Poston, J. Edwin, (BV) … '48 '84 C.246 B.A. L.862 J.D. [J.E.Poston]
Poston, Jack Edwin, P.L.L.C., (BV) … P.O. Box 903
Sullivan, Lovell Wayne … '57 '82 C.375 B.S. L.378 J.D. [W.Sullivan]
Sullivan, Wayne, Attorney at Law … 108 N. 2nd
Tollette, Steven R. … '52 '91 C&L.862 B.S.E.E., J.D. P.O. Box 232 (Pat.)
Williams, Gerald G., (BV) … '47 '75 C.553 B.A. L.616 J.D. [Gerkin&W.]

JONES, 2,424, *Oklahoma Co.*

Dean, Bill V., Jr., (BV) … '57 '82 C.1147 B.S. L.616 J.D. [Dean&Assoc.]
Dean, Christine P., (BV) … '54 '87 C.350 B.A. L.616 J.D. [Dean&Assoc.]
Dean & Associates, (BV) … 110 W. Main St.
Dean & Associates, Law Offices of, (BV) … 110 W. Main St.
Weaver, Bill R., II, (AV) … '59 '84 C&L.623 B.A., J.D. 8600 NE129th St.

KETCHUM, 263, *Craig Co.*

Hochberger, Donald E. '28 '56 C.513 B.S. L.546 J.D.
(adm. in NE; not adm. in OK) P.O. Box 840‡

KINGFISHER, * 4,380, *Kingfisher Co.*

Atkins & Markoff
(See Oklahoma City)

Baker, Thomas E., (AV) … '23 '50 C&L.623 B.S., LL.B. [Baker,L.S.&G.]
Baker, Logsdon, Schulte & Gibson, (AV) … 302 North Main Street

Boeckman, Sara Jane, Law Office of '51 '87 C.420 B.S. L.615 J.D. 1125 S. 8th St.
Gibson, Patrick J., (BV) '60 '94 C.768 B.S. L.616 J.D. [Baker,L.S.&G.]
Harrison, Ralph Edward, (AV) '49 '75 C.612 B.S. L.623 J.D. [Harrison&M.]
Harrison & Mecklenburg, Inc., (AV) Sixth and Miles
Lindsey, E. H. '22 '65 C.921 B.S. L.69 LL.B. P.O. Box RR 2 Box 118
Logsdon, Harold L., (AV) '40 '64 C&L.623 B.A., J.D. [Baker,L.S.&G.]
Mecklenburg, Randy, (AV) '51 '80 C.612 B.S. L.616 J.D. [Harrison&M.]
Miller, Doyle '42 '71 C.1147 B.A. L.623 J.D. P.O. Box 28
Oppel, Matthew Robert, (BV) '70 '95 C.622 B.S. L.615 J.D. [M.R.Oppel]
Oppel, Matthew R., (BV) 117 N. Main
Pritchett, Mary Sue '41 '71 C&L.623 B.A., J.D. Assoc. Dist. J.
Pritchett, Susie, (BV) '41 '72 C&L.623 B.S., J.D. Assoc. Dist. J.
Schulte, Paul I., (AV) '57 '82 C.612 B.S. L.623 J.D. [Baker,L.S.&G.]

LANGLEY, 582, *Mayes Co.*

Rogers, Chris Ellen '53 '91 C.1288 B.A. L.862 J.D. [Rogers&Assoc.]
Rogers & Associates, P.C. P.O. Box 68

LAVERNE, 1,097, *Harper Co.*

Armor, G. W., (AV) '31 '55 C&L.623 B.A., LL.B. 103 West Jayroe Street
Armor, Vance W. '65 '92 C.859 B.A. L.623 J.D. P.O. Box 267‡
Harkins, Jim Neil, (BV) '43 '73 C.622 B.A. L.623 J.D. [Holcomb&H.] ⊙
Holcomb, M. Marcus, (AV) '32 '56 C.612 L.623 LL.B. [Holcomb&H.] ⊙
Holcomb & Harkins, (AV) 120 E. Jane Jayroe Blvd (⊙Buffalo)

LAWTON, * 92,757, *Comanche Co.*

Ashton, Alfred J., Jr., (AV) '20 '48 C&L.623 LL.B. 4704 N.W. 47th Place
Ashton, Mark A., (AV) '44 '69 C&L.623 B.B.A., J.D. [Ashton,W.&M.]
Ashton, Wisener & Munkacsy, P.C., (AV) 711 S.W. C Ave.

Atkins & Markoff
(See Oklahoma City)

Aycock, Keith B., (BV) '47 '73 C&L.623 B.B.A., J.D. Dist. J.
Babbitt, Jerry R., (CV) '41 '69 C.612 B.S. L.862 J.D. 1111 W. Gore Blvd.
Bassel, Rodney A., (AV) '46 '73 C.622 B.A. L.616 J.D. P.O. Box 328
Bledsoe, Chad '35 '66 C&L.623 B.B.A., J.D. 616 N.W. Waterford Drive‡

Booker, Steven R., P.C., Law Office of
(See Wichita Falls, Texas)

Brown, Carole J., (BV) '45 '80 C.1375 A.B. L.845 J.D. [C.J.Brown]
Brown, Carole J., Inc., (BV) 601 S.W. C Ave.
Burgess, Bill W., Jr., (BV) '56 '81 C.1300 B.A. L.623 J.D. [Burgess,B.B.&H.]
Burgess, Brad W., (BV) '57 '83 C.1300 B.A. L.623 J.D. [Burgess,B.B.&H.]
Burgess, Sylvia M., (BV) '57 '82 C.1300 B.A. L.623 J.D. [Burgess,B.B.&H.]

Burgess, Burgess, Burgess & Hightower, (BV)
A Partnership of Professional Corporations
21 N.W. 44th Street, Suite 201, 73505
Telephone: 580-355-8920 Fax: 580-355-8999
Email: legal@burgess-hightower.com
Bill W. Burgess, Jr.; Brad W. Burgess; Sylvia M. Burgess; M. Monty Hightower.
See Professional Biographies, LAWTON, OKLAHOMA

Butler, David, (BV) '— '97 C.612 B.S. L.623 J.D. [Butler&B.]
Butler, Dennis, (AV) '44 '71 C.612 B.A. L.862 J.D. [Butler&B.]

Butler & Butler, (AV)
A Partnership
810 C Avenue, 73501
Telephone: 580-355-8081 Fax: 580-353-5387
Dennis Butler; David Butler.
General Civil Trial Practice, Criminal, Personal Injury, Eminent Domain.
Reference: City National Bank of Lawton.

Calvert, Roy M. L., (BV) '44 '84 C.1300 B.S. L.623 J.D. Asst. Dist. Atty.
Carter, David W., (BV) '40 '71 C.766 B.A. L.623 J.D. 632 S.W. D Ave.
Caudle, Dietmar K. H., (BV) '46 '77 C.623 B.A. L.616 J.D. 702 A Ave., S.W.
Cook, Max, (BV) '18 '41 C&L.623 B.A., LL.B. P.O. Box 3017‡
Copeland, Hyman Z., (BV) '55 '80 C.617 B.S. L.616 J.D. 525 S.W. C Ave.
Cousins, Barry Wayne, (BV) '47 '72 C.622 B.A. L.623 J.D. 802 "D" Ave.
Cramer, John, (BV) '61 '87 C&L.623 B.B.A., J.D. 2109 N.W. Cache Rd.
Cruz, Felix A. D., (BV) '35 '82 C.201 B.A. L.616 J.D. City Atty.
Cude, Jerry C., (BV) '37 '66 C.621 L.616 LL.B. 315 S.W. 5th Street
Davis, Don C. '43 '69 C&L.623 B.A., J.D. Pres., Cameron Univ.
Davis, John Randolph '59 '85 C.861 B.A. L.846 J.D. City Natl. Bk. & Tr. Co.
Doerfel, Ken Sue, (BV) '44 '78 C.623 B.A. L.616 J.D. Route 1
Doolin, J. W., (AV) '47 '73 C.620 B.A. L.862 J.D. 802 "D" Ave.
Dugger, Richard L., (BV) '38 '64 C&L.616 B.S.B., J.D. Asst. Dist. Atty.
Dutcher, J. Blake, Jr., (BV) '57 '82 C.934 B.A. L.623 J.D. [Godlove,M.D.D.&E.]
Dzialo, Edward W., Jr., (BV) '48 '78 C.1300 B.S. L.616 J.D. [Godlove,M.D.D.&E.]

Ellis, Leonard & Buckholts
(See Duncan)

Erwin, Shon T., (AV) '61 '86 C.1288 B.A. L.623 J.D. [Godlove,M.D.D.&E.]

Flanagan, Michael C., Attorney at Law
(See Walters)

Fox, Fred T., Jr., (BV) '42 '69 C&L.623 B.S., J.D. [Firm of F.T.Fox]
Fox, Fred T., Law Firm of, (BV) 808 W. Gore Blvd.
Fullerton, James M. '35 '67 C&L.623 B.B.A., J.D. P.O. Box 804
Garrett, Nicholas D., (AV) '41 '67 C.612 B.S. L.623 J.D. [Garrett&H.]
Garrett & Hamlin, (AV) 431 "C" Avenue, Suite 101
Godlove, Ernest F., (AV) '41 '66 C.228 B.A. L.623 J.D. [Godlove,M.D.D.&E.]

Godlove, Mayhall, Dzialo, Dutcher & Erwin, A Professional Corporation, (AV) BB
802 "C" Avenue, P.O. Box 29, 73502
Telephone: 580-353-6700 Fax: 580-353-2900
Email: gmdde@sirinet.net
W. W. Godlove (1908-1982); Ernest F. Godlove; Michael C. Mayhall; Edward W. Dzialo, Jr.; J. Blake Dutcher, Jr.; Shon T. Erwin.
Litigation, Collections, Corporate, Banking, Real Estate, Estate Planning, Probate, Personal Injury, Workers Compensation, Taxation, Bankruptcy and Domestic Relations, Courts-Martial and Military Administrative Law. General Civil, Trial and Appellate Practice in all State and Federal Courts.
Representative Clients: International Bank of Commerce; Arvest Bank; Wells-Fargo Bank; Southwest Abstract Company; Comanche County Industrial Development Authority; EZ Go Foods, Inc.; Goodyear Tire & Rubber Company; Jan-L Construction, Inc.; Sears Roebuck and Co.
See Professional Biographies, LAWTON, OKLAHOMA

Graham, Ken J., (BV) '45 '81 C.622 B.A. L.623 J.D. 810 SW C Avenue
Hamlin, Joe W., (AV) '45 '73 C&L.623 B.B.A., J.D. [Garrett&H.]

Haupt Brooks Vandruff, PLLC
(See Oklahoma City)

Highsaw, Robert
(See Oklahoma City)

Hightower, M. Monty, (BV) '55 '90 C&L.623 B.B.A., J.D. [Burgess,B.B.&H.]
Holmes Ray, Chandra L., (BV) '65 '90 C&L.862 B.S., J.D. [A J.P.Zelbst]
Hoskins, Max E., (CV) '58 '90 C.1300 B.S. L.623 J.D. 608 S.W. D Ave.
Hutcherson, Daniel L., (CV) '43 '93 C.1147 B.S. L.615 J.D. [Hutcherson]
Hutcherson Law Offices, (CV) 715 S.W. A. Ave.
Jennings, R. Keith, (BV) '48 '76 C.1300 B.A. L.616 J.D. 802 "D" Avenue
Jensen, Franklin V. '59 '85 C.1300 B.a. L.862 J.D. Dep. City Atty.★
Johnson, H. Allen, Law Office of, (BV) '36 '77 C.623 B.S. L.616 J.D.
816 W. Gore Blvd.
Johnson, Larry W. '61 '85 C.612 B.S. L.623 J.D. Asst. City Atty.
Johnson, Sam H., (AV) '37 '63 C&L.623 B.A., LL.B. 501 S.W. C Ave.

Johnston & Associates
(See Chickasha)

Jones, Russell G., (AV) '12 '38 C&L.623 B.A., LL.B. 3502 N.W. Arlington‡
Jordan, Robert P., (BV) '43 '71 C.896 B.A. L.623 J.D. 750 N.W. 16th St.
Kinslow, John, Law Offices of, (BV) '41 '65 C.613 B.A. L.623 J.D.
501 S.W. "C" Street
Kriegel, Andrew M. '72 '00 C.560 B.A. L.623 J.D. 802 SW D Avenue

Leach, Sullivan, Sullivan & Watkins
(See Duncan)

Leyja, Vickie C. '57 '99 C.1300 B.S. L.623 J.D. 802 Sw D Ave
Lowenfield, Frances Sears '67 '94 C.859 B.A. L.228 J.D. 903 NW Becontree Place
Mackey, John C., (AV) '44 '69 C&L.623 B.A., J.D. [Wade&M.]
Manning, Inez '12 '52 C.615 A.B. L.623 LL.B. 715 Bell St.‡
Mata, Art G., (BV) '55 '80 C&L.623 B.A., J.D. 609 S.W. East Ave.
Mayhall, Michael C., (AV) '48 '75 C&L.623 B.B.A., J.D. [Godlove,M.D.D.&E.]
McCall, C. Allen, Jr. '54 '79 C&L.623 B.A., J.D. Chf. Dist. J.
Mcclure, Kade A., (BV) '— '76 C&L.623 B.A., J.D. 621 D Ave.
Meyers, O. Christopher, (AV) '44 '69 C&L.623 B.B.A., J.D. [O.C.Meyers]

Meyers, O. Christopher, Inc., (AV)
15 N.W. 44th Street, 73505
Telephone: 580-355-0341 Fax: 580-355-0359
Email: cmeyers@sirinet.net URL: http://www.lawyers.com/cmeyerslaw
O. Christopher Meyers.
Tax Planning, Tax Litigation, Living Trusts, Estate Planning, Probate Administration, Real Estate Exchanges, Pension & Profit Sharing Plans, Buying and Selling Businesses.
See Professional Biographies, LAWTON, OKLAHOMA

Moore, Roy D. '40 '70 C.614 B.A. L.616 J.D. Dist. J.
Moyano, Lillian M. '67 '91 C.623 B.A. L.602 J.D. 207 Lakeview Circle
Munkacsy, John, (AV) '44 '70 C.97 B.S. L.608 J.D. [Ashton,W.&M.]
Neuwirth, Gerald F., (AV) '46 '71 C.612 B.S. L.623 J.D. 812 W. Gore Blvd., Ste. A
Newcombe, Ralph W., (AV) '31 '60 C.1050 B.S. L.623 LL.B. [Newcombe,R.R.&N.]
Newcombe, Stephen K., (BV) '56 '83 C&L.623 B.S., J.D. [Newcombe,R.R.&N.]

Newcombe, Redman, Ross & Newcombe, P.C., A Professional Corporation, (AV)
513 C Avenue, 73501
Telephone: 580-355-8000 FAX: 580-355-8007
Ralph W. Newcombe; Manville Redman; Eddie Y. Newcombe (1940-1992); Robert L. Ross; Stephen K. Newcombe; Joel A. Perlmutter.
General Civil Practice. Trials. Insurance Defense, Probate, Criminal, Domestic Relations, Real Estate and Oil and Gas Law.
Representative Clients: Caddell Transit Corp., Lawton, Oklahoma; Kennedy & Co. Lawton, Oklahoma.
See Professional Biographies, LAWTON, OKLAHOMA

Oaks, J. Merle '27 '51 C&L.623 B.S., LL.B. 408 N.W. 6th St.‡

Parrish Law Firm, The, A Professional Corporation
(See Oklahoma City)

Pereira, John, (BV) '46 '94 C.1145 B.S.B.A. L.615 J.D. [J.A.Pereira]
Pereira, John A., (BV) 611 S.W. E Ave.
Perlmutter, Joel A. '56 '87 C.161 B.B.A. L.1003 J.D. [Newcombe,R.R.&N.]
Porter, George L., III '60 '88
C.170 B.A. L.623 J.D. V.P., Tr. Offr., City Natl. Bk. & Tr. Co.
Prince, Robert E., (BV) '44 '71 C.612 B.A. L.623 J.D. 632 S.W. "D" Ave.
Ramsey, William J., (CV) '36 '81 C.627 B.G.S. L.623 J.D.
Assoc. Prof., Cameron Univ.‡
Ray, G. Scott, (AV) '55 '82 C.623 B.A. L.616 J.D. [Scott R.]
Redman, Manville, (AV) '25 '49 C&L.623 B.A., LL.B. [Newcombe,R.R.&N.]
Reeves, Joe B., (BV) '45 '71 C.622 B.S. L.616 J.D. 2805 North East Heritage Drive
Rhoads, Githen K., (AV) '20 '48 C&L.623 LL.B. 411 SW 6th Street
Riley, William C., (BV) '47 '82 C.612 B.S. L.615 J.D. Asst. Dist. Atty.
Ross, Robert L., (BV) '52 '77 C&L.623 B.A., J.D. [Newcombe,R.R.&N.]
Schacher, Robert C., Jr., (AV) '40 '65 C&L.623 B.A., J.D. 511 SW "C" Ave
Schmulbach, G. Barry '45 '88 C.836 B.B.A. L.1015 J.D.
Gen. Mgr., Oklahoma Abstract Co. of Lawton, Inc.
Schulte, Robert C., (AV) '47 '77 C.1300 B.A. L.616 J.D. Dist. Atty.

Scott Ray Law Firm, (AV) BB
P.O. Box 1676, 73502
Telephone: 580-248-5557 Fax: 580-248-5556
URL: http://www.lawtonlawyer.com
G. Scott Ray.
General Civil Litigation, Medical Malpractice, Family Law, Children, Federal Practice, Civil Practice, Traffic Violations, Wrongful Death, Negligence, Trial Practice, Products Liability, Premises Liability, Torts, Criminal Law.
See Professional Biographies, LAWTON, OKLAHOMA

Shaw, Jeffrey Lee, (BV) '58 '84 C.1300 B.A. L.623 J.D.
City Bank Bldg., 5th & D Ave.
Sims, Tommy L., (BV) '54 '88 C.1300 B.S. L.623 J.D. [A J.P.Zelbst]

Smith, Don L., (AV) '47 '72 C.612 B.S. L.623 J.D.
612 SW "D" Avenue, 73501-4570
Telephone: 580-248-7525 Telefax: 580-248-7557
Email: dlsatty@sirinet.net
General Civil Practice. Real Estate, Banking, Probate, Commercial Law, Corporate, Litigation.
Approved Attorney for: Resolution Trust Corp.; Federal Deposit Insurance Corp.; Security Union Title Insurance Co.; Chicago Title Insurance; Ticor Title Insurance Inc.; American-First Title & Trust Co.; First American Title Insurance Co.; Stewart Title Guaranty Co.; Lawyer's Title Insurance Co.; Farmers Home Administration.
See Professional Biographies, LAWTON, OKLAHOMA

Smith, Fred C., Jr., (BV) '53 '82 C.612 B.S. L.616 J.D. Asst. Dist. Atty..
Smith, Mark R. '51 '75 C.612 B.S. L.616 J.D. Dist. J.
South, Arthur R., (AV) '45 '74 C&L.616 B.A., J.D. 802 "D" Avenue
Stabler, Jeffrey C. '56 '81 C.1300 B.S. L.623 J.D. 304 NW 19th St.

Stein, Taylor C., (BV) .... '53 '78 C.623 B.A. L.862 J.D. Asst. Dist. Atty.
Stevens, Donald T. .... '67 '92 C&L.623 B.A., J.D. 3 N.W. 59th★
Stratton, C. William .... '35 '64 C.622 B.A. L.421 LL.B. Dist. J.
Sullivan, Carol S., (BV) .... '39 '92 C.1300 B.S. L.623 J.D. [Sullivan]
Sullivan, Patrick N., (AV) .... '30 '60 C&L.623 B.A., LL.B. [Sullivan]
Sullivan, Sean P., (BV) .... '63 '89 C.1300 B.S. L.862 J.D. [Sullivan]
Sullivan Law Office, (AV) .... 501 W. Gore Blvd.
Sullivan Law Office, P.C., (BV) .... 501 W. Gore Blvd.
Tannery, Dick W., (CV) .... '44 '76 C.612 B.S. L.623 J.D. 602 S.E. D Ave.
Tayloe, D. Emmit, (BV) .... '57 '83 C.1300 B.A. L.623 J.D. 716 S.W. A Avenue
Vincent, John Hollis, Jr., (BV) '46 '75
C.1147 B.B.A. L.612 J.D. City Atty.; Lawton Atty. Off.
Wade, Charles E., Jr., (AV) .... '40 '65 C.734 B.S. L.623 J.D. [Wade&M.]

Wade and Mackey, A Professional Corporation, (AV)
431 "C" Avenue, P.O. Box 2515, 73502
Telephone: 580-357-7700 Fax: 580-357-7706 URL: http://www.wademackey.com
URL: http://www.lawyers.com/wademackey
Charles E. Wade, Jr.; John C. Mackey.
General Civil and Trial Practice in State and Federal Courts. Banking, Estate Planning, Probate, Real Estate, School, Health Care, Corporate and Business Law.
Representative Clients: City National Bank and Trust Co.; Comanche County Hospital Authority; Fort Sill National Bank; Liberty National Bank; Lawton Public Schools; Altus Public Schools; Great Plains Technology Center; Lawton Metropolitan Area Airport Authority; Stewart Escrow & Title Service, Inc.; P-A Chevrolet.
See Professional Biographies, LAWTON, OKLAHOMA

Walker, Jay Stanley, (BV) .... '52 '82 C.1300 B.S. L.623 J.D. [Walker,J.S.]
Walker, Ferguson & Ferguson
(See Oklahoma City)
Walker, Jay S., (BV) .... 527 C Ave.
West, Neil S. .... '69 '97 C.556 B.A. L.615 J.D. 208 S.W. 3rd St.
Willson, James Ray, (BV) .... '49 '82 C.620 B.S. L.45 J.D. [J.R.Willson]
Willson, James Ray, (BV) .... 608 S.W. D Ave., Ste. 1
Wilson, William H., (CV) .... '22 '59 C.846 B.B.A. L.862 J.D. 606 S.W. D Ave.
Wisener, Thomas W., (AV) .... '42 '67 C.612 B.A. L.623 J.D. [Ashton,W.&M.]
Youngblood, Karen N. .... '50 '75 C&L.623 B.A., J.D. Cameron Univ.
Youngblood, Kenneth L. .... '26 '50 C.1300 L.623 J.D. 303 N.W. 33rd Place‡
Zaugg, Gary '62 '91 C&L.878 B.A., J.D.
(adm. in UT; not adm. in OK) Special Agent, F.B.I.
Zelbst, John P., (AV) .... '54 '80 C.1300 B.A. L.862 J.D. [J.P.Zelbst]

Zelbst, John P., Law Firm, (AV)
411 S.W. 6th, P.O. Box 365, 73502-0365
Telephone: 580-248-4844 Fax: 580-248-6916
Email: ZelbstLawFirm@cs.com
John P. Zelbst. Associates: Tommy L. Sims; Chandra L. Holmes Ray.
Personal Injury Trial Practice and General Civil Trial Practice. Medical Malpractice. Criminal Trial Practice.
Reference: City National Bank.
See Professional Biographies, LAWTON, OKLAHOMA

Zwaan, Susan Garnett, (CV) .... '51 '97 C.1300 B.S. L.623 J.D. 716 S.W. A Avenue

LEBANON, 327, *Marshall Co.*

Catron, James W. .... '48 '74 C&L.560 B.A., J.D. P.O. Box 58

LINDSAY, 2,947, *Garvin Co.*

Barber, Wilfred L., (BV) .... '29 '59 C&L.623 B.A., LL.B. 1010 W. Choctaw‡
Elkins, Von B., (BV) .... '50 '76 C.1147 B.A. L.616 J.D. City Atty. [Elkins&H.]
Elkins & Hart, A Professional Corporation, (BV) .... P.O. Box 428
Frankenberg, Don, (BV) .... '46 '71 C.612 B.S. L.623 J.D. 502 S. Main St.
Hart, Thomas H., (BV) .... '49 '76 C&L.623 B.S.Ch.E., J.D. [Elkins&H.]

LUTHER, 612, *Oklahoma Co.*

Craig, Nancy G., (AV) .... '44 '76 C&L.623 B.A., J.D. P.O. Box 358

MADILL, * 3,410, *Marshall Co.*

Ables, Lyn E., (AV) .... '41 '71 C&L.623 B.B.A., J.D. P.O. Box 205
Godfrey, Peter .... '56 '88 C.623 B.B.A. L.616 J.D. P.O. Box G
Haggerty, Paule' Thrift ... '71 '96 C.1147 B.B.A. L.623 J.D. Marshall Co. Dist. Attys. Off.
Landgraf, Jeffrey S. .... '77 '02 C.612 B.S. L.623 J.D. [Little,L.L.W.C.O.&G.]
Little, Dan, (AV) '42 '68 C.309 B.A. L.623 J.D.
[Little,L.L.W.C.O.&G.] (⊙Joplin, MO; Tishomingo, OK)
Little, Prudence Mae, (AV) '42 '68 C.914 B.A. L.623 J.D.
[Little,L.L.W.C.O.&G.] (⊙Joplin, MO; Tishomingo, OK)
Little, Little, Little, Windel, Coppedge, Oliver & Gallagher, P.L.L.C., (AV)
202 West Lillie Boulevard (⊙Ardmore, Tishomingo)
Maxwell, Alfred L. .... '36 '68 C.810 B.S. L.862 J.D. Route 2, Box 66
Miller, Floyd, Jr., (BV) .... '25 '50 C.612 L.623 LL.B. 214 Plaza
Miller, Richard A. .... '53 '78 C.593 B.S. L.616 J.D. Assoc. Dist. J.
Scaggs, John H. .... '46 '74 C.616 B.A. L.623 J.D. Dist. J.
Thompson, Sherry P. '57 '97 C&L.560 B.A., J.D.
(adm. in NM; not adm. in OK) 202 W. Lillie
Watson, Millicent McClure .... '53 '87 C.612 B.S. L.623 J.D. [Watson,M.M.]
Watson, Millicent McClure, P.C. .... 216 Plaza
Windel, Jerry Lynn, (BV) '43 '68
C&L.623 B.A., J.D. [Little,L.L.W.C.O.&G.] (⊙Tishomingo)

MANGUM, * 2,924, *Greer Co.*

Horton, Charles P. .... '49 '77 C.623 B.B.A. L.616 J.D. [Horton&Assoc.] ⊙

Horton & Associates
122 North Oklahoma Avenue, 73554 ⊙
Telephone: 580-782-3348 Facsimile: 580-782-2836
Email: chorton@pacer.com
Charles P. Horton.
General Civil Practice, Trusts, Probate, Estate Planning, Personal Injury, Real Estate, Business, Divorce, Interstate Custody, Military, Municipal, Public Finance and Aviation Law.
Altus Office: 216 West Commerce Street. Telephone: 580-482-3355. Fax: 580-482-0363
See Professional Biographies, MANGUM, OKLAHOMA

McDaniel, Yonne P., (BV) .... '21 '46 C.999 A.B. 125 N. Oklahoma Ave.
Mclemore, Heidi Baier .... '67 '96 C.839 B.A. L.623 J.D. State Indigent Def. Sys.
Schwabe, Charles L. .... '43 '72 C.612 B.S. L.862 J.D. Assoc. Dist. J.
Stumbaugh, Paul D., (BV) .... '31 '60 C&L.862 B.A., LL.B. 122 N. Oklahoma
Tyner, Wayna Lynn .... '70 '97 C.1300 B.A. L.623 J.D. State Indigent Def. Sys.
Yarborough, Eric G. .... '60 '97 C.622 B.A. L.900 J.D. State's Atty.

MANNFORD, 2,095, *Creek, Pawnee & Tulsa Cos.*

Baker, Robert D. .... '51 '76 C.862 B.S. L.623 J.D. Mannford Fam. Clinic‡
Hobaugh, Gary L. .... '51 '77 C.705 B.A. L.616 J.D. 136 Lakeview Drive

MARIETTA, * 2,445, *Love Co.*

Barton, L. Jack, (BV) .... '40 '66 C.614 B.A. L.616 J.D. 1st Asst. Dist. Atty
Caldwell, Gary L., (BV(T)) '37 '72 C.999 A.A. L.1095 B.L.
(adm. in CA; not adm. in OK) P.O. Box 356
Cochran, Richard A., Jr., (BV) .... '52 '77 C.1147 B.A. L.616 J.D. 309 W. Main
Delashaw, Kenneth L., Jr., (AV) .... '46 '73 C.623 B.B.A. L.616 J.D. 204 W. Chickasaw
Roberts, Charles E. .... '52 '79 C.942 B.S. L.623 J.D. Assoc. Dist. J.

MARLOW, 4,592, *Stephens Co.*

Bills, Russell G., (CV) .... '53 '79 C.612 B.S. L.616 J.D. Maple St., R.R. 3

MAUD, 1,204, *Pottawatomie Co.*

Zeller, Ralph James .... '35 '90 C.618 B.A. L.615 J.D. P.O. Box 160‡

MAYSVILLE, 1,313, *Garvin Co.*

Henson, William H. .... '56 '82 C.623 B.B.A. L.659 J.D. Farmers & Merchants Bank

McALESTER, * 17,783, *Pittsburg Co.*

Allford, John A., (AV) .... '29 '56 C&L.623 B.B.A., LL.B. [Allford,A.I.Z.&G.]
Allford, Ashmore, Ivester, Zellmer & Green, (AV) .... 10 East Washington Street
Ashmore, Anthony D., (BV) .... '39 '65 C.612 B.S. L.623 J.D. [[C] Allford,A.I.Z.&G.]
Bartheld, Thomas M. .... '57 '84 C.612 B.S. L.623 J.D. Assoc. Dist. J.
Belote, Jeffry L., (BV) .... '60 '87 C&L.623 B.A., J.D. 209 E. Wyandotte
Bishop, Paul B. .... '46 '75 C&L.623 B.B.A., J.D. Admin., The McAlester Clinic, Inc.
Bland, James D. .... '56 '82 C.314 B.S. L.45 J.D. Assoc. Dist. J.
Boyer, Ronald L., (CV) .... '44 '79 C.375 B.S. L.900 J.D. Asst. Dist. Atty.
Brown, Monte R., (BV) .... '52 '77 C.623 B.S. L.616 J.D. [Brown&B.]
Brown, Wesley, (AV) .... '48 '73 C&L.623 B.A., J.D. [Brown&B.]
Brown & Brown, (AV) .... 417 E. Cherokee
Cable, Brett D. .... '71 '02 C.802 B.B.A. L.862 J.D. [[A] Steidley&N.]
Clayton, Mark A., (CV) .... '65 '91 C&L.623 B.B.A., J.D. [Steidley&N.]
Constantikes, John J., (CV) .... '50 '79 C.623 B.A. L.616 J.D. 10 E. Washington, Ste. 110
Cornish, Richard P. .... '42 '66 C.612 B.S. L.623 J.D. U.S. Mag.
Crain, Billie W., P.C. .... '23 '49 C.618 L.623 LL.B. 2207 Mockingbird Ln.‡
Dobbins, Amy Beth .... '75 '01 C.1147 B.A.Ed. L.623 J.D. [[A] Steidley&N.]
Eaton, Walter Ross .... '63 '92 C.620 B.A. L.623 J.D. State Farm Ins.
Edwards, Mark L., (CV) .... '69 '96 C.1315 B.S. L.623 J.D. [[A] Stipe,H.L.U.E.&B.]
Edwards, Tony W., (BV) .... '56 '82 C.618 B.A. L.623 J.D. [Stipe,H.L.U.E.&B.]
Ervin, William J., (BV) .... '40 '69 C&L.623 B.A., J.D. [Ervin&E.]
Ervin, William J., Jr., (CV) .... '69 '96 C&L.623 B.S., J.D. [Ervin&E.]
Ervin & Ervin, (BV) .... 215 East Choctaw, Suite 104 A
Eschenheimer, Whitney M. .... '70 '96 C.378 B.A. L.623 J.D. [Steidley&N.] ⊙
Evans, Bruce L. '20 '50 C.612 A.B. L.862 J.D.
Admin. Law J., Off. of Hearings & App., SSA
Faling, James Richard, Jr., (BV) '63 '92
C.623 B.B.A. L.615 J.D. 122 East Carl Albert Parkway, Suite B
Fields, Mark E. .... '74 '01 C&L.623 B.A., J.D. [[A] Steidley&N.]
Furlong, Trevor J. .... '73 '05 C.999 B.S. L.623 J.D. [[A] Stipe,H.L.U.E.&B.]
Gaylor, Guy A. .... '— '02 C&L.862 B.A., J.D. [[A] Steidley&N.]
Gotcher, Paul Warren, (AV) .... '47 '71 C&L.623 B.A., J.D. 209 E. Wyandotte
Green, Elaine, (CV) .... '54 '91 C.618 B.S. L.623 J.D. [Allford,A.I.Z.&G.]
Hackler, Deborah L., (BV) .... '62 '93 C.623 B.B.A. L.616 J.D. [Hackler&H.]
Hackler, Donald R., (AV) .... '29 '60 C.618 B.S. L.616 LL.B. [Hackler&H.]
Hackler and Hackler, (AV) .... 19 E. Carl Albert Pkwy.
Harper, Eddie, (AV) .... '38 '63 C&L.623 B.S., LL.B. [Stipe,H.L.U.E.&B.]
Harris, Michelle .... '71 '00 C.1050 B.A. L.862 J.D. [[A] Steidley&N.] ⊙
Hendrix, Angela Renee, (CV) .... '62 '92 C.999 B.A. L.421 J.D. 3430 N. Hwy 69 Pass
Herrick, Jeff P., (BV) .... '66 '92 C.619 B.A. L.615 J.D. 426 E. Wyandotte Avenue
Hogan, Michael W., (BV) .... '58 '86 C.619 B.S. L.616 J.D. [Steidley&N.]
Ivester, Robert L., (BV) .... '40 '65 C&L.623 B.B.A., J.D. [Allford,A.I.Z.&G.]
Janzen, Eric D., (BV) .... '64 '90 C&L.623 B.A., J.D. [Steidley&N.]
Konsure, M. Todd .... '65 '90 C&L.623 B.B.A., J.D. 1st National Ctr.
Lalli, Daniel F., (CV) .... '41 '90 C.618 B.S. L.862 J.D. 405 E. Wyandotte
Layden, Bill, (BV) .... '50 '76 C.1182 B.A. L.623 J.D. [Layden]
Layden, Joseph L., (CV) .... '54 '82 C.619 B.A. L.616 J.D. [Layden]
Layden, Patrick T. .... '61 '87 C.623 B.S. L.616 J.D. [P.Layden]
Layden, Robert A. .... '22 '52 C&L.62 B.Sc., LL.B. Ret. Dist. J.
Layden, William H., (AV) .... '22 '53 C.602 B.S. L.623 LL.B. [Layden]
Layden, Inc., (AV) .... 320 E. Carl Albert Pky.
Layden, Pat, Law Office of .... 320 E. Carl Albert Pkwy.
Martin, James B. .... '30 '54 C.619 L.192 LL.B. 1201 E. Wyandotte
Maxcey, Timothy D., (BV) .... '63 '89 C.1315 B.S. L.845 J.D. [[A] Stipe,H.L.U.E.&B.]
May, Ronnie, (BV) .... '58 '83 C.619 B.A. L.45 J.D. [May]
May Law Office, (BV) .... P.O. Box 846
McDonald, Scott D., (AV(T)) .... '66 '91 C&L.846 B.A., J.D [[C] Steidley&N.]
McKelvey, Sean M., (CV) .... '70 '96 C.1142 B.A. L.615 J.D. [Steidley&N.]
McKnight, Gary L., (BV) .... '42 '66 C&L.623 B.S., J.D. [G.L.McKnight]
McKnight, Gary L., Inc., (BV) .... 11 E. Carl Albert Pkwy.
Mercer, Tod S., (BV) .... '58 '91 C.623 B.A. L.616 J.D. [Mercer]

Mercer Law Firm, P.C., (BV)
2626 S. 14th Street, Suite C-20, 74501
Telephone: 918-420-5850 Fax: 918-420-5855
Email: tod@todmercerlaw.com URL: http://www.lawyers.com/mercerlawfirm
Tod S. Mercer.
Insurance Bad Faith, Personal Injury, Insurance, Extra Contractual Insurance Claims, Accident Insurance, Catastrophic Injury, Mediation.
Representative Client: Southeast Oklahoma Box Company, Inc.
See Professional Biographies, MCALESTER, OKLAHOMA

Miller, Jim B., (CV) .... '60 '89 C.623 B.B.A. L.616 J.D. 118 E. Carl Albert Pkwy
Neal, Charles D. "Buddy", Jr., (AV) .... '49 '75 C.612 B.S. L.616 J.D. [Steidley&N.]
Parks, Michael D., (BV) .... '55 '80 C&L.623 B.A., J.D. 109 East Carl Albert Parkway
Quinton, Ellen Clare, (CV) .... '68 '93 C.618 B.A. L.862 J.D. 10 E. Washington, Ste. 103
Raunikar, F. Nils, (BV) .... '61 '91 C.618 B.A. L.623 J.D. [Steidley&N.]
Roberts, Don R., (CV) .... '37 '66 C.619 B.A. L.623 J.D. Dist. Atty.
Steidley, W. G. "Gil", Jr., (AV) .... '44 '69 C&L.623 B.B.A., J.D. [Steidley&N.] ⊙‡

Steidley & Neal, (AV)
100 East Carl Albert Parkway, P.O. Box 1165, 74502 ⊙
Telephone: 918-423-4611 Fax: 918-423-4620
Senior Members of Firm: W. G. "Gil" Steidley, Jr.; Charles D. "Buddy" Neal, Jr. Members of Firm: Mark A. Clayton; Michael W. Hogan; Eric D. Janzen; F. Nils Raunikar; Whitney M. Eschenheimer; Sean M. McKelvey. Associates: Mark E. Fields; Michelle Harris; Brett D. Cable; Guy A. Gaylor; Amy Beth Dobbins. Of Counsel: Scott D. McDonald; Jerry E. Truster (Resident Tulsa Office).
Insurance Defense and Personal Injury Law, Medical and Legal Malpractice, Municipal Law, Insurance Law, Civil Rights and Employment Law.

(This Listing Continued)

Steidley & Neal (Continued)

Tulsa, Oklahoma Office: Exchange Tower, Suite 800. 4500 South Garnett Road. 74146. Telephone: 918-664-4612. Fax: 918-664-4133.

See Professional Biographies, MCALESTER, OKLAHOMA

Stipe, Clyde, (BV) .... '29 '57 C.999 L.616 LL.B. [Ⓒ Stipe,H.L.U.E.&B.]

Stipe, Harper, Laizure, Uselton, Edwards & Belote, LLP, (AV)
343 East Carl Albert Parkway, P.O. Box 1369, 74502 ⊙
Telephone: 918-423-0421 Fax: 918-423-0266
URL: http://www.stipelaw.com
Members of Firm: Eddie Harper; Russell G. Uselton; Tony W. Edwards; Anthony M. Laizure (Resident, Tulsa Office); James A. Belote (Resident, Oklahoma City Office);—Timothy D. Maxcey; Mark L. Edwards; Trevor J. Furlong. Of Counsel: Clyde Stipe.
General Civil and Criminal Trial Practice. Personal Injury, Workers Compensation, Probate, Federal Employers Liability, Medical Malpractice, Products Liability Law, Mass Torts, Class Actions.
Representative Clients: Sooner Federal Savings & Loan Assn.; Safeway Stores, Inc.; U.M.W.A. (State); AFL-CIO (State); Kiamichi Electric Cooperative.
Muskogee, Oklahoma Office: 384 South 33rd Street. Telephone: 918-683-5050. Telefax: 918-682-5700
Oklahoma City, Oklahoma Office: 4111 North Lincoln Boulevard. Telephone: 405-524-2268.
Tulsa, Oklahoma Office: 2417 E. Skelly Drive. Telephone: 918-749-0749.

See Professional Biographies, MCALESTER, OKLAHOMA

Taylor, Steven W. .... '49 '74 C.612 B.A. L.623 J.D. Dist. J.
Truster, Jerry E., (BV) .... '43 '70 C.608 B.S. L.862 J.D. [Ⓒ Steidley&N.] ⊙
Uselton, Russell G., (BV) .... '55 '83 C.621 B.S. L.45 J.D. [Stipe,H.L.U.E.&B.]

Wagner & Wagner, P.C.
(See Oklahoma City)

Webb, Thomas B., (BV) .... '51 '75 C.648 B.S. L.64 J.D. [Ⓐ Layden]
Weber, Larry M. '42 '67 C&L.623 B.B.A., J.D.
Admin. Law J., Dept. of Health & Human Servs.
Wiley, Roger, (BV) .... '55 '85 C.623 B.A. L.1143 J.D. 216 East Choctaw Avenue
Wynn, Donnita Weinkauf, (BV) ...... '57 '83 C&L.862 B.S., J.D. 19 E. Carl Albert Pkwy.
Zellmer, George, (CV) .... '51 '79 C.623 B.A. L.616 J.D. [Allford,A.I.Z.&G.]

McLOUD, 3,548, *Pottawatomie Co.*

Ingraham, Sandra Jo .... '47 '94 C.1147 B.A. L.623 J.D. [Ingraham P.&Assoc.]
Ingraham & Associates, PLLC ....Rte. 2, 369-B

MEDFORD, * 1,172, *Grant Co.*

Bramlett, Rick M., (BV) .... '51 '77 C.612 B.S. L.623 J.D. [Bramlett&B.]
Bramlett & Bush, (AV) .... 123 N. Main
Bush, Harvey J., (AV) .... '50 '77 C.612 B.S. L.623 J.D. [Bramlett&B.]
Dayton, Michael R. .... '50 '77 C&L.623 B.A., J.D. Assoc. Dist. J.
Drennan, J. C., (AV) .... '32 '59 C&L.623 B.B.A., LL.B. 124 N. Main
Falkenberg, Denny W., (AV) .... '11 '38 C&L.623 100 E. Cherokee
Hammontree, Jack D., (BV) .... '57 '83 C&L.623 B.B.A., J.D. 112 E. Guthrie
Redway, Melissa Lynn '76 '01
C.225 B.A. L.862 J.D. Asst. Dist. Atty., Grant Co. Dist. Atty. Off.
Reed, Joseph H. .... '30 '57 C.612 B.S. L.276 J.D. Chmn. & CEO, Grant Co. Bk.

MIAMI, * 13,704, *Ottawa Co.*

Beauchamp, Glenn, (CV) .... '47 '84 C.623 B.A. L.616 J.D. [Beauchamp&B.]

Beauchamp and Beauchamp, (CV)
Not a Partnership
201 East Central, 74355
Telephone: 918-542-2860 Fax: 918-542-7100
Herschel G. E. Beauchamp (1910-1998); Glenn Beauchamp.
General Civil Practice and State Courts. Trials. Real Estate, Probate, Social Security and Workers Compensation Law, Personal Injury, Family, Divorce, General Negligence and Products Liability Law, Criminal Defense, Driving While Intoxicated.

See Professional Biographies, MIAMI, OKLAHOMA

Beilke, Marilyn A. .... '52 '01 C.612 B.S. L.862 J.D. 27 B. St. S.E.
Breaune, Joseph G. .... '15 '45 C&L.623 B.A., L.L.B. Ret. Dist. J.
Brown, T. Logan, (CV) .... '48 '73 C.623 B.S. L.616 J.D. 101 A St., S.E.
Chesnut, Charles W., (AV) .... '52 '77 C&L.623 B.B.A., J.D. 34 1st Avenue NE
Coiner, R. H., Jr. ... '55 '84 C.623 B.A. L.862 J.D. Instr., Northeastern Okla. A & M Coll.
Connor, Winston H., II, (BV) .... '64 '90 C.619 B.S. L.45 J.D. 2 N. Main St., Ste. 600
Culver, William Eugene .... '56 '95 C.618 B.A. L.623 J.D. Ottawa Co. Ct.
Edwards, Scott Nesbitt, (CV) .... '61 '93 C.612 B.S. L.862 J.D. 2 N. Main
Fullerton, Samuel C., III .... '31 '59 C.674 A.B. L.623 LL.B. Dist. J.
Garrette, Merle K. .... '42 '72 C.1147 B.S. L.616 J.D. 2 N. Main‡
Greer, Francis Owen .... '34 '72 C.377 B.S. L.616 J.D. 631 H St. N.E.
Greer, Frank A., (AV) .... '23 '59 C.1043 B.A. L.862 J.D. 101 A St. SE
Haney, Robert G. .... '50 '75 C.612 B.S. L.623 J.D. Dist. J.
Hanson, Orvan J., Jr. .... '41 '73 C.56 B.S. L.862 J.D. 103 E. Central Ave.
Hudson, Robert Aaron, II, (BV) .... '68 '95 C.619 B.A. L.623 J.D. Asst. Dist. Atty.
James, Richard D., (BV) '58 '82 C.610 A.B. L.862 J.D.
[Wallace,O.L.G.M.W.W.&J.] ⊙

Logan & Lowry, LLP
(See Vinita)

Morrow, Coy Dean, (AV) .... '42 '68 C.612 A.B. L.623 J.D. [Wallace,O.L.G.M.W.W.&J.]
Reavis, Robert E., II .... '61 '87 C.378 B.A. L.900 J.D. 5300 S. 500 Rd.‡
Reed, James, (AV) .... '19 '48 L.623 J.D. 127 B St. N.W.‡
Sharp, William R., (BV) .... '55 '82 C.1310 B.S. L.862 J.D. 2 N. Main, Suite 506 (Pat.)
Smith, Jack L., (BV) .... '51 '78 C.623 B.A. L.616 J.D. [J.L.Smith]
Smith, Marvin L. .... '46 '70 C&L.45 B.S., J.D. 2 N. Main, Ste. 414
Smith, Jack L., P.C., (BV) .... 123 E. Central
Stockwell, Ronald B., (BV) .... '44 '69 C&L.862 B.S., J.D. 2 N. Main St., Ste. 600
Wallace, Owens, Landers, Gee, Morrow, Wilson, Watson & James, A Professional Corporation, (AV)
21 South Main Street (⊙Jay)
Watson, Dennis J., (AV) ..... '52 '77 C.621 B.A. L.623 J.D. [Wallace,O.L.G.M.W.W.&J.]
Wilson, W. Neil, (BV) .... '44 '69 C&L.623 B.B.A., J.D. [Wallace,O.L.G.M.W.W.&J.]
Yohn, Richard L. .... '56 '93 C.619 B.S. L.616 J.D. 103 Eat Central

MIDWEST CITY, 54,088, *Oklahoma Co.*

Bailey, David J., (BV) .... '49 '77 C.1147 B.A. L.616 J.D. [Morris,B.&Assoc.]
Bates, John Roddy, (AV) .... '60 '86 C.612 B.S. L.616 J.D. Gen. Coun., Century Inc.
Childers, Bridget M. .... '74 '00 C&L.623 B.A., J.D. [Ⓐ Rice&R.]
Crosthwait, M. Joe, Jr., (AV) .... '48 '74 C.623 B.A. L.616 J.D. [Crosthwait]

Crosthwait Law Firm, The, A Professional Corporation, (AV)
Attorneys and Counselors at Law
The Timbers Office Park, 1384 South Douglas Boulevard, 73130
Telephone: 405-733-1683 Fax: 405-741-1688
Email: joe.crosthwait@lawoklahoma.com URL: http://www.crosthwaitlaw.com
M. Joe Crosthwait, Jr.;—Traci L. Soderstrom.

(This Listing Continued)

Crosthwait Law Firm, The, A Professional Corporation (Continued)

Estate Planning, Wills, Trust Law, Elder Law, Probate, Estate Litigation, Serious or Complex Personal Injury, Automobile Accidents, Motorcycle Accidents, Slip and Fall, Wrongful Death, Real Estate, Family Law, Divorce, Child Custody, Child Support.

See Professional Biographies, MIDWEST CITY, OKLAHOMA

Eischen, Anna M. .... '61 '00 C.612 B.S. L.616 J.D 1800 S. Midwest Blvd.
Fletcher, G. Russell .... '23 '59 L.615 J.D. 1013 W. Silver Meadow Dr
Flies, Matthew Brian .... '72 '97 C&L.623 B.S., J.D. P.O. Box 10798
Forbes, John C., (AV) .... '52 '79 C.269 B.A. L.616 J.D. 1800 S. Midwest Blvd.
Gust, Terence F., (BV) .... '48 '74 C.623 B.A. L.616 J.D. 2801 Parklawn St.
Gust, Terry .... '48 '74 C.623 B.A. L.615 J.D. 2801 Parklawn, Suite 400 C
Hammett, Taylor K., (BV) .... '39 '67 C.502 A.B. L.616 J.D. 6920 E. Reno St.
Hemphill, Harry G. '22 '49 C.911 B.A. L.986 LL.B.
(adm. in KS; not adm. in OK) 207 Orchard Dr.‡
Herndon, J. Hugh, and Associates .... '26 '57 L.623 LL.B. 2101 S. Air Depot
Howell, David F., (AV) .... '62 '88 C.612 B.S. L.616 J.D. [J.F.Howell&Assoc.]
Howell, James F., (AV) .... '34 '63 C.613 B.S. L.623 LL.B. [J.F.Howell&Assoc.]
Howell, James F., Inc. & Associates, (AV) .... 1840 S. Douglas Boulevard
Hunt, Brady R., (BV) .... '50 '75 C.612 B.A. L.623 J.D. 8000 S.E., 15th Fl.
Massie, Allen B., (BV) .... '40 '68 C.1147 L.616 LL.B. 1840 S. Douglas
McDonald, Richard A. .... '48 '78 C.612 B.S. L.623 J.D. 3225 N. Peebly★
Meston, Steven M. .... '53 '78 C&L.546 B.S., J.D. Century Private Capital
Monks, Terrell, (BV) .... '63 '97 C&L.616 B.A., J.D. 1840 S. Douglas Boulevard
Morris, Gary, (BV) .... '50 '75 C&L.623 B.S., J.D. [Morris,B.&Assoc.]
Morris, Bailey & Associates, (BV) .... 351 N. Air Depot
Munkres, Raymond D., (BV) .... '45 '76 C&L.500 B.A., J.D. 123 Chevy Chase Drive
Price, Alton B. .... '10 '54 C&L.616 LL.B. 113 W. Coe Dr.‡
Reneau, Roger T., (AV) .... '67 '93 C.623 B.A. L.616 J.D. [Rice&R.]
Rice, Richard R. .... '66 '93 C.1109 B.A. L.615 J.D. [Rice&R.]
Rice & Reneau, (AV) .... 2801 Parklawn Drive
Rodgers, Beverly, (BV) .... '54 '91 C.612 B.A. L.862 J.D. Asst. City Atty.
Soderstrom, Traci L. .... '73 '03 C.618 B.S. L.616 J.D. [Ⓐ Crosthwait]
Steiner, Stacey R. .... '76 '01 [Ⓐ Rice&R.]
Taylor, Gerald L. .... '41 '73 C.619 B.S. L.616 J.D. 728 E. Bouse St.
Tesio, Albert J., (BV) .... '41 '67 C&L.616 LL.B. 1401 S. Douglas Blvd.
Tesio, Mike, Jr., (BV) .... '34 '64 C&L.616 B.S., LL.B. 1212 S. Airport Depot 23
Toland, Deborah R. .... '56 '81 C.1300 B.A. L.623 J.D. [D.Toland]
Toland, Deborah, Law Office of .... 351 N. Air Depot, Ste. J
Walker, M. Kevin .... '62 '02 C.82 B.S. L.616 J.D. 1840 S. Douglas Boulevard
Walker, Robert W. .... '27 '56 C.871 B.S. L.273 LL.B. 3212 Bella Vista‡
Wood, Paula Davidson, (BV) ...... '52 '83 C.612 B.S. L.616 J.D. 3020 Shadybrook Drive

MINCO, 1,672, *Grady Co.*

Handke, Melissa G. .... '75 '04 C.1245 B.S./B.A. L.615 J.D. [Handke]
Handke Law Firm .... P.O. Box 42

MOODYS, 150, *Cherokee Co.*

Davis, Kenneth E. .... '34 '66 C.623 L.862 LL.B. P.O. Box 99‡

MOORE, 41,138, *Cleveland Co.*

Barrick-Pizzo, Victoria A. .... '53 '89 C&L.623 B.A., J.D. 801 NW 5th St.
Cotner, Paul Stephen '50 '76
C&L.623 B.B.A., J.D. V.P., Southwest Title and Trust Company
Dean, Wilbur R. .... '10 '49 C.612 B.S. L.623 LL.B. 1521 N.E. 1st St.
Estes, Steve, (BV) .... '52 '81 C&L.623 B.A.J., J.D. 110 W. Main
Good, Joyce Ann .... '46 '91 C.612 B.A. L.616 J.D. 1705 Smoking Tree Rd.
Halbrook, Donald E., (BV) .... '45 '75 C.663 B.S.B.A. L.616 J.D. [Halbrook&Assoc.]
Halbrook & Associates, (BV) .... 121 W. Main St., Ste. 102
Moore, Andrew J., Jr. .... '33 '60 C.1147 B.A. L.623 LL.B. City College, Inc.‡
Moore, Kevin Glen .... '63 '89 C.623 B.A. L.616 J.D. [K.G.Moore]
Moore, Kevin G. .... 2300 Kings Road
Morris, Rosalee Estella .... '56 '82 C.616 B.S.B. L.615 J.D. 600 N. Morgan Drive
Pipkin, William A., (BV) .... '34 '57 C.623 L.192 J.D. 110 W. Main St.
Simpson, Michael W. .... '59 '86 C.623 B.A. L.615 J.D. 105 S. Iriving Dr.

MOORELAND, 1,157, *Woodward Co.*

Thomas, Gerald W. .... '28 '52 C&L.623 B.A., LL.B. Mun. J.

MOUNTAIN VIEW, 880, *Kiowa Co.*

Caruso, Mike A., Jr. .... '16 '38 C&L.623 B.A., LL.B. P.O. Box 458‡

MUSKOGEE, * 38,310, *Muskogee Co.*

Abbott, Teddy J. .... '51 '91 C.623 B.S. L.862 J.D. P.O. Box 1635
Adair, Robin Watt .... '56 '83 C.619 B.A. L.862 J.D. Spec. Dist. J.
Alford, Thomas H. .... '49 '76 C&L.623 B.B.A., J.D. Assoc. Dist. J.
Anthis, Ernest R., Jr., (AV) .... '23 '47 C.999 L.192 LL.B. P.O. Box 1251

Atkins & Markoff
(See Oklahoma City)

Ball, Terrence L., (BV) .... '51 '90 C.619 B.A. L.862 J.D. Asst. City Atty.
Bates, John Francis ... '50 '79 C.801 B.A. L.615 J.D. [Ⓐ Garrett] (⊙Oklahoma City, Tulsa)
Bean, David C. ... '45 '88 C.896 B.A. L.862 J.D. [Ⓐ Garrett] (⊙Oklahoma City, Tulsa)
Been, Brian C., (CV) .... '69 '94 C&L.45 B.S.B.A., J.D. [Ⓐ B.A.Smith]
Berlin, Lee F. '72 '00 C.1012 B.S. L.623 J.D.
(adm. in NM; not adm. in OK) Dept. of Vet. Affairs
Blakeburn, Dave L. '32 '59 C&L.623 B.B.A., LL.B.
Exec. V.P. & Tr. Offr., Commercial Bk. & Tr. Co.
Blood, Robert K. .... '28 '58 C.612 B.S. L.616 LL.B. 2505 Hayes St.‡
Boettcher, Wayne M., (CV) .... '57 '91 C.619 B.A. L.623 J.D. 1502 E Okmulgee St.
Bonds, A. Camp, (AV) .... '06 '29 C&L.623 LL.B. 444 Court Street
Bonds, A. Camp, Jr., (AV) .... '42 '68 C&L.623 B.S., J.D. [Bonds&M.]
Bonds, Jeff M., (CV) .... '69 '94 C.934 B.S. L.615 J.D. [Ⓐ Bonds&M.]

Bonds & Matthews Law Firm, P.L.L.C., (AV)
444 Court Street, P.O. Box 1906, 74402-1906
Telephone: 918-683-2911 Fax: 918-687-0846
Members of Firm: Albert R. Matthews; A. Camp Bonds, Jr. Associates: Juliet N. Brennan; Jeff M. Bonds; Martha J. Cherbini.
General Practice in all Oklahoma State and Federal Courts, Trial and Appellate Practice, Personal Injury and Wrongful Death actions, Products Liability claims, Civil Rights Litigation, including Wrongful Discharge, Discrimination and Excessive Force, Governmental and Municipal Law, Railroad Defense, Insurance Defense, School Law, Business Litigation, Banking, Administrative Law, Real Estate, Probate and Estates, Domestic Relations, Bankruptcy, Criminal Defense, Equine (including Racing Commission), OSHA Related Injury and Death, Franchise Law, Nursing Home Negligence, Employment.
Representative Clients: Anderson Wholesale Co.; Griffin Grocery Co.; Missouri-Kansas-Texas Railroad; Muskogee Regional Medical Center Hospital; Great American Insurance Co.; Lake Country Bank; Hopes & Dreams Futurity; Fast Food Systems.

See Professional Biographies, MUSKOGEE, OKLAHOMA

Bonney, William Mark, (AV) ... '61 '87 C&L.623 B.A., J.D. P.O. Box 2757
Brandon, Susan Stidham, (BV) ... '55 '87 C.623 B.A. L.276 J.D. Asst. U.S. Atty.
Brennan, Juliet N., (BV) ... '60 '87 C.383 B.A. L.500 J.D. [A Bonds&M.]
Broderick, Sherril Elder ... '59 '97 C&L.862 B.S.B.A., J.D. 2399 S. 79th St. E.
Brook, Rodney L., (CV) ... '55 '94 C.619 B.S. L.862 J.D. [Settle,L.&B.]
Brooks, Sejin C. ... '71 '00 C.623 B.A. L.862 J.D. 220 State Street
Burris, Carol A. T. ... '37 '84 C.619 B.S. L.862 J.D. 2311 Michael Rd.‡
Burris, Gregory Dean ... '70 '96 C.101 B.A. L.862 J.D. Asst. Dist. Atty.
Burris, Lyle ... '37 '70 C.619 B.A. L.615 J.D. Dist. J.
Cate, Clifford K., Jr., (AV) ... '40 '65 C&L.623 B.A., J.D. 323 W. Broadway, Ste. 200
Cherbini, Martha J., (CV) ... '48 '89 C&L.1209 B.A., J.D. [A Bonds&M.]
Choate, Ben P., Jr. ... '28 '55 L.623 J.D. Spec. Dist. J.
Cook, Jay ... '44 '72 C.619 B.S. L.862 J.D. 620 W. Broadway St.
Cousparis, Steven Gus ... '49 '76 C.992 B.A. L.623 J.D. City Atty.
Crow, Nelson T. ... '13 '35 C&L.623 P.O. Box 1369‡
Cunningham, Jan Marie ... '69 '94 C.862 B.A. L.623 J.D. Law Clk., U.S. Dist. Ct.
DeSilvey, Jared A. ... '70 '97 C.499 B.S. L.862 J.D. [A Garrett] (⊙Oklahoma City, Tulsa)

Dorwart, Frederic
(See Tulsa)

Edge, David Wilfred ... '39 '93 C.569 B.A. L.862 J.D. Legal Serv.(s)
Edmondson, James E. ... '45 '74 C.619 B.A. L.276 J.D. Dist. J.
Elliott, Douglass R. '62 '93 C.623 B.B.A. L.862 J.D.
[A Garrett] (⊙Oklahoma City, Tulsa)
Engleman, Danita Gay, (CV) ... '57 '93 C.618 B.A. L.862 J.D. Off. of Co. Dist. Atty.
Epperley, Linda A., (BV) ... '60 '87 C&L.623 B.A., J.D. 1200 W. Okmulgee
Finerty, Michael Arthur, (BV) ... '60 '87 C.187 B.S.S. L.862 J.D. [M.A.Finerty]
Finerty, Michael A., (BV) ... 436 Court St.
Fite, C. Bart, (AV) ... '59 '84 C.612 B.S. L.623 J.D. [Wright,S.F.&W.]
Frix, Paige Lane, (BV) ... '61 '87 C&L.623 B.B.A., J.D. P.O. Box 284
Gage, Edwin L., (AV) ... '40 '66 C&L.623 B.A., J.D. [Gage&W.]

Gage & Williams Law Firm, (AV) BR
530 Court Street, P.O. Box 87, 74401
Telephone: 918-687-5424 Fax: 918-687-0761
Members of Firm: Edwin L. Gage; Betty Outhier Williams;—Edith M. Gregory.
General Civil Practice before State and Federal Courts. Insurance, Negligence, Corporation, Real Estate and Probate Law.
Representative Clients: Nationwide Insurance Co.; Oklahoma Municipal Assurance Group; Golden Rule Insurance Co.; Tastee Freeze International, Inc.; Security Alarms Co., Inc.
See Professional Biographies, MUSKOGEE, OKLAHOMA

Gannaway, Robert A. ... '28 '65 C&L.623 B.S., J.D. 2724 Robin Lane St.‡
Garrett, Amber Peckio ... '— '03 C.621 B.S. L.862 J.D. [A Garrett] (⊙Tulsa)
Garrett, David M., (AV) '41 '69 C.619 B.S. L.862 J.D.
[Garrett] (⊙Oklahoma City, Tulsa)
Garrett Law Office, P.C., (AV)
215 State St., 10th FL (⊙Fayetteville, AR; Oklahoma City, Tulsa, OK)
Graham, M. Denise, (BV) '57 '82 C&L.862 B.S.B.A., J.D.
Staff Atty., U.S. Dist. Ct., Eastern Dist. of OK
Green, Bruce, (AV) ... '34 '57 C.619 B.A. L.623 LL.B. Asst. U.S. Atty

Green, Mark, (AV) '53 '78 C&L.623 B.B.A., J.D.
706 West Okmulgee, P.O. Box 2362, 74402
Telephone: 918-683-0309 Fax: 918-687-5964
Email: green@azalea.net
General Civil and Criminal Trial and Appellate Practice in all State and Federal Courts. Negligence, Personal Injury, Products Liability, Bankruptcy Law.
See Professional Biographies, MUSKOGEE, OKLAHOMA

Gregory, Edith M., (CV) ... '45 '87 C.612 B.S. L.862 J.D. [A Gage&W.]
Haugland, Richard C. '35 '61 C.118 A.B. L.494 LL.B.
(adm. in MN; not adm. in OK) Sr. V.P., Bank of Oklahoma
Haxton, Harold K. ... '31 '61 C.612 B.S. L.623 LL.B. 3421 Gulick‡
Hayes, D. D., (AV) ... '47 '74 C.619 B.A. L.862 J.D. 444 Court Street
Heater, Jeffrey A. ... '69 '05 C.836 B.S. L.862 J.D. [A Garrett]
Hildebrand, Vicky R. ... '52 '91 C.586 B.A. L.862 J.D. Law Clerk
Hilfiger, Roger, (AV) ... '45 '72 C.619 B.S. L.862 J.D. 620 W. Broadway
Howe, Lowell G. ... '77 '03 C.1012 B.B.A. L.862 J.D. 417 W. Broadway
Howerton, E. Kay ... '49 '80 C.47 B.A. L.623 J.D. 416 Court St.
Howerton, Michael C. ... '49 '80 C.612 B.S. L.623 J.D. 416 Court St.
Isbell, William C. ... '62 '87 C.1147 B.B.A. L.623 J.D. P.O. Box 2757
Jacobs-Seward, Gail A. ... '57 '89 C&L.623 B.A., J.D. Law Clk., U.S. Mag. J.
James, Robert M. ... '26 '65 C.623 B.S. L.616 J.D. 407 W. Robb‡
Jones, Preston W., Jr., (AV) ... '45 '72 C.612 B.A. L.623 J.D. 627 W. Broadway
Jones, Ronald L. ... '41 '69 C&L.623 B.B.A., J.D. 2511 South Woodland Road
Keaney, Patrick M. ... '60 '85 C.612 B.S. L.862 J.D. Law Clk., U.S. Dist. Ct.
Keen, Ralph F., (CV) ... '34 '72 C.619 B.A. L.862 J.D. Asst. U.S. Atty.
Kelly, Michael E., (BV) ... '37 '63 C&L.623 B.B.A., LL.B. 502 Court St.
Kennedy, Joe R., (AV) ... '39 '63 C&L.623 B.A., LL.B. 306 Kingsbury Dr.‡
Landrum, Terrill V., (BV) ... '50 '75 C&L.623 B.S., J.D. [Settle,L.&B.]
Langer, Steven F. ... '— '92 C&L.623 B.A., J.D. [A Garrett] ⊙
Littlefield, David M., (AV) ... '50 '79 C.619 B.A. L.623 J.D. Asst. U.S. Atty.
Littlefield, Kristin A. ... '76 '04 C.619 B.S. L.862 J.D. Asst. Dist. Atty.
Locke, Robert, (AV) ... '43 '70 C.612 B.S. L.862 J.D. [Locke&M.]

Locke & Moore, (AV)
314 West Broadway, P.O. Box 1468, 74402
Telephone: 918-687-4900 Fax: 918-687-5969
Email: lockenmoore@yahoo.com
Members of Firm: Robert Locke; Larry Dean Moore. Of Counsel: Corrine O'Day.
General Practice including Family Law, Criminal Law, Business Law, Bankruptcy, Personal Injury, Wills, Trusts and Estates, Probate.
See Professional Biographies, MUSKOGEE, OKLAHOMA

Loge, Orvil Lee, Jr., (BV) ... '68 '94 C.999 B.S. L.615 J.D. 624 W. Bway St.
Luton, John D., (BV) ... '22 '50 C&L.623 B.L., J.D. [A Riggs,A.N.T.O.&L.]
Matthews, Albert R., (AV) ... '30 '60 C.612 B.S. L.623 LL.B. [Bonds&M.]
McClure, James R., (BV) ... '58 '85 C.880 B.S. L.862 J.D. [J.McClure]
McClure, Jim, Attorney at Law, (BV) ... 502 Court St.
Means, Yasodhara M. Mohanty, (BV) ... '52 '81 C&L.623 B.A., J.D. [Y.M.Means]

Means, Yasodhara "Mitty" Mohanty, P.C., (BV)
Seres Building, 215 State Street, Suite 503, 74401
Telephone: 918-686-6255 Fax: 918-686-5503 URL: http://www.meanslawoffice.com
Email: mittymohanty0186@sbcglobal.net URL: http://www.mittymohantylaw.com
Yasodhara M. Mohanty Means (Of Counsel to Locke & Moore).
Mediation, Federal Litigation, Civil Litigation, Representation of Nurses and other Health Care Professionals, Administration Law, Corporate Law, Business Litigation, Estate Plan, Probate, Insurance and Surety Law.
See Professional Biographies, MUSKOGEE, OKLAHOMA

Meyer, K. L., Jr., (AV) ... '26 '50 L.623 LL.B. P.O. Box 2325
Miller, Gerald R., (BV) ... '53 '79 C.623 B.B.A. L.616 J.D. 627 W. Broadway St.
Moore, Larry Dean, (BV) ... '59 '88 C.619 B.A. L.862 J.D. [Locke&M.]
Nolen, Lynn D., (CV) ... '40 '64 C.618 B.A. L.623 LL.B. 501 W. Okmulgee St.
Norman, Michael T., (BV) ... '43 '68 C&L.862 B.A., J.D. City J.
O'Day, Corrine ... '62 '03 C&L.862 B.S.B.A., J.D. [© Locke&M.]
Payne, James H. ... '41 '66 C&L.623 B.S., J.D. Chf. U.S. Dist. J.
Paynter, Rick ... '— '85 C&L.623 B.A., J.D. [© Garrett] (⊙Tulsa)
Payton, Lloyd ... '33 '61 C.619 L.862 LL.B. 417 W. Broadway
Pearson, Don, (BV) ... '34 '60 C.819 B.S. L.862 LL.B. 25 W. Okmulgee
Pierce, David K., (BV) ... '57 '90 C.619 B.A. L.862 J.D. 620 W. Bway.
Primomo, Gene V., (BV) ... '57 '85 C.1145 B.S. L.862 J.D. [Wilcoxen&W.]
Rackley, Victoria L., (BV) ... '48 '82 C.619 B.S. L.862 J.D. [A Riggs,A.N.T.O.&L.]
Ranallo, Paula Anne ... '62 '87 C.623 L.862 J.D. P.O. Box 707

Riggs, Abney, Neal, Turpen, Orbison & Lewis, A Professional Corporation, (AV)
First National Severs Building, Suite 508, 215 State Street, 74402 ⊙
Telephone: 918-687-5404; Toll Free: 800-722-1332 Fax: 918-687-1128
URL: http://www.riggsabney.com
Associates: John D. Luton; Victoria L. Rackley.
General Civil, Trial and Appellate Practice before all State and Federal Courts and Agencies, Alternative Dispute Resolution, Banking, Corporate, Securities, Anti-trust, Administrative, Government Relations, Real Estate, Commercial Transactions, Oil and Gas, Estate Planning, Probate, Taxation, Employment and Discrimination, Employee Benefits, Social Security, Bankruptcy and Reorganization, Family Law, Healthcare, Negligence, Personal Injury, Products Liability, Medical Malpractice, Transportation, and Indian Law.
Tulsa, Oklahoma Office: Frisco Building, 502 West Sixth Street, 74119. Telephone: 918-587-3161. Fax: 918-587-9708.
Oklahoma City, Oklahoma Office: Paragon Building, Suite 101. Telephone: 405-843-9909. Facsimile: 405-842-2913.
Denver, Colorado Office: 621 17th St., Ste. 1900. Telephone: 303-298-7392. Facsimile: 303-398-7398.
See Professional Biographies, MUSKOGEE, OKLAHOMA

Robinson, A. Carl, (AV) ... '26 '50 C.613 L.623 LL.B. Spec. Dist. J.
Ruby, Russell, (AV) ... '11 '39 C.502 B.J. L.862 LL.B. 4500 Girard St.‡

Sanders & Associates, P.C.
(See Tulsa)

Sandlin, R. Forney, (AV) ... '34 '58 C&L.623 B.B.A., LL.B. 330 N. 4th St.
Scales, William D. '52 '79 C&L.69 B.A., J.D.
(adm. in TX; not adm. in OK) Dept. of Vet. Affs.
Schumacher, Matthew A. P., (BV) '33 '83 C.612 B.S. L.616 J.D.
323 E. Bway., Suite 301
Seay, Frank Howell ... '38 '63 C&L.623 B.A., LL.B. Sr. J.‡
Settle, Bill, (AV) ... '37 '66 C.619 B.A. L.862 J.D. [Settle,L.&B.]
Settle, Lisa A., (BV) ... '62 '87 C&L.623 B.A., J.D. Dept. of Vet. Affs.
Settle, Wm John Earle ... '37 '66 C.619 B.A. L.862 J.D. P.O. Box 1368
Settle, Landrum and Brook, (AV) ... 110 North Sixth Street
Shreder, Steven P. ... '56 '84 C&L.623 B.A., J.D. U.S. Dist. Ct.
Smith, Bret A., (BV) ... '64 '91 C.623 B.A. L.862 J.D. 417 West Broadway
Smith, Louis ... '20 '49 L.623 LL.B. 517 S. Junction St.‡
Sperling, Sheldon J., (BV) '49 '79 C.619 B.A. L.862 J.D.
Jus. Dept., U.S. Atty. Off. Eastern Dist. of OK
Stipe, Gene, (AV) ... '26 '49 C.484 L.623 LL.B. State Sen. [Stipe,H.L.U.E.&B.] ⊙
Stipe, Harper, Laizure, Uselton, Edwards & Belote, LLP, (AV)
384 South 33rd Street (⊙McAlester, Oklahoma City)
Stout, Justin C. ... '76 '02 C&L.623 B.A., J.D. [A Wright,S.F.&W.]
Stout, Weldon W., (AV) ... '49 '74 C.623 B.A. L.616 J.D. [Wright,S.F.&W.]
Surles, Tia J. Baker ... '70 '98 C&L.45 B.A., J.D. [A Garrett] (⊙Tulsa)
Taylor, Ernest Lee '49 '00 C.59 B.A. L.862 J.D.
V.P., Muskogee Regional Medical Center
Thetford, Mark S., (BV) ... '56 '88 C.623 B.B.S. L.616 J.D. [A Stipe,H.L.U.E.&B.]
Watkins, Max D., (BV) ... '41 '67 C&L.862 B.A., J.D. 428 Court St.
Wells, Roy H. ... '30 '59 C.621 L.623 LL.B. 12164 S. 35th St. E.‡
West, Kimberly E., (AV) ... '— '83 C.623 B.A. L.616 J.D. P.O. Box. 2999
White, Harold L. ... '24 '60 L.862 Vet. Admn.
White, Ronald A. ... '61 '86 C&L.623 B.A., J.D. U.S. Dist. J.
Wilburn, Paula A. Ranallo, (BV) ... '62 '87 C.623 B.S. L.862 J.D. [Wright,S.F.&W.]
Wilcoxen, Andrew C., III, (AV) ... '48 '79 C.623 L.616 J.D. [Wilcoxen&W.]
Wilcoxen, James G., (AV) ... '53 '79 C.623 B.A. L.616 J.D. [Wilcoxen&W.]
Wilcoxen & Wilcoxen, (AV) ... 112 North Fifth Street
Williams, Betty Outhier, (AV) ... '47 '72 C.616 B.A. L.880 J.D. [Gage&W.]
Williams, Gregory P., (AV) ... '45 '81 C.502 B.J. L.862 J.D. [© Garrett] (⊙Tulsa)
Williams, John A. ... '39 '70 C&L.616 B.A., J.D. U.S. Dept. of Vet. Affairs
Williams, John C., III ... '63 '89 C.612 B.S. L.623 J.D. City of Muskogee
Wilson, Joseph F., (BV) ... '55 '80 C.618 B.A. L.862 J.D. Asst. U.S. Atty.
Wilson, Kay, Jr., (AV) ... '20 '42 C.612 A.B. L.623 LL.B. 319 Court St.
Wright, J. Ron, (AV) ... '44 '69 C&L.623 B.A., J.D. [Wright,S.F.&W.]

Wright, Stout, Fite & Wilburn, (AV) BR
300 West Broadway, P.O. Box 707, 74402-0707
Telephone: 918-682-0091 Fax: 918-683-6340
Email: weldon@wsfw-ok.com
Members of Firm: J. Ron Wright; Weldon W. Stout; C. Bart Fite; Paula A. Ranallo Wilburn.
Associate: Justin C. Stout.
General Civil Practice in all State and Federal Courts. Trials, Insurance, Real Estate, Corporate, Banking, Bankruptcy, Civil Rights, Family and Probate Law, Eminent Domain, Employment Law and Mediation Services.
Counsel for: Bank of America, N.A. (Muskogee); Ft. James Paper Co.; Arkhola Sand & Gravel Co.; Equity Mutual Insurance Co.; Home Insurance Co.; United Services Auto Assn.; Equitable Life & Casualty; Universal Underwriters Insurance Co; Oklahoma Turnpike Authority; Oklahoma Department of Transportation.
See Professional Biographies, MUSKOGEE, OKLAHOMA

MUSTANG, 13,156, *Canadian Co.*

Arledge, Christopher A., (BV) ... '68 '94 C.82 B.S. L.623 J.D. P.O. Box 355
Arnold, Elaine Kay ... '52 '94 C.1359 B.B.A. L.616 J.D. 501 N. Mustang
Denton, Michael D., Jr., (BV) ... '63 '91 C.622 B.S. L.623 J.D. [Denton]
Denton Law Firm, (BV) ... 1102 East 5H 152
Henley, Martha N. E. ... '42 '85 C.623 B.A. L.616 J.D. 1638 E. Longview Ln.
Stevens, Linda Louise ... '48 '00 C.1147 B.S. L.616 J.D. 925 W Hwy 152
Williford, Valerie ... '73 '99 C&L.616 B.A., J.D. [V.Williford]
Williford, Valerie, P.C. ... 13500 S.W. 104th Street

NEWALLA, 214, *Oklahoma Co.*

Day, Lauren LeBlanc, Attorney at Law, (BV) '44 '87 C.586 B.A. L.616 J.D.
P.O. Box 500

NEWCASTLE, 5,434, *McClain Co.*

Brinkley, Alan, (BV) ... '52 '76 C&L.623 B.A., J.D. 101 Corp. Ctr.
Harting, David B., (BVⓣ) ... '50 '79 C.390 B.A. L.1202 J.D. 405 S. Hwy. 76

NEWKIRK, * 2,168, *Kay Co.*

Boyd, D. W. ....'50 '75 C.612 B.S. L.880 J.D. Co. J.
Galbraith, Robert H. ....'48 '74 C.1147 B.B.A. L.623 J.D. Dist. J.
Gibson, Mark L., (BV) ....'61 '87 C&L.623 B.B.A., J.D. 8th Dist Atty
Goodman, Edgar G., (BV) ....'55 '80 C.623 B.A. L.45 J.D. Asst. Dist. Atty.
Jacobs, Dave ....'41 '66 C&L.623 A.B., J.D. Courthouse‡
Layton, Jennifer Adina ....'68 '94 C.612 B.A. L.862 J.D. 811 Oakwood Ln.
Marsh, Bettie J., (Ms.), (BV) ....'41 '67 C&L.966 B.S., J.D. Asst. Dist. Atty.
McCarty, Jack De, (AV) ....'41 '68 C.612 B.S. L.623 J.D. [McCarty&R.]
McCarty & Rigdon, (AV) ....116 S. Main
Page, Leslie D., Jr. ....'42 '67 C&L.623 B.B.A., J.D. Assoc. Dist. J.
Revard, Douglas ....'43 '75 C.612 B.S. L.616 J.D. Spec. Dist. J.
Rigdon, Thomas M., (AV) ....'47 '75 C.934 B.A. L.623 J.D. [McCarty&R.]
Ross, Philip A., (BV) ....'53 '84 C.623 B.B.A. L.862 J.D. 1st Asst. Dist Atty.
Welch, Donald C. ....'28 '53 C&L.623 B.A., LL.B. Spec. Dist. Ct. J.
Wideman, Joseph A. ....'38 '63 C&L.623 B.B.A., LL.B. Courthouse‡

NICHOLS HILLS, 4,020, *Oklahoma Co.*

Jones, Warren E., (AV) ....'46 '73 C&L.623 B.A., J.D. 1129 Glenwood Ave.
Laughlin, Thomas G. ....'48 '74 C&L.623 B.B.A., J.D. 7311 Lancet Ln.
Rivers, Julie Simmons, (AV) ....'61 '92 C.612 B.S. L.623 J.D. [J.S.Rivers]
Rivers, Julie Simmons, P.C., (AV) ....6440 Avondale Drive, Suite 208

NOBLE, 5,260, *Cleveland Co.*

Charles, Margaret W. '30 '81 C&L.705 B.A., J.D.
(adm. in PA; not adm. in OK) P.O. Box 1289
Clayton, Cheryl Ann, (BV) ....'51 '76 C.375 B.S. L.623 J.D. 110 S. Main
Clinton, Robert M. ....'51 '79 C&L.623 B.B.A., J.D. V.P., Fin., United Design Corp.
Ellis, Warren H., (BV) ....'31 '79 C.627 B.S. L.623 J.D. P.O. Box 249
Pichot, Cindee, (BV) ....'60 '86 C.999 B.B.A. L.623 J.D. P.O. Box 88
Stead, Robin, (BV) ....'55 '85 C&L.623 B.B.A., J.D. 107 48th Street

NORMAN, * 95,694, *Cleveland Co.*

Adair, Christal Dianne ....'64 '99 C&L.623 B.A., J.D. [C.D.Adair]
Adair, Christal D. ....510 S. Webster, Ste. A
Adwon, Cole E. ....'63 '01 C&L.623 B.S., J.D. 4712 Pinon Ct.
Aktansel, Vera, (CV) ....'44 '82 C&L.623 B.A., J.D. [Aktansel&Assoc.]
Aktansel & Associates, (CV) ....2419 Wilcox Dr.
Allen, Cindy Loree ....'— '97 C&L.623 B.A., J.D. [C.Allen]
Allen, Cindy, Attorney at Law ....114 E. Main St.
Anderson, Owen L. '49 '75 C&L.585 B.A., J.D.
(adm. in ND; not adm. in OK) Univ. of Okla., Coll. of Law

Atkins & Markoff
(See Oklahoma City)

Bachrach, Osher ....'39 '88 C.623 B.A. L.616 J.D. P.O. Box 2442
Bailey, R. Lindsay, (AV) ....'51 '76 C&L.623 B.A., J.D. [Bailey]
Bailey, Robert L. ....'22 '48 C&L.623 J.D. Ret. Dist. J.
Bailey Law Offices, (AV) ....303 East Eufaula
Barnum, Cathy Clinton, (BV) ....'55 '81 C&L.623 B.A., J.D. [C.C.Barnum]
Barnum, Cathy C., P.C., (BV) ....1011 24th Avenue N.W.
Barr, Joel W., (BV) ....'44 '72 C.612 B.A. L.623 J.D. 231 S. Peters Ave.
Barr, T. Leslie ....'62 '98 C&L.623 B.A., J.D. 2320 Westpark Dr.
Barrett, Lydia JoAnn, (BV) ....'58 '86 C.616 B.S. L.623 J.D. 870 Coppefield Drive
Barrett, Mark H., (BV) ....'50 '80 C.846 B.A. L.623 J.D. Asst. Appl. Pub. Def.
Base, Elizabeth Ann ....'69 '94 C&L.623 B.A., J.D. [E.Base]
Base, Elizabeth, Attorney at Law ....114 S. Peters Ave., Ste. 206
Batton, David J., & Associates, Law Office of, (BV) '51 '86
C.612 B.S. L.623 J.D. 209 South Crawford
Bauman, Del Louis ....'54 '80 C&L.623 B.A., J.D. 1325 W. Lindsey Street
Bauman, Marion C., (AV) ....'43 '68 C.623 B.A. L.309 J.D. [M.C.Bauman]
Bauman, Marion C., P.C., (AV) ....2600 Van Buren St., Ste. 2604
Beadles, Gary, (BV) ....'47 '73 C.612 B.S. L.623 J.D. 3111 Meadow Ave.
Beck, Robert M. ....'47 '78 C.612 B.S. L.623 J.D. 1321 Eastgate Dr.
Beckett, Lewis W. '51 '79 C.44 B.S. L.45 J.D.
(adm. in AR; not adm. in OK)
Sr. V.P. & Tr. Offr., The Security Natl. Bk. & Tr. Co. of Norman
Bell, Nicole ....'67 '94 [R.A.Bell]
Bell, Richard A., P.C. ....1225 W. Main St.
Benedum, Ben T., (AV) ....'36 '65 C&L.623 B.B.A., J.D. [Benedum&B.]

Benedum & Benedum, Inc., (AV)
131 E. Main Street, Suite 200, 73069
Telephone: 405-321-2212 Fax: 405-321-5438
Email: benbenedum@hotmail.com
T. R. Benedum (1905-1991); Ben T. Benedum.
General Practice. Business Law, Commercial Litigation, Insurance, Probate, Oil and Gas, Personal Injury and Real Estate Law. Trials. Collections over $10,000.00.
Representative Clients: Oklahoma Gas & Electric Co.; First Fidelity Bank, N.A.; Prudential Insurance Co. of America; Jefferson Standard Life Insurance Co.; The Equitable Life Assurance Society of the United States; Travelers Indemnity Co.; CDP Corporation; Laidlaw Waste Systems, Inc.
See Professional Biographies, NORMAN, OKLAHOMA

Bernier, A. Kenneth ....'35 '70 C.309 A.B. L.616 J.D. 1603 Cambridge

Bernstein, David '58 '83 C.378 B.A. L.623 J.D.
Bernstein Law Building, 104 West Gray Street, P.O. Box 1692, 73070-1692
Telephone: 405-329-1484 Toll Free: 1-800-235-0529 Facsimile: 405-329-5949 URL: http://www.lawyers.com/dblaw
Email: dbnormanok@aol.com URL: http://www.dblaw.net
Complex Personal Injury, Airplane Crashes, Product Liability, Medical Malpractice, Unsafe Products, Workers Compensation, Nursing Home Abuse, Insurance, Automobile Accidents, Dog Bites, Slip and Fall, Wrongful Death.
See Professional Biographies, NORMAN, OKLAHOMA

Block, Deborah S. '62 '87 C&L.623 B.B.A., J.D.
Gen. Coun., Associated Metallurgists, Engineering Consulting Firm‡
Bode, Jane, P.C. ....1125 Westbrooke Ter.
Bogan, Donald T., (AVⓣ) '52 '79 C.103 A.B. L.896 J.D.
(adm. in NC; not adm. in OK) Univ. of Oklahoma
Bonner, Stephen W., (BV) ....'44 '70 C&L.623 B.B.A., J.D. [S.W.Bonner]
Bonner, Stephen W., P.C., (BV) ....2119 Forister Ct.
Boswell, William E., Jr., (BV) ....'37 '69 C&L.623 B.B.A., J.D. Asst. Dist. Atty.
Bowlan, Russell T. ....'65 '93 C.1147 B.S. L.623 J.D. 3621 Peregrine Dr.
Broadway, Charles L. ....'55 '85 C&L.623 B.B.A., J.D. 1014 Thistlewood Drive
Brock, William L., (AV) ....'36 '67 C.612 B.S. L.623 J.D. [W.L.Brock]
Brock, William L., Inc., (AV) ....2533 Osborne Dr.
Brockman, David Marion ....'56 '96 C.618 B.A. L.623 J.D. 1212 Burkshire Terr.
Brown, Elvin J., (BV) ....'22 '49 C.467 L.623 J.D. 117 East Main Street
Brown, J. Scott, (AV) ....'38 '67 C.870 B.S. L.623 J.D. [Brown] (⊙Oklahoma City)
Brown Firm, The, P.C., (AV) ....2313 Crestmont, Suite 100
Bruehl, Sheryn Lee Anne ....'69 '94 C&L.623 B.A., J.D. 309 W. Main St.
Bryant, Jeffery Harley ....'61 '86 C.1315 B.A. L.623 J.D. City Atty.'s Off.
Bublis, James Fredric ....'54 '94 C.845 B.A. L.615 J.D. Lexis-Nexis
Burns, Douglas E., (AV) ....'52 '78 C&L.623 B.A., J.D. [Burns&S.]
Burns & Stowers, P.C., (AV) ....1300 W. Lindsey
Burr, Sally A. ....'40 '88 C.1004 B.A. L.616 J.D. 305 Stonehaven Dr.
Burton, Ron D. ....'46 '74 C&L.623 B.B.A., J.D. P.O. Box 721260
Bussey, Susan ....'49 '85 C&L.623 B.A., J.D. Admin. Law J., State Merit Protec. Coml.
Bystrom, Keith ....'50 '75 C.546 B.S. L.276 J.D. Prof. of Law, Univ. of Okla.
Cain, Tamara Beam, (BV) ....'58 '91 C.622 B.S. L.623 J.D. 3750 W. Main, Ste. 240
Carpino, Robert Anthony ....'61 '95 C&L.623 B.A., J.D. W4G Industries
Castillo, Ruth Furman ....'49 '86 C.823 B.A. L.623 J.D. Legal Aid Western Okla.
Chesley, Patrick J., (CV) ....'51 '77 C&L.623 B.A., J.D. 629 24th Street S.W.
Christensen, Ronald E. ....'51 '82 C.612 B.S. L.623 J.D. 104 E. Eufaula St.
Clark, J. Brent, (BV) ....'48 '75 C&L.623 B.A., J.D. [Floyd]
Clark, Stakem, Wood & Patten, P.C., (AV) ....103 W. Boyd (⊙Oklahoma City)
Clifton, John L., IV ....'60 '85 C&L.623 B.A., J.D. 3917 Sparkle St.★
Cline, Van H., (AVⓣ) ....'44 '79 C.623 B.A. L.1065 J.D. 501 Merrywood Lane
Conrad-Legler, Katrina Susanna ....'— '96 C.378 B.A. L.623 J.D. OK Indigent Def. Sys.
Coogan-Sutter, Sandee, Law Office of '50 '88
C&L.623 B.S., J.D. 115 S. Peters Ave., Ste. 4
Cooper, Mark S. ....'63 '88 C&L.623 B.B.A., J.D. [M.S.Cooper]
Cooper, Mark S., A Professional Corporation ....225 North Peters Avenue
Couch, Alan J. ....'35 '63 C.663 B.S. L.616 J.D. Dist. J.
Coyne, Randall T. E. '58 '87 C.454 B.Mus. L.276 J.D.
(adm. in MA; not adm. in OK) Assoc. Prof. of Law, Univ. of Okla.
Crowder, Douglas S. ....'63 '90 C.622 B.S. L.623 J.D. [Talley,C.&G.]

Crowe & Dunlevy, A Professional Corporation, (AV) 🅱🅻
2500 South McGee, Suite 140, 73072-6705 ⊙
Telephone: 405-321-7317 Fax: 405-360-4002
Email: bryantd@crowedunlevy.com URL: http://www.crowedunlevy.com
Robert L. Pendarvis; Gary C. Rawlinson; Mary Robertson; Christopher R. Graves;—John H. Sparks.
General Practice. Litigation of all types in both state and federal court. All types of alternative dispute resolution methodologies. Administrative Law, Antitrust, Appellate, Aviation, Bankruptcy and Creditors' Rights, Business Organizations, Commercial Real Estate, Commercial Transactions, Consumer Credit, Corporate and Securities Finance, Environmental, ERISA, Estates and Trusts, Family Law, Financial Institutions and Finance, Franchising and Distribution, Healthcare, Initiative Petition, Insurance Litigation and Regulation, Intellectual Property and Technology, International Business, Labor and Employment, Medicare/Medicaid Fraud and Abuse, Medical Malpractice Defense, Mergers and Acquisitions, Oil and Gas, Oklahoma Corporation Commission, Patent, Trademark, Copyright and Related Matters, Products Liability, Public Finance, School Law, Small Business and Venture Capital, Taxation, White Collar Crime.
Oklahoma City, Oklahoma Office: 20 North Broadway, Suite 1800, 73102-8273. Telephone: 405-235-7700. Fax: 405-239-6651.
Tulsa, Oklahoma Office: 500 Kennedy Building, 321 South Boston Avenue, 74103-3313. Telephone: 918-592-9800. Fax: 918-592-9801.
See Professional Biographies, NORMAN, OKLAHOMA

Cubberley, Douglas B., (BV) ....'53 '91 C.378 B.S.W. L.623 J.D. [Ⓐ Redwine&Assoc.]
Davenport, Bettite Jean ....'64 '97 C&L.623 B.A., J.D. 1707 Ridgemont Cir.
Davis, J. Stark, (CV) ....'61 '90 C.1070 B.S. L.616 J.D. 2900 E. Lake Dr.
DeBolt, Helen Thayer '47 '74 C&L.623 B.A., J.D.
Dir., Oklahoma Scholarship-Leadership Enrichment Program
DeKalb, Lori Ann Williams ....'65 '90 C.612 B.S. L.623 J.D. 808 24th Ave., N.W.
Dill, William R., (BV) ....'47 '73 C.332 B.A. L.623 J.D. 401 West Main, Suite 380
Dimery, Velmer J., (BV) ....'32 '60 C&L.623 B.A., LL.B. 116 S. Peters
Doty, William C. ....'44 '69 1225 W. Main St., Ste. 201
Douglas, Charles E., (AV) ....'50 '75 C.1147 B.A. L.616 J.D. P.O. Box 472
Driver, B. Lynne, (BV) ....'58 '94 C&L.623 B.S., J.D. [Floyd]
Drummond, James Alexander ....'48 '76 C.918 B.A. L.623 J.D. Okla. Indigent Def. Sys.
Edgar, Glynis C., (AV) ....'54 '88 C&L.623 B.A., J.D. 213 W. Main St.
Elkouri, Edna Asper '22 '53 C.665 A.B. L.273 J.D.
(adm. in DC; not adm. in OK) 1001 Whispering Pines Dr.‡
Elkouri, Frank ....'21 '47 C.623 B.A. L.477 S.J.D. Prof. of Law, Univ. of Oklahoma‡
English, Bill J., (AV) ....'46 '77 C.612 B.S. L.623 J.D. [English]
English, Linda K. ....'56 '00 C.623 B.A. L.615 J.D. [English]
English Law Firm, The, P.C., (AV) ....404 S. Peters Ave.
Entzeroth, Lyn Suzanne '59 '87 C.966 B.A. L.861 J.D.
(adm. in MD; not adm. in OK) Pub. Def.
Evans, Sarah, (CV) ....'62 '91 C&L.625 B.A., J.D. [S.A.Evans]
Evans, Sarah A., P.C. Law Office, (CV) ....1800 N. Interstate Dr., Ste. 121
Evers, Randy D. ....'56 '87 C.623 B.S. L.616 J.D. Coun., State Indigent Def. Sys.
Ezzell, Hal William ....'70 '96 C.1147 B.S. L.623 J.D. [H.W.Ezzell]
Ezzell, Hal Wm., P.C. ....3500 W. Robinson, Ste. 203
Fisher, Jill L. ....'71 '96 C&L.623 B.A., J.D. 660 Parrington Oval
Fitzgerald, Patrick W. ....'50 '82 C.1142 B.B.A. L.623 J.D. [Fitzgerald&Assoc.]
Fitzgerald & Associates, Inc. ....4417 Green View Circle
Flagler, Rita M., (BV) ....'58 '90 C&L.623 B.B.A., J.D. [Flagler&F.]
Flagler, Robert A., (BV) ....'41 '70 C&L.623 B.B.A., J.D. [Flagler&F.]
Flagler & Flagler, P.C., (BV) ....3625 W. Main
Floyd, Glenn E., (AV) ....'37 '67 C.618 B.S. L.623 J.D. [Floyd]

Floyd Law Firm, P.C., (AV) 🅱🅻
118 East Main Street, P.O. Box 396, 73070
Telephone: 405-364-6660 Fax: 405-360-5076
Email: floydpc@swbell.net
Glenn E. Floyd; B. Lynne Driver; J. Brent Clark; Jeff F. Raley. Of Counsel: Charles P. Rainbolt; Philip R. Russ.
Municipal and Public Authority Financing. Securities and Corporate Financing Law. Banking Law. Municipal and Local Government Law.
Representative Client: Bank First, Oklahoma City, Oklahoma.
See Professional Biographies, NORMAN, OKLAHOMA

Foor, Tracy L., (CV) ....'61 '86 C&L.623 B.S., J.D. 4809 Wellman Way
Ford, Jana Edwards ....'69 '98 C&L.623 B.B.A., J.D. Asst. Dist. Atty.
Foster, Carrie L. ....'60 '85 C&L.623 B.A., J.D. [P.Foster]
Foster, Paul R. ....'59 '84 C&L.623 B.A., J.D. [P.Foster]
Foster, Paul, Law Offices, P.C. ....2600 Van Buren Drive
Frank, Jonella J. ....'52 '79 C&L.623 B.A., J.D. 1001 Joe Keeley Dr.‡
Frank, Loraine ....'27 '74 C.612 M.S. L.623 J.D. 2514 Boxwood‡
Gallagher, Tatum ....'74 '00 C.613 B.A. L.623 J.D. [Talley,C.&G.]
Gardner, Julie Lynn ....'— '95 C.619 B.A. L.623 J.D. P.O. Box 926
Garrett, Terry J., (BV) ....'47 '90 C.1147 B.B.A. L.623 J.D. [T.J.Garrett&Assoc.]
Garrett, Terry J., & Associates, P.C., (BV) ....421 East Comanche
Garrison, Sally Elizabeth ....'73 '00 C.154 B.A. L.623 J.D. Univ. of OK, Legal Coun. Off.

Gatewood, Frank C. .... '42 '68 C&L.623 B.B.A., J.D. 222 E. Main St.
Gatlin, John C. .... '46 '76 C&L.623 B.A., J.D. Contl. Fed. Svgs. & Loan
Gibbens, Daniel G. '33 '59 C.976 B.A. L.623 J.D.
Regents' Prof. of Law, Univ. of Okla.
Gillett, Mark R. '52 '78 C.945 B.A. L.36 J.D.
(adm. in IA; not adm. in OK) Prof., Univ. of Okla., Coll. of Law
Gipson, Fred A., (AV) .... '36 '60 C&L.623 B.B.A., LL.B. Gen. Coun., Univ. of Okla.
Goddard, Ginger D., (CV) .... '55 '81 C&L.623 B.A., J.D. 224 West Gray, Suite 202
Goodspeed, Steven Don .... '72 '00 C&L.623 B.A., J.D. Diocide Intl.
Goree, Christopher W., (BV) .... '68 '94 C.623 B.A. L.616 J.D. [Goree&G.]
Goree & Goree, P.C., (BV) .... 1212 Leslie Lane
Grant Johnson, Jan, (BV) .... 629 24th Ave. S.W.
Grant-Johnson, Janis ("Jan"), (BV) .... '36 '85 C&L.623 B.A., J.D. [J.GrantJohnson]
Graves, Christopher R., (BV) .... '55 '92 C&L.623 B.B.A., J.D. [Crowe&D.]
Graves, Peter E. '55 '80 C.840 B.A. L.802 J.D.
(adm. in TX; not adm. in OK) Univ. of Okla. Coll. of Law
Grider, Hal L., (AV) .... '29 '62 C.921 B.B.A. L.623 J.D. 206 Roserock Dr.
Gunning, S. Gail '44 '91 C.663 B.S. L.623 J.D.
Appl. Def. Coun., State Indigent Def. Sys.
Hackett, Stephen Beaty .... '48 '96 C.1111 B.A. L.615 J.D. State Indigent Def. Sys.
Hall, Wilburn C., Jr. .... '41 '75 C&L.623 B.S.E., J.D. Drawer B
Hallman, Dawn Desirae .... '74 '00 C&L.623 B.B.A., J.D. [Hallman&Assoc.]
Hallman & Associates, P.C. .... 2424 Springer Dr., Ste. 202
Harroz, Joseph, Jr. .... '67 '93 C.623 B.A. L.276 J.D. Gen. Coun., Univ. of Okla.
Harvey, Derrick Wade .... '74 '01 C.612 B.S. L.623 J.D. 3750 West Main St. (Pat.)
Harvey, Harvey F., III .... '46 '93 C.277 B.S. L.615 J.D. 3750 W. Main St., Ste. 130
Harvey, James F., III, (BV) .... '46 '93 C.277 B.S. L.616 J.D. [Harvey&Assoc.] (Pat.)
Harvey & Associates, P.C., (BV) .... 3750 West Main Street, Suite 130 (Pat.)
Hastie, John D., (AV) .... '39 '64 C&L.623 B.A., LL.B. [⊡ Phillips M.M.M.&M.]
Heiple, Harold L., (AV) .... '35 '61 C&L.623 B.B.A., LL.B. [Heiple]
Heiple Law Offices, Inc., (AV) .... 218 E. Eufaula
Heiser, Gregory Mark .... '59 '93 C.645 L.623 J.D. Asst. Provost, Univ. of Oklahoma
Henning, Randy W. .... '57 '85 C.623 B.A. L.616 J.D. P.O. Box 882

Henricksen & Henricksen Lawyers, Inc.
(See El Reno)

Henson, Virginia D., (AV) ..... '56 '80 C&L.623 B.A., J.D. 314 E. Comanche St., Ste. 102
Herbst, Henry Nicholas, Law Office of '57 '84 C.613 B.A. L.623 J.D.
115 S. Peters, Ste. 5
Hetherington, William C., Jr. .... '47 '80 C.623 B.A. L.616 J.D. Dist. J., Hetherington Off.

Highsaw, Robert
(See Oklahoma City)

Hill, Charles L., (BV) .... '47 '75 C&L.623 B.B.A., J.D. 303 E. Eufaula St.
Hobbs, Wyndi Thomas '68 '93
C.612 B.S. L.862 J.D. Appl. Def. Coun., OK Indigent Def. Sys.
Holden, Virgil Leornard .... '45 '75 C.623 B.B.A. L.615 J.D. [Holden&Assoc.]
Holden & Associates .... 2321 W. Park
Honeywell, Elizabeth A. .... '57 '82 C.621 B.A. L.616 J.D. P.O. Box 1204
Hoover, Don .... '67 '99 C.1147 B.A. L.615 J.D. [⊡ D.G.Pope&Assoc.]
Housley, Roger O., (AV) .... '45 '70 C&L.623 B.B.A., J.D. [Pence&H.]
Howard, James E. .... '53 '82 C&L.623 B.A., J.D. P.O. Box 1204
Hudson, Perry W. .... '72 '97 C.999 B.A. L.623 J.D. State Indigent Def. Sys.
Hull, Richard L. .... '24 '49 C&L.623 LL.B. 2401 Tropicana Ave.
Hunt, Gary M., (CV) .... '50 '93 C.45 B.A. L.615 J.D. 309 S. Peters Ave.
Hunt, Gary Neal .... '55 '86 C.618 B.S. L.1288 J.D. 2608 Ridgefield Dr.
Iker, Holly R. .... '73 '00 C.1044 B.S. L.623 J.D. 1800 N. Interstate Dr., Ste. 122
Jackson, Robert Wade .... '63 '91 C&L.623 B.A., J.D. P.O. Box 5392
Jameson, Molly A. .... '42 '89 C.846 B.A. L.616 J.D. 1011 Woodland Dr.
Jarmon, Gary M. '41 '66 C&L.623 B.B.A., J.D.
Pres., Agar-Ford, Jarmon & Muldrow Ins. Co.

Johnston & Associates
(See Chickasha)

Kappel, Henry Wilde, (BV) .... '49 '80 C&L.623 B.A., J.D. 224 W. Gray
Kauffman, Brande' Michelle .... '73 '98 C&L.623 B.A., J.D. [B.M.Kauffman]
Kauffman, Brande M. .... 108 E. Main
Kernal, Todd E. .... '69 '97 C.556 B.S. L.623 J.D. [Shaeffer,S.&K.]
Kershen, Drew L. .... '44 '69 C.602 B.A. L.846 J.D. Prof. of Law, Univ. of Oklahoma
Kiecolt, Edward H. .... '16 '54 C.623 B.S. L.616 LL.B. 1630 Holliday Dr.‡

Koop & Medley
(See Oklahoma City)

Kruger, Treva K., (CV) .... '49 '84 C.620 B.A.Ed. L.623 J.D. P.O. Box 1333
Kutner, Peter B. '48 '72 C.188 A.B. L.309 J.D.
(adm. in CO; not adm. in OK) Prof.of Law, Univ. of OK, Coll. of Law
Kuykendall, Timothy D., (BV) .... '58 '84 C&L.623 B.S., J.D. Dist. Atty.
Lamberty, Lynn B. .... '55 '80 C.546 B.A. L.602 J.D. Asst. App. Pub. Def.
Lawter, Joe B., (BV) '58 '83 C.612 B.S. L.623 J.D.
Gen. Coun., United Bk. & Tr. Co. of Norman
Leavey, Jana Kay .... '57 '97 C&L.623 B.A., J.D. American-First Abstract Co.
Ledgerwood, Thomas D. .... '20 '51 C&L.623 B.S., LL.B. 823 Mockingbird Lane
Leeper, Bob J. .... '30 '64 C.942 B.A. L.623 LL.B. P.O. Box 5858
Little, Patrick D. .... '37 '62 C&L.378 B.A., LL.B. 3828 Apex Court
Livingston, Clint G. .... '18 '48 C&L.623 J.D. 1151 Robinhood Lane‡
Livingston, D. Mark, (CV) .... '45 '80 C.999 B.S. L.623 J.D. 911 S. Lahoma Ave.★
Lockard, James Harry .... '68 '98 C.1300 B.A. L.623 J.D. Okla. Indigent Def. Sys.
Lockhart, James H., (AV) .... '47 '76 C&L.623 B.A., J.D. 3750 W. Main St., Ste. 136
Loeffelholz, Debra D., (CV) .... '66 '92 C.623 B.A. L.615 J.D. 117 E. Main St.
Loftis, Jim D., (AV) .... '58 '88 C.621 B.S. L.623 J.D. [J.Loftis]

Loftis, Jim, P.C., (AV)
225 North Peters, 73069
Telephone: 405-366-1400 Fax: 405-366-0041
Email: jimloftis@coxinet.net URL: http://www.lawyers.com/loftislaw
Jim D. Loftis.
Personal Injury, Medical Malpractice, Products Liability, Workers Compensation.
See Professional Biographies, NORMAN, OKLAHOMA

Logan, Marcy Renea .... '73 '98 C.616 B.S. L.623 J.D. Dist. Atty.'s Off.
Logan, Robert E. .... '45 '72 C&L.623 B.B.A., LL.B. 1175 Merrymen Green‡
Lohmann, Danny G. '54 '92
C.620 B.S.B.A. L.615 J.D. App. Coun., State Indigent Def. Sys.
Long, Golda Renee .... '75 '01 C.612 B.A. L.623 J.D. Asst. Dist. Atty.
Long, Joseph C. .... '39 '63 C&L.502 B.A., LL.B. Prof. of Law, Univ. of Okla.
Louden, Pete David .... '66 '98 C.15 B.S. L.616 J.D. [Louden]
Louden Law Firm, P.C. .... 2300 McKown Drive

Lowrey, Jeremy Booth, (CV) '65 '92 C.862 B.A. L.945 J.D.
Cap. Post Conviction Apps. Div., Indigent Def. Sys.
Lucas, Tom A. .... '34 '64 C.612 B.A. L.623 LL.B. Dist. J.
Marshall, Mary Beth .... '63 '88 C.846 B.B.A. L.802 J.D. 309 W. Main Street
Martin, Mike D., (BV) .... '42 '67 C&L.623 B.B.A., LL.B. 2322 Westpark Dr.
Mattoon, William H., (BV) .... '30 '59 C.612 B.S. L.623 LL.B. [Mattoon]
Mattoon Law Offices, (BV) .... 132 West Main Street
Maute, Judith L. .... '49 '81 C.347 A.B. L.665 J.D. Prof., Univ. of OK Coll. of Law
Maynard, Allison J. .... '75 '03 C&L.623 B.A., J.D. [⊡ D.G.Pope&Assoc.]

McBride Law Firm
(See Oklahoma City)

McCarty, Lisbeth L. .... '53 '84 C&L.623 B.A., J.D. The Oklahoma Indigent Def. Sys.

McCoy Law Firm
(See Oklahoma City)

McCurdy, David K., (BV) .... '50 '75 C&L.623 B.A., J.D. U.S. Rep.
McDanel, Mike, (BV) .... '43 '73 C&L.623 B.B.A., J.D. Assistant District Attorney
McFall, Sara W., (BV) .... '53 '92 C.312 B.F.A. L.623 J.D. 309 S. Peters St.
McFarland, Carl C., (AV) .... '41 '72 C.1300 B.S. L.623 J.D. [C.C.McFarland]
McFarland, Carl C., PC, (AV) .... 220 E. Eufaula
McGraw, Jamie J. .... '60 '90 C&L.623 B.A., J.D. 100 E. Main
McIlroy, Robert N., (BV) .... '47 '74 C&L.623 B.A., J.D. 307 E. Eufaula St.
McLawhorn, Melissa Dail ..... '69 '94 C&L.623 B.A., J.D. Dep. Dir., Okla. Sheriffs Assn.
Mclerran, Bradley Dwayne .... '63 '97 C&L.623 B.A., J.D. 900 E. Main
McNichols, William J. .... '37 '62 C.116 A.B. L.276 LL.B. Prof. of Law, Okla. Univ.
Meadows, Jan, (BV) .... '54 '79 C.623 B.A. L.616 J.D. P.O. Box 1243
Miller, Fred H. .... '37 '62 C&L.477 A.B., J.D. Prof., Univer. of Okla. Coll. of Law
Miller, Mark V. .... '46 '78 C&L.623 B.B.A., J.D. P.O. Box 795
Miller, Michael J., (BV) '51 '82
C.906 B.S. L.615 J.D. Staff Atty., Legal Aid of Western Okla., Inc.
Morehead, Michael D. '63 '98 C&L.45 B.A., J.D.
Appl. Def. Coun., Okla. Indigent Defense System
Morse, David, (BV) .... '52 '79 C&L.623 B.A., J.D. [⊡ Pitchlynn&Assoc.]
Mortimer, Steven T. .... '70 '03 C&L.623 BBA, J.D. 2909 Edinburg Drive
Moseley, Jimmy A. .... '31 '61 L.615 LL.B. Cleveland Co. Dist. Atty.
Moses, Amos N., Jr. .... '42 '67 C&L.623 B.B.B., J.D. 2322 Westpark Dr.
Mouser, James W. .... '39 '65 C&L.623 B.B.A., J.D. 307 W. Brooks St.
Mulinix, Russell L., (AV) .... '55 '80 C.612 B.S. L.623 J.D. [Mulinix O.H.A.&L.] ⊙
Mulinix Ogden Hall Andrews & Ludlam, A Professional Limited Liability Company, (AV)
905 24th, NW, Suite B-1 (⊙Oklahoma City)
Mullins, Gail Hedrick .... '54 '93 C.612 B.S. L.623 J.D. 1007 Greenway Circle
Mullins, Susan L. .... '53 '86 C&L.623 B.S., J.D. 4808 Kathy Lynn Dr.
Murray, Cindy H. .... '65 '98 C&L.623 B.S., J.D. [⊡ Phillips M.M.M.&M.]
Naifeh, Clifton D., (AV) .... '50 '77 C.612 B.S. L.616 J.D. [Naifeh&Assoc.]
Naifeh, Lawrence E., (BV) ...... '53 '79 C&L.623 B.A., J.D. Coun., Oklahoma University
Naifeh, Robert N. .... '21 '50 C&L.623 B.A., J.D. 307 E. Eufaula Street

Naifeh & Associates, A Professional Corporation, (AV)
870 Copperfield Drive, Suite B, 73072
Telephone: 405-292-2244 Telefax: 405-292-2288
Email: naifehlaw@coxinet.net
Clifton D. Naifeh.
General Civil Litigation Practice: Insurance, Personal Injury, Products Liability, Negligence, Banking, Commercial.

Napoli, Jequita Harmon .... '57 '82 C&L.623 B.B.A., J.D. Dist. J.

Nash, Cohenour & Kelley, P.C.
(See Oklahoma City)

Nesbitt, Weldon E., (CV) .... '50 '91 C.839 B.S. L.623 J.D. [W.E.Nesbitt]
Nesbitt, Weldon E., PC, (CV) .... 224 W. Gray, Ste. 203
Nettles, Sheila Pyle .... '47 '00 C.621 B.A. L.623 J.D. Dist. Atty., OK Dist. Attys. Off.
Nicar, Reo E. .... '20 '69 C.663 A.B. L.616 J.D. 823 Annie Ct.‡
Noland, Rhonda Virginia, (BV) .... '64 '91 C.1300 B.S. L.623 J.D. P.O. Box 6597
Nuttle, R. Marc, (BV) .... '49 '75 C&L.623 B.A., J.D. 900 36th Ave. N.W., Ste. 202
Ockershauser, Kurt F. .... '41 '71 C.966 B.S. L.623 J.D. Coun., Univ. of Okla.
Odom, Benjamin H., (BV) .... '59 '84 C.1147 B.A. L.623 J.D. 1905 Brookhaven Blvd.
Olson, Rebecca J. McGee .... '53 '80 C&L.623 B.S., J.D. 616 Shadow Grove Ct.
Ostas, Daniel T. '56 '80 C.679 B.S. L.347 J.D.
(adm. in IN; not adm. in OK) Prof. Legal Studies, Univ. of Oklahoma
Ott, Sam D., (AV) .... '50 '74 C.612 B.S. L.623 J.D. [⊡ Phillips M.M.M.&M.]
Owens, Brian '— '00 C.172 B.A. L.615 J.D.
(adm. in ME; not adm. in OK) [⊡ Velie&V.]
Pain, William F., Law Office of, (BV) '48 '76
C&L.623 B.A., J.D. 207 W. Main St., Ste. 200
Palk, Scott L., (BV) .... '67 '92 C.612 B.S. L.623 J.D. First Assistant District Attorney
Palomar, Joyce Dickey '53 '86 C&L.546 B.S., J.D.
(adm. in NE; not adm. in OK) Assoc. Prof. of Law, Univ. of Okla. Coll. of Law
Pape, Donald A., (AV) .... '45 '74 C&L.623 B.A., J.D. [D.A.Pape] (⊙Oklahoma City)
Pape, Donald A., P.C., (AV) .... Suite B 232 E. Main
Parkinson, Jerry R. '54 '85 C.590 B.S. L.352 J.D.
(adm. in OR; not adm. in OK) Prof. of Law, Univ. of Okla. Coll. of Law
Parsons, Randy A., (BV) .... '53 '88 C.569 B.A. L.615 J.D. [Parsons&Assoc.]

Parsons & Associates Law Firm, A Corporation, (BV)
227 East Gray Street, P.O. Box 1265, 73070-1265
Telephone: 405-321-7887 Fax: 405-321-7715
URL: http://www.lawyers.com/parsonsassociates
Randy A. Parsons.
Banking Litigation, Business Litigation, Business Torts, Commercial Collections, Commercial Litigation, Corporate Contracts, Creditors Rights, Lawsuits, Lender Liability, Internet Violations, Oklahoma Lottery, Employer Defense and Trial Practice in All Courts.
Representative Clients: Citizens Bank; Security National Bank and Trust Company; Harding Glass Industries; Laidlaw Waste Systems, Inc.; Redbud Glass Company; Norman Motors Lincoln-Mercury; Gordon's Heat & Air Service Experts.
See Professional Biographies, NORMAN, OKLAHOMA

Patten, Rebecca J., (AV) .... '52 '77 C.623 B.A. L.145 J.D. [Clark,S.W.&P.]
Pearson, Thomas Dawson, Jr. .... '39 '86 C.870 B.S. L.1209 J.D. 3121 Pine Hill Rd.
Pecore, Jama H., (BV) .... '58 '86 C.651 B.A. L.623 J.D. 301 E. Eufala St.
Pence, James E., (AV) .... '43 '70 C&L.623 B.B.A., J.D. [Pence&H.]
Pence & Housley, (AV) .... 314 East Comanche
Pendarvis, Robert L., (AV) .... '29 '57 C&L.623 B.A., LL.B. [Crowe&D.]
Pennington, Jane L. .... '45 '92 C.532 B.S. L.623 J.D. Legal Aid of Western Okla.
Penrose, Mary M. '65 '93 C.1142 B.A. L.990 J.D.
(adm. in TX; not adm. in OK) Univ. of OK Coll. of Law
Peters, Lee Ann Jones .... '56 '83 C&L.623 B.A., J.D. Oklahoma Indigent Defense System
Petersen, Catherine Holland, (AV) .... '51 '76 C.310 B.A. L.623 J.D. [Petersen]
Petersen Associates, Inc., (AV) .... 314 E. Comanche

Petrone, Alison A. ....'78 '03 C&L.623 B.A., J.D. [R.D.Watson&Assoc.]
Phillips McFall McCaffrey McVay & Murrah, P.C., (AV)
232 E. Main, Suite B (Oklahoma City)
Pierce, Terry Lynn ....'61 '90 C&L.623 B.B.A., J.D. [Pierce]
Pierce Law Firm, P.C. .... 106 1/2 E. Main
Pitchlynn, Gary S., (AV) ....'47 '77 C.623 B.A. L.616 J.D. [Pitchlynn&Assoc.]

Pitchlynn & Associates, P.A., (AV)
124 East Main Street, P.O. Box 427, 73070
Telephone: 405-360-9600 Fax: 405-447-4219
URL: http://www.pitchlynnlaw.com
Patrick A. Morse (1956-2004); Gary S. Pitchlynn;—O. Joseph Williams; David Morse.
Indian Gaming Law, Business and Corporate Law, Insurance Litigation, Criminal Defense, General Litigation.
See Professional Biographies, NORMAN, OKLAHOMA

Pitsiri, Andreas Tasso .... '71 '01 C.616 B.S. L.623 J.D. Oklahoma Indigent Def. Sys.
Poarch, David A., (AV) '48 '77
C.614 B.A. L.623 J.D. Asst. Dean, Univ. of OK Coll. of Law
Polston, Roderick Heath ....'74 '01 C.612 B.A. L.616 J.D. 3280 Marshall Avenue
Ponder, David E., (CV) ....'55 '93 C&L.623 B.A., J.D. [D.Ponder]
Ponder, David, The Law Office of, (CV) .... P.O. Box 5027
Pope, Don G., (BV) .... '52 '78 C.623 B.A. L.616 J.D. [D.G.Pope&Assoc.]
Pope, Don G., & Associates, P.C., (BV) ....2424 Springer Drive, Suite 201
Presson, Steven Michael .... '56 '89 C&L.623 B.A., J.D. P.O. Box 5392
Price, King F. ....'56 '88 [K.Price]
Price, King ....101 E. Gray, Ste. A
Primrose, Turner O. ....'32 '65 C&L.623 B.B.A., LL.B. 115 S. Peters
Puckett, Lori A. ....'69 '94 C.612 B.A. L.623 J.D. Asst. Dist. Atty.
Rainbolt, Charles P., (AV) ....'48 '74 C&L.623 B.A., J.D. [Floyd]
Raley, Jeff F., (BV) .... '47 '72 C&L.623 B.S., J.D. [Floyd]
Rambo, G. Dan, (BV) ....'28 '65 C&L.623 B.B.A., J.D. 303 S. Peters Ave.
Ratliff, Marianne Shimanek, (BV) .....'56 '86 C.622 B.S. L.623 J.D. 813 Landsdowne Dr.
Rawlinson, Gary C., (AV) .... '41 '66 C.623 B.A. L.188 LL.B. [Crowe&D.]
Redwine, Philip Warren, (BV) .... '42 '68 C.619 B.A. L.623 J.D. [Redwine&Assoc.]
Redwine & Associates, (BV) ....400 S. Crawford

Resides & Resides, PLLC
(See Oklahoma City)

Reynolds, Osborne M., Jr. '40 '64 C&L.37 B.A., LL.B.
(adm. in AZ; not adm. in OK) Prof. of Law, Univ. of Oklahoma‡
Richardson, Robert E. L. '32 '60 C.622 B.A. L.623 J.D.
Prof. of Law, Univ. of Oklahoma‡
Ridgeway, Judith A., (CV) .... '50 '75 C.620 B.A. L.623 J.D. 901 N. Peters Ave.
Ridgeway, Michael William ....'57 '94 C&L.623 B.A., J.D. 901 N. Peters Ave.
Ring, Rodney D. .... '49 '87 C.1300 B.A. L.623 J.D. Spec. Dist. J.
Ripley, Terry Lensgraf, (AV) ....'54 '81 C&L.623 B.A., J.D. 2404 Lusriston Dr.
Ritter, Ted, (BV) ....'51 '76 C&L.623 B.A., J.D. 3102 Tall Oaks Cir.
Roane, Marjorie A. ....'39 '86 C.1201 B.A. L.1035 J.D. 316 Millbrook Dr.
Roberts, Theodore P. ....'39 '64 C&L.623 B.S., LL.B. Presiding Judge
Robertson, Mary, (AV) ....'58 '83 C.802 B.S. L.623 J.D. [Crowe&D.]
Robinson, James T. .... '45 '90 C.616 B.S.Chem. L.623 J.D. 222 E. Main St. (Pat.)
Royse, Robert R. ....'41 '69 C.813 B.A. L.1049 J.D. 4300 Briarcrest Dr.
Ruggiers, Christopher M., (BV) .... '52 '83 C&L.623 B.A., J.D. 400 Baker St.
Russ, Philip R., (BV) ....'43 '67 C.845 B.A. L.623 J.D. [Floyd] (Amarillo, TX)
Ryan, Henry G., III, (AV) ....'50 '75 C.623 B.A. L.846 J.D. P.O. Box 888
Salem, Micheal C., (AV) .... '49 '75 C&L.623 B.S.E.E., J.D. [Salem]

Salem Law Offices, (AV)
111 North Peters, Suite 100, 73069-7235
Telephone: 405-366-1234 Fax: 405-366-8329; 405-"FON-UFAX"
Email: mcsalem@swbell.net
Micheal C. Salem.
Constitutional Law and Civil Rights, General Civil, Criminal Trial and Appellate Practice. State and Federal Courts. Personal Injury, Product Safety, Domestic Relations, Guardianship, Probate Law.
See Professional Biographies, NORMAN, OKLAHOMA

Saunders, Kevin W. '47 '85 C.264 A.B. L.477 J.D.
(adm. in DC; not adm. in OK) Prof. of Law, Univ. of Okla. Coll. of Law
Scaperlanda, Michael A. '60 '84 C&L.846 B.A., J.D.
(adm. in TX; not adm. in OK) Prof. of Law, Univ. of Okla.
Schmidt, Joey D. ....'60 '85 C&L.623 B.A., J.D. Legal Aid
Schumacher, Tracy Erin ....'70 '95 C.612 B.S. L.623 J.D. Off. of Dist. Atty.
Scott, Steven R. ....'61 '86 C&L.623 B.B.A., J.D. P.O. Box 722400
Shaeffer, Fred J., (AV) ....'52 '78 C&L.623 B.S., J.D. [Shaeffer,S.&K.]
Shaeffer, Laura A., (BV) .... '64 '92 C&L.623 B.A., J.D. [Shaeffer,S.&K.]
Shaeffer, Shaeffer & Kernal, (AV) ....231 South Peters
Sherry, Janet Brenan, (BV) ....'47 '85 C.182 B.A. L.623 J.D. P.O. Box 720516
Silkey, Al E. ....'45 '79 C&L.623 B.B.A., J.D. [Silkey]
Silkey Law Offices ....P.O. Box 727
Singleton, Alma Nickell '47 '79 C&L.790 B.A., J.D.
(adm. in SC; not adm. in OK) Libr. Dir., Univ. of OK Coll. of Law

Sisson, B. David, (AV) '51 '90 C.1367 B.M. L.623 J.D.
Old Towne Square, 224 West Gray, Suite 202, P.O. Box 534, 73070-0534
Telephone: 405-447-2521 Fax: 405-447-2552 URL: http://www.lawyers.com/sissonlawoffice
Email: sisson@sissonlawoffice.com URL: http://www.sissonlawoffice.com
Bankruptcy, Domestic, Probate and Estate Planning, Family Law, Divorce, Child Custody Modifications.
See Professional Biographies, NORMAN, OKLAHOMA

Sitzman, R. Richard, (AV) ....'49 '77 C.154 B.A. L.623 J.D. Asst. Dist. Atty.
Smith, Barbara Ann .... '51 '77 C.494 B.A. L.1066 J.S.D. Appellate Def.
Smith, David D., (BV) ....'57 '82 C&L.623 B.A., J.D. [D.D.Smith]
Smith, Douglas J. ....'61 '90 C.999 B.S. L.623 J.D. [Smith]
Smith, Ralph Allen '63 '89 C.45 B.A. L.862 J.D.
Appl. Def. Coun., Oklahoma Indigent Def. Sys.
Smith, Robert Barr ...... '33 '59 C&L.813 B.A., J.D. Prof., Univ. of Okla. College of Law
Smith, David D., P.C., (BV) .... 216 East Eufaula

Smith Law Office, P.C.
104 East Eufaula, 73069
Telephone: 405-360-2660 Fax: 405-360-6702
Email: djsmithlaw@aol.com URL: http://www.dougsmithlaw.com
Douglas J. Smith.
Criminal, Personal Injury, Family Law, Driving While Intoxicated, Traffic Violations, Automobile Accidents, Divorce, Child Custody.
See Professional Biographies, NORMAN, OKLAHOMA

Snider, Jeanne Meacham ....'58 '01 C&L.623 B.A., J.D. City Attys. Office
Sparks, John H., (BV) ....'69 '94 C.309 A.B. L.623 J.D. [Crowe&D.]

Spector, Robert G. '41 '68 C&L.966 B.S., J.D.
(adm. in WI; not adm. in OK) Prof. of Law, Univ. of Okla.
Stevens, Richard D., (BV) ....'57 '83 C&L.623 B.A., J.D. Asst. Dist. Atty.
Stice, Steven Lee, (BV) ....'69 '96 C.612 B.S. L.623 J.D. [S.Stice]
Stice, Steve, (BV) .... 303 S. Peters Ave.
Stockwell, Dave, (BV) ....'56 '89 C&L.623 B.S., J.D. [Stockwell]
Stockwell, Peggy, (BV) ....'54 '83 C&L.623 B.A., J.D. [Stockwell]

Stockwell Law Offices, A Professional Corporation, (BV)
119 East Main Street, P.O. Box 519, 73070
Telephone: 405-321-9414 Fax: 405-321-9416 Toll Free: 800-360-9414
Email: stockwelllaw@stockwelllaw.com URL: http://www.stockwelllaw.com
Benjamin E. Stockwell (1931-1990); Peggy Stockwell; Dave Stockwell.
Personal Injury, Family Law, Criminal, Wills and Probate, Expungement Law, DUI Defense, Drivers License Revocation, Elder Law.
References: City National Bank and Trust Co., Norman; Interactive Communications, Norman.
See Professional Biographies, NORMAN, OKLAHOMA

Stout, John H., (BV) ....'61 '86 C&L.623 B.B.A., J.D. 2429 Westport Dr.
Stowers, Terry Lee ....'64 '99 C.620 B.S. L.615 J.D. [Burns&S.]
Sugarman, David B. .... '44 '72 C&L.623 B.B.A., J.D. P.O. Box 5091
Swank, David '31 '59 C.612 B.A. L.623 LL.B.
Prof. of Law, Univ. of Okla. Coll. of Law
Sweeney, Law Office, (BV) .... 123 East Tonhawa Street
Sweeney, Everett J., (BV) .... '45 '70 C.622 B.S. L.623 J.D. [Sweeney]
Sweeney, Paul L., Jr. '60 '94 C.1057 B.A. L.1389 J.D.
(adm. in MA; not adm. in OK)
Gen. Coun. & Secy., Yamanouchi Pharma Technologies, Inc.
Talley, Richard B., (AV) ....'47 '72 C&L.623 B.B.A., J.D. [Talley,C.&G.]
Talley, Crowder & Gallagher, (AV) ....219 East Main Street

Tawwater & Slama, LLP
(See Oklahoma City)

Telley, Murlene Worth '35 '57 C&L.623 B.A., LL.B.
Secy. & Treas., Overseas Enterprises & Servs., Inc.
Tharp, Paul A. ....'38 '63 C&L.623 B.S., LL.B. Univ. of Okla.
Timmons, Cheryl F. ....'69 '94 C&L.623 B.A., J.D. Asst. Dist. Atty.
Tontz, Gregory T., (BV) ....'67 '94 C.612 B.S. L.623 J.D. [Bailey]
Townsend, Chiles E., (BV) .... '54 '85 C.612 B.S. L.623 J.D. 3300 Hillview Dr.

Travis, Mary A., Attorney at Law
(See Oklahoma City)

Traw, John M., (BV) ....'44 '74 C&L.623 B.S.E.E., J.D. P.O. Box 546
Trimble, Preston A. ....'30 '60 C&L.623 B.A., LL.B. Ret. Dist. J.
Trost-Walker, Kelly Jo .... '68 '97 C.612 B.S. L.623 J.D. 5205 Rhodes Dr.
Uphoff, Rodney J. '50 '76 C&L.966 B.A., J.D.
Prof. of Law, Univ. of Oklahoma Law Ctr.
Valley, Marina S. ....'55 '93 C.618 B.A. L.615 J.D. 629 24th Ave. S.W.
Vaughan, Robert L. ....'37 '62 C&L.623 LL.B. 915 S. Lahoma‡
Velie, Jonathan T. ....'65 '93 C.112 B.A. L.623 J.D. [Velie&V.]
Velie, William Place ....'68 '95 C.1375 L.623 J.D. [Velie&V.]
Velie & Velie, P.C. ....210 East Main Street
Virgin, Blake, (BV) ....'55 '81 C.1147 B.A. L.623 J.D. Mun. J.
Vittitow, Jon R., (BV) ....'— '90 C&L.623 B.A., J.D. [Vittitow]
Vittitow, Katherine E., (BV) ....'66 '92 C.623 B.A. L.1209 J.D. 714 Jona Kay Terr.
Vittitow Law Office, P.C., (BV) .... 330 W. Gray, Suite 207
Wadsack, Charles E., (BV) ....'48 '73 C&L.623 B.B.A., J.D. 415 W. Gray St.
Walker, Salliann Parker, (CV) ....'47 '93 C.314 B.A. L.623 J.D. [Petersen]
Wall, Douglas, (CV) ....'66 '93 C&L.623 B.A., J.D. 216 E. Eufaula
Wall, Richard, (CV) ....'68 '93 C&L.623 B.A., J.D. [Wall]
Wall Law Office, (CV) .... 216 E. Eufaula
Walters, Robin L. ....'60 '85 C.246 B.S. L.900 J.D. Asst. City Atty.
Ward, Stanley M., (AV) .... '39 '66 C.612 B.A. L.623 J.D. 629 24th Avenue, S.W.
Warner, Eric Paul ....'50 '77 C.623 B.B.A. L.616 J.D. P.O. Box 721615

Watley, Kevin "D", (AV) '55 '81 C&L.623 B.Ac., J.D.
Suite 202-A, 224 West Gray Street, P.O. Box 1304, 73070-1304
Telephone: 405-321-5858
Federal Income, Estate and Gift Taxation, Federal and State Tax Representation and Litigation, Estate Planning, Probate and Trusts Law.
See Professional Biographies, NORMAN, OKLAHOMA

Watson, Rodney D. ....'53 '83 C&L.623 B.A., J.D. [R.D.Watson&Assoc.]
Watson, William R. ....'52 '80 C.1237 B.G.S. L.846 J.D. Univ. of Okla. Coll. of Law‡

Watson, Rodney D., & Associates, P.C.
The Republic Building, 401 West Main, Suite 310, 73069
Telephone: 405-364-9480 Facsimile: 405-364-0425
Email: rwatson@rodneywatsonassociates.com URL: http://www.rodneywatsonassociates.com
Rodney D. Watson;—Alison A. Petrone.
Slip and Fall, Sex Crimes, Discrimination, Personal Injury, Family Law, Civil Litigation, Criminal Litigation, Automobile Accidents, DUI, Trucking Accidents, Medical Malpractice, Family, Divorce, Child Custody, Visitation Rights, Dog Bites, Adoption Law, Wills, Trust Law, Estate Planning.
See Professional Biographies, NORMAN, OKLAHOMA

Welcher, Gayle ....'41 '66 C&L.623 B.B.A., J.D. 1311 Sunset Dr.
Whinery, Ken, (BV) .... '32 '73 C&L.623 B.S., J.D. 6519 Crooked Oak Dr.
Williams, Gary W., (BV) ....'33 '58 C&L.623 B.B.A., J.D. 629 24th Ave., S.W.
Williams, Laurie Anne, (BV) ....'57 '81 C.228 A.B. L.623 J.D. 730 South Ponca
Williams, O. Joseph ....'75 '01 C.621 B.S. L.615 J.D. [Pitchlynn&Assoc.]
Willis, Lu, (BV) ....'56 '85 C.10 B.S. L.623 J.D. Staff Atty., Ct. of Civ. App.
Wilson, Dane T. ....'55 '99 C.859 B.S. L.623 J.D. 421 East Comanche, Suite C
Wise, Matthew Tate .... '63 '94 C.612 B.S. L.615 J.D. 2201 McKown Dr., Ste. 3
Wofford, Michelle, (CV) ....'59 '91 C&L.623 B.S., J.D. 404 S. Peters
Wolf, Silas C. ....'19 '52 C.800 L.623 LL.B. [Wolf&W.]
Wolf, Silas C., Jr., (BV) ....'49 '75 C&L.623 B.S., J.D. [Wolf&W.]
Wolf & Wolf, P.C., (BV) .... 225 N. Peters Ave., Ste. 2
Woodall, Arthur L. ....'40 '71 C.1147 B.A. L.616 J.D. 131 E. Main
Woods, William C. ....'46 '72 C&L.623 B.A., J.D. 2301 W. Main St.
Woodson, William E., (AV) ....'45 '71 C.1147 B.A. L.862 J.D. [W.E.Woodson]

Woodson, William E., PLLC, (AV)
307 East Eufaula Street, 73069
Telephone: 405-360-1222 Fax: 405-360-1269
William E. Woodson.
Practice includes Personal Injury, Medical Malpractice, Products Liability, Workers Compensation, Litigation State and Federal Courts.
See Professional Biographies, NORMAN, OKLAHOMA

Worth, Murlene '35 '57 C&L.623 B.S., LL.B.
In-House Coun., Overseas Enterprises & Serv., Inc.
Wrede, Jane Bode ....'60 '90 C.612 B.S. L.623 J.D. [J.B.Wrede]

Young, Eileen Beth, (BV) ....'51 '79 C.477 B.A. L.623 J.D. 2604 Barry Switzer St.

NOWATA, * 3,896, *Nowata Co.*

Grazier, G. Roy, Sr. ....'36 '75 C.623 B.A. L.616 J.D. 717 E. Seneca Ave.
Hamit, Charles Lee ....'44 '88 C.927 B.A. L.862 J.D. [Hamit]
Hamit Law Office ....P.O. Box 739

Logan & Lowry, LLP
(See Vinita)

Maddux, W. E., (AV) ....'28 '51 C&L.623 A.B., LL.B. 114 E. Delaware
Sontag, James L. ....'31 '60 C.711 L.862 LL.B. Dist. J.

OCHELATA, 441, *Washington Co.*

Preston, Thomas B. ....'30 '59 C.612 B.A. L.623 LL.B. P.O. Box 120‡

OKARCHE, 1,110, *Canadian & Kingfisher Cos.*

Davis, Robert E., (CV) ....'46 '76 C.678 B.A. L.616 J.D. P.O. Box 117

OKEENE, 1,240, *Blaine Co.*

Davis, Elise D. ....'79 '05 C&L.623 B.B.A., J.D. [A Traynor,L.W.&W.] ⊙
Long, James F., (AV) ....'48 '74 C.663 B.A. L.900 J.D. [Traynor,L.W.&W.] ⊙
Traynor, Timothy R., (AV) ....'43 '68 C&L.623 B.B.A., J.D. [Traynor,L.W.&W.] ⊙
Traynor, Long, Wynne & Woodward, P.C., A Professional Corporation, (AV)
214 S. Main St. (⊙Enid)
Woodward, Paul K., (BV) ....'59 '85 C.1315 B.S. L.616 J.D. [Traynor,L.W.&W.] ⊙
Wynne, John H., (AV) ....'49 '74 C.612 B.S. L.862 J.D. [Traynor,L.W.&W.] ⊙

OKEMAH, * 3,085, *Okfuskee Co.*

Coker, Bruce A., (CV) ....'62 '90 C&L.623 B.A., J.D. 318 W. Broadway
Craig, Oral C. ....'21 '56 C&L.623 LL.B. Ret. Assoc. Dist. J.
Garrison, Michael W. '45 '82 C.612 B.S. L.862 J.D.
Assistant General Counsel, Occidental Petroleum Corporation
Martin, David N. ....'54 '80 C.619 B.S. L.623 J.D. Assoc. Dist. J.
McFarland, Don W. ....'67 '93 C.619 B.S. L.616 J.D. [McFarland]
McFarland Law Office ....307 W. Broadway
Meyer, Regina Ann ....'65 '00 C.616 B.S. L.623 J.D. 318 W. Broadway
Pittman, Jeremy T. ....'73 '00 C.612 B.S. L.623 J.D. [A J.T.Pittman]
Pittman, Jeremy T., PLC ....127 North Fourth Street
Rahhal, Franklin D. ....'33 '57 L.623 LL.B. Dist. J.

OKLAHOMA CITY, 506,132, *Canadian, Cleveland, Oklahoma & Pottawatomie Cos.*

Abbott, W. Rogers, II, (AV) .....'35 '61 C.623 B.B.A. L.477 LL.B. 5009 N. Pennsylvania
Abel, Ed, (AV) ....'42 '66 C&L.623 B.A., J.D. [Abel,M.S.M.&K.]

Abel, Musser, Sokolosky, Mares & Kouri, (AV)
One Leadership Square, Suite 600, 211 North Robinson, 73102
Telephone: 405-239-7046 Fax: 405-272-1090
Email: contactus@abelmusser.com URL: http://www.abellawfirm.com
Ed Abel; Sidney A. Musser, Jr.; Jerry D. Sokolosky; Lynn Brusin Mares; Harry J. (Trey) Kouri, III. Associates: Kelly S. Bishop; Barry R. Davis; Steven T. Horton; Brent L. Neighbors; Lynne C. Zaccaria. Of Counsel: John A. Alberts; Warner E. Lovell, Jr.; Leo H. Whinery.
General Civil and Criminal Practice in all Courts. Personal Injury. Family. Workers Compensation. Products Liability Law. Trials. Medical Malpractice, Insurance Litigation, Automobile Accidents, Insurance Bad Faith.
See Professional Biographies, OKLAHOMA CITY, OKLAHOMA

Abernathy, Robert S., (BV) '65 '93 C.623 B.A. L.616 J.D.
3555 N.W. 58th Street, Suite 510, 73112
Telephone: 405-946-8022 Fax: 405-942-8362
URL: http://www.lawyers.com/abernathy
Real Property, Oil and Gas Law, Corporate Law, Probate, General Practice.
See Professional Biographies, OKLAHOMA CITY, OKLAHOMA

Ablah, George M. ....'27 '50 C&L.623 B.A., LL.B. 5900 Mosteller Dr.
Ables, J. Angela, (AV) ....'50 '76 C.618 B.A. L.616 J.D. [Kerr,I.R.&A.]
Abowitz, Murray E., (AV) ....'41 '71 C.659 B.S. L.766 J.D. [Abowitz,T.&D.]

Abowitz, Timberlake & Dahnke, P.C., (AV) BR
10th Floor Hightower Building, 105 North Hudson, 73102
Mailing Address: P.O. Box 1937, Oklahoma City, OK 73101
Telephone: 405-236-4645 Facsimile: 405-239-2843
Email: mainmail@abowitzlaw.com URL: http://www.abowitzlaw.com
Murray E. Abowitz; Sarah Jackson Timberlake; George W. Dahnke; Kayce L. Gisinger;—Lisa Luschen Dietrich; Blake A. Bittel; Mary B. Scott; Henry A. Meyer, III; Jonathan C. Horton; Ms. Christine M. Cave. Of Counsel: William C. McAlister.
Civil Trial and Appellate Practice in all State and Federal Courts, including General Tort, Business and Securities Litigation, Products Liability, Insurance, Professional Liability, Workers Compensation and Antitrust Law, Employment and Civil Rights Law.
Representative Clients: Admiral Insurance Co.; Carolina Casualty Insurance Co.; Certain Underwriters at Lloyds of London; Liberty Mutual Insurance Co.; National Farmers Union Insurance Co.; Oklahoma Attorneys Mutual Insurance Co.; Oklahoma Farmers Union Mutual Insurance Co.; Progressive Insurance Companies; The UNITRIN Companies; VIACOM.
See Professional Biographies, OKLAHOMA CITY, OKLAHOMA

Ackley, Gary L., (BV) ....'54 '81 C&L.623 B.B.A., J.D. Asst. Dist. Atty., Dist. Atty. Off.
Acquaviva, Joseph T., Jr., (AV) ....'59 '86 C.415 B.A. L.616 J.D. [Wilson,C.&A.]
Adams, Candyce S. ....'51 '85 C.1147 B.S. L.623 J.D. P.O. Box 892517
Adams, Daniel D., Jr. '42 '67 C.198 B.A. L.623 J.D.
V.P. & Investment Off., Amer. Fidelity Assur. Co.
Adams, Edgar W. ....'17 '41 L.623 LL.B. 9524 Northland Rd.‡
Adams, Givens L., (BV) '35 '62
C.502 B.A. L.623 LL.B. Asst. Gen. Coun., State Tax Comm.
Adams, Glenn D. ....'50 '77 C.361 B.S.E. L.623 J.D. Appl. Ct. J.
Adams, R. Scott, (AV) ....'63 '89 C.614 B.B.A. L.616 J.D. [Adams&Assoc.]
Adams, Rebecca L. ....'50 '75 C.1322 B.A. L.802 J.D. Gen. Coun., State Ethics Comm.
Adams, Woodrow W. ....'18 '55 C.361 B.S. L.616 J.D. I.R.S.

Adams & Associates, P.C., (AV)
City Place Building, 204 North Robinson Twenty-Fifth Floor, 73102
Telephone: 405-232-9100 Fax: 405-232-9114
Email: Adams44@swbell.net URL: http://www.lawyers.com/adams-associates
R. Scott Adams.
General Civil and Criminal Trial and Appellate Practice in State and Federal Courts, Administrative, Automobile, Banking, Bankruptcy, Commercial, Corporate, Estate Planning, Equine, Health Care, Insurance Defense and Regulatory, International Law, Oil & Gas, Probate, Personal Injury, Real Estate, Taxation, Telecommunications and Transportation.
See Professional Biographies, OKLAHOMA CITY, OKLAHOMA

Addison, Roger G., (AV) '51 '77 C.174 B.A. L.623 J.D.
V.P., Chemical Legal Servs. & Asst. Gen. Coun., Kerr-McGee Corp.
Adelson, Jeffrey M. ....'52 '77 C.1109 B.A. L.1137 J.D. [Adelson,T.&B.] ⊙
Adelson, Testan & Brundo
3601 Classen Boulevard, Suite 103 (⊙Calabasas, Concord, Fresno, Glendale, Grover

(This Listing Continued)

Adelson, Testan & Brundo (Continued)
Beach, Long Beach, Oxnard, Sacra., San Bernardino, San Diego, San Fran., San Jose, Santa Ana, Santa Rosa, CA; Hartford, CT; Chgo., IL; Berkeley Heights, Princeton, NJ; Austin, Dallas, Hous., TX)
Adkins, M. Craig, (BV) ....'68 '96 C&L.623 B.A., J.D. [A McAfee&T.]
Adler, Kathleen J., (BV) ....'47 '83 C&L.623 B.A., J.D. [A Merritt&Assoc.]
Adler, S. Thomas, (AV) ....'48 '74 C&L.623 B.B.A., J.D. [C Kline,K.E.&B.]
Akins, Johnny J., (AV) ....'44 '74 C.1147 B.A. L.623 J.D. [C R.H.Mitchell&Assoc.]
Albert, Barry, (AV) ....'36 '63 C&L.623 B.B.A., J.D. Asst. Pub. Def.
Albert, Gregory W. ....'49 '78 C.53 B.S. L.623 J.D. Supm. Ct. Ref.

Albert, John B., (AV) '67 '92 C&L.623 B.A., J.D. BR
204 North Robinson, Suite 3030, 73102
Telephone: 405-232-3906; Mobile: 405-834-2409 Fax: 405-928-2889
URL: http://www.johnalbertlaw.com
Associate: Joshua A.L. Lee.
Criminal Defense, Civil Practice, Driving While Intoxicated, Traffic Violations, Driving Under the Influence, Drug Trafficking, Homicide, Felonies and White Collar Crime.
See Professional Biographies, OKLAHOMA CITY, OKLAHOMA

Albert, Victor F., (AV) ....'60 '87 C.623 B.B.A. L.616 J.D. [Conner&W.]
Alberts, John A., (AV) ....'64 '90 C.612 B.S. L.616 J.D. [C Abel,M.S.M.&K.]
Alcorn, R. Daniel, Jr ....'45 '75 C.613 B.A. L.615 J.D. OK Health Care Auth.
Alcorn, Stephen Paul ....'67 '00 C.1213 B.F.A. L.616 J.D. Dist. Atty.
Alden, Amy L., (AV) ....'71 '96 C.612 B.A. L.623 J.D. [A Durbin,L.&B.]
Alden, Charles F., III, (AV) ....'47 '73 C.612 B.A. L.616 J.D. [Hudson,A.&L.]
Alexander, Linda G., (BV) ....'53 '78 C.1209 B.A. L.623 J.D. [Niemeyer,A.A.&P.]
Alexander, Robert H., Jr., (BV) '51 '77
C.329 B.A. L.309 J.D. [R.H.,.a.C.A.L.Alexander,Jr.]
Alexander, Stanley J., (BV) '38 '71 C.1147 B.S. L.616 J.D.
Asst. Gen. Coun., Tax Comm.

Alexander, Robert H., Jr., Attorneys and Counselors At Law, p.c., The Law Office of, (BV)
First National Center, 24th Floor, 120 North Robinson, P.O. Box 868, 73101-0868
Telephone: 405-232-0803 Facsimile: 405-232-0519
Email: alexattys@productlaw.com URL: http://www.productlaw.com
Robert H. Alexander, Jr.; Annita M. Bridges. Associates: Robert W. Ivy (Not admitted in OK); Carmen M. Palomo; Marilyn S. Morphis. Of Counsel: John J. Love.
Pharmaceutical, Automotive, Mechanical and General Products Liability Defense, General Civil Trial and Appellate Practice.
See Professional Biographies, OKLAHOMA CITY, OKLAHOMA

Allen, Charles I. ....'22 '51 C.623 L.615 LL.B. 2112 N.W. 47th St.
Allen, Douglas B., (BV) ....'51 '78 C.612 B.A. L.616 J.D. Sr. House Leadership Asst.
Allen, Douglas Reese, (BV) ....'54 '80 C.623 B.A. L.615 J.D. 10300 Greenbriar Pl.
Allen, Ethan, III, Law Offices of, (BV) '54 '82 C.612 B.S. L.616 J.D.
2601 Northwest Expressway, Suite 815, East Tower
Allen, Hilary S., (BV) ....'70 '96 C&L.623 B.A., J.D. [A Durbin,L.&B.]
Allen, R. Reagan D. ....'— '03 C.1347 B.S. L.1218 J.D. [A Crowe&D.]
Allen, Robert D., (AV) ....'28 '48 C&L.623 B.A., LL.B. Assit. Gen. Coun.
Allen, Zachary W., (AV) ....'63 '88 C&L.623 B.B.A. L.802 J.D. [Mock,S.W.E.R.&B.]
Alley, Wayne E. ....'32 '57 C&L.813 A.B., J.D. 200 N.W. 4th St.‡
Alonso, Beth M. ....'54 '81 C.550 B.S. L.1202 J.D. Staff Atty., OK Ct. of Civil App.
Altshuler, Ashley L. ....'69 '99 C.623 B.A. L.615 J.D. [A Coyle]
Alvis, Whitney ....'77 '05 C&L.623 B.S., J.D. [A Mock,S.W.E.R.&B.]
Amick, John M. ....'23 '48 C.612 L.623 LL.B. Dist. J.
Amini, Gordon C., (AV) '48 '77 C.249 B.S.E.E. L.616 J.D.
Genn. Coun., C.L. Frates and Company (Legal Department)
Anderson, J. Steve, III ....'41 '66 C.197 B.A. L.623 J.D. 5809 N.W. Grand Blvd.
Anderson, Merlaine ....'54 '80 C&L.623 B.A., J.D. Law Clk. to Supm. Ct. Jus.
Anderson, Michael A., (BV) ....'59 '85 C.1147 B.A. L.616 J.D. [Anderson,M.&O.]
Anderson, Mikel K. ....'61 '87 C.233 B.S. L.862 J.D. U.S. Dept. H.U.D.
Anderson, Nancy K ....'41 '81 C.350 B.S. L.623 J.D. [A Pierce C.H.B.&G.]
Anderson, Philip W., (BV) ....'48 '96 C&L.616 B.A., J.D. [Whitten,N.M.T.&R.]
Anderson, R. Wayne, (AV) ....'57 '82 C&L.623 B.A., J.D. [Grimes,G.A.&D.]
Anderson, Richard W., (BV) ....'56 '83 C.1143 B.S. L.616 J.D. 1021 N.W. 16th St.
Anderson, Robert H., (BV) ....'28 '58 C.862 B.A. L.623 LL.B. 5901 N. Western
Anderson, Scott Michael ....'72 '01 C.663 B.S.B.A. L.615 J.D. Pub. Def. Off.

Anderson, McCoy & Orta, A Professional Corporation, (AV)
2600 Bank One Center, 100 North Broadway, 73102
Telephone: 405-236-0003 Facsimile: 405-236-1448
Email: amo@amopc.com URL: http://www.amopc.com
Michael A. Anderson; J. Michael McCoy; Vanessa A. Orta;—Kimberlee Taggart Spady; Mark J. Peregrin; Jeanette A. Oates; Hilary M. Nolan; Ben F. Meek, III.
Commercial Mortgage Backed Securities Transactions, Real Estate Finance, Securitization Document Management, Loan Servicing Transactions, Commercial and Residential Real Estate Litigation, Real Estate Foreclosures and Bankruptcy.
See Professional Biographies, OKLAHOMA CITY, OKLAHOMA

Andrews, Cynthia L. ....'65 '94 C.623 B.B.A. L.616 J.D. [Crowe&D.]
Andrews, J. Don, (AV) ....'64 '89 C.623 B.F.A. L.615 J.D. [Mulinix O.H.A.&L.]
Andrews, R. Greg ....'72 '01 C&L.623 B.A., J.D. [A Mullins,H.&J.]

Andrews Davis, A Professional Corporation, (AV) BR
Chase Tower, 100 N. Broadway Avenue, Suite 3300, 73102-8812
Telephone: 405-272-9241 Fax: 405-235-8786
Email: andrewsdavis@andrewsdavis.com URL: http://www.andrewsdavis.com
L. Karlton Mosteller (1895-1966); John C. Andrews (1926-2001); Mona S. Lambird (1938-1999); J. Edward Barth; Kennis M. Bellmard II; C. Temple Bixler; James F. Davis; Alan C. Durbin; John F. Fischer, II; Matthew H. Griffith; Timothy M. Larason; Mark H. Price; D. Joe Rockett; Anne E. Zachritz;—Valerie R. Devol; L. Matthew Dobson; Sandra Benischek Harrison; Jennifer Henshaw McBee; Jennifer B. Scott; Leif E. Swedlow. Of Counsel: Lynn O. Holloman; Robert B. Milsten; Stephen J. Moriarty.
Administrative, Aircraft Finance and Leasing, Alternative Dispute Resolution, Antitrust, Appellate Practice, Banking, Bankruptcy, Blue Sky, Broker-Dealer Registration, Business, Casinos and Gambling, Commercial, Commercial Real Estate, Computers and Software, Construction Contracts, Corporate, Corrections, Creditors Rights, Debt and Equity Finance, E-Commerce, Employee Benefits, Employment Law, Environmental, Equipment Leasing, ERISA, Estate Planning, Finance, Gaming, Health Care, Historic Preservation, Indian Gaming, Insurance, Initial Public Offerings, Intellectual Property, International Business, Investment Banking, Landlord and Tenant, Limited Liability Company Law, Limited Partnerships, Litigation, Local Government Contracts, Media, Mergers and Acquisitions, Mortgages, Municipal Bonds, Native American, Oil and Gas, Partnership, Private Placement, Probate, Professional Liability, Public Corporations, Real Estate Title Insurance, Real Property, Regulatory, Securities, Shareholder Agreements, Surety, Taxation, Technology, Trade Association, Trade Mark Registration, Trial Practice, Trusts and Estates, Venture Capital.
See Professional Biographies, OKLAHOMA CITY, OKLAHOMA

Angus, Joseph, (BV) ....'47 '87 C&L.623 B.A., J.D. [Angus]
Angus Associates, P.C., (BV) ....1720 N. Shartel Ave.
Anspaugh, Rex H. ....'12 '35 C&L.900 LL.B., J.D. 3032 Drakestone‡
Anthis, Joe M., (AV) ....'42 '66 C&L.862 B.S., J.D. [J.M.Anthis]
Anthis, Joe M., P.C., (AV) ....4808 N. Classen Blvd.

Anthony, Robert M., (AV) ....'54 '79 C.612 B.U.S. L.623 J.D. [🄲 Pierce C.H.B.&G.]
Antonioli, Vincent .... '56 '93 C.16 B.A. L.615 J.D. 500 N. Walker Ave., Ste. B
Archibald, J. William, (AV) .... '54 '81 C.612 B.S. L.623 J.D. [Holloway,D.&B.]
Argo, Doyle W. .... '47 '76 C&L.623 B.A., J.D. U.S. Mag. J.
Armstrong, Frances J. .... '48 '87 C.1147 B.S. L.862 J.D. [🄰 Wilson,C.&A.]
Arnett, M. Michael ....'53 '87 C.612 B.S. L.615 J.D. [Arnett]
Arnett Law Firm .... 3133 N.W. 63rd St.
Arnold, Shawn E. '58 '87 C&L.623 B.A., J.D.
Sr. Trial Specialist, Hartford Fire Insurance Co.
Artus, Andrew A., (BV) ....'65 '94 C.805 B.B.A. L.623 J.D. [🄰 Collins,Z.&W.]
Ashbaker, Joseph L. ....'69 '02 C.612 B.S. L.623 J.D. [Ashbaker&M.]
Ashbaker & McKay, P.C. .... 228 Robert S. Kerr Avenue, Suite 220
Ashley, Kim D., (AV) '56 '90 C.623 B.S. L.616 J.D.
Asst. Gen. Coun., State Tax Comm.
Ashmore, Steven S. ....'63 '98 C.612 B.S. L.623 J.D. [🄰 Mansell&E.]
Askins, Jari ....'53 '80 C&L.623 B.A., J.D. Dep. Gen. Coun.
Assaf, R. Robyn, Law Offices of .... '59 '92 C.054 B.A. L.615 J.D. 1317 Glenbrook Drive
Atkins, Jeffrey R., (BV) ....'68 '93 C.1147 B.B.A. L.623 J.D. [Atkins&M.]

Atkins & Markoff, (BV)
9211 Lake Hefner Parkway Suite 104, 73120
Telephone: 405-607-8757 Fax: 405-607-8749 URL: http://oklalawyer.com
URL: http://www.lawyers.com/atkinsandmarkoff
Member of Firm: Jeffrey R. Atkins.
Personal Injury, Automobile Accidents, Wrongful Death, Trucking Accidents, Slip and Fall, Nursing Home Abuse, Head and Spinal Injuries, Dog Bites, Sexual Abuse, Criminal Law, Drug Crimes, DUI/DWI, Juvenile Crimes, General Practice, Family , Divorce, Adoptions, Child Custody, Child Support, Domestic Violence, Visitation Rights, Elder Law, Legal Malpractice, Medical Malpractice, Social Security, Social Security Disability, Taxation, IRS Audits, Property Tax Appeals, Tax Planning, Toxic Torts, Trust and Estate, Wills and Probate.
See Professional Biographies, OKLAHOMA CITY, OKLAHOMA

Atkinson, Haskins, Nellis, Brittingham, Gladd & Carwile
(See Tulsa)

Austin, Howard B. ....'20 '50 C&L.623 LL.B. 3200 W. Britton Rd.
Austin, Kathryn Barr, (AV) ....'62 '90 C.1147 B.S. L.615 J.D. Gen. Coun. to Admr.
Austin, Norman F., (BV) ....'53 '89 C.623 B.A. L.616 J.D. [Niemeyer,A.A.&P.]
Auston, Kirk D., Law Office of, (CV🅃) '58 '87 C&L.378 B.A., J.D.
(adm. in KS; not adm. in OK) 8517 N.W. Expwy.
Autry, Lorrie Gray ....'57 '89 C.623 B.S. L.744 J.D. 1601 S.W. 89th Street, Building C
Babb, Charles K., (BV) '52 '83
C.663 B.S. L.862 J.D. Asst. Gen. Coun., State Dept. of Corrections
Babb, D. Lynn, (AV) ....'53 '80 C.612 B.A. L.623 J.D. [Pierce C.H.B.&G.]
Bacharach, Robert E., (AV) ....'59 '85 C.623 B.A. L.910 J.D. U.S. Mag. J.
Bachman, Gary C., (AV) ....'43 '70 C.614 B.S. L.616 J.D. [Holloway,D.&B.]
Bachman, James M. ....'41 '67 C&L.616 B.A., J.D. P.O. Box 96265
Bachman, Stephen D., (AV) ....'64 '90 C.614 B.A. L.616 J.D. [Holloway,D.&B.]
Baer, Gary D., (AV) ....'38 '62 C&L.623 B.B.A., LL.B. [Baer,T.C.&C.]

Baer, Timberlake, Coulson & Cates, P.C., (AV)
Suite 300, 5901 North Western, 73118-1237 ⊙
Telephone: 405-842-7722 Fax: 405-848-9349
Email: james@baer-timerlake.com
Gary D. Baer; Donald J. Timberlake; James P. Cates; Donald J. Timberlake, Jr.; Scott E. Coulson (Resident, Tulsa Office);—Steven A. Heath (Resident, Tulsa Office); Matthew J. Hudspeth (Resident, Tulsa Office); Richard A. Chapman; Spencer B. Housley; Rosemary Clinton; James H. Thiessen.
General Civil Practice. Real Estate, Mortgage, Corporate Law and Creditor Bankruptcy Practice.
Tulsa, Oklahoma Office: 6846 South Canton, Suite 100, 74136. Telephone: 918-491-3100. Fax: 918-497-5927.
See Professional Biographies, OKLAHOMA CITY, OKLAHOMA

Baggett, Bryce A., (AV) ....'32 '56 C&L.623 A.B., LL.B. 5817 N.W. Grand Blvd.
Bailey, Burck, (AV) ....'34 '61 C.934 B.A. L.569 LL.B. [🄲 Fellers,S.B.B.&T.]
Bailey, Richard R., (AV) ....'33 '58 C&L.623 A.B., LL.B. [🄲 Bellingham,C.&L.]
Bailey, Robert C., (AV) '31 '57
C&L.623 A.B., LL.B. 2050 Oklahoma Tower, 210 Park Ave.‡
Baird, Jack ....'09 '37 C.947 L.374 LL.B. 11000 N. May Ave.‡
Baker, Dessa J. ....'80 '05 C.623 B.B.A. L.228 J.D. [🄰 Hall,E.H.G.G.&N.]
Baker, J. Randy, (AV) ....'55 '80 C.612 B.S. L.616 J.D. [🄰 Hiltgen&B.]
Baker, John R., III ....'52 '77 C&L.623 B.B.A., J.D. 3315 NW 63rd Street
Baker, Robert S., (AV) ....'37 '61 C&L.623 LL.B. [🄲 Day,E.P.&C.]
Baker, Valerie L., (BV) ....'70 '97 C.225 B.A. L.615 J.D. 200 N. Harvey
Balaban, Donald E. ....'32 '62 C.375 B.S. L.616 LL.B. Heritage Tr. Co., N.A.
Balentine, Jerry D., (BV) ....'40 '75 C.623 B.S.Phar. L.616 J.D. [Balentine&B.]
Balentine, Margie, (BV) ....'53 '78 C.16 B.A. L.192 J.D. [Balentine&B.]
Balentine & Balentine, P.C., (BV) .... 6303 N. Portland Ave.
Balkenbush, Joseph P., (AV) ....'54 '87 C.537 B.B.A. L.616 J.D. [Kirk&C.]
Ball, Larry G., (AV) ....'62 '87 C&L.623 B.B.A., J.D. [Hall,E.H.G.G.&N.]
Ball, Leonard Frank ....'39 '65 C&L.623 B.B.A., L.L.B. 707 N. E. 42
Ballard, Greg K. ....'61 '90 C.618 B.S. L.623 J.D. [Fenton,F.S.R.&M.]
Ballard, John B., II, (BV) ....'49 '76 C.612 B.S. L.616 J.D. 3015 N.W. 59th
Bane, Mary Elizabeth, (AV) ....'46 '72 C&L.623 B.A., J.D. 2017 Carey Place
Banks, T.R. ....'72 '00 C.612 B.S. L.616 J.D. [🄰 Burton&Assoc.] ⊙
Barber, James M. ....'61 '02 C.1147 B.S. L.615 J.D. [🄰 Haupt B.V.]
Barber, Lewis, Jr., (BV) ....'39 '74 C.623 B.B.A. L.615 J.D. [L.Barber]
Barber & Bartz, A Professional Corporation, (AV)
204 North Robinson, 25th Floor (⊙Tulsa)
Barber, Lewis, Law Office of, (BV) ....528 N.E. 23rd St., Ste 410
Barefoot, Bert B., Jr., (AV) .... '13 '37 C&L.623 B.A., LL.B. 6051 N. Brookline Ave.
Barghols, Steven L., (AV) ....'51 '76 C.623 B.A. L.846 J.D. [Gable&G.]
Barlow, Alan '67 '92 C&L.623 B.A., J.D.
Labor Rel. Consultant, Barlow & Assocs., Inc.
Barnard, Nathan E. .... '67 '92 C&L.612 B.S., J.D. 4323 NW 63rd St.
Barnes, Ben .... '— '94 C.1271 B.A. L.615 J.D. [🄲 Beeler,W.&W.]
Barnes, David R., (BV) ....'59 '92 C.114 B.A. L.616 J.D. 116 S. Walker Ave.
Barnes, E. Carole, (AV) ....'55 '80 C.623 B.A. L.846 J.D. [🄲 Phillips M.M.M.&M.]
Barnes, F. Smith, (AV) ....'38 '68 C&L.623 B.A., J.D. [F.S.Barnes]
Barnes, Robert N., (AV) ....'49 '74 C&L.623 B.A., J.D. [Barnes&L.]
Barnes, Sheila D. ....'77 '02 C.1147 B.A. L.623 J.D. [🄰 Walker,F.&F.]

Barnes, F. Smith, P.C., (AV)
1012 Northwest Grand Boulevard, 73118
Telephone: 405-848-1776 Fax: 405-840-1164
URL: http://www.fsmithbarnes.com
F. Smith Barnes.
Practice including Corporate, Real Estate, Estate Planning and Probate Law, Commercial and Residential Real Estate, Contracts.
See Professional Biographies, OKLAHOMA CITY, OKLAHOMA

Barnes & Lewis, P.C., (AV) .... 701 NW 63rd St.
Barnett, James R., (AV) ....'42 '67 C&L.623 B.A., J.D. [Kerr,I.R.&A.]
Barnett, Jerry ....'59 '85 C.613 B.A. L.623 J.D. Staff Atty., OK Water Res. Bd.
Baron, Robert D., (AV) ....'43 '68 C.352 B.A. L.623 J.D. [🄲 Coyle]
Barragree, Jack, (BV) ....'47 '73 C&L.623 B.B.A., J.D. [J.Barragree]
Barragree, Jack, P.C., (BV) .... 9004 N. May Ave.
Barrett, Gayle L., (AV) ....'47 '83 C.623 B.S. L.616 J.D. [Crowe&D.]
Barrett, Terry R., (AV) ....'44 '73 C&L.623 B.B.A., J.D. [McAfee&T.]
Barringer, Marilyn Dyda, (BV) ......'51 '85 C.999 B.S. L.616 J.D. 4901 Richmond Square
Barth, J. Edward, (AV) ....'37 '62 C.976 B.A. L.477 J.D. [Andrews D.]
Bartley, John W. ....'70 '95 C.612 B.S. L.623 J.D. 4334 N.W. Expressway, Ste. 174
Bartmess, Duchess, (BV) ....'39 '66 C.494 B.A. L.616 J.D. P.O. Box 12344
Bartz, Robert J., (AV) ....'55 '80 C&L.862 B.S., J.D. [Barber&B.] ⊙
Basey, Kelly Kee, (BV) ....'65 '95 C.612 B.S. L.623 J.D. Asst. Dist. Atty.
Basler, Stanley L. '48 '77 C.623 B.A. L.378 J.D.
(adm. in KS; not adm. in OK) 1540 Kingsgate Rd.‡
Bass, Kathryn .... '49 '84 C&L.623 B.A., J.D. Dep. Gen. Coun., State Tax Comm.
Bastow, Edward C. (Ned), Jr., (AV) '41 '83
C.476 A.B. L.623 J.D. Gen. Coun., State Regents for Higher Educ.
Batchelor, James D. "Dan", (AV) .... '36 '61 C.621 B.S. L.623 LL.B. [Batchelor&P.]
Batchelor, Leslie V., (AV) '66 '93 C.103 A.B. L.893 J.D.
Center for Econ. Develop. Law
Batchelor and Powers, Professional Corporation, (AV) ....301 N. Harvey
Bates, John Francis ....'50 '79 C.801 B.A. L.615 J.D. [🄰 Garrett] (⊙Muskogee, Tulsa)
Bates, Julie E., (AV) ....'57 '83 C.840 B.A. L.623 J.D. [Postic&B.]
Bates, Thomas A. ....'69 '94 C&L.616 B.A., J.D. Asst. Atty. Gen., OK Atty. Gen.'s Off.
Batson, Christine A. ....'67 '00 C&L.623 B.S., J.D. [Hester,S.H.&B.]
Batt, Niki S. ....'78 '04 C.612 B.A. L.623 J.D. [🄰 Johnson&H.]
Baulch, Trent A., (BV) ....'47 '75 C.621 B.S.Ed. L.616 J.D. Stream Energy, Inc.
Baum, John, (AV) ....'44 '70 C&L.623 B.A., J.D. 4901 Richmond Square, Suite 104
Bauman, Randy Alan ....'56 '82 C&L.623 B.B.A., J.D. Pub. Def. Off.
Baumann, Eugenia Tremaine, (BV) ......'49 '76 C.612 B.A. L.862 J.D. Asst. Pub. Def.
Baxter, Charles L. ....'26 '49 C.612 L.623 J.D. 11705 N. Victoria Dr.
Baxter, J. Lamont ....'12 '54 C.623 B.S. L.616 J.D. 2421 N.W. 46th St.‡

Bays, Ray, & Associates, (BV) '44 '79 C.612 B.S. L.616 J.D.
6444 South Western Avenue, 73139-1710
Telephone: 405-632-4494 Fax: 405-632-0273
Email: raybays@aol.com URL: http://www.lawyers.com/raybays
Associate: Chris D. Caldwell.
General Civil Trial Practice in State and Federal Courts. Mediation, Personal Injury, Probate, Commercial, Criminal, Insurance Plaintiff/Defense, Wrongful Death, Nursing Injury, Products Liability, Social Security and Workers Compensation Law. Divorce/Custody, Construction Injury, Agricultural Injury, Medical Malpractice.
See Professional Biographies, OKLAHOMA CITY, OKLAHOMA

Baysinger, Hugh A., (AV) ....'38 '66 C.976 B.E. L.623 J.D. [Pierce C.H.B.&G.]
Baze, William J. ....'72 '01 C&L.623 B.A., J.D. [🄰 Pierce C.H.B.&G.]
Beadle, Christine, (BV) .... '— '85 C&L.623 B.A., J.D. 2821 N. Robinson Ave.
Beadles, Richard T., Jr., (AV) ....'52 '77 C.612 B.S. L.616 J.D. [Biscone&B.]
Beal, David O., (BV) ....'46 '74 C&L.616 B.S., J.D. [Love,B.&N.]
Bean, David C. ....'45 '88 C.896 B.A. L.862 J.D. [🄰 Garrett] (⊙Muskogee, Tulsa)
Beaty, Susan Renee .... '69 '94 C&L.623 B.A., J.D. Jud. Staff Atty., OK Ct. of Civil App.
Beavin, Jerry V., (BV) ....'37 '73 C&L.616 B.S., J.D. 3721 Classen Blvd.
Bednar, Alexander L. '70 '03 C.880 B.A. L.623 J.D.
20 N Broadway Ave, 1800 Mid America Tower
Bednar, James D., (AV) .... '41 '75 C.612 B.S. L.623 J.D. Atty. Gen.
Beeler, Blake D. ....'75 '03 C&L.623 B.A., J.D. [🄰 Foliart,H.O.&B.]
Beeler, Jeff R., (AV) ....'49 '75 C&L.623 B.A., J.D. [Beeler,W.&W.]

Beeler, Walsh & Walsh P.L.L.C., (AV)
4508 N. Classen Boulevard, 73118
Telephone: 405-843-7600; 405-810-9339 Facsimile: 405-606-7050
URL: http://www.beelerwalsh.com
Jeff R. Beeler; Michael Allen Walsh; Regena McNeill Walsh;—James B. Buxton. Of Counsel: Ben Barnes.
Insurance Defense, Automobile Accidents, Personal Injury, Medical Malpractice, Products Liability, Nursing Home Negligence.
See Professional Biographies, OKLAHOMA CITY, OKLAHOMA

Beets, Timothy David ....'72 '99 C.612 B.A. L.616 J.D. [Beets&Y.]
Beets & Yanda, PLLC .... 2629 West I-44 Service Road, Suite 214
Behenna, Vicki Zemp, (AV) '59 '84 C.623 B.A. L.616 J.D.
Asst. U.S. Atty., Western Dist. of OK, U.S. Atty. Off.
Behrens, Verland E. (Buddy), (AV) '50 '75 C.612 B.A. L.616 J.D.
[Behrens,T.W.&C.]

Behrens, Taylor, Wheeler & Chamberlain, (AV)
Suite 400 6 Northeast 63rd, 73105-1014
Telephone: 405-848-1014 Fax: 405-848-3155
Verland E. (Buddy) Behrens; K. David Taylor; Cheri Marie Wheeler; Rick D. Chamberlain.
Civil Practice including Trials in all State and Federal Courts. Appellate, Oil and Gas, Environmental, Corporation Commission, Energy, Telecommunications, Public Utility, Corporate, Bankruptcy and Reorganization, Banking, Real Estate, Title Examination, Commercial, Administrative, Federal and State Taxation, Financing, Estate Planning and Probate, Arbitration, Employment, Securities, Personal Injury and Family Law.
See Professional Biographies, OKLAHOMA CITY, OKLAHOMA

Belanger, Michael ....'40 '65 C&L.623 B.B.A., J.D. [🄲 R.H.Mitchell&Assoc.]
Bell, Michael C. ....'66 '94 C.612 B.S. L.862 J.D. [🄰 McGivern,G.&C.]
Bell, Morris R., (BV) ....'50 '77 C.612 B.A. L.623 J.D. Legal Aid of Western Okla.
Bellingham, James H., (AV) ....'46 '71 C&L.623 B.A., J.D. [Bellingham,C.&L.]
Bellingham, Collins & Loyd, P.C., (AV) .... 210 Park Avenue
Bellmard, Kennis M., II ....'58 '90 C.612 b.s. L.623 j.d. [Andrews D.]
Belote, James A., (AV) ....'62 '88 C&L.623 B.B.A., J.D. [Stipe,H.L.U.E.&B.]
Benischek, Sandra D. ..... '69 '00 C.560 B.A. L.623 J.D. 2300 N. Lincoln Blvd., Ste. 109
Bennett, Mark H., (AV) ....'64 '90 C.210 B.A. L.615 J.D. [Conner&W.]
Benson, Harry J. ....'41 '71 C.623 B.A. L.146 J.D. 4201 NW 34th St.
Benson, John Martin ....'76 '01 C&L.623 B.A., J.D. [🄰 Gable&G.]
Benson, Sheila R. .... '76 '01 C.172 B.A. L.623 J.D. [🄰 Edmonds,C.H.G.R.&W.]
Bentwood, Venessa ....'70 '97 C.783 B.A. L.623 J.D. 245 Edgemere Ct.
Berger, Richard Fred, (BV) '45 '74
C.556 B.B.A. L.616 J.D. 1330 N. Classen Blvd., Ste. 109
Bergin, Christopher J., (BV) .... '55 '83 C.602 B.A. L.424 J.D. [C.J.Bergin]
Bergin, Christopher J., PC, (BV) .... 4312 N. Classen Blvd.
Berglan, Angela K. ....'73 '98 C&L.623 B.B.A., J.D. Asst. Atty. Gen.
Bergner, William J., (AV) ....'48 '81 C.585 B.S. L.623 J.D. [Nash,C.&K.]
Berman, James M. ....'53 '78 C&L.623 B.B.A., J.D. 8312 N.W. 105th Ter.
Bernard, Phyllis E. '54 '82 C.104 A.B. L.659 J.D.
(adm. in DC; not adm. in OK) Prof. of Law, Oklahoma City Univ. School of Law

Bernstein, David
(See Norman)

Berry, Charles N., Jr., (AV) ....'18 '48 C.976 A.B. L.309 J.D. 1401 Classen Dr.

Berry, Howard K., (AV) ... '06 '32 C.616 1923 N. Classen Blvd.
Berry, Howard K., III, (AV) ... '53 '78 C.800 B.A. L.809 J.D. [Berry&V.]
Berry, Howard K., Jr., (AV) ... '31 '58 C&L.623 B.A., LL.B. 1923 Classen Blvd
Berry, Jennifer L. ... '— '03 C.862 B.S.B.A. L.615 J.D. [Ⓐ Crowe&D.]
Berry, William A., (AV) ... '15 '40 C.612 B.A. L.623 LL.B. [Berry&M.]
Berry & McKee, (AV) ... 805 Northwest 63rd Street
Berry & Van Meter, (AV) ... 1923 North Classen Blvd.
Bertman, Eugene K. ... '72 '02 C.612 B.S. L.616 J.D. [Wallace&B.]
Best, Marilyn Dianne ... '47 '87 C.82 B.S. L.616 J.D. Dept. of Health
Bethea, Kenyatta R. ... '74 '00 C&L.623 B.A., J.D. [Ⓐ Holloway,D.&B.]
Beuch, C. Scott, (BV) ... '48 '75 C.612 B.S. L.616 J.D. 3801 N. Classen Blvd.
Beverage, Roger M. ... '45 '70 C&L.546 B.A., J.D. Pres., Okla. Bankers Assn.
Beveridge, Norwood P. '36 '63 C&L.309 A.B., LL.B.
(adm. in NY; not adm. in OK) Okla. City Univ. School of Law
Bewley, Lillie B. ... '11 '43 L.615 LL.B. 3313 N.W. 62nd St.‡
Bialick, Mark E., (AV) ... '56 '81 C&L.623 B.A., J.D. [Durbin,L.&B.]
Bickford, Michael A., (AV) ... '58 '83 C&L.623 B.B.A., J.D. [Ⓒ Fuller,T.P.&S.]
Bickford, Warren F., IV, (AV) ... '49 '74 C&L.623 B.B.A., J.D. [Fellers,S.B.B.&T.]
Billings, Michael D. ... '55 '98 C.619 B.S. L.615 J.D. 200 N. Harvey, Ste. 1300
Bingham, Park A. ... '23 '54 C.623 B.S. L.616 LL.B. 3101 N.W. 19th St.
Birch, Linda Jean ... '47 '95 C&L.623 B.S., J.D. U.S. Dist. Ct.
Bird, Jerri K. ... '73 '01 C.840 B.S. L.616 J.D. [Norman&E.]
Birdsong, Jimmy ... '25 '54 C&L.616 LL.B. Pres., Jimmy Birdsong, Inc.
Birdwell, Dwight W., (AV) ... '48 '76 C.619 B.A. L.623 J.D. [Birdwell]
Birdwell, Robt. L. ... '22 '49 C.616 B.A. L.623 LL.B. V.P., Morgan Stanley Dean Witter

Birdwell Law Office, (AV)
Suite 200 Investors Capital Building, 217 North Harvey, 73102
Telephone: 405-236-4675 Fax: 405-235-1209
Email: dwbirdwell@aol.com
Dwight W. Birdwell.
Indian Law, Oil and Gas, Probate, Real Estate Law, Personal Injury and Commercial Litigation.
References: Available upon request.
See Professional Biographies, OKLAHOMA CITY, OKLAHOMA

Biscone, Joseph C., II, (AV) ... '49 '75 C.264 B.A. L.616 J.D. [Biscone&B.]
Biscone & Biscone, Attorneys at Law, (AV) ... 105 N. Hudson, Ste. 100
Bisher, Rick W., (AV) ... '58 '87 C.798 B.S. L.862 J.D. [Boettcher,R.M.&B.]
Bishop, Kelly S., (BV) ... '65 '93 C.612 B.S. L.623 J.D. [Ⓐ Abel,M.S.M.&K.]
Bishop, Kim D. ... '60 '90 C.612 B.S. L.616 J.D. State House of Reps.
Bittel, Blake A. ... '71 '97 C.263 B.A. L.616 J.D. [Ⓐ Abowitz,T.&D.]
Bixler, C. Temple, (AV) ... '30 '56 C&L.623 B.A., LL.B. [Andrews D.]
Black, Jeffrey D., (BV) ... '64 '90 C.623 B.B.A. L.616 J.D. [Bonham&H.]
Black, Teresa Marie ... '48 '74 C&L.623 B.A., J.D. U.S. Atty. Off.
Black, Virgil C. ... '45 '77 C&L.616 B.S., J.D. Dist. J.
Blackburn, Mitchell D., (AV) ... '61 '87 C.1147 B.S. L.623 J.D. [Conner&W.]
Blackman, Melinda S. ... '71 '00 C.880 B.A. L.623 J.D. [Ⓐ McAfee&T.]
Blaik, Catherine S. ... '71 '99 C.822 B.S. L.623 J.D. [C.S.Blaik]
Blaik, William M., Jr. ... '69 '00 C.623 B.A. L.615 J.D. [Ⓒ Pritchett&S.]
Blaik, Catherine S., P.C. ... 625 N.W. 13th Street
Blake, T. Michael ... '— '96 C.228 A.B. L.623 J.D. [McAfee&T.]
Blakeburn, J. Robert, (AV) ... '53 '85 10325 Greenbriar Pl.
Blakley, Kenneth H., (AV) ... '59 '85 C&L.623 B.B.A., J.D. [Edinger&B.]
Blalock, Thomas J., (AV) ... '61 '86 C.612 B.S. L.623 J.D. [Commercial]
Blan-Byford, Linda J. ... '70 '03 C.612 B.S. L.616 J.D. [Ⓐ Elias,B.B.&N.]
Blaney, J. Kevin, (AV) ... '52 '77 C.532 B.A. L.616 J.D. [J.K.Blaney]

Blaney, J. Kevin, P.C., (AV)
2601 City Place, 204 North Robinson, P.O. Box 657, 73102
Telephone: 405-235-8445 Fax: 405-236-3410
Email: kblaney@kevinblaney.com URL: http://www.lawyers.com/jkevinblaney
J. Kevin Blaney.
Commercial Litigation, Banking Law, Real Estate.
See Professional Biographies, OKLAHOMA CITY, OKLAHOMA

Blank, Audrey D. ... '52 '00 C.237 B.A. L.615 J.D. [Williams,B.F.&B.]
Blankenship, G. T., (AV) ... '28 '54 C&L.623 B.A., LL.B. 6412 Avondale Dr.
Blankenship, Jap W., (AV) ... '35 '63 C&L.623 B.A., LL.B. [Ⓒ Fellers,S.B.B.&T.]
Blankinship, Melody Ruth ... '74 '01 C.1147 B.A. L.615 J.D. 4549 N.W. 36th St.
Blaschke, Michael J., (AV) ... '49 '78 C&L.623 B.A., J.D. [M.J.Blaschke]

Blaschke, Michael J., P.C., (AV)
825 Robinson Renaissance, 119 N. Robinson, 73102
Telephone: 405-319-0400 Fax: 405-319-0404
Email: mjblaschke@aol.com
Michael J. Blaschke.
Oil and Gas Litigation, Commercial Litigation, Oil and Gas Law.
See Professional Biographies, OKLAHOMA CITY, OKLAHOMA

Blasdel, W. Todd ... '77 '02 C.806 B.A. L.623 J.D. [Ⓐ Short W.M.&B.]
Bleakley, William P., (AV) ... '43 '72 C&L.623 B.A., J.D. [CenterForEducationLaw]
Blessington, G. Michael, (P.C.), (BV) ... '43 '75 C.623 B.A. L.616 J.D. 4111 N. Lincoln
Blevins, Gary L., (BV) ... '45 '73 C&L.623 B.A., J.D. 6701 Broadway Ext., Suite 240
Blevins, James B. ... '27 '57 C&L.616 B.A., J.D. Dist. J.‡
Blevins, James B., Jr., Attorney at Law '53 '79
C.612 B.S. L.616 J.D. 5609 N. Barnes Ave.
Bloom, Gary L. ... '37 '81 C.663 B.S. L.616 J.D. I.R.S.
Blue, Michael M., (AV) ... '62 '89 C.623 B.A. L.616 J.D. [Ⓐ Merritt&Assoc.]
Blumenthal, Jerome H., (BV) ... '28 '56 C&L.623 B.B.A., LL.B. 2232 S.W. 59th St.
Boatright, Peter L. ... '— '60 C&L.623 B.B.A., J.D. 4932 N.W. 31st. Street
Boaz, Stephen S., (AV) ... '48 '84 C.612 B.A. L.623 J.D. [Boaz&Assoc.]
Boaz & Associates, P.C., (AV) ... 3613 N.W. 56th Street, Suite 300
Bock, William H., (AV) ... '64 '90 C.614 B.S. L.615 J.D. [W.H.Bock]

Bock, William H., Inc., (AV) BR
6402 N. Santa Fe Avenue, Suite A, 73116
Telephone: 405-848-5400 Fax: 405-848-5479
Email: bocklaw@sbcglobal.net URL: http://www.lawyers.com/bocklaw
William H. Bock. Associate: Michelle Greene.
Criminal Defense in State and Federal Court, Personal Injury, Trial Practice, Driving While Intoxicated, Drug Crimes, Juvenile Law, Military Court Marshal.
See Professional Biographies, OKLAHOMA CITY, OKLAHOMA

Bocock, Joseph H., (AV) ... '54 '78 C.197 A.B. L.623 J.D. [McAfee&T.]
Boesch, Jason '71 '03 C.612 M.B.A. L.615 J.D.
Credit Union Manager, OKRET Credit Union
Boettcher, Ryan, Martin & Bisher, (AV)
4323 NW 63rd, Suite 110 (ⓞPonca City, Tulsa)
Boghetich, Antonio '54 '78 C.802 B.B.A. L.623 J.D.
Secy. & Treas., Omar B. Milligan Enterprises, Inc.
Bohanon, Philip L., (BV) ... '66 '91 C.378 B.S.B.A. L.623 J.D. [P.L.Bohanon]
Bohanon, Richard L. ... '35 '60 C.197 A.B. L.623 LL.B. Bkrptcy. J.
Bohanon, Philip L., P.C., (BV) ... 120 N. Robinson Ave.
Bollinger, Gerald A., (AV) ... '50 '76 C&L.508 B.A., J.D. [Kunzman&B.]
Bomhoff, Margaret A., (AV) ... '62 '87 C&L.623 B.A., J.D. [Fellers,S.B.B.&T.]
Bomhoff, Timothy J., (AV) ... '62 '88 C.612 B.S. L.623 J.D. [Ryan,W.&C.]
Bond, Gregory W., (BV) ... '52 '82 C.622 B.S. L.616 J.D. 4528 N. Clasen Blvd.
Bond, Jay R., (AV) ... '32 '59 C&L.623 B.A., LL.B. 903 N.W. 13th Street
Bond, John M., (AV) ... '47 '75 C.623 B.S. L.616 J.D. 4301 N.W. 63rd St.
Bonham, J. Ted, (BV) ... '36 '67 C.612 B.S. L.623 J.D. [Bonham&H.]

Bonham & Howard, (BV)
An Association of Professional Associates
Not A Partnership
Land Mark Towers West, Suite 200, 3555 NW 58th Street, 73112 ⊙
Telephone: 405-943-6650 Facsimile: 405-943-6655
URL: http://www.bonhamandhoward.com
J. Ted Bonham; James W. Swank, Jr.; Jeffrey D. Black; Wesley E. Combs. Of Counsel: David L. Thomas.
General, Civil and Trial Practice in Federal Courts and all State Courts, Insurance Defense, Property and Casualty, Workers' Compensation, Products Liability, Surety, Civil Rights Defense, Regulatory and Administrative Law, Corporate, Estate Planning, Probate.
Tulsa, Oklahoma Office: 15 W. 6th Street, 74119. Telephone: 918-744-7440. Fax: 918-744-9358.
See Professional Biographies, OKLAHOMA CITY, OKLAHOMA

Bonner, Lewis Mark, (AV) ... '61 '92 C&L.623 B.A., J.D. 127 N.W. 10th St.
Bonner, Mark ... '61 '92 C&L.623 B.A., J.D. [Norman&E.]
Bonsall, Bradley P. ... '64 '93 C&L.623 B.B.A., J.D. 3555 N.W. 58th St., Ste. 130

Booker, Steven R., P.C., Law Office of
(See Wichita Falls, Texas)

Bookout, Linda K. '51 '76
C.614 B.B.A. L.623 J.D. Gen. Coun., Tinker Federal Credit Union
Books, Richard K., (AV) ... '52 '77 C.663 B.A. L.623 J.D. [Elias,B.B.&N.]
Boone, Charlene Louise ... '56 '98 C.1147 B.A. L.623 J.D. P.O. Box 75525
Boone, William W., (AV) ... '52 '78 C.623 B.B.A. L.616 J.D. [Helm&B.]
Booth, Clay P., (BV) ... '59 '86 C.612 B.S. L.616 J.D. [Ⓐ Kline,K.E.&B.]
Borden, William Lee, Jr. ... '49 '77 C&L.623 B.A., J.D. U.S. Atty.'s Off.
Boren, Bart A., (AV) ... '54 '80 C.802 B.B.A. L.623 J.D. [Williams,B.&Assoc.]
Boren, Rebecca P. ... '50 '92 C.623 B.S.N. L.615 J.D. 6502 N. Western Ave.
Boren, Robert G., (BV) ... '46 '83 C.1147 B.S. L.616 J.D. 6502 N. Western Ave.
Bosler, Christy ... '61 '91 C.623 B.A. L.615 J.D. 9309 May Park Dr.
Bost, Merrilee J., (BV) ... '51 '78 C.862 B.A. L.616 J.D. 6204 S. Shore Dr.
Bost, Robert K. ... '49 '74 C.602 A.B. L.623 J.D. 515 N.W. 14th St.★
Bostick, Blake M., (CV) ... '53 '90 C.814 B.S. L.615 J.D. 2805 Lakeside Dr.
Boston, William C., Jr., (AV) ... '34 '61 C.612 B.S. L.623 LL.B. 1701 Camden Way
Bottom, Monty B., (AV) ... '57 '82 C.622 B.S. L.602 J.D. [Foliart,H.O.&B.]
Boudreau, Daniel J. ... '47 '76 C.93 B.A. L.862 J.D. Supm. Ct. Jus.
Boughton, Scott D., (AV) '54 '79
C.612 B.S. L.623 J.D. Asst. Atty. Gen., OK Atty. Gen. Off.
Boul, John L. ... '41 '90 C.134 A.B. L.616 J.D. 2103 North Walker Avenue
Bova, Gary ... '52 '81 C.556 B.A. L.615 J.D. [Mancillas]
Bowen, Ashley A. ... '80 '05 C.616 B.S. L.615 J.D. [Ⓐ Hall,E.H.G.G.&N.]
Bower, David H., (BV) ... '67 '93 C.1147 B.S. L.616 J.D. [Bower&B.]
Bower, Walter M., P.C., (AV) ... '37 '61 C&L.623 B.A., LL.B. [Bower&B.]
Bower & Bower, (AV) ... 3721 North Classen Boulevard
Bowers, Brock C., (BV) ... '69 '94 C&L.623 B.A., J.D. [Ⓐ Hiltgen&B.]
Bowlby, William C., (AV) ... '41 '72 C.1147 B.S. L.623 J.D. [W.C.Bowlby]

Bowlby, William C., A Professional Corporation, (AV)
Suite 105, Atrium Building, 3601 North Classen Boulevard, 73118
Telephone: 405-528-8783 Fax: 405-528-1625
Email: bowlbylaw@aol.com URL: http://www.bowlbylaw.com
William C. Bowlby.
General Civil Litigation in State and Federal Courts, Divorce, Custody, Bankruptcy, Mechanics Liens, Debtor and Creditor, Landlord and Tenant, Personal Injury.
See Professional Biographies, OKLAHOMA CITY, OKLAHOMA

Bowling, Michael W. ... '— '03 C.228 B.A. L.475 J.D. [Ⓐ Crowe&D.]
Bowman, Alfred Lee ... '40 '69 C&L.623 B.A., J.D. 7013 N. Roff Ave.
Bowman, Byrne A., (AV) ... '05 '27 C.623 L.192 LL.B. 1141 N.W. 63rd St.‡
Box, Dennis R., (AV) ... '53 '78 C.612 B.S. L.616 J.D. [Williams,B.F.&B.]
Box, Dwain D. ... '16 '40 L.192 LL.B. Ret. Ct. of App. J.
Boxeur, Dennis S., (AV) ... '51 '78 C.749 B.S. L.623 J.D. [Nash,C.&K.]
Bozarth, Lisa Dianne '70 '96 C.622 B.A. L.615 J.D.
Chf. Legal Offr. & Gen. Coun., Gulfport Energy Corp.
Bracklein, Steven E. ... '60 '93 C.612 B.S. L.616 J.D. Law Clk., U.S. Dist. Ct.
Bradford, Peter B., (AV) ... '36 '61 C.293 B.A. L.862 J.D. [Ⓒ Conner&W.]
Bradford, Robert A., (BV) ... '48 '83 C&L.623 B.A., J.D. Asst. U.S. Atty.
Brady, Michael H., (P.C.), (BV) ... '50 '75 C.621 B.A. L.616 J.D. [Brady,S.&F.]
Brady, Schaulat & Falsetti, Professional Association, (AV) ... 719 N. Shartel
Bragg, Susan W. ... '49 '80 C.942 B.A. L.623 J.D. 321 Park Ave., Ste. 321
Branch, Douglas A., (AV) ... '57 '82 C&L.623 B.B.A., J.D. [Ⓒ Phillips M.M.M.&M.]
Brandenburg, Adam C. ... '72 '05 C.623 B.B.A. L.616 J.D. [Ⓐ Haupt B.V.]
Brandon, Jack L. '30 '54 C&L.846 B.A., LL.B.
(adm. in TX; not adm. in OK) Kerr-McGee Ctr.‡
Brandt, Charles A., (AV) ... '43 '84 C&L.616 B.S., J.D. [Pierce C.H.B.&G.]
Branham, Seth Shannon ... '72 '98 C.862 B.A. L.623 J.D. Atty. Gen. Off.
Branscum, David A., (AV) ... '60 '86 C.747 B.A. L.623 J.D. [Foliart,H.O.&B.]
Braun, Charles G., (AV) ... '53 '78 C&L.616 B.A., J.D. [Hornbeek,K.V.&B.]
Brawner, Jacque J., (AV) ... '53 '77 C.612 B.S. L.616 J.D. [Ⓒ McAfee&T.]
Brawner, Larry C., (P.C.), (AV) ... '44 '73 C.618 B.A. L.623 J.D. [Brawner]
Brawner Law Firm, A Professional Corporation, (AV)
301 Northwest 63rd Street, Suite 225
Breathwit, John J., (AV) ... '53 '81 C.420 B.S. L.623 J.D. [Breathwit&P.]
Breathwit & Patton, P.C., (AV) ... 101 Park Avenue, Suite 460
Brennan, Joseph T. '31 '59 C.321 B.A. L.374 J.D.
(adm. in MO; not adm. in OK) 3426 S. Lakeside Dr., Ste. 9
Breshears, Randall A., (AV) ... '54 '79 C.612 B.A. L.862 J.D. [Monnet,H.B.T.&E.]
Brett, William T., (BV) '55 '82
C.623 B.B.A. L.616 J.D. 4801 North Classen Boulevard, Suite 155
Brewer, John Nathan, Law Office of, (BV) '44 '74
C&L.623 B.A., J.D. 3033 N.W. 63rd Street, Suite 150
Brewer, Kathryn Boyle ... '67 '96 C&L.612 B.S., J.D. Asst. Dist. Atty.
Brewer, Michael W., (AV) ... '60 '86 C&L.623 B.S.M.E., J.D. [Hiltgen&B.]
Brickell, Bradley D., (AV) ... '51 '76 C.612 B.S. L.623 J.D. [Brickell&Assoc.]
Brickell & Associates, P.L.C., (AV) ... 105 North Hudson
Bridges, Annita M. ... '51 '76 C.329 B.A. L.276 J.D. [R.H.,a.C.A.L.Alexander,Jr.]
Briggs, M. Courtney, (BV) ... '60 '91 C.918 B.A. L.623 J.D. [Derrick&B.]
Bright, Mark Edward ... '69 '97 C.1111 B.A. L.623 J.D. [Bright]
Bright, Robert C., (AV) ... '43 '68 C&L.623 B.A., J.D. [R.C.Bright] ⊙

Bright Law Firm
204 N. Robinson, Suite 2625, 73102
Telephone: 405-232-8001: 405-210-7483 Fax: 405-232-3641
Email: mbright@earthlink.net URL: http://www.brightlawfirm.com
Mark Edward Bright.
Criminal Defense, Drug Crimes, DUI, DWI, Domestic Violence, White Collar Crime, Larseny, Traffic Violations, Misdemeanors, Felonies, Assault, Assault and Battery, Family Law, Personal Injury, Bankruptcy, Environmental Law.
See Professional Biographies, OKLAHOMA CITY, OKLAHOMA

Bright, Robert C., A Professional Corporation, Law Offices of, (AV) 211 North Robinson, Suite 1900 (⊙Santa Fe, NM)
Brink, Randy C., (BV) .... '56 '82 C.1349 B.A. L.616 J.D. [Eulberg]
Britton, Charles Ronald .... '39 '82 C&L.208 B.A., J.D. 3133 N.W. 63rd St.
Britton, James E., (AV) .... '46 '74 C.612 B.S. L.623 J.D. [Britton,R.&G.]

Britton, Ramsey and Gray, P.C., (AV)
700 Corporate Tower, 101 North Robinson Street, 73102
Telephone: 405-239-2393 Fax: 405-232-5135
Email: firm@lawbrg.com URL: http://www.lawbrg.com
James E. Britton; Rodney C. Ramsey; Michael D. Gray;—Andrew D. Schwartz. Of Counsel: W. Samuel Dykeman; Christa B. Richardson.
General Civil Litigation in State and Federal Courts. Corporate, Insurance Law, Commercial Law, Bankruptcy, Banking, Real Estate, Corporate and Business Law, Estate Planning, Trusts and Probate, Copyrights and Trademarks, Business Litigation, Employment and Health Care.
Representative Clients: BancFirst; Union Bank and Trust Company; Community Action Agency of Oklahoma City and Oklahoma/Canadian, Inc.; NationsBank; Poteau State Bank; Trigen Energy Corporation; Mitsubishi Acceptance Corporation; Total Waste Systems, Inc.; City of Ardmore and City of Oklahoma City.
See Professional Biographies, OKLAHOMA CITY, OKLAHOMA

Brockett, B. J., (AV) .... '30 '62 C&L.623 B.A., LL.B. [Brockett&J.]
Brockett & Jackson, P.C., (AV) .... 719 N. Shartel
Brockhaus, Marc A. .... '68 '98 C&L.623 B.S., J.D. [Dunlap,C.&R.] (See Pat. Sect.)
Brogden, William H., (BV) .... '40 '66 C.622 B.A. L.616 J.D. 10400 N. Hassett Rd.
Brokaw, Kenneth A., (AV) .... '51 '83 C&L.623 B.A., J.D. [Day,E.P.&C.]
Brooks, Allan Arthur, III, (AV) .... '60 '85 C.612 B.S. L.623 J.D. [Fagin,B.B.T.&K.]
Brooks, Ann, (BV) .... '62 '94 C.1147 B.A. L.623 J.D. [G.L.Brooks&Assoc.]
Brooks, Carson M. .... '76 '01 C.612 B.S. L.615 J.D. [Haupt B.V.]
Brooks, Deborah Lynn .... '67 '94 C&L.623 B.A., J.D. 5500 N. Western
Brooks, Gary L., (AV) .... '50 '75 C&L.623 B.A., J.D. [G.L.Brooks&Assoc.]
Brooks, Rex D., (BV) .... '37 '67 C&L.623 B.B.A., LL.B. 1900 N.W. 23rd St.

Brooks, Gary L., and Associates, P.L.L.C., (AV)
7100 North Classen Boulevard, Suite 300, 73116-7101
Telephone: 405-840-1066 Fax: 405-843-8446
Email: GLB@medlaws.com URL: http://www.medlaws.com
Gary L. Brooks; Ann Brooks.
Plaintiffs Medical Malpractice, Products Liability, Personal Injury, Catastrophic Injury, Automobile Accidents, Brain Injuries, State and Federal Courts.
See Professional Biographies, OKLAHOMA CITY, OKLAHOMA

Brooks-Jimenez, Michael, (BV) '70 '95 C.612 B.A. L.623 J.D. 228 Robert S. Kerr, Ste. 940
Brower, D.E., Jr., (BV) .... '48 '75 C.618 B.S. L.616 J.D. 501 N.W. 13th
Brown, Benjamin Charles, (AV) .... '62 '93 C.560 B.A. L.615 J.D. Asst. Pub. Def.
Brown, Craig E. .... '70 '98 C.69 B.A. L.615 J.D. [Brown&R.]
Brown, Dean, (AV) .... '27 '57 C.623 B.S. L.616 J.D. [Dimick,G.B.&S.]
Brown, Dorothy J. Lindsey .... '47 '81 C.623 B.A. L.615 J.D. Asst. Atty. Gen.
Brown, Elizabeth Kemp, (AV) .... '57 '83 C&L.623 B.A., J.D. [Phillips M.M.M.&M.]
Brown, H. Blanton, (AV) .... '54 '79 C.622 B.S. L.623 J.D. [H.B.Brown&Assoc.]
Brown, Harry E., Jr., (AV) .... '30 '59 C.612 B.S. L.623 J.D. 2335 N.W. 12th St.
Brown, Heidi L. ....'58 '83 C.860 B.A. L.94 J.D. V.P. & Mng. Coun., LSB Indus., Inc.
Brown, J. Scott, (AV) .... '38 '67 C.870 B.S. L.623 J.D. [Fagin,B.B.T.&K.] (⊙Norman)‡
Brown, Jane A. Johanningsmeier, (BV) .... '59 '85 C.249 B.S. L.616 J.D. Asst. Dist. Atty.
Brown, Jerry D., (BV) .... '68 '96 C.623 B.A. L.615 J.D. [Pappas,B.&Assoc.]
Brown, L. Vance, (AV) .... '59 '84 C&L.623 B.S., J.D. [Elias,B.B.&N.]
Brown, Linda Prine .... '45 '89 C.612 B.S. L.616 J.D. [Pierce C.H.B.&G.]
Brown, Michael H. .... '79 '05 C.802 B.A. L.846 J.D. [Fellers,S.B.B.&T.]
Brown, Michael L. ....'63 '88 C&L.623 B.B.A., J.D. Sr. Tax Atty., State Tax Comm.
Brown, Michael N., (AV) .... '54 '83 C.346 B.A. L.623 J.D. [Brown]
Brown, Owen S. .... '42 '66 C.861 B.B.A. L.846 LL.B. Pres., Atlas Investment Corp.
Brown, Ronald L., (AV) .... '58 '83 C&L.623 B.A., J.D. [Burnett&G.]
Brown, Sidney D., (AV) .... '47 '79 C.614 B.A. L.615 J.D. [Morgan&Assoc.]
Brown Law Firm, (AV) .... 8112 N.W. 129th Pl.
Brown & Roberts, P.L.L.C. .... 1012 N.W. Grand Boulevard, Suite A
Browne, James B. .... '35 '59 C.862 B.A. L.623 J.D. 2335 N.W. 12th St.
Browne, John R. .... '14 '39 C&L.623 A.B., LL.B. 4029 Neptune St.‡
Bruce, Deborah J., (BV) .... '45 '88 C.1147 B.A.Ed. L.616 J.D. Dir. Jud. Educ.
Bruehl, Jamie K. .... '76 '02 C&L.623 B.B.A., J.D. [Rife&W.]
Brummitt, Daniel T. .... '49 '79 C&L.623 B.S., J.D. Asst. Mun. Coun.
Bruno, Tsinena, (BV) .... '60 '97 C.616 B.S. L.615 J.D. [Miller D.]
Brust, Jerry L. .... '41 '01 C&L.623 B.A., J.D. [Crowe&D.]
Bryan, Jerry E., (AV) .... '59 '85 C.679 B.A. L.616 J.D. [Bryan&R.]
Bryan & Robinson, Inc., (AV) .... 3715 N. Classen Blvd.
Bryant, G. David, (AV) .... '49 '75 C.623 B.A. L.616 J.D. [Kline,K.E.&B.]
Bryant, Gary A., (AV) .... '51 '77 C.623 B.B.A. L.846 J.D. [Mock,S.W.E.R.&B.]
Buchanan, Brandon L. .... '74 '00 C&L.623 B.A., J.D. [McAfee&T.]
Buchanan, Vickie J. .... '73 '99 C.619 B.S. L.623 J.D. [Phillips M.M.M.&M.]
Buck, Robert R. .... '28 '56 C.612 B.S. L.623 J.D. [McGrew,B.&Assoc.]
Buckelew, R. L., (BV) '40 '68 C.614 B.A. L.616 J.D. 5500 N. Western Plaza, 1 Western Plaza
Buckles, Joseph A., II, (BV) .... '51 '76 C.747 B.A. L.616 J.D. [J.A.Buckles,II]
Buckles, Joseph A., II, PC .... 6725 NE 63rd Street
Buergler, Whitney E. .... '76 '01 C.612 B.A. L.623 J.D. [Foliart,H.O.&B.]
Buettner, Kenneth L. ...... '50 '75 C.840 B.A. L.802 J.D. Civil App. Ct. J., Civil App. Ct.
Bugg, Steven W., (AV) .... '56 '82 C&L.623 B.B.A., J.D. [McAfee&T.]
Bullard, Donald A., (AV) .... '59 '84 C.622 B.S. L.623 J.D. [Bullard&H.]
Bullard, William J., (AV) .... '48 '75 C&L.623 B.B.A., J.D. [Williams,B.F.&B.]

Bullard & Hoehner, P.C., (AV)
312 N.W. 13th Street, P.O. Box 780, 73101-0780
Telephone: 405-604-5000 Facsimile: 405-604-5005
Email: mail@bullard-hoehner.com URL: http://www.lawyers.com/bullard-hoehner
Donald A. Bullard; Daniel J. Hoehner;—Robert C. Simpson, Jr.; Elizabeth Honeywell Gray; Michael T. Egan. Of Counsel: Lee Endicott.
Workers Compensation Defense, Litigation, Insurance Coverage, Environmental, Products Liability.
See Professional Biographies, OKLAHOMA CITY, OKLAHOMA

Bumgarner, Randy, (BV) .... '58 '84 C.337 B.A. L.616 J.D. 435 N. Walker Ave., Ste. 102
Bump, Kim Sook '74 '01 C&L.623 B.S., J.D. Staff Atty., Oklahoma Indian Legal Svc., Inc.
Bunn, Jimmy D., Jr., (BV) '64 '91 C.612 B.S. L.36 J.D. Asst. Gen. Coun., OK St. Bur. of Investigation
Bunting, Larry A., (BV) ..... '48 '86 C.623 B.S. L.615 J.D. 3721 North Classen Boulevard
Buratti, Barbara K., (BV) .... '51 '87 C.831 B.A. L.623 J.D. [Wilson,C.&A.]
Burch, Derek K., (AV) .... '61 '89 C.612 B.S. L.615 J.D. [Burch&G.]
Burch, Jonathan W., (AV) .... '40 '69 C.309 B.A. L.623 J.D. [J.W.Burch]

Burch & George, A Professional Corporation, (AV)
1500 City Place Building, 204 North Robinson, 73102
Telephone: 405-239-7711 Toll Free: 1-877-239-7711 Fax: 405-239-7795
Email: derekburch@burch-george.com URL: http://www.lawyers.com/burchgeorge
Derek K. Burch; Kelly A. George. Of Counsel: Kenneth G. Cole. Associate: DeeAnn L. Germany.
General Civil Trial Practice in all State and Federal Courts, Personal Injury, Products Liability, Medical Malpractice and Insurance Litigation.
See Professional Biographies, OKLAHOMA CITY, OKLAHOMA

Burch, Jonathan W., P.C., (AV) .... 825 N.W. 58th
Burchett, Jennifer M. .... '77 '03 C.623 B.A. L.862 J.D. Legis. Liaison
Burdick, Ben L., (AV) .... '19 '48 C.623 A.B. L.976 LL.B. 20 N. Broadway
Burdick, Glen M. .... '37 '66 C&L.623 B.S., J.D. [Dunlap,C.&R.] (See Pat. Sect.)
Burget, Mark E., (AV) .... '54 '79 C&L.623 B.B.A., J.D. [McAfee&T.]
Burget, Melissa Shelton .... '73 '99 C&L.623 B.A., J.D. [Shelton]
Burke, Bob, (AV) .... '48 '80 C.623 B.A. L.616 J.D. 5101 N. Classen Blvd.
Burke, John L., (AV) '23 '48 C.810 B.B.A. L.802 LL.B. (adm. in TX; not adm. in OK) Admin. Law J.
Burkett, William R., (AV) .... '25 '49 C.999 L.623 LL.B. Municipal Counselor
Burkett-O'Hern, Linda, Law Office of .... '45 '81 C.623 B.A. L.615 J.D. P.O. Box 891737
Burnett, George F. '55 '87 C.612 B.S. L.616 J.D. Asst. Dist. Atty., 7th Jud. Dist. Atty's Off.
Burnett, Kevin W., (AV) .... '60 '85 C.612 B.S. L.862 J.D. [Burnett&G.]
Burnett, LeAnne, (AV) .... '49 '89 C.802 B.A. L.623 J.D. [Crowe&D.]

Burnett & Gelnar, PLLC, (AV)
13838 Quail Pointe Drive, Suite C, 73134-1020
Mailing Address: P.O. Box 21387, Oklahoma City, OK 73156-1387
Telephone: 405-302-0400 Fax: 405-302-0411
Email: info@burnettgelnar.com URL: http://www.burnettgelnar.com
Kevin W. Burnett; Stephen C. Gelnar;—Ronald L. Brown; Dawn M. Kissinger-Christel.
Business Law, Commercial Transactions, Banking, Real Estate, Taxation, Trusts and Estates, Estate Planning, Mergers and Acquisitions, Charitable and Non-Profit Organizations.
See Professional Biographies, OKLAHOMA CITY, OKLAHOMA

Burns, Dennis R. .... '61 '89 C.1147 B.S. L.616 J.D. Acrs Inc.
Burnsed, Carrie L. .... '77 '02 C.259 B.S. L.615 J.D. [N.R.Giles]
Burris, Michael E., (AV) .... '48 '74 C.623 B.A. L.616 J.D. 229 S. Eagle Ln.
Burton, Brandon J., (AV) .... '68 '97 C.612 B.S. L.616 J.D. [Burton&Assoc.] ⊙
Burton, Catherine M., (AV) .... '64 '90 C&L.623 B.A., J.D. 500 N. Walker Ave., Ste. B
Burton, James L. .... '32 '59 C.623 A.B. L.477 J.D. 805 N.W. 63rd St.

Burton & Associates, P.C., (AV)
308 NW 13th, Suite 100, P.O. Box 2666, 73103 ⊙
Telephone: 405-232-0555; 800-257-5533 Fax: 405-232-1849
Email: okc@burtonlaw.com URL: http://www.burtonlaw.com
Lew Gravitt (1954-2005); Brandon J. Burton;—T.R. Banks. Of Counsel: Gregory R. Rasnake; Steve Davis; William A. Robinson.
Workers Compensation, Wrongful Termination, Personal Injury, Automobile Accidents, Bankruptcy, Social Security.
Tulsa Office: 1861 East 15th Street, 74104. Telephone: 918-747-4600. Fax: 918-744-6300. Email: Tulsa@burtonlaw.com.
Walters, Office: 122 North Broadway, 73572. Telephone: 580-875-2200. Fax: 580-875-2202. Email: Walters@burtonlaw.com.
See Professional Biographies, OKLAHOMA CITY, OKLAHOMA

Busey, Phil G., (AV) ...... '52 '78 C&L.616 B.A., J.D. 13208 North MacArthur Boulevard
Bush, Gary M., (AV) .... '43 '68 C&L.623 B.S., J.D. [Fagin,B.B.T.&K.]
Bush, Jack G., (AV) .... '— '59 C.1147 B.A. L.616 J.D. [Kirk&C.]
Bussert, Ronald E. '55 '92 C.612 B.S. L.616 J.D. V.P. & Asst. Gen. Coun., Boatmen's First Natl. Bk. of Okla.
Bussett, Curtis W. .... '72 '99 C.1142 B.A. L.615 J.D. [Bussett&W.]
Bussett, Rachel L. .... '— '03 C.612 B.S. L.615 J.D. [Rainey,R.R.&B.]
Bussett & Winters P.C. .... 5100 N. Brookline Ave., Suite 825
Bussey, Helen Susan Diane .... '49 '85 C&L.623 B.A., J.D. OK Merit Protec. Comm.
Butkin, Robert A., (AV) .... '52 '79 C.976 B.A. L.659 J.D. Asst. Atty. Gen.
Butler, R. Kevin, (BV) .... '65 '91 C.612 B.S. L.615 J.D. 4700 N.W. 23rd St., Ste. 112
Butts, Benjamin J., (AV) .... '58 '83 C.902 B.S. L.623 LL.B. [Short W.M.&B.]
Butts, J. Crawford .... '20 '53 C.623 B.S. L.616 J.D. 5701 N. Virginia Ave.
Buxton, James B. .... '75 '01 C.500 B.A. L.616 J.D. [Beeler,W.&W.]
Byars, Karen E. .... '64 '90 C.800 P.S.C. L.862 J.D. 6608 N. Western Ave., Ste. 616
Byers, Jeffrey M. .... '71 '98 C&L.623 B.S., J.D. 228 Robert S. Kerr
Byrd, Charles J., (BV) .... '44 '72 C&L.623 B.B.A., J.D. 3555 NW 58th St.
Byrd, Dan R., (CV) '58 '88 C.623 B.B.A. L.615 J.D. Sr. Coun., Law & Govt. Affrs., American Fidelity Corp.
Byrne, Justin '75 '00 C.862 B.A. L.846 J.D. (adm. in TX; not adm. in OK) Assoc. Staff Coun., Kerr-McGee Corp.
Byrom, Chris Scott .... '64 '89 C.612 B.S. L.623 J.D. 3134 N.W. 23rd St.
Cail, Paula Fuhrman, (AV) .... '51 '78 C.623 B.A. L.616 J.D. [Brawner]
Cain, Bernest H., Jr. .... '49 '89 C.613 B.A. L.623 J.D. State Senator
Cain, Marty G., (BV) .... '65 '91 C&L.623 B.A., J.D. 300 Northeast First Street
Cain, Monty Lynn, (BV) .... '— '95 C.623 B.S. L.615 J.D. [Foshee&Y.]
Cain, Timothy D., (AV) .... '61 '86 C.623 B.B.A. [Wilson,C.&A.]
Caldwell, Chris D., (BV) .... '53 '77 C.622 B.A. L.616 J.D. [R.Bays&Assoc.]
Caldwell, M. Dan, (AV) .... '49 '77 C&L.623 B.B.A., J.D. [Caldwell&R.]
Caldwell, Scott .... '72 '00 C.622 B.M.E. L.623 J.D. [Cathcart&D.]

Caldwell & Russell, P.C., (AV)
201 Robert S. Kerr, Suite 800, 73102
Telephone: 405-232-1456 Fax: 405-232-1450
M. Dan Caldwell; Kristi Bynum Russell;—Angela D. Thompson.
Workers Compensation Defense.
See Professional Biographies, OKLAHOMA CITY, OKLAHOMA

Callahan, Jennifer H., (AV) .... '68 '96 C.1074 B.S. L.623 J.D. [McAfee&T.]
Callahan, Kelley C., (AV) .... '52 '80 C.165 B.A. L.623 J.D. [Day,E.P.&C.]
Callaway, Charles C., Jr., (AV) .... '56 '81 C&L.623 B.A., J.D. [Fellers,S.B.B.&T.]
Calloway, James Andrew, (AV) '56 '81 C.619 B.A. L.623 J.D. 1901 N. Lincoln Boulevard
Calvert, Carey C., (CV) .... '68 '93 C.612 B.S. L.623 J.D. [Pierce C.H.B.&G.]
Calvert, Horace K. .... '15 '39 C&L.623 B.A., LL.B. Pres., The Calvert Co.
Calvert, Randall K., (AV) .... '58 '90 C.612 B.S. L.616 J.D. [Calvert]

Calvert Law Firm, (AV)
1041 N.W. Grand Boulevard, 73118
Telephone: 405-848-5000 Fax: 405-848-5052
URL: http://www.calvertlaw.com

(This Listing Continued)

Calvert Law Firm (Continued)

Randall K. Calvert; W. Brett Willis; Monica J. Hoenshell; John W. Swinford, Jr.
Business & Complex Litigation, Mergers & Acquisitions, Taxation, Real Estate, Debtor, Creditor & Insolvency; Securities Arbitration.

See Professional Biographies, OKLAHOMA CITY, OKLAHOMA

Calvey, Kevin J., (BV) ....'66 '94 C.1105 B.A. L.276 J.D. 3909 S.E. 29th St.
Camp, George, (BV) .... '26 '50 C&L.623 J.D. 2200 N.W. 50
Campbell, Allen, (AV) .... '— '83 C.623 B.B.A. L.616 J.D. [Kirk&C.]
Campbell, Catherine L., (BV) ...'65 '91 C.174 B.A. L.623 J.D. [Ⓐ Phillips M.M.M.&M.]
Campbell, Odell D. ....'66 '95 C.1335 B.A. L.615 J.D. [Ⓐ Morgan&M.]
Campbell, Robert J., Jr., (AV) ....'52 '80 C.623 B.A. L.616 J.D. [Phillips M.M.M.&M.]
Campbell, William H., (BV) ....'49 '82 C&L.616 B.A., J.D. 925 N.W. 6th Street
Campney, A. Michelle, (BV) .... '63 '88 C&L.623 B.B.A., J.D. [Ⓒ McKinney&S.]
Canada, Denise D., (BV) ....'56 '96 C&L.623 B.A., J.D. [Foliart,H.O.&B.]
Canon, William L., (BV) '57 '88
C.623 B.B.A. L.616 J.D. 4101 Perimeter Center Dr., Ste. 115
Cantrell, Charles L. '48 '72 C.846 L.69 J.D.
(adm. in TX; not adm. in OK) Prof. of Law, Okla. City Univ.
Cantrell, Robert M. .... '43 '68 L.615 LL.B. 1414 S.W. 89th St.
Caporal, John P. .... '26 '49 L.623 1100 Classen Dr.
Capra, Toni Himes .... '56 '96 C.614 B.S. L.615 J.D. [Ⓐ Haupt B.V.]
Caraher, Tarquin J. '71 '00 C&L.02 B.Sc., LL.B.
(adm. in AB; not adm. in OK) Devon Energy Corporation (⊙Calgary, AB)
Carel, Robert Douglas ....'67 '94 C.1147 B.A. L.623 J.D. [D.Carel]
Carel, Dough, PC ....10326 Greenbriar Pkwy.
Carey, Susan ....'77 '03 C.612 B.A. L.623 J.D. [Ⓐ Kline,K.E.&B.]
Cargill, Stephen C., (AV) '51 '80
C&L.623 B.A., J.D. Atty., Dominion Exploration Production, Inc.
Carlson, David W. .... '70 '00 C&L.623 B.B.A., J.D. [Ⓐ Crowe&D.]
Carlson, Robert J. ....'69 '02 C&L.862 B.S.B.A., J.D. [Ⓐ Day,E.P.&C.]
Carman, Caroleen '54 '92 C.623 M.A. L.615 J.D.
Asst. Gen. Coun., State Dept. of Mines
Carnell, Joseph L., (AV) ....'51 '80 C.663 B.A. L.616 J.D. 3535 N.W. 58th
Carola, Inc. ....3101 Classen Blvd., Ste. 201
Carrier, Edward B., Jr., (AV) ....'37 '69 C.614 B.S. L.616 J.D. [Carrier,E.]
Carrier, Kymala B., (AV) .... '57 '98 C&L.623 B.A., J.D. [Ⓐ McAfee&T.]
Carrier, Ed, P.C., (AV) .... P.O. Box 890960
Carroll, Elizabeth W. .... '80 '05 C&L.623 B.A., J.D. [Ⓐ Doerner,S.D.&A.] ⊙
Carroll, Patricia L. .... '26 '56 L.615 J.D. 3632 NW 51st Street
Carroll, Stanley F., (AV) .... '54 '83 C&L.623 B.A., J.D. [S.F.Carroll]

Carroll, Stanley F., P.C., (AV)
1900 N.W. Expressway, Suite 1300, 73118
Telephone: 405-848-2255 Fax: 405-840-4701
Email: stan4law@aol.com URL: http://www.stan4law.com
Stanley F. Carroll.
General Civil Litigation in State and Federal Courts, Contracts, Commercial Real Estate, Landlord and Tenant, Real Estate Law, Construction Law, Business Law, Family Law, Divorce, Child Custody, Wills, Probate, Trusts and Estates.

See Professional Biographies, OKLAHOMA CITY, OKLAHOMA

Carson, Joel L., (AV) ....'37 '61 C&L.623 B.A., LL.B. [Carson,M.S.&A.&Assoc.]
Carson, Mueller, Sparks & Abernathy, (AV) .... Suite 510, 3555 Northwest 58th Street
Carter, Douglas Alan .... '50 '87 C.929 B.A. L.623 J.D. Soc. Sec. Admn.
Carter, H. A. Bud, (AV) ....'31 '62 C.612 B.S. L.616 LL.B. 2548 N.W. Expwy.
Carter, H.A., III, (BV) ....'59 '92 C.612 B.S. L.616 J.D. 2548 N.W. Expressway, Ste. 104
Carter, Jeanne M. ....'18 '67 C&L.615 A.B., J.D. 3835 N.W. 63rd St.‡
Carter, Jeremy Z. .... '77 '03 C.612 B.S. L.623 J.D. [Ⓐ Hiltgen&B.]
Carter, Mark Edward ....'66 '03 C.999 B.S. L.615 J.D. [Marshall&C.]
Carter, Michael D., (AV) ....'57 '82 C&L.623 B.A., J.D. [Ⓒ Phillips M.M.M.&M.]
Carter, Robert D. .... '34 '60 C&L.623 B.B.A., LL.B. Fed. Aviation Admn.
Carter, Tammy T. '58 '85
C.1042 B.A. L.329 J.D. Assoc. Gen. Coun., Okla. City Pub. Sch.
Carver, Harry .... '24 '50 C&L.623 A.B., LL.B. Hall Production Co.
Carver, Sherri Ann .... '65 '91 C.616 B.A. L.615 J.D. [Ⓐ Eddy&J.]
Casey, Jodi Sue ....'— '97 C.616 B.A. L.615 J.D. [Ⓐ Collins,Z.&W.]
Casey, Katherine L. .... '68 '94 C.616 B.S. L.623 J.D. [Ⓐ T.W.Hosty]
Casey, Orben J. ....'17 '58 C.623 B.S. L.616 J.D. 14901 N. Pennsylvania Ave.‡
Cashion, Charles L., (AV) ....'42 '68 C&L.623 B.S., J.D. 3121 Harriet St.
Cashion, Edw. H. ....'24 '50 C&L.45 LL.B. 3409 N.W. 45th St.‡
Cashner, Josie Carolyn '— '01 C.619 B.S. L.623 J.D.
4200 Perimeter Center Dr., Ste. 222
Caskey, Joseph K. '20 '48 C.1125 L.45 J.D.
(adm. in AR; not adm. in OK) Pres., Joseph K. Caskey, Inc.‡
Cason, Len, (AV) .... '47 '72 C&L.623 B.A., J.D. [Hartzog C.C.&N.]
Cassil, Larry G., (AV) .... '32 '64 C.612 B.S. L.616 J.D. 3315 NW 63rd St.
Cassil, Larry G., Jr., (BV) ....'63 '88 C.880 B.A. L.178 J.D. [Ⓐ Pierce C.H.B.&G.]
Castleberry, Elizabeth Riley, (AV) .... '58 '83 C.612 B.S. L.623 J.D. [Miller D.]
Castleberry, Patrick M., (AV) .... '57 '83 C.612 B.S. L.623 J.D. [Ⓒ Kline,K.E.&B.]
Castor, William Franklin .... '— '94 C.612 B.S. L.623 J.D. Off. of Chf. Coun.
Castro, Gregory A., (AV) .... '61 '86 C.612 B.S. L.623 J.D. [Fellers,S.B.B.&T.]
Caswell, Susan P. ....'54 '79 C.134 B.S. L.615 J.D. 321 Park Ave., Ste. 814
Cates, James P., (AV) ....'64 '89 C&L.623 B.A., J.D. [Baer,T.C.&C.]
Cathcart, William R., (AV) ....'45 '71 C.695 B.A. L.616 J.D. [Cathcart&D.]

Cathcart & Dooley, A Professional Corporation, (AV)
Cornett Building, 2807 Classen Boulevard, 73106
Telephone: 405-524-1110 Fax: 405-524-4143
William R. Cathcart; Cary D. Dooley;—Virginia Cathcart Holleman; Scott Caldwell; Laurie J. Miller; James S. Dilbeck.
Insurance Defense, Insurance and Subrogation, Property Insurance, Fire and Casualty and Insurance Law. Negligence Trial Practice.

See Professional Biographies, OKLAHOMA CITY, OKLAHOMA

Catlett, Stanley B., Jr. .... '28 '58 C&L.623 B.A., LL.B. 3225 Canyon Rd.
Catron, Gary W., (AV) ....'44 '76 C.473 B.A. L.309 Ph.D. [Ⓒ McAfee&T.]
Cauthron, Robin J. .... '50 '77 C&L.623 B.A., J.D. Chf. U.S. Dist. J.
Cave, Christine M. ....'72 '03 C.908 B.A. L.623 J.D. [Ⓐ Abowitz,T.&D.]
Caves, Matthew A. '74 '01
C.612 B.S. L.623 J.D. Env. Atty., Oklahoma Dept. of Env. Quality
Cazes, Dale B. ....'72 '98 C.260 B.S.B.A. L.615 J.D. [Ⓐ Phillips M.M.M.&M.]
Cecil, Gordon B., (AV) .... '41 '66 C&L.862 B.A., J.D. U.S. Atty. Off.
Cejda, Kirk Joseph, (BV) ....'60 '87 C&L.623 B.B.A., J.D. 770 N.E. 63rd
Center For Education Law, The, Inc., (AV) .... 900 North Broadway, Suite 300
Chaffin, Ryan R. ....'74 '02 C&L.623 B.A., J.D. [Ⓐ Fenton,F.S.R.&M.]
Chamberlain, Rick D., (AV) .... '54 '85 C&L.862 B.S., J.D. [Behrens,T.W.&C.]
Chambers, James R. .... '54 '90 C.309 Ed.M. L.623 J.D. Asst. Dist. Atty.
Champlin, Richard H., (AV) .... '35 '61 C&L.623 B.B.A., LL.B. 5005 Lincoln Blvd.

Chancellor, Angela D. .... '65 '90 C&L.623 B.B.A., J.D. [Dobbs&M.]
Chandler, James C., (AV) ....'36 '63 C.612 B.S. L.623 LL.B. [Lytle S.&C.]
Chandler, Roy W. ....'35 '61 C&L.616 B.S., J.D. Peters & Chandler CPA's
Chaney, James M., (AV) ....'— '80 C.616 B.A. L.623 J.D. [Kirk&C.]
Chansolme, Beverly W. ....'48 '79 C.612 B.A. L.616 J.D. 3208 N.W. 19th
Chapel, Charles S. ....'41 '69 C.763 B.S. L.862 J.D. Ct. of Crim. App. J.
Chapel, Jennifer Marie ....'— '94 C.378 B.S. L.623 J.D. Co. Pub. Def. Off.
Chapman, C. Hayden, (AV) '50 '89
C&L.623 B.A., J.D. Gen. Coun., First Amer. Title Ins. Co.
Chapman, Richard A. .... '65 '98 C.801 B.A. L.862 J.D. [Ⓐ Baer,T.C.&C.]
Chapman, Stephanie P. .... '76 '02 C&L.623 B.A., J.D. [Ⓐ McAfee&T.]
Chase, Melissa M. ....'69 '00 C.1175 B.A. L.1339 J.D. [Ⓐ McKinney&S.]
Chastain, Charles C. ....'35 '67 C.623 B.S. L.615 J.D. 2904 N. Dittmer
Cheatham, Charles E., (AV) ....'49 '79 C.612 B.A. L.309 J.D. [Cheatham&W.]
Cheatham & Womble, P.C., (AV) .... 1222 N.W. 19th St.
Cheek, David A., (AV) ....'48 '74 C.859 B.A. L.623 J.D. [McKinney&S.]
Cheek, John D., (AV) ....'20 '43 C&L.623 B.A., LL.B. [Cheek]
Cheek, Tim N., (AV) ....'58 '85 C.941 B.A. L.623 J.D. [Cheek]

Cheek Law Firm, The, (AV) BB
(Formerly Cheek, Cheek & Cheek)
Law Center Building, 311 North Harvey, 73102
Telephone: 405-272-0621 Fax: 405-232-1707 Email: triddles@cheeklaw.com
Email: tcheek@cheeklaw.com
James C. Cheek (1885-1960); Alex Cheek (1916-1996); William C. Cheek (1923-1997); Tim N. Cheek; John D. Cheek. Associates: Darin Todd Riddles; Scott M. Inman.
General Civil Practice in all State and Federal Courts. Personal Injury Defense, Insurance Defense, Products Liability Defense, Automobile Injury Defense, Motor Carrier Liability, Medical Malpractice Defense, Corporation, Aircraft Titles, Insurance and Probate Law, Labor and Employment Law (Management), Commercial Litigation. Trials in all Courts.
Representative Insurance Clients: American Insurance Co.; Protective Insurance Co.

See Professional Biographies, OKLAHOMA CITY, OKLAHOMA

Chiaf, Joey, (BV) .... '57 '83 C.612 B.S. L.616 J.D. [Chiaf]
Chiaf Law Offices, P.C., (BV) ....1717 North Broadway
Childers, Adam W. .... '73 '00 C&L.623 B.A., J.D. [Ⓐ Crowe&D.]
Childers, Nancy L. '45 '85 C.621 B.A. L.616 J.D.
State Alcoh. Beverage Laws Enforce. Comm.
Chiles, Robert K., (AV) ....'30 '57 C&L.623 B.B.A., LL.B. 11609 Heritage Sq. Rd.‡
Chilton, Gary S., (AV) ....'54 '81 C&L.378 B.S., J.D. [Holladay,C.&D.]
Christensen, Cathy M. ....'57 '87 C.612 B.S. L.616 J.D. 2932 N.W. 122nd St., Ste. 10
Christensen, D. Wade, (AV) ....'54 '83 C.612 B.S. L.862 J.D. [Day,E.P.&C.]
Christensen, J. Clay, (AV) ....'61 '86 C.612 B.S. L.623 J.D. [Day,E.P.&C.]
Christian, William N., (AV) ....'22 '49 C&L.623 LL.B. 101 Park Avenue
Christiansen, Mark D., (AV) ....'55 '80 C&L.623 B.A., J.D. [Crowe&D.]
Christopher, Angela R. '68 '98 C&L.623 B.A., J.D.
Oklahoma Farm Bur. & Aff. Comps.
Christopher, Kristi Lee ....'69 '94 C&L.623 J.D. U.S. Pub. Def.
Chubbuck, Gary Mitchell, (AV) '48 '75
C.682 B.S. L.623 J.D. 211 N. Robinson Ave., Ste. 800 N.
Chubbuck, June L., (AV) '51 '76
C.612 B.S. L.623 J.D. 211 N. Robinson Ave., Ste. 800 N.
Clark, Carolyn, (AV) ....'55 '79 C.623 B.A. L.802 J.D. 1701 Bedford Drive
Clark, Jack G. (Chip), Jr., (AV) ....'45 '69 C&L.623 B.A., J.D. [Clark,S.W.&P.]
Clark, Robert Alden, Jr. ...... '64 '97 C&L.623 B.A., J.D. 6801 S. Western Ave., Ste. 203
Clark, Steven E., (AV) ....'50 '75 C&L.623 B.A., J.D. [Clark&M.]

Clark & Mitchell, P.C., (AV)
101 Park Avenue, Suite 210, 73102
Telephone: 405-235-8488 Fax: 405-235-7979
Email: clark@clarkmitchell.com URL: http://www.lawyers.com/clarkmitchell
Steven E. Clark; Heather Johnson Mitchell.
Trials State and Federal Courts. Medical Malpractice, Nursing Home Malpractice, Legal Malpractice, Automobile Accidents, Personal Injury, Professional Liability.

See Professional Biographies, OKLAHOMA CITY, OKLAHOMA

Clark, Stakem, Wood & Patten, P.C., (AV)
Suite 400, 101 Park Avenue, 73102 ⊙
Telephone: 405-232-4271 Fax: 405-232-4275
URL: http://www.cswp-law.com
Jack G. (Chip) Clark, Jr.; Ronald E. Stakem; Betty Garrett Wood; Rebecca J. Patten (Resident, Norman Office).
Business Planning, Commercial, Corporate, Federal and State Taxation, School Law, Real Estate Administration, Telecommunications Regulation, Civil Rights, Domestic Relations, Employment, Officers and Directors Liability, Securities Litigation, Torts, Estate Planning, Probate, Elder Law, Arbitration and Mediation, Trials and Appeals in all State and Federal Courts.
Norman, Oklahoma Office: 103 West Boyd, Suite K, 73069. Telephone: 405-321-0610. Fax: 405-321-7571.

See Professional Biographies, OKLAHOMA CITY, OKLAHOMA

Clarke, Edward J. ....'71 '00 L.623 J.D. [Ⓒ Walker&W.]
Clarke, Stephen O. .... '67 '97 C&L.623 B.A., J.D. [Ⓒ Walker&W.]
Clarke, Thomas J. .... '63 '99 C.1147 B.A. L.623 J.D. 931 N.W. 7th, Suite 207
Claro, John Anthony, (AV) .... '41 '65 C&L.623 B.A., J.D. 4027 Spyglass Road
Claro, Joseph A., (BV) ....'43 '71 C&L.623 B.B.A., J.D. 2900 Wilton Lane
Clay, Peggy L., (AV) .... '51 '89 C.862 B.S. L.623 J.D. 20 N. Broadway, Ste. 1800
Clayborne, Mark A., (BV) ....'62 '95 C.511 B.A. L.574 J.D. 200 North Harvey
Clemens, Robert Lyle, (AV) .... '57 '85 C.101 B.A. L.616 J.D. [Clemens&Assoc.]
Clemens & Associates, (AV) .... 128 W. Hefner
Clifton, Cara Lousia Epps .... '62 '88 C.921 B.S. L.616 J.D. Dept. of Pub. Safety
Clifton, Lowell E. ....'23 '49 C.612 L.623 LL.B. P.O. Box 76476‡
Cline, Heather M., (AV) .... '66 '92 C.502 B.A. L.615 J.D. [Cline]
Cline, Jeffrey L., (BV) ....'66 '92 C.623 B.B.A. L.615 J.D. [Cline]
Cline Law Offices, (AV) .... 1403 Classen Drive
Clinton, Rosemary ....'48 '89 C&L.862 B.F.A., J.D. [Ⓐ Baer,T.C.&C.]
Cloud, William M. ....'33 '60 C.623 B.B.A. L.862 LL.B. 12008 Quail Creek Rd.
Coates, John J., III '64 '90 C.800 B.S. L.623 J.D.
Exec. V.P. & Gen. Coun., Coates Field Service, Inc.
Coates, John J., Jr. ....'39 '64 C&L.623 B.B.A., LL.B. Pres., Coates Field Service, Inc.
Coats, Andrew M., (AV) ....'35 '63 C&L.623 B.A., J.D. [Crowe&D.]
Cochran, Thomas R. .... '24 '51 C.197 B.A. L.813 LL.B. Kerr-McGee Ctr.
Cocon, A. Terry, Attorney at Law ....'50 '01 C.623 B.A. L.616 J.D. P.O. Box 2492
Codding, Charles A., (AV) '39 '70
C.612 B.S.E.E. L.616 J.D. [Dunlap,C.&R.] (See Pat. Sect.)
Cody, J. Derrill ....'38 '64 C.618 B.A. L.623 J.D. [Ⓒ McKinney&S.]
Coe, Allen B. ....'63 '88 C.902 B.S. L.623 J.D. Jud. Law Clk., U.S. Bkrptcy. Ct.
Coe, Jeffrey Stuart ....'70 '96 C&L.623 B.A., J.D. 2200 N Classen, Ste 710
Coffee, V. Glenn, (AV) ..'67 '93 C.619 B.A. L.623 J.D. [Ⓒ Phillips M.M.M.&M.]
Coffey, John M., (AV) ....'41 '66 C&L.623 B.B.A., J.D. [White,C.&F.]
Coffey, Kevin M., (AV) ....'60 '86 C.612 B.S. L.623 J.D. 435 N. Walker Avenue
Coffman, Mary Jane ....'64 '00 C.623 B.A. L.893 J.D. Midland Mortgage Co.

Cohen, Abe ....'15 '43 C.616 B.S. L.623 LL.B. 2533 N.W. 51st St.
Cohenour, Cynthia, (AV) ....'52 '87 C&L.623 B.S., J.D. [Nash,C.&K.]
Cohlmia, Lana, (BV) ....'59 '85 C.612 B.S. L.616 J.D. 4312 N. Classen Blvd.
Coit, Stephen G., (BV) ....'51 '76 C.612 B.S. L.623 J.D. Gen. Coun.
Coker, Michael G., (AV) ....'50 '75 C&L.623 B.A., J.D. [Oldfield,C.&G.]
Colbert, Julia Markovna ....'52 '00 L.615 J.D. 1109 N. Francis
Coldiron, Brent D., Attorney At Law, (BV) '51 '76
C&L.623 B.B.A., J.D. 1800 E. Memorial Rd., Ste. 106
Coldiron, Mark D., (AV) ....'45 '72 C&L.623 B.S.C.E., J.D. [Ryan,W.&C.]

Cole, C. Craig, & Associates, (AV) '44 '72 C.1147 B.S. L.616 J.D.
317 Northwest Twelfth Street, 73103-3704
Telephone: 405-232-8700 Fax: 405-232-1655 URL: http://www.lawyers.com/colelaw
Email: thefirm@ccc-a.com URL: http://www.ccc-a.com
Antitrust, Arbitration, Aviation, Banking Law, Bankruptcy, Civil Liability, Commercial Law, Commercial Collections and Litigation, Commercial Insurance Defense, Consumer Finance, Corporate Law, Covenants Not to Compete, Creditors Rights, Dealership Law, Debtor and Creditor, Defense Litigation, Ecclesiastical Law, Employment Law, Environmental Law, Federal Civil, Franchise Law, Health Care Law, Land Use Litigation, Mediation, Oil and Gas, Partnerships, Personal Injury Defense, Personal Property, Probate, Products Liability Defense, Real Estate, Subrogation, Wage and Hour Law, Workers Compensation Defense, Wrongful Termination Defense.
See Professional Biographies, OKLAHOMA CITY, OKLAHOMA

Cole, David H., (AV) ....'47 '73 C&L.623 B.B.A., J.D. [Edmonds,C.H.G.R.&W.]
Cole, Holly, (BV) ....'66 '92 C&L.623 B.A., J.D. 210 Park Avenue
Cole, Kecia Khae ....'68 '94 C.612 B.S. L.616 J.D. [Robertson&W.]
Cole, Kenneth G., (AV) ....'61 '86 C.622 B.A. L.623 J.D. [Burch&G.]
Cole, Kimberly F. '57 '90 C.612 B.S. L.378 J.D.
Assoc. Corp. Coun., Dobson Communications Corp.
Cole, Regan Wade ....'65 '91 C.622 B.S. L.616 J.D. Liberty Mutual Ins. Grp.
Cole, Steven P., (AV) ....'60 '85 C&L.623 B.B.A., J.D. [McAfee&T.]
Coleman, Cece Lynn Goodrich ....'62 '88 C.1012 B.S. L.615 J.D. Asst. Atty. Gen.
Coleman, Myron S. ....'51 '81 C&L.623 B.A., J.D. Co. Health Dept.
Coleman, Stephen A., (BV) ....'48 '74 C.880 B.A. L.616 J.D. [S.A.Coleman]
Coleman, W. Chris, (AV) ....'56 '82 C&L.623 B.A., J.D. [McAfee&T.]
Coleman, Stephen A., P.C., (BV) ....3904 E. Reno
Coley, Mickey C., (BV) ....'42 '68 C&L.616 B.S., J.D. 3501 NW 36th St.
Collier, Ronald V., (BV) ....'38 '69 C.622 B.A. L.616 J.D. 917 N. Robinson
Collins, Christopher J., (AV) ....'53 '80 C.1147 B.A. L.623 J.D. [Collins,Z.&W.]
Collins, James V., (BV) ....'48 '73 C&L.623 B.B.A., J.D. Pres., Combined Res. Corp.
Collins, William F., III, (AV) ....'48 '73 C&L.623 B.B.A., J.D. [Bellingham,C.&L.]

Collins, Zorn & Wagner, P.C., (AV)
429 N.E. 50th, Second Floor, 73105-1815
Telephone: 405-524-2070 1-800-916-0676 Facsimile: 405-524-2078
Email: czwg@czwglaw.com
Christopher J. Collins; Daniel K. Zorn; Jason C. Wagner;—Robert Ray Jones, Jr.; Andrew A. Artus; Stephen L. Geries; Stephen R. Palmer; Jodi Sue Casey; Timothy E. Lurtz.
Trial Practice State and Federal Courts. Appellate Practice. Civil Rights, Employment Law. Insurance Defense, Manufacturers' Products Liability, Workers Compensation.
See Professional Biographies, OKLAHOMA CITY, OKLAHOMA

Collinsworth, John L., (BV) '41 '74
C.1147 B.A. L.616 J.D. 5101 N. Classen Blvd., Ste. 504
Collum, Hugh H. ....'21 '60 C.612 A.B. L.623 LL.B. Asst. Atty. Gen.
Collum, Leslie Anne, (BV) ....'57 '81 C.616 B.A. L.623 J.D. Asst. Atty. Gen.
Combs, Lori, (CV) ....'62 '89 C&L.623 B.A., J.D. 4400 Woodland Dr.
Combs, Melvin, Jr., (BV) ....'41 '73 C.1147 B.S. L.616 J.D. P.O. Box 18782
Combs, Roland V., III ....'50 '85 C.1362 B.S. L.623 J.D. [Firm of R.V.Combs,III&Assoc.]
Combs, Wesley E. ....'54 '88 C.619 B.A. L.45 J.D. [Bonham&H.]
Combs, Roland V., III, & Associates, PLC, The Law Firm of .... 1316 N.W. 10th St.
Comingdeer, Ronald, (AV) ....'51 '79 C.82 B.S. L.862 J.D. 6011 N. Robinson Ave.

Commercial Law Group, P.C., (AV)
2725 Oklahoma Tower, 210 Park Avenue, 73102-5643
Telephone: 405-232-3001 Fax: 405-232-5553
Email: postmaster@clgroup.org
Thomas J. Blalock; C. Ray Lees; Shannon T. Self;—Michael D. Meleen; Kendra D. Parsons. Of Counsel: Theresa B. Lewis.
Banking, Bankruptcy, Complex Commercial Transactions, Corporate Law, Energy, Entrepreneur Representation, Equine Law, Mergers and Acquisitions, Oil and Gas, Real Estate, Venture Capital, Complex Commercial Credit Workouts and Reorganization.
See Professional Biographies, OKLAHOMA CITY, OKLAHOMA

Condren, John Christopher, (AV) ....'52 '76 C.378 B.A. L.623 J.D. [Pierce C.H.B.&G.]
Conger, J. William, (AV) ....'45 '71 C&L.623 B.A., J.D. [Hartzog C.C.&N.]
Conison, Nancy Jo '56 '81 C&L.494 B.A., J.D.
(adm. in IL; not adm. in OK) Dir. Legal Research, Oklahoma City Univ. Sch. of Law
Connally, Dan Michael ....'52 '88 C.663 B.A. L.623 J.D. Asst. Jud. Asst., Ct. of Crim. App.
Connell, Keith, (BV) ....'62 '87 C&L.623 B.B.A., J.D. 1601 N.W. Expy., Ste. 1515
Conner, Claudia Cole ....'54 '81 C.623 B.A. L.616 J.D. Commrs. of Land Off.
Conner, Randy Patrick, (BV) ....'59 '88 C.623 B.B.A. L.616 J.D. [R.P.Conner]
Conner, Scot A., (AV) ....'57 '86 C&L.623 B.B.A., J.D. [Vaught&C.]
Conner, Randy P., P.C., (BV) ....2601 N.W. Expressway, Ste. 601

Conner & Winters, LLP, (AV)
One Leadership Square, 211 North Robinson, Suite 1700, 73102-7101
Telephone: 405-272-5711 Facsimile: 405-232-2695
Email: postmaster@cwlaw.com URL: http://www.cwlaw.com
Irwin H. Steinhorn; John W. Funk; Jared D. Giddens; Kiran A. Phansalkar; Victor F. Albert; Mitchell D. Blackburn; Mark H. Bennett; Bryan J. Wells; Laura L. McCasland Holbrook. Associates: John E. Gatliff II; J. Dillon Curran; William M. ("Billy") Lewis. Of Counsel: Peter B. Bradford; Shelia M. Darling.
General Civil Practice. Trial and Appeals of Civil Cases in all State and Federal Courts. Administrative Proceedings, Alternative Dispute Resolution, Bankruptcy and Reorganization, Construction, Corporate and Securities, Employee Benefits, Employment and Labor Relations, Energy, Environmental, Estate Planning, Trust and Probate, Federal and State Taxation, Federal White Collar Criminal Defense, Financial Services and Banking, Governmental Affairs, Insurance and Risk Management, International, Litigation and Antitrust, Products Liability, Propane, Real Estate, Tax Exempt Organizations and Charitable Foundations and Workers' Compensation.
Tulsa, Oklahoma Office: 3700 First Place Tower, 15 East 5th Street, 74103-4344. Telephone: 918-586-5711. Facsimile: 918-586-8982.
Fayetteville, Arkansas Office: 100 West Center Street, Suite 200, 72701-6081. Telephone: 479-582-5711. Facsimile: 479-587-1426.
Santa Fe, New Mexico Office: 303 Paseo De Peralta, 87501. Telephone: 505-983-6497. Facsimile: 505-983-6478.
Jackson, Wyoming Office: 155 East Pearl Street, Suite 200, P.O. Box 4099, 83001-4099. Telephone: 307-733-2547. Fax: 307-733-3947.
Washington, DC Office: 1627 I Street, N.W., Suite 900, 20006. Telephone: 202-887-5711. Fax: 202-887-6999.
Houston, Texas Office: 1000 Louisiana, Suite 1301, 77002-5005. Telephone: 713-355-5711. Fax: 713-651-3929.
See Professional Biographies, OKLAHOMA CITY, OKLAHOMA

Conrad, Kyle D., (BV) '58 '83 C&L.862 B.S.B.A., J.D.
V.P. & Asst. Corp. Coun., Reserve Natl. Ins. Co.
Conrad, Susan Dennehy ....'59 '87 C.862 B.S. L.623 J.D. Corp. Comr., OK Corp. Comm.
Consumer Legal Counseling Center, P.C., (AV) .... 1400 North Shartel Avenue, Suite 100
Conway, Vaughn B. ....'56 '87 C.469 B.A. L.616 J.D. 3140 W. Britton Rd., Ste. 200
Conyers, Howard W. ....'49 '75 C.347 B.S. L.623 J.D. Admin. Dir. of the Cts.
Conyers, Susan Witt, (AV) ....'61 '88 C.614 B.B.A. L.623 J.D. 1915 N. Stiles
Cook, Darren R. ....'71 '97 C&L.623 B.A., J.D. [Helms&U.]
Cook, David T., (AV) '42 '70
C.623 B.A. L.616 J.D. 1001 Northwest 63rd Street, Suite 290
Cook, Gayle Freeman, (AV) ....'49 '75 C.623 B .S. L.616 J.D. [Monnet,H.B.T.&E.]
Cook, Lee W. ....'21 '49 C.612 B.S. L.623 LL.B. 5908 N.W. 81st‡
Cook, Rodney L., (AV) ....'57 '83 C&L.623 B.S., J.D. [Jennings C.H.&T.]
Cook, Rodney L., (AV) ....'— '74 C&L.623 B.B.A., J.D. [Rainey,R.R.&B.]
Cook, Russell, (AV) ....'52 '82 C.623 B.A. L.616 J.D. [Hartzog C.C.&N.]
Cook, Thomas R., (BV) ....'48 '74 C.1147 B.A.E. L.616 J.D. 625 N.W. 13th Street
Cook, Timothy Lee ....'59 '00 C.234 B.A. L.615 J.D. [T.L.Cook]
Cook, Vinson L. ....'28 '73 C&L.616 B.I.A., J.D. 1544 S.W. 31st St.
Cook, William C., (AV) ....'69 '98 C.1147 B.S. L.615 J.D. [W.C.Cook]
Cook, William R., II, (AV) ....'52 '78 C.623 B.B.A. L.846 J.D. [W.R.Cook,II]
Cook, Timothy L., Law Office of .... 5613 S. Pennsylvania
Cook, William C., P.C., (AV) ....1001 N.W. 63rd Street, Suite 290

Cook, William R., II, PLLC, (AV)
1900 N.W. Expressway Suite 1350, 73118-1805
Telephone: 405-858-1920 Facsimile: 405-858-1921
Email: williamcook@wrciilaw.com URL: http://www.wrcooklaw.com
William R. Cook II.
Federal and State Income Taxation, Estate and Gift Taxation Law, Tax Controversies and Tax Litigation. Probate, Estate Planning, Trust Law, Wills.
See Professional Biographies, OKLAHOMA CITY, OKLAHOMA

Cooke, Laura J. ....'51 '85 C&L.623 B.B.A., J.D. P.O. Box 436‡
Cooley, Tenal S., III, (AV) ....'50 '77 C.131 B.A. L.616 J.D. [Looney,N.&J.]
Cooley, Tenal S., Jr. ....'23 '56 C.612 B.A. L.616 LL.B. P.O. Box 25125
Coon, Audrey T. ....'50 '01 C.623 B.A. L.616 J.D. 2901 Classen Blvd.
Cooper, B. J., Law Offices of, (AV) '35 '59
C&L.623 B.B.A., LL.B. 124 Northwest Tenth Street
Cooper, Donald L., (AV) ....'32 '59 C.612 B.S. L.623 LL.B. 3713 N.W. 70th‡
Cooper, H. C., (BV) ....'38 '64 C&L.616 B.A., J.D. 105 N. Hudson Ave.
Cooper, Jeffrey M., (BV) ....'67 '94 C.623 B.B.A. L.616 J.D. [Homsey,C.H.&Assoc.]
Cooper, R. Thompson, (BV) ....'68 '93 C&L.623 B.A., J.D. [Pignato&C.]
Cooper, Teresa Lee, Attorney At Law, (AV) '48 '77
C.478 B.A. L.623 J.D. 12817 Plum Hollow Dr.

Cooper, McKinney & Woosley, PLLP
(See Tulsa)

Coppedge, Darrell Wayne ....'50 '86 C&L.616 B.A., J.D. 11133 Springhollow Ct.
Corbin, Lorrie A., (BV) ....'70 '95 C.1050 B.A. L.615 J.D. [Kirschner K.L.]
Corbyn, George S., Jr., (AV) ....'47 '73 C.813 B.A. L.623 J.D. [Corbyn]

Corbyn Law Firm, (AV)
Two Leadership Square, 211 North Robinson, Suite 1120, 73102
Telephone: 405-239-7055 Telefax: 405-239-2436
Email: gcorbyn@corbynlaw.com URL: http://www.lawyers.com/georgecorbyn
George S. Corbyn, Jr.;—Kathryn M. Zynda.
Civil Trial and Appellate Practice, State and Federal Courts.
See Professional Biographies, OKLAHOMA CITY, OKLAHOMA

Corn, Danny M., (BV) ....'46 '77 C.614 B.S. L.623 J.D. 4312 N. Classen Blvd.
Cornelius, Kelley L., (BV) ....'58 '88 C.623 B.B.A. L.616 J.D. [K.L.Cornelius]
Cornelius, Kelley L., P.C., (BV) ....1800 N. Eagle Lane
Cornett, Clydine, (BV) ....'43 '68 C&L.623 B.B.A., J.D. 5800 Rosebay Ct.‡
Corona, Johnny C., (BV) ....'34 '63 C&L.623 B.B.A., LL.B. 6800 Newman Drive
Corum, William R., (AV) '44 '77
C.357 B.S.B.A. L.616 J.D. V.P. & Sr. Coun., Amer. Fidelity Co.
Costello, Mary Alice '53 '93 C.378 B.S.J. L.326 J.D.
(adm. in TX; not adm. in OK) 12901 N. Macarthur Blvd., Apt. 117
Cottingham, Dale E., (AV) ....'56 '82 C.613 B.A. L.802 J.D. [Moricoli,H.&C.]
Couch, Dean A. ....'53 '82 C.1147 B.A. L.623 J.D. Gen. Coun., State Water Res. Bd.
Couch, Melissa A. ....'77 '02 C.623 B.A. L.615 J.D. [Short W.M.&B.]
Couch, Valerie K. ....'51 '83 C.1097 B.A. L.623 J.D. U.S. Mag. J.
Coulter, Terri Anne, (BV) ....'55 '85 C.623 B.A. L.615 J.D. 3955 N. W. 23rd
Courbois, Francis, (AV) ....'41 '69 C.375 B.A. L.616 J.D. 120 North Robinson, 29th Floor
Court, H. Leonard ....'47 '73 C.612 B.A. L.309 J.D. 20 N. Broadway, Ste. 1800
Court, Leonard, (AV) ....'47 '73 C.612 B.A. L.309 J.D. [Crowe&D.]
Court, Todd ....'74 '02 C.612 B.S. L.616 J.D. [McAfee&T.]
Coury, John Douglas ....'64 '93 C.623 B.B.A. L.615 J.D. [J.D.Coury]
Coury, John D., Law Office ....306 N.W. 13th Street
Covey, Keith H. ....'53 '87 C.612 B.S. L.615 J.D. 2200 Classen Blvd., Ste. 1130
Cox, Alton B. ....'56 '84 C.1300 B.A. L.623 J.D. 3240 N.W. Grand Blvd.
Cox, Charles Foster, Jr., (BV) ....'44 '69 C.45 B.S.B.A. L.623 J.D. 434 N.W. 11th St.
Cox, Christopher H., (BV) ....'46 '74 C.575 B.A. L.616 J.D. 217 N. Harvey
Cox, James C., (BV) '40 '83
C.1147 B.B.A. L.616 J.D. 3601 North Classen Boulevard, Suite 102
Cox, Mark A. ....'62 '90 C.1147 B.B.A. L.616 J.D. [Norman&E.]
Cox, Martha ....'57 '97 C.616 B.S. L.615 J.D. Asst. Gen. Coun, OK Ins. Dept.
Cox, Mary E. ....'23 '48 C&L.623 A.B., LL.B. 3100 Brookhollow Rd.‡
Cox, Randall Lee ....'60 '92 C&L.623 B.S., J.D. 4308 N. Libby
Cox, Robert L. ....'07 '31 C&L.623 A.B., LL.B. 1808 Huntington Ave.‡
Cox, Shirley A. ....'50 '81 C.612 B.A. L.623 J.D. Catholic Charities
Coyle, John W., III, (AV) ....'48 '74 C&L.616 B.A., J.D. [Coyle]
Coyle, John W. "Billy", IV ....'74 '04 C.259 B.S. L.623 J.D. [Coyle]

Coyle Law Firm, (AV)
119 North Robinson, Suite 320, 73102
Telephone: 405-232-1988 Fax: 405-272-9859
Email: email@coylelaw.com
John W. Coyle, III;—James L. Hankins; Ashley L. Altshuler; John W. "Billy" Coyle, IV. Of Counsel: Robert D. Baron.
Criminal Trial and Appellate Practice in all State and Federal Courts. Grand Jury Investigations, White Collar and Complex Crimes, Drugs, DUI, Murder, Sex Crimes, Obscenities, Securities Fraud, Personal Injury, Condemnation, Driving While Intoxicated, Criminal Records Expungements, Civil Rights.
See Professional Biographies, OKLAHOMA CITY, OKLAHOMA

Crabb, Jerry J., (AV) ....'41 '68 C.1147 B.S. L.616 J.D. [Crabb,F.&R.]
Crabb, Ferguson & Riesen, (AV) .... 5101 N. Classen Blvd.
Craig, Jeri B. '41 '67 C.378 B.S.B.A. L.900 J.D.
(adm. in KS; not adm. in OK) Coun., Express Servs., Inc.
Craig, Michele O'Neill ....'— '83 C.228 B.A. L.623 J.D. P.O. Box 52000
Craig, Richard D., (AV) ....'57 '84 C.618 B.S. L.623 J.D. [McAfee&T.]
Crain, Jeffrey I. ....'71 '04 C.198 B.A. L.616 J.D. [Pierce C.H.B.&G.]

Crane, Warren H., (AV) ... '25 '53 C.619 B.A. L.623 J.D. 5513 N.W. 111th St.
Crawford, Gregory J. ... '63 '97 C.813 A.B. L.623 J.D. [Ⓐ Day,E.P.&C.]
Crawley, Patrick T., (AV) ... '43 '91 C.614 B.S. L.623 J.D. Asst. Atty. Gen.
Creasey, Marjorie ... '74 '99 C.1147 B.S. L.623 J.D. [Ⓐ Elias,B.B.&N.]
Croll, Billy M., (AV) ... '54 '79 C.612 B.S. L.623 J.D. [Hartzog C.C.&N.]
Crosby, Durand H. ... '64 '92 C&L.623 B.A., J.D. 1200 N.E. 13th St.
Cross, Freda J. ... '52 '90 C.1147 B.A.E. L.616 J.D. 4808 N. Classen Blvd.
Cross, Laura L., (AV) ... '45 '88 C.623 B.S.N. L.616 J.D. [Scoggins&C.]

Crosthwait Law Firm, The, A Professional Corporation
(See Midwest City)

Crow, Steven Wayne ... '68 '94 C.1300 B.B.A L.615 J.D. [Delluomo&C.]
Crowe, R. Denning, (BV) ... '42 '67 C.133 B.A. L.623 J.D. [Crowe&C.]
Crowe & Crowe, Inc., (BV) ... 3113 Classen Blvd.

Crowe & Dunlevy, A Professional Corporation, (AV) BR
20 North Broadway, Suite 1800, 73102-8273 ⊙
Telephone: 405-235-7700 Fax: 405-239-6651
Email: bryantd@crowedunlevy.com URL: http://www.crowedunlevy.com
V. P. Crowe (1897-1974); Fred W. Dunlevy (1914-1994); Gary W. Davis; Andrew M. Coats; Allen D. Evans; D. Kent Meyers; Preston G. Gaddis II; Clyde A. Muchmore; William G. Paul; Arlen E. Fielden; Harry A. Woods, Jr.; Jimmy Goodman; Earl A. Skarky; James H. Holloman, Jr.; Richard C. Ford; John J. Griffin, Jr.; Brooke Smith Murphy; Michael M. Stewart; Leonard Court; Cynda C. Ottaway; Judy Hamilton Morse; Mark D. Christiansen; Michael S. Laird; Mack J. Morgan III; Anton J. Rupert; Karen S. Rieger; Harvey D. Ellis, Jr.; Gayle L. Barrett; L. Mark Walker; Stephen L. DeGiusti; Mark S. Grossman; Kevin D. Gordon; Reeder E. Ratliff; Todd Taylor; Roger A. Stong; LeAnne Burnett; Paul D. Trimble; Timila S. Rother; Tamela R. Hughlett; Rustin J. Strubhar; Phillip L. Free, Jr.; Cynthia L. Andrews; C. Robert Stell; William H. Hoch, III; Jeremy Tubb; J. Robert Kalsu; William L. Teague; Eric S. Fisher; John M. Thompson;—Mary Hirth Tolbert; Charles B. Goodwin; Stacey D. Spivey; Courtney K. Warmington; David W. Carlson; Adam W. Childers; David M. Sullivan; David V. Stewart; William E. van Egmond; James W. Larimore; R. Reagan D. Allen; Jennifer L. Berry; Michael W. Bowling; Jennifer A. Dutton; Alison Howard; Marie Johnston; Justin C. Sullivan; John W. Garrett; Daniel P. Johnson; Jonathan D. Echols. Of Counsel: Bruce H. Johnson; Lawrence E. Walsh; Val R. Miller; James C. Gibbens; James A. Peabody (Retired); James W. George; Robert A. Reece; Kenni B. Merritt; Terry R. Hanna; Jerry L. Brust; Henry Rheinberger; Robert M. Johnson; James F. Hartmann, Jr.
General Practice. Litigation of all types in both state and federal court. All types of alternative dispute resolution methodologies. Administrative Law, Antitrust, Appellate, Aviation, Bankruptcy and Creditors' Rights, Business Organizations, Commercial Real Estate, Commercial Transactions, Consumer Credit, Corporate and Securities Finance, Environmental, ERISA, Estates and Trusts, Family Law, Financial Institutions and Finance, Franchising and Distribution, Healthcare, Initiative Petition, Insurance Litigation and Regulation, Intellectual Property and Technology, International Business, Labor and Employment, Medicare/Medicaid Fraud and Abuse, Medical Malpractice Defense, Mergers and Acquisitions, Oil and Gas, Oklahoma Corporation Commission, Patent, Trademark, Copyright and Related Matters, Products Liability, Public Finance, School Law, Small Business and Venture Capital, Taxation, White Collar Crime.
Tulsa, Oklahoma Office: 500 Kennedy Building, 321 South Boston Avenue, 74103-3313. Telephone: 918-592-9800. Fax: 918-592-9801.
Norman, Oklahoma Office: 2500 South McGee, Suite 140, 73072-6705. Telephone: 405-321-7317. Fax: 405-360-4002.

See Professional Biographies, OKLAHOMA CITY, OKLAHOMA

Croy, James B. ... '46 '80 C.623 B.A. L.615 J.D. Dist. Ct. J., Oklahoma Co.
Crum, C. Bruce, (AV) ... '50 '77 C.165 A.B. L.623 J.D. [McAfee&T.]
Crumpley, James L., (AV) ... '64 '95 C.1315 B.S. L.616 J.D. [McKinney&S.]
Cryer, Rebecca ... '46 '77 C&L.623 B.A., J.D. Enforce. Atty., State Dept. of Sec.
Cubbage, Thomas (T.L.), III, (AVⓉ) '66 '92
C.802 B.A. L.846 J.D. Sr. Coun., Kerr-McGee Corp.
Culp, Dudley H., (AV) ... '09 '34 C&L.623 J.D. 1219 Classen Dr.
Cummings, Tom M. ... '53 '78 C.951 B.A. L.623 J.D. [T.M.Cummings]
Cummings, Tom M., P.C. ... 4528 N. Classen Blvd.
Cummins, Carolyn Crawford, (AV) ... '57 '83 C&L.623 B.A., J.D. Sonic Industries
Cunningham, Clell I., III, (AV) ... '53 '80 C.173 B.A. L.37 J.D. [Dunn,S.&C.]
Cunningham, Myron K., (AV) '55 '80
C.620 B.A. L.623 J.D. Sr. Coun., Kerr-McGee Corp.
Cunningham, Ryan Yerger ... '70 '96 L.623 J.D. 228 Robert S. Kerr, Ste. 200
Cunningham, Stanley L., (AV) ... '38 '63 C&L.623 B.S., LL.B. [Ⓒ McAfee&T.]
Cunnyngham, Maxine Brown, (AV) '49 '80
C.1147 B.B.A. L.616 J.D. [Lamun,M.C.&D.]
Curran, J. Dillon ... '77 '02 C.612 B.S. L.623 J.D. [Ⓐ Conner&W.]
Curry, Caran, (BVⓉ) ... '54 '80 C&L.45 B.A., J.D. Pros. Coordinator
Curtin, T. Shane, (BV) ... '66 '91 C.1147 B.B.A. L.623 J.D. [Ⓐ Hiltgen&B.]
Custar, David B., (AV) ... '61 '87 C&L.623 M.B.A., J.D. [McCarty&C.]
Dace, Robert W., (AV) ... '53 '83 C.870 B.S. L.623 J.D. [McAfee&T.]
Dahnke, George W., (AV) ... '40 '65 C.934 B.A. L.597 J.D. [Abowitz,T.&D.]
Dalley, Paula J. '63 '89 C.674 A.B. L.309 J.D.
(adm. in NY; not adm. in OK)
Assoc. Prof. of Law, Oklahoma City Univ. School of Law
Dalton, Henry, (BV) ... '63 '93 C.35 B.S. L.616 J.D. 101 N. Robinson Ave.
Daniel, Susan Estelle ... '67 '92 C&L.623 B.A., J.D. Oklahoma Municipal League, Inc.
Daniel IV, Thomas J., (AV) ... '— '86 C&L.623 B.B.A., J.D. [Kirk&C.]
Daniels, J. Christopher ... '72 '98 C.275 B.A. L.616 J.D. 204 N. Robinson Ave., Ste. 3030
Daniels, Keith A. ... '72 '03 C.1147 B.A. L.623 J.D. [Ⓐ Morgan&Assoc.]
Daniels, Steven W., (BV) ... '62 '87 C&L.623 B.A., J.D. [Ⓐ Lawson,K.&S.]
Dansby, Janice M., (AV) ... '49 '82 C&L.623 B.A., J.D. 435 N.W. 20th St.
Darks, H. Maxwell ... '25 '51 C&L.623 LL.B. Admin. Law J., H.E.W.
Darling, Shelia M., (AV) ... '59 '88 C&L.623 B.A., J.D. [Ⓒ Conner&W.]
Darrah, Micheal L., (AV) ... '51 '77 C.1147 B.A. L.616 J.D. [Durbin,L.&B.]
Darrow, George E. '24 '59
C.912 B.B.A. L.623 LL.B. Pres., George E. Darrow Appraisal Co., Inc.
Darrow, Laurel Susan ... '65 '90 C&L.623 B.A., J.D. [Martin]
Dasovich, W. Jeffrey, (AV) '43 '73
C.190 A.B. L.616 J.D. 11914 North Pennsylvania Avenue Suite B2
Daugherty, Phil E., (AV) ... '04 '28 C.616 L.192 LL.B. 6308 Avalon Lane‡

Daugherty, Fowler, Peregrin & Haught, A Professional Corporation, (AV)
204 North Robinson 900 City Place, 73102-6800
Telephone: 405-232-0003 Facsimile: 405-232-0865
Email: dfph@dfph.com URL: http://www.dfph.com
Daniel J. Fowler (Retired); Robert M. Peregrin; Susan H. Haught; Robin D. Jenson. Of Counsel: R. Steven Haught.
Aircraft Title, Aircraft Finance and Leasing, Civil Litigation and Arbitration.

See Professional Biographies, OKLAHOMA CITY, OKLAHOMA

Davenport, David M. '57 '83 C.1147 B.A. L.623 J.D.
(adm. in TX; not adm. in OK) 6414 N. Santa Fe Ave.‡
Davis, Allene D. ... '21 '69 C.612 L.616 LL.B. 5961 N.W. 27th Street
Davis, Barry R., (AV) ... '49 '75 C.623 B.A. L.616 J.D. [Ⓐ Abel,M.S.M.&K.]
Davis, Bret D. ... '68 '93 C.612 B.S. L.623 J.D. [Lamun,M.C.&D.]
Davis, Carl W. ... '20 '53 C&L.623 B.A., LL.B. 3009 Huntleigh Dr.
Davis, Charles B. ... '42 '73 C.612 B.S. L.623 J.D. [C.B.Davis]
Davis, Daniel M., (BV) ... '61 '87 C.616 B.S. L.862 J.D. 525 NW 13th St.
Davis, David A., Attorney at Law, (AV) '45 '71
C.1147 B.A. L.615 J.D. 5101 N. Classen Blvd., Ste. 412
Davis, Donald W. ... '34 '69 C.174 B.A. L.972 J.D. P.O. Box 14750‡
Davis, Gary W., (AV) ... '31 '57 C&L.378 B.A., J.D. [Crowe&D.]
Davis, George D., (AV) ... '44 '70 C.612 A.B. L.623 J.D. [McKinney&S.]
Davis, James F., (AV) ... '33 '57 C&L.623 B.B.A., LL.B. [Andrews D.]
Davis, John B., (PLLC), (BV) ... '59 '85 C&L.623 B.B.A., J.D. [Mitchell,D.K.&P.]
Davis, Kenneth R., (AV) ... '64 '90 C.612 B.S. L.623 J.D. [Ⓒ Hartzog C.C.&N.]
Davis, Lawrence E. ... '56 '83 C.425 B.B.A. L.802 J.D. [Davis,L.E.]
Davis, Lisa Tipping, (AV) ... '59 '84 C&L.623 B.B.A., J.D. Coun.
Davis, Steve ... '71 '98 C.893 B.A. L.569 J.D. [Ⓒ Burton&Assoc.] ⊙
Davis, Steven C., (AV) ... '58 '83 C.612 B.S. L.623 J.D. [Hartzog C.C.&N.]
Davis, Steven R., (BV) ... '46 '92 C.623 B.B.A. L.615 J.D. [Ⓐ Tawwater&S.]
Davis, Teresa B., (BV) ... '54 '94 C.925 B.S. L.623 J.D. [Ⓐ Brawner]
Davis, William R., (BV) ... '31 '60 C&L.623 B.B.A., LL.B. 1001 N.W. 63rd
Davis, Charles B., P.C. ... 2601 N.W. Expressway
Davis, Lawrence E., P.C. ... 2728 N.W. 39th St., Ste. 200
Dawson, Gary M., (BV) ... '47 '74 C.45 B.S. L.623 J.D. [G.M.Dawson]
Dawson, Jack S., (AV) ... '40 '72 L.616 J.D. [Miller D.]
Dawson, James William ... '49 '77 C&L.623 B.S., J.D. P.O. Box 95146
Dawson, Gary M., P.C., (BV) ... 2601 N.W. Expressway
Day, Bruce W., (AV) ... '45 '72 C&L.623 B.A., J.D. [Day,E.P.&C.] ⊙
Day, Jerry, (AV) ... '55 '80 C.843 B.S. L.623 J.D. [Grimes,G.A.&D.]
Day, Michelle R. Loy '62 '89
C.1147 B.S. L.623 J.D. Asst. Chief Coun., Dept. of Pub. Safety

Day, Edwards, Propester & Christensen, P.C., (AV) BR
Suite 2900 Oklahoma Tower, 210 Park Avenue, 73102-5605 ⊙
Telephone: 405-239-2121 Telecopier: 405-236-1012
URL: http://www.dayedwards.com
Bruce W. Day; Joe E. Edwards; Richard P. Propester; D. Wade Christensen; J. Clay Christensen; Jeanette C. Timmons; Joel Warren Harmon; Bill Powell Guest;—D. Michael O'Neil, Jr.; P. David Newsome, Jr.; Kelley C. Callahan; Thomas Pitchlynn Howell, IV; Nick C. Linholm; Myra Palevsky Kaufman; Gary L. Farnum; Jeffrey E. Tate; Gregory J. Crawford; L. Nazette Zuhdi; Tara A. LaClair (Not admitted in OK); A. Ainslie Stanford, II; Lisa Michele Molsbee; Robert J. Carlson. Of Counsel: Robert S. Baker; Herbert F. (Jack) Hewett; Kenneth A. Brokaw.
General Civil Trial. Trial of Civil Cases in all State and Federal Courts. Administrative Law, Agribusiness, Anti-Trust Law, Arbitration and Mediation of disputes, Banking Regulation and Transactions, Bankruptcy and Insolvency Law, Commercial Law, Corporate Law, Employment Law, Energy Law, Environmental Law, Franchising Regulation and Transactions, Health Care Law, Insurance Law, International Law, Labor Relations, Litigation, Mergers and Acquisitions, Natural Resources, Products Liability, Professional Malpractice, Real Estate Law, Securities Regulation and Transactions and Workers Compensation.
Representative Clients: AIG Aviation, Inc.; Aztec Specialty Co., Inc.; Aztec Rig Equipment Company; BancFirst Corporation.
Tulsa, Oklahoma Office: 320 South Boston Avenue, Suite 805, 74103. Telephone: 918-592-2121. Facsimile: 918-388-6601.

See Professional Biographies, OKLAHOMA CITY, OKLAHOMA

Deason, Donald L., (AV) ... '53 '79 C&L.623 B.A., J.D. Asst. Dist. Atty.
Deason, Tina Taylor, (AV) '66 '94 C.201 B.A. L.615 J.D.
9400 Broadway Ext., Ste. 500
DeBee, H. Edward, III, (AV) ... '52 '78 C.612 B.S. L.623 J.D. [DeBee G.]

DeBee Gilchrist, A Professional Corporation, (AV)
100 North Broadway Avenue Suite 1500, 73102
Telephone: 405-232-7777 Facsimile: 405-232-9898
Email: firm@debeegilchrist.com URL: http://www.debeegilchrist.com
H. Edward DeBee, III; Jack P. Gilchrist;—Brian Thomas Fagan; Barrett J. Knudsen; Lawn B. Gardner; Blaine M. Peterson; Carole L. Houghton; Steven R. McConnell. Of Counsel: Don Hager.
Acquisitions and Divestitures, Administrative Law; Aircraft Title Law; Aircraft Financing Law; Aviation Law; Banking Law, Commercial Transactions; Commercial Aircraft Leasing; Charitable and Exempt Organizations, Corporation, Estate Planning, Federal and State Taxation Law, General Civil Law, Municipal Law; Partnership Law, Privatization Law; Probate and Estate Administration, Real Property Transactions, Public Private Partnerships, and Commercial Litigation.

See Professional Biographies, OKLAHOMA CITY, OKLAHOMA

DeCaulp, Bobara E. '47 '75 C.643 B.A. L.1019 J.D.
(adm. in NY; not adm. in OK) 12316 Windsong Way‡
Dech, Janet E., (BV) ... '51 '89 C.999 B.S. L.623 J.D. [McGivern,G.&C.]
Decker, Michael L., (AV) '53 '78 C&L.616 B.A., J.D.
Dep. Gen. Coun., Gen. Coun. Off., OK Corp. Comm.
DeFilippo, Diane ... '52 '78 C&L.623 B.A., J.D. [Ⓐ Hampton&M.]
DeGiusti, Anthony D., (BV) ... '49 '92 C.623 B.A. L.615 J.D. [Ⓒ Homsey,C.H.&Assoc.]
DeGiusti, Stephen L., (AV) ... '58 '83 C.1147 B.A. L.623 J.D. [Crowe&D.]
DeGiusti, Timothy D., (AV) ... '62 '88 C&L.623 B.A., J.D. [Holladay,C.&D.]
DeGraffenreid, Paul E. '31 '59 C.1147 B.A. L.616 LL.B.
Gen. Coun., Comrs. of Land Off.
Delaney, Casey Tippens ... '80 '05 C.612 B.A. L.623 J.D. [Ⓐ Fellers,S.B.B.&T.]
Deligans, Julianna G. ... '77 '03 C.612 B.S. L.623 J.D. [Ⓐ Dunlap,C.&R.]
Deligans, Ryan ... '77 '03 C.556 B.A. L.623 J.D. [Ⓐ Durbin,L.&B.]
Dell, Brian M., (BV) ... '41 '77 C.616 B.S. L.623 J.D. [B.M.Dell]
Dell, Brian M., A Professional Corporation, (BV) ... 501 N.W. 13th Street
Delluomo, Daniel Monty ... '61 '86 C.623 B.B.A. L.615 J.D. [Delluomo&C.]
Delluomo & Crow ... 2601 N.W. Expy., Ste. 100 W
Demastus, Julie A. ... '56 '89 C.53 B.S. L.616 J.D. [Demastus]
Demastus Law Office ... 12460 Saint Andrews Dr., Ste. B
Denker, Rick L., (BV) ... '52 '80 C.1315 B.S. L.615 J.D. 4700 N.W. 23rd St.
Denman, Don ... '46 '77 C.976 B.A. L.616 J.D. 4513 N. Classen Boulevard
Denneny, John R., (AV) ... '56 '81 C.612 B.S. L.63 J.D. [Ⓐ Lawson,K.&S.]
Dennis, Frank ... '26 '51 C&L.623 A.B., LL.B. 3900 S.E. 29th St.‡
Dennis, Patricia Sellers, (AV) ... '37 '69 C.623 L.616 LL.B. Dep. Mun. Counselor
Dennis, Robert D. ... '43 '73 C.612 B.S. L.616 J.D. Clk., U.S. Dist. Ct.
Denny, Richard J., III ... '70 '03 C.618 B.S. L.623 J.D. [Ⓐ Elias,B.B.&N.]
Denson, Orenthel James ... '68 '03 C.623 B.A. L.615 J.D. [Denson&H.]
Denson & Haworth Law Firm LLP ... 4334 Northwest Expressway, Suite 273
Denwalt, Lisa K. Hammond, (BV) ... '58 '89 C&L.623 B.A., J.D. Asst. Dist. Atty.
Derouen, Jon Louis, Jr ... '70 '98 C.839 B.A. L.616 J.D. [Ⓐ Walker,F.&F.]
Derrick, Gary W., (AV) ... '53 '79 C.612 B.A. L.623 J.D. [Derrick&B.]

Derrick & Briggs, LLP, (AV)
A Professional Partnership
Chase Tower, 28th Floor, 100 North Broadway Avenue, 73102-8831
Telephone: 405-235-1900 Facsimile: 405-235-1995
URL: http://www.derrickandbriggs.com
Gary W. Derrick; M. Courtney Briggs.
Business Law, including Corporations, Limited Liability Companies and Partnerships, Mergers and Acquisitions, Securities Regulation, Business and Oil and Gas Financing, Publishing Law, Probate and Estate Planning, Entertainment Law; No Trial Work.

See Professional Biographies, OKLAHOMA CITY, OKLAHOMA

Derryberry, Larry, (AV) ... '39 '63 C&L.623 B.A., LL.B. [Derryberry,Q.S.&N.]

Derryberry, Quigley, Solomon & Naifeh, P.A., (AV)
4800 North Lincoln Boulevard, 73105
Telephone: 405-528-6569 Fax: 405-528-6462 URL: http://www.Derryberrylaw.com URL: http://www.lawyers.com/derryberrylaw
Email: Derryberry@Derryberrylaw.com URL: http://www.statecapitallaw.org
Larry Derryberry; Stephen G. Solomon; Robert N. Naifeh, Jr.; Patrick D. Shore; Jerome S. Sepkowitz; Donald B. Nevard; George W. Velotta II; Douglas A. Rice; Stephen L. McCaleb; Caleb J. Muckala; Sherri T. Fleming. Of Counsel: Paul E. Quigley; J. Eric Turner; Justin A. Whitefield.
Civil Trial Practice, Administrative and Governmental, Commercial, Insurance Regulatory and Defense. Workers' Compensation, Construction, Probate, Estates and Trusts, Real Estate, Bankruptcy, Public Utility, Personal Injury, Corporation, Taxation, Banking, Health and Hospital, Professional Licensing, Oil and Gas, Municipal and Public Authority Finance, Transportation, Common Carrier, Educational Law, Employment Law, Environmental Law, Arbitration and Mediation.

See Professional Biographies, OKLAHOMA CITY, OKLAHOMA

DeSilvey, Jared A. ....'70 '97 C.499 B.S. L.862 J.D. [Ⓐ Garrett] (⊙Muskogee, Tulsa)
DeSpain, Donald E., (AV) .... '45 '73 C&L.623 B.B.A., J.D. [Ⓒ Mulinix O.H.A.&L.]
Devol, Valerie R. .... '66 '97 C.623 B.B.A. L.986 J.D. [Ⓐ Andrews D.]
DeVore, Allan, (AV) ....'52 '78 C.612 B.A. L.623 J.D. [DeVore]

DeVore Law Firm, The, A Professional Corporation, (AV)
1318 North Robinson, 73103-4822
Telephone: 405-232-4997 Fax: 405-236-3940
Email: devorelaw@devorelawfirm.com
Allan DeVore;—Jane G. Rowe; Jacquelyn L. Thompson.
Oil and Gas, Commercial Litigation, Class Actions, Aircraft Litigation, Environmental/Pollution, Real Property, Contracts, Personal Injury, Products Liability.

See Professional Biographies, OKLAHOMA CITY, OKLAHOMA

Dewbre, Kenneth, (AV) ....'32 '60 C&L.623 B.S., LL.B. [Dewbre&D.]
Dewbre, Ross J., (BV) .... '63 '88 C&L.623 B.B.A., J.D. [Dewbre&D.]
Dewbre & Dewbre, P.C., (AV) .... 2220 Shadowlake Dr.
Dewitt, Derrick T., (BV) ....'73 '98 C.612 B.A. L.615 J.D. [Whitten,N.M.T.&R.]
Dick, Jerry, (A Professional Corporation), (BV) '31 '56
C&L.623 B.B.A., LL.B. 209 S.W. 89th St.
Dick, Jerry W. ....'47 '74 C&L.623 B.B.A., J.D. 535 NW 34th St.
Dickey, David R., (AV) ....'34 '63 C.612 B.S. L.623 LL.B. [Dickey&D.]
Dickey, Steven M., (AV) ....'47 '73 C.612 B.S. L.623 J.D. [Dickey&D.]

Dickey & Dickey, (AV)
1012 North West Grand Boulevard, 73118
Telephone: 405-848-1775 Fax: 405-840-1164
Members of Firm: David R. Dickey; Steven M. Dickey.
Banking, Commercial, Corporation, Insurance, Mortgage, Probate and Real Estate Law, Estate Planning, Trusts and Estates. Litigation.
Representative Clients: Reserve National Insurance Co.; First National Bank, Thomas, OK; Southwest National Bank, Weatherford, OK; Hill & Co. Plumbing and Heating; Smith Farm and Garden, Inc.; Jett Distributing Co.; Coppermark Bank; AMS Health Sciences, Inc.
Other Oklahoma City Office: 211 NW 67th Street. Telephone: 405-840-1644.

Dickson, Charles A., III ....'69 '99 C.1147 B.A. L.615 J.D. [Niemeyer,A.A.&P.]
Dickson, Richard L. ....'37 '80 C.623 B.A. L.616 J.D. State Farm Ins. Co.
Diesselhorst, Jacob D. .... '76 '02 C.612 B.A. L.623 J.D. [Ⓐ Nix&M.]
Dietrich, Lisa Luschen, (BV) ....'60 '85 C.1322 B.A. L.623 J.D. [Ⓐ Abowitz,T.&D.]
Diggs, James B. ....'10 '34 C.674 A.B. L.976 LL.B. 1510 W. Wilshire Blvd.‡
Dilbeck, James S. ....'79 '04 C.621 B.A. L.623 J.D. [Ⓐ Cathcart&D.]
Dillard, Stacie Rene' ....'71 '00 C.1147 B.B.A. L.623 J.D. 1800 E. Memorial, Ste. 106
Dillingham, Carol Price ....'52 '84 C.339 B.A. L.616 J.D. [Turner,T.B.&G.]
Dillon, Peter Gardner '45 '73 C.823 B.A. L.262 J.D.
(adm. in CO; not adm. in OK) Assoc. Prof. of Law, Oklahoma City Univ. Sch. of Law
Dills, Patrice Raye ....'62 '87 C.1315 B.S. L.623 J.D. P.O. Box 14709
Dimery, Carlton Wayne .... '72 '97 C&L.623 B.A., J.D. 120 N. Robinson, Suite 2300
Dimick, Green, Brown & Stark, A Professional Corporation, (AV) .. 3717 NW 63rd Street
Ditto, Steven M., (AV) ....'50 '78 C.612 B.A. L.623 J.D. [S.M.Ditto]
Ditto, Steven M., P.C., (AV) .... 1800 East Memorial Road, Suite 106
Dixon, Bryan C. ....'52 '77 C&L.623 B.A., J.D. Dist. J., Judge Dixon Chambers
Dixon, Jane Ann .... '67 '95 C&L.623 B.A., J.D. Child Abuse Response & Evaluation Ctr.
Dixon, Karen L., (CV) ..... '57 '83 C.612 B.A. L.623 J.D. Dir., Wrkrs. Comp. Fraud Unit
Dizikes, Pamela B. '47 '75 C.339 A.B. L.608 J.D.
(adm. in OH; not adm. in OK) State Agency
Doak, D. Fred, (AV) ....'47 '72 C.616 B.A. L.623 J.D. Dist. Ct.
Dobbs, James W., (BV) ....'65 '91 C&L.623 B.A., J.D. [Smith R.S.&E.]
Dobbs, Steven, (AV) ....'47 '80 C.502 B.A. L.623 J.D. [Dobbs&M.]
Dobbs & Middleton, (AV) ....100 North Broadway
Dobelbower, Peter M., (AV) '59 '85 C.934 B.A. L.616 J.D.
V.P., Chf. Legal Off., Asst. Sec. & Gen. Coun., Hobby Lobby Stores, Inc.
Dobson, David H., (AV) ....'60 '87 C.623 B.A. L.616 J.D. [Ⓒ Holloway,D.&B.]
Dobson, Frederick Page '35 '59
C&L.623 B.A., LL.B. One Leadership Sq., 211 N. Robinson
Dobson, L. Matthew ....'75 '05 C.942 B.G.S. L.615 J.D. [Ⓐ Andrews D.]
Dobson, Page, (AV) ....'35 '59 C&L.623 B.A., LL.B. [Holloway,D.&B.]
Dodson, Catherine S., (Mrs.) ....'18 '39 C.734 L.615 2416 N.W. 55th St.‡

Doerner, Saunders, Daniel & Anderson, L.L.P., (AV)
One Leadership Square, Suite 501, 73102 ⊙
Telephone: 405-319-3500 Fax: 405-319-3509
URL: http://www.dsda.com
Partners in Tulsa, Oklahoma: Sam P. Daniel; William C. Anderson; G. Michael Lewis; Lawrence T. Chambers, Jr.; Dallas E. Ferguson; Sam G. Bratton II; Gary M. McDonald; H. Wayne Cooper; Kevin C. Coutant; Richard P. Hix; William F. Riggs; Lewis N. Carter; Linda Crook Martin; James Patrick McCann; Richard H. Foster; Charles S. Plumb; Leonard I. Pataki; S. Douglas Dodd; Elise Dunitz Brennan; Jon E. Brightmire; Tom Q. Ferguson; Richard J. Eagleton; Rebecca McCarthy Fowler; Michael C. Redman; Steven K. Metcalf; Russell W. Kroll; Rachel Blue; James C. Milton. Associates: Audra K. Hamilton; William H. Spitler; Young Pei; Chad M. Hinrichs; Johnathan D. Horton; Robert Spoo; Lesley Ford Richer; David L. Iandiorio; N. Lance Bryan; Chad J. Kutmas; Heather D. Flynn; Elizabeth W. Carroll; E. McLaine DeWitt Herndon; Steven P. Tepera; Raymond H. Tipton III. Of Counsel: Michael Minnis; David McCullough.
Federal Civil Practice, State Civil Practice, Administrative Law, Appellate Practice, Antitrust, Bankruptcy, Creditors' Rights and Loan Workouts, Construction Law, Consumer Credit, Corporate, Commercial and Securities, Employment and Labor, Environmental, ERISA and Employee Benefits, Estates, Trusts and Probate, Family Law, General Litigation, Health Care, Indian Law, Intellectual Property, Patents, Trademarks, Copyrights, International Business, Mediation and Arbitration, Media and First Amendment Law, Medicare/Medicaid Fraud and Abuse, Mergers and Acquisitions Law, Oil and Gas, Oklahoma Corporation Commission, Products Liability, Public Trust and Tax Exempt Financing, Real Estate, Rural Water District Competition, Securities Litigation, Small Business and Venture Capital, Taxation, Telecommunications, Toxic Tort Litigation and Workers' Compensation.
Tulsa, Oklahoma Office: Suite 500, 320 South Boston Avenue. Telephone: 918-582-1211. Fax: 918-591-5360. URL: http://www.dsda.com.

See Professional Biographies, OKLAHOMA CITY, OKLAHOMA

Dollarhide, Charles L., II, (AV) ....'43 '74 C.612 B.S. L.616 J.D. [Ⓒ Miller D.]
Donahoe, Laurence K., (BV) ....'44 '81 C&L.616 B.S., J.D. [L.K.Donahoe]
Donahoe, Laurence K., P.C., (BV) .... 200 N. Harvey Ave, #1315
Donaldson, Earl R., (AV) ....'47 '74 C&L.616 B.S., J.D. [Wheeler,W.M.F.&D.]
Donaldson, Randi A. ....'74 '99 C&L.221 B.A., J.D. [Ⓐ Pierce C.H.B.&G.]

Donchin, David B., (AV) ....'59 '84 C&L.623 B.A., J.D. [Durbin,L.&B.]
Donelson, Kevin R., (AV) ....'61 '88 C.622 B.A. L.623 J.D. [Fellers,S.B.B.&T.]
Donnell, Bradley K., (AV) ....'68 '94 C.623 B.B.A. L.615 J.D. [McAfee&T.]
Dooley, Cary D., (AV) ....'63 '88 C.69 B.A. L.623 J.D. [Cathcart&D.]
Dooley, Daniel P. ....'48 '00 C.494 B.M.E. L.616 J.D. [Fellers,S.B.B.&T.] (Pat.)
Doray, Walter Francis, Jr. ....'52 '00 C.612 B.S. L.615 J.D. Currency Comptroller

Dorwart, Frederic
(See Tulsa)

Dotter, Stephen A. ....'55 '98 C.560 B.A. L.615 J.D. [Niemeyer,A.A.&P.]
Dougherty, C. Clark, Jr., (AV) '35 '66
C.623 B.S.Ch.E. L.616 J.D. [Ⓒ McAfee&T.] (Pat.)
Dougherty, Clifford Clark, III, (AV) .... '60 '85 C&L.623 B.S., J.D. [McAfee&T.] (Pat.)

Dougherty & Hessin
(See McAfee & Taft, A Professional Corporation)

Doughty, Stefan K., (BV) ....'69 '94 C.613 B.A. L.623 J.D. 4545 N. Lincoln, Ste. 260
Douglas, Patrice Raye Dills ....'62 '87 C.1315 B.S. L.623 J.D. P.O. Box 14709
Douglas-Talley, Rita ....'57 '85 C.623 B.A. L.616 J.D. Asst. Mun. Counselor
Dowd, Pamela Jane ....'54 '80 C.623 B.A. L.862 J.D. 2505 N. W. 121st St.
Dowd, Timothy C., (AV) ....'53 '79 C.623 B.A. L.862 J.D. [Ⓒ Elias,B.B.&N.]
Dowd, W. Timothy ....'27 '57 C.973 L.862 LL.B. P.O. Box 770474‡
Dowell, Jim D. ....'71 '02 C.1 B.A. L.623 J.D. [Ⓐ Gum,P.&M.]
Dowling, Elaine M., (BV) .... '64 '90 C&L.623 B.A., J.D. 11032 Quail Creek Road
Dowling, Mathew M. .... '31 '57 C&L.623 B.B.A., LL.B. Dowlings Inc.
Downing, Marjorie Mosburg ....'33 '59 C&L.623 B.A., LL.B. [Ⓒ Howick&Assoc.]
Dozier, Russell W., Jr. ....'27 '53 L.623 J.D. 8622 Waverly‡
Dratz, Mary C. ....'51 '78 C.508 B.A. L.862 J.D. Staff Atty., House of Rep.
Drennan, James S., (AV) ....'50 '77 C.612 B.S. L.623 J.D. [Monnet,H.B.T.&E.]
Drew, Rollin E., (AV) ....'33 '65 C.623 L.616 LL.B. Gen. Coun., Midland Financial Co.
Driskill, Kevin, (AV) ....'57 '82 C&L.623 B.A., J.D. 100 N. Broadway, Ste. 2300
Driskill, Linda R., (AV) .... '37 '77 C.623 B.A. L.616 J.D. 100 N. Broadway
Driskill, Sylva Tsinena .... '60 '97 C.616 B.S. L.615 J.D. 100 Park Avenue
Dubberstein, Mark J., (AV) .... '53 '78 C.612 B.A. L.623 J.D. [Dubberstein H.&M.]

Dubberstein Heinen & Morris PC, (AV)
777 N.W. Grand Boulevard Suite 150, 73118
Telephone: 405-942-8700 Facsimile: 405-608-0447
Email: dhm@dhmlaw.net
Mark J. Dubberstein; Gary J. Heinen; Stephen M. Morris.
Civil Litigation, Business Transactions, Oil and Gas Litigation, Oil and Gas Acquisitions, Oil and Gas Contracts, Oil and Gas Title Examination.

See Professional Biographies, OKLAHOMA CITY, OKLAHOMA

Duckworth, Gary F., (AV) .... '46 '73 C&L.623 B.A., J.D. 401 N. Hudson Ave.
Dudley, Carter G. ....'18 '49 C.846 B.A. L.623 J.D. 2619 Clermont Pl.‡
Dudley, Chas. D. .....'30 '55 C&L.623 B.B.A., LL.B. Admin. Law J., State Corp. Comm.
Dudman, Paul W., (AV) .... '49 '75 L.999 LL.B. [Ⓒ Fellers,S.B.B.&T.]
Dunagan, Sidney G., (AV) ....'43 '68 C&L.862 B.A., J.D. [Gable&G.]
Duncan, Jerry S., Law Office, (AV) '36 '65
C.623 B.S. L.616 J.D. 3715 N. Classen Blvd., Ste. B
Duncan, Laney, (CV) ....'68 '95 C.623 B.A. L.616 J.D. [Ⓐ J.S.Duncan]
Duncan, Michael D., (AV) ....'58 '85 C&L.623 B.A., J.D. [Fenton,F.S.R.&M.]
Duncan, Paul C., Jr., (AV) '40 '64 C&L.623 B.A., LL.B.
Gen. Coun., State Employees Group Insurance Program
Dunlap, Gary S. '50 '75 C.418 B.A. L.420 J.D.
(adm. in LA; not adm. in OK) P.O. Box 54712
Dunlap, Jerry J., (AV) '25 '52
C.623 B.S.M.E. L.862 J.D. [Dunlap,C.&R.] (See Pat. Sect.)
Dunlap, Jerry J., II, (AV) ....'49 '75 C.623 B.B.A. L.616 J.D. P.O. Box 75404

Dunlap, Codding & Rogers, P.C., (AV) BR
1601 Northwest Expressway, Suite 1000, 73118
Telephone: 405-607-8600 Fax: 405-607-8686
URL: http://www.okpatents.com
Jerry J. Dunlap; Charles A. Codding; G. Neal Rogers; Marc A. Brockhaus; Nicholas D. Rouse; Douglas J. Sorocco; Joseph P. Titterington; R. Trent Pipes;—Glen M. Burdick; Richard Nelson; Michael Hoyt Smith; Julianna G. Deligans.
Patent, Trademark, Unfair Competition, Trade Secret, Antitrust and Copyright Practice and related trial practice, Complex Civil Litigation.
Reference: Local Oklahoma Bank, Oklahoma City.

See Professional Biographies, OKLAHOMA CITY, OKLAHOMA

Dunlevy, F. W. "Rick", Jr., (AV) .... '41 '67 C&L.623 B.A., J.D. [F.W.Dunlevy,Jr.]
Dunlevy, F.W., Jr., A Professional Corporation, (AV) ....9816 Lakeshore Dr.
Dunn, John W., Jr., (BV) ....'63 '89 C.612 B.A. L.623 J.D. 6303 Waterford Blvd.
Dunn, Michael E., (AV) .... '46 '72 C.1147 B.S. L.623 J.D. [Dunn,S.&C.]
Dunn, Teena P., (BV) ....'59 '94 C.1147 B.A. L.616 J.D. [Ⓐ McAfee&T.]
Dunn, Travis .... '70 '95 C.612 B.S. L.623 J.D. [Ⓐ Wilson,C.&A.]

Dunn, Swan & Cunningham, P.C., (AV)
2800 Oklahoma Tower, 210 Park Avenue, 73102-5604
Telephone: 405-235-8318 Fax: 405-235-9605
Michael E. Dunn; Sheldon B. Swan; Clell I. Cunningham III. Of Counsel: Jackie L. Hill, Jr.
Corporate, Securities, State and Federal Tax, Commercial, Construction, Banking, Real Estate, Oil and Gas, Trusts, Wills and Probate Law. General Civil Practice in State and Federal Courts, and Administrative Agencies.

See Professional Biographies, OKLAHOMA CITY, OKLAHOMA

Dupre, James T., (BV) '49 '82
C.1147 B.A. L.616 J.D. Asst. Gen. Coun., Comrs. of Land Off.
Duran, Robert S., Jr. '76 '01 C.613 B.B.A. L.880 J.D.
(adm. in TX; not adm. in OK) [Ⓐ Hartzog C.C.&N.]
Durbin, Alan C., (AV) .... '42 '72 C&L.623 B.A., J.D. [Andrews D.]
Durbin, Gerald E., II, (AV) ....'44 '71 C&L.623 B.B.A., J.D. [Durbin,L.&B.]

Durbin, Larimore & Bialick, P.C., (AV)
920 North Harvey, 73102-2610
Telephone: 405-235-9584 Fax: 405-235-0551
Email: dlb@dlb.net URL: http://www.dlb.net
Gerald E. Durbin, II; James K. Larimore; Mark E. Bialick; David B. Donchin; Micheal L. Darrah; J. Logan Johnson; Rodney D. Stewart; R. Brad Miller; Katherine Taylor Loy;—Hilary S. Allen; E. Edd Pritchett, Jr.; Glen Mullins; Amy L. Alden; Ryan Deligans; Charles B. Williams; James M. Siderias.
Casualty and Insurance, Fire, Product Liability, Personal Injury, Litigation, Federal and State, Corporate, Real Estate, Banking and Commercial Law.

See Professional Biographies, OKLAHOMA CITY, OKLAHOMA

Dutton, Jennifer A. ....'— '03 C.616 B.A. L.615 J.D. [Ⓐ Crowe&D.]
Duty, John C. '58 '90 C.1004 B.B.A. L.326 J.D.
Asst. V.P. & Tr. Offr., Boatmen's First Natl. Bk. of Okla.
Duvall, Mark E., (AV) ....'61 '86 C.136 B.S. L.623 J.D. [Holloway,D.&B.]

Dyke, William H. '51 '76 C.840 B.A. L.280 J.D.
Assoc. Gen. Coun. & Asst. Secy., Sonic Corporation (Legal Department)
Dykeman, David B., (BV) ..... '60 '86 C.845 B.A. L.616 J.D. Sr. Atty., OK Corp. Comm.
Dykeman, W. Samuel, (AV) .... '28 '53 C.612 B.S. L.623 LL.B. [Britton,R.&G.]
Eads, Susan Lynn, (BV) ...... '73 '98 C.339 B.A. L.623 J.D. [Edmonds,C.H.G.R.&W.]

Eagleton & Nicholson, P.C., (AV)
3100 Bank One Center, 100 N. Broadway Avenue, 73102
Telephone: 405-236-0550 Fax: 405-236-0560
Email: eaglenk@coxinet.net
James R. Eagleton (1903-1990); Don R. Nicholson II; W. Davidson Pardue;—Jeffrey M. Love; Ronald R. Tracy. Of Counsel: Robert V. Varnum.
Litigation, Civil Practice, Commercial Law, Business Law, Bankruptcy, Contracts, Real Estate, Commercial Collections, Business Entities, Oil and Gas, Banks and Banking, Trusts and Estates, Construction Litigation, Children, Family Law.
Chandler, Oklahoma Office: 109 W. 9th, 74834. Telephone: 405-258-5301. Fax: 405-258-5302. Email: pordos@brightok.net
See Professional Biographies, OKLAHOMA CITY, OKLAHOMA

Earley, William P., (BV) .... '60 '85 C.612 B.S. L.623 J.D. Asst. Fed. Pub. Def.
Earnheart, Chas. E., Jr., (AV) .... '05 '28 C.616 A.B. L.623 LL.B. 4325 N.W. 56th St.‡
Easley, Blair, Jr. .... '43 '76 C.618 B.A. L.616 J.D. Dept. of Instit., Soc. & Rehab. Servs.
Eason, Douglas G., (AV) .... '51 '76 C.623 B.B.A. L.802 J.D. [Lawrence&E.]
Eason, Loutitia Denison, (AV) .... '45 '79 C&L.623 B.S., J.D. [Lawrence&E.]
Easter, Donald L., (BV) .... '48 '80 C.1142 B.A. L.616 J.D. 228 Robert S. Kerr Ave.
Eberle, Edward J. '55 '83 C.178 B.A. L.597 J.D.
(adm. in MA; not adm. in OK) Prof. of Law, Okla. City Univ. Sch. of Law
Eberle, John T., Law Offices of, (AV) '42 '67
C.276 A.B. L.623 J.D. 120 North Robinson Avenue Suite 1710
Echols, David W., (AV) .... '50 '79 C.623 B.A. L.616 J.D. [Echols&Assoc.]
Echols, Jonathan D. .... '79 '05 C.623 B.A. L.615 J.D. [Crowe&D.]
Echols, M. Eileen .... '51 '79 C.1147 B.S. L.616 J.D. [Echols&Assoc.]
Echols & Associates, (AV) .... 10001 Pennsylvania Ave., Ste. 190
Eddington, Gregory Neil '56 '87 C&L.623 B.B.A., J.D.
Legal Research & Writing Instr., Oklahoma City Univ. Sch. of Law
Eddy, Rand C., (AV) .... '61 '86 C.264 B.A. L.616 J.D. [Eddy&J.]

Eddy & Jones, P.C., (AV)
Court Plaza Building, 228 Robert S. Kerr, Suite 220, 73102
Telephone: 405-239-2524 Fax: 405-239-2665
Email: ejlaw@eddyjoneslaw.com URL: http://www.eddyjoneslaw.com
Rand C. Eddy; Kindanne C. Jones;—Linda Samuel-Jaha; Sherri Ann Carver.
Employment Discrimination, Criminal Law, Civil Rights, Employment Law, Disability Rights, Guardianships, Children's Rights, Education Law, General Practice, Contract Law.
See Professional Biographies, OKLAHOMA CITY, OKLAHOMA

Edem, Emmanuel E., (AV) .... '52 '82 C.06 B.S. L.616 J.D. [Norman&E.]
Edinger, Robert D., (AV) .... '52 '79 C.616 B.A. L.623 J.D. [Edinger&B.]

Edinger & Blakley, P.C., (AV)
Possum Creek Place, 6301 N. Western, Suite 150, 73118-1058
Telephone: 405-286-0251 Facsimile: 405-286-0893
Robert D. Edinger; Kenneth H. Blakley.
Civil Litigation and Regulatory Proceedings in the areas of Telecommunications, Antitrust, Energy and Environmental Law.
See Professional Biographies, OKLAHOMA CITY, OKLAHOMA

Edmonds, David W., (AV) .... '38 '65 C.446 L.623 J.D. [Edmonds,C.H.G.R.&W.]

Edmonds, Cole, Hargrave, Givens, Ryan & Woodson, P.C., (AV)
One North Hudson, Suite 200, 73102
Telephone: 405-272-0322 Fax: 405-235-4654
Email: echgwrw@edmonds-cole.com
David W. Edmonds; David H. Cole; John R. Hargrave; Greg D. Givens; Michael S. Ryan; Michael Woodson;—Clinton D. Whitworth; Scott R. Farris; Sheila R. Benson; Susan Lynn Eads; Brandon P. Wilson; Nevin R. Kirkland; Kelsie M. Sullivan.
General Civil Practice. Insurance, Casualty and Surety Law, Negligence Trial Practice, Environmental Law, Employment Law, Civil Rights Law, Lender Liability Law.
Southeast Oklahoma Office: 117 1/2 S. Wewoka, P.O. Box 1342, Wewoka, Oklahoma 74884. Telephone: 405-257-5550.
See Professional Biographies, OKLAHOMA CITY, OKLAHOMA

Edmondson, W. A. Drew, (AV) .... '46 '79 C.619 B.A.E. L.862 J.D. Atty. Gen.
Edmonson, Randy D. .... '67 '98 C.618 B.S. L.862 J.D. [P.A.Scott]
Edwards, Donald E. .... '46 '83 C.612 B.A. L.623 J.D. Sr. Atty. IRS Dist. Coun.
Edwards, Gordon W., Jr., (BV) ...... '44 '70 C.612 B.A. L.623 J.D. 4823 S. Western St.
Edwards, J. O., Jr. .... '33 '57 C&L.623 B.A., LL.B. Pres. & CEO, Enogex Inc.
Edwards, Joe E., (AV) .... '49 '74 C.623 B.B.A. L.616 J.D. [Day,E.P.&C.]
Edwards, John T., (AV) .... '27 '51 C&L.623 B.A., LL.B. [Monnet,H.B.T.&E.]
Edwards, Marc, (AV) .... '55 '83 C.804 B.S. L.862 J.D. [Phillips M.M.M.&M.]
Edwards, Roberta M. .... '30 '82 C.999 M.D. L.615 J.D. P.O. Box 12245
Edwards, Sally Ketchum, (AV) '53 '79 C.1147 B.A. L.623 J.D.
[Mulinix O.H.A.&L.]
Edwards, Shannon L., (AV) .... '60 '87 C.112 A.B. L.276 J.D. [Monnet,H.B.T.&E.]
Egan, Michael T., (AV) .... '58 '84 C.623 B.A. L.616 J.D. [Bullard&H.]
Ehlers, Patrick J., Jr. .... '67 '94 C.454 B.A. L.623 J.D. Pub. Def.
Eichner, Gregg B., (BV) .... '69 '94 C.575 B.S. L.910 J.D. [McAfee&T.]
Eilers, Justin P. .... '78 '04 C.612 B.S. L.623 J.D. [Johnson&H.]
Eisel, Timothy David, (CV) .... '66 '92 C&L.623 B.S., J.D. [Whitten,N.M.T.&R.]
Eissenstat, Eric S., (AV) .... '58 '83 C.612 B.S. L.623 J.D. [Fellers,S.B.B.&T.]
Elam, Theodore M., (AV) .... '34 '59 C&L.623 B.B.A., LL.B. [McAfee&T.]
Elder, A. Thomas, Jr., (AV) .... '43 '70 C.612 B.S. L.623 J.D. [Smith R.S.&E.]
Elder, David Allen .... '76 '02 C.806 B.A. L.1565 J.D. [Hartzog C.C.&N.]
Elder, James C., (AV) .... '47 '72 C&L.623 B.A., J.D. [Mock,S.W.E.R.&B.]
Elder, Mary E. .... '57 '92 C.174 B.S. L.616 J.D. [Elder,M.E.]
Elder, Mary Elizabeth, A Professional Corporation .... 5801 N.W. Grand Blvd., Ste. C
Eldridge, Clarence Kent .... '49 '76 C&L.623 B.A., J.D. [K.Eldridge]
Eldridge, David S. .... '36 '67 C.305 B.A. L.616 J.D. 6401 Brentford Pl.‡
Eldridge, Gregory S., (BV) .... '61 '92 C.1219 B.A. L.616 J.D. 5236 N.W. 111th Ter.
Eldridge, Kent, (AV) .... '49 '76 C&L.623 B.A., J.D. [K.Eldridge]

Eldridge, Kent, P.C., (AV)
1100 North Shartel, 73103-2618
Telephone: 405-235-6565 Fax: 405-236-1814
Email: kent@kenteldridge.com URL: http://www.kenteldridge.com
Kent Eldridge.
Criminal Law, Federal Criminal Law, White-Collar Crime, Drug Defense, Felonies, Insanity Defense, DUI, Juvenile, Divorce, Personal Injury, Workers Compensation, Administrative Adjudications.
See Professional Biographies, OKLAHOMA CITY, OKLAHOMA

Eldridge, Kent, PC .... 1100 N. Shartel
Elias, William K., (AV) .... '55 '81 C.612 B.A. L.862 J.D. [Elias,B.B.&N.]

Elias, Books, Brown & Nelson, P.C., (AV)
Two Leadership Square, 211 North Robinson, Suite 1300, 73102-7114
Telephone: 405-232-3722 Fax: 405-232-3746
URL: http://www.eliasbooksbrown.com

(This Listing Continued)

Elias, Books, Brown & Nelson, P.C. (Continued)
William K. Elias; Richard K. Books; L. Vance Brown; Lyle R. Nelson;—Marjorie Creasey; Richard J. Denny, III; Linda J. Blan-Byford. Of Counsel: Timothy C. Dowd.
Civil Practice including Trials in all State and Federal Courts, Appellate, Oil and Gas, Ad Valorem Taxation, Administrative, Corporation Commission, Environmental, Corporate, Bankruptcy and Reorganization, Commercial, State and Local Taxation, Financing, Real Estate, Title Examination, Banking Law, Commercial Litigation.
See Professional Biographies, OKLAHOMA CITY, OKLAHOMA

Elkouri, Joe M., (BV) '50 '75 C.612 B.A. L.616 J.D.
Admin. Law J., State Protec. Comm. & Dept. of Health
Ellingson, Darren T. .... '72 '02 C.999 L.615 J.D. Asst. Gen. Coun.
Ellington, Toni J. '56 '99 C.623 B.F.A. L.312 J.D.
Assoc. Staff Coun., Kerr-McGee Corp.
Elliott, Douglass R. ...... '62 '93 C.623 B.B.A. L.862 J.D. [Garrett] (Muskogee, Tulsa)
Elliott, Kenneth W., (AV) .... '53 '79 C&L.623 B.S., J.D. [Elliott&P.]
Elliott, Ray C., (AV) .... '51 '81 C.622 B.A. L.615 J.D. Asst. Dist. Atty.
Elliott, Stephen W., (AV) .... '54 '81 C&L.862 B.S., J.D. [Kline,K.E.&B.]

Elliott & Pederson, (AV)
City Place Building Twenty-Second Floor, 204 North Robinson Avenue, 73102
Telephone: 405-236-3600 Fax: 405-239-2265
Email: firm@kwelliott.com URL: http://www.kwelliott.com
Members of Firm: Kenneth W. Elliott; Devan A. Pederson.
ERISA, Premises Liability, Insurance Bad Faith, Insurance Subrogation, Fire Insurance Law, Inland Marine and Casualty Law, Medical Malpractice, Nursing Home Litigation, Toxic Substances, Environmental Law, Fidelity and Surety, Products Liability, Construction Law, Defense Law, Civil Trials in all Courts.
Reference: Bank One.
See Professional Biographies, OKLAHOMA CITY, OKLAHOMA

Ellis, Harvey D., Jr., (AV) .... '54 '82 C&L.623 B.A., J.D. [Crowe&D.]
Ellis, Nathan D. .... '73 '00 C&L.623 B.S./M.B.A., J.D. [Fagin,B.B.T.&K.]
Ellsworth, Arthur, (AV) .... '17 '41 C&L.623 B.A., LL.B. P.O. Box 54308
Elmore, Brant Matthew .... '72 '98 C&L.623 B.A., J.D. Off. of OK Atty. Gen.
Ely, John J., Jr., (BV) .... '56 '81 C&L.623 B.A., J.D. P.O. Box 53025
Embry, Donna .... '44 '76 C.531 B.S. L.615 J.D. Jud. Asst.; OK Supm. Ct.
Emerson, George Marvin, (AV) ...... '64 '89 C&L.623 B.A., J.D. [Riggs,A.N.T.O.&L.]
Emerson, Marvin C. .... '28 '53 C&L.623 A.B., J.D. Exec. Dir., State Bar Assn.
Emerson, Sandra L. .... '44 '77 C.623 L.615 J.D. Chf. Coun., Dept. of Human Servs.
Emmons, Michael A., (AV) '44 '73
C.612 B.A. L.623 J.D. 6301 Waterford Blvd., Suite 401
Emmons, Shannon K., (AV) .... '60 '90 C&L.623 B.A., J.D. [Phillips M.M.M.&M.]
Emmons, Stuart W., (BV) ...., '61 '87 C&L.623 B.B.A., J.D. [Federman&S.] (Pat.)
Empie, Robt. Y. .... '19 '50 C.623 L.615 LL.B. 6719 Avondale Dr.‡
Endicott, Lee, (AV) .... '59 '84 C.612 B.S. L.623 J.D. [Bullard&H.]
Enegren, Allen C. .... '42 '73 C.82 A.B. L.616 J.D. 4200 Perimeter Ctr., Ste. 245
Engel, Mark A., (AV) .... '59 '84 C&L.623 B.B.A., J.D. [Mansell&E.]
Engle, Niles S. .... '13 '53 C.608 B.S. L.616 LL.B. 6825 N.W. 135th Circle‡
Enis, Thomas J., (AV) .... '37 '66 C.698 B.S. L.502 J.D. [Fellers,S.B.B.&T.]
Entz, J. Michael, The Law Office of, (BV) '56 '87
C.612 B.S. L.623 J.D. 2816 N.W. 58th St., Ste. 103
Ephraim, Allan M. .... '32 '62 C.623 B.B.A. L.273 LL.B. 3141 N.W. 63rd St.
Epperson, Kraettli Q., (AV) .... '49 '79 C.623 B.A. L.616 J.D. [Rolston,H.E.M.&N.]
Epstein, Jon A., (AV) .... '63 '88 C.846 B.A. L.623 J.D. [Hall,E.H.G.G.&N.]
Erbar, Maria Tully, (CV) .... '55 '81 C&L.623 B.A., J.D. 5500 N. Western, Ste. 152
Erdoes, Peter A., (BV) .... '60 '85 C.612 B.S. L.623 J.D. [Peck,E.&W.]
Estes, Todd, (BV) .... '— '90 C&L.623 B.A., J.D. [Pierce C.H.B.&G.]
Eulberg, Chris H., (AV) .... '46 '78 C&L.616 B.S., J.D. [Eulberg]
Eulberg, Jane S., (AV) .... '49 '85 C.1147 B.S. L.616 J.D. Clk., U.S. Dist. Ct.
Eulberg, Jeff A., (BV) .... '68 '95 C.612 B.S. L.616 J.D. [Eulberg]
Eulberg Law Offices, (AV) .... 925 N.W. 6th
Evans, Allen D., (AV) .... '38 '63 C.623 B.A. L.477 J.D. [Crowe&D.]
Evans, Bryan Neil .... '75 '01 C.622 B.S. L.623 J.D. [Evans L.]
Evans, Daniel Leroy, (BV) '47 '78 C.842 B.A. L.616 J.D.
Dir., State of OK Corp. Comm., Off. of Admin. Proceedings
Evans, Edward Earl .... '68 '93 C&L.623 B.A., J.D. State Employ. Sec. Comm.
Evans, Jenny L. .... '72 '99 C.621 B.A. L.623 J.D. [Federman&S.]
Evans, Justin T. '— '01 C.424 B.S. L.329 J.D.
(adm. in IL; not adm. in OK) U.S. Ct.house, 200 N.W. 4th St., Rm. 5011
Evans, Kirby Byron .... '60 '00 C.1147 M.B.A. L.616 J.D. [Evans]
Evans, Marie Weston, (AV) .... '38 '82 C.059 B.Mus. L.623 J.D. 612 N.W. 39th‡

Evans, Rees T., (AV) '45 '71 C.893 B.A. L.623 J.D.
501 Northwest 13th Street, 73103
Telephone: 405-232-4311 Fax: 405-232-4315
Email: r.t.evans@att.net URL: http://www.lawyers.com/reestevanslaw
Practice Limited to Family Law including Trials, Appeals, and Mediations in Divorce, Alimony, Child Support and Child Custody Matters.
See Professional Biographies, OKLAHOMA CITY, OKLAHOMA

Evans, Sue R. .... '54 '78 C.69 B.A. L.623 J.D. V.P., Coates Field Service, Inc.
Evans Law .... Nichols Hill Plz., Ste. 200
Evans Law Firm, The, P.C. .... P.O. Box 2323
Everest, Claude Randolph '29 '54
C&L.623 B.A., LL.B. Exec. V.P., First Natl. Bk. & Tr. Co.
Everett, Dale M., (BV) .... '35 '62 C&L.623 B.B.A., LL.B. 1708 N. Bway.
Fabian, Stephen G., Jr., (BV) .... '45 '73 C.942 B.M.E. L.616 J.D. [Fabian&Assoc.]

Fabian & Associates, Inc., P.C., (BV)
228 Robert S. Kerr, Suite 700, 73102
Telephone: 405-232-4384 Fax: 405-232-5334 Toll Free: 1-877-435-7384
Email: sfabian@sbcglobal.net URL: http://www.lawyers.com/okc-dui
Stephen G. Fabian, Jr.
Driving Under The Influence, Traffic Violations, Criminal Defense.
See Professional Biographies, OKLAHOMA CITY, OKLAHOMA

Fagan, Brian Thomas .... '70 '97 C&L.862 B.S.B.A., J.D. [DeBee G.]
Fagin, Arnold D., (AV) .... '33 '58 C&L.623 B.A., LL.B. [Fagin&F.]
Fagin, Charles L., (AV) .... '37 '61 C&L.623 B.B.A., LL.B. [C.L.Fagin]

Fagin, Brown, Bush, Tinney & Kiser, A Professional Corporation, (AV)
120 N. Robinson, 1900 First National Center West, 73102
Telephone: 405-235-3413 Fax: 405-235-7436; 405-235-2807
Email: fbbtk@faginfirm.com
Gary M. Bush; Wm. Don Kiser; Allan Arthur Brooks, III; Nathan D. Ellis; George J. Fagin (1908-1994); Michael D. Tinney (1944-1989); J. Scott Brown (Retired).
Municipal and Public Authority Finance, Securities and Corporate Financing Law.
See Professional Biographies, OKLAHOMA CITY, OKLAHOMA

Fagin, Charles L., P.L.L.C., (AV) .... 100 Park Avenue, Suite 400
Fagin & Fagin, P.C., (AV) .... 210 Park Avenue
Falcone, John P. .... '71 '96 C.1044 B.A. L.262 J.D. [McKinney&S.]

Falsetti, Louis P., (BV) ....'57 '83 C.705 B.A. L.616 J.D. [Brady,S.&F.]
Farabow, Loraine Dillinder, (AV) ..... '66 '93 C.232 B.A. L.575 J.D. The State Bar Assn.
Farber, Joseph W., (BV) ....'57 '84 C.145 B.A. L.623 J.D. [Farber]
Farber, M. Jay, (AV) ....'55 '80 C.025 B.A. L.615 J.D. Asst. U.S. Atty.
Farber Law Office, (BV) .... 8524 S. Western Ave., Ste. 118
Farha, Geo. S. ....'18 '55 C.623 L.616 LL.B. 12824 Cedar Springs Rd.‡
Farha, James T. .... '41 '66 C&L.623 B.B.A., J.D. Oklahoma Student Loan Authority
Farnum, Gary L., (BV) ....'54 '96 C&L.618 B.A., J.D. [Ⓐ Day,E.P.&C.]
Farris, Rebecca A. ....'72 '99 C.612 B.A. L.623 J.D. [Ⓐ Helms&U.]
Farris, Richard L., (BV) .... '48 '73 C.612 B.B.A. L.623 J.D. 641L Avondale Dr., Ste. 320
Farris, Scott R., (BV) ....'70 '97 C.840 B.S. L.615 J.D. [Ⓐ Edmonds,C.H.G.R.&W.]
Farzaneh, Amir M., (BV) ....'63 '96 C.623 B.S. L.615 J.D. [Ⓒ McKinney&S.]
Fashimpaur, Jay Jon, (BV) ....'44 '71 C.1147 B.S. L.616 J.D. 6801 N. Bway. Ext.
Faught, Irving L., (AV) .... '40 '65 C.623 B.A. L.893 J.D. Admr., State Secs. Comm.
Fauss, Edw. J., (AV) .... '24 '49 C.861 L.623 J.D. 6416 W. Rambridge Dr.‡
Feagins, Ken .... '60 '89 C.623 B.L.S. L.880 J.D. [K.Feagins]
Feagins, Ken, P.C. .... 1000 N.E. 10th St., Ste. 206
Fears, John G. .... '46 '75 C.612 B.A. L.615 J.D. Asst. Gen. Coun., Dept. of Human Servs.
Featherly, Henry F., (AV) ....'30 '57 C.612 B.A. L.623 LL.B. [Ⓒ Lamun,M.C.&D.]
Feaver, M. Ellen, (BV) ....'50 '84 C&L.623 B.A., J.D. P.O. Box 53025
Federman, William B., (AV) ....'58 '82 C.94 B.A. L.862 J.D. [Federman&S.]

Federman & Sherwood, (AV)
120 North Robinson, Suite 2720, 73102
Mailing Address: Attn: Nancy Beatty, 120 North Robinson, Suite 2720, Oklahoma City, OK 73102
Telephone: 405-235-1560 Fax: 405-239-2112
URL: http://www.federmanlaw.com
William B. Federman; John Charles Sherwood (Not admitted in OK; Board Certified, Civil Trial Law; Personal Injury Trial Law, Texas Board of Legal Specialization);—Stuart W. Emmons; W. Todd Ver Weire; Jenny L. Evans; Jennifer F. Sherrill. Of Counsel: A. Daniel Woska; Rodney J. Heggy; William P. Wasson.
Litigation, Arbitration, Securities Litigation, Products Liability, Class Actions.
Dallas, Texas Office: 2926 Maple Avenue, Suite 200, 75201. Telephone: 214-696-1100. Facsimile: 214-740-0112.
See Professional Biographies, OKLAHOMA CITY, OKLAHOMA

Felkner, Stacey Haws, (BV) ....'66 '91 C&L.623 B.A., J.D. [Ⓒ Fenton,F.S.R.&M.]

Fellers, Snider, Blankenship, Bailey & Tippens, A Professional Corporation, (AV) BR
Bank One Tower, 100 North Broadway, Suite 1700, 73102-8820 ⊙
Telephone: 405-232-0621 Fax: 405-232-9659
Email: fsbb&t@icnet.net URL: http://www.fellerssnider.com
James D. Fellers (1913-1997); John Joseph Snider (1928-1997); Terry W. Tippens; K. Nicholas Wilson; Harry H. Selph, II; Warren F. Bickford, IV; John B. Heatly; Michael R. Ford; Eric S. Eissenstat; Stephen R. Stephens; Doneen Douglas Jones; Thomas J. Enis; Joe C. Lewallen, Jr.; Gregory A. Castro; Kevin R. Donelson; Mark K. Stonecipher; Andrew L. Walding; Bryan N.B. King; Brent M. Johnson; Charles C. Callaway, Jr.; William H. Whitehill, Jr.; Randall K. McCarthy; Jay P. Walters; Margaret A. Bomhoff; Brooks A. Richardson; Daniel P. Dooley;—Kelli M. Masters; N. Janine Wheeler; Lance E. Leffel; Nicholas V. Merkley; Michael H. Brown; Casey Tippens Delaney. Of Counsel: Jap W. Blankenship; Burck Bailey; Paul W. Dudman; Bill D. McCarthy; Mitchell K. McCarthy.
General Practice. Trial of all Cases in State and Federal Courts. Commercial, Corporate, Oil and Gas, Banking and Banking Regulation, Administrative, Probate, Estate Planning, Transportation, Bankruptcy, Securities, Insurance, Federal and State Taxation, Unfair Competition, Aircraft Finance and Leasing, Aircraft Sales, Aircraft Title, Real Property, Employment, Workers' Compensation, Intellectual Property, and Antitrust Law.
Representative Clients: A.S.C. Incorporated; Chrysler Financial Corp.; Corken, Inc.; Doug Carson & Associates, Inc.; Filtrex, Inc.; General Electric Capital Corp; Halliburton Co.; Harold Simpson, Inc.; Hertz Corp.; Little Giant Pump Company.
Tulsa, Oklahoma Office: The Kennedy Building, 321 South Boston, Suite 800. Telephone: 918-599-0621. Fax: 918-583-9659.
See Professional Biographies, OKLAHOMA CITY, OKLAHOMA

Felty, Michael C., (AV) ....'54 '84 C.1300 B.S. L.623 J.D. [Foliart,H.O.&B.]
Fent, Jerry R., (BV) ....'34 '66 C.614 B.S. L.615 J.D. 1830 N.W. 18th St.
Fenton, Elliott C., (AV) ....'14 '37 C&L.623 B.A., LL.B. [Ⓒ Fenton,F.S.R.&M.]

Fenton, Fenton, Smith, Reneau & Moon, (AV)
211 North Robinson, Suite 800 N, 73102
Telephone: 405-235-4671 Telecopier: 405-235-5247
Email: mail@fentonlaw.com
Edgar Fenton (1890-1977); Milton R. Moon (1921-1988); Wm. G. Smith (1919-1993); Dale Reneau; Donald R. Wilson; Stephen Peterson; John A. McCaleb; C. William Threlkeld; Tom E. Mullen; Brenda K. Peterson; Beverly S. Pearson; Michael D. Duncan; Michael S. McMillin; Greg K. Ballard; C. Todd Ward; John B. Vera; Albert Lewis Tait, Jr.;—John Mark Mcalester; Brion Hitt; Ryan R. Chaffin; John C. Kmetz. Of Counsel: Stacey Haws Felkner; Elliott C. Fenton; James P. Kelley; Gerald E. Kelley; J. Mitchell Gregory, Jr.; Ross L. Gregory; Susan Ann Knight; Robert Edward Manchester.
General Civil Practice. Casualty, Surety and Insurance Law, Workers Compensation, Employers Liability, Medical and Hospital Malpractice, Products Liability, Toxic Tort and Environmental Law, School Law, Real Property, Title Examination, Title Insurance, Probate, Mortgage Foreclosure, Corporate, Commercial, Zoning, Planning and Subdivision, Real Estate Development, Municipal Law. Trials in all State and Federal Courts.
Representative Clients: The Alliance Insurance Cos.; American Fidelity Insurance Co.; Chrysler Corp.; The Hartford Insurance Group; Insurance Company of North America; Roadway Express Inc.; The St. Paul Insurance Cos.; The Travelers Insurance Cos.; United States Fidelity & Guaranty Co.
See Professional Biographies, OKLAHOMA CITY, OKLAHOMA

Ferguson, James C., (AV) ....'51 '85 C.902 B.S. L.623 J.D. [Walker,F.&F.]
Ferguson, Steven E., (BV) ....'55 '80 C.623 B.A. L.615 J.D. [Crabb,F.&R.]
Ferguson, Thomas G., Jr., (AV) ....'48 '73 C.885 B.A. L.902 J.D. [Walker,F.&F.]
Ferrell, Joan E. ....'50 '92 C.612 B.S. L.623 J.D. 1330 N. Classen Blvd., Ste. 306
Ferrell, Shannon L. ....'75 '03 C.612 B.A. L.615 J.D. [Ⓐ McKinney&S.]
Field, Leslie M. ..... '68 '96 C.966 B.A. L.623 J.D. Compl. Coun., Midland Financial Co.
Fielden, Arlen E., (AV) ....'41 '65 C.612 B.S. L.623 J.D. [Crowe&D.]
Fields, Roberta Browning, (AV) ...... '— '84 C.1288 B.A. L.623 J.D. [Rainey,R.R.&B.]
Fields, Robin F., (AV) ....'55 '84 C.1083 B.A. L.623 J.D. [Ryan,W.&C.]
File, Diane P., (BV) '49 '80
C.623 B.A. L.615 J.D. Asst. Gen. Coun., Dept. of Human Servs.
Findeiss, Nancy, (BV) ....'50 '78 C.1322 B.A. L.623 J.D. Atty., Ct. of App.
Fischer, Amy Sherry, (BV) ....'70 '95 C.862 B.A. L.623 J.D. [Foliart,H.O.&B.]
Fischer, John F., II, (AV) ....'48 '76 C&L.623 B.A., J.D. [Andrews D.]
Fisher, Eric S., (BV) ....'65 '96 C.378 B.S. L.623 J.D. [Crowe&D.]
Fisher, R. Darryl ....'39 '89 C.618 B.S. L.615 J.D. 3340 Oak Hollow Rd.
Fist, David L., (AV) ....'31 '55 C&L.623 B.A., LL.B. [Rosenstein,F.&R.] ⊙

Fitch, Mark K., (AV) '57 '83 C&L.623 B.A., J.D.
1900 N.W. Expressway, Suite 1300, 73118-1822
Telephone: 405-848-7100 Fax: 405-848-8241
Email: mfitch@ilinkusa.net
Estate Planning, Wills and Probate, Trusts, Elder Law, Real Property, Federal and State Taxation Law, including Individual, Estate and Gift, Corporations, Partnerships, Fiduciary and Trust Litigation.
See Professional Biographies, OKLAHOMA CITY, OKLAHOMA

Fite, Jack P., (AV) ....'51 '76 C.623 B.A. L.616 J.D. [White,C.&F.]
Fitzpatrick, Jeremy R. ....'77 '04 C&L.623 B.B.A., J.D. [Ⓐ Moricoli,H.&C.]

Flaugher, W. Terry, (BV) ....'43 '73 C.1147 B.A. L.615 J.D. [W.T.Flaugher]
Flaugher, W. Terry, P.C., (BV) ....Fifty Penn Place, Suite 507
Fleetwood, Judy Lynn ....'52 '84 C.173 B.S. L.616 J.D. Okla. Tax Comm.
Fleischaker, David S. '44 '70 C.1036 B.A. L.846 J.D.
(adm. in TX; not adm. in OK) 100 N. Broadway Ste. 2460
Fleming, Kent, (AV) ....'37 '65 C&L.623 B.S., J.D. [Huckaby,F.G.&O.]
Fleming, Sherri T. ....'71 '02 C.1183 B.A. L.1187 J.D. [Derryberry,Q.S.&N.]
Fletcher, Cheri D. ....'66 '99 C.1147 B.B.A. L.616 J.D. [C.D.Fletcher]
Fletcher, George R. ....'23 '59 C.612 B.S. L.616 LL.B. 708 N.W. 27th St.‡
Fletcher, Cheri D., P.C. .... 6909 N. Robinson
Flood, Kathryn K. '59 '85 C.951 B.A. L.94 J.D.
(adm. in MA; not adm. in OK) OK Ct. of App.
Flores, Mikel Walter, (BV) ....'67 '94 C.556 B.A. L.615 J.D. [M.Flores&Assoc.]
Flores, Mikel & Associates, P.C., (BV) ....6440 Avondale Dr., Ste. 200
Flowers, Toby Gene ....'75 '01 C&L.623 B.A., J.D. 317 N.W. 12th St.
Floyd, P. Kay ....'58 '83 C.612 B.S. L.623 J.D. Okla. Horse Racing Comm.
Flynn, Heather D. ....'75 '02 C&L.862 B.S., J.D. [Ⓐ Doerner,S.D.&A.]
Fogarty, Michael O. ....'48 '85 C.613 B.A. L.616 J.D. Okla. Dept. of Human Servs.
Foley, John J. ....'— '81 C.613 B.A. L.623 J.D. [J.J.Foley]
Foley, John J., P.C. ....205 N.W. 63rd St., Ste. 330
Folger, Mark D. ....'76 '05 C.210 B.A. L.615 J.D. [Ⓐ McAfee&T.]
Foliart, James D., (AV) ....'— '48 C.620 A.B. L.623 LL.B [Foliart,H.O.&B.]

Foliart, Huff, Ottaway & Bottom, A Professional Corporation, (AV)
The Bank of Oklahoma Plaza, 201 Robert S. Kerr Avenue, 12th Floor, 73102
Telephone: 405-232-4633 FAX: 405-232-3462
Email: foliartfirm@oklahomacounsel.com
James D. Foliart; Glen D. Huff; Larry D. Ottaway; Monty B. Bottom; Michael C. Felty; Susan A. Short; David A. Branscum; David K. McPhail; Michael T. Maloan; Robert D. Hoisington; Amy Sherry Fischer; Denise D. Canada;—Steven James Johnson; Whitney E. Buergler; Amanda F. Miller; Jason T. Rogers; Larry H. Harden; Blake D. Beeler.
General Civil, Trial and Appellate Practice in State and Federal Courts. Insurance Defense, Medical Malpractice, Professional Liability, Products Liability, Personal Injury, Health Care, Employment, Intellectual Property and Negligence Law. Complex Litigation, including Class Actions and Environmental Law.
See Professional Biographies, OKLAHOMA CITY, OKLAHOMA

Foltz, Howard P. ....'25 '53 C.623 B.A. L.616 J.D. 3317 Red Rock Rd.‡
Forbes, Robert A., Jr., (BV) ....'48 '75 C.307 B.A. L.616 J.D. 1120 S. Douglas Blvd.
Ford, Claire M. ....'46 '90 C.617 B.S. L.616 J.D. 4800 W. I-40
Ford, Kenneth L., (CV) '47 '85
C.942 B.A. L.616 J.D. Mng. Atty., Legal Aid of Western Okla.
Ford, Michael R., (AV) ....'45 '70 C&L.623 B.A., J.D. [Fellers,S.B.B.&T.]
Ford, Richard C., (AV) ....'46 '75 C.674 A.B. L.623 J.D. [Crowe&D.]
Ford, Richard D., (BV) ....'46 '81 C.612 B.S. L.616 J.D. 6 N.E. 63rd St.
Foreman, Linda S. '50 '89
C.619 B.S.Ed. L.612 J.D. Staff Atty., State Ins. Fund [Hoffman K.]
Forrow, Yolanda Rachelle '68 '00
C&L.623 B.A., J.D. Legal Aid Services of Oklahoma, Inc.
Forshee, Richard D., (AV) ....'51 '80 C.612 B.S. L.616 J.D. [Williams,B.F.&B.]
Fortune, Deborah E., (BV) ....'51 '79 C&L.623 B.S., J.D. 4528 N. Classen Blvd.
Fosdyke, Clyde E. ....'43 '68 C.612 B.S. L.623 J.D. 2725 N.W. 111
Foshee, Jerry ....'47 '76 C.1147 B.A. L.615 J.D. [Foshee&Y.]
Foshee & Yaffe, (AV) .... P.O. Box 890420
Foss, David Nile ....'65 '93 C.612 B.A. L.623 J.D. Fleming Cos., Inc.
Foster, Michael J., (AV) '67 '93 C.339 B.S. L.862 J.D.
Staff Coun., Kerr-McGee Corp.
Foster, Stan L., (AV) '43 '69
C&L.623 B.B.A., J.D. Exec. Dir., Legal Aid of Western Okla.
Fouts, Michael F., (BV) ....'49 '79 C.1070 B.S. L.616 J.D. Asst. Mun. Coun.
Fowler, Daniel J., (AV) ....'33 '65 C&L.623 B.S., J.D. [Daugherty,F.P.&H.] ‡
Fowler, George E., Jr. ....'47 '78 C.999 B.A. L.383 J.D. Ky. Ct. of App.
Fox, David N. ....'30 '65 C.623 B.B.A. L.616 LL.B. Int. Rev. Serv.
Francis, Monroe C. ....'28 '56 C.612 A.B. L.623 LL.B. 1401 Dorchester Dr.
Frank, Virginia L. ....'66 '92 C.623 B.A. L.615 J.D. 5350 S. Western Ave., Ste. 617
Franklin, Inks ....'31 '72 C.502 B.A. L.616 J.D. 6108 S. McKinley Ave.
Franz, Patricia L. ....'— '98 C.611 B.A. L.608 J.D. [Ⓐ Rainey,R.R.&B.]
Frates, Kent F., (AV) ....'38 '64 C.813 B.A. L.37 LL.B. [Ⓒ Hartzog C.C.&N.]
Fredrick, Dustin R. ....'— '01 C.612 B.A. L.623 J.D. [Ⓐ Rainey,R.R.&B.]
Fredrickson, Kirk D., (AV) ....'50 '76 C.623 B.A. L.846 J.D. [Ⓒ R.C.Bright]
Free, Phillip L., Jr., (BV) ....'66 '93 C.622 B.S. L.623 J.D. [Crowe&D.] (Pat.)
Freede, Charles L., Jr., (BV) '46 '73
C&L.623 B.A., J.D. Gen. Coun., Capitol Abstract & Title Co.
Freeman, Howard S. ....'19 '55 C.188 B.A. L.616 J.D. 1218 Belford Avenue‡
Freeman, Louis J. ....'56 '91 C.1147 B.S. L.615 J.D. 2548 N.W. Expy.
Freeman, Richard W., Jr. ....'52 '77 C&L.623 B.A., J.D. Dept. of Human Servs.
French, Robert A., (AV) ....'59 '93 C&L.623 B.A., J.D. [Ⓐ Monnet,H.B.T.&E.]
Friend, Rex D., (BV) ....'54 '84 C.620 B.A. L.623 J.D. 3801 N. Classen Blvd., Ste. 8
Fries, Ann C. ...... '58 '84 C.802 B.A. L.502 J.D. Mng. Atty., Hartford Fire Insurance Co.
Fries, Robert C. .... '71 '96 C.1243 B.A. L.623 J.D. 1101 Soverign Row, Suite A
Friot, Stephen P. ....'47 '72 C&L.623 B.A., J.D. U.S. Dist. J.
Fritze, Christine R. ....'55 '91 C.1147 B.A. L.623 J.D. [Ⓐ Brickell&Assoc.]
Frogge, Gregory, (BV) ....'64 '89 C.502 B.A. L.623 J.D. [Ⓒ McAfee&T.]
Fudge, Randall S. ....'53 '94 C.623 B.B.A. L.616 J.D. [R.S.Fudge]
Fudge, Randall S., P.C. .... P.O. Box 60872
Fugitt, F. Andrew, (AV) .... '58 '83 C&L.623 B.B.A., J.D. [Ⓐ CenterForEducationLaw]
Fulkerson, Ronald D., (BV) ....'32 '62 C.1147 B.S. L.616 LL.B. P.O. Box 780
Fulkerson, Sam R., (AV) ....'59 '91 C&L.623 B.A., J.D. [McAfee&T.]
Fulkerson, Shawn D., (BV) ....'63 '91 C&L.623 B.B.A., J.D. 10444 Greenbriar Pl.
Fuller, Gary F., (AV) ....'36 '59 C&L.623 B.A., LL.B. [McAfee&T.]

Fuller, Tubb, Pomeroy & Stokes, A Professional Corporation, (AV)
1000 Bank of Oklahoma Plaza, 201 Robert S. Kerr Avenue, 73102
Telephone: 405-235-2575 Fax: 405-232-8384
Email: ftps@ftpslaw.com URL: http://www.ftpslaw.com
G. M. Fuller (1920-1999); Jerry Tubb; L. David Pomeroy; Terry Stokes. Of Counsel: Michael A. Bickford; Thomas J. Kenan; Roland Tague; Dan M. Peters.
General Practice, Litigation, Bankruptcy, Bankruptcy Reorganization, Commercial Workouts, Corporate, Corporate Finance, Real Estate, Probate, Estate Planning, Administrative Law, Commercial Law, Alternative Dispute Resolution, Arbitration, Mediation, Securities, Appellate Practice, Employment Law, Insolvency, Debtor/Creditor Rights.
Representative Clients: French Petroleum Corp.; Oklahoma Association of Insurance Agents; LTV Energy Products Co.; Northwestern National Life Insurance Co.; Purina Mills, Inc.; Sequa Corp.; Halliburton Oil Producing Co.; Chemical Bank/Chemical Financial Corporation; Pitney Bowes, Inc.; Norwest Banks.
See Professional Biographies, OKLAHOMA CITY, OKLAHOMA

Fulmer, Simone Gosnell ....'67 '96 C.613 B.M.E. L.623 J.D. [Whitten,N.M.T.&R.]
Fulp, Ray R., Jr., (BV) .... '37 '74 C.69 B.B.A. L.615 J.D. 2828 N.W. 57th, Ste. 310
Funk, John W., (AV) ....'53 '78 C&L.623 B.B.A., J.D. [Conner&W.]

Funnell, Donald K., (AV) ....'55 '84 C.1147 B.B.A. L.623 J.D. [Lytle S.&C.]
Funston, Bob, (AV) '38 '65
C.613 B.S. L.862 J.D. Exec. Dir., State Employ. Security Comm.
Furr, Carol J., (BV) ....'— '84 C.620 B.A. L.616 J.D. OK Crim. Jus. Admin.
Fuson, James R. ....'34 '61 C.623 B.A. L.846 LL.B. 3630 N.W. 47th‡

Gable & Gotwals, A Professional Corporation, (AV)
Fifteenth Floor, One Leadership Square, 211 North Robinson Avenue, 73102-7101
⊙
Telephone: 405-235-5500 Fax: 405-235-2875
Email: info@gablelaw.com URL: http://www.gablelaw.com
Leadership Square Office Personnel: Steven L. Barghols; Sidney G. Dunagan; David L. Kearney; Eric R. King; Rob F.M. Robertson; Leasa M. Stewart. Associates: John Martin Benson; Daniel A. Nickel; Amy M. Stipe; Jeremy K. Webb (Not admitted in OK). Of Counsel: Linda A. King; Joseph T. Thai.
Administrative Law, Alternative Dispute Resolution, Antitrust, Bankruptcy, Banks and Banking, Class Actions, Commercial Law, Communications and Media, Copyright, Corporate Law, Employee Benefits, Energy, Environmental Law, Family Law, Finance, Franchises and Franchising, General Practice, Guardianship and Conservatorship, Insurance, Intellectual Property, Labor and Employment, Litigation, Mergers, Acquisitions and Divestitures, Natural Resources, Patents, Personal Injury, Probate, Property Law, Real Estate, RICO, Regulatory Law, Securities, Software Licensing, Taxation, Trademarks, Torts, Utility Law, Workers Compensation.
Tulsa, Oklahoma Offices: 1100 Oneok Plaza, 100 West Fifth Street 74103-4217. Telephone: 918-595-4800. Fax: 918-595-4990.
See Professional Biographies, OKLAHOMA CITY, OKLAHOMA

Gaddis, Preston G., II, (AV) ....'38 '62 C&L.623 A.B., LL.B. [Crowe&D.]
Gaines, B. Gore, (AV) ....'69 '95 C.623 B.B.A. L.616 J.D. [Lytle S.&C.]
Galier, Anthony C., The Law Office of ....'61 '91 C.1147 B.S. L.623 J.D. P.O. Box 1011
Gallegos, Luis H. ....'73 '01 C&L.623 B.A., J.D. 3211 S Western Ave.
Galyon, Justin Brent, (BV) ....'50 '87 C.623 B.A. L.615 J.D. 200 N. Harvey
Gamble, Gerald L. ....'41 '68 C.623 B.A. L.616 J.D. 204 N. Robinson
Gamino, Daniel J., (AV) ....'47 '73 C.1147 B.A. L.623 J.D. 3315 N.W. 63rd St.
Garbrecht, Robert L., (AV) ....'64 '90 C&L.623 B.B.A., J.D. [McAfee&T.]
Gardner, John S., (BV) ....'55 '93 C.871 B.S. L.623 J.D. [Ⓒ Mulinix O.H.A.&L.]
Gardner, Kent W. ....'78 '04 C.612 B.S. L.623 J.D. [Ⓐ Hartzog C.C.&N.]
Gardner, Lawn B., (BV) ....'62 '94 C.1147 B.A. L.623 J.D. [Ⓐ DeBee G.]
Garnett, Wm. K., (BV) ....'11 '37 C&L.623 B.S., LL.B. 13216 Cedar Springs Rd.
Garrett, Bryan G., (BV) ....'72 '98 C.802 B.A. L.623 J.D. [Holloway,D.&B.]
Garrett, David M., (AV) ......'41 '69 C.619 B.S. L.862 J.D. [Garrett] (⊙Muskogee, Tulsa)
Garrett, James P. ....'22 '48 C&L.623 B.S., J.D. Ct. of Civil App. J.
Garrett, John W. ....'78 '04 C.802 B.B.A. L.615 J.D. [Ⓐ Crowe&D.]
Garrett, Lisa A. ....'77 '02 C.1300 B.A. L.623 J.D. [Ⓐ Moricoli,H.&C.]
Garrett, Robert D. ......'37 '67 C.623 B.A. L.616 J.D. 4334 N.W. Expressway, Suite 297
Garrett, Stephen P., (AV) '44 '76 C.623 B.B.A. L.616 J.D.
Sr. V.P., Law & Govt. Affs., Amer. Fidelity Corp.
Garrett Law Office, P.C., (AV)
4000 N. Classen Boulevard, Suite 110-S (⊙Fayetteville, AR; Muskogee, Tulsa, OK)
Garrison, Edwin F., (AV) ....'39 '67 C.622 B.S. L.862 J.D. [Looney,N.&J.]
Garside, Steven "L" ....'57 '83 C.1085 B.A. L.615 J.D. Asst. Municipal Coun.
Garvey, John J. ....'55 '81 C.612 B.A. L.623 J.D. [J.J.Garvey]
Garvey, John J., PC ....1724 Dorchester Place

Garvin, Agee, Carlton & Mashburn, L.L.P., (AV)
2100 City Place Tower, 204 North Robinson Avenue, 73102 ⊙
Telephone: 405-232-9996 Fax: 405-232-9979
URL: http://www.attysatlaw.com
John D. Mashburn.
General Civil Practice. Personal Injury, Property Damage, Products Liability, Insurance and Commercial Litigation. Real Estate, Probate, Estate Planning and Trusts. Oil and Gas, Business, Commercial, Banking, Bankruptcy, Collections, Employment, School and Municipal Law.
Representative Clients: Banks: Paul Valley National Bank; First National Bank, Maysville; Farmers Home Administration Insurance: Loftin Humphrey & Menefee, Inc. Real Estate: Humphrey Realty, Inc. Oil & Gas: Norman Bros. Tank Trucks, Inc. Other: City of Pauls Valley, Oklahoma; Royal Coach Manufacturing; James Supplies & Rental Co.
Pauls Valley Office: 101 E. Grant Avenue, P.O. Box 10, 73075. Telephone: 405-238-5559. Fax: 405-238-5666.
See Professional Biographies, OKLAHOMA CITY, OKLAHOMA

Gaston, James L., Jr., (BV) ....'54 '79 C.831 B.A. L.615 J.D. [Ⓐ McGivern,G.&C.]
Gatewood, Evan Blake, (AV) ....'64 '89 C&L.623 B.A., J.D. [Ⓐ Hayes&M.]
Gatliff, John E., II ....'60 '98 C&L.623 B.A., J.D. [Ⓐ Conner&W.]
Gautreaux, Mark E. ....'55 '81 C.1147 B.S. L.623 J.D. 3008 Brownestone Rd.‡
Geary, Edmond F., Jr., (AV) ....'42 '72 C&L.623 B.A., J.D. [E.F.Geary]
Geary, Edmond F., (AV) ....5601 N.W. 72nd St., Ste. 178
Geer, Kurt A., (BV) ....'55 '87 C.608 B.A. L.616 J.D. Asst. Pub. Def.
Geiger, Jerrod S. ....'76 '02 C&L.623 B.A., J.D. [Ⓐ Pierce C.H.B.&G.]
Geister, Charles E., III, (AV) ....'55 '80 C&L.623 B.A., J.D. [Hartzog C.C.&N.]
Geitgey, Jonna S., (BV) '56 '81 C&L.623 B.A., J.D.
Asst. Gen Coun., State Dept. of Human Servs.
Gelders, John B., (P.C.), (AV) ....'51 '78 C.612 B.S. L.623 J.D. [Grimes,G.A.&D.]
Gelnar, Stephen C., (AV) ....'66 '99 C.612 B.S. L.616 J.D. [Burnett&G.]
Gelvin, (Pete) K., Jr., (BV) ......'54 '79 C.1300 B.A. L.615 J.D. Crim. App. Ct. Jud. Asst.
Gentry, D. Sharon ....'52 '94 C.623 B.A. L.616 J.D. [Ⓐ Riggs,A.N.T.O.&L.]
George, Cindy Jo ....'52 '88 C&L.623 B.S., J.D. OK Supm. Ct.
George, David C. ....'21 '48 C&L.623 LL.B. Sr. V.P., Wilshire Oil Co. of Texas
George, James W., (AV) ....'30 '57 C&L.623 B.A., LL.B. [Ⓒ Crowe&D.]
George, Kelly A., (AV) ....'62 '89 C.1315 B.S. L.623 J.D. [Burch&G.]
George, Tracy L. ....'68 '04 C.714 B.A. L.615 J.D. P.O. Box 60367
Geries, Stephen L. ....'70 '01 C.921 B.S. L.615 J.D. [Ⓐ Collins,Z.&W.]
Germany, DeeAnn L. ....'71 '99 C.612 B.S. L.623 J.D. [Ⓐ Burch&G.]
Gerrish, Jennifer C. '— '97 C.174 B.A. L.623 J.D.
Law Ref. Libr., Oklahoma City Univ. Law Libr.
Geurin, Stan P. '61 '93 C.623 B.S. L.615 J.D.
Coun. - Marketing and Midstream, Devon Energy Corp.
Ghosh, Shubha '64 '96 C.31 B.A. L.813 J.D.
(adm. in CA; not adm. in OK) Asst. Prof., Oklahoma City Univ. Sch. of Law
Gibbens, James C., (AV) ....'23 '50 C.976 B.A. L.309 LL.B. [Ⓒ Crowe&D.]
Gibbons, Nicole Marie Nantois ....'71 '96 C&L.623 B.A., J.D. OK Health Care Authority
Gibson, Joe Fred ....'12 '36 C&L.623 B.S., LL.B. 2521 Cummings Dr.‡
Gibson, Keith R., (AV) ....'54 '84 C.1047 B.A. L.616 J.D. [Williams,B.F.&B.]
Gibson, Michael T. '58 '82 C.546 B.A. L.976 J.D.
(adm. in NE; not adm. in OK) Prof. of Law, Oklahoma City Univ. Sch. of Law
Giddens, Jared D., (AV) ....'56 '81 C.1147 B.S. L.623 J.D. [Conner&W.]
Gieger, Gayland G. ....'66 '92 C.1315 B.A. L.615 J.D. Co. Dist. Atty.'s Off.
Gierhart, Douglas M., (CV) '56 '82
C.623 B.A. L.616 J.D. 2629 W. I 44 Service Rd., Ste. 214
Giessmann, Gary L., (BV) ....'52 '85 C.623 B.A. L.616 J.D. [Nash,C.&K.]
Gifford, Lisa ....'68 '95 C.1147 B.A. L.623 J.D. OK Health Care Auth.
Gigger, Helen C. ....'44 '70 C&L.325 B.A., J.D. Asst. Mun. Counselor
Gigger, Nathan J., (BV) ....'44 '70 C.1362 B.A. L.325 J.D. 732 N. E. 36th
Gilbert, Barbara Snow, (AV) ....'54 '80 C.170 B.A. L.846 J.D. Fed. Law Clk.
Gilbert, E. Harry, III, (AV) ......'52 '79 C&L.623 B.S.E.E., J.D. [Ⓒ McAfee&T.] (Pat.)
Gilbert, Olin Dudley '66 '92 C.612 B.S. L.616 J.D.
4545 N. Lincoln Boulevard, Ste. 164
Gilbert, Sally, (AV) ....'54 '80 C.429 B.A. L.1035 J.D. 9400 Broadway Ext., Ste. 500‡
Gilchrist, Jack P., (AV) ....'61 '89 C&L.623 B.A., J.D. [DeBee G.]
Gile, C. Merle, (AV) ....'44 '72 C.1147 B.S. L.616 J.D. [Ⓒ McCaffrey&Assoc.]
Giles, Nita R., (BV) ....'49 '74 C.612 B.A. L.623 J.D. [N.R.Giles]
Giles, Nita R., Inc., (BV) ....5101 N. Classen Blvd., Suite 400
Gilliland, Kent A., (AV) ....'59 '87 C.612 B.S. L.616 J.D. [Hall,E.H.G.G.&N.]
Gilliland, Robert H., Jr., (AV) ....'41 '66 C.840 B.A. L.623 J.D. [McAfee&T.]
Gingrich, Gary A., (BV) ....'53 '80 C.623 B.B.A. L.616 J.D. 401 N. Hudson
Gisinger, Kayce L., (AV) ....'62 '88 C.1300 B.A. L.615 J.D. [Abowitz,T.&D.]
Gist, J. Fred, (AV) ....'51 '76 C.623 B.A. L.846 J.D. [Hall,E.H.G.G.&N.]
Givens, Greg D., (AV) ....'58 '83 C&L.623 B.A., J.D. [Edmonds,C.H.G.R.&W.]
Givens, Jimmy D., (BV) ....'55 '81 C&L.623 B.A., J.D. Gen. Coun., Dept. of Envir. Qual.
Givens, Juston Robert ....'75 '01 C.612 B.A. L.615 J.D. [Ⓐ Pierce C.H.B.&G.]
Glasgow, Paula R. ....'59 '85 C.612 B.S. L.623 J.D. State Dept. of Secs.
Glasgow, Richard M., (AV) ....'— '90 C.1147 B.S. L.616 J.D. [Ⓐ King]
Glover, Daniel J., (AV) ....'61 '87 C.612 B.S. L.623 J.D. [Hall,E.H.G.G.&N.]
Goble, Cynthia Jean, (CV) ....'61 '93 C&L.623 B.B.A., J.D. 3020 S.W. 100th Street
Gockel, Ashford R. '25 '48 C&L.976 B.E., LL.B.
Exec., V.P., Kerr-McGee Refining Corp.
Goerke, Joseph K., (AV) ....'64 '89 C.612 B.S. L.623 J.D. [Ⓒ Mulinix O.H.A.&L.]
Goerke, Kyle Edward ....'59 '87 [Ⓒ Mulinix O.H.A.&L.]
Goetzinger, Steven J., (AV) ....'58 '83 C.623 B.B.A. L.616 J.D. [Ⓒ Kline,K.E.&B.]
Goff, Gary, (BV) '46 '82 C.1147 B.S. L.616 J.D.
State & Educ. Employees Grp. Ins. Bd.
Gofton, Roger K., (BV) ....'56 '82 C.1040 B.A. L.616 J.D. 4200 Perimeter Center
Goins, Larry E. ....'59 '92 C.619 B.S. L.623 J.D. 5216 S. Land Avenue
Golden, James E., Jr., (AV) ....'55 '79 C&L.802 B.A., J.D. 1109 North Francis
Golden, Jennifer K., (BV) ....'56 '98 C.174 B.S. L.623 J.D. [Ⓐ Phillips M.M.M.&M.]
Goldfield, Robert E. ....'41 '74 C.619 B.S. L.623 J.D. Admin. Law J., State Corp. Comm.
Goldman, Edward, (AV) ....'45 '71 C&L.616 B.A., J.D. [Goldman&G.]
Goldman, Robert M., (BV) ....'49 '73 C.873 B.A. L.862 J.D. [Goldman&G.]
Goldman, Thomas ....'74 '01 C.612 B.S. L.615 J.D. [Ⓐ Goldman&G.]
Goldman & Goldman, (AV) ....416 N.W. 23rd St.
Goldschmidt, Diane S., (BV) ....'47 '79 C.502 B.S. L.615 J.D. Okla. Gas & Elec. Co.
Gonzales, Bonner J. ....'77 '04 C&L.623 B.B.A., J.D. [Ⓐ Phillips M.M.M.&M.]
Gooch, Ambre Camille, (BV) ....'70 '96 C&L.623 B.B.A., J.D. [Lee&G.]
Goodin, Matthew C. ....'71 '02 C.618 B.S. L.615 J.D. 209 Southwest 89th
Gooding, O. Clifton, (AV) ....'59 '83 C.612 B.S. L.623 J.D. [Gooding]

Gooding Law Firm, The, A Professional Corporation, (AV) BB
1200 City Place Building, 204 N. Robinson, 73102
Telephone: 405-948-1978 Telecopier: 405-948-0864
Email: cgooding@goodingfirm.com URL: http://www.goodingfirm.com
O. Clifton Gooding.
General, Civil, Criminal, Commercial, Bankruptcy, Personal Injury and Insurance Litigation.
See Professional Biographies, OKLAHOMA CITY, OKLAHOMA

Goodman, Jerry L., (AV) ....'39 '64 C.862 B.A. L.276 J.D. Cabinet Secy.
Goodman, Jimmy, (AV) ....'45 '71 C.623 B.A. L.813 J.D. [Crowe&D.]
Goodman, John N., (AV) ....'45 '71 C&L.623 B.A., J.D. [J.N.Goodman]
Goodman, John N., A Professional Corporation, (AV) ....Suite 210, 301 North Harvey
Goodwin, Charles B. ....'70 '97 C&L.623 B.A., J.D. [Ⓐ Crowe&D.]
Goodwin, Deborah ....'53 '89 C.1147 B.S. L.616 J.D. P.O. Box 95252
Goodwin, Kyle W., (AV) ....'68 '96 C.612 B.S. L.623 J.D. [Hughes&G.]
Goodwin, Richard K., (BV) ....'45 '72 C&L.623 B.S., J.D. [Rainey,G.M.&M.]
Goolsby, Robert Todd, (AV) ....'60 '88 C.623 L.616 J.D. 701 North Broadway Avenue
Goralewicz, Richard J., (AV) ....'57 '82 C.1113 A.B. L.616 J.D. [Turner,T.B.&G.]
Gorden, William W., Jr., (BV) ....'48 '75 C.623 B.A. L.616 J.D. 6321 Kingston Rd.
Gordon, Kenneth ....'12 '42 C.103 Ph.B. L.724 LL.B. Gen. Coun., Midwest Mtge. Co.
Gordon, Kevin D., (AV) ....'58 '84 C.934 B.A. L.910 J.D. [Crowe&D.]
Gordon, Mary Lu T. ....'35 '75 C.623 B.A. L.616 J.D. Asst. Mun. Coun.
Gore, Richard J., (AV) ....'44 '75 C&L.623 B.A., J.D. [Mahaffey&G.]
Gorelick, Jacquita R., (BV) ....'43 '82 C.1147 B.A. L.623 J.D. 200 N. Harvey Ave.
Gorelick, Sidney J. ....'37 '61 C&L.623 B.B.A., LL.B. 3829 Classen Blvd.
Goresen, Thomas Patrick, (AV) '55 '81
C.1044 B.S. L.615 J.D. Asst. Gen. Coun., Kerr-McGee Corp.
Goresen, Virginia K. ....'60 '87 C&L.623 B.A., J.D. State Wkrs. Comp. Ct.
Gosney, J. Wayne '46 '78 C.1147 B.S. L.616 J.D.
Dir., Employ. Rel., Kerr-McGee Corp.
Gottshall, Kevin L., (AV) ....'64 '89 C&L.623 B.A., J.D. Kerr-McGee Ctr.
Gould, Douglas N., (AV) ....'57 '82 C.612 B.S. L.616 J.D. [Gould]
Gould & Company, (AV) ....210 Park Avenue
Gowdy, J. L. ....'05 '28 L.623 LL.B. 901 S.W. 94th St.‡
Gowens, Marcus Anthony .....'70 '97 C.602 B.A. L.623 J.D. 701 N.W. 63rd St., Ste. 506
Grable, Lawrence F. ....'74 '01 C.619 B.S. L.862 J.D. [Ⓐ McKinney&S.] (Pat.)
Graham, Chanda R. ....'69 '98 C.1147 B.S. L.623 J.D. 2101 N. Lincoln, Rm. 400
Graham, R. William ....'62 '90 C&L.623 B.S., J.D. 3340 Rosewood Lane (Pat.)
Gramlich, Raymond, (AV) ....'18 '41 C&L.623 B.A., LL.B. 12401 Trail Oaks Dr.‡
Grantham, Robert E., (BV) '44 '79 C.1143 B.S. L.623 J.D.
200 N.E. 21st St. Room D1/3
Grau, Randy J. ....'75 '01 C.1117 B.A. L.623 J.D. [Ⓐ McKinney&S.]
Graven, David L. '50 '78 C&L.623 J.D.
2601 Northwest Expressway, Suite 815 East Tower
Graves, James D. ....'75 '04 C&L.623 B.A., J.D. [Ⓐ Johnson&H.]
Graves, Matthew J., (BV) ....'62 '88 C.992 B.A. L.623 J.D. [Oldfield,C.&G.]
Graves, William D., (BV) ....'37 '68 C.623 B.A. L.616 J.D. State Rep.
Gray, Dan T. ....'25 '58 C.614 B.A. L.623 LL.B. 4312 N.W. 59 Ter.‡
Gray, Elizabeth Honeywell, (BV) ....'57 '82 C.621 B.A. L.616 J.D. [Ⓐ Bullard&H.]
Gray, Jack E. ....'30 '56 C&L.623 B.A., LL.B. 1601 S. W. 89th St.
Gray, Lorrie C. ....'57 '89 C.623 B.S. L.744 J.D. [Gray]
Gray, Michael D., (AV) ....'60 '85 C.1300 B.A. L.623 J.D. [Britton,R.&G.]
Gray, Mitchell A. ....'60 '88 C&L.623 B.A., J.D. [Gray]
Gray, Robert D. ....'53 '90 C.623 B.B.A. L.615 J.D. 3015 N.W. 59th St.
Gray, Twyla Mason ....'54 '89 C.1147 B.S. L.862 J.D. Dist. J.
Gray, Walter L., Jr. ....'24 '50 C.846 B.A. L.623 J.D. 817 N.W. 39th‡
Gray Law Firm, The, P.C. ....1601 S.W. 89, Building C, Suite 300
Green, Charles C., (AV) ....'34 '58 C&L.623 B.A., LL.B. [Ⓒ McKinney&S.]
Green, Gerald P., (AV) ....'52 '76 C&L.623 B.A., J.D. [Pierce C.H.B.&G.]
Green, Joan M. ....'52 '90 C.623 B.S.N. L.616 J.D. 921 N.E. 13th Street
Green, John A., (AV) ....'21 '52 C.623 B.S. L.616 J.D. [Dimick,G.B.&S.]
Green, John E., (BV) ....'29 '57 C.511 B.A. L.623 LL.B. 1st Asst. U.S. Atty.

Green, Louis Mitchell, (BV) '62 '88 C.846 B.A. L.615 J.D.
3555 N.W. 58th Street, Suite 510, 73112
Telephone: 405-942-8292 Fax: 405-942-8362
Email: lmitchgreen@netscape.net URL: http://www.okclemonlaw.com
Lemon Law, Consumer Fraud, Consumer Protection, Warranties, Mobile Homes, Odometer Fraud, Fair Debt Collection, Fair Credit Reporting, Equal Credit Opportunity Act.
See Professional Biographies, OKLAHOMA CITY, OKLAHOMA

Green, William O., III .... '40 '64 C&L.623 B.B.A., LL.B. P.O. Box 25861‡

Green, James & Williams, (AV)
601 N.W. 13th Street, P.O. Box 2248, 73101-2248
Telephone: 405-525-0033 Fax: 405-525-0528
Email: gjw@flash.net
Clarence P. Green (1921-1999); Earl G. Williams (1926-2003); Mickey James; Marcie James.
Fire, Inland Marine, Casualty and Insurance Law. Toxic Substances and Structural Failures, including Toxic Mold, Defense Law. Products Liability, Personal Injury, Probate, Family Law, Civil Trials in all Courts and Adoption.
Representative Clients: Farmers Alliance Mutual Insurance Co.; Employers Mutual Cos.; Interstate Ins. Group; Daimler Chrysler Ins. Co.; Allianz Ins. Co.
See Professional Biographies, OKLAHOMA CITY, OKLAHOMA

Greene, Michelle .... '71 '97 C.623 B.A. L.615 J.D. [Ⓐ W.H.Bock]
Greenhaw, Joshua Clark .... '73 '01 C&L.623 B.Arch., J.D. [Ⓐ Mee,M.&H.]
Greenwood, William D., (AV) ....'51 '82 C.1147 B.S. L.623 J.D. [Huckaby,F.G.&O.]
Gregory, J. Mitchell, Jr., (AV) .... '44 '74 C.613 B.A. L.623 J.D. [Ⓒ Fenton,F.S.R.&M.]
Gregory, Ross L., (BV) .... '68 '96 C.197 A.B. L.1009 J.D. [Kelley,K.&G.]
Grennan, Jim, (BV) .... '33 '61 C&L.862 B.A., LL.B. P.O. Box 60871
Grider, Victor R., (BV) ....'53 '78 C&L.623 B.B.A., J.D. 204 N. Robinson, Ste. 1235
Gridley, Daniel Duke, Jr. ....'70 '98 C.840 B.B.A. L.623 J.D. Asst. Dist. Atty.
Griffeth, Tobin Curtis ....'67 '97 C.1142 B.A. L.1340 J.D. U.S. Air Force
Griffin, Billy D. ....'72 '99 C.619 B.S. L.615 J.D. [Griffin,R.&Assoc.]
Griffin, Brian C. ....'53 '78 C.309 B.A. L.623 J.D. Sec. of Envir.
Griffin, John J., (AV) ....'14 '48 C&L.616 B.S., LL.B. 5009 N. Pennsylvania Ave.
Griffin, John J., Jr., (AV) .... '50 '75 C.623 B.A. L.569 J.D. [Crowe&D.]
Griffin, Warren L., (AV) ..... '41 '67 C.1147 B.S. L.623 J.D. 5101 N. Classen Boulevard

Griffin, Reynolds & Associates
416 S.W. 79th Street Suite 200, 73139-8121
Telephone: 405-721-9500 Fax: 405-721-9503
Billy D. Griffin; Jason B. Reynolds.
Personal Injury, Insurance Bad Faith, Family Law, Wills, Trust Law, Probate, Bankruptcy, Auto Accidents, Trucking Accidents, Motorcycle Accidents, Wrongful Death, Products Liability, Nursing Home Abuse, Medical Malpractice, Divorce, Child Custody, Adoptions, Child Support and Workers Compensation Law.
See Professional Biographies, OKLAHOMA CITY, OKLAHOMA

Griffith, Matthew H. .... '70 '00 C.1147 B.A. L.623 J.D. [Andrews D.]
Grimes, Richard A., (P.C.), (AV) .... '49 '77 C.612 B.S. L.623 J.D. [Grimes,G.A.&D.]
Grimes, Gelders, Anderson & Day, (AV) .... 101 Park Avenue
Groeneveld, Lee D. ....'69 '94 C.802 B.S. L.846 J.D. [Mahaffey&G.]
Groom, Donald K. ....'20 '57 C.623 B.S. L.616 LL.B. 4505 NW 36th Street
Groom, M. Thad, (AV) ....'60 '85 C.612 B.S. L.616 J.D. [Groom]
Groom, Sid M., Jr., (AV) ....'25 '51 C&L.623 B.S., LL.B. [Ⓒ Groom]

Groom Law Firm, The, P.C., (AV)
100 North Broadway, Suite 3000, 73102
Telephone: 405-235-1440 Fax: 405-235-1708
M. Thad Groom;—Tava Seifert Jones. Of Counsel: Sid M. Groom, Jr.; James M. Kaufman.
Insurance Defense, Workers' Compensation Defense, Bankruptcy, Employment and Labor Law, Commercial and Business Litigation, Personal Injury Litigation.
See Professional Biographies, OKLAHOMA CITY, OKLAHOMA

Groshon, Robert F., Jr. '50 '93 C.623 B.S. L.615 J.D.
1603 West Memorial Road Suite A
Grossman, Mark S., (AV) ....'57 '83 C.976 B.A. L.800 J.D. [Crowe&D.]
Grotta, Jeff C., (CV) ....'61 '93 C&L.623 B.A., J.D. [Ⓐ Hiltgen&B.]
Grove, Robert G., (AV) ....'26 '55 C&L.623 B.B.A., LL.B. [R.G.Grove&Assoc.]
Grove, Robert Lake, (BV) ....'40 '66 C&L.623 B.A., J.D. 6412 Avondale Dr.
Grove, Roger A., (AV) ....'50 '75 C&L.623 B.B.A., J.D. [Horning,G.H.&C.]
Grove, Robert G. and Associates, PLLC, (AV) ....1321 North Robinson Avenue

Groves, Eric J., & Associates, (AV) '42 '70 C.216 B.A. L.623 J.D. 🅱🅱
The Robinson Renaissance Building, 119 North Robinson, Suite 777, 73102
Telephone: 405-236-5303 Fax: 405-236-5309
Email: ejg777@aol.com URL: http://www.lawyers.com/groves&associates
General Civil and Criminal Trial Practice. Municipal, Zoning and Land Use, Commercial Litigation, White Collar Crime, Family Law, Development Real Estate.
See Professional Biographies, OKLAHOMA CITY, OKLAHOMA

Gruber, Thomas William, (BV) '48 '77
C.620 B.A. L.623 J.D. 1st Asst. Atty. Gen., OK Atty. Gen. Off.
Guajardo, Leslie Diane ....'76 '02 C.622 B.A. L.615 J.D. [Ⓐ Pierce C.H.B.&G.]
Guarasci, Daniel J., (AV) '57 '84
C.567 B.S. L.616 J.D. Staff Coun., Allstate Insurance Company
Guest, Bill Powell, (AV) ....'63 '94 C&L.623 B.B.A., J.D. [Day,E.P.&C.]
Guhl, Lauren F. ....'79 '04 C&L.623 B.A., J.D. [Ⓐ Whitten,N.M.T.&R.]
Gum, Robert G., (AV) ....'52 '77 C.612 B.A. L.623 J.D. [Gum,P.&M.]

Gum, Puckett & Mackechnie, L.L.P., (AV)
105 North Hudson, Suite 900, 73102
Telephone: 405-488-1212 Fax: 405-488-1216
Members of Firm: Robert G. Gum; Charles L. Puckett, Jr.; John A. Mackechnie. Associates: Jim D. Dowell; Meredith A. Wegener.
Oil and Gas, Insurance Defense, Personal Injury, General Civil Practice in all State and Federal Courts, Oklahoma Corporation Commission.
See Professional Biographies, OKLAHOMA CITY, OKLAHOMA

Gunter, John M. ....'48 '78 C.1283 B.A. L.615 J.D. Reg. Coun., Marathon Oil Co.
Gunter, Teena G. '67 '92 C.01 B.A. L.45 J.D.
(adm. in AR; not adm. in OK) P.O. Box 780
Gurich, Noma Diane ....'52 '78 C.346 A.B. L.623 J.D. Dist. J.
Gutteridge, Don J., Jr., (AV) ....'42 '67 C&L.378 B.A., J.D. 5900 Mosteller Drive
Guzzy, J. Christian, (BV) ....'70 '96 C.309 B.A. L.623 J.D. [Hartzog C.C.&N.]
Gwartney, Aaron Don ....'72 '97 C.613 B.A. L.623 J.D. Atty., Integris Health
H. Blanton Brown & Associates, P.C., (AV) ....100 North Broadway
Haave, Christian Rollow ....'71 '99 C.66 B.A. L.276 J.D. Asst. Atty. Gen.

Hackett, Benjamin F., & Associates
(See Edmond)

Hackler, Donald R., Jr. ....'58 '84 C.612 B.S.B.A. L.623 J.D. State Off. OK Dept. of Com.
Hackler, Nolan R., (BV) ....'40 '76 C.614 B.A. L.616 J.D. 7928 NW 83rd St.
Hadden, John D. ....'68 '00 C.1147 B.A. L.615 J.D. 119 North Robinson
Haddock, Melissa Carol ....'62 '01 C&L.623 B.S., J.D. [Ⓐ Berry&V.]
Haddock, Peter, (BV) ....'60 '90 C.1432 B.A. L.616 J.D. OK Asst. Dist. Atty.

Hadrava, Ann K. .... '70 '02 C.612 B.S., B.A. L.615 J.D. [Ⓐ Ogle&W.]
Hadzellis, Nicholas B. ....'77 '03 C.556 B.A./B.C.J. L.615 J.D. 1219 N. Classen Drive

Hafar, Barry L., Law Office of, (CV) '56 '93 C.1147 B.B.A. L.623 J.D.
One North Hudson Avenue, Suite 700, 73102-5011
Telephone: 405-236-1994 Fax: 405-236-1861
Email: blhafar@swbell.net
Family Law, Adoptions, Step Parent Adoptions, Child Custody, Children, Post-Decree Modifications, Guardianships, Probate, Bankruptcy, General Practice.
See Professional Biographies, OKLAHOMA CITY, OKLAHOMA

Hager, Clay Steven ....'58 '87 C.663 B.A. L.623 J.D. OK Indian Legal Servs.
Hager, Don, (BV) ....'40 '68 C.612 B.S. L.862 J.D. [Ⓒ DeBee G.]
Haiges, Robert W. ....'68 '96 C.612 B.S. L.623 J.D. 9301 Cedar Lake Ave.
Haines, Spencer W. ....'75 '04 C.612 B.S. L.623 J.D. [Ⓐ McAfee&T.]
Hale, Jeannine ....'53 '83 C&L.623 B.S., J.D. Asst. Atty. Gen
Hall, Joel C., (AV) ....'63 '89 C&L.623 B.B.A., J.D. [Mulinix O.H.A.&L.]
Hall, Melvin C., (AV) ....'56 '82 C.1362 B.A. L.623 J.D. [Riggs,A.N.T.O.&L.]
Hall, Russell D., (AV) ....'49 '78 C.623 B.A. L.616 J.D. 1979 Leslie Beachler Ln.
Hall, Sarah Alexander, (AV) .... '64 '89 C&L.623 B.B.A., J.D. [Mock,S.W.E.R.&B.]
Hall, William D. ....'62 '90 C.294 B.S. L.8 J.D. [Ⓒ McAfee&T.]

Hall, Estill, Hardwick, Gable, Golden & Nelson, A Professional Corporation, (AV)
Bank One Center Suite 2900, 100 North Broadway, 73102-8827 ⊙
Telephone: 405-553-2828 Facsimile: 405-553-2855
URL: http://www.HallEstill.com
Robert D. Nelon; J. Fred Gist; Michael E. Smith; Ralph E. Seals, Jr.; Robert D. Looney, Jr.; Sharon T. Thomas; Michael J. Massad; Daniel J. Glover; Kent A. Gilliland; Jon A. Epstein; Elaine R. Turner (Resident); Larry G. Ball; Stephen R. Pitcock; Christian S. Huckaby; Susanna Gattoni Voegeli; J. Todd Woolery; Sarah K. Oberndorfer; Dessa J. Baker; Ashley A. Bowen.
General Civil Practice. Trials and proceedings before all State and Federal Courts and Agencies. Antitrust, Bankruptcy, Banking, Construction, Corporate, Commercial, Securities, Employee Benefits, Executive Compensation, Energy, Natural Resources, Energy Regulatory, Environmental, Estate Planning, Probate, Family Law, Domestic, Healthcare, Medical Malpractice, Indian Law, Intellectual Property, International Law and Trade, Labor, Employment, Legislative, Administrative Law, Litigation, Media, Real Estate, Taxation, Telecommunications, Tort, Insurance Defense, Utility Law.
Tulsa, Oklahoma Office: 320 South Boston Avenue, Suite 400, 74103. Telephone: 918-594-0400. Facsimile: 918-294-0505.
Washington, D.C. Office: Suite 700, North Building, 1120 20th Street N.W., 20036-3406. Telephone: 202-973-1200. Facsimile: 202-973-1212.
Fayetteville, Arkansas Office: One East Center Street, Suite 315, 72701. Telephone: 479-973-5200. Facsimile: 479-973-0520.
See Professional Biographies, OKLAHOMA CITY, OKLAHOMA

Halley, Duke, (AV) ....'48 '73 C.622 B.A. L.623 J.D. [D.Halley] ⊙
Halley, Duke, Law Firm, P.L.L.C., (AV) ....500 Colcord Drive (⊙Woodward)
Hamill, James G., (AV) ....'29 '55 C.612 B.S. L.623 LL.B. [Rolston,H.E.M.&N.]
Hamill, Tom P. ....'22 '49 C.612 B.S. L.623 LL.B. 12617 Green Valley Dr
Hamilton, Andrew L., (AV) ......'22 '54 C.846 B.S. L.616 LL.B. 3029 Lamp Post Lane‡
Hamilton, Frank O. ....'15 '39 C&L.623 A.B., LL.B. 1114 Sherwood Lane‡
Hammack, E. Eugene ....'21 '54 C.612 B.S. L.616 LL.B. 2604 Cummings Dr.‡
Hammert, J. Kord, (BV) ....'67 '93 C.612 B.S. L.616 J.D. [J. .K.Hammert]
Hammert, John Kord, (BV) .... 3721 N. Classen Blvd.
Hammonds, Glen D., (AV) '56 '81
C.612 B.A. L.623 J.D. Asst. Atty. Gen.; OK Atty. Gen. Off.
Hammons, Mark E., (BV) .....'50 '75 C.623 B.B.A. L.616 J.D. 325 Dean A. McGee Ave.
Hammons, S. Paul, (AV) ....'42 '68 C&L.623 B.A., J.D. 10617 Eastlake Circle
Hampton, J. David, (AV) ....'55 '80 C&L.623 B.A., J.D. [Hampton&M.]
Hampton, Joe M. ....'61 '86 C&L.623 B.B.A., J.D. [Ryan,W.&C.]
Hampton, Richard D. ....'25 '50 L.623 LL.B. 1400 N. Shartel‡

Hampton and Milligan, (AV)
119 North Robinson Avenue Suite 225, 73102-4613
Telephone: 405-235-5620 Fax: 405-232-4901
Email: AttysHandM@aol.com
J. David Hampton; Daniel A. Milligan. Associate: Diane DeFilippo.
Oil and Gas Title Examination, Oil and Gas Litigation, Riparian Rights, Real Estate Title, Probate Administration, Condemnation.
See Professional Biographies, OKLAHOMA CITY, OKLAHOMA

Hanan, Mary B., (AV) ....'54 '83 C.612 B.S. L.623 J.D. [Johnson&H.]
Hankins, James L., (BV) ....'68 '93 C.620 B.S. L.623 J.D. [Ⓐ Coyle]
Hanna, Terry R., (AV) ....'47 '72 C&L.623 B.B.A., J.D. [Ⓒ Crowe&D.]
Hansen, Carol M. ....'29 '75 C&L.616 B.A., J.D. App. Ct. J.
Hanson, Mary ....'55 '88 C.614 B.A. L.616 J.D. Admr., Tax Comm.
Hanson, Patricia J., (AV) ....'55 '81 C&L.623 B.A., J.D. [Lytle S.&C.]
Harbour, David M. ....'39 '66 C.623 B.B.A. L.616 J.D. Spec. Dist. Ct. J.
Harbour, John W., Jr. ....'40 '67 C.623 B.B.A. L.616 J.D. Harbour Law Services‡
Hardberger, J. Derek ....'68 '94 C.623 B.B.A. L.862 J.D. [McKinney&S.]
Hardeman, John Tolbert, (BV) ....'48 '91 C.623 B.A. L.615 J.D. P.O. Box 1948
Harden, Larry H. ....'72 '00 C.612 B.S. L.615 J.D. [Ⓐ Foliart,H.O.&B.]
Hardin, Lloyd T., Jr., (AV) ....'49 '77 C&L.623 B.A., J.D. [Phillips M.M.M.&M.]
Hargis, Vaden Burns ....'45 '70 C.612 B.S. L.623 J.D. V. Chmn., Bank of Oklahoma
Hargrave, John R., (AV) ....'55 '80 C.618 B.A. L.623 J.D. [Edmonds,C.H.G.R.&W.] ⊙
Hargrave, Rudolph ....'25 '49 C.618 L.623 LL.B. Chf. Jus., Supm. Ct.
Harkey, Byron E., Jr. ....'42 '73 C.1147 B.A. L.616 J.D. Okla. Tax Comm.
Harkey, Michael J., (AV) '51 '77 C.623 B.A. L.616 J.D.
3601 N. Classen Blvd., Ste. 100
Harkins, Lynnell A., (BV) ....'39 '82 C.174 B.S. L.616 J.D. [Ⓐ Kline,K.E.&B.]
Harley, Kay, (AV) ....'52 '79 C.623 B.A. L.616 J.D. Gen. Coun., Dept. of Educ.
Harlton, April, (AV) ....'66 '91 C.623 B.B.A. L.862 J.D. Midland Financial Co.
Harmon, Joel Warren, (AV) ....'60 '85 C.1315 B.S. L.623 J.D. [Day,E.P.&C.]
Harness, Gordon A., Attorney at Law, (BV) '47 '79
C.942 B.S. L.616 J.D. 10015 S. Pennsylvania, Ste. B
Harness, Inona Jane, (AV) ....'47 '81 C.612 B.S. L.623 J.D. [Pierce C.H.B.&G.]
Harr, Donald J., (BV) ....'29 '56 C.618 L.616 LL.B. P.O. Box 32505
Harrah, Michael K., (AV) ....'53 '81 C.225 A.B. L.623 J.D. 6301 Gaelic Glen Drive
Harrell, Shawn E., (BV) ....'70 '95 C.802 B.A. L.623 J.D. [McAfee&T.]
Harrington, Jay L. ....'57 '83 C.612 B.A. L.45 J.D. 2608 Kings Way
Harrington, John C., Jr., (AV) '30 '55
C.976 B.A. L.623 LL.B. 2809 Northwest Expressway
Harrington, Michelle C. ....'59 '92 C&L.623 B.B.A., J.D. [M.Harrington]
Harrington, Michelle .... P.O. Box 1219
Harris, Benjamin ....'75 '00 C.616 B.S. L.623 J.D. [Ⓐ Reynolds,R.V.&M.]
Harris, Gretchen Grover, (AV) ....'47 '81 C&L.623 B.A., J.D. Asst. Atty. Gen.
Harris, Jonathan ....'50 '93 C.605 B.A. L.615 J.D. 4901 Richmond Sq., Ste. 104
Harris, Maxwell D. ....'23 '48 C.393 L.623 LL.B. 12113 Camelot Pl.‡
Harris, Michael G., (AV) ....'51 '78 C&L.623 B.A., J.D. [Moricoli,H.&C.]
Harris, Richard J., (BV) ....'65 '95 C.612 B.S. L.188 J.D. [McKinney&S.]
Harrison, Richard D. '23 '50 C.813 B.A. L.477 LL.B.
(adm. in UT; not adm. in OK) Chmn. of the Bd., Fleming Cos., Inc.
Harrison, Sandra Benischek ....'69 '00 C.560 B.A. L.623 J.D. [Ⓐ Andrews D.]

Harrison, Victoria Ann .... '61 '90 C&L.623 B.A., J.D. 2409 N. Kelly Annex
Harrod, Marsha Dee Debord .... '55 '80 C.612 B.S. L.615 J.D. Off. of Mun. Counselor
Harry, Virgil M., III, (BV) '56 '81 C&L.623 B.B.A., J.D.
Gen. Coun., Harry Mortgage Co.
Hart, Philip D., (AV) ....'36 '60 C&L.623 B.A., LL.B. [McAfee&T.]
Hart, Theresa L. ....'53 '00 C.663 B.A. L.615 J.D. [Chiaf]
Hartmann, James F., Jr., (AV) .... '44 '69 C.494 B.A. L.477 J.D. [C Crowe&D.]
Hartmann, Jeff L., (AV) .... '42 '66 C.612 L.623 LL.B. [A Kerr,I.R.&A.]
Hartshorn, Scott R. .... '61 '90 C.226 B.S. L.616 J.D. 2809 N.W. Expressway St.
Hartzog, Larry D., (AV) ....'34 '59 C&L.623 B.B.A., LL.B. [Hartzog C.C.&N.]

Hartzog Conger Cason & Neville, A Professional Corporation, (AV) BR
1600 Bank of Oklahoma Plaza, 201 Robert S. Kerr, 73102
Telephone: 405-235-7000 Facsimile: 405-996-3403
URL: http://www.hartzoglaw.com
Larry D. Hartzog; Len Cason; Jack L. (Drew) Neville, Jr.; David E. Pepper; Steven C. Davis; Russell Cook; Joseph P. Hogsett; John D. Robertson; Laura Haag McConnell; William A. Johnson; Susan B. Shields; Billy M. Croll; Ryan S. Wilson; Amy J. Sine; Jon H. Trudgeon; Charles E. Geister, III; Armand Paliotta; Richard B. Kells; J. Christian Guzzy; Bernard J. Rothbaum;—Michael J. Novotny; Byron K. Linkous; Kevin B. Ratliff; J. Leslie LaReau; Alix Lormand Samara (Not admitted in OK); Kurt M. Rupert; Kent W. Gardner; Robert S. Duran, Jr. (Not admitted in OK); David Allen Elder. Of Counsel: J. William Conger; Kent F. Frates; Kenneth R. Davis; James D. Kallstrom.
Administrative Law, Appellate Practice, Business Transactions, Civil Litigation, Commercial Lending, Commercial Real Estate, Corporate and Securities, Employee Benefits/ERISA, Employment Law, Family Law, Federal and State Taxation, Healthcare Law, Insurance, Intellectual Property, Products Liability, Tax-Exempt Organizations, Trusts and Estates, Wealth Transfer Planning, Oil and Gas.
See Professional Biographies, OKLAHOMA CITY, OKLAHOMA

Harvey, James Daniel, Jr. .... '67 '96 C.1147 B.A. L.616 J.D. [C.A.Wood&Assoc.]
Hasbrook, Edward D., (AV) '56 '86
C.663 B.S. L.616 J.D. Police Legal Advsr., Mun. Counselors Off.
Hasenfratz, Sally A., (AV) ....'60 '86 C&L.623 B.B.A., J.D. [Phillips M.M.M.&M.]
Hasley, Richard L., (BV) ....'39 '68 C.622 B.S. L.616 J.D. 3535 NW 58th, Ste. 1000
Hasty, Jason C., (BV) ....'69 '94 C.622 B.A. L.623 J.D. [A Lytle S.&C.]
Hatamyar, Patricia W. '57 '83 C.597 B.A. L.145 J.D.
Asst. Prof. of Law, Oklahoma City Univ. Sch. of Law
Hatfield, Carlyle Ronald ....'43 '92 C.608 B.A. L.616 J.D. [Hatfield]
Hatfield Law Office .... 217 North Harvey
Hathaway, John S. '48 '75 C.845 B.S.M.E. L.846 J.D.
(adm. in TX; not adm. in OK) Assoc. Gen. Coun., Devon Energy Corp.
Hatley, Marvin G. '33 '61 C&L.802 B.B.A., J.D.
(adm. in TX; not adm. in OK) Unit Parts Co.
Hatley, Morris L. .... '43 '68 C&L.623 B.A., J.D. P.O. Box 24128‡
Haubrich, Greg, (AV) .... '52 '86 C.804 B.S. L.623 J.D. [C Holloway,D.&B.]
Haught, R. Steven, (AV) ....'53 '78 C.276 A.B. L.623 J.D. [C Daugherty,F.P.&H.]
Haught, Susan H., (AV) .... '55 '85 C.623 B.S. L.616 J.D. [Daugherty,F.P.&H.]
Haupt, Robert J. ....'61 '01 C.613 B.A. L.616 J.D. [Haupt B.V.]

Haupt Brooks Vandruff, PLLC
One North Hudson, Ninth Floor, 73102
Telephone: 405-231-4600 Facsimile: 405-231-4601
Email: info@hauptbrooks.com URL: http://www.hbvlawyers.com
Robert J. Haupt; Carson M. Brooks; Joel Wayne Vandruff;—James M. Barber; Toni Himes Capra; Bradford A. Mazo; Ruth Lawrence Mor; Charles W. Wright; Adam C. Brandenburg. Of Counsel: Lawrence R. Scott; Richard D. Morrissette.
Administrative/Agency, Agricultural, Bankruptcy (Chapter 7, 11, 12, 13), Civil Rights, Criminal, Domestic & Family, Employment, Estate Planning (Wills & Trusts), Finance, Debtor and Creditor Law, General Corporate and Business (Organization, Product Liability, Mergers and Acquisition, Litigation), General Trial Practice, Insurance, Medical and Nursing Home Malpractice and Probate, Personal Injury, Real Estate, Taxation (Personal and Corporate), Workers Compensation, Wrongful Death.
Edmond, Oklahoma Office: 200 East 10th Street Plaza, Suite A, 73034. Telephone: 405-348-2529. Facsimile: 405-330-4872.
Lawton, Oklahoma Office: 5 N.W. 16th Street, 73507. Telephone: 580-355-4000. Facsimile: 405-231-4600.
See Professional Biographies, OKLAHOMA CITY, OKLAHOMA

Hawkins, Harold .... '14 '39 C&L.623 B.A., LL.B. 10213 Major Ave.‡
Hawkins, Kerry Ray ....'68 '94 C.616 B.S.B. L.615 J.D. I.R.S.
Hawkins, Terry L., (AV) ....'56 '81 C.612 B.S. L.623 J.D. [Phillips M.M.M.&M.]
Haworth, Timothy Dean .... '77 '03 C.622 B.A. L.615 J.D. [Denson&H.]
Hayes, Amy S. ....'79 '03 C.10 B.A. L.616 J.D. [A Pierce C.H.B.&G.]
Hayes, Gaylon C., (BV) ....'49 '91 C.622 B.A. L.615 J.D. 6616 S.Western Ave.
Hayes, John B., (AV) ....'38 '62 C.612 B.S. L.623 LL.B. [Hayes&M.]
Hayes, Rodney A., (BV) ....'51 '78 C.882 B.A. L.862 J.D. State Ins. Fund
Hayes & Liddell, P.C. ....6616 South Western Ave.
Hayes & Magrini, (AV) .... 1220 North Walker
Haynes, R. Stephen, (AV) .... '52 '77 C.612 B.S. L.616 J.D. [Haynes&M.]
Haynes & Montgomery, (AV) .... 6307 Waterford Boulevard Suite 150
Heady, Kenneth, (AV) .... '24 '49 C&L.623 LL.B. 2 Leadership Sq.
Healy, Richard M., III, (AV) ....'50 '79 C.623 B.A. L.616 J.D. [C Kline,K.E.&B.]
Heath, Donald F., Jr., (AV) ....'57 '82 C.293 B.A. L.623 J.D. [A Mullins,H.&J.]
Heatly, John B., (AV) .... '50 '76 C.612 B.S. L.623 J.D. [Fellers,S.B.B.&T.]
Heaton, Joe .... '51 '76 C.620 B.A. L.623 J.D. U.S. Dist. J.
Hebert, Carolyn K. ....'66 '95 C.435 B.A. L.615 J.D. [A Walker,F.&F.]
Heefner, Timothy A., (BV) '71 '98 C&L.623 B.B.A., J.D.
701 N. Broadway Ave., Ste. 400
Hefner, Hal L., (BV) .... '25 '77 C.623 B.S. L.616 J.D. 8301 John Robert Dr.
Hefner, Jona Rae .... '70 '96 C.623 B.S. L.615 J.D. [Hefner&Assoc.]
Hefner, Kenneth, (BV) .... '29 '60 C.623 B.B.A. L.616 LL.B. 6224 Beaver Creek Rd.
Hefner & Associates .... 3441 W. Memorial Rd., Ste. 4
Heggy, Rodney J., (AV) .... '55 '81 C.621 B.A. L.326 J.D. [Heggy&Assoc.]

Heggy & Associates, LLC, (AV)
2716W First National Center, 120 North Robinson, 73102
Telephone: 405-235-1551 Fax: 866-858-0358
Rodney J. Heggy.
Commercial Litigation and Arbitration, Securities Litigation, Employment Law, Insurance Law, Fraud Investigations, Broker-Dealer Arbitration.
See Professional Biographies, OKLAHOMA CITY, OKLAHOMA

Heinen, Gary J., (AV) ....'58 '87 C.1147 B.B.A. L.623 J.D. [Dubberstein H.&M.]
Helbert, David P. .... '51 '80 C.959 B.B.A. L.616 J.D. Okla. State Ins. Fund
Heller, Ulf R. "Ron", (AV) ....'45 '78 C.475 B.A. L.616 J.D. 1900 Northwest Expressway
Hellman, Gay Linn .... '50 '80 C.938 B.A. L.615 J.D. [G.L.Hellman]
Hellman, Lawrence K. '44 '70 C.902 B.S. L.597 J.D.
Dean & Prof. of Law, Oklahoma City Univ. Sch. of Law
Hellman, Gay L., Attorney at Law .... P.O. Box 20089
Helm, Charles L., (AV) .... '51 '78 C.623 B.A. L.616 J.D. [Helm&B.]
Helm & Boone, (AV) .... 105 N. Hudson
Helms, Conner L., (AV) .... '61 '87 C.900 B.A. L.616 J.D. [Helms&U.]
Helms, Julian D., (AV) ....'32 '56 C.845 B.B.A. L.846 LL.B. [C Helms&U.]
Helms, Louise A., (BV) .... '36 '80 C.835 B.S. L.616 J.D. P.O. Box 26910

Helms & Underwood, (AV)
2500 First National Center, 120 North Robinson Avenue, 73102
Telephone: 405-319-0700 Fax: 405-319-9292
Email: conner@helmsunderwood.com
Conner L. Helms; Gary R. Underwood; Darren R. Cook. Associates: Rebecca A. Farris; Rachel K. McCombs. Of Counsel: Julian D. Helms.
Litigation, Commercial Law, Oil and Gas Law, Corporate Law, Mergers and Acquisitions, Intellectual Property, Copyright and Trademarks, Internet Law, Entertainment Law, Employment Law, Family Law, Probate, Trusts, Estate Planning, Immigration Law, Intellectual Property.
See Professional Biographies, OKLAHOMA CITY, OKLAHOMA

Hemry, Gene H., (AV) .... '09 '32 C.616 B.A. L.623 LL.B. 531 Couch Dr.‡
Hemry, Jerome E., (AV) ....'05 '28 C.616 B.A. L.309 J.D. 401 N. Hudson
Hemry, Jerry L., (AV) ....'37 '61 C.623 B.B.A. L.477 LL.M. [Hemry,H.&M.]
Hemry, Kenneth M., (AV) .... '42 '67 C&L.623 B.A., LL.B. [Hemry,H.&M.]
Hemry, Hemry & McDoniel, P.C., The Law Offices of, (AV)
531 Couch Drive, Suite 100
Henderson, Paula M. ....'51 '83 C&L.623 B.A., J.D. 8121 N.W. 119th St.
Henderson, Susan Moebius, (AV) ....'61 '86 C&L.623 B.A., J.D. Intergris Health
Hendrick, Howard H., (AV) ....'54 '80 C.82 B.S. L.623 J.D. [C Thom,H.&D.]
Hendrick, Robert ....'32 '63 C.612 B.S. L.616 J.D. 12500 St. Andrews Dr.
Hendricks, David G. '39 '80 C&L.45 B.A., J.D.
(adm. in AR; not adm. in OK) Sr. Tax Atty., I.R.S.
Hendrickson, Russell L., (AV) ....'59 '84 C.612 B.S. L.623 J.D. [Pierce C.H.B.&G.]
Hendrickson, Steven, (BV) .... '56 '81 C.352 B.A. L.616 J.D. 5909 N.W. Exwy., Ste. 236
Hendryx, Gina L., (BV) .... '58 '83 C&L.616 B.A., J.D. P.O. Box 53036
Henley, L. Gaylene .... '46 '88 C.1147 B.B.A. L.623 J.D. Jud. Asst.
Henricksen, Lanita, (BV) .... '48 '92 C.999 B.A. L.615 J.D. [Henricksen&H.] ⊙
Henricksen & Henricksen Lawyers, Inc., (AV)
6440 Avondale Drive, Suite 200 (⊙El Reno)
Henry, David P., (BV) .... '60 '85 C.502 B.S. L.615 J.D. 3315 N.W. 63rd St.
Henry, Robert H. ....'53 '77 C&L.623 B.A., J.D. U.S. Cir. J.
Henson, Warren W., III, (BV) ....'62 '89 C&L.623 B.B.A., J.D. 6308 N. Drexel
Hentges, Harlan G. ....'65 '92 C.612 B.S. L.846 J.D. [C Mulinix O.H.A.&L.]
Henthorn, Rick J. ....'55 '98 C.1147 B.B.A. L.615 J.D. [A Mullins,H.&J.]
Hermansen, Eric H., (BV) ....'44 '82 C.1050 B.B.A. L.615 J.D. [E.H.Hermansen]
Hermansen, Eric H., A Professional Corporation, The Law Office of, (BV)
7200 S. Pennsylvania Ave., Ste. F

Hermanson, Brian T.
(See Ponca City)

Hermes, John N., (AV) .... '46 '75 C.694 A.B. L.623 J.D. [McAfee&T.]
Hernando, Orlando M. '27 '83 C.662 A.B. L.999 LL.B.
(adm. in IN; not adm. in OK) 3535 N.W. 58th Street
Herndon, E. McLaine DeWitt ...... '75 '05 C&L.862 B.A., J.D. [A Doerner,S.D.&A.] ⊙
Herren, Richard D. '64 '90 C.612 B.A. L.623 J.D.
General Counsel & Assistant Executive Director, Oklahoma Farm Bureau Mutual Insurance Co.
Herring, Donald A. ....'64 '90 C&L.623 B.A., J.D. [Schnetzler&H.]
Hester, Jon L., (AV) ....'48 '73 C.999 B.A. L.623 J.D. [Hester,S.H.&B.]
Hester, Scott A. ....'73 '00 C&L.623 B.A., J.D. [Hester,S.H.&B.]

Hester, Schem, Hester & Batson, (AV) BR
5400 North Grand Boulevard, Suite 265, 73112
Telephone: 405-947-8866 Fax: 405-947-1140 URL: http://www.hesterlaw.net
URL: http://www.okcfamilylaw.com
Jon L. Hester; Charles O. Schem; Scott A. Hester; Christine A. Batson.
Family Law including: Divorce, Child Custody, Adoptions, Spousal Support, Premarital Agreements, Child Support and Post Decree Modifications.
See Professional Biographies, OKLAHOMA CITY, OKLAHOMA

Hetrick, Stephen M. .... '78 '03 C.1147 B.S. L.623 J.D. [A McAfee&T.]
Hewett, Herbert F. (Jack), (AV) ...... '26 '50 C.623 B.A. L.976 LL.B. [C Day,E.P.&C.]
Hickman, William H. ....'68 '99 C.1070 B.S. L.623 J.D. [Moricoli,H.&C.]
Hiersche, G. Rudy, Jr., (BV) .... '46 '73 C&L.623 B.A., J.D. [Hiersche]
Hiersche Law Firm, (BV) ....15 N. Robinson
High, David R., (AV) ....'50 '78 C.623 B.A. L.616 J.D. 3601 North Classen Boulevard
High, Patricia Leigh .... '64 '89 C&L.623 B.A., J.D. Off. of Dist. Atty.

Highsaw, Robert, (BV) '53 '79 C.399 B.A. L.862 J.D.
3801 N. Classen Boulevard, 73118
Telephone: 405-525-7680 Fax: 405-525-8038
Email: highsaw@sbcglobal.net URL: http://www.roberthighsaw.com
Workers Compensation, Federal Workers Compensation, Workers Compensation Appeals, Workers Compensation Defense, Workers Compensation Self-Insurance, Workers Compensation Subrogation, Immigration and Naturalization, Business Immigration, Citizenship, Consular Law, Deportation, Diplomatic Immunity, Employment Authorization, Employment Immigration, Employment Visas, Family Immigration Law, Immigration Discrimination, Immigration Law, Investor Visas, Labor Certifications, Permanent Visas, Political Asylum, Refugee Law, Religious Visas, Visas, Social Security, Social Security Appeals, Social Security Disability, Social Security Disability Insurance, Supplemental Security Income, Administrative Law, Longshore and Harbor Workers Compensation.
See Professional Biographies, OKLAHOMA CITY, OKLAHOMA

Hilbert, Douglas R., (BV) .... '37 '72 C.1147 B.S. L.616 J.D. [Shumake&H.]
Hill, Frank D., (AV) .... '40 '66 C.623 B.B.A. L.846 LL.B. [McAfee&T.]

Hill, Jackie L., Jr., (AV) '61 '86 C.612 B.S. L.623 J.D.
2800 Oklahoma Tower, 210 Park Avenue, 73102-5604
Telephone: 405-232-4456 Fax: 405-232-4457
Email: jackie@jhilllaw.com
Of Counsel To: Dunn, Swan & Cunningham, Oklahoma City, Oklahoma.
Bankruptcy, Banking Law, Real Estate, Business Litigation, Corporate Law.
See Professional Biographies, OKLAHOMA CITY, OKLAHOMA

Hill, John B. ....'72 '03 C.621 B.A. L.616 J.D. [A Johnson&H.]
Hill, Kevin E., (BV) ....'65 '92 C.1147 B.B.A. L.615 J.D. [Homsey,C.H.&Assoc.]
Hill, Marny Joell, (BV) .... '68 '97 C.612 B.A. L.623 J.D. Off. of Co. Dist. Atty.
Hill, Sam ....'18 '43 C&L.623 A.B., LL.B. Okla. State Ins. Fund
Hill, Victor G., Jr., (BV) .... '38 '70 L.615 J.D. [V.Hill]
Hill, William J. ....'52 '83 C.1147 B.B.A. L.616 J.D. 2715 NW 24th St.
Hill, Victor, (BV) ....1141 N. Robinson Ave., Ste. 204
Hillerman, Holly M. ....'70 '96 C.612 B.A. L.623 J.D. [A Miller D.]
Hiltgen, Cary E., (AV) ....'54 '81 C.593 B.S. L.616 J.D. [Hiltgen&B.]

Hiltgen & Brewer, P.C., (AV) BR
One Benham Place, Suite 800, 9400 N. Broadway Extension, 73114-7401
Telephone: 405-605-9000 Facsimile: 405-605-9010
Email: administrator@hiltgenbrewer.com URL: http://www.hiltgenbrewer.com
Cary E. Hiltgen; Michael W. Brewer;—Brock C. Bowers; T. Shane Curtin; Jennifer E. Jackson; Norman Lemonik; Scott C. Sublett; Jeremy Z. Carter; Jeff C. Grotta; J. Randy Baker; Lynne F. Saunders.
Civil Litigation, Insurance Defense, Manufacturers' Products Liability, Negligence, Premises Liability, Environmental Law, Construction and Complex Commercial Litigation, Trucking Law, Employment and Labor Law, Insurance and Workers' Compensation.
See Professional Biographies, OKLAHOMA CITY, OKLAHOMA

Hines, Harold D., (AV) .... '24 '49 C&L.623 B.S., LL.B. 6488 Avondale Dr.
Hintz, Heather L., (BV) ....'61 '88 C.747 B.A. L.880 J.D. [Ⓐ Phillips M.M.M.&M.]
Hirlinger, Charles L. .... '29 '59 C.846 B.B.A. L.623 LL.B. P.O. Box 26030
Hirsch, Karl F., (AV) .... '52 '78 C&L.623 B.B.A., J.D. [Mullins,H.&J.]
Hitt, Brion .... '74 '01 C.1300 B.S. L.623 J.D. [Ⓐ Fenton,F.S.R.&M.]
Hoang, My My Khanh .... '75 '00 C&L.623 B.A., J.D. 510 E. Memorial, Suite D-1
Hobbs, Straus, Dean & Walker, LLP
117 Park Avenue, Second Floor (⊙Wash., DC; Port., OR)
Hoch, William H., III, (AV) .... '66 '93 C&L.128 B.A., J.D. [Crowe&D.]
Hocker, Keith J., (BV) .... '59 '85 C&L.623 B.A., J.D. Gen. Coun., Taco Mayo
Hodge, Randall P. .... '60 '90 C.612 B.A. L.623 J.D. 4312 N. Classen Blvd.
Hodges, Ralph B. .... '30 '54 C.613 B.A. L.623 LL.B. Supm. Ct. Jus.
Hoehn, Melissa J. .... '59 '04 C.623 B.A. L.616 J.D. [Ⓐ Pierce C.H.B.&G.]
Hoehner, Daniel J., (AV) .... '58 '84 C.612 B.S. L.623 J.D. [Bullard&H.]
Hoenig, Karl Blake .... '42 '75 C&L.623 B.A., J.D. P.O. Box 61265
Hoenshell, Monica J. .... '78 '03 C.612 B.A. L.623 J.D. [Ⓐ Calvert]
Hoffman Kelley, L.L.P.
3030 NW Expressway, Suite 625 (⊙Albuquerque, NM; Austin, TX)
Hoge, Arthur F., III, (AV) .... '53 '81 C.934 B.A. L.802 J.D. [Mee,M.&H.]
Hogsett, Joseph P., (AV) .... '60 '86 C.859 B.S. L.846 J.D. [Hartzog C.C.&N.]
Hogue, Darrell L. .... '41 '75 C.39 B.S. L.616 J.D. 724 W. Britton Road
Hoisington, Carrie Palmer, (AV) ..... '68 '93 C.375 B.S. L.623 J.D. [Jennings C.H.&T.]
Hoisington, Robert D., (BV) .... '68 '93 C.612 B.A. L.623 J.D. [Foliart,H.O.&B.]
Holbrook, L. Win, (AV) .... '42 '71 C&L.616 B.S., J.D. [Holbrook&T.]
Holbrook, Lisa D. .... '70 '96 C.622 B.A. L.615 J.D. VP, Gen. Coun.

Holbrook & Toffoli, (AV)
An Association of Attorneys
2205 First National Center, 120 North Robinson, 73102
Telephone: 405-232-3664 Telefacsimile: 405-236-1286
Members of Firm: L. Win Holbrook; Mark B. Toffoli; Mark E. Monfort.
Creditor Bankruptcy, Creditors Rights in Bankruptcy, Debtor and Creditor Bankruptcy, Debtor and Creditor Reorganization, Debtor and Creditor Workouts, Debtor Bankruptcy, Secured Creditors Rights, Unsecured Creditors Rights and General Business Transactions.
Representative Clients: Furnished Upon Request.
See Professional Biographies, OKLAHOMA CITY, OKLAHOMA

Holden, Steven M., (CV) .... '70 '96 C.130 B.A. L.862 J.D. [S.Holden]

Holden & Carr
(See Tulsa)

Holden, Steven, PC, (CV) .... 1420 Linwood Blvd.
Holdstock, Charles .... '45 '91 C.618 B.A. L.862 J.D. P.O. Box 61125
Holl, Alfred O. .... '21 '49 C.263 A.B. L.900 J.D. 3033 Hemingford Ln.‡
Holladay, Don G., (AV) .... '44 '69 C&L.623 B.A., J.D. [Holladay,C.&D.]

Holladay, Chilton & DeGiusti, PLLC, (AV)
City Place, Suite 1550, 204 North Robinson, 73102
Telephone: 405-236-2343 Facsimile: 405-236-2349
URL: http://www.hcdattorneys.com
Don G. Holladay; Gary S. Chilton; Timothy D. DeGiusti; Heidi J. Long;—Gideon A. Lincecum; James E. Warner, III.
Complex Commercial and Business Litigation, Insurance Coverage, Securities Fraud, Class Action Suits, Banking, Real Estate, Business Torts, Bankruptcy, Environmental and General Business Contract Litigation in State and Federal Courts.
See Professional Biographies, OKLAHOMA CITY, OKLAHOMA

Hollar, Bradley T. .... '67 '93 C.378 B.G.S. L.616 J.D. 11212 N. May Ave., Ste. 401
Hollar, Michele Sharon .... '— '94 C.378 B.A. L.615 J.D. [Hollar]
Hollar Law Firm .... 11212 N. May Ave., Ste. 401
Holleman, Virginia Cathcart, (BV) ...... '66 '93 C&L.623 B.B.A., J.D. [Ⓐ Cathcart&D.]
Hollingsworth, Norman Earl .... '53 '01 L.616 J.D. 6616 S. Western
Holloman, James H., Jr., (AV) .... '46 '69 C&L.623 B.B.A., J.D. [Crowe&D.]
Holloman, Lynn O., (AV) .... '44 '69 C.612 B.A. L.623 J.D. [ⓒ Andrews D.]
Holloway, Alan G., (BV) .... '— '96 C.999 B.S. L.623 J.D. [Ⓐ McAfee&T.]
Holloway, Dan L., (AV) .... '49 '83 C&L.623 B.S., J.D. [Holloway,D.&B.]
Holloway, William J., Jr. .... '23 '50 C.623 A.B. L.1565 LL.B. Sr. U.S. Cir. J.

Holloway, Dobson & Bachman, A Professional Corporation, (AV) BB
Suite 900 One Leadership Square 211 North Robinson, 73102-7102
Telephone: 405-235-8593 Fax: 405-235-1707
URL: http://www.hollowaydobson.com
Page Dobson; Gary C. Bachman; Dan L. Holloway; Mark E. Duvall; J. William Archibald; Stephen D. Bachman; Michael E. Smith; Bryan G. Garrett;—Lu Ann Stout; Kenyatta R. Bethea; Marissa T. Osenbaugh. Of Counsel: Russell B. Holloway (1920-2004); David H. Dobson; Greg Haubrich.
Litigation, Appellate Practice, Alternate Dispute Resolution, Mediation, Aviation Law, Bankruptcy, Banks and Banking, Lender Liability, Business Law, Anti-trust and Unfair Competition, Mergers and Acquisitions, Civil Rights, Commercial Law, Construction Law, Corporate Law, Oil and Gas Law, Personal Injury, Products Liability, Labor and Employment Law, Municipal and other Governmental Subdivisions, Workers' Compensation, Professional Malpractice, Medical Malpractice, Toxic Torts, Health Law, Trusts and Estates, Probate, Wills, Negligence, Casualty and Surety Insurance, Real Estate and Environmental Law.
Representing: AIG Aviation, Inc.; Blue Cross Blue Shield of Oklahoma; Chubb Group of Insurance Cos.; Church Mutual Insurance Co.; Ford Motor Credit Co.; General Motors Corp.; Halliburton Energy Services, Inc.; Hobby Lobby Stores, Inc.; Nissan North America; Volvo North America.
See Professional Biographies, OKLAHOMA CITY, OKLAHOMA

Holmes, Jerome A. .... '61 '88 C.896 B.A. L.276 J.D. 210 W. Park Avenue
Holmes, Laura L. .... '64 '91 C.918 B.A. L.623 J.D. [CenterForEducationLaw]
Holmes, Lee M., & Associates, (AV) '39 '63 C&L.623 B.A., LL.B.
501 N.W. 13th Street
Holmes, Mark L. .... '63 '93 C&L.623 B.B.A., J.D. [Ⓐ L.M.Holmes&Assoc.]
Holmes, Philip, (BV) .... '34 '65 C.616 B.S.B. L.623 J.D. 3109 N. Pa. St.
Holmes, William R. (Bill), (BV) ...... '55 '86 C.1147 B.A. L.623 J.D. State Capitol Bldg.
Holshouser, Ted P., (AV) .... '31 '64 C&L.623 B.S., LL.B. 128 W. Hefner Rd.
Holton, William R., Jr. ... '51 '79 C.612 B.S. L.616 J.D. Attorney, Marathon Oil Company
Homburg, Randal D., (BV) .... '58 '89 C.621 B.S. L.616 J.D. [ⓒ Niemeyer,A.A.&P.]

Homsey, Gary B., (AV) '49 '74 C.612 B.S. L.616 J.D. BB
Homsey Law Center, 4816 Classen Boulevard, 73118 ⊙
Telephone: 405-843-9923 Telecopier: 405-848-4223; Toll Free 1-800-845-9923
Email: gbh@homseylawcenter.com URL: http://www.homseylawcenter.com
Trial Practice and Civil Litigation in Negligence Actions, Insurance Litigation, Personal Injury, Automobile/Trucking Litigation (18-Wheeler), Trucking Accidents, Motorcycle Accidents, Railroad Accidents, Dog Bites, Dog Attacks, Consumer Fraud, Deceptive Trade Practices, Product Liability, Workers' Compensation, Environmental Law, Nursing Home Negligence, Dram Shop and Liquor Liability and Wrongful Death.
See Professional Biographies, OKLAHOMA CITY, OKLAHOMA

Homsey, Gary B., (AV) '49 '74
C.612 B.S. L.616 J.D. [Homsey,C.H.&Assoc.] (⊙Oklahoma City)
Homsey, Joseph R., Jr., (BV) .... '47 '74 C.622 B.A. L.615 J.D. 4528 N. Classen Blvd.
Homsey, Michael S., (AV) .... '51 '76 C.612 B.A. L.616 J.D. [M.S.Homsey&Assoc.]
Homsey, Cooper Hill & Associates, (AV) .... 4816 Classen Boulevard

Homsey, Michael S. "Mickey", & Associates, Inc., (AV)
719 North Shartel, 73101-0718
Telephone: 405-235-6622 Fax: 405-236-0096
Email: mhomsey@swbell.net
Michael S. Homsey;—Terry R. McMillan.
Criminal Law, Personal Injury, Family Law, Workers Compensation, Automobile Accidents and Injuries, Wrongful Death, Child Custody, Divorce, Child Support.
See Professional Biographies, OKLAHOMA CITY, OKLAHOMA

Honeywell Gray, Elizabeth .... '57 '82 C.621 B.A. L.615 J.D. 312 N.W. 13th St.
Hood, Henry John, (AV) '60 '85 C.228 A.B. L.623 J.D.
Chesapeake Energy Corporation
Hood, Vivien McC. .... '10 '41 C&L.623 LL.B. 7105 N. Independence St.‡

Hood & Raynolds, P.C.
(See Tulsa)

Hoover, Michael R., (BV) .... '48 '81 C.614 B.A. L.616 J.D. [Robinson&H.]
Hopkins, Daniel R. .... '17 '47 C.378 B.S. L.900 J.D. 11300 N. Penn‡
Hopper, David T. .... '45 '76 C.613 B.A. L.623 J.D. State Employ. Sec. Comm.
Horn, Patricia D., (AV) ...... '58 '89 C.82 B.S. L.623 J.D. V.P., Gen. Coun., Enogex Inc.
Hornbeek, Richard E., (AV) .... '57 '84 C.623 B.B.A. L.616 J.D. [Hornbeek,K.V.&B.]
Hornbeek, Krahl, Vitali & Braun, PLLC, (AV) .... 3711 N. Classen Boulevard
Horner, Russell G., Jr., (AV) .... '39 '63 C&L.623 B.A., LL.B. Kerr-McGee Ctr.
Horning, Philip F., (AV) .... '41 '68 C&L.623 B.A., J.D. [Horning,G.H.&C.]
Horning, Grove, Hulett,Thompson & Comstock, A Professional Corporation, (AV)
119 North Robinson
Horton, Jonathan C. .... '74 '02 C.999 B.S. L.615 J.D. [Ⓐ Abowitz,T.&D.]
Horton, Steven T., (AV) .... '66 '92 C.612 B.S. L.623 J.D. [Ⓐ Abel,M.S.M.&K.]
Hoss, Henry D., (AV) .... '60 '85 C.623 B.S.E. L.862 J.D. [McAfee&T.]
Hosty, Thomas W., (BV) .... '67 '92 C.1147 B.B.A. L.425 J.D. [T.W.Hosty]

Hosty, Thomas W., P.C., (BV)
204 N. Robinson, Suite 1717, P.O. Box 20685, 73156-0685
Mailing Address: P.O. Box 20685, Oklahoma City, OK 73156-0685
Telephone: 405-235-4040 Fax: 405-553-9925 Cell: 405-210-3462
Email: twhoklaw@aol.com URL: http://www.hostylaw.com
Thomas W. Hosty;—Katherine L. Casey.
Criminal Defense, Driving While Intoxicated, DPS, City Tickets, Traffic Violations, Felonies, Misdemeanors, Drug Charges.
See Professional Biographies, OKLAHOMA CITY, OKLAHOMA

Houghton, Carole L. .... '70 '98 C.1077 B.A. L.615 J.D. [Ⓐ DeBee G.]
Housley, Spencer B. .... '77 '04 C&L.623 B.A., J.D. [Ⓐ Baer,T.C.&C.]
Houston, Robert B. .... '65 '91 C.138 B.S. L.862 J.D. [Ⓐ Pierce C.H.B.&G.]
Hoverson, Ronald A. '37 '61 C&L.585 Ph.B., J.D.
(adm. in ND; not adm. in OK) F.B.I.
Hovis, Richard .... '45 '77 C.612 B.S. L.862 J.D. 905 N.W. 12th St.
Howard, Alison .... '— '03 C&L.602 B.A., J.D. [Ⓐ Crowe&D.]
Howard, William R., Jr. .... '36 '65 C&L.378 B.S., J.D. Deputy General Counsel
Howell, Thomas Pitchlynn, IV, (AV) .... '51 '83 C.309 A.B. L.623 J.D. [Ⓐ Day,E.P.&C.]
Howick, Karen L., (BV) .... '45 '78 C.477 B.F.A. L.616 J.D. [Howick&Assoc.]
Howick & Associates, (BV) .... 4508 Classen Blvd.
Howland, Ronald L. .... '34 '64 C.623 B.B.A. L.616 J.D. U.S. Mag.
Howland-Butler, Ann '66 '91 C.623 B.B.A. L.615 J.D.
Sr. Claims Rep., State Farm Insurance Company
Hoyt, Frederick J., (BV) .... '13 '37 C&L.623 B.A., LL.B. 625 N.W. 13th
Hubbard, Carol Partee '45 '83
C.82 B.A. L.615 J.D. Chambers of Judge Carol Partee Hubbard
Hubbard, Janis '56 '93 C.612 B.S. L.615 J.D.
Oklahoma Bar Association, Gen. Coun. Off.
Huckaby, Christian S., (BV) .... '70 '95 C&L.623 B.A., J.D. [Hall,E.H.G.G.&N.]
Huckaby, Robert L., (AV) .... '40 '64 C&L.623 B.A., LL.B. [Huckaby,F.G.&O.]

Huckaby, Fleming, Greenwood & Olsson, LLP, (AV) BB
1215 Classen Drive, P.O. Box 60130, 73103
Telephone: 405-235-6648 Fax: 405-235-1533
URL: http://www.hfgolaw.com
Members of the Firm: Robert L. Huckaby; Kent Fleming; William D. Greenwood; Brently C. Olsson.
Associate: Christopher M. Murphy.
State and Federal Civil Litigation and Appellate Practice. Insurance Defense, Subrogation, Arbitration, Mediation, Tort Law, Product Liability, Vehicular Negligence, Premises Liability.
See Professional Biographies, OKLAHOMA CITY, OKLAHOMA

Hudson, David, P.C., (AV) ...... '35 '60 C.612 B.S. L.623 LL.B. 5304 N. Walker Avenue
Hudson, J. Clifford, (AV) .... '54 '81 C.623 B.A. L.276 J.D. Sonic Industries
Hudson, John .... '49 '73 C.613 B.A. L.623 J.D. 5400 N. Classen Blvd.
Hudson, Ronald R., (AV) .... '42 '67 C.614 B.A. L.623 J.D. [Hudson,A.&L.]
Hudson, Stephanie C. '66 '94 C.616 B.S.B. L.615 J.D.
Staff Atty., Oklahoma Indian Legal Services, Inc.
Hudson, Alden & Leonard, (AV) .... Suite 850 211 North Robinson
Huff, Brenda J., (BV) ...... '50 '81 C.339 B.A. L.616 J.D. 5801 N.W. Grand Blvd., Ste. B
Huff, Glen D., (AV) .... '49 '75 C&L.623 B.A., J.D. [Foliart,H.O.&B.]
Huffman, Laurence M., (AV) .... '49 '74 C&L.623 B.A., J.D. [McAfee&T.]
Hughes, Carl D., (AV) .... '46 '71 C&L.623 B.B.A., J.D. [Hughes&G.]
Hughes, James L., Jr. .... '48 '90 C&L.623 B.A., J.D. [J.L.Hughes,Jr.]
Hughes, Marilyn K. .... '49 '76 C.612 B.A. L.862 J.D. Ethics Comm.
Hughes, Tina A. .... '56 '90 C.82 B.A. L.616 J.D. Asst. Mun. Counselor
Hughes & Goodwin, (AV) .... 5801 N. Broadway Extension, Ste. 302
Hughes, James L., Jr., Attorney at Law, P.C. .... 200 North Harvey, Suite 920
Hughey, John Robert .... '36 '61 C&L.623 B.A., J.D. 2516 Warwick Drive
Hughlett, Tamela R., (BV) .... '65 '92 C.1147 B.A. L.623 J.D. [Crowe&D.]
Hulett, Carrie S., (AV) .... '52 '78 C&L.616 B.A., J.D. [Horning,G.H.&C.]
Hullum, Patrick L. .... '77 '03 C.612 B.A. L.623 J.D. [Ⓐ Pignato&C.]
Humble, Charles G. .... '36 '63 C.624 L.623 J.D. Spec. Dist. J.
Hummel, Timothy B. .... '66 '95 C.623 B.B.A. L.846 J.D. 325 Dean A. McGee
Hunsinger, Rodney Kent, III '77 '03 C.619 B.B.A. L.623 J.D.
[Ⓐ Phillips M.M.M.&M.]
Hunsucker, John E., (CV) .... '66 '98 C.623 B.A. L.615 J.D. [J.E.Hunsucker]
Hunsucker, John E., LLC, (CV) .... P.O. Box 60931
Hunt, Christopher Michael .... '60 '89 C.623 B.S. L.616 J.D. State Dept. of Secs.
Hunt, David D., II, (AV) .... '57 '82 C&L.623 B.A., J.D. [D.D.Hunt,II]
Hunt, Jake, (AV) .... '20 '50 C&L.623 LL.B. 1408 Canterbury
Hunt, Lewis E., Jr. .... '34 '62 C.623 B.B.A. L.616 LL.B. 3101 Castle Rock Rd.

Hunt, David D., II, A Professional Corporation, (AV)
1428 Northwest 35th Street, P.O. Box 18896, 73154-0896
Telephone: 405-528-0168 Fax: 405-528-3508
URL: http://www.hunt-law.com
David D. Hunt, II.
Oil and Gas, Oil and Gas Title Examination, Commercial Real Estate Finance.
See Professional Biographies, OKLAHOMA CITY, OKLAHOMA

Hunter, Betty Elrod ... '29 '82 C.1147 B.S. L.616 J.D. 508 N.W. 15th
Hunter, Cheryl P., (AV) ... '— '82 C.612 B.S. L.623 J.D. [Kirk&C.]
Hunter, Stewart M. ... '27 '62 C.612 B.S. L.616 J.D. Ct. of App. J.
Hurley, Kahla R. ... '61 '89 C.92 B.S. L.616 J.D. Law Clk. to U.S. Bkrptcy. J.
Hurley, Kay Allen, (AV) ... '64 '90 C.612 B.J. L.615 J.D. 6440 Avondale Dr.
Hurt, John Roger, (AV) ... '58 '84 C.862 B.S. L.623 J.D. [Pierce C.H.B.&G.]
Hurtt, Philip Anthony ... '66 '94 C.623 B.A. L.616 J.D. 4912 S. Western
Hyatt, Bonita J., (BV) '48 '83
C.1086 B.A.E. L.616 J.D. Sr. Staff. Atty., Hartford Fire Insurance Co.
Hyde, Herbert K., Jr. ... '31 '61 C.623 B.A. L.273 LL.B. 1804 Coventry Lane
Hyde, James Dudley, (AV) ... '44 '69 C.623 B.A. L.802 J.D. [McAfee&T.]
Hyde, Vernon D., (AV) ... '53 '81 C.1147 B.S. L.616 J.D. [V.D.Hyde&Assoc.]

Hyde, Vernon D., & Associates, PLLC, (AV)
1120 Northwest 63rd Street, Suite 116, 73116-6500
Telephone: 405-842-1177 Fax: 405-842-1884
Email: vhydeatty@aol.com URL: http://www.vhydelaw.com
Vernon D. Hyde.
Estate Planning, Trusts and Estates, Probate, Tax Litigation, Estate and Gift Taxation, Wills.

Ice, Kristi Jo ... '75 '00 C&L.612 B.A., J.D. Gov. Off.
Ihrig, Chad E. ... '76 '02 C.612 B.S. L.623 J.D. [Ⓐ Whitten,N.M.T.&R.]
Ingham, Richard G., (AV) ... '48 '78 C.612 B.A. L.802 J.D. Legal Serv. Developer
Inman, Scott M. ... '78 '04 C&L.623 B.A., J.D. [Ⓐ Cheek]
Irby, Bobby G. ... '77 '03 C.1142 B.S. L.615 J.D. [Ⓐ Morgan&Assoc.]
Ircink, J.D. ... '68 '94 C.958 B.S. L.615 J.D. [Ircink&M.]
Ircink & Miller, P.C. ... 3037 N.W. 63rd St., Ste. 206
Irvine, Francis S., (AV) ... '23 '50 C.612 B.A. L.623 LL.B. 1936 N.W. 56th Terrace‡
Isaacs, Garvin A., (AV) ... '45 '74 C.840 B.A. L.616 J.D. [G.A.Isaacs]

Isaacs, Garvin A., Inc., (AV)
Rainy Mountain Building, 123 N.W. Eighth Street, 73102-5804
Telephone: 405-232-2060 Fax: 405-232-9035
Garvin A. Isaacs;—Nancy A. Zerr.
Medical Malpractice, Nursing Home Negligence, Products Liability, Bad Faith Insurance, Toxic Torts, Oil and Gas Fraud, Murder Cases and White Collar Crime.
See Professional Biographies, OKLAHOMA CITY, OKLAHOMA

Ison, Randy K. ... '67 '93 C.612 B.S. L.623 J.D. 211 N. Robinson
Israel, Howard F., (BV) ... '45 '76 C&L.616 B.A., J.D. [H.F.Israel]
Israel, Jay G., (BV) ... '48 '74 C&L.616 B.A., J.D. [J.G.Israel]
Israel, Howard F., A Professional Corporation, (BV) ... 401 N. Hudson Ave.
Israel, Jay G., A Professional Corporation, (BV) ... 401 N. Hudson Ave.
Istook, Ernest J., Jr., (BV) '50 '77 C.69 B.A. L.616 J.D.
120 N. Robinson Ave., Ste. 100
Ivy, Robert W. '64 '90 C.597 B.S. L.602 J.D.
(adm. in IL; not adm. in OK) [Ⓐ R.H.,.a.C.A.L.Alexander,Jr.]
Jackson, Anthony L., (AV) ... '60 '87 C&L.623 B.A., J.D. P.O. Box 892541
Jackson, Benjamin Brown ... '55 '81 C.145 A.B. L.623 J.D. State Corp. Comm.
Jackson, Charles M. ... '63 '88 C&L.623 B.A., J.D. Asst. Gen. Coun., Dept. Human Servs.
Jackson, Donna J., (AV) ... '57 '88 C.612 B.S. L.615 J.D. 2812 North West 57th Suite 101
Jackson, Guy W., (AV) ... '55 '81 C.1315 B.S.E. L.623 J.D. [Jackson&Assoc.]
Jackson, Jennifer E. ... '77 '02 C.613 B.A. L.623 J.D. [Ⓐ Hiltgen&B.]
Jackson, Justin L. ... '75 '00 C&L.623 B.B.A., J.D. [Ⓐ McAfee&T.]
Jackson, Kerry Ann Painton ... '60 '88 C&L.623 B.A., J.D. 8809 Stoneleigh Ct.
Jackson, Scott R. ... '71 '98 C.45 B.A. L.623 J.D. 4323 NW 63rd St.
Jackson, T. Michael, (AV) ... '45 '72 C.1147 B.A. L.616 J.D. 700 Couch Dr.
Jackson & Associates, P.C., (AV) ... 2200 NW 50th St.
Jacobsen, John McClellan ... '58 '86 C.101 B.A. L.616 J.D. Asst. Mun. Coun.
Jaffery, Syeda Sehra '74 '02 C.862 B.A. L.446 J.D.
V.P. & Legal Coun., Bluebonnett Resources Corporation
James, Gary J., and Associates, (AV) '62 '88
C.1023 B.A. L.616 J.D. 701 N. Broadway, Ste. 410
James, Harry ... '17 '49 C.623 B.A. L.615 LL.B. 4304 N.W. 23rd St.
James, Jon D., (BV) ... '41 '71 C.1147 B.A. L.616 J.D. 6521 N.W. 95th
James, Marcie, (AV) ... '40 '82 C&L.623 B.B.A., J.D. [Green,J.&W.]
James, Mickey, (AV) ... '40 '66 C&L.615 B.A., J.D. [Green,J.&W.]
James, Philippa C. ... '— '92 C.477 B.A. L.615 J.D. Mun. J.
Jantzen, Stephen L. ... '68 '94 C.935 B.A. L.616 J.D. [Ryan,W.&C.]
Jarnigan, Jami ... '68 '94 C&L.623 B.B.A., J.D. Juv. Pros.
Jarvis, William J. ... '71 '03 C.623 B.B.A. L.616 J.D. [Ⓐ Phillips M.M.M.&M.]
Jaworsky, Stephen ... '21 '53 C&L.616 LL.B. 41 S.E. 51st St.
Jenks, Terry James ... '58 '85 C.623 B.A. L.616 J.D. Exec. Dir., Pardon & Parole Bd.
Jennings, James A., III, (AV) ... '49 '74 C.612 B.A. L.623 J.D. [Jennings C.H.&T.]

Jennings Cook Hoisington & Teague, P.C., (AV) BR
204 North Robinson, Suite 1000, 73102
Telephone: 405-609-6000 Facsimile: 405-609-6501
Email: JCH@JCHLaw.com URL: http://www.jchlaw.com
James A. Jennings, III; Rodney L. Cook; Carrie Palmer Hoisington; J. Derrick Teague. Associates: Jeffrey W. Miller; Linda G. Kaufmann.
Product Liability Defense, Insurance Defense, Personal Injury Defense, Employment Law, Civil Rights Law, Personal Injury, General Civil Litigation, Transportation..
See Professional Biographies, OKLAHOMA CITY, OKLAHOMA

Jennings-Johnson, W. Kay ... '— '93 C.1147 B.S. L.623 J.D. 3433 N.W. 56th St., Ste. 660
Jenson, Robin D., (AV) ... '57 '87 C.612 B.S. L.616 J.D. [Daugherty,F.P.&H.]
Jernigan, Robert M., (AV) ... '35 '67 C&L.623 B.A., J.D. 4301 N.W. 63rd St., Ste. 109
Jester, Melanie J., (AV) ... '66 '92 C&L.623 B.A., J.D. 1600 Bank of Oklahoma Plz.
Johannes, Ryan J. ... '62 '96 C.612 B.S. L.623 J.D. [R.J.Johannes]
Johannes, Ryan J., PLLC, The Law Offices of ... One North Hudson, 9th Floor
Johanning, Paul, (AV) ... '34 '58 C.612 B.A. L.623 LL.B. 3134 N.W. 23rd Street
Johnson, A. Scott, (AV) ... '50 '79 C.36 B.S. L.616 J.D. [Johnson&H.]
Johnson, Barry L. '63 '90 C.597 B.A. L.477 J.D.
(adm. in IL; not adm. in OK) Asst. Prof., Oklahoma City Univ. Sch. of Law
Johnson, Barry W., (AV) ... '36 '67 C.347 B.A. L.616 J.D. [B.W.Johnson]
Johnson, Brent M., (BV) ... '69 '96 C.813 B.A. L.623 J.D. [Fellers,S.B.B.&T.]
Johnson, Bruce H., (AV) ... '13 '36 C.108 A.B. L.1119 J.D. [Ⓒ Crowe&D.]
Johnson, Bryce B., (AV) ... '58 '85 C.508 B.S.B.A. L.615 J.D. [Biscone&B.]
Johnson, Burton J., (AV) ... '20 '50 L.616 [Looney,N.&J.]
Johnson, Celeste T. ... '70 '02 C.846 B.B.A. L.623 J.D. [Ⓐ Phillips M.M.M.&M.]
Johnson, Charles A. ... '31 '55 C&L.623 B.A., LL.B. Presiding J., Crim. App. Ct.
Johnson, Daniel P. ... '79 '05 C.1147 B.A. L.623 J.D. [Ⓐ Crowe&D.]
Johnson, Darlene Parker ... '65 '91 C&L.623 B.A., J.D. [P.Johnson]
Johnson, Debbie Sue ... '59 '99 C&L.623 B.A., J.D. 4312 N. Classen Blvd.
Johnson, Eric L. ... '69 '94 C.612 B.S. L.616 J.D. [Ⓐ Phillips M.M.M.&M.]
Johnson, Ernest G., (BV) ... '57 '83 C&L.623 B.A., J.D. 401 NE 60th
Johnson, J. Logan, (AV) ... '63 '88 C&L.623 B.B.A., J.D. [Durbin,L.&B.]
Johnson, J. Terry '42 '69 C.1315 B.A. L.802 J.D.
Pres., Okla. Christian Univ. of Science & Arts

Johnson, John G., (BV) ... '49 '75 C.623 B.S. L.616 J.D. 3904 E. Reno Ave.
Johnson, Robert M., (AV) ... '42 '67 C.612 B.S. L.623 J.D. [Ⓒ Crowe&D.]
Johnson, Stephen R., (AV) ... '56 '82 C.37 B.A. L.862 J.D. [J.P.Linn]
Johnson, Steven James, (BV) ... '70 '95 C.612 B.B.A. L.623 J.D. [Ⓐ Foliart,H.O.&B.]
Johnson, Walter O. ... '28 '51 C&L.793 LL.B. Int. Rev. Ser.
Johnson, Wayne L., (BV Ⓣ) ... '34 '71 C.304 B.A. L.208 J.D. P.O. Box 268812
Johnson, William A., (BV) ... '51 '77 C.623 B.A. L.616 J.D. [Hartzog C.C.&N.]
Johnson, Barry W., P.C., (AV) ... 120 N. Robinson

Johnson and Hanan, P.C., (AV)
Bank One Center, Suite 2750, 100 North Broadway Avenue, 73102
Telephone: 405-232-6100 Fax: 405-232-6105
Email: jhht@johnsonhanan.com
A. Scott Johnson; Mary B. Hanan;—Alexander C. Vosler; Jon M. Williford; Bryan E. Stanton; Justin P. Eilers; James D. Graves; Niki S. Batt; John B. Hill.
General Civil, Trial and Appellate Practice in all State and Federal Courts. Insurance and Casualty, Medical, Legal and Professional Malpractice, Negligence, and Personal Injury Law. Health Law in State and Federal Agencies.
See Professional Biographies, OKLAHOMA CITY, OKLAHOMA

Johnson, Parker, Legal Services ... 3200 S. Anderson Rd.
Johnston, D. Craig '58 '85
C.1147 B.A. L.616 J.D. Vice-Presiding J., State Wkrs. Comp. Ct.
Johnston, David C., Jr., (AV) ... '31 '60 C&L.616 B.S., J.D. [Ⓒ Smith R.S.&E.]
Johnston, John Michael, (BV) '48 '74
C&L.623 B.B.A., J.D. 228 Robert S. Kerr Ave., Ste. 620
Johnston, Marie ... '— '03 C.612 B.S. L.623 J.D. [Ⓐ Crowe&D.]
Johnston, Norman B. ... '52 '79 C.95 A.B. L.623 J.D. P.O. Box 721473
Johnston, Stanley P. ... '40 '67 C.623 L.616 LL.B. Coun. to the Comr., State Tax Comm.
Jones, A.J. ... '54 '99 C.623 M.A. L.616 J.D. 325 Dean A. McGee
Jones, Cathleen Ann ... '63 '88 C&L.623 B.Acct., J.D. Atty., I.R.S.
Jones, Daniel K. ... '70 '97 C&L.623 B.A., J.D. [Ⓐ Mills]
Jones, Doneen Douglas, (AV) ... '51 '81 C&L.623 B.S., J.D. [Fellers,S.B.B.&T.]
Jones, Gary ... '62 '92 C.840 B.B.A. L.616 J.D. [Ⓐ R.G.Grove&Assoc.]
Jones, Glenn M., (AV) ... '51 '77 321 Park Ave.
Jones, Jake, III, (AV) ... '57 '82 C.1147 B.B.A. L.623 J.D. 100 N. Broadway
Jones, James Lynn ... '66 '94 C&L.623 B.A., J.D. 1327 N. Robinson Ave.
Jones, Jay L. ... '66 '94 C&L.623 B.F.A., J.D. [Ⓒ McKinney&S.]
Jones, Jerry D. ... '39 '68 C.622 B.S. L.616 J.D. 6700 S. Western
Jones, K. Nicholle, (BV) ... '69 '97 C&L.623 B.B.A, J.D. [Mullins,H.&J.]
Jones, Kenneth I., Jr., (AV) ... '50 '76 C.623 B.B.A. L.616 J.D. [K.Jones]
Jones, Kindanne C., (AV) ... '60 '85 C.623 B.A. L.93 J.D. [Eddy&J.]
Jones, Mark Lawton, (BV) ... '55 '80 C&L.623 B.A., J.D. OK Atty. Gen.
Jones, Mickey K. ... '21 '48 C&L.623 LL.B. V.P., Mid-Continent Life Ins. Co.
Jones, Orval Edwin, (AV) ... '59 '84 C.910 A.B. L.623 J.D. 200 N. Walker, Ste. 400
Jones, Phyllis Stevenson ... '41 '77 4400 Hemingway Dr., Ste. 173
Jones, Ray L. ... '48 '78 C.1147 B.A. L.623 J.D. [Ⓒ R.H.Mitchell&Assoc.]
Jones, Robert Ray, Jr. ... '70 '04 C.418 B.S. L.615 J.D. [Ⓐ Collins,Z.&W.]
Jones, Tava Seifert, (BV) ... '69 '96 C.612 B.S. L.623 J.D. [Ⓐ Groom]
Jones, Thomas Scott ... '46 '80 C.174 B.A. L.616 J.D. Asst. Mun. Coun.

Jones, Andrews & Ortiz
21 E. Main Street, Suite 101, 73104 ⊙
Telephone: 405-601-8713 Fax: 405-232-8330
URL: http://www.jao-law.com
Associate: Bruce A. Robertson.
Civil Trial Law and Insurance Defense.
San Antonio, Texas Office: 10100 Reunion Place, Suite 600, 78216. Telephone: 210-344-3900. Telecopier: 210-366-4301.
See Professional Biographies, OKLAHOMA CITY, OKLAHOMA

Jones, Kenneth, P.C., (AV) ... 321 Dean McGee
Joosten, Stephen D. ... '50 '76 C.608 B.S.E. L.616 J.D. Star Mfg. Co.
Jordan, H. Dale ... '16 '48 C.623 L.615 LL.B. 5901 N. Western‡
Jordan, Marion E. ... '25 '49 C.615 L.999 LL.B. 710 N.E. 19th‡
Joseph, Jeb Emmet ... '74 '01 C&L.623 B.A., J.D. [Ⓐ Hughes&G.]
Joseph, Michael E., (AV) ... '51 '76 C&L.623 B.A., J.D. [McAfee&T.]
Kaestner, Steven D., (AV) ... '56 '82 C.793 B.S. L.623 J.D. [S.P.Kaestner]
Kaestner, Steven P., P.C., (AV) ... 2601 N.W. Expwy. St.
Kallstrom, James D., (AV) ... '50 '76 C.385 B.A. L.930 J.D. [Ⓒ Hartzog C.C.&N.]
Kalsu, J. Robert, (BV) ... '70 '95 C.623 B.B.A. L.802 J.D. [Crowe&D.]
Kane, Matthew C. ... '76 '02 C&L.623 B.A., J.D. [Ryan,W.&C.]
Kane, Susan F. ... '76 '02 C&L.623 B.A., J.D. [Ⓐ Smith R.S.&E.]
Kanelopoulos, George James, Jr. ... '61 '88 C.1111 B.A. L.1288 J.D. [Kanelopoulos]
Kanelopoulos Law Firm, P.C. ... 4549 N.W., 36th Street
Karey, Gus J. ... '22 '59 C.623 B.S. L.616 LL.B. 3000 Pelham Dr.
Karim, Andrew E., (BV) ... '54 '85 C.1147 B.S. L.862 J.D. 10325 Greenbriar Place
Kasper, Kris D. ... '57 '83 C.612 B.S. L.616 J.D. Admin. Law J., Okla. Tax Comm.
Kaufman, James M., (AV) ... '51 '76 C&L.623 B.B.A., J.D. [Ⓒ Groom]
Kaufman, Katheryn K., (BV) '50 '83
C.623 B.S. L.616 J.D. Staff Coun., Allstate Insurance Company
Kaufman, Myra Palevsky ... '71 '95 C.30 B.A. L.472 J.D. [Ⓐ Day,E.P.&C.]
Kaufman, Perry ... '62 '88 C.612 B.S. L.616 J.D. Commissioners Land Off.
Kaufmann, Linda G. ... '64 '91 C.623 B.S. L.615 J.D [Ⓐ Jennings C.H.&T.]
Kearney, David L., (AV) ... '60 '85 C&L.623 B.B.A., J.D. [Gable&G.]
Keating, Francis A., II ... '44 '69 C.276 B.A. L.623 J.D. Gov.
Keef, Marian F., and Associates ... '49 '94 C.623 B.F.A. L.615 J.D. 4801 Classen Blvd.
Keel, Robert T., (BV) ... '36 '68 C.82 B.S. L.616 J.D. State Capitol Building, Suite 114
Keel, William Louis, (BV) ... '50 '80 C&L.616 B.A., J.D. Asst. Dist. Atty.
Keith, Craig B. ... '57 '82 C.1044 B.A. L.616 J.D. Asst. Mun. Coun.
Keller, E. W., (BV) ... '36 '60 C&L.623 B.A., LL.B. [Keller&K.]
Keller, Trenton W., (BV) ... '59 '84 C.35 B.S. L.623 J.D. [Keller&K.]
Keller & Keller, (BV) ... 101 N. Robinson Ave.
Kelley, Gerald E., (AV) ... '52 '78 C&L.623 B.A., J.D. [Kelley,K.&G.]
Kelley, James P., (AV) ... '44 '70 C.623 B.A. L.616 J.D. [Kelley,K.&G.]
Kelley, Kevin, (AV) ... '62 '88 C.1147 B.A. L.623 J.D. [Nash,C.&K.]
Kelley, William B. ... '59 '85 C.929 B.A. L.616 J.D. 6 N.E. 63rd St.
Kelley, Kelley & Gregory, (AV) ... 211 N. Robinson
Kellogg, Robert D., (AV) ... '46 '78 C.623 B.S. L.616 J.D. [Shipley&K.]
Kells, Richard B., (AV) ... '53 '78 C.829 B.S. L.616 J.D. [Hartzog C.C.&N.]
Kelly, Michael P. ... '59 '85 C.623 B.B.A L.615 J.D. [Ⓒ Pignato&C.]
Kelly, Robert Dale, Sr. ... '49 '87 C.618 B.A. L.623 J.D. Jud. Law Clk., U.S. Dist. Ct.
Kelly, Robert W., II ... '58 '89 C.623 B.B.A. L.616 J.D. 3100 Hickory Stick Rd.
Kelly, Ronald "Skip" ... '50 '82 C&L.612 B.S., J.D. 200 North Harvey, Suite 810
Kelsay, Kenneth E. ... '38 '68 C&L.616 LL.B. Gen. Coun., Okla. State Med. Assn.
Keltch, Peter M. ... '47 '72 C.619 B.A. L.623 J.D. Admin. Law J., Soc. Sec. Admn.
Keltner, Thomas N. ... '17 '47 C&L.623 B.A., LL.B. 9636 N. May‡
Kemether, Redmond P., (BV) ... '59 '84 C.645 B.A. L.616 J.D. [R.P.Kemether]

Kemether, Redmond P., A Professional Corporation, (BV) 437 Northwest 5th Street, Suite 201
Kempf, John Frederick, Jr., (AV) '51 '77 C.612 B.A. L.616 J.D. [Pate,K.&K.]
Kempton, J. Wayne '25 '50 C&L.623 LL.B. Pres., The Kempton Company
Kenan, Thomas J., (AV) '32 '58 C&L.623 A.B., LL.B. [Fuller,T.P.&S.]
Kenderdine, Nancy I. '42 '73 C.228 B.A. L.623 J.D. Prof of Law, Oklahoma City Univ. Sch. of Law
Kendrick, Thomas Rowe, (BV) '71 '98 C.1147 B.A. L.615 J.D. [Looney,N.&J.]
Kennedy, Brigid F., (AV) '61 '87 C&L.616 B.A., J.D. [Kennedy]
Kennedy, David D., (AV) '58 '84 C.587 B.S. L.623 J.D. [Spradling,K.&M.]
Kennedy, Neal R., (AV) '45 '83 C.623 B.S.M.E. L.616 J.D. [McAfee&T.] (Pat.)
Kennedy Law Firm, A Professional Corporation, (AV) 4334 Northwest Expressway, Suite 151
Kenney, Herbert, (AV) '47 '74 C.691 B.A. L.623 J.D. Assoc. Corp. Coun., Dobson Communications Corp.
Kenney, John A., (AV) '48 '75 C&L.623 B.S.I.E., J.D. [McAfee&T.]
Kerr, Aubrey M., Jr., (BV) '39 '64 C&L.623 B.A., LL.B. P.O. Box 2016
Kerr, Elizabeth A. '69 '93 C.612 B.S. L.623 J.D. [Shelton]
Kerr, Elizabeth H., (BV) '61 '87 C.802 B.A. L.616 J.D. Asst. City Atty.
Kerr, Ken D., Jr., (BV) '66 '95 C&L.623 B.B.A., J.D. [Pate,K.&K.]
Kerr, Robert Bruce '54 '81 C&L.623 J.D. Isotek Laboratories
Kerr, Steven S., (BV) '60 '85 C.802 B.A. L.616 J.D. 12501 N. May Ave.

Kerr, Irvine, Rhodes & Ables, A Professional Corporation, (AV)
201 Robert S. Kerr Avenue, Suite 600, 73102-4267
Telephone: 405-272-9221 Fax: 405-236-3121
URL: http://www.kiralaw.com
Robert S. Kerr, Jr. (1926-2004); Horace G. Rhodes; J. Angela Ables; James W. Rhodes; James R. Barnett; R. Thomas Lay;—Jeff L. Hartmann. Of Counsel: Robert A. Miller.
General Civil Practice in all State and Federal Courts. Corporation, Probate, Insurance, Banking, Administrative, Employment, Water, Environmental, Oil and Gas, Agricultural Law, Commercial Litigation, and Insurance Law.
Representative Clients: Bethany-Warr Acres; Public Works Authority; City of Crescent; Fort James Corp.; 66 Federal Credit Union.
See Professional Biographies, OKLAHOMA CITY, OKLAHOMA

Ketelsleger, David J., (AV) '64 '90 C.508 B.A. L.623 J.D. [McAfee&T.]
Keyl, Mark David '50 '88 C.869 B.S. L.616 J.D. Gen. Coun., AmeriResource Grp. Inc.
Khuu, Tuan Anh '69 '97 C.910 B.A. L.623 J.D. 3010 N. Classen
Kickingbird, Kirke '44 '69 C&L.623 B.A., J.D. [Hobbs,S.D.&W.] (Wash., DC)
Kifer, James E. '50 '74 C.618 B.A. L.862 J.D. 5601 N.W. 72nd St.
Kilpatrick, Don W., (BV) '39 '63 C&L.616 LL.B. Comr., Okla. Tax Comm.
Kilpatrick, Tammie Thomas '60 '85 C.612 B.S. L.623 J.D. Kilpatrick Consulting, Inc.
Kimball, Paul M., (AV) '42 '69 C.623 B.S. L.616 J.D. 3208 Lamp Post Ln.
Kimbrough, Pamela Jean King, (BV) '60 '88 C.1300 B.S. L.616 J.D. 4901 Richmond Sq.
King, Bryan N.B., (AV) '70 '95 C.990 B.A. L.623 J.D. [Fellers,S.B.B.&T.]
King, Eric R., (AV) '46 '76 C.1315 B.S.E. L.623 J.D. [Gable&G.]
King, Jamelle Ritsch '70 '98 C.619 B.S. L.615 J.D. Five Corp. Plz., 3625 N.W., 56th St.
King, James Edward '68 '98 C.618 B.A. L.615 J.D. 10300 Greenbriar Pl.
King, Justin T. '72 '00 C.902 B.A. L.623 J.D. [King]
King, Kenneth '20 '54 C.623 B.S. L.616 LL.B. [K.King] ‡
King, Linda A., (AV) '47 '77 C.1315 B.A. L.623 J.D. [Gable&G.]
King, Ricky H. '60 '85 C.1300 B.A. L.285 J.D. Title Coun., Amer. Guaranty Title Co.
King, Tom L., (AV) '43 '70 C&L.623 B.S., J.D. [King]
King, Kenneth, P.C. 2400 N.W. 30th Street

King Law Firm, (AV)
15 North Robinson, Suite 1100, 73102
Telephone: 405-239-6143 Fax: 405-236-3934 Email: King@King-Lawfirm.com
Email: king@king-lawfirm.com
Tom L. King. Associates: Richard M. Glasgow; Justin T. King.
General Civil and Trial Practice in all State and Federal Courts, Insurance Defense, Bad Faith, Negligence, Products Liability, Workers' Compensation, Labor and Employment, and Business Law. Litigation in all State and Federal Courts.
References: BankOne; BancFirst.
See Professional Biographies, OKLAHOMA CITY, OKLAHOMA

Kinney, David L. '58 '84 C.1147 B.S. L.623 J.D. Univ. of Okla. Health Science Ctr.
Kinsey, Letitia '64 '99 C.1147 B.A. L.623 J.D. [Kinsey&Assoc.]
Kinsey & Associates, PLLC 510 E. Memorial, Suite D-1
Kirby, R. Gregory '67 '96 C.1147 B.A. L.615 J.D. [Whitten,N.M.T.&R.]
Kirk, D. Benham, Jr. '57 '82 C.859 B.A. L.623 J.D. [Pignato&C.]
Kirk, David W., (AV) '57 '85 C.945 B.A. L.623 J.D. [Lytle S.&C.]
Kirk, Edward C., (BV) '51 '84 C.621 B.A. L.616 J.D. Asst. Atty. Gen., OK Atty. Gen. Off.
Kirk, James A., (AV) '— '68 C&L.623 B.B.A., J.D. [Kirk&C.]
Kirk, Kaye M., (BV) '59 '85 C.612 B.S. L.623 J.D. State Dept. of Human Servs.

Kirk & Chaney, (AV)
101 Park Avenue, Suite 800, 73102-7202
Telephone: 405-235-1333 Fax: 405-235-5914
Members of Firm: James A. Kirk; James M. Chaney; Allen Campbell; Matthew L. Standard; Thomas J. Daniel IV; Cheryl P. Hunter; Joseph P. Balkenbush. Associate: Katherine H. Pence. Of Counsel: Jack G. Bush.
Civil Trial Practice in all State and Federal Courts. Oil and Gas, Real Estate, Securities, Administrative, Commercial Law and Family Law.
References: First Interstate Bank (Trust Department); The Oklahoma Bank.
See Professional Biographies, OKLAHOMA CITY, OKLAHOMA

Kirkland, Nevin R. '72 '03 C.1147 B.A. L.615 J.D. [Edmonds,C.H.G.R.&W.]
Kirkpatrick, Jennifer Heald '73 '02 C.1300 B.A. L.616 J.D. [Phillips M.M.M.&M.]
Kirschner, Michael Paul, (AV) '43 '68 C&L.616 B.A., J.D. [Kirschner K.L.]

Kirschner Kisner Lee, P.L.L.C., (AV)
Chase Center, 100 North Broadway Avenue, Suite 3030, 73102-8838
Telephone: 405-239-3300; Toll Free: 888-978-3300 Facsimile: 405-235-3352
URL: http://www.kirschnerlaw.com
Michael Paul Kirschner; David W. Kisner; Jim W. Lee;—Lorrie A. Corbin.
Commercial Law, General Civil and Appellate Practice in State and Federal Courts. Bankruptcy and Commercial Transactions, Business Law, Contracts, Corporate Law, Banks and Banking, Insurance Defense, Workers' Compensation, Alternative Dispute Resolution, Labor and Employment, Health Care, International Law, Arbitration, Mediation, Mergers, Acquisitions and Divestitures, Personal Injury, Product Liability, Malpractice, Family Law, Partnership Law, Finance, Real Estate, Wills, Trusts and Estates, and Construction Law.
Representative Clients: Available Upon Request.
See Professional Biographies, OKLAHOMA CITY, OKLAHOMA

Kiser, Wm. Don, (AV) '43 '71 C.612 B.S. L.623 J.D. [Fagin,B.B.T.&K.]
Kisner, David W., (BV) '40 '68 C.619 B.S. L.862 J.D. [Kirschner K.L.]
Kissinger-Christel, Dawn M. '73 '01 C.746 B.A. L.615 J.D. [Burnett&G.]
Kite, Charles Thomas, (BV) '45 '75 C&L.616 B.S., J.D. [C.T.Kite]
Kite, Jerry D., (BV) '47 '80 C.618 B.S. L.616 J.D. 3721 Classen Blvd.
Kite, C. Thomas, P.C., (BV) 620 N. Robinson, Suite 207
Kivel, Franklin Jay, (AV) '42 '74 C.800 B.A. L.616 J.D. 1434 Duffner Dr.
Klaus, Lester Anthony, (AV) '36 '61 C.502 B.S.B.A. L.734 LL.B. 6809 N.W. Grand Boulevard
Klein, Bruce F., (P.C.), (BV) '55 '85 C.1044 B.A. L.616 J.D. [Mitchell,D.K.&P.]
Klein, Hali Jane '61 '92 C&L.862 B.S., J.D. State Farm Ins.
Klein, Keith J. '52 '84 C.674 B.A. L.1049 J.D. [Ryan,W.&C.]
Klepper, James Bradley '67 '01 C.623 B.Arch. L.615 J.D. [McAfee&T.]
Klepper, Jim C. '49 '91 C.622 B.S. L.616 J.D. 1101 Sovereign Row
Kline, David A., (AV) '23 '49 C.616 L.623 LL.B. [Kline,K.E.&B.]
Kline, John Frank '46 '88 C.497 B.S. L.615 J.D. 4200 Perimeter Ctr., Ste. 245
Kline, Timothy D., (AV) '49 '76 C&L.623 B.A., J.D. [Kline,K.E.&B.]

Kline, Kline, Elliott & Bryant, P.C., (AV)
Kline Law Building, 720 N.E. 63rd Street, 73105
Telephone: 405-848-4448 Fax: 405-842-4539
Email: kline@klinefirm.org URL: http://www.klinefirm.org
David A. Kline; Timothy D. Kline; G. David Bryant; Stephen W. Elliott;—Clay P. Booth; Lisa M. Mueggenborg; Christopher T. Stein; Susan Carey; Lynnell A. Harkins. Of Counsel: Richard M. Healy, III; Patrick M. Castleberry; S. Thomas Adler; Steven J. Goetzinger.
General Trial and Appellate Practice in all State and Federal Courts. Civil and Criminal, Bankruptcy and Commercial Law. Employment and Civil Rights Litigation.
See Professional Biographies, OKLAHOMA CITY, OKLAHOMA

Klinge, Richard M., (AV) '49 '74 C.1283 B.S. L.900 J.D. [R.M.Klinge&Assoc.]

Klinge, Richard M., & Associates, P.C., (AV)
3555 Northwest 58th Street Suite 1000, 73112
Telephone: 405-917-0398 Fax: 405-917-0323
Email: rklinge@klingelaw.com
Richard M. Klinge.
Transactional Practice including Health Law, Computer Law, Electronic Commerce, Intellectual Property, Information Law, Contracts, Commercial, Internet Law, and Corporate Law.
See Professional Biographies, OKLAHOMA CITY, OKLAHOMA

Klingenberg, Kenneth W., (AV) '47 '73 C&L.623 B.B.A., J.D. [K.W.Klingenberg]
Klingenberg, K. W., Inc., (AV) 330 N.W. 13th St.
Kmetz, John C. '66 '04 C.858 B.A. L.623 J.D. [Fenton,F.S.R.&M.]
Knarr, Stuart Alan, (AV) '61 '89 C.838 B.S.Mech.E. L.616 J.D. [Pate,K.&K.]
Knight, Gerald G. '29 '60 C&L.616 B.S., LL.B. 3825 N.W. 23rd St.
Knight, Susan Ann, (BV) '57 '92 C&L.623 B.A., J.D. [Fenton,F.S.R.&M.]
Knudsen, Barrett J. '71 '98 C.1288 B.S. L.623 J.D. [DeBee G.]
Kohlman, Lou Ann '60 '87 C.691 B.A. L.309 J.D. Jud. Asst., OK Ct. of Crim. Apps.
Kolar, Maria T., (AV) '69 '95 C.602 B.A. L.976 J.D. 1600 Bank of Oklahoma Plz.
Kolker, Paul M., (BV) '74 '00 C.418 B.A. L.623 J.D. [Pignato&C.]
Kolker, Raymond F. '42 '73 C.1147 B.S. L.623 J.D. Bk. of Oklahoma, N.A.
Koop, Stanley '69 '97 C&L.632 B.B.A., J.D. [Koop&M.]

Koop & Medley, (BV)
The Maney Historic District, 725 Northwest Eleventh, 73103
Telephone: 405604-5953 Fax: 405-604-9775
Email: billmedley@coxinet.net
Stanley Koop; William C. Medley, IV.
Litigation, Negligence, Products Liability.
See Professional Biographies, OKLAHOMA CITY, OKLAHOMA

Kordelski, Terry D., II '— '98 C&L.623 B.S., J.D. [Riggs,A.N.T.O.&L.]
Kornfeld, Julian P., (AV) '34 '58 C&L.846 B.B.A., LL.B. [Kornfeld F.R.&R.]

Kornfeld Franklin Renegar & Randall, A Professional Corporation, (AV)
4100 Perimeter Center Drive, Suite 150, 73112
Telephone: 405-840-2731 Fax: 405-946-0376
Email: kfrr@swbell.net
Harvey L. Harmon (1920-1990); Ben Franklin (1912-2002); Julian P. Kornfeld; Clarke L. Randall; Gregg R. Renegar; Joan A. Renegar. Of Counsel: Marcelo M. Puiggari.
General Civil Practice. Class Action Litigation, Federal and State Taxation, Oil and Gas, Corporate, Estate Planning, Banking, Employment Law, Bankruptcy, Communications, Real Estate, Pollution Litigation, Railroad and Insurance Law. Trials and Appellate Practice in all State and Federal Courts before Mediation and Arbitration Panels and Administrative Agencies.
Representative Clients: Borg Warner Financial Service; Bunte Candies, Inc.; Federal Savings & Loan Insurance Corp.; First Texas Savings & Loan; Griffin Television, Inc.; Meridian Oil Co.; Mobil Oil Corp.; Phillips Petroleum Co.; Red Eagle Resources.
Edmond, Oklahoma Office: 2964 Via Esperanza, 73013. Telephone: 405-285-8118. Facsimile: 405-285-8119. Email: grenegar@lawyer.com
See Professional Biographies, OKLAHOMA CITY, OKLAHOMA

Koss, Mark T., Law Office of, (BV) '54 '81 C.1046 B.S. L.616 J.D. P.O. Box 720804
Koss, Theodore, Jr., (BV) '56 '85 C.1046 B.A. L.616 J.D. 2525 N.W. Expressway, Ste. 201
Kouri, Harry J. (Trey), III, (AV) '65 '90 C.378 B.S.B. L.616 J.D. [Abel,M.S.M.&K.]
Krahl, Kevin E., (AV) '58 '85 C.623 B.A. L.616 J.D. [Hornbeek,K.V.&B.]
Kramer, Julie A. '67 '92 C&L.846 B.B.A., J.D. Asst. Atty. Gen.
Kramer, Karl Franklin '56 '96 C.499 B.S. L.616 J.D. OK Ins. Dept.
Krasnow, Michael E., (AV) '39 '67 C&L.623 B.B.A., LL.B. 211 N. Robinson
Kreiter, Ron L., (BV) '48 '77 C.608 B.A. L.616 J.D. Gen. Coun., State Ins. Fund
Krepps, Ethel C. '37 '79 C&L.862 B.S., J.D. State Dept. of Health
Krieger, Lane O. '78 '04 C.612 B.B.A. L.623 J.D. [Short W.M.&B.]
Krise, Stephen James '66 '99 C&L.623 B.A., J.D. Asst. Mun. Counselor
Kriz, Karin Michelle '61 '89 C.612 B.S. L.615 J.D. Off. of Atty. Gen.
Krug, Sandra Willis '— '78 C.586 B.Ed. L.615 J.D. 2525 N.W. Expressway St., Ste. 333
Krug, Susan Damron '58 '93 C.622 B.A. L.615 J.D. 4545 N. Lincoln Blvd., Ste. 260
Kubier, Julius E., Jr. '23 '48 C.755 B.A. L.494 J.D. 1612 N.W. 38th
Kulmacz, Martha Ruth '— '78 C&L.623 B.S., J.D. 1412 S. Agnew
Kumiega, Edward J., (AV) '55 '81 C.98 B.A. L.862 J.D. Asst. U.S. Atty.
Kunkle, J. Richard '35 '59 C&L.623 B.B.A., LL.B. P.O. Box 26048
Kuntz, Eugene, (AV) '13 '38 C&L.69 A.B., J.D. 2 Leadership Sq.
Kunzman, Wallace W., Jr., (AV) '49 '76 C.560 B.B.A. L.603 J.D. [Kunzman&B.]

Kunzman & Bollinger, Inc., (AV)
Suite 600 5100 North Brookline, 73112
Telephone: 405-942-3501 Fax: 405-942-3527
Email: Kunzboll@sbcglobal.net
Wallace W. Kunzman, Jr.; Gerald A. Bollinger.
Business and Corporation Law. Securities, Oil and Gas, Federal Taxation.
See Professional Biographies, OKLAHOMA CITY, OKLAHOMA

Kutak Rock LLP, (AV)
Suite 475 6305 Waterford Boulevard, 73118-1116
Telephone: 405-848-2475 FAX: 405-842-5748
URL: http://www.kutakrock.com
Partner: Mark F. Selvidge.
Civil Litigation and Bankruptcy, Public Finance, Corporate and Structured Finance, Banking and Commercial Lending, Real Estate Law, Taxation Law, Health Care and Hospital Law.
Atlanta, Georgia Office: Suite 2100, 225 Peachtree Street, NE, 30303-1731. Telephone: 404-222-4600. Facsimile: 404-222-4654.

(This Listing Continued)

Kutak Rock LLP (Continued)

Denver, Colorado Office: Suite 3100, 1801 California Street, 80202-2658. Telephone: 303-297-2400. Facsimile: 303-292-7799.
Des Moines, Iowa Office: Suite 124, Highland Building, 4201 Westown Parkway, Des Moines, 50266-6720. Telephone: 515-224-1266. Facsimile: 515-457-7669.
Kansas City, Missouri Office: Valencia Place, Suite 200, 444 West 47th Street, 64112-1914. Telephone: 816-960-0090. Telefax: 816-960-0041.
Fayetteville, Arkansas Office: The Three Sisters Building, 214 West Dickson Street, 72701-5221. Telephone: 501-973-4200. Facsimile: 501-973-0007.
Little Rock, Arkansas Office: Suite 1100, 425 West Capitol Avenue, 72201-3409. Telephone: 501-975-3000. Facsimile: 501-975-3001.
Los Angeles, California Office: Suite 3000, 555 West Fifth Street, 90013-1010. Telephone: 213-996-8478. Fascimile: 213-996-8479.
Lincoln, Nebraska Office: Suite 314, Meridian Park Office Building, 6940 O Street, 68510-2499. Telephone: 402-464-8200. Facsimile: 402-464-8204.
Omaha, Nebraska Office: The Omaha Building, 1650 Farnam Street, 68102-2186. Telephone: 402-346-6000. Facsimile: 402-346-1148.
Scottsdale, Arizona Office: Suite 300, 8601 N. Scottsdale Road, 85253-2742. Telephone: 480-429-5000. Facsimile: 480-429-5001.
Washington, D.C. Office: Suite 1000, 1101 Connecticut Avenue, NW, 20036-4374. Telephone: 202-828-2400. Facsimile: 202-828-2488.
Irvine, California Office: Suite 1100, 18201 Von Karman Avenue, 92612-1077. Telephone: 949-417-0999. Facsimile: 949-417-5394.
Pasadena, California Office: Suite 308, 201 South Lake Avenue, 91101-3004. Telephone: 626-432-1630. Facsimile: 626-432-1614.
Richmond, Virginia Office: Bank of America Center, Suite 800, 1111 East Main Street, 23219-3103. Telephone: 804-644-0313. Facsimile: 804-644-0313.
Chicago, Illinois Office: One South Wacker Drive, 60606-4614. Telephone: 312-602-4100. Facsimile: 312-602-4101.
Wichita, Kansas Office: Suite 370, 8301 East 21st Street North, 67206-2935. Telephone: 316-609-7900. Facsimile: 316-630-8021.

See Professional Biographies, OKLAHOMA CITY, OKLAHOMA

Kutmas, Chad J. .... '75 '02 C.45 B.A. L.862 J.D. [Ⓐ Doerner,S.D.&A.] ⊙
Kuykendall, Charles Fox .... '60 '96 C.1147 B.S. L.623 J.D. 4436 Nw 50th St., Ste 102
Kyte, Donald J., (AV) .... '68 '93 C&L.623 B.A., J.D. Gen. Coun., Balon Corp.
Labarthe, Patricia McCarthy, (AV) ... '58 '83 C.1147 B.S. L.623 J.D. Okla. Dept. of Secs.
Labarthe, Richard C., (AV) .... '56 '85 C.612 B.S. L.623 J.D. [Schneider&L.]
LaBrie, Michael J., (AV) .... '68 '94 C.623 B.S. L.616 J.D. [McAfee&T.] (Pat.)
Lackey, Kester D., Jr., (AV) .... '48 '75 C.623 B.B.A. L.616 J.D. 6 N.E. 63rd St., Ste. 275
LaClair, Tara A. '— '99 C.476 B.B.A. L.1117 J.D.
(adm. in CA; not adm. in OK) [Ⓐ Day,E.P.&C.]
Lacy, Paul Antonio, (AV) .... '56 '81 C&L.616 B.A., J.D. Asst. Fed. Pub. Def.
Lafferrandre, Robert S., (AV) .... '60 '86 C.882 B.A. L.623 J.D. [Pierce C.H.B.&G.]
Laird, Jeff R., Jr., (AV) .... '46 '76 C.623 B.B.A. L.616 J.D. [Foshee&Y.]
Laird, Michael S., (AV) .... '51 '79 C.309 B.A. L.623 J.D. [Crowe&D.]
Laity, Eric T. '53 '79 C&L.309 A.B., J.D.
(adm. in TX; not adm. in OK) Prof. of Law, Okla. City Univ. Sch. of Law
Lake, Heather Dawn, (BV) .... '71 '96 C.612 B.A. L.623 J.D. [Ⓐ Lawson,K.&S.]
Lambert, Donald R. .... '46 '75 C.1147 B.A. L.616 J.D. Dept. of Human Servs.
Lambert, Harry O. ...... '12 '39 C&L.623 B.A., LL.B. 14901 North Pennsylvania Avenue
Lamiell, Timothy J., (AV) .... '52 '76 C.312 B.B.A. L.862 J.D. [Ⓐ Walker,F.&F.]
Lampkin, Ben T., (AV) .... '28 '54 C.839 L.623 J.D. 3037 N.W. 63rd St.
Lamson, JoAn .... '57 '00 C.623 B.A. L.615 J.D. [Ⓐ Phillips M.M.M.&M.]

Lamun, Mock, Cunnyngham & Davis, (AV)
5900 N.W. Grand Boulevard (Grand at N. Western), 73118
Telephone: 405-840-5900 FAX: 405-842-6132
Byron Lamun (1902-1988). Members of Firm: Barry D. Mock; Maxine Brown Cunnyngham; Bret D. Davis. Associates: Charles B. Sexson; O. Saul Reid. Of Counsel: Henry F. Featherly.
General Civil and Trial Practice. Real Estate, Mortgage, Probate, Insurance, Bankruptcy, Workers Compensation and Corporate Law.

Lane, C. Wesley, II, (AV) .... '55 '81 C&L.623 B.A., J.D. Asst. Dist. Atty.
Lane, E. Marissa, (AV) .... '61 '88 C&L.623 B.S.N., J.D. 100 Park Ave., Ste. 400
Lane, James F. .... '31 '54 C.613 B.A. L.623 LL.B. Ct. App. J.
Lane, Mark M. '69 '98 C.623 B.B.A. L.615 J.D.
Asst. Gen. Coun., Okla. State Bur. of Narcotics
Langer, Steven F. .... '— '92 C&L.623 B.A., J.D. [Ⓐ Garrett] ⊙
Lankford, E. Joe, (BV) .... '47 '72 C&L.623 B.A., J.D. [E.J.Lankford]
Lankford, E. Joe, P.C., (BV) .... 115 E. California Street, Suite 350
Larason, Timothy M., (AV) .... '39 '69 C.623 B.B.A. L.616 J.D. [Andrews D.]
LaReau, J. Leslie .... '64 '94 C&L.623 B.B.A., J.D. [Ⓐ Hartzog C.C.&N.]
Larimore, James K., (AV) .... '49 '74 C&L.623 B.A., J.D. [Durbin,L.&B.]
Larimore, James W. .... '75 '01 C.623 B.B.A. L.846 J.D. [Ⓐ Crowe&D.]
Larsen, Elaine Murphree, (AV) '57 '82
C&L.623 B.A., J.D. Asst. V.P. & Sr. Coun., Amer. Fidelity Corp.
Lasher, Cheryl D., (BV) .... '44 '78 C.623 B.A. L.616 J.D. 532 Waterview Rd.
Latham, Gretchen M. .... '72 '98 C.1147 B.S. L.616 J.D. [Love,B.&N.]
Latham, Myrna Schack, (AV) .... '56 '85 C.82 B.A. L.623 J.D. [McAfee&T.]
Latimer, Henry Woodley, Sr. '55 '89
C.623 B.B.A. L.615 J.D. 2601 N.W. Expressway, Ste. 700 E.
Latrobe, Osmun R. .... '47 '75 C&L.623 B.B.A., J.D. Sr. Atty., U.S. Treas.
Latting, Trimble B. .... '15 '39 C&L.623 A.B., LL.B. 3600 Harvey Pkwy.‡
Lauderdale, Michael F., (AV) .... '65 '90 C&L.623 B.B.A., J.D. [McAfee&T.]
Lavender, Robert E. .... '26 '53 C&L.862 LL.B. Supm. Ct.Jus.
Law, Scott A., (BV) .... '63 '88 C.612 B.S. L.623 J.D. [Pierce C.H.B.&G.]
Lawler, Betty L. .... '38 '83 C&L.623 B.L.S., J.D. 12008 Camelot Ct.‡
Lawrence, Jack R., (AV) .... '35 '62 C&L.623 B.S., J.D. [Lawrence&E.] ‡
Lawrence & Eason, A Professional Association, (AV) .... 4900 Richmond Square
Laws, Marvin .... '68 '00 C.623 B.A. L.796 J.D. 1220 N Walker
Lawson, Steve L. .... '62 '87 C.623 B.S. L.616 J.D. [Lawson,K.&S.]

Lawson, King & Shelton, PLLC, (AV)
2501 North Stiles, 73105 ⊙
Telephone: 405-523-2501 Fax: 405-523-2324
Members of Firm: Steve L. Lawson; Jeffrey A. King (Resident, Tulsa Office); Tami J. Shelton;— Heather Dawn Lake; M. Christian Tolen (Resident, Tulsa Office); Richard B. Selman (Resident, Tulsa Office); Steven W. Daniels; John R. Denneny.
General Civil Practice before all State and Federal Courts, Trials, Insurance Defense, Personal Injury, Negligence, Workers' Compensation and Products Liability.
Tulsa, Oklahoma Office: 10777 S. Memorial Drive, Suite C, 74133-7351. Telephone: 918-369-9980. Fax: 918-369-9981.

See Professional Biographies, OKLAHOMA CITY, OKLAHOMA

Lay, R. Thomas, (AV) .... '48 '73 C.612 B.S. L.615 J.D. [Kerr,I.R.&A.]
Le, Vi T. .... '73 '97 C.612 B.A. L.623 J.D. Lucent Technologies
Leader, Cornelius, (AV) '45 '75 C.612 B.S. L.623 J.D.
Sr. Asst. Atty. Gen.; OK State Atty. Gen. Off.
Leaf, Kelli Jo Laker '69 '01
C.839 B.S. L.615 J.D. OK. Corp. Comm., Office of Gen. Coun.
LeBoeuf, MaryGaye, (BV) .... '58 '89 C.1147 B.A. L.616 J.D. 6704 Parkwood Lane
Ledgerwood, Shaun Dexter .... '67 '90 C.623 B.A. L.846 J.D. 5555 N. Grand Blvd.
Ledgerwood, Steven T., (AV) .... '66 '92 C&L.623 B.A., J.D. [McAfee&T.]
Lee, David W., (AV) .... '47 '73 C&L.623 B.A., J.D. [Lee&G.]
Lee, Jeffrey A. .... '57 '89 C.714 B.A. L.616 J.D. 228 Robert S. Kerr, Ste. 500
Lee, Jim W., (AV) .... '39 '68 C.69 B.B.A. L.616 J.D. [Kirschner K.L.]
Lee, Joshua A.L. .... '76 '03 C.612 B.S. L.623 J.D. [Ⓐ J.B.Albert]
Lee, Lydia Kaye Heimer .... '— '83 C.1147 B.A. L.616 J.D. 1120 N.W. 63rd St., Ste. 200
Lee, Maribob L. .... '53 '86 C&L.623 B.A., J.D. Law Clerk to U.S. Dist. J.
Lee, Mary Ellen, (BV) .... '27 '86 C.623 B.A. L.616 J.D. 3208 Elmwood Ave.
Lee, Richard J. .... '26 '50 L.623 LL.B. 3609 Nw 67‡
Lee, Richd. J. .... '26 '50 C&L.623 LL.B. 3609 N.W. 67th St.‡

Lee & Gooch, P.C., (AV)
6011 North Robinson, 73118-7425
Telephone: 405-848-1983 Fax: 405-848-4978 Toll Free: 800-717-1983
Email: leelawok@swbell.net URL: http://www.lawyers.com/leegoochpc
David W. Lee; Ambre Camille Gooch.
Trial Practice State and Federal Courts. Civil Rights, Employment Law. Discrimination. Appellate Practice and Insurance Defense.

See Professional Biographies, OKLAHOMA CITY, OKLAHOMA

Leeman, Don J. .... '28 '71 C.623 B.S. L.616 J.D. 50 Penn Pl.
Lees, C. Ray, (AV) .... '54 '79 C.622 B.A. L.623 J.D. [Commercial]
Lees, Donald H., (BV) .... '43 '68 C.934 B.A. L.623 J.D. Big D Industries, Inc.
Lefebvre, Paul E., (AV) .... '52 '95 C.623 B.A. L.616 J.D. [Williams,B.F.&B.]
Leffel, Lance E. .... '75 '02 C&L.623 B.A., J.D. [Ⓐ Fellers,S.B.B.&T.]
LeFrancois, Arthur G. '51 '78 C.72 B.A. L.145 J.D.
(adm. in PA; not adm. in OK) Prof. of Law, Okla. City Univ. Sch. of Law
Legate, Clifford W. .... '42 '68 C&L.623 B.S., J.D. 400 N.E. 16th St.‡
Lehrter, Richard John .... '56 '92 C.475 B.A. L.213 J.D. UMB Oklahoma Bk.
Leibrock, Fred A., (AV) .... '65 '90 C.840 B.A. L.615 J.D. [Phillips M.M.M.&M.]
Lemonik, Norman, (BV) .... '54 '80 C.823 B.S. L.564 J.D. [Ⓐ Hiltgen&B.]
Lentz, Harry A., Jr., (AV) .... '44 '69 C.815 B.S. L.862 J.D. [Works&L.] ⊙
Leonard, Alvin R., (AV) .... '43 '74 C.623 B.S. L.616 J.D. [Hudson,A.&L.]
Leonard, Timothy D. .... '40 '65 C&L.623 B.A., J.D. U.S. Dist. J.
Levine, James M. .... '50 '77 C.623 B.A. L.616 J.D. 105 North Hudson, Suite 202
Levine, Jodi B. .... '57 '82 C.846 B.A. L.862 J.D. Admin. Law J., Soc. Sec. Admn.
Lewallen, Joe C., Jr., (AV) .... '60 '85 C.612 B.S. L.623 J.D. [Fellers,S.B.B.&T.]
Lewis, Benj. F., (BV) .... '21 '48 C&L.623 B.A., LL.B. 2040 Liberty Twr. Bldg.‡
Lewis, David B. .... '58 '84 C.612 B.B.A. L.623 J.D. Ct. of Crim. App. J.
Lewis, Diane, (AV) .... '47 '74 C&L.623 B.A., J.D. Dep. Mun. Coun.
Lewis, Frederick D., Jr. '43 '77 C.472 B.A. L.208 J.D.
(adm. in CO; not adm. in OK) Asst. Prof. of Law, Oklahoma City Univ.
Lewis, Marvel E. .... '66 '02 C.614 B.A. L.615 J.D. [Ⓐ White&W.]
Lewis, Michael D., (AV) .... '60 '87 C.612 B.S. L.1288 J.D. [Lewis,W.P.&M.]
Lewis, Patranell Britten, (AV) .... '62 '87 C.612 B.S. L.623 J.D. [Barnes&L.]
Lewis, Robert L., (AV) .... '39 '68 C.623 B.B.A. L.616 J.D. [R.L.Lewis&Assoc.]
Lewis, Theresa B. .... '62 '97 C.612 B.S.M.E. L.802 J.D. [Ⓒ Commercial]
Lewis, William M. ("Billy") .... '76 '03 C.616 B.B.A. L.615 J.D. [Ⓐ Conner&W.]
Lewis, Robert L., & Associates, P.C., (AV) .... 3717 N.W. 63rd
Lewis, White, Porter & Merchant, Law Offices of, (AV) .... 6114 N.W. 63rd
Ley, David Cress .... '55 '82 C.612 B.S. L.615 J.D. 6305 Waterford Blvd., Ste. 450
Liddell, Janet Marie .... '59 '01 C.623 B.A. L.616 J.D. [Hayes&L.]
Liddell, Tomilou Gentry, (BV) ...... '52 '81 C.623 B.A. L.616 J.D. Jud. Asst., Ct. of App.
Liebel, William E., (AV) .... '56 '81 C.1147 B.A. L.616 J.D. [W.Liebel]
Liebel, William, (AV) .... 119 N. Robinson, Ste. 1000
Liedtke, William C., III '51 '77 C.31 B.A. L.846 J.D.
(adm. in TX; not adm. in OK) Castle Energy Corp.
Lienhard, Tammie T. .... '60 '85 C.612 B.S. L.623 J.D. Okla. Tax Comm.
Lieppman, Liessa, (AV) '47 '85
C.94 M.Ed. L.616 J.D. Asst. Gen. Coun. Okla. Tax Comm.
Ligon, Duke R. '41 '69
C.934 B.S. L.846 J.D. Sr. V.P. & Gen. Coun., Devon Energy Corp.
Lile, Stephen E., (AV) .... '47 '73 C&L.623 B.S., J.D. J., OK Ct. of Crim. App.
Lillard, Ross N., III, (AV) .... '47 '76 C.623 B.S. L.616 J.D. 210 W. Park Ave.

Lilly, John T. '60 '86 C&L.623 B.B.A., J.D.
1900 N.W. Expressway, Suite 1300, 73118
Telephone: 405-286-2110 Fax: 405-840-4701
Email: jtlilly10@aol.com
Business and Corporate Law, Oil and Gas, Venture Capital, Business Litigation, Oil and Gas Litigation, Tax Law, Real Estate Planning, Estate, Probate and Trust Litigation, Property Tax Litigation.

See Professional Biographies, OKLAHOMA CITY, OKLAHOMA

Lincecum, Gideon A. .... '72 '03 C.1237 B.G.S. L.615 J.D. [Ⓐ Holladay,C.&D.]
Lindsey, Lori D. .... '72 '97 C&L.623 B.A., J.D. 200 N. W. 4th Rm. 5011
Lindsey, Paul B. .... '31 '57 C&L.623 B.B.A., LL.B. U.S. Bkruptcy. J.
Linholm, Nick C., (BV) .... '62 '90 C.612 B.S. L.616 J.D. [Ⓐ Day,E.P.&C.]
Linkous, Byron K. .... '69 '99 C&L.623 B.A., J.D. [Ⓐ Hartzog C.C.&N.]
Linn, James P., (AV) .... '26 '50 C.839 L.846 LL.B. [J.P.Linn]
Linn, Richard R. .... '14 '38 C.616 L.623 LL.B. 14901 N. Pennsylvania Avenue‡

Linn, James P., Law Firm, P.L.L.C., (AV)
The Tower, 1601 NW Expressway Suite 1710, 73118
Telephone: 405-239-6781 Facsimile: 405-516-5525
James P. Linn; Stephen R. Johnson. Of Counsel: John D. Singleton.
Civil Trial Practice in all State and Federal Courts, White Collar Criminal Defense, Commercial and Business Litigation, Business Law, Estate Planning, Taxation, Corporate and Real Property.

See Professional Biographies, OKLAHOMA CITY, OKLAHOMA

Lisle, Donald R., (AV) .... '35 '65 C&L.616 B.B.A., J.D. [Lisle&W.]
Lisle & Woodward, (AV) .... Ste 201W, 3037 N.W. 63rd St.
Lissuzzo, Russell C., II, (AV) .... '60 '87 C.97 B.S. L.615 J.D. 6406B N. Santa Fe
Little, David W., (BV) .... '60 '91 C.623 B.B.A. L.616 J.D. [D.W.Little]
Little, James M., (AV) .... '32 '56 C&L.623 LL.B. [Little,M.&P.]
Little, John L. .... '42 '73 C.1147 B.S. L.615 J.D. State Ins. Fund
Little, Steven Louis .... '56 '87 C.1082 B.A. L.616 J.D. 2549 NW 21st Street
Little, Susan C. '59 '91 C.587 B.S.N. L.734 J.D.
(adm. in TX; not adm. in OK) 4732 N.W. 76th Street
Little, David W., P.C., Law Offices of, (BV) .... 115 E. California, Ste. 350
Little, Miner & Petersen, (AV) .... 3035 Northwest 63rd Street, Suite 200
Livingston, David Neil .... '54 '86 C.623 B.B.A. L.616 J.D. 5400 Nw Grand Blvd.
Locke, Kevin, (BV) .... '66 '91 C.934 B.A. L.623 J.D. 1132 N. Bdway.
Loeffler, Pauli D. .... '56 '82 C&L.623 B.A., J.D. Oklahoma Bankers Association
Logan, Edward Anderson .... '53 '79 C.622 B.S. L.623 J.D. 2108 Carey Pl.
Long, Gary D., (BV) .... '51 '76 C.620 B.A.Ed. L.616 J.D. 701 N.W. 63, Ste. 201
Long, Heidi J., (BV) .... '72 '97 C.622 B.A. L.623 J.D. [Holladay,C.&D.]
Longley, Michael F. '48 '74
C.623 B.A. L.616 J.D. Asst. Gen. Coun., Midland Financial Co.
Looney, Robert D., Jr., (AV) .... '46 '70 C&L.623 B.A., J.D. [Hall,E.H.G.G.&N.]
Looney, Robert Dudley, (AV) .... '19 '42 C.623 B.A. [Looney,N.&J.]

Looney, Nichols & Johnson, PLLC, (AV) BR
528 Northwest 12th, 73103
Telephone: 405-235-7641 Fax: 405-239-2050; 239-2052
Email: firm@lnjlaw.com
Ned Looney (1886-1965); Clyde J. Watts (1907-1975); Willard R. Bergstrasser (1922-1993); Henry W. Nichols (1923-2002); Robert Dudley Looney; Burton J. Johnson; Edwin F. Garrison; Tenal S. Cooley, III; Timothy L. Martin; H. Grady Parker, Jr.; Brandon S. Nichols;—Thomas Rowe Kendrick; Kenneth L. Wood; Charles F. Moser.
General Civil Practice in all State and Federal Courts, Workers Compensation. Insurance, Aircraft, Trials. Drug and Medical Device Claims, Products Liability, Environmental Law, Bad Faith Litigation, Appellate Practice.
Representative Clients: U.S. Aviation Insurance Underwriters; CNA Insurance Co.; Home Insurance Co.; The Maryland Insurance Group; Travelers Property & Casualty Co.; Jefferson Insurance Group; Michelin North America, Inc.
See Professional Biographies, OKLAHOMA CITY, OKLAHOMA

Lott, Dean .... '68 '98 C.1147 B.A. L.616 J.D. [Ⓐ Brawner]
Loudenback, Douglas, (BV) ...... '43 '68 C.612 B.A. L.623 J.D. 200 N. Harvey, Ste. 500
Loughridge, Amy L. .... '70 '98 C.802 B.A. L.862 J.D. [Ⓐ Wilson,C.&A.]

Loughrin, Brian T. '62 '98 C.475 B.A. L.213 J.D.
115 S.W. 89th Street, 73139
Telephone: 405-634-2100 Fax: 405-634-6870
Email: donatio@aol.com
Criminal Defense, Bankruptcy Chapter 7, Driving While Intoxicated, Felonies, Sexual Assault, Federal Criminal Law, Personal Bankruptcy, Criminal Law, Sex Crimes.
See Professional Biographies, OKLAHOMA CITY, OKLAHOMA

Love, Jeffrey M., (BV) .... '70 '95 C&L.623 B.A., J.D. [Ⓐ Eagleton&N.]
Love, John J., (AV) .... '50 '76 C.276 B.S.F.S. L.623 J.D. [Ⓒ R.H.,.a.C.A.L.Alexander,Jr.]
Love, Beal & Nixon, P.C., (BV) .... 6613 N. Meridian Ave.
Lovelace, J. Mark, (AV) .... '55 '82 C.228 B.A. L.623 J.D. [Phillips M.M.M.&M.]
Lovell, Warner E., Jr., (BV) .... '44 '70 C&L.623 B.A., J.D. [Ⓒ Abel,M.S.M.&K.]
Lowe, Bill G. .... '27 '50 C&L.623 LL.B. P.O. Box 57507‡
Lowe, Lyle Justin .... '73 '01 C&L.616 B.A., J.D. 2601 N.W. Expressway
Lowes, Albert C., II, (BVⓉ) '65 '94
C&L.502 B.S.B.A., J.D. 6608 N. Western Ave., Ste. 175
Loy, Katherine Taylor, (BV) .... '67 '92 C&L.623 B.B.A., J.D. [Durbin,L.&B.]
Loyd, Janice D., (AV) .... '59 '86 C&L.623 B.A., J.D. [Bellingham,C.&L.]
Lucky, Grant M., (BV) .... '71 '97 C.862 B.A. L.615 J.D. [Ⓐ Lytle S.&C.]
Lucus, Charles R. .... '50 '84 C&L.801 B.A., J.D. Asst. Atty. Gen.
Ludlam, Jeffery S. .... '73 '99 C&L.623 B.B.A., J.D. [Mulinix O.H.A.&L.]
Ludlum, Marvin Paul, II '64 '89
C&L.623 B.A., J.D. Prof., Oklahoma City Community Coll.
Luker, William H. .... '48 '76 C.934 B.A. L.45 J.D. 2500 S.W. 124th St.
Lumpkin, Gary L. .... '46 '74 C.622 B.S. L.623 J.D. Ct. App. J., OK Ct. of Crim. App.
Lurtz, Timothy E., (BV) .... '64 '91 C&L.623 B.A., J.D. [Ⓐ Collins,Z.&W.]
Luther, Gregg W., (AV) ..... '66 '92 C.616 B.S. L.615 J.D. 116 E. Sheridan Ave., Ste. 107
Luttrell, Robert T., III, (AV) .... '46 '73 C&L.623 B.A., J.D. [R.T.Luttrell,III]

Luttrell, Robert T., III P.C., (AV)
100 Park Avenue, Second Floor, 73102-8099
Telephone: 405-235-1946 Fax: 405-235-2046 URL: http://www.luttrell-lawfirm.com
Email: robert.luttrell@luttrell-law.com URL: http://www.luttrell-law.com
Robert T. Luttrell, III.
Commercial Law, Contracts, Real Estate, Consumer Finance Law, Banking Law.
See Professional Biographies, OKLAHOMA CITY, OKLAHOMA

Lutz, Charles B., Jr., (AV) .... '39 '68 C&L.623 B.A., LL.B. [Speck P.]
Lynch, Leslie L. .... '65 '93 C.613 B.B.A. L.616 J.D. Law Clerk, U.S. Dist. Ct.
Lynn, Dick .... '15 '51 L.616 J.D. Wkrs. Comp. J.
Lynn, Donald B. .... '63 '89 C&L.623 B.B.A., J.D. Jud. Asst., Supm. Ct.
Lyon, Jim A., (BV) .... '47 '82 C.921 B.S. L.616 J.D. 2200 Northwest 50th Street

Lytle Soulé & Curlee, P.C., (AV)
1200 Robinson Renaissance, 119 North Robinson, 73102
Telephone: 405-235-7471 Telecopy: 405-232-3852
Email: info@lytlesoule.com URL: http://www.lytlesoule.net
Roy Cobb Lytle (1902-1982); Edward E. Soulé (1924-1984); William D. Curlee (1929-1992); James C. Chandler; Donald K. Funnell; G. David Ross; Gordon D. Ryan; Patricia J. Hanson; David W. Kirk; B. Gore Gaines;—Jason C. Hasty; Grant M. Lucky.
General Civil Practice. Employment Law, Labor Relations, Civil Litigation, Business Organization, Taxation, Oil and Gas, Civil Rights, ERISA Litigation, Probate, Trust Law, Banking, Real Estate, Construction, Insurance Defense, Aircraft Title and Financing Law and Environmental Law.
Representative Clients: Aetna U.S. Health Care, Inc.; Aetna Life Insurance Company; AIG; Amoco Production Company; Asset Management Advisors, L.L.C.; Association of Plumbing, Heating & Cooling Contractors of Oklahoma; BP America Production Company; Bricktown Wire Company, L.L.C.; Chromalloy Division-Oklahoma; Chromalloy Gas Turbine Corp.; CMH Manufacturing, Inc.; CMH Parks, Inc.; Conoco Inc.; Continental Resources, Inc.; CUNA Mutual Insurance; Del Rancho, Inc.; Del Rancho USA, Inc.; Dewberry & Davis; Dewberry Design Group Incorporated; Dulaney Bros. Investments; Elson Oil Co.; Environmental Management, Inc.; Farmers Insurance Group of Companies; Great American Insurance Company; Hanna Oil and Gas Company; Harco National Insurance Company; Heritage Communications, Inc.; The Heritage Group; Honeywell Information Systems, Inc.; Household Finance Corp.; Ingram Industries, Inc.; Jackson National Life Insurance Company; Marathon Oil Co.; Municipal Employees Credit Union of Oklahoma City; Oklahoma City University; Oklahoma Industries Authority; Oklahoma Housing Finance Agency; Oklahoma Medical Research Foundation, Inc.; Oklahoma Municipal Assurance Group; Photographic Society of America, Inc.; Pratt Discount Foods, Inc.; Rife Oil Properties, Inc.; R.M. Barton Company; Roberts Truck Center, Inc.; Shawver & Son, Inc.; Shawver Electric, Inc.; State of Oklahoma; Stevens Trucking, Co.; St. Gregory's College; Tex-Ok Energy, L.L.C.; Union Oil Company of California; Vanderbilt Mortgage & Finance; Waste Management of Oklahoma, Inc.; Weyerhaeuser Company; Wynn Construction Company, Inc.
See Professional Biographies, OKLAHOMA CITY, OKLAHOMA

MacDougall, Vicki Lawrence '52 '77
C.623 B.A. L.616 J.D. Prof. of Law, Okla. City Univ.Sch. of Law
Mackechnie, John A., (AV) .... '50 '78 C&L.616 B.S., J.D. [Gum,P.&M.]
Macy, Robert H., (AV) .... '30 '61 C.231 B.A. L.623 J.D. Dist. Atty.
Magrini, Lorri Duncan, (BV) .... '65 '92 C.834 B.S. L.616 J.D. [Ⓐ J.S.Duncan]
Magrini, Robert L., (AV) .... '62 '87 C&L.623 B.A., J.D. [Hayes&M.]
Mahaffey, Gregory L., (AV) .... '50 '75 C.845 B.S.I.E. L.623 J.D. [Mahaffey&G.]

Mahaffey & Gore, A Professional Corporation, (AV) BR
Suite 1100 Two Leadership Square, 211 North Robinson, 73102-7107
Telephone: 405-236-0478 FAX: 405-236-1520
Email: lawfirm@mahaffeygore.com
Gregory L. Mahaffey; Richard J. Gore; Arthur W. Schmidt; Bruce R. Rooker; Lee D. Groeneveld;—Deena Tyler; Ryan W. Sears.
General Civil Trial and Appellate Practice. Oil and Gas, Real Property, Land Titles, Environmental, *Employment, Trust and Business Law.*
Reference: Bank of America, Oklahoma City.
See Professional Biographies, OKLAHOMA CITY, OKLAHOMA

Mahoney, Patricia E., (AV) .... '57 '82 C.560 B.B.A. L.623 J.D. [Speck P.]
Mahoney, Richard E. .... '54 '81 C.623 B.A. L.615 J.D. Asst. Mun. Coun.
Maillard, Kenneth G. .... '57 '85 C.623 B.A. L.329 J.D. Dir., Dept. of Sec.
Majors, Warren D., (AV) .... '52 '78 C&L.616 B.A., J.D. Asst. U.S. Atty.
Majors, Wm. M., Jr. .... '10 '34 C&L.623 B.A., J.D. Pres., Cal-Ray Petro. Corp.
Makohin, George M. ..... '51 '78 C.309 A.B. L.930 J.D. 1140 N.W. 63rd Street, Suite 402
Makohin, Lundy .... '— '91 C.409 B.S. L.615 J.D. P.O. Box 20357
Mallett, J. C. .... '21 '60 C.45 B.S.E.E. L.616 LL.B. 2821 Guilford Ln.‡
Maloan, Michael T., (BV) .... '67 '93 C.859 B.A. L.623 J.D. [Foliart,H.O.&B.]
Malone, Mark W. .... '67 '02 C.840 B.S. L.615 J.D. [Ⓐ McAfee&T.]
Manchester, Robert A., III, (AV) ... '41 '77 C.641 B.A. L.616 J.D. 1136 N. Robinson Ave.
Manchester, Robert Edward, (AV) '36 '67 C.614 B.A. L.623 J.D.
[Ⓒ Fenton,F.S.R.&M.]
Manchester, Susan, (AV) .... '50 '80 C.612 B.A. L.623 J.D. 1412 N. Dewey Ave.
Mancillas, J. Michael, (BV) .... '49 '74 C&L.623 B.B.A., J.D. [Mancillas]
Mancillas Law Office, (BV) .... 301 N.W. 63rd Street, Ste. 230
Mann, Patricia Ivester, (BV) '65 '91 C.623 B.A. L.616 J.D.
House Coun., First American Title & Trust Co.
Mann, Richard N. .... '58 '85 C.1090 B.S. L.616 J.D. Asst. Mun. Coun.
Manners, Don .... '28 '58 C.1147 B.A. L.616 LL.B. 1400 N. Shartel Ave.
Manning, Hugh A., (AV) .... '53 '81 C.225 B.A. L.616 J.D. [Manning&Assoc.]
Manning, Thomas P., (BV) '57 '95 C.1142 B.B.A. L.616 J.D.
[Ⓐ Phillips M.M.M.&M.]
Manning & Associates, (AV) .... 330 N.W. Tenth St., Ste. 101
Mansell, Steven S., (AV) .... '58 '84 C.1300 B.S. L.623 J.D. [Mansell&E.]
Mansell & Engel, P.C., (AV) .... 101 Park Ave.
Maples, L. Ray, II, (BV) '71 '00
C.1377 B.B.S. L.615 J.D. 701 N. Broadway Ave., Ste. 510
Marble, John Dexter, (AV) .... '44 '88 C.813 A.B. L.623 J.D. [Smith R.S.&E.]
March, John P. .... '40 '69 C.612 B.S. L.616 J.D. [Ⓒ Pate,K.&K.]
Marcussen, Carin L. '77 '03 C.612 B.S. L.623 J.D.
(adm. in TN; not adm. in OK) [Ⓐ Whitten,N.M.T.&R.]
Marek, Kristina S. .... '51 '83 C.679 B.A. L.615 J.D. 1924 N.W. 17th St.
Mares, Lynn Brusin, (AV) .... '45 '85 C.1143 B.S. L.623 J.D. [Abel,M.S.M.&K.]
Margo, Robert C., (AV) .... '49 '74 C.802 B.A. L.616 J.D. [Short W.M.&B.]
Markoff, Daniel Pines, (BV) '64 '92
C.846 B.A. L.615 J.D. 9211 Lake Hefner Parkway, Suite 104
Marks, Joey, (BV) .... '55 '87 C.623 B.A. L.616 J.D. 3711 N. Classen
Marks, Mary Whitten .... '53 '77 C.613 B.A. L.623 J.D. 800 N. Harvey, Rm. 310
Markum, Todd, (AV) .... '38 '65 C&L.623 B.A., J.D. Suite 205, 6801 North Broadway
Marr, James Anderson, (BV) .... '57 '82 C.802 B.B.A. L.623 J.D. 3141 N.W. 63rd
Marr, Jeff D. .... '61 '95 C.623 B.A. L.616 J.D. 210 Park Ave., Ste. 1130
Marrs, Perry T., Jr., (AV) .... '60 '86 C&L.623 B.A., J.D. [Short W.M.&B.]
Marsh, Regina M. .... '70 '04 C.616 B.S. L.623 J.D. [Ⓐ McKinney&S.]
Marshall, Ann Dudley .... '45 '74 C&L.623 B.A., J.D. Law Clk., U.S. Mag. J.
Marshall, Bert E. .... '55 '81 C&L.623 B.A., J.D. Asst. V.P., United Ins. Cos., Inc.
Marshall, Kirk A. .... '55 '01 C.1164 B.S.N. L.616 J.D. [Marshall&C.]
Marshall, Martha L., (AV) .... '57 '82 C&L.623 B.A., J.D. 701 Cedar Lake Boulevard
Marshall & Carter, P.L.L.C. .... P.O. Box 82984
Marston, Stephanie A. .... '73 '02 C.623 B.A. L.615 J.D. [Brady,S.&F.]
Martin, G. Stephen, II, (AV) .... '69 '96 C.619 B.S. L.615 J.D. [Strong,M.&Assoc.]
Martin, James Richard (Rick), Jr., (AV) '61 '86 C.82 B.S. L.623 J.D.
[Rainey,G.M.&M.]
Martin, Lindsey E. .... '15 '44 C&L.623 B.S., LL.B. 420 W. Main St.
Martin, Mack K., (AV) .... '53 '79 C.1300 B.A. L.616 J.D. [Martin]
Martin, Syble H. .... '18 '60 L.616 LL.B. P.O. Box 12627
Martin, Timothy L., (AV) .... '47 '83 C.623 B.B.A L.616 J.D. [Looney,N.&J.]

Martin Law Office, (AV) BR
Suite 360, 119 North Robinson Avenue, 73102
Telephone: 405-236-8888 Fax: 405-236-8844
Email: mack@martinlawoffice.net URL: http://www.martinlawoffice.net
Mack K. Martin; Laurel Susan Darrow.
Criminal Defense. White Collar Fraud, Homicide, Grand Jury Practice, Trial and Appellate Practice in all Courts.
See Professional Biographies, OKLAHOMA CITY, OKLAHOMA

Martin-Diehl, Lyn Kelley '61 '99
C.846 B.A. L.615 J.D. Off. of Gen. Coun., OK Tax Comm.
Mashburn, John D., (BV) .... '59 '88 C&L.623 B.Acct., J.D. [Garvin,A.C.&M.]
Mason, Richard G. .... '45 '75 C.808 B.S. L.623 J.D. Wrkrs. Comp. J.
Mason, Ron R. .... '64 '92 C.613 B.A. L.623 J.D. [Dobbs&M.]
Massad, Michael J., (AV) .... '60 '85 C&L.623 B.B.A., J.D. [Hall,E.H.G.G.&N.]
Massey, Jack T. .... '27 '57 C&L.623 B.B.A., LL.B. 5900 Mosteller Dr.‡
Masters, C. Richard .... '44 '69 C&L.623 B.B.A., J.D. 3217 N.W. 63rd St.
Masters, Kelli M. .... '73 '00 C&L.623 B.A., J.D. [Ⓐ Fellers,S.B.B.&T.]
Mastin, Tony L. .... '61 '87 C.1147 B.A. L.616 J.D. Okla. Tax Comm.
Matchette, June E. .... '64 '01 C.347 B.S. L.862 J.D. [Ⓐ Phillips M.M.M.&M.]
Mather, Stephanie J., (AV) .... '52 '81 C&L.616 B.A., J.D. [CenterForEducationLaw]
Mathews, Eugene H. .... '28 '54 C.623 L.734 J.D. Dist. J.
Mathews, Mark A., (BV) .... '60 '85 C.613 B.A. L.616 J.D. [M.A.Mathews]
Mathews, Mark A., PLLC, (BV) .... 6303 N. Portland Ave., Ste. 300
Matlock, Malinda S., (BV) .... '66 '91 C&L.623 B.B.A., J.D. [Ⓒ Pierce C.H.B.&G.]
Matlock, Ronald Lee, (AV) .... '51 '79 C.623 B.B.A. L.616 J.D. Sonic Industries
Mattax, Kevyn Gray, Law Office .... '58 '92 C.614 B.S. L.623 J.D. P.O. Box 780468
Matthews, James S., Jr. .... '52 '81 C.383 B.A. L.862 J.D. 3524 Northwest 50th Street
Matula, Brian R. .... '67 '91 C.612 B.A. L.378 J.D. [Moricoli,H.&C.]
Maule, Byrona J., (AV) .... '61 '93 C&L.502 B.S., J.D. [Ⓐ Phillips M.M.M.&M.]
Mayberry, Leisa Prather .... '55 '88 C.622 B.S. L.616 J.D. Law Clk., U.S. Bkrptcy. J.
Mayberry, Michael E. .... '54 '88 C.623 B.A. L.616 J.D. Dept. of Trans.
Maye, Kieran D., Jr., (AV) .... '58 '85 C.612 B.S. L.623 J.D. [Miller D.]
Mayfield, Kenneth G., (BV) .... '45 '70 C.620 B.S. L.623 J.D. 13304 Green Valley Dr.
Maynard, Glen C. .... '61 '87 C.612 B.S. L.623 J.D. Coun., Devon Energy Corp.
Mays, Jimanne Harris, (AV) .... '52 '78 C.69 B.A. L.623 J.D. [Speck P.]
Mazo, Bradford A. .... '49 '81 C.912 B.A. L.464 J.D. [Ⓐ Haupt B.V.]

McAfee & Taft, A Professional Corporation, (AV) BR
211 North Robinson, 73102-7103
Telephone: 405-235-9621 Facsimile: 405-235-0439
URL: http://www.mcafeetaft.com
Kenneth E. McAfee (1903-1986); Richard G. Taft (1913-1999); Joseph G. Rucks (1913-1988); Reford Bond (1930-1989); Stewart W. Mark (1915-1993); Judson S. Woodruff (1925-1997); Terry R. Barrett; T. Michael Blake; Joseph H. Bocock; Steven W. Bugg; Jennifer H. Callahan; Steven P. Cole; W. Chris Coleman; Richard D. Craig; C. Bruce Crum; Robert W. Dace; Bradley K. Donnell; Clifford Clark Dougherty, III; Gregg B. Eichner; Sam R. Fulkerson; Gary F. Fuller; Robert L. Garbrecht; Robert H. Gilliland, Jr.; Shawn E. Harrell; Philip D. Hart; John N. Hermes; Frank D. Hill; Henry D. Hoss; Laurence M. Huffman; James Dudley Hyde; Michael E. Joseph; John A. Kenney; David J. Ketelsleger; Michael J. LaBrie; Myrna Schack Latham; Michael F. Lauderdale; Steven T. Ledgerwood; Scott D. McCreary; James C. McMillin; Sally Mock; Mark Richard Mullins; Richard D. Nix; J. Michael Nordin; John A. Papahronis; Ross A. Plourde; Frank L. Polk; Louis J. Price; Tony G. Puckett; Anthony L. Rahhal; Dee A. Replogle, Jr.; Richard A. Riggs; Reid E. Robison; John E. Sargent, Jr.; John N. Schaefer; Scott W. Sewell; James W. Sharrock; Mark D. Spencer; C. David Stinson; Jeff L. Todd; Elizabeth Dalton Tyrrell; Peter T. Van Dyke; Erin M. Van Laanen; Joseph Walters; Jerry A. Warren; Drew D. Webb; James R. Webb; Steven R. Welch; Nathan L. Whatley;

(This Listing Continued)

McAfee & Taft, A Professional Corporation (Continued)

Jennifer Wheeler; Elizabeth Scott Wood; Sheryl N. Young. Associates: M. Craig Adkins; Melinda S. Blackman; Brandon L. Buchanan; Kymala B. Carrier; Stephanie P. Chapman; Todd Court; Teena P. Dunn; Mark D. Folger; Spencer W. Haines; Stephen M. Hetrick; Alan G. Holloway; Justin L. Jackson; James Bradley Klepper; Mark W. Malone; Michael D. McClintock; Charles L. McLawhorn, III; M. Brandon Meyer; Beauchamp M. Patterson; Jean L. Pinkston; Jennifer Beth Rader; Natalie K. Ramsey; David Ridgway; Patricia A. Rogers; Paul A. Ross; Richard J. Salamy; Ronald T. Shinn, Jr.; Joshua D. Smith; Spencer F. Smith; W. Blake Sonne, Jr.; Abbey B. Stallings; John D. Stiner; Cheryl Vinall; Amy D. White. Of Counsel: Jacque J. Brawner; Mark E. Burget; Gary W. Catron; Stanley L. Cunningham; C. Clark Dougherty, Jr.; Theodore M. Elam; Gregory Frogge; E. Harry Gilbert, III; William D. Hall; Neal R. Kennedy; John M. Mee; James C. Prince; William W. Rodgers; Jay Shanker (Not admitted in OK); Mary Ellen Ternes.
General Civil Practice. Administrative Law, Aircraft Financing and Leasing, Antitrust Law, Banking and Financial Institutions, Bankruptcy Law, Business Organizations and Transactions, Construction Law, Corporate and Securities Law, Creditors Rights, Employee Benefits, Energy Law, Entertainment Law, Environmental Law, Federal Aviation Administration and Aviation Title Law, Franchising, Health Care, Insurance, Intellectual Property, International Law, Labor and Employment Law, Mergers and Acquisitions, Nonprofit and Tax Exempt Organizations, Oil and Gas Coverage, Products Liability, Real Estate, Tax Law, Trust, Estate Planning and Probate, Workers' Compensation Defense. General Civil Trial Practice and Appellate Practice, including trials and proceedings in all federal and state courts, before mediation and arbitration panels and administrative agencies.
A list of representative clients will be furnished upon request.
Reviser of the Oklahoma Law Digest for this Directory.

See Professional Biographies, OKLAHOMA CITY, OKLAHOMA

Mcalester, John Mark ... '73 '98 C.1147 B.B.A. L.623 J.D. [🄰 Fenton,F.S.R.&M.]
McAlister, William C., (AV) ... '38 '69 C.623 B.S. L.616 J.D. [🄲 Abowitz,T.&D.]

McAlister, McAlister, McKinnis & Tuggle, P.C.
(See Edmond)

McAnally, Perry A. '48 '77 C&L.623 B.B.A., J.D.
V.P. & Land Atty., Wilshire Oil Co. of Texas
McAtee, Michael G., (AV) ... '60 '85 C.804 B.S. L.616 J.D. [McAtee&W.]
McAtee & Woods, P.C., (AV) ... 410 Northwest 13th Street
McBee, Jennifer Henshaw ... '76 '01 C.612 B.A. L.623 J.D. [🄰 Andrews D.]
McBride, Kenneth E., (BV) ... '48 '74 C.1147 B.A. L.616 J.D. [🄲 Phillips M.M.M.&M.]
McBride, L. David, (BV) ... '64 '96 C&L.623 B.S., J.D. [McBride&Assoc.]
McBride, Michael David ... '67 '94 C.623 B.B.A. L.615 J.D. [McBride]
McBride & Associates, P.C., (BV) ... 3035 Northwest 63rd Street

McBride Law Firm
204 North Robinson, Suite 3030, 73102
Telephone: 405-232-3906 Fax: 405-232-3641
Email: mcblaw@cox.net URL: http://www.mcbridelawyers.com
Michael David McBride.
Criminal Law, DUI, Drug Crimes, Felonies, Misdemeanors, Personal Injury, Automobile Accidents, Trucking Accidents, Wrongful Death, Family Law, Divorce, Child Custody.

See Professional Biographies, OKLAHOMA CITY, OKLAHOMA

McCaffree, Sheridan A., (BV) ... '61 '86 C.612 B.S. L.616 J.D. 517 NW 40th St.
McCaffrey, George J., (AV) ... '37 '62 C&L.623 B.B.A., J.D. [McCaffrey&Assoc.]
McCaffrey, James A., (AV) ... '39 '64 C&L.623 B.B.A., LL.B. [Phillips M.M.M.&M.]
McCaffrey & Associates, P.L.L.C., (AV) ... 6301 Waterford Boulevard, Suite 401
McCaleb, John A., (AV) ... '51 '76 C&L.623 B.A., J.D. [Fenton,F.S.R.&M.]
McCaleb, Stephen L., (BV) ... '68 '94 C&L.623 B.A., J.D. [Derryberry,Q.S.&N.]
McCampbell, Robert G., (AV) ... '57 '83 C.880 B.A. L.976 J.D. 210 W. Park, Ste. 400
McCandless, John R., (AV) ... '35 '63 C&L.623 B.A., LL.B. 2525 N.W. Expressway
McCarthy, Bill D., (AV) ... '34 '72 C.623 B.S. L.616 J.D. [🄲 Fellers,S.B.B.&T.] (Pat.)
McCarthy, Mitchell K. ... '60 '99 C.623 B.S.M.E. L.616 J.D. [🄲 Fellers,S.B.B.&T.] (Pat.)
McCarthy, Randall K. ... '65 '95 C.623 B.S.E.E. L.616 J.D. [Fellers,S.B.B.&T.] (Pat.)
McCarty, Kevin E., (AV) ... '61 '91 C.1147 B.A. L.615 J.D. [McCarty&C.]
McCarty & Custar, PLLC, (AV) ... 3108 E. Hefner Road
McCaskill, Austin, III '50 '76 C.902 B.A. L.1243 J.D.
(adm. in AR; not adm. in OK) 13500 Green Valley Dr.
McCasland Holbrook, Laura L., (AV) ... '71 '97 C.612 B.A. L.616 J.D. [Conner&W.]
McClain, Gwendolyn Kay ... '50 '86 C.623 B.A. L.616 J.D. Asst. Advocate Gen.
McClelland, Bruce, (AV) '18 '42 C.893 B.A. L.623
2050 Oklahoma Tower, 210 Park Ave.
McClintock, Matthew Thomas '72 '00 C.1147 B,A, L.623 J.D.
3717 N.W. 63rd, Ste. 100
McClintock, Michael D., (BV) ... '70 '98 C.1027 B.S. L.615 J.D. [🄰 McAfee&T.]
McCombs, Don W., Jr. ... '47 '71 C&L.623 B.A., J.D. 100 N. Bway., Ste. 2460
McCombs, Rachel K. ... '75 '01 C&L.623 B.A., J.D. [🄰 Helms&U.]
McConnell, Jeffery H. ... '60 '95 C.623 B.S. L.1187 J.D. 3441 W. Memorial Rd., Ste. 4
McConnell, Laura Haag, (AV) ... '61 '87 C.613 B.S. L.623 J.D. [Hartzog C.C.&N.]
McConnell, Steven R. ... '67 '94 C.623 B.A. L.615 J.D. [🄰 DeBee G.]
McConnell, Woodrow H. ... '16 '54 C&L.623 B.S., LL.B. 3620 N.W. 66th St.‡
McCorkell, Don, Jr. ... '47 '74 C&L.862 B.A., J.D. State Congressman
Mccormick, Joellyn Alicia W. '69 '99 C.1362 B.A. L.862 J.D.
Oklahoma Co. Dist. Atty.
McCormick, John M., (AV) ... '47 '79 C.623 B.A. L.615 J.D. Okla. City Pub. Sch.
McCormick, Joseph L., IV '59 '89 C.1147 B.A. L.623 J.D.
Atty., Oklahoma Natural Gas
McCormick, Thomas D. ... '47 '74 C.1027 B.S. L.862 J.D. 313 Hightwr. Bldg.
McCormick, Timothy E., (AV) ... '48 '77 C.494 B.A. L.862 J.D. [McCormick S.&G.] ⊙
McCormick Schoenenberger & Gish, A Professional Association, (AV)
4312 Classen Drive (⊙Tulsa)
Mccowan, Philip Edward ... '41 '90 C.623 B.B.A. L.615 J.D. P.O. Box 23254
McCown, Jay F., (BV) ... '47 '73 C.1147 B.S. L.616 J.D. [J.McCown]
McCown, Jay, (BV) ... 4117 N.W. 122nd, Ste. B
McCoy, Gloyd L., (AV) ... '56 '82 C.1147 B.A. L.623 J.D. [McCoy]
McCoy, J. Michael, (AV) ... '58 '86 C.623 B.B.A. L.616 J.D. [Anderson,M.&O.]
McCoy, J. Tully, (BV) ... '48 '73 C&L.623 B.A., J.D. Asst. Atty. Gen.
McCoy, Kenneth C., (BV) ... '48 '77 C.623 B.B.A. L.616 J.D. Amer. Bkrptcy. Atty.

McCoy Law Firm, (AV)
120 N. Robinson, Suite 1816, 73102
Telephone: 405-602-5405
Email: GloydMcCoy@coxinet.net
Gloyd L. McCoy.
Criminal Trials and Appeals, Civil Rights Litigation and Appeals, Civil Litigation and Appeals, Habeas Corpus Litigation, Stock Market Arbitration.

See Professional Biographies, OKLAHOMA CITY, OKLAHOMA

McCracken, Gregory E., (BV) ... '56 '81 C.1300 B.A. L.616 J.D. [G.McCracken&Assoc.]
McCracken, Greg, & Associates, (BV) ... 210 Park Ave.
McCreary, Scott D., (AV) ... '65 '92 C.612 B.S. L.623 J.D. [McAfee&T.]
McCullough, David, (BV) ... '53 '84 C&L.623 B.A., J.D. [🄲 Doerner,S.D.&A.] ⊙
McDaniel, Mark B., (AV) ... '63 '90 C&L.623 B.B.A., J.D. Devon Energy Corp.
McDaniel, Melvin L. ... '45 '74 C.376 B.S. L.616 J.D. 100 N. Bwy.
McDaniel, Stacy Cole, (AV) '65 '90 C.612 B.S. L.623 J.D.
Sr. V.P. & Corp. Coun., Reserve National Insurance Co.

McDevitt, Matthew J.G. ... '79 '04 C.839 B.A. L.616 J.D. [🄰 Pierce C.H.B.&G.]
McDonald, Fred J. '17 '55 C.616 L.623 LL.B.
Prof. of Law, Emeritus, Okla. City Univ. Sch. of Law
McDonald, William M. '49 '74 C&L.500 B.B.A., J.D.
(adm. in MS; not adm. in OK) Triad Energy
McDoniel, William P., (AV) ... '57 '82 C&L.623 B.B.A., J.D. [Hemry,H.&M.]
Mcdown, Becky D. '60 '89
C.623 B.S. L.615 J.D. Sr. Trial Atty. Oklahoma Dept. of Transp.
McElwee, Roma M., (AV) ... '46 '75 C.623 B.F.A. L.616 J.D. [R.McElwee]
McElwee, Roma, (AV) ... 1317 N.E. 55th St.
Mcentire, Clifford Donald ... '39 '89 L.615 J.D. 1700 Exchange Avenue.
McFall, D. Keith, (AV) ... '57 '82 C&L.623 B.B.A., J.D. [Phillips M.M.M.&M.]
McFall, Martha Louise, (BV) ... '56 '83 C&L.623 B.A., J.D. Fleming Cos. Inc.
McFarland, Mel A. '58 '88
C.69 B.S. L.616 J.D. Tinkere AFB, 7460 Arnold Street, S.E. Wing
McGinley, Brandon T. ... '73 '01 C&L.623 B.S., j.d. Atty., Devon Energy Corp.
McGivern, Gilliard & Curthoys, Professional Corporation, (AV)
701 N.W. 63rd Street, Suite 201 (⊙Tulsa)
McGrew, Michael D., (AV) ... '64 '88 C&L.623 B.S., J.D. [McGrew,B.&Assoc.]
McGrew, Buck & Associates, (AV) ... 308 NW 13th Street, Suite 200
McGuffee, Neil P., (BV) ... '54 '81 C&L.623 B.A., J.D. 209 S.W. 89th St.
McGuigan, Bruce F. ... '28 '71 C&L.616 B.S., J.D. 612 N.W. 45th‡
McGuire, Julia Lynne Race ... '64 '89 C.623 B.B.A. L.616 J.D. Co. Dist. Atty.
McGuire, Kent R., (AV) ... '63 '89 C.618 B.S. L.616 J.D. [Whitten,N.M.T.&R.]
McIlvain, Alan M., (BV) ... '47 '80 C.612 B.S. L.623 J.D. CompSource Oklahoma
McIntire, Lee S., (BV) ... '64 '89 C&L.623 B.B.A., J.D. Asst. Atty. Gen.
McIntyre, John R. '47 '73 C.645 B.S. L.846 J.D.
(adm. in PA; not adm. in OK) 3000 Lamp Post Lane‡
McIntyre, Noble K., (BV) ... '70 '95 C.613 B.B.A. L.623 J.D. [Nix&M.]
McIntyre, Thomas Francis, (AV) ... '15 '51 C.597 L.615 LL.B. 5000 N.W. 61st Pl.‡
McKay, Stan, (BV) ... '53 '78 C&L.623 B.A., J.D. Stewart Abstract and Title
McKay, Waynette Lynn ... '64 '00 C.612 B.A. L.623 J.D. [Ashbaker&M.]
McKee, John R., (BV) ... '36 '61 C&L.623 B.B.A., LL.B. [Berry&M.]
McKenzie, Clovis A., (AV) ... '21 '49 C&L.339 B.S., J.D. 3832 Spyglass Road‡
McKesson, Anthony B., (BV) ... '61 '88 C&L.623 B.A., J.D. Legal Aid of Western Okla.
McKinney, Debbie Cannon, (BV) '55 '89 C.921 B.S. L.615 J.D.
6709 N. W. Grand Blvd.
McKinney, Kenneth N., (AV) ... '36 '62 C&L.623 B.S., LL.B. [McKinney&S.]
McKinney, William R., (AV) ... '54 '80 C.612 B.S. L.616 J.D. Asst. Pub. Def.

McKinney & Stringer, A Professional Corporation, (AV)
Corporate Tower, 101 North Robinson Suite 1300, 73102-5510 ⊙
Telephone: 405-239-6444 Telecopier: 405-239-7902
URL: http://www.McKinneyStringer.com
Directors: Kenneth N. McKinney; N. Martin Stringer; George D. Davis; David A. Cheek; Ronald L. Walker; Robert D. Tomlinson; Robert L. Roark; Mary E. Nelson; David A. Walls; Philip B. Sears; Connie M. Wolfe; Richard J. Harris; Jefferson I. Rust; James L. Crumpley; Sean V. O'Connell; Toby M. McKinstry; J. Derek Hardberger. Of Counsel: J. Derrill Cody; Charles C. Green; Jay L. Jones; Philip L. (Larry) Savage; Robert C. Thompson; A. Michelle Campney; Amir M. Farzaneh. Associates: Keith D. Tracy; Cody J. McPherson; John P. Falcone; Lawrence F. Grable; Randy J. Grau; Lance E. Schneiter; Shannon L. Ferrell; Benjamin E. Russ; Regina M. Marsh; Melissa M. Chase.
Litigation; Appellate Practice; Alternate Dispute Resolution; Administrative Law; Antitrust and Trade Regulation; Aviation Law; Bankruptcy; Banks and Banking; Business Law; Civil Rights; Commercial Law; Computer and Technology Issues; Corporate Law; Mergers and Acquisitions; Energy; Oil and Gas Law; Environmental Law; Government Agency Practice; Health Care; Immigration Law; Insurance; Intellectual Property; Trademarks; Patent Litigation; Labor and Employment; Workers Compensation; Medical Malpractice; Personal Injury; Toxic Torts; Products Liability; Probate; Real Estate; Securities Law; Taxation; Trusts and Estates; Wills.
Representative Clients: Allstate Insurance Co.; AT&T/Lucent Technologies; Bank of Oklahoma, N.A.; Duke Energy Corp.; Holcim, Inc.; Kerr-McGee Corporation; State Stores, Inc.; The Charles Machine Works, Inc.; W.H. Braum, Inc.
Tulsa, Oklahoma Office: Mid Continent Tower, 401 S. Boston, Suite 600. Telephone: 918-582-3176. Fax: 918-582-1403.

See Professional Biographies, OKLAHOMA CITY, OKLAHOMA

McKinney-Foster, Rozia Marie, (AV) ... '54 '81 C.674 B.A. L.616 J.D. Asst. U.S. Atty.
McKinstry, Toby M. ... '72 '98 C.845 B.S. L.616 J.D. [McKinney&S.]
McLain, Richard S., (AV) '57 '83 C.228 A.B. L.623 J.D.
Legal Coun., Mull Corporation
McLane, Larry ... '30 '58 C&L.623 B.B.A., LL.B. 1619 Fox Hollow Ridge
McLawhorn, Charles L., III ... '76 '02 C&L.623 B.S., J.D. [🄰 McAfee&T.]
McLoughlin, C. Glenn ... '53 '78 C.623 B.A. L.846 J.D. Int. Rev. Serv.
McLoughlin, Charles M., (AV) ... '51 '78 C&L.623 B.A., J.D. Asst. Atty. Gen.
McLoughlin, Christopher G. ... '53 '77 C.623 B.A. L.846 J.D. I.R.S.
McManes, Alison Ann ... '60 '85 C.616 B.Mus. L.623 J.D. Judicial Asst., Okla. Supr. Ct.
McMillan, Harold B., Jr., (AV) ... '35 '72 C.1147 B.A. L.616 J.D. [H.B.McMillan]
McMillan, Terry R. ... '64 '90 C.612 B.S. L.616 J.D. [🄰 M.S.Homsey&Assoc.]
McMillan, H. B., (AV) ... 9636 N. May Ave., Ste. 200
McMillin, James C., (AVⓉ) ... '49 '77 C.623 B.A. L.569 J.D. [McAfee&T.]
McMillin, Michael S., (AV) ... '62 '87 C&L.623 B.B.A., J.D. [Fenton,F.S.R.&M.]

McMorrow-Love, Margaret, (AV) '51 '77 C.856 B.A. L.623 J.D.
228 Robert S. Kerr Avenue Suite 540, 73102
Telephone: 405-235-3848 Facsimile: 405-235-3863
Email: mcmorrowlove@sbcglobal.net
Civil Rights Law, Employment Law, Litigation, Municipal Law, Products Liability and General Civil Practice.

See Professional Biographies, OKLAHOMA CITY, OKLAHOMA

McMurry, John C., (AV) ... '44 '71 C.902 B.A. L.623 J.D. [J.C.McMurry]

McMurry, John C., P.C., (AV)
Suite 215, 301 North Harvey, 73102
Telephone: 405-236-0038 Fax: 405-232-5010
Email: jcmcmurry@sbcglobal.net
John C. McMurry.
Civil Trials and Appeals. Trials in all State and Federal Courts.

See Professional Biographies, OKLAHOMA CITY, OKLAHOMA

McNaughton, Michele S. ... '72 '98 C.619 B.S. L.616 J.D. [McNaughton]
McNaughton Legal Services, P.C. ... 2629 W. I-44 Service Road, Suite 214
McPhail, David K., (AV) ... '64 '89 C&L.623 B.B.A., J.D. [Foliart,H.O.&B.]
McPhail, Mark R., (BV) ... '67 '92 C&L.623 B.B.A., J.D. [Spradling,K.&M.]
McPherson, Cody J. ... '77 '04 C.623 B.A. L.615 J.D. [🄰 McKinney&S.]
McVay, Melvin R., Jr., (AV) ... '54 '82 C.502 B.S. L.862 J.D. [Phillips M.M.M.&M.]
Meacham, Scott A., (AV) ... '63 '88 C&L.623 B.B.A., J.D. 3001 Quail creek Rd.
Meade, K. T., Jr. ... '28 '65 C.276 B.S.S. L.616 J.D. Snee & Eberly Oil & Gas Producers
Medley, William C., IV, (BV) ... '70 '97 C&L.623 B.B.A., J.D. [Koop&M.]
Medlin, Virgil D. ... '43 '80 C&L.616 B.A., J.D. 2125 Turner Dr.
Mee, John M., (AV) ... '30 '54 C.668 A.B. L.623 LL.B. [🄲 McAfee&T.]
Mee, John W., III, (AV) ... '65 '90 C&L.623 B.B.A., J.D. [Mee,M.&H.]
Mee, John W., Jr., (AV) ... '39 '64 C&L.623 B.A., LL.B. [Mee,M.&H.]

Mee, Patrick H., (AV) .... '46 '71 C&L.623 B.A., J.D. [Rainey,G.M.&M.]

Mee, Mee & Hoge, (AV)
A Professional Limited Liability Partnership
50 Penn Place, Suite 1400, 1900 Northwest Expressway, 73118
Telephone: 405-848-9100 Fax: 405-848-9101
Email: E-mail@meehoge.com URL: http://www.lawyers.com/meehoge
John W. Mee, Jr.; John W. Mee, III; Arthur F. Hoge III;—Brinda K. White; Joshua Clark Greenhaw.
Civil Litigation, Creditor Collections and Bankruptcy, Financial Institution Defense, Real Estate, Contracts, Commercial Law, Business Organizations and Transactions, Estate and Charitable Planning, Tax Law, Wills, Trusts and Probate.

See Professional Biographies, OKLAHOMA CITY, OKLAHOMA

Meek, Ben F., III, (BV) .... '58 '86 C.69 B.A. L.616 J.D. [🄰 Anderson,M.&O.]
Meek, Gary .... '52 '82 C.1147 B.S. L.616 J.D. 531 Couch Dr.‡
Meier, Robert S., (BV) .... '55 '79 C.412 B.S. L.616 J.D. [Meier&Assoc.]
Meier & Associates, (BV) .... 10015 S. Pennsylvania, Ste. B
Melders, Eric .... '57 '83 C.1350 B.A. L.616 J.D. [🄰 R.G.Grove&Assoc.]
Meleen, Michael D. .... '71 '98 C.1288 B.S. L.623 J.D. [🄰 Commercial]
Melton, Timothy M., (AV) .... '57 '86 C.612 B.S. L.623 J.D. [T.M.Melton]
Melton, Timothy M., PLC, (AV) .... 116 South Walker Avenue
Mendoza, Heather Elizabeth .... '74 '99 C&L.623 B.A., J.D. Okalhoma Co. Dist. Atty.
Mendros, Jaye .... '70 '94 C&L.623 B.A., J.D. [Mendros]

Mendros Law Office, PLLC
d/b/a Mendros & Stout
The Hightower Building, 105 N. Hudson, Suite 540, 73102
Mailing Address: PO Box 1725, Oklahoma City, OK 73101-1725
Telephone: 405-605-8639; 405-408-1561 Fax: 405-605-8640 URL: http://www.jayemendros.com
Email: jayemendros@cox.net URL: http://www.mendroslawoffice.com
Jaye Mendros.
Languages: Greek and French.
Criminal Defense, DUI/DWI, Drug Crimes, Homicide, Juvenile Crimes, Appeals.

See Professional Biographies, OKLAHOMA CITY, OKLAHOMA

Meneely, Bruce K. '57 '83 C.282 B.A. L.851 J.D.
(adm. in PA; not adm. in OK) I.R.S.
Meoli, Linda M., (AV) .... '47 '84 C.4 B.B.A. L.616 J.D. [CenterForEducationLaw]
Merchant, Paul Michael, (BV) .... '50 '96 C.623 B.S. L.273 J.D. [Lewis,W.P.&M.]
Merkley, Nicholas V. .... '79 '04 C&L.623 B.B.A., J.D. [🄰 Fellers,S.B.B.&T.]
Merritt, Barbara Anne .... '52 '90 C.623 B.S. L.615 J.D. [🄰 Merritt&Assoc.]
Merritt, Carolyn L., (BV) .... '47 '89 C&L.616 B.S., J.D. Pub. Def.
Merritt, John M., (AV) .... '38 '68 C.616 L.615 LL.B. [Merritt&Assoc.] ⊙
Merritt, Kenni B., (AV) .... '50 '80 C&L.623 B.A., J.D. [🄲 Crowe&D.]

Merritt & Associates, P.C., (AV) [BR]
917 North Robinson, P.O. Box 1377, 73101 ⊙
Telephone: 405-236-2222 Nationwide Toll Free: 1-800-690-2277 Fax: 405-232-8630 URL: http://www.merrittfirm.com
Email: referralattorney@merrittfirm.com URL: http://www.lawyers.com/merritt&associatespc
John M. Merritt;—Michael M. Blue; Anthony D. Phelps; Barbara Anne Merritt; Kathleen J. Adler.
Practice Limited to Personal Injury Law, including Products Liability, Medical Malpractice, Aviation Litigation, Truck Accidents, Fires and Explosions.
Houston, Texas Office: 10101 Southwest Freeway, Suite 400. Telephone: 713-690-77074; 1-800-690-2277.

See Professional Biographies, OKLAHOMA CITY, OKLAHOMA

Merson, Harry, (AV) .... '37 '61 C&L.623 B.A., LL.B. [H.Merson]
Merson, Herman, (AV) .... '08 '30 C&L.623 LL.B. 4229 Royal Ave.‡
Merson, Harry, P.C., (AV) .... 4229 Royal Ave.
Mertens, Carl G. .... '17 '69 C.934 A.B. L.616 J.D. 1102 Hemstead Pl.‡
Mesigh, Herbert J. .... '26 '65 C.862 B.S. L.616 J.D. Mun. J.
Metheny, Steven P., (AV) .... '48 '75 C&L.616 B.S., J.D. 101 Park Ave., Ste. 200
Meyer, Henry A., III .... '48 '77 C.623 B.A. L.276 J.D. [🄰 Abowitz,T.&D.]
Meyer, M. Brandon .... '69 '01 C.612 B.B.S. L.615 J.D. [🄰 McAfee&T.]
Meyers, D. Kent, (AV) .... '38 '64 C&L.623 B.B.A., LL.B. [Crowe&D.]
Meyers, Maria Robles, (AV) .... '— '88 C.767 B.S. L.623 J.D. [M.R.Meyers&Assoc.]

Meyers, M.R., & Associates, P.C., (AV)
3421 N.W. 50th Street, 73112
Telephone: 405-843-6000 1-800-293-7472 Fax: 405-604-0329
Email: mrobles-kropp@coxinet.net
Maria Robles Meyers.
Employee Benefits, Retirement Plans, ERISA.

See Professional Biographies, OKLAHOMA CITY, OKLAHOMA

Middleton, Paul B., (AV) .... '57 '82 C.612 B.S. L.623 J.D. [Dobbs&M.]
Mikkanen, Arvo Q., (AV) .... '61 '86 C.197 B.A. L.976 J.D. Asst. U.S. Atty.
Milam, William T. "Tom", Jr. '54 '81
C.734 B.A. L.623 J.D. V.P. & Gen. Coun., The Inglesrud Corp.
Mildren, Richard A., (AV) .... '52 '77 C&L.623 B.A., J.D. [Riggs,A.N.T.O.&L.]
Miles-La Grange, Vicki .... '53 '82 C.881 B.A. L.329 J.D. U.S. Dist. J.
Miley, John Edward '59 '86
C&L.623 B.Acct., J.D. Dep. Gen. Coun., OK Employ. Sec. Comm.
Miller, Amanda F. .... '75 '01 C&L.623 B.A., J.D. [🄰 Foliart,H.O.&B.]
Miller, Andrea Digilio .... '70 '96 C.446 B.A. L.623 J.D. [A.Miller]
Miller, George, (AV) .... '12 '38 C&L.623 A.B., LL.B. [🄲 Miller D.]
Miller, Jeffrey W. .... '66 '94 C.612 B.S. L.623 J.D. [🄰 Jennings C.H.&T.]
Miller, Jennifer Lynn .... '76 '03 C.612 B.S. L.616 J.D. [🄰 Phillips M.M.M.&M.]
Miller, Kevin Louis, (CV) '60 '85
C.623 B.A. L.616 J.D. 6701 N. Broadway Extension, Suite 240
Miller, Larry Noel .... '62 '95 C.612 B.S. L.616 J.D./M.B.A. [Ircink&M.]
Miller, Laurie J. .... '65 '03 C.616 B.A. L.615 J.D. [🄰 Cathcart&D.]
Miller, R. Brad, (AV) .... '60 '85 C.618 B.A. L.623 J.D. [Durbin,L.&B.]
Miller, Richard G. .... '56 '90 C.82 B.A. L.623 J.D. Tax Policy Analyst
Miller, Robert A., (AV) .... '43 '68 C&L.623 B.B.A., J.D. [🄲 Kerr,I.R.&A.]
Miller, Thomas J. '43 '67 C&L.326 B.S., LL.B.
(adm. in TX; not adm. in OK) I.R.S.
Miller, Val R., (AV) .... '22 '49 C&L.623 LL.B. [🄲 Crowe&D.]
Miller, William B.. .... '61 '87 C.623 B.S. L.205 J.D. Coun., Kerr-McGee
Miller, Andrea, PLLC .... 228 South Robert S. Kerr

Miller Dollarhide, A Professional Corporation, (AV)
100 Park Avenue, Second Floor, 73102-8099
Telephone: 405-236-8541 Facsimile: 405-235-8130
URL: http://www.millerdollarhide.com
Elizabeth Riley Castleberry; Jack S. Dawson; Kieran D. Maye, Jr.; James A. Scimeca; James C. Shaw;—*Tsinena Bruno; Holly M. Hillerman;* Richard L. Rose. Of Counsel: Charles L. Dollarhide, II; George Miller; Robert E. Norman.
General Civil, Trial and Appellate Practice in all State and Federal Courts. Banking, Estate Planning, Negligence, Personal Injury, Probate, Real Estate, Corporation, Trusts, Business Entity, Employment Law, Insurance Defense.
Representative Clients: The Baptist Foundation of Oklahoma; Baptist General Convention of the State of Oklahoma; Deaconess Hospital.

See Professional Biographies, OKLAHOMA CITY, OKLAHOMA

Milligan, Daniel A. .... '60 '87 C&L.623 B.A., J.D. [Hampton&M.]
Milligan, Michael J. .... '55 '80 C.602 B.B.A. L.623 J.D. Milligan Enterprises
Mills, Brent L., (AV) .... '64 '89 C&L.623 B.B.A., J.D. [🄲 Phillips M.M.M.&M.]
Mills, Earl D., (AV) .... '31 '59 C.1147 B.S. L.616 J.D. [Mills]
Mills, Leah Lowder .... '65 '89 C&L.623 B.A., J.D. 14209 Rouen Ct.
Mills, Robert B., (AV) .... '57 '82 C&L.623 B.A., J.D. [Mills]
Mills, W. Wayne, (AV) .... '54 '83 C.1147 B.A. L.616 J.D. [Mills] (⊙Oklahoma City)
Mills, W. Wayne, (AV) '54 '83
C.1147 B.A. L.616 J.D. [W.W.Mills&Assoc.] (⊙Oklahoma City)

Mills Law Firm, The, P.C., (AV)
Robinson Renaissance, Suite 500, 119 North Robinson, 73102
Telephone: 405-239-2501 Fax: 405-239-2575
Email: attymail@millsfirm.com
Earl D. Mills; Robert B. Mills; W. Wayne Mills;—Margaret K. Myers; Daniel K. Jones.
General Civil Practice. Trials in all State and Federal Courts. Insurance Defense, Products Liability, Bad Faith, Civil Rights, Commercial Litigation, Uninsured Motorist Coverage, Employment Law, Professional Liability, Personal Injury, Insurance Coverage, Nursing Home Defense.

See Professional Biographies, OKLAHOMA CITY, OKLAHOMA

Mills, W. Wayne, & Associates, P.C., (AV) .... 119 North Robinson Avenue
Milsten, Robert B., (AV) .... '32 '56 C.347 B.S. L.623 LL.B. [🄲 Andrews D.]
Miner, Joseph B., (AV) .... '54 '82 C.172 B.A. L.616 J.D. [Little,M.&P.]
Minnis, Michael, (AV) .... '44 '69 C&L.623 B.A., J.D. [🄲 Doerner,S.D.&A.] ⊙
Minx-Bays, Lisa Gayle '65 '92 C.623 B.A. L.615 J.D.
Asst. Gen. Coun., C.L. Frates and Company (Legal Department)
Miskovsky, George, Jr. .... '34 '62 C.623 B.A. L.615 LL.B. 210 Park Ave., Ste. 2700
Mitchell, Alice S., (BV) .... '50 '75 C&L.16 B.S., J.D. Atty. Gen's. Off.
Mitchell, Brian, (BV) '63 '88 C.616 B.S. L.623 J.D.
V.P. & Assoc. Gen. Coun., Globe Life & Accident Ins. Co.
Mitchell, Caroline Emerson .... '58 '85 C&L.623 B.A., J.D. Jud. Asst., Crim. App. Ct.
Mitchell, Heather Johnson, (AV) .... '65 '90 C.623 B.A. L.616 J.D. [Clark&M.]
Mitchell, Mark D., (P.C.), (AV) .... '55 '80 C&L.623 B.A., J.D. [Mitchell,D.K.&P.]
Mitchell, Pamela L. .... '58 '92 C.942 B.S. L.623 J.D. Internal Coun., Okla. Blood Inst.
Mitchell, Robert H., (AV) .... '38 '65 C&L.623 B.B.A., J.D. [R.H.Mitchell&Assoc.]
Mitchell, Robert L., (BV) .... '54 '78 C&L.623 B.A., J.D. 205 N.W. 63rd St., Ste. 330
Mitchell, Suzanne .... '68 '97 C.276 B.S.F.S. L.273 J.D. Law Clerk
Mitchell, Davis, Klein & Pickens, (AV) .... 101 Park Avenue, Suite 250
Mitchell, Robert H., & Associates, P.C., (AV) .... 4101 Perimeter Center Dr., Ste. 250
Mitts, Eric, (BV) .... '58 '87 C.623 B.A. L.616 J.D. Gen. Coun., Dept. of Com.
Mixon, Susan Thomas '58 '87
C.612 B.S. L.623 J.D. Dep. Dir., State Horse Racing Comm.
Mizirl, Christina Lee .... '— '95 C.623 B.B.A. L.616 J.D. 2101 S.W. 61st St.
Moates, Bruce Arnold .... '41 '75 C.623 B.B.A. L.615 J.D. 30 SW 97th St.
Moates, Edith F. .... '45 '91 C.623 B.A. L.615 J.D. I.R.S.
Mock, Barry D., (AV) .... '35 '59 C.612 B.A. L.623 LL.B. [Lamun,M.C.&D.]
Mock, Randall D., (AV) .... '43 '68 C&L.623 B.B.A., J.D. [Mock,S.W.E.R.&B.]
Mock, Sally, (AV) .... '43 '73 C&L.623 B.S., J.D. [McAfee&T.]

Mock, Schwabe, Waldo, Elder, Reeves & Bryant, (AV) [BR]
A Professional Limited Liability Company
Fourteenth Floor, Two Leadership Square, 211 North Robinson Avenue, 73102
Telephone: 405-235-1110 Fax: 405-235-0333
URL: http://www.mswerb.com
Randall D. Mock; G. Blaine Schwabe, III; James R. Waldo; James C. Elder; John R. Reeves; Gary A. Bryant; Sarah Alexander Hall; Zachary W. Allen (Board Certified, Real Estate Law, Texas Board of Legal Specialization); J. Matthew Thompson. Associate: Whitney Alvis.
General Civil, Trial Practice and Appellate Practice in all State and Federal Courts. Business Entities, Construction Law, Commercial Law and Transactions, Bankruptcy, Debtor and Creditor, Banking, Real Property, Eminent Domain, Oil and Gas, Energy, Products Liability, Employment Law, Insurance, Estate Planning, Probate, Administrative, Federal and State Taxation Law, Telecommunications and Environmental Law.

See Professional Biographies, OKLAHOMA CITY, OKLAHOMA

Moeder, Randy E. .... '60 '87 C.375 B.S. L.861 J.D. 1318 N. Robinson
Moershel, Diane C., (AV) .... '46 '75 C.112 B.A. L.623 J.D. [D.C.Moershel]
Moershel, Diane C., P.C., (AV) .... 120 N. Robinson Avenue
Mogan, Matthew S. .... '78 '04 C&L.623 B.B.A., J.D. [🄰 Morgan&Assoc.]
Moler, Edward H., (AV) .... '23 '48 C&L.623 B.A., LL.B. 204 North Robinson
Molinsky, William J., Jr., (AV) '63 '88 C.612 B.S. L.623 J.D.
511 Couch Drive, Suite 200
Molsbee, Lisa Michele .... '74 '02 C.814 B.A. L.615 J.D. [🄰 Day,E.P.&C.]
Monarch, Kammie .... '61 '94 C.613 B.S.N. L.616 J.D. [🄲 Brady,S.&F.]
Monard, Larry R., (AV) .... '50 '75 C.622 B.A. L.616 J.D. P.O. Box 54403
Monfort, Mark E., (AV) .... '48 '73 C&L.623 B.A., J.D. [Holbrook&T.]
Monk, Patricia Rodi '46 '75 C.623 B.A. L.734 J.D.
(adm. in MO; not adm. in OK) Assoc. Dir., Okla. City Univ. Law Library
Monnet, John B. .... '56 '82 C&L.623 B.B.A., J.D. 1000 W Wilshire Boulevard

Monnet, Hayes, Bullis, Thompson & Edwards, (AV)
Suite 1719 First National Center West, 120 North Robinson, 73102
Telephone: 405-232-5481 Fax: 405-235-9159
Email: office@monnethayes.com
Members of Firm: Claude Monnet (1899-1980); Lynn J. Bullis, Jr. (1910-1984); Coleman H. Hayes (1903-1985); Russell F. Thompson (1920-1985); John T. Edwards; James M. Peters; James S. Drennan; Randall A. Breshears; Sarah H. Stuhr; Gayle Freeman Cook; Robert C. Smith, Jr.; Shannon L. Edwards;—Christopher J. Perry; Michael S. Peters; Robert A. French.
General Civil Practice in all State and Federal Courts, Appellate Practice, Insurance, Banking, Bankruptcy, Business Law, Class Action Defense, Corporation, Partnership Law, Oil and Gas, Commercial Planning, Personal Injury, Real Estate, Oil and Gas Title Examination, Real Estate Title Examination, Tax Planning and Litigation, Environmental, Estate Planning, Trusts, Wills, Probate Law, Guardianship and Family Law.
Representative Clients: Chevron USA, Inc.; Toys R Us; Firemen's Fund Insurance Co.; Globe Life & Accident Insurance Company; Apache Corporation; Chase Manhattan Bank; OXY USA, Inc.; Kerr McGee Corporation; Signature Properties International, L.P.; Crosstimbers Oil Company.

See Professional Biographies, OKLAHOMA CITY, OKLAHOMA

Monroe, Stanley D., & Associates
(See Tulsa)

Montgomery, James T. M. .... '53 '83 C.902 B.S. L.623 J.D. [Haynes&M.]
Moon, Larry Horton .... '36 '71 C.616 B.S. L.615 J.D. Asst. Gen. Coun., Tax Comm.
Moore, Bobbie A., (BV) .... '44 '70 C&L.616 B.S., J.D. Staff Lawyer, Suprm. Ct.
Moore, Gloria J., Law Office of, (BV) '52 '86
C.561 B.S. L.616 J.D. 1900 N.W. Expressway, Suite 315
Moore, James R., (AV) .... '51 '78 C&L.623 B.A., J.D. [J.R.Moore&Assoc.]
Moore, Patrick E., (BV) .... '47 '76 C&L.623 B.A., J.D. [Consumering]
Moore, R. P. (Bob), Jr., (BV) .... '42 '68 C.623 B.B.A. L.616 J.D. 311 N. Harvey Ave.
Moore, Steven E. '46 '71 C&L.623 B.B.A., J.D.
V.P., Law & Pub. Affs., Okla. Gas & Elec. Co.
Moore, James R., & Associates, P.C., (AV) .... 301 N.W. 63rd St., Ste. 550

Moorman, Jeffrey H., Law Office of, (AV) '48 '73
C.623 B.B.A. L.616 J.D. 7100 North Classen Boulevard
Mor, Ruth Lawrence, (BV) '54 '85 C.1147 B.A. L.616 J.D. [Ⓐ Haupt B.V.]
Moran, Nancy M. '49 '87 C.719 B.S. L.862 J.D. U.S. Vet. Admin.

Moran, Susan P., (AV) '53 '78 C&L.623 B.B.A., J.D.
4200 Perimeter Center Drive Suite 120, 73112
Telephone: 405-947-2024 Fax: 405-947-2252
Estate Planning, Probate, Trusts and Estates and Real Estate, Asset Protection, State and Federal Taxation, Corporate and Business Law.
See Professional Biographies, OKLAHOMA CITY, OKLAHOMA

Morgan, Arthur J. '23 '54 C.623 B.S. L.616 LL.B. 6304 N.W. 82nd St.
Morgan, Daniel J. '44 '70 C&L.972 B.A., J.D.
Prof. of Law, Oklahoma City Univ. Sch. of Law
Morgan, David D., (AV) '47 '81
C.623 B.A. L.208 J.D. Gen. Coun., Midland Financial Co.
Morgan, Douglas H. '48 '76 C.616 B.A. L.623 J.D. Asst. Dir., Minerals Mgmt. Div.
Morgan, Fred S., (AV) '54 '80 C.734 B.A. L.616 J.D. [Reynolds,R.V.&M.]
Morgan, John P., (BV) '42 '70 C.619 B.S. L.615 J.D. 10300 Greenbriar Pl.
Morgan, Judith A. '39 '82 C.746 B.A. L.1209 J.D.
Prof. of Law & Law Libr., Okla. City Univ. Sch. of Law
Morgan, Larry A., (BV) '47 '73 C&L.623 B.B.A., J.D. [Morgan&M.]
Morgan, Mack J., III, (AV) '55 '80 C.880 B.A. L.383 J.D. [Crowe&D.]
Morgan, Page P. '53 '80 C.612 B.S. L.615 J.D. Asst. Municipal Coun.
Morgan, Porter H., III, (AV) '45 '71 C&L.623 B.A., J.D. [Morgan&Assoc.]
Morgan, Russell L., (BV) '15 '39 C&L.623 A.B., J.D. [Morgan&M.]

Morgan & Associates, P.C., (AV)
The Oil Center, Suite 205E, 2601 Northwest Expressway, 73112
Telephone: 405-425-0700 Fax: 405-425-0739
Email: maa@ionet.net
Porter H. Morgan, III;—Bobby G. Irby; Matthew S. Mogan; Keith A. Daniels. Of Counsel: Sidney D. Brown.
Litigation Practice, includes Collections, Commercial and Creditor Rights Law. State and Federal Courts.
See Professional Biographies, OKLAHOMA CITY, OKLAHOMA

Morgan and Morgan, (BV) 11912 N. Pennsylvania Avenue
Moriarty, Stephen J., (AV) '57 '82 C.1505 B.A. L.862 J.D. [Ⓒ Andrews D.]
Moricoli, John C., Jr., (AV) '45 '74 C&L.623 B.S.M.E., J.D. [Moricoli,H.&C.]

Moricoli, Harris & Cottingham, A Professional Corporation, (AV) BR
Two Leadership Square, Suite 1200, 211 North Robinson, 73102-7114
Telephone: 405-235-3357 Fax: 405-232-6515
Email: mhcok@mhcok.com
John C. Moricoli, Jr.; Michael G. Harris; Dale E. Cottingham; Brian R. Matula; Philip A. Schovanec; William H. Hickman;—Lisa A. Garrett; Jeremy R. Fitzpatrick.
Mineral Law, Oil and Gas Law, Civil Litigation, Complex Litigation, Federal Civil Litigation, Regulatory Agency Practice.
See Professional Biographies, OKLAHOMA CITY, OKLAHOMA

Morozuk, John Jay '50 '76 C&L.623 B.A., J.D. 3440 Hemlock Lane
Morphis, Marilyn S. '63 '88 C.612 B.S. L.862 J.D. [Ⓐ R.H.,a.C.A.L.Alexander,Jr.]
Morris, Dwayne A. '— '84 C.604 B.A. L.597 J.D.
Asst. Gen. Coun., Kerr-McGee Corp.
Morris, Matthew O., (CV) '48 '89 C.101 B.S. L.616 J.D. 3708 S. Douglas Avenue
Morris, Richard, (BV) '38 '67 C.614 B.A. L.616 LL.B. 2208 S.W. 59th
Morris, Stephen M., (AV) '59 '84 C&L.623 B.B.A., J.D. [Dubberstein H.&M.]
Morrison, James Michael '74 '99 C&L.623 B.A., J.D. [Love,B.&N.]
Morrissette, Richard D. '56 '85 C.550 B.A. L.862 J.D. [Ⓒ Haupt B.V.]
Morrissey, Gary L., (AV) '44 '72 C.1147 B.A. L.615 J.D. [Consumering]
Morrow, Janice '— '87 C.612 B.S. L.623 J.D. [Ⓐ Riggs,A.N.T.O.&L.]
Morrow, Mark J. '43 '76 C.612 B.S. L.616 J.D.
Dep. Gen. Coun., Comrs. of the Land Off.
Morse, Judy Hamilton, (AV) '46 '79 C&L.623 B.A., J.D. [Crowe&D.]
Morton, Derrick L. '73 '99 C.845 B.B.A. L.623 J.D. [Ⓐ Whitten,N.M.T.&R.]
Moser, Charles F., (AV) '64 '90 C.263 B.B.A. L.616 J.D. [Ⓐ Looney,N.&J.]
Moslander, Carl E., (BV) '25 '51 C&L.623 LL.B. 5100 N.W. 27th St.‡
Moulton, Max, (BV) '42 '67 C&L.623 B.A., J.D. [M.Moulton]
Moulton, Max, PC, (BV) 50 Penn Pl., Ste. 520
Mounts, Walter W. '26 '56 C&L.623 B.A., LL.B. 3932 N.W. 34th‡
Muchmore, Clyde A., (AV) '42 '67 C.691 A.B. L.623 J.D. [Crowe&D.]
Muckala, Caleb J. '79 '04 C.623 B.A. L.615 J.D. [Derryberry,Q.S.&N.]
Mudd, Chris '44 '90 C.842 B.S. L.615 J.D. 2637 N.W. 65th St.
Mueggenborg, Lisa M. '69 '00 C.1147 B.B.A. L.615 J.D. [Ⓐ Kline,K.E.&B.]
Muehleisen, H. Richard '51 '75 C.612 B.S. L.616 J.D. 12809 Park Hill Rd.
Mueller, Diana G., (BV) '46 '79 C.613 B.A. L.623 J.D. 410 W. Main Street
Mueller, Karen A. Pepper, (AV) '54 '79 C.597 B.A. L.623 J.D.
[Carson,M.S.&A.&Assoc.]
Muise, Judith Ann '64 '93 C.1142 B.A. L.615 J.D.
V.P., Assoc. Gen. Coun., LSB Industries, Inc.
Mulinix, Russell L., (AV) '55 '80 C.612 B.S. L.623 J.D. [Mulinix O.H.A.&L.] ⊙

Mulinix Ogden Hall Andrews & Ludlam, A Professional Limited Liability Company, (AV)
3030 Oklahoma Tower, 210 West Park Avenue, 73102 ⊙
Telephone: 405-232-3800 Telecopier: 405-232-8999
URL: http://www.lawokc.com
Russell L. Mulinix; Richard C. Ogden; Joel C. Hall; J. Don Andrews; Jeffery S. Ludlam. Associates: James W. Shepherd; Russell A. Wantland; T. Matthew Smith. Of Counsel: John S. Gardner; Sally Ketchum Edwards; Armando J. Rosell; Travis W. Watkins; Harlan G. Hentges; Donald E. DeSpain; Joseph K. Goerke; Kyle Edward Goerke.
General Civil and Criminal Trial and Appellate Practice in State and Federal Courts. Business and Commercial Litigation, Appellate Litigation, Eminent Domain, Administrative, Banking, Bankruptcy, Business Transactions, Corporate, Trust and Estate Planning, Probate, Health Care, Insurance Defense and Regulatory, Construction Law, Environmental Law, Oil and Gas, Real Estate, Taxation, Telecommunications and Transportation, Aviation Law.
Norman, Oklahoma Office: 905 24th Avenue, NW, Suite B-1. Telephone: 405-329-0003.
See Professional Biographies, OKLAHOMA CITY, OKLAHOMA

Mullen, Tom E., (AV) '54 '79 C&L.623 B.A., J.D. [Fenton,F.S.R.&M.]
Mullendore, Patricia Ann '62 '87 C.859 B.A. L.862 J.D.
Gen. Coun., V.P., & Secy., American Mercury Insurance Company
Mullens, Charles Lee, Jr. '56 '82 C.623 B.B.A. L.862 J.D. 6201 NW 85th Street
Mullins, Glen, (AV) '48 '76 C&L.623 B.A., J.D. [Ⓐ Durbin,L.&B.]
Mullins, Mark Richard, (AV) '63 '88 C&L.623 B.A., J.D. [McAfee&T.]
Mullins, Michael L., (AV) '64 '90 C&L.623 B.B.A., J.D. [Mullins,H.&J.]
Mullins, Steven K., (AV) '52 '82 C&L.623 B.S., J.D. Asst. U.S. Atty.

Mullins, Hirsch & Jones, P.C., (AV)
100 Park Avenue Suite 400, 73102
Telephone: 405-235-2335 Fax: 405-232-7930
Email: lawyers@mhj-law.com URL: http://www.oklahomafamilylaw.com

(This Listing Continued)

Mullins, Hirsch & Jones, P.C. (Continued)
Michael L. Mullins; Karl F. Hirsch; K. Nicholle Jones;—Donald F. Heath, Jr.; Rick J. Henthorn; R. Greg Andrews; Blake C. Parrott.
Civil Litigation, Oil and Gas, Corporation Commission, Title Examinations, Employment, Banks and Banking Law, Products Liability, Family Law, Adoption, Child Custody, Child Support, Wills and Probate, Guardianships, Trusts and Estates Law.
See Professional Biographies, OKLAHOMA CITY, OKLAHOMA

Mungle, Constance Ford '47 '85 C.612 B.S. L.284 J.D. 621 N.W. 42nd Street
Murphy, Andrew P. '61 '95 C.588 B.S. L.616 J.D. [A.P.Murphy]
Murphy, Brooke Smith, (AV) '45 '75 C.623 B.A. L.966 J.D. [Crowe&D.]
Murphy, Christopher M. '74 '00 C.623 B.B.A. L.862 J.D. [Ⓐ Huckaby,F.G.&O.]
Murphy, Laura Elizabeth, (BV) '— '89 C.616 B.S. L.615 J.D. [L.B.Murphy]
Murphy, Linda Williams '53 '87 C.475 B.S. L.1187 J.D. P.O. Box 76058
Murphy, Sara G. '77 '03 C.618 B.S. L.623 J.D. [Ⓐ W.W.Mills&Assoc.]
Murphy, William S., Jr., (BV) '39 '69 C&L.615 B.S., J.D. 2728 N.W. 39th Expressway
Murphy, William W., (BV) '44 '70 C.1350 B.A. L.1009 J.D. P.O. Box 61044
Murphy, Andrew P., Attorney At Law, P.C. 3601 N. Classen Blvd.
Murphy, Laura Beth, (BV) 2345 Nw 1st Terrace
Murrah, Alfred P., Jr., (AV) '33 '61 C.976 B.A. L.623 LL.B.
[Ⓒ Phillips M.M.M.&M.]
Murray, James W., III, (BV) '56 '81 C.612 B.S. L.623 J.D.
Asst. V.P. & Assoc. Gen. Coun., LSB Indus., Inc.
Murray, Susan T. '56 '83 C&L.623 B.A., J.D. Admin. Law J.
Musser, R. Clark, (AV) '45 '70 C&L.623 B.B.A., J.D. [R.C.Musser]
Musser, Sidney A., Jr., (AV) '40 '69 C&L.623 B.A., J.D. [Abel,M.S.M.&K.]
Musser, R. Clark, P.C., (AV) 6506 N.W. Grand Boulevard
Myers, Margaret K. '66 '95 C.1147 B.A. L.617 J.D. [Ⓐ Mills]
Myers, William S., Jr. '24 '49 C.623 B.S. L.309 LL.B. District Judge‡
Myles, James L., (AV) '55 '89 C.612 B.S. L.616 J.D. [Rolston,H.E.M.&N.]
Myles, John L., (AV) '57 '89 C.612 B.S. L.623 J.D. [Rolston,H.E.M.&N.]
Naifeh, Robert N., Jr., (AV) '57 '83 C.623 B.A. L.616 J.D. [Derryberry,Q.S.&N.]
Nalagan, Ernest R., III '66 '98 C&L.623 B.A., J.D. Asst. Pub. Def.
Nance, Kenneth Robert '41 '68 C&L.616 B.A., J.D. 5224 S. Western Ave.
Nance, Odie Allen '40 '65 C&L.623 B.B.A., J.D. 6107 N.W. 48‡
Nance, Robert A., (AV) '53 '78 C.612 B.A. L.276 J.D. [Riggs,A.N.T.O.&L.]
Nantois, Robert J. '46 '75 C.623 B.A. L.616 J.D. 5504 Mackelman
Nash, Kenneth A. '30 '56 C.623 B.A. L.616 LL.B. Asst. Mun. Coun.
Nash, Rollin, Jr., (AV) '55 '80 C.612 B.S. L.623 J.D. [Nash,C.&K.]

Nash, Cohenour & Kelley, P.C., (AV) BR
4101 Perimeter Center Drive Suite 200, 73112
Telephone: 405-917-5000 Fax: 405-917-5005
Email: INFO@NASHFIRM.COM URL: http://www.NASHFIRM.COM
Members of Firm: Rollin Nash, Jr.; Cynthia Cohenour; Kevin Kelley; Dennis S. Boxeur; Gary L. Giessmann; William J. Bergner.
Commercial and Bankruptcy Law (Creditors only). Civil Litigation, Insurance Defense, Real Property, Foreclosures, Corporations, Partnerships, Fiduciary and Trust Litigation, Collections, Estate Planning and Probate, Trusts, Federal and State Taxation Law.
See Professional Biographies, OKLAHOMA CITY, OKLAHOMA

Nayfa, Paula Jean '62 '99 C.1147 B.A. L.615 J.D. 7101 Lakeway Dr.
Necco, A. David, (BV) '36 '65 C.549 B.A. L.616 J.D. 3555 NW 58th Street
Neighbors, Brent L., (AV) '68 '94 C.69 B.A. L.616 J.D. [Ⓐ Abel,M.S.M.&K.]
Neisent, Tracy Speck, (AV) '68 '93 C.612 B.S. L.623 J.D. [Ⓐ L.M.Holmes&Assoc.]
Neller, Corey A. '76 '02 C.1147 B.A. L.623 J.D. [Ryan,W.&C.]
Nelon, Robert D., (AV) '46 '71 C.597 B.A. L.623 J.D. [Hall,E.H.G.G.&N.]
Nelson, Kathy Lynne '55 '92 C.612 B.S. L.616 J.D. [Rolston,H.E.M.&N.]
Nelson, Kevin '65 '90 C.602 B.B.A. L.623 J.D. Gen. Coun., State Ins. Fund
Nelson, Lyle R., (BV) '59 '84 C.619 B.A. L.623 J.D. [Elias,B.B.&N.]
Nelson, Mary E., (BV) '60 '86 C&L.623 B.A., J.D. [McKinney&S.]
Nelson, Richard, (BV) '53 '81 C.98 B.S. L.615 J.D. [Ⓐ Dunlap,C.&R.] (See Pat. Sect.)
Nelson, Robert W., (AV) '55 '80 C.618 B.S. L.623 J.D. [Whitten,N.M.T.&R.]
Nesbit, Douglas C., (AV) '52 '79 C.976 B.S. L.623 J.D. 600 N.W.-15th St.
Nesbitt, Charles, (AV) '21 '47 C.623 B.A. L.976 J.D. 1703 N. Hudson Ave.
Nevard, Donald B., (BV) '47 '73 C.610 B.B.A. L.608 J.D. [Derryberry,Q.S.&N.]
Neville, Jack L. (Drew), Jr., (AV) '47 '72 C&L.623 B.B.A., J.D. [Hartzog C.C.&N.]
Newhouse, William G., III '53 '78 C.616 B.S.B. L.623 J.D. [W.G.Newhouse]
Newhouse, William G. 425 N. Meridian
Newsome, P. David, Jr., (AV) '47 '76 C.614 B.A. L.623 J.D. [Ⓐ Day,E.P.&C.] ⊙
Nguyen, Kim Ngan '71 '00 C.612 B.A. L.623 J.D. 228 Robert S. Kerr, Ste. 940
Nicholas, Fred, Jr. '30 '55 C.612 B.A. L.623 LL.B.
(adm. in OH; not adm. in OK) [Ⓒ R.G.Grove&Assoc.]
Nichols, Brandon S. '75 '01 C.619 B.A. L.616 J.D. [Looney,N.&J.]
Nichols, Danny B., (BV) '53 '80 C.1147 B.S. L.616 J.D. 4308 N.W. 23rd St.
Nichols, Donna A. '— '94 C&L.623 B.A., J.D. [D.Nichols]
Nichols, Heidi M. '76 '02 C.354 B.A. L.734 J.D. [Ⓐ Pierce C.H.B.&G.]
Nichols, John M., (AV) '46 '72 C.612 B.S.M.E. L.1035 J.D. P.O. Box 1096
Nichols, Donna 4901 Richmond Sq., Ste. 104

Nichols, Wolfe, Stamper, Nally, Fallis & Robertson, Inc.
(See Tulsa)

Nicholson, Don R., II, (AV) '35 '65 C&L.623 B.B.A., J.D. [Eagleton&N.]
Nickel, Daniel A. '79 '04 C.942 B.B.A. L.623 J.D. [Ⓐ Gable&G.]
Nicklas, Cara Sue '65 '90
C.623 B.A. L.615 J.D. Asst. Gen. Coun., State Employ. Sec. Comm.
Niece, Stanley '40 '66 C.612 B.S. L.623 J.D. 1330 N. Classon, Ste. 110
Niemeyer, John C., (AV) '35 '62 C.839 B.B.A. L.802 J.D. [Niemeyer,A.A.&P.]

Niemeyer, Alexander, Austin & Phillips, A Professional Corporation, (AV)
Three Hundred North Walker, 73102
Telephone: 405-232-2725 Fax: 405-239-7185
Email: staff@niemeyerfirm.com URL: http://www.niemeyerfirm.com
John C. Niemeyer; Linda G. Alexander; Norman F. Austin; Harris A. Phillips, III; Stephen A. Dotter; Charles A. Dickson, III. Of Counsel: Randal D. Homburg.
General Civil Practice. Products Liability Law, Environmental, Insurance, Casualty and Surety Law. Trials in all State and Federal Courts.
See Professional Biographies, OKLAHOMA CITY, OKLAHOMA

Nix, Glendell D., (BV) '64 '89 C.1147 B.B.A. L.862 J.D. [Nix&M.]
Nix, Richard D., (AV) '60 '85 C&L.623 B.B.A., J.D. [McAfee&T.]

Nix & McIntyre LLP, (BV)
1300 South Meridian, Suite 501, 73108-1700
Telephone: Toll Free: 866-917-5200 800-4-Injury (Oklahoma) 866-917-5200 (Nationwide) Fax: 405-917-5405 URL: http://www.oklahomainjurylaw.com
Email: counsel@oklahoma-law.com URL: http://www.oklahoma-law.com
Members of Firm: Glendell D. Nix; Noble K. McIntyre. Associates: Jacob D. Diesselhorst; Jeremy A. Thurman.
Litigation practice including Personal Injury, Automobile Accidents and Injuries, Product Liability, Medical Malpractice, Nursing Home Negligence, Mass Torts.
See Professional Biographies, OKLAHOMA CITY, OKLAHOMA

Nixon, William L., Jr., (BV) ....'60 '88 C&L.623 B.B.A., J.D. [Love,B.&N.]
Noble, Carolyn A. ....'48 '89 C.280 B.A. L.616 J.D. 12706 N. Macarthur Blvd.‡
Noble, Jeffrey B., (AV) '53 '79
C&L.623 B.B.A., J.D. Sr. V.P. & Gen. Coun., Amer. Guaranty Title
Nolan, Hilary M. ....'70 '02 C.1574 M.B.A. L.615 J.D. [Ⓐ Anderson,M.&O.]
Noland, Michael L., (AV) ....'50 '78 C.999 B.S. L.616 J.D. [Noland,U.&W.]
Noland, Upton & Wenzel, P.C., (AV) .... 119 N. Robinson Avenue, Suite 550
Nordin, J. Michael, (AV) ....'57 '82 C&L.623 B.A., J.D. [McAfee&T.]
Norman, Bradley E. ....'71 '00 C.999 B.A. L.616 J.D. [Norman&E.]
Norman, John B., (AV) ....'64 '88 C.69 B.A. L.623 J.D. [Norman&E.]
Norman, John W., (AV) ....'44 '68 C&L.623 B.A., LL.B. [Norman&E.]
Norman, Robert E., (BV) ....'65 '91 C&L.623 B.A., J.D. [Ⓒ Miller D.]
Norman, William R., Jr. ....'66 '93 C.999 B.B.A. L.623 J.D. [Hobbs,S.D.&W.]

Norman & Edem, P.L.L.C., (AV)
127 Northwest 10th Street, 73103-4927
Telephone: 405-272-0200 Fax: 405-235-2949 Toll Free: 866-272-0201
URL: http://www.nemw.com
John W. Norman; Emmanuel E. Edem; Thomas A. Wallace; John B. Norman; Mark A. Cox; Bradley E. Norman; Jerri K. Bird; Mark Bonner.
Civil Trial and Appellate Practice, Personal Injury, Negligence, Aviation, Products Liability and Professional Negligence.
References: IBC Bank; Bank of Oklahoma.
See Professional Biographies, OKLAHOMA CITY, OKLAHOMA

Novotny, Michael J., (BV) ....'59 '92 C.174 B.S. L.623 J.D. [Ⓐ Hartzog C.C.&N.]
Nowakowski, John R., (AV) ....'60 '87 [Dobbs&M.]

Nunn, David L., P.C.
(See Edmond)

Oates, Jeanette A. ....'67 '02 C.1147 B.A. L.623 J.D. [Ⓐ Anderson,M.&O.]
O'Bannon, Robert O., (AV) ....'54 '79 C.623 B.A. L.616 J.D. [Phillips M.M.M.&M.]
Obee, Mary Jo ....'56 '91 C.37 B.S. L.615 J.D. Chf. Dep. Clk., U.S. Bkrptcy. Ct.
Oberndorfer, Sarah K. ....'78 '02 C.82 B.S. L.623 J.D. [Ⓐ Hall,E.H.G.G.&N.]
O'Brien, Michael J. '46 '71 C.1268 B.A. L.846 J.D.
(adm. in TX; not adm. in OK) I.R.S.
O'Brien, William F. ....'53 '83 C.425 B.A. L.615 J.D. Atty. Gen. Off.
O'Bryan, W. Howard, Jr. '25 '53 C&L.616 B.S., J.D.
Admin. Law J., U.S. Dept. of Health & Human Servs.
O'Connell, Sean V., (BV) ....'66 '97 C.602 B.S.E.E. L.190 J.D. [McKinney&S.]
O'Connor, Richard B., Law Office of '29 '83 C.502 B.A. L.616 J.D.
2501 Somerset Place‡
Offutt, Robt. B. ....'14 '37 C&L.623 B.A., LL.B. 3336 N.W. 25‡
Ogden, Richard C., (AV) ....'63 '89 C.612 B.S. L.623 J. D. [Mulinix O.H.A.&L.]
Ogle, David, (BV) ....'68 '97 C.612 B.A. L.616 J.D. [Ogle&W.]

Ogle & Welch, P.C., (BV)
117 Park Avenue, Third Floor, 73102
Telephone: 405-232-9800 Facsimile: 405-232-1608
Email: josh@joshwelchlaw.com URL: http://www.joshwelchlaw.com
David Ogle; Josh T. Welch;—Ann K. Hadrava. Of Counsel: Hack Welch.
Criminal Trial and Appellate Practice in all State and Federal courts. Grand Jury Investigations, White Collar and Complex Crimes, Drugs, Driving Under the Influence, Murder, Sex Crimes, Obscenities, Security Fraud, Personal Injury, Auto Accidents, Trucking Accidents, Driving While Intoxicated, Criminal Record Expungements, Civil Rights.
See Professional Biographies, OKLAHOMA CITY, OKLAHOMA

Ogletree, L. Earl, (BV) ....'71 '99 C.1377 B.S. L.616 J.D. [Ⓐ Short W.M.&B.]
O'Hara, G. Patrick "Pat", (AV) ....'50 '92 C.622 B.S. L.623 J.D. [Whitten,N.M.T.&R.]
O'Hara, Patrick, Jr., (BV) ....'69 '95 C.612 B.S. L.623 J.D. [Whitten,N.M.T.&R.]
O'Laughlin, Frederick J. ....'54 '82 C&L.45 B.A., J.D. [O'Laughlin,F.J.] ⊙
O'Laughlin, Frederick J. ....5900 Mosteller Dr., Ste. 1510 (⊙Dallas, TX)
Oldfather, Chad M. ....'68 '94 C.309 A.B. L.893 J.D. Asst. Prof.
Oldfield, John S., Jr., (AV) ....'45 '73 C.1115 B.A. L.623 J.D. [Oldfield,C.&G.]

Oldfield, Coker & Graves, (AV)
4808 North Classen Boulevard, 73118
Telephone: 405-840-0555 Fax: 405-840-4808
Members of Firm: John S. Oldfield, Jr.; Michael G. Coker; Matthew J. Graves. Associate: Cynthia Wood Welch.
General Civil Practice. Trials in all State and Federal Courts. Corporation, Insurance, Workers Compensation, Personal Injury and Oil and Gas Law.
See Professional Biographies, OKLAHOMA CITY, OKLAHOMA

Oliver, Edward, (CV) '39 '67 C.612 B.A. L.616 J.D.
217 North Harvey Avenue, Suite 107
Olsen, B. Joan ....'34 '92 C.990 B.S. L.623 J.D. Staff Atty., State Ins. Fund
Olson, Kirk Alan, (AV) ...'66 '92 C.612 B.S. L.623 J.D. 701 N. Broadway Ave., Ste. 400
Olson, Stephen L., (AV) ....'51 '77 C&L.623 B.A., J.D. [Pierce C.H.B.&G.]
Olsson, Brently C., (BV) ....'63 '88 C.1288 B.A. L.862 J.D. [Huckaby,F.G.&O.]
O'Neal, Michael D. ....'77 '04 C.1315 B.S. L.1117 J.D. [Williams,B.F.&B.]
O'Neil, D. Michael, Jr., (BV) ....'47 '72 C.770 B.A. L.623 J.D. [Ⓐ Day,E.P.&C.]
Onken, Judith Slayman, (AV) ....'51 '79 C.859 B.A. L.616 J.D. 408 N.W. 42nd St.
Opala, Marian P. ....'21 '53 C&L.616 B.S.B., J.D. OK Supm. Ct. Jus.,
Orndorff, Terry O. ....'50 '75 C&L.623 B.B.A., J.D. Okla. Ins. Comm.
O'Roke, Sharon, (AV) '57 '84 C.1147 B.A. L.616 J.D.
Law Clerk, Hon. Doyle W. Argo
Orta, Vanessa A., (BV) ....'63 '89 C.840 B.A. L.623 J.D. [Anderson,M.&O.]
Osenbaugh, Marissa T. ....'78 '03 C.268 B.S. L.623 J.D. [Ⓐ Holloway,D.&B.]
Oshel, David B. '53 '78 C.623 B.B.A. L.615 J.D.
Gen. Coun., Louis Dreyfus Natural Gas Corp.
Oswalt, Robert D. '11 '37 C.845 L.192 LL.B.
(adm. in TX; not adm. in OK) 6201 N. Ann Arbor Ave.‡
Ottaway, Cynda C., (AV) ....'53 '78 C&L.623 B.A., J.D. [Crowe&D.]
Ottaway, Larry D., (AV) ....'48 '74 C&L.623 B.A., J.D. [Foliart,H.O.&B.]
Owen, Robert I., (BV) ....'47 '77 C&L.623 B.B.A., J.D. 818 N.W. 31st St.
Owens, Charles L. ....'30 '60 C.410 B.S. L.862 J.D. 5208 N. Stonewall Dr.
Owens, Daniel L. ....'43 '81 C.1147 Bus. L.616 J.D. Co. J.
Owens, Margaret W., (BV) ....'51 '85 C.623 B.S.N. L.616 J.D. 817 N.W. 41st St.
Oyler, Mac, (AV) ....'37 '64 C.612 B.S. L.616 J.D. 1 North Hudson Avenue
Ozinga, Martin G., (BV) '64 '90 C.802 B.S. L.616 J.D.
[Ⓒ Phillips M.M.M.&M.] (Pat.)
Pack, Lelin E. ....'21 '52 L.862 LL.B. 1717 N.W. 41st St.
Paddleford, James H. ....'38 '68 C.614 B.A. L.615 J.D. Dist. Ct. J.
Paden, Larry J. ....'57 '95 C&L.616 Ph.D., J.D. 1501 Oakhill Lane
Padley, Pamela K. ....'45 '79 C&L.616 B.A., J.D. Dept. of Human Services
Page, John V., (BV) ....'34 '68 C&L.623 B.B.A., J.D. 4101 Perimeter Ctr. Dr.
Pain, Betsy M. ....'50 '77 C&L.623 B.A., J.D. Chf. Legal Ofr., Atkins Benham Inc.
Paliotta, Armand, (AV) ....'67 '92 C&L.623 J.D. [Hartzog C.C.&N.]
Pallotta, Howard J., (AV) '58 '85
C.506 B.S. L.616 J.D. Gen. Coun., Okla. Health Care Auth.
Palmatary, Ronald C. .....'58 '86 C&L.623 B.A., J.D. V.P., Amer. Institute of Discussion
Palmer, Beverly A., (BV) ....'61 '92 C.845 B.S. L.615 J.D. Asst. Dist. Atty.
Palmer, Harry R., Jr., (AV) ....'27 '52 C&L.615 LL.B. 2728 N.W. 39th Expwy.
Palmer, Stephen R. ....'71 '96 C.613 B.A. L.616 J.D. [Ⓐ Collins,Z.&W.]
Palomo, Carmen M. ....'69 '97 C.1073 B.S. L.1067 J.D. [Ⓐ R.H.,a.C.A.L.Alexander,Jr.]
Pankey, Charles H., (BV) ....'46 '74 C.1147 B.A. L.623 J.D. 903 N.W. 13th St.
Panter, C. K. ....'— '93 C.612 B.S. L.862 J.D. First American Title & Trust Co.
Papahronis, John A., (AV) ....'58 '83 C.623 B.A. L.597 J.D. [McAfee&T.]
Pape, Donald A., (AV) '45 '74 C&L.623 B.A., J.D.
[Ⓒ Phillips M.M.M.&M.] (⊙Norman)
Pappas, Jon N. ....'58 '94 C.613 B.A. L.862 J.D. [Pappas,B.&Assoc.]
Pappas, Brown & Associates, (BV) ....5500 North Western, Suite 150
Pardue, W. Davidson, (AV) ....'47 '72 C&L.623 B.S., J.D. [Eagleton&N.]
Parker, H. Grady, Jr., (BV) ....'61 '91 C.623 B.B.A. L.616 J.D. [Looney,N.&J.]
Parker, Stephen S., (AV) ....'60 '87 C&L.623 B.S., J.D. 416 S.W. 79th St., Ste. A100
Parker, William P. ....'45 '72 C.612 B.A. L.623 J.D. [W.P.Parker]
Parker, William P., P.C. ....2212 N.W. 50th St.
Parkinson, Joshua L. ....'77 '04 C.619 B.S. L.623 J.D. [Ⓐ White&W.]
Parman, Larry V. ....'47 '74 C.502 B.S. L.986 J.D. [Parman&Assoc.]
Parman & Associates ....3545 N.W. 58th St., Ste. 400 (⊙Kansas City, MO)

Parr, Douglas L. '51 '79 C.612 B.S. L.623 J.D.
228 Robert S. Kerr, Suite 550, 73102
Telephone: 405-528-1018 Fax: 405-528-1035
Email: douglas.parr@parrlawoffice.com URL: http://www.parrlawoffice.com
Criminal Law, Criminal Defense, Post-Conviction Remedies, Police Misconduct, Civil Rights, Drug Trafficking, Assault and Battery, Sexual Assault, Homicide, Felonies, Misdemeanors, White Collar Crime, Forensic, DNA, Theft, Driving While Intoxicated.
See Professional Biographies, OKLAHOMA CITY, OKLAHOMA

Parr, Jack R. ....'26 '50 C&L.623 B.A., LL.B. Ret. Dist. J.‡
Parr, Patrick S. ....'70 '00 C.621 B.A. L.862 J.D. [Ⓐ Pierce C.H.B.&G.]
Parrish, Ashley Anne D. ....'52 '78 C.788 B.A. L.616 J.D. 1707 Drakestone
Parrish, Gary L., (BV) ....'58 '83 C.619 B.A. L.623 J.D. 115 S.W. 89th St.
Parrish, Kendall W., (BV) .....'61 '92 C.616 B.S.B. L.862 J.D. 6011 N. Robinson Avenue
Parrish, Kim D., (AV) ....'53 '80 C.612 B.S. L.616 J.D. J., Soc. Sec. Admn.
Parrish, Murry J., (BV) ....'69 '95 C.612 B.A. L.623 J.D. [Parrish]
Parrish, Patricia G., (AV) ....'56 '82 C.612 B.A. L.623 J.D. 100 Park Ave.
Parrish, Richard E. ....'55 '80 C.612 B.S. L.623 J.D. Staff Atty, Okla. State Sen.
Parrish, Sarah Lee, (AV) ....'62 '86 C&L.623 B.A., J.D. OK Supm. Ct.

Parrish Law Firm, The, A Professional Corporation, (BV)
One North Hudson, Suite 700, 73102
Telephone: 405-232-1985; Toll Free: 800-270-1980 Facsimile: 405-232-4679
Email: mparrish@parrishlaw.org
Member of Firm: Murry J. Parrish.
Personal Injury, Slip and Fall, Automobile Accidents, Trucking Accidents, Wrongful Death, Workers Compensation, Nursing Home Abuse.
See Professional Biographies, OKLAHOMA CITY, OKLAHOMA

Parrott, Blake C. ....'73 '00 C&L.623 B.B.A., J.D. [Ⓐ Mullins,H.&J.]
Parrott, Nancy S. ....'44 '84 C.623 B.A. L.616 J.D. Okla. Supm. Ct. Marshal
Parsons, Kendra D. ....'78 '03 C.1147 B.A. L.623 J.D. [Ⓐ Commercial]

Parsons & Associates Law Firm, A Corporation
(See Norman)

Paruolo, Thomas A. ....'74 '99 C.69 B.A. L.823 J.D. [Ⓐ Whitten,N.M.T.&R.]
Passmore, Joe Richard, II ....'59 '00 C&L.623 B.A., J.D. 317 N.W. 12th St.
Pate, Collier H., (AV) ....'39 '69 C.840 B.S. L.616 J.D. [Pate,K.&K.]
Pate, Kandi K. Jepsen, (AV) '51 '84
C.1300 B.S. L.616 J.D. 1900 N.W. Expressway St., Ste. 1300
Pate, Marc Steven ....'54 '84 C.1147 B.S. L.615 J.D. Asst. OK Atty. Gen.

Pate, Kempf & Knarr, A Professional Corporation, (AV)
Two Leadership Square, 211 North Robinson, Suite 418, P.O. Box 1907, 73102
Telephone: 405-235-4211 Fax: 405-232-3930
Email: sknarr@pkklawyers.com
Collier H. Pate; John Frederick Kempf, Jr.; Stuart Alan Knarr; Ken D. Kerr, Jr. Of Counsel: John P. March.
Civil Practice which includes: Trial and Appellate Practice in State and Federal Courts. Insurance Defense, Banking Law, Telecommunication Law, Real Estate, Federal and State Taxation, Bankruptcy and Creditor's Rights, Probate, Oil and Gas.
See Professional Biographies, OKLAHOMA CITY, OKLAHOMA

Patridge, James C. '50 '81 C.45 B.S.B.A. L.616 J.D.
V.P., Admin., Okla. Energies Corp.
Patterson, Beauchamp M. ....'— '01 C.560 B.A. L.615 J.D. [Ⓐ McAfee&T.]
Patterson, J. Phillip, (BV) ....'45 '74 L.616 J.D. 6403 N.W. Grand Blvd.
Patterson, James W., (BV) ....'49 '77 C.1147 B.A. L.616 J.D. Clk. Supm. Ct.
Patterson, John E., Jr., (BV) ....'31 '60 C&L.623 B.B.A., LL.B. [J.E.Patterson,Jr.]
Patterson, John E., Jr., P.C., (BV) ....5555 North Grand Boulevard, Suite 210
Patton, Babette, (AV) ....'57 '84 C.198 B.A. L.623 J.D. [Breathwit&P.]
Patton, Frances E., (AV) ....'59 '84 C&L.623 B.A., J.D. [Pierce C.H.B.&G.]
Patton, Nan J. ....'46 '71 C.612 B.A. L.623 J.D. Assoc. Dist. J. OK Co. Juv. Center
Pauchnik, Elizabeth A. ....'59 '93 C.1147 B.S. L.616 J.D. Integris Health
Paul, William G., (AV) ....'30 '56 C&L.623 B.A., J.D. [Crowe&D.]
Paull, Debra Woods, (AV) ....'53 '78 C.613 B.A. L.623 J.D. Asst. U.S. Atty.
Paulson, Suzanne Denise Shiff ....'74 '01 C.1147 B.S. L.615 J.D. Mun. Coun.'s Off.
Payne, Elizabeth Mee ....'62 '87 C&L.623 B.A., J.D. The Okla. Publishing Co.
Payne, Gary E., (AV) ....'44 '69 C.612 B.S. L.623 J.D. [G.E.Payne]
Payne, Gary E., Inc., (AV) ....11212 N. May, Ste. 206
Peabody, George E. ....'22 '54 C&L.900 B.B.A., J.D. 2929 Huntleigh Dr.
Peabody, James A., (AV) ....'29 '53 C&L.623 A.B., LL.B. [Ⓒ Crowe&D.] ‡
Peace, Jerry A. ....'62 '90 C.613 B.B.A. L.616 J.D. Clinton Gas Transmission
Peacher, Kenneth L., II, (BV) '50 '76 C.623 B.A. L.616 J.D.
4808 N. Classen Boulevard
Pearce, Patrick R., Jr. ....'75 '00 C.45 B.A. L.862 J.D. [Ryan,W.&C.]
Pearson, Beverly S., (AV) ....'50 '83 C.618 B.A. L.1049 J.D. [Fenton,F.S.R.&M.]

Pearson, Jim, (AV) '46 '73 C.612 B.A. L.623 J.D. ⒷⒷ
Penn Park, Suite 304, 5001 North Pennsylvania, 73112
Telephone: 405-858-8500 Fax: 405-858-8585
Email: jpearsonpc@aol.com URL: http://www.lawyers.com/jimpearson
Divorce and Family Law, including Child Law, Child Custody and Child Support.
See Professional Biographies, OKLAHOMA CITY, OKLAHOMA

Peck, James C., (AV) ....'47 '74 C.623 B.A. L.616 J.D. 101 Park Ave., Ste. 250
Peck, Scott W., (BV) ....'60 '85 C.612 B.S. L.623 J.D. [Peck,E.&W.]
Peck, Erdoes & Wenzel, P.A., (BV) ....21 E. Main St., Ste. 101
Pederson, Devan A., (BV) ....'69 '96 C.612 B.A. L.623 J.D. [Elliott&P.]
Peek, Thomas L. ....'51 '89 C.612 B.S. L.616 J.D. 4320 McAuley Blvd.‡
Pence, Katherine H. ....'— '98 C&L.623 B.A., J.D. [Ⓐ Kirk&C.]

Pennell, Nancy H., (BV) .....'57 '86 C.612 B.S. L.623 J.D. Acct. Mgr., First Maintenance
Peoples, A. V., III, (BV) ....'45 '75 C&L.616 B.A., J.D. [🄰 Phillips M.M.M.&M.]
Pepper, David E., (AV) ....'50 '75 C.623 B.B.A. L.616 J.D. [Hartzog C.C.&N.]
Percival, Cindy J. ....'52 '88 C&L.623 B.S., J.D. Staff Atty., Supm. Ct.
Percival, John F., (AV) ......'47 '75 C.1077 B.A. L.623 J.D. 210 Park Avenue, Suite 3030
Peregrin, Mark J., (AV) ....'61 '87 C.761 B.S. L.623 J.D. [🄰 Anderson,M.&O.]
Peregrin, Robert M., (AV) ....'57 '82 C.1147 B.A. L.623 J.D. [Daugherty,F.P.&H.]
Perri, Michael R., (AV) ....'61 '86 C.602 B.B.A. L.623 J.D. [Phillips M.M.M.&M.]
Perry, Christopher J. ....'66 '91 C&L.623 B.B.A., J.D. [🄰 Monnet,H.B.T.&E.]
Perry, Douglas L., Attorney at Law, (AV) '54 '79
C.623 B.S. L.616 J.D. 4508 Blackberry Run
Perry, Giovanni Isabel '67 '92
C&L.623 B.B.A., J.D. Legal Aid of Western Oklahoma, Inc.
Perry, Justin Wade ....'72 '99 C.234 B.A. L.616 J.D. [J.Perry]
Perry, Justin ....114 E. Sheridan, Ste. 102
Perryman, Gisele ....'— '99 C&L.623 B.A., J.D. [🄰 Riggs,A.N.T.O.&L.]
Persons, Louis Delaney, II ....'42 '79 C.612 B.A. L.623 J.D. 200 NE. 21st St.
Peters, Dan M., (AV) ....'57 '82 C.612 B.S. L.623 J.D. [🄲 Fuller,T.P.&S.]
Peters, James M., (AV) ....'39 '65 C.612 B.A. L.623 J.D. [Monnet,H.B.T.&E.]
Peters, Michael A. ....'66 '92 C&L.623 B.A., J.D. [Ryan,W.&C.]
Peters, Michael S., (BV) ....'66 '92 C.934 B.A. L.616 J.D. [🄰 Monnet,H.B.T.&E.]
Petersen, Christopher J. ....'65 '91 C&L.623 B.A., B.A. [Little,M.&P.]
Peterson, Blaine M. ....'71 '99 C&L.623 B.B.A., J.D. [🄰 DeBee G.]
Peterson, Brenda K., (AV) ....'57 '83 C.612 B.S. L.616 J.D. [Fenton,F.S.R.&M.]
Peterson, Brian L., (AV) ....'60 '85 C.976 B.A. L.69 J.D. [B.L.Peterson]
Peterson, Deborah A. ......'55 '81 C.375 B.S. L.900 J.D. 1012 NW Grand Blvd., Suite A
Peterson, Gary, (AV) ....'53 '77 C.111 B.S. L.174 J.D. 101 N. Robinson (Pat.)
Peterson, Lesli Bailey, (AV) ......'63 '90 C.623 B.B.A. L.616 J.D. [🄰 Bellingham,C.&L.]
Peterson, Stephen, (AV) ....'50 '75 C&L.623 B.A., J.D. [Fenton,F.S.R.&M.]
Peterson, William L., (AV) ....'30 '54 C&L.623 B.A., LL.B. 6430 N. Western

Peterson, Brian L., P.C., (AV)
101 Park Avenue, Suite 275, 73102-7206
Telephone: 405-232-1857 Fax: 405-232-1665
Email: bpeterson@blppc.com
Brian L. Peterson.
Aviation, Oil and Gas, Environmental Law, Civil Litigation, Litigation, Commercial, Corporate, Financing, Transactions.
See Professional Biographies, OKLAHOMA CITY, OKLAHOMA

Petherick, J. T. '72 '99 C.619 B.B.A. L.623 J.D.
Deputy Dir. of Legislative Affs., National Indian Health Board
Petroff, Dragan D. ....'32 '59 C.999 A.B. L.309 LL.B. 907 N.W. 9thh
Pettigrew, William D., (AV) ....'61 '90 C.618 B.A. L.616 J.D. [Dobbs&M.]
Phansalkar, Kiran A., (AV) ....'60 '85 C.612 B.S. L.623 J.D. [Conner&W.]
Phelps, Anthony D. ....'63 '94 C&L.623 B.A., J.D. [🄰 Merritt&Assoc.]
Philbin, Donald R., (AV) ....'37 '66 C.612 B.S. L.616 J.D. [D.R.Philbin]
Philbin, John A., (AV) ....'34 '61 C.623 B.B.A. L.616 J.D. [Speck P.]
Philbin, Donald R., A Professional Corporation, (AV) .... 1040 W. Hefner Rd.
Phillips, Doran C. ....'24 '67 C.480 B.S. L.616 J.D. 5801 N.W. 67‡
Phillips, Harris A., III, (BV) ....'66 '91 C.612 B.S. L.623 J.D. [Niemeyer,A.A.&P.]

Phillips, Lance Boyd, (BV) '71 '96 C.840 B.B.A. L.623 J.D.
1 North Hudson, Suite 700, 73102
Telephone: 405-235-5944 Mobile: 405-641-3869 Fax: 405-232-4679
Email: lancebp2000@yahoo.com URL: http://www.lawyers.com/lancephillips
Language: Spanish.
Criminal Law, Family Law, Adoption Law, Civil Practice, Workers Compensation, Divorce, DUI, Auto Accidents.
See Professional Biographies, OKLAHOMA CITY, OKLAHOMA

Phillips, Michael W. ....'64 '91 C.612 B.S. L.862 J.D. 4323 NW 63rd St.
Phillips, T. Ray, III, (AV) ....'39 '66 C&L.623 B.B.A., J.D. [Phillips M.M.M.&M.]

Phillips McFall McCaffrey McVay & Murrah, P.C., (AV) 🄱🅁
One Leadership Square, 12th Floor, 211 North Robinson, 73102 ⊙
Telephone: 405-235-4100 Fax: 405-235-4133
URL: http://www.phillipsmcfall.com
Elizabeth Kemp Brown; Robert J. Campbell, Jr.; Marc Edwards; Lloyd T. Hardin, Jr.; Sally A. Hasenfratz; Terry L. Hawkins; Fred A. Leibrock; J. Mark Lovelace; James A. McCaffrey; D. Keith McFall; Melvin R. McVay, Jr.; Robert O. O'Bannon; Michael R. Perri; T. Ray Phillips, III; Sandra Leah Schovanec; Robert N. Sheets; Douglas M. Todd; Thomas G. Wolfe; Ray E. Zschiesche;—Vickie J. Buchanan; Catherine L. Campbell; Dale B. Cazes; Jennifer K. Golden; Bonner J. Gonzales; Heather L. Hintz; Rodney Kent Hunsinger, III; William J. Jarvis; Celeste T. Johnson; Eric L. Johnson; Jennifer Heald Kirkpatrick; JoAn Lamson; Thomas P. Manning; June E. Matchette; Byrona J. Maule; Jennifer Lynn Miller; A. V. Peoples, III; Dawn M. Rahme; Marcia A. Rupert; Beverly I. Vilardofsky; Lyndon W. Whitmire. Of Counsel: E. Carole Barnes; Douglas A. Branch; Michael D. Carter; V. Glenn Coffee; Shannon K. Emmons; John D. Hastie (Resident, Norman, Oklahoma Office); Kenneth E. McBride; Brent L. Mills; Alfred P. Murrah, Jr.; Cindy H. Murray (Resident, Norman, Oklahoma Office); Sam D. Ott (Resident, Norman, Oklahoma Office); Martin G. Ozinga; Donald A. Pape; Bill Price; Ellen K. Spiropoulos; D. Craig Story.
Administrative, Antitrust, Banking, Bankruptcy and Reorganization, Commercial, Consumer Financial Services, Corporate and Partnership, Employment, Environmental, Estate Planning and Probate, Federal and State Taxation, Financial Institution Regulation, Franchise, Health Care, Insurance Defense, International, Litigation, Municipal Finance, Oil and Gas, Product Liability, Public Pension, Real Estate, Securities Regulation and Telecommunications.
Representative Clients: AT&T Communications of Southwest, Inc.; American Home Products Corp.; Bank of America, N.A.; Daimler Chrysler Corp.; Employers Reinsurance Corp.; Federal Employees Credit Union; General Electric Capital Corp.; Local Oklahoma Bank, N.A.; Oklahoma Firefighters Pension and Retirement System; Oklahoma Gas & Electric.
Other Oklahoma City Office: 1001 N.W. 63rd Street, Suite 200, 73116. Telephone: 405-840-5240; Fax: 405-840-2136.
Norman, Oklahoma Office: 232 E. Main, Suite B., 73069. Telephone: 405-346-3346. Fax: 405-364-4666.
Other Norman Office: 401 W. Main, Suite 444, 72067. Telephone: 405-292-4445. Fax: 405-292-4446.
See Professional Biographies, OKLAHOMA CITY, OKLAHOMA

Phipps, Stephanie L. ....'70 '95 C.612 B.S. L.623 J.D. [Rischard&P.]
Pickens, Travis A., (P.C.), (AV) ....'58 '84 C&L.623 B.S., J.D. [Mitchell,D.K.&P.]
Pickering, Millard C. ....'55 '85 C.1314 B.A. L.862 J.D. Off. of U.S. Atty.
Pierce, Amy J. ....'74 '99 C.612 B.S L.615 J.D. [Ryan,W.&C.]
Pierce, Melvin F., (AV) ....'24 '52 C.893 L.623 LL.B. 2935 Acropolis St.

Pierce Couch Hendrickson Baysinger & Green, L.L.P., (AV)
1109 North Francis, P.O. Box 26350, 73126 ⊙
Telephone: 405-235-1611 Fax: 405-235-2904
URL: http://www.PierceCouch.com
Clayton B. Pierce (1889-1981); John R. Couch (1915-1993); Calvin W. Hendrickson (1921-2001); James B. Durant (1934-2004). Members of Firm: Hugh A. Baysinger; Gerald P. Green; Stephen L. Olson; D. Lynn Babb; Inona Jane Harness; Russell L. Hendrickson; John Roger Hurt; Frances E. Patton; Charles A. Brandt; Robert S. Lafferrandre; John Christopher Condren; Peter L. Wheeler; G. Calvin Sharpe; Todd Estes; Leah P. Keele (Resident, Tulsa Office); Scott A. Law. Associates: Haven Tobias; Victoria D. Tindall; Linda Prine Brown; Angela Reinstein; John R. Schneider; Randi A. Donaldson; Jason M. Henderson (Resident, Tulsa Office); Robert B. Houston; Juston Robert Givens; Leslie Diane Guajardo; Larry G. Cassil, Jr.; Jamie Messina Beller (Resident, Tulsa Office); Nancy K Anderson; Jerrod S. Geiger; Carey C. Calvert; Amy S. Hayes; Heidi M. Nichols; Lori R. Whitworth

(This Listing Continued)

Pierce Couch Hendrickson Baysinger & Green, L.L.P. (Continued)
(Resident, Tulsa Office); John L. Shears; Jeffrey I. Crain; Melissa J. Hoehn; William J. Baze; Matthew J.G. McDevitt; Patrick S. Parr; Amy R. Steele. Of Counsel: James E. Golden, Jr.; Malinda S. Matlock; Robert M. Anthony.
General Civil Practice. Insurance, Surety, Corporation, Aviation Law, Medical and Dental Malpractice, Professional Liability, Workers Compensation, Bad Faith Law, Arson, Construction Law, Municipal Liability, Civil Rights, Employment Law, Business Torts and Business Litigation, Insurance Coverage Issues and Automobile/Vehicle Liability. Trial of Cases in all Courts in Oklahoma.
Representative Clients: American Society of Composers, Authors and Publishers; Chubb Insurance Group; CNA/Insurance; Insurance Company of North America; Lloyd's of London; Oklahoma Natural Gas Co.; Physicians Liability Insurance Co.; Shelter Insurance Co.; Sears, Roebuck & Co.; Well Tech., Inc.
Tulsa, Oklahoma Office: 624 South Boston, Suite 500, 74119. Telephone: 918-583-8100. Fax: 918-583-8107.
See Professional Biographies, OKLAHOMA CITY, OKLAHOMA

Pignato, Gerard F., (AV) .... '59 '85 C.103 B.A. L.623 J.D. [Pignato&C.]

Pignato & Cooper, P.C., (AV)
1120 Robinson Renaissance, 119 North Robinson, 73102
Telephone: 405-606-3333 Fax: 405-606-3334
Email: firm@pclaw.com URL: http://www.pignatocooper.com
Gerard F. Pignato; R. Thompson Cooper;—Paul M. Kolker; Brad L. Roberson; Adrienne Babette Roberson; Patrick L. Hullum. Of Counsel: Michael P. Kelly; D. Benham Kirk, Jr.
See Professional Biographies, OKLAHOMA CITY, OKLAHOMA

Pilcher, Gregory F., (AV) '60 '88 C.612 B.S. L.623 J.D.
Sr. Vice Pres., Gen. Coun. & Corp. Secy., Kerr-McGee Corp.

Pinkerton & Finn, P.C.
(See Tulsa)

Pinkston, Jean L., (AV) ....'66 '97 C&L.623 B.S., J.D. [🄰 McAfee&T.] (Pat.)
Pipes, R. Trent, (AV) ....'57 '85 C&L.616 B.M., J.D. [Dunlap,C.&R.]
Pippin, Tra C., (Mr.) ....'51 '77 C.623 B.A. L.616 J.D. Pres., Perfection Properties
Pirrong, Cary Merritt ....'65 '90 C&L.616 B.S., J.D. Oklahoma Pardon & Parole Brd.
Pitcock, Stephen R., (AV) ....'57 '83 C.862 B.S. L.802 J.D. [Hall,E.H.G.G.&N.]
Pitt, Brent W., (BV) ....'58 '83 C&L.623 B.A., J.D. 3109 N. Pennsylvania
Plank, Lynda E. ....'48 '77 C.347 B.S. L.623 J.D. 6135 Graham Rd.
Plater, Frederick Oliver, (BV) .... '49 '81 C.616 B.S. L.623 J.D. [F.Plater]
Plater, Fred, Attorney at Law, (BV) .... P.O. Box 60832
Platt, Bonnie Ruth '41 '88 C.228 B.A. L.190 J.D.
(adm. in NE; not adm. in OK) 300 NW 38th St.
Plourde, Ross A., (AV) ....'56 '82 C.431 B.A. L.616 J.D. [McAfee&T.]
Poe, Wellon B., Jr., (BV) ....'62 '87 C.619 B.A. L.623 J.D. Asst. Atty. Gen.
Poffenberger, Max V. ....'22 '66 C.612 B.S. L.616 J.D. 3413 N.W. 65th Ter.‡
Pointer, Jack Dempsey, (CV) .... '45 '70 C.1147 B.S. L.623 J.D. [J.D.Pointer]
Pointer, Jack Dempsey, P.C., (CV) ....1136 North Robinson Avenue
Polk, Frank L., (AV) ....'54 '81 C.623 B.A. L.228 J.D. [McAfee&T.]
Polley, Kent A. ....'34 '58 C&L.623 B.B.A., LL.B. 11904 Camelot Dr.‡
Pomeroy, L. David, (AV) .... '41 '66 C&L.623 B.B.A., LL.B. [Fuller,T.P.&S.]
Pool, Garrett N., (BV) ....'69 '94 C&L.602 B.A., B.A. [Pool,B.V.&P.] ⊙
Pool, Ted N., (AV) .... '39 '64 C.612 B.S. L.623 J.D. [Pool,B.V.&P.] ⊙
Pool, Blankenship, Vincent & Pool, A Professional Association, (AV)
430 Northwest 11th Street (⊙Del City)
Poole, Heather M. ....'65 '98 C.623 B.S. L.862 J.D. [🄰 Scoggins&C.]
Pope, Janet Childers, (BV) .... '43 '80 C.623 B.S. L.616 J.D. 4705 N Virginia Avenue
Porch, William W. .... '45 '70 C&L.623 B.B.A., J.D. Pres., Porch School Supply, Inc.
Porta, Michelle G. ....'48 '78 C&L.616 B.A., J.D. Asst. Mun. Coun.
Porter, Delmer W., (AV) .... '48 '78 C.612 B.A. L.623 J.D. 10325 Greenbriar Pl.
Porter, James D., (BV) .... '30 '61 C.586 B.B.A. L.616 LL.B. 3711 N. Classen Blvd.
Porter, James S., (BV) .... '52 '85 C.623 B.A. L.616 J.D. [Lewis,W.P.&M.]
Porter, Joel A. ....'62 '88 C.832 B.S. L.325 J.D. [Porter]
Porter, Michael John ....'53 '84 C.612 B.S. L.616 J.D. 700 Couch Dr.
Porter, Paul E. ....'54 '86 C&L.616 B.S., J.D. 11226 Twisted Oak Road
Porter, Sonja Roxanne ....'72 '99 C.92 B.A. L.615 J.D. 610 Colcord Drive
Porter, William P., (BV) ....'41 '66 C.616 B.S. L.623 J.D. 1135 Southwest 44th Street
Porter Law Firm ....527 Northwest 23rd Street
Portis, Jerry Lee, Jr. ....'45 '79 C.1147 B.A. L.623 J.D. [J.Portis]
Portis, Jerry ....3601 N. Classen Blvd., Ste. 102
Postic, Martin, Jr., (AV) ....'56 '80 C&L.623 B.B.A., J.D. [Postic&B.]

Postic & Bates, A Professional Corporation, (AV)
2212 Shadowlake Drive, 73159-7440
Telephone: 405-691-5080 Telecopier: 405-691-6329
URL: http://www.posticbates.com
Martin Postic, Jr.; Julie E. Bates.
Estate Planning, Real Estate Law, Adoption Law, Probate, Guardianship.
See Professional Biographies, OKLAHOMA CITY, OKLAHOMA

Potts, Ray H. ....'32 '65 C.502 B.A. L.616 J.D. 100 N. Bwy.
Powell, Rick Ellis ....'— '79 C.622 B.S. L.615 J.D. [Foshee&Y.]
Powers, Janis S., (AV) ....'55 '84 C.1147 B.A. L.616 J.D. [Batchelor&P.]
Powers, LeRoy A., (BV) ....'14 '40 C.612 L.615 3413 E. Cardinal Dr.
Powley, Brian E. ....'57 '97 C.623 B.S. L.615 J.D. [B.E.Powley]
Powley, Brian E., P.L.L.C. .... P.O. Box 720415
Pratt, Jack S. ....'43 '68 C&L.623 B.B.A., J.D. 1204 Glenwood Ave.‡
Prentice, Dara Derryberry ....'70 '98 C.623 B.A. L.615 J.D. 433 N.W. 15th St.
Prescott, Michael R. ....'53 '82 C.101 B.A. L.616 J.D. 101 Park Ave Ste 101
Preslar, Janis Wood, (BV) '58 '87 C.839 B.S. L.616 J.D.
Asst. Atty. Gen.; OK Atty. Off.
Price, Bill, (AV) .... '48 '73 C.276 B.S.F.S. L.623 J.D. [🄲 Phillips M.M.M.&M.]
Price, Brenda Elaine ....'46 '82 C.1243 B.A. L.861 J.D. Senate Staff Attorney
Price, Douglas F., (AV) ....'57 '83 C.612 B.S. L.623 J.D. Asst. Atty. Gen.
Price, Hadley ....'16 '56 C.613 B.A. L.623 LL.B. 3305 N. Glenoaks Dr.
Price, James R., (AV) ....'50 '78 C.623 B.B.A. L.616 J.D. 3035 N.W. 63rd St.
Price, Louis J., (AV) ....'53 '78 C.597 B.S. L.623 J.D. [McAfee&T.]
Price, Mark H., (AV) ....'41 '66 C.597 B.S. L.623 J.D. [Andrews D.]
Priest, Jim T., (AV) ....'55 '80 C.324 B.A. L.823 J.D. [Whitten,N.M.T.&R.]
Prigmore, Gene ....'44 '80 C.620 B.A. L.623 J.D. Wkrs. Comp. J., Wkrs. Comp. Ct.
Prince, Annette Hooper, (AV) ....'46 '78 C.1147 B.A. L.623 J.D. P.O. Box 22306
Prince, James C., (AV) ....'52 '81 C.612 B.S. L.623 J.D. [🄲 McAfee&T.]
Pringle, Laura Nan Smith, (AV) ....'52 '77 C.961 B.S. L.352 J.D. [Pringle&P.]
Pringle, Lynn A., (AV) ....'51 '77 C.623 B.A. L.273 J.D. [Pringle&P.]

Pringle & Pringle, A Professional Corporation, (AV)
4101 North Classen Boulevard Suite A, 73118-2432
Telephone: 405-848-4810 Fax: 405-848-4819
Email: pringle@pringleandpringle.com URL: http://www.pringleandpringle.com
Lynn A. Pringle; Laura Nan Smith Pringle. Of Counsel: Michael P. Sullivan.

(This Listing Continued)

Pringle & Pringle, A Professional Corporation (Continued)

Banking and Financial Law, Mergers and Acquisitions, Commercial Litigation, Corporate Law, Bankruptcy and Commercial Law, Association and Legislative Law, Oil and Gas and Real Estate Law, Franchise Law, Probate and Estate Planning.
Representative Clients: Provided upon Request.

Pritchett, E. Edd, (BV) .... '41 '67 C.612 B.S. L.616 J.D. [Pritchett&S.]
Pritchett, E. Edd, Jr., (BV) .... '69 '95 C.612 B.A. L.623 J.D. [Ⓐ Durbin,L.&B.]
Pritchett & Snyder, A Professional Association, (BV) .... P.O. Box 16462
Probst, David G., (BV) .... '31 '59 C&L.862 B.S., LL.B. 2809 N.W. Expwy.
Prochaska, Gary G., (BV) .... '51 '76 C.121 B.S.Ch. L.623 J.D. [Foshee&Y.]
Proctor, Shawnae E. .... '75 '01 C.1300 B.S. L.616 J.D. [M.C.Tuepker]
Propester, Richard P., (AV) .... '52 '78 C.696 B.A. L.616 J.D. [Day,E.P.&C.]
Propps, Floyd K., (CV) .... '50 '90 C.663 B.S. L.616 J.D. P.O. Box 42466
Pruet, Boyd C. .... '23 '50 C&L.623 B.S., LL.B. 3024 NW 66th‡
Pruett, William H. '28 '53 C.591 B.S. L.472 J.D.
(adm. in FL; not adm. in OK) Pres., Southwest Spec. Risks, Inc.
Pruitt, Mark E., (BV) .... '57 '84 C.623 B.B.A. L.616 J.D. 6 Ne 63rd St Ste 250
Puckett, Charles L., Jr., (AV) .... '49 '77 C&L.623 B.B.A., J.D. [Gum,P.&M.]
Puckett, Jennifer Tubb, (AV) .... '61 '87 C.170 B.A. L.623 J.D. 6503 N. Lenox Ave.
Puckett, Larry J. .... '46 '71 C&L.623 B.A., J.D. 4802 S. Western
Puckett, Tony G., (AV) .... '61 '88 C.170 B.A. L.623 J.D. [McAfee&T.]
Puckett, W. Brian .... '63 '88 C&L.623 B.B.A., J.D. Equity Financial Mgmt., L.L.C.
Pugh, John Thomas .... '43 '75 C.616 B.A. L.615 J.D. 1900 N. MacArthur
Pugsley, Charles L. .... '24 '51 C&L.623 LL.B. 3009 Hickory Stick Rd.
Puiggari, Marcelo M., (BV) .... '58 '84 C.910 A.B. L.616 J.D. [Ⓒ Kornfeld F.R.&R.]
Purcell, Gary M. .... '50 '76 C.623 B.A. L.616 J.D. U.S. Mag. J.
Puttroff, Paul A. .... '17 '52 C.375 B.S. L.616 LL.B. P.O. Box 279‡
Pyle, Ronny D., (BV) .... '44 '69 C&L.623 B.S., J.D. U.S. Attys. Off.
Querry, Jack .... '36 '61 C&L.623 LL.B. 6209 N.W. 83rd St.
Quigley, Miranda J. .... '77 '04 C.1147 B.A. L.616 J.D. [Ⓐ Delluomo&C.]
Quigley, Paul E., (AV) .... '51 '78 C.612 B.S. L.623 J.D. [Ⓒ Derryberry,Q.S.&N.]
Quinn, Marvin E. ..... '48 '92 C.383 B.A. L.615 J.D. 2601 N.W. Expressway St., #100W-B
Race, Richard K. .... '32 '62 C.612 B.S. L.623 LL.B. Okla. State Ins. Comm.
Rader, Jennifer Beth .... '72 '01 C.82 B.S. L.623 J.d. [Ⓐ McAfee&T.]
Raftery, Robert W., (AV) '51 '84
C.321 B.A. L.616 J.D. 211 North Robinson Avenue, Suite 900
Rahhal, Anthony L., (AV) .... '60 '91 C.622 B.S. L.623 J.D. [McAfee&T.] (Pat.)
Rahhal, Susan J. .... '48 '81 C.793 B.A. L.616 J.D. Law Clk. to U.S. Dist. J.
Rahme, Dawn M. .... '75 '01 C.862 B.S.B.A. L.623 J.D. [Ⓐ Phillips M.M.M.&M.]
Raines, June "Jill" C. '64 '93 C&L.623 B.A., J.D.
University of Oklahoma Health Sciences Center
Rainey, Robert Lee .... '60 '86 C.101 B.A. L.623 J.D. [Rainey,G.M.&M.]
Rainey, Goodwin, Mee & Martin, LLP, (AV) .... 3030 N.W. Expressway

Rainey, Ross, Rice & Binns, P.L.L.C., (AV)
735 First National Center West, 73102-7405
Telephone: 405-235-1356 Telecopier: 405-235-2340
Robert M. Rainey (1882-1971); Streeter Blanton Flynn (1892-1971); Gordon F. Rainey (1913-1975); H. D. Binns, Jr. (1944-1997); Hugh D. Rice; Rodney L. Cook; Roberta Browning Fields;—William P. Tunell, Jr.; Patricia L. Franz; Kenneth A. Tillotson; Dustin R. Fredrick; Rachel L. Bussett. Of Counsel: William J. Ross; Robert D. Stewart, Jr.
General Practice. Trials in all State and Federal Courts, Corporation, Public Utility, Commercial, Bankruptcy, Administrative, Probate, Negligence, Oil and Gas, Products Liability, Railroad, Aircraft Title Law.
General Attorneys for Oklahoma: Santa Fe Pacific Corp.; Burlington Northern Santa Fe Railway Co. Attorneys for: OG&E; The Circle K Corp.; Dover Elevator Co.; Dover Industries Acceptance, Inc.
See Professional Biographies, OKLAHOMA CITY, OKLAHOMA

Rakes, Gerald S. .... '47 '76 C.815 B.A. L.339 J.D. Asst. Mun. Coun.
Ralstin, G. Todd, (BV) .... '50 '79 C.623 B.B.A. L.616 J.D. [G.T.Ralstin]
Ralstin, G. Todd, Inc., (BV) .... 5131 Classen Boulevard, Suite 207

Ramey & Tharp
(See Yukon)

Ramsey, David M. .... '69 '95 C&L.623 B.A., J.D. [Ramsey]
Ramsey, Natalie K. .... '76 '02 C.612 B.S. L.623 J.D. [Ⓐ McAfee&T.]
Ramsey, Rodney C., (AV) .... '56 '82 C.612 B.A. L.623 J.D. [Britton,R.&G.]
Ramsey Law Office .... 5350 S. Western Ave., Ste. 105
Randall, Arlene M. .... '61 '03 C.620 B.S. L.615 J.D. [Ⓐ Scoggins&C.]
Randall, Clarke L., (AV) .... '48 '76 C.347 A.B. L.623 J.D. [Kornfeld F.R.&R.]
Rasnake, Gregory R. .... '72 '00 C.889 B.S. L.623 J.D. [Ⓒ Burton&Assoc.] ⊙
Ratheal, Donelle H. .... '57 '92 C.208 B.M. L.623 J.D. [D.Ratheal]

Ratheal, Donelle, P.C.
5909 N.W. Expressway, Suite 300, 73132
Telephone: 405-842-6342 Fax: 405-842-6708
Email: donelleratheal@yahoo.com URL: http://www.lawyers.com/donelleratheal
Donelle H. Ratheal.
Languages: English and Spanish.
Domestic Relations/ Contested and Uncontested, Family Law Litigation, Family Law Mediation, Collaborative Divorce, Child Custody and Support.
See Professional Biographies, OKLAHOMA CITY, OKLAHOMA

Ratliff, Kevin B. .... '71 '98 C.623 B.B.A. L.616 J.D. [Ⓐ Hartzog C.C.&N.]
Ratliff, Reeder E., (AV) .... '60 '85 C&L.623 B.B.A., J.D. [Crowe&D.]
Rauch, Barbara .... '44 '76 C.623 B.S. L.615 J.D. Oklahoma Dept. of Envir. Quality
Ray, Kimberly Robinson .... '56 '80 C.616 B.S. L.208 J.D. 4300 N. Lincoln Blvd.
Rayburn, Kermit O. .... '13 '60 C.1147 B.A. L.616 LL.B. Dir., Law Enf. Training Council‡
Rayburn, Scott M., (AV) .... '52 '77 C.623 B.B.A. L.846 J.D. [S.M.Rayburn]
Rayburn, Scott M., P.C., (AV) .... 211 N. Robinson
Rean, Susan Palmer, (BV) '54 '79
C.134 B.S. L.616 J.D. Asst. Gen. Coun., State Tax Comm.
Reece, Robert A., (AV) .... '44 '69 C&L.623 B.B.A., J.D. [Ⓒ Crowe&D.]
Reed, Sherman A., (BV) .... '58 '86 C.1315 B.S.Acct. L.616 J.D. 6 N.E. 63rd St., Ste. 400
Reed, Tracy Cotts, (BV) .... '65 '90 C&L.623 B.A., J.D. [T.C.Reed]
Reed, Tracy Cotts, P.C., (BV) .... 6440 Avondale, Suite 200
Reel, Stephen E., (BV) .... '48 '77 C.612 B.A. L.616 J.D. Okla. Mun. Assn. Grp.
Reeves, Earl Leslie, Jr. .... '39 '84 C.1196 B.S. L.623 J.D. Dept. of Pub. Safety
Reeves, John R., (AV) .... '49 '74 C.623 B.B.A. L.259 J.D. [Mock,S.W.E.R.&B.]
Rehl, Kevin Dean .... '64 '91 C.1315 L.45 J.D. 701 N.W. 63rd St., Ste. 506
Reichenberger, John F., (AV) '52 '77 C.620 B.S. L.623 J.D.
Corp. V.P., Dep. Gen. Coun. & Asst. Secy., Kerr-McGee Corp.
Reid, O. Saul .... '74 '04 C&L.623 B.A., J.D. [Ⓐ Lamun,M.C.&D.]
Reiff, Jonathan D., (AV) .... '38 '68 C.309 B.A. L.896 J.D. [J.D.Reiff]

Reiff, Jonathan D., P.C., (AV)
Center 3000, Suite 136, 3000 United Founders Boulevard, 73112
Telephone: 405-848-8474 Fax: 405-848-4114
Jonathan D. Reiff.
Estate Planning and Tax, Probate and Trust Law, Business, Oil and Gas.

Reinke, Joseph J., (AV) .... '50 '77 C.623 B.B.A. L.796 J.D. [J.J.Reinke]
Reinke, Joseph J., P.C., Attorney and Counselor at Law, (AV)
5101 N. Classen, Ste. 100
Reinstein, Angela .... '71 '97 C&L.623 B.A., J.D. [Ⓐ Pierce C.H.B.&G.]
Remmers, Richard F. .... '22 '52 C&L.623 B.S., J.D. 9636 N. May Ave.
Reneau, Dale, (AV) .... '31 '56 C&L.623 B.A., LL.B. [Fenton,F.S.R.&M.]
Renegar, Gregg R., (AV) .... '49 '75 C.612 B.S. L.616 J.D. [Kornfeld F.R.&R.]
Renegar, Joan A., (BV) .... '50 '79 C.623 B.A. L.616 J.D. [Kornfeld F.R.&R.]
Renegar, O. Blanchard .... '27 '55 C&L.616 B.B.S., LL.B. State Farm Mut. Auto. Ins. Co.
Replogle, Dee A., Jr., (AV) .... '43 '68 C.813 B.A. L.623 J.D. [McAfee&T.]
Resides, Laure M. .... '75 '02 C.612 B.A. L.615 J.D. [Resides&R.]
Resides, W. Devin .... '67 '02 C.35 B.S. L.615 J.D. [Resides&R.]

Resides & Resides, PLLC
114 NW Sixth Street, Suite 203, 73102
Telephone: 405-605-6547 Fax: 405-605-6577
Email: wdresides@resideslaw.com URL: http://www.resideslaw.com
W. Devin Resides; Laure M. Resides. Of Counsel: Dr. Barbara K. Yuill.
General Practice.
See Professional Biographies, OKLAHOMA CITY, OKLAHOMA

Reynolds, Jason B. .... '73 '98 C.45 B.A. L.623 J.D. [Griffin,R.&Assoc.]
Reynolds, Joe Brett .... '67 '92 C.623 B.A. L.616 J.D. [J.B.Reynolds]
Reynolds, Rhonda Murphy, (AV) ... '52 '83 C.763 B.S. L.623 J.D. Law Clk., U.S. Dist. J.
Reynolds, Joe Brett, P.C. .... 204 North Robinson, 25th Floor

Reynolds, Ridings, Vogt & Morgan, (AV)
2200 First National Center, 120 North Robinson, 73102
Telephone: 405-232-8131 Fax: 405-232-7911
Email: rrvm@rrvmlaw.com
Members of Firm: Norman E. Reynolds (1888-1953); W. Otis Ridings (1899-1970); James W. Vogt; Fred S. Morgan. Associates: Lisa A. Robertson; Benjamin Harris.
Commercial and Civil Litigation, Bankruptcy, Collections, Business Law, Banks and Banking, Creditor Rights.
See Professional Biographies, OKLAHOMA CITY, OKLAHOMA

Rheinberger, Henry, (AV) .... '33 '61 C.602 B.S. L.623 LL.B. [Ⓒ Crowe&D.]
Rhodes, Avery England .... '71 '97 C.1147 B.A. L.623 J.D. 12320 St. Andrews Dr. #A
Rhodes, Gary C., (AV) ...... '41 '69 C.612 B.S. L.616 J.D. 2200 NW 50th St., Suite 127E
Rhodes, Horace G., (AV) .... '27 '55 C&L.623 B.S., J.D. [Kerr,I.R.&A.]
Rhodes, James W., (AV) .... '58 '84 C.918 B.A. L.623 J.D. [Kerr,I.R.&A.]
Rhodes, Mary Kathleen, (BV) .... '48 '76 C&L.623 B.A., J.D. P.O. Box 2266
Rhodes, Rebecca G. .... '64 '89 C.293 B.A. L.623 J.D. Asst. Atty. Gen.
Rhodes, Scott M., (AV) .... '52 '79 C&L.623 B.A., J.D. [Smith R.S.&E.]
Rhodes, Timothy E. .... '57 '90 C&L.623 B.A., J.D. 805 N.W. 42nd St.

Rhodes, Hieronymus, Jones, Tucker & Gable, P.L.L.C.
(See Tulsa)

Rice, Douglas A., (BV) .... '69 '94 C.612 B.S. L.623 J.D. [Derryberry,Q.S.&N.]
Rice, Hugh D., (AV) .... '— '64 C.623 B.A. L.893 LL.B. [Rainey,R.R.&B.]
Rice, James H., (AV) ...... '39 '71 C.623 B.S. L.309 J.D. 1012 N.W. Grand Blvd., Ste. A
Richard, Bert A., Jr., (AV) .... '48 '77 C&L.616 B.A., J.D. Asst. Pub. Def.

Richards, Elizabeth A., (BV) '— '87 C.675 B.A. L.615 J.D.
112 West Commerce, 73109-6020
Telephone: 405-319-9696 Fax: 405-319-9464
Email: richardslawfirm@aol.com URL: http://www.lawyers.com/richardslawfirm
Probate, Bankruptcy, Family Law, Divorce, Child Support, Real Estate, Residential Real Estate, Guardianships, Adoptions, Child Custody, Wills, Workers Compensation, Collections.
See Professional Biographies, OKLAHOMA CITY, OKLAHOMA

Richardson, Brooks A., (CV) .... '70 '98 C.228 B.A. L.623 J.D. [Fellers,S.B.B.&T.]
Richardson, Christa B., (AV) .... '71 '97 C.802 B.A. L.623 J.D. [Ⓒ Britton,R.&G.]
Richie, Michael Sherwood, (BV) '47 '80
C.1096 B.A. L.861 J.D. 2300 Lincoln Boulevard, Room 208
Ricks, Bob A. '44 '69 C&L.69 B.B.A., J.D.
(adm. in TX; not adm. in OK) F.B.I.
Riddles, Darin Todd, (AV) .... '67 '94 C&L.623 M.B.A., J.D. [Ⓐ Cheek]
Ridenour, Craig Wicker .... '46 '89 C.375 B.A. L.616 J.D. [C.W.Ridenour]
Ridenour, Craig W. .... 9636 N. May Ave., Ste. 272
Ridgway, David .... '73 '03 C&L.623 B.B.A., J.D. [Ⓐ McAfee&T.]
Ridle, Robert A. .... '36 '66 C.502 B.S. L.616 J.D. 3721 N. Classen Blvd.
Rieger, Karen S., (AV) .... '56 '81 C&L.623 B.A., J.D. [Crowe&D.]
Riesen, Thomas C., (AV) .... '59 '85 C.623 B.A. L.616 J.D. [Crabb,F.&R.]
Rieves, L. Michael, (BV) .... '43 '68 C.612 B.A. L.623 J.D. 4808 N. Classen Boulevard
Rife, Gary A., (AV) .... '53 '78 C&L.623 B.B.A., J.D. [Rife&W.]

Rife & Walters, (AV)
BankOne Center, 100 North Broadway Avenue, Suite 2730, 73102
Telephone: 405-235-3800 Fax: 405-235-5800
Email: rwstaff@rifewalters.com
Members of Firm: Gary A. Rife; Hilton H. Walters. Associates: Jamie K. Bruehl; Travis K. Siegel.
Medical, Legal and Professional Malpractice, Professional Discipline, Insurance Defense Law. Trial Practice State and Federal Courts.
See Professional Biographies, OKLAHOMA CITY, OKLAHOMA

Riggs, Richard A., (AV) .... '49 '74 C.623 B.A. L.477 J.D. [McAfee&T.]

Riggs, Abney, Neal, Turpen, Orbison & Lewis, A Professional Corporation, (AV)
5801 Broadway Extension, Paragon Building, Suite 101, 73118-7489 ⊙
Telephone: 405-843-9909 Fax: 405-842-2913
URL: http://www.riggsabney.com
Members of the Firm: Michael C. Turpen; Richard A. Mildren; Robert A. Nance; Melvin C. Hall; George Marvin Emerson. Associates: D. Sharon Gentry; Terry D. Kordelski, II; Janice Morrow; Gisele Perryman; Gary W. Wood.
General Civil, Trial and Appellate Practice before all State and Federal Courts and Agencies, Alternative Dispute Resolution, Banking, Corporate, Securities, Anti-trust, Administrative, Government Relations, Real Estate, Commercial Transactions, Oil and Gas, Estate Planning, Probate, Taxation, Employment and Discrimination, Employee Benefits, Social Security, Bankruptcy and Reorganization, Family Law, Healthcare, Negligence, Personal Injury, Products Liability, Medical Malpractice, Transportation, and Indian Law.
Tulsa, Oklahoma Office: 502 West Sixth Street, 74119. Telephone: 918-587-3161. Fax: 918-587-9708.
Muskogee, Oklahoma Office: 215 State Street, First National Severs Building, Suite 508. Telephone: 918-687-5404; 800-722-1332. Fax: 918-687-1128.
Denver, Colorado Office: 621 Seventeenth Street, Suite 1900. Telephone: 303-298-7392. Fax: 303-298-7398.
See Professional Biographies, OKLAHOMA CITY, OKLAHOMA

Rinderer, William P., Jr. '21 '69 C&L.767 B.S., J.D.
(adm. in CA; not adm. in OK) 3104 Raintree Rd.‡
Rinehart, Sandra Dianne .... '59 '86 C.1315 B.S. L.623 J.D. 2300 N. Lincoln, Ste. 112
Ringer, Frank M., (AV) .... '43 '70 C&L.623 B.A., J.D. Asst. U.S. Atty.
Ringold, A. F., (AV) .... '31 '55 C&L.477 A.B., LL.B. [Rosenstein,F.&R.] ⊙
Ripley, Ronald L., (AV) '46 '72 C&L.623 B.B.A., J.D.
Sr. Corp. Coun., Dobson Communications Corp.
Ripperger, Rhonda L. McNutt ..... '61 '88 C&L.623 B.A., J.D. Legal Aid of W. Okla., Inc.
Rischard, Denis P., (AV) .... '61 '86 C.602 B.B.A. L.623 J.D. [Rischard&P.]

Rischard & Phipps P.C., (AV)
120 N. Robinson Avenue, Suite 2320, 73102
Telephone: 405-235-2393 Fax 405-235-2347
Email: admin@rischardphipps.com
Denis P. Rischard; Stephanie L. Phipps.
General Civil Litigation, Business Litigation, Health Care Law, Nursing Home Litigation, Contract Litigation, Corporate and Insurance Defense, Oil and Gas Litigation, Employment Litigation, Federal Civil Litigation, Estate Planning, Adoption Law.
See Professional Biographies, OKLAHOMA CITY, OKLAHOMA

Roach, Pamela M. .... '49 '95 C.614 M.Ed. L.1363 J.D. 325 Dean A. McGee Ave.
Roark, Robert L., (AV) .... '45 '75 C.612 B.S. L.623 J.D. [McKinney&S.]
Roberson, Adrienne Babette .... '75 '00 C.623 B.A L.615 J.D. [[A] Pignato&C.]
Roberson, Brad L. ....'75 '00 C.80 B.A. L.623 J.D. [[A] Pignato&C.]
Roberts, Bana Burkett .... '48 '77 C&L.623 B.A., J.D. U.S. Mag. J.
Roberts, Bill M., (AV) ....'53 '80 C.1147 B.B.A. L.616 J.D. [[A] Wilson,C.&A.]
Roberts, James W. ....'20 '49 C&L.623 B.A., J.D. 2444 N.W. 46th St.‡
Roberts, K. David, (AV) ....'46 '71 C&L.623 B.A., J.D. [[C] McCaffrey&Assoc.]
Roberts, Lori R. .... '64 '91 C&L.623 B.B.A., J.D. Integris Health
Roberts, Mary Ann ....'67 '97 C&L.623 B.B.A., J.D. Asst. Atty Gen.
Roberts, Shawn J. .... '72 '98 C.336 B.A. L.615 J.D. [Brown&R.]
Robertson, Bruce A., (AV) ....'60 '89 C&L.623 B.B.A., J.D. [[A] Jones,A.&O.]
Robertson, James B. ....'64 '91 C&L.623 B.B.A., J.D. 101 North Broadway
Robertson, Jayne J., (AV) .... '58 '83 C&L.623 B.B.A., J.D. [J.J.Robertson]
Robertson, John D., (AV) ....'61 '86 C.612 B.S. L.623 J.D. [Hartzog C.C.&N.]
Robertson, Kenneth J. ....'28 '61 C.623 B.F.A. L.796 J.D. 7004 Nichols Rd.‡
Robertson, Lisa A., (AV) ....'65 '95 C.623 B.A. L.616 J.D. [[A] Reynolds,R.V.&M.]
Robertson, Mark A., (AV) .... '50 '75 C.210 B.A. L.623 J.D. [Robertson&W.]
Robertson, Michelle M., (BV) ....'65 '91 C&L.623 B.A., J.D. Hammons & Assoc.
Robertson, Rob F.M., (AV) .... '61 '87 C&L.623 B.B.A., J.D. [Gable&G.]
Robertson, Vicki .... '49 '79 C.623 B.S. L.616 J.D. Dist. J.

Robertson, Jayne Jarnigan, P.C., (AV) [BB]
119 North Robinson, Suite 825, 73102
Telephone: 405-319-0400 Fax: 405-319-0404
Email: jaynerobertson@cs.com URL: http://www.lawyers.com/jaynerobertson
Jayne J. Robertson.
Commercial Litigation, Environmental Law, Oil and Gas Law, Contracts.
See Professional Biographies, OKLAHOMA CITY, OKLAHOMA

Robertson & Williams, Inc., (AV) [BB]
3033 N.W. 63rd Street, Suite 200, 73116-3607
Telephone: 405-848-1944 Fax: 405-843-6707
Email: marobert@robertsonwilliams.com
Mark A. Robertson; Thomas C. Williams; R. Pope Van Cleef, Jr.; James D. Tack, Jr.; Kecia Khae Cole; Charles E. Wetsel.
Business and Corporate Law, Oil and Gas, Civil Litigation, Securities, Mergers, Acquisitions and Divestitures, Commercial Law, Real Estate, Trusts and Estates, International Trusts, Franchising, Aircraft Title, Consumer Law.
See Professional Biographies, OKLAHOMA CITY, OKLAHOMA

Robinson, Brett ...... '64 '89 C.623 B.A. L.862 J.D. Mng. Dir., Public Issue Advisers, Inc.
Robinson, Harold L.R. "Bob", (BV) '54 '81
C.131 B.A. L.616 J.D. 3829 N. Classen Blvd., Ste. 105
Robinson, James F., (AV) .... '44 '73 C.663 B.A. L.616 J.D. Asst. U.S. Atty.
Robinson, James M., (AV) ....'39 '66 C&L.623 B.B.A., J.D. 6211 Diane Drive
Robinson, Randall P., (AV) ....'56 '82 C.612 B.A. L.623 J.D. [Bryan&R.]
Robinson, Richard A., (BV) ....'47 '81 C.976 B.A. L.616 J.D. [Robinson&H.]
Robinson, William A., (AV) ..... '40 '74 C.1089 B.A. L.616 J.D. [[C] Burton&Assoc.] ⊙‡
Robinson, William J., (AV) ....'31 '55 C&L.623 A.B., LL.B. [[C] Shirk W.&R.]
Robinson & Hoover, (BV) ....119 N. Robinson
Robison, Reid E., (AV) .... '44 '68 C&L.623 B.A., J.D. [McAfee&T.]
Robles, Robert R., (BV) ....'53 '81 C.326 B.A. L.811 J.D. 428 N.5th, Suite A
Rockett, D. Joe, (AV) .... '42 '67 C&L.623 B.A., J.D. [Andrews D.]
Rockett, David Montgomery .... '64 '94 C&L.623 B.A., J.D. [Rockett]
Rockett Law Firm .... 6801 S. Western Ave., Ste. 203
Rodgers, John Jeffrey ....'67 '96 C.1145 B.S. L.623 J.D. [Rodgers]
Rodgers, Michelle ....'71 '98 C.623 B.A. L.615 J.D. Asst. Dist. Atty.
Rodgers, William W. ....'37 '64 C.623 B.A. L.802 LL.B. [[C] McAfee&T.]
Rodgers Law Firm, P.L.L.C. ....1207 S.W. 44th St.
Rodriguez, Alonso J. '51 '79 C.842 B.A. L.846 J.D.
(adm. in TX; not adm. in OK) F.A.A.
Rogalin, Michael Paul ....'54 '80 C.1174 B.A. L.623 J.D. 1 N. Hudson, Ste. 1050
Rogers, Charles S., (BV) '53 '78 C.612 B.A. L.623 J.D.
Asst. Atty. General, Multicounty Grand Jury Unit
Rogers, Cleeta J. .... '30 '55 C.614 B.A. L.616 J.D. Gen. Coun., Okla. City Pub. Sch.
Rogers, G. Neal, (AV) ....'49 '81 C.1147 B.A. L.616 J.D. [Dunlap,C.&R.]
Rogers, Jason T. ....'74 '99 C.612 B.S. L.623 J.D. [[A] Foliart,H.O.&B.]
Rogers, Lynn C., (AV) .... '39 '75 C&L.623 B.S., J.D. Asst. Atty. Gen.
Rogers, Patricia A. ....'60 '99 C.665 B.A. L.616 J.D. [[A] McAfee&T.]
Rogers, Rosemary Myles, (BV) .... '58 '83 C&L.623 B.A., J.D. 601 N.W. 13th St.
Rogers, William B., (AV) '30 '55 C&L.623 B.A., LL.B.
Bank IV Nichols Hills 6412 Avondale Dr., Ste. #200
Rolston, Joe S., III, (AV) ....'32 '62 C.612 B.S. L.616 LL.B. [Rolston,H.E.M.&N.]
Rolston, Shirley D. ....'38 '96 C.82 B.A. L.623 J.D. [Rolston,H.E.M.&N.]
Rolston, Hamill, Epperson, Myles & Nelson, P.A., (AV)
4334 N.W. Expressway, Suite 174
Romano, Enrico J. .... '24 '57 C&L.616 B.A., J.D. 3801 N.W. 63rd St., Ste. 200
Romano, Rick E., (BV) ....'58 '83 C&L.623 B.A., J.D. [Romano&R.]
Romano, Rick J., (BV) ....'24 '57 C&L.616 B.A., LL.B. [Romano&R.]
Romano & Romano, P.C., (BV) .... 3801 N.W. 63rd St., Ste. 200
Romberger, Warren O. .... '20 '51 C.623 L.615 LL.B. 904 N.W. 59th St.
Rooker, Bruce R., (AV) .... '54 '79 C.618 B.A. L.623 J.D. [Mahaffey&G.]
Rops, Mia C., (BV) ....'67 '93 C.623 B.A. L.846 J.D. [[C] Walker,F.&F.]
Rorie, Julie Louise '55 '80 C.225 A.B. L.623 J.D.
Ct. Admr., State of OK, Ct. Admin. Off.
Rose, Richard L. ....'69 '04 C.82 B.S. L.615 J.D. [[A] Miller D.]
Rose, Teresa M. .... '56 '93 C.616 B.S. L.615 J.D. [CenterForEducationLaw]
Roselius, Jason E., (BV) ....'69 '95 C.921 B.A. L.623 J.D. [Whitten,N.M.T.&R.]
Rosell, Armando J. ....'72 '00 C.802 B.B.A. L.615 J.D. [[C] Mulinix O.H.A.&L.]
Roselle, Joe L. ....'30 '59 L.616 J.D. 1603A W. Memorial Rd.
Rosenstein, Fist & Ringold, A Professional Corporation, (AV)
2801 N. Lincoln Blvd, Suite 224 (⊙Tulsa)
Ross, Don W. .... '15 '47 C.612 B.S. L.192 Law Clk., Supm. Ct.
Ross, G. David, (AV) .... '54 '79 C.612 B.S. L.623 J.D. [Lytle S.&C.]
Ross, Paul A. .... '75 '02 C.612 B.S. L.616 J.D. [[A] McAfee&T.]
Ross, Susan Elizabeth, (BV) ....'55 '80 C&L.623 B.A., J.D. 13124 Oak Cliff Road
Ross, William J., (AV) ....'— '54 C&L.623 B.B.A., LL.B. [[C] Rainey,R.R.&B.]
Roth, James Anthony .... '68 '94 C.375 B.A. L.615 J.D. Staff Atty., Co. Comr.'s Off.

Rothbaum, Bernard J., (AV) .... '45 '70 C&L.623 B.A., J.D. [Hartzog C.C.&N.]
Rother, Timila S., (AV) .... '64 '90 C&L.623 B.A., J.D. [Crowe&D.]
Rouse, Charles R. ....'54 '82 C.612 B.S. L.616 J.D. 1330 N. Classen
Rouse, Nicholas D. .... '64 '90 C&L.623 B.S., J.D. [Dunlap,C.&R.] (See Pat. Sect.)
Roush, Raymond Bryan, (AV⊤) .... '46 '76 C.418 B.S. L.616 J.D. P.O. Box 18496
Rowan, James T., (AV) '44 '72
C.375 B.A. L.623 J.D. 228 Robert S. Kerr Avenue, Suite 220
Rowan, William J. '57 '83 C.691 B.A. L.846
(adm. in TX; not adm. in OK) 12129 Thorn Ridge Rd.‡
Rowe, Jane G. .... '59 '85 C&L.623 B.A., J.D. [[A] DeVore]
Rowland, Geremy A. ....'72 '00 C.623 B.A. L.615 J.D. [[A] Short W.M.&B.]
Rowntree, John M., (AV) .... '24 '52 C.623 L.616 LL.B. 6421 Avondale Dr.‡
Royer, Charles W., (AV) ....'31 '55 C&L.623 B.B.A., LL.B. 3717 N.W. 63rd.
Rozin, Mitchell D. .... '59 '87 C&L.623 B.B.A., J.D. 4045 N.W. 64th St., Ste. 510
Rudy, Daron Allen ....'60 '85 C.620 B.S. L.623 J.D. 1st Union Securities, Inc.
Rueb, Mary W., (BV) .... '— '80 C.736 B.A. L.616 J.D. 3033 N.W. 63rd Street, Suite 150
Ruiz, Chas. W. ....'10 '53 C&L.616 B.S., LL.B. 2517 N.W. 12th St.‡
Rupert, Anton J., (AV) .... '55 '81 C.309 A.B. L.813 J.D. [Crowe&D.]
Rupert, Kurt M., (AV) .... '60 '86 C&L.623 B.A., J.D. [[A] Hartzog C.C.&N.]
Rupert, Marcia A., (BV) .... '58 '87 C&L.623 B.A., J.D. [[A] Phillips M.M.M.&M.]
Russ, Benjamin E. .... '74 '04 C.612 B.S. L.615 J.D. [[A] McKinney&S.]
Russell, David L. ....'42 '65 C.613 B.S. L.623 J.D. U.S. Dist. J.
Russell, Kristi Bynum, (BV) .... '70 '96 C.616 B.A. L.623 J.D. [Caldwell&R.]
Russell, Ralph W. .... '21 '44 L.623 LL.B. 312 W. Odom Rd.
Russell, W. Ryan .... '15 '43 C.623 L.616 3220 Wilshire Ter.‡
Rust, Jefferson I., (AV) .... '57 '95 C.956 B.S. L.615 J.D. [McKinney&S.]
Ryan, Gordon D. ....'36 '61 C&L.378 B.A., LL.B. [Lytle S.&C.]
Ryan, Gregory J. ....'57 '82 C.823 B.A. L.616 J.D. Spec. Dist. Ct. J., Oklahoma Co.
Ryan, Jason A. ....'73 '00 C&L.616 B.S., J.D. [Ryan,W.&C.]
Ryan, Michael S., (BV) .... '57 '90 C.1147 B.A. L.616 J.D. [Edmonds,C.H.G.R.&W.]
Ryan, Patrick C., (AV) .... '35 '69 C.1023 B.S. L.616 J.D. 4323 NW 63rd St.
Ryan, Patrick M., (AV) ....'45 '69 C&L.623 B.A., J.D. [Ryan,W.&C.]
Ryan, Philip D., (AV) .... '58 '87 C.1147 B.B.A. L.616 J.D. [Boettcher,R.M.&B.]

Ryan, Whaley & Coldiron, (AV) [BB]
119 N. Robinson Avenue, Suite 900, 73102-4617
Telephone: 405-239-6040 Fax: 405-239-6766
URL: http://www.ryanwhaley.com
Patrick M. Ryan; Phillip G. Whaley; Mark D. Coldiron; Joe M. Hampton; Timothy J. Bomhoff; Robin F. Fields; Daniel G. Webber, Jr.; Keith J. Klein; Michael A. Peters; Stephen L. Jantzen; Amy J. Pierce; Patrick R. Pearce, Jr.; Jason A. Ryan; Matthew C. Kane; Corey A. Neller; Coree L. Stevenson.
Civil Litigation, Disability Insurance, Products Liability, Environmental and Energy Law and Litigation, Securities, Business Litigation, Drug and Medical Device Litigation, Complex Litigation, Franchise Litigation, Arbitration, Commercial Litigation, Employment Law, White Collar Criminal Defense, Civil Practice, Trial Practice, Appellate Practice, Medical Malpractice.
See Professional Biographies, OKLAHOMA CITY, OKLAHOMA

Rysted, Karl M., (BV) '61 '92 C.170 B.A. L.615 J.D.
Staff Atty., Legal Aid Services of Oklhamoa, Inc.
Sachs, Andrew '65 '92 C.1044 B.S. L.823 J.D.
V.P. & Dir. of Pers., Coates Field Service, Inc.
Saied, William R. ....'21 '49 C&L.623 B.A., LL.B. 2529 N.W. 60th St.‡
Salalati, Aimée D. M. ....'74 '99 C&L.623 B.S., J.D. [[A] Scoggins&C.]
Salamy, Richard J. .... '66 '92 C&L.69 B.A., J.D. [[A] McAfee&T.]
Sales, Jimmy R. '29 '54
C&L.623 B.B.A., LL.B. Gen. Coun., State Employment Sec. Comm.
Sallusti, Ralph A., (AV) .... '46 '74 C.623 B.A. L.616 J.D. [R.A.Sallusti]
Sallusti, Ralph A., P.C., (AV) ....3015 Northwest 59th
Salyer, Jerry L. ....'36 '61 C&L.623 B.A., J.D. Wkrs. Comp. J.
Samara, Alix Lormand '77 '02 C.802 B.A. L.273 J.D.
(adm. in TX; not adm. in OK) [[A] Hartzog C.C.&N.]
Samuel-Jaha, Linda ....'— '92 C.614 B.S. L.615 J.D. [[A] Eddy&J.]
Sanders, Anita F. ....'49 '83 C.612 B.S. L.616 J.D. 410 W. Main St.
Sanders, Elaine .... '68 '93 C.862 B.A. L.623 J.D. Asst. Atty. Gen.
Sanders, William S. ....'51 '78 C.1300 B.S. L.615 J.D. 13317 Pinehurst Rd.
Sanger, Brett D., (AV) .... '62 '93 C.612 B.S. L.616 J.D. [B.D.Sanger&Assoc.]
Sanger, Jerry Jean .... '55 '96 C.1147 B.S. L.623 J.D. P.O. Box 805
Sanger, Brett D., & Associates, (AV) .... 200 N. Harvey Ave., Ste. 100
Sargent, John E., Jr., (AV) .... '43 '70 C.884 B.S. L.623 J.D. [McAfee&T.]
Satterfield, Grey W., Jr., (AV) '33 '59
C&L.623 B.A., LL.B. Jud. Asst. & Info. Sys. Coord.
Saunders, Lynne F. ....'56 '94 C.446 B.S. L.615 J.D. [[A] Hiltgen&B.]
Savage, Malcolm M. ....'69 '98 C.59 B.A. L.616 J.D. [M.M.Savage]
Savage, Philip L. (Larry), (AV) ...... '38 '64 C.197 A.B. L.623 LL.B. [[C] McKinney&S.]
Savage, Malcolm M., P.C. ....200 N. Harvey, Suite 810
Schaefer, John N., (AV) .... '40 '66 C.623 B.B.A. L.846 LL.B. [McAfee&T.]

Schaffer, Peter K., Law Office of, (AV) '43 '74 C.1155 B.S. L.616 J.D.
204 N. Robinson Avenue Suite 2305, 73102-6891
Telephone: 405-239-7707 Fax: 405-239-6800
Email: pschaffer@adoptionattorneys.org
Adoption Law.
See Professional Biographies, OKLAHOMA CITY, OKLAHOMA

Scharnberg, Charles J. .... '48 '79 C&L.623 B.A., J.D. 800 N. Harvey
Schatz, Steven R. '52 '78 C.612 B.A. L.623 J.D.
Hazelwood Production and Exploration Company, L.L.C.
Schaulat, Ronald A., (AV) ....'58 '83 C.337 A.B. L.616 J.D. [Brady,S.&F.]
Schem, Charles O., (BV) .... '54 '80 C&L.623 B.A., J.D. [Hester,S.H.&B.]
Scherry, Richard J. '32 '57 C.569 L.94 LL.B.
(adm. in NY; not adm. in OK) P.O. Box 12312‡
Schindler, Charles S. .... '51 '98 C.1147 B.A. L.615 J.D. 12405 Abbotts Way
Schmidt, Arthur W., (AV) ....'52 '79 C.663 B.S. L.623 J.D. [Mahaffey&G.]
Schmidt, H. Lee, (AV) ....'50 '78 C.173 B.S. L.623 J.D. Asst. U.S. Atty.
Schmidt, Howard L., (BV) ....'37 '71 C.1147 B.S. L.616 J.D. 4301 N. McArthur St.
Schneider, David B., (AV) ....'44 '69 C&L.846 B.B.A., J.D. [Schneider&L.]
Schneider, John R., (BV) ....'51 '83 C.801 B.S. L.616 J.D. [[A] Pierce C.H.B.&G.]
Schneider, Rebecca K. ....'50 '84 C.623 B.A. L.616 J.D. 4901 Richmond Sq

Schneider & Labarthe, P.A., (AV)
304 Northwest 13th Street Suite 120, 73103
Mailing Address: P.O. Box 1147, Oklahoma City, OK 73101
Telephone: 405-232-9990 Fax: 405-232-9992
URL: http://www.okielaw.com
David B. Schneider; Richard C. Labarthe.
Civil Litigation in all State and Federal Courts, Transportation, Immigration Law, Motor Carrier, Truck Accidents, Cargo Claims, Products Liability, Bankruptcy, Estate Planning, Employment Law, Civil Business Litigation, Corporate Law, Real Estate Law, Estate and Trust Law.
See Professional Biographies, OKLAHOMA CITY, OKLAHOMA

Schneiter, Lance E. ....'— '02 C.1147 B.A. L.623 J.D. [[A] McKinney&S.]

Schnetzler, Martin K., (BV) .... '51 '75 C.614 B.S. L.616 J.D. [Schnetzler&H.]
Schnetzler, Nancy J., (BV) .... '52 '82 C.846 B.S. L.616 J.D. [Schnetzler&H.]
Schnetzler & Herring, A Professional Corporation, (BV) .... 3109 Carlton Way
Schooler, Don A. .... '67 '93 C.612 B.A. L.623 J.D. Dept. of Labor
Schovanec, Philip A. .... '68 '94 C.612 B.S. L.623 J.D. [Moricoli,H.&C.]
Schovanec, Sandra Leah, (AV) .... '59 '84 C.663 B.S. L.623 J.D. [Phillips M.M.&M.]
Schrameck, Marilyn Kay .... '50 '74 C&L.623 B.A., J.D. 12912 Fox Forest Circle
Schrempp, Albert F. .... '21 '57 C.623 B.S. L.616 J.D. 2938 Carlton Way‡
Schumacher, James S. '32 '57 C&L.793 B.A., LL.B.
(adm. in SD; not adm. in OK) 409 N.W. 46th St.‡
Schurr, Thomas R. .... '63 '96 C.902 B.A. L.623 J.D. 2901 N. Classen Boulevard
Schuster, E. Elaine, (BV) .... '36 '68 C.822 B.A. L.623 J.D. [E.E.Schuster]
Schuster, E. Elaine, P.C., (BV) .... 515 NW 13th Street
Schwabe, G. Blaine, III, (AV) .... '47 '74 C&L.623 B.B.A., J.D. [Mock,S.W.E.R.&B.]
Schwartz, Andrew D., (CV) .... '68 '94 C.846 B.S. L.862 J.D. [A Britton,R.&G.]
Schwartz, Debra .... '58 '99 C.623 B.L.S. L.615 J.D. Atty. Gen. Off.
Schwartz, Frederic S. '51 '76 C.813 B.S. L.309 J.D.
(adm. in CA; not adm. in OK) Prof. of Law, Oklahoma City Univ. Sch. of Law
Scimeca, James A., (AV) .... '60 '84 C&L.623 B.A., J.D. [Miller D.]
Scivally, Kristie D. .... '67 '92 C.621 B.S. L.623 J.D. 830 N.W. 10th
Scoggins, Linda G., (AV) .... '47 '81 C&L.623 B.A., J.D. [Scoggins&C.]

Scoggins & Cross, PLLC, (AV)
3100 City Place, 204 N. Robinson, 73102
Telephone: 405-239-4300 Fax: 405-239-4305
URL: http://www.okhealthlawyer.com
Members of Firm: Linda G. Scoggins; Laura L. Cross. Associates: Heather M. Poole; Arlene M. Randall; Aimée D. M. Salalati.
Civil Litigation, Healthcare Law, Employment Law, Administrative Law, Regulatory Law, Employment Litigation, Bioethics, General Corporate Law, Mergers and Acquisitions, Guardianship, Elder Law.
See Professional Biographies, OKLAHOMA CITY, OKLAHOMA

Scott, Dennis L. .... '49 '80 C.612 B.A. L.425 J.D. Okla. City Police Dept.
Scott, Jennifer B. .... '77 '03 C&L.623 B.A., J.D. [A Andrews D.]
Scott, Lawrence R., (BV) .... '56 '81 C.663 B.A. L.623 J.D. [B Haupt B.V.]
Scott, Mary B. .... '60 '88 C.612 B.S.B.A. L.615 J.D. [A Abowitz,T.&D.]
Scott, Paul A., (BV) .... '56 '87 C&L.623 B.S.Ed., J.D. [P.A.Scott]
Scott, Tamar Graham '57 '84 C&L.623 B.A., J.D.
Dep. Gen. Coun., Okla. Dept. of Transp.
Scott, Paul A., P.C., (BV) .... 7301 North Broadway, Suite 226
Seale, Sandi S. .... '64 '94 C.1012 B.S. L.615 J.D. [Seale]
Seale Law Office .... 2525 N.W. Expwy., Ste. 330
Seals, Ralph E., Jr., (AV) .... '49 '75 C.612 B.S. L.623 J.D. [Hall,E.H.G.G.&N.]
Seamans, Susan G., (AV) '48 '75 C.788 A.B. L.623 J.D.
Assoc. Gen. Coun., University of Oklahoma Health Sciences Center
Sears, Philip B., (AV) .... '48 '77 C.645 B.S. L.616 J.D. [McKinney&S.]
Sears, Ryan W. .... '78 '04 C&L.623 B.A., J.D. [A Mahaffey&G.]
Secrest, Mark Christopher .... '55 '84 C&L.862 B.S., J.D. OK Dept. of Mines
Seitsinger, Daniel W. .... '36 '66 C.614 B.S. L.623 J.D. Okla. Nat. Gas Co.
Seitsinger, Mark Wendell .... '61 '87 C.623 B.A. L.616 J.D. 409 Brookside Terr.★
Self, Anna L. .... '61 '92 C.621 B.S. L.623 J.D. [A.Self]
Self, James F., Jr., (BV) .... '55 '81 C.36 B.S. L.862 J.D. [J.F.Self,Jr.&Assoc.]
Self, Shannon T., (AV) .... '56 '84 C.623 B.B.A. L.597 J.D. [Commercial]
Self, Anna .... 5350 S. Western, Ste. 101
Self, James F., Jr., & Assocs., Inc., The Law Office of, (BV) .... 8720 S. Pennsylvania
Selph, Harry H., II, (AV) .... '42 '70 C.612 B.S. L.623 J.D. [Fellers,S.B.B.&T.]
Selvidge, Mark F., (AV) .... '47 '73 C&L.623 B.A., J.D. [Kutak R.]
Semtner, Bernard L., III .... '51 '75 C.623 B.A. L.616 J.D. Pres., Semco Inc.
Sengel, Randal A., (AV) .... '48 '86 C&L.623 B.A., J.D. U.S. Atty. Off.
Sepkowitz, Jerome S., (AV) .... '47 '73 C&L.623 B.A., J.D. [Derryberry,Q.S.&N.]
Sewell, Frank R. .... '66 '91 C.623 B.A. L.615 J.D. Jud. Asst., Supm. Ct.
Sewell, Kay D., (AV) .... '59 '84 C.911 B.A. L.623 J.D. Asst. U.S. Atty.
Sewell, Randall L., (AV) .... '59 '84 C&L.623 B.A., J.D. [Short W.M.&B.]
Sewell, Scott W., (AV) .... '56 '82 C.612 B.S. L.623 J.D. [McAfee&T.]
Sewell, Sheila J., (AV) .... '54 '79 C&L.623 B.A., J.D. Trial Ct. Admr.
Sexson, Charles B. .... '78 '03 C.347 B.S. L.623 J.D. [A Lamun,M.C.&D.]
Sexton, T. Grant, Jr. .... '79 '04 C.16 B.A. L.615 J.D. [A Smith R.S.&E.]
Shadid, Chas. A. '29 '52 C.616 B.S. L.623 LL.B.
222 Victoria Bldg. 1901 Classen Blvd.
Shadid, Danny K., (AV) .... '53 '79 C.623 B.A. L.616 J.D. 6307 Waterford Blvd., Ste. 133
Shadid, Ellen Darlene ...... '44 '91 C.613 B.S. L.623 J.D. Legal Aid of Western Okla., Inc.
Shanahan, Richard A. .... '31 '68 C.612 B.S.I.E. L.616 J.D. 1208 W. Britton Rd.
Shandy, Donald K., (AV) .... '60 '85 C&L.623 B.A., J.D. Kerr-McGee Corporation
Shanker, Jay '53 '81 C.976 B.A. L.569 J.D.
(adm. in CA; not adm. in OK) [B McAfee&T.]

Shannonhouse, Joseph G., IV, (AV) '45 '70 C.1147 B.S. L.623 J.D. BB
500 North Walker, Suite C-100, 73102
Telephone: 405-415-1700 Fax: 405-415-1703
Email: JS@Shannonhouselaw.com URL: http://www.lawyers.com/shannonhouse
Tax Controversies, Tax Litigation, Criminal Taxation, Taxation, White Collar Criminal Defense, Criminal Trial Practice - Federal.
See Professional Biographies, OKLAHOMA CITY, OKLAHOMA

Shapard, Edwin J., (AV) .... '40 '65 C.612 B.A. L.623 J.D. [Shapard&S.]
Shapard & Shapard, Inc., (AV) .... 820 NE 63rd St.
Sharpe, Carla J., (AV) .... '59 '84 C&L.623 B.S.E., J.D. Enogex Inc.
Sharpe, G. Calvin, (BV) .... '60 '86 C&L.623 B.B.A., J.D. [Pierce C.H.B.&G.]
Sharrock, Elizabeth R. .... '71 '97 C&L.623 B.A., J.D. Asst. Atty. Gen.
Sharrock, James W., (AV) .... '47 '73 C&L.623 B.A., J.D. [McAfee&T.]
Shaw, Dirk M., (AV) .... '53 '82 C&L.616 B.S., J.D. [D.M.Shaw]
Shaw, James C., (AV) .... '49 '78 C.673 B.S. L.790 J.D. [Miller D.]
Shaw, Judy L., Attorney at Law, (BV) .... '49 '78 C&L.623 B.A., J.D. P.O. Box 22306
Shaw, Leo H. .... '34 '64 C.614 B.A. L.616 LL.B. 2632 Guilford Lane
Shaw, Dirk M., Inc., (AV) .... 1001 N.W. 63rd Street, Suite 290
Shawareb, Tammer .... '— '02 C.612 L.615 J.D. [A Kinsey&Assoc.]
Shear, David M., (AV) '59 '85 C.1036 B.A. L.94 J.D.
V.P., Gen. Coun., LSB Indus., Inc.
Shear, Heidi Brown .... '58 '84 C.860 B.A. L.94 J.D. LSB Industries, Inc.
Shears, John L. .... '75 '01 C.612 B.A. L.623 J.D. [A Pierce C.H.B.&G.]
Sheets, Robert N., (AV) .... '54 '79 C.910 A.B. L.616 J.D. [Phillips M.M.&M.]
Shelton, Douglas J., (AV) .... '56 '81 C&L.623 B.A., J.D. [Shelton]
Shelton, Tami J. .... '68 '94 C.618 B.S. L.623 J.D. [Lawson,K.&S.]

Shelton Law Group, (AV) BB
7701 S. Western Avenue, Suite 201, 73139
Telephone: 405-605-8800 Fax: 405-601-0677
Email: dshelton@sheltonlawok.com URL: http://www.okshelton.com
(This Listing Continued)

Shelton Law Group (Continued)
Member of Firm: Douglas J. Shelton. Associates: M. Daniel Weitman; Melissa Shelton Burget; Elizabeth A. Kerr.
Litigation and Trial Practice, Personal Injury, Insurance Law, Insurance Defense, Construction Defects, Mold Litigation, Consumer Law, Employment Law, Real Estate, Trusts and Estates.
See Professional Biographies, OKLAHOMA CITY, OKLAHOMA

Shepherd, James W. .... '75 '03 C.623 B.A. L.615 J.D. [A Mulinix O.H.A.&L.]
Sherman, Stephen A., (AV) ...... '53 '81 C.477 B.G.S. L.770 J.D. [S.A.Sherman&Assoc.]

Sherman, Stephen A., & Associates, (AV) BB
117 Park Avenue Building, Fourth Floor, 73102
Telephone: 405-235-0707 Fax: 405-235-0712
Email: ssherman@shermanfirm.com
Stephen A. Sherman.
General Civil Practice, Real Estate, Landlord-Tenant, Commercial, Corporate, Partnership and Probate Law, Litigation, Business Litigation, Contracts.
Representative Clients: CMH Parks, Inc.; Gungall Exploration; Hogan Property Corp.; Irish Realty Corp.; Kaiser-Francis Oil Co.; Price-Edwards; Realtech Development & Construction Co.; Realty Operating Company; B.F. Saul Co.; U.S. Food Service, Inc.; Western Industries, Inc.
See Professional Biographies, OKLAHOMA CITY, OKLAHOMA

Sherrill, Jennifer F. .... '74 '03 C.315 B.A. L.862 J.D. [A Federman&S.]
Sherrod, J. Michael, (BV) .... '54 '86 C&L.623 B.B.A., J.D. [Sherrod]
Sherrod Law Firm, P.C., (BV) .... 10324 Greenbriar Pl., Ste. A
Sherwood, John Charles, (AVⓉ) '58 '84 C.840 B.B.A. L.69 J.D.
(adm. in TX; not adm. in OK) [Federman&S.] (ⓞDallas, TX)
Shields, Susan B., (AV) .... '63 '89 C.813 B.A. L.1068 J.D. [Hartzog C.C.&N.]
Shiles, Jerry E., (AV) .... '— '74 C.549 B.S. L.878 J.D. 3545 N.W. 58th St., Ste. 400
Shinn, Carmelita Reeder .... '57 '83 C&L.629 B.S., J.D. Law Clk., Dist J.
Shinn, Ronald T., Jr. .... '74 '02 C.473 B.A. L.623 J.D. [A McAfee&T.]

Shipley & Kellogg, P.C., (AV)
Two Leadership Square, 211 North Robinson, Suite 1300, 73102-7114 ⊙
Telephone: 405-235-0808 Fax: 405-232-3746
Email: rkellogg@shipleylaw.net
Robert D. Kellogg (Resident).
General Civil Practice in all State and Federal Courts, with emphasis in Environmental Law, Water Rights, Business and Commercial Litigation, Class Actions, Alternative Dispute Resolution and Native American Law.
Reference: Nations Bank.
Tulsa, Oklahoma Office: 1648 South Boston Avenue, Suite 100, 74119-4416. Telephone: 918-582-1720. Facsimile: 918-584-7681. Email: firm@shipleylaw.net
See Professional Biographies, OKLAHOMA CITY, OKLAHOMA

Shirk Work & Robinson, P.C., (AV) BB
15 North Robinson Avenue, Suite 500, 73102
Telephone: 405-236-3571 FAX: 405-236-8028
Email: shirklawfirm@swbell.net
James E. Work. Of Counsel: William J. Robinson; J. Kelly Work.
Municipal Bond, Corporate, Probate, Land Use and Real Property.
Representative Clients: Oklahoma County Finance Authority; Southeastern Oklahoma Industries Authority; Oklahoma City Chamber of Commerce; Weyerhaeuser Co.; Federal Corp.; Little Giant Corp.; Denny's Restaurants; Black-Eyed Pea U.S.A.; AMF Bowling Centers, Inc.; Aviation Title Insurance Co.
See Professional Biographies, OKLAHOMA CITY, OKLAHOMA

Shore, Patrick D., (AV) .... '54 '81 C.623 B.A.J. L.616 J.D. [Derryberry,Q.S.&N.]
Shores, Gary, (BV) .... '31 '60 C&L.623 B.A., LL.B. 500 N.W. 13th St.
Shores, Mark A., (AV) .... '57 '83 C.618 B.S. L.616 J.D. P.O. Box 2955
Short, George F., (AV) .... '27 '50 C.418 L.623 LL.B. [Short W.M.&B.]
Short, Jacqueline M. .... '52 '90 C.1147 B.S. L.623 J.D. 5500 North Western
Short, Roy Benjamin .... '43 '90 C.44 B.S. L.623 J.D. 5500 North Western
Short, Susan A., (AV) .... '53 '85 C&L.623 B.S.N., J.D. [Foliart,H.O.&B.]

Short Wiggins Margo & Butts, (AV)
3100 Oklahoma Tower, 210 Park Avenue, 73102
Telephone: 405-232-1211 Telecopier: 405-235-7025
Email: swmb@swmb.net
Members of Firm: George F. Short; John E. Wiggins; Robert C. Margo; Benjamin J. Butts; Randall L. Sewell; Perry T. Marrs, Jr.; Cynthia L. Sparling. Associates: L. Earl Ogletree; Kevin K. Trout; Geremy A. Rowland; Melissa A. Couch; W. Todd Blasdel; Lane O. Krieger.
General Civil Litigation Practice, Medical Liability, Products Liability, Employment Law, Appellate Practice. Trial of Cases in all Courts in Oklahoma.
Representative Clients: CIGNA Companies; Johnson & Johnson; Kemper Group Insurance Cos.; Liberty Mutual Insurance Co.; Physicians Liability Insurance Co.
See Professional Biographies, OKLAHOMA CITY, OKLAHOMA

Shrader, Glenn J., Jr. .... '52 '78 C.473 A.B. L.616 J.D. [B Walker&W.]
Shreffler, S. Gordon .... '21 '44 C&L.623 B.S., LL.B. P.O. Box 12610
Shropshire, Kenneth Leroy .... '55 '82 C.813 A.B. L.178 J.D. 101 N. Robinson, Ste. 1300
Shumake, David S., (BV) .... '25 '50 C.616 L.623 LL.B. [Shumake&H.]
Shumake & Hilbert, (BV) .... P.O. Box 1237
Siderias, James M. .... '73 '99 C.613 B.A. L.623 J.D. [A Durbin,L.&B.]
Siegel, Travis K. .... '77 '02 C.616 B.S. L.623 J.D. [A Rife&W.]
Simmons, Teresa .... '50 '89 C.612 B.A. L.616 J.D. [T.Simmons]
Simmons, Teresa, PC, Law Office of .... 1308 S.W. 110th Place
Simms, Barry R. .... '31 '59 C&L.623 B.B.A., LL.B. 4141 N.W. Expressway
Simons, Charles T. .... '72 '98 C.437 B.A. L.615 J.D. 4323 NW 63rd St.
Simpson, John L. '45 '73 C&L.846 B.A., J.D.
(adm. in TX; not adm. in OK) I.R.S.
Simpson, Robert C., Jr. .... '72 '01 C.767 B.A. L.623 J.D. [A Bullard&H.]
Sine, Amy J., (AV) .... '62 '88 C.623 B.A. L.880 J.D. [Hartzog C.C.&N.]
Singletary, Robert D. '— '01
C.839 B.B.A. L.862 J.D. Environ. Atty., OK Dept. of Environ. Quality
Singleton, John D., (AV) .... '52 '77 C.612 B.S. L.616 J.D. [B J.P.Linn]

Sisson, B. David
(See Norman)

Skarky, Earl A., (AV) .... '44 '72 C&L.623 B.B.A., J.D. [Crowe&D.]
Slama, Jo Lynn, (AV) .... '61 '90 C.546 B.S. L.616 J.D. [Tawwater&S.]
Slane, David .... '67 '93 C.1147 B.A. L.615 J.D. [A Kinsey&Assoc.]
Slater, Carol Dennis .... '53 '89 C.1147 B.A. L.616 J.D. State Election Bd.‡

Slater, Lee, (AV) '43 '88 C.623 B.B.A. L.616 J.D.
2601 Northwest Expressway, Suite 210-West, P.O. Box 14785, 73113-0785
Telephone: 405-608-0914 Fax: 405-608-0907
Email: leeslater@coxinet.net URL: http://www.lawyers.com/leeslater
General Practice.
See Professional Biographies, OKLAHOMA CITY, OKLAHOMA

Slayton, James A., (AV) .... '53 '87 C.623 B.B.A. L.616 J.D. [J.A.Slayton]
Slayton, James A., P.C., (AV) .... 4808 North Classen
Sleeper, Gary W., (BV) '45 '75
C.623 B.S. L.616 J.D. Managing Atty., Oklahoma State Ins.

Sloan, Rose M. J., (AV) '58 '83
C.612 B.A. L.623 J.D. Sr. Staff. Atty., Hartford Fire Insurance Co.
Sloop, Everett E. ... '24 '49 L.623 LL.B. 3301 Brookhollow Road‡
Smalley, Richard E., (AV) ... '48 '88 C.623 B.A. L.616 J.D. [Smalley&Assoc.]
Smalley & Associates, P.C., (AV) ... 620 North Robinson Avenue, Suite 207
Smethers, Jess J., (BV) ... '51 '79 C.612 B.S. L.616 J.D. 8611 S. Camay St.
Smith, Benjamin E. ... '22 '56 C.612 B.A. L.615 J.D. 2748 Sw 44th‡
Smith, Bill ... '60 '93 C.339 B.A. L.623 J.D. 925 North West Sixth Street
Smith, Bob A. ... '30 '60 C.612 B.A. L.616 J.D. [Smith&S.]
Smith, Carl Michael, (AV) ... '44 '69 C&L.623 B.A., J.D. Asst. Secy. for Fossil Energy
Smith, Charles C., (BV) ... '49 '75 C.623 B.A. L.616 J.D. Chesapeake Energy Corp.
Smith, Curtis L., (AV) ... '51 '76 C&L.623 B.A., J.D. [Smith R.S.&E.]
Smith, Derek B., (CV) ... '71 '98 C.839 B.B.A. L.616 J.D. [D.B.Smith]
Smith, Donald J., (AV) ... '33 '69 C&L.616 B.S., J.D. [Smith&W.]
Smith, Fern L., (AV) ... '44 '82 C.617 B.S. L.616 J.D. Asst. Dist. Atty.
Smith, Gomer, Jr., (AV) ... '19 '42 C&L.623 B.A., LL.B. 9636 N. May Avenue
Smith, Gretchen Zumwalt ... '61 '86 C&L.623 B.A., J.D. 4545 N. Lincoln Blvd., Ste. 260
Smith, John Tolleson ... '18 '54 C.614 B.S. L.616 J.D. Kerr-McGee Corp.
Smith, Joshua D. ... '80 '05 C&L.623 B.A., J.D. [🄰 McAfee&T.]
Smith, Lesley Dione ... '58 '83 C&L.623 B.A., J.D. [Smith&S.]
Smith, Linda McCarrell '— '91
C.614 B.A. L.616 J.D. V.P. & Coun., Bank of Oklahoma, N.A.
Smith, Mary Margaret ... '48 '81 C.612 B.A. L.623 J.D. 210 Park Ave., Ste. 400
Smith, Michael E., (AV) ... '46 '75 C.870 B.S. L.623 J.D. [Hall,E.H.G.G.&N.]
Smith, Michael E., (AV) ... '50 '78 C.623 B.A. L.616 J.D. [Holloway,D.&B.]
Smith, Michael Hoyt ... '68 '01 C.613 B.S. L.623 J.D. [🄰 Dunlap,C.&R.] (See Pat. Sect.)
Smith, Ralph R. ... '22 '50 C&L.623 LL.B. 2348 N.W. 58th St.‡
Smith, Richard C., (BV) ... '55 '82 C.1329 B.A. L.616 J.D. City Atty.
Smith, Robert B., (BV) ... '42 '71 C.1147 B.A. L.616 J.D. 105 N. Hudson Ave.
Smith, Robert C., Jr., (AV) ... '50 '80 C.577 B.S. L.616 J.D. [Monnet,H.B.T.&E.]
Smith, Robert Dean ... '50 '75 C.1147 B.S. L.616 J.D. P.O. Box 2286
Smith, Robt. H. ... '30 '64 C&L.616 B.S., LL.B. 5224 S. Western Ave.
Smith, Sherry L., (AV) ... '56 '84 C.616 B.A. L.623 J.D. [Welch&S.]
Smith, Spencer F. ... '71 '98 C.623 B.A. L.846 J.D. [🄰 McAfee&T.]
Smith, Steven Scott, (BV) ... '59 '84 C.234 B.A. L.616 J.D. [🄰 Stipe,H.L.U.E.&B.]
Smith, T. Matthew ... '78 '05 C&L.623 B.A., J.D. [🄰 Mulinix O.H.A.&L.]
Smith, Thomas C., Jr. ... '17 '46 C.838 B.A. L.623 LL.B. Dist. J.
Smith, Travis Calvin ... '53 '79 C&L.623 B.A., J.D. 2901 Classen Blvd.
Smith, Derek B., P.C., (CV) ... 2601 N.W. Expwy., 601 Oil Ctr. W.

Smith Rhodes Stewart & Elder, P.L.L.C., (AV)
Robinson Renaissance, Suite 820, 119 North Robinson, 73102
Telephone: 405-236-8282 Fax: 405-236-2828
Email: lawyers@srselaw.com URL: http://www.srselaw.com
Curtis L. Smith; Scott M. Rhodes; John Dexter Marble; James W. Dobbs;—Kelly L. Whitworth; T. Grant Sexton, Jr.; Susan F. Kane. Of Counsel: A. Thomas Elder, Jr.; David C. Johnston, Jr.; Michael C. Stewart.
Litigation in State and Federal Courts. Products Liability, Negligence, Aircraft Accident, Environmental, Insurance Law and Coverage, Asbestos Litigation, Employment Law, Commercial Transactions, Business and Corporate Law, Bankruptcy, Asset Protection, Entertainment Law, Mediation Services.
See Professional Biographies, OKLAHOMA CITY, OKLAHOMA

Smith, Shew, Scrivner, Corbin & Watts, (AV)
6520 N. Western Ave. (⊙Ada, Tishomingo)
Smith & Smith ... 4208 S. Goff Ave.
Smith & Warren, (AV) ... 3131 N.W. 63rd Street
Snapp, Maribeth D., (AV) '56 '79
C.845 B.B.A. L.616 J.D. Dep. Gen. Coun., Okla. Corp. Comm.

Sneed Lang, P.C.
(See Tulsa)

Snider, Scott F., (BV) '62 '87 C&L.623 B.B.A., J.D.
V.P. & Asst. Claims Mgr., Reserve Natl. Ins. Co.
Snow, Wayne B. ... '20 '47 C&L.623 B.A., LL.B. Sr. Supm. Ct. Ref.
Snyder, Charles Edward, (BV) '56 '82
C.999 B.A. L.616 J.D. Atty., U.S. Trustee Off., Dept. of Jus.
Snyder, Riki R., (BV) ... '59 '84 C.663 B.S. L.623 J.D. [Pritchett&S.]
Snyder, Steven K., (BV) ... '57 '82 C&L.623 B.A., J.D. Asst. Atty. Gen.
Sobral, Courtenay Parrott ... '— '96 C&L.623 B.A., J.D. 11816 Blue Sage Rd.
Sokolosky, Jerry D., (AV) ... '37 '62 C&L.623 B.B.A., LL.B. [Abel,M.S.M.&K.]
Solomon, Stephen G., (AV) ... '48 '77 C.623 B.B.A. L.616 J.D. [Derryberry,Q.S.&N.]
Sonne, W. Blake, Jr. ... '77 '04 C.1266 B.S. L.623 J.D. [🄰 McAfee&T.]
Sopher, John P. ... '41 '72 C.1147 B.S. L.616 J.D. 4513 N. Classen Blvd.
Sorenson, Brett B. ... '69 '95 C&L.623 B.B.A., J.D. 6005 N. Covington Ln.
Sorocco, Douglas J. ... '70 '96 C.108 B.S. L.201 J.D. [Dunlap,C.&R.] (See Pat. Sect.)
Southwick, Jeffrey P., (CV) ... '51 '89 C.559 B.A. L.616 J.D. P.O. Box 1131
Spady, Kimberlee Taggart, (BV) ... '68 '93 C.612 B.S. L.615 J.D. [🄰 Anderson,M.&O.]

Sparks, Leslie Gene '— '01 C.1147 M.A.Ed. L.616 J.D.
3555 N.W. 58th Street, Suite 510, 73112
Telephone: 405-946-8022 Fax: 405-942-8362
URL: http://www.lawyers.com/lessparks
Appellate Practice, Family Law, Divorce, Child Custody, Spousal Support, Guardianship, Adoption Law, Contracts.
See Professional Biographies, OKLAHOMA CITY, OKLAHOMA

Sparling, Cynthia L., (AV) ... '47 '78 C.802 B.A. L.616 J.D. [Short W.M.&B.]
Spears, Kenneth L., (AV) ... '41 '71 C.1147 B.S. L.623 J.D. [K.L.Spears]
Spears, Larry M., (AV) ... '47 '73 C.1147 B.A. L.616 J.D. [Spears]
Spears, Kenneth L., P.C., (AV) ... P.O. Box 687
Spears Law Firm, The, (AV) ... 501 Northwest Thirteenth
Specht, Randolph Stephen '51 '81
C.612 B.S. L.623 J.D. Appl. Admin. Law J., State Corp. Comm.
Speck, Michael W. ... '68 '00 C.623 B.A. L.801 J.D. 317 N.W. 12th

Speck Philbin Attorneys, A Professional Corporation, (AV)
204 North Robinson, Suite 800, 73102-6885
Telephone: 405-235-1603 Fax: 405-232-0587
Email: SPTFL1@aol.com
Arnold T. Fleig (1902-1993); John K. Speck (1904-1983); Joseph A. Elbow (1915-2001); John A. Philbin; Charles B. Lutz, Jr.; Jimanne Harris Mays; Patricia E. Mahoney.
General Civil Practice in all State and Federal Courts. Corporation, Taxation, Probate, Estate Planning, Commercial, Real Estate, Employee Benefits Law, ERISA, Wills and Trusts, Litigation, Health Law.
Representative Clients: First Bank of Apache, Oklahoma; National Car Rental of Oklahoma City; Broce Construction Co., Inc.; Morris Investment Co.; W & W Steel Co.; B.C. Clark, Inc.; The Oklahoma Medical Research Foundation; Radiology Associates, Inc.; Radiology Group, Inc.; Anadarko Publishing Co.
See Professional Biographies, OKLAHOMA CITY, OKLAHOMA

Spencer, Garold L. ... '47 '90 C&L.616 M.S., J.D. City Police Dept.
Spencer, Mark D., (AV) ... '59 '87 C.861 B.A. L.365 J.D. [McAfee&T.]
Spencer, Melvin J., (BV) ... '23 '50 C&L.477 A.B., J.D. 5910 N. Shawnee
Spencer, Sarah Carmack, (BV) ... '49 '78 C.623 B.A. L.616 J.D. 5623 N.Western Ave.
Spiropoulos, Andrew C. '62 '88 C.118 B.A. L.145 J.D.
(adm. in IL; not adm. in OK) Prof. of Law, Oklahoma City Univ. Sch. of Law
Spiropoulos, Ellen K., (BV) ... '64 '94 C.118 B.A. L.597 J.D. [🄱 Phillips M.M.M.&M.]
Spivey, Stacey D., (BV) ... '70 '97 C&L.623 B.A., J.D. [🄰 Crowe&D.]
Spoo, Robert ... '57 '01 C.399 B.A. L.976 J.D. [🄰 Doerner,S.D.&A.] ⊙
Spradling, T. Scott, (AV) ... '48 '75 C.893 B.A. L.623 J.D. [Spradling,K.&M.]

Spradling, Kennedy & McPhail, L.L.P., (AV)
The Tower, 1601 NW Expressway, Suite 1750, 73118
Telephone: 405-418-2700 Facsimile: 405-418-2705
Email: firm@spradlinglaw.com
Members of Firm: T. Scott Spradling; David D. Kennedy; Mark R. McPhail.
General Civil Practice in all State and Federal Courts. Administrative, Aviation, Banking, Construction, Corporate Law, Business Organization, Employment, Health Care, Insurance, Lending, Product Liability, Real Estate, and Zoning Law.
See Professional Biographies, OKLAHOMA CITY, OKLAHOMA

Staats, Marilyn Kay ... '48 '73 C.612 B.S. L.615 J.D. Legal Aid of Western Okla.
Stakem, Ronald E., (AV) ... '47 '75 C.309 B.A. L.623 J.D. [Clark,S.W.&P.]
Stallings, Abbey B. ... '77 '04 C&L.623 B.A., J.D. [🄰 McAfee&T.]
Stallings, Susan Camille, (BV) ... '60 '91 C.612 B.A. L.623 J.D. Asst. Dist. Atty.
Stallsworth, Bruce A. '52 '81 C.375 B.A. L.378 J.D.
(adm. in KS; not adm. in OK) Dir., Govt. & Pub. Affs., Phillips Petroleum Co.
Standard, Matthew L., (AV) ... '— '86 C&L.623 B.B.A., J.D. [Kirk&C.]
Stanfield, E. Neil ... '37 '62 C&L.623 B.B.A., LL.B. Pres., The Stanfield Co.
Stanford, A. Ainslie, II ... '75 '00 C&L.623 B.B.A., J.D. [🄰 Day,E.P.&C.]
Stanley, Brian J., (AV) '54 '85 C.623 B.A. L.616 J.D.
V.P. & Gen. Coun., Hefner Company, Inc., The
Stanley, Julie D. ... '72 '00 C&L.623 B.B.A., J.D. 12204 Hickory Creek Boulevard
Stanton, Bryan E. ... '75 '01 C.623 B.A. L.862 J.D. [🄰 Johnson&H.]
Stark, Stephen L., (AV) ... '46 '77 C&L.623 B.B.A., J.D. [Dimick,G.B.&S.]
Starke, Henry C. ... '17 '69 C.476 B.S.B.A. L.616 J.D. 3106 N.W. 63rd‡
Steece, Thomas J., (BV) ... '58 '85 C.1247 B.A. L.616 J.D. Sr. Partner, OK Legal Servs.
Steele, Amy R. ... '78 '04 C.1271 B.A. L.623 J.D. [🄰 Pierce C.H.B.&G.]
Stein, Christopher T. ... '64 '00 C.651 B.S. L.615 J.D. [🄰 Kline,K.E.&B.]
Stein, Rance G., (AV) ... '61 '88 C.618 B.S. L.623 J.D. 2200 N.W. 50th St., Ste. 240
Steinhorn, Irwin H., (AV) ... '40 '64 C&L.846 B.B.A., LL.B. [Conner&W.]
Stell, C. Robert, (AV) ... '68 '94 C.612 B.S. L.623 J.D. [Crowe&D.]
Stephens, L. Michelle ... '66 '92 C.1315 B.S. L.623 J.D. Asst. Atty. Gen.
Stephens, Stephen R., (AV) ... '58 '83 C.612 B.S. L.623 J.D. [Fellers,S.B.B.&T.]
Sterling, Timothy F. ... '68 '96 C.346 B.S. L.862 J.D. Midland Financial Co.
Stevens, James D. '45 '69 C&L.502 B.S., J.D.
Dep. Gen. Coun., Okla. Employ. Sec. Comm.
Stevenson, Coree L. ... '73 '99 C.612 B.A. L.616 J.D. [Ryan,W.&C.]
Stewart, David V. ... '69 '01 C&L.623 B.A., J.D. [🄰 Crowe&D.]
Stewart, Janet Elizabeth ... '60 '86 C&L.623 B.A., J.D. Staff Atty., Dept. of Vet. Affairs
Stewart, Janet Marie ... '69 '94 C.622 B.S. L.862 J.D. Dir. Legal Servs.
Stewart, Leasa M., (AV) ... '66 '91 C.623 B.S. L.276 J.D. [Gable&G.]
Stewart, Michael C., (AV) ... '38 '64 C&L.623 B.S., LL.B. [🄱 Smith R.S.&E.]
Stewart, Michael M., (AV) ... '47 '77 C.976 B.A. L.623 J.D. [Crowe&D.]
Stewart, Robert D., Jr. ... '— '72 C&L.623 B.A., J.D. [🄱 Rainey,R.R.&B.]
Stewart, Rodney D., (AV) ... '68 '93 C.1300 B.B.A. L.623 J.D. [Durbin,L.&B.]
Stiner, John D., (AV) ... '71 '98 C.276 B.S.F.S. L.623 J.D. [🄰 McAfee&T.]
Stinson, C. David, (AV) ... '46 '76 C.612 B.A. [McAfee&T.]
Stipe, Amy M., (AV) ... '73 '99 C&L.623 B.A., J.D. [🄰 Gable&G.]
Stipe, Gene, (AV) ... '26 '49 C.484 L.623 LL.B. [Stipe,H.L.U.E.&B.] ⊙
Stipe, Jack ... '72 '99 C&L.623 B.A., J.D. [🄰 Stipe,H.L.U.E.&B.]

Stipe, Harper, Laizure, Uselton, Edwards & Belote, LLP, (AV)
4111 North Lincoln Boulevard, P.O. Box 53567, 73105 ⊙
Telephone: 405-524-2268 Fax: 405-525-3231
Email: jstipe@stipelawokc.com URL: http://www.stipelaw.com
Members of Firm: Gene Stipe; James A. Belote. Resident Associates: Steven Scott Smith; Jack Stipe.
General Civil and Criminal Trial Practice. Personal Injury, Workers Compensation, Probate, Real Estate, Federal Employers Liability, Medical Malpractice and Products Liability Law.
McAlester, Oklahoma Office: 343 East Carl Albert Parkway. Telephone: 918-423-0421.
Muskogee, Oklahoma Office: 384 S. 33rd St. Telephone: 918-683-5050. Telefax: 918-682-5700.
Tulsa, Oklahoma Office: 2417 E. Skelly Drive. Telephone: 918-749-0749.
See Professional Biographies, OKLAHOMA CITY, OKLAHOMA

Stokes, Terry, (AV) ... '59 '85 C.1315 B.S. L.616 J.D. [Fuller,T.P.&S.]
Stone, Jacqueline G. ... '64 '90 C&L.623 B.A., J.D. 4601 N. Portland Ave.
Stone, Jerry L., (AV) ... '55 '82 C&L.623 B.A., J.D. Gen. Coun., Co. Treas.
Stone, Kenneth C., Jr. ... '54 '88 C.612 B.S. L.616 J.D. State Conserv. Dist.
Stone, Whitney G. ... '77 '04 C.882 B.A. L.623 J.D. 100 North Broadway, Suite 1700
Stonecipher, Mark K., (AV) ... '57 '83 C.616 B.S. L.623 J.D. [Fellers,S.B.B.&T.]
Stoner, Daniel Justus ... '69 '96 C&L.623 B.B.A., J.D. 5350 S. Western Ave., Ste. 606
Stoner, Kenneth Morgan ... '68 '01 C.618 B.S. L.623 J.D. Co. Dist. Atty. Off.
Stong, Roger A., (AV) ... '62 '86 C.893 B.A. L.1119 J.D. [Crowe&D.]
Storm, Clifton E., Jr. '21 '48 C.846 L.69 LL.B.
(adm. in TX; not adm. in OK) 4997 N.W. 30th Pl.‡
Stormont, Robert, (BV) ... '41 '66 C.612 B.S. L.623 J.D. 912 S.W. 50th St.
Story, D. Craig, (AV) ... '55 '80 C.228 A.B. L.623 J.D. [🄱 Phillips M.M.M.&M.]
Stout, Lu Ann, (AV) ... '57 '87 C&L.623 B.A., J.D. [🄰 Holloway,D.&B.]
Stout, R. Mark '59 '89 C.623 B.B.A. L.616 J.D.
Mgr., Land & Mktg., Rio Algom Mining Corporation
Stout, William H. ... '63 '92 C.623 B.A. L.615 J.D. 233 W. Park
Strasner, Stuart B. ... '29 '54 C.639 A.B. L.623 LL.B. P.O. Box 54887
Stratton, H. Duane, (AV) ... '24 '48 C.612 L.623 LL.B. 11800 Camelot Dr.‡
Stratton, Stephen L., (AV) ... '47 '78 C.378 B.S. L.616 J.D. [S.L.Stratton]
Stratton, Stephen L., P.C., (AV) ... 4101 Parimeter Center Drive Suite 110
Strawn, James R. '56 '81 C.612 B.A. L.862 J.D.
Assoc. Gen. Coun., Devon Energy Corp.
Street, John G. ... '23 '52 C.616 B.A. L.615 LL.B. 4317 Tamarisk
Stricklin, G. Gail ... '55 '79 C.298 B.A. L.862 J.D. FDIC
Stringer, N. Martin, (AV) ... '40 '64 C&L.623 B.S., LL.B. [McKinney&S.]
Strong, Don S., (AV) ... '47 '90 C&L.623 B.A., J.D. [Strong,M.&Assoc.]

Strong, Martin & Associates, P.L.L.C., (AV)
A Professional Limited Liability Company
Attorneys and Counselors at Law
2700 First National Center, 120 North Robinson, 73102
Telephone: 405-604-7500 Fax: 405-604-7503 Toll Free: 1-866-859-7500
Email: info@strongmartin.com URL: http://www.strongmartin.com
Don S. Strong; G. Stephen Martin, II.

(This Listing Continued)

Strong, Martin & Associates, P.L.L.C. (Continued)

Nursing Home, Wrongful Death, Pharmaceutical and Personal Injury Litigation, Commercial and Insurance Litigation, Products Liability, Consumer, Corporate, Class Action and Multi Plaintiff Litigation and General Civil Litigation, Practice in State and Federal Courts in Oklahoma and other jurisdictions.
Representative Clients: Furnished upon request.
See Professional Biographies, OKLAHOMA CITY, OKLAHOMA

Strubhar, Reta M. Chaney ... '43 '81 L.616 J.D. Appl. Ct. J.
Strubhar, Rustin J., (BV) ... '67 '93 C.613 B.S. L.623 J.D. [Crowe&D.]
Struble, Robert B., (AV) '54 '82
C.612 B.S. L.615 J.D. 211 N. Robinson Avenue, Suite 1200
Stubbs, Charles W. ... '18 '49 C.616 L.623 LL.B. 6115 N. Shawnee‡
Stuhr, Sarah H., (AV) ... '56 '81 C.862 B.A. L.623 J.D. [Monnet,H.B.T.&E.]
Stump, T. Douglas, (AV) '57 '83
C.618 B.A. L.616 J.D. 1900 N.W. Expwy., Ste. 1320 (⊙Tulsa)
Sturm, J. Christopher ... '42 '68 C.902 B.A. L.623 J.D. P.O. Box 20956
Sublett, Scott C., (AV) ... '52 '79 C.174 B.S. L.862 J.D. [[A] Hiltgen&B.]
Suchy, Scott K., (BV) ... '67 '94 C.623 B.A. L.616 J.D. 1319 Classen Dr.
Suenram, Lester L. ... '19 '48 C.614 L.615 Pres., Kiamichi Resources, Inc.
Sullivan, David M. ... '74 '00 C.612 B.S. L.623 J.D. [[A] Crowe&D.] (Pat.)
Sullivan, John G. ... '23 '50 C&L.623 A.B., LL.B. 909 S. Meridian St.
Sullivan, Justin C. ... '73 '00 C.893 B.S. L.228 J.D. [[A] Crowe&D.]
Sullivan, Kelsie M. ... '79 '04 [[A] Edmonds,C.H.G.R.&W.]
Sullivan, Scott Randall, (AV) ... '57 '85 C.623 B.A. L.616 J.D. 300 Northeast First Street
Sullivan, Sheryl S., (BV) ... '50 '75 C.881 A.B. L.623 J.D. [S.S.Sullivan]
Sullivan, William H., (AV) ... '40 '66 C.612 B.A. L.623 J.D. 1901 N. Lincoln Blvd.
Sullivan, Sheryl S., P.C., (BV) ... 117 Park Avenue, 4th Floor
Summars, Paul G., (AV) '57 '82 C&L.623 B.B.A., J.D.
10015 South Pennsylvania, Suite B
Summers, Hardy ... '33 '57 C&L.623 B.A., LL.B. Supm. Ct. Chief Jus.
Summers, Julia Clare ... '64 '93 C&L.623 B.A., J.D. Off. of Co. Pub. Def.
Sund, John W. ... '28 '58 C&L.623 B.B.A., LL.B. 3116 Windsor Terrace
Sureck, Philip ... '10 '33 C&L.623 LL.B. Ret. Adm. Law J., H. E. & W.
Sutter, W. Craig '62 '88 C&L.623 B.B.A., J.D.
Gen. Coun., Mental Health & Substance Abuse Servs.
Suttle, Walter E. ... '— '78 C.616 B.A. L.615 J.D. [Foshee&Y.]
Sutton, Lois Michelle ... '71 '97 C.612 B.S. L.623 J.D. State Dept. of Agric.
Sutton, Wendell Blair ... '61 '86 C.612 B.S. L.623 J.D. Asst. Pub. Def., OK Co. Pub. Def.
Swafford, Cheri K. ... '63 '92 C.614 B.A. L.615 J.D. Superior Ins.
Swan, Sheldon B., (AV) ... '60 '85 C.612 B.S. L.623 J.D. [Dunn,S.&C.]
Swank, James W., Jr., (BV) ... '43 '72 C.623 B.B.A. L.802 J.D. [Bonham&H.]
Swarts, Russell E., Jr. ... '30 '54 C&L.623 B.A., LL.B. 2600 Elmhurst Ave.
Swatek, Wendy S. ... '71 '01 C.586 B.S. L.623 J.D. [[A] Berry&V.]
Swedlow, Leif E. ... '70 '97 C&L.616 B.A., J.D. [[A] Andrews D.]
Swimley, Barbara L., (AV) ... '53 '85 C.608 B.A. L.623 J.D. Supm. Ct.
Swinford, John W., Jr., (AV) ... '44 '69 C.918 B.A. L.623 J.D. [[C] Calvert]
Swinton, Barbara Green ... '60 '91 C.612 B.S. L.1059 J.D. Dist. Ct. J.
Swisher, Arthur Kyle ... '71 '97 C&L.623 B.A., J.D. 330 N.W. 13th St.
Switzer, Regina Ann ... '63 '92 C&L.623 B.A., J.D. P.O. Box 3000
Sykes, Anthony Wade ... '72 '00 C&L.623 B.A., J.D. [[A] Kinsey&Assoc.]
Tack, James D., Jr., (AV) ... '51 '78 C.188 B.S. L.900 J.D. [Robertson&W.]
Tague, Roland, (AV) ... '40 '65 C&L.623 B.B.A., J.D. [[C] Fuller,T.P.&S.]
Tait, Albert Lewis, Jr., (AV) ... '50 '80 C&L.623 B.B.A., J.D. [Fenton,F.S.R.&M.]
Taliaferro, Henry B., Jr. ... '32 '56 C&L.623 B.A., J.D. 1908 Huntington Ave.‡
Talley, Rita Douglas ... '57 '85 C.623 B.A. L.615 J.D. P.O. Box 149
Tapp, George Michael ... '25 '53 C&L.623 B.A., J.D. 4715 Hemlock Lane‡
Tardibono, Timothy Nick '— '01
C.1315 B.S. L.1339 J.D. OK St. Health Dept., Off. of Gen. Coun.
Tarpley, Francis M., (BV) ... '27 '58 C.623 B.B.A. L.616 LL.B. P.O. Box 21555‡
Tate, Jeffrey E., (BV) ... '70 '96 C.612 B.A. L.623 J.D. [[A] Day,E.P.&C.]
Tawwater, Darren M. ... '72 '00 C.840 B.S. L.615 J.D. [[A] Tawwater&S.]
Tawwater, Larry A., (AV) ... '47 '72 C&L.623 B.A., J.D. [Tawwater&S.]

Tawwater & Slama, LLP, (AV)
Suite 1950, One Leadership Square, 211 North Robinson, 73102-7124
Telephone: 405-319-7300 Fax: 405-319-7350
Email: help@tawlaw.com URL: http://www.tawlaw.com
Members of Firm: Larry A. Tawwater; Jo Lynn Slama. Associates: Darren M. Tawwater; Steven R. Davis.
Civil Trial Practice. Negligence, Products Liability, Medical Malpractice, Insurance Bad Faith, Personal Injury, Wrongful Death, HMO Law, Nursing Home Negligence, Automobile Accidents, Construction Injuries, Pharmaceutical Litigation, Mass Torts, Class Action Torts.
See Professional Biographies, OKLAHOMA CITY, OKLAHOMA

Taylor, Barney D., (BV) ... '40 '85 C.619 B.S. L.616 J.D. P.O. Box 891857
Taylor, Floyd W., (BV) ... '43 '68 C&L.623 B.A., J.D. 625 N.W. 13th St.
Taylor, Gregory L. '65 '00 C.82 B.S. L.615 J.D.
V.P. & Gen. Coun., DCA Services, Inc.
Taylor, K. David, (AV) ... '50 '80 C.612 B.S. L.616 J.D. [Behrens,T.W.&C.]
Taylor, Kathryn L., (AV) ... '55 '81 C&L.623 B.A., J.D. Secy., OK Dept. of Com.
Taylor, Michael A., (BV) ... '53 '81 C.1300 B.A. L.623 J.D. 311 N. Harvey Ave.
Taylor, Sam E. ... '30 '54 C.862 B.A. L.623 LL.B. Admn. Law J., U.S. Dept. of Interior
Taylor, Todd, (AV) ... '61 '86 C.622 B.S. L.623 J.D. [Crowe&D.]
Teague, J. Derrick, (AV) ... '67 '93 C.612 B.S. L.616 J.D. [Jennings C.H.&T.]
Teague, William L., (AV) ... '63 '94 C.616 A.B. L.82 J.D. [Crowe&D.]
Tehan, Martha V., (CV) ... '50 '94 C.787 B.A. L.615 J.D. [M.Tehan]
Tehan, Martha, (CV) ... 601 N.W. 13th St.
Temple, Judson L. '46 '74 C.506 B.S. L.508 J.D.
(adm. in MT; not adm. in OK) Prof. of Law, Okla. City Univ. Sch. of Law
Templeton, Michael K., (AV) ... '51 '83 C.502 B.S. L.616 J.D. 12000 N. Century Dr.
Tepera, Steven P. ... '79 '05 C&L.846 B.S., J.D. [[A] Doerner,S.D.&A.] ⊙
Ternes, Mary Ellen, (BV Ⓣ) ... '62 '95 C.880 B.E.Ch.E. L.1243 J.D. [[C] McAfee&T.]
Terry, Douglas A., (BV) ... '67 '93 C.619 B.A. L.623 J.D. [Whitten,N.M.T.&R.]
Terry, Judy Ann ... '69 '93 C.619 B.A. L.623 J.D. Dist. Atty.
Terry, Kathryn D. ... '71 '96 C&L.623 B.A., J.D. [[A] Whitten,N.M.T.&R.]
TeSelle, John ... '22 '51 C.260 B.M.E. L.273 J.D. U.S. Bkrptcy. J.
Thai, Joseph T. ... '— '98 C&L.309 A.B., J.D. [[C] Gable&G.]
Thetford, F. William, (AV) ... '53 '78 C.623 B.A. L.615 J.D. [F.W.Thetford]
Thetford, Rachel K. ... '71 '96 C.623 B.A. L.616 J.D. [F.W.Thetford]
Thetford, F. William, Attorneys at Law, A.P.C., (AV) ... 1319 N. Shartel Ave.
Thiessen, James H. ... '73 '04 C&L.623 B.S., J.D. [[A] Baer,T.C.&C.]
Thom, Michael W., (AV) ... '54 '77 C&L.623 B.S., J.D. [Thom,H.&D.]
Thom, Hendrick & Doak, P.C., (AV) ... 4301 N.W. 63rd St.
Thomas, D. C., Law Firm, (AV) '— '60
C.623 B.S. L.616 J.D. 211 N. Robinson, No. Leadership Sq.
Thomas, David L., (AV) ... '54 '78 C.621 B.A. L.623 J.D. [[C] Bonham&H.]
Thomas, James D., (AV) ... '43 '70 C&L.846 B.A., J.D. [J.D.Thomas]
Thomas, Kyle F., (AV) ... '56 '81 C&L.623 B.B.A., J.D. 2932 N.W. 122nd St., Ste. F
Thomas, Robert J., Jr. ... '72 '97 C.934 B.S. L.862 J.D. Off. of State Ins. Comr.
Thomas, Sharon T., (AV) ... '54 '81 C.623 B.A. L.23 J.D. [Hall,E.H.G.G.&N.]
Thomas, James D., P.C., (AV) ... 6 N.E. 63rd St., Ste. 410
Thompson, Angela D. ... '71 '96 C&L.623 B.A., J.D. [[A] Caldwell&R.]
Thompson, Carolyn S., (AV) ... '49 '84 C.861 B.S. L.616 J.D. [Horning,G.H.&C.]
Thompson, Edward L. ... '58 '83 C&L.623 B.B.A., J.D. Admin. Law J., Soc. Sec. Admn.
Thompson, Eleanor Joyce Darden, (BV) '50 '74 C.429 B.A. L.329 J.D.
606 N.E. 17th St.
Thompson, J. Matthew, (AV) ... '69 '95 C.197 A.B. L.623 J.D. [Mock,S.W.E.R.&B.]
Thompson, Jacquelyn L. ... '78 '03 C.622 B.B.A. L.623 J.D. [[A] DeVore]
Thompson, Jennifer Lee ... '74 '00 C.802 B.A. L.623 J.D. [[A] Horning,G.H.&C.]
Thompson, John M. ... '72 '98 C&L.623 B.A., J.D. [Crowe&D.]
Thompson, Judith J. ... '52 '80 C.788 A.B. L.623 J.D. Law Clk., U.S. Dist. J.
Thompson, Kathryn Leola ... '54 '94 C.619 B.A. L.862 J.D. 8613 N.W. 116th St.
Thompson, Ralph G. ... '34 '61 C&L.623 B.B.A., LL.B. U.S. Dist. J.
Thompson, Robert C., (BV) ... '47 '75 C.622 B.S. L.623 J.D. [[C] McKinney&S.]
Thompson, Robert E., Jr., (BV) ... '47 '74 C.616 B.A. L.615 J.D. 2833 S.W. 76th
Thompson, Robert W. ... '52 '87 C.612 B.S. L.616 J.D. State Senate
Thompson, Stephen L., (CV) ... '58 '81 C.921 B.S. L.378 J.D. 6437 Brandywine Lane
Thomson, Carolyn H., (AV) '46 '85
C&L.623 B.A., J.D. Asst. Gen. Coun., State Tax Comm.
Threlkeld, C. William, (AV) ... '50 '76 C&L.623 B.S., J.D. [Fenton,F.S.R.&M.]
Thurman, Jeremy A. ... '76 '02 C.621 B.S. L.623 J.D. [[A] Nix&M.]
Thweatt, C. Harold, (AV) ... '10 '33 C&L.623 A.B., LL.B. 20 n. Broadway
Thygesen, Norman D. '46 '80
C.619 B.A. L.616 J.D. State Dept. of Econ. & Community Affairs
Tiller, Julia K. ... '66 '01 C.1147 B.S. L.862 J.D. 4334 N.W. Expressway, Suite 174
Tillotson, Kenneth A. ... '— '01 C.619 B.A. L.623 J.D. [[A] Rainey,R.R.&B.]
Timberlake, Donald J., (AV) ... '41 '66 C.612 B.S. L.623 J.D. [Baer,T.C.&C.]
Timberlake, Donald J., Jr., (AV) ... '67 '93 C.802 B.B.A. L.616 J.D. [Baer,T.C.&C.]
Timberlake, Sarah Jackson, (AV) ... '54 '80 C&L.623 B.A., J.D. [Abowitz,T.&D.]
Timberman, Gena R. ... '74 '99 C.612 B.A. L.623 J.D. 211 N. Robinson, Ste 900
Timmons, Aletia Haynes, (BV) ... '61 '86 C.612 B.S. L.623 J.D. [Timmons&Assoc.]
Timmons, Jeanette C., (AV) ... '— '79 C&L.623 B.B.A., J.D. [Day,E.P.&C.]
Timmons & Associates, L.L.C., (BV) ... 527 N.W. 23rd Street Suite 200
Tindall, Victoria D. ... '56 '97 C&L.623 B.A., J.D. [[A] Pierce C.H.B.&G.]
Tinney, Michael L., (AV) ... '54 '83 C.622 B.A. L.623 J.D. 1001 NW 63rd
Tippens, Terry W., (AV) ... '45 '71 C.612 B.S. L.623 J.D. [Fellers,S.B.B.&T.]
Tipton, Milissa R. ... '69 '04 C.942 B.S. L.615 J.D. [[A] Davis,L.E.]
Tipton, Raymond H., III ... '79 '05 C&L.623 B.S., J.D. [[A] Doerner,S.D.&A.] ⊙
Titterington, Joseph P., (AV) ... '54 '80 C.612 B.S. L.623 J.D. [Dunlap,C.&R.]
Tobias, Haven, (AV) ... '42 '74 C.560 B.A. L.623 J.D. [[A] Pierce C.H.B.&G.]
Todd, Douglas M. ... '67 '93 C.1274 B.S. L.615 J.D. [Phillips M.M.M.&M.]
Todd, Jeff L., (AV) ... '72 '97 C.620 B.A. L.623 J.D. [McAfee&T.]
Todd, Sherry Abbott ... '48 '89 C.618 B.A. L.623 J.D. Asst. Dist. Atty.
Toffoli, Mark B., (AV) ... '54 '82 C.506 B.S. L.615 J.D. [Holbrook&T.]
Tolbert, Mary Hirth, (AV) ... '— '94 C.477 B.A. L.976 J.D. [[A] Crowe&D.]
Tomerlin, Granville, (AV) '12 '38
C.277 B.S. in Ch.E. L.623 LL.B. 3601 N. Classen Boulevard
Tomlinson, Robert D., (AV) ... '46 '75 C.612 B.S. L.616 J.D. [McKinney&S.]
Tompkins, Raymond E., (AV) ... '34 '63 C.612 B.S. L.623 J.D. 1001 N.W. 63rd Street
Towery, Curtis K., (AV) '54 '80
C.859 B.A. L.623 J.D. Asst. Gen. Coun., State Corp. Comm.
Townley, Sam A. ... '35 '63 C.623 L.616 LL.B. 511 Couch Dr., Suite 333
Tracy, Keith D. ... '71 '96 C.612 B.A. L.616 J.D. [[A] McKinney&S.]
Tracy, Ronald R. ... '68 '95 C.112 B.A. L.426 J.D. [[A] Eagleton&N.]
Trautmann, Victor Franz ... '59 '95 C.861 B.S. L.615 J.D. 5500 N. Western Avenue
Travis, Margaret E., (BV) ... '62 '91 C&L.623 B.A., J.D. 500 Colcord Drive

Travis, Mary A., Attorney at Law, (AV) '66 '92 C&L.623 B.A., J.D.
500 Colcord Drive, 73102
Telephone: 405-610-2280 Fax: 405-737-1595
Email: mary@marytravis.com
Bankruptcy, Family Law, Criminal Law and Insurance.
See Professional Biographies, OKLAHOMA CITY, OKLAHOMA

Travis, Rex K., (AV) '38 '62 C&L.623 B.A., LL.B.
500 Colcord Drive, 73102-2279
Telephone: 405-236-5400 Fax: 405-236-5499
Email: RexTravis@TravisLawOffice.com URL: http://www.TravisLawOffice.com
Practice Limited to Plaintiffs Personal Injury and Insurance Litigation, Products Liability and Appellate.
See Professional Biographies, OKLAHOMA CITY, OKLAHOMA

Treadway, Keith R. ... '29 '62 C.347 B.S. L.616 LL.B. 1536 S.W. 44th
Treece, Aimee S. ... '59 '85 C.623 B.A. L.616 J.D. Liberty Mutual Ins. Grp.
Treece, Robert D. ... '57 '90 C.623 B.S. L.616 J.D. 3400 Partridge Rd.
Trimble, Paul D., (AV) ... '62 '89 C&L.623 B.B.A., J.D. [Crowe&D.]
Trotter, Patsy A., (BV) ... '37 '90 C.623 B.S. L.615 J.D. Libr. Admr., Dir. of Research
Trout, Kevin K. ... '69 '94 C&L.623 B.B.A., J.D. [[A] Short W.M.&B.]
Trudgeon, Jon H., (AV) ... '39 '64 C&L.623 B.B.A., LL.B. [Hartzog C.C.&N.]
Truex, Mark E., (AV) ... '60 '86 C.1315 B.S. L.623 J.D. 50 Penn Pl., Ste. 1300
Tubb, James F., (AV) ... '43 '73 C.623 B.A. L.796 J.D. P.O. Box 18431
Tubb, Jeremy, (AV) ... '69 '95 C.183 B.A. L.623 J.D. [Crowe&D.]
Tubb, Jerry, (AV) ... '39 '64 C&L.623 B.A., LL.B. [Fuller,T.P.&S.]
Tuck-Richmond, Doletta ... '66 '91 C.621 B.S. L.623 J.D. Asst. U.S. Atty.
Tudor, Gay Abston, (BV) ... '41 '80 C.1 B.A. L.623 J.D. 4545 N. Lincoln, Suite 260
Tuepker, Max C., (AV) ... '53 '80 C.1147 B.S. L.862 J.D. [M.C.Tuepker]

Tuepker, Max C., P.C., (AV)
204 North Robinson, 25th Floor, 73102
Telephone: 405-235-1700 Fax: 405-232-9114
URL: http://www.lawyers.com/tuepkerlaw
Max C. Tuepker; Shawnae E. Proctor.
Civil Litigation Practice in State and Federal Courts. Commercial, Contracts, Corporate, Employment, Probate, Insurance, Oil and Gas Law, Creditors' Rights, Intellectual Property Litigation, Business Litigation.
See Professional Biographies, OKLAHOMA CITY, OKLAHOMA

Tullius, Michael John ... '46 '72 C.612 B.A. L.623 J.D. [M.J.Tullius]
Tullius, Michael J. ... 401 North Hudson
Tullos, Hugh S., III ... '60 '89 C.623 B.S. L.615 J.D. 100 N. Broadway
Tunell, William P., Jr. ... '— '96 C.659 B.A. L.602 J.D. [[A] Rainey,R.R.&B.]
Turnell, Valeria B., (Mrs.) ... '17 '49 C.617 B.A. L.615 LL.B. 2809 Windsor Terr.‡
Turner, Elaine R., (AV) ... '— '89 C.623 B.B.A. L.615 J.D. [Hall,E.H.G.G.&N.]
Turner, J. Eric, (AV) ... '58 '83 C.59 B.A. L.623 J.D. [[C] Derryberry,Q.S.&N.]
Turner, Kenneth W., (AV) ... '38 '65 C.612 B.S. L.623 J.D. [Turner,T.B.&G.]
Turner, Mista Lizabeth ... '69 '97 C.612 B.S. L.623 J.D. 707 N. Robinson St.

Turner, Turner, Braun & Goralewicz, A Professional Corporation, (AV) 1319 Classen Drive
Turpen, Michael C., (AV) .... '49 '75 C&L.862 B.A., J.D. [Riggs,A.N.T.O.&L.]
Twardy, Stan, (BV) ....'27 '74 L.365 J.D. 3721 North Classen Boulevard
Tyler, Deena ....'72 '00 C&L.623 B.B.A., J.D. [A Mahaffey&G.]
Tyree, Lana Jeanne, (BV) .... '45 '71 C.616 B.A. L.623 J.D. 3101 NW Expressway St.
Tyrrell, Elizabeth Dalton, (AV) .... '59 '85 C.893 B.A. L.802 J.D. [McAfee&T.]
Tytanic, Chris A., (BV) .... '61 '86 C&L.623 B.A., J.D. Coun., Devon Energy Corp.
Underwood, Gary R., (AV) .... '45 '75 C.623 B.B.A. L.616 J.D. [Helms&U.]
Upp, Brian H., (AV) ....'38 '63 C.612 B.A. L.623 J.D. 1505 Westchester Drive
Urbach, Eric Allen, (BV) '73 '00 C.1315 B.A. L.615 J.D. 701 N. Broadway Ave., Ste. 510
Utter, Michael E., (AV) .... '48 '77 C&L.623 B.A., J.D. 921 N.W. 13th St.
Vallejo, Richard H. B., (BV) .... '41 '73 C.612 B.S. L.616 J.D. 625 N.W. 13th
Van Antwerp, Patricia A. .... '38 '78 C.612 B.S. L.616 J.D. State Student Loan Auth.
Van Cleef, R. Pope, Jr., (AV) .... '52 '77 C.623 B.A. L.616 J.D. [Robertson&W.]
Vandruff, Joel Wayne ....'69 '01 C.612 B.S. L.616 J.D. [Haupt B.V.]
Van Dyke, Peter T., (AV) .... '42 '68 C.690 B.S. L.982 J.D. [McAfee&T.]
van Egmond, William E. .... '73 '01 C.692 B.A. L.846 J.D. [A Crowe&D.]
Van Laanen, Erin M., (AV) ....'60 '91 C.1147 B.B.A. L.623 J.D. [McAfee&T.]
VanMerlin, Taye K ....'52 '84 C.880 B.S.N. L.616 J.D. 1724 N. Davis Avenue
VanMeter, David W., (BV) .... '60 '91 C.814 B.S. L.623 J.D. [Berry&V.]
Varnum, Robert V. ....'46 '73 C.613 B.A. L.276 J.D. [C Eagleton&N.]
Vassar, William A., III, (AV) ....'48 '74 C.862 B.S. L.623 J.D. 1001 N.W. 63rd.
Vaughan-Reynolds, Kathryn ....'61 '88 C&L.623 B.A., J.D. Jud. Clk., Ct. App.
Vaughn, Lyle S., (AV) ....'52 '85 C.112 A.B. L.309 J.D. 912 NW 41st St
Vaughn, Robt. H. ....'27 '56 C.623 L.616 LL.B. 5712 N.W. 36th St.
Vaught, Cheryl A., (AV) ....'59 '85 C&L.623 B.A., J.D. [Vaught&C.]

Vaught & Conner, (AV)
A Professional Limited Liability Company
50 Penn Place, Suite 1300, 73118
Telephone: 405-848-2255 Fax: 405-840-4701
Email: sconner@vcokc.com
Cheryl A. Vaught; Scot A. Conner.
Commercial, Corporate and Business, Real Estate, Energy, Cogeneration, Utility Law, Employment, Healthcare Law, Estates and Trusts, Litigation in State and Federal Courts.
See Professional Biographies, OKLAHOMA CITY, OKLAHOMA

Velotta, George W., II, (AV) .... '53 '78 C.612 B.S. L.623 J.D. [Derryberry,Q.S.&N.]
Venters, Harley E. .... '22 '53 C.870 B.S. L.623 LL.B. # 219, 2801 N Lincoln Blvd
Vera, John B., (AV) ....'63 '91 C&L.623 B.B.A., J.D. [Fenton,F.S.R.&M.]
Verity, G. L. Jidge, (BV) .... '46 '73 C&L.623 B.B.A., J.D. Big D Industries, Inc.
Verity, George L., (AV) .... '14 '37 C&L.623 LL.B. 5620 S.W. 29th St.‡
Verity, Joanne LeBlanc, (AV) '55 '83 C&L.623 B.A., J.D. Instr., Legal Res. & Writing, Okla. City Univ. Sch. of Law‡
Vernier, Douglas Duane ....'65 '00 C.1257 B.A. L.615 J.D. 301 N.W. 63rd St.
Vernier-Gelven, Nicole Marie '70 '96 C.734 B.A. L.615 J.D. Dep. Gen. Coun., OK Dept. Mental Health & Substance
Ver Weire, W. Todd, (CV T) .... '66 '93 C.840 B.B.A. L.692 J.D. [A Federman&S.]
Vilardofsky, Beverly I. ....'70 '95 C.690 B.A. L.616 J.D. [A Phillips M.M.M.&M.]
Vinall, Cheryl .... '74 '00 C.613 B.A. L.276 J.D. [A McAfee&T.]
Vincent, Raymond A., (AV) .... '51 '86 C.101 B.S. L.616 J.D. [Pool,B.V.&P.] ⊙
Vitali, John E., (AV) ....'56 '86 C.93 A.B. L.616 J.D. [Hornbeek,K.V.&B.]
Voegeli, Susanna Gattoni, (BV) ....'72 '97 C&L.623 B.A., J.D. [Hall,E.H.G.G.&N.]
Vogt, James W., (AV) ....'50 '75 C.622 B.A. L.616 J.D. [Reynolds,R.V.&M.]
Vogt, Julie Lynn ....'70 '97 C.958 B.S. L.616 J.D. 2801 N Lincoln Blvd
Vosler, Alexander C. ....'74 '02 C.235 B.S. L.1187 J.D. [A Johnson&H.]
Waddell, Cody B., (AV) ....'47 '75 C&L.623 B.A., J.D. [C.B.Waddell]
Waddell, Cody B., PC, (AV) ....2212 N.W. 50th, Ste. 163
Wagner, Amy R. .... '68 '92 C&L.623 B.A., J.D. Southwestern Bell Tele. Co.
Wagner, Jason C., (BV) ....'65 '91 C&L.623 B.A., J.D. [Collins,Z.&W.]
Wagner, John E., (AV) .... '26 '54 C&L.623 B.A., LL.B. 8500 Waverly Ave.
Wagner, Kerry L., (BV) ....'56 '92 C.502 M.E.D. L.615 J.D. [Wagner&W.]
Wagner, Robert J. ....'60 '96 C.616 B.S. L.615 J.D. [Wagner&W.]

Wagner & Wagner, P.C., (BV)
4000 N. Classen Boulevard, Suite 101-N, P.O. Box 60924, 73146-0924
Telephone: 405-521-9105;1-800-453-9890 Fax: 405-521-8994 Email: rjw@wagnerfirm.com Email: klw@wagnerfirm.com
Email: info@wagnerfirm.com
Kerry L. Wagner; Robert J. Wagner.
Family Law, Personal Injury, Automobile Accidents, Truck Accidents, Wrongful Death, Divorce, Alimony, Child Support, Workers Compensation, Social Security Disability, Employment, Employment Discrimination, Wrongful Termination, Adoptions.
See Professional Biographies, OKLAHOMA CITY, OKLAHOMA

Wakely, Nancy K., (BV) .... '49 '90 C.1147 B.A. L.616 J.D. 1436 S.W. 44th
Wakely, Thomas M., (BV) ....'34 '61 C&L.623 B.A., LL.B. [T.Wakely]
Wakely, Tom, (BV) ....1436 S.W. 44th St.
Walding, Andrew L., (AV) ....'53 '90 C&L.623 B.B.A., J.D. [Fellers,S.B.B.&T.]
Waldo, James R., (AV) ....'46 '74 C.228 A.B. L.623 J.D. [Mock,S.W.E.R.&B.]
Waldron, Andrew J. ....'72 '97 C.1147 B.A. L.623 J.D. [A Walker&W.]
Walker, Barth P., (AV) ....'14 '39 C&L.623 B.S., LL.B. 13313 Oakcliff Rd.‡
Walker, David A., (BV) '37 '69 C.1147 B.S. L.616 J.D. 6701 N. Broadway Extension, Suite 240
Walker, Gina Kay ....'63 '93 C.623 B.B.A. L.616 J.D. Co. Pub. Def. Off.
Walker, James E. (Jim), (AV) ....'44 '74 C&L.623 B.B.A., J.D. [Walker,F.&F.]
Walker, L. Mark, (AV) ....'57 '83 C&L.623 B.B.A., J.D. [Crowe&D.]
Walker, Lucile J. ....'16 '42 C&L.623 B.S., LL.B. 1709 Elmhurst Ave.‡
Walker, Ronald L., (AV) ....'53 '79 C.663 B.A. L.623 J.D. [McKinney&S.]
Walker, Russell James, (AV) ....'46 '74 C.976 B.A. L.623 J.D. [Walker&W.]

Walker, Ferguson and Ferguson, (AV)
Suite 400 301 N.W. 63rd Street, 73116
Telephone: 405-843-8855 Fax: 405-843-8934
Email: walkerl@okc.coxatwork.com
Members of Firm: James E. (Jim) Walker; Thomas G. Ferguson, Jr.; James C. Ferguson. Associates: Timothy J. Lamiell; Jon Louis Derouen, Jr; Carolyn K. Hebert; Sheila D. Barnes. Of Counsel: Bruce V. Winston; Mia C. Rops.
General Civil Practice. Insurance Defense, Banking and Commercial Law, Federal, State and Local Taxes, Real Estate, Oil and Gas, Probate, Administrative and Legislative Law. Transportation, Communications, Cable TV, Workers Compensation Law, Employer Liability Law, Employment (Management), Telecommunications, Commercial Litigation, Taxation, Subrogation, Trials in State and Federal Courts.
Reference: Bank of Oklahoma N.A.
See Professional Biographies, OKLAHOMA CITY, OKLAHOMA

Walker & Walker, (AV)
950 Landmark Towers East, 3535 N.W. 58th Street, 73112
Telephone: 405-943-9693 Fax: 405-949-1505
URL: http://www.lawyers.com/walkerwalker
(This Listing Continued)

Walker & Walker (Continued)
Members of Firm: Russell James Walker;—Andrew J. Waldron. Of Counsel: Glenn J. Shrader, Jr.; Stephen O. Clarke; Edward J. Clarke.
General Civil Practice. Trials. Oil and Gas including International Oil and Gas Transactions, Real Property, Environmental, Probate, Trusts, Corporations and Partnerships, Complex Litigation, Personal Injury and Products Liability.
See Professional Biographies, OKLAHOMA CITY, OKLAHOMA

Wallace, R. Brown, (AV) ....'44 '70 C&L.623 B.A., J.D. [Wallace&B.]
Wallace, Ronald L., (AV) ....'56 '81 C.623 B.B.A. L.616 J.D. 1 N. Hudson
Wallace, Thomas A., (AV) ....'23 '52 C&L.178 B.S., J.D. [Norman&E.]

Wallace & Bertman, PC, (AV)
100 N. Broadway Avenue, Suite 2270, 73102
Telephone: 405-605-6100 Fax: 405-606-8403
Email: lawfirm@wallacebertman.com URL: http://www.wallacebertman.com
R. Brown Wallace; Eugene K. Bertman.
Civil Litigation, Indian Law, Aircraft Finance and Leasing, Litigation, Commercial Law, Administrative Law, Contracts, Business, Construction Law, Corporate, Partnership, Family Business, Professional Licensing, Municipal Law, Native American Law, Appellate Practice.
See Professional Biographies, OKLAHOMA CITY, OKLAHOMA

Wallis, Kathy Eileen .... '61 '99 C.617 B.S. L.616 J.D. Bob Howard Automitive Group
Walls, David A., (AV) ....'58 '88 C.846 B.B.A. L.616 J.D. [McKinney&S.]
Walls, S. Marc, (AV) '51 '81 C.1147 B.A. L.616 J.D. Staff Coun., Allstate Insurance Company
Walos, Kevin M. ....'67 '93 C.107 B.A. L.623 J.D. [A Wilson,C.&A.]
Walsh, Lawrence E., (AV) ....'12 '36 C&L.178 A.B., LL.B. [C Crowe&D.]
Walsh, Michael Allen, (AV) ....'54 '80 C.623 B.A. L.616 J.D. [Beeler,W.&W.]
Walsh, Regena McNeill, (AV) ....'64 '90 C.612 B.S. L.623 J.D. [Beeler,W.&W.]
Walsingham, Carl B., Jr., (CV) ....'35 '72 C.259 B.S. L.616 J.D. Asst. Mun. Coun.
Walter, Jenny W. ....'57 '83 C.911 B.A. L.615 J.D. Asst. Atty. Gen.
Walters, Hilton H., (AV) .... '55 '87 C.269 B.S. L.616 J.D. [Rife&W.]
Walters, Jay P. ....'68 '96 C.59 B.A. L.273 J.D. [Fellers,S.B.B.&T.]
Walters, Joseph, (AV) ....'50 '86 C.1044 B.A. L.623 J.D. [McAfee&T.]
Wangrud, Carole A. ....'— '79 C.86 B.A. L.615 J.D. [Carola]
Wantland, Russell A. .... '76 '03 C&L.623 B.B.A., J.D. [A Mulinix O.H.A.&L.]
Ward, C. Todd, (AV) ....'63 '90 C&L.623 B.S., J.D. [Fenton,F.S.R.&M.]
Ward, Charles C. ....'63 '89 C.82 B.S. L.615 J.D. 770 N.E. 63rd
Ward, Kurtis J., Esq. ....'65 '05 C.612 L.615 J.D. 9225 Lake Hefner Pkwy., Ste. 101
Warmington, Courtney K. ....'74 '99 C.612 B.A. L.615 J.D. [A Crowe&D.]
Warner, James E., III ....'76 '02 C.619 B.S. L.623 J.D. [A Holladay,C.&D.]
Warren, James G. ....'48 '77 C.1019 B.B.A. L.616 J.D. [Smith&W.]
Warren, Jerry A., (AV) ....'43 '68 C&L.623 B.A., J.D. [McAfee&T.]
Warren, Loyde H., (BV) ....'39 '69 C.612 B.S.B.A. L.623 J.D. [L.H.Warren]
Warren, Winford Mike ....'54 '81 C.802 B.B.A. L.862 J.D. Dist. J.
Warren, Loyde H., P.C., (BV) ....719 N. Shartel
Washington, Gary Russell ....'70 '00 C.616 B.A. L.615 J.D. 233 W. Park Ave.
Wasson, William P. ....'71 '01 C.326 B.A. L.623 J.D. [C Federman&S.]
Waters, Richard L., (AV T) '50 '76 C.502 B.S. L.862 J.D. Sr. Coun., Kerr McGee Corp.
Watkins, Travis W. ....'73 '99 C.947 B.A. L.616 J.D. [C Mulinix O.H.A.&L.]
Watson, Kenneth C., (BV) '44 '76 C.1362 B.A. L.1003 J.D. 200 N. Harvey Ave., Ste. 300
Watt, Joseph M. ....'47 '72 C.845 B.A. L.846 J.D. Supm. Ct. Jus.
Watts, Beverley Q., (AV) ....'59 '86 C.621 B.A. L.616 J.D. [Watts&W.]
Watts, Charles J., (AV) ....'46 '73 C.612 B.A. L.623 J.D. [C Smith,S.S.C.&W.]
Watts, Philip O., (AV) ....'59 '84 C.621 B.A.B.S. L.623 J.D. [Watts&W.]
Watts, William D., (AV) ....'33 '60 C.623 B.B.A. L.802 LL.B. 14200 N. May Avenue
Watts & Watts, (AV) ....101 North Robinson, Suite 501
Webb, Barbara G. '51 '85 C.612 B.S. L.1209 J.D. Dir., Legis. Servcs., OK Farmers Union
Webb, Drew D., (AV) ....'60 '85 C.623 B.A. L.309 J.D. [McAfee&T.]
Webb, James R., (AV) ....'67 '93 C.59 B.A. L.910 J.D. [McAfee&T.]
Webb, Jeremy K. '76 '02 C.623 B.A. L.893 J.D. (adm. in TX; not adm. in OK) [A Gable&G.]
Webber, Daniel G., Jr., (BV) ....'66 '94 C.612 B.S. L.276 J.D. [Ryan,W.&C.]
Weber, James W., (AV) ....'50 '79 C.859 B.S. L.846 J.D. 1125 N.W. 50th
Weddle, Charles C., III, (BV) .... '73 '00 C.623 B.A. L.616 J.D. [White&W.]
Weeks, Joseph Righton '48 '77 C.280 B.B.A. L.893 J.D. Prof. of Law, Oklahoma City Univ. Sch. of Law
Wegener, Meredith A. ....'77 '03 C.859 B.A. L.623 J.D. [A Gum,P.&M.]
Weichbrodt, Karen S. ....'53 '90 C.616 B.S. L.623 J.D. Pub. Def. Off.
Weimer, Mark L. ....'60 '87 C.376 B.A. L.615 J.D. [M.L.Weimer]
Weimer, Mark L., PA .... 309 N.W. 9th St.
Weitman, M. Daniel ....'67 '97 C&L.623 B.A., J.D. [A Shelton]
Welch, Allen John ....'56 '85 C.618 B.A. L.623 J.D. Oklahoma Bar Assn.
Welch, Cynthia Wood, (BV) .... '62 '90 C&L.623 B.A., J.D. [A Oldfield,C.&G.]
Welch, Hack, (BV) ....'46 '73 C.623 B.B.A. L.862 J.D. [C Ogle&W.]
Welch, Josh T., (CV) ....'68 '97 C.612 B.S. L.615 J.D. [Ogle&W.]
Welch, Marjorie L., (BV) ......'55 '84 C.338 B.S. L.623 J.D. Dep. Gen., State Tax Comm.
Welch, Mort G., (AV) ....'50 '75 C.623 B.A. L.846 J.D. [Welch&S.]
Welch, Ruston C., (AV) ....'64 '89 C.82 B.S. L.623 J.D. [Welch]
Welch, Steven R., (AV) .... '50 '79 C&L.623 B.A., J.D. [McAfee&T.]

Welch Law Firm, P.C., (AV)
722 North Broadway Suite 301, 73102-6025
Telephone: 405-236-5222 Fax: 405-231-5222
Email: RWelch@WelchLawPC.com
Ruston C. Welch.
Corporate Law, Commercial Law, Financial Transactions, Commercial Litigation, Bankruptcy Law, Creditors Rights.
See Professional Biographies, OKLAHOMA CITY, OKLAHOMA

Welch & Smith, P.C., (AV) BR
6440 Avondale Drive, Suite 206, 73116
Telephone: 405-286-0801 Fax: 405-286-0301 Email: mwelch@welchsmith.com
Email: ssmith@welchsmith.com
Mort G. Welch; Sherry L. Smith.
Civil Trial and Appellate Practice in all State and Federal Courts, including Insurance Coverage, Professional Liability, Business Torts, Employment, Products Liability and Negligence.
Representative Clients: Jefferson Insurance Company of New York; Admiral Insurance Co.; Liberty Mutual Insurance Co.; Mazda Distributors (West), Inc.; National Farmers Union Insurance Co.; Oklahoma Farmers Union Mutual Insurance Co.; Trinity Universal Insurance Co.
See Professional Biographies, OKLAHOMA CITY, OKLAHOMA

Wells, Bryan J., (AV) .... '63 '88 C&L.623 B.B.A., J.D. [Conner&W.]
Wells, Joseph L., (BV) ....'46 '74 C&L.616 B.M.E., J.D. 3955 N.W. 23rd
Wenzel, Stefan, (AV) ....'61 '95 C.556 B.C.J. L.616 J.D. 21 E. Main St., Ste. 101
Werneke, Vicki Ruth Adams '63 '89 C.616 B.A. L.623 J.D. Jud. Clk., Ct. of Crim. App.

West, Allen G. ....'11 '40 C&L.623 B.A., J.D. 9708 N. Council Rd.
West, Barbara S. ....'48 '88 C.622 B.S. L.616 J.D. Staff Atty.
West, James R., (AV) ....'27 '55 C&L.623 LL.B. Legal Aid of Western Okla.
West, Laurie R. ....'49 '93 C.1147 B.A. L.623 J.D. 501 N.W. 13
West, Lee R. ....'29 '56 C&L.623 B.A., J.D. U.S. Dist. J.
Westerman, Helen K. ....'29 '62 C&L.616 B.A., J.D. 6612 Stinchcomb Dr.
Wetsel, Charles E. ....'56 '86 C.1315 B.S. L.623 J.D. [Robertson&W.]
Whaley, Phillip G., (AV) ....'61 '88 C&L.623 B.B.A., J.D. [Ryan,W.&C.]
Whatley, Nathan L., (AV) ....'67 '92 C&L.623 B.A., J.D. [McAfee&T.]
Wheeler, Albert L., III, (BV) '54 '90
C.1147 B.ME. L.615 J.D. 9400 North Broadway Suite 515
Wheeler, Allison Ann ....'54 '89 C&L.862 B.A., J.D. CompSource Oklahoma
Wheeler, Cheri Marie, (BV) ....'52 '81 C.623 B.S. L.616 J.D. [Behrens,T.W.&C.]
Wheeler, Jennifer, (BV) ....'72 '97 C.862 B.A. L.623 J.D. [McAfee&T.]
Wheeler, Joe D., Jr., (AV) ....'48 '75 C&L.616 B.A., J.D. [Wheeler,W.M.F.&D.]
Wheeler, N. Janine, (BV) ....'66 '91 C&L.623 B.B.A., J.D. [Fellers,S.B.B.&T.]
Wheeler, Peter L., (AV) ....'60 '88 C&L.623 B.A., J.D. [Pierce C.H.B.&G.]
Wheeler, Robert L. (Duke), (P.C.), (AV) '35 '63
C&L.623 B.B.A., LL.B. 7819 Old Hickory Ln
Wheeler, Wheeler, Morgan, Faulkner & Donaldson, A Professional Association, (AV)
1900 Northwest Expressway Suite 450
Whinery, Leo H. ....'26 '51 C&L.986 A.B., LL.B. [Abel,M.S.M.&K.]
White, Amy D. ....'75 '01 C.838 B.A. L.616 J.D. [McAfee&T.]
White, Brinda K., (AV) ....'51 '82 C&L.623 Ph.D., J.D. [Mee,M.&H.]
White, Charles F. ....'17 '42 C&L.623 B.A., LL.B. 2643 N.W. 45th St.
White, Daniel L. ....'62 '96 C.1310 B.S. L.623 J.D. 1136 N. Robinson
White, Edward L., (AV) ....'67 '95 C.612 B.S. L.616 J.D. 50 Penn Place, 4th Floor (Pat.)
White, Glenn M., (BV) ....'62 '87 C.612 B.S.B.A. L.623 J.D. [Lewis,W.P.&M.]
White, James U., Jr., (AV) ....'49 '74 C.976 B.A. L.623 J.D. [White,C.&F.]
White, Joe E., Jr., (AV) ....'62 '88 C.1147 B.A. L.623 J.D. [White&W.]
White, Paul Wayne ....'50 '82 C.1315 B.A. L.623 J.D. 2300 N. Lincoln Blvd., Rm. 244
White, Peter S., (AV) ....'38 '73 C.1147 B.S. L.616 J.D. [P.S.White]
White, Travis Keith ....'57 '01 C.618 B.S. L.623 J.D. P.O. Box 720291

White, Coffey & Fite, P.C., (AV)
1001 N.W. 63rd St., Suite 100, 73116-7335
Telephone: 405-842-7545 Fax: 405-840-9890
John M. Coffey; Jack P. Fite; James U. White, Jr.
General Civil Practice. Trials of Civil Cases in all State and Federal Courts. Corporation, Commercial, Oil and Gas, Environmental, Agriculture, Public Utility, Real Property, Title and Probate, Taxation, Banking and Bankruptcy Law.
See Professional Biographies, OKLAHOMA CITY, OKLAHOMA

White, Peter S., PC, (AV) .... P.O. Box 2535

White & Weddle, P.C., (AV)
5532 North Western, 73118
Telephone: 405-858-8899 Fax: 405-858-8844
Joe E. White, Jr.; Charles C. Weddle III. Associates: Marvel E. Lewis; Joshua L. Parkinson.
Criminal State and Federal, Personal Injury, Education Law, General Civil Practice.
See Professional Biographies, OKLAHOMA CITY, OKLAHOMA

Whitefield, Justin A. ....'73 '97 C.612 B.A. L.623 J.D. [Derryberry,Q.S.&N.]
Whitehill, William H., Jr., (AV) ....'60 '86 C.1300 B.S. L.623 J.D. [Fellers,S.B.B.&T.]
Whitmire, Lyndon W., (AV) ....'71 '96 C.612 B.A. L.623 J.D. [Phillips M.M.M.&M.]
Whittaker, Robert Lee, (BV) ....'53 '81 C.612 B.A. L.615 J.D. Asst. Atty. Gen.
Whittaker, Zona ....'39 '87 C.613 B.A. L.612 LL.D. 4323 NW 63rd St.
Whitten, Hal S., Jr., (BV) ....'34 '61 C.616 LL.B. 3721 N. Classen Blvd.
Whitten, Reggie N., (AV) ....'55 '80 C&L.623 B.A., J.D. [Whitten,N.M.T.&R.]

Whitten, Nelson, McGuire, Terry & Roselius, (AV)
A Professional Limited Liability Company
Suite 400, One Leadership Square, 211 North Robinson, 73102
Telephone: 405-239-2522 Fax: 405-239-2573
Email: whitten@whitten-nelson.com URL: http://www.whitten-nelson.com
Reggie N. Whitten; Robert W. Nelson; Kent R. McGuire; Douglas A. Terry; Jason E. Roselius; Jim T. Priest; G. Patrick "Pat" O'Hara; Patrick O'Hara, Jr.; Philip W. Anderson; Simone Gosnell Fulmer; Derrick T. Dewitt; Timothy David Eisel;—R. Gregory Kirby; Derrick L. Morton; Thomas A. Paruolo; Kathryn D. Terry; Guy R. Wood; Carin L. Marcussen (Not admitted in OK); Chad E. Ihrig; Lauren F. Guhl.
Products Liability, Civil Rights, Business & Commercial Litigation, Casualty and Fire Loss Insurance, Underinsured Motorist Coverage, Labor and Employment Law, Environmental Law, Professional Liability, Personal Injury, RICO, ERISA, Workers' Compensation. Trials in all State, Federal and Appellate Courts, Automobile and Trucking Defense, Construction Accidents, Insurance Coverage Disputes; ERISA Litigation.
Representative Clients: The St. Paul Insurance Cos.; Crum & Forster Commercial Insurance Co.; OML Municipal Assurance Group; Progressive Casualty; Biomet, Inc.; Eagle Manufacturing Co.; Ferno Manufacturing Co.; Great West Casualty; Liberty Mutual; Manhattan Construction Co.
See Professional Biographies, OKLAHOMA CITY, OKLAHOMA

Whitworth, Clinton D. ....'71 '00 C.616 B.S. L.862 J.D. [Edmonds,C.H.G.R.&W.]
Whitworth, Kelly L. ....'78 '03 C.862 B.A. L.623 J.D. [Smith R.S.&E.]
Wiebelt, Stacey Anne ....'73 '99 C.128 B.A. L.623 J.D. [Wiebelt P.&Assoc.]
Wiebelt & Associates, PLLC .... 1802 N. Shartel
Wiens, Terry T., (BV) ....'43 '72 C.623 B.A. L.616 J.D. 3015 North West 59th Street
Wiggins, John E., (AV) ....'49 '74 C.612 B.A. L.623 J.D. [Short W.M.&B.]
Wilcox, Jack W. ....'21 '50 C&L.623 A.B., LL.B. 11625 Leaning Elm‡
Wiley, Eddie Carroll ....'57 '87 L.623 J.D. 200 North Harvey Avenue
Wilguess, Douglas D. ....'69 '94 C.612 B.S. L.623 J.D. [H.B.Brown&Assoc.]
Wilke, Monica Leah '73 '99
C.612 B.S. L.623 J.D. Oklahoma Farm Bureau and Affiliated Cos.
Williams, Bill E. D. ....'24 '73 C.627 B.A. L.615 J.D. [Williams]
Williams, Charles B. ....'76 '03 C&L.623 B.B.A., J.D. [Durbin,L.&B.]
Williams, Freda L. ....'58 '94 C.82 B.A. L.623 J.D. Chesapeake Energy
Williams, James M. '49 '77 C.976 B.S. L.659 J.D.
(adm. in NY; not adm. in OK) 2701 N. Windser Blvd.
Williams, John K., (AV) ....'46 '74 C.612 B.S. L.616 J.D. [Williams,B.&Assoc.]
Williams, John Michael, (AV) ....'49 '74 C.612 B.S. L.623 J.D. [Williams,B.F.&B.]
Williams, P. M., (AV) ....'25 '54 C&L.623 B.B.A., LL.B. 201 Robert S. Kerr
Williams, Patricia Dare '66 '92 C&L.623 B.S., J.D.
Asst. Prof., Univ. of Oklahoma Health Servs. Ctr.
Williams, Teresa Ann Goode, (BV) '59 '91
C.1147 B.B.A. L.623 J.D. Ste 800, 3366 N W Expy
Williams, Thomas C., (AV) ....'51 '76 C&L.616 B.S., J.D. [Robertson&W.]
Williams, Tyson Lane '73 '97
C.619 B.S. L.45 J.D. Staff Atty., Oklahoma State Sch. Bd. Assoc.
Williams, Wiley L. ....'52 '82 C.622 B.S. L.616 J.D. Asst. Mun. Coun.
Williams, Boren & Associates, P.C., (AV) .... 401 North Hudson

Williams, Box, Forshee & Bullard, P.C., (AV)
522 Colcord Drive, 73102-2202
Telephone: 405-232-0080 Telecopier: 405-236-5814
(This Listing Continued)

Williams, Box, Forshee & Bullard, P.C. (Continued)
John Michael Williams; Dennis R. Box; Richard D. Forshee; Keith R. Gibson; Paul E. Lefebvre; Audrey D. Blank; Michael D. O'Neal. Of Counsel: William J. Bullard.
Municipal Law, Zoning, Planning and Land Use, Real Estate, Eminent Domain, Municipal Redevelopment, Municipal Bonds, Public Finance, Corporate Law, Banks and Banking, Trust Law, Commercial Law, Business Litigation, Utility Law, Telephone Utility Regulation, Administrative Law, Public Law.
See Professional Biographies, OKLAHOMA CITY, OKLAHOMA

Williams Law Office .... 1801 N.W. 17th
Williams-Harris, LaRonna '52 '85
C.475 B.A. L.615 J.D. Asst. Gen. Coun., State Tax Comm.
Williamson, Charles Dean, (BV) ....'33 '62 C.612 B.S. L.623 LL.B. 3030 N.W. Expwy.
Williamson, Creston B. ....'21 '57 2717 Winston Rd.
Williamson, Wilburn L., (AV) ....'31 '59 C.612 B.S. L.623 LL.B. 3030 Northwest Expwy.
Williford, Jon M. ....'76 '02 C&L.623 B.B.A., J.D. [Johnson&H.]
Willis, Ozella M. ....'33 '82 C.1362 B.A. L.1288 J.D. 1915 N. Stiles
Willis, W. Brett, (AV) ....'68 '93 C&L.623 B.B.A., J.D. [Calvert]
Wilmarth, Marjorie I. ....'15 '45 L.615 LL.B. 540 N. W. 40th St.
Wilson, Alma ....'— '41 C&L.623 A.B., LL.B. Supm. Ct. Jus.
Wilson, Brandon P. ....'76 '02 C.999 B.A. L.623 J.D. [Edmonds,C.H.G.R.&W.]
Wilson, David D., (AV) ....'44 '70 C&L.623 B.B.A., J.D. [Wilson,C.&A.] ⊙
Wilson, Donald R., (AV) ....'42 '67 C&L.623 B.A., J.D. [Fenton,F.S.R.&M.]
Wilson, Howard L. '23 '52 C&L.378 B.A., LL.B.
(adm. in KS; not adm. in OK) P.O. Box 2872
Wilson, K. Nicholas, (AV) ....'43 '68 C&L.616 B.A. L.623 J.D. [Fellers,S.B.B.&T.]
Wilson, Montgomery J., (BV) ....'60 '85 C&L.623 B.A., J.D. 1521 S.W. 89th St.
Wilson, Ryan S., (AV) ....'65 '90 C.612 B.S. L.623 J.D. [Hartzog C.C.&N.]
Wilson, Timothy E. ....'71 '97 C&L.623 B.A., J.D. Asst. Pub. Def.

Wilson, Cain & Acquaviva, (AV)
300 N.W. 13th Street, Suite 100, 73103-3739 ⊙
Telephone: 405-236-2600 Fax: 405-236-2607
Email: wcaokc@swbell.net URL: http://www.wca-law.com
Members of Firm: David D. Wilson; Timothy D. Cain; Joseph T. Acquaviva, Jr. Associates: Amy L. Loughridge; Barbara K. Buratti; Bill M. Roberts; Travis Dunn; Frances J. Armstrong; Kevin M. Walos.
General Civil Trial Practice State and Federal Courts. Products Liability, Fire and Casualty Insurance Defense, Insurance Coverage, Uninsured Motorist, Bad Faith Law, Professional Malpractice Defense, Veterinary and Insurance Defense, Workers Compensation, Subrogation Insurance Defense, including Personal Injury, Automobile Accidents, Wrongful Death.
Tulsa Office: 1717 South Boulder Avenue, Suite 801, 74119-4805. Telephone: 918-583-4777. Fax: 918-583-0774.
See Professional Biographies, OKLAHOMA CITY, OKLAHOMA

Winans, Nancy Ann '60 '88 C.623 B.A. L.616 J.D.
Child Support Enforce. Atty., Dept. of Human Servs.
Winblad, Richard S., (BV) '61 '92 C.612 B.S. L.623 J.D.
204 N. Robinson Ave., Ste. 1100
Windham, David B., (BV) ....'42 '74 C&L.616 B.S., J.D. 1327 N. Robinson Avenue
Winger, Brian Neil ....'67 '96 C.1315 B.S. L.615 J.D. Okla. Christian Univ.
Winn, Virginia '— '81 C.665 B.A. L.229 J.D.
(adm. in TX; not adm. in OK) Atty., Devon Energy Corp.

Winningham, E. Vance, (AV) '42 '66 C.612 B.S. L.623 J.D.
2200 N.W. 50th Street, Suite 240, 73112
Telephone: 405-843-1037 Fax: 405-848-2463
URL: http://www.americanvisas.com
Immigration Law.
See Professional Biographies, OKLAHOMA CITY, OKLAHOMA

Winn-Mcgee, Mary Anne ....'50 '76 C&L.623 B.A., J.D. 1001 N.W. 63rd St.
Winston, Bruce V., (AV) ....'47 '73 C.623 B.B.A. L.616 J.D. [Walker,F.&F.]
Wintory, Richard M., (AV) '58 '84 C&L.623 B.A., J.D.
Chf. Dep. Atty. Gen., Crim. Div.
Wittrock, Monica A., (AV) ....'57 '82 C.612 B.A. L.623 J.D. 133 N.W. 8th
Wolf, Carol J. ....'39 '78 C&L.623 B.A., J.D. 10213 Island View Dr.‡
Wolf, Ramona Lee ....'57 '01 C.305 B.A. L.615 J.D. 12833 Knight Hill Rd.
Wolfe, Charles W., (AV) ....'35 '67 C.418 B.S. L.616 J.D. P.O. Box 25861‡
Wolfe, Connie M., (AV) ....'65 '91 C.1147 B.S. L.623 J.D. [McKinney&S.]
Wolfe, Deborah A., (BV) '52 '85
C.1147 B.A. L.616 J.D. Asst. Gen. Coun., Midland Financial Co.
Wolfe, Mark A., (BV) ....'62 '87 C&L.623 B.A., J.D. 128 W. Hefner Rd.
Wolfe, Thomas G., (AV) ....'57 '85 C&L.623 B.S., J.D. [Phillips M.M.M.&M.]
Womble, Michael A., (AV) ....'60 '87 C.623 B.B.A. L.846 J.D. [Cheatham&W.]
Wood, Betty Garrett, (AV) ....'51 '80 C&L.623 B.A., J.D. [Clark,S.W.&P.]
Wood, Christopher A., (BV) ....'63 '88 C.1147 B.S. L.623 J.D. [C.A.Wood&Assoc.]
Wood, Elizabeth Scott, (AV) ....'50 '80 C&L.623 B.A., J.D. [McAfee&T.]
Wood, Gary W., (AV) ....'70 '95 C&L.623 B.S., J.D. [Riggs,A.N.T.O.&L.]
Wood, Guy R. ....'68 '93 C.1300 B.B.A. L.623 J.D. [Whitten,N.M.T.&R.]
Wood, Kenneth L., (BV) ....'— '93 C.623 B.A. L.615 J.D. [Looney,N.&J.]
Wood, Randall J., (BV) '58 '83
C.612 B.S. L.623 J.D. Gen. Coun., Avalon Correctional Servs., Inc.
Wood, Victor C., Jr. ....'42 '69 C.612 B.A. L.623 J.D. 3601 North Classen Boulevard
Wood, Christopher A., & Associates, P.C., (BV) .... 1303 N. Western
Woods, Harry A., Jr., (AV) ....'41 '70 C.612 B.A. L.569 J.D. [Crowe&D.]
Woods, Maurice G., II, (AV) ....'71 '96 C&L.623 B.B.A., J.D. [McAtee&W.]
Woodson, Mark R. ....'61 '89 C&L.623 B.A., J.D. 6317 Plum Thicket Rd.
Woodson, Michael, (AV) ....'68 '94 C.620 B.S. L.623 J.D. [Edmonds,C.H.G.R.&W.]
Woodward, Charles N., (AV) ....'47 '72 C&L.623 B.B.A., J.D. [Lisle&W.]
Woolery, J. Todd ....'74 '00 C&L.623 B.A., J.D. [Hall,E.H.G.G.&N.]

Work, J. Kelly, (AV) '55 '80 C&L.623 B.B.A., J.D.
Hightower Building, 105 N. Hudson, Suite 304, 73102
Telephone: 405-232-2790 Fax: 405-232-3966
Email: jkwork@sbcglobal.com URL: http://www.lawyers.com/kellywork
Real Property, Business and Commercial. Employment, Litigation, Municipal, Land Use, Landlord/Tenant, Municipal Bond Law.
See Professional Biographies, OKLAHOMA CITY, OKLAHOMA

Work, James E., (AV) ....'27 '53 C&L.623 B.A., LL.B. [Shirk W.&R.]
Works & Lentz, Inc., A Prof. Corp., (AV) .... 3030 N.W. Expwy. (⊙Tulsa)
Woska, A. Daniel, (AV) ....'52 '78 C.623 B.A. L.616 J.D. [Federman&S.]
Wright, Angela C. '71 '97 C.612 B.A. L.623 J.D.
Asst. Dist. Atty., OK Co. Dist. Atty. Off.
Wright, Charles W., (BV) ....'43 '83 C.614 B.A. L.616 J.D. [Haupt B.V.]
Wright, Clifford A., (AV) ....'50 '77 C.911 B.A. L.616 J.D. [C.A.Wright]
Wright, Fredric H., III, (AV) ....'32 '60 C&L.623 B.B.A., LL.B. 2200 Classen Blvd.
Wright, Thornton, Jr., (AV) ....'30 '54 C&L.623 B.B.A., LL.B. 9636 N. May Ave.
Wright, William G. ....'45 '71 C&L.623 B.B.A., J.D. Pres., Gil Wright Properties, Inc.

Wright, Clifford A., P.C., (AV)
Suite 1300, Two Leadership Square, 211 North Robinson, 73102-7114
Telephone: 405-235-5880 Fax: 405-235-5664
Email: cawpclaw@aol.com URL: http://www.cliffordawrightpc.com
Clifford A. Wright.
General Civil Trial Practice, Appellate Practice in all Courts in Oklahoma, including Business, Commercial, Oil and Gas Contracts, Securities, Collections, Bankruptcy, Insolvency Law, Creditors Rights, Domestic Relations, Family Law, Real Estate, Corporations, Limited Liability Companies, Federal and State Taxation, Insurance, Estate Planning, Probate and Estate Administration, Health Care Law, Administrative Law, Torts (including Negligence, and Personal and Business Injuries), Taxing Agencies, Elder Law, Employment Law.
See Professional Biographies, OKLAHOMA CITY, OKLAHOMA

Wulff, Geo. W. ....'21 '50 C.616 L.615 J.D. 7716 N.W. 14th St.‡
Wyatt, Robert L., IV, (AV) ....'64 '89 C.621 B.S. L.623 J.D. [Wyatt]

Wyatt Law Office, (AV) BB
501 North Walker Avenue, Suite 110, P.O. Box 1947, 73101
Telephone: 405-234-5500 Fax: 405-232-4556
Email: bobwyatt@wyattlaw.com URL: http://www.wyattlaw.com
Robert L. Wyatt, IV.
Statewide criminal practice in Oklahoma and in federal courts nationwide. Focus on sex crimes and pornography, drug crimes, conspiracy, homicide and violence, white collar crimes (such as mail fraud, bank crimes, embezzlement), grand jury investigations, appeals and expungement.
See Professional Biographies, OKLAHOMA CITY, OKLAHOMA

Wymer, Richard D. ....'50 '76 C&L.616 B.A., J.D. 340 Court Plz.‡
Yaffe, M. Blake ....'— '77 C.623 B.A. L.615 J.D. [Foshee&Y.]
Yancey, Mark A. '60 '87 C.259 B.S. L.192 J.D.
(adm. in FL; not adm. in OK) Asst. U.S. Atty.
Yanda, Christopher T. ....'69 '99 C.1147 B.B.A. L.615 J.D. [Beets&Y.]
Yeary, Carl L. ....'56 '87 C&L.623 B.A., J.D. Regis. Coun., State Dept. of Secs.
Yeary, Janice L. ....'54 '84 C&L.623 B.S., J.D. Clk., U.S. Mag.
Young, Joseph A., (AV) ....'32 '60 C&L.623 B.B.A., LL.B. Kerr-McGee Ctr.
Young, Karen L., (BV) ....'58 '85 C.1147 B.S. L.616 J.D. Law Clk., Dist. J.
Young, Lawrence E. '46 '69 C.432 B.A. L.477 J.D.
(adm. in MO; not adm. in OK) Sr. Coun., Kerr-McGee Corp.
Young, Marilyn Ann ....'62 '91 C&L.623 B.A., J.D. Staff Coun., Kerr-McGee Corp.
Young, Sheryl N., (AV) ....'50 '90 C.1147 B.S. L.615 J.D. [McAfee&T.]
Yuill, Barbara K. ....'54 '02 C.37 B.S. L.616 J.D. [Ⓒ Resides&R.] (Pat.)
Zaccaria, Lynne C. ....'58 '00 C.884 MSN L.623 J.D. [Ⓐ Abel,M.S.M.&K.]
Zachritz, Anne E., (AV) ....'63 '91 C.172 B.A. L.1035 J.D. [Andrews D.]
Zeaman, Christian M. ....'74 '00 C&L.623 B.A., J.D. [Ⓐ G.J.James&Assoc.]
Zerr, Nancy A. ....'55 '94 C.1125 B.S. L.972 J.D. [Ⓐ G.A.Isaacs]
Zorn, Daniel K., (AV) ....'52 '77 C.963 B.S. L.616 J.D. [Collins,Z.&W.]
Zrenda, Stephen A., Jr., (BV) ....'45 '74 C.853 B.A. L.383 J.D. [S.A.Zrenda,Jr.]
Zrenda, Stephen A., Jr., P.C., A Prof. Corp., (BV) .... 100 N. Bdwy.
Zschiesche, Ray E., (AV) ..'59 '85 C.612 B.S. L.623 J.D. [Phillips M.M.M.&M.]
Zuhdi, L. Nazette ....'72 '97 C&L.623 B.A., J.D. [Ⓐ Day,E.P.&C.]
Zuhdi, Nabil (Bill), (BV) ....'55 '82 C.1147 B.S. L.623 J.D. [B.Zuhdi]
Zuhdi, Bill, P.C., (BV) .... P.O. Box 1077
Zynda, Kathryn M. ....'66 '93 C&L.623 B.A., J.D. [Ⓐ Corbyn]

OKMULGEE, * 13,022, *Okmulgee Co.*

Barksdale, Bill, (AV) ....'47 '73 C&L.623 B.A., J.D. [Barksdale]

Barksdale Law Firm, The, P.C., (AV)
310 East Seventh Street, P.O. Box 1366, 74447
Telephone: 918-756-0900 Fax: 918-756-0943 URL: http://www.barksdalelawfirm@hotmail.com
URL: http://www.lawyers.com/brwlaw
Dale F. Rainey (1907-1987); John H. W. Barksdale (1915-1999); Bill Barksdale.
Civil Trial Practice, Business Organization and Litigation, Probate, Oil and Gas, Real Estate, Bankruptcy-Creditor only, Estate Planning-Trusts.
Representative Clients: Citizens Bank & Trust Co.; Okmulgee School District; Okmulgee Creek Conservancy District; Emergency Medical Service; OMH Medical Center, Inc.; Chamber of Commerce of Okmulgee; Morris State Bank.
See Professional Biographies, OKMULGEE, OKLAHOMA

Boatman, Edgar R. ....'24 '50 C&L.623 LL.B. Ret. Dist. J.‡
Cornish, Tom R. ....'44 '68 C.612 B.S. L.623 J.D. U.S. Bkrptcy. J.
Cozzoni, Shannon Bears ....'— '96 C.59 B.A. L.862 J.D. 1st Asst. Atty. Gen.
Deer, Montie R. '40 '72 C.972 B.A. L.900 J.D.
(adm. in KS; not adm. in OK) 1600 E. Lake Shore Dr.
Fugate, Robert Allen '46 '75 C&L.862 B.S.B.A., J.D.
Staff Atty., OK Indigent Def. Sys.
Gaither, Luke ....'72 '98 C.619 B.A. L.862 J.D [Inglish&G.] ⊙
George, Terry Lee, (CV) ....'47 '74 C.504 B.A. L.862 J.D. 118 E. 8th St.
Gibbon, Richard D., (AV) ....'25 '54 C&L.862 LL.B. [Gibbon&Assoc.] ⊙
Gibbon & Associates, P.A., (AV) .... P.O. Box 1211 (⊙Tulsa)
Giulioli, Thomas C., (AV) ....'51 '80 C.612 B.S. L.862 J.D. Dist. Atty.
Henson, Donald W., (BV) ....'52 '77 C.622 B.S. L.623 J.D. Hwy. 75 N.
Humphrey, Charles M., III ....'49 '75 C.612 B.S. L.623 J.D. Dist. J.
Inglish, Robert, (AV) ....'54 '79 C.612 B.S. L.623 J.D. [Inglish&G.]

Inglish & Gaither, Professional Corporation, (AV)
McCulloch Building, 114 North Grand, Suite 408, P.O. Box 130, 74447 ⊙
Telephone: 918-756-5274 Fax: 918-756-0502
Email: ig@inglishgaither.com
George R. Inglish (1912-1998); Robert Inglish; Luke Gaither.
General Civil Practice in all State and Federal Courts. Probate, Oil and Gas, Real Estate, Banking, Bankruptcy (Creditor), Corporation, Mortgage Foreclosures, Estate Planning Law, Title Insurance, Family Law, Personal Injury.
General Counsel for: The First National Bank and Trust Co. of Okmulgee; American Exchange Bank, Henryetta.
Representative Clients: Pine Properties, Inc.; Okmulgee Ready-Mix Concrete Co.; Okmulgee Land Title Co.; Brewer Communications, Inc.; Morris State Bank, American Heritage Bank, Beggs Branch; Sam K. Viersan Jr. Trust; First United Bank, Henryetta; First Family Credit Union, Henryetta.
Henryetta, Oklahoma Office: 405 West Trudgeon Street, P.O. Box 1090, 74437. Telephone: 918-652-4402. Facsimile: 918-652-4487.
See Professional Biographies, OKMULGEE, OKLAHOMA

Jennings, George M. ....'50 '79 C.45 B.A. L.862 J.D. 806 N. Grand Ave.‡
Mabrey, W. Carlisle, III ......'44 '69 C&L.623 B.A., J.D. Pres., Citizens Bk. & Trust Co.
Maley, John D. ....'30 '59 C&L.623 B.A., J.D. Dist. J.
Martin, Billy L. ....'25 '67 C&L.425 J.D. Assoc. Dist. J.
Moore, Patrick Edward, (BV) ....'42 '77 C.623 B.B.A. L.616 J.D. [Moore]
Moore, Thos. E., (BV) ....'11 '48 C.947 A.B. L.623 LL.B. [Moore]
Moore Law Firm, The, (BV) ....206 W. Seventh Street
Neal, Bryan D. ....'56 '82 C&L.623 B.B.A., J.D. P.O. Box 250
Proctor, David Dale ....'60 '90 C&L.623 B.S., J.D. 1004 Plainview
Ramirez, Javier ....'72 '00 C.197 A.B. L.862 J.D. [Moore]
Ramirez, Pandee Ayne Moore ....'72 '99 C.623 B.A. L.862 J.D. [Moore]
Robinson, Hugh M., (BV) ....'54 '81 C&L.623 B.B.A., J.D. [Robinson W.]
Robinson Wiemer, (BV) ....114 North Grand, Suite 200
Romine, Mary B. ....'29 '64 C.618 B.A. L.623 LL.B. 408 W. 6th, Ste. 300‡
Seacat, Carol Ann, (BV) ....'44 '78 C&L.862 B.S., J.D. P.O. Box 1259
Seacat, Dennis F., (BV) ....'38 '77 C.623 B.A. L.862 J.D. P.O. Box 1259
Wiemer, Rod W., (BV) ....'65 '90 C&L.862 B.S.B.A., J.D. [Robinson W.]

OVERBROOK, 443, *Love Co.*

Hester, Michael J., Inc.
(See Ardmore)

OWASSO, 18,502, *Tulsa Co.*

Baysinger, Laura Hancock ....'63 '93 C.612 B.S. L.862 J.D. [Resolution R.]
Charney, Harold, (BV) ....'30 '55 C&L.623 B.A. 202 S. Cedar
Charney, Randee F., (AV) ....'62 '88 C.976 B.A. L.862 J.D. P.O. Box 240
Cummings, Gordon L. '48 '75 C&L.45 B.A., J.D.
(adm. in AR; not adm. in OK) P.O. Box 171
Cummings, Maupin '10 '35 C&L.45 B.A.
(adm. in WA; not adm. in OK) P.O. Box 171
Elias, Philip D. ....'48 '79 C.93 B.S. L.623 J.D. 10102 N. 147th. E. Ave.
Holmes, Randall T. ....'52 '79 C&L.623 B.A., J.D. P.O. Box 115
Johnson, Timothy E., (BV) ....'49 '76 C.619 B.S. L.862 J.D. P.O. Box 807
Johnston, Dean S. ....'23 '58 C.694 B.A. L.986 LL.B. 12706 East 82nd Street North‡
Moriarty, Sandra A. ....'64 '89 C.612 B.S. L.862 J.D. 9009 N. 135th E. Ave.
Resolution Resources, PLLC ....202 E. First St.
Sokolosky, Dominic, III, (AV) ....'57 '83 C.612 B.S. L.623 J.D. P.O. Box 1800

Spence Law Office
(See Tulsa)

Whalen, Thomas ....'35 '72 C.436 B.S. L.862 J.D. P.O. Box 621‡

PAULS VALLEY, * 6,256, *Garvin Co.*

Agee, Alan, (AV) ....'34 '72 C&L.623 B.B.A., J.D. [Garvin,A.C.&M.]
Agee, Brett, (BV) ....'63 '88 C&L.623 B.Acct., J.D. [Garvin,A.C.&M.]
Balcerak, L. ....'67 '92 C.612 B.S. L.623 J.D. [L.Balcerak]
Balcerak, L., Attorney PLLC ....211 N. Walnut Street
Blake, John A., (BV) ....'44 '74 C.210 B.A. L.623 J.D. 100 East Paul
Blalock, Candace L. ....'43 '76 C.623 B.A. L.615 J.D. Dist. J.
Carlton, James W., Jr., (BV) ....'62 '88 C&L.623 B.Acct., J.D. [Garvin,A.C.&M.]
Day, Ralph E., Jr. ....'47 '76 C&L.986 B.S., J.D. 102 Willow Spring Circle

Garvin, Agee, Carlton & Mashburn, L.L.P., (AV)
101 East Grant Avenue, 73075 ⊙
Telephone: 405-238-5559; 888-238-5559 Fax: 405-238-5666
URL: http://www.attysatlaw.com
R.B. Garvin (1906-1975); Alan Agee; Brett Agee; James W. Carlton, Jr.; John D. Mashburn (Resident, Oklahoma City Office); Steven C. Kendall.
Litigation, Personal Injury, Medical Malpractice, Automobile Accidents, Slip and Fall, Wrongful Death, Nursing Home Abuse, Unsafe Products, Toxic Torts, Legal Malpractice, Insurance, Professional Liability, Business Law, Commercial Law, Contracts, Corporate Law, Education Law, Banking Law, Bankruptcy, Debtor and Creditor, Taxation, Tax Planning, Consumer Law, Consumer Fraud, Warranties, Natural Resources, Energy, Elder Law, Wills and Probate, Trusts and Estates, Estate Planning, Guardianship, Real Estate, Buying or Selling a Home, Construction Law, Landlord and Tenant, General Practice, Appellate Practice.
Oklahoma City Office: 2100 City Place Tower, 204 North Robinson Avenue, 73102. Telephone: 405-232-9996. Fax: 405-232-9979.
See Professional Biographies, PAULS VALLEY, OKLAHOMA

Ham, Glen, (AV) ....'19 '49 C.623 L.615 LL.B. P.O. Box 188
Hart, Dean, Jr., (AV) ....'44 '73 C&L.623 B.A., J.D. [Hart&H.]
Hart, Walter D., (AV) ....'16 '41 C&L.623 B.A., LL.B. [Hart&H.] ‡
Hart & Hart, (AV) ....105 N. Willow St.
Helvey, Sandra, (BV) ....'52 '79 C.612 B.A. L.623 J.D. P.O. Box 1045
Hope, Garland ....'11 '42 C&L.623 B.S., J.D. Rte. 3, Box 4‡
Kendall, Steven C. ....'66 '94 C.999 B.A. L.623 J.D. [Garvin,A.C.&M.]
Lance, Lisa Watson ....'68 '96 C.1300 B.S. L.623 J.D. 104 Grandview Ave.
McClain, Richard B. ....'39 '64 C&L.623 B.A., LL.B. Assoc. Dist. J.
Meinders, Hildred McCants ....'08 '42 C.617 L.999 405 N. Chickasaw‡
Misak, Trisha Ann ....'72 '97 C&L.623 B.A., J.D. Spec. Dist. Ct. J.
Readnour, Keith ....'67 '93 C.612 B.A. L.623 J.D. [K.Readnour]
Readnour, Keith, P.C. ....108 W. Paul
Rennie, Robert T., (BV) ....'29 '53 C&L.623 B.A., LL.B. P.O. Box 1212
Sampson, Philip Scot ....'66 '99 C.613 B.A. L.623 J.D. Dist. Atty. Off.
Scarce, Max H. ....'23 '62 C.622 B.A. L.623 LL.B. Ret. Asso. Dist. J.
Shumate, Joe D. ....'14 '38 C&L.623 B.A., LL.B. Ret. Dist. J.

Sisson, B. David
(See Norman)

Sprouse, Daniel T., (BV) ....'52 '79 C.338 B.S. L.616 J.D. 105 S. Willow
Sprowls, John R., (AV) ....'44 '72 C.921 B.S. L.623 J.D. 211 N. Walnut St.
Tillery, Edward T., Law Office of, (BV) ...'50 '84 C.612 B.B.A. L.623 J.D. 210 W. Grant
Tipton, Virgil ....'40 '73 C.618 B.A. L.623 J.D. Spec. Dist. J.
Vandever, Billy ....'62 '91 C.621 B.A. L.623 J.D. P.O. Box 82

PAWHUSKA, * 3,629, *Osage Co.*

Boggs, John S., Jr., (BV) ....'43 '73 C.934 B.A. L.862 J.D. Asst. Dist. Atty.

Brewer, Worten, Robinett, (AV)
204 First National Bank Building, 74005 ⊙
Telephone: 918-287-2200
Member of Firm: Jesse J. Worten, III.
General Civil Practice. State and Federal Litigation. Corporate, Banking, Real Estate, Oil and Gas, Probate, Trust and Estate Planning, Family and Employment Law, Personal Injury and Insurance Defense.
Bartlesville, Oklahoma Office: 117 W. 5th Street, 500 Professional Building, P.O. Box 1066, 74005-1066. Telephone: 918-336-4132. Fax: 918-336-9009.
See Professional Biographies, PAWHUSKA, OKLAHOMA

Briggs, John Thomas ....'56 '82 C.623 B.A. L.862 J.D. [J.T.Briggs]
Briggs, John T. ....106 W. Main
Daniel, Noble D., (BV) ....'48 '74 C.623 B.B.A. L.616 J.D. [Daniel]
Daniel Law Firm, (BV) ....211 E. Main St.
Gambill, B. David ....'56 '81 C.623 B.S. L.616 J.D. Spec. Dist. Ct. J.
Gambill, Bruce, (AV) ....'30 '57 C&L.623 B.S., J.D. 525 Kihekah
Haney, William E. '27 '51 C&L.900 B.A., LL.B.
(adm. in KS; not adm. in OK) Dept. of Interior
Hukill, Sheree Lee ....'61 '98 C.612 B.S. L.862 J.D. 606 Kihekah‡
Jones, Jeff Steven ....'58 '99 C.612 B.A. L.862 J.D. Osage Co. Dist. Atty.
Kane, M. John, IV, (BV) ....'62 '87 C.612 B.S. L.623 J.D. [Kane] ⊙
Kane Law Offices, P.C., (BV) ....120 East Sixth Street (⊙Skiatook)
Kelly, Robert P., (AV) ....'26 '52 C&L.502 A.B., LL.B. 6th Ave.‡
Lamirand, Stephen A., (BV) ....'50 '77 C&L.623 B.S., J.D. [Lamirand&P.]
Lamirand & Palmer, (BV) ....520 Leahy

Mattingly, William H. ....'30 '58 C&L.623 B.A., LL.B. Assoc. Dist. J.
Palmer, Patti, (BV) ....'52 '77 C&L.623 B.S., J.D. [Lamirand&P.]
Payne, Harvey, (AV) ....'47 '73 C.612 B.S. L.862 J.D. [Wilson&P.]
Pearman, J.R. ....'40 '68 C.613 B.A. L.616 J.D. Dist. J.
Shoemake, Bransford, (BV) ....'56 '82 C&L.623 B.A., J.D. [Shoemake]
Shoemake, Shockley T. ....'22 '47 C&L.623 B.A., LL.B. 106 W. Main St.‡
Shoemake Law Office, (BV) ....106 W. Main
Standing Bear, Geoffrey M., (BV) ... '53 '80 C.623 B.A. L.862 J.D. [G.M.StandingBear]

Standing Bear, Geoffrey M., (BV)
715 Kihekah, P.O. Box 1049, 74056
Telephone: 918-287-4700 Fax: 918-287-4711
Email: ndnlawyer@sbcglobal.net URL: http://www.geoffreystandingbear.com
Geoffrey M. Standing Bear.
Civil Litigation, Federal Indian Law, Criminal Defense, Governmental Law, Personal Injury, Family Law, Probate.
Representative Clients: Muscogee (Creek) Nation; Oklahoma Indian Gaming Association; Oklahoma Nursing Homes, Ltd.

Stuart, Larry D., (AV) ....'48 '73 C.612 B.S. L.623 J.D. Dist. Atty.
Wilson, W. Robert, (AV) ....'35 '62 C&L.623 B.B.A., LL.B. [Wilson&P.]
Wilson & Payne, (AV) ....Suite 400 First National Building
Woodyard, L. Wayne, (BV) ....'46 '76 C.170 B.A. L.862 J.D. 1221 Lynn Street
Worten, Jesse J., III, (AV) ....'50 '76 C.612 B.S. L.616 J.D. [Brewer,W.R.] ⊙

PAWNEE, * 2,197, *Pawnee Co.*

Buchanan, Bob D., (BV) ....'60 '91 C.612 B.S. L.862 J.D. P.O. Box 445
Ellington, Billy Joe, (CV) ....'56 '83 C.612 B.S. L.616 J.D. 613 Illinois (⊙Cushing)
Foster, Alan B., (BV) ....'48 '77 C.612 B.A. L.616 J.D. Asst. Dist. Atty.
Henry, Matthew D. ....'52 '77 C.663 B.S. L.616 J.D. Assoc. Dist. J.
Henry, Rene P., Jr., (BV) '50 '76
C.612 B.A. L.862 J.D. Asst. Dist. Atty., The Dist. Atty. Off.

Perry, William J., (AV) '41 '66 C.612 B.S. L.623 LL.B.
522 Illinois, P.O. Box 372, 74058-0372
Telephone: 918-762-2501 Fax: 918-762-2502
General Civil Trial Practice. Real Property, Probate, Wills, Corporate, Oil and Gas Law.
Reference: First National Bank of Pawnee, Pawnee, Oklahoma.
See Professional Biographies, PAWNEE, OKLAHOMA

Privett, Kenneth B. ....'49 '76 C&L.623 B.B.A., J.D. 524 5th St.
Scott, Robert J., (AV) ....'24 '53 C&L.623 B.B.A., LL.B. P.O. Box 7

PERKINS, 2,272, *Payne Co.*

Thompson, Patrick A. ....'52 '77 C.612 B.A. L.615 J.D. [P.Thompson]
Thompson, Patrick ....RR 1

PERRY, * 5,230, *Noble Co.*

Allen, Danny G. ....'52 '77 C&L.623 B.S., J.D. Assoc. Dist. J.
Beier, Vicky Jean, (CV) ....'49 '90 C.82 B.A. L.623 J.D. 409 6th St.
Debord, Sherry Wallace ....'53 '88 C.623 B.A. L.616 J.D. P.O. Box 481
Kasper, Robert L., (AV) ....'29 '57 C.378 B.A. L.623 LL.B. 633 Delaware

Spence Law Office
(See Tulsa)

Yost, Donna Occhipinti, (BV) ....'59 '89 C.645 B.S. L.612 J.D. Asst. Dist. Atty.
Yost, Harvey D., II, (AV) ....'46 '71 C.612 B.A. L.623 J.D. 623 Delaware St.

PIEDMONT, 3,650, *Canadian Co.*

Allen, Gordon K. ....'36 '71 C.622 B.S. L.616 J.D. 1618 Rolling Ct., N.W.‡
Durall, Harold M., (BV) ....'23 '51 C&L.616 B.S., LL.B. 3019 Turkey Creek Lane
Hurst, Guy L. ....'50 '80 C&L.862 B.S., J.D. 415 Wash. Ave. E.
Lawter, Jack W. ....'28 '55 C.616 B.A. L.623 LL.B. 106 Monroe Ave., N.E.
McInnis-Nixon, R. Amanda, (AV) ....'62 '87 C.612 B.S. L.623 J.D. 13201 Blair Dr.
Patton, Wilbur P. ....'20 '48 L.623 LL.B. Fireman's Fund Ins. Co.
Ready, Charles Mark ....'54 '94 C.845 B.B.A. L.623 J.D. 2425 Richland Rd., N.W.

PONCA CITY, 25,919, *Kay Co.*

Armstrong, Chester, (AV) ....'26 '49 C&L.623 LL.B. 113A N. 4th St.

Atkins & Markoff
(See Oklahoma City)

Bailey, James M., (BV) ....'55 '80 C.1147 B.S. L.623 J.D. 222 E. Grand
Basham, Marshall D., (BV) ....'43 '80 C.1147 B.A. L.623 J.D. 116 N. 5th St.
Baumert, L. Enloe, (AV) ....'33 '59 C.612 B.A. L.623 LL.B. [Baumert,C.H.&Y.]

Baumert, Cummings, Hiatt & Young, (AV)
Home National Bank Building, Suite 205, P.O. Box 470, 74602
Telephone: 580-762-2403 Fax: 580-762-3166
URL: http://www.bchylawfirm.com
Members of Firm: L. Enloe Baumert; David S. Cummings; Derrin K. Hiatt; Lori L. Young.
General Civil Practice in all Courts. Real Estate, Family Law, Probate, Banking, Taxation, Bankruptcy, Employment, Corporation, Insurance, Personal Injury and Negligence Law. Trials.
Representative Clients: First National Bank & Trust Co., Ponca City; Ponca Plaza, Ltd.; Nickles Industrial Manufacturing Corp.; Conoco Inc.; Educational Data Services, Inc. (ADPC); Allied Producers Inc.; Kay County Development Authority; Ratliff, Inc.
Reference: First National Bank and Trust Co., Ponca City.
See Professional Biographies, PONCA CITY, OKLAHOMA

Boettcher, Ryan, Martin & Bisher, (AV)
116 North Fifth Street (⊙Oklahoma City, Tulsa)
Bracken, Gary L., (AV) ....'56 '81 C.60 B.S. L.378 J.D. 1223 E. Highland, Ste. 311
Brune, Walter F., Jr., (AV) ....'53 '79 C.339 B.A. L.623 J.D. 400 E. Central, Ste. 406
Burlie, Todd R., (BV) ....'69 '95 C.612 B.S. L.623 J.D. [Turner&B.]

Carmichael, Karen L., P.C.
(See Tulsa)

Casey, Charles W., (BV) ....'32 '59 C&L.623 B.B.A., LL.B. 1223 E. Highland
Clark, Guy P., (AV) ....'40 '65 C.612 B.S. L.623 J.D. [Northcutt,C.G.H.&T.]
Coleman, Robert B., Jr. ....'16 '52 C.576 B.Ch.E. L.87 LL.B. 1601 Academy Rd.‡
Collins, Michael R., (BV) ....'46 '72 C.620 B.S. L.623 J.D. 222 E. Grand, Suite 300
Collins, Richard W. ....'34 '62 C.612 B.S. L.273 LL.B. 2305 Skylark‡
Cummings, David S., (AV) ....'52 '77 C.1147 B.S. L.623 J.D. [Baumert,C.H.&Y.]

DeLacerda, Melissa, Law Office of
(See Stillwater)

Ealick, Perry L. '37 '79 C.871 B.S. L.796 J.D.
(adm. in TX; not adm. in OK) 1933 Mary St.‡
Emig, James M., (BV) ....'50 '80 C&L.623 B.A., J.D. 114 N. 3rd St.
Evans, Douglas Ellsworth ....'71 '00 C.490 B.S. L.612 J.D. [Evans]
Evans, Thomas S., (BV) ....'58 '84 C.494 B.A. L.862 J.D. [Evans]
Evans Law Center, (BV) ....115 E. Grand Ave.

Franseen, Craig J., (BV) ....'55 '80 C.623 B.A. L.615 J.D. 612 N. 3rd. St.
Gardner, John J., II, (AV) ....'46 '71 C.612 B.S. L.623 J.D. [Northcutt,C.G.H.&T.]
Garrison, David R., (AV) ....'37 '67 C.612 B.S. L.623 J.D. 612 North 3rd
Hammer, Bruce E., (BV) ....'54 '79 C.622 B.M.E. L.862 J.D. Asst. Dist. Atty.

Hermanson, Brian T., (AV) '52 '78 C.121 B.A. L.623 J.D.
620 E. Comanche, Suite 3, P.O. Box 2110, 74602
Telephone: 580-762-0020 Fax: 580-762-5620
Email: bhermanson@oklawhoma.com
Litigation, Criminal Law, Family Law, Divorce, Personal Injury.
See Professional Biographies, PONCA CITY, OKLAHOMA

Hiatt, Derrin K., (BV) ....'64 '89 C.1315 B.A. L.623 J.D. [Baumert,C.H.&Y.]
Holmes, Kenneth E., (AV) ....'34 '63 C&L.623 B.S., LL.B. 222 E. Grand, Ste. 4B
Hron, John W., Jr., (AV) ....'47 '73 C.612 B.S. L.623 J.D. [Northcutt,C.G.H.&T.]
Huth, Henry H. ....'20 '54 C.339 B.S. L.986 LL.B. 1704 Monument Rd. (Pat.)‡
Jean, Kenneth N., (BV) ....'62 '93 C&L.623 B.A., J.D. P.O. Box 1588
Kirkpatrick, William E. ....'45 '71 C.612 B.A. L.862 J.D. 2501 Wildwood
Kotarski, Joseph C. '24 '52 C.679 B.S. L.209 LL.B.
(adm. in IL; not adm. in OK) 2309 Meadowbrook‡
Lee, K. Wayne, (AV) ....'67 '93 C.618 B.A. L.616 J.D. 2016 Huntington Pl.
Leonard, Tom, (AV) ....'46 '73 C.612 B.S. L.623 J.D. 1926 Lake Road
Lobaugh, Russell D. ....'70 '01 C.1147 B.A. L.862 J.D. P.O. Box 1588
Martin, Paul S., (BV) ....'56 '87 C.612 B.S.B.A. L.623 J.D. [Boettcher,R.M.&B.]
Miller, Barbara A. ....'56 '81 C.612 B.A. L.862 J.D. [Miller]
Miller, Carolyn A. ....'53 '86 C.612 B.S.Ed. L.862 J.D. [Miller]
Miller, Geraldene Y. ....'28 '58 C.378 B.A. L.986 LL.B. [Miller] ⊙
Miller, William J. ....'24 '58 C.378 B.S.E.E. L.986 LL.B. [Miller] (Pat.)
Miller Law Office ....120 N. 2nd St. (Pat.) (⊙Galena, KS)
Morris, Thomas J., III, (BV) ....'43 '79 C&L.616 B.S., J.D. 400 E. Central Ave.
Murphy, Kevin J., (BV) ....'50 '75 C.612 B.A. L.623 J.D. City Atty.
Northcutt, Clarence D., (AV) ....'16 '38 C&L.623 B.A., LL.B. [Northcutt,C.G.H.&T.]
Northcutt, Paul E., (AV) ....'25 '50 C&L.623 LL.B. [Northcutt,C.G.H.&T.]

Northcutt, Clark, Gardner, Hron & Tate, (AV) 🄱🄱
Fourth Floor, Commercial Federal Bank, P.O. Drawer 1669, 74602
Telephone: 580-762-1655 Fax: 580-765-4142
URL: http://www.northcuttlawfirm.com
Members of Firm: Clarence D. Northcutt; Paul E. Northcutt; Guy P. Clark; John J. Gardner, II; John W. Hron, Jr.; Stuart L. Tate. Of Counsel: John W. Raley, Jr.
General Civil Practice in all State and Federal Courts. Trials and Appeals. Personal Injury, Probate, Real Estate, Family Law, Corporate, Business and Business Litigation and Workers Compensation Law. No collections.
See Professional Biographies, PONCA CITY, OKLAHOMA

Phipps, Kent C., (AV) ....'30 '57 C&L.623 B.A., LL.B. P.O. Box 388
Powell, Cleve W., (BV) ....'55 '80 C.802 B.S. L.273 J.D. 400 East Central Avenue
Raley, John W., Jr., (AV) ....'32 '59 C.613 A.B. L.623 J.D. [🄱 Northcutt,C.G.H.&T.]
Shears, Jack L., (BV) ....'49 '74 C.620 B.A. L.192 J.D. [Shears&S.]
Shears & Shears, (BV) ....1932 Lake Rd.
Smith, Carolyn S., (BV) ....'47 '90 C.1080 B.S. L.623 J.D. 107 N. 4th
Stout, W. Lee ....'61 '98 C.999 B.S. L.615 J.D. 400 E. Central Ave., Ste. 505
Tate, Stuart L., (BV) ....'62 '92 C.1147 B.A. L.616 J.D. [Northcutt,C.G.H.&T.]
Trewitt, Michael C., Jr., (BV) ....'49 '82 C.999 B.A. L.623 J.D. [M.C.Trewitt]
Trewitt, Michael C., (BV) ....1926 Lake Rd.
Turner, Lee, (BV) ....'57 '95 C.1300 B.S. L.623 J.D. [Turner&B.]
Turner & Burlie, P.C., (BV) ....1914 Lake Road
Westphal, David W. '59 '88 C.886 B.S. L.128 J.D.
Sr. Coun., ConocoPhillips Co. (Pat.)
Wicker, Bradley Wayne, (CV) ....'70 '97 C.612 B.S. L.623 J.D. 116 N. 5th St.
Yates, Grace Katharine ....'74 '99 C.612 B.A. L.623 J.D. 222 E. Grand, Ste. 4B
Young, Lori L., (BV) ....'60 '97 C.1147 B.S. L.615 J.D. [Baumert,C.H.&Y.]

POTEAU, * 7,939, *Le Flore Co.*

Allen, Sara H. ....'48 '77 C.101 B.A. L.208 J.D. Legal Servs. of Eastern Okla.
Amend, Terry L., Attorney at Law, (BV) ....'48 '74 C&L.623 B.A., J.D. 406 Dewey

Atkins & Markoff
(See Oklahoma City)

Barber, Belva Brooks, (BV) ....'56 '82 C.612 B.S. L.862 J.D. [Barber&B.]
Barber, Russell V., (BV) ....'57 '83 C.45 B.S.B.A. L.862 J.D. [Barber&B.]
Barber and Barber, P.C., (BV) ....107 Beard Street
Barnes, Samuel Stephen, (BV) ....'56 '91 C.1310 B.S. L.862 J.D. Off. of Dist. Atty.
Bovos, Marc L., (BV) ....'63 '88 C.619 B.S. L.616 J.D. [Hamilton,W.&B.]
Cundiff, Shelley A., (CV) ....'58 '90 C.612 B.S. L.862 J.D. [Waren&C.]
Curtis, Benjamin J., (BV) ....'36 '71 C.612 B.S. L.616 J.D. [Curtis]

Curtis Law Firm, The, (BV)
900 North Broadway, P.O. Box 767, 74953
Telephone: 918-647-9191 Fax: 918-647-9688
Email: curtisandsides@alltel.net
Benjamin J. Curtis.
General Civil and Criminal Practice. Real Estate, Probate, Wills and Trusts, Personal Injury, Corporation and Commercial, Matrimonial, Family Law, Bankruptcy.

Dunagan, Michael Patrick ....'60 '86 C.623 B.A. L.862 J.D. P.O. Box 935
Fry, Marion D. ....'74 '99 C.612 B.S. L.862 J.D. P.O. Box 880
Garland, Stanley Keith ....'56 '86 C.623 B.S. L.862 J.D. [Garland,S.K.]
Garland, Stanley K. ....P.O. Box 27

Hamilton, Warren & Bovos, A Professional Corporation, (BV)
Delivery Address: 101 North Broadway, P.O. Box 660, 74953-9998
Telephone: 918-647-9171 Fax: 918-647-9175
URL: http://www.lawyers.com/hwb
Dean E. Warren; Marc L. Bovos. Associate: Kevin S. Merritt.
General Civil and Trial Practice. Real Estate, Oil and Gas, Probate, Corporate, Negligence, Insurance and Mining Law. No collections under $25,000.00.
Representative Clients: Central National Bank, Poteau; First State Bank, Wister; First National Bank, Heavener; State National Bank, Heavener; Ollies Lumber Co., Poteau; Bob Smedley Chevrolet-Olds, Inc., American Title and Trust Co.
See Professional Biographies, POTEAU, OKLAHOMA

Knight, Ted A. ....'50 '75 C.619 B.S. L.616 J.D. Assoc. Dist. J.
Lee, Michael D. ....'41 '72 C.621 B.A. L.623 J.D. Spec. Dist. J.
Lucas, Larry B., (BV) ....'39 '64 C&L.623 B.S., LL.B. 112 N. Witte
McBee, George H. ....'42 '67 C&L.623 B.S., J.D. Dist. J.
McCroskey, Eddie A., (BV) ....'43 '73 C.619 B.A. L.616 J.D. P.O. Box 785
Merritt, Kevin S. ....'77 '03 C.999 B.S. L.862 J.D. [🄰 Hamilton,W.&B.]
Mixon, Jeffrey L., (BV) ....'53 '85 C&L.623 B.A., J.D. Asst. Dist. Atty.
Nicholson, Margaret Sheldon ....'67 '98 C.1271 B.A. L.623 J.D. 224 Dewey
Pate, Pat ....'31 '60 C.819 B.S. L.45 LL.B. 109 Beard‡
Pate, Whit, (AV) ....'24 '53 C.623 M.A. L.45 LL.B. 109 Beard
Poole, Anita K. ....'67 '99 C.38 B.A. L.1243 J.D. P.O. Box 588

Sanders, Douglas W., Jr., (BV) .... '58 '84 C.612 B.S. L.616 J.D. Mun. J.
Schmuck, Douglas Wayne ....'70 '97 C.612 B.A. L.862 J.D. [D.W.Schmuck]
Schmuck, Douglas W. .... 102 Fleener Ave.

Sides, Desmond, (CV) '55 '94 C.619 B.S. L.862 J.D.
100 Fleener Avenue, P.O. Box 995, 74953
Telephone: 918-647-3442 Fax: 918-647-0649
General Civil and Criminal Practice. Real Estate, Probate, Wills and Trusts, Personal Injury, Corporation and Commercial, Matrimonial, Family Law, Bankruptcy.
See Professional Biographies, POTEAU, OKLAHOMA

Smith, Jeffrey C., (CV) '59 '85
C.473 B.S.Ed. L.862 J.D. 109 Beard, Professional Building, Suite 108
Sullivan, Don, (BV) .... '44 '73 C.619 B.A.Ed. L.862 J.D. 106 Mozell Street
Sullivan, Jonathan K., (BV) ....'62 '87 C.612 B.S.B.A. L.45 J.D. 104 S. Church
Sullivan, Mike, (BV) .... '38 '65 C.1023 L.862 LL.B. Dist. Atty.
Thompson, Elton E. .... '25 '51 C.612 L.45 J.D. [Thompson&T.] ‡
Thompson, Glenn E., (BV) .... '49 '73 C&L.862 B.S., J.D. [Thompson&T.]
Thompson & Thompson, (BV) ....101 North Church Street
Wallace, Robert A., (BV) ....'63 '88 C&L.623 B.A., J.D. Dist. Atty.
Ward, Farley W., (CV) .... '54 '80 C.612 B.A. L.623 J.D. Dist. J.
Waren, Drucilla E., (CV) .... '50 '83 C.619 B.A. L.862 J.D. [Waren&C.]
Waren & Cundiff, P.C., (CV) ....1809 N. Broadway
Warren, Dean E., (BV) ....'39 '69 C.619 B.S. L.623 J.D. [Hamilton,W.&B.]

PRAGUE, 2,138, *Lincoln Co.*

Bykerk, Donald N., (BV) ....'26 '50 C&L.546 B.S.L., LL.B. 905 Main St.
Hamm, Christopher P. .... '52 '90 C.1164 L.615 J.D. 902 Jim Thorpe Blvd.
Morrison, Walter M. .... '11 '35 C&L.623 P.O. Box 623‡

PROCTOR, —, *Adair Co.*

Tate, Tom .... '36 '60 C.612 B.S. L.623 LL.B. Mgr., Tate Ranch, L.L.C.

PRYOR, * 8,659, *Mayes Co.*

Blevins, Nancy Nesbitt, (BV) ....'50 '77 C.623 B.A. L.862 J.D. [Blevins&S.]
Blevins, Paul E., (AV) ....'48 '73 C.612 B.S. L.862 J.D. [Blevins&S.]
Blevins & Sordahl, Inc., A Professional Corporation, (AV) .... 110 N. Adair
Bohannan, Lisa M. .... '67 '93 C.619 B.S. L.616 J.D. [Bohannan]
Bohannan Law Office, The ....103 S. Vann St.
Crockett, John M., (BV) .... '50 '76 C.619 B.A. L.862 J.D. [J.M.Crockett]
Crockett, John M., Attorney at Law, PC, (BV) .... 226 E. Graham Ave.
Dean, Gary J. ....'40 '66 C&L.623 B.B.A., J.D. Spec. Dist. J.
Dennis, Jerrold R., (BV) ....'51 '81 C.504 B.A. L.862 J.D. 108 N. Adair
Dodson, Kevin Lee ....'74 '01 C.612 B.S. L.862 J.D [Dodson]
Dodson Law Office ....308A N.E. 1st St.
Dunker, Steven J. '63 '96 C.1310 B.S. L.986 J.D.
(adm. in MO; not adm. in OK) 108 N. Rowe St.
Elliott, Randall, (AV) ....'51 '76 C.612 B.A. L.623 J.D. [Elliott&S.]

Elliott & Sherrer, P.C., (AV)
112 B North Vann, P.O. Box 1165, 74362
Telephone: 918-825-6711 Fax: 918-825-0080
URL: http://www.lawyers.com/elliott
Randall Elliott; R. Benjamin Sherrer;—Danny L. Littlefield, Jr.
Condemnation/Eminent Domain, Criminal Law, Family Law, Corporate Law, Estate Planning, Probate, Personal Injury and Real Estate.
See Professional Biographies, PRYOR, OKLAHOMA

Goodpaster, James D. .... '42 '66 C&L.623 B.B.A., LL.B. 1 Court Pl., Ste. 240
Jones, Robert B. ....'37 '90 C.862 B.S. L.616 J.D. Ret. Col. U.S.A.F.
Lamb, Dana Leigh Lyons ....'48 '79 C.45 B.A. L.862 J.D. 38 Stone Forest‡
Lamb, Nash ....'42 '74 C.882 B.A. L.862 J.D. Gen. Coun., Williams Construction Co.
Lee, Gerald R., (BV) ....'51 '78 C&L.862 B.A., J.D. P.O. Box 1101
Littlefield, Danny L., Jr. .... '77 '02 C.619 B.S. L.862 J.D. [Ⓐ Elliott&S.]

Logan & Lowry, LLP
(See Vinita)

Longmire, Carl W., (BV) .... '24 '52 C&L.623 B.B.S., J.D. 226 E. Graham Ave.
Lyons, Christopher B., (BV) .... '51 '81 C.45 B.A. L.862 J.D. 207 N.E. 1st St.
Lyons, Tony Jack, (AV) '24 '52
C.612 L.623 LL.B. 207 N.E. lst, Northside Courthouse Sq.
McBride, Terry H. ....'50 '79 C.612 B.S. L.862 J.D. Assoc. District Judge
Moore, Darrell L., (BV) ....'54 '79 C&L.623 B.B.A., J.D. [J.R.Moore]
Moore, J. Ralph, (AV) ....'28 '53 C&L.623 B.A., J.D. [J.R.Moore] ‡

Moore, J. Ralph, PC, (BV)
Court Place at N. Vann, P.O. Box 368, 74362
Telephone: 918-825-0332
Email: jrmpc@swbell.net URL: http://www.jrmpclaw.com
J. Ralph Moore (Retired); Darrell L. Moore; Julia L. Neftzger.
Civil Litigation, Insurance Defense, Workers Compensation, Civil Rights, Litigation, Employment and Labor Law, Estate Planning, Medicaid Planning, Real Estate, Probate and Adoptions.
See Professional Biographies, PRYOR, OKLAHOMA

Neftzger, Julia L. ....'66 '91 C.612 B.S. L.862 J.D. [J.R.Moore]
Ritchie, K. Ellis, (BV) ....'62 '92 C.619 B.S. L.862 J.D. [K.E.Ritchie]

Ritchie, K. Ellis, P.C., (BV)
2 1/2 South Adair, 74361
Mailing Address: P.O. Box 246, Pryor, OK 74362
Telephone: 918-825-4558 Fax: 918-825-1623
Email: kim-kellispc@swbell.net URL: http://www.ritchielawok.com
K. Ellis Ritchie;—Shawn Scott Taylor.
Practice includes Eminent Domain/Condemnation/Property Rights.
See Professional Biographies, PRYOR, OKLAHOMA

Sherrer, R. Benjamin, (CV) ....'68 '97 C.612 B.S. L.616 J.D. [Elliott&S.]
Sordahl, Fredrick H., Jr., (AV) ....'55 '80 C.339 B.A. L.862 J.D. [F.H.Sordahl]
Sordahl, Fred H., Inc., (AV) ....110 N. Adair
Taylor, Shawn Scott ....'65 '91 C.612 B.S. L.623 J.D. [Ⓐ K.E.Ritchie]

Taylor, Burrage, Foster, Mallett, Downs & Ramsey, P.C.
(See Claremore)

Thomas, Wm. M., Jr. ....'26 '52 C&L.623 A.B., LL.B. Assoc. Dist. J.
Van Horn, David R. ....'37 '69 C.691 B.A. L.862 J.D. 21 N. Vann St.
Williams, Byron E., Jr. .... '37 '72 C.616 B.S. L.862 J.D. 28 S. Adair St.

PURCELL, * 5,571, *McClain Co.*

Barger, Gary ....'47 '89 C&L.623 B.S., J.D. P.O. Box 774
Barry, William G. ....'15 '49 C&L.623 B.A., LL.B. 900 Lovers Lane‡
Bonnell, Larry, (BV) ....'57 '83 C&L.623 B.A., J.D. [L.Bonnell]
Bonnell, Larry, PC, Law Office of, (BV) ....120 N. 2nd St.
Dixon, Greg ....'66 '94 C&L.623 B.S.B.A., J.D. [Montgomery&D.]
Ewing, Noah H., Jr. ....'47 '73 C&L.623 B.B.A., J.D. 121 N. 2nd Ave., Ste. 225
Farnan, Joe, (BV) ....'50 '77 C.1109 B.A. L.623 J.D. P.O. Box 770
Ford, Darrell G. ....'59 '86 C.612 B.S. L.846 J.D. 118 N. 2nd, Ste. C
Gardner, Michael L., (CV) .... '66 '92 C.612 B.A. L.623 J.D. [Ⓐ J.Farnan]
Gonzalez, Jose, (BV) ....'50 '86 C.623 B.S. L.1300 J.D. P.O. Box 429
Gray, Charles N., (CV) ....'54 '82 C.623 B.A. L.616 J.D. P.O. Box 249
Haxel, Ted W., (AV) .... '48 '75 C&L.623 B.B.A., J.D. 108 North Second Street
Langer, Steven ....'64 '92 C&L.623 B.A., J.D. [Ⓐ J.Farnan]
Lester, Billy Carl ....'50 '80 C&L.623 B.B.A., J.D. [B.C.Lester]
Lester, Billy C., PC ....223 W. Main

Mantooth, John, (AV) '47 '73 C&L.623 B.A., J.D.
111 North Third Street, P.O. Box 667, 73080-0667
Telephone: 405-527-2137 Facsimile: 405-527-3440
Civil Litigation, Probate Law, Personal Injury Law, Wills, Trusts and Estate Planning.
References: First American Bank, Purcell, Oklahoma; American Abstract Company of Purcell, Oklahoma; Guaranty Abstract Company of Purcell, Oklahoma.

McCasland, Linda K., (CV) ....'47 '82 C&L.623 B.B.A., J.D. 309 W. Main
Montgomery & Dixon ....212 West Main
Oliphant, L. Dee, (BV) ....'39 '66 C&L.623 B.B.A., J.D. P.O. Box 996
Shilling, Leland Woodyard, (CV) ....'52 '96 C.1044 B.S. L.615 J.D. [L.W.Shilling]
Shilling, Leland W., PC, (CV) ....P.O. Box 614
Tracy, Jack F. ....'49 '86 C.639 B.S. L.623 J.D. 201 W. Main
Woodrow, Suzanne, (CV) ....'56 '93 C.612 B.S. L.623 J.D. 309 W. Main St.

RUSH SPRINGS, 1,229, *Grady Co.*

Mileur, Alfred Donald ....'25 '50 C.623 L.273 J.D. P.O. Box 67‡
Williams, Danny C. ....'52 '85 C.1061 B.S.C.E. L.744 J.D. P.O. Box 761

SALINA, 1,422, *Mayes Co.*

Jay, Gary M., (AV) ....'37 '60 C&L.862 B.A., LL.B. P.O. Box 557

SALLISAW, * 7,989, *Sequoyah Co.*

Condit, Thomas W., (BV) ....'41 '67 C.766 B.A. L.1065 J.D. [Ⓐ H.Scoufos]
Cripps, John T., (BV) .... '45 '75 C&L.623 B.S., J.D. [J.T.Cripps]

Cripps, John T., Inc., Law Offices of, (BV)
104-A South Oak, P.O. Box 606, 74955
Telephone: 918-775-9142 Fax: 918-775-7588
Email: crippslaw@sbcglobal.net
John T. Cripps.
General Civil Practice. Real Estate, Probate, Family, Workers Compensation, Bankruptcy and Commercial Law, Social Security.
Approved Attorney for: Farmers Home Administration; American First Title Insurance Co.; Chicago Title Insurance Co.; St. Paul Title Insurance Co.
References: First National Bank, Sallisaw; Sequoyah State Bank of Muldrow; Cimarron Savings and Loan Association.
See Professional Biographies, SALLISAW, OKLAHOMA

Cunningham, Don ....'27 '53 L.616 J.D. 302 S. Oak St.
Daffin, Michael A., (BV) ....'56 '79 C.698 B.A. L.862 J.D. [M.A.Daffin]
Daffin, Michael A., Inc., The Law Office of, (BV) ....131 East Chickasaw
Dodson, William H., Sr., (CV) ....'50 '82 C.612 B.A. L.809 J.D. [Dodson]
Dodson Law Office, (CV) ....P.O. Box 682
Gean, David A., III, Law Office of, (CV) ... '61 '87 C&L.45 B.A., J.D. 212 E. Chickasaw

Gean, Gean & Gean
(See Fort Smith, Arkansas)

Ghahremani, Kent S. ....'56 '87 C.560 B.B.A. L.862 J.D. P.O. Box 1524
Green, Fred D. (Jack) ....'25 '52 C.623 L.615 LL.B. Ret. Assoc. Dist. J.
Henshaw, A.J., Jr. ....'46 '81 C.619 B.A. L.616 J.D. Assoc. Dist. J.
Hickman, T. Scott, (BV) ....'58 '85 C.612 B.S. L.1288 J.D. Asst. Dist. Atty.
Jones, Jim, (AV) .... '32 '61 C.619 B.S. L.900 J.D. 204 North Elm Street
Martin, Nancy A., (BV) ....'52 '82 C.623 B.A. L.45 J.D. 201 N. Main St.
Montgomery, John Robert, (AV) '41 '71
C.623 B.B.A. L.616 J.D. City Atty. [Montgomery&M.]
Montgomery, Medessa Cook, (BV) '57 '89 C.619 B.A.Ed. L.862 J.D.
[Montgomery&M.]
Montgomery and Montgomery, P.C., (AV) .... 123 E. Choctaw
Orendorff, William K., (BV) ....'51 '86 C.623 B.B.A. L.616 J.D. 206 North Oak Street
Rogers, Bill E. ....'41 '66 C.619 L.862 LL.B. Dist. J.
Rogers, J. Neal ....'58 '92 C.623 B.A. L.862 J.D. 100 N. Oak
Scoufos, Harry G., III, (AV) ....'43 '71 C.618 B.A. L.616 J.D. [H.Scoufos]
Scoufos, Harry G. ("Fourth"), IV, (BV) '70 '96 C.623 B.B.A. L.616 J.D.
[Ⓐ H.Scoufos]

Scoufos, Harry, P.C., Law Offices of, (AV)
Creek & Elm Streets, P.O. Box 787, 74955
Telephone: 918-775-5546 Toll Free: 888-775-5546 Fax: 918-775-4990
Email: scoufos3@iamerica.net
Harry G. Scoufos, III;—Thomas W. Condit; Harry G. ("Fourth") Scoufos, IV.
Trial Practice. Negligence, Personal Injury, Products Liability, Medical Malpractice, Insurance, Workers Compensation, Family, Criminal Defense, Admiralty Law, Aviation Law, Class Action.
See Professional Biographies, SALLISAW, OKLAHOMA

Sprouse, Dennis M. ....'52 '78 C.1288 B.A. L.862 J.D. Spec. Dist. J.
Steele, James R. ....'19 '70 C.612 B.S. L.862 J.D. Route 3
Sullivan, Frank, Jr., (BV) ....'52 '77 C.1288 B.A. L.623 J.D. 105 N. Oak

Taylor, Burrage, Foster, Mallett, Downs & Ramsey, P.C.
(See Claremore)

Wood, Clark S., (BV) ....'50 '82 C.612 B.S. L.615 J.D. 115 E. Choctaw, Ste. 201

SAND SPRINGS, 17,451, *Osage & Tulsa Cos.*

Adams, Ryan L. ....'72 '97 C.619 B.B.A. L.623 J.D. Fin. Dir.
Collins, John E. ....'53 '90 C.612 B.S. L.862 J.D. P.O. Box 898
Drummond, I. Michele, (BV) ....'54 '93 C.613 B.A. L.862 J.D. 9108 Country Road
Henson, E. Bryan, Jr., (AV) ....'30 '64 C&L.862 B.S., J.D. 1208 E. 8th Street
Lloyd, Jim, (BV) ....'49 '75 C.612 B.S. L.862 J.D. [Lloyd&L.]
Lloyd, Nancy, (BV) ....'51 '87 C.612 B.S. L.862 J.D. [Lloyd&L.]
Lloyd & Lloyd, (BV) .... 200 N. Main St.
Munn, James M., (BV) ....'35 '69 C.619 B.S. L.862 J.D. 16 Rawson Place
Mushrush, Leroy, (BV) ....'30 '59 C.862 B.A. L.623 LL.B. 108 E. Bway.
Phillips, Cynthia A., (BV) ....'65 '90 C.612 B.S. L.862 J.D. 207 N. Main St.
Phillips, David W., (BV) ....'33 '65 C&L.862 B.A., J.D. 200 Roosevelt St.
Phillips, Erwin D., (BV) ....'28 '61 C&L.862 B.A., J.D. 200 Roosevelt Ave.
Thomas, Paul George ....'19 '42 C&L.623 B.A., J.D. 1001 N Main
Williams, Joe A. ....'36 '61 C.639 A.B. L.623 LL.B. Pres., Sand Springs Home

SAPULPA, * 19,166, *Creek Co.*

Allen, Sam T., III, (AV) ....'23 '50 C&L.623 A.B., LL.B. [Loeffler A.&H.]
Allen, Sam T., IV, (BV) ....'52 '77 C&L.623 B.S., J.D. [Loeffler A.&H.]

Atkins & Markoff
(See Oklahoma City)

Branscum, Valley M., (CV) .....'50 '89 C.612 B.S. L.862 J.D. 510 S. Main St.
Brown, C. Clifton, (BV) .....'27 '69 C.623 A.B. L.862 J.D. 208 E. Dewey Ave.

Carmichael, Karen L., P.C.
(See Tulsa)

Carson, Russell D., P.C.
(See Tulsa)

Cook, D. Max, (BV) '49 '88 C.612 B.S. L.862 J.D. Dist. Atty., Creek Co. Dist. Atty. Off.
Corbridge, Richard M. .....'32 '59 C&L.208 B.S.L., J.D. 2714 W. 126th St.‡
Corgan, Craig D., (BV) .....'52 '78 C.623 B.A. L.862 J.D. Dist. Atty.
Dimmitt, William W., Jr. .....'17 '51 C&L.900 A.B., LL.B. 1306 E. Fairview Ave.‡
Dormont, April Denise .....'65 '91 C.619 B.S. L.862 J.D. P.O. Box 190
Erickson, William E., (BV) .....'53 '89 C.134 B.S. L.862 J.D. 111 E. Lee Ave.
Filbeck, Tom, (BV) .....'44 '69 C&L.623 B.A., J.D. 7 S. Park
Frazier, Sandra J. .....'60 '99 C.999 B.A. L.862 J.D. [Frazier&L.]
Frazier & Lockhart, P.C. .....102 S. Poplar St.
Gardner, Dale Ray, (BV) .....'46 '79 C.801 B.A. L.862 J.D. 7 S. Park St.
Gilbertson, Melvin L., (BV) .....'50 '78 C&L.623 B.B.A., J.D. 21 S. Park
Ham, C. Keith, (AV) .....'54 '79 C&L.862 B.A., J.D. [Loeffler A.&H.] ⊙
Hammers, Pamela B., (BV) .....'71 '97 C.804 B.S. L.862 J.D. Off. of Dist. Atty.
Harlan, John L., (AV) .....'48 '77 C.347 B.A. L.862 J.D. [J.L.Harlan&Assoc.]
Harlan, John L., & Associates, P.C., (AV) .....404 E. Dewey St.
Henderson, Lester D., (AV) .....'37 '61 C.612 B.S. L.623 LL.B. [L.D.Henderson]

Henderson, Lester D., P.C., (AV)
16 North Park, P.O. Box 205, 74067
Telephone: 918-227-2733 FAX: 918-227-2051
Lester D. Henderson.
Probate, Estate Planning, Real Estate, General Civil, Municipal Law, Personal Injury, Oil and Gas and Contract Law.
References: American National Bank & Trust, Sapulpa; Citizens Bank, Sapulpa.

See Professional Biographies, SAPULPA, OKLAHOMA

Holdsclaw, Frank Lynn .....'58 '00 C.623 B.S.C.S. L.862 J.D. [F.L.Holdsclaw]
Holdsclaw, Frank L. .....7 S. Park St.
Lane, Tom C., (BV) .....'48 '88 C.839 B.B.A. L.862 J.D. P.O. Box 384
Lockhart, Frank .....'51 '96 C.33 B.A. L.862 J.D. [Frazier&L.]
Loeffler, Michael S., (BV) .....'63 '88 C&L.623 B.B.A., J.D. [Loeffler A.&H.] ⊙
Loeffler Allen & Ham, (AV) .....Loeffler-Allen Building (⊙Bristow)
Lorbiecki, Stefanie, (BV) .....'59 '86 C.961 B.S. L.862 J.D. 208 E. Dewey, Ste. 305
Lowe, Joseph Charles .....'52 '00 C.612 B.S. L.862 J.D. P.O. Box 1331
Mitchell, Allen B., (AV) .....'44 '68 C.612 B.A. L.862 J.D. [A.B.Mitchell]
Mitchell, Allen B., A Professional Corporation, (AV) .....111 E. Dewey St.
Neil, Nicki Sue .....'48 '97 C.376 B.A. L.862 J.D. Trial Atty., Okla. Indigent Def. Sys.
Nelson, Don I., (AV) .....'44 '73 C.84 B.S. L.862 J.D. 1st Asst. Dist. Atty.
Redding, Sherry A., (BV) .....'63 '88 C&L.862 B.A., J.D. [⊡ J.L.Harlan&Assoc.]
Root, Carla Mullins .....'76 '02 C.612 B.S. L.623 J.D. [Root]
Root Law Office .....20 N. Elm St.
Ryan, Melinda Johnson .....'65 '91 C.612 B.A. L.623 J.D. [M.J.Ryan]
Ryan, Melinda Johnson, P.C. .....16 N. Park street
Saviers, Allen Boyd .....'66 '94 C.616 B.S. L.623 J.D. 3935 Hillside Dr.‡
Schultz, J. Bruce, (BV) .....'51 '80 C&L.862 B.M.E., J.D. Asst. Dist. Atty.
Sellers, Jack B., (AV) .....'28 '51 C&L.623 LL.B. [J.B.Sellers]
Sellers, W. C. (Bill), (AV) .....'30 '59 C.614 B.A. L.623 LL.B. [W.C.Sellers]
Sellers, Jack B., Law Associates, Inc., (AV) .....208 E. Dewey, Suite 400
Sellers, W. C. (Bill), Inc., (AV) .....600 S. Main
Sherrill, Lisa Ann Boyer .....'71 '98 C.612 B.S. L.623 J.D. 7 S. Park St.
Thompson, Donald D. .....'46 '71 C&L.623 B.A., J.D. Dist. J.‡
Thompson, Wesley R., (BV) .....'48 '74 C.623 B.S.I.E. L.862 J.D. Asst. Dist. Atty.
Wallace, W. Creekmore, II, (AV) .....'44 '73 C.623 B.A. L.862 J.D. 15 S. Poplar
White, April Sellers .....'51 '76 C.910 A.B. L.862 J.D. Assoc. Dist. J.
Widdoes, David R. .....'64 '89 C.1147 B.A. L.616 J.D. 1201 E. Fairview St.
Wilson, William L. .....'26 '56 C.623 B.B.A. L.862 LL.B. Spec. Dist. J.
Woolery, Richard A. .....'51 '77 C.1147 B.A.Ed. L.862 J.D. Spec. Dist. Ct. J.
Young, David, (AV) .....'21 '49 C.623 B.A. L.477 LL.B. 12 Woodland Rd.‡
Young, John M., (BV) .....'50 '75 C&L.623 B.B.A., J.D. [Young&Y.]
Young, John W., (BV) .....'23 '50 C.861 B.B.A. L.623 [Young&Y.]
Young & Young, (BV) .....2 N. Main (⊙Agawam, MA; Bloomfield, NJ)

SAYRE, * 4,114, *Beckham Co.*

Alexander, Dorothy Y. .....'34 '75 C.1147 B.A. L.616 J.D. P.O. Box 117
Blevins, Michael W., (AV) .....'47 '72 C.612 B.S. L.616 J.D. 129 East Main Street
Brooks, David, (BV) .....'53 '78 C.622 B.A. L.862 J.D. [Brooks&I.]

Brooks & Israel, (BV)
119 East Main Street, 73662-2913
Telephone: 580-928-5593 Fax: 580-928-2648
David Brooks; Timothy P. Israel.
General Trial Practice, Domestic Relations, Divorce, Family, Adoption, Probate, Real Estate, Collections, Commercial and Criminal Law, Driving Under the Influence, Trusts and Estates, Estate Planning.

See Professional Biographies, SAYRE, OKLAHOMA

Haught, Doug .....'50 '80 C.622 B.A. L.616 J.D. Assoc. Dist. J.
Israel, Timothy P., (BV) .....'54 '79 C&L.623 B.B.A., J.D. [Brooks&I.]
Ivester, Jack W., (AV) .....'47 '73 C&L.623 B.B.A., J.D. [Ivester,I.&I.]
Ivester, John Ed T., (BV) .....'33 '65 C.623 B.A. L.616 J.D. [Ivester,I.&I.] ⊙
Ivester, Thomas S. .....'69 '00 C.840 B.B.A. L.623 J.D. [Ivester,I.&I.]

Ivester, Ivester & Ivester, (AV)
115 W. Main Street, P.O. Box 160, 73662-0160 ⊙
Telephone: 580-928-2116; 1-800-891-2319 Fax: 580-928-5353
Email: ivesterlaw@itlnet.net URL: http://www.ivesterlaw.com
Members of Firm: H. C. Ivester (1901-1975); John Ed T. Ivester; Jack W. Ivester; Thomas S. Ivester.
Civil Litigation, Business Law, Commercial Law, Corporate Law, Partnership Law, Insurance, Real Estate, Family Law, Oil & Gas, Probate, Taxation, Trusts and Estates.
Elk City Office: 114 N. Adams, P.O. Box 1950, 73648-1950. Telephone: 580-225-6525. Fax: 580-225-2806.

See Professional Biographies, SAYRE, OKLAHOMA

Lakey, J. Robert W. .....'50 '77 C.69 B.B.A. L.623 J.D. Pres., Interbank Sayre
Whinery, R. Kent, (BV) .....'56 '89 C.622 B.A. L.616 J.D. 213 E. Main St.
Willsie, Leon W., (AV) .....'44 '75 C.622 B.S. L.616 J.D. 121 N. 4th St.
Wilson, Charles M. .....'22 '48 C.622 B.A.E. L.623 LL.B. 1109 N. 3rd‡

SEMINOLE, 6,899, *Seminole Co.*

Boren, Molly Shi .....'43 '74 C.618 B.A. L.623 J.D. 4 Harber Ct.‡
Cadenhead, Ed, (BV) .....'50 '80 C&L.862 B.S., J.D. [Elsener&C.]
Carter, Mac Bradley, (BV) .....'70 '95 C.623 B.B.A. L.615 J.D. 207 E. Oak Ave.
Choate, James A. .....'67 '95 C.612 B.A. L.616 J.D. RR 1
Choate, John I.M. .....'46 '71 C.623 B.A. L.976 LL.B. [Choate&C.] (⊙Stamford, CT)
Choate, William W. .....'39 '74 C.623 B.S.G.E. L.615 J.D. [Choate&C.]
Choate & Choate, P.C. .....209 E. Oak St.
Colclazier, Amie Rose .....'65 '91 C&L.616 B.S.B., J.D. 404 N. Main St.
Colclazier, Jerry L., (AV) .....'56 '90 C.623 B.S. L.616 J.D. [Colclazier&Assoc.]
Colclazier & Associates, (AV) .....404 N. Main Street
Elsener, G. Dale, (AV) .....'51 '76 C.612 B.S. L.623 J.D. [Elsener&C.]

Elsener & Cadenhead, P.C., (AV)
300 East Seminole, P.O. Box 2067, 74818-2067
Telephone: 405-382-6341; 257-2773 Fax: 405-382-5513
Email: cadnhead@swbell.net URL: http://www.lawyers.com/e&claw
G. Dale Elsener; Ed Cadenhead.
General Civil Trial Practice. Probate, Real Estate, Indian Land Title, Oil and Gas Law, Foreclosure, Municipal.

See Professional Biographies, SEMINOLE, OKLAHOMA

Johnston, McMains & Walker, A Professional Association, (BV) .....201 N. 2nd St.
Mattingly, Jack A., (AV) .....'43 '68 C&L.623 B.A., J.D. [Mattingly]
Mattingly, Jack A., Jr., (BV) .....'69 '95 C.1315 B.A. L.623 J.D. [⊡ Mattingly]
Mattingly Law Firm, The, P.C., (AV) .....215 East Oak Street
Melson, Gordon R. .....'35 '63 C&L.623 B.A., LL.B. Executive Director
Phelps, J. Mark, (BV) .....'51 '81 C.612 B.A. L.623 J.D. 416 N. Main
Pyron, Rob L., (BV) .....'49 '79 C.613 B.S. L.616 J.D. 207 E. Oak
Walker, Kevin J., (BV) .....'57 '85 C.612 B.S. L.623 J.D. [Johnston,M.&W.]
Wantland, William C. .....'34 '64 C.312 B.A. L.615 J.D. P.O. Box 1692

SHATTUCK, 1,274, *Ellis Co.*

Barton, Samuel K., (CV) .....'22 '54 C.620 L.616 205 S. Main St.
Herber, Darrell F., (CV) .....'53 '83 C.620 B.S. L.623 J.D. 332 S. Main
Klem, M. Cecil, (AV) .....'30 '62 C&L.623 B.A., J.D. 312 S. Main St.

SHAWNEE, * 28,692, *Pottawatomie Co.*

Berry, James D. .....'62 '88 C.618 B.A. L.862 J.D. P.O. Box 3908
Butler, Robert A., (BV) .....'57 '87 C.623 B.A. L.616 J.D. 320 N. Bway.
Cale, Stephen Leroy .....'68 '99 C.623 B.A. L.1339 J.D. 23 E. 9th St., Ste. 323
Canavan, John G., Jr., (AV) .....'54 '79 C&L.623 B.A., J.D. City Atty. [Henry,C.&H.]
Carter, Glenn Dale .....'36 '63 C.613 B.A. L.623 LL.B. Dist. J.
Cawthon, James David, (AV) .....'62 '87 C.1182 B.A. L.623 J.D. [West]
Christiansen, Barbara Kay, (BV) .....'38 '90 C.613 B.A. L.623 L.D. Dist. Atty.
Clarke, Sidney R., III .....'37 '61 C.612 B.A. L.623 LL.B. [Clarke&V.]
Clarke & Van Wagner, Inc., (AV) .....130 N. Bway., Suite 200
Clover, Michael D., (AV) .....'55 '90 C.1147 B.S. L.616 J.D. [Stuart&C.]
Combs, Douglas L. .....'51 '76 C.623 B.A. L.616 J.D. 3822 N. Broadway
Conaway, Michael Cameron .....'47 '74 C.618 B.A. L.623 J.D. Dep. Gen. Couns.
Defenbaugh, George .....'21 '48 C&L.623 LL.B. 1900 N. Beard St.
Elrod, Ronald L. .....'48 '82 C.959 B.A. L.616 J.D. 23 E. 9th, Ste. 329
Engle, Dawson R. .....'73 '98 C.612 B.S. L.623 J.D. Asst. Dist. Atty.
Field, Jesse R. .....'11 '34 C.623 L.616 LL.B. Spec. Dist. J.
Flowers, Jon D., (BV) .....'50 '78 C.618 B.A. L.623 J.D. 102 E. Highland
Freed, Rodney K., (BV) .....'47 '77 C.579 B.S. L.623 J.D. 318 N. Broadway
Freeman, Larry Joe .....'62 '95 C.621 B.S. L.862 J.D. [Freeman]
Freeman Law Office .....316 N. Broadway
Gardner, John .....'56 '81 C&L.623 B.A., J.D. Assoc. Dist. J.
Haddox, Carla Dawn .....'68 '96 C&L.623 B.A., J.D. Dist Atty. Off.
Hargus, Curtis D., (CV) .....'65 '90 C&L.623 B.B.A., J.D. 19 E. Severn st.
Harris, B.C. .....'35 '61 C&L.623 B.B.A., LL.B. 109 N. Beard St.
Haselwood, William Scott, (BV) .....'48 '92 C.623 B.S. L.615 J.D. 400 N Broadway
Henry, Canavan & Hopkins, P.L.L.C., (AV) .....4419 N. Bryan
Henson, Almon E., (AV) .....'19 '48 C&L.623 LL.B. [Henson,H.H.M.&M.]
Henson, J. Roger, (AV) .....'51 '76 C.613 B.A. L.623 J.D. [Henson,H.H.M.&M.]
Henson, Karen Ann, (AV) .....'54 '79 C.613 B.A. L.623 J.D. [Henson,H.H.M.&M.]

Henson, Henson, Henson, Marshall & Milburn, LLP, (AV) ⊡
101 West Ninth, P.O. Box 3488, 74802-3488
Telephone: 405-275-2550 Fax: 405-275-2588
Members of Firm: Almon E. Henson; J. Roger Henson; Karen Ann Henson; James R. Marshall; Kermit M. Milburn.
General Civil Practice. Probate, Real Property, Family, Banking, Bankruptcy, Insurance, Oil and Gas and Negligence Law. Trials in State and Federal Courts.
General Counsel for: Oklahoma Baptist University; Canadian Valley Electric Cooperative, Inc.; Bell Federal Credit Union; Carney State Bank.
Representative Clients: Arvest Bank; First United Bank and Trust Company.
Approved Attorneys for: First American Title & Trust Co.; American First Title & Trust Co.

See Professional Biographies, SHAWNEE, OKLAHOMA

Hopkins, D. Matt, (BV) .....'67 '95 C.613 B.A. L.623 J.D. [Henry,C.&H.]
Howard, M. Elaine .....'52 '88 C&L.623 B.S., J.D. 4310 Blaise Drive
Ingram, David T., (AV) .....'41 '68 C.623 L.616 LL.B. 231 N. Bway.
Jay, Gary K., (BV) .....'39 '72 C.612 B.S. L.623 J.D. 320 N. Broadway
Jeter, Laura C. Macdonald, (BV) .....'65 '93 C.802 B.B.A. L.615 J.D. Off. of Dist. Atty.
Jones, Robert H., (AV) .....'31 '56 C.612 B.S. L.623 J.D. 122 N. Bell
Laster, Charles M., (AV) .....'54 '79 C.612 B.S. L.623 J.D. 102 E. Highland
Livermon, Merrilyn B., (BV) .....'45 '80 C.623 B.A. L.616 J.D. Attorney General
Marshall, James R., (BV) .....'50 '79 C&L.623 B.A., J.D. [Henson,H.H.M.&M.]
Martin, D. Neal, (BV) .....'56 '80 C&L.623 B.S., J.D. 322 N. Broadway
McCullar, Benjamin .....'53 '92 [B.McCullar]
McCullar, Benjamin, P.C. .....316 N. Broadway Ave., Ste. G
McDaniel, Tracy .....'— '00 C.201 B.A. L.623 J.D. [Henry,C.&H.]
McKimmey, Joseph E., (BV) .....'37 '74 C.623 L.616 LL.B. [McKimmey]
McKimmey Law Office, P.C., (BV) .....24 E. Highland
McKinney, Paul, (BV) .....'25 '62 C.621 B.A. L.616 J.D. 9-11 East 9th Street
Milburn, Kermit M., (BV) .....'59 '84 C.612 B.S. L.623 J.D. [Henson,H.H.M.&M.]
Miller, Marianne .....'60 '96 C.623 B.A. L.615 J.D. 118 N. Broadway
Owen, Irvin .....'10 '38 C.616 L.623 316 N. Bway.
Palinkas, James E. .....'54 '92 C.614 B.S. L.615 J.D. 23 E. 9th St., Ste 429
Parsons, Alfred M. .....'23 '57 C.618 L.623 LL.B. 118 N. Broadway

Parsons & Associates Law Firm, A Corporation
(See Norman)

Peters, Lindsay, (AV) .....'25 '53 C&L.623 B.B.A., LL.B. 128 N. Bway‡
Pettis, Jim Cole, (CV) .....'56 '96 C&L.623 B.L.S., J.D. 4405 Lilly Valley St.
Romberg, Carolyn Walker .....'54 '85 C&L.623 B.Badm., J.D. 2025 S. Gordon Cooper Dr.
Sill, James D., Jr. .....'44 '69 C.622 B.A. L.623 J.D. [J.D.Sill]
Sill, James D., Inc. .....231 N. Broadway
Simpson, William D., (BV) .....'52 '78 C&L.623 B.A., J.D. 316 N. Bway, 2nd Fl.
Stephens, Pamela M. Snider, (CV) '64 '90 C.623 B.S. L.615 J.D. 1523 N. Oklahoma Ave.

Stuart, James T., (AV) ....'53 '79 C.1147 B.B.A. L.862 J.D. [Stuart&C.]

Stuart & Clover, (AV)
Formerly Miller, Peters, Diamond & Stuart
128 North Broadway, P.O. Box 1925, 74802-1925
Telephone: 405-275-0700 Telecopy: 405-275-6805
URL: http://www.lawyers.com/stuart&clover
Members of Firm: James T. Stuart; Michael D. Clover.
General Corporate, Banking, Commercial Law and Litigation, Real Property, Probate, Oil and Gas, Estate Planning, General Civil Practice.
Representative Clients: Oklahoma Gas & Electric Co.; Shawnee Urban Renewal Authority; TDK Ferrites Corp.; Mobil Chemical Co.
General Counsel: BancFirst, Shawnee; Central Plastics Co.
Approved Examining Attorneys for: Southwest Title & Trust Co., Oklahoma City; Lawyers Title Insurance Corp.; American First Title & Trust Co., Oklahoma City.
See Professional Biographies, SHAWNEE, OKLAHOMA

Sutton, Paul E., Attorney at Law, (BV) '46 '78 C.620 B.S. L.615 J.D. 639 N. Kickapoo St.
Terry, H. Edward, (BV) ....'49 '81 C.623 B.A. L.616 J.D. 639 N. Kickapoo
Thompson, Rex L. ....'30 '66 C.613 L.615 J.D. City Atty.
Van Wagner, George, (AV) .... '41 '65 C&L.623 B.A., J.D. [Clarke&V.]
Van Wagner, Harris, (AV) .... '11 '35 C&L.623 B.A., J.D. 23 E. 9th St.
Warwick, Michael P., (BV) ....'49 '74 C&L.623 B.A., J.D. [M.P.Warwick]
Warwick, Michael P., Inc., (BV) ....318 N. Broadway St.
Webb, Cregg Dale ....'70 '96 C&L.623 B.A., J.D. 320 N. Broadway
West, Bradley C., (BV) .... '63 '90 C.613 B.A. L.623 J.D. [West]
West, Terry W., (AV) ....'38 '66 C.623 L.862 LL.B. [West]
West Law Firm, The, (AV) .... 124 West Highland
White, Angela M., (BV) ....'65 '92 C&L.623 B.S., J.D. 231 N. Bway.
Wiley, Randall J., (BV) .... '54 '79 C&L.623 B.A., J.D. 1501 N. Beard
Wilson, Gregory Scott ....'69 '98 C.612 Acct. L.616 J.D. [Wilson]
Wilson Law Firm ....322 North Broadway
Winterringer, J. C., (AV) ....'32 '59 C.612 B.S. L.623 J.D. 109 N. Beard

SKIATOOK, 5,396, *Osage & Tulsa Cos.*

Barnaby, Joel William .... '70 '98 C.619 B.B.A. L.623 J.D. P.O. Box 311
Kane, M. John, IV, (BV) ....'62 '87 C.612 B.S. L.623 J.D. [Kane] ⊙
Kane Law Offices, P.C., (BV) ....520 W. Rogers Blvd. (⊙Pawhuska)
Nelson, Kathy Sherwood .... '69 '03 C&L.862 B.A., J.D. [K.S.Nelson] ⊙
Nelson, K. S., Law Firm, P.L.L.C. ....205 E. Rogers Boulevard (⊙Tulsa)

SNYDER, 1,509, *Kiowa Co.*

McLaury, Shane, The Law Office of, (BV) ....'50 '79 C.623 B.A. L.616 J.D. 715 Main St.

SPENCER, 3,746, *Oklahoma Co.*

Roper, Fred Dwight .... '62 '95 C&L.623 B.A., J.D. P.O. Box 417

SPERRY, 937, *Tulsa Co.*

Baker, Bradford S., (BV) .... '49 '76 C&L.862 B.A., J.D. [B.S.Baker]
Baker, Bradford S., Inc., (BV) ....8030 North Cincinnati Drive

SPIRO, 2,146, *Le Flore Co.*

Lawson, Ronald H., (BV) ....'50 '81 C.614 B.A. L.623 J.D. 101 N. Main

STIGLER, * 2,731, *Haskell Co.*

Blankenship, Chris Wayne .... '61 '91 C.619 B.S. L.623 J.D. [Blankenship]
Blankenship Law Offices, P.C. ....P.O. Box 69
Henderson, John N. ....'47 '72 C.619 B.A. L.862 J.D. Assoc. Dist. J., Haskell Co.
McLaughlin, Brian Ray ....'60 '97 C.619 B.A. L.862 J.D. [McLaughlin]
McLaughlin Law Offices ....109 E. Main St.
Nunn, Bill J., (CV) ....'51 '78 C.612 B.S. L.623 J.D. 111 S. Bway.
Poteete, Troy Wayne ....'55 '01 C.619 B.S. L.862 J.D. 109 E. Main St.
Scott, McCurtain ....'14 '48 C&L.623 LL.B. P.O. Box 370‡
Smith, James W., (BV) ....'40 '68 C&L.862 B.S., J.D. 121 E. Main St.
Striegel, Louis E. ....'32 '62 C.947 B.S. L.502 J.D. 115 E. Main
Volz, James T. .... '38 '84 C.1122 B.B.A. L.616 J.D. Assist. Dist. Atty.
Wilson, David L., (CV) .... '49 '85 C.621 B.A. L.623 J.D. 202 N. Broadway St.

STILLWATER, * 39,065, *Payne Co.*

Astle, Doris J. "Dorie", (AV) ....'48 '82 C.612 B.S. L.862 J.D. 4712 W. 8th Ave.

Atkins & Markoff
(See Oklahoma City)

Baker, William J., (AV) ....'47 '72 C.612 B.A. L.623 J.D. [Hert,B.&K.]
Barto, Lowell A., (BV) ....'56 '81 C.612 B.A. L.862 J.D. [L.A.Barto]

Barto, Lowell A., A Professional Corporation, (BV)
Suite 210 Seventh Avenue Center, 123 West Seventh Avenue, 74074
Telephone: 405-372-4371 Fax: 405-372-4420
Lowell A. Barto.
General Civil Trial Practice. Commercial, Probate, Estate Planning and Real Estate Law, Elder Care Law.
See Professional Biographies, STILLWATER, OKLAHOMA

Belden, Lois L. ....'25 '78 C.612 B.A. L.623 J.D. Spec. Dist. Ct. J.
Boyce, Sherry L. ....'58 '95 C.612 B.S. L.623 J.D. [Boyce&B.]
Boyce, William H. ....'65 '95 C.502 B.S. L.623 J.D. [Boyce&B.]
Boyce & Boyce .... P.O. Box 2055
Brown, Robert A., (CV) .... '47 '85 C.999 B.S.L. L.862 J.D. [R.Brown]
Brown, S. Teresa Bell ....'49 '94 C.612 B.A. L.623 J.D. 123 W. 7th, Ste. 102
Brown, Robert, (CV) ....123 W. 7th Ave., Ste. 102
Bryson, Terry W. ....'50 '89 C.623 L.615 J.D. 2129 N. Crescent Dr.
Campbell, Charles E., (BV) ....'45 '74 C.612 B.S. L.616 J.D. 713 S. Husband St.
Corley, Phillip Craig ....'63 '90 C.612 B.A. L.623 J.D. Spec. Dist. J.

Couch, John R., Jr., (BV) '42 '70 C.691 B.A. L.623 J.D.
123 W. 7th, Suite 102, P.O. Box 984, 74076
Telephone: 405-377-9383 Fax: 405-377-8187
Email: couchlaw@provalue.net URL: http://www.couch-lawfirm.com
Probate, Estate Planning, Environmental Law, General Practice, Personal Injury.
See Professional Biographies, STILLWATER, OKLAHOMA

DeLacerda, Melissa, Law Office of, (BV) '52 '79 C.836 B.S. L.862 J.D.
301 South Duck, P.O. Box 1252, 74076
Telephone: 405-624-8383 Fax: 405-624-8385
Email: melissde@aol.com URL: http://www.stillwater-law.com
Family Law, Bankruptcy, Divorce, Child Custody, Adoptions, Criminal Law and Probate, Driving While Intoxicated, Wills Trusts and Estates.
See Professional Biographies, STILLWATER, OKLAHOMA

Drake, Charles E., (BV) .... '40 '66 C.612 B.S. L.623 J.D. Legal Coun. Off.
Draper, Daniel D., Jr. .... '40 '64 C.612 B.S. L.273 LL.B. 222 S. Kings St.‡
Drummond, LeAnn Page, (BV) ....'65 '91 C.612 B.S. L.623 J.D. [Ellis&D.]
Dunivan, John D. ....'60 '02 C.502 M.S. L.615 J.D. 919 South Main Street
Ellis, Hal Wm., (AV) ....'48 '74 C.1147 B.B.A. L.623 J.D. [Ellis&D.]

Ellis & Drummond, (AV)
An Association of Professional Limited Liability Companies.
711 South Husband Street, 74074
Telephone: 405-743-3770 Fax: 405-743-3773
Email: hwellis@ellisanddrummond.com URL: http://www.EllisandDrummond.com
Hal Wm. Ellis; LeAnn Page Drummond.
Wills and Trusts, Tax and Estate Planning, Probate, Business Formations, Non-profit Organizations, Tax Litigation, Corporate and Business Law.
See Professional Biographies, STILLWATER, OKLAHOMA

Forsyth, Cubbage & Associates, P.C.
(See Cushing)

Fowler, Joe W. ....'37 '66 C.612 B.S. L.616 J.D. Prof.of Law, Okla. State Univ.
Headrick, Charles H. ....'37 '68 C.612 B.S. L.616 J.D. Assoc. Dist. J.‡
Hert, Robert L., Jr., (AV) ....'44 '69 C.612 B.A. L.623 J.D. [Hert,B.&K.]

Hert, Baker & Koemel, A Professional Corporation, (AV)
222 East Seventh, P.O. Box 668, 74076
Telephone: 405-377-8644 FAX: 405-377-6363
Robert L. Hert, Jr.; William J. Baker; Tina Mooney Koemel; John E. Koemel, Jr.
Civil Practice. Banking Law, Commercial Law, Family Law, Probate, Trusts and Estates, Wills, Real Estate, Corporate Law, Personal Injury, Oil and Gas Law, Labor and Employment, Criminal Law, Elder Law, Social Security, Franchise Law, Trademarks, Collections, General Practice.
See Professional Biographies, STILLWATER, OKLAHOMA

Hobbs, Royce A., (AV) '52 '77 C.612 B.A. L.862 J.D.
801 South Main, P.O. Box 1455, 74076
Telephone: 405-377-8989 Fax: 405-377-8979
URL: http://www.rhobbsatty@aol.com
Criminal Trial Practice including Criminal Defense, General Civil Practice, Domestic Relations including Family Law Divorce, Child Custody and Modifications, Commercial, Personal Injury, Probate, Wills and Real Estate Law.

Houston, Winfrey D., (AV) ....'26 '50 C.612 B.A. L.623 J.D. [Houston&O.]

Houston & Osborn, PC, (AV)
123 West 7th Avenue, P.O. Box 1118, 74076
Telephone: 405-377-7618; 377-8233 Telecopier: 405-377-8234
Email: losborn@Houston-Osborn.com URL: http://www.houston-osborn.com
Members: Winfrey D. Houston; Lynn R. Osborn.
General Civil and Trial Practice. Probate, Estate Planning, Real Estate, Banking, Business, Commercial and Oil and Gas Law, Civil Litigation, Commercial Litigation, Business Law.
Representative Clients: Payne County Bank, Perkins, Okla.; Citizens State Bank of Morrison, Oklahoma; Stillwater National Bank, BancFirst; Sumpter-Barker Drilling Co.; Stillwater School District.
Approved Attorneys for: American First Title & Trust Co.; Southwest Title & Trust Co.
See Professional Biographies, STILLWATER, OKLAHOMA

Huddle, Robert L. ....'57 '82 C.612 B.S. L.623 J.D. U.S. Dept. of Agric.
Irwin-Smith, Mozella Beth, Law Office of '70 '01 C.612 B.A. L.623 J.D. 824 South Adams
Johnson, Paula D., (BV) ....'50 '77 C.623 B.A. L.616 J.D. Legal Coun. Off.
Karns, Mary Ann, (BV) ....'47 '76 C&L.616 B.A., J.D. City Atty.
Koemel, John E., Jr., (CV) ....'63 '88 C.839 B.S. L.69 J.D. [Hert,B.&K.]
Koemel, Tina Mooney, (BV) ....'60 '86 C&L.69 B.B.A., J.D. [Hert,B.&K.]
Laughlin, Glenn E. ....'21 '46 C.612 A.B. L.623 J.D. P.O. Box 1304‡
Love, Jon F. '40 '68 C.807 B.A. L.900 J.D. (adm. in KS; not adm. in OK) Coun., New Dominion, L.L.C.
McBride, Charles L., (AV) ....'42 '69 C.612 B.A. L.623 J.D. 301 S. Duck
McMillian, Roger L., (BV) ....'47 '73 C.612 B.S. L.862 J.D. 715 S. Husband, Ste. 3
Miller, George W., Jr. ....'55 '80 C&L.623 B.A., J.D. 2013 Arrowhead Dr.★
Muret, Frank, (BV) ....'45 '72 C.1147 B.S. L.616 J.D. 301 S. Duck St., Ste. 1
Murphy, Robert M. ....'20 '43 C.612 L.45 LL.B. 118 W. 8th St.‡
Murphy, Robert M., Jr. ....'49 '75 C.612 B.A. L.623 J.D. Dist. J.
Murray, James V., & Associates, (BV) ....'58 '85 C.612 B.S. L.623 J.D. 919 S. Main
Nipp, Brenda Kay Jenkins .... '62 '91 C.612 B.S. L.862 J.D. [Nipp,B.]
Nipp, Brenda ....920 S. Main St.
Osborn, Lynn R., (AV) ....'47 '72 C.612 B.S. L.623 J.D. [Houston&O.]
Price, John A. '68 '96 C.612 B.A. L.862 J.D. Dir., Gift Planning, Oklahoma State University Foundation
Ramsey, Cheryl A., (AV) .... '51 '77 C.612 B.S. L.616 J.D. [Szlichta&R.]
Raun, Tanya Colclasure, (CV) .... '58 '89 C.612 B.S. L.569 J.D. P.O. Box 1718
Rossander, Jeff ....'53 '83 C&L.612 B.A., J.D. 713 S. Husband
Schott, Albert J., (AV) ....'15 '40 C.612 B.S. L.615 601 W. Harned Ave.‡
Severe, John T., (BV) ....'51 '78 C.612 B.S. L.616 J.D. 715 S. Husband, Ste. 11

Solomon, G. Michael, (AV Ⓣ) '57 '82 C.612 B.S. L.862 J.D.
711 South Husband Street, 74074 ⊙
Telephone: 405-743-3770 Fax: 405-743-3773
Email: gmsolomonlaw@aol.com
General Business, Transactions, Commercial Litigation, Banking Including Lending Practices, Creditor Bankruptcy, Commercial and Corporate Law.
Woodland Hills, California Office: 22151 Ventura Boulevard, Suite 200. Telephone: 818-348-4470. Telecopier: 818-992-7687.
See Professional Biographies, STILLWATER, OKLAHOMA

Springer, James M., Jr., (AV) '13 '39 C.612 B.S. L.192 LL.B. 1215 W. 10th Ave., Ste. 216‡
Stano, Michael ....'47 '90 C.494 PH.D L.616 J.D. Spec. Dist. Ct. J.
Szlichta, Christopher D., (AV) ....'49 '76 C.612 B.A. L.616 J.D. [Szlichta&R.]

Szlichta & Ramsey, (AV)
8 Main Place, P.O. Box 1206, 74076
Telephone: 405-377-3393 Fax: 405-377-4775
Email: ramseyc911@aol.com
Members of Firm: Christopher D. Szlichta; Cheryl A. Ramsey.
General Practice. Trials. Family, School, Municipal, Administrative Law and Criminal Defense Law.
References: Stillwater National Bank and Trust Co.; First Bank and Trust Co., Yale, Oklahoma.
See Professional Biographies, STILLWATER, OKLAHOMA

Teter, Michael L., (BV) '56 '83 C&L.623 B.B.A., J.D. 808 South Main Street, Suite 306
Thomas, Laura Austin, (BV) ....'57 '84 C.612 B.A. L.623 J.D. Asst. Dist. Atty.
Thomas, W. Keith, (AV) ....'39 '68 C.612 B.S. L.623 LL.B. 715 S. Husband
Tilley, Marcia L. ....'50 '80 C.350 B.S. L.260 J.D. Oklahoma State Univ.
Watkins, Sherrin ....'54 '84 C.377 B.A. L.862 J.D. 113 S. Lewis St.
Wheat, Donald R., (BV) ....'53 '79 C.612 B.S. L.616 J.D. [Wheat&Assoc.]
Wheat & Associates PC, (BV) .... P.O. Box 721473
Williams, Sidney ....'18 '41 C&L.623 B.A., LL.B. 122 E. 5th St.
Wisner, Kevin R. ....'69 '97 C.619 B.S. L.623 J.D. 424 S. Squires Street, Suite 200-A
Worthington, Donald L. ....'26 '50 C.999 L.623 J.D. Dist. J.

Worthington, Susan C., (BV) '53 '84 C.612 B.A. L.623 J.D. 715 South Husband, Suite 9

STILWELL, * 3,276, *Adair Co.*

Cole, Lloyd E., Jr., (AV) ... '28 '51 C.612 L.623 LL.B. 120 W. Division
Crawley, Monica Kay ... '72 '98 C.45 B.S.B.A. L.596 J.D. Rt. 2 Box 1060
Garrett, John C., (BV) ... '41 '73 C.623 B.B.A. L.862 J.D. 220 Division Street
Hembree, Jenine Lawlor, (BV) ... '67 '92 C.1049 B.A. L.602 J.D. [Hembree&H.]
Hembree, Todd, (BV) ... '65 '91 C.619 B.A. L.602 J.D. [Hembree&H.]
Hembree and Hembree, (BV) ... 17 N. 2nd St.
Limore, Kenneth Earl ... '55 '98 C.619 B.S. L.352 J.D. Rt 5
Starr, Rex Earl, (BV) ... '44 '73 C.612 B.S. L.862 J.D. 108 North 1st Street

STRATFORD, 1,404, *Garvin Co.*

Prater, Claude J. ... '38 '67 C&L.623 B.A., J.D. RR 1

STROUD, 2,666, *Lincoln Co.*

Ball, David T. ... '60 '89 C.1147 B.A. L.623 J.D. [D.T.Ball]
Ball, David Tipton, Law Office of ... 411 W. Main
Beltz, Danny R., (BV) ... '41 '66 C&L.623 B.A., J.D. 503 W. 4th Street
Burleson, Ned, II ... '57 '96 C&L.623 B.A., J.D. [Hodgens&B.]
Hodgens, James J., (BV) ... '54 '83 C.612 B.S. L.862 J.D. [Hodgens&B.]
Hodgens & Burleson, P.A., (BV) ... 301 W. Main St.
James, Richard, (AV) ... '26 '49 C.861 B.S. L.623 LL.B. [Richards,J.]
Richards, James, P.C., (AV) ... 301 W. Main Street

SULPHUR, * 4,824, *Murray Co.*

Albright, W. Joe ... '27 '57 C&L.616 B.S., LL.B. 2000 Williams Dr.
Colbert, D. Scott, (BV) ... '55 '83 C&L.616 B.S., J.D. [Colbert&D.]
Colbert, Timothy K. ... '50 '76 C.623 B.A. L.616 LL.B. Assoc. Dist. J.
Colbert & Duck, (BV) ... 1801 West Broadway
Duck, Aaron ... '74 '99 C.618 B.S. L.623 J.D. [Colbert&D.]
Fulton, W. R. ... '20 '50 C&L.623 LL.B. Ret. Assoc. Dist. J.
Gibbard, Elaine, (BV) ... '45 '69 C&L.623 B.A., J.D. 1016 W. 3rd St.
Gibbard, Frank, (AV) ... '14 '41 C.621 B.S. L.623 LL.B. W. 3rd & Vinita Sts.
Gordon, Laura K., (CV) ... '62 '88 C.612 B.A. L.623 J.D. [Hurst,M.&G.]
Hurst, Phil S., (AV) ... '34 '63 C.612 B.S. L.623 LL.B. [Hurst,M.&G.]
Hurst, McNeil & Gordon, (AV) ... 1020 West Second Street (⊙Davis)
Jones, Fob F., (BV) ... '66 '92 C.618 B.S. L.615 J.D. 1010 W. 2nd St.
McNeil, Edd R., (AV) ... '45 '71 C&L.623 B.A., J.D. [Hurst,M.&G.] ⊙
Wade, Jerry D., (BV) ... '44 '77 C.1147 B.A. L.616 J.D. 1016 W. 3rd St.

TAHLEQUAH, * 14,458, *Cherokee Co.*

Allen, Jo Nan ... '42 '97 C.615 B.A. L.623 J.D. 219 W Keetoowah
Allen, Steven K., (BV) ... '50 '75 C.473 B.A. L.862 J.D. 210 S. Muskogee Ave.
Baker, Donn F., (AV) ... '49 '80 C.619 B.S. L.615 J.D. 239 W. Keetoowah St.
Baker, Tim K., & Associates, (AV) ... '47 '73 C.619 B.S. L.616 J.D. 303 West Keetoowah
Barker, Dianne, (BV) ... '51 '87 C.619 B.S.W. L.862 J.D. Dist. Atty.
Barker-Jones, Angela, (BV) ... '69 '95 C.619 B.S. L.862 J.D. 110 Harrison Ave.
Bigby, Terry D., (CV) ... '60 '86 C.619 B.S. L.623 J.D. [Bigby]
Bigby Law Office, (CV) ... 429 S. Muskogee
Burris, Lynn ... '37 '68 C.619 B.A. L.623 J.D. Assoc. Dist. J.
Chaffin, Harvey L., (AV) ... '41 '68 C&L.623 B.B.A., J.D. 215 W. Shawnee St.
Chapman-Plumb, Susan ... '64 '91 C.623 B.A. L.862 J.D. Vice Pres., Bk. of Cherokee Co.
Clark, Jeffrey S. ... '75 '02 C&L.378 B.A., J.D. [⊠ T.K.Baker&Assoc.]
Combs, Gregory N., (BV) ... '47 '78 C.619 B.A. L.69 J.D. Dist. Atty.
deSteiguer, Darla R. '63 '89 C.619 B.S. L.990 J.D.
(adm. in TX; not adm. in OK) 314 W. Keetoowah St.‡
Dobbins, Mark L., (BV) ... '56 '89 C.588 B.S. L.862 J.D. Asst. Dist. Atty.
Donelson, Linda L. ... '55 '95 C.619 B.S. L.862 J.D. Cherokee Nation, Law & Jus. Dept.
Ewart, John D., (BV) ... '20 '49 C.612 L.802 LL.B. 120 E. Keetoowah St.
Fishinghawk, Diana Dry, (CV) ... '49 '77 C.619 B.A. L.623 J.D. Asst. Dist. Atty.
Garcia, A.J. ... '71 '01 C.619 B.S. L.862 J.D. [Garcia]
Garcia Law Office ... 307 S. Muskogee Ave., Ste. C

Garrett Law Office, P.C.
(See Tulsa)

Hale, Mary Jeannine, Law Office of ... '53 '83 C&L.623 B.S., J.D. P.O. Box 491
Harrold, Dianne Barker, (BV) ... '51 '87 C.619 B.S.W. L.862 J.D. Mun. J.
Hazen, Kristi L. ... '76 '03 C.1147 B.A. L.623 J.D. [⊠ T.K.Baker&Assoc.]
Johnson, Becky Michelle ... '70 '99 C.197 B.A. L.174 J.D. Jus. Dept., Cherokee Nation
Johnson, Elton L., Jr., (BV) ... '40 '66 C&L.623 B.S., J.D. 205 W. Shawnee St.
Jones, Chester Randall, (CV) ... '50 '81 C&L.623 B.B.A., J.D. 106 W. Delaware St.
Jordan, Tina, Law Office of ... '56 '81 C.612 B.S. L.862 J.D. 111 N. College
Kingfisher, Cheryl Rios '64 '94 C.1004 B.S.N. L.900 J.D.
(adm. in MO; not adm. in OK) P.O. Box 948‡

Locke & Moore
(See Muskogee)

Means, Yasodhara "Mitty" Mohanty, P.C.
(See Muskogee)

Medearis, Frank M., (BV) ... '67 '93 C.619 B.S. L.862 J.D. 226 W. Choctaw St.
Medearis, Robert Park, Jr., (BV) ... '62 '86 C&L.623 B.A., J.D. 226 W. Choctaw St.
Miller, Wesley ... '18 '45 C.619 B.A. L.623 214 S. Muskogee St.
Moore, Jerry S., (BV) ... '60 '91 C.999 B.S. L.623 J.D. Asst. Dist. Atty.
Otteson, Peggy E. Shannon ... '58 '01 C.719 B.S. L.862 J.D. [OttesonP]

Otteson Law PLLC
236 South Muskogee Avenue, 74464
Telephone: 918-456-7000 Fax: 918-456-5800
Email: ottesonlaw@sbcglobal.net
Member of Firm: Peggy E. Shannon Otteson.
Civil and Criminal Trial Practice, Family Law, Bankruptcy and Employment Law. Licensed Family and Divorce Mediator.
See Professional Biographies, TAHLEQUAH, OKLAHOMA

Parris, John Everett ... '— '01 C.613 B.S.Ed. L.862 J.D. Cherokee Nation Justice Dept.
Purcell, Janice Walters, (BV) ... '— '86 C.623 B.A. L.616 J.D. 219 N. Muskogee Ave.
Pursley, Holli O. ... '67 '96 C.619 B.S. L.623 J.D. 213 W. Delaware
Sewell, Bruce ... '53 '80 C.612 B.S. L.862 J.D. Dist. J.
Smith, Chadwick, (AV) ... '50 '79 C.280 B.S. L.862 J.D. P.O. Box 1716
Teague, Bertha Faye ... '39 '95 C.619 B.A. L.862 J.D. Dist. Atty. Off.
Wales, Deanna Michelle ... '74 '99 C.619 B.S. L.326 J.D. [D.M.Wales]
Wales, Deanna M. ... 226 South Muskogee
Willis, H. Doak, (CV) ... '54 '79 C.619 B.A. L.862 J.D. [Willis]
Willis, William P., Jr. ... '50 '75 C.619 B.S. L.862 J.D. [B.Willis]
Willis, Bill, Law Office of ... 400 S. Muskogee Avenue
Willis Law Firm, (CV) ... 220 S. Muskogee

TALIHINA, 1,297, *Le Flore Co.*

Coleman, Mary Ann ... '43 '75 C.612 B.A. L.623 J.D. 407 Dallas St.

TALOGA, * 415, *Dewey Co.*

Bozarth, Rick, (AV) ... '50 '76 C.622 B.A. L.616 J.D. [Ruble&B.]
Collier, Robert W. ... '38 '63 C.612 B.S. L.623 LL.B. Assoc. Dist. J.
Foster, Roger W., (BV) ... '45 '89 C.620 B.S. L.616 J.D. [⊠ Rodolph&F.] ⊙
Rodolph & Foster, (AV) ... Collier Building (⊙Clinton)
Ruble, Tom J., (AV) ... '26 '51 L.623 LL.B. [Ruble&B.]
Ruble and Bozarth, (AV) ... Bway. & Ruble Sts.

TECUMSEH, 6,098, *Pottawatomie Co.*

Atkins & Markoff
(See Oklahoma City)

Elliott, Janette C., (CV) ... '59 '84 C&L.623 B.S., J.D. P.O. Box 207
Hillerman, Gerald D. ... '39 '82 C.613 B.S. L.616 J.D. RR3
Murray, Sherman Dee, (CV) ... '53 '93 C.623 B.S. L.615 J.D. [S.Murray]
Murray, Sherman, Law Office, (CV) ... P.O. Box 417
Parker, Steven L., (BV) ... '41 '78 C.619 B.A. L.623 J.D. City Atty.

THOMAS, 1,246, *Custer Co.*

Dickey, Jack W. '38 '63 C.612 B.S. L.623 LL.B.
Pres. & Chmn. of the Bd., First Natl. Bk.
Graft, C. B., (AV) ... '41 '66 C.622 B.A. L.623 J.D. [Graft&C.] ⊙
Graft & Cabaniss, (AV) ... P.O. Box 508 (⊙Clinton)

TISHOMINGO, * 3,116, *Johnston Co.*

Coppedge, Jack W., II, (BV) ... '60 '86 C.613 B.A. L.616 J.D. [Little,L.L.W.C.O.&G.]
Corbin, Laura J., (CV) ... '72 '96 C.618 B.S. L.616 J.D. [Smith,S.S.C.&W.] (⊙Ada)
Highsmith, Robert M. ... '50 '76 C.1147 B.A. L.616 J.D. Assoc. Dist. J.
Little, Dan V., (AV) '42 '68 C.309 B.A. L.623 J.D.
[Little,L.L.W.C.O.&G.] (⊙Joplin, MO; Madill, OK)
Little, Prudence Mae, (AV) '42 '68 C.914 B.A. L.623 J.D.
[Little,L.L.W.C.O.&G.] (⊙Joplin, MO; Madill, OK)
Little, Little, Little, Windel, Coppedge, Oliver & Gallagher, P.L.L.C., (AV)
224 West Main Street (⊙Ardmore, Madill)
Rowe, Dustin P. ... '75 '01 C.618 B.A. L.623 J.D. [Little,L.L.W.C.O.&G.]
Savage, Bob E., (BV) ... '50 '79 C.621 B.S. L.623 J.D. 708 W. Main
Smith, Shew, Scrivner, Corbin, & Watts, P.C., (AV)
109 W. Main (⊙Ada, Oklahoma City)
Windel, Jerry Lynn, (BV) '43 '68 C&L.623 B.A., J.D.
[Little,L.L.W.C.O.&G.] (⊙Madill)

TONKAWA, 3,299, *Kay Co.*

Colombe, Robt. N., (AV) ... '20 '54 L.623 LL.B. 207 E. Grand
McMurtrie, Shaen M. ... '64 '90 C.663 B.S. L.623 J.D. Northern Oklahoma College

TULSA, 393,049, *Osage & Tulsa Cos.*

Aamodt, Jason B. ... '69 '96 C.1044 B.S. L.862 J.D. [Aamodt&T.]
Aamodt & Tobey, P.C. ... 406 South Boulder, Suite 101
Abbott, Russell D. ... '71 '98 C.378 B.A. L.623 J.D. [⊠ Strickland]
Abel, Kevin M., (AV) ... '49 '75 C.420 B.S. L.862 J.D. Gen. Coun., OK Dept. of Labor
Abernathy, Chris L. ... '70 '98 C.206 B.A. L.500 J.D. [Abernathy]
Abernathy Law Firm, The, P.C. ... 406 South Boulder
Abney, Benjamin P., (AV) '45 '68 C&L.862 B.S., J.D.
Case & Associates Properties, Inc.

Abrahamson, A. Craig, (BV) '54 '79 C.494 B.A. L.862 J.D.
706 Beacon Building, 406 S. Boulder Avenue, 74103
Telephone: 918-584-0318 Fax: 918-582-6106
Email: craiga@abrahamsonlaw.com URL: http://www.abrahamsonlaw.com
Family Law, Divorce, Child Custody, Visitation Rights, Child Support, Alimony, Spousal Support, Post Decree Modification and Enforcement, Premarital Agreements, Bankruptcy Creditors, Bankruptcy Debtor Ch. 7, Bankruptcy Debtor Ch. 11, Bankruptcy Debtor Ch. 13, Business Law, Commercial Transactions, Business Litigation, Commercial Litigation, Real Estate Transactions, Landlords.
See Professional Biographies, TULSA, OKLAHOMA

Acord, Stacy L. ... '74 '00 C.612 B.A. L.623 J.D. [⊠ Joyce,P.&M.]
Acun, C. Mengu '62 '00 C.1537 L.862 J.D.
Domestic Violence Intervention Servs. (DVIS)
Adams, David M. '62 '98 C.473 B.A. L.1035 J.D.
(adm. in MN; not adm. in OK) Sr. Atty., The Williams Companies, Inc.
Adams, Elmer W., (AV) ... '11 '38 C&L.862 LL.B. 3763 E. 48th Pl.‡

Adams, Kevin D., (BV) '73 '01 C&L.862 B.S., J.D.
1717 South Cheyenne Avenue, 74119
Telephone: 918-587-8100 Fax: 918-582-7830
Email: kevin@oklahomacriminallaw.com URL: http://www.oklahomacriminallaw.com
Criminal Defense, Felonies, White Collar, Drug Crimes, Driving While Intoxicated, Assault and Battery, Manslaughter, Sex Crimes, Murder.
See Professional Biographies, TULSA, OKLAHOMA

Adams, Patrick L. ... '73 '02 C.612 B.A. L.862 J.D. [Adams,P.]
Adams, Randal J. '50 '74 C.377 B.S.B.A. L.378 J.D.
(adm. in KS; not adm. in OK) 3223 E. 31st‡
Adams, Steven J., (AV) ... '53 '79 C.612 B.S. L.862 J.D. [Fellers,S.B.&T.]
Adams Law Office, The, PLLC ... 2 West 6th Street, Suite 500
Adamson, J. Philip, (AV) ... '44 '72 C&L.623 B.B.A., J.D. 624 S. Boston
Adams-Webb, Lonna ... '70 '96 C.619 B.S. L.862 J.D. 1639 S. Carson Ave.
Adwan, Teresa B., (AV) ... '43 '75 C.276 B.S.F.S. L.862 J.D. 2946 E. 57th Pl.
Adwon, Nicholas A. ... '18 '56 C.623 B.S. L.616 LL.B. 6828 E. 57th Pl.
Affeldt, Thomas M., (AV) '46 '72
C.352 B.B.A. L.862 J.D. [O'Donnell,M.&A.d/b/a.S.O.M.&A.]
Albers, Lindsey E. ... '75 '02 C.112 B.A. L.862 J.D. [Barkley]
Alberty, Greg ... '70 '97 C&L.862 B.A., J.D. [⊠ Riggs,A.N.T.O.&L.]
Albright, Kenneth F., (AV) ... '56 '81 C.612 B.A. L.623 J.D. [Albright,R.&H.]

Albright, Rusher & Hardcastle, A Professional Corporation, (AV)
2600 Bank of America Center, 15 West Sixth Street, 74119
Telephone: 918-583-5800 Fax: 918-583-8665
Email: arhlaw@arhlaw.com URL: http://www.arhlaw.com
Kenneth F. Albright; James W. Rusher; Heath E. Hardcastle.
General Civil Trial Practice, Trials and Appeals of Civil Cases in State and Federal Courts, Construction Litigation, Federal and State Taxation, Corporate and Securities, Mergers and Acquisitions, Bankruptcy and Creditors' Rights, Commercial Bankruptcy, Debtor and Creditor, Collections, Oil and Gas, Real Estate, Probate and Estate Planning, Family Law, Alternative Dispute Resolution, Limited Liability Company Law, Business Formation, Closely Held Business Law, Tax Exempt Organizations, Asset Protection.
See Professional Biographies, TULSA, OKLAHOMA

Alexander, Todd, (BV) '54 '80 C.145 B.A. L.623 J.D.
2121 South Columbia Suite 500, Parkland Plaza Building, 74114-3519
Telephone: 918-744-0201 Facsimile: 918-747-8820
Email: todd@toddalexanderlaw.com URL: http://www.toddalexanderlaw.com
Family Law, Divorce, Child Custody, Adoptions, Guardianship, Visitation Rights, Premarital Agreements, Spousal Support, Probate, Wills, Trusts, Business Litigation, Civil Litigation.
See Professional Biographies, TULSA, OKLAHOMA

Alexander, Robert H., Jr., Attorneys and Counselors At Law, p.c., The Law Office of
(See Oklahoma City)

Allbritten, Phillip L., (BV) ... '52 '88 C.612 B.S. L.846 J.D. 15 E. 5th St.
Allen, Bobbi L. ... '77 '05 C.612 B.S. L.623 J.D. [Hall,E.H.G.G.&N.]
Allen, Carol J. ... '65 '99 C.619 B.S. L.862 J.D. [Atkinson,H.N.B.G.&C.]
Allen, Dewayne, Law Office of, (BV) '51 '92 C&L.862 B.S.B.A., J.D. 1718 S. Cheyenne
Allen, Mark H., (AV) '56 '82 C.623 B.B.A. L.802 J.D. Pres., TV Guide Affiliate Sales, Inc.
Allen, Scott, (BV) ... '65 '90 C.612 B.A. L.862 J.D. [Stipe,H.L.U.E.&B.]
Allen, Stephen B., (BV) ... '73 '98 C.613 B.A. L.880 J.D. [Gable&G.]
Allen, Teddi Lewis ... '55 '90 C&L.862 B.A., J.D. [Kivell,R.&F.]
Allis, Daniel F., Law Offices of, (AV) '34 '67 C&L.862 B.S.B.A., J.D. 6915 S. 77th East Ave.
Allison, Ann E., (AV) ... '63 '88 C.612 B.S. L.623 J.D. [Rhodes,H.J.T.&G.]
Allison, Gale Graham, (AV) ... '51 '76 C.280 B.A. L.838 J.D. [Allison] (⊙Knoxville, TN)
Allison Firm, The, (AV) ... 1831 East 71st Street, Suite 415
Allred, Howard W. '11 '34 C&L.352 B.A., J.D. (adm. in IA; not adm. in OK) 4530 E. 103rd St.‡
Allred, Raymond S., (BV) ... '59 '86 C.466 B.A. L.1339 J.D. 2619 E. 15th St.
Alred, Charles Bryan, (BV) ... '58 '87 C.612 B.S. L.378 J.D. [C.B.Alred]

Alred, Charles Bryan, P.C., (BV)
3242 East 30th Place Suite B, 74114
Telephone: 918-745-9960 Fax: 918-745-9965 URL: http://www.tulsaautoaccidentslaw.com
Email: bryanalred@hotmail.com URL: http://www.tulsaautoaccident.com
Charles Bryan Alred.
Automobile Accidents, Personal Injury, Wrongful Death, Insurance Disputes, Criminal Defense, Driving While Intoxicated, Workers' Compensation, Negligence, General Civil Litigation. Trial in State and Federal Courts, Trucking Accidents, Motorcycle Accidents, Boating Accidents, Dog Bites, Products Liability and Driving While Under the Influence.
See Professional Biographies, TULSA, OKLAHOMA

Amatucci, Richard D., (CV) ... '34 '65 C&L.862 B.A., J.D. 4644 S. Vandalia
Amrine, Danny A., (BV) ... '51 '83 C.623 B.S. L.862 J.D. 1701 S. Boston Ave.
Amundsen, Dawn '68 '93 C.663 B.A. L.623 J.D. Staff Atty., Oklahoma Disability Law Center, Inc.
Anderson, Jack R., (AV) ... '44 '68 C&L.862 B.S., J.D. [Riggs,A.N.T.O.&L.]
Anderson, Jan Slater, (BV) '53 '91 C.630 B.A. L.862 J.D. Corp. Legal Coun., St. John Med. Ctr.
Anderson, John W., Jr., (BV) ... '62 '89 C&L.878 B.S., J.D. [J.W.Anderson,Jr.]
Anderson, Pamela S., (AV) ... '59 '86 C&L.862 B.A., J.D. [Hall,E.H.G.G.&N.]
Anderson, Peer L., (AV) '44 '69 C&L.623 B.A., J.D. V.P. & Gen. Coun., Citgo Petro. Corp.
Anderson, Russell L., (BV) ... '58 '84 C.305 B.A. L.862 J.D. Tulsa Co. Courthouse
Anderson, Sidney L., (BV) ... '47 '72 C&L.623 B.B.A., J.D. 2339 S. Delaware Pl.
Anderson, William C., (AV) ... '41 '66 C.604 B.A. L.477 J.D. [Doerner,S.D.&A.]

Anderson, John W., Jr., P.C., (BV)
7318 South Yale Avenue, Suite A, 74136-7000
Telephone: 918-481-5552 Fax: 918-481-5558
Email: johnanderson@abanet.org URL: http://www.lawyers.com/johnanderson
John W. Anderson, Jr.
General and Commercial Litigation in Federal and State Courts. Judgment Domestication and Collection, Contract Analysis, Drafting and Litigation, Contingency Business Litigation, Appellate Practice, General Corporate Work, White Collar Criminal Law, Grand Jury Practice, Insurance Defense, Insurance Coverage, International Contract and Distribution Agreements, Dealer and Distributor Termination, Risk Management and Legal Research and Writing on a contract basis.
See Professional Biographies, TULSA, OKLAHOMA

Andrew, Stephen L., (AV) ... '44 '73 C.732 B.S. L.862 J.D. [Andrew,W.&I.]

Andrew, Williams & Ikenberry, A Professional Corporation, (AV)
125 West Third Street, 74103
Telephone: 918-583-1111 Fax: 918-587-4414
Email: info@awlaw.net URL: http://www.awlaws.com
Stephen L. Andrew; Renee Williams; D. Kevin Ikenberry.
Labor Law, Equal Employment Law, Civil Trials.
See Professional Biographies, TULSA, OKLAHOMA

Annis, Jennifer, (CV) ... '72 '98 C&L.623 B.A., J.D. [Atkinson,H.N.B.G.&C.]
Anton, William J., (BV) ... '50 '83 C.724 B.A. L.862 J.D. 717 S. Houston Ave., Ste. 402
Applegate, Robert E., (CV) ... '72 '98 C.623 B.B.A. L.616 J.D. [Holden&C.]
Arbogast, Oliver W., Jr., (BV) ... '54 '84 C.922 B.A. L.862 J.D. P.O. Box 8417
Area, Steven E. ... '51 '79 C.45 B.A. L.862 J.D. Samson Resources Co.
Armstrong, Craig R., (BV) ... '55 '83 C&L.1288 B.A., J.D. [Armstrong&L.]
Armstrong, Richard Volker ... '36 '61 C.623 B.L. L.273 LL.B. [R.V.Armstrong]
Armstrong, Tom L., (AV) ... '40 '71 C.112 B.A. L.1066 J.D. [Gibbs A.B.M.&H.]
Armstrong & Lowe, (AV) ... 1401 South Cheyenne
Armstrong, Richard V. ... 125 E. 34th St.
Arnold, Teresa E. ... '53 '79 C.612 B.S. L.862 J.D. [Hanson&H.]
Arnold, Will B. ... '16 '43 C&L.862 LL.B. 2134 E. 60th St.‡
Arras, Kurt G., (BV) ... '58 '94 C.502 B.S. L.862 J.D. 1756 South Utica Avenue
Arrington, John L., Jr., (AV) ... '31 '56 C.674 A.B. L.309 J.D. [Gable&G.]
Ash, Edwin W., (AV) ... '35 '65 C.759 B.S. L.862 J.D. [Ash]
Ash, M. Scott, (BV) ... '63 '89 C.623 B.A. L.862 J.D. [Ash]

Ash Law Firm, The, (AV)
2500 Mid-Continent Tower, 401 South Boston Avenue, 74103-4016
Telephone: 918-599-0001; 1-800-700-0715 Fax: 918-599-0101
Email: info@ashlawfirm.net URL: http://www.ash-law.com
Members of Firm: Edwin W. Ash; M. Scott Ash.
Trials in all State and Federal Courts. Personal Injury, Medical Malpractice, Product Liability, Insurance, Workers' Compensation Law and Social Security Disability.
See Professional Biographies, TULSA, OKLAHOMA

Ashbaugh, Judith A., (CV) ... '39 '91 C.623 B.A. L.862 J.D. [Leblang,S.&A.]
Ashcraft, Carole Anne, (BV) ... '40 '91 C&L.862 B.S.B.A., J.D. 1861 E. 15th St.
Ashe, Sharon E., (BV) ... '54 '81 C.880 B.A. L.862 J.D. [Firm of S.Ashe]
Ashe, Sharon, Law Firm of, (BV) ... 403 S. Cheyenne, Ste. 500-2
Ashley, Everett L. '35 '65 C.862 B.S. L.208 J.D. (adm. in CO; not adm. in OK) 7318 S. Yale Ave.
Askew, Bryant R. ... '30 '60 C&L.862 B.B.A., LL.B. 3712 S. Winston Ave.
Askew, Thomas M., (AV) ... '64 '90 C.612 B.S. L.862 J.D. [Pray,W.J.W.&M.]
Assink, Ryan James ... '71 '97 C&L.862 B.S., J.D. [Riggs,A.N.T.O.&L.]

Astle, Dale L., (AV) '47 '74 C.612 B.S. L.623 J.D. Exec. V.P. & Gen. Coun., Guaranty Abstract Co.
Aston, H. I., (BV) ... '39 '65 C&L.862 B.A., J.D. 3242 E. 30th Place
Astor, Peter C. ... '70 '97 C&L.623 B.A., J.D. [Gibbs A.B.M.&H.]
Athens, Everett ... '15 '41 C&L.623 LL.B. 2115 E. 25th St.
Atherton, Susan V., (BV) ... '52 '77 C&L.862 B.A., J.D. FirsTitle & Abstract Servs., Inc.
Atkins, Donald B., (AV) ... '29 '58 C.623 B.B.A. L.862 LL.B. [Atkins&A.]
Atkins, R. Blake, (BV) ... '59 '87 C.896 B.S. L.862 J.D. 1406 Terrace Dr.
Atkins & Atkins, P.C., (AV) ... 1406 Terrace Drive

Atkins & Markoff
(See Oklahoma City)

Atkinson, Michael P., P.C., (AV) '46 '72 C&L.623 B.A., J.D. [Atkinson,H.N.B.G.&C.]
Atkinson, Thomas M., Law Offices, (AV) '49 '74 C.802 B.B.A. L.615 J.D. 715 Mid Continent Twr.

Atkinson, Haskins, Nellis, Brittingham, Gladd & Carwile, (AV)
1500 ParkCentre, 525 South Main Street, 74103
Telephone: 918-582-8877 Fax: 918-585-8096
Email: ahnmail@ahn-law.com
Michael P. Atkinson, P.C.; Walter D. Haskins, P.C.; Gregory D. Nellis, P.C.; Galen Lee Brittingham, P.C.; John S. Gladd; John J. Carwile; William A. Fiasco; James N. Edmonds; Scott R. Hall; Mark W. Maguire; Jennifer Annis; Martha J. Phillips; Jon D. Starr; Marthanda J. Beckworth; Kirsten E. Pace; Eric J. Begin;—Carol J. Allen; Gabe W. Lawson; Rachel D. Parrilli; Andrew C. Jayne; James Craig Buchan; Stacie L. Hixon; Jamie A. Rogers; Bart Jay Robey. Of Counsel: K. Clark Phipps.
Medical and Legal Malpractice, Negligence, Insurance, General Civil Practice, Trials and Appeals, Product Liability, Environmental, Oil and Gas, Aviation, Corporation and Antitrust, Securities, Broker-Dealer Disputes, Workers' Compensation, Civil Rights, Employment Law, Pharmaceutical Defense, Commercial Litigation, Construction Litigation, Bankruptcy, Antitrust.
Representative Clients: Allstate Insurance Co.; Bayer Corp.; Crum & Forster Insurance Co.; Hartford Insurance Company; National American Insurance Co.; Federated Insurance Co.; Liberty Mutual Insurance Co.; Physicians Liability Insurance Co.; State Farm Mutual Automobile Insurance Co.; United States Aviation Underwriters.
See Professional Biographies, TULSA, OKLAHOMA

Atteberry, Beverly A., (BV) ... '67 '92 C.613 B.A. L.862 J.D. 1408 S. Denver Ave.
Azam, Syma S. ... '72 '98 C.804 B.A. L.862 J.D. [Secrest,H.&B.]
Baber, Charles S., (BV) ... '55 '80 C.612 B.S. L.862 J.D. 320 S. Boston
Baber, Cheryl L., (BV) ... '64 '93 C.1050 B.A. L.178 J.D. 333 W. Fourth St., Rm. 411
Back, Ann Wright, (BV) ... '53 '96 C.859 B.A. L.623 J.D. 406 S. Boulder Ave., Ste. 400
Backer, Larry Cata '55 '82 C.1036 B.A. L.178 J.D. (adm. in CA; not adm. in OK) Prof., Univ. of Tulsa Coll. of Law
Bacon, Kenneth D. ... '38 '63 C.621 B.S. L.623 LL.B. Ret. Presiding J., Ct. of App.
Baer, Timberlake, Coulson & Cates, P.C., (AV) ... 6846 South Canton (⊙Oklahoma City)
Bailey, Charlotte Mortson, (AV) ... '30 '83 C.112 B.A. L.862 J.D. 8201 S. New Haven
Bailey, P. Craig ... '54 '80 C.804 B.S. L.862 J.D. [Bridger-Riley&Assoc.]
Bainbridge, Robert L., (AV) ... '30 '76 C.623 B.B.A. L.862 J.D. P.O. Box 35771‡
Baker, Ben F., (AV) ... '23 '58 C&L.862 B.A., LL.B. 1st Asst. Dist. Atty.
Baker, Jay C., (AV) ... '34 '59 C.880 B.A. L.623 LL.B. 4825 South Peoria Ave., Suite 5
Baker, Jodi Johnson ... '77 '02 C&L.623 B.A., J.D. [Gassaway]
Baker, Thomas E., (AV) ... '58 '85 C&L.862 B.A., J.D. [Morgan,B.M.M.F.&K.]
Baker, Wyn Dee, (AV) ... '52 '77 C&L.623 B.A., J.D. Asst. U.S. Atty.
Baldwin, Dana Yeatman ... '59 '00 C.45 B.S.B.A. L.862 J.D. 2864 E. 35th Place
Balman, Steven K., (AV) ... '56 '81 C.309 A.B. L.846 J.D. [Sneed L.]
Balogh, Bernadetta ... '58 '97 C.1362 B.S. L.862 J.D. [Balogh,C.M.&W.]
Balogh, Cherry, Mitchell & Williams ... 324 S. Main Street, Suite 601
Banks, T.R. ... '72 '00 C.612 B.S. L.616 J.D. [Burton&Assoc.] ⊙
Banner, Mark, (AV) ... '58 '88 C.623 B.A. L.276 J.D. [Hall,E.H.G.G.&N.]
Barber, Ron B., (AV) ... '54 '80 C.45 B.S.B.A. L.862 J.D. [Barber&B.]

Barber & Bartz, A Professional Corporation, (AV)
525 South Main Street, Suite 800, 74103 ⊙
Telephone: 918-599-7755 Fax: 918-599-7756
Email: email@barberbartz.com
Ron B. Barber; Robert J. Bartz; Nancy Hanania Jones; John M. Hickey; Joe M. Fears; Curtis J. Shacklett;—Robert Lee Bearer; Lynn Summers Lugibihl; Matt David Matheson; Richard P. Clarke. Counsel: Richard D. White, Jr.
Business Organizations and Transactions, Securities, Taxation, Estate Planning, Probate, Commercial Litigation, Real Property, Domestic Relations, Bankruptcy, Labor and Employment, Franchising and Civil Practice.
Representative Client: Metals, Inc.
Oklahoma City, Oklahoma Office: 204 North Robinson, 25th Floor, 73102. Telephone: 405-235-6677. Fax: 405-235-6679.
See Professional Biographies, TULSA, OKLAHOMA

Barker, Jack Steven ... '— '79 C.621 B.S. L.862 J.D. [Riggs,A.N.T.O.&L.]
Barker, Terry J., (BV) ... '60 '88 C.612 B.S. L.862 J.D. [Pezold,B.&W.]
Barkett, Cassie M. ... '75 '00 C.840 B.S. L.862 J.D. [Brewster&D.]
Barkett, Michael L., (BV) ... '68 '94 C&L.623 B.A., J.D. [Graves&B.]
Barkley, C. Michael, (AV) ... '48 '73 C.612 B.S. L.862 J.D. [Barkley]

Barkley Law Firm, The, (AV)
401 South Boston Avenue, Suite 2700, 74103
Telephone: 918-599-9991 Fax: 918-584-1110
URL: http://www.thebarkleylaw.com
C. Michael Barkley; Fred Will DeMier; David G. Graves; Brad Smith; Jeffrey L. Wilson; Lindsey E. Albers; Ashley R. Melson.
Trial Practice, Civil Litigation in State and Federal Courts. Hospital Law, Labor and Employment, Administrative, Corporate, Probate, Estate Planning, Real Estate, Litigation, Medical Malpractice, Securities, Drug and Products Liability Law, Environmental Law, Communications Law, Negligence, Insurance, Business Reorganization, Arbitration, Mediation, Alternative Dispute Resolution.
See Professional Biographies, TULSA, OKLAHOMA

Barlow, James W., (BV) ... '50 '75 C.623 B.B.A. L.862 J.D. 5644 S. Yorktown Pl.
Barnes, Carl A., (BV) ... '51 '77 C&L.862 B.S.B.A., J.D. 4401 S. Harvard Ave.
Barnes, Claudine S. ... '22 '67 C&L.862 U.S. Dept. of the Interior
Barnes, Gerald H., (AV) ... '42 '66 C&L.623 B.A., LL.B. 5234 S. Toledo Ave.
Barnes, Lou Ann Rountree ... '60 '95 C.639 B.A. L.862 J.D. [L.A.R.Barnes]
Barnes, Ronald Merrill, (AV) ... '53 '80 C.623 B.B.A. L.616 J.D. [Crutchmer,B.&B.]
Barnes, Lou Ann R. ... 9102 E. 66th St.
Barnett, Adam S. ... '— '94 C.804 B.A. L.623 J.D. Asst. Pub. Def.
Barnett, Loretha M. ... '71 '00 C.619 B.S.W. L.623 J.D. OK. Ct. of Civil App.
Barnhart, John G., (AV) ... '62 '89 C.612 B.S. L.623 J.D. [Layman P.B.B.&W.]
Barrett, Tammy D. ... '64 '90 C.376 B.S. L.623 J.D. Staff Atty., U.S. Dist. Ct.
Barron, Bradford D. ... '71 '97 C.376 B.S. L.862 J.D. [Gibbon,B.&B.]
Barron, Zachary T. ... '76 '01 C.60 B.S. L.862 J.D. [Gibbon,B.&B.]
Barrow, Allen E., Jr., (AV) ... '44 '70 C.623 B.B.A. L.862 J.D. [Barrow&G.]
Barrow, Christopher A. ... '75 '01 C.347 B.S. L.245 J.D. [Barrow&G.]

Barrow & Grimm, P.C., (AV)
610 South Main, Suite 300, 74119-1258
Telephone: 918-584-1600 Fax: 918-585-2444
Email: EMAIL@BGGG.com URL: http://www.BGGG.com

(This Listing Continued)

Barrow & Grimm, P.C. (Continued)

Allen E. Barrow, Jr.; William R. Grimm; William E. Farrior; Robert B. Sartin. Associates: Wm. Brad Heckenkemper; Christopher A. Barrow; Adam K. Marshall.
Civil Trial and Appellate Practice. General Business Practice. Corporate, Commercial Litigation, Employment Law, Finance, Bankruptcy, Contract, Insurance, Real Estate, Mineral, Probate, Taxation, Estate Planning and Health Law.
Reference: NationsBank.

See Professional Biographies, TULSA, OKLAHOMA

Barrowman, Fred W., (AV) '46 '81
C.619 B.S. L.862 J.D. Sr. Atty. - Risk & Claims, ONEOK, Inc.
Barry, David L. ... '36 '65 C&L.862 B.S., J.D. Sr. V.P. & Tr. Offr., State Bk. & Tr., N.A.
Barry, Sara E. ... '74 '00 C.612 B.A. L.69 J.D. [Ⓐ Gable&G.]
Barrydavid, Lawrence ... '36 '65 C&L.862 B.S., J.D. Arvest Trust Co., N.A.

Bartlett, Barbara Ann, (AV) '57 '85 C.877 B.S. L.623 J.D. BB
406 South Boulder, Suite 642, 74103
Telephone: 918-584-1894 Fax: 918-584-1891
Email: bab@babartlett.com
Family Law.

See Professional Biographies, TULSA, OKLAHOMA

Bartmann, William R. ... '48 '76 C.177 B.A. L.221 J.D. 10901 S. Louisville Ave.
Bartz, Robert J., (AV) ... '55 '80 C&L.862 B.S., J.D. [Barber&B.] ⊙
Bashaw, Catharine M., (BV) ... '62 '88 C.770 B.A. L.623 J.D. [Ⓒ Rosenstein,F.&R.]
Basi, Rajpreet S. '68 '94 C.999 B.A. L.596 J.D.
(adm. in AK; not adm. in OK) Sr. Atty., The Williams Companies, Inc.
Basnett, Patricia M., Attorney at Law, (BV) '53 '79
C.340 B.A. L.862 J.D. 5514 S. Lewis Ave.
Bass, James D., (BV) ... '28 '55 C&L.862 B.A., LL.B. 1820 S. Cincinnati
Bass, Michael T., (BV) ... '60 '86 C.420 B.S. L.802 J.D. MCI
Bass, Sandra Stephenson '58 '86 C.612 B.S. L.802 J.D.
(adm. in TX; not adm. in OK) 4160 Oak Rd.‡
Bates, John Francis '50 '79
C.801 B.A. L.615 J.D. [Ⓐ Garrett] (⊙Muskogee, Oklahoma City)
Batow, David P., (AV) ... '52 '77 C.602 B.B.A. L.597 J.D. 8516 S. Winston
Baum, Dawn Sturdevant '76 '01
C.72 B.A. L.966 J.D. Assoc., Univ. of Tulsa, Boesche Legal Clinic
Baum, Jeffrey C. ... '69 '96 C&L.623 B.A., J.D. [Ⓐ Richards&C.]
Baumgarten, Julie P. '72 '99 C&L.326 B.B.A., J.D.
(adm. in TX; not adm. in OK) Sr. Atty, The Williams Companies, Inc.
Bayliss, Jann S. ... '56 '86 C.845 B.S. L.862 J.D. 11016 Jamestown Ave.
Bayouth, Philip O. ... '53 '79 C&L.862 B.A., J.D. 7044 S Sandusky Avenue
Beach, Toni Ann ... '— '99 C&L.862 B.A., J.D. P.O. Box 52755
Bean, David C. '45 '88 C.896 B.A. L.862 J.D.
[Ⓐ Garrett] (⊙Muskogee, Oklahoma City)
Bearden, Stan K., Law Office of, (BV) '62 '89
C.623 B.S. L.862 J.D. 9246 S. Sheridan Rd.
Bearer, Robert Lee, (BV) ... '49 '82 C.623 B.A. L.862 J.D. [Ⓐ Barber&B.]
Beasley, B. R. ... '34 '68 C&L.862 B.S., J.D. Chf. Juv. J.
Beasley, Bradley K., (AV) ... '56 '80 C.623 B.A. L.862 J.D. [Boesche M.]
Beauchamp, James H., (BV) ... '42 '68 C.612 B.S. L.861 J.D. [J.H.Beauchamp]
Beauchamp, James H., P.C., (BV) ... 7233 S. 85th E. Ave.
Beaver, Kelly, (AV) '51 '77 C&L.45 B.S.B.A., J.D.
V.P., Legal & Gen. Coun., Hilti, Inc.
Beckert, James A., (BV) ... '61 '87 C.1147 B.S. L.862 J.D. [Layman P.B.B.&W.]
Beckworth, Marthanda J., (AV) '49 '83 C.588 B.A. L.862 J.D.
[Atkinson,H.N.B.G.&C.]
Bednar, Stephen J. '47 '74 C.502 B.S. L.378 J.D.
(adm. in KS; not adm. in OK) Sr. Corp. Coun., Citgo Petro. Corp.
Beeby, Richard D., (CV) ... '40 '75 C.612 B.S. L.862 J.D. 2206 S. 83rd East Avenue

Beeler, Walsh & Walsh P.L.L.C.
(See Oklahoma City)

Begin, Eric J., (BV) ... '69 '94 C.1315 B.S. L.616 J.D. [Atkinson,H.N.B.G.&C.]
Behling, Richard W. ... '47 '77 C.959 B.S. L.862 J.D. Behling Petroleum
Beirute, James Daniel ... '71 '96 C.804 B.A. L.309 J.D. [J.D.Beirute]
Beirute, J. Daniel ... 2448 E. 81st St., Ste. 5900
Beitel, Remsen H., III '67 '92 C.228 A.B. L.846 J.D.
Gen. Coun., Community Care Managed Healthcare Plans of OK
Bell, Eugene G. ... '21 '48 C&L.923 LL.B. MAPCO Inc.
Bell, Sharon J., (AV) ... '51 '85 C.183 B.A. L.862 J.D. [Rogers&B.]
Beller, Jamie Messina ... '77 '02 C&L.862 B.A., B.A. [Ⓐ Pierce C.H.B.&G.]
Belsky, Martin Henry ... '44 '69 C.831 B.A. L.178 J.D. 3125 E. 4th Place
Bender, Gerald M., (AV) ... '53 '91 C&L.900 B.A., J.D. [Smiling,B.&R.]
Bender, James J., (AVⓉ) '56 '81 C.747 B.A. L.494 J.D.
(adm. in MN; not adm. in OK) Sr. V.P. & Gen. Coun., The Williams Cos., Inc.
Bendure, P. Bradley ... '76 '01 C.388 B.A. L.623 J.D. [Ⓐ Conner&W.]
Benedict, Shelton L., (AV) ... '56 '84 C.263 B.A. L.900 J.D. 406 S. Boulder Avenue
Beneke, Ron '44 '69 C&L.744 B.A., J.D.
(adm. in TX; not adm. in OK) Property Co. of America
Bennett, Allen ... '— '02 C&L.45 B.S., J.D. [Head,J.&K.] (See Pat. Sect.)
Bennett, Claudia N. ... '45 '89 C&L.862 B.S.Ed., J.D. 406 S. Boulder‡
Bennett, Everett R., Jr., (BV) ... '59 '85 C.623 B.S. L.862 J.D. [Frasier,F.&H.]
Bennett-White, Kristina E. ... '66 '99 C.438 b.a. L.862 J.D. 3720 S. Birmingham
Bentley, Royce H. ... '48 '87 C.621 B.S. L.862 J.D. 7419 E. 30th Place
Bereolos, Demetrius ... '54 '87 C.623 B.A. L.285 J.D. 1929 S. Cheyenne
Berman, Mark D. ... '56 '81 C.1169 A.B. L.878 J.D. [Conner&W.]
Berman, Stephen '— '97 C&L.107 B.A., J.D.
(adm. in AZ; not adm. in OK) Vice Pres., Regulatory Affs., Envirosolve LLC
Bernbaum, Jennie Marie '65 '96 C.208 B.A. L.862 J.D.
V.P. & Gen. Coun., Oklahoma Lighting Distributos, Inc.

Bernert, Martin Benjamin, (AV) '49 '79 C.623 B.A. L.862 J.D.
3314 East 51st Street, Suite 218, 74135-3527
Telephone: 918-749-4222 Fax: 918-743-3377
Email: mberlaw@aol.com
Estate Planning, Probate and Trust Law, Real Estate, Business, Commercial and Franchise Law.

See Professional Biographies, TULSA, OKLAHOMA

Bernhardt, Peter, (AV) ... '43 '76 C&L.862 B.A., J.D. 7531 S. Knoxville Ave.‡
Berry, Brent D. ... '— '98 C.621 B.A. L.623 J.D. [Carr&C.]
Berry, Kevin D., (AV) ... '61 '86 C.502 B.A. L.862 J.D. [Perrine,M.R.R.B.&T.]
Besly, Helen Frances ... '20 '50 C.612 B.A. L.623 LL.B. 3904 E. 31st St.
Besore, Kort A. ... '67 '91 C&L.623 B.A., J.D. [Ⓐ Harris,M.P.T.&S.]
Best, Joseph M., (AV) ... '25 '50 C.612 L.862 LL.B. [Best&S.]
Best, Timothy G., (AV) ... '60 '88 C.612 B.S. L.862 J.D. [Best&S.]

Best & Sharp, A Professional Corporation, (AV) BB
Oneok Plaza, 100 W. 5th, Suite 808, 74103-4225
Telephone: 918-582-1234 Fax: 918-585-9447
URL: http://www.bestsharp.com
Joseph M. Best; Joseph A. Sharp; Timothy G. Best; Daniel S. Sullivan; Amy E. Kempfert; Thomas A. Le Blanc; Sean H. McKee; Dan W. Ernst;—Matthew B. Free; Steven W. Simcoe; Bob D. James; John Jay Bowling; J. Spencer Bryan; Trevor A. Dennis. Of Counsel: William E. Patten.
Medical Malpractice, Legal Malpractice, Professional Liability, Accountants Malpractice, Products Liability, Insurance Defense, Architects and Engineers Liability, General Civil Practice, Appellate Law, Labor and Employment, Directors and Officers Liability, Civil Rights Defense, Probate, Workers' Compensation, Environmental Law, Taxation and Estate Planning.

See Professional Biographies, TULSA, OKLAHOMA

Betow, Gary L., (AV) ... '54 '79 C.623 B.A. L.309 J.D. [Crowe&D.]
Bettis, R. Mack ... '34 '68 C.619 B.A. L.616 J.D. Chief Dep. Assessor
Betzer, J. Paul ... '69 '03 C.1288 B.A. L.1049 J.D. [Ⓐ Norman W.C.&D.]
Beustring, Glenn R., (AV) ... '41 '67 C.1 B.S. L.862 J.D. 2624 East 21st Street
Bibb, Ashley M., (BV) ... '72 '97 C.619 B.A. L.862 J.D. [Ⓐ King,T.&R.]
Bickell, C. Matthew ... '72 '98 C.862 B.B.A. L.623 J.D. [Ⓐ Doyle H.D.&H.]
Bilderback, Heather Holt ... '74 '02 C&L.45 B.A., J.D. [Ⓐ Conner&W.]
Bingham, Donald M., (AV) ... '47 '77 C.674 A.B. L.862 J.D. [Riggs,A.N.T.O.&L.]
Bingham, Thomas M., (AV) ... '52 '78 C.862 B.A. L.623 J.D. 1515 S. Denver
Biolchini, Robert F., (AV) ... '39 '65 C.602 B.A. L.273 LL.B. [Stuart,B.&T.]
Biolchini, Tobin M. ... '74 '01 C.602 B.A. L.599 J.D. [Ⓐ Stuart,B.&T.]
Bircher, Molly A. ... '78 '03 C.999 B.A. L.378 J.D. [Ⓐ Hall,E.H.G.G.&N.]
Birmingham, Thomas F., (BV) ... '36 '69 C&L.862 B.A., J.D. [Birmingham,M.W.&P.]
Birmingham, Morley, Weatherford & Priore, (AV) ... 1141 East 37th Street
Bishop, Douglas ... '31 '61 C&L.862 LL.B. 4815 S. Harvard
Bitting, Terry H., (BV) ... '54 '79 C&L.862 B.S., J.D. Spec. Dist. J.
Bivens, Cull, (BV) ... '30 '61 C.623 L.862 LL.B. 3010 S. 94th E. Ave.
Black, Diane M. ... '68 '00 C&L.862 B.A., J.D. [Ⓐ Buckman&R.]
Black, Thomas E., Jr., (AV) '56 '81
C.846 B.B.A. L.802 J.D. Sr. Coun., The Williams Cos., Inc.
Blackstock, Charles L. ... '74 '99 C.612 B.S.B.A L.623 J.D. [Ⓐ C.Blackstock]
Blackstock, Craig, (AV) ... '42 '67 C.902 B.A. L.862 J.D. 320 South Boston, Suite 2000
Blackstock, LeRoy, (AV) ... '14 '38 C.999 L.862 J.D. 7213 S. Atlanta‡
Blackstock, Vincent Craig ... '42 '67 C.902 B.A. L.862 J.D. 320 S. Boston, Ste. 2000
Blackwell, Debbie L., (AV) ... '56 '86 C&L.862 B.S., J.D. [Concordia B.]
Blackwell, Monta Sharon '42 '75
C.618 B.A. L.560 J.D. U.S. Dept. of Interior, Field Solr. Off.
Blades, David R., (BV) ... '61 '92 C&L.862 B.S.E., J.D. [Ⓐ Armstrong&L.]
Blair, D. Marianne '52 '82
C.210 B.A. L.608 J.D. Assoc. Prof., Univ. of Tulsa Coll. of Law
Blake, Glen J. ... '70 '00 C&L.862 B.A., J.D. [Blake]
Blake, Helen Holt, (BV) ... '54 '93 C.879 B.S. L.862 J.D. Staff Atty.
Blake Law Firm ... P.O. Box 50001
Blakeley, Dick A., (BV) ... '37 '65 C&L.616 B.A., J.D. Chf. Civil Asst.
Blakemore, Robert ... '73 '00 C&L.623 B.A., J.D. [Ⓐ Miller,K.&B.]
Blanchard, Richard L., (BV) ... '49 '76 C&L.862 B.A., J.D. 444 S. Houston, Ste. 210

Blaschke, Michael J., P.C.
(See Oklahoma City)

Bledsoe, D. Gregory, (AV) ... '53 '79 C.1288 B.A. L.862 J.D. 1717 S. Cheyenne Avenue
Blongewicz, Mark K., (AV) ... '55 '80 C.546 B.S. L.228 J.D. [Hall,E.H.G.G.&N.]
Bloomfield, Melvin C. ... '41 '66 C&L.378 B.S., LL.B. 6144 S New Haven Avenue
Blough, Philip K., II, (BV) ... '56 '83 C&L.862 B.S., J.D. 6966 S. Utica Ave.
Blue, Rachel, (AV) ... '63 '88 C.846 B.A. L.862 J.D. [Doerner,S.D.&A.] (Pat.)
Bodenhamer, Katrina S., (BV) ... '58 '92 C&L.862 B.A., J.D. [Bodenhamer&L.]
Bodenhamer, Kenneth D., (BV) ... '34 '82 C.302 B.A. L.1288 J.D. [Bodenhamer&L.]

Bodenhamer & Levinson, P.C., (AV)
Southbridge Office Park, 1743 E. 71st Street, 74136-5108
Telephone: 918-492-4433 Fax: 918-492-6224
Email: ken@bodenhamer.com
Kenneth D. Bodenhamer; Lee I. Levinson; Katrina S. Bodenhamer; Rick D. Westcott. Of Counsel: Kenny Joe Smith.
General Civil Practice in all State and Federal Courts. Oil and Gas, Corporate, Construction, Administrative, Family, Divorce, Child Custody and Probate Law, Environmental.

See Professional Biographies, TULSA, OKLAHOMA

Bodine-Keely, Michelle Lee ... '62 '95 C.612 B.S. L.862 J.D. 500 S. Denver
Boerner, Gene G., III ... '71 '97 C.862 B.A. L.623 J.D. [Ⓐ Pezold,B.&W.]

Boesche McDermott LLP, (AV)
Suite 800 Oneok Plaza, 100 West Fifth Street, 74103
Telephone: 918-583-1777 Fax: 918-592-5809
Email: bme@bme-law.com URL: http://www.bme-law.com
Members of Firm: Fenelon Boesche (1910-1993); Richard B. McDermott (1905-1977); Bradley K. Beasley; David A. Johnson. Of Counsel: Linda McQuillen Kulp; Michael S. Forsman; Rodger A. Randle.
General Civil Practice, State and Federal Civil Trials. Banking, Bankruptcy, Corporation, Oil and Gas, Probate, Real Property, Insurance, Employment, Sports Law, Aviation, Insurance, Negligence, Environmental, International, Estate Planning, Commercial Litigation, Mergers and Acquisitions.
Representative Clients: Apache Corp.; Aetna Insurance; Cogentriy Energy; Houlihan-Parnes; Adesa; Williams Cos.; Barbre Groul Investments; Term Insurance; Helmerich Payne; Metropolitan Life.

See Professional Biographies, TULSA, OKLAHOMA

Boettcher, Cynthia J., (BV) ... '58 '85 C.546 B.A. L.190 J.D. [Boettcher&D.]
Boettcher, Thomas D. ... '44 '74 C.1070 B.S. L.623 J.D. 4111 S. Darlington, Ste. 1075
Boettcher & Drummond, (BV) ... 5200 S. Yale Ave.
Boettcher, Ryan, Martin & Bisher, (AV)
4111 South Darlington, Suite 1075 (⊙Oklahoma City, Ponca City)
Bogatko, John D. ... '73 '02 C.804 B.A. L.862 J.D. [Ⓐ Glendening]
Bogie, Dana Lynn ... '71 '96 C.612 B.A. L.862 J.D. 7015 E. 85th St.
Bohannon, Joe M., (BV) ... '36 '88 C.612 B.S. L.862 J.D. 4157 S. Harvard, Ste. 130
Bolden, Stephen R. ... '66 '91 C.315 B.A. L.999 J.D. [Mysock&C.]
Bollinger, Catherine Parker, (BV) '64 '92 C.846 B.A. L.862 J.D.
MCI Legal Department
Bolt, Donald B., III, (BV) ... '67 '93 C.623 B.A. L.862 J.D. [Ⓐ Corley&G.]
Bomer, Jesse N. ... '78 '03 C&L.862 B.S.B.A., J.D. [Ⓐ Johnson,J.D.C.&S.]

Bonham & Howard, (BV)
An Association of Professional Associates
Not A Partnership
15 W. 6th Street, 74119 ⊙
Telephone: 918-744-7440 Fax: 918-744-9358
URL: http://www.bonhamandhoward.com
Members of Firm: Gene C. Howard; P. Gae Widdows; Joseph F. Bufogle. Associates: David C. Fisher; Martin Franklin Halstead; Andrew B. Morsman; Kymberly J. Watt; Malcolm D. Smith, Jr. (Also practicing individually); Mark T. Hamby (Also practicing individually).
General, Civil and Trial Practice in Federal Courts and all State Courts, Insurance Defense, Property and Casualty, Workers' Compensation, Products Liability, Surety, Civil Rights Defense, Personal Injury, Regulatory and Administrative Law, Corporate, Estate Planning, Probate.

(This Listing Continued)

Bonham & Howard (Continued)
Oklahoma City Office: 3555 NW 58th Street, 73112. Telephone: 405-943-6650. Fax: 405-943-6655.
See Professional Biographies, TULSA, OKLAHOMA

Boone, Smith, Davis, Hurst & Dickman, A Professional Corporation, (AV) BB
500 Oneok Plaza, 100 West 5th Street, 74103
Telephone: 918-587-0000 Fax: 918-599-9317
URL: http://www.boonesmith.com
Byron V. Boone (1908-1988); Teresa Meinders Burkett; John A. Burkhardt; Reuben Davis; Garry M. Gaskins; Charles Greenough; Larry D. Henry; Gerald L. Hilsher; William C. Kellough; Donald A. Lepp; Michael J. McDaniel; Angela McSpadden Paulsen; Frederic N. (Nick) Schneider III; Stephen A. Schuller; L. K. Smith (1934-2001). Of Counsel: Edwin S. Hurst; Bill Freudenrich.
Litigation in State and Federal Courts. Employment and Labor, ERISA, Healthcare and Hospital Law, Antitrust, Product Liability, Municipal and Zoning, Securities Transactions and Litigation, Business Organization, Banking, Bankruptcy, Estate Planning, Probate, Energy Law, Environmental, Intellectual Property, Media Law, International Transactions, White Collar Crime, Arbitration/ Mediation, Alternative Dispute Resolution, Trademarks, Copyrights, Telecommunications.
Representative Clients: American Airlines; BP Amoco Corp.; Chevron U.S.A., Inc.; Ford Motor Co.; PricewaterhouseCoopers; Phillips Petroleum Co.; The Boeing Company; Sears, Roebuck & Co.; World Publishing Co; Whirlpool Corp.
See Professional Biographies, TULSA, OKLAHOMA

Borchardt, Katherine Evans, (BV) .... '44 '76 C.623 B.A. L.862 J.D. [K.E.Borchardt]
Borchardt, Kathy Evans, (BV) .... 3701 S. Harvard Ave., No. 193
Borders, William D., (BV) .... '30 '59 C&L.623 LL.B. 1302 S. Guthrie
Borochoff, Douglas M., (BV) .... '55 '90 C.623 B.A. L.862 J.D. [Gibbs A.B.M.&H.]
Boss, Fred L., Jr., (BV) '36 '70 C.45 B.S.B.A. L.862 J.D.
3223 East 31st Street, Suite 101
Bost, James A., (AV) '42 '68 C.612 B.S. L.862 J.D.
V.P. & Gen. Coun., Midwesco Industries, Inc.
Bostwick, James S., (AVⓉ) '43 '69 C.911 B.S. L.1065 J.D.
(adm. in CA; not adm. in OK) [Bostwick&Assoc.] ⊙
Bostwick & Associates, (AVⓉ)
5310 E. 31st. Street, Penthouse Suite II (⊙San Fran., CA; Honolulu, HI)
Botsko, Dennis M., (BV) .... '46 '77 C.679 B.S. L.862 J.D. 1503 E. 35th St.
Boudreaux, Paul T., (AV) .... '55 '80 C.616 B.A. L.623 J.D. [Feldman,F.W.F.&B.]
Boulden, Patrick T., (BV) .... '53 '83 C&L.862 B.S., J.D. Asst. City Atty.
Boutot, Michael W. .... '67 '02 C&L.862 B.A., J.D. [Ⓐ Secrest,H.&B.]
Bowden, Stephanie M.L. '63 '89 C.846 B.B.A. L.45 J.D.
(adm. in AR; not adm. in OK) [Ⓐ Young]
Bowen, James Carl, (BV) '53 '89 C.1147 B.A. L.623 J.D.
State Capital Trial Def. Coun.
Bowker, Robert W. .... '26 '64 C.612 B.S. L.862 J.D. [McKee&B.]
Bowles, Margo L., (BV) ...... '49 '85 C.612 B.S. L.862 J.D. 2021 S. Lewis Ave., Ste. 640
Bowles, William A., (BV) .... '45 '80 C&L.862 B.A., J.D. [Ⓐ Riggs,A.N.T.O.&L.]
Bowling, John Jay, (BV) .... '70 '96 C.679 B.A. L.862 J.D. [Ⓐ Best&S.]
Bowman, David W., (AV) '40 '67 C&L.352 B.A., J.D.
(adm. in IA; not adm. in OK)
Senior Vice President, General Counsel & Secy., MAPCO Inc.
Boyd, Douglas L., (AV) .... '42 '67 C.612 B.A. L.623 J.D. 1717 E. 15th St.
Boyd, Jamie Taylor, (AV) .... '64 '89 C.612 B.S. L.862 J.D. [Shipley&K.]
Boyd, Jeffrey G., (BV) .... '56 '83 C.623 B.B.A. L.862 J.D. 4115 E. 47th Pl
Braden, Paul E., (AV) .... '42 '80 C.430 B.A. L.900 J.D. [Conner&W.]
Bradley, Sheila M., (BV) .... '40 '89 C.659 B.A. L.862 J.D. [Graham&F.]
Bradshaw, Gatra Marvin, (BV) .... '40 '67 C&L.862 B.A., J.D. 1717 E. 15th St.
Bradshaw, Scott W., (AV) .... '37 '77 C.602 B.A. L.862 J.D. 1717 E. 15th St.
Brady, Brian H. .... '60 '85 C.612 B.S. L.616 J.D. 3771 E. 78 St.★
Brady, Ginger K. .... '54 '87 C.619 B.A. L.862 J.D. 5563 S. Lewis St., Ste. 300
Braly, Cynthia J., (BV) .... '60 '86 C&L.623 B.A., J.D. 8086 S. Yale Ave.
Brame, Wendy J. .... '71 '99 C.101 B.S. L.378 J.D. [Ⓐ King,T.&R.]
Brandon, James E., (AV) .... '55 '82 C&L.623 B.A., J.D. 406 Co. Courthouse
Bransford, Mark H. .... '55 '87 C.840 B.A. L.45 J.D. 406 S. Boulder, Ste. 400
Bratcher, Kelly L., (BV) .... '69 '96 C.880 B.A. L.623 J.D. [Ⓐ Riggs,A.N.T.O.&L.]
Bratton, Paula W. .... '45 '77 C.560 B.S. L.862 J.D. 2160 South Owasso Avenue
Bratton, Sam G., II, (AV) .... '46 '74 C&L.560 B.B.A., J.D. [Doerner,S.D.&A.]
Breedlove, Roy C., (AV) .... '52 '77 C&L.900 B.A., J.D. [Fellers,S.B.B.&T.]
Brejcha, Robert Allen '54 '79 C.801 B.A. L.734 J.D.
(adm. in IL; not adm. in OK) P.O. Box 21348
Brennan, Elise Dunitz, (AV) .... '54 '83 C.861 A.B. L.802 J.D. [Doerner,S.D.&A.]
Brennan, Terence P., (BV) .... '57 '82 C&L.966 B.A., J.D. 15 E. 5th Street, Suite 3630
Brett, Thomas R. .... '31 '57 C&L.623 B.B.A., J.D. [Ⓒ Crowe&D.]

Brewer, Worten, Robinett
(See Bartlesville)

Brewster, Clark O., (AV) .... '56 '81 C.136 B.S. L.862 J.D. [Brewster&D.]

Brewster and De Angelis, P.L.L.C., (AV) BB
2617 East 21st Street, 74114-1707
Telephone: 918-742-2021 Facsimile: 918-742-2197
URL: http://www.brewsterlaw.com
Members of Firm: Clark O. Brewster; Jennifer L. De Angelis; Guy A. Fortney; Montgomery Loyd Lair; Cassie M. Barkett; Robert Nigh, Jr.; Mark B. Jennings.
General Civil Trial Practice in State and Federal Courts. Personal Injury, Medical Malpractice, Products Liability, Taxation, Probate, Real Estate, Bankruptcy, Family Law, Selected Criminal Defense.
See Professional Biographies, TULSA, OKLAHOMA

Bridger-Riley, N. Kay, (AV) .... '51 '75 C.36 B.A. L.862 J.D. [Bridger-Riley&Assoc.]
Bridger-Riley & Associates, P.C., (AV) .... 7030 South Yale Avenue, Suite 306
Briggs, Dale J., (AV) .... '26 '50 C.134 L.862 LL.B. [Briggs,P.&Assoc.]
Briggs, James R. .... '54 '93 C.619 B.S. L.862 J.D. [Ⓐ Riggs,A.N.T.O.&L.]
Briggs, Michael P. .... '49 '92 C.934 B.A. L.862 J.D. 3808 E 108th
Briggs, Patterson & Associates, (AV) .... 1717 E. 15th St.
Brightmire, Jon E., (AV) .... '60 '86 C.612 B.S. L.846 J.D. [Doerner,S.D.&A.]
Brightmire, Paul W., (AV) .... '24 '51 C&L.862 B.A., LL.B. Ret. Ct. of App. J.‡
Brightmire, William Paul, (BV) .... '54 '90 L.862 J.D. [W.P.Brightmire]
Brightmire, William P., (BV) .... 1831 E. 71st St., Ste. 119
Brittingham, Galen Lee, P.C., (AV) '54 '87
C.804 B.S. L.900 J.D. [Atkinson,H.N.B.G.&C.]
Brolick, Peter W., (CV) .... '70 '98 C&L.623 B.A., J.D. [Ⓐ Riggs,A.N.T.O.&L.]
Brooks, Wendy S., (BV) '64 '94 C.612 B.A. L.623 J.D.
Sr. Atty., The Williams Cos., Inc.
Broussard, Steven A., (AV) .... '62 '88 C.880 B.S. L.862 J.D. [Hall,E.H.G.G.&N.]
Browers, Deborah B., (AV) .... '54 '84 C.623 B.A. L.616 J.D. [Crutchmer,B.&B.]
Brown, Darrell E. .... '46 '91 C.623 B.B.A. L.862 J.D. 7204 E. 90th Pl. S.
Brown, Darven L., (AV) .... '25 '52 C.942 B.A. L.45 LL.B. [D.L.Brown]
Brown, Dennis D., (AV) .... '57 '89 C.839 B.S.Ch.E. L.862 J.D. [Fellers,S.B.B.&T.] (Pat.)
Brown, Everette T., Jr., (BV) .... '25 '56 C.612 B.S. L.862 J.D. 2226 E. 35th St.
Brown, Georgenia A., (BV) .... '56 '86 C.1288 B.S. L.862 J.D. P.O. Box 52541
Brown, Heather E., (BV) ...... '64 '93 C.822 B.A. L.61 J.D. Sr. Atty., The Williams Cos.
Brown, Jack L., (AV) .... '57 '84 C.623 B.A. L.862 J.D. [Jones,G.&B.]
Brown, Martin Allen .... '70 '00 C&L.862 B.A., J.D. [Ⓐ Joyce,P.&M.]
Brown, Robert G., (BV) .... '33 '58 C&L.862 B.A., LL.B. 6216 S. Lewis Ave.
Brown, Vernon A. .... '21 '53 L.862 LL.B. 1624 S. St. Louis
Brown, Darven L., P.C., (AV) .... Suite 100, 5561 South Lewis
Browne, Matthew James, III, (AV) .... '52 '91 C.131 B.S. L.45 J.D. 124 E. 4th St.
Brownson, Richmond Jay .... '38 '93 C.935 A.B. L.862 J.D. 2530 East 71st Street
Bruce, Tammy Lesta .... '60 '91 C&L.862 B.S., J.D. DHS Child Supp. Enforce.
Brumbaugh, Wm. M. .... '30 '55 C&L.862 B.A., LL.B. 2815 E. Skelly Dr.
Brune, Kenneth L., (AV) .... '45 '75 C.707 B.A. L.862 J.D. [Brune]

Brune Lawyers, (AV)
900 Reunion Center, Nine East Fourth Street, 74103
Telephone 918-599-8600 Facsimile: 918-599-8673
Email: nancypascoe@bruneneff.com
Kenneth L. Brune;—David M. Messer. Of Counsel: Jonathan C. Neff.
General Civil Litigation, International and Domestic Business Transactions, Commercial, Corporate and Contract Law, Securities and Finance, Trademarks, Energy, Transportation, Real Estate and Construction.
See Professional Biographies, TULSA, OKLAHOMA

Bruner, Tom H., (BV) .... '44 '70 406 S. Boulder Ave., Ste. 610
Brunton, Paul D., (AV) .... '44 '71 C.623 B.A. L.862 J.D. U.S. Pub. Def.
Bryan, J. Spencer .... '— '02 C.37 B.A. L.623 J.D. [Ⓐ Best&S.]
Bryan, N. Lance .... '77 '03 C.612 B.A. L.846 J.D. [Ⓐ Doerner,S.D.&A.]
Bryant, Craig, (CV) .... '57 '83 C.663 B.S. L.911 J.D. Off. of Pub. Def.
Bryant, David L., (AV) .... '55 '81 C.623 B.A. L.846 J.D. [Bryant P.]
Bryant, Hubert Hale .... '31 '56 C.254 B.A. L.329 LL.B. 2623 N. Peoria Avenue

Bryant, James D., (BV) '59 '87 C.1147 B.S. L.623 J.D.
7633 E. 63rd Place, Suite 510, 74133
Telephone: 918-392-1985 Fax: 918-392-1955
Email: jim@jbryantlaw.com URL: http://www.jbryantlaw.com
Commercial Litigation, Family Law, Divorce, Taxation, Bankruptcy.
See Professional Biographies, TULSA, OKLAHOMA

Bryant, John L., Jr. .... '52 '81 C&L.45 B.A., J.D. P.O. Box 52155

Bryant Law Firm PLLC, (AV) BB
950 Kennedy Building, 321 South Boston Avenue, 74103-3313
Telephone: 918-587-4200 Fax: 918-587-4217
URL: http://www.bryantlaw.com
David L. Bryant; Craig A. Fitzgerald.
Business Litigation and Trials in Federal and State Courts including Business Torts, Contract Litigation, Securities Litigation, Oil & Gas Litigation, Intellectual Property Litigation, Unfair Competition, Fraud and Deceit, Banking Litigation and Professional Liability.
Representative Clients: ACE Capital Re; ExxonMobil; First North American National Bank; ING Investment Management, Inc.; Johnson & Johnson; National Farms, Inc; ONEOK, Inc.; Shell Oil Company; Union Oil Company of California; Wal-Mart.
See Professional Biographies, TULSA, OKLAHOMA

Buchan, James Craig .... '76 '02 C&L.623 B.B.A., J.D. [Ⓐ Atkinson,H.N.B.G.&C.]
Buchner, Mark E. .... '48 '75 C.225 B.A. L.623 J.D. 5153 East 51, Suite 105
Bucholtz, Barbara .... '39 '80 C.518 B.A. L.879 J.D. Univ. of Tulsa College of Law
Buck, Rodney L., (AV) '48 '79
C.612 B.A. L.862 J.D. Corp Cnsl, St. Francis Health Sys., Inc.
Buckley, Julie Griffith .... '57 '86 C.862 B.A. L.36 J.D. 1301 Terrace Drive
Buckman, Steven V., (BV) .... '60 '84 C.612 B.S. L.616 J.D. [Buckman&R.]

Buckman & Roach, A Professional Corporation, (AV) BB
Park Centre, Suite 660, 525 South Main Street, 74103-4521
Telephone: 918-587-1525 Fax: 918-587-1535
URL: http://www.lawyers.com/buckman&roach
Loyal J. Roach, III; Steven V. Buckman;—Diane M. Black.
General Civil and Trial Practice in all State and Federal Courts. Insurance, Negligence, Bad Faith Litigation, Trade Secrets, Products Liability, Fire, Life and Casualty, Employment Law, and Business Torts.
Reference: Bank of America, Tulsa.
See Professional Biographies, TULSA, OKLAHOMA

Budd, Toni Turner .... '63 '97 C.619 B.B.A. L.602 J.D. [Ⓐ Stuart,B.&T.]
Bufogle, Joseph F., (BV) .... '53 '83 C.1 B.S. L.862 J.D. [Bonham&H.]
Buford, Daniel S., (BV) .... '37 '61 C.612 B.S. L.862 LL.B. Beacon Bldg.

Bullard & Hoehner, P.C.
(See Oklahoma City)

Bullock, Louis W., (AV) .... '48 '75 C.612 B.S. L.623 J.D. [Miller,K.&B.]
Bullock, Patricia W., (AV) .... '52 '77 C.183 B.A. L.623 J.D. [Bullock&B.]
Bullock and Bullock Law Office, (AV) .... 222 S. Kenosha Ave.
Bunting, Steven K., (AV) .... '52 '77 C&L.623 B.A., J.D. [Ⓒ Newton,O.T.&K.]
Burch, Dana A., (AV) .... '54 '79 C.691 B.A. L.846 J.D. Sr. Coun., Citgo Petro. Corp.
Burgess, Shena Elaine .... '75 '00 C.125 B.A. L.862 J.D. Pub. Def. Off.
Burk, Jana R. '70 '97 C&L.846 B.A., J.D.
(adm. in TX; not adm. in OK) [Ⓒ Rosenstein,F.&R.]
Burk, Robert A., (BV) .... '57 '94 C.804 B.S. L.45 J.D. Energy Transfer Partners

Burke, Robbie Emery, (AV) '52 '82 C.623 B.A. L.862 J.D.
320 S. Boston Avenue, Suite 1030, 74103
Telephone: 918-592-9003 Fax: 918-592-9006
Email: rburkelaw@aol.com URL: http://www.robbieburke.com
Elder Law, Guardianship, Decedents Estates, Contested Wills, Contested Trusts and Estates, Estate Planning, Real Property, Real Estate Title Examination, Oil and Gas Law.
See Professional Biographies, TULSA, OKLAHOMA

Burke, Thomas J. .... '55 '82 C.966 B.S. L.623 J.D. P.O. Box 614
Burkett, Teresa Meinders, (AV) .... '59 '85 C&L.623 B.S., J.D. [Boone,S.D.H.&D.]
Burkhardt, John A., (AV) .... '55 '80 C&L.862 B.A., J.D. [Boone,S.D.H.&D.]
Burns, Sherlene E. '51 '81 C.378 B.G.S. L.862 J.D.
(adm. in KS; not adm. in OK) 6536 E. 85th Street
Burress, Robin L. .... '60 '00 C&L.862 B.A., J.D. 1802 E. 72nd St., Apt. 1514
Burton, Brandon J., (AV) .... '68 '97 C.612 B.S. L.616 J.D. [Burton&Assoc.] ⊙
Burton, C. Robert, IV, (BV) .... '65 '90 C.187 B.A. L.950 J.D. [Seymour]
Burton & Associates, P.C., (AV) .... 1861 East 15th Street (⊙Oklahoma City, Walters)
Buss, Everett R., III .... '64 '91 C.804 B.A. L.862 J.D. 1743 E. 71st Street
Butler, John M., & Associates .... '38 '69 C.619 B.S. L.862 J.D. 6846 South Canton Street
Butler, Robert C., III .... '73 '00 C&L.862 B.A., J.D. [Butler M.]
Butler, Robert M., (BV) .... '31 '59 C.612 B.S. L.623 LL.B. 1714 S. Boston
Butler, Roger N., Jr., (AV) .... '64 '89 C&L.623 B.A., J.D. [Secrest,H.&B.]
Butler McMurray, (BV) .... 5508 South Lewis, Ste. 200
Butterfield, Steven B., (AV) .... '64 '90 C&L.623 B.B.A., J.D. [Pray,W.J.W.&M.]
Buxton, Fred M., (AV) .... '59 '87 C.612 B.S. L.862 J.D. [Hall,E.H.G.G.&N.]
Buzzard, Gene C., (AV) .... '46 '74 C.976 B.A. L.910 J.D. [Gable&G.]
Byars, Roy William .... '40 '69 L.623 J.D. 815 S. Denver
Byers, David E. .... '38 '62 C&L.352 B.A., J.D. 4337 E. 72nd St.
Byrd, Scott Wallace .... '71 '02 C&L.623 B.A., J.D. [Ⓐ Riggs,A.N.T.O.&L.]

Cain, Deborah Gayle .....'50 '78 C.1375 B.A. L.862 J.D. Legal Aid Services of Oklahoma
Caldwell, Catherine Mary ....'55 '89 C&L.862 J.D. 3214 S. Louisville
Caldwell, Excetral K. ....'57 '83 C&L.831 B.A., J.D. Sr. Atty., The Williams Cos, Inc.
Caldwell, Robt. E. ....'27 '53 C&L.862 LL.B. Ret. Dist. J.
Caldwell, Terry Joe, (BV) ....'54 '96 C.16 B.S. L.862 J.D. [T.J.Caldwell]
Caldwell, Terry J., Attorney at Law, (BV) .... 3105 E. Skelly Dr., Ste. 520
Cale, Randall C. '63 '90 C.45 B.A. L.862 J.D.
(adm. in AR; not adm. in OK) Bus. & Estate Solutions
Callahan, Karen L., (AV) ....'65 '91 C&L.862 B.A., J.D. [Rodolf&T.]
Callahan-Freeberg, Bobbie, Law Office of, (BV) '49 '81
C.679 B.A. L.862 J.D. 2021 S. Lewis, Ste. 640
Callicoat, F. Bennett ....'62 '00 C&L.862 B.A., J.D. [Jarboe&S.]
Calvarese, Stephen C. '47 '73 C.457 B.A. L.260 J.D.
(adm. in FL; not adm. in OK) Chf. Admin. Law J., Soc. Sec. Admn.
Calvert, Gregory A., (BV) ....'66 '93 C.612 B.S. L.623 J.D. [Robinett&M.]
Cameron, David C., (AV) ....'55 '80 C&L.623 B.A., J.D. [Riggs.A.N.T.O.&L.]
Cameron, Dennis C., (AV) ....'62 '87 C&L.623 B.S.M.E., J.D. [Gable&G.]
Cameron, Donald D., (AV) ....'19 '50 C.612 B.S. L.623 LL.B. 5849 S. Irvington‡
Campbell, John A.L., (BV) ....'67 '97 C.612 B.S. L.862 J.D. [Richards&C.]
Campbell, Philip R., (BV) ....'35 '59 C&L.902 A.B., LL.B. 2651 E. 21st St.
Campbell, Stuart D., (AV) ....'60 '85 C.663 B.S. L.623 J.D. [Sneed L.]
Campbell, Tiffany Arend, (BV) ....'68 '96 C.840 B.S. L.861 J.D. [Sneed L.]
Campbell, Vanessa Darlene ....'67 '00 2021 S. Lewis,Ste. 640
Canada, W. Deke, (BV) ....'69 '98 C.1331 B.S. L.861 J.D. [Hall,E.H.G.G.&N.]
Cannon, John W., (AV) ....'67 '93 C.1288 B.S. L.862 J.D. [Jones,G.&B.]
Cannon, Scott D., (BV) ....'51 '84 C&L.862 B.A., J.D. [Wagner,S.&C.]
Canon, Jack A. '49 '77
C.1082 B.S. L.862 J.D. V.P. & Gen. Coun., Samson Investment Co.
Carlson, Jeffery E., (AV) ....'55 '91 C.508 B.S. L.862 J.D. 15 W. 6th Street Suite 2800
Carlson, Ronald J. ....'36 '66 C.688 B.Ch.E. L.276 J.D. Conoco Inc. (Pat.)
Carmichael, Karen L., (BV) ....'58 '85 C.612 B.A. L.862 J.D. [K.L.Carmichael]

Carmichael, Karen L., P.C., (BV)
2727 E. 21st., Suite 402, 74114
Telephone: 918-493-4939 Fax: 918-488-1573
Email: trustkaren@juno.com URL: http://www.lawyers.com/karencarmichael
Karen L. Carmichael.
Estate Planning, Living Trusts, Living Wills, Wills and Probate, Trusts and Estates, Probate, Business Counseling, Irrevocable Trusts, Asset Protection, Charitable Giving, Health Care, Power of Attorney, HIPAA.
See Professional Biographies, TULSA, OKLAHOMA

Carney, Timothy A., (AV) ....'60 '86 C.804 B.S. L.862 J.D. [Gable&G.]
Carpenter, David A., (AV) .... '54 '77 C.862 B.S. L.623 J.D. 10514 South Erie Avenue
Carpenter, Harvey C., (BV) ....'27 '51 C.862 L.623 LL.B. 7262 S. Jamestown
Carpenter, Leah P. ....'71 '04 C.623 B.S. L.862 J.D. [McKinney&S.]
Carpenter, Richard L., Jr., (BV) ...... '38 '64 C.862 B.A. L.623 LL.B. [Carpenter,M.&M.]
Carpenter, Mason and McGowan, (AV) .... Suite 205 1516 South Boston
Carr, Eddie L., (BV) ....'61 '89 C.1147 B.S. L.616 J.D. [Gibbs A.B.M.&H.]
Carr, Michael L. ....'72 '99 C&L.623 B.A., J.D. [Holden&C.]
Carr, Patrick E., (AV) ....'48 '73 C&L.623 B.A., J.D. [Carr&C.]

Carr & Carr, (AV)
4416 S. Harvard Avenue, 74135-2605
Telephone: 918-747-1000 Fax: 918-747-7284
URL: http://www.carrcarrlaw.com
Members of the Firm: Patrick E. Carr; Guy A. Thiessen; Randall Kent Gause; A. Laurie Koller; Brian R. Huddleston; Bradley W. Wallace; Robert N. Ylla, Jr.; Tye H. Smith; Jeremy D. West; Brent D. Berry; Phillip Votaw.
Brain Injury, Personal Injury, Insurance Bad Faith, Nursing Home Negligence, Products Liability, Trucking Law, Toxic Exposure, Accidents, Wrongful Death, Negligence.
See Professional Biographies, TULSA, OKLAHOMA

Carrasquillo, George, (BV) ....'30 '63 C&L.862 LL.B. 1518 South Norfolk Avenue
Carrigan, Gina J. ....'66 '94 C.623 B.A. L.378 J.D. 1408 S. Denver Ave.
Carrington, James E., (AV) '60 '85 C.612 B.S. L.862 J.D.
Dir., Bus. Dev., The Williams Companies, Inc.
Carroll, Elizabeth W. ....'80 '05 C&L.623 B.A., J.D. [Doerner,S.D.&A.]
Carroll, Robert W., (AV) ....'45 '71 C.347 B.S. L.893 LL.B. [Carroll&M.]

Carroll & Miller, (AV)
A Professional Limited Liability Company
3130 N. Wild Mountain Road, 74127
Telephone: 918-299-6914 Fax: 918-298-6915
Email: joemiller@jwmweb.com URL: http://www.carroll-miller.com
Members of Firm: Robert W. Carroll; Joseph W. Miller.
Corporate Law, Commercial Transactions, Technology Transfer, Software Licensing, Telecommunications, Business Law, Energy, Due Diligence Reviews.
See Professional Biographies, TULSA, OKLAHOMA

Carson, Beverly P. ....'29 '69 C.378 B.S. L.862 J.D. [Carson&C.]
Carson, Davis S. ....'22 '50 C&L.900 A.B., LL.B. P.O. Box 1993
Carson, Kainor ....'25 '68 C.378 A.B. L.862 J.D. [Carson&C.]
Carson, Richard M., (BV) '66 '91
C.862 B.S. L.623 J.D. Sr. Atty., The Williams Cos., Inc.
Carson, Russell D., (BV) ....'55 '85 C.375 B.S. L.1288 J.D. [R.D.Carson]
Carson, Tami L., (BV) ...'64 '89 C.612 B.S. L.623 J.D. Sr. Atty., The Williams Cos. Inc.
Carson & Carson .... 239 W. 16 Pl.

Carson, Russell D., P.C., (BV)
The Adams Building Penthouse, 403 South Cheyenne, 74103
Telephone: 918-582-5490 Fax: 918-582-5063
Russell D. Carson.
Family Law, Child Custody, High Conflict Divorce, Child Support, Adoptions, Step-Parent Adoption, Mediation.
See Professional Biographies, TULSA, OKLAHOMA

Carter, Cason P. ....'77 '03 C.228 B.A. L.276 J.D. [Gable&G.]
Carter, Craig H. ....'71 '97 C.591 B.A. L.862 J.D. [Carter]
Carter, Lewis N., (AV) ....'51 '80 C.197 B.A. L.623 J.D. [Doerner,S.D.&A.]
Carter, Michelle M. ....'73 '99 C.839 B.S. L.1243 J.D. [Riggs,A.N.T.O.&L.]
Carter, Michelle Marie ....'70 '99 C.942 B.S. L.900 J.D. Dist. Atty.
Carter, R. Michael, (AV) ....'48 '73 C.612 B.S. L.862 J.D. ORU Athletic Dept.
Carter, Shelley L. ....'78 '03 C.228 B.A. L.276 J.D. [Conner&W.]
Carter Law Office, P.C. ....2431 E. 51st St., Ste. 601
Cartledge, Jonathan D. ....'76 '01 C.1288 B.A. L.862 J.D. [Gibbs A.B.M.&H.]
Caruso, Dennis A., (AV) ....'60 '86 C.999 B.S. L.862 J.D. [Caruso]

Caruso Law Firm, P.C., (AV)
The Colonial Building, 1325 East 15th Street, Suite 201, 74120
Telephone: 918-583-5900 Fax: 918-583-5902
Email: dcaruso@carusolawfirm.com URL: http://www.carusolawfirm.com
Dennis A. Caruso.

(This Listing Continued)

Caruso Law Firm, P.C. (Continued)
Business and Commercial Trial and Appellate Practice in Federal and State Courts, including Arbitration, Contract Litigation, Energy Litigation, General Civil Litigation, Intellectual Property Litigation, Oil and Gas Litigation, Real Estate Litigation and Unfair Trade Practices Litigation; Business Organization, Planning and Review.
See Professional Biographies, TULSA, OKLAHOMA

Carwile, John J., (AV) .... '54 '84 C.871 B.S. L.309 J.D. [Atkinson,H.N.B.G.&C.]
Casey, Jama L. '52 '78 C.900 B.A. L.846 J.D.
(adm. in TX; not adm. in OK) 6309 S. 72nd East Pl.‡
Casey, Joseph H. ....'51 '98 C.1108 B.S. L.862 J.D. 403 S. Cheyenne Ave., Ste. 1100
Casey, N. Franklyn, (AV) ....'42 '66 C&L.862 B.A., J.D. [Casey&J.]
Casey, Wesley G., Attorney at Law, (AV) '58 '88
C.612 B.S. L.862 J.D. 11 W. 5th St. Ste. 500
Casey & Jones, P.C., (AV) .... 3140 South Winston Avenue, Suite 2
Cassody, James B., (BV) ....'63 '94 C.623 B.A. L.616 J.D. [McGivern,G.&C.]
Castor, William H., (AV) '43 '68 C.612 B.A. L.623 J.D.
5115 S. Norfolk Ave., Apt. 203
Catalano, Frank J. ....'42 '69 C&L.215 B.E.E., J.D. [Gable&G.] (Pat.)
Cathcart & Dooley, A Professional Corporation
(See Oklahoma City)
Catterlin, Ben Dale, (CV) ....'53 '87 C.802 B.B.A. L.862 J.D. 6216 S. Lewis
Cavert, Wm. C. ......'21 '49 C&L.378 A.B., LL.B. Pres., Triangle Blue Print & Supply Co.
Chambers, Lawrence T., Jr., (AV) .....'45 '72 C&L.623 B.B.A., J.D. [Doerner,S.D.&A.]
Champ, Harry William, (BV) ....'58 '96 C.612 B.S. L.862 J.D. [Davis,C.&Assoc.]
Champlin, Jennifer A. ....'77 '02 C.612 B.A. L.188 J.D. [Crowe&D.]
Chandler, R. Jay, (AV) ....'49 '79 C.1310 B.A. L.862 J.D. [Norman W.C.&D.]
Chapman, Marguerite A. '— '76 C&L.45 B.A., J.D.
(adm. in AR; not adm. in OK) Univ. of Tulsa Coll. of Law
Chappelle, Carlos J., (AV) ....'51 '81 C.623 B.B.A. L.862 J.D. P.O. Box 1165
Chasen, Jeffrey I. '62 '87 C&L.273 B.A., J.D.
(adm. in MO; not adm. in OK) General Counsel & Senior Vice President, AGOS Group
Chastain, Holly '— '95 C&L.16 B.S., J.D.
(adm. in AL; not adm. in OK) [McQueen,R.&T.]
Cheadle, Grant E., (AV) ....'57 '82 C.911 B.A. L.1288 J.D. [Cheadle&Assoc.]

Cheadle & Associates, (AV)
7318 South Yale Avenue Suite A, 74136-7000
Telephone: 918-585-8500 Fax: 918-592-3030
Email: gecesq@ionet.net
Grant E. Cheadle. Associate: Dana M. McDaniel.
Estate Planning, Oil and Gas Law, Creditor and Debtor Bankruptcy, Probate, Real Estate, Contracts, Corporate Law, Civil Trial Practice.
See Professional Biographies, TULSA, OKLAHOMA

Cherry, Sara A. ....'74 '01 C.340 B.A. L.862 J.D. [Balogh,C.M.&W.]
Chevaillier, William C., Jr., (AV) ....'55 '82 C&L.45 B.S.B.A., J.D. [Mysock&C.]
Chien, Julie C. ....'— '98 C.813 B.A. L.309 J.D. [McQueen,R.&T.]
Chiga, George C. ....'13 '51 C.612 B.S. L.615 B.L. 7319 E. 62nd St. S.‡
Childers, Robert J. ....'21 '56 C.619 L.862 LL.B. P.O. Box 9041033‡
Childers, Tamera A. ....'64 '03 C.612 B.S. L.862 J.D. 1800 S. Baltimore, Suite 1000
Chlouber, Steven E., (BV) ....'66 '91 C.612 B.S. L.623 J.D. [Fuller,C.&F.]
Christie, Brenda S., Attorney at Law '67 '99
C.619 B.S. L.862 J.D. 1304 S. Knoxville Ave.
Christofferson, David B. ....'48 '74 C&L.623 B.B.A., J.D. Bank of Okla., N.A.
Chronister, John ....'31 '62 C&L.862 B.A., LL.B. 3830 E. 82nd Pl.‡
Chronos, William J. ....'27 '62 C.612 B.S. L.862 LL.B. 6525 E. 24th Street
Church, Donald, (AV) ....'19 '42 C&L.862 LL.B. 3715 S. Granite‡
Cinocca, Hillary E., (BV) '72 '98
C.1365 B.A. L.862 J.D. Sr. Atty, The Williams Cos., Inc.
Cinocca, Holly Breese, (BV) ....'69 '94 C&L.862 B.A., J.D. [McCormick F.&C.]
Cinocca, James Edward, Jr., (BV) '68 '95 C.846 B.B.A. L.862 J.D.
[McCormick F.&C.]
Cinocca, Jonathan M., (BV) '72 '98
C&L.623 B.Acc., J.D. Atty., Helmerich & Payne, Inc.
Cinocca, Tracy A. ....'72 '98 C.623 B.A. L.862 J.D. [Cinocca&Assoc.]

Cinocca & Associates, P.C.
9710 E. 55th Place, 74146
Telephone: 918-488-9117 Facsimile: 918-488-9198 URL: http://www.cinoccalaw.com
Email: tcinocca@cinoccalaw.com URL: http://www.lawyers.com/cinocca
Tracy A. Cinocca.
Corporate and Business Law, Corporations and Limited Business Formations, Liability Companies, Contracts, Employment Law, Family, Divorce, Child Custody, Premises Liability, Auto Accidents, Personal Injury, and Criminal, Assault and Battery; DUI.
See Professional Biographies, TULSA, OKLAHOMA

Cipolla, Patrick W., (AV) ....'65 '92 C.612 B.S. L.623 J.D. [Gable&G.]
Cipolla, Richard J., Jr., (AV) ....'62 '89 C.862 B.S. L.378 J.D. [F.Dorwart]
Cirdekk, Barbara Ellen ....'72 '04 C.880 B.A. L.862 J.D. [Eldridge C.S.&L.]
Clancy, Herbert L. ....'28 '55 C&L.846 B.A., J.D. 110 W. 7th St.
Clancy, Timothy P., (AV) ....'58 '90 C.45 B.S., B.A. L.862 J.D. [Clancy]
Clancy Law Firm, (AV) ....5801 East 41st Street, Suite 507
Clark, Diana H. ....'50 '92 C&L.862 B.S., J.D. [Johnson,J.D.C.&S.]
Clark, Gary C., (AV) ....'47 '75 C.612 B.S. L.846 J.D. [Crowe&D.]
Clark, Joseph F., Jr., (AV) ....'49 '74 C.884 A.B. L.862 J.D. [J.F.Clark,Jr.]
Clark, Kimberly N. ....'71 '99 C.619 B.A., B.S. L.862 J.D. [Secrest,H.&B.]
Clark, Larry D., (BV) ....'56 '84 C&L.623 B.B.A., J.D. 9829 E. 85th St.
Clark, Nathan E., (BV) ....'71 '97 C&L.69 B.A., J.D. [Rhodes,H.J.T.&G.]
Clark, Stephen R., (BV) ...'47 '72 C.612 B.S. L.862 J.D. 1924 S. Utica Avenue, Suite 110
Clark, Wendell W., (AV) ....'44 '68 C&L.862 B.A., J.D. [Clark&W.]
Clark, Joseph F., Jr., P.C., (AV) ....1622 S. Denver Ave.

Clark & Williams, (AV)
Suite 600 Fox Plaza Office Center, 5416 South Yale Avenue, 74135
Telephone: 918-496-9200 Fax: 918-496-3851
Email: CLAWIL96@aol.com
Members of Firm: Wendell W. Clark; Darrell E. Williams. Associates: Mark R. Reents; Michael DeCarlo; Kathryn A. Herwig.
General Civil and Criminal Trial Practice. Corporate, Oil and Gas, Personal Injury, Workers Compensation, Domestic Relations, Probate, Commercial, Real Estate, Corporate Real Estate, Commercial and Residential Landlord and Tenant Law, Zoning, Creditor's Rights, Bankruptcy, Family Law, Divorce, Wills and Trusts, and Child Custody.
References: Bank of Oklahoma; Peoples State Bank.
See Professional Biographies, TULSA, OKLAHOMA

Clarke, Margaret M., (BV) ....'71 '96 C.623 B.A. L.616 J.D. [Rhodes,H.J.T.&G.]
Clarke, Richard P., (CV) ....'60 '85 C.942 B.B.A. L.862 J.D. [Barber&B.]
Clausing, W. Kirk, (AV) '44 '69 C&L.623 B.B.A., J.D.
2021 South Lewis Avenue, Suite 240, 74104
Telephone: 918-745-0417 Telecopier: 918-745-9909
Email: clausing@swbell.net

(This Listing Continued)

Clausing, W. Kirk (Continued)

Taxation, Estate and Gift Taxation, Wills, Probate, Trusts and Estate Planning, Corporations, Business Transactions, Private Foundations; Non Profit, Asset Protection; Business Organization and Formation.
Representative Clients: Furnished Upon Request.

See Professional Biographies, TULSA, OKLAHOMA

Clay, Michael D., (CV) .... '56 '91 C.623 B.A. L.862 J.D. 2431 E. 51st St., Ste. 502
Clayman, John D., (AV) ....'60 '86 C.846 B.B.A. L.862 J.D. [F.Dorwart]
Cleary, Paul J. ....'50 '81 C.971 B.S. L.862 J.D. U.S. Mag. J.
Clegg, Gwendolyn L. .... '72 '00 C.619 B.S. L.862 J.D. 4733 S. Evanston Avenue
Cleveland, Charles R. ....'39 '70 C.622 B.S. L.623 J.D. 8364 S. Urbana Ave.
Clouser, Stephen R., (BV) ....'55 '81 C.623 B.B.A. L.862 J.D. [Covington&P.]
Cluck, Sharail L. .... '72 '98 C.623 B.A. L.615 J.D. Legal Servs. of Eastern Oklahoma
Coates, John A., (BV) ....'59 '87 C.976 B.A. L.880 J.D. [Stauffer,G.&N.]
Coates, Stephanie R. ....'69 '96 C.69 B.A. L.796 J.D. [Richards&C.]
Coates, Stephen M., (BV) ....'67 '96 C.378 B.A. L.623 J.D. [Wilson,C.&A.]
Cochrane, Don ....'05 '30 P.O. Box 52874‡
Coffey, Robert P., Jr., (AV) ....'66 '92 C.623 B.B.A. L.862 J.D. [LaCourse,D.C.&G.]
Coffman, W. Thomas, (AV) .... '40 '66 C&L.862 B.S.B.A., J.D. [Johnson,J.D.C.&S.]
Coil, Roger M. ....'63 '96 C&L.623 B.A., J.D. [Works&L.]
Cole, David W., (BV) ....'52 '77 C.45 B.A. L.862 J.D. 624 E. Archer St.
Cole, R. Michael, (BV) ....'66 '91 C.623 B.S. L.309 J.D. [Fuller,C.&F.]
Collier, Mark L., (BV) .... '62 '88 C.612 B.S. L.602 J.D. [Richardson,S.R.&W.]
Collingsworth, William J., (AV) .... '30 '53 C.804 L.502 J.D. 3419 E. 59th St.‡
Collins, Amy Elizabeth ....'71 '98 C.628 B.S. L.862 J.D. [Kivell,R.&F.]
Collinson, Stephen A., (BV) ....'42 '71 C.612 B.A. L.623 J.D. 1639 South Cheyenne
Collver, Gary A. '42 '74 C.1051 B.S. L.184 J.D.
(adm. in CO; not adm. in OK) 3805 E. 97th St.‡
Colpitts, Greggory T. ....'65 '91 C.612 B.S. L.862 J.D. 6130 S. Maplewood, Ste. B
Comfort, Richard E., (AV) ....'37 '70 C.38 B.S.E. L.862 J.D. [R.E.Comfort]
Comfort, Richard E., A Professional Corporation, (AV) ....5517 South Peoria Avenue
Commercial Litigation Group, (BV) .... 1502 S. Boulder Ave., Suite 205
Conard, Lynn A., (AV) '58 '83
C.612 B.S. L.862 J.D. Sr. Coun., Wiltel Communications Group

Concordia Benefits Group, P.C., (AV)
320 South Boston, Suite 2000, 74103-4713
Telephone: 918-583-5700 Fax: 918-583-5341
URL: http://www.concordiabenefits.com
Debbie L. Blackwell; Eric S. Smith; C. Gordon Harris.
ERISA, Employee Benefits Law.

See Professional Biographies, TULSA, OKLAHOMA

Conley, Marc F., (AV) ....'47 '79 C.612 B.S. L.862 J.D. [Conley&M.]
Conley & Mitrani, P.C., (AV) ....100 West Fifth Street, Suite 610

Conner & Winters, LLP, (AV)
3700 First Place Tower, 15 East 5th Street, 74103-4344
Telephone: 918-586-5711 Fax: 918-586-8982
Email: postmaster@cwlaw.com URL: http://www.cwlaw.com
Henry G. Will; Joseph J. McCain, Jr.; Lynnwood R. Moore, Jr.; Robert A. Curry; Steven W. McGrath; D. Richard Funk; Randolph L. Jones, Jr.; J. Ronald Petrikin; Larry B. Lipe; James E. Green, Jr.; Martin R. Wing; John W. Ingraham; Andrew R. Turner; Gentra Abbey Sorem; R. Kevin Redwine; Tony W. Haynie; Bruce W. Freeman; David R. Cordell; John N. Hove; C. Raymond Patton, Jr.; Paul E. Braden; Robert J. Melgaard; P. Scott Hathaway; Lawrence A. Hall; Timothy T. Trump; Mark E. Dreyer; Nancy E. Vaughn; Gregory D. Renberg; Mark D. Berman; Katherine G. Coyle; Beverly K. Smith; Melodie Freeman-Burney; R. Richard Love, III; Robert D. James; Stephen R. Ward; Jeffrey R. Schoborg; Anne B. Sublett; J. Ryan Sacra; Jason S. Taylor;—Katy Day Inhofe; Julia Forrester-Sellers; Melinda L. Kirk; P. Bradley Bendure; Kathryn J. Kindell; Amy Monsour Santee; Cara M. Hair; Alissa A. Hurley; Heather Holt Bilderback; Debra Renae Stockton; Shelley L. Carter; Jed W. Isbell; Travis L. Wright; Jason B. Coutant; Allison C. McGrath Gardner; Kerrilee E. Kobbeman. Of Counsel: Bob F. McCoy; William G. Von Glahn.
General Civil Practice. Trial and Appeals of Civil Cases in all State and Federal Courts. Administrative Proceedings, Alternative Dispute Resolution, Bankruptcy and Reorganization, Construction, Corporate and Securities, Employee Benefits, Employment and Labor Relations, Energy, Environmental, Estate Planning, Trust and Probate, Federal and State Taxation, Federal White Collar Criminal Defense, Financial Services and Banking, Governmental Affairs, Insurance and Risk Management, International, Litigation and Antitrust, Products Liability, Propane, Real Estate, Tax Exempt Organizations and Charitable Foundations and Workers' Compensation.
Oklahoma City, Oklahoma Office: One Leadership Square, 211 North Robinson, Suite 1700, 73102-7101. Telephone: 405-272-5711. Facsimile: 405-232-2695.
Fayetteville, Arkansas Office: 100 West Center Street, Suite 200, 72701-6081. Telephone: 479-582-5711. Facsimile: 479-587-1426.
Santa Fe, New Mexico Office: 303 Paseo De Peralta, 87501. Telephone: 505-983-6497. Facsimile: 505-983-6478.
Jackson, Wyoming Office: 155 East Pearl Street, Suite 200, P.O. Box 4099, 83001-4099. Telephone: 307-733-2547. Fax: 307-733-3947.
Washington, DC Office: 1627 I Street, N.W., Suite 900, 20006. Telephone: 202-887-5711. Fax: 202-887-6999.
Houston, Texas Office: 1000 Louisiana, Suite 1301, 77002-5005. Telephone: 713-355-5711. Fax: 713-651-3929.

See Professional Biographies, TULSA, OKLAHOMA

Connor, James W., Jr., (AV) ....'61 '87 C&L.862 B.S.B.A., J.D. [Richards&C.]
Conway, John H., Jr., (AV) '24 '49 C.602 B.S. L.623 LL.B.
Vice Chmn., J.E. and L.E. Mabee Foundation
Conyers, Henry W., Jr. .... '16 '51 C&L.862 B.A., LL.B. 2240 S. St. Louis Ave.
Cook, Colby ....'— '00 C.999 B.A. L.623 J.D. [Riggs,A.N.T.O.&L.]
Cook, Harold Dale ....'24 '50 C&L.623 B.S., LL.B. Sr. U.S. Dist. J.

Cook, William R., II, PLLC
(See Oklahoma City)

Cooke, Michael D., (AV) .... '51 '80 C.225 B.A. L.862 J.D. [Hall,E.H.G.G.&N.]
Cooper, Catherine Gatchell ....'51 '77 C.846 B.J. L.616 J.D. 406 S. Boulder, Ste. 400
Cooper, Frank V., (AV) .... '61 '86 C.880 B.A. L.862 J.D. 2929 S. Utica Ave.
Cooper, H. Wayne, (AV) .... '45 '75 C.623 B.S.M.E. L.862 J.D. [Doerner,S.D.&A.]
Cooper, Harold H., Jr. ....'40 '67 C&L.862 B.A., J.D. 5147 South Harvard, Suite 219
Cooper, John D. ....'64 '97 C.210 B.A. L.862 J.D. 1 Williams Center
Cooper, Mary Quinn, (AV) .... '60 '86 C.45 B.A. L.862 J.D. [Eldridge C.S.&L.]
Cooper, R. Casey, (AV) .... '43 '67 C&L.862 B.S.B.A., J.D. [Cooper,M.&W.]
Cooper, Sam ....'11 '35 C&L.623 A.B., LL.B. 4821 S. Joplin St.

Cooper, McKinney & Woosley, PLLP, (AV)
401 South Boston, 74103
Telephone: 918-592-3302 Fax: 918-592-7816
URL: http://www.coopermckinney.com
R. Casey Cooper; David B. McKinney; Christopher K. Woosley;—Andrea D. Stailey. Of Counsel: T. Hillis Eskridge; C. Eric Pfanstiel; Kenneth E. Crump Jr.; Monica A. Plake.
General Civil Practice, Civil Litigation, Major Transactions, Business Organization, Employment Law, Health Care, Employee Benefits, Banking, Estate Planning, Education Law, Construction, Oil and Gas, Real Estate and Environmental Law.

See Professional Biographies, TULSA, OKLAHOMA

Copeland, C. Michael, (AV) ....'63 '88 C&L.623 B.B.A., J.D. [Jones,G.&B.]
Copeland, Gregory V. .... '66 '94 C.619 B.A. L.862 J.D. 403 S. Cheyenne, Ste. 1200
Copeland, Wayne M., (BV) .... '53 '90 C.69 B.S. L.862 J.D. [W.M.Copeland&Assoc.]
Copeland, Wayne M., & Associates, (BV) ....1602 S. Main St.
Corbitt, Sharon L., (AV) ....'46 '82 C.619 B.S. L.862 J.D. [Sneed L.]
Cordell, David R., (AV) ....'59 '85 C.902 B.A. L.623 J.D. [Conner&W.]
Core, M. Allen ....'48 '88 C&L.623 B.S., J.D. P.O. Box 35751
Corley, E. Terrill, (AV) ....'42 '72 C.1147 B.A. L.862 J.D. [Corley&G.]

Corley & Ganem, (AV)
1809 East 15th Street, 74104
Telephone: 918-745-9200 FAX: 918-747-4921
Email: cna@corleyganem.com URL: http://www.corleyganem.com
Members of Firm: E. Terrill Corley; Thomas F. Ganem. Associate: Donald B. Bolt, III.
Personal Injury, Products Liability, Medical Malpractice, Insurance, State and Federal Court Litigation, Nursing Home Negligence.

See Professional Biographies, TULSA, OKLAHOMA

Corn, Burton N. ....'15 '41 C.623 L.615 LL.B. 6229 S. Fulton‡
Cornelison, Corey ....'72 '03 C.619 B.S. L.862 J.D. [Gibbs A.B.M.&H.]
Cornell, Melissa F. ....'67 '04 C.1201 B.S. L.862 J.D. [Wagner&G.]
Cornish, Frederick Cabell, (AV) .... '45 '74 C&L.734 B.A., J.D. [Eldridge C.S.&L.]
Corns, Jasen R. ....'71 '04 C.627 B.A. L.862 J.D. [Feldman,F.W.F.&B.]
Corral, Francis S. .... '18 '46 C.477 M.A. L.221 LL.B. 4306 E. 58th Pl.‡
Cortright, Stephen P., (BV) .... '41 '73 C.612 B.S. L.862 J.D. 4724 S. Evanston Pl.
Costin, Suzanne H. '66 '94 C.623 B.A. L.862 J.D.
Corp. Sec. & Sr. Atty., Magellan Midstream Partners
Cottom, Karissa K. ....'74 '01 C.612 B.A. L.69 J.D. [Hall,E.H.G.G.&N.]
Coulson, Scott E., (BV) ....'63 '88 C.623 B.S. L.862 J.D. [Baer,T.C.&C.]
Coulter, Jean Walpole, (AV) '53 '81 C&L.862 B.S., J.D.
1638 S. Carson Ave., Ste. 1107
Coulter, Michael Ryan ....'74 '01 C&L.862 B.A., J.D. [Coulter]
Coulter Law Firm, P.C. ....1703 East Skelly Drive
Coulter Tucker, P.C. ....1638 South Carson, Suite 1107
Coury, Malleck G. ....'19 '49 C.612 L.862 LL.B. 3757 E. 47th St.‡
Coutant, Jason B. ....'80 '05 C.612 B.S. L.846 J.D. [Conner&W.]
Coutant, Kevin C., (AV) ....'52 '77 C.612 B.S. L.846 J.D. [Doerner,S.D.&A.]
Covey, Michael L., Jr. '71 '99
C.225 B.A. L.862 J.D. Asst. Gen. Coun., Vintage Petroleum

Covington & Poe, (AV)
Suite 740, 111 West Fifth Street, 74103-4267
Telephone: 918-585-5537 Fax: 918-585-5530
A. M. Covington; James E. Poe. Associate: Stephen R. Clouser.
General Civil Practice. Insurance, Negligence and Products Liability. Trials and Appeals.
Representative Client: Hartford Accident & Indemnity Co.

See Professional Biographies, TULSA, OKLAHOMA

Cowan, Robert E. ....'— '95 C.999 A.S. L.862 J.D. [Gibbs A.B.M.&H.]
Cowdery, Allen C. ....'43 '68 C&L.623 B.B.A., J.D. 6540 South Lewis
Cowdery, Jane R., (BV) ....'47 '90 C.623 B.A. L.862 J.D. [Smiling,B.&R.]
Cox, B. Kenneth, Jr., (AV) ....'56 '81 C.45 B.S. L.228 J.D. [Hall,E.H.G.G.&N.]
Cox, Charles Robert ....'49 '74 C&L.623 B.B.A., J.D. 1432 S. Carson Avenue
Cox, Gary ....'46 '74 C.619 B.A. L.862 J.D. Asst. Dir., City Health Dept.
Cox, Robert W., (BV) '45 '70
C.862 B.S. L.477 J.D. V.P. -Gen. Coun., Vintage Petroleum, Inc.
Cox, Samuel M., (BV) ....'46 '89 C.619 B.S. L.862 J.D. 7743 S. Irvington Ave.
Cox, Vicki Allane, (BV) '55 '84 C&L.862 B.A., J.D.
Mng. Atty., Dept. of Human Servs.
Coyle, Katherine G., (AV) ....'47 '72 C.320 B.A. L.862 J.D. [Conner&W.]
Cozzoni, Philip James ....'67 '96 C.587 B.A. L.862 J.D. Tulsa Police Dept.
Craft, Joseph W., III '50 '76 C&L.383 B.S., J.D.
(adm. in KY; not adm. in OK) Pres., MAPCO Coal Inc.
Craig, Curtis L., (AV) ... '55 '80 C.612 B.S. L.862 J.D. Corp. Secy., Explorer Pipeline Co.
Craige, Mark A., (AV) ....'57 '82 C.621 B.S. L.862 J.D. [Morrel,W.S.C.&H.]
Crain, Charles H., (BV) ....'51 '83 C.388 B.A. L.45 J.D. [C.H.Crain]
Crain, Charles H., P.C., (BV) ....2421 E. Skelly Drive
Craine, Robert E., Jr., (AV) '48 '75
C.378 B.S. L.802 J.D. Exec. V.P., T/SF Communications Corp.
Crane, Charles Bretton, (AV) ....'58 '84 C&L.862 B.S., J.D. [Pray,W.J.W.&M.]
Cravens, Louise Dickson ....'44 '77 C.683 A.B. L.862 J.D. 5323 S. Sandusky Ave.‡
Crawford, B. Hayden, (AV) ....'22 '49 C&L.477 A.B., J.D. 401 South Boston Avenue
Crawford, Daniel L., (BV) ....'58 '85 C.619 B.S. L.862 J.D. [Elias&C.]
Crawford, Rachel B. ....'80 '05 C&L.623 B.A., J.D. [Newton,O.T.&K.]
Creekmore, Thomas A., III, (AV) ....'57 '82 C&L.623 B.A., J.D. [Hall,E.H.G.G.&N.]
Cremin, J. Patrick, (AV) ....'44 '74 C&L.862 B.S., J.D. [Hall,E.H.G.G.&N.]
Crews, Gary W., (BV) ....'53 '90 C.10 B.A. L.862 J.D. [G.W.Crews]
Crews, Jack D., (AV) ....'46 '75 C.45 B.S. L.862 J.D. 5508 South Lewis Avenue
Crews, Gary W., PLLC, (BV) .... 7318 S. Yale Ave.
Crewson, Thomas S. ....'33 '62 C.612 B.A. L.862 J.D. Dist. J.
Crockett, Ed R., (BV) ....'42 '66 C.612 B.S. L.862 LL.B. 6380-A E. 31st Street
Crook, Matthew T. ....'74 '02 C&L.623 B.B.A., J.D. [Hall,E.H.G.G.&N.]
Crosby, Joseph H. ....'39 '63 C&L.623 B.A., LL.B. OXY USA Inc.
Crow, Timothy F. '61 '90
C.612 B.F.A. L.862 J.D. Sr. Trial Atty., Farmers Insurance Company
Crowe, Harry M., Jr., (AV) ....'19 '48 C&L.378 B.S., LL.B. 406 S. Boulder Ave.

Crowe & Dunlevy, A Professional Corporation, (AV)
500 Kennedy Building, 321 South Boston Avenue, 74103-3313
Telephone: 918-592-9800 Fax: 918-592-9801
Email: bryantd@crowedunlevy.com URL: http://www.crowedunlevy.com
James L. Kincaid; Craig W. Hoster; Gary R. McSpadden; Gary C. Clark; Gary L. Betow; Malcolm E. Rosser IV; Michael J. Gibbens; Terry M. Thomas; Madalene A. B. Witterholt; Randall J. Snapp; Victor E. Morgan; Jeffrey T. Hills;—Gerald L. Jackson; Alexander F. King; Kayci Bair Hughes; Susan E. Huntsman; Christopher J. Kirt; Christopher B. Woods; Jennifer A. Champlin; Nora R. O'Neill; Paige N. Shelton-Vanderyt; Jeran E. Steuart. Of Counsel: The Hon. (Ret.) Thomas R. Brett.
General Practice. Litigation of all types in both state and federal court. All types of alternative dispute resolution methodologies. Administrative Law, Antitrust, Appellate, Aviation, Bankruptcy and Creditors' Rights, Business Organizations, Commercial Real Estate, Commercial Transactions, Consumer Credit, Corporate and Securities Finance, Environmental, ERISA, Estates and Trusts, Family Law, Financial Institutions and Finance, Franchising and Distribution, Healthcare, Initiative Petition, Insurance Litigation and Regulation, Intellectual Property and Technology, International Business, Labor and Employment, Medicare/Medicaid Fraud and Abuse, Medical Malpractice Defense, Mergers and Acquisitions, Oil and Gas, Oklahoma Corporation Commission, Patent, Trademark, Copyright and Related Matters, Products Liability, Public Finance, School Law, Small Business and Venture Capital, Taxation, White Collar Crime.
Oklahoma City, Oklahoma Office: 20 North Broadway, Suite 1800, 73102-8273. Telephone: 405-235-7700. Fax: 405-239-6651.
Norman, Oklahoma Office: 2500 South McGee, Suite 140, 73072-6705. Telephone: 405-321-7317. Fax: 405-360-4002.

See Professional Biographies, TULSA, OKLAHOMA

Crump, Kenneth E., Jr., (AV) .... '58 '86 C.623 B.A. L.862 J.D [Cooper,M.&W.]
Crutchfield, B. Darlene ....'50 '90 C&L.862 B.A., J.D. Co. J.
Crutchmer, Clyde V., (AV) ....'53 '82 C.174 B.S. L.862 J.D. [Crutchmer,B.&B.]

Crutchmer, Browers & Barnes, P.L.L.C., (AV)
1112 S. Boston Avenue, 74119
Telephone: 918-382-8686 Fax: 918-382-8685
URL: http://www.cbb-law.com
Clyde V. Crutchmer; Ronald Merrill Barnes; Deborah B. Browers.
Securities Law, Banking, Oil and Gas Law, Real Estate, Commercial Transactions.
Representative Clients: Bank of America; Bank of Oklahoma; Braum's Ice Cream & Dairy Stores; First Fidelity Bank; M-D Building Products, Inc.; MidFirst Bank; Samson Resources Company; Unit Petroleum Corporation; Vintage Petroleum Company.
See Professional Biographies, TULSA, OKLAHOMA

Culver, Wm. Eric, (AV) ...... '51 '75 C&L.623 B.A., J.D. 20 East Fifth Street, Suite 1402
Cundiff, James N., (AV) '54 '79 C.612 B.S. L.862 J.D.
Sr. Atty., The Williams Cos., Inc.
Cupp, Heather L., (BV) .... '69 '97 C.619 B.A. L.862 J.D. [Hall,E.H.G.G.&N.]
Curry, Robert A., (AV) .... '47 '75 C.375 B.S. L.846 J.D. [Conner&W.]
Curthoys, Brian A., Law Offices of, (BV) '59 '88
C.188 B.S. L.862 J.D. 601 South Boulder Ave.
Curthoys, Karen McGivern, (BV) .... '57 '88 C.623 B.B.A. L.862 J.D. [McGivern,G.&C.]
Curtis, Nancy C. ....'53 '91 C.623 B.A. L.124 J.D. [Ⓐ Holden&C.]
Custer, Johnson W. .... '79 '05 C.802 B.A. L.880 J.D. [Ⓐ Hall,E.H.G.G.&N.]
Cyran, Matt P., (BV) .... '66 '97 C.37 B.A. L.862 J.D. [Ⓐ Rosenstein,F.&R.]
Dabner, Jack .... '26 '56 C.597 B.S. L.862 J.D. 4423 E. 13th Pl.
Daffern, Eric Mitchell, (AV) ....'62 '89 C&L.623 B.S., J.D. 1719 E. 71st St.
Dailey, Erin K. ....'78 '04 C.623 B.A. L.862 J.D. [Ⓐ Gable&G.]
Dale, Angelyn L., (AV) .... '59 '84 C.623 B.B.A. L.802 J.D. [Hall,E.H.G.G.&N.]
Dale, John D. ....'77 '03 C.425 B.A. L.862 J.D. [Ⓐ Gable&G.]
D'Alessandro, Peter A. '63 '93
C.612 B.S. L.623 J.D. Assoc. Gen. Coun., Vintage Petroleum, Inc.
Dalrymple, Dwight A., (CV) .... '57 '88 C.805 B.S. L.796 J.D. Sr. Atty., Tejas Gas Corp.
Dalrymple, Shelly, (BV) .... '58 '92 C.216 B.A. L.999 J.D. [Ⓐ Eldridge C.S.&L.]
Dalton, Andrew T., Jr., (BV) .... '37 '62 C.674 A.B. L.623 LL.B. 1437 S. Main St.
Daniel, James C. "Chris", (BV) ..... '51 '84 C.619 B.A. L.862 J.D. 5440 S. 101St E. Ave.
Daniel, Michael G. .... '62 '88 C.612 B.S. L.623 J.D. Samson Investment Co.
Daniel, Sam P., (AV) .... '32 '59 C.276 B.S. L.623 LL.B. [Doerner,S.D.&A.]
Daniel, Samuel P., III, (AV) ....'53 '80 C.276 B.A. L.623 J.D. [S.P.Daniel,III]

Daniel, Sam P., III, P.L.L.C., (AV)
1756 South Utica Avenue, 74104-5336
Telephone: 918-749-9007 Telecopier: 918-749-9023
Email: sam.daniel@samdaniellaw.com URL: http://www.samdaniellaw.com
Samuel P. Daniel III.
General Civil Litigation, Family, Construction, Oil and Gas, Real Estate, Business, Condemnation, Employment, Mechanic's Liens, Collections.
Representative Clients: Manhattan Construction Co.; Federal Bank Centre; Keith F. Walker Oil & Gas Company, LLC.; Oklahoma Department of Transportation.
See Professional Biographies, TULSA, OKLAHOMA

Danielson, Kevin, (AV) .... '49 '87 C.494 B.A. L.862 J.D. Asst. U.S. Atty.
Danz, Don W. .... '66 '92 C.339 B.A. L.862 J.D. [Ⓐ Secrest,H.&B.]
Darr, Stephanie R. ....'67 '93 C.69 B.B.A L.1339 J.D. Ronald D. Wood & Assoc.
Darrah, Mark S., (AV) ....'56 '82 C.800 A.B. L.623 J.D. 2121 South Columbia
Dart, Gary W. .... '47 '73 C&L.623 B.A., J.D. Legal Servs. of Eastern Okla., Inc
Davidson, James G., (AV) .... '21 '47 C.623 B.A. L.976 J.D. 3336 E. 32nd St.
Davidson, Miles E. '42 '74 C&L.420 J.D.
(adm. in LA; not adm. in OK) Sr. Coun., Citgo Petro. Corp.
Davies, Edward E., (BV) .... '25 '58 L.862 LL.B. 2406 E. 72nd St.
Davis, David W., (BV) ....'48 '74 C&L.378 B.S., J.D. [Davis,C.&Assoc.]
Davis, J. Christopher, (AV) ....'65 '95 C.1288 B.A. L.623 J.D. [LaCourse,D.C.&G.]
Davis, Leon P. .... '49 '89 C.619 B.A. L.623 J.D. 1503 E. 21st Street
Davis, Michael D. ....'56 '85 C.610 B.S. L.862 J.D. [Doyle H.D.&H.]
Davis, Nancy Lynn .... '67 '92 C.668 B.A. L.623 J.D. Hillcrest Health Care System
Davis, Reuben, (AV) ....'43 '73 C.934 B.A. L.623 J.D. [Boone,S.D.H.&D.]
Davis, Richard H., Jr. ....'39 '70 C&L.45 B.S.C.E., J.D. P.O. Box 702061
Davis, Steve ....'71 '98 C.893 B.A. L.569 J.D. [Ⓒ Burton&Assoc.] ⊙
Davis, Champ and Associates, Inc., (BV) ....601 S. Boulder Avenue, Suite 100
Day, Bruce W., (AV) ....'45 '72 C&L.623 B.A., J.D. [Day,E.P.&C.] ⊙
Day, Ernest B., Jr., (BV) .... '37 '62 C&L.623 B.B.A., LL.B. 1861 E. 15th St.
Day, Victor R. .... '36 '64 C.845 B.A. L.846 LL.B. 8714 S. 70th. E. Ave.

Day, Edwards, Propester & Christensen, P.C., (AV)
320 South Boston Avenue 805, 74103 ⊙
Telephone: 918-592-2121 Facsimile: 918-388-6601
URL: http://www.dayedwards.com
Bruce W. Day; Joe E. Edwards;—P. David Newsome, Jr.
General Civil Trial. Trial of Civil Cases in all State and Federal Courts. Administrative Law, Agribusiness, Anti-Trust Law, Arbitration and Mediation of disputes, Banking Regulation and Transactions, Bankruptcy and Insolvency Law, Commercial Law, Corporate Law, Employment Law, Energy Law, Environmental Law, Franchising Regulation and Transactions, Health Care Law, Insurance Law, International Law, Labor Relations, Litigation, Mergers and Acquisitions, Natural Resources, Products Liability, Professional Malpractice, Real Estate Law, Securities Regulation and Transactions and Workers Compensation.
Representative Clients: AIG Aviation, Inc.; BancFirst Corporation.
Oklahoma City, Oklahoma Office: 210 Park Avenue, 73102-5605. Telephone: 405-239-2121. Telecopier: 405-236-1012.
See Professional Biographies, TULSA, OKLAHOMA

De Angelis, Jennifer L., (BV) .... '62 '87 C.612 B.S. L.862 J.D. [Brewster&D.]
Deaton, Jo Anne, (AV) .... '55 '81 C.623 B.A. L.862 J.D. [Rhodes,H.J.T.&G.]
Deaton, Steven A., (BV) ....'58 '83 C.1311 B.S. L.862 J.D. Tulsa Jr. Coll.
DeCarlo, Michael, (BV) .... '58 '88 C&L.862 B.S., J.D. [Ⓐ Clark&W.]
Decker, John R., (AV) .... '54 '85 C.798 B.S. L.862 J.D. [Richey&D.]
Dees, Don L., (BV) .... '32 '57 C&L.862 LL.B. 1700 Southwest Blvd.
Deisenroth, Craig '52 '78 C&L.862 B.A., J.D.
(adm. in TX; not adm. in OK) Pres., Deisenroth Gas Products, Inc.
DeMier, Fred Will, (BV) ....'56 '89 C&L.862 B.S., J.D. [Barkley]
DeMoss, Renee, (AV) ....'58 '84 C.612 B.A. L.623 J.D. [Gable&G.]
DeMuro, Paul, (AV) ....'65 '93 C.647 B.A. L.560 J.D. [Ⓐ F.Dorwart]
Denney, Gregory J. ....'70 '98 C.1310 B.S. L.862 J.D. [G.J.Denney&Assoc.]
Denney, John S. "Steve", (BV) ....'49 '76 C.1320 B.A. L.862 J.D. [J.S.Denney]
Denney, Gregory J., & Associates, P.C. ....1204 South Cheyenne
Denney, John S., P.C., (BV) ....3140 S. Winston
Dennis, Trevor A. ....'76 '03 C.375 B.S. L.862 J.D. [Ⓐ Best&S.]
Denslow, Gretchen B. ....'72 '00 C.800 B.A. L.862 J.D. 1520 S. Gary Place
Des Barres, John Brian, (BV) .... '61 '87 C&L.862 B.S.B.A., J.D. [Ⓐ Wilson,C.&A.]
DeSilvey, Jared A. '70 '97
C.499 B.S. L.862 J.D. [Ⓐ Garrett] (⊙Muskogee, Oklahoma City)
Detrich, Donald, (AV) .... '51 '76 C&L.862 B.S., J.D. [Eller&D.]
de Verges, Eugene P., (BV) ....'53 '80 C.612 B.A. L.846 J.D. 6792 S. Atlanta Avenue
Dewitt, Phyllis A., (BV) .... '44 '81 C&L.862 B.S., J.D. 9726 E. 42nd St., Ste. 221
Dexter, Deirdre O., (AV) ....'56 '84 C.663 B.S. L.623 J.D. [Ⓐ F.Dorwart]
Dick, Robert N. ....'39 '73 C&L.862 B.S., J.D. Co. Comr.
Dickerson, Frank S., III '39 '67 C.31 B.A. L.477 J.D.
(adm. in NY; not adm. in OK) Sr. V.P., CFO & Treas., MAPCO Inc.
Dickman, J. Scott, (BV) .... '60 '92 C&L.862 B.A., J.D. [Titus H.R.D.&M.]
Dillsaver, Joe D. .... '45 '78 C.1321 B.A. L.623 J.D. 5010 East 75th Place
Dilschneider, Henry Adolphus .... '68 '96 C&L.862 B.A., J.D. P&H Properties, L.L.C.
Dismukes, D. E., (AV) .... '52 '86 C.810 B.A. L.862 J.D. [Ⓒ Shipley&K.]
Dittrich, Brian E., (BV) .... '67 '93 C.612 B.S.M.E. L.616 J.D. [Dittrich]
Dittrich Law Firm, P.L.L.C., (BV) .... 406 South Boulder, Suite 416
Dixon, Mark W., (AV) .... '50 '82 C.352 B.A. L.862 J.D. [Works&L.]
Dobbins, Amy Beth ....'75 '01 C.1147 B.A.Ed. L.623 J.D. [Ⓐ Steidley&N.]
Dobbs, Tanya L. ....'— '88 L.616 J.D. 406 S. Boulder
Dodd, S. Douglas, (AV) ....'49 '82 C&L.862 B.S., J.D. [Doerner,S.D.&A.]
Doenges, William S. .... '38 '66 C.612 B.S. L.862 J.D. Pres., Doenges Bros. Ford

Doerner, Saunders, Daniel & Anderson, L.L.P., (AV) [BB]
Suite 500, 320 South Boston Avenue, 74103-3725 ⊙
Telephone: 918-582-1211 Fax: 918-591-5360
URL: http://www.dsda.com
Partners: Erwin J. Doerner (1897-1980); Dickson M. Saunders (1920-2001); Sam P. Daniel; William C. Anderson; G. Michael Lewis; Lawrence T. Chambers, Jr.; Dallas E. Ferguson; Sam G. Bratton II; Gary M. McDonald; H. Wayne Cooper; Kevin C. Coutant; Richard P. Hix; William F. Riggs; Lewis N. Carter; Linda Crook Martin; James Patrick McCann; Richard H. Foster; Charles S. Plumb; Leonard I. Pataki; S. Douglas Dodd; Elise Dunitz Brennan; Jon E. Brightmire; Tom Q. Ferguson; Richard J. Eagleton; Rebecca McCarthy Fowler; Michael C. Redman; Steven K. Metcalf; Russell W. Kroll; Rachel Blue; James C. Milton. Associates: Audra K. Hamilton; William H. Spitler; Young Pei; Chad M. Hinrichs; Johnathan D. Horton; Robert Spoo; Lesley Ford Richer; David L. Iandiorio; N. Lance Bryan; Chad J. Kutmas; Heather D. Flynn; Elizabeth W. Carroll; E. McLaine DeWitt Herndon; Steven P. Tepera; Raymond H. Tipton III. Of Counsel: Michael Minnis; David McCullough.
Federal Civil Practice, State Civil Practice, Administrative Law, Appellate Practice, Antitrust, Bankruptcy, Creditors' Rights and Loan Workouts, Construction Law, Consumer Credit, Corporate, Commercial and Securities, Employment and Labor, Environmental, ERISA and Employee Benefits, Estates, Trusts and Probate, Family Law, General Litigation, Health Care, Indian Law, Intellectual Property, Patents, Trademarks, Copyrights, International Business, Mediation and Arbitration, Media and First Amendment Law, Medicare/Medicaid Fraud and Abuse, Mergers and Acquisitions Law, Oil and Gas, Oklahoma Corporation Commission, Products Liability, Public Trust and Tax Exempt Financing, Real Estate, Rural Water District Competition, Securities Litigation, Small Business and Venture Capital, Taxation, Telecommunications, Toxic Tort Litigation and Workers' Compensation.
Oklahoma City, Oklahoma Office: One Leadership Square, Suite 501. Telephone: 405-319-3500. Fax: 405-319-3509. URL: http://www.dsda.com.
See Professional Biographies, TULSA, OKLAHOMA

Dohnalek, Charles W. .... '14 '37 C&L.602 B.C.S., J.D. 4192 S. Zunis Ave.
Dohnalek, Marilyn Ann, (AV) .... '53 '78 C.612 B.S. L.862 J.D. 4192 S. Zunis Ave.
Domin, Ann C. .... '53 '87 C&L.862 B.S., J.D. Indian Nations Council of Govts.
Donnelly, John E. '44 '73 C.862 B.A. L.276 J.D.
(adm. in CT; not adm. in OK) Sr. Legal Coun., Hilti, Inc.
Donovan, Erin, (AV) ....'53 '81 C.602 A.B. L.862 J.D. [Wright&D.]
Donovan, Gerard K. ....'19 '49 C.602 A.B. L.862 J.D. 717 S. Houston Ave.
Dooley, Ann ....'51 '92 C.225 B.A. L.862 J.D. U.S. Atty's Office
Dorman, John Edward, II ....'58 '85 C.1147 B.A. L.623 J.D. City Attys Off.
Dorman, William S., (AV) ....'24 '53 C.971 B.S. L.273 J.D. [Dorman&G.] (Pat.)
Dorman & Gilbert, P.A., (AV) ....Fourth and Boulder (Pat.)
Dornblaser, Kenneth E., (AV) .... '55 '80 C.612 B.S. L.623 J.D. [Johnson,J.D.C.&S.]
Dorris, Glenna S. ....'— '91 C.619 B.S. L.862 J.D. [Ⓐ Riggs,A.N.T.O.&L.]
Dorwart, Erica Anne ....'68 '99 C.880 B.A. L.862 J.D. [Ⓐ F.Dorwart]

Dorwart, Frederic, (AV) '37 '66 C.871 B.S. L.309 LL.B. [BB]
Old City Hall, 124 East Fourth Street, 74103-5010
Telephone: 918-583-9922 Fax: 918-583-8251
Email: fdorwart@fdlaw.com URL: http://www.fdlaw.com
—J. Michael Medina; Richard J. Cipolla, Jr.; Matthew James Browne, III; Paul DeMuro; Tamara R. Wagman; John D. Clayman; Erica Anne Dorwart; Tori M. Snyder; Kenneth Benjamin Watt; Steven M. Kobos; Deirdre O. Dexter; Eric R. Schelin.
General Civil Practice including Oil and Gas, Banking and Business Planning, Securities Regulation, Technology Sales and Licensing, Mergers and Acquisitions, Corporation, White Collar Crime, Environmental, Employment Law, Health Care Law, Securities fraud, Securities Arbitration, Commercial Litigation, Business Litigation.
Representative Clients: BOK Financial Corp.; Bank of Oklahoma, N.A.; Bank of Texas, N.A.; Bank of Albuquerque, N.A.; Kaiser-Francis Oil Co.; The Williford Companies; Williford Energy Co.; Williford Building Corp.; Safety Training Systems, Inc.; Sooner Southwest Bancshares, Inc.
See Professional Biographies, TULSA, OKLAHOMA

Doss, Glennella P., (AV) ....'49 '80 C.623 B.A. L.862 J.D. [Doss]
Doss, Julie C., (BV) .... '60 '99 C.82 B.A. L.862 J.D. Asst. Dist. Atty.
Doss Law Office, (AV) .... 720 East Marshall
Doty, Sharon Womack, (BV) .... '44 '91 C&L.623 B.M., J.D. 1322 S. Houston Ave.
Doud, Catherine Marie .... '68 '96 C.375 B.A. L.862 J.D. Assoc.
Dougherty, Robert F., (BV) ....'65 '91 C&L.623 B.B.A., J.D. [Hall,E.H.G.G.&N.]
Doverspike, Terry R., (AV) .... '51 '76 C.623 B.A. L.862 J.D. [Pray,W.J.W.&M.]
Dow, Steven H. ....'63 '90 C&L.976 B.A., J.D. Dir., Project Get-Together
Dowdell, John E., (AV) .... '55 '83 C.896 B.A. L.862 J.D. [Norman W.C.&D.]
Downes, Sean P., (BV) ....'68 '97 C.612 B.A. L.862 J.D. [Shook&D.]
Downie, R. Hayden, (AV) ....'41 '66 C&L.900 B.B.A., J.D. [R.H.Downie]
Downie, R. Hayden, P.C., (AV) ....7017 E. 52nd St.
Downing, Andrew D., (AV) .... '69 '96 C.691 B.A. L.862 J.D. [Rhodes,H.J.T.&G.]
Doyle, Kevin Pierce, (AV) .... '63 '88 C.623 B.A. L.862 J.D. [Pray,W.J.W.&M.]
Doyle, Ronald E., (BV) ....'60 '98 C.140 B.A. L.862 J.D. P.O. Box 3345
Doyle, Stan P., (AV) ......'39 '64 C&L.862 LL.B. [Doyle H.D.&H.] & [Ⓒ James,P.&W.]
Doyle, William J., (AV) .... '38 '63 C.623 B.A. L.862 LL.B. [Doyle&S.]

Doyle Harris Davis & Haughey, A Professional Corporation, (AV) [BB]
1350 Boulder, Suite 700, P.O. Box 1679, 74101-1679
Telephone: 918-592-1276 Fax: 918-592-4389
Email: D&H@CommercialLaw.com URL: http://www.CommercialLaw.com
Stan P. Doyle; Steven M. Harris; Michael D. Davis; Douglas R. Haughey;—C. Matthew Bickell.
Federal Practice, Business Torts/Commercial Litigation, Anti-Trust, Securities, Environmental, Insurance Coverage Litigation, Patent and Copyright Litigation. Trial Practice.
Reference: Peoples State Bank.
See Professional Biographies, TULSA, OKLAHOMA

Doyle & Salisbury, (AV)
100 West 5th Street, Suite 550, 74103-4288
Telephone: 918-583-7766 Fax: 918-583-9251
William J. Doyle III; Harold W. Salisbury.
Real Estate, Employment Law and General Civil Litigation.
See Professional Biographies, TULSA, OKLAHOMA

Dreiling, Theresa G. .... '61 '87 C.900 B.B.A. L.862 J.D. Ct. of Civil App.
Drewyor, Jill Grimsley ....'76 '01 C.840 B.S. L.861 J.D. [Pray,W.J.W.&M.]
Drewyor, Pine G. ....'74 '01 C&L.45 B.S., J.D. [Ⓐ Latham,S.W.S.&L.]
Dreyer, Mark E., (AV) .... '63 '88 C.910 B.A. L.862 J.D. [Conner&W.]
Driskill, Timothy W., (BV) ....'45 '79 C.612 B.S. L.862 J.D. 5611 E. 113th St.
Drummond, Bryan K., (BV) .... '67 '95 C.612 B.S. L.623 J.D. [Rosenstein,F.&R.]
Drummond, Cecil G., (BV) ....'40 '67 C.612 B.S. L.623 J.D. [Boettcher&D.]

Drummond, Douglas Earl .... '59 '92 C.612 B.S. L.862 J.D. Dist. Atty.'s Off.
Drummond, Gentner F., (AV) .... '63 '95 C.612 B.S. L.276 J.D. [Drummond]
Drummond, Thomas E., (BV) .... '45 '71 C.623 B.B.A. L.862 J.D. [Drummond]

Drummond Law Firm, The, (AV)
1500 South Utica, Suite 400, 74104
Telephone: 918-749-7378 Fax: 918-749-7869
Email: gfd@drumlaw.com URL: http://www.drumlaww.com
Thomas E. Drummond; Gentner F. Drummond. Associates: Max C. Myers, Jr.; Will K. Wright, Jr.; Loretta (Lori) K. Roberts; Rebecca R. Hert. Of Counsel: Randall S. Pickard (P.C.); Alan J. Oxford, II; Max K. Naegler; J. Peter Messler.
General Civil Practice in State and Federal Courts. Corporate, Banking, Insurance Defense, Bankruptcy, Estate Planning, Probate, Oil & Gas, Real Estate, Employment, Environmental, Indian and Criminal Law.

See Professional Biographies, TULSA, OKLAHOMA

Dryer, David Mitchell .... '63 '93 C.1314 L.045 J.D. [Dryer&Assoc.]
Dryer & Associates, P.C. .... 5110 S. Yale Ave., Ste. 430
Duensing, Emily Y. .... '53 '84 C&L.862 B.A., J.D. Jud. Asst., OK Ct. of Civil App.
Dukelow, Cornelius P. .... '74 '01 C.375 B.S. L.862 J.D. [🄰 James,P.&W.]
Dumont, Janet S., (AV) .... '50 '87 C.623 B.F.A. L.862 J.D. [Riggs,A.N.T.O.&L.]
Duncan, Randall T., (AV) .... '63 '90 C.619 B.S. L.862 J.D. [🄰 Harris,M.P.T.&S.]

Dunham, James W., Jr., (AV) '52 '78 C&L.862 B.S., J.D.
2112 Bank of America Center, 15 West 6th Street, 74119
Telephone: 918-592-1144 Fax: 918-592-1149
Email: elawyer@swbell.net URL: http://www.nursingneglect.com
Commercial Litigation, Personal Injury, Nursing Home Abuse and Neglect.

See Professional Biographies, TULSA, OKLAHOMA

Dunkelberg, Ryk A., (BV) '47 '80
C.612 B.S. L.862 J.D. Gen. Coun., Barnard Dunkelberg & Co.
Dunn, F. L., III, (AV) .... '41 '66 C.910 B.A. L.623 J.D. P.O. Box 1424
Dupler, Bryan L. .... '66 '92 C.1300 B.A. L.623 J.D. P.O. Box 701196
Eagleton, E. John, (AV) .... '32 '56 C&L.623 B.B.A., LL.B. [Eagleton,E.&H.]
Eagleton, James R., (AV) .... '24 '51 C&L.623 A.B., J.D. [Eagleton,E.&H.]
Eagleton, John M., (BV) '59 '86 C.934 B.A. L.1288 J.D.
1718A South Cheyenne Avenue
Eagleton, Norma, (AV) .... '34 '88 C.623 B.A. L.615 J.D. [🄲 Eagleton,E.&H.]
Eagleton, Richard J., (BV) .... '62 '88 C&L.880 B.A., J.D. [Doerner,S.D.&A.]
Eagleton, T. Paul, (BV) '63 '89 C.623 B.A. L.846 J.D.
4200 East Shelly Drive, Suite 1000
Eagleton, William L., IV, (AV) .... '55 '81 C.623 B.A. L.862 J.D. [Pray,W.J.W.&M.]

Eagleton, Eagleton & Harrison, Inc., (AV) BR
Suite 1700, 320 South Boston Avenue, 74103-4706
Telephone: 918-584-0462 Fax: 918-584-3724
Email: eaglelaw@swbell.net URL: http://www.eehlaw.com
E. John Eagleton; James R. Eagleton; Charles D. Harrison;—L. Michele Nelson. Of Counsel: Norma Eagleton.
Administrative and Judicial Resolution of Tax Controversy, Civil and Criminal, State and Federal; Estate Planning and Probate, Business Transactions, Employee Benefits, Family Law.

See Professional Biographies, TULSA, OKLAHOMA

Eakens, Laura L. .... '79 '04 [🄰 Gibbs A.B.M.&H.]
Earl, Leslie R., Jr., (BV) .... '37 '66 C&L.862 B.S., J.D. 3223 E. 31st St.
Eaton, Gary A., (AV) .... '49 '75 C&L.862 B.S.P.E., J.D. [Sparks&E.]
Ebersole, Jenny R., (BV) .... '73 '99 C.648 B.A. L.862 J.D. [🄰 Secrest,H.&B.]
Echols, John D., (AV) .... '49 '78 C.976 B.A. L.862 J.D. P.O. Box 701196
Eck, Lonnie D., (AV) .... '51 '77 C&L.862 B.S.B.A., J.D. P.O. Box 2038
Economou, Chris, Law Offices of, (BV) '56 '82 C&L.862 B.S., J.D.
6315 S. Memorial Dr.
Ede, Daniel R. .... '55 '88 C.1288 B.A. L.362 J.D. Coun., TruVision, INc.
Eden, Van N., (BV) .... '45 '71 C.934 B.A. L.862 J.D. 1717 S. Cheyenne
Edgar, James L., (BV) .... '35 '63 C.612 B.S. L.862 LL.B. 4867 S. Sheridan, Ste. 701
Edgar, Steven E., (AV) .... '51 '77 C.1125 B.S. L.45 J.D. [Edgar&P.]

Edgar & Perigo, P.C., (AV)
2615 East Fifteenth Street, 74104-4711
Telephone: 918-748-9444 Fax: 918-748-9464
Email: eph.law@cox.net URL: http://www.lawyers.com/ephlaw
Steven E. Edgar; Jerry E. Perigo.
Family, Child Custody, Divorce, Adoptions, General Business, Guardianships, Real Estate, Probate, Estate Planning, Wills and Trusts, Civil Law, Juvenile Law.
References: Bank IV Oklahoma, N.A.; Guaranty Abstract Co., Tulsa, Oklahoma

See Professional Biographies, TULSA, OKLAHOMA

Edge, D. Bruce .... '— '03 C.814 B.B.A. L.862 J.D. [Edge]
Edge Law Firm .... 717 S. Houston, Ste. 500
Edmiston, Mark A., (BV) .... '55 '82 C.612 B.S. L.862 J.D. 4614 E. 105th Place
Edmiston, Robert R., (AV) .... '45 '72 C.619 B.A. L.862 J.D. City Atty. Off.
Edmonds, James N., (BV) .... '61 '93 C&L.378 B.A., J.D. [Atkinson,H.N.B.G.&C.]
Edmonds, Mary Frances, (BV) '65 '93
C&L.378 B.A., J.D. Sr. Atty., The Williams Cos., Inc.
Edmonson, Richard L. '51 '77 C.612 B.A. L.846 J.D.
Sr. V.P., Gen. Coun. & Corp. Secy., Syntroleum Corp.
Edwards, Ellen Caslavka, (BV) .... '59 '85 C.170 B.A. L.623 J.D. 440 S. Houston
Edwards, Ira L., Jr., (AV) .... '49 '76 C.1147 B.S. L.623 J.D. [Riggs,A.N.T.O.&L.]
Edwards, Joe E., (AV) .... '49 '74 C.623 B.B.A. L.616 J.D. [Day,E.P.&C.] ⊙
Edwards, Rodney A., (AV) .... '51 '76 C.623 B.A. L.862 J.D. [Edwards&M.]
Edwards, Timothy C. .... '77 '02 C&L.623 B.A., J.D. [🄰 Perrine,M.R.R.B.&T.]

Edwards & Mailath, L.L.P., (AV)
6226 East 101st Street, Suite 100, 74137
Telephone: 918-299-9360 Facsimile: 918-299-9369
URL: http://www.lawyers.com/edwards&huffman
Members of Firm: Rodney A. Edwards; Melissa D. Mailath.
Commercial Transactions, Commercial Litigation, Real Estate, Title Insurance, Banking, Bankruptcy Reorganizations and Creditor's Rights, Loan Documentation and Lending Transactions, Administrative, Public Utility, General Corporate Law and Estate Planning.

See Professional Biographies, TULSA, OKLAHOMA

Ehlen, Susan Kathleen .... '50 '83 C.623 B.S. L.862 J.D. 7906E.33rdst.stE100
Elder, James R., (AV) .... '46 '72 C.619 B.A. L.862 J.D. [Fry&E.]
Eldredge, Roger K., (BV) .... '62 '92 C.612 B.S. L.862 J.D. [Norman W.C.&D.]
Eldridge, Richard M., (AV) .... '51 '76 C.612 B.A. L.862 J.D. [Eldridge C.S.&L.]

Eldridge Cooper Steichen & Leach P.L.L.C., (AV) BR
110 West Seventh Street, Suite 200, 74119
Mailing Address: P.O. Box 3566, Tulsa, OK 74101-3566
Telephone: 918-388-5555 Fax: 918-388-5654 URL: http://www.ecsloklaw.com
Email: general_delivery@ecslok.com URL: http://www.ecslok.com
Richard M. Eldridge; Mary Quinn Cooper; Thomas E. Steichen; William S. Leach (Board Certified, Civil Trial Law and Personal Injury Trial Law, Texas Board of Legal Specialization); Harold C. Zuckerman; Andrew L. Richardson; Kathy R. Neal; Michael F. Smith; Frederick Cabell Cornish. Associates: Lynda Dianne Riker; Vani Singhal; Dwain S. Shaw; Jennifer D. Lee; Shelly Dalrymple; Selim K. Flagome; Barbara Ellen Cirdekk. Of Counsel: Brita Haugland-Cantrell.

(This Listing Continued)

Eldridge Cooper Steichen & Leach P.L.L.C. (Continued)
Appellate Practice, Business Law, Civil Trial Practice, Class Actions, Commercial Litigation, Construction Law, Environmental Law, Insurance Law, Labor and Employment Law, Personal Injury, Product Liability Law.

See Professional Biographies, TULSA, OKLAHOMA

Elias, Cynthia K., (AV) .... '63 '89 C.172 B.S. L.862 J.D. [Elias&C.]
Elias, Herbert E. .... '36 '63 C.623 L.862 LL.B. 7906E.33rdst.stE100
Elias, Herbert E., Jr., (BV) .... '64 '89 C&L.862 B.A., J.D. [Elias&C.]
Elias & Crawford, (AV) .... 1519 S. Utica Ave.
Eliot, Judith Seymour, (AV) '54 '79
C.682 A.B. L.616 J.D. Gen. Coun., T.D. Williamson, Inc.
Eliot, Theodore Q., (AV) .... '54 '79 C.221 B.A. L.623 J.D. [Gable&G.]
Eller, Philip J., (AV) .... '50 '76 C&L.862 B.S.B.A., J.D. [Eller&D.]

Eller and Detrich, A Professional Corporation, (AV) BR
Midway Building, 2727 E. 21st Street, Suite 200, 74114-3533
Telephone: 918-747-8900 Toll Free: 866-547-8900 Fax: 918-747-2665
URL: http://www.ellerdetrich.com
Philip J. Eller; Donald Detrich; Kevin H. Wylie; R. Louis Reynolds; James C. Hodges; Shanann Pinkham Passley; Paul A. Kane. Associate: Rebecca W. Hunter. Of Counsel: John H. Lieber; Philip R. Feist (Certified Specialist, Estate Planning, Trust and Probate Law, The State Bar of California Board of Legal Specialization); Jerry M. Snider.
General Civil Practice, Mergers and Acquisitions, Commercial Transactions, Real Property, Construction, Financial Services and Banking, Corporation, Employment, Oil and Gas, Estate Planning and Probate, Bankruptcy and Creditor's Rights, Commercial, Tort, Insurance and Zoning Law, Trials and Appeals in State and Federal Courts.
Representative Clients: U.S. Home Corp.; Statewide General Agency, Inc.; Patterson Realtors.

See Professional Biographies, TULSA, OKLAHOMA

Elliott, Douglass R. '62 '93
C.623 B.B.A. L.862 J.D. [🄰 Garrett] (⊙Muskogee, Oklahoma City)
Ellis, Gerald B. .... '32 '68 C&L.862 B.S.B.M., J.D. Intl. Union of Operating Engrs.
Ellison, James O. .... '29 '51 C&L.623 B.A., LL.B. Sr. U.S. Dist. J.
Embrey, Douglas R. .... '43 '93 C.612 B.A. L.862 J.D. 2316-D S. Garnett
England, Donald W. .... '48 '83 C.621 B.A. L.623 J.D. Mgr., ONEOK, Inc.
English, Jack B. .... '19 '59 C.839 B.S. L.862 LL.B. 6730 E. 24th St.
Enlow, J. Andrew, (BV) .... '47 '96 C.508 B.S.B.A. L.862 J.D. 1508 S. Carson Ave.
Epp, Kandi D. .... '76 '03 C.619 B.B.A. L.862 J.D. [🄰 Latham,S.W.S.&L.]
Epperson, J. Barry, (AV) .... '38 '68 C.902 B.A. L.862 J.D. [Epperson&J.]
Epperson & Johnsen, (AV) .... 201 West Fifth, Suite 501
Epstein, Helen T. .... '35 '85 C&L.862 B.S., J.D. Law Clk., Ct. of App.
Erickson, Robert S., (AV) '60 '86
C.1193 B.A. L.623 J.D. Dollar Thrifty Automotive Group, Inc.
Ernst, Dan W., (AV) .... '55 '80 C.473 B.S. L.862 J.D. [Best&S.]
Erwin, James E., (BV) .... '61 '97 C.1147 B.A. L.862 J.D. [🄰 Strecker&Assoc.]
Eschenheimer, Whitney M. .... '70 '96 C.378 B.A. L.623 J.D. [Steidley&N.] ⊙
Eskridge, T. Hillis, (AV) .... '20 '48 C&L.623 B.S., LL.B. [🄲 Cooper,M.&W.]
Esmond, Michael E. .... '72 '05 C.623 B.B.A. L.862 J.D. [🄰 Moyers,M.S.I.&T.]
Estill, John S., Jr., (AV) .... '19 '48 C.840 B.S. L.802 J.D. [🄲 Hall,E.H.G.G.&N.] ‡
Evans, Gomer A., Jr., (BV) .... '44 '69 C.623 B.B.S. L.862 J.D. 2840 E. 51st Street
Evans, John Robert, Jr., Law Office '68 '94
C.612 B.S. L.623 J.D. 2727 E. 21st. St. Ste. 204.
Evans, Julie A., (AV) .... '— '89 C.612 B.S. L.862 J.D. [J.A.Evans]
Evans, Larry E., (AV) .... '48 '75 C.339 B.A. L.862 J.D. [🄲 Moyers,M.S.I.&T.]
Evans, Owen T., (AV) .... '57 '85 C.823 B.S. L.862 J.D. [McGivern,G.&C.]
Evans, Valerie Williams, (BV) .... '64 '93 C&L.623 B.S., J.D. Off. of City Atty.
Evans, Wm. O. .... '21 '56 C&L.862 B.A., LL.B. 406 S. Boulder Ave.‡

Evans, Julie A., P.C., (AV)
624 South Denver, Suite 202, 74119
Telephone: 918-592-5566 Fax: 918-582-5022
Email: Julie@EvansEstateLaw.com URL: http://www.lawyers.com/julieaevans
Julie A. Evans.
Practice includes Wills and Probate, Trust and Estates, Guardianship, Estate Litigation and Estate Planning.

See Professional Biographies, TULSA, OKLAHOMA

Fallin, Joseph C. '46 '73 C.612 B.A. L.623 J.D.
Staff Atty., Oklahoma Disability Law Center, Inc.
Fallis, S. M., Jr., (AV) .... '34 '60 C&L.862 B.A., LL.B. [Nichols,W.S.N.F.&R.]
Farish, Leah Waldorf .... '53 '84 C.228 B.A. L.69 J.D. 2834 E. 26th Place
Farmer, M. Lynn, (BV) .... '48 '87 C.134 B.S. L.862 J.D. 1611 S. Utica Ave., Ste. 336
Farrar, Greg A., (AV) .... '57 '82 C.623 B.B.S. L.862 J.D. [Farrar&F.]
Farrar, Gus A., (AV) .... '52 '77 C&L.623 B.A., J.D. [Farrar&F.]
Farrar & Farrar, (AV) .... 717 S. Houston
Farrell, John L., Jr. '29 '56 C.749 B.A. L.724 LL.B.
(adm. in NY; not adm. in OK) The Morgan Investment Grp.
Farrior, William E., (AV) .... '50 '76 C.880 B.A. L.16 J.D. [Barrow&G.]
Farris, Joseph R., (AV) .... '47 '76 C.502 A.B. L.862 J.D. [Feldman,F.W.F.&B.]
Farris, Robert S., (AV) .... '50 '76 C&L.862 B.S.M.E., J.D. [Rogers&B.]
Fatigante, James, (BV) '69 '96
C.1287 B.A. L.862 J.D. 4815 S. Harvard Avenue, Suite 426

Faulkner, Benjamin C., (AV) '46 '76 C&L.623 B.A., J.D. BR
1111 Park Centre Building, 525 South Main Street, 74103
Telephone: 918-582-8801 FAX: 918-582-8803
Email: benfaulkner@lawyers.com URL: http://www.bcfaulkner.com
General Civil Practice, Business Litigation, Civil Litigation, Probate Litigation, Contested Trusts and Estates, Trust Litigation, Family Law, Divorce, Child Custody, Adoption Law, Private Adoptions, Indian Child Welfare Act.

See Professional Biographies, TULSA, OKLAHOMA

Fay, Thomas R. .... '41 '66 C.362 B.A. L.260 J.D. P.O. Box 54054
Feamster, James W., III, (BV) .... '45 '74 C.612 B.S. L.862 J.D. 2130 E. 15th Street
Fears, Joe M., (BV) .... '55 '80 C.619 B.S.B.A. L.1066 J.D. [Barber&B.]
Feist, Philip R., (AV) .... '50 '92 C.112 A.B. L.1049 J.D. [🄲 Eller&D.]
Feldman, Nancy G. .... '22 '45 C&L.145 A.B., J.D. 2120 E. 46th St.‡
Feldman, Raymond G., (AV) ..... '22 '46 C.623 B.S. L.145 J.D. [🄲 Feldman,F.W.F.&B.]
Feldman, Stephen M. '55 '82 C.299 B.A. L.629 J.D.
(adm. in CA; not adm. in OK) Univ. of Tulsa Coll. of Law

Feldman, Franden, Woodard, Farris & Boudreaux, (AV) BR
1000 Park Centre, 525 South Main, 74103-4514
Telephone: 918-583-7129 Telecopier: 918-584-3814
Email: feldman@tulsalawyer.com URL: http://www.tulsalawyer.com
Members of Firm: W. E. Green (1889-1977); William S. Hall (1930-1991); Robert A. Franden; John R. Woodard, III; Joseph R. Farris; Paul T. Boudreaux; Paula J. Quillin. Associates: Thayla Painter Bohn; Paul F. Prather; F. Jason Goodnight; Curtis J. Roberts; Victor R. Wandres; Jasen R. Corns. Of Counsel: Raymond G. Feldman.
General Civil Practice. Trials. Corporation, Insurance, Negligence, Products Liability, Toxic Torts, Environmental Law, Securities, Oil and Gas, Real Estate, Probate, Fidelity and Surety, Aviation, School Law, Professional Liability. Estate Planning, Business, Bankruptcy and Medical Malpractice Law, Securities Fraud, Employment Law, White Collar Criminal Defense.

(This Listing Continued)

Feldman, Franden, Woodard, Farris & Boudreaux (Continued)

Representative Clients: The Equitable Life Assurance Society of the United States; Browning-Ferris Industries, Inc.; Oklahoma Bar Professional Liability Insurance Co.; Aviation Underwriters Inc.; Progressive Casualty Insurance Co.; ACE/USA; AIG; Schneider National Transportation; Arrow Truck Lines; Metris Companies, Inc.

See Professional Biographies, TULSA, OKLAHOMA

Fell, Melissa Beth ....'64 '97 C&L.862 B.A., J.D. 6575 Eagles Nest
Fell, Riley B. ....'21 '47 C.418 B.S. L.861 LL.B. 4231 S. Sandusky Ave.‡

Fellers, Snider, Blankenship, Bailey & Tippens, A Professional Corporation, (AV)
The Kennedy Building, 321 South Boston, Suite 800, 74103-3318 ⊙
Telephone: 918-599-0621 Fax: 918-583-9659
Email: fsbb&t@icnet.net URL: http://www.fellerssnider.com
Roy C. Breedlove; Todd A. Nelson; Dennis D. Brown; R. Alan Weeks; R. Daniel Scroggins; Terry L. Watt; Scott R. Zingerman; Curtis M. Long; Steven J. Adams; John D. Russell; James F. Lea; Tracy A. Poole; Charles R. Willing;—Travis A. Fulkerson; Robert Todd Waddell; Deborah V. Melikian. Of Counsel: Jack E. Phillips; Lon Foster, III; Fred H. Holmes.
General Practice. Trial of all Cases in State and Federal Courts. Commercial, Corporate, Oil and Gas, Banking and Banking Regulation, Administrative, Probate, Estate Planning, Transportation, Bankruptcy, Securities, Insurance, Federal and State Taxation, Unfair Competition, Aircraft Title, Aircraft Finance and Leasing, Aircraft Sales, Real Property, Employment, Workers' Compensation, Intellectual Property, and Antitrust Law.
Representative Clients: Adams Investment Company, Inc.; Bank of America, N.A.; Bayliner Marine Corporation; BellSouth Communication Systems, Inc.; BP America, Inc.; Brunswick Corporation; CenterPoint Energy Arkla, a division of CenterPoint Resources Group; Chevron U.S.A., Inc.; Cingular Wireless, LLC.
Oklahoma City, Oklahoma Office: Bank One Tower, 100 North Broadway, Suite, 1700. Telephone: 405-232-0621. Fax: 405-232-9659.

See Professional Biographies, TULSA, OKLAHOMA

Fenton, Fenton, Smith, Reneau & Moon
(See Oklahoma City)

Ferguson, Dallas E., (AV) ....'45 '71 C.187 B.A. L.178 J.D. [Doerner,S.D.&A.]
Ferguson, Tom Q., (AV) ....'62 '87 C.619 B.A. L.623 J.D. [Doerner,S.D.&A.]
Ferris, James H., (AV) ....'49 '75 C.623 B.A. L.862 J.D. [Moyers,M.S.I.&T.] ⊙
Fiasco, William A., (BV) ....'61 '88 C&L.623 B.A., J.D. [Atkinson,H.N.B.G.&C.]
Field, Stewart E., (AV) ....'56 '82 C&L.862 B.S., J.D. [McCormick F.&C.]
Fields, Jeffrey G. ....'71 '00 C.235 B.A. L.862 J.D. [A Gibbs A.B.M.&H.]
Filer, Jere R. '35 '61 C&L.326 B.S.
(adm. in TX; not adm. in OK) 5523 E. 51st‡
Filosa, Jim ....'49 '79 C.804 B.S. L.862 J.D. Wkrs. Comp. Ct. J.
Fincher, Joseph D., (BV) ....'59 '84 C.602 B.A. L.228 J.D. [Hall,E.H.G.G.&N.]
Finkelman, Byrgen P. ....'58 '86 C&L.846 B.A., J.D. 1621 E. 36th Ct.
Finlayson, Mac D., (AV) ....'51 '76 C.225 B.A. L.862 J.D. [C Morrel,W.S.C.&H.]
Finn, Judith A., (BV) ....'40 '81 C.966 B.A. L.862 J.D. [Pinkerton&F.]
Fischer, Jeffrey D., (BV) ....'50 '75 C.105 B.S. L.862 J.D. 403 S. Cheyenne Ave.
Fisher, Curtis W., Law Office of, (AV) .... '49 '81 C.663 B.S. L.862 J.D. 1861 E. 15th St.
Fisher, David C. ....'68 '02 C.612 L.862 J.D. [A Bonham&H.]
Fisher, Kristin Blue, (AV) ....'69 '94 C&L.862 B.A., J.D. [Fisher&F.]
Fisher, Timothy A., (BV) ....'— '94 C&L.862 B.A., J.D. [Fisher&F.]

Fisher & Fisher, (AV)
8177 South Harvard Avenue, #333, 74137
Telephone: 918-296-9898 Fax: 918-296-9880
Email: tfisheresq@sbcglobal.net URL: http://www.tulsaattorneyslaw.com
Partners of Firm: Timothy A. Fisher; Kristin Blue Fisher.
Commercial Law, Commercial Collections, Litigation, Criminal Defense, General Practice, Workers Compensation, Products Liability, Insurance Law, Professional Liability Law, Appellate Practice, Medical Malpractice.

See Professional Biographies, TULSA, OKLAHOMA

Fist, David L., (AV) ....'31 '55 C&L.623 B.A., LL.B. [Rosenstein,F.&R.] ⊙
Fitzgerald, Craig A., (AV) ....'67 '92 C.1315 B.S. L.880 J.D. [Bryant P.]
Fitzgerald, Mary F., (BV) ....'51 '90 C.612 B.S. Ed. L.862 J.D. 2729 E. 22nd St.
Fitz-Patrick, Robert P., (BV) ....'57 '91 C.94 B.S. L.862 J.D. [Hall,E.H.G.G.&N.]
Flagome, Selim K. ....'79 '04 C&L.862 B.A, J.D. [A Eldridge C.S.&L.]
Flasch, Donald A. ....'35 '67 C.612 B.S. L.862 J.D. 6520 S. Lewis Ave.
Flippo, John W., (BV) ....'48 '78 C.613 B.M. L.862 J.D. [Frasier,F.&H.]
Floren, Charles M. .... '46 '74 C.623 B.A. L.1065 J.D. Sr. Corp. Coun., Citgo Petro. Corp.
Flores, Joseph A. ....'60 '03 C.846 B.S. L.862 J.D. [A Francy]
Flowers, Steven P., (BV) ....'50 '75 C&L.862 B.S., J.D. [Flowers&Assoc.]

Flowers & Associates, P.C., Law Offices of, (BV)
810 South Cincinnati, Suite 400, 74105
Telephone: 918-742-4000 Fax: 918-749-0164
Email: Info@flowersandfisher.com URL: http://www.lawyers.com/flowerslaw
Steven P. Flowers.
General Civil Practice. Civil Trial Practice in all State and Federal Courts. Collections, Commercial Law, Corporation, Probate, Guardianship Litigation, Taxation and Estate Planning, Wills and Trusts, Commercial Litigation.

See Professional Biographies, TULSA, OKLAHOMA

Flynn, Heather D. ....'75 '02 C&L.862 B.S., J.D. [A Doerner,S.D.&A.]
Flynn, Robert A., (BV) ....'50 '83 C.862 B.A. L.1288 J.D. [Flynn]
Flynn Law Firm, (BV) .... 610 South Main, Suite 200
Fogleman, Amelia A., (BV) ....'69 '94 C.612 B.A. L.893 J.D. [Gable&G.]
Folks, John M., (BV) ....'71 '97 C.225 B.A. L.623 J.D. [A Holloway&M.]
Follansbee, Muriel H. ....'13 '41 L.669 LL.B. 6536 S. Louisville Ave.‡
Folluo, Dan S., (AV) ....'60 '85 C.804 B.S. L.862 J.D. [Rhodes,H.J.T.&G.]
Folluo, Rick A., (AV) ....'54 '79 C.587 B.S. L.862 J.D. 1408 S. Denver Ave.
Fontanez, Noah J. ....'74 '02 C.143 B.S. L.862 J.D. 1831 E. 71st Street
Forrester-Sellers, Julia ....'75 '00 C.623 B.A. L.862 J.D. [A Conner&W.]
Forsman, Michael S., (AV) ....'45 '71 C&L.623 B.B.A., J.D. [C Boesche M.]
Fortney, Guy A., (BV) ....'64 '96 C&L.862 B.S., J.D. [Brewster&D.]
Foster, Lon, III, (AV) ....'42 '68 C.623 B.A. L.477 J.D. [C Fellers,S.B.B.&T.]
Foster, Richard H., (AV) ....'57 '82 C.378 B.S. L.228 J.D. [Doerner,S.D.&A.]
Foster, Rita A., (BV) ....'43 '80 C.45 B.S.B.A. L.862 J.D. 1500 S. Frisco Ave.
Fowler, Rebecca McCarthy, (AV) .....'47 '89 C&L.326 B.B.A., J.D. [Doerner,S.D.&A.]
Fox, D. Sentell ....'38 '71 C.612 B.S. L.862 J.D. 3530 S. Florence Ave.
Frame, Lynn Edward, (BV) ..... '50 '87 C.623 B.S. L.862 J.D. 1919 S. Wheeling, Ste. 402
Francis, Joe, (AV) ....'21 '48 C.623 A.B. L.276 J.D. [Francis&F.]
Francis, Joe B., (AV) ....'56 '82 C.612 B.S. L.862 J.D. [Kivell,R.&F.]
Francis, Keith S. '62 '88 C.1315 B.A. L.862 J.D.
Asst. Dist. Coun., U.S. Army Corps. of Engrs.
Francis, Martha M. ....'51 '81 C.679 B.S. L.862 J.D. [Francis&F.]
Francis, Randy, (BV) ....'55 '83 C.767 B.A. L.862 J.D. [Francis&F.]
Francis & Francis, (AV) .... 4733 S. Harvard Avenue
Francy, David G. ....'75 '04 C.619 B.A. L.862 J.D. [A Francy]
Francy, J. Kenton, (AV) ....'50 '76 C&L.862 B.S., J.D. [Francy] ⊙

Francy Law Firm, (AV)
1861 East 15th Street, 74104-4610 ⊙
Mailing Address: P.O. Box 2048, Broken Arrow, OK 74013
Telephone: 918-747-1295 Fax: 918-744-6300
Email: jkenton.francy@francylaw.com URL: http://www.francylaw.com
J. Kenton Francy. Associates: Michael F. McCann; Joseph A. Flores; David G. Francy. Of Counsel: Lucy S. Kroblin.
Collaborative Law, Family Law, Divorce, Child Support Collection, Visitation Rights, Protective Orders, Premarital Agreements, Grandparents Rights, Guardianship, Post Decree Modifications, Violations of Protection Orders, Criminal Law, Driving Under the Influence, Drug Crimes, Estate Planning, Trusts and Estates, Wills and Probate, Living Wills, Advanced Directives, Mediation, Arbitration.
Broken Arrow, Oklahoma Office: 110 South Main Street, 74012. Telephone: 918-251-7373. Fax: 918-258-4606.

See Professional Biographies, TULSA, OKLAHOMA

Franden, Robert A., (AV) ....'39 '64 C&L.623 B.A., LL.B. [Feldman,F.W.F.&B.]
Franks, Jerry L., Jr., (BV) ....'64 '90 C.45 B.S.B.A. L.862 J.D. [Frasier,F.&H.]
Fransein, Doris L. ....'54 '81 C.225 B.A. L.862 J.D. Dist. J.
Fransein, Jim, (AV) ....'38 '67 C&L.862 B.A., J.D. 201 W. 5th St., Ste. 555
Frasier, Frank W, III, (BV) ....'66 '98 C.273 B.A. L.1364 J.D. [Frasier,F.&H.]
Frasier, James E., (AV) ....'40 '65 C&L.862 B.A., J.D. [Frasier,F.&H.]

Frasier, Frasier & Hickman, LLP, (AV)
1700 Southwest Boulevard, 74107
Telephone: 918-584-4724 Fax: 918-583-5637
Email: frasier@tulsa.com URL: http://www.frasierlaw.com
Members of Firm: Thomas Dee Frasier (1924-2001); James E. Frasier; Steven R. Hickman; John W. Flippo; Everett R. Bennett, Jr.; Jerry L. Franks, Jr.; Frank W Frasier, III; George M. Miles. Associates: Michael A. Shiflet; Tomy W. McDonald; Laurie Phillips.
General Civil, Criminal and Trial Practice. Personal Injury, Medical Mal-practice, Labor, Products Liability, Workers Compensation, FELA, Transportation, Commercial, Probate, Corporate, Real Estate and Administrative Law.
References: Community State Bank, Tulsa, Oklahoma; American Exchange Bank, Tulsa, Oklahoma; The Bank of Oklahoma, Tulsa, Oklahoma.

See Professional Biographies, TULSA, OKLAHOMA

Frazier, Lisa Renee, (BV) ....'— '93 C&L.623 B.A., J.D. Asst. Pub. Def.
Frazier, Phil, (AV) ....'34 '65 C.623 B.B.A. L.862 J.D. [Frazier&P.]
Frazier & Phillips, (AV) .... 1424 Terrace Drive
Fredenberger, J. Kent, (CV) ....'59 '93 C.616 B.S. L.326 J.D. [Smiling,B.&R.]
Free, Matthew B., (BV) ....'73 '98 C.612 B.S. L.623 J.D. [A Best&S.]
Freeman, Bruce W., (AV) ....'59 '84 C.976 B.A. L.623 J.D. [Conner&W.]
Freeman, Kyle D. ....'69 '98 C.1147 B.A. L.862 J.D. [A Hall,E.H.G.G.&N.]
Freeman, Michael Hays, (BV) ....'52 '77 C.612 B.S. L.862 J.D. [Freeman]
Freeman, R. Jack, (AV) ....'48 '82 C.377 B.S. L.862 J.D. [Graham&F.]
Freeman Law Firm, (BV) .... 1701 S. Carson Ave.
Freeman-Burney, Melodie, (AV) ....'54 '88 C.613 B.A. L.862 J.D. [Conner&W.]
Freese, John Markham, (AV) ....'28 '50 C&L.623 A.B., LL.B. [Freese&M.]

Freese & March, P.A., (AV)
4510 East 31st Street, 74135
Telephone: 918-749-9331 Fax: 918-749-9336
Email: jackfreese@aol.com
Charles H. March (1912-1997); John Markham Freese.
General Civil Practice in all State and Federal Courts. Trials. Probate, Real Estate, Corporation, Oil and Gas, Family, Commercial, Administrative and Labor Law, Estate Planning.

See Professional Biographies, TULSA, OKLAHOMA

Freije, Lance, (BV) ....'70 '96 C&L.378 B.A., J.D. [A Latham,S.W.S.&L.]
French, Michael Allen ....'58 '97 C.831 B.A. L.862 J.D. 403 S. Cheyenne Ave.
Freudenrich, Bill, (BV) ....'61 '88 C.612 B.A. L.862 J.D. [C Boone,S.D.H.&D.]
Frey, Cecil H. ....'17 '48 C&L.378 A.B., J.D. 5125 S. Birmingham Pl.‡
Frey, Martin A. .... '39 '65 C.597 B.S.M.E. L.910 J.D. Prof. of Law, Univ. of Tulsa
Frizzell, Blaine G., (AV) .... '62 '89 C.612 B.S. L.862 J. D. [Fuller,C.&F.]
Frizzell, Gregory K. ....'56 '85 C.862 B.A. L.477 J.D. Dist. J.
Froeb, Charles H., (BV) ....'22 '50 C&L.623 B.A., LL.B. 2161 E. 27th‡
Frossard, Laura Emily, (BV) ....'52 '80 C.623 B.A. L.862 J.D. 1616 S. Trenton Ave.
Fry, Robert G., Jr., (AV) ....'41 '68 C.475 B.A. L.862 J.D. [Fry&E.]
Fry, Thomas L., (BV) '48 '77 C&L.623 B.A., J.D.
Assoc. Gen. Coun., Blue Cross & Blue Shield of Oklahoma (Legal Department)

Fry & Elder, (AV)
906 South Cheyenne, 74119
Telephone: 918-585-1107 Fax: 918-592-2410
Members of Firm: Robert G. Fry, Jr.; James R. Elder.
Family Law, Domestic Relations including Divorce, Custody, Marital Estates, Visitation.

See Professional Biographies, TULSA, OKLAHOMA

Fulkerson, Travis A. ....'75 '00 C&L.623 B.A., J.D. [A Fellers,S.B.B.&T.]
Fuller, Brad D., (AV) ....'62 '87 C&L.623 B.B.A., J.D. [Fuller,C.&F.]
Fuller, Gregg G., (BV) ....'64 '92 C.612 B.S.B.A. L.862 J.D. [Fuller,C.&F.]

Fuller, Chlouber & Frizzell, L.L.P., (AV)
Twenty East Fifth Street, Suite 200, 74103-4407
Telephone: 918-585-9155 Facsimile: 918-585-9414
URL: http://www.legalok.com
Brad D. Fuller; Steven E. Chlouber; Blaine G. Frizzell; Gregg G. Fuller; R. Michael Cole.
Banking, Bankruptcy, Business Law, Commercial Transactions, Corporate, Creditor's Rights, Criminal Law, Energy and Regulatory Law, Family Law, Federal, General Civil Litigation, Health Care Law, Insurance Defense, Labor and Employment Law, Oil & Gas, Private Foundations, Probate, Products Liability, State and Local Taxation of Businesses and Individuals, Trial Practice, Wills and Estates, Workers' Compensation, Telecommunications and Real Estate.

See Professional Biographies, TULSA, OKLAHOMA

Fulton, Kenton Wade ....'60 '85 C.446 B.A. L.790 J.D. 444 S. Houston, Ste. 210
Fulton, Larry J. ....'39 '64 C.623 B.A. L.309 LL.B. 2135 Terwilliger Blvd.
Fumia, Joan C. '45 '90 C.104 A.B. L.184 J.D.
(adm. in MI; not adm. in OK) 3207 S. Evanston Ave.
Funk, D. Richard, (AV) ....'46 '73 C.401 B.S. L.1017 J.D. [Conner&W.]
Funk, Karen M., (BV) ....'46 '76 C.840 B.A. L.862 J.D. [A Kivell,R.&F.]
Funk, R. V. Terry ....'45 '77 C.378 B.S. L.862 J.D. [C Lundy]
Gaberino, John A., Jr., (AV) '41 '66
C&L.276 A.B., J.D. Sr. V.P. & Gen. Coun., ONEOK, Inc.
Gable, Richard W., (AV) ....'38 '63 C&L.623 B.S.M.E., J.D. [C Gable&G.]
Gable, Thomas D., (AV) ....'42 '67 C&L.623 B.B.A., J.D. [C Hall,E.H.G.G.&N.] ‡

Gable & Gotwals, A Professional Corporation, (AV)
1100 Oneok Plaza, 100 West Fifth Street, 74103-4217 ⊙
Telephone: 918-595-4800 Fax: 918-595-4990
Email: info@gablelaw.com URL: http://www.gablelaw.com
Stephen B. Allen; Gene C. Buzzard; Dennis C. Cameron; Timothy A. Carney; Patrick W. Cipolla; Renee DeMoss; Theodore Q. Eliot; Amelia A. Fogleman; Jeffrey D. Hassell; Oliver S. Howard; David E. Keglovits; Thomas J. Kirby; Stephen W. Lake; Douglas J. May; Sheppard F. Miers, Jr.; J. Daniel Morgan; Joseph W. Morris; Elizabeth R. Muratet; Richard B. Noulles; Michael L. Pate; Terry D. Ragsdale; Jeffrey C. Rambach; Ronald N. Ricketts; Scott R. Rowland; Lisa Traylor Silvestri; M. Benjamin Singletary; James M. Sturdivant; Sidney K. Swinson; Ramon L. Watkins. Associates: Sara

(This Listing Continued)

Gable & Gotwals, A Professional Corporation (Continued)

E. Barry; Cason P. Carter; Erin K. Dailey; John D. Dale; John J. Griffin, III; Rania Nasreddine; Mason G. Patterson; Tyson D. Schwerdtfeger; Mia Vahlberg; Bradley W. Welsh. Of Counsel: John L. Arrington, Jr.; Frank J. Catalano; G. Ellis Gable (1905-2001); Richard W. Gable; Charles P. Gotwals, Jr.; Chad M. Hinrichs; Paul H. Johnson; Donald A. Kihle; Michael E. Sellers.
Administrative Law, Alternative Dispute Resolution, Antitrust, Bankruptcy, Banks and Banking, Class Actions, Commercial Law, Communications and Media, Copyright, Corporate Law, Employee Benefits, Energy, Environmental Law, Family Law, Finance, Franchises and Franchising, General Practice, Guardianship and Conservatorship, Insurance, Intellectual Property, Labor and Employment, Litigation, Mergers, Acquisitions and Divestitures, Natural Resources, Patents, Personal Injury, Probate, Property Law, Real Estate, RICO, Regulatory Law, Securities, Software Licensing, Sports Law, Taxation, Technology Law, Torts, Trademarks, Utility Law, Workers Compensation.
Oklahoma City, Oklahoma Offices: Fifteenth Floor, One Leadership Square, 211 North Robinson, 73102-7101. Telephone: 405-235-5500. Fax: 405-235-2875.

See Professional Biographies, TULSA, OKLAHOMA

Gaddis, William E., (BV) ....'48 '73 C&L.623 B.A., J.D. 2431 E. 51st St., Ste. 602
Gage, Jake W. '47 '84 C.619 B.A. L.862 J.D.
Pub. Util. Specialist, Southwestern Power Administration
Gainer, Leslie M. .... '61 '87 C.860 B.A. L.309 J.D. 2401 Terwillegger Blvd.
Gaither, Jack I., (AV) .... '24 '50 C.862 L.623 LL.B. 2605 S. St. Louis
Gallant, Robert M., (BV) ....'63 '94 C.150 B.A. L.862 J.D. [Ⓐ Latham,S.W.S.&L.]
Gallegos, Joanna L. .... '71 '00 C.112 B.A. L.770 J.D. 333 W. 4th St.
Gammie, John C., (BV) '60 '92
C.821 B.A. L.862 J.D. Sr. Coun., The Williams Cos., Inc.
Gan, Cheryl S. ....'54 '91 C.623 B.A. L.862 J.D. [Ⓐ Perrine,M.R.R.B.&T.]
Ganem, Thomas F., (AV) .... '47 '75 C&L.623 B.S., J.D. [Corley&G.]
Gann, Richard A., (AV) ....'49 '75 C.612 B.S. L.862 J.D. [Riggs,A.N.T.O.&L.]
Gann, Tom R., (BV) ....'44 '70 C.612 B.A. L.862 J.D. 2504 E. 21st St., Ste. A
Gardner, B. R., Jr. .... '20 '75 C&L.862 B.S.B.A., J.D. 10959 S. Quebec Pl.‡
Gardner, Bernard Richard, III .... '48 '88 C&L.862 B.S., J.D. 11242 S. Kingston Ave.
Gardner, Richd. E. .... '18 '54 C.862 B.S. L.904 LL.B. 3419 E. 58th St.‡
Garland, James C., III, (BV) ....'61 '87 C.619 B.S. L.616 J.D. [Commercial L.]
Garland, James Clinton, (BV) ....'37 '81 C&L.862 B.A., J.D. [Commercial L.]
Garland, William Joseph .... '72 '98 C.619 B.A. L.1363 J.D. [Commercial L.]
Garner, Robert H., (BV) ....'56 '81 C&L.862 B.S., J.D. Sr. Asst. City Atty.
Garren, Richard T., (AV) .... '48 '75 C&L.862 B.A., J.D. [Riggs,A.N.T.O.&L.]
Garrett, Amber Peckio ....'— '03 C.621 B.S. L.862 J.D. [Ⓐ Garrett] (⊙Muskogee)
Garrett, Cynthia K., (BV) .... '58 '94 C&L.862 B.S., J.D. [C.Garrett]
Garrett, David M., (AV) '41 '69
C.619 B.S. L.862 J.D. [Garrett] (⊙Muskogee, Oklahoma City)
Garrett, Cynthia, Law Firm, (BV) .... P.O. Box 9250

Garrett Law Office, P.C., (AV)
111 West Fifth Street, Suite 800, 74103 ⊙
Telephone: 918-622-9292
URL: http://www.garrettlawoffice.com
David M. Garrett;—Douglass R. Elliott; Jared A. DeSilvey; David C. Bean; John Francis Bates; Amber Peckio Garrett; Steven F. Langer; Tia J. Baker Surles; Jeffrey A. Heater. Of Counsel: Rick Paynter; Gregory P. Williams.
Personal Injury, Insurance Litigation, Products Liability, Workers Compensation, Securities, Bankruptcy.
Muskogee, Oklahoma Office: 215 State Street, 10th Floor, Suite 1000 74401. Telephone: 918-683-3288. Fax: 918-683-8445.
Oklahoma City, Oklahoma Office: 4000 N. Classen Boulevard, Suite 110-S, 73118. Telephone: 405-634-2500.
Fayetteville, Arkansas Office: One West Mountain Street, Suite 302, 72701.

See Professional Biographies, TULSA, OKLAHOMA

Garvin, Agee, Carlton & Mashburn, L.L.P.
(See Pauls Valley)

Gaskill, Brian S., (AV) ....'44 '68 C.315 B.A. L.309 J.D. [Sneed L.]
Gaskins, Garry M. ....'78 '04 C.623 B.A. L.862 J.D. [Ⓐ Boone,S.D.H.&D.]
Gassaway, Jim F., (AV) '27 '55 C.618 B.A. L.623 LL.B.
4111 South Darlington Avenue
Gassaway, Kevin T., (AV) .... '55 '80 C&L.623 B.A., J.D. [Gassaway]
Gassaway, Rita J., (AV) .... '59 '84 C.612 B.S. L.623 J.D. [Gassaway]

Gassaway Law Firm, (AV)
Thompson Building, 20 East Fifth Street, Suite 600, 74103-4441
Telephone: 918-592-6800 Fax: 918-592-1800
URL: http://www.lawyers.com/gassawaylaw
Kevin T. Gassaway; Rita J. Gassaway;—Jodi Johnson Baker.
Civil Litigation, Family Law, Divorce Child Custody, Child Support, Visitation Rights, Domestic Violence, Alimony, Spousal Support, Premarital Agreements, Post Decree Modifications, Adoptions, Guardianships, Estate Planning, Trusts, Probate and Wealth Transfer.

See Professional Biographies, TULSA, OKLAHOMA

Gassett, J. Michael .... '52 '78 C.623 B.B.A. L.862 J.D. Dist. J.
Gassett, John D. ....'24 '52 C.623 B.S. L.862 J.D. 810 S. Cincinnati Avenue (Pat.)
Gatchell, Catherine A. ....'51 '77 C.846 B.J. L.616 J.D. 406 S. Boulder Ave.
Gault, William Hibbard ...... '70 '97 C&L.378 B.A., J.D. Atty., The Williams Cos., Inc.
Gause, Randall Kent ....'62 '90 C&L.623 B.A., J.D. [Carr&C.]
Gavras, Dian L. .... '59 '85 C.802 B.A. L.862 J.D. Tr. Offr., Utica Natl. Bk. & Tr. Co.
Gavras, Leon C. ....'27 '52 C.813 L.623 LL.B. 2121 S. Yorktown‡
Gebetsberger, Leisa Michelle, (BV) '57 '83
C.862 B.S. L.623 J.D. Asst. Gen. Coun., State Tax Comm.
Gee, R. Paul ....'60 '92 C.839 B.S. L.862 J.D. 5222 E. 69th Place
Geffen, Barbara F., (AV) '46 '75
C.802 B.A. L.734 J.D. Gen. Coun., The University of Tulsa
Gehres, Tony L., (AV) '57 '82 C.893 B.A. L.378 J.D.
Asst. Gen. Coun., The Williams Companies, Inc.
Gentges, Alan W., P.C., (BV) '53 '85
C.804 B.A. L.862 J.D. 406 S. Boulder Mezzanine, S.W.
Gentges, Delilah Christine Zarate ..... '54 '87 C.878 B.S.N. L.862 J.D. 1517 S. Newport‡
Gentry, Stephanie T. ....'73 '98 C&L.37 B.S., J.D. [Ⓐ Hall,E.H.G.G.&N.]
Getchell, Robert J., (BV) .... '60 '85 C&L.1288 B.A., J.D. [R.J.Getchell]
Getchell, Robert J., P.C., (BV) .... 2250 E. 73rd Street
Gibbens, Michael J., (AV) ....'56 '81 C.691 B.A. L.846 J.D. [Crowe&D.]
Gibbon, Richard D., (AV) .... '25 '54 C&L.862 LL.B. [Gibbon,B.&B.] ⊙

Gibbon, Barron & Barron, P.A., (AV)
2 W. 6th Street, Suite 320, 74119-1215 ⊙
Telephone: 918-745-0687 Fax: 918-745-0821
Richard D. Gibbon; Cindy L. McVey; Bradford D. Barron; Zachary T. Barron.
General Civil Practice in all Courts. Workers Compensation, Personal Injury, Products Liability, Surety, Aviation and Insurance Law. Trials.
Representative Clients: Mid-Continent Casualty Co.; State Farm Insurance Co.; Unigard Insurance Group; Mutual Service Insurance Co.; Equity Mutual Insurance.
Okmulgee, Oklahoma Office: P.O. Box 1211. Telephone: 918-756-7772.

See Professional Biographies, TULSA, OKLAHOMA

Gibbs, Charles A., III, (BV) '56 '82 C.612 B.S. L.862 J.D.
Beacon Building-SW Mezzanine, 406 South Boulder Avenue, 74103-3821
Telephone: 918-599-9000 Fax: 918-599-9001
Email: LAW4HIRE@morelaw.com URL: http://www.law4hire.com
Construction Law, Corporate and Business Practice. Commercial Law, Real Estate, Leases, Evictions, Landlord/Tenant, Mechanics Liens. General Civil Practice State and Federal Courts, Indian Gaming Law.

See Professional Biographies, TULSA, OKLAHOMA

Gibbs, George, (BV) .... '54 '86 C.1321 B.A. L.616 J.D. [Gibbs A.B.M.&H.]

Gibbs Armstrong Borochoff Mullican & Hart, P.C., (AV)
500 Petroleum Club Building, 601 South Boulder Avenue, 74119
Telephone: 918-587-3939 Fax: 918-582-5504
Email: ggibbs@tulsacounsel.com URL: http://www.gibbsandarmstrong.com
George Gibbs; Tom L. Armstrong; Douglas M. Borochoff; George Robert Mullican; Robert D. Hart; Christopher D. Wolek;—Jeffrey G. Fields; Robert E. Cowan; Charles A. McSoud; Kevin S. Hoskins; Jonathan D. Cartledge; Karla M. Rogers; Eddie L. Carr; Peter C. Astor; January J. Windrix; Corey Cornelison; Laura L. Eakens.
General Civil Trial Practice including Corporate, Commercial, Railroad, Personal Injury, Bad Faith, Professional Malpractice, Nursing Home Malpractice, Medical Malpractice, Premises Liability, Automobile Negligence, Private and Commercial Trucking Negligence, Catastrophic Injury cases; Environmental Liability, Domestic Law and Workers Compensation; Governmental Tort Claims; Civil Rights Litigation; Military Justice; Business Planning and Municipal Law.

See Professional Biographies, TULSA, OKLAHOMA

Gibson, A. T. .... '28 '63 C.619 B.S. L.616 LL.B. 6732 E. 66th Pl. S.‡
Gibson, Theodore P., (AV) ....'31 '60 C.103 A.B. L.862 LL.B. [Ⓒ Jarboe&S.]
Gilbert, Fred P., (AV) ....'37 '65 C&L.309 A.B., LL.B. [Dorman&G.] (Pat.)
Gill, Randall A., Law Office of, (BV) '58 '83 C&L.862 B.S., J.D.
2512 E. 21st St., #100
Gillert, Thomas C. .... '47 '74 C.616 B.A. L.862 J.D. Dist. J.
Gillett, Sarah Jane, (AV) ....'67 '93 C.914 B.A. L.93 J.D. [Hall,E.H.G.G.&N.]
Gilliard, Lori .... '57 '90 C&L.862 B.A., J.D. [Ⓐ Holloway&M.]
Gilliard, Michael D., (AV) ....'51 '78 C&L.862 B.S., J.D. [McGivern,G.&C.]
Gilpin, Timothy S., (BV) ....'60 '86 C.273 B.A. L.862 J.D. 1717 S. Cheyenne Ave.
Gilsinger, Dale Joseph, (AV) '51 '84
C.679 B.S. L.862 J.D. 320 South Boston Avenue Suite 1030
Gish, Dana L., (AV) ....'65 '90 C.623 B.A. L.862 J.D. [McCormick,S.&G.]
Givens, Blake R., (BV) .... '63 '92 C.326 B.S. L.862 J.D. [Givens&G.P.]
Givens, Jack R., (AV) ....'28 '58 C.612 B.S. L.623 LL.B. [Givens&G.P.]
Givens & Givens, PLLC, (AV) .... One West 3rd Street
Gladd, John A., (AV) ....'38 '67 C&L.862 B.S., J.D. 9535 S. College Avenue
Gladd, John S., (AV) .... '61 '87 C.612 B.S. L.862 J.D. [Atkinson,H.N.B.G.&C.]
Glass, Jason L., (BV) ....'71 '97 C.802 B.A. L.846 J.D. [Ⓐ Richards&C.]
Glass, Robert S., (AV) ....'59 '84 C&L.846 B.B.A., J.D. [Glass]
Glass Law Firm P.C., (AV) ....2118 South Atlanta Place, Suite 100
Glassco, Kurt G., (BV) ....'55 '82 C.612 B.S. L.862 J.D. [McCollam&G.]
Gleason, George E. '25 '52 L.500 LL.B.
(adm. in MS; not adm. in OK) MAPCO Inc.
Glendening, Jeffrey A., (AV) ....'60 '86 C&L.623 B.A., J.D. [Glendening]

Glendening Law Firm, The, (AV)
8816 South Sheridan Road, 74133
Telephone: 918-494-7037 Fax: 918-494-0766
Member of Firm: Jeffrey A. Glendening. Associates: John D. Bogatko; James A. Higgins; Angie A. Sumner.
General Practice.

See Professional Biographies, TULSA, OKLAHOMA

Godlove, Joan, (BV) .... '39 '77 C.228 B.A. L.345 J.D. 2121 S. Columbia, Ste. 500
Goetting, Ralph W., Jr. '44 '72 C&L.436 B.S., J.D.
(adm. in WI; not adm. in OK) 7927 S. Oswego Pl.‡
Goins, Karen, (BV) ....'48 '90 C.97 B.L.S. L.862 LL.B. [Ⓐ Stipe,H.L.U.E.&B.]
Goins, Ronald E., (AV) .... '57 '82 C.277 B.S. L.45 J.D. [Tomlins&G.]
Goldberg, Pamela H., (AV) ....'55 '87 C.102 B.A. L.862 J.D. [Hall,E.H.G.G.&N.]
Golden, Thomas F., (AV) ....'42 '68 C.612 B.S. L.862 J.D. [Ⓒ Hall,E.H.G.G.&N.] ‡
Gomez, Matthew P., (BV) .... '63 '94 C.698 B.S.B.A. L.862 J.D. 1444 South Carson Ave.
Goodman, Aaron J. '73 '98
C.112 B.A. L.862 J.D. Asst. Pub. Def., Tulsa Co. Pub. Def. Off.
Goodnight, F. Jason, (CV) ....'75 '00 C&L.45 B.A., J.D. [Ⓐ Feldman,F.W.F.&B.]
Goodnight, Tara P. ....'75 '01 C&L.45 B.A., J.D. [Ⓐ Secrest,H.&B.]
Goodpaster, Scott A. ....'60 '88 C&L.862 B.A., J.D. 3642 E. 49th Place
Goodwin, Dan Luke, (BV) ....'56 '82 C.612 B.S. L.862 J.D. P.O. Box 521166
Goodwin, James O., (AV) ....'39 '65 C.602 B.A. L.862 J.D. 624 E. Archer
Gordon, G. David ....'61 '88 C.69 B.B.A. L.862 J.D. [G.D.Gordon&Assoc.]
Gordon, G. David, & Associates, P.C. ....7633 East 63rd Place, Suite 210
Goree, Brian J., (BV) ....'64 '89 C.623 B.S. L.862 J.D. [Ⓐ Latham,S.W.S.&L.] (Pat.)
Goree, Jack Y., (AV) .... '39 '70 C.619 B.A. L.862 J.D. [Ⓐ Secrest,H.&B.]
Gorrell, Michael K. '50 '75 C&L.900 B.B.A., J.D.
(adm. in KS; not adm. in OK) 6307 S. Richmond
Goss, Douglas L. ..... '44 '70 C.935 B.A. L.862 J.D. V.P. & Tr. Offr., Bank of Okla., N.A.
Goss, Michael D. .... '68 '95 C.593 B.S. L.862 J.D. [Ⓐ Secrest,H.&B.]
Gottschalk, Debbra J. ....'52 '76 C.377 B.A. L.862 J.D. 2530 E. 71st St.
Gotwals, Charles P., Jr., (AV) .... '17 '40 C&L.623 B.A., J.D. [Ⓒ Gable&G.]
Gotwals, James R., (AV) ....'50 '75 C&L.623 B.B.A., J.D. [J.R.Gotwals&Assoc.]

Gotwals, James R., and Associates, Inc., A Prof. Corp., (AV)
1130 Park Centre, 525 South Main Street, 74103-4512
Telephone: 918-599-7088 Fax: 918-599-7153 URL: http://www.jrgotlaw.com
Email: jim.gotwals@jrgotlaw.com URL: http://www.gotwalslaw.com
James R. Gotwals;—Mary L. Gutierrez. Of Counsel: Arthur E. Rubin.
General Civil and Trial Practice. Family, Personal Injury, Real Estate, Probate, Corporate, Oil and Gas, Criminal Law, Business Formations, Business Litigation, Commercial Litigation, Contingent Business Litigation, Securities Litigation, Mediation.

See Professional Biographies, TULSA, OKLAHOMA

Gourley, Nancy Glisan, (AV) ....'48 '83 C.612 B.A. L.862 J.D. 1861 E. 15th Street
Grabel, Ralph, (BV) ....'21 '63 C.693 L.862 LL.B. 4746 E. 54th St.
Graddy, Catherine J. .... '75 '04 C.174 B.A. L.862 J.D. [Ⓐ Joyce&P.]
Graddy, Mark K. .... '76 '04 C.225 B.A. L.862 J.D. [Ⓐ Joyce&P.]
Graham, Scott A. ....'70 '03 C.1083 B.S. L.862 J.D. [Ⓐ Seymour]
Graham, Tony M., (AV) ....'49 '77 C.502 B.S. L.862 J.D. [Graham&F.]
Graham, Warren D. ....'51 '80 C.184 B.A. L.862 J.D. Prof. of Law, Tulsa Jr. Coll.

Graham & Freeman, PLLC, (AV)
6226 E. 101st Street, Suite 300, 74137
Telephone: 918-298-1716 Fax: 918-298-1728
Email: info@grahamfreeman.com URL: http://www.grahamfreeman.com
Tony M. Graham; R. Jack Freeman; William F. Smith; Sheila M. Bradley.
Litigation, Business Litigation, Business Arbitration, Products Liability, White Collar Criminal Defense, Civil Trial Law, Insurance Bad Faith Litigation, Native American Law, Insurance Defense.

See Professional Biographies, TULSA, OKLAHOMA

Grant, Floyd Patrick .... '45 '72 C&L.862 B.A., J.D. P.O. Box 4980

Graves, Daniel B., (AV) '69 '95 C&L.862 B.A., J.D. [Graves&B.]
Graves, David G., (BV) '66 '91 C.623 B.B.A. L.902 J.D. [Barkley]
Graves, Gregg L., (BV) '60 '89 C&L.623 B.B.A., J.D. [Stauffer,G.&N.]
Graves, Michael D., (AV) '46 '73 C.862 B.A. L.910 J.D. [Hall,E.H.G.G.&N.]
Graves, Michael Lon, (AV) '46 '72 C&L.623 B.A., J.D. Acquis. Mgr., Calumet Oil Co.

Graves & Barkett, PLLC, (AV)
1010 Boulder Towers, 1437 South Boulder Avenue, 74119
Telephone: 918-582-6900 Fax: 918-582-6907
Email: dgraves@webzone.net URL: http://www.gblaw.org
Daniel B. Graves; Michael L. Barkett;—William McLain.
Civil Practice, Medical Negligence, Personal Injury, Medical Malpractice, Products Liability, Business Litigation, Commercial Law, Employment Litigation, Criminal Defense.
See Professional Biographies, TULSA, OKLAHOMA

Gravis, Marylinn M., (BV) '60 '86 C&L.862 B.A., J.D. 8908 S. Yale Ave.
Gray, Gregory A., (BV) '54 '86 C&L.862 B.S.B.A., J.D. [Rogers&B.]
Gray, Stephen P., (AV) '55 '80 C.612 B.A. L.862 J.D. [S.P.Gray&Assoc.]
Gray, Stephen P., & Associates, (AV) 4530 S. Sheridan Rd.
Grayless, Stephen M., (BV) '51 '86 C.804 B.S. L.900 J.D. 1718 S. Cheyenne Avenue
Graziano, Mark A., (BV) '60 '86 C&L.862 B.A., J.D. 616 S. Main St.
Greaves, Linda Kay, (BV) '50 '95 C.921 B.S. L.862 J.D. Asst. Dist. Atty.
Green, James E., Jr., (AV) '49 '77 C&L.862 B.S., J.D. [Conner&W.]
Green, Robert G., (BV) '38 '65 C&L.623 B.B.A., J.D. 3723 S. Delaware Pl.
Greenough, Charles, (AV) '62 '87 C.856 B.A. L.623 J.D. [Boone,S.D.H.&D.]
Greenough, Kelly M., (BV) '— '92 C.612 B.S. L.862 J.D. [Ⓐ Perrine,M.R.R.B.&T.]
Greenstreet, John R. '29 '61 C&L.802 B.A., LL.B. 2650 E. 45th St.‡
Greubel, Stephen J., (AV) '59 '82 C.619 B.A. L.500 J.D. 423 South Boulder, Suite 300
Griffin, Gene Edward '39 '91 C.1147 B.B.A. L.862 J.D. 2617 E. 21st Street
Griffin, John J., III '80 '05 C&L.623 B.A., J.D. [Ⓐ Gable&G.]
Griffin, Sue, (BV) '— '93 C.612 B.S. L.862 J.D. ONEOK, Inc. (Legal Department)

Griffin, Reynolds & Associates
(See Oklahoma City)

Grigg, Bert M., (BV) '19 '55 C.619 L.862 LL.B. 3010 S. 94th E. Ave.
Grimaldi, Jack P. '46 '73 C.1004 B.A. L.378 J.D. [Ⓐ McQueen,R.&T.]
Grimm, William R., (AV) '47 '73 C&L.623 B.B.A., J.D. [Barrow&G.]
Grimshaw, Eric, (AV) '52 '77 C.174 B.A. L.862 J.D. 100 W. Fifth St.
Grisso, Gary G., (BV) '60 '89 C.45 B.S.B.A. L.1243 J.D. 10346 E. 21st St.
Grissom, Marijo Copeland '51 '96 C.862 B.S. L.623 J.D. [M.C.Grissom]

Grissom, Marijo Copeland, P.C.
Two Main Plaza, 616 South Main, Suite 301, 74119
Telephone: 918-582-4848 Fax: 918-582-4846
Email: mcgrissom@sbcglobal.net
Marijo Copeland Grissom.
Family Law, Wills, Probate, Personal Injury.
See Professional Biographies, TULSA, OKLAHOMA

Groenendyke, Richard A., Jr., (AV) '45 '70 C.16 B.A. L.192 J.D. [Hall,E.H.G.G.&N.]
Grundy, Bradley A., (AV) '65 '90 C.802 B.A. L.602 J.D. [Wagner&G.]
Grundy, Karen M., (AV) '64 '90 C.59 B.A. L.602 J.D. [Ⓐ Nichols,W.S.N.F.&R.]
Gudgel, Tom H., III, (AV) '56 '90 C.623 B.B.A. L.862 J.D. [LaCourse,D.C.&G.]
Gudgel, Trent A., (AV) '63 '90 C&L.623 B.B.A., J.D. [Nichols,W.S.N.F.&R.]
Guerrero, Gregory A., (AV) '53 '78 C.862 B.S. L.846 J.D. 1120 S. Boston
Gulbis, Janet '51 '98 C.388 B.A. L.862 J.D. Williams Cos.
Gustafson, Del L., (AV) '54 '79 C.546 B.A. L.880 J.D. [Hall,E.H.G.G.&N.]
Guten, David A. '78 '04 C.616 B.S. L.862 J.D. [Ⓐ LaCourse,D.C.&G.]
Gutierrez, Mary L., (BV) '51 '99 C&L.862 B.A., J.D. [Ⓐ J.R.Gotwals&Assoc.]
Guy, Don J., (BV) '53 '80 C&L.862 B.S., J.D. 5205 S. Kingston
Hack, Charles W., (BV) '29 '74 C.846 M.S. L.862 J.D. Ste 400, 111 W 5th St
Hackler, Bonnie N., (CV) '74 '99 C&L.623 B.A., J.D. [Ⓐ Hall,E.H.G.G.&N.]
Hagedorn, Frank M., (AV) '38 '68 C&L.862 B.A., J.D. [Hall,E.H.G.G.&N.]
Haglund, Jacqueline O'Neil, (AV) '51 '76 C&L.862 B.A., J.D.
Gen. Coun., Blue Cross & Blue Shield of Oklahoma (Legal Department)
Haines, Lewis J., Jr. '21 '47 C.36 L.352 LL.B. 7216 E. 55th Pl.‡
Hair, Cara M. '76 '02 C.612 B.S. L.623 J.D. [Ⓐ Conner&W.]
Hale, Stephen E., (BV) '— '93 C.612 B.S. L.862 J.D. [Ⓐ Riggs,A.N.T.O.&L.]
Hall, Carl D., Jr., (AV) '28 '53 C.862 A.B. L.276 J.D. 693 S. Delaware Pl.‡
Hall, Elizabeth K., (BV) '69 '95 C&L.623 B.B.A., J.D. [Rodolf&T.]
Hall, John Vincent, (BV) '70 '96 C.619 B.S. L.616 J.D. [Hall&H.]
Hall, Kim Majors '69 '94 C.999 B.A. L.623 J.D.
Case Mgr., Big Brothers & Sisters of Green Country
Hall, Lawrence A., (AV) '65 '90 C.623 B.B.A. L.309 J.D. [Conner&W.]
Hall, Linda A. '45 '79 C.823 A.B. L.862 J.D.
(adm. in IA; not adm. in OK) 1425 W. Virgin St.
Hall, Scott R., (AV) '68 '94 C.612 B.S. L.623 J.D. [Atkinson,H.N.B.G.&C.]
Hall, Terese A., (BV) '53 '83 C&L.623 B.A., J.D. 5272 S. Lewis Avenue, Suite 112
Hall, Terry A., (BV) '54 '84 C&L.623 B.A., J.D. [Ⓐ Armstrong&L.]

Hall, Estill, Hardwick, Gable, Golden & Nelson, A Professional Corporation, (AV) BR
320 South Boston Avenue, Suite 400, 74103 ⊙
Telephone: 918-594-0400 Facsimile: 918-594-0505
URL: http://www.HallEstill.com
Walter B. Hall (1923-1986); Fred S. Nelson (1928-1987); James C. T. Hardwick; Larry W. Sandel; Andrew M. Wolov; Frank M. Hagedorn; J. Patrick Cremin; J. Kevin Hayes; Michael D. Graves; James D. Satrom; Richard A. Groenendyke, Jr.; Graydon Dean Luthey, Jr.; Del L. Gustafson; Mark K. Blongewicz; Michael D. Cooke; Kenneth L. Hunt; B. Kenneth Cox, Jr.; D. Kenyon Williams, Jr.; Thomas P. Schroedter; James J. Proszek; James M. Reed; Thomas A. Creekmore, III; Stephen W. Ray; Margaret A. Swimmer; Michael T. Keester; Ronald O. Ray, Jr.; Fred M. Buxton; Steven A. Broussard; Steven W. Soulé; Michael L. Nemec; Joseph D. Fincher; Angelyn L. Dale; R. Mark Petrich; Pamela H. Goldberg; Mark Banner; Robert F. Dougherty; T. Lane Wilson; Betsy Grabel Jackson; Robert P. Fitz-Patrick; Sarah Jane Gillett; John F. Heil, III; Pamela S. Anderson; Timothy S. Posey; Marshall J. Wells; Anthony J. Jorgenson; Heather L. Cupp; Michael J. Lissau; Kyle D. Freeman; W. Deke Canada; Bonnie N. Hackler; Kimberly R. Schutz; Matthew T. Crook; John T. Richer; Genevieve L. Schmook; Stephanie T. Gentry; Stephanie A. Horton; Molly A. Bircher; Karissa K. Cottom; Kimberly L. Watkins; Maren K. Minnaert; Bobbi L. Allen; Johnson W. Custer; Elisabeth R. Higham. Of Counsel: John S. Estill, Jr.; Thomas D. Gable; Thomas F. Golden; William W. Pritchard; Clive A. Seymour; Ronald L. Jones.
General Civil Practice. Trials and proceedings before all State and Federal Courts and Agencies. Antitrust, Bankruptcy, Banking, Construction, Corporate, Commercial, Securities, Employee Benefits, Executive Compensation, Energy, Natural Resources, Energy Regulatory, Environmental, Estate Planning, Probate, Family Law, Domestic, Healthcare, Medical Malpractice, Indian Law, Intellectual Property, International Law and Trade, Labor, Employment, Legislative, Administrative Law, Litigation, Media, Real Estate, Taxation, Telecommunications, Tort, Insurance Defense, Utility Law.
Oklahoma City Office: Bank One Center, Suite 2900, 100 North Broadway, 73102-8827. Telephone: 405-553-2828. Facsimile: 405-553-2855.
Washington, D.C. Office: Suite 700 North Building, 1120 20th Street N.W. 20036-3406. Telephone: 202-973-1200. Facsimile: 202-973-1212.
Fayetteville, Arkansas Office: One East Center Street, Suite 315, 72701. Telephone: 479-973-5200. Facsimile: 479-973-0520.
See Professional Biographies, TULSA, OKLAHOMA

Hall & Hall, P.C., (BV) 406 S. Boulder, Ste. 400
Halstead, Martin Franklin '59 '03 C.619 B.S. L.862 J.D. [Ⓐ Bonham&H.]
Hamby, Mark T., (BV) '60 '89 C&L.208 B.A., J.D. 15 West 6th Street, Suite 1500
Hamernik, Robert '22 '50 C&L.436 Ph.B., J.D. 4932 E. 27th‡
Hamill, Luanna L., (BV) '46 '82 C&L.862 B.S.B.A., J.D. 616 S. Main St.
Hamilton, Audra K., (BV) '70 '96 C.315 B.A. L.45 J.D. [Ⓐ Doerner,S.D.&A.]
Hamilton, Ray F., III, (AV) '36 '66 C&L.623 B.S., J.D. [R.F.Hamilton]
Hamilton, Scott, (AV) '53 '78 C.862 B.A. L.902 J.D.
Mng. Atty., Legal Servs. of Eastern Okla., Inc.
Hamilton, Ray F., P.C., (AV) 2141 E. 25th St.
Hammond, Joe P. '22 '49 C.612 B.S. L.178 LL.B. 4013 S. Birmingham Ave.‡
Hamor, Lillian M., (BV) '45 '81 C.623 B.A. L.862 J.D. 3314 E. 51st St., Ste. 214W
Hampton, Amy E. '76 '04 C&L.862 B.A., J.D. [Ⓐ Richards&C.]
Hampton, Robert J. '28 '80 C&L.862 B.S., J.D. 4821 S. 69th E. Ave.
Haney, Philip S., (AV) '46 '71 C&L.999 A.B., J.D. [P.S.Haney]

Haney, Philip S., Associates, (AV) BR
1437 South Boulder, Suite 1050, Boulder Towers, 74119
Telephone: 918-744-1023 Facsimile: 918-583-7170
Email: pshaney@swbell.net URL: http://www.lawyers.com/churchlaw
Philip S. Haney.
Tax Exempt, Nonprofit and Charitable Organizations, Public Charities, Churches, Religious Ministries, Charitable Giving, Estate Planning.
See Professional Biographies, TULSA, OKLAHOMA

Hansel, Sarah E., (AV) '61 '89 C.234 B.A. L.623 J.D. [Nichols,W.S.N.F.&R.]
Hansen, Carl Douglas '63 '98 C.612 B.S. L.326 J.D. Unit Corp.
Hanson, Charles O., (AV) '44 '76 C.352 B.B.A. L.862 J.D. [Hanson&H.]
Hanson & Holmes, L.L.P., (AV) 5918 E. 31st St.
Hanton, Rena C. '11 '36 L.862 1516 N. Harvard‡
Harbison, William T., II, (BV) '41 '83 C.627 B.S. L.862 J.D. 1408 S. Denver Ave.
Hardcastle, Heath E., (BV) '67 '90 C&L.45 B.A., J.D. [Albright,R.&H.]
Hardgrave, Meredith E., (Mr.) '31 '59 C.621 B.S. L.616 J.D. 6012 E. 114th St.‡
Hardin, Mark Edward '68 '93 C.612 B.S. L.623 J.D. [Ⓐ Rodolf&T.]
Hardwick, James C. T., (AV) '38 '63 C&L.623 B.S., LL.B. [Hall,E.H.G.G.&N.]
Hardwick, Martha Moody, (AV) '41 '76 C.623 B.A. L.862 J.D. [Hardwick]
Hardwick Law Office, (AV) P.O. Box 35975
Hargis, Zachery R. '— '02 C.900 B.A. L.1202 J.D. [Ⓐ Riggs,A.N.T.O.&L.]
Harlin, John K., Jr., (BV) '31 '60 C&L.862 B.A., LL.B. 810 S. Cincinnati Ave.
Harlton, Bruce H., Jr. '31 '60 C&L.862 LL.B. 4537 S. Lakewood Ave.
Harlton, Hilda C. '57 '82 C&L.862 B.S.B.A., J.D. Law Clk. to Ct. of App. J.
Harmon, Judith Elaine, (BV) '39 '90 C.82 B.A. L.862 J.D.
315 S. Gilcrease Museum Road
Harmon, Timothy S., (AV) '60 '85 C&L.1288 B.A., J.D. [Ⓐ Secrest,H.&B.]
Harper, John E., Jr. '73 '97 C&L.623 B.A., J.D. [Nichols,W.S.N.F.&R.]
Harper, Ryan C., (BV) '72 '99 C.198 B.A. L.862 J.D. [Ⓐ King,T.&R.]
Harral, Larry S., Attorney at Law, (BV) '46 '71 C&L.623 B.S., J.D.
3127 S. Rockford Dr.
Harrington, John C., (AV) '42 '69 C&L.861 B.A., J.D. [Harrington&M.]
Harrington, William A., (AV) '17 '48 C.862 B.A. L.623 LL.B. [Harrington&M.]
Harrington & Mann, (AV) 406 South Boulder Avenue Suite 400
Harris, C. Gordon '66 '05 C.623 B.A. L.900 J.D. [Concordia B.]
Harris, Imogene H., (BV) '30 '58 C.619 B.S. L.862 LL.B. 3324 E. 76th St.
Harris, Jesse S., (AV) '54 '79 C.103 B.A. L.273 J.D. 1423 N. Main St.
Harris, Joseph W., Attorney at Law '51 '96
C.802 B.M. L.862 J.D. 4867 S. Sheridan Rd., Ste. 701
Harris, Michelle '71 '00 C.1050 B.A. L.862 J.D. [Ⓐ Steidley&N.] ⊙
Harris, Richard L., (AV) '32 '62 C.839 B.B.A. L.208 LL.B. [Harris,M.P.T.&S.]
Harris, Steven M., (BV) '50 '75 C.378 B.A. L.882 J.D. [Doyle H.D.&H.]
Harris, Timothy H., (AV) '52 '84 C.966 B.A. L.999 J.D. 1st Asst. Dist. Atty.

Harris, McMahan, Peters, Thompson & Stall P.C., (AV) BR
Suite 900 1800 South Baltimore, 74119
Telephone: 918-743-6201 Fax: 918-747-2965
URL: http://www.hmptsfirm.com
Richard L. Harris; John A. McMahan; Stephen Q. Peters; R. Lynn Thompson; Eric W. Stall;—Todd William Singer; Randall T. Duncan; Kort A. Besore. Of Counsel: William D. Toney; John W. Moody.
General Civil and Federal Practice. Oil and Gas, Real Estate and Corporation Law.
References: Bank IV; Valley National Bank.
See Professional Biographies, TULSA, OKLAHOMA

Harrison, Charles D., (AV) '54 '81 C.98 B.S. L.862 J.D. [Eagleton,E.&H.]
Hart, Elizabeth A., (BV) '75 '00 C.45 B.A. L.862 J.D. [Ⓐ Richards&C.]
Hart, Frank L. '31 '66 C.612 B.S.M.E. L.623 J.D. 8911 S. 73rd East Ave. (Pat.)

Hart, Martin G., (AV) '53 '79 C.612 B.S. L.862 J.D.
318 W. 14th Place, 74119
Telephone: 918-582-5888 Fax: 918-582-4443
Email: mgh9393@hotmail.com
Trial Practice State and Federal Courts, including Medical Malpractice, Personal Injury, Criminal Defense, Environmental Investigations and Defense.
See Professional Biographies, TULSA, OKLAHOMA

Hart, Robert D. '69 '95 C.619 B.B.A. L.623 J.D. [Gibbs A.B.M.&H.]
Hart, Yvette B. '74 '02 C.634 B.S.W. L.862 J.D. [Ⓐ Strecker&Assoc.]
Hartman, Denise G. '55 '81 C&L.623 B.A., J.D. 7271 S. College Ave.
Harvell, Steven Charles '67 '93 C.612 B.A. L.623 J.D. 2727 E. 21st Street
Harvey, Raymond L. '59 '89 C.612 B.S. L.623 J.D. Atty., Citgo Petroleum Corp.
Harward, Amy '71 '97 C.878 B.A. L.94 J.D.
(adm. in MA; not adm. in OK) Atty., The Williams Cos., Inc.
Haskins, Kyle B. '60 '88 C.612 B.S. L.862 J.D. Dist. J.
Haskins, Walter D., P.C., (AV) '56 '80 C.225 B.A. L.378 J.D.
[Atkinson,H.N.B.G.&C.]
Haslam, George D., Jr. '59 '98 C.145 A.B. L.862 J.D. [Haslam,P.]
Haslam Law Firm, The, PLLC 406 S. Boulder, Ste. 450
Hass, Russell Perry, (BV) '50 '80 C.375 B.S. L.862 J.D. Tulsa Co. Courthouse
Hassell, Jeffrey D., (AV) '62 '87 C&L.623 B.B.A., J.D. [Gable&G.]
Hasseman, Dean M. '46 '71
C.588 B.A. L.893 J.D. Sr. Corp. Coun., Citgo Petroleum Corp.
Hastings, J. Christopher '55 '91 C.602 B.B.A. L.862 J.D. 1323 East 71st Street
Hastings, Laurie Lynn '67 '96 C.619 B.S. L.862 J.D. 1408 S. Denver Avenue
Hatfield, Jack K. '22 '54 C.663 B.S. L.616 LL.B. 7060 S. Yale‡
Hathaway, P. Scott, (AV) '64 '89 C.880 B.A. L.802 J.D. [Conner&W.]
Hathcoat, Richard L., (BV) '63 '91 C&L.862 B.S.B.A., J.D. [Ⓐ Richards&C.]
Hatley, Jerry F. '44 '81 C.82 B.A. L.623 J.D. 3836 S. St. Louis
Haugen, Nicholas G. '77 '05 C.340 B.A. L.862 J.D. [Ⓐ LaCourse,D.C.&G.]
Hauger, Leslie S., Jr. '30 '68 C.691 L.862 LL.B. Admin. Law J., Soc. Sec. Admin.
Haughey, Douglas R., (BV) '56 '88 C.338 B.A. L.862 J.D. [Doyle H.D.&H.]
Haugland-Cantrell, Brita, (AV) '62 '87 C.914 B.A. L.623 J.D. [Ⓒ Eldridge C.S.&L.]
Hawkins, Francis G. '17 '55 C.804 A.B. L.862 J.D. 4410 S. Louisville‡

Hawkins, Phillip C., (BV) .... '63 '93 C.1281 B.A. L.862 J.D. [Hawkins]
Hawkins Law Firm, (BV) .... 1800 S. Baltimore Ave., Ste. 1020
Hayes, J. Kevin, (AV) .... '50 '75 C&L.862 B.S., J.D. [Hall,E.H.G.G.&N.]
Haynie, Tony W., (AV) .... '55 '85 C.623 B.A. L.862 J.D. [Conner&W.]

Hays, Kimberly K., (BV) '67 '93 C.612 B.A. L.378 J.D.
248 West 16th Street, 74119-4212
Telephone: 918-592-2800 Fax: 918-592-4143
Email: kimberlyhayslaw@aol.com URL: http://www.divorcelaw-firm.com
Family Law, Divorce, Child Custody, Child Support, Paternity, Visitation Rights.
See Professional Biographies, TULSA, OKLAHOMA

Head, James R., (AV) '28 '57
C.612 B.S.M.E. L.862 LL.B. [Head,J.&K.] (See Pat. Sect.)‡

Head, Johnson & Kachigian, (AV)
228 West 17th Place, Moore Manor, 74119-4694
Telephone: 918-587-2000; 1-800-627-4323 Telefax: 918-587-5603 URL: http://www.lawyers.com/hjklaw
Email: hjklaw.com URL: http://www.hjklaw.com
James R. Head (Retired); Mark G. Kachigian; Allen Bennett.
Domestic and International Patent, Trademark, Copyright and Intellectual Property Law.
See Professional Biographies, TULSA, OKLAHOMA

Heater, Jeffrey A. .... '69 '05 C.836 B.S. L.862 J.D. [A Garrett]
Heath, Steven A., (AV) .... '51 '82 C.352 B.A. L.862 J.D. [Baer,T.C.&C.]
Heaver, Barry A., (BV) .... '41 '75 C.105 A.B. L.862 J.D. 2706 S. 98th E. Ave.
Heckenkemper, Wm. Brad, (AV) .... '— '80 C.612 B.A. L.623 J.D. [A Barrow&G.]
Hedges, H. Ric .... '52 '79 C&L.623 B.B.A., J.D. Pres., Bird Creek Resources Inc.
Hedges, Leslie Joe .... '58 '93 C.377 B.G.S. L.862 J.D. Sr. Corp. Coun., TV Guide, Inc.
Hegenbart, Frederick J., (AV) .... '59 '84 C.350 B.A. L.862 J.D. [Rosenstein,F.&R.]
Heil, John F., III .... '— '94 C.612 B.S. L.862 J.D. [Hall,E.H.G.G.&N.]
Heinen, Steven G., (BV) '65 '91 C.623 B.A. L.309 J.D.
Sr. Atty. & Corp. Coun., WilTel Communications, Legal Dept.
Heister, Jan L. .... '73 '98 C.612 B.A. L.623 J.D. 2278 S. Delaware Court
Helton, Scott R. .... '76 '03 C.613 B.S. L.862 J.D. [B McKinney&S.]
Henderson, Jason M. .... '68 '95 C.623 B.A. L.862 J.D. [A Pierce C.H.B.&G.]
Henderson, Robert '30 '69 C.839 B.S. L.425 J.D.
(adm. in LA; not adm. in OK) P.O. Box 702335
Henke, Frank X., III, (AV) .... '41 '68 C.597 B.A. L.862 J.D. 3449 S. Atlanta Pl.
Henke, Frank X., IV .... '77 '03 C.597 B.A. L.862 J.D. American Bank & Trust
Henry, Jeannie C., (BV) '61 '87
C.623 B.B.A. L.862 J.D. Corp. Atty., Thrifty Rent-A-Car System, Inc.
Henry, Larry D., (AV) .... '46 '70 C&L.352 LL.B. [Boone,S.D.H.&D.]
Henry, R. Paul .... '17 '40 C.69 A.B. L.846 LL.B. 2113 E. 60th St.‡

Henshaw, Todd Maxwell, (AV) '50 '76 C.118 A.B. L.910 J.D.
320 South Boston Suite 1130, 74103
Telephone: 918-583-7500 Fax: 918-583-7542
Email: thenshaw@swbell.net URL: http://www.henshawlaw.com
Bankruptcy, Commercial Litigation and Corporate Law, State and Federal Courts.
See Professional Biographies, TULSA, OKLAHOMA

Herndon, E. McLaine DeWitt .... '75 '05 C&L.862 B.A., J.D. [A Doerner,S.D.&A.] ⊙
Heroux, Christopher S., (AV) .... '58 '86 C.424 A.B. L.862 J.D. [B McKinney&S.]
Herrold, David H., (AV) .... '69 '96 C.846 B.A. L.862 J.D. 100 W. 5th St., Ste. 300
Herrold, Donald E., (AV) .... '40 '66 C.623 B.A. L.862 J.D. 5310 E. 31st Street
Herrold, Jack N., (AV) .... '47 '82 C&L.862 B.A., J.D. 100 W. 5th St., Ste. 300
Hert, Rebecca R. .... '70 '02 L.615 J.D. [A Drummond]
Herwig, Kathryn A., (BV) .... '51 '90 C&L.862 B.S, J.D. [A Clark&W.]
Hess, Cynthia D., (BV) .... '59 '85 C&L.862 B.S.B.A., J.D. [C.D.Hess]
Hess, Forrest B. .... '65 '99 C.612 B.S. L.862 J.D. [A Young]
Hess, Cynthia D., P.C., (BV) .... 5801 East 41st Street - Suite 801
Hickey, Elizabeth '74 '99 C.339 B.A. L.221 J.D.
(adm. in IA; not adm. in OK) 1607 S. Delaware Ave.
Hickey, John M., (AV) .... '56 '85 C.347 B.A. L.862 J.D. [Barber&B.]
Hickman, Frank Robt., (BV) .... '23 '49 C.1027 L.862 LL.B. [Hickman&H.]
Hickman, Steven R., (AV) .... '54 '81 C&L.101 B.S., J.D. [Frasier,F.&H.]
Hickman, William L., (BV) .... '53 '78 C.612 B.S. L.616 J.D. [Hickman&H.]
Hickman & Hickman, (BV) .... 1601 S. Main St.
Hicks, Edward J., III .... '50 '75 C&L.623 B.A., J.D. Spec. Dist. J.
Hicks, James R., (AV) .... '60 '85 C.623 B.B.A. L.862 J.D. [Morrel,W.S.C.&H.]
Hicks, John F. '42 '67 C&L.69 B.A., LL.B.
(adm. in TX; not adm. in OK) Prof. of Law, Univ. of Tulsa
Hiddle, William Joseph .... '54 '81 C&L.862 B.S., J.D. 2840 E. 51st St.
Higginbotham, R. E. .... '11 '38 C.711 L.862 LL.B. 2025 E. 71st St.‡
Higgins, James A. .... '70 '00 C&L.862 B.A., J.D. [A Glendening]
Higham, Elisabeth R. .... '76 '05 C.383 B.A. L.45 J.D. [A Hall,E.H.G.G.&N.]
Hightower, J. Vince, (BV⊙) .... '58 '83 C&L.862 B.S., J.D. 320 South Boston, Suite 1030
Hilborne, Thomas G., Jr., (AV) .... '46 '71 C&L.623 B.B.A., J.D. [Hilborne&W.]
Hilborne & Weidman, A Professional Corporation, (AV) .... 2405 East 57th Street
Hill, Bryce A., Law Offices of, (BV) '59 '85 C.623 B.A. L.862 J.D.
1418 East 71st Street
Hill, Scott .... '41 '80 C.1333 B.S. L.862 J.D. Dir., Contracts, John Zink Company, LLC
Hill, Theresa Noble .... '70 '99 C.039 B.A. L.623 J.D. [A Rhodes,H.J.T.&G.]
Hill, W. Michael, (AV) .... '47 '74 C.69 B.A. L.862 J.D. [Secrest,H.&B.]
Hillis, Clay Rankin, (CV) .... '62 '93 C.1300 B.A. L.623 J.D. [B W.B.Lee]
Hillis, R. Tom, (AV) .... '62 '87 C&L.623 B.B.A., J.D. [Titus H.R.D.&M.]
Hills, Jeffrey T., (BV) .... '64 '91 C.612 B.S. L.862 J.D. [Crowe&D.]
Hilsabeck, Michael D., (AV) .... '52 '80 C.1288 B.A. L.862 J.D. 2615 E. 15th
Hilsher, Gerald L., (AV) .... '53 '79 C.619 B.S. L.846 J.D. [Boone,S.D.H.&D.]
Hinds, Collin McDermitt .... '69 '97 C.378 B.A. L.623 J.D. [Hinds]
Hinds, James M., (AV) .... '43 '68 C.698 A.B. L.862 J.D. [Hinds]
Hinds Law Firm, (AV) .... 1611 S. Denver Ave.
Hinkle, E. Diane .... '52 '91 C.619 B.A. L.862 J.D. [A Richardson,S.R.&W.]
Hinrichs, Chad M. .... '67 '95 C.378 B.S.M.E. L.862 J.D. [A Doerner,S.D.&A.] (Pat.)
Hird, Thomas D., (BV) .... '62 '90 C.1315 B.S. L.623 J.D. [Richards&C.]
Hix, Richard P., (AV) .... '48 '77 C.623 B.A. L.228 J.D. [Doerner,S.D.&A.]
Hixon, Philip D. .... '66 '01 C.1147 B.B.A. L.616 J.D. [A Joyce,P.&M.]
Hixon, Stacie L. .... '74 '02 C.612 B.A. L.862 J.D. [A Atkinson,H.N.B.G.&C.]
Hjelm, Scott Douglas, (BV) .... '67 '94 C.612 B.S. L.862 J.D. 7 S. Houston, Ste. 300
Hjelm, Steven Erik, (BV) .... '64 '98 C.612 B.S. L.862 J.D. 1503 S. Denver
Hobza, Christopher R. '73 '99 C.612 B.A. L.862 J.D.
Mgr. Contracts & Compl., USIS Commercial Services, Inc.
Hodges, James C., (AV) .... '50 '75 C.970 B.A. L.802 J.D. [Eller&D.]
Hodges, P. Jay .... '41 '66 C&L.623 B.B.A., J.D. P.O. Box 3248
Hodgson, Paul R., (AV) .... '24 '63 C.378 B.S. L.862 J.D. [B Morrel,W.S.C.&H.]
Hoffman, Kurt Karl .... '64 '91 C.616 B.S. L.623 J.D. 403 S. Cheyenne, Ste 1200
Hoffman, Richard A., Attorney at Law, (BV) '49 '75
C.367 B.A. L.862 J.D. 1701 S. Boston Ave.

Holden, David W., (AV) '42 '68 C&L.623 B.A., J.D.
4146 S. Birmingham Place, 74105
Telephone: 918-742-3985 Fax: 918-742-4617
Email: dwh@dwhweb.com URL: http://www.dwhweb.com
Business Law, Mergers, Acquisitions and Divestitures, Corporate Law and Securities.
See Professional Biographies, TULSA, OKLAHOMA

Holden, Steven E., (AV) .... '55 '81 C.804 B.S. L.862 J.D. [Holden&C.]

Holden & Carr, (AV) BB
Holden Professional Corporation
200 Reunion Center, 9 East Fourth Street, Suite 200, 74103
Telephone: 918-295-8888 Facsimile: 918-295-8889
Email: hm@holdenokla.com URL: http://www.holden-okla.com
Steven E. Holden; Michael L. Carr;—Robert E. Applegate; Nancy C. Curtis; Derek S.A. Lawrence; Michelle D. Skeens; Rhonda G. Thomas.
Insurance Defense, Medical Malpractice Defense, Nursing Home Defense, Toxic Mold Defense, Casualty Insurance, Commercial Litigation, Banking, Appeals, Coverage Opinions, Labor and Employment Litigation, Contracts.
See Professional Biographies, TULSA, OKLAHOMA

Holder, Randall J., (AV) '53 '79 C&L.616 B.A., J.D.
V.P. & Gen. Coun., Thrifty Rent-A-Car System, Inc.
Holdgrafer, Michael E., (AV) '58 '84 C.352 B.G.S. L.862 J.D.
Corp. Atty., Dollar Thrifty Automotive Group, Inc.
Holeman, Daniel E., (AV) .... '61 '86 C&L.623 B.A., J.D. [Holeman]

Holeman Law Firm, PLLC, (AV) BB
320 South Boston Avenue, Suite 1500, 74103
Telephone: 918-585-2225 Fax: 918-585-2224
Email: dholeman@holemanlaw.com URL: http://www.lawyers.com/dholeman
Daniel E. Holeman.
Civil Litigation in all State and Federal Courts, Certified Mediator.
See Professional Biographies, TULSA, OKLAHOMA

Holladay, Charles R. .... '58 '99 C&L.862 B.S., J.D. [Pray,W.J.W.&M.]
Holland, David P., (BV) .... '38 '64 C&L.862 B.A., J.D. 1504 East 34th St.
Holland, Tom L. .... '38 '71 C.268 B.A. L.862 J.D. [B Nichols,W.S.N.F.&R.]
Holliman, Joe M., (AV) .... '21 '46 C.612 B.A. L.623 LL.B. [Holliman L.&R.]
Holliman Langholz & Runnels, P.C., (AV) .... Ten East Third Street, Suite 400
Hollingsworth, William G. .... '37 '69 C&L.260 B.S.B.A., J.D. Prof. of Law, Univ. of FL.
Holloway, K. Jack, (AV) .... '60 '85 C&L.862 B.S., J.D. [Holloway&M.]
Holloway & Monaghan, (AV) .... 4111 South Darlington, Suite 900
Holmes, Fred H., (BV) .... '57 '96 C.623 B.S.E.E. L.862 J.D. [B Fellers,S.B.B.&T.]
Holmes, M. Jean .... '43 '72 C.483 B.A. L.1529 J.D. 2448 E. 81st Street
Holmes, Richard Kent, (AV) .... '50 '75 C.623 B.A. L.862 J.D. [Hanson&H.]
Holt, Vic E. .... '44 '72 C&L.623 B.A., J.D. 3754 E. 47th Place
Holtmann, Harold L. .... '44 '79 C.619 B.S. L.862 J.D. [H.L.Holtmann]
Holtmann, H. L., Law Office, P.C. .... 5232 E. 69th Place
Holtz, Lloyd K., (BV) .... '33 '66 C.188 B.S. L.862 J.D. 5314 S. Yale Ave.
Honn, Richard C., (AV) .... '34 '63 C&L.862 LL.B. [Secrest,H.&B.]

Hood & Raynolds, P.C., (AV) BB
1914 South Boston, 74119
Telephone: 918-583-5825 Fax: 918-583-6872
Email: info@hoodandraynoldspc.com URL: http://www.hood-raynolds.com
William W. Hood (1941-1999); William F. Raynolds, II.
Matrimonial Law, Family Law, Child Custody, Divorce, Child Support, Litigation, Trials and Appeals.
See Professional Biographies, TULSA, OKLAHOMA

Hooper, Angela Knight '70 '98
C.1142 B.A. L.802 J.D. Sr. Atty., The Williams Cos., Inc.
Hooper, George G., (BV) .... '43 '73 C.840 B.B.A. L.862 J.D. 601 S. Boulder Ave., #400
Hoover, Marilyn K. .... '— '83 C.612 B.A. L.862 J.D. U.S. Army Corp. of Engrs.
Hopkins, Donald G., (AV) .... '31 '58 C.378 B.S. L.623 J.D. 4606 S. Garnett St., Ste. 310
Hoplight, Jacklynn Grace .... '67 '01 C&L.862 B.A., J.D. Joint Dissolution Services
Hopper, Clifford E. .... '26 '65 C&L.862 B.S., J.D. Dist. J.
Hopper, Orlin Woodie .... '35 '60 C&L.862 B.S., LL.B. 3140 S. Winston Ave.
Horkey, W. R., (AV) '25 '50
C.352 B.A. L.623 LL.B. Chairman, Woolslayer Companies, Inc.‡
Horn, R. Steven, (BV) .... '52 '79 C.612 B.S. L.862 J.D. 3701-A S. Harvard Ave., Ste. A
Horton, Johnathan D. .... '76 '01 C.999 B.A. L.40 J.D. [A Doerner,S.D.&A.]
Horton, Rick J., (AV) .... '68 '95 C.69 B.A. L.862 J.D. [Latham,S.W.S.&L.]
Horton, Stephanie A. .... '73 '03 C.862 B.A. L.623 J.D. [A Hall,E.H.G.G.&N.]
Hoskins, Kevin S. .... '66 '96 C.620 B.S. L.862 J.D. [A Gibbs A.B.M.&H.]
Hoster, Craig W., (AV) .... '46 '73 C&L.623 B.B.A., J.D. [Crowe&D.]
Hough, F. Eugene .... '48 '88 C&L.260 B.S.B.A., J.D. 6968 S. Utica Ave.
Houghton, Erik .... '73 '00 C.942 B.A. L.862 J.D. [A Riggs,A.N.T.O.&L.]
Houston, Sondra Fogley, (AV) .... '39 '70 C&L.862 B.A., J.D. [Houston&W.]
Houston and Witt, (AV) .... 502 W. 6th St.
Hove, John N. .... '47 '72 C.862 B.S.B.A. L.802 J.D. [Conner&W.]
Howard, Gene C., (BV) .... '26 '50 C&L.623 LL.B. [Bonham&H.]
Howard, John W. .... '16 '52 C.882 A.B. L.976 J.D. 3156 S. Gary Pl.‡
Howard, Joseph T. .... '57 '92 C.623 B.B.A. L.862 J.D. 111 W. 5th Street
Howard, L. Richard, (BV) .... '45 '70 C&L.900 B.A., J.D. 2431 E. 61st St., Ste. 100
Howard, Oliver S., (AV) .... '45 '79 C.1315 B.A. L.150 J.D. [Gable&G.]
Howard, Robert E. .... '43 '83 C.336 B.S. L.862 J.D. [A Riggs,A.N.T.O.&L.]
Howell, Jason L. .... '76 '01 C.612 B.S. L.623 J.D. [A Kivell,R.&F.]
Howland, Jennifer Hayes .... '56 '83 C.821 B.A. L.1009 J.D. 3171 S. Madison Avenue
Howland, John E., (AV) .... '50 '78 C&L.623 B.A., J.D. [Rosenstein,F.&R.]
Hrbek, Joseph William '48 '84 C.674 A.B. L.1026 J.D.
(adm. in CA; not adm. in OK) 5421 Oak Forest Lane
Huber, James R. .... '68 '93 C.623 B.A. L.862 J.D. 1924 S. Utica
Huckabee, Brian W., (BV) .... '56 '81 C.612 B.A. L.623 J.D. [Huckabee&H.]
Huckabee, Darita DeLoach, (BV) .... '56 '82 C.612 B.S. L.623 J.D. [Huckabee&H.]
Huckabee and Huckabee, Inc., (BV) .... 406 S. Boulder Ave.

Huckaby, Fleming, Greenwood & Olsson, LLP
(See Oklahoma City)

Huckin, William P., Jr., (BV) .... '20 '47 C&L.623 B.A., LL.B. 6706 S. Florence Ave.
Huddleston, Brian R., (BV) .... '60 '88 C.880 B.A. L.45 J.D. [Carr&C.]
Hudgins, R. Carl .... '43 '68 C.612 B.A. L.623 J.D. 6130 E. 81st St.
Hudson, Jean Ann, (AV) .... '63 '89 C.612 B.S. L.623 J.D. Asst. City Atty., Atty. City Off.
Hudspeth, Matthew J., (BV) .... '66 '92 C.802 B.A. L.862 J.D. [Baer,T.C.&C.]
Huffman, Michelle Clarice, (BV) .... '69 '95 C.619 B.A. L.623 J.D. [M.Huffman]
Huffman, Robert A., (AV) .... '21 '52 C&L.37 J.D. 5808 S. Delaware Ave.
Huffman, William H., (AV) .... '55 '82 C.623 B.B.A. L.862 J.D. [Huffman&T.]
Huffman, Michelle, Attorney at Law, (BV) .... 7412 W. 39th St.

Huffman & Thomas, (AV) .... 406 S. Boulder Ave., Ste., 400
Hughes, Kayci Bair .... '74 '99 C&L.623 B.A., J.D. [A Crowe&D.]
Hulett, D. Joel .... '55 '84 C&L.862 B.S.B.A., J.D. [Hulett]
Hulett Law Firm .... 2727 E. 21st Street, Suite 100
Hull, Joseph L., III, (BV) .... '46 '71 C.934 B.A. L.623 J.D. [J.L.Hull]
Hull, Joseph L., Jr., (AV) .... '19 '42 C&L.623 A.B., LL.B. [J.L.Hull]
Hull, Joseph L., A Professional Corporation, (AV) .... 1717 South Cheyenne
Humphreys, R. David, (BV) .... '61 '87 C.1125 B.S. L.862 J.D. [Humphreys W.H.]
Humphreys, Tanya D., (CV) .... '64 '92 C.1125 B.A. L.862 J.D. [Humphreys W.H.]
Humphreys Wallace Humphreys, P.C., (BV) .... 1724 E. 15th St.
Humphries, Tommy W. .... '73 '01 C.1147 B.A. L.862 J.D. [A Stipe,H.L.U.E.&B.]
Hunt, Kenneth L., (AV) .... '55 '81 C&L.101 B.S., J.D. [Hall,E.H.G.G.&N.]
Hunter, Carolyn R. .... '60 '99 C.612 B.S. L.862 J.D. Wiltel
Hunter, Rebecca W. .... '76 '02 C.862 B.S.B.A. L.623 J.D. [A Eller&D.]
Huntsman, Susan E. .... '73 '99 C.45 B.A. L.309 J.D. [A Crowe&D.]
Hurley, Alissa A. .... '77 '02 C&L.862 B.A., J.D. [A Conner&W.]
Hurst, Edwin S., (AV) .... '19 '42 C&L.623 A.B., LL.B. [C Boone,S.D.H.&D.]
Hutchison, A. Colleen .... '43 '79 C&L.862 B.S., J.D. 5639 S. Winston Ave.
Hutchison, Dan C. ....'50 '76 C&L.862 B.A., J.D. 3101 Charles Page Blvd., Ste. 101
Hyman, David J., (AV) .... '52 '81 C.880 B.A. L.192 J.D. [Sneed L.]
Iandiorio, David L. ....'70 '01 C.1374 B.S. L.1218 J.D. [A Doerner,S.D.&A.] (Pat.)
Ikenberry, D. Kevin, (BV) .... '54 '83 C&L.1288 B.A., J.D. [Andrew,W.&I.]
Imel, John M., (AV) .... '32 '59 C&L.623 B.S., J.D. [Moyers,M.S.I.&T.]
Inbody, Brian T., (AV) .... '64 '90 C&L.623 B.B.A., J.D. [Sneed L.]
Ingle, J. Derek, (BV) .... '67 '95 C&L.862 B.S.B.A., J.D. 4111 S. Darlington, Ste. 1050
Ingraham, John W., (AV) .... '48 '76 C.918 B.A. L.262 J.D. [Conner&W.]
Ingram, R. Carl .... '46 '89 C.619 B.S. L.862 J.D. Sun Refining & Mktg. Co.
Inhofe, Douglas L., (AV) .... '46 '71 C.623 B.A. L.188 J.D. [Sneed L.]
Inhofe, Katy Day, (AV) .... '65 '92 C.910 B.A. L.862 J.D. [A Conner&W.]
Inman, Gerri Anne .... '57 '98 C.1362 B.B.A. L.862 J.D. [G.A.Inman]
Inman, Gerri Anne, LLC .... 1719 E. 71st St.
Insabella, John, (BV) ...... '49 '75 C.755 B.A. L.616 J.D. 2815 E. Skelly Drive, Suite 818
Iola, Mark H., (AV) .... '58 '82 C.276 B.A. L.623 J.D. [Stanley,M.&I.] (⊙Dallas, TX)
Iola, Randall L., (AV) .... '64 '89 C.659 B.A. L.623 J.D. [C Stanley,M.&I.]
Isbell, Jed W. .... '75 '04 C.612 B.S. L.862 J.D. [A Conner&W.]
Iski, David Thomas, (BV) '51 '88
C&L.862 B.A., J.D. Asst. Dist. Atty., Tulsa Co. Dist. Atty. Off.
Iwata, Jere D. ....'47 '77 C.768 B.A. L.862 J.D. Liberty Bk. & Tr. Co. of Tulsa, N.A.
Jack, Tara K. .... '73 '01 C.619 B.A. L.616 J.D. Tulas Co. Dist. Atty.
Jackere, Alan L., (AV) '44 '71 C&L.623 B.A., J.D.
Sr. Asst. City Atty. & Mgr. Real Prop. Div., City Attys. Off.
Jackson, Betsy Grabel, (AV) ...... '65 '91 C.802 B.B.A. L.862 J.D. [Hall,E.H.G.G.&N.]
Jackson, Bradley A., (BV) .... '67 '92 C.612 B.S. L.862 J.D. [Rhodes,H.J.T.&G.]
Jackson, Gary L. .... '47 '75 C.612 B.S. L.623 J.D. 6928 S. 32nd W. Ave.
Jackson, Gerald L., (BV) .... '64 '90 C.804 B.S. L.862 J.D. [A Crowe&D.]
Jacobs, C. W. Daimon .... '47 '91 C.1362 B.A. L.623 J.D. 406 S. Boulder Ave., Ste. 450
Jacobson, Russell M., Jr. .... '61 '91 C.612 B.S. L.862 J.D. [A Latham,S.W.S.&L.]
Jacobus, D. Wm., Jr., (AV) .... '35 '59 C.623 B.A. L.862 LL.B. [Jacobus&Assoc.]
Jacobus & Associates, (AV) .... 1508 S. Carson Ave.
James, Bart C., (BV) .... '53 '77 C&L.802 B.B.A., J.D. 8908 S. Yale Ave.
James, Bob D., (BV) .... '65 '92 C&L.623 B.S., J.D. [A Best&S.]
James, David F., (AV) .... '40 '64 C&L.862 B.S.B.A., LL.B. [C James,P.&W.]
James, E. Carleton, (AV) .... '32 '74 C.623 B.S. L.862 J.D. [Lang,J.&W.]
James, Robert D., (AV) .... '68 '95 C&L.45 B.S.B.A., J.D. [Conner&W.]

James, Potts and Wulfers, Inc., (AV) BB
Suite 2600, Mid-Continent Tower, 401 South Boston Avenue, 74103-4015
Telephone: 918-584-0881 Fax: 918-584-4521
URL: http://www.jpwlaw.com
Thomas G. Potts; David W. Wulfers;—Cornelius P. Dukelow. Of Counsel: David F. James; Pamela K. Wheeler-Norberg.
General Practice. Trial and Appellate Practice in Federal and State Courts, including Defense of Criminal and Civil State and Federal Tax Claims. Commercial Law, Commercial Litigation, Business Law, Corporation Law and Planning, Financial Institutions, Real Estate, Oil and Gas, Estate Planning, Trust Planning, Wealth Transfer Planning, Probate, Administrative and Tax Law.
See Professional Biographies, TULSA, OKLAHOMA

Jarboe, John B., (AV) .... '40 '65 C.623 B.A. L.862 J.D. [Jarboe&S.]

Jarboe & Stoermer, A Professional Corporation, (AV)
18th Floor, Mid-Continent Tower, 401 South Boston, Suite 1810, 74103
Telephone: 918-582-6131 Fax: 918-584-4213
John B. Jarboe; Jeffrey D. Stoermer. Associate: F. Bennett Callicoat. Of Counsel: Theodore P. Gibson.
General Civil and Federal Practice. Antitrust, Bankruptcy and Reorganization, Corporate, Private and Public Contract, State and Federal Taxation, Tax Controversies, Estate Planning and Probate Law, Wills, Trusts, Business Organizations and Formation, State and Federal Administrative Law, Water Law, Real Estate, Commercial Litigation, Asset Protection.
Reference: American Bank & Trust.
See Professional Biographies, TULSA, OKLAHOMA

Jarvis, Sandra G. .... '59 '90 C.623 B.B.A. L.862 J.D. Staff Atty., Ct. of App.
Jayne, Andrew C. .... '76 '02 C.934 B.A. L.623 J.D. [A Atkinson,H.N.B.G.&C.]
Jeffers, Dalinda J. .... '— '91 C&L.862 B.A. [A Stauffer,G.&N.]
Jeka, Eugene J. '46 '71 C&L.424 B.A., J.D.
(adm. in IL; not adm. in OK) Gen. Coun., UNO-VEN Co.
Jenkins, James Patrick .... '53 '95 C.999 B.S. L.862 J.D. Laufen USA
Jennings, Mark B., (BV) .... '54 '83 C.612 B.S. L.45 J.D. [Brewster&D.]
Jeter, Jo Lynn .... '79 '04 C.612 B.S. L.623 J.D. [A Norman W.C.&D.]
Jimerson, Carlye O., (BV) .... '57 '97 C.612 B.S. L.862 J.D. [A Rhodes,H.J.T.&G.]
Johnsen, Roy D., (AV) .... '41 '67 C.612 B.S. L.862 J.D. [Epperson&J.]
Johnson, Blake Allen .... '62 '93 C.623 B.S.A. L.862 J.D. [B.A.Johnson]
Johnson, Brent '64 '91 C&L.846 B.A., J.D.
(adm. in TX; not adm. in OK) 7121 S. College Ave.
Johnson, Candace Merifield .... '65 '92 C.378 B.A. L.862 J.D. State Ins. Fund
Johnson, Cornelius R. .... '63 '96 C.840 B.S. L.862 J.D. 200 Civic Center
Johnson, Curtis Marland, Jr. '60 '92
C.623 B.S. L.862 J.D. Admin. Law J., OK Corp. Com.
Johnson, David A., (AV) .... '44 '69 C&L.623 B.A., J.D. [Boesche M.]
Johnson, Denise, (BV) .... '52 '81 C&L.862 B.S., J.D. P.O. Box 8533
Johnson, E. Andrew .... '69 '95 C.612 B.S. L.623 J.D. [Johnson,J.D.C.&S.]
Johnson, J. Richard, Jr., (BV) ... '44 '73 C.623 B.B.A. L.862 J.D. 717 South Houston Ave.
Johnson, James D., (BV) '50 '87
C.351 B.A. L.616 J.D. Coun., Mid-Continent Casualty Company
Johnson, Jennifer A. .... '— '03 C&L.862 B.A., J.D. [A Perrine,M.R.R.B.&T.]
Johnson, John B., Jr., (AV) .... '33 '57 C&L.623 B.B.A., J.D. [Johnson,J.D.C.&S.]
Johnson, Kendall W., (BV) .... '60 '94 C.1288 B.S. L.862 J.D. [K.W.Johnson]
Johnson, Lawrence A. G., (BV) .... '32 '58 C.902 B.S. L.623 LL.B. 2535 E. 21st St.
Johnson, N. Scott, (AV) .... '66 '92 C.612 B.S. L.862 J.D. [Sneed L.]

Johnson, Paul H., (AV) .... '26 '57 C.612 B.S.E.E. L.862 LL.B. [C Gable&G.] (Pat.)
Johnson, Wesley E., (BV) .... '42 '77 C.205 B.A. L.862 J.D. 125 West 15th
Johnson, Blake A., LPA .... 2616 E. 66th Place

Johnson, Jones, Dornblaser, Coffman & Shorb, (AV)
A Professional Corporation
2200 Bank of America Center, 15 West Sixth Street, 74119-5416
Telephone: 918-584-6644 Fax: 918-584-6645
W. Thomas Coffman; Kenneth E. Dornblaser; E. Andrew Johnson; John B. Johnson, Jr.; C. Robert Jones; Randy R. Shorb;—Jesse N. Bomer. Of Counsel: Richard D. Jones; Paul D. Kingsolver; Diana H. Clark.
General Practice of Business Law with emphasis on Business Organizations, Business and Commercial Transactions and Planning, Non-Profit and Professional Corporations, Securities Law, Federal, State and Local Taxation, Tax Controversies, Health Law, Municipal Finance, Tax Exempt Bonds, Governmental Law, Real Estate, Estate Planning, Probate and Trust Administration.
See Professional Biographies, TULSA, OKLAHOMA

Johnson, Kendall W., P.C., (BV)
601 South Boulder, Suite 600, 74119
Telephone: 918-583-9000 Fax: 918-585-1079
Email: kwjohnson4@sbcglobal.net URL: http://www.kwjohnsonlaw.com
Kendall W. Johnson.
Family Law, Divorce, Child Custody, Child Support, Spousal Support, Personal Injury, Auto Accidents, Wrongful Death, Estate Planning, Wills, Trusts, Probate, Bankruptcy, Criminal Law, Driving While Intoxicated, Driving Under the Influence, Traffic Violations, Garnerships, Adoptions, Business Law, Entertainment Law.
See Professional Biographies, TULSA, OKLAHOMA

Johnston, Eric O. .... '71 '97 C&L.623 B.A., J.D. Asst. Dist. Atty.
Johnstone, Deborah .... '— '98 C&L.623 B.A., J.D. [A Riggs,A.N.T.O.&L.]
Jones, Annabel M., (AV) '53 '79
C&L.623 B.A., J.D. Asst. Gen. Coun., Samson Investment Co.
Jones, Bert M., (AV) .... '32 '59 C&L.623 B.A., LL.B. [Rhodes,H.J.T.&G.]
Jones, C. Bruce, (AV) .... '49 '76 C.612 B.A. L.623 J.D. [C Pray,W.J.W.&M.]
Jones, C. Robert, (AV) .... '36 '61 C.612 B.S. L.623 J.D. [Johnson,J.D.C.&S.]
Jones, David M. .... '42 '83 C.623 B.S. L.862 J.D. Realty Splst
Jones, Jack D. .... '25 '55 C.871 B.S. L.862 LL.B. 3413 E. 58th Pl.‡
Jones, Jas. K. .... '24 '49 C&L.623 B.A., J.D. P.O. Box 702100
Jones, Jeri L. .... '67 '98 C.612 B.S. L.862 J.D. [A Stipe,H.L.U.E.&B.]
Jones, Kiemonn .... '— '01 C.999 B.A. L.623 J.D. [A Riggs,A.N.T.O.&L.]
Jones, Michael S. .... '66 '94 C.612 B.S. L.862 J.D. 4143 E. 31st St.
Jones, Nancy Hanania, (BV) .... '56 '81 C.509 B.A. L.862 J.D. [Barber&B.]
Jones, Nik, (AV) .... '49 '74 C.612 B.A. L.862 J.D. 902 S. Boulder Ave.
Jones, Randolph L., Jr., (AV) '47 '74
C&L.494 B.A., J.D. [Conner&W.] (⊙Jackson, WY)
Jones, Richard D., (AV) .... '39 '64 C.612 B.S. L.623 J.D. [C Johnson,J.D.C.&S.]
Jones, Robert E. .... '23 '58 C.45 B.S.B.A. L.862 LL.B. [Casey&J.] ‡
Jones, Ronald L. .... '42 '73 C.340 B.A. L.61 J.D. [C Hall,E.H.G.G.&N.]
Jones, S. Frank .... '22 '50 C.839 B.A. L.69 LL.B. 2619 E. 73rd Street‡
Jones, Sharon Cole .... '69 '99 C.999 B.A. L.862 J.D. [S.C.Jones]
Jones, Susan H. .... '64 '89 C&L.862 B.A., J.D. 5810 E. Skelly Dr.‡
Jones, William B., (AV) .... '25 '51 C.575 L.623 LL.B. [Jones,G.&B.]
Jones, Wilson, (BV) .... '46 '76 C&L.862 B.S., J.D. [W.Jones]

Jones, Gotcher & Bogan, A Professional Corporation, (AV) BB
3800 First Place Tower, 74103
Telephone: 918-581-8200 Fax: 918-583-1189 or 918-583-6652
URL: http://www.jonesgivens.com
Deryl Lee Gotcher (1922-2001); Neil E. Bogan (1945-1990); William B. Jones; James E. Weger; Thomas L. Vogt; Jack L. Brown; William G. LaSorsa; C. Michael Copeland; Robert R. Peters II; Michael Alan Joyce;—Adam J. Strange. Of Counsel: John W. Cannon.
General Civil Practice and Appeals before all State and Federal Courts. Corporate, Banking, Administrative, Bankruptcy, Probate, Employment Law, Insurance, Real Estate, Construction, Zoning, Oil and Gas, Family, Employee Relations, Communications, Trademark, Copyright, Environmental, E-Commerce and Estate Planning Law.
Representative Clients: Local America Bank of Tulsa; Tulsa National Bank; BancOklahoma Mortgage Corporation; Kansas City Life Insurance Company; Liberty Mortgage Company; Clear Channel Communications; Tulsa Community College; BankOne N.A.; Professional Services: KPMG, Peat Marwick; Williams Bros. Engineering.
See Professional Biographies, TULSA, OKLAHOMA

Jones, Sharon Cole, P.L.L.C. .... 624 E. Archer
Jones, Wilson, P.C., (BV) .... 5810 E. Skelly Dr.
Jordan, Eric M., (BV) .... '68 '97 C.802 B.A. L.862 J.D. [A Rodolf&T.]
Jorgenson, Anthony J. .... '71 '96 C.350 B.B.A. L.623 J.D. [Hall,E.H.G.G.&N.]
Jorgenson, J. David, (AV) .... '53 '78 C.613 B.A. L.846 J.D. [C Pinkerton&F.]
Jorgenson, Jandra Susanne .... '70 '96 C.612 B.S. L.623 J.D. Premier Legal Res.
Joyce, J. C., (AV) .... '40 '66 C.612 B.A. L.862 J.D. [Joyce&P.]
Joyce, John C. .... '66 '93 C.859 B.A. L.862 J.D. [A Joyce&P.]
Joyce, Kevin B. .... '77 '04 C.174 B.A. L.862 J.D. [A Joyce&P.]
Joyce, Michael Alan .... '62 '87 C&L.862 B.S.B.A., J.D. [Jones,G.&B.]
Joyce, Robert J., (AV) .... '58 '88 C&L.862 B.S., J.D. [Joyce,P.&M.]

Joyce, Paul & McDaniel, P.C., (AV)
200 Mapco Plaza, 1717 South Boulder Avenue, 74119-4833
Telephone: 918-599-0700 Facsimile: 918-732-5370
URL: http://www.jpm-law.com
Robert J. Joyce; Chris A. Paul; A. Scott McDaniel;—Stacy L. Acord; Nicole M. Longwell; Philip D. Hixon; Martin Allen Brown; David M. vonHartitzsch.
Administrative Law, Class Actions, Commercial Law, Construction Law, Contracts, Eminent Domain, Energy, Environmental Law, Labor and Employment, Litigation, Mergers, Acquisitions and Divestitures, Natural Resources, Oil and Gas Transportation, Natural Gas Pipelines, Hazardous Materials Transportation, Occupational Safety and Health, Real Estate, Regulatory Law, Torts, Transportation, Immigration and Nationality Law.
See Professional Biographies, TULSA, OKLAHOMA

Joyce and Pollard, (AV) BB
515 South Main Street, Suite 300, 74103-4475
Telephone: 918-585-2751 Fax: 918-582-9308
Email: contact@joycepollard.com URL: http://www.joycepollard.com
Dwayne C. Pollard (1939-1999); J. C. Joyce;—Ted J. Nelson; John C. Joyce; Michael A. Pollard; Mark K. Graddy; Kevin B. Joyce; Catherine J. Graddy.
Litigation, Trials, Appeals, Estate and Gift Taxation, Corporate Law, Business Law, Real Estate, Estate Planning, Wills and Probate, Trusts and Estates, First Amendment Law, Constitutional Law, Tax Exempt Organizations, Nonprofit and Charitable Organizations, Religious Ministries, Church Law.
Representative Clients: Furnished Upon Request.
See Professional Biographies, TULSA, OKLAHOMA

Joyner, Elizabeth A., (AV) '61 '92
C.1300 B.A. L.862 J.D. Sr. Atty., The Williams Companies, Inc.
Joyner, Samuel, III .... '41 '66 C.273 A.B. L.623 J.D. U.S. Mag. J.
Justice, George A., Jr. .... '53 '82 C&L.623 B.Acct., J.D. Univ. of Tulsa Coll. of Law
Kachigian, Mark G., (AV) '— '78 C.693 B.S. L.862 J.D.
[Head,J.&K.] (See Pat. Sect.)
Kaiser, Curtis W., (BV) .... '47 '82 C.1060 B.A. L.862 J.D. [Layon,C.&K.]

Kalbfleisch, Jolie H. ....'39 '77 C.623 B.A. L.862 J.D. 7102 E. 101st St.
Kallenberger, Paul E. .... '45 '70 C.623 B.B.A. L.862 J.D. Sr. V.P., Trust Co. of Okla.
Kallsnick, Richard J. ....'43 '71 C&L.623 B.S., J.D. U.S. Admin. Law J., Soc. Sec. Admn.
Kane, Paul A., (BV) ....'66 '92 C.602 B.A. L.623 J.D. [Eller&D.]

Kania, Charles J., Law Offices of '59 '05 C.612 B.S. L.862 J.D.
4860 South Lewis Avenue, Suite 105, 74105
Telephone: 918-743-2233 Fax: 918-743-2244
Email: cjkania@cox.net URL: http://www.lawyers.com/charleskania
General Practice, Criminal Law, Personal Injury, Family Law, Business Law.
See Professional Biographies, TULSA, OKLAHOMA

Kastner, Lori Moon ....'63 '92 C&L.862 B.S.B.A., J.D. OK Ct. of Civil App.
Kaufman, Ronald C., (BV) ....'69 '97 C.1113 B.A. L.862 J.D. [Kaufman&Assoc.]
Kaufman & Associates, (BV) .... 624 South Boston Avenue, Suite 1070
Keele, Garry L., II ....'65 '94 C.623 B.B.A. L.862 J.D. [Ⓒ McKinney&S.]
Keele, Leah P. ....'65 '94 C.619 B.S. L.862 J.D. [Pierce C.H.B.&G.]
Keesling, David Royce ....'70 '98 C.804 B.A. L.862 J.D. [D.Keesling]
Keesling, Dave .... 601 S. Boulder, Suite 704
Keester, Michael T., (AV) ....'59 '84 C&L.623 B.A., J.D. [Hall,E.H.G.G.&N.]
Keglovits, David E., (AV) ....'63 '90 C.602 B.B.A. L.846 J.D. [Gable&G.]
Keil, John S. ....'34 '70 C&L.862 B.S.B.A., J.D. Getty Oil Co.
Keith, Scott David, Law Office of '52 '78 C.612 B.S. L.862 J.D.
1515 S. Denver Avenue
Keller, Vickie D. .... '57 '88 C.815 B.A. L.862 J.D. Legal Servs. of Eastern OK Inc.
Kelley, Kevin R., Law Offices of, (BV) .... '61 '86 C.612 B.S. L.862 J.D. 1861 E. 15th St.
Kellough, William C., (AV) ....'49 '75 C&L.846 B.A., J.D. [Boone,S.D.H.&D.]
Kelsey, Darrel A., (AV) ....'38 '63 C.1182 A.B. L.900 J.D. 1916 E. 58th
Kelson, John W., (BV) .... '47 '79 C.1147 B.A. L.616 J.D. [Ⓒ Richards&C.]
Kempfert, Amy E., (AV) ....'50 '81 C.963 B.S. L.862 J.D. [Best&S.]
Kendrick, Bert M. .... '61 '87 C.621 B.S. L.623 J.D. P.O. Box 4630
Kennedy, Kurt M., Attorney at Law, (BV) '57 '82
C.16 B.A. L.862 J.D. 7912 E. 31st Ct., Ste. 110
Kern, Jennifer K. .... '— '03 C.1079 B.A. L.862 J.D. [Ⓐ Newton,O.T.&K.]
Kern, Terence C. .... '44 '69 C.612 B.S. L.623 J.D. Chf. J., U.S. Dist. Ct.
Kernan, Patrick H., (AV) .... '48 '75 C.612 B.S. L.616 J.D. [McKinney&S.]
Ketchum, Daniel R., II, (BV) ....'64 '93 C.612 B.S. L.623 J.D. [Newton,O.T.&K.]
Kihle, Donald A., (AV) .... '34 '67 C.585 B.S. L.623 J.D. [Ⓒ Gable&G.]
Kimery, Brenda Gail '53 '98 C&L.862 B.A., J.D.
Dom. Violence Intervention Servs., Inc.
Kincaid, James L., (AV) ....'36 '61 C&L.309 A.B., LL.B. [Crowe&D.]
Kindell, Kathryn J. .... '54 '01 C.619 B.S. L.862 J.D. [Ⓐ Conner&W.]
King, Alexander F., (BV) .... '71 '98 C.378 B.A. L.276 J.D. [Ⓐ Crowe&D.]
King, Dennis D., (AV) .... '48 '79 C.927 B.A. L.862 J.D. [King,T.&R.]
King, Jeffrey A., (AV) ....'46 '72 C.934 B.A. L.623 J.D. [Lawson,K.&S.]
King, Michael J., (AV) .... '56 '82 C.845 B.A. L.1288 J.D. 2448 E. 81st, Ste. 5900
King, Nicole A. .... '73 '00 C&L.862 B.S.B.A., J.D. [Ⓐ Lyons&C.]

King, Taylor & Ryan, P.C., (AV)
Boulder Towers, Suite 850, West Tower 1437 South Boulder, 74119
Telephone: 918-749-5566 FAX: 918-749-9531
Email: ktr@kingtaylorryan.com
Dennis D. King; Robert H. Taylor; James M. Scott Ryan; Melissa Minton Schmidt; Neil D. Van Dalsem;—Ashley M. Bibb; Ryan C. Harper; Wendy J. Brame.
General Civil Practice in all Courts. Insurance Defense, Civil Litigation, Workers Compensation, Corporate, Products Liability, Personal Injury Law and Appellate Practice.

Kingsolver, Paul D., (BV) ....'58 '83 C&L.862 B.S., J.D. [Ⓒ Johnson,J.D.C.&S.]
Kinsey, Leah McCaslin, (BV) ....'70 '95 C.388 B.A. L.862 J.D. [Ⓐ Paul]
Kirby, Thomas J., (AV) ....'51 '76 C&L.623 B.A., J.D. [Gable&G.]
Kirk, Chad Micah ....'75 '01 C.612 B.S. L.623 J.D. [Ⓐ Wilson,C.&A.]
Kirk, Melinda L. ....'64 '01 C&L.862 B.S., J.D. [Ⓐ Conner&W.]
Kirkland, Connie Lee, (AV) '56 '90
C.622 B.S. L.862 J.D. Asst. Gen. Coun., The Williams Cos., Inc.
Kirkley, Douglas A., (BV) .... '62 '92 C.618 B.A. L.615 J.D. [Ⓐ Boettcher,R.M.&B.]
Kirkpatrick, Neal, (BVⓉ) '49 '74 C.623 B.A. L.45 J.D.
(adm. in AR; not adm. in OK) 333 West 4th, 3460 U.S. Courthouse
Kirt, Christopher J. ....'70 '00 C.859 B.B.A. L.623 J.D. [Ⓐ Crowe&D.]
Kirtley, Scott P., (AV) .... '58 '85 C.612 B.S. L.1288 J.D. [Riggs,A.N.T.O.&L.]
Kivell, Thomas D., (AV) .... '48 '76 C.475 B.A. L.862 J.D. [Kivell,R.&F.]

Kivell, Rayment and Francis, P.C., (AV)
Suite 240, Triad Center One, 7666 East 61st Street, 74133
Telephone: 918-254-0626 Fax: 918-254-7915
Email: tkivell@kivell.com URL: http://www.kivell.com
Thomas D. Kivell; Brian J. Rayment; Joe B. Francis;—Karen M. Funk; Jeffrey Darin Lower; Jason L. Howell; Amy Elizabeth Collins; Teddi Lewis Allen; Michael W. McCoy; A. Grant Schwabe; Shannon Taylor.
General Civil Trial Practice. Commercial and Residential Real Estate, Corporations, Partnerships, Estate Planning, Bankruptcy, Mortgage Foreclosure, and Automobile Finance Law.
Representative Client: GMAC Mortgage Corporation of Iowa.
References: Triad Bank, N.A.; Bank of Oklahoma; Bank IV.
See Professional Biographies, TULSA, OKLAHOMA

Klein, Allen ....'31 '75 C.645 B.S. L.862 J.D. Spec. Dist. J.

Klenda, Thomas M., (AV) '55 '80 C.612 B.S. L.862 J.D.
15 East 5th Street, Suite 3900, 74103-4306
Telephone: 918-587-9191 Fax: 918-587-3064 URL: http://www.tmklaw.com
Email: tklenda@shapexpress.com URL: http://www.lawyers.com/tmklaw
Corporate, Business Transactions, Estate and Business Planning, Wills, Trust Law, Franchises, Real Estate, Probate and Commercial Litigation.
Representative Franchise Clients: Ron's Hamburgers & Chili, Inc.; ShapeXpress, Inc.
See Professional Biographies, TULSA, OKLAHOMA

Klinzing, Robert J. ....'29 '61 C&L.862 B.S., LL.B. 7806 S. 66th E. Avenue
Kneafsey, John G. ....'32 '59 C&L.884 A.B., J.D. 6941 S. Birmingham Pl.
Knight, Chris L., (BV) .... '60 '85 C&L.1288 B.A., J.D. [Knight,C.L.]
Knight, Chris L., P.C., (BV) ....1418 East 71st Street
Knorr, Stephen J., (AV) '51 '79 C.276 B.S. L.597 J.D.
(adm. in IL; not adm. in OK) Fed. Pub. Def.
Knudson, Maureen J. ....'53 '83 C.381 B.A. L.862 J.D. 1150 E. 61st St.
Kobbeman, Kerrilee E. ....'75 '05 C.467 B.S. L.45 J.D. [Ⓐ Conner&W.]
Kobos, Steven M., (AV) ....'65 '90 C&L.623 B.A., J.D. [Ⓐ F.Dorwart]
Koepsel, Kristopher .... '— '01 C.388 B.A. L.862 J.D. [Ⓐ Riggs,A.N.T.O.&L.]
Kohler, Thomas Wayne '52 '88 C.619 B.A. L.862 J.D.
Staff Atty., Oklahoma Disability Law Center, Inc.
Kole, Karen V. '54 '81 C.800 B.S. L.597 J.D.
(adm. in IL; not adm. in OK) Prof., Univ. of Tulsa College of Law
Koller, A. Laurie ....'65 '91 C&L.228 B.A., J.D. [Carr&C.]
Kollmorgen, Terry M., (AV) ....'64 '89 C&L.623 B.B.A., J.D. [Moyers,M.S.I.&T.]
Korens, Joel A., (CV) ....'60 '89 C.260 B.A. L.862 J.D. 6968 S. Utica

Kornfeld Franklin Renegar & Randall, A Professional Corporation
(See Oklahoma City)

Kraft, Michael A. ....'60 '89 C&L.862 B.A., J.D. P.O. Box 472023
Kramer, Dan R., (BV) ....'46 '74 C&L.862 B.A., J.D. 1408 S. Denver
Kriete, Vance R. ....'41 '65 C&L.862 B.S., J.D. 2919 E. 28th St.
Kroblin, Lucy S. ....'47 '87 C.741 B.A.Soc. L.862 J.D. [Ⓒ Francy]
Kroll, Russell W., (AV) ....'59 '92 C&L.862 B.S., J.D. [Doerner,S.D.&A.]
Kronfeld, Edwin, (AV) ....'31 '59 C&L.309 LL.B. Pres., Plymouth Resources, Inc.
Kruger, Joel L., (BV) ....'55 '82 C.620 B.A. L.862 J.D. [Kruger&Assoc.]
Kruger & Associates, P.C., (BV) .... 8816 S. Sheridan Road
Kulp, Linda McQuillen, (AV) ....'44 '69 C&L.623 B.S., J.D. [Ⓒ Boesche M.]
Kulp, Victor K., (BV) '43 '68 C&L.862 B.S.B.A., J.D.
Sr. Atty. Advisor, Soc. Sec. Admin.
Kumpe, Billy Eugene ....'49 '00 C.619 B.S. L.862 J.D. [B.Kumpe]
Kumpe, Billy, Attorney at Law ....406 S. Boulder, Ste. 400
Kunkel, Andrea R., (BV) .... '61 '86 C&L.862 B.A., J.D. [Rosenstein,F.&R.]
Kunkel, Elmer M. .... '24 '60 C.237 B.S. L.862 LL.B. 1619 E. 62nd St.
Kupetsky, Adam L. '66 '92 C.264 B.A. L.569 J.D.
(adm. in NY; not adm. in OK) Dir. of Regulatory, WilTel Comm.
Kurtz, Edward T. .... '42 '68 C.623 B.B.A. L.862 J.D. 2758 E. 44th Pl‡
Kutmas, Chad J. ....'75 '02 C.45 B.A. L.862 J.D. [Ⓐ Doerner,S.D.&A.] ⊙
Kyle, Philip W., (AV) ....'37 '63 C&L.623 B.B.A., LL.B. 1918 E. 51st St.
LaCourse, Joel A., (BV) ....'62 '96 C.1288 B.S. L.1339 J.D. [LaCourse,D.C.&G.]

LaCourse, Davis, Coffey & Gudgel, P.L.C., (AV)
2250 East 73rd Street, Suite 600, 74136
Telephone: 918-744-7100 Fax: 918-477-2299 URL: http://www.lacoursedavis.com
Email: administrator@lacoursedavis.com URL: http://www.lacourse-davis.com
Joel A. LaCourse; J. Christopher Davis; Robert P. Coffey, Jr.; Tom H. Gudgel, III. Associates: David A. Guten; Nicholas G. Haugen.
General Civil Trial Practice including Commercial Litigation, Business Transactions, Corporate Law, Wills and Trusts, Estate Planning, Securities Offerings, Employment Law, Insurance Defense, Family Law, Divorce, Commercial Transportation, Products Liability, Nursing Home Litigation.
See Professional Biographies, TULSA, OKLAHOMA

Ladd, B. Ernest ....'34 '69 C.1147 B.S. L.862 J.D. [B.E.Ladd]
Ladd, Bill E. ....3223 E. 31st, Ste. 101
Ladner, John A., (AV) .... '28 '56 C.862 B.A. L.623 LL.B. 2512 S. Columbia Ave.‡
Ladner, Thomas M., (AV) ....'55 '81 C&L.734 A.B., J.D. [Norman W.C.&D.]
LaFevers, J. Gregory, (AV) .... '58 '84 C&L.862 B.S., J.D. 5314 South Yale Avenue
LaFortune, William D., (AV) ....'57 '86 C.112 B.A. L.862 J.D. Mayor
Lair, Eric G., (CV) ....'66 '95 C.613 B.B.A. L.862 J.D. [E.G.Lair]
Lair, Montgomery Loyd ....'72 '97 C.613 B.A. L.862 J.D. [Brewster&D.]
Lair, Eric G., pllc, Law Offices of, (CV) .... 320 S. Boston Ave., Ste. 1130
Laizure, Anthony M., (AV) ....'55 '80 C&L.623 B.S., J.D. [Stipe,H.L.U.E.&B.]
Lake, Stephen W., (AV) ....'63 '91 C.880 B.A. L.623 J.D. [Gable&G.]
Lamb, James M., (BV) ....'44 '79 C.623 B.S. L.862 J.D. [Lamb]
Lamb, Patricia A., (BV) ....'45 '82 C.623 B.A. L.862 J.D. [Lamb]
Lamb Law Firm, P.C., (BV) ....1408 S. Denver Ave.
Lambert, James M. ....'35 '63 C.612 B.A. L.623 LL.B. 3147 S. Zunis Ave.
Lamkin, Rita J., (BV) ....'48 '80 C.619 B.S. L.862 J.D. 1640 S. Boston Ave.
Lamprich, Julie E., (AV) '51 '76
C&L.862 B.A., J.D. Assoc. Gen. Coun., Guaranty Abstract Co.
Lander, Larry D. ....'47 '92 C.352 B.S. L.862 J.D. 6132 E. 61st. St.
Lander, Melanie D. ....'73 '02 C&L.862 B.A., J.D. [Ⓐ Edge]
Landers, David S., (BV) '62 '87
C.947 B.A. L.862 J.D. Sr. Trial Atty., Farmers Insurance Company
Lane, Stanford C., (BV) ....'58 '87 C.612 B.S. L.862 J.D. Asst. Pub. Def.
Lanford, Annelle S. ....'27 '57 C.623 B.A. L.846 LL.B. 2651 E. 21st St.
Lang, James C., (AV) ....'40 '64 C&L.862 B.A., J.D. [Sneed L.]
Lang, R. Michael, (AV) ....'39 '64 C.276 L.862 LL.B. [Lang,J.&W.]
Lang, James & Wheeler, Inc., A Professional Corporation, (AV)
5314 South Yale, Suite 400
Langenkamp, R. Dobie '36 '62 C.813 B.A. L.309 LL.B.
College of Law, 3120 E Fourth Pl
Langer, Steven F. ....'— '92 C&L.623 B.A., J.D. [Ⓐ Garrett] ⊙
Langholz, Robert W., (AV) .... '30 '56 C&L.352 B.A., J.D. [Holliman L.&R.]
Langston, Pamela D. ....'64 '97 C&L.862 B.S., J.D. [Pray,W.J.W.&M.]
Larey, Lance L. ....'39 '70 C.612 B.S. L.862 J.D. 4901 S. Sheridan
Larkin, Lloyd G. ....'21 '50 C&L.623 B.A., J.D. 3105 E. Skelly Dr.
LaSorsa, William G., (AV) ....'45 '74 C.436 B.A. L.862 J.D. [Jones,G.&B.]
Latham, Bobby L., Jr., (AV) ....'66 '93 C&L.623 B.A., J.D. [Latham,S.W.S.&L.]

Latham, Stall, Wagner, Steele & Lehman, (AV)
Spirit Tower - Suite 500, 1800 South Baltimore, 74119
Telephone: 918-382-7523 Fax: 918-382-7541
URL: http://www.lswsl.com
Bobby L. Latham, Jr.; Douglas E. Stall; Kenneth E. Wagner; Mark T. Steele; Scott F. Lehman; Rick J. Horton. Associates: Roni S. Rierson; Brian J. Goree; Marcus N. Ratcliff; Pine G. Drewyor; Robert M. Gallant; Samantha Weyrauch; Kandi D. Epp; Russell M. Jacobson, Jr.; Lance Freije; Allison L. Thompson. Of Counsel: Neal F. Lehman; E. Scott Pruitt.
General Civil Litigation including Insurance Law, Corporate Law, Professional Liability Defense, Medical Malpractice Defense, Premises Liability Defense, Products Liability Defense, Commercial Litigation, Banking, Construction Litigation, Commercial Transactions, Nursing Home Litigation, Creditors Rights, Bankruptcy, Pharmacy Liability, Civil Rights, Media Law, Bad Faith Litigation, Real Estate Zoning, Automobile Liability, Class Action, Antitrust.
See Professional Biographies, TULSA, OKLAHOMA

Latimer, Caesar C. ....'26 '54 C.347 A.B. L.1119 LL.B. 2611 N. St. Louis
Lauer, Mark M., (BV) ....'67 '92 C&L.623 B.A., J.D. Atty., Samson Investment Co.
Lawrence, Derek S.A. ....'56 '02 C.808 B.A. L.862 J.D. [Ⓐ Holden&C.]
Lawrence, Robert Neil ....'70 '99 C.623 B.B.A. L.846 J.D. [Ⓐ Pezold,B.&W.]
Lawson, Gabe W. ....'76 '01 C.810 B.A. L.862 J.D. [Ⓐ Atkinson,H.N.B.G.&C.]

Lawson, King & Shelton, PLLC, (AV)
10777 S. Memorial Drive, Suite C, 74133-7351 ⊙
Telephone: 918-369-9980 Fax: 918-369-9981
Jeffrey A. King (Resident);—M. Christian Tolen (Resident); Richard B. Selman (Resident).
General Civil Practice before all State and Federal Courts, Trials, Insurance Defense, Personal Injury, Negligence, Workers' Compensation, Products Liability.
Oklahoma City, Oklahoma Office: 2501 North Stiles, 73105. Telephone: 405-523-2501. Fax: 405-523-2324.
See Professional Biographies, TULSA, OKLAHOMA

Layman Padgett Barnhart Beckert & Williams, (AV)
324 South Main, Suite 818, 74103
Telephone: 918-293-0903 Fax: 918-293-0901 Email: nlayman@lpblaw.com Email: ppadgett@lpblaw.com Email: jbarnhart@lpblaw.com
Email: landp@ionet.net
Members of Firm: Neil F. Layman (1932-2004); Pat A. Padgett; John G. Barnhart; James A. Beckert; Kimberlee Dawn Williams.
Workers Compensation Defense, Civil Practice and Insurance Defense Law.

(This Listing Continued)

Layman Padgett Barnhart Beckert & Williams (Continued)

Representative Clients: Alexis, Inc.; Berkley Administrators; Crawford & Co.; Gallagher Basset Services; Consolidated Benefits Resources; The Travelers Ins. Co.; Wausau Ins. Co.

See Professional Biographies, TULSA, OKLAHOMA

Layon, Thomas A., Jr., (AV) .... '48 '74 C.579 B.S. L.862 J.D. [Layon,C.&K.]
Layon, Cronin & Kaiser, P.L.L.C., (AV) .... 125 West 15th, #600
Lea, James F. .... '67 '94 C&L.623 B.S., J.D. [Fellers,S.B.B.&T.] (Pat.)
Leach, William S., (AV) .... '56 '82 C.612 B.S. L.623 J.D. [Eldridge C.S.&L.]
Leake, James C., Jr. .... '43 '68 C.45 B.S.B.A. L.862 J.D. P.O. Box 3569
LeBlanc, James B. .... '64 '90 C.612 B.A. L.862 J.D. 2 W. 2nd St., 16th Fl.
LeBlanc, Robert F. .... '31 '60 C.623 B.S. L.420 J.D. 4469 Oak Rd.‡
Le Blanc, Thomas A., (AV) .... '65 '91 C.420 B.A. L.446 J.D. [Best&S.]
Leblang, Mark J., (AV) .... '53 '77 C.823 B.A. L.862 J.D. [Leblang,S.&A.]

Leblang, Solano & Ashbaugh, P.L.L.P., (AV) BB
7615 East 63rd Place, Suite 200, 74133
Telephone: 918-254-1414; 877 Visa Law Fax: 918-254-1888; 888-650-1888 URL: http://www.tulsalaw.com
Email: leblang@tulsalaw.com URL: http://www.lawyers.com/lsa
Members of Firm: Mark J. Leblang; R. Mark Solano; Judith A. Ashbaugh;—Kevin Y. Litz.
Languages: Spanish, Portuguese.
Citizenship, Immigration and Naturalization, Visa Law, International Law, Foreign Investors.

See Professional Biographies, TULSA, OKLAHOMA

Ledford, Kris T., (BV) .... '72 '97 C.1300 B.A. L.862 J.D. [McKinney&S.]
Lee, G. Diane .... '57 '01 C.623 B.A. L.862 J.D. [Ⓐ Riggs,A.N.T.O.&L.]
Lee, Jennifer D. .... '68 '93 C.880 B.A. L.616 J.D. [Ⓐ Eldridge C.S.&L.]
Lee, William B. .... '40 '70 C.861 B.C.S. L.862 J.D. [W.B.Lee]
Lee, William B., Inc. .... 2310 E. 15th St.
Legg, Sonya Kay .... '54 '98 C.612 B.M.E. L.862 J.D. Amer. Bk. & Tr. Co.
Lehman, Neal F. .... '43 '71 C.294 B.A. L.744 J.D. [Ⓒ Latham,S.W.S.&L.]
Lehman, Scott F., (AV) .... '67 '95 C&L.862 B.A., J.D. [Latham,S.W.S.&L.]
Leitch, Deborrah Ludi, Law Office of '54 '84
C.560 B.A. L.623 J.D. 3819 S. Troost Avenue
Leitch, Kevin C., (AV) .... '52 '77 C.546 B.A. L.309 J.D. Asst. U.S. Atty.
Leiter, William, (AV) .... '28 '52 C.145 B.S. L.813 J.D. 427 South Boston Avenue
Leithead, R. James .... '28 '53 C&L.174 B.A., LL.B. 7436 E. 49th St.
Lennart, Joseph P., (BV) .... '46 '81 C&L.862 B.S., J.D. [Riggs,A.N.T.O.&L.]
Lentz, Harry A., Jr., (AV) .... '44 '69 C.815 B.S. L.862 J.D. [Works&L.] ⊙
Lenz, Leslie Edward .... '64 '91 C.612 B.S. L.623 J.D. [Ⓐ Works&L.]
Leonard, Edward L. .... '25 '59 C.612 B.S. L.862 LL.B. 9141 S. Lakewood Ave.
Leonard, Larry D., (AV) .... '48 '74 C&L.378 B.S., J.D. [Leonard&R.]
Leonard, Tyler D. .... '— '03 C&L.862 B.A., J.D. [Ⓐ Riggs,A.N.T.O.&L.]

Leonard & Rineer, P.C., (AV)
1921 South Boston Avenue, 74119-5221
Telephone: 918-583-8700 Fax: 918-582-3838 URL: http://www.lawyers.com/leonardlaw
Email: thefirm@leonardrineer.com URL: http://www.leonardrineer.com
Larry D. Leonard; Hugh V. Rineer.
General Civil and Appellate Practice. Business and Commercial Litigation, Business Planning, Estate Planning, Guardianship, Trust and Probate Law, Personal Injury Law, Environmental Law, Business, Corporate and Commercial Transactions, Real Estate Law, Domestic Relations, Mediation.
Reference: Bank IV, Oklahoma, N.A.

See Professional Biographies, TULSA, OKLAHOMA

Lepp, Donald A., (BV) .... '67 '93 C.623 B.B.A. L.477 J.D. [Ⓐ Boone,S.D.H.&D.]
Leslie, Mickey K., (BV) '56 '94
C.623 B.B.A. L.862 J.D. 8988-L S. Sheridan Rd., Ste. 132
Lester, Laine R. .... '70 '96 C.613 B.A. L.464 J.D. Staff Atty., ODEN Ins. Servs., Inc.
Lester, Michelle .... '— '97 C.1078 B.A. L.464 J.D. [Ⓐ Riggs,A.N.T.O.&L.]
Levinson, Lee I., (AV) .... '51 '76 C.623 B.A. L.862 J.D. [Bodenhamer&L.]
Levy, Louis, (AV) .... '31 '55 C&L.623 B.A., LL.B. [L.Levy]
Levy, Phyllis, (BV) .... '47 '89 C&L.862 B.S., J.D. 5314 S. Yale Ave.
Levy, Louis, Inc., A Professional Corporation, (AV) .... 5314 S. Yale Ave.
Lewis, C.S., III, (AV) .... '46 '71 C.910 B.A. L.623 J.D. [Riggs,A.N.T.O.&L.]
Lewis, G. Michael, (AV) .... '42 '67 C&L.623 B.A., J.D. [Doerner,S.D.&A.]
Lewis, Harold A. .... '63 '90 C.188 B.A. L.802 J.D. 4719 S. Columbia Pl.
Lewis, Kerry R., (BV) .... '65 '94 C.82 B.S. L.862 J.D. [Rhodes,H.J.T.&G.]
Lewis, Larry A. .... '47 '73 C.612 B.S. L.276 J.D. [Ⓒ Rosenstein,F.&R.]
Lewis, Marichiel A. .... '72 '99 C.339 B.A. L.623 J.D. [Ⓒ Norman W.C.&D.]
Lewis, Mary B., (BV) .... '38 '82 C.188 B.A. L.862 J.D. 6657 s. New Haven Ave.
Lewis, Stephen Charles, (BV) .... '43 '67 C.613 B.A. L.623 J.D. 610 S. Main, Suite 300
Lieber, John H., (AV) .... '53 '78 C&L.862 B.S., J.D. [Ⓒ Eller&D.]
Limas, Vicki J., (AV) ... '52 '84 C.339 B.A. L.597 J.D. Asst. Prof. of Law, Univ. of Tulsa
Limekiller, David P., (BV) .... '63 '89 C.94 B.A. L.276 J.D. [Ⓐ Stuart,B.&T.]
Lindsey, Camilla J. .... '58 '87 C.921 B.S. L.862 J.D. Tr. Offr., Boatmen's Trust Co.
Lindsey, Edward G. .... '67 '92 C&L.862 B.A., J.D. 403 S. Cheyenne Ave., Ste. 905
Linger, James C., (BV) .... '51 '77 C.923 B.S. L.862 J.D. [Linger&Assoc.]
Linger & Associates, (BV) .... 1710 S. Boston Ave.
Linker, Russell R., II, (BV) .... '33 '58 C.862 B.A. L.623 LL.B. [Linker&N.]
Linker & Northcutt, (AV) .... 406 S. Boulder
Linscott, Lynda Burris .... '59 '84 C&L.623 B.A., J.D. 8922 S. Sandusky Avenue‡
Linscott, Michael S., (AV) .... '59 '91 C.623 B.S. L.862 J.D. [McKinney&S.]
Lipe, Larry B., (AV) .... '51 '76 C.45 B.S. L.802 J.D. [Conner&W.]
Lissau, Michael J., (BV) .... '71 '98 C.934 B.G.S. L.862 J.D. [Hall,E.H.G.G.&N.]
Litchfield, Allen, (AV) .... '58 '84 C.59 B.A. L.862 J.D. Off. of U.S. Atty.
Litchfield, E.P., Jr. .... '19 '47 C&L.623 A.B., LL.B. 1129 S. Owasso Ave.‡
Little, Christine D., (BV) .... '68 '95 C&L.623 B.A., J.D. [Norman W.C.&D.]
Little, Mary Jean .... '58 '93 C&L.862 B.A., J.D. [Ⓐ Riggs,A.N.T.O.&L.]
Little, Ronald W., (AV) .... '63 '92 C.839 B.B.A. L.862 J.D. [Sneed L.]
Litz, Kevin Y., (AV) .... '61 '89 C.877 B.A. L.878 J.D. [Ⓐ Leblang,S.&A.]
Livingood, Matthew G., (AV) .... '51 '80 C&L.421 B.A., J.D. 6211 S. Jamestown Ave.
Livingston, John J., (AV) .... '36 '62 C.623 B.B.A. L.477 J.D. 1831 E. 71st.
Loeffler, David H., Jr., (BV) .... '46 '71 C&L.623 B.A., J.D. 610 S. Main St., Ste. 300
Lofton, J. Heath .... '72 '98 C.612 B.S. L.623 J.D. [Ⓐ McGivern,G.&C.]

Logan & Lowry, LLP
(See Vinita)

Lollman, Joseph F. .... '44 '69 C&L.623 B.B.A., J.D. Sr. V.P., Century Natl. Bk.
Lombardi, Julie Trout .... '61 '86 C&L.623 B.A., J.D. 6846 S. Trenton Ave.
Lombardi, Philip Bryan .... '53 '86 C.619 B.A. L.623 J.D. 333 W. 4th St., Ste. 411
Long, Curtis M., (AV) .... '48 '74 C&L.623 B.A., J.D. [Fellers,S.B.B.&T.]
Long, Karen L., (AV) .... '52 '79 C.1329 B.A. L.616 J.D. [Rosenstein,F.&R.]
Longwell, Nicole M. .... '70 '00 C.619 B.S. L.862 J.D. [Ⓐ Joyce,P.&M.]
Lorenz, Lewis C. .... '57 '88 C.621 B.S. L.862 J.D. [L.Lorenz]
Lorenz, Lewis .... 1219 S. Galveston Ave.
Loud, Kelley G. .... '64 '89 C.616 B.A. L.623 J.D. [Ⓐ Titus H.R.D.&M.]

Loughrin, Brian T.
(See Oklahoma City)

Love, James M., (AV) '58 '84 C.612 B.S. L.862 J.D.
First Place Tower, 15 E. 5th Street
Love, R. Richard, III, (AV) .... '66 '91 C&L.623 B.A., J.D. [Conner&W.]
Lovell, Kenneth D., (AV) '54 '81
C.101 B.A. L.862 J.D. V.P., ONEOK Res. Co., ONEOK, Inc.
Lovoi, Gerald J., (BV) .... '60 '87 C.602 B.B.A. L.862 J.D. 324 S. Main St.
Lovoi-Nieves, Lori T. .... '59 '88 C.1380 B.A. L.1040 J.D. [Ⓐ Riggs,A.N.T.O.&L.]
Low, Frederick Charles '43 '94 C.280 B.S.F. L.862 J.D.
Coord., Regulatory & Right of Way Compl., Explorer Pipeline Co.
Lowe, Daniel W., (AV) .... '54 '79 C.612 B.S. L.424 J.D. [Armstrong&L.]
Lowell, James E., (BV) .... '49 '78 C.800 B.S. L.862 J.D. 7030 S. Yale Ave., Suite 100
Lower, Jeffrey Darin, (BV) .... '61 '86 C&L.862 B.S., J.D. [Ⓐ Kivell,R.&F.]

Lowrey, George H., (AV) '58 '84 C.623 B.A. L.188 J.D. BB
The Beacon Building, 406 South Boulder Avenue Suite 400, 74103-3800
Telephone: 918-599-9788 Fax: 918-582-6106
Email: glowlaw@mac.com URL: http://www.georgelowrey.com
Civil Litigation including Arbitration. Civil Trial Practice and Commercial Litigation.
References: Available Upon Request.

See Professional Biographies, TULSA, OKLAHOMA

Lucy, Patricia Alden, (AV) .... '32 '78 C.623 B.S. L.862 J.D. 2882 E. 29th St.
Lugibihl, Lynn Summers, (BV) .... '59 '84 C.612 B.S. L.910 J.D. [Ⓐ Barber&B.]
Lundy, Jerry D., (BV) .... '69 '95 C.1310 B.A. L.862 J.D. [Lundy]
Lundy Law Firm, PLLC, (BV) .... 4500 S. Garnett, Ste. 906
Luthey, Graydon D., (AV) .... '30 '54 C.378 A.B. L.900 J.D. 5661 S. Evanston Place‡
Luthey, Graydon Dean, Jr., (AV) .... '55 '79 C&L.623 B.A., J.D. [Hall,E.H.G.G.&N.]
Lutz, Edward J., Attorney at Law, (BV) '57 '84 C.415 B.A. L.1202 J.D.
1421 S. Yale Ave.
Lyons, Mark D., (AV) .... '54 '80 C.623 B.S. L.862 J.D. [Lyons&C.]

Lyons & Clark, (AV)
Two Main Plaza, 616 South Main, Suite 201, 74119
Telephone: 918-599-8844 Fax: 918-599-8585
URL: http://www.lawyers.com/lyons&clark
Cary W. Clark (1950-1988); Mark D. Lyons. Associates: Nicole A. King; C. Alison Wade.
General Civil and Criminal Practice in Federal and State Courts. Commercial/Business Litigation, Construction Law, Negligence, Employment, Civil Rights, Probate, Appeals.

See Professional Biographies, TULSA, OKLAHOMA

MacKenzie, John N., (BV) .... '51 '80 C.612 B.A. L.623 J.D. [J.N.MacKenzie&Assoc.]
MacKenzie, John N., & Associates, P.C., (BV) .... 1820 South Boulder Place
Mackey, Steven R., (AV) '50 '76 C.612 B.S. L.602 J.D.
V.P., Secy. & Gen. Coun., Helmerich & Payne, Inc.
Maddux, Gary L., (AV) .... '54 '82 C.612 B.S. L.802 J.D. [G.Maddux]
Maddux, Howard A. .... '29 '65 C.377 B.S. L.378 J.D. 2431 E. 61st St.
Maddux, Gary, Law Office of, (AV) .... 2642 E. 21st Street, Suite 150
Madison, Gary D., (BV) '46 '72 C.612 B.A. L.862 J.D.
1350 S. Boulder Ave., Ste. 1200
Magee, Clifford R., (BV) .... '59 '88 C.1333 B.S. L.862 J.D. P.O. Box 701800
Magee, Rebecca, (CV) .... '68 '94 C&L.623 B.B.A., J.D. [Ⓒ P.F.McTighe,Jr.]
Maguire, Mark W., (AV) .... '63 '89 C.612 B.B.A. L.623 J.D. [Atkinson,H.N.B.G.&C.]
Maier, Willard James .... '68 '95 C.861 B.A. L.623 J.D. 616 S Boston
Mailath, Melissa D. .... '69 '97 C.861 B.A. L.623 J.D. [Edwards&M.]
Main, Edward John, (BV) .... '47 '86 C&L.862 B.A., J.D. [Secrest,H.&B.]
Main, Ronald, (AV) .... '40 '64 C&L.862 B.A., J.D. [R.Main]

Main, Ronald, P.C., (AV)
Center 2800, Suite 821, 2815 East Skelly Drive, 74105-6251
Telephone: 918-742-1990 Fax: 918-742-2004
Email: rmainbtl@aol.com
Ronald Main.
General Civil Trial and Appellate Practice in all State and Federal Courts. Real Estate, Financial Institutions, Corporations, Creditors' Rights, Insurance, Personal Injury, Probate, Guardianship and Estate Planning Law, Wills, Trusts, Matrimonial Law, Divorce, Employment.
Representative Clients: Brumbaugh & Fulton, Co.; Miles Shipping Co.; H.S. Boyd, Co.; Kemco Fuels, Inc.; McDonnell-Douglas Corp.; Oklahoma Bar Professional Liability Insurance Co.; Sawyer Manufacturing Co.
References: Bank of Oklahoma, N.A.; Tulsa National Bank.

See Professional Biographies, TULSA, OKLAHOMA

Mains, David S. .... '47 '73 C.612 B.S. L.862 J.D. 5828 E. 79th St.
Major, Susan E. .... '— '92 C.612 B.S. L.862 J.D. [Ⓐ Miller,K.&B.]
Mallow, Janet G. .... '56 '95 C&L.862 B.A., J.D. [Ⓐ Riggs,A.N.T.O.&L.]
Malloy, Patrick J., III, (AV) .... '46 '72 C.602 B.A. L.623 J.D. [Malloy&M.]
Malloy, Terry P., & Associates, (BV) .... '47 '74 C.602 B.A. L.862 J.D. 1924 S. Utica

Malloy & Malloy, Inc., (AV)
111 West Fifth, Suite 700, 73103
Telephone: 918-747-3491 Fax: 918-743-6103
Email: psmiiim@aol.com
Pat Malloy, Jr. (1916-2004); Patrick J. Malloy, III.
General Trial Practice. Civil Wrongful Termination, F.E.L.A., Insurance, Bankruptcy, Real Estate, Appellate Practice.

See Professional Biographies, TULSA, OKLAHOMA

Malone, Allen Robinson .... '60 '85 C.1015 B.A. L.862 J.D. [Malone]
Malone Law Firm, P.C. .... 601 S. Boulder Ave., Ste. 100
Maloy, John R. .... '62 '89 C.612 B.S. L.45 J.D. [Ⓐ Riggs,A.N.T.O.&L.]
Maner, C. Jack, (AV) .... '26 '65 C.802 B.Ed. L.862 J.D. 3626 E. 70th Place
Manipella, Samuel P., (BV) .... '21 '62 C&L.862 B.A., LL.B. 3242 30th Pl.
Manke, Robert B. .... '32 '56 C&L.623 B.S., LL.B. 1516 N. Harvard St.
Mann, J. Douglas, (AV) .... '48 '73 C.612 B.A. L.846 J.D. [Rosenstein,F.&R.]
Maple, Monica L., (BV) .... '69 '98 C.999 B.S. L.862 J.D. 4500 S. Garnett, Suite 230
Mareshie, Eric A. .... '66 '99 C.801 B.S. L.862 J.D. [Ⓐ Secrest,H.&B.]
Marlar, Donald F., (AV) .... '44 '69 C.43 B.S. L.862 J.D. [Pray,W.J.W.&M.]
Marlow, Hubert A., (BV) .... '17 '51 C&L.862 LL.B. 1123 E. 26th
Marrs, Richard D., (BV) .... '51 '76 C&L.623 B.A., J.D. [Ⓐ Richardson,S.R.&W.]
Marsh, David T., (BV) .... '64 '91 C.623 B.S. L.862 J.D. [Marsh&M.]
Marsh, Thomas G., (AV) .... '30 '57 C&L.862 B.S., LL.B. [Marsh&M.]
Marsh & Marsh, P.C., (AV) .... 5727 S. Lewis, Suite 200
Marshall, Adam K. .... '— '03 C.862 B.A. L.623 J.D. [Ⓐ Barrow&G.]
Martin, C. Rabon, (BV) .... '44 '69 C&L.862 B.A., LL.B. [Martin&Assoc.]
Martin, Jack Alan, (BV) .... '49 '87 C.838 B.S. L.862 J.D. [J.A.Martin]
Martin, Jeffrey A., (CV) .... '56 '93 C&L.862 B.S., J.D. [J.Martin&Assoc.]
Martin, Joseph W., Law Office of, (AV) '47 '72
C.612 B.S. L.862 J.D. 1437 S. Boulder Ave., Ste. 1050
Martin, Linda Crook, (AV) .... '49 '80 C&L.838 B.A., J.D. [Doerner,S.D.&A.]
Martin, Melinda J., (AV) .... '55 '81 C.560 B.B.A. L.623 J.D. 6520 S. Lewis Ave., Ste. 15
Martin, Robert F., Jr. .... '25 '55 C.381 B.A. L.7 LL.B. Ret. Dist. Ct. J.‡

Martin & Associates, (BV) 15 W. 6th St., Ste. 2626
Martin, Jack Alan, Attorney at Law, (BV) 2761 E. Skelley Dr., Ste. 700
Martin, Jeffrey, & Associates, (CV) 320 S. Boston, Ste. 725
Martin-Farris, Melodie Leigh '72 '00 C.378 B.S. L.862 J.D Crawford & Company
Mason, J. Thomas, (AV) '40 '66 C.612 B.S. L.862 J.D. [Carpenter,M.&M.]
Massa, Robert E. '20 '63 C.910 A.B. L.862 J.D. 1535 S. Memorial Dr. (Pat.)
Masterson, Michael J., (AV) '56 '81 C.620 B.S. L.623 J.D. [Wilburn&M.]
Matheson, John M., (AV) '65 '92 C.623 B.Ac. L.276 J.D.
Gen. Coun., Global Power Equipment Grp. Inc.
Matheson, Matt David '65 '90 C.612 B.A. L.862 J.D. [Ⓐ Barber&B.]
Mathis, Rachel Carver, (BV) '70 '95 C.612 B.S. L.623 J.D. [Richards&C.]
Mathis, Stephan S. '68 '01 C.612 B.S.B.A. L.862 J.D. [Robinett&M.]
Matlock, Darell R., Jr. '42 '71 C.612 B.S. L.862 J.D. 4410 S. 33rd W. Ave.
Matthews, Carl T., Jr., (AV) '18 '42 C&L.623 B.A., LL.B. Atlas Life Bldg.
Matthews, Catherine E., (CV) '59 '86 C.1271 B.A. L.862 J.D. 6210 S. 69th. E. Pl.
Matthews, Thomas O. '52 '77 C&L.862 B.S., J.D. 6901 S. Yorktown Ave., Ste. D (Pat.)
Matthies, Mary Constance T., (Ms.), (AV) '48 '73 C.623 B.S. L.862 J.D. [Matthies]

Matthies Law Firm, A Professional Corporation, (AV)
Suite 310, Thompson Building, 20 East Fifth Street, 74103-4435
Telephone: 918-582-4400 Fax: 918-584-4453
Email: mattlawfrm@aol.com URL: http://www.members.aol.com/mattlawfrm/mattlaw.htm
Mary Constance T. Matthies (Ms.).
Labor and Employment Law (Management) and Corporate Civil Litigation, Employment Discrimination, ERISA.
Representative Clients: ENRON Corp; MAPCO Inc; Dowell Schlumberger, Inc.; General Motors Co.; Zurich-American Insurance Co.

See Professional Biographies, TULSA, OKLAHOMA

Maupin, James E., (AV) '66 '92 C.619 B.A. L.862 J.D. [Moyers,M.S.I.&T.]
Maurer, Mitchell C. '— '95 C.612 B.S. L.862 J.D. [Ⓐ McGivern,G.&C.]
Maxwell, Todd E. '73 '00 C.840 B.S. L.846 J.D. Flint Industries
May, Douglas J., (BV) '70 '95 C.502 B.A. L.862 J.D. [Gable&G.]
Mayer, Thomas R., (CVⓉ) '41 '71 C&L.352 B.A., J.D. [Mayer]
Mayer Law Firm, (CVⓉ) P.O. Box 702035

McAlister, McAlister, McKinnis & Tuggle, P.C.
(See Edmond)

McAllister, Gordon D., Jr. '46 '73 C.999 B.S. L.862 J.D. Spec. Dist. J.
McAllister, Sherrie Thompson, (AV) '52 '84
C.577 B.S. L.862 J.D. [S.ThompsonMcAllister]
McArtor, Keith O., (AV) '58 '91 C.612 B.S. L.862 J.D. 406 S. Boulder SW Mezzanine
McAtee, R. Jay, (AV) '56 '83 C.612 B.S. L.862 J.D. [McAtee]

McAtee Law Office, (AV)
1115 South Cincinnati, 74119
Mailing Address: P.O. Box 50611, Tulsa, OK 74150-0611
Telephone: 918-746-4332 Fax: 918-746-4334
Email: jmcatee@mcateelawoffice.com URL: http://www.mcateelawoffice.com
R. Jay McAtee. Associate: Valerie L. Sparks.
State Workers Compensation Law, Insurance Defense, Immigration Law.
Representative Clients: J.B. Hunt; Love's Country Stores; OK Foods; A.I.G.; John Christner Trucking; Risk Enterprise Management.

See Professional Biographies, TULSA, OKLAHOMA

McAuliff, James A., (BV) '60 '85 C&L.862 B.S., J.D. 1515 Ltd.
McBride, D. Michael, III, (AV) '65 '93 C.859 B.A. L.623 J.D. [Sneed L.]
McCain, Joseph J., Jr., (AV) '42 '67 C&L.802 B.B.A., J.D. [Conner&W.]
McCalmon, Jack S. '64 '89 C&L.623 B.A., J.D. [Titus H.R.D.&M.]
McCann, James Patrick, (AV) '51 '75 C&L.767 B.A., J.D. [Doerner,S.D.&A.]
McCann, Michael F. '59 '92 C.612 B.S. L.862 J.D. [Ⓐ Francy]
McCarthy, Frank H. '52 '77 C.754 B.A. L.862 J.D. U.S. Mag.
McCarthy, W. James '51 '79 C.623 B.S. L.1187 J.D. Citgo Petro. Corp.
McClellan, Stephen L., (BV) '67 '94 C&L.623 B.A., J.D. [Ⓐ Robinson]
McCloud, Howard D. '25 '50 C.862 L.623 LL.B. 6014 E. 57th Pl.‡
McCollam, M. E. (Malcolm), (BV) '54 '82 C.378 B.S. L.900 J.D. [McCollam&G.]
McCollam & Glassco, P.A., (BV) 1640 S. Boston Ave.
McCord, Brenda Henson, (CV) '— '94 C&L.862 B.S.N., J.D.
4530 S. Sheridan, Ste. 205
McCormick, John F., Jr., (AV) '44 '74 C.602 B.A. L.623 J.D. [Pray,W.J.W.&M.]
McCormick, Joseph A., (AV) '42 '67 C.612 L.862 LL.B. [McCormick F.&C.]
McCormick, Stephen E. '69 '02 C.69 B.B.A. L.862 J.D. [McCormick F.&C.]
McCormick, Timothy E., (AV) '48 '77 C.494 B.A. L.862 J.D. [McCormick,S.&G.] ⊙

McCormick Field & Cinocca, P.L.L.C., (AV)
Bridgeport II, Suite 100, 6440 South Lewis Avenue, 74136-1039
Telephone: 918-488-8000 Facsimile: 918-481-8751
Members of Firm: Joseph A. McCormick; Stewart E. Field; James Edward Cinocca, Jr.; Holly Breese Cinocca; Stephen E. McCormick.
General Trial Practice in all State and Federal Courts. Real Estate, General Corporate, Probate and Estate Planning, Wills and Probate, Trusts and Estates, Corporation, Commercial, Class Action Litigation, Bankruptcy, Civil Litigation, Personal Injury, Automobile Accidents, Wrongful Death and Products Liability.

See Professional Biographies, TULSA, OKLAHOMA

McCormick, Schoenenberger & Gish, A Professional Association, (AV)
1441 South Carson Avenue, 74119-3417 ⊙
Telephone: 918-582-3655 Facsimile: 918-582-3657
URL: http://www.tulsaoklawfirm.com
Timothy E. McCormick; Thomas R. Schoenenberger; Dana L. Gish.
General Civil Practice before all State and Federal Courts including, Insurance Defense, Personal Injury, Business Litigation, Corporation, Oil and Gas Law and Acquisitions, Title Examination, Employment Law, Sports Law, Family Law, Guardianship, Adoption Law, Divorce, Child Custody, Paternity, Social Security Disability.
Reference: Bank of Oklahoma, Bank of Oklahoma Tower.
Oklahoma City, Oklahoma Office: 4312 Classen Drive, 73118. Telephone: 405-525-0777. Fax: 405-557-0777.

See Professional Biographies, TULSA, OKLAHOMA

McCoy, Bob F., (AV) '42 '72 C.870 B.S. L.477 J.D. [Ⓒ Conner&W.]
McCoy, Michael W. '52 '95 C.1288 B.S. L.862 J.D. [Ⓐ Kivell,R.&F.]
McCoy, Timothy E., (BV) '54 '81 C&L.900 B.A., J.D.
Sr. Atty., The Williams Cos., Inc.
McCullough, David, (BV) '53 '84 C&L.623 B.A., J.D. [Ⓒ Doerner,S.D.&A.] ⊙
McCune, Mitchell M., (BV) '67 '94 C.623 B.A. L.862 J.D. [McCune&P.]
McCune, Phyllis L., (BV) '63 '89 C.619 B.A. L.862 J.D. [McCune]
McCune Law Office, PC, (BV) 5200 South Yale Avenue, Suite 202
McCune & Penney, P.C., (BV) 406 S. Boulder
McDaniel, A. Scott, (AV) '58 '95 C.576 B.S. L.862 J.D. [Joyce,P.&M.]
McDaniel, Dana M. '66 '05 C.1245 B.A. L.862 J.D. [Ⓐ Cheadle&Assoc.]
McDaniel, Michael J. '68 '99 C&L.862 B.A., J.D. [Ⓐ Boone,S.D.H.&D.]
McDonald, Gary M., (AV) '50 '75 C&L.45 B.A., J.D. [Doerner,S.D.&A.]
McDonald, Tomy W. '— '03 C.1362 B.A. L.862 J.D. [Ⓐ Frasier,F.&H.]

McDougal, M. M., (AV) '22 '58 C.613 B.S. L.862 LL.B. 5401 E. 110 Pl.‡
McDowell, Lindsay J. '77 '03 C.612 B.A. L.623 J.D. [Ⓐ Rhodes,H.J.T.&G.]
McElroy, Trecia Annette '61 '99 C&L.862 M.A., J.D. 1204 S. Cheyenne Ave.
McGivern, Michael W., (AV) '52 '80 C&L.862 B.S., J.D. [Perrine,M.R.R.B.&T.]
McGivern, Paul V., Jr., (AV) '30 '61 C&L.862 B.S., LL.B. [McGivern,G.&C.]
McGivern, Gilliard & Curthoys, Professional Corporation, (AV)
1515 South Boulder (⊙Oklahoma City)
McGowan, Linda Cole, (BV) '50 '75 C&L.623 B.S., J.D. [Carpenter,M.&M.]
McGowan, Philip James, (AV) '50 '75 C.623 B.A. L.862 J.D. [Carpenter,M.&M.]
McGranahan, F. Michael, (BV) '57 '85 C.1034 B.S. L.61 J.D. 1861 E. 15th Street
McGrath, Steven W., (AV) '48 '74 C.446 B.S. L.945 J.D. [Conner&W.]
McGrath Gardner, Allison C. '80 '05 C.893 B.A. L.623 J.D. [Ⓐ Conner&W.]
McGraw, Joseph Robert, Jr. '32 '60 C.602 L.862
McGraw-Davisson-Stewart Realtors, Inc.
McGrew, Jeffrey Dean '55 '94 C.616 B.S. L.862 J.D. [J.McGrew]
McGrew, Jeff, Attorney at Law 3315 S. 88th E. Ave.
McGuire, Michael G., (AV) '51 '85 C.502 B.S. L.862 J.D. [M.McGuire]
McGuire, Michael, (AV) 717 S. Houston Ave., Ste. 400
McKay, Molly D., (AV) '54 '90 C.1321 B.S. L.862 J.D. [M.D.McKay]
McKay, Molly D., P.C., (AV) 3207 E. 22nd St.
McKee, Charles H., (AV) '49 '75 C.612 B.S. L.623 J.D. [McKee&B.]
McKee, Sean H., (AV) '65 '90 C.1281 B.A. L.862 J.D. [Best&S.]
McKee & Bowker, (AV) 4137 S. Harvard Ave.
McKenna, Bruce A., (AV) '55 '80 C.415 B.A. L.862 J.D. 100 W. 5th Street
McKenzie, Milton D. '37 '65 C.862 B.S. L.208 J.D. 5727 S. Lewis Ave.‡
McKinney, David B., (AV) '51 '75 C.691 B.A. L.178 J.D. [Cooper,M.&W.]
McKinney, James R., (AV) '41 '72 C&L.862 B.S., J.D. P.O. Box 794

McKinney & Stringer, A Professional Corporation, (AV)
Mid Continent Tower, 401 South Boston, Suite 600, 74103 ⊙
Telephone: 918-582-3176 Telecopier: 918-582-1403
URL: http://www.McKinneyStringer.com
Directors: Patrick H. Kernan; Michael S. Linscott; Kris T. Ledford. Of Counsel: Christopher S. Heroux; Garry L. Keele, II. Associates: Scott R. Helton; Leah P. Carpenter.
Litigation; Appellate Practice; Alternate Dispute Resolution; Administrative Law; Antitrust and Trade Regulation; Aviation Law; Bankruptcy; Banks and Banking; Business Law; Civil Rights; Commercial Law; Computer and Technology Issues, Corporate Law; Mergers and Acquisitions; Energy; Oil and Gas Law; Environmental Law; Government Agency Practice; Health Care; Insurance; Intellectual Property; Trademarks; Patent Litigation; Labor and Employment; Workers Compensation; Medical Malpractice; Personal Injury; Toxic Torts; Products Liability; Probate; Real Estate; Securities Law; Taxation; Trusts and Estates; Wills.
Oklahoma City, Oklahoma Office: Corporate Tower, 101 North Robinson, Suite 1300. Telephone: 405-239-6444. Telecopier: 405-239-7902.

See Professional Biographies, TULSA, OKLAHOMA

McKnight, Marianna Ellen '67 '00
C.999 B.S. L.862 J.D. 717 S Houston Avenue, Suite 404
McLain, William '69 '02 C.968 B.A. L.862 J.D. [Ⓐ Graves&B.]
McMahan, John A., (BV) '53 '78 C.802 B.S. L.862 J.D. [Harris,M.P.T.&S.]
McMahon, Julie K. '63 '91 C.839 B.A. L.862 J.D. Asst. Pub. Def.
McMahon, Lawrence P. '47 '85 C.724 B.S. L.862 J.D. [L.P.McMahon]
McMahon, Lawrence P., P.C. 8086 S. Yale
McMurray, Kurston P., (BV) '72 '98 C.763 B.S. L.862 J.D. [Butler M.]
McNair, R. Nancy '48 '74 C&L.862 B.S., J.D. Asst. City Atty.
McNamara, Stephen R., (AV) '53 '79 C.602 B.A. L.862 J.D. [Sneed L.]
McNeely, Cynthia Lynn "Cindy", (BV) '53 '88 C.623 B.S.N. L.862 J.D.
2624 E. 21st St.
McNeill, Neal E. '27 '50 C&L.902 LL.B. 3724 S. Florence Ave.‡
McNulty, Jack L., Jr., (AV) '35 '61
C.734 B.S. L.862 LL.B. [O'Donnell,M.&A.d/b/a.S.O.M.&A.]
McQueen, John J. '21 '57 C.375 B.S. L.862 LL.B. 4815 S. Harvard Ave.
McQueen, L. Dru, (AV) '55 '83 C.802 B.F.A. L.862 J.D. [McQueen,R.&T.]

McQueen, Rains & Tresch, LLP, (AV)
6100 S. Yale Avenue, Suite 618, 74136
Telephone: 918-728-7800 Fax: 918-728-7899
L. Dru McQueen; Stuart A. Rains; W. Kyle Tresch; Jack P. Grimaldi; Julie C. Chien; Eugene L. Riccetti (Not admitted in OK); Jennifer E. Mustain; Amit K. Misra (Not admitted in OK); Holly Chastain (Not admitted in OK).
Commercial Law, Commercial Finance, Consumer Credit, Corporate Banking Law, Secured Lending, Emergency Response Transactions, General Civil Litigation, Commercial Litigation, Products Liability, Energy Litigation, Refining and Marketing, Contracts, International Transactions, Joint Ventures, Investment Funds, Energy Law, Oil and Gas Law, Labor and Employment, Litigation.

See Professional Biographies, TULSA, OKLAHOMA

McSoud, Charles A. '71 '00 C.934 B.A. L.862 J.D. [Ⓐ Gibbs A.B.M.&H.]
McSoud, Lawrence A., (BV) '33 '59 C.612 B.S. L.862 LL.B. [L.A.McSoud&Assoc.]
McSoud, Lawrence A., and Associates, (BV) 134 E. 26th Place
McSpadden, Gary R., (AV) '47 '72 C&L.623 B.A., J.D. [Crowe&D.]
McTighe, Paul F., Jr., (BV) '48 '73 C.665 B.A. L.862 J.D. [P.F.McTighe,Jr.]
McTighe, Paul F., Jr., Inc., (BV) 2448 East 81st Street
McVey, Cindy L. '59 '88 C&L.862 B.S.B.A., J.D. [Gibbon,B.&B.]
McWilliams, Bryan Scott '72 '01 C.1332 B.S. L.862 J.D. [Ⓐ S.P.Gray&Assoc.]
McWilliams, J.Scott, (AV) '58 '86 C.623 B.B.A. L.862 J.D. 1612 S. Cincinnati
Means, William W. '33 '61 C.623 L.863 LL.B. 5519 S. Marion Ave
Medina, J. Michael, (AV) '50 '75 C.807 B.A. L.623 J.D. [Ⓐ F.Dorwart]
Mefford, Howard R. '33 '63 C.619 B.S. L.862 LL.B. 3930 S. 61st West Avenue
Meier, Gregory G., (BV) '48 '73 C.602 B.A. L.623 J.D. 1524 S. Denver Ave.
Melgaard, Robert J., (AV) '59 '85 C.506 B.S. L.546 J.D. [Conner&W.]
Melikian, Deborah V. '75 '04 C&L.862 B.A., J.D. [Ⓐ Fellers,S.B.B.&T.]
Melone, Jerry M., (BV) '26 '52 C&L.862 LL.B. 1718 S. Cheyenne Ave.
Melone, Matt Allan, Law Office of, (BV) '62 '86
C&L.273 B.A., J.D. 5824 S. Louisville Ave.
Melson, Ashley R. '— '04 C.623 B.S. L.862 J.D. [Barkley]
Mensching, J. Patrick, Jr., (AV) '57 '82
C.1505 B.A. L.862 J.D. 610 South Main, Suite 300
Mensching, John P. '57 '82 C.1505 B.S. L.862 J.D. 610 S. Main, Ste. 300
Meredith, James R., (AV) '20 '50 C&L.862 LL.B. 4737 S. Birmingham
Merrill, Stephen J. '51 '78 C.612 B.S. L.623 J.D. [Merrill&Assoc.]
Merrill & Associates 7170 S. Braden Ave., Ste. 195-B
Messenger, Jason C. '— '03 C.45 B.S. L.862 J.D. [Smiling,B.&R.]
Messer, David M. '63 '01 C.999 B.S. L.862 J.D. [Ⓐ Brune]
Messler, J. Peter '40 '71 C.612 B.S. L.862 J.D. [Ⓒ Drummond]
Metcalf, Steven K., (BV) '58 '91 C.612 B.S.M.E. L.862 J.D. [Doerner,S.D.&A.]
Metz, Donald P. '31 '56 C&L.352 B.A., LL.B.
(adm. in IA; not adm. in OK) 110 W. 7th St.‡
Meyer, Lewis '13 '37 C.197 B.A. L.477 J.D. 1308 E. 19th St.
Michael, Terrence L. '58 '83 C.218 B.A. L.800 J.D.
(adm. in NE; not adm. in OK) U.S. Bkrptcy. J.
Michaels, Elizabeth A. '64 '97 C&L.45 B.A., J.D. The Money Store

Michalak, William S. '47 '76 C&L.326 B.A., J.D. Bird Creek Res. Inc.
Midland Professional Associates 4815 S. Harvard, Suite 380
Miers, Sheppard F., Jr., (AV) '41 '66 C&L.623 B.A., J.D. [Gable&G.]
Miles, George M., (BV) '60 '85 C.612 B.S. L.862 J.D. [Frasier,F.&H.]
Miles, Kenneth G., (BV) '46 '81 C.640 B.A. L.846 J.D. 2626 E. 34th Street
Miller, Beth A. '59 '96 C.1322 B.A. L.862 J.D. [Ⓐ Richardson,S.R.&W.]
Miller, D. Berry, (BV) '41 '68 C&L.623 B.B.A., J.D. Sr. V.P., UMB Bank
Miller, J. Anthony, (BV) '57 '83 C.37 B.S. L.1288 J.D. 1722 S. Carson Ave.
Miller, J. Randall, (AV) '51 '77 C&L.862 B.S., J.D. [Miller,K.&B.]
Miller, John S. '14 '38 C&L.972 A.B., LL.B. 1835 E. 32nd St.‡
Miller, Joseph W., (AV) '56 '85 C&L.502 A.B., J.D. [Carroll&M.]
Miller, Sarah C., (BV) '71 '97 C.612 B.A. L.616 J.D.
Sr. Atty., The Williams Cos., Inc.

Miller, Keffer & Bullock, PC, (AV)
222 South Kenosha Avenue, 74120 ☉
Telephone: 918-743-4460 Fax: 918-743-6689
J. Randall Miller; Louis W. Bullock;—David P. Page; Susan E. Major; Robert Blakemore.
Environmental, Oilfield Pollution, Expert Witness Support.
Dallas, Texas Office: Miller, Keffer & Pedigo, P.C., 8401 North Central Expressway, Suite 630, 75225. Telephone: 214-696-2050. Fax: 214-696-2482.

See Professional Biographies, TULSA, OKLAHOMA

Milligan, Stephen Alan '47 '75 C&L.862 B.A.B.S., J.D. Spirit Bank, N.A.
Mills, Cathlyn J., (P.C.), (BV) '63 '89 C.1147 B.A. L.862 J.D. [Mills]
Mills Law Office, (BV) 2431 East 51st Street, Suite 401
Milton, James C., (AV) '66 '95 C.612 B.S.B.A. L.846 J.D. [Doerner,S.D.&A.]
Mincher, Brian Lee, (CV) '74 '99
C.618 B.A. L.623 J.D. Staff Atty., Farmers Insurance Company
Minnaert, Maren K. '78 '04 C.612 B.S. L.276 J.D. [Ⓐ Hall,E.H.G.G.&N.]
Minnis, Michael, (AV) '44 '69 C&L.623 B.A., J.D. [Ⓒ Doerner,S.D.&A.] ☉
Minshall, Richard E. '— '66 C.623 B.A. L.893 LL.B. Pres., Capital Advsrs., Inc.
Misra, Amit K. '72 '96 C.273 B.A. L.846 J.D.
(adm. in TX; not adm. in OK) [Ⓐ McQueen,R.&T.]
Mitchell, Kathleen M. '54 '88 C.1116 B.A. L.678 J.D.
(adm. in WA; not adm. in OK) 4814 E. 112th St.
Mitchell, Mark '— '97 [Balogh,C.M.&W.]
Mitchell, Mark A. '61 '92 C&L.494 B.S., J.D. [Mitchell&Assoc.]
Mitchell, William C. '61 '87 C.770 B.S.C. L.862 J.D. [W.C.Mitchell]
Mitchell & Associates 6215 S. Trenton Ave.
Mitchell, William C., A Professional Corporation 16 E. 16th Street
Mitrani, Ada L., (CV) '54 '98 C.999 B.A. L.862 J.D. [Conley&M.]
Moeller, William D. '57 '85 C.350 B.S. L.352 J.D. [Ⓐ Stuart,B.&T.]
Moffett, J. Denny, (AV) '47 '72 C.623 B.B.A. L.273 J.D. [Moffett&Assoc.] (☉Tulsa)

Moffett & Associates, P.C., (AV)
1722 South Carson Avenue Suite 3203, 74119-4665
Telephone: 918-587-5700 Fax: 918-587-1242
J. Denny Moffett.
Civil Practice including Trials in all State and Federal Courts, Appellate, Arbitration, Insurance Coverage and Bad Faith, Corporate, Bankruptcy and Reorganization, Commercial, Federal and State Taxation, Ad Valorem Taxation, Financing.
Reference: Charles Schwab & Co., Inc.
Jackson, Wyoming Office: 215 South Willow, P.O. Box 4797, 83001. Telephone: 307-733-8734. Fax: 307-733-3994.

Molenda, Francis A. '45 '88 C.424 B.S. L.862 J.D. Natl. Labor Relations Bd.
Momeni, Kamran K. '73 '01 C&L.862 B.A., J.D. [Ⓐ Wagner,S.&C.]
Monaghan, Kelly F., (AV) '60 '86 C.804 B.S. L.862 J.D. [Holloway&M.]
Monnet, Burford D. '23 '53 C.862 B.S. L.623 LL.B. 3731 S. Trenton Ave.‡
Monnet, Edward O., (AV) '27 '51 L.623 LL.B. 616 S. Main, Ste. 308

Monroe, Stanley D., & Associates, (AV) '53 '78 C.623 B.A. L.862 J.D. BR
Bank of America Center, Suite 2112, 15 W. 6th Street, 74119
Telephone: 918-592-1144 Fax: 918-592-1149 Email: sdmonroe@swbell.net
Email: stanley.monroe@monroe-associates.com URL: http://www.monroe-associates.com
Associate: Trevor L. Reynolds.
General Trial Practice in State and Federal Courts, Criminal Appellant Practice-10th Circuit; Criminal Law, Family Law, Juvenile Law, Personal Injury, Medical Malpractice.

See Professional Biographies, TULSA, OKLAHOMA

Moody, Chad H. '70 '98 C&L.862 B.S., J.D. [Ⓐ Rodolf&T.]
Moody, John W., (BV) '43 '69 C.612 B.A. L.862 J.D. [Ⓒ Harris,M.P.T.&S.]
Moore, Jack C., (BV) '65 '90
C&L.623 B.B.A., J.D. Gen. Coun., Computek Computing Corp.
Moore, Lola Wells '35 '90 C&L.862 B.A., J.D. P.O. Box 580206
Moore, Lynnwood R., Jr., (AV) '45 '70 C.674 A.B. L.623 J.D. [Conner&W.]
Moore, Richd. C. '13 '41 C&L.862 LL.B. 1360 E. 25th St.
Moore, Samuel E. '14 '47 C.623 B.A. L.862 J.D. 7110 S. Indianapolis Ave.‡
Moore-Shrier, Pansy C. '76 '04 C.739 B.S. L.862 J.D. [Robinett&M.]
Moran, Lisa L., (BV) '50 '89 C.612 B.S. L.862 J.D. 4500 S. Garnett, Ste. 906
Morehead, J. Lyon, (AV) '47 '76 C&L.862 B.A., J.D. [Riggs,A.N.T.O.&L.]
Morgan, J. Daniel, (AV) '50 '78 C.880 B.A. L.836 J.D. [Gable&G.]
Morgan, Pamela K. '64 '99 C.619 B.S. L.616 J.D. 5801 E. 41st St., Ste. 305
Morgan, Susan K., (BV) '50 '77 C.210 B.A. L.862 J.D. U.S. Attys. Off.
Morgan, Victor E., (AV) '62 '87 C&L.623 B.B.A., J.D. [Crowe&D.]
Morgan, William Borden, (AV) '44 '72 C.529 A.B. L.862 J.D. 1923 S. Utica Avenue
Morgan, Baker, Morgan, Meyers, Folks & Kerr, PLC, (AV)
2431 East 51st Street, Suite 306
Morlan, Alfred K., (AV) '43 '72 C.804 B.S. L.502 J.D. [Morlan&Assoc.]
Morlan & Associates, P.C., (AV) 406 South Boulder, Suite 450
Morley, Randal D., (BV) '54 '79 C.942 B.G.S. L.862 J.D. [Birmingham,M.W.&P.]
Morrel, Reece B., (AV) '40 '66 C.1147 B.S. L.862 J.D. [Morrel,W.S.C.&H.]
Morrel, Reece B., Jr., (BV) '62 '91 C.612 B.S. L.862 J.D. [Morrel,W.S.C.&H.]

Morrel, West, Saffa, Craige & Hicks, Inc., (AV)
3501 South Yale Avenue, 74135-8014
Telephone: 918-664-0800 Fax: 918-663-1383
URL: http://www.law-office.com
Reece B. Morrel; Barry G. West; Ronald J. Saffa; Mark A. Craige (Certified in Business Bankruptcy Law by the American Board of Certification); James R. Hicks; Reece B. Morrel, Jr. Of Counsel: Paul R. Hodgson; Mac D. Finlayson.
General Civil, Criminal and Trial Practice in all State and Federal Courts. Taxation, Personal Injury, Administrative, Real Estate, Commercial, Corporate, Estate Planning, Pension and Profit Sharing, Bankruptcy, Corporate Reorganization, Oil and Gas, Family and Probate Law.

See Professional Biographies, TULSA, OKLAHOMA

Morris, Ann H. '64 '91 C.623 B.B.A. L.862 J.D. 2021 S. Lewis Ave., Ste. 450
Morris, Joseph W., (AV) '— '47 C&L.900 A.B., J.D. [Gable&G.]
Morris, Warren G. '23 '50 C&L.623 B.S., LL.B. 2532 E. 46th Pl.
Morrissey, Linda G. '53 '80 C.612 B.S. L.623 J.D. Dist. Judge
Morrow, George W. '22 '48 C.802 B.B.A. L.846 LL.B. 4021 E. 51st Pl.‡
Morrow, Jeffrey L., (BV) '54 '82 C.619 B.A. L.45 J.D. P.O. Box 1

Morse, David Charles, (BV) '50 '94 C.59 B.A. L.862 J.D. 5153 East 51st Street
Morsman, Andrew B., (BV) '59 '84 C.612 B.S. L.623 J.D. [Ⓐ Bonham&H.]
Mortensen, Thomas Andrew '70 '01 C.612 B.A. L.862 J.D. 2727 E. 21st St., Ste. 504
Morton, J. Craig, (BV) '65 '90 C.612 B.S. L.862 J.D. 1638 S. Denver Ave.
Morton, Sheldon E. '49 '74 C.80 B.A. L.900 J.D. 10338 E. 21 St.
Moseley, Warren G. '45 '73 C.502 B.S. L.734 J.D.
(adm. in MO; not adm. in OK) Pres., Physicians Total Care, Inc.
Moss, William R. '47 '72 C&L.862 B.S., J.D. 1310 S. Denver Ave.
Moyer, John G., Jr., (AV) '45 '75 C&L.862 B.S., J.D. [Rosenstein,F.&R.]

Moyers, Martin, Santee, Imel & Tetrick, L.L.P., (AV) BR
Formerly Moyers, Martin, Conway, Santee & Imel
1100 Mid-Continent Tower, 401 South Boston Avenue, 74103 ☉
Telephone: 918-582-5281 Fax: 918-585-8318
Email: info@moyersmartin.com URL: http://www.moyersmartin.com
Members of Firm: Villard Martin (1889-1965); Garrett Logan (1901-1975); Donald P. Moyers (1907-1995); Villard Martin, Jr. (1918-2002); Jack H. Santee; John M. Imel; Steven A. Stecher; James H. Ferris; Patrick D. O'Connor; John E. Rooney, Jr.; Terry M. Kollmorgen; James E. Maupin;—Michael E. Esmond. Of Counsel: Charles B. Tetrick; Larry E. Evans.
Civil Practice, Banks and Banking, Bankruptcy, Business Law, Commercial Law, Construction Law, Corporate Law, Education Law, Energy, Federal Practice, Insurance, Labor and Employment, Leases and Leasing, Litigation, Mergers, Acquisitions and Divestitures, Natural Resources, Personal Injury, Probate, Real Estate, Taxation, Trusts and Estates.
Bixby, Oklahoma Office: 113 West Dawes, Suite 100, 74408. Telephone: 918-366-3935. Fax: 918-366-3936.

See Professional Biographies, TULSA, OKLAHOMA

Muller, Timothy W. '69 '95 C&L.623 B.A., J.D. Sr. Atty., The Williams Cos., Inc.
Mullican, George Robert '70 '95 C.619 B.B.A L.623 J.D. [Gibbs A.B.M.&H.]
Mundell, Lynn A., (AV) '48 '76 C.502 B.S. L.862 J.D. 5561 S. Lewis
Muratet, Elizabeth R., (AV) '54 '83 C.612 B.A. L.862 J.D. [Gable&G.]
Murphy, Lawrence R., Jr., (AV) '72 '97 C.708 B.A. L.862 J.D. [Robinett&M.]
Murphy, Thomas W., (AV) '45 '76 C.93 A.B. L.982 J.D.
1350 South Boulder, Suite 400
Murray, Jo Ann E. '41 '92
C&L.862 B.A., J.D. Corp. Atty., Thrifty Rent-A-Car System, Inc.
Muscari, Susan A., (BV) '57 '95 C.136 B.S. L.862 J.D. [Muscari&Assoc.]
Muscari & Associates, P.C., (BV) 6440 South Lewis Avenue, Suite 2700
Mustain, Jennifer E., (BV) '66 '91 C&L.623 B.A., J.D. [Ⓐ McQueen,R.&T.]
Myers, Deanna Cochran '53 '79 C.612 B.S. L.623 J.D. 403 S. Cheyenne St.
Myers, Max C., Jr., (BV) '66 '97 C.612 B.S. L.862 J.D. [Ⓐ Drummond]
Mysock, Edward J., Jr., (AV) '47 '77 C.659 B.S. L.862 J.D. [Mysock&C.]

Mysock & Chevaillier, L.L.P., (AV)
Suite 700, 2021 South Lewis, 74104
Telephone: 918-747-6099 Telecopier: 918-747-6299
Edward J. Mysock, Jr.; William C. Chevaillier, Jr.; Stephen R. Bolden.
Practice includes Taxation, Tax Audits, Like Kind Exchanges, General Business Law, Estate Planning, Wills and Probate, Trusts and Estates, Employee Benefits, Asset Protection, Business Transactions, NASD Arbitration, Sports Law.

See Professional Biographies, TULSA, OKLAHOMA

Naegler, Max K., (BV) '41 '66 C.804 B.A. L.910 J.D. [Ⓒ Drummond]
Naifeh, Jack E. '21 '50 C&L.862 B.S., LL.B. 624 S. Denver Ave.
Naifeh, Sheila J., (BV) '65 '91 C&L.862 B.A., J.D. 1408 South Denver Avenue
Nally, Thomas P., (AV) '51 '76 C&L.862 B.S., J.D. [Nichols,W.S.N.F.&R.]
Nance, J. D., Jr. '19 '47 C&L.623 A.B., LL.B. 2807 S. 88th E. Ave.‡
Nasreddine, Rania '80 '05 C.1365 B.A. L.623 J.D. [Ⓐ Gable&G.]
Nathan, Jody R., (AV) '57 '86 C.685 B.A. L.623 J.D. [Stauffer,G.&N.]

Nay, William D., (AV) '43 '71 C.612 B.S. L.862 J.D.
4444 East 66th Street, 74136-4206
Telephone: 918-492-8481
Email: william.nay@lawoklahoma.com
Corporate, Business, Commercial, Wills and Probate, Trusts and Estate.

See Professional Biographies, TULSA, OKLAHOMA

Neal, Gary L., (AV) '46 '75 C.619 B.A. L.623 J.D. [Riggs,A.N.T.O.&L.]
Neal, Kathy R., (AV) '57 '82 C.623 B.A. L.862 J.D. [Eldridge C.S.&L.]
Neal, Wylie J. '47 '79 C&L.862 B.S.B.A., J.D. 7060 S. Yale Ave.
Neel, Patricia, (AV) '50 '80 C.612 B.A. L.862 J.D. Carreer Law Clk., Dist. J.
Neely, Thomas W. '56 '87 C.1147 B.A. L.623 J.D. Universal Field Servs.
Neff, Jonathan C., (AV) '51 '85 C.112 B.A. L.45 J.D. [Ⓒ Brune]
Neill, Dennis R. '52 '77 C.612 B.A. L.846 J.D. Sr. V.P., Samson Investment Co.
Nellis, Gregory D., P.C., (AV) '55 '80 C.622 B.A. L.623 J.D. [Atkinson,H.N.B.G.&C.]
Nelms, Mark L. '65 '96 C.623 B.S. L.962 J.D. [Ⓐ Riggs,A.N.T.O.&L.]
Nelson, Eric P., (AV) '57 '86 C.45 B.A. L.862 J.D. [Rosenstein,F.&R.]
Nelson, J. Barlow, (AV) '37 '65 C.197 A.B. L.862 J.D. [J.B.Nelson]
Nelson, Kathy Sherwood '69 '03 C&L.862 B.A., J.D. [K.S.Nelson] ☉
Nelson, L. Michele '64 '96 C.623 B.B.A. L.862 J.D. [Ⓐ Eagleton,E.&H.]
Nelson, Ted J., (AV) '55 '83 C.679 B.A. L.1288 J.D. [Ⓐ Joyce&P.]
Nelson, Todd A., (BV) '64 '92 C.375 B.S. L.623 J.D. [Fellers,S.B.B.&T.]
Nelson, J. Barlow, Inc., (AV) 1924 South Utica Avenue

Nelson, K. S., Law Firm, P.L.L.C.
320 South Boston Avenue, Suite 1030, 74103 ☉
Telephone: 918-230-2708; Toll Free: 866-414-0529 Fax: 866-414-0529
Kathy Sherwood Nelson.
Family Law.
Tulsa Office: 320 South Boston Avenue, Suite 1030, 74103.

See Professional Biographies, TULSA, OKLAHOMA

Nemec, Michael L., (AV) '49 '76 C&L.862 B.A., J.D. [Hall,E.H.G.G.&N.]
Nesbit, Gordon '29 '56 C.132 B.A. L.221 LL.B.
(adm. in IA; not adm. in OK) 2533 E. Skelly Dr.‡
Nester, Tracy P., (AV) '60 '88 C&L.623 B.B.A., J.D. [Ⓐ McGivern,G.&C.]
Nestor, Andrew, III, (BV) '60 '89 C.1376 B.S. L.862 J.D.
4815 S. Harvard Ave., Ste. 322
Newberry, Getulio C. "Bud" '38 '95 C.1243 B.S.A. L.616 J.D. 6208 Jamestown
Newsome, P. David, Jr., (AV) '47 '76 C.614 B.A. L.623 J.D. [Ⓐ Day,E.P.&C.] ☉
Newton, G. W. (Bill), (AV) '37 '62 C&L.623 B.A., LL.B. [Newton,O.T.&K.]

Newton, O'Connor, Turner & Ketchum, A Professional Corporation, (AV)
Bank of America Center, 15 West 6th Street, Suite 2700, 74119-5421
Telephone: 918-587-0101 Fax: 918-587-0102
Email: joconnor@newtonoconnor.com URL: http://www.newtonoconnor.com
G. W. (Bill) Newton; John M. O'Connor; W. Kirk Turner; Daniel R. Ketchum, II; Keith A. Wilkes;—Christopher S. Thrutchley; Jennifer K. Kern; Jon M. Payne; Rachel B. Crawford. Of Counsel: Michael L. Willis; Steven K. Bunting.
Employment counsel and training, Labor and Employment Litigation, Worker's Compensation, Business Law counsel and litigation, Business Formation, Business Development, Commercial Transactions, Business Succession Planning, Banking, Real Estate, Estate Planning, Probate and Adoption.
Reference: WestStar Bank, Tulsa, Oklahoma.

See Professional Biographies, TULSA, OKLAHOMA

Nichols, Carol S., (AV) '48 '79 C.931 B.A. L.862 J.D. [Nichols&N.]

Nichols, David M., (AV) ....'50 '81 C.663 B.S. L.862 J.D. [Nichols&N.]
Nichols, Elizabeth C. ....'71 '02 C.619 B.A. L.862 J.D. [A Strickland]
Nichols, Jerry R., (AV) ....'42 '69 C.612 B.S. L.862 J.D. [Nichols,W.S.N.F.&R.]

Nichols, Robert J., (AV) '49 '75 C.823 B.A. L.862 J.D.
400 Petroleum Club Building, 601 South Boulder Avenue, 74119
Telephone: 918-582-3222 Fax: 918-582-2705
Email: nicholsatty@worldnet.att.net
General Civil Practice before all State and Federal Courts. Trials, Eminent Domain, Condemnation, Municipal, Real Estate, Zoning, Real Estate Brokerage.
Representative Clients: Greater Tulsa Association of Realtors; McGraw Davisson and Stewart Realtors; Oral Roberts Ministries; Sitrin Petroleum Corp.; State Bank; Wal-Mart Stores, Inc.
References: State Bank; Bank IV; John Hausam Realtors.
See Professional Biographies, TULSA, OKLAHOMA

Nichols & Nichols, (AV) ....2506A E. 21st St.

Nichols, Wolfe, Stamper, Nally, Fallis & Robertson, Inc., (AV)
Suite 400, Old City Hall Building, 124 East Fourth Street, 74103-5010
Telephone: 918-584-5182 Fax: 918-582-9321
URL: http://www.nicholswolfe.com
Jerry R. Nichols; Frank B. Wolfe, III; Gerald G. Stamper; Thomas P. Nally; S. M. Fallis, Jr.; Thomas D. Robertson; Sarah E. Hansel; Trent A. Gudgel; John E. Harper, Jr.;—Karen M. Grundy; Stuart E. Van De Wiele. Of Counsel: Tom L. Holland.
Corporate Law, Business Law, Management Labor and Employment Law, Construction Law, Banks and Banking, Financial Institutions Law, Software Licensing (or Computer Law), Real Estate Law, Surety Law, Wills, Trusts, Estates and Probate, Product Liability Defense, Civil Litigation Practice in all Federal and State Courts and before Government Agencies.
Special Labor Relations Counsel for: Axelson, Inc., Division of USI.
See Professional Biographies, TULSA, OKLAHOMA

Nickel, Dennis R. ....'53 '78 C.747 B.A. L.502 J.D. 3336 East 32nd Street
Nicks, John B., (AV) ....'52 '80 C&L.623 B.S.I.E., J.D. 1448 S. Carson
Niedermeyer, James P., (AV) '49 '75 C.934 B.A. L.862 J.D.
Assoc. Gen. Coun., Magellan Midstream Partners
Nigh, Robert, Jr. ....'59 '86 C.947 B.S. L.623 J.D. [Brewster&D.]
Nightingale, Rebecca Brett, (AV) ....'65 '90 C.612 B.S. L.623 J.D. 500 South Denver
Norman, Charles E., (AV) ....'30 '53 C&L.623 B.A., LL.B. [Norman W.C.&D.]

Norman Wohlgemuth Chandler & Dowdell, (AV) BB
2900 Mid Continent Tower, 74103
Telephone: 918-583-7571 Fax: 918-584-7846
Email: postmaster@nwcdlaw.com
Members of Firm: Charles E. Norman; Joel L. Wohlgemuth; R. Jay Chandler; John E. Dowdell; Thomas M. Ladner; William W. O'Connor; Roger K. Eldredge; Christine D. Little; Angela F. Porter. Associates: David R. Ross; J. Paul Betzer; Jo Lynn Jeter; Melanie M. Pouncey. Of Counsel: Marichiel A. Lewis.
General Civil Practice. Trials and Appeals in all State and Federal Courts. Business Organizations, General Corporate, Banking, Communications, Real Estate, Commercial Transactions, Oil and Gas, Energy Acquisitions, Municipal and Zoning, Antitrust, Probate, Arbitration and Mediation, Securities Fraud Litigation, Securities Arbitration, Commercial Litigation, Telecommunications, Energy Litigation, Insurance Litigation, Tort Litigation.
See Professional Biographies, TULSA, OKLAHOMA

Norris, Robert D., Jr. '46 '71
C.934 B.A. L.502 J.D. V.P. & Gen. Coun., Galloway Resources
Norris, William F. ....'21 '72 C.800 B.E. L.862 J.D. 10024 S. Norwood Ave.‡
Northcutt, William M., (AV) ....'34 '60 C&L.862 B.A., LL.B. [Linker&N.]
Norton, Mallie M., (BV) ....'29 '68 C.1125 B.A. L.862 J.D. 2835 E. Skelly Dr.
Noulles, Richard B., (AV) ....'49 '75 C.691 B.A. L.862 J.D. [Gable&G.]
Noulles, Thomas G., (AV) '47 '75 C&L.575 B.A., J.D.
Sr. Atty., The Williams Cos, Inc.
Novick, Steven A., (AV) ....'47 '73 C.912 B.A. L.623 J.D. [S.A.Novick]
Novick, Steven A., P.C., (AV) ....1717 S. Cheyenne Avenue
Nowinski, Matthew John, (BV) ....'57 '87 C.645 B.A. L.862 J.D. 5800 S. Lewis Ave.
O'Connell, Julia Lynn Bisbee ....'58 '90 C.585 B.S. L.862 J.D. Fed. Pub. Def.
O'Connor, John M., (AV) ....'54 '80 C.612 B.A. L.862 J.D. [Newton,O.T.&K.]
O'Connor, Patrick D., (AV) ....'52 '77 C.352 B.G.S. L.862 J.D. [Moyers,M.S.I.&T.]
O'Connor, William W., (AV) ....'64 '89 C.612 B.S. L.623 J.D. [Norman W.C.&D.]
O'Donnell, Mitchell D., (AV) '34 '61
C.618 B.S. L.862 J.D. [O'Donnell,M.&A.d/b/a.S.O.M.&A.]
O'Donnell, McNulty & Affeldt, P.C., d/b/Savage O'Donnell McNulty &, (AV)
601 S. Boulder, Ste. 600
Oglesby, Patricia L. ....'54 '82 C.861 B.A. L.809 J.D. V.P., Oak Resources, Inc.
Olaniyan, Cathy Cheney, (AV) '58 '85
C.1315 B.S. L.623 J.D. Sr. Atty., Helmerich & Payne, Inc.
O'Leary, Catherine Ann, (AV) ....'51 '82 C.612 B.S. L.862 J.D. 907 S. Detroit Ave.
Oliver, Larry L., (AV) ....'35 '64 C&L.862 B.A., LL.B. [L.L.Oliver&Assoc.]
Oliver, Terry E., (BV) ....'62 '88 C.620 B.S.B.A. L.862 J.D. Off. of Pub. Def.
Oliver, Larry L., & Associates, P.C., (AV) ....2840 E. 51st Street, Suite 105
Oltman, Glenn W., (BV) ....'44 '81 C.234 B.S.Ed. L.862 J.D. 1809 E. 15th
O'Meilia, David E., (AV) ......'51 '76 C.612 B.S. L.862 J.D. 616 South Main, Suite 201
O'Neill, Nora R. ....'— '03 C.665 B.A. L.659 J.D. [A Crowe&D.]
Orbison, James C., (AV) ....'43 '68 C&L.862 B.A., J.D. [Riggs,A.N.T.O.&L.]
Orlowski, D. Faith, (AV) ....'54 '78 C&L.846 B.A., J.D. [Sneed L.]
Osborn, Joel ....'67 '98 C.1 B.S., B.A. L.623 J.D. [A Holloway&M.]
Osmond, William K., (BV) '67 '92
C.612 B.S. L.623 J.D. 1800 S. Baltimore, Ste. 1000, 10th Fl.
Otey, George N., III '51 '90
C.623 B.A. L.862 J.D. Mgr, Prop. Admin., Communications Inc.
Owens, Floyd Wesley ....'56 '94 C.619 B.S. L.862 J.D. P.O. Box 4566
Owens, George W., (AV) ....'26 '51 C&L.846 B.A., LL.B. [Owens]
Owens, Robyn, (AV) ....'54 '79 C.859 B.A. L.862 J.D. [Owens]
Owens, Victor R., & Associates ....'59 '87 C.612 B.A. L.616 J.D. 2738 E. 51st Street

Owens Law Firm, The, P.C., (AV)
234 W. 13th Street, 74119-3026
Telephone: 918-587-0021 Fax: 918-587-6111
Email: olf@owenslawfirmpc.com
George W. Owens; Robyn Owens;—Randall E. Rose.
General Civil Trial Practice in all State and Federal Courts. Probate, Corporation, Real Estate, Oil and Gas, Taxation, International, Bankruptcy, Business Law, Estate Planning, Elder Law and Guardianship Law.
See Professional Biographies, TULSA, OKLAHOMA

Oxford, Alan J., II ....'61 '97 C.613 B.A. L.623 J.D. [C Drummond]
Pace, Kirsten E., (BV) ....'65 '90 C.228 A.B. L.623 J.D. [Atkinson,H.N.B.G.&C.]
Pack, Jerry D. ....'38 '76 C.619 B.S. L.862 J.D. 5626 S. 75th Ave.
Paden, Lee W. ....'42 '67 C.613 B.A. L.623 J.D. [L.W.Paden]
Paden, Lee W., Law Offices of, P.C. ....1201 East 33rd. St.
Padgett, Pat A., (BV) ....'42 '87 C&L.862 B.S.B.A., J.D. [Layman P.B.B.&W.]
Page, Connie Kaye ....'52 '98 C&L.862 B.S., J.D. 315 S. Gilcrease Muse
Page, David P., (AV) ....'54 '81 C.768 B.A. L.862 J.D. [A Miller,K.&B.]
Painter Bohn, Thayla, (CV) ....'72 '98 C.862 B.A. L.45 J.D. [A Feldman,F.W.F.&B.]

Palik, Donald L. ....'61 '00 C.859 B.A. L.862 J.D. Pub. Def.
Palmer, Lisa J. McNair ....'63 '91 C.612 B.S. L.846 J.D. 1831 E. 71st Street
Palmer, Wilma L., (BV) ....'64 '89 C&L.862 B.S., J.D. P.O. Box 48600
Pansius, Jonathan E., (BV) '55 '80 C&L.477 A.B., J.D.
717 S. Houston Ave. K, Ste. 102
Pappas, Louis C., (CV) ....'50 '80 C.205 B.A. L.45 J.D. 2520 S. Oswego Ave.
Parham, Candace Jeanne ....'68 '93 C&L.623 B.B.A., J.D. 1440 S. Marion Ave.
Parker, Edwin W., II ....'39 '69 C.616 B.S. L.862 J.D. 8110 S. 70th East Pl.‡
Parker, Robert E., and Associates, (AV) ....'34 '64 C&L.862 LL.B. 2431 E. 61st. St.
Parmele, Laura M. ....'45 '84 C&L.862 B.A., J.D. P.O. Box 702214
Parr, Royse M., (AV) ....'35 '64 C.612 B.S. L.862 J.D. 2521 E. 31st Street
Parrilli, Nathan Guy ....'75 '00 C.339 B.A. L.862 J.D. [A Stauffer,G.&N.]
Parrilli, Rachel D. ....'75 '00 C.1288 B.A. L.862 J.D. [A Atkinson,H.N.B.G.&C.]
Parrish, Harry A., (BV) ....'51 '85 C.378 B.A. L.862 J.D. [Pray,W.J.W.&M.]
Passley, Shanann Pinkham, (AV) ....'49 '90 C.263 B.A. L.862 J.D. [Eller&D.]
Pataki, Leonard I., (AV) ....'53 '78 C.665 B.S. L.616 J.D. [Doerner,S.D.&A.]
Pate, C. W. (Bill), (BV) ....'27 '65 C.502 B.S. L.862 J.D. 2835 E. Skelly Dr.
Pate, Michael L. ....'53 '79 C.477 A.B. L.347 J.D. [Gable&G.]
Patten, Gordon L., (BV) ....'26 '51 C&L.862 LL.B. 3005 E. Skelly Dr.
Patten, William E., (BV) ....'48 '87 C.1310 B.S. L.862 J.D. [C Best&S.]
Patterson, Laurie A., (BV) ....'55 '84 C.612 B.S. L.862 J.D. 10126 S. Toledo
Patterson, Mason G. ....'75 '00 C.612 B.S. L.893 J.D. [A Gable&G.]
Patterson, W. Ralph, (BV) ....'32 '64 C.616 B.S. L.862 LL.B. [Briggs,P.&Assoc.]
Patterson, William John, (BV) ....'50 '85 C.804 B.S. L.862 J.D. 403 S. Cheyenne Ave.
Patterson, William Lin ....'41 '69 C.1012 B.S. L.623 J.D. 1800 S. Baltimore Ave.
Patton, C. Raymond, Jr., (AV) ....'50 '76 C&L.623 B.B.A., J.D. [Conner&W.]
Patton, Jon Reece ....'61 '97 C.619 B.S. L.862 J.D. [Patton]
Patton Law Office ....406 South Boulder, Ste. 810
Paul, Chris A., (AV) ....'58 '83 C.216 B.A. L.945 J.D. [Joyce,P.&M.]
Paul, John R., (AV) ....'49 '75 C.138 B.A. L.862 J.D. [Paul]

Paul Law Firm, The, A Professional Corporation, (AV) BB
Suite 400, Reunion Center, 9 East 4th Street, 74103
Telephone: 918-584-2583 Telefax: 918-587-8521 URL: http://www.paulfirm.com
URL: http://www.paullawfirm.com
E. Lee Griggs (Deceased); John R. Richards (Deceased); John R. Paul;—Leah McCaslin Kinsey.
General Civil and Trial Practice in State and Federal Courts, including Medical Malpractice, Insurance Defense, Commercial, Negligence, Professional Liability, General Liability, Products Liability, Employment, Employee Discrimination, Insurance Law and Environmental Law.
Reference: Bank of Oklahoma, Tulsa, Oklahoma.
See Professional Biographies, TULSA, OKLAHOMA

Pauling, David L., (BV) ....'43 '71 C.623 B.A. L.862 J.D. City Atty.
Paulk, Joseph H., (AV) ....'55 '83 C.45 B.S.B.A. L.902 J.D. 1602 South Main Street
Paulsen, Angela McSpadden, (BV) ......'61 '94 C&L.862 B.A., J.D. [Boone,S.D.H.&D.]
Payden, Robert C. ....'46 '77 C.804 B.S. L.862 J.D. 717 S. Houston
Payne, Jon M., (BV) ....'66 '92 C.674 A.B. L.802 J.D. [A Newton,O.T.&K.]
Paynter, Frank R., (BV) ....'59 '85 C&L.623 B.A., J.D. [A Stipe,H.L.U.E.&B.]
Paynter, Rick ....'— '85 C&L.623 B.A., J.D. [C Garrett] ((O)Muskogee)
Payton, Edgar Lee ....'50 '84 C.1152 B.A. L.986 J.D. Celebrity Attractions, Inc.
Payton, Mark F., III, (P.C.) ....'55 '81 C&L.623 B.A., J.D. 3015 E. Skelly
Pearson, Thomas L. '54 '80 C.210 B.A. L.352 J.D.
(adm. in OH; not adm. in OK)
Sr. V.P.-Law & Admn., Gen. Coun. & Secy., Alliance Resource Partners, L.P.
Peaster, Richard L., (BV) ....'40 '71 C.377 B.S. L.862 J.D. [Peaster&Assoc.]
Peaster & Associates, (BV) ....4500 South Garnett Road, Suite 900
Peckio, Amber N. ....'77 '03 C.621 B.S. L.862 J.D. 4100 S. Darlington, Ste. 1075
Pei, Young ....'71 '00 C.94 B.A. L.623 J.D. [A Doerner,S.D.&A.]
Pence, Mark E. ....'43 '76 C.502 B.S. L.862 J.D. 1727 S. 140 E. Ave.
Penick, Giles A., Jr. ....'10 '34 C.893 L.623 LL.B. 6955 S. Birmingham Pl.‡
Penney, Jed E., (BV) ....'69 '96 [McCune&P.]
Perigo, Jerry E., (AV) ....'46 '76 C.623 B.A. L.862 J.D. [Edgar&P.]
Perkins, Howard D., Jr., (BV) ....'53 '82 C&L.862 B.S., J.D. P.O. Box 690355
Perrault, Margaret M., (BV) ....'56 '81 C&L.862 B.A., J.D. [M.M.Perrault]
Perrault, Margaret M., P.C., (BV) ....3140 S. Winston
Perrine, William D., (AV) ....'51 '86 C.623 B.S. L.862 J.D. [Perrine,M.R.R.B.&T.]

Perrine, McGivern, Redemann, Reid, Berry & Taylor, PLLC, (AV)
1437 South Boulder Avenue, Suite 620, P.O. Box 1710, 74101-1710
Telephone: 918-382-1400 Fax: 918-382-1499 URL: http://www.pmrlaw.com
Email: rredemann@pmrlaw.net URL: http://www.pmrlaw.net
William D. Perrine; Michael W. McGivern; Robert P. Redemann; David P. Reid; Kevin D. Berry; Catherine C. Taylor; Victor R. Seagle;—Kelly M. Greenough; Cheryl S. Gan; L. Brad Taylor; Jennifer L. Struble; Timothy C. Edwards; David C. Senger; Jennifer A. Johnson. Of Counsel: Lawrence W. Zeringue.
Civil Litigation, Products Liability, Insurance Defense, Professional Liability, Workers Compensation, Toxic Tort Law, Insurance Receivership, Insurance Law, Insurance Bad Faith, Labor and Employment Law, Wrongful Death, Personal Injury, Social Security Appeals.
See Professional Biographies, TULSA, OKLAHOMA

Perugino, Robert ....'53 '79 C.705 B.A. L.862 J.D. Spec. Dist. J.
Peters, Robert R., II, (BV) ....'62 '92 C.378 B.A. L.862 J.D. [Jones,G.&B.]
Peters, Stephen Q., (AV) ....'58 '85 C.802 B.A. L.623 J.D. [Harris,M.P.T.&S.]
Petersen, Victoria A., (BV) '52 '80 C.326 B.S. L.862 J.D.
Law Clk., Sr. J., U.S. Dist. Ct.
Peterson, Aaron C., (BV) ....'53 '85 C.1111 B.A. L.862 J.D. [Peterson&R.]
Peterson, David L. ....'43 '73 C.101 B.A. L.623 J.D. Dist. J.
Peterson & Ramirez, P.A., (BV) ....P.O. Box 52680
Petrich, R. Mark, (AV) ....'59 '86 C.312 B.B.A. L.862 J.D. [Hall,E.H.G.G.&N.]
Petrikin, J. Ronald, (AV) ....'46 '73 C.502 B.A. L.734 J.D. [Conner&W.]
Pezold, R. K., (AV) ....'44 '75 C.893 B.S. L.862 J.D. [Pezold,B.&W.]

Pezold, Barker & Woltz, (AV)
A Partnership of Professional Corporations
15 West Sixth Street, Suite 2800, 74119-5415
Telephone: 918-584-0506 Fax: 918-584-0720
Email: mail@pbwtulsa.com URL: http://www.pbwtulsa.com
Members of Firm: R. K. Pezold; Terry J. Barker; Joseph C. Woltz. Associates: Gene G. Boerner, III; Robert Neil Lawrence.
General Civil Practice. Business Litigation. Oil and Gas Law. Oil and Gas Litigation. Environmental Litigation. Class Actions. Corporation. Banking, Securities Regulation and Litigation. General Appellate Practice.
See Professional Biographies, TULSA, OKLAHOMA

Pfanstiel, C. Eric, (BV) ....'68 '95 C.317 B.A. L.862 J.D. [C Cooper,M.&W.]
Phillips, David C., III, (CV) ....'50 '90 C.665 B.A. L.623 J.D. [D.C.Phillips&Assoc.]
Phillips, Jack E. ....'33 '61 C.575 A.B. L.273 J.D. [C Fellers,S.B.B.&T.] (Pat.)
Phillips, Laurie ....'62 '03 C&L.862 B.A., J.D. [A Frasier,F.&H.]
Phillips, Martha J., (BV) ....'49 '86 C.612 B.S. L.862 J.D. [Atkinson,H.N.B.G.&C.]
Phillips, Sharon K., (AV) ....'44 '86 C&L.862 B.S., J.D. [Frazier&P.]
Phillips, D.C., & Associates, P.C., (CV) ....3014 S. 121st East Ave.
Phipps, K. Clark, (AV) ....'57 '86 C.623 B.S. L.861 J.D. [C Atkinson,H.N.B.G.&C.]

Phoenix, James T. ....'53 '78 C.276 B.S.B.A. L.862 J.D. Deloitte & Touche LLP
Pickard, Randall S., (P.C.), (BV) ....'58 '83 C.621 B.A. L.1288 J.D. [⊡ Drummond]
Pickard, W. Joseph ....'75 '02 C&L.623 B.A., J.D. [⊡ Secrest,H.&B.]
Piel, Bernard W., Jr. ....'45 '73 C.502 B.A. L.862 J.D. P.O. Box 2147
Pielsticker, J. W. ....'38 '63 C.602 B.B.A. L.623 LL.B. Pres., Arrow Trucking Co.
Pierce, H. Cynthia '53 '78 C&L.623 B.A., J.D.
Right of Way Admr., Williams Communications, Inc.

Pierce Couch Hendrickson Baysinger & Green, L.L.P., (AV)
624 South Boston, Suite 500, 74119 ⊙
Telephone: 918-583-8100 Fax: 918-583-8107
URL: http://www.PierceCouch.com
James B. Durant (1934-2004). Member of Firm: Leah P. Keele (Resident). Associates: Jason M. Henderson; Jamie Messina Beller; Lori R. Whitworth.
General Civil Practice. Insurance, Surety, Corporation, Aviation Law, Medical and Dental Malpractice, Professional Liability, Workers Compensation, Bad Faith Law, Arson, Construction Law, Municipal Liability, Civil Rights, Employment Law, Business Torts and Business Litigation, Insurance Coverage Issues and Automobile/Vehicle Liability. Trial of Cases in all Courts in Oklahoma.
Oklahoma City, Oklahoma Office: 1109 North Francis, P.O. Box 26350, 73126. Telephone: 405-235-1611. Fax: 405-235-2904.
See Professional Biographies, TULSA, OKLAHOMA

Pilgrim, Gary Wayne, (BV) ......'53 '96 C.612 B.S. L.862 J.D. 1700 S.W. Blvd., Ste. 100
Pinkerton, Harlan, Jr. ....'42 '75 C.623 B.S. L.615 J.D. [⊡ Morgan,B.M.M.F.&K.]
Pinkerton, James C., (AV) ....'36 '60 C.674 A.B. L.623 LL.B. [Pinkerton&P.]
Pinkerton, Laurence L., (AV) ....'46 '76 C.623 B.A. L.178 J.D. [Pinkerton&F.]

Pinkerton & Finn, P.C., (AV)
2000 First Place 15 East Fifth Street, 74103-4367
Telephone: 918-587-1800 Facsimile: 918-582-2900
URL: http://www.pinkerton-finn.com
Laurence L. Pinkerton; Judith A. Finn. Of Counsel: J. David Jorgenson.
Civil Trial and Appellate Practice, State and Federal Courts, Commercial, Securities and Intellectual Property Litigation, Securities Fraud, Health Law, Contract Litigation, Non-Compete Agreements, Business Litigation.
See Professional Biographies, TULSA, OKLAHOMA

Pinkerton and Pinkerton, A Professional Corporation, (AV) ....1722 S. Boston
Pinnell, Philip E., (AV) ....'50 '75 C&L.862 B.A., J.D. Asst. U.S. Atty.
Pizzo, Richard A., (BV) ....'57 '86 C.502 B.S.B.A. L.616 J.D. 1515 S. Denver
Plake, Monica A., (BV) ....'66 '97 C.1142 B.A. L.862 J.D. [⊡ Cooper,M.&W.]
Plake, Susan ....'68 '99 C&L.862 B.A., J.D. The University of Tulsa
Plumb, Charles S., (AV) ....'57 '82 C.802 B.B.A. L.608 J.D. [Doerner,S.D.&A.]
Poe, James E., (AV) ....'35 '59 C&L.862 B.A., LL.B. [Covington&P.]
Polan, James R., (AV) ....'47 '87 C.862 B.F.A. L.188 J.D. [Riggs,A.N.T.O.&L.]
Pollard, Michael A., (BV) ....'70 '98 C.174 B.S. L.862 J.D. [⊡ Joyce&P.]
Pollard, Stephanie A. ....'73 '02 C.1262 B.A. L.862 J.D. P.O. Box 4494
Pool, Jo Anne ....'52 '90 C.845 B.S. L.8 J.D. 1861 E. 15th St.
Pool, Tilman E., Jr., (BV) ....'46 '72 L.862 J.D. 1638 S. Denver Ave.
Poole, Tracy A., (BV) ....'67 '93 C.612 B.S. L.623 J.D. [Fellers,S.B.B.&T.]
Porter, Angela F. ....'70 '97 C.320 B.A. L.862 J.D. [Norman W.C.&D.]
Porter, Scott L. ....'65 '96 C.172 B.A. L.862 J.D. 1207 E. 27th Place
Posey, Timothy S., (AV) ....'63 '89 C&L.623 B.A., J.D. [Hall,E.H.G.G.&N.]

Postic & Bates, A Professional Corporation
(SeeOklahoma City)

Pottorf, Fred A., (AV) ....'46 '75 C.604 B.A. L.862 J.D. [Works&L.]
Potts, Roberta. J. ....'50 '87 C&L.1288 B.A., J.D. Oral Roberts Univ.
Potts, Thomas G., (AV) ....'48 '77 C.623 B.A. L.862 J.D. [James,P.&W.]
Pouncey, Melanie M. ....'79 '04 C.499 B.S. L.623 J.D. [⊡ Norman W.C.&D.]
Powell, Michael A. '59 '86 C&L.446 B.A., J.D.
(adm. in PA; not adm. in OK) Univ. of Tulsa
Powers, Bruce N., (BV) '59 '88
C.612 B.S. L.623 J.D. 4867 South Sheridan Road Suite 701
Powers, William K., (AV) ....'13 '36 C&L.623 B.A., LL.B. 2602 E. 16th‡
Prather, Jon Lee, (AV) '39 '64 C&L.623 B.A., LL.B.
Sr. V.P. & Gen. Coun., Columbian Chemicals Co.
Prather, Paul F., (BV) ....'64 '90 C.861 B.A. L.623 J.D. [⊡ Feldman,F.W.F.&B.]
Pratt, Dawn E., (CV) ....'65 '92 C.619 B.A. L.862 J.D. 9432 S. Florence Avenue
Pratt, Stacy J., (BVⓉ) ....'69 '98 C.1359 B.B.A. L.862 J.D. [Pratt,P.]
Pratt Law Firm, PLLC, (BVⓉ) ....5153 E. 51st Street
Pray, Donald E., (AV) ....'32 '63 C.862 B.S. L.623 LL.B. [⊡ Pray,W.J.W.&M.]

Pray, Walker, Jackman, Williamson & Marlar, A Professional Corporation, (AV) ⊞
900 ONEOK Plaza, 100 West 5th Street, 74103-4218
Telephone: 918-581-5500 Fax: 918-581-5599
URL: http://www.praywalker.com
J. Warren Jackman (1934-2002); W. Bland Williamson, Jr.; Donald F. Marlar; Terry R. Doverspike; John F. McCormick, Jr.; Frank D. Spiegelberg; John L. Randolph, Jr.; William L. Eagleton, IV; Wm. Gregory James; Donald S. Smith; Randall G. Vaughan; Charles Bretton Crane; Kevin Pierce Doyle; Thomas M. Askew; Robert J. Winter; Steven B. Butterfield; Pamela D. Langston; Kimberly A. Vojvoda; Harry A. Parrish; Charles R. Holladay; Chad C. Taylor; Jill Grimsley Drewyor; Scott C. Weatherholt; David A. Warta. Of Counsel: Donald E. Pray; Floyd L. Walker; C. Bruce Jones.
General Civil Trial Practice in all State and Federal Courts; Corporate, Oil and Gas, Taxation, Labor and Employment Law, Employee Benefits, Securities, Real Estate, Banking, Commercial, Probate, Trusts, Insurance, Bankruptcy, Personal Injury, Products Liability, Entertainment and Administrative Law.
See Professional Biographies, TULSA, OKLAHOMA

Prescott, Harris Howard, (AV) ....'53 '78 C.94 B.A. L.862 J.D. Asst. City Atty.
Price, Arthur G., (CV) ....'41 '70 C&L.862 B.A., J.D. 6735 S. Oswego Ave.
Price, James Townley, (BV) ....'42 '89 C.623 B.S. L.862 J.D. 1700 Southwest Blvd.
Price, Robert B. ....'60 '90 C.1165 B.A. L.862 J.D. First Natl. Bk. of Tulsa
Priddy, John E., (BV) ....'63 '90 C.623 B.S. L.862 J.D. [Rosenstein,F.&R.]
Priore, Donna J., (BV) ....'54 '79 C.612 B.S. L.862 J.D. [Birmingham,M.W.&P.]
Pritchard, William W. ....'51 '76 C.378 B.A. L.862 J.D. [⊡ Hall,E.H.G.G.&N.]
Pritchett, Monty C. "Cutter", (BV) ....'51 '92 C.845 B.S. L.862 J.D. 223 E. 21st
Proszek, James J., (AV) ....'53 '83 C&L.862 B.S., J.D. [Hall,E.H.G.G.&N.]
Pruitt, E. Scott, (BV) ....'68 '93 C.275 B.A. L.862 J.D. [⊡ Latham,S.W.S.&L.]
Pruitt, Nancy C., (AV) '52 '78 C&L.623 B.A., J.D.
Asst. Gen. Coun., Blue Cross & Blue Shield of Oklahoma (Legal Department)
Puhl, Helen D., (AV) ....'60 '87 C.804 B.S. L.502 J.D. 11010 S. Erie Ave.
Purser, Charles A., (AV) ....'40 '65 C&L.623 B.S.P.E. J.D. Ste 1578, 110 W 7th St
Quandt, Eric W., (BV) ....'63 '88 C.966 B.A. L.862 J.D. 5200 S. Yale
Quillin, Paula J., (AV) ....'56 '81 C.612 B.S. L.846 J.D. [Feldman,F.W.F.&B.]
Quinn, Camille M., (BV) ....'57 '89 C.612 B.S. L.862 J.D. [C.M.Quinn]
Quinn, *Camille M., P.C.*, (BV) ....*5800 East Skelly Dr., Suite 1230*
Ragsdale, Terry D., (BV) ....'62 '92 C.862 B.S. L.802 J.D. [Gable&G.]
Rahal, Fred, Jr., (AV) ....'39 '63 C&L.862 B.A., J.D. [Riggs,A.N.T.O.&L.]
Rainey, Craig L., (AV) '52 '77 C&L.623 B.A., J.D.
Asst. Gen. Coun., Williams Companies, Inc., The
Rainey, Jessica E. ....'74 '99 C&L.221 B.A., J.D. [⊡ Titus H.R.D.&M.]
Rainey, Kent "Bo", (BV) ....'65 '92 C.378 B.S.B.A. L.862 J.D. [⊡ Rosenstein,F.&R.]

Rains, Charles E., (AV) ....'44 '69 C.623 B.B.A. L.846 J.D. [Rains&S.]
Rains, Mark S., (BV) ....'58 '84 C.352 B.A. L.862 J.D. [Rosenstein,F.&R.]
Rains, Stuart A., (AV) ....'56 '81 C&L.623 B.A., J.D. [McQueen,R.&T.]

Rains & Saunders, PLC, (AV) ⊞
A Professional Limited Liability Company
Midway Building, 2727 E. 21st Street, Suite 402, 74114
Telephone: 918-747-3727 URL: http://www.rstaxlaw.com
URL: http://www.tulsaestateplanner.com
Charles E. Rains; Katherine Saunders.
Trusts and Estates, Wills, Probate, Guardianship and Conservatorship, Taxation, Medicare and Medicaid, Business Law, Contracts, Corporate Law, Partnership Law, Nonprofit and Charitable Organizations, International Law.
See Professional Biographies, TULSA, OKLAHOMA

Rambach, Jeffrey C., (AV) ....'61 '86 C.94 B.S. L.861 J.D. [Gable&G.]
Ramirez, Eddie D., (BV) ....'59 '85 C.639 B.S. L.1339 J.D. [⊡ Richardson,S.R.&W.]
Ramsey, Mari Strong, (BV) '64 '91
C.612 B.S. L.862 J.D. Sr. Atty., The Williams Cos., Inc.
Randle, Rodger A. ....'43 '78 C.623 B.A. L.862 J.D. [⊡ Boesche M.]
Randolph, John L., Jr., (AV) ....'53 '79 C.198 B.A. L.862 J.D. [Pray,W.J.W.&M.]
Rankin, Randy A., (AV) ....'53 '78 C.174 B.A. L.862 J.D. 1515 Ltd.
Rankin, Stephen S., (AV) ....'55 '83 C.184 B.S. L.862 J.D. 2431 E. 61st St., Ste. 100
Rapp, Walter Keith ....'34 '68 C.804 B.S. L.862 J.D. Civil App. Ct. J.
Rasnake, Gregory R. ....'72 '00 C.889 B.S. L.623 J.D. [⊡ Burton&Assoc.] ⊙
Rasure, Dana L. ....'52 '77 C.900 B.A. L.477 J.D. U.S. Bkrptcy. J.
Ratcliff, Marcus N. ....'75 '01 C.999 B.A. L.862 J.D. [⊡ Latham,S.W.S.&L.]
Ratcliff, Susan Lentz, (BV) ....'74 '00 C.613 BB.A. L.623 J.D. [Works&L.]
Ravits, Richard ....— '82 C.228 B.A. L.862 J.D. 52 N Delaware
Ray, Kurt A., (BV) ....'51 '76 C.1086 B.A. L.862 J.D. 406 S. Boulder, Ste. 400
Ray, Ronald O., Jr., (AV) ....'58 '84 C.612 B.A. L.623 J.D. [Hall,E.H.G.G.&N.]
Ray, Stephen W., (AV) ....'57 '82 C&L.623 B.B.A., J.D. [Hall,E.H.G.G.&N.]
Rayment, Brian J., (AV) ....'57 '82 C.612 B.A. L.862 J.D. [Kivell,R.&F.]
Raymond, Elam Jewett, (BV) '42 '69 C.612 B.S. L.623 J.D.
1500 S. Utica Ave., Ste. 400
Raynolds, Ronald G., (AV) ....'38 '63 C.309 A.B. L.862 LL.B. 1625 E. 43rd Pl.‡
Raynolds, William F., II, (AV) ....'48 '76 C&L.862 B.S., J.D. [Hood&R.]
Reaves, Leigh A. ....'62 '87 C.934 B.A. L.623 J.D. 224 S. Boulder
Reavis, Edwin R. ....'50 '78 C&L.862 B.A., J.D. 2313 S. Florence Pl.
Redemann, Linda G., (AV) ......'52 '78 C&L.862 B.S., J.D. One Technology Center, 15B
Redemann, Robert P., (AV) ....'51 '78 C.966 B.S. L.862 J.D. [Perrine,M.R.R.B.&T.]
Redman, Michael C., (AV) ....'61 '88 C&L.623 B.B.A., J.D. [Doerner,S.D.&A.]
Redwine, R. Kevin, (AV) ....'58 '84 C&L.623 B.B.A., J.D. [Conner&W.]
Reed, James M., (AV) ....'56 '82 C.1285 B.A. L.45 J.D. [Hall,E.H.G.G.&N.]
Reed, Jerry, (Inc.), (AV) ....'41 '65 C.612 B.S. L.623 J.D. 1828 E. 47th Pl.
Reents, Mark R., (AV) ....'53 '78 C&L.862 B.S., J.D. [⊡ Clark&W.]
Rees, Andrew Thomas, (BV) ....'68 '93 C.612 B.S. L.862 J.D. Off. of City Atty.
Reid, David P., (AV) ....'54 '79 C.999 B.B.A. L.623 J.D. [Perrine,M.R.R.B.&T.]
Reif, John F. ....'51 '78 C&L.862 B.S., J.D. Ct. of App. J.
Reincke, Janet Woehl, (BVⓉ) ....'47 '86 C&L.862 B.S., J.D. Asst. U.S. Atty.
Reis, Robert R., (AV) ....'39 '64 C&L.623 B.A., J.D. P.O. Box 520954
Rembisz, Eugene R. ....'30 '61 C.229 B.S. L.862 LL.B. 5626 S. 75th Ave.
Renberg, Gregory D., (BV) '57 '85 C&L.862 B.S.B.A., J.D.
[Conner&W.] (⊙Hous., TX)
Renfrow, Kent E., Attorney at Law, (BV) '46 '76
C.813 B.A. L.623 J.D. 8906 E. Skelly Dr., Ste. B
Renkes, Robert N. '52 '78 C.967 B.S. L.896 J.D.
Exec. V.P. & Gen. Coun., Petroleum Equipment Institute
Replin, Ricki M., (BV) ....'53 '75 C.174 B.A. L.862 J.D. [R.M.Replin]
Replin, Ricki M., P.C., (BV) ....5200 S. Yale Ave.
Reynolds, Barry G., (AV) ....'63 '89 C.499 B.S. L.623 J.D. [Titus H.R.D.&M.]
Reynolds, Elizabeth S. ....'74 '00 C.339 B.A. L.221 J.D. [⊡ Rodolf&T.]
Reynolds, R. Louis, (AV) ....'56 '82 C&L.862 B.S., J.D. [Eller&D.]
Reynolds, Trevor L. ....'71 '99 C.843 B.A. L.221 J.D. [⊡ S.D.Monroe&Assoc.]
Rhodes, Chris L., III, (AV) ....'32 '59 C&L.623 B.B.A., LL.B. [Rhodes,H.J.T.&G.]
Rhodes, Jeffrey K., (AV) ....'63 '92 C&L.862 B.S.B.A., J.D. [Riseling&R.]

Rhodes, Hieronymus, Jones, Tucker & Gable, P.L.L.C., (AV) ⊞
ONEOK Plaza, 100 West 5th Street, Suite 400, 74103-4287
Mailing Address: P.O. Box 21100, Tulsa, OK 74121-1100
Telephone: 918-582-1173 Fax: 918-592-3390
URL: http://www.rhodesokla.com
E. D. Hieronymus (1908 -1994); George W. Gable (1918-2000);—Chris L. Rhodes, III; Bert M. Jones; John H. Tucker; Jo Anne Deaton; Dan S. Folluo; Ann E. Allison; Andrew D. Downing; Bradley A. Jackson; Colin H. Tucker; Kerry R. Lewis; Leslie J. Southerland;—Nathan E. Clark; Theresa Noble Hill; Carlye O. Jimerson; Bradley S. Shelts; Lindsay J. McDowell; Margaret M. Clarke; Denelda L. Richardson.
General Civil Trial and Appellate Practice in all State and Federal Courts. General and Extra-contractual Liability Insurance, Negligence, Products Liability, Medical, Legal and Professional Liability, Employment, Workers' Compensation, Environmental, Aviation, Suretyship, Common Carriers, Toxic Torts, ERISA, Construction.
Representative Clients: Bechtel; Chubb Group; General Motors; Nissan; Pfizer; Volkswagen, A.G.; Zurich.
See Professional Biographies, TULSA, OKLAHOMA

Ribner, Clifford N., (AV) ......'51 '79 C.188 B.A. L.569 J.D. 320 South Boston Suite 1130
Riccetti, Eugene L. '68 '94 C.846 B.A. L.796 J.D.
(adm. in TX; not adm. in OK) [⊡ McQueen,R.&T.]
Rice, Delbert L. ....'53 '85 C.376 B.A. L.862 J.D. Dir., Human Res., Crosby Grp., Inc.
Richard, S. Joe ....'23 '50 C.862 B.A. L.623 LL.B. 7317 S. Canton Ave.
Richards, Phil R., (AV) ....'58 '83 C&L.623 B.A., J.D. [Richards&C.]

Richards & Connor, (AV) ⊞
12th Floor, Park Centre Building, 525 South Main, Suite 1250, 74103-4509
Telephone: 918-585-2394 Fax: 918-585-1449
Email: prichards@richardsconnor.com URL: http://www.richardsconnor.com
Members of Firm: Phil R. Richards; James W. Connor, Jr.; Rachel Carver Mathis; Thomas D. Hird. Associates: Jason L. Glass; John A.L. Campbell; Richard L. Hathcoat; Jeffrey C. Baum; Stephanie R. Coates; Elizabeth A. Hart; Oliver L. Smith; Amy E. Hampton. Of Counsel: John W. Kelson.
General Civil and Trial Practice in State and Federal Courts, including Medical Malpractice, Insurance Defense, Commercial, Negligence, Professional Liability, General Liability, Physical Damage, Bodily Injury, Products Liability, Employment, Insurance Law and Environmental Law.
See Professional Biographies, TULSA, OKLAHOMA

Richardson, Andrew L., (BV) ....'68 '94 C.612 B.A. L.623 J.D. [Eldridge C.S.&L.]
Richardson, Charles L., (BV) .....'63 '90 C.623 B.B.A. L.862 J.D. [Richardson,S.R.&W.]
Richardson, Denelda L. ....'63 '04 C.82 B.S. L.862 J.D. [⊡ Rhodes,H.J.T.&G.]
Richardson, Gary L., (AV) ....'41 '72 C.82 B.S. L.796 J.D. [Richardson,S.R.&W.]
Richardson, Jerry A., (AV) ....'58 '83 C&L.45 B.A., J.D. [⊡ Rosenstein,F.&R.]
Richardson, Stoops, Richardson & Ward, (AV) ....6555 S. Lewis Ave., Ste. 200
Richer, John T. ....'71 '02 C.862 B.A. L.374 J.D. [⊡ Hall,E.H.G.G.&N.]
Richer, Lesley Ford ....'76 '02 C.602 B.A. L.802 J.D. [⊡ Doerner,S.D.&A.]

Richey, Danny P., (AV) .... '54 '83 C.43 B.A. L.45 J.D. [Richey&D.]
Richey & Decker, LLP, (AV) .... 5555 E. 71st Street
Rickel, Peter L. .... '44 '69 C.578 B.A. L.623 J.D. F.B.I.
Ricketts, Ronald N., (AV) .... '43 '69 C.623 B.A. L.862 J.D. [Gable&G.]
Riddle, Jason .... '67 '96 C.612 B.S. L.623 J.D. P.O. Box 52234
Riddle, Richard W., (AV) .... '44 '73 C.612 B.S.E.E. L.502 J.D. [Riddle&W.]
Riddle & Wimbish, P.C., (AV) .... 5314 South Yale, Suite 200
Ridout, William D., (CV) .... '55 '81 C.846 B.A. L.802 J.D. 6716 S. Saint Louis Ave.
Rierson, Roni S., (BV) .... '68 '97 C.840 B.A. L.623 J.D. [Ⓐ Latham,S.W.S.&L.]
Riggin, Matthew E. .... '63 '92 C.612 B.S. L.862 J.D. 1700 S.W. Boulevard
Riggs, Lisa R., (AV) .... '60 '87 C.623 B.S. L.276 J.D. [Riggs,A.N.T.O.&L.]
Riggs, M. David, (AV) .... '37 '69 C.663 B.A. L.862 J.D. [Riggs,A.N.T.O.&L.]
Riggs, William F., (AV) .... '53 '79 C&L.45 B.S.P.A., J.D. [Doerner,S.D.&A.]

Riggs, Abney, Neal, Turpen, Orbison & Lewis, A Professional Corporation, (AV)
502 West Sixth Street, 74119 ⊙
Telephone: 918-587-3161 Fax: 918-587-9708
URL: http://www.riggsabney.com
Members of Firm: M. David Riggs; Gary L. Neal; C.S. Lewis, III; James C. Orbison; Donald M. Bingham; Joseph P. Lennart; Kenneth M. Smith; Stephen B. Riley; Scott P. Kirtley; Richard A. Gann; Harley W. Thomas; Janet S. Dumont; Lisa R. Riggs; J. Lyon Morehead; Richard T. Garren; Jack R. Anderson; Stephanie L. Jones Theban; Fred Rahal, Jr.; Gretchen M. Widdig Schilling; Rex Wade Thompson; Beverly A. Stewart; James R. Polan; Karen Carden Walsh; Douglas A. Wilson; David C. Cameron; Ira L. Edwards, Jr.; Robert P. Skeith. Associates: Greg Alberty; Ryan James Assink; Jack Steven Barker; William A. Bowles; Kelly L. Bratcher; James R. Briggs; Peter W. Brolick; Scott Wallace Byrd; Michelle M. Carter; Colby Cook; Glenna S. Dorris; Stephen E. Hale; Zachery R. Hargis; Erik Houghton; Robert E. Howard; Deborah Johnstone; Kiemonn Jones; Kristopher Koepsel; G. Diane Lee; Tyler D. Leonard; Michelle Lester; Mary Jean Little; Lori T. Lovoi-Nieves; Janet G. Mallow; John R. Maloy; Mark L. Nelms; Mary J. Rounds; William C. Searcy; Linda Van Arkel-Greubel; Sharon K. Weaver; Jerry Witt; Courtney Wolin; Michael P. Womack.
General Civil, Trial and Appellate Practice before all State and Federal Courts and Agencies, Alternative Dispute Resolution, Banking, Corporate, Securities, Anti-trust, Administrative, Government Relations, Real Estate, Commercial Transactions, Oil and Gas, Estate Planning, Probate, Taxation, Employment and Discrimination, Employee Benefits, Social Security, Bankruptcy and Reorganization, Family Law, Healthcare, Negligence, Personal Injury, Products Liability, Medical Malpractice, Transportation and Indian Law.
Oklahoma City, Oklahoma Office: The Paragon Building, Suite 101, 73118-7489. Telephone: 405-843-9909. Fax: 405-842-2913.
Muskogee, Oklahoma Office: 215 State Street, First National Severs Building, Suite 508, 74402. Telephone: 918-687-5404; 800-722-1332. Fax: 918-687-1128.
Denver, Colorado Office: 621 Seventeenth Street, Suite 1900, 80293. Telephone: 303-298-7392. Fax: 303-298-7398.

See Professional Biographies, TULSA, OKLAHOMA

Riker, Lynda Dianne .... '57 '00 C.612 B.S. L.862 J.D. [Ⓐ Eldridge C.S.&L.]
Riley, Stephen B., (BV) .... '45 '72 C&L.623 B.S., J.D. [Riggs,A.N.T.O.&L.]
Rineer, Hugh V., (AV) .... '48 '75 C.649 B.A. L.862 J.D. [Leonard&R.]
Ringold, A. F., (AV) .... '31 '55 C&L.477 A.B., LL.B. [Rosenstein,F.&R.] ⊙
Riseling, Ted M., (AV) .... '42 '70 C&L.862 B.S., J.D. [Riseling&R.]
Riseling & Rhodes, P.C., (AV) .... 2510 E. 21st Street
Risk, Richard B., Jr. .... '41 '02 C.612 B.A. L.862 J.D. [Risk]
Risk Law Firm .... 3417 E. 76th St.

Ritchie, K. Ellis, P.C.
(See Pryor)

Ritter, Dennis D., Jr. '52 '77 C&L.420 J.D.
(adm. in LA; not adm. in OK) Contour Energy Co. EP LLC
Rizley, Robert S., (AV) .... '23 '53 C.623 B.A. L.477 LL.B. 4209 E. 98th
Roach, Bruce E., Jr., (BV) .... '70 '96 C.840 B.B.A. L.900 J.D. [Carpenter,M.&M.]
Roach, Loyal J., III, (AV) .... '39 '70 C&L.623 B.F.A., J.D. [Buckman&R.]
Roberson, R. Lawrence, (BV) .... '52 '91 C&L.862 B.S., J.D. [Roberson]
Roberson Law Office, (BV) .... 7030 S. Lewis Avenue, Suite C
Roberts, C. Clay, III, (BV) .... '47 '76 C.197 A.B. L.623 J.D. 4444 E. 66th St.
Roberts, Curtis J. .... '77 '03 C.623 B.B.A. L.862 J.D. [Ⓐ Feldman,F.W.F.&B.]
Roberts, Joseph R., (BV) .... '31 '60 C&L.862 B.A., J.D. [Ⓒ Stauffer,G.&N.]
Roberts, Loretta (Lori) K. .... '63 '96 C&L.862 B.A., J.D. [Ⓐ Drummond]
Robertson, James J., (BV) .... '61 '95 C.1362 B.S. L.862 J.D. [Ⓐ Toon]
Robertson, James M. .... '31 '54 C&L.623 B.A., LL.B. 3005 E. Skelly Dr.
Robertson, Jason A., (BV) .... '71 '97 C.619 B.S. L.615 J.D. [Secrest,H.&B.]
Robertson, Moura A.J., (BV) .... '60 '92 C.1044 B.A. L.862 J.D. [Robertson,P.]
Robertson, Thomas D., (AV) .... '53 '78 C.59 B.A. L.245 J.D. [Nichols,W.S.N.F.&R.]

Robertson Law Firm, The, PLLC, (BV)
2000 Bank of America Center, 15 E. 6th Street, 74119
Telephone: 918-382-9332 Fax: 918-382-9319
Email: moura@robertsonlawfirm.net URL: http://www.tulsadivorce.com
Moura A.J. Robertson.
Matrimonial and Family Law, including Antenuptial Agreements, Divorce, Child Custody, Domestic Torts, Adoption, Guardianship.

See Professional Biographies, TULSA, OKLAHOMA

Robey, Bart Jay .... '78 '03 C.30 B.A. L.537 J.D. [Ⓐ Atkinson,H.N.B.G.&C.]
Robinett, Susan Markham .... '63 '92 C&L.623 B.S., J.D. 1365 E. 43rd Pl.
Robinett, Tracy W., (AV) .... '64 '89 C.623 B.B.A. L.862 J.D. [Robinett&M.]

Robinett & Murphy, (AV)
624 South Boston, Suite 900, 74119
Telephone: 918-592-3699 Fax: 918-592-0963
Tracy W. Robinett; Lawrence R. Murphy, Jr.; Gregory A. Calvert; Kelly A. Smakal; Stephan S. Mathis; Pansy C. Moore-Shrier.
General Civil Practice Before all State and Federal Courts.

See Professional Biographies, TULSA, OKLAHOMA

Robinowitz, Marcialyn G. .... '47 '74 C.783 B.A. L.930 J.D. 3303 S. Florence Ave.‡
Robinson, Cooper Brett, (BV) .... '64 '89 C.623 B.A. L.862 J.D. 502 W. 6th St.
Robinson, Eugene, (AV) .... '57 '83 C&L.862 B.S., J.D. [Robinson]
Robinson, H. Murray .... '19 '57 C.309 A.B. L.262 LL.B. 3836 S. 134th E. Ave.‡
Robinson, James A., (AV) .... '29 '53 C.612 B.S. L.623 LL.B. 1924 S. Utica
Robinson, Mark R. .... '58 '92 C.586 B.B.A. L.862 J.D. 6202 S. Lewis, Ste. A
Robinson, Michael M. .... '69 '94 C.612 B.S. L.862 J.D. 1 Technology Center
Robinson, William A., (AV) .... '40 '74 C.1089 B.A. L.616 J.D. [Ⓒ Burton&Assoc.] ⊙‡

Robinson Law Firm, The, (AV)
5810 East Skelly Drive Suite 1100, 74135
Telephone: 918-587-2311 Fax: 918-587-2317
Email: grobinson@webzone.net URL: http://www.grobinson.com
Eugene Robinson. Associates: Kenneth M. Yates; Stephen L. McClellan.
Insurance Defense, Premises Liability, Tort, General Civil Practice in all courts.

See Professional Biographies, TULSA, OKLAHOMA

Robison, Coleman L., (AV) .... '43 '67 C&L.623 B.B.A., J.D. [Rosenstein,F.&R.]
Rode, Robert Lee, (CV) .... '63 '90 C.579 B.A. L.862 J.D. 324 S. Main St.
Rodolf, Sandra F., (AV) .... '54 '84 C&L.623 B.A., J.D. 1145 E. 26th St.
Rodolf, Stephen J., (AV) .... '48 '79 C&L.623 B.A., J.D. [Rodolf&T.]

Rodolf & Todd, (AV)
401 South Boston, 20th Floor, 74103
Telephone: 918-295-2100
Stephen J. Rodolf; Terry Todd; Karen L. Callahan; Leslie Custer Weeks; Elizabeth K. Hall; David A. Russell. Associates: Elizabeth S. Reynolds; Mark Edward Hardin; Eric M. Jordan; Brent L. Thompson; Chad H. Moody; Beth Anne Wilkening.
General Civil Practice, Trials in all State and Federal Courts. Medical Malpractice Defense, Products Liability, Employment Litigation.

See Professional Biographies, TULSA, OKLAHOMA

Roesler, Robert J. '30 '67 C&L.616 B.S., J.D.
Sr. V.P. & Tr. Offr., Bank IV Oklahoma, N.A.
Roffers, Juley M., (AV) .... '54 '80 C&L.623 B.A., J.D. 1603 S. Boulder
Rogers, Dan A., (AV) .... '23 '50 C.862 L.623 J.D. [D.A.Rogers&Assoc.]
Rogers, Jamie A. .... '77 '03 C.612 B.S. L.623 J.D. [Ⓐ Atkinson,H.N.B.G.&C.]
Rogers, Karla M. .... '67 '00 C.845 B.S. L.862 J.D. [Ⓐ Gibbs A.B.M.&H.]
Rogers, Marsha Lee '71 '96
C.619 B.A. L.862 J.D. Asst. Pub. Def., Tulsa Co. Pub. Def. Off.

Rogers & Bell, (AV)
320 South Boston Building, Suite 801, 74103
Telephone: 918-582-5201 Fax: 918-582-1751
Members of Firm: John Rogers (1890-1977); William H. Bell (1926-1988); Sharon J. Bell; Robert S. Farris; Gregory A. Gray.
Probate, Wills, Trusts, Estate Planning, Oil and Gas, Real Estate and Taxation Law, Charitable Organizations.
General Counsel for: Chapman-McFarlin Interests.
Representative Client: BancOklahoma Trust Co.

See Professional Biographies, TULSA, OKLAHOMA

Rogers, Dan A. & Associates, P.A., (AV) .... 5310 E. 31st Street, PH2
Romer, Trudy Maria .... '47 '94 C.619 B.A. L.862 J.D. P.O. Box 1
Romig, Michael, (AV) .... '51 '76 C.258 B.A. L.862 J.D. 200 Civic Ctr., Ste. 316
Rooney, John E. .... '27 '51 C&L.276 B.S., J.D. Chmn. of the Bd., The Rooney Corp.
Rooney, John E., Jr., (AV) .... '56 '81 C.602 B.A. L.276 J.D. [Moyers,M.S.I.&T.]
Rose, Randall E., (AV) .... '51 '78 C&L.862 B.A., J.D. [Ⓐ Owens]
Rose, Raymond K. .... '49 '74 C.976 B.A. L.910 J.D. Pres., Rose Company

Rosenstein, Fist & Ringold, A Professional Corporation, (AV)
525 South Main, Suite 700, 74103 ⊙
Telephone: 918-585-9211 Facsimile: 918-583-5617
URL: http://www.rfrlaw.com
Members of Firm: David L. Fist; A. F. Ringold; Coleman L. Robison; J. Douglas Mann; John G. Moyer, Jr.; John E. Howland; Jerry L. Zimmerman; Mark S. Rains; Frederick J. Hegenbart; Andrea R. Kunkel; Eric P. Nelson; Karen L. Long; John E. Priddy; Bryan K. Drummond. Of Counsel: Jerry A. Richardson; Larry A. Lewis; Kent "Bo" Rainey; Catharine M. Bashaw; Jana R. Burk (Not admitted in OK);—Matt P. Cyran; Eric D. Wade; Cassandra L. Wilkinson.
General Civil Practice in all State and Federal Courts. Corporation, Bankruptcy Reorganization, Education, Environmental, Health Care, Labor and Employment, Oil and Gas, Real Estate, Taxation, Wills and Probate, Workers' Compensation Law and Estate Planning.
Oklahoma City Office: 2801 N. Lincoln Blvd., Suite 224, 73105. Telephone: 405-521-0202. Facsimile: 405-521-1515.

See Professional Biographies, TULSA, OKLAHOMA

Ross, Alan B. .... '45 '82 C.1070 B.S. L.862 J.D. 2519 E. 21
Ross, David R., (AVⓉ) .... '42 '69 C.1044 B.A. L.823 J.D. 2900 Mid Continent Tower
Ross, David R. .... '76 '03 C.347 B.A. L.910 J.D. [Ⓐ Norman W.C.&D.]
Rosser, Malcolm E., IV, (AV) .... '55 '81 C.612 B.S. L.623 J.D. [Crowe&D.]
Rothbaum, Julian J. .... '13 '38 C&L.623 A.B., LL.B. P.O. Box 21468
Rothman, John D., (AV) .... '55 '81 C.309 B.A. L.94 J.D. OK Mediation/Arbitration Serv.
Rounds, Mary J., (AV) .... '— '82 C&L.862 B.S., J.D. [Ⓐ Riggs,A.N.T.O.&L.]
Rounds, Philard L., Jr., (AV) .... '52 '77 C.1288 B.A. L.616 J.D. [Smiling,B.&R.]
Rouse, Harry V., (AV) .... '55 '85 C.871 B.S. L.309 J.D. [H.V.Rouse]
Rouse, Steve L., (BV) .... '59 '84 C.612 B.S. L.862 J.D. 1503 S. Denver Ave.

Rouse, Harry V., P.C., Law Office of, (AV)
1408 South Denver, 74119
Telephone: 918-583-2227 Fax: 918-584-1129
Email: hvrouse@aol.com URL: http://www.harryvrouse.com
Harry V. Rouse.
Tax, Estate Planning, Probate, Wills, Complex Trusts and Estates, Trusts, Elder Law, Guardianships, ERISA, Employee Benefits, Medicaid Planning, Non Profit Organizations, Business Formations.

See Professional Biographies, TULSA, OKLAHOMA

Routh, Barbara L. .... '59 '92 C&L.862 B.S.N., J.D. 744 W. 9th Street
Rowland, Scott R., (AV) .... '60 '85 C.839 B.S. L.862 J.D. [Gable&G.]
Rubin, Arthur E., (AV) .... '21 '50 C&L.623 J.D. [Ⓒ J.R.Gotwals&Assoc.]
Rucker, Truman B., Jr., (AV) .... '50 '77 C&L.862 B.S., J.D. [Ⓒ Wilson,C.&A.]
Runnels, Gail R., (AV) .... '36 '60 C&L.862 B.S., LL.B. [Holliman L.&R.]
Runnels, Joseph Arnold, Jr. .... '56 '81 C.499 B.S. L.500 J.D. 401 S. Boston Ave.
Running, Jon R., (BV) .... '43 '71 C&L.623 B.B.A., J.D. [J.R.Running]
Running, Jon R., P.C., (BV) .... 2512 E. 71st St.
Rusher, James W., (BV) .... '60 '85 C&L.802 B.A., J.D. [Albright,R.&H.]
Russell, David A., (AV) .... '68 '93 C.378 B.A. L.623 J.D. [Rodolf&T.]
Russell, James J. .... '22 '51 C&L.862 LL.B. 750 N. 41 W. Ave.
Russell, John D., (AV) .... '63 '88 C.612 B.S. L.623 J.D. [Fellers,S.B.B.&T.]
Rutherford, S. Morton, III .... '20 '47 C.623 A.B. L.976 LL.B. 2419 E. 24th St.‡
Rutledge, William E. .... '23 '51 C.608 B.A. L.930 LL.B. 15 E. 5th St.
Ryan, James M. Scott, (BV) .... '65 '91 C&L.623 B.A., J.D. [King,T.&R.]
Sachse, Robert G., (AV) '49 '76
C.859 B.S. L.862 J.D. Pres., MAPCO Nat. Gas. Liquids Inc.
Sacra, J. Ryan, (BV) .... '71 '96 C&L.623 B.B.A., J.D. [Conner&W.]
Sacra, Jeffrey C., (AV) '67 '92
C.623 B.S. L.880 J.D. Gen. Coun., St. Francis Health Sys., Inc.
Saffa, Ronald J., (BV) .... '48 '82 C&L.612 B.S., J.D. [Morrel,W.S.C.&H.]
Sakelaris, S. J. .... '20 '60 C&L.862 B.A., LL.B. 5200 S. Yale
Salisbury, Harold W., (BV) .... '62 '88 C.623 B.B.A. L.862 J.D. [Doyle&S.]
Salle, Frank E. .... '40 '66 C&L.623 B.B.A., J.D. 302 S. Cheyenne
Sandel, Larry W., (AV) .... '43 '69 C&L.800 B.A., J.D. [Hall,E.H.G.G.&N.]
Sanders, David H., Jr., (AV) .... '43 '69 C.623 B.A. L.862 J.D. [Sanders&S.]
Sanders, Esther M., (BV) .... '64 '93 C.225 B.A. L.615 J.D. [Sanders&Assoc.]
Sanders, William J. .... '52 '93 C.401 B.S. L.426 J.D. 4706 E. 87th Street

Sanders & Associates, P.C., (BV)
2727 E. 21st Street, Suite 303, 74114
Telephone: 918-745-2000; 800-745-2006 Fax: 918-745-0575
Email: esther@sanderslawoffice.com
Esther M. Sanders;—Tana Fredrick Smith.
Personal Injury, Workers Compensation, Social Security, Automobile Insurance Coverage.

See Professional Biographies, TULSA, OKLAHOMA

Sanders & Sanders, P.C., (AV)
Denver Building, 624 South Denver, 74119
Telephone: 918-582-5181 Fax: 918-582-5022
Email: dsandersjr@sandersok.com

(This Listing Continued)

Sanders & Sanders, P.C. (Continued)

David H. Sanders (1915-2004); David H. Sanders, Jr.
General Civil Practice, Commercial Real Estate, Commercial Loans, Bank Law, Corporation, Wills, Probate, Surety Law.

See Professional Biographies, TULSA, OKLAHOMA

Sanditen, Scott A. .... '53 '79 C.623 B.A. L.862 J.D. 3314 E. 51st St.‡
Sanford, Raymond F. .... '17 '41 C&L.352 J.D. 5898 S. Joplin Ave.‡
Santee, Amy Monsour .... '71 '01 C&L.623 B.A., J.D. [A Conner&W.]
Santee, Jack H., (AV) .... '31 '56 C&L.623 B.S., LL.B. [Moyers,M.S.I.&T.] ⊙
Sappenfield, Keith M., II '48 '82
C.701 B.S.C.E. L.215 J.D. Mgr., Rates & Reg. Affs., Transok, Inc.
Sartin, Robert B., (AV) .... '63 '88 C&L.623 B.B.A., J.D. [Barrow&G.]
Satrom, James D., (AV) .... '52 '77 C.861 B.A. L.893 J.D. [Hall,E.H.G.G.&N.]
Saunders, James E., (CV) .... '52 '87 C.304 B.S. L.846 J.D. Divorce Ctr. of Tulsa
Saunders, Katherine, (AV) .... '54 '91 C.859 B.A. L.862 J.D [Rains&S.]
Savage, Dale G., (BV) .... '11 '49 C.378 B.S. L.862 LL.B. 6411 S. 90th E. Ave.
Savage, Robert Scott, (AV) '53 '78 C&L.623 B.A., J.D.
Gen. Coun., Amer. Central Gas Technologies Inc.
Schaffer, David J. .... '74 '01 C.276 B.S.B.A. L.623 K.D. [Schaffer,P.]
Schaffer Law Firm, The, PLLC .... 406 S. Boston Ave., Ste. 450
Schelin, Eric R. .... '76 '02 C.505 B.S. L.862 J.D. [A F.Dorwart]
Schell, Kent Alan .... '48 '79 C.375 B.S. L.862 J.D. City of Tulsa
Schell, Mark E., (AV) '57 '83 C.36 B.S. L.862 J.D.
Secy., Gen. Coun. & Sr. V.P., Unit Corporation
Schilling, Gretchen M. Widdig, (BV) '65 '92
C.1300 B.Acct. L.862 J.D. [Riggs,A.N.T.O.&L.]
Schmidt, Melissa Minton, (BV) .... '67 '94 C.378 B.A. L.862 J.D. [King,T.&R.]
Schmook, Genevieve L. .... '75 '02 C.612 B.S. L.862 J.D. [A Hall,E.H.G.G.&N.]
Schneider, Ann Makela .... '58 '86 C&L.862 B.S., J.D. Law Clk. to U.S. Mag. J.
Schneider, Frederic N. (Nick), III, (AV) '48 '73 C&L.862 B.A., J.D.
[Boone,S.D.H.&D.]
Schneider, Stephen E., (AV) .... '55 '81 C.612 B.S. L.846 J.D. 403 S. Cheyenne, Ste. 1200
Schoborg, Jeffrey R., (BV) .... '56 '84 C.623 B.S. L.862 J.D. [Conner&W.]
Schoenenberger, Thomas R., (AV) .... '50 '77 C.94 B.S. L.862 J.D. [McCormick,S.&G.]
Schofield, Martin P. '59 '86 C.506 B.S.A.E. L.37 J.D.
(adm. in IL; not adm. in OK) V.P. Product Safety/Liability, Hilti, Inc.
Schooley, Sharon K. .... '59 '84 C.623 B.A. L.862 J.D. Staff Atty.
Schroeder, Donald E., (AV) '49 '80
C.542 B.A. L.616 J.D. Mng. Atty., Farmers Insurance Company
Schroedter, Thomas P., (AV) .... '54 '79 C.228 B.A. L.862 J.D. [Hall,E.H.G.G.&N.]
Schuler, John D. .... '27 '58 C&L.862 LL.B. Ste 700, 2021 South Lewis
Schuller, Stephen A., (AV) .... '51 '76 C.597 B.A. L.862 J.D. [Boone,S.D.H.&D.]
Schutz, Kimberly R. .... '75 '00 C.378 B.B.A. L.623 J.D. [A Hall,E.H.G.G.&N.]
Schwabe, A. Grant .... '76 '05 C.623 B.A. L.862 J.D. [A Kivell,R.&F.]
Schwartz, Bernard '23 '45 C.563 B.S.S. L.569 LL.B.
(adm. in NY; not adm. in OK) Prof. of Law, Univ. of Tulsa
Schwartz, Joshua L. .... '73 '00 C.659 B.A L.861 J.D. 2000 S. Wheeling, Ste. 401 (Pat.)
Schwerdtfeger, Tyson D. .... '76 '02 C.1315 B.A. L.880 J.D. [A Gable&G.]
Scott, Douglas R. .... '79 '04 C.612 B.S. L.623 J.D. [A Morgan,B.M.M.F.&K.]
Scott, John P., (AV) .... '30 '61 C.560 B.B.A. L.862 LL.B. 406 S. Boulder SW Mezzanine
Scott, Marcia A., (AV) '53 '80
C&L.862 B.A., J.D. Corp. Atty., Thrifty Rent-A-Car System, Inc.

Scott, Roger R., (AV) '35 '60 C&L.862 B.A., J.D.
Eleven Eleven Park Centre, 525 South Main Street, 74103
Telephone: 918-583-8201 FAX: 918-582-8803
Email: rogrescott@web2one.net
Civil Litigation, Oil and Gas, Corporation and Real Estate Law. Probate, Trusts, Estate Planning and Antitrust Law. Trials in all State and Federal Courts.

Scroggins, R. Daniel, (AV) .... '66 '93 C.586 B.B.A. L.862 J.D. [Fellers,S.B.B.&T.]
Seagle, Victor R., (AV) .... '45 '76 C&L.862 B.A., J.D. [Perrine,M.R.R.B.&T.]
Searcy, William C. .... '— '99 C.69 B.A. L.623 J.D. [A Riggs,A.N.T.O.&L.]
Seay, Harry L., III, (AV) .... '37 '65 C.674 A.B. L.976 LL.B. 320 S. Boston Bldg.
Secrest, James K., II, (AV) .... '47 '72 C&L.862 B.S.B.A., J.D. [Secrest,H.&B.]
Secrest, James Keith, III, (BV) .... '72 '00 C.612 M.I.S. L.862 J.D. [Secrest,H.&B.]

Secrest, Hill & Butler, (AV) BB
7134 South Yale, Suite 900, 74136-6342
Telephone: 918-494-5905 Fax: 918-494-2847
Email: rbutler@secresthill.com URL: http://www.secresthill.com
Members of Firm: James K. Secrest, II; W. Michael Hill; Roger N. Butler, Jr.; Richard C. Honn; Edward John Main; James Keith Secrest, III; Jason A. Robertson;—Syma S. Azam; Timothy S. Harmon; Don W. Danz; Jack Y. Goree; Michael D. Goss; Eric A. Mareshie; Jenny R. Ebersole; Kimberly N. Clark; W. Joseph Pickard; Michael W. Boutot; Tara P. Goodnight.
General Civil Practice. Trials. Insurance, Negligence, Corporation, Aviation, Medical/Dental Malpractice, Architectural/Engineer Malpractice, Products Liability Law, Accounting Malpractice, Construction Defect, Insurance Coverage, Insurance Bad Faith, Nursing Home/Long Term Care Malpractice, Employment Practice, Appellate Oractice, Nursing Malpractice, Environmental Law, Mass Tort Litigation. .

See Professional Biographies, TULSA, OKLAHOMA

Seibert, Steven D. .... '65 '91 C.225 B.A. L.910 J.D. Sr. Atty., The Williams Cos., Inc.
Seifert, Lisa Mans .... '63 '93 C.623 B.A. L.862 J.D. P.O. Box 3066
Sell, Howard William .... '43 '78 C.399 B.A. L.862 J.D. 5352 E. 47th Pl.
Sellers, Jefferson D. .... '55 '80 C.188 B.A. L.862 J.D. Dist. J., Tulsa Co. Courthouse
Sellers, Keith F., (BV) .... '48 '81 C.992 B.A. L.623 J.D. 7134 S. Yale Ave., Ste. 110
Sellers, Michael E. .... '62 '94 C&L.45 B.S.E.E., J.D. [B Gable&G.] (Pat.)
Selman, Richard B. .... '75 '00 C&L.623 B.B.A., J.D. [A Lawson,K.&S.]
Selman, William B., (AV) .... '45 '73 C.597 B.S. L.623 J.D. [Selman&Assoc.]
Selman & Associates, P.C., (AV) .... 601 South Boulder
Semler, J. Dennis, (BV) .... '56 '81 C.1288 B.A. L.862 J.D. Asst. Dist. Atty.
Senger, David C. .... '74 '00 C.1362 B.S. L.862 J.D. [A Perrine,M.R.R.B.&T.]
Seward, Larry E. .... '46 '80 C.623 B.B.A. L.862 J.D. 2761 E. Skelly Dr.
Seymour, Clive A. .... '46 '78 C&L.846 B.A., J.D. [B Hall,E.H.G.G.&N.]
Seymour, Michael L., (AV) .... '50 '80 C&L.862 B.S., J.D. 1717 East 15th Street
Seymour, R. Thomas, (AV) .... '42 '67 C&L.309 A.B., LL.B. [Seymour]
Seymour, Stephanie K. .... '40 '65 C.788 B.A. L.1565 J.D. U.S. App. Ct. J.

Seymour Law Firm, (AV)
100 West Fifth Street, Suite 550, 74103-4288
Telephone: 918-583-5791 FAX: 918-583-9251 Email: rtseymour1@aol.com
Email: robtburton@aol.com URL: http://www.seymourlawfirm.com
R. Thomas Seymour; C. Robert Burton, IV. Associate: Scott A. Graham.
General Civil Practice in all State and Federal Courts. Trials and Appeals. White Collar Criminal, Corporate, Bankruptcy, Securities, Securities Fraud, Commercial Litigation, Banking Law, Civil RICO Litigation, Civil Rights.

See Professional Biographies, TULSA, OKLAHOMA

Shacklett, Curtis J., (AV) .... '44 '79 C&L.862 B.S., J.D. [Barber&B.]
Shafer, John L., III, (AV) .... '50 '75 C.45 B.A. L.862 J.D. [J.L.Shafer,III]
Shafer, John L., III, P.C., (AV) .... 5918 E. 31st St.
Shaffer, Ronald L. .... '36 '64 C&L.862 LL.B. Dist. J.
Shallcross, Richard A., (AV) .... '47 '82 C.701 B.S. L.862 J.D. [Shallcross]

Shallcross Law Firm, (AV)
The Wrightsman Manor, 1645 South Cheyenne, 74119
Telephone: 918-592-1645 Fax: 918-585-9137
Email: ADVOCATUS@AOL.COM URL: http://www.shallcrosslaw.com
Richard A. Shallcross.
General Civil Trial Practice in State and Federal Courts. Personal Injury and Medical Malpractice.

See Professional Biographies, TULSA, OKLAHOMA

Shamas, Mitchell E., (BV) .... '48 '73 C&L.623 B.A., J.D. 6863 S. Canton Ave.
Sharbrough, DeVan .... '34 '91 C.623 B.S. L.862 J.D. P.O. Box 35858
Sharma, Rohit C. .... '— '03 C.1213 B.S. L.862 J.D. [Sharma]

Sharma Law Firm, PLLC
403 South Cheyenne Suite 1100, 74103
Telephone: 918-398-0327 Fax: 918-516-0232
Email: rohit@sharmalawfirm.com URL: http://www.sharmalawfirm.com
Rohit C. Sharma.
General Practice. Business Organization, Business Transactions, Securities Litigation, Securities Arbitration, Bankruptcy, Estate Planning, Family Law, Divorce, Immigration and Criminal Law.

See Professional Biographies, TULSA, OKLAHOMA

Sharp, David P. .... '48 '73 C&L.37 B.A., J.D. 1647 E. 3rd St.
Sharp, John M., (AV) '41 '68 C.623 B.A. L.862 J.D.
Managing Atty., Child Supp. Enfor. Div., Dept. of HHS
Sharp, John S., (AV) .... '56 '82 C&L.623 B.B.A., J.D. 1831 E. 71st Street
Sharp, Joseph A., (AV) .... '21 '49 C.862 B.A. L.623 LL.B. [Best&S.]
Shaw, Dwain S. .... '62 '03 C.1341 M.P.H. L.862 J.D. [A Eldridge C.S.&L.]
Sheehan, Mary M. .... '23 '50 C.856 B.A. L.862 LL.B. 8887 S. Lewis Ave.‡
Sheil, William B., II .... '60 '85 C&L.862 B.A., J.D. 3701 S. Peoria Ave.‡
Shelton, J. Charles, (BV) .... '45 '70 C.612 B.A. L.862 J.D. [B Richardson,S.R.&W.]
Shelton, Leslie, (BV) .... '53 '85 C.612 B.A. L.862 J.D. 6226 E. 101st St., Ste. 100
Shelton, Pamela Dowell, (AV) '— '84
C&L.378 B.A., J.D. Sr. Coun., The Williams Cos., Inc.
Shelton-Vanderyt, Paige N. .... '76 '04 C.880 B.A. L.862 J.D. [A Crowe&D.]
Shelts, Bradley S. .... '74 '02 C.612 B.S. L.862 J.D. [A Rhodes,H.J.T.&G.]
Shepherd, Robert L., (BV) .... '23 '49 C&L.623 LL.B. 222 W. 8th St.
Sherman, Mark, (BV) .... '58 '81 C.986 B.A. L.862 J.D. Pres., MAPCO Inc.
Sherwood, Charles L. '53 '78 C.170 B.A. L.208 J.D.
(adm. in CO; not adm. in OK) Lariat Petroleum, Inc.
Sherwood, Ted C., (AV) .... '55 '83 C.862 B.S.B.A. L.623 J.D. 15 W. 6th St., Ste. 2112
Shiflet, Michael A. .... '69 '00 C.663 B.S. L.862 J.D. [A Frasier,F.&H.]
Shipley, Charles W., (AV) .... '43 '71 C.612 B.S. L.273 J.D. [Shipley&K.]
Shipley, Sally A. .... '49 '91 C.623 B.L.S. L.862 J.D. 5859 S. 81st W. Avenue

Shipley & Kellogg, P.C., (AV) BB
1648 South Boston Avenue, Suite 100, 74119-4416 ⊙
Telephone: 918-582-1720 Fax: 918-584-7681
Email: firm@shipleylaw.net
Charles W. Shipley; Jamie Taylor Boyd. Of Counsel: D. E. Dismukes.
General Civil Practice in all State and Federal Courts, with emphasis in Environmental Law, Water Rights, Business and Commercial Litigation, Class Actions, Alternative Dispute Resolution and Native American Law.
Reference: Bank of America.
Oklahoma City, Oklahoma Office: Two Leadership Square, 211 North Robinson, Suite 1300, 73102-7114. Telephone: 405-235-0808. Facsimile: 405-232-3746. Email: rkellogg@shipleylaw.net

See Professional Biographies, TULSA, OKLAHOMA

Shirley, Shannon Rochelle .... '68 '96 C.931 B.A. L.862 J.D. 1915 S. Boston Ave.
Shook, Jonathan E., (BV) .... '60 '97 C.623 B.A. L.862 J.D. [Shook&D.]
Shook & Downes, P.L.L.C., (BV) .... 2121 S. Columbia Ave., Ste. 405
Shorb, Randy R., (AV) .... '59 '85 C.263 B.A. L.802 J.D. [Johnson,J.D.C.&S.]
Shore, Brian K. .... '64 '89 C&L.862 B.S.B.A., J.D. Corp. Secy., The Williams Cos., Inc.
Short, Jack Marwood, (AV) .... '24 '58 C.861 B.A. L.623 LL.B. 1709 Utica Square
Shotts, Ron, (BV) .... '46 '72 C&L.623 B.B.A., J.D. P.O. Box 52233‡
Shoup, David D. .... '59 '84 C&L.477 B.A., J.D. Community Action Proj. of Tulsa Co.
Sibley, Margaret J. Hamlett, (BV) '59 '87 C&L.862 B.S.B.A., J.D.
Gen. Coun., Mental Health Assoc. of Tulsa, Inc.
Sigler, Jared Paul .... '75 '01 C.612 B.A. L.615 J.D. Dist. Atty. Off.
Silva, Pete, Jr., (AV) .... '47 '75 C&L.862 B.S., J.D. 3716 S. Braden Pl.
Silvestri, Lisa Traylor .... '70 '96 C&L.846 B.A., J.D. [Gable&G.]
Simcoe, Steven W., (AV) .... '65 '92 C.623 B.A. L.276 J.D. [A Best&S.]
Simmons, Larry Vernon, (AV) .... '56 '84 C.612 L.862 J.D. Dep. City Atty.
Simonson, Terry A., (BV) .... '51 '89 C.80 B.A. L.862 J.D. [Vestal&S.]
Singer, Todd William, (BV) .... '61 '90 C.1036 B.A. L.862 J.D. [A Harris,M.P.T.&S.]
Singhal, Vani .... '71 '96 C.612 B.A. L.276 J.D. [A Eldridge C.S.&L.]
Singletary, M. Benjamin, (AV) .... '48 '77 C.575 B.A. L.862 J.D. [Gable&G.]
Skalnik, Brinton .... '65 '90 C.612 B.S. L.862 J.D. [Skalnik]
Skalnik Law Office .... 1613 E. 32nd St.
Skeens, Michelle D. .... '75 '99 C&L.923 B.A., J.D. [A Holden&C.]
Skeith, Robert P., (AV) .... '65 '94 C&L.862 B.A., J.D. [Riggs,A.N.T.O.&L.]
Skrzypczak, Julie A. .... '65 '92 C.612 B.S. L.862 J.D. P.O. Box 52833
Slater, John M. .... '25 '56 C&L.862 B.A., LL.B. Sr. Admin. Law J., Soc. Sec. Admn.
Slicker, Frederick K., (AV) .... '43 '68 C&L.378 B.A., J.D. [Slicker]

Slicker Law Firm, P.C., (AV)
4444 East 66th, Suite 201, 74136-4206
Telephone: 918-496-9020 Facsimile: 918-496-9024 URL: http://www.tulsalaw-firm.com
Email: fslicker@swbell.net URL: http://www.slickerlawfirm.com
Frederick K. Slicker.
Mergers, Acquisitions, Business Purchases and Sales, Corporate Finance, Securities Offerings and Compliance, Franchise Compliance, Corporations, Partnerships, LLCs, Joint Ventures, General Business Law, Problem Solving and Dispute Resolution.

See Professional Biographies, TULSA, OKLAHOMA

Sloan, Betty H. .... '41 '78 C&L.862 B.S., J.D. [B Hanson&H.]
Smakal, Kelly A., (BV) .... '70 '97 C&L.45 B.A., J.D. [Robinett&M.]
Smallwood, Allen M., (AV) .... '47 '75 C.612 B.S. L.862 J.D. [A.Smallwood]
Smallwood, Allen, (AV) .... 1310 S. Denver Ave.
Smiling, A. Mark, (AV) .... '58 '84 C&L.999 B.S., J.D. [Smiling,B.&R.]

Smiling, Bender & Rounds, P.A., (AV) BB
Bradford Place, 9175 South Yale Avenue, Suite 300, 74137
Telephone: 918-477-7500 Fax: 918-477-7510 URL: http://www.smilinglaw.com
Email: slf@smilinglaw.com URL: http://www.smilinglawfirm.com
A. Mark Smiling; Gerald M. Bender; Philard L. Rounds, Jr.; Stephan A. Wangsgard; Jane R. Cowdery; J. Kent Fredenberger; Jason C. Messenger.
General Insurance Defense in all State and Federal Courts, Insurance Law with First and Third Party Claims, Products Liability, Medical and Legal Malpractice, Hospital, Nursing Home and Health Care Law, Civil Rights, Employment Law, Workers' Compensation, Premises Liability, Subrogation, Environmental Law, Transportation and Common Carriers, Arson, Property and Casualty, Com

(This Listing Continued)

Smiling, Bender & Rounds, P.A. (Continued)

mercial Litigation, Mediation/Arbitration, Construction Law, Estate Planning, Business Planning, Charitable Gift Tax Planning, Business Litigation, Personal Injury, Wrongful Death, Wills, Trusts and Estates, Contracts, Transactions, Equine Law, Aviation Law.

See Professional Biographies, TULSA, OKLAHOMA

Smith, Aundrea R. ... '72 '99 C.612 B.S. [Townsend&S.]
Smith, B. Jack, (BV) ... '57 '82 C&L.623 B.A., J.D. [Works&L.]
Smith, Beverly K., (AV) ... '48 '88 C.623 B.A. L.862 J.D. [Conner&W.]
Smith, Brad, (AV) ... '51 '77 C&L.862 B.S., J.D. [Barkley]
Smith, Bryan L., (BV) ... '59 '85 C&L.1288 B.A., J.D. 201 W. 5th St., Ste. 530
Smith, Charlotte A., (AV) '57 '85
C.623 B.S. L.862 J.D. Staff Atty., St. Francis Health Sys., Inc.
Smith, D. Rustin ... '76 '02 C&L.623 B.A., J.D. [Ⓐ Wilburn&M.]
Smith, David S. ... '— '02 C&L.623 B.A., J.D. Crawford & Company
Smith, Dean H., (BV) ... '12 '47 C.900 A.B. L.862 LL.B. [Smith&S.] ‡

Smith, Dianne L., (AV) '47 '79 C.315 B.A. L.862 J.D.
2502 East 21st Street, 74114-1706
Telephone: 918-743-5151 Telecopier: 918-743-4695
Email: dsmith@gutheryandsmith.com
Banking Law, Bankruptcy, Real Estate, Business Law, Corporate, Contracts, Commercial and Probate Law.

See Professional Biographies, TULSA, OKLAHOMA

Smith, Donald S., (AV) ... '57 '82 C.804 B.A. L.862 J.D. [Pray,W.J.W.&M.]
Smith, Dwight L., (AV) ... '56 '81 C&L.862 B.S., J.D. Ste 1030, 1800 S Baltimore
Smith, Eric S. ... '73 '98 C.612 B.S. L.623 J.D. [Concordia B.]
Smith, Jerry L., (BV) ... '43 '71 C.612 B.A. L.862 J.D. State Sen.
Smith, Kenneth M., (AV) ... '42 '72 C.612 B.S.C.E. L.862 J.D. [Riggs,A.N.T.O.&L.]
Smith, Kenny Joe, (BV) ... '54 '81 C.612 B.A. L.862 J.D. [Ⓒ Bodenhamer&L.]
Smith, Kim Renee, (BV) ... '57 '84 C&L.862 B.M.E., J.D. Neighbor for Neighbor
Smith, Malcolm D., Jr., (BV) ... '48 '81 C.612 B.S.B.A. L.862 J.D. 15 W. 6th Street
Smith, Michael F., (BV) ... '64 '91 C.612 B.S. L.862 J.D. [Eldridge C.S.&L.]
Smith, Oliver L. ... '78 '03 C.623 B.A. L.862 J.D. [Ⓐ Richards&C.]
Smith, Patricia, (BV) ... '— '84 C&L.862 B.A., J.D. 1700 S.W. Blvd.
Smith, Phillip K., (BV) ... '57 '82 C.1315 B.S. L.1288 J.D. [Smith&S.]
Smith, Robert L., (BV) ... '57 '86 C.221 B.S.B.A. L.862 J.D. [R.L.Smith]
Smith, Robert Steen ... '23 '71 C.623 B.S. L.862 J.D. 129 E. 26th Ct.‡
Smith, Sarah Day ... '55 '83 C.500 B.A. L.45 J.D. Spec. Dist. Ct. J.
Smith, Steven E. ... '29 '57 C.1243 B.S. L.623 J.D. 2930 E. 51st Street
Smith, Tana Fredrick, (BV) ... '57 '95 C.619 B.S. L.862 J.D. [Ⓐ Sanders&Assoc.]
Smith, Terence W. ... '41 '67 C&L.862 LL.B. 3743 E. 82nd Street
Smith, Tye H., (AV) ... '67 '92 C&L.623 B.A., J.D. [Carr&C.]
Smith, William F., (AV) ... '52 '77 C.612 B.A. L.862 J.D. [Graham&F.]
Smith, Robert L., P.C., (BV) ... 717 S. Houston Ave., Ste. 400
Smith & Smith, (BV) ... 8906 E. Skelly Dr.
Smolen, Donald E. ... '50 '76 C.966 B.A. L.862 J.D. 201 W. 5th St.
Snapp, Randall J., (AV) ... '59 '85 C&L.378 B.A., J.D. [Crowe&D.]
Sneed, James L., (AV) ... '38 '63 C.309 A.B. L.623 J.D. [J.L.Sneed]
Sneed, James L., Law Offices, A Professional Corporation, (AV)
427 South Boston, Suite 309

Sneed Lang, P.C., (AV) BR
1700 Williams Center Tower I, One West Third Street, 74103
Telephone: 918-583-3145 Telecopier: 918-582-0410
URL: http://www.sneedlang.com
James C. Lang; D. Faith Orlowski; Brian S. Gaskill; G. Steven Stidham; Stephen R. McNamara; Patrick O. Waddel; Douglas L. Inhofe; Steven K. Balman; David J. Hyman; Sharon L. Corbitt; Stuart D. Campbell; Brian T. Inbody; D. Michael McBride III; N. Scott Johnson; Ronald W. Little; Tiffany Arend Campbell. Of Counsel: James L. Sneed.
Civil Litigation, White Collar Criminal Defense Litigation. Oil and Gas Law, Securities, Securities Fraud. Qui Tam Litigation, Antitrust, Bankruptcy, Negligence, Insurance, Banking, Corporate, Real Estate Law and Title Examination. Environmental Law, Health Care Law, Federal Indian Law and Policy. Family Law, Divorce, Child Custody. Guardianships, Probate, Estate Planning, Sports Law and Transportation.
Representative Clients: Bank One, Texas; BP Pipeline N.A., Inc.; Halliburton Energy Services; Helmerich & Payne, Inc.; ChevronTexaco Corporation; Wells Fargo Bank; The Williams Companies.

See Professional Biographies, TULSA, OKLAHOMA

Snider, Jerry M., (AV) ... '51 '76 C.623 B.S. L.862 J.D. [Ⓒ Eller&D.]
Snoke, Kenneth P. ... '41 '71 C.668 B.A. L.862 J.D. Asst. U.S. Atty.
Snyder, Tori M. ... '59 '00 C.839 B.B.A. L.862 J.D. [Ⓐ F.Dorwart]
Sobel, David L., (AV) ... '46 '72 C.623 B.B.A. L.192 J.D. 2431 E. 51st St., Ste. 601
Sohn, Rina L. ... '72 '97 C.645 B.S. L.862 J.D. Tech. Coun., McLeodUSA, Inc.
Solano, R. Mark, (AV) ... '51 '81 C.1044 B.A. L.982 J.D. [R.M.Solano]
Solano, R. Mark, P.L.L.C., (AV) ... 7615 East 63rd Place, Suite 210
Sorem, Gentra Abbey, (AV) ... '58 '83 C&L.378 B.A., J.D. [Conner&W.]
Sorenson, S. Brent ... '56 '89 C.101 B.S. L.862 J.D. Asst. Dist. Atty.
Soulé, Steven W., (AV) ... '64 '89 C&L.623 B.B.A., J.D. [Hall,E.H.G.G.&N.]
Sousa, Vicki J. ... '56 '91 C.999 B.S. L.862 J.D. 1518 S. Cheyenne
Southerland, Leslie J., (BV) ... '60 '87 C&L.862 B.A., J.D. [Rhodes,H.J.T.&G.]
Sparks, Valerie L. ... '73 '04 C.619 B.S. L.862 J.D. [Ⓐ McAtee]
Sparks, W. E. "Bill", (AV) ... '56 '83 C.616 B.S. L.862 J.D. [Sparks&E.]
Sparks & Eaton, (AV) ... P.O. Box 52548
Speaker, Susan J., (BV) '46 '85 C&L.45 B.A., J.D.
Exec. Dir., Properties and Concessions, Dollar Thrifty Automotive Group, Inc.
Spears, Marvin E., (BV) ... '40 '67 C&L.623 B.B.A., J.D. P.O. Box 54220
Spence, Bruce A., (CV) ... '56 '94 C.375 B.S. L.862 J.D. [Spence]

Spence Law Office, (CV)
1440 South Harvard Avenue Suite 100, 74112
Telephone: 918-582-3266 Fax: 918-582-3271
Email: brucespence@sbcglobal.net URL: http://www.tulsaconstructionlaw.com
Managing Attorney: Bruce A. Spence.
Commercial and Civil Litigation, Construction Law, Real Property Law, General Practice Litigation, Trust and Estate Litigation, Bankruptcy.

See Professional Biographies, TULSA, OKLAHOMA

Spiegelberg, Frank D., (AV) ... '48 '73 C.381 B.A. L.228 J.D. [Pray,W.J.W.&M.]
Spillers, G. C., Jr., (AV) ... '17 '42 C.197 A.B. L.846 LL.B. 3836 S. Birmingham Pl.‡
Spitler, William H. ... '74 '00 C.234 B.A. L.1243 J.D. [Ⓐ Doerner,S.D.&A.]
Spoo, Robert ... '57 '01 C.399 B.A. L.976 J.D. [Ⓐ Doerner,S.D.&A.] ⊙
Squire, Harris G. '12 '37 C.942 L.900 LL.B.
(adm. in KS; not adm. in OK) 3150 E. 34th St.‡
Staggs, Dawn Lei ... '66 '97 C.446 B.A. L.862 J.D. 2727 E. 21st St., Ste. 305
Stailey, Andrea D. ... '78 '05 C.619 B.A. L.862 J.D. [Ⓐ Cooper,M.&W.]
Stainer, Kenneth L., (BV) ... '17 '50 C.862 L.623 LL.B. 7030 So. Yale
Stall, Douglas E., (AV) ... '63 '89 C.612 B.S. L.862 J.D. [Latham,S.W.S.&L.]
Stall, Eric W., (BV) ... '65 '90 C.612 B.A. L.862 J.D. [Harris,M.P.T.&S.]
Stallard, Diana Renee ... '63 '97 C.612 B.S.B.A. L.862 J.D. [Stallard]
Stallard Law Firm, PLLC ... 5521 S. Lewis Avenue

Stamper, Gerald G., (AV) ... '36 '59 C&L.623 B.A., LL.B. [Nichols,W.S.N.F.&R.]
Stamper, James W., (BV) ... '56 '88 C.612 B.S. L.862 J.D. [Harrington&M.]
Stangeland, L. Alan ... '27 '60 C&L.862 B.A., J. D. 1611 S. Denver Ave.

Stanley, Mandel & Iola, L.L.P., (AV)
1323 East 71st Street, Suite 315, 74136-5068
Telephone: 918-524-5005 Fax: 918-524-5006
URL: http://www.smi-dallas.com
Mark H. Iola. Of Counsel: Randall L. Iola.
Asbestos Litigation.

See Professional Biographies, TULSA, OKLAHOMA

Stanton, Robert J., (AV) ... '13 '37 C&L.623 B.A., LL.B. 4150 S. Harvard Ave.‡
Starr, Jon D., (AV) ... '64 '91 C.612 B.S. L.623 J.D. [Atkinson,H.N.B.G.&C.]
Stauffer, James S. ... '17 '41 C&L.623 A.B., LL.B. 8919 E. 62nd St.‡
Stauffer, Neal E., (AV) ... '56 '89 C&L.623 B.B.A., J.D. [Stauffer,G.&N.]

Stauffer, Graves & Nathan, (AV) BR
2816 East 51st Street, Suite 200, 74105
Mailing Address: P.O. Box 702860, Tulsa, OK 74170-2860
Telephone: 918-592-7070 Facsimile: 918-592-7071 URL: http://www.nealstaufferlawyers.com
Email: nstauffer@staufferlaw.com URL: http://www.lawyers.com/nealstauffer
Neal E. Stauffer; Gregg L. Graves; Jody R. Nathan;—Nathan Guy Parrilli; Dalinda J. Jeffers. Of Counsel: John A. Coates; Joseph R. Roberts.
Insurance coverage, including First and Third Party Claims, Bad Faith Claims, Insurance Defense, Products Liability Defense, Personal Injury, Commercial Litigation, and General Civil Litigation. Trial and Appellate practice in State and Federal Courts.
Representative Clients: Mt. Hawley Insurance Company; RLI Insurance Company; National American Insurance Company; Shelter Insurance Companies; Oklahoma Attorneys Mutual Insurance Company; State Farm Fire and Casualty Company; Oklahoma Farm Bureau Mutual Insurance Company; State Farm Mutual Insurance Company.

See Professional Biographies, TULSA, OKLAHOMA

Stecher, Steven A., (AV) ... '48 '73 C.623 B.B.A. L.846 J.D. [Moyers,M.S.I.&T.] ⊙
Steele, Mark T., (AV) ... '65 '91 C.1288 B.A. L.862 J.D. [Latham,S.W.S.&L.]
Steele, Perry L. '52 '89 C.880 B.A. L.326 J.D.
(adm. in TX; not adm. in OK) Contract Atty., Tejas Gas Corp.
Steelman, J. D., Jr., (AV) '46 '76 C.294 B.A. L.69 J.D.
General Counsel, Williams International Co., L.L.C.
Steichen, Thomas E., (AV) ... '48 '75 C&L.734 A.B., J.D. [Eldridge C.S.&L.]
Steidley, W. G. "Gil", Jr., (AV) ... '44 '69 C&L.623 B.B.A., J.D. [Steidley&N.] ⊙‡

Steidley & Neal, (AV)
Exchange Tower, Suite 800, 4500 South Garnett Road, P.O. Box 1165, 74146 ⊙
Telephone: 918-664-4612 Fax: 918-664-4133
W. G. "Gil" Steidley, Jr.; Whitney M. Eschenheimer. Associates: Amy Beth Dobbins; Michelle Harris. Of Counsel: Jerry E. Truster.
Civil Litigation in all State and Federal Courts. Insurance Defense and Personal Injury Law.
McAlester, Oklahoma Office: 100 East Carl Albert Parkway, P.O. Box 1165, 74502. Telephone: 918-423-4611. Fax: 918-423-4620

See Professional Biographies, TULSA, OKLAHOMA

Steinmetz, Martin R. ... '51 '90 C.326 B.S. L.862 J.D. Atty., U.S. Dept. of Interior
Steinmetz, Roberta F. ... '48 '80 C&L.378 B.S., J.D. 4247 S. 76th Ave.
Steuart, Jeran E. ... '78 '05 C&L.623 B.A., J.D. [Ⓐ Crowe&D.]
Stewart, Beverly A., (BV) ... '— '88 C&L.862 B.A., J.D. [Riggs,A.N.T.O.&L.]
Stewart, Robert B. '37 '61 C&L.352 B.A., J.D.
(adm. in IA; not adm. in OK) P.O. Box 1650
Stidham, G. Steven, (AV) ... '54 '79 C.170 B.A. L.477 J.D. [Sneed L.]
Stipe, Gene, (AV) ... '26 '49 C.484 L.623 LL.B. [Stipe,H.L.U.E.&B.] ⊙

Stipe, Harper, Laizure, Uselton, Edwards & Belote, LLP, (AV)
2417 East Skelly Drive, 74114 ⊙
Telephone: 918-749-0749
URL: http://www.stipelaw.com
Gene Stipe; Anthony M. Laizure (Resident). Associates: Frank R. Paynter; John M. Thetford; Karen Goins; Jeri L. Jones; Scott Allen; Tommy W. Humphries.
General Civil and Criminal Trial Practice. Personal Injury, Workers Compensation, Probate, Real Estate, Federal Employers Liability, Medical Malpractice and Products Liability Law.
Representative Clients: Sooner Federal Savings & Loan Assn.; Safeway Stores, Inc.; U.M.W.A. (State); AFL-CIO (State); Kiamichi Electric Cooperative.
McAlester, Oklahoma Office: 343 East Carl Albert Parkway. Telephone: 918-423-0421.
Muskogee, Oklahoma Office: 384 South 33rd Street. Telephone: 918-683-5050. Telefax: 918-682-5700
Oklahoma City, Oklahoma Office: 4111 North Lincoln Boulevard. Telephone: 405-524-2268.

See Professional Biographies, TULSA, OKLAHOMA

Stites, Jef T., (BV) ... '59 '83 C&L.862 B.S.B.A., J.D. 3400 E. 33rd St.
Stock, Jamie Alicia ... '68 '96 C.966 B.A. L.862 J.D. 5801 E. 41st St., Ste. 305
Stock, Susan Hilary ... '70 '97 C.232 B.A. L.862 J.D. 1524 S. Denver Ave.
Stockton, Debra Renae ... '69 '94 C.619 B.A. L.862 J.D. [Ⓐ Conner&W.]
Stockwell, Lance, (AV) '42 '68
C.623 B.B.A. L.862 J.D. College of Law, 3120 E Fourth St
Stoermer, Jeffrey D., (AV) ... '52 '79 C.197 A.B. L.862 J.D. [Jarboe&S.]
Stone, Samuel C., (AV) ... '42 '66 C.378 B.A. L.862 J.D. [Stone J.]

Stone Jessup, P.C., (AV)
320 South Boston, 74103-4736
Telephone: 918-583-1178 Fax: 918-583-0277
Email: stonejes@sw.bell.net
Samuel C. Stone; James R. Jessup (1936-1991).
Municipal Law, Public Authority Financing, Tax Exempt Finance, Economic Development, Project Finance, Real Estate, Financing, Mortgage Law and Indian Law.

See Professional Biographies, TULSA, OKLAHOMA

Stoops, Fred E., Sr., (BV) ... '55 '81 C.63 B.S. L.862 J.D. [Richardson,S.R.&W.]
Story, John David ... '51 '99 C.92 B.S. L.862 J.D. 1503 S. Denver
Stovall, Michael C., Jr. ... '51 '76 C.575 B.A. L.896 J.D. Pres., Genie Oil & Gas Corp.
Stover, Kim R. ... '49 '84 C&L.862 B.S., J.D. Mgr., Prod. Develop., T.D. Williamson, Inc.
Strange, Adam J. ... '— '04 C.1105 B.S. L.615 J.D. [Ⓐ Jones,G.&B.]
Strecker, David E., (AV) ... '50 '76 C.934 B.A. L.188 J.D. [Strecker&Assoc.]

Strecker & Associates, P.C., (AV) BR
2150 Mid-Continent Tower, 401 South Boston Avenue, 74103-4009
Telephone: 918-582-1716; 918-582-1734 Fax: 918-582-1780
Email: mail@streckerlaborlaw.com URL: http://www.streckerlaborlaw.com
David E. Strecker;—James E. Erwin; Yvette B. Hart.
Labor and Employment Law (Management).

See Professional Biographies, TULSA, OKLAHOMA

Strickland, Dean W. '54 '88 C.945 B.A. L.472 J.D.
V.P., Prop. & Concessions, Dollar Rent A Car Systems, Inc.
Strickland, Gray M., (BV) ... '61 '87 C&L.623 B.A., J.D. [Strickland]

Strickland Law Firm, The, P.C., (BV)
320 South Boston, Suite 1107, 74103
Telephone: 918-584-3744 Fax: 918-584-3745
Email: Gray@strickland-law-firm.com URL: http://www.Strickland-Law-Firm.com
Gray M. Strickland. Associates: Elizabeth C. Nichols; Russell D. Abbott. Of Counsel: J. Barak White.

(This Listing Continued)

Strickland Law Firm, The, P.C. (Continued)

Languages: French and Spanish.
Insurance Defense, Personal Injury, Construction, Commercial Transactions and Litigation, Bankruptcy and Real Estate.

See Professional Biographies, TULSA, OKLAHOMA

Struble, Jennifer L. .... '71 '03 C.612 B.S. L.862 J.D. [Ⓐ Perrine,M.R.R.B.&T.]
Stuart, Harold C., (AV) .... '12 '36 C&L.893 J.D. [Stuart,B.&T.]
Stuart, John B., (AV) .... '48 '74 C&L.862 B.S., J.D. [Wagner,S.&C.]

Stuart, Biolchini & Turner, (AV)
First Place Tower, Suite 3300 15 East 5th Street, 74103-4334
Telephone: 918-582-3311 Fax: 918-582-3033
C. B. Stuart (1857-1936). Members of Firm: Harold C. Stuart; Robert F. Biolchini; John B. Turner. Associates: William D. Moeller; David P. Limekiller; Toni Turner Budd; Tobin M. Biolchini.
General Civil Practice, State and Federal Courts, Aviation, Aerospace, Corporation, Securities, Joint Ventures, Mergers and Acquisitions, Banking, Taxation, Estates and Trusts, Oil and Gas, Antitrust, Intellectual Property, Internet and E-Business, Technology, False Advertising, Secured Transactions, Labor Relations and Bankruptcy.
Representative Clients: The NORDAM Group, Inc.; PennWell Corporation; Oil & Gas Journal; Women Energy Corporation; World Publishing Company; Oxley Petroleum; Manhattan Construction Company; Valley National Bank; Bank of the Lakes; Bank of Jackson Hole.

See Professional Biographies, TULSA, OKLAHOMA

Stubblefield, Patricia L. '43 '75
C.621 B.A. L.623 J.D. Southeastern Oklahoma State University
Stubblefield, Robert J., (BV) .... '42 '68 C&L.862 B.A., J.D. 1924 E. 6th Street
Stubblefield, Ronald J. .... '46 '75 C&L.623 B.A., J.D. Ct. of App. J.
Studenny, J. Richard, (AV) .... '46 '70 C&L.862 B.A., J.D. [J.R.Studenny]
Studenny, J. Richard, P.C., (AV) .... 2504 East 21st Street
Stump, T. Douglas, (AV) '57 '83
C.618 B.A. L.616 J.D. 7136 S. Yale, Suite 300 (⊙Oklahoma City)
Stumps, Deborah Ann Joseph .... '63 '88 C&L.623 B.A. 3324 E. 100th Pl.
Sturdivant, James M., (AV) .... '37 '64 C&L.623 B.B.A., J.D. [Gable&G.]
Sublett, Anne B., (AV) .... '46 '80 C.862 B.A. L.276 J.D. [Conner&W.]
Sublett, Charles M., (AV) ... '46 '75 C.103 B.A. L.623 J.D. 320 South Boston, Suite 1020
Sublett, Melissa Kay .... '66 '92 C&L.862 B.A., J.D. OK Disability Ctr.
Sullivan, Daniel S., (AV) .... '63 '88 C.619 B.S. L.862 J.D. [Best&S.]
Sullivan, John F. '29 '54 C.691 B.A. L.846 LL.B.
Div. Atty., Getty Oil Co., Cen. Expl. & Prod. Div.
Sullivan, Stuart C. '68 '94 C&L.862 B.A., J.D.
Gen. Coun. & Corp. Secy., QuikTrip Corp.
Sumner, Angie A. .... '70 '02 C.69 B.B.A. L.862 J.D. [Ⓐ Glendening]
Supernaw, Kathleen R. .... '49 '92 L.623 J.D. Trial Atty., U.S. Dept. of Int.
Suppes, George B., Jr. .... '43 '69 C&L.862 B.S.B.A., J.D. [G.Suppes]
Suppes, George .... 7823 S. 88th E. Ave.
Surles, Tia J. Baker .... '70 '98 C&L.45 B.A., J.D. [Ⓐ Garrett] (⊙Muskogee)
Sutton, Jonathan M., (BV) .... '59 '93 C.136 B.S. L.862 J.D. 4401 South Harvard
Swanson, Gerald D. .... '26 '55 C&L.862 B.S., LL.B. 111 W. 5th St.
Swartz, James L. .... '38 '63 C.126 B.S. L.862 LL.B. 4319 E. 70th St.
Swatek, Susan S., (BV) .... '41 '79 C.623 B.L. L.862 J.D. 5729 S. Utica Ave.
Swenson, Carol L. .... '47 '82 C&L.862 B.S., J.D. 2535 E. 21st St.
Swimmer, Margaret A., (AV) .... '44 '83 C.623 B.A. L.862 J.D. [Hall,E.H.G.G.&N.]
Swiney, Mark D., (BV) .... '52 '85 C.602 B.A. L.862 J.D. 200 Civic Ctr., Rm. 316
Swinson, Sidney K., (AV) .... '55 '80 C.602 B.A. L.862 J.D. [Gable&G.]
Symanski, Stan .... '18 '51 C&L.623 LL.B. 1330 S. 87th E. Ave.
Tacker, D. Stanley, (AV) .... '54 '81 C.623 B.A. L.862 J.D. P.O. Box 702588

Taliaferro, Bruce O., (BV) '47 '72 C.45 B.A. L.862 J.D.
Elmcrest Park Office Center, Suite 220, 2738 East 51st Street, 74105-6225
Telephone: 918-742-9555 Fax: 918-742-8138
Taxation, Probate, Estate Planning, Commercial, Workers Compensation, Personal Injury Law, General Trial and Appellate Practice.
Representative Clients: Sentry Insurance; Affiliated F.M. Insurance; Mission Insurance; Bell Stations, Inc.
Reference: Bank of Oklahoma.

Talley, Claude E. .... '19 '56 C&L.862 B.A., LL.B. 3105 S. 88th E. Ave.‡
Tanaka, Winona M. '45 '71 C.914 B.A. L.178 J.D.
(adm. in NY; not adm. in OK) Assoc. Prof. of Law, Univ. of Tulsa Coll. of Law
Tanner, John J. .... '30 '57 C.612 B.S. L.862 LL.B. 3315 E. 39th St.
Taubman, Michael P. .... '70 '04 C&L.862 B.A., J.D. Corp. Coun., Syntroleum Corp.
Taylor, Catherine C., (AV) .... '61 '90 C.623 B.A. L.862 J.D. [Perrine,M.R.R.B.&T.]
Taylor, Chad C., (BV) .... '71 '99 C.623 B.B.A. L.862 J.D. [Pray,W.J.W.&M.]
Taylor, Jason S., (CV) .... '70 '98 C&L.623 B.A., J.D. [Conner&W.]
Taylor, Joe Clinton .... '42 '68 C.612 B.A. L.623 J.D. Appl. Ct. J.
Taylor, L. Brad, (BV) .... '65 '94 C.69 B.B.A. L.862 J.D. [Ⓐ Perrine,M.R.R.B.&T.]
Taylor, Larry G., (AV) .... '47 '82 C&L.502 B.S., J.D. 624 Boston Avenue, #500
Taylor, Lawrence D., (BV) .... '44 '74 C.503 B.S. L.862 J.D. 3223 E. 31st St., Ste. 211
Taylor, Michael C., Attorney at Law, (BV) '55 '82
C.225 B.S. L.862 J.D. 2021 S. Lewis Ave., Ste. 420
Taylor, Robert H., (AV) .... '50 '76 C.612 B.S. L.862 J.D. [King,T.&R.]
Taylor, Shannon .... '— '04 C.612 B.S. L.862 J.D. [Ⓐ Kivell,R.&F.]
Tegeler, W. Charles, Jr., (BV) .... '39 '65 C.612 B.S. L.862 J.D. 3242 E. 30th Pl.
Tepera, Steven P. .... '79 '05 C&L.846 B.S., J.D. [Ⓐ Doerner,S.D.&A.] ⊙
Terrell, Teri R. .... '— '87 L.862 J.D. 423 S. Boulder, Ste. 300
Tetrick, Charles B., (AV) ..... '33 '65 C.623 B.B.A. L.862 J.D. [Ⓒ Moyers,M.S.I.&T.] ⊙
Thames, Gerry G. .... '46 '81 C&L.862 M.B.A., J.D. 2202 S. 65th West Ave.
Theban, Stephanie L. Jones, (AV) '58 '83 C.612 B.A. L.862 J.D.
[Riggs,A.N.T.O.&L.]
Thetford, John M., (BV) .... '— '88 C.612 B.S. L.615 J.D. [Ⓐ Stipe,H.L.U.E.&B.]
Thiessen, Guy A., (BV) .... '63 '89 C.612 B.S. L.616 J.D. [Carr&C.]
Thigpen, Cheryl Minnix .... '63 '96 C.623 B.S. L.45 J.D. 6217 South Lewis
Thomas, Dan C. .... '23 '53 C&L.862 B.S., J.D. 4198 E. 47th Pl.‡
Thomas, Dixie .... '33 '83 C.619 B.A. L.862 J.D. 2637 ER. 36th Street‡
Thomas, Harley W., (AV) .... '54 '78 C.880 B.A. L.862 J.D. [Riggs,A.N.T.O.&L.]
Thomas, Jill Nelson, (AV) .... '56 '87 C&L.862 B.S., J.D. 2251 E. 39 St.
Thomas, Julie Hird, (AV) .... '58 '84 C.1315 B.A. L.862 J.D. 8511 S. Jamestown Ave.
Thomas, Larry D., (AV) .... '56 '82 C.612 B.S. L.862 J.D. [Huffman&T.]
Thomas, Michelle A., (BV) .... '— '92 C.862 B.S. L.910 J.D. Corp. Coun., TV Guide, Inc.
Thomas, Paul R., (BV) .... '56 '85 C.21 A.B. L.862 J.D. U.S. Trustees
Thomas, Ralph C. .... '25 '50 C.862 B.A. L.623 LL.B. 6861 E. 56th St.‡
Thomas, Rhonda G. .... '67 '99 C.620 B.S. L.616 J.D. [Ⓐ Holden&C.]
Thomas, Terry M., (AV) .... '51 '81 C.621 B.S. L.846 J.D. [Crowe&D.]

Thomas, Glass, Atkinson, Haskins, Nellis & Boudreaux
(See Atkinson, Haskins, Nellis, Brittingham, Gladd & Carwile)

Thompson, Allison L., (BV) ...... '69 '97 C.1147 B.S. L.862 J.D. [Ⓐ Latham,S.W.S.&L.]
Thompson, Brent L. .... '70 '95 C.623 B.B.A. L.862 J.D. [Ⓐ Rodolf&T.]
Thompson, Frank L. .... '44 '71 C.612 B.S. L.623 J.D. 4162 E. 46th St.
Thompson, J. Patrick, (P.C.), (BV) .... '35 '69 C&L.862 B.A., J.D. [J.P.Thompson]
Thompson, R. Lynn, (BV) .... '62 '90 C.921 B.A. L.862 J.D. [Harris,M.P.T.&S.]
Thompson, Rex Wade, (AV) .... '63 '89 C&L.862 B.A., J.D. [Riggs,A.N.T.O.&L.]
Thompson, J. Patrick, P.C., (BV) .... 124-B N. Greenwood Ave.
Thompson McAllister, Sherrie, P.C., (AV) .... 1861 East 15th Street
Thornbrugh, P. Thomas .... '46 '74 C.376 B.A. L.862 J.D. Dist J.
Thornton, David M. (Mike), Jr., (AV) ...... '48 '74 C&L.276 A.B., J.D. [Thornton&T.]
Thornton, Patrick W., (BV) .... '50 '77 C&L.602 B.A., J.D. 525 S. Main Mall
Thornton, William Thomas .... '52 '78 C.103 A.B. L.602 J.D. 525 S. Main St., Ste. 660

Thornton and Thornton, A Professional Corporation, (AV)
Suite 660, 525 South Main, 74103-4507
Telephone: 918-587-2544 Fax: 918-582-0551
Email: dmthornton@sbcglobal.net
David M. (Mike) Thornton, Jr.
Business Law, Commercial Law, Civil Litigation, Probate, Real Estate, Trust and Estates, Family Law.

See Professional Biographies, TULSA, OKLAHOMA

Thrutchley, Christopher S., (AV) '67 '93 C.1281 B.A. L.862 J.D.
[Ⓐ Newton,O.T.&K.]
Thurston, Mark O., & Associates, (AV) '50 '76
C&L.623 B.A., J.D. 6108 South Memorial Drive
Tiernan, Tracy Lynn .... '63 '90 C.802 B.A. L.862 J.D. [Tracy T.]
Tilly, James W., (AV) .... '53 '79 C.612 B.A. L.862 J.D. [Tilly]

Tilly Law Firm, The, (AV)
One West Third Street, Suite 109, P.O. Box 3645, 74101-3645
Telephone: 918-583-8868 Facsimile: 918-584-3162
Email: jwtilly@tilly.com URL: http://www.tilly.com
James W. Tilly.
General Civil Trial Practice in State and Federal Courts. Corporate Representation, Commercial Litigation, Intellectual Property, Insurance, Bankruptcy, Real Property and Oil and Gas Law.
References: Bank of Oklahoma, Sand Springs, Okla.; The Trust Company of Oklahoma.

See Professional Biographies, TULSA, OKLAHOMA

Tips, Robert H., (AV) .... '35 '60 C&L.623 B.A., J.D. [R.H.Tips]
Tips, Robert H., Law Office, (AV) .... 2804 E. 29th
Tipton, Raymond H., III .... '79 '05 C&L.623 B.S., J.D. [Ⓐ Doerner,S.D.&A.] ⊙
Titus, J Schaad, (AV) .... '53 '78 C.802 B.F.A. L.623 J.D. [Titus H.R.D.&M.]

Titus Hillis Reynolds Dickman & McCalmon, (AV)
First Place Tower, Suite 2750, 15 East 5th Street, 74103-4334
Telephone: 918-587-6800 Facsimile: 918-587-6822
URL: http://www.titushillis.com
J Schaad Titus; R. Tom Hillis; Barry G. Reynolds; J. Scott Dickman; Jack S. McCalmon;—Kelley G. Loud; Jessica E. Rainey.
Trial Practice, Civil Litigation, Federal Litigation, Labor and Employment, Hospital Law, Banking Law, Administrative, Corporate, Probate, Estate Planning, Real Estate, Securities Litigation, Medical Malpractice, Products Liability Law, Environmental Law, Aviation Law, Oil and Gas Law, Communications Law, Negligence, Insurance, Antitrust, Mergers and Acquisitions, Bankruptcy, Business Reorganization, Arbitration, Mediation, Alternative Dispute Resolution.

See Professional Biographies, TULSA, OKLAHOMA

Tobey, Rayanne Griffin .... '70 '95 C.802 B.A. L.862 J.D. [Aamodt&T.]
Todd, Byron D., (BV) .... '30 '59 C.612 B.S. L.862 J.D. 3140 S. Winston Ave.
Todd, R. Terry, (AV) .... '53 '79 C.612 B.S. L.616 J.D. 401 S. Boston, Ste. 2000
Todd, Robert A., (CV) .... '57 '82 C&L.862 B.S., J.D. 10202 E. 41st St.
Todd, Terry, (AV) .... '53 '79 C.612 B.S. L.616 J.D. [Rodolf&T.]
Toedter, Dennis L. .... '48 '76 C.339 B.B.A. L.862 J.D. U.S. Army Corps. of Engrs.
Tolen, M. Christian .... '75 '01 C.999 B.S. L.502 J.D. [Ⓐ Lawson,K.&S.]
Toliver, Tolie .... '52 '89 C&L.862 B.S., LL.B. 3657 S. Gary Pl.‡
Tom, Paul R., (BV) .... '53 '80 C.347 A.B. L.45 J.D. 2727 E. 21st Street, Suite 304
Tomlins, Edward E., Jr. .... '28 '56 C.623 B.S. L.862 LL.B. [Ⓒ Tomlins&G.]
Tomlins, Neal, (AV) .... '58 '83 C.802 B.B.A. L.623 J.D. [Tomlins&G.]

Tomlins & Goins, A Professional Corporation, (AV)
Utica Plaza Building, 2100 South Utica Avenue, Suite 300, 74114
Telephone: 918-747-6500 Fax: 918-749-0874
URL: http://www.tomlinsandgoins.com
Neal Tomlins; Ronald E. Goins. Of Counsel: Edward E. Tomlins, Jr.
Litigation Practice, State and Federal Courts, Bankruptcy, Corporate, Employment and Commercial.

See Professional Biographies, TULSA, OKLAHOMA

Toney, William D., (AV) .... '27 '57 C.612 B.S. L.623 LL.B. [Ⓒ Harris,M.P.T.&S.]
Toon, Richard S., Jr., (BV) .... '69 '94 C.802 B.A. L.862 J.D. [Toon]
Toon Law Firm, A Professional Corporation, (BV)
1800 S. Baltimore 10th Floor, Suite 1000
Totten, Larry T. .... '35 '68 C.375 B.S. L.862 J.D. V.P., G.C. Broach Co.
Townsend, Andrew R. .... '69 '98 C.623 B.A. L.862 J.D. [Townsend&S.]
Townsend, Bruce Miller, (BV) ...... '29 '57 C.619 B.S. L.623 LL.B. 3221 S. Braden Ave.
Townsend & Smith, P.L.L.C. .... 1719 East 71st Street
Tracy, David A., (AV) .... '55 '83 C.612 B.S. L.862 J.D. 1701 S. Boston Ave.
Tracy Tiernan .... 320 S. Boston Ave., Ste. 1130
Tresch, W. Kyle, (BV) .... '64 '89 C.613 B.A. L.902 J.D. [McQueen,R.&T.]
Troutman, Gayle L., (BV) .... '49 '93 C.623 B.A. L.862 J.D. [Ⓒ P.F.McTighe,Jr.]
Troutman, Steve Alan .... '50 '99 C.623 B.S. L.862 J.D. 717 South Houston
Trower, Thomas H., (AV) .... '19 '42 C&L.623 B.A., LL.B. 2936 E. 84th St.‡
Troy, Scott Anthony, (AV) .... '56 '86 C.623 B.A. L.615 J.D. 406 S. Boulder, Ste. 405
Trump, Timothy T., (AV) .... '58 '84 C&L.378 B.S., J.D. [Conner&W.]
Truster, Jerry E., (BV) .... '43 '70 C.608 B.S. L.862 J.D. [Ⓒ Steidley&N.] ⊙
Tuck, D. Sue .... '66 '91 C.621 B.S. L.623 J.D. 500 Kennedy Bldg.
Tuck, Tim, Attorney at Law, (BV) '54 '88 C.612 B.S. L.862 J.D.
111 W. 5th St., Ste 500
Tucker, Colin H., (AV) .... '67 '94 C.197 B.A. L.178 J.D. [Rhodes,H.J.T.&G.]
Tucker, John H., (AV) .... '42 '66 C&L.623 B.A., J.D. [Rhodes,H.J.T.&G.]
Tucker, Roy D. .... '76 '03 C.1147 B.A. L.862 J.D. [Coulter T.]
Tucker, Wm. F., Jr., (AV) .... '21 '50 C&L.862 B.A., LL.B. 1211 E. 21st
Turner, Andrew R., (AV) .... '56 '81 C.623 B.A. L.802 J.D. [Conner&W.]
Turner, Anna L. .... '22 '62 C.45 L.862 3210 S. Quebec Ave.
Turner, John B., (AV) .... '43 '67 C&L.862 B.A., J.D. [Stuart,B.&T.]
Turner, W. Kirk, (AV) .... '64 '89 C.1125 B.S. L.45 J.D. [Newton,O.T.&K.]
Tyler, Merle L., (BV) .... '39 '89 C.862 B.F.A. L.999 J.D. 10920 E. 66th St.
Underwood, George W. .... '16 '57 C.619 B.S. L.862 LL.B. 6363 E 31st St.
Underwood, Ken R., (BV) .... '51 '76 C&L.862 B.S., J.D. [K.R.Underwood]
Underwood, Ken Ray, (BV) .... 111 W. 5th St., Ste. 400
Ungerman, Maynard I., (AV) .... '29 '53 C&L.813 B.A., J.D. [M.I.Ungerman]
Ungerman, Maynard I., Law Offices of, (AV) .... 6203 S. Jamestown Ave.
Unruh, R. James, (AV) .... '29 '54 C&L.862 B.A., J.D. 9 E. 4th St.
Unterschuetz, Bret Alexander ...... '65 '91 C.612 B.A. L.623 J.D. 7130 S. Lewis, Ste. 852
Upton, Howard B. .... '22 '48 C&L.623 B.A., LL.B. Petro. Equipment Institute‡
Urich, Tara Fitzgerald .... '64 '92 C.112 B.A. L.809 J.D. Duloitte & Touche, LLP
Vahlberg, Mia .... '59 '04 C.623 B.B.A. L.862 J.D. [Ⓐ Gable&G.]

Valanty, Burton J. '49 '77 C.475 B.S. L.215 J.D.
(adm. in MI; not adm. in OK)
Dir. Human Resources, Delphi Automotive/ASEC Manufacturing-Subsidiary
Van Arkel-Greubel, Linda ..... '59 '97 C.804 B.B.A. L.862 J.D. [Ⓐ Riggs,A.N.T.O.&L.]
Vance, Katherine McCormick '53 '79
C.732 B.A. L.862 J.D. Asst. U.S. Trustee, U.S. Trustees Off.
Van Dall, William W., (BV) .... '41 '66 C&L.623 B.S., J.D. 9515 S. Canton Ave.
Van Dalsem, Neil D., (BV) .... '69 '94 C.612 B.A. L.862 J.D. [King,T.&R.]
Van De Wiele, Stuart E. ..... '72 '99 C.623 B.B.A. L.862 J.D. [Ⓐ Nichols,W.S.N.F.&R.]
Van Dusen, Virgil R. .... '55 '83 C.612 B.S. L.862 J.D. 2445 E. 81st St.‡
Van Eerten, Emily .... '64 '90 C.691 B.A. L.862 J.D. 111 W. 5th‡
Vaniman, Vicki J., (AV) '56 '83 C.612 B.S. L.623 J.D.
Exec. V.P. & Gen. Coun., Dollar Thrifty Automotive Group, Inc.
Van Valkenburgh, Janine H., (AV) .... '48 '75 C.272 B.A. L.862 J.D. [Ⓐ Epperson&J.]
Vaughan, Cynthia K. ....'63 '89 C.172 B.S. L.862 J.D. 7751 S. Memorial Dr.‡
Vaughan, Randall G., (AV) .... '54 '85 C.1288 B.A. L.862 J.D. [Pray,W.J.W.&M.]
Vaughn, Nancy E., (AV) .... '47 '74 C.800 A.B. L.862 J.D. [Conner&W.]
Vaught, Charles C. .... '76 '03 C.619 B.S. L.862 J.D. [Ⓐ Armstrong&L.]
Vestal, Paul E., (BV) .... '28 '68 L.862 LL.B. [Vestal&S.]
Vestal & Simonson, P.A., (BV) ....1515 E. 71st St., Ste. 309
Viles, Philip H., Jr., (BV) '46 '75 C.893 B.A. L.862 J.D.
Chief Jus., Cherokee Nation Jud. App. Tribunal
Vincent, Carl, Jr. ....'64 '91 C.1288 B.S. L.862 J.D. Dir. Opers., Ruffin Properties
Vining, Pamela Jo Craigo .... '57 '95 C.421 B.S.B.A. L.436 J.D. [P.C.Vining]
Vining, Pamela C. ....1924 S. Utica, Ste. 805
Vogt, Thomas L., (AV) ....'59 '84 C&L.623 B.B.A., J.D. [Jones,G.&B.]
Vojvoda, Kimberly A. ....'62 '93 C&L.623 B.B.A., J.D. [Pray,W.J.W.&M.]
Von Glahn, William G., (AV) .... '43 '74 C.575 B.A. L.910 J.D. [Ⓒ Conner&W.]
vonHartitzsch, David M. .... '70 '00 C.802 B.A. L.862 J.D. [Ⓐ Joyce,P.&M.]
Voseles, Charles A., (AV) ....'43 '72 C.697 B.S. L.862 J.D. 3336 E. 32nd St.
Votaw, Phillip ....'— '99 C.619 B.B.A. L.623 J.D. [Carr&C.]
Vyhnal, Nancy L. ....'43 '79 C&L.862 B.A., J.D. Law Clk., U.S. Ct. of App.
Waddel, Patrick O., (AV) .... '41 '67 C.862 B.A. L.802 LL.B. [Sneed L.]
Waddell, Robert Todd .... '63 '98 C.623 B.S. L.616 J.D. [Ⓐ Fellers,S.B.B.&T.]
Wade, Amber Lee ....'— '01 C.16 B.A. L.862 J.D. [Midland&Assoc.]
Wade, C. Alison ....'73 '01 C.69 B.A. L.862 J.D. [Ⓐ Lyons&C.]
Wade, Eric D. .... '76 '01 C.612 B.S. L.862 J.D. [Ⓐ Rosenstein,F.&R.]
Wagman, Tamara R., (AV) ....'70 '95 C.546 B.A. L.1194 J.D. [Ⓐ F.Dorwart]
Wagner, Kenneth E., (AV) ....'64 '94 C.623 B.A. L.862 J.D. [Latham,S.W.S.&L.]
Wagner, Richard A., II, (AV) .... '47 '72 C.862 B.S.B.A. L.602 J.D. [Wagner&G.]
Wagner, Richard D. (Dan), (AV) ....'37 '63 C&L.862 B.S., LL.B. [Wagner,S.&C.]

Wagner and Grundy, L.L.P., (AV) BR
2000 Bank of America Center, Fifteen West Sixth, 74119-5414
Telephone: 918-587-2547 Fax: 918-587-2886
Email: wagnerandgrundy@aol.com
Members of Firm: Richard A. Wagner, II; Bradley A. Grundy. Associate: Melissa F. Cornell.
Family and Matrimonial Law.
See Professional Biographies, TULSA, OKLAHOMA

Wagner, Stuart & Cannon, (AV) .... 902 South Boulder Avenue
Waits, J. Kirk ....'61 '87 C.623 B.S.B.A. L.862 J.D. 3211 S. Florence Ave.★
Waldman, Gilbert D. ..... '31 '60 C.566 A.B. L.862 LL.B. Pres., Superior Linen Serv. Inc.
Walker, Floyd L., (AV) .... '19 '49 C&L.862 LL.B. [Ⓒ Pray,W.J.W.&M.]
Walker, William T., (AV) '57 '85 C.575 B.A. L.623 J.D.
Corp. Atty., Dollar Thrifty Automotive Group, Inc.

Walker, Ferguson & Ferguson
(See Oklahoma City)

Wallace, Bradley W. .... '73 '02 C.305 B.A. L.45 J.D. [Carr&C.]
Wallace, Lucius "Luke" James, (BV) ... '68 '94 C.663 B.A. L.862 J.D. [Humphreys W.H.]
Wallace, Ronald Ray ....'50 '79 L.862 J.D. Pub. Def. Off.
Wallace, Russell W. .... '57 '82 C.63 B.S. L.1288 J.D. [R.W.Wallace]
Wallace, Russell W., Inc. .... 2448 E. 81st St., E.
Wallis, Jon B., (BV) .... '45 '73 C.619 B.A. L.862 J.D. 1310 S. Denver
Walsh, Karen Carden, (AV) ....'66 '91 C.862 B.S. L.623 J.D. [Riggs,A.N.T.O.&L.]
Wandres, Victor R. ....'74 '02 C.861 B.S. L.623 J.D. [Ⓐ Feldman,F.W.F.&B.]
Wangsgard, Stephan A., (BV) ....'67 '97 C.36 B.A. L.862 J.D. [Smiling,B.&R.]
Ward, Keith A., (AV) ....'50 '76 C.1147 B.A. L.623 J.D. [Richardson,S.R.&W.]
Ward, Stephen R., (AV) .... '56 '90 C.612 B.S. L.862 J.D. [Conner&W.]
Warman, Mark A., (AV) .... '61 '88 C.906 B.A. L.615 J.D. [Wilkerson,W.&W.]
Warner, Dale, (AV) ....'42 '70 C.377 B.S. L.862 J.D. [D.Warner]
Warner, Valerie M. .... '69 '94 C&L.878 B.A., J.D. 7319 E. 91st Pl.
Warner, Dale, Inc., (AV) ....2624 E. 21st St., Ste. 1
Warren, Delores W....................'56 '92 C.999 B.S. L.861 J.D. MCI/WORLDCOM
Warren, Sandra Marie '50 '86 C.612 B.S. L.585 J.D.
(adm. in ND; not adm. in OK) Asst. Atty. Gen.
Warta, David A. .... '68 '04 C.378 B.A. L.862 J.D. [Pray,W.J.W.&M.]
Warzynski, Richard E., (BV) .... '53 '91 C&L.862 B.S., J.D. [Ⓐ Layon,C.&K.]
Wassall, Richard W., (AV) .... '56 '83 C&L.1288 B.A., J.D. [Wilkerson,W.&W.]
Watkins, Kimberly L. ....'77 '04 C.39 B.S. L.45 J.D. [Ⓐ Hall,E.H.G.G.&N.]
Watkins, Ramon L. ....'70 '98 C.188 B.S. L.329 J.D. [Gable&G.]
Watkins, Theresa R., (CV) ....'53 '89 C&L.862 B.S., J.D. 7155 S. 77th East Ave.
Watt, Adrienne L. ....'77 '04 C.813 A.B. L.276 J.D. Staff Atty.
Watt, Bryan S. ....'42 '67 C&L.623 B.B.A., J.D. 2706 S. Birmingham Pl.
Watt, Kenneth Benjamin ....'65 '93 C.91 B.S.B.A. L.862 J.D. [Ⓐ F.Dorwart]
Watt, Kymberly J., (BV) ....'65 '93 C&L.862 B.S.B.A., J.D. [Ⓐ Bonham&H.]
Watt, Terry L. ....'52 '95 C&L.862 B.A., J.D. [Fellers,S.B.B.&T.] (Pat.)
Watts, Gary L., (BV) .... '47 '78 C.674 A.B. L.862 J.D. 502 W. 6th
Weatherford, David L., (AV) ......'57 '82 C.612 B.S. L.862 J.D. [Birmingham,M.W.&P.]
Weatherholt, Scott C. ....'77 '03 C&L.623 B.B.A., J.D. [Pray,W.J.W.&M.]
Weaver, Sharon K. ....'— '01 C.1362 B.A. L.862 J.D. [Ⓐ Riggs,A.N.T.O.&L.]
Webb, Daniel M., (AV) ....'57 '84 C.623 B.A. L.862 J.D. [Works&L.]
Webb, Kent Randall, (BV) ....'69 '95 C.612 B.S.B.A. L.862 J.D. [K.Webb]
Webb, Kent, (BV) .... 401 S. Boston Ave., Ste. 2500
Weber, Terry L., (BV) ....'52 '83 C.612 B.S. L.862 J.D. 406 S. Boulder, Suite 417
Weeks, Leslie Custer, (AV) ....'66 '91 C.840 B.S. L.846 J.D. [Rodolf&T.]
Weeks, R. Alan, (AV) ....'64 '90 C.839 B.S. L.846 J.D. [Fellers,S.B.B.&T.] (Pat.)
Weger, James E., (AV) ....'56 '82 C&L.623 B.B.A., J.D. [Jones,G.&B.]
Weidman, John David, (AV) ....'59 '84 C&L.623 B.A.C., J.D. [Hilborne&W.]
Weiner, Howard M. '18 '77 C.415 B.S. L.776 J.D.
(adm. in NJ; not adm. in OK) 1241 E. 27th Pl.‡
Weintraub, Adam Scott, (AV) ....'64 '89 C&L.623 B.S., J.D. [A.S.Weintraub]
Weintraub, Adam Scott, P.C., (AV) ....Twenty East Fifth Street, Suite 410
Welch, William J. ....'34 '58 C&L.623 B.B.A., LL.B. 2100 S. Utica Avenue‡
Wells, Marshall J., (BV) ....'71 '96 C.210 B.A. L.862 J.D. [Hall,E.H.G.G.&N.]
Welsh, Bradley W. .... '71 '99 C.623 M.A. L.846 J.D. [Ⓐ Gable&G.]
Welsh Law Ltd., PC .... 1831 E. 71st Place
Werner, Jas. H. ....'27 '56 C.597 B.S. L.862 J.D. 3105 E. Skelly Dr.
West, Barry G., (BV) ....'46 '74 C.612 B.S. L.862 J.D. [Morrel,W.S.C.&H.]
West, Jeremy D. ....'— '96 C.619 B.S. L.623 J.D. [Carr&C.]
West, Newell E. ....'18 '53 C&L.862 LL.B. 1144 S. 76 East Ave.‡
Westcott, Rick D., (BV) ....'54 '93 C.1288 B.A. L.862 J.D. [Bodenhamer&L.]
Westlake, Joseph D. ....'32 '63 C.378 B.S.E. L.862 J.D. 6244 S. Hudson Avenue‡
Weyrauch, Samantha ....'73 '01 C&L.862 B.A., J.D. [Ⓐ Latham,S.W.S.&L.]
Wheaton, Elvis L. ....'57 '83 C.355 B.A. L.329 J.D. [E.Wheaton]
Wheaton, Elvis, Law Office .... 1638 S. Carson, Ste. 1118
Wheeler, Brian Edward ....'68 '00 C.870 B.S. L.623 J.D. U.S. Dist. Ct.
Wheeler, David Keith, (AV) ....'60 '85 C.622 B.A. L.623 J.D. [Lang,J.&W.]
Wheeler, Robert S., (AV) ....'34 '70 C.623 B.S. L.862 J.D. [R.S.Wheeler]
Wheeler, Robert S., Inc., (AV) ....20 E. 5th St.
Wheeler-Norberg, Pamela K. ....'— '74 C.683 B.S. L.623 J.D. [Ⓒ James,P.&W.]
White, J. Barak ....'59 '83 C&L.378 B.S., J.D. [Ⓒ Strickland]
White, Kevin B., (BV) ....'63 '89 C.623 B.A. L.862 J.D. [K.B.White]
White, Richard D., Jr., (BV) ....'55 '80 C.1042 B.S. L.862 J.D. [Ⓒ Barber&B.]
White, Robert Stanley, Jr. ....'65 '97 C.902 B.A. L.862 J.D. 2559 E. 26th Pl.
White, Timothy M. ....'52 '81 C.614 B.A. L.862 J.D. 2526 E. 71st St.
White, Wilson T., (AV) ....'61 '90 C.802 B.B.A. L.862 J.D. P.O. Box 4716
White, Yvonne C. ....'51 '78 C.612 B.S. L.862 J.D. Sr. Corp. Coun., Citgo Petro. Corp.
White, Kevin B., Attorney at Law, PLLC, (BV) .... 2619 E. 15th St.
Whitebook, Charles A. ....'08 '35 C&L.352 B.A., J.D. 2431 E. 51st St.‡
Whitehill, David B., (AV) '45 '74 C.575 B.A. L.862 J.D.
Gen. Coun., William K. Warren Foundation, The
Whitman, Charles, (BV) '45 '73
C.1147 B.B.A. L.862 J.D. 403 S. Cheyenne Ave., Ste. 1200
Whitman, James Earl ....'42 '67 L.862 J.D. 5811 E. 62nd
Whitman, O. Charles ....'45 '73 C&L.862 B.B.A., J.D. 403 S. Cheyenne, Ste. 1200
Whitney, David M. ....'50 '76 C.934 B.A. L.862 J.D. Pres., Cayman Resources Corp.
Whitney, Edwin J. ....'31 '60 C.623 B.B.A. L.862 LL.B. P.O. Box 472146
Whitt, Arthur F. ....'23 '51 C&L.623 B.S., LL.B. 2709 E. 42nd St.‡
Whitten, Chad R., (BV) ....'57 '89 C&L.623 B.A., J.D. [Whitten]
Whitten, Dale F., (AV) ....'27 '52 C.162 B.A. L.623 LL.B. [Whitten]
Whitten Firm, (AV) ....4111 S. Darlington, Ste. 400
Whitworth, Lori R. ....'78 '03 C&L.623 B.A., J.D. [Ⓐ Pierce C.H.B.&G.]
Widdows, P. Gae, (BV) ....'54 '79 C.45 B.S.B.A. L.862 J.D. [Bonham&H.]
Wienecke, Emil A., Jr. ....'16 '48 C.378 B.S.M.E. L.623 LL.B. 3408 E. 75th Pl.‡
Wilburn, Ray H., (AV) ....'28 '53 C.862 A.B. L.623 LL.B. [Ⓒ Wilburn&M.]
Wilburn, Rhett Henry ....'61 '89 C&L.862 B.S., J.D. 4528 S. Sheridan Rd., Ste. 220

Wilburn & Masterson, (AV)
5800 E. Skelly Drive, Suite 250, 74135-6439
Telephone: 918-494-0414 Fax: 918-493-3455
Email: mike.masterson@wilburnmasterson.com URL: http://www.wilburnandmasterson.com
Michael J. Masterson. Of Counsel: Ray H. Wilburn. Associate: D. Rustin Smith.
General Civil Practice in all Courts. Insurance (Every Aspect), Personal Injury, Insurance Defense, Bad Faith, Property and Casualty, Products Liability, Premises Liability, Defamation, Appellate Practice, Nursing Home Law, Civil Rights, Wrongful Termination, Workers Compensation, Subrogation, Sexual Harassment, Wrongful Death.
See Professional Biographies, TULSA, OKLAHOMA

Wilkening, Beth Anne .... '68 '93 C&L.623 B.A., J.D. [Ⓐ Rodolf&T.]
Wilkerson, Brian S., (BV) .... '70 '96 C.859 B.A. L.623 J.D. [Ⓐ Wilkerson,W.&W.]
Wilkerson, Stephen C., (AV) .... '47 '74 C&L.623 B.A., J.D. [Wilkerson,W.&W.]
Wilkerson, Wassall & Warman, P.C., (AV) .... 15 West Sixth Street, Suite 2301
Wilkes, Keith A., (BV) ....'62 '95 C.612 B.S. L.862 J.D. [Newton,O.T.&K.]
Wilkin, R. Charles, III, (AV) .....'67 '99 C&L.45 B.A., J.D. 2118 S. Atlanta Pl., Ste. 100
Wilkinson, Bill V., (AV) ....'44 '69 C.623 B.S. L.862 J.D. [Wilkinson]
Wilkinson, Cassandra L. ....'— '04 C&L.623 B.S., J.D. [Ⓐ Rosenstein,F.&R.]
Wilkinson, Ronald D. ....'49 '93 C.612 B.A. L.862 J.D. P.O. Box 2207

Wilkinson Law Firm, The, (AV) BR
Suite 400, 7625 East 51st Street, 74145
Telephone: 918-663-2252 Fax: 918-663-2254 URL: http://www.wilklaw.com
Email: wilklaw@wilklaw.com URL: http://www.wilkinson-law.com
Member of Firm: Bill V. Wilkinson.
General Civil Trial Practice, State and Federal Courts. Education, Franchise, Commercial and Employment Law, Employment Discrimination, Harassment, Wrongful Discharge, Wrongful Termination, Covenants Not to Compete.
See Professional Biographies, TULSA, OKLAHOMA

Will, Henry G., (AV) ....'40 '65 C&L.976 B.A., LL.B. [Conner&W.]
Williams, Bencile H., Jr., (BV) ... '31 '62 C.923 B.S. L.862 LL.B. 1612 S. Cincinnati Ave.
Williams, Bradford J., Jr. '44 '70
C.623 B.A. L.862 J.D. Sr. V.P. & Gen. Coun., Mazzio's Corp.
Williams, Carlos L. ....'73 '00 C&L.45 B.A., J.D. 2530 E. 71st St., Ste. L
Williams, D. Kenyon, Jr., (BV) ....'52 '77 C&L.862 B.S., J.D. [Hall,E.H.G.G.&N.]
Williams, Darrell E., (AV) ....'47 '74 C.619 B.A. L.862 J.D. [Clark&W.]
Williams, Don E., (AV) ....'42 '68 C&L.862 B.S.B.A., J.D. 1701 S. Boston AVe.
Williams, Gregory P., (AV) ..... '45 '81 C.502 B.J. L.862 J.D. [Ⓒ Garrett] (⊙Muskogee)
Williams, Jacob ....'74 '03 C.999 B.S. L.862 J.D. [J.Williams]
Williams, Jerry G. ....'47 '75 C.553 B.A. L.615 J.D. [Balogh,C.M.&W.]
Williams, Kimberlee Dawn ....'62 '94 C&L.623 B.A., J.D. [Layman P.B.B.&W.]
Williams, Otis W., Jr., (BV) .... '48 '76 C.623 B.S. L.862 J.D. 345 E. Apache St.
Williams, Paul R., III, (AV) '48 '84
C.861 B.A. L.862 J.D. Of Coun., CB Richard Ellis, Inc.
Williams, Renee ....'— '88 C.942 B.G.S. L.45 J.D. [Andrew,W.&I.]
Williams, Robert Theron ....'74 '01 C.1288 B.S. L.862 J.D. 4401 S. Harvard
Williams, Roger R., (AV) ....'40 '73 C.1147 B.A. L.862 J.D. 252 W. 16 Street
Williams, Jacob, Law Firm, PLLC .... 320 S. Boston Ave., Ste. 1130
Williamson, Dana Freiburger, (BV) ....'55 '80 C.862 B.S. L.623 J.D. 1228 E. 19th St.
Williamson, James A., (BV) ....'51 '75 C&L.862 B.S., J.D. 1515 E. 71st St.
Williamson, Tracie Anne '— '99 C.30 B.A. L.904 J.D.
U.S. Dept. of Interior, Off. of Tulsa Field Solr.
Williamson, W. Bland, Jr., (AV) ....'38 '63 C.362 B.S. L.245 J.D. [Pray,W.J.W.&M.]
Willing, Charles R. ....'62 '93 C.623 B.S.P.E. L.616 J.D. [Fellers,S.B.B.&T.]
Willis, Michael L. ....'67 '92 C.612 B.S. L.862 J.D. [Ⓒ Newton,O.T.&K.]
Wilson, David D., (AV) ....'44 '70 C&L.623 B.B.A., J.D. [Wilson,C.&A.] ⊙
Wilson, Douglas A., (BV) ....'57 '89 C.612 B.A. L.862 J.D. [Riggs,A.N.T.O.&L.]
Wilson, Jeffrey L., (BV) ....'61 '86 C.612 B.S. L.623 J.D. [Barkley]
Wilson, Kathleen Lynn ....'56 '89 C.612 B.A. L.862 J.D. P.O. Box 14082
Wilson, Mickey D. .... '31 '56 C.862 B.A. L.623 LL.B. Ret. Chf. J., U.S. Bkrptcy. Ct.‡
Wilson, T. Lane, (AV) ....'67 '94 C&L.862 B.S.E.E., J.D. [Hall,E.H.G.G.&N.]

Wilson, Cain & Acquaviva, (AV)
1717 South Boulder Avenue, Suite 801, 74119-4410 ⊙
Telephone: 918-583-4777 Fax: 918-583-0774
Email: wcatulsa@swbell.net URL: http://www.wca-law.com

(This Listing Continued)

Wilson, Cain & Acquaviva (Continued)

Member of Firm: David D. Wilson. Associates: John Brian Des Barres; Stephen M. Coates; Chad Micah Kirk. Of Counsel: Truman B. Rucker, Jr.
General Civil Trial Practice State and Federal Courts. Products Liability, Fire and Casualty Insurance Defense, Insurance Coverage, Uninsured Motorist, Bad Faith Law, Professional Malpractice Defense, Veterinary and Insurance Defense, Workers Compensation, Subrogation Insurance Defense, including Personal Injury, Automobile Accidents, Wrongful Death, Mediation and Settlement Services.
Oklahoma City Office: 300 N.W. 13th, Suite 100, 73103-3739. Telephone: 405-236-2600. Fax: 405-236-2607.

See Professional Biographies, TULSA, OKLAHOMA

Wimbish, John B., (AV) '47 '72 C.859 B.A. L.623 J.D. [A Riddle&W.]
Wimbish, Philip R. '12 '37 C.618 A.B. L.623 LL.B. 2834 E. 34th St.
Winburn, Henry C., Jr. '43 '68 C&L.623 B.B.A., LL.B. 7637 S. 26th W. Ave.
Windrix, January J. '76 '04 C.619 B.S. L.862 J.D. [A Gibbs A.B.M.&H.]
Wing, Martin R., (AV) '54 '78 C.691 B.A. L.178 J.D. [Conner&W.]
Winn, Jack, (BV) '29 '63 C&L.862 LL.B. [J.Winn]
Winn, Jack, Inc., (BV) 1408 South Denver
Winter, Robert J., (BV) '69 '95 C.101 B.A. L.862 J.D. [Pray,W.J.W.&M.]
Wisne, Gerald '46 '79 C.602 B.B.A. L.215 J.D.
(adm. in FL; not adm. in OK) 6120 South Yale
Witt, Jerry '— '97 C&L.862 B.S., J.D. [A Riggs,A.N.T.O.&L.]
Witt, Jerry L. '45 '76 C&L.862 B.S., J.D. [Houston&W.]
Witterholt, Madalene A. B., (AV) '59 '83 C&L.862 B.A., J.D. [Crowe&D.]
Wohlgemuth, Joel L., (AV) '45 '70 C.103 A.B. L.910 J.D. [Norman W.C.&D.]
Wolek, Christopher D., (BVⓣ) '70 '95 C.861 B.S. L.623 J.D. [Gibbs A.B.M.&H.]
Wolfe, Frank B., III, (AV) '39 '67 C.902 B.S. L.862 J.D. [Nichols,W.S.N.F.&R.]
Wolfe, Jeffrey S. '51 '76 C.112 A.B. L.61 J.D. U.S. Admin. Law J., Soc. Sec. Adm.
Wolfe, Stephen C., (AV) '40 '65 C.934 B.A. L.623 J.D. 59205 Atlanta Place
Wolin, Courtney '— '03 C&L.623 B.B.A., J.D. [A Riggs,A.N.T.O.&L.]
Wolov, Andrew M., (AV) '41 '66 C.645 B.S. L.884 J.D. [Hall,E.H.G.G.&N.]
Woltz, Joseph C. '63 '90 C.623 B.A. L.862 J.D. [Pezold,B.&W.]
Womack, Michael P. '— '05 C.623 B.A. L.602 J.D. [A Riggs,A.N.T.O.&L.]
Wood, Ronald D., (BV) '45 '74 C.352 B.A. L.862 J.D. 111 W. 5th St.
Woodard, John R., III, (AV) '43 '68 C&L.862 B.A., J.D. [Feldman,F.W.F.&B.]
Woodcock, Alan R. '56 '80 C.82 B.A. L.623 J.D. U.S. Dept. of the Int.
Woods, Christopher B. '74 '00 C&L.623 B.B.A., J.D. [A Crowe&D.]
Woods, Nancy L., (AV) '47 '80 C.814 B.A. L.862 J.D. 333 W. 4th St., Rm 411
Woodstock, Charles L., (BV) '46 '72 C.1281 B.A. L.862 J.D. 1518 S. Cheyenne Ave.
Woosley, Christopher K., (AV) '69 '94 C.612 B.S. L.990 J.D. [Cooper,M.&W.]

Works & Lentz, Inc., A Professional Corporation, (AV)
1437 South Boulder, Suite 900, 74119-8609 ⊙
Telephone: 918-582-3191 Fax: 918-592-2709
Email: wl@workslentz.com URL: http://www.workslentz.com
Wilton W. Works (1925-2004); Harry A. Lentz, Jr.; Fred A. Pottorf; Mark W. Dixon; B. Jack Smith; Daniel M. Webb; Susan Lentz Ratcliff;—Roger M. Coil; Leslie Edward Lenz.
General Civil Practice in all State and Federal Courts, Probate, Trust and Estates, Real Estate, Title Examination, Mortgage Foreclosure, Landlord Tenant, Bankruptcy, Creditors Rights, Business, Family, Personal Injury, Corporate and Commercial Law, Retail Collections, Commercial Collections, Fair Debt Collection Practices Act, Construction, Creditors Rights.
Representative Clients: Hillcrest Medical Center; Emergency Medical Services Authority; The University of Tulsa; St. Francis Hospital.
Oklahoma City, Oklahoma Office: Union Plaza, Suite 225, 3030 Northwest Expressway. Telephone: 405-942-2211. Fax: 405-942-2370.

See Professional Biographies, TULSA, OKLAHOMA

Wright, Gerald W. "Ged", (BV) '42 '78 C.612 B.S. L.862 J.D. State Sen.
Wright, Marcus S., (BV) '62 '87 C.612 B.S. L.45 J.D. 4815 S. Harvard Ave.
Wright, Richard E., III, (AV) '39 '64 C&L.623 B.B.A., LL.B. [Wright&D.]
Wright, Travis L. '74 '05 C.260 B.A. L.862 J.D. [A Conner&W.]
Wright, Will K., Jr. '62 '94 C.1288 B.S. L.862 J.D. [A Drummond]
Wright & Donovan, (AV) 2021 South Lewis, Suite 760
Wulfers, David W., (AV) '54 '81 C.798 B.S.B.A. L.862 J.D. [James,P.&W.]
Wyatt, Martin E. '33 '58 L.862 LL.B. P.O. Box 771‡
Wylie, Kevin H., (AV) '57 '83 C.612 B.S. L.862 J.D. [Eller&D.]
Wynn, Rowe C., Jr. '36 '62 C&L.862 B.S. in B.A., J.D. U.S. Army Corps of Engrs.
Yadon, Laurence J., II '48 '74
C.862 B.A. L.623 J.D. Williams Tower One West Third, Ste. 1668
Yates, Kenneth M., (BV) '66 '92 C.1315 B.S. L.862 J.D. [A Robinson]
Yeagley, Laurence A., (BV) '44 '71 C.1024 B.S. L.862 J.D.
V.P. & Gen. Coun., International Chemical Company
Yeksavich, Michael E., (BV) '43 '69 C.612 B.S. L.862 J.D.
4137 S. Harvard Ave., Ste. H
Ylla, Robert N., Jr. '70 '97 C&L.623 B.A., J.D. [Carr&C.]
Young, Carl H., III '41 '67 C.802 B.A. L.862 J.D. 11644 S. Hudson Court
Young, Stephen R., (BV) '43 '75 C.612 B.S. L.862 J.D. 3739 E. 31st St.
Young, T. Reid, (BV) '52 '77 C.612 B.A. L.862 J.D. 1006 E. 17th Pl.
Young, Warren F., (BV) '37 '66 C.623 B.B.A. L.862 J.D. [Young]
Young Law Firm, Inc., (BV) 415 South Boston Avenue
Zacharias, C. Michael, (AV) '39 '71 C&L.862 B.S., J.D. Dist. J.
Zanerhaft, Jackson M., (BV) '56 '81 C.102 B.A. L.1194 J.D. [Zanerhaft&Assoc.]
Zanerhaft & Associates, (BV) 2642 E. 21st St., Ste. 150

Zannotti, Mark A., (BV) '61 '94 C.612 B.S. L.862 J.D.
525 South Main, Suite 1111, 74103-4512
Telephone: 918-583-6964 Fax: 918-582-8803
Email: mark.zannotti@jrgotlaw.com
Family Law, Adoptions, Probate, Commercial, Collections, Criminal, White Collar Crime, General Litigation.

See Professional Biographies, TULSA, OKLAHOMA

Zeligson, Samuel L. '16 '49 C.623 L.862 LL.B. 2025 E. 71st St.‡
Zeligson, Stephen J. '35 '59 C&L.623 B.B.A., LL.B. Sr. V.P., Crane Carrier Co.
Zeringue, Lawrence W., (AV) '46 '75 C.352 B.S. L.862 J.D. [B Perrine,M.R.R.B.&T.]
Zieren, Leslie, (AV) '53 '82 C.150 B.M. L.862 J.D. 321 S. Boston, Ste. 900
Zilahy Welsh, Catherine G. '70 '99 C.326 B.S. L.846 J.D. [Welsh]
Zimmerman, Jerry L., (AV) '54 '79 C.187 B.A.Pol.Sc. L.862 J.D. [Rosenstein,F.&R.]

Zimmerman, Phyllis L., (AV) '31 '63 C.862 B.S.B.A. L.904 J.D.
1220 Bank of America Center, 15 West 6th Street, 74119-5406
Telephone: 918-582-6151 Fax: 918-582-6153
Email: phyzim@swbell.net
Adoptions, General Civil Practice.
Reference: Bank One.

See Professional Biographies, TULSA, OKLAHOMA

Zingerman, Scott R. '63 '90 C.1288 B.S. L.862 J.D. [Fellers,S.B.B.&T.] (Pat.)
Zirkle, R. Kent, (AV) '46 '74 C.616 B.S. L.623 J.D. [R.K.Zirkle]
Zirkle, R. Kent, P.C., (AV) 2021 S. Lewis, Suite 450
Zuckerman, Harold C., (AV) '59 '85 C&L.862 B.S., J.D. [Eldridge C.S.&L.]

Zurawik, Jack G., (AV) '58 '85 C.1172 B.A. L.862 J.D. P.O. Box 35346

VIAN, 1,414, *Sequoyah Co.*

Humphrey, Joseph H. '33 '64 C&L.623 B.S., LL.B. HC 68

VINITA, * 6,472, *Craig Co.*

Clanton, Jess B., Jr. '42 '72 C.612 B.A. L.862 J.D. Assoc. Dist. J.
Curnutte, Mark W., (AV) '54 '79 C&L.623 B.B.A., J.D. [Logan&L.] ⊙
Gardner, Joseph M., (BV) '67 '93 C&L.862 B.A., J.D. [Jones&G.]
Hartley, Thomas Jot, (BV) '52 '77 C.612 B.S. L.623 J.D. [Hartley]
Hartley Law Firm, The, P.L.L.C., (BV) 106 E. Canadian
Jahnke, Tamara E., (BV) '68 '94 C.132 B.S. L.862 J.D. [A Jones&G.]
Johnson, Deann D. '41 '67 C.412 B.A. L.999 J.D. P.O. Box 69
Johnston, O. B., III, (AV) '41 '66 C.69 B.B.A. L.862 J.D. [Logan&L.] ⊙
Jones, David E., (BV) '65 '90 C&L.378 B.S., J.D. [Logan&L.] ⊙
Jones, Karl D., (BV) '60 '86 C.623 B.A. L.862 J.D. [Jones&G.]

Jones & Gardner, (BV)
244 South Scraper, P.O. Box 866, 74301
Telephone: 918-256-8791 Fax: 918-256-8794
Email: karl@junct.com
Karl D. Jones; Joseph M. Gardner. Associates: Tamara E. Jahnke; Adrian M. Wilkerson.
Real Estate, Probate, Wills and Trusts, Estate Planning, Banking Law, Condemnation.

See Professional Biographies, VINITA, OKLAHOMA

Kolczun, Todd E. '69 '94 C.262 B.S. L.802 J.D. [Logan&L.]
Langston, Ryan P. '77 '05 C.612 B.S.B.A. L.862 J.D. [A Logan&L.]
Logan, J. Duke, (AV) '31 '55 C&L.623 B.A., LL.B. [Logan&L.] ⊙
Logan, Leonard M., IV, (AV) '57 '85 C.623 B.B.A. L.862 J.D. [Logan&L.] ⊙

Logan & Lowry, LLP, (AV)
101 South Wilson Street, P.O. Box 558, 74301-0558 ⊙
Telephone: 918-256-7511 Fax: 918-256-3187
Email: vinitaoffice@loganlowry.com
Members of Firm: J. Duke Logan; O. B. Johnston, III; Thomas J. McGeady; Mark W. Curnutte; Leonard M. Logan, IV; Donna L. Smith; Robert Alan Rush; David E. Jones; Todd E. Kolczun. Associates: Steve Neas; Martha L. Londagin; Ryan P. Langston. Of Counsel: Richard W. Lowry; Charles E. West.
General Practice, Including Trials in all State and Federal Courts, Eminent Domain, Environmental and Coal, Banking, Commercial Transactions, Creditors' Rights and Bankruptcy, Corporation, Public Utility, Real Estate, Estate Planning and Probate, Criminal, Domestic Relations, Civil Rights, Employment, Appellate Practice and Administrative Law.
General Counsel: First National Bank & Trust Company of Vinita; Northeast Oklahoma Electric Cooperative, Inc.
Representative Clients: Northeast Area Vo-Tech Schools; Afton Cooperative Assn.; C & L Supply, Inc.; Oklahoma Wildlife Federation; Craig General Hospital; Alternate Fuels, Inc.
Grove, Oklahoma Office: 19 East 3rd Street. P.O. Box 452469. 74345-2469. Telephone: 918-786-7511. Fax: 918-786-5687.

See Professional Biographies, VINITA, OKLAHOMA

Londagin, Martha L., (BVⓣ) '65 '93 C&L.45 B.S., J.D. [A Logan&L.]
Lowry, Richard W., (AV) '37 '63 C.623 B.A. L.862 LL.B. [B Logan&L.] ⊙
Maxey, Gary Lee '55 '82 C.612 B.S. L.862 J.D. Assoc. Dist. J.
McGeady, Thomas J., (AV) '51 '76 C.893 B.A. L.276 J.D. [Logan&L.] ⊙
Neas, Steve '74 '03 C&L.862 B.S., J.D. [A Logan&L.]
Pease, Allen B., (AV) '43 '72
C.616 B.A. L.623 J.D. Gen. Coun., Grand River Dam Authority
Pitcher, George P., (AV) '19 '42 C&L.623 A.B., J.D. P.O. Box 964‡
Pitcher-Hartley, Pamela R., (BV) '50 '91 C.586 B.A. L.862 J.D. 244 S. Scraper St.
Rush, Robert Alan, (BV) '63 '88 C.543 B.S. L.378 J.D. [Logan&L.] ⊙
Ryals, Kent '44 '75 C&L.616 B.A., J.D. 215 S. Wilson St., Ste. A
Smith, Donna L., (BV) '50 '88 C.377 B.S.Ed. L.862 J.D. [Logan&L.] ⊙
Sullivan, Robert W., (BV) '47 '75 C.612 B.A. L.862 J.D. Grand River Dam Auth.

Taylor, Burrage, Foster, Mallett, Downs & Ramsey, P.C.
(See Claremore)

Von Drehle, Mary E., (CV) '50 '76 C.484 B.A. L.862 J.D.
Asst. Gen. Coun., Grand River Dam Authority
Ward, Clint, (BV) '61 '86 C.612 B.S. L.862 J.D. Asst. Dist. Atty.
West, Charles E., (AV) '47 '78 C.619 B.S. L.862 J.D. [B Logan&L.] ⊙
Wilkerson, Adrian M. '77 '03 C.602 B.B.A. L.436 J.D. [A Jones&G.]
Wyatt, H. M. "Bud", III, (AV) '49 '80 C.802 B.B.A. L.862 J.D. Assoc. Dist. J.

WAGONER, * 7,669, *Wagoner Co.*

Abrahamson, A. Craig
(See Tulsa)

Adair, Joe Dean, (BV) '57 '86 C.619 B.S. L.45 J.D. [Littlejohn,A.&G.]
Craig, Terri Raye '68 '95 C.619 B.S. L.862 J.D. 318 E. Cherokee
Dobbs, Donovan D., (CV) '66 '91 C.619 B.S. L.623 J.D. P.O. Box 274
Gephart, John M., (AV) '16 '40 C&L.893 B.S., LL.B. 808 N. Parkinson Ave.
Gray, Richard Loy, Jr. '60 '96 C.619 B.S. L.862 J.D. [Littlejohn,A.&G.]
Hicks, Kenneth A., (AV) '45 '71 C&L.623 B.A., J.D. 318 E. Cherokee
Jones, Angelyn A. '25 '49 C.619 B.S. L.597 J.D. 912 E. 3rd‡
Landon, Scott, (BV) '51 '78 C&L.862 B.S., J.D. 110 North Main Street
Langley, Larry '46 '78 C.612 B.A. L.616 J.D. Spec. Dist. J.
Littlejohn, Junior Dewayne, (BV) '43 '76 C.619 B.A. L.273 J.D. [Littlejohn,A.&G.]
Littlejohn, Adair & Gray, P.C., (BV) 322 E. Cherokee
McLaughlin, Richard L., (BV) '56 '89 C&L.862 B.S., J.D. 318 E. Cherokee
Nelson, David '39 '65 C&L.623 B.S., J.D. Spec. Dist. J.
Raley, Robert Thames, (BV) '63 '88 C&L.623 B.A., J.D. Asst. Dist. Atty.
Russell, John W., Jr., (AV) '23 '48 L.623 LL.B. P.O. Box 597‡
Saffari, Karen Youree, (BV) '48 '74 C&L.623 B.S., J.D. [K.Saffari]
Saffari, Karen, (BV) 216 E. Cherokee
Sewell, G. Bruce '53 '80 C.612 B.S. L.862 J.D. Dist. J., Wagoner Co. Dist. Ct.
Shook, Dennis N., (BV) '53 '80 C.352 B.A. L.862 J.D. [D.Shook]
Shook, Dennis, The Law Office of, (BV) 320 E. Cherokee

Spence Law Office
(See Tulsa)

Taylor, Burrage, Foster, Mallett, Downs & Ramsey, P.C.
(See Claremore)

Youree, Earl, (AV) '20 '49 C&L.623 LL.B. 216 E. Cherokee

WALTERS, * 2,657, *Cotton Co.*

Aubrey, David J. '18 '47 C&L.623 A.B., LL.B. Ret. Assoc. Dist. J.
Banks, T.R. '72 '00 C.612 B.S. L.616 J.D. [A Burton&Assoc.] ⊙
Burton, Brandon J., (AV) '68 '97 C.612 B.S. L.616 J.D. [Burton&Assoc.] ⊙
Burton & Associates, P.C., (AV) 122 North Broadway (⊙Oklahoma City, Tulsa)
Callaway, Charles C., (BV) '24 '56 C.273 A.B. L.904 LL.B. Asst. Dist. Atty.
Davis, Steve '71 '98 C.893 B.A. L.569 J.D. [B Burton&Assoc.] ⊙

Dolman, Carl L. . . . . '16 '48 C.623 L.192 LL.B. Ret. Assoc. Dist. J.
Fitzsimons, Hugh F., (AV) . . . . '25 '52 C&L.623 B.A., J.D. 208 N. Bway.
Flanagan, Kathleen, (CV) . . . . '42 '76 C.612 B.S. L.616 J.D. 310 N. 5th

Flanagan, Michael C., Attorney at Law, (AV) '54 '80 C.612 B.S. L.616 J.D.
Not a Partnership
217 North Broadway, P.O. Box 5, 73572-0005
Telephone: 580-875-2121, 875-3113 Fax: 580-875-2135
Email: michaelcflanagan@sbcglobal.net
General Practice in all Federal and State Courts. Trials. Probate, Real Estate, Taxation, Bankruptcy, Estate Planning, Family Law, Education Law, Oil and Gas Law, Commercial Law.
Representative Clients: Waurika National Bank; Walters Bank & Trust Co.
References: Walters Bank & Trust Co.; Waurika National Bank.

See Professional Biographies, WALTERS, OKLAHOMA

Rasnake, Gregory R. . . . . '72 '00 C.889 B.S. L.623 J.D. [Ⓒ Burton&Assoc.] ⊙
Robinson, William A., (AV) . . . . . . '40 '74 C.1089 B.A. L.616 J.D. [Ⓒ Burton&Assoc.] ⊙‡
Watson, Leo A., Jr. . . . . '45 '73 C&L.260 B.S.B.A., J.D. Assoc. Dist. J.

WARR ACRES, 9,735, *Oklahoma Co.*

Ellis, Charles W., (AV) . . . . '35 '62 C&L.623 B.B.A., LL.B. [C.W.Ellis]
Ellis, Charles W., PLLC, (AV) . . . . 5601 N.W. 72nd St., Ste. 178I
Pitts, James B., III . . . . '48 '76 C.623 B.F.A. L.615 J.D. [Pitts]
Pitts Law Firm . . . . 5830 N.W. Expressway, Ste. 342

WASHINGTON, 520, *McClain Co.*

Love, J. Kenneth . . . . '27 '67 C.618 B.S. L.623 J.D. Ret. Dist. J.

WATONGA, * 4,658, *Blaine Co.*

Benson, Jerry Earl . . . . '46 '78 C.622 B.S. L.616 J.D. 119 E. 2nd
Daugherty, Veva, (BV) . . . . '47 '77 C.612 B.A. L.616 J.D. 120 W. A
Goerke, Earl E. . . . . '26 '52 C.1147 B.A. L.623 LL.B. Courthouse
Hopper, S. David, (BV) . . . . '42 '73 C.663 B.A. L.616 J.D. 205 W. Main
Lafferty, Todd O., (BVⓉ) '66 '92
C.840 B.B.A. L.623 J.D. Gen. Coun., Wheeler Brothers Grain Co.
Moore, Mark A. . . . . '58 '85 C.612 B.S. L.623 J.D. Assoc. Dist. J.
Morgan, Tom, (AV) . . . . '28 '53 C.612 L.623 J.D. 109 N. Weigel Ave.
Shirley, F. Douglas, (BV) . . . . '48 '76 C.623 B.B.A. L.616 J.D. [F.D.Shirley]

Shirley, F. Douglas, P.C., (BV)
207 West Main Street, P.O. Box 717, 73772
Telephone: 580-623-7336 Facsimile: 580-623-7340
Email: dshirley@pldi.net
F. Douglas Shirley; Fred V. Shirley (1916-1990).
General Civil Practice. Probate, Trusts and Estate Planning, Real Estate and Negligence.

Tolbert, H. G., (AV) . . . . '15 '39 C.623 L.192 LL.B. P.O. Box 139‡

WATSON, —, *McCurtain Co.*

Ballard, Bill J. '26 '68 C.846 B.A. L.802
(adm. in TX; not adm. in OK) HC 15

WAURIKA, * 2,088, *Jefferson Co.*

Gay, Dennis Lynn . . . . '64 '95 C.619 L.623 J.D. Dist. Atty. Off.
Ivy, James Harley, (AV) . . . . '18 '41 C&L.623 B.A., LL.B. 521 E. B Ave.
Largent, Pinkney C., Jr. . . . . '24 '49 C&L.623 J.D. 109 N. Main‡
Scott, Phillip R., Attorney at Law, (AV) . . . '43 '69 C&L.623 B.B.A., J.D. 105 S. Main St.
Staton, Jon T. . . . . '33 '80 C.613 B.S. L.616 J.D. Assoc. Dist. J.
Stone, Richard D. . . . . '19 '48 C&L.623 B.A., LL.B. 110 N. Main

WEATHERFORD, 9,859, *Custer Co.*

Arney, John, (AV) . . . . '20 '48 C.622 B.A. L.623 LL.B. [Arney&W.]
Arney & Weedn LLC, (AV) . . . . 1101 N. Washington

Atkins & Markoff
(See Oklahoma City)

Beam, Stephen D., (AV) '58 '82 C.612 B.A. L.623 J.D.
110 South Broadway, P.O. Box 31, 73096
Telephone: 580-772-2900 Telecopier: 580-772-6879
Email: sbeam@ionet.net URL: http://www.lawyers.com/beamlaw
General Civil and Criminal Practice in all State and Federal Courts. Trusts and Estates, Real Estate, Commercial, Banking, Oil and Gas, Personal Injury, Bankruptcy, and Family Law.
Representative Clients: BancFirst; First Bank & Trust Company, Clinton, Oklahoma; Bank of Hydro, Hydro, Oklahoma; Hydro Cooperative Assn., Hydro, Oklahoma; Federal Deposit Insurance Corp.; ANR Pipeline Co.; Transok, Inc.; Southern Natural Gas; Resolution Trust Corp.; Texaco; United Auto Workers.

See Professional Biographies, WEATHERFORD, OKLAHOMA

Dirickson, Donna Lynn, (BV) . . . . '66 '96 C.622 B.S. L.615 J.D. [Duncan&D.]
Donley, John W., (AV) . . . . '27 '54 C&L.623 B.A., LL.B. 300 N. State
Duncan, David D., (AV) . . . . '51 '78 C.612 B.S. L.623 J.D. [Duncan&D.]
Duncan & Dirickson, (AV) . . . . 1100 E. Main, Ste. 305
Elwick, Donald D. . . . . '71 '98 C.619 B.A. L.623 J.D. 300 North State St.
Minton, (AV) . . . . 400 E. Main
Minton, M.L., III, (AV) . . . . '55 '81 C&L.623 B.A., J.D. [Minton]
Schomp, Bonnie J., (BVⓉ) . . . . '53 '77 C.612 B.S. L.623 J.D. 301 S. 7th St.
Tate, James Oliver '49 '94
C.1300 B.A. L.623 J.D. Southwestern Oklahoma State University
Weedn, John Maurice . . . . '74 '00 C.1310 B.S. L.623 J.D. [Arney&W.]

WELEETKA, 1,112, *Okfuskee Co.*

Hammond, Dean . . . . '42 '69 C.612 B.A. L.862 Rte. 2‡

WELLING, 669, *Cherokee Co.*

Carter-White, Kathy, (CV) . . . . '57 '83 C.623 B.A. L.862 J.D. P.O. Box 36

WELLSTON, 912, *Lincoln Co.*

Paull, George W., Jr., (AV) . . . . '47 '78 C.352 B.B.A. L.616 J.D. RR 3

WEWOKA, * 3,562, *Seminole Co.*

Brown, Gary R. . . . . '44 '78 C.622 B.A. L.616 J.D. Dist. J.
Butner, George W., (AV) . . . . '49 '76 C&L.623 B.S., J.D. Dist. J.
Butner, Richard E., (BV) . . . . '50 '76 C&L.623 B.A., J.D. P.O. Box 1460

Edmonds, Cole, Hargrave, Givens, Ryan & Woodson, P.C., (AV)
117 1/2 S. Wewoka, P.O. Box 1342, 74884 ⊙
Telephone: 405-257-5550
Email: jhargrave@edmonds-cole.com
John R. Hargrave.
General Civil Practice. Insurance, Casualty and Surety Law, Negligence Trial Practice, Environmental Law, Employment Law, Civil Rights Law, Lender Liability Law.
Oklahoma City Office: One North Hudson, Suite 200, 73102. Telephone: 405-272-0322. Fax: 405-235-4654.

See Professional Biographies, WEWOKA, OKLAHOMA

Hargrave, John R., (AV) . . . . . '55 '80 C.618 B.A. L.623 J.D. [Edmonds,C.H.G.R.&W.] ⊙
Huser, William D., (BV) . . . . '40 '66 C&L.623 B.A., J.D. 107 Wewoka Avenue
Kennemer, R. Victor, III, (BV) . . . . '44 '73 C.623 B.A. L.615 J.D. 315 S. Wewoka Ave.
Lively, John Edward, (AV) . . . . '51 '82 C.846 B.A. L.616 J.D. 107 Wewoka Ave.
Olsen, Timothy L., (BV) '61 '87 C.623 B.A. L.862 J.D.
Asst. Dist. Atty., Dist. Atty. Off.
Smith, Paul B., (BV) . . . . '60 '86 C.612 B.S. L.862 J.D. Asst. Dist. Atty.

WILBURTON, * 2,972, *Latimer Co.*

Johnston, Ray A. . . . . '29 '67 C.839 B.S. L.616 J.D. [Johnston]
Johnston Law Firm . . . . 103 W. Main St.
Negen, Gary E., (CV) . . . . '53 '80 C.494 B.S. L.862 J.D. 131 W. Main St.

WOODWARD, * 11,853, *Woodward Co.*

Alley, Aric A. . . . . '76 '05 C.101 B.A. L.623 J.D. [Ⓐ Mitchel,G.R.&R.]
Annis, Jack M., (BV) . . . . '27 '61 C.620 B.S. L.616 J.D. 2411 Williams Avenue #111
Benbrook, Sheryl S., (BV) . . . . '54 '80 C.612 B.S. L.623 J.D. 1117 10th St.
Billings, Barbara R. . . . . '53 '78 C&L.623 B.A., J.D. [Billings&B.]
Billings, Bryan L., (BV) . . . . '53 '77 C&L.623 B.A., J.D. [Billings&B.]
Billings & Billings, (BV) . . . . 1114 Hillcrest
Bouse, Bartlett A. . . . . '68 '93 C.620 B.S. L.623 J.D. [B.A.Bouse]
Bouse, Bartlett A., P.L.L.C. . . . . 2201 S.W. Main
Cheap, Jeffrey Joe . . . . '63 '96 C.612 B.S. L.616 J.D. 8 Horseshoe Road
Christian, David B., (BV) . . . . '61 '88 C&L.623 B.A., J.D. 1416 Main Street
Cook, Vickie Leigh, (BV) . . . . '59 '86 C.839 B.A. L.616 J.D. [V.L.Cook]
Cook, Vickie L., (BV) . . . . 1403 Main St.
Gaston, Donald C., (AV) . . . . '42 '75 C.612 B.S. L.616 J.D. [Mitchel,G.R.&R.]
Halley, Duke, (AV) . . . . '48 '73 C.622 B.A. L.623 J.D. [D.Halley] ⊙

Halley, Duke, Law Firm, P.L.L.C., (AV)
1703 Main Street, P.O. Box 509, 73802-0509 ⊙
Telephone: 580-254-9131 Facsimile: 580-254-2738
Email: dukehalley@sbcglobal.net URL: http://www.lawyers.com/dukehalley
Duke Halley.
Civil Trial Practice, Appellate Practice in all State and Federal Courts, Personal Injury, Workers' Compensation, Product Defects, Insurance, Oil and Gas, Iodine Law, Environmental Law, Toxic Litigation.
Reference: First State Bank of Mooreland.
Oklahoma City, Oklahoma Office: 500 Colcord Drive, 73102. Telephone: 405-602-5600. Facsimile: 405-236-5499.

See Professional Biographies, WOODWARD, OKLAHOMA

Hallren, Kathleen Lies, (BV) . . . . '57 '82 C.971 B.S. L.623 J.D. [Hodgden,H.S.&H.]
Hodgden, Bryce, (AV) . . . . '42 '67 C.612 B.S. L.623 J.D. [Hodgden,H.S.&H.]
Hodgden, Cody B., (BV) . . . . '70 '95 C.612 B.S. L.623 J.D. [Hodgden,H.S.&H.]

Hodgden, Hallren, Smithton & Hodgden, P.L.L.C., (AV)
1002 Ninth Street, P.O. Box 529, 73802
Telephone: 580-256-5517 Fax: 580-256-8459
Email: hodgdenh@sbcglobal.net
Bryce Hodgden; Kathleen Lies Hallren; W. Shane Smithton; Cody B. Hodgden.
General Civil and Criminal Practice, State and Federal Courts. Trials. Real Property, Probate, Oil and Gas, Personal Injury, Workers Compensation, Family Law, Pollution, Environmental, Iodine, Personal Injury.
Approved Examining Attorneys for: Chicago Title Co.; Lawyers Title Insurance Co.; American First Title & Trust Co.; Farmers Home Administration.
Attorneys for: First American Bank; John Hancock Mutual Life Insurance Co.
References: Central National Bank of Alva; Stock Exchange Bank; First American Bank, Woodward, Okla.

See Professional Biographies, WOODWARD, OKLAHOMA

Jackson, Ray D., (BV) . . . . '40 '70 C.1315 B.S. L.616 J.D. Dist. Atty.
Laubhan, Alan J., (BV) . . . . '47 '73 C.623 B.A. L.893 J.D. 3220 Robin Ridge Road
Liles, Donald R., (BV) . . . . '37 '66 C&L.623 B.S., LL.B. [Liles&S.]
Liles & Sims, PLLC, (BV) . . . . 1517 Main St.
Marak, Joseph P., Jr. . . . . '47 '77 C.1004 B.A. L.616 J.D. Assoc. Dist. J.
McVay, Dalen D. . . . . '77 '05 C.1147 B.S. L.616 J.D. [Ⓐ Mitchel,G.R.&R.]
Meinders, John R., (BV) . . . . '67 '92 C.612 B.S. L.616 J.D. [J.Meinders]
Meinders, John, (BV) . . . . 2201 S.W. Main
Mitchel, Michael W., (AV) . . . . '48 '73 C.620 B.S. L.623 J.D. [Mitchel,G.R.&R.] (⊙Alva)

Mitchel, Gaston, Riffel & Riffel, P.L.L.C., (AV)
1725 Oklahoma Avenue, 73801 ⊙
Mailing Address: P.O. Box 887, Woodward, OK 73802-0887
Telephone: 580-254-3447 Fax: 580-254-5314
Email: lawyers@westoklaw.com URL: http://www.westoklaw.com
Michael W. Mitchel; Donald C. Gaston; Katresa J. Riffel; Craig Riffel. Associates: Lynn M. Retz; Aric A. Alley; Dalen D. McVay.
Banks and Banking, Bankruptcy, Civil Rights, Collections, Contracts, Corporate Law, Criminal Law, Family Law, Federal Estate and Gift Taxation, Income Tax, Insurance, Oil and Gas Law, Personal Injury, Probate, Real Estate, Torts, Utility Law, Workers Compensation. .
Enid, Oklahoma Office: 201 N. Grand, Fourth Floor, 73701. Telephone: 580-234-8447.
Fairview, Oklahoma Office: 124 E. Broadway, Suite 6, 73737. Telephone: 580-234-8447.
Alva, Oklahoma Office: 907 Oklahoma Boulevard, 73717. Telephone: 580-254-3447.

See Professional Biographies, WOODWARD, OKLAHOMA

Mossman, Romain S., (BV) . . . . '28 '56 C.612 B.S. L.623 LL.B. 1846 20th St.
Parker, Donna . . . . P.O. Box 1963
Price, Ryan E. . . . . '75 '02 C.612 B.A. L.615 J.D. [Price L.]
Price Law, P.L.L.C. . . . . 1211 34th St., Ste. 14
Retz, Lynn M. . . . . '66 '92 C.942 B.S. L.616 J.D. [Ⓐ Mitchel,G.R.&R.] (⊙Enid)
Riffel, Craig, (BV) '67 '95 C.612 B.S. L.616 J.D.
[Mitchel,G.R.&R.] (⊙Enid, Fairview)
Riffel, Katresa J., (CV) . . . . '67 '92 C.612 B.S. L.616 J.D. [Mitchel,G.R.&R.] (⊙Enid)
Rizley, Jerry W., (AV) . . . . '34 '62 C&L.623 B.B.A., LL.B. 924 Main Street
Savage, Donna Parker . . . . '60 '85 C.679 B.S. L.896 J.D. [D.Parker]
Sims, Aaron R. . . . . '73 '98 C.612 B.S. L.623 J.D. [Liles&S.]
Smithton, W. Shane, (BV) . . . . '66 '91 C.612 B.S. L.602 J.D. [Hodgden,H.S.&H.]
Williams, J. Douglas '42 '68 C&L.623 B.B.A., J.D.
Pres. & Gen. Mgr., K-101, Omni Media Group, Inc.
Work, Charla Renee . . . . '55 '79 Mng. Atty., Dept. of Human Servs., State of OK

WYNNEWOOD, 2,451, *Garvin Co.*

James, Frank W., Law Office of, (BV) '53 '77
C.639 B.S. L.616 J.D. 101 N. Dean A. Mcgee
Kennedy, Kay Karen, (BV) . . . . '47 '72 C.623 B.S. L.616 J.D. P.O. Box 635

YALE, 1,392, *Payne Co.*

Lee, Tom, (BV) . . . . '47 '80 C.620 B.S. L.615 J.D. Pub. Def.

YUKON, 21,043, *Canadian Co.*

Bill James, (BV) . . . . 800 W. Main St.
Bradley, Will, (CV) . . . . '54 '87 C.623 B.A. L.616 J.D. 725 Chateau

Chatman, Stan .....'44 '74 C.1042 B.A. L.616 J.D. 200 S. Ranchwood Boulevard, Suite 12
Clair, Robert J., Law Office of ....'55 '79 C.477 B.A. L.213 J.D. 11824 S.W. 2nd St.
Cosentino, Lisa K., (CV) ....'58 '86 C&L.616 B.A., J.D. 800 W. Main
Coulson, Marilyn Olivo .... '52 '85 C.616 M.B.A. L.615 J.D. 11113 Coachman Rd.
Crampton, Elizabeth Dianne .... '70 '95 C&L.623 B.B.A., J.D. 13330 Big Cedar Trl.
Cunningham, Peggy Bevard, (BV) ....'52 '79 C.862 B.A. L.623 J.D. P.O. Box 850564
Darley, Janis Flanagan ....'57 '84 11145 Folkstone Drive
Davis, Dana R. ....'56 '81 C&L.623 B.A., J.D. 1804 Mackenzie Way
Everett, Roger D., (AV) ....'53 '80 C.921 B.S. L.615 J.D. 1400 S. Holly
Glandon, Donna C., (CV) .... '58 '89 C.1300 B.S. L.616 J.D. 112 S. 4th St.
Hanes, H. David, (BV) .... '56 '82 C&L.623 B.B.A., J.D. 1400 S. Holly, Suite 115
Henthorn, B. Christopher, (CV) '— '97
C.1147 B.B.A. L.615 J.D. 1400 S. Holly Avenue, Suite 115
Hixson, Wendell M., (BV) .... '66 '92 C.999 B.A. L.623 J.D. 800 W. Main St.
James, William Hugh, (BV) ....'46 '73 C&L.623 B.B.A., J.D. [Bill J.]
Lyman, Silas R. ....'32 '60 C&L.972 B.S.L., LL.B. 11924 Somerville Drive‡
McCurdy, Jack D., II, Law Office of, (BV) .... '57 '83 C.623 B.B.A. L.615 J.D. 112 S. 4th
Miller, Duane H., (BV) ....'41 '65 C.612 B.S. L.623 J.D. 5 S. 5th St.
Miller, Jonathan Eric, (AV) .... '59 '84 C.612 B.S. L.623 J.D. P.O. Box 850126
Mize, Timothy I. ....'50 '80 C&L.623 B.A., J.D. 108 E. Snowmass Dr.‡
Nelson, Janice Sue ....'60 '91 C.1147 B.B.A. L.623 J.D. 3920 Tori Pl.
Osby, Mark W., (CV) ....'68 '94 C.623 B.B.A. L.615 J.D. [A Wheatley&W.]
Phelps, Ronald W. ....'47 '79 C.1097 B.A. L.623 J.D. [R.Phelps]
Phelps, Ronald, Inc., Law Office .... P.O. Box 850374
Ramey, Fenton R., (AV) .... '35 '59 C&L.623 B.A., LL.B. [F.R.Ramey]
Ramey, George H., (AV) .... '43 '69 C.612 B.A. L.862 J.D. [Ramey&T.]
Ramey, Fenton R., Inc., (AV) .... 5 S. Fifth

Ramey & Tharp, (AV)
3 South Fifth Street, 73099
Telephone: 405-354-1987 Telecopier: 405-354-1992
Email: rameytharp@msn.com URL: http://www.lawyers.com/rameytharp
Members of Firm: George H. Ramey; William D. Tharp.
General Civil Trial and Criminal Practice in all State and Federal Courts. Real Property, Medical Malpractice, Personal Injury, Child Custody, Products Liability, Probate, Corporate, Banking and Commercial Law, Family Law.
Representative Clients: Canadian State Bank of Yukon, OK; Bank of Chelsea, Chelsea, OK; Bank of Commerce N.A., Catoosa, OK; Jackie Cooper Olds-GMC Truck, Inc.; Jackie Cooper Ford, Inc.; Jackie Cooper Lincoln-Mercury of Oklahoma City; Title Insurance Company of Minnesota; Jackie Cooper Buick-Mazda-Suzucki of Norman; Jackie Cooper Mercedes Benz and Volvo of Tulsa, Oklahoma.
See Professional Biographies, YUKON, OKLAHOMA

Segler, Michael D., (BV) .... '58 '84 C&L.623 B.B.A., J.D. [C Wheatley&W.]
Spears, Robert R. ....'28 '52 C.623 L.616 LL.B. 10708 Ashford Dr.
Stout, James Ray, (BV) .... '46 '72 C&L.623 B.B.A., J.D. 1221 S. Holly Ave.
Strubhar, Richard D. ....'41 '69 C.663 B.A. L.616 J.D. 403 Vandament
Struckle, Joe Jay ....'63 '89 C.620 B.S. L.623 J.D. 400 S. Mustang Road
Tharp, William D., (BV) .... '62 '90 C&L.623 B.B.A., J.D. [Ramey&T.]
Theus, Harold C. ....'15 '48 C.82 Th.B. L.623 LL.B. 11720 Hastings Street‡
Tipps, Shelley A., (BV) ....'54 '90 C.623 B.A. L.615 J.D. 508 W. Vandament Ave.
Wheatley, John E., (AV) ....'26 '50 C&L.623 LL.B. [Wheatley&W.]
Wheatley, Matthew L., (BV) .... '59 '91 C.612 B.S. L.623 J.D. [Wheatley&W.]
Wheatley & Wheatley, P.C., (AV) ....501 W. Main St.

OREGON

CAPITAL: SALEM

Oregon State Bar
5200 S.W. Meadows Road
P.O. Box 1689
Lake Oswego, Oregon 97035
Telephone: 503-620-0222
Fax: 503-684-1366

Index of Towns and Cities Listed by County

*Indicates County Seat

Baker County
* Baker City
Haines

Benton County
Albany
* Corvallis
Monroe
Philomath

Clackamas County
Beavercreek
Canby
Clackamas
Estacada
Gladstone
Lake Oswego
Marylhurst
Milwaukie
Molalla
Oak Grove
* Oregon City
Portland
Sandy
Tualatin
Welches
West Linn
Wilsonville

Clatsop County
* Astoria
Cannon Beach
Gearhart
Seaside
Tolovana Park
Warrenton

Columbia County
Clatskanie
Rainier
* St. Helens
Scappoose
Warren

Coos County
Bandon
Coos Bay
* Coquille
Myrtle Point
North Bend

Crook County
Post
Powell Butte
* Prineville

Curry County
Brookings
* Gold Beach
Harbor
Port Orford
Wedderburn

Deschutes County
* Bend
Black Butte Ranch
Redmond
Sisters
Sunriver

Douglas County
Drain
Myrtle Creek
Reedsport
* Roseburg
Sutherlin
Winchester
Winston

Gilliam County
* Condon

Grant County
* Canyon City
John Day
Mount Vernon

Harney County
* Burns

Hood River County
* Hood River

Jackson County
Ashland
Central Point
Eagle Point
Jacksonville
* Medford
Phoenix
Rogue River
White City

Jefferson County
* Madras

Josephine County
Cave Junction
* Grants Pass

Klamath County
Chiloquin
* Klamath Falls

Lake County
* Lakeview

Lane County
Cottage Grove
Creswell
* Eugene
Florence
Junction City
Springfield
Veneta
Vida

Lincoln County
Depoe Bay
Gleneden Beach
Lincoln City
* Newport
Seal Rock
South Beach
Toledo
Waldport
Yachats

Linn County
* Albany
Brownsville
Lebanon
Lyons
Scio
Sweet Home

Malheur County
Nyssa
Ontario
* Vale

Marion County
Aurora
Hubbard
Jefferson
Keizer
Mount Angel
St. Paul
* Salem
Silverton
Stayton
Woodburn

Morrow County
* Heppner

Multnomah County
Fairview
Gresham
Lake Oswego
* Portland
Troutdale

Polk County
* Dallas
Grand Ronde
Independence
Monmouth
Salem

Sherman County
* Moro

Tillamook County
Garibaldi
Manzanita
Netarts
Oceanside
Pacific City
* Tillamook

Umatilla County
Athena
Hermiston
Milton-Freewater
* Pendleton

Union County
* La Grande

Wallowa County
* Enterprise
Joseph
Wallowa

Wasco County
* The Dalles
Maupin

Washington County
Aloha
Banks
Beaverton
Cornelius
Forest Grove
* Hillsboro
King City
Lake Oswego
North Plains
Portland
Sherwood
Tigard
Tualatin

Wheeler County
* Fossil
Mitchell

Yamhill County
Carlton
Dayton
Dundee
Lafayette
* McMinnville
Newberg
Sheridan
Yamhill

ALBANY, 40,852, *Benton & Linn Cos.*

Alexander, Dell A., (BV) ....'46 '75 C.628 B.S. L.950 J.D. [Kryger,A.E.E.&C.]
Ashenfelter, Dennis D., (AV) '44 '71 C.628 B.S. L.950 J.D. [⊡ Weatherford,T.C.B.&S.]
Baisinger, Glen D. ....'47 '74 C.678 B.A. L.950 J.D. Cir. J.
Bean, Andrew J. ....'69 '99 C.770 B.S. L.950 J.D. [⊡ Weatherford,T.C.B.&S.]
Beckham, David B., (AV) ....'43 '74 C.628 B.S. L.950 J.D. 319 6th Ave. S.W.
Black, Thomas L., (BV) ....'47 '77 C.1042 B.A. L.1051 J.D. [Weatherford,T.C.B.&S.]
Bodtker, Willard, (AV) ....'25 '53 C.546 B.S. L.911 J.D. 1643 NW Hwy. 20
Boock, John A. ....'15 '43 C.494 B.A. L.273 LL.B. 433 S.W. 4th Ave.‡
Boock, John A., Jr. ....'44 '71 C.628 B.S. L.596 J.D. 433 S.W. 4th St.
Brady, Nancy M. ....'68 '95 C.628 B.S. L.285 J.D. [Brady]
Brady Law Offices ....810 S. Lyon St.
Brink, Michael B., (BV) ....'53 '79 C.1051 B.A. L.950 J.D. [Weatherford,T.C.B.&S.]

Brittle, Tim, Attorney at Law
(See Corvallis)

Burgess-Thompson, Gwenen ....'67 '98 C.1071 B.A. L.629 J.D. P.O. Box 1003
Carlile, Jason S., (BV) ....'52 '80 C.628 B.S. L.629 J.D. Dist. Atty.
Carlson, Robert D. ....'65 '99 C.950 B.S. L.101 J.D. [⊡ Kryger,A.E.E.&C.]
Chytraus, Brett R., (BV) ....'61 '90 C.506 B.A. L.596 J.D. [⊡ Weatherford,T.C.B.&S.]

Clark, Lindauer, Fetherston, Edmonds, Lippold & Collier, LLP
(See Salem)

Colville, Stephen E. '49 '88 C.112 B.S. L.464 J.D. (adm. in CA; not adm. in OR) P.O. Box 1119
Corr, Thomas Nathan ....'43 '87 C.1109 B.A. L.629 J.D. Co. Coun.
Cowgill, Michael G., (BV) ....'53 '78 C.628 B.S. L.629 J.D. [Weatherford,T.C.B.&S.]
Crow, Jonathan D. ....'70 '98 L.950 J.D. Dep. Dist. Atty.
Delapoer, James V. B., (AV) ....'51 '76 C&L.629 B.S., J.D. [Long,D.H.M.&N.]
Denham, James H. ....'52 '77 C.911 B.A. L.629 J.D. Gen. Coun., Wah Chang
Egan, James C., (BV) ....'56 '85 C.950 B.S. L.629 J.D. [Kryger,A.E.E.&C.]
Frost, Jackson L. ....'34 '63 C&L.477 A.B., LL.B. Cir. J.
Goode, James C. ....'29 '55 C&L.629 B.S., J.D. Sr. Cir. J.
Hackett, James Allen ....'58 '87 C.1071 B.S. L.950 J.D. 1250 Queen Ave. SE
Healy, F. James, (BV) ....'54 '78 C.1181 B.S. L.950 J.D. [Long,D.H.M.&N.]
Hendricks, Nicole M. ....'71 '96 C.950 B.A. L.494 J.D. Dep. Dist. Atty.
Hickam, Kent L., (BV) ....'50 '80 C.813 B.A. L.950 J.D. [K.L.Hickam]
Hickam, Kent L., P.C., (BV) ....250 Broadalbin S.W.
Houchin, Larry K., (BV) ....'39 '63 C.1056 B.S. L.629 J.D. Dep. Dist. Atty.
Hsu, Eric ....'72 '97 C.05 B.COMM. L.629 J.D. Dist. Atty. Off.
Jackson, Brian P. ....'28 '68 C.05 B.A.S. L.950 J.D. 1735 Belmont Loop SW‡
Jewel, Christine M. '68 '95 C.608 B.A. L.879 J.D. Staff Atty., Legal Aid Servs. of Oregon
Johnson, Dustan E. ....'52 '78 C&L.629 B.S., J.D. [D.E.Johnson]
Johnson, Dustan E., P.C. ....425 S.W. 2nd Ave.
Jordan, James H., (AV) ....'35 '60 C.628 B.S. L.178 J.D. 100 Calapooia Street, S.W.
Kalberer, Joel D. ....'72 '01 C.939 B.A. L.629 J.D. [⊡ Weatherford,T.C.B.&S.]
Karandy, Eugene J., II ....'71 '97 C.1049 B.A. L.950 J.D. 104 4th Sw Rm 123
Kropp, Richard T., (AV) ....'37 '62 C.628 B.S. L.950 J.D. 507 S.W. Washington‡
Kryger, J. David, (AV) ....'40 '65 C.735 B.A. L.950 J.D. [Kryger,A.E.E.&C.]
Kryger, Alexander, Egan, Elmer & Carlson, P.C., (AV) 507 Washington St. S.W. (⊙Salem)
Long, Merle A., (AV) ....'20 '48 C.628 B.S. L.950 J.D. [Long,D.H.M.&N.] ‡

Long, Delapoer, Healy, McCann & Noonan, P.C., (AV)
201 West First Avenue, P.O. Box 40, 97321
Telephone: 541-926-5504 Fax: 541-926-7167
Email: thefirm@longdel.com URL: http://www.longdel.com
Merle A. Long (Retired); James V. B. Delapoer; F. James Healy; Robert C. McCann, Jr.; Andrew S. Noonan;—Kristen Sager-Kottre.
Business and Corporate Law, Insurance, Domestic Relations, Municipal Law, Land Use and Zoning, Real Property, Trial Practice and Probate Law, Personal Injury.
Representative Clients: City of Albany, Oregon; City of Harrisburg, Oregon; Linn-Benton Community College; Linn-Benton Housing Authority; Scio Mutual Telephone Association; Fisher Implement Co.; Boshart Trucking, Inc.; SWS Manufacturing, Inc.; Stalford Seed Farms, Inc.; Ram Trucking, Inc.

MacNeil, Christopher E., (BV) ....'53 '84 C&L.629 B.S., J.D. [Nelson&M.]
Marshall, James A. ....'53 '84 C.636 B.A. L.629 J.D. [J.A.Marshall]
Marshall, James A., P.C. ....240 First Avenue W, Suite A
Martines, Sue B. '62 '93 C.170 B.A. L.560 J.D. (adm. in NM; not adm. in OR) 510 N.W. Thornton Lake Dr.
Mayo, Terri A. ....'61 '92 C.888 B.A. L.107 J.D. Dep. Dist. Atty.
McCann, Robert C., Jr., (AV) ....'55 '81 C.629 B.S. L.285 J.D. [Long,D.H.M.&N.]
McClain, Michael F. ....'37 '62 C.629 B.S. L.950 J.D. 34295 Oakville Rd. S.W.‡
McCormick, John, (BV) ....'46 '76 C&L.629 B.S., J.D. Cir. Ct. J.
McCormick, Rick J. ....'48 '74 C.628 B.S. L.596 J.D. Cir. J.
Moore, Douglas W. ....'46 '73 433 4th St. S.W.
Murphy, Daniel R. ....'54 '81 C.628 B.S. L.950 J.D. Cir. J.
Nelson, James G., (AV) ....'46 '74 C.628 B.S. L.950 J.D. [Nelson&M.]
Nelson & MacNeil, P.C., (AV) ....213 Water Ave., N.W., Suite 100
Noonan, Andrew S., (BV) ....'68 '93 C.628 B.S. L.336 J.D. [Long,D.H.M.&N.]
Norman, Gary E., (BV) ....'40 '69 C&L.352 B.B.A., J.D. [Scott&N.]
Ohlsen-Johnson, Jonathan ....'67 '93 C.330 B.S. L.1358 J.D. 2450 14th Ave Se

Peterson Law Offices, PC
(See Portland)

Poole, Arnold W., (CV) ....'56 '89 C.690 B.A. L.950 J.D. [A.W.Poole]
Poole, Arnold W., P.C., (CV) ....204 Ellsworth SW
Post, Daniel A. ....'43 '70 C.1074 B.S. L.950 J.D. Pres., Valley Pacific, Inc.
Reid, Roger H., (BV) ....'30 '61 C&L.629 B.S., LL.B. P.O. Box 665
Reiling, Donald P., (BV) ....'36 '62 C.628 B.S. L.950 LL.B. [D.P.Reiling]
Reiling, Donald P., P.C., (BV) ....138 7th Ave. S.W.
Reiter, Garvin ....'67 '97 C.685 B.A. L.1051 J.D. Legal Aid Svcs. of Oregon
Rollema, Melvin T., (CV) ....'52 '78 C.1259 B.S. L.629 J.D. 135 5th Ave., S.W.
Sager-Kottre, Kristen ....'64 '00 C.330 B.A. L.950 J.D. [⊡ Long,D.H.M.&N.]
Schultz, Edward F., Jr., (AV) ....'46 '72 C&L.629 B.S., J.D. [Weatherford,T.C.B.&S.]
Scott, Robert T., (BV) ....'41 '67 C.629 B.A. L.950 J.D. [Scott&N.]
Scott & Norman, (BV) ....433 S.W. 3rd St.
Smith, Allison E. ....'33 '68 C&L.1051 J.D. Co. Coun.
Stevenson, F. David '41 '70 C.813 B.A. L.1049 J.D. (adm. in CA; not adm. in OR) 2145 NW Crocker Lane‡
Suver, Katie A. ....'71 '97 C.911 B.A. L.629 J.D. P.O. Box 100
Taleff, Mark A., (BV) ....'48 '78 C.508 B.A. L.950 J.D. 433 S.W. 4th
Tibbetts, Kirk E., Jr., (CV) ....'64 '91 C.1051 B.S. L.950 J.D. 135 W. 5th Ave.
Tripp, Susan M., (BV) ....'61 '89 C.273 B.A. L.1209 J.D. P.O. Box 1749

Weatherford, Thompson, Cowgill, Black & Schultz, P.C., (AV)
130 West First Avenue, P.O. Box 667, 97321
Telephone: 541-926-2255 Fax: 541-967-6579
Email: legal@wtlegal.com URL: http://www.wtlawyer.com
Michael G. Cowgill; Thomas L. Black; Edward F. Schultz, Jr.; Michael B. Brink. Associates: Joel D. Kalberer; Andrew J. Bean. Counsel: Brett R. Chytraus; Dennis D. Ashenfelter.
General Civil and Trial Practice, Business and Corporate Law, Pension and Profit Sharing, Banks and Banking, Taxation, Probate, Estate Planning, Elder Law, Real Property, Agricultural Law, Land Use and Zoning, Securities, Creditors Rights, Commercial Law, Personal Injury, Environmental and Natural Resources.
Representative Clients: Citizens Bank; Linn-Benton Bank; Willamette Industries, Inc.; Oregon Metallurgical Corp.; Morse Bros., Inc.; Teledyne Wah Chang Albany; Willamette Seed Co.
Reference: Linn-Benton Bank.

See Professional Biographies, ALBANY, OREGON

ALOHA, 41,741, *Washington Co.*

Allred, Jonathan D., (AV) ....'60 '87 C&L.101 B.A., J.D. 1650 S.W. Sahnow Dr.
Brask, Gerald, Jr. ....'51 '76 C.589 B.A. L.585 J.D. 4475 S.W. 185th Ave.
Carter, Russ ....'43 '84 C.1056 B.S. L.596 J.D. 6080 S.W. Cross Creek Dr.‡
Fairchild, Michael H. '40 '88 C.1056 M.S. L.1051 J.D. 21785 S.W. Tualatin Valley Hwy., Ste. P
Grant, Amy P. ....'56 '99 7193 S.W. 184th Pl.
Gray, Gerald B. ....'11 '37 C&L.629 B.A., LL.B. 17590 S.W. Blanton St.‡
Hobson, David N., Jr., (BV) ....'58 '85 C.976 B.A. L.629 J.D. [Hobson&H.]
Hobson, David N., Sr. ....'32 '59 C.976 B.A. L.893 LL.B. [Hobson&H.]
Hobson & Hobson, P.C., (BV) ....18255 S.W. Tualatin Valley Hwy.
Marinello, Deborah Kae ....'65 '93 C.108 B.S. L.879 J.D. 420 S.W. 207th Ave.‡
Overfelt, Gary, (BVⓉ) ....'51 '78 C.197 B.A. L.1051 J.D. 18230 S.W. Jaylee St.
Schmidt, Michael A., (BV) ....'49 '78 C.263 B.A. L.1051 J.D. [Schmidt&Y.]
Schmidt & Yee, P.C., (BV) ....18525 S.W. Vincent St.
Yee, Pamela, (BV) ....'60 '87 [Schmidt&Y.]

ASHLAND, 19,522, *Jackson Co.*

Ainsworth, Sidney E. ....'27 '53 C&L.629 B.S., LL.B. 515 E. Main St.‡
Axon, Gary L. ....'42 '66 C.106 B.A. L.221 J.D. P.O. Box 190
Balocca, Michael G. ....'54 '83 C.1103 B.A. L.950 J.D. 149 ClearCreek Drive
Barr, Lawrence J. '43 '68 C.472 B.B.A. L.192 J.D. (adm. in FL; not adm. in OR) 110 Pine St.‡
Bastian, Ted A., Jr., (BVⓉ) ....'44 '73 C.767 B.A. 1257 Siskiyou Blvd.
Berk, Gail A. '48 '82 C.1097 B.A. L.1136 J.D. (adm. in CA; not adm. in OR) 137 Manzanita St.‡
Boesche, Philip Windsor, (AVⓉ) '46 '74 C.813 B.A. L.477 J.D. (adm. in CA; not adm. in OR) 1121 Old Hwy 99 S.
Bridges, Jennifer Ann ....'70 '01 C.878 B.S. L.1051 J.D. [⊡ Davis,G.H.S.&S.]
Carreon, Charles Hernan ....'56 '87 C.1071 B.A. L.1068 J.D. [Online M.L.]
Clark, Amy Ahrendt ....'58 '84 C.896 B.A. L.597 J.D. 159 Nob Hill Street
Clark, Paul S. '56 '82 C.105 B.A. L.273 J.D. (adm. in CA; not adm. in OR) 159 Nob Hill St.
Cottle, Richard C., (AV) ....'26 '53 C&L.900 B.S., LL.B. 607 Siskiyou Blvd.
Davis, Jack, (BV) ....'50 '75 C.705 B.A. L.04 LL.B. [Davis,G.H.S.&S.]
Davis, Sam B. ....'23 '50 C&L.494 B.S., J.D. 515 E. Main St.‡
Davis, Gilstrap, Hearn, Saladoff & Smith, A Professional Corporation, (AV) 515 East Main Street
Dietz, James, (BV) ....'47 '86 C.1071 M.S. L.629 J.D. 815 Tolman Creek Rd.
Drescher, Allen G., (CV) ....'46 '72 C&L.178 B.A., J.D. [A.G. .P.Drescher]
Drescher, Allen G., PC, (CV) ....21 S. 2nd St.
Foster, John D. '45 '77 C&L.629 B.A., J.D. (adm. in AK; not adm. in OR) 189 Myer Creek Rd.‡

Foster Denman, LLP
(See Medford)

Freund, Henry L., Jr. '43 '69 C.228 B.A. L.910 J.D. (adm. in MO; not adm. in OR) 903 Pinecrest Terr.‡
Gilstrap, David V., (BV) ....'40 '76 C.174 B.S. L.208 J.D. [Davis,G.H.S.&S.]
Good, Robert W., (BV) ....'55 '93 C.1124 B.A. L.285 J.D. 622 Siskiyou Boulevard
Greenleaf, Stephen H. '42 '68 C.118 B.A. L.1066 J.D. (adm. in CA; not adm. in OR) 6 Beach Ave.‡
Harrell, Bruce B., Law Office of ....'54 '82 C.1042 B.A. L.112 J.D. 564 Liberty St.
Hearn, Christian E., (BV) ....'61 '88 C.112 B.A. L.1065 J.D. [Davis,G.H.S.&S.]
Holtey, Jud, (BV) ....'49 '74 C.352 B.A. L.36 J.D. 622 Siskiyou Blvd
Hopkins, Randall A., (AVⓉ) ....'49 '74 C.612 B.A. L.846 J.D. [R.A. .P.Hopkins]
Hopkins, Randall A., PC, (AVⓉ) ....735 S. Mountain Ave.
Howser, Thomas C., (AV) ....'— '61 C&L.629 B.S., J.D. [T.C.Howser]

Howser, Thomas C., P.C., (AV)
607 Siskiyou Boulevard, P.O. Box 640, 97520
Telephone: 541-482-2621 Fax: 541-482-1512
Email: info@ashlandlaw.com URL: http://www.ashlandlaw.com
Thomas C. Howser;—Judith H. Uherbelau.
Accidents, Adoptions, Appeals, Assault and Battery, Auto Accidents, Business Law, Civil Practice, Commercial Litigation, Corporations, Criminal Damages, Damages, Easements, Elder Law, Employment Discrimination, Estate Planning, General Practice, Insurance, Land Use, Landlord Tenant Law, Leasing, Litigation, Malpractice, Medical Malpractice, Modification, Municipal Law, Partnerships, Personal Injury, Probate Law, Property, Real Estate, Trial Practice, Trusts, Water Rights, Wills Wrongful Death, Zoning.

See Professional Biographies, ASHLAND, OREGON

Jacobson, Thierolf & Dickey, P.C.
(See Medford)

Jarvis, Barbara A., (BV) ....'34 '79 C&L.36 B.S., J.D. 1159 Emma St.‡
Jensen, Leslie W. '31 '54 C.145 A.B. L.546 J.D. (adm. in SD; not adm. in OR) 1845 Dragonfly Ln.‡
King, John R. ....'44 '74 C.976 B.A. L.309 J.D. Owner, Blue Feather Products, Inc.‡

Kochlacs, Charles George
(See Medford)

Krasner, Fred '40 '73 C.197 B.A. L.284 J.D. (adm. in CA; not adm. in OR) 950 Neil Creek Rd.‡
Kuenzel, Robert V., (AVⓉ) ....'49 '76 C.674 A.B. L.597 J.D. [Kuenzel&Assoc.] ⊙

Kuenzel & Associates, (AVⓉ)
98 Pine Street, 97520 ⊙
Telephone: 541-552-0142 Fax: 541-552-0145
Email: kuenzel@aol.com URL: http://www.lawyers.com/kuenzel&associates
Robert V. Kuenzel.
Business Law, Business Litigation, Employment Law, Intellectual Property, Arbitration and Mediation.
San Rafael, California Office: 4040 Civic Center Drive, Suite 200, 94903. Telephone: 415-492-8100. Fax: 415-492-8174.

See Professional Biographies, ASHLAND, OREGON

Lloyd, Thomas W., (BV) ....'44 '74 C.629 B.S. L.596 J.D. 125 N. 2nd

Lombardi, Robert J. '54 '85 C.112 A.B. L.312 J.D.
(adm. in HI; not adm. in OR) P.O. Box 1265‡
Marsh, Ray T. '14 '38 C.112 A.B. L.1066 LL.B.
(adm. in CA; not adm. in OR) 1065 Beswick Way‡
Munsell, Glenn H., (BV) .... '33 '65 C&L.950 B.S., J.D. 7696 Hyatt Prairie Rd.‡
Nolte, Paul, (BV) .... '44 '69 C&L.629 B.S., J.D. City Atty.
Online Media Law, PLLC .... 1131 Barrington Circle
Packer, Alexis J., (CV) .... '49 '94 C.569 M.A. L.1148 J.D. [A.Packer]
Packer, Alexis, (CV) .... 585 A St., Ste. 3
Pavlich, Paul A. '52 '82 C.945 A.B. L.1066 J.D.
Asst. Prof., Southern Ore. State College
Powers, Dennis M. .... '42 '67 C.174 A.B. L.208 J.D. 521 Thornton Way
Robison, Thornton E. '42 '71 C.813 B.A. L.1066 J.D.
(adm. in CA; not adm. in OR) P.O. Box 822‡
Saladoff, Susan Vogel, (AV) .... '59 '83 C.188 B.A. L.273 J.D. [Davis,G.H.S.&S.]
Sawyer, Loren L. .... '30 '59 C.950 B.A. L.629 LL.B. Cir. J.
Seulean, David P. A., (BV) .... '51 '84 C.992 B.A. L.345 J.D. [D.P.A.Seulean]
Seulean, David P. A., P.C., (BV) .... 622 Siskiyou Blvd.
Shulster, Stanley Anthony, (BVⓉ) '38 '65 C.319 A.B. L.1065 LL.B.
165 Pilot View Rd.
Skerry, Harry, Jr., (BV) .... '21 '45 C&L.629 LL.B. 290 N. Main Street
Skibinski, J. Michael, (BVⓉ) .... '49 '81 C.629 B.S. L.966 J.D. 425 Merrill Circle
Smith, David L. .... '47 '77 C.112 B.A. L.990 J.D. [Davis,G.H.S.&S.]
Thompson, David J. '30 '74 C.1043 B.S. L.1190 J.D.
(adm. in CA; not adm. in OR) 2230 Green Meadows Way‡
Turner, Garrison F., (BV) .... '47 '72 C.112 B.A. L.1065 J.D. 108 N. Second St.
Uherbelau, Judith H., (BV) .... '— '81 C.63 B.S. L.1068 J.D. [Ⓐ T.C.Howser]
Vote, Robert M. '19 '47 C&L.174 B.A., LL.B.
(adm. in CO; not adm. in OR) 1372 Woodland Dr.
Watson, Charles R., (CV) .... '52 '81 C.118 B.A. L.596 J.D. 850 Siskiyou Blvd.
Weisler, Faye L. .... '55 '82 C.208 B.A. L.420 J.D. 2305 Ashland St
Westerman, Paul '42 '74 C.679 B.S. L.1049 J.D.
(adm. in CA; not adm. in OR) 420 Sheridan St.‡

ASTORIA, * 9,813, *Clatsop Co.*

Alvey, Martin L., (AV) .... '59 '87 C.950 B.A. L.1051 J.D. [M.L.Alvey] ⊙
Alvey, Martin L., P.C., (AV) ..... Suite 3A #1 Portway, Port of Astoria Bldg. (⊙Portland)
Autio, Michael A., (BV) .... '64 '91 C.628 B.A. L.950 J.D. [M.A.Autio]
Autio, Michael A., LLC, Law Office of, (BV) .... P.O. Box 389
Bourn, Kathryn D. .... '65 '95 C.629 B.S. L.188 J.D. [K.Bourn]
Bourn, Kathryn .... 10 Sixth St., Ste. 201
Bugas, Theodore T. '24 '50 C.174 L.602 J.D.
(adm. in WY; not adm. in OR) 1608 Irving‡
Cole, George F. .... '26 '59 C.628 B.S. L.596 LL.B. Dist. J.
Edison, Thomas E. .... '30 '57 C.628 B.S. L.629 LL.B. Cir. J.
Fischer, D. Richard, (BV) .... '44 '69 C.210 B.A. L.1119 J.D. [Larson&F.]
Haller, Don H., III, (BV) .... '50 '76 C.1056 B.S. L.950 J.D. No. 10 6th St., Ste. 204
Henningsgaard, Blair J., (BV) .... '52 '78 C&L.629 B.A., J.D. Pier 11 Mall
Hook, Laurel P. .... '74 '99 C.629 B.S. L.1358 J.D. [Stahancyk,K.J.&H.] (⊙Portland)
Hoxie, Ronald P. .... '33 '58 C&L.950 B.S., LL.B. 280 3rd St.
Kaino, Kristopher A. .... '63 '89 C&L.950 B.S., J.D. P.O. Box 294
Lang, Mark J. '70 '97 C.770 B.S. L.585 J.D.
Dep. Dist. Atty., Clatsop Co. Dist. Atty. Off.
Larson, W. Louis, (BV) .... '43 '69 C.1056 B.S. L.950 J.D. [Larson&F.]
Larson & Fischer, (BV) .... 990 Astor St.
Leonard, Edward W., Jr. .... '38 '83 C.1070 B.S. L.846 J.D. P.O. Box 771‡
Marquis, Joshua K., (BV) .... '52 '81 C&L.629 B.A., J.D. Dist. Atty.
Matyas, Cindee S. .... '58 '89 C.932 L.1051 J.D. P.O. Box 1026
Nelson, Philip L., (BV) .... '51 '76 C.950 B.A. L.629 J.D. P.O. Box 603
Orr, John F., (CV) .... '56 '90 C.37 B.A. L.1051 J.D. [J.F.Orr]
Orr, William R., (BV) .... '49 '78 C.347 L.1026 LL.B. [Snow&S.]
Orr, John F., P.C., (CV) .... P.O. Box 354
Reynolds, Heather, (CV) .... '55 '81 C.939 B.A. L.950 J.D. P.O. Box 145
Snow, Harold A., (AV) .... '41 '68 C&L.629 B.S., J.D. [Snow&S.]
Snow, Jeanyse R., (AV) .... '45 '70 C.629 B.A. L.950 J.D. [Snow&S.]
Snow & Snow, (AV) .... 801 Commercial Street
Stahancyk, Kent, Johnson & Hook P.C., (AV) ..... 552 Commercial St. (⊙Bend, Portland)
Zafiratos, Nicholas D., (BV) .... '26 '55 C&L.950 B.S., LL.B. 552 Commercial

ATHENA, 1,221, *Umatilla Co.*

Duncan, Donald R. .... '17 '51 C.608 A.B. L.273 LL.B. E. 339 Main St.‡

AURORA, 567, *Marion Co.*

Auxier, James E., (BV) .... '36 '71 C.800 B.S. L.596 J.D. 25875 N.E. Butteville Rd.
Chez, Steve P., (CV) .... '45 '71 C&L.629 B.S., J.D. 24325 N.E. Boones Ferry Rd.
Cox, Thomas W. '53 '83 C.906 B.S., B.A. L.285 J.D.
(adm. in WA; not adm. in OR) 22740 Mooney Ave., N.E.
Oscar, Leonard .... '29 '53 C&L.608 B.S., J.D. V.P., Oscar Plumbing & Heating Co.
Rice, James M. '51 '82 C.36 B.S. L.61 J.D.
(adm. in AZ; not adm. in OR) 25124 N.E. Prairie View Dr.‡
Youngstrom, Susan L. '52 '80 C.1051 B.A. L.629 J.D.
(adm. in MT; not adm. in OR) 28241 S. Barlow Rd.‡

BAKER CITY, * 9,860, *Baker Co.*

Baxter, Gregory L. .... '59 '89 C.101 B.S. L.596 J.D. Cir. Ct. J.
Bergland, Kathleen E., (BV) .... '50 '76 C.112 B.A. L.284 J.D. Pub. Def.
Collins, Timothy M., (CV) .... '47 '73 C.285 B.A. L.629 J.D. City Atty.
Corcoran, Anne L. .... '63 '91 C.999 B.A. L.629 J.D. Legal Coun.

Corey, Byler, Rew, Lorenzen & Hojem, L.L.P.
(See Pendleton)

Coughlin, J. David, (AV) .... '44 '70 C.197 B.A. L.950 J.D. [Coughlin,L.&M.] ⊙
Coughlin, Leuenberger & Moon, P.C., (AV) .... 1650 Dewey Avenue (⊙Ontario)
Leuenberger, Martin, (AV) .... '49 '75 C.628 B.S. L.629 J.D. [Coughlin,L.&M.] ⊙
Marlette, Gary L., (BV) .... '39 '68 C.735 L.596 J.D. 2031 Court Ave., Apt. 8
Moon, J. Robert, Jr., (AV) .... '55 '81 C.207 B.A. L.851 J.D. [Coughlin,L.&M.] ⊙

Peterson Law Offices, PC
(See Portland)

Pope, Milo, (AV) .... '36 '61 C.629 L.336 LL.B. [Yervasi P.]
Shirtcliff, Matthew B., (BV) .... '67 '94 C.628 B.S. L.285 J.D. Asst. Dist. Atty.
Tomlinson, Mary B., (BV) .... '52 '80 C.276 B.S.F.S. L.1051 J.D. 905 Lund Lane
Triplett, Linda, (AV) .... '43 '76 C.629 B.A. L.596 J.D. 13748 Red Fox Lane
Van Duyn, Pamela C., (BV) .... '51 '81 C.629 B.S. L.596 J.D. [P.C.Van Duyn]
Van Duyn, Pamela C., P.C., (BV) .... 2195 Main St.
Whitnah, Robert W. .... '66 '01 L.629 J.D. Dist. Atty. Off.

Yervasi, Damien R., (BV) .... '66 '95 C.152 B.S. L.596 J.D. [Yervasi P.]
Yervasi, Lise F. .... '64 '93 C.972 B.S. L.596 J.D. [Yervasi P.]

Yervasi Pope, P.C., (AV)
1990 Third Street, P.O. Box 50, 97814-0050
Telephone: 541-523-7973 Fax: 541-523-7993
URL: http://www.lawyers.com/yervasicoltman
Damien R. Yervasi; Milo Pope; Lise F. Yervasi.
Personal Injury, Civil and Criminal Litigation, Wrongful Death, Probate, Estate Planning, Bankruptcy.
See Professional Biographies, BAKER CITY, OREGON

Zuercher, Christopher W. '68 '00
C.832 B.S. L.7 J.D. Dist. Atty.'s Off. [Ⓐ Coughlin,L.&M.]

BANDON, 2,833, *Coos Co.*

Allen, David R., (AVⓉ) .... '42 '69 C.813 A.B. L.800 J.D. [Atherton&A.] ⊙

Atherton & Allen, (AVⓉ) ⊞
P.O. Box 1256, 97411 ⊙
Telephone: 541-347-8315 Fax: 541-347-7620
Email: daveallen@estplanlaw.com
Member of Firm: David R. Allen (Certified Specialist, Estate Planning, Trust and Probate Law, The State Bar of California Board of Legal Specialization).
General Civil Practice. Estate Planning, Trusts and Estates, Wills, Probate Law, Corporate and Real Estate Law.
Chula Vista, California Office: 210 Towne Centre Professional Building, 345 "F" Street, 91910. Telephone: 619-420-6869.
See Professional Biographies, BANDON, OREGON

Carleton, Frederick J., (BV) .... '51 '77 C.670 B.A. L.629 J.D. 301 Hwy. 101
Cook, Jeffrey W. '45 '70 C.293 B.A. L.352 J.D.
(adm. in IA; not adm. in OR) P.O. Box 1096★
Hernandez, Manuel C. .... '49 '79 C&L.629 B.A., J.D. [M.C.Hernandez]
Hernandez, Manuel C., LLC .... 1212 Alabama
Lundgren, David R. .... '55 '87 C.1032 B.A. L.1162 J.D. P.O. Box 1433
McCorkle, Elizabeth Sue .... '50 '91 C.629 B.S. L.880 J.D. 1212 Alabama
O'Dwyer, Michael P., Attorney at Law, (BV) '46 '76
C.629 B.S. L.1051 J.D. P.O. Box 2052

BANKS, 1,286, *Washington Co.*

Guist, Carolyn L. .... '53 '78 C.1169 B.A. L.1049 J.D. 15845 N.W. Harry's Place
Lucas, Jim L. .... '57 '94 C.608 B.S. L.950 J.D. 630 South Main Street
Steinbach, Roch .... '61 '89 C.813 B.A. L.629 J.D. 42280 NW Banks Rd.

BEAVERCREEK, —, *Clackamas Co.*

Ried, Joshua .... '51 '82 C.184 B.A. L.596 J.D. 19497 S. Logan Dr.

BEAVERTON, 76,129, *Washington Co.*

Aaby, Barbara J., (BV) .... '50 '93 C.608 B.A. L.1051 J.D. 4915 Sw Griffith Dr #100
Adams, Rodney C., (AV) .... '35 '60 C&L.950 B.A., J.D. [Adams&U.]

Adams & Uffelman LLP, (AV)
Hall Street Station, 4500 S.W. Hall Boulevard, 97005-0504
Telephone: 503-644-2146 Fax: 503-646-2227
Email: info@beavertonlaw.com URL: http://www.beavertonlaw.com
Members of Firm: Rodney C. Adams; John E. Uffelman.
General Civil and Trial Practice in all State and Federal Courts. Business, Corporate, Estate Planning and Probate Law, Entertainment Law, Family Law, Divorce, Real Estate Law, Contracts, Criminal Law, Criminal Trials and Appeals in all State and Federal Courts.
Reference: United States National Bank of Oregon (Beaverton Branch).
See Professional Biographies, BEAVERTON, OREGON

Andersen, Thomas A. '52 '80 C.588 B.S. L.1051 J.D.
Mng. Trial Atty., National Insurance Enterprise
Anderson, Richard T., Jr., (AV) '53 '83
C.628 B.S. L.1051 J.D. 10700 S.W. Bvtn-Hlsdale Hwy., Ste. 460
Anderson, Vincent H. '74 '03
C.101 B.S.E.E. L.950 J.D. [Ⓐ Blakely,S.T.&Z.] (See Pat. Sect.)
Azari, Cameron R. '68 '97 C.999 B.S. L.596 J.D.
Dir. Huntington Legal Advertising, Poorman-Douglas Corp.
Bailey, D. Charles .... '66 '97 C&L.629 B.S. 15345 SW Riddle Ct.
Bell, Robert P., (BV) .... '43 '68 C.705 B.A. L.1017 J.D. [Myatt&B.]
Bellis, Jeffrey W., (BV) .... '46 '75 C.629 B.S. L.596 J.D. [Ⓐ Moomaw,M.&H.]
Berner, William E., Jr. '67 '93 C.150 B.S.M.E. L.800 J.D.
(adm. in CA; not adm. in OR; Pat.) Asst. Gen. Coun., Nike, Inc.

Blakely, Sokoloff, Taylor & Zafman
A Limited Liability Partnership
1925 NW AmberGlen Parkway, Suite 230, 97006 ⊙
Telephone: 503-439-8778 Facsimile: 503-439-6073
Email: BSTZ_mail@bstz.com URL: http://www.bstz.com
Gregory D. Caldwell; Paul A. Mendonsa;—Mark C. Van Ness (Not admitted in OR); Vincent H. Anderson.
Intellectual Property Law, including Patents, Trademarks, Copyrights, Related Prosecution and Litigation.
Sunnyvale, California Office: 1279 Oakmead Parkway. Telephone: 408-720-8300. Facsimile: 408-720-8383.
Los Angeles, California Office: 7th Floor, 12400 Wilshire Boulevard. Telephone: 310-207-3800. Facsimile: 310-820-5988.
Costa Mesa, California Office: 3200 Park Center Drive, Suite 700. Telephone: 714-557-3800. Facsimile: 714-557-3347.
Denver, Colorado Office: 8055 E. Tufts Avenue, 13th Floor. Telephone: 303-740-1980. Facsimile: 303-740-6962.
Seattle, Washington Office: 601 Union Street, Suite 3000. Telephone: 206-292-8600. Facsimile: 206-292-8606.
San Jose, California Office: 60 S. Market Street, Suite 510. Telephone: 408-947-8200. Facsimile: 408-947-8280.
See Professional Biographies, BEAVERTON, OREGON

Blaufus, Daniel A. .... '58 '93 C.1181 B.S. L.569 J.D. Asst. Gen. Coun., Nike, Inc.
Blyth, Bradley C., (BV) .... '58 '84 C.629 B.S. L.1051 J.D. [Blyth&B.]
Blyth, Peter R., (BV) .... '25 '53 C.629 L.596 J.D. [Blyth&B.]
Blyth & Blyth, (BV) .... 10700 S.W. Beaverton-Hillsdale Highway
Borgeson, William B. ..... '27 '57 C.629 B.S. L.276 J.D. 10090 S.W. Beaverton Hwy 10‡
Brooke, Kathryn '53 '98 C.735 B.A. L.705 J.D.
Gen. Coun., RE/MAX Equity Group, Inc.
Brown, Daniel A. '53 '79 C.1044 B.A. L.966 J.D.
(adm. in WI; not adm. in OR) 11310 S.W. Meadowlark Ln.
Brown, Kevin R. .... '47 '73 C&L.930 B.A., J.D. Asst. Gen. Coun., Nike Inc.
Brown, Susan Jane McKibben ..... '74 '01 C.880 B.A. L.1051 J.D. 14893 S.W. Linda Ct.
Bruech, Valerie M., (BV) .... '49 '76 C.991 B.A. L.365 J.D. 14950 Satelluride Terrace
Burke, Richd. J. .... '12 '39 L.596 LL.B. Sr. State Ct. J.
Burton, Paul H. .... '62 '88 C&L.950 B.A., J.D. Coun., GemStone Systems, Inc.
Bush, Allen B., (BV) .... '52 '77 C.112 B.A. L.950 J.D. 13825 S.W. 33rd Pl.

Caldwell, Gregory D. ... '63 '95 C.999 B.S. L.770 J.D. [Blakely,S.T.&Z.] (See Pat. Sect.)
Caldwell, John L. '48 '83 C.476 B.S. L.1206 J.D.
(adm. in FL; not adm. in OR) Sequest Computer Systems, Inc.
Campbell, Michael A. ... '48 '78 C&L.800 B.A., J.D. N.W. Law Publishing Co., Inc.
Carlson, Gary M., Law Office of '40 '64
C&L.508 B.S., J.D. 12725 S.W. Millikan Way, Ste. 260
Caro, Michael J., (AV) ... '50 '79 C.768 B.A. L.629 J.D. 4085 SW 109th Ave.
Carter, James C., (AV) '48 '76
C.813 A.B. L.629 J.D. Gen. Coun.-USA/Americas Reg., Nike, Inc.
Case, James D., (AV) ... '45 '73 C.906 B.S. L.596 J.D. [Case&D.]

Case & Dusterhoff, LLP, (AV) BR
9800 SW Beaverton Hillsdale Highway, Suite 200, 97005
Telephone: 503-641-7222 Facsimile: 503-643-6522
Email: info@case-dusterhoff.com URL: http://www.case-dusterhoff.com
James D. Case; R. Bruce Dusterhoff;—Leo A. Reinikka; Margaret H. Leek Leiberan.
Business and Business Litigation, Insurance, Asbestos Defense, Construction Litigation, Probate and Real Property Law, Taxation. General Civil and Trial Practice, Products Liability, Casualty, Surety and Fidelity, Errors and Omissions, Employment, Estate Planning and Wills and Trusts, Personal Injury, Medical and Legal Malpractice, Family Law and Mediation.
See Professional Biographies, BEAVERTON, OREGON

Cheyne, Jeffrey M., (BV) ... '46 '75 C.629 B.A. L.1049 J.D. [Myatt&B.]
Civey, Sara D. ... '76 '02 C.1051 B.A. L.950 J.D. [A Helzer&C.]
Coad, Michael R. ... '58 '93 C.1056 B.S. L.950 J.D. [M.R.Coad]
Coad, Michael R., P.C. ... 4220 S.W. 109th Ave.
Coburn, John F., III '61 '87
C.309 A.B. L.893 J.D. Asst. Gen. Coun. & Asst. Secy., Nike, Inc.
Cockle, John R. '21 '47 C.546 A.B. L.190 LL.B.
(adm. in NE; not adm. in OR) 14645 S.W. Farmington Rd.‡
Cornilles, Fredrick R., (BV) ... '37 '61 C&L.629 B.S., LL.B. 8625 S.W. Cascade Ave.
Creasing, Thomas John ... '59 '94 C.1028 B.A. L.596 J.D. 4500 S.W. Hall Boulevard
Cromar, James S. ... '64 '91 C.477 B.A. L.910 J.D. [Helzer&C.]
Dalton, James F., (AV) '58 '85
C.454 B.A. L.93 J.D. V.P., Gen. Coun. & Secy., Tektronix, Inc.
Davis, C. Thomas, (BV) ... '51 '81 C.628 B.S. L.596 J.D. 12220 SW 1st. Street
Davis, Carl K. ... '48 '73 C.1032 B.A. L.878 J.D. Dir. Intl. Trade, Nike, Inc.
Davis, Julianne R., (AV) '52 '84 C.629 B.S. L.1051 J.D.
Asst. Gen. Coun., Nike, Inc. (Legal Department)

DeBast, McFarland & Richardson, LLP
(See Portland)

de la Forest, John M. ... '47 '73 C.813 B.A. L.284 J.D. Gen. Mgr.-Soccer Div., Nike, Inc.
Del Balzo, Mary D. ... '61 '85 C.188 A.B. L.950 J.D. eFusion, Inc.
Deurwaarder, Barbara G. ... '54 '92 C.911 B.A. L.1358 J.D. [Myatt&B.]
Diamond, Nancy H. ... '59 '86 C.309 A.B. L.893 J.D. Asst. Gen. Coun., Nike, Inc.

Drakulich & Carlson, P.C.
(See Portland)

Druce, Michelle S. ... '63 '90 C.878 B.S. L.950 J.D. AVP Compl., Wilshire Credit Corp.
Dunn, Timothy P., (BV) ... '52 '79 C&L.352 B.A., J.D. 4475 S.W. 185th Ave.
Dusterhoff, R. Bruce, (BV) ... '45 '75 C&L.629 B.A., J.D. [Case&D.]
Ebner, Susan D., (BV) ... '42 '81 C.629 B.B.A. L.339 J.D. 15460 N.W. Perimeter Dr.
Edelson, Charles Z., (BV) ... '57 '83 C&L.629 B.S., J.D. 9900 S.W. 135th Ave.
Fiereck, Stephanie Jost ... '72 '97 C.492 B.A. L.629 J.D. Poorman-Douglas Corporation
Ford, Kelly E. ... '51 '87 C.685 B.A. L.846 J.D. [K.E.Ford]
Ford, Kelly E., PC ... 4800 S.W. Griffith Dr., Ste. 320
Fowler, Margo S. ... '67 '93 C.188 B.S. L.273 J.D. Asst. Gen. Coun., Nike, Inc.
Fredericks, Barbara H. ... '48 '73 C.416 B.A. L.209 J.D. Researcher‡
Furrer, Patrick J., (AV) ... '42 '71 C.629 B.S. L.464 J.D. [P.J.Furrer]
Furrer, Patrick J., P.C., (AV) ... 9900 S.W. Wilshire
Garnett, Pryor A. '57 '86 C.453 B.S. L.911 J.D.
(adm. in WA; not adm. in OR; Pat.) Coun, Intell. Prop., IBM Corporation
Gleeson, J. Michael, (BV) ... '44 '70 C&L.629 B.S., J.D. 12450 S.W. 1st St.
Godfrey, Frank J., III ... '61 '00 C.861 B.A. L.596 J.D. [A Moomaw,M.&H.]
Goodman, Michael L. ... '64 '89 C.911 B.S. L.309 J.D. Asst. Gen. Coun., Nike, Inc.
Goss, Robert L. ... '53 '80 C.629 B.S. L.950 J.D. Hearing Offr., State Dept. of Transp.
Gray, Francis I. '39 '71
C.188 B.E.E. L.770 J.D. Sr. Intell. Prop. Coun., Tektronix, Inc. (Pat.)
Grey, Herbert G., (BV) ... '55 '81 C&L.950 B.S., J.D. 4800 S.W. Griffith Dr., Ste. 320
Groce, Robert J. ... '23 '58 C.911 B.A. L.596 J.D. 15250 N.W. Oak Hills Dr.‡
Gunderson, Paul H., (BV) ... '48 '77 C.35 B.S. L.596 J.D. 12275 S.W. 2nd St.
Guzman, Michael, (BV) ... '57 '86 C.1056 B.S. L.596 J.D. 8075 S.W. 187th Ave.
Hammack, Marsha C. ... '53 '83 C.1056 M.A. L.596 J.D. State Div. Motor Vehicles
Harbolt, Thomas P. ... '66 '93 C.628 B.S. L.950 J.D. 5925 S.W. Spruce Ave., Ste. 100
Harrasser, Ian Michael ... '62 '99 C.147 B.A. L.950 J.D. Corp. Coun., Avant Corporation
Hartvig, Donald H. ... '20 '71 C.999 L.1065 J.D. 12275 S.W. Second St.‡
Helfant, Adam S. '64 '89 C.453 B.S. L.309 J.D.
(adm. in NY; not adm. in OR) 1 Bowerman Dr.
Helzer, Richard G., (AV) ... '39 '69 C.628 B.S. L.596 J.D. [Helzer&C.]

Helzer & Cromar, LLP, (AV)
4900 S.W. Griffith Drive, Suite 245, 97005
Telephone: 503-626-2889 Fax: 503-626-9944 URL: http://www.helzercromar.com
URL: http://www.helzercromarlaw.com
Richard G. Helzer; James S. Cromar. Associates: Roger Dale Scarbrough; Sara D. Civey.
Criminal Law, Family Law, Divorce, Child Custody, Spousal Support, Personal Injury, Automobile Accidents, Criminal Law, Driving While Intoxicated, Felonies, Drug Crimes, Juvenile Crimes, Parole and Probation, Sexual Abuse, Traffic Violations, Estate Litigation, Guardianship and Conservatorship, Employment Law, Discrimination, Sexual Harassment.
See Professional Biographies, BEAVERTON, OREGON

Hensen, Virginia G. ... '53 '83 C.174 B.S. L.596 J.D. Dir., Pub. Affs., Nike, Inc.
Hess, Raymond W. ... '48 '74 C.546 A.B. L.1051 J.D. 12450 S.W. 1st St.
Hildebrand, Brien F. ... '52 '83 C&L.629 B.A., J.D. [Moomaw,M.&H.]
Hirsch, Jeffrey, (AVⓉ) '50 '75 C&L.861 B.A., J.D.
(adm. in NY; not adm. in OR) Gen. Coun., Retail Div., Nike, Inc.
Holady, Mark John, Law Office of, (BV) '64 '90
C.1056 B.A. L.596 J.D. 4800 SW Griffith Dr., Ste. 320
Holmes, Patricia Kathleen '69 '01 C.839 B.B.A. L.1360 J.D.
(adm. in NM; not adm. in OR) 9085 S.W. Trigger Ct.
Howe, Robert R. ... '37 '70 C.911 B.A. L.629 J.D. 13925 S.W. Cherryhill Dr.
Huffman, Lois K. ... '— '86 C.506 B.S. L.596 J.D. 12725 SW Millikan Way, Ste. 300
Hutterli, Conrad G., (BV) ... '54 '83 C.966 B.A. L.950 J.D. 4240 S.W. Cedar Hills Blvd.
Isaacs, Susan D., (BV) '54 '79 C.205 B.A. L.1051 J.D.
4915 SW Griffith Drive, Suite 105
Isaak, Charles N. ... '30 '57 C.629 B.S. L.309 J.D. 14325 S.W. Lisa Lane
Joseph, Thomas P., Jr., (AV) '30 '55
C&L.950 B.A., J.D. 10700 S.W. Bvtn-Hlsdale Hwy., Bldg. 3
Kane, Henry, (BV) ... '26 '61 C.629 B.S. L.596 J.D. 12677 SW Camden Lane
Kane, Philip M. '36 '95 C.186 B.E.E. L.765 J.D.
(adm. in CA; not adm. in OR) 6595 SW Elm Ave.
Kang, Scott S. ... '70 '97 C.629 B.S. L.596 J.D. [S.S.Kang]
Kang, Scott S., P.C. ... 9800 Beaverton Hillsdale Hwy.
Kempton, Timothy R. ... '63 '89 C.950 B.A. L.596 J.D. City Pros., City Atty.'s Off.
Kirby, William B., (BV) '58 '84
C.154 B.A. L.950 J.D. Asst. City Atty., Beaverton City Atty.'s Off.
Knaupp, Benjamin D. ... '68 '97 C&L.101 B.A., J.D. [B.D.Knaupp]
Knaupp, Benjamin D., P.C. ... 4900 S.W. Griffith Dr., Ste 165
Knowles, Pamela Stebbeds, (BV) ... '55 '83 C.628 B.S. L.596 J.D. Jud. Fit. Com.
Kwartler, Kenneth M. ... '56 '84 C.1044 B.A. L.94 J.D. Asst. Gen. Coun., Nike, Inc.
Leiberan, Margaret H. Leek, (AV) ... '50 '77 C.629 B.S. L.309 J.D. [A Case&D.]
Lenihan, Thomas F. '47 '88 C.397 B.S.E.Ph. L.776 J.D.
Chf. Intell. Prop. Coun., Tektronix, Inc. (Pat.)
Lewis, Edward J. ... '39 '64 C.628 B.S. L.950 J.D. Sr. Coun., Tektronix, Inc.
Madsen, Elizabeth C., (BV) '52 '79
C.605 A.B. L.145 J.D. 10700 SW Beaverton Hillsdale Highway 450
Manning, John P., Attorney at Law, (BV) '48 '76
C&L.629 B.A., J.D. 8196 S.W. Hall Blvd., Ste. 203
Manske, Karen Laree '70 '94 C.335 B.A. L.285 J.D.
Area Atty., Nextel Communications
Marshall, Abigail V. ... '69 '95 C.425 B.A. L.861 J.D. Nationwide Enterprise Trial Div.
Mason, Beth, (AV) ... '51 '77 C.549 B.A. L.950 J.D. [Mason&Assoc.]
Mason & Associates, (AV) ... 4915 S.W. Griffith Drive, Suite 100
Mayfield, John H., III ... '48 '74 C.880 B.A. L.420 J.D. [J.Mayfield]
Mayfield, John ... 12275 S.W. 2nd St.

McNeil Law Office LLC
(See Hillsboro)

Mendonsa, Paul A. '71 '97 C.101 B.S.E.E. L.770 J.D.
[Blakely,S.T.&Z.] (See Pat. Sect.)
Merten, Charles J., (AV) ... '37 '63 C.112 A.B. L.629 J.D. 1905 N.W. 169th Pl.‡
Mesirow, Nicholas A. ... '74 '00 C&L.629 B.A., J.D. [A Moomaw,M.&H.]
Miller, Douglas G. ... '58 '86 C.477 B.A. L.861 J.D. [D.G.Miller]
Miller, Eranda L. ... '65 '99 C.563 B.A. L.950 J.D. 11515 S.W. Center St., Apt. 17
Miller, R. Joseph, Jr. ... '70 '97 C.629 B.S. L.950 J.D. [A Moomaw,M.&H.]
Miller, Robert J., Sr., (BV) ... '43 '73 C.1056 B.S. L.596 J.D. [Moomaw,M.&H.]
Miller, Douglas G., PC ... 14780 S.W. Osprey Dr., Ste. 240
Mitchell, Virginia G., (BV) ... '58 '84 C.169 B.A. L.112 J.D. 12100 Sw Allen
Monson, Miles D. '62 '92 C.101 B.S. L.1035 J.D.
10700 SW Beaverton-Hillsdale Hwy., Ste. 460
Montgomery, H. Paul, (AV) '52 '80
C&L.629 B.S., J.D. Sr. Coun. & Asst. Secy., Tektronix, Inc.
Moomaw, Larry D., (BV) ... '48 '73 C.1051 B.S. L.596 J.D. [Moomaw,M.&H.]
Moomaw, Miller & Hildebrand, L.L.P., (BV) ... 12275 Southwest Second Avenue
Moore, Martin H. ... '58 '83 C.628 B.S. L.1051 J.D. 9989 S.W. 175th
Muir, Phillip R., (BV) ... '48 '75 C.1056 B.A. L.464 J.D. [Muir&T.]
Muir & Troutman, (BV) ... 16100 N.W. Cornell Rd., Ste. 200
Myatt, Lewis E., (BV) ... '33 '60 C&L.950 B.A., J.D. [Myatt&B.]
Myatt & Bell, P.C., (BV) ... 4240 Southwest Cedar Hills Boulevard
Naemura, Theodore R. '67 '95 C.860 B.A. L.629 J.D.
Asst. City Atty., City of Beaverton
North, Philip E. '48 '74 C.169 B.A. L.950 J.D.
(adm. in WI; not adm. in OR) 7725 S.W. Wilson Ave.
Novak, Pamela R. ... '64 '94 C.1077 B.S. L.809 J.D. 6800 SW 105th Avenue
Olsen, Richard W. '46 '75 C.907 B.A. L.285 J.D.
V.P. & Gen. Coun., Shari's Mgmt. Corp.
Palka, Bonnie M. ... '52 '77 C.454 B.A. L.818 J.D. 17207 S.W. Soren Ct.
Parker, Eugene L., (BV) ... '30 '65 C.911 B.A. L.596 J.D. 21145 N.W. Quatama Rd.
Perkins-Reed, Marcia A. ... '56 '85 C.1181 B.S. L.596 J.D. 14153 S.W. Daphne St.‡
Perry, Richard T. ... '41 '82 C.1056 B.A. L.596 J.D. 1905 N.W. 169th Place

Peterson Law Offices, PC
(See Portland)

Pilliod, Mark E., (BV) ... '53 '78 C.597 B.A. L.596 J.D. City Atty.
Polk, Arnold S., (BV) ... '47 '81 C.966 B.B.A. L.629 J.D. 5150 S.W. Griffith
Potempa, Eryn ... '68 '04 C&L.1051 B.A., J.D. Immig., Nike, Inc.
Powers, Leonard R. '39 '67 C.966 B.B.A. L.436 J.D.
(adm. in WI; not adm. in OR) 13320 S.W. Hyland Ter.‡

Raivio, Kohlmetz & Steen, P.C.
(See Portland)

Reel, Allen, (BV) ... '44 '74 C.506 B.S. L.596 J.D. 7300 S.W. Bel Aire Dr.
Reinikka, Leo A., (BV) ... '45 '70 C.907 B.A. L.950 J.D. [A Case&D.]
Richmond, Allan E. ... '14 '66 C.999 L.596 J.D. 7360 S.W. 101st Ave.‡
Rink, Les, (BV) ... '47 '87 C.628 B.S. L.285 J.D. 12220 S.W. 2nd St.
Rowe, Stephanie Davis '69 '94 C.95 B.A. L.94 J.D.
(adm. in MA; not adm. in OR) Nike
Saathoff, Mardilyn ... '56 '91 C&L.1051 B.A., J.D. Coun., Tektronix, Inc.
Scannell, Terry, (BV) '54 '85
C.1051 B.S. L.629 J.D. Gen. Coun., Color & Design Exhibits, Inc.
Scarbrough, Roger Dale ... '55 '91 C.845 B.A. L.1463 J.D. [A Helzer&C.]
Scheiderich, William J. W. ... '50 '79 C.976 B.A. L.596 J.D. Asst. City Atty.
Schouten, Dick A. ... '52 '79 C.770 B.S. L.1068 J.D. 6105 S.W. 148th
Schrock, Bradley J. ... '61 '87 C.475 B.A. L.596 J.D. 4500 SW Hall Blvd., 2nd Fl.
Shepherd, Tasaneeya P. ... '76 '02 C.999 L.285 J.D. [B.a.T.P.S.Wang]

Shertz, Laurie, LLC
(See Portland)

Sloan, Andrea ... '60 '87 C&L.770 B.S., J.D. Admin. Law J., Off. of Admin. Hearings
Smith, Duncan C. '37 '64 C.674 B.A. L.976 J.D.
(adm. in CT; not adm. in OR) 16645 SW Estuary Dr.
Spencer, Karen Y. '64 '90 C.453 B.S. L.309 J.D.
(adm. in CA; not adm. in OR) Asst. Gen. Coun., Nike, Inc.
Stamm, Douglas A., (BV) '53 '80
C.813 B.S. L.596 J.D. Assoc. Dir., Sports Mktg., Nike, Inc.
Stewart, Lindsay D. '47 '73 C&L.950 B.A., J.D.
V.P., Law & Corp. Affs., & Chf. of Staff, Nike, Inc.
Stinson, Richard B., Jr. ... '38 '68 C.1056 B.S. L.596 J.D. 12275 S.W. 2nd Ave.
Stolpman, Preethi G. '68 '98
C.494 B.S.B. L.1035 J.D. Staff Atty., Oregon Credit Union League
Sutherland, Norman E., (AV) ... '15 '47 C.629 L.596 J.D. 7300 S.W. Kimberly Ct.‡
Teppola, Susan Ertle ... '51 '77 C.629 B.S. L.208 J.D. Admin. Law J.
Terwilliger, Connie L. F., (BV) ... '46 '76 C.629 B.A. L.982 J.D. 12125 S.W. 2nd St.
Thomas, Brian G. ... '41 '70 C.604 B.A. L.608 J.D. 4080 SW 193rd Avenue
Thomashow, Mark H. ... '49 '80 C.454 B.A. L.629 J.D. Mgr. Bus. Affs., Nike, Inc.

Thompson Law Firm, The
(See Portland)

Troutman, Ted A., (BV) . . . '57 '84 C.1056 B.S. L.569 J.D. [Muir&T.]
Udziela, Robert K., (AV) . . . '44 '77 C.742 B.A. L.596 J.D. P.O. Box 5310
Uffelman, John E., (BV) . . . '48 '73 C.285 B.A. L.629 J.D. [Adams&U.]
VanderWeele, Mary, (AV) . . . '61 '86 C.373 B.A. L.477 J.D. Asst. Gen. Coun., Nike, Inc.
Van Ness, Mark C. '58 '83 C.174 B.A. L.276 J.D.
(adm. in CO; not adm. in OR; See Pat. Sect.) [Ⓐ Blakely,S.T.&Z.]
Vardavas, Stephanie J. '56 '86 C.976 B.A. L.262 J.D.
(adm. in NY; not adm. in OR) Coun., Endorsement & League Affrs., Nike, Inc.
Varela, Raul De Assis . . . '29 '87 17964 N.W. Maudsley Ct.‡
Volchok, Larry R. . . . '42 '66 C.911 B.S. L.950 J.D. Sr. V.P., National Assoc. Inc., N.W.
VonBergen, Paul K., (BV) . . . '48 '76 C.674 A.B. L.596 J.D. 12440 S.W. 1st Street
Walsh, Thomas P. . . . '53 '90 C.697 B.A. L.345 J.D. 4085 S.W. 109th Ave.
Wang, Baoqin . . . '68 '00 C.999 L.101 J.D. [B.a.T.P.S.Wang]

Wang, Baoqin and Tanya P. Shepherd
4900 SW Griffith Drive, Suite 165, 97005
Telephone: 503-626-7051 Fax: 503-626-7950
Email: immigration@askwang.com URL: http://www.askwang.com
Baoqin Wang; Tasaneeya P. Shepherd.
Languages: Chinese, Thai, Japanese.
Immigration Law, Corporate Law.
See Professional Biographies, BEAVERTON, OREGON

Way, Gary D. '58 '84 C.705 B.A. L.569 J.D.
(adm. in NY; not adm. in OR) Coun., Endorsement & League Affrs., Nike, Inc.
Webster, Alison Greene . . . '— '87 C.1494 B.A. L.1522 J.D. Admin. Law J.
Wenzlick, Grant . . . '61 '99 C.1056 B.S. L.950 J.D. 4085 S.W. 109th Avenue, Ste. 100
Whalen, Jeffrey B. '57 '85 C.228 A.B. L.30 J.D.
(adm. in DC; not adm. in OR) Coun., Customs & Intl. Trade, Nike, Inc.
Yaksich, Kelly D. '54 '91 C&L.831 B.A., J.D.
(adm. in DC; not adm. in OR) Poorman-Douglas Corporation
Yoakum, Grant F. . . . '61 '92 C.628 B.S. L.596 J.D. [Myatt&B.]
Zikes, Denny Z., (AV) . . . '28 '59 C.1051 B.A. L.596 J.D. 4085 S.W. 109th Ave.‡

BEND, * 52,029, *Deschutes Co.*

Adler, A. Michael . . . '53 '80 C.170 B.A. L.1051 J.D. Cir. J.
Albertazzi, Anthony V. . . . '62 '94 C.813 B.A. L.1065 J.D. [Albertazzi]
Albertazzi Law Firm . . . 1070 N.W. Bond St., Ste. 202
Alexander, J. Brendon, (CV) . . . '59 '86 C.966 B.A. L.629 J.D. [Alexander&D.]
Alexander & DeHoog, P.C., (CV) . . . 17 N.W. Hawthorne Street, Suite #2
Allen, Jennifer A. . . . '73 '01 C.339 B.S. L.734 J.D./M.H.A. P.O. Box 1151
Anderson, Philip R. . . . '66 '95 C.1375 B.A. L.629 J.D. [Elliott A.]
Arnett, Howard G., (AV) . . . '47 '77 C.813 B.A. L.629 J.D. [Karnopp P.]
Ash, Jonathan G., (AVⓉ) '45 '72
C.401 L.1095 LL.B. 44 N.W. Irving Ave. (⊙Tarzana, CA)
Ash, Seana McMann . . . '52 '78 C.112 B.A. L.398 J.D. 44 N.W. Irving
Atchison, Donald, (AV) . . . '32 '59 C.1051 B.S. L.596 LL.B. 61793 Tam Macarthur Loop
Austin, Erin '62 '93 C.941 B.A. L.596 J.D.
Corporate Counsel, David Evans And Associates
Austin, Stanley D., (CV) . . . '61 '91 C.907 B.A. L.596 J.D. [Ⓐ Hurley,L.&R.]
Babb, Ray A., (BV) . . . '40 '65 C.170 B.A. L.629 J.D. [Babb H.]

Babb Heatherman LLP, (BV)
960 SW Disk Drive, P.O. Box 8, 97709
Telephone: 541-389-1010 Fax: 541-382-6875
Email: paul@bendattorneys.com URL: http://bendattorneys.com
Partners: Ray A. Babb; Paul B. Heatherman. Associate: Lillah McBride. Of Counsel: Katharine A. Miller.
Business Law, Commercial Law, Contracts, Collections, Construction Law, Real Estate, Commercial Leasing, Family Law, Divorce, Child Custody, Estate Planning, Wills, Probate, Personal Injury, Lawsuits, Litigation.
See Professional Biographies, BEND, OREGON

Bagley, Christopher A. . . . '71 '97 C.629 B.A. L.494 J.D. [Ⓐ Bryant,L.&J.]

Ball Janik LLP, (AV)
15 SW Colorado Avenue, Suite 3, 97702 ⊙
Telephone: 541-617-1309 Telecopy: 541-617-8824
Email: info@balljanik.com URL: http://www.balljanik.com
Partners of Firm: Nancy Craven (Also at Portland, Oregon Office); Laura Craska Cooper (Also at Portland, Oregon Office). Special Counsel: Robert A. Stout (Also at Portland, Oregon Office). Associates: Reagan L.B. Desmond (Also at Portland, Oregon Office); Kristin L. Udvari (Also at Portland, Oregon Office).
Real Estate and Land Use Law, Business and Corporate Law, Construction, Environmental and Natural Resources Law, Zoning Law, Health Care, Securities.
Portland, Oregon Office: One Main Place, 101 SW Main Street, Suite 1100, 97204-3219. Telephone: 503-228-2525. Telecopy: 503-295-1058.
Washington, D.C. Office: 1455 F Street, NW, Suite 225, 20005-1004. Telephone: 202-638-3307. Telecopy: 202-783-6947.
See Professional Biographies, BEND, OREGON

Balyeat, Andrew C., (BV) . . . '60 '85 C.150 B.A. L.607 J.D. 920 N.W. Bond Street
Basham, Jonathan G., (CV) '50 '87
C.112 B.A. L.629 J.D. 2542 North East Courtney Drive, Suite 200
Bauhofer, Donald N. '51 '77 C.813 B.A. L.1067 J.D.
(adm. in CA; not adm. in OR) 516 N.W. Drake Rd.‡
Bemis, Richard C., (AV) . . . '32 '57 C.1051 B.S. L.629 J.D. 2607 N.W. Foley Ct.
Berge, John A., (AV) . . . '61 '87 C.628 B.S. L.950 J.D. [Bryant,L.&J.]
Bertalan, Lisa N. . . . '65 '91 C.174 B.A. L.629 J.D. [Hendrix,B.&B.]
Bischof, Bruce, (AV) . . . '40 '67 C&L.623 B.A., J.D. 747 S.W. Millview Way
Brady, Alta J. . . . '55 '83 C.911 B.A. L.950 J.D. Cir. J.
Bregenzer, Neil S., (BV) . . . '49 '90 C.502 B.A. L.629 J.D. Dep. Dist. Atty.
Brewster, Susan Aileen, (CV) . . . '53 '85 C.475 B.S. L.950 J.D. 63333 W Hwy 20
Brinich, Ken, (BV) . . . '55 '82 C.878 B.S. L.1051 J.D. [Hendrix,B.&B.] (Pat.)
Brockett, Phillip R. . . . '55 '81 C.805 B.B.A. L.802 J.D. 388 SW Bluff Drive
Brothers, Barbara Beth '53 '88 C.678 B.A. L.1137 J.D.
(adm. in CA; not adm. in OR) 60579 Bozeman Trail
Brothers, Bruce J., & Associates, (AV) '42 '70
C&L.629 B.S., J.D. 974 N.W. Riverside Boulevard
Brown, Glenn C., (BV) '51 '91 C.628 B.Ch.E. L.950 J.D.
777 Northwest Wall Street (Pat.)
Bryant, Lon N. . . . '31 '62 C&L.629 B.S., J.D. 18215 Pinehurst Road
Bryant, Neil R., (AV) . . . '48 '73 C.1058 B.A. L.950 J.D. [Bryant,L.&J.]
Bryant, Thomas V., Jr. . . . '25 '54 C&L.188 A.B., J.D. 537 N.W. Wall St.

Bryant, Lovlien & Jarvis, P.C., (AV) BB
591 SW Mill View Way, P.O. Box 1151, 97709-1151
Telephone: 541-382-4331 Fax: 541-389-3386
Email: bljadmin@bljlawyers.com URL: http://www.bljlawyers.com
Neil R. Bryant; Robert S. Lovlien; Lynn F. Jarvis; John A. Berge; Sharon R. Smith; John D. Sorlie; Mark G. Reinecke; Melissa P. Lande; Kitri C. Ford;—Paul J. Taylor; Christopher A. Bagley; Jeremy M. Green; Kelly L. Schukart.

(This Listing Continued)

Bryant, Lovlien & Jarvis, P.C. (Continued)

General Civil and Trial Practice, Corporations, Creditor's Rights in Bankruptcy, Taxation, Estate Planning, Probate, Elder Law, Real Estate, Land Use Planning, Natural Resource Law, Water Rights, Insurance Defense and Family Law.
Representative Clients: Bend-Lapine School District; Bend Metroparks and Recreation District; City of Madras; Sisters School District; Arnold Irrigation District; Western Communications, dba The Bulletin; Eagle Crest Resort; Western Title & Escrow Company; Bend Broadband; Jack Robinson & Sons Construction, Inc.
See Professional Biographies, BEND, OREGON

Buchanan, William F. . . . '66 '93 C.628 B.S. L.273 J.D. [Karnopp P.]
Byers, Ira L. '43 '91 C.1265 B.A. L.930 J.D.
(adm. in AZ; not adm. in OR) 1532 N.W. Albany Ave.
Charbonneau, Robert L. . . . '40 '66 L.1522 J.D. 20060 Rodeo Dr.
Cherzan, Deidre' . . . '56 '92 C.628 B.A. L.911 J.D. 708 N.E. 11th St.
Clark, L. Thomas, Jr., (BV) . . . '44 '70 C&L.629 B.A., J.D. [L.T.Clark,Jr.]
Clark, L. Thomas, Jr., P.C., (BV) . . . 521 N.W. Harriman St.

Clark, Lindauer, Fetherston, Edmonds, Lippold & Collier, LLP
(See Salem)

Conway, Myles A. . . . '60 '88 C.112 B.A. L.629 J.D. [Schwabe,W.&W.]
Cooper, Laura Craska . . . '66 '91 C.502 B.A. L.1066 J.D. [Ball J.] (⊙Portland)
Copenhaver, John M. . . . '24 '50 C&L.950 A.B., LL.B. [Ⓒ Merrill O.]
Corbett, Alfred H. . . . '15 '40 C.309 B.S. L.976 LL.B. 19175 Tumalo Reservoir Rd.‡
Costello, Donald O., (BV) . . . '48 '77 C.112 A.B. L.1051 J.D. P.O. Box 8370
Coyner, Craig C., (BV) . . . '21 '50 C&L.950 A.B., J.D. 780 N.E. Dyer Dr.
Coyner, Craig C., III, (BV) '47 '74 C.1056 B.S. L.596 J.D.
115 N.W. Oregon Ave., Ste. 21
Crabtree, Thomas J., (BV) . . . '50 '75 C.388 B.A. L.596 J.D. 215 N.W. Greenwood.
Craghead, Laurie E. . . . '59 '92 C.999 B.S. L.596 J.D. Legal Coun.
Craven, Nancy, (AV) . . . '54 '79 C.399 B.A. L.801 J.D. [Ball J.] (⊙Portland)
Dale, Lorna Gene . . . '42 '82 C.1253 B.A. L.809 J.D. 162 S.E. Piper Dr.

D'Amore & Associates, P.C.
(See Portland)

Davis, Paul K., (BV) . . . '38 '63 C.1051 B.S. L.950 LL.B. City Comr.
DeKock, Bruce W., (BV) . . . '63 '91 C.112 B.S. L.1066 J.D. Bend Research, Inc. (Pat.)
Desmond, Reagan L.B. . . . '67 '97 C.651 B.S. L.878 J.D. [Ⓐ Ball J.] (⊙Portland)
Dewey, Paul . . . '50 '78 C.378 B.A. L.893 J.D. 1539 NW Vicksburg
Dickson, Elizabeth A., (CV) . . . '57 '96 C.1051 B.A. L.599 J.D. [Ⓐ Hurley,L.&R.]
Dillard, Michael L., (AVⓉ) . . . '48 '73 C.112 B.A. L.1068 J.D. [Karnopp P.]
Dillingham, James W. . . . '41 '67 C&L.378 B.S., J.D. 1030 N.W. Bond
Dixon, Stephen D., (AV) . . . '48 '73 C.1051 B.A. L.585 J.D. [Merrill O.]
Doyle, Robert Paul . . . '70 '99 C.478 B.A. L.629 J.D. 142 N.W. Hawthorne Avenue
Duerst, Jonathan R., (BV) . . . '53 '79 C.628 B.S. L.629 J.D. 111 N.W. Oregon Ave.
Dugan, Michael T., (BV) . . . '51 '76 C.629 B.S. L.1051 J.D. Dist. Atty.
Dvorak, Louis B., (CV) . . . '44 '75 C.668 B.A. L.1068 J.D. 1123 N.W. Bond St.
Dwyer, Roy, Law Office of, (BV) . . . '33 '62 C&L.629 B.S., LL.B. 725 N.W. Broadway
Eager, Jeffrey T. . . . '75 '04 C.950 B.A. L.629 J.D. [Ⓐ Karnopp P.]
Edwards, Craig K., (BV) . . . '51 '80 C.1111 B.A. L.1051 J.D. [Edwards W.]
Edwards Widmer, LLP, (BV) . . . 225 N.W. Franklin Ave., Ste. C
Elliott, Timothy G., (BV) . . . '66 '95 C.112 B.A. L.950 J.D. [Elliott A.]
Elliott Anderson, LLP, (BV) . . . 42 NW Greeley Avenue
Emerson, Philip . . . '56 '90 C.629 B.A. L.596 J.D. [Lage F.E.]
Erwin, Lawrence W., (BV) . . . '48 '73 C.629 B.S. L.596 J.D. 221 N.W. Lafayette Ave.
Eves, Valerie, (CV) . . . '43 '89 C.611 B.A. L.950 J.D. 215 N.W. Greenwood
Fancher, Elizabeth L., (BV) . . . '55 '81 C.222 B.A. L.950 J.D. Asst. City Atty.
Farra, Roxanne L., (BV) . . . '62 '90 C.628 B.A. L.596 J.D. [R.L.Farra]

Farra, Roxanne L., P.C., (BV)
17 N.W. Irving Avenue, 97701
Telephone: 541-385-3017 Fax: 541-330-1556
Email: rfarra@bendbroadband.com URL: http://www.lawyers.com/roxannefarra
Roxanne L. Farra.
Employment Litigation and Consultation, Business Litigation, Employment Law, Wage and Hour Law, Discrimination, Sexual Harassment, Wrongful Termination and Disability Accommodation.
See Professional Biographies, BEND, OREGON

Fennell, Dennis E. . . . '49 '74 C.629 B.A. L.950 J.D. [D.Fennell]
Fennell, Dennis . . . 1195 N.W. Wall St.
Flinn, William E., (AV) . . . '42 '67 C.768 B.A. L.629 J.D. [Hurley,L.&R.]
Foley, Robert H. . . . '11 '35 C&L.629 LL.B. 1305 Columbia St., N.W.‡
Forcum, Richard E., (BV) '39 '64 C&L.950 B.S., LL.B.
141 N.W. Greenwood, Suite 101
Ford, Kitri C., (BV) . . . '52 '89 C.628 B.S. L.878 J.D. [Bryant,L.&J.]
Forte, Stephen P., (BV) . . . '53 '83 C.589 B.S. L.336 J.D. P.O. Box 1148
Francis, C. E. "Win", (BV) . . . '48 '77 C.813 A.B. L.1051 LL.B. [Francis,H.&M.]

Francis, Hansen & Martin, LLP, (AV)
1148 N.W. Hill Street, 97701
Telephone: 541-389-5010 Fax: 541-382-7068
URL: http://www.francishansenmartin.com
Members of Firm: C. E. "Win" Francis; Martin E. Hansen; Gerald A. Martin;—Michael H. McGean; Gregory J. Stuman.
Real Estate, Probate, Personal Injury, Workers Compensation, Business, Corporate, Limited Liability Companies, Estate Planning, Homeowners Association Law and Civil Litigation.
Reference: Wells Fargo & Co.
See Professional Biographies, BEND, OREGON

Gardner, Christopher H., (CV) . . . '46 '81 C&L.347 B.S., J.D. Dep. Dist. Atty.
Gill, Rockne, (AV) . . . '31 '55 C&L.629 B.S., LL.B. [Schwabe,W.&W.] (⊙Portland)‡
Gingerich, Brian L., (BV) . . . '64 '92 C.950 B.A. L.629 J.D. [Schwabe,W.&W.]
Glass, Foster A. . . . '42 '75 C.629 B.S. L.446 J.D. [F.A.Glass]
Glass, Foster A., A Professional Corporation, Law Offices of
339 SW Century Drive, Suite 101
Graham, Bethany C. . . . '73 '02 C.1058 B.A. L.508 J.D. [Ⓐ Schwabe,W.&W.]
Gray, Alvin J., (AV) . . . '20 '48 C&L.629 B.S., LL.B. U.S. Mag.
Greaney, Mark R. . . . '65 '93 C&L.602 B.A., J.D. American Express Financial
Green, Jeremy M. . . . '77 '04 C.999 B.S. L.629 J.D. [Ⓐ Bryant,L.&J.]
Green, Karen H. . . . '50 '77 C.629 B.A. L.950 J.D. 1331 N.W. West Hills Ave.
Gregory, Julie L. . . . '60 '86 C.260 B.A. L.902 J.D. 920 N.W. Bond Street

Groener, Bethany Flint, Law Offices of '76 '03 C.112 B.A L.1148 J.D.
360 Northwest Vermont Place Suite 500, 97701
Telephone: 541-318-0221 Fax: 541-318-7274
Email: beth@bendfamilylaw.com
Litigation, Family Law, Domestic Relations, Divorce, Child Custody.
See Professional Biographies, BEND, OREGON

Grover, Ellen H. . . . '70 '99 C.140 B.A. L.1051 J.D. [Ⓐ Karnopp P.]
Gruetter, Bryan W., (BV) . . . '58 '86 C.1056 B.S. L.950 J.D. [Hurley,L.&R.]
Haase, Linda Reed, (BV) . . . '46 '81 C&L.629 B.A., J.D. 960 S.W. Disk Dr., Ste. 101

Handy, Paul Donald .... '46 '75 C.843 B.S. L.900 J.D. [P.D.Handy]
Handy, Paul D. .... 327 N.W. Greenwood Ave., Ste. 302
Hansen, Mark B., (BVⓉ) '56 '83 C.352 B.G.S. L.596 J.D.
(adm. in WA; not adm. in OR) [M.B.Hansen]
Hansen, Martin E., (AV) ....'55 '79 C.1071 B.S. L.678 J.D. [Francis,H.&M.]
Hansen, Mark B., P.S., (BVⓉ) .... P.O. Box 8754
Haslinger, Barbara ....'54 '81 C.628 B.S. L.629 J.D. Cir. Ct. J.
Hatfield, Christopher D., (CV) ....'59 '87 C.629 B.S. L.596 J.D. [Hurley,L.&R.]
Heatherman, Patricia L., (BV) ....'64 '93 C.508 B.A. L.950 J.D. [Merrill O.]
Heatherman, Paul B. ....'62 '93 C.330 B.S. L.950 J.D. [Babb H.]
Hellis, Lori A. G. ....'56 '92 C.670 B.A. L.1051 J.D. [L.A.G.Hellis]
Hellis, Lori A.G., P.C. .... 327 NW Greenwood St., Ste. 300
Henderson, Michael.......................'41 '69 C.629 B.A. L.596 J.D. [M.Henderson]
Henderson, Philip G., (CV) ....'55 '89 C.976 B.A. L.629 J.D. [Henderson]
Henderson Law Office, (CV) ....61517 S.E. Orion Dr.
Henderson, Michael, PC ....360 Northwest Vermont Place, Suite 100
Hendrix, Greg, (BV) ....'53 '83 C.763 B.A. L.950 J.D. [Hendrix,B.&B.]

Hendrix, Brinich & Bertalan, LLP, (BV)
716 N.W. Harriman Street, 97701
Telephone: 541-382-4980 Fax: 541-382-9060
Email: gh@bendcable.com URL: http://www.hxbri.com
Greg Hendrix; Ken Brinich; Lisa N. Bertalan.
General Civil and Trial Practice, Business, Corporate, Real Estate, Construction Law, Land Use, Trademarks, Copyrights, Intellectual Property, Probate and Estate Planning.
See Professional Biographies, BEND, OREGON

Hepburn, Heather J. .... '77 '03 C&L.629 B.S., J.D. [Ⓐ Karnopp P.]
Hill, Thomas A. .... '58 '96 C.767 B.S.P.A. L.950 J.D. [Ⓐ B.J.Brothers&Assoc.]
Hohengarten, Alison G. .... '72 '01 C.174 B.A. L.950 J.D. 225 N.W. Franklin
Holmes, William M., (AV) ..... '28 '56 C.629 B.S. L.596 LL.B. Gen. Coun., Baney Corp.
Hopp, Carl W., Jr., (BV) ....'50 '75 C.880 B.E. L.596 J.D. 168 N.W. Greenwood
Hummel, John J. ....'69 '95 C.695 B.A. L.1243 J.D. 142 Nw Hawthorne Ave
Hurley, James V., (AV) .... '34 '61 C.424 B.S.C. L.966 LL.B. [Ⓒ Hurley,L.&R.]

Hurley, Lynch & Re, P.C., (AV) BR
747 S.W. Mill View Way, 97702 ⊙
Telephone: 541-317-5505 Fax: 541-317-5507
Email: info@hlr-law.com URL: http://www.hlandr.com
Gregory P. Lynch; Daniel C. Re; Bryan W. Gruetter; William E. Flinn; Christopher D. Hatfield. Of Counsel: James V. Hurley; Brian J. MacRitchie;—Stanley D. Austin; Elizabeth A. Dickson; Todd J. Winegar; Gary R. Johnson.
General Civil and Trial Practice, Business, Corporate, Real Estate and Land Use, Leasing, Insurance Defense, Commercial Litigation, Water Rights Law, Taxation, Intellectual Property, Licensing, Probate and Estate Planning, Health Law, Employment Law.
Representative Clients: David Evans & Associates; Bend Research; Quality Materials, Inc.; Brooks Resources Corporation; Central Oregon Irrigation District; Scottsdale Insurance Co.; USAA; Bend Memorial Clinic.
Prineville Office: 446 NW 3rd Street, Suite 230, 97754. Telephone: 541-447-5777. Fax: 541-447-5755.
See Professional Biographies, BEND, OREGON

Hutchens, Terri, (CV) '60 '86 C.911 B.A. L.596 J.D.
1735 S.W. Chandler Avenue, Suite 3
Jarvis, Lynn F., (AV) ....'43 '79 C.628 B.S. L.336 J.D. [Bryant,L.&J.]
Johansen, Kirk, (AV) .... '49 '74 C&L.629 B.S., J.D. [Schwabe,W.&W.] (⊙Portland)
Johnson, Gary R. ....'64 '93 C.911 B.S. L.1051 J.D. [Ⓐ Hurley,L.&R.]
Johnson, Ronald M., (BV) ....'56 '88 C&L.1051 B.A., J.D. [Stahancyk,K.J.&H.]
Karnopp, Dennis C., (AV) ....'42 '67 C&L.546 B.A., J.D. [Karnopp P.]

Karnopp Petersen LLP, (AV)
1201 NW Wall Street, Suite 300, 97701
Telephone: 541-382-3011 Fax: 541-388-5410
Email: mail@karnopp.com URL: http://www.karnopp.com
Lyman C. Johnson (1929-1986); Dennis C. Karnopp; James E. Petersen; James D. Noteboom; Howard G. Arnett; Thomas J. Sayeg; Ronald L. Roome; Michael L. Dillard; Brent S. Kinkade; William F. Buchanan; Tamara E. MacLeod. Of Counsel: A. Reed Marbut;—Josh Newton; Jon J. Napier; Ellen H. Grover; Cynthia J. Starke; Heather J. Hepburn; Jeffrey T. Eager.
General Civil, Trial and Appellate Practice, including Plaintiff's Personal Injury and Tort Litigation. General Business, Banking, Creditor Bankruptcy, Tax, Estate Planning, Probate, Real Estate and Land Use, Employment Law, Water Law, Utility/Energy, Environmental and Indian Affairs Law.
Representative Clients: City of Bend; Confederated Tribes of the Warm Springs Reservation of Oregon; First Interstate Bank; Bank of the Cascades; FDIC; Allstate Insurance Co.; U.S.F. & G.; North Pacific Insurance.
See Professional Biographies, BEND, OREGON

Keillor, Kevin J., (BV) ....'59 '87 C&L.629 B.S., J.D. Gen. Coun., Edge Wireless
Kent, Joel J., (BV) ....'69 '96 C.678 B.S. L.1358 J.D. [Stahancyk,K.J.&H.]
Kinkade, Brent S. ....'66 '93 C.101 B.A. L.911 J.D. [Karnopp P.]
Lage, Rita L. ....'61 '94 C.477 B.A. L.596 J.D. [Lage F.E.]
Lage Fisher Emerson, LLP ....1045 N.W. Bond St., Ste. 4
Lande, Melissa P., (BV) ....'66 '91 C.569 B.A. L.902 J.D. [Bryant,L.&J.]
Larson, Kristin M. ....'70 '02 C.668 B.A. L.596 J.D. [Ⓐ Stahancyk,K.J.&H.]
Larsson, Dan R. '62 '94 C.629 B.A. L.1358 J.D.
(adm. in WA; not adm. in OR) 243 S.W. Scalehouse Loop
Lasken, Glen J., (BV) ..... '58 '83 C.339 B.A. L.629 J.D. 777 N.W. Wall Street Suite 308
Leach, Edmund J., Jr. '22 '53 C.112 B.A. L.1065
(adm. in CA; not adm. in OR) Ret. Supr. Ct. J.‡
Lee, Angela T. ....'68 '97 C.112 B.A. L.629 J.D. Pub. Def.
Leventhal, Steven H. .... '47 '72 C.588 B.A. L.818 J.D. 855 S.W. Yates Drive Suite 104
Lewis, Tia M., (BV) ....'65 '93 C.576 B.A. L.596 J.D. [Schwabe,W.&W.]
Lohrey, Christopher Thomas, (BV) ....'70 '96 C.37 B.A. L.596 J.D. 817 N.W. Hill St.
Lovlien, Robert S., (AV) ....'49 '74 C.911 B.A. L.629 J.D. [Bryant,L.&J.]

Lowry, Robert D., Law Offices of
(See Eugene)

Lynch, Gregory P., (AV) ....'49 '75 C.767 B.A. L.596 J.D. [Hurley,L.&R.]
MacLeod, Tamara E. ....'68 '95 C.549 B.A. L.950 J.D. [Karnopp P.]
MacRitchie, Brian J., (BV) ....'52 '79 C.475 B.S. L.950 J.D. [Ⓒ Hurley,L.&R.]
Marbut, A. Reed ....'34 '87 C.172 D.V.M. L.1051 J.D. [Ⓒ Karnopp P.]
Martin, Gerald A., (BV) ....'43 '69 C&L.352 B.A., J.D. [Francis,H.&M.]
Mattei, Lyn O. ....'48 '94 C.1375 B.A. L.1051 J.D. [L.Mattei]
Mattei, Lyn ....61487 Elder Ridge St.
McBride, Lillah ....'77 '03 C.499 B.A. L.950 J.D. [Ⓐ Babb H.]
McCabe, Duane J., (AV) ....'47 '74 C.911 B.A. L.950 J.D. 44 N.W. Irving
McCarty, Kevin J., (BV) ....'57 '89 C&L.950 B.S., J.D. P.O. Box 1245
McCord, Michael B., (BV) ....'54 '78 C&L.629 B.S., J.D. 65 N.W. Greeley Ave.
McGean, Michael H. ....'70 '00 C.685 B.A. L.1065 J.D. [Ⓐ Francis,H.&M.]
Merrill, Edward A., Law Office of '70 '01
C.628 B.S. L.602 J.D. 243 S.W. Scalehouse Loop, Ste 1B
Merrill, Max, (AV) ....'41 '66 C&L.950 B.A., J.D. [Merrill O.]
Merrill O'Sullivan, LLP, (AV) ....1070 Northwest Bond Street, Suite 303
Mierjeski, Edward '50 '82
C.354 B.A. L.1051 J.D. Crabtree & Rahmsdorff Def. Servs., Inc.

Miller, Katharine A. .... '55 '87 C.678 B.S. L.1148 J.D. [Ⓒ Babb H.] (⊙Pasadena, CA)
Miller, Roy '30 '61 C.911 B.S. L.273 LL.B.
(adm. in CA; not adm. in OR) 16690 Stagestop Dr.‡
Mock, Rodney P. ....'72 '03 C.112 B.A. L.629 J.D. [Ⓐ Merrill O.]
Mosgrove, Thomas M. ....'29 '53 C&L.629 B.S., J.D. Sr. Cir. J.
Napier, Jon J. ....'72 '98 C.413 B.S. L.950 J.D. [Ⓐ Karnopp P.]
Nash, Robert L. ....'46 '73 C&L.629 B.A., J.D. 15 S.W. Colorado Ave.
Newton, Josh ....'72 '98 C.628 B.S. L.950 J.D. [Ⓐ Karnopp P.]
Nielsen, Erwin C. '25 '57 L.1026 LL.B.
(adm. in CA; not adm. in OR) P.O. Box 6055‡
Noteboom, James D., (AV) ....'45 '77 C.628 B.S. L.629 J.D. [Karnopp P.]
Nye, Bradley I. ....'64 '92 C.629 B.A. L.911 J.D. 2008 North West 4th Street
Olson, Allan J. ....'53 '79 C.628 B.S. L.629 J.D. 65770 Tweed Rd.‡
O'Neill, Greg, (BV) .... '53 '81 C.352 B.A. L.1051 J.D. 296 S.W. Columbia St.
O'Sullivan, Terrence B., (AV) ....'43 '68 C&L.629 B.S., J.D. [Merrill O.]
Parker, Leonard C., (CV) ....'51 '79 C&L.950 B.S., J.D. 1150 N.E. Revere Ave.
Paulson, David E., (BV) .... '55 '82 C.585 B.S. L.629 J.D. 168 N.W. Greenwood Ave.
Perkins, Edward L. ....'43 '74 C.629 B.S. L.950 J.D. Cir. J.
Peterkin, Michael W. ....'51 '82 C.1060 B.A. L.950 J.D. [Peterkin&Assoc.]
Peterkin & Associates ....222 N.W. Irving Ave.
Peters, Lisa A. ....'62 '94 C.1044 B.A. L.1170 J.D. [L.A.Peters]
Peters, Lisa A., P.C., Law Office of .... 115 NW Oregon Ste 19
Petersen, David E., (BV) ....'55 '82 C.628 B.S. L.678 J.D. [Merrill O.]
Petersen, James ....'53 '87 C.878 B.A. L.596 J.D. 205 NW Franklin Ave.
Petersen, James E., (AV) ....'40 '64 C&L.629 B.A., J.D. [Karnopp P.]
Phillips, Gordon E. ....'72 '00 C.911 B.A. L.596 J.D. [Ⓐ Stahancyk,K.J.&H.]
Piccolo, V. Brian, (BVⓉ) ....'64 '92 C.705 B.S. L.1051 J.D. 19979 Heron Loop
Re, Daniel C., (BV) ....'49 '80 C.629 B.S. L.285 J.D. [Hurley,L.&R.]
Reinecke, Mark G., (BV) ....'62 '91 C.363 B.S.B.A. L.902 J.D. [Bryant,L.&J.]
Roome, Ronald L., (BV) ....'51 '82 C.1060 B.A. L.1065 J.D. [Karnopp P.]
Saalfeld, Robert J., (AV) ....'49 '74 C.767 B.A. L.950 J.D. [Saalfeld G.] ⊙

Saalfeld Griggs PC, (AV)
1001-B SW Disk Drive, Suite 102, 97702-1995 ⊙
Telephone: 541-322-1822 Fax: 541-322-1823
Email: contactus@sglaw.com URL: http://www.sglaw.com
Robert J. Saalfeld.
Business, Taxation, Intellectual Property, Real Estate and Land Use, Employment, Construction, Banking, Creditors' Rights, Estate Planning and Probate Law, Pension and Profit Sharing, Environmental Law, Labor and Employment, Commercial and Tax Litigation in all Courts.
Salem, Oregon Office: 250 Church Street, SE, P.O. Box 470, 97308. Telephone: 503-399-1070. Fax: 503-371-2927.
See Professional Biographies, BEND, OREGON

Sarancik, Karen L. '54 '85 C.763 B.S. L.1049 J.D.
(adm. in CA; not adm. in OR) 61470 Admiral Wy.‡
Sayeg, Thomas J., (AV) ....'56 '82 C.770 B.S.C. L.1065 J.D. [Karnopp P.]
Scheiderman, Patricia J. '47 '92 L.1370 J.D.
(adm. in CA; not adm. in OR) [P.J.Scheiderman]
Scheiderman, Patricia J., P.C. .... 2626 N.W. Pilot View Ct.
Schukart, Kelly L. .... '79 '05 C.629 B.A. L.150 J.D. [Ⓐ Bryant,L.&J.]

Schwabe, Williamson & Wyatt, P.C., (AV)
A Partnership including Professional Corporations
354 SW Upper Terrace Drive, Suite 101, 97702 ⊙
Telephone: 541-749-4044 Fax: 541-330-1153
Email: info@schwabe.com URL: http://www.schwabe.com
Shareholders: Donald Joe Willis; Kirk Johansen; Tia M. Lewis; Katherine C. Tank; Thomas M. Triplett; Myles A. Conway; Brian L. Gingerich. Associates: Bethany C. Graham; Isa A. Taylor. Retired Shareholder: Rockne Gill.
Admiralty and Maritime Law, Antitrust, Appellate, Bankruptcy and Creditor's Rights, Business Law, Condemnation, Commercial Litigation, Complex Litigation, Construction Law, Energy and Environmental Law, Financial Institutions, Forest Products, Health Care Industry, Intellectual Property, International Law, Labor Relations, Land Use, Malpractice and Insurance Defense, Product Liability, Real Estate, Securities, Taxation, Workers' Compensation.
Portland, Oregon Office: Suites 1600-1900 Pacwest Center, 1211 S.W. Fifth Avenue. Telephone: 503-222-9981.
Seattle, Washington Office: U.S. Bank Centre, Suite 3010, 1420 Fifth Avenue. Telephone: 206-622-1711. Fax: 206-292-0460.
Vancouver, Washington Office: Suite 410, Main Place Building, 1111 Main Street. Telephone: 360-694-7551; 696-0241.
See Professional Biographies, BEND, OREGON

Shamberg, Stephen C., (AVⓉ) .... '39 '64 C.861 B.A. L.309 J.D. [S.Shamberg]
Shamberg, Stephen, Law Office of, (AVⓉ) .... 16657 Wagon Trail
Sheasby, Robert H., P.C. ....'58 '93 C.228 B.S.E. L.629 J.D. [R.H.Sheasby]
Sheasby, Robert H., P.C. .... P.O. Box 1274
Sheehy, R. Michael .... '45 '92 C.1077 L.809 J.D. 1050 N.E. Butler Market Road
Slothower, Jim N., (BV) ....'45 '74 C.1056 B.A. L.1119 J.D. 205 North West Franklin
Smiley, David W. ....'62 '95 C.101 B.S. L.629 J.D. [Ⓐ Merrill O.]
Smith, Ralph H., Jr. ....'33 '58 C&L.502 A.B., LL.B. 44 N.W. Irving
Smith, Sharon R., (BV) ....'58 '86 C&L.629 B.S., J.D. [Bryant,L.&J.]
Sorlie, John D., (CV) ....'63 '93 C.118 B.A. L.596 J.D. [Bryant,L.&J.]

Speck, Paul J., (BV) '45 '72 C.112 B.A. L.629 J.D.
1123 N.W. Bond Street, 97701
Telephone: 541-388-1107 Fax: 541-388-7370
Email: pspeck@youroregonlawyer.com URL: http://www.lawyers.com/pauljspeck
General Practice. Criminal Law, Driving While Intoxicated, Drug Crimes, Juvenile, Parole and Probation, Traffic Violations. Employment Law, Sexual Harassment and Wrongful Termination. Family Law including Adoptions, Child Custody, Child Support, Divorce, Domestic Violence and Visitation Rights. Real Estate including Buying or Selling, Commercial Leasing, Construction, Eminent Domain, Environmental, Landlord and Tenant, Zoning and Land Use. Trusts and Estates, Estate Planning, Guardianship, Wills and Probate. Business Enterprises, Closely Held Businesses, Corporate, Franchises, Limited Liability Companies, Partnerships, Small Business, Buying or Selling a Business, General Business, Business Planning, Contracts, Lawsuits. Debt and Credit, Collections and Creditors Rights.
See Professional Biographies, BEND, OREGON

Stahancyk, Kent, Johnson & Hook P.C., (AV)
225 NW Franklin Avenue, Suite 3, 97701 ⊙
Telephone: 541-318-9115 Fax: 541-318-9116
Email: info@stahancyk.com URL: http://www.oregondivorce.com
Joel J. Kent (Resident); Ronald M. Johnson (Resident);—Gordon E. Phillips; Kristin M. Larson.
Adoptions, Child Custody, Child Support, Divorce, Domestic Violence, Visitation Rights, Wills and Probate, Trusts and Estates, Asset Protection, Guardianship, Family Law, Estate Planning.
Portland, Oregon Office: Athena Plaza, 808 S.W. 15th Avenue, 97205-1907. Telephone: 503-222-9115. Facsimile: 503-222-4037.
Astoria, Oregon Office: 552 Commercial Street, 97103. Telephone: 503-325-9117.
Prineville, Oregon Office: 105 SW Beaver Street, 97754. Telephone: 541-416-9312.
Vancouver, Washington Office: 411 West 11th Street, 98660. Telephone: 360-750-9115.
See Professional Biographies, BEND, OREGON

Stark, Thomas A. '33 '61 C.951 B.A. L.37 J.D.
(adm. in AZ; not adm. in OR) P.O. Box 8058‡

Starke, Cynthia J. ....'71 '01 C.446 B.A. L.309 J.D. [Ⓐ Karnopp P.]
Steele, Arnold O. '16 '41 C&L.174 B.S., J.D.
(adm. in CA; not adm. in OR) 19930 Juniper Ln.‡
Steelhammer, Daniel C. ....'56 '81 C&L.629 B.S., J.D. 61307 Mount Vista Dr.‡
Stinson, Jill Sensenbach '48 '01 C.628 B.A. L.629 J.D.
Pub. Def., Crabtree & Rahmsdorf Defense Servs., Inc.
Stout, Robert A., (AV) ....'46 '74 C.475 B.A. L.976 J.D. [Ⓐ Ball J.] (⊙Portland)
Straley, Deidre C. ....'56 '93 708 N.E. 11th St.
Strausbaugh, P. Daniel .... '76 '02 C&L.629 B.A., J.D. [Ⓐ B.J.Brothers&Assoc.]
Stuman, Gregory J. ....'67 '93 C.950 B.S. L.1049 J.D. [Ⓐ Francis,H.&M.]
Sullivan, Michael C. ....'48 '73 C.910 B.S. in B.A. L.629 J.D. Cir. J.
Tank, Katherine C., (BVⓉ) '62 '88 C&L.629 B.S., J.D.
[Schwabe,W.&W.] (⊙Portland)
Taylor, Isa A. .... '77 '04 C.629 B.A. L.174 J.D. [Ⓐ Schwabe,W.&W.]
Taylor, Paul J. ....'68 '98 C&L.629 B.A., J.D. [Ⓐ Bryant,L.&J.]
Thalhofer, Jos. J. ....'24 '52 C&L.309 A.B., LL.B. Ret. Dist. J.
Tiktin, Stephen N. ....'47 '73 C&L.629 B.S., J.D. Cir. J., Cir. Ct.
Townsend, Cara P. ....'73 '99 C.881 L.629 215 N.W. Greenwood
Triplett, Thomas M., (AV) '40 '65
C.976 A.B. L.813 LL.B. [Schwabe,W.&W.] (⊙Portland)
Udvari, Kristin L. ....'74 '99 C.976 B.A. L.596 J.D. [Ⓐ Ball J.] (⊙Portland)
Van Vactor, Dan, (CV) ....'46 '72 C.629 B.S. L.950 J.D. [VanVactor,D.]
Van Vactor, Dan, P.C., (CV) ....P.O. Box 1524
West, Warren John, (AV) ....'43 '68 C&L.339 A.B., J.D. [W.J.West]
West, Warren John, P.C., (AV) ....160 N.W. Irving
Whatley, Milly ....'53 '79 C.673 B.A. L.309 J.D. [M.Whatley]
Whatley, Milly, P.C. ....2445 N.E. Division St., Ste. 202
White, Bruce W., (BV) ....'56 '85 C.860 B.A. L.629 J.D. P.O. Box 1278
Widmer, Patrick J. ....'61 '93 C.629 B.S. L.1051 J.D. [Edwards W.]
Willis, Donald Joe, (AV) .... '40 '71 C&L.629 B.S., J.D. [Schwabe,W.&W.] (⊙Portland)
Williver, Sterling D. ....'38 '65 C.629 L.336 J.D. Dist. Atty. Off.
Wilson, John R. ....'52 '84 C.1060 B.A. L.1067 J.D. Dep. Dist. Atty.
Wilson, L. Todd ....'72 '97 C.770 B.A. L.950 J.D. [Ⓐ B.J.Brothers&Assoc.]
Winegar, Todd J. ....'68 '98 C.101 B.A. L.45 J.D. [Ⓐ Hurley,L.&R.]

BLACK BUTTE RANCH, 100, *Deschutes Co.*

Swaner, Jack D. '25 '62 C.112 B.S. L.767 J.D.
(adm. in CA; not adm. in OR) P.O. Box 8173‡

BROOKINGS, 5,447, *Curry Co.*

Babin, John C., (BV) ....'50 '75 C.893 B.A. L.950 J.D. 517 Chetco Ave
Beaman, Cynthia Lynnae ....'67 '98 C.502 B.S.B.A. L.464 J.D. [C.L.Beaman]
Beaman, Cynthia Lynnae, P.C. ....609 Chetco Ave Ste B
Foertmeyer, Ross L. '23 '58 C.976 B.A. L.477 J.D.
(adm. in PA; not adm. in OR; Pat.) P.O. Box 4118
Fortier, David R. ....'22 '49 C&L.494 B.S.L., LL.B. P.O. Box 1043‡
Georgeff, Gary M., (AV) ....'54 '80 C.161 B.A. L.596 J.D. P.O. Box 847
Keusink, Christopher ....'51 '84 C.813 B.S. L.950 J.D. 517 Chetco Ave
Margolis, Jesse C. ....'66 '92 C.1060 B.A. L.1051 J.D. [Olin&M.]
Maxwell, W. Stirling '22 '49 C&L.477 A.B., J.D.
(adm. in IL; not adm. in OR) 1241 Collis Lane‡
Nishioka, Bruce Matsuo ....'60 '91 C.629 B.S. L.1049 J.D. P.O. Box 1450
Nokes, William G. ....'40 '66 C.628 L.1051 LL.B. P.O. Box 6998
Olin, Kim R. ....'— '90 C.628 B.S. L.950 J.D. [Olin&M.]
Olin & Margolis, PC ....586 5th Street, Suite 200
Pierson, Paul L. ....'50 '88 C&L.629 B.A., J.D. [P.Pierson]
Pierson, Paul, Attorney at Law ....16210 E. Hoffeldt Ln., Ste. 6
Smith, Dudley B. ....'22 '50 C.111 B.S. L.273 LL.B. 17328 La Bonte Lane‡
Spratt, Peter C., Attorney at Law ....'55 '80 C.629 B.S. L.678 J.D. P.O. Box 1344

BROWNSVILLE, 1,449, *Linn Co.*

Lemhouse, Jad B., (CV) ....'43 '89 C.628 B.S. L.629 J.D. 714 Loucks Way
Tressler, Jonathan H. ....'47 '76 C&L.629 B.A., J.D. 258 N. Main St.

BURNS, * 3,064, *Harney Co.*

Colahan, Timothy J., (BV) ....'58 '85 C.1181 B.S. L.629 J.D. Dist. Atty.
Cramer, W. D., Jr. ....'54 '81 C.309 A.B. L.629 J.D. Cir. J.
Finlayson, Stephen D., (BV) .... '44 '74 C.593 B.S. L.986 J.D. 709 Ponderosa Vil.
Lamborn, John B., (CV) ....'60 '90 C.629 B.S. L.464 J.D. [Mallon&L.]
Mallon, Gordon, (BV) ....'57 '84 C&L.629 B.S., J.D. [Mallon&L.]
Mallon & Lamborn, (BV) ....90 West Washington Street
Raschio, Robert S. ....'73 '01 C.1056 B.S. L.629 J.D. [Ⓐ Mallon&L.]
Saad, Summer ....'76 '00 C&L.629 B.A., J.D. Dist. Atty. Off.

CANBY, 12,790, *Clackamas Co.*

Bell, Aaron J. ....'62 '87 C.1056 B.S. L.950 J.D. 273 N. Grant St.
Bettis, Wade P., (AV) ....'22 '53 C.950 L.596 J.D. 160 N.W. 3rd Ave.
Clancy, Michael J. ....'46 '76 C.1051 B.S.Ec. L.596 J.D. [Clancy&S.]
Clancy & Slininger, (BV) ....181 N. Grant St.
Cross, Amy J. '74 '00 C.670 B.A. L.629 J.D.
(adm. in NY; not adm. in OR) 1246 S.E. 17th Ave.‡

Hutchison & Walsh, A Professional Corporation
(See West Linn)

Kauffman, Andrew ....'61 '99 C.1056 B.S. L.1051 J.D. 675 N.W. 2nd
Kelley, John H., (BV) ....'47 '77 C.629 B.A. L.596 J.D. City Atty.
La Follett, Thomas L., (BV) ....'45 '87 C.950 B.A. L.1051 J.D. 181 N. Grant St.
Magee, Robert M. ....'33 '69 C.684 B.A. L.426 J.D. 12241 S. Adkins Cir.
McNichols, Michael D. ....'53 '92 C.861 B.S. L.950 J.D. 181 N. Grant St., Ste. 206A
Reif, R. Roger, (BV) ....'48 '75 C&L.950 B.A., J.D. 273 N. Grant St.
Reif, Raymond R., (BV) ....'24 '64 C.628 B.S. L.596 J.D. 273 N. Grant St.
Slininger, Arthur P., (BV) ....'51 '79 C.678 B.A. L.1051 J.D. [Clancy&S.]
Thalhofer, Paul T. ....'54 '86 C.174 B.A. L.629 J.D. 273 N. Grant St.

CANNON BEACH, 1,588, *Clatsop Co.*

Bennett, J. William, (BV) ....'35 '72 C.629 B.S. L.596 J.D. [J.W.Bennett]
Bennett, J. William, P.C., (BV) ....363 Elk Creek Rd., Unit Q
Comisky, Clifford C. ....'16 '40 C&L.596 LL.B. Mun. J.
Corwin, Brent E., (AVⓉ) ....'51 '76 C&L.36 B.S., J.D. [B.E.Corwin] ⊙
Corwin, Brent E., P.C., (AVⓉ) ........................P.O. Box 1336 (⊙Scottsdale, AZ)
Hillestad, Charles, Law Offices of, (AVⓉ) '45 '72
C.629 B.S. L.477 J.D. 1347 South Hemlock
McIntosh, Dawn M. ....'66 '92 C.950 B.S. L.596 J.D. 271 North Hemlock, Suite 208
Schwab, Herbert M. ....'15 '40 L.596 LL.B. P.O. Box 216‡

CANYON CITY, * 648, *Grant Co.*

Sario, Markku A., Law Office of, (BV) '44 '82 C.628 B.S. L.678 J.D.
206 S. Humbolt St.
Williams, Grace K., (CV) .... '17 '42 C.629 B.S. L.596 LL.B. 146 Izee St.

CARLTON, 1,514, *Yamhill Co.*

Polite, David C ....'55 '84 C.685 B.A. L.1051 J.D. 11511 NW Cummins Rd
Wood, Rollin B. ....'24 '47 C&L.629 B.S., LL.B. 10400 Riverwood Ln.‡

CAVE JUNCTION, 1,363, *Josephine Co.*

Cleary, Mansfield R., (CV) .... '52 '80 C.330 B.S. L.950 J.D. P.O. Box 234
Savord, George Hugh, (A Professional Law Corporation) '29 '72 C&L.1137 B.S., J.D.
(adm. in CA; not adm. in OR) 164 Simmons Cut Dr.‡
Versteeg, Ronald B., (BV) ....'55 '86 C.950 B.S. L.629 J.D. 435 Junction Avenue

CENTRAL POINT, 12,493, *Jackson Co.*

Deems, Mark F. '61 '93 C.338 B.S. L.767 J.D.
Gen. Coun. & Corp. Secy., Erickson Air-Crane, Inc.
Francis, Richard L., (BVⓉ) '48 '76 C.112 B.A. L.1065 J.D.
(adm. in CA; not adm. in OR) [Francis&I.] ⊙
Francis & Idiart, Law Offices of, (BVⓉ) ....55 South Fifth Street (⊙Oxnard, CA)
Hall, Risa L., (BV) ....'59 '87 C.1071 B.S. L.950 J.D. 55 N. 3rd St.
Heisel, Manville M., (AV) ....'20 '49 C.628 L.629 J.D. P.O. Box 3546
Idiart, Damian M. ....'74 '01 C.101 B.A. L.770 J.D. [Francis&I.] ⊙

CHILOQUIN, 673, *Klamath Co.*

Ullman, Carl V. ....'48 '76 C.388 B.A. L.911 J.D. 116 Chocktoot St

CLACKAMAS, 5,177, *Clackamas Co.*

Culver, Virgilia S. ....'49 '79 C.972 B.A. L.629 J.D. 8800 S. E. Sunnyside Road
Dolton, Robert G., (CV) ....'56 '81 C.1169 B.A. L.950 J.D. 13100 S.E. Sunnyside Rd.
Erdmann, Stephen S. ....'50 '75 C&L.878 B.S., J.D. Safeway Inc.
Falk, Theodore C., (AV) '46 '82 C.685 B.A. L.976 J.D.
Vice President, Legal & Secretary, QualMed Oregon Health Plan, Inc.
Findlay, Suzanne M. '— '95 C&L.112 J.D.
(adm. in CA; not adm. in OR) 13701 S.E. 127th Ave.
Fitzwater, Wesley D. ....'55 '81 C.950 B.S. L.1358 J.D. [Fitzwater&M.]

Fitzwater & Meyer, LLP
Three Town Center, 10121 S.E. Sunnyside Road, Suite 140, 97015
Telephone: 503-786-8191 Fax: 503-786-3785
Email: wfitzwater@fitzwatermeyer.com URL: http://www.fitzwatermeyer.com
Members of Firm: Wesley D. Fitzwater; Donna R. Meyer.
Estate Planning, Trusts and Estate, Estate and Gift Taxation, Wills and Probate, Elder Law, Medicaid.
See Professional Biographies, CLACKAMAS, OREGON

Gibson, K. William, (BV) '49 '79
C.629 B.A. L.1051 J.D. 10121 SE Sunnyside Road, Suite 325
Hildum, Robert M. ....'59 '87 C.373 B.A. L.596 J.D. 10121 S.E. Sunnyside Rd.

James Law Group LLC, The
(See Portland)

Kaspari, John T. ....'23 '55 C.629 B.S. L.596 LL.B. P.O. Box 495
Kobelin, Jerry F., (BV) ....'34 '68 C.911 B.A. L.596 J.D. 20340 S.E. Hwy. 212
Laughlin, Ronald L., Jr. ....'60 '88 C.101 B.S. L.950 J.D. P.O. Box 1930
Matesi, Michele M. '60 '98 C.35 B.S. L.285 J.D.
(adm. in WA; not adm. in OR) Emmert Develop. Co.
Meyer, Donna R. ....'51 '76 C.670 B.S. L.629 J.D. [Fitzwater&M.]
O'Brien, Michael D., Jr. '68 '95 C.629 B.S. L.966 J.D.
9200 Se Sunnybrook Blvd, Ste 150
Schnidrig, Veronica M. '55 '85
C.1056 B.S. L.1051 J.D. 10121 S.E. Sunnyside Rd., Ste. 325
Sunderland, Brian J. ....'60 '92 C.1051 B.A. L.1209 J.D. [Sunderland&Assoc.]
Sunderland & Associates ....10121 S.E. Sunnyside Rd., Ste. 300
Thorpe, Thomas K., (AV) .... '30 '58 C.629 B.S. L.596 J.D. 13276 S.E. 122nd. Ave.‡
Tourville, Heather R. ....'73 '01 C.897 B.A. L.950 J.D. [H.Tourville]
Tourville, Heather, LLC ....15431 S.E. 82nd Drive, Suite J
Urness, Craig '65 '94 C.629 B.S. L.950 J.D.
Legal Counsel & Resource Manager, Dulcich Inc.
Zimmerman, Timothy J. ....'56 '87 C.1056 B.S. L.596 J.D. P.O. Box 2108

CLATSKANIE, 1,528, *Columbia Co.*

Grove, Ted E., (BV) ....'53 '80 C.350 B.S. L.1051 J.D. P.O. Box 443
Olsen, Heidi L., (CV) ....'66 '92 C.221 B.A. L.596 J.D. [Salisbury&O.]
Salisbury, John P., (BV) ....'56 '82 C.309 A.B. L.800 J.D. [Salisbury&O.]
Salisbury & Olsen, (BV) ....P.O. Box 288

CONDON, * 759, *Gilliam Co.*

Weatherford, Marion T. .... '60 '96 C.628 B.S. L.1051 J.D. P.O. Box 727

COOS BAY, 15,374, *Coos Co.*

Bodkin, Michael N., (BV) ....'54 '79 C.208 B.S.B.A. L.629 J.D. [Foss,W.L.M.&B.]
Corrigall, Malcolm J., (BV) .... '48 '73 C&L.629 B.S., J.D. [Corrigall&M.]
Corrigall & McClintock, LLP, (AV) ....P.O. Box 1178
De Plois, Jacques P., (BV) ....'59 '92 C&L.950 B.S., J.D. P.O. Box 3159
Dials, William D. ....'51 '78 C.1056 B.S. L.629 J.D. [W.D.Dials]
Dials, William D., Attorney at Law, P.C. ....63357 Boat Basin Drive
Dorsey, David A., (AV) ....'54 '79 C.112 B.S. L.950 J.D. [D.A.Dorsey]
Dorsey, David A., P.C., (AV) ....243 W. Commercial
Eaton, John M. .... '16 '50 C&L.174 B.S., J.D. 3340 Sandpiper Dr.‡
Finneran, Lawrence F., (BV) ....'53 '78 C.285 B.A. L.629 J.D. [Lesan&F.]
Foss, John T., (AV) ....'29 '56 C.56 B.A. L.352 J.D. [Foss,W.L.M.&B.]

Foss, Whitty, Littlefield, McDaniel & Bodkin, LLP, (AV)
444 North Fourth Street, P.O. Box 1120, 97420-2222
Telephone: 541-267-2156 Fax: 541-269-0839
Email: info@coosbaylaw.com URL: http://www.coosbaylaw.com
Members of Firm: John T. Foss; John W. Whitty; Jon R. Littlefield; William A. McDaniel; Michael N. Bodkin.
General Civil and Trial Practice in all State and Federal Courts. Business, Corporation and Commercial Law, Estate Planning, Probate and Taxation Law, Real Property, Timber, Creditor's Rights, Personal Injury Law.
Representative Clients: Al Peirce Co.; Tower Motor Co.; North Bend Medical Center, Inc.; Stamper's J & J Tire Co.; Coos Bay Towboat Co.; Oregon State Bar Professional Liability Fund; Tico Title Insurance Co.; International Contractors, Inc.
See Professional Biographies, COOS BAY, OREGON

Gould, Adam Q. ....'76 '02 C.906 B.S. L.629 J.D. [Ⓐ R.W.Gould]
Gould, Roger W., (BV) ....'47 '72 C&L.629 B.S., J.D. [R.W.Gould]

Gould, Roger W., P.C., (BV)
243 W. Commercial Street, P.O. Box 29, 97420
Telephone: 541-269-5566 Fax: 541-269-0670
Email: rwgould@gte.net
Roger W. Gould;—Adam Q. Gould.
Personal Injury, Automobile Accidents, Probate, Estate Planning, Wills and Trusts, Conservatorship, General Trials, Business Law.

Hinrichs, Daniel M. .... '65 '92 C.769 B.A. L.1051 J.D. [D.M. .P.Hinrichs]
Hinrichs, Daniel M., PC .... 590 Commercial

Hutchinson, Cox, Coons, DuPriest, Orr & Sherlock, P.C.
(See Eugene)

Jaqua & Wheatley, LLC
(See Eugene)

Joelson, Gordon A., (BV) .... '43 '70 C.629 B.B.A. L.596 J.D. [G.A.Joelson]
Joelson, Gordon A., P.C., (BV) .... 243 W. Commercial
Laird, Robert D. .... '43 '75 C.1056 B.S. L.596 J.D. 650 Newmark Avenue‡
Landes, Donald H., (BV) .... '45 '74 C.629 B.S. L.597 J.D. 200 S. 4th St.
Lehman, Michael R., (BV) .... '53 '78 C.413 B.A. L.950 J.D. Coun., Cardinal Servs., Inc.
Lesan, Jerry O., (AV) .... '42 '67 C&L.629 B.S., J.D. [Lesan&F.]
Lesan & Finneran, (AV) .... 405 N. 5th
Littlefield, Jon R., (AV) .... '44 '74 C.813 A.B. L.950 J.D. [Foss,W.L.M.&B.]

Lowry, Robert D., Law Offices of
(See Eugene)

McClintock, Nathan B., (BV) .... '56 '82 C.112 B.A. L.767 J.D. [Corrigall&M.]
McDaniel, William A., (BV) .... '50 '76 C.112 A.B. L.629 J.D. [Foss,W.L.M.&B.]
McNutt, Lynne W. .... '23 '52 C.378 B.A. 345 N. 5th
McNutt, Scott M., (BV) .... '50 '77 C.1071 B.S. L.596 LL.B. 345 N. 5th St.
Melvin-Davidson, Margaret K., (CV) .... '— '89 C.628 B.S. L.629 895 Commercial

Muhlheim Boyd
(See Eugene)

Nelson, Kristi A., (BVⓉ) ...... '56 '83 C.1060 B.A. L.1067 J.D. 89954 Cape Arago Hwy.
Newhouse, Andrew J., (AV) .... '14 '38 C&L.629 B.S., LL.B. 444 N. 4th St.‡
Ormsbee, Orrin R., (AV) .... '39 '63 C&L.950 A.B., J.D. P.O. Box 1178
Pennington, Richard D., (BVⓉ) '40 '74 C.999 B.A. L.596 J.D.
89954 Cape Arago Hwy.
Plinski, Steven W., (BV) .... '50 '77 C&L.285 B.A., J.D. P.O. Box 1347
Scannell, Jeremiah J. .... '53 '89 C.950 B.S. L.596 J.D. 334 N. Front St.
Thom, Cameron C. .... '28 '56 C&L.629 B.S., LL.B. 590 Commercial St.‡
Tilton, David S., (BV) .... '50 '84 C.33 B.A. L.1051 J.D. 590 Commercial
Whitty, John W., (AV) .... '33 '56 C&L.629 B.S., LL.B. [Foss,W.L.M.&B.]
Wilgers, Steven L., (AV) .... '44 '74 C&L.629 B.S., J.D. [S.Wilgers]
Wilgers, Steven, P.C., (AV) .... 243 W. Commercial

COQUILLE, * 4,121, *Coos Co.*

Barron, Rick .... '45 '70 C.1056 B.A. L.950 J.D. Cir. J.
Burch, Robert J., (CV) .... '42 '75 C&L.339 A.B., J.D. 56965 Gladewood Rd.
Burgett, Paul R., (BV) .... '48 '75 C.763 B.A. L.629 J.D. Dist. Atty.
Cyphers, Carol Poli, (CV) .... '43 '91 C.330 B.A. L.629 J.D. 222 E. 2nd St.
Gillespie, Michael J. .... '53 '78 C.629 B.S. L.336 J.D. Cir. J.
Herzog, Karen Rose .... '70 '95 C.1058 B.A. L.950 J.D. Asst. Dist. Atty.
Irwin, Beth M., (BV) .... '73 '97 C.112 B.A. L.494 J.D. Dist. Atty. Off.
Keutzer, Stephen H., (BV) .... '38 '63 C.336 B.A. L.629 LL.B. Chf. Dep. Dist. Atty.
Meynink, John P., Jr., (BV) .... '45 '79 C.1056 B.A. L.1051 J.D. Asst. Pub. Def.
Norman, James A. .... '14 '38 C&L.352 B.A., J.D. Ret. Cir. J.
Reeves, Charles H. .... '29 '53 C.629 B.S.L. L.950 LL.B. Ret. Dist. J.
Ris, David R., (BV) .... '58 '83 C.1071 B.A. L.629 J.D. Co. Coun.
Slack, Harry A., Jr. .... '29 '55 C.629 B.S. L.950 LL.B. 222 East 2nd Street‡
Stone, Martin E., (BV) .... '52 '77 C.950 B.A. L.629 J.D. 222 East 2nd Street
Walberg, Robert F. .... '34 '62 C.629 B.S. L.950 J.D. Cir. J.
Walsh, Alfred C., Jr., (BV) .... '32 '59 C.770 B.S. L.629 LL.B. 280 N. Collier St.‡

CORNELIUS, 9,652, *Washington Co.*

Wolf, Elizabeth J. .... '72 '01 C.1056 B.S. L.596 J.D. 1180 S. 12th Ave., Suite C

CORVALLIS, * 49,322, *Benton Co.*

Adkins, Steven L., (BV) .... '54 '80 C.628 B.S. L.629 J.D. [Adkins&Assoc.]
Adkins & Associates, P.C., (BV) .... 200 S.W. 4th Street, Suite 201
Armstrong, Dan C. .... '60 '88 C.1193 B.A. L.950 J.D. [▣ Cable H.B.H.&L.]
Audrain, Linda A. .... '47 '82 C.1181 B.S. L.629 J.D. Dist. Atty. Off.
Barker, Michael D., (BV) .... '34 '72 C.575 A.B. L.629 J.D. [Petersen,B.&D.]
Barlow, John L., (AV) .... '55 '81 C.596 B.A. L.813 J.D. [Barnhisel,W.B.&S.]
Barnhisel, Peter L., (AV) .... '39 '66 C.813 B.S. L.629 J.D. [Barnhisel,W.B.&S.]

Barnhisel, Willis, Barlow & Stephens, P.C., (AV)
123 N.W. Seventh Street, P.O. Box 396, 97339
Telephone: 541-757-0575 Fax: 541-757-2031
Email: barnhisel@bwbslaw.com URL: http://www.bwbslaw.com
Peter L. Barnhisel; R. Tim Willis; John L. Barlow; Cary B. Stephens;—Mark R. May.
General Civil and Trial Practice in State and Federal Courts and Administrative Agencies. Appeals, Arbitration and Dispute Resolution. Banking, Business and Corporate, Charitable Trusts and Foundations, Communications, Construction, Estate Planning and Administration, Living Trusts, Family, Labor and Employment Relations and Real Estate Law.
Representative Clients: CH2M/Hill, Inc. (Consulting Engineers); Truax Corp.; Town and Country Realtors; Oregon State University Foundation; Hewlett-Packard, Inc.; Wood Castle, Ltd.; Videx, Inc.; TRC Communications, Inc.; Evanite Fiber Corp.
See Professional Biographies, CORVALLIS, OREGON

Black, Steven W. .... '47 '78 C&L.629 B.S., J.D. 226 S.W. 8th St.

Brittle, Tim, Attorney at Law, (BV) '49 '77 C.878 B.S. L.770 J.D.
343 N.W. 7th Street, 97330
Telephone: 541-738-8303 Fax: 541-753-2009 URL: http://www.brittle-law.com
Email: tim@brittle-law.com URL: http://www.lawyers.com/brittlelaw
Elder Law, Trusts and Estates, Estate Planning, Estate Litigation, Wills, Probate, Insurance, Nursing Home Abuse, Guardianship and Conservatorship, Asset Protection, Business Law, Corporate Law, Closely Held Business, Limited Liability Company Law, Partnership Law, Small Business Law, Buying or Selling a Business, Contracts, Business Start-Ups, Business Planning, Real Estate, Buying or Selling a Home, Residential Real Estate, Landlord and Tenant, Commercial Leasing.
See Professional Biographies, CORVALLIS, OREGON

Brookes, Thomas B. .... '62 '89 C.629 B.A. L.911 J.D. Timberhill Corp.

Cable Huston Benedict Haagensen & Lloyd LLP, (AV)
582 N.W. Van Buren, 97339 ☉
Telephone: 541-754-7477 Facsimile: 541-754-0051
URL: http://www.cablehuston.com
Of Counsel: George B. Heilig (Resident); Dan C. Armstrong.
Administrative, Agricultural, Banking, Bankruptcy, Commercial, Corporate, Complex Litigation, Creditors' Rights, Legislative, Employment, Energy, Environmental, Estate Planning, General Business, Land Use, Mining, Municipal, Natural Resource, Probate, Real Property, Taxation, Telecommunications, Trust Administration, Utility and Water Law.

(This Listing Continued)

Cable Huston Benedict Haagensen & Lloyd LLP (Continued)

Portland, Oregon Office: Suite 2000, 1001 S.W. Fifth Avenue, 97204. Telephone: 503-224-3092. Facsimile: 503-224-3176.
See Professional Biographies, CORVALLIS, OREGON

Callahan, CeeAnn ...... '58 '85 C.942 B.B.A. L.378 J.D. Sr. Coun., Hewlett-Packard Co.
Christensen, Gregory J., (BV) .... '49 '77 C.589 B.A. L.629 J.D. 730 S.W. 4th St.
Cihak, Raymond M., (BV) .... '68 '93 C.602 B.A. L.1067 J.D. [Evashevski,E.C.&H.]

Clark, Lindauer, Fetherston, Edmonds, Lippold & Collier, LLP
(See Salem)

Cohnstaedt, William, (CV) .... '45 '76 C.966 B.S. L.284 J.D. 561 N.W. Jackson Ave.
Connell, David B., (BV) .... '48 '74 C.906 B.A. L.950 J.D. 343 N.W. 7th St.
Conroy, J. Britton .... '52 '77 C.628 B.S. L.629 J.D. 7750 N.W. Oxbow Dr.‡
Corl, Robert D., Jr., (CV) .... '51 '76 C.628 B.S. L.950 J.D. 455 S.W. Madison Ave.
Coulombe, David E. .... '58 '02 C.635 B.A. L.950 J.D. 456 S.W. Monroe Ave.
Croney, Vance M., (BV) .... '60 '92 C.846 B.J. L.950 J.D. Benton Co.
Demarest, Joan Elaine .... '70 '98 C.788 B.A. L.629 J.D. Dep. Dist. Atty.
Dickerson, Henry R., Jr. .... '42 '70 C&L.950 B.A., J.D. Dist. J.
Dickman, Don B. .... '55 '95 C.1111 B.S. L.972 J.D. [D.B.Dickman]
Dickman, Don B., PC .... 525 S.W. 4th St.
Donahue, Mark D., (BV) .... '48 '75 C.878 B.A. L.629 J.D. 344 N.W. 6th St.
Dunfield, Chris W., (BV) .... '50 '76 C.378 B.A. L.477 J.D. [Petersen,B.&D.]
Edinger, Pamela K. '58 '84 C.112 B.A. L.1067 J.D.
(adm. in WA; not adm. in OR) 4025 SW West Hills Rd.
Elliott, Thomas E., (BV) .... '53 '78 C.1181 B.S. L.629 J.D. [Evashevski,E.C.&H.]
Ensor, Stephen R., (BV) .... '55 '81 C.347 B.A. L.629 J.D. [Ringo,S.E.&H.]
Evashevski, Forest, Jr., (BV) .... '42 '68 C.477 B.A. L.352 J.D. [Evashevski,E.C.&H.]
Evashevski, Jean Fee .... '44 '68 C&L.352 B.A., J.D. 2505 S.W. Whiteside
Evashevski, Elliott, Cihak & Hediger, P.C., (BV) .... 745 N.W. Van Buren St.
Eves, S. David, (AV) .... '43 '67 C.628 B.Sc. L.629 J.D. [S.D.Eves]
Eves, S. David, P.C., (AV) .... 305 S.W. C St.
Feeney, Daniel J. .... '68 '96 C.436 B.S.C.E. L.950 J.D. Hemlett-Packard Co.
Fewel, Scott A., (AV) .... '46 '72 C&L.629 B.S., J.D. 456 S.W. Monroe Ave.
Frohnmayer, John E., (AV) .... '42 '72 C.813 B.A. L.629 J.D. 1356 S.W. Timian St.
Gallagher, Thomas L., Jr., (BV) .... '43 '68 C.628 B.S. L.309 J.D. 527 N.W. 3rd St.
Gardner, Robert S. .... '42 '67 C.372 B.A. L.659 J.D. Sr. J.
Gomez, Angelo, (BV) .... '50 '78 L.629 J.D. 2941 NW Hayes Avenue
Hadlock, Patrick L., (BV) .... '56 '83 C.685 B.A. L.629 J.D. [Ringo,S.E.&H.]
Haines, Candace A. .... '53 '85 C.628 B.A. L.770 J.D. Co. Coun.
Hansen, George A. '14 '41 L.365 LL.B.
(adm. in IL; not adm. in OR) 7795 N.W. Oxbow Dr.‡
Hart, Debra K. .... '56 '95 C.1056 B.S. L.950 J.D. Comm. Serv.'s Consortium
Hediger, Pamela S., (BV) .... '63 '91 C.1201 B.S. L.285 J.D. [Evashevski,E.C.&H.]
Heilig, George B., (BV) .... '44 '73 C.1056 B.S. L.950 J.D. [▣ Cable H.B.H.&L.]
Heinrich, Steven A., (CV) .... '62 '94 C.037 B.A. L.911 J.D. 527 N.W. Third St.
Heiser, Scott A., (BV) .... '60 '87 C.628 B.S. L.596 J.D. Dep. Dist. Atty.
Holcomb, Janet Schoenhard .... '52 '86 C.628 B.S. L.629 J.D. Cir. J.
Jenski, Raymond A. '45 '89
C.339 B.S.E.E. L.146 J.D. Sr. Coun., Hewlett-Packard Co. (Pat.)
Johnson, LaVerne M., (AV) ...... '27 '52 C&L.629 B.S., LL.B. 3993 S.W. Fairhaven Ct.‡
Johnson, Roderick L., (BV) .... '52 '76 C.628 L.950 J.D. 5800 NW Highland Pl.
Joiner, J. Alfred .... '15 '41 C.999 L.421 J.D. 3345 SW Cascade Avenue‡
Jolly, Thomas A. '62 '97 C.1356 B.S.E.E. L.208 J.D.
Coun., Hewlett-Packard Co. (Pat.)
Kerl, Caroline A. .... '49 '74 C.1375 A.B. L.1065 J.D. Gen. Coun.
Kimball, Katharine W. .... '55 '85 C.494 B.A. L.1119 J.D. 26658 Sulphur Springs Rd.
Knight, Frank D. .... '35 '62 C&L.950 B.S., LL.B. Cir. J.
Krag, Donald R. '27 '52 C.112 L.809 J.D.
(adm. in CA; not adm. in OR) 2715 N.W. Glenwood Pl.‡
Lacy, Patricia A. .... '52 '00 C.438 B.A. L.629 J.D. Of Coun.
Lanker, Alan S. .... '64 '95 C.1060 B.S. L.950 J.D. [▣ R.L.Marek]

Lowry, Robert D., Law Offices of
(See Eugene)

Marek, Ronald L., Law Office of, (BV) '44 '69
C.350 B.S. L.494 J.D. 810 Southwest Madison Avenue
May, Mark R. .... '71 '05 C.950 B.A. L.1051 J.D. [▣ Barnhisel,W.B.&S.]
Mengler, Richd. .... '11 '52 C&L.629 M.A., LL.B. 3557 N.W. Van Buren Ave.‡
Morgan, Ann Louise .... '53 '85 C.628 B.S. L.629 J.D. Town & Country Realty
Morris, Gretchen R. .... '38 '73 C.813 B.A. L.629 J.D. 6315 N.W. Ponderosa Avenue‡
Morrow, Alice M. .... '40 '74 C.454 B.S. L.421 J.D. Oregon State Univ.
Mukatis, W. Alfred .... '37 '76 C.597 B.S. L.339 J.D. Assoc. Prof., Ore. State Univ.
Myers, Noeline J. .... '40 '79 C.1264 B.S. L.208 J.D. 3205 N.W. Deer Run‡
O'Brien, Joseph E., Jr. '33 '64 C&L.276 B.S., J.D.
(adm. in MD; not adm. in OR) 3931 N.W. Clarence Circle‡
Ortiz, Nicolas .... '72 '98 C.1060 B.A. L.596 J.D. 312 SW Jefferson Ave.
Petersen, Gerald K., (BV) .... '23 '51 C&L.508 J.D. [Petersen,B.&D.]
Petersen, Barker & Dunfield, (BV) .... 213 N.W. 5th

Peterson Law Offices, PC
(See Portland)

Reeves, Meg, (BV) '52 '82 C.1044 B.A. L.629 J.D.
Dir., Policy & Legal Serv., Oregon State University
Rich, John C. .... '68 '96 C.628 B.S. L.629 J.D. [J.Rich]
Rich, John .... 455 S.W. Madison Ave.
Ringo, Robert G., (AV) .... '24 '51 C.629 B.S. L.596 LL.B. [Ringo,S.E.&H.]

Ringo, Stuber, Ensor & Hadlock, P.C., (AV) ▣
605 S.W. Jefferson Avenue, P.O. Box 1108, 97339
Telephone: 541-757-1414 FAX: 541-753-0884
Email: ringoseh@peak.org URL: http://www.ringostuber.com
Robert G. Ringo; Larry W. Stuber; Stephen R. Ensor; Patrick L. Hadlock.
General Civil and Trial Practice. Plaintiff's Personal Injury, Family, Malpractice, Products Liability, Negligence, Criminal.
References: Citizens Bank of Corvallis; Wells Fargo Bank.
See Professional Biographies, CORVALLIS, OREGON

Rodeman, Richard D. .... '53 '78 C.330 B.A. L.950 J.D. 1100 Nw Vanburen Ave
Rose, Curtis G. '59 '88 C.679 B.S.E.E. L.273 J.D.
Mng. Corp. Coun., Hewlett-Packard Co. (Pat.)
Sandrock, Peter F., Jr., (BV) .... '46 '74 C.178 B.A. L.629 J.D. Dist. Atty.
Saunders, V. Denise .... '63 '90 C.882 B.A. L.596 J.D. P.O. Box 1416
Schaeffer, Virginia K. .... '59 '89 C.477 B.B.A. L.174 J.D. 7540 NW Valley View Dr.
Snyder, Thompson, (BV) .... '32 '58 C&L.546 B.S., J.D. 3175 N.W. Greenwood Ave.
Stephens, Cary B., (BV) .... '69 '95 C&L.629 B.S., J.D. [Barnhisel,W.B.&S.]

Street, Robert D., (BV) .... '54 '83 C.628 B.S. L.629 J.D. P.O. Box 1869
Stuber, Larry W., (BV) .... '52 '78 C.911 B.A. L.629 J.D. [Ringo,S.E.&H.]
Sullivan, Terry Anne .... '56 '83 C&L.623 B.A., J.D. 1658 N.W. Polk‡
Swanson, David L. .... '42 '70 C.813 B.A. L.596 J.D. Pioneer Natl. Title Ins. Co.

Weatherford, Thompson, Cowgill, Black & Schultz, P.C.
(See Albany)

Wehmeyer, Richard L., (BV) .... '45 '73 C.763 B.A. L.1049 J.D. 344 N.W. 6th St.
Willes, Clark Smith .... '58 '86 C.1071 B.A. L.950 J.D. 312 S.W. Jefferso Ave.
Willis, R. Tim, (AV) .... '48 '76 C.187 B.A. L.950 J.D. [Barnhisel,W.B.&S.]
Wood, Kathryn Ann .... '41 '77 C.628 B.S. L.1051 J.D. 344 N.W. 6th St.
Wright, Mark Alan .... '52 '99 C&L.546 B.A., J.D. Oregon State Univ Foundation
Zorn, Karen Johnson, (BV) .... '42 '85 C.289 B.A. L.629 J.D. Dep. Dist. Atty.

COTTAGE GROVE, 8,445, *Lane Co.*

Ackley, Gary R., (BV) .... '40 '66 C&L.629 B.S., J.D. 30 N 5th St
Genna, Michael Ray .... '44 '72 C.950 B.A. L.629 J.D. 11 S. 6th St.
Gifford, Milton Earl, (CV) .... '48 '86 C.36 B.S. L.629 J.D. [M.E.Gifford]
Gifford, Milton E., P.C., (CV) .... P.O. Box 247
Irvine, Ronald A., (BV) .... '48 '79 C&L.629 B.S., J.D. [R.A.Irvine]
Irvine, Ronald A., P.C., (BV) .... 210 S. 5th St.
Kelly, Sean David .... '69 '97 C&L.629 B.A., J.D. 30 N. 5th Street
Melendy, Patrick S., (BV) .... '71 '97 C.1181 B.S. L.629 J.D. 30 N 5th St
Trunnell, Tracy, (BV) .... '72 '99 C&L.629 B.S., J.D. [Trunnell&Assoc.]
Trunnell & Associates, P.C., (BV) .... P.O. Box 627

CRESWELL, 3,579, *Lane Co.*

Cohen, Jeri-Anne .... '49 '75 C&L.629 B.S., J.D. 595 Pine Ct.‡
Fadeley, Edward N. .... '29 '57 C.502 A.B. L.629 J.D. Assoc. Jus., Supm. Ct.‡

DALLAS, * 12,459, *Polk Co.*

Berg, Doug, (BV) .... '47 '84 C.628 B.S. L.950 J.D. 236 Sw Mill

Clark, Lindauer, Fetherston, Edmonds, Lippold & Collier, LLP
(See Salem)

Doyle, David, (BV) .... '61 '86 C.426 B.A. L.464 J.D. [Doyle]
Doyle Law Firm PC, (BV) .... 140 SE Mill St.
Fisher, John W., (BV) .... '50 '78 C&L.378 B.G.S., J.D. Dist. Atty. Off.
Hayter, Philip, (AV) .... '13 '39 C.629 B.S. L.950 LL.B. 840 S.E. Fir Villa Rd.‡
Heslinga, Mark A., (CV) .... '58 '85 C&L.352 B.A., J.D. Dep. Dist. Atty.
Hooste, David A. .... '70 '00 C.877 B.S. L.950 J.D. 189 Sw Academy St
Horner, William M. .... '43 '69 C.112 A.B. L.950 J.D. Cir. J.
Irick, Mark K., (BV) .... '52 '79 C.63 B.S. L.950 J.D. [Irick,S.&O.]
Irick, Shetterly & Ozias, (BV) .... 189 S.W. Academy
Johnson, Robert B. .... '35 '97 L.950 J.D. Dir., Willamette Valley Ctr.
Lillegard, Chris L., (BV) .... '51 '76 C.906 B.A. L.950 J.D. [C.L.Lillegard]
Lillegard, Chris L., PC, (BV) .... 236 Sw Mill
Mannenbach, Stephen F., (BV) .... '48 '80 C.629 B.A. L.950 J.D. 133 S.W. Academy
Ozias, Teresa, (CV) .... '63 '90 C.1071 B.A. L.950 J.D. [Irick,S.&O.]
Shetterly, Lane P., (BV) .... '55 '81 C.1181 B.S. L.596 J.D. [Irick,S.&O.]
Smith, Laurence N. '05 '32 L.336 LL.B.
(adm. in ID; not adm. in OR) 310 W. Ellendale Ave.‡
Williams, Darrell J. .... '21 '51 C.670 L.596 LL.B. Ret. Cir. J.

THE DALLES, * 12,156, *Wasco Co.*

Bailey, Bridget .... '66 '97 C.309 A.B. L.596 J.D. Orchard View Farms, Inc.
Carter, Andrew W., (BV) .... '58 '84 C.906 B.A. L.629 J.D. [Dunn,T.&C.]
Coats, J. Thomas, (BV) .... '43 '72 C&L.629 B.S., J.D. 113 "B" E. 2nd St.
Corey, Jason R., (BV) .... '65 '94 C.101 B.A. L.950 J.D. [Dick,D.&T.]
Dick, Roger L., (AV) .... '22 '49 C&L.629 B.S., J.D. [Dick,D.&T.]
Dick, William G., II, (BV) .... '52 '78 C.629 B.A. L.950 J.D. [Dick,D.&T.]

Dick, Dick & Timmons, (AV) BB
601 Washington Street, 97058
Telephone: 541-296-2152 FAX: 541-296-4220
William G. Dick (1916-1992); Roger L. Dick; William G. Dick, II; Edgar M. Dick (1924-1986); Bradley V. Timmons; Jason R. Corey.
General Civil and Trial Practice in all Courts. Negligence, Probate and Estate Planning, Corporation and Real Property Law.
References: U.S. Bank (The Dalles); Wells Fargo (The Dalles).

Donnell, James C. .... '39 '64 C&L.950 B.A., LL.B. Dist. J.‡
Dunn, Donald F., (AV) .... '30 '54 C&L.629 B.S., J.D. [⊙ Dunn,T.&C.]
Dunn, Toole & Carter, LLP, (BV) .... 112 West 4th Street
Foster, James R., (BV) .... '47 '72 [Foster,P.&Y.]
Foster, Peachey & Young, (BV) .... 420 E. 3rd. St.
Gouge, Linda K., (CV) .... '— '92 C.999 B.S. L.1051 J.D. 203 W. 4th St.
Habberstad, James M., (AV) '43 '73
C.906 B.A. L.950 J.D. 106 East Fourth Street Second Floor
Hashizume, Kevin J. .... '71 '99 C.1494 B.A. L.352 J.D. [VanValkenburgh&H.]
Heisler, Donald E. .... '13 '37 C&L.629 B.S., LL.B. 204 E. 4th St.‡
Hinkley-Lawrence, Tara .... '72 '99 C.670 B.A. L.950 J.D. [Ⓐ VanValkenburgh&H.]
Hinman, Jennifer .... '73 '01 C.1056 B.A. L.596 J.D. [J.Hinman]
Hinman, Jennifer, P.C. .... 502 Washington St., Rm. 204
Kelly, John V. .... '49 '77 C.628 B.A. L.285 J.D. Cir. Ct. J.
Parker, Gene E., (BV) .... '55 '82 C.950 B.A. L.1358 J.D. City Atty.
Peachey, Thomas C., (BV) .... '53 '78 C.112 B.A. L.950 J.D. [Foster,P.&Y.]
Rathkey, Rita L. .... '49 '80 C.629 B.S. L.345 J.D. [R.Rathkey] ‡
Rathkey, Rita, P.C. .... 1010 East 7th Street
Smith, Bernard L. .... '40 '71 C.911 B.A. L.629 J.D. Cir. J.
Somers, Ronald M., (BV) .... '37 '62 C.1051 B.S. L.950 LL.B. [Somers&W.]

Somers & Wolf, (BV)
106 East Fourth Street, P.O. Box 1578, 97058
Telephone: 541-296-2181 FAX: 541-296-9382 URL: http://www.somersandwolf.com
Email: susanchof@sbcglobal.net URL: http://www.lawyers.com/somersandwolf
Ronald M. Somers; John A. Wolf.
General Civil and Trial Practice. Family Law, Civil Litigation, Business Law, Real Estate, Probate, Trusts and Estates, Wills, Guardianships and Conservatorships, Partnership Law, Bankruptcy, Criminal Law, Personal Injury and Civil Drug Forfeiture.
Reference: United States National Bank.

See Professional Biographies, THE DALLES, OREGON

Timmons, Bradley V., (BV) .... '64 '90 C.1056 B.S. L.950 J.D. [Dick,D.&T.]
Toole, Charles K., (BV) .... '49 '75 C.629 B.S. L.950 J.D. [Dunn,T.&C.]
Van Valkenburgh, M. D., (BV) ... '27 '53 C.623 B.A. L.950 LL.B. [VanValkenburgh&H.]
Van Valkenburgh & Hashizume, P.C., (BV) .... 204 East Fourth Street
Wolf, John A., (BV) .... '70 '95 C.628 B.S. L.950 J.D. [Somers&W.]
Wolf, Leslie C., (BV) .... '69 '96 C.112 B.A. L.950 J.D. Dist. Atty. Off.
Young, Katherine J., (BV) .... '55 '80 C&L.629 B.A., J.D. [Foster,P.&Y.]

DAYTON, 2,119, *Yamhill Co.*

Craig, Elaine Hartung, (CV) '32 '87
C.629 B.A. L.950 J.D. 18465 S.E. Weston Landing Ln.
Francis, Carl .... '15 '37 C.950 L.596 LL.B. P.O. Box 97‡

DEPOE BAY, 1,174, *Lincoln Co.*

Langdon, Betty J. '29 '75 L.1095 J.D.
(adm. in CA; not adm. in OR) 95 Pacific St.‡
Poling, Dan W. .... '27 '56 C.628 B.S. L.950 LL.B. P.O. Box 35

DRAIN, 1,011, *Douglas Co.*

De La Vergne, Warren T. .... '28 '51 C&L.629 J.C., LL.B. P.O. Box 517‡
Trump, Russell G., (CV) .... '54 '84 C.628 B.S. L.629 J.D. 135 2nd St.

DUNDEE, 2,598, *Yamhill Co.*

Cain, Jessica S. .... '71 '98 C.744 B.A. L.190 J.D. 974 SW Tomahawk Place
Goldschmidt, Neil .... '40 '67 C.629 B.A. L.1066 LL.B. P.O. Box 9
Johnson, Jesse H., Jr. .... '43 '68 C.897 B.A. L.950 J.D. Pres., Newberg Care Ctr., Inc.

EAGLE POINT, 4,797, *Jackson Co.*

Parrott, Bruce R. .... '48 '78 C&L.616 B.S., J.D. 649 Oakwood Dr.

ENTERPRISE, * 1,905, *Wallowa Co.*

Harman, Rebecca J. .... '76 '01 C.1056 B.A. L.950 J.D. D. Rahn Hostetter, PC
Hostetter, D. Rahn .... '52 '78 C.1053 B.A. L.1051 J.D. 203 E. Main St.
Kirby, William B. .... '31 '59 C&L.629 B.B.A., LL.B. Hwy. 82 Crossroads, Ste. 3
Ousley, Daniel .... '46 '73 C.188 B.A. L.629 J.D. 101 S. River St., Ste. 201‡
Purnell, Sandra E. .... '43 '85 C.912 B.S. L.112 J.D. [Transitions D.]
Reynolds, William L. .... '28 '62 C.108 B.S. L.209 LL.B. P.O. Box 333
Transitions Divorce Service .... 81964 Black Marble Lane
Williams, Mona K., (BV) .... '53 '89 C.1104 B.S. L.336 J.D. [M.K.Williams]
Williams, Mona K., P.C., (BV) .... 117 E Main St

ESTACADA, 2,371, *Clackamas Co.*

Tommas, Jacqueline A. .... '37 '68 C.629 B.S. L.1355 J.D. 19288 S. Mattoon Rd.

EUGENE, * 137,893, *Lane Co.*

Adler, Ellen D., (BV) .... '56 '89 C.260 B.A. L.629 J.D. [Speer,H.J.F.P.W.&G.]
Alberty, Steven C., (AV) .... '47 '73 C&L.174 B.A., J.D. 581 Covey Ln.
Aldave, Barbara Bader .... '38 '66 C.813 B.A. L.1066 J.D. 1221 University of Oregon
Alderman, Karla H. .... '56 '99 C.1071 B.S. L.950 J.D. [Ⓐ Harrang L.G.R.]
Alderman, Thomas O. .... '49 '74 C&L.629 B.S., J.D. [T.O.Alderman]
Alderman, Thomas O., P.C. .... 132 East Broadway, Suite 400
Alderson, Frank R. .... '25 '51 C&L.629 B.S., LL.B. Dist. J.
Allen, Edwin E. .... '26 '49 C&L.629 B.S., LL.B. Sr. Cir. J.
Allen, Wayne E., (BV) .... '44 '68 C&L.629 B.S., J.D. Mun. J.
Alley, Frank R., III .... '49 '77 C.918 B.A. L.1358 J.D. U.S. Bkrptcy. J.
Allison, Hushek J. '73 '98
C.112 B.A. L.61 J.D. Dir., Business Affairs, Chambers Productions
Anderson, Beverly .... '51 '95 P.O. Box 2626
Anderson, Bruce H., (BV) .... '41 '66 C&L.228 B.A., LL.B. 4240 Hilyard
Anderson, Howard J. .... '42 '76 C.210 B.A. L.1051 J.D. 1027 West Broadway

Anderson, Kent, & Associates, (BV) '49 '78 C&L.629 B.S., J.D.
888 West Park Street, 97401
Telephone: 541-683-5100 Telefax: 541-484-1754 URL: http://www.kentandersonlaw.com
Email: kentanderson@compuserve.com URL: http://www.lawyers.com/kentanderson
Bankruptcy, Business Transactions, Construction, Creditor's Rights, Real Estate, Taxation, Tax Liens, Business Law, Contracts, Mechanics Liens, Foreclosures, Small Business, Buying or Selling a Business, Commercial Leasing, IRS Audits.

See Professional Biographies, EUGENE, OREGON

Anderson, Larry J., P.C., (BV) .... '34 '59 C&L.629 Suite 2, 1358 Oak St.
Andrews, David N., (AV) .... '30 '59 C&L.629 B.S., J.D. [Hershner H.]
Ard, Marlin D. .... '48 '76 C.637 B.S. L.629 J.D. [⊙ Hershner H.]
Armbrust, Julie Gentili .... '73 '99 C.911 B.A. L.629 J.D. 399 E. 10th Ave.
Armstrong, Donald K., (BV) .... '43 '73 C&L.629 B.S., J.D. [D.K.Armstrong]
Armstrong, Gavin W., (BV) .... '42 '69 C&L.378 B.B.A., J.D. 440 E. Broadway
Armstrong, Donald K., P.C., (BV) .... 450 Country Club Rd., Ste. 340
Arnold, John B., (AV) .... '47 '73 C.813 A.B. L.477 J.D. [Arnold G.S.P.R.&P.]

Arnold Gallagher Saydack Percell Roberts & Potter, P.C., (AV) BB
800 Willamette Street, Suite 800, P.O. Box 1758, 97440-1758
Telephone: 541-484-0188 Fax: 541-484-0536
Email: info@agsprp.com URL: http://www.arnoldgallagher.com
John B. Arnold; Donald A. Gallagher, Jr.; Roger M. Saydack; Dennis W. Percell; Rohn M. Roberts; William R. Potter; Bradley S. Copeland; Bryon L. Land; Joseph G. Schwarte; Catherine D. Susman;—Susan B. Bock; Gregory T. Lusby; Andrew P. Parks; Megan McAlpin; Diane M. Weisheit; Aaron J. Noteboom.
General Civil Practice, Banking, Business, Mergers and Acquisitions, Construction, Corporate, Creditors' Rights and Commercial Bankruptcy, Labor and Employment, Environmental, Estate Planning and Probate, Insurance, Media, Real Estate, Partnerships, Taxation, Timber and Trial Practice in Oregon State and Federal Courts.
References: LibertyBank; Farmers Insurance Group; Frontier Resources, LLC; Timber Products Group; The Papé Group; Troutman Investment Co.; Lane Transit District; Obie Industries, Inc.; PeaceHealth Oregon Region; Washington Mutual Bank.

See Professional Biographies, EUGENE, OREGON

Atherly, Darst B., (AV) '30 '59 C.932 B.S. L.477 J.D.
1200 Executive Pkwy., Suite 440‡
Augur, M. Janise .... '53 '81 C.112 B.A. L.1051 J.D. Pub. Def. Servs. of Lane Co.
Bader, Gregory V., (AVⓉ) '48 '79 C.506 B.A. L.309 J.D.
(adm. in TX; not adm. in OR) 4035 Donald St., Apt. J
Baker, Sheryl Hansen, (BV) '65 '91
C&L.629 B.A., J.D. 440 East Broadway, Suite 300 (⊙Eugene)
Baker, Wendy J. .... '53 '02 C.911 BA. L.629 J.D. [Ⓐ Harrang L.G.R.]
Baldwin, Steve C., (BV) .... '52 '83 C&L.629 B.S., J.D. [Watkinson L.R.B.&B.]
Balthrop, Sheryl, (BV) .... '65 '91 C&L.629 B.A., J.D. [Gaydos,C.&B.] (⊙Eugene)
Bandiero, Emilio F., (BV) .... '38 '91 C.994 B.A. L.629 J.D. [E.F.Bandiero]
Bandiero, Emilio F., P.C., (BV) .... 975 Oak Street, Suite 625
Bannon, Sean M. .... '69 '05 C&L.629 B.A., J.D. [Ⓐ Gleaves S.P.&S.]
Barber, John L., Jr. .... '08 '34 C.627 A.B. L.546 LL.B. 92803 Prairie Rd.‡
Barnhart, Philip N. .... '46 '71 C&L.629 B.A., J.D. 291 W. 12th Ave.‡
Baron, Robert A. .... '61 '89 C.966 B.A. L.209 J.D. [Cram,H.W.&B.]
Barton-Russell, Rachel L. .... '61 '99 C.999 B.A. L.629 J.D. 110 E. 14th Ave
Bassinger, Scott G. .... '65 '91 C.628 B.S. L.950 J.D. 1200 Executive Pkwy., Ste. 320
Batson, Frederick A., (BV) .... '57 '82 C.35 B.S. L.1051 J.D. [Gleaves S.P.&S.]
Bauer, Elizabeth W. .... '77 '03 C&L.629 B.A., J.D. [Ⓐ Watkinson L.R.B.&B.]
Bear, Steven F. .... '48 '74 C.1077 B.S. L.809 J.D. Admin. Law J., State Employ. Dept.
Beck, Melvin J., (BV) ...... '46 '75 C&L.629 B.A., J.D. Assoc. Coun., Centennial Bancorp

Becker, Ronald C., (BV) .... '53 '83 C&L.629 B.S., J.D. 400 E 2nd Ste 229
Beckett, William A. .... '28 '54 C&L.477 A.B., LL.B. Sr. Cir. J.‡
Beckley, Kelly R., (BV) .... '49 '74 C.906 B.A. L.629 J.D. [Beckley&L.]

Beckley & Longtin, P.C., (BV)
1257 High Street, Suite 2, P.O. Box 11098, 97440-3298
Telephone: 541-683-0888 Fax: 541-683-0889
Email: lawyers@beckleyandlongtin.com URL: http://www.beckleyandlongtin.com
Kelly R. Beckley; Matthew D. Longtin.
Federal Criminal Law and State Criminal Defense. Corporate Law, Family Practice, Divorce, Child Support, Domestic Violence, Drug Crimes, Felonies, Sexual Assault, Commercial, Estate Planning, Probate Law, and Domestic Relations.
Representative Clients: Betts Telcom, Inc.; New Horizons Home Care Resources, Inc.; Reed's Fuel & Trucking; Papa's Pizza, Inc.; Lane Forest Products, Inc.; Professional Credit Services, Inc.; H&J Construction, Inc.
See Professional Biographies, EUGENE, OREGON

Behrends, Stephen L., (BV) .... '52 '79 C.112 B.S. L.629 J.D. 1445 Willamette St., Ste. 9
Bellows, Scott .... '61 '87 C&L.112 B.A., J.D. P.O. Box 51197
Beneke, Paul G. .... '68 '96 C.966 B.S. L.629 J.D. Univ. of OR
Bergland, John H. .... '47 '77 C.436 B.A. L.145 J.D. 4392 N. Shasta Loop
Bevans, Russell D. .... '42 '73 C.101 B.S. L.629 J.D. 895 Country Club Rd., Ste. C-175
Billings, Jack A. .... '46 '71 C.350 B.S. L.352 J.D. Cir. J.
Billington, John W. .... '47 '73 C&L.629 B.A., J.D. [J.W.Billington]
Billington, John W., P.C., Law Office of .... 91 Madison Street
Bischoff, Strooband & Ousey, P.C., (BV) .... 1127 Lincoln St.
Bjerre, Carl S. .... '59 '89 C.1375 B.A. L.188 J.D. Univ. of Oregon Sch. of Law
Blackwell, Barbara J. Cullen, (CV) .... '39 '75 C.339 B.S. L.629 LL.B. Univ. of Oregon
Blixseth, Stephen R. '46 '71 C.950 B.A. L.629 J.D.
Sr. Asst. Atty. Gen., OR Dept. of Jus.
Bloom, Duff, (BV) .... '61 '91 C.911 B.A. L.950 J.D. [Cary,W.B.&E.]
Bocci, Frank E., Jr., (CV) .... '55 '81 C.628 B.S. L.950 J.D. [Ⓐ Luvaas C.]
Bock, Susan B. .... '68 '93 C.104 A.B. L.228 J.D. [Ⓐ Arnold G.S.P.R.&P.]
Bodie, Gary J. .... '53 '82 C.939 B.A. L.596 J.D. 765 Mimosa Ave.
Boiler, Jeffrey H. .... '52 '83 C&L.629 B.S., J.D. [Boiler]
Boiler Law Firm .... 925 Country Club Road, Suite 125
Bond, Peggy A., (BV) .... '46 '90 C.1109 B.A. L.629 J.D. [P.A.Bond]
Bond, Peggy A., P.C., Law Offices of, (BV) .... 40 East Broadway, Suite 200
Botsios, Cynthia A. .... '59 '97 C.589 B.A. L.629 J.D. State Dept. of Jus.
Bourassa, Donald R. .... '39 '80 C.871 B.S. L.629 J.D. 1749 Ferry St.‡
Boyd, Keith Y., (BV) .... '50 '76 C.628 B.S. L.629 J.D. [Muhlheim B.]
Bradley, Ralph A., (BV) .... '47 '80 C.628 B.S. L.629 J.D. 470 W. Bway.
Bradley, Raymond J. .... '44 '70 C.339 B.A. L.629 J.D. 700 Lawrence St.
Brewer, Timothy Fraser, (BV) .... '51 '84 C.293 B.A. L.629 J.D. [T.F.Brewer]
Brewer, William D., (AV) .... '47 '85 C.950 B.A. L.1051 J.D. [Hershner H.] ⊙
Brewer, Timothy F., P.C., (BV) .... 590 W. 13th Ave.
Britt, James W., (CV) .... '63 '96 C&L.629 B.A., J.D. P.O. Box 10554
Broadhurst, Mary E., (CV) .... '59 '91 C.330 B.A. L.629 J.D. P.O. Box 11377
Bromley, William W., (BV) .... '46 '74 C.475 B.S. L.629 J.D. [Bromley N.]
Bromley Newton, LLP, (BV) .... 627 Country Club Rd., Ste. 200
Brotherton, Kathryn P., (BV) .... '72 '98 C.37 B.A. L.629 J.D. [Ⓐ Harrang L.G.R.]
Brown, Joseph J. .... '29 '56 C&L.546 B.A., LL.B. 84400 Boods Rd.‡
Brown, Larry A., (AV) .... '42 '68 C&L.629 B.S., J.D. [Brown,R.L.M.&K.]
Brown, Todd G., (BV) .... '43 '68 C&L.502 A.B., J.D. Asst. Atty. Gen.

Brown, Roseta, Long, McConville & Kilcullen, (AV) BR
210 Northbank Building, 44 Club Road, 97401
Telephone: 541-686-1883 Fax: 541-686-2008
Email: lawfirm@brownroseta.com
Members of Firm: Larry A. Brown; Michael H. Long; Philip R. McConville; John F. Kilcullen. Of Counsel: Richard A. Roseta.
Civil Trial and Appellate Practice. Insurance Defense. Insurance Law.
Representative Clients: All Nation Insurance Co.; Allstate Insurance Co.; American States Insurance Co.; Crawford & Co.; Grange Mutual Insurance; Heritage Life Insurance Co.; Insurance Corp. of America; Mutual of Enumclaw; Northwest Physicians Mutual Insurance Co.
See Professional Biographies, EUGENE, OREGON

Browne, Elizabeth W., (CV) .... '26 '66 C.494 B.A. L.629 LL.B. 2719 W. 29th Ave.
Brownhill, Thomas E., (AV) .... '21 '50 C&L.629 B.S., J.D. P.O. Box 70328‡
Bruce, Jillian R., (CV) .... '59 '85 C.1051 B.S. L.464 J.D. [Harrang L.G.R.]
Bruce, Michael M., (BV) .... '55 '82 C&L.629 B.S., J.D. 941 Lawrence
Brucker, Nancy J. '51 '86 C.112 A.B. L.1066 J.D.
(adm. in CA; not adm. in OR) Univ. of Ore. Foundation
Bryson, Randall, (AV) .... '48 '77 C&L.629 B.S., J.D. [Bryson&B.]
Bryson, Richard, (AV) .... '16 '41 C&L.629 B.A., J.D. [Bryson&B.]
Bryson & Bryson, (AV) .... 399 E. 10th Ave.
Buchalter, Alan Roy .... '54 '92 C.881 B.A. L.629 J.D. 399 E. 10th Avenue
Budge, Hamilton W., Jr., (AV) .... '54 '80 C.813 B.A. L.1065 J.D. [Gardner,H.P.B.&F.]
Buerstatte, Jon V., (BV) .... '56 '82 C.906 B.A. L.629 J.D. [Gleaves S.P.&S.]
Burgess, B. Kevin, (BV) .... '54 '88 C.1320 B.A. L.629 J.D. [Watkinson L.R.B.&B.]
Burgott, George A., (AV) .... '49 '74 C&L.477 B.S.Ch.E., J.D. [Luvaas C.]
Burgott, Susan L., (CV) .... '49 '79 C.477 B.S. L.629 J.D. 2955 Wolf Meadows Lane
Busby, Carol A., (CV) .... '51 '90 C.112 B.A. L.629 J.D. 141 W. 39th Ave.
Buseman, Michael J. .... '70 '97 C&L.629 B.A., J.D. 199 E 5th Ave.
Bush, Ronald P. '41 '76 C.267 B.A. L.426 J.D.
(adm. in CA; not adm. in OR) P.O. Box 7842
Busley, Melissa F. .... '79 '04 C.906 B.A. L.629 J.D. [Ⓐ Hershner H.]
Butler, Edward M., (CV) .... '56 '87 C.628 B.S. L.629 J.D. P.O. Box 51476
Butler, Richard W., (AV) .... '34 '60 C&L.629 B.S., J.D. [Ⓒ Luvaas C.]
Calkins, Judy Ann, (BV) .... '49 '91 C&L.629 B.A., J.D. [Calkins&C.]
Calkins, Win, (AV) .... '44 '71 C.629 B.A. L.950 J.D. [Calkins&C.]

Calkins & Calkins, (AV) BR
101 East 14th Avenue, 97401-3517
Telephone: 541-345-0371 FAX: 541-342-1220
Email: win@calkinslaw.com URL: http://www.lawyers.com/calkinslaw
Members of Firm: Windsor Calkins (1910-1989); S. M. Calkins (1872-1969); W. W. Calkins (1860-1945); Win Calkins; Judy Ann Calkins;—Eric S. DeFreest. Of Counsel: Josephine H. Mooney.
General Litigation including Civil Trial, Medical Malpractice Defense, Insurance Defense, Contracts, Construction Law, Construction Defense, Hospital Law, Utility Law, Trusts and Estates, Asset Protection, Charitable Giving, Estate Litigation, Estate Planning, Guardianship and Conservatorship, Wills and Probate.
Counsel for: Eugene Water & Electric Board; Sacred Heart Medical Center; Lane County Medical Society; Oregon Automobile Insurance Co.; North Pacific Insurance Co.; St. Paul Insurance Cos.; Safeco; Northwest Physicians Mutual Insurance Co.; General Accident Insurance Co.; Farmers Insurance Group.
See Professional Biographies, EUGENE, OREGON

Capon, Craig J., (BV) .... '73 '98 C.112 B.A. L.911 J.D. [Ⓐ Harrang L.G.R.]
Carlson, Charles D. .... '54 '80 C.645 B.A. L.629 J.D. Cir. Ct. Judge
Carlson, Cynthia D. .... '52 '77 C&L.629 B.A., J.D. Cir. J.
Carmichael, David E., (BV) .... '48 '73 C&L.629 B.S., J.D. 777 High St.
Carp, Ted .... '43 '70 C.910 B.A. L.112 J.D. Cir. J.
Carpenter, William Charles, Jr., (BV) .... '51 '90 C.174 B.S. L.629 J.D. 474 Willamette St.
Carroll, Tami S. P., (CV) .... '62 '96 C.150 B.A. L.1051 J.D. 399 East 10th Avenue
Carusone, Judson M .... '66 [Bromley N.]
Cary, Nancy K., (BV) .... '62 '90 C&L.950 B.A., J.D. [Hershner H.]
Cary, Thomas M., (BV) .... '52 '82 C.1056 B.A. L.494 J.D. [Cary,W.B.&E.]
Cary, Wing, Bloom & Edmunson, P.C., (BV) .... 1600 Executive Pkwy.
Casby, James J., Jr. .... '34 '60 C.276 B.S. L.659 LL.B. Special Asst. Atty. Gov.
Chandler, Stephanie T. .... '69 '99 C.939 B.S. L.629 J.D. [Ⓐ Watkinson L.R.B.&B.]
Chaney, James C., (BV) .... '58 '83 C.813 B.A. L.1068 J.D. [Chaney]
Chaney Firm, The, LLC, (BV) .... 777 High Street, Suite 280
Chanti, Suzanne Bradley, (BV) .... '58 '88 C.1071 B.S. L.629 J.D. [Walters R.C.&D.]
Chapman, Patricia L., (BV) .... '56 '83 C.112 A.B. L.767 J.D. [Hershner H.] ⊙
Childs, Will .... '72 '98 C.823 B.A. L.629 J.D. 399 East 10th Avenue
Churnside, Donald J., (AV) .... '54 '79 C.413 B.A. L.629 J.D. [Gaydos,C.&B.]
Clark, Arthur J., (AV) .... '50 '76 C&L.629 B.A., J.D. [Hershner H.]
Clark, Joshua A., (CV) .... '69 '98 C.911 B.A. L.629 J.D. [Gleaves S.P.&S.]
Clark, Laurie L., (BV) .... '62 '88 C.429 B.A. L.629 J.D. 975 Oak St., Ste. 610
Clark, Roger Lee .... '51 '97 C.1071 B.S. L.629 J.D. P.O. Box 10243
Clarke, Gary R. .... '65 '94 C.610 B.B.A. L.7 J.D. P.O. Box 287
Clayton, Paul D., (BV) .... '37 '61 C&L.629 B.S., LL.B. 1358 Oak St., Ste. 1
Clemmens, William B., Jr. '48 '73 C.645 B.A. L.421 J.D.
(adm. in KY; not adm. in OR) V.P., Bus. Dev., SunBurst, Inc.
Clifton, Jacob K., Jr., (AV) .... '45 '74 C.1056 B.A. L.629 J.D. [Johnson C.L.&S.]
Clinkinbeard, Karl .... '21 '58 C.628 B.S. L.950 J.D. 2742 Elysium Ave.‡
Cobb, Ralph F., (AV) .... '21 '48 C.977 B.A. L.793 LL.B. [Luvaas C.]
Coffin, Thomas M. .... '45 '70 C.711 B.A. L.309 J.D. U.S. Mag. J.
Cohen, Marilyn .... '37 '62 C.183 B.A. L.976 LL.B. Asst. Dir., Global Resources Institute

Coit & Dean, P.C.
(See Portland)

Coles-Bjerre, Andrea '63 '88 C.66 B.A. L.1009 J.D.
(adm. in NY; not adm. in OR) University of Oregon School of Law
Collin, Robin Morris .... '54 '80 C.170 B.A. L.36 J.D. Prof. of Law, Oregon Sch. of Law
Collins, Simon R. '62 '90 C.906 B.A. L.336 J.D.
(adm. in WA; not adm. in OR) Soc. Sec. Admn.
Commissiong, Nicole R. .... '73 '02 C&L.629 B.A., J.D. [Ⓐ Harrang L.G.R.]
Connelly, Carolyn H., (BV) .... '68 '95 C.197 B.A. L.1194 J.D. [Ⓐ Speer,H.J.F.P.W.&G.]
Connelly, Joe, (BV) .... '52 '93 C.184 B.A. L.629 J.D. 1361 Pearl St.
Conner, Daniel K. .... '44 '85 C.145 B.A. L.629 J.D. 4820 Garnet St.‡
Cooley, Lawrence F., (BV) .... '43 '68 C&L.629 B.S., J.D. P.O. Box 50655
Coons, Allan H. .... '39 '67 C.813 A.B. L.1065 J.D. 3480 Bardell Ave.‡
Coons, James K., (BV) .... '49 '76 C.309 A.B. L.629 J.D. [Hutchinson,C.C.D.O.&S.]
Cooper, Laura D. .... '56 '86 C.629 B.S. L.911 J.D. 808 Lariat Drive
Cooper, Michael L. .... '58 '84 C&L.629 B.S., J.D. 895 Country Club Rd.
Copeland, Bradley S., (BV) .... '56 '87 C.205 B.A. L.1051 J.D. [Arnold G.S.P.R.&P.]
Cornacchia, P. Steve .... '50 '80 C&L.629 B.S., J.D. [Ⓒ Hershner H.]
Correll, Kathleen J., (BV) .... '56 '89 C.575 B.S. L.629 J.D. Asst. Dist. Atty.

Corson, Don, (AV) '56 '85 C&L.629 B.S., J.D.
101 East Broadway, Suite 303, 97401
Telephone: 541-484-2525 Fax: 541-484-2929
Email: dcorson@doncorsonlaw.com URL: http://www.doncorsonlaw.com
Personal Injury, Wrongful Death, Products Liability, Medical Negligence, Industrial Accidents, Electrical Injury.
See Professional Biographies, EUGENE, OREGON

Courchaine, Christine M. .... '58 '89 C.475 B.S.N. L.629 J.D. 3711 Lawrence St.‡
Cox, Brian D., (CV) .... '58 '90 C.1253 B.S. L.950 J.D. [Cox&Assoc.]
Cox, John G., (BV) .... '— '69 C.629 B.A. L.950 J.D. [Hutchinson,C.C.D.O.&S.]
Cox, Matthew J., (CV) .... '69 '98 C&L.629 B.A., J.D. Dist. Atty.
Cox & Associates LLC, (CV) .... 142 W. 8th Ave.
Crabtree, Dale T. .... '16 '54 C&L.950 A.B., LL.B. 1243 Woodside Dr.‡
Cram, Stanley, (BV) .... '52 '78 C.966 B.A. L.629 J.D. [Cram,H.W.&B.]
Cram, Harder, Wells & Baron, (BV) .... 474 Willamette
Crider, Kay Michele '64 '89 C.112 B.A. L.146 J.D.
(adm. in IL; not adm. in OR) P.O. Box 11615
Critchlow, William J., (BV) .... '62 '91 C.506 B.S. L.629 J.D. 1445 Willamette St Ste 9
Crumme, Douglas C. .... '52 '78 C.629 B.A. L.950 J.D. Wkrs. Comp. Bd.
Darnielle, Gary L. .... '46 '74 C&L.629 B.S., J.D. 1130 President St.
Daugirda, John P., (BV) .... '50 '75 C.367 B.A. L.64 J.D. [Roost&D.]
Daum, Carter A., (CV) .... '43 '81 C.401 B.A. L.629 J.D. P.O. Box 10924
Davies, Anne C., (BV) .... '64 '90 C.674 B.A. L.629 J.D. 800 Willamette St.
Davis, Andrea M. .... '74 '99 C.417 B.A. L.420 J.D. [Ⓐ Harrang L.G.R.]
Davis, Barry S. .... '53 '83 C.36 B.S. L.1009 J.D. P.O. Box 5883
Day, Lois Ann .... '56 '86 C.012 B.S. L.629 J.D. Lane Co. Legal Aid Servs., Inc.
Deal, Gary F., (CV) .... '50 '77 C&L.629 B.S., J.D. 750 Lawrence
Deckman, Lawrence G. .... '53 '85 C&L.629 B.S., J.D. Legal Mediation Serv.
DeFreest, Eric S., (BV) .... '63 '92 C.472 B.S. L.629 J.D. [Ⓐ Calkins&C.]
Dennett, Douglas J., (AV) .... '44 '69 C&L.629 M.S., J.D. [D.J.Dennett]
Dennett, Douglas J., P.C., (AV) .... 199 E. 5th Avenue, Suite 35
DePaolis, Diane Mary, (BV) .... '49 '76 C.813 B.A. L.629 J.D. [DePaolis&S.]
DePaolis & Shepard, (BV) .... 767 Willamette
deVilleneuve, David Andrew, (CV) .... '66 '94 C.101 B.S. L.629 J.D. [Shlesinger&d.]
DeVore, Joel S., (AV) .... '51 '82 C.33 B.A. L.629 J.D. [Luvaas C.]
Dickens, David, (BV) .... '48 '77 C.691 B.A. L.629 J.D. [Walters R.C.&D.]
Dickinson, Robert G. .... '40 '66 C&L.477 B.A., J.D. 2121 Franklin Blvd.‡
Diment, Donald D., Jr., (AV) .... '42 '68 C.1056 B.S. L.950 J.D. [Diment&W.]

Diment & Walker, (AV)
Suite 208, 767 Willamette Street, 97401
Telephone: 541-484-2422 FAX: 541-484-9395
URL: http://www.dimentwalker.com
Members of Firm: Donald D. Diment, Jr.; Theodore L. Walker.
Civil Litigation, Criminal Law, Driving While Intoxicated, State and Federal Courts, Corporate, Construction, Personal Injury Automobile Accidents, Family Law, Divorce, Child Custody, Visitation Rights, Child Support, Real Estate Law, Probate Law.
See Professional Biographies, EUGENE, OREGON

Divita, Fred A. A., (BV) .... '44 '69 C.628 B.S. L.629 J.D. [F.A.A.Divita]
Divita, Fred A. A., (Professional Corporation), (BV) .... 1147 High St.
Doolittle, Roger T. .... '30 '54 C&L.629 B.S., LL.B. 132 E. Bway.
Doyle, Michael W., (AV) .... '43 '69 C.112 B.A. L.1066 J.D. [Doyle,G.N.M.&W.]

Doyle, Gartland, Nelson, McCleery & Wade, P.C., (AV)
44 Club Road, Suite 200, 97401
Mailing Address: P.O. Box 11230, Eugene, OR 97440
Telephone: 541-344-2174 Fax: 541-344-0209
Michael W. Doyle; John C. Gartland; Douglas A. Nelson; P. Scott McCleery; David Wade;—Mindy L. Wittkop; Heather M. Walloch; Emily S. Hill.

(This Listing Continued)

Doyle, Gartland, Nelson, McCleery & Wade, P.C. (Continued)

General Civil and Trial Practice in all State and Federal Courts. Corporate, Business Litigation, Bankruptcy, Creditors Rights, Family, Mediation, Real Property, Construction, Estate Planning and Probate Law, Intellectual Property Law.
Reference: Pacific Continental Bank.

See Professional Biographies, EUGENE, OREGON

Dugan, Marianne G., (BV) .... '59 '93 C.174 B.A. L.629 J.D. 485 E. 13th Ave.
Dugdale, Robert B., (BV) .... '44 '74 C.549 B.A. L.629 J.D. Suite 100, 915 Oak St.
Duncan, Charles G., (BV) .... '41 '71 C.976 B.A. L.188 J.D. [C.G.Duncan]
Duncan, Charles G., P.C., (BV) .... 700 Lawrence St.
DuPriest, Douglas M., (BV) ... '51 '77 C.604 A.B. L.629 J.D. [Hutchinson,C.C.D.O.&S.]

Duvall, Hubert G., Jr., (AV) '60 '88 C.628 B.S. L.629 J.D.
Citizens Building, 975 Oak Street, Suite 610, 97401
Telephone: 541-349-9909 Fax: 541-349-9799 URL: http://www.oregoncriminalattorney.com
Email: hughduvall@oregoncriminalattorney.com URL: http://www.lawyers.com/hgduvall
Criminal Law, Drug Crimes, Measure II, Sex Offenses, Stalking, Assault, Harassment, Theft, Forgery, Drug Crimes, DUI, Shoplifting, Driving While Intoxicated, Felonies, Juvenile Law, Misdemeanors, Parole and Probation, Sexual Assault, Business Crimes, Juvenile, Traffic Violations, Sexual Abuse, Sexual Harassment.

See Professional Biographies, EUGENE, OREGON

Easton, Thomas '35 '83 C&L.629 B.S., J.D.
(adm. in CA; not adm. in OR) 2890 Emerald St.
Eberly, John H., Jr. '42 '67 C.602 B.A. L.128 LL.B.
(adm. in VA; not adm. in OR) 2647 Ter. View Dr.‡
Edmunson, James L. .... '51 '83 C.628 B.S. L.629 J.D. [Cary,W.B.&E.]
El-Jourbagy, Jehan Y. .... '78 '03 C&L.280 A.B.J., J.D. [▣ M.J.McKeown]
Elmore, Kenneth B., (BV) .... '59 '85 C.801 B.S. L.629 J.D. [Jensen,E.&S.]
Endicott, Bruce .... '48 '97 C&L.629 B.S., J.D. 1524 Mckinley St.
Eng, Fern, (BV) .... '50 '82 C.813 B.A. L.629 J.D. [Neal&E.]
Engelmann, Therese .... '32 '58 C&L.339 B.S., LL.B. 2185 Tyler St.‡
Evans, H. Thomas .... '40 '68 C.628 B.S. L.629 J.D. 750 Lawrence
Evans, Herbert G., (BV) .... '43 '91 C.494 B.A. L.629 J.D. [▣ Boiler] ‡
Fadeley, Charles N., (BV) .... '56 '81 C.911 B.A. L.629 J.D. 875 Country Club Rd.
Fagan, Thomas L., (BV) '48 '73 C&L.629 B.S., J.D.
Staff Atty., Pub. Def. Servs. of Lane Co., Inc.
Faulhaber, Dwight L. .... '43 '71 C.629 B.S. L.950 J.D. 400 E. 2nd Ave.
Feinman, Howard F., (BV) .... '49 '75 C.390 B.A. L.910 J.D. [Speer,H.J.F.P.W.&G.]
Feldman, Kenneth N., (BV) .... '43 '72 C.898 B.A. L.629 J.D. [K.N. .P.Feldman]
Feldman, Kenneth N., PC, (BV) .... 3266 Lakemont Dr.
Ferrari, Gerald B. '24 '57 C&L.813 B.S., LL.B.
(adm. in CA; not adm. in OR) [Ferrari&F.] ‡
Ferrari, Maria A., (BVⓥ) '58 '84 C.1051 B.A. L.770 J.D.
(adm. in CA; not adm. in OR) [Ferrari&F.]
Ferrari & Ferrari, A Law Corporation, (BVⓥ) .... 87087 Kellmore St.
Fetherstonhaugh, Jill R., (CV) '61 '98 C.1056 B.A. L.629 J.D.
399 E. 10th Ave., Ste. 101
Fine, Laura Anne .... '61 '88 C&L.378 B.A., J.D. [L.A.Fine]
Fine, Laura A., P.C., Law Office of .... 541 Willamette St., Ste. 403
Fink, Marc D. .... '70 '96 C.1086 B.A. L.1051 J.D. Western Environ. Law Ctr.
Fisher, John C., (BV) .... '51 '77 C&L.629 B.S., J.D. 975 Oak St.
Fisher, Katherine C. .... '73 '05 C.508 B.A. L.629 J.D. [▣ Hershner H.]
Fishlen, Michael '43 '88 C.388 B.A. L.629 J.D.
Dept. Head, East Asian Languages & Lit., Univ. of Oregon
Fitzgerald, William E., (BV) .... '55 '85 C.870 B.S. L.228 J.D. Asst. U.S. Atty.
Flanagan, John K. .... '68 '94 C.174 B.A. L.188 J.D. [Flanagan&F.]
Flanagan, John R. .... '41 '70 C.504 B.A. L.128 J.D. [Flanagan&F.] (Pat.)
Flanagan & Flanagan .... P.O. Box 2629 (Pat.)
Fogarty, Danna C., (AVⓥ) .... '52 '79 C&L.285 B.A., J.D. [Skillman,F.]

Force, David C., (CV) '46 '82 C&L.629 B.S., J.D.
96 East Broadway, Suite 2, P.O. Box 10972, 97440
Telephone: 541-343-2956 Fax: 541-686-1594
Email: forcelaw@aol.com URL: http://www.lawyers.com/forcelaw
Government Agency Practice, Civil Rights, Libel, Slander and Defamation, Employment Law, Wrongful Termination, Discrimination, Gay and Lesbian Rights, Workers Compensation, Sexual Harassment, Family and Medical Leave Act, Employee Rights, Appellate Law, Federal Civil Law, Administrative Law.

See Professional Biographies, EUGENE, OREGON

Ford, Michael E., P.C., (BV) .... '51 '85 C&L.629 B.S., J.D. [Gardner,H.P.B.&F.]
Ford, Robert A., (BV) .... '49 '74 C.668 A.B. L.629 J.D. [Kurtz,F.&J.]
Forsyth, Will .... '70 '99 C.602 B.A. L.629 J.D. [Hershner H.]
Fowler, Lindsay H. .... '74 '02 C&L.923 B.A., J.D. [▣ Veralrud&Assoc.]
Fox, Michael F., (BV) .... '46 '74 C.321 A.B. L.629 J.D. 975 Oak St.
Frank, Jay W., (BV) .... '50 '79 C.628 B.A. L.215 J.D. [Moule&F.]
Fraser, Robert H., (AV) .... '29 '59 C.827 B.A. L.1119 J.D. [▣ Luvaas C.] ‡
Friedman, Marc P., (BV) .... '53 '89 C.17 B.A. L.629 J.D. 245 W. 13th Avenue
Froemming, Holli .... '— '05 C.1081 B.A. L.477 J.D. [▣ Jaqua&W.] ⊙
Frohnmayer, David B., (AV) '40 '67
C.309 A.B. L.1066 J.D. Pres. & Prof. of Law, Univ. of Ore.
Furtick, William A., (BV) .... '47 '75 C.33 B.A. L.629 J.D. 1262 Lawrence, Ste. 1-A
Fussner, Eileen Tuhy .... '47 '74 C.605 B.A. L.1068 J.D. Pub. Def. Servs., Inc.
Gallagher, Donald A., Jr., (AV) .... '46 '74 C.628 B.S. L.629 J.D. [Arnold G.S.P.R.&P.]
Gallagher, Douglas L. .... '72 '97 C&L.629 B.A., J.D. [▣ Scott H.] ⊙
Galose, William Brian .... '60 '87 C.980 B.A. L.800 J.D. 2188 W. 17th Court
Gardner, Alexander R., (BV) .... '61 '91 C&L.629 B.A., J.D. Dist. Atty.
Gardner, Allen E., (BV) .... '51 '80 C&L.629 B.A., J.D. [Gardner,H.P.B.&F.]
Gardner, Honsowetz, Potter, Budge & Ford, LLP, (AV) .... 725 Country Club Road
Garrick, Paul J., (BV) .... '53 '82 C.112 B.A. L.1051 J.D. 115 W. 8th Ave.
Gartland, John C., (AV) .... '52 '77 C.628 B.A. L.629 J.D. [Doyle,G.N.M.&W.]
Gary, Susan N. .... '55 '81 C.976 B.A. L.178 J.D. Asst. Prof. of Law, Univ. of Oregon
Gary, William F., (AV) ... '50 '76 C.629 B.A. L.1065 J.D. [Harrang L.G.R.] (⊙Portland)
Gaydos, Gerry, (AV) .... '47 '72 C.608 B.A. L.930 J.D. [Gaydos,C.&B.]

Gaydos, Churnside & Balthrop, P.C., (AV)
440 East Broadway, Suite 300, P.O. Box 1499, 97440
Telephone: 541-343-8060 Fax: 541-343-1599
Email: gcb@gcbpc.com URL: http://www.gcb@gcbpc.com
***Sheryl Balthrop; Donald J. Churnside; Gerry Gaydos;*—P. Rebecca Kamitsuka. Of Counsel: Jonathan R. Miko.**
General Civil and Trial Practice in State and Federal Courts. Business, Commercial, Banking, Corporate, Construction, Real Property, Bankruptcy, Estate Planning, Trusts, Probate, Alternate Dispute Resolution.

See Professional Biographies, EUGENE, OREGON

Geiger, Gail Brehm '— '83 C.285 L.950
(adm. in WA; not adm. in OR) U.S. Trustee, Dept. of Jus., Fed. Govt.
Geller, Randolph '64 '92 C.1331 B.A. L.911 J.D.
Dir. of Policy & Leg. Affairs, Univ. of Oregon
Gerl, Dennis M., (BV) .... '54 '85 C.112 B.A. L.629 J.D. [Johnson C.L.&S.]
Gibbons, Edward Paul, (CVⓥ) .... '51 '83 C.1059 B.A. L.280 J.D. 2055 Sunrise Boulevard
Gibbs, J. David, (AVⓥ) '54 '79 C.692 B.A. L.245 J.D.
(adm. in GA; not adm. in OR) [▣ Harrang L.G.R.]
Gibson, Frank C., (BV) .... '50 '79 C.112 B.A. L.629 J.D. [Hutchinson,C.C.D.O.&S.]
Giers, Judith A., (BV) .... '60 '91 C.174 B.A. L.818 J.D. [▣ Hershner H.]
Gilbert, Gerald D. .... '35 '62 C&L.629 B.S., LL.B. 3175 Bailey Hill Rd.‡
Gildea, Larry O., (BV) .... '36 '62 C&L.950 LL.B. 324 E. 12th Ave., #2
Giustina, Ansel J., (AV) .... '43 '73 C&L.629 B.S.B.A. L.950 J.D. [▣ Gleaves S.P.&S.]

Gleaves Swearingen Potter & Scott LLP, (AV) BB
975 Oak Street, 8th Floor, 97401
Telephone: 541-686-8833 Fax: 541-345-2034
Email: info@orbuslaw.com URL: http://www.orbuslaw.com
Members of Firm: Frederick A. Batson; Jon V. Buerstatte; Joshua A. Clark; Thomas P. E. Herrmann; Kristin E. Kernutt; Stephen O. Lane; William H. Martin; Laura T.Z. Montgomery; Standlee G. Potter; Ian T. Richardson; Martha J. Rodman; Douglas R. Schultz; Malcolm H. Scott; James W. Spickerman; Kate A. Thompson. Associates: Sean M. Bannon; Tanya C. O'Neil; Jane M. Yates. Special Counsel to the Firm: Ansel J. Giustina.
General Civil Practice. Trial and Appellate Practice in all State and Federal Courts and Administrative Agencies, Antitrust, Banking, Bankruptcy, Business and Commercial, Construction, Computer, Corporations and Corporate Financing, Partnerships, Creditors Rights, Domestic Relations, Estate Planning, Government Contract, Labor and Employment, Media, Municipal, Probate, Trusts, Professional Negligence Defense, Real Property, Taxation, Timber, Trade Regulation and Natural Resource Law.
Representative Clients: Cascade Title Co.; Giustina Land & Timber Co.; Eugene Association of Realtors; Pacific Continental Bank; PWPipe; Seneca Sawmill Co.; Sherman Bros. Heavy Trucking; University of Oregon Foundation, Valley River Center.

See Professional Biographies, EUGENE, OREGON

Goldberg, Janice C., (BV) .... '44 '82 C&L.629 B.A., J.D. [▣ Hershner H.]
Goldstein, Michael B. .... '49 '76 C.188 A.B. L.629 J.D. 474 Willamette
Goodman, Jerry C., (CV) .... '42 '85 C&L.629 B.A., J.D. [J.C.Goodman]
Goodman, Jerry C., P.C., (CV) .... 399 E. 10th Ave., Ste. 201
Gough, A. Kenneth, (CV) .... '39 '70 C&L.629 B.A., J.D. 541 Willamette St., Ste. 304
Gough, Terrance P., (CV) .... '46 '74 C&L.336 B.A., J.D. 96 E. Broadway
Graebner, Paul M., (BV) .... '59 '85 C.763 B.A. L.629 J.D. Dep. Dist. Atty.
Green, Larry S. .... '57 '83 C.112 A.B. L.1067 J.D. 65WI Division Avenue, #300
Grier, Melinda W. .... '47 '88 C.813 B.A. L.629 J.D. Bd. of Higher Educ.
Griffith, Gwendolyn, (BV) .... '57 '81 C.699 B.A. L.813 J.D. [Speer,H.J.F.P.W.&G.]
Grubbe, Nelson H. .... '22 '48 C&L.629 B.S., LL.B. 455 Alexander Loop
Guarrasi, Robert J., (BV) .... '55 '81 C.178 B.A. L.629 J.D. 678 Country Club Rd.
Hagen, Edward I., Jr., (BV) .... '51 '76 Dep. Dist. Atty.
Haines, Cyndee C., (BV) .... '51 '91 C.768 B.A. L.629 J.D. 1445 Willamette St Ste 9
Halpern, John, Jr., (BV) .... '45 '75 C.112 A.B. L.629 J.D. [J.H.Halpern,Jr.]
Halpern, John H., Jr., (BV) .... 130 S. Park St.
Hammons, Terence J., (AV) .... '45 '69 C&L.629 B.S., J.D. [Hammons&M.]
Hammons & Mills, (AV) .... 115 W. 8th Ave., Ste. 280
Han, James W. .... '54 '83 C.112 A.B. L.1065 J.D. 888 W. Park St.
Hancock, Cary E. .... '61 '89 C&L.629 B.A., J.D. 2660 Spring Blvd.‡
Hansen, Marc .... '27 '59 C.629 B.S. L.950 J.D. 1601 Olive St.‡
Hansen, Robert C. '48 '74 C&L.629 B.A., J.D.
Staff Atty., Pub. Def. Servs. of Lane Co., Inc.
Harcleroad, F. Douglass, (AV) .... '48 '73 C.352 B.A. L.629 J.D. Dist. Atty.
Harder, Rick A., (BV) .... '57 '84 C&L.629 B.A., J.D. [Cram,H.W.&B.]
Harrang, James P., (AV) .... '23 '51 C&L.629 B.S., LL.B. [Harrang L.G.R.]

Harrang Long Gary Rudnick P.C., (AV) BB
360 East 10th Avenue, Suite 300, 97401 ⊙
Mailing Address: P.O. Box 11620, Eugene, OR 97440-3820
Telephone: 541-485-0220 Fax: 541-686-6564
URL: http://www.harrang.com
Jillian R. Bruce; William F. Gary; James P. Harrang; Emily Newton Jerome; Glenn Klein; Jerome Lidz; Stanton F. Long; Jeffery J. Matthews; Walter W. Miller; Christine Cusick Nesbit; Arden J. Olson; Sharon A. Rudnick; Jens Schmidt;—Karla H. Alderman; Wendy J. Baker; Kathryn P. Brotherton; Craig J. Capon; Nicole R. Commissiong; Andrea M. Davis; Kirk A. Moore; Ross M. Williamson; Justin Wirth. Of Counsel: J. David Gibbs (Not admitted in OR); Judith A. Recchio.
General Civil Trial and Appellate Practice in all State and Federal Courts, Governmental and Business Law, Corporate Law, Administrative Law, Financial Services, Securities Law, Creditors Rights, Partnership Law, Real Estate, State and Local Government Law, Environmental Law, Zoning, Planning and Land Use, Estate Planning and Probate, Insurance Law, Civil, Business, Complex and Tort Litigation, Alternative Dispute Resolution, Labor and Employment Law, Employee Benefits, Intellectual Property, Health Law, Nonprofit Law.
Representative Clients: Schering-Plough Corp.; Philip Morris USA Inc.; Providence Health Plan; PeaceHealth; Les Schwab Tire Centers, Inc.; Taco Time International; City of Eugene.
Portland, Oregon Office: 1001 S.W. 5th Avenue, Suite 1650. Telephone: 503-242-0000. Fax: 503-241-1458.
Salem, Oregon Office: 333 High Street, N.E., Suite 200. Telephone: 503-371-3330. Fax: 503-371-5336.

See Professional Biographies, EUGENE, OREGON

Harrison, Pamela A., (BV) .... '48 '82 C.604 B.A. L.629 J.D. 1158 High St., Ste. 202
Hartstrom, Frederick A., (CV) ..... '39 '66 C&L.629 B.S., LL.B. Chief Dep. Dist. Atty.
Hasselman, Erik V., (BV) .... '68 '94 C.629 B.A. L.950 J.D. Asst. Dist. Atty.
Hays, Charles J. '10 '40 C.966 Ph.B. L.436 LL.B.
(adm. in WI; not adm. in OR) 65 W. 30th Ave.‡
Heid, Edward P. ..... '44 '73 C.1051 B.A. L.629 J.D. Dir. Labor Rel., Eugene School Dist.
Heiken, Marilyn, (CV) .... '61 '92 C&L.629 B.A., J.D. [Johnson C.L.&S.]
Heilbrun, Emily .... '55 '81 C.66 A.B. L.178 J.D. 3440 Harris St.‡
Helfenstein, Allegra .... '52 '89 C.172 B.S. L.802 J.D. Legal Coun., Molecular Probes, Inc.
Helikson, Lloyd W., (BV) .... '55 '81 C.154 B.A. L.629 J.D. 2440 Suncrest Avenue
Hendershott, Herman P. .... '13 '36 C&L.629 LL.B. 2288 Potter St.‡
Hendershott, James A., (CV) .... '53 '79 C&L.629 B.S., J.D. 132 E. Broadway
Henderson, John L., (CV) .... '33 '76 C.629 B.S. L.1051 J.D. [▣ Bromley N.]
Hendriksen, Margie, (CV) .... '43 '75 C.494 B.A. L.596 J.D. Asst. Co. Coun.
Henner, Martin E. .... '40 '69 L.966 J.D. 2675 Baker Blvd.
Henry, Eveleen .... '48 '85 C.436 B.A. L.629 J.D. Dist. J.
Herrigel, A. Warren '26 '49 C&L.705 LL.B.
(adm. in NJ; not adm. in OR) 5320 Fox Hollow Road‡
Herrmann, Thomas P. E., (BV) .... '63 '88 C&L.629 B.S., J.D. [Gleaves S.P.&S.]
Hershner, James L., (AV) .... '29 '54 C&L.629 B.B.A., LL.B. 180 East 11th Avenue

Hershner Hunter, LLP, (AV) BB
180 East 11th Avenue, P.O. Box 1475, 97440 ⊙
Telephone: 541-686-8511 Fax: 541-344-2025
Email: info@hershnerhunter.com URL: http://www.hershnerhunter.com
Members of Firm: David N. Andrews; William D. Brewer; Nancy K. Cary; Patricia L. Chapman; Arthur J. Clark; Will Forsyth; Jeffrey D. Kirtner; Andrew G. Lewis; Sheryl S. McConnell; Everett R. Moreland; K. Patrick Neill; Robert S. Quinney; Craig A. Smith; Wm. Randolph Turnbow; Paul V. Vaughan. Of Counsel: Marlin D. Ard; P. Steve Cornacchia; Judith A. Giers; Janice C. Goldberg; Linda J. Kessel; Norman J. LeCompte, Jr.; Patrick W. Wade. Associates: Todd R. Johnston; Sylvia M. Van Dyke; Gabriela Sanchez-Amparan; Nathan S. Snow; Vicki L. Rees; Melissa F. Busley; Katherine C. Fisher.
Business, Banking, Corporate, Timber, Estate Planning, Probate Trust Administration, Taxation, Creditors' Rights, Bankruptcy, Construction, Real Property, Land Use, Employee Benefits, Health Care, Employment and Litigation.

(This Listing Continued)

Hershner Hunter, LLP (Continued)
Representative Clients: U.S. Bank National Association; Union Bank of California; Western Pioneer Title Co.; Cascade Title Co.; Delta Sand & Gravel Co.; John Hyland Construction, Inc.; Country Coach, Inc.
Florence, Oregon Office: 1441 7th Street. Telephone: 541-997-1997. Fax: 541-344-2025.
See Professional Biographies, EUGENE, OREGON

Hilderbrand, Sarah R. .... '73 '97 C.629 B.S. L.950 J.D. [Speer,H.J.F.P.W.&G.]
Hildreth, Richard G. .... '43 '69 C&L.477 B.S.E., J.D. Prof. of Law, Univ. of Ore.
Hill, David A., (BV) .... '48 '79 C&L.629 B.S., J.D. 1147 High Street
Hill, David K. .... '49 '74 C.668 B.A. L.629 J.D. 2753 Riverwalk Loop
Hill, Emily S. .... '79 '04 C&L.1375 B.A., J.D. [Doyle,G.N.M.&W.]
Hoag, Rush M., II, (BV) '47 '73
C.950 B.A. L.629 J.D. Atty., Pub. Def. Servs. of Lane Co.
Hoar, Sean B., (AV) .... '58 '87 C.413 B.A. L.629 J.D. Asst. U.S. Atty.
Hodges, Bryan T. .... '40 '65 C&L.629 B.A., LL.B. Cir. J.
Hoffman, James W., (BV) .... '46 '71 C.602 B.A. L.629 J.D. [J.W.Hoffman]
Hoffman, Lewis .... '17 '40 C&L.629 J.D. 975 Oak St.‡
Hoffman, James W., P.C., (BV) .... 975 Oak St., Ste. 600
Holland, Daniel M., (AV) .... '48 '73 C&L.502 A.B., J.D. [Loomis&H.]
Holland, Lauren S. .... '52 '78 C&L.629 B.A., J.D. Cir. Ct. J.
Hollis, Orlando John .... '04 '28 C&L.629 B.S., J.D. 975 Oak St.
Honsowetz, F. William, (P.C.), (BV) '44 '72 C.906 B.A. L.629 J.D.
[Gardner,H.P.B.&F.]
Hopkins, Stephen T. '50 '86 C.36 B.A. L.61 J.D.
(adm. in CA; not adm. in OR) P.O. Box 40638
Horn, John H., (BV) .... '27 '51 C&L.629 B.S., LL.B. 875 Country Club Rd.
Horton, William P. '43 '68 C&L.623 B.A., J.D.
Admin. Law J., U.S. Dept. of Health & Human Servs.
Hoyt, Thomas H., (AV) .... '40 '66 C.629 B.S. L.950 J.D. [Speer,H.J.F.P.W.&G.]
Hudson, John A., (BV) .... '46 '73 C&L.37 B.A., J.D. 66 Club Rd.
Hughes, Patrick T., (CV) .... '65 '98 C&L.629 B.S., J.D. 576 Olive Street
Hugi, Frederick A. .... '45 '73 C.705 B.S. L.629 J.D. Asst. Dist. Atty.
Hunt, Greg Allen, (BV) .... '52 '78 C&L.629 B.S., J.D. 2296 Oakmont Way
Hunt, James L., (AV) .... '45 '77 C.1047 B.A. L.950 J.D. Asst. Dist. Atty.
Hunter, Garland D., (AV) .... '32 '61 C&L.629 B.A., J.D. 180 E. 11th Ave.‡
Hutchinson, Stephen A., (BV) '40 '67 C.628 B.S. L.629 J.D.
[Hutchinson,C.C.D.O.&S.]

Hutchinson, Cox, Coons, DuPriest, Orr & Sherlock, P.C., (BV)
200 Forum Building, 777 High Street, 97401-2782
Telephone: 541-686-9160 Fax: 541-343-8693
Email: info@eugene-law.com URL: http://www.eugene-law.com
James K. Coons; John G. Cox; Douglas M. DuPriest; Frank C. Gibson; Stephen A. Hutchinson; Thomas Michael Orr; William H. Sherlock;—E. Bradley Litchfield; Zack P. Mittge; Patrick L. Stevens.
General Practice in all Courts. Business Law, Contracts, Corporate Law, Environmental Law, Land Use, Real Estate, International Business, Civil Litigation, Personal Injury, Probate, Estate Planning, Copyright and Trademark, Family Law, Arbitration and Mediation, Tax Law, Creditors Rights.
A list of Representative Clients is available upon request.
See Professional Biographies, EUGENE, OREGON

Hyde-Patton, Kay, Law Office of '68 '03
C.1332 B.A. L.629 J.D. 767 Willamette St., Ste. 203
Hynes, Kathleen M. .... '51 '86 C.494 B.S. L.629 J.D. 630 Spencer Ct.
Ierulli, Frank M., (BV) .... '24 '53 C.629 B.S. L.596 LL.B. 1441 E. 22nd Ave.
Ing, Michelle L.H. .... '76 '01 C.312 B.A. L.950 J.D. Co. Cir. Ct.
Ingram, Claud A., Jr. .... '33 '61 C&L.629 B.S., LL.B. P.O. Box 2937
Jacobs, David A., (BV) .... '63 '94 C&L.629 B.A., J.D. [Luvaas C.]
Jagger, James C. .... '45 '70 C.594 B.A. L.950 J.D. [J.C.Jagger]
Jagger, James C., P.C. .... 540 Oak St.
Jaqua, John E., (AV) .... '20 '50 C.668 B.A. L.629 LL.B. [Jaqua&W.] ‡

Jaqua & Wheatley, LLC, (AV)
825 East Park, 97401-2909
Telephone: 541-686-8485 Fax: 541-343-0701
Email: bwheatley@jaquawheatly.com URL: http://www.jaquawheatly.com
John E. Jaqua (Inactive); William G. Wheatley;—Holli Froemming; Elizabeth Watson; Patrick A. Lynd.
General Practice in all Courts. Insurance Defense, Casualty and Surety Insurance Law. Litigation, Corporate Law, Partnerships, Business Litigation, Products Liability, Construction Law, Environmental Law, Professional Malpractice, Premises Liability, Estate Planning, Employment Law.
Representative Insurance Clients: Fireman's Fund Insurance Cos.; Industrial Indemnity Co.; Kemper Insurance Co.; Safeco Insurance Cos.; State Farm Insurance Cos.; Zurich-American Insurance Co.; United States Fidelity & Guaranty Co.
Representative Corporate Clients: Ford Motor Corp.; General Motors Corp.; Michelin Tire Corp. Portland, Oregon
See Professional Biographies, EUGENE, OREGON

Jensen, Christine, (CV) .... '49 '85 C.628 B.S. L.629 J.D. [Malagon,M.&J.]
Jensen, David L., (AV) .... '44 '69 C.911 B.A. L.629 J.D. [Jensen,E.&S.]
Jensen, Elmore & Stupasky, P.C., (AV) .... 199 E. 5th Ave., Ste. 25
Jerome, Emily Newton, (BV) .... '70 '95 C.927 B.A. L.629 J.D. [Harrang L.G.R.]
Johns, Varner Jay, III, (AV) .... '53 '79 C.1163 B.A. L.950 J.D. [Luvaas C.]
Johnson, Arthur C., (AV) .... '28 '53 C.629 B.S. L.309 LL.B. [Johnson C.L.&S.]
Johnson, Derek C., (BV) .... '59 '85 C.951 B.A. L.1068 J.D. [Johnson C.L.&S.]
Johnson, Donald E., (BV) .... '59 '86 C&L.629 B.A., J.D. [Kurtz,F.&J.]
Johnson, Drew L., (BV) .... '50 '75 C&L.629 B.S., J.D. [D.L.Johnson]
Johnson, Matthew S., (CV) .... '— '96 C&L.629 B.A., J.D. P.O. Box 23033

Johnson Clifton Larson & Schaller, P.C., (AV)
10th Floor, Citizens Building, 975 Oak Street, 97401-3124
Telephone: 541-484-2434 Fax: 541-484-0882
Email: jclc@jclc.com URL: http://www.jclc.com
Arthur C. Johnson; Jacob K. Clifton, Jr.; Richard L. Larson; Douglas G. Schaller; Derek C. Johnson; Dennis M. Gerl; Scott C. Lucas; Marilyn Heiken; Michele C. Smith.
Civil Litigation Practice in Personal Injury, Product Liability, Environmental Law, Employment Law, Civil Rights, Medical Malpractice, Taxation, Appellate, Real Estate, Trusts and Estates, Wills and Probate, Business Law.
See Professional Biographies, EUGENE, OREGON

Johnson, Drew L., PC, (BV) .... 1700 Valley River Dr.
Johnston, J. Christopher .... '75 '00 C.300 B.A. L.339 J.D. 2852 Willamette
Johnston, Todd R. .... '74 '99 C.170 B.A. L.629 J.D. [Hershner H.]
Jones, J. Kenneth, (BV) .... '47 '72 C.906 B.A. L.629 J.D. [Speer,H.J.F.P.W.&G.]
Judy, Lee J. .... '— '91 C.670 B.S.N. L.629 J.D. 1158 High St.
Kamitsuka, P. Rebecca, (CV) .... '57 '93 C.502 B.A. L.629 J.D. [Gaydos,C.&B.]
Kardell, Marc, (CV) .... '56 '82 C.1071 B.S. L.1049 J.D. Off. of Legal Coun.
Kaufman, Dean Stewart, (BV) .... '45 '69 C.112 B.A. L.629 J.D. [Kaufman&S.]
Kaufman & Stewart, (BV) .... 270 Oakway Ctr.
Kearney, Michael P., (BV) .... '45 '74 C.549 B.S. L.767 J.D. [M.P.Kearney]
Kearney, Michael P., P.C., (BV) .... 260 Country Club Rd.
Kelly, George W. .... '— '82 C.604 B.A. L.846 J.D. [G.W.Kelly]
Kelly, George W., P.C. .... 303 W. 10th Ave.
Kent, William N., (CV) .... '51 '78 C.628 B.S.Pol. Sc. L.629 J.D. [W.N.Kent]
Kent, William N., PC, (CV) .... 91 Madison St.
Kernutt, Kristin E. .... '65 '99 C.678 B.A. L.629 J.D. [Gleaves S.P.&S.]
Kessel, Linda J., (BV) .... '51 '90 C&L.629 B.S., J.D. [Hershner H.]
Kilby, Patrick M. .... '48 '72 C.1071 B.S. L.629 J.D. [Kilby R.E.]
Kilby Real Estate Services .... P.O. Box 51059
Kilcullen, John F., (BV) .... '46 '83 C&L.629 B.S., J.D. [Brown,R.L.M.&K.]
Kim, John H., (BV) .... '63 '90 C.311 B.A. L.629 J.D. 1200 Executive Pkwy., Ste. 320
King, Donald Claude .... '66 '96 C&L.629 B.A., J.D. 1805 Garden Ave., #6★
Kirkpatrick, Laird C. .... '43 '68 C.309 A.B. L.629 J.D. Prof. of Law, Univ. of Oregon
Kirtner, Jeffrey D. .... '59 '96 C.145 B.A. L.846 J.D. [Hershner H.]
Klein, Glenn, (BV) .... '56 '83 C.112 B.A. L.629 J.D. [Harrang L.G.R.]
Klinect, Abigail A. .... '76 '02 C.172 B.A. L.629 J.D. [Watkinson L.R.B.&B.]
Kloos, Bill, (BV) .... '47 '80 C&L.312 M.A., J.D. [B.Kloos]
Kloos, Bill, Law Office of, PC, (BV) .... 576 Olive St Ste 300
Kneeland, Ann B. .... '66 '99 C.228 B.A. L.276 J.D. Lane Co. Legal Aid Serv., Inc.
Knudsen, K. Sam, (CV) .... '43 '85 C&L.629 B.A., J.D. [S.Knudsen]
Knudsen, Sam, (CV) .... 875 Country Club Rd.
Kocher, James K. .... '47 '72 C&L.378 B.A., J.D. 376 E. 11th Ave.
Kolego, John J., (BV) .... '50 '85 C&L.629 B.A., J.D. [J.J.Kolego]
Kolego, John J., P.C., (BV) .... 804 Pearl St.
Kouba, Patrick J., (BV) .... '58 '83 C.813 B.A. L.1066 J.D. [P.J.Kouba]

Kouba, Patrick J., A Professional Corporation, (BV)
158 East 14th Avenue, 97401
Telephone: 541-687-0409 Fax: 541-687-0293
URL: http://www.sharkesq.com
Patrick J. Kouba.
Civil Litigation, including Insurance Defense and Plaintiff's Personal Injury, Contracts, Commercial Litigation, Small Business Formation, and Estate Planning.
See Professional Biographies, EUGENE, OREGON

Kunath, Dwayne '41 '78 C.766 B.A. L.765 J.D.
(adm. in CA; not adm. in OR) 2315 Bailey Hill Rd.‡
Kurtz, Louis L., (AV) .... '47 '74 C.686 B.S.B.A. L.190 J.D. [Kurtz,F.&J.]

Kurtz, Ford & Johnson, LLP, (AV)
400 East 2nd Avenue, Suite 101, 97401
Telephone: 541-484-1273 Fax: 541-683-1815
Louis L. Kurtz; Robert A. Ford; Donald E. Johnson. Associate: R. Scott Weiland.
Civil Litigation, Insurance Law, Insurance Defense, Legal Malpractice Defense, Product Liability Defense, Construction Law, Domestic Relations, Real Estate Law.
See Professional Biographies, EUGENE, OREGON

Laidlaw, Trina Eubank '54 '84
C&L.629 B.A., J.D. Asst. Co. Coun., Lame Co. Off., Legal Coun.
Laing, Wendy L. .... '66 '95 C.145 A.B. L.629 J.D. [Luvaas C.]
Laird, Donald R., (AV) .... '47 '75 C.628 B.S. L.629 J.D. [Watkinson L.R.B.&B.]
Land, Bryon L. .... '66 '94 C&L.950 B.S., J.D. [Arnold G.S.P.R.&P.]
Lane, Robert D., (BV) .... '61 '86 C.1071 B.S. L.629 J.D. Asst. Dist. Atty.
Lane, Stephen O., (AV) .... '47 '75 C.939 B.A. L.950 J.D. [Gleaves S.P.&S.]
Larson, Darryl L. .... '45 '71 C.793 B.A. L.629 J.D. Cir. J.
Larson, Richard L., (AV) .... '51 '77 C.813 B.A. L.629 J.D. [Johnson C.L.&S.]
Larson, Robert J., (CV) .... '43 '71 C.30 B.A. L.629 J.D. 399 E. 10th Ave.
Larsson, John A. .... '24 '52 C&L.629 B.S., LL.B. 811 Willamette St.
Lashway, J. Lee, (BV) .... '51 '79 C.813 B.A. L.1068 J.D. 295 West Broadway
Lawlor, E. Scott, (BV) .... '40 '65 C.735 L.950 J.D. [E.S.Lawlor]
Lawlor, E. Scott, P.C., (BV) .... 895 Country Club Rd.
LeCompte, Norman J., Jr., (AV) .... '50 '76 C.911 B.A. L.629 J.D. [Hershner H.]
Lee, Darren W. .... '67 '93 C.1077 B.A. L.629 J.D. Liberty Northwest Ins. Co.
Leistner, Mary Porter .... '25 '80 767 Willamette‡
Leonard, Kip W. .... '48 '75 C.629 B.S. L.950 J.D. Cir. J.
Lerner, Judith .... '48 '74 C.102 B.A. L.1065 J.D. 2510 Kincaid St.
Leslie, Lann D., (BV) .... '55 '82 C&L.629 B.S., J.D. [Luvaas C.]
Levin, Richard W. '46 '74 C.388 B.A. L.424 J.D.
(adm. in IL; not adm. in OR) P.O. Box 5491‡
Lewis, Andrew G., (BV) .... '63 '90 C.112 B.S. L.629 J.D. [Hershner H.]
Lewis, Michael A. .... '47 '76 C.477 B.G.S. L.94 J.D. 96 E. Broadway, Ste. 3
Lidz, Jerome, (BV) .... '47 '77 C.976 B.A. L.629 J.D. [Harrang L.G.R.]
Liepe, Winfrid K. F. .... '26 '52 C.977 B.A. L.145 J.D. Sr. Dist. J.
Lindberg, Roberta J. .... '47 '74 C.914 B.A. L.564 J.D. 376 E. 11th St.
Litchfield, E. Bradley, (BV) '65 '93 C.101 B.A. L.05 LL.B.
[Hutchinson,C.C.D.O.&S.]
Livesley, George P. .... '42 '73 C.629 B.S. L.950 J.D. Admin. Law J., Wkrs. Comp. Bd.
Long, Michael H., (AV) .... '51 '76 C&L.629 B.S., J.D. [Brown,R.L.M.&K.]
Long, Stanton F., (AV) .... '41 '67 C.629 B.S. L.950 J.D. [Harrang L.G.R.]
Longtin, Matthew D., (BV) .... '65 '98 C.637 B.A. L.629 J.D. [Beckley&L.]
Loomis, Donald A., (BV) .... '41 '69 C.628 B.S. L.950 J.D. [Loomis&H.]

Loomis & Holland, (AV)
801 East Park Street, 97401-2980
Telephone: 541-344-8333 Fax: 541-344-8075
Members of Firm: Daniel M. Holland; Donald A. Loomis; Ronald B. Terzenbach.
Trial practice in State and Federal Courts, Medical Malpractice, Professional Liability, Insurance, Products Liability, Pharmaceutical and Toxic Tort Litigation, Business Litigation, Real Property, Family, Probate Law, Unsafe Products, Legal Malpractice, Personal Injury, Wrongful Death.
See Professional Biographies, EUGENE, OREGON

Loschiavo, Chris. '73 '98 C&L.260 B.A., J.D.
(adm. in FL; not adm. in OR) Univ. of Ore.

Lowry, Robert D., Law Offices of, (AV) '49 '80 C&L.629 B.A., J.D.
Citizens Building, 975 Oak Street, Suite 790, P.O. Box 12010, 97440
Telephone: 541-687-7592 Cellular: 541-954-4451 Fax: 541-687-0805
Email: rdlowry@lowry-law.com
Insurance Defense, Products Liability Defense, Medical Malpractice, Hospital Malpractice, Business Litigation, Construction Law and Civil Litigation.
See Professional Biographies, EUGENE, OREGON

Loya, Mervyn H. .... '40 '68 C.504 B.A. L.339 J.D. Univ. of Ore. Sch. of Law
Lucas, Scott C., (BV) .... '65 '97 C.112 B.A. L.629 J.D. [Johnson C.L.&S.]
Lundeen, Ernest W. .... '21 '50 C.494 B.A. L.309 LL.B. 132 E. Broadway
Lusby, Gregory T., (BV) .... '67 '93 C.911 B.A. L.950 J.D. [Arnold G.S.P.R.&P.]
Luvaas, John L., (AV) .... '18 '42 C&L.629 B.A., LL.B. [Luvaas C.] ‡

Luvaas Cobb, P.C., (AV)
300 Forum Building, 777 High Street, P.O. Box 10747, 97401
Telephone: 541-484-9292 Fax: 541-343-1206
URL: http://www.luvaascobb.com
John L. Luvaas (Retired); Robert H. Fraser (Retired); Ralph F. Cobb; Joe B. Richards; J. Dominic Monahan; Varner Jay Johns, III; Joel S. DeVore; David A. Jacobs; Lann D. Leslie; George A. Burgott;—Wendy L. Laing; Frank E. Bocci, Jr.; Greg M. Womer. Of Counsel: Richard W. Butler.
General Civil Trial and Appellate Practice in all State and Federal Courts and Administrative Agency. Taxation, Business, Domestic Relations, Corporate, Commercial, Computer, Construction, Environ

(This Listing Continued)

Luvaas Cobb, P.C. (Continued)

mental, Media, Probate, Insurance, Estate Planning, Real Estate and Municipal Law. Legal and Medical Malpractice Defense. Intellectual Property, Copyright and Trademark.
Representative Clients: Farmers Insurance Group; Professional Liability Fund of the Oregon State Bar; Radio-One Broadcast Group; Sunbelt Broadcasting Co.; Eagle Broadcasting Co.
Local Counsel for: Bi-Mart Corp.; CIT Financial Services Group.
General Counsel for: Romania Enterprises, Inc.; Combined Communications, Inc.
Public Corporation Client: School District Eugene 4J.
See Professional Biographies, EUGENE, OREGON

Lynd, Patrick A., (CV) .... '61 '98 C&L.629 B.A., J.D. [🄰 Jaqua&W.]
Madden, Norine G. '48 '74 C.1110 B.A. L.1065 J.D.
(adm. in CA; not adm. in OR) 1574 Coburg Rd.‡
Malagon, Evohl F., (BV) .... '38 '66 C&L.629 B.A., LL.B. [Malagon,M.&J.]
Malagon, Moore & Jensen, (BV) .... 678 Country Club Road
Manders, Robert P., (BV) .... '54 '89 C.705 B.A. L.629 J.D. 259 E. 5th Ave.
Manela, Julia I. .... '72 '02 C&L.629 B.A., J.D. [🄰 Muhlheim B.]
Manning, Mark A. .... '69 '00 C.172 B.A. L.629 J.D. 474 Willamette St.
Marcus, Gary P. .... '50 '81 C.1331 B.A. L.629 J.D. Pres., Frontier Technology, Inc.
Martin, William H., (AV) .... '48 '74 C.678 B.S. L.629 J.D. [Gleaves S.P.&S.]
Matthews, Jeffery J. .... '54 '89 C.1071 B.S. L.986 J.D. [Harrang L.G.R.]
Matthews, Karl B., (BV) .... '49 '95 C&L.629 B.S., J.D. Staff Atty., Lane Co. Dist. Off.
Mattson, Floyd C. .... '— '94 C.932 B.S. L.629 J.D. [B.Mattson&Assoc.]
Mattson, Buz, & Associates, P.C. .... 399 E. 10th Avenue
Maybee, Lisa A., (BV) .... '61 '87 C.911 B.A. L.629 J.D. 423 Lincoln St.
McAlpin, Megan .... '78 '03 C.1181 B.S. L.950 J.D. [🄰 Arnold G.S.P.R.&P.]
McCleery, P. Scott, (BV) .... '52 '85 C.112 B.A. L.629 J.D. [Doyle,G.N.M.&W.]
McConnell, Sheryl S., (BV) .... '60 '95 C.628 B.S. L.112 J.D. [Hershner H.] ⊙
McConville, Philip R., (AV) .... '52 '78 C&L.629 B.A., J.D. [Brown,R.L.M.&K.]
McCoy, Bert, Jr., (CV) .... '14 '39 C&L.793 LL.B. [E.S.Lawlor]
McCrea, P.C., (AV) .... 1147 High St.
McCrea, Robert J., (AV) .... '32 '56 C&L.950 A.B., LL.B. [McCrea]
McCrea, Shaun S., (BV) .... '56 '83 C&L.629 B.A., J.D. [McCrea]
McGavic, Derrick E., (BV) .... '38 '63 C.31 L.352 LL.B. 941 W. Third Avenue
McKeown, Martin J., (BV) .... '43 '75 C.285 A.B. L.950 J.D. [M.J.McKeown]
McKeown, Martin J., P.C., (BV) .... 909 Lawrence St.
McMahon, Fredk. E., Jr. '22 '51 C&L.477 A.B., LL.B.
Chm. of the Bd., Cascade Title Co.
McMahon, Thomas M. .... '52 '77 C.629 B.S. L.596 J.D. Pres., Cascade Title Co.
McWilliams, Claudette Mirassou '53 '77
C&L.629 B.A., J.D. Admin. Law J., State Wkrs. Comp. Bd.
Meisner, William S. .... '47 '84 C.502 A.B. L.629 J.D. 66 N. Adams
Melevin, Douglas L., (CV) .... '33 '65 C&L.629 B.S., LL.B. 750 Lawrence
Merten, Maurice K. .... '45 '69 C&L.629 B.S., J.D. Cir. J.
Miko, Jonathan R. .... '71 '98 C.705 B.A. L.564 J.D. [🄲 Gaydos,C.&B.]
Miller, David K., (AV) .... '55 '82 C&L.629 B.S., J.D. [Miller&W.]
Miller, Gretchen L. .... '50 '76 C.378 B.A. L.629 J.D. 2510 Oakmont Way
Miller, Robert A., (BV) .... '48 '73 C&L.629 B.S., J.D. [Miller&W.]
Miller, Walter W., (BV) .... '54 '82 C.424 B.B.A. L.209 J.D. [Harrang L.G.R.]
Miller & Wagner, (AV) .... 400 Country Club Road Suite 350
Mills, David B., (AV) .... '49 '77 C&L.629 B.S., J.D. [Hammons&M.]
Minger, Douglas E., (CV) .... '49 '93 C.1073 B.A. L.629 J.D. 541 Willamette St., Ste. 110
Mitchell, Douglas S., (AV) '47 '83 C.267 B.A. L.629 J.D.
Lane Cnty. DA Fam. Law Div.
Mitchell-Lizars, Jane P. '35 '73 C.188 B.A. L.146 J.D.
(adm. in IL; not adm. in OR) 329 W. 17th Ave.‡
Mittge, Zack P. .... '76 '04 C.911 B.A. L.629 J.D. [🄰 Hutchinson,C.C.D.O.&S.]
Molly, Kenneth R. .... '38 '81 C.627 B.G.S. L.629 J.D. 2105 Hubbard Ln.
Monahan, J. Dominic .... '38 '68 C.670 B.A. L.276 J.D. [Luvaas C.]
Monks, Edward T., (BV) .... '48 '77 C.178 B.A. L.776 J.D. [Morrow,M.&S.]
Montgomery, David Robert, (BV) .... '61 '93 C&L.629 B.S., J.D. Asst. Dist. Atty.
Montgomery, Laura T.Z., (BV) .... '66 '93 C&L.629 B.A., J.D. [Gleaves S.P.&S.]
Moon, David C. .... '53 '79 C.170 B.A. L.336 J.D. [Moon]
Moon Firm .... P.O. Box 82
Mooney, Josephine H., (BV) .... '62 '88 C.959 B.A. L.629 J.D. [🄲 Calkins&C.]
Moore, Bruce C., (BV) .... '55 '80 C&L.629 B.S., J.D. 96 E. Bway., Suite 7
Moore, Christopher D., (BV) .... '56 '82 C.145 A.B. L.629 J.D. [Malagon,M.&J.]
Moore, Kirk A. .... '— '04 C.950 B.S. L.629 J.D. [🄰 Harrang L.G.R.]
Moore, Sidney E., Jr. .... '70 '99 C&L.629 B.S., J.D. Off. of Affirmative Action and EO
Moreland, Everett R., (AV) .... '46 '76 C.1056 B.S. L.950 J.D. [Hershner H.]
Mori, Mary Jane .... '54 '81 C.174 B.A. L.629 J.D. 399 E. 10th Street
Morrow, Monks & Sharp, P.C., (BV) .... 1342 High St.
Morse, F. Davis '72 '98 C.1090 B.A. L.893 J.D.
(adm. in TN; not adm. in OR) Consumer Justice Group
Mortimore, P. Kent, (BV) .... '57 '82 C&L.629 B.A., J.D. Dep. Dist. Atty.
Moule, David M., (CV) .... '50 '76 C&L.629 B.A., J.D. [Moule&F.]
Moule & Frank, (BV) .... 259 E. Fifth Ave.
Muhlheim, Wilson C., (AV) .... '44 '68 C.999 B.S. L.629 J.D. [Muhlheim B.]

Muhlheim Boyd, (AV)
A Partnership of Professional Corporations
88 East Broadway, 97401
Telephone: 541-868-8005 Fax: 541-868-8004
Email: linen@mbclawoffice.com URL: http://www.mbclawoffice.com
Keith Y. Boyd; Wilson C. Muhlheim. Associates: Julia I. Manela; Loren S. Scott. Of Counsel: Todd H. Tinker.
Creditor/Debtor Representation; Commercial Litigation; Workouts and Bankruptcy Reorganizations; Bankruptcy Litigation; Creditors' Rights; Foreclosure; Commercial Law; Business Litigation; Business Transactions; Litigation; Estate and Probate.
See Professional Biographies, EUGENE, OREGON

Mullen, Robert G. '23 '49 C&L.911 B.S., LL.B.
(adm. in WA; not adm. in OR) 31008 Lanes Turn Rd.‡
Mumford, William P. .... '20 '49 C&L.339 B.S., LL.B. 1960 Alder St.‡
Murphy, Alexander B. '54 '81 C.976 B.A. L.178 J.D.
(adm. in IL; not adm. in OR) Univ. of Ore., Dept. of Geography
Nagler, Robert H., (CV) .... '50 '78 C&L.629 B.A., J.D. 1143 Oak St.
Naslund, Robert K., (BV) .. '39 '66 C&L.629 B.S., LL.B. 1200 Executive Pkwy., Ste. 330
Neal, Dan E., (AV) .... '52 '77 C&L.629 B.S., J.D. [Neal&E.]
Neal & Eng, (AV) .... 1361 Pearl St.
Neill, K. Patrick, (AV) .... '46 '71 C.318 B.A. L.800 J.D. [Hershner H.]
Nelson, Douglas A., (BV) .... '49 '78 C.629 B.S. L.990 J.D. [Doyle,G.N.M.&W.]
Nesbit, Christine Cusick, (BV) .... '66 '95 C.1169 B.A. L.1067 J.D. [Harrang L.G.R.]
Newton, Bruce W., (CV) .... '53 '80 C&L.629 B.S., J.D. [Bromley N.]
Nobel, Barry, (BV) .... '— '80 C.674 B.A. L.629 J.D. 2570 Jackson St.

Nollkamper, William H., III Law Offices of '44 '71
C.218 B.A. L.900 J.D. 372 W. 12th Ave.
Noteboom, Aaron J. .... '73 '03 C.628 B.A. L.629 J.D. [🄰 Arnold G.S.P.R.&P.]
Novkov, Julie L. '66 '92 C.309 A.B. L.569 J.D.
(adm. in NY; not adm. in OR) Asst. Prof., Univ. of Oregon, Dept. of Political Sci.
O'Connor, Robert J., (CV) .... '37 '73 C.1097 B.A. L.800 J.D. 440 Charnelton St., Ste 5
Odell, Marilyn K., (CV) .... '53 '81 C&L.629 B.A., J.D. 750 W. Broadway St.
Olson, Arden J., (AV) .... '52 '78 C.1058 B.A. L.911 J.D. [Harrang L.G.R.]
O'Neil, Tanya C. .... '75 '04 C.169 B.A. L.950 J.D. [🄰 Gleaves S.P.&S.]
O'Reilly, Edward V. .... '18 '52 C&L.629 B.S., LL.B. 3260 Brycelen Dr.‡
Orr, Thomas Michael, (BV) .... '55 '88 C&L.16 B.A., J.D. [Hutchinson,C.C.D.O.&S.]
Oswald, Mark G. .... '57 '82 C.659 B.A. L.629 J.D. 87275 Windward Pl.★
Ousey, Roger William, (BV) .... '61 '86 C.112 B.A. L.629 J.D. [Bischoff,S.&O.]
Palmer, Barbara M., (BV) .... '56 '96 C.1056 B.A. L.629 J.D. [B.M.Palmer]
Palmer, James A. .... '49 '75 C.629 B.A. L.285 J.D. 96 E. Broadway
Palmer, R. Scott, (BV) .... '51 '76 C.174 B.A. L.629 J.D. [Watkinson L.R.B.&B.]
Palmer, Barbara M., P.C., (BV) .... 310 East 11th Avenue
Papagni, Frank R., Jr. .... '50 '76 C&L.629 B.S., J.D. Asst. Dist. Atty.
Paris, Margaret L. '55 '85 C&L.597 B.A., J.D.
(adm. in IL; not adm. in OR) Asst. Prof., Univ. of Ore. Sch. of Law
Parks, Andrew P. .... '74 '02 C.678 B.A. L.629 J.D. [🄰 Arnold G.S.P.R.&P.]

Parrish, Laura A., (AV) '51 '76 C&L.629 B.S., J.D. 🄱🄱
975 Oak Street, Suite 670, 97401
Telephone: 541-485-6162 Fax: 541-686-0114
URL: http://www.parrishor.com
Family Law, Divorce, Spousal Support, Child Support, Child Custody, Domestic Relations, Mediation, Collaborative Law, Negotiation and Settlement, Arbitration, Wills.
See Professional Biographies, EUGENE, OREGON

Parrott, John R. .... '46 '76 C.388 B.A. L.352 J.D. P.O. Box 651
Paulus, Sandra K. .... '47 '81 C.352 B.A. L.629 J.D. Admin. Law J., State Employ. Div.
Pearson, James A., (BV) .... '31 '57 C.629 B.S. L.276 J.D. 2902 Metolius Dr.
Pease, Susan R. .... '— '78 C&L.629 B.S., J.D. 1158 High Street, Ste. 202
Percell, Dennis W., (AV) .... '50 '75 C.1188 B.A. L.950 J.D. [Arnold G.S.P.R.&P.]
Perrin, Marc D., (BV) .... '57 '82 C&L.629 B.A., J.D. [Perrin,M.D.]
Perrin, Mark W., (AV) .... '41 '66 C&L.846 B.A., J.D. [Perrin&T.]
Perrin, Marc D., P.C., (BV) .... 777 High St.
Perrin & Thayer LLP, (AV) .... 975 Oak Street
Perry, E. Jay, (BV) .... '47 '73 C&L.629 B.A., J.D. 2201 Birchwood Ave.
Peters, Robert N., (BV) .... '30 '80 C.1051 B.A. L.629 J.D. Pub. Def. Serv. of Lane Co.

Peterson Law Offices, PC
(See Portland)

Phelps, Mark M. .... '50 '75 C&L.629 B.S., J.D. Univ of Ore. School of Mgmt.
Phillips, David J., (BV) .... '52 '76 C.112 B.A. L.629 J.D. Pub. Def.
Phillips, Michael, (AV) .... '43 '69 C&L.629 B.S.E., J.D. 1158 High Street, Suite 102
Philpott, Steven L., (BV) .... '51 '78 C&L.629 B.A., J.D. Gen. Coun., Centennial Bancorp
Platt, Arlene A., (BV) .... '53 '78 C.629 B.S. L.1051 J.D. 777 High St., Ste. 260
Pocock, Brian L., (BV) .... '42 '66 C&L.058 B.A., LL.B. 132 E. Broadway
Poppe, Russell D., (BV) .... '53 '80 C.378 B.A. L.629 J.D. [Speer,H.J.F.P.W.&G.]
Porter, Chas. O. .... '19 '48 C&L.309 A.B., LL.B. 132 E. Bway.
Potter, Jeffrey E., (P.C.), (AV) .... '46 '79 C.918 B.A. L.629 J.D. [Gardner,H.P.B.&F.]
Potter, Richard, Law Office of '47 '98
C.427 B.A. L.128 J.D. 115 West Eighth Avenue, Suite 380
Potter, Standlee G., (AV) .... '40 '65 C&L.629 B.S., LL.B. [Gleaves S.P.&S.]
Potter, William R., (AV) .... '53 '78 C.628 B.S. L.629 J.D. [Arnold G.S.P.R.&P.]
Powers, Melissa Ann '70 '02 C.1375 B.A. L.596 J.D.
Western Enviromental Law Center
Pries, John Putnam .... '50 '91 C.20 A.B. L.629 J.D. [J.P.Pries]
Pries, John P., LLC .... 862 Olive St.
Prozanski, Floyd F., Jr., (BV) .... '54 '83 C.839 B.S. L.796 J.D. P.O. Box 11511
Pugh, D. Michael, (AV) .... '49 '85 C.347 B.A. L.629 J.D. Dep. Dist. Atty.
Quinn, Richard K., (BV) .... '29 '55 C&L.911 B.A., J.D. [R.K.Quinn]
Quinn, Richard K., P.C., (BV) .... P.O. Box 10282
Quinney, Robert S., (BV) .... '43 '71 C.101 B.S. L.629 J.D. [Hershner H.]
Radcliffe, Albert E. .... '47 '72 C&L.629 B.A., J.D. U.S. Bkrptcy. J.
Radostitz, Rita J., (BV) .... '59 '85 C.629 B.A. L.884 J.D. Fed. Pub. Def.
Rasmussen, Karsten H., (AV) '57 '83
C&L.629 B.A., J.D. 125 E. 8th Ave., Lane County Courthouse
Rauch, Nick E., (BV) .... '47 '72 C&L.629 B.S., J.D. 875 Country Club Rd.
Ravella, Peter A., II .... '59 '86 C.839 B.S. L.596 J.D. Editor, Oregon Insider
Rawlins, Benjamin E. .... '50 '76 C.369 B.A. L.276 J.D. 1431 Johnson Ln
Ray, John C., (AV) .... '44 '68 C&L.16 B.A., J.D. U.S. Atty. Off.
Recchio, Judith A. .... '64 '92 C.112 B.A. L.770 J.D. [🄲 Harrang L.G.R.]
Rees, Vicki L. .... '66 '04 C.836 M.S. L.629 J.D. [🄰 Hershner H.]
Reid, Robert W., (CV) .... '53 '81 C.475 B.A. L.629 J.D. Pub. Def.
Richards, Joe B., (AV) .... '29 '54 C.629 B.A. L.950 LL.B. [Luvaas C.]
Richardson, Ian T. .... '65 '97 C.112 B.A. L.596 J.D. [Gleaves S.P.&S.]
Richmond, Robert D. .... '40 '64 C&L.629 B.A., LL.B. Pres., Baseball Opportunities, Inc.
Ridder, Daniel H., Jr. .... '49 '80 C.768 B.A. L.770 J.D. P.O. Box 5770
Riddle, Dale A., (BV) '56 '81 C&L.629 B.A., J.D.
V.P. Legal Affs., Seneca Sawmill Co.
Robert, William J. .... '18 '41 C&L.629 B.A., LL.B. 2366 McMillan St.‡
Roberts, Jack R., (BV) .... '52 '78 C&L.629 B.S., J.D. Co. Comr.
Roberts, Martha L. .... '46 '89 C&L.629 B.S., J.D. [🄰 Shepard]
Roberts, Rohn M., (AV) .... '54 '79 C&L.629 B.S., J.D. [Arnold G.S.P.R.&P.]
Rodman, Keith, (BV) .... '21 '49 C&L.629 LL.B. 132 E. Broadway
Rodman, Martha J., (BV) .... '51 '77 C&L.629 B.A., J.D. [Gleaves S.P.&S.]
Roloff, Larry R. .... '46 '72 C&L.629 B.S., J.D. 132 E. Broadway
Romm, Jacquelyn .... '48 '81 C.102 B.A. L.629 J.D. [Walters R.C.&D.] ‡
Rooke-Ley, Ilisa, (BV) '60 '89 C.319 B.A. L.1206 J.D.
Pub. Def. Servs. of Lane Co., Inc.
Roost, Eric R.-T., (BV) .... '44 '71 C.112 B.A. L.1066 J.D. [Roost&D.]
Roost & Daugirda, (BV) .... 1234 Pearl St.
Rosas, Jeffrey J., (CV) .... '57 '93 C.508 B.A. L.569 J.D. 132 East Broadway, Suite 516
Roseta, Richard A., (AV) .... '47 '72 C&L.629 B.S., J.D. [🄲 Brown,R.L.M.&K.]
Ross, Lawrence W., Jr. .... '24 '52 C.823 A.B. L.145 J.D. Prof., Univ. of Ore.
Rosta, Anthony T., (BV) .... '55 '80 C&L.608 B.A., J.D. 1361 Pearl St.
Rubenstein, Barry, (AV) .... '42 '68 C.911 B.S. L.1065 J.D. [Watkinson L.R.B.&B.]
Rubin, Sheldon I., (BV) .... '54 '80 C.273 B.A. L.146 J.D. 440 East Broadway, Ste. 300
Rudnick, Sharon A., (AV) .... '56 '81 C.478 B.A. L.1068 J.D. [Harrang L.G.R.]
Ryer, Charles W. '40 '68
C.804 B.A. L.910 J.D. Asst. Dir., Lane Co. Dept. of Youth Servs.
Sahlstrom, E. B., (AV) .... '18 '47 C&L.629 B.S., J.D. Suite 100, 915 Oak St.‡

Salisbury, Jeffrey S., Law Office of, (BV) '55 '82
C&L.101 B.S., J.D. 4725 Village Plz. LP, Ste. 200
Salyer, Jeannie .... '63 '00 C.950 B.S. L.629 J.D. 1680 Olive St.
Sanchez-Amparan, Gabriela .... '74 '03 C.843 B.S. L.629 J.D. [Ⓐ Hershner H.]
Saydack, Roger M., (AV) .... '47 '80 C.1154 B.A. L.629 J.D. [Arnold G.S.P.R.&P.]
Schaller, Douglas G., (BV) .... '52 '85 C.112 B.A. L.629 J.D. [Johnson C.L.&S.]
Schmidt, Jens, (AV) .... '58 '84 C&L.629 B.S., J.D. [Harrang L.G.R.]
Schons, Larry H., (BV) .... '41 '78 C&L.629 B.S., J.D. [L.H.Schons]
Schons, Larry H., P.C., (BV) .... Suite B150, 895 Country Club Road
Schultz, Douglas R., (AV) .... '45 '73 C&L.629 B.A., J.D. [Gleaves S.P.&S.]
Schultz, Martin T. .... '55 '86 C.174 B.A. L.629 J.D. Gen. Coun., Vitus Elec.
Schultz, R. Conrad, (P.C.), (BV) ..... '38 '65 C&L.629 B.S., LL.B. 969 Willagillespie Rd.
Schwarte, Joseph G., (BV) .... '63 '92 C.174 B.A. L.950 J.D. [Arnold G.S.P.R.&P.]
Schwartz, David James '72 '00
C.966 B.A. L.280 J.D. Dist. Atty., Lane Co. Dist. Atty. Off.
Scott, Loren S. .... '76 '02 C.36 B.A. L.629 J.D. [Ⓐ Muhlheim B.]
Scott, Malcolm H., (AV) .... '35 '64 C&L.629 B.S., LL.B. [Gleaves S.P.&S.]

Scott Hookland LLP, (AV)
423 Lincoln Street, 97401 ⊙
Telephone: 541 284-5820; 503 754-4700 Fax: 541 284-5821
Email: dlg@scott-hookland.com URL: http://www.scott-hookland.com
Associate: Douglas L. Gallagher.
Construction, Design, Civil and Trial Practice. Commercial Collections, Business, Real Estate, Mediations, Arbitrations, Creditors Rights.
Tigard, Oregon Office: 9185 S.W. Burnham Street, P.O. Box: 23414, 97223. Telephone: 503-620-4540. Toll Free: 800-334-8986. Fax: 503-620-4315.
See Professional Biographies, EUGENE, OREGON

Scotti, Joel P., (BV) .... '47 '89 C.686 B.S. L.1049 J.D. Co. Pub. Def.
Seip, Maria .... '72 '01 C.352 B.A. L.629 J.D. 111 West 7th Avenue
Seligson, Alan G., (BV) .... '55 '88 C.645 B.S. L.629 J.D. [A.G.Seligson]
Seligson, Alan G., P.C., (BV) .... 142 West 8th Avenue
Sermak, Thomas S., (BV) .... '48 '78 C.477 B.A. L.629 J.D. 1143 Oak St.
Sharp, Bill R., (BV) .... '52 '78 C&L.629 B.A., J.D. [Morrow,M.&S.]
Shepard, Lynn .... '51 '79 C&L.629 B.A., J.D. [Shepard]
Shepard, Ross M., (BV) '46 '72 C.165 B.A. L.608 J.D.
Pub. Def. Servs. of Lane Co., Inc.
Shepard, Stephen J. R., (BV) .... '47 '73 C.285 A.B. L.950 J.D. [DePaolis&S.]
Shepard Law Offices, P.C. .... 66 Club Road, Suite 200
Sherlock, William H., (CV) ... '62 '90 C.1169 B.A. L.629 J.D. [Hutchinson,C.C.D.O.&S.]
Shields, Barbara Roman '56 '81
C.610 B.S. L.629 J.D. Gen. Coun., Pacific Continental Bank
Shlesinger, Itzik, (BV) .... '71 '96 C.112 B.A. L.950 J.D. [Shlesinger&d.]
Shlesinger & deVilleneuve Attorneys, P.C., (BV) .... 576 Olive Street, Suite 305
Shugar, Kamala Hollander .... '71 '96 C&L.629 B.A., J.D. Asst. Dist. Atty.
Shurts, Patricia L. '49 '85 C.629 B.L.A. L.1051 J.D.
(adm. in CO; not adm. in OR) 2260 Kincaid‡
Sihler, John C., (BV) .... '30 '55 C.31 B.A. L.309 LL.B. 4235 Brae Burn Dr.
Silvis, Michael J. .... '47 '71 C&L.629 B.S., J.D. 529 Covey Ln.
Simmons, Derek D. .... '69 '00 C.378 B.S. L.596 J.D. [Ⓐ Watkinson L.R.B.&B.]
Simpson, Clinton D., (BV) '52 '77 C.906 B.A. L.629 J.D.
627 Country Club Rd., Ste. 201
Singer, Edward J. .... '64 '90 C.112 B.S. L.426 J.D. 180 East 11th Avenue
Singer, Ellen M., (BV) .... '52 '79 C.1349 B.A. L.284 J.D. 1025 Elkay Dr.
Skelton, Steven M., (BV) .... '45 '74 C&L.629 B.S., J.D. Dep. Dist. Atty.
Skillman, Gregory E., (BV) .... '49 '87 C&L.629 B.A., J.D. [Skillman,F.]
Skillman Fogarty, P.C., (AVⓉ) .... 576 Olive Street, Suite 200
Slayton, Donald R., (CV) .... '59 '86 C&L.950 B.S., J.D. 142 W. 8th Avenue
Sloan, Glenda R. .... '77 '02 C.628 B.S. L.629 J.D. [Ⓐ Watkinson L.R.B.&B.]
Smejkal, Robert A., (BV) .... '53 '78 C&L.629 B.S., J.D. 696 Country Club Rd.
Smith, Craig A., (AV) .... '45 '73 C.494 B.S. L.477 J.D. [Hershner H.]
Smith, Irvin D., (BV) .... '27 '60 C.285 L.596 LL.B. P.O. Box 10121
Smith, Jay H. '16 '42 C.238 B.A. L.146 J.D.
(adm. in CA; not adm. in OR) 2287 Greiner St.‡
Smith, Kim R. '54 '80 C.336 B.S. L.273 J.D.
(adm. in DC; not adm. in OR) P.O. Box 5505
Smith, Michele C. .... '64 '02 C&L.629 B.A., J.D. [Johnson C.L.&S.]
Smith, Robert J. .... '51 '76 C&L.629 B.S., J.D. [R.J.Smith]
Smith, Robert J., P.C. .... 310 East 11th Avenue
Smurthwaite, Richard .... '25 '53 C&L.629 B.A., LL.B. Pub. Def.‡
Sneirson, Judd F. .... '70 '96 C.951 B.A. L.659 J.D. Prof., Univ. OR Sch. Law
Snelling, Derek D. .... '69 '98 C&L.629 B.A., J.D. [Ⓐ Shlesinger&d.] ‡
Snow, Nathan S. .... '77 '04 C.950 B.A. L.629 J.D. [Ⓐ Hershner H.]
Sobol, Marjorie R.S. .... '55 '81 C.103 A.B. L.94 J.D. P.O. Box 5606
Sobol, Michael R. .... '51 '78 C.103 A.B. L.94 J.D. Exec. Dir., Advanced Legal Studies
Solomon, Jennifer Lynn .... '66 '94 C.1044 B.S. L.30 J.D. PSC Inc.
Sorenson, C. Peter .... '51 '82 C&L.629 B.A., J.D. P.O. Box 10836‡
Speer, Howard E., (AV) .... '36 '61 C&L.950 B.A., LL.B. [Speer,H.J.F.P.W.&G.]

Speer, Hoyt, Jones, Feinman, Poppe, Wolf & Griffith, P.C., (AV)
975 Oak Street Suite 700, 97401
Telephone: 541-485-5151 Fax: 541-485-5168
Email: inquiry@speerhoyt.com URL: http://www.speerhoyt.com
Howard E. Speer; Thomas H. Hoyt; J. Kenneth Jones; Howard F. Feinman; Russell D. Poppe; John A. Wolf; Gwendolyn Griffith; Ellen D. Adler;—Carolyn H. Connelly; Sarah R. Hilderbrand.
Business Law, Formation of Business Entities, Business Buying and Selling, Employee Benefits, Conflict Resolution, Taxation, Trusts and Estates, Wills and Probate, Estate Planning, Real Estate, Tax Planning, Estate Tax, Tax Conflict Resolution, Collaboration, Family Law, Divorce, Separation, Prenuptial Agreements, Adoption, Custody, Paternity, Municipal Law, Government.
See Professional Biographies, EUGENE, OREGON

Spencer, Douglas R. .... '23 '49 C&L.309 A.B., J.D. Sr. Cir. J.
Spickard, Devon M., (CV) .... '69 '96 C.426 B.A. L.629 J.D. [Gardner,H.P.B.&F.]
Spickerman, James W., (BV) .... '43 '68 C&L.629 B.S., J.D. [Gleaves S.P.&S.]

Spooner, Much & Ammann, P.C.
(See Salem)

Starr, Craig A., (BVⓉ) .... '49 '74 C.112 B.A. L.477 J.D. [C.A.Starr]
Starr, J. Michael, (AV) .... '37 '62 C.735 B.A. L.629 J.D. [Starr&V.]
Starr, Craig A., P.C., (BVⓉ) .... 4916 Larkwood Lane
Starr & Vinson, P.C., (AV) .... 132 E. Broadway
Stater, William J. .... '48 '77 2151 Birchwood Ave.
Steckbeck, Jane A. .... '61 '89 C.347 B.A. L.629 J.D. Univ. of Oregon Sch. of Law.
Steers, Lester L. B. .... '13 '39 C.339 L.809 J.D. 5320 Fox Hollow Rd.‡
Stevens, Patrick L. .... '71 '98 C.839 B.A. L.629 J.D. [Ⓐ Hutchinson,C.C.D.O.&S.]
Stewart, Jane Lauren Buel, (BV) .... '40 '75 C.813 A.B. L.629 J.D. [Kaufman&S.]
Sticka, Ronald R., (BV) .... '47 '72 C.950 B.A. L.629 J.D. [R.R.Sticka]
Sticka, Ronald R., P.C., (BV) .... 401 E. 10th St., Ste. 470
Stotter, Daniel J .... '61 [Bromley N.]
Strickland, James R., (BV) .... '42 '67 C.193 B.A. L.629 J.D. [J.R.Strickland]
Strickland, James R., PC, (BV) .... 96 E. Broadway, Ste. 3
Strooband, Michael, (BV) .... '45 '74 C.339 B.A. L.365 J.D. [Bischoff,S.&O.]
Stuart, Margaret Mary ...... '44 '90 C&L.629 B.S., J.D. Ore. State System of Higher Educ.
Stupasky, Tina M., (BV) .... '62 '87 C&L.629 B.S., J.D. [Jensen,E.&S.]
Sugahara, T. Kenji .... '73 '00 C.197 B.A. L.629 J.D. Counterclaim.com
Susman, Catherine D. .... '72 '97 C.419 B.A. L.420 J.D. [Arnold G.S.P.R.&P.]
Sutherland, James L., (AV) .... '43 '68 C.629 B.S. L.112 J.D. Asst. U.S. Atty.
Svoboda, John L., (BV) .... '41 '66 C.637 B.A. L.950 J.D. 875 Country Club Rd.
Sycamore, Sylvia .... '41 '00 C.610 A.B. L.629 J.D. [S.Sycamore]
Sycamore, Sylvia, P.C. .... 132 E. Broadway, Ste. 410
Tassinari, Kathryn E. .... '52 '80 C.112 B.A. L.950 J.D. [Ⓒ Cram,H.W.&B.]
Taylor, Stanley N., (CV) .... '51 '78 1285 Mclean Blvd
Tebbutt, Charles M. .... '59 '88 C.1044 B.A. L.823 J.D. [Western E.]
Terzenbach, Ronald B., (BV) .... '52 '78 C&L.629 B.A., J.D. [Loomis&H.]
Thayer, Alan J., Jr., (BV) .... '59 '85 C.628 B.S. L.596 J.D. [Perrin&T.]
Thompson, Edward P., (BV) .... '46 '71 C.373 B.A. L.477 J.D. 875 Country Club Rd.
Thompson, Kate A. .... '68 '00 C.170 B.A. L.966 J.D. [Gleaves S.P.&S.]
Thomsen, Donald P., (CV) .... '36 '70 C.966 B.S. L.629 J.D. 541 Willamette St., Ste. 304
Thwing, Randall E., (BV) .... '45 '70 C.629 B.A. L.950 J.D. [Thwing&T.]
Thwing, Sidney E., (AV) .... '14 '41 C&L.494 B.S., LL.B. 975 Oak Street‡
Thwing & Thwing, (BV) .... 975 Oak St.
Tinker, Todd H. .... '62 '89 C.477 B.G.S. L.802 J.D. [Ⓒ Muhlheim B.]
Tomlinson, R. (Richard) Sande, (AV) ..... '42 '72 C.950 B.A. L.629 J.D. [R.S.Tomlinson]
Tomlinson, R. Sande, P.C., (AV) .... 101 East Broadway
Tozer, Robert Cole, (BV) .... '57 '85 C.378 B.A. L.629 J.D. [R.C.Tozer]
Tozer, Robert Cole, P.C., (BV) .... 96 E. Broadway
Triem, Susan M., (BV) .... '62 '92 C.629 B.A. L.336 J.D. Dep. Dist. Atty.
Trigueiro, Gary L. .... '47 '72 C.549 B.S. L.1066 J.D. 401 E. 10th Ave.
Tufts, William L., (BV) .... '47 '79 C&L.629 B.A., J.D. Trial Atty.
Turnbow, Wm. Randolph, (AV) .... '52 '80 C.813 B.A. L.629 J.D. [Hershner H.]
Vallerand, Patricia A., (BV) .... '51 '79 C&L.629 B.A., J.D. 3835 Blanton Rd.
Van Dyke, Sylvia M. .... '78 '03 C.988 B.A. L.629 J.D. [Ⓐ Hershner H.]
Van Landingham, John H., IV '46 '79
C.885 B.A. L.629 J.D. Lane Co. Legal Aid Servs., Inc.
Van Rysselberghe, Pierre L. .... '34 '60 C.813 B.A. L.911 J.D. Sr. Cir. J.
Vaughan, Paul V., (BV) .... '55 '80 C.174 B.A. L.629 J.D. [Hershner H.]
Velure, Lyle C. .... '41 '66 C&L.629 B.S., J.D. Cir.J.‡
Veralrud, Gregory E., (AV) .... '52 '78 C&L.629 B.A., J.D. [Veralrud&Assoc.]

Veralrud & Associates, Attorneys, P.C., (AV)
625 Citizens Building, 975 Oak Street, 97401
Telephone: 541-345-3333 Fax: 541-342-1908 URL: http://www.oregonattorney.com
Email: Veralrud@Oregonattorney.com URL: http://www.EugeneAttorney.com
William F. Frye (1929-1988); Gregory E. Veralrud;—Lindsay H. Fowler.
Plaintiff's Personal Injury. Automobile Accidents, Aviation Accidents, Wrongful Death, Slip and Fall, Medical Malpractice, Products Liability, Legal Malpractice, Civil Rights, Business Litigation, Criminal Law, White Collar Crime, Drug Defense, Sex Offenses, DUI.
See Professional Biographies, EUGENE, OREGON

Vetri, Dominick R. .... '38 '65 C.570 B.S.M.E. L.659 LL.B. Univ. of Ore. Sch. of Law
Vincent, Charles H., (CV) .... '61 '94 C&L.629 B.S., J.D. 1342 High St., Ste. 200
Vinson, Bradford A. .... '69 '01 C&L.629 B.S., J.D. 132 E. Broadway
Vinson, David A., (BV) .... '40 '67 C&L.629 B.S., J.D. [Starr&V.]
von Hippel, James A., (CV) .... '61 '89 C.629 B.A. L.950 J.D. 399 East 10th Avenue
Vorhes, Stephen L., (BV) .... '53 '81 C.182 B.A. L.596 J.D. Off. of Legal Coun.
Wach, Michael .... '57 '94 C.188 B.S. L.629 J.D. Western Envir. Law Ctr.
Wade, David, (AV) .... '51 '77 C&L.309 A.B., J.D. [Doyle,G.N.M.&W.]
Wade, Patrick W., (BV) .... '44 '84 C.112 A.B. L.629 J.D. [Ⓒ Hershner H.]
Wagner, Robert S., (AV) .... '56 '84 C&L.950 B.S., J.D. [Miller&W.]
Walker, Darrell D. .... '48 '80 C&L.629 B.S., J.D. Hearing Officer, DHR Hearings Unit
Walker, Theodore L., (BV) .... '56 '83 C&L.629 B.S., J.D. [Diment&W.]
Walloch, Heather M. .... '71 '96 C.678 B.A. L.629 J.D. [Ⓐ Doyle,G.N.M.&W.]
Walro, Ronald A., (BV) .... '49 '81 C.602 B.A. L.629 J.D. 2050 W. 29th Ave.
Walsh, James Kelsey .... '57 '86 C.629 B.S. L.950 J.D. 151 W. 7th Ave., Ste. 550
Walters, Martha Lee, (AV) .... '50 '77 C.477 B.A. L.629 J.D. [Walters R.C.&D.]
Walters Romm Chanti & Dickens, P.C., (AV) .... 245 East 4th Avenue
Wang, Benjamin Beijing, (BV) .... '67 '98 C.988 B.A. L.629 J.D. [B.B.Wang]
Wang, Benjamin Beijing, P.C., (BV) .... 1672 Willamette Street
Warburg, Peter F. M., (BV) '52 '78 C&L.629 B.A., J.D.
Pub. Def. Servs. of Lane Co., Inc.
Watkins, H. Eric, Attorney at Law .... '48 '97 C.870 B.S. L.629 J.D. 405 Brookside Dr.
Watkinson, John C., (AV) .... '43 '68 C.628 B.S. L.1119 J.D. [Watkinson L.R.B.&B.]

Watkinson Laird Rubenstein Baldwin & Burgess, P.C., (AV) BB
101 East Broadway, Suite 200, P.O. Box 10567, 97440
Telephone: 541-484-2277 Fax: 541-484-2282
URL: http://www.wlrlaw.com
Steve C. Baldwin; B. Kevin Burgess; Donald R. Laird; R. Scott Palmer; Barry Rubenstein; John C. Watkinson;—Stephanie T. Chandler; Derek D. Simmons; Abigail A. Klinect; Elizabeth W. Bauer; Glenda R. Sloan. Of Counsel: R. Sande Tomlinson.
Representative Clients: Lane Individual Practice Association; Whittaker Realty Group; Gateway Mall Shopping Center; Douglas County Independent Practice Association, Inc.; East Earth Herb, Inc.; Far West Fibers, Inc.; Advantage Dental Plan, Inc.; Valley River Plaza Shopping Center; Coastwide Laboraties, Inc.
See Professional Biographies, EUGENE, OREGON

Watson, Elizabeth .... '— '94 C.907 B.A. L.629 J.D. [Ⓐ Jaqua&W.] ⊙
Webb, Don R. .... '52 '97 2630 Elinor St.
Wechsler, Terry J. .... '55 '98 C.1273 B.B.A. L.208 J.D. 850 W. 38th Ave.
Weiland, R. Scott .... '74 '02 C&L.629 B.S., J.D. [Ⓐ Kurtz,F.&J.]
Weinstein, Dana M., (AV) .... '54 '80 C.169 B.A. L.629 J.D. 777 High St., Ste. 260
Weintraub, Mark B., (AV) .... '56 '83 C.696 B.A. L.596 J.D. Asst. Fed. Pub. Def.
Weisheit, Diane M. .... '79 '04 C.895 B.A. L.629 J.D. [Ⓐ Arnold G.S.P.R.&P.]
Wekselblatt, Mindy, (BV) .... '56 '90 C.330 B.A. L.629 J.D. 767 Willamette Street
Wells, Brent, (BV) .... '60 '85 C.585 B.A. L.629 J.D. [Cram,H.W.&B.]
Wells, D. Michael, (BV) .... '46 '79 C.94 B.A. L.629 J.D. 199 East 5th Avenue
Western Environmental Law Ctr. .... 1216 Lincoln St.
Westling, Wayne T. .... '43 '69 C.605 A.B. L.569 J.D. Univ. of Oregon
Wheatley, William G., (AV) .... '33 '59 C&L.629 B.A., J.D. [Jaqua&W.] ⊙
Wheeler, Robert Wakeley .... '50 '76 C.813 B.A. L.597 J.D. P.O. Box 5757
Whitney, Robynne A., (BV) .... '70 '97 C&L.629 B.S., J.D. [Ⓐ McCrea]
Wiley, Diane Karen .... '56 '85 C.1071 B.A. L.629 J.D. Univ. of Ore.
Williams, David B., (AV) .... '40 '76 C.112 B.A. L.629 J.D. Asst. Co. Coun.
Williams, Phillip M. .... '67 '97 C.793 B.S. L.629 J.D. 310 E. 11th Avenue
Williamson, Ross M. .... '73 '01 C.907 B.A. L.629 J.D. [Ⓐ Harrang L.G.R.]
Wills, Jerald A. .... '28 '58 L.596 LL.B. 450 N. 2nd‡
Wilson, David O. .... '49 '85 C.118 B.A. L.629 J.D. Liberty Northwest Ins. Co.
Wilson, Teresa J. .... '50 '75 C.939 B.A. L.629 J.D. County Counsel

Wilson, Virgil James, III, (BVⓉ) '53 '81
C.1169 B.A. L.770 J.D. 440 East Broadway, Suite 300
Wing, Jeffrey C., (BV) ....'54 '90 C.431 B.A. L.629 J.D. [Cary,W.B.&E.]
Wirth, Justin ....'72 '00 C.174 B.A. L.629 J.D. [A Harrang L.G.R.]
Wiswall, William, (AV) ....'35 '62 C&L.629 B.S., J.D. 151 W 7th Ave Ste 550
Wittkop, Mindy L., (BV) ....'71 '97 C.670 B.S. L.629 J.D. [A Doyle,G.N.M.&W.]
Wolf, John A., (BV) ....'48 '80 C.628 B.S. L.1051 J.D. [Speer,H.J.F.P.W.&G.]
Womer, Greg M. ....'70 '03 C&L.629 B.S., J.D. [A Luvaas C.]
Wood, Mary C. ....'62 '89 C.911 B.A. L.813 J.D. Univ. of Ore. Sch. of Law
Wood, Terri, (AV) ....'54 '82 C&L.260 B.S., J.D. [T.Wood]
Wood, Terri, P.C., Law Office of, (AV) ....730 Van Buren St.
Woodrich, George J. ....'27 '55 C.629 B.S. L.950 LL.B. Sr. Cir. J.
Woodworth, John S. ....'69 '96 C.350 B.B.A. L.629 J.D. [J.S.Woodworth]
Woodworth, John S., P.C. .......................P.O. Box 747
Wylie, Gordon K. ....'32 '56 C&L.950 LL.B. 1147 High St.
Wynd, Gladys B. '06 '51 C.629 B.A.
(adm. in AK; not adm. in OR) 494 W. 10th Ave.‡
Yates, Gloria D. ....'48 '91 C&L.629 B.S., J.D. P.O Box 51089
Yates, Jane M. ....'— '05 C.999 B.A. L.629 J.D. [A Gleaves S.P.&S.]
Yates, Steven C., (BV) ....'49 '77 C.801 B.A. L.424 J.D. 1400 High St.
Yeager, Steven R. ....'57 '92 C&L.629 B.A., J.D. 1147 High St.
Zennaché, Charles M., (BV) ....'60 '88 C.184 B.S. L.629 J.D. [Walters R.C.&D.]

FAIRVIEW, 7,561, *Multnomah Co.*

Cornelius, Darrell L., (BV) ....'39 '65 C&L.629 B.S., J.D. [D.L.Cornelius]
Cornelius, Darrell L., PC, (BV) .......................P.O. Box 1929

FLORENCE, 7,263, *Lane Co.*

Berg, Bradley Burton ....'65 '92 C.1070 B.S. L.629 J.D. [j.Berg]
Berg, jBradley, P.C. ....733 Highway 101
Brewer, William D., (AV) ....'47 '85 C.950 B.A. L.1051 J.D. [Hershner H.] ⊙
Chapman, Patricia L., (BV) ....'56 '83 C.112 A.B. L.767 J.D. [Hershner H.] ⊙
Clark, David L., (CV) ....'46 '75 C&L.629 B.S., J.D. [D.L.Clark]
Clark, David L., P.C., (CV) ....1245 Rhododendron Dr.
Haws, Eric ....'40 '73 C.376 B.S. L.629 J.D. P.O. Box 1473

Hershner Hunter, LLP, (AV)
1441 7th Street, P.O. Box K, 97439 ⊙
Telephone: 541-997-1997 Fax: 541-344-2025
Email: info@hershnerhunter.com URL: http://www.hershnerhunter.com
Partners: Sheryl S. McConnell; William D. Brewer; Patricia L. Chapman. Associate: Todd R. Johnston.
Business, Banking, Timber, Estate Planning, Probate and Trust Administration, Taxation, Creditors' Rights, Bankruptcy, Construction, Real Property, Land Use, Employee Benefits, Health Care, Employment and Litigation.
Eugene, Oregon Office: 180 East 11th Avenue. Telephone: 541-686-8511. Fax: 541-344-2025.
See Professional Biographies, FLORENCE, OREGON

Hess, Douglas S., (BV) ....'42 '67 C.629 L.950 J.D. 616 38th Pl.
Johnston, Todd R. ....'74 '99 C.170 B.A. L.629 J.D. [A Hershner H.] ⊙
McConnell, Sheryl S., (BV) ....'60 '95 C.628 B.S. L.112 J.D. [Hershner H.] ⊙
Nicholson, Thomas C., (P.C.), (BV) ....'56 '81 C.628 B.S. L.629 J.D. 552 Laurel St.
Riley, Patricia ...... '44 '85 C.1056 B.A. L.1051 J.D. Sr. VP, Oregon Pacific Banking Co.
Sanford, Gene '43 '75 C.284 B.A. L.1065 J.D.
(adm. in CA; not adm. in OR) 88700 Shoreline Loop‡

Speer, Hoyt, Jones, Feinman, Poppe, Wolf & Griffith, P.C.
(See Eugene)

Young, Leo F., (AV) ....'17 '62 C&L.629 B.S., LL.B. 342 Northridge Dr.‡

FOREST GROVE, 17,708, *Washington Co.*

Ballard, Douglas D., (BV) ....'51 '83 C.871 B.S. L.596 J.D. [Moore L.&B.]
Browning, Robert A., (CV) ....'44 '79 C.1056 B.S. L.596 J.D. [Browning&C.]
Browning & Colas Attorneys, P.C., (CV) ....3012-B Pacific Ave.
Bump, Ellen Arnold ....'14 '37 C.637 B.S. L.596 LL.B. 1421 Rosearden Dr.‡
Colas, Leon S., (CV) ....'53 '92 C.1181 B.A. L.629 J.D. [Browning&C.]
Lommen, Stephanie M., (BV) ....'64 '89 C&L.950 B.A., J.D. [Moore L.&B.]
Lynch, Tonya L. ....'67 '93 C.950 B.S. L.112 J.D. 3333 22nd Ave.
Moore, Michael M., (BV) ....'47 '72 C.1056 B.S. L.629 J.D. [Moore L.&B.]
Moore Lommen & Ballard, (BV) ....2002 Pacific Ave.
Musick, Albert R. ....'11 '36 C&L.339 B.S., LL.B. Cir. J.‡
Post, Joseph C., (CV) ....'42 '72 C.679 B.A. L.569 J.D. [J.Post]
Post, Joseph, Law Office of, (CV) ....2609 Pacific Ave.
Reynolds, James G. '43 '68 C.207 A.B. L.145 J.D.
(adm. in IL; not adm. in OR) Chmn. of the Bd., Gray & Co.
Ringholm, Sally ....'54 '94 C.999 B.S. L.1051 J.D. 2178 NW Gales Creek Rd.
Sardinia, Lisa M. ....'57 '98 C.941 B.S. L.1065 J.D. Pacific Univ.
Tebbet, Sally A. ....'47 '76 C.172 B.A. L.1051 J.D. 3226 Valley Crest Way‡

FOSSIL, * 399, *Wheeler Co.*

Cutsforth, Thomas William, (CV) ....'53 '88 C.628 B.S. L.629 J.D. Dist. Atty.

GARIBALDI, 877, *Tillamook Co.*

Dolan, Timothy M., (BV) '57 '84 C.628 B.S. L.596 J.D.
206 Garibaldi Avenue, 97118
Telephone: 503-322-3742 Fax: 503-322-3238
Email: timothymdolan@oregoncoast.com
Real Estate, Trusts and Estates, General Litigation, Criminal Law, Bankruptcy.
See Professional Biographies, GARIBALDI, OREGON

GEARHART, 1,027, *Clatsop Co.*

Coumont, Frank J. ....'12 '64 C.999 L.950 LL.B. P.O. Box 2191‡
Hodges, Charles E., Jr., (BV) ....'31 '61 C.735 B.A. L.596 J.D. P.O. Box 2372
Shea, Charles A., III ....'35 '62 C.813 B.A. L.770 J.D. P.O. Box 2274

GLADSTONE, 11,438, *Clackamas Co.*

Henricksen, Jon S., (BV) ....'42 '73 C.154 B.A. L.950 J.D. [J.S. .P.Henricksen]
Henricksen, Jon S., PC, (BV) ....725 Portland Ave.
Henriksen, John R. ....'44 '70 C&L.950 B.A., J.D. 82nd Drive★

Peterson Law Offices, PC
(See Portland)

Richard, John E. ....'21 '56 C.670 A.B. L.596 LL.B. 18555 Columbia Ave.
Strock, Jon F. ....'51 '79 C.188 B.A. L.950 J.D. 725 Portland Ave.

GLENEDEN BEACH, 4,198, *Lincoln Co.*

Douglas, Wayne W. '18 '50 C.826 L.800
(adm. in CA; not adm. in OR) P.O. Box 471‡
Mulee, Annette, (AV) ....'53 '84 C.188 B.A. L.1051 J.D. [A.M.Mulee]
Mulee, A.M., (AV) .......................P.O. Box 850

GOLD BEACH, * 1,897, *Curry Co.*

Downer, Hugh C., Jr. ....'46 '71 C.477 B.S.E. L.813 J.D. Cir. J.
Herbage, Cathleen B. ....'55 '80 C.628 B.A. L.629 J.D. Mun. J.
Herbage, Michael G., (CV) ...'54 '81 C.628 B.A. L.629 J.D. Co. Coun. & Dep. Dist. Atty.
Mickelson, Richard K. ....'47 '74 C.988 B.A. L.629 J.D. Cir. J.
Patterson, Cynthia Lynnae ....'67 '98 C.502 B.S.B.A. L.464 J.D. Pub. Def. Services
Pitney, Ernest W. '07 '31 L.809
(adm. in CA; not adm. in OR) 96155 N. Bk. of the Rogue‡
Spicer, M. John, (CV) ....'42 '72 C.1075 B.S.I.E. L.61 J.D. [M.J.Spicer]
Spicer, M. John, P.C., (CV) ....94211 Gauntlett St.
Starkweather, Frederic H., Jr. ....'17 '49 C.823 B.C.E. L.629 LL.B. Ret. Cir. J.
Steak, Charles A., (CV) ....'— '90 C.112 B.A. L.1065 J.D. Dep. Dist. Atty.
Streich, Alexandria Chris ....'72 '98 C.112 B.A. L.336 J.D. Dist. Atty. Off.
Wallace, William N., (BV) ....'33 '62 C&L.629 B.S., J.D. Dist. Atty.

GRAND RONDE, 271, *Polk Co.*

Aubertin, Deneen M. ....'61 '93 C.909 B.S. L.911 J.D. 9615 Grand Ronde Rd.
Estensen, Lisa Jean ....'70 '97 C.280 B.A. L.1051 J.D. Conf Tribes of Grand Ronde
Thomas, Bruce A., (BV) ...'53 '84 C.629 B.S. L.950 J.D. Pres., Spirit Mt. Develop. Corp.

GRANTS PASS, * 23,003, *Josephine Co.*

Adams, Richard D., (BV) ....'54 '80 C.543 B.A. L.950 J.D. [Davis,A.&D.]
Baker, Lindi L. ....'52 '84 C.1071 B.S. L.767 J.D. Cir. Ct. J. Pro Tem
Berlant, Gary A., (CV) .... '51 '92 C.112 B.A. L.629 J.D. Southern OR Pub. Defs. Off.
Bird, Michael J., (BV) ....'42 '71 C.263 B.S. L.629 J.D. [Brown,H.B.R.W.&B.]
Boyer, Robert W. ....'48 '74 C.464 B.A. L.1132 J.D. 980 S.W. 6th St., Ste. 28
Brouhard, Jason ....'— '98 C&L.950 B.S., J.D. [Brown,H.B.R.W.&B.]

Brown, Hughes, Bird, Rote, Wetmore & Brouhard, LLP, (BV)
612 N.W. Fifth Street, P.O. Box 10, 97528
Telephone: 541-479-2678 Fax: 541-479-7485 URL: http://www.southernoregonlawyer.com
Email: brown_hughes@charterinternet.com URL: http://www.lawyers.com/bhbrw
Gene L. Brown (1921-1999). Members of Firm: Daniel F. Hughes; Michael J. Bird; Frank C. Rote, III; LaDonna S. Wetmore; Jason Brouhard.
General Civil and Trial Practice. Appellate Practice. Personal Injury, Family Law, Divorce, Custody, Child Support, Trusts and Estates, Wills and Probate, Contracts, Business, Corporate, Commercial, Employment Law, Real Estate, Bankruptcy, Land Use, Mining, Estate Planning, Federal and State Taxation, Civil Litigation, Creditors Rights, Landlord-Tenant.
See Professional Biographies, GRANTS PASS, OREGON

Browne, Claudia E., (BV) ....'51 '81 C&L.629 J.D. 236 N.W. E. St.
Calvert, Jesse R., Jr. ....'22 '48 C&L.813 A.B., LL.B. P.O. Box 1298‡
Campbell, Stephen D., (BV) ....'53 '80 C&L.629 B.A., J.D. Asst. Dist. Atty.
Cauble, Christopher L., (CV) ....'70 '96 C.950 B.A. L.285 J.D. [Cauble,D.&S.]
Cauble, Walter L., (AV) ....'41 '67 C&L.950 B.A., J.D. [Cauble,D.&S.]

Cauble, Dole & Sorenson, (AV)
One Eleven Building, 111 S.E. 6th Street, P.O. Box 398, 97526
Telephone: 541-476-8825 Fax: 541-471-1704 Toll Free: 888-870-8825
Email: rvlaw@qwest.net URL: http://www.roguevalleylaw.com
Members of Firm: Walter L. Cauble; James R. Dole; Christopher L. Cauble; Deborah L. Sorenson. Associate: Willard L. Ransom.
General Civil and Trial Practice in State and Federal Courts. Business, Construction Law, Corporate, Creditors' Rights, Elder Law, Employment Law, Estate Planning, Land Use Law, Mining, Probate, Real Property, School Law, Timber and Logging, Water and Natural Resources Law.
Representative Clients: Grants Pass School District; First American Title Co.; Grants Pass Clinic; Rough & Ready Lumber Co.; Valley of the Rogue Bank; Environmental Container Systems; Copeland Sand and Gravel; Copeland Paving.
See Professional Biographies, GRANTS PASS, OREGON

Coon, Allan H. ....'44 '72 C&L.629 B.S., J.D. Cir. J.
Coulter, Donald H., (AV) ....'21 '48 C&L.629 B.S., LL.B. [Davis,A.&D.] ‡
Cushing, Laur. A. ....'25 '52 C&L.629 B.S. Ret. Cir. J.
Dahlin, Eric T., (CV) ....'64 '94 C&L.112 B.A., J.D. Grants Pass Office, 207 Sw G St #C
Davis, John E., (BV) ....'49 '75 C.629 B.S. L.678 J.D. [Davis,A.&D.]
Davis, Adams & Day, (BV) ....600 N.W. Fifth Street
Day, Gregory T., (CV) ....'64 '95 C.330 B.A. L.629 J.D. [Davis,A.&D.]
DeCourcey, James M. '44 '70
C.813 B.A. L.629 J.D. Pres., Josephine-Crater Title Cos., Inc.
Dole, James R., (BV) ....'64 '89 C&L.629 B.A., J.D. [Cauble,D.&S.]
Farmer, Gene, (BV) ....'38 '78 C.941 B.A. L.285 J.D. 432 N.W. 6th St., Ste. 101
Fong, Douglas W., (BV) ....'56 '84 C.668 B.A. L.629 J.D. Asst. U.S. Atty.
Freudenberg, Ben, (BV) ....'52 '77 C.950 B.S. L.629 J.D. 600 N.W. 5th St.
Galli, Matthew Gregory ....'65 '92 C.628 B.S. L.950 J.D. [A Davis,A.&D.]
Hathaway, Homer C., (AVⓉ) '26 '54 C.605 L.426 LL.B.
(adm. in CA; not adm. in OR) 4413 Foothill Blvd.
Holley, Lee A. '33 '58 C&L.276 B.S., J.D.
(adm. in WA; not adm. in OR) 964 1/2 N.E. 11th St.‡
Holt, Heather L., (CV) ....'62 '94 C&L.629 B.B.A., J.D. 777 N.E. 7th St.
Hughes, Daniel F., (BV) ....'43 '69 C.173 B.A. L.950 J.D. [Brown,H.B.R.W.&B.]
Hull, Thomas M., (BV) ....'52 '77 C.1071 B.S. L.629 J.D. 236 N.W. E. St.

Jacobson, Thierolf & Dickey, P.C.
(See Medford)

James, Dennis D., (BV) ....'48 '77 C&L.744 B.A., J.D. [Nelson&J.]
Jenner, J. Kirkham '15 '40 C&L.911 A.B., J.D.
(adm. in WA; not adm. in OR) Claim Coun., State Farm Mutual Automobile Ins. Co.‡
Johnson, Clay E., (BV) ....'47 '75 C&L.629 B.A., J.D. Dist. Atty.Off.
Jordan, Kim L., (BV) ....'37 '67 C.101 B.S. L.273 LL.B. 228 N.W. B St.
Killoran, Michael S. ....'36 '62 C.1051 B.S. L.629 130 N.W. D St.‡
Lane, Richard K., (BV) ....'47 '72 C.108 B.S. L.345 J.D. [R.K.Lane]
Lane, Richard K., P.C., (BV) ....219 Northwest E. Street
Lansing, Mark A., (BV) ....'57 '88 C.629 B.A. L.911 J.D. [M.Lansing]
Lansing, Mark, P.C., (BV) ....307 N.W. East St.
Luckey, Clarence E. ....'19 '42 C&L.629 B.S., J.D. 1631 N.W. Olmar St.‡
Mackay, William J. ....'43 '84 C.1071 B.S.Ed L.950 J.D. Cir. J.
Maier, Joseph G., (CV) ....'66 '94 C&L.629 B.S., J.D. Southern OR Pub. Def.
Martin, Wally P. ....'26 '50 C&L.629 LL.B. 119 N.W. E St.‡
Mecca, Christopher D. ....'51 '76 C.602 B.A. L.285 J.D. Dist. J.
Morey, Neil C. ....'76 '00 C.477 B.A. L.1065 J.D. Dist. Atty.
Myrick, Donald F., (AV) ....'23 '51 C&L.629 B.S., LL.B. 133 N.W.D St.
Nealy, Oscar R. ....'42 '68 C&L.629 B.S., J.D. 224 Northwest "B" St.
Nelson, Philip L., (BV) ....'38 '68 C.813 A.B. L.1065 J.D. [C Nelson&J.]
Nelson & James, (BV) ....130 N.W. "D" St.
O'Neal, J. Loyd ....'44 '74 C.1042 B.A. L.1051 J.D. Cir. J.
Peterson, Rebecca L. ....'64 '97 C.556 B.A. L.629 j.D. [A Nelson&J.]

Peterson Law Offices, PC
(See Portland)

Phillips, Floyd M. '31 '65 C&L.276 B.S.S., J.D. (adm. in MD; not adm. in OR) 107 Harmony Circle, S.E.‡
Pitts, Rolf M. '25 '61 C&L.800 B.S.E.E., LL.B. (adm. in CA; not adm. in OR) P.O. Box 451‡
Preslar, Holly A., (BV) '66 '92 C.1071 B.A. L.629 J.D. 245 NW "B" Street
Price, Virginia S. '48 '75 C.449 B.A. L.724 J.D. 1210 Kubli Rd.
Ransom, Willard L. '78 '03 C.375 B.A. L.378 J.D. [Ⓐ Cauble,D.&S.]
Reade, John E., (CV) '59 '85 C.1044 B.S. L.950 J.D. 127 1/2 N.W. "D" Street
Rote, Frank C., III, (CV) '54 '82 C.973 B.S. L.8 J.D. [Brown,H.B.R.W.&B.]
Scannell, Jerry '26 '57 C.28 B.A. L.93 J.D. 777 N.E. 7th St.
Schultz, Duane Wm., (BV) '45 '70 C.187 B.A. L.36 J.D. [D.W.Schultz]
Schultz, Duane Wm., P.C., (BV) 219 N.W. "E" Street
Seagraves, Charles H., Jr., (AV) '32 '62 C&L.950 B.A., LL.B. [Davis,A.&D.] ‡
Simcoe, Daniel, (BV) '48 '80 C.112 B.A. L.464 J.D. 242 N.W. E St.
Sloan, William M., (AV) '30 '56 C&L.629 B.S., LL.B. 220 S.E. H St.
Sniffen, Carl R. J., (AVⓉ) '52 '77 C.378 B.S. L.502 J.D. 405 Parkhill Pl.
Sorenson, Deborah L. '77 '02 C.906 B.A. L.285 J.D. [Cauble,D.&S.]
Spletter, Lori Lynn, (CV) '71 '97 C.628 B.A. L.1148 J.D. Dist. Atty. Off.
Stanley, Meta K. '15 '55 C.483 A.B. L.767 J.D. (adm. in CA; not adm. in OR) 220 Larkin Rd.‡
Stapleton, Ulys J., (CV) '49 '74 C.628 B.S. L.629 J.D. City Atty.
Swift, Jack H. '39 '95 C.276 B.A. L.1137 J.D. (adm. in CA; not adm. in OR) 134 Rossier Lane
Swint, Thomas W. '47 '73 C.988 B.A. L.950 J.D. P.O. Box 5047
Thompson, Timothy R., (BV) '50 '78 C.629 B.S. L.464 J.D. Dist. Atty.
Titzler, Scott K., (BV) '49 '87 C.112 B.S. L.596 J.D. Asst. Dist. Atty.
Wetmore, LaDonna S., (CV) '— '95 C&L.972 B.S., J.D. [Brown,H.B.R.W.&B.]
Wolke, Pat, (BV) '49 '75 C.629 B.S. L.1051 J.D. 119 N.W. "E" St.
Woodburn, Kris '69 '98 C.413 B.A. L.1051 J.D. Dist. Atty. Off.

GRESHAM, 90,205, *Multnomah Co.*

Anderson, Richard M., Law Office of '48 '97 C.1060 B.S. L.836 J.D. 2665 N.E. Cleveland Ave
Arno, Margaret E. '53 '91 C.774 B.A. L.596 J.D. 1217 N.E. Burnside St.
Baines, Matthew R., (AV) '48 '77 C.154 B.A. L.629 J.D. Dep. City Atty.
Barrie, Stephanie L.H. '68 '94 C&L.950 B.A., J.D. 406 N.E. 4th St.
Bartels, Sidney A., (BV) '30 '62 C.629 L.596 LL.B. 21440 S.E. Stark St.
Blake, Rick '57 '85 C.966 B.A. L.436 J.D. 2460 N.E. Division St.
Cook, Vernon '25 '52 C.685 B.A. L.629 LL.B. 519 N.E. 4th
Downing, Scott T., (AV) '53 '80 C.1051 B.A. L.596 J.D. [S.Downing]
Downing, Scott, P.C., (AV) 510 N.E. Roberts, Suite 200
Echols, M. Patton '— '93 C.244 B.A. L.950 J.D. 510 NE Roberts Ave.
Egner, Richard, Jr., (BV) '33 '59 C&L.629 B.S., J.D. 1550 N.W. Eastman Pkwy.
Fjelstad, Eric J. '62 '89 C.1058 B.A. L.911 J.D. [Smith&F.]
Foraker, Peggy S., (BV) '49 '78 C&L.383 B.G.S., J.D. [Jennings&F.]
Freeman, Brian J., (BV) '40 '69 C.628 B.S. L.1051 J.D. [Ⓒ S.Downing]
Freyer, Frank L. '48 '81 C.1056 B.S. L.1051 J.D. 184 S.W. Sandlewod Loop
Fryar, Michael S., (BV) '47 '72 C.101 B.A. L.597 J.D. [M.S.Fryar]
Fryar, Michael S., PC, (BV) 1300 N.E. Linden
Howe, Jack D. '27 '57 L.596 LL.B. 21459 S.E. Stark St.
Jennings, James R., (BV) '45 '74 C.36 B.S. L.950 J.D. [Jennings&F.]
Jennings & Foraker, LLP, (BV) 1550 N.W. Eastman Pkwy.
Johnson, Steven C., (BV) '51 '78 C.112 B.A. L.1051 J.D. 21825 S.E. Stark St.
Joseph, Michael S. '64 '91 C.508 B.S. L.950 J.D. 21459 S.E. Stark St.
Loacker, John R. '41 '93 C.1056 B.S. L.596 J.D. 510 N.E. Roberts
Masaoy, Donato B., III '65 '96 C.988 B.A. L.950 J.D. 519 N.E. 4th
Melville, Thomas A. '67 '96 C.882 B.S. L.336 J.D. [T.Melville]
Melville, Thomas, PC 1300 N.E. Linden Ave.
Mettler, Greg L., (AV) '56 '84 C&L.629 B.S., J.D. [G.L.Mettler]
Mettler, Greg L., P.C., (AV) 200 E. Powell Boulevard, Suite #200
Nelson, Robert E. '28 '64 C.629 B.S. L.596 J.D. 2053 E. Burnside‡

O'Rourke, James F., Jr., & Associates
(See Portland)

Patterson, S. Jane, (BV) '50 '79 C.1051 B.A. L.629 J.D. 2460 N.E. Division St.

Peterson Law Offices, PC
(See Portland)

Rindfusz, Robert D., (BV) '46 '71 C.347 A.B. L.477 J.D. 1217 N.E. Burnside St.
Robertson, Donald K. '27 '58 C.999 L.596 LL.B. 21459 S.E. Stark St.
Skofstad, Philip G. '28 '64 C.629 B.B.A. L.695 LL.B. 250 N.W. Blaine Lane‡
Smith, Kerry M. '60 '88 C.436 B.A. L.950 J.D. [Smith&F.]
Smith & Fjelstad 722 N. Main Ave.
Trammell, M. Lyle '31 '68 C.112 B.S. L.596 J.D. 21903 S.E. Borges Rd.‡
Twedt, Mark S., (BV) '51 '78 C.629 B.S. L.1051 J.D. 1300 N.E. Linden Ave.
Vanagas, Timothy J. '51 '76 C.1051 B.A. L.596 J.D. [T.Vanagas]
Vanagas, Timothy 21440 S.E. Stark St.
Young, David W. '20 '53 C.670 B.A. L.596 LL.B. P.O. Box 809‡
Young, Gary '57 '87 C.1165 B.S.B.A. L.1051 J.D. Reg. Mgr., Pioneer Consolidated Corp.‡
Young, R. Eric, (BV) '45 '73 C.950 B.A. L.596 J.D. [E.Young]
Young, Eric, P.C., (BV) 1300 N.E. Linden Ave.

HAINES, 426, *Baker Co.*

Jacobson, John L., (BV) '39 '65 C.628 B.S. L.950 J.D. [J.L.Jacobson]
Jacobson, John L., P.C., (BV) 14504 S. Rock Creek Ln.

HARBOR, 2,622, *Curry Co.*

Foley, Patrick, Law Offices of, (CV) '43 '75 C.29 L.1240 J.D. 97900 Shopping Center Avenue

HEPPNER, * 1,412, *Morrow Co.*

Hallman & Dretke
(See Pendleton)

Kuhn, William J., (BV) '51 '76 C.645 B.A. L.1051 J.D. [Kuhn,S.&M.]
Kuhn, Spicer & Mills, (BV) 267 N. Main
Mills, Michael A., (CV) '57 '90 C.628 B.S. L.878 J.D. [Kuhn,S.&M.]
Spicer, Annetta L., (CV) '50 '77 C.1056 B.S. L.1051 J.D. [Kuhn,S.&M.]

HERMISTON, 13,154, *Umatilla Co.*

Anderson, George L., (AV) '— '76 C.939 B.A. L.1051 J.D. [Anderson H.]

Anderson Hansell, P.C., (AV)
475 East Main Street, 97838
Telephone: 541-567-7800 Fax: 541-567-7656
Email: sally@andersonhansell.com

(This Listing Continued)

Anderson Hansell, P.C. (Continued)

George L. Anderson; Sally Anderson-Hansell.
General Civil and Trial Practice, Agriculture, Business Litigation, Creditor's Rights, Real Estate, Estate Planning and Probate.

See Professional Biographies, HERMISTON, OREGON

Anderson-Hansell, Sally '— '00 C&L.629 B.A., J.D. [Anderson H.]
Bendixsen, Kurt C., (BV) '57 '88 C.1056 B.S. L.1187 J.D. [K.C.Bendixsen]
Bendixsen, Kurt C., P.C., (BV) 245 E. Main St.
Brewer, Rustin A., (BV) '24 '57 C.906 A.B. L.596 LL.B. 245D E. Main
Delaney, Patrick J. '50 '77 C.629 B.S. L.208 J.D. (adm. in CO; not adm. in OR) 955 S.W. 10th Pl.‡
Hadley, David Wm., (BV) '53 '81 C.36 B.S. L.336 J.D. [D.W.Hadley]
Hadley, David W., (BV) 130 S.E. 3rd St.
Luisi, Gary R., (BV) '45 '71 C&L.629 B.A., J.D. 230 S.E. 4th St.
Smallmon, John W., (BV) '34 '62 C&L.950 B.S.L., B.L. [J.W.Smallmon]
Smallmon, John W., P.C., (BV) 410 E. Hurlburt Ave.
Smith, Dale L., (CV) '46 '79 C.629 B.A. L.596 J.D. 913 N. 1st. St.
Wallace, Jeffrey M. '49 '76 C.629 B.S. L.950 J.D. Dist. J.

HILLSBORO, * 70,186, *Washington Co.*

Adams, Joseph T. '59 '85 C.350 B.A. L.494 J.D. (adm. in NY; not adm. in OR) 2111 N.E. 25th Ave.

Adams & Uffelman LLP
(See Beaverton)

Aldous, Alan K. '57 '88 C.878 B.S.E.E. L.800 J.D. 2111 N.E. 25th Ave. (Pat.)
Alexander, Timothy P. '47 '72 C.880 B.A. L.846 J.D. Cir. J.
Allen, Sara Lynn '72 '99 C.628 B.S. L.950 J.D. Co. Dist. Atty. Off.
Anderson, Robert D. '65 '91 C.339 B.S. L.273 J.D. (adm. in CO; not adm. in OR; Pat.) Sr.Licensing Atty., Intel Corp.
Arntt, Steven E. '67 '97 C.628 B.A. L.950 J.D. 4660 North East Belknap Court, Suite 101K
Atwood, Gina M. '67 '95 C&L.101 B.A., J.D. 2373 N.W. 185th Ave., Ste. 134‡
Audet, David M., (BV) '51 '79 C.228 B.A. L.596 J.D. 249 N.E. Lincoln
Bassel, Raymond B., (BV) '58 '85 C.528 B.A. L.596 J.D. 249 N.E. Lincoln St.
Beaves, Martha E. '— '96 C.145 B.A. L.352 J.D. 1294 NE Creeksedge Dr.
Becker, Mark L. '54 '78 C.112 B.A. L.37 J.D. 5555 N.E. Moore Court (Pat.)
Berrien, James D., (BV) '48 '75 C&L.1051 B.A., J.D. P.O. Box 543
Blough, Lynn E. '57 '89 C.1051 B.A. L.911 J.D. Sr. Coun., Intel Corp.
Bonebrake, Alan C. '42 '67 C.1056 B.S. L.629 J.D. Cir. J.
Breckon, Garry L. '44 '97 C.145 B.A. L.596 J.D. [Garland,G.L.S.H.e.a.]
Brenden, Kevin D. '— '02 C.17 B.A. L.596 J.D. [Ⓐ McNeil]
Brink, Bernard B., (BV) '42 '71 C.629 B.S. L.950 J.D. 330 NE Lincoln St.
Brisbee, Larry A., (AV) '41 '67 C.628 B.S. L.950 J.D. [Brisbee&S.]
Brisbee & Stockton, (AV) 139 N.E. Lincoln Street
Brooke, Thomas M.L. '62 '90 C.770 B.S. L.629 J.D. Gen. Coun., Corillian Corp.
Buchér, Erik M. '74 '00 C.628 B.A. L.629 J.D. [Ⓐ McNeil]
Burns, Stephanie M. '69 '95 C.597 B.S. L.770 J.D. Sr. Corp. Coun., Merant, Inc.
Cadiz, Patrick G. '72 '02 C.770 B.S. L.1398 J.D. [Ⓐ Brisbee&S.]
Campbell, Nancy W. '46 '79 C.1056 B.S. L.1051 J.D. Cir. J.
Carda, Gayle Kay '62 '89 C.1051 B.A. L.596 J.D. In House Coun., Intel Corp.
Carlson, Darin W. '70 '98 C&L.101 B.A., J.D. Assoc. Coun., Intel Corp.
Carman, Frederick S., (BV) '50 '75 C.628 B.S. L.950 J.D. [Ⓐ Karpstein&V.]
Castro, Lisa W. E. '72 '00 C.429 B.A. L.1051 J.D. [Garland,G.L.S.H.e.a.]
Christensen, Daniel K. '66 '96 C.101 B.A. L.878 J.D. (adm. in UT; not adm. in OR) Intel Corp.
Cimini, Christine N. '67 '92 C.156 B.A. L.306 J.D. Ore. Legal Servs.
Cobb, Rita Batz '54 '81 C.679 B.A. L.596 J.D. Cir. J.
Collins, Tom, (BV) '51 '81 C.1056 B.A. L.596 J.D. 249 N.E. Lincoln
D'Agostino, Diane M., (CV) '60 '89 C.1056 B.A. L.880 J.D. Co. Dep. Dist. Atty.
Daigle, James M. '65 '94 C&L.629 B.S., J.D. [Brisbee&S.]
Darr, J. W. '35 '63 C&L.629 B.S., LL.B. 1341 NW Jackson School Rd.‡
Deggendorf, Rose M. '57 '85 C.454 B.A. L.818 J.D. Sr. Atty., Intel Corp.
Dehmer, Wendy C. Battias '68 '94 C.222 B.A. L.1018 J.D. Assoc. Coun., Intel Corp.
Domokos, Marius '72 '00 C.800 B.S. L.1375 J.D. (adm. in CA; not adm. in OR) Sr. IP Atty., Intel. Corp.
Doyle, James P. '67 '92 C.888 B.S. L.1209 J.D. [Garland,G.L.S.H.e.a.]
Dyess, Carl F. '46 '91 C.336 B.A. L.1051 J.D. 4660 NE Belknap Court, Suite 101
Eagar, James, Law Office of '52 '98 C.999 B.S. L.596 J.D. 247 SE Washington Street, Suite 200

Edling, Shelley K., (BV) '51 '80 C&L.101 B.S., J.D.
134 S.E. 5th Avenue, Suite A, P.O. Box 728, 97123
Telephone: 503-648-2900 Fax: 503-846-9110
Email: info@shelleyedling.com URL: http://www.shelleykedling.com
Language: French.
Practice Limited to Workers Compensation Law.

See Professional Biographies, HILLSBORO, OREGON

Eisenstein, Scott L., (BV) '65 '92 C.30 B.A. L.596 101 S.W. Washington St.
Elliott, Harry F., (BV) '30 '56 C&L.629 B.A., LL.B. 122 N.E. 3rd St.
Elliott, John M., (CV) '59 '91 C.1056 B.S. L.678 J.D. 122 N.E. 3rd
Elliott, Robert M. '45 '73 C.174 B.A. L.30 J.D. 247 S.E. Washington St.
Erwin, Andrew R. '66 '96 C.628 B.S. L.950 J.D. Dist. Atty. Off.
Farrell, Douglas C., (BV) '50 '77 C.477 B.A. L.629 J.D. 3000 NW Stucki Pl.
Finkelstein, Paul H. '71 '98 C.956 B.A. L.950 J.D. 232 NE Lincoln Street
Flaherty, Thomas J., (BV) '43 '74 C&L.734 B.S., J.D. 3032 Rood Bridge Road Drive
Flug, Robert K. '45 '90 C.860 B.A. L.1051 J.D. Oregon Legal Servs. Corp.
Force, Michael A. '48 '74 C.1056 B.S. L.950 J.D. 22920 N.W. Chestnut St.
Freerksen, Karl W., Jr. '36 '63 C.950 B.A. L.596 J.D. Dist. J.
Friedman, Mark F. '62 '88 C.478 B.A. L.846 J.D. (adm. in NY; not adm. in OR) Sr. Counsel, Intel Corp.
Frisella, Barbara Anne, (BV) '59 '86 C.670 B.B.A. L.602 J.D. Dep. Dist. Atty.
Frost, David G., (AV) '35 '60 C&L.950 B.A., LL.B. 217 E. Main
Fun, James Lee, Jr., (BV) '61 '88 C.972 B.S. L.950 J.D. Dep. Dist. Atty.
Garcia, Oscar '69 '95 230 N.E. 2nd St., Ste. D
Gardner, James K., (BV) '21 '47 C.878 L.596 LL.B. 122 N.E. 3rd
Gardner, Mark '49 '74 C.169 B.Pol.S. L.1065 J.D. Cir. J.
Garland, Barbara J., (BV) '— '90 C.1056 B.S. L.1051 J.D. [B.J.Garland]
Garland, Marvin J., (BV) '42 '73 C.1056 B.S. L.596 J.D. [Garland,G.L.S.H.e.a.]

Garland, Barbara J., Law Office, P.C., (BV)
230 Northeast Second Avenue, Suite H, 97124
Telephone: 503-615-8233 Fax: 503-693-0139
Email: bjgarland@verizon.net URL: http://www.lawyers.com/bgarlandlaw
Barbara J. Garland.

(This Listing Continued)

Garland, Barbara J., Law Office, P.C. (Continued)

Family Law, Divorce, Child Custody, Paternity, Parenting Rights, Grandparents Visitation Rights, Support, Criminal Law, All State Court Offenses (non-Federal) including Aggravated Murder.

See Professional Biographies, HILLSBORO, OREGON

Garland, Griffiths, Lay, Suwada, Hilborn et al.., A Professional Corporation, (BV) 254 North First Avenue
Gillingham, John W. '52 '92 C.1130 B.A. L.502 J.D. 121 N.E. 75th Ave.
Gillins, Peter W., (CV) '48 '93 C.878 B.S. L.1051 J.D. 247 S.E. Washington St., Ste. 200
Gimre, Jon K. '53 '85 C.1051 B.A. L.629 J.D. Gimres Shoes, Inc.
Ginsburg, Richard M., (BV) '45 '74 C.930 B.A. L.273 J.D. [R.Ginsburg]
Ginsburg, Richard, LLC, Law Office of, (BV) 1049 S.W. Baseline
Gluesenkamp, Cary A., (BV) '49 '74 C&L.378 B.A., J.D. P.O. Box 1866
Goldstein, James A., Jr., (CV) '68 '95 C.1349 B.A. L.596 J.D. [Ⓐ McNeil]
Green, Boyd Andrew, (CV) '72 '96 C&L.502 B.A., J.D. Metro. Pub. Def.
Griffiths, Dennis V., (BV) '39 '76 C.1056 B.S. L.596 J.D. [Garland,G.L.S.H.e.a.]
Hall, Marlene Wylde '48 '74 C&L.629 B.A., J.D. [Hall]
Hall, Terrance A., (AV) '47 '73 C&L.950 A.B., J.D. 106 E Main St
Hall, Marlene Wylde P.O. Box 280
Hanlon, Roger Michael, (BV) '52 '88 C.763 B.S. L.1051 J.D. Dep. Dist. Atty.
Harrington, Jennifer L., (BV) '61 '90 C.685 B.A. L.629 J.D. Metro Pub. Def. Servs., Inc.
Harris, Robert J., (BV) '58 '86 C.911 B.A. L.596 J.D. [Harris]
Harris Law Firm, P.C., (BV) 165 S.E. 26th Ave.
Hathaway, Paul L., III '60 '90 C.628 B.S. L.596 J.D. Asst. Co. Coun.
Hayashida, Sheryl '49 '79 C.999 B.A. L.678 J.D. 155 N.1st Ave.
Healy, Scott Patrick '64 '92 C&L.950 B.A., J.D. Judicial Clk., Washington Co. Crt.

Helzer & Cromar, LLP
(See Beaverton)

Hermann, Robert W., (AV) '49 '74 C&L.950 B.A., J.D. Chf. Dep. Dist. Atty., Dist. Attys. Off.
Hernández, Marco A. '57 '86 C.1181 B.A. L.911 J.D. Oregon Legal Servs. Corp.
Hieber, Glen '11 '35 L.629 LL.B. Sr. Cir. J.
Hilborn, James C. '48 '77 C.418 B.A. L.464 J.D. [Garland,G.L.S.H.e.a.]
Hinds, Thomas M. '56 '82 C.305 B.A. L.1243 J.D. Gen. Coun., Hinds Instruments, Inc.
Hood, Drake A. '67 '95 C.1056 B.A. L.596 J.D. [Brisbee&S.]
Hoyt, Joanne McGilvra '38 '85 C&L.950 B.A., J.D. Wash. Co. E.M.S.
Hughes, Steven H. '43 '70 C.1051 B.A. L.813 J.D. [S.H.Hughes]
Hughes, Steven H., P.C. 1060 S.E. Oak St.
Hull, Robert Martin, (BV) '62 '87 C.249 B.S. L.347 J.D. Sr. Dep. Dist. Atty.
Jensen, Kit A., (AV) '47 '74 C&L.950 B.A., J.D. P.O. Box 157
Karpstein, Gregory A., (BV) '46 '73 C.628 B.S. L.596 J.D. [Karpstein&V.]
Karpstein & Verhulst, P.C., (BV) 220 NW 3rd Ave.
Karr, Ted Douglas '67 '00 C.628 B.S. L.464 J.D. (adm. in CA; not adm. in OR) Corp. Coun., Intel Corp.
Kassar, Jude N. '75 '02 C.494 B.A. L.608 J.D. [Ⓐ Ridehalgh&Assoc.]
Kehoe, Matthew H., (BV) '60 '90 C.1056 B.S. L.629 J.D. 330 NE Lincoln, Ste. 200
Kent, Wendy M. '62 '88 C.174 B.A. L.596 J.D. [Ⓒ Brisbee&S.]
Killian, Douglas P. '55 '83 C.877 B.S. L.546 J.D. 400 E. Main St.
Knapp, Rick, (BV) '54 '83 C.1051 B.S. L.1049 J.D. Dep. Dist. Atty.
Knupp, Emily Lynn '45 '71 C&L.629 B.S., J.D. 230 N.E. 2nd Ave., Ste. I
Kuennen, Tamara L. '69 '96 C.605 B.A. L.588 J.D. Legal Aid Soc. of OR
Law, David S. '67 '92 C.112 B.A. L.1065 J.D. Intel Corp.
Lay, Mark D. '62 '95 C.629 B.S. L.950 J.D. [Garland,G.L.S.H.e.a.]
Lewis, John B. '46 '75 C.1056 B.S., M.A. L.596 J.D. Cir. Ct. J.
Linder, Gerald P. '55 '89 C.911 B.A. L.426 J.D. 155 N. First Ave.
Litch, Erich J. '71 '97 C.112 B.A. L.426 J.D. (adm. in CA; not adm. in OR) 3400 N.W. John Olsen Place
Lund, Jon B. '41 '66 C.629 B.S. L.950 J.D. Sr. Cir. J.
Maloney, Paul T. '71 '01 C.602 B.A. L.596 J.D. Dist. Atty. Off.
McElligott, Michael J. '46 '73 C.1056 B.S. L.276 J.D. Cir. J.
McKey, Bracken Duane '71 '98 C.897 B.A. L.950 J.D. Dep. Dist. Atty.
McNeil, Kenneth W., (BV) '65 '91 C.939 B.A. L.629 J.D. [McNeil]

McNeil Law Office LLC, (BV)
1323 N.E. Orenco Station, Suite 310, 97124
Telephone: 503-615-8336 Fax: 503-726-2220
Email: ken@mcneillawoffice.com URL: http://www.mcneillawoffice.com
Kenneth W. McNeil;—Kevin D. Brenden; Erik M. Buchér; James A. Goldstein, Jr.
Family, Criminal, Wills, Personal Injury, Business Litigation.

See Professional Biographies, HILLSBORO, OREGON

Milstead, Byron W., (BV) '56 '82 C.685 B.A. L.878 J.D. Gen. Coun./V.P., Credence Systems Corp.
Minson, Douglas L., (BV) '44 '69 C.1239 A.B. L.950 J.D. 247 SE Washington
Morgan, Janice R. '58 '83 C.518 B.A. L.276 J.D. (adm. in DC; not adm. in OR) Dir., Migrant Legal Action Prog.
Munsey, David N. '52 '78 C.628 B.S. L.1051 J.D. Intel Corp.
Nachtigal, Fred C., (BV) '51 '79 C.1071 B.A. L.596 J.D. 101 S.W. Washington St.
Nachtigal, Gayle A. '52 '79 C.97 B.L.S. L.596 J.D. Cir. J.
Noren, David C. '52 '85 C.502 B.A. L.1051 J.D. Sr. Asst. Co. Coun.
Olsen, Dan R., (BV) '52 '80 C.1056 B.S. L.950 J.D. 155 N. First, Ste. 340
Petersen, Virginia A. '— '95 C.145 B.A. L.911 J.D. [Ⓐ Harris]
Peterson, Douglas Neal '75 '01 C.628 B.S. L.629 J.D. [Peterson&P.]
Peterson, John D., (AV) '47 '73 C.628 B.S. L.950 J.D. [Peterson&P.]
Peterson & Peterson, Attorneys, L.L.P., (AV) 330 N.E. Lincoln, Suite 200
Pihl, Holger M., Jr. '28 '55 C.629 B.S. L.597 J.D. Cir. J.
Polaski, Alan P. '66 '95 C.119 B.S.M.E. L.596 J.D. Coun., Intel Corp.
Price, Steven L. '49 '80 C.659 B.A. L.1051 J.D. Cir. J.
Ravelo, Theresa '69 '94 C.670 B.B.A. L.1051 J.D. Intel Corp.
Ray, Scott D. '69 '01 C.1056 B.S. L.1051 J.D. [VanTrease&R.]
Rich, Andrew M., (BV) '47 '77 C.628 B.S. L.1051 J.D. [Zenger&R.]
Rich, David L., (BV) '49 '79 C.1056 B.S. L.596 J.D. 101 S.W. Washington
Ridehalgh, Ronald L. '71 '96 C&L.950 B.S., J.D. [Ridehalgh&Assoc.]
Ridehalgh & Associates, LLC 233 E. Main, Ste. 200
Rini, Michele C., (CV) '67 '92 C.1056 B.S. L.1051 J.D. [Ⓐ Karpstein&V.]
Salisbury, Michael J. '54 '92 *C.188 A.B. L.1051 J.D. Supvr., Co. Dept. of Assessment & Taxation*
Schumacher, Gregory B. '66 '00 C.1109 B.A. L.999 J.D. 1066 N.E. Creeksedge Dr.
Schwenn, W. C., (AV) '14 '41 C&L.966 Ph.B., J.D. 100 S.W. Baseline‡

Scott Hookland LLP
(See Tigard)

Shadden, John L., (CV) '46 '89 C.413 B.A. L.596 J.D. 126 N.E. 2nd St.
Shannon, Marcy S., (CV) '67 '95 C&L.629 B.S., J.D. Dep. Dist. Atty.

Shertz, Laurie, LLC
(See Portland)

Short, Jason Glenn '72 '00 C.877 B.S. L.950 J.D. Dist. Atty. Off.
Sirtori, Michael J. '66 '95 C.1044 B.A. L.602 J.D. Intel Corp.
Smith, P. McCoy '62 '91 C.174 B.S. L.893 J.D. Intel Corp. (Pat.)
Spencer, Douglas F., (BV) '49 '75 C.1181 B.S. L.629 J.D. 217 East Main Street
Stewart, Steven C. '60 '89 C.277 B.E.E. L.1202 J.D. (adm. in MA; not adm. in OR; Pat.) Sr. Patent Atty., Intel Corp.
Stockton, Grant D. '73 '02 C&L.950 B.S., J.D. [Ⓐ Brisbee&S.]
Stockton, William H., (AV) '47 '74 C.1056 B.A. L.596 J.D. [Brisbee&S.]
Suwada, Suzanne J. '70 '97 C.769 B.A. L.464 J.D [Garland,G.L.S.H.e.a.]
Thies, Bradley J. '60 '87 C.950 B.A. L.178 J.D. Gen. Coun., FEI Co.
Tintera, Thomas J., (BV) '49 '81 C.434 B.A. L.1051 J.D. Co. Dist. Atty.
Tyner, John J., III, (BV) '54 '82 C.950 B.S. L.285 J.D. 330 N.E. Lincoln Street, Suite 300
Upham, Donald Scott, (AV) '45 '72 C.1056 B.S. L.629 J.D. Dist. Atty.
Upton, Suzanne M. '— '90 C.931 B.A. L.629 J.D. Cir. Ct. J.
Van Kommer, Gerritt, (CV) '50 '78 C.774 B.A. L.911 J.D. 247 SE Washington St., Ste. 200
VanTrease, Philip D. '72 '00 C.859 B.S. L.629 J.D. [VanTrease&R.]
VanTrease & Ray, LLC 4660 NE Belknap Court, Suite 101
Veillet, Raymond M. '64 '91 C.629 B.S. L.950 J.D. Picojet Inc.
Verhulst, Steven L., (BV) '47 '75 C.1056 B.S. L.629 J.D. [Karpstein&V.]
Veverka, David M. '74 '00 C.629 B.A. L.950 J.D. [Ⓐ Harris]
Watkins, Michael M. '42 '69 C.628 L.629 J.D. 230 Ne 2nd Ave Ste D
Wiggins, Paul S., Jr. '31 '57 C&L.629 B.S., LL.B. 366 N.E. 18th Ave.‡

Wilkinson, Merlin D., Attorney at Law, (BV) '57 '91 C.101 B.S. L.596 J.D.
100 S.W. Baseline, 97123
Telephone: 503-693-6641 Fax: 503-615-8687
Email: merlinwilkinson@att.net URL: http://www.merlinwilkinson.com
Divorce, Child Custody, Child Support, Visitation Rights and Family Law.

See Professional Biographies, HILLSBORO, OREGON

Williams, Zografos & Peck, A Professional Corporation
(See Lake Oswego)

Wilson, Karen M. '63 '94 C.330 B.A. L.284 J.D. [Garland,G.L.S.H.e.a.]
Winkle, Robert G. '61 '94 C.336 B.S. L.1051 J.D. Coun., Intel Corp. (Pat.)
Wipper, Janelle Factora '69 '96 C.628 B.S. L.950 J.D. 150 N. 1st Ave.
Wiseman, Charles J., (AV) '42 '73 C.1051 B.S. L.596 J.D. [Wiseman]

Wiseman Law Office, P.C., (AV)
473 S. First Avenue, 97123
Telephone: 503-681-4626 Fax: 503-681-2171 URL: http://www.charleswiseman.com
Email: wisemancj@aol.com URL: http://www.lawyers.com/wisemanlawoffices
Charles J. Wiseman.
Bankruptcy, Business Start-Ups, Personal Injury, Automobile Accidents, Dog Bites, Slip and Fall, Wrongful Death, Domestic Relations, Child Custody, Child Support, Divorce, Premarital Agreements, Business Law, Criminal Law, Driving While Intoxicated, Drug Crimes, Aviation Law.

See Professional Biographies, HILLSBORO, OREGON

Woodard, John H. '47 '84 C.597 B.S. L.950 J.D. Sr. Coun., Intel Corp.
Yates, Steven D. '— '93 C.94 B.A.M.A. L.309 J.D. (adm. in MA; not adm. in OR; Pat.) Pat. Atty., Intel Corp.
Zenger, H. Kenneth, (AV) '33 '60 C&L.629 B.S., J.D. [Zenger&R.]
Zenger & Rich, P.C., (AV) P.O. Box 487

HOOD RIVER, * 5,831, *Hood River Co.*

Aaron, Brian D., (BV) '59 '90 C.766 B.A. L.770 J.D. [Aaron&Assoc.]
Aaron & Associates, (BV) 212 Front St.
Abraham, Kenneth M., (AV) '16 '40 C&L.629 B.S., LL.B. 216 Cascade St.‡
Annala, Wayne C., (AV) '32 '57 C&L.629 B.S., LL.B. [Annala,C.,.&T.]
Annala, Carey,VanKoten & Thompson, P.C., (AV) 305 Cascade St.
Apple, Lesley, (CV) '69 '96 C.575 B.S. L.1051 J.D. 216 Columbia
Benton, Charles K., III '44 '75 C.628 B.S. L.629 Rt. 5‡
Bofferding, Todd, (CV) '61 '88 C.1071 B.S. L.284 J.D. [T.Bofferding]
Bofferding, Todd, P.C., (CV) P.O. Box 539
Bonansinga, Tim J. '44 '72 C.337 B.A. L.339 J.D. (adm. in IL; not adm. in OR) U.S. Tel. Co. of the N.W.
Bowe, Larry S., (BV) '50 '76 C&L.1051 B.S., J.D. Hood River Memorial Hospital
Carey, Wilford K., (BV) '41 '72 C.877 B.A. L.629 J.D. [Annala,C.,.&T.]
Crowley, Paul G. '58 '85 C.589 B.S. L.950 J.D. Dist. J.
Crowley, Susan Garrett, (CV) '45 '82 C.220 B.A. L.588 J.D. P.O. Box 963
Dezurick, Bradford Lawrence '64 '92 C.112 B.A. L.767 J.D. V.P. & Gen. Coun., Advanced Navigation & Positioning Corp.
Einhorn, Eric Carl '60 '89 C.197 B.A. L.112 J.D. 216 Columbia Ave.
FitzSimons, Michael B., (BV) '67 '95 C.399 B.A. L.365 J.D. [Jaques,S.S.&F.]
Franke, Scott D., (CV) '56 '90 C.629 B.A. L.911 J.D. 212 Front St.
Garrabrant, Hugh '32 '73 C.629 B.S. L.596 J.D. Dist. J.
Geller, Marc S., (BV) '62 '87 C.188 B.S. L.1068 J.D. [M.Geller]
Geller, Marc, P.C., (BV) 417 Sherman Avenue, Suite 5
Hendricks, William E., III '71 '99 C.907 B.S. L.1358 J.D. Sprint
Hull, Donald W. '44 '70 C&L.629 B.B.A., J.D. Cir. J.
Jaques, Jerry J., (BV) '49 '75 C&L.629 B.S., J.D. [Jaques,S.S.&F.]
Jaques, Sharp, Sherrerd & FitzSimons, (BV) 205 Third St.
Macht, William P. '41 '68 C.674 A.B. L.893 J.D. (adm. in DC; not adm. in OR) Adj. Prof, Portland State Univ.
Mason, James M., (BV) '68 '97 C.629 B.S. L.285 J.D. 216 Columbia Ave.
Mulford, Sharon N. '35 '85 C.627 B.S.N. L.174 J.D. (adm. in CO; not adm. in OR) Exec. V.P., The Wilderness Land Tr.
Phillips, Deborah M., (BV) '54 '83 C.107 B.A. L.596 J.D. [Phillips,R.&S.]
Phillips, Reynier & Sumerfield, (BV) 718 State Street
Reynier, Ronald H., Jr., (BV) '59 '86 C.105 B.A. L.596 J.D. [Phillips,R.&S.]
Sewell, John T., (CV) '54 '79 C.670 B.A. L.1051 J.D. Co. Dist. Atty.
Sharp, B. Gil, (BV) '51 '77 C.813 B.A. L.629 J.D. [Jaques,S.S.&F.]
Sherrerd, John J. F., Jr., (BV) '59 '87 C.112 B.S. L.629 J.D. [Jaques,S.S.&F.]
Smale, Carolyn R. '69 '94 512 Cascade, Ste. 100
Smith, A. V. Lonny, III, (BV) '50 '87 C.259 B.S. L.362 J.D. 2550 Reed Road
Starns, Brian Michael, (BV) '72 '98 C&L.546 B.A., J.D. 116 Oak St.
Sumerfield, William H., (BV) '60 '85 C.57 B.A. L.678 J.D. [Phillips,R.&S.]
Thompson, Michael J., (CV) '61 '91 C.1051 B.A. L.629 J.D. [Annala,C.,.&T.]
Van Koten, Vickie E. '46 '71 C.1051 B.A. L.629 J.D. 2790 Hwy. 35‡
Webb, Shelley A., (CV) '70 '95 C.112 B.A. L.629 J.D. Dep. Dist. Atty.
Womble, Mark S., (BV) '49 '75 C.1097 B.A. L.596 J.D. [M.S.Womble]
Womble, Mark S., P.C., (BV) P.O. Box 1307
Wyers, Teunis J., Jr., (BV) '46 '76 C.629 B.A. L.1051 J.D. [T.Wyers]
Wyers, Teunis, PC, (BV) 216 Columbia

HUBBARD, 2,483, *Marion Co.*

Bolland, Marvin O., (BV) '33 '61 C.1058 B.A. L.950 J.D. 31501 Yoder Rd.

INDEPENDENCE, 6,035, *Polk Co.*

Poole, Kathleen M., (CV) '48 '81 C.1181 B.S. L.950 J.D. 240 Monmouth St.
Russell, Maurice L., II '50 '78 C.1169 B.A. L.1068 J.D. P.O. Box 96
Tish, Eugene C., (AV) '48 '74 C.635 B.S. L.1051 J.D. Pres. & CEO, Schuler Corp.

JACKSONVILLE, 2,235, *Jackson Co.*

Cox, Condé T., (AVⓉ) '54 '81 C.802 B.A. L.846 J.D.
(adm. in TX; not adm. in OR) P.O. Box 1506‡
Herson, Alan R., (AVⓉ) '46 '71 C.563 B.B.A. L.1068 J.D. 196 Eastside Rd.
James, Ronald M. '25 '63 C.628 B.S. L.950 J.D. 125 Beekman Sq.‡
Lewis, James W. '45 '74 C&L.945 B.A., J.D.
(adm. in VA; not adm. in OR) P.O. Box 1198‡
Piazza, Eugene J., Law Office of, (BV) '55 '89 C.1056 B.S. L.596 J.D. 205 Surrey Dr.
Reed, Shane A., (CV) '62 '92 C.1071 B.A. L.950 J.D. P.O. Box 452
Schwimmer, Alec M. '64 '93 C.910 B.A. L.678 J.D. P.O. Box 1105
Wise, Ellen J. '53 '80 C.788 B.A. L.770 J.D.
(adm. in CA; not adm. in OR; Pat.) 11777 Highway 238

JEFFERSON, 2,487, *Marion Co.*

Clark, Margaret Andrews '47 '99 C.112 B.A. L.911 J.D.
(adm. in WA; not adm. in OR) Oregon Tilth

JOHN DAY, 1,836, *Grant Co.*

Carpenter, Jim '68 '00 C.1071 B.S. L.796 J.D. 601 South Canyon Boulevard
Cronin, Daniel L., (P.C.), (BV) '52 '81 C.628 B.S. L.585 J.D. 235 S. Canyon Blvd.

JOSEPH, 1,073, *Wallowa Co.*

Whiting, Geoffrey M. '64 '95 C.918 B.A. L.893 J.D. 61062 Lake Shore Road

JUNCTION CITY, 4,721, *Lane Co.*

Beach, David R. '36 '83 C&L.629 B.A., J.D. 92984 River Rd.‡
Bower, Barbara K. '59 '85 C.628 B.S. L.629 J.D. [B.K.Bower]
Bower, Barbara K., P.C. P.O. Box 688
Cooney, Stephen M. '63 '98 C.174 B.A. L.629 J.D. 180 W. Sixth Ave.
Trudeau, K. Joseph, (BV) '56 '92 C.851 B.A. L.629 J.D. P.O. Box 428

KEIZER, 32,203, *Marion Co.*

Forster, Sharon S. '59 '94 C.1181 B.S. L.950 J.D. 3824 River Rd. N.
Higashi, Thomas Y., (BV) '35 '59 C&L.629 B.S., LL.B. P.O. Box 21749
Jensen, Eric D. '67 '00 C.1056 B.A. L.629 J.D. [Walsh&Assoc.]
Johnson, E. Shannon, (AV) '54 '85 C.1056 B.S. L.950 J.D. 4855 River Rd., N.
Kaffun, Howard '20 '51 C.950 L.596 LL.B. 770 Ivy Way N.E.‡
Lent, Berkeley '21 '50 C.685 L.950 LL.B. Sr. Jus., Supm. Ct.
Lien, John A. '45 '75 C.628 B.S. L.950 J.D. 4855 River Rd., N.
Miller, Albert C. '47 '75 C.1104 B.S. L.950 J.D. [A.C.Miller]
Miller, Albert C., P.C. 3975 River Rd. N.
Park, James R. '37 '64 C.897 A.B. L.145 J.D. 390 Weeks Dr. N.‡
Park, Rupert E. '17 '47 C&L.950 LL.B. 7693 Wheatland Rd. N.‡
Pesola, Taisto A. '35 '62 C.280 L.950 LL.B. 1350 Rafael Ave., N.
Stevens, Sharon Cox, (BV) '48 '77 C.906 B.A. L.464 J.D. P.O. Box 20937
Walsh, Richard M., (BV) '58 '86 C.1056 B.S. L.629 J.D. [Walsh&Assoc.]
Walsh & Associates, (BV) 5845 Shoreview Lane North
Watson, Gerald G., (BV) '45 '83 C.950 B.A. L.174 J.D. [G.G.Watson]
Watson, Gerald G., P.C., (BV) P.O. Box 20758

KING CITY, 1,949, *Washington Co.*

O'Neil, Michael D., (BV) '39 '64 C.813 B.A. L.309 J.D. 11875 S.W. King James Pl.

KLAMATH FALLS, * 19,462, *Klamath Co.*

Aspell, Bradford J., (BV) '49 '74 C.413 B.A. L.596 J.D. [Aspell,D.&R.]
Aspell, Della-Rose & Richard, (BV) 122 S. 5th St.
Bailey, Timothy A., (BV) '46 '71 C&L.629 B.S., J.D. Pres., Klamath Med. Serv. Bur.
Ball, Jeffrey D., (BV) '50 '78 C.118 B.A. L.966 J.D. City Mgr., City Admn.
Barnes, Hollis E. '41 '00 C.999 A.B. L.629 J.D. 5413 Brentwood Dr.
Beesley, Richard C. '22 '52 C.475 B.A. L.213 J.D. Cir. J.
Blair, Wayne H. '28 '54 C.208 B.S. L.950 LL.B. Ret. Dist. J.

Boivin, Uerlings & DiIaconi, P.C., (BV)
803 Main Street, Suite 201, 97601-6070
Telephone: 541-884-8101 FAX: 541-884-8498
Email: bud2025@qwest.net
Harry D. Boivin (1903-1999); Robert D. Boivin (1937-1999); James R. Uerlings; Barbara M. DiIaconi.
General Civil and Trial Practices in State and Federal Courts. Arbitration, Business Law, Bankruptcy, Banking and Commercial Law, Corporate Law, Trusts and Estates, Wills and Probate, Estate and Trust Planning, Family Law, Divorce, Health Care Law, Hospital Defense, Insurance Defense, Municipal Law, Professional Liability Defense, Real Estate, Foreclosures, Collections.
Representative Clients: Basin Transit Service Transportation District; Carolina Casualty Insurance Co.; Huston General Insurance Co.; Klamath County School District; Merle West Medical Center.
See Professional Biographies, KLAMATH FALLS, OREGON

Bozgoz, Enver, (BV) '30 '66 C.1056 L.596 7629 Donegal Ave.
Brandsness, Andrew C., (BV) '57 '83 C&L.629 B.S., J.D. [Brandsness,B.R.&B.]
Brandsness, William P., (AV) '33 '62 C&L.629 B.A., LL.B. [Brandsness,B.R.&B.]

Brandsness, Brandsness, Rudd & Bunch, P.C., (AV)
411 Pine Street, 97601-6020
Telephone: 541-882-6616 FAX: 541-882-8819
Email: info@brandsnessrudd.com URL: http://www.brandsnessrudd.com
William P. Brandsness; Andrew C. Brandsness; Michael Patrick Rudd; William D. Bunch.
Trusts and Estates, Wills and Probate, Estate Planning, Real Estate, Zoning, Planning and Land Use, Corporate Law, Business Law, Buying and Selling of Businesses, Partnership Law, Commercial Law, Banking, Business Acquisitions, Timber Law, Contracts, Financial, Construction Law, Creditors Rights, Bankruptcy, Collections, Complex Civil Litigation.
See Professional Biographies, KLAMATH FALLS, OREGON

Brant, Michael L. '28 '68 C.628 L.596 J.D. 945 Hanks St.‡

Buchanan, Neal G., (BV) '49 '77 C.628 B.S. L.1051 J.D.
435 Oak Avenue, 97601
Telephone: 541-882-6607 Fax: 541-882-2029
Email: buchananneal@msn.com
General Civil and Trial Practice. Family, Probate, Estate Planning, Commercial, Business, Real Estate, Personal Injury, Bankruptcy Law, Collections.

Bunch, William D., (CV) '65 '90 C.301 B.A. L.893 J.D. [Brandsness,B.R.&B.]
Caleb, Edwin I., (CV) '47 '79 C.1044 B.S. L.629 J.D. Dist. Atty.
Cherry, Ruth A., (CV) '50 '91 C.999 B.S. L.950 J.D. 2300 Clairmont Dr., Ste. 1
Crane, Donald R., (AV) '40 '64 C&L.629 B.A., LL.B. 303 Pine, Ste. 201
Cummins, Marla J. '59 '00 C.1071 B.A. L.629 J.D. [M.J.Cummins]
Cummins, Marla J., PC 204 N. 3rd St.
Dalrymple, Richard A., Jr. '60 '93 C.628 B.A. L.950 J.D. Dep. Dist. Atty.
Davis, Reginald R., (BV) '33 '87 C.870 B.S. L.950 J.D. Co. Coun.
Della-Rose, Thomas F., (BV) '50 '76 C.629 B.S. L.221 J.D. [Aspell,D.&R.]
deSchweinitz & Hamilton, (AV) 409 Pine Street, Suite 301 (⊙Medford)
DiIaconi, Barbara M., (BV) '49 '89 C&L.285 B.A., J.D. [Boivin,U.&D.]
duPont, Ann S. '39 '81 C&L.629 B.A., J.D. 3610 Pine Grove Rd.‡
Fairclo, Richard, (BV) '50 '75 C.628 B.S.B.A. L.190 J.D. 280 Main St.
Ferguson, Melvin D., (CV) '56 '85 C.628 B.S. L.629 J.D. 514 Walnut Ave.
Foltyn, Robert J., (BV) '51 '76 C.1071 B.S. L.678 J.D. 514 Walnut Ave.
Ganong, William M., (BV) '52 '78 C.413 B.A. L.1051 J.D. 514 Walnut Ave.
Ganong, Wm., Sr., (AV) '21 '48 L.629 LL.B. 204 Garden Circle‡
Garbutt, Richard L., (BV) '46 '74 C.966 B.B.A. L.950 J.D. 110 N. 7th
Giacomini, J. Anthony, (AV) '30 '56 C.670 A.B. L.813 J.D. [Giacomini]
Giacomini Law Office, (AV) 115 North 5th Street, Suite 202
Gilman, Julie A. '58 '86 C.378 B.S. L.221 J.D.
(adm. in CA; not adm. in OR) Sr. Corp. Coun., Jeld-Wen Inc.
Hamilton, Robert S., (AV) '42 '67 C.197 B.A. L.629 J.D. [deSchweinitz&H.] ⊙
Hedlund, Gary L., (BV) '47 '73 C.628 B.S. L.950 J.D. 303 Pine St.
Henderson, Blair M., (AV) '42 '69 C&L.950 B.A., J.D. 426 Main Street
Henderson, Robert K. '58 '89 C.154 B.A. L.950 J.D. 4711 Hwy. 39‡
Hoots, D. L. '26 '63 L.596 LL.B. P.O. Box 8081‡
Isaacson, Rodger J. '49 '75 C.665 B.A. L.464 J.D. Cir. J.

Jacobson, Thierolf & Dickey, P.C.
(See Medford)

Jones, Stanley C., (AV) '22 '49 C&L.629 B.S., J.D. 5452 Brentwood‡
Knieps, Karla J. '44 '82 C.1051 B.S. L.1065 J.D. Cir. J.
Lam, Bonnie A., (CV) '71 '97 C.37 B.A. L.284 J.D. [B.A.Lam]
Lam, Bonnie A., P.C., Law Office of, (CV) 111 North 7th Street
LeBourveau, Lisette M. '63 '96 [Spencer R.&L.]

Lowry, Robert D., Law Offices of
(See Eugene)

Mac Arthur, Scott D., (CV) '58 '89 C.768 B.A. L.950 J.D. [S.D.MacArthur]
Mac Arthur, Scott D., PC, (CV) 280 Main St.
Matzen, Bonham J. '42 '70 C.628 B.S. L.950 J.D. 435 Oak St.
Molatore, Jerry M., (AV) '45 '70 C.629 B.A. L.770 J.D. 426 Main St.
Moore, Craig M. '57 '93
C.1193 B.A. L.1051 J.D. Klamath First Federal Savings & Loan Assn.

Muhlheim Boyd
(See Eugene)

Oden, Dennis, (CV) '59 '92 C.1071 B.S. L.950 J.D. 3922 Lakeport Boulevard
Oldenkamp, EveLyn A. '70 '98 C&L.629 B.S., J.D. [E.Oldenkamp]
Oldenkamp, EveLyn 200 Pine St.
Osborne, Douglas V., (BV) '45 '72 C.549 B.S. L.464 J.D. 439 Pine St.
Osborne, Roxanne Burgett '54 '79 C.628 B.S. L.629 J.D. Cir. J.
Piper, Donald A. W. '22 '50 C.31 L.596 LL.B. Ret. Cir. J.
Porter, Samuel D. '60 '86 C.350 B.B.A. L.221 J.D.
(adm. in CA; not adm. in OR) Gen. Coun., Jeld-Wen, Inc.
Potter, Thomas L., IV '77 '02 C.629 B.A. L.208 J.D. 905 Main St., Ste. 610
Rambo, Richard B. '48 '77 C&L.629 B.S., J.D. Cir. Ct. J.
Ratliff, Donald M. (Mike), (BV) '49 '75 C.628 B.S. L.596 J.D. [Ratliff&R.]
Ratliff, Michael '49 '75 C.628 B.A. L.596 J.D. 905 Main Street
Ratliff, Nathan J. '77 '03 C.628 B.A. L.629 J.D. [Ratliff&R.]

Ratliff & Ratliff, P.C., (BV)
905 Main Street, Suite 200, 97601
Telephone: 541-882-6331; 882-6334 Fax: 541-883-8494
URL: http://www.ratliffandratliff.com
Members of Firm: Donald M. (Mike) Ratliff; Nathan J. Ratliff.
Language: Spanish.
General Civil and Criminal Trial Practice. Real Estate, Family, Divorce, Probate, Corporate. Traffic Matters. Personal Injury.
See Professional Biographies, KLAMATH FALLS, OREGON

Richard, Peter J., (BV) '46 '74 C.1056 B.S. L.596 J.D. [Aspell,D.&R.]
Rodger, Robert Charbonneau '62 '01 C&L.629 B.A., J.D. Dist. Atty. Off.
Rudd, Michael Patrick, (BV) '67 '93 C.911 B.A. L.950 J.D. [Brandsness,B.R.&B.]
Runnels, Mark L., (CV) '49 '80 C.1071 B.S. L.1051 J.D. [Spencer R.&L.]
Smith, Herman F. (Bud), (AV) '25 '54 C.629 L.596 LL.B. 1636 Worden Ave.‡
Spencer, Michael L. '52 '83 C.628 B.S. L.629 J.D. [Spencer R.&L.]
Spencer Runnels & LeBourveau, (CV) 419 Main St.
Stork, David G., (AVⓉ) '62 '86 C.427 B.S. L.494 J.D. Sr. Corp. Coun., Jeld-Wen Inc.
Studenberg, Philip W., (BV) '52 '77 C&L.793 B.A., J.D. 200 Pine St.
Sturm, C. Robert '67 '92 C.188 B.S. L.94 J.D. Sr. Corp. Coun., Jeld-Wen Inc.
Uerlings, James R., (BV) '50 '76 C.1071 B.S. L.678 J.D. [Boivin,U.&D.]
Whitney-Smith, Rebecca, (BV) '56 '95 C.1073 B.S.N. L.629 J.D. 635 Main St.
Wogan, Cameron F. '55 '84 C.628 B.S. L.629 J.D. Cir. J.

LAFAYETTE, 2,586, *Yamhill Co.*

Helm, Ann '53 '97 C.999 B.S.N. L.596 J.D. 1007 Third Street

LA GRANDE, * 12,327, *Union Co.*

Anderson, Bruce E., (BV) '54 '82 C.297 B.A. L.1051 J.D. 2115 Washington Ave.
Baum, David C., (BV) '49 '75 C.1104 B.A. L.950 J.D. [Mautz B.&O.]
Bettis, Wade P., Jr. '44 '72 C&L.950 B.A., J.D. [W.P.Bettis,Jr.]
Bettis, Wade P., Jr., P.C. 1906 4th St.
Blaser, Dawn H. '71 '99 C&L.629 B.S., J.D. Dist. Atty. Off.
Carey, Willard K., (AV) '29 '56 C.629 B.S. L.950 J.D. 3 Pine Crest Dr.‡
Cater, Charles R. '13 '39 C&L.950 A.B., LL.B. 492 Modelaire Dr.‡

Corey, Byler, Rew, Lorenzen & Hojem, L.L.P.
(See Pendleton)

Hallman & Dretke
(See Pendleton)

Hamner, John Alton, II '71 '97 C.1104 B.A. L.950 J.D. 1502 Bonneville Lane★
Hearing, Ross E. '21 '51 C.1104 B.S. L.596 LL.B. 1112 Adams‡
Joseph, Steven J., (BV) '50 '75 C.1104 B.S. L.629 J.D. [S.J.Joseph]
Joseph, Steven J., P.C., (BV) 901 Washington Avenue
Kemp, M. Mark, (CV) '54 '84 C.1104 B.S. L.596 J.D. [M.M.Kemp]
Kemp, M. Mark, P.C., (CV) 901 Washington Ave.
Ledridge, Sam H., (CV) '32 '76 C.1104 B.S. L.596 J.D. 10702 S. McAlister Rd.
Mammen, D. Dale, (CV) '39 '67 C.335 B.A. L.950 J.D. [D.Mammen]
Mammen, Dale, (CV) 1602 6th St.

Mautz Baum & O'Hanlon, LLP, (AV)
1902 4th Street, P.O. Box 967, 97850 ⊙
Telephone: 541-963-3104 Fax: 541-963-9254
Email: mbolg@mautzeltal.com

(This Listing Continued)

Mautz Baum & O'Hanlon, LLP (Continued)

Resident Partner: David C. Baum.
General Litigation and Appellate Practice in all State and Federal Courts. Administrative, Agriculture, Bankruptcy, Business, Commercial, Creditors' Rights, Estate Planning and Probate, Insurance, Personal Injury, Professional Malpractice Defense and Real Estate.
Pendleton, Oregon Office: 101 S.E. Byers Avenue, P.O. Box 628. 97801. Telephone: 541-276-2811. Fax: 541-276-0543.

See Professional Biographies, LA GRANDE, OREGON

Mendiguren, Phillip A. . . . '50 '78 C.629 B.S. L.285 J.D. Cir. J.

Peterson Law Offices, PC
(See Portland)

Ricker, Jonel K., (BV) . . . '54 '79 C.1104 B.S. L.950 J.D. [Ricker&R.]
Ricker & Roberson, (BV) . . . 1005 Adams Avenue
Roberson, Kippy, (CV) . . . '60 '97 C.628 B.S. L.1194 J.D. [Ricker&R.]
Tipperman, Mark, (BV) . . . '48 '74 C.184 B.A. L.1019 J.D. 1108 Adams Avenue
Valentine, Eric W. . . . '43 '72 C&L.813 A.B., J.D. Cir. J.
Wasley, Warner V. . . . '42 '68 C.473 B.S. L.629 J.D. Sr. J.‡
Weishaar, Steven F. '51 '77 C.628 B.S. L.1137 J.D.
(adm. in CA; not adm. in OR) 2005 Linda Ln.‡
West, Russell B., (BV) . . . '53 '81 C.174 B.A. L.629 J.D. Dist. Atty.
Williams, Wes . . . '60 '96 C.1056 B.S. L.629 J.D. 115 Elm St.

LAKE OSWEGO, 35,278, *Clackamas, Multnomah & Washington Cos.*

Abramowitz, Kay Wakefield, (BV) . . . '40 '84 C.878 B.S. L.596 J.D. [Buckley L.]
Alvey, Kathryn L. . . . '57 '84 C.508 B.S. L.1051 J.D. 3 Monroe Parkway, Suite P
Angus, Jane E., (AV) . . . '47 '73 C.1056 B.S. L.950 J.D. The OR State Bar
Avison, David B. . . . '45 '74 C.1051 B.A. L.950 J.D. 14523 S.W. Westlake Dr.
Bailey, William David . . . '51 '76 C.413 B.A. L.596 J.D. [W.D.Bailey]
Bailey, William D., P.C. . . . 5 Centerpointe Dr.
Baker, Bradley O., (AV) . . . '50 '78 C.1056 B.S. L.950 J.D. 15545 Village Park Court
Bartsch, Ann . . . '50 '77 C.813 A.B. L.145 J.D. Oregon State Bar
Baum, Victoria Short . . . '48 '77 C.1056 B.S. L.596 J.D. Ore. State Bar
Beck, Alan R., (AV) . . . '50 '80 C.911 B.A. L.596 J.D. OR State Bar Prof. Liability Fund
Bedor, Stephen J. . . . '57 '82 C.494 B.A. L.1018 J.D. 155 B Avenue, Suite 240
Bennett, James P. '54 '79 C.37 B.A. L.990 J.D.
(adm. in CA; not adm. in OR) 18383 Old River Dr.‡
Berentson, David J. . . . '44 '73 C.747 B.A. L.596 J.D. P.O. Box 507
Berne, Craig R., (AV) . . . '62 '87 C.911 B.A. L.1066 J.D. [Harris,B.C.]
Binkley, Kristin R. . . . '74 '01 C.1044 B.A. L.215 J.D. [Ⓐ Williams,Z.&P.]
Bittner, Brandon C. . . . '71 '00 C.941 B.S. L.629 J.D. [Ⓐ Bittner&H.]
Bittner, J. Terrence, (AV) . . . '46 '71 C.629 B.S. L.1065 J.D. [Bittner&H.]

Bittner & Hahs, P.C., (AV)
4949 SW Meadows Road, Suite 260, 97258-2085
Telephone: 503-228-5626 FAX: 503-228-8566
URL: http://www.bittner-hahs.com
J. Terrence Bittner; Andrew D. Hahs;—Brandon C. Bittner; Mark J. McGranaghan; Leah Colette Sykes.
General Civil and Trial Practice in all State and Federal Courts. Corporate, Business, Employment, Construction, Estate Planning, Probate and Real Estate Law.

See Professional Biographies, LAKE OSWEGO, OREGON

Blankenship, Aaron . . . '72 '99 C.413 B.A. L.1051 J.D. [Ⓐ Buckley L.]

Blunck & Walhood, LLC
(See West Linn)

Boone, Evan P., (BV) . . . '53 '78 C.637 B.A. L.950 J.D. 380 A Ave
Bosshardt, John P. . . . '44 '72 C.112 B.A. L.1065 J.D. P.O. Box 2206
Brady, Laura J. . . . '72 '97 C.1060 B.S. L.950 J.D. [Ⓐ Buckley L.]
Brask, Gretchen M. '65 '91 C.939 B.A. L.596 J.D.
Sr. Staff Atty., Greenbrier Companies
Brookshire, Dennis P., (BV) . . . '56 '82 C.628 B.S. L.629 J.D. [Buckley L.]
Brown, Jeffrey M. . . . '69 '97 C.966 B.A. L.950 J.D. [Cooney&C.]
Brown, Walter F. . . . '26 '52 C&L.800 A.B., J.D. Consumer Jus. Alliance
Brustad, George H. . . . '20 '50 L.629 LL.B. 72 S. W. Condolea Way
BTI International Law Office, (BV) . . . 5285 S.W. Meadows Rd., Ste. 370
Buckley, William T., (BV) . . . '43 '73 C.629 B.S. L.1051 J.D. [Buckley L.]

Buckley LeChevallier, P.C., (AV)
Three Centerpointe Drive, Suite 250, 97035
Telephone: 503-620-8900 Telecopier: 503-620-4878
Email: ncp@buckley-law.com URL: http://www.buckley-law.com
Dennis P. Brookshire; William T. Buckley; William E. Gaar; Robert LeChevallier; Richard A. Mario; Jaye Wickham Taylor; Richard A. Uffelman; Kay Wakefield Abramowitz. Of Counsel: Jay A. Richardson. Associates: Aaron Blankenship; Laura J. Brady; Shawn A. Nolan; June M. Wiyrick.
Business, Real Estate, Commercial, Corporate, Land Law, Environmental Law, Bankruptcy, Trusts, Probate, Wills.

See Professional Biographies, LAKE OSWEGO, OREGON

Buehler, John W., (AV) . . . '50 '77 C.112 B.A. L.950 J.D. [Buehler&B.]
Buehler, Karen J., (BV) . . . '58 '91 C.1056 B.S. L.950 J.D. [Buehler&B.]
Buehler & Buehler, (AV) . . . 340 Oswego Pointe Drive, Suite 204
Burke, Steven Charles '69 '00 C.1056 B.S. L.596 J.D.
(adm. in WA; not adm. in OR) [S.C.Burke]
Burke, Steven C., P.C. . . . 4248 Galewood
Bussman, David L., (AV) . . . '51 '80 C&L.629 B.S., J.D. 4101 S.W. Kruse Way, Ste. 201
Capener, Jeffery Howard . . . '68 '98 C.101 B.A L.190 J.D. [Ⓐ Wallace,K.&M.]
Carlson, Eric H. . . . '40 '75 C&L.629 B.A., J.D. 907 Oak St.
Carr, John T. . . . '64 '92 C.1058 B.A. L.950 J.D. 155 B Avenue
Charles, Alan F. '37 '64 C.112 A.B. L.309 LL.B.
(adm. in CA; not adm. in OR) 6950 Childs Rd.‡
Choban, Steven L. . . . '47 '90 C.766 B.A. L.284 J.D. Gen. Coun., US Mortgage, LLC
Christensen, Milt, P.C., (AV) . . . '56 '85 C&L.101 B.S., J.D. [Harris,B.C.]
Churchill, Leonard, Lodine & Hendrie, (AV)
Two Centerpointe Drive, Suite 580 (⊙Salem)

Clark, Lindauer, Fetherston, Edmonds, Lippold & Collier, LLP
(See Salem)

Coady, Larry T., (BV) . . . '50 '75 C.628 B.A. L.950 J.D. PMB 452, 3 Monroe Pkwy
Cohen, Martin R., (BV) . . . '51 '77 C.597 B.S. L.1051 J.D. 4040 Douglas Way
Colett, Charles D., (BV) . . . '55 '79 C.813 B.A. L.1051 J.D. [Galton,S.&C.]
Colett, Rose Sahlberg . . . '54 '79 C.813 B.A. L.596 J.D. 849 F Ave.
Combs, Charles W. '48 '74 C.813 B.A. L.846 J.D.
(adm. in TX; not adm. in OR) P.O. Box 2237‡
Cooney, Paul A. . . . '60 '92 C.628 B.S. L.629 J.D. [Cooney&C.]
Cooney, Thomas E., (AV) . . . '31 '56 C.670 B.A. L.950 J.D. [Cooney&C.]
Cooney, Thomas M., (AV) . . . '57 '87 C.1051 B.S. L.596 J.D. [Cooney&C.]

Cooney & Crew, LLP, (AV)
4949 Meadows Road Suite 460, 97035
Telephone: 503-607-2700 Fax: 503-607-2702

(This Listing Continued)

Cooney & Crew, LLP (Continued)

Members of Firm: Paul A. Cooney; Thomas E. Cooney; Thomas M. Cooney; Michael D. Crew; Charles A. Sinsel; David J. Madigan; Brent M. Crew; Jeffrey M. Brown.
General Insurance and Civil Trial Practice, Professional Liability, Products Liability, General Corporate, Aviation, Real Property, Motor Carrier Law, Health and Employment Law and Administrative Law.
Representative Clients: Oregon Medical Assn.; Underwriters at Lloyds; Amica Mutual Insurance Co.; Elect Mutual Liability Ins. Co.; Norcal Mutual Ins. Co.; McDonald Douglas Corp.; Canal Ins. Co.; Oregon Insurance Guaranty Assn.; The Doctors Co.; Everest National Ins. Co.

See Professional Biographies, LAKE OSWEGO, OREGON

Cowan, Katherine H. . . . '59 '86 C.112 B.A. L.1065 J.D. Juvenile Diabetes Found.
Craig, Debbie F., (BV) . . . '50 '78 C.170 B.A. L.208 J.D. Trustee, Meyer Memorial Trust
Crew, Brent M. . . . '65 '92 C.950 B.S. L.596 J.D. [Cooney&C.]
Crew, Michael D., (AV) . . . '46 '72 C.335 B.A. L.950 J.D. [Cooney&C.]
Cronlund, Jayne Renee '— '95
C.831 B.A. L.588 J.D. Exec. Dir., Three Rivers Conservancy
Dalton, Steven L. . . . '56 '01 C.1056 B.A. L.596 J.D. 4040 Douglas Way
Dardano, David W. . . . '25 '51 C.999 L.629 LL.B. 14584 Pfeifer Way‡
Davies, David C. . . . '34 '60 C.813 A.B. L.309 LL.B. P.O. Box 443★
DeFrank, Maureen A., (BV) '65 '92
C.628 B.A. L.629 J.D. Claims Atty., Professional Liability Fund
Delta Counsel, P.C. . . . P.O. Box 751
Ellmaker, Michael L. . . . '43 '72 C&L.629 B.S., LL.B. 13814 Regency Ct.
Engrav, Gregory W. . . . '64 '89 C.972 B.S. L.190 J.D. [BTI I.]
Ervin, Douglas L. . . . '49 '85 C.965 B.S. L.596 J.D. Safeco Ins. Co.
Ferrero, Edward L. . . . '65 '90 C.770 B.A. L.911 J.D. 12740 S.W. Boones Ferry Rd.
Fischer, Joel . . . '43 '92 C.724 Ph.D. L.1051 J.D. 730 Boca Ratan
Fleissner, Pierre D. . . . '26 '71 C.906 B.S. L.596 J.D. Oregon Assn. of Hospitals
Foote, John S., (AV) . . . '50 '79 C.970 B.A. L.1051 J.D. 17447 Blue Heron Rd.
Ford, Richard G. '40 '73 C.1056 B.S. L.596 J.D.
(adm. in HI; not adm. in OR) 13410 S.W. Fielding Rd.‡
Forde, Richard C. '53 '79 C.684 B.A. L.1137 J.D.
(adm. in CA; not adm. in OR) 2366 Palisades Crest Dr
Forte, Alexa L. . . . '66 '91 C.1365 B.A. L.966 J.D. [BTI I.]
Frisbee, Denise S. . . . '48 '76 C.788 B.A. L.596 J.D. 1860 Egan Way
Fulsher, Allan A., (AV) . . . '52 '79 C.629 B.A. L.464 J.D. [Fulsher&W.]
Fulsher & Weatherhead, P.C., (AV) . . . 18945 Bryant Rd.
Gaar, William E., (CV) . . . '61 '89 C.375 B.A. L.596 J.D. [Buckley L.]
Gabin, Sara L. . . . '57 '81 C.477 B.A. L.950 J.D. [S.L.Gabin]

Gabin, Sara L., P.C.
Five Centerpointe Drive - Suite 400, 97035
Telephone: 503-620-3171 Fax: 503-620-3365
Email: slgabin@pacifier.com URL: http://www.lawyers.com/gabinlaw
Sara L. Gabin.
Social Security Disability and SSI, Personal Injury, Workers Compensation, Family Law.

See Professional Biographies, LAKE OSWEGO, OREGON

Galitz, Keith G. . . . '45 '69 C.586 B.B.A. L.69 J.D. 17406 Brookhurst Drive
Galton, Gary M., (BV) . . . '44 '70 C&L.629 B.S., J.D. [Galton,S.&C.]
Galton, Scott & Colett, LLP, (AV) . . . 5285 S.W. Meadows Rd., Ste. 333

Garrett, Hemann, Robertson, Jennings, Comstock & Trethewy, P.C.
(See Salem)

Gilroy, John . . . '71 '98 C.770 B.S. L.629 J.D. [Gilroy&N.]
Gilroy & Napoli . . . 5335 S.W. Meadows Road Suite 261
Glazer, Peter K., (BV) . . . '52 '78 C&L.629 B.A., J.D. 4500 Kruse Way
Guyer, George H. . . . '72 '97 C&L.950 B.A., J.D. 16325 Boones Ferry Rd., Ste. 205
Haessler, Eric R. . . . '21 '50 C.197 A.B. L.309 LL.B. 15530 Diamond Head‡
Hahs, Andrew D., (BV) . . . '56 '81 C.1060 B.A. L.1067 J.D. [Bittner&H.]
Hall, Kirk R. '53 '80 C.309 A.B. L.596 J.D.
CEO, Oregon State Bar Prof. Liability Fund
Hanway, Kevin L. '53 '78 C.350 B.A. L.352 J.D.
Coun., Home Builders Assn. of Metro. Portland
Harnish, Jonathan T., (AV) . . . '46 '71 C.950 B.A. L.174 J.D. 890 Lake Shore Rd.
Harris, Roger K., (AV) . . . '47 '78 C.628 B.S. L.596 J.D. [Harris,B.C.]
Harris Berne Christensen, LLP, (AV) . . . 5000 Meadows Road, Suite 400
Haslett, George A., Jr. . . . '23 '53 C.629 L.596 LL.B. 3 Masaryk St.
Hatch, Victoria E. . . . '63 '86 C&L.911 B.A., J.D. 18225 River Edge Court
Hatfield, Chandra R. . . . '— '02 C.637 B.S. L.950 J.D. [Ⓐ Williams,Z.&P.]
Hebert, Thomas B., (AV) . . . '41 '74 C.1056 B.S. L.596 J.D. 4090 S.W. Virginia Wy.
Hendrie, Richard L., Jr., (BV) . . . '56 '81 C.629 B.S. L.950 J.D. [Churchill,L.L.&H.] ⊙
Hewitt, Stephen W. . . . '46 '72 C.475 B.A. L.477 J.D. Oregon State Bar
Hicks, Martha M. '50 '75 C.685 B.A. L.705 J.D.
Asst. Disciplinary Coun., OR State Bar
Hitchcock, Wendy S. '55 '86 C.454 B.A. L.629 J.D.
Publications Atty., Oregon State Bar
Hohbach, Susan K. . . . '64 '94 4000 Kruse Way Pl., Ste. 340
Horowitz, Lisa D. . . . '57 '85 C.454 B.A. L.276 J.D. 13537 Fielding Rd.
Hubbard, Rose . . . '61 '89 C.685 B.A. L.596 J.D. 4248 Galewood
Hull, Pamela K. '51 '81 L.1230 LL.B.
(adm. in CA; not adm. in OR) 17337 Bergis Farm Dr.
Hylland, Mark David '65 '00
C.907 B.S. L.950 J.D. Home Builders Assn. of Metro Portland
Hyne, Joyce A., (BV) . . . '51 '83 C.112 B.A. L.596 J.D. 4101 Kruse Wy., Ste. 201
Isaacs, Fred M. . . . '54 '82 C.63 B.A. L.602 J.D. 14130 Knaus Rd.
Johnson, R. Erick, (AV) . . . '52 '80 C.477 A.B. L.813 J.D. [R.E.Johnson]

Johnson, R. Erick, PC, (AV)
5285 S.W. Meadows Road, Suite 230, 97035
Telephone: 503-684-9658 Fax: 503-968-6159
Email: EJohnson@rejpc.com
R. Erick Johnson.
Energy and Telecommunications, Regulatory, Administrative and Environmental Law, Directors and Officers, Complex Litigation.

See Professional Biographies, LAKE OSWEGO, OREGON

Jordan Schrader PC, Attorneys at Law
(See Portland)

Karson, Keir Thomas . . . '57 '83 C.118 B.A. L.1051 J.D. Seminar Mgr., Ore. State Bar
Keller, Matt W. . . . '61 '89 C.505 B.S.B.A. L.208 J.D. [M.W.Keller]
Keller, Matt W., CPA, LLC . . . 4248 Galewood St
Kendall, Stuart O. . . . '39 '72 C.628 B.S. L.1051 J.D. P.O. Box 1708
Klor, John L., (AV) . . . '50 '75 C.383 B.A. L.221 J.D. [Wallace,K.&M.]

Knudsen, Kris D., Law Offices of ...... '50 '75 C.597 B.S. L.813 J.D. 4248 Galewood St.
Kohlhoff, Michael E., (AV) ....'44 '69 C.1051 B.S. L.629 J.D. 3122 Diane Dr.
Kohlhoff, Theresa M. ....'47 '80 C.1056 B.A. L.1051 J.D. 3122 Diane Dr.
Kranovich, Thomas E., (BV) '49 '82 C.629 B.Mus. L.596 J.D.
5 Centerpointe Dr., Ste. 400
Kruschke, Linda L. ....'64 '91 C.939 B.A. L.596 J.D. 227 5th St.
Kwitman, William H. ... '48 '79 C.178 B.A. L.596 J.D. 5335 S.W. Meadows Rd., Ste. 300
Lachman, Theodore D. .... '24 '50 C&L.813 B.A., J.D. 16984 Alder Circle‡
Lawson, Jerry L., Jr. .... '63 '91 C.1181 B.S. L.596 J.D. [Delta]
LeChevallier, Robert, (AV) ....'53 '78 C.950 B.A. L.629 J.D. [Buckley L.]
Lederer, Dean J. ....'68 '00 C.16 B.A. L.1339 J.D. [Ⓐ Scheminske&L.]
LeFeber, Sally '60 '86 C.518 B.A. L.145 J.D.
(adm. in WA; not adm. in OR) 5272 Westfield Ct.
Leonetti, Douglas .... '41 '67 C&L.309 A.B., J.D. 17898 S.W. Blue Heron Dr.
Leuenberger, James E. ....'57 '87 C.36 B.S. L.336 J.D. [J.E.Leuenberger]
Leuenberger, James E., PC .... 4800 S.W. Meadows, Ste. 300
Levine, David P., (AV) ....'54 '84 C.170 B.A. L.596 J.D. 1 Centerpointe Dr., Ste. 560
Lindley, Mark R., (BV) ....'57 '82 C.1056 B.S. L.596 J.D. [M.R.Lindley]
Lindley, Mark R., LLC, (BV) .... 1850 Egan Way
Loewy, John H. '47 '74 C.473 B.A. L.966 J.D.
(adm. in WI; not adm. in OR) 790 Terrace Dr.‡
Lorenzen, Shelley A. ....'52 '81 C.911 B.A. L.276 J.D. 1920 Northshore Road
Lorenzini, Paul G. ....'42 '76 C.1027 B.S. L.426 J.D. Law Clerk
Lundeen, John W., (BV) '47 '79 C.477 B.G.S. L.1051 J.D.
15942 S.W. Boones Ferry Rd.
Lyons, Allen W., (BV) ....'47 '73 C.911 B.A. L.950 J.D. [Scheminske&L.]
Lyons, Clifton A., Jr '57 '82 C&L.309 B.A., J.D.
(adm. in MA; not adm. in OR) Silicon Forest Research
Madigan, David J. ....'64 '01 C.1056 B.S. L.596 J.D. [Cooney&C.]
Mann, Lawrence E. ....'61 '89 C.637 B.A. L.190 J.D. [Wallace,K.&M.] ⊙
Marandas, John J. ....'72 '97 C.770 B.S. L.950 J.D. [J.J.Marandas]
Marandas, John J., P.C. .... 16325 Boones Ferry Road, Suite 206
Mario, Richard A., (BV) ....'52 '79 C.628 B.A. L.285 J.D. [Buckley L.]
Marsh, Steven D. ....'— '01 C.1555 B.S. L.950 J.D. [Marsh&Assoc.]
Marsh & Associates, P.C. ....4248 Galewood Street
Maughan, Kevin C. '62 '89 C&L.101 B.S., J.D.
Associate General Counsel, Greenbrier Companies
May, Earle C. '17 '42 C&L.966 B.A., LL.B.
(adm. in WI; not adm. in OR) Pres., May & Camp, Inc.
McCord, Cheryl L. ....'48 '79 C.1056 B.A. L.1051 J.D. Oregon State Bar
McGranaghan, Mark J. ....'54 '95 C.1078 B.A. L.1051 J.D. [Ⓐ Bittner&H.]
Merrick, Jeffrey S., (BV) .... '— '84 C.813 B.A. L.494 J.D. [J.Merrick]
Merrick, Jeff, P.C., (BV) .... P.O. Box 2348
Mickelson, Lon M. ....'47 '73 C.800 A.B. L.813 J.D. 975 Schukart Ln.
Miller, Timothy E. ....'54 '82 C.494 B.S. L.596 J.D. [Miller&Assoc.]
Miller & Associates ....5005 Meadows Rd., Ste. 405
Miska, Edward P. ....'29 '69 C.1056 L.596 J.D. 745 3rd St.
Moller, James W. ....'55 '80 C.813 B.A. L.880 J.D. [Ⓒ Scheminske&L.]
Moore, John C. ....'48 '92 C.1056 Th.D. L.1051 J.D. [J.C.Moore&Assoc.]
Moore, Stephen R., (AV) ....'42 '74 C.966 B.S. L.477 J.D. 8 N. State St.
Moore, John C., & Associates, P.C. ....4248 Galewood St.
Morey, Michael S., (AV) ....'51 '79 C.637 B.A. L.596 J.D. 8 N. State St.
Mullmann, Chris L., (AV) ....'46 '72 C.629 B.A. L.1065 J.D. OR State Bar
Napoli, Jeff ....'71 '98 C.950 B.A. L.285 J.D. [Gilroy&N.]
Neer, Lawrence A. ....'28 '71 C.629 B.S. L.596 J.D. 4261 Chapman Way‡
Neese, Paul .... '70 '03 C.1375 B.A. L.767 J.D. 5 Centerpointe Drive, Suite 400
Nelson, Paul M. ....'53 '80 C.629 B.A. L.813 J.D. 4040 Douglas Way
Nevin, James F. ....'37 '62 C.594 B.A. L.950 J.D. 40 Morningview Cir.‡
Nicholls, Samuel J., (BV) ....'54 '81 C.477 B.A. L.596 J.D. 4040 Douglas Way
Nolan, Shawn A. ....'74 '01 C.34 B.S. L.1051 J.D. [Ⓐ Buckley L.]
Norville, Gerald J., (AV) ....'18 '47 C&L.629 B.A., J.D. 50 Condolea Ct.‡
Oberst, Mary J. ....'52 '84 C.138 B.A. L.629 J.D. 5200 Sw Meadows Rd
O'Kain, Alan N., (AVⓣ) '51 '76 C.112 B.A. L.990 J.D.
(adm. in CA; not adm. in OR) 18225 River Edge Ct.
Paisner, Jonah H. ....'71 '00 C.273 B.A. L.1051 J.D. 4040 Douglas Way
Pakula, Jennifer Lynn ....'63 '88 C.174 B.A. L.596 J.D. Prudential NW Properties
Parks, Gary Abbott ....'45 '93 C.1241 B.B.A. L.596 J.D. 4040 Douglas Way
Parrilli, Tifani M. ....'64 '94 C.770 B.S. L.950 J.D. [BTI I.]
Peck, Kathy A., (AV) ....'52 '77 C.906 B.A. L.950 J.D. [Williams,Z.&P.]
Peterson, Lawrence K., (BV) .... '54 '83 C.147 B.A. L.596 J.D. 8 North State Street
Phillips, James D. ....'35 '67 C.813 L.596 J.D. P.O. Box 1600
Phinney, W. Scott ....'58 '82 C.976 B.A. L.950 J.D. Hearings Offr., Dept. of Rev.
Pippin, James M., (AV) ....'45 '71 C.1051 B.S. L.596 J.D. 385 1st Ave. 215
Pixton, J. Thomas ....'46 '76 C.101 B.A. L.767 J.D. [J.T.Pixton]
Pixton, J. Thomas, P.C. .... 4040 Douglas Way
Powell, David D., (BV) ....'52 '78 C&L.629 B.S., J.D. City Atty. Off.
Pyron, Paula E., (BV) ....'57 '83 C.1271 B.S. L.862 J.D. 4113 Wolf Berry Ct.
Quenelle, Tim ....'68 '93 C&L.629 B.S., J.D. 4248 Galewood St.
Quinn, Lillian ....'61 '92 C.508 B.A. L.1051 J.D. [J.C.Moore&Assoc.]
Rasmussen, Richard R., (AV) '46 '73 C&L.629 B.S., J.D.
Exec. V.P., Gen. Coun. & Secy., West Coast Bancorp
Rathje, Karen E. '58 '86 C.605 A.B. L.800 J.D.
(adm. in CA; not adm. in OR) [Rathje&R.]
Rathje, William John ....'45 '70 C.112 B.A. L.1065 J.D. [Rathje&R.]
Rathje & Rathje .... 5 Centerpointe Dr.
Rayburn, Ralph F., (AV) ....'54 '80 C.966 B.A. L.546 J.D. [Rayburn]

Rayburn Law Offices, (AV)
17685 S.W. 65th Avenue, Suite 300, 97035
Telephone: 503-968-5820 Fax: 503-670-0441
Email: rayburn@pacifier.com
Ralph F. Rayburn.
Litigation, Personal Injury, Automobile Accidents and Injuries, Wrongful Death Employment Law, Sexual Harassment.
See Professional Biographies, LAKE OSWEGO, OREGON

Reeves, Beth Ellen, (BV) '56 '81
C.881 B.A. L.629 J.D. Atty., SAFECO Prop. & Cas. Ins. Co.
Richardson, Jay A., (AV) ....'57 '82 C.1335 B.S. L.950 J.D. [Ⓒ Buckley L.]
Riemer, George A., (AV) ....'50 '75 C.1058 B.A. L.879 J.D. Gen. Coun., Ore. State Bar
Roberts, Penny K. ....'48 '78 C.1044 B.A. L.569 J.D. 100 Kerr Pkwy., Apt. 57
Robertson, Douglas S. ....'47 '73 C.628 B.A. L.208 J.D. Pres., The Robertson Group
Rochette, Edward C., III ....'47 '78 C.963 B.S. L.596 J.D. NERCO Minerals Co.
Rosenbaum, Steven E., P.C. ....'63 '89 C&L.477 B.A., J.D. [S.E.Rosenbaum]
Rosenbaum, Steven E., P.C. .... 4040 Douglas Way
Rubanoff, Dian S. ....'61 '91 L.1148 J.D. [Williams,Z.&P.]

Russell, Howard ....'62 '89 C&L.101 B.S., J.D. 16869 S.W. 65th Ave., Ste. 15 (Pat.)
Sacco, Russell N. ....'35 '74 C.966 B.S. L.1051 J.D. 1159 Lake Front Rd.‡
Saito, Jacquilyn E. ....'65 '94 C.1168 B.A. L.596 J.D. 4040 Douglas Way
Sapiro, Jeffrey D., (AV) ....'52 '78 C&L.966 B.A., J.D. OR State Bar
Schafer, Bruce L., (BV) ....'51 '77 C.881 B.A. L.245 J.D. Claims Dir., OR State Bar
Scharfstein, Steven R. ....'57 '93 C.1067 B.S. L.596 J.D. 4248 Galewood Street
Schaus, Margaret E. '56 '84 C.911 B.A. L.1065 J.D.
(adm. in CA; not adm. in OR) 17849 Upper Cherry Ln.‡
Scheminske, Bradley R., (BV) .... '47 '76 C&L.629 B.S., J.D. [Scheminske&L.]
Scheminske & Lyons, LLP, (BV) .... 5285 Meadows Rd.
Schmidt, Ludwig C. ....'47 '94 C.705 M.S.C.S. L.596 J.D. [Schmidt]
Schmidt Law Firm ....4248 Galewood Street
Schwartz, Todd E. .... '62 '91 C.950 B.A. L.629 J.D. 155 B Ave., Ste. 240
Scott, Alan M., (AV) ....'45 '71 C&L.629 B.A., J.D. [Galton,S.&C.]
Shertz, Laurie, LLC
(See Portland)
Sideras, Leah D., (BV) ....'54 '82 C&L.950 B.A., J.D. [Ⓐ Wallace,K.&M.]
Sienkiewicz, Raymond J. ....'52 '00 C.839 B.S. L.1051 J.D. Social Sec. Admn.
Sinsel, Charles A. ....'68 '99 C.923 B.A. L.950 J.D. [Cooney&C.]
Smith, Cecial C. '14 '60 C.508 B.A. L.981 LL.B.
(adm. in MT; not adm. in OR) 1530 S.W. Spruce St.
Smith, Rex Q. ....'47 '74 C.911 B.A. L.596 J.D. P.O. Box 757
Smith, Stuart W. '60 '04 C.910 B.S.B.A. L.1049 J.D.
5005 S.W. Meadows Rd., Ste. 405
Solomon, Kenneth S. ....'28 '62 C.446 L.596 J.D. 4018 Coho‡
Spiegel, Laurence H. ....'47 '81 C.1188 B.A. L.1051 J.D. 4040 Douglas Way
Stevens, Sylvia E., (AV) '48 '81 C.628 B.S. L.596 J.D.
Asst. Gen. Coun., Ore. State Bar
Stirek, Kathryn Nelson ....'60 '87 C.628 B.S. L.950 J.D. 2775 Arrowhead Ct
Stone, Michael N. ....'53 '79 C&L.629 B.S., J.D. Ste 265, 5285 Sw Meadows Rd‡
Stratton, Richard V. ....'29 '59 C&L.950 B.A., LL.B. 13 Masaryk‡
Street, Jeffrey L. ....'67 '98 C.69 B.A. L.596 J.D. 5005 SW Meadows Road, Ste. 405
Studebaker, Kent E. ....'45 '71 C&L.629 B.A., J.D. 4137 Westbay Rd.‡
Stutz, Benjamin R. ....'56 '85 C.197 A.B. L.477 J.D. 1128 Englewood Dr.
Suwanjindar, Tony, Law Offices of ....'44 '88 C.999 B.A. L.1051 J.D. 4040 Douglas Way
Sykes, Leah Colette ....'74 '02 C.043 B.A. L.596 J.D. [Ⓐ Bittner&H.]
Taylor, Jaye Wickham, (CV) ....'51 '94 C.112 B.A. L.596 J.D. [Buckley L.]
Taylor, Paul S., (BV) ....'59 '86 C.101 B.A. L.178 J.D. [BTI I.]

Taylor, Priscilla, Attorney at Law '53 '86 C.1109 B.A. L.1051 J.D.
4248 Galewood Street, 97035
Telephone: 503-675-4340 Fax: 503-675-4399 URL: http://www.ptaylorlawfirm.com
Email: prismt_53@yahoo.com URL: http://www.ptaylorlaw.com
Trusts and Estates, Estate Planning, Wills, Probate and Corporate Law.
See Professional Biographies, LAKE OSWEGO, OREGON

Thwing, James B. ....'44 '73 C.629 B.S. L.596 J.D. 4565 Carman Dr.
Tuppan, Sharon Barton ....'57 '86 C.605 A.B. L.809 J.D. 680 Iron Mountain Blvd.
Uffelman, Richard A., (BV) ....'41 '66 C.1051 B.A. L.950 J.D. [Buckley L.]

Urban, Jay '44 '92 C.112 B.A. L.1051 J.D.
4248 Galewood Street, 97035
Mailing Address: P.O. Box 1947, Lake Oswego, Or 97035
Telephone: 503-655-1800 Fax: 503-675-8651
Email: jayurban@comcast.net URL: http://www.jayurban.com
Taxation, Domestic Relations, Business Law, Financial Law, Business Planning, Personal Injury.
See Professional Biographies, LAKE OSWEGO, OREGON

Vetto, Jane E. .... '66 '91 C&L.629 B.A., J.D. Atty., SAFECO Prop. & Cas. Ins. Co.
Wallace, Schuyler T., Jr., (AV) ....'57 '82 C.112 B.A. L.950 J.D. [Wallace,K.&M.]
Wallace, Klor & Mann, P.C., (AV) .... 5800 S.W. Meadows Rd. (⊙Seattle, WA)
Webb, Norriss M. ....'39 '68 C&L.911 B.A., J.D. Exec. V.P., Greenbrier Companies
Weisensee, Lloyd W., (AV) '33 '57
C&L.629 B.S., LL.B. State Bar Professional Liability Fund
Welsh, Edwin J., (AV) ....'15 '39 C&L.629 LL.B. 4500 Kruse Way
Westenhaver, Dana A. ....'60 '89 C.101 B.A. L.596 J.D. Newton Cottle, et.al.
Whitaker, Kent C., (BV) ....'44 '70 C.629 B.A. L.596 J.D. P.O. Box 755
Williams, Ronald J., (AV) ....'48 '73 C.629 B.S. L.1051 J.D. [Williams,Z.&P.]

Williams, Zografos & Peck, A Professional Corporation, (AV) 🅱🅱
334 Third Street, P.O. Box 547, 97034
Telephone: 503-699-1300 Fax: 503-699-4111
URL: http://www.wzplaborlaw.com
Ronald J. Williams; Dean T. Zografos; Kathy A. Peck; Dian S. Rubanoff;—Chandra R. Hatfield; Kristin R. Binkley.
Limited Exclusively to the representation of Employers in Labor and Employment Matters, including Union-Management Relations, Labor Negotiations, Employment Discrimination, Wrongful Discharge, Wage and Hour, Preventive Labor Relations, Before Federal and State Courts and Administrative Agencies.
See Professional Biographies, LAKE OSWEGO, OREGON

Wiser, Ralph E., III, (AV) '52 '81 C.1056 B.A. L.629 J.D.
Kruse Woods One, 5285 S.W. Meadows Road, Suite 333, 97035
Telephone: 503-620-5577 Fax: 503-598-4646 URL: http://www.ralphwiser.com
Email: ralph@wiserlaw.com URL: http://www.lawyers.com/ralphewiser
Languages: Spanish.
Personal Injury, Medical Malpractice, Disability Insurance Issues, Sexual Abuse, Products Liability, Automobile Accidents and Injuries, Wrongful Death, Negligence, Torts, Employment Law, ERISA, Discrimination, Labor Law, Professional Licensing Issues, Civil Litigation, Business Litigation, Professional Sports Agency Issues, Trial Practice.
See Professional Biographies, LAKE OSWEGO, OREGON

Wiyrick, June M. ....'72 '97 C.908 B.A. L.596 J.D. [Ⓐ Buckley L.]
Wolf, Thomas K. ....'53 '79 C.36 B.S. L.37 J.D. [T.K.Wolf]
Wolf, Thomas K., LLC ....4550 S.W. Kruse Way Suite 125
Wolfe, Randall J., (BV) ....'64 '89 C.112 B.A. L.770 J.D. [R.J.Wolfe]
Wolfe, Randall J., P.C., (BV) ....4500 Kruse Way, Ste. 270
Wyman, Richard A., (AV) '46 '74
C.813 A.B. L.629 J.D. 5335 S.W. Meadows Rd., Ste. 300
Yeager, Walter W., (BV) ....'21 '53 C.629 L.596 LL.B. 8 N. State St.
Zografos, Dean T., (AV) ....'50 '76 C.906 B.A. L.950 J.D. [Williams,Z.&P.]

LAKEVIEW, * 2,526, *Lake Co.*

Bogardus, John H., (BV) ....'49 '74 C&L.950 B.A., J.D. [Bogardus&N.]
Bogardus & Nichols, P.C., (BV) .... 35 "G" St., S.

Brandsness, Brandsness, Rudd & Bunch, P.C.
(See Klamath Falls)

Lynch, James C., (AV) .... '36 '61 C&L.629 B.S., LL.B. [Lynch&V.]

Lynch & Vandenberg, (AV)
620 North First Street, P.O. Box 351, 97630
Telephone: 541-947-2196 Fax: 541-947-5234

(This Listing Continued)

Lynch & Vandenberg (Continued)

James C. Lynch; David M. Vandenberg.
General Practice. Probate, Trusts and Estate Planning. Real Estate and Water Law. Corporate, and Government Law.
Representative Clients: Fremont Sawmill Co.; Lake County Education Service District; Lake District Hospital; Lakeview Water Users, Inc.; Summer Lake Irrigation District; Collins Motors, Inc.
References: Klamath First Federal, Lakeview, Oregon.

See Professional Biographies, LAKEVIEW, OREGON

Monaco, Albert M., Jr. ....'38 '64 C.112 B.S. L.1066 LL.B. [Ⓐ Bogardus&N.]
Nichols, Robert F., Jr., (BV) ....'48 '78 C.628 B.S. L.950 J.D. [Bogardus&N.]

Ratliff & Ratliff, P.C.
(See Klamath Falls)

Simpson, Lane W. ....'50 '77 C.1071 B.S. L.596 J.D. Cir. J.
Vandenberg, David M., (BV) ....'63 '89 C.1071 B.S. L.950 J.D. [Lynch&V.]
Watts, Sandra K. ....'42 '73 C&L.629 B.S., J.D. 95781 Sunny Slope Lane

LEBANON, 12,950, *Linn Co.*

Cox, Lynne A. ....'56 '90 C.628 B.A. L.950 J.D. 799 Mountain River Drive
Harris, Kathleen M. ....'49 '83 C.1056 B.S. L.1051 J.D. 621 W. Oak St.
Kingsley, Richard E. ....'27 '59 C.628 B.S. L.596 LL.B. 80 E. Maple St.‡
Kuntz, Joel D., (AV) '46 '72 C.311 B.A. L.976 J.D.
V.P. & Gen. Coun., Entek Manufacturing Inc.
McHill, Thomas A., (BV) ....'53 '81 C.950 B.A. L.678 J.D. [Morley,T.M.&P.]
Morley, Thomas, McHill & Phillips, LLC, (AV) ....80 East Maple Street

Peterson Law Offices, PC
(See Portland)

Phillips, Joseph K., (CV) ....'50 '92 C.999 B.S. L.950 J.D. [Morley,T.M.&P.]
Thomas, William R., (AV) ....'19 '43 C&L.950 B.S., J.D. [Morley,T.M.&P.]
Triska, Richard E. ....'32 '68 C.424 B.S. L.209 J.D. Co. J.
Zimmerman, Natasha Annika ....'71 '99 C&L.336 B.A., J.D. [Ⓐ Morley,T.M.&P.]

LINCOLN CITY, 7,437, *Lincoln Co.*

Andrews, Alan, (CV) ....'46 '81 C.112 L.1137 J.D. [Andrews&C.]
Andrews & Cramer, LLC, (CV) ....2015 N.W. 39th Street
Arant, Gene W., (AVⓉ) '20 '50 C.628 B.S.E.E. L.800 J.D.
(adm. in CA; not adm. in OR; Pat.) P.O. Box 269
Baldwin, Russell L. ....'63 '89 C.939 B.A. L.629 J.D. P.O. Box 1242
Bjornsen, James A. ....'58 '94 C&L.878 B.S., J.D. [Ⓐ Pridgeon&Assoc.] ⊙
Cerebalaw ....6435 N.E. Neptune Drive (Pat.)
Chambers, Joan M., (CV) ....'52 '78 C.413 B.A. L.950 J.D. City Atty.
Cramer, David V. ....'66 '99 C.1085 B.A. L.629 J.D. [Andrews&C.]
Elliott, Scott, (BV) ....'57 '87 C.1079 B.A. L.629 J.D. 2137 N.W. Highway, Suite B
Ernst, Gregory ....'52 '92 C.1331 B.A. L.950 J.D. P.O. Box 1181
Krom, David B. ....'31 '65 C.966 B.S. L.37 LL.B. P.O. Box 65‡
Lovell, William S. ....'33 '72 C.1056 B.S.B.A. L.950 J.D. [Cerebalaw] (Pat.)
McCrum, Bruce L., (CV) ....'58 '88 C.1109 B.A. L.629 J.D. [Ⓐ Pridgeon&Assoc.] ⊙
Payne, Martha J., (AV) '42 '85
C.1056 B.S. L.596 J.D. 103 Coronado Shores 225 Escondido
Pewsey, Wilmar A. ....'29 '51 C&L.585 B.S., LL.B. 2126 N.E. Quay Pl.‡
Pridgeon, Jeffrey C., (BV) ....'52 '77 C.477 B.A. L.629 J.D. [Pridgeon&Assoc.] ⊙
Pridgeon & Associates, LLC, (BV) ....2604 N.E. Hwy. 101, Ste. A (⊙Newport)
Rich, Matthew L. ....'67 '95 C.296 B.S. L.629 J.D. [Ⓐ Pridgeon&Assoc.]
Ronnau, Frederick J. ....'46 '75 C&L.629 B.S., J.D. 4488 Devils Lake Blvd.‡
Schaub, Scott J., (CV) ....'57 '89 C&L.950 B.S., J.D. 4488 Devils Lake Blvd.
Stimac, Patrick J. ....'56 '81 C.1181 B.S. L.950 J.D. [Pridgeon&Assoc.] ⊙

LYONS, 938, *Linn Co.*

Larson, Theadore A. ....'50 '84 C.147 B.A. L.950 J.D. P.O. Box 172
Lulay, Patricia C., (BV) ....'59 '91 C.1201 B.S. L.950 J.D. P.O. Box 607
Stroud, Ramey ....'47 '91 C.1181 B.Sc. L.950 J.D. [R.R.Stroud]
Stroud, Ramey R., P.C. ................P.O. Box 428

MADRAS, * 5,078, *Jefferson Co.*

Allen, David C. ....'65 '92 C.378 B.A. L.629 J.D. 205 S.E. Fifth St.
Glenn, David C., (BV) ....'46 '73 C.911 B.A. L.629 J.D. [Glenn,S.&R.]
Glenn, Sites & Reeder, (BV) ....205 S.E. Fifth Street
Kimble, Jennifer Frances ....'64 '91 C.35 B.A. L.37 J.D. 242 S.W. 4th St.
Laws, James W., (BV) ....'47 '78 C.637 B.S. L.629 J.D. [J.Laws]
Laws, James, (BV) ....449 Hood Ave.
Neilson, George W. ....'48 '73 C&L.629 B.S., J.D. Cir. J.
Reeder, Donald V., (BV) ....'53 '81 C.628 B.S. L.950 J.D. [Glenn,S.&R.]
Rodriguez, Sumner C., (AV) ....'20 '49 C.685 B.A. L.813 J.D. 375 S.E. 6th St.‡
Silvertooth-Stewart, John ....'52 '88 C&L.629 B.S., J.D. 185 S.W. B St.
Sites, Edward E., (CV) ....'47 '73 C&L.629 B.S., J.D. [Glenn,S.&R.]
Sumner, Paul F., (CV) ....'52 '78 C.178 A.B. L.629 J.D. 185 S.W. B St.

MANZANITA, 564, *Tillamook Co.*

Martin, Stewart A., (BV) ....'50 '77 C.112 B.S. L.1051 J.D. P.O. Box 909
Sacks, Joel D., (AVⓉ) ....'36 '63 C.30 B.P.S. L.446 J.D. 298 Laneda Ave.

MARYLHURST, —, *Clackamas Co.*

Blackford, Sheila Maloney ....'54 '00 C.483 B.A. L.169 J.D. P.O. Box 4
Smith, Olivia Lee '46 '77 C.628 B.A. L.1051 J.D.
Contracts Mgr., Clackamas Co. Mental Health Center

MAUPIN, 456, *Wasco Co.*

Langtry, Virgil ....'11 '34 L.629 LL.B. P.O. Box 3‡

McMINNVILLE, * 26,499, *Yamhill Co.*

Albus, Glenn L. '40 '82 C.1056 B.S. L.596 J.D.
V.P. & Gen. Coun., Evergreen International Aviation, Inc.
Anderson, Thomas H., (BV) ....'54 '81 C.478 A.B. L.629 J.D. [T.H.Anderson]
Anderson, Thomas H., P.C., (BV) ....426 N.E. Third Street
Berry, Bradley C., (BV) ....'54 '80 C.628 P.S. L.285 J.D. Yamhill Co. Dist. Atty.
Bierly, Mark F., (BV) ....'54 '79 C&L.950 B.A., J.D. 525 Ne 4th St Ste C
Brady, Stephan D. ....'60 '90 C.670 B.A. L.629 J.D. Dist. Atty's. Off.

Clark, Lindauer, Fetherston, Edmonds, Lippold & Collier, LLP
(See Salem)

Collins, John L. ....'47 '72 C.628 B.S. L.950 J.D. Cir. J.
Coukoulis, Lori L., (CV) '60 '90 C.629 B.A. L.596 J.D.
414 North East Galloway Street
Craig, James E., (AV) ....'21 '47 C&L.502 A.B., J.D. 330 N. Evans St.‡

Cummins, Goodman, Fish, Denley & Vickers, P.C.
(See Newberg)

Cushing, Willard L., (AV) ....'20 '51 C.629 B.S. L.596 LL.B. 2133 St. Andrews Dr.‡
DeAndreis, Peter ....'60 '92 C.1320 B.A. L.629 J.D. Law Clk., Cir. Ct.
Dielschneider, Janmarie ....'59 '90 C.1056 B.S. L.1051 J.D. 2162 N.E. Grandhaven St.
Drabkin, Jules, (AV) ....'40 '71 C.1068 B.A. L.426 J.D. [Drabkin&T.]
Drabkin & Tankersley, (AV) ....701 N. Evans St.
Farag, Denise M. ....'66 '92 C.413 B.S. L.950 J.D. 1337 Villard St.‡
Fox, Jill R. ....'65 '93 C.413 B.A. L.950 J.D. [J.R.Fox]
Fox, Jill R., P.C. ....327 NE Fifth
Fredrick, Carol J., (CV) ....'61 '88 C.685 B.A. L.596 J.D. 2046 N. Highway 99W, Ste. D
Fredricks, Douglas S., (BV) '53 '80 C.629 B.A. L.1095 J.D.
[Haugeberg,R.G.F.H.&M.]
Goldberg, Anita Meg ....'61 '89 C.1051 B.A. L.596 J.D. Oregon Legal Servs. Corp.
Goodfellow, Brent, P.C. ....'75 '03 C.101 B.A. L.950 J.D. [Johnstone&G.]
Gowell, Walter R., (AV) ....'52 '79 C.685 B.A. L.1051 J.D. [Haugeberg,R.G.F.H.&M.]
Gray, John M., Jr. ....'55 '81 C&L.629 B.A., J.D. Co. Coun.
Hansen, Bernt "Al", (BV) ....'41 '72 C.1056 B.S. L.629 J.D. P.O. Box 597
Hanson, Eric L. ....'49 '77 C.101 B.A. L.950 J.D. [E.Hanson]
Hanson, Eric ....405 E. 3rd St., Ste. 4
Harris, Wayne R. ....'35 '69 C.950 B.A. L.596 J.D. Ret. Cir. J.‡
Haugeberg, David C., (AV) '40 '65 C.950 B.A. L.629 LL.B.
[Haugeberg,R.G.F.H.&M.]
Haugeberg, Dianne L. ....'75 '00 C.950 B.S. L.770 J.D. [Ⓐ Haugeberg,R.G.F.H.&M.]

Haugeberg, Rueter, Gowell, Fredricks, Higgins & McKeegan, P.C., (AV)
620 NE Fifth Street, P.O. Box 480, 97128
Telephone: 503-472-5141 Fax: 503-472-4713
URL: http://www.haugebergandrueter.com
David C. Haugeberg; Gary A. Rueter; Walter R. Gowell; Douglas S. Fredricks; Robert G. Higgins; John N. McKeegan; Dianne L. Haugeberg.
General, Civil and Trial Practice, State and Federal Courts. Municipal, Insurance, Corporation, Timber and Logging, Federal and State Taxation, Estate Planning and Probate Law, Family Law, School Law.

See Professional Biographies, MCMINNVILLE, OREGON

Higgins, Robert G., (BV) ....'52 '82 C.1163 B.A. L.950 J.D. [Haugeberg,R.G.F.H.&M.]
Hitchcock, John W. ....'48 '74 C.629 B.S. L.1065 J.D. Cir. J.
Hunt, Ryan ....'76 '02 C.906 B.A. L.629 J.D. [Ⓐ G.G.Norris]
Johnstone, Robert M., P.C., (AV) ....'44 '72 C.911 B.A. L.950 J.D. [Johnstone&G.]

Johnstone & Goodfellow, (AV) BR
1215 North Adams, P.O. Box 626, 97128-0626
Telephone: 503-472-9555; 800-409-3555 Fax: 503-472-9550
Email: rmjohnstone@johnstone-law.com URL: http://www.johnstone-law.com
Robert M. Johnstone, P.C.; Brent Goodfellow, P.C.
General Practice, Litigation, Federal and State Courts, Business, Corporate, Probate, Family Law, Divorce, Child Custody Law, Personal Injury, Alternative Dispute Resolution, Mediation and Arbitration, Construction Law, Debtor/Creditor Law, School, Insurance Law, Real Estate, International Law, Wills and Estate Planning.
Moscow, Russia Office: Novoslabodskaya #33, Suite 17, Moscow 130030, Russia. Telephone: 972-61-84.

See Professional Biographies, MCMINNVILLE, OREGON

Jones, Carol E. ....'55 '85 C.1071 B.S. L.596 J.D. 235 E. 3rd St.
Justice, Samuel R., (BV) ....'62 '93 C.1056 B.A. L.596 J.D. 2046 N. Hwy. 99 W., Ste. D
King, C. W. ....'09 '35 C.628 B.S. L.659 LL.B. 859 N.W. Meadowood Cir.‡
Leighton, Patricia A. '58 '96
C.1175 B.S.B.A. L.846 J.D. Evergreen International Aviation, Inc.
Lisle, Charles L., (BV) ....'56 '86 C.101 B.S. L.950 J.D. 315 North Evans, Suite 9
Marthaller, Chris R. ....'25 '52 C.629 B.S. L.596 LL.B. 229 Atlantic St.‡
McKeegan, John N. ....'62 '88 C.105 B.A. L.602 J.D. [Haugeberg,R.G.F.H.&M.]
Mendenhall, Cynthia Kaufman ....'59 '92 C.823 B.F.A. L.950 J.D. Bus Book Pub., Inc.

Norris, Gary G., Law Office of, (BV) '53 '82 C&L.629 B.S., J.D.
2235 N.E. Evans Street, 97128
Telephone: 503-472-3770 Fax: 503-472-2349
Email: garyg.norris@verizon.net
Associate: Ryan Hunt.
General Civil Trial Practice, Automobile and General Liability Insurance Defense, Insurance Coverage Disputes, Products Liability Defense, Business Litigation, Insurance Litigation and Commercial Litigation .
Representative Clients: Safeco/American States Insurance; Ohio Casualty Group; Oregon Mutual Insurance; Fleetwood Retail Corp.

See Professional Biographies, MCMINNVILLE, OREGON

Peterson, John R., (BV) ....'47 '72 C.717 B.A. L.128 J.D. [Peterson&P.]
Peterson & Prause, L.L.P., (BV) ....408 S. Baker St.
Prause, Carol J., (BV) ....'62 '88 C.878 B.A. L.950 J.D. [Peterson&P.]

Richardson, Beverly D., (AV) '43 '79 C.813 B.A. L.184 J.D.
414 N. Galloway, 97128
Telephone: 503-472-3347 Fax: 503-472-3559
Criminal and Civil Trial Practice, Personal Injury, Criminal Defense and Family Law.

Rueter, Gary A., (AV) ....'45 '69 C&L.950 B.A., J.D. [Haugeberg,R.G.F.H.&M.]
Schroy, Paul H. '18 '42 C&L.339 A.B., LL.B.
(adm. in IL; not adm. in OR) 2278 N.W. Victoria Ct.‡
Schultz, Gary, (BV) ....'50 '80 C&L.629 B.A., J.D. 205 E. 6th
Sparks, Jerry G. ....'38 '74 C.628 B.S. L.1051 J.D. 301 W. 18th Pl.‡
Stern, Mary P. ....'59 '91 C.462 B.S. L.818 J.D. 1863 NW Doral Street
Stone, Ronald W., (AV) ....'46 '77 C.8 B.A. L.7 J.D. 535 NE 5th Street
Suchy, Robert F., (CV) ....'56 '85 C.413 B.A.B.S. L.596 J.D. 4201 SE Riverside Loop
Tankersley, Thomas Channing, (AV) ....'49 '75 C.112 B.A. L.1068 J.D. [Drabkin&T.]
Thompson, Robert S. ....'30 '56 C.299 B.A. L.477 J.D. City J.
Tichenor, Carroll J. ....'39 '64 C&L.629 B.S., J.D. Dep. Dist. Atty.★
Wright, Catherine A. ....'71 '00 C.999 L.L.B. L.950 J.D. [Ⓐ Drabkin&T.]

MEDFORD, * 63,154, *Jackson Co.*

A A Bankruptcy Clinic, (CV) ....303 W. 5th Street
Abel, Gregory M. ....'68 '99 C.1071 B.S. L.285 J.D. [Ⓐ Grantland,B.&S.]
Abel, Robert L., (CV) ....'39 '70 C.629 B.S. L.950 J.D. 10 Crater Lake Ave.
Aebi, Fred M., (AV) ....'41 '67 C.1056 L.596 J.D. [Ⓒ Hornecker,C.H.&H.]
Allan, Karen C., (AV) ....'43 '75 C.681 B.A. L.629 J.D. [Foster D.]
Allmaras, Jacob H., (BVⓉ) '47 '74 C.755 B.A. L.190 J.D.
(adm. in MN; not adm. in OR) [J.H.Allmaras]
Allmaras, Jacob H., P.C., (BVⓉ) ....2847 Bailey Ave.
Almaguer, John A. '68 '99 C.769 B.A. L.37 J.D.
(adm. in CA; not adm. in OR) 1133 S. Riverside Drive, Suite 5-C
Amborn, Candace ....'69 '94 C.112 B.A. L.1051 J.D. P.O. Box 580
Andersen, Kelly L., (AV) ....'52 '79 C&L.101 B.A., J.D. [K.L.Andersen]

Andersen, Kelly L., P.C., (AV) BR
1730 E. McAndrews Road, Suite A, 97504-5575
Telephone: 541-773-7000 Fax: 541-608-0535 URL: http://www.lawyers.com/klandersenlaw
Email: kelly@andersenlaw.com URL: http://www.andersenlaw.com
Kelly L. Andersen.

(This Listing Continued)

Andersen, Kelly L., P.C. (Continued)

Plaintiff's Personal Injury, Product Liability, Medical Malpractice, Wrongful Death, Sexual Abuse.
See Professional Biographies, MEDFORD, OREGON

Anderson, Eugene V. .... '61 '97 C.999 B.A. L.629 J.D. 220 N. Oakdale
Anderson, Glen C. '44 '74 C.172 B.S. L.950 J.D.
(adm. in AK; not adm. in OR) 2387 Gene Cameron Way‡
Anderson, Jason M., (CV) .... '70 '95 C&L.629 B.A., J.D. [Foster D.]
Anderson, Robert L., (AVⓉ) '38 '66 C.791 B.S. L.174 J.D.
(adm. in NE; not adm. in OR) 601 Summerwood Drive‡
Annand, Megan B., (AVⓉ) .... '51 '82 C.112 A.B. L.1065 J.D. 800 West Eighth Street
Antholz, Shane J., LL.M. .... '75 '02 C.375 B.S. L.629 J.D. [Ⓐ Hornecker,C.H.&H.]
Arant, Michael, (BV) .... '— '76 C&L.950 B.S., J.D. 312 S. Ivy
Armosino, Thomas F., Jr., (BV) '65 '91 C.147 B.A. L.61 J.D.
[Frohnmayer,D.P.J.C.&M.]
Austin, Penny Lee, (BV) ....'53 '81 C.494 B.S. L.950 J.D. 925 W. 8th St.
Barrows, Gayla K. '54 '85 C.1147 B.S. L.623 J.D.
(adm. in OK; not adm. in OR) 2020 Martin Dr.
Bartholomew, Mark S. .... '75 '03 C.628 B.S. L.596 J.D. [Ⓐ Hornecker,C.H.&H.]
Berg, John N. .... '63 '92 C&L.629 B.S., J.D. Dep. Dist. Atty.
Billin, Richard L. ....'65 '90 C.939 B.A. L.950 J.D. [Ⓐ Hornecker,C.H.&H.]
Black, Dennis H., (AV) .... '45 '70 C.262 B.A. L.976 LL.B. [Black,C.W.S.&P.]
Black, Chapman, Webber, Stevens & Petersen, (AV) .... 930 West 8th Street
Blackhurst, John, (BV) .... '53 '79 C.629 B.S. L.596 J.D. [Kellington,K.R.B.&G.]
Blodgett, Bryan E., (BV) .... '58 '85 C&L.1288 B.A., J.D. [Grantland,B.&S.]
Bloom, Benjamin M., (CV) ....'66 '93 C.299 A.B. L.596 J.D. [Hornecker,C.H.&H.]
Bluth, Robert E., (BV) '52 '90
C.101 B.A. L.950 J.D. Sr. V.P./Gen. Coun., Bear Creek Corp.
Boehmer, Colette, (BV) .... '53 '82 C.1056 B.A. L.629 J.D. 201 W. Main, Ste. 3B
Bolen, Charles E. .... '66 '96 C.736 B.A. L.285 J.D. [Hornecker,C.H.&H.]
Bolen, Kimberly S. T., (CV) .... '69 '96 C.308 B.A. L.285 J.D. [Ⓐ Fowler&M.]
Bondurant, John W., (BV) ....'56 '85 C.950 B.A. L.861 J.D. Chf. Dep. Dist. Atty.
Brian, Michael, (BV) .... '44 '70 C.466 B.B.A. L.846 J.D. 1611 E. Barnett Rd.
Bridges, Rachel D. '69 '00 C.610 B.A. L.629 J.D.
Dist. Atty., Jackson Co. Dist. Atty. Off.
Broesder, Jason C. .... '70 '99 C&L.972 B.S., J.D. 312 South Ivy
Brophy, Timothy E., (BV) ....'52 '78 C.813 B.A. L.629 J.D. [Brophy,M.S.G.B.&P.]

Brophy, Mills, Schmor, Gerking, Brophy & Paradis, LLP, (AV) BB
A Limited Liability Partnership
Park Place Building, Fifth Floor, 201 West Main Street, P.O. Box 128, 97501
Telephone: 541-772-7123 Fax: 541-772-7249
URL: http://www.brophymills.com
Members of Firm: Lee A. Mills; Douglass H. Schmor; Timothy C. Gerking; Timothy E. Brophy; David B. Paradis; Todd B. Maddox; Mark R. Weaver; Thaddeus G. Pauck. Associates: Tamara L. Gledhill; Dominic M. Campanella.
General Practice. Trial Practice in all State and Federal Courts. Corporations, Business Transactions, Insurance, Trusts, Estate Planning and Probate, Real Property and Land Use, Real Estate, Timber Law, Creditors' Rights, Construction Law, Employment Law and School Law.
General Counsel for: California Oregon Broadcasting, Inc.; Medford Moulding Co.; Southern Oregon Sales, Inc.
Local Counsel for: Charter Communications; Farmers Insurance Group; Rogue Valley Sewer Services; State Farm Mutual Automobile Insurance Company; State Farm Fire & Casualty Co.
See Professional Biographies, MEDFORD, OREGON

Brown, Stephen D. .... '47 '72 C.221 B.S. L.629 J.D. Admin. Law J., Wkrs. Comp. Bd.
Burke, Stefanie L. .... '— '03 C.763 B.S. L.1370 J.D. [Ⓐ Hornecker,C.H.&H.]
Burkhalter, Mark W. .... '46 '73 C.388 B.A. L.424 J.D. Dep. Dist. Atty.
Campanella, Dominic M. ....'76 '04 C.1236 B.A. L.629 J.D. [Ⓐ Brophy,M.S.G.B.&P.]
Campbell, G. Jefferson, Jr., (CV) ....'50 '75 C.684 B.A. L.94 J.D. [Bankruptcy]
Carini, Peter J. .... '62 '93 C.1040 B.B.A. L.950 J.D. [P.Carini]
Carini, Peter, P.C. .... 800 W. 8th St.
Carter, William G., (AV) .... '40 '65 C&L.629 B.S., LL.B. 900 W. 8th St.‡
Chapman, Robert Lee, (BV) .... '48 '74 C&L.629 B.A., J.D. [Black,C.W.S.&P.]
Charter, Joseph M., (BV) .... '57 '85 C.477 B.G.S. L.1066 J.D. 220 N. Oakdale
Cherkoss, Arne I. ....'71 '03 C.1131 B.A. L.629 J.D. [Ⓐ Frohnmayer,D.P.J.C.&M.]
Cherry, Jason S. .... '— '97 C.670 B.A. L.1209 J.D. 604 W. Main St.
Clarke, Mark D., (AV) .... '56 '83 C.1071 B.S. L.629 J.D. [Frohnmayer,D.P.J.C.&M.]
Cogdell, Laura G. .... '56 '86 C.629 B.S. L.950 J.D. 711 Medford Ctr., PMB 205
Collins, Hugh B., (AV) .... '— '41 C&L.629 J.D. 2442 Dellwood Ave.
Conroy, Evelyn M. ....'49 '84 C&L.629 B.A., J.D. [E.Conroy&Assoc.]
Conroy, Evelyn & Associates, PC ....916 West 10th Street
Cooney, John Patrick .... '32 '62 C.934 L.950 J.D. U. S. Mag. J.
Courtright, Richard W. ....'28 '57 C.629 B.S. L.950 J.D. 226 Olwell Way‡
Cowling, Robert L., (AV) .... '40 '65 C&L.629 B.S., LL.B. [Hornecker,C.H.&H.]
Crain, Patricia, (BV) .... '47 '77 C&L.629 B.A., J.D. 100 S. Oakdale
Dahlin, Lewis W., (AV) .... '47 '72 C.628 B.S. L.629 J.D. [Foster D.]
Daley, Gordon R. '13 '38 C.112 B.S. L.309 J.D.
(adm. in CA; not adm. in OR) 115 Sheffel Ave.‡
Dames, Robert D. .... '11 '46 C.494 L.748 LL.B. 33 N. Barneburg‡
Dames, William S. ....'44 '74 C.629 B.A. L.564 J.D. 243 S. Holly St.
Daniels, Georgia Lynn, (CV) .... '52 '83 C.605 B.A. L.678 J.D. Asst. Co. Coun.
Davis, Ross G. .... '42 '67 C.399 B.A. L.950 J.D. Cir. J.
Deatherage, William V., (AV) '27 '54 C&L.629 B.S., LL.B.
[Frohnmayer,D.P.J.C.&M.]
De Forest, Russell W. .... '20 '52 C.136 B.A. L.477 J.D. 1542 Grand Dr.‡
Deichler, Clark Ludlow .... '69 '01 C.767 B.A. L.596 J.D. 1818 E. McAndrews
Denman, Donald K., (AV) .... '33 '62 C.628 B.S. L.950 J.D. [Foster D.]
deSchweinitz, Allan B., (AV) ....'43 '67 C&L.950 B.S., J.D. [deSchweinitz&H.]
deSchweinitz & Hamilton, (AV) .... 821 E. Jackson Street (ⓒKlamath Falls)
De Simone, Frank L., (AV) ....'43 '72 C.1097 B.A. L.800 J.D. 219 S. Holly St.
Dibb, Alfred W. '22 '54 C.605 A.B. L.809 LL.B.
(adm. in CA; not adm. in OR) P.O. Box 38‡
Dickey, Robert R., Jr., (BV) .... '53 '78 C&L.629 B.S., J.D. [Jacobson,T.&D.]
Dreyer, Sydnee B., (BV) ....'69 '95 C.112 B.S. L.629 J.D. [Ⓐ Huycke,O.&J.]
Duhaime, William E., (AV) .... '27 '53 C&L.629 B.S., J.D. 261 Black Oak Dr.‡
Dzieman, Thomas J., (CV) .... '49 '76 C.1071 B.S. L.629 J.D. [T.J.Dzieman]
Dzieman, Tom J., Attorney, P.C., (CV) .... 10 Crater Lake Avenue
Engle, Douglas M., (BV) ....'55 '82 C.999 B.S.E.E. L.174 J.D. 219 S. Holly Street
Fawcett, Matthew G., (CV) ....'52 '90 C.1071 B.S. L.629 J.D. [M.Fawcett]
Fawcett, Matt, (CV) ....916 W. 10th St.
Ferguson, L. Lee, (CV) .... '53 '89 C.999 B.S.N. L.629 J.D. 408 S. Oakdale
Ferguson, William H., (BV) .... '36 '61 C&L.629 B.S., LL.B. 5200 Pioneer Rd.
Ferris, John E., (BV) ....'41 '66 C.336 B.S. L.477 J.D. [Ⓐ Jacobson,T.&D.]
Fliegel, J. F., Jr. .... '30 '60 C.629 B.S. L.950 J.D. 22 N. Modoc Ave.‡
Foster, Eric R. .... '74 '02 C&L.629 B.S., J.D. [Ⓐ Foster D.]
Foster, Stuart E., (AV) .... '42 '67 C.629 B.S. L.950 J.D. [Foster D.]

Foster Denman, LLP, (AV) BB
3521 East Barnett Road, P.O. Box 1667, 97501
Telephone: 541-770-5466 Facsimile: 541-770-6502
URL: http://www.fosterdenman.com
Members of Firm: Donald K. Denman; Stuart E. Foster; Karen C. Allan; Gary C. Peterson; Lewis W. Dahlin; Jason M. Anderson; Timothy L. Jackle. Associate: Eric R. Foster.
Business Litigation in all State and Federal Courts. Corporate Law, Business Law, Real Property, Land Use, Estate Planning, Estate Administration, Probate, Trusts Law, Nonprofit Organizations Law, Health Law, Construction Law, Tax Law.
Representative Clients: Asante Health System; Britt Festivals; Cardiology Consultants, P.C.; The Carpenter Foundation; Cascade Wood Products, Inc.; Erickson Air-Crane; LTM Incorporated (construction); Mail Tribune; Oregon Shakespeare Festival; Pulver & Leever Real Estate, Inc.
See Professional Biographies, MEDFORD, OREGON

Fowler, William H., (AV) ....'43 '68 C.629 B.S. L.950 J.D. [Fowler&M.]

Fowler & McNair, LLP, (AV)
705 West Tenth Street, P.O. Box 1746, 97501
Telephone: 541-779-4075 Fax: 541-779-8742
Members of Firm: William H. Fowler; Charles M. McNair. Associate: Kimberly S. T. Bolen.
Business Transactions, Real Property, Creditors Rights, Estate and Trust Planning and Administration, Arbitration, Commercial and Family Law.
See Professional Biographies, MEDFORD, OREGON

Foxx, Jeffrey W., (BV) .... '51 '82 C.970 B.A. L.285 J.D. P.O. Box 4218
Francis, William .... '51 '94 C.1071 B.S. L.950 J.D. [W.Francis]
Francis, William, Attorney at Law, P.C. .... 1237 N. Riverside Ave., Ste. 228

Frohnmayer, Deatherage, Pratt, Jamieson, Clarke & Moore, P.C., (AV) BB
Larson Creek Professional Center, 2592 E. Barnett Road, 97504
Telephone: 541-779-2333 Fax: 541-779-6379
Email: fdfirm@fdfirm.com URL: http://www.lawyers.com/fdfirm
Otto J. Frohnmayer (1905-2000); William V. Deatherage; Steven H. Pratt; Stephen G. Jamieson; Mark D. Clarke; Bernard S. Moore; Thomas F. Armosino, Jr.; Tracy M. McGovern;—Kenneth M. Tharp; Edward H. Talmadge; Arne I. Cherkoss; Jodee L. Scott.
General Civil and Trial Practice in all State and Federal Courts. Corporate Law, Business Law, Real Estate, Probate, Trust, Estate Planning, Federal Tax Law, Construction Law, Civil Rights, Commercial Litigation, Insurance Law, Professional Malpractice, Medical Malpractice, Personal Injury, Products Liability, Premises Liability, Wrongful Death, Criminal Law, Domestic Relations, Employment Law, Divorce, Family Law.
Local Counsel for: State Farm Insurance Company; CNA; Farmers Insurance Group; Northwest Physicians Mutual Insurance Company; Professional Liability Fund.
General Counsel for: Lithia Motors, Inc.; Premier West Bank; Radiology Oncology Group, P.C.
See Professional Biographies, MEDFORD, OREGON

Galpern, Craig S., (BV) .... '49 '78 C.902 B.S. L.950 J.D. [C.S.Galpern]
Galpern, Craig S., PC, (BV) .... 1237 North Riverside, Suite 30
Gerking, Timothy C., (AV) ....'49 '74 C.37 B.A. L.36 J.D. [Brophy,M.S.G.B.&P.]
Glatte, Erik J. ....'63 '92 C.678 B.A. L.629 J.D. [Kellington,K.R.B.&G.]
Gledhill, Tamara L. ....'75 '02 C.628 B.S. L.285 J.D. [Ⓐ Brophy,M.S.G.B.&P.]
Gonser, Carl A. '49 '80 C.813 B.A. L.1065 J.D.
(adm. in CA; not adm. in OR) 1901 Wildflower Cir.
Grant, Robert H., (AV) .... '32 '56 C&L.629 B.S., LL.B. 2413 Republic Way‡
Grantland, James L., Jr., (BV) .... '51 '78 C.1071 B.S. L.950 J.D. [Grantland,B.&S.]
Grantland, Blodgett & Shaw, (BV) .... 1818 E. McAndrews
Greif, Lisa C. .... '73 '98 C&L.629 B.A., J.D. Southern OR Pub. Def., Inc.
Grensky, Ronald D., (CV) .... '54 '80 State Sen.
Guy, Michael S., (CV) .... '46 '92 C&L.629 B.S., J.D. 916 W. 10th St., Ste. 101
Guyer, Thad M., (BV) .... '50 '78 C.276 B.S.F.S. L.1162 J.D. [T.M.Guyer&F.]
Guyer, T.M., & Friends, P.C., (BV) .... P.O. Box 1061
Haberlach, William P., (BV) '43 '68
C.628 B.A. L.950 J.D. 201 West Main Street, Suite 3B
Hamilton, Robert S., (AV) ....'42 '67 C.197 B.A. L.629 J.D. [deSchweinitz&H.] ⓒ
Hammack, Larry C., (BV) .... '42 '69 C&L.629 B.S., J.D. [Stark&H.]
Hansen, Donald .... '26 '52 C.339 A.B. L.930 LL.B. 1024 Winchester Ave.‡
Hanson, John R., (BV) ....'51 '77 C.950 B.A. L.1051 J.D. [Werdell&H.]
Harbison, Sam B. ....'14 '40 C&L.950 A.B., LL.B. 1717 View Pl.‡
Harper, Alan D.B., (CV) .... '67 '94 C&L.950 B.A., J.D. [Hornecker,C.H.&H.]
Hart, Eugene F., Jr., (BV) ....'43 '68 C&L.893 B.A., LL.B. 1625 Stardust Way
Hassen, John R., (AV) .... '39 '65 C.309 A.B. L.813 LL.B. [Hornecker,C.H.&H.]
Haviland, Paul W. .... '14 '39 C.629 L.596 LL.B. 201 W. Main St.‡
Haynes, Gerald D. ....'58 '85 C.1051 B.A. L.273 J.D. [Ⓐ Jacobson,T.&D.] (Pat.)
Heffernan, Robert D., Jr., (AV) .... '30 '58 C.629 B.S. L.950 J.D. 705 W. 10th St.‡
Heil, Dennis J. ....'58 '83 C.684 B.A. L.596 J.D. [D.J.Heil]
Heil, Dennis J., P.C. .... P.O. Box 1147
Henault, Martial E., (BV) .... '53 '83 C.882 B.A. L.629 J.D. 244 S. Grape St.
Heysell, R. Ray, (AV) ....'45 '73 C.1051 B.S. L.596 J.D. [Hornecker,C.H.&H.]
Hollowell, William E. '52 '84 C.492 B.A. L.494 J.D.
(adm. in MN; not adm. in OR) 1666 Edgevale Ave.‡
Hoover, Franklin (Cal) .... '46 '73 C.618 B.A. L.623 J.D. P.O. Box 4636
Hoppe, David G. ....'67 '95 C.477 B.A. L.1051 J.D. [Ⓐ D.Richardson&Assoc.]
Hornecker, Gregory T., (AV) ......'33 '58 C.628 B.S. L.629 LL.B. [Hornecker,C.H.&H.]

Hornecker, Cowling, Hassen & Heysell, L.L.P., (AV) BB
717 Murphy Road, 97504
Telephone: 541-779-8900 Fax: 541-779-2982; 541-773-2635
Email: hchh@roguelaw.com URL: http://www.roguelaw.com
Members of Firm: Gregory T. Hornecker; Robert L. Cowling; John R. Hassen; R. Ray Heysell; H. Scott Plouse; P. David Ingalls; Adam T. Stamper; Joseph E. Kellerman; James A. Wallan; Benjamin M. Bloom; Charles E. Bolen; Alan D.B. Harper; Ryan J. Vanderhoof. Of Counsel: Fred M. Aebi. Associates: Richard L. Billin; Shane J. Antholz, LL.M.; Stefanie L. Burke; Mark S. Bartholomew.
Hornecker, Cowling, Hassen & Heysell, L.L.P., is the largest firm in Southern Oregon and endeavors to be a full service provider of legal services for all of our clients. The firm specializes in Business, Estate Planning and Probate, Real Estate, Land Use, Workers Compensation, Medical and Professional Malpractice, Products Liability, Premises Liability, Automobile, Commercial Litigation and Employee/Employer Relations, Personal Injury, Domestic Relations and Adoption, Municipal and Government, Health Care, Intellectual Property, Computer Law and Civil Trial and Appellate Practice in all State and Federal Courts.
See Professional Biographies, MEDFORD, OREGON

Huddleston, Mark D., (BV) '49 '79
C.705 B.S. L.336 J.D. Dist. Atty., Jackson Co. Dist. Attys. Off.
Hunter, Robert G., (BV) .... '53 '78 C&L.477 B.S., J.D. 2 N. Oakdale Ave.
Huttl, John R., (CV) ....'61 '95 C.112 B.A. L.950 J.D. City Atty. Off.
Huycke, Patrick G., (BV) ....'49 '75 C.629 B.S. L.950 J.D. [Huycke,O.&J.]
Huycke, O'Connor & Jarvis, LLP, (BV) .... 502 West Main Street, Suite 102
Ingalls, P. David, (BV) .... '51 '78 C.112 A.B. L.596 J.D. [Hornecker,C.H.&H.]
Ingram, Dennis R., Attorney at Law ....'52 '78 C.1163 B.A. L.950 J.D. 1216 E. Main St.
Jackle, Timothy L. .... '70 '98 C.413 B.S. L.629 J.D. [Foster D.]
Jacobson, Jerry A., (BV) ....'48 '76 C.1071 B.S. L.596 J.D. [Jacobson,T.&D.]

Jacobson, Thierolf & Dickey, P.C., (BV)
Two North Oakdale Avenue, P.O. Box 4687, 97501
Telephone: 541-773-2727 Fax: 541-734-7269
URL: http://www.jacobsonthierolfdickey.com

(This Listing Continued)

Jacobson, Thierolf & Dickey, P.C. (Continued)
Jerry A. Jacobson; Richard B. Thierolf, Jr.; Robert R. Dickey, Jr.;—Gerald D. Haynes. Of Counsel: John E. Ferris.
General Litigation and Office Practice, Civil and Criminal Trials and Appeals in State and Federal Courts, Bankruptcy and Collections, Real Estate and Land Use, Probate, Estate Planning, Business, Domestic Relations. Indian and Environmental Law, Water Law, Immigration, Patents, Trademarks, Copyrights, Licensing, Wills, Trusts.
See Professional Biographies, MEDFORD, OREGON

Jamieson, Stephen G., (BV) ..... '44 '71 C.31 B.A. L.94 J.D. [Frohnmayer,D.P.J.C.&M.]
Jarvis, Darrel R., (CV) .... '68 '95 C.112 B.A. L.629 J.D. [Huycke,O.&J.]
Jewett, Michael, (BV) .... '48 '78 C.1071 B.A. L.596 J.D. Co. Atty
Johnson, Steven B. .... '60 '94 C.1051 B.S. L.950 J.D. [S.B.Johnson]
Johnson, Steven B., P.C. .... 120 Mistletoe Street
Karaman, Mitchell A. .... '35 '62 C&L.629 B.S., LL.B. Cir. J.
Kellerman, Joseph E., (BV) .... '65 '92 C.260 B.A. L.629 J.D. [Hornecker,C.H.&H.]
Kellington, Bruce, (AV) .... '38 '62 C&L.629 B.S., J.D. [Kellington,K.R.B.&G.]
Kellington, Daniel F., (BV) .... '36 '65 C.629 B.S. L.596 J.D. [Kellington&K.]
Kellington, Michael E., (CV) .... '66 '96 C.1071 B.A. L.1358 J.D. [Kellington&K.]

Kellington & Kellington, (BV)
901 West 8th Street, P.O. Box 357, 97501
Telephone: 541-773-8436 Fax: 541-773-8940
Email: dkellingtn@aol.com URL: http://www.lawyers.com/kellington&kellington
Members of Firm: Daniel F. Kellington; Michael E. Kellington.
Personal Injury, Automobile Accidents, Wrongful Death, Criminal Law, Felonies, Drug Crimes, Wills, Probate, Estate Planning.
See Professional Biographies, MEDFORD, OREGON

Kellington, Krack, Richmond, Blackhurst & Glatte, LLP, (AV)
23 Newtown Street, 97501
Telephone: 541-779-5175 Fax: 541-779-5585
URL: http://www.kkrbg.com
Members of Firm: Bruce Kellington; Carl R. Krack; Douglas J. Richmond; John Blackhurst; Erik J. Glatte.
General Civil and Trial Practice. Corporation, Business, Real Property, Land Use Planning, Construction, Trusts, Estate Planning, Probate, Negligence, Creditor's Rights, Collections, Family Law, Employment Law, Appellate Practice and Wireless Communications.
See Professional Biographies, MEDFORD, OREGON

Kerr, Larry L. .... '37 '70 C.629 B.S. L.596 J.D. 116 Mistletoe St.

Kochlacs, Charles George, (BV) '62 '89 C.112 B.A. L.629 J.D.
308 Howard Street, 97504
Telephone: 541-608-9122 Fax: 541-779-0705
Email: divorce@cdsnet.net URL: http://www.lawyers.com/kochlacs
Family Law, Divorce, Child Custody, Child Support, Spousal Support, Domestic Violence, Premarital Agreements, Criminal Law and Juvenile Law, Driving While Intoxicated, Drug Crimes, Felonies, Misdemeanors, Sexual Assault, Traffic Violations, Parole and Probation.
See Professional Biographies, MEDFORD, OREGON

Krack, Carl R., (BV) .... '46 '72 C&L.879 B.A., J.D. [Kellington,K.R.B.&G.]
Kristiansen, Sandra Skains '57 '94
C.3 B.A. L.629 J.D. Community Dispute Resolution Ctr.

Kuenzel & Associates
(See Ashland)

Lanier, Angie, (BV) .... '50 '86 C.1071 B.A. L.629 J.D. 916 W. 10th St.
Leister, Donald D. .... '31 '71 C.112 A.B. L.284 J.D. 108 Kensington Sq.
Lipton, Jeremie .... '74 '01 C.1058 B.A. L.597 J.D. 717 Murphy Road
Lohman, David H. .... '47 '81 C.976 B.A. L.477 J.D. [Ⓐ Huycke,O.&J.]
Loomis, Karen S., (CV) .... '52 '91 C.398 L.809 J.D. Dep. Dist. Atty.

Loomis & Holland
(See Eugene)

Lowry, Robert D., Law Offices of
(See Eugene)

Lundblade, Frederick H., III, (BV) ... '62 '96 C.813 A.B. L.950 J.D. [Ⓐ Black,C.W.S.&P.]
Maddox, Todd B., (BV) .... '57 '91 C.1071 B.S. L.950 J.D. [Brophy,M.S.G.B.&P.]
Main, Jas. M. .... '16 '49 L.596 LL.B. Ret. Cir. J.
Mansfield, William A., (BV) .... '29 '53 C&L.629 B.S., J.D. [W.A.Mansfield]
Mansfield, William A., P.C., (BV) .... 408 South Oakdale
Marshall, Jeannette, (CV) .... '21 '43 L.629 J.D. 246 E. 10th St.
Mayer, Deborah K. .....'64 '95 C.112 B.A. L.464 J.D. Ctr. for Nonprofit Legal Servs., Inc.
McCauley, Matthew R., (BV) ....'66 '95 C.101 B.A. L.629 J.D. Off. of the Dist. Atty.
McGaughey, Morgain Faye ....'54 '99 C.999 B.S. L.950 J.D. 916 West Tenth Street
Mc Geary, Douglas M. .... '56 '88 C.1056 B.S. L.596 J.D. Co. Coun.
McGovern, Tracy M., (AV) ...'67 '93 C.128 B.A. L.273 J.D. [Frohnmayer,D.P.J.C.&M.]
McNair, Charles M., (AV) .... '43 '75 C.629 B.A. L.596 J.D. [Fowler&M.]
Merryman, Lavaughn A. .... '34 '63 C&L.629 B.S., LL.B. Cir. J.‡
Miller, David L., (BV) ... '50 '93 C.785 B.A. L.146 J.D. 916 West Tenth Street, Suite 201
Mills, Lee A., (AV) .... '48 '75 C.628 B.S.E. L.950 J.D. [Brophy,M.S.G.B.&P.]
Minder, Debbie V. .... '56 '96 C.1071 B.A. L.629 J.D. 10 Crater Lake Avenue
Moore, Bernard S., (AV) .... '58 '84 C.27 B.A. L.596 J.D. [Frohnmayer,D.P.J.C.&M.]
Morehouse, Michael L. .... '26 '60 C&L.597 B.A., LL.B. 633 Pierce Rd.‡
Mueller, James L., (BV) .... '51 '76 C&L.629 B.S., J.D. 220 Laurel St.

Muhlheim Boyd
(See Eugene)

Mullen, Brian B., (BV) .... '31 '54 C.798 B.A. L.502 J.D. 123 Black Oak
Naumes, Susan F. ....'48 '75 C.770 B.A. L.950 J.D. Secy. & Treas., Naumes, Inc.
Nelson, Lowell Y. '50 '81 C.628 B.S. L.300 J.D.
(adm. in ND; not adm. in OR) 1900 N. Keene Way‡
Nunley, Walter D., Jr. .... '19 '50 C.437 L.508 J.D. P.O. Box 1076‡
O'Connor, Allie .... '57 '02 C.273 B.A. L.629 J.D. 915 West Tenth Street
O'Connor, Daniel .... '67 '95 C.907 B.A. L.629 J.D. [Huycke,O.&J.]

Orf, David M., (BV) '50 '76 C&L.500 B.A., J.D.
900 W. Eighth Street, 97501
Telephone: 541-772-8494 Fax: 541-773-6790
Email: davidorf@charterinternet.com URL: http://www.lawyers.com/dmorf
Criminal Defense in all State and Federal Courts. Criminal Law, Driving While Intoxicated, Drug Crimes, Sexual Assault, Felonies, Misdemeanors.
See Professional Biographies, MEDFORD, OREGON

Orf, Rebecca Gordon .... '50 '77 C&L.500 B.A.E., J.D. Cir. Ct. J.
Paradis, David B., (BV) ....'59 '85 C.1071 B.A. L.950 J.D. [Brophy,M.S.G.B.&P.]
Parker, Laurance W., (CV) .... '58 '88 C.1071 B.S. L.629 J.D. 116 Mistletoe Street
Parks, Thomas S. .... '41 '73 C.813 B.S. L.228 J.D. 815 E. Jackson‡
Patridge, Robert W. .... '68 '93 C&L.950 B.S., J.D. 1200 Mira Mar Ave.
Patronik, Susan T. .... '53 '91 C.608 B.S. L.884 J.D. 117 Meadowview Drive
Pauck, Thaddeus G. .... '68 '98 C.1071 B.S. L.629 J.D. [Brophy,M.S.G.B.&P.]

Pendleton, Alan R. '40 '69 C.112 A.B. L.1065 J.D.
(adm. in CA; not adm. in OR) 4386 Pioneer Rd.
Petersen, Thomas N., (BV) .... '51 '82 C.112 B.A. L.809 J.D. [Black,C.W.S.&P.]
Peterson, Gary C., (BV) .... '45 '77 C&L.1051 B.S., J.D. [Foster D.]

Peterson Law Offices, PC
(See Portland)

Plouse, H. Scott, (BV) .... '51 '82 C.608 B.A. L.117 J.D. [Hornecker,C.H.&H.]
Pratt, Steven H., (AV) .... '46 '77 C.546 B.S. L.893 J.D. [Frohnmayer,D.P.J.C.&M.]
Putney, Herbert A., (BV) .... '42 '70 C.1071 B.S. L.950 J.D. Off. of Pub. Def.
Rankin, Linda L. '47 '74 C.1056 B.A. L.94 J.D.
Sr. V.P. & Gen. Coun., Bear Creek Corp.
Reeder, Joel B., (BV) .... '28 '58 C&L.629 B.S., J.D. 116 Mistletoe St.
Reeder, Thos. J. .... '25 '50 C.619 L.623 LL.B. 705 W. 10th. St.‡
Richardson, Dennis M., (BV) .... '49 '79 C&L.101 B.A., J.D. [D.Richardson&Assoc.]
Richardson, Dennis, & Associates, P.C., (BV) .... 55 South 5th Street
Richmond, Douglas J., (BV) ..... '50 '76 C.628 B.S. L.629 J.D. [Kellington,K.R.B.&G.]
Rinkle, Steven R. ..... '59 '90 C.221 B.A. L.1066 J.D. Co. Coun., Jackson Co. Courthouse
Robertson, Robert C., (BV) .... '39 '66 C.1 B.S. L.950 J.D. 1175 E. Main St.
Rudolph, R. D., Jr. .... '69 '97 C.628 B.A. L.273 J.D. Federal Emergency Management
Salter, Ronald L. .... '33 '62 C.999 L.800 LL.B. 1952 Dale St.
Sanz, Cristina P., (BV) .... '60 '89 C.112 B.A. L.629 J.D. P.O. Box 443
Scales, Donald L. .... '66 '97 C.101 B.A. L.629 J.D. 604 W. Main St.
Schieber, David, (CV) .... '59 '88 C.1169 B.A. L.1051 J.D. Spec. Asst. Atty. Gen.
Schireman, William E. .... '58 '84 C.629 B.A. L.950 J.D. [W.E.Schireman]
Schireman, William E., P.C. .... 210 Laurel Street
Schiveley, Mark .... '48 '75 C.629 B.S. L.950 J.D. Dist. J.
Schmor, Douglass H., (AV) ....'51 '76 C.950 B.A. L.309 J.D. [Brophy,M.S.G.B.&P.]
Schott, David R. .... '47 '73 C.629 B.A. L.950 LL.B. Pres., Forestglen Lumber Co.
Scott, Jodee L. .... '77 '05 C.591 B.S. L.629 J.D. [Ⓐ Frohnmayer,D.P.J.C.&M.]
Shaw, Barry N., (BV) .... '40 '66 C&L.705 B.S., LL.B. [Grantland,B.&S.]
Shean, Gerald M., III, Law Offices of, (BV) '62 '93
C.628 B.S. L.629 J.D. 145 S Holly Ste B
Smith, Bruce D., (BV) .... '45 '72 C.629 B.A. L.950 J.D. 710 Cardley Ave.
Smith, Holly N., (CV) .... '64 '89 C&L.629 B.A., J.D. Dep. Dist. Atty.
Smith, Justin M., (BV) .... '34 '62 C.629 B.S. L.950 LL.B. Pub. Def. Off.
Stamper, Adam T., (AV) .... '64 '89 C.1042 B.S. L.1065 J.D. [Hornecker,C.H.&H.]
Stark, Eric R., (CV) .... '66 '92 C&L.629 B.A., J.D. [Stark&H.]
Stark, Richard A., (BV) .... '43 '69 C&L.629 B.S., J.D. [Stark&H.]

Stark and Hammack, P.C., (BV)
201 West Main Street, Suite 1B, 97501
Telephone: 541-773-2213; 779-2133 Fax: 541-773-2084
Email: ers@starkhammack.com URL: http://www.lawyers.com/starkhammack
Richard A. Stark; Larry C. Hammack; Eric R. Stark.
Corporate Commercial Law, Corporate Real Estate, Commercial Leasing, Real Property, Real Estate Development, Employment Defense, Estate Planning, Elder Law, Mechanics Liens, Contracts, Corporate Law, Divorce, Foreclosures, Business Law, Partnership Law, Landlord and Tenant Law, Mortgages, Commercial Real Estate, Wills and Probate, Zoning, Planning and Land Use.
References: Washington Mutual, Medford Branch; South Valley Bank and Trust.
See Professional Biographies, MEDFORD, OREGON

Stevens, Arthur W., III, (AV) .... '55 '85 C.939 B.A. L.596 J.D. [Black,C.W.S.&P.]
Stevens, George R. '37 '76 C.1097 B.A. L.1148 J.D.
(adm. in CA; not adm. in OR) 5299 Pioneer Rd.‡
Stone, Robert M., (CV) .... '46 '94 C.1071 B.S. L.629 J.D. 916 W. 10th
Sullivan, Constance E., (BV) .... '40 '92 C.787 B.A. L.629 J.D. 925 West 8th Street
Talmadge, Edward H. .... '68 '01 C&L.629 B.A., J.D. [Ⓐ Frohnmayer,D.P.J.C.&M.]
Tharp, Kenneth M. .... '71 '00 C.911 B.A. L.950 J.D. [Ⓐ Frohnmayer,D.P.J.C.&M.]
Thierolf, Richard B., Jr., (BV) .... '48 '76 C.178 B.A. L.629 J.D. [Jacobson,T.&D.]
Thorndike, Daniel C., (BV) ....'55 '80 C.170 B.A. L.911 J.D. Gen. Coun., C S C, Inc.
Vanderhoof, Ryan J. .... '72 '98 C.629 B.S. L.596 J.D. [Hornecker,C.H.&H.]
Waliser, Vance M. .... '61 '87 C&L.629 B.S., J.D. 219 S. Holly Street
Wallan, James A., (BV) .... '57 '86 C.1181 B.A. L.950 J.D. [Hornecker,C.H.&H.]
Wallan, Kimberly D. .... '61 '86 C&L.950 B.S., J.D. 200 S. Modoc Ave.‡
Weaver, Alissa Migliore .... '68 '96 C.16 B.A. L.950 J.D. 225 W. Main St.
Weaver, Mark R. .... '69 '96 C&L.950 B.A., J.D. [Brophy,M.S.G.B.&P.]
Webber, Robert F., (BV) .... '44 '71 C.413 B.A. L.950 J.D. [Black,C.W.S.&P.]
Wells, Michael H., (CV) .... '53 '82 C.147 B.A. L.284 J.D. [M.H.Wells]
Wells, Michael H., P.C., (CV) .... 900 W. 8th St.
Werdell, Lee S., (BV) .... '40 '64 C&L.629 B.S., LL.B. [Werdell&H.]
Werdell & Hanson, (BV) .... 800 W. 8th St.
Whatley, Susanne Marie .... '56 '99 C.1071 B.S. L.629 J.D. [Werdell&H.]
White, Raymond B. .... '46 '72 C.1071 B.S. L.629 J.D. Cir. J.
Wickre, James A., (BV) .... '46 '74 C&L.629 B.S., J.D. 201 W. Main St., Ste. 3B
Workman, Larry B. .... '48 '86 C.838 B.A. L.813 J.D. 835 E. Main St., Ste. D
Yost, Claudette L., (CV) .... '— '84 C.909 B.A. L.629 J.D. 916 W. 10th St.

MILTON-FREEWATER, 6,470, *Umatilla Co.*

Coblens, Robert P. .... '39 '64 C.629 B.S. L.950 LL.B. [R.P.Coblens]
Coblens, Robert P., P.C. .... 618 N. Main
Eden, Melinda S., (AV) .... '48 '81 C.446 B.S. L.629 J.D. 85170 March Rd.
Grove, John U., (AV) .... '33 '62 C&L.629 B.S., LL.B. 105 N. Main St.
Lieuallen, Jonathan S. .... '68 '00 C.637 B.A. L.336 J.D. [Ⓐ Monahan,G.&T.]
Millar, R. A. "Andy", (CV) .... '46 '89 C.1104 B.S. L.285 J.D. [R.A.Millar]
Millar, R. A. "Andy", P.C., (CV) .... 920 S. Main St.

Monahan, Grove & Tucker, (AV)
105 North Main Street, 97862
Telephone: 541-938-3377 FAX: 541-938-6112
Email: tuckers@bmi.net URL: http://www.lawyers.com/monahangrovetucker
Member of Firm: Samuel E. Tucker. Associate: Jonathan S. Lieuallen.
General Trial Practice, State Courts. Corporation, Probate, Real Estate, Water, Municipal Law, Estate Planning, Criminal Law, Domestic Relations.
See Professional Biographies, MILTON-FREEWATER, OREGON

Peery, W. W. .... '31 '59 C&L.502 B.S., LL.B. Pres. & CEO, Bank of Commerce
Tucker, Samuel E., (AV) .... '51 '76 C.950 B.A. L.228 J.D. [Monahan,G.&T.]
Williams, Ray, (CV) .... '51 '81 C.813 B.A. L.596 J.D. P.O. Box 79

MILWAUKIE, 20,490, *Clackamas Co.*

Bassett, John .... '40 '65 C&L.629 B.S., LL.B. 2700 S.E. Harrison St.
Bond, Thomas D. .... '48 '74 C.273 B.A. L.596 J.D. [T.D.Bond]
Bond, Thomas D., P.C. .... 4664 S.E. King Rd.
Borden, Judith L. .... '44 '70 C&L.339 B.S., J.D. 10120 S.E. Cambridge Ln.
Boston, Julia L., (BV) .... '15 '63 C.972 L.596 2705 S.E. Courtney Rd.
Breck, William H. .... '43 '67 C&L.629 B.S., J.D. [W.H.Breck]
Breck, William H., P.C. .... 16578 S.E. Key Court

Connors, Hollis Gay '12 '52 L.596 LL.B.
(adm. in MT; not adm. in OR) 125 S.E. River Forest Dr.‡
Covington, Kim '70 '99 C.628 B.S. L.629 J.D. 4035 S.E. Hillside Dr.
Eades, Gregory A. '50 '75 C&L.36 B.A., J.D. City Atty.
Eivers, George J. '14 '37 L.596 LL.B. 12345 Stanley Ave.‡

Gabin, Sara L., P.C.
(See Lake Oswego)

Halton, Richard D. '52 '77 C.966 B.S. L.930 J.D. 2647 S.E. Lake Rd.
Hull, Sander Marcus '70 '99 C&L.629 B.S., J.D. Fin. Advsr., Am. Express
Huston, James H. '43 '74 C.24 B.S. L.596 J.D. 6090 Detkin Rd.‡
Ives, Mari Redman '54 '00 C.628 B.A. L.596 J.D. [Redman]
Jahnke, Frederick A. '20 '49 C&L.508 LL.B. 911 S.E. River Forest Ct.
Kinsman, Keith '46 '71 C&L.950 B.A., J.D. 8989 S.E. 42nd
Kovac, Leonard J., Jr., (BV) '51 '79 [Mundorff,M.&K.]
Lankford, Howell L. '44 '77 C.685 B.A. L.629 J.D. P.O. Box 22331
Lent, Gerri Sue, (CV) '44 '84 C.1056 B.A. L.596 J.D. [Lent]
Lent Law Office, (CV) 10565 S.E. 23rd Ave.
Lizzi, Kenneth A. '69 '97 C.1056 B.A. L.1051 J.D. Dark Horse Comics, Inc.
Lundy, Leroy J. '34 '67 C&L.596 B.S., LL.B. First State Bk. of Ore.
Majors, Carrie A. '68 '98 C.628 B.S.B.A. L.596 J.D. 5536 S.E. Harlow
McClain, J. Gary, (BV) '36 '61 C.1104 L.950 LL.B. [Mundorff,M.&K.]
McDonald, William D., (BV) '25 '55 C&L.950 B.S., LL.B. 10851 S.E. Main St.
McDonald, William S., (BV) '40 '71 C.336 B.A. L.596 J.D. 4585 S.E. Aldercrest Rd.
Mundorff, Roger P., (BV) '40 '68 C&L.1051 B.A., J.D. [Mundorff,M.&K.]
Mundorff, McClain & Kovac, (BV) 11073 S.E. Main St.
Nash, Kendall E. M. '26 '57 C.637 B.S. L.629 LL.B. 12600 S.E. Freeman Way‡
Oetken, Randy P. '58 '87 C.950 B.A. L.464 J.D. [R.P.Oetken]
Oetken, Randy P., P.C. 2647 S.E. Lake Road
Redman, James E., (AV) '32 '63 C.1051 B.A. L.596 J.D. [Redman]

Redman Law Firm, (AV)
10565 S.E. 23rd Avenue, 97222
Telephone: 503-659-5335 Fax: 503-659-5568
Email: mail@redmanlaw.com
James E. Redman; Mari Redman Ives (Managing Partner).
Personal Injury, Automobile Accidents, Wrongful Death, Trusts and Estates, Business Law, Corporate Law, Wills and Probate, Guardianship and Conservatorship, Real Estate, Eminent Domain and Condemnation Law.
See Professional Biographies, MILWAUKIE, OREGON

Rook, Roger N. '28 '55 C&L.950 B.S., LL.B. 4005 S.E. Risley‡
Schockner, Leslie T. '47 '97 C.1275 B.A. L.596 J.D. 4316 S.E. Fieldcrest Dr.
Sugahiro, William Y. '39 '71 C.628 B.S. L.596 J.D. 4664 S.E. King Rd.
Turner, Ted E. '49 '74 C&L.352 B.A., J.D. 4664 S.E. King Rd.
Van Bergen, Vincent G., (BV) '25 '57 C.999 L.596 LL.B. 2336 S.E. Washington St.
Viuhkola, David T., (BV) '48 '73 C.1075 B.S. L.596 J.D. 675 S.E. Thiesen Rd.
Wills, Russell M. '16 '57 C.506 B.S. L.596 J.D. 15010 E. McLoughlin Blvd.

MITCHELL, 163, *Wheeler Co.*

Ferenstein, Marvin L. '37 '63 C.453 B.S. L.477 LL.B.
(adm. in CA; not adm. in OR) 38559 S. Twickenham Rd.‡

MOLALLA, 5,647, *Clackamas Co.*

Price, Gordon H., (CV) '30 '54 C.629 B.S. L.950 LL.B. 101 S. Molalla Ave.

MONMOUTH, 7,741, *Polk Co.*

Dealy-Browning, Deborah '50 '81 C.628 B.S. L.950 J.D. 110 N. Atwater
Henderson, Bruce '47 '75 C.112 B.A. L.990 J.D.
(adm. in CA; not adm. in OR) P.O. Box 267
McArthur, K. Scott, (BV) '32 '66 C.678 A.B. L.1051 J.D. [K.S.McArthur]
McArthur, K. Scott, P.C., (BV) 112 N. Atwater St.
Penna, Joseph E., (BV) '50 '75 C&L.629 B.A., J.D. 207 W. Main St.

MONROE, 607, *Benton Co.*

Cleeton, Bruce Cameron '50 '75 C.629 B.S. L.596 J.D. 96350 Territorial Rd.
Latta, William A. '44 '71 C.112 B.A. L.1068 J.D.
(adm. in CA; not adm. in OR) Route 1‡

MORO, * 292, *Sherman Co.*

English, Ray '39 '65 C.723 B.S. L.585 J.D. Dist. Atty.

MOUNT ANGEL, 3,121, *Marion Co.*

Fournier, James D., (BV) '32 '62 C.629 B.A. L.596 LL.B. 195 Main St.

MOUNT VERNON, 538, *Grant Co.*

Kilpatrick, Mike, (BV) '52 '78 C.1104 B.S. L.596 J.D. [Kilpatricks]
Kilpatricks, (AV) Highway 395 N.

MYRTLE CREEK, 3,419, *Douglas Co.*

Pollock, Jeffrey R. '68 '95 C.911 B.S. L.1358 J.D.
(adm. in WA; not adm. in OR) P.O. Box 755
Sanborn, Albert Beckwith, II '50 '78 C.1049 B.A. L.1051 J.D. [A.B.Sanborn,II]
Sanborn, A. Beckwith, II, P.C. 1110 Arburnia Street
Twitchell, Dennis W. '42 '72 C.112 B.A. L.426 J.D. 113 S. Main‡

MYRTLE POINT, 2,451, *Coos Co.*

Hogan, Walter B. '49 '74 C.629 B.A. L.1051 J.D. 706 Ash St.

NETARTS, 744, *Tillamook Co.*

Dyson, Deborah A. '60 '89 C.999 B.A. L.276 J.D. P.O. Box 47

NEWBERG, 18,064, *Yamhill Co.*

Bridges, John, (BV) '65 '90 C&L.347 B.A., J.D. [Brown,T.&B.]
Brown, Allyn E., (BV) '44 '69 C&L.629 B.S., J.D. [Brown,T.&B.]
Brown, Tarlow & Bridges, P.C., (AV) 515 E. 1st Street
Bunn, Stanley E. '46 '72 C&L.950 B.A., J.D. State Leg.
Capell, Fredrick G., (BV) '41 '66 C&L.629 B.S., LL.B. 29875 Mtn. Top Rd.
Cummins, Elliott C., (AV) '41 '79 C.413 B.A. L.1051 J.D. [Cummins,G.F.D.&V.]

Cummins, Goodman, Fish, Denley & Vickers, P.C., (AV)
100 S. College Street, P.O. Box 609, 97132
Telephone: 503-476-8200 Fax: 503-476-8201
Email: lat@cumminsgoodman.com
Elliott C. Cummins; George W. Goodman; Reuel K. Fish; Matthew F. Denley; Damon L. Vickers;— Stephen E. Verotsky; Samuel A. Kubernick.
Insurance Defense, Employment Law, Workers' Compensation Defense, OSHA Defense, General Litigation, Business Law.
See Professional Biographies, NEWBERG, OREGON

Denley, Matthew F., (BV) '59 '86 C.182 B.A. L.950 J.D. [Cummins,G.F.D.&V.]
Fish, Reuel K., (CV) '50 '86 C.966 B.A. L.1051 J.D. [Cummins,G.F.D.&V.]
Funk, David A., (BV) '19 '53 L.596 LL.B. 1103 N. Springbrook Rd.
Goodman, George W., (AV) '49 '79 C.966 B.A. L.596 J.D. [Cummins,G.F.D.&V.]
Goodwin, Robert W. '29 '77 C.628 B.S. L.596 J.D. 11723 N.E. Lauren Lane‡

Johnstone & Goodfellow
(See McMinnville)

Kubernick, Samuel A. '73 '01 C.112 B.A. L.276 J.D. [Cummins,G.F.D.&V.]
Mahr, Terrence D., (BV) '47 '73 C.1080 B.A. L.420 J.D. City Atty.
McNulty, J. P. '61 '97 C.424 M.S.W. L.1051 J.D. 3101 Aldersgate Dr.
Mock, Ronald L. '56 '82 C.635 B.A. L.477 J.D. George Fox College
Moeller, Donald R. '41 '73 C.589 B.A. L.629 J.D. 1925 Westlake Loop
Palmer, Stephen C. '67 '94 C.121 B.A. L.629 J.D. [Brown,T.&B.]
Platt, Gene L., and Associates, (BV) '50 '77
C.999 B.A. L.101 J.D. 901 N. Brutscher, Ste. D383
Stone, Truman A. '67 '92 C.1144 L.596 [Brown,T.&B.]
Swift, Robert E., (BV) '33 '62 C.413 B.A. L.596 LL.B. [Swift&S.]
Swift & Swift, (BV) 210 S. College St.
Tarlow, Donald O., (AV) '44 '69 C.668 B.A. L.629 J.D. [Brown,T.&B.]
Verotsky, Stephen E. '75 '01 C.645 B.S. L.838 J.D. [Cummins,G.F.D.&V.]
Vickers, Damon L. '66 '92 C.285 B.A. L.950 J.D. [Cummins,G.F.D.&V.]
Whittaker, Kathryn Dessayer '66 '92 C.112 A.B. L.477 J.D. P.O. Box 302
Wingfield, Keith W. '51 '87 C.446 B.A. L.1051 J.D. 4204 Bird Haven Loop

NEWPORT, * 9,532, *Lincoln Co.*

Allen, David Nathan '58 '87 C.678 B.A. L.1051 J.D. [Macpherson,G.G.&D.]
Baldwin, Scott E. '66 '96 C.629 B.A. L.950 J.D. 56 Sw Nye St
Bandonis, Michael J., (BV) '55 '80 C&L.629 B.S., J.D. [Minor,B.&C.]
Bartoldus, Dennis L., Attorney at Law, (BV) '52 '77 C&L.950 B.A., J.D. 380 SW 2nd
Barton, William A., (AV) '48 '72 C.637 B.S. L.950 J.D. [Barton&S.]

Barton and Strever, P.C., (AV)
214 South West Coast Highway, P.O. Box 870, 97365
Telephone: 541-265-5377 Fax: 541-265-5614 URL: http://www.bartonstrever.com
Email: attorneys@bartonstrever.com URL: http://www.lawyers.com/barton&strever
William A. Barton; Kevin K. Strever.
Civil Litigation, Plaintiffs Trial Practice. Psychological and Physical Injury Claims including Sexual Exploitation. Sexual Abuse, Personal Injury, Insurance Bad Faith, Wrongful Death, Medical Malpractice, Psychiatric Malpractice. Criminal Defense, DUI Defense.
Reference: Bank of the West, Newport, Oregon.
See Professional Biographies, NEWPORT, OREGON

Baxter-Jones, Melinda, (CV) '56 '85 C.1051 B.S. L.950 J.D. P.O. Box 270
Beckstead, Scott, (CV) '66 '91 C.877 B.S. L.878 J.D.
236 West Olive Street (⊙Waldport)
Beeson, Richard D., (BV) '46 '71 C&L.629 B.S., J.D. [R.D.Beeson]
Beeson, Richard D., P.C., (BV) P.O. Box 510
Belmont, Wayne '54 '84 C.413 B.A. L.629 J.D. Co. Legal Coun.
Biedermann, Alan H. '57 '87 C&L.188 A.B., J.D. 615 Sw Hurbert St
Bjornsen, James A. '58 '94 C&L.878 B.S., J.D. [Pridgeon&Assoc.] ⊙
Bovett, Robert E. '65 '91 C.398 B.A. L.1051 J.D. Asst. Co. Coun., Lincoln Co.
Branchfield, Edward '14 '42 C&L.477 A.B., J.D. 149 N.E. 35th St.‡
Branford, Thomas O. '46 '73 C&L.950 B.A., J.D. Cir. J.
Brant, Judith Ann, (BV) '54 '82 C.150 B.S. L.1051 J.D. Dist. Atty. Off.
Carstens, Kurt, (BV) '47 '72 C&L.629 B.A., J.D. [Litchfield&C.]
Chadwick, Wes '71 '00 C.101 B.S. L.629 J.D. 423 North Coast Hwy.

Clark, Lindauer, Fetherston, Edmonds, Lippold & Collier, LLP
(See Salem)

Collard, Clifford G., (BV) '51 '77 C.628 B.S. L.464 J.D. [D.L.Bartoldus]
Connell, Robert W., (BV) '54 '81 C.880 B.A. L.1051 J.D. [Minor,B.&C.]
Dailey, Margaret E., (CV) '55 '82 C.1051 B.A. L.464 J.D. 15 S.W. Lee St.
Diaz, Richard S. '56 '86 C.851 B.B.A. L.629 J.D. [Macpherson,G.G.&D.]
Dunn, Kathleen Erin '71 '97 C.500 B.A. L.339 J.D. Oregon Legal Servs.
Eder, Michele Longo '54 '79 C.367 B.A. L.596 J.D. [Macpherson,G.G.&D.]
Escobar, Braulio, (CV) '49 '78 C.174 B.A. L.629 J.D. 530 N.W. 3rd Ste. 7
Fahy, Peter B., (BV) '49 '86 C.628 B.S. L.629 J.D. Chf. Dep. Dist. Atty.
Fetsch, Elizabeth A. '57 '96 C.1051 B.S. L.596 J.D. [Minor,B.&C.]
Flaherty, Patrick James '56 '88 C&L.629 B.S., J.D. Dep. Dist. Atty.
Gintner, Peter, (CV) '54 '82 C.494 B.A. L.1035 J.D. [Macpherson,G.G.&D.]
Gordon, David M. '55 '81 C.813 B.A. L.629 J.D. [Macpherson,G.G.&D.]
Greco, Guy B., (BV) '51 '76 C.705 A.B. L.1292 J.D. 111 S.E. Douglas, Ste. C
Hadley, Kenneth C., Jr., (BV) '38 '67 C.1056 L.596 J.D. 1055 N.E. Avery
Haggerty, Brian '56 '98 C.475 B.A. L.596 J.D. [Minor,B.&C.]
Hogg, Susan '56 '86 C.1505 B.A. L.629 J.D. P.O. Box 537
Holbrook, Douglas R., (CV) '62 '87 C.336 B.S. L.1051 J.D. [Litchfield&C.]
Huckleberry, Robert J. '48 '74 C.878 B.S. L.1051 J.D. Cir. J.
Jade, Rose '58 '95 C.453 B.S. L.588 J.D. P.O. Box 2104
Jebousek, Nyla Lynn '51 '98 C&L.629 B.A., J.D. [N.L.Jebousek]
Jebousek, Nyla L., Law Office of P.O. Box 642
Konowalchuk, Thomas William '55 '99 C.630 M.D. L.629 J.D. 1070 NE 7th Dr.
Larsen, David B. '54 '02 C.897 B.A. L.950 J.D. [Pridgeon&Assoc.]
Litchfield & Carstens LLP, (BV) 407 N. Coast Highway
Littlehales, Charles P. '41 '69 C.1056 B.S. L.629 J.D. Cir. J.

Lowry, Robert D., Law Offices of
(See Eugene)

Macpherson, Gintner, Gordon & Diaz, (CV) 423 N. Coast Hwy.
Mason, John C. '62 '96 C.623 B.B.A. L.1339 J.D. Dist. Atty. Off.
McCrum, Bruce L., (CV) '58 '88 C.1109 B.A. L.629 J.D. [Pridgeon&Assoc.] ⊙
McMullen, Albert R., Jr. '25 '52 C&L.950 B.A., B.L. Sr. Cir. J.
Minor, J. Christopher, (BV) '42 '67 C&L.950 B.S., J.D. [Minor,B.&C.]
Minor, Bandonis & Connell, P.C., (BV) 236 W. Olive St.
Ouderkirk, James F., (BV) '50 '75 C.103 A.B. L.629 J.D. P.O. Box 1167
Pridgeon, Jeffrey C., (BV) '52 '77 C.477 B.A. L.629 J.D. [Pridgeon&Assoc.] ⊙
Pridgeon & Associates, LLC, (BV) 515 W. Olive St. (⊙Lincoln City)
Raymer, Brian Todd, (CV) '63 '92 C.958 B.S. L.831 J.D. Dep. Dist. Atty.
Reed, Scott W., (BVⓉ) '53 '83 C.878 B.S. L.678 J.D. [Litchfield&C.]
Reim, Paul E. '71 '98 C.685 B.A. L.629 J.D. 626 S.W. Hurbert St.
Rich, Matthew L. '67 '95 C.296 B.S. L.629 J.D. [Pridgeon&Assoc.]
Savee, Timothy J. '52 '92 C.147 B.A. Dep. Dist. Atty.
Segel, Amy, (AV) '52 '80 C.117 B.G.S. L.608 J.D. P.O. Box 2374
Seifert, Ronald H., (BV) '52 '79 C&L.629 B.S., J.D. [Litchfield&C.]
Selich, Judith N., Law Office of, (CV) '48 '77 C.112 B.A. L.990 J.D. P.O. Box 745
Stimac, Patrick J. '56 '81 C.1181 B.S. L.950 J.D. [Pridgeon&Assoc.] ⊙
Strever, Kevin K., (AV) '60 '85 C.1071 B.S. L.629 J.D. [Barton&S.]
Townsend, Richard T. '50 '77 C.112 B.A. L.276 J.D. 380 S.W. 2nd

Waarvick, Jeffrey D., (BV) .... '48 '75 C.668 B.A. L.629 J.D. [Waarvick&W.]
Waarvick, Louise Smith, (BV) .... '49 '83 C.668 B.A. L.629 J.D. [Waarvick&W.]
Waarvick & Waarvick, (BV) .... 924 S.W. Hurbert Street
Warner, Alice .... '60 '85 C.976 B.A. L.94 J.D. Oregon Legal Servs.
Yeck, Fred A. .... '46 '71 C.628 B.S. L.629 J.D. 236 W. Olive St.‡

NORTH BEND, 9,614, *Coos Co.*

Bauder, Steven W., (BV) .... '54 '89 C&L.629 B.S., J.D. 880 California St
Bechtold, Paula M. .... '46 '75 C.1051 B.A. L.596 J.D. Cir. J.
Burke, Thomas F., (BV) .... '41 '73 C.1056 B.A. L.596 J.D. 1611 Virginia Ave.
Coffey, James C., (BV) .... '49 '74 C.197 B.A. L.629 J.D. [Stebbins&C.]
Flaxel, Benton C., (BV) .... '34 '58 C.629 B.S. L.950 J.D. [Flaxel&N.]
Flaxel & Nylander, (BV) .... 880 California St.
Holcombe, Glenn D. '60 '85 C.911 B.A. L.477 J.D.
(adm. in AK; not adm. in OR) General Manager, Menasha Corporation
Jones, Robt. E. .... '24 '52 C&L.629 B.S., LL.B. Dist. J.
Nylander, Nickolas C., (BV) .... '47 '73 C.628 B.S. L.629 J.D. [Flaxel&N.]
Stebbins, Michael R., (BV) .... '48 '75 C.960 B.A. L.596 J.D. [Stebbins&C.]
Stebbins & Coffey, (BV) .... 745 California St.
Thomas, Robert L., (AV) .... '23 '50 C&L.174 LL.B. 1935 Union Ave.
Todd, Roger B., (AV) .... '25 '50 C&L.950 LL.B. 50 E. Bya Dr.‡

NORTH PLAINS, 1,605, *Washington Co.*

Bolton, Averill H., (CV) .... '46 '81 C.1051 B.A. L.61 J.D. P.O. Box 788
Hughes, Shalas J. .... '67 '94 C.1056 B.S. L.596 J.D. P.O. Box 328
Warren, Jeffrey Scott .... '57 '97 23545 N.W. Skyline Boulevard

NYSSA, 3,163, *Malheur Co.*

Asay, Don A. '44 '73 C.101 B.A. L.878 J.D.
(adm. in UT; not adm. in OR) 302 N. 4th St.
Fonda, Stephen B., (BV) .... '36 '66 C&L.629 B.S., LL.B. [Stunz,F.K.&H.] ⊙
Horton, Michael W., (BV) .... '63 '89 C&L.950 B.A., J.D. [Stunz,F.K.&H.] ⊙
Kiyuna, Gary K., (CV) .... '49 '82 C.312 B.A. L.1119 J.D. [Stunz,F.K.&H.] ⊙
Stunz, Fonda, Kiyuna & Horton, LLP, (BV) .... 106 Main Street (⊙Ontario)

OAK GROVE, 12,808, *Clackamas Co.*

Barnes, Walter A. .... '44 '69 C.1051 B.S. L.950 J.D. P.O. Box 68288
Beck, Rodney J., (AV) .... '48 '75 C.628 B.S. L.596 J.D. [R.J.Beck]

Beck, Rodney J., P.C., (AV)
16239 SE McLoughlin Boulevard, Suite 204, 97267
Mailing Address: P.O. Box 68447, Oak Grove, OR 97268-0447
Telephone: 503-656-5888 Fax: 503-656-0588
Email: beckrodneyjpc@qwest.net
Rodney J. Beck.
Probate, Guardianship and Conservatorship, Estate Planning, Agricultural Law, Wills, Elder Law, Real Property, Contracts and General Litigation.
See Professional Biographies, OAK GROVE, OREGON

Sweeney, Patrick J. .... '51 '78 C.950 B.A. L.285 J.D. 2905 S.E. Oak Grove Blvd.‡

OCEANSIDE, 326, *Tillamook Co.*

Balsiger, Richard M. '22 '48 C&L.793 LL.B.
(adm. in SD; not adm. in OR) P.O. Box 409
Pommier, Raneen '37 '83 C.691 B.A. L.326 J.D.
(adm. in TX; not adm. in OR) P.O. Box 403‡

ONTARIO, 10,985, *Malheur Co.*

Auxier, David R. .... '— '90 C.336 B.S. L.950 J.D. [Yturri R.]
Bentz, Cliff S., (AV) .... '— '77 C.1104 B.S. L.1051 J.D. [Yturri R.]
Burnham, Carl, Jr., (AV) .... '— '64 C&L.629 B.S., LL.B. [Yturri R.]
Coughlin, J. David, (AV) .... '44 '70 C.197 B.A. L.950 J.D. [Coughlin,L.&M.] ⊙
Coughlin, Leuenberger & Moon, P.C., (AV) .... 153 S.W. First Street (⊙Baker City)
Embrey, M. Gregory '— '00 C.939 B.A. L.285 J.D.
(adm. in ID; not adm. in OR) [Ⓐ Yturri R.]
Fonda, Stephen B., (BV) .... '36 '66 C&L.629 B.S., LL.B. [Stunz,F.K.&H.] ⊙
Helfrich, Timothy J., (AV) .... '— '76 C&L.629 B.A., J.D. [Yturri R.]
Horton, Michael W., (BV) .... '63 '89 C&L.950 B.A., J.D. [Stunz,F.K.&H.] ⊙
Jagelski, Bruno J., (AV) .... '— '90 C.1104 B.S. L.950 J.D. [Yturri R.]
Kiyuna, Gary K., (CV) .... '49 '82 C.312 B.A. L.1119 J.D. [Stunz,F.K.&H.] ⊙
Leuenberger, Martin, (AV) .... '49 '75 C.628 B.S. L.629 J.D. [Coughlin,L.&M.] ⊙
Linhart, Lisa A. .... '60 '88 C.783 B.A. L.846 J.D. Oregon Legal Servs. Corp.
Moon, J. Robert, Jr., (AV) .... '55 '81 C.207 B.A. L.851 J.D. [Coughlin,L.&M.] ⊙
Oakes, Charles S., (BV) .... '59 '86 C.1104 B.S. L.950 J.D. 522 S.W. 4th St.
Okai, Thomas K., (CV) .... '57 '85 C.950 B.S. L.61 J.D. [Okai]

Okai Law Office, P.C., (CV)
475 Southwest 12th Street, 97914
Telephone: 541-889-7810 Fax: 541-889-7840
Email: tokai@qwest.net URL: http://www.lawyers.com/okai
Thomas K. Okai.
Civil Litigation, Employment Law, Sexual Harassment, Discrimination, Business Law, Government Law, Agriculture, Personal Injury Law.
See Professional Biographies, ONTARIO, OREGON

Peterson, Shawna D. .... '— '02 C.285 B.A. L.596 J.D. [Ⓐ Yturri R.]

Peterson Law Offices, PC
(See Portland)

Rader, Mark S. .... '47 '73 C.628 B.S. L.596 J.D. 381 W. Idaho
Reynolds, Lorena M. .... '73 '98 C.174 B.A. L.1068 J.D. Legal Aid Servs. of OR
Rock, Douglas J., (BV) .... '63 '91 C.101 B.A. L.950 J.D. [Ⓐ Coughlin,L.&M.]
Rose, Gene C., (AV) .... '28 '53 C&L.629 B.A., LL.B. P.O. Box 1500‡
Stoddard, Steven M., (BVⓉ) .... '50 '79 C.1193 B.S. L.285 J.D. 381 W. Idaho Ave.
Stunz, Fonda, Kiyuna & Horton, LLP, (BV) .... 40 S. Oregon St. (⊙Nyssa)
Taggart, Max S., II, (BV) .... '40 '68 C&L.950 B.A., J.D. 399 S. Oregon
Van Atta, William E., (BV) .... '52 '78 C.1104 B.S. L.629 J.D. 142 S.W. 3rd Street
Warner, Scott K., (BV) .... '— '93 C.628 L.629 J.D. [Yturri R.]
Wheeler, Jeffrey R. .... '— '02 C.1181 B.S. L.950 J.D. [Ⓐ Yturri R.]
Wilk, Mark J. .... '56 '81 C.610 A.B. L.629 J.D. Reg. Dir., Ore. Legal Servs. Corp.

Yturri Rose, LLP, (AV)
89 S.W. Third Avenue, P.O. Box S, 97914-2721
Telephone: 541-889-5368 Telecopier: 541-889-2432
Email: law@yturrirose.com URL: http://www.yturrirose.com
Carl Burnham, Jr.; Cliff S. Bentz; Timothy J. Helfrich; Bruno J. Jagelski; Scott K. Warner; David R. Auxier;—Jeffrey R. Wheeler; Shawna D. Peterson; M. Gregory Embrey (Not admitted in OR).
General Civil and Trial Practice. Medical and Legal Malpractice, Insurance Defense, Insurance Law, Personal Injury, Business Litigation, Commercial Law, Corporations, Estate Administration, Estate Planning, Foreclosures, Debtor and Creditor, Zoning and Land Use, Real Estate, Farm and Ranch Law, Labor and Employment Law.

(This Listing Continued)

Yturri Rose, LLP (Continued)

Attorneys for: United States National Bank of Oregon (Ontario Branch); Cascade Natural Gas Inc.; Idaho Power Co.; Liberty Mutual Insurance Corp.; Interstate Production Credit Assn.; State Farm Insurance Co.; Farmers Insurance Exchange; Professional Liability Fund of the Oregon State Bar Association; Mountain Bell Telephone; American Hardware Insurance Company.
See Professional Biographies, ONTARIO, OREGON

Zanotelli, Brian T. .... '66 '98 C.1056 B.A. L.285 J.D. 650 Fortner St.

OREGON CITY, * 25,754, *Clackamas Co.*

Anderson, David W. .... '54 '79 C.939 B.A. L.1066 J.D. Co. Coun.
Aughenbaugh, Donald .... '50 '75 C.628 B.S. L.846 J.D. 17431 S. Holcomb Rd.‡
Averill, James D. .... '48 '73 C&L.950 B.A., J.D. 14137 Conway Dr.
Bagley, Raymond R., Jr. .... '41 '66 C&L.352 B.A., J.D. Cir. J.
Bayless, John D. .... '52 '81 C.1056 B.S. L.1051 J.D. 16205 S. Holcomb Blvd.

Beck, Rodney J., P.C.
(See Oak Grove)

Belknap, Wendell L., (BV) .... '60 '85 C.629 B.A. L.596 J.D. 411 5th St.
Bernstein, James E., (BV) .... '48 '75 C.678 B.A. L.596 J.D. [Schumaker&B.]
Bliven, Michael A. .... '68 '94 C.602 B.A.L. L.950 J.D. [M.A.Bliven]
Bliven, Michael A., P.C. .... 419 5th St.

Blunck & Walhood, LLC
(See West Linn)

Boutin, Roderick A., (AV) .... '56 '82 C.154 B.A. L.596 J.D. [Bowerman&B.]
Bowerman, Donald B., (AV) .... '34 '59 C.628 L.1051 J.D. [Bowerman&B.]
Bowerman & Boutin, LLP, (AV) .... 1001 Molalla Ave., Ste. 208
Burke, Ginger Enden .... '68 '95 C&L.950 B.A., J.D. Clackamas Co. Dist. Atty.'s Off.
Burris, Christopher Edward .... '52 '77 C.823 B.A. L.851 J.D. 720 McLoughlin Blvd.
Caldwell, John C., (AV) .... '24 '50 C&L.629 B.A., J.D. [Hibbard C.S.S.&O.] ‡
Canning, Frederic D., (AV) .... '30 '59 C.629 B.S. L.596 J.D. 294 Warner Milne Rd.‡
Coleman, James M. .... '46 '76 C.1056 B.S. L.629 J.D. 906 Main St.
Combs, Charles H. .... '48 '75 C&L.629 B.A., J.D. 454 S. Center St.
Coulter, Charles E. .... '52 '89 C.508 B.A. L.596 J.D. 411 5th St.
Cross, Mark Austin, (AV) .... '46 '73 C&L.966 B.A., J.D. [M.A.Cross]
Cross, Mark Austin, P.C., (AV) .... 294 Warner Milne Rd.
Czaiko, Michael, Law Office of, (CV) .... '57 '92 C.1056 B.S. L.629 J.D. 219 7th St.
Darling, Deanne L. .... '53 '81 C.172 B.S.W. L.1051 J.D. 807 Main St.
David, Kristen S. .... '75 '00 C.1051 B.A. L.596 J.D. [Ⓐ Bowerman&B.]
Fitting, James T. .... '33 '69 C.336 B.S. L.596 LL.B. 14667 S. Holcomb‡

Gabin, Sara L., P.C.
(See Lake Oswego)

Gilroy, Patrick D. .... '32 '60 C.670 B.A. L.767 J.D. Cir. J.
Gray, Ronald L., (BV) .... '54 '79 C.1071 B.S. L.950 J.D. 615 Main Street, Suite 201
Guinn, James T. .... '60 '93 [Mitchell&G.]
Hedges, William J., (CV) .... '49 '81 C.678 B.A. L.950 J.D. 503 High St.

Helzer & Cromar, LLP
(See Beaverton)

Hensley, William E., (CV) .... '46 '85 C.1235 B.A. L.596 J.D. [Ⓐ Hergert&Assoc.]
Hergert, Ronald E., (AV) .... '43 '69 C&L.1051 B.S., J.D. [Hergert&Assoc.]
Hergert & Associates, P.C., (AV) .... 1001 Molalla Ave.
Herndon, Robert D. .... '44 '68 C&L.629 B.S., J.D. Cir. J.
Hibbard Caldwell Schultz Stalnaker & O'Brien LLP, (AV)
1001 Molalla Avenue, Suite 200
Hill, Gary D., (BV) .... '52 '82 C.413 B.A. L.596 J.D. [Ⓐ Hergert&Assoc.]
Hingson, John Henry, III, (AV) .... '46 '71 C.802 B.A. L.846 J.D. [J.H.Hingson,III]
Hingson, John Henry, III, P.C., (AV) .... 409 Center St.
Hungerford, Nancy .... '47 '81 C.627 B.A. L.1051 J.D. 615 High St
Hunt, J. Kevin, (BV) .... '— '84 C.508 B.A. L.596 J.D. 1145 Sunny Ln.

Hutchison & Walsh, A Professional Corporation
(See West Linn)

Huva, Susie L., (BV) .... '64 '91 C.790 B.A. L.596 J.D. Asst. Co. Coun.
Jack, Alan R. .... '33 '60 C&L.950 B.A., LL.B. Cir. J.
Jastak, Steffany Hergert, (CV) .... '69 '94 C.629 B.S. L.1051 J.D. [Ⓐ Hergert&Assoc.]
Johnson, Mary W., (CV) .... '53 '84 C.610 B.S. L.950 J.D. [M.E.Johnson]
Johnson, Mary Ebel, P.C., (CV) .... 500 Abernethy Road, Suite 4
Jonasson, W. Bradford, Jr., (BV) .... '46 '76 C.976 B.A. L.629 J.D. 1317 7th Street
Karabeika, Heather L., (CV) .... '67 '94 C.906 B.A. L.950 J.D. Dep. Dist. Atty.
Kelly, Stephen Robert, (BV) .... '56 '82 C.205 B.A. L.596 J.D. 720 McLoughlin Blvd.
Knauss, Arthur B., (AV) .... '45 '73 C.629 B.A. L.596 J.D. 294 Warner Milne Rd.
Lampkin, Margy J. .... '22 '65 C.950 L.596 LL.B. 707 Main St.
Landers, Christine L. .... '66 '92 C.878 b.a. L.1051 J.D. 807 Main St., Rm. 7
Latourette, Edward D., (BV) .... '43 '72 C.629 B.S. L.596 J.D. 503 High St.
Long, Melissa .... '69 '98 C.1169 B.A. L.629 J.D. Dist. Atty. Off.
Lowe, John K. .... '49 '74 C.629 B.S. L.596 J.D. Cir. J.
Lowe, Kathleen Dugi, (CV) .... '49 '84 C.629 B.S. L.596 J.D. Dep. Dist. Atty.
Lyell, Heather Hansen .... '70 '96 C.315 B.A. L.1051 J.D. 294 Warner Milne Road
Mattox, Matthew H., (BV) .... '61 '87 C.577 B.A. L.259 J.D. 807 Main St.
Maurer, Steven L. .... '49 '75 C.1104 B.S. L.596 J.D. Circuit Judge
McFarland, Carol Anne, (CV) .... '51 '78 C.628 B.S. L.1137 J.D. Dep. Dist. Atty.
McNiece, Laraine, (BV) .... '48 '90 C.447 B.A. L.596 J.D. [Schneider&M.]
Miller, Eve L., (BV) .... '56 '81 C.147 B.A. L.596 J.D. 807 Main Street
Miller, S. Dennis .... '38 '66 C&L.950 B.S.L., J.D. Chief Dep. Dist. Atty.
Mills, Robert L. .... '22 '63 C.939 B.A. L.596 LL.B. Dist. J.
Mitchell, Charles F., (BV) .... '52 '81 C.1058 B.A. L.629 J.D. [Mitchell&G.]
Mitchell & Guinn, (BV) .... 1419 7th St.
Morgan, Robert J. .... '34 '64 C.317 B.A. L.950 LL.B. Cir. J.
Munns, Jeffrey D. .... '73 '98 C.489 B.A. L.596 J.D. [Ⓐ Mitchell&G.]
Nove, Michael J., (CV) .... '55 '85 C.1168 B.A. L.950 J.D. [M.J.Nove]
Nove, Michael J., PC, (CV) .... 714B Main St Ste 202
O'Brien, Todd W. .... '68 '96 C.575 B.A. L.596 J.D. [Hibbard C.S.S.&O.]
O'Leary, James W. .... '33 '65 L.596 LL.B. Dist. Atty.
Oster, Warren .... '46 '75 C.446 B.A. L.273 J.D. Coord., Co. Juv. Dept.
Parker, Scott H. .... '42 '67 C.629 B.S. L.813 LL.B. Co. Coun.
Parkinson, S. Lynn .... '43 '74 14956 S. Redland Rd.
Rastetter, Thomas J., (AV) .... '55 '84 C.945 B.A. L.1051 J.D. [T.J.Rastetter]
Rastetter, Thomas J., P.C., (AV) .... 294 Warner Milne Rd.
Regan, Michael P. .... '57 '82 C&L.629 B.S., J.D. Dist. Attys. Off.
Ringle, Phil H., Jr., (BV) ...... '31 '57 C&L.950 B.A., J.D. 1001 Molalla Avenue, Suite 214
Ruonala, Arnold W. .... '25 '56 C.629 L.596 LL.B. 20248 S. Molalla Ave.
Schaleger, Rebecca Suzanne .... '67 '00 C.629 B.A. L.596 J.D. Dist. Atty. Off.
Schermer, David W., (CV) .... '50 '78 C.475 B.A. L.596 J.D. 712 Main St.
Schilling, John Leslie, (CV) .... '55 '89 C.908 B.A. L.596 J.D. Dep. Dist. Atty.

Schneider, Anne K., (Mrs.), (BV) ... '31 '71 C.629 B.B.A. L.596 J.D. [Schneider&M.]
Schneider & McNiece, (BV) ... 1317 7th St.
Schramm, Kenneth R. ... '12 '38 C&L.629 B.A., LL.B. 21851 Somerset Dr. S.‡
Schultz, Paul D., (AV) ... '35 '60 C.336 B.A. L.629 LL.B. [Hibbard C.S.S.&O.]
Schumaker, William E. ... '27 '56 C.629 B.S. L.596 LL.B. [Schumaker&B.] ‡
Schumaker & Bernstein, (BV) ... 219 7th St.

Scott Hookland LLP
(See Tigard)

Selander, Robert R. ... '46 '72 C&L.950 B.A., J.D. Cir. J.
Shebley, Floyd H. ... '44 '78 C.1042 B.A. L.1065 J.D. P.O. Box 1717
Shepley, Wm. Bruce, (AV) ... '51 '84 C.98 B.S. L.1051 J.D. [W.B.Shepley]
Shepley, Wm. Bruce, PC, (AV) ... 615 Main St., Ste. 202
Smith, Monica M. ... '62 '87 C.280 A.B. L.629 J.D. Dep. Dist. Atty., Admin. Hearing Off.
Stalnaker, William J. ... '44 '76 C.1056 B.S. L.596 J.D. [Hibbard C.S.S.&O.]
Stangell, Sherrie Lyn ... '52 '91 C.1056 B.S. L.596 J.D. Stangell & Stangell
Steele, Kathie F., (BV) ... '53 '81 C.813 B.A. L.596 J.D. [K.F.Steele]
Steele, Kathie F., PC, (BV) ... 421 High St.
Tait, Eric J. ... '70 '95 C.629 B.S. L.950 J.D. [Ⓐ Tait&Assoc.]
Tait, James C., (AV) ... '44 '71 C&L.629 B.S., J.D. [Tait&Assoc.]
Tait & Associates, (AV) ... 294 Warner Milne Road
Thom, Ronald D., (BV) ... '37 '64 C.628 L.596 LL.B. 715 5th St.
Thompson, Scott K. ... '51 '90 C.1104 B.S. L.1051 J.D. 503 High St
Tosney, Terrance J. ... '43 '83 C.629 Ph.D. L.950 J.D. 11998 S. Criteser Rd.
Uney, Harold ... '12 '37 L.596 J.D. 205 Masonic Bldg.
Ward, Miles A., (BV) ... '52 '77 C.198 B.A. L.629 J.D. Asst. Co. Coun.
Watson, Joseph Guild, (BV) ... '55 '88 C.878 B.S. L.596 J.D. [J.G.Watson]
Watson, Joseph G., P.C., (BV) ... 216 7th St.
Welch, Donald D. ... '32 '66 C.112 L.1051 LL.B. Dir., Clackamas Co. Juv. Ct.‡

PACIFIC CITY, 1,027, *Tillamook Co.*

Paulus, John C. ... '20 '48 C&L.350 B.A., J.D. P.O. Box 640

PENDLETON, * 16,354, *Umatilla Co.*

Abrams, Robert B. ... '25 '52 C.813 B.A. L.629 LL.B. Cir. J.
Blanc, David M., (BV) ... '60 '86 C.939 B.A. L.285 J.D. [Corey,B.R.L.&H.]
Bloom, Stephen M., (AV) ... '48 '77 C.813 B.A. L.950 J.D. [Kottkamp&O.]
Brauer, Christopher R., (BV) ... '53 '81 C.950 B.A. L.285 J.D. 216 S.E. 4th St.
Burford, Christopher Linton ... '64 '92 C.929 B.A. L.629 J.D. Leg. Coun.
Burns, Justin J. ... '73 '00 C.628 B.A. L.950 J.D. [Corey,B.R.L.&H.]
Burton, Grant Richard ... '75 '01 C.260 B.A. L.37 J.D. Pub. Def.
Byler, Alex M., (AV) ... '32 '58 C.629 B.S. L.950 J.D. 1234 N.W. Ingram Ave.
Capps, Jeffrey D. ... '66 '95 C.1193 B.B.A. L.285 J.D. 310 S.E. 2nd St., Ste. 200‡
Collins, Michael B., (BV) ... '53 '80 C.138 B.A. L.1194 J.D. [Collins&C.]
Collins, Robert W., (AV) ... '21 '51 C.138 L.880 LL.B. [Ⓒ Collins&C.]
Collins, Robert W., Jr., (BV) ... '51 '81 C.138 B.A. L.365 J.D. [Collins&C.]
Collins & Collins, (BV) ... 326 S.E. Second Street
Corey, George H., (AV) ... '16 '40 C&L.629 B.S., J.D. 200 N.W. Gilliam Ave.‡
Corey, Steven H., (AV) ... '46 '72 C.976 A.B. L.813 J.D. [Corey,B.R.L.&H.]

Corey, Byler, Rew, Lorenzen & Hojem, L.L.P., (AV)
222 Southeast Dorion Street, P.O. Box 218, 97801
Telephone: 541-276-3331 Facsimile: 541-276-3148
URL: http://www.corey-byler.com
Members of Firm: Steven H. Corey; Henry C. Lorenzen; Douglas E. Hojem; David M. Blanc; Timothy P. O'Rourke; Steven N. Thomas; Justin J. Burns. Associates: Patricia Sullivan; J. T. Lieuallen. Of Counsel: Lawrence B. Rew; Robert E. O'Rourke.
General Civil and Trial Practice. Agriculture and Agricultural Cooperatives, Domestic Relations, Banking, Business, Municipal, Zoning, Condemnation, School, Corporation, Insurance, Tax, Estate Planning, Probate, Water and Real Estate Law.
Representative Clients: Port of Umatilla; Farmers Insurance Group; St. Anthony Hospital; Pendleton Grain Growers; Pendleton School District 16R; J. R. Simplot Company (Food Processing); East Oregonian Publishing Co.; McCormack Construction Co.; Umatilla Electric Cooperative Association.

See Professional Biographies, PENDLETON, OREGON

Courson, Richard J. ... '23 '54 L.596 LL.B. Sr. Dist. J.‡
Dretke, Brian Craig, (BV) ... '59 '93 C.1237 B.G.S. L.862 J.D. [Hallman&D.]
Eyre, Brandon J. ... '73 '01 C&L.101 B.A., J.D. [Ⓐ Mautz B.&O.]
Fabre, Harold A., (AV) ... '20 '49 C.911 L.950 J.D. 27 S.E. Third St.‡
Fine, J. David, (AV) ... '51 '87 C.276 B.S.F.S. L.012 LL.B. 1412 SW 18th St.
Fisher, L. Kent, (CV) ... '60 '91 C.1104 B.A. L.629 J.D. Dep. Dist. Atty.
Fogelson, Steven ... '56 '83 C&L.629 B.S., J.D. 17 S.W. Frazer St., Ste. 310
Gallaher, David D., (BV) '49 '74
C.1104 B.S. L.596 J.D. 34 Southeast Dorion Avenue, Suite 200
Grable, Michele, (BV) ... '51 '77 C.604 B.A. L.950 J.D. 334 S.E. 2nd Street
Gushwa, Dean F. '57 '98 C&L.585 B.A., J.D.
Dep. Dist. Atty., Umatilla Co. Dist. Atty. Off.
Hachler, Dennis A., (BV) ... '35 '70 C.939 B.A. L.950 J.D. 245 S.E. 4th St.
Hagey, Kristi L., (CV) ... '67 '92 C.628 B.S. L.950 J.D. Dep. Dist. Atty.
Hallman, W. Eugene, (AV) ... '49 '74 C.1056 B.S. L.950 J.D. [Hallman&D.]

Hallman & Dretke, (AV)
104 S.E. 5th Street, P.O. Box 308, 97801
Telephone: 541-276-3857 FAX: 541-276-7620
Email: Office@hallmandretke.com URL: http://www.lawyers.com/hallmandretke
Members of Firm: W. Eugene Hallman; Brian Craig Dretke.
Civil Litigation, Personal Injury and Wrongful Death Litigation and Appellate Practice.

See Professional Biographies, PENDLETON, OREGON

Hampton, John, (CV) ... '50 '77 C.112 B.A. L.629 J.D. Shearson Lehman Bros. Inc.
Hampton, Lynn Wolgamott, (CV) ... '54 '78 C&L.629 B.A., J.D. 73303 July Grounds Ln
Hill, Robert E., (BV) ... '49 '76 C.628 B.S. L.508 J.D. Dist. Atty. Off.
Hill, Steven L. ... '64 '93 C.604 B.A. L.124 J.D. 310 S.E. Second St., Ste. 200
Hojem, Douglas E., (AV) ... '51 '80 C.907 B.A. L.911 J.D. [Corey,B.R.L.&H.]
Jones, William C., II ... '48 '78 C.628 B.S. L.629 J.D. Trial Ct. Admr.
Klahn, Robert G. ... '53 '80 C.950 B.S. L.285 J.D. Pub. Def. Off.
Klahn-Kerns, Nancy Elizabeth, (BV) ... '56 '81 C.628 B.S. L.862 J.D. Dep. Dist. Atty.
Kottkamp, John H., (AV) ... '30 '57 C&L.629 B.S., LL.B. 331 S.E. 2nd St.‡
Kottkamp & O'Rourke, LLP, (AV) ... 331 S.E. 2nd Street
Lieuallen, J. T. ... '78 '04 C.413 B.S. L.629 J.D. [Ⓐ Corey,B.R.L.&H.]
Lorenzen, Henry C., (AV) ... '44 '76 C.628 B.S.E.E. L.596 J.D. [Corey,B.R.L.&H.]

Lowry, Robert D., Law Offices of
(See Eugene)

Mautz, Robert T., (AV) ... '40 '64 C&L.813 B.S., J.D. [Mautz B.&O.]

Mautz Baum & O'Hanlon, LLP, (AV) BR
101 S.E. Byers Avenue, P.O. Box 628, 97801 ⊙
Telephone: 541-276-2811 Fax: 541-276-0543
Email: mbo@mautzetal.com URL: http://www.mautzetal.com
Members of Firm: Robert T. Mautz; Timothy J. O'Hanlon; David C. Baum (Resident Partner, La Grande Office);—Eva Jo Temple; Brandon J. Eyre.

(This Listing Continued)

Mautz Baum & O'Hanlon, LLP (Continued)

General Litigation and Appellate Practice in all State and Federal Courts. Administrative, Agriculture, Bankruptcy, Business, Commercial, Creditors' Rights, Estate Planning and Probate, Insurance, Personal Injury, Professional Malpractice Defense, Real Estate and Wrongful Death.
La Grande, Oregon Office: 1902 4th Street, P.O. Box 967. 97850. Telephone: 541-963-3104. Fax: 541-963-9254. Email: mbolg@mautzeltal.com.

See Professional Biographies, PENDLETON, OREGON

McCormmach, Maureen, (CV) ... '45 '86 C.483 B.A. L.1238 J.D. 225 S.W. Emigrant Ave.
McLeod, Wade Michael ... '65 '98 C.585 B.A. L.596 J.D. Dist. Atty. Off.
Murgo, Rudy M. ... '49 '75 C.911 B.A. L.950 J.D. Cir. J.
O'Hanlon, Timothy J., (BV) ... '62 '87 C.770 B.S. L.596 J.D. [Mautz B.&O.]
Olsen, Jack F. ... '31 '64 C.1051 B.S. L.596 J.D. Cir. J.
O'Rourke, Robert E., (AV) ... '37 '61 C.670 L.596 LL.B. [Ⓒ Corey,B.R.L.&H.]
O'Rourke, Timothy P., (BV) ... '58 '87 C.670 B.B.A. L.950 J.D. [Corey,B.R.L.&H.]
Pahl, Ronald J., (CV) ... '52 '89 C.628 B.S. L.1339 J.D. Cir.J.

Peterson Law Offices, PC
(See Portland)

Rew, Lawrence B., (BV) ... '36 '61 C.939 B.A. L.950 J.D. [Ⓒ Corey,B.R.L.&H.]
Reynolds, Garry L. ... '48 '75 C.1056 B.S. L.596 J.D. Cir. J.
Ridgway, Robert E., (BV) ... '41 '71 C.766 B.A. L.950 J.D. [R.E.Ridgway]
Ridgway, Robert E., P.C., (BV) ... 410 Se Dorion
Roloff, Shannon R. ... '74 '01 C&L.629 B.S., J.D. Dist. Atty's Off.
Shepherd, Harold S. ... '61 '90 C.172 B.S. L.629 J.D. 73239 Confederated Way
Stacy, Naomi ... '69 '99 C.911 B.A. L.900 J.D. P.O. Box 638
Stephens, Daniel E. ... '61 '96 C.999 B.A. L.285 J.D. Intermountain Public Defender, Inc.
Struve, John G. ... '41 '66 C.628 B.S. L.950 J.D. P.O. Box 429‡
Sullivan, Patricia, (BV) ... '46 '78 C.424 B.S. L.280 J.D. [Ⓐ Corey,B.R.L.&H.]
Temple, Eva Jo ... '68 '96 C&L.629 B.A., J.D. [Ⓐ Mautz B.&O.]
Thomas, Steven N., (BV) ... '54 '80 C.112 B.A. L.1097 J.D. [Corey,B.R.L.&H.]
Walsh, Edward M. ... '42 '68 L.629 J.D. P.O. Box 1628
Weinstein, Marc Alan ... '71 '96 C.112 B.A. L.629 J.D. Dep. Dist. Atty.
Wells, William W. ... '16 '41 C.939 A.B. L.178 J.D. Sr. Cir. J.
Woodward, Christie A. ... '72 '97 C.628 B.S.L.A. L.629 J.D. Dep. Dist. Atty.

PHILOMATH, 3,838, *Benton Co.*

Enz, Jonathan K., (BV) ... '46 '71 C.678 B.A. L.950 J.D. P.O. Box 670

PHOENIX, 4,060, *Jackson Co.*

Falls, Edward J., (AVⓉ) '20 '47 C&L.724 B.S., J.D.
(adm. in NY; not adm. in OR) 300 Luman Rd.‡

PORTLAND, 529,121, *Clackamas, Multnomah & Washington Cos.*

Aamodt, David A. ... '50 '75 C.628 B.S. L.1051 J.D. Portland Gen. Elec. Corp.
Aarnas, Laila E. ... '53 '78 C&L.629 B.A., J.D. Fred Meyer, Inc.
Aaron, Clifford V. '45 '71 C.659 B.S. L.569 J.D.
(adm. in NY; not adm. in OR) Pinnacle Acceptance Corp.‡
Abbassian, Jennifer H. ... '69 '94 C.1051 B.A. L.596 J.D. [Ⓐ MacMillan,S.&M.]
Abbe, Chas. Cleveland, (AV) '49 '81 C.860 B.A. L.902 J.D.
V.P. & State Coun., Lawyers Title Insurance Corp.
Abbott, Gary V., (AV) ... '43 '72 C.1056 B.S. L.596 J.D. [Abbott&P.]

Abbott & Prange, P.C., (AV)
111 SW Fifth Avenue, Suite 2650, 97204
Telephone: 503-241-1254 Fax: 503-241-1245
URL: http://www.abbottprange.com
Gary V. Abbott; David E. Prange;—Annalie M. Faddis; Nicholas A. Nardi; Klarice A. Kolbe; Jennifer L. Gates; Kevin Brague; Theodore F. Sumner.

See Professional Biographies, PORTLAND, OREGON

Abel, Kirstin L. ... '77 '03 C.413 B.A. L.365 J.D. [Ⓐ Keating J.B.&H.]
Abel, Steven W., (AV) ... '53 '83 C.1056 B.S. L.596 J.D. [Stoel R.]
Abere, Kenneth J., Jr ... '— '94 C.856 B.A. L.950 J.D. [Cosgrave V.K.]
Abney, James R. ... '59 '97 C.112 B.S. L.1051 J.D. [Kolisch H.] (Pat.) (⊙Palo Alto, CA)
Abraham, Laurie, (AV) ... '57 '84 C&L.629 B.S., J.D. Dep. Dist. Atty.
Abraham, Philip T. ... '28 '57 C.629 B.S. L.596 LL.B. Cir. J.
Abrams, Marc, (AV) ... '57 '82 C.918 A.B. L.477 J.D. 2868 N.W. Wardway St., Apt. 11
Abrams, Paula L. '53 '79
C.477 B.G.S. L.1066 J.D. Assoc. Prof., Northwestern School of Law
Abravanel, Allan R., (AV) ... '47 '72 C.976 B.A. L.309 J.D. [Perkins C.]
Acker, Randal B. ... '66 '92 C.154 B.A. L.188 J.D. [R.B.Acker]
Acker, Randal B., P.C. ... 806 S.W. Broadway
Ackerman, Stark, (AV) ... '51 '79 C.31 B.A. L.273 J.D. [Black H.]
Ackerman, Susan K., (AV) '57 '83 C.56 B.A. L.1051 J.D.
Mgr. Regul. Affs. & Assoc. Coun., Northwest Nat. Gas Co.
Adams, Charles F., (AV) ... '47 '75 C.628 B.S. L.1066 J.D. [Stoel R.]
Adams, Cynthia Croft, (BV) ... '53 '83 C.658 B.A. L.596 J.D. [Ⓐ Dunn C.A,H.&T.]
Adams, Hub ... '67 '01 C.339 B.A.U.P. L.596 J.D. 905 Ne 11th LC-7
Adams, Ronald T., (AV) ... '42 '76 C.174 B.S. L.770 J.D. [Black H.]
Adams, Spencer S. '73 '01 C&L.101 B.A., J.D.
(adm. in CA; not adm. in OR) [Ⓐ Gordon&P.]
Adams Lien, Sarah ... '71 '02 C.771 B.A. L.1051 J.D. [Ⓐ Stoel R.]

Adams & Uffelman LLP
(See Beaverton)

Adler, David J. ... '52 '82 C.1350 B.A. L.596 J.D. Bonneville Power Admn.
Adler, James R. '51 '77 C&L.629 B.S., J.D.
Oper. Coun., G.E. Capital Colonial Pacific Leasing
Agosti, Elizabeth Clark ... '54 '93 C.188 B.A. L.861 J.D. 7037 SW 33 Place
Aguilar, Elvia ... '73 '00 C&L.629 B.A., J.D. [Pickett D.R.]
Ainsworth, Harry D., (BV) ... '63 '90 C.860 B.A. L.94 J.D. 1033 SW Yamhill St.
Aitchison, William B., (AV) ... '51 '77 C.629 B.A. L.276 J.D. 3021 Ne Broadway
Akers, Richard J. ... '19 '48 C.336 B.A. L.596 LL.B. 4809 S.W. Vermont St.‡
Alan, Lisa Carey ... '69 '00 C.911 B.A. L.596 J.D. [Ⓐ Schwabe,W.&W.]
Alba, Susana, (BV) ... '60 '89 C.1158 B.S. L.596 J.D. 6340 SE Brownlee Road
Albrecht, Cheryl, (BV) ... '65 '93 C.420 B.A. L.596 J.D. 1021 S.W. 4th Ave.
Alcantar, Michael Peter, (AVⓉ) ... '50 '75 C&L.800 B.A., J.D. [Alcantar&K.] ⊙
Alcantar and Kahl LLP, (AVⓉ) ... 1300 SW 5th Ave. (⊙San Fran., CA)
Alderson, W. David, (BV) ... '31 '65 C.336 B.S. L.1003 J.D. 2809 S.E. 122nd Ave.
Alderton, Donald L., (BV) ... '22 '49 C&L.950 B.A., J.D. [D.L.Alderton]
Alderton, Donald L., P.C., (BV) ... P.O. Box 231117
Aldisert, Robert L. ... '56 '89 C.178 A.B. L.426 J.D. [Perkins C.]
Aldrich, Dean E., (AV) ... '65 '94 C.628 B.S. L.861 J.D. [Aldrich]
Aldrich Law Office PC, (AV) ... 522 S.W. 5th Ave., Ste. 1230
Alexander, Dina E. ... '70 '96 C.911 B.A. L.950 J.D. [Ball J.]
Alexander, Jason W., (BV) ... '69 '96 C.169 B.S. L.950 J.D. [Sussman S.]
Alexander, Richard E., (AV) ... '44 '69 C.628 B.S. L.629 J.D. [Stoel R.]

Alexander, Tonya M., Law Office of '74 '01
C.1056 B.S. L.1051 J.D. 1500 SW 1st Ave., Suite 920
Alexanderson, Alvin '47 '72
C.317 B.S. L.477 J.D. Sr. V.P. & Gen. Coun., Portland Gen. Corp.
Alfred, Roger A., (BV) ... '66 '93 C.37 B.A. L.1051 J.D. [🄰 Perkins C.]
Allan, Richard H., (AV) ... '59 '88 C.112 B.S. L.1066 J.D. [Ball J.]
Alleman, Mark D. '71 '98 C.813 B.S. L.629 J.D.
[🄰 Kolisch H.] (Pat.) (⊙Palo Alto, CA)
Allen, Beth A. ... '— '96 C.1056 B.S. L.950 J.D. [🄰 Lane P.]
Allen, Brenda ... '68 '94 C.134 B.S. L.1051 J.D. Dep. Dist. Atty.
Allen, F. Gordon, III, (AV) ... '47 '74 C.31 B.A. L.145 J.D. [McEwen G.]
Allen, Robert L., (AV) ... '37 '65 C.813 A.B. L.1066 LL.B. [Dunn C.A.H.&T.]
Allen, Russell M., (AV) ... '39 '65 C.813 A.B. L.770 J.D. [Allen,S.&M.]
Allen, Warner E., (BV) ... '43 '69 C&L.950 B.S., J.D. [Warren A.]
Allen, Sheridan & McClanahan, LLP, (AV) ... 190 S.W. Harrison Street
Alley, Walter D., (BV) ... '29 '60 C.629 B.S. L.596 LL.B. 1205 NW 25th Avenue
Alli, Richard J., Jr., (BV) ... '54 '80 C.629 B.S. L.950 J.D. [Bullard S.J.W.]
Allport, Michael G. ... '52 '83 C.685 B.A. L.629 J.D. Pres., Allport Editions
Alpern, Amy R., (AV) ... '58 '84 C.800 B.A. L.596 J.D. [Amburgey&R.]
Alterman, Dean N., (AV) ... '— '89 C.309 A.B. L.596 J.D. [Lane P.]
Alton, Janis K. ... '55 '81 C.174 B.A. L.596 J.D. Lewis and Clark Law Sch.
Altschul, Andrew ... '70 '95 C.293 B.A. L.477 J.D. [Altschul]

Altschul Law Office, PC
117 SW Taylor Street, Suite 200, 97204
Telephone: 503-417-0444 Fax: 503-417-0501
Email: andrew@portlandemploymentlaw.com URL: http://www.portlandemploymentlaw.com
Andrew Altschul.
Employment Law, Human Resources, Employment Contracts, Employee Benefits.
See Professional Biographies, PORTLAND, OREGON

Alvey, Martin L., (AV) ... '59 '87 C.950 B.A. L.1051 J.D. [M.L.Alvey] ⊙

Alvey, Martin L., P.C., (AV)
Suite 100, 140 S.W. Arthur Street, 97201 ⊙
Telephone: 503-229-0895 Fax: 503-229-1094 URL: http://www.martinalveylaw.com
Email: malvey@qwest.net URL: http://www.martinalvey.com
Martin L. Alvey.
Personal Injury, Automobile Accidents, Workers Compensation, Longshore and Harbor Workers Compensation Act, Social Security Disability.
Astoria, Oregon Office: #1 Portway, Port of Astoria Building, Suite 3A, 97103. Telephone: 503-325-5509.
See Professional Biographies, PORTLAND, OREGON

Aman, David S. ... '71 '96 C&L.1051 B.A., J.D. [Tonkon T.]
Ambrose, Christopher R., (AV) ... '61 '87 C.112 B.A. L.1049 J.D. [Ambrose]
Ambrose, David R., (AV) ... '53 '79 C.602 B.S. L.596 J.D. [Ambrose]
Ambrose, James F., (AV) ... '— '79 C.602 B.B.A. L.426 J.D. [Davis W.T.]

Ambrose Law Group LLC, (AV)
An Oregon Limited Liability Company
1670 Koin Center, 222 S.W. Columbia Street, 97201-6616
Telephone: 503-222-0552 Facsimile: 503-222-0984
Email: admin@ambroselaw.com URL: http://www.ambroselaw.com
Members: David R. Ambrose; Christopher R. Ambrose. Senior Counsel: Douglas B. Gordon.
Banking, Business and Corporate Transactions, Business Tax and Estate Planning, Finance, Real Estate Secured Finance, Asset-Based Lending, Real Estate Transactions, Technology, Internet and E-Commerce Strategies.
See Professional Biographies, PORTLAND, OREGON

Amburgey, Larry K., (AV) ... '47 '75 C.939 B.A. L.596 J.D. [Amburgey&R.]

Amburgey & Rubin, P.C., (AV)
Riverplace Office Building, 1750 S. W. Harbor Way, Suite 450, 97201-0104
Telephone: 503-221-0309 Fax: 503-242-2457
Email: general@amburgeyrubin.com
Larry K. Amburgey; Howard Rubin; Amy R. Alpern; Patricia Ann Haim; Scott Talmage Cliff; Ursula A. Kienbaum.
Practice Limited to Representing Management in Labor and Employment Law, including Practice before State and Federal Courts and Administrative Agencies, and Business Immigration.
See Professional Biographies, PORTLAND, OREGON

Amiton, Marshall L. ... '45 '70 C.1056 B.S. L.950 J.D. Cir. J.
Anderly, Andrea J. ... '48 '90 C.629 B.S. L.596 J.D. [Gevurtz,M.L.&H.]
Andersen, Steven B., (BV) ... '49 '87 C.966 B.A. L.1051 J.D. 210 S.W. Morrison St.

Andersen, Susan K. '47 '85 C.950 B.A. L.1051 J.D.
2686 Southwest Vista Avenue, 97201-1777
Telephone: 503-222-1996 Fax: 503-274-9945
Email: suzyander@aol.com URL: http://www.lawyers.com/ska
Wills and Probate, Asset Protection, Trust Law, Estate Planning, Guardianship and Conservatorship.
See Professional Biographies, PORTLAND, OREGON

Anderson, Dana A. ... '50 '75 C.629 B.S. L.950 J.D. Tri-Met Legal Servs.
Anderson, Douglas P. ... '57 '84 Louisiana-Pacific Corporation
Anderson, Edward B. ... '47 '80 C.628 B.S.E.E. L.1051 J.D. [🄰 Kolisch H.] (Pat.)
Anderson, Jennifer M. ... '70 '96 C.939 B.A. L.1194 J.D. Cust. Mngr., Freightliner LLC
Anderson, John A., (BV) ... '50 '75 C.950 B.A. L.629 J.D. [Anderson&Y.]
Anderson, John P., (BVⓉ) ... '63 '89 C.427 B.A. L.1035 J.D. Metro. Public Def.
Anderson, Kenneth E., (BV) ... '44 '73 C.1056 B.S. L.596 J.D. 1737 NE Broadway
Anderson, Mark A., (BV) ... '53 '79 C.800 A.B. L.976 J.D. P.O. Box 8154
Anderson, Norman E., (AV) ... '20 '49 C.629 B.S. L.309 J.D. [N.E.Anderson] ‡
Anderson, Ronald P., (AV) ... '39 '65 C&L.629 B.S., LL.B. [Schulte,A.D.A.&B.]
Anderson, Samuel K. ... '75 '03 C.1169 B.A. L.629 J.D. [🄰 Davis R.E.&X.]
Anderson, Suzanne D. ... '56 '85 C&L.629 B.A., J.D. Law Clk. to Sr. Dist. J.
Anderson, Traci ... '64 '98 C.1056 B.A. L.950 J.D. Dist. Atty. Off.
Anderson, Norman E., P.C., (AV) ... 4850 S.W. Scholls Ferry Rd.
Anderson and Yamada, P.C., (AV) ... 1515 S.W. 5th Ave.
Andres, Douglas R., (AV) ... '52 '78 C.105 B.A. L.273 J.D. [Bullivant H.B.]
Andrews, Alvin L. ... '27 '56 C.629 B.B.A. L.596 LL.B. 3210 N. Lombard St.‡
Andrews, Frank '38 '68 C&L.560 B.A., J.D.
(adm. in NM; not adm. in OR) Sr. Coun., Harland Fin. Solutions, Inc.
Angeli, Courtney W., (BV) ... '67 '94 C.280 B.A. L.477 J.D. [Stoel R.]
Angeli, David H. ... '67 '97 C.94 B.S. L.276 J.D. [Stoel R.]
Angello, Paul S., (AV) ... '50 '81 C.659 B.S.E.E. L.800 J.D. [Stoel R.] (See Pat. Sect.)
Angius, Christopher W., (AV) ... '53 '81 C.178 B.A. L.309 J.D. [Holland&K.]
Animal Law Practice, The ... 5331 S.W. Macadam Ave., Ste. 299
Antell, Kenneth S., (AV) ... '59 '86 C.477 B.A. L.629 J.D. [Dunn C.A.H.&T.]
Antell, Rhonda Lee ... '57 '87 C.628 B.S. L.629 J.D. Deloitte & Touche
Anuta, Karl G., (AV) ... '59 '86 C.1051 B.S. L.596 J.D. [Sokol&A.]
Apolito, Fabio ... '68 '96 C.282 B.A. L.285 J.D. Native American Prog., OR Legal Servs.
Appleman, Wayne R. ... '— '75 L.629 J.D. I.R.S.
Archer, Stephen E. ... '58 '96 C.770 B.A. L.950 J.D. 1001 SW Fifth Avenue, Ste. 1700
Archie, Peter B., (AVⓉ) ... '40 '66 C.575 B.S. L.228 LL.B. [Perkins C.] (⊙Seattle, WA)

Arellano, Joseph C., (AV) ... '53 '79 C.209 B.A. L.1051 J.D. [Kennedy,W.A.&R.]
Arenz, Thomas J. ... '68 '96 C.629 B.S. L.285 J.D. [Brownstein,R.S.K.G.D.&H.]
Armstrong, Craig R., P.C., (AV) ... '66 '92 C.112 B.A. L.426 J.D. [Miller N.]
Arnold, Joshua L. '74 '00
C.860 B.A. L.596 J.D. Jud. Clerk to the Hon. Kimberly C. Frankel
Arntz, Rickee N. ... '55 '92 C.37 B.A. L.190 J.D. [🄲 Keating J.B.&H.]
Aronson, Lee S., (AV) ... '50 '77 C.33 B.A. L.596 J.D. [Schulte,A.D.A.&B.]
Arthur, Randy L., (AV) ... '55 '85 C.605 A.B. L.1019 J.D. [Bullivant H.B.]
Artz, David J. ... '50 '75 C.112 B.A. L.1065 J.D. [🄰 Peterson]
Ashe, Richard Theodore ... '71 '02 C.804 B.A. L.1051 J.D. [🄰 Dunn C.A.H.&T.]
Ashmanskas, Donald C. ... '35 '68 C.705 A.B. L.569 J.D. U.S. Mag. J.
Ashton, David ... '62 '90 C.1475 LL.B. L.472 J.D. Asst. Gen. Coun., Port of Portland
Ashton, Derek J. ... '— '87 C&L.629 B.S., J.D. [🄰 Cosgrave V.K.]
Ashworth, John P., (AV) ... '54 '82 C.813 B.A. L.569 J.D. [Bullivant H.B.]
Ater, Jonathan A., (AV) ... '40 '66 C&L.976 B.A., LL.B. [Ater W.]

Ater Wynne LLP, (AV) 🄱🅁
222 S.W. Columbia, Suite 1800, 97201-6618 ⊙
Telephone: 503-226-1191 Telecopier: 503-226-0079
URL: http://www.aterwynne.com
Partners/Shareholders: Jonathan A. Ater; Steven K. Blackhurst; Ernest G. Bootsma; Leslie G. Bottomly; William C. Campbell; Fred J. Coccodrilli; L. David Connell; Alice Cuprill-Comas; James B. Davidson; Valerie D. Fisher; Kirk H. Gibson; Wallace A. Glausi; Gregg D. Johnson; Randal A. Johnson; Frank V. Langfitt, III; Daniel P. Larsen; Douglas C. MacCourt; Stacey E. Mark; Brenda L. Meltebeke; Claudia Kay Powers; Lisa Rackner; Michael J. "Sam" Sandmire; Ronald L. Saxton; John M. Schultz; Michael W. Shackelford; Gregory E. Struxness; Mark A. Turner. Retired Partner: Steven E. Wynne. Associates: Rukaiyah Adams (Resident, Menlo Park, California Office); James M. Barrett; James C. Bradshaw; Amie Jamieson; Nathan A. Karman; James N. McDermott; Alia S. Miles; Douglas D. Morris; Jenny L. Trieu; Sarah K. Wallace. Of Counsel: Lori Irish Bauman; Akana K. J. Ma; John D. Walch; Laurie M. Younger.
Business, Civil Litigation, Corporation Law, Emerging Business, Employment and Labor Law, Energy, Environmental, Global Trade, Indian Law, Intellectual Property, International Law, Mergers and Acquisitions, Public/Private Ventures and Finance, Real Estate, Securities and Corporate Finance, Tax, Technology, Telecom, Venture Capital.
Representative Clients: AT&T Wireless; ATOFINA; Advanced Silicon Materials Inc.; Bank of America, N.A.; Bank of New York; Bechtel Enterprises, Inc.; BOC Group, Inc.; Cascade General; Cascade Microtech, Inc.; Cascade Station Development, LLC.
Seattle, Washington Office: Two Union Square, 601 Union Street, Suite 5450, Seattle, WA 98101-2327. Telephone: 206-623-4711. Telecopier: 206-467-8406.
Menlo Park, California Office: 525 Middlefield Road, Suite 150, Menlo Park, CA 94025-3441. Telephone: 650-566-1443. Telecopier: 650-325-2340.
See Professional Biographies, PORTLAND, OREGON

Atkin, Nelson D., II, (AV) ... '49 '74 C.1044 B.S. L.823 J.D. [Barran L.]
Atkins, Jeanne Paquette ... '49 '79 C.911 B.A. L.629 J.D. 1525 S.W. Wynwood Ave.
Atkins, Riley J., (AV) ... '52 '78 C.154 B.A. L.1067 J.D. U. S. Attorneys Office
Atwood, Ronald W., (AV) ... '50 '78 C.1051 B.A. L.629 J.D. [R.W.Atwood]
Atwood, Ronald W., P.C., (AV) ... 333 S.W. Fifth Avenue
Auerbach, Harry Michael ... '55 '82 C.112 B.A. L.284 J.D. Off. of City Atty.
Auerbach, Valerie Tomasi, (AV) ... '58 '84 C.690 B.A. L.596 J.D. [Farleigh W.]
Augee, Joel L. ... '67 '92 C&L.950 B.S., J.D. Fred Meyer, Inc.
Austin, Greg, (BV) ... '43 '84 C.1109 B.A. L.1051 J.D. 101 S.W. Main Street, Suite 700
Austin, Jeffrey D., P.C., (AV) ... '51 '83 C.1056 B.A. L.596 J.D. [Miller N.]
AuYeung, Al ... '50 '90 C.1056 B.S. L.770 J.D. [Schwabe,W.&W.] (Pat.)
Axelrod, David W., (AV) ... '50 '75 C.1097 B.A. L.1067 J.D. [Schwabe,W.&W.]
Ayres, Jason M. ... '74 '00 C.893 B.A. L.596 J.D. [🄰 Field&Assoc.]
Babener, Jeffrey A., (AV) ... '48 '74 C.605 A.B. L.800 J.D. [Babener&Assoc.]

Babener & Associates, (AV)
1020 Bank of America Financial Center, 121 S.W. Morrison, 97204-3140
Telephone: 503-226-6600 FAX: 503-226-4290
Email: contact@mlmlegal.com URL: http://www.mlmlegal.com
Jeffrey A. Babener;—Mitchell A. Goldstein.
General Civil and Trial Practice in all State and Federal Courts. Direct Selling, Marketing and Distribution, Commercial, Trade Regulation, Taxation, International, Corporation, Intellectual Property, Food and Drug, International Expansion.
Reference: Key Bank of Oregon.
See Professional Biographies, PORTLAND, OREGON

Babka, Nancy A., (BV) ... '49 '83 C.339 B.A. L.596 J.D. 610 S.W. Alder St., Ste. 1000
Babson, Stephen E., (AV) ... '50 '78 C&L.813 B.A., J.D. Endeavour Capital
Baca, David C., (AV) ... '— '82 C.413 B.A. L.309 J.D. [Davis W.T.]
Bacci, Bethany A. ... '73 '01 C.813 B.A. L.596 J.D. [🄰 Stoel R.]
Bachman, Craig D., (AV) ... '— '78 C.1056 B.S. L.596 J.D. [Lane P.]
Bachman, Ellen C., (AV) ... '49 '74 C.813 A.B. L.911 J.D. [Preston G.&E.]
Back, Jean Ohman ... '61 '91 C.112 B.A. L.629 J.D. [🄲 Schwabe,W.&W.]
Back, William D. '51 '76 C.813 B.A. L.36 J.D.
(adm. in AZ; not adm. in OR) Dep. Reg. Solr., U.S. Dept. of Interior
Backlar, Byron '25 '56 C&L.910 A.B., J.D.
(adm. in MO; not adm. in OR) 4160 S.W. Greenleaf Dr.‡
Bader, Jeremy R. ... '— '02 C.911 B.A. L.1355 J.D. [🄰 Foster P.T.]
Bahrman, Thomas E. ... '— '00 C.678 B.A. L.950 J.D. [🄰 Newcomb,S.S.&L.]
Bailey, Ron D., (AV) ... '36 '66 C.628 B.S. L.596 J.D. [🄲 Duffy K.]
Bailey, Ronald E., (AV) ... '37 '63 C.629 B.S. L.950 J.D. [Bullivant H.B.]
Baird, Gregory L. ... '64 '92 C.1056 B.S. L.596 J.D. [Gordon&P.]
Baird, Susan J. '— '01 C.112 B.A. L.1494 J.D.
(adm. in CA; not adm. in OR) [🄰 Lane P.]
Baisch, Jan Thomas, (AV) '49 '74
C.629 B.S. L.596 J.D. 1000 Southwest Broadway, Suite 2450
Baisden, Fred R., Jr. ... '43 '69 C.575 A.B. L.260 J.D. 4902 SW 1st Avenue
Baker, Aaron W., Attorney at Law '66 '92
C&L.629 B.S., J.D. 888 S.W. 5th Ave., Ste. 650
Baker, Audrey A. ... '— '96 C.267 B.A. L.285 J.D. [🄰 Harrang L.G.R.]
Baker, John H., Jr., (BV) ... '46 '86 C.188 B.Arch. L.629 J.D. [Jordan S.]
Baker, Leslie K., (AV) ... '53 '78 C&L.629 B.S., J.D. Asst. U.S. Atty.
Baker, Mandy M. Parkinson ... '— '02 C.763 B.A. L.596 J.D. [🄰 James]
Baker, Mitchell C. ... '70 '98 C.907 B.A. L.1051 J.D. [🄲 Fisher&P.]
Baker, Randall H. ... '59 '91 C.1051 B.A. L.629 J.D. [🄰 Casteel&C.]
Baker, Sarah L., (AV) '50 '75 C.560 B.A. L.608 J.D.
10121 S.E. Sunnyside Road, Ste. 140
Baker, Terry W., (AV) ... '41 '68 C.628 B.S. L.800 J.D. [Tonkon T.]
Baker, Theodore W. ... '76 '03 C&L.37 B.S., J.D. [🄰 Klarquist S.]
Bakkensen, John Reser, (AV) ... '43 '69 C.309 A.B. L.813 J.D. 1141 S.W. Mitchell Lane
Bakker, Tyl W., (BV) ... '64 '90 C.259 B.A. L.596 J.D. [T.W.Bakker]
Bakker, Tyl W., P.C., Law Offices of, (BV) ... 621 SW Alder St., Ste. 621
Balasubramani, Krishna, (BV) ... '68 '94 C.112 B.A. L.596 J.D. [Sather,B.&H.]
Balcom, E. Clarke ... '50 '01 C.1056 B.S. L.1051 J.D. [C.Balcom]
Balcom, Clarke, PC ... 5125 S.W. Macadam Ave., Ste. 210
Baldwin, Richard C. ... '47 '81 C.760 B.S. L.796 J.D. Co. Ct. J., Multnomah Co. Cir. Ct.
Baldwin-Sayre, J. Nicholas ... '— '97 C.112 B.A. L.596 J.D. [🄰 Cosgrave V.K.]
Balenger, Victoria L. ... '56 '87 C.293 B.A. L.596 J.D. [🄰 S.V.Rizzo]
Balfour, Clark I. ... '54 '79 C.413 B.A. L.596 J.D. [Cable H.B.H.&L.]

Ball, Robert S., (AV) .... '41 '67 C.939 B.A. L.1066 J.D. [Ⓒ Ball J.]

Ball Janik LLP, (AV) ⒷⓋ
One Main Place, 101 SW Main Street, Suite 1100, 97204-3219 ⊙
Telephone: 503-228-2525 Telecopy: 503-295-1058
Email: info@balljanik.com URL: http://www.balljanik.com
Partners of Firm: Dina E. Alexander; Richard H. Allan; James A. Beall (Also at Washington, D.C. Office); Bruce H. Cahn; Laura Craska Cooper (Also at Bend, Oregon Office); Nancy Craven (Also at Bend, Oregon Office); David W. Criswell; John J. Dunbar; Jeffrey C. Gardner; Robert G. Hayes (Not admitted in OR; Resident, Washington, D.C. Office); Stephen T. Janik; Phillip E. Joseph; Sally C. Landauer; James T. McDermott; Bradley S. Miller; Jack L. Orchard, Jr.; Timothy M. Parks; Barbara W. Radler; Irene Ringwood (Not admitted in OR; Resident, Washington, D.C. Office); Sarah J. Ryan; Leon Simson; Brad T. (Tony) Summers; Christopher M. Walters; Christen Carlson White. Senior Counsel: Robert S. Ball. Special Counsel: Craig A. Crotteau (Also at Washington, D.C. Office); Robert A. Stout (Also at Bend, Oregon Office). Of Counsel: William H. Perkins; Richard J. Stone. Associates: Amy S. Campbell; Denise R. Case (Not admitted in OR); Dwain M. Clifford; Reagan L.B. Desmond (Also at Bend, Oregon Office); Renee M. France; Aaron D. Goldstein (Not admitted in OR); Jessica T. Hamilton; Dana L. Krawczuk; Kevin S. Mapes; Jeana M. McGlasson; James C. Prichard; Robert L. Taylor; Rebecca Biermann Tom; Kristin L. Udvari (Also at Bend, Oregon Office); Robert W. Wilkinson.
Real Estate, Land Use, Commercial Litigation, Business, Corporate, Government Relations, Financing, Bankruptcy, Business Workouts and Reorganizations, Environmental, Natural Resources, Creditors' Remedies, Taxation, Estate Planning and Probate, Administrative, Health Care, Employment, Construction, Insurance Recovery.
Representative Clients: Charles Schwab & Co., Inc.; Norris Beggs & Simpson; Oregon Health & Science University; PG&E National Energy Group; Trammell Crow Co.
Washington, D.C. Office: 1455 F Street, NW, Suite 225, 20005-1004. Telephone: 202-638-3307. Telecopy: 202-783-6947.
Bend, Oregon Office: 15 SW Colorado Avenue, Suite 3, 97702. Telephone: 541-617-1309. Telecopy: 541-617-8824.
See Professional Biographies, PORTLAND, OREGON

Ballo, Nicole Louise Faith '72 '99
C.604 B.A. L.208 J.D Dept. of Human Serv., Child Welfare
Ballou, Vicki A., (AV) .... '— '86 C.897 B.A. L.846 J.D. [Tonkon T.]
Balske, Dennis N., (AVⓉ) .... '49 '74 C.97 B.S. L.608 J.D. Asst. Fed. Pub. Def.
Bangay, Peter, Jr. .... '59 '89 C&L.950 B.A., J.D. 140 S.W. Arthur St.
Banks, Robert S., Jr., (AV) .... '55 '82 C.685 B.A. L.966 J.D. [Banks]
Banks, Roland F. (Jerry), Jr., (AV) '32 '58 C&L.629 B.S., LL.B.
[Schwabe,W.&W.] ‡

Banks Law Office, P.C., (AV)
200 S.W. Market Street, Suite 1600, 97201
Telephone: 503-222-7475 Telecopier: 503-248-0138 URL: http://www.investordefender.com
Email: info@investordefender.com URL: http://www.lawyers.com/investordefender
Robert S. Banks, Jr.
Securities Fraud, Stockbroker Arbitration, Investor Rights, Investment Fraud, Business Torts, Securities Arbitration, Legal Malpractice in State and Federal Courts and before NASD, NYSE and AAA Arbitration Panels.
Reference: Bank of America.
See Professional Biographies, PORTLAND, OREGON

Banner & Witcoff, Ltd.
Established In 1920 - Predecessor Parent
601 SW Second Avenue Suite 1900, 97204 ⊙
Telephone: 503-425-6800 Fax: 503-425-6801
Email: info@bannerwitcoff.com URL: http://www.bannerwitcoff.com
Thomas L. Evans; Byron S. Kuzara.
Intellectual Property including Procurement of Patents, Trademarks, Copyrights, Trade Secrets, Counseling & Opinions, Unfair Competition, Interferences, Licensing, Antitrust and International Trade Matters. Litigation including Trials and Appeals in Federal and State Courts and International Trade Commission.
Chicago, Illinois Office: Ten South Wacker Drive, Suite 3000. Telephone: 312-463-5000. Facsimile: 312-463-5001.
Washington, D.C. Office: 1001 G Street, N.W., Suite 1100 Telephone: 202-824-3000. Facsimile: 202-824-3001.
Boston, Massachusetts Office: 28 State Street, 28th Floor. Telephone: 617-720-9600. Fax: 617-720-9601.
See Professional Biographies, PORTLAND, OREGON

Bannon, Albert J., (AV) .... '44 '69 C.728 A.B. L.602 J.D. [Bannon M.]
Bannon Mediation, LLC, (AV) .... 101 S. W. Main Street
Baptiste, Remi A. .... '65 '94 C.433 B.A. L.1051 J.D. [Black H.]
Barbur, William .... '69 '98 C.280 B.A. L.1051 J.D. [Ⓐ Rycewicz&C.]
Barg, Jonathan V., (AV) .... '60 '85 C.154 B.A. L.800 J.D. [Barg H.]
Barg Horvat PC, (AV) .... 121 SW Morrison Street Suite 600
Barger, Glenn E. .... '71 '97 C.112 B.A. L.950 J.D. [Ⓐ Smith F.&E.]
Barhoum, John R. .... '— '04 L.1051 J.D. [Ⓐ Lane P.]
Barker, Anthony J., (AV) .... '37 '66 C.165 A.B. L.477 LL.B. 3003 N.E. 25th Avenue
Barker, Catherine E. .... '78 '03 C&L.378 B.S., J.D. [Ⓐ Stahancyk,K.J.&H.]
Barker, Heidi Heim .... '77 '99 C.940 B.A. L.629 J.D. Co. Dist. Atty. Off.
Barker, John R., (AV) .... '47 '73 C.950 B.A. L.629 J.D. [Barker]
Barker, Kurt Eric .... '71 '01 C.629 B.A. L.813 J.D. [Ⓐ Stoel R.]
Barker Law Firm, (AV) .... One Southwest Columbia Street
Barnes, Dana L., (BV) .... '58 '85 C.1051 B.S. L.596 J.D. [Ⓐ Kell,A.&R.]
Barnes, Gretchen S. .... '71 '03 C.285 B.A. L.1051 J.D. [Ⓐ Cable H.B.H.&L.]
Barnes, Kenton R., (BV) .... '51 '79 C&L.966 B.A., J.D. [K.R.Barnes]
Barnes, Kenton R., P.C., (BV) .... 222 S.W. Columbia St., Ste. 1625
Barnett, Kerry E. .... '57 '87 C.696 B.A. L.976 J.D. The ODS Companies
Barnhart, Daniel R. .... '64 '91 C&L.629 B.A., J.D. [Bullard S.J.W.]
Barnicle, Brendan J. .... '67 '93 C.309 A.B. L.911 J.D. 2894 N.W. Ariel Terrace
Barnum, Gary R., (AV) .... '54 '81 C.629 B.A. L.911 J.D. [Stoel R.]
Barnwell, Francis T., (AV) .... '54 '81 C.197 B.A. L.273 J.D. [Bullard S.J.W.]
Baroff, David L. '61 '91 C.787 B.A. L.184 J.D.
(adm. in NH; not adm. in OR) 1531 S.E. Pershing St.
Barofsky, Andrew D. .... '71 '02 C.629 B.S. L.93 J.D. [Ⓐ Schwabe,W.&W.]
Baron, Lawrence, (AV) .... '50 '75 C.373 B.A. L.912 J.D. [L.Baron]

Baron, Lawrence, PC, Law Office of, (AV)
1515 S.W. Fifth Avenue, Suite 808, 97201
Telephone: 503-417-1117 Fax: 503-417-1118 URL: http://www.lawyers.com/baron
Email: baron@baronlawfirm.com URL: http://www.baronlawfirm.com
Lawrence Baron.
Product Liability, Medical Malpractice, Lasik Eye Surgery, Air Bag Injuries, Automobile Defect Claims (Crash Worthiness) Wrongful Death, Maritime and Railroad Injuries.
See Professional Biographies, PORTLAND, OREGON

Baroway, Richard, (AV) .... '58 '83 C.330 B.A. L.950 J.D. [Garvey S.B.]
Barquin, William K. .... '73 '98 C&L.285 B.A., J.D. [Haglund,K.H.&J.]
Barrack, Martin J. .... '— '89 C.188 B.S. L.1068 J.D. [Barrack]

Barrack Law Firm, P.C.
1675 S.W. Marlow Avenue Suite 340, 97225
Telephone: 971-222-3646 Fax: 971-275-1023
Email: info@barrack.net URL: http://www.barrack.net
Martin J. Barrack.

(This Listing Continued)

Barrack Law Firm, P.C. (Continued)
Technology and Computer Law, Outsourcing, Strategic Alliances, Corporate Law, Finance, Real Estate, Intellectual Property, Mergers, Acquisitions and Divestitures, Arbitration, Mediation and Corporate Training.
See Professional Biographies, PORTLAND, OREGON

Barragar, Anne L., (AV) .... '— '87 C.668 B.A. L.911 J.D. [Davis W.T.]
Barram, Stephen H. .... '56 '81 C.999 B.A. L.596 J.D. 12242 S.W. Garden Pl.
Barran, Paula A., (AV) .... '49 '80 C.945 B.A. L.029 LL.B. [Barran L.]

Barran Liebman LLP, (AV) ⒷⓋ
601 SW Second Avenue, Suite 2300, 97204-3159
Telephone: 503-228-0500 Fax: 503-274-1212
Email: clientservices@barran.com URL: http://www.barran.com
Members of Firm: Nelson D. Atkin II; Paula A. Barran; Brenda K. Baumgart; Lisa C. Brown; Robert L. Carey; Todd A. Hanchett; Edwin A. Harnden (Managing Partner); Richard C. Hunt; Allyson S. Krueger; Richard F. Liebman; Bradley F. Tellam; Richard N. VanCleave; Maryann Yelnosky;— Kristin L. Bremer; Kimberly C. Capobianco; Karen L. O'Connor; Andrew M. Schpak; Kimberly A. Sordyl.
Labor and Employment Law.
Representative Clients: Frito-Lay; Health Future LLC; Hollywood Entertainment Corp.; Intel Corp.; Lloyds of London; Louisiana-Pacific Corporation; Pacific Maritime Association; The Oregonian; Tri-Met; Xerox Corporation.
See Professional Biographies, PORTLAND, OREGON

Barrett, Cynthia L., (AV) .... '49 '76 C.659 B.A. L.596 J.D. [C.L.Barrett]
Barrett, James M. .... '— '01 C.911 B.A. L.893 J.D. [Ⓐ Ater W.]
Barrett, Cynthia L., P.C., (AV) .... 1500 S.W. First Ave., Ste. 760
Barrie, Walter L. .... '34 '61 C&L.950 B.S., LL.B. Asst. Atty. Gen.
Barrow, David R. ..... '56 '85 C.629 B.A. L.596 J.D. 522 Southwest 5th Avenue, Suite 710
Barrows, David S., (BV) .... '35 '61 C&L.950 B.A., LL.B. 1201 S.W. 12th Ave.
Barsocchini, Kathleen '55 '81 C.1169 B.A. L.1051 J.D.
Assoc. Gen. Coun., Harland Fin. Solutions, Inc.
Barsocchini, Robert J., (BV) '50 '80
C.112 A.B. L.1051 J.D. Gen. Coun., Goodwill Industries
Barteld, Allen .... '66 '97 C.174 B.A. L.950 J.D. Gen. Coun., Associates
Bartels, James E., (AV) .... '47 '74 C.734 B.S. L.145 J.D. [Meyer&W.]
Bartoloni, Andrea, (AV) .... '50 '82 C.907 B.A. L.950 J.D. [Bartoloni]
Bartoloni Law Group, P.C., (AV) .... 1 World Trade Ctr., Ste. 1030
Barton, Kevin E. .... '— '02 C.285 B.A. L.602 J.D. [Ⓐ Bullivant H.B.]
Barton, Michelle E. .... '— '04 C&L.602 B.A., J.D. [Ⓐ Miller N.]
Barton, Rachelle Hong .... '— '02 C.1375 B.A. L.602 J.D. [Ⓐ Fisher&P.]
Barton, Robert E., (AV) .... '— '72 C.734 A.B. L.602 J.D. [Cosgrave V.K.]

Barton and Strever, P.C.
(See Newport)

Bartsch, Duane A. .... '27 '58 C.911 B.B.A. L.596 J.D. 2001 N.E. 64th Ave.‡
Bartz, David F., Jr., (AV) .... '57 '82 C.475 B.A. L.629 J.D. [Schwabe,W.&W.]
Basic, Anne Marie '60 '85 C.518 B.A. L.30 J.D.
(adm. in NJ; not adm. in OR) General Counsel, Sulzer Bingham Pumps, Inc.
Bass, Sally Forbes .... '47 '78 C.1208 B.A. L.201 J.D. Asst. Coun., Standard Ins. Co.
Bass, Shirley A., (AV) '38 '80
C.1056 B.A. L.596 J.D. 4380 S.W. Macadam Avenue, Suite 500
Batchelor, Jeffrey M., (AV) .... '46 '72 C.101 B.S. L.950 J.D. [Markowitz,H.G.&M.]
Bateman, Randall B., (AV) ...... '55 '80 C&L.950 B.S., J.D. 888 S.W. 5th Ave., Ste. 1150
Batson, F. Blair .... '58 '86 C.298 B.A. L.861 J.D. 1000 Friends of Oregon
Bauer, H. Stephen, (CV) .... '58 '84 C.628 B.S. L.629 J.D. [H.L.Bauer&Assoc.]
Bauer, Henry L., (AV) .... '28 '53 C.628 B.S. L.629 J.D. [H.L.Bauer&Assoc.]
Bauer, Henry L., & Associates, A Prof. Corp., (AV) ..... 5440 S.W. Westgate Drive, #170
Baum, Gregory H., (BV) '47 '76 C.188 B.S. L.1051 J.D.
V.P., Sec. & Gen. Coun., Harsch Investment Corp.
Baum, Richard L., (AV) .... '56 '82 C.165 B.A. L.276 J.D. [Perkins C.]
Bauman, Frank A., (AV) .... '21 '50 C.813 A.B. L.976 J.D. 1331 S.W. Broadway‡
Bauman, Kenneth C. .... '43 '69 C&L.629 B.S., J.D. State Atty. Off.
Bauman, Lori Irish, (AV) .... '59 '84 C.674 A.B. L.145 J.D. [Ⓒ Ater W.]
Bauman, Todd A., (AV) .... '56 '84 C.813 A.B. L.145 J.D. [Stoel R.]
Baumann, Merrill J., Jr., (AV) .... '— '86 C.197 A.B. L.800 J.D. [Davis W.T.]
Baumgart, Brenda K. .... '73 '99 C&L.950 B.A., J.D. [Barran L.]
Baumgartner, James M., (AV) .... '58 '86 C.1181 B.S. L.950 J.D. [Black H.]

Baumgartner, Nelson & Price, P.L.L.C.
(See Vancouver, Washington)

Baxendale, James C. L., (AV) .... '45 '71 C&L.705 B.A., J.D. 1209 S.W. 6th Ave.
Bayern, Douglas C. .... '53 '78 C.446 B.S. L.629 J.D. 12030 S.W. Bowmont
Bayless, Richard V., (AV) .... '31 '60 C.628 B.S. L.596 LL.B. [Bayless&M.]
Bayless & Murphy, (AV) .... 1300 S.W. 5th Ave.
Beall, James A., (AV) .... '50 '76 C.628 B.A. L.629 J.D. [Ball J.] (⊙Wash., DC)
Bean, David I. .... '72 '01 C.174 B.A. L.596 J.D. [Ⓐ Meyer&W.]
Bean, James H., (AV) .... '34 '67 C.101 B.A. L.273 J.D. [Lindsay,H.N.&W.]
Bearden, Frank L. .... '41 '71 C.169 B.A. L.208 J.D. Cir. J.
Beasley, Heather C., (BV) .... '66 '91 C.860 B.A. L.904 J.D. [Davis R.E.&X.]
Beattie, Jay W., (AV) .... '57 '87 C.768 B.A. L.596 J.D. [Lindsay,H.N.&W.]
Beatty, John C., Jr., (AV) .... '19 '48 C.674 A.B. L.178 J.D. Sr. J.‡
Beatty-Walters, Christina L. .... '71 '98 C.437 B.A. L.629 J.D. [Ⓐ Stoll S.B.L.&S.]
Beauchamp, Neil A. .... '50 '83 C.629 B.S. L.285 J.D. 900 S.W. 5th Ave.
Beck, Lawrence J., (BV) .... '53 '86 C.546 A.B. L.596 J.D. 621 S.W. Morrison Street
Becker, Dylan T. .... '— '02 C.907 B.A. L.629 J.D. [Ⓐ James]
Becker, Millard M., (BV) .... '28 '57 [Ⓒ Hunt&Assoc.]
Beckman, Douglas G. .... '44 '72 C.976 B.A. L.1066 J.D. Cir. J.
Bedell, Daniel J., (BV) .... '46 '80 C.628 B.S.E.E. L.1051 J.D. [Smith-Hill&B.] (Pat.)
Beer, Donald E., (BV) ...... '50 '78 C.911 B.A. L.1051 J.D. 1500 S.W. First Ave., Ste. 1050
Beery, Pamela J., (BV) .... '53 '80 C.1056 B.A. L.596 J.D. [Beery&E.]
Beery & Elsner LLP, (AV) .... 1750 SW Harbor Way, Suite 380
Bell, Rodland G. .... '36 '66 C.628 B.S. L.284 LL.B. 5017 S.E. 36th Ave.
Bellanca, Robin .... '78 '05 C.95 B.A. L.1565 J.D. [Ⓐ Cable H.B.H.&L.]
Belloni, Robt. C. .... '19 '51 C&L.629 B.A., J.D. U.S. Sr. Dist. Ct. J.
Belnavis, Clarence M. .... '69 '94 C.1086 B.A. L.329 J.D. [Fisher&P.]
Belsheim, Edmund O. '05 '31 C.585 B.A. L.145 S.J.D.
(adm. in IL; not adm. in OR) Lewis & Clark Law Sch.
Bemis, Kenneth E., (AV) .... '64 '89 C.675 B.A. L.950 J.D. [Bullard S.J.W.]
Benazzi, John B. .... '76 '04 C.902 B.S. L.629 J.D. [Ⓐ McEwen G.]

Bender, Brett N. '57 '88 C.629 B.S. L.596 J.D.
1000 S.W. Broadway, Suite 2400, 97205-3054
Telephone: 503-223-6337 Fax: 503-241-2249
Email: brett@benderlaw.us URL: http://www.lawyers.com/brettbender
Family Law, Child Custody, Child Support, Divorce, Visitation Rights, Domestic Violence.
See Professional Biographies, PORTLAND, OREGON

Bender, Carmel .... '64 '02 C&L.629 B.A., J.D. [C.Bender]

Bender, Laurie, (BV) .... '59 '88 C.999 B.S. L.596 J.D. [L.Bender]

Bender, Carmel, PC
610 S.W. Broadway, Suite 303, 97205
Telephone: 503-222-3116 Fax: 503-222-3116
Email: carmelbender@comcast.net URL: http://www.lawyers.com/carmelbender
Carmel Bender.
General Practice.

See Professional Biographies, PORTLAND, OREGON

Bender, Laurie, P.C., (BV) ....735 SW 1st Ave 2nd Flr
Benderly, Danielle .... '69 '96 C.914 B.A. L.1066 J.D. [🄰 Perkins C.]
Benedict, James E., (AV) .... '46 '76 C.628 B.S.Ch.E. L.326 J.D. [Cable H.B.H.&L.]
Benke, Thomas R. .... '61 '92 C.846 B.S. L.596 J.D. 7845 Sw Capitol Hwy Ste 8
Benn, Travis J. '75 '03 C.198 B.A. L.1128 J.D.
Corp. Coun., Harland Financial Solutions, Inc.
Benner, Ray R., (AV) .... '37 '66 C.1051 B.S. L.596 LL.B. [Benner&Assoc.]
Benner & Associates, P.C., (AV) .... 121 S.W. Morrison Street Suite 1010
Bennett, Burton H., (AV) ....'29 '58 C.413 B.A. L.596 J.D. [B.H.Bennett]
Bennett, Gregory C., (BV) ....'46 '75 C.228 A.B. L.966 J.D. 2314 N.E. 56th Ave.
Bennett, J. David, (AV) ....'41 '71 C.413 B.A. L.950 J.D. [Landye B.B.]
Bennett, Jeffrey J., (AV) .... '52 '81 C.966 B.S. L.596 J.D. [Jordan S.]
Bennett, Jeffrey S., (BV) ....'61 '89 C.10 B.A. L.596 J.D. [Warren A.]
Bennett, John A., (AV) ....'50 '75 C.629 B.A. L.596 J.D. [Bullivant H.B.]
Bennett, Jonathan A., (AV) .... '59 '86 C&L.629 B.S., J.D. [Dunn C.A.H.&T.]
Bennett, Joseph F. '34 '76 C.260 B.S. L.1051 J.D.
(adm. in WA; not adm. in OR) Asst. Gen. Coun., Bonneville Power Admn.
Bennett, Philip R., (AV) ....'— '84 C&L.629 B.A., J.D. [Cosgrave V.K.]
Bennett, Robert A., (AV) .... '31 '60 C&L.629 B.B.A., LL.B. [🄲 Bennett,H.M.&K.]
Bennett, Steven R., (AV) ....'52 '78 C.629 B.A. L.770 J.D. [Powers,M.&B.]
Bennett, Burton H., P.C., (AV) ....1001 S.W. 5th Ave.
Bennett, Hartman, Morris & Kaplan, LLP, (AV) .... 111 S.W. 5th Ave., Ste. 1650
Benson, Fred O. .... '17 '41 C.18 L.596 LL.B. P.O. Box 14652
Benson, Reed D. '62 '88 C.350 B.S. L.477 J.D.
Reclamation Issues Dir., Water Watch of Oregon
Benson, Steven E. ....'47 '73 C.685 B.A. L.596 J.D. P.O. Box 15036
Bentley, Philip S. ....'72 '01 C&L.629 B.S., J.D. [🅂 Rose,S.&B.]
Berg, Patrick R. .... '44 '70 C.670 B.A. L.602 J.D. 11040 S.W. Berkshire
Berg, William A. '54 '79 C.813 B.A. L.309 J.D.
Pres., Sigma Investment Management Company
Berger, Leland R., (BV) ..... '56 '83 C.216 B.A. L.596 J.D. 3527 N.E. 15th Ave., Ste. 103
Bergeson, Nancy ....'51 '81 C&L.878 B.S., J.D. Fed. Pub. Def. Off.
Berkowitz, Karen A. .... '51 '77 C.1044 B.A. L.209 J.D. Legal Aid Serv.(s) of OR
Berkshire, William C. ....'50 '80 C.207 B.A. L.629 J.D. [W.C.Berkshire]
Berkshire, William C., P.C. ....1216 SE Belmont
Berman, Steven C. ....'66 '95 C.31 B.A. L.309 J.D. [🄲 Stoll S.B.L.&S.]
Bernabei, Vincent James, (BV) ....'58 '84 C.549 B.A. L.596 J.D. [V.J.Bernabei]
Bernabei, Vincent James, LLC, (BV) ....9900 SW Greenburg Road
Bernard, William F., (AV) .... '21 '47 C&L.629 B.S., J.D. 1100 S.W. Sixth Avenue‡
Bernardi, Edward P. ....'53 '81 C.1051 B.S. L.678 J.D. [Bernardi&S.]
Bernardi & Spencer ....3331 S.E. Milwaukie Ave.
Berne, Gary M., (AV) ....'51 '77 C&L.659 B.A., J.D. [Stoll S.B.L.&S.]
Bernhard, Edward A. ....'69 '95 C.674 B.A. L.950 J.D. [🄰 Stoel R.]
Bernhard, Milton E., (AV) .... '32 '58 C.674 B.A. L.1009 LL.B. 121 S.W. Morrison
Bernick, Carol J., (AV) ....'— '89 C.695 B.A. L.893 J.D. [Davis W.T.]
Berning, Bruce G., (AV) .... '— '77 C.347 A.B. L.309 J.D. [Tonkon T.]
Bernstein, Harlan, (AV) .... '49 '74 C.966 B.A. L.209 J.D. [Jolles&B.]
Bernstein, Lloyd ....'69 '96 C.999 B.A. L.61 J.D. [🄰 Bullivant H.B.]
Bernstine, Daniel O. ....'47 '73 C.1375 B.A. L.597 J.D. Florida State Univ.
Berres-Paul, Toni '47 '86 C.966 B.A. L.596 J.D.
Legal Writing Instuctor, Northwestern Sch. of Law
Berry, Karen ....'45 '75 C.112 B.A. L.1051 J.D. Dept. of Vet. Affairs
Bertolino, Michelle M. ....'63 '91 C&L.950 B.S., J.D. [🄰 Farleigh W.]
Bertoni, Gary B., (AV) ....'51 '78 C.243 B.A. L.596 J.D. [Bertoni&T.]
Bertoni & Todd, (AV) .... 520 S.W. Yamhill St.
Beshears, Charles D., Law Offices of, (BV) '52 '79
C.605 B.A. L.596 J.D. 1500 S.W. 1st Ave., Ste. 700
Bethlahmy, Aliza D. .... '53 '78 C.911 B.A. L.336 J.D. 800 N.E. Oregon St., Ste. 340
Bethune, Downing M., (BV) .... '57 '86 C.280 B.A. L.950 J.D. 519 S.W. Park Ave.
Betz, Jan V. V., (AV) .....'46 '85 C.763 B.A. L.1202 J.D. Dep. City Atty., City Atty. Off.
Beutler, Toija J., (AV) '54 '82 C.629 B.A. L.596 J.D.
Asst. V.P. & Gen. Coun., Fidelity Natl. Title Co. of Ore.
Beyer, Ruth A., (AV) ....'55 '80 C.628 B.S. L.602 J.D. [Stoel R.]
Bibb, Benjamin C., Jr. '54 '81
C&L.893 B.A., J.D. Prog. Analyst, U.S. Fish & Wildlife Serv.
Bible, Patrick M. ....'74 '99 C.950 B.A. L.170 J.D. [🄰 Klarquist S.]
Bierly, Paul S. ....'60 '90 C.911 B.A. L.678 J.D. [Markowitz,H.G.&M.]
Biggs, Hugh L., (AV) ....'04 '31 C&L.629 B.A., J.D. 900 S.W. 5th Ave.‡
Biggs, Richard L., (AV) ....'26 '58 C.685 B.A. L.596 LL.B. 3517 S.W. Santa Monica Ct.‡
Bikus, Christopher M. ....'69 '96 C.57 B.A. L.546 J.D. [🄲 Tonkon T.]
Bildstein, Jeffrey W., (AV) .... '57 '82 C.923 B.S. L.629 J.D. [Keating J.B.&H.]
Bilyeu, Amy E. .... '73 '01 C&L.629 B.A., J.D. [🄰 Samuels Y.K.S.&S.]
Bird, A. Jeffery ....'55 '81 C.902 B.A. L.893 J.D. [Garvey S.B.]
Birdwell, William A., (AV) '46 '73
C.628 B.S.E.E. L.174 J.D. [Birdwell&J.] (See Pat. Sect.) ⊙

Birdwell & Janke LLP, (AV) BR
1400 Standard Plaza, 1100 S.W. Sixth Avenue, 97204-1221
Telephone: 503-228-1841 Fax: 503-228-2635
Email: portland@birdwelljanke.com URL: http://www.birdwelljanke.com
William A. Birdwell; Garth Janke (Resident). Associates: Allen W. Field; Richard A. Wilhelm; Geoffrey K. Cooper.
Intellectual Property including: Patent, Trademark, Copyright, Trade Secret and Unfair Competition Law, Licensing, Trials in State and Federal Courts, Practice before U.S. Patent and Trademark Office.
Tucson, Arizona Office: 2301 E. Seventh Street, 85719. Telephone: 520-795-1446.

See Professional Biographies, PORTLAND, OREGON

Birk, Robert A., (CV) .... '53 '84 C&L.339 B.S., J.D. 1318 S.W. 12th Ave.
Birkland, Wendell R., (AV) '46 '72
C.1109 B.A. L.950 J.D. 1211 S.W. Fifth Avenue, Suite 1460
Birmingham, Pat, (AV) ....'47 '75 C.1056 B.S. L.1137 J.D. [Birmingham&M.]

Birmingham & Mackeson, LLP, (AV) BR
1001 SW Fifth Avenue, Suite 2175, 97204
Telephone: 503-224-2310 Fax: 503-224-4533
Email: pmbirm@teleport.com URL: http://www.lawyers.com/patbirmingham
Pat Birmingham; Wayne Mackeson.
Criminal Trial Practice in State and Federal Courts. Drug Crimes, Felonies, Misdemeanors, Juvenile Law, White Collar Crime.

See Professional Biographies, PORTLAND, OREGON

Birnie, George E. ....'12 '37 C&L.629 B.S., J.D. 621 S.W. Morrison‡
Bisaccio, Gary A., (BV) .... '46 '73 P.O. Box 2926
Bishop, Marilyn Roorda .... '55 '80 C.350 B.S. L.273 J.D. Robert Randall Co.
Bitner, R. Hunter, II ....'68 '94 C.10 B.A. L.802 J.D. 1000 SW Bway., Ste. 2000
Bittner, Thomas A., (AV) .... '60 '90 C&L.1051 B.S., J.D. [Schulte,A.D.A.&B.]

Bittner & Hahs, P.C.
(See Lake Oswego)

Blachly, Victoria D. .... '— '97 C.906 B.S. L.596 J.D. [🄰 Lane P.]
Black, Harvey N., Jr. '32 '64 C.976 A.B. L.1066 J.D.
(adm. in CA; not adm. in OR) Mediation Servs,
Black, Val J. McLam '56 '79 C&L.336 B.A., J.D.
(adm. in ID; not adm. in OR) Off. of Gen. Coun., USDA

Black Helterline LLP, (AV)
1900 Fox Tower, 805 S.W. Broadway, 97205-3359
Telephone: 503-224-5560 Telecopier: 503-224-6148
URL: http://www.bhlaw.com
Members of Firm: Stark Ackerman; Ronald T. Adams; Remi A. Baptiste; James M. Baumgartner; Robert W. Donaldson; Clarence H. Greenwood; John A. Hirschy; Paul R. Hribernick; John M. McGuigan; Michael B. Merchant; Michael O. Moran; David G. Newhall; Adam S. Rittenberg; David P. Roy; Steven R. Schell; David R. Simon; Kenneth A. Williams. Associates: Margaret E. Schroeder; Andrew T. Reilly; David C. Streicher; Kelly R. Tilden; Steven M. Zipper; Jennifer M. Morrissey; Brooke M. Burns; Nathan R. Gerhardt; Erin L. Donald. Of Counsel: Robert E. Glasgow; Lewis B. Hampton; Gerald H. Robinson (Retired).
Banking, Bankruptcy, Business and Corporate, Computer, Construction, Creditors' Rights, Employee Benefits, Employment and Discrimination, Environmental, Forest Products, Immigration, Insurance, International Transactions, Land Use and Development, Litigation in all Courts, Probate, Real Estate, Securities, Taxation, Technology Licensing, Trade Regulation and Antitrust, Trust and Estate Law, Venture/Technology Law.

See Professional Biographies, PORTLAND, OREGON

Blackhurst, Steven K., (AV) ....'46 '73 C.668 B.A. L.629 J.D. [Ater W.]
Blacklidge, Gary L., (BV) .... '54 '90 C.628 B.A. L.596 J.D. [Greene&M.]
Blackman, Marc D., (AV) ....'47 '73 C.309 B.A. L.976 J.D. [Ransom B.]
Blackman, Stephen E., (AV) '55 '91
C.1056 B.A. L.1051 J.D. [Brownstein,R.S.K.G.D.&H.]
Blackmore, Robert F., (BV) .... '52 '81 C.629 B.A. L.1051 J.D. [Jordan S.]
Blackmore, Steven C. '61 '86 C.732 B.A. L.665 J.D.
1420 N.W. Lovejoy Street, Apt. 601
Blackwell, Pamela T. ....'66 '00 L.596 J.D. [🄰 Miller N.]
Blair, Bowen, Jr., (BV) '54 '80 C.976 B.A. L.596 J.D.
Sr. V.P., Trust for Public Land, The
Blake, Larry Jay ....'59 '87 C.911 B.A. L.596 J.D. Blake & Duckler, LLP

Blakely, Sokoloff, Taylor & Zafman
(See Lake Oswego)

Blanchard, Vye, (AV) ....'39 '89 C.1056 B.S. L.1051 J.D. 5125 SW Macadam Ave.
Blank, Alan R., (AV) ....'56 '81 C&L.910 A.B., J.D. [Stoel R.]
Blank, Harold J., (AV) ....'34 '58 C.1051 B.S. L.950 J.D. 1021 S.W. 4th Ave.
Blank, Owen D., (AV) ....'— '73 C&L.813 A.B., J.D. [Tonkon T.]
Blatt, Janine C., (AV) ....'65 '92 C&L.950 B.A., J.D. [J.J.Druckman]
Blattmachr, Jonathan G. '45 '73 C.105 A.B. L.178 J.D.
(adm. in NY; not adm. in OR) [🄲 Hanna S.] (⊙New York, NY)
Blattner, Christopher C. S., (AV) .....'56 '82 C.950 B.S. L.596 J.D. [Motschenbacher&B.]
Bledsoe, David A., (AV) .... '54 '85 C.309 A.B. L.1066 J.D. [Perkins C.]
Bledsoe, John P., (AV) .... '— '48 C.45 A.B. L.309 LL.B. [Lane P.]
Bliesner, Lawrence D. .... '47 '76 C.1056 B.S. L.1051 J.D. Sr. Acct., ESCO Corp.
Blitz, C. Akin, (BV) ....'49 '75 C.950 B.A. L.1051 J.D. [Bullard S.J.W.]
Block, Lainie ....'68 '94 C.112 B.A. L.629 J.D. [🄰 Larkins V.]
Block, Mark B. .... '53 '82 C.330 B.A. L.629 J.D. Bkrptcy. Recovery Sys.
Block, Patrick L., (BV) '66 '92
C.629 B.S. L.1051 J.D. 200 S.W. Market Street, Suite 1698
Bloom, Barbara A., (BV) .... '67 '92 C.770 B.S. L.950 J.D. [Bullard S.J.W.]

Bloom, Michael H., (AV) '54 '81 C&L.629 B.S., J.D.
522 South West 5th Avenue, Suite 1125, 97204-2128
Telephone: 503-223-2128
Email: bloompc@easystreet.com
Personal Injury, Medical Malpractice, Products Liability, Construction Law, Business Litigation.

See Professional Biographies, PORTLAND, OREGON

Blount, David L., (AV) ....'54 '80 C.945 B.S. L.1051 J.D. [Landye B.B.]
Blubaugh, Timothy A. .... '66 '01 C.610 B.S.M.E. L.7 J.D. Freightliner LLC
Blumm, Michael '50 '76 C.951 B.A. L.273 J.D.
(adm. in PA; not adm. in OR) Prof. of Law, Northwestern Sch. of Law

Blunck & Walhood, LLC
(See West Linn)

Boardman, Charles T. ....'47 '75 C.112 B.A. L.1051 J.D. 1607 N.E. 41st Ave.
Bobbitt, Barton C., (BV) ....'44 '71 C&L.629 B.S., J.D. [B.C.Bobbitt]
Bobbitt, Barton C., P.C., (BV) ....4380 SW Macadam Avenue, Suite 500
Bocci, Paul R., Jr., (AV) ....'47 '78 C.605 B.A. L.950 J.D. [Bocci&H.]
Bocci & Hoffmann, (AV) .... 111 S.W. Columbia St., Ste. 1000
Bock, Jeffrey W., (AV) ....'50 '75 C.197 A.B. L.145 J.D. [Perkins C.]
Bodie, Jeffrey C., (BV) .... '51 '78 C.597 B.A. L.596 J.D. [Grenley,R.E.B.&B.]
Bodin, Philippe ....'41 '69 C.813 B.A. L.893 LL.B. 2151 S.W. Laurel
Bodyfelt, E. Richard, (AV) .... '40 '69 C.628 B.S. L.629 J.D. 65 S.W. Yamhill St.‡

Bodyfelt Mount Stroup & Chamberlain LLP, (AV) BR
707 S.W. Washington Street, Suite 1100, 97205
Telephone: 503-243-1022 Fax: 503-243-2019
Members of Firm: Barry M. Mount; Peter R. Chamberlain; Richard A. Lee; Mark A. Hiefield; Molly Jo Mullen; Eric "Skip" Winters. Associates: Andrew D. Glascock; Deanna L. Wray; Vicki M. Smith; Jennifer A. Durham. Of Counsel: Cathy E. Crandall; Farrand "Randy" M. Livingston.
Civil Trial and Appellate Practice in all State and Federal Courts. Products Liability, Professional Liability including Medical Malpractice, Insurance and Commercial Litigation.
Representative Clients: American International Group; Catholic Health Initiatives; Federated Mutual Insurance Co.; Genuine Parts Co.; Georgia-Pacific Corp.; Hartford Insurance Co.; Oregon Mutual Insurance Co.; Otis Elevator Co.; Safeway Stores, Inc.; Tokio Marine Insurance Co.

See Professional Biographies, PORTLAND, OREGON

Bogdanski, John A., (AV) '54 '78
C.749 A.B. L.813 J.D. Prof. of Law, Northwestern Sch. of Law
Boge, Melissa A. ....'73 '99 C.474 B.S. L.1051 J.D. [🄰 Schwabe,W.&W.]
Bohy, Ronald L. .... '56 '82 C.169 B.A. L.950 J.D. [Radler,B.R.&M.]
Boileau, Guy D. ....'51 '86 C.1051 B.A. L.596 J.D. P.O. Box 23547
Boise, Whitney P., (AV) ....'58 '85 C.569 B.A. L.950 J.D. [Hoevet,B.&O.]
Boland, William H., (BV) ....'14 '51 C.670 B.A. L.596 LL.B. 888 S.W. 5th Ave.
Bolliger, Ralph W., (AV) ....'31 '55 C&L.950 B.A., J.D. 1815 SW Marlow Ave.
Bomarito, Douglas M., (BV) .... '45 '76 C.871 B.S. L.1051 J.D. [D.M.Bomarito]
Bomarito, Douglas M., P.C., (BV) ....1001 S.W. 5th
Bonanno, Mark A. .... '64 '94 C.882 B.S. L.1051 J.D. [M.A.Bonanno]

Bonanno, Mark A., LLC ... P.O. Box 5486
Bonaparte, Nell Hoffman ... '55 '81 C.112 B.A. L.893 J.D. [Shenker&B.]
Bonaparte, Robert E. L., (AV) ... '55 '81 C.813 B.A. L.893 J.D. [Shenker&B.]
Bonnett, Mark L. ... '64 '90 C.112 A.B. L.1068 J.D. 3817 S.W. Pasadena Street
Booth, Brian G., (AV) ... '36 '62 C.629 B.S. L.813 LL.B. [Tonkon T.]
Boothe, Ferris F. ... '23 '50 C&L.813 A.B., LL.B. 4025 S.W. 75th Ave.
Boothe, Thomas S., (BV) ... '51 '79 C&L.813 A.B., J.D. 7635 S.W. Westmoor Way
Bootsma, Ernest G., (BV) ... '64 '90 C.628 B.S. L.950 J.D. [Ater W.]
Borden, Gary ... '66 '95 C.112 B.A. L.1051 J.D. Cathcart & Borden PC
Borg, C. Lane, (AV) ... '59 '85 C.668 B.A. L.596 J.D. [Borg S.&G.]

Borg Strom & Greenlick, (AV)
400 SW 6th Avenue, Suite 600, 97204
Telephone: 503-224-2595 Fax: 503-224-3203
URL: http://www.bsg-attys.com
Members: C. Lane Borg; Trina J. Strom; Michael A. Greenlick.
Criminal Law and Criminal Defense, Driving While Intoxicated, Drug Crimes, Juvenile Crimes, Parole and Probation, Traffic Violations, Family Law, Adoptions, Child Custody, Child Support, Divorce, Domestic Violence, Visitation Rights, Business Law, Business Planning, Buying or Selling a Business, Contracts, Starting a Business and Small Business Law.
See Professional Biographies, PORTLAND, OREGON

Borgwardt, John P. ... '31 '55 C&L.813 A.B., J.D. 3466 S.W. Doschview Ct.‡
Bosworth, Duane A., II, (AV) ... '— '82 C.976 B.A. L.629 J.D. [Davis W.T.]
Bothello, Deena B. '72 '02 C.945 B.A. L.629 J.D.
(adm. in CA; not adm. in OR) [Ⓐ Perkins C.]
Bottini, Bruce A., (AV) ... '48 '74 C&L.770 B.S.C., J.D. [Bottini,B.&O.]
Bottini, Marianne, (BV) ... '46 '76 [Bottini,B.&O.]
Bottini, Bottini & Oswald, P.C., (AV) ... 6420 SW Macadam Avenue
Bottomly, Leslie G., (AV) ... '62 '91 C.813 B.A. L.596 J.D. [Ater W.]
Bouman, Jennifer Lyn ... '71 '98 C&L.845 B.A., J.D. [Ⓐ Bullard S.J.W.]
Bouneff, Bobby B., (AV) ... '32 '59 C&L.629 B.S., LL.B. [Bouneff&C.]
Bouneff & Chally, (AV) ... 825 N. E. Multnomah, Ste. 1125
Bovarnick, Paul S., (AV) ... '52 '79 C.154 B.A. L.629 J.D. [Ⓒ Rose,S.&B.]
Bow, James T., II ... '49 '81 C&L.629 B.A., J.D. 8655 White Pine Lane
Bowers, Charles R., (AV) ... '56 '85 C&L.629 B.S., J.D. [Delo&B.]
Bowker, Leanne M., (AV) ... '61 '86 C.897 B.A. L.596 J.D. [Harris&B.]
Bowler, Carson D. ... '65 '95 C&L.629 B.A., J.D. [Ⓐ Schwabe,W.&W.]
Bowles, George H., Jr. ... '24 '56 C.670 B.A. L.596 LL.B. [Kennedy B.] ‡
Bowman, Andrew J. ... '69 '95 C.112 B.A. L.1065 J.D. Law Ck. U.S. Dist. J.
Bowser, David Hunter ... '70 '01 C.645 B.A. L.950 J.D. [Ⓐ Yazbeck,C.&H.]
Boyke, Stephen T., (AV) ... '52 '88 C.339 B.M. L.629 J.D. [Greene&M.]
Boylan, Ann T. ... '74 '04 C.1356 B.A. L.596 J.D. [Ⓐ Swanson,T.&C.]
Boyle, Ryan P. ... '79 '05 C.678 B.A. L.629 J.D. [Ⓐ Bullivant H.B.]
Boylston, Patrick G., (AV) ... '52 '77 C.197 B.A. L.596 J.D. [Stoel R.]
Boysen, Douglas R. '71 '98
C.351 B.A. L.352 J.D. Asst. Gen. Coun., Legacy Health System
Bracanovich, Judith Ann, (BV) '47 '76 C.188 B.A. L.629 J.D.
9079 Se Mcloughlin Blvd
Bradach, John F., Sr., (AV) ... '51 '79 C.629 B.A. L.596 J.D. [Bradach]

Bradach Law Offices, (AV)
Lloyd 700 Building, Suite 900, 700 N.E. Multnomah Street, 97232
Telephone: 503-238-7170 Facsimile: 503-238-7127
URL: http://www.bradachlaw.com
John F. Bradach, Sr. Associate: Danelle C. Forseth.
Construction and Design Law, Contracts, Government Contracts, Real Estate, Land Use, Arbitration, Mediation and General Litigation in State and Federal Courts.
See Professional Biographies, PORTLAND, OREGON

Bradley, Carrell F., (AV) ... '24 '50 C&L.629 B.S., LL.B. 2221 S.W. 1st‡
Bradley, John C., (AV) ... '45 '71 C.1056 B.S. L.950 J.D. Dep. Dist. Atty., Dist. Atty. Off.
Bradley, Todd A., (AV) ... '51 '77 C.605 B.A. L.1051 J.D. [Ⓐ Gaylord&E.]
Bradshaw, James C. ... '71 '01 C.878 B.S. L.950 J.D. [Ⓐ Ater W.]
Bragdon, Peter J., (AV) '62 '93
C.31 B.A. L.813 J.D. Asst. Gen. Coun., Columbia Sportswear Co.
Bragg, Michael J., (AV) ... '49 '76 C.628 B.S. L.464 J.D. [Grenley,R.E.B.&B.]
Brague, Kevin ... '67 '05 C.36 B.A. L.1117 J.D. [Ⓐ Abbott&P.]
Brainard, Barbara A., (AV) ... '54 '80 C.705 B.A. L.950 J.D. [Stoel R.]
Brand, Thomas B., (AV) ... '26 '53 C.813 B.A. L.629 LL.B. 111 S.W. Harrison‡
Brann, Heather A. '— '00 C.1032 B.A. L.878 J.D.
(adm. in ID; not adm. in OR) [Ⓐ Gordon&P.]
Brannon, Kevin E. ... '55 '84 C.813 A.B. L.950 J.D. [Schwabe,W.&W.]
Brant, Larry J., (AV) ... '59 '84 C.1056 B.S. L.950 J.D. [Garvey S.B.]
Braun, Richard H. ... '50 '85 C&L.629 B.A., J.D. 1001 S.W. 5th Ave
Brauser, Jason M. ... '69 '94 C.813 A.B. L.597 J.D. [Stoel R.]
Bray, Shantel P. '77 '05 C.101 B.A. L.878 J.D.
(adm. in WA; not adm. in OR) [Ⓐ Stahancyk,K.J.&H.]

Brayton Purcell, LLP
The American Bank Building, 621 Southwest Morrison, Suite 950, 97205-3824 ⊙
Telephone: 503-295-4931 Fax: 503-241-2573
Email: portland@braytonlaw.com URL: http://www.braytonlaw.com
Associate: Elaine J. Brown.
Personal Injury including Asbestos, Toxic Torts, Automobile Accidents, Products Liability, Premises Liability.
Novato, California Office: 222 Rush Landing Road, 94948. Telephone: 415-898-1555. Fax: 415-898-1247. Email: novato@braytonlaw.com.
Los Angeles, California Office: 2401 El Segundo Boulevard, Suite 440, 90245. Telephone: 310-727-1900. Fax: 310-727-1904. Email: elsegundo@braytonlaw.com.
Salt Lake City, Utah Office: Parkview Tower, 215 S. State Street, Suite 900. 84111. Telephone: 801-366-9100. Fax: 801-350-0065.
See Professional Biographies, PORTLAND, OREGON

Breathouwer, James G., (AV) ... '34 '62 C.629 B.S. L.596 LL.B. [Breathouwer&G.]

Breathouwer & Gilman, (AV)
2125 S.W. Fourth Avenue, Suite 600, 97201
Telephone: 503-450-9331 Fax: 503-525-5680
Members of Firm: James G. Breathouwer; Scott F. Gilman.
General Civil and Trial Practice in all Courts. Insurance, Negligence, Products Liability and Workers Compensation Law.

Brecheen, Cole D. ... '57 '83 C.1 B.B.A. L.309 J.D. Claris, Inc.
Brecht, Jeff C. Duncan ... '61 '96 C.338 B.S. L.589 J.D. [Ⓐ Sussman S.]
Breck, Stephanie M. ... '69 '99 C.1060 B.S. L.950 J.D. 111 S.W. Fifth Avenue, Suite 3500
Breiling, John J. '41 '74 C.517 L.276 J.D.
Sr. Asst. Dist. Coun., U.S. Army Corps of Engrs.
Bremer, Kristin L. ... '73 '03 C.846 B.A. L.950 J.D. [Ⓐ Barran L.]
Brewster, William M., (BV) '61 '92 C.628 B.A. L.1051 J.D.
555 Benjamin Franklin Plaza, One S.W. Columbia
Bricken, Kathleen C. ... '68 '94 C.769 B.A. L.602 J.D. [Garvey S.B.]
Bricker, Jennie L. ... '63 '97 C.629 B.A. L.596 J.D. [Ⓐ Stoel R.]
Bricker, Monte, (AV) ... '36 '63 C.674 A.B. L.813 J.D. 1020 S.W. Taylor Street
Brindle, Theodore M., (BV) ... '49 '85 C.999 M.A. L.1051 J.D. [McKeown&B.]
Briney, Michael D. ... '49 '81 C.988 B.A. L.1051 J.D. App. Off., I.R.S. App. Div.
Brinkman, Catherine B. ... '74 '00 C.682 B.A. L.1051 J.D. [Ⓐ Kilmer,V.&L.]
Brischetto, Stephen L., (AV) ... '52 '77 C&L.602 B.A., J.D. 520 SW Yamhill
Bristol, David G., P.C., (AV) ... '61 '92 C.629 B.S. L.880 J.D. [Miller N.]
Brock, Bryan J. ... '65 '96 C.171 B.S. L.596 J.D. Jud. Clk., State Jud. Dept.
Brockley, Sidney A. ... '41 '66 C&L.477 A.B., J.D. Sr. Cir. J.‡
Bronson, Shannon I. ... '59 '85 C.629 B.S. L.950 J.D. Law Clk., Mag. J.
Brook, Doris J. ... '59 '89 C.1044 B.A. L.596 J.D. 1933 N.E. Alameda‡
Brookhyser, Donald E., (BVⓉ) ... '51 '76 C.629 B.A. L.276 J.D. [Ⓐ Alcantar&K.]
Brooks, Hillary Anne ... '70 '95 C.911 B.A. L.802 J.D. [Marger J.&M.] (See Pat. Sect.)
Brooksby, Scott A. ... '62 '95 C.101 B.A. L.128 J.D. [Bullivant H.B.]
Brown, Aaron, Jr. ... '26 '59 Dist. J.
Brown, Anna J. ... '52 '80 C.1056 B.S. L.596 J.D. U.S. Dist. J.
Brown, Bradley L., (BVⓉ) ... '57 '85 C.950 B.A. L.1049 J.D. 522 SW 5th Ave. Ste. 1110
Brown, Cedric R. ... '53 '91 C.499 B.A. L.1051 J.D. 720 N.E. Flanders St., Ste. 204
Brown, Christine P., (AV) ... '51 '77 C.1115 B.A. L.180 J.D. [Garvey S.B.]
Brown, Christopher T. L. ... '72 '00 C&L.950 B.A., J.D. [Ⓐ Hanna S.]
Brown, Christopher W. ... '74 '02 C.628 B.S. L.1051 J.D. [Ⓐ DuBoff]
Brown, David W., (AV) ... '55 '80 C&L.629 B.S., J.D. Obsidian Fin. Grp.
Brown, Elaine J. ... '55 '93 C.549 B.A. L.596 J.D. [Ⓐ Brayton P.]
Brown, Garthe, (AV) ... '14 '41 L.596 LL.B. [Ⓒ Wetzel D.&S.] ‡
Brown, Jolynn M. ... '— '99 C.174 B.A. L.900 J.D. [Ⓐ Harrang L.G.R.]
Brown, Kelly Kennedy, (BV) ... '54 '83 C.685 B.A. L.464 J.D. [K.K.Brown]
Brown, Lawrence R., (BV) ... '47 '72 C.813 A.B. L.1066 J.D. [Ⓒ Newcomb,S.S.&L.]
Brown, Lisa C., (AV) ... '54 '79 C.597 B.A. L.273 J.D. [Barran L.]
Brown, Michael J., (AV) ... '47 '74 C.770 B.A. L.1066 J.D. U. S. Attorneys Office
Brown, Patricia G. ... '53 '78 C.915 B.A. L.1003 J.D. 5535 N.W. Deschutes Dr.‡
Brown, Richard D. '52 '79
(adm. in NE; not adm. in OR) Assoc. Claim Atty., Amer. Fam. Ins.
Brown, Stuart M., (AV) ... '45 '76 C.628 B.S. L.629 J.D. [Gordon&R.]
Brown, Thomas W., (AV) ... '— '80 C.846 B.S. L.596 J.D. [Cosgrave V.K.]
Brown, Trish M. ... '56 '81 C.659 B.S. L.902 J.D. Bnkruptcy J.
Brown, William C. ... '43 '69 C.813 A.B. L.178 J.D. 10928 S.W. Collina Ave.‡
Brown, Kelly K., (BV) ... 520 S.W. Yamhill St., Ste. 420
Browning, Robert L. ... '47 '82 C.637 B.A. L.1015 J.D. Bur. of Labor & Ind. Civil Rights
Browning, Ronald D., P.C. ... '43 '74 C.878 B.S. L.596 J.D. [R.D.Browning]
Browning, Sheri C. ... '69 '97 C.586 B.A. L.596 J.D. [Keating J.B.&H.]
Browning, Ronald D., P.C. ... 1906 SW Madison St., Ste. 1A
Brownstein, Richard J., (AV) '30 '53 C.685 L.950 LL.B.
[Brownstein,R.S.K.G.D.&H.]

Brownstein, Rask, Sweeney, Kerr, Grim, DeSylvia & Hay, LLP, (AV)
1200 S.W. Main Building, 97205
Telephone: 503-221-1772 Facsimile: 503-221-1074
Email: general@brownrask.com
Members of Firm: John H. Arenz (1940-1999); Richard J. Brownstein; Raymond M. Rask; Miles Sweeney; Andrew P. Kerr; Douglas R. Grim; Terry DeSylvia; David J. Sweeney; Kirkham E. Hay; Scott L. Jensen; James W. Hendry; Paul G. Dodds; Stephen E. Blackman; Douglas J. Raab; Stephen H. Buckley; Thomas J. Arenz. Associates: Frank O. Diarmit; Cary R. Cadonau; Engred K. Chai; Angela M. Russell; Jay B. Derum; Rebekah L. Stiles; Joseph M. Mabe; Kent D. Johnson.
General Practice. Trial Practice in all State and Federal Courts. Antitrust, Cooperatives, Corporations, Securities, Taxation, Real Estate, Insurance, Municipal, Pension and Profit Sharing, Estate Planning, Probate, Family, Television and Radio Law.
See Professional Biographies, PORTLAND, OREGON

Brugman, John W. ... '09 '41 C.813 B.A. L.596 LL.B. 3560 S.W. Vista Dr.‡
Brunet, Edward J. '44 '69 C.597 B.A. L.339 J.D.
Prof. of Law, Northwestern Sch. of Law
Brunner, William L., (BV) '— '53 C.685 B.A. L.1051 J.D.
1001 S.W. 5th Ave., Ste. 1520
Brush, Bart Anderson ... '60 '93 C.477 B.A. L.1051 J.D. 621 SW Morrison Street
Bruun, Larry K., (AV) ... '— '67 C.629 B.A. L.950 J.D. [Welch,B.&G.]
Brydolf, Ingrid ... '— '93 C.950 B.A. L.596 J.D. [Ⓒ Davis W.T.]
Buccino, Anthony A., (BV) ... '47 '75 C.112 B.A. L.596 J.D. [A.A.Buccino]
Buccino, Anthony A., P.C., (BV) ... 1211 S.W. 5th Ave., Ste. 1100
Buchal, James L., (BV) ... '59 '86 C.309 A.B. L.976 J.D. [Murphy&B.]
Buchanan, Paul C., (AV) ... '64 '90 C.881 A.B. L.93 J.D. [Stoel R.]
Buck, William P., (BV) ... '45 '75 C.228 B.A. L.596 J.D. [Ⓒ MacMillan,S.&M.]
Buckle, Eugene H., (AV) ... '— '76 C.228 B.A. L.893 J.D. [Cosgrave V.K.]
Buckler, Michael L. ... '74 '00 C.188 B.S. L.228 J.D. [Ⓐ Klarquist S.]
Buckley, Jerome B., Jr., (AV) ... '42 '71 C.1056 B.A. L.629 J.D. [Carney,B.H.&M.]
Buckley, Kim T., (AV) ... '48 '78 C&L.911 B.A., J.D. [Esler,S.&B.]
Buckley, Stephen H., (AV) '55 '80 C.172 B.A. L.950 J.D.
[Brownstein,R.S.K.G.D.&H.]
Buley, Joseph E., (AV) ... '26 '51 C.120 L.508 LL.B. Asst. U.S. Dist. Atty.
Bullard, Garry R., (AV) ... '34 '59 C&L.597 B.A., J.D. [Bullard S.J.W.]

Bullard Smith Jernstedt Wilson, A Professional Corporation, (AV) BR
1000 S.W. Broadway, Suite 1900, 97205
Telephone: 503-248-1134 Fax: 503-224-8851
Email: laborlaw@bullardlaw.com URL: http://www.bullardlaw.com
Garry R. Bullard; Jim D. Korshoj (Retired); Lester V. Smith, Jr.; Kenneth E. Jernstedt; David H. Wilson, Jr.; Richard J. Alli, Jr.; Robert J. Lee; Francis T. Barnwell; Alan M. Lee; David J. Riewald; Kathryn M. Hindman; Kenneth E. Bemis; C. Akin Blitz; Barbara A. Bloom; Kirk S. Peterson; Daniel R. Barnhart; Michael G. McClory; Jacqueline M. Damm; J. Kent Pearson, Jr.; Thomas I. Kramer;—Adam S. Collier; Jennifer Lyn Bouman.
Practice Restricted to Labor and Employment Law, representing management and Business Interests including Litigation Practice before Federal and State Courts and Administrative Agencies.
Representative Corporate Labor Clients: Mid-Columbia Medical Center; Nike, Inc.; Portland General Electric Co.; Schnitzer Industries; United Grocers, Inc.; Weyerhaeuser.
Representative Public Labor Clients: Mt. Hood Community College; Port of Portland.
See Professional Biographies, PORTLAND, OREGON

Bullivant Houser Bailey PC, (AV)
300 Pioneer Tower, 888 S.W. Fifth Avenue, 97204-2089 ⊙
Telephone: 503-228-6351 Facsimile: 503-295-0915
URL: http://www.bullivant.com
Shareholders: Douglas R. Andres; Randy L. Arthur; John P. Ashworth; Ronald E. Bailey; John A. Bennett; Scott A. Brooksby; Howard W. Carsman; Ronald J. Clark; Stephen F. Cook; Clay D. Creps; Dianne K. Dailey; James G. Driscoll; Jeffrey S. Eden; Stephen F. English; David A. Ernst; Kimball H. Ferris; David R. Foster; Douglas G. Houser; Thomas L. Hutchinson; Stuart D. Jones; John M. Junkin; John T. Kaempf; Lisa E. Lear; R. Daniel Lindahl; Jeanne F. Loftis; Robert B. Lowry; Francis J. Maloney, III; Chrys A. Martin; Stanley E. Martinson; Daniel F. McNeil; Robert B. Miller; Robert A. Moore; John R. Osburn; Loren D. Podwill; Renée E. Rothauge; Beth Skillern; Katherine S. Somervell; Ronald G. Stephenson; David D. VanSpeybroeck; Margaret M. Van Valkenburg; Karen M. Vickers; Peter J. Viteznik; Timothy J. Wachter; Joseph W. West; Richard J. Whittemore; Joel Wilson. Associates: Kevin E. Barton; Lloyd Bernstein; Ryan P. Boyle; Timothy J. Calderbank; Matthew Craig Casey; Darin Christensen; Dayna J. Christian; Nancy M. Cooper; Beth Cupani; Nicholas L. Dazer; Stephen Forrest Deatherage; Allen E. Eraut; Susan L. Ford; Marianne M. Ghim; Leta E. Gorman; Chelsea L. Grimmius; Krista N. Hardwick; DeLyne Klein; John M. Kreutzer; J. Riley Lagesen; Andrew C. Lauersdorf; Brad J. Lewis; Michael J. Mayerle; Robert C. Muth; Kristin

(This Listing Continued)

Bullivant Houser Bailey PC (Continued)
L. Olson; Dain Paulson; Todd M. Peck; Holly E. Pettit; Sheila H. Potter; Anthony Reiner; Blake Robinson; Sara Van Loh; Tonya Van Walleghem; Michael Yimesgen. Of Counsel: Thomas A. Gerber; Stephen B. Hill; Henry "Chip" Lazenby; Walter H. Pendergrass; Jeffrey G. Robertson; Donald R. Stark; Mark L. Stermitz.
Multiservice Business and Trial law firm offering Civil Litigation and Appellate Practice in all State and Federal Courts. Alternative Dispute Resolution, Mediation and Arbitration. Commercial Litigation; Bankruptcy, Finance and Banking; Creditors' Rights; Intellectual Property; International Business; Food and Beverage; Securities; Insurance Coverage and Insurance Defense; Bad Faith; Environmental; Products Liability; Life, Health and Disability; Errors and Omissions; Directors and Officers; Professional Liability, Fire, Inland Marine, Fidelity and Surety, Municipal Liability; Insurance Regulation; General Business and Corporate; S Corporations and Limited Liability Partnerships; Tax; Real Estate and Construction; Estate Planning and Probate; Employment Law; ERISA.
Seattle, Washington Office: 1601 Fifth Avenue, Suite 2300, 98101-1618. Telephone: 206-292-8930. Facsimile: 206-386-5130.
Vancouver, Washington Office: 805 Broadway Street, Suite 400, 98660-3310. Telephone: 360-693-2424. Facsimile: 360-695-8504.
Gold River, California Office: 11335 Gold Express Drive, Suite 105, 95670-6310. Telephone: 916-852-9100. Fax: 916-852-5777.
San Francisco, California Office: 601 California Street, Suite 1800, 94108-2823. Telephone: 415-352-2700. Fax: 415-352-2701.
Las Vegas, Nevada Office: 3980 Howard Hughes Parkway, Suite 550, 89109. Telephone: 702-650-6565. Facsimile: 702-650-2995.

See Professional Biographies, PORTLAND, OREGON

Bullock, Brentley M., (AV) ... '61 '86 C.628 B.S. L.813 J.D. [Perkins C.]
Bullock, Gary M., (BV) ... '37 '66 C.628 B.S. L.596 J.D. [G.M.Bullock&Assoc.]

Bullock, Gary M., and Associates, P.C., (BV)
1001 S.W. Fifth Avenue, Suite 1500, 97204
Telephone: 503-228-6277 Fax: 503-228-6280
Email: garybullock@qwest.net URL: http://www.lawyers.com/bullockandregier
Gary M. Bullock;—Arthur Baird Fowler, V; Eric S. Postma; Joanna L. Dorchuck.
General Civil and Trial Practice. Family Law, Personal Injury, Negligence, Corporate, Real Estate and Condemnation Law.

See Professional Biographies, PORTLAND, OREGON

Bunch, Peter, (CV) ... '50 '94 C.1131 B.A. L.285 J.D. [Zimmer&B.]
Bunker, Cynthia L. ... '58 '83 C&L.950 B.S., J.D. Multnomah Defenders
Bunnell, Gregory A., (BV) ... '65 '91 C.629 B.S. L.1051 J.D. [Preston B.&F.]
Bunnenberg, Ann, (CV) ... '56 '80 C.813 B.A. L.629 J.D. [A.Bunnenberg]
Bunnenberg, Ann, P.C., (CV) ... 700 NE Multnomah St.
Buono, David J., (AV) ... '43 '68 C&L.629 B.S., J.D. [Dunn C.A.H.&T.]
Burdett, James E. ... '13 '36 C&L.950 A.B., LL.B. 1209 S.W. 6th Ave.‡
Burke, Lawrence B., (AV) ... '— '89 C.602 B.S. L.426 J.D. [Davis W.T.]
Burkholder, Kurt B., (AV) ... '54 '80 C.645 B.S. L.629 J.D. Asst. Atty. Gen.
Burnett, Chris ... '72 '99 C.908 B.A. L.950 J.D. 10260 SW Greenburg Road, Suite. 400
Burns, Andrew T., (BV) ... '— '88 C.629 B.S. L.596 J.D. [Cosgrave V.K.]
Burns, Brooke M. ... '75 '00 C.628 B.A. L.629 J.D. [Ⓐ Black H.]
Burns, Donald A., P.C., (AV) ... '46 '73 C.475 B.A. L.228 J.D. [Miller N.]
Burns, James M. ... '24 '50 C.670 B.A. L.424 J.D. U.S. Sr. Dist. J.
Burns, John D., (AV) ... '36 '62 C.602 B.A. L.276 J.D. [Ⓟ Miller N.]
Burns, Keith, (AV) ... '27 '58 C.1051 B.S. L.596 J.D. 1100 S.W. 6th Ave.
Burns, Susan Ford, Law Office of ... '56 '91 C.1104 L.1051 J.D. 1406 S.E. 12th Ave.
Burris, Marianne Onett ... '53 '78 C.25 B.A. L.851 J.D. Dep. Dist. Atty.
Burrows, Ernest J., (BV) ... '08 '34 C&L.629 B.S., LL.B. 12640 N.E. Rose Pkwy.
Burt, Robert G., (AV) ... '44 '72 C&L.37 B.A., J.D. [R.G.Burt]

Burt, Robert G., P.C., (AV)
The 1515 Building, Suite 600, 1515 S.W. Fifth Avenue, 97201-5449
Telephone: 503-223-3600 Fax: 503-274-0778
Email: rgb@burtfirm.com URL: http://www.burtfirm.com
Robert G. Burt.
Tax Law (including Business Tax Planning, Tax-Exempt Charitable Organizations, Administrative Proceedings with the Internal Revenue Service and Oregon Department of Revenue, and Tax Litigation (Civil and Criminal)); Business Law (including Corporations, Partnerships, Limited Liability Companies/Partnerships, Business Trusts, Cooperatives and Sole Proprietorships, particularly Closely-Held and Emerging Growth Businesses); Corporate Law; Partnership Law; Mergers (and other Major Business Transactions including Acquisitions, Reorganizations, and Sales); Nonprofit and Tax Exempt Organizations; Intellectual Property Law; Trademark, Copyright and Unfair Competition (including Registrations, Trade Secret Agreements, Non-Compete Agreements and Licensing Agreements); Trusts and Estates, Wills and Probate (including Wills, Trusts, Probates, Guardianships, Conservatorships, and Asset Protection/Preservation).

See Professional Biographies, PORTLAND, OREGON

Burton, Brian T. ... '62 '90 C.878 B.S. L.596 J.D. Corp. Coun., Freightliner LLC
Burton, Susan, (AV) ... '62 '87 C.1494 B.A. L.950 J.D. [Ⓟ Holland&K.]
Busch, Eric S. ... '44 '70 C.385 A.B. L.339 J.D. Assoc. Gen. Coun., Regence Group
Busch, Mark L. ... '64 '91 C.336 B.A. L.950 J.D. 4380 S.W. Macadain Ave., Ste. 500
Busch, Thomas P. ... '59 '88 C.670 B.A. L.596 J.D. [VavRosky M.O.]
Bush, L. Leslie, (AV) ... '49 '78 C.813 B.A. L.1051 J.D. [Parker,B.&L.]
Bush, Stephen C. ... '75 '02 C.112 B.A. L.800 J.D. [Ⓐ Schwabe,W.&W.]
Bushaw, Amy C. '58 '84 C.674 A.B. L.976 J.D.
(adm. in TX; not adm. in OR) Assoc. Prof. of Law, Northwestern Sch. of Law
Buss, Donald A., (BV) ... '30 '53 C.629 L.950 LL.B. 2225 N.E. 49th St.
Busse, Richard C., Jr., (AV) ... '48 '74 C.763 B.S. L.1065 J.D. [Busse&H.]

Busse & Hunt, (AV)
521 American Bank Building, 621 SW Morrison Street, 97205
Telephone: 503-248-0504 Fax: 503-248-2131 URL: http://www.busseandhuntlaw.com
URL: http://www.busseandhunt.com
Richard C. Busse, Jr.; Scott N. Hunt. Associate: Matthew B. Duckworth.
Employment Law.

See Professional Biographies, PORTLAND, OREGON

Bustany, Brady M. ... '— '01 C.477 A.B. L.1494 J.D. [Ⓐ Lane P.]
Butkovsky, Gwenn F. ... '51 '87 [Ⓐ Squires&L.]
Butterfield, Lisanne M. ... '— '91 C.208 B.A. L.950 J.D. [Ⓟ James]
Buttler, John H. ... '23 '50 C.197 B.A. L.178 LL.B. Sr. J.‡
Byerly, Bruce L., (AV) ... '45 '72 C&L.629 B.A., J.D. [Sather,B.&H.]
Byrne, Christopher S. ... '66 '93 C.37 B.A. L.1051 J.D. [Ⓐ Motschenbacher&B.]
Byrne, Gregory W., (AV) '39 '71
C.790 A.B. L.309 J.D. 5550 S.W. Macadam Avenue, Suite 220
Cable, Abraham J.B. ... '75 '00 C.678 B.A. L.309 J.D. [Ⓐ Miller N.]
Cable, Brian R. ... '71 '01 C.906 B.A. L.596 J.D. [Ⓐ Dunn C.A.H.&T.]
Cable, J. Franklin, P.C., (AV) ... '41 '67 C.813 A.B. L.309 LL.B. [Miller N.]
Cable, J. Laurence, (AV) ... '45 '71 C.813 B.A. L.950 J.D. [Cable H.B.H.&L.]

Cable Huston Benedict Haagensen & Lloyd LLP, (AV)
1001 S.W. Fifth Avenue, Suite 2000, 97204 ⊙
Telephone: 503-224-3092 Facsimile: 503-224-3176
URL: http://www.cablehuston.com
Members of Firm: Clark I. Balfour; James E. Benedict; J. Laurence Cable; Susan Trump Felstiner; Edward A. Finklea; Thomas M. Grim; Anita H. Grinich; Donald A. Haagensen; G. Frank Hammond; Robert T. Huston; G. Kevin Kiely; James S. Kincaid; William J. Lehman; Don K. Lloyd; Richard G. Lorenz; Margaret B. Stern; Laura J. Walker; J. Stephen Werts. Associates: Gretchen S. Barnes;

(This Listing Continued)

Cable Huston Benedict Haagensen & Lloyd LLP (Continued)
Lindsay R. Kandra; Carla S. Rhoden; Chad M. Stokes; Robin Bellanca. Of Counsel: Dan C. Armstrong; Tamara L. Faucette; George B. Heilig (Resident, Corvallis Office); David K. McAdams.
Administrative, Agricultural, Banking, Bankruptcy, Commercial, Corporate, Complex Litigation, Creditors' Rights, Legislative, Employment, Energy, Environmental, Estate Planning, General Business, Land Use, Mining, Municipal, Natural Resource, Probate, Real Property, Taxation, Telecommunications, Trust Administration, Utility and Water Law.
Representative Clients: Bank of Tokyo-Mitsubishi, Ltd.; Chemical Waste Management, Inc.; Clatskanie People's Utility District; Eugene Water & Electric Board; Rhône-Poulenc, Inc.; SimmCo Properties, Inc.; Waste Management, Inc.
Corvallis, Oregon Office: 582 N.W. Van Buren, 97339. Telephone: 503-754-7477. Facsimile: 503-754-0051.

See Professional Biographies, PORTLAND, OREGON

Cacciottoli, Vincent P., (AV) ... '50 '76 C.569 B.A. L.262 J.D. [V.P.Cacciottoli]

Cacciottoli, Vincent P., A Prof. Corp., Law Offices of, (AV)
121 Southwest Morrison Street Suite 1010, 97204
Telephone: 503-220-1933 Facsimile: 503-220-1974
Email: vince@vpcpc.com
Vincent P. Cacciottoli.
Employee Benefits Law, Executive Compensation, Employment Law and Corporate and Business Planning.

See Professional Biographies, PORTLAND, OREGON

Cadonau, Cary R. ... '72 '00 C.426 B.A. L.596 J.D. [Ⓐ Brownstein,R.S.K.G.D.&H.]
Cadzow, Linda K. '47 '74 C.696 A.B. L.950 J.D.
Louisiana-Pacific Corporation (⊙Nashville, TN)
Cahn, Bruce H., (AV) ... '63 '90 C.1077 B.A. L.426 J.D. [Ball J.]
Cairns, J. H., (BV) ... '23 '54 C.629 B.S. L.596 LL.B. 3553 S.E. Division
Calderbank, Timothy J. ... '64 '97 C.907 B.A. L.1051 J.D. [Ⓐ Bullivant H.B.]
Caldwell, Lance A., (AV) ... '49 '77 C.628 B.S. L.1051 J.D. U. S. Attorneys Office
Caldwell, Lisa M. ... '62 '94 C.768 B.S. L.950 J.D. [Klarquist S.] (See Pat. Sect.)
Callaghan, Hannah M. '50 '75 C.988 B.A. L.602 J.D.
Supvr., Civil Lit. Unit, Legal Aid Servs. of OR
Callahan, James M., (AV) ... '50 '78 C.696 B.A. L.823 J.D. [Callahan&S.]
Callahan, Patrick K., (AV) ... '54 '81 C.1051 B.A. L.629 J.D. Sr. Dep. Dist. Atty.

Callahan & Shears, P.C., (AV)
4215 Southeast King Road, P.O. Box 22677, 97269-2677
Telephone: 503-513-5130 Fax: 503-513-5915
URL: http://www.callahanandshears.com
James M. Callahan; Melia M. Shears;—Susan D. Cardoni.
Insurance Coverage Litigation, Professional Liability and Personal Injury Defense. General Civil and Trial Practice.

See Professional Biographies, PORTLAND, OREGON

Callier, Michael E. ... '78 '04 C&L.629 B.A., J.D. [Ⓐ Tonkon T.]
Calo, Robert R. '— '85 C.1145 B.S.B.A. L.94 J.D.
(adm. in MA; not adm. in OR) [Lane P.]
Calzacorta, Carmen M., (AV) ... '57 '84 C&L.629 B.A., J.D. [Schwabe,W.&W.]
Calzaretta, Victor, (BV) ... '42 '82 C.988 B.S. L.596 J.D. Ste 440, 621 Sw Morrison St
Cameron, John A., Jr. ... '— '73 C.477 B.A. L.273 J.D. [Davis W.T.]
Campbell, Alison Kean ... '63 '90 C.930 B.A. L.477 J.D. Metro Off. of Gen. Coun.
Campbell, Amy S. ... '71 '02 C.670 B.A. L.596 J.D. [Ⓐ Ball J.]
Campbell, Bruce L., P.C., (AV) ... '57 '90 C.629 B.S. L.477 J.D. [Miller N.]
Campbell, Dana M. '61 '89 C.628 B.S. L.596 J.D.
Director, Special Prosecuter Program, Animal Legal Defense Fund
Campbell, David C. ... '— '03 L.629 J.D. [Ⓐ Williams,K.&G.P.]
Campbell, George B., (AV) ... '17 '41 C&L.813 A.B., J.D. 520 S.W. Yamhill St.
Campbell, James, (AV) ... '34 '61 C.174 B.S.E.E. L.273 LL.B. 121 S.W. Salmon St. (Pat.)
Campbell, Madeleine S., (BV) ... '55 '81 C&L.05 B.A., LL.B. [Dunn C.A.H.&T.]
Campbell, Mary Koch ... '56 '84 C.118 B.A. L.629 J.D. Hearings Ref.
Campbell, Michael Roame ... '59 '87 C.685 B.A. L.911 J.D. [Stoel R.]
Campbell, Neva T., (AV) ... '33 '73 C.628 B.A. L.596 J.D. [Schwabe,W.&W.]
Campbell, Sandra ... '46 '80 C.475 B.A. L.596 J.D. Assisted Living Concepts
Campbell, William C., (AV) ... '54 '79 C&L.976 B.A., J.D. [Ater W.]
Campf, Brian S. ... '67 '92 C.685 B.A. L.950 J.D. [Ⓐ Williams L.O.C.&P.]
Canaday, Richard A., (AV) ... '47 '73 C.813 A.B. L.1066 J.D. [Miller N.]
Canary, David L., (AV) ... '50 '76 C.413 B.A. L.1051 J.D. [Garvey S.B.]
Cann, Frederic E. ... '53 '78 C.197 A.B. L.93 J.D. [Cann]

Cann Lawyers
1300 S.W. Fifth Avenue, Suite 2750, 97201-5617
Telephone: 503-226-6529 Fax: 503-228-6529
Email: fec@cannlawyersusa.com URL: http://www.cannlawyersusa.com
Member: Frederic E. Cann.
Construction Contract Litigation, Construction Defect Litigation.

See Professional Biographies, PORTLAND, OREGON

Cannady, Michael R. ... '42 '71 C.413 B.A. L.950 J.D. Asst. Atty. Gen.
Cantlin, Richard A., (AV) ... '46 '73 C.276 B.A. L.178 J.D. [Perkins C.]
Cantrell, M. Caroline ... '47 '91 C.1056 B.S. L.596 J.D. [M.C.Cantrell&Assoc.]

Cantrell, M. Caroline, & Assoc., PC
1500 NE Irving Street, Suite 100, 97232
Telephone: 503-236-9211 Fax: 503-236-0209 URL: http://www.bankruptcyoregon.com
Email: info@bankruptcyoregon.com URL: http://www.lawyers.com/ccantrell
M. Caroline Cantrell;—Michael S. Scott.
Bankruptcy Chapter 7, Bankruptcy Chapter 13.

See Professional Biographies, PORTLAND, OREGON

Caplan, Barry P., (AV) ... '40 '65 C.911 B.A. L.112 LL.B. [Sussman S.]
Capobianco, Donato C. ... '72 '02 C.602 B.B.A. L.569 J.D. [Ⓐ Stoel R.]
Capobianco, Kimberly C. ... '76 '01 C.839 B.A. L.569 J.D. [Ⓐ Barran L.]
Capps, Douglas L. ... '43 '73 C.1056 B.S. L.596 J.D. 2260 N.E. 32nd Ave.‡
Capriotti, F.J. (Franco), III ... '50 '78 C.429 B.A. L.300 J.D. [Capriotti&Assoc.] ⊙
Capriotti & Associates ... P.O. Box 2792 (⊙Outing, MN)
Cardoni, Susan D., (BV) ... '46 '83 C.475 B.A. L.596 J.D. [Ⓐ Callahan&S.]
Carey, Gordon T., Jr., (AV) ... '50 '75 C.629 B.A. L.477 J.D. [G.T.Carey,Jr.]
Carey, Jeffrey C. '49 '77
C.285 A.B. L.1051 J.D. Asst. V.P. & Assoc. Coun., Standard Ins. Co.
Carey, Rachel C. ... '69 '96 C.629 B.A. L.285 J.D. 1000 Sw Broadway Ste 2000
Carey, Robert L., (AV) ... '61 '87 C.309 B.A. L.950 J.D. [Barran L.]

Carey, Gordon T., Jr., P.C., (AV)
A Partnership of Professional Corporations
721 Southwest Oak, Second Floor, 97205
Telephone: 503-222-1415 FAX: 503-222-1923
URL: http://www.careylaw-firm.com
Gordon T. Carey, Jr.
Civil Trial and Appellate Practice in State and Federal Courts. Personal Injury, Business, Commercial, Maritime, Environmental, Securities Litigation.

See Professional Biographies, PORTLAND, OREGON

Carlough, Leslie A. ... '60 '93 C.280 Ph.D. L.1051 J.D. Dept. of Envir. Quality

Carlson, Richard A., (BV) ... '49 '75 C.339 B.A. L.596 J.D. [Drakulich&C.]
Carlton, Amy J., (BV) ... '— '92 L.596 J.D. [Williams,K.&G.P.]
Carlton, Marc M. ... '— '99 L.629 J.D. [Ⓐ Williams,K.&G.P.]
Carlton, Robert L., (AV) ... '53 '85 C.174 B.A. L.1051 J.D. [Sussman S.]
Carnese, Charles W., (AV) ... '44 '69 C.309 A.B. L.1066 J.D. [C.W.Carnese]
Carnese, Charles W., P.C., (AV) ... 1500 S.W. 1st Ave., Ste. 1170
Carney, George V. ... '34 '64 C.1051 B.S. L.596 LL.B. 7039 S.W. Brenne Lane‡
Carney, Richard R., (AV) ... '22 '49 C.670 B.A. L.629 J.D. [Carney,B.H.&M.] ‡
Carney, Robert A. '35 '69 C.238 B.S. L.146 J.D.
(adm. in IL; not adm. in OR) P.O. Box 25111‡
Carney, Buckley, Hays & Marsh, (AV) ... 811 S.W. Naito Parkway

Caron Colven Robison & Shafton P.S.
(See Vancouver)

Carpenter, Jessica ... '62 '97 C.378 B.A. L.36 J.D. [Ⓐ Martin,B.T.L.&H.]
Carr, Kathleen M. ... '61 '92 C.447 B.A. L.950 J.D. Off. of Solr., Dept. of Interior
Carraway, J. Christopher ... '70 '96 C.659 B.S. L.228 J.D. [Klarquist S.]
Carroll, Catherine N., (BV) ... '48 '75 C.722 B.A. L.560 J.D. [C.N.Carroll]
Carroll, Catherine N., P.C., (BV) ... 3718 Southwest Condor Avenue
Carsman, Howard W., (AV) ... '53 '79 C.1077 B.A. L.1067 J.D. [Bullivant H.B.]
Carson, Brett S., (AV) ... '52 '79 C.629 B.S. L.285 J.D. [Casteel&C.]
Carson, Christopher T., (AV) ... '58 '84 C.170 B.A. L.950 J.D. [Kilmer,V.&L.]
Carter, Don G., (AV) ... '53 '79 C.628 B.A. L.629 J.D. [McEwen G.]
Carter, Eric H. ... '68 '96 C.911 B.S. L.1051 J.D. Bonneville Power
Carter, Jordan A. ... '78 '04 C.628 B.A. L.629 J.D. [Ⓐ Stahancyk,K.J.&H.]
Carter, Julie A. ... '69 '89 C.1051 B.A. L.30 J.D. Policy Analyst
Carter, Thomas C. ... '51 '79 C.502 B.S. L.629 J.D. Law Clk. to Cir. Ct. of App. J.
Carter, Thomas O., (BV) ... '39 '66 C.628 B.S. L.596 LL.B. 3718 S.W. Condor St
Cartwright, and Associates, (AV) ... 1000 SW Broadway, Suite 1750
Cartwright, James R., (AV) ... '47 '75 C.966 B.A. L.629 J.D. [Cartwright&Assoc.]
Carty, Kim R. '72 '99 C.1058 B.A. L.596 J.D.
4888 Northwest Bethany Boulevard, Suite K5#353
Casad, Kurt R. ... '54 '79 C.939 B.A. L.950 J.D. Atty., Adv.
Case, Denise R. '78 '03 C.911 B.A. L.1292 J.D.
(adm. in NJ; not adm. in OR) [Ⓐ Ball J.]
Case, Gary L. '46 '73 C.628 B.S. L.169 J.D.
Exec. V.P. & Gen. Legal Coun., Associated Admin., Inc. (E.R.I.S.A.)

Case & Dusterhoff, LLP
(See Beaverton)

Casey, Bob, Attorney '54 '83 C.939 B.A. L.988 J.D.
1205 NW 25th Avenue, 97210-2422
Telephone: 503-221-9700 Fax: 503-226-3131
Email: bcasey@rsblaw.net URL: http://www.bobcaseylaw.com
Estate Planning, Probate, Trust Administration, Contested Wills, Guardianships and Conservatorships.

See Professional Biographies, PORTLAND, OREGON

Casey, Craig J., (AV) ... '43 '68 C.670 B.A. L.629 J.D. Asst. U.S. Atty.
Casey, John Michael "Mike", (AV) ... '49 '85 C.884 B.A. L.1051 J.D. [J.M.Casey]
Casey, Matthew Craig ... '73 '98 C.770 B.S. L.950 J.D. [Ⓐ Bullivant H.B.]
Casey, J. Michael, P.C., (AV) ... 1515 SW 5th Ave.
Castagna, Robert J., (BV) '47 '75 C.262 B.A. L.128 J.D.
Gen. Coun. & Exec. Dir., Oregon Catholic Conference
Castanza, Jason D. ... '70 '97 C.97 B.S., B.A. L.950 J.D. [Ⓐ Squires&L.]
Casteel, James L., (BV) ... '45 '71 C.628 B.S. L.629 J.D. [Casteel&C.]

Casteel & Carson, (AV)
2035 N.E. 42nd Avenue, 97213
Telephone: 503-288-9291 FAX: 503-288-4576
Members of Firm: James L. Casteel; Brett S. Carson. Associate: Randall H. Baker.
Business, Business Enterprises, Buying and Selling a Business, Real Estate, Contracts, Probate, Estate Planning and Trusts, Wills, Conservatorships, Guardianships, Commercial Law, Collections, Personal Injury, Automobile Accidents, Slip and Fall, Dog Bites, Wrongful Death, Professional Liability, Family Law, Step-Parent Adoptions, Divorce, Child Custody, Child Support, Visitation Rights, Elder Law, Neglect, Elder Abuse, Medical Malpractice, Trademarks, Tax Planning,

See Professional Biographies, PORTLAND, OREGON

Cathcart, Kevin L. ... '64 '91 C.939 B.A. L.1051 J.D. 12790 S.E. Stark St.
Cavanagh, John S., (BV) '41 '74 C.629 B.S. L.950 J.D.
Ste 710, 10260 Sw Greenburg Rd
Cavanaugh, Heather K. ... '74 '02 C.628 B.S. L.629 J.D. [Ⓐ Miller N.]
Cavanaugh, James C., (AV) ... '57 '87 C.375 B.S. L.900 J.D. 888 S.W. 5th Ave.
Chadsey, Phillip D., (AV) ... '36 '66 C.629 B.S. L.950 J.D. [Stoel R.]
Chaffin, Mary D., (AV) ... '54 '82 C.103 B.A. L.280 J.D. Legal Coun., Mercy Corps.
Chai, Engred K. ... '68 '01 C.628 B.S. L.596 J.D. [Ⓐ Brownstein,R.S.K.G.D.&H.]
Chaimov, Gregory A., (AV) ... '— '82 C.118 B.A. L.596 J.D. [Ⓒ Davis W.T.]
Chaivoe, Nick, (AV) ... '11 '63 C.1056 L.596 J.D. 720 S. W. Washington‡
Chally, John, (AV) ... '50 '75 C.169 B.A. L.464 J.D. [Bouneff&C.]
Chamberlain, Jeanne M., (AV) ... '52 '85 C.999 B.F.A. L.629 J.D. [Tonkon T.]
Chamberlain, Peter R., (AV) ... '50 '78 C.1074 B.S. L.596 J.D. [Bodyfelt M.S.&C.]
Chamberlain, Stacy J. ... '75 '01 C.1056 B.S. L.950 J.D. 1500 Ne Irving St Ste 370
Chambers, Chad R. ... '71 '99 C.823 B.S. L.276 J.D. [Ⓐ Stoel R.]
Chambers, John H., (BV) ... '65 '92 C.477 B.A. L.629 J.D. [Dunn C.A.H.&T.]
Chamness, Robert P. '53 '78 C.894 A.B. L.345 J.D.
(adm. in IN; not adm. in OR) CFI ProService, Inc.
Chandler, Cindi L. ... '70 '95 C.597 B.A. L.770 J.D. 11600 S.W. Barnes Rd.
Chapman, Ann K., (AV) ... '— '82 C.494 B.S. L.1035 J.D. [VandenBos&C.]
Charles, Mark D. ... '48 '84 C.592 B.A. L.30 J.D. 8265 S.W. Wilderland Ct.
Chase, Gerald M., (BV) ... '52 '78 C.309 B.A. L.629 J.D. [Chase&W.]
Chase & Weil, LLP, (AV) ... 722 S.W. 2nd Avenue, Suite 240
Chaudoin, Cheryl L. ... '54 '80 C.1056 B.S. L.1051 J.D. [Kinsley&C.]
Chen, Baolin, Law Office of '55 '93
C.999 B.A. L.596 J.D. 1000 S.W. Broadway, Suite 2150
Chenoweth, Andrew K., (AV) '50 '76
C.174 B.A. L.1067 J.D. 13118 N.W. Old Germantown Rd.
Chenoweth, Brian D., (BV) ... '67 '94 C.629 B.A. L.904 J.D. [Rycewicz&C.]

Chernoff, Vilhauer, McClung & Stenzel, LLP, (AV) BR
1600 ODS Tower, 601 S.W. Second Avenue, 97204
Telephone: 503-227-5631 Facsimile: 503-228-4373
Email: postmaster@chernofflaw.com URL: http://www.chernofflaw.com
Members of Firm: Daniel P. Chernoff (1935-1995); Jacob E. Vilhauer, Jr.; Dennis E. Stenzel; Charles D. McClung; Donald B. Haslett; J. Peter Staples; William O. Geny; Nancy J. Moriarty; Kevin L. Russell;—Tim A. Long; Kurt A. Rohlfs; Brenna K. Legaard; Susan D. Pitchford; J. Douglas Wells.
Intellectual Property Law and Litigation Relating to Patent, Trademark, Copyright, Trade Secrets, Licensing, Computer Technology. Franchising, Unfair Competition, Trade Dress and False Advertising.
Representative Clients: Bend Research, Inc.; Cascade Corp.; Columbia Sportswear Co.; Gunderson, Inc.; Leatherman Tool Group, Inc.; Pfizer, Inc.; Planar Systems, Inc.; Sharp Laboratories of America, Inc.

See Professional Biographies, PORTLAND, OREGON

Chestler, Stuart, (AV) ... '57 '82 C.629 B.A. L.1066 J.D. [Stoel R.]
Chestnut, Amy ... '73 '99 C.112 B.S. L.629 J.D. [Ⓐ Schwabe,W.&W.]
Chiapuzio, Douglas S., (BV) ... '60 '85 C.1051 B.S. L.950 J.D. [D.S.Chiapuzio]
Chiapuzio, Douglas S., P.C., (BV) ... 5125 S.W. Macadam Avenue, Suite 210
Chicoine, Jeffrey P., (AV) ... '56 '81 C&L.339 B.A., J.D. [Newcomb,S.S.&L.]
Childs, Kenneth P., (AV) ... '53 '83 C.165 B.A. L.966 J.D. [Ⓐ Stoel R.]
Childs, Sandra J. ... '61 '88 C.685 B.A. L.1044 J.D. 3034 N.E. Davis St.
Chin, Bill Y. ... '63 '95 C.1056 B.S. L.1051 J.D. Legal Writing Prof.
Chin, Elleanor H. '— '99 C.104 A.B. L.477 J.D.
(adm. in OH; not adm. in OR) [Ⓐ Davis W.T.]
Chipman, Kerry D., (BV) '51 '76 C.959 B.A. L.966 J.D.
2125 SW Fourth Street, Suite 600
Chisholm, Craig M. ... '43 '71 C.976 B.A. L.629 J.D. Stewart Title Ins. Co. of Oregon
Chock, Jay R., (AV) ... '55 '83 C.645 B.A. L.596 J.D. [Dunn C.A.H.&T.]
Choi, Jim ... '69 '97 C.1056 B.S. L.950 J.D. [J.Choi&Assoc.]
Choi, Jim & Associates, P.C. ... 16323 S.E. Stark Street, Suite 3
Chor, Patricia ... '48 '92 C.999 B.A. L.596 J.D. 2930 N.W. Bauer Woods Dr.
Chorzempa, Janelle E. ... '— '90 C.494 B.A. L.1051 J.D. [Marvin,C.&L.]
Christ, Thomas M., (AV) ... '— '83 C&L.629 B.S., J.D. [Cosgrave V.K.]
Christensen, D. Gary, P.C., (AV) ... '62 '88 C&L.101 B.A., J.D. [Miller N.]
Christensen, Darin ... '67 '97 C&L.101 B.S., J.D. [Ⓐ Bullivant H.B.]
Christensen, Steven L. ... '67 '97 C.101 B.S. L.276 J.D. [Ⓐ Miller N.]
Christian, Dayna J. ... '— '03 C.30 B.A. L.596 J.D. [Ⓐ Bullivant H.B.]
Christy, Alex, (BV) ... '33 '71 C.267 B.S. L.596 J.D. 1130 S.W. Morrison Street
Church, Brian F. ... '73 '00 C.628 B.S. L.629 J.D. [Ⓐ Davis R.E.&X.]

Church, James D., (BV) '43 '73 C.950 B.A. L.1051 J.D.
1001 S.W. Fifth Avenue, Suite 1520, 97204
Telephone: 503-228-6449 Fax: 503-228-1058
URL: http://www.lawyers.com/jamesdchurch
General Trial Practice, Family Law, Domestic Relations, Interstate Child Custody, Mediation, Personal Injury, Probate Law, Adoptions, Child Custody, Child Support, Divorce, Domestic Violence, Visitation Rights, Automobile Accidents, Wills and Probate.

See Professional Biographies, PORTLAND, OREGON

Churchill, Bryan K., (CV) ... '62 '96 C.112 B.A. L.950 J.D. 1011 S.W. 5th Avenue
Cienfuegos, Jose ... '67 '01 C.172 B.A. L.1051 J.D. 520 Sw Yamhill St Ste 430
Cieslik, Sheila L. '70 '03 C.546 B.S.B.A. L.190 J.D.
Assoc. Staff Atty., Amer. Fam. Ins.
Clark, Delos R. ... '69 '96 C.902 B.S. L.950 J.D. [Ⓐ Dunn C.A.H.&T.]
Clark, Gordon T., (BV) ... '55 '83 C.1051 B.A. L.596 J.D. [Reinisch,M.H.&W.]
Clark, Jonathan A. ... '65 '02 C.1181 B.S. L.950 J.D. [Ⓐ O'Donnell&C.]
Clark, Kelly (W.G.), (BV) ... '57 '83 C.1051 B.S. L.596 J.D. [O'Donnell&C.]
Clark, Ronald J., (AV) ... '60 '88 C.1181 B.S. L.596 J.D. [Bullivant H.B.]

Clark, Lindauer, Fetherston, Edmonds, Lippold & Collier, LLP
(See Salem)

Clarke, Richd. T., (BV) ... '23 '50 L.596 LL.B. 5225 S.E. 33rd Pl.
Claus, Jane Marie ... '65 '90 C.801 B.S. L.596 J.D. 520 SW 6th Ave., Ste. 600
Clausen, Amity L. ... '— '04 C.629 B.S. L.878 J.D. [Ⓐ Cosgrave V.K.]
Claussen, Steven M., (BV) '61 '87
C.285 B.A. L.950 J.D. 650 N.E. Holladay Street, Ste. 1400
Cleary, Thomas Patrick '65 '92 C.120 B.A. L.1051 J.D.
Dep. Dist. Atty., Multnomah Co. Dist. Atty.'s Off.
Cleek, W. Todd ... '68 '94 C.205 B.A. L.950 J.D. [Ⓐ Dunn C.A.H.&T.]
Cleveland, Kristin L. ... '69 '96 C.65 B.A. L.273 J.D. [Klarquist S.]
Cliff, Scott Talmage, (BV) ... '57 '87 C.1051 B.S. L.596 J.D. [Amburgey&R.]
Clifford, Dwain M. ... '66 '00 C.556 B.A. L.846 J.D. [Ⓐ Ball J.]
Cline, Christopher, (AV) ... '60 '91 C.766 B.A. L.1065 J.D. [Holland&K.]
Cline, Elizabeth M. ... '— '94 C.645 B.A. L.665 J.D. [Ⓐ Rosen]
Cloran, William F., (AV) ... '47 '72 C.670 B.A. L.950 J.D. [Yazbeck,C.&H.]
Close, Bertrand J., (AV) ... '25 '52 C.628 B.A. L.950 LL.B. 888 S.W. Fifth Ave.
Clostermann, Adelbert G. ... '14 '55 L.596 LL.B. 2314 N.E. 32nd Ct.‡
Clydesdale, William L. ... '67 '94 C.918 B.A. L.309 J.D. [Stoel R.]
Coan, Thomas K. ... '58 '89 C.95 B.A. L.596 J.D. 715 S.W. Morrison Street, Suite 504
Cobb, Philip G., (BV) ... '54 '81 C.679 B.S. L.596 J.D. 6501 S.W. Macadam
Coccodrilli, Fred J., (AV) ... '59 '85 C.569 B.S. L.262 J.D. [Ater W.]
Coers-Mitchell, Christine, (BV) ... '— '92 C.1169 B.A. L.285 J.D. [Cosgrave V.K.]
Coffey, Meldon R., (BV) ... '33 '62 C.1051 B.S. L.596 LL.B. 1430 S.E. Water Ave.
Cogan, Mark C. ... '56 '83 C.629 B.A. L.569 J.D. [M.C.Cogan]
Cogan, Mark C., P.C. ... 815 S.W. 2nd Ave.
Cogen, Mitchell J. ... '63 '00 C.882 B.A. L.306 J.D. 4747 N. Channel Ave.
Cohen, Emily S., (BV) ... '49 '87 C.628 B.S. L.1051 J.D. P.O. Box 20996
Cohen, Jonathan E., (BV) ... '61 '88 C.174 B.A. L.596 J.D. Prudential NW Properties
Cohen, Joseph D., (AV) ... '48 '80 C.999 B.A. L.659 J.D. [Stoel R.]
Cohen, Michael A. ... '67 '96 C.145 B.A. L.629 J.D. [Schwabe,W.&W.]
Cohen, Mitchel R., (AV) ... '51 '76 C.165 B.A. L.285 J.D. [Landye B.B.]
Cohen, Nathan L., (AV) ... '13 '38 C.685 B.A. L.629 LL.B. 851 S.W. 6th Ave.
Cohen, Richard D., (BV) ... '53 '79 C.763 B.A. L.596 J.D. 3431 S.E. Rex St.
Cohen, Stuart K., (BV) ... '60 '85 C.939 B.A. L.596 J.D. [Landye B.B.]
Cohen, Susan N. ... '50 '82 C.145 A.B. L.629 J.D. P.O. Box 29094
Coit, Andrew ... '68 '97 C.769 B.A. L.596 J.D. [Coit&D.]

Coit & Dean, P.C.
1211 SW 5th Avenue, Suite 2350, 97204
Telephone: 503-546-3178 Fax: 503-213-6023
Email: adeanattorneyatlaw@hotmail.com URL: http://www.lawyers.com/adamldean
Adam L. Dean; Andrew Coit.
Family Law, Divorce, Child Custody, Child Support, Visitation Rights, Spousal Support, Modifications, Restraining Orders, Criminal Law, Personal Injury.

See Professional Biographies, PORTLAND, OREGON

Colby, John D., (BV) ... '47 '76 C.1071 B.S. L.596 J.D. Dep. Dist. Atty.
Cole, Bartlett F. ... '16 '40 C.629 L.950 LL.B. 1201 S.W. 12th Ave.‡
Cole, Neil A. ... '71 '96 C.1181 B.S. L.596 J.D. [Schwabe,W.&W.]
Cole, Norman D. ... '49 '74 C.154 B.A. L.629 J.D. [Ⓐ Sather,B.&H.]
Coleman, Robert B. ... '69 '00 C.685 B.A. L.1209 J.D. [Ⓐ Stewart S.&G.]
Coleman, Thomas A. ... '51 '82 C.1236 B.A. L.596 J.D. P.O. Box 14285
Coleman, Timothy J., (AV) ... '— '84 C&L.629 B.S., J.D. [Cosgrave V.K.]
Coletti, John M., (AV) ... '68 '94 C.911 B.A. L.950 J.D. [Tichenor D.&C.]
Colletta, Dominic G. ... '48 '75 C.670 B.A. L.426 J.D. 1727 N.W. Hoyt Street
Collier, Adam S. ... '70 '97 C.101 B.A. L.800 J.D. [Ⓐ Bullard S.J.W.]
Collins, Calvin ... '58 '86 C.101 B.A. L.999 J.D. Esco Corp.
Collins, Jack G., (AV) ... '30 '58 C.674 A.B. L.309 LL.B. Asst. U.S. Atty.
Collins, James L., (AV) ... '50 '79 C.1058 B.A. L.1051 J.D. U. S. Attorneys Office
Collmeyer, Michael K. ... '44 '96 1000 Friends of Oregon
Colombo, Virgil, (BV) ... '17 '47 C.670 A.B. L.596 LL.B. 12705 N.E. Shaver St.
Combs, Mariel J. ... '74 '00 C&L.1051 B.S., J.D. Dept. of Interior, Off. of the Solr.
Compa, Gary P. ... '45 '73 C.276 A.B. L.30 J.D. [Kell,A.&R.]

Conable, Paul W. .... '66 '97 C.860 B.A. L.596 J.D. [Ⓐ Tonkon T.]
Condit, Jeffrey G., (AV) ....'56 '82 C.911 B.A. L.950 J.D. [Miller N.]
Conklin, Robert B. ....'38 '65 C.197 B.A. L.1066 J.D. Pres. & CEO, Timber Press, Inc.
Connall, Des, (AV) .... '30 '57 C.629 B.A. L.1051 J.D. [D.&S.Connall]
Connall, Shannon K. .... '68 '97 L.1051 J.D. [D.&S.Connall]

Connall, Des & Shannon, LLP, (AV)
1000 SW Broadway, Suite 1220, 97205
Telephone: 503-227-2688 Fax: 503-227-2687
URL: http://www.des-shannonconnall-llp.com
Members of Firm: Des Connall; Shannon K. Connall.
Federal and State Criminal Trial and Appellate Practice, Family Law including Divorce, Child Custody, Visitation Rights, Spousal Support, Child Support, Pre-nuptial Agreements, Domestic Relations, Juvenile Law.
See Professional Biographies, PORTLAND, OREGON

Connell, L. David .... '68 '95 C&L.101 B.S., J.D. [Ater W.]
Connolly, Janet Frances ....'67 '94 C.228 B.A. L.1051 J.D. Off. of Pub. Def.
Connolly, Stephen J., (AV) .... '52 '78 C.628 B.S. L.285 J.D. [Garvey S.B.]
Connors, E. Michael ....'— '95 C.112 B.A. L.629 J.D. [Davis W.T.]
Connors, John J., (AV) ....'56 '82 C.162 B.A. L.596 J.D. Pub. Def.
Conratt, Linda D. ....'67 '95 C.950 B.A. L.209 J.D. [Ⓐ Sather,B.&H.]
Conratt, Robert C. ....'64 '89 C.767 B.S. L.36 J.D. 13765 N.W. Cornell Rd.
Conti, Philip O. ....'47 '76 C.871 B.S. L.446 J.D. 3107 N.E. Rodney
Conway, Timothy J., (AV) .... '59 '85 C.1060 B.A. L.596 J.D. [Tonkon T.]
Conway, Wendy H. '64 '91 C.354 B.A. L.1202 J.D.
(adm. in MA; not adm. in OR) 3902 SE 68th Ave.
Coogan, Alan D. ....'55 '80 C.597 B.A. L.1051 J.D. 3617 NW Bluegrass Place
Cook, Christine M. .... '52 '85 C.610 A.B. L.276 J.D. 1207 S.W. 6th Ave.
Cook, H. Lee, (BV) ....'56 '86 C&L.629 B.A., J.D. [Stewart S.&G.]
Cook, Nena, (AV) ....'66 '91 C.285 B.A. L.950 J.D. [Sussman S.]
Cook, Stephen F., (AV) ....'58 '83 C.197 B.A. L.813 J.D. [Bullivant H.B.]
Cooke, Roger A., (AVⓉ) ....'48 '74 C&L.276 A.B., J.D. Precision Castparts Corp.
Coon, Cheryl F. ......'52 '77 C.104 B.A. L.94 J.D. Sr. Asst. Atty. Gen., State Dept. of Jus.
Coon, James S., (AV) ....'49 '77 C.976 B.A. L.596 J.D. [Swanson,T.&C.]
Cooper, David P. ... '58 '87 C.436 B.S.Chem. L.966 J.D. [Kolisch H.] (Pat.) (⊙Boise, ID)
Cooper, Geoffrey K. ....'49 '03 L.629 J.D. [Ⓐ Birdwell&J.]
Cooper, George J., (AV) ....'47 '72 C.950 B.A. L.228 J.D. [Dunn C.A.H.&T.]
Cooper, Jerome S. ....'44 '70 C&L.950 B.A., J.D. Co. J.
Cooper, Laura Craska ....'66 '91 C.502 B.A. L.1066 J.D. [Ball J.] (⊙Bend)
Cooper, Nancy M., (AV) .... '58 '95 C.37 B.S. L.596 J.D. [Ⓐ Bullivant H.B.]
Cooper, Sally Anne '60 '90
C.628 B.A. L.950 J.D. Sr. Trial Coun., Liberty Northwest Ins. Corp.
Coppock, Caroline ....'— '02 C.790 B.S. L.596 J.D. [Ⓐ Keating J.B.&H.]
Corbett, Sherrill A. ....'70 '95 C.740 B.A. L.1065 J.D. [Tonkon T.]
Corbin, Greg D. ....'65 '00 C.973 B.S. L.596 J.D. [Ⓐ Stoel R.]
Cordon, Bruce W. ....'58 '87 C.629 B.A. L.911 J.D. 3046 SW Bennington Dr.
Coreson, Latricia K. ....'70 '96 C.629 B.A. L.950 J.D. Flying Rhinoceros, Inc.
Correll, Kathleen M. ....'61 '87 C.604 B.A. L.588 J.D. [Curtis&C.]
Corrigan, Charles E., (AV) ....'48 '76 C.659 B.S. L.629 J.D. [Ramis C.C.]

Cosgrave Vergeer Kester LLP, (AV)
805 S.W. Broadway, 8th Floor, 97205
Telephone: 503-323-9000 Fax: 503-323-9019
Email: cvk@cvk-law.com URL: http://www.cvk-law.com
Members of Firm: Randall B. Kester; Walter H. Sweek; Frank H. Lagesen; Eugene H. Buckle; David P. Morrison; Thomas W. Brown; David H. Williams; Jeffrey A. Johnson; Robert E. Barton; Charles J. Huber (President Elect); Timothy J. Coleman; Michael C. Lewton; Andrew T. Burns; Philip R. Bennett; Thomas M. Christ; Kenneth J. Abere, Jr; Wendy M. Margolis; Michael K. Walton; Christine Coers-Mitchell; Jill D. Laney; Richard Miller. Associates: Robert E. Sabido; Peter S. Willcox-Jones; Jason Pistacchio; J. Nicholas Baldwin-Sayre; Glenn W. Robles; Derek J. Ashton; Amity L. Clausen; Gretchen L. Mandekor; Nicholas E. Wheeler.
Civil, Trial and Appellate Practice. Casualty, Corporate, Construction, Environmental Law, Labor, Employment and Discrimination, Occupational Health and Safety, Probate, Trusts and Estates, Fire. Insurance Defense, Liability and Coverage. Life, Professional Malpractice, Products Liability, Railroad Federal Employer's Liability Act, Transportation Law and Business and Corporate Law.
Counsel for: Boise Cascade Corp.; Farmers Insurance Co. of Oregon; North Pacific Insurance Co.; Professional Liability Fund; State Farm Fire and Casualty Co.; State Farm Mutual Insurance Co.; Union Pacific Railroad Co.; Valley Insurance Co.
See Professional Biographies, PORTLAND, OREGON

Cosgrove, Paul S., (AV) ....'52 '81 C.907 B.A. L.596 J.D. [Ⓒ Lindsay,H.N.&W.]
Courser, D. Jeffrey ....'56 '85 C.685 B.A. L.596 J.D. [Stoel R.] (⊙Vancouver, WA)
Courtnage, Emily ....'75 '02 C.976 B.A. L.575 J.D. [Ⓐ Stoll S.B.L.&S.]
Courtney, Aaron C. ....'67 '93 C&L.893 B.A., J.D. [Ⓒ Perkins C.]
Cousineau, Sharon Dawn ....'61 '00 C.907 B.A. L.1051 J.D. [S.Cousineau]
Cousineau, Sharon .... 3842 NE 76th Ave.
Covington, Warren A., (BV) ....'47 '79 C.1056 B.S. L.629 J.D. 4130 S. W. Lee St.
Cowger, Graciela Gomez, (BV) '66 '97
C.763 B.S.E.E. L.911 J.D. [Marger J.&M.] (See Pat. Sect.)
Cowgill, Nancy L., (AV) ....'51 '76 C.813 A.B. L.911 J.D. [Stoel R.]
Cowley, Craig M. ....'51 '85 C.169 B.A. L.629 J.D. [Ⓐ Gevurtz,M.L.&H.]
Cox, F. Kim, (BV) '52 '80 C&L.950 B.S., J.D.
Exec. V.P., Strategic Planning, Rentrak Corp.
Cox, Lawrence E. ....'33 '61 C.1056 L.950 LL.B. Reg. Solr., U.S. Dept. of Interior
Cox, Michael A., (AV) .... '63 '89 C.112 B.A. L.1065 J.D. 522 S.W. 5th Ave.
Cox, Ryan R. ....'72 '99 C.694 B.A. L.221 J.D. 10260 S.W. Greenburg Rd.
Cox, William C. ....'45 '76 C.629 M.B.A. L.1051 J.D. 244 SW California Street
Coxey, Gregory B. ....'— '03 C&L.101 B.A., J.D. [Ⓐ Vial F.]
Coyne, Arthur E. ....'70 '97 C.108 B.A. L.344 J.D. [Ⓐ Powers,M.&B.]
Craig, Barbara D., (AV) ....'53 '88 C.628 B.S. L.596 J.D. [Stoel R.]
Craig, William E., (AV) '37 '62 C.813 A.B. L.37 LL.B.
Sr. Coun., Georgia-Pacific Corp.
Craine, Diana, (AV) ....'56 '82 C.907 B.A. L.950 J.D. [Williams L.O.C.&P.]
Crandall, Cathy E., (BV) ....'57 '85 C.878 B.S. L.596 J.D. [Ⓒ Bodyfelt M.S.&C.]
Crane, James S., (AV) ....'48 '76 C.1169 B.A. L.588 J.D. [Landye B.B.]
Crane, Liann ....'66 '92 C.475 B.A. L.589 J.D. 621 Sw Alder St Ste 621
Crane, Peggy L. ....'77 '01 C.69 B.A. L.861 J.D. [Ⓐ Perkins C.]
Craven, John P., Jr. '31 '59 C.494 B.A. L.585 LL.B.
(adm. in ND; not adm. in OR) 8007 S.E. 30th Ave.‡
Craven, Nancy, (AV) ....'54 '79 C.399 B.A. L.801 J.D. [Ball J.] (⊙Bend)
Crawford, John G., Jr., (AV) ....'43 '73 C.911 B.A. L.629 J.D. [Schwabe,W.&W.]
Crawshaw, Eugene P. ....'57 '85 C.164 B.A. L.1065 J.D. 1021 S.W. 4th Ave.
Cray, Rex H. ....'51 '81 C&L.629 B.S., J.D. Dept. of Vet. Affs.
Creamer, Neale E., (AV) ....'37 '61 C&L.813 A.B., LL.B. [Foster P.T.]
Creasman, Jason ....'74 '02 C.506 B.S. L.1051 J.D. [Ⓐ Kolisch H.] (Pat.)
Creem, Sarah B. ....'76 '03 C.999 B.B.A. L.477 J.D. [Ⓐ Gevurtz,M.L.&H.]
Creighton, Beth ....'69 '97 C.025 B.A. L.966 J.D. 815 SW. 2nd
Creps, Clay D., (AV) ....'60 '86 C.602 B.A. L.309 J.D. [Bullivant H.B.]
Crew, Mitchell ....'22 '57 C.670 L.596 LL.B. 1410 N.E. 106th Ave.
Crew, Stephen F., (AV) .... '51 '78 C.629 B.B.A. L.1051 J.D. [Ramis C.C.]
Crim, Gordon E. ....'54 '93 C.813 B.A. L.596 J.D. [Foster P.T.]
Crispin, Craig A., (AV) ....'51 '81 C.801 B.S. L.950 J.D. [Crispin R.R.R.]

Crispin Russell Rissberger Rohny PC, (AV) BB
d/b/a Crispin Employment Lawyers
9600 Southwest Oak Street Suite 500, 97223
Telephone: 503-293-5770 Fax: 503-293-5766 URL: http://www.lawyers.com/employmentlaw-nw
Email: crispin@employmentlaw-nw.com URL: http://www.employmentlaw-nw.com
Craig A. Crispin; Shelley D. Russell; Patty T. Rissberger; Charese A. Rohny.
Employment and Civil Rights Litigation before State and Federal Agencies and Courts of Oregon and Washington, including Americans with Disabilities Act, Sexual Harassment, Discrimination, Wage and Hour, Employee Benefits, Executive Employment Law, Executive Severance Contracts, Wrongful Termination, Civil Rights, Disability Accommodation, Personal Injury.
See Professional Biographies, PORTLAND, OREGON

Criswell, David W., (AV) .... '63 '89 C.197 B.A. L.966 J.D. [Ball J.]
Critchlow, Carey L., (BV) '56 '82
C.629 B.A. L.1068 J.D. Oregon Health Sciences University
Crofoot, Betty I. ....'25 '53 C.629 B.A. L.596 LL.B. 16775 SW Matador Lane
Crofoot, Emory J. ....'19 '58 L.596 LL.B. 16775 S.W. Matador Lane‡
Cromwell, William T., (AV) ....'36 '65 C&L.629 B.S., LL.B. 15110 N.E. Brazee St.‡
Cronan, James P. .... '10 '39 C&L.976 B.A., LL.B. 3048 S.W. Santa Monica St.
Crone, Jessica ....'— '02 C.297 B.A. L.879 J.D. [Ⓐ Davis W.T.]
Cronn, Jeffrey S. ....'— '94 C.112 B.A. L.477 J.D. [Tonkon T.]
Cronn, Leah B. ....'— '98 C.477 B.A. L.596 J.D. [Ⓐ Lane P.]
Crooks, Sarah J. ....'71 '97 C.549 B.S. L.629 J.D. [Ⓐ Perkins C.]
Cropp, Nicholas ....'77 '99 [Ⓐ J.L.Hoffman]
Crothers, Sarie K. .... '76 '02 C&L.629 B.A., J.D. [Ⓐ Samuels Y.K.S.&S.]
Crotteau, Craig A. ... '54 '87 C.285 B.S.C.E. L.273 J.D. [Ⓒ Ball J.] (Pat.) (⊙Wash., DC)
Crow, William B., (AV) ....'31 '61 C.629 B.S. L.950 J.D. [Schwabe,W.&W.]
Crowe, Austin W., Jr., (AV) ....'39 '65 C.860 B.A. L.188 LL.B. [Perkins C.]
Crowell, John B., Jr., (AV) ....'— '58 C.197 A.B. L.309 LL.B. [Lane P.]

Crowell, John P., (AV) '55 '82 C.197 B.A. L.629 J.D.
870 Pioneer Tower, 888 S.W. Fifth Avenue, 97204-2019
Telephone: 503-222-4455 Facsimile: 503-243-2717
Email: john@jpcrowell.com
General Civil Law; Trial Practice in State and Federal Courts. Commercial, Securities, Personal Injury and Pension Litigation.
See Professional Biographies, PORTLAND, OREGON

Crumpacker, John W. ....'57 '83 C.174 B.A. L.1051 J.D. [Northwest]
Crutchley, Raymond Dean ....'68 '01 C.994 B.A. L.596 J.D. [Hartfield&C.]
Cruz, Gustavo J., Jr., (BV) ....'— '93 C.629 B.S. L.596 J.D. [Davis W.T.]
Cruz, Serena M. ....'67 '96 C.1051 B.A. L.1066 J.D. Co. Comr.
Culpepper, David C., P.C., (AV) ....'46 '74 C.770 B.A. L.629 J.D. [Miller N.]
Cumfer, Cynthia ....'49 '78 C.1275 B.A. L.1051 J.D. 316 N.E. 28th Ave.
Cunningham, Thomas A., Law Office of '51 '89
C.1056 B.A. L.629 J.D. 812 NW 17th Ave.
Cupani, Beth ....'— '96 C.267 B.A. L.596 J.D. [Ⓐ Bullivant H.B.]
Cupani, Thomas V. ....'60 '89 C.273 B.A. L.1117 J.D. [Ⓐ Kilmer,V.&L.]
Cuprill-Comas, Alice ....'70 '95 C.846 B.A. L.1051 J.D. [Ater W.]
Curley, Kieran J. ....'70 '01 C.423 B.B.A. L.911 J.D. [Ⓐ Miller N.]
Currey-Wilson, Robert T., (BV) ....'58 '87 C.629 B.S. L.596 J.D. 3800 Se 22nd
Curtis, George G., (BV) ....'57 '82 C.966 B.S. L.678 J.D. [Zbinden&C.]
Curtis, James H. .... '48 '79 C.1056 B.A. L.596 J.D. Bonneville Power Admn.
Curtis, Michael ....'49 '77 C.178 B.A. L.950 J.D. [Curtis&C.]

Curtis & Correll
4300 North East Fremont Street, Suite 230, 97213-1100
Telephone: 503-230-9285 Fax: 503-282-4106
URL: http://www.curtiscorrell.com
Members of Firm: Michael Curtis; Kathleen M. Correll.
Criminal Law, Sex Crimes, Sexual Abuse, Sexual Assault, Parole and Probation, Homicides, Death Penalty, Drug Crimes, Felonies, Post Conviction, Juvenile.
See Professional Biographies, PORTLAND, OREGON

Cushing, Douglas P., (BV) ....'45 '70 C.813 A.B. L.950 J.D. [Jordan S.]
Cushing, Keith A. ....'57 '82 C&L.629 B.S., J.D. P.O. Box 19809 (Pat.)
Custis, Robert J., (BV) ....'53 '79 C.249 B.S. L.950 J.D. [Kent C.] ⊙
Cutler, Stuart J. .... '45 '70 C.112 A.B. L.1066 J.D. Metropolitan Pub. Def.
Cyr, Steven M., (AV) ....'48 '79 C.628 B.S. L.1051 J.D. 4850 S.W. Scholls Ferry Rd.
Dagle, C. Paul, (AV) ....'44 '69 C&L.352 B.A., J.D. [Holland&K.]
Dahl, Christine Stebbins ....'63 '86 C.94 B.A. L.472 J.D. Asst. Fed. Def.
Dahl, Jeffrey C. ....'60 '85 C.174 B.A. L.472 J.D. [Ⓐ Gordon&P.]
Dahl, Joyle C., (AV) ....'35 '59 C&L.629 B.S., LL.B. [Schwabe,W.&W.]
Dahlin, Eric L. ....'— '96 C.293 B.A. L.629 J.D. [Davis W.T.]
Dailey, Dianne K., (AV) ....'50 '82 C.1056 B.S. L.596 J.D. [Bullivant H.B.]
Daily, Matthew Cole ....'67 '92 C.1181 B.S. L.950 J.D. [M.C.Daily]
Daily, Matthew C. ....7160 S.W. Fir Loop, Ste. 103
Dall, Anne .... '47 '80 C.1059 B.A. L.425 J.D. CFI Bankers Serv. Grp., Inc.
Dalton, Jason A. ....'75 '02 C.678 B.A. L.309 J.D. [Ⓐ Stoel R.]

Dames, Robert D., Jr., (AV) '48 '75 C.1494 B.A. L.596 J.D.
1000 S.W. Broadway, Suite 1510, 97205
Telephone: 503-228-2700 FAX: 503-228-5341
Email: damesjr@aol.com
Plaintiff's Medical Malpractice and Pharmaceutical Liability.
See Professional Biographies, PORTLAND, OREGON

Damiano, Michael ....'43 '96 C.112 B.A. L.808 J.D. 10260 S.W. Greenburg Rd.
Damis, James J., (AV) ....'35 '62 C.309 A.B. L.178 LL.B. 620 S.W. 5th Ave.
Damm, Jacqueline M. ....'65 '92 C.966 B.A. L.494 J.D. [Bullard S.J.W.]
Damore, Shelly M. ....'— '02 C.35 B.A. L.596 J.D. [Ⓐ Lehner&R.]
D'Amore, Thomas D., (AV) ..... '61 '90 C.549 B.A./B.S. L.990 J.D. [D'Amore&Assoc.]

D'Amore & Associates, P.C., (AV)
506 S.W. 6th Avenue, Suite 700, 97204
Telephone: 503-222-6333 Vancouver Telephone: 360-696-3437 Fax: 503-224-1895 URL: http://www.damorelaw.com
Email: help@damorelaw.com URL: http://www.lawyers.com/damorelaw
Thomas D. D'Amore;—Linda M. Weimar.
Medical Malpractice, Plaintiff's Personal Injury, Wrongful Death, Automobile Collisions and Injuries, Consumer Class Actions, Automobile Negligence, Insurance Litigation, Automobile Insurance Coverage, Insurance Bad Faith, Insurance Fraud, Insurance Premium Fraud, Unfair Insurance Practices, Uninsured Motorists, Property Damage Insurance Coverage, Brain Injury, Catastrophic Injury, Vehicular Homicide, Premises Liability, Medical Negligence, Motorcycle and Bicycle Accidents, Toxic Torts, ERISA and HMO Litigation, Employment Law and Discrimination, Wrongful Termination, Sexual Harassment, Workers Compensation, Dog Bites, Nursing Home Abuse, Trucking Accidents.
See Professional Biographies, PORTLAND, OREGON

Dane, Frank '— '88 L.770 J.D.
(adm. in CA; not adm. in OR) CEO, Exec. Advsry. Servs. Inc.

Danford, Mary Thurston, (AV) .... '51 '78 C.822 A.B. L.1051 J.D. City Atty.'s Off.
Dang, Samantha N., Law Office of '74 '02 C.988 B.A. L.629 J.D.
6919 SE 82nd Avenue
Daniels, Brad .... '74 '02 C.629 B.A. L.976 J.D. [🄰 Stoel R.]
Daraee, Hafez, Attorney at Law, (BV) '65 '93
C.629 B.S. L.1051 J.D. 601 S.W. 2nd, Ste. 1940
Dartt, Donald D. .... '61 '89 C.1051 B.A. L.596 J.D. 1515 S.W. 5th Ave., suite 1022
D'Ascenzo, David S. .... '71 '96 C.691 B.S. L.846 J.D. [Kolisch H.] (Pat.)
Dauenhauer, Lorne O. .... '— '02 C.285 B.S. L.596 J.D. [🄰 Lane P.]
David, Phillip A. .... '41 '77 C&L.629 B.S., J.D. Standard Ins. Co.
Davidson, Ilene Dobrow, (AVⓉ) '50 '75 C.298 B.A. L.910 J.D.
(adm. in IL; not adm. in OR) Gen. Coun., The Schnitzer Group‡
Davidson, James B., (AVⓉ) .... '50 '75 C.339 B.A. L.910 J.D. [Ater W.]
Davis, Andrew I., (AV) .... '62 '93 C.280 B.B.A. L.596 J.D. [Stoel R.]
Davis, Anthony E. .... '71 '95 C.628 B.A. L.813 J.D. [Davis D.K.]
Davis, Donna D. .... '39 '64 C.939 B.A. L.950 J.D. 1616 S.W. Harbor Wy., Apt. 601
Davis, Elizabeth A. '63 '93 C.628 B.S. L.596 J.D.
Dir. of Career Servs., Northwestern School of Law of Lewis & Clark College
Davis, I. Kenneth, (AV) .... '50 '88 C.178 A.B. L.596 J.D. [Dunn C.A.H.&T.]
Davis, Jeffrey S. .... '64 '95 C.878 B.S. L.629 J.D. [🄰 Schwabe,W.&W.]
Davis, Karen Wetherell, (AVⓉ) .... '66 '91 C.823 B.Mus. L.813 J.D. [Elliott,O.&P.] ⊙
Davis, Kenneth Ray, II .... '— '92 C.939 B.A. L.678 J.D. [Lane P.] (Pat.)
Davis, Penny L. .... '53 '77 C.188 B.A. L.94 J.D. 111 S.W. 5th Ave., Ste. 1890
Davis, Peter C. .... '42 '71 C.767 A.B. L.1065 J.D. 10260 S.W. Greenburg Rd.
Davis, Richard Wm., (BV) .... '37 '60 L.596 LL.B. 1 Centerpointe Dr.
Davis, Scott E. '73 '00 C.628 B.S. L.1494 J.D.
(adm. in CA; not adm. in OR) [S.E.Davis]
Davis, Scott E. .... '73 '00 C.628 B.S. L.1068 J.D. [🄰 Klarquist S.]
Davis, Thomas A., (BV) .... '40 '67 C.629 B.S. L.596 J.D. [Smith&G.]
Davis, William Alan, (AV) .... '52 '77 C.813 B.A. L.629 J.D. [Davis R.E.&X.]
Davis Dixon Kirby .... 519 SW Third, Suite 601

Davis Rothwell Earle & Xochihua P.C., (AV)
1900 Wells Fargo Center, 1300 Southwest Fifth Avenue, 97201-5604 ⊙
Telephone: 503-222-4422 Telecopier: 503-222-4428
Email: inquiry@davisrothwell.com URL: http://www.davisrothwell.com
Heather C. Beasley; William Alan Davis; Christopher J. Drotzmann; William G. Earle; Alan Gladstone; John S. Knowles; Nicole M. Rhoades; Paul R. Xóchihua;—Samuel K. Anderson; Brian F. Church; Gina M. Delahunt; Kevin A. Eike; Elizabeth E. Lampson; Cari Waters.
Litigation Practice Concentrating on Insurance Defense, Personal Injury and Tort Claims, Environmental Law, Construction, Products Liability, Employment Law and the Defense of Professionals.
Seattle, Washington Office: 2850 Bank of America Tower, 701 Fifth Avenue, 98104-7047. Telephones: 206-622-2295; Toll-Free: 1-800-370-8399. Telecopier: 206-340-0724.
See Professional Biographies, PORTLAND, OREGON

Davis, Scott E., PC .... 7117 S.W. 7th Ave.

Davis Wright Tremaine LLP, (AV)
Suite 2300, 1300 S.W. Fifth Avenue, 97201-5682 ⊙
Telephone: 503-241-2300 FAX: 503-778-5299
URL: http://www.dwt.com
Partners: James F. Ambrose; David C. Baca; Anne L. Barragar; Merrill J. Baumann, Jr.; Carol J. Bernick; Duane A. Bosworth, II; Lawrence B. Burke; John A. Cameron, Jr.; E. Michael Connors; Gustavo J. Cruz, Jr.; Eric L. Dahlin; Kathleen Dent; John DiLorenzo; Timothy Dozois; Richard M. Glick; Eugene Grant; Patrick J. Green; Mark J. Hackett; Stuart C. Harris; Gregory S. Hathaway; Thomas S. Hillier; Jay D. Hull; Everett W. Jack, Jr.; Christopher P. Koback; Wendell G. Kusnerus; Peter S. Leichtfuss; Rodney E. Lewis, Jr.; Jesse D. Lyon; George M. Mardikes; D. Charles Mauritz; Michael McArthur-Phillips; Christopher F. McCracken; Patricia McGuire; John F. McGrory, Jr.; James M. Mei; William R. Miller, Jr.; James K. Neill; Robert D. Newell; Dennis M. Paterson, III; Phillip C. Querin; Coni S. Rathbone; Carmen J. SantaMaria; Erik S. Schimmelbusch; Michael H. Schmeer; Peter A. Sergienko; James Stuart Smith; Milton R. Stewart; Kent B. Thurber; Mark P. Trinchero; Joseph Vance; Joseph M. VanLeuven; Timothy R. Volpert; James C. Waggoner; James D. Zupancic. Resident Associates: Elleanor H. Chin (Not admitted in OR); Jessica Crone; Anne E. Denecke; Jeff N. Evans; Kristen M. Gurdin; Thomas M. Jones; Nanci Klinger; Elizabeth Knight; Kevin Kono; Jeni L. Lassell; Devon T. Lyon (Not admitted in OR); Sean B. Malcolm (Not admitted in OR); Joe Mattoon; P. Andrew McStay, Jr.; William D. Miner; Rita Molina; Jenna Leigh Mooney; Sheila Fox Morrison (Not admitted in OR); Carol Noonan; David C. Rocker; Aaron K. Stuckey; Trinh Tran; Scott E. Warnick (Not admitted in OR). Counsel: Ingrid Brydolf; Gregory A. Chaimov; Jacob A. Heth; David J. Krieger; Milton C. Lankton; Daniel E. O'Leary; Dean M. Phillips; Ronald K. Ragen; Thomas S. Smith; H. Stewart Tremaine (Retired).
Antitrust, Business and Corporate, Communications, Media and Information Technologies, Construction and Government Contracts, Credit Recovery and Bankruptcy, Education, eHealth Law, Emerging Business and Technology, Employee Benefits, Employment, Energy, Environmental and Natural Resources, Finance and Commercial Transactions, Food and Agriculture, Government Contracts, Healthcare, Hospitality, Immigration, Intellectual Property, International Law, Internet and eCommerce, Legislation, Litigation, Mergers and Acquisitions, Municipal Finance, Newspapers and Publishing, Real Estate and Land Use, Retail, Securities, Shanghai and China, State and Local Tax, Tax Exempt Organizations, Taxes, Technology, Telecommunications and Regulatory, Trusts and Estates.
Offices also at: Anchorage, Alaska, Bellevue, Washington, Los Angeles, California, New York, New York, San Francisco, California, Washington, D.C., Seattle, Washington, Shanghai, China.
See Professional Biographies, PORTLAND, OREGON

Davison, Melinda J., (BV) .... '60 '86 C.208 B.A. L.1165 J.D. [Davison V.]
Davison Van Cleve, P.C., (AV) .... 333 S.W. Taylor St., Ste. 400
Dawson, John R. '64 '92 C.475 B.S.M.E. L.678 J.D.
805 S.W. Broadway, Ste. 2740 (Pat.)
Dawson, Sheryl Westfall '— '83 C.1181 B.A. L.950 J.D.
Mgr., Corp. Secy. Div.; Asst. Secy., U.S. Bancorp
Day, Bartley F., (AV) .... '48 '77 C.894 B.A. L.910 J.D. [B.F.Day]
Day, Kirsten J. .... '65 '93 C.860 B.A. L.1065 J.D. Gen. Coun., Pacific Realty Assoc., L.P.
Day, Michael A. .... '70 '03 C&L.629 B.S., J.D. [Discount B.]
Day, Bartley F., A Prof. Corp., Law Offices of, (AV)
1001 S.W. Fifth Avenue, Suite 1100
Dayton, Robert D., (AV) .... '44 '68 C&L.950 B.S.L., J.D. [Schwabe,W.&W.]
Daywitt, Jason H. .... '68 '99 C.902 B.A. L.629 J.D. [🄰 Keating J.B.&H.]
Dazer, Nicholas L. .... '74 '00 C.17 B.A. L.596 J.D. [🄰 Bullivant H.B.]
Dean, Adam L. .... '67 '95 C.957 B.S.W. L.436 J.D. [Coit&D.]
Dean, David E. .... '56 '81 C.373 B.A. L.1051 J.D. [Grenley,R.E.B.&B.]
Dean, E. Joseph, (AV) .... '49 '74 C.629 B.A.B.A. L.309 J.D. [Stoel R.]
Deatherage, Stephen Forrest .... '69 '98 C.629 B.A. L.950 J.D. [🄰 Bullivant H.B.]
Deavours, Carrie .... '71 '99 [🄰 Rycewicz&C.]
DeBast, Paul J., (AV) .... '46 '72 C.911 B.A. L.950 J.D. [DeBast,M.&R.]

DeBast, McFarland & Richardson, LLP, (AV)
9600 Building, 9600 Southwest Barnes Road, Suite 325, 97225
Telephone: 503-297-9600 Fax: 503-297-9500
URL: http://www.dmr-law.com
Partners of Firm: Paul J. DeBast; Barbara P. McFarland; James B. Richardson.
Family Law, Divorce, Premarital Agreements, Child Support, Property Settlements, Spousal Support, Child Custody, Domestic Violence, Visitation Rights, Estate Planning, Wills, Trusts, Probate, Civil Litigation, Criminal Law, Personal Injury, Driving While Intoxicated, Drug Crimes, Guardianships and Conservatorship.
See Professional Biographies, PORTLAND, OREGON

DeBlasio, David H., (BV) .... '45 '74 C.1056 B.S. L.596 J.D. P.O. Box 12669
de Boer, Saskia .... '75 '03 C.881 A.B. L.813 J.D. [🄰 Stoel R.]
DeChaine, Dean D., P.C., (AV) .... '36 '64 C.1056 B.S. L.893 LL.B. [Miller N.]
Deckelbaum, Gerald E. .... '55 '84 C.1036 B.A. L.472 J.D. 1137 SE 52nd Ave.‡
Decker, Heather Wright .... '71 '96 C&L.629 B.S., J.D. Contract Atty.
DeCristo, Joshua S. .... '74 '99 C.670 B.A. L.950 J.D. [🄰 Schwabe,W.&W.]
DeDobbelaere, Lori K. .... '65 '94 C.629 B.A. L.1051 J.D. [🄰 Lachenmeier E.R.&H.]
Deering, Nicole Lynn .... '68 '94 C.1056 B.A. L.1051 JD. 1500 N.E. Irving St., Ste. 370
DeFrancq, Donald J., (AV) '37 '63 C.629 B.S. L.1066 LL.B.
4331 S.W. Twombly Ave.‡
DeFrang, Gary R., (AV) .... '41 '69 C.136 B.S. L.208 J.D. [Wetzel D.&S.]
Deiz, Mercedes F. .... '17 '60 C.331 L.596 J.D. Sr. Cir. J.‡
DeJong, Timothy, (AV) .... '65 '91 C.907 B.A. L.629 J.D. [Stoll S.B.L.&S.]
Delahunt, Gina M. .... '65 '04 C.670 B.B.A. L.1051 J.D. [🄰 Davis R.E.&X.]
Delaney, Justin R. '— '96 C.37 B.A. L.596 J.D.
2nd VP & Asst. Gen. Coun., Standard Ins. Co.
DeLapp, Mark L., (BV) .... '58 '83 C.629 B.S. L.950 J.D. [M.L.DeLapp]
DeLapp, Mark L., P.C., (BV) .... 1627 N.E. Alberta Street
Delehant, Klarissa G. .... '— '03 C.602 B.A. L.596 J.D. [🄰 Welch,B.&G.]
De Leo, Shelley (Barber) '61 '87 C.629 B.A. L.1066 J.D.
Asst. Gen. Coun., KinderCare Learning Centers, Inc.
Dell, Martitia M. .... '59 '93 C.911 B.A. L.596 J.D. 2416 SW Fifth Avenue
Dellett, John P., (AV) .... '28 '59 C.350 B.S. L.273 J.D. 310 S.W. 4th Ave. (Pat.)
Delo, Donna S., (AV) .... '44 '80 C.911 B.S. L.1051 J.D. [Delo&B.]
Delo, Lew E., (AV) .... '44 '74 C.906 B.A. L.596 J.D. [Delo&B.]

Delo & Bowers, LLP, (AV)
2400 SW Fourth Avenue, Suite 210, 97201
Telephone: 503-228-3299 Fax: 503-228-1890
URL: http://www.delo-bowers.com
Members of Firm: Lew E. Delo; Charles R. Bowers; Donna S. Delo.
General Business, E-commerce, Computer and Internet Law, Intellectual Property and Business, Tax and International Commercial Litigation.
Reference: Wells Fargo Bank.
See Professional Biographies, PORTLAND, OREGON

Demary, Robert F., (BV) '56 '89 C.112 B.A. L.596 J.D.
1000 S.W. Broadway, Ste. 2400
Demer, Kevin .... '63 '96 C&L.1059 B.B.A., J.D. Multnomah Co. Dist. Atty.
Denecke, Anne E., (AV) .... '— '87 C&L.950 B.S., J.D. [🄰 Davis W.T.]
Denecke, David R., (AV) .... '49 '78 C.629 B.A. L.596 J.D. [Harrang L.G.R.]
Dent, Kathleen .... '— '96 C.950 B.A. L.546 J.D. [Davis W.T.]
Denton, Aaron C. .... '71 '02 C.378 B.A. L.494 J.D. [🄰 Martin,B.T.L.&H.]
Denton, Justin B. .... '— '97 C&L.101 B.A., J.D. [Tonkon T.]
Deras, Warren C., (AV) .... '44 '71 C.112 A.B. L.976 J.D. 1400 S.W. Montgomery St.
Derr, Lawrence R., (AV) .... '44 '69 C.629 B.A. L.950 J.D. [🄲 Josselson,P.&R.]
Derum, Jay B. .... '63 '97 C.629 B.A. L.596 J.D. [🄰 Brownstein,R.S.K.G.D.&H.]
DeShaw, Aaron C. .... '69 '00 C&L.950 D.C., J.D. Siren Publishing LLC
DeSimone, Samuel R., Jr., (AV) '59 '85
C.31 B.A. L.569 J.D. 601 SW 2nd Avenue, Suite 2100
Desmond, James L. '56 '81 C.602 B.A. L.880 J.D.
(adm. in IL; not adm. in OR) The Trust for Public Land
Desmond, Reagan L.B. .... '67 '97 C.651 B.S. L.878 J.D. [🄰 Ball J.] (⊙Bend)
DeSylvia, Terry, (AV) .... '43 '69 C&L.813 A.B., J.D. [Brownstein,R.S.K.G.D.&H.]
Deterling, Sheri L. '64 '90 C.802 B.B.A. L.846 J.D.
(adm. in TX; not adm. in OR) 2810 N.W. Beuhla Vista Terrace
Detlefsen, Jeffrey E. .... '53 '80 C&L.629 B.S., J.D. [Detlefsen]
Detlefsen Law Office, P.C. .... 621 S.W. Alder St.
Deveny, Lori E., (AV) .... '65 '89 C.594 B.A. L.950 J.D. 1020 SW Taylor
Devers, Douglas P., (BV) .... '45 '72 C.629 B.A. L.950 J.D. 25 N.W. 23rd Pl.
DeVoe, Charles H. .... '63 '93 C.674 B.S.M.E. L.945 J.D. [Kolisch H.] (Pat.)
DeWald, Jennifer K. .... '70 '98 C.1051 B.A. L.596 J.D. 2121 S.W. Broadway
Dewey, Eric S. .... '58 '96 C.1056 B.S. L.629 J.D. 5425 SW Seymore St.
DeWitt, Julia A., P.C., (AV) .... '69 '94 C.629 B.S. L.1065 J.D. [Miller N.]
Diamond, Barbara J., (BV) .... '58 '85 C.1349 B.A. L.569 J.D. [Smith,G.D.&O.]
Diamond, Peter C., (BV) .... '61 '92 C.174 B.A. L.950 J.D. 850 N.E. 122nd Ave.
Diarmit, Frank O. .... '49 '81 C.1181 B.S. L.950 J.D. [🄰 Brownstein,R.S.K.G.D.&H.]
Dickas, William D., (BV) .... '41 '74 C.999 A.B. L.608 J.D. [Kell,A.&R.]
Dickson, Russell M. .... '25 '53 C.813 B.A. L.477 LL.B. 319 S.W. Washington
Dierking, Roger F. .... '27 '69 C.999 L.596 J.D. [Dierking&S.]
Dierking & Schuster .... 3565 N.E. Broadway St.
Dietrich, Howard N. .... '10 '40 C.629 B.S. L.596 LL.B. 10300 S.W. Greenburg Rd.

Dillon, Helen C., (BV) '44 '80 C.1051 B.A. L.596 J.D.
210 S.W. Morrison, Suite 600, 97204-3150
Telephone: 503-223-7884 FAX: 503-273-8591
Email: helen@helendillon.com URL: http://www.lawyers.com/hdillon
Family, Domestic Relations, Divorce, Child Custody, Parenting Time, Visitation Rights, Child Support Modifications, Spousal Support, Adoption, Premarital Agreements, Domestic Violence.
See Professional Biographies, PORTLAND, OREGON

DiLorenzo, John, (AV) .... '— '80 C&L.950 B.S., J.D. [Davis W.T.]
DiPiero, Deborah S., Attorney at Law .... '73 '98 C.610 B.B.A. L.94 J.D. [D.S.DiPiero]
DiPiero, Deborah S., Attorney at Law .... 2290 S.W. 106th Pl.
Dippel, Courtney C. .... '76 '02 C.323 B.A. L.966 J.D. [🄰 Holland&K.]
Discount Bankruptcy Law Center .... 521 S.W. Clay, Suite 204
Dixon, Andrea Contreras .... '68 '96 C.813 B.A. L.904 J.D. [🄲 Davis D.K.]
Dixon, Frank J., (BV) .... '51 '79 C.602 B.A. L.1051 J.D. 2205 N.W. Johnson, Ste. A
Dixon, R. Dale, Jr. .... '69 '95 C.228 A.B. L.30 J.D. [Davis D.K.]
Dobbins, Jeffrey C. .... '67 '94 C.309 A.B. L.228 J.D. [🄰 Perkins C.]
Doblie, Gerald C., (AV) .... '34 '68 C.628 B.S. L.596 J.D. [Doblie&Assoc.]
Doblie & Associates, P.C., (AV) .... 1015 S.W. Yamhill St.
Dobson, John D., (AV) '50 '76 C.950 B.A. L.629 J.D.
Assoc. Coun., First Amer. Title Ins. Co. of Ore.
Dobson, Kenneth P. .... '69 '00 C.972 B.S. L.1194 J.D. [Dobson]

Dobson Law Firm, The, LLC
1000 S.W. Broadway, Suite 2400, 97205
Telephone: 503-295-6888 Fax: 503-241-2249
Email: ken@oregonenvironmentallaw.com URL: http://www.oregonenvironmentallaw.com
Member of Firm: Kenneth P. Dobson.
Environmental Law, Complex Litigation, Solid and Hazardous Waste, Indian Law, Water Law, Toxic Torts, Zoning, Planning and Land Use, Bankruptcy, Commercial, Business Law, Business Litigation, Construction Law, Construction Defects, Mechanics Liens, Debtor and Creditor, Creditors Rights, Real Estate, Commercial Real Estate, Landlord and Tenant Law, Residential Real Estate, Agricultural Law, Eminent Domain, Condemnation, Natural Resources Law, Endangered Species Law, Contaminated Site Litigation.
See Professional Biographies, PORTLAND, OREGON

Dodds, Paul G., (AV) .... '60 '87 C.1056 B.S. L.596 J.D. [Brownstein,R.S.K.G.D.&H.]
Dodson, Mark S., (AV) '45 '73 C.309 B.A. L.1066 J.D.
Sr. V.P. & Gen. Coun., Northwest Nat. Gas Co.

Doherty, Brian B., P.C., (AV) ....'52 '78 C.602 B.A. L.596 J.D. [Miller N.]
Dolan, Martin, (AV) ..... '47 '87 C.602 B.A. L.352 J.D. 1130 S.W. Morrison St., Ste. 630
Doll, Kathleen J. ....'— '03 C.911 B.A. L.1051 J.D. [Ⓐ Stoel R.]
Donaca, Thomas C. ....'27 '59 C.813 B.A. L.596 LL.B. Pres., Donaca Enterprises, Inc.
Donahe, Heidi Pederson '66 '92
C.747 B.A. L.1035 J.D. Dir. of Marketing, M Financial Group

Donahue, Sean, (AV) '54 '79 C.178 B.A. L.629 J.D.
Suite 1625, Benj. Franklin Plaza, One S.W. Columbia, 97258-2098
Telephone: 503-226-1084 Fax: 503-227-6366
Email: sdonalaw@aol.com
General Business, Labor Law and Civil Litigation including Employment and Commercial Litigation, Employment Discrimination, Sexual Harassment, Wrongful Termination.
See Professional Biographies, PORTLAND, OREGON

Donald, Erin L. ....'75 '04 C.429 B.A. L.629 J.D. [Ⓐ Black H.]
Donaldson, Robert W., (AV) ....'46 '74 C.628 B.S. L.950 J.D. [Black H.]
Donis, Emi A. '64 '89
C.602 B.B.A. L.112 J.D. Dep. Gen. Coun., Precision Castparts Corp.
Donnelly, Maxwell, (BV) ....'14 '39 C.629 L.596 LL.B. 912 S.W. Moss St.
Dorchuck, Joanna L. .... '74 '01 C.637 B.A. L.793 J.D. [Ⓐ G.M.Bullock&Assoc.]
Dormire, Kornelia ....'— '01 C.174 B.A. L.1051 J.D. [Ⓐ Miller N.]
Dorn, Peter E. ....'51 '83 C.494 B.A. L.596 J.D. 888 S.W. 5th Ave.
Dorr, Christopher C. ....'70 '99 C.911 B.S. L.596 J.D. [Ⓐ Schwabe,W.&W.]
Dorsay, Craig J., (AV) ....'53 '79 C.477 B.S. L.629 J.D. 2121 S.W. Broadway
Dost, Patricia M., (BV) ....'65 '90 C.911 B.A. L.477 J.D. [Schwabe,W.&W.]
Dougherty, Robert C., (BV) '60 '87
C.1104 B.S. L.950 J.D. 1130 S.W. Morrison St., Ste. 210
Douthwaite, David T., (AV) '47 '78
C.575 A.B. L.893 J.D. VP Admin., J. E. Dunn Northwest, Inc.
Dowell, James R. ....'77 '02 C.1142 B.A. L.69 J.D. [Tombleson&D.]
Downes, Gile R., (AV) ....'43 '69 C.988 B.A. L.813 J.D. [Ⓢ Schulte,A.D.A.&B.]
Doyle, Kelly Michael, (BV) ....'56 '84 C.685 B.A. L.950 J.D. [Doyle]
Doyle, Thomas K. ....'71 '97 C.685 B.A. L.596 J.D. [Ⓐ Bennett,H.M.&K.]
Doyle Law, PC, (BV) ....5806 SE 41st St.
Dozois, Timothy ....'— '89 C.628 B.S. L.629 J.D. [Davis W.T.]
Drake, Eileen, (AV) ....'46 '80 C.530 B.A. L.477 J.D. Atty., PCC Structurals Inc.
Drake, Robin J. '71 '99 C.999 B.A. L.900 J.D.
(adm. in TX; not adm. in OR) 5830 S.W. Florida St.
Drakulich, Nick A., (BV) ....'50 '75 C.950 B.A. L.596 J.D. [Drakulich&C.]

Drakulich & Carlson, P.C., (BV)
1500 Southwest 1st Avenue, Suite 1170, 97201
Telephone: 503-224-0871 Fax: 503-224-4215 URL: http://www.drakulichcarlson.com
Email: rich@teleport.com URL: http://www.lawyers.com/drakulich&carlson
Nick A. Drakulich; Richard A. Carlson.
General Civil and Trial Practice. Family Law, Child Custody, Child Support, Divorce, Domestic Violence, Visitation Rights, Personal Injury, Automobile Accidents, Dog Bites, Sexual Abuse, Slip and Fall, Wrongful Death, Medical Malpractice, Insurance, Health Care, Construction Law, Contracts, Lawsuits, Real Estate Buying and Selling, Residential Real Estate, Commercial Real Estate, Criminal Law, Driving While Intoxicated, Drug Crimes, Parole and Probation.
See Professional Biographies, PORTLAND, OREGON

Draneas, John H., (AV) ....'51 '77 C.112 B.S. L.950 J.D. [Draneas&H.]
Draneas & Huglin, P.C., (AV) ....222 S.W. Columbia St., Ste. 1625
Draudt, James P., (AV) ....'53 '82 C.197 B.A. L.596 J.D. [Jensen D.]
Drazan, Daniel J. ....'73 '98 C.1051 B.A. L.950 J.D. [Ⓐ Dunn C.A.H.&T.]
Dressler, Robert L. ....'21 '49 C.174 B.A. L.309 LL.B. 12701 S.E. Salmon Ct.‡
Drew, William A. ....'66 '95 C.950 B.S. L.309 J.D. [Elliott,O.&P.]
Driscoll, James G., (AV) ....'48 '77 C.178 B.A. L.1051 J.D. [Bullivant H.B.]
Driscoll, Neil Joseph, III, (BV) ....'48 '78 C.670 B.S. L.1051 J.D. [N.J.Driscoll]
Driscoll, Neil J., P.C., (BV) ....140 S.W. Arthur St., Ste. 300
Driver, Joan L., (AV) ....'53 '79 C.318 B.A. L.950 J.D. 3702 S.W. Cullen Blvd.
Driver, Susan K., (AV) ....'54 '82 C&L.629 B.S., J.D. [Mediation]
Drotzmann, Christopher J. ....'71 '96 C.906 B.A. L.950 J.D. [Davis R.E.&X.]
Druckman, Jeffrey J., (AV) ....'54 '79 C.813 B.A. L.94 J.D. [J.J.Druckman]
Druckman, Jeffrey J., P.C., Law Office of, (AV) ....424 S.W. Iowa St.
Drummonds, Henry H., (AV) '45 '72 C.629 A.B. L.309 J.D.
Assoc. Prof. of Law, Northwestern Sch. of Law
Duarte, Alex M., (BVⓉ) '59 '85
C.339 B.A. L.813 J.D. Corp. Coun., Qwest Communications, Inc.
Dubanevich, Keith S., (AV) ....'57 '83 C.588 B.S. L.861 J.D. [Garvey S.B.]
DuBay, John L. ....'31 '60 C.628 B.S. L.950 J.D. Chf. Asst. Co. Coun.
DuBoff, Leonard D., (AV) ....'41 '72 C.1019 B.E.S. L.1009 J.D. [DuBoff]

DuBoff Law Group, The, LLC, (AV)
6665 S.W. Hampton Street, Suite 200, 97223
Telephone: 503-968-8111 Fax: 503-968-7228
Email: info@dubofflaw.com URL: http://www.dubofflaw.com
Members of Firm: Leonard D. DuBoff; Christy O. King. Associates: Abigail R. Michels; Christopher W. Brown; Marisa N. James.
General Business, Art Law, Publishing Law, Copyright, Trademark and High Tech Law, Estate Planning, Civil Litigation, Intellectual Property, Licensing Agreements, Trade Secrets, Trademarks, Internet, E-Commerce, Business Planning, Contracts, Lawsuits, Entertainment, Starting A Business.
See Professional Biographies, PORTLAND, OREGON

Duckler, Geordie ....'59 '87 C.628 B.S. L.596 J.D. [AnimalPractice]
Duckworth, Matthew B. ....'71 '02 C.813 B.A. L.596 J.D. [Ⓐ Busse&H.]
Duden, Paul R., (AV) ....'— '66 L.629 LL.B. [Williams,K.&G.P.]
Dudley, J. Jeffrey, (BV) '48 '74 C.477 B.S.Ch.E. L.813 J.D.
Coun., Portland Gen. Corp.
Dudley, Paul W., (BV) ....'54 '82 C.784 B.A. L.1051 J.D. [P.Dudley]
Dudley, Paul, (BV) ....1020 S.W. Taylor St., Ste. 375
Dudrey, John, (AV) ....'48 '73 C&L.813 A.B., J.D. [Williams F.]
Duffy, Peter J., (AV) ....'58 '87 C.911 B.A. L.629 J.D. [Duffy K.]
Duffy, Sandra N. '47 '82
C.1056 B.S. L.596 J.D. Chf. Asst. Co. Coun., Multnomah Co. Atty.

Duffy Kekel LLP, (AV)
1200 Standard Plaza, 1100 S.W. Sixth Avenue, 97204
Telephone: 503-226-1371 Telecopier: 503-226-3574
URL: http://www.duffykekel.com
Members of Firm: Charles P. Duffy (1915-2001); David A. Kekel (1938-1999); Philip N. Jones; Steven A. Nicholes; Donna M. Muehleck; Peter J. Duffy; Eric H. Vetterlein. Associate: Holly N. Mitchell. Of Counsel: Dana R. Taylor; Ron D. Bailey.
Taxation, Estate Planning, Tax Planning, Tax Litigation, Business Law, Timber Matters, Probate, Real Property, Wills, Trusts, Deferred Compensation, Exempt Organizations, Elder Law, Estate and Trust Litigation, Commercial Litigation, Special Education, Guardianships, Conservatorships.
See Professional Biographies, PORTLAND, OREGON

Dukelow, Kyle B. ....'66 '94 C.475 B.S. L.629 J.D. [K.Dukelow]
Dukelow, Owen W. '61 '96
C.999 B.S.E.T. L.464 J.D. [Ⓐ Kolisch H.] (Pat.) (ⓞPalo Alto, CA)

Dukelow, Kyle, PC, Law Office of ....6226 N.E. Halsey
Dulcich, James F., (AV) ....'54 '82 C.629 B.S. L.893 J.D. [Schwabe,W.&W.]
Dulcich, Thomas V., (AV) ....'53 '80 C.629 B.S. L.145 J.D. [Schwabe,W.&W.]
Dummigan, R. Brendan ....'65 '93 C.174 B.A. L.1051 J.D. [Pickett D.R.]
Dunaway, Susan Marie ....'49 '97 C.341 B.A. L.1522 J.D. Co. Atty. Off.
Dunbar, John J., (AV) ....'57 '84 C.602 A.B. L.911 J.D. [Ball J.]
Duncan, James T. ....'18 '58 C.999 L.596 LL.B. 2133 N.E. Bway.
Duncan, M. Elizabeth, (AV) ....'57 '87 C.893 B.A. L.596 J.D. [Ⓐ Greene&M.]
Duncan, Randall L., (BV) ....'57 '85 C.112 B.A. L.464 J.D. [Dunn C.A.H.&T.]
Dunn, James T., (AV) ....'46 '71 C.93 B.S. L.602 J.D. [Martin,B.T.L.&H.]
Dunn, Randall L. ....'50 '75 C.597 B.A. L.813 J.D. U.S. Bkrptcy. J.
Dunn, Terence H. ....'49 '74 C.628 B.S. L.596 J.D. Bkrptcy. Clk.

Dunn Carney Allen Higgins & Tongue LLP, (AV)
Pacific First Federal Building, 851 S.W. Sixth Avenue Suite 1500, 97204
Telephone: 503-224-6440 FAX: 503-224-7324
Email: info@dunn-carney.com URL: http://www.dunncarney.com
Partners of Firm: Robert L. Allen; Kenneth S. Antell; Jonathan A. Bennett; David J. Buono; Madeleine S. Campbell; John H. Chambers; Jay R. Chock; George J. Cooper; I. Kenneth Davis; Randall L. Duncan; Susan C. Glen; James M. Hillas; Frank H. Hilton, Jr.; Jack D. Hoffman; Charles Scott Howard; Scott A. Jonsson; JoDee K. Keegan; Eric A. Kekel; Robert A. Kerr; Marsha Murray-Lusby; Gilbert E. Parker; Renee R. Stineman; Brian R. Talcott; Donald E. Templeton; Thomas Healy Tongue; Daniel F. Vidas; Robert K. Winger;—Cynthia Croft Adams; Richard Theodore Ashe; Brian R. Cable; Delos R. Clark; W. Todd Cleek; Daniel J. Drazan; Paul G. Ellis; Samantha Fair; Stefan Feuerherdt; Anne D. Foster; Heather L. Guthrie; Tim Hering; Misti K. Johnson; Tamara B. Maher; John G. O'Neil (Not admitted in OR); Pierre L. Robert; David P. Rossmiller; Melissa M. Ryan; Damien J. Sinnott; Eric A. Smith; Kyle J. Stinchfield; Kjersten H. Turpen; Gail P. Vore. Of Counsel: Ty K. Wyman; J. David Zehntbauer.
General Civil and Trial Practice in all State and Federal Courts. General Business, Antitrust, Appellate Practice, Banking Law, Bankruptcy, Construction Law, Contracts, Corporate, Creditors Rights, Employee Benefits,Employment Law, ERISA, Estate Planning, Federal and State Tax Law, Guardianship and Conservatorship, Health Care, Insurance, Intellectual Property, Medical Malpractice, Mergers, Acquisitions and Divestitures, Nonprofit and Charitable Organizations, Partnership Law, Probate, Products Liability, Real Estate, Retirement Plans, Trust Administration, and Zoning, Planning and Land Use.
Representative Clients: Allstate Insurance Co.; Gerding/Edlen Development Co.; Kuni Enterprises, Inc.; North Pacific Group, Inc.; Pan Pacific Retail Properties, Inc.; Shelter Products, Inc; South Coast Lumber Co.
See Professional Biographies, PORTLAND, OREGON

Duong-Tran, Hien C. ....'66 '98 C.629 B.A. L.273 J.D. Regulatory Serv. Mngr.
Dupuy, Howard M., Jr. ....'29 '56 C.670 B.A. L.596 LL.B. 1205 N.W. 25th Ave.‡
Durham, Jennifer A. ....'79 '05 C.106 B.S. L.596 J.D. [Ⓐ Bodyfelt M.S.&C.]
Durkee, Joe ....'— '97 C.1058 B.A. L.950 J.D. Staff Atty., Amer. Fam. Ins.
Durkheimer, John H., (AV) ....'53 '79 C.668 B.A. L.629 J.D. [Ⓢ M.G.Hanlon]
Dutton, Julie E. ....'68 '00 C.629 B.A. L.950 J.D. [Ⓐ Lachenmeier E.R.&H.]
Du Val, William C. ....'59 '92 C.941 B.A. L.950 J.D. [DuVal B.]
Du Val Business Law PC ....1012 S.W. King Ave., Ste. 103
Duyck, Daniel L. ....'65 '97 C.628 B.A. [Ⓐ Schwabe,W.&W.]
Dwyer, J. Michael, (AV) ....'52 '77 C.112 B.A. L.426 J.D. [Dwyer&M.]
Dwyer, James P., (BV) ....'60 '88 C.629 L.61 J.D. [D.Heiling&Assoc.]

Dwyer & Miller, LLP, (AV)
215 S.W. Washington Street, Suite 200, 97204
Telephone: 503-241-9456 Fax: 503-241-7708
Email: attys@dwyermiller.com URL: http://www.dwyerandmiller.com
J. Michael Dwyer; Lisa Almasy Miller.
Arbitration and Mediation, Family Law, Domestic Relations, Personal Injury.
See Professional Biographies, PORTLAND, OREGON

Dyer, Constance E. '47 '80 C.347 B.A. L.1119 J.D.
(adm. in IN; not adm. in OR) Nityananda Institute Inc.
Dziuba, Daniel C., (AV) ....'48 '75 C.1122 B.A. L.982 J.D. [Tichenor D.&C.]
Eads, Scott D. ....'56 '91 C.834 B.S. L.846 J.D. [Perkins C.] (Pat.)
Eakins, Eileen G. ....'62 '94 C.1060 B.A. L.596 J.D. [Jordan S.]
Earle, William G., (AV) ....'55 '83 C.112 A.B. L.596 J.D. [Davis R.E.&X.]
Easley, Saville W., (BV) ....'62 '92 C.17 B.A. L.629 J.D. [Ⓐ Gevurtz,M.L.&H.]
Eaton, Kristin Winnie ....'69 '96 C&L.1051 B.A., J.D. [Ⓐ Yates,M.&Assoc.]
Ebbett, Patrick M. ....'68 '97 C.882 B.A. L.1051 J.D. 610 S.W. Broadway
Eberhard, Jeffrey D., (BV) ....'61 '87 C.629 B.S. L.950 J.D. [Smith F.&E.]
Eberhardt, Paul E., (AV) '61 '88
C.453 B.S. L.145 J.D. 805 S.W. Broadway, Ste. 1560 (Pat.)
Eckelman, Eugene M., (BV) ....'19 '55 C.999 L.596 LL.B. 2400 S.W. 4th Ave. (Pat.)
Eckert, C. Marie, (AV) ....'57 '88 C.477 B.A. L.597 J.D. [Miller N.]
Eckstein, Lisa Newman ....'55 '89 C.976 B.A. L.477 J.D. P.O. Box 25446
Edelman, Laurence H. ....'49 '74 C.705 B.A. L.1165 J.D. Dept. of Jus.
Edelson, Jeffrey M., (AV) ....'61 '86 C.390 A.B. L.884 J.D. [Markowitz,H.G.&M.]
Eden, Jeffrey S., (AV) ....'60 '85 C.629 B.S. L.596 J.D. [Bullivant H.B.]
Eder, H. Philip, (BV) ....'27 '69 C.911 B.A. L.596 J.D. [Reeves,K.&H.]
Edmonds, Thomas H., (AV) ....'61 '90 C.611 B.A. L.1051 J.D. U.S. Atty. Off.
Edwards, Amy ....'72 '02 C.597 B.A. L.911 J.D. [Ⓐ Stoel R.]
Edwards, Dirk L. ....'54 '79 C&L.950 M.Ad., J.D. 5550 S.W. MacAdam Ave.
Edwards, Richard A., (AV) ....'38 '68 C.628 B.S. L.950 J.D. 111 S.W. Fifth Ave.‡
Edwardsen, J. Chris, (AV) '43 '75
C.911 B.B.A. L.596 J.D. Assoc. Gen. Coun., Freightliner LLC
Eggum, Susan K., (AV) ....'53 '82 C.1375 B.A. L.276 J.D. [S.K.Eggum]

Eggum, Susan K., P.C., Attorneys at Law, (AV)
621 SW Alder, Suite 600, 97205
Telephone: 503-228-9607 Fax: 503-228-5790 Email: susan@eggum.com Email: catherine@eggum.com
Email: stephen@eggum.com URL: http://www.eggum.com
Shareholder: Susan K. Eggum. Associate: Catherine D. Lawson. Of Counsel: Stephen D. Leggatt.
Trial and Appellate Practice in Federal and State Courts. Employment Litigation, Age Discrimination, Sexual Harassment, Construction Defect Litigation, Contract Litigation and Professional Malpractice.
Representative Clients: Geopier Foundation Company Northwest, Inc.; Helix Homes; Al Frank Asset Management, Inc.; Mt. Hood Group, Inc.; Professional Liability Fund.
See Professional Biographies, PORTLAND, OREGON

Egnor, Susan T., (BV) ....'41 '79 C.104 A.B. L.911 J.D. OR Dept. of Jus.
Ehrlich, Paul R. .... '67 '92 C.629 B.S. L.602 J.D. General Coun., Adidas America, Inc.
Eichen, Richard L. ....'54 '78 C.107 B.A. L.596 J.D. Atty., I.R.S.
Eighmey, George V., (BV) ....'41 '72 C&L.339 B.S., J.D. State Legis. Rep.
Eike, Kevin A. ....'75 '01 C.350 B.S. L.546 J.D. [Ⓐ Davis R.E.&X.]
Einowski, Edward D., (AV) ....'53 '78 C&L.477 B.A., J.D. [Stoel R.]
Elfers, Robert J., (AV) ....'36 '61 C.628 B.S. L.629 LL.B. 1211 S.W. 5th Ave.
Elkanich, David J. ....'73 '99 C.37 B.A. L.629 J.D. [Ⓐ Hinshaw&C.]
Elkins, Julie D., (AV) ....'57 '86 L.1051 J.D. 10260 S.W. Greenburg Rd., Ste. 710
Elliott, Amy ....'53 '78 L.1051 J.D. 2455 N.W. Marshall St., Ste. 5
Elliott, Dennis H., (AV) ....'46 '74 C.668 B.A. L.596 J.D. [Elliott&P.]
Elliott, Jerome F., (AV) ....'59 '85 C.339 B.S. L.477 J.D. [Elliott,O.&P.]

Elliott, Ostrander & Preston, P.C., (AV)
Union Bank of California, 707 S.W. Washington Street, Suite 1500, 97205 ⊙
Telephone: 503-224-7112 Fax: 503-224-7819
Email: attorneys@eoplaw.com URL: http://www.eoplaw.com
Karen Wetherell Davis; William A. Drew; Jerome F. Elliott; Matthew W. McClellan (Not admitted in OR); John D. Ostrander; Robert J. Preston. Associates: Harshi M. Liyanage; Sonia A. Montalbano; Jennifer L. Rollins.
General Civil, Trial, and Appellate Practice in State and Federal Courts. Business and Finance Law, Mergers and Acquisitions, Real Estate, Employment, Commercial, Environmental, Insurance, Intellectual Property, Internet Law, Entertainment Law, Personal Injury, Trusts and Estates, and Taxation, Insurance, Copyrights, Licensing, Trademarks, Immigration and Nationality.
Seattle, Washington Office: 707 East Harrison Street, 98102. Telephone: 206-325-2171. Fax: 206-325-3269.
See Professional Biographies, PORTLAND, OREGON

Elliott & Park, (AV)
0324 SW Abernethy Street, 97239-4356
Telephone: 503-227-1690 Fax: 503-274-8384
Members of Firm: Dennis H. Elliott; David D. Park.
General Civil and Trial Practice in State and Federal Courts. Business Litigation, Personal Injury, Communications, Commercial Law, Professional Negligence, Product Liability, Consumer and Securities Fraud, Wrongful Termination, Employment, Auto Accidents, Wrongful Death, Civil Rights.
See Professional Biographies, PORTLAND, OREGON

Ellis, Barnes H., (AV) .... '40 '64 C.976 B.A. L.309 LL.B. [Stoel R.]
Ellis, Daniel C. .... '37 '69 C.893 L.596 J.D. 6915 S.W. Alden St.
Ellis, James R. .... '30 '56 C&L.950 B.A., J.D. Cir. J.
Ellis, Jane E. .... '57 '87 C.629 B.A. L.1051 J.D. [J.Ellis]
Ellis, Joy .... '69 '95 C.976 B.A. L.1051 J.D. [⊠ Garvey S.B.]
Ellis, Paul G., (BV) .... '49 '85 C.352 B.B.A. L.1051 J.D. [⊠ Dunn C.A.H.&T.]
Ellis, Jane .... 621 S.W. Morrison, Ste. 1414
Elmquist, Mareesa M. .... '— '99 C.878 B.A. L.1051 J.D. [⊠ Miller N.]
Elsen, Lura P. .... '56 '81 C.813 B.A. L.770 J.D. 1885 NW Ramsey Drive
Elsner, Paul C., (AV) .... '50 '82 C.385 A.B. L.596 J.D. [Beery&E.]
Elzinga, Ronald H. .... '59 '91 C.774 B.A. L.596 J.D. [Elzinga&Assoc.]
Elzinga & Associates LLC .... 1020 S.W. Taylor St., 8th Fl.
Emery, Chandra .... '— '94 C.893 B.A. L.273 J.D. [⊠ Tonkon T.]
Emory, Carol A., (AV) .... '44 '72 C.438 B.A. L.1066 J.D. [Emory]
Emory Law Group, P.C., (AV) .... 1 South West Columbia
Empey, Dolores J. '53 '88 C.878 B.S. L.596 J.D.
Assoc. Health Plan Coun., Kaiser Found. Health Plan of the Northwest
Enfield, Stephen H. '50 '80 C.911 B.A. L.285 J.D.
(adm. in WA; not adm. in OR) P.O. Box 850
Engel, Brett E., (BV) .... '65 '95 C.882 B.A. L.950 J.D. [Gearing,R.&E.]
Engel, Edward I., (AV) .... '26 '55 C.670 B.A. L.596 J.D. 6209 S.W. Tower Way‡
Engelstad, Kurt .... '37 '72 C.628 B.S. L.596 J.D. WABS
Englander, Beth Shara .... '70 '98 C.454 B.A. L.629 J.D. Friends of the Columbia Gorge
English, Stephen F., (AV) .... '48 '73 C.629 B.A. L.1065 J.D. [Bullivant H.B.]
English, Trisha J. .... '80 '05 C.911 B.A. L.1117 J.D. [⊠ Stahancyk,K.J.&H.]
Englund, Gregory J., (AV) .... '56 '81 C&L.950 B.S., J.D. [Hooper,E.&W.]
Enloe, Jay D., (AV) .... '51 '76 C&L.629 B.A., J.D. [Lachenmeier E.R.&H.]
Enos, P. Beth '52 '81 C&L.836 B.A., J.D.
Inst. Legal Writing, Northwestern Sch. of Law
Epstein, Edward L., (AV) .... '36 '62 C.813 A.B. L.309 LL.B. [Stoel R.]
Epstein, Lawrence L. .... '52 '79 C.645 B.S. L.575 J.D. [L.Epstein]
Epstein, Larry, P.C. .... 1020 S.W. Taylor St., Ste. 730
Eraut, Allen E. .... '— '99 C.770 B.S. L.629 J.D. [⊠ Bullivant H.B.]
Erfle, Nancy M., (AV) .... '65 '90 C.86 B.A. L.950 J.D. [Schwabe,W.&W.]
Erickson, Arthur W. .... '41 '75 C.629 B.S. L.1066 J.D. P.O. Box 14868
Erickson, Burdette W., (Mr.) .... '12 '34 L.596 LL.B. 3311 N.E. 12th St.‡
Erickson, Christopher D. .... '74 '01 C&L.629 B.S., J.D. [⊠ Tonkon T.]
Ericsson, Robert J., (AV) .... '53 '78 C&L.629 B.A., J.D. [Ericsson R.]
Ericsson Ridgeway, P.C., (AV) .... 222 S.W. Columbia St.
Eriksen, Thomas B., (BVⓉ) .... '57 '84 C.628 B.S. L.950 J.D. [Jordan S.]
Eriksson, Xan Marie .... '75 '98 C.154 B.A. L.629 J.D. 1 Sw Columbia St Ste 555
Erland, Alan S. .... '51 '76 C.628 B.S. L.629 J.D. 3622 S.W. Iowa St.
Ernst, David A., (AV) .... '60 '85 C.628 B.S. L.569 J.D. [Bullivant H.B.]
Esler, Michael J., (AV) .... '45 '71 C&L.145 B.A., J.D. [Esler,S.&B.]

Esler, Stephens & Buckley, (AV)
700 Pioneer Tower, 888 SW Fifth Avenue, 97204-2021
Telephone: 503-223-1510 Fax: 503-294-3995
Members of Firm: Michael J. Esler; John W. Stephens; Kim T. Buckley.
General Civil, Trial and Appellate Practice. Complex Litigation, Private, Business and Non-Profit Corporations, Securities, Franchises, Banking, Energy and Telecommunications, Patent Litigation and Intellectual Property Law, Antitrust, Public Utility, Municipal, Real Estate, Administrative and Commercial Law.
See Professional Biographies, PORTLAND, OREGON

Esterkin, James .... '53 '80 C.1168 B.A. L.1051 J.D. [J.N.Esterkin]
Esterkin, James N. .... 210 S.W. Morrison, Ste. 600
Estes, Ernest E. '51 '76 C.312 B.A. L.950 J.D.
U.S. Dept. of Energy/Bonneville Power Admin.-Gen. Coun. Off.
Etter, John C., (BV) .... '51 '78 C.911 B.A. L.285 J.D. 921 S.W. Washington St., Ste. 755
Ettinger, Lainie Keslin '67 '96 C.112 B.A. L.659 J.D.
(adm. in CO; not adm. in OR) Lewis & Clark College
Evans, Cary Christopher .... '67 '95 C.154 B.A. L.1358 J.D. Field Dir.
Evans, Charles S. .... '22 '59 C.112 A.B. L.596 LL.B. Admin. Law J., Soc. Sec. Admn.
Evans, George L. .... '21 '61 C.629 A.B. L.596 LL.B. 2527 N.E. Brazee St.‡
Evans, James F. .... '62 '89 C&L.950 B.S., J.D. 200 S.W. Carey Lane
Evans, Jeff N. .... '— '03 C.635 B.S. L.1117 J.D. [⊠ Davis W.T.]
Evans, Lawrence, (BV) .... '50 '75 C.629 B.S. L.569 J.D. [Grenley,R.E.B.&B.]
Evans, Michael S., (BV) '59 '85 C&L.629 B.S., J.D.
5331 S.W. Macadam Ave., Ste. 299
Evans, Thomas L. .... '— '94 C.893 B.S.E.E. L.1209 J.D. [Banner&W.] (See Pat. Sect.)
Evans, Walter H., III, (AV) .... '41 '67 C.629 B.S. L.950 J.D. [Schwabe,W.&W.]

Evans, Kathleen A., Attorney at Law
(See Salem)

Everhart, Tad .... '56 '84 C.813 A.B. L.629 J.D. Asst. Dist. Atty.
Evers, Erin Michele .... '65 '01 C.1056 B.S. L.1051 J.D. 2722 Ne 33rd Ave
Eves, Mark W., (BV) .... '50 '75 C.56 B.A. L.190 J.D. [Eves&W.]
Eves & Wade, (AV) .... 3236 S.W. Kelly Ave.
Ewert, Lowell M. '53 '78 C.999 B.A. L.900 J.D.
(adm. in KS; not adm. in OR) Mercy Corps Intl.
Eyerman, Linda K., (AV) .... '48 '76 C.239 B.A. L.629 J.D. [Gaylord&E.]
Fabrizio, Thomas A. '49 '79 C.860 B.A. L.1202 J.D.
(adm. in MA; not adm. in OR) 1025 N.E. 33rd Ave.‡
Faddis, Annalie M. .... '72 '99 C.950 L.629 J.D. [⊠ Abbott&P.]
Fagan, David G. .... '67 '98 L.596 J.D. [⊠ Schwabe,W.&W.]
Fair, Samantha .... '64 '90 C.685 B.A. L.1051 J.D. [⊠ Dunn C.A.H.&T.]
Fallgren, Burton J., (BV) .... '28 '53 C.581 L.596 LL.B. 7318 N. Leavitt Ave.
Falls, Wm. David .... '49 '76 C.835 B.S. L.845 S.J.D. [W.D.Falls]
Falls, Wm. David, P.C. .... 5410 S.W. Macadam, Ste. 270
Farleigh, F. Scott, (AV) .... '46 '74 C&L.629 B.S., LL.B. [Farleigh W.]

Farleigh Witt, Attorneys at Law, (AV)
121 SW Morrison Street, Suite 600, 97204
Telephone: 503-228-6044 FAX: 503-228-1741
Email: farleighwitt.com URL: http://www.farleighwitt.com
F. Scott Farleigh; Brian R. Witt; Karen E. Saul; Dean T. Sandow; Valerie Tomasi Auerbach; Peter C. McKittrick; Brad C. Stanford; Harold B. Scoggins, III; David R. Ludwig; Kathryn P. Salyer; Tara J. Schleicher;—Michelle M. Bertolino; Robert N. Muraski; Kimberley A. Hanks Mc Gair; Michelle Holman Kerin; Connie L. Speck. Of Counsel: Laury H. Hennings.
Banking, Bankruptcy, Commercial Litigation, Corporate, Electronic Commerce, Employment, Environmental, Estate Planning and Administration, Financial Services, Insurance Defense, Mediation/Arbitration, Real Estate, Securities, Trademark and General Business Practice.
See Professional Biographies, PORTLAND, OREGON

Farley, Eugene D., (AV) .... '10 '45 C.966 A.B. L.262 J.D. 2400 S.W. 4th Ave. (Pat.)
Farnell, Michael E. .... '64 '92 C.950 B.A. L.988 J.D. [Parsons F.&G.]

Farr, Mary Ellen Page, (AV) '48 '82 C.1056 B.A. L.1051 J.D.
0324 S.W. Abernethy Street, 97239
Telephone: 503-224-9133 Fax: 503-827-5060
Email: mefarr@qwest.net
Litigation, Business Litigation, Employment Law, Sexual Harassment, Wrongful Termination, Personal Injury, Insurance Coverage, Discrimination, Automobile Accidents, Premises Liability, Negligence, Wrongful Death, Slip and Fall, Contracts, Business Law.
See Professional Biographies, PORTLAND, OREGON

Farrell, Michael J. .... '64 '89 C.629 B.A. L.180 J.D. [Martin,B.T.L.&H.]
Farver, William M. '48 '83 C.951 B.A. L.1051 J.D.
Exec. Asst., Multnomah Co. Comm.
Fassell, Mary M. .... '49 '89 C.112 B.S. L.1065 J.D. 714 S.E. Franklin St.
Faucette, Tamara L. .... '69 '95 C.101 B.A. L.596 J.D. [⊠ Cable H.B.H.&L.]
Faust, John R., Jr., (AV) .... '32 '58 C&L.629 B.S., J.D. [Schwabe,W.&W.]
Faveluke, Martin, (BV) .... '40 '73 C&L.596 B.S., J.D. [Martindale&F.]
Fay, Claire M. '55 '81 C.1044 B.A. L.107 J.D.
(adm. in DC; not adm. in OR) 2938 S.W. Comus St.‡
Fedde, G. Bernhard .... '09 '36 C.951 A.B. L.629 J.D. 1919 N.W. Ramsey Crest‡
Feichtinger, Mark R., (AV) '48 '78 C.597 B.A. L.477 J.D.
[Stoel R.] (⊙Vancouver, WA)
Feldman, Stephen M. .... '67 '95 C.103 B.A. L.596 J.D. [⊠ Perkins C.]
Feldman, Steven .... '54 '89 L.809 J.D. 5550 S.W. Macadam Ave., Ste. 330
Feldman, Steven H. .... '52 '79 C.629 B.A. L.950 J.D. 931 SW King Ave.
Fell, James F., (AV) .... '44 '70 C.602 B.A. L.608 J.D. [Stoel R.]
Fellows, Douglas M., (BV) .... '40 '68 C.629 L.596 J.D. 6110 S.W. Lesser Way
Felstiner, Susan Trump .... '65 '94 C.1051 B.A. L.596 J.D. [Cable H.B.H.&L.]
Feltz, Eugene E., (AV) .... '27 '51 C.670 L.770 LL.B. 110 S.W. 6th Ave.‡
Fennell, Michael V., (AV) '57 '83
C&L.629 B.S., J.D. V.P. & Gen. Coun., Trail Blazers Inc.
Fernández, Richard M. .... '57 '96 C.999 B.A. L.1066 J.D. V.P., US Bank
Ferreira, Aaron S. .... '72 '00 C.1074 B.A. L.596 J.D. 806 Sw Broadway Ste 550
Ferreira, Louis A., IV, (AV) '63 '90
C.906 B.A. L.336 J.D. [Stoel R.] (⊙Vancouver, WA)
Ferris, Kassim M. .... '68 '96 C.172 B.S.M.E. L.950 J.D. [⊠ Stoel R.] (See Pat. Sect.)
Ferris, Kimball H., (AV) .... '47 '78 C.976 B.A. L.950 J.D. [Bullivant H.B.]
Feuerherdt, Stefan .... '63 '92 C.1111 B.A. L.259 J.D. [⊠ Dunn C.A.H.&T.]
Feuerstein, Howard M., (AV) .... '39 '63 C&L.880 B.A., J.D. [Stoel R.]
Field, Allen W. .... '60 '88 C.685 B.A. L.629 J.D. [⊠ Birdwell&J.]
Field, Daniel J. .... '62 '90 C.950 B.A. L.629 J.D. Kaiser Permanente
Field, Joseph A., (BV) .... '57 '94 C.4 B.A. L.596 J.D. [Field&Assoc.]
Field & Associates, (BV) .... 610 SW Alder Street, Suite 910
Fife, Christiane R. .... '77 '04 C.911 B.A. L.629 J.D. [⊠ Schwabe,W.&W.]
Fig, William G. .... '67 '95 C.575 B.A. L.1051 J.D. [⊠ Sussman S.]
Filippi, David E. .... '69 '96 C.375 B.S. L.596 J.D. [Stoel R.]
Finders, Lee, (BV) .... '22 '50 C.352 B.A. L.273 J.D. 7235 N.E. Sandy Blvd.
Fink, Karen L. .... '45 '77 C.476 B.S. L.1051 J.D. 1915 N.W. Yorkshire Lane‡
Finklea, Edward A., (AV) .... '51 '84 C.494 B.A. L.1051 J.D. [Cable H.B.H.&L.]
Finn, James M., (AV) .... '47 '79 C.1209 B.A. L.893 J.D. [Schwabe,W.&W.]

Fiorino, Margaret, (AV) '49 '82 C.628 B.A. L.629 J.D.
P.O. Box 14068, 97293-0068
Mailing Address: P.O. Box 14068, Portland, OR 97293-0068
Telephone: 503-224-1551 Facsimile: 503-233-0785
Email: mfiorino@easystreet.com URL: http://www.lawyers.com/fiorinolaw
Trust and Estate Litigation, Insurance Coverage Litigation, Elder Financial Abuse Litigation, Guardianship and Conservatorship Litigation, Contested Wills, Medical Malpractice, Appellate Practice, Wrongful Death, Probate Litigation.
See Professional Biographies, PORTLAND, OREGON

Firestone, Gary, (AV) .... '52 '87 C.012 B.A. L.37 J.D. 1727 N.W. Hoyt Street
Fischer, Danielle L. .... '— '97 C.97 B.S. L.273 J.D. 1000 Sw Broadway Ste 1100

Fischer, Justine, (AV) '46 '72 C.788 A.B. L.145 J.D.
720 S.W. Washington Street, Suite 750, 97205
Telephone: 503-222-4326 Telecopier: 503-222-6567
Email: jfattyor@aol.com
Securities, Antitrust and Business Litigation and Class Actions in Federal and State Courts.
See Professional Biographies, PORTLAND, OREGON

Fish, Jeff .... '63 '88 C.945 B.A. L.128 J.D. Metro. Pub. Def.
Fish, Jerry R., (AV) .... '49 '82 C.674 A.B. L.1051 J.D. [Stoel R.]
Fish, Nicholas S., (AV) .... '58 '87 C.309 B.A. L.588 J.D. [Meyer&W.]

Fisher, Ann L., (AV) '48 '84 C.628 B.S. L.950 J.D.
AF Legal and Consulting Services
2005 SW 71st Avenue, 97225-3705
Telephone: 503-721-0181 Fax: 503-223-2305 Email: afisherl@qwest.net
Email: enerGlaw@aol.com URL: http://www.lawyers.com/annfisher
General Business and Commercial Law, Contracts and Litigation, Real Estate, Energy and Utility Law, Mediation Services.
See Professional Biographies, PORTLAND, OREGON

Fisher, George P., Attorney at Law '49 '91 C.323 B.A. L.585 J.D.
3635 S.W. Dosch Road, 97239-1427
Telephone: 503-224-7730 Fax: 503-227-2429
Email: george.fisher@gpf-law.com URL: http://www.gpf-law.com
Labor Law, Employment Law, Contracts.
See Professional Biographies, PORTLAND, OREGON

Fisher, Kelsey L. .... '71 '96 C.629 B.A. L.1051 J.D. [⊠ Schulte,A.D.A.&B.]
Fisher, Melvin Jack, Jr. .... '51 '91 C.629 B.S. L.596 J.D. 1300 Sw 5th Ave Ste 1700
Fisher, Valerie D., (AV) .... '49 '74 C.813 B.A. L.629 J.D. [Ater W.]

Fisher & Phillips LLP, (AV) BB
Suite 1600, 1001 S.W. Fifth Avenue, 97204 ⊙
Telephone: 503-242-4262 Fax: 503-242-4263
Email: fp@laborlawyers.com URL: http://www.laborlawyers.com
Members of Firm: Clarence M. Belnavis; Richard R. Meneghello. Senior Counsel: Corbett Gordon. Of Counsel: Mitchell C. Baker. Associates: Rachelle Hong Barton; Heidi Guettler; Joseph J. Haddad.
Labor and Employment, Alternative Dispute Resolution, Arbitration, Business Immigration, Collective Bargaining, Employment Discrimination, Labor Relations, Mergers, Acquisitions and Divestitures, Occupational Safety and Health, Pension and Benefits, Sexual Harassment, Wage and Hour, Whistleblower Litigation, Wrongful Termination.
Atlanta, Georgia Office: 1500 Resurgens Plaza, 945 East Paces Ferry Road, 30326-1125. Telephone: 404-231-1400. Fax: 404-240-4249.
Charlotte, North Carolina Office: Suite 2020, 227 West Trade Street, 28202. Telephone: 704-334-4565. Fax: 704-334-9774.
Chicago, Illinois Office: 1000 Marquette Building, 140 South Dearborn Street, 60603. Telephone: 312-346-8061. Fax: 312-346-3179.
Columbia, South Carolina Office: Suite 1400, 1901 Main Street, 29201. Telephone: 803-255-0000. Fax: 803-255-0202.
Dallas, Texas Office: 4343 Thanksgiving Tower, 1601 Elm Street, 75201. Telephone: 214-220-9100. Fax: 214-220-9122.
Fort Lauderdale, Florida Office: Suite 800, 450 East Las Olas Boulevard, 33301. Telephone: 954-525-4800. Fax: 954-525-8739.
Irvine, California Office: Suite 400, 18400 Von Karman Avenue, 92612. Telephone: 949-851-2424. Fax: 949-851-0152.
Kansas City, Missouri Office: Suite 400, 104 West Ninth Street, 64105. Telephone: 816-842-8770. Fax: 816-842-8767.
Las Vegas, Nevada Office: Suite 650, 3993 Howard Hughes Parkway, 89109. Telephone: 702-252-3131. Fax: 702-252-7411.
New Orleans, Louisiana Office: Suite 3710, 201 St. Charles Avenue, 70170. Telephone: 504-522-3303. Fax: 504-529-3850.
Oakland, California Office: City Center, Suite 200, 501 Fourteenth Street, 94612. Telephone: 510-763-4411. Fax: 510-763-4418.
Orlando, Florida Office: 1250 Lincoln Plaza, 300 South Orange Avenue, 32801. Telephone: 407-541-0888. Fax: 407-541-0887.
San Diego, California Office: 4225 Executive Square, Suite 950, La Jolla, California, 92037. Telephone: 858-597-9600. Fax: 858-597-9601.
Somerset, New Jersey Office: Corporate Park III, Third Floor, 580 Howard Avenue, 08873. Telephone: 732-560-7100. Fax: 732-560-0788.
Tampa, Florida Office: Suite 2525, 401 East Jackson Street, 33602. Telephone: 813-769-7500. Fax: 813-769-7501.

See Professional Biographies, PORTLAND, OREGON

Fishleder, Barbara S., (BV) .... '54 '79 C.477 B.B.A. L.365 J.D. 533 S.W. Colony Dr.
Fitzhenry, James A., (AV) '55 '81 C.629 B.A. L.950 J.D.
Sr. V.P., Gen. Coun. & Secy., FLIR Systems, Inc.
Fitzpatrick, Brian Casey .... '73 '01 C.629 B.A. L.336 J.D. [Ⓐ Klarquist S.]
Fitzsimon, Kenneth M. .... '45 '72 C.145 L.1148 J.D. 1730 N. E. Brazee St.
Fjordbeck, Marvin D., (BV) .... '57 '83 C&L.629 B.A., J.D. 600 Ne Grand Ave
Flanagan, Brien J. .... '74 '02 C.602 B.A. L.276 J.D. [Ⓐ Schwabe,W.&W.]
Fletcher, Michael W. .... '70 '97 C&L.502 B.S., J.D. [Ⓐ Tonkon T.]
Flynn, Frank M. .... '48 '92 C.70 B.A. L.1051 J.D. [Ⓒ Perkins C.]
Flynn, Meagan, (AV) .... '67 '92 C.950 B.A. L.285 J.D. [Ⓐ Preston B.&F.]
Fogarty, Jean .... '54 '81 C.112 B.A. L.629 J.D. Dept. of Jus.
Fogg, George K., (AV) .... '47 '73 C.165 A.B. L.966 J.D. [Perkins C.]
Folawn, John S., (AV) .... '— '71 C.629 B.S. L.1065 J.D. [Kirklin F.]
Foldes, Katherine .... '49 '76 C.104 A.B. L.629 J.D. 13360 N.W. Northrup St.
Foley, Ridgway K., Jr., (AV) .... '37 '63 C.1051 B.S. L.629 J.D. [Ⓒ Greene&M.]
Follansbee, Julia A. .... '49 '86 C.508 B.A. L.629 J.D. Law Clk. for U.S. Appellate J.
Follett, Herald M. .... '39 '72 C.999 B.A. L.950 J.D. P.O. Box 3092
Fontana, Ronald A., (BV) .... '51 '76 C.112 B.A. L.629 J.D. 721 Sw Oak St 2nd Flr
Foote, Jeffrey P., (AV) .... '49 '74 C.629 B.S. L.1051 J.D. [J.Foote&Assoc.]

Foote, Jeffrey, & Associates, P.C., (AV) BB
1515 S.W. Fifth Avenue, Suite 808, 97201
Telephone: 503-228-1133 Fax: 503-228-1556
Email: jfoote@footelaw.com URL: http://www.footelaw.com
Jeffrey P. Foote;—Ronald F. Webster.
Civil Trial Practice including Personal Injury, Vehicle Rollover and Auto Products Liability, Professional Negligence, Medical Malpractice, Products Liability, Automobile Accidents, Wrongful Death, Legal Malpractice.

See Professional Biographies, PORTLAND, OREGON

Foraker, David A., (AV) .... '56 '81 C.492 B.S. L.629 J.D. [Greene&M.]
Ford, Charles A. '53 '84
C.1027 B.S. L.911 J.D. Corp. Coun., Schnitzer Steel Industries, Inc.
Ford, Patrick, (BV) .... '32 '58 C&L.770 A.B., LL.B. [P.Ford]
Ford, Stephen S. .... '60 '92 C.906 B.S.E.E. L.950 J.D. [Marger J.&M.] (See Pat. Sect.)
Ford, Susan L. .... '65 '94 C.597 B.S. L.276 J.D. [Ⓐ Bullivant H.B.]
Ford, Susan S., (AV) .... '58 '84 C.1051 B.A. L.596 J.D. [Sussman S.]
Ford, Patrick, P.C., (BV) .... 0305 S.W. Montgomery St.
Forester, J. Richard .... '44 '70 C.569 B.A. L.262 J.D. 728 N.W. Skyline Blvd.
Forman, David Copley, (AV) .... '— '89 C&L.477 B.A., J.D. [Ⓒ Tonkon T.]
Forrest, Brian G .... '— '02 C.911 B.S.M.E. L.596 J.D. [Ⓐ Marger J.&M.]
Forseth, Danelle C. .... '73 '04 C.906 B.S. L.1051 J.D. [Ⓐ Bradach]
Forst, Mary C. .... '41 '72 C.1150 B.A. L.213 J.D. Confluence Northwest
Fortino, Paul T., (AV) .... '45 '75 C.477 B.B.A. L.602 J.D. [Perkins C.]
Fortner, Richard L., (AV) '62 '92
C.628 B.S.N.E. L.950 J.D. Corp. Coun, Freightliner LLC
Forum 500, (BV) .... 4380 S.W. Macadam Ave., Ste. 500
Foster, Anne D. .... '70 '99 C&L.629 B.A., J.D. [Ⓐ Dunn C.A.H.&T.]
Foster, David R., (AV) .... '52 '79 C.1275 B.A. L.37 J.D. [Bullivant H.B.]
Foster, David S. .... '69 '03 C.629 B.A. L.596 J.D. [Ⓐ Sokol&A.]
Foster, Mark E., (AV) .... '48 '81 C.27 B.A. L.1065 J.D. 4250 S.W. Dosch Road
Foster, Randolph C., (AV) .... '52 '78 C.678 B.A. L.276 J.D. [Stoel R.]
Foster, Teresa L. .... '66 '97 C&L.36 B.S.W., J.D. [Ⓐ Stahancyk,K.J.&H.]

Foster Pepper Tooze LLP, (AV)
601 S.W. Second Avenue, Suite 1800, 97204-3171 ⊙
Telephone: 503-221-0607 Facsimile: 503-221-1510
URL: http://www.foster.com
New Address Effective October 25, 2003: 601 SW Second Avenue, Suite 1800, Portland, Oregon 97204-3171.
James P. Weter (1877-1959); F. M. Roberts (1880-1973); W. V. Tanner (1881-1953); John P. Garvin (1888-1972); Harold S. Shefelman (1898-1984); James C. Harper (1915-1993); Arthur S. Quigley (Not admitted in OR; Retired); Thomas B. Foster (1915-1999); Willard Hatch (Not admitted in OR; Retired). Resident Partners of Firm: Neale E. Creamer; Gordon E. Crim; Michael J. Gentry; Paul B. George; Curt B. Gleaves; William P. Hutchison; Joel S. Kaplan; Janet Knauss Larsen; Carter M. Mann; Walter W. McMonies, Jr.; Andrew J. Morrow, Jr.; Tod A. Northman; Nancie K. Potter; Gregory L. Powell; Kenneth E. Roberts; Michael R. Silvey. Resident Associates: Jeremy R. Bader; H. Faith Graham; Andrew H. Ognall; Elia E. Popovich; Kathleen Profitt; Marisol Ricoy; Charmin B. Shiely; Cliff E. Spencer.
Banks and Banking, Business Law, Business Acquisitions, Divestitures and Reorganizations, Civil Litigation, Cooperative Law, Corporate Finance, Corporate Law, Creditor's Rights and Bankruptcy, Emerging Companies and High Growth Companies, Environmental Law, Estate Planning, Health Care, Intellectual Property, Labor and Employment, Land Use, Real Estate, Securities, Sports Law, Taxation.

(This Listing Continued)

Foster Pepper Tooze LLP (Continued)
Seattle, Washington Office: Foster Pepper & Shefelman PLLC, 34th Floor, 1111 Third Avenue. Telephone: 206-447-4400. Facsimile: 206-447-9700.
Spokane, Washington Office: Foster Pepper & Shefelman PLLC, W. 422 Riverside Avenue, Suite 1310. Telephone: 509-777-1600. Facsimile: 509-777-1616.

See Professional Biographies, PORTLAND, OREGON

Fotheringham, Robert C. '59 '86 C.878 B.A. L.101 J.D.
(adm. in UT; not adm. in OR) [Vial F.]
Fowler, Arthur Baird, V ...... '70 '98 C.282 B.A. L.1348 J.D. [Ⓐ G.M.Bullock&Assoc.]
Fowlks, Richard E., (BV) .... '49 '75 C.628 B.S. L.1051 J.D. 1607 NE 41st Ave.
Fox, Kenneth H. .... '55 '85 C.112 B.A. L.596 J.D. Portland State Univ.
Fox, Kevin T. .... '70 '05 C.112 B.S. L.1066 J.D. [Ⓐ Stoel R.]
Frager, Larry N. .... '44 '70 C.629 B.A. L.1068 J.D. 720 S.W. Washington St.
France, Renee M. .... '72 '00 C.769 B.A. L.596 J.D. [Ⓐ Ball J.]
Francesconi, James L., (AV) .... '52 '78 C.813 B.A. L.629 J.D. [Ⓒ Haglund,K.H.&J.]
Franco, Deanna L. .... '75 '01 C.1056 B.S. L.950 J.D. [Ⓐ Smith&D.]
Frank, Lawrence S. .... '53 '86 C.352 B.S. L.1051 J.D. Standard Ins. Co.
Frank, Stephen R., (AV) .... '— '67 L.950 J.D. [Ⓒ Williams,K.&G.P.]
Franklin, Holley Young .... '57 '83 C.628 B.S. L.950 J.D. Standard Ins. Co.
Frantz, Julie E. .... '48 '75 C.813 B.A. L.596 J.D. Cir. J.
Frantz, Mary Ann, P.C., (AV) .... '53 '78 C&L.813 B.A., J.D. [Miller N.]
Franzke, Richard A., (AV) .... '35 '60 C&L.950 B.S., J.D. [Stoel R.]
Frasch, Pamela D. .... '58 '85 C.494 B.A. L.1035 J.D. Animal Legal Defense Fund
Fraser, Cynthia M. .... '— '87 C&L.629 B.A., J.D. [Ⓒ Garvey S.B.]
Fraser, George H., (AV) .... '17 '47 C.966 B.A. L.309 LL.B. [Stoel R.] ‡
Fraser, Sara V. Aiken .... '45 '88 C.628 B.A. L.950 J.D. Sr. Atty., Standard Ins. Co.
Fraser, Thomas J., (AV) .... '51 '85 C&L.629 B.S., J.D. [Hagen O.]
Frassetto, Eugene A., (AV) .... '50 '84 C.628 B.S. L.950 J.D. [Stoel R.]
Fredrickson, Floyd A., (AV) .... '27 '52 C&L.813 A.B., LL.B. [Williams F.] ‡
Freed, Dennis N., (AV) .... '48 '74 C.628 B.S. L.1051 J.D. [Smith F.&E.]
Freeman, Clifford L., (AV) .... '44 '77 C&L.629 B.S., J.D. Cir.J.
Freeman, Roxane J. .... '45 '80 C.208 B.A. L.596 J.D. Bonneville Power Admin.
French, Pilar Cortwright .... '— '96 C.597 B.A. L.347 J.D. [Ⓐ Lane P.]
Friedenberg, Samuel C., (AV) '57 '85
C.860 B.A. L.596 J.D. 6500 S.W. Macadam Ave., Ste. 300
Friedman, Eric R., (AV) .... '53 '78 C.668 B.A. L.596 J.D. 2839 S.W. 2nd Ave., Ste. B
Friedman, Jonathan M., (BV) .... '58 '84 C.118 B.A. L.596 J.D. [J.Friedman]
Friedman, Mark E., (AV) .... '47 '73 C&L.339 B.S., J.D. [Garvey S.B.]
Friedman, Michele L. .... '58 '85 C.628 B.S. L.596 J.D. 1020 S.W. Taylor St.
Friedman, Jon, (BV) .... 1020 S.W. Taylor, Ste. 430
Friel, Mark A. .... '73 '00 C.950 B.A. L.1375 J.D. [Ⓐ Stoll S.B.L.&S.]
Frink, Norman W., (AV) .... '52 '77 C.393 B.A. L.902 J.D. Chief Dep. Dist. Atty.
Frisch, Paul R., (AV) ..... '49 '75 C.169 B.A. L.629 J.D. Gen. Coun., Oregon Med. Assn.
Fritz, Kathryn J.S. '57 '96 C.791 B.S.N. L.596 J.D.
Corp. Coun., Northwest Permanente, P.C., Physicians & Surgeons
Friz, Richard M., (BV) .... '46 '75 C.312 B.B.A. L.1051 J.D. [R.M.Friz]
Friz, Richard M., PC, (BV) .... Suite 902, 620 SW, 5th Avenue
Froebe, Gerald A., (AV) ..... '35 '62 C&L.629 B.B.A., LL.B. 1109 S.W. Ardmore Avenue
Froemming, Holli .... '— '05 C.1081 B.A. L.477 J.D. [Ⓐ Jaqua&W.] ⊙
Fruchtengarten, Zachary J. .... '74 '01 C&L.629 B.S., J.D. [Ⓐ Gevurtz,M.L.&H.]
Frye, Helen J. .... '30 '66 C&L.629 B.A., LL.B. U.S. Sr. Dist. J.
Fuchs, Alicia A., (AV) ..... '61 '87 C&L.285 B.A., J.D. 2125 SW Fourth Street, Suite 600
Fuchs, Mark A. '63 '93 C.1051 B.S. L.950 J.D.
Louisiana-Pacific Corporation (⊙Nashville, TN)
Fullem, Greg D .... '68 '95 C.858 B.A. L.950 J.D. [Ⓐ Schwabe,W.&W.]
Fullerton, Ky .... '74 '02 C.276 A.B. L.629 J.D. [Ⓐ Miller N.]
Fulop, Eugene I., (BV) .... '23 '52 C.629 B.S. L.596 LL.B. 424 N.W. 19th
Funk, Richard W. .... '48 '86 C.927 B.A. L.596 J.D. [Ⓐ Gevurtz,M.L.&H.]
Funk, William F. '45 '74 C.309 B.A. L.178 J.D.
(adm. in NY; not adm. in OR) Prof. of Law, Northwestern Sch. of Law
Furlong, Michael D. .... '73 '02 C.37 B.A. L.950 J.D. [Ⓐ Schwabe,W.&W.]
Furnanz, Kari .... '70 '96 C.628 B.S. L.950 J.D. 1000 S.W. Broadway, Ste. 2000
Furness, Paulette A. .... '44 '85 C.452 B.A. L.93 J.D. Archdiocese of Portland
Furniss, Anthony W., (AV) .... '47 '73 C&L.950 B.S., J.D. [Furniss,S.&L.]
Furniss, Shearer & Leineweber, (AV) .... 1500 S.W. First Avenue, Suite 700
Gabin, Sara L., P.C.
(See Lake Oswego)
Gabriel, Craig J. .... '71 '01 C.178 B.S. L.276 J.D. [Ⓐ Ransom B.]
Gadd, Michael S. .... '64 '90 C.790 B.A. L.477 J.D. [Ⓐ Perkins C.]
Gadinas, Peter J. .... '56 '84 9780 S.W. Shady Lane
Gadon, John H., (AV) .... '— '83 C.103 A.B. L.911 J.D. [Lane P.]
Galbi, Elmer W. '— '61 C.705 B.S. L.276 J.D.
(adm. in NY; not adm. in OR; See Pat. Sect.) [Ⓒ Marger J.&M.]
Galbreath, William A. .... '30 '59 C&L.950 B.A., LL.B. [Ⓒ Tichenor D.&C.]
Galen, Morris J., (AV) .... '— '50 C&L.629 B.S., J.D. [Tonkon T.]
Gallagher, Stephen L., Jr. .... '39 '68 C.103 A.B. L.629 J.D. Cir. J.
Galloway, George M., (AV) .... '48 '75 C.165 A.B. L.477 J.D. [Stoel R.]
Galton, Sidney A. .... '47 '72 C.813 A.B. L.1066 J.D. Cir. J.
Galton, Zanley F., (BV) .... '40 '65 C.597 A.B. L.1066 LL.B. [Ⓒ Opton&U.]
Gamblin, Amanda T. .... '68 '02 C.610 B.A. L.1051 J.D. [Ⓐ Schwabe,W.&W.]
Game, Rachel .... '70 '97 C.35 B.G.S. L.950 J.D. 2724 S.E. 20th Ave.
Gamson, Paul B., (AV) .... '50 '82 C.1071 B.S. L.596 J.D. [Smith,G.D.&O.]
Gangle, Michael L. .... '58 '97 C.629 B.S. L.950 J.D. [Ⓐ Opton&U.]
Gann, Steve D. .... '27 '56 C.629 B.S. L.596 LL.B. Gann Publishing Co.
Gannett, David G. .... '58 '93 C.172 B.S. L.596 J.D. [Meyer,E.&G.]
Gannicott, Gordon S., (AV) ..... '59 '84 C&L.893 B.A., J.D. 1500 S.W. 1st Ave., Ste. 700
Ganz, Bradley M. .... '61 '89 C.112 B.S. L.426 J.D. P.O. Box 10105 (Pat.)
Ganz, Mark B. '60 '86 C&L.276 A.B., J.D.
Vice President & Chief Legal Officer, Regence Group
Garber, Bradley G., (CV) .... '54 '87 C.958 B.S. L.629 J.D. [Ⓐ Radler,B.R.&M.]
García Tagle, Ricardo Alberto '68 '96
C.1273 B.S. L.1051 J.D. Atty., Housing Auth. of Portland
Gardiner, Gloria ....'52 '85 C.477 B.F.A. L.629 J.D. 2806 N.E. 63rd Ave.‡
Gardner, Andrew R., (AV) .... '53 '79 C&L.893 B.A., J.D. [Stoel R.]
Gardner, James N., (AV) .... '46 '74 C&L.976 B.A., J.D. 111 S.W. Columbia Street
Gardner, Jeffrey C. .... '52 '98 C.670 B.A. L.596 J.D. [Ball J.]
Gardner, Lynda Nelson, (AV) '48 '76
C.112 A.B. L.1065 J.D. 111 S.W. Columbia St., Ste. 810
Garner, Daniel T. .... '54 '91 C.629 B.S. L.1051 J.D. Freightliner Corp.
Garone, Michael T., (AV) .... '56 '80 C.1349 B.A. L.629 J.D. [Schwabe,W.&W.]
Garrahan, Paul A. .... '65 '98 C&L.893 B.A., J.D. 600 NE Grand Avenue
Garrett, Christopher L. '73 '01 C.685 B.A. L.145 J.D.
(adm. in NY; not adm. in OR) [Ⓐ Perkins C.]
Garrett, Jeffry S. .... '— '00 C.629 B.A. L.950 J.D. [Ⓐ Lane P.]

Garrett, Hemann, Robertson, Jennings, Comstock & Trethewy, P.C.
(See Salem)

Garten, Allan M., (AV) .... '50 '75 C.197 B.A. L.260 J.D. Asst. U.S. Atty.

Garvey Schubert Barer, (AV)
Eleventh Floor, 121 S.W. Morrison Street, 97204 ⊙
Telephone: 503-228-3939 Fax: 503-226-0259
URL: http://www.GSBlaw.com
Owners: Richard Baroway; A. Jeffery Bird; Larry J. Brant; Kathleen C. Bricken; Christine P. Brown; David L. Canary; Stephen J. Connolly; Keith S. Dubanevich; Mark E. Friedman; Robert R. Griffith; Eric A. Lindenauer; Jeffrey F. Nudelman; Michael M. Ratoza; Alec J. Shebiel; Edward J. Sullivan; Robert C. Weaver, Jr. Of Counsel: Cynthia M. Fraser; William K. Kabeiseman; Samuel C. Kauffman; Paul J. Kelly, Jr.; Timothy D. Smith. Associates: Joy Ellis; Adam R. Kelly; Michael R. O'Connor; Carrie A. Richter; Laura Caldera Taylor; Adrienne W. Whitworth.
General Practice in Business, Litigation and Government Relations. Administrative, Admiralty, Affordable Housing and Community Development, Antitrust, Banking, Bankruptcy and Creditors' Rights, Class Action Litigation, Commercial and Secured Transactions, Communications and Media Law, Construction Law, Corporate Finance and Securities, E-Commerce and Emerging Technologies, Employee Benefits, Entertainment, Sports and Arts, Environmental, Estate Planning and Probate, Federal Taxation, Global Customs and Trade, Government Contracts, Health and Safety Regulation, Healthcare Law, Immigration, Indian Law, Insurance Coverage and Defense, Intellectual Property, International Practice, Labor and Employment Law, Land Use and Condemnation, Maritime, Mergers and Acquisitions, Municipal, Natural Resources, Nonprofit and Tax-Exempt Organizations, Products Liability, Public Policy, Lobbying and Political Law, Real Estate, State and Local Taxation, Sustainable Business, Transportation Law, White-Collar Criminal Defense.
Representative Clients: DirecTV; Foss Maritime Company; InFocus Corporation; NIKE, Inc.; Regence BlueCross BlueShield of Oregon; Regence HMO Oregon; St. John Medical Center; TriQuint Semiconductor, Inc.
Beijing, China Office: 820 South Tower, Beijing Kerry Center, 1 Guang Hua Road, Chaoyang District, Beijing, PRC 100020. Telephone: 8610-8529-9880. Fax: 8610-8529-9881.
New York, New York Office: Eighth Floor, 599 Broadway, 10012. Telephone: 212-431-8700. Fax: 212-334-1278.
Seattle, Washington Office: 1191 Second Avenue, 18th Floor, 98101. Telephone: 206-464-3939. Fax: 206-464-0125.
Washington, D.C. Office: Fifth Floor, 1000 Potomac Street, N.W., 20007. Telephone: 202-965-7880. Fax: 202-965-1729.

See Professional Biographies, PORTLAND, OREGON

Gary, Paul R., (AV) ....'50 '76 C&L.597 B.A., J.D. [Gary]
Gary, William F., (AV) .... '50 '76 C.629 B.A. L.1065 J.D. [Harrang L.G.R.] (⊙Eugene)

Gary Law Group, The, (AV)
2000 One Main Place, 101 SW Main Street, 97204
Telephone: 503-227-8424 Facsimile: 503-227-8412
Email: rachel@prgarylaw.com URL: http://www.prgarylaw.com
Paul R. Gary;—Steve Norman.
Litigation and Management of Construction, Product Defects and Business Claims, Insurance and Insurance Coverage.

See Professional Biographies, PORTLAND, OREGON

Gates, Jennifer L. ....'75 '01 C&L.352 B.A., J.D. [Ⓐ Abbott&P.]
Gauger, Charles S., (BV) .... '54 '81 C.1051 B.A. L.596 J.D. [C.S.Gauger]
Gauger, Charles S., P.C., Attorney at Law/CPA, (BV) ....1437 S.W. Columbia St.
Gautier, B. Elise ....'57 '86 C.976 B.A. L.1066 J.D. 4341 S.W. 54th Place‡
Gay, Sean C. ....'69 '04 L.950 J.D. [Ⓐ Stoel R.]
Gaylord, William A., (AV) .... '47 '73 C.628 B.S. L.596 J.D. [Gaylord&E.]
Gaylord & Eyerman, P.C., (AV) ....1400 S.W. Montgomery
Gazzola, Charles D., (AV) ....'57 '84 C.723 B.A. L.629 J.D. [Gazzola&H.]

Gazzola & Hull, P.C., (AV)
210 Morgan Building, 720 S.W. Washington Street, 97205
Telephone: 503-295-3025 Fax: 503-248-0295 Email: chip@gazzolahull.com
Email: david@gazzolahull.com
Charles D. Gazzola; David E. Hull.
Domestic Relations, Family Law, Juvenile Law, Child Custody, Visitation Rights.

Gearing, David C., (AV) .... '57 '84 C.1044 B.A. L.629 J.D. [Gearing,R.&E.]

Gearing, Rackner & Engel LLP, (AV)
811 SW Naito Parkway, 97204
Telephone: 503-222-9116 Fax: 503-222-9118
URL: http://www.gre-lawfirm.com
Members of Firm: David C. Gearing; Laura E. Rackner; Brett E. Engel; Craig Wymetalek; Michael T. McGrath.
Family Law, Custody Law, Juvenile Law, Estate Planning.

See Professional Biographies, PORTLAND, OREGON

Gebhardt, Robert A. .... '52 '78 C.506 B.A. L.629 J.D. U.S. Bancorp
Geddes, Robert D. '38 '63
C.629 B.A. L.1066 LL.B. Exec. V.P. & Corp. Coun., U.S. Bancorp
Gelineau, Jill S., (AV) ....'60 '85 C&L.629 B.S., J.D. [Schwabe,W.&W.]
Gentry, Michael J., (AV) .... '46 '71 C.502 B.S. L.477 J.D. [Foster P.T.]
Geny, William O., (AV) '47 '74
C.861 B.S. L.880 J.D. [Chernoff,V.M.&S.] (See Pat. Sect.)
George, Erika J. .... '— '97 L.629 J.D. [Ⓒ Williams,K.&G.P.]
George, Paul B., (AVⓉ) .... '47 '73 C.629 B.S. L.767 J.D. [Foster P.T.]
George, Peter Warren '48 '74 C.950 B.A. L.1165 J.D.
(adm. in WA; not adm. in OR) Holman D.C. Oregon, Inc.
Georges, Katherine G. ....'50 '84 C.560 B.A. L.629 J.D. Dept. of Jus.
Gerber, Thomas A., (AV) ....'47 '74 C.1056 B.S. L.596 J.D. [Ⓒ Bullivant H.B.]
Gerber, Walter P. ....'12 '34 L.595 2805 N.W. Westover Rd.‡
Gerdes, Ellis E. .... '25 '61 C.911 B.B.A. L.596 LL.B. 4233 S.E. Oak St.‡
Gerhardt, Nathan R. ....'72 '03 C.911 B.A. L.629 J.D. [Ⓐ Black H.]
Gerhardt, Paul, (AV) .... '27 '52 C.453 B.S. L.597 J.D. 1 S.W. Columbia St.
Gericke, Justin D. ....'68 '99 C.210 B.A. L.596 J.D. [Ⓐ Jordan S.]
Geringer, James E., (BV) .... '61 '90 C.112 B.A. L.309 J.D. [Klarquist S.]
Gerlt, Danny H. .... '49 '85 C.628 B.S.M.E. L.596 J.D. 8600 S.W. 30th Ave.
Gernant, David ....'43 '69 C.932 B.A. L.309 J.D. Cir. J.
Gevurtz, Ronald I., (AV) '36 '60 C&L.950 B.S., LL.B.
111 S.W. Fifth Avenue, Suite 900‡

Gevurtz, Menashe, Larson & Howe, P.C., (AV)
111 S.W. Fifth Avenue Suite 900, 97204-3604
Telephone: 503-227-1515 Fax: 503-243-2038
URL: http://www.gevurtzmenashe.com
Albert A. Menashe; Eric C. Larson; William J. Howe, III; Marshal P. Spector (Resident); Ruth E. Pekelder; Andrea J. Anderly; Julia M. Hagan; Kathryn L. Villa-Smith;—Craig M. Cowley; Saville W. Easley; Catherine A. Tappel; Drake A. Lightle; Richard W. Funk; Zachary J. Fruchtengarten; Robin J. Wright; Shawn N. Menashe; Sarah B. Creem.
Practice Limited to Family Law, including Divorce Spousal Support, Prenuptial Agreements, Palimony, Paternity, Parenting, Custody and Visitation Issues, Adoption and Surrogacy, Name Changes, International Custody, Domestic Partnerships, Juvenile Issues, Grandparents Rights.

See Professional Biographies, PORTLAND, OREGON

Ghastin, Jon Jay, (AV) .... '61 '89 C.373 B.A. L.1051 J.D. 521 S.W. Clay St.
Ghazi, David Darius ....'65 '99 C.235 B.A. L.421 J.D. [Ⓐ Smith F.&E.]
Ghim, Marianne M., (BV) ....'64 '92 C.629 B.A. L.950 J.D. [Ⓐ Bullivant H.B.]

Giampa, Kelly A. '63 '90 C.597 B.A. L.424 J.D.
(adm. in IL; not adm. in OR) 1000 Sw Broadway Ste 2000
Gibbon, John T. .... '53 '79 C.637 B.A. L.1051 9822 S.W. Quail Post Rd.
Gibbon, Steven Charles ....'69 '00 C.506 B.A. L.878 J.D. Dist. Atty. Off.
Gibbons, William J. .... '30 '59 C.563 B.A. L.724 LL.B. 1313 N.W. 19th Ave.
Gibert, Christine .... '78 '04 C.691 B.A. L.1565 J.D. [Ⓐ Miller N.]
Gibson, Giles, (BV) ....'55 '91 C.766 B.A. L.767 J.D. [Goldberg,M.S.&G.]
Gibson, Kirk H., (BV) ....'53 '85 C.693 B.S. L.1170 J.D. [Ater W.]
Gidley, James H., (AV) ....'42 '67 C.972 B.S. L.629 J.D. [Perkins C.]
Gilbert, Bruce R. ....'69 '95 C.911 B.S. L.1358 J.D. [Ⓐ Smith F.&E.]
Gilbertson, John R., (AV) .... '23 '50 C&L.629 B.S., J.D. 1200 S.W. Main St.‡
Gilbertson, Michael A., (AV) ....'63 '89 C.1175 B.A. L.596 J.D. [Ransom&G.]
Gill, Jacob S. ....'75 '03 C.1056 B.A. L.629 J.D. [Ⓐ Stoll S.B.L.&S.]
Gill, Rockne, (AV) .... '31 '55 C&L.629 B.S., LL.B. [Schwabe,W.&W.] (⊙Bend)‡
Gilles, Paul Joseph ....'61 '97 C.628 B.S. L.596 J.D. Industrial Design Corp.
Gillespie, Laura M. '74 '02 C.966 B.A. L.1051 J.D.
555 Benjamin Franklin Plaza, One S.W. Columbia
Gilman, Scott F., (AV) ....'46 '74 C.1051 B.S. L.596 J.D. [Breathouwer&G.]
Gilmore, Chris A. .... '67 '98 C.588 B.S. L.1194 J.D. [Ⓐ Beery&E.]
Gilroy, Patrick D., Jr., (AV) ....'56 '83 C&L.770 B.S., J.D. [Gilroy]
Gilroy Law Firm, The, PC, (AV) .... 5100 S.W. Macadam Avenue, Suite 240
Ginsberg, Mark J. ....'70 '95 C.1036 B.A. L.596 J.D. 1001 S.W. 5th Ave., Ste. 1900
Giorgetti, Lucinda R. ....'48 '95 C.888 B.A. L.596 J.D. 222 SW Columbia Street
Giovanini, L. M. ....'24 '53 C&L.950 B.S., J.D. 5104 S.W. Scholls Fry Rd.‡
Gipson, Gary R. '44 '69 C.35 B.S. in Ed. L.37 J.D.
(adm. in AZ; not adm. in OR) Supr. Spec. Agent, F.B.I.
Girard, Leonard A., (AV) .... '42 '67 C.629 B.S. L.813 LL.B. 2169 S.W. Kings Ct.
Girard, Michael P. .... '68 '94 C.446 B.S. L.893 J.D. [Klarquist S.] (See Pat. Sect.)
Gisvold, Dean P., (AV) ....'41 '66 C.350 B.S. L.494 LL.B. [McEwen G.]
Glade, Peter H., (AV) ....'51 '79 C.347 A.B. L.596 J.D. [Markowitz,H.G.&M.]
Gladstone, Alan ....'48 '94 C.186 B.S. L.1051 J.D. [Davis R.E.&X.]
Glascock, Andrew D. .... '73 '99 C.1032 B.B.A. L.950 J.D. [Ⓐ Bodyfelt M.S.&C.]
Glaser, Erica C. ....'69 '97 C.1307 B.A. L.629 J.D. Ste 710, 10260 Sw Greenburg Rd
Glasgow, Robert E., (AV) .... '44 '69 C&L.273 B.A., J.D. [Ⓒ Black H.]
Glass, Caitlin J. ....'70 '96 C.178 B.A. L.596 J.D. Atty., Legal Aid Services of Oregon
Glassman, Dina ....'73 '99 C.165 B.A. L.569 J.D. [Ⓐ Perkins C.]
Glausi, Wallace A., (CV) ....'63 '92 L.629 J.D. [Ater W.]
Glazer, Anne W., (AV) .... '— '92 C&L.911 B.A., J.D. [Lane P.]
Gleason, Richard S., (AV) ....'51 '81 C.813 B.A. L.336 J.D. [Stoel R.]
Gleaves, Curt B., (AV) ....'57 '82 C.813 A.B. L.1065 J.D. [Foster P.T.]
Glen, Susan C. .... '64 '94 C.118 B.A. L.494 J.D. [Dunn C.A.H.&T.]
Glick, Richard M., (AV) .... '— '76 C.112 B.A. L.800 J.D. [Davis W.T.]
Glikbarg, Andrew S. '67 '95 C.1494 B.A. L.1051 J.D.
Asst. Gen. Coun., KinderCare Learning Centers, Inc., Corp. & Regulatory Affs.
Glisson, Gary W., (AV) ....'59 '88 C.502 B.A. L.597 J.D. [Stoel R.]
Glor, Megan E., (AV) ....'63 '90 C&L.705 B.A., J.D. [Ⓐ Swanson,T.&C.]
Glover, James A. .... '50 '79 C.1056 B.S. L.1051 J.D. 520 S.W. Yamhill St.
Go, Jimmy W., (AV) ....'55 '81 C&L.629 B.S., J.D. [Go&L.]
Go, Sivhwa ....'— '03 C.950 B.A. L.629 J.D. [Ⓐ Harrang L.G.R.]
Go & Laster, (AV) ....621 S.W. Morrison St., Ste. 1150
Godwin, Diana E., (AV) .... '47 '76 C.112 A.B. L.629 J.D. 1000 S.W. Broadway
Goe, Douglas E., (AV) ....'— '81 C.1051 B.S. L.950 J.D. [Orrick,H.&S.]
Goebel, Helen Elizabeth ....'53 '79 C.352 B.A. L.950 J.D. Tri-Co. Metro. Trans. Dist.
Goff, Jared S. ....'72 '99 C&L.101 M.E., J.D. [Ⓐ Klarquist S.] (See Pat. Sect.)
Goff, Starla Jean ....'71 '97 C.635 B.A. L.950 J.D. [Ⓐ Smith F.&E.]
Gold, Ivan, (BV) ....'— '72 C.665 B.A. L.569 J.D. [Perkins C.]
Goldberg, Deborah B. .... '60 '88 C.685 B.A. L.436 J.D. Asst. Secy., U.S. Bancorp
Goldberg, Steven, (AV) ....'47 '72 C.477 B.A. L.309 J.D. [Goldberg,M.S.&G.]
Goldberg, Mechanic, Stuart & Gibson LLP, (AV) ....621 S.W. Morrison Street, Suite 1450
Golding, Mark A., (AV) ....'46 '76 C.390 B.S. L.1009 J.D. [Ⓒ Parsons F.&G.]
Goldsmith, Gerson F., (AV) ....'20 '47 C&L.813 B.A., J.D. 1600 S.W. 4th Ave.
Goldstein, Aaron D. '77 '03 C.188 B.A. L.800 J.D.
(adm. in WA; not adm. in OR) [Ⓐ Ball J.]
Goldstein, Gersham, (AV) ....'38 '63 C.563 B.B.A. L.659 LL.B. [Stoel R.]
Goldstein, Mitchell A. ....'59 '87 C.207 B.A. L.596 J.D. [Ⓐ Babener&Assoc.]
Gonzales, Daniel E. .... '55 '85 C.950 B.A. L.1066 J.D. Law Clk., U.S. Sr. Dist. Ct. J.
Gonzales, Ellen M. '72 '99 C.453 S.B. L.813 J.D.
[Ⓐ Kolisch H.] (Pat.) (⊙Palo Alto, CA)
Gonzales, Jeffrey Charles .... '54 '82 C.1056 B.S. L.911 J.D. [J.C.Gonzales]
Gonzales, Jeffrey C. .... 888 S.W. 5th Ave., Ste. 650
Gonzalez, Rene G. ....'74 '00 C&L.950 B.A., J.D. [Ⓐ Stoel R.]
Goode, William R. ....'47 '84 C.1111 B.A. L.362 J.D. 4224 S.W. Melville Ave.
Goodling, Jonathon L., P.C., (AV) .... '53 '79 C&L.629 B.S., J.D. [Miller N.]
Goodman, Edmund J. .... '— '89 C.1044 B.A. L.309 J.D. Oregon Legal Servs. Corp.
Gorciak, G. Joseph, III .... '53 '87 C.425 B.S. L.1051 J.D. [G.J.Gorciak]
Gorciak, G. Joseph, Law Offices .... 129A N.E. 102nd Avenue
Gorder, Charles F., Jr., (AV) .... '52 '77 C.112 B.A. L.1066 J.D. Asst. U.S. Atty.
Gordon, Corbett, (AV) ....'46 '82 C.33 B.A. L.309 J.D. [Ⓒ Fisher&P.]
Gordon, Debra A. ....'— '98 C.907 B.S. L.37 J.D. [Ⓐ Klarquist S.]
Gordon, Douglas B., (BV) ....'47 '73 C.610 A.B. L.966 J.D. [Ⓒ Ambrose]
Gordon, Kim D. .... '55 '86 C.1322 B.A. L.596 J.D. 5125 S.W. Macadam Ave.
Gordon, Michael F. ....'54 '85 C.502 B.S. L.596 J.D. [Gordon]
Gordon, Noah J. .... '61 '87 C.311 B.A. L.978 J.D. 6303 S.E. Harrison St.
Gordon, Thomas A., (AV) ....'48 '74 C.1056 B.S. L.596 J.D. [Gordon&P.]
Gordon Law Offices .... 5125 SW Macadam Avenue

Gordon & Meneghello, P.C.
(See Fisher & Phillips LLP)

Gordon & Polscer, LLC, (AV)
9755 SW Barnes Road, Suite 650, 97225 ⊙
Telephone: 503-242-2922 Fax: 503-242-1264
URL: http://www.gordon-polscer.com
Members of Firm: Thomas A. Gordon; Diane L. Polscer; Gregory L. Baird. Associates: Russell W. Pike; Andrew S. Moses; Jeffrey C. Dahl; Robert Spajic; Heather A. Brann (Not admitted in OR); Spencer S. Adams (Not admitted in OR).
Insurance Coverage and Defense Law, Bad Faith Law, Professional Liability Law, Products Liability Law, General Civil Litigation and Appellate Practice.
Seattle, Washington Office: 1000 Second Avenue, Suite 1500, 98104. Telephone: 206-223-4226; Fax: 206-223-5459.

See Professional Biographies, PORTLAND, OREGON

Gordon & Rees LLP, (AV)
1001 S.W. Fifth Avenue, Suite 1100, 97204 ⊙
Telephone: 503-220-1679 Fax: 503-907-6636
Email: info@gordonrees.com URL: http://www.gordonrees.com
Partners of Firm: Stuart M. Brown; Thomas A. Packer. Senior Counsel: Mark P. Pihl.
Business and Corporate Litigation, Business and Technology, Construction, Commercial, Environmental Law, Estate Planning and Probate, Health Care, International, Maritime, Intellectual Prop

(This Listing Continued)

Gordon & Rees LLP (Continued)

erty, Product Liability, Property Insurance, Real Estate, Real Property Litigation, Reinsurance, Tort Injury Defense, Toxic Tort, Insurance Coverage and Bad Faith, Medical Device Litigation, Professional Liability, Employment Law.
Phoenix, Arizona Office: 2375 E. Camelback Road, Suite 500. Telephone: 602-265-4700. Fax: 602-265-4700.
San Francisco, California Office: Embarcadero Center West, Twentieth Floor, 275 Battery Street. Telephone: 415-986-5900. Fax: 415-986-8054; 415-296-9287; 415-677-9673.
San Diego, California Office: 101 West Broadway, Suite 1600. Telephone: 619-696-6700. Fax: 619-696-7124.
Los Angeles, California Office: 633 West Fifth Street, Suite 4900. Telephone: 213-576-5000. Fax: 213-680-4470.
Sacramento, California Office: 655 University Avenue, Suite 200. Telephone: 916-565-2900. Fax: 916-920-4402.
Newport Beach, California Office: 4675 MacArthur Court, Suite 800. Telephone: 949-255-6950. Fax: 949-474-2060.
Las Vegas, Nevada Office: 221 North Buffalo Drive, Suite A. Telephone: 702-577-9300. Fax: 702-255-2858.
New York, New York Office: One Liberty Plaza, 14th Floor. Telephone: 212-201-6777. Fax: 212-201-6778.
Houston, Texas Office: 3D/International Tower, 1900 West Loop South, Suite 1100. Telephone: 713-961-3366. Fax: 713-961-3938.

See Professional Biographies, PORTLAND, OREGON

Gores, Hala J., (AV) '63 '89 C.1056 B.S. L.1051 J.D.
621 S.W. Morrison, Suite 1218, 97205
Telephone: 503-295-1940 Fax: 503-295-2651
Email: hala@goreslaw.com URL: http://www.goreslaw.com
Personal Injury, Wrongful Death, Medical Malpractice, Therapy Malpractice, Automobile Accidents and Catastrophic Injuries, Dog Bites, Sexual Abuse, Insurance Law.

See Professional Biographies, PORTLAND, OREGON

Gorin, Lawrence D., (AV) . . . . . . '45 '73 C.1097 B.A. L.1051 J.D. [L.D.Gorin]
Gorin, L. D., Law Offices of, (AV) . . . . . . 521 S.W. Clay St., Ste. 205
Gorman, Leta E. . . . . . . '67 '94 C.911 B.A. L.988 J.D. [Ⓐ Bullivant H.B.]
Gottlieb, Ira L., (AV) . . . . . . '38 '69 C.563 B.A. L.966 J.D. 621 S.W. Morrison St.
Goulder, David N., (AV) . . . . . . '50 '79 C.1036 B.A. L.309 J.D. [Landye B.B.]
Grabe, Timothy, (AV) . . . . . . '54 '83 C.629 B.A. L.1051 J.D. 2722 NE 33rd Ave.
Graber, Susan P. . . . . . . '49 '72 C.914 B.A. L.976 J.D. U.S. Cir. J.
Grade, Andrew A. . . . . . . '68 '98 C.107 B.S. L.950 J.D. [Ⓐ S.V.Rizzo]
Graf, Alan Stuart, (BV) . . . . . . '50 '92 C.1350 B.A. L.1051 J.D. 1020 S.W. Taylor Street
Graff, John Paul, (AV) . . . . . . '35 '76 C.976 B.A. L.629 J.D. [Graff&O.]
Graff & O'Neil, (AV) . . . . . . 2121 S.W. Broadway, Suite 100
Gragg, J. Daniel . . . . . . '69 '96 C.35 B.S. L.472 J.D. [Seifer,Y.M.&Z.]
Graham, H. Faith . . . . . . '73 '01 C.911 B.A. L.588 J.D. [Ⓐ Foster P.T.]
Graham, Hunter S. . . . . . . '62 '95 C.378 B.A. L.1051 J.D. 5963 S.W. Terwilliger Blvd.
Gramp, Lisa M. . . . . . . '— '04 L.588 J.D. [Ⓐ Marvin,C.&L.]
Granata, Fred A., (BV) . . . . . . '31 '57 C&L.629 B.A., J.D. [Ⓐ McKeown&B.]
Grant, Donald K. . . . . . . '49 '81 C.645 B.A. L.596 J.D. Fed. Pub. Def.
Grant, Eugene, (AV) . . . . . . '— '79 C&L.629 B.A., J.D. [Davis W.T.]

Grant, Richard L., (AV) '52 '83 C.477 B.S. L.596 J.D.
The Gadsby House, 1205 NW 25th Avenue, 97210-2497
Telephone: 503-222-7343 Fax: 503-226-3131
Email: rgrant@rsblaw.net
Business Law, Creditor Rights, Collections, Business Enterprises, Corporate, Limited Liability Companies, Partnerships, Small Business, Debt and Credit, General Business, Business Planning, Lawsuits, Contracts, Wills and Probate, Trusts and Estates, Estate Planning, Civil Litigation.

See Professional Biographies, PORTLAND, OREGON

Grasberger, Eric A., (AV) . . . . . . '65 '91 C.602 B.A. L.575 J.D. [Stoel R.]
Graser, Laura . . . . . . '51 '79 C.685 B.A. L.1051 J.D. Dep. Dist. Atty.
Gravdal, Janet M., (AV) . . . . . . '59 '87 C.906 B.A. L.336 J.D. [McEwen G.]
Gray, Arnold L., (AV) . . . . . . '54 '79 C&L.37 B.S., J.D. [Stewart S.&G.]
Gray, Ben T. . . . . . . '23 '53 C.966 L.174 LL.B. 3345 N.W. Vaughn St.‡
Grayson, Joel E., (AV) . . . . . . '46 '71 C.629 B.S. L.950 J.D. [Maylie&G.]
Greaves, Robert D., (BV) . . . '48 '82 C.112 B.A. L.596 J.D. 2121 S.W. Broadway, Ste. 100
Grebe, Walter H., (AV) . . . . . . '38 '64 C&L.629 B.S., LL.B. [Schwabe,W.&W.]
Greeff, Charles M. . . . . . . '63 '89 C.882 B.A. L.1048 J.D. [C.Greeff]
Greeff, Charles, PC, Law Office of . . . . . . 720 S.W. Washington Street #210
Green, David W., (AV) . . . . . . '51 '76 C.999 B.A. L.309 J.D. [Stoel R.]
Green, Donald W., III, (BV) . . . . . . '41 '66 C&L.629 B.S., LL.B. 1300 S.W. 5th Ave.
Green, Douglas S., (AV) . . . . . . '— '68 C.1051 B.A. L.950 J.D. [Welch,B.&G.]
Green, Patrick J., (AV) . . . . . . '— '74 C&L.629 B.S., J.D. [Davis W.T.]
Greenberg, Joel . . . . . . '49 '94 C.685 B.A. L.1051 J.D. 630 S.W. 5th Ave.
Greene, Michael A., (AV) . . . . . . '46 '72 C&L.813 A.B., J.D. [Rosenthal&G.]
Greene, S. Ward, (AV) . . . . . . '47 '73 C.259 B.S. L.228 J.D. [Greene&M.]

Greene & Markley, P.C., (AV)
1515 S.W. Fifth Avenue, Suite 600, 97201
Telephone: 503-295-2668 Fax: 503-224-8434
URL: http://www.greenemarkley.com
S. Ward Greene; Charles R. Markley; David A. Foraker; Sanford R. Landress; Stephen T. Boyke; Gary L. Blacklidge; Jeffrey M. Wong;—M. Elizabeth Duncan; Heather E. Harriman; Daniel L. Steinberg; Aaron M. Wigod. Of Counsel: Ridgway K. Foley, Jr.; David P. Weiner (P.C.).
All Facets of Bankruptcy and Commercial Law including Reorganization, Trustee Representation, Litigation, Creditors' Rights and UCC, Real Estate, Tax Controversy, Collection, Corporate Matters, Appellate Law.

See Professional Biographies, PORTLAND, OREGON

Greenfield, Julia T. . . . . . . '71 '98 C.767 B.A. L.976 J.D. OR Legal Aid Servs.
Greening, Robert, (AV) . . . . . . '44 '72 C&L.813 B.A., J.D. 655 S.E. Saint Andrews Dr.
Greenlick, Michael A., (AV) . . . . . . '59 '85 C.668 B.A. L.1051 J.D. [Borg S.&G.]
Greenman, Ronald L., (AV) . . . . . . '46 '74 C&L.629 B.S., J.D. [Tonkon T.]
Greenspan, Jeffrey M. . . . . . . '78 '03 C.628 B.A. L.629 J.D. [Ⓐ Stahancyk,K.J.&H.]
Greenwood, Clarence H., (AV) . . . . . . '47 '75 C&L.508 B.A., J.D. [Black H.]
Greenwood, Myrtle Rae, (BV) '50 '75
C&L.508 B.A., J.D. Corp. Coun., Willamette Svgs. & Loan Assn.
Greer, Anne Toland '61 '89
C.813 A.B. L.1065 J.D. Asst. Gen. Coun., Legacy Health System
Gregores, George J., (AV) . . . . . . '48 '73 C.629 B.S. L.596 J.D. [Holland&K.]
Gregory, Alexander I. . . . . . . '67 '94 C.951 B.A. L.1051 J.D. 4004 SE Woodstock Blvd.
Gregory, Betsy A. . . . . . . '76 '03 C.477 B.S. L.904 J.D. [Ⓐ Samuels Y.K.S.&S.]
Gregory, Jana T., (BV) . . . . . . '42 '70 C.629 B.A. L.596 J.D. 2805 N.E. 26th Ave.
Greif, Thomas J., (AV) . . . . . . '44 '70 C.629 B.A. L.950 J.D. [T.J.Greif]

Greif, Thomas J., P.C., (AV)
4519 S.W. Coronado, P.O. Box 80458, 97280
Telephone: 503-244-4822 Fax: 503-244-5745
Email: GreifPC@aol.com URL: http://www.lawyers.com/tjgreif
Thomas J. Greif.
General Business, Corporations, Partnerships, Franchises, Licensing Agreements, Joint Ventures, Limited Liability Companies, Transactions, Real Estate Purchases/Sales, Commercial Leases, Con-

(This Listing Continued)

Greif, Thomas J., P.C. (Continued)

struction Liens, Partitions, Commercial Litigation, Debtor-Creditor, Probate and Estate Planning, Will Contests, Guardianship/Conservatorships, Elder Law, Vessel Documentation Sales, and Maritime Ship Financing.

See Professional Biographies, PORTLAND, OREGON

Grein, David E. . . . . . . '62 '90 C.118 B.A. L.378 J.D. [Parsons F.&G.]
Grenham, E. Bradley . . . . . . '66 '95 C.197 B.A. L.1051 J.D. U.S. Dept. of Interior
Grenley, Gary I., (AV) . . . . . . '47 '75 C.678 B.A. L.596 J.D. [Grenley,R.E.B.&B.]

Grenley, Rotenberg, Evans, Bragg & Bodie, P.C., (AV)
Suite 1100 PacWest Center, 1211 S.W. Fifth Avenue, 97204-3737
Telephone: 503-241-0570 Facsimile: 503-241-0914
URL: http://www.grebb.com
Jeffrey C. Bodie; Michael J. Bragg; David E. Dean; Lawrence Evans; Gary I. Grenley; Laura L. Hammond; Kelly Meltzer; Stan N. Rotenberg;—James F. Marron; David L. Shawcross; Nicholas J. Slinde; Paul H. Trinchero; Joseph A. Tripi. Of Counsel: Norman A. Rickles.
Business and Corporate Law, Real Estate and Land Use, Taxation (State and Federal), Pension and Profit Sharing, Estate Planning and Probate, Employment Relations and Benefits, Securities and Venture Capital, Franchising and Trade Regulation, Intellectual Property, Government and Regulatory Affairs, Municipal Law, Charitable Organizations, Alternative Dispute Resolution and related Commercial, Business, Class Actions and Civil Trial and Appellate Litigation in State and Federal Courts in Oregon and Washington.
Reference: Key Bank of Oregon.

See Professional Biographies, PORTLAND, OREGON

Gresham, C. Brandon, Jr. '45 '75 C.1070 B.S. L.893 J.D.
(adm. in VA; not adm. in OR) Owner, Ad Hoc Enterprises
Gress, James L. . . . . . . '66 '91 C&L.950 B.A., J.D. [Reinisch,M.H.&W.]
Grewe, Todd M. . . . . . . '62 '96 C.911 B.A. L.823 J.D. [Ⓐ Schwabe,W.&W.]
Griffin, James E., (AV) . . . . . . '41 '66 C&L.477 B.A., J.D. Asst. Atty. Gen.
Griffin, Philip S. . . . . . . '— '87 C&L.629 B.A., J.D. [James]
Griffith, Norman N., (AV) . . . . . . '21 '49 C&L.309 S.B., LL.B. 1020 S.W. Taylor St.
Griffith, Phyllis Ann . . . . . . '47 '76 C&L.629 B.A., J.D. 14648 N.E. San Rafael
Griffith, Robert R., (AV) . . . . . . '52 '85 C.628 B.S. L.1051 J.D. [Garvey S.B.]
Griffith, Stephen L., (AV) . . . . . . '45 '77 C.309 B.A. L.813 J.D. [Stoel R.]
Griggs, David H. . . . . . . '63 '98 C.629 B.S. L.950 J.D. 710 S.W. Madison Street, 4th Floor
Grillo, Phillip E., P.C., (AV) . . . . . . '56 '85 C.475 B.A. L.596 J.D. [Miller N.]
Grim, Douglas R., (AV) . . . . . . '44 '70 C.906 B.S. L.950 J.D. [Brownstein,R.S.K.G.D.&H.]
Grim, Thomas M., (AV) . . . . . . '62 '88 C.112 B.A. L.770 J.D. [Cable H.B.H.&L.]
Grimmius, Chelsea L. . . . . . . '— '03 C.101 B.A. L.273 J.D. [Ⓐ Bullivant H.B.]
Grinfas, Dan . . . . . . '66 '94 C.112 B.S. L.950 J.D. [Ⓒ Stoel R.]
Grinich, Anita H., (BV) . . . . . . '56 '83 C.1051 B.A. L.596 J.D. [Cable H.B.H.&L.]
Griswold, James B., (AV) . . . . . . '23 '50 C.629 L.596 LL.B. 806 S.W. Broadway, Ste. 1000
Groce, Barry L., (AV) . . . . . . '54 '80 C&L.112 B.A., J.D. [McEwen G.]
Groner, P. Campbell, III, (AV) '49 '86 C.976 B.A. L.596 J.D.
Sr. V.P. & Chf. Exec. Offr., Legacy Health System
Gross, William N., (AV) . . . . . . '43 '68 C.734 B.S. L.477 J.D. 117 S.W. Taylor St.
Grossblatt, Fred J. '53 '78 C.112 B.A. L.809 J.D.
(adm. in CA; not adm. in OR) 10940 S.W. Barnes Rd., Ste. 101
Grossmann, Ronald S., (AV) . . . . . . '44 '69 C.597 B.A. L.477 J.D. [Stoel R.]
Grover, Diane L. . . . . . . '54 '01 C.1056 B.A. L.997 J.D. [D.L.Grover]
Grover, Diane L., P.C., Law Office of . . . . . . 317 S.W. Alder St., 9th Fl.
Grube, Edwin H., (AV) . . . . . . '61 '90 C.629 B.A. L.678 J.D. [Ⓐ Kobin&K.]
Grundfossen, Peter '35 '77 C.1056 B.S. L.878 J.D.
(adm. in UT; not adm. in OR) Assoc. of OR Housing Auth.

Gudger, Gregory L. '51 '87 C.629 B.S. L.950 J.D.
140 SW Arthur Street, Suite 200, 97201
Telephone: 503-228-1170 Fax: 503-228-1173
Email: dcglg@hotmail.com
Family Law, Criminal Law, Civil Rights Law, Employment Law, Torts, DUI, Real Estate, Litigation, Probate.

See Professional Biographies, PORTLAND, OREGON

Guest, Caroline R., (BV) . . . . . . '59 '94 C.788 A.B. L.629 J.D. [Harrang L.G.R.]
Guettler, Heidi, (AV) . . . . . . '66 '94 C.285 B.A. L.950 J.D. [Ⓐ Fisher&P.]
Guilbert, Thomas G. P., (AV) . . . '42 '72 C.31 B.A. L.976 J.D. 2370 S.W. Montgomery Dr.
Guinasso, Charles B. . . . . . . '31 '63 C.988 B.A. L.596 LL.B. Dist. J.
Guinasso, John D., (AV) . . . . . . '58 '83 C.1051 B.A. L.813 J.D. [Schwabe,W.&W.]
Guldager, Amanda Nicole Hill . . . . . . '78 '03 C.629 B.A. L.94 J.D. [A.H.Guldager]
Guldager, Amanda Hill, Law Office of . . . . . . 10260 S.W. Greenburg Rd., Ste. 400
Gumusoglu, Shea . . . . . . '65 '01 C.629 B.A. L.1051 J.D. [Tarlow N.&S.]
Gundle, Ruth E. . . . . . . '47 '75 C.33 B.A. L.705 J.D. 624 SE 29th Ave.
Gunter, Raymond W. . . . . . . '28 '63 C.906 B.A. L.596 LL.B. Bonneville Power Admin.‡
Gurdin, Kristen M. . . . . . . '— '00 C.103 A.B. L.831 J.D. [Ⓐ Davis W.T.]
Guse, James L. . . . . . . '74 '99 C.670 B.A. L.602 J.D. [Ⓐ Parsons F.&G.]
Gustafson, Karna R. . . . . . . '68 '94 C.1369 B.S. L.950 J.D. [Landye B.B.]
Guthrie, Heather L. . . . . . . '68 '00 C.1056 B.A. L.1051 J.D. [Ⓐ Dunn C.A.H.&T.]
Gutzler, Michael N., (AV) . . . . . . '52 '77 C&L.950 B.S., J.D. [Gutzler&H.]
Gutzler & Hudson, (AV) . . . . . . 5200 Southwest Macadam Avenue Suite 500
Guyol, Deborah S., (AV) . . . . . . '46 '83 C.685 B.A. L.800 J.D. 5161 N.E. Wistaria Dr.
Haagensen, Donald A., (AV) . . . . . . '45 '77 C.335 B.S. L.472 J.D. [Cable H.B.H.&L.]
Haan, Pamela . . . . . . '72 '99 C.910 B.A. L.596 J.D. Co. Legal Aid Servs.
Haas, Harl H. . . . . . . '32 '61 C&L.950 B.S., LL.B. Cir. J.
Habernigg, Charles H., (AV) '33 '60
C.604 A.B. L.976 LL.B. 121 S.W. Salmon, Suite 1160
Hackett, Mark J. . . . . . . '— '92 C.112 A.B. L.188 J.D. [Davis W.T.]
Haddad, Joseph J. . . . . . . '74 '00 C.477 B.A. L.629 J.D. [Ⓐ Fisher&P.]
Haendler, Jeffrey Brian . . . . . . '71 '00 C.446 B.S. L.950 J.D. [Ⓐ Klarquist S.]
Hagan, Julia M., (AV) . . . . . . '56 '85 C.770 B.S. L.1051 J.D. [Gevurtz,M.L.&H.]
Hagan, Kelly T., (AV) . . . . . . '52 '81 C.813 B.A. L.629 J.D. [Schwabe,W.&W.]
Hagen, Cathryn C. . . . . . . '50 '76 C.670 B.A. L.629 J.D. 2806 N.E. 14
Hagen, Douglas D., (AV) . . . . . . '48 '74 C.1056 B.A. L.950 J.D. 1205 N.W. 25th Ave.
Hagen, Joseph T., (AV) . . . . . . '45 '72 C.517 B.A. L.276 J.D. [Hagen O.]

Hagen O'Connell LLP, (AV)
Bank of America Building Suite 1500, 121 SW Morrison Street, 97204-3160
Telephone: 503-227-2900 Fax: 503-227-3870 URL: http://www.hagenoconnell.com
Email: shval@hagenoconnell.com URL: http://www.lawyers.com/hagenoconnell
Joseph T. Hagen; Kevin P. O'Connell; Steven B. Hval; Thomas J. Fraser;—Paul D. Migchelbrink. Of Counsel: John C. Ramig; Diane C. Kerns.
Taxation Law, Corporate Law, Mergers and Acquisitions, Business Law, Estate Planning, Executive Compensation, Estate Administration, Probate, Business Transactions, Real Estate, Litigation.

See Professional Biographies, PORTLAND, OREGON

Hager, Laurie R. . . . . . . '75 '01 C.184 B.A. L.174 J.D. [Ⓐ Sussman S.]
Haggerty, Ancer L. . . . . . . '44 '73 C.629 B.S. L.1065 J.D. Chief J.
Haggerty, Patchen M. . . . . . . '75 '01 C.679 B.A. L.347 J.D. [Ⓐ Schwabe,W.&W.]
Haglund, Michael E., (AV) . . . . . . '52 '77 C.1181 B.A. L.94 J.D. [Haglund,K.H.&J.]

Haglund, Kelley, Horngren & Jones LLP, (AV)
One Main Place, 101 S.W. Main, Suite 1800, 97204
Telephone: 503-225-0777 Facsimile: 503-225-1257 URL: http://www.hk-law.com
URL: http://www.lawyers.com/hk-law
Members of Firm: Michael E. Haglund; Michael K. Kelley; Scott W. Horngren; Timothy J. Jones; Michael G. Neff; Shay S. Scott; Julie A. Weis; LeRoy W. Wilder; William K. Barquin. Associates: Danica K. Hibpshman; Christopher G. Lundberg. Counsel: James L. Francesconi.
Commercial Litigation, Business (including Forest Products Industry), Contracts, Antitrust, Public Lands, Land Use, Products Liability, Personal Injury, Probate, Admiralty, Administrative Law, Employment Law, Indian Law.
See Professional Biographies, PORTLAND, OREGON

Hahn, Spencer J. .... '79 '04 C.763 B.A. L.1051 J.D. Multnomah Defenders, Inc.
Haim, Patricia Ann, (AV) ....'48 '84 C.999 B.A. L.602 J.D. [Amburgey&R.]
Haley, George P. ....'22 '58 C.950 A.B. L.596 LL.B. P.O. Box 16454
Haley, Kathleen '52 '80
C.1044 B.A. L.1202 J.D. Exec. Dir., Oregon Psychiatric Sec. Rev. Bd.
Hall, Bruce MacGregor, (P.C.), (AV) '24 '52 C.674 A.B. L.1066 J.D.
101 S.W. Main St.‡
Hall, David E. .... '74 '00 C&L.150 B.S., J.D. [Ⓐ Kolisch H.] (Pat.)
Hall, Gordon L., (BV) .... '44 '73 C.870 B.S. L.629 J.D. 10260 S.W. Greenburg Rd.
Hall, M. Christopher ....'67 '97 C.475 B.A. L.94 J.D. [Perkins C.]
Hall, M. Matthews .... '68 '99 C.896 B.S. L.174 J.D. [Ⓐ Kolisch H.] (Pat.)
Hall, Nelson R., (AV) .... '54 '85 C.628 B.S. L.596 J.D. [Bennett,H.M.&K.]
Hall, Stephen C. ....'67 '97 C.932 B.B.A. L.602 J.D. [Stoel R.]
Hall, Stuart A., (AV) ....'40 '65 C&L.950 B.A., J.D. Liberty Northwest Ins. Corp.
Halle, Barbara W., (BV) '52 '88
C.860 B.A. L.596 J.D. Asst. Gen. Coun., Portland Gen. Corp.
Halle, John J., (AV) ....'47 '78 C.629 B.A. L.818 J.D. [Stoel R.]
Halley, James F. .... '54 '83 C.112 B.S. L.596 J.D. [J.F.Halley]
Halley, James F., P.C. .... 735 Southwest First Avenue
Halligan, Michael G., (BV) ....'54 '82 C.1181 B.S. L.596 J.D. [Sussman S.]
Hallinan, Michael B. ....'73 '01 C.145 B.A. L.950 J.D. [Ⓐ Stoel R.]
Halpern, Robert ....'68 '96 C.1307 B.A. L.588 J.D. Metropolitan Public Defender, Inc.
Halvorson, Omar W. ....'22 '51 C.670 A.B. L.950 J.D. 1127 S.E. 53rd Ave., N.W.‡

Hamalian, A. Alexander, Law Offices of '69 '96 C.147 B.A. L.1051 J.D.
714 SW 20th Place, 97205
Telephone: 503-222-3641 Fax: 503-274-7975
Email: mistrial@teleport.com URL: http://www.lawyers.com/ahamalian
Criminal Defense.
See Professional Biographies, PORTLAND, OREGON

Hamilton, Douglas M. .... '48 '75 1500 S.W. Taylor St.
Hamilton, Douglass M., (AV) ....'42 '68 C&L.502 B.A., J.D. [Hamilton M.&A.]
Hamilton, Jessica T. .... '74 '03 C.112 B.A. L.911 J.D. [Ⓐ Ball J.]
Hamilton Mediation and Arbitration, (AV) ....1500 S.W. Taylor St.
Hamlin, Bruce C., (AV) ....'— '79 C.939 B.A. L.629 J.D. [Lane P.]
Hammer, Susan M., (AV) .... '48 '76 C.678 B.A. L.950 J.D. 25 N.W. 23rd Pl., Ste. 6
Hammond, G. Frank .... '59 '85 C.1051 B.S. L.188 J.D. [Cable H.B.H.&L.]
Hammond, John H., Jr., (AV) '43 '68 C&L.629 B.S., J.D.
1750 S.W. Harbor Wy., Ste. 380
Hammond, Laura L. ....'70 '95 C&L.629 B.A., J.D. [Grenley,R.E.B.&B.]
Hammond, Paula Biggs ....'44 '85 C.629 B.A. L.596 J.D. [P.B.Hammond]
Hammond, Susan K., (AV) ....'47 '77 C.1058 B.S. L.596 J.D. [Ⓐ Anderson&Y.]
Hammond, Paula B., LLC .... 9843 S.W. Second Ave.
Hampton, Karen R. ....'61 '88 C&L.629 B.S., J.D. Oregon Legal Serv. Corp.
Hampton, Lewis B., (AV) .... '33 '60 C&L.950 B.A., J.D. [Ⓒ Black H.]
Hanchett, Todd A. ....'74 '99 C.897 B.S. L.950 J.D. [Barran L.]
Hancock, Douglas D. '56 '91 C.1056 B.S. L.628 J.D.
805 S.W. Broadway, Ste. 2740 (Pat.)
Handy, Jeffrey K. .... '46 '84 C.112 B.A. L.596 J.D. U.S. Dist. Atty.
Hanf, Russell Scott ....'69 '94 C.112 B.A. L.950 J.D. [R.S.Hanf]
Hanf, Russell S. .... 510 S.W. Third Ave., Ste. 425
Hanlon, Michael G., (AV) ....'53 '79 C.629 B.A. L.1051 J.D. [M.G.Hanlon]

Hanlon, Michael G., A Professional Corporation, Law Offices of, (AV)
1300 Congress Center, 1001 S.W. Fifth Avenue, 97204
Telephone: 503-228-9787 Facsimile: 503-224-4200
Email: mgh@hanlonlaw.com URL: http://www.hanlonlaw.com
Michael G. Hanlon. Of Counsel: John H. Durkheimer.
Business Litigation including Antitrust, Securities and other Complex Business Litigation. General Corporate, Business and Real Estate. Creditors Rights, Bankruptcy and Commercial Law.
See Professional Biographies, PORTLAND, OREGON

Hanna, Harry M., (AV) .... '36 '66 C.629 B.S. L.596 J.D. [Ⓒ Sussman S.]
Hanna, Joseph J., Jr., (AV) ....'38 '63 C.670 B.B.A. L.276 J.D. [Hanna S.]
Hanna Strader, A Professional Corporation, (AV) .... 1300 S.W. Sixth Avenue
Hannam, Jack R., (BV) ....'24 '57 C.629 B.A. L.596 LL.B. 4015 N.E. Davis
Hannigan, Penelope J. '48 '86 C.1056 B.A. L.1051 J.D.
Dept. Chmn., Legal Asst. Prog., Portland Community College
Hansberger, Sandra A. .... '56 '83 C.1168 B.A. L.596 J.D. Northwestern Sch. of Law
Hansen, Jeffrey W., (BV) ....'65 '92 C.670 B.S. L.221 J.D. [Smith F.&E.]
Hansen, Kurt F., (AV) ....'53 '84 C.628 B.S. L.629 J.D. [Schwabe,W.&W.]

Hansen, Peter O., Law Offices of, (AV) '50 '75 C.629 B.S. L.950 J.D.
620 S.W. Fifth Avenue, Suite 1210, 97204
Telephone: 503-228-6040 Fax: 503-226-0457
URL: http://www.peterohansenlawyers.com
Workers Compensation, Personal Injury, Maritime Law, Social Security Disability.
See Professional Biographies, PORTLAND, OREGON

Hansen, Richard K., (AV) ....'54 '83 C.1056 B.S. L.596 J.D. [Schwabe,W.&W.]
Hanson, Jeffrey K., (BV) ....'65 '90 C.1051 B.A. L.596 J.D. [Yazbeck,C.&H.]
Harbolt, James B., (AV) '62 '89
C.628 B.S. L.629 J.D. Asst. V.P. & Assoc. Coun., Standard Ins. Co.
Harding, Robert B. .... '49 '78 C.768 B.A. L.1051 J.D. 4130 S.W. Alice St.
Harding, Simon Jonathon .... '66 '92 C.1051 B.A. L.629 J.D. [Ⓐ Schulte,A.D.A.&B.]
Harding, Tanya M., Ph.D. '68 '99 C.705 B.S. L.188 J.D.
[Ⓐ Klarquist S.] (See Pat. Sect.)

Hardman, Christopher R., (AV) '54 '79 C.303 B.A. L.950 J.D.
909 Southwest St. Clair, 97205
Telephone: 503-916-1787 Fax: 503-916-1789
Email: crhardman@crhardman.com URL: http://www.lawyers.com/crhardman
Attorney Professional Responsibility and Ethics Defense, Professional Licensing, Corporate Planning, Business Litigation, Consumer Fraud, Litigation, Insurance Defense, Criminal Defense.
See Professional Biographies, PORTLAND, OREGON

Hardman, Janis L. .... '47 '91 C.1056 B.S. L.1051 J.D. 1 S.W. Columbia St., Ste. 680
Hardwick, Krista N. ....'79 '05 C.549 B.A. L.950 J.D. [Ⓐ Bullivant H.B.]
Harmon, Timothy R., (AV) ....'— '79 C.238 B.A. L.494 J.D. [Lane P.]
Harms, Charles D., (BV) ....'52 '77 C.1056 B.S. L.629 J.D. [Mitchell,L.&S.]
Harnden, Edwin A., (AV) ....'46 '72 C&L.178 A.B., J.D. [Barran L.]
Harper, Brad J. ....'68 '93 C.659 B.A. L.950 J.D. 4201 N.E. 19th Ave.

Harrang Long Gary Rudnick P.C., (AV)
1001 S.W. 5th Avenue, Suite 1650, 97204 ⊙
Telephone: 503-242-0000 Fax: 503-241-1458
URL: http://www.harrang.com
David R. Denecke; William F. Gary; Caroline R. Guest; Susan D. Marmaduke; Frank A. Moscato; James E. Mountain, Jr. (Resident); Mark R. Wada;—Audrey A. Baker; Jolynn M. Brown; Sivhwa Go; Craig L. Leis; Adina Matasaru; Jona J. Maukonen; C. Robert Steringer; Sean T. Waters. Of Counsel: Douglas S. Chiapuzio; K. Bruce Knivila.
General Civil Trial and Appellate Practice in all State and Federal Courts, Governmental and Business Law, Corporate Law, Administrative Law, Financial Services, Securities Law, Creditors Rights, Partnership Law, Real Estate, State and Local Government Law, Environmental Law, Zoning, Planning and Land Use, Estate Planning and Probate, Insurance Law, Civil, Business, Complex and Tort Litigation, Alternative Dispute Resolution, Labor and Employment Law, Employee Benefits, Intellectual Property, Health Law, Nonprofit Law.
Representative Clients: Hyundai Semiconductor America; Schering-Plough Corp.; Philip Morris Companies, Inc.; CheckPoint Software Tech Inc.; Providence Health Plan; PeaceHealth; Les Schwab Tire Centers, Inc.; Echo Spring Dairy, Inc.
Eugene, Oregon Office: 300 East 10th Avenue, Suite 300. Telephone: 541-485-0220. Fax: 541-686-6564.
Salem, Oregon Office: 333 High Street, N.E., Suite 200. Telephone: 503-371-3330. Fax: 503-371-5336.
See Professional Biographies, PORTLAND, OREGON

Harrell, Gary P., (BV) .... '52 '91 C.846 B.S. L.596 J.D. 1515 S.W. 5th Ave., Ste. 1022
Harriman, Heather E. .... '74 '99 C.629 B.A. L.1048 J.D. [Ⓐ Greene&M.]
Harriman, Victoria A. .... '59 '89 C&L.508 B.A., J.D. 3445 N.W. Loriann Dr.
Harrington, John Daniel '71 '95 C.1029 B.S. L.1009 J.D.
(adm. in NY; not adm. in OR) Standard Ins. Co.
Harrington, Robert L., (AV) ...... '36 '61 C&L.585 B.S., J.D. [Schwabe,W.&W.] (Pat.)
Harris, Cheryl B. .... '59 '84 C.957 B.B.A. L.597 J.D. I.R.S.
Harris, Gregory E., (AV) ....'53 '79 C.1051 B.A. L.629 J.D. [Harris&B.]
Harris, Mary M. .... '42 '83 C.1331 B.A. L.1051 J.D. 10250 S.W. Greenburg Rd., Ste. 102
Harris, Robert, (BV) .... '45 '69 C&L.629 B.S., J.D. 1618 S.W. 1st Ave.
Harris, Stuart C., (AV) ....'— '86 C.101 B.A. L.188 J.D. [Davis W.T.]
Harris, Wayne E., (AV) ....'55 '84 C.502 A.B. L.1051 J.D. [Wayne E.H.]
Harris & Bowker, LLP, (AV) .... 10300 S.W. Greenburg Rd.
Harris Crowne, Caroline .... '75 '02 C.691 B.A. L.569 J.D. [Ⓐ Tonkon T.]
Harrison, Penny H. ....'44 '88 C.103 A.B. L.596 J.D. Asst. Atty. Gen.
Hart, Harold C., (AV) .... '29 '56 C.629 B.S. L.596 J.D. 2323 S.W. Park Pl.‡
Hart, Holly .... '47 '75 C.685 B.A. L.1066 J.D. 1300 E. Burnside‡
Hartfield, Sean .... '67 '02 C.1142 B.A. L.596 J.D. [Hartfield&C.]
Hartfield & Crutchley, LLC .... 6021 NE Martin Luther King, Jr., Boulevard
Hartman, Gregory A., (AV) ....'49 '74 C.145 B.A. L.629 J.D. [Bennett,H.M.&K.]
Hartwell, Darius L. ....'71 '00 C.205 B.A. L.596 J.D. [Ⓐ Schwabe,W.&W.]
Hartwell, Shannon .... '70 '00 C.1331 B.A. L.596 J.D. [Ⓐ Perkins C.]
Hartzell, Lynda J., (AV) ....'— '93 C.1356 B.S.Ed. L.1051 J.D. [Tonkon T.]
Hasche, Tilman, (AV) .... '50 '84 C.276 B.S. L.285 J.D. [Parker,B.&L.]
Hashimoto, Takashi ....'54 '88 C.685 B.A. L.950 J.D. 520 S.W. Sixth Ave., Ste. 1010
Haskins, Robert L. .... '43 '69 C.629 A.B. L.309 J.D. Asst. Atty Gen.
Haslach, Timothy F., (AV) .... '61 '91 C&L.770 B.S., J.D. [Schwabe,W.&W.]
Haslett, Donald B., (AV) '45 '77
C.871 B.S. L.188 J.D. [Chernoff,V.M.&S.] (See Pat. Sect.)
Hass, Fredrick R., Attorney at Law ... '52 '81 C.629 B.A. L.285 J.D. 824 N.W. Everett St.
Hasson, Jeffrey I., (BV) .... '58 '87 C.629 B.S. L.1051 J.D. 12707 N.E. Halsey St.
Hatch, Willard '— '48
(adm. in WA; not adm. in OR) [Foster P.T.] ⊙‡
Hathaway, Gregory S., (AV) ....'— '73 C.950 B.A. L.596 J.D. [Davis W.T.]
Hattenhauer, Richard R., (BV) '49 '75 C.629 B.S. L.1051 J.D.
5550 S.W. Macadam Ave.
Hatton, Nikki C., (AV) .... '49 '77 C.911 B.A. L.260 J.D. [Schwabe,W.&W.]
Hattrick, David L. ....'39 '69 C.285 B.A. L.276 J.D. Sr. Dep. Dist. Atty.
Haub, Johnathan S. .... '48 '76 C.352 B.S. L.1051 J.D. U.S. Atty. Off.
Hauck, Terry C., (AV) ....'41 '71 C.1056 B.S. L.950 J.D. [Schwabe,W.&W.]
Hausafus, Karl E. ....'71 '00 C.629 B.S. L.1051 J.D. [Ⓐ Preston G.&E.]
Havel, Paul L. ....'68 '96 C.207 B.A. L.146 J.D. [Ⓐ Miller N.]
Haver, Kohel M., (BV) .... '54 '86 C.33 B.S. L.596 J.D. [Haver&Assoc.]
Haver & Associates, (BV) ....621 S.W. Morrison St., Ste. 1417
Hay, Kirkham E., (AV) ...'48 '75 C.629 B.B.A. L.464 J.D. [Brownstein,R.S.K.G.D.&H.]
Hay, Lisa C. ....'63 '91 C.976 B.A. L.309 J.D. Fed. Pub. Def. Off.
Hayes, Gerald R., (BV) ....'26 '58 C.1051 B.S. L.596 LL.B. 1001 S.W. 5th Ave.
Hayes, Kevin M. .... '74 '01 C.678 B.S. L.628 J.D. [Ⓐ Klarquist S.] (See Pat. Sect.)
Haynie, Erick J. ....'— '98 C.670 B.A. L.597 J.D. [Ⓐ Perkins C.]
Hays, Paul C., (AV) ....'49 '75 C.906 B.A. L.950 J.D. [Carney,B.H.&M.]
Hayward, Joshua Paul .... '74 '01 C.628 B.A. L.1117 J.D. [Ⓐ Smith F.&E.]
Heady, Stephen '46 '75 C.350 B.S. L.352 J.D.
(adm. in NE; not adm. in OR) V.P. & Mgr., Bus. Tr. Servs., Union Bk. of Calif.
Healey, R. Michael, (BV) ....'50 '75 C.546 B.S. L.190 J.D. [Reinisch,M.H.&W.]
Healy, Therasa A., (AV) ..... '66 '93 C.1212 B.A. L.1051 J.D. 650 Ne Holladay St #1400
Heap, Theodore H., (BV) .... '44 '70 C.1109 B.A. L.950 J.D. 121 S.W. Salmon St.
Heath, Amelia ....'— '02 C.774 B.A. L.950 J.D. [Ⓐ Holland&K.]
Heath, C. Craig ....'54 '80 C&L.950 B.S., J.D. Sr. VP, U.S. Bank
Hedberg, Steven M., (AV) .... '58 '84 C.1056 B.A. L.596 J.D. [Perkins C.]
Heekin, Katherine R. ....'67 '94 C.674 A.B. L.629 J.D. [Heekin]

Heekin Law Firm
121 SW Morrison Street, Suite 600, 97204
Telephone: 503-222-5578 Fax: 503-914-1889
Email: katherine@heekinlawoffice.com URL: http://www.heekinlawoffice.com
Katherine R. Heekin.
Commercial Litigation, Employment Law, Electronic Discovery.
See Professional Biographies, PORTLAND, OREGON

Hefferin, Victor C., (BV) .... '23 '59 C.1056 L.596 LL.B. 4804 S. E. 118th
Heffernan, James Patrick '59 '89 C.172 B.S. L.596 J.D.
Policy Asst., Columbia River Inter-tribal Fish Comm.
Heiling, Dean, (AV) ....'45 '71 C.911 B.A. L.950 J.D. [D.Heiling&Assoc.]
Heiling, Dwyer, & Associates, (AV) .... 1220 S.W. Morrison
Heinrich, Thomas A. ....'65 '90 C.1051 B.A. L.911 J.D. [Ⓐ Mitchell,L.&S.]
Heinson, Timothy J. ....'58 '87 C.670 B.B.A. L.596 J.D. [Lachenmeier E.R.&H.]
Heinzel, James T. .... '49 '76 C.339 B.S. L.209 J.D. P.O. Box 3287
Heitkemper, Allard J. .... '30 '61 C&L.276 B.S.S., J.D. 2665 S.W. Vista Ave.
Heitman, Perry S. ....'58 '03 C.1098 B.S. L.596 J.D. [Ⓐ Larkins V.]
Heller, James W. "Mike", (BV) .... '39 '86 C.645 B.S. L.1051 J.D. Freightliner LLC
Helm, Kenneth D. ....'65 '94 C&L.950 B.A., J.D. Asst. Coun., Metro
Helmer, M. Christie, P.C., (AV) ....'49 '74 C.906 B.A. L.596 J.D. [Miller N.]
Heltzel, Timothy W., (AV) '46 '71 C.629 B.S. L.950 J.D.
209 S.W. Oak Street, 5th Floor

Helzer & Cromar, LLP
(See Beaverton)

Hemmingway, Leroy H., (AV) ......'46 '72 C.813 B.A. L.976 J.D. 01030 S.W. Comus St.
Henderson, William A. ....'55 '81 C.637 B.A. L.629 J.D. 1726 Se Umatilla St.
Hendon, Jeremy N. ....'73 '98 C&L.629 B.S., J.D. Law Clk., Dist. Ct.
Hendricks, Stephanie ....'— '03 C.1059 B.I.S. L.950 J.D. [A Lane P.]
Hendricks, Stephen C., (AV) ....'54 '79 C.188 B.A. L.629 J.D. [Hendricks]
Hendricks Law Firm, P.C., (AV) .... 4614 SW Kelly Avenue, Suite 200
Hendry, James W., (BV) ... '58 '83 C.1074 B.S. L.950 J.D. [Brownstein,R.S.K.G.D.&H.]
Henke, Susanna ....'69 '02 C.66 B.A. L.178 J.D. [A Stoll S.B.L.&S.]
Hennessy, Peggy, (BV) ....'54 '87 C.413 B.A. L.596 J.D. [Reeves,K.&H.]
Henning, Sonja L. ....'— '95 C.813 B.A. L.228 J.D. [A Tonkon T.]
Hennings, James D., (AV) '42 '68
C.393 B.A. L.950 J.D. Dir., Metropolitan Public Defenders
Hennings, Laury H. ....'46 '76 C.950 B.A. L.596 J.D. [B Farleigh W.]
Henry, Louis G., P.C., (AV) ....'55 '81 C.629 B.S. L.596 J.D. [Miller N.]
Henzel, D. Ben ....'67 '95 C&L.629 B.S., J.D. [D.B.Henzel]
Henzel, D. Ben, PC ....224 S.W. Hamilton St., Ste. 300
Hepburn, Rodger M. ....'64 '92 C.907 B.A. L.950 J.D. [Reinisch,M.H.&W.]
Hepler, David A. ....'69 '02 C.112 B.A. L.1049 J.D. [A Schwabe,W.&W.]
Hercher, David W., P.C., (AV) ....'55 '81 C.629 B.A. L.1066 J.D. [Miller N.]
Hergenhan, Kenneth W., P.C., (AV) '31 '58 C.401 B.S. L.309 LL.B.
111 S.W. 5th Ave.‡
Hering, Tim .... '— '05 C.911 B.A. L.629 J.D. [A Dunn C.A.H.&T.]
Hermann, Christopher R., (AV) ....'53 '82 C.95 B.A. L.629 J.D. [Stoel R.]
Hermann, Dale M., (AV) ....'42 '69 C&L.950 B.A., J.D. [Hermann]
Hermann & Company, P.C., (AV) ....No. 271 25 NW 23rd Place., Suite 6
Hern, Jeffrey D. ....'76 '04 C.207 B.A. L.950 J.D. [A Schwabe,W.&W.]
Hernández, Román D. ....'— '01 C.628 B.A. L.596 J.D. [A Schwabe,W.&W.]
Herrell, Stephen B. ....'38 '66 C.880 B.A. L.276 LL.B. Ret. Sr. Cir. J.
Herrick, Christine T., (AV) .....'49 '75 C.771 B.A. L.596 J.D. [B Markowitz,H.G.&M.]
Herriges, Nicholas P. '57 '83 C.188 A.B. L.508 J.D.
Sr. Corp. Coun., Cadence Design Systems, Inc.
Hershey, Lisa L. ....'— '82 C.629 B.A. L.950 J.D. Atty., U.S. Bancorp
Herzog, Theodore G. ....'— '89 C.906 B.A. L.846 J.D. [Tonkon T.]
Heskett, Sara C. ....'66 '00 C.914 B.A. L.260 J.D. [A Holland&K.]
Hess, Henry L., Jr. ....'24 '49 C&L.629 B.S., J.D. Ret. Chf. U.S. Bkrptcy. J.
Hess, Lee M., (BV) ....'48 '77 C&L.911 B.S., J.D. [L.M.Hess]

Hess, Lee M., P.C., (BV)
1000 S.W. Broadway, Suite 1780, 97205
Telephone: 503-273-8674 Fax: 503-273-8803
Email: lee@lmhpc.net URL: http://www.lawyers.com/leehess
Lee M. Hess.
Business and Commercial Litigation. Creditors Rights, Secured Transactions, Real Estate. Trial and Appellate Practice, Corporate, Contracts, Debt and Credit Collections, Commercial Leasing, Construction, Environmental, Trusts and Estates, Wills and Probate.
See Professional Biographies, PORTLAND, OREGON

Hester, Thomas Jeffrey ....'62 '91 C.383 B.A. L.705 J.D. Pub. Def. Off.
Heth, Jacob A. ....'— '94 C.112 B.A. L.950 J.D. [B Davis W.T.]
Heth, Sharon O. ....'68 '93 C.911 B.A. L.950 J.D. 1121 Sw Salmon St Ste 200
Heuer, Christopher K., (AV) ....'59 '90 C.813 A.B. L.309 J.D. [Stoel R.]
Heuser, Peter E., (AV) ....'49 '76 C.1027 B.S. L.966 J.D. [Kolisch H.] (Pat.) ⊙
Hewitt, Henry H., (AV) ....'41 '69 C.976 A.B. L.950 J.D. [Stoel R.]
Hibbs, Carol Dey, (AV) ....'48 '78 C.629 B.A. L.813 J.D. [Tonkon T.]
Hibpshman, Danica K. ....'76 '03 C.17 B.A. L.950 J.D. [A Haglund,K.H.&J.]
Hickman, Molly E. ....'— '98 L.596 J.D. 1645 N.E. 146
Hickok, Harold M. ....'50 '84 C.629 B.A. L.477 J.D. 10720 N.W. Lost Park Dr.
Hicks, Graham M., P.C., (AV) ....'49 '73 C&L.950 B.A., J.D. [Miller N.]
Hiefield, Mark A., (AV) ....'51 '77 C.906 B.S. L.285 J.D. [Bodyfelt M.S.&C.]
Hiefield, Preston C., Jr. ....'31 '55 C&L.629 B.S., J.D. 200 S.W. Market St.
Hilgenfeld, Chris ....'73 '00 C.942 B.S. L.596 J.D. [A Jolles&B.]
Hill, Anne Pendergrass, (BV) '54 '80
C.950 B.A. L.596 J.D. First Interstate Bk. of Ore., N.A.
Hill, Christopher T. ....'71 '97 C.375 B.A. L.1051 J.D. [C.T.Hill]
Hill, Edward J. ....'61 '94 C.276 B.A. L.1051 J.D. [Hill&W.]
Hill, Jeffrey V., (AV) ....'55 '81 C.906 B.A. L.678 J.D. [Zarosinski&H.]
Hill, John S. '08 '35 L.999 LL.B.
(adm. in TX; not adm. in OR) 3325 NW 131st Pl.‡
Hill, John W., (AV) ....'25 '49 C&L.629 B.S., J.D. [Miller N.] ‡
Hill, Stephen B., (AV) ....'41 '66 C.339 B.S. L.813 J.D. [B Bullivant H.B.]
Hill, Steven F., (BV) ....'60 '93 [Miller N.] (⊙Vancouver, WA)
Hill, Thomas K. ....'48 '74 C.813 B.A. L.629 J.D. 4015 N.E. 12th‡
Hill, Wilmer B. ....'28 '56 C.197 A.B. L.276 J.D. Admin. Law J., Soc. Sec. Admn.
Hill, Christopher T., PC ....1020 S.W. Taylor St.
Hill & Wren, LLP, (AV) ....1826 N.E. Broadway
Hillas, James M. ....'66 '94 C.1307 B.A. L.596 J.D. [Dunn C.A.H.&T.]
Hiller, James L., (AV) ....'52 '77 C.1044 B.A. L.477 J.D. [Hitt H.&M.]
Hillier, Thomas S., (AV) ....'— '80 C&L.629 B.S., J.D. [Davis W.T.]
Hilton, Frank H., Jr., (AV) ....'41 '66 C.813 A.B. L.629 LL.B. [Dunn C.A.H.&T.]
Hilzer, John J. '45 '73 C.1056 B.S. L.336 J.D.
(adm. in WA; not adm. in OR) 2313 S.E. Eliott‡
Hindley, R. Craig ....'50 '78 C.645 L.1051 J.D. [R.C.Hindley]
Hindley, R. Craig, LLC ....9900 S.W. Greenburg Road, Suite 130
Hindman, Kathryn M., (AV) ....'58 '87 C.911 B.A. L.285 J.D. [Bullard S.J.W.]
Hines, Stephanie K. ....'— '02 C.785 B.A. L.1051 J.D. [A Perkins C.]
Hinkle, Charles F., (AV) ....'42 '71 C.813 B.A. L.976 J.D. [Stoel R.]

Hinshaw & Culbertson LLP, (AV)
Hinshaw & Culbertson LLP is an Illinois registered limited liability partnership that has elected to be governed by the Illinois Uniform Partnership Act (1997)
1000 SW Broadway Suite 1950, 97205-3078 ⊙
Telephone: 503-243-3243 Fax: 503-243-3240 Telex: 880248
Email: kfox@hinshawlaw.com URL: http://www.hinshawlaw.com
Partner: Peter R. Jarvis. Associates: David J. Elkanich; René C. Holmes.
Appellate, Banking & Financing, Bankruptcy & Creditors' Rights, Class Action Litigation, Civil Rights Defense, Commercial Litigation, Corporate, Construction Law, Director & Officer Liability, Employee Benefits, Environmental, Fidelity & Surety, General Liability Litigation, Government, Health Care, Insurance Coverage, Insurance and Reinsurance, Labor & Employment, Legal Malpractice, Medical Malpractice, Mergers & Acquisitions, Municipal Liability, Personal Injury Defense, Public Law, Products Liability Litigation, Professional Liability, Regulatory, Real Estate, School Law, Securities, Taxation, Transportation, White Collar Crime and Workers' Compensation Defense.
Representative Clients: Aetna Life & Casualty Co.; Allstate Insurance Co.; Continental Insurance; Farmers Insurance Group; Fireman's Fund American; Hartford Insurance Group; Maryland Casualty Co.; Unigard Security; U.S. Fidelity & Guaranty Co.
Other Office Locations: Chicago, Illinois; Appleton, Wisconsin; Belleville, Illinois; Boston, Massachusetts; Champaign, Illinois; Crystal Lake, Illinois; Edwardsville, Illinois; Fort Lauderdale, Florida; Jacksonville, Florida; Joliet, Illinois; Lisle, Illinois; Los Angeles, California; Miami, Florida; Milwaukee, Wisconsin; Minneapolis, Minnesota; New York, New York; Peoria, Illinois; Phoenix, Ari-

(This Listing Continued)

Hinshaw & Culbertson LLP (Continued)
zona; Providence, Rhode Island; Rockford, Illinois; St. Louis, Missouri; San Francisco, California; Schererville, Indiana; Springfield, Illinois; Tampa, Florida; Waukegan, Illinois.
See Professional Biographies, PORTLAND, OREGON

Hinton, Floyd, (BV) ....'23 '58 C.629 B.S. L.596 LL.B. Oregon Central Credit Union
Hirsch, Janice L. Holtorf, (AV) ....'50 '93 C.906 B.A. L.1051 J.D. [Jordan S.]
Hirschy, John A., (AV) ....'53 '82 C.473 B.S. L.260 J.D. [Black H.]
Hirshon, Robert E., (AV) '48 '73 C&L.477 B.A., J.D.
(adm. in ME; not adm. in OR) [Tonkon T.]
Hitt, Danny L., Jr., (BV) ....'57 '83 C.966 B.A. L.629 J.D. [Hitt H.&M.]

Hitt Hiller & Monfils LLP, (AV)
510 Southwest Third Avenue, Suite 309, 97204
Telephone: 503-228-8870 Fax: 503-228-4250
URL: http://www.hittandhiller.com
Danny L. Hitt, Jr.; James L. Hiller; Scott P. Monfils; Brian B. Williams.
Civil Litigation, Personal Injury, Wrongful Death, Insurance Coverage, Products Liability, Transportation, Employment Law, Discrimination, and Business Litigation.
See Professional Biographies, PORTLAND, OREGON

Ho, Cheryl Lee, (BV) '45 '75
C.312 B.E. L.596 J.D. Admin. Law J., State Liquor Control Comm.
Hoarfrost, Daniel G., (BV) ....'48 '75 C.197 B.A. L.629 J.D. 9600 SW Barnes Rd.
Hobbs, Straus, Dean & Walker, LLP
806 S.W. Broadway, Ste. 900 (⊙Wash., DC; Oklahoma City, OK)
Hochberg, Sam, (BV) ....'50 '83 C.35 B.S. L.596 J.D. [S.Hochberg]
Hochberg, Samuel, (BV) ....720 S.W. Washington St., Ste. 750
Hocken, Natalie L. ....'69 '94 C.911 B.A. L.629 J.D. Sr. Coun., PacifiCorp
Hodge, William C. ....'42 '71 C.309 B.A. L.813 J.D. Prof., Northwestern Sch. of Law
Hodges, Carlton W., (AV) '37 '67 C&L.629 B.A., J.D.
1000 S.W. Broadway, Suite 1770
Hodgson, Sandra L., (BV) ....'54 '85 C&L.352 B.A., J.D. [Bouneff&C.]
Hoevet, Ronald H., (AV) ....'46 '75 C.950 B.A. L.228 J.D. [Hoevet,B.&O.]

Hoevet, Boise & Olson, PC, (AV)
1000 S.W. Broadway, Suite 1500, 97205
Telephone: 503-228-0497 Fax: 503-228-7112
Email: attys@hoevet-boise.com
Ronald H. Hoevet; Whitney P. Boise;—Per C. Olson.
Criminal Defense in State and Federal Court, White Collar/Business Crimes, Drug Crimes, Vehicular Homicide, Sex Crimes, Tax and Securities Fraud, Civil Forfeiture.
See Professional Biographies, PORTLAND, OREGON

Hoffinger, Julie M. H. ....'70 '96 C.629 B.A. L.911 J.D. 9725 NW Fleischner St.
Hoffman, David A. .... '68 '94 C.299 A.B. L.228 J.D. Coun. & Dir. of Privacy, Intel Corp.
Hoffman, Jack D., (AV) ....'47 '76 C.906 B.S. L.596 J.D. [Dunn C.A.H.&T.]

Hoffman, Janet Lee, (AV) '51 '77 C.684 B.A. L.93 J.D.
1000 S.W. Broadway Suite 1500, 97205
Telephone: 503-222-1125 Fax: 503-222-7589
Email: janet@jhoffman.com URL: http://www.janetleehoffman.com
Associates: Carrie Menikoff; Catherine M. Tosswill; Nicholas Cropp.
Criminal Trial and Appellate Practice in State and Federal Courts. Administrative Defense of Professional Licenses. Civil Forfeiture.
See Professional Biographies, PORTLAND, OREGON

Hoffman, Jonathan M., (AV) ......'48 '75 C.309 A.B. L.629 J.D. [Martin,B.T.L.&H.] ⊙
Hoffman, Susan E., (BV) ....'54 '80 C.813 A.B. L.950 J.D. 2838 S.W. Dickinson St.
Hoffmann, Erich H., (AV) ....'47 '76 C.628 B.S. L.596 J.D. [Bocci&H.]
Hoffmann, Margaret A. O'Connor, (AV) '53 '83
C.1042 B.A. L.809 J.D. [Schwabe,W.&W.]
Hoguet, Albert W., (BV) .....'42 '68 C.604 A.B. L.930 J.D. Ref., State Wkrs. Comp. Bd.
Hohimer, Ashley S. ....'77 '03 C.629 B.A. L.245 J.D. [A Miller N.]
Holden, John G., (AV) ....'30 '56 C&L.629 B.S., LL.B. 1001 S.W. Fifth Ave.
Holeman, Jacob J. ....'45 '73 C.413 B.A. L.629 J.D. 3540 S.W. 87th Ave.‡

Holland & Knight LLP, (AV) [BB]
2300 U.S. Bancorp Tower, 111 Southwest Fifth Avenue, 97204 ⊙
Telephone: 503-243-2300 Telecopier: 503-241-8014
URL: http://www.hklaw.com
Portland Members: Christopher W. Angius; Christopher Cline; C. Paul Dagle; George J. Gregores; J. Alan Jensen; Joel P. Leonard; Louis A. Santiago; Mark A. von Bergen. Senior Counsel: Susan Burton; Charles P. Starkey. Associates: Courtney C. Dippel; Amelia Heath; Sara C. Heskett; Joshua E. Husbands; David A. Koempel; Benjamin Leedy; David C. Wang.
Litigation, Government Law, Business Law, Real Estate Law and Private Wealth Services.
Annapolis, Maryland Office: State Circle Building, 47 State Circle, Suite 400, 21401. Telephone: 410-263-7800. Fax: 410-263-3768.
Atlanta, Georgia Office: One Atlantic Center, 1201 West Peachtree Street, N.E., Suite 2000, 30309. Telephone: 404-817-8500. Fax: 404-881-0470.
Beijing, China Office: No. 33, 14th Floor, IBM Tower, Pacific Century Place, 2 A Workers Stadium Road North, Chaoyang District, 100027. Telephone: 86-10-653-91232. Fax: 86-10-653-91060.
Bethesda, Maryland Office: 3 Bethesda Metro Center, Suite 800, 20814. Telephone: 301-654-7800. Fax: 301-656-3978.
Boston, Massachusetts Office: 10 St. James Avenue, 11th Floor, 02116. Telephone: 617-523-2700. Fax: 617-523-6850.
Bradenton, Florida Office: Bradenton Financial Center, 1401 West Manatee Avenue, Suite 1200, 34205. Telephone: 941-748-7076. Fax: 941-747-9774.
Chicago, Illinois Office: 131 South Dearborn Street, 30th Floor, 60603. Telephone: 312-263-3600. Fax: 312-578-6666.
Fort Lauderdale, Florida Office: One East Broward Boulevard, Suite 1300, 33301. Telephone: 954-525-1000. Fax: 954-463-2030.
Jacksonville, Florida Office: 50 North Laura Street, Suite 3900, 32202. Telephone: 904-353-2000. Fax: 904-358-1872.
Lakeland, Florida Office: 92 Lake Wire Drive, 33815. Telephone: 863-682-1161. Fax: 863-688-1186.
Los Angeles, California Office: 633 West Fifth Street, 21st Floor, 90071. Telephone: 213-896-2400. Fax: 213-896-2450.
Mexico City, Mexico Office: Holland & Knight - Gallastegui y Lozano, S.C., Edificio Arcos Bosques Corporativo, Paseo de los Tamarindos 400-B, Piso 2, Delegación Cuajimalpa, Bosques de las Lomas, 05120. Telephone: 525-55-261-1866. Fax: 525-55-261-1867.
Miami, Florida Office: 701 Brickell Avenue, Suite 3000, 33131. Telephone: 305-374-8500. Fax: 305-789-7799.
New York, New York Office: 195 Broadway, 10007. Telephone: 212-513-3200. Fax: 212-385-9010.
Northern Virginia: 1600 Tysons Boulevard, Suite 700, McLean, Virginia, 22102. Telephone: 703-720-8600. Fax: 703-720-8610.
Oakbrook Terrace, Illinois Office: One Mid America Plaza, Suite 1000, 60181. Telephone: 630-954-2100. Fax: 630-954-2112.
Orlando, Florida Office: SunTrust Building, Suite 2600, 200 South Orange Avenue, 32801. Telephone: 407-425-8500. Fax: 407-244-5288.
Providence, Rhode Island Office: One Financial Plaza, Suite 1800, 02903. Telephone: 401-751-8500. Fax: 401-553-6850.
Rancho Santa Fe, California Office: 6050 El Tordo, 92067. Telephone: 858-756-4410. Fax: 858-756-4386.
Sacramento, California Office: 1215 K Street, 17th Floor, 95814. Telephone: 916-503-1695. Fax: 916-503-2401.
San Antonio, Texas Office: Weston Centre, 112 East Pecan Street, Suite 2700, 78205. Telephone: 210-229-3000. Fax: 210-229-1194.
San Francisco, California Office: 50 California Street, Suite 2800, 94111. Telephone: 415-743-6900. Fax: 415-743-6910.

(This Listing Continued)

Holland & Knight LLP (Continued)

Seattle, Washington Office: 2600 Pike Tower, 520 Pike Street, 98101. Telephone: 206-340-1825. Fax: 206-623-4363.
St. Petersburg, Florida Office: 200 Central Avenue, Suite 1600, 33701. Telephone: 727-896-7171. Fax: 727-822-8048.
Tallahassee, Florida Office: 315 South Calhoun Street, Suite 600, 32301. Telephone: 850-224-7000. Fax: 850-224-8832.
Tampa, Florida Office: 100 North Tampa Street, Suite 4100, 33602-3644. Telephone: 813-227-8500. Fax: 813-229-0134.
Tokyo, Japan Office: Tokyo Ginko Kyokai Building, 15th Floor, 1-3-1 Marunouchi, Chiyoda-ku, 100-0005. Telephone: 813-3216-7206. Fax: 813-3216-7286.
Washington, D.C. Office: 2099 Pennsylvania Avenue, N.W., Suite 100, 20006. Telephone: 202-955-3000. Fax: 202-955-5564.
West Palm Beach, Florida Office: 222 Lakeview Avenue, Suite 1000, 33401. Telephone: 561-833-2000. Fax: 561-650-8399.
Representative Offices:
Caracas, Venezuela Office: Tinoco, Travieso, Planchart & Núñez, Avenida Francisco De Miranda, Torre Country Club, Pisos 1 y 2, Chacaito, 1050. Telephone: 582-12-952-9033 (Master). Fax: 582-12-953-1053/8365/7583. Email: ttpn@ttpn.com.ve.
Helsinki, Finland Office: Holland & Knight Oy, Pohjoisesplanadi 33, FIN-00100. Telephone: 358-9-684-1520. Fax: 358-9-6841-5252.
Tel Aviv, Israel Office: Haim Samet, Steinmetz, Haring & Co. Advocates, 23 Begin Road, 18th Floor, 66814. Telephone: 972-3-567-0100. Fax: 972-3-567-01010.

See Professional Biographies, PORTLAND, OREGON

Hollander, David J., (BV) '51 '77 C.102 B.A. L.1009 J.D. 1500 S.W. First Ave., Ste. 700
Hollis, Robert R., (AV) '27 '51 C&L.629 J.D. 520 S.W. Yamhill St.
Holloway, Charles R., III, (AV) '40 '65 C&L.629 B.S., LL.B. [C.R.Holloway]
Holloway, Ronald C., (AV) '46 '79 C.628 B.S. L.950 J.D. [Sather,B.&H.]
Holloway, Charles R., Attorney at Law, (AV) 1000 S.W. Broadway, Ste. 1060
Holm Jensen, Paula '64 '94 C.918 B.A. L.770 J.D. [Holm J.]
Holm Jensen Law LLC P.O. Box 4825
Holma, Paul J., (BV) '64 '93 C.911 B.S. L.629 J.D. [B Motschenbacher&B.]
Holmes, John H., (AV) '38 '65 C&L.629 B.S., J.D. [B Mersereau&S.]
Holmes, René C., (CV) '72 '98 C.1181 B.A. L.950 J.D. [A Hinshaw&C.]
Holmes, Sherman W. '27 '54 C&L.629 B.S., LL.B. 10414 N.E. Sandy Blvd.
Holmes, William H., (AV) '60 '86 C.846 B.A. L.477 J.D. [Stoel R.]
Holmes-Gaar, Elizabeth G. '59 '90 C.628 B.S. L.1051 J.D. Natl. Marine Fisheries Serv.
Holsinger, Pamala R. '64 '89 C.1051 B.A. L.950 J.D. U.S. Attys. Off.
Honn, Darin D., (AV) '62 '88 C.547 B.S. L.546 J.D. [Sussman S.]
Hook, Laurel P. '74 '99 C.629 B.S. L.1358 J.D. [Stahancyk,K.J.&H.] (⊙Astoria)
Hooper, Thomas K., (AV) '52 '77 C.878 B.S. L.629 J.D. [Hooper,E.&W.]

Hooper, Englund & Weil LLP, (AV)
Suite 1507, Standard Plaza, 1100 Southwest Sixth Avenue, 97204-1016
Telephone: 503-226-0500 Fax: 503-226-7192
Members of Firm: Thomas K. Hooper; Gregory J. Englund; John W. Weil;—Chelsea S. Lewandowski.
General Civil and Trial Practice in all State and Federal Courts. Corporate, Business and Commercial Law, Uniform Commercial Code, Mergers and Acquisitions, Securities, Estate Planning and Probate, Bankruptcy Litigation, Personal Injury.

See Professional Biographies, PORTLAND, OREGON

Hoover, John K., (BV) '47 '72 C&L.950 B.A., J.D. Dep. Dist. Atty.
Hoover, Ronald C., (BV) '48 '74 C.103 B.A. L.596 J.D. 7235 N.E. Sandy Blvd.
Hopkins, Robert B., (AV) '48 '73 C.604 B.A. L.145 J.D. [Landye B.B.]
Hornecker, Mitchell E., (AV) '60 '86 C.629 B.S. L.1051 J.D. [Schwabe,W.&W.]
Horngren, Scott W., (BV) '55 '88 C.628 B.S. L.596 J.D. [Haglund,K.H.&J.]
Hornik, Philip, (AV) '50 '77 C.569 B.A. L.678 J.D. 520 S.W. 6th Ave., Ste. 1010
Horning, Fred A. '45 '75 C.813 B.A. L.950 J.D. (adm. in WA; not adm. in OR) 9535 N.E. Colfax‡
Horowitz, Lewis M., (AV) '— '85 C.178 B.A. L.276 J.D. [Lane P.]
Horton, William Patrick, (BV) '51 '79 C.629 B.S. L.678 J.D. 101 South West Main Street
Hortsch, Stephanie '65 '98 C.1071 B.S. L.950 J.D. Jud. Clk., Cir. Ct.
Horvat, Robert J., (AV) '55 '86 C.446 B.A. L.629 J.D. [Barg H.]
Hosenpud, David G., (AV) '— '83 C.769 B.A. L.629 J.D. [Lane P.]
Hossaini, Kelly Shafer '64 '01 C.1056 B.A. L.596 J.D [A Miller N.]
Houser, Douglas G., (AV) '35 '60 C.950 B.A. L.813 J.D. [Bullivant H.B.]
Houze, Stephen A., (AV) '46 '72 C.103 A.B. L.880 J.D. 1211 S.W. 5th Ave., Ste. 1190
Howard, Charles Scott, (AV) '53 '78 C.605 B.A. L.1148 J.D. [Dunn C.A.H.&T.]
Howard, Daniel W. '69 '00 C.546 B.A. L.629 J.D. [A Lindsay,H.N.&W.]
Howe, Gregory J., (BV) '42 '72 C.976 B.A. L.309 J.D. [B D.F.Tripp]
Howe, James C., (AV) '55 '80 C.629 B.S. L.911 J.D. [Martin,B.T.L.&H.]
Howe, William J., III, (AV) '48 '75 C.911 B.A. L.950 J.D. [Gevurtz,M.L.&H.]
Howitt, David M. '68 '94 C.207 B.A. L.1051 J.D. Assoc. Coun., adidas America, Inc.
Hribernick, Paul R., (AV) '54 '80 C&L.629 B.S., J.D. [Black H.]
Hu, Yi-Kang '— '05 C.685 B.A. L.596 J.D. [A Preston G.&E.] (Pat.)
Hubel, Dennis J. '47 '76 C.188 B.S.E.E. L.596 J.D. Mag. J., U.S. Dist. Ct.
Huber, Charles J., (AV) '— '76 C&L.629 B.B.A., J.D. [Cosgrave V.K.]
Hubert, Mark S. '56 '98 C.999 R.E. L.596 J.D. [M.S.Hubert]
Hubert, Mark S., PC 516 S.E. Morrison, Ste. 420
Hudson, Charles F., (AV) '— '83 C&L.893 B.A., J.D. [Lane P.]
Huegli, James D., (AV) '47 '72 C.628 B.S. L.950 J.D. 101 SW Main Street, Suite 1800‡
Huffman, James L. '45 '88 C.506 B.S. L.145 J.D. (adm. in MT; not adm. in OR) Dean, Lewis and Clark Law School‡
Hughes, Lindsey H., (AV) '56 '81 C.336 B.A. L.950 J.D. [Keating J.B.&H.]
Hughes, Robert M. '51 '80 C.911 B.A. L.596 J.D. 5125 S.W. Macadam Ave., Ste. 200
Hughey, Patrick W. '52 '83 C.1044 B.S. L.1051 J.D. 805 S.W. Broadway, Ste. 2740 (Pat.)
Huglin, Mark L. '56 '88 C.628 B.S. L.950 J.D. [Draneas&H.]
Hull, David E., (BV) '61 '86 C.477 B.A. L.608 J.D. [Gazzola&H.]
Hull, Gerit F. '66 '96 C.318 B.A. L.273 J.D. Atty., PacifiCorp
Hull, Jay D. '— '84 C.685 B.A. L.1051 J.D. [Davis W.T.]
Hull, Mary P. '72 '97 C.31 B.A. L.861 J.D. [A Stoel R.]
Hull, Steven H. '67 '97 C.103 B.A. L.596 J.D. [Stoel R.]
Hummel, Holly Jane, (BV) '57 '84 C.1214 B.A. L.629 J.D. 522 S.W. 5th Ave.
Humphreys, Richard H., Jr. '40 '65 C&L.911 B.A., J.D. Gen. Coun. & Corp. Secy., Columbia Helicopters Inc.
Hunt, Brian L. '63 '93 C.1071 B.S. L.596 J.D. Staff Atty., American Family Insurance Group
Hunt, Lawrence B., (BV) '50 '75 C.597 B.A. L.629 J.D. [Hunt&Assoc.]
Hunt, Richard C., (AV) '42 '67 C.813 B.A. L.1066 J.D. [Barran L.]
Hunt, Scott N., (AV) '54 '92 C.293 B.A. L.596 J.D. [Busse&H.]
Hunt, Steven B. '46 '86 C.208 B.A. L.1051 J.D. Lewis & Clark College
Hunt, Terrance C., (BV) '42 '72 C.1056 B.A. L.767 J.D. [Parker,B.&L.]

Hunt & Associates, PC, (BV)
805 One Main Place, 101 S.W. Main Street, 97204
Telephone: 503-226-1162 FAX: 503-223-5442
Email: admin@huntpc.com
Lawrence B. Hunt; Millard M. Becker (Retired). Associates: Brad A. Macomber; Kevin J. Tillson.
Business and Commercial Litigation. Commercial and Creditors Rights Law, Real Estate. Trial and Appellate Practice, Corporate, Contract, Employment Law, Negligence, Plaintiffs Personal Injury, Wills, Probate, and Family Law.

See Professional Biographies, PORTLAND, OREGON

Hurd, Paul G., (AV) '46 '76 C.1056 B.S. L.1051 J.D. Gen. Coun. & Secy., Freightliner LLC
Hurtig, Robt. L., (BV) '27 '53 C.629 B.S. L.596 LL.B. 2756 S.W. Boundary St.
Husbands, Joshua E. '73 '99 C.846 B.B.A. L.596 J.D. [A Holland&K.]
Huston, Michael B. '50 '75 C.668 B.A. L.910 J.D. Dept. of Jus.
Huston, Robert T., (AV) '41 '68 C&L.629 B.A., J.D. [Cable H.B.H.&L.]
Hutchinson, Donald K. '45 '75 C&L.629 B.S., J.D. 2109 S.E. Ash St.
Hutchinson, Scott M. '71 '97 C.911 B.A. L.629 J.D. [Hutchinson]
Hutchinson, Thomas L. '63 '92 C.494 B.S. L.420 J.D. [Bullivant H.B.]
Hutchinson Legal Services, P.C. 819 S.E. Morrison Street, Suite 160
Hutchison, William P. '— '69 C.629 B.S. L.950 J.D. [Foster P.T.]
Hutchison & Walsh, A Professional Corporation
(See West Linn)
Huynh, Hong N. '73 '98 C.637 B.S. L.629 J.D. [A Miller N.]
Hval, Steven B. '65 '93 C.911 B.A. L.629 J.D. [Hagen O.]
Hyatt, Townsend, (AV) '— '89 C.575 B.A. L.228 J.D. [Orrick,H.&S.]
Hybertsen, Paul S. '21 '52 L.596 J.D. 12114 N.E. Fargo Ct.‡
Hytowitz, David A., (AV) '50 '75 C&L.629 B.S., J.D. 10324 S.W. 14th Dr.
Idea Advocates Law Group, LLC 322 NW 5th Street, Suite 310 (Pat.)
Ifversen, Thomas '69 '00 C.629 B.A. L.596 J.D. 415 N.W. 18th Avenue
Igielski, Christopher T. '63 '98 C.911 B.S. L.1358 J.D. (adm. in WA; not adm. in OR) 1127 NW Irving St.
Ihnat, Patricia A., (AVⓉ) '55 '81 C.265 B.A. L.37 J.D. Sr. V.P. & Gen. Coun., Fidelity National Company of Oregon
Imperati, Samuel J., (AV) '51 '79 C.770 B.A. L.1067 J.D. Dir., Institute for Conflict Mgmt., Inc.
Inforzato, Valerie Fogel, (BV) '59 '86 C.659 B.A. L.623 J.D. Gen. Coun. & JD Electronic Discovery Consultant, Pacific Legal Litigation Support Services
Ingram, Kristin M. '71 '96 C.112 B.S. L.629 J.D. Oregon Pub. Broadcasting
Iniguez, Ruben L. '62 '90 C.976 B.A. L.1066 J.D. 101 S.W. Main St., Ste. 1700
Irving, Richard H., III '43 '68 C.597 B.S. L.309 LL.B. (adm. in IL; not adm. in OR) Sr. V.P., Gen. Coun. & Secy., Blount International, Inc.
Isgro, Connie L. '53 '83 C.1056 B.S. L.596 J.D. Juv. Ct. Ref.
Itkin, Gerald H. '48 '74 C.696 B.A. L.30 J.D. Co. Atty.
Iverson, Craig E., (AV) '45 '71 C.629 B.S. L.813 J.D. 1001 S.W. 5th, Ste. 1415
Iverson, Todd J. '— '02 C.174 B.S.E.E. L.629 J.D. [A Marger J.&M.]
Jack, Everett W., Jr., (AV) '— '89 C.670 B.B.A. L.796 J.D. [Davis W.T.]
Jacklin, Pamela L., (AV) '45 '78 C.340 B.A. L.336 J.D. [Stoel R.]
Jackson, Kathryn E., (BV) '— '87 C.339 B.S. L.629 J.D. [K.E.Jackson] ⊙
Jackson, Neil W., (BV) '51 '78 C.1056 B.S. L.1051 J.D. [N.Jackson]
Jackson, Ronald D., Law Office of '56 '81 C.97 B.A. L.659 J.D. 1001 S.W. 5th Ave.

Jackson, Kathryn E., Law Office, (BV)
1515 Southwest 5th Avenue, Suite 1010, 97201 ⊙
Telephone: 503-222-4070 Fax: 503-399-9315
URL: http://www.kathrynjacksonlawfirm.com
Kathryn E. Jackson.
Personal Injury, Wrongful Death, Premises Liability.

See Professional Biographies, PORTLAND, OREGON

Jackson, Neil, & Partners, (BV) 2450 S.E. Belmont St.
Jacobson, Barbara Ann '— '82 C.492 B.S. L.950 J.D. Sr. Asst. Gen. Coun., Port of Portland
Jacobson, Craig A. '67 '95 C.629 B.A. L.596 J.D. [A Hobbs,S.D.&W.]
Jacobson, James A. '46 '73 C.347 A.B. L.502 J.D. (adm. in MO; not adm. in OR) Dir., Product Litig., Freightliner LLC
Jakubek, Joseph T. '62 '88 C.980 B.E. L.608 J.D. [Klarquist S.] (See Pat. Sect.)
James, Alvin C., Jr. '48 '76 C.628 B.S. L.1051 J.D. I.R.S.
James, Christopher, (AV) '— '74 C&L.629 B.S., J.D. [James]
James, Forrest T. '20 '57 C.1051 B.A. L.596 LL.B. 2821 S.W. Collins Ct.‡
James, Marisa N. '77 '02 C.118 B.A. L.1051 J.D. [A DuBoff]
James, Michael H., (Ms.) '46 '71 C&L.846 B.A., J.D. (adm. in TX; not adm. in OR) Lee Koehn Associates, Inc.

James Law Group LLC, The, (AV)
121 Southwest Morrison Street, Suite 900, 97204
Telephone: 503-228-5380 Fax: 503-228-5381
Email: info@jameslawgroup.com URL: http://www.jameslawgroup.com
Members of the Firm: Christopher James; Ronald J. Miller; Philip S. Griffin. Associates: Dylan T. Becker; Mandy M. Parkinson Baker. Of Counsel: Mary Jo Naples Miller (Not admitted in OR); Lisanne M. Butterfield.
Business Law and Planning, Corporate Law, Corporate Finance, Mergers and Acquisitions, Real Estate, Securities, Banking, Employment Litigation, Emerging Companies, Software Licensing, Corporate Finance, Commercial Leasing, Business Litigation.

See Professional Biographies, PORTLAND, OREGON

Jamieson, Amie '75 '05 C.431 B.A. L.1051 [A Ater W.]
Janasak, Gerald A., Law Offices of '53 '94 C.966 B.A. L.748 J.D. (adm. in WA; not adm. in OR) P.O. Box 15197
Janik, Stephen T., (AV) '47 '74 C&L.309 A.B., J.D. [Ball J.]
Janke, Garth '55 '94 C.112 M.S. L.813 J.D. [Birdwell&J.] (See Pat. Sect.)
Jansa, Mark C. '53 '78 C&L.190 B.S.B.A., J.D. (adm. in NE; not adm. in OR) Deloitte & Touche
Jaqua, Martin W., (BV) '60 '86 C.413 B.A. L.629 J.D. [A Rickles]
Jaqua & Wheatley, LLC, (AV) One SW Columbia, Suite 1110 (⊙Eugene)
Jaquillard, S. Joy '49 '79 C.679 B.S. L.596 J.D. 2440 N.E. 25th
Jarrett, Noah '73 '99 C.906 B.A. L.629 J.D. [A Schwabe,W.&W.]
Jarvis, Constance Canfield, (AV) '30 '56 C.939 B.A. L.911 J.D. 2309 S.W. 1st Ave.‡
Jarvis, Peter R., (AV) '50 '76 C.309 B.A. L.976 J.D. [Hinshaw&C.]
Jasaitis, Jennifer C., (BV) '50 '77 C.813 B.A. L.188 J.D. 2701 N.W. Cornell Rd.
Jauch, Roger P. '52 '78 C.276 B.S. L.659 J.D. V.P., Rex L Walker, Plbg. & Htg. Co.
Jayne, Louise '29 '52 C.659 B.A. L.976 LL.B. P.O. Box 8189
Jefferson, Brian Lee '— '89 L.596 J.D. Metropolitan Pub. Defs. Off.
Jefferson, Theressa '69 '98 C.413 B.A. L.950 J.D. [A Scalf&O.]
Jeffery, Donald C., (BV) '33 '64 3715 N.E. Wistaria Dr.
Jelderks, John A. '38 '64 C&L.950 B.A., LL.B. U.S. Mag.‡
Jenkins, Edwin L. '17 '53 C.637 B.A. L.596 LL.B. 2211 S.W. 1st Ave.‡
Jennings, Jay T., (BV) '65 '91 C.897 b.A. L.950 J.D. Sr. Compl. Coun., Harland Financial Solutions, Inc.

Jensen, J. Alan, (AV) .... '38 '63 C.118 B.A. L.477 LL.B. [Holland&K.]
Jensen, Jeffrey D. .... '55 '84 C.1193 B.B.A. L.596 J.D. Pres., Jensen Properties, Inc.
Jensen, Patrick H., (AV) .... '44 '73 C.911 B.A. L.950 J.D. [Jensen D.]
Jensen, Scott L., (CV) ...... '55 '86 C.1181 B.S. L.564 J.D. [Brownstein,R.S.K.G.D.&H.]
Jensen, Sylvia L. .... '50 '75 C&L.950 B.A., J.D. Bonneville Power Admn.
Jensen Draudt LLP, (AV) .... 9755 S.W. Barnes Rd., Ste. 695
Jepsen, Carl F. .... '49 '74 C.629 B.B.A. L.950 J.D. [Warren A.]
Jeremiah, Velma, (AV) .... '21 '68 C.629 L.596 J.D. 2309 S.W. 1st Ave.‡
Jergovic, Nicole Marie .... '75 '00 C.961 B.A. L.436 J.D. [Ⓐ Smith F.&E.]
Jernstedt, Kenneth E., (AV) .... '44 '70 C.813 A.B. L.1066 J.D. [Bullard S.J.W.]
Jewell, Stephanie Francis '52 '85 C.770 B.S. L.1051 J.D.
(adm. in CA; not adm. in OR) 01309 SW Corbett Hill Cir
Joachims, Bert E., (BV) .... '22 '52 C.911 B.A. L.596 LL.B. 1596 N.W. 14th Ave.
Jockin, Mark .... '66 '93 C.732 B.S. L.107 J.D. 1917 SE Morrison
Johansen, Kirk, (AV) .... '49 '74 C&L.629 B.S., J.D. [Schwabe,W.&W.] (⊙Bend)
Johansen, Steve '56 '87 C.1056 B.S. L.596 J.D.
Asst. Prof. of Law, Northwestern Sch. of Law
Johnson, Alexander C., Jr., (AV) '48 '78
C.152 B.S.E.E. L.101 J.D. [Marger J.&M.] (See Pat. Sect.)
Johnson, Allen L., (AV) .... '43 '73 C.118 B.A. L.629 J.D. [Johnson&S.]
Johnson, David P. '46 '78 C.608 B.S. L.1051 J.D.
Sr. Coun., U.S. Army Corps of Engrs.
Johnson, Edward B. .... '67 '94 C.473 B.A. L.178 J.D. Atty., Legal Aid Svcs.
Johnson, Elaine N., (AV) .... '49 '79 C.242 B.A. L.101 J.D. [E.N.Johnson]
Johnson, Gregg D., (AV) .... '53 '83 C.174 B.A. L.276 J.D. [Ater W.]
Johnson, Jeffrey A., (AV) .... '— '82 C&L.629 B.S., J.D. [Cosgrave V.K.]
Johnson, Jennifer J. '51 '77
C.483 B.A. L.976 J.D. Prof. of Law, Northwestern Sch. of Law
Johnson, Kent D. .... '65 '96 C.747 B.A. L.508 J.D. [Ⓐ Brownstein,R.S.K.G.D.&H.]
Johnson, Kevin A. '73 '99 C.1365 B.A. L.502 J.D.
(adm. in MO; not adm. in OR) Corp. Coun., Harland Fin. Solutions, Inc.
Johnson, Leslie S. .... '56 '95 C.1056 B.S. L.596 J.D. [Kent C.]
Johnson, Mark A., (AV) .... '59 '87 C.685 B.A. L.1066 J.D. [Johnson R.&L.]
Johnson, Misti K. .... '— '01 C.628 B.A. L.629 J.D. [Ⓐ Dunn C.A.H.&T.]
Johnson, Nely L. .... '47 '72 C&L.966 B.A., J.D. Cir. J.
Johnson, Randal A., (AV) .... '61 '87 C.475 B.A. L.790 J.D. [Ater W.]
Johnson, Rees C., (AV) .... '38 '67 C&L.976 B.A., J.D. 6720 SW Macadam Ave.
Johnson, Robert P., (BV) .... '43 '73 C.1056 B.A. L.596 J.D. 1437 S.W. Columbia St.
Johnson, Thomas H. .... '52 '81 C.494 B.S. L.629 J.D. Liberty N.W. Ins. Corp.
Johnson, Thomas Russell .... '71 '98 C.477 B.B.A. L.575 J.D. [Perkins C.]
Johnson, Wallace A. '10 '35
(adm. in NE; not adm. in OR) 3433 N.E. Morris St.‡

Johnson Clifton Larson & Schaller, P.C.
(See Eugene)

Johnson, Elaine N., P.C., (AV) .... 888 S.W. Fifth Avenue, Suite 650
Johnson Renshaw & Lechman-Su, PC, (AV) .... 516 SE Morrison Street, Suite 420

Johnson & Sherton, P.C., (AV)
2303 S.E. Grant Street, 97214 ⊙
Telephone: 503-233-1533 Fax: 503-236-8216
Email: js@orlanduse.com URL: http://www.orlanduse.com
Allen L. Johnson; Corinne C. Sherton (Resident, Salem Office).
Land Use Law, Plan and Zone Changes, Environmental Law, Resource Regulation, Water Law.
Salem, Oregon Office: 247 Commercial Street, N.E., Suite 205, 97301. Telephone: 503-391-7446. Fax: 503-391-7403. Email: sherton@teleport.com.
See Professional Biographies, PORTLAND, OREGON

Johnston, Jenifer .... '69 '95 C.259 B.S. L.596 J.D. City Atty. Off.
Johnston, Ronald Allen, (AV) .... '50 '76 C.637 B.A. L.128 J.D. [Johnston,R.&L.]

Johnston, Root & Leibenguth, P.C., (AV)
920 Crown Plaza, 1500 S.W. First Avenue, 97201
Telephone: 503-226-7986 Fax: 503-223-0743 URL: http://www.johnstonroot.com
Email: lawoffice@johnstonroot.com URL: http://www.lawyers.com/johnston&rootlaw
Ronald Allen Johnston; Kathryn Smith Root; M. Scott Leibenguth.
Family Law, Interstate and International Custody and Support, Marital Dissolution, Modifications, Child and Spousal Support, Property, Father's and Mother's Rights, Pre-Marriage Agreements, Appeals, Family Law Practice.
See Professional Biographies, PORTLAND, OREGON

Johnstone, David L., (BV) .... '53 '86 C.670 B.A. L.596 J.D. [VavRosky M.O.]

Johnstone & Goodfellow
(See McMinnville)

Joiner, Sona Jean .... '55 '84 C&L.629 B.A., J.D. 2729 N.W. Savier Street
Jolles, Bernard, (AV) .... '28 '63 C.569 B.A. L.596 LL.B. [Jolles&B.]
Jolles & Bernstein, P.C., (AV) .... 721 Southwest Oak Street, Second Floor
Joncus, Stephen J. .... '59 '95 C.696 B.S. L.326 J.D. [Ⓐ Klarquist S.] (See Pat. Sect.)
Jones, Andrew R. .... '66 '99 C.1056 B.S. L.596 J.D. Pacific Realty Assoc LP
Jones, Brian R. .... '60 '88 C.1071 L.596 J.D. 12707 NE Halsey St.
Jones, Douglas W., Jr. .... '49 '74 C.629 B.S. L.596 J.D. 6955 S.W. Canyon Dr.
Jones, Edward J. .... '47 '75 C.685 B.A. L.596 J.D. Multnomah County Circuit Court
Jones, Harlan E., (AV) .... '48 '79 C.939 A.B. L.178 J.D. [Jordan S.]
Jones, Jeffrey R. .... '73 '01 C.911 B.A. L.950 J.D. [Ⓐ Schwabe,W.&W.]
Jones, Karen E. .... '58 '84 C.846 B.M. L.326 J.D. [Ⓒ Stoel R.]
Jones, Keith N. .... '47 '76 C.579 B.A. L.585 J.D. Atty., U.S. Bancorp
Jones, Michael D. .... '50 '97 C.910 A.B. L.596 J.D. [Klarquist S.] (See Pat. Sect.)
Jones, Milton T. .... '48 '77 C&L.629 B.A., J.D. [Ⓒ Perkins C.]
Jones, Nikola Lyn .... '67 '94 C.1165 B.A. L.1187 J.D. [Lindsay,H.N.&W.]
Jones, Philip N., (AV) .... '51 '76 C.1051 B.A. L.596 J.D. [Duffy K.]
Jones, Robert E. .... '27 '53 C.312 B.A. L.596 LL.B. U.S. Dist. J.
Jones, Robert P. .... '27 '52 L.950 J.D. Cir. J.
Jones, Steven P., (AV) .... '51 '78 C.628 B.S. L.596 J.D. [Keating J.B.&H.]
Jones, Stuart D., (AV) .... '54 '84 C&L.1051 B.S., J.D. [Bullivant H.B.]
Jones, Thomas M. .... '— '98 C.768 B.S. L.629 J.D. [Ⓐ Davis W.T.]
Jones, Timothy J., (AV) .... '58 '89 C.628 B.S. L.950 J.D. [Haglund,K.H.&J.]
Jonsson, Scott A., (BV) .... '51 '83 C&L.629 B.S., J.D. [Dunn C.A.H.&T.]
Joondeph, Robert C. .... '50 '76 C.103 A.B. L.930 J.D. Exec. Dir., Ore. Advocacy Ctr.
Jordan, E. Andrew, (BV) .... '44 '72 C&L.629 B.A., J.D. [Jordan S.]
Jordan, Jan Alden .... '46 '80 C&L.846 B.A., J.D. 210 S.W. Morrison St.
Jordan, Michael R., (BV) '49 '74
C.628 B.S. L.629 J.D. 921 S.W. Washington St., Ste. 755

Jordan Schrader PC, Attorneys at Law, (AV)
P.O. Box 230669, 97281-0669
Telephone: 503-598-7070 Fax: 503-598-7373
Email: info@jordanschrader.com URL: http://www.jordanschrader.com
E. Andrew Jordan; Charles R. Schrader; Jeffrey J. Bennett; Christopher L. Reive; John H. Baker, Jr.; Robert F. Blackmore; Thomas B. Eriksen; Harlan E. Jones; Douglas P. Cushing; Janice L. Holtorf Hirsch; Edward H. Trompke; Christine M. Meadows; Steven L. Shropshire; Jeremy T. Vermilyea; Eileen G. Eakins;—Peter O Watts; Justin D. Gericke.
(This Listing Continued)

Jordan Schrader PC, Attorneys at Law (Continued)
Business, Construction Contracting and Claims, Real Estate Law, Land Use and Development, Environmental and Natural Resources Law, Water Law, Bankruptcy Creditors' Rights Law, Employment Law, Municipal Law, General Corporate and Commercial Law, Banking and Finance, Mediation, Arbitration and Litigation in all Federal and State Courts.
See Professional Biographies, PORTLAND, OREGON

Jorgenson, Neil T., (BV) '47 '72 C.605 A.B. L.276 J.D.
520 S.W. Sixth Avenue Suite 820 (⊙Vancouver, WA)
Jorling, David L. .... '46 '72 C&L.436 A.B., J.D. Dep. Dist. Atty., City Atty. Off.
Jory, Marcia L. .... '55 '80 C.678 B.A. L.629 J.D. U.S. Trust Co. NA
Joseph, George M. .... '30 '55 C.685 B.A. L.145 J.D. 7110 S.E. 29th Ave.‡
Joseph, Phillip E. .... '60 '88 C.629 B.A. L.911 J.D. [Ball J.]
Joseph, Robert E., (AV) .... '35 '65 C&L.950 B.A., LL.B. [Schwabe,W.&W.]
Joseph, William R. .... '69 '96 C.94 B.A. L.273 J.D. [Ⓐ Mitchell,L.&S.]
Josephson, Richard C., (AV) .... '47 '73 C.930 A.B. L.945 J.D. [Stoel R.]

Josselson, Potter & Roberts, (AV)
425 NW 10th Avenue, Suite 306, 97209
Telephone: 503-228-1455 Facsimile: 503-228-0171
Email: office@jprlaw.com
Members of Firm: Frank Josselson (1944-1998); Irving W. Potter; Leslie M. Roberts. Of Counsel: Lawrence R. Derr.
Real Estate, Finance, Land Use, Environmental, Administrative, Municipal, Health Care, General Business, Surety, Construction, Business Litigation.
See Professional Biographies, PORTLAND, OREGON

Joyce, William M., (BVⓉ) .... '61 '87 C.93 B.A. L.1040 J.D. 133 NW 18th Ave.
Juba, George E. .... '28 '56 C&L.950 A.B., J.D. 620 S. W. Main St.
Jubb, David R. .... '49 '76 C.413 B.A. L.596 J.D. Coopers & Lybrand
Judd, Kenneth M. .... '25 '59 C.505 B.S. L.813 LL.B. 1500 S.W. 5th St.
Judy, Alan D., (AVⓉ) .... '— '75 C.208 B.A. L.596 J.D. [Karr T.C.] ⊙
Junewick, Walter J., Jr., (BVⓉ) .... '42 '74 C.473 B.A. L.1340 J.D. 14415 S.W. Stark
Junkin, John M., (AV) .... '49 '74 C.628 B.S. L.464 J.D. [Bullivant H.B.]
Jurinski, James John .... '49 '80 C.299 A.B. L.1051 J.D. Coopers & Lybrand
Jurva, Mark A. .... '69 '96 C.475 B.S. L.950 J.D. [Ⓐ Smith F.&E.]
Justice, Samuel C., (BV) '52 '78
C.685 B.A. L.1119 J.D. 5125 S.W. Macadam Ave., Ste. 200
Kabacy, Robert E. .... '68 '93 C.678 B.A. L.436 J.D. [Kell,A.&R.]
Kabeiseman, William K. .... '65 '94 C.945 B.A. L.629 J.D. [Ⓒ Garvey S.B.]
Kadish, Joshua, (AV) .... '51 '79 C.311 B.A. L.813 J.D. [Meyer&W.]
Kaempf, John T., (BV) .... '66 '92 C.1056 B.S. L.1051 J.D. [Bullivant H.B.]
Kafoury, Gregory, (AV) ...... '46 '74 C.629 B.S. L.1065 J.D. 320 S.W. Stark St., Ste. 202
Kahn, Garry L., (AV) .... '36 '62 C.670 L.596 LL.B. [Kahn&K.]
Kahn, Gary K., (AV) .... '55 '81 C.608 B.S. L.629 J.D. [Reeves,K.&H.]
Kahn, Steven A., (BV) .... '63 '88 C.112 B.A. L.596 J.D. [Kahn&K.]

Kahn & Kahn, P.C., (AV)
1210 Cascade Building, 520 S.W. Sixth Avenue, 97204-1510
Telephone: 503-227-4488 Fax: 503-227-0753 URL: http://www.kahnattorneys.com
Email: steven@kahnattorneys.com URL: http://www.lawyers.com/kahn&kahn
Garry L. Kahn; Steven A. Kahn.
Civil Trials, Negligence, Products Liability, Professional Liability, Premises Liability, Personal Injury, Auto Accidents, Wrongful Death, Slip and Fall, Insurance Claims.
See Professional Biographies, PORTLAND, OREGON

Kalmanson, Matthew J. .... '72 '00 C.454 B.A. L.976 J.D. [Ⓐ Stoel R.]
Kamin, Scott A., (BV) .... '48 '76 C.629 B.S. L.596 J.D. [Martin,B.T.L.&H.]
Kaminash, Benjamin H., (AV) .... '50 '82 C.562 B.A. L.846 J.D. [Kaminash&Assoc.]

Kaminash & Associates, LLC, (AV)
805 SW Broadway, Suite 2440, 97205
Telephone: 503-224-3241 Fax: 503-224-3581
Email: bkaminash@kaminashlaw.com URL: http://www.kaminashassociates.com
Benjamin H. Kaminash.
Intellectual Property, Copyrights, Trade Secrets, Trademarks, Intellectual Property Licensing, Advertising, Internet Law, E-Commerce, Business Law, Business Formation, Venture Capital, Acquisitions, Breach of Contract, Antitrust and Trade Regulation.
See Professional Biographies, PORTLAND, OREGON

Kaminski, Kimberly A., Law Office of ..... '65 '94 C.339 B.A. L.36 J.D. P.O. Box 13307
Kampsula, Jennifer .... '72 '99 C.988 B.A. L.911 J.D. [Ⓐ Kell,A.&R.]
Kandra, Lindsay R. .... '77 '04 C.413 B.A. L.629 J.D. [Ⓐ Cable H.B.H.&L.]
Kane, Christopher J. .... '68 '95 C.1056 B.S. L.596 J.D. 424 NW 19th Avenue
Kane, Mary .... '61 '98 C.518 B.A. L.893 J.D. Juv. Rights Proj.
Kaner, Lisa A., (AV) .... '60 '86 C.659 B.A. L.884 J.D. [Markowitz,H.G.&M.]
Kanter, Stephen, (AV) '46 '71
C.453 B.S. L.976 J.D. Prof. of Law, Northwestern Sch. of Law
Kantor, Henry .... '54 '79 C.659 B.A. L.596 J.D. Cir. J.
Kantor, Stephen E., (P.C.), (AV) .... '49 '74 C.629 B.S. L.596 J.D. [Samuels Y.K.S.&S.]
Kanwit, Marianna, (AV) ...... '52 '83 C.685 B.A. L.596 J.D. Dep. Dir., Human Resources
Kaplan, Henry J., (AV) .... '55 '83 C.674 B.A. L.569 J.D. [Bennett,H.M.&K.]
Kaplan, Joel S., (AV) .... '54 '79 C.1109 B.A. L.629 J.D. [Foster P.T.]
Kaplan, Matthew D. .... '70 '98 C.454 B.A. L.1522 J.D. [M.D.Kaplan]
Kaplan, Ronald M., (AVⓉ) '46 '71 C&L.352 B.A., J.D.
(adm. in IA; not adm. in OR) 2661 S.W. Buena Vista Dr.
Kaplan, Scott J., (AV) .... '64 '89 C.685 B.A. L.1066 J.D. [Stoel R.]
Kaplan, Matthew D., LLC .... 621 S.W. Morrison Street Suite 1218
Karlin, Benjamin M. .... '57 '82 C.813 A.B. L.1097 J.D. 2410 S.E. 121st.
Karlin, Harvey, (BV) .... '17 '48 C.665 B.S. L.309 J.D. 1100 SW 6th Ave.
Karman, Nathan A. .... '— '04 C.959 B.A. L.228 J.D. [Ⓐ Ater W.]
Karmel, Ivan M., (BV) .... '55 '80 C.1349 B.A. L.596 J.D. 1023 S.W. Yamhil Street

Karnopp Petersen LLP
(See Bend)

Karnstein, Walter W. .... '65 '90 C.597 B.S.E.E. L.950 J.D. [Kolisch H.] (Pat.)
Karpinski, Alan W., (BV) .... '53 '88 C.628 B.S. L.596 J.D. [A.W.Karpinski]
Karpinski, Alan W., PC, (BV) .... 621 S.W. Alder St Ste 621
Karplus, Lisa '58 '88 C.976 B.A. L.1065 J.D.
(adm. in CA; not adm. in OR) P.O. Box 12439
Karr, Emily V., (AV) .... '64 '90 C.597 B.A. L.228 J.D. [Stoel R.]
Karr Tuttle Campbell, A Professional Service Corporation, (AVⓉ)
888 S.W. Fifth Avenue, Suite 650 (⊙Seattle, WA)
Karter, Thomas G., (BV) .... '40 '65 C.679 B.A. L.1119 J.D. 3565 N.E. Bway.
Kasameyer, James W., (AV) .... '47 '72 C.197 A.B. L.309 J.D. 3940 SW Jerald Ct.
Kasting, Peter Alan .... '53 '78 C.347 B.A. L.629 J.D. City Atty. Off.
Kaston, Warren D. '59 '87 C.604 A.B. L.966 J.D.
(adm. in WI; not adm. in OR) 1005 S.E. Center St.

Kauffman, Samuel C. '67 '94
C.172 B.S. L.950 J.D. 121 S.W. Morrison St., Ste. 11 (⊙Portland)
Kauffman, Samuel C. '67 '94 C.172 B.S. L.950 J.D.
[Ⓒ Garvey S.B.] & [S.C.Kauffman] (⊙Portland)
Kaufman, Lissa K. ....'67 '97 C.705 B.A. L.911 J.D. Metro. Pub. Def.
Kay, Leslie N. ....'53 '84 L.950 J.D. Legal Servs. of OR
Kayser, Bruce D., (BV) ....'35 '63 C.1056 L.596 J.D. [Ⓒ Smith F.&E.]
Keaney, Kevin N., (BV) ....'54 '87 C.415 B.A. L.262 J.D. [K.Keaney]
Keaney, Kevin, P.C., (BV) ....825 N.E. Multnomah St., Ste. 960
Kearney, James M. ....'68 '98 C.154 B.A. L.911 J.D. [Ⓐ Stoel R.]
Kearns, Daniel H. ....'59 '89 C.980 B.S. L.596 J.D. [Reeve K.]
Keating, Robert M., (AV) ....'43 '68 C.602 B.A. L.597 J.D. [Keating J.B.&H.]

Keating Jones Bildstein & Hughes, P.C., (AV)
800 Benjamin Franklin Plaza, One Southwest Columbia, 97258-2095
Telephone: 503-222-9955 Fax: 503-796-0699
Jeffrey W. Bildstein; Sheri C. Browning; Lindsey H. Hughes; Steven P. Jones; Robert M. Keating; Scott G. O'Donnell;—Kirstin L. Abel; Caroline Coppock; Jason H. Daywitt; Monica A. Wells; Devon Zastrow Newman; Peter O. Tuenge. Of Counsel: Molly K. Marcum; Rickee N. Arntz.
Civil Litigation Practice Concentrating on the Defense of Professionals, including Physicians, Hospitals and other Health Care Providers and Attorneys, Health Care Antitrust, Medical Device and Drug Products Liability Claims, Health Care Law, Employment Law.
See Professional Biographies, PORTLAND, OREGON

Keegan, JoDee K. ....'71 '97 C.1193 B.A. L.950 J.D. [Dunn C.A.H.&T.]
Keeley, Pierre ....'74 '01 C.800 B.S.B.A. L.770 J.D. [Ⓐ Schwabe,W.&W.]
Keene, Jerald P., (BV) ....'55 '81 C.629 B.A. L.1051 J.D. [Reinisch,M.H.&W.]
Keeney, Jeffrey H., (AV) ....'58 '83 C.882 B.A. L.596 J.D. [Tonkon T.]
Keeney, Karen L., (BV) ....'47 '85 C.1056 B.S. L.596 J.D. 1112 N.E. 21st Ave., Ste. 1
Keenon, Wade R., (AV) ....'53 '85 C&L.629 B.A., J.D. [Gilroy]
Keith, Calvin L., (AV) ....'52 '78 C.37 B.S. L.477 J.D. [Perkins C.]
Keith, Corinne ....'70 '99 C.454 B.A. L.596 J.D. [Ⓐ Smith F.&E.]
Kekel, Eric A., (AV) ....'61 '92 C.628 B.S. L.950 J.D. [Dunn C.A.H.&T.]
Kell, Lee Davis, (AV) ....'39 '67 C.629 B.A. L.569 LL.B. [Kell,A.&R.]

Kell, Alterman & Runstein, LLP, (AV)
520 S.W. Yamhill, Suite 600, 97204
Telephone: 503-222-3531 Fax: 503-227-2980
Email: webmaster@kelrun.com URL: http://www.kelrun.com
Members of Firm: Raymond M. Kell (1911-1991); Clifford B. Alterman (1925-1995); Ted E. Runstein; Lee Davis Kell; Wayne D. Palmer; William D. Dickas; Gary P. Compa; Charles R. Williamson; Eric Sogge; Thomas R. Rask, III; Robert E. Kabacy; Dennis Steinman;—Dana L. Barnes; Jennifer Kampsula; John A. Kodachi. Of Counsel: Lloyd R. Summers.
General Business and Trial Practice, including Corporate, Tax and Real Estate Law, Litigation in all State and Federal Courts of Business, Personal Injury, Employment, Environmental, Divorce and Maritime cases, Estate Planning and Probate Law, Health Care Law, Construction Law, Bankruptcy, Debtor-Creditor Law, Government Relations, Secured Transactions, Business Acquisitions and Mergers and Franchise Law.
References: Union Bank of California, N.A. (Portland Branch); The Bank of Tokyo-Mitsubishi, Ltd. (Portland Branch); US Bank (Portlano Branch); (5th S. Main Branch).
See Professional Biographies, PORTLAND, OREGON

Kelleigh, Melissa Budden ....'72 '00 C.145 B.A. L.1051 J.D. [Ⓐ Kennedy,W.A.&R.]
Keller, Harvey W. ....'22 '49 C&L.209 LL.B. 621 S.W. Morrison St.‡
Keller, John M., (AV) ....'55 '79 C.670 B.B.A. L.1051 J.D. [Keller&K.]
Keller, Shelley ....'71 '97 C.305 B.A. L.309 J.D. Dist. Atty.
Keller, William M., (AV) ....'25 '51 C.670 A.B. L.276 J.D. [Keller&K.]
Keller & Keller, P.C., (AV) ....1025 S.E. Morrison Street
Kelley, Carla L., (AV) ....'45 '87 C.966 B.A. L.596 J.D. Gen. Coun., Port of Portland
Kelley, Jennifer J. '49 '92 C.1071 B.S. L.629 J.D.
US Dept of the Interior, 500 Ne Multnomah St #607
Kelley, Michael K., (AV) ....'59 '85 C.120 B.A. L.602 J.D. [Haglund,K.H.&J.]
Kelley, Scott M. ....'26 '52 C.629 B.S. L.596 J.D. 2127 S.W. Elm‡
Kelly, Adam R. ....'75 '02 C.174 B.A. L.629 J.D. [Ⓐ Garvey S.B.]
Kelly, David M. ....'71 '96 C.1058 B.A. L.596 J.D. 6305 S.E. 43rd Ave.
Kelly, Jodee K ....'— '95 C.628 B.S. L.950 J.D. [Landye B.B.]
Kelly, John C. ....'51 '82 C.276 B.S.F.S. L.596 J.D. Bonneville Power Admin.
Kelly, Paul J., Jr., (AV) ....'— '70 C.602 B.A. L.276 J.D. [Ⓒ Garvey S.B.]
Kelly, Sharon E., (BV) '53 '80 C.685 B.A. L.1051 J.D.
111 S.W. Columbia St., Ste. 1000
Kelsey, Joan S. ....'51 '94 C.881 B.A. L.596 J.D. [Ⓐ Beery&E.]
Kemp, Dorothy Lendaris ....'64 '95 C.773 B.A. L.950 J.D. 1220 S.W. Morrison
Kemper, Thomas J. '52 '79 C.1056 B.S. L.1051 J.D.
V.P., PacifiCorp Harbor Capital, Inc.
Kennedy, Albert N., (AV) ....'51 '76 C.103 A.B. L.880 J.D. [Tonkon T.]
Kennedy, Jack L., (AV) ....'24 '51 C.809 L.596 J.D. [Ⓒ Kennedy,W.A.&R.]
Kennedy, James M., (AV) ....'50 '76 C&L.477 B.A., J.D. [Kennedy&K.]
Kennedy, Michael D., (AV) ....'52 '78 C&L.950 B.A., J.D. [Kennedy B.]
Kennedy, Olywn E., (BV) ....'25 '53 L.596 LL.B. [Kennedy B.]
Kennedy, Rhonda W., (AV) ....'51 '76 C&L.477 B.A., J.D. [Kennedy&K.]
Kennedy, Thos. A. ....'22 '57 C.629 B.S. L.596 LL.B. 7252 S.W. Benz Park Ct.‡
Kennedy Bowles, P.C., (AV) ....111 SW Fifth Avenue

Kennedy & Kennedy LLP, (AV)
601 SW Second Avenue, Suite 2050, 97204
Telephone: 503-226-6555 Telecopier: 503-226-6466
Members of Firm: James M. Kennedy; Rhonda W. Kennedy.
Business and Corporate Law, Acquisitions, Insurance Regulation and Real Estate.
See Professional Biographies, PORTLAND, OREGON

Kennedy, Watts, Arellano & Ricks LLP, (AV)
(As Kennedy & King)
2850 Pacwest Center, 1211 S.W. Fifth Avenue, 97204
Telephone: 503-228-6191 FAX: 503-228-0009
Email: kwar@kwar.com URL: http://www.kwar.com
Of Counsel: Jack L. Kennedy. Members of Firm: Susan E. Watts; Joseph C. Arellano; Daniel M. Ricks; Todd L. Van Rysselberghe; Daniel L. Keppler. Associates: Xin Xu; Melissa Budden Kelleigh.
Civil Litigation in State and Federal Courts including Business, Securities, Professional Liability, Products Liability, Drug and Medical Device Defense, Insurance and Family Law.
Reference: United States National Bank of Oregon.
See Professional Biographies, PORTLAND, OREGON

Kenny, William J. '43 '73 C.911 B.A.B.A. L.285 J.D.
(adm. in WA; not adm. in OR) Portland State Univ.
Kent, Amy R. ....'60 '90 C.112 B.A. L.596 J.D. Jud. Law Clk. to Sr. U.S. Dist. J.
Kent, Christopher H., (AV) ....'55 '85 C.1090 B.A. L.629 J.D. [Kent C.]

Kent Custis LLP, (AV)
1500 S.W. Taylor Street, 97205 ⊙
Telephone: 503-220-0717 Facsimile: 503-220-4299
URL: http://www.kentlaw.com
Christopher H. Kent; Robert J. Custis; Leslie S. Johnson.
Civil Litigation emphasizing Business, Commercial, First Party Insurance, Real Estate, Construction, Shareholder Disputes, Franchise and Securities, Business Organizations and Transactions, Accoun-

(This Listing Continued)

Kent Custis LLP (Continued)
tant and Attorney Malpractice and Employment Law, General Business, Discrimination, Wrongful Termination, Employment Contracts, Wrongful Death, Personal Injury, Eminent Domain, Commercial Leasing, Buying or Selling A Business, Business Enterprises, Closely Held Business, Limited Liability Companies, Partnerships, Small Business, Business Planning, Contracts, Intellectual Property, Licensing Agreements, Trade Secrets, Trademarks, Strategic Alliances, Joint Ventures, Mergers, Internet, E-Commerce.
See Professional Biographies, PORTLAND, OREGON

Keppler, Daniel L., (AV) ....'67 '92 C.950 B.A. L.285 J.D. [Kennedy,W.A.&R.]
Kerin, Michelle Holman ....'— '96 C.112 B.A. L.1051 J.D. [Ⓐ Farleigh W.]
Kerns, Diane C., (AV) ....'49 '78 C.436 B.A. L.596 J.D. [Ⓒ Hagen O.]
Kerr, Andrew P., (AV) ......'44 '69 C.197 A.B. L.950 J.D. [Brownstein,R.S.K.G.D.&H.]
Kerr, Robert A. ....'70 '96 C&L.101 B.A., J.D. [Dunn C.A.H.&T.]
Kerstiens, Kevin F., (AV) ....'53 '81 C.678 B.A. L.910 J.D. [Schwabe,W.&W.]
Kester, Randall B., (AV) ....'— '40 C.950 A.B. L.178 J.D. [Cosgrave V.K.]
Ketterling, Keith A., (AV) ....'62 '87 C.932 B.B.A. L.352 J.D. [Stoll S.B.L.&S.]
Key, Philip '58 '89 C.685 B.A. L.1051 J.D.
Bonneville Power Admn., Off. of Gen. Coun.
Keyes, Christopher M., (BV) '51 '81 C.813 A.B. L.464 J.D.
(adm. in AK; not adm. in OR) Louisiana-Pacific Corporation
Kiely, G. Kevin, (AV) ....'58 '83 C&L.629 B.A., J.D. [Cable H.B.H.&L.]
Kienbaum, Ursula A. ....'74 '04 C.508 B.A. L.1051 J.D. [Amburgey&R.]
Kieper, Karyl S. ....'53 '90 C.897 B.S. L.1051 J.D. [K.Kieper]
Kieper, Karyl, LLC ....851 S.W. Sixth Avenue
Kierstead, Andrew, Law Office of .....'62 '87 C.367 B.A. L.800 J.D. 1001 S.W. 5th Ave.
Kilkenny, Russell R., (AV) ....'50 '75 C.629 B.S. L.1051 J.D. [Scarborough,M.O.&K.]
Kilmer, Jeffrey M., (AV) ....'41 '69 C.604 B.A. L.150 J.D. [Kilmer,V.&L.]

Kilmer, Voorhees & Laurick, A Professional Corporation, (AV)
732 N.W. Nineteenth Avenue, 97209
Telephone: 503-224-0055 FAX: 503-222-5290
Email: kvl@teleport.com URL: http://www.lawyers.com/kvl
Jeffrey M. Kilmer; Stephen C. Voorhees; James P. Laurick; Gregory B. Snook; Carolyn L. Larson; Christopher T. Carson; Pamela J. Stendahl;—Mary L. Pool; Thomas V. Cupani; Catherine B. Brinkman.
Civil litigation in State and Federal courts, including Business, Construction, Insurance, ERISA, Professional Liability, Banking, Product Liability and General Casualty.
See Professional Biographies, PORTLAND, OREGON

Kim, Candice Y. ....'77 '04 C.911 B.A. L.94 J.D. [Ⓐ Parsons F.&G.]
Kimmelfield, Neil D., (AV) ....'— '79 C.881 A.B. L.309 J.D. [Lane P.]
Kimmell, P. Adam ....'51 '79 C.178 B.A. L.1066 J.D. 6532 S.W. Firlock Way‡
Kincaid, James S., (AV) ....'61 '87 C.629 B.S. L.596 J.D. [Cable H.B.H.&L.]
Kindley, Raymond S., (BV) ....'57 '92 C.911 B.S. L.596 J.D. [Schwabe,W.&W.]
King, Brian J., (AV) ....'53 '80 C.172 B.A. L.174 J.D. [Schwabe,W.&W.]
King, Christy O. ....'69 '93 C.420 B.A.J. L.1051 J.D. [DuBoff]
King, Garr M., (AV) ....'36 '63 C.878 L.596 J.D. U.S. Dist. J.
King, Jean M. ....'19 '53 C.628 B.S. L.596 LL.B. 3407 S.E. Steele St.
King, Richard L., (BV) ....'47 '72 C&L.339 B.A., J.D. [Warren A.]
Kinsey, William W. ....'49 '75 C.813 B.A. L.309 J.D. Bonnevelle Power Admn.
Kinsley, Curtis D., (BV) ....'55 '80 C.1056 B.S. L.950 J.D. [Kinsley&C.]
Kinsley & Chaudoin, P.C., (BV) ....9900 S.W. Greenburg Rd.
Kirby, Kimberly '65 '00
(adm. in CA; not adm. in OR) [Davis D.K.]
Kirchhof, Anton C., (AV) '45 '71 C.1056 B.A. L.813 J.D.
Sr. Atty. & Corp. Secy., Louisiana-Pacific Corporation
Kirk, James J. ....'45 '80 C.1056 B.A. L.950 J.D. Asst. Gen. Coun., Port of Portland
Kirk, Monica M. ....'49 '81 C.627 B.A. L.629 J.D. Spec. Coun., U.S. E.P.A.
Kirklin, George L., (AV) ....'— '62 C&L.309 A.B., LL.B. [Kirklin F.]

Kirklin Folawn LLP, (AV)
1125 Yeon Building, 522 SW 5th Avenue, 97204
Telephone: 503-222-1640 Fax: 503-227-5251
URL: http://www.lawyers.com/lawyercomkirklinfolawnllp
George L. Kirklin; John S. Folawn; Bonnie Richardson.
Securities, Intellectual Property, Lender Liability, Business Torts, Contracts, Finance, Accounting and Auditing, Personal Injury, Product Liability, Professional Liability, Commercial Litigation, Civil Litigation, Probate, Wills.
See Professional Biographies, PORTLAND, OREGON

Kirkpatrick, Bryan D. ....'69 '04 C.628 B.S. L.1051 J.D. [Ⓐ Marger J.&M.]
Kirkpatrick, C. Rodney (Rod), (AV) '42 '68
C.1056 B.A. L.950 J.D. 8030 N.E. Clackamas St.
Kirtley, Wesley Williams (Bill), (AV) '41 '68
C.309 A.B. L.893 LL.B. 1300 S.W. Fifth Avenue
Kisch, Victor J., (AV) ....'— '86 C.352 B.B.A. L.831 J.D. [Tonkon T.]
Kiss, Carl G., (AV) ....'56 '83 C.188 B.A. L.569 J.D. 888 S.W. 5th Ave., Ste. 650
Kitchel, Chris, (AV) ....'50 '81 C.494 B.S.B. L.1051 J.D. [Stoel R.]
Kitchel, Jan K., (AV) ....'51 '78 C.628 B.S. L.950 J.D. [Schwabe,W.&W.]
Klang, Lawrence C., (BV) ....'47 '72 C&L.629 B.S., J.D. 5550 S.W. Macadam Ave.
Klarquist, Kenneth S., (AV) '21 '50
C.494 B.Ch.E. L.276 J.D. [Ⓒ Klarquist S.] (See Pat. Sect.)
Klarquist, Kenneth S., Jr., (AV) ....'48 '74 C.674 A.B. L.629 J.D. [Zalutsky&K.]
Klarquist, Stephen J., (AV) ....'56 '85 C.628 B.S. L.596 J.D. [Ⓐ Zalutsky&K.]

Klarquist Sparkman, LLP, (AV) BB
One World Trade Center, Suite 1600, 121 S.W. Salmon Street, 97204 ⊙
Telephone: 503-226-7391 FAX: 503-228-9446
Email: inquiry@klarquist.com URL: http://www.klarquist.com
Members of Firm: Lisa M. Caldwell; J. Christopher Carraway; Kristin L. Cleveland; James E. Geringer; Michael P. Girard; Joseph T. Jakubek; Michael D. Jones; Ramon A. Klitzke, II; Gregory L. Maurer; Dr. William D. Noonan; David P. Petersen; Richard J. Polley; Kyle B. Rinehart; Wayne W. Rupert; Stacey C. Slater; Donald L. Stephens, Jr.; John D. Vandenberg; Stephen A. Wight; Garth A. Winn. Senior Counsel: Kenneth S. Klarquist; James S. Leigh; Arthur L. Whinston. Counsel: Jeffrey S. Love. Of Counsel: Michael N. Zachary. Associates: Theodore W. Baker; Patrick M. Bible; Michael L. Buckler; Scott E. Davis; Brian Casey Fitzpatrick; Jared S. Goff; Debra A. Gordon; Jeffrey Brian Haendler; Tanya M. Harding, Ph.D.; Kevin M. Hayes; Stephen J. Joncus; Richard D. McLeod (Not admitted in OR); Sunjay Y. Mohan (Not admitted in OR); Todd Siegel; A. Jonathan Vance; Justin D. Wagner; Gwynedd Warren, Ph.D.
Patent, Trademark, Copyright Law, Trials, Unfair Competition Law.
Clients available upon request.
Reno, Nevada Office: 800 South Meadows Parkway, Suite 700. Telephone: 775-824-0104. Fax: 775-824-0107.
Seattle, Washington Office: Wells Fargo Center, 999 Third Avenue, Suite 4200. Telephone: 206-264-2960.
See Professional Biographies, PORTLAND, OREGON

Klatt, August E., (CVⓉ) ....'49 '76 C.629 B.S.Psych. L.596 J.D. [Ⓐ D.M.Bomarito]
Klein, DeLyne ....'68 '04 C.413 B.S.N. L.596 J.D. [Ⓐ Bullivant H.B.]
Klein, Steven E. ....'69 '97 C.696 B.A. L.468 J.D. [Ⓒ Stoel R.]
Kleinman, Jeffrey L., (BV) ....'50 '74 C.188 B.S. L.629 J.D. 1207 S.W. 6th Ave.
Kleinsmith, Kenneth L. ....'26 '53 C&L.188 B.A., LL.B. [Ⓐ Radler,B.R.&M.]
Klepser, Mary ....'43 '80 C.373 B.A. L.976 J.D. 110 S.E. 129th Ave.

Kliks, Bernard B. . . . . '15 '39 C&L.629 B.S., J.D. 418 S.W. Washington St.
Klingbeil, Rick, (BV) . . . . '61 '93 C.839 B.S.C.E. L.1051 J.D. 520 S.W. 6th Ave., Ste. 950
Klinger, Dustin R. . . . . '70 '99 C.602 B.A. L.911 J.D. [🄰 Miller N.]
Klinger, Nanci . . . . '— '94 C.1331 B.S. L.1051 J.D. [🄰 Davis W.T.]
Klitzke, Ramon A., II, (AV) '55 '80 C.790 B.S. L.436 J.D.
[Klarquist S.] (See Pat. Sect.)
Kloss Hogan, Sharon L. '56 '88 C.398 B.A. L.596 J.D.
Major and Planned Giving Dir., The Salvation Army
Kmetz, Heather A. . . . . '71 '00 C.597 B.S.J. L.596 J.D. [🄰 Sussman S.]
Knapp, Jeffrey W., (AV) . . . . '— '89 C.902 B.A. L.659 J.D. [🄲 Lane P.]
Knapp, Michael J., (AV) . . . . . . '55 '83 C.902 B.A. L.950 J.D. 1 Sw Columbia St Ste 920
Knappenberger, Allan F., (BV) . . . . . . '47 '73 C&L.602 A.B., J.D. 1318 S.W. 12th Ave.
Knauerhase, Karen M. W. . . . . '69 '02 C.670 B.S. L.596 J.D. [Knauerhase]
Knauerhase Law Office . . . . 8403 S.W. 8th Ave.
Kneeland, Janet . . . . '35 '78 C.629 B.A. L.1051 J.D. I.R.S.
Kneeland, John P., (AV) . . . . '41 '67 C&L.629 B.S., LL.B. Gen. Coun., Shilo Inns
Knight, Elizabeth . . . . '— '99 C.174 B.A. L.629 J.D. [🄰 Davis W.T.]
Knight, Ethan D. . . . . '74 '99 C.228 A.B. L.629 J.D. Co. Dist. Atty. Off.
Knivila, K. Bruce . . . . '62 '92 C.1209 B.A. L.276 J.D. [🄲 Harrang L.G.R.]
Knivila, Kelly, (AV) . . . . '63 '90 C.1181 B.A. L.276 J.D. [🄲 Stoel R.]
Knoll, James L., (AV) . . . . '42 '67 C.103 A.B. L.145 J.D. [J.L.Knoll]

Knoll, James L., P.C., (AV)
1500 S.W. Taylor Street, 97205
Telephone: 503-222-9000 Fax: 503-222-9003
Email: Jim@knollmediation.com URL: http://www.knollmediation.com
James L. Knoll.
Mediation and Arbitration.
See Professional Biographies, PORTLAND, OREGON

Knottnerus, John W., (AV) . . . . '64 '89 C.508 B.A. L.629 J.D. [Martin,B.T.L.&H.] ⊙
Knowles, John S., (AV) . . . . '50 '84 C.927 B.S. L.596 J.D. [Davis R.E.&X.]
Knox, Daniel F., (AV) . . . . '48 '78 C.174 B.A. L.326 J.D. [Schwabe,W.&W.]
Knox, William C., III . . . . '62 '00 C.301 B.A. L.950 J.D. 317 SW Alder, 9th Floor
Knudsen, William J., Jr. '21 '48
C.724 B.S. L.178 J.D. Prof. of Law, Lewis & Clark Law Sch.
Knuths, William R., (AV) . . . . '55 '83 C&L.629 B.A., J.D. [🄲 Miller N.]
Koback, Christopher P. . . . . '— '88 C.963 B.A. L.966 J.D. [Davis W.T.]
Kobin, Charles L., (AV) . . . . '39 '64 C&L.629 B.S., LL.B. [Kobin&K.]
Kobin & Kobin, (AV) . . . . 610 S.W. Alder Street
Koblegarde, B. Rupert, (BV) '37 '70
C.1056 B.S. L.1051 J.D. 1130 S.W. Morrison, Ste. 510
Koch, Anne E. . . . . '72 '01 C.787 B.A. L.596 J.D. [🄰 Motschenbacher&B.]
Koch, Jacqueline L., (AV) '49 '87 C.685 B.A. L.1051 J.D.
1500 N.E. Irving St., Ste. 370
Koch, Shawn L. '64 '91
C.629 B.A. L.596 J.D. Corp. Benefits Mgr., Louisiana-Pacific Corp.
Kocher, Scott F. . . . . '75 '01 C&L.309 A.B., J.D. [🄰 Stoel R.]
Kocher-Moar, Leslie A. . . . . '68 '93 C.112 B.A. L.629 J.D. [🄰 MacMillan,S.&M.]
Kodachi, John A. . . . . '66 '92 C.604 B.A. L.1051 J.D. [🄰 Kell,A.&R.]
Koempel, David A. . . . . '— '01 C.276 B.S. L.596 J.D. [🄰 Holland&K.]
Kohlmetz, Andrew M., (BV) . . . . . . '67 '96 C.319 B.A. L.629 J.D. [Raivio,K.&S.]
Kohn, Sandra L., (AV) . . . . '49 '83 C.508 B.A. L.629 J.D. [🄰 Stoll S.B.L.&S.]
Kolbe, Klarice A. . . . . '78 '03 C.911 L.577 J.D. [🄰 Abbott&P.]
Koliner, Kevin M. . . . . '75 '01 C.494 B.A. L.893 J.D. [🄰 Miller N.]
Kolisch, J. Pierre, (AV) . . . . '18 '46 C.178 A.B. L.188 LL.B. [🄲 Kolisch H.] (Pat.)
Kolisch Hartwell, P.C., (AV)
520 S.W. Yamhill Street (Pat.) (⊙Palo Alto, CA; Boise, ID)
Kolodzie, Annette T. . . . . . . '59 '85 C&L.846 B.A., J.D. 1515 SW 5th Ave., Suite 600
Kono, Kevin . . . . '— '02 C&L.629 B.A., J.D. [🄰 Davis W.T.]
Korshoj, Jim D., (AV) . . . . '44 '69 C.546 B.S. L.477 J.D. [Bullard S.J.W.] ‡
Kosloff, Laura H. . . . . '56 '85 C.33 B.A. L.112 J.D. Atty., Trexler & Assoc., Inc.
Kosydar, Christine A., (AV) . . . . . . '51 '81 C.1056 B.S. L.1051 J.D. [Stoel R.]
Koury, Robert G., II . . . . '— '98 C.800 B.A. L.950 J.D. [Lane P.]
Kraemer, J. Kurt . . . . '71 '98 C&L.285 B.A., J.D. [🄰 McEwen G.]
Kraemer, Kenneth, (AV) . . . . '18 '46 C&L.309 A.B., J.D. 7175 S.W. Dogwood Pl.‡
Krage, Roger L. . . . . '47 '74 C.1056 B.S. L.285 J.D. Gen. Coun., Crown Pacific, Ltd.
Krages, Bert P., II '57 '87
C.597 B.S. L.629 J.D. 6665 S.W. Hampton Street, Suite 200 (Pat.)
Krahmer, Donald L., Jr., (AV) . . . . . '57 '88 C&L.950 B.S., J.D. [Schwabe,W.&W.]
Kramer, Mark, (BV) . . . . '57 '81 C.188 B.A. L.588 J.D. 520 S.W. 6th Ave., Ste. 1010
Kramer, Michael L. '67 '97 C.870 B.S. L.1294 J.D.
(adm. in ME; not adm. in OR) 40 Wellington Rd.★
Kramer, Thomas I., (AV) . . . . '54 '81 C.154 B.A. L.976 J.D. [Bullard S.J.W.]
Kraus, Gregory Robert . . . . '64 '96 Pamplin Communications
Krause, Darcia, (BV) . . . . '49 '75 C.685 B.A. L.1066 J.D. 620 S.W. 5th Ave., Ste. 602
Krauss, Michael D. . . . . '52 '77 C.846 B.B.A. L.802 J.D. 2807 NE Mason St.
Kraut, Lory J. . . . . '55 '90 C.877 B.S. L.629 J.D. Dep. City Atty.
Krawczuk, Dana L. . . . . '74 '99 C.280 B.A. L.596 J.D. [🄰 Ball J.]
Kreisler, David . . . . '59 '94 C.1248 B.A. L.930 J.D. Six City Center
Krem, Janice . . . . '52 '77 C.665 B.A. L.950 J.D. 10260 S.W. Greenburg Rd., Ste. 400
Kreutzer, John M. . . . . '66 '97 C.628 B.S. L.950 J.D. [🄰 Bullivant H.B.]
Krieger, David J., (AV) . . . . '— '58 C&L.629 B.A., J.D. [🄲 Davis W.T.]
Kripalani, Eva M., (AV) '59 '86 C.1056 B.S. L.950 J.D.
V.P., Gen. Coun. & Secy., Kindercare Learning Ctrs., Inc.
Kronick, Geoffrey M. '54 '85 C.629 B.S. L.596 J.D.
Sr. Atty., Bonneville Power Admin.
Kropitzer, Harold . . . . '23 '50 C.563 B.S. L.94 LL.B. 11220 N.W. Ridge Rd.‡
Krueger, Allyson S. . . . . '65 '96 C.112 B.A. L.629 J.D. [Barran L.]
Krueger, Jeffrey M. . . . . '71 '96 C&L.910 A.B., J.D. [Stoel R.]
Krull, Julie . . . . '66 '96 C.1056 B.A. L.1051 J.D. [🄰 Squires&L.]
Krumbholz, Walter O., Jr. '50 '84
C.911 B.S. L.596 J.D. Pres., Marine & Environ. Testing, Inc.‡
Kuffner, Charles A., Jr. '37 '65 C.262 B.S. L.564 LL.B.
(adm. in NY; not adm. in OR) Supm. Ct. Jus.‡
Kuhn, Jas. R., Jr. . . . . '22 '50 C&L.339 B.S., LL.B. 4122 N.E. 136th Ave.
Kuhn, Richard J., (AV) . . . . '56 '81 C.629 B.A. L.950 J.D. 1000 S.W. Broadway, Ste. 2000
Kuhn, Steven James . . . . '70 '98 C.231 B.A. L.950 J.D. [🄰 Meyer&W.]
Kurshner, Paula J. . . . . '46 '76 C.629 B.A. L.596 J.D. Dist. J.
Kushner, Margaret Baumgardner, (AV) . . . . . '53 '78 C.475 B.A. L.309 J.D. [Stoel R.]
Kusnerus, Wendell G. . . . . '— '79 C.475 B.S. L.629 J.D. [Davis W.T.]
Kuykendall, Glen R. . . . . . . '36 '66 C.629 B.S. L.1066 J.D. 6975 S.W. Gable Pkway.
Kuzara, Byron S. . . . . '— '00 C&L.972 B.S.M.E., J.D. [Banner&W.]
Kuzmich, James A. . . . . '66 '00 C.35 B.S. L.623 J.D. [Davis D.K.]
Kyle, Carol J., (AV) . . . . '42 '79 C.36 B.A. L.1051 J.D. 1515 SW 5th Ave.
Kyung, James H. . . . . '65 '93 C.112 B.A. L.950 J.D. [J.H.Kyung]
Kyung, James H., PC . . . . 888 S.W. 5th Ave., Ste. 650
Lacampagne, Suzanne C., P.C., (AV) . . . . . . '— '83 C.914 B.A. L.93 J.D. [Miller N.]
Lachenmeier, Rudy R., (AV) . . . . '50 '75 C.629 B.S. L.1051 J.D. [Lachenmeier E.R.&H.]

Lachenmeier Enloe Rall & Heinson, (AV)
9600 S.W. Capitol Highway, 97219
Telephone: 503-768-9600 FAX: 503-768-9133
Email: ler@lerlaw.com URL: http://www.lerlaw.com
Members of Firm: Jay D. Enloe; Rudy R. Lachenmeier; Martin M. Rall; Timothy J. Heinson;—Julie E. Dutton; Brian S. Ruff; Lori K. DeDobbelaere.
General Civil, Trial and Appellate Practice in all State and Federal Courts. Insurance Law. Products Liability and Professional Liability.
See Professional Biographies, PORTLAND, OREGON

LaFrance, Arthur B. '39 '64
C.197 B.A. L.976 LL.B. Prof. of Law, Northwestern Sch. of Law
Lagesen, Frank H., (AV) . . . . '— '69 C.1056 B.S. L.629 J.D. [Cosgrave V.K.]
Lagesen, J. Riley . . . . '— '03 C.800 B.F.A. L.596 J.D. [🄰 Bullivant H.B.]
Lai, Corinne J., (BV) . . . . '50 '84 C.629 B.S. L.596 J.D. 520 S.W. 6th Ave., Ste. 825
Laing, John C., Jr., (AV) '53 '82
C.1056 B.S. L.1051 J.D. Asst. U.S. Atty., U.S. Attys. Off.
LaMar, Kristena A. . . . . '48 '73 C.679 B.A. L.477 J.D. Cir. J.
LaMarche, Clara . . . . '— '78 C.446 B.S. L.596 J.D. 3963 N.E. 14th Ave.
Lamb, Bradford H., (BV) . . . . '57 '87 C.628 B.S. L.596 J.D. [🄰 Zarosinski&H.]
Lamb, Colin D., (BV) . . . . '44 '69 C&L.950 B.A., J.D. 7410 S.W. Oleson Rd.
Lambert, Kristine M. '69 '95 C&L.260 B.S., J.D.
(adm. in TN; not adm. in OR) 222 S.W. Columbia, Ste. 1600
Lambert, Roy D., (AV) . . . . '46 '72 C.188 B.S. L.178 J.D. [Schwabe,W.&W.]
Lamborn, Josh . . . . '71 '97 C.147 B.A. L.596 J.D. Dep. Dist. Atty.
Lampros, R. G. Wilmot '53 '81 C.604 B.A. L.569 J.D.
(adm. in NY; not adm. in OR) Pres., Machine Tool Finance Corp.
Lampson, Elizabeth E. . . . . '67 '93 C.112 B.A. L.809 J.D. [🄰 Davis R.E.&X.]
Lamvik, Nancy M. '48 '83 C.1056 B.S. L.596 J.D.
Mgr., Crim. Div., Multnomah Co. Cts.
Lance, Clayton J. . . . . '59 '83 C&L.629 B.A., J.D. [C.Lance]

Lance, Clayton, LLP
610 S.W. Alder Street, Suite 915, 97204
Telephone: 503-241-2242 Fax: 503-227-4136
Email: clayton_lance@qwest.net
Clayton J. Lance.
Criminal Defense, Family Law.
See Professional Biographies, PORTLAND, OREGON

Land, Dean P. . . . . '69 '97 C.696 B.A. L.861 J.D. Law Clerk, Co. Ct.
Landauer, Sally C., (AV) . . . . '39 '78 C.939 B.A. L.596 J.D. [Ball J.]

Landis, David C., (AV) '37 '62 C.950 B.A. L.1066 LL.B.
1515 Southwest 5th Avenue, Suite 844, 97201
Telephone: 503-224-5680 Fax: 503-224-5826
Email: landis@dclandis.com
Civil Litigation, Professional Liability Defense including Attorney Malpractice and Medical Malpractice, Insurance Coverage and Personal Injury before State and Federal Courts.

Landon, Abby Wool, (P.C.) . . . . . '56 '91 C.783 B.A. L.1051 J.D. [🄲 Samuels Y.K.S.&S.]
Landress, Sanford R., (AV) . . . . '53 '81 C&L.629 B.S., J.D. [Greene&M.]
Landsverk, Wayne D., (AV) . . . . '46 '72 C&L.966 B.A., J.D. [Newcomb,S.S.&L.]
Landye, Thomas M., (AV) . . . . '39 '69 C.685 A.B. L.145 J.D. [Landye B.B.]

Landye Bennett Blumstein LLP, (AV)
1300 Southwest Fifth Avenue, Suite 3500, 97201 ⊙
Telephone: 503-224-4100 Facsimile: 503-224-4133
Email: info@landye-bennett.com URL: http://www.landye-bennett.com
J. David Bennett; David L. Blount; Philip Blumstein (Resident, Anchorage, Alaska Office); David S. Case (Resident, Anchorage, Alaska Office); Mitchel R. Cohen; Stuart K. Cohen; James S. Crane; Kim Dunn (Resident, Anchorage, Alaska Office); David N. Goulder; Karna R. Gustafson; Robert B. Hopkins; Robert H. Hume, Jr. (Resident, Anchorage, Alaska Office); Jodee K Kelly; Thomas M. Landye; Michelle K. McClure; Orlando Medina; Jeffrey S. Mutnick; Glen Price (Resident, Wasilla, Alaska Office); P. Stephen Russell, III; Thane W. Tienson; Richard S. Yugler. Associates: Cynthia M. Hora (Resident, Anchorage, Alaska Office); Cheryl L. McKay (Resident, Anchorage, Alaska Office); Kyle D. Sciuchetti.
General Practice and Litigation in State and Federal Courts. Business Entities and Business Finance, Real Estate, Taxation, Securities, Bankruptcy, Administrative Practice before Governmental Departments, Agencies and Commissions, Land Use Planning, Federal Land Law, Condominium and Community Association Law, Products Liability, Personal Injury and Aviation Law, Environmental and Hazardous Substances Law, Intellectual Property and Computer Law.
Anchorage, Alaska Office: 701 West Eighth Avenue, Suite 1200, 99501. Telephone: 907-276-5152. Facsimile: 907-276-8433.
Wasilla, Alaska Office: 1981 E. Palmer Wasilla Highway, Suite 220, 99654. Telephone: 907-746-5971. Facsimile: 907-746-5972.
See Professional Biographies, PORTLAND, OREGON

Lane, James L., (AV) . . . . '31 '83 C.679 B.S. L.1051 J.D. [Parker,B.&L.]
Lane, Richard A., (AV) . . . . '59 '86 C.629 L.1051 J.D. [🄰 L.Wobbrock]

Lane Powell PC, (AV)
601 SW Second Avenue, Suite 2100, 97204-3158 ⊙
Telephone: 503-778-2100 Facsimile: 503-778-2200
Email: information@lanepowell.com URL: http://www.lanepowell.com
Shareholders: Dean N. Alterman; Craig D. Bachman; Robert R. Calo (Not admitted in OR); Kenneth Ray Davis, II; John H. Gadon; Anne W. Glazer; Bruce C. Hamlin; Timothy R. Harmon; Lewis M. Horowitz; David G. Hosenpud; Charles F. Hudson; Neil D. Kimmelfield; Robert G. Koury, II; Robert E. Maloney, Jr.; Stephen P. McCarthy; Lee C. Nusich; Paul M. Ostroff; Milo P. Petranovich; Claire J. Philpott; Bryan E. Powell; Donald H. Pyle; Vicki L. Smith; Thomas W. Sondag; Leigh D. Stephenson-Kuhn; John C. Stevason; Catherine S. Travis; Steven B. Ungar; Jack Walsh; Karen M. Williams; Richard H. Williams; Jeffrey C. Wolfstone. Emeritus Members: John P. Bledsoe; John B. Crowell, Jr.; Stanley R. Loeb; William F. Lubersky; Frank H. Spears. Counsel: Jeffrey W. Knapp. Associates: Beth A. Allen; Susan J. Baird (Not admitted in OR); John R. Barhoum; Victoria D. Blachly; Brady M. Bustany; Leah B. Cronn; Lorne O. Dauenhauer; Pilar Cortwright French; Jeffry S. Garrett; Stephanie Hendricks; Benjamin G. Lenhart; Parna A. Mehrbani; William T. Patton; Christopher B. Storey.
Alternative Dispute Resolution; Admiralty and Maritime Law; Antitrust and Trade Regulation; Appellate Practice; Aviation; Banking; Bankruptcy and Reorganizations; Business Law; Creditor Rights; Architects; Engineers; Construction and Design Law; Class Actions; Corporate Finance and Securities; Emerging Companies and Venture Investment; Director and Officer Liability; Employee Benefits; Employment; ERISA Litigation; Energy Law; Environmental Law; Estate and Gift Taxation; Estate Planning; Federal and State Tax Planning, Litigation and Controversies; Franchising; Governmental Law; Hospital and Healthcare; Immigration and Naturalization; Intellectual Property and Technology; International Business, Trade Regulation; Labor and Employment Law, Counseling and Litigation; Land Use; Litigation; Local Government; Long-Term Care and Senior Housing; Mergers and Acquisitions; Natural Resources; Products Liability; Professional Liability; Real Estate, Land Use Development and Finance; Securities Litigation; Taxation and Tax Controversies; Toxic Torts; Transportation; Trusts and Estates; Trademarks; Utilities; White Collar Criminal Defense and Regulatory Compliance; Wood Products and Forest Resources.
Other Offices at: Seattle, Washington; Anchorage, Alaska; Olympia, Washington; and London, England.
See Professional Biographies, PORTLAND, OREGON

Laney, Jill D. . . . . '— '93 C.670 B.S. L.950 J.D. [Cosgrave V.K.]

Lang, James D., (AV) '53 '81 C.1331 B.A. L.596 J.D.
1020 S.W. Taylor, Suite 375, 97205-2554
Telephone: 503-227-4533 Facsimile: 503-248-9776
Email: jlang@teleport.com URL: http://www.lawyers.com/jlang
Criminal and Juvenile Law. Trials in all State and Federal Courts.
See Professional Biographies, PORTLAND, OREGON

Lang, Richard L., (AV) '33 '62 C.670 B.A. L.596 J.D. [Mitchell,L.&S.]
Langfitt, Frank V., III, (AV) '47 '73 C.813 B.A. L.629 J.D. [Ater W.]
Langford, Liza '59 '88 C.1056 B.A. L.596 J.D. 520 SW Yamhill
Langford, Shonee D. '75 '04 C.1056 B.A. L.950 J.D. [Ⓐ Schwabe,W.&W.]
Langslet, John L., (AV) '44 '72 C.1056 B.S. L.1066 J.D. [Martin,B.T.L.&H.]
Lankton, Milton C., (AV) '— '57 C.894 A.B. L.976 J.D. [Ⓒ Davis W.T.]
Lansing, Ronald B. '32 '60
C.879 B.A. L.950 J.D. Prof. of Law, Northwestern Sch. of Law
Large, Donald W. '42 '67 C&L.188 B.A., LL.B.
(adm. in DE; not adm. in OR) Prof. of Law, Northwestern Sch. of Law
Larkin, Linda J., (AV) '51 '79 C.966 B.A. L.596 J.D. [Ⓒ Bennett,H.M.&K.]
Larkin, Thomas A., (BV) '67 '92 C.477 B.A. L.208 J.D. [Stewart S.&G.]
Larkins, William L., Jr., (AV) '55 '81 C.813 A.B. L.1066 J.D. [Larkins V.]

Larkins Vacura, LLP, (AV)
808 S.W. Third Avenue, Suite 540, 97204
Telephone: 503-222-4424 Facsimile: 503-827-7600 Email: jvacura@larkinsvacura.com
Email: wlarkins@larkinsvacura.com URL: http://www.lawyers.com/vacuralarkins-llp
William L. Larkins, Jr.; Julie R. Vacura. Associates: Lainie Block; Perry S. Heitman.
Litigation Practice in Federal and State Courts, emphasizing Business and Real Estate Disputes, Real Estate and Banking Transactions.
See Professional Biographies, PORTLAND, OREGON

Larpenteur, James A., Jr., (AV) '35 '61 C&L.629 B.S., LL.B. [Schwabe,W.&W.]
Larsen, Daniel P. '68 '94 C.966 B.S. L.596 J.D. [Ater W.]
Larsen, Janet Knauss '— '95 C.939 B.A. L.1051 J.D. [Foster P.T.]
Larson, Amy L. '70 '99 C.118 B.A. L.966 J.D. [Ⓐ Parsons F.&G.]
Larson, Carolyn L., (AV) '— '77 C.174 B.A. L.208 J.D. [Kilmer,V.&L.]
Larson, Eric C., (AV) '47 '72 C&L.629 B.A., J.D. [Gevurtz,M.L.&H.]
Larson, Jon C. '— '89 C.723 B.A. L.494 J.D. [Marvin,C.&L.]
Larson, Matthew D. '75 '03 C.906 B.A. L.596 J.D. [Ⓐ Markowitz,H.G.&M.]
Larson, Stephen R. '47 '79 C.959 J.D. L.596 J.D. Bonneville Power Admn.
Larson, Steve D., (AV) '57 '86 C.494 B.S. L.629 J.D. [Stoll S.B.L.&S.]
LaRue, Dan F., (BV) '48 '73 C.336 B.S. L.596 J.D. 2125 S.W. 4th Avenue, Suite 600
LaRue, Janis M. '48 '80 C.932 B.S. L.215 J.D.
Gen. Coun., National College of Neuropathic Medicine
LaSasso, James F., (BV) '54 '81 C.1056 B.S. L.629 J.D. 807 Ne Alberta St
Laskowski, Robert C., (AV) '46 '71 C&L.477 B.A., J.D. 520 S.W. Yamhill, Suite 600
Lassell, Jeni L. '— '04 C.188 B.A. L.629 J.D. [Ⓐ Davis W.T.]
Laster, Alan M., (AV) '55 '83 C.629 B.S. L.596 J.D. [Go&L.]
Latcu, Misty M. '74 '00 C.1056 B.S. L.950 J.D. Asst. Dist. Coun.
Later, William N. '53 '89 C.629 B.S. L.596 J.D. [Steenson,S.T.L.&R.]
Latto, Harrison, (AV) '52 '81 C.156 B.A. L.629 J.D. 400 SW 6th Avenue, Suite 600
Lau, Robert K. '57 '93 C.563 B.Ch.E. L.809 J.D. [Ⓒ Yazbeck,C.&H.]
Lauersdorf, Andrew C. '66 '98 C.966 B.A. L.596 J.D. [Ⓐ Bullivant H.B.]
Launer, Jeannette M., (BV) '50 '75 C&L.629 B.A., J.D. 5216 S.W. Burton Dr.
Laurick, James P., (AV) '54 '82 C.173 B.S. L.596 J.D. [Kilmer,V.&L.]
Law, Karen K. '67 '93 C.112 B.A. L.767 J.D. [Ⓑ Schwabe,W.&W.]
Law, Linda S. '67 '94 C.145 B.A. L.596 J.D. Dep. City Atty.
Lawrence, R. Ryan, (BV) '43 '70 C.911 B.A. L.596 J.D. 2301 N.W. Thurman St.
Lawson, Catherine D. '— '85 C.629 B.A. L.950 J.D. [Ⓐ S.K.Eggum]
Lawton, Donald P. '33 '65 C.569 B.S. L.950 J.D. 4303 S.W. 68th Ave.‡
Laybourn, Ross L. '49 '74 C&L.813 B.A., J.D. Jus. Dept.
Layne, Richard M., (AV) '46 '78 C.1193 B.A. L.950 J.D. [Layne&L.]

Layne & Lewis, LLP, (AV)
111 SW Columbia Street, Suite 1000, 97201
Telephone: 503-295-1882 Facsimile: 503-295-2057
Email: mlayne@layne-lewis.com URL: http://www.layne-lewislaw.com
Richard M. Layne.
Securities Arbitration and Litigation, Legal Malpractice, Shareholder Litigation.
See Professional Biographies, PORTLAND, OREGON

Lazar, Richard A., (BV) '54 '85 C.629 B.S. L.596 J.D. Fios, Inc.
Lazenby, Henry "Chip", (AV) '— '82 C.309 A.B. L.629 J.D. [Ⓒ Bullivant H.B.]
Leadroot, Don '49 '82 C.210 B.A. L.596 J.D. Fidelity Natl. Exch. Servs., Inc.
Lear, Lisa E., (AV) '59 '85 C.174 B.A. L.596 J.D. [Bullivant H.B.]
Leavy, Edward '29 '53 C.670 A.B. L.602 LL.B. U.S. Sr. Cir. J.‡
Lechman-Su, Bradley C., (AV) '52 '87 C.549 B.S. L.502 J.D. [Johnson R.&L.]
LeCoq, Mark M., (AV) '55 '82 C.950 B.S. L.1051 J.D. [Schwabe,W.&W.]
Ledwidge, Chris P., (BV) '42 '67 C.285 B.A. L.629 J.D. [Ledwidge&L.]
Ledwidge & Ledwidge, (BV) 520 S.W. Yamhill, Suite 400
Lee, Alan M., (BV) '42 '68 C&L.950 B.S., J.D. [Bullard S.J.W.]
Lee, Andrew J. '75 '02 C.293 B.A. L.629 J.D. [Ⓐ Schwabe,W.&W.]
Lee, Byung Min '66 '96 [Ⓐ McKeown&B.]
Lee, Grace Y. '76 '01 C&L.37 B.S., J.D. [Ⓐ Stahancyk,K.J.&H.]
Lee, Hosoon '64 '98 C&L.999 B.S., J.D. [Marger J.&M.] (See Pat. Sect.)
Lee, Richard A., (AV) '58 '84 C.293 B.A. L.629 J.D. [Bodyfelt M.S.&C.]
Lee, Robert J., (BV) '56 '81 C.911 B.A. L.1051 J.D. [Bullard S.J.W.]
Lee, Shelly D. '74 '00 C.556 B.A. L.596 J.D. 1825 Sw Broadway
Lee, Vivian Me-Hae '— '95 C.860 B.A. L.629 J.D. Sr. Atty.
Leeds, Terence C. '51 '79 C.259 B.A. L.629 J.D. P.O. Box 19411
Leedy, Benjamin '78 '05 C.670 B.A. L.1051 J.D. [Ⓐ Holland&K.]
Legaard, Brenna K. '73 '00
C.1032 B.A. L.124 J.D. [Ⓐ Chernoff,V.M.&S.] (See Pat. Sect.)
Legernes, Norman W. '22 '58 C.637 B.A. L.596 LL.B. 11020 S.W. Butner Rd.‡
Leggatt, Stephen D. '— '96 C.103 A.B. L.477 J.D. [Ⓒ S.K.Eggum]
Lehman, William J. '69 '98 C.754 B.A. L.602 J.D. [Cable H.B.H.&L.]
Lehner, Michael A., (AV) '42 '74 C.629 B.S. L.1051 J.D. [Lehner&R.]

Lehner & Rodrigues, PC, (AV) BR
Suite 1015 Crown Plaza, 1500 S.W. First Avenue, 97201
Telephone: 503-226-2225 Facsimile: 503-226-2418
Michael A. Lehner; Carl R. Rodrigues;—Thomas C Patton; Shelly M. Damore.
Insurance Defense Practice including Civil Trial and Appellate Practice, Casualty, Fire, Auto, Insurance Coverage, Products Liability, Professional Liability, Environmental and Hazardous Waste, Motor Carrier and Transportation Insurance Law, Municipal and Governmental Liability.
See Professional Biographies, PORTLAND, OREGON

Leibenguth, M. Scott '62 '94 C.74 B.S. L.950 J.D. [Johnston,R.&L.]
Leichtfuss, Peter S. '— '95 C.966 B.A. L.629 J.D. [Davis W.T.]
Leier, Glenn A. '58 '83 C.585 B.A. L.878 J.D. [McKeown&B.]
Leigh, James S., (AV) '35 '61 C.475 B.S. L.477 J.D. [Ⓒ Klarquist S.] (See Pat. Sect.)
Leineweber, Gregory J., (AV) '49 '74 C.629 B.S. L.596 J.D. [Furniss,S.&L.]
Leineweber, Robert J., (AV) '53 '80
C.629 B.A. L.300 J.D. Dep. Dist. Atty., Multnomah Co. Courthouse
Leis, Craig L. '— '02 C.608 B.A. L.117 J.D. [Ⓐ Harrang L.G.R.]
Leisure, Sally R., (AV) '48 '83 C.483 B.A. L.629 J.D. 520 S.W. Yamhill St.
Lekas, Gary J. '33 '62 C&L.950 LL.B. 1001 S.W. 5th Ave.
Lekas, Thomas J., (BV) '30 '60 C.629 B.S. L.596 J.D. 812 S.W. Washington St.
Le Meitour, Deborah L. '48 '77 C.1529 B.A. L.596 J.D. 3203 SW Hamilton St
Lenhart, Benjamin G. '— '96 C.939 B.A. L.596 J.D. [Ⓐ Lane P.]
Lenzser, Frederick, (AV) '49 '76 C&L.629 B.A., J.D. Chf. Dep. Dist. Atty.
Leo, Roger J., (BV) '45 '73 C&L.629 B.A., J.D. 520 S.W. Yamill Street
Leonard, Joel P. '61 '88 C.309 A.B. L.966 J.D. [Holland&K.]
Leonard, Justin D. '77 '03 C.813 B.A. L.596 J.D. [Ⓐ Parsons F.&G.]
LeRoux, Mark F., (AV) '— '82 C&L.950 B.A., J.D. [Tonkon T.]
Lesage, Lisa M., (AV) '56 '85 10015 Sw Terwilliger Blvd
Lesh, David N. '64 '90 C&L.629 B.A., J.D. 1916 S.W. Madison
Levak, Thomas F., (AV) '38 '64 C.629 B.A. L.950 LL.B. P.O. Box 82639
Levelle, Michael D., (AV) '51 '90 C.508 B.A. L.950 J.D. [Ⓒ Sussman S.]
Levin, Charles G. '59 '86 C.118 B.A. L.629 J.D. Oregon Advocacy Ctr.
Levin, Matthew A. '68 '95 C&L.477 B.S., J.D. [Markowitz,H.G.&M.]
Levine, Howard M., (AV) '54 '80 C.1108 B.S. L.851 J.D. [Sussman S.]

Levine, Michael R., Law Office of, (AVⓉ) '44 '74 C.699 A.B. L.1066 J.D. BR
400 SW Sixth Avenue, Suite 600, 97204
Telephone: 503-546-3927 Fax: 503-224-3203 URL: http://www.lawyers.com/michaelrlevine
Email: michael@levinedefenders.com URL: http://www.levinedefenders.com
Associate: Matthew G. McHenry.
Criminal Law, Drug Crimes, Trial Practice, Appellate Practice, Post-Conviction Remedies.
See Professional Biographies, PORTLAND, OREGON

Levy, Jack, (BV) '68 '93 C.569 B.A. L.629 J.D. [Smith F.&E.]
Levy, Jonathan A., (AV) '54 '83 C.309 A.B. L.477 J.D. 888 S.W. 5th Ave., Ste. 650
Levy, Victor, (BV) '36 '61 C.1056 L.596 J.D. Dept. of Jus.
Lew, Ted M. '— '93 C.1056 B.S. L.596 J.D. [Welch,B.&G.]
Lewandowski, Chelsea S. '72 '99 C.1171 B.S. L.1051 J.D. [Ⓐ Hooper,E.&W.]
Lewis, Brad J., (BV) '59 '89 C.628 B.S. L.1051 J.D. [Ⓐ Bullivant H.B.]
Lewis, Christopher J. '70 '00 C.911 B.S.Che L.596 J.D. [Ⓐ Schwabe,W.&W.]
Lewis, F. Jackson '— '00 C.309 B.A. L.477 J.D. [Ⓐ Tonkon T.]
Lewis, Katherine A., (CV) '50 '82
C.906 B.A. L.1051 J.D. 111 SW Columbia Street, Suite 1000
Lewis, Marilyn Gail, (AV) '49 '85 C.629 B.A. L.596 J.D. Nationwide Ins.
Lewis, Rodney E., Jr., (AV) '— '74 C.813 B.A. L.629 J.D. [Davis W.T.]
Lewis, Wayne E. '30 '72 C.226 B.S. L.596 J.D. 903 N.E. 125th St.
Lewis, William, (BVⓉ) '43 '72 C.821 B.A. L.966 J.D. [W.Lewis&Assoc.]
Lewis, William, & Associates, P.C., (BVⓉ) 1000 SW Vista Avenue, Suite 1214
Lewton, Michael C. '— '87 C.35 B.S. L.950 J.D. [Cosgrave V.K.]
Leybold, Dennis, (AV) '54 '79 C.813 A.B. L.93 J.D. [Stoel R.]
Lezak, Sidney I., (AV) '24 '49 C&L.145 Ph.B., J.D. [Ⓒ Newcomb,S.S.&L.]
Liberty, Robert L., (AV) '53 '81 C.629 B.A. L.309 J.D. 1000 Friends of Oregon
Liebe, Annette I. '65 '96 C.174 B.A. L.629 J.D. State Dept. of Envir. Quality
Lieber, Katherine B., (BV) '66 '93
C.788 B.A. L.347 B.A. Dep. Dist. Atty., Dist. Atty. Off.
Liebman, Richard F., (AV) '47 '72 C.112 B.A. L.1066 J.D. [Barran L.]
Liebman-Alperson, Laura '71 '02 C.1036 B.A. L.596 J.D. [Ⓐ Tonkon T.]
Liebowitz, Bruce A. '53 '79 C.94 B.S. L.1051 J.D. 522 S.W. 5th, Ste. 1000
Lightle, Drake A. '69 '99 C.502 B.A. L.596 J.D. [Ⓐ Gevurtz,M.L.&H.]
Lilly, Marie J. '54 '84 C.685 B.A. L.596 J.D. Atty., U.S. Bancorp
Lilly, Michael J., (AV) '48 '75 C&L.629 B.A., J.D. 101 SW Main Street, Suite 805
Lindahl, R. Daniel, (AV) '58 '84 C.629 B.S. L.596 J.D. [Bullivant H.B.]
Lindau, Mose S. '10 '33 C&L.793 J.D.
(adm. in SD; not adm. in OR) Ret. Dist. J.
Lindberg, Gary W., (AV) '41 '70 C&L.629 B.S., LL.B.
First Interstate Bk. of Ore., N.A.
Lindenauer, Eric A., (AV) '53 '83 C.112 A.B. L.950 J.D. [Garvey S.B.]
Lindley, Thomas E., (AV) '48 '77 C.339 B.A. L.880 J.D. [Perkins C.]
Lindsay, Dennis J., (AV) '18 '41 C.604 B.A. L.477 J.D. [Lindsay,H.N.&W.]

Lindsay, Hart, Neil & Weigler, LLP, (AV)
3400 Wells Fargo Center, 1300 S.W. Fifth Avenue, 97201-5640 ⊙
Telephone: 503-226-7677 Telecopier: 503-226-7697
Email: LHNW@lindsayhart.com URL: http://www.lindsayhart.com
Members of Firm: Gunther F. Krause (1895-1967); Carmie R. Dafoe, Jr. (1920-1975); Donald G. Krause (1921-1986); C. Allan Hart, Jr. (1909-2002); Leslie F. Darby (1958-2002); Dennis J. Lindsay; Carl R. Neil; Jerard S. Weigler; James H. Bean; Glen P. McClendon; Robert W. Palmer; Thomas E. McDermott; William M. Tomlinson; Jay W. Beattie; Roy E. Pulvers; Paul Silver; Nikola Lyn Jones. Associates: Edward T. Tylicki; Daniel W. Howard; Corinne Sam; Jenni E. Marsh; James P. McCurdy. Of Counsel: Paul S. Cosgrove; Peter A. Friedmann (Resident, Washington, D.C. Office).
Litigation, Products Liability, Corporate, Maritime, Employment, Professional Liability, Regulatory and Insurance.
Washington, D.C. Office: 1201 Pennsylvania Avenue, N.W., Suite 315, 20004. Telephone: 202-783-3333. Fax: 202-783-4422.
See Professional Biographies, PORTLAND, OREGON

Lindstedt, Norman L., (AV) '31 '58 C.629 B.S. L.596 LL.B. [N.L.Lindstedt]
Lindstedt, Norman L., P.C., (AV) 4081 N. Overlook Blvd.
Lipton, David D. '52 '78 C.311 B.A. L.1051 J.D. 800 N.E. Oregon St., Ste. 340
Little, Mark W. '69 '97 C.911 B.A. L.188 J.D.
(adm. in ME; not adm. in OR)
V.P., Prod. Develop. & Compliance Legal, Harland Financial Solutions, Inc.
Littlefield, J. Bradley, (AV) '39 '69 C.550 B.S. L.596 J.D. 1515 S.W. Fifth‡
Litzenberger, Marilyn E. '56 '88 C.628 B.S. L.596 J.D. Cir.J.
Livingston, Farrand "Randy" M., (AV) '41 '67
C.385 B.A. L.228 J.D. [Ⓒ Bodyfelt M.S.&C.]
Livingston, Peter, (AV) '51 '82 C.31 B.A. L.339 J.D. [Schwabe,W.&W.]
Liyanage, Harshi M. '67 '91 C&L.999 LL.B., J.D. [Ⓐ Elliott,O.&P.]
Lloyd, Don K., (AV) '44 '73 C.1056 B.A. L.596 J.D. [Cable H.B.H.&L.]
Locke, Douglas L. '54 '79 C.629 B.A. L.950 J.D. Coopers & Lybrand
Locke, Lawrence A. '49 '90 C.685 B.A. L.976 J.D. 1001 SW 5th Avenue, Suite 1100
Lockwood, Robert W. '49 '74 C.373 B.A. L.629 J.D.
Prof., Admin. of Jus. Dept., Portland State Univ.‡
Loeb, Stanley R., (AV) '— '60 C&L.309 A.B., LL.B. [Lane P.]
Loennig, Carlton P., (BV) '32 '70 C.629 B.B.A. L.596 J.D. P.O. Box 55814
Lofgren, David E., Jr. '17 '51 C.685 B.A. L.596 LL.B. Bonneville Power Admin.
Loftis, Jeanne F., (AV) '63 '91 C.112 B.S. L.464 J.D. [Bullivant H.B.]
Logan, Paul Sandberg '72 '01 C.228 B.A. L.813 J.D. [Ⓐ Stoel R.]
Lohn, D. Robert '48 '76 C.309 B.A. L.508 J.D.
(adm. in MT; not adm. in OR) Gen. Coun., N.W. Power Planning Council
Loiselle, Darien S., (BV) '65 '92 C.950 B.A. L.629 J.D. [Schwabe,W.&W.]
Loiselle, Sabrina P., (AV) '67 '92 C.950 B.S. L.629 J.D. [Ⓐ Miller N.]
Lokting, David A., (AV) '53 '80 C.1056 B.A. L.629 J.D. [Stoll S.B.L.&S.]

Londer, Donald H. ... '25 '64 C.629 L.596 J.D. Cir. J.
Lonergan, Clint A., (BV) ... '50 '76 [Lonergan&L.]
Lonergan, James F. ... '15 '47 C.629 B.S. L.596 LL.B. 2375 S.W. Burbank St.‡
Lonergan, Richard L., (AV) ... '54 '79 C&L.629 B.A., J.D. [Lonergan&L.]
Lonergan & Lonergan, (AV) ... 620 S.W. 5th Ave.
Long, Jeffrey A. ... '60 '86 C.1056 B.S. L.950 J.D. 1500 SW 1st Avenue
Long, Mark A., (AV) ... '53 '82 C.154 B.A. L.904 J.D. [Schwabe,W.&W.]
Long, Tim A. ... '45 '74 C.336 B.S. L.596 J.D. [🄰 Chernoff,V.M.&S.] (See Pat. Sect.)

Loomis & Holland
(See Eugene)

Lopez, Angel, (Mr.), (AV) ... '53 '79 C.605 B.A. L.950 J.D. [Squires&L.]
Loprinzi, Arusi R. ... '— '03 C.1051 B.A. L.1068 J.D. [🄰 Schwabe,W.&W.]
Loren, Lydia Pallas '66 '92 C&L.477 A.B., J.D.
(adm. in MI; not adm. in OR) Assoc. Prof., Northwestern Sch. of Law
Lorenz, Daniel C., (AV) ... '54 '78 C.813 B.A. L.1051 J.D. 521 S.W. Clay
Lorenz, Richard G. ... '75 '00 C.413 B.A. L.309 J.D. [Cable H.B.H.&L.]
Love, Jeffrey S., (AV) ... '58 '87 C.112 B.A. L.1066 J.D. [🄲 Klarquist S.]
Love, Linda C., (BV) ... '54 '81 C.173 B.A. L.950 J.D. [Williams L.O.C.&P.]
Love, William E., (AV) ... '26 '52 C.602 B.N.S. L.629 J.D. [Schwabe,W.&W.]
Lovett, Steven T., (AV) ... '57 '89 C.861 B.A. L.262 J.D. [Stoel R.]
Lovinger, Jeffrey Scott ... '67 '96 C.911 B.A. L.596 J.D. [🄰 T.H.Nelson&Assoc.]
Low, David G., (BV) ... '54 '81 C.628 B.A. L.678 J.D. 18445 E. Burnside
Lowe, Gregg A., (BV) ... '38 '64 C.988 B.A. L.950 LL.B. Dep. Dist. Atty.
Lowe, Matthew D. ... '69 '00 C.884 B.A. L.950 J.D. [🄰 O'Donnell&C.]
Lowinger, Sarah ... '71 '02 C.629 B.A. L.893 J.D. [🄰 Miller N.]
Lowry, Robert B., (AV) ... '51 '85 C.670 B.A. L.596 J.D. [Bullivant H.B.]
Lowthian, Philip H., (AV) '36 '65 C&L.629 B.S., LL.B.
828 S.W. First Avenue, Suite 200
Loy, Michael S. ... '52 '76 C&L.950 B.S., J.D. Cir. J.
Lubersky, William F., (AV) ... '— '40 C&L.629 A.B., LL.B. [Lane P.]
Lucas, Mitchell V. '— '87 C.628 B.S. L.1051 J.D.
(adm. in WA; not adm. in OR) Mng. Sr. Compl. Coun., Harland Financial Solutions, Inc.
Lucas, Robert C., (BV) ... '38 '64 C&L.174 B.A., J.D. 10252 NW Alpenglow Way
Luce, James O., III, (BV) '44 '74 C.906 B.A. L.629 J.D.
(adm. in WA; not adm. in OR) Asst. Gen. Coun., Bonneville Power Admn.
Lucey, Kevin Edward ... '58 '92 C.859 B.A. L.146 J.D. 621 S.W. Morrison St. #1412
Ludwig, David R., (AV) ... '52 '78 C&L.629 B.A., J.D. [Farleigh W.]
Luedtke, Roger A., (AV) ... '42 '74 C&L.966 B.S., J.D. [Schwabe,W.&W.] ‡
Lundberg, Christopher G. ... '66 '94 C.802 B.A. L.596 J.D. [🄰 Haglund,K.H.&J.]
Lusk, Robert M., (BV) ... '52 '78 C.312 B.A. L.950 J.D. 9900 S.W. Wilshire
Lusky, John A., (AV) ... '51 '77 C.309 B.A. L.813 J.D. [Miller N.]
Luther, Richelle Tustin ... '68 '97 C.950 B.A. L.1051 J.D. NW Natural Gas
Luu, Nhi ... '73 '98 C.950 B.S. L.596 J.D. Dist. Coun., I.R.S.
Lyman, Helen T. ... '44 '81 C.112 A.B. L.596 J.D. 7425 S.E. 20th Ave.
Lynch, Brian D., (AVⓉ) '50 '75 C.767 A.B. L.276 J.D.
(adm. in CA; not adm. in OR) Chapter 13 Trustee
Lynott, Bradley C. ... '48 '75 C.1056 B.S. L.596 J.D. U.S. Bancorp
Lyon, Barbee B., (AV) ... '40 '71 C.880 B.A. L.976 J.D. [Tonkon T.]
Lyon, Devon T. '— '03 C.413 B.A. L.990 J.D.
(adm. in CA; not adm. in OR) [🄰 Davis W.T.]
Lyon, Jesse D. ... '— '98 C.906 B.S. L.1209 J.D. [Davis W.T.]
Lysne, Matthew J. ... '76 '02 C&L.911 B.A., J.D. [🄰 Preston G.&E.]
Ma, Akana K. J. ... '56 '84 C.860 B.A. L.93 J.D. [🄲 Ater W.]
Mabe, Joseph M. ... '75 '01 C.629 B.S. L.306 J.D. [🄰 Brownstein,R.S.K.G.D.&H.]
MacColl, E. Kimbark, Jr., (AV) ... '50 '75 C.674 B.A. L.629 J.D. [VavRosky M.O.]
MacCourt, Douglas C., (BV) ... '59 '89 C.330 B.S. L.629 J.D. [Ater W.]
MacDonald, Terry S. ... '51 '78 C.1056 B.S. L.629 J.D. CNF Transp., Inc.
MacDougal, Douglas W., (AVⓉ) ... '45 '73 C.882 B.S. L.902 J.D. [Schwabe,W.&W.]
Mac Haffie, Dale S. ... '47 '86 C.628 B.S. L.1051 J.D. Tax Mgr., Esco Corp.
Mack, Mitchell W. ... '41 '68 C.602 B.A. L.950 J.D. 4380 S.W. Macadam Ave.
Mackenzie, Leslie J., (AV) ... '50 '80 C.911 B.S. L.596 J.D. [Reinisch,M.H.&W.]
Mackeson, Wayne, (AV) ... '53 '82 C.594 B.S. L.596 J.D. [Birmingham&M.]
Mackin, Patrick K. ... '— '77 C.629 B.A. L.1051 J.D. 4511 S.E. Hawthorne Blvd.
MacLaren, Caroline Emma '71 '99 C.881 B.A. L.629 J.D.
1000 Friends of Oregon, 534 SW 3rd Avenue
MacLaren, Gordon M., (BV) ... '32 '60 C.1056 L.596 LL.B. 1122 N.E. 122nd Ave.
MacMillan, John R. ... '70 '97 C.112 B.A. L.1051 J.D. [🄰 MacMillan,S.&M.]
MacMillan, Roderic S., (AV) ... '46 '76 C.112 B.A. L.767 J.D. [MacMillan,S.&M.]
MacMillan, Scholz & Marks, P.C., (AV) ... 101 S.W. Main St., Ste. 1000
MacMurray, Frank G., Jr. ... '44 '72 C.674 B.A. L.893 LL.B. 8312 N. Edison
Macomber, Brad A. ... '75 '03 C.878 B.S. L.950 J.D. [🄰 Hunt&Assoc.]
Macpherson, Gregory H., (AV) ... '50 '75 C.309 A.B. L.276 J.D. [Stoel R.]
Macpherson, Victoria L. ... '56 '86 C.628 B.A. L.950 J.D. [🄲 Miller N.]
Macy, Jed C. ... '51 '76 C.1349 B.A. L.107 J.D. Deloitte & Touche
Madkour, Stephen Lewis, (BV) ... '62 '94 C.999 B.A. L.1187 J.D. [Madkour&M.]
Madkour & Mottram, P.C., (BV) ... 522 S.W. Fifth Ave., Ste. 925
Maffei, Laura ... '66 '99 C.112 B.S. L.596 J.D. [🄰 Schwabe,W.&W.]
Magee, Frank E. ... '16 '54 C.1279 M.C.S. L.596 LL.B. 205 N.W. 86th‡
Magee, John E. ... '51 '76 C.628 B.S. L.596 J.D. 5125 S.W. Macadam
Magliana, John A., Jr. ... '57 '84 C.628 B.S. L.950 J.D. 222 S. W. Columbia St., Ste. 1625
Maguire, Margaret M., (AV) ... '63 '91 C.399 B.A. L.1051 J.D. The Regence Group
Mahalic, Drew ... '53 '83 C.602 B.B.A. L.309 J.D. Proj. Dir., Portland State Univ.
Maher, James L. ... '54 '85 C.170 B.A. L.508 J.D. U.S. Dept. of Agric.
Maher, Tamara B. ... '— '91 C.1349 B.A. L.950 J.D. [🄰 Dunn C.A.H.&T.]
Maier, Bradley D. ... '67 '03 C.1056 B.S. L.596 J.D. [🄰 Schwabe,W.&W.]
Maizels, Richard, (AV) ... '38 '66 C.911 B.A. L.596 J.D. 1001 SW 5th Ave. Ste. 1625
Majkut, Paul Stevenson '50 '76
C&L.911 B.A., J.D. Asst. Gen. Coun., Bonneville Power Admn.
Maki, Nathan R. ... '— '03 C.502 B.S. L.596 J.D. [🄰 Schwabe,W.&W.]
Makler, Mark J., (BV) ... '64 '91 C.1056 B.S. L.596 J.D. 5530 Sw Kelly Ave
Makuch, Joseph S. ... '65 '95 C.124 B.S.E.E. L.596 J.D. [Marger J.&M.] (See Pat. Sect.)
Malcolm, David J. '60 '99 C.1060 B.A. L.950 J.D.
Financ. Advis., The Strategic Alliance
Malcolm, Sean B. '— '05 C.039 B.Sc. L.911 J.D.
(adm. in WA; not adm. in OR) [🄰 Davis W.T.]
Mallory, Gregory W. ... '68 '94 C.628 B.S. L.950 J.D. [🄰 Schwabe,W.&W.]
Malm, Stephen M. '42 '67 C.939 B.A. L.950 J.D.
Asst. Secy. & Asst. Gen. Coun., NACCO Materials Handling Grp., Inc.
Maloney, Francis J., III ... '67 '95 C.93 B.A. L.629 J.D. [Bullivant H.B.]
Maloney, Robert E., Jr., (AV) ... '— '67 C.670 B.A. L.950 J.D. [Lane P.]
Mandekor, Gretchen L. ... '73 '00 C.012 B.A. L.629 J.D. [🄰 Cosgrave V.K.]
Mandiberg, Susan F. '47 '75
C.604 B.A. L.112 J.D. Prof. of Law, Northwestern Sch. of Law
Mandt, Heidi L. ... '69 '95 C.906 B.S. L.950 J.D. [Schwabe,W.&W.]

Manicke, Robert T. ... '62 '92 C.950 B.A. L.339 J.D. [Stoel R.]
Manishan, Anita G. ... '48 '86 C.685 B.A. L.596 J.D. 215 S.W. Washington St., Ste. 201
Manlove, William Woodrow ... '59 '89 C.1051 B.A. L.112 J.D. Dep. City Atty.
Mann, Carter M. ... '62 '92 C.165 B.A. L.107 J.D. [Foster P.T.]
Manne, William S., P.C., (AV) ... '51 '85 C.1213 B.S. L.1051 J.D. [Miller N.]
Manning, James V. ... '61 '86 C.190 B.A. L.629 J.D. P.O. Box 33042
Mansfield, Johnathan E., (AVⓉ) '62 '93 C.629 B.Mus. L.188 J.D.
(adm. in PA; not adm. in OR) [Schwabe,W.&W.]
Manulik, Mark A., (AV) ... '52 '78 C.846 B.A. L.326 J.D. [Schwabe,W.&W.]
Mapes, Jeffrey Colin, (AV) ... '56 '84 C.347 B.A. L.629 J.D. 4370 N.E. Halsey
Mapes, Kevin S. ... '67 '94 C.678 B.A. L.1051 J.D. [🄰 Ball J.]
Mapes, Laurie B. ... '59 '84 C.813 B.A. L.1051 J.D. Lewis & Clark Law School
Marandas, John S., (BV) ... '40 '66 C.1051 B.S. L.950 J.D. [Marandas,P.M.A.&D.]
Marandas, Perdue, Marandas, Alexander & Durham, LLC, (BV)
1500 S.W. First Ave., Ste. 840
Marcum, Molly K., (AV) ... '54 '83 C.1056 B.S. L.1051 J.D. [🄲 Keating J.B.&H.]
Marcus, Michael H. ... '43 '70 C.112 A.B. L.1066 J.D. Cir. J.
Marcy, Gary L. ... '64 '95 C.1056 B.A. L.1051 J.D. [🄰 Snyder&Assoc.]
Mardikes, George M. ... '— '84 C.145 A.B. L.502 J.D. [Davis W.T.]
Marger, Jerome S., (AV) '41 '71
C.570 B.S.Ch.E L.7 J.D. [🄲 Marger J.&M.] (See Pat. Sect.)

Marger Johnson & McCollom, P.C., (AV) 🄱🅁
210 S.W. Morrison Street, Suite 400, 97204
Telephone: 503-222-3613 FAX: 503-274-4622
Email: info@techlaw.com URL: http://www.techlaw.com
Alexander C. Johnson, Jr.; Alan T. McCollom; Stephen S. Ford; Scott A. Schaffer; Joseph S. Makuch; Graciela Gomez Cowger; Craig R. Rogers; Julie L. Reed (Not admitted in OR); Ariel S. Rogson; Hosoon Lee; Hillary Anne Brooks;—Todd J. Iverson; Jeffrey John Richmond; Brian G Forrest; Bryan D. Kirkpatrick. Of Counsel: Jerome S. Marger; Elmer W. Galbi (Not admitted in OR).
Intellectual Property Law, Patents, Trademarks, Copyrights, Computers and Software, Trade Secrets, Licensing Agreements, Nanotechnology, Technology Licensing and Litigation.
Vancouver, Washington Office: 5123 N.E. 94th Avenue, Suite C, 98662. Telephone: 360-260-3613. Fax: 360-695-0271.

See Professional Biographies, PORTLAND, OREGON

Margiloff, Susan G., (CV) ... '64 '89 C.1365 B.A. L.904 J.D. 9600 Sw Barnes Rd Ste 200
Margolin, Daniel S., Law Offices of '75 '02
C.1375 B.A. L.569 J.D. 621 SW Morrison Street, Suite 1425
Margolin, Doreen Stamm, Law Offices of, (AV) '47 '81
C.569 B.A. L.596 J.D. 621 S.W. Morrison St.
Margolin, Phillip M., (AV) ... '44 '72 C.30 B.A. L.569 J.D. 1020 S.W. Taylor St.‡
Margolis, Wendy M. ... '— '94 C.112 B.A. L.629 J.D. [Cosgrave V.K.]
Marino-Blair, Bonnie B. ... '50 '05 C.1051 L.596 J.D. 3404 S.E. 45th Ave., Ste. 1
Mark, Stacey E., (AV) ... '56 '87 C.831 B.F.A. L.596 J.D. [Ater W.]
Markley, Charles R., (AV) ... '44 '75 C.911 B.A. L.1051 J.D. [Greene&M.]
Markley, Julia E. ... '74 '00 C.813 B.A. L.911 J.D. [🄰 Perkins C.]
Markowitz, David B., (AV) ... '49 '74 C.1074 B.S. L.464 J.D. [Markowitz,H.G.&M.]

Markowitz, Herbold, Glade & Mehlhaf, P.C., (AV)
3000 Pacwest Center, 1211 SW Fifth Avenue, 97204-3730
Telephone: 503-295-3085 FAX: 503-323-9105
URL: http://www.MarkowitzHerbold.com
Shareholders: David B. Markowitz; Peter H. Glade; William N. Mehlhaf; Lynn R. Stafford; Lisa A. Kaner; Lynn R. Nakamoto; Jeffrey M. Edelson; Kerry J. Shepherd; Jeffrey M. Batchelor; Paul S. Bierly; Matthew A. Levin;—Charles J. Paternoster; Matthew D. Larson. Of Counsel: Christine T. Herrick.
Civil Litigation including Commercial, Insurance, Employment and Real Estate.

See Professional Biographies, PORTLAND, OREGON

Marks, Christopher B., (AV) ... '56 '83 C.911 B.A. L.629 J.D. [MacMillan,S.&M.]
Marks, J. Barrett (Barry), (AV) ... '46 '75 C.309 B.A. L.1066 J.D. [J.B.Marks]
Marks, Steven G. ... '52 '78 C.112 B.S. L.1068 J.D. [S.G.Marks]
Marks, J. Barrett, P.C., (AV) ... 442 S.E. 33rd Ave.
Marks, Steven G., P.C. ... 3735 S.E. Clay St.
Marmaduke, Don H., (AV) ... '26 '51 C.976 B.E. L.309 LL.B. [Tonkon T.]
Marmaduke, Susan D., (AV) ... '52 '78 C.1056 B.A. L.1066 J.D. [Harrang L.G.R.]
Marmion, Melanie E. ... '69 '96 C.93 B.A. L.776 J.D. 4333 NE Beech Street
Marquoit, J. Jason, Law Office of '74 '99
C.670 B.A. L.190 J.D. 7830 S.W. 40th Ave., Ste. 8
Marron, James F. ... '72 '00 C.1058 B.A. L.221 J.D. [🄰 Grenley,R.E.B.&B.]
Marsh, James O., (BV) ... '51 '80 C.576 B.A. L.596 J.D. [Carney,B.H.&M.]
Marsh, Jenni E. ... '76 '02 C.629 B.S. L.93 J.D. [🄰 Lindsay,H.N.&W.]
Marsh, John H. '54 '86
C.628 B.S. L.1051 J.D. Dir. Fisheries/ESA Program, Parametrix, Inc.
Marsh, Kimberly A., (BVⓉ) ... '62 '91 C.112 B.A. L.596 J.D. 1205 NW 25th Street
Marsh, Malcolm F. ... '28 '54 C&L.629 B.S., LL.B. Sr. U.S. Dist. J.

Marsh, Higgins, Beaty & Hatch, P.C.
(See Vancouver, Washington)

Marshall, Christopher J., (AV) ... '— '85 C.628 B.S. L.950 J.D. Cir.J.
Martin, Adian ... '64 '97 C.1111 B.A. L.596 J.D. [🄰 Ransom&G.]
Martin, Chrys A., (AV) ... '53 '81 C.628 B.A. L.596 J.D. [Bullivant H.B.]
Martin, Nancy E. ... '60 '90 C.893 B.A. L.629 J.D. Dep. City Atty.
Martin, Robert E., (BV) ... '43 '71 C.1056 B.A. L.596 J.D. 1920 S.W. 13th Ave.
Martin, William A., (AV) ... '12 '38 C&L.629 J.D. 6200 S.W. Arrow Wood Lane‡

Martin, Bischoff, Templeton, Langslet & Hoffman, LLP, (AV)
900 Pioneer Tower, 888 S.W. Fifth, 97204 ⊙
Telephone: 503-224-3113 Fax: 503-224-9471
URL: http://www.martinbischoff.com
Members of Firm: John L. Langslet; Jonathan M. Hoffman; James C. Howe; John W. Knottnerus; Mary-Anne S. Rayburn; James T. Dunn; Douglas G. Pickett; Philip A. Rush; Michael J. Farrell; Scott A. Kamin; Justin M. Thorp. Associates: Jessica Carpenter; Marja E. Selmann; Aaron C. Denton; Camille Tourjé; Stephen P. Yoshida.
General Civil and Trial Practice in all State and Federal Courts of Oregon, Washington and Alaska. Insurance Defense and Coverage, Aviation, Products Liability, Business Planning, Employment, Estate Planning and Probate, Tax, Real Estate, Financial Institutions, Creditors Rights, Admiralty, Commercial and Real Property Litigation and Transactions and Federal and State Civil Appeals.
Representative Insurance Clients: Aviation & General Insurance Co.; Lloyds of London.
References: The Oregon Bank; First National Bank of Oregon.
Anchorage, Alaska Office: 425 G Street, Suite 910, 99501. Telephone: 907-276-1277.

See Professional Biographies, PORTLAND, OREGON

Martindale, Dorothy M. ... '10 '44 C.629 L.596 J.D. [Martindale&F.]
Martindale & Faveluke, (BV) ... 1714 S.E. Ankeny St.
Martinson, Stanley E., (AV) ... '35 '70 C&L.1051 B.S., J.D. [Bullivant H.B.]
Martson, William F., Jr., (AV) ... '47 '72 C.901 B.A. L.477 J.D. [Tonkon T.]
Marvin, James H., (BV) ... '— '72 C.906 B.S. L.596 J.D. [Marvin,C.&L.]

Marvin, Chorzempa & Larson, P.C., (BV)
Sellwood Building, Suite 300, 380 S.E. Spokane Street, 97202-6464
Telephone: 503-232-1410 Fax: 503-234-1824
Email: jhmarvin@mca-law.com URL: http://www.lawyers.com/marvinchorzempa

(This Listing Continued)

Marvin, Chorzempa & Larson, P.C. (Continued)

James H. Marvin; Janelle E. Chorzempa; Jon C. Larson;—Lisa M. Gramp.
Civil Trial in Federal And State Courts representing the Design and Construction Industry. Products Liability, Subsurface Litigation, Toxic Torts, Professional Liability, Estate Planning, Personal Injury, Mediation and Arbitration.

See Professional Biographies, PORTLAND, OREGON

Mascal, Christine .... '64 '90 C.801 B.S. L.879 J.D. Dist. Atty. Off.
Mason, Christine B. Miller, (BV) '61 '93
C.93 B.A. L.734 J.D. Asst. Atty. Gen., Charitable Activities Sect.
Mason, Tammy English ....'60 '87 C&L.950 B.A., J.D. 900 SW 5th Ave
Masters, William J. .... '19 '48 C.813 A.B. L.629 J.D. 2404 N.E. 23rd Ave.‡
Matarazzi, William H. '53 '78 C.602 B.B.A. L.900 J.D.
(adm. in KS; not adm. in OR) P.O. Box 8792‡

Matarazzo, Harris S., (AV) '57 '86 C.103 A.B. L.596 J.D.
121 S.W. Morrison Avenue, Suite 1020, 97204
Telephone: 503-226-0306 FAX: 503-226-4290
Mental Health Issues related to Criminal Defense; Administrative Law; Appellate; Probate and Estate Planning.

See Professional Biographies, PORTLAND, OREGON

Matarazzo, Judith Hudson, (AV) ....'59 '85 C.300 L.950 J.D. [Gutzler&H.]
Matasar, Lawrence, (AV) ....'49 '74 C&L.659 B.S., J.D. [L.Matasar]

Matasar, Lawrence, P.C., (AV)
Suite 1025, 621 Southwest Morrison Street, 97205
Telephone: 503-222-9830 Fax: 503-274-8575
Email: larry@pdxlaw.com URL: http://www.lawyers.com/matasar
Lawrence Matasar.
Criminal Defense, Fraud Environmental Crimes, White Collar Crimes, Narcotics Drug Crimes, Appellate Practice.

See Professional Biographies, PORTLAND, OREGON

Matasaru, Adina ....'— '03 C.670 B.A. L.950 J.D. [Ⓐ Harrang L.G.R.]
Matheson, David S., (AV) ....'64 '91 C.813 B.A. L.112 J.D. [Perkins C.]
Mathews, Charles W., III '44 '69 C&L.421 B.A., J.D.
(adm. in KY; not adm. in OR) FBI
Matthews, Christopher T., (AV) .... '54 '89 C.766 B.A. L.1065 J.D. [Perkins C.]
Matthews, Jeffrey S., (AV) .... '53 '82 C&L.629 B.A., J.D. [Yates,M.&Assoc.]
Matthews, Kendra Marie ....'71 '96 C.678 B.A. L.276 J.D. [Ⓐ Ransom B.]
Matthys, Shelly ....'61 '95 C.628 B.A. L.678 J.D. 807 N.E. Alberta St.
Mattingly, John Michael ....'68 '95 C.280 B.B.A. L.596 J.D. [Ⓐ S.V.Rizzo]
Mattis, James M. '42 '67 C.909 B.A. L.911 J.D.
Sr. Assoc. Gen. Coun., Oregon Health Sciences Univ.
Mattoon, Joe ....'— '03 C.1290 B.A. L.1509 J.D. [Ⓐ Davis W.T.]
Maukonen, Jona J. ....'— '04 C.628 B.S. L.629 J.D. [Ⓐ Harrang L.G.R.]
Maurer, Gregory L. ....'67 '96 C.1083 B.S. L.893 J.D. [Klarquist S.] (See Pat. Sect.)
Mauritz, D. Charles, (AV) ....'— '69 C.170 B.A. L.846 J.D. [Davis W.T.]
Mautner, Paul F., (AV) '58 '83 C.154 B.S. L.950 J.D.
Dep. Gen. Coun., Tri-County Metro Transp. Dist.
Maxfield, Lisa, (AV) '53 '81
C&L.878 B.S., J.D. 621 Southwest Morrison Street, Suite 1025
Mayerle, Michael J. ....'— '03 C.1051 B.S. L.596 J.D. [Ⓐ Bullivant H.B.]
Maylie, Joseph W., (AV) .... '41 '69 C.628 B.S. L.950 J.D. [Maylie&G.]
Maylie & Grayson, (AV) .... 7959 S.E. Foster Rd.
Maynard, Katherine B. '52 '84 C.575 B.A. L.284 J.D.
(adm. in CA; not adm. in OR) 6555 N. Boston Avenue
Maynard, Sharon ....'61 '92 C.1494 B.A. L.982 J.D. [Ⓐ Swanson,T.&C.]
Mayor, Richard H. .... '44 '75 C.1056 B.S. L.1051 J.D. 1826 N.E. Broadway St.
McAdams, David K., (AV) .... '45 '75 C&L.629 B.B.A., J.D. [Ⓒ Cable H.B.H.&L.]
McAllister, Conway C. ....'54 '94 C.999 B.S. L.596 J.D. Liberty Northwest Ins. Corp.
McAllister, William M., (AV) ....'33 '62 C.309 A.B. L.950 J.D. [Stoel R.] ‡
McAlpine, Gwyneth .... '71 '00 C.112 B.A. L.1068 J.D. [Ⓐ Perkins C.]
McArthur, Douglas W. ....'75 '03 C.878 B.S. L.101 J.D. 520 S.W. Yamhill, Ste. 200
McArthur-Phillips, Michael, (AV) ....'— '82 C.477 B.A. L.596 J.D. [Davis W.T.]
McAvity, Thomas Adams .... '65 '00 C.37 B.A. L.596 J.D. 621 SW Morrison, Suite 1060
McBurney, Mari F. .... '62 '91 C.911 B.A. L.339 J.D. Flying Rhinoceros, Inc.
McCain, Richard J. '46 '74
C.637 B.A. L.893 J.D. Secy. & Gen. Coun., Zidell Marine Corp.
McCandlish, James E., (AV) .... '45 '75 C.309 A.B. L.596 LL.B. P.O. Box 10767
McCarrel, Steven F. '— '76 C.878 B.S. L.950 J.D.
Asst. Gen. Coun., Enron Broadband Servs., Inc.
McCarthy, Joseph J., (BV) ....'35 '69 C.1056 L.1051 1500 S.W. 1st Ave.
McCarthy, Michael P. '47 '75 C.670 B.A. L.678 J.D.
Dist. Coun., U.S. Dept. Vet. Affairs
McCarthy, Stephen P., (AV) ....'— '85 C.1074 B.S. L.464 J.D. [Lane P.]
McCarthy, Stephen R., (AV) .... '43 '69 C.685 B.A. L.569 J.D. 1646 N.W. 32nd St.
McCaslin, J. Clay, Law Office of '72 '01
C.88 B.A. L.861 J.D. 1001 S.W. Fifth Ave., Ste. 1100
McCaslin, Michael C., (AV) ... '61 '89 C.629 B.S. L.596 J.D. 8700 S.W. 26th Ave., Ste. 2
McCauley, Jennifer Anne ....'71 '01 C.454 B.S. L.596 J.D. [Ⓐ Smith F.&E.]
McCaulley, Carol L. Catherine '50 '01 C.906 M.A. L.596 J.D.
(adm. in WA; not adm. in OR) [Ⓐ Schwabe,W.&W.] (⊙Vancouver, WA)
McCaw, Kenneth M., Jr., (AV) ....'37 '62 C&L.813 B.A., J.D. Esco Corp.
McClanahan, Mark C., (AV) ....'30 '54 C&L.950 B.A., J.D. [Ⓒ Vial F.]
McCleary, Standish, III ....'48 '75 C.880 B.A. L.64 J.D. 231 N.W. Seblar Dr.‡
McClellan, Matthew W. '65 '92 C.276 B.A. L.128 J.D.
(adm. in PA; not adm. in OR) [Elliott,O.&P.]
McClendon, Glen P., (AV) ....'48 '73 C.1056 B.S. L.629 J.D. [Lindsay,H.N.&W.]
McClory, Michael G. .... '63 '89 C&L.602 B.A., J.D. [Bullard S.J.W.]
McClung, Charles D., (AV) '39 '75
C.911 B.S.M.E. L.285 J.D. [Chernoff,V.M.&S.] (See Pat. Sect.)
McClure, Michelle K. ....'68 '95 C.154 B.A. L.770 J.D. [Landye B.B.]
McClurg, James W., (AV) ....'43 '71 C.628 B.S. L.596 J.D. 1834 S.W. 58th Ave.
McCollom, Alan T., (AV) '50 '77
C.612 B.S.E.E. L.623 J.D. [Marger J.&M.] (See Pat. Sect.)
McCoog, Carol J. ....'72 '97 C&L.911 B.A., J.D. [Ⓐ Preston G.&E.]
McCord, Peter C., (BV) .... '47 '72 C.629 B.A. L.1065 J.D. [Ⓐ Scarborough,M.O.&K.]
McCormack, John M. '44 '75 C.628 B.S.M.E. L.30 J.D.
(adm. in DC; not adm. in OR; Pat.) [Ⓒ Kolisch H.] (⊙Palo Alto, CA)
McCormick, John E., (AV) ....'53 '80 C.629 B.S. L.950 J.D. [Sussman S.]
McCoy, B. Anna ....'73 '00 C.685 B.A. L.1051 J.D. [Ⓐ Kolisch H.] (Pat.)
McCracken, Christopher F. ....'— '89 C.385 B.A. L.629 J.D. [Davis W.T.]
McCravey, Mary A. '21 '47 C&L.280 A.B., J.D.
(adm. in GA; not adm. in OR) 3625 S.W. 60th Pl.‡
McCulloch, Mark M., (AV) ....'42 '67 C&L.629 B.A., J.D. [Powers,M.&B.]
McCulloch, Sue-Del '65 '95 C.483 B.A. L.1051 J.D.
710 S.W. Madison Street, 4th Floor

McCune, Kevin J. .... '54 '81 C.763 P.E. L.950 J.D. Penthse. 210 SW Morrison★
McCurdy, James P. ....'73 '04 C.988 B.A. L.629 J.D. [Ⓐ Lindsay,H.N.&W.]
McCurdy, Mary Kyle ....'57 '86 C.813 B.A. L.1067 J.D. 1000 Friends of Oregon
McDermott, Daniel M. '53 '78
C.884 B.A. L.161 J.D. Asst. U.S. Trustee; U.S. Dept. of Jus.
McDermott, James N. ....'71 '00 C.112 B.A. L.1065 J.D. [Ⓐ Ater W.]
McDermott, James T., (AV) ....'60 '86 C.823 B.S. L.893 J.D. [Ball J.]
McDermott, Thomas E., (AV) ...... '47 '76 C.884 A.B. L.1065 J.D. [Lindsay,H.N.&W.]
McDonald, David Thomas ....'58 '86 C.896 B.A. L.596 J.D. 808 S.W. 3rd Ave., Suite 425
McDonald, Gregg A. '— '91
C.1071 B.S. L.629 J.D. 888 Southwest 5th Avenue, Suite 650
McDonald, Joseph D., (AV) ....'54 '84 C.1056 B.S. L.596 J.D. [Smith&M.]
McDonnell, Brendan R., (AV) .... '62 '87 C.426 B.S. L.1067 J.D. [Preston G.&E.]
McDougal, Mark G. .... '63 '89 C&L.861 B.A., J.D. 320 S.W. Stark St., Ste. 202
McDowell, Katherine A., (AV) ....'60 '85 C.352 B.A. L.362 J.D. [Stoel R.]

McEwen Gisvold LLP, (AV)
(Founded as Cake & Cake-1886)
1600 Standard Plaza, 1100 S.W. Sixth Avenue, 97204
Telephone: 503-226-7321 FAX: 503-243-2687
Email: contact@mcewengisvold.com URL: http://www.mcewengisvold.com
Donald W. McEwen (1920-2000). Senior Partners: Dean P. Gisvold; F. Gordon Allen, III. Partners: Don G. Carter; James Ray Streinz; Janet M. Gravdal; Barry L. Groce; Jonathan M. Radmacher; Janice Nystrom Turner; Johnston A. Mitchell; Robert L. O'Halloran. Of Counsel: Robert D. Rankin. Associates: J. Kurt Kraemer; Hertsel Shadian; Trung D. Tu; John B. Benazzi; Erin Moak Lillis.
Real Estate, Real Estate Finance, Commercial Real Estate, Leases and Leasing, Corporate Law, Business Law, Bankruptcy, Debtor and Creditor, Low Income Housing, Estate Planning, Probate, Taxation, Nonprofit and Charitable Organizations, Litigation, Commercial Litigation, Legal Malpractice Defense, Products Liability Defense, Real Estate Litigation, Real Estate Title Insurance, Construction, Public Contracts, Surety Bond Claims and Defense and Mechanic's Liens.
General Counsel for: Standard Insurance Co.; Northwest Food Processors Assn.
Local Counsel for: Safeway Inc.; John Deere Co.; Travelers Insurance Co. (Real Estate Investment Dept.); Transnation Title Insurance Co.; Bank of America, N.A.; GE Security, Inc.; Protective Life Insurance Company; Allianz Life Insurance Company of North America.

See Professional Biographies, PORTLAND, OREGON

McFaddin, Dwight E. ....'17 '56 C.629 B.S. L.596 LL.B. 6316 S.W. Peyton Rd.‡
McFarland, Barbara P., (AV) .... '34 '74 C.1056 B.A. L.1051 J.D. [DeBast,M.&R.]
Mc Gair, Kimberley A. Hanks .... '73 '98 C.629 B.A. L.596 J.D. [Ⓐ Farleigh W.]

McGaughey, Robert J., (AV) '49 '80 C.422 B.S. L.8 J.D.
111 S.W. Columbia Street, Suite 1000, 97201-5855
Telephone: 503-223-7555 Fax: 503-525-4833
Email: bob@law7555.com
Securities, Shareholder, Partnership, LLC Litigation.

See Professional Biographies, PORTLAND, OREGON

McGill, Liam ....'50 '93 C&L.215 B.A., J.D. 700 Ne Multnomah Ste 533
McGill, Kapranos & Wynn .... 1734 Northeast Broadway Street
McGinnis, Charles I. .... '38 '63 C.629 B.B.A. L.950 J.D. First Interstate Bk. of Ore., N.A.
McGirr, Charles H. .... '15 '38 L.629 LL.B. 6385 S.W. Arrowwood Lane‡
McGlasson, Jeana M. ....'71 '03 C.628 B.S. L.629 J.D. [Ⓐ Ball J.]
McGrath, Michael T. .... '76 '01 C.413 B.A. L.1051 J.D. [Gearing,R.&E.]
McGrew, R. Scott ....'47 '82 C.825 B.S. L.823 J.D. 3612 S.W. Multnomah Blvd.
McGrory, John F., Jr., (AV) ....'— '81 C.494 B.A. L.596 J.D. [Davis W.T.]
McGuigan, John M., (AV) ....'54 '79 C&L.629 B.S., J.D. [Black H.]
McGuire, Patricia ....'— '96 C.628 B.A. L.596 J.D. [Davis W.T.]
McHenry, Matthew G. ....'75 '04 C.477 B.B.A. L.1051 J.D. [Ⓐ M.R.Levine]
McIlhenny, John K., Jr., (AV) '48 '79
C.906 B.A. L.596 J.D. [Sorensen-Jolink,T.W.M.&W.]
McIntosh, Jock G. '47 '75 C.629 B.S. L.285 J.D.
Multnomah Co. Facilities & Prop. Mgmt.
McIntyre, Jane M. '22 '46 C.777 B.A. L.659 J.D.
(adm. in PA; not adm. in OR) 13633 N.E. Fremont St.‡
McIntyre, Shelley K., (AV) '45 '84
C.112 B.A. L.596 J.D. Asst. Atty. Gen., OR Dept. of Jus.
McKallip, George W., Jr., (AV) ....'58 '84 C.25 B.A. L.596 J.D. [Sussman S.]
McKallip, Kerry Kent ....'56 '84 C.174 B.A. L.1051 J.D. 475 N.E. Hazelfern Pl.
McKean, Douglas A. '53 '82 C.1056 B.S. L.629 J.D.
Admin. Law J., Bur. of Labor & Ind.
McKelvey, Donald D. '41 '67 C.629 B.A. L.950 J.D.
V.P. & Coun., First Amer. Title Ins. Co. of Ore.
Mckelvey, Lowell P. ....'71 '99 C.810 B.A. L.508 J.D. [Ⓐ Mitchell,L.&S.]
McKeown, Scott A., (BV) ....'49 '85 [McKeown&B.]
McKeown & Brindle, P.C., (BV) .... 8700 S.W. 26th Ave., Ste. S
McKercher, Karin ....'64 '00 C.1400 B.S. L.596 J.D. [Idea A.]
McKey, Ray E. ....'12 '36 C&L.950 LL.B. 2578 N.E. 32nd Ave.‡
McKillop, Christopher ....'63 '88 C.1239 B.A. L.1065 J.D. Rogers Machinery Co.
McKittrick, Peter C., (AV) ....'59 '85 C.1051 B.S. L.950 J.D. [Farleigh W.]
McLaughlin, Bruce D. ....'60 '97 C.273 B.A. L.596 J.D. P.O. Box 25059
McLaughlin, Vincent A. ....'10 '37 L.588 LL.B. 7540 S.E. 32nd St.
McLean, Holly R. ....'57 '84 C&L.629 B.A., J.D. Off. of Gen. Coun., USDA
McLennan, Janet .... '26 '72 C.629 B.A. L.1051 J.D. 5252 SW Northwood Ave.‡
McLennan, William S. ....'23 '52 C.629 B.S. L.273 J.D. Sr. Cir. J.
McLeod, Richard D. '— '00 C.326 B.S. L.846 J.D.
(adm. in TX; not adm. in OR; See Pat. Sect.) [Ⓐ Klarquist S.]
McMahan, Timothy L. .....'61 '86 C.678 B.A. L.950 J.D. [Stoel R.] (⊙Vancouver, WA)
McManus, Marilyn C. '53 '79
C.112 B.A. L.809 J.D. Portland State Univ., Reg. Resch. Institue
McMenamin & Taylor, (BV) .... P.O. Box 19855
McMonies, Walter W., Jr., (AV)................'47 '73 C&L.976 B.A., J.D. [Foster P.T.]
McMullen, Colleen L., P.C. ....'67 '95 C.118 B.A. L.596 J.D. [Miller N.]
McMurchie, Charles J., (AV) ....'31 '59 C.939 A.B. L.911 LL.B. [Stoel R.] ‡
McMurry, Garry P. ....'34 '58 C&L.629 B.S., LL.B. 435 Benjamin Franklin Plaza
McNally, Yone C. ....'60 '88 C.529 B.A. L.596 J.D. Coord., Dept. of Envir. Quality
McNamara, Wesley F. .....'55 '82 C.145 B.A. L.1051 J.D. U.S. Treas., I.R.S. Dist. Coun.
McNamee, Heather ....'74 '00 C.970 B.A. L.124 J.D. [Ⓐ Yazbeck,C.&H.]
McNeese, A. John, (AV) ....'46 '77 C.629 B.S. L.596 J.D. [Scarborough,M.O.&K.]
McNeil, Daniel F., (AV) .... '54 '80 C.882 B.S. L.602 J.D. [Bullivant H.B.]
McNeil, Tim ....'68 '98 C.602 B.A. L.1051 J.D. 520 Sw 6th Ave Ste 1130

McNeil Law Office LLC
(See Hillsboro)

McPherson, Thomas W., (BV) ....'46 '73 C.813 A.B. L.1066 J.D. [Mersereau&S.]
McShane, Michael, (AV) ....'61 '88 C.285 L.596 J.D. Metro Pub. Def.
McStay, P. Andrew, Jr. ....'— '03 C.976 B.A. L.846 J.D. [Ⓐ Davis W.T.]
McSwain, Peter W., (AV) '43 '73 C.629 A.B. L.950 J.D.
800 N.E. Oregon Street, #1160
McTaggart, Ingrid M. .... '65 '92 C&L.36 B.S.Ch.E., J.D, 1816 S.E. 54th Ave. (Pat.)
McVittie, James D. ....'61 '88 C.906 B.A. L.596 J.D. 2310 NW Everett St., Ste. 200

Meabe, Gary J., (AV) ....'57 '82 C&L.950 B.S., J.D. Sr. Dep. Dist. Atty.
Meadows, Christine M. ....'69 '96 C.339 B.S. L.596 J.D. [Jordan S.]
Meagher, Anne LaLonde ....'56 '93 C.477 B.A. L.596 J.D. Standard Ins. Co.
Mechanic, Gene B., (AV) ....'47 '73 C.696 B.A. L.273 J.D. [Goldberg,M.S.&G.]
Medeiros, Martin F. ....'— '95 C.30 B.S. L.862 J.D. [Ⓐ Preston G.&E.]
Medford, Kimberly Anne ....'72 '99 C&L.950 B.A., J.D. [Ⓐ Stoel R.]
Mediation Services, (AV) ....2121 S.W. Broadway, Ste. 100
Medina, Orlando ....'74 '00 C.839 B.B.A. L.596 J.D. [Landye B.B.]
Meekcoms, Yvonne P., (BV) '56 '84
C.629 B.S. L.1051 J.D. Gionet Investment/Milestone Mngt. Co.
Mehlhaf, William N., (AV) .... '50 '75 C.628 B.S. L.596 J.D. [Markowitz,H.G.&M.]
Mehrbani, Parna A. ....'— '05 C.339 B.A. L.1051 J.D. [Ⓐ Lane P.]
Mei, James M. ....'— '89 C.999 B.A. L.950 J.D. [Davis W.T.]
Melkonian, Bruce L. ....'32 '72 C&L.800 B.E., J.D. P.O. Box 55036
Meltebeke, Brenda L. ....'56 '87 C.1056 B.S. L.94 J.D. [Ater W.]
Meltzer, Kelly ....'69 '97 C.174 B.S. L.1051 J.D. [Grenley,R.E.B.&B.]
Meltzer, Michael W., P.C., (AV) ....'— '85 C.951 B.A. L.976 J.D. [M.W.Meltzer]

Meltzer, Michael W., P.C., (AV)
4225 S.W. Huber Street, Suite 410, 97219
Telephone: 503-892-6615 Fax: 503-892-8851 URL: http://www.immigrationcases.com
Email: mmeltzer@firstam.com URL: http://www.lawyers.com/meltzer
Michael W. Meltzer, P.C.
Languages: Spanish and Vietnamese.
Immigration and Naturalization.
See Professional Biographies, PORTLAND, OREGON

Menashe, Albert A., (AV) ....'50 '77 C.629 B.S. L.950 J.D. [Gevurtz,M.L.&H.]
Menashe, Albert L. ....'38 '65 C.1056 B.S. L.596 LL.B. Admin. Law J., Wkrs. Comp. Bd.
Menashe, Shawn N. ....'78 '03 C&L.629 B.S., J.D. [Ⓐ Gevurtz,M.L.&H.]
Menchaca, Ricardo Jay ....'69 '00 C.628 B.A. L.1187 J.D. 630 Sw 5th Ave Ste 500
Mendelson, Michael B. ....'42 '81 C.472 B.S.C.E. L.950 J.D. 888 S.W. 5th Ave.
Mender, Samantha L. ....'72 '01 C.659 B.A. L.37 J.D. [Ⓐ Parsons F.&G.]
Meneghello, Kirsten Cook ....'70 '95 C.260 B.S. L.1059 J.D. U.S. Trust Co., Pacific N.W.
Meneghello, Richard R., (AV) ....'71 '96 C.823 A.B. L.1059 J.D. [Fisher&P.]
Meng, Linda J., (AV) ....'49 '79 C.445 B.A. L.446 J.D. Chf. Dep. City Atty.
Menikoff, Carrie ....'67 '97 C.659 B.A. L.930 J.D. [Ⓐ J.L.Hoffman]
Mercer, John C., (AV) ....'49 '74 C.1167 B.S. L.629 J.D. [Wood T.S.&M.]
Mercer, Robert M., (BV) ....'30 '57 C.1051 B.Sc. L.596 LL.B. 1122 N.E. 122nd Ave.
Merchant, Michael B., (BV) ....'63 '88 C.911 B.A. L.629 J.D. [Black H.]
Merrill, Erich W., Jr., P.C., (AV) ....'57 '83 C.880 B.E. L.309 J.D. [Miller N.]
Merrill, Ian G. ....'70 '05 C.790 B.A. L.1009 J.D. [Ⓐ Stoel R.]
Mersereau, Peter R., (AV) ....'48 '73 C.976 B.A. L.188 J.D. [Mersereau&S.]
Mersereau & Shannon LLP, (AV) ....One S.W. Columbia Street
Merten, Eric H. ....'67 '97 C.766 B.A. L.596 J.D. 7135 S.E. 16th Ave.
Meserve, Leslie M. ....'42 '83 C.873 A.B. L.596 J.D. 111 S.W. 5th Ave. (⊙Portland)
Meyer, Andrea R., (BV) '65 '93
C.604 B.A. L.1051 J.D. Legis. Dir./Coun., ACLU of Oregon
Meyer, David P., (BV) ....'59 '89 C.429 B.A. L.629 J.D. [D.P.Meyer]
Meyer, Paul R., (AV) ....'25 '53 C.178 A.B. L.976 J.D. 1325 S.W. Myrtle Dr.
Meyer, Roger L., (AV) ....'32 '57 C.604 B.A. L.976 LL.B. [Meyer&W.]
Meyer, Scott J., (AV) ....'56 '81 C.339 B.S. L.596 J.D. [Mitchell,L.&S.]
Meyer, William Aring, (BV) ....'61 '87 C&L.629 B.S., J.D. [Meyer,E.&G.]
Meyer, William R., (AV) ....'45 '71 C.813 A.B. L.309 J.D. 4511 S.E. 39th Ave.
Meyer, David P., P.C., (BV) ....621 S.W. Morrison St., Ste. 1300
Meyer, Elzinga & Gannett, P.C., (BV) ....1211 S.W. Fifth Avenue

Meyer & Wyse LLP, (AV)
American Bank Building, 621 S.W. Morrison Street Suite 1300, 97205-3816
Telephone: 503-228-8448 Fax: 503-273-9135
Email: law@meyerwyse.com URL: http://www.meyerwyse.com
Members of Firm: Roger L. Meyer; Scott C. Wyse; Joshua Kadish; Bruce H. Orr; Helen Rives Pruitt; James E. Bartels; Nicholas S. Fish;—Steven James Kuhn; David I. Bean.
General Civil Trial and Appellate Practice in State and Federal Courts. Business, Real Property, Estate Planning, Probate, Mediation, Family Law, Creditors' Rights, Bankruptcy, Secured Transactions, Community Associations and Architectural, Engineering and Construction Law.
See Professional Biographies, PORTLAND, OREGON

Meyers, Daniel L., (BV) ....'46 '76 C.628 B.S. L.596 J.D. [Radler,B.R.&M.]
Meyers, Martin P. ....'56 '86 C.37 B.A. L.879 J.D. [Ⓒ Sussman S.]
Meysing, Leo S., (P.C.), (BV) ...'29 '53 C&L.378 B.A., LL.B. 921 S.W. Washingtopn St.
Michels, Abigail R. ....'75 '01 C.911 B.A. L.950 J.D. [Ⓐ DuBoff]
Michels, Frank Stephen ....'61 '96 C.112 B.S. L.1051 J.D. 1924 S. W. Palatine St.
Michie, Preston D. ....'48 '80 C.966 B.S. L.596 J.D. Bonneville Pwr. Ad.
Middlebrook, Krista Marie ....'68 '94 C.112 B.A. L.629 J.D. Jud. Clk., Cir. Ct.
Migchelbrink, Paul D. ....'65 '93 C.336 B.S. L.950 J.D. [Ⓐ Hagen O.]
Miholer, Jeff S. ....'71 '01 C&L.629 B.S., J.D. [J.Miholer]
Miholer, Jeff, Law Office of ....1515 S.W. 5th Ave., Ste. 1022
Miles, Alia S. ....'— '98 C.112 B.A. L.1051 J.D. [Ⓐ Ater W.]
Millar, Susan B. ....'51 '89 C.273 B.S. L.861 J.D. 905 Ne 11th St
Millard, Frederick M. ....'52 '98 C.1206 B.S. L.770 J.D. [F.Millard]
Millard, Fred ....621 S.W. Alder St., Ste. 621
Millender, Michael ....'— '03 C.228 B.A. L.352 J.D. [Ⓐ Tonkon T.]
Miller, Bradley K. '56 '82 C.112 A.B. L.1065 J.D.
(adm. in CA; not adm. in OR) 101 SW Main St.
Miller, Bradley S., (AV) ....'61 '87 C.821 B.A. L.145 J.D. [Ball J.]
Miller, Carolyn W., (AV) ....'53 '78 C.112 B.A. L.950 J.D. [C.W.Miller]
Miller, Clair ....'46 '97 C.628 B.S. L.950 J.D. 1826 N.E. Broadway
Miller, David P., II, (AV) ....'42 '67 C&L.813 A.B., LL.B. [Stoel R.]
Miller, Donald C. ....'44 '75 C.107 B.A. L.1051 J.D. 400 S.W. 6th Ave.‡
Miller, Eric R. ....'52 '87 C.112 B.A. L.596 J.D. [Radler,B.R.&M.]
Miller, Fred B., (AV) .....'40 '66 C&L.813 B.A., LL.B. 111 S.W. Columbia St., Ste. 260
Miller, Judith Leonie '53 '81 C.897 B.A. L.1051 J.D.
Northwestern Sch. of Law of Lewis and Clark Coll.
Miller, Lisa Almasy, (AV) ....'55 '83 C.112 B.A. L.770 J.D. [Dwyer&M.]
Miller, Marilyn G. ....'42 '71 C.1056 B.S. L.596 J.D. Standard Ins. Co.
Miller, Marjorie ....'53 '94 C&L.629 M.B.A., J.D. Coopers & Lybrand, L.L.P.
Miller, Mary Jo Naples '— '95 C.363 B.S. L.602 J.D.
(adm. in IL; not adm. in OR) [Ⓒ James]
Miller, Max M., Jr., (AV) ....'57 '83 C.1168 B.A. L.1051 J.D. [Tonkon T.]
Miller, Peter, (BV) ....'50 '82 C.170 B.A. L.596 J.D. [Miller,P.]
Miller, Richard, & Associates, (AV) '50 '76
C.170 B.A. L.950 J.D. 805 S.W. Broadway, Ste. 800
Miller, Robert B., (AV) ....'59 '91 C.1175 B.A. L.472 J.D. [Bullivant H.B.]
Miller, Robert J. ....'51 '91 C.1104 B.S. L.596 J.D. Lew & Clark N.W. Sch. of Law
Miller, Ronald J. ....'— '95 C.906 B.A. L.602 J.D. [James]
Miller, Ted M., (BV) ....'52 '78 C&L.950 B.A., J.D. 1805 N. W. Glisan
Miller, Todd J. ....'63 '01 C.35 B.S. L.1151 J.D. Atty. Advsr.
Miller, W. Randy ....'70 '04 C.413 B.S. L.950 J.D. [Ⓐ Schwabe,W.&W.]
Miller, William R., Jr., (AV) ....'— '75 C.668 B.A. L.596 J.D. [Davis W.T.]

Miller, Carolyn W., P.C., (AV)
The River Forum, Suite 525, 4380 S W Macadam, 97239
Telephone: 503-241-2801 Fax: 503-241-2811
Email: carolyn@cwmillerpc.com URL: http://www.lawyers.com/cwmillerlaw
Carolyn W. Miller.
Estate Planning, Probate, Trusts, Taxation, Tax Exempt Organization.
See Professional Biographies, PORTLAND, OREGON

Miller Nash LLP, (AV) BB
A Limited Liability Partnership including Professional Corporations
111 S.W. Fifth Avenue, Suite 3400, 97204-3699 ⊙
Telephone: 503-224-5858 Facsimile: 503-224-0155
Email: clientservices@millernash.com URL: http://www.millernash.com
Portland, Oregon Partners: Craig R. Armstrong, P.C.; Jeffrey D. Austin, P.C.; David G. Bristol, P.C.; Donald A. Burns, P.C.; J. Franklin Cable, P.C.; Bruce L. Campbell, P.C.; Richard A. Canaday; D. Gary Christensen, P.C.; Jeffrey G. Condit; David C. Culpepper, P.C.; Dean D. DeChaine, P.C.; Julia A. DeWitt, P.C.; Brian B. Doherty, P.C.; C. Marie Eckert; Mary Ann Frantz, P.C.; Jonathon L. Goodling, P.C.; Phillip E. Grillo, P.C.; M. Christie Helmer, P.C.; Louis G. Henry, P.C.; David W. Hercher, P.C.; Graham M. Hicks, P.C.; Steven F. Hill (Also at Vancouver, Washington Office); Suzanne C. Lacampagne, P.C.; John A. Lusky; William S. Manne, P.C.; Colleen L. McMullen, P.C.; Erich W. Merrill, Jr., P.C.; John Casey Mills, P.C.; Conrad L. Moore; David M. Munro; John F. Neupert, P.C.; Teresa H. Pearson, P.C.; David G. Post, P.C.; John F. Purcell, P.C.; Dennis P. Rawlinson, P.C.; Peter C. Richter, P.C.; Bruce A. Rubin, P.C.; Thomas C. Sand, P.C.; Joshua M. F. Sasaki, P.C.; Catherine A. Shaw, P.C.; Ronald A. Shellan, P.C.; Michelle Slater, P.C.; Jeffrey C. Thede, P.C. Portland, Oregon Of Counsel: John D. Burns. Portland, Oregon Special Counsel: William R. Knuths; William H. Walters. Portland, Oregon Counsel: Victoria L. Macpherson. Portland, Oregon Retired Partners: John W. Hill; Norman J. Wiener. Portland, Oregon Associates: Michelle E. Barton; Pamela T. Blackwell; Abraham J.B. Cable; Heather K. Cavanaugh; Steven L. Christensen; Kieran J. Curley; Kornelia Dormire; Mareesa M. Elmquist; Ky Fullerton; Christine Gibert; Paul L. Havel; Ashley S. Hohimer; Kelly Shafer Hossaini; Hong N. Huynh; Dustin R. Klinger; Kevin M. Koliner; Sabrina P. Loiselle; Sarah Lowinger; Clifton Molatore; Ryan R. Nisle; J. Michael Porter; Jennifer J. Roof; Tamara E. Russell; Jeffrey T. Sagalewicz; Justin Clark Sawyer; Amy Silliman; Gena A. Stone; Alyssa Eve Thirsk Tormala; Erin E. Truax; Connie Tsai.
General Civil Practice and Litigation in all State and Federal Courts and before Federal and State Administrative Tribunals. Agricultural Cooperatives; Antitrust and Trade Regulation; Appellate Practice; Banking and Financial Institutions; Bankruptcy; Biotechnology; Business; Communications and Media; Computers and Software; Construction; Contracts; Corporate Governance Litigation; Corporate; Debtor/Creditor; Education; Employee Benefits; Employment and Labor Relations Litigation; Energy; Entity Structuring; Environmental and Natural Resources; Finance; Gaming; Government; Healthcare and Hospitals; High-Tech; Homeland Security; Housing; Immigration; Insurance, Intellectual Property; International Litigation and Arbitration; International Trade; Land Use; Litigation, Arbitration and Mediation; Maritime; Mergers and Acquisitions; Municipal; Nonprofit and Charitable Organizations; Products Liability; Public Finance and Bonds; Real Estate; Securities, Corporate, Shareholder Disputes Litigation; Taxation; Technology and Science; Telecommunications; Trademarks; Transportation and Utilities; and Trusts and Estates.
Representative Clients: HemCon, Inc.; Merrill Lynch; Portland Public Schools; Potlatch Corporation; R.B. Pamplin Corporation; Rentrak Corporation; Siltronic Corporation; UBS Financial Services, Inc.; U.S. Bancorp; Widmer Brothers Brewing Company.
Seattle, Washington Office: 4400 Two Union Square, 601 Union Street, 98101-2352. Telephone: 206-622-8484. Facsimile: 206-622-7485.
Vancouver, Washington Office: 500 East Broadway, Suite 400, P.O. Box 694, 98660-3324. Telephone: 360-699-4771; 503-289-2643. Facsimile: 360-694-6413.
Reviser of the Oregon Law Digest for this Directory.
See Professional Biographies, PORTLAND, OREGON

Miller, Peter, A Professional Corporation, (BV) ....915 N.E. 25th Ave.
Millner, Jeffrey B., P.C., (AV) ....'51 '81 C.768 B.A. L.309 J.D. 111 S.W. Fifth Avenue‡
Mills, John Casey, P.C., (AV) ....'58 '84 C.103 B.A. L.1051 J.D. [Miller N.]
Mills, Rodney R., (BV) ....'57 '82 C.629 B.S. L.1068 J.D. [Seifer,Y.M.&Z.]
Mindlin, Jessica E. ....'59 '90 C.156 B.A. L.911 J.D. Legal Aid Serv(s). of OR
Miner, William D. ....'— '04 C.629 B.A. L.911 J.D. [Ⓐ Davis W.T.]
Minetto, Steven L. ....'55 '88 C.101 B.A. L.596 J.D. Jud. Clk., Cir. Ct.
Minger, John S. ....'51 '76 C.605 B.A. L.629 J.D. U.S. Army Corps. of Engrs.
Mionske, Robert C. ....'62 '99 C.966 B.S. L.950 J.D. 1747 N.E. Multnomah Street
Misley, Jeffrey C., (AV) ....'55 '85 C.1051 B.S. L.596 J.D. [Sussman S.]
Mitchell, Holly N., (AV) ....'52 '84 C.1051 B.A. L.596 J.D. [Ⓐ Duffy K.]
Mitchell, Jennifer ....'71 '99 C.378 B.A. L.950 J.D. [Ⓐ Smith F.&E.]
Mitchell, John Bruce '46 '74 C.588 B.S. L.94 J.D.
V.P. & Assoc. Area Coun., Ticor Title Ins. Co.
Mitchell, Johnston A. ....'59 '92 C.112 B.A. L.285 J.D. [McEwen G.]
Mitchell, William H., (AV) ....'29 '65 C.911 B.A. L.596 J.D. [Mitchell,L.&S.] ‡

Mitchell, Lang & Smith, (AV)
A Law Firm Partnership
2000, One Main Place, 101 S.W. Main Street, 97204 ⊙
Telephone: 503-221-1011 Fax: 503-248-0732
Email: portlandoffice@mls-law.com URL: http://www.MLS-law.com
Members of Firm: Charles T. Smith; Wm. Kelly Olson; Bruce M. White; Scott J. Meyer; Charles D. Harms; Candace H. Weatherby; Shawn M. O'Neil; Matthew T. Boyle (P.S.C.) (Not admitted in OR; Resident at Seattle, Washington Office); Robert C. Levin (Not admitted in OR; Resident at Seattle, Washington Office); William H. Mitchell; Richard L. Lang. Associates: James E. Oliver; Raylynna J. Peterson; Lowell P. Mckelvey; William R. Joseph; Barton J. Wachsteter; Thomas A. Heinrich.
General Civil Trial and Appellate Practice in all State and Federal Courts. General Insurance Defense Practice, including Auto, Bad Faith Fire Coverage, Casualty, Professional Liability, Products Liability, Toxic Tort, Environmental Liability, Hazardous Waste, Uninsured and Underinsured Motorists, Trucking Liability, Premises Liability, Employment Defense, Insurance Coverage, Insurance Litigation, Liquor Liability.
Seattle, Washington Office: 1001 Fourth Avenue, Suite 3714, 98154. Telephone: 206-292-1212. Fax: 206-682-4687.
See Professional Biographies, PORTLAND, OREGON

Mize, Franklin H., (AV) ....'29 '56 C.546 B.S. L.477 LL.B. 1001 S.W. 5th Ave
Mlodinoff, David J. '68 '95 C&L.178 B.A., J.D.
(adm. in NY; not adm. in OR) 321 SW 4th Avenue, Suite 603
Moak Lillis, Erin ....'79 '05 C.602 B.A. L.276 J.D. [Ⓐ McEwen G.]
Moede, J. Scott, III, (BV) '63 '88 C.118 B.A. L.494 J.D.
Dep. City Atty., City Atty. Off.
Moen, Stephen A., (BV) ....'42 '69 C&L.629 B.S., J.D. 2125 S.W. 4th Ave.
Mohan, Sunjay Y. '66 '01 C.277 B.S.E.E. L.280 J.D.
(adm. in GA; not adm. in OR) [Ⓐ Klarquist S.]
Mohrman, Jennifer L. '71 '00
C.967 B.A. L.893 J.D. 707 S.W. Washington Street, Suite 1500
Molatore, Clifton ....'75 '00 C&L.629 B.A., J.D. [Ⓐ Miller N.]
Molina, Rita ....'— '03 C&L.629 B.S., J.D. [Ⓐ Davis W.T.]
Moline, Mark ....'55 '81 C.118 B.A. L.1051 J.D. City Atty.
Moll, Martin D. ....'63 '90 C.629 B.S. L.1051 J.D. Arthur Andersen, LLP
Mones, Paul A. '52 '78 C.567 B.A. L.575 J.D.
(adm. in CA; not adm. in OR) P.O. Box 10241
Monfils, Scott P., (AV) ....'51 '80 C.1056 B.S. L.285 J.D. [Hitt H.&M.]
Montague, Malcolm J., (AV) ....'29 '54 C&L.629 B.S., J.D. 3960 S.W. Wapato Ave.‡
Montalbano, Sonia A. ....'69 '97 C.331 B.A. L.596 J.D. [Ⓐ Elliott,O.&P.]
Montaño, Alfonso J. '52 '82 C.557 B.A. L.1355 J.D.
(adm. in FL; not adm. in OR) Admin. Law J., Soc. Sec. Admn.
Montgomery, Gerald E., (BV) ....'46 '73 C.628 B.S. L.950 J.D. [G.E.Montgomery]
Montgomery, Gerald E., PC, (BV) ....9900 S.W. Greenburg Rd.

Mooney, Jenna Leigh .... '— '99 C.1068 B.A. L.629 J.D. [Ⓐ Davis W.T.]
Moore, Conrad L., (AV) .... '37 '62 C.950 A.B. L.1066 J.D. [Miller N.]
Moore, James R., (AV) .... '31 '55 C&L.629 B.S., LL.B. [Schwabe,W.&W.] ‡
Moore, Kathleen Kelly ....'52 '79 C.112 A.B. L.1051 J.D. 1 S.W. Columbia Street
Moore, Renee S. .... '55 '97 C.184 B.A. L.564 J.D. 3735 SW Clay
Moore, Robert A., (AV) .... '55 '82 C.112 B.A. L.893 J.D. [Bullivant H.B.]
Moore, Steven A., (AV) .... '67 '92 C.1051 B.A. L.629 J.D. [Stoel R.]
Moore, Thomas S., (AV) .... '37 '62 C&L.950 B.A., J.D. [T.S.Moore]

Moore Smith Buxton & Turcke, Chartered
(See Boise, Idaho)

Moore, Thomas S., P.C., (AV) .... 5901 S.W. Macadam
Moorman, Robert J., (AV) .... '51 '80 C.659 A.B. L.976 J.D. [Stoel R.]
Moran, Christine E. .... '51 '80 C.629 B.S. L.1051 J.D. 1100 S.W. 6th Ave.‡
Moran, Michael O., (AV) .... '45 '76 C.685 B.A. L.1066 J.D. [Black H.]
Morford, J. Mark, (AV) .... '57 '83 C.277 B.S. L.893 J.D. [Stoel R.]
Morgan, Donald J., (AV) .... '33 '60 C.939 B.A. L.1066 LL.B. 8450 S.W. Homewood St.‡

Morgan, Lynne B., (AV) '60 '89 C.629 B.A. L.1051 J.D.
1 SW Columbia Street, Suite 1110, 97258
Telephone: 503-417-7746 Fax: 503-227-7829
Email: lbmorgan@worldnet.att.net URL: http://www.lawyers.com/lynnebmorgan
Federal Crimes, White Collar Crimes, Murder, Aggravated Murder, Sex Crimes, Drug Crimes, Parole and Probation, Fraud.
See Professional Biographies, PORTLAND, OREGON

Morgan, Michael M., (AV) .... '47 '72 C.605 B.A. L.145 J.D. [Tonkon T.]
Morgenstern, Ann R., (AV) .... '40 '71 C.208 B.A. L.1051 J.D. 5935 SW Kelly Ave.‡
Moriarty, Nancy J., (AV) '52 '84
C.112 B.S. L.352 J.D. [Chernoff,V.M.&S.] (See Pat. Sect.)
Morrell, Mark, (AV) .... '49 '78 C.629 B.S. L.596 J.D. [M.J.Morrell]
Morrell, Mark J., (AV) .... 806 S.W. Broadway, Ste. 1200
Morrill, Angela '72 '96 C.909 B.A. L.911 J.D.
(adm. in WA; not adm. in OR) Corp. Coun., Columbia Sportswear Co.
Morris, Douglas D. .... '69 '96 C.112 B.A. L.1051 J.D. [Ⓐ Ater W.]
Morris, Michael J., (AV) .... '47 '77 C.112 B.A. L.950 J.D. [Bennett,H.M.&K.]
Morrison, David P., (AV) .... '— '77 C.629 B.A. L.596 J.D. [Cosgrave V.K.]
Morrison, Sheila Fox '— '98 C.112 B.A. L.767 J.D.
(adm. in CA; not adm. in OR) [Ⓐ Davis W.T.]
Morrissey, Jennifer M. .... '71 '03 C.352 B.A. L.1051 J.D. [Ⓐ Black H.]
Morrow, Andrew J., Jr., (AV) .... '52 '80 C.629 B.A. L.813 J.D. [Foster P.T.]
Morrow, Kimberlee Collins, (BV) '55 '83
C.138 B.A. L.596 J.D. 1000 Sw Broadway Ste 2000
Moscato, Frank A., (AV) .... '43 '72 C.1056 B.S. L.950 J.D. [Harrang L.G.R.]
Moses, Andrew S. .... '69 '98 C.813 B.S. L.629 J.D. [Ⓐ Gordon&P.]
Mosman, Michael W., (AV) .... '56 '84 C.877 B.S. L.101 J.D. U.S. Dist. J.
Mostow, Peter D. .... '64 '95 C.685 B.A. L.976 J.D. [Stoel R.]
Motley, John C. .... '66 '97 C.1331 B.A. L.145 J.D. [Ⓐ Stoel R.]
Motley, Peter David .... '69 '01 C&L.629 B.A., J.D. [Ⓐ Smith F.&E.]
Motschenbacher, Anthony J., (BV) ... '65 '90 C.629 B.S. L.950 J.D. [Motschenbacher&B.]
Motschenbacher & Blattner, LLP, (AV) .... 117 S.W. Taylor St., Ste. 200
Mottram, John F. .... '72 '97 C.911 B.A. L.950 J.D. [Madkour&M.]
Mount, Barry M., (AV) .... '44 '69 C.1051 B.A. L.629 J.D. [Bodyfelt M.S.&C.]
Mountain, James E., Jr., (AV) .... '48 '75 C.629 B.A. L.1051 J.D. [Harrang L.G.R.]
Mowe, Gregory Robert, (AV) .... '46 '74 C.629 B.A. L.309 J.D. [Stoel R.]
Mozena, Peter J. '48 '77 C&L.988 B.S., J.D.
4411 N.E. Tillamook St. (ⓞVancouver, WA)
Mudrow, Michael T., (AV) '53 '79
C.629 B.S. L.1051 J.D. V.P. & Gen. Coun., Regence Group
Muehleck, Donna M., (AV) .... '53 '86 C.1056 B.S. L.569 J.D. [Duffy K.]
Mueller, Lane .... '48 '92 C.208 B.A. L.284 J.D. 2000 Northeast 42nd Avenue

Muhlheim Boyd
(See Eugene)

Muir, H. Stanley, III '49 '77 C.886 B.S. L.945 J.D.
(adm. in VA; not adm. in OR; Pat.)
V.P. & Gen. Coun., Harland Financial Solutions, Inc.
Mullen, Karl I. .... '60 '85 C.800 B.S.A.E. L.477 J.D. 8225 S.W. Fairway Dr., Ste. 100
Mullen, Molly Jo, (BV) .... '65 '91 C.629 B.A. L.767 J.D. [Bodyfelt M.S.&C.]
Muller, Richard H. .... '33 '61 C.685 B.A. L.911 LL.B. Ret. Col., U.S.M.C.‡
Mullin, Joel A., (AV) .... '57 '81 C.145 B.A. L.910 J.D. [Stoel R.]
Munro, David M., (AV) .... '41 '66 C&L.813 A.B., J.D. [Miller N.]
Munson, Carol Farley .... '47 '82 C.183 B.A. L.216 J.D. Asst. Atty. Gen.
Munson, John B., (BV) '45 '81
C.976 B.A. L.1017 J.D. U.S. Dept. of Agric., Gen. Coun. Off.
Muraski, Courtney C. .... '— '99 C.188 B.A. L.629 J.D. [Ⓐ Orrick,H.&S.]
Muraski, Robert N. .... '— '00 C.209 B.S. L.629 J.D. [Ⓐ Farleigh W.]
Murchison, James H. .... '47 '76 C.950 B.A. L.596 J.D. Actg. Adm. Cir. Ct.
Murphy, Bryan P. .... '62 '89 C.770 B.S. L.629 J.D. [Bayless&M.]
Murphy, Craig C., (AV) .... '46 '73 C.668 B.A. L.629 J.D. [Wood T.S.&M.]
Murphy, Paul M., (AV) .... '46 '74 C&L.966 B.A., J.D. [Murphy&B.]

Murphy & Buchal, LLP, (AV)
2000 S.W. First Avenue, Suite 320, 97201
Telephone: 503-227-1011 Fax: 503-227-1034
Email: pmurphy@mbllp.com
Members of Firm: Paul M. Murphy; James L. Buchal.
Electric Energy, Utility, Commercial Litigation, Contracts, Natural Resources, Administrative Law, Appellate Litigation and Endangered Species Law.
See Professional Biographies, PORTLAND, OREGON

Murr, William .... '40 '88 C.197 A.B. L.596 J.D. [W.H.Murr]
Murr, William H., P.C., Law Offices of .... 9820 E. Burnside Street
Murray, Ronald D., (AV) .... '54 '84 C.909 B.S. L.629 J.D. [R.D.Murray]
Murray, Ronald D., P.C., (AV) .... 9999 S.W. Wilshire Street, Suite 202
Murray-Lusby, Marsha, (AV) ..... '57 '84 C.508 B.A. L.950 J.D. [Dunn C.A.H.&T.]
Muth, Robert C. .... '63 '88 C.484 B.A. L.902 J.D. [Ⓐ Bullivant H.B.]
Mutnick, Jeffrey S., (AV) .... '47 '72 C.861 B.A. L.597 J.D. [Landye B.B.]
Myers, Jane Barbara '43 '85 C.628 B.S. L.950 J.D.
Dir., Govt. Affs., Oregon Dental Assn.
Myers, Robt. L., (AV) '26 '50 C.1051 B.S. L.629 LL.B.
Prof. of Law, Lewis & Clark Coll.
Myles, Kevin M., (BV) .... '48 '74 C&L.339 B.A., J.D. [Myles&M.]
Myles, Phylis C., (BV) .... '49 '92 C.339 B.S. L.596 J.D. [Myles&M.]
Myles & Myles, (BV) .... 0232 S.W. Lane St.
Nachtigal, Kathleen B. .... '32 '68 C.1056 L.596 J.D. Ret. Cir. J.
Nagasako, Lynn T., (BV) '47 '74 C.674 A.B. L.178 J.D.
First Interstate Bk. of Ore., N.A.

Nagle, Eric W. '57 '86 C.446 B.A. L.893 J.D.
(adm. in VA; not adm. in OR) Dept. of Interior
Naglins, Lisa M. .... '67 '92 C.999 B.A. L.596 J.D. 150 S.E. 80th Ave.
Nahstoll, R. W., (AV) .... '18 '46 C.475 A.B. L.477 LL.B. 9706 S.W. Quail Post Rd.‡
Naito, Steven L., (BV) .... '55 '80 C.855 B.S. L.629 J.D. [Tarlow N.&S.]
Nakamoto, Lynn R., (AV) .... '60 '86 C.914 A.B. L.569 J.D. [Markowitz,H.G.&M.]
Nakata, Nancy K. .... '49 '76 C&L.629 B.A., J.D. 870 S.W. 84th Ct.
Namiki, James J. '58 '00 C.911 B.S. L.823 J.D.
(adm. in VA; not adm. in OR; Pat.) [Ⓐ Schwabe,W.&W.]
Nardi, Nicholas A. .... '72 '98 C.860 B.A. L.596 J.D. [Ⓐ Abbott&P.]
Nash, Thomas K. '44 '70 C.597 B.A. L.813 J.D.
(adm. in CA; not adm. in OR) 1885 N.W. Ramsey Dr.‡
Nash, Valerie .... '61 '88 C&L.950 B.A., J.D. 4620 N.E. Ainsworth St.
Nathanson, Neil .... '60 '92 C.477 B.S. L.813 J.D. [Perkins C.]
Navarra, James K. .... '18 '50 C&L.276 B.S., J.D. 1234 S.E. River Forest Ln.
Nay, Barbara L., (AV) .... '51 '79 C.813 B.A. L.174 J.D. [Stoel R.]
Neal, Fred R., III .... '50 '76 C.668 B.A. L.1051 J.D. Intergovernmental Rel. Offr.
Neal, Spencer M., (AV) .... '48 '77 C&L.911 B.A., J.D. [Oregon]
Nebel, David W. .... '47 '73 C.951 B.A. L.94 J.D. Oregon Law Ctr. Inc.
Needham, Gerald M. .... '56 '82 C.724 B.S. L.285 J.D. Asst. Fed. Def.
Neely, C. Richard ...... '27 '53 C.629 B.S. L.477 J.D. Off. of Solr. Gen. U.S. Dept. of Int.
Neff, Michael G. .... '60 '92 C.939 B.A. L.629 J.D. [Haglund,K.H.&J.]
Neidig, John W. .... '48 '88 C.685 B.A. L.1051 J.D. P.O. Box 14462
Neil, Carl R., (AV) .... '33 '58 C.976 B.A. L.178 LL.B. [Lindsay,H.N.&W.]
Neill, James K., (AV) .... '— '71 C.628 B.S. L.950 J.D. [Davis W.T.]
Neiman, Eric J., (AV) .... '— '82 L.629 J.D. [Williams,K.&G.P.]
Neiswanger, Ted .... '55 '80 C.767 B.A. L.629 J.D. Sr. Atty., Soc. Sec. Admin.

Nellor Retsinas & Crawford
(See Vancouver)

Nelson, Adrienne C. .... '67 '96 C.45 B.A. L.846 J.D. [Ⓐ Bennett,H.M.&K.]
Nelson, Gregory L. .... '42 '67 C&L.950 B.A., J.D. Legal Coun., Chicago Title Ins.
Nelson, J. Robt. .... '13 '40 L.596 J.D. 4524 S.E. 45th Ave.‡
Nelson, James A. .... '20 '48 C&L.629 B.S., J.D. 2565 N.E. 28th Ave.‡
Nelson, James C. '47 '77 C.629 B.S. L.1137 J.D.
(adm. in CA; not adm. in OR) 6211 S.E. Division St.
Nelson, Kristen A. '73 '01
C.579 B.A. L.950 J.D. U.S. Dept. of Vet. Affs., Off. of Reg. Coun.
Nelson, Luella E. .... '52 '76 C.429 B.S. L.309 J.D. 4306 N.E. Mason St.
Nelson, Richard D., (BV) .... '20 '52 C.670 L.596 LL.B. 240 N.E. 148th Ave.
Nelson, Roscoe C., Jr., (AV) .... '48 '73 C.939 B.A. L.950 J.D. [Nelson&N.]
Nelson, Thomas H., & Associates, Law Offices, (AV) '44 '74
C.911 B.A. L.879 J.D. 825 NE Multnomah, Suite 925

Nelson & Nelson, (AV)
Suite 1620, Umpqua Bank Plaza, One S.W. Columbia, 97258-2098
Telephone: 503-222-1081 FAX: 503-222-6441
Email: mail@roscoecnelson.com
Members of Firm: Roscoe C. Nelson (1913-1987); Roscoe C. Nelson, Jr.
General Civil, Criminal and Trial Practice. Probate and Estate Planning, Wills, Trusts, Guardianship, Asset Protection, Corporate, Business and Real Estate Law.
References: Wells Fargo Bank of Oregon; U.S. Bank of Oregon.
See Professional Biographies, PORTLAND, OREGON

Nemirow, Steven J., (AV) .... '49 '86 C.685 B.A. L.1065 J.D. 3335 N.E. 20th
Nepom, David R., (BV) ...... '53 '80 C.976 B.A. L.1051 J.D. 3718 S.W. Condor, Ste. 100
Nepom, Marvin S., (AV) .... '26 '62 C.911 B.B.A. L.596 J.D. 3718 S.W. Condor
Nesbit, Roger W. .... '50 '76 C.339 B.S. L.596 J.D. 500 NE Multnomah Street
Nesler, Robert D., (AV) .... '50 '76 C.934 B.A. L.276 J.D. Asst. U.S. Atty.
Ness, Gretel Margaret .... '70 '94 C.705 B.A. L.982 J.D. 1336 E. Burnside St.
Nesting, Richard O., (BV) .... '42 '72 C.670 L.1051 J.D. 4370 N.E. Halsey St.
Nettleton, Alan T. .... '45 '74 C.1056 B.A. L.596 J.D. 4023 S.E. 33rd Pl.

Neuberger, Robert J., (AV) '53 '80 C.1164 B.A. L.1051 J.D.
700 Jackson Tower, 806 SW Broadway, 97205-3309
Telephone: 503-228-1221 Toll Free: 877-631-5126 Fax: 503-228-2556
Email: rjn@robertneuberger.com URL: http://www.lawyers.com/neuberger
Personal Injury, Dog Bites, Slip and Fall, Automobile Accidents, Wrongful Death, Products Liability, Automotive Products Liability, Professional Liability, Admiralty and Maritime, Maritime Injuries, Medical Malpractice, Insurance, Legal Malpractice, Consumer, Unsafe Products.
See Professional Biographies, PORTLAND, OREGON

Neupert, John F., P.C., (AV) .... '52 '78 C&L.629 B.S., J.D. [Miller N.]
Newcomb, Elizabeth, (AV) '54 '82 C.1331 B.A. L.596 J.D.
Secy & Gen Coun., UEA, Inc.
Newcomb, Verne W., (AV) .... '24 '51 C.112 A.B. L.178 LL.B. [Newcomb,S.S.&L.]

Newcomb, Sabin, Schwartz & Landsverk, LLP, (AV)
Suite 4040, 111 S.W. Fifth Avenue, 97204
Telephone: 503-228-8446 Fax: 503-228-5472
Email: office@nsslaw.com URL: http://www.nsslaw.com
Members of Firm: Robert L. Sabin (1894-1985); John R. Sabin (1927-1990); Verne W. Newcomb; Jack B. Schwartz; Wayne D. Landsverk; Richard S. Pope; Jeffrey P. Chicoine. Counsel: Brian S. Thompson. Of Counsel: Sidney I. Lezak; Lawrence R. Brown. Associate: Thomas E. Bahrman.
General Civil and Trial Practice. Emphasizing Corporations and General Business, Labor and Employment Law, Employee Benefits, Business Litigation, Real Property, Estate Planning and Insurance Coverage Litigation. Federal and State Tax Planning.
General or Special Counsel for: Cascade Corp.; Simpson Timber Co.; United Employers' Assn.
See Professional Biographies, PORTLAND, OREGON

Newell, Douglas K. '40 '66
C.668 B.A. L.309 J.D. Prof. of Law, Northwestern Sch. of Law
Newell, Robert D., (AV) .... '— '77 C.309 A.B. L.629 J.D. [Davis W.T.]
Newhall, David G., (AV) .... '56 '87 C.605 B.A. L.596 J.D. [Black H.]
Newman, Devon Zastrow ...... '72 '01 C.556 B.S., B.A. L.188 J.D. [Ⓐ Keating J.B.&H.]
Newman, Patricia A. .... '56 '83 C.1044 B.A. L.629 J.D. 1012 S.W. King Ave.
Newman Eckstein, Lisa '55 '89 C.976 B.A. L.477 J.D.
(adm. in WA; not adm. in OR) 6126 S.W. Seymour St.‡
Newton, Cynthia F., (AVⓣ) .... '60 '87 C.906 B.A. L.1065 J.D. [Ⓐ Swanson,T.&C.]
Newton, Paul W. .... '55 '89 C.1056 B.S. L.770 J.D. Admin. Clk., Co. Ct.
Newton, Ronalds S. .... '48 '76 C.705 B.A. L.884 J.D. 1826 N.E. Broadway
Neyman, Craig T. .... '64 '91 C.659 B.S. L.629 J.D. 111 S.W. Columbia‡
Nguyen, Lan D. .... '67 '98 C.112 B.S. L.809 J.D. [Ⓐ Hanna S.]
Nguyen, Toan-Hao B. '75 '01 C.112 B.S. L.464 J.D
(adm. in WA; not adm. in OR) PacifiCorp
Nichol, Anne L. .... '68 '97 C.806 B.A. L.629 J.D. Co. J., Multnomah Co. Courthouse
Nicholes, Steven A., (AV) .... '52 '80 C.628 B.A. L.285 J.D. [Duffy K.]
Nichols, Craig Allen, (AV) .... '54 '83 C.1056 B.S. L.285 J.D. [Nichols&Assoc.]
Nichols, Douglas R., (BV) '42 '73
C.628 B.S. L.208 J.D. Gen. Coun., Portland General Electric
Nichols, John D., (AV) ..... '20 '49 C.352 B.A. L.950 LL.B. 1795 S.W. Montgomery Dr.‡

Nichols & Associates, (AV) .... 4614 SW Kelly Ave.
Nickel, Jon W., (AV) .... '45 '73 C.605 B.A. L.309 J.D. [Tonkon T.]
Nickerson, Heyke G. '62 '98 C.790 B.S. L.596 J.D.
1300 S.W. 5th Ave., MAC P6101-162, 16th Fl.
Nicolai, Thomas R., (AV) .... '43 '72 C.373 B.A. L.477 J.D. [Stoel R.]
Niedermeyer, James C., (BV) .... '34 '61 C.670 B.A. L.276 J.D. P.O. Box 4078
Niehaus, Russell R., (AV) .... '26 '52 C.602 L.767 LL.B. 101 S. W. Morrison St.
Nielsen, Howard R. .... '53 '82 C.1056 B.S. L.950 J.D. [Ⓐ Gilroy]
Nisle, Ryan R. .... '75 '01 C.350 B.S. L.629 J.D. [Ⓐ Miller N.]

Noland, Suzanne J. '45 '75 C.629 B.A. L.596 J.D.
1000 S. W. Broadway Suite 2400, 97205
Telephone: 503-228-7591 Fax: 503-241-2249
Email: nolandsuzannej@qwest.net URL: http://www.lawyers.com/portlandfamilylaw
Family Law, Divorce, Premarital Agreements, Child Support, Child Custody, Guardianships, Spousal Support, Domestic Relations, Visitation Rights.
See Professional Biographies, PORTLAND, OREGON

Noonan, Carol .... '— '02 C.228 B.A. L.276 J.D. [Ⓐ Davis W.T.]
Noonan, Frank, (AV) .... '43 '70 C.112 B.A. L.629 J.D. Asst. U.S. Atty.
Noonan, William D. .... '55 '80 C.674 A.B. L.986 J.D. [Klarquist S.] (See Pat. Sect.)
Norby, Mark A., (AV) .... '55 '80 C.628 B.S. L.477 J.D. [Stoel R.]
Norling, Jonathan M. .... '69 '97 C.478 B.A. L.1051 J.D. [Ⓐ T.H.Nelson&Assoc.]
Norman, Steve .... '69 '96 C.629 B.S. L.1067 J.D. [Ⓐ Gary]
Norr, Paul, (AV) .... '48 '75 C.477 B.B.A. L.608 J.D. 5550 S.W. Macadam Ave., Ste. 330
Norris, Alan R. .... '61 '95 C.999 B.A. L.1051 J.D. 522 S.W. 5th Ave., Ste. 1500
North, W. A. Jerry, (AV) .... '40 '75 C.871 B.S. L.813 J.D. [Schwabe,W.&W.]
Northman, Tod A. .... '66 '94 C.1056 B.A. L.930 J.D. [Foster P.T.]
Northwest Law Firm, (AV) .... 121 SW Morrison Street, Sixth Floor
Northwest Legal Counsel, P.C. .... 1001 S.W. Fifth Avenue
Norton, Katherine L. .... '61 '90 3121 S.W. Evelyn St.
Norton, Rodney K. .... '52 '77 C.906 B.A. L.950 J.D. Oregon Health Sciences Univ.
Norville, Darcy M., (AV) .... '— '85 C.147 B.A. L.1066 J.D. [Tonkon T.]
Norville, Oliver I., (AV) .... '28 '54 C&L.813 B.A., J.D. One S.W. Columbia Street
Norwood, Timothy D., (BV) .... '47 '72 C.454 B.A. L.659 J.D. [Underwood&N.]
Noto, Ingolf, (AV) .... '48 '78 C.101 B.S. L.878 J.D. [Tonkon T.]
Noto, Margaret Hill, (AV) .... '53 '78 C.685 B.A. L.1066 J.D. [Stoel R.]
Novack, Kenneth M., (AV) ..... '46 '70 C.154 A.B. L.800 J.D. Schnitzer Investment Corp.
Nudelman, Jeffrey F., (AV) .... '61 '86 C.629 B.S. L.596 J.D. [Garvey S.B.]
Nunn, Robert W., (AV) .... '50 '76 C.950 B.S. L.629 J.D. [Ⓒ Sussman S.]
Nusich, Lee C., (AV) .... '— '77 C.585 B.S. L.629 J.D. [Lane P.]
Oberdorfer, S. Patricia .... '69 '99 C.112 B.A. L.1051 J.D. [Oberdorfer]
Oberdorfer Law Firm LLC .... 210 SW Morrison Street, Suite 600
O'Brien, Brian W. .... '23 '58 C.897 L.596 LL.B. 1912 N.E. 33rd Ave.
O'Brien, John C., Jr., (BV) .... '50 '75 C&L.285 B.A., J.D. 4511 S.E. Hawthorne Blvd.
O'Brien, Kathleen, (BV) .... '56 '83 C.628 B.A. L.629 J.D. [Wittrock&O.]
O'Brien, Monica M., (AV) .... '52 '78 C.881 B.A. L.596 J.D. [Scarborough,M.O.&K.]
O'Brien, Robert V., Jr. ..... '52 '79 C.309 A.B. L.1294 J.D. Exec. Dir., Health Choice, Inc.
O'Connell, Kevin P., (AV) .... '42 '66 C&L.262 B.A., J.D. [Hagen O.]
O'Connor, Karen L. .... '66 '95 C.518 B.A. L.629 J.D. [Ⓐ Barran L.]
O'Connor, Michael R. .... '72 '97 C.976 B.A. L.629 J.D. [Ⓐ Garvey S.B.]
O'Connor, Paul L'Roy .... '15 '42 L.596 LL.B. 522 S.W. 5th Ave.
Oden-Orr, Melvin D. .... '67 '96 C.112 B.A. L.339 J.D. 710 N.E. Holladay Street
Odman, Dennis M., (BV) .... '45 '74 C.906 B.A. L.596 J.D. 1000 S.W. Broadway
O'Donnell, Mark P., (AV) .... '43 '68 C.285 B.A. L.950 J.D. [O'Donnell&C.]
O'Donnell, Scott G., (BV) .... '66 '93 C&L.629 B.S., J.D. [Keating J.B.&H.]

O'Donnell & Clark LLP, (AV)
Fremont Place II, Suite 302, 1650 NW Naito Parkway, 97209-2534
Telephone: 503-306-0224 Fax: 503-306-0257 URL: http://www.oandc.com URL: http://www.odonnellclark.com
Email: wendyd@oandc.com URL: http://www.lawyers.com/odonnellandclark
Members of Firm: Mark P. O'Donnell; Kelly (W.G.) Clark. Associates: Matthew D. Lowe; Kristian Spencer Roggendorf; Jonathan A. Clark.
Administrative Law, Agency and Distributorships, Business Law, Business Transactions, Commercial Law, Commercial Real Estate, Consumer Law, Contracts, Corporate Law, Debtor and Creditor, Education Law, Election Campaign and Political Law, Estate Planning, Franchises and Franchising, Government Agency Practice, Government Law, Labor and Employment Law, Litigation, Nonprofit Corporations, Nonprofit Charitable Organizations, Real Estate, Resorts and Leisure, Taxation, Hospitality Law, Trade Associations.
See Professional Biographies, PORTLAND, OREGON

Oelke, Christian .... '71 '98 C.629 B.S. L.950 J.D. [Ⓐ Scarborough,M.O.&K.]
Oetter, Jennifer K. .... '69 '95 C.629 B.S. L.950 J.D. 1000 S.W. Broadway, Ste. 2000
Ognall, Andrew H. .... '71 '97 C.188 B.A. L.1051 J.D. [Ⓐ Foster P.T.]
O'Halloran, Robert L., (AV) .... '57 '82 C.629 B.S. L.596 J.D. [McEwen G.]
O'Halloran, Sean, (BV) .... '47 '75 C.1056 B.S. L.629 J.D. [Scalf&O.]
O'Hara, John J. .... '43 '68 C.285 B.A. L.1065 J.D. [Warren A.]
Ohle, William J. .... '62 '91 C.999 B.A. L.950 J.D. [Schwabe,W.&W.]
O'Leary, Daniel E., (AV) .... '— '63 C.285 B.A. L.596 LL.B. [Ⓒ Davis W.T.]
O'Leary, James C. '47 '77 C.602 B.A. L.809 J.D.
(adm. in CA; not adm. in OR) 10701 SE Stevens Way‡
O'Leary, Lawrence F. '37 '66 C.755 B.A. L.190 J.D.
(adm. in IA; not adm. in OR) Pres., Larry O'Leary, Inc.
O'Leary, Leslie W. .... '59 '99 C.508 B.A. L.596 J.D. [Williams L.O.C.&P.]
Oliver, James E. .... '61 '94 C.420 B.S. L.950 J.D. [Ⓐ Mitchell,L.&S.]
Olney, Kathryn .... '— '87 C.629 B.A. L.950 J.D. Liberty Northwest Ins. Corp.
Olney, Margaret S., (AV) .... '58 '88 C.951 B.A. L.588 J.D. [Smith,G.D.&O.]
Olsen, Christine V. .... '51 '82 C.112 B.A. L.596 J.D. I.R.S.
Olsen, Clifford B. .... '21 '49 C.569 L.950 LL.B. 111 S.W. 5th Ave.
Olsen, Neil N. .... '75 '05 C.846 B.A. L.1051 J.D. [Ⓐ Stewart S.&G.]
Olshin, Andrew Matthew '65 '94 C.401 B.S. L.284 J.D.
(adm. in CA; not adm. in OR) 3728 N.W. Thurman
Olson, David C. '52 '80 C.685 B.A. L.1051 J.D.
Dir., City Off. of Cable Commun. & Franchise Mgt.
Olson, Edward C. '48 '76 C.1056 B.S. L.596 J.D.
Sr. Claims Coun., North Pacific Ins. Co.
Olson, Erin K. '64 '93 C.813 B.A. L.306 J.D.
600 Multnomah Co Crthouse, 1021 Sw 4th Ave
Olson, Karli L., (AV) .... '51 '77 C.628 B.S. L.596 J.D. [VavRosky M.O.]
Olson, Kristin L. .... '— '03 C.285 B.A. L.629 J.D. [Ⓐ Bullivant H.B.]
Olson, Kristine .... '47 '73 C.914 B.A. L.976 J.D. Congressman Earl Blumenauer
Olson, Per C. .... '66 '93 C.950 B.A. L.596 J.D. [Ⓐ Hoevet,B.&O.]
Olson, Roger J. .... '54 '81 C.950 B.S. L.629 J.D. 18445 E. Burnside
Olson, Steven D. .... '68 '00 C.999 B.S. L.494 J.D. [Ⓐ Tonkon T.]
Olson, Wm. Kelly, (AV) .... '48 '74 C.629 B.A. L.596 J.D. [Mitchell,L.&S.]
O'Malley, Dennis, (AV) .... '52 '81 C.685 B.A. L.1051 J.D. 1500 N.E. Irving Street
O'Malley, J. Patrick, (AV) .... '50 '78 C&L.629 B.A., J.D. 1500 S.W. Taylor St.

O'Neil, John G. '70 '01 C.1056 B.S. L.1065 J.D.
(adm. in CA; not adm. in OR) [Ⓐ Dunn C.A.H.&T.]
O'Neil, Katherine H., (AV) .... '38 '77 C.813 B.A. L.596 J.D. [Graff&O.]
O'Neil, Shawn M. .... '63 '91 C.94 B.A. L.950 J.D. [Mitchell,L.&S.]
O'Neill, Chris P. .... '61 '93 C.197 B.A. L.1051 J.D. 2728 N. Jessup St.
O'Neill, John R. .... '54 '02 C.1056 B.S. L.596 J.D. 1400 SW Montgomery
Opton, Michael P., (AV) .... '43 '70 C.31 B.A. L.569 J.D. [Opton&U.]
Opton & Underwood, P.C., (AV) .... 621 South West Morrison
Orchard, Jack L., Jr., (AV) .... '47 '72 C.906 B.A. L.629 J.D. [Ball J.]
Orcutt, Steven Y., (BV) .... '47 '75 C.1051 B.A. L.1358 J.D. [S.Y.Orcutt]

Orcutt, Steven Y., P.C., (BV)
Suite 500 River Forum I, 4380 SW Macadam Avenue, 97239-6412
Telephone: 503-228-9350 Fax: 503-228-6993
Email: yaleo@aol.com URL: http://www.lawyers.com/stevenyorcutt
Steven Y. Orcutt.
Real Estate (Buying or Selling), Commercial Real Estate, Commercial Leasing, Starting a Business, General Business, Contracts, Business Planning, Closely Held Business, Corporate, Limited Liability Companies, Small Business, Family Business, Estate Planning, Guardianship and Conservatorships, Trusts and Estates, Asset Protection, Wills and Probate, Elder Law.
See Professional Biographies, PORTLAND, OREGON

Oregon Law Center, (AV) .... 921 S.W. Washington St., Ste. 516
Orloff, Monford A. '14 '40 C.813 B.A. L.309 LL.B.
(adm. in WA; not adm. in OR) 2323 S.W. Park Pl.‡

O'Rourke, James F., Jr., & Associates, (BV) '51 '78 C.629 B.A. L.285 J.D.
522 Southwest 5th Avenue, Suite 710, 97204
Telephone: 503-221-1425 Fax: 503-221-1497
Email: jfo@jfolaw.com URL: http://www.lawyers.com/jfolaw
Criminal Law, Driving While Intoxicated, Drug Crimes, Parole and Probation, Major Traffic Violations, Assault, Property Crimes, Domestic Violence, Personal Injury, Automobile Accidents, Wrongful Death, Truck, Motorcycle, Bicycle, Pedestrian Accidents, Asset Protection, Estate Planning, Guardianship, Wills, Trusts and Probate, Elder Law.
See Professional Biographies, PORTLAND, OREGON

Orr, Bruce H., (BV) .... '54 '81 C.1074 B.S. L.596 J.D. [Meyer&W.]

Orrick, Herrington & Sutcliffe LLP, Pacific Northwest Office, (AV)
1125 N.W. Couch Street, Suite 800, 97209 ⊙
Telephone: 503-943-4800 Telecopier: 503-943-4901
URL: http://www.orrick.com
Resident Partners: Douglas E. Goe; Townsend Hyatt. Resident Associates: Courtney C. Muraski; Christine Reynolds; Melissa M. Robertson. Of Counsel: Scott E. Schickli; Michael E. Schrader.
General Practice, including Corporate and Municipal Finance, Domestic and International Commercial Law, Banking and Commercial Finance, Project Finance, Structured Finance, Mergers and Acquisitions, Commercial Litigation, Insurance, Insurance Insolvency, White Collar Criminal Defense, Tax, Employee Benefits and Personal Estates, Antitrust, Distribution, and Trade Regulation, Intellectual Property, Real Estate, Environmental and Energy, Labor and Employment Law and Bankruptcy.
San Francisco, California Office: The Orrick Building, 405 Howard Street. Telephone: 415-773-5700. Telecopier: 415-773-5759.
Los Angeles, California Office: 777 South Figueroa Street, Suite 3200. Telephone: 213-629-2020. Telecopier: 213-612-2499.
New York, New York Office: 666 Fifth Avenue. Telephone: 212-506-5000. Telecopier: 212-506-5151.
Sacramento, California Office: 400 Capitol Mall. Telephone: 916-447-9200. Telecopier: 916-329-4900.
Washington, D.C. Office: Washington Harbour, 3050 K Street, N.W. Telephone: 202-339-8400. Telecopier: 202-339-8500.
Menlo Park, California Office: 1000 Marsh Road. Telephone: 650-614-7400. Telecopier: 650-614-7401.
Tokyo, Japan Office: Izumi Garden Tower, 28th Floor, 6-1 Roppongi 1-Chome, Minato-ku. Telephone: +81-3-3224-2900. Telecopier: +81-3-3224-2901.
London, England Office: Tower 42, 25 Old Broad Street. Telephone: +44-20-7562-5000. Telecopier: +44-20-7628-0078.
Pacific Northwest Office: Seattle, Washington Office: 719 Second Avenue, Suite 900. Telephone: 206-839-4300. Telecopier: 206-839-4301.
Irvine, California Office: 4 Park Plaza, Suite 1600. Telephone: 949-567-6700. Telecopier: 949-567-6710.
Paris, France Office: 47 rue de Monceau. Telephone: +33-1-53-53-7500. Telecopier: +33-1-53-53-7501.
Milan, Italy Office: Via Visconti di Modrone, 12. Telephone: +39-02-45-41-3800. Telecopier: +39-02-45-41-3801.
Rome, Italy Office: Via del Consolato, 6. Telephone: +39 0668600751. Telecopier: +39 0668192393.
See Professional Biographies, PORTLAND, OREGON

Orth, Beverly J. '52 '78 C.1167 B.S. L.309 J.D.
Assoc., William M. Mercer, Incorporated‡
Osaka, Gordon L., (AV) ... '48 '75 C.911 B.A. L.596 J.D. 1000 S.W. Broadway, Ste. 1660
Osborn, Harvey J. .... '28 '55 C.670 B.A. L.596 LL.B. P.O. Box 19036
Osborne, Peter L., (AV) .... '47 '73 C.911 B.A. L.950 J.D. [Schwabe,W.&W.]
Osburn, John R., (AV) .... '55 '89 C&L.629 B.S., J.D. [Bullivant H.B.]
Osburn, John W., (P.C.), (AV) .... '33 '59 C.1058 B.A. L.629 LL.B. [Ⓒ Mersereau&S.]
O'Scannlain, Brendan N. .... '67 '97 C.321 B.A. L.276 J.D. [Stoel R.]
O'Scannlain, Diarmuid F. .... '37 '64 C.724 B.A. L.309 J.D. U.S. Cir. J.
Osoinach, Ellen .... '71 '02 C.806 B.A. L.596 J.D. Asst. U.S. Dist. Atty.
Osterink, Camellia L. '76 '03 C.629 B.A. L.950 J.D.
Suite 2300, 1300 S.W. Fifth Avenue
Ostrander, John D., (AV) .... '62 '87 C.293 B.A. L.910 J.D. [Elliott,O.&P.]
Ostroff, Paul M. .... '— '75 C.112 A.B. L.1065 J.D. [Lane P.]
Oswald, John Michael, (BV) .... '67 '92 C&L.285 B.B.A.D., J.D. [Bottini,B.&O.]
O'Toole, E. Susan '60 '03 C.906 B.A. L.629 J.D.
(adm. in CA; not adm. in OR) [Ⓐ Stewart S.&G.]
Otto, Angela M. .... '73 '99 C.1058 B.A. L.629 J.D. [Ⓐ Stewart S.&G.]
Otto, Darren L. .... '60 '86 C.112 B.A. L.950 J.D. Admin. Law J., Wkrs. Comp. Bd.
Otto, Stephan K. .... '— '00 C.763 B.A. L.596 J.D. Coun.
Overgaard, Mary A. '51 '75 C&L.546 B.S., J.D.
(adm. in NE; not adm. in OR) Dep. City Atty.
Owens, David W., (BV) .... '45 '75 C.1056 B.S. L.1051 J.D. [D.W.Owens&Assoc.]

Owens, David W., P.C. & Associates, (BV)
101 SW Main Street, Suite 700, 97201
Telephone: 503-224-3100 Fax: 503-274-8660
URL: http://www.lawyers.com/owens-law
David W. Owens.
General Practice.
See Professional Biographies, PORTLAND, OREGON

Owren, Turid L., (AV) .... '— '84 C.685 B.A. L.1051 J.D. [Tonkon T.]
Packer, Thomas A., (AV Ⓣ) '57 '82
C.112 B.A. L.1065 J.D. [Gordon&R.] (⊙San Fran., CA)
Padilla, Anthony Alan .... '59 '94 C&L.878 B.S., J.D. Standard Ins. Co.
Page, Thomas R., (AV) .... '51 '78 C.378 B.A. L.629 J.D. [Stoel R.]
Pagel, Martha O'Donnell, (AV) .... '53 '83 C.763 B.A. L.950 J.D. [Schwabe,W.&W.]
Pagnano, Richard A. .... '57 '89 C.770 B.S. L.596 J.D. 111 S.W. 5th Ave., Ste. 1890
Pahl, Douglas R. .... '63 '95 C.909 B.A. L.950 J.D. [Perkins C.]
Paine, James C. .... '47 '72 C&L.546 B.A., J.D. [Ⓒ Stoel R.]
Palmer, Joshua L. ..... '67 '93 C.705 B.A. L.629 J.D. Assoc. Gen. Coun., Freightliner LLC

Palmer, Louise M. ....'58 '90 [McKeown&B.]
Palmer, Robert W., (AV) ....'46 '74 C&L.477 B.B.A., J.D. [Lindsay,H.N.&W.]
Palmer, Thomas P., (AV) ....'51 '77 C.299 A.B. L.188 J.D. [Tonkon T.]
Palmer, Wayne D., (AV) ....'55 '81 C.1056 B.S. L.1051 J.D. [Kell,A.&R.]
Palmquist, Jennifer L., (AV) ....'48 '79 C&L.629 B.A., J.D. [Northwest]
Panarella, Samuel J. ....'69 '00 C.508 B.A. L.1051 J.D. [A Stoel R.]
Pancoast, Terrence R., (AV) ....'42 '68 C.939 A.B. L.309 LL.B. [Stoel R.]
Panner, Owen M. ....'24 '49 C&L.623 LL.B. Sr. U.S. Dist. J.
Parcel, Howard E. ....'11 '34 L.629 LL.B. 3102 S.E. Holgate Blvd., #D320‡
Parelius, M. Ronald ....'31 '62 C.629 B.B.A. L.596 LL.B. Ore. Health Sciences Univ.‡
Paretchan, Lynne M. ....'— '02 C.1375 B.S. L.560 J.D., [A Perkins C.]
Parisi, Frank M., (AV) ....'48 '79 C.685 B.A. L.629 J.D. [Parisi&P.]
Parisi, Robin B., (AV) ....'54 '81 C.813 A.B. L.336 J.D. [Parisi&P.]

Parisi & Parisi, P.C., (AV)
Suite 100, The Annand Building, 1630 SW Morrison Street, 97205
Telephone: 503-417-1144 Fax: 503-721-2300
Email: admin@parisi-parisi.com
Robin B. Parisi; Frank M. Parisi.
Finance, Antitrust, Real Estate, Land Use, Environmental, Business Transactions, Mining, Commercial Leasing, Zoning and Land Use.
See Professional Biographies, PORTLAND, OREGON

Park, David D., (AV) ....'55 '80 C.112 B.A. L.950 J.D. [Elliott&P.]
Park, Herbert W. ....'30 '57 C.855 B.A. L.145 J.D. 2885 S.W. Fairview Blvd.‡
Parker, Douglas S., (AVⓉ) ....'53 '82 C.628 B.A. L.950 J.D. [Preston G.&E.]
Parker, Gilbert E., (AV) ....'50 '75 C.1051 B.A. L.1065 J.D. [Dunn C.A.H.&T.]
Parker, Jack G. '16 '47 C&L.911 B.A., LL.B.
(adm. in WA; not adm. in OR) 3635 S.W. 48th Pl.‡
Parker, Joel A. ....'73 '00 C.347 B.A. L.629 J.D. [A Schwabe,W.&W.]
Parker, Richard J., (BV) ....'53 '78 C.685 B.A. L.284 J.D. [Parker,B.&L.]
Parker, Bush & Lane, P.C., (AV) ....1400 S.W. 5th Ave., Suite 670
Parkhurst, John M., (BV) ....'44 '70 C.207 B.A. L.629 J.D. 610 S.W. Alder St., Ste. 1000
Parks, Timothy M. ....'66 '93 C&L.950 B.S., J.D. [Ball J.]
Parsons, John D., (AV) ....'64 '92 C.877 B.A. L.101 J.D. [Parsons F.&G.]

Parsons Farnell & Grein LLP, (AV) BB
805 S.W. Broadway, Suite 1560, 97205
Telephone: 503-222-1812 Fax: 503-274-7979
URL: http://www.pfglaw.com
Partners: Michael E. Farnell; David E. Grein; John D. Parsons. Of Counsel: Mark A. Golding. Associates: Samantha L. Mender; James L. Guse; Candice Y. Kim; Amy L. Larson; Justin D. Leonard; Emily S. Robertson.
Appellate Practice, Business and Corporate Law, Commercial Litigation, Construction Litigation, Estate Planning, Insurance Coverage Litigation, Probate and Trust Administration and Litigation, Real Estate, Tax Planning and Controversies.
See Professional Biographies, PORTLAND, OREGON

Passannante, Mark G. ....'68 '94 C.629 B.S. L.1051 J.D. 888 S.W. 5th Ave., Ste. 650
Pasternack, Alan L. ....'61 '89 C.165 A.B. L.188 J.D. [A Schwabe,W.&W.]
Paternoster, Charles J. ....'71 '98 C.165 B.A. L.665 J.D. [A Markowitz,H.G.&M.]
Paterson, Dennis M., III, (AV) ....'— '82 C.1060 B.A. L.1051 J.D. [Davis W.T.]
Patrick, Clayton C., (BV) ....'44 '70 C.939 B.A. L.1066 J.D. [C.C.Patrick]
Patrick, Frank G. ....'48 '76 C.628 B.S. L.629 J.D. 17437 S.E. Pilgrim Ct., Suite A
Patrick, Clayton C., P.C., (BV) ....1030 S.W. Jefferson St., Apt. 530
Patterson, Sarah B., (BVⓉ) '43 '77 C.436 B.A. L.421 J.D.
(adm. in KY; not adm. in OR) [S.Patterson&Assoc.]
Patterson, Stephen W., (AVⓉ) '57 '84 C&L.846 B.B.A., J.D.
(adm. in TX; not adm. in OR) President, Portland Trail Blazers
Patterson, Sarah, Associates, (BVⓉ) ....1610 SE 32 Ave.
Patton, Thomas C ....'59 '96 C.999 L.1051 J.D. [A Lehner&R.]
Patton, William T. ....'— '97 C.605 B.A. L.273 J.D. [A Lane P.]
Paul, David, (AV) ....'57 '86 C.1169 B.A. L.1051 J.D. [Paul&S.]
Paul & Sugerman, P.C., (AV) ....520 Southwest Sixth Avenue, Suite 920
Paulson, Charles, (AV) ....'31 '58 C.685 L.596 J.D. [Paulson]
Paulson, Dain ....'70 '97 C&L.629 B.A., J.D. [A Bullivant H.B.]
Paulson, Jane, (AV) ....'65 '91 C.347 B.S. L.893 J.D. [Paulson]

Paulson Law Firm, (AV)
1000 S.W. Broadway, Suite 1660, 97205-3068
Telephone: 503-226-6361 Fax: 503-226-6276
Email: chuck@paulsonlawfirm.com URL: http://www.lawyers.com/paulsonlawfirm
Charles Paulson; Jane Paulson.
Civil Trials in all State and Federal Courts. Personal Injury, Medical and Dental Malpractice, Negligence, Products Liability, Wrongful Death, Automobile and Trucking Accidents, Sexual Abuse, Nursing Home Abuse, Unsafe Products.
See Professional Biographies, PORTLAND, OREGON

Payne, Jeff ....'61 '05 C.94 B.A. L.1051 J.D. [A VandenBos&C.]
Pearce, Richard C., (BV) '50 '76 C.629 B.S. L.596 J.D.
921 S.W. Washington St., Ste. 755
Pearlman, Leonard W., (BV) ....'32 '59 C.1051 B.S. L.950 LL.B. 7154 S.W. Nevada Terr.
Pearman, Beverly C. ....'70 '99 C.269 B.A. L.575 J.D. [A Stoel R.]
Pearson, J. Kent, Jr., (BV) ....'57 '82 C.896 B.A. L.902 J.D. [Bullard S.J.W.]
Pearson, Kevin T. ....'69 '96 C.413 B.S. L.285 J.D. [A Stoel R.]
Pearson, Teresa H., P.C. ....'70 '95 C.112 B.A. L.228 J.D. [Miller N.]
Pearson, Wayne C., (AV) ....'47 '72 C.628 B.S. L.950 J.D. Dep. Dist. Atty.
Peck, Todd M. ....'67 '92 C.906 B.A. L.823 J.D. [A Bullivant H.B.]
Pecknold, J. Kristen ....'64 '90 C.550 B.S. L.596 J.D. [A Reeves,K.&H.]
Ped, Thomas A., (BV) ....'— '95 L.950 J.D. [A Williams,K.&G.P.]
Pedersen, A. W. ....'17 '46 C.878 B.S. L.309 LL.B. 1500 S.W. 5th Ave.
Pedersen, Amy Joseph, (AV) ....'58 '85 C.629 B.A. L.893 J.D. [Tonkon T.]
Peek, William D., (AV) ....'39 '64 C&L.629 B.S., LL.B. [C Schwabe,W.&W.]
Peifer, Stephen F., (AV) ....'49 '74 C.812 B.A. L.602 J.D. U. S. Attorneys Office
Pekelder, Ruth E., (AV) ....'57 '84 C.114 B.A. L.596 J.D. [Gevurtz,M.L.&H.]
Pendergrass, Walter H., (AV) ....'25 '50 C&L.813 A.B., J.D. [C Bullivant H.B.]
Perdue, Lance D., (BV) ....'54 '84 [Marandas,P.M.A.&D.]
Perkins, Matthew ....'74 '01 C.839 B.S. L.596 J.D. [A Davison V.]
Perkins, Robert S. ....'55 '83 C.1051 B.S. L.950 J.D. [C Draneas&H.]
Perkins, William H., (AV) ....'51 '79 C.951 B.A. L.276 J.D. [C Ball J.]

Perkins Coie LLP, (AV)
1120 N.W. Couch Street, 10th Floor, 97209-4128 ⊙
Telephone: 503-727-2000 Facsimile: 503-727-2222
Email: perkins@perkinscoie.com URL: http://www.perkinscoie.com
Partners: Allan R. Abravanel; Robert L. Aldisert; Peter B. Archie; Richard L. Baum; David A. Bledsoe; Jeffrey W. Bock; Brentley M. Bullock; Richard A. Cantlin; Austin W. Crowe, Jr.; Scott D. Eads; George K. Fogg; Paul T. Fortino; James H. Gidley; Ivan Gold; M. Christopher Hall; Steven M. Hedberg; Thomas Russell Johnson; Calvin L. Keith; Thomas E. Lindley; David S. Matheson; Christopher T. Matthews; Neil Nathanson; Douglas R. Pahl; Steven L. Pfeiffer; Lawrence H. Reichman; Michael C. Robinson; Elizabeth Schwartz; Michael H. Simon; Patrick J. Simpson; David P. R. Symes; Roy W. Tucker; Mark D. Whitlow; Jay A. Zollinger. Of Counsel: Aaron C. Courtney; Frank M. Flynn; Milton T. Jones; Jeanette Thomas. Resident Associates: Roger A. Alfred; Danielle Benderly; Deena

(This Listing Continued)

Perkins Coie LLP (Continued)
B. Bothello (Not admitted in OR); Peggy L. Crane; Sarah J. Crooks; Jeffrey C. Dobbins; Stephen M. Feldman; Michael S. Gadd; Christopher L. Garrett (Not admitted in OR); Dina Glassman; Shannon Hartwell; Erick J. Haynie; Stephanie K. Hines; Julia E. Markley; Gwyneth McAlpine; Lynne M. Paretchan; Kevin Sali; Andrew H. Solomon; Cody Weston.
General Civil Trial and Appellate Practice in Federal and State Courts and before various Federal and State Administrative Tribunals. Administrative; Antitrust and Trade Regulation; Aviation and Aerospace; Banks and Banking; Bankruptcy; Biotechnology; Business Law; Corporate Law; Employee Benefits; Energy; Environmental; Estate Planning; Federal Indian Law; Franchising; General Litigation; Government Contracts; Government Relations; Immigration; Intellectual Property; International Trade; International Law; Internet and Electronic Commerce; Labor and Employment; Land Use; Life Sciences; Mergers, Acquisitions and Divestitures; Municipal/Public Finance; Natural Resources; Nonprofit and Charitable Organizations; Probate; Patents; Product Liability; Project Finance; Political Law; Public Utility; Real Estate; School Law; Securities Law and Litigation; Taxation; Technology; Telecommunications; Toxic Torts; Trademarks and Copyrights; Venture Capital and Investment Funds; Water Rights; White-Collar Criminal Representation; Workers' Compensation.
Other Offices: Anchorage, Alaska; Bellevue, Washington; Boise, Idaho; Chicago, Illinois; Denver, Colorado; Los Angeles, California; Menlo Park, California; Olympia, Washington; Phoenix, Arizona; San Francisco, California; Seattle, Washington; Washington, D.C.
Reviser of the Washington Law Digest for this Directory.
See Professional Biographies, PORTLAND, OREGON

Perko, Brian M., (AV) ....'53 '78 C&L.950 B.A., J.D. [Sather,B.&H.]
Perris, Elizabeth L. ....'51 '76 C.112 A.B. L.1067 J.D. U.S. Bkrptcy. J.
Perron, Brian John '75 '01 C.1058 B.A. L.945 J.D.
Staff Atty., Off. of the Solicitor, U.S. Dept. of the Interior
Perry, Edwin C., (AV) ....'— '84 C.911 B.A. L.629 J.D. [Tonkon T.]
Perry, Kenneth R. ....'60 '91 C.705 B.A. L.477 J.D. 310 S.W. 4th. Ave.
Perry, Lynne A. ....'62 '90 C.915 B.A. L.893 J.D. Nat. Res. Gen. Coun.
Perry, R.W. ....'38 '69 C.612 B.S.C.E. L.615 J.D. [R.W.Perry]
Perry, Tatiana A. ....'— '00 C.999 M.Ed. L.950 J.D. [A Tonkon T.]

Perry, R.W. (Reg)
7420 SW Bridgeport Road, Suite 204, 97224
Telephone: 503-670-0443 Fax: 503-443-3793
Email: rwperry@perrywingar.com URL: http://www.perrywinegar.com
Member: R.W. Perry.
General Civil Litigation, Arbitration and Mediation, Construction, Business Law, Real Estate, Estate Planning and Probate, Wills, Trusts, Guardianships.
See Professional Biographies, PORTLAND, OREGON

Peters, Daniel B. ....'59 '85 C.311 B.A. L.878 J.D. 720 S.W. Washington St., Ste. 210
Peters, Sharon C. ....'— '01 L.421 J.D. [A Williams,K.&G.P.]
Petersen, David J. ....'— '98 C.823 B.A. L.1066 J.D. [A Tonkon T.]
Petersen, David P., (AV) '50 '75 C.628 B.S.E.E. L.629 J.D.
[Klarquist S.] (See Pat. Sect.)
Petersen, John M., (BV) ....'50 '76 C&L.629 B.A., J.D. Supvr., Bk. of America‡
Peterson, Gary N. ....'39 '68 C.950 B.A. L.596 J.D. 800 Ne Oregon St Ste 340
Peterson, Kirk S. ....'55 '93 C.1235 B.S. L.546 J.D. [Bullard S.J.W.]
Peterson, Mark A. '49 '76
C.1056 B.A. L.851 J.D. Clinical Prof., Lewis and Clark Legal Clinic
Peterson, P. Lynn '55 '82 C.104 B.A. L.309 J.D.
(adm. in MA; not adm. in OR) Reg. Sol.; U.S. Dept. of Interior
Peterson, Raylynna J. ....'67 '97 C.629 B.A. L.1148 J.D. [A Mitchell,L.&S.]
Peterson, Ronald A., (BVⓉ) '39 '65 C.170 B.A. L.174 J.D.
(adm. in CO; not adm. in OR) 423 S.E. Gilham Ave.
Peterson, Todd A. ....'63 '91 C.610 B.A. L.596 J.D. [Peterson]

Peterson Law Offices, PC
825 NE 20th Avenue, Suite 340, 97232
Telephone: 503-280-0888 Fax: 503-231-9500 URL: http://injurylaworegon.com
Email: toddpeterson@coho.net URL: http://injurylawfirmoregon.com
Todd A. Peterson;—David J. Artz.
Personal Injury, Premises Liability, Automobile Accidents and Injuries, Dog Bites and Wrongful Death.
See Professional Biographies, PORTLAND, OREGON

Petranovich, Milo P., (AV) ....'— '77 C.30 B.A. L.477 J.D. [Lane P.]
Petrowsky, Duane K. ....'60 '01 C.1077 B.S. L.596 J.D. 8700 S.W. 26th Ave., Ste. S
Petterson, Paul S., (AV) ....'51 '79 C.878 B.S. L.1051 J.D. 522 S.W. Fifth Ave., Ste. 1500
Pettit, Holly E. ....'75 '00 C.1051 B.A. L.596 J.D. [A Bullivant H.B.]
Pettit, Richard R. '14 '41 C.674 A.B. L.976 LL.B.
(adm. in NY; not adm. in OR) 9760 SW Imperial Dr.‡
Pfeifer, Stephen L. ....'63 '92 C.602 B.A. L.285 J.D. [VavRosky M.O.]
Pfeiffer, Eugene L. ....'24 '53 C.629 L.596 LL.B. 5404 N.E. 112 St.‡
Pfeiffer, Steven L., (AV) ....'53 '81 C.1051 B.S. L.629 J.D. [Perkins C.]

Phelan, Margaret Madison, P.S.
(See Vancouver)

Philbrook, Julia A. ....'54 '80 C.1044 B.A. L.596 J.D. Metro. Pub. Def.
Phillips, Dean M., (AV) ....'— '75 C.1056 B.S. L.1051 J.D. [C Davis W.T.]
Phillips, Matthew C. ....'69 '01 C.878 B.A. L.276 J.D. [A Stoel R.]
Philpott, Claire J. ....'— '92 C.112 B.A. L.1068 J.D. [Lane P.]
Pickett, Douglas G., (BV) ....'53 '81 C.1056 B.A. L.629 J.D. [Martin,B.T.L.&H.]
Pickett, J. Randolph, (BV) ....'46 '72 C.37 B.A. L.629 J.D. [Pickett D.R.]

Pickett Dummigan Rhodes LLP, (BV)
621 SW Morrison Street, Suite 900, 97205
Telephone: 503-223-7770 Fax: 503-227-2530
URL: http://www.pickettdummiganrhodes.com
Partners: J. Randolph Pickett; R. Brendan Dummigan; Laura Lee Rhodes; Elvia Aguilar.
Litigation Practice including Personal Injury, Products Liability, Professional Liability and Toxic Tort Litigation.
See Professional Biographies, PORTLAND, OREGON

Piekarski, Christopher ....'74 '00 C.939 B.A. L.950 J.D. Dep. Dist. Atty.
Pierce, Harold W. ....'22 '52 C&L.950 LL.B. 8011 N. St. Louis St.
Pierce, Jan R. '43 '71 C&L.900 B.S., J.D.
(adm. in KS; not adm. in OR) Asst. Dist. Coun., I.R.S.
Pieretti, Gino G., Jr., (AV) ....'34 '58 C&L.950 B.A., J.D. 1012 S.W. King, Room 201
Pierznik, William R. ....'73 '99 C.311 B.A. L.1068 J.D. [A Stoel R.]
Pihl, Mark P. ....'56 '90 C.1056 B.S. L.950 J.D. [C Gordon&R.]
Pijanowski, Michael A. ....'66 '00 C.37 B.A. L.596 J.D. 1606 S.E. Glenwood
Pike, Russell W. ....'46 '81 C.112 B.A. L.426 J.D. [A Gordon&P.]
Pilorget, Debbie L. ....'64 '00 C.1056 B.S. L.596 J.D. [A Smith F.&E.]
Pinkerton, A. Duane ....'11 '35 C&L.629 J.D. 8709 S.E. Causey Ave.‡
Pinkstaff, John C., (CV) ....'45 '75 C.629 B.S. L.1065 J.D. 1727 N.W. Hoyt Street
Pinto, Russell G. '49 '76 C.800 B.A. L.988 J.D.
(adm. in WA; not adm. in OR) The Trust For Pub. Land
Pionk, Nancy L. '64 '89 C.476 B.A. L.424 J.D.
(adm. in IL; not adm. in OR) 5221 E. Burnside‡
Pistacchio, Jason ....'— '00 C.906 B.A. L.629 J.D. [A Cosgrave V.K.]
Pitcher, George S. ....'— '96 L.950 J.D. [Williams,K.&G.P.]

Pitchford, Susan D. '71 '96
C&L.285 B.S.,B.A., J.D. [Ⓐ Chernoff,V.M.&S.] (See Pat. Sect.)
Pitzer, Jeff S. .... '63 '90 C.378 B.A. L.966 J.D. [Pitzer L.]

Pitzer Law
101 S.W. Main Street, Suite 805, 97204
Telephone: 503-227-1477 Fax: 503-227-5839
Email: jpitzer@pitzerlaw.net URL: http://www.pitzerlaw.net
Jeff S. Pitzer.
Complex Commercial Litigation, Intellectual Property Litigation (Patents, Trademarks, Copyrights), Technology Law, White Collar Criminal Defense, Antitrust, Eminent Domain, Products Liability Defense, Employment Litigation.
See Professional Biographies, PORTLAND, OREGON

Piucci, Stephen V., (AV) .....'54 '82 C.339 B.A. L.285 J.D. 900 S.W. 13th Ave., Ste. 200
Pizzuti, Kristine M. ....'68 '95 C.629 B.S. L.884 J.D. [Schwabe,W.&W.]
Plaster, T. Chad ....'71 '97 C.911 B.A. L.596 J.D. 1727 N.W. Hoyt Street
Playfair, M. Brian, (AV) '45 '75 C.413 B.A. L.1051 J.D.
Gen. Coun., Tri-Met Legal Servs.

Podemski, Marilyn R., (BV) '46 '76 C.629 B.A. L.145 J.D.
2477 S.W. Arden Road, 97201
Telephone: 503-228-5229 Fax: 503-224-5451
Email: mrp@podemski.com URL: http://www.lawyers.com/podemski
Bankruptcy, Collections, Commercial Law, Litigation
See Professional Biographies, PORTLAND, OREGON

Podwill, Loren D., (AV) ....'56 '84 C.172 B.A. L.950 J.D. [Bullivant H.B.]
Poff, Randall E., (BV) .... '52 '78 C.1056 B.S. L.596 J.D. 1618 S.W. 1st Avenue
Polance, Jack, (BV) ....'50 '75 C.347 B.A. L.813 J.D. 888 S.W. 5th Ave.
Poland, James E. ....'56 '96 C.150 B.S. L.8 J.D. Mgr. & Sr. Atty., Standard Ins. Co.
Polley, Richard J., (AV) '48 '75 C&L.950 B.A.Chem., J.D.
[Klarquist S.] (See Pat. Sect.)
Polscer, Diane L., (AV) ....'60 '84 C.645 B.A. L.629 J.D. [Gordon&P.]
Pomeroy, Ronald K. ....'46 '73 C.1056 B.S. L.596 J.D. [Sather,B.&H.]
Pool, Mary L., (BV) ....'62 '92 C.339 B.S. L.209 J.D. [Ⓐ Kilmer,V.&L.]
Pope, Richard S., (AV) ....'52 '79 C&L.339 B.S., J.D. [Newcomb,S.S.&L.]
Pope, Robin Elizabeth, (AV) ....'53 '81 C.1213 B.S. L.1051 J.D. [R.E.Pope]
Pope, Robin E., (AV) .... 1834 S.W. 58th Ave., Ste. 101
Popkin, Nancy J., (AV) '56 '82
C.112 B.A. L.596 J.D. Dep. Dist. Atty., Multnomah Co. Courthouse
Popovich, Elia E. ....'— '98 C.478 B.A. L.1035 J.D. [Ⓐ Foster P.T.]
Popperl, M. Vivienne, (AV) ....'51 '85 C.999 B.A. L.596 J.D. U.S. Trustee Atty.
Porter, J. Michael ....'70 '00 C.375 B.S. L.378 J.D. [Ⓐ Miller N.]
Porter, Janis Sue '46 '85 C.685 B.A. L.596 J.D.
Exec. Dir., U.S. Arbitration & Mediation of Oregon
Porter, Richard F. ....'29 '54 C.309 A.B. L.813 J.D. 2006 S.W. Montgomery Dr.‡
Portnoy, Lois J., (AV) ....'47 '74 C.104 B.A. L.629 J.D. 2427 N.W. Pinnacle Dr.
Portwood, Daniel M. ....'14 '46 L.596 LL.B. 11915 S.W. Foothills Dr.
Posewitz, Brian J., (AV) ....'60 '91 C.950 B.S. L.629 J.D. [Tonkon T.]
Posner, Jason L. ....'69 '98 C.241 B.F.A. L.629 J.D. 806 S.W. Broadway, Ste. 800
Post, David G., P.C. ....'67 '96 C.188 A.B. L.309 J.D. [Miller N.]
Postlewaite, Ann C., (BV) ....'54 '89 C.1056 B.S. L.950 J.D. P.O. Box 92112
Postma, Eric S. ....'72 '99 C.1109 B.A. L.950 J.D. [Ⓐ G.M.Bullock&Assoc.]
Poteet, Mary '52 '79 C.518 B.A. L.1065 J.D.
(adm. in AK; not adm. in OR) 2005 N.W. Wheatfield Way
Potter, Aaron J. ....'71 '99 1000 S.W. Broadway, 20th Fl.
Potter, Donald B., Law Offices of ....'54 '84 C.344 B.A. L.596 J.D. 522 SW 5th Ave.
Potter, Irving W., (AV) ....'48 '74 C.154 B.A. L.950 J.D. [Josselson,P.&R.]
Potter, Nancie K., (AV) ....'53 '79 C.1051 B.A. L.596 J.D. [Foster P.T.]
Potter, Sheila H. ....'71 '99 C.945 B.A. L.174 J.D. [Ⓐ Bullivant H.B.]
Poust, Alex I., (BV) ....'63 '92 C.668 B.A. L.629 J.D. [Schwabe,W.&W.]
Powell, Bruce R., (AV) ....'53 '78 C&L.378 B.A., J.D. [Susak&P.]
Powell, Bryan E., (BV) ....'— '88 C.911 B.A. L.1065 J.D. [Lane P.]
Powell, Gregory L. ....'63 '90 C.629 B.A. L.1051 J.D. [Foster P.T.]
Powers, Claudia Kay, (AV) ....'47 '83 C.629 B.S. L.596 J.D. [Ater W.]
Powers, John, (AV) ....'50 '74 C.605 B.A. L.596 J.D. 421 S.W. 6th Avenue, Ste. 1111
Powers, Teri L. ....'55 '85 C&L.280 B.A., J.D. 38504 N.W. Reeder Road
Powers, Thomas B. ....'60 '98 C.259 B.S. L.569 J.D. [Williams L.O.C.&P.]
Powers, William T., (BV) ....'38 '68 C.629 B.S. L.596 LL.B. 8006 S.E. 17th Ave.

Powers, McCulloch & Bennett, LLP, (AV)
3000 Wells Fargo Center, 1300 S.W. Fifth Avenue, 97201
Telephone: 503-228-8588 Facsimile: 503-228-0057
URL: http://www.lawyers.com/pmblaw
Partners of Firm: Mark M. McCulloch; Steven R. Bennett. Associates: Arthur E. Coyne; Walter Weiss, Jr.
Appellate Practice; Business Law; Construction Law; Family Law; Guardianship and Conservatorship; Insurance; Litigation; Medical Malpractice; Personal Injury; Probate; Products Liability; Professional Liability; Real Estate; Trusts and Estates; Wills.
See Professional Biographies, PORTLAND, OREGON

Prange, David E., (AV) ....'59 '87 C.172 B.S. L.596 J.D. [Abbott&P.]
Pratt, Kathryn Mary ....'64 '94 C.685 B.A. L.596 J.D. 6586 N.W. McGregor Terrace
Pratt, Scott O., (AV) ....'55 '81 C.957 B.A. L.950 J.D. 806 S.W. Broadway
Preg, Theodore L., (AVⓉ) '45 '74 C.197 B.A. L.629 J.D.
[Preg O.&G.] (⊙Seattle, WA)
Preg O'Donnell & Gillett PLLC, (AV)
111 S.W. 5th, Suite 1650 (⊙Anchorage, AK; Seattle, WA)
Prentice, William H. ....'49 '89 C.1036 B.A. L.950 J.D. Sr. Coun., PacifiCorp
Prescott, Christopher A. ....'45 '77 C.629 B.A. L.1051 2112 S. E. Main St.‡
Preston, Kevin D. '65 '00 C.670 B.B.A. L.596 J.D.
10211 S.W. Baubur Blvd., Ste. 206A
Preston, Peter W., (AV) ....'54 '82 C.685 B.A. L.838 J.D. [Preston B.&F.]
Preston, Robert J., (AV) ....'57 '85 C.1375 A.B. L.911 J.D. [Elliott,O.&P.]
Preston Bunnell & Flynn, LLP, (AV) .... 1500 S.W. 1st Ave., Ste. 770

Preston Gates & Ellis LLP, (AV)
1400 KOIN Tower, 222 S.W. Columbia Street, 97201-6632 ⊙
Telephone: 503-228-3200 Facsimile: 503-248-9085
Email: info@prestongates.com URL: http://www.prestongates.com
Resident Partners: Ellen C. Bachman; Brendan R. McDonnell; Douglas S. Parker; Jeffery W. Ring; Harvey W. Rogers; Timothy J. Sercombe; Ann L. Sherman; Harvard P. Spigal; Philip S. Van Der Weele. Of Counsel: Richard G. Price. Senior Associate: Martin F. Medeiros. Resident Associates: Karl E. Hausafus; *Yi-Kang Hu; Matthew J. Lysne; Carol J. McCoog; Gulgun Ugur.*
Languages: Chinese, French, German, Japanese, Korean, Russian, Spanish and Taiwanese.
General Practice. Administrative, Affordable Housing Finance, Americans with Disabilities Act, Bankruptcy Litigation, Business Transactions and Business Planning, Business Reorganization and Bankruptcy, Commercial Transactions and Litigation, Construction, Corporate, Corporate Financing, Creditors' Rights, Emerging Business, Employment, Environmental, Governmental Relations, Insurance, Technology and Intellectual Property (domestic and international, includes copyrights, trademarks, trade secrets, licensing and internet/e-commerce); International Business Transactions, Internet/E-Commerce Law, Labor, Land Use, Leasing, Legislative, Litigation, Mergers and Acqui-

(This Listing Continued)

Preston Gates & Ellis LLP (Continued)
sitions, Municipal (general and finance), Natural Resources, Probate, Products Liability, Public Law, Real Estate, Real Estate Financing and Leasing, Securities, Solid Waste, Tax, Telecommunications, Uniform Commercial Code, Energy, Utilities and Transportation Law.
Anchorage, Alaska Office: 420 L Street, Suite 400, 99501-1937. Telephone: 907-276-1969. Facsimile: 907-276-1365.
Coeur d'Alene, Idaho Office: 1200 Ironwood Drive, Suite 315, 83814. Telephone: 208-667-1839. Facsimile: 208-765-2494.
Washington, D.C. Office: Preston Gates Ellis & Rouvelas Meeds LLP, 1735 New York Avenue, N.W., Suite 500, 20006-5209. Telephone: 202-628-1700. Facsimile: 202-331-1024.
Irvine, California Office: 1900 Main Street, Suite 600, 92614-7319. Telephone: 949-253-0900. Facsimile: 949-253-0902.
San Francisco, California Office: 55 Second Street, Suite 1700, 94105. Telephone: 415-882-8200. Facsimile: 415-882-8220.
Seattle, Washington Office: 925 Fourth Avenue, Suite 2900, 98104-1158. Telephone: 206-623-7580. Facsimile: 206-623-7022.
Spokane, Washington Office: 601 West Riverside Avenue, Suite 1400, 99201-0636. Telephone: 509-624-2100. Facsimile: 509-456-0146.
Beijing, China Office: Preston Gates & Ellis, Suite 1003, Tower E3, Oriental Plaza, No. 1 East Chang An Avenue. Telephone: +86 10 8518 8528. Facsimile: +86 10 8518 9299.
Hong Kong Office: Preston Gates & Ellis, 35th Floor, Two International Finance Centre, 8 Finance Street, Central, Hong Kong. Telephone: 852-2511-5100. Facsimile: 852-2511-9515.
Taipei, Taiwan Office: Preston Gates & Ellis, 2/F, No. 131, Min Sheng E. Rd., Sec. 3. Telephone:+886 (2) 2717 6657. Facsimile:+886 (2) 2712-8264.
See Professional Biographies, PORTLAND, OREGON

Prewitt, Steven J. '74 '99 C.893 B.A. L.1209 J.D.
(adm. in VA; not adm. in OR; Pat.) [Ⓐ Schwabe,W.&W.]
Pribbanow, Norman B. ....'— '90 C.1056 B.S. L.950 J.D. Asst. Gen. Coun., Tri-Met
Price, Anne R. '65 '94 C.477 B.G.S. L.273 J.D.
(adm. in MD; not adm. in OR) Dept. of Environmental Quality
Price, Richard G., (BV) .... '52 '89 C.629 B.S. L.188 J.D. [Ⓑ Preston G.&E.]
Prichard, James C. ....'74 '99 C&L.629 B.S., J.D. [Ⓐ Ball J.]
Priestley, Kimberly J. .... '66 '93 213 S.W. Ash, Ste. 208
Probst, Leo R., (BV) ....'39 '65 C.629 B.S. L.950 LL.B. 2938 N.W. Montana Ct.
Profitt, Kathleen ....'— '04 C&L.1051 B.A., J.D. [Ⓐ Foster P.T.]
Prokopenko, Vladimir I. ....'67 '95 1500 Se Waverly Dr
Proppe, Phyllis S. ....'26 '50 C&L.813 B.A., J.D. 6719 S.E. 29th Ave.‡
Pruitt, Helen Rives, (AV) ....'54 '80 C.914 A.B. L.629 J.D. [Meyer&W.]
Prunty, James A. ....'55 '84 C.437 B.S. L.1162 J.D. Asst. Atty. Gen.
Pulley, Daryl M., (BV) ....'45 '76 C.56 B.A. L.596 J.D. 1924 N.E. 45th Ave.
Pulvers, Roy E., (AV) ....'55 '83 C.477 A.B. L.178 J.D. [Lindsay,H.N.&W.]
Purcell, John F., P.C., (AV) ....'54 '80 C.813 A.B. L.596 J.D. [Miller N.]
Purcell, Michael T. ....'60 '85 C.208 B.A. L.1051 J.D. [M.T.Purcell]
Purcell, Michael T., P.C., Law Offices of ....520 S.W. Yamhill St., Ste. 422
Pyle, Donald H., (AV) ....'— '76 C.674 A.B. L.831 J.D. [Lane P.]
Qdro-Law, (AV) ....1937 NE Multnomah
Querin, Douglas S., (AV) ....'46 '71 C&L.629 B.S., J.D. [Zakovics T.&R.]
Querin, Phillip C., (AV) ....'— '72 C&L.629 B.S., J.D. [Davis W.T.]
Quigley, Arthur S., (AVⓉ) '16 '42 C&L.911 A.B., LL.B.
(adm. in WA; not adm. in OR) [Foster P.T.] ⊙‡
Raab, Douglas J., (BV) ...... '68 '93 C.629 B.S. L.950 J.D. [Brownstein,R.S.K.G.D.&H.]
Rabenold, Keith M. '64 '89 C&L.608 B.S.B.A., J.D.
(adm. in OH; not adm. in OR) Assoc. Gen. Coun., Harland Financial Solutions, Inc.
Rackner, Laura E., (AV) ....'56 '84 C&L.629 B.S., J.D. [Gearing,R.&E.]
Rackner, Lisa, (AV) ....'58 '87 C.685 B.A. L.569 J.D. [Ater W.]
Radler, Barbara W., (AV) ....'57 '82 C.352 B.A. L.273 J.D. [Ball J.]
Radler, Robert J. ....'57 '82 C.350 B.A. L.273 J.D. [Radler,B.R.&M.]
Radler, Bohy, Replogle & Miller, (AV) ....9445 S.W. Locust St.
Radmacher, Jonathan M., (AV) ....'65 '92 C.950 B.S. L.273 J.D. [McEwen G.]
Rafter, John A., Jr. ....'56 '86 C.602 B.S.M.E. L.426 J.D. [Stoel R.] (See Pat. Sect.)
Ragen, Ronald K., (AV) ....'— '61 C.976 B.A. L.813 J.D. [Ⓑ Davis W.T.]
Ragland, Andrew J. ....'47 '79 C.1056 B.S. L.596 J.D. 1621 N.E. 41st Ave.
Raivio, H. Scott, (BV) ....'50 '75 C.927 B.A. L.365 J.D. [Raivio,K.&S.]

Raivio, Kohlmetz & Steen, P.C., (BV)
400 SW 6th Avenue, Suite 914, 97204
Telephone: 503-224-1104 Fax: 503-224-9417
Email: andy@rkslawyers.com URL: http://www.rkslawyers.com
H. Scott Raivio; Andrew M. Kohlmetz; Jason A. Steen.
Criminal Law, Personal Injury, Civil Rights, Driving While Intoxicated, Weapons Charges, Drug Crimes, Auto Accidents, Slip and Fall, Dog Bites, Wrongful Death, Assault, Homicide, Robbery, Measure II, White Collar Crime, Sexual Accusations.
See Professional Biographies, PORTLAND, OREGON

Rall, Martin M., (AV) ....'56 '84 C.988 B.S. L.950 J.D. [Lachenmeier E.R.&H.]
Ramfjord, Per A., (AV) ....'58 '84 C&L.477 A.B., J.D. [Stoel R.]
Ramig, John C., (BV) ....'58 '85 C.309 A.B. L.893 J.D. [Ⓑ Hagen O.]
Ramis, Timothy V., (AV) ....'50 '75 C.813 A.B. L.629 J.D. [Ramis C.C.]

Ramis Crew Corrigan, LLP, (AV)
Ballow & Wright Building, 1727 N.W. Hoyt Street, 97209
Telephone: 503-222-4402 Fax: 503-243-2944
Email: info@rcclawyers.com URL: http://www.rcclawyers.com
Principals: Timothy V. Ramis; Stephen F. Crew; Charles E. Corrigan.
General Civil Litigation in all State and Federal Courts. Administrative, Antitrust, Business Law, Condemnation, Environmental, Governmental Relations, Inverse Condemnation, Land Use, Legislative, Municipal, Personal Injury, Public Lands, Real Estate, Water and Zoning Law.
See Professional Biographies, PORTLAND, OREGON

Ramras, Christopher Andrew ....'66 '96 C.112 B.A. L.950 J.D. [Ⓐ Smith F.&E.]★
Randles, Guy A., (AV) ....'52 '77 C.602 A.B. L.1066 J.D. [Stoel R.]
Raney, Paul A. ....'59 '85 C&L.893 B.A., J.D. 2308 N.E. 28th Ave.
Rankin, Howard A., (AV) ....'20 '48 C&L.378 B.S., J.D. 222 S.W. Columbia St.
Rankin, Robert D., (AV) ....'43 '68 C.350 B.S. L.597 J.D. [Ⓑ McEwen G.]
Ransom, Hollis C., Jr. ....'32 '58 C&L.629 B.A., LL.B. [Ransom&G.]
Ransom, John S., (AV) ....'42 '68 C.838 B.S. L.276 J.D. [Ransom B.]

Ransom Blackman LLP, (AV)
1001 S.W. Fifth Avenue Suite 1400, 97204-1144
Telephone: 503-228-0487 Telecopier: 503-227-5984
Members of Firm: John S. Ransom; Marc D. Blackman;—Kendra Marie Matthews; Craig J. Gabriel. Federal and State Civil and Criminal Trial and Appellate Practice. Complex Business Litigation. Administrative Law. Professional Licensing.
See Professional Biographies, PORTLAND, OREGON

Ransom & Gilbertson, (AV) ....317 S.W. Alder St.
Rapoport, Simeon D., (BV) '57 '87
C.174 B.A. L.1051 J.D. Standard Insurance Co., Law Dept.
Rappaport, Richard I. ....'47 '77 C.477 B.A. L.596 J.D. 2725 N.E. 49th
Rask, Paul J., (BV) ....'27 '67 C.670 B.A. L.596 J.D. 4610 Belmont St.
Rask, Raymond M., (BV) ....'36 '61 C.1056 L.596 J.D. [Brownstein,R.S.K.G.D.&H.]
Rask, Thomas R., III, (AV) ....'68 '93 C.602 B.B.A. L.950 J.D. [Kell,A.&R.]
Rasmussen, Dale ....'59 '88 C.101 B.S. L.145 J.D. Sr. Coun., Enron North America Corp.

Rasmussen, Stephen R. ....'58 '84 C.1056 B.S. L.1065 J.D. 1000 S.W. Bway., Ste. 2000
Rasskazova, Larisa Z. '53 '95 C&L.999 M.A., J.D.
(adm. in WA; not adm. in OR) 1020 SW Taylor Street, Suite 425
Rathbone, Coni S. ....'— '88 C.336 B.S. L.950 J.D. [Davis W.T.]
Ratliff, Jeffrey S., (BV) ....'63 '89 C.1365 B.A. L.596 J.D. Dep. Dist. Atty.
Ratoza, Michael M., (AV) ....'51 '76 C&L.629 B.S., J.D. [Garvey S.B.]
Ratto, John Russell, (AV) ....'53 '79 C.413 B.A. L.950 J.D. Dep. Dist. Atty.
Raven, Terrence J., II '72 '98
C.932 B.B.A. L.912 J.D. Land Amer. Nat'l. Commercial Servs.
Rawlinson, David A. ....'40 '65 C&L.629 B.S., LL.B. 432 N.E. 10th Ave.‡
Rawlinson, Dennis P., P.C., (AV) ....'47 '76 C.602 A.B. L.188 J.D. [Miller N.]
Rayburn, Mary-Anne S., (AV) ...... '55 '80 C.1056 B.A. L.950 J.D. [Martin,B.T.L.&H.]

Rayburn Law Offices
(See Lake Oswego)

Raymond, Laurie A., (BV) ....'54 '80 C&L.1051 B.S., J.D. 1207 S.W. 6th Ave.
Rayne, Steven T. ....'65 '91 C.966 B.S. L.596 J.D. 520 SW 6th Ave.
Reagan, Patrick A. ....'50 '77 C.629 B.S. L.596 J.D. 1826 N. E. Broadway
Redden, James A. ....'29 '54 C.94 L.93 LL.B. U.S. Sr. Dist. J.
Redden, Michael A., (BV) .... '53 '80 C.628 B.A. L.1051 J.D. 2722 N.E. 33rd Ave.
Redding, Earl L. ....'26 '60 L.596 LL.B. 13221 S.E. Blackberry Cir.
Redding, Robert W. .... '42 '67 C.629 B.S. L.950 J.D. 3831 S.W. Dosch Road‡

Redman Law Firm
(See Milwaukie)

Redshaw, Stephen A., (CV) ....'61 '94 C.629 B.A. L.705 J.D. [Stoel R.]
Reece, Marilyn Cranley '44 '79 C.856 B.A. L.151 J.D.
(adm. in OH; not adm. in OR) 7 Highland Dr.‡
Reed, Julie L. '66 '95 C.906 B.S.E.E. L.802 J.D.
(adm. in TX; not adm. in OR; See Pat. Sect.) [Marger J.&M.]
Reed, Michael V. '46 '76 C.413 B.A. L.477 J.D.
Asst. Admr., State Liquor Control Comm.
Rees, David F. ....'67 '94 C.813 B.S. L.112 J.D. [Stoll S.B.L.&S.]
Rees, Linly Ferris ....'67 '94 C.813 A.B. L.1066 J.D. 1221 SW 4th Ave.
Rees, Michael A. ....'64 '00 C.774 B.A. L.596 J.D. 630 SW 5th Ave.
Reese, Sharon A. '71 '98 C.773 B.A. L.477 J.D.
Assoc. Coun., Litig. & Employ., KinderCare Learning Centers, Inc.
Reese, Susan Elizabeth, (AV) ....'46 '73 C.604 B.A. L.309 J.D. [S.E.Reese]
Reese, Susan Elizabeth, P.C., (AV) .... 1 S.W. Columbia St., Ste. 1800
Reeve, Mark P., (AV) ....'60 '85 C.309 B.A. L.911 J.D. [Reeve K.]
Reeve, Tracy Pool, (AV) ....'60 '85 C.1051 B.A. L.911 J.D. [Reeve K.]
Reeve Kearns PC, (AV) ....610 S.W. Alder Street
Reeves, Edward J., (AV) ....'56 '83 C.976 B.A. L.94 J.D. [Stoel R.]
Reeves, Martin W., (AV) ....'53 '81 C.907 B.A. L.629 J.D. [Reeves,K.&H.]
Reeves, Kahn & Hennessy, (AV) .... 4035 S.E. 52nd Avenue
Reichman, Lawrence H., (AV) ....'59 '85 C&L.188 B.A., J.D. [Perkins C.]
Reid, Michael K. ....'61 '89 C.1044 B.A. L.893 J.D. Career Law Clk., U.S. Dist. Ct.
Reifenberg, Arno ....'22 '50 C.112 A.B. L.1066 LL.B. Reg. Atty., U.S. Dept. of Agric.
Reilly, Andrew T. ....'67 '96 C.790 B.S. L.1051 J.D. [Ⓐ Black H.]
Reimer, B. LaVonne, (AV) ....'52 '80 C.950 B.A. L.1065 J.D. 8945 N.W. Kaiser Rd.
Reiner, Anthony ....'65 '96 C.1051 B.S. L.950 J.D. [Ⓐ Bullivant H.B.]
Reinhart, Joseph L. ....'57 '83 C.950 B.S. L.596 J.D. [Ⓐ Zalutsky&K.]
Reinisch, Steven R., (AV) ....'52 '77 C&L.950 B.A., J.D. [Reinisch,M.H.&W.]
Reinisch, Mackenzie, Healey & Wilson, P.C., (AV) .... 10260 S.W. Greenburg Rd.
Reinke, Cecil E. '33 '59 C&L.585 Ph.B., J.D.
Div. Coun., N. Pacific Div., U.S. Army Corps of Eng.
Reisman, Joanne ....'58 '83 C.112 B.A. L.596 J.D. 732 S.W. 3rd Ave.
Reive, Christopher L., (AV) ....'51 '83 C.477 B.S. L.596 J.D. [Jordan S.]
Renecker, Stanley G. ....'55 '81 C.909 B.A. L.950 J.D. Price Waterhouse
Reniche-Smith, Cecil A. ....'61 '96 C.112 B.A. L.1194 J.D. [Ⓐ Zimmer&B.]
Renison, Brent W., (AV) .... '— '96 C.629 B.A. L.312 J.D. [Tonkon T.]
Renn, Thomas M., (AV) ....'59 '84 C.297 B.A. L.494 J.D. P.O. Box 91397
Renshaw, Jeffrey F., (BV) ....'63 '93 C.112 B.A. L.1051 J.D. [Johnson R.&L.]
Replogle, William H., (AV) .... '46 '71 C.347 B.S. L.1119 J.D. [Radler,B.R.&M.]
Resch, Timothy J. ....'70 '98 C.629 B.A. L.596 J.D. [Ⓐ Samuels Y.K.S.&S.]
Reynolds, Christine ....'— '01 C.911 B.A. L.596 J.D. [Ⓐ Orrick,H.&S.]
Reynolds, JoAnn B., (AV) .... '42 '78 C.586 B.S. L.802 J.D. [Ⓒ Yates,M.&Assoc.]
Reynolds, MacDaniel E. ....'72 '98 C.565 B.S. L.596 J.D. Dep. Dist. Atty.
Reynolds, Stephen D. ....'55 '81 C&L.629 B.A., J.D. [S.D.Reynolds]
Reynolds, Stephen D., P.C. ....811 SW Naito Pkwy., Ste 500
Rezvani, Shouka D. ....'— '94 C.685 B.A. L.950 J.D. [Tonkon T.]
Rhoades, Gary E., (AV) ....'45 '70 C.628 B.S. L.950 J.D. [G.E.Rhoades]
Rhoades, Nicole M. ....'73 '99 C.628 B.S. L.950 J.D. [Davis R.E.&X.]
Rhoades, Gary E., P.C., (AV) .... 5200 Southwest Macadam Avenue
Rhoden, Carla S. ....'71 '02 C&L.629 B.A., J.D. [Ⓐ Cable H.B.H.&L.]
Rhodes, Laura Lee ....'— '91 C&L.560 B.A., J.D. [Pickett D.R.]
Ricciardelli, Kathryn M. ....'54 '88 C.629 B.S. L.950 J.D. P.O. Box 4400
Rice, James G., (AV) ....'48 '77 C&L.201 B.A., J.D. Deputy City Atty.
Rice, Randall George ....'52 '82 C.950 B.A. L.1051 J.D. 3718 SW Condor
Rice-Kent, Mary K. ....'55 '85 C.1090 B.A. L.629 J.D. 6476 SW Burlingame Pl.
Rich, Christopher W. ....'64 '92 C.112 B.A. L.208 J.D. [Rycewicz&C.]
Richardson, Bonnie ....'— '97 C&L.623 B.A., J.D. [Kirklin F.]
Richardson, Donald S., (AV) ....'17 '41 C&L.629 B.S., J.D. 7400 S.W. Newton Pl.‡
Richardson, James B., (BV) ....'47 '77 C.1056 B.S. L.1051 J.D. [DeBast,M.&R.]
Richardson, Steven F. .... '55 '83 C&L.285 B.A., J.D. 11621 S.E. Fuller Road, Apt. 301
Richman, Jennifer R. '71 '02 C.112 B.A. L.273 J.D.
(adm. in CA; not adm. in OR) Asst. Div. Coun.
Richmond, Jeffrey John ....'— '01 C.628 B.S. L.950 J.D. [Ⓐ Marger J.&M.]
Richter, Carrie A. ....'71 '00 C.1051 B.A. L.596 J.D. [Ⓐ Garvey S.B.]
Richter, Peter C., P.C., (AV) ....'44 '71 C&L.629 B.S., J.D. [Miller N.]
Rickard, Scott M. ....'71 '04 C.399 B.A. L.950 J.D. [Ⓐ Stoel R.]

Rickles, Norman A., (AV) '50 '79 C.629 B.A. L.1051 J.D.
Suite 1100, Pacwest Center, 1211 S.W. Fifth Avenue, 97204
Telephone: 503-241-0570 Facsimile: 503-241-0914
Email: nrickles@grebb.com
(Also Of Counsel, Grenley, Rotenberg, Evans, Bragg & Bodie, P.C.).

Rickles, Stephen P., (AV) .... '53 '79 C.629 B.A. L.596 J.D. [Rickles]

Rickles Law Firm, The, PC, (AV)
One SW Columbia Street, Suite 1850, 97258-2001
Telephone: 503-229-1850 Facsimile: 503-229-1856 Toll Free: 1-800-669-1850
URL: http://www.rickles-law.com
Stephen P. Rickles;—Martin W. Jaqua; Lawrence Schuckman.
Civil Trial Practice. Litigation and Insurance Defense including Casualty, Auto, Fire, Medical and Legal Malpractice. Construction Litigation, Complex Litigation, Products Liability, Employment, Liquor Liability, Public Tort Liability, Auto Dealer Law, Business Litigation and Personal Injury.
See Professional Biographies, PORTLAND, OREGON

Ricks, Daniel M., (AV) ....'51 '78 C.264 A.B. L.1051 J.D. [Kennedy,W.A.&R.]
Ricoy, Marisol .... '72 '02 C.475 B.S. L.950 J.D. [Ⓐ Foster P.T.]
Ridgeway, T. Ericsson ....'58 '96 C.1056 B.S. L.596 J.D. [Ericsson R.]
Ridler, Robyn E. .... '74 '00 C.860 B.A. L.309 J.D. [Ⓐ Tonkon T.]
Riebe, Frank D., (AV) ....'31 '55 C&L.950 B.S.L., J.D. 806 S.W. Broadway
Riedlinger, Meegan L. .... '76 '01 C.413 B.A. L.950 J.D. [Ⓐ MacMillan,S.&M.]
Riedlinger, Stephen P., (BV) ....'48 '77 C.628 B.A. L.1051 J.D. [Susak&P.]
Riewald, David J., (AV) ....'58 '83 C.20 B.A. L.629 J.D. [Bullard S.J.W.]
Riffe, Catherine, (BV) .... '52 '80 C&L.629 B.A., J.D. City Atty. Off.
Riherd, John A., (BVⓉ) ....'46 '74 C&L.352 B.A., J.D. [J.A.Riherd]
Riherd, John A., LLC, (BVⓉ) .... 9541 N.W. Shadywood Ln.
Rimbey, Lori Lin ....'66 '94 C.1181 B.S. L.950 J.D. 0245 S.W. Bancroft
Rinehart, Kyle B. ....'71 '98 C.378 B.A. L.309 J.D. [Klarquist S.] (See Pat. Sect.)
Ring, Jeffery W., (AV) .... '51 '76 C&L.629 B.S., J.D. [Preston G.&E.]
Rinks, Kathleen Y. .... '63 '88 C.629 B.A. L.1292 J.D. 1123 SW Yamhill Street
Rissberger, Patty T. ....'60 '87 C.116 B.A. L.823 J.D. [Crispin R.R.R.]
Ritchey, Michael L., (BV) .... '56 '83 C.629 B.A. L.950 J.D. [Zakovics T.&R.]
Rittenberg, Adam S. ....'62 '93 C.629 B.A. L.1051 J.D. [Black H.]
Ritter, Suzanne C., (BV) .... '63 '91 C.629 B.S. L.1051 J.D. Off. of Dist. Atty.
Rizzo, Steven V., (AV) ....'55 '84 C.1376 B.A. L.221 J.D. [S.V.Rizzo]

Rizzo, Steven V., P.C., (AV)
(Formerly, Seidl & Rizzo)
Lincoln Place, Suite 350, 1620 S.W. Taylor Street, 97205
Telephone: 503-229-1819 Fax: 503-229-0630
Steven V. Rizzo;—John Michael Mattingly; Andrew A. Grade; Victoria L. Balenger.
Civil Trial Practice in State and Federal Courts in Oregon, Washington and California. Commercial Litigation and Personal Injury Litigation including Business Torts, Labor and Employment, Medical Malpractice, Torts, Professional Liability, Products Liability, Insurance, Drug and Medical Device, Employment, Insurance, Negligence, Products Liability, Premises Liability, Toxic Torts, Environmental Law.
See Professional Biographies, PORTLAND, OREGON

Roach, Donald P., (BV) .... '50 '75 C.602 A.B. L.1051 J.D. 140 S.W. Arthur St.
Roach, Randy Alan '53 '78 C.911 B.S. L.285 J.D.
(adm. in WA; not adm. in OR) Bonneville Power Admn.
Robben, Janine O'Neill ....'51 '80 C.906 B.A. L.1051 J.D. Asst. Atty. Gen.
Robeck, Paul G. ....'53 '78 C.670 B.B.A. L.602 J.D. Assoc. Dist. Coun., IRS
Robert, Pierre L. ....'58 '92 C.373 B.A. L.950 J.D. [Ⓐ Dunn C.A.H.&T.]
Roberts, Allison C. ....'— '97 C.112 B.A. L.1051 J.D. NACM Oregon, Inc.
Roberts, Alvin G. ....'31 '75 C.1056 B.S. L.596 J.D. 16000 S.E. River Forest Pl.
Roberts, C. Kent, (AV) ....'54 '80 C.575 B.A. L.596 J.D. [Schwabe,W.&W.]
Roberts, Gary, (AV) ....'47 '74 C.629 B.S. L.569 J.D. [Schwabe,W.&W.]
Roberts, Kenneth E., (AV) .... '44 '69 C.628 B.S. L.309 J.D. [Foster P.T.]
Roberts, Kenneth E., (AV) .... '22 '51 L.596 J.D. [Schwabe,W.&W.] ‡
Roberts, Kirkland T. .... '54 '81 C.173 B.A. L.596 J.D. 6501 S.W. Macadam Ave.
Roberts, Leslie M., (AV) .... '47 '72 C.685 B.A. L.976 J.D. [Josselson,P.&R.]
Roberts, R. Kenney, (AV) ....'43 '70 C.101 B.S. L.950 J.D. [Radler,B.R.&M.]
Roberts, Robb F. ....'56 '86 C.906 B.A. L.629 J.D. Bonneville Power Admin.
Robertson, Emily S. ....'77 '03 C.629 B.A. L.94 J.D. [Ⓐ Parsons F.&G.]
Robertson, Jeffrey G. ....'73 '00 C.911 B.A. L.1119 J.D. [Ⓐ Bullivant H.B.]
Robertson, Melissa M. .... '— '97 C&L.846 B.A., J.D. [Ⓐ Orrick,H.&S.]
Robinowitz, Charles, (AV) '42 '69
C.188 B.A. L.893 LL.B. 1211 Southwest 5th Avenue, Suite 1150
Robinson, Blake ....'79 '05 C.1555 B.A. L.950 J.D. [Ⓐ Bullivant H.B.]
Robinson, Gerald H., (AV) .... '27 '52 C.685 A.B. L.178 J.D. [Ⓒ Black H.] ‡
Robinson, Michael C., (AV) ....'55 '89 C.623 B.A. L.596 J.D. [Perkins C.]
Robles, Glenn W. .... '— '96 C.1169 B.A. L.596 J.D. [Ⓐ Cosgrave V.K.]
Rocker, David C. ....'— '94 C&L.629 B.A., J.D. [Ⓐ Davis W.T.]
Rocker, Ruth Casby ....'67 '94 C.1051 B.A. L.629 J.D. 1000 Sw Broadway Ste 2000
Rodrigues, Carl R., (AV) ....'51 '82 C.1042 B.A. L.596 J.D. [Lehner&R.]
Roels, Starla K. .... '69 '96 C.36 B.A. L.596 J.D. [Ⓐ Hobbs,S.D.&W.]
Rogers, Craig R. ....'70 '98 C&L.101 B.S.M.E., J.D. [Marger J.&M.] (See Pat. Sect.)
Rogers, Harvey W., (AV) ....'45 '75 C.1073 B.A. L.629 J.D. [Preston G.&E.]
Rogers, Jeffrey L., (AV) .... '44 '73 C.197 A.B. L.976 J.D. City Atty.
Rogers, Kristine O., (AV) '47 '73 C.914 B.A. L.976 J.D.
Assoc. Dean & Prof., Lewis & Clark N.W. Sch. of Law
Rogers, Richard M., (BV) ....'50 '75 C.768 B.A. L.1051 J.D. [R.M.Rogers]
Rogers, Terry Ann, (AV) .... '43 '71 C.289 B.A. L.569 J.D. Legal Aid Serv.
Rogers, Richard M., P.C., (BV) .... 200 SW Market St. Ste. 1698
Roggendorf, Kristian Spencer ....'— '01 C.1111 B.A. L.596 J.D. [Ⓐ O'Donnell&C.]
Roghair, Wallace Armand .... '52 '83 C.413 B.A. L.596 J.D. U.S. Dept. of Energy
Rogoway, Edie M. ....'70 '00 C.800 B.A. L.809 J.D. Pub. Def., Pub. Def. Off.
Rogson, Ariel S. .....'69 '97 C.112 B.S.B.S. L.1067 J.D. [Marger J.&M.] (See Pat. Sect.)
Rohlf, Daniel J. '61 '87 C.170 B.A. L.813 J.D.
(adm. in CO; not adm. in OR) Environ. Law Inst., Northwestern Sch. of Law
Rohlfs, Kurt A. .....'67 '97 C.544 B.S. L.1051 J.D. [Ⓐ Chernoff,V.M.&S.] (See Pat. Sect.)
Rohny, Charese A., (BV) ....'65 '95 C.330 B.A. L.950 J.D. [Crispin R.R.R.]
Rohr, Erin Galli ....'69 '95 C.966 B.A. L.596 J.D. Chilton, Ebbett & Rohr, LLC
Rollins, Jennifer L. ....'71 '00 C.967 B.A. L.893 J.D. [Ⓐ Elliott,O.&P.]
Romain, Paul R., (AV) ....'47 '72 C.112 B.A. L.1066 J.D. 805 S.W. Broadway
Roof, Jennifer J. ....'72 '00 C.911 B.S. L.629 J.D. [Ⓐ Miller N.]
Root, Kathryn Smith, (AV) ....'58 '85 C.1051 B.S. L.596 J.D. [Johnston,R.&L.]
Rosacker, J. Warren, (BV) ....'17 '49 C.246 A.B. L.986 LL.B. 2772 S.W. Talbot
Rose, Adam D. ....'73 '97 C.243 B.A. L.309 J.D. [Rose]
Rose, Joanne Mcgilvra ....'38 '86 C&L.950 B.A., J.D. 15677 N.W. Clubhouse Dr.‡
Rose, Krystin Draper ....'65 '93 C.1275 B.A. L.596 J.D. 317 Sw Alder 9th Flr
Rose, Michael E. ....'52 '75 C.597 B.A. L.339 J.D. [Steenson,S.T.L.&R.]
Rose, S. Michael ....'70 '98 C.769 B.A. L.596 J.D. 2210 N.W. Flanders
Rose, Steven M., (AV) ....'49 '74 C.597 B.A. L.629 J.D. [Rose,S.&B.]
Rose Law Firm ....1211 S.W. Fifth Ave., Ste. 2300

Rose, Senders and Bovarnick, LLP, (AV)
1205 N.W. 25th Avenue, 97210
Telephone: 503-227-2486 Fax: 503-227-4172
Steven M. Rose; Richard D. Senders. Of Counsel: Paul S. Bovarnick;—Philip S. Bentley.
Business, Real Estate, Civil Litigation, Personal Injury, Workers Compensation, Employment Law and Federal Employees Liability Act Law. Trial and Appellate Practice in all State and Federal Courts.
See Professional Biographies, PORTLAND, OREGON

Rosen, Steven O., (AV) .... '— '77 C.107 B.S. L.596 J.D. [Rosen] ⊙

Rosen Law Firm, The, (AV)
Old Federal Courthouse, Suite 702, 620 S.W. Main Street, 97205 ⊙
Telephone: 503-525-2525 Fax: 503-525-2526
Email: Rosen@RosenLawFirm.com URL: http://www.RosenLawFirm.com
Steven O. Rosen. Associate: Elizabeth M. Cline.
Trial practice, Aviation and Aerospace Law, Products Liability, Unsafe Products, Business Litigation, Wrongful Death, Automobile Accidents, Medical Malpractice Lawsuits.

(This Listing Continued)

Rosen Law Firm, The (Continued)
Salem, Oregon Office: 512 State Street, 97301.
See Professional Biographies, PORTLAND, OREGON

Rosenbaum, Katherine K. .....'73 '98 C.228 A.B. L.596 J.D. [Ⓐ Stoel R.]
Rosenbaum, Lois Omenn, (AV) .....'50 '74 C.914 A.B. L.813 J.D. [Stoel R.]
Rosenbaum, Michael L., (AV) .....'50 '76 C.309 B.A. L.178 J.D. 1826 N.E. Broadway
Rosenberg, Judith N. .....'59 '98 [Ⓐ Bertoni&T.]
Rosenblum, Ellen F. .....'51 '75 C&L.629 B.S., J.D. Cir. J.
Rosenfeld, John H., (AV) .....'52 '77 C.659 B.S. L.629 J.D. [Tonkon T.]
Rosenhouse, Daniel H. .....'51 '77 C.145 B.A. L.629 J.D. Asst. Atty. Gen.
Rosenthal, Benjamin, (BV) .....'56 '83 C.339 B.S. L.1051 J.D. 1023 S.W. Yamhill St.
Rosenthal, Elden M., (AV) .....'47 '72 C.112 B.A. L.813 J.D. [Rosenthal&G.]
Rosenthal, Richard A. '— '86 C.1375 B.A. L.1066 J.D.
(adm. in CA; not adm. in OR) City of Portland, Indep. Police Review Div.
Rosenthal, Robert, (AV) .....'47 '72 C.352 B.B.A. L.339 J.D. [R.Rosenthal]

Rosenthal & Greene, P.C., (AV)
1001 S.W. Fifth Avenue, Suite 1907, 97204
Telephone: 503-228-3015 FAX: 503-228-3269
Elden M. Rosenthal; Michael A. Greene.
Personal Injury, Wrongful Death, Legal and Medical Malpractice, Employee Termination, Civil Rights. Trial and Appellate Practice in State and Federal Courts.
See Professional Biographies, PORTLAND, OREGON

Rosenthal, Robert, P.C., (AV) .....6931 S.W. Arranmore Way
Ross, Joshua L. .....'72 '03 C.846 B.A. L.1051 J.D. [Ⓐ Stoll S.B.L.&S.]
Ross, Michael J. .....'65 '91 C.999 B.S. L.950 J.D. 1 S.W. Columbia St., Ste. 1850
Ross, Virginia L. .....'59 '90 C.999 B.A. L.1051 J.D. [Ross,V.L.]
Ross, Virginia L., P.C. .....8830 SW Woodside Dr.
Rossmiller, David P. .....'61 '98 C.584 B.A. L.477 J.D. [Ⓐ Dunn C.A.H.&T.]
Rost, Barbara Bennie .....'50 '92 C.1056 B.S. L.1051 J.D. Classroom Law Project
Rotenberg, Kyle W., (BV) '52 '87
C.629 B.S. L.596 J.D. 6500 S.W. Macadam Ave., Ste. 300
Rotenberg, Stan N., (AV) .....'49 '77 C.629 B.S. L.678 J.D. [Grenley,R.E.B.&B.]
Roth, Phillip J. .....'20 '48 C.670 B.A. L.596 J.D. Ret. Cir. J.
Rothauge, Renée E., (AV) .....'63 '90 C.276 B.S.F.S. L.950 J.D. [Bullivant H.B.]
Rothman, Bruce J., (AV) .....'33 '63 C.1056 L.596 LL.B. 1733 S.W. Clifton‡
Roumell, Jennifer R. .....'66 '93 C.477 B.A. L.1051 J.D. [Sather,B.&H.]
Rowe, Gerard P., (AVⓇ) .....'43 '70 C.893 B.A. L.692 J.D. 2728 S.W. Summit Dr.
Roy, David P., (AV) .....'51 '76 C.906 B.A. L.309 J.D. [Black H.]
Royce, Michael D., (AV) .....'46 '79 C.569 B.A. L.596 J.D. 621 S.W. Morrison‡
Rubin, Bruce A., P.C., (AV) .....'51 '76 C.976 B.A. L.813 J.D. [Miller N.]
Rubin, Howard, (AV) .....'55 '83 C.597 B.A. L.596 J.D. [Amburgey&R.]
Ruby, Frederick C., (AV) .....'57 '84 C.309 A.B. L.629 J.D. Asst. Atty. Gen.
Rudd, Michelle .....'63 '95 C.813 B.S.C.E. L.1066 J.D. [Ⓐ Stoel R.]
Rudolph, Francis R. '47 '76 C.150 B.A. L.838 J.D.
(adm. in WA; not adm. in OR) Columbia Management Co.
Ruff, Brian S. .....'70 '98 C.1075 B.A. L.950 J.D. [Ⓐ Lachenmeier E.R.&H.]
Ruhnke, Lyndon .....'64 '99 C.546 B.S. L.596 J.D. [Ruhnke,L.]
Ruhnke, Lyndon, P.C. .....6350 Pamela St.
Runnymede Brown, Karen E. '58 '83 C.880 B.A. L.1292 J.D.
Dept. of Interior Reg. Solr.
Runstein, Ted E., (AV) .....'39 '66 C.911 B.A. L.950 J.D. [Kell,A.&R.]
Runzler, Kurt William .....'62 '88 C.866 B.A. L.596 J.D. Bonneville Power Admin.
Rupert, Wayne W. .....'63 '89 C.645 B.S. L.273 J.D. [Klarquist S.] (See Pat. Sect.)
Rush, Philip A. .....'56 '88 C.1250 B.S. L.284 J.D. [Martin,B.T.L.&H.] ⊙
Russell, Angela M. .....'76 '00 C.1071 B.A. L.596 J.D. [Ⓐ Brownstein,R.S.K.G.D.&H.]
Russell, John D. .....'— '03 C.608 B.S. L.477 J.D. [Ⓐ Kolisch H.]
Russell, Karen A. .....'62 '90 C.911 B.A. L.1051 J.D. Asst. Dir., Water Watch of Oregon
Russell, Kevin L. '67 '93 C.906 B.S.E.E. L.950 J.D.
[Chernoff,V.M.&S.] (See Pat. Sect.)
Russell, P. Stephen, III, (AV) .....'56 '81 C.276 B.S.F.S. L.950 J.D. [Landye B.B.]
Russell, Robert A. .....'53 '80 C.1229 B.M.E. L.1051 J.D. 4370 N.E. Halsey Street
Russell, Shelley D. .....'67 '94 C.668 B.A. L.1051 J.D. [Crispin R.R.R.]
Russell, Susan A. .....'60 '88 C.350 B.A. L.054 LL.B. Metro. Pub. Def.
Russell, Tamara E. .....'70 '97 C.783 B.A. L.94 J.D. [Ⓐ Miller N.]
Russell, William B., Jr. .....'54 '79 C.147 B.A. L.336 J.D. 222 NW Couch St.
Russillo, Craig G. .....'71 '97 C.267 B.S. L.950 J.D. [Ⓐ Schwabe,W.&W.]
Russo, Jolie A. .....'58 '88 C.1051 B.S. L.596 J.D. Clk., Dist. Ct. J.
Rutledge, Robert B. '35 '59 C.999 L.37 LL.B.
(adm. in AZ; not adm. in OR) Reg. Coun., Fed. Hwy. Admin.
Ruttum, Kurt W. .....'— '86 C.174 B.A. L.145 J.D. [Tonkon T.]
Ruyle, James B., (AV) .....'38 '66 C.339 A.B. L.477 LL.B. 2714 S.W. Sherwood Dr.‡
Ryan, David J. .....'— '95 L.1051 J.D. [Ⓑ Williams,K.&G.P.]
Ryan, John D., (AV) .....'20 '50 C.262 B.S. L.596 J.D. [J.D.Ryan]
Ryan, Matthew Owen .....'58 '86 C.1056 B.S. L.1051 J.D. Asst. Co. Coun.
Ryan, Melissa M. .....'69 '98 C.93 B.A. L.972 J.D. [Ⓐ Dunn C.A.H.&T.]
Ryan, Sarah J., (AV) .....'58 '83 C.546 B.A. L.629 J.D. [Ball J.]
Ryan, Shawn P., Law Office of, (AV) '63 '89
C.906 B.A. L.678 J.D. 620 S.W. Main St., Ste. 612
Ryan, John D., PC, (AV) .....503 S.W. Colony Dr.
Rycewicz, Christopher A., (BV) .....'53 '86 C.172 B.S. L.596 J.D. [Rycewicz&C.]
Rycewicz & Chenoweth, (BV) .....601 SW Second Avenue, Suite 1940

Rylander, Kurt M., Trial & Patent Attorney At Law PC
(See Vancouver, Washington)

Rynerson, S. Diane '52 '85 C.1056 B.A. L.770 J.D.
Exec. Dir., Nat. Conf. of Women's Bar Assns.
Sabido, Peter David G. .....'— '03 C.800 B.S. L.596 J.D. [Ⓐ Kolisch H.]
Sabido, Robert E. .....'— '96 C.800 B.A. L.990 J.D. [Ⓐ Cosgrave V.K.]
Sacks, Jeremy D. .....'69 '94 C.918 B.A. L.276 J.D. [Stoel R.]
Sacks, Robert A., (AV) .....'50 '74 C.477 B.A. L.629 J.D. 510 NW 23rd Ave.
Sadlo, Timothy S. (Todd) .....'55 '81 1532 S.E. 36th Ave.
Sady, Stephen Reese, (AV) '51 '77
C.33 B.A. L.1051 J.D. Chf. Dep. U.S. Pub. Def., Pub. Def. Off.
Sagalewicz, Jeffrey T. .....'71 '05 C&L.629 B.S., J.D. [Ⓐ Miller N.]
Sahm, S. Cary .....'45 '76 C.766 B.A. L.596 J.D. 9905 S.W. Quail Post Rd.
St. Louis, Gary M., (BV) .....'47 '74 C.628 B.S. L.629 J.D. 1606 S.E. Glenwood St.
Saitas, Katherine E. .....'— '02 C.788 B.A. L.228 J.D. [Ⓐ Tonkon T.]
Sali, Kevin .....'— '04 C.937 B.S. L.228 J.D. [Ⓐ Perkins C.]
Salvi, Vincent P., (BV) '52 '78 C.800 B.A. L.596 J.D.
Asst. Gen. Coun., Port of Portland
Salyer, Kathryn P., (AV) .....'59 '88 C.446 B.A. L.629 J.D. [Farleigh W.]
Sam, Corinne .....'73 '00 C.112 B.A. L.1051 J.D. [Ⓐ Lindsay,H.N.&W.]
Sample, John P. .....'57 '93 C.999 B.A. L.629 J.D. Sr. Coun., PacifiCorp

Samuels Yoelin Kantor Seymour & Spinrad LLP, (AV)
A Partnership including Professional Corporations
200 Willamette Wharf, 4640 S.W. Macadam Avenue, 97239-4232
Telephone: 503-226-2966 Telecopier: 503-222-2937
URL: http://www.samuelslaw.com
Members of Firm: Stephen E. Kantor (P.C.); Hy Samuels (1904-1992); Steven W. Seymour; Alan M. Spinrad; Michael D. Walker (P.C.); Van M. White, III; Merritt S. Yoelin (P.C.). Associates: Amy E. Bilyeu; Sarie K. Crothers; Betsy A. Gregory; Timothy J. Resch; Edward L. "Ted" Simpson. Of Counsel: Abby Wool Landon (P.C.).
Taxation, Business Ventures, Closely Held Business, Corporations, Limited Liability Companies, Mergers and Acquisitions, Family Business Entities, Commercial Leasing Real Estate Transactions and Construction Law, Retirement Plans, Employment Litigation, Discrimination, Employee Benefits, Employee Contracts, Sexual Harassment, Wrongful Termination, Real Estate Litigation and Other General Civil Litigation, Construction, Eminent Domain, Commercial Landlord and Tenant, IRS Audits, Tax Planning, Trusts and Estates, Asset Protection, Estate Planning, Guardianship, Wills, Business Enterprises, Probate, Trust Administration, Estate Planning, Business Transactions, Buying or Selling of Businesses, and Mediation and Arbitration of the same.
See Professional Biographies, PORTLAND, OREGON

Sand, Thomas C., P.C., (AV) .....'52 '77 C.629 B.A. L.596 J.D. [Miller N.]
Sanders, Nathan D., (BV) .....'49 '79 C.347 B.M. L.1051 J.D. [Siegel&S.]
Sanders, Robert I., (AV) .....'42 '69 C.1027 B.S. L.174 J.D. [Wood T.S.&M.]
Sandmire, Michael J. "Sam" .....'61 '90 C&L.813 A.B., J.D. [Ater W.]
Sandor, Russell A., (AV) .....'48 '82 C.629 B.A. L.596 J.D. [Wetzel D.&S.]
Sandoval, Michael R., (AV) .....'48 '81 C.560 B.B.A. L.950 J.D. 1123 S.W. Yamhill St.
Sandow, Dean T., (AV) .....'58 '84 C.636 B.S. L.950 J.D. [Farleigh W.]
Sanger, Irion .....'72 '00 C.1230 B.A. L.596 J.D. [Ⓐ Davison V.]
SantaMaria, Carmen J., (AV) .....'— '76 C.665 B.S. L.285 J.D. [Davis W.T.]
Santiago, Louis A., (AV) .....'50 '78 C.260 B.S.I.E. L.1051 J.D. [Holland&K.]
Sarant, Jeremy V., (AV) .....'46 '83 C.1056 B.S. L.1051 J.D. 603 SE 69th
Sargent, Brandy A. .....'73 '99 C.424 B.A. L.146 J.D. [Ⓐ Stoel R.]
Sasaki, Joshua M. F., P.C. .....'71 '96 C.197 A.B. L.1051 J.D. [Miller N.]
Sather, Deborah L., (AV) .....'52 '81 C.629 B.S. L.596 J.D. [Sather,B.&H.]
Sather, John S., (CV) .....'40 '84 C.629 B.A. L.1051 J.D. [Sather i.&Assoc.]
Sather & Association, (CV) .....222 SW Columbia St.

Sather, Byerly & Holloway, LLP, (AV)
621 Southwest Morrison Street, Suite 600, 97205
Telephone: 503-225-5858 Fax: 503-721-9272
URL: http://www.sbhlegal.com
Deborah L. Sather; Bruce L. Byerly; Ronald C. Holloway; Krishna Balasubramani; Jennifer R. Roumell; Ronald K. Pomeroy; Brian M. Perko; Robb A. Schotthoefer;—Linda D. Conratt; Karen S. Varney; Rebecca Watkins; Norman D. Cole.
Employer Defense, Workers Compensation Law, OSHA, WISHA, Employment Law, Legal Malpractice, and Appellate.
See Professional Biographies, PORTLAND, OREGON

Saul, Karen E., (AV) .....'57 '83 C.1051 B.A. L.950 J.D. [Farleigh W.]
Sause, H. Richard '52 '78 C.628 B.S. L.988 J.D.
4380 S.W. Macadam Avenue, Suite 500
Savage, John William, (AV) .....'51 '77 C.1051 B.A. L.596 J.D. [J.W.Savage]

Savage, J. William, P.C., (AV)
620 S.W. Fifth Avenue, Suite 1125, 97204
Telephone: 503-452-5858 Fax: 503-248-0200
Email: jwsavage@earthlink.net
John William Savage.
Personal Injury, Medical Malpractice, Legal Malpractice.
See Professional Biographies, PORTLAND, OREGON

Sawyer, Dianne L., (AV) .....'53 '79 C.347 B.A. L.1119 J.D. [Reinisch,M.H.&W.]
Sawyer, Justin Clark .....'75 '01 C.170 B.S. L.596 J.D. [Ⓐ Miller N.]
Saxena, Neisha A. .....'67 '92 C.914 B.A. L.276 J.D. 3316 N.E. Alameda St.
Saxton, Ronald L., (AV) .....'54 '79 C.950 B.S. L.893 J.D. [Ater W.]
Scalf, William D. .....'39 '67 L.596 J.D. [Scalf&O.]
Scalf & O'Halloran, (BV) .....18445 E. Burnside St.
Scanlon, Robert A. .....'45 '71 C&L.629 B.A., J.D. 2800 N.W. Beuhla Vista Terr.‡
Scarborough, William E., Jr., (AV) '38 '67
C.1056 B.S. L.596 J.D. [Scarborough,M.O.&K.]
Scarborough, McNeese, O'Brien & Kilkenny, P.C., (AV) .....5410 S.W. Macadam Avenue
Schaffer, Scott A. .....'67 '94 C.813 B.S. L.623 J.D. [Marger J.&M.] (See Pat. Sect.)
Schantz, William T. .....'34 '60 C.629 B.S. L.950 J.D. 2215 S.W. 84th Ave.
Schatz, Christopher J., (BV) .....'50 '77 C.112 B.A. L.1049 J.D. Pub. Def. Off.
Schauermann, Scott T. .....'71 '96 C.36 B.A. L.629 J.D. 1000 S.W. Bway, Ste. 2000
Schedler, Martin, (AV) .....'19 '51 C.629 B.S. L.596 J.D. [M.Schedler]
Schedler, Martin, P.C., (AV) .....222 S.W. Harrison
Scheele, Dana Shenker .....'74 '00 C.966 B.A. L.494 J.D. Fl 20, 1000 Sw Broadway
Scheldrup, Linda J. '43 '83 C.675 B.A. L.1051 J.D.
(adm. in WA; not adm. in OR) Field Atty., N.L.R.B.
Schell, L. Otto, (BVⓇ) .....'55 '84 C.473 B.S. L.345 J.D. 3611 N.E. Klickitat St.
Schell, Steven R., (AV) .....'39 '68 C&L.629 B.A., J.D. [Black H.]
Scher, Linda Rose '60 '86 C.454 B.S. L.911 J.D.
(adm. in WA; not adm. in OR) 3282 S.E. Hawthorne Blvd.
Schermerhorn, Lee R. .....'07 '33 C.273 B.S. L.904 M.P.L. 2400 S. W. 4th
Scherzer, Robert T., (AV) '52 '79 C&L.629 B.S., J.D.
1020 Southwest Taylor, Suite 880
Schickli, Scott E., (AV) .....'— '81 C.118 B.A. L.494 J.D. [Ⓑ Orrick,H.&S.]
Schiefelbein, Scott M. .....'70 '96 C.575 B.A. L.228 J.D. [Ⓐ Hanna S.]
Schimmelbusch, Erik S. .....'— '95 C.101 B.A. L.464 J.D. [Davis W.T.]
Schleicher, Tara J. .....'— '95 C.628 B.S. L.950 J.D. [Farleigh W.]
Schleuning, Elizabeth A., (AV) .....'60 '85 C.668 B.A. L.950 J.D. [Schwabe,W.&W.]
Schmeer, Michael H., (AV) .....'— '59 C&L.813 B.A., LL.B. [Davis W.T.]
Schmidt, Owen L. '47 '78 C.492 B.A. L.1051 J.D.
U.S. DA Office of the General Counsel
Schmitz, Frank B. .....'35 '76 C.629 A.B. L.770 J.D. P.O. Box 25504
Schneider, Alan L., (BV) .....'43 '68 C.767 B.A. L.813 J.D. 1437 S.W. Columbia St.
Schneider, Alexander .....'08 '34 C&L.629 B.S., LL.B. 3310 N.E. 36th Ave.‡
Schneider, Jill .....'50 '97 C.628 B.S. L.831 J.D. [Ⓐ Schwabe,W.&W.]
Schneider, Merrill .....'51 '77 C.107 B.A. L.629 J.D. [Schneider]
Schneider, Nicole L. .....'74 '01 C&L.546 B.A., J.D. [Schneider]
Schneider, Richard B. .....'51 '82 C.347 A.B. L.1119 J.D. [R.B.S.Llc]
Schneider, Susan K. .....'48 '82 C.950 B.A. L.596 J.D. 1220 S.W. 5th Ave.
Schneider Law Offices .....14415 S.E. Stark
Schneider Law Offices .....14415 Se Stark
Schneider, Richard B., LLC, Law Offices of .....2455 N. W. Marshall Street, Suite 11
Schnitzer, Dori, (BV) .....'53 '81 C.1051 B.S. L.596 J.D. V.P., Admin., Lasco Shipping Co.
Schoen, Ava .....'73 '02 C.299 B.A. L.262 J.D. [Ⓐ Tonkon T.]
Schoen, Douglas A. .....'51 '76 C.629 B.A. L.950 J.D. [Ⓢ Schwabe,W.&W.]
Schofield, Dale H. (Hal) .....'46 '82 C.1056 B.S. L.101 J.D. 1000 S.W. Vista Avenue
Scholz, Robert D., (AV) .....'51 '77 C.597 B.S. L.1051 J.D. [MacMillan,S.&M.]
Schornstein, Jay M. .....'53 '80 C.354 B.S. L.1051 J.D. 1609 S.E. 48th Ave.

Schotthoefer, Robb A. ... '71 '97 C.628 B.A. L.1358 J.D. [Sather,B.&H.]
Schouboe, Lee M., (AV) ... '20 '50 L.596 LL.B. 1500 S.W. 1st Ave.
Schpak, Andrew M. ... '80 '04 C.685 B.A. L.1556 J.D. [Ⓐ Barran L.]
Schrader, Charles R., (AV) ... '47 '77 C.813 B.S. L.629 J.D. [Jordan S.]
Schrader, Michael E. ... '— '91 C.101 B.A. L.347 J.D. [Ⓒ Orrick,H.&S.]
Schreck, George C., (AV) ... '52 '82 C.1155 B.S. L.94 J.D. Senior Counsel, PacifiCorp
Schreyer, Frederic E. '53 '78 C.477 B.B.A. L.1068 J.D.
(adm. in CA; not adm. in OR) 11110 S.W. Collina Ave.
Schroeder, Katherine J. ... '60 '86 C.276 B.S.F.S. L.596 J.D. 6411 S.E. 29th Ave.‡
Schroeder, Laura A., (AV) ... '51 '87 C.629 B.A. L.596 J.D. [Schroeder]
Schroeder, Margaret E. ... '74 '02 C.269 B.A. L.629 J.D. [Ⓐ Black H.]

Schroeder Law Offices, P.C., (AV)
A Professional Corporation
1915 NE 39th Ave., P.O. Box 12527, 97212-0527
Telephone: 503-281-4100 Fax: 503-281-4600
Email: schroeder@water-law.com URL: http://www.water-law.com
Laura A. Schroeder.
Environmental Law including Water Law, Irrigation Law, Water Districts, Agricultural Law, Property Rights, Administrative Litigation. Matters pertaining to the Clean Water Act, NEPA and Title Transfer.
See Professional Biographies, PORTLAND, OREGON

Schrunk, Michael D., (AV) ... '42 '67 C.1056 B.S. L.629 J.D. Dist. Atty.
Schuckman, Lawrence ... '63 '92 C.1044 B.S. L.1009 J.D. [Ⓐ Rickles]
Schulhof, Robert P., Jr. ... '69 '94 C.347 B.A. L.801 J.D. 811 SW Naito Pkwy., Suite 500
Schulte, Frances K. ... '17 '54 C.623 B.A. L.596 LL.B. 4509 S.W. Vermont‡
Schulte, William F., (AV) ... '41 '66 C.939 A.B. L.950 J.D. [Schulte,A.D.A.&B.]
Schulte, Anderson, Downes, Aronson & Bittner, P.C., (AV)
811 S.W. Naito Pkwy., Ste. 500
Schultz, Adam J. ... '— '91 C.629 B.S. L.1194 J.D. 2128 N.E. 23rd Ave.
Schultz, John M. ... '49 '78 C.976 B.A. L.893 J.D. [Ater W.]
Schultz, Pamela A. ... '56 '84 C&L.629 B.A., J.D. 948 N.E. 102nd Ave.‡

Schumacher, David B. '64 '96 C.1058 B.A. L.950 J.D.
3422 N.E. Forty First Avenue, 97212
Telephone: 503-249-8384 Fax: 503-249-8406
Email: schumacherdavid@hotmail.com URL: http://www.lawyers.com/dbschumacher
Creditors' Rights, Business, Collections, Commercial Bankruptcy, Foreclosures.
See Professional Biographies, PORTLAND, OREGON

Schumann, Michael ... '41 '69 C&L.912 B.S., J.D. [Steenson,S.T.L.&R.]
Schuster, Jeanette C. ... '68 '02 C.35 B.S. L.1051 J.D. [Ⓐ Stoel R.]
Schuster, Philip F., II ... '45 '72 C.911 B.A. L.950 J.D. [Dierking&S.]
Schwab, Mildred A. ... '17 '39 L.596 LL.B. 900 S.W. 5th Ave.‡
Schwabe, John L., (AV) ... '19 '48 C.612 B.A. L.608 LL.B. [Schwabe,W.&W.] ‡

Schwabe, Williamson & Wyatt, P.C., (AV) BR
Suites 1600-1900 Pacwest Center, 1211 S.W. Fifth Avenue, 97204-3795 ⊙
Telephone: 503-222-9981 Fax: 503-796-2900 Telex: 4937535 SWK UI
Email: info@schwabe.com URL: http://www.schwabe.com
Shareholders: Al AuYeung (Resident); David W. Axelrod; David F. Bartz, Jr.; Kevin E. Brannon; Carmen M. Calzacorta; Michael A. Cohen; Neil A. Cole; John G. Crawford, Jr.; William B. Crow; Joyle C. Dahl; Robert D. Dayton; Patricia M. Dost; James F. Dulcich; Thomas V. Dulcich; Nancy M. Erfle; Walter H. Evans, III; John R. Faust, Jr.; James M. Finn; Michael T. Garone; Jill S. Gelineau; Walter H. Grebe; John D. Guinasso; Kelly T. Hagan; Kurt F. Hansen; Richard K. Hansen; Robert L. Harrington; Timothy F. Haslach; Nikki C. Hatton; Terry C. Hauck; Margaret A. O'Connor Hoffmann; Mitchell E. Hornecker; Kirk Johansen; Robert E. Joseph; Kevin F. Kerstiens; Raymond S. Kindley; Brian J. King; Jan K. Kitchel; Daniel F. Knox; Donald L. Krahmer, Jr.; Roy D. Lambert; James A. Larpenteur, Jr.; Mark M. LeCoq; Peter Livingston; Darien S. Loiselle; Mark A. Long; William E. Love; Douglas W. MacDougal; Heidi L. Mandt; Johnathan E. Mansfield (Not admitted in OR); Mark A. Manulik; W. A. Jerry North; William J. Ohle; Peter L. Osborne; Martha O'Donnell Pagel; Kristine M. Pizzuti; Alex I. Poust; C. Kent Roberts; Gary Roberts; Elizabeth A. Schleuning; Marc K. Sellers; Robert G. Simpson; Mark A. Stayer; Anne M. Talcott; Katherine C. Tank; Thomas M. Triplett; Jay T. Waldron; Donald Joe Willis. Of Counsel/Contract Attorneys: Jean Ohman Back; Karen K. Law; William D. Peek; Douglas A. Schoen. Associates: Lisa Carey Alan; Andrew D. Barofsky; Melissa A. Boge; Carson D. Bowler; Stephen C. Bush; Amy Chestnut; Jeffrey S. Davis; Joshua S. DeCristo; Christopher C. Dorr; Daniel L. Duyck; David G. Fagan; Christiane R. Fife; Brien J. Flanagan; Greg D Fullem; Michael D. Furlong; Amanda T. Gamblin; Todd M. Grewe; Patchen M. Haggerty; Darius L. Hartwell; David A. Hepler; Jeffrey D. Hern; Román D. Hernández; Noah Jarrett; Jeffrey R. Jones; Pierre Keeley; Shonee D. Langford; Andrew J. Lee; Christopher J. Lewis; Arusi R. Loprinzi; Laura Maffei; Bradley D. Maier; Nathan R. Maki; Gregory W. Mallory; Carol L. Catherine McCaulley (Not admitted in OR); W. Randy Miller; James J. Namiki (Not admitted in OR); Joel A. Parker; Alan L. Pasternack; Steven J. Prewitt (Not admitted in OR); Craig G. Russillo; Jill Schneider; Neda D. Soofi; Ryan P. Steen; Joshua P. Stump; Timothy M. Sullivan; Nathan A. Schwartz Sykes; Thomas M. Tongue; Katherine O. VanZanten; Allyssa J. Walton; B. Scott Whipple; Carrie M. Wood. Retired Shareholders: Roland F. (Jerry) Banks, Jr.; Neva T. Campbell; Rockne Gill; Roger A. Luedtke; James R. Moore; Kenneth E. Roberts; John L. Schwabe; Douglas M. Thompson; Douglas J. White, Jr.; Wayne A. Williamson; Wendell Wyatt (Semi-Retired).
Business and Corporate Law, Joint Ventures, Partnerships, LLC's, Securities, Mergers and Acquisitions, Banking and Financial Institutions, Trusts and Estate Planning, Intellectual Property, Patents and Trademarks, Nanotechnology, White Collar Criminal Law, Real Estate and Land Use, Business, Commercial, and General Litigation, Bankruptcy, Reorganizations and Workouts, Hospital and Health Law, Forest Products, Franchise Law, Immigration, Insurance, Workers' Compensation and Insurance Defense, Employment Relations, Labor Law, Antitrust, Product Liability, Employee Benefits, Construction, Environmental, Energy and Utilities Law, Mining, Natural Resources, State and Local Taxation, Appellate Law, Government Relations, Professional Malpractice Defense, Indian Law, Insurance Coverage Litigation, International Law, eCommerce, Trade and Ports, Landlord & Tenant Law, Transportation, Entertainment & Media, Water Rights Law, Municipal Law and Public Entity Law .
Representative Clients: KeyBank NA; Oregon Steel Mills; Columbia Forest Products; DuPont.
Bend, Oregon Office: 354 SW Upper Terrace Drive, Suite 101, 97702. Telephone: 541-749-4044. Fax: 541-330-1153.
Seattle, Washington Office: U.S. Bank Centre, Suite 3010, 1420 Fifth Avenue. Telephone: 206-622-1711. Fax: 206-292-0460.
Vancouver, Washington Office: Suite 410, Main Place Building, 1111 Main Street. Telephone: 360-694-7551; 696-0241.
See Professional Biographies, PORTLAND, OREGON

Schwartz, Diane ... '70 '98 C.112 B.A. L.629 J.D. [Ⓒ Squires&L.]
Schwartz, Elizabeth, (AV) ... '68 '94 C.691 B.A. L.846 J.D. [Perkins C.]
Schwartz, Jack B., (AV) ... '37 '61 C.813 A.B. L.309 LL.B. [Newcomb,S.S.&L.]
Schwarz, Leigh E. ... '54 '82 C.610 B.S. L.1051 J.D. Paccom Leasing Corp.
Schweitzer, John M., (AV) '44 '72
C&L.966 B.B.A., J.D. 900 S.W. Fifth Avenue, Suite 2600‡
Schwimmer, John A., (AVⓉ) ... '— '83 C.103 B.A. L.1066 J.D. [Ⓒ Sussman S.]
Schwindt, Christopher ... '74 '01 C.907 B.A. L.1051 J.D. 1915 Ne 39th Ave
Sciuchetti, Kyle D. ... '70 '96 C.911 B.A. L.1051 J.D. [Ⓐ Landye B.B.]
Scoggins, Harold B., III ... '62 '91 C.301 B.A. L.1209 J.D. [Farleigh W.]
Scott, Brian J. ... '56 '81 C.911 B.A. L.1067 J.D. Sr. Staff Atty., Amer. Fam. Ins.
Scott, Christian H. ... '75 '02 C.629 B.A. L.597 J.D. [Ⓐ Stoel R.]
Scott, Michael S. ... '70 '97 C.473 B.A. L.596 J.D. [Ⓐ M.C.Cantrell&Assoc.]
Scott, Shay S. ... '64 '93 C.36 B.M. L.629 J.D. [Haglund,K.H.&J.]

Scott Hookland LLP
(See Tigard)
Scott-Brier, Barbara '— '82 C.942 B.A. L.352 J.D.
(adm. in IA; not adm. in OR) Dept. of Interior, Off. of Solr.
Scoumperdis, Kristopher '44 '76
C.1056 B.S. L.596 J.D. V.P., Human Rel., Good Samaritan Hospital
Scruggs, J. Richard, (CV) ... '48 '76 C.846 B.A. L.950 J.D. Asst. U.S. Atty.
Scully, Jason David '— '96 C.1375 B.A. L.1065 J.D.
(adm. in CA; not adm. in OR) 7214 SE 32nd Ave.
Scurlock, Mary C. ... '63 '89 C.228 A.B. L.94 J.D. Pacific Rivers Council

Seaborg, Priscilla L., (BV) '55 '81 C&L.347 B.A., J.D.
1906 S.W. Madison Street, 97205
Telephone: 503-417-7744 Fax: 503-221-1908
Email: plslaw@qwest.net URL: http://www.lawyers.com/plslaw
Federal and State Courts, Criminal Law, Family Law, Divorce, Child Custody, Child Support, Domestic Violence, Visitation Rights, Homicide, Murder, Self Defense, Battered Women, White Collar Crimes, Drug Crimes, Parole and Probation, Adoptions, Juvenile Law.
See Professional Biographies, PORTLAND, OREGON

Sechrist, Shana W. ... '73 '99 C.112 B.A. L.1565 J.D. [Ⓐ Stoel R.]
Seelig, Robert L. ... '48 '86 C.629 B.S. L.1051 J.D. Liberty Northwest Ins. Corp.
Seeronen, John R. '47 '72
C.767 B.A. L.878 J.D. Asst. Div. Coun., U.S. Army Corps of Engrs.
Seidenwurm, Robert S. '71 '96 C.951 B.A. L.112 J.D.
Gen. Coun., Fairway Commercial Mortgage Corp.
Seidl, Michael R., (AV) ... '57 '83 C.957 B.S. L.950 J.D. 806 Sw Broadway Ste 400
Seidman, Scott G., (AV) ... '— '81 C&L.339 A.B., J.D. [Tonkon T.]
Seifer, Daniel J., (AV) ... '44 '69 C.477 A.B. L.145 J.D. [Seifer,Y.M.&Z.]
Seifer, Yeats, Mills & Zwierzynski, LLP, (AV) ... 121 S.W. Morrison Street Suite 850
Seims, Charles G. ... '44 '87 C.800 B.A. L.810 J.D. St. Andrew Legal Clinic
Selby, William R., (BV) ... '40 '66 C.670 B.S. L.950 J.D. Dep. City Atty.
Self, Steven M. ... '73 '99 C.1185 B.A. L.836 J.D. 1000 Sw Broadway Ste 1950
Sellers, Marc K., (AV) ... '53 '78 C.684 B.S. L.426 J.D. [Schwabe,W.&W.]
Selmann, Marja E. ... '70 '96 C.1058 B.A. L.911 J.D. [Ⓐ Martin,B.T.L.&H.] ⊙
Semler, Elizabeth A., (BV) ... '64 '92 C.165 B.A. L.245 J.D. [Ⓐ Sussman S.]
Senders, Richard D., (AV) ... '49 '74 C.178 B.A. L.629 J.D. [Rose,S.&B.]
Sepenuk, Norman, (AV) ... '33 '60 C.674 B.A. L.309 LL.B. [N.Sepenuk]

Sepenuk, Norman, P.C., (AV)
520 S.W. Yamhill Street Suite 600, 97204
Telephone: 503-221-1633 Fax: 503-227-2980
Email: nsepenuk@aol.com
Norman Sepenuk.
Federal Practice. Criminal Trials and Appeals in Federal Courts, Corporate Compliance.
See Professional Biographies, PORTLAND, OREGON

Sercombe, Timothy J., (AV) ... '49 '76 C.597 B.A. L.629 J.D. [Preston G.&E.]
Sergienko, Peter A. ... '— '88 C.309 A.B. L.629 J.D. [Davis W.T.]
Serkin, Bonnie P., (AV) ... '49 '78 C.788 B.A. L.950 J.D. 333 S.W. 5th Ave.
Serrurier, Penny H., (AV) ... '64 '91 C.478 B.A. L.188 J.D. [Stoel R.]
Serrurier, Peter L., (BV) ... '58 '90 C.628 B.S. L.596 J.D. [Stoel R.]
Sewell, Travis Taylor '68 '95
C.228 B.A. L.629 J.D. Dep. Dist. Atty., Multnomah Co. DA Off.
Seymour, Steven W., (AV) ... '45 '75 C.352 B.A. L.950 J.D. [Samuels Y.K.S.&S.]
Shackelford, Michael W., (AV) ... '56 '81 C&L.950 B.S., J.D. [Ater W.]
Shadduck, James E., (BV) ... '59 '87 C.999 B.A. L.596 J.D. 1000 S.W. Broadway
Shade, Dean H. ... '53 '81 C.112 B.S. L.1051 J.D. 13765 N.W. Cornell Rd., Ste. 250
Shadian, Hertsel ... '67 '98 C.312 B.A. L.285 J.D. [Ⓐ McEwen G.]
Shaffer, Michelle L. ... '71 '98 C.347 B.A. L.596 J.D. Jud. Clk.
Shain, Bernard L. ... '26 '55 C.999 L.596 J.D. 7625 S.W. Green Valley Terr.‡
Shank, Jerome B., (AV) ... '20 '54 C.629 A.B. L.1051 LL.B. [Sussman S.]
Shannon, James P. ... '49 '75 C&L.215 A.B., J.D. [Mersereau&S.]
Shannon, Scott H. ... '66 '93 C&L.629 B.S., J.D. 1200 S.W. Main Bldg.
Shapiro, David J. ... '52 '78 C.477 B.A. L.1051 J.D. 2121 NW York Street‡
Sharp, Stanley E. ... '36 '66 C.871 B.S. L.911 LL.B. 7812 S.E. Reed College Pl.‡
Shartel, James R., (BV) ... '41 '74 C.1056 B.S. L.596 J.D. P.O. Box 219271
Shatzer, William W. ... '44 '73 C.628 B.S. L.188 J.D. Hearings Officer, City of Portland
Shaver, Peter Vaughan ... '62 '99 C.477 B.A. L.629 J.D. 621 S.W. Morrison St., Ste. 1417
Shaw, Catherine A., P.C., (AV) ... '61 '88 C&L.911 B.A., J.D. [Miller N.]
Shaw, D. Jean, (BVⓉ) '50 '75 C.911 B.A. L.285 J.D.
Asst. Gen. Coun., Kindercare Learning Ctrs., Inc.
Shaw, David D. ... '67 '96 C.629 B.S. L.911 J.D. [Ⓐ Hobbs,S.D.&W.]
Shawcross, David L. ... '75 '04 C.906 B.A. L.596 J.D. [Ⓐ Grenley,R.E.B.&B.]
Shearer, Glen S., (AV) ... '50 '78 C.629 B.A. L.285 J.D. [Furniss,S.&L.]
Shearin, Leah M., (AV) ... '50 '83 C.1056 B.S. L.596 J.D. 520 S.W. 6th Ave., Ste. 820
Shears, Melia M., (AV) ... '57 '86 C.911 B.A. L.678 J.D. [Callahan&S.]
Shebiel, Alec J. ... '67 '94 C.966 B.S. L.94 J.D. [Garvey S.B.]
Sheehan, Daniel C. '47 '73 C.629 B.A. L.188 J.D.
(adm. in MA; not adm. in OR) COO & CFO, Crabbe Huson Grp., Inc.
Sheely, Paul E., (CVⓉ) ... '59 '91 C.909 B.S. L.589 J.D. [Ⓐ Smith F.&E.]
Shellan, Ronald A., P.C., (AV) ... '49 '75 C.911 B.A. L.950 J.D. [Miller N.]
Shenker, Arden E., (AV) ... '38 '62 C.813 A.B. L.976 LL.B. [Shenker&B.]

Shenker & Bonaparte, LLP, (AV)
One S.W. Columbia Street, Suite 475, 97258
Telephone: 503-294-1118 Fax: 503-294-0015
URL: http://www.ashenkeresq.com
Arden E. Shenker; Robert E. L. Bonaparte; Nell Hoffman Bonaparte.
Complex Litigation, Insurance Coverage, Energy Law, Environmental Law, Professional Liability.
See Professional Biographies, PORTLAND, OREGON

Shepherd, Kerry J. ... '63 '89 C.1181 B.S. L.950 J.D. [Markowitz,H.G.&M.]
Shepherd, Ralph J., (BV) ... '21 '51 L.596 LL.B. Spalding Bldg.
Sherar, Reed L. ... '51 '77 C&L.629 B.A., J.D. [R.L.Sherar]
Sherar, Reed L., P.C ... 11512 S.W. Streamside Court
Sheridan, William G., Jr., (AV) ... '41 '68 C.911 B.A. L.950 J.D. [Allen,S.&M.]
Sherlag, Steven J. ... '66 '91 C&L.477 B.A., J.D. [S.Sherlag]
Sherlag, Steven, Law Office of ... 522 S.W. Fifth Ave., Ste. 800
Sherman, Ann L., (AV) ... '53 '88 C.339 B.F.A. L.1051 J.D. [Preston G.&E.]
Sherman, Paul F., Law Offices of ... '61 '88 C.560 B.A. L.770 J.D. 2125 S.W. 4th Ave.
Sherrett, Maryhelen ... '53 '88 C.1056 B.A. L.596 J.D. Marion-Polk Legal Aid Servs., Inc.
Sherris, Lawrence E., (BV) ... '49 '79 C.1056 B.S. L.1051 J.D. 3550 S.E. Hillside Dr.
Sherry, Leo C., Jr., (AV) ... '28 '65 C.670 B.A. L.596 LL.B. 2230 S.W. 77th Pl.
Shertz, Laurie ... '70 '95 C.911 B.A. L.988 J.D. [L.Shertz]

Shertz, Laurie, LLC
World Trade Center, 121 SW Salmon, 11th Floor, 97204
Telephone: 503-471-1332 Fax: 503-296-5669 URL: http://www.LShertzlaw.com
Email: Laurie@lshertzlaw.com URL: http://www.lawyers.com/lshertz
Laurie Shertz.

(This Listing Continued)

Shertz, Laurie, LLC (Continued)
Criminal Defense, Trial Practice, Felonies, Homicide and Assault, Self Defense, Weapons Charges, Sex Offenses, Drug Crimes, Theft and Fraud. Practice in Federal and State Courts.
See Professional Biographies, PORTLAND, OREGON

Sherwood, Ray D. .... '46 '73 C&L.950 B.A., J.D. 5254 N.E. 21st Ave.
Sherwood, Thomas A. .... '42 '66 C.1051 B.S. L.37 J.D. 888 Sw 5th Ave Ste 900
Shevach, Bernard, (BV) .... '20 '49 C.685 A.B. L.1066 LL.B. 2017 S.E. 24th Ave.
Shiely, Charmin B. .... '— '00 C.228 B.A. L.575 J.D. [Ⓐ Foster P.T.]
Shifrin, Gerald B., (AV) '29 '51 C.859 L.744 J.D.
(adm. in TX; not adm. in OR) 736 S.W. Burlingame Ter.‡
Shinn, Michael R., (AV) .... '47 '73 C&L.950 B.A., J.D. 621 Southwest Morrison
Shiroishi, G. Kenneth, (AV) '41 '74 C.112 B.S. L.1066 J.D.
1631 NE Broadway St. # 112
Shishido, Nolan M. .... '55 '85 C.1051 B.S. L.596 J.D. Dept. of Interior
Shively, J. Mack, (AV) '50 '80
C.906 B.A. L.596 J.D. Asst. Gen. Coun., Portland Gen. Corp.
Shlachter, Robert A., (AV) .... '47 '74 C.976 B.A. L.276 J.D. [Stoll S.B.L.&S.]
Shoemaker, John Robert '49 '83 C.347 B.S. L.1119 J.D.
(adm. in IN; not adm. in OR) Pres., Productivity, Inc.‡
Shorr, Scott A. .... '68 '96 C.881 A.B. L.112 J.D. [Stoll S.B.L.&S.]
Short, Lisa R. .... '53 '79 C.846 B.A. L.1067 J.D. 4110 Se Hawthorne Pmb 422
Shropshire, Steven L. .... '67 '94 C.174 B.A. L.1051 J.D. [Jordan S.]
Shulevitz, Mel '33 '58 C.475 B.A. L.262 LL.B.
(adm. in MI; not adm. in OR) P.O. Box 17555
Shyshlak, Dean M. .... '64 '90 C.1051 B.S. L.767 J.D. [D.M.Shyshlak]
Shyshlak, Dean M., P.C. .... 10490 S.W. Eastridge St., Ste. 110B
Sidman, John R. .... '30 '58 C.629 B.S. L.596 J.D. 1618 S.W. 1st Ave.‡
Siegel, Roberta A., (BV) .... '53 '81 C.685 B.A. L.596 J.D. [Siegel&S.]
Siegel, Sol, (AV) .... '14 '40 C.685 B.A. L.596 J.D. 1211 S.W. 5th Ave., 30th Fl
Siegel, Todd .... '69 '96 C.502 B.S. L.1439 J.D. [Ⓐ Klarquist S.]
Siegel & Sanders, P.C., (BV) .... 2303 E. Burnside
Silberman, Todd J. .... '50 '78 C.610 B.B.A. L.326 J.D. 2646 N.W. Cornell Rd.
Silliman, Amy .... '68 '96 C.813 B.A. L.309 J.D. [Ⓐ Miller N.]
Silver, Arnold B. .... '33 '58 C.1056 B.S. L.596 LL.B. 1515 S.W. 5th Ave.‡
Silver, Geoffrey S., (BV) .... '53 '83 C.221 B.A. L.596 J.D. 520 Sw Yamhill St Ste 330
Silver, Gregory F. .... '52 '93 C.645 B.A. L.665 J.D. 630 S.W. Fifth Ave.
Silver, Paul, (AV) .... '51 '78 C.27 B.A. L.950 J.D. [Lindsay,H.N.&W.]
Silverman, David .... '65 '01 C.976 B.A. L.813 J.D. [Ⓐ Stoel R.]
Silverman, Geoffrey B. .... '71 '00 C.734 B.S. L.616 J.D. 608 S.E. Tacoma Street
Silvey, Michael R., (AVⓉ) .... '45 '72 C.769 A.B. L.1065 J.D. [Foster P.T.]
Simko, Joshua K. .... '— '03 C.1239 B.A. L.228 J.D. [Ⓐ Tonkon T.]

Simmons, E. J., (AV) '47 '75 C.575 B.S.B.A. L.477 J.D.
621 SW Morrison, Suite 1300, 97205
Telephone: 503-221-2000 Fax: 971-223-4733
Email: ejs@ejsimmons.com URL: http://www.ejsimmons.com
Trial Practice, Personal Injury, Business Litigation, Technology Litigation, Intellectual Property Litigation.
See Professional Biographies, PORTLAND, OREGON

Simmons, Forrest W., (AV) .... '24 '52 C.628 B.S. L.477 J.D. P.O. Box 2400
Simon, David R., (AV) .... '56 '82 C.939 B.A. L.880 J.D. [Black H.]
Simon, Emily, (AV) .... '53 '79 C.299 B.A. L.1009 J.D. 26 NE 11th Avenue
Simon, Michael H., (AV) .... '56 '81 C.112 B.A. L.309 J.D. [Perkins C.]
Simon, Robert S. .... '64 '90 C.299 B.A. L.596 J.D. [R.Simon]
Simon, Robert, Law Firm .... P.O. Box 6059
Simpson, Edward L. "Ted" .... '68 '97 C.908 B.A. L.285 J.D. [Ⓐ Samuels Y.K.S.&S.]
Simpson, Ian Ronald .... '64 '01 C.1494 B.A. L.950 J.D. 2116 S.E. 28th Place
Simpson, James F., (AV) .... '36 '82 C.628 B.S. L.678 J.D. 3235 S.E. Ash St.‡
Simpson, Patrick J., (AV) .... '44 '71 C.112 A.B. L.1066 J.D. [Perkins C.]
Simpson, Robert G., (AV) .... '32 '59 C.629 B.S. L.950 LL.B. [Schwabe,W.&W.]
Simson, Leon, (AV) .... '46 '75 C.604 B.A. L.966 J.D. [Ball J.]
Sinclair, Amy Sousley .... '72 '00 C.947 B.A. L.862 J.D. MBL Grp., Inc.
Sinnott, Damien J. .... '71 '96 C.939 B.A. L.823 J.D. [Ⓐ Dunn C.A.H.&T.]
Sipprell, Ralph C. .... '35 '62 C.629 B.A. L.596 J.D. 9011 S. Beaverton Hillsdale Hwy.‡
Sitnick, Stanley A., (AV) .... '44 '69 C.276 A.B. L.145 J.D. 14819 N.W. McNamee
Skalak, William H., (BV) .... '50 '79 C.549 B.A. L.950 J.D. 6234 N. Greeley Ave.

Skarstad, Dennis W., (AV) '41 '68 C.906 B.A. L.629 J.D.
520 SW Sixth Avenue, Suite 820, 97204-1514
Telephone: 503-223-3334 FAX: 503-224-9875
Email: dws@skarstadlaw.com
Trial Practice including Personal Injury, Medical Malpractice, Products Liability, Professional Liability and Wrongful Death, Automobile Accidents, Unsafe Products, Legal Malpractice.
See Professional Biographies, PORTLAND, OREGON

Skerritt, Daniel H., (AV) .... '43 '68 C&L.950 B.A., J.D. [Tonkon T.]
Skillern, Beth, (AV) .... '44 '86 C.1071 B.A. L.596 J.D. [Bullivant H.B.]
Skopil, Otto R., Jr. .... '19 '46 C&L.950 B.A., J.D. U.S. Sr. App. Ct. J.‡
Slader, David L., Law Office of, (AV) '46 '71
C.339 B.S. L.597 J.D. 806 SW Broadway Ste 400
Slansky, David L. '49 '75 C.821 B.A. L.659 J.D.
Hearings Exam., State Liquor Control Comm.
Slater, Michelle, P.C. .... '69 '96 C.881 B.A. L.596 J.D. [Miller N.]
Slater, Stacey C. .... '61 '90 C.174 B.A. L.629 J.D. [Klarquist S.] (See Pat. Sect.)
Slezak, Ingrid E., (BVⓉ) '45 '81 C.309 A.B. L.93 J.D.
(adm. in CO; not adm. in OR) 1220 Sw Morrison St
Slinde, Nicholas J. .... '74 '00 C.352 B.A. L.629 J.D. [Ⓐ Grenley,R.E.B.&B.]
Sloane, Maureen R., P.C., (AV) .... '43 '84 C.473 B.S. L.596 J.D. 501 N. Dixon St.
Slominski, Michael J. .... '— '98 C.628 B.S.M.S. L.950 J.D. [M.J.Slominski]
Slominski, Michael J., P.C. .... 7150 S.W. Hampton St., Ste. 201
Slottee, Richard A. .... '47 '72 C&L.629 B.A., J.D. 310 S.W. 4th Ave., Ste. 1018

Sly, Richard A., (AV) '35 '63 C.629 B.B.A. L.950 J.D.
1001 S.W. Fifth Avenue, Suite 310, 97204
Telephone: 503-224-0436 Fax: 503-226-1227
Email: rsly@teleport.com
Social Security Disability, Workers Compensation (OR).
See Professional Biographies, PORTLAND, OREGON

Smith, Brice L. .... '20 '49 C.939 B.A. L.950 J.D. 1001 S. W. Fifth Ave.‡
Smith, Cara Johns .... '75 '01 L.950 J.D. [Ⓐ Bertoni&T.]
Smith, Charles T., (AV) .... '37 '65 C.628 B.S. L.596 J.D. [Mitchell,L.&S.]
Smith, Cynthia L. .... '61 '89 C.678 B.A. L.629 J.D. Law Clk., Cir. Ct.
Smith, D. Gordon '62 '91 C.101 B.S. L.145 J.D.
(adm. in DE; not adm. in OR) Asst. Prof., Northwestern Sch. of Law
Smith, Dean Arthur .... '58 '92 C.999 B.A. L.1051 J.D. Metro. Pub. Def., Pub. Defs. Off.
Smith, Deborah C. .... '66 '93 C.855 B.A. L.184 J.D. [Ⓐ Bertoni&T.]
Smith, Eric A. .... '— '99 C&L.629 B.A., J.D. [Ⓐ Dunn C.A.H.&T.]

Smith, Francis I., (BV) .... '13 '35 L.596 LL.B. 3236 S.W. Kelly Ave.
Smith, Frederick T., (BV) .... '36 '65 C.446 A.B. L.276 LL.B. 1437 S.W. Columbia
Smith, Helen T., (AV) .... '47 '77 C.610 B.S.Ed. L.161 J.D. Chf. Dep. Dist. Atty.
Smith, James Stuart .... '— '84 C.1056 B.A. L.800 J.D. [Davis W.T.]
Smith, Joshua W. .... '69 '05 C.1070 B.S. L.1051 J.D. [Ⓐ Stoel R.]
Smith, Lester V., Jr., (AV) .... '40 '65 C.228 A.B. L.575 J.D. [Bullard S.J.W.]
Smith, Levi J., (AV) .... '38 '67 C.628 B.S. L.1066 J.D. [L.J.Smith]
Smith, M. Robert F., (AV) .... '49 '75 C&L.629 B.S., J.D. [Smith F.&E.]
Smith, Molly K., (BV) .... '57 '84 C.999 B.S.N. L.629 J.D. [Smith&S.]
Smith, Monica A., (AV) .... '51 '82 C.145 B.A. L.596 J.D. [Smith,G.D.&O.]
Smith, Nancy A. .... '57 '84 C.1056 B.A. L.596 J.D. 2121 S.W. Broadway
Smith, Nyle B., Law Office of .... '57 '93 C.101 B.A. L.1051 J.D. 8410 S.W. 37th Ave.
Smith, Philip .... '62 '96 C.838 B.S.C. L.575 J.D. 208 SW 1st Ave., Ste. 260
Smith, R. P. (Joe), (BV) .... '35 '66 C&L.273 B.A., J.D. 2211 N.E. 21st
Smith, Robert B., (AV) .... '44 '70 C.629 B.A. L.950 J.D. [Smith&D.]
Smith, Steven Allen, (BV) .... '43 '74 C.629 B.A. L.596 J.D. [S.A.Smith]
Smith, Steven Charles '49 '78
C.1077 B.A. L.809 J.D. 10260 S.W. Greenburg Rd., Ste. 400
Smith, Steven H., (BV) .... '47 '73 C&L.629 B.A., J.D. [Smith&M.]
Smith, Thomas S. .... '— '78 C.1375 B.A. L.1065 J.D. [Ⓒ Davis W.T.]
Smith, Timothy D. .... '64 '91 C.602 B.A. L.309 J.D. [Ⓒ Garvey S.B.]
Smith, Vicki L., (AV) .... '— '85 C.629 B.A. L.30 J.D. [Lane P.]
Smith, Vicki M. .... '75 '01 C.908 B.A. L.950 J.D. [Ⓐ Bodyfelt M.S.&C.]
Smith & Davis, (AV) .... 610 S.W. Broadway, Ste. 310
Smith Freed & Eberhard, PC, (AV) .... 1001 S.W. Fifth Ave., Ste. 1700
Smith, Gamson, Diamond & Olney, (AV) .... 1500 N.E. Irving Street, Ste. 370
Smith, Levi J., P.C., (AV) .... 1001 S.W. 5th Ave.
Smith & McDonald, LLP, (AV) .... 1100 S.W. 6th Ave.
Smith & Smith, P.C., (BV) .... 1001 S.W Fifth Ave., Ste. 1100
Smith, Steven Allen, P.C., (BV) .... 5745 N.E. Glisan St.
Smith-Hill, John, (AV) .... '45 '79 C.999 B.S. L.262 J.D. [Smith-Hill&B.] (Pat.)
Smith-Hill & Bedell, (AV) .... 12670 N.W. Barnes Rd. (Pat.)
Smitke, Raymond T. .... '53 '79 C.773 B.A. L.1051 J.D. Liberty NW Ins. Corp.
Smolak, Mark E., (AV) .... '52 '79 C.1044 B.A. L.1051 J.D. [M.Smolak]
Smolak, Mark, (AV) .... 806 S.W. Broadway, Ste. 1200
Smucker, Steven R., (AV) .... '54 '81 C.685 B.A. L.629 J.D. [S.Smucker]
Smucker, Steve, (AV) .... 806 SW Broadway, Suite 1200
Smythe, Seth L. .... '75 '00 C.950 B.A. L.893 J.D. [Ⓐ Stoel R.]
Snarskis, John E., (AV) '49 '80
C.350 B.S. L.1051 J.D. Mng. Atty., Industrial Indemnity Co.
Snider, Timothy W. .... '76 '03 C.938 B.A. L.950 J.D. [Ⓐ Stoel R.]
Snook, Gregory B., (BV) .... '50 '77 C.1056 B.S. L.309 J.D. [Kilmer,V.&L.]
Snow, Nancy J., (AV) .... '22 '69 C.604 Mus.B. L.596 J.D. Legal Aid Serv.

Snyder, Daniel, Law Offices of, (BV) '52 '78 C.920 B.A. L.602 J.D.
1000 S.W. Broadway Suite 2400, 97205
Telephone: 503-241-3617 FAX: 503-241-2249
Email: dansnyder@qwest.net URL: http://www.lawyers.com/snyderlaw
Civil Litigation in State and Federal Courts, Civil Rights, Personal Injury, Automobile Accidents, Legal Malpractice, Sexual Abuse, Wrongful Death, Employment, Disability Accommodation, Discrimination, Employee Benefits, Sexual Harassment, Workers Compensation, Wrongful Termination, Labor and Employment, Insurance.
See Professional Biographies, PORTLAND, OREGON

Snyder, Joan P., (AV) .... '56 '84 C.205 B.S. L.477 J.D. [Stoel R.]
Snyder, Judy Danelle, (AV) '48 '73
C.920 B.A. L.602 J.D. 1000 S.W. Broadway, Ste. 1500
Snyder, Kent V. .... '52 '78 C.375 B.S. L.1051 J.D. [Snyder&Assoc.]
Snyder, Robin .... '71 '99 C.797 B.A. L.596 J.D. Dist. Atty's. Off.
Snyder & Associates .... 424 N.W. 19th Ave.
Sobkowski, Mary H. .... '53 '78 C&L.477 B.G.S., J.D. Multnomah Co. Legal Aid Serv.
Sogge, Eric, (BV) .... '43 '72 C.309 A.B. L.629 J.D. [Kell,A.&R.]
Sokol, Jan D., (AV) .... '52 '78 C.705 B.S. L.596 J.D. [Stewart S.&G.]
Sokol, Larry Nides, (AV) .... '46 '72 C.659 B.A. L.930 J.D. [Sokol&A.]
Sokol & Anuta, P.C., (AV) .... 735 S.W. First Avenue
Sola, Robert S., (AV) .... '53 '84 C.966 B.A. L.629 J.D. 8835 S.W. Canyon Ln., Ste. 130
Solodky, Brian .... '72 '97 C.656 B.S. L.596 J.D. [Ⓐ Radler,B.R.&M.]
Solomon, Andrew H. .... '68 '01 C.95 B.A. L.596 J.D. [Ⓐ Perkins C.]
Soltero, Nona M. .... '55 '82 C.112 B.S. L.596 J.D. Fred Meyer, Inc.
Somers, Holly J. .... '68 '97 C.1056 B.S. L.596 J.D. 3309 S.W. Arnold Heights Ter.
Somers, Jocelyn B., (BV) .... '55 '84 C.216 B.A. L.629 J.D. Gen. Coun. Off., USDA
Somervell, Katherine S. .... '63 '95 C.112 B.A. L.596 J.D. [Bullivant H.B.]
Sommers, Michael S., (BV) .... '48 '73 C.950 B.A. L.629 J.D. 610 SW Broadway Ste. 510
Sondag, Thomas W., (AV) .... '— '84 C.112 A.B. L.1066 J.D. [Lane P.]
Sonderen, John W. .... '23 '54 C.502 L.629 5300 N.E. Cully # 26‡
Soofi, Neda D. .... '63 '98 C.1461 B.S. L.1051 J.D. [Ⓐ Schwabe,W.&W.]
Sordyl, Kimberly A. .... '69 '99 C.477 B.A. L.215 J.D. [Ⓐ Barran L.]
Sorensen-Jolink, Scott, (AV) '50 '77 C.427 B.A. L.596 J.D.
[Sorensen-Jolink,T.W.M.&W.]
Sorensen-Jolink, Trubo, Williams, McIlhenny & Williams, (AV) .... 1020 S.W. Taylor
Soriano, Gregory B., (AV) .... '47 '73 C.911 B.A. L.596 J.D. [Soriano&Assoc.]
Soriano and Associates, (AV) .... 9900 S.W. Wilshire St., Ste. 100
Soublet, Erika E. .... '— '98 C.285 B.A. L.596 J.D. 1021 S.W. 4th Ave.
Soule, Jeffrey A. .... '56 '86 C.347 A.B. L.93 J.D. 2807 NE Hoyt Street
Souther, John B. .... '32 '59 C.813 A.B. L.477 LL.B. Souther Co.
Southwell, Wm. G., (AV) .... '30 '58 C.629 B.B.A. L.950 J.D. 2400 S.W. Fourth Ave.
Sowle, Agnes, (AV) .... '48 '82 C&L.336 B.A., J.D. Co. Atty.
Spajic, Robert .... '64 '93 C.768 B.A. L.285 J.D. [Ⓐ Gordon&P.]
Sparkman, Joseph B., (AV) .... '19 '47 C.691 B.S. L.273 J.D. 121 S.W. Salmon St.‡
Sparks, Charles H., (AV) .... '56 '85 C&L.629 B.S., J.D. Dep. Dist. Atty., Dist. Atty. Off.
Spears, Frank H., (AV) .... '— '39 C.629 B.S. L.309 LL.B. [Lane P.]
Speck, Connie L., (BV) .... '63 '96 C&L.629 B.S., J.D. [Ⓐ Farleigh W.]
Spector, Marshal P., (AV) .... '60 '86 C.446 B.A. L.64 J.D. [Gevurtz,M.L.&H.]
Speight, Richard, Law Offices of .... '44 '74 C.1071 B.S. L.596 J.D. 2416 S.W. 5th Ave.
Speirs, Marjorie Anne .... '49 '78 C.1174 B.A. L.1051 J.D. 1000 SW Broadway‡
Spence, Martha W. '49 '86
C.922 B.A. L.1051 J.D. Assoc. Dean, Northwestern Sch. of Law
Spencer, Clarinda S. .... '53 '82 C.413 B.A. L.629 J.D. Metropolitan Pub. Def.
Spencer, Cliff E. .... '— '95 C.506 B.S. L.950 J.D. [Ⓐ Foster P.T.]
Spencer, George C., (AV) .... '— '66 C&L.629 B.S., LL.B. [Tonkon T.]
Spencer, Jesse Neal .... '53 '81 C.1056 B.A. L.678 J.D. [Bernardi&S.]
Spere, Jeffrey R., (AV) .... '50 '75 C.1058 B.B.A. L.950 J.D. [Sussman S.]
Spere, Kathryn McFerron, (AV) .... '51 '80 C&L.678 B.A., J.D. Bank of the Northwest
Spetter, Ruth M., (AV) .... '50 '77 C.1349 B.A. L.596 J.D. Sr. Dep. City Atty.
Spiegel, David M. .... '16 '39 L.596 J.D. 4010 S.W. Westdale Dr.‡
Spier, Richard G., (AV) .... '48 '76 C.813 B.A. L.188 J.D. 2536 N.E. 28th Ave.

Spiers, William A. '53 '86 C.136 B.S. L.1209 J.D.
(adm. in MI; not adm. in OR) 222 S.E. 16th Ave.‡
Spigal, Harvard P. .... '45 '70 C&L.911 B.A., J.D. [Preston G.&E.]
Spinrad, Alan M., (AV) .... '50 '78 C.119 B.S. L.629 J.D. [Samuels Y.K.S.&S.]
Sponsler, Thomas, (AV) .... '44 '68 C&L.950 B.S., J.D. Co. Coun.

Spooner, Much & Ammann, P.C.
(See Salem)

Springer, Richard S., (BV) .... '48 '77 C.674 A.B. L.629 J.D. P.O. Box 9158
Squier, Anne W. .... '38 '84 C.685 B.A. L.596 J.D. 13402 N.W. Marina Way
Squires, Wendy Jo, (BV) .... '54 '79 C.1331 B.A. L.950 J.D. [Squires&L.]
Squires & Lopez, P.C., (AV) ....621 S.W. Morrison Street, Suite 1250
Stacey, Robert E., Jr., (AV) '49 '75
C.685 B.A. L.629 J.D. Executive Dir. Policy and Planning, Tri-Met
Stadum, Steven D., (AV) '55 '81 C.1051 B.S. L.596 J.D.
Gen. Coun., Oregon Health Sciences University
Stafford, Lynn R., (AV) .... '49 '80 C.112 B.A. L.1209 J.D. [Markowitz,H.G.&M.]
Stafford, Robert P., (BV) .....'48 '80 C.999 B.A. L.1209 J.D. 5870 S.W. Terwilliger Blvd.
Stahancyk, Jody L., (AV) .... '48 '73 C.413 B.A. L.629 J.D. [Stahancyk,K.J.&H.]

Stahancyk, Kent, Johnson & Hook P.C., (AV) BB
Athena Plaza, 808 S.W. 15th Avenue, 97205-1907 ⊙
Telephone: 503-222-9115 Fax: 503-222-4037
Email: info@stahancyk.com URL: http://www.oregondivorce.com
Jody L. Stahancyk; Joel J. Kent (Resident, Bend Office); Ronald M. Johnson (Resident, Bend Office); Laurel P. Hook;—Teresa L. Foster; Gordon E. Phillips (Resident Bend Office); Grace Y. Lee; Kristin M. Larson (Resident Bend Office); Catherine E. Barker; Jeffrey M. Greenspan; Trisha J. English; Shantel P. Bray (Not admitted in OR); Jordan A. Carter.
Adoptions, Child Custody, Child Support, Divorce, Domestic Violence, Visitation Rights, Wills and Probate, Trusts and Estates, Asset Protection, Guardianship, Family Law, Estate Planning.
Bend, Oregon Office: 225 NW Franklin Ave., Suite 3, 97701. Telephone: 541-318-9115. Fax: 541-318-9116.
Astoria, Oregon Office: 552 Commercial Street, 97103. Telephone: 503-325-9117.
Prineville, Oregon Office: 105 SW Beaver Street, 97754. Telephone: 541-416-9312.
Vancouver, Washington Office: 411 West 11th Street, 98660. Telephone: 360-750-9115.
See Professional Biographies, PORTLAND, OREGON

Stalnaker, Thurl, Jr. .... '51 '77 C.823 B.A. L.184 J.D. [T.Stalnaker,Jr.]
Stalnaker, Thurl, Jr., P.C. ....405 N.W. 18th Ave.
Stampfer, Noam, (BV) .... '51 '78 C.178 B.A. L.569 J.D. 7135 S.W. 34th Ave.
Stanford, Brad C., (AV) ....'59 '85 C.629 B.S. L.911 J.D. [Farleigh W.]
Stanke, Samuel T. .... '74 '03 C.966 B.A. L.1051 J.D. [S.T.Stanke]

Stanke, Samuel T., Attorney at Law, LLC
1400 SW Montgomery Street, 97201
Telephone: 503-224-1127 Fax: 503-228-4454
Email: sstatty@qwest.net URL: http://www.lawyers.com/samueltstankelaw
Samuel T. Stanke.
See Professional Biographies, PORTLAND, OREGON

Stanton, David R. .... '49 '85 C.670 B.A. L.596 J.D. Sgt./Criminalist
Staples, J. Peter, (AV) '47 '79 C.870 B.S. L.596 J.D.
[Chernoff,V.M.&S.] (See Pat. Sect.)
Stark, Donald R., (AV) .... '28 '54 C&L.629 B.S., J.D. [Ⓒ Bullivant H.B.]
Stark, Gary R. .... '40 '65 C&L.629 B.S., LL.B. U.S. Dept. of Int.
Stark, Justin W. .... '64 '97 C.1051 B.A. L.508 J.D. [Stark]
Stark Law Office LLC ....1826 NE Broadway
Starkey, Charles P., (AV) .... '49 '75 C.178 B.A. L.1065 J.D. [Ⓒ Holland&K.]
Staropoli, Michael W., (AV) '58 '83 C.628 B.S. L.596 J.D.
1211 SW 5th Ave., Ste. 1460
Starr, Renee E. ....'68 '04 C.629 B.A. L.950 J.D. [Ⓐ Stoel R.]
Starrs, Thomas J. '62 '88 C.112 B.A. L.1066 J.D.
(adm. in WA; not adm. in OR) 4535 S.W. 60th Pl.

Statler, Teresa A. '56 '91 C.945 A.B. L.596 J.D.
The Yeon Building, 522 Southwest 5th Avenue, Suite 812, 97204
Telephone: 503-220-4185 Fax: 503-281-2624
Email: tstatler@easystreet.com URL: http://www.lawyers.com/statlerlaw
Languages: French, Spanish and Italian.
Emphasizing Deportation Defense, Family Immigration Law, Naturalization and Asylum, Citizenship, Visas, Green Cards.
See Professional Biographies, PORTLAND, OREGON

Stayer, Mark A., (AV) .... '54 '85 C.960 B.B.A. L.950 J.D. [Schwabe,W.&W.]
Stearns, Douglas H. .... '29 '58 C.950 B.A. L.178 J.D. 333 S.W. 5th Ave.‡
Stedman, Randy M. '54 '89 C.1073 B.A. L.880 J.D.
V.P., Human Res. & Legal Affs., Copeland Lumber Yards, Inc.
Steele, Nathan G. .... '72 '00 C&L.629 B.A., J.D. Staff Atty., Amer. Fam. Ins.
Steen, Jason A. .... '67 '93 C.610 B.A. L.678 J.D. [Raivio,K.&S.]
Steen, John C. "Pete" .... '41 '87 C.629 Ph.D. L.1051 J.D. Shared Communications
Steen, Ryan P. .... '— '03 C.911 B.S. L.596 J.D. [Ⓐ Schwabe,W.&W.]
Steenson, Tom, (AV) .... '48 '74 C.911 B.A. L.596 J.D. [Steenson,S.T.L.&R.]
Steenson, Schumann, Tewksbury, Later & Rose, P.C., (AV) .... 815 S.W. 2nd
Steffen, Jeffrey C. '48 '73 C.1056 B.S. L.596 J.D.
Div. Coun., Transnation Title Ins. Co.
Steiger, John W. '56 '91 C.37 B.S. L.878 J.D.
(adm. in UT; not adm. in OR) Dept. of Interior
Steinberg, Daniel L. ....'71 '99 C.1056 B.S. L.629 J.D. [Ⓐ Greene&M.]
Steinman, Dennis, (BV) ....'55 '95 C.831 B.A. L.596 J.D. [Kell,A.&R.]
Stendahl, Pamela J. .... '61 '89 C.112 B.A. L.596 J.D. [Kilmer,V.&L.]
Stenzel, Dennis E., (AV) '42 '72
C.101 B.S. L.273 J.D. [Chernoff,V.M.&S.] (See Pat. Sect.)
Stephens, C. Sean .... '69 '94 C.629 B.S. L.950 J.D. [C.S.Stephens]
Stephens, Donald L., Jr. ... '49 '90 C.1109 B.S. L.596 J.D. [Klarquist S.] (See Pat. Sect.)
Stephens, Elizabeth M. .... '47 '79 C.024 B.A. L.025 LL.B. 620 Sw Main St Ste 706
Stephens, John W., (AV) .... '52 '77 C.813 A.B. L.1068 J.D. [Esler,S.&B.]
Stephens, Kenneth D., (AV) .... '42 '67 C&L.629 B.S., J.D. [Tonkon T.]

Stephens, C. Sean, P.C.
1211 SW 5th Avenue, Suite 2350, 97204
Telephone: 503-546-6374; Toll Free: 866-336-9346 Fax: 503-546-6376 URL: http://www.lawyers.com/stephensfamilylaw
Email: info@stephensfamilylaw.com URL: http://www.stephensfamilylaw.com
C. Sean Stephens.
Family Law, Divorce, Child Custody, Paternity, Child Support, Modification of Custody and Child Support, Visitation Rights, Premarital Agreements.
See Professional Biographies, PORTLAND, OREGON

Stephenson, Ronald G., (AV) .... '42 '67 C.1051 B.S. L.950 J.D. [Bullivant H.B.]
Stephenson-Kuhn, Leigh D., (AV) .... '— '62 C.976 A.B. L.178 LL.B. [Lane P.]
Steringer, C. Robert .... '69 '98 C&L.629 B.A., B.A. [Ⓐ Harrang L.G.R.]
Sterling, Kristin H. .... '75 '00 C.37 B.A. L.596 J.D. [Ⓐ Stoel R.]
Stermitz, Mark L., (BVⓉ) .... '53 '83 C&L.508 B.A., J.D. [Ⓒ Bullivant H.B.]
Stern, Denise L., (BV) .... '57 '86 C.1044 B.A. L.285 J.D. 7430 S.E. Milwaukie Ave.
Stern, Margaret B. .... '65 '93 C&L.276 B.S., J.D. [Cable H.B.H.&L.]
Stevason, John C., (AV) .... '— '74 C.674 A.B. L.569 J.D. [Lane P.]
Stevens, Julie A. ....'49 '73 C.629 B.S. L.178 J.D. Multnomah Co. Legal Aid Serv.
Stevens, Randolph J. ....'50 '81 C&L.629 B.A., J.D. 2918 N. Lombard
Steverson-Wright, Janet W. '61 '87 C.1044 B.A. L.309 J.D.
(adm. in NY; not adm. in OR) Asst. Prof., Northwestern Sch. of Law
Stewart, James G. .... '51 '84 C.1165 B.S. L.678 J.D. [Idea A.] (Pat.)
Stewart, Janice M. .... '51 '75 C.813 A.B. L.145 J.D. U.S. Mag. J.
Stewart, John Spencer, (AV) .... '46 '71 C.905 B.S. L.950 J.D. [Stewart S.&G.]
Stewart, Milton R., (AV) .... '— '71 C.347 A.B. L.1119 J.D. [Davis W.T.]

Stewart Sokol & Gray, LLC, (AV) BB
2300 SW First Avenue, Suite 200, 97201
Telephone: 503-221-0699 Facsimile: 503-223-5706 URL: http://www.wwwlawssg.com
URL: http://www.lawssg.com
Members of Firm: John Spencer Stewart; Jan D. Sokol; Arnold L. Gray; Susan Z. Whitney; H. Lee Cook; Jeffrey B. Wilkinson; Thomas A. Larkin. Associates: Angela M. Otto; Matthew A. Wand; Robert B. Coleman; Lawrence A. Wagner; Tyler J. Storti; Neil N. Olsen; E. Susan O'Toole (Not admitted in OR).
General Civil and Trial Practice. Construction, Bankruptcy, Corporation, Insurance, Fidelity and Surety and Real Estate Law.
See Professional Biographies, PORTLAND, OREGON

Stibolt, Victor D., (AV) .... '51 '76 C.197 A.B. L.678 J.D. Gen. Coun., Jubitz Corp.
Stiles, Rebekah L. .... '77 '03 C.910 A.B. L.1051 J.D. [Ⓐ Brownstein,R.S.K.G.D.&H.]
Stiles, William N., (AV) .... '38 '64 C&L.976 B.A., LL.B. [Sussman S.]
Stilley, Thomas W., (AV) .... '54 '88 C.846 B.B.A. L.326 J.D. [Sussman S.]
Stinchfield, Kyle J. .... '75 '02 C.678 B.A. L.629 J.D. [Ⓐ Dunn C.A.H.&T.]
Stineman, Renee R. .... '68 '94 C.1060 B.A. L.464 J.D. [Dunn C.A.H.&T.]
Stiner, Alonzo P., (BV) .... '34 '60 C&L.629 B.S., J.D. 2630 S,.W. Chelmsford
Stoel, Caroline P. .... '14 '37 C&L.228 A.B., J.D. Prof. of Law, Portland State Univ.
Stoel, Thomas B., (AV) .... '13 '37 C.319 A.B. L.228 LL.B. [Stoel R.] ‡

Stoel Rives LLP, (AV) BB
900 S.W. Fifth Avenue Suite 2600, 97204-1268 ⊙
Telephone: 503-224-3380 Facsimile: 503-220-2480 Cable Address: "Lawport"
URL: http://www.stoel.com
Members of Firm: Steven W. Abel; Charles F. Adams; Richard E. Alexander; Courtney W. Angeli; David H. Angeli; Paul S. Angello; Gary R. Barnum; Todd A. Bauman; Ruth A. Beyer; Alan R. Blank; Patrick G. Boylston; Barbara A. Brainard; Jason M. Brauser; Paul C. Buchanan; Michael Roame Campbell; Phillip D. Chadsey; Stuart Chestler; William L. Clydesdale; Joseph D. Cohen; D. Jeffrey Courser; Nancy L. Cowgill; Barbara D. Craig; Andrew I. Davis; E. Joseph Dean; Edward D. Einowski; Barnes H. Ellis; Edward L. Epstein; Mark R. Feichtinger; James F. Fell; Louis A. Ferreira, IV; Howard M. Feuerstein; David E. Filippi; Jerry R. Fish; Randolph C. Foster; Richard A. Franzke; Eugene A. Frassetto; George M. Galloway; Andrew R. Gardner; Richard S. Gleason; Gary W. Glisson; Gersham Goldstein; Eric A. Grasberger; David W. Green; Stephen L. Griffith; Ronald S. Grossmann; Stephen C. Hall; John J. Halle; Christopher R. Hermann; Christopher K. Heuer; Henry H. Hewitt; Charles F. Hinkle; William H. Holmes; Steven H. Hull; Pamela L. Jacklin; Richard C. Josephson; Scott J. Kaplan; Emily V. Karr; Chris Kitchel; Christine A. Kosydar; Jeffrey M. Krueger; Margaret Baumgardner Kushner; Dennis Leybold; Steven T. Lovett; Gregory H. Macpherson; Robert T. Manicke; Katherine A. McDowell; Timothy L. McMahan; David P. Miller, II; Steven A. Moore; Robert J. Moorman; J. Mark Morford; Peter D. Mostow; Gregory Robert Mowe; Joel A. Mullin; Barbara L. Nay; Thomas R. Nicolai; Mark A. Norby; Margaret Hill Noto; Brendan N. O'Scannlain; Thomas R. Page; Terrence R. Pancoast; John A. Rafter, Jr.; Per A. Ramfjord; Guy A. Randles; Stephen A. Redshaw; Edward J. Reeves; Lois Omenn Rosenbaum; Jeremy D. Sacks; Penny H. Serrurier; Peter L. Serrurier; Joan P. Snyder; Micah D. Stolowitz; John R. Thomas; Robert H. Thomson; Robert D. Van Brocklin; James M. Van Nostrand; E. Walter Van Valkenburg; Stephen S. Walters; Jere M. Webb; James N. Westwood, P.C.; Marcus Wood; Thomas R. Wood; James A. Zehren. Of Counsel: Karen E. Jones; Dan Grinfas; Steven E. Klein; Kelly Knivila; James C. Paine. Retired Members: George H. Fraser; William M. McAllister; Charles J. McMurchie; Thomas B. Stoel. Associates: Sarah Adams Lien; Bethany A. Bacci; Kurt Eric Barker; Edward A. Bernhard; Jennie L. Bricker; Donato C. Capobianco; Chad R. Chambers; Kenneth P. Childs; Greg D. Corbin; Jason A. Dalton; Brad Daniels; Saskia de Boer; Kathleen J. Doll; Amy Edwards; Kassim M. Ferris; Kevin T. Fox; Sean C. Gay; Rene G. Gonzalez; Michael B. Hallinan; Mary P. Hull; Matthew J. Kalmanson; James M. Kearney; Scott F. Kocher; Paul Sandberg Logan; Kimberly Anne Medford; Ian G. Merrill; John C. Motley; Samuel J. Panarella; Beverly C. Pearman; Kevin T. Pearson; Matthew C. Phillips; William R. Pierznik; Scott M. Rickard; Katherine K. Rosenbaum; Michelle Rudd; Brandy A. Sargent; Jeanette C. Schuster; Christian H. Scott; Shana W. Sechrist; David Silverman; Joshua W. Smith; Seth L. Smythe; Timothy W. Snider; Renee E. Starr; Kristin H. Sterling; Ellen Theodorson; Paul M. Tiger; Jennifer K.T. Warner; Kyle D. Wuepper.
General Corporate Counsel and Litigation. Antitrust and Trade Regulation, Bankruptcy, Construction and Design, Corporate Finance and Securities, Employee Benefits, Energy, Environmental, Estates and Trusts, Financial Institutions, Healthcare, Intellectual Property, International Trade and Transactions, Labor and Employment, Mergers and Acquisitions, Natural Resources, Real Estate and Land Use, Reorganizations and Workouts, Taxation, Technology, White Collar Criminal Law.
Counsel for: Columbia Sportswear Company; PacifiCorp; Precision Castparts Corp.; Tektronix, Inc.; Electro Scientific Industries; Northwest Natural Gas Company; Oregon Steel Mills, Inc.; NIKE, Inc.
Seattle, Washington Office: Suite 3600, One Union Square, 600 University. Telephone: 206-624-0900.
Vancouver, Washington Office: Suite 725, 805 Broadway. Telephone: 360-699-5900.
Boise, Idaho Office: Suite 1900, 101 S. Capitol Boulevard. Telephone: 208-389-9000.
Salt Lake City, Utah Office: Suite 1100, One Utah Center, 201 South Main Street. Telephone: 801-328-3131.
San Francisco, California Office: 111 Sutter Street, Suite 700. Telephone: 415-617-8900.
Sacramento, California Office: 770 L Street, Suite 800. Telephone: 916-447-0700.
Tahoe City, California Office: 3000 N. Lake Boulevard, Suite 1, P.O. Box 7336. Telephone: 530-583-2116.
Fresno, California Office: 1233 W. Shaw Avenue, Suite 103. Telephone: 559-228-9900.
See Professional Biographies, PORTLAND, OREGON

Stokes, Chad M. .... '71 '00 C.769 B.A. L.1051 J.D. [Ⓐ Cable H.B.H.&L.]
Stokes, Stacy M. .... '71 '00 L.596 J.D. 630 Sw 5th Ave Ste 500
Stoll, N. Robert, (AV) .... '42 '69 C.966 B.S. L.309 LL.B. [Stoll S.B.L.&S.]

Stoll Stoll Berne Lokting & Shlachter, P.C., (AV)
209 S.W. Oak Street, 5th Floor, 97204
Telephone: 503-227-1600 Telecopier: 503-227-6840
URL: http://www.ssbls.com
Gary M. Berne; Keith A. Ketterling; Steve D. Larson; David A. Lokting; Robert A. Shlachter; N. Robert Stoll; Timothy DeJong; David F. Rees; Scott A. Shorr;—Sandra L. Kohn; Christina L. Beatty-Walters; Mark A. Friel; Susanna Henke; Jennifer A. Wagner; Emily Courtnage; Jacob S. Gill; Joshua L. Ross. Of Counsel: Steven C. Berman.
Major Business Litigation, including Securities, Antitrust, Intellectual Property and Unfair Competition in Federal and State Courts. Real Estate, Corporation, Environmental, Estate Planning, and Taxation Law.
See Professional Biographies, PORTLAND, OREGON

Stoloff, Alfred H., (AV) .... '21 '49 C.659 B.A. L.976 LL.B. Chinook Capital Corp.‡
Stoloff, Peter F., (AV) .... '51 '78 C.813 A.B. L.629 J.D. [P.F.Stoloff]

Stoloff, Peter F., P.C., (AV)
Bank of America Financial Center, Suite 600, 121 S.W. Morrison Street, 97204
Telephone: 503-224-4664 Fax: 503-224-3673
Email: pstoloff@aol.com URL: http://www.lawyers.com/stoloff
Peter F. Stoloff.
Business Law, Health Care Law, Buying and Selling Businesses, Securities and Investments, Creditors Rights, Employee Benefits, Employment Contracts, Business Planning, Contracts, Antitrust, Insurance, Commercial Leasing, Real Estate, Business Start-Ups, Joint Ventures, Mergers, Tax Planning.
See Professional Biographies, PORTLAND, OREGON

Stolowitz, Micah D., (AV) '54 '81 C.112 B.S.E.E. L.596 J.D. [Stoel R.] (See Pat. Sect.)
Stolzberg, Karen Gale ....'49 '82 C.1294 B.S. L.596 J.D. 4370 N.E. Halsey Street
Stone, Gena A. ....'— '02 C.897 B.A. L.950 J.D. [🄰 Miller N.]
Stone, John S., (AV) ....'49 '75 C.629 B.S. L.950 J.D. 1500 S.W. First Ave., Ste. 770
Stone, Richard J., (AVⓉ) ....'45 '71 C.145 B.A. L.1068 J.D. [🄲 Ball J.]
Stone, Robt. S. ....'24 '55 C&L.950 LL.B. 790 S.E. Webber‡
Storch, Tyson Ernst ....'66 '94 C.628 B.A. L.596 J.D. 1717 N.W. 21st Ave.
Storey, Christopher B. ....'— '00 C.950 B.S. L.569 J.D. [🄰 Lane P.]
Storti, Tyler J. ....'77 '03 C.861 B.A. L.629 J.D. [🄰 Stewart S.&G.]
Stout, Richard Alan ....'48 '77 C.1056 B.S. L.596 J.D. 1500 S.W. 1st Ave.
Stout, Robert A., (AV) ....'46 '74 C.475 B.A. L.976 J.D. [🄲 Ball J.] (ⓒBend)
Strader, Charles J., (BV) ......'28 '60 C.629 B.S. L.596 LL.B. 4386 S.W. Macadam Ave.
Strader, Timothy R., (AV) ....'56 '81 C.602 B.B.A. L.950 J.D. [Hanna S.]
Strange, Cecil B., III ....'51 '89 C.976 B.A. L.629 J.D. 222 S.W .Columbia
Strasser, Robert J. ....'47 '72 C.950 B.A. L.1066 J.D. 1500 S.W. 5th Ave.‡
Stratton, Karen E. ....'57 '82 C.373 B.A. L.477 J.D. I.R.S.
Streicher, David C., (AV) ....'57 '84 C.1056 B.S. L.629 J.D. [🄰 Black H.]
Streicker, Gail ....'56 '82 C&L.629 B.A., J.D. 3122 N.E. 40th Ave.‡
Streinz, James Ray, (AV) ....'55 '79 C.413 B.A. L.309 J.D. [McEwen G.]
Streisinger, Cory, (AV) ....'55 '80 C.188 A.B. L.813 J.D. 3279 N.E. Alameda
Stride, Jon P., (AV) ....'52 '90 C.1181 B.S. L.629 J.D. [Tonkon T.]
Strom, Trina J., (AV) ....'59 '87 C.30 B.A. L.1051 J.D. [Borg S.&G.]
Strommer, Geoffrey D. ....'62 '90 C.112 B.A. L.276 J.D. [Hobbs,S.D.&W.]
Struxness, Gregory E. ....'52 '83 C.628 B.S. L.950 J.D. [Ater W.]
Stuart, Diana I. ....'51 '77 C.222 B.A. L.950 J.D. [Goldberg,M.S.&G.]
Stuckey, Aaron K. ....'— '95 C.36 B.A. L.596 J.D. [🄰 Davis W.T.]
Stump, Joshua P. ....'72 '97 C.990 B.A. L.945 J.D. [🄰 Schwabe,W.&W.]
Stutsman, Eli D., (BV) ....'57 '92 C.628 B.S. L.596 J.D. [E.D.Stutsman]
Stutsman, Eli D., P.C., (BV) ....621 SW Morrison 13th Flr.
Su, Ann Y. ....'71 '96 C.893 B.A. L.273 J.D. 123 Ne 3rd Ste 310
Sugerman, David F., (AV) ....'59 '86 C.846 B.A. L.596 J.D. [Paul&S.]
Sullivan, Brian M., (BV) ....'51 '76 C&L.508 B.A., J.D. [Sullivan&T.]
Sullivan, Cornelius G. '16 '53 C.659 B.S. L.831 LL.B.
(adm. in PA; not adm. in OR) 0308 S.W. Montgomery St.‡
Sullivan, Cornelius G. '40 '66 C.659 B.A. L.846 J.D.
(adm. in TX; not adm. in OR) V.P. & Gen. Coun., Lasco Shipping Co.
Sullivan, Donal D. ....'31 '57 C.424 L.209 LL.B. 1001 S.W. 5th Avenue, Suite 900‡
Sullivan, Edward J., (AV) ....'45 '69 C.724 B.A. L.950 J.D. [Garvey S.B.]
Sullivan, Robert J., (BV) ....'56 '83 C.1056 B.S. L.950 J.D. [🄲 Mersereau&S.]
Sullivan, Timothy M. ....'71 '00 C.1030 B.A. L.596 J.D. [🄰 Schwabe,W.&W.]
Sullivan & Terranova, (BV) ....3526 S.W. Corbett Ave.
Sulmonetti, Alfred T. ....'14 '35 C&L.221 A.B., J.D. Sr. Cir. J.
Summers, Brad T. (Tony), (AV) ....'57 '83 C.602 B.A. L.1068 J.D. [Ball J.]
Summers, Brent G., (AV) ....'56 '82 C&L.629 B.S., J.D. [Tarlow N.&S.]
Summers, Lloyd R., (BV) ....'39 '67 C.897 B.A. L.174 J.D. [🄲 Kell,A.&R.]
Summers, Robert S. ....'33 '59 C.629 B.S. L.309 LL.B. [🄲 Tarlow N.&S.]
Summers, Steven P. ....'52 '77 C.628 B.S. L.1206 J.D. 8305 S. E. Monlerey Ave.
Sumner, Theodore F. ....'69 '00 C.869 B.S. L.596 J.D. [🄰 Abbott&P.]
Sundby, Herbert C., (AV) '45 '72 C.628 B.S. L.1051 J.D.
Asst. U.S. Atty., U.S. Atty. Off.
Supperstein, Scott M., (AV) ....'57 '84 C.170 B.A. L.1051 J.D. [S.M.Supperstein]
Supperstein, Scott M., P.C., Law Offices of, (AV) .... 620 SW 5th Avenue, Suite 1125
Susac, Karen L. Komlos '49 '80
C.339 B.A. L.365 J.D. Acct. Exec., Management Comp. Grp.
Susak, Frank J., (AV) ... '43 '70 C.988 B.A. L.1051 J.D. 2151 S W 4th Avenue, Suite 600
Susak, Gary J., (AV) ....'46 '72 C.988 B.A. L.1051 J.D. [Susak&P.]
Susak & Powell, P.C., (AV) ....2125 S.W. Fourth Avenue
Sussman, Gary Y., (AV) ....'55 '87 C.475 B.S. L.596 J.D. Asst. U.S. Atty.
Sussman, Marc, (AV) ....'50 '77 C.705 B.A. L.950 J.D. [M.Sussman]

Sussman, Marc, P.C., (AV)
1906 Southwest Madison Street, Suite 1B, 97205
Telephone: 503-221-0520; 1-866-230-1906 Fax: 503-221-1908
Email: sussmarc@qwest.net URL: http://www.marcsussmanlaw.com
Marc Sussman.
Criminal Defense in State & Federal Courts at Trial, Appellate, Post-Conviction and Habeas Corpus Levels, Capital Crimes, Homicides, White Collar, RICO, Sex Crimes, Drug Crimes and other Major Felonies, Parole and Probation.
See Professional Biographies, PORTLAND, OREGON

Sussman Shank, LLP, (AV)
1000 S.W. Broadway Suite 1400, 97205
Telephone: 503-227-1111 Telecopier: 503-248-0130
Email: info@sussmanshank.com URL: http://www.sussmanshank.com
Members of Firm: Gilbert Sussman (1905-1985); Jerome B. Shank (Retired); Norman Wapnick (Retired); Barry P. Caplan; William N. Stiles; Jeffrey R. Spere; Howard M. Levine; Stuart I. Teicher; Jeffrey C. Misley; John E. McCormick; Michael G. Halligan; Robert L. Carlton; Thomas W. Stilley; Nena Cook; George W. McKallip, Jr.; Susan S. Ford; Jason W. Alexander; Jeffrey S. Tarr; Darin D. Honn. Associates: Dallas G. Thomsen; Elizabeth A. Semler; Michael C. Wetzel; William G. Fig; Laurie R. Hager; Jeff C. Duncan Brecht; Heather A. Kmetz. Special Counsel: Robert W. Nunn; Martin P. Meyers; Michael D. Levelle; John A. Schwimmer; Harry M. Hanna.
Full Service Commercial Practice including: Business, Tax and Real Estate; Business Organization and Transactions; Litigation and Dispute Resolution in all Courts; Construction Law, Employment Law, Environmental Law, Toxic Torts, Creditors' Rights and Bankruptcy Reorganization; Business Succession Planning, Estate and Wealth Preservation Planning and Probate.
See Professional Biographies, PORTLAND, OREGON

Sutter, John A. ....'61 '87 C.309 B.A. L.494 J.D. AFT Locals 2277 & 3922
Swan, Ronald Edward '49 '74 C.347 B.A. L.893 J.D.
(adm. in VA; not adm. in OR) Asst. Reg. Solr., U.S. Dept. of Interior
Swanson, Judith Lynn ....'60 '92 C.37 B.S. L.1051 J.D. Juvenile Rights Project
Swanson, Les, Jr., (AV) ....'40 '66 C.57 B.A. L.629 J.D. 527 SW Hall Street

Swanson, Thomas & Coon, (AV)
Thomas Mann Building, 820 SW Second Avenue, Suite 200, 97204
Telephone: 503-228-5222 Fax: 503-273-9175
URL: http://www.stc-law.com
Members of Firm: Douglas A. Swanson (1953-2004); Raymond F. Thomas; James S. Coon. Associates: Megan E. Glor; Margaret F. Weddell; Sharon Maynard; Cynthia F. Newton; Ann T. Boylan.
Personal Injury and Products Liability (Vehicles machinery, construction accidents, bicycles, tobacco, asbestos), Medical Malpractice, Automobile Accidents, Wrongful Death, Employee Benefits, Workers' Compensation, (including Longshore), Social Security, Environmental Litigation, Public Sector Labor and Pensions, Long Term Disability (ERISA), Legal Malpractice, Class Actions, Trial and Appellate.
See Professional Biographies, PORTLAND, OREGON

Sweek, Walter H., (AV) ....'— '62 C&L.629 B.A., LL.B. [Cosgrave V.K.]
Sweeney, David J., (AV) ....'48 '75 C.178 A.B. L.596 J.D. [Brownstein,R.S.K.G.D.&H.]
Sweeney, Michael J. '49 '76 C.629 B.S. L.285 J.D.
Prog. Atty., Oregon State Bar Prof. Liability Fund
Sweeney, Miles, (AV) ....'41 '66 C.1056 L.596 J.D. [Brownstein,R.S.K.G.D.&H.]
Sweitzer, Graham M. ....'74 '02 C.911 B.A. L.1051 J.D. [🄰 Gilroy]
Swenson, Ingrid L., (AV) ....'44 '73 C.57 B.A. L.1065 J.D. Metro. Pub. Def.
Swider, Robert A., (AV) ....'53 '82 C.776 B.A. L.596 J.D. 621 S.W. Morrison Street
Swindells, Charles ....'64 '93 C.464 B.A. L.596 J.D. 1207 S.W. 6th Ave.
Swink, Don G., (AV) ....'20 '50 C.629 B.S. L.596 LL.B. 4850 S.W. Scholls Ferry Rd.‡
Sykes, Nathan A. Schwartz ....'68 '95 C.172 B.A. L.629 J.D. [🄰 Schwabe,W.&W.]
Symes, David P. R., (AV) ....'66 '93 C.747 B.A. L.910 J.D. [Perkins C.]
Symons, Wade A. .....'70 '95 C.659 B.A. L.629 J.D. Mercer Human Resource Consulting
Takaro, Martha, (BV) ....'52 '80 C.478 B.A. L.596 J.D. Metropolitan Pub. Def.
Talcott, Anne M. ....'69 '96 C.112 B.A. L.629 J.D. [Schwabe,W.&W.]
Talcott, Brian R. ....'68 '96 C.112 B.A. L.629 J.D. [Dunn C.A.H.&T.]
Talmadge, W. Wells, (AV) '58 '83
C.165 B.A. L.188 J.D. Assoc. Gen. Coun., Freightliner LLC
Tandan, Kurt Nath '67 '92
C.1036 B.A. L.276 J.D. Assoc. Gen. Coun., adidas America, Inc.
Tank, Katherine C., (BVⓉ) ....'62 '88 C&L.629 B.S., J.D. [Schwabe,W.&W.] (ⓒBend)
Tanner, Grant, P.C., (AV) ....'48 '77 C.1078 B.A. L.1067 J.D. [G.E.Tanner]
Tanner, Grant E., P.C., (AV) ....12057 S.E. Mt. Scott Boulevard
Tanzer, Jacob B., (AV) ....'35 '59 C&L.629 B.A., LL.B. 4405 S.W. Warrens Way‡
Tanzosh, Brenna A. ....'73 '99 C.30 B.A. L.446 J.D. [🄰 Yates,M.&Assoc.]
Tappel, Catherine A. ....'58 '87 C.1074 B.S. L.1065 J.D. [🄰 Gevurtz,M.L.&H.]
Tarlow, Arthur L., (AV) ....'42 '66 C.939 B.S. L.629 LL.B. [Tarlow N.&S.]
Tarlow Naito & Summers, LLP, (AV) ....6650 SW Redwood Lane #215
Tarr, Jeffrey S., (AV) ....'63 '89 C.112 B.A. L.426 J.D. [Sussman S.]
Tassin, Terry J., Jr. ....'63 '98 C.911 B.A. L.596 J.D. [🄰 Scarborough,M.O.&K.]
Tauman, Charles S., (AV) ....'44 '77 C.813 A.B. L.596 J.D. [C.S.Tauman]
Tauman, Nancy S., (AV) ....'45 '78 C.813 A.B. L.1051 J.D. 1727 N.W. Hoyt Street
Tauman, Charles S., PC, (AV) ....P.O. Box 19631
Taylor, Dana R., (AV) ....'50 '77 C.800 A.B. L.596 J.D. [🄲 Duffy K.]
Taylor, Laura Caldera ....'68 '99 C.147 B.A. L.950 J.D. [🄰 Garvey S.B.]
Taylor, Robert L. ....'77 '04 C.103 B.A. L.950 J.D. [🄰 Ball J.]
Taylor, Steven B., (BV) ....'55 '82 C.670 B.A. L.596 J.D. [McMenamin&T.]
Teicher, Stuart I., (AV) ....'48 '76 C.569 B.A. L.1051 J.D. [Sussman S.]
Tellam, Bradley F., (AV) ....'57 '82 C.154 B.A. L.426 J.D. [Barran L.]
Teller, Susan E., Law Office of, (AVⓉ) '53 '80
C.1078 B.A. L.1065 J.D. 1123 S.W. Yamhill St.
Templeton, Donald E., (AV) ....'59 '84 C.629 B.S. L.911 J.D. [Dunn C.A.H.&T.]
Tenenbaum, Gilah ... '48 '78 C.94 B.A. L.1051 J.D. Ref., Hearings Div. Wkrs. Comp. Bd.
Tennant, Joseph P. ....'52 '78 C&L.276 B.A., J.D. Pres., Northern Pacific Capital Corp.
Terranova, Greg ....'46 '77 C.599 B.B.A. L.629 J.D. [Sullivan&T.]
Tewksbury, Zan E., (BV) ....'— '91 [Steenson,S.T.L.&R.]
Thede, Jeffrey C., P.C., (AV) ....'54 '79 C.629 B.S. L.950 J.D. [Miller N.]
Theodorson, Ellen ....'68 '99 C&L.629 B.A., J.D. [🄰 Stoel R.]
Thies, Pamela McCarroll, (BV) '49 '75 C.773 B.A. L.426 J.D.
830 N.W. Powhatan Terr.
Thomas, Christopher P., (AV) ....'45 '69 C.31 B.A. L.569 J.D. [C.Thomas]
Thomas, Jeanette ....'— '94 C.415 B.A. L.1019 J.D. [🄲 Perkins C.]
Thomas, John R. ....'60 '91 C.678 B.A. L.1051 J.D. [Stoel R.]
Thomas, John S. .....'48 '78 C.813 B.A. L.1051 J.D. Asst. Co. Coun., Multnomah Co. Off.
Thomas, Kevin S. ....'73 '98 C.894 A.B. L.880 J.D. Corp. Atty., ESCO Corp.
Thomas, Raymond F., (AV) ....'51 '79 C.1082 B.A. L.596 J.D. [Swanson,T.&C.]
Thomas, Wm. F., (BV) ....'26 '52 C.629 B.S. L.273 J.D. 812 S.W. Washington
Thomas, Christopher, (AV) ....2611 N.E. 12th Ave.
Thompson, Anne M., (AV) ....'58 '88 C.1365 B.A. L.280 J.D. [Thompson]
Thompson, Brian S. ....'59 '86 C.628 B.S. L.629 J.D. [🄲 Newcomb,S.S.&L.]

Thompson, Bruce G., (AV) '51 '81 C.871 B.S. L.1494 J.D.
111 S.W. Columbia Street, Suite 1000, 97201
Telephone: 503-226-6491 Fax: 503-228-6392 URL: http://www.btelderlaw.com
Email: bruce@btelderlaw.com URL: http://www.lawyers.com/btelderlaw
Elder Law, Wills and Probate (in OR, WA and CA), Wills and Trusts, Estate and Gift Tax Planning, Guardianship (in OR, WA and CA), Estate Taxation, Medicaid Planning.
See Professional Biographies, PORTLAND, OREGON

Thompson, Cynthia A. '45 '87 C.1060 B.A. L.1051 J.D.
Exec. Dir., Children's Trust Fund of OR Foundation
Thompson, Douglas M., (AV) ....'29 '55 C&L.813 A.B., LL.B. [Schwabe,W.&W.] ‡
Thompson, Karen Gillison '59 '86 C.350 B.A. L.596 J.D.
Asst. V.P., Dir., Claims Admin., Fred Meyer, Inc.
Thompson, Karen R., (BVⓉ) ....'56 '89 C.846 B.A. L.326 J.D. 520 SW Sixth Avenue
Thompson, Mark R. ....'77 '04 C.101 B.S. L.596 J.D. Atty., Public Power Council
Thompson, Patricia L., (BV) ....'51 '81 C.1056 B.S. L.629 J.D. 15234 S.E. Stark
Thompson, Robert E., (AV) '28 '58
C.628 B.S. L.950 J.D. 9400 SW Barnes Road, Suite 300
Thompson, Stephen C., (AV) ....'51 '76 C&L.629 B.A., J.D. [Zakovics T.&R.]

Thompson Law Firm, The, (AV)
9400 SW Barnes Road, Suite 300, 97225-6658
Telephone: 503-292-8990 Fax: 503-292-9040 URL: http://www.amthompsonlawfirm.com
Email: anne@amthompsonlawfirm.com URL: http://www.ttlf.com
Anne M. Thompson.
Wills, Trusts and Estates, Estate Planning, Probate, Taxation, Tax Planning, Guardianship, Conservatorships, Contracts, Closely Held Business, Small Business Law, Partnership Law, Limited Liability Company Law, Business Planning.
See Professional Biographies, PORTLAND, OREGON

Thomsen, Dallas G. ....'76 '02 C.906 B.A. L.285 J.D. [🄰 Sussman S.]
Thomson, Robert H., (AV) ....'44 '75 C.950 B.A. L.477 J.D. [Stoel R.]
Thornton, Cynthia Rosebaugh '56 '83
C.1347 B.A. L.285 J.D. Employ. Rels. Mgr., Fred Meyer, Inc.
Thorp, Justin M. ....'72 '97 C.950 B.A. L.629 J.D. [Martin,B.T.L.&H.] ⊙
Thrush, Rose ....'39 '80 C.629 B.A. L.1051 J.D. Admin. Analyst, U.S. Bkrptcy. Ct.
Thuemmel, Robert G., (AV) ....'51 '77 C&L.629 B.A., J.D. [Thuemmel&U.]
Thuemmel & Uhle, (AV) ....210 S.W. Morrison
Thurber, Kent B. ....'— '75 C.813 A.B. L.950 J.D. [Davis W.T.]
Thye, Gary A. ....'39 '67 C.800 B.S. L.629 J.D. Admin. Law J., Wkrs. Comp. Bd.
Tice, John E. '25 '72 C.800 B.A. L.61 J.D.
(adm. in CA; not adm. in OR) 7425 S.E. Market St.‡
Tichenor, Keith E., (AV) ....'44 '69 C.918 B.A. L.911 J.D. [Tichenor D.&C.]
Tichenor, Roberta A. ....'44 '82 C.75 B.A. L.596 J.D. 7834 S.W., Capitol Hwy.‡

Tichenor Dziuba & Coletti LLP, (AV)
1100 S.W. 6th Avenue, Suite 1450, 97204
Telephone: 503-224-3333 Fax: 503-224-2949
URL: http://www.tdcinjurylaw.com
Keith E. Tichenor; Daniel C. Dziuba; John M. Coletti. Of Counsel: William A. Galbreath.
Personal Injury, Product Liability, Maritime Injuries, Medical Malpractice, Construction Accidents.
See Professional Biographies, PORTLAND, OREGON

Tienson, Thane W., (AV) ....'46 '77 C.770 B.A. L.596 J.D. [Landye B.B.]

Tiger, Paul M. ....'76 '04 C.629 B.A. L.813 J.D. [🄰 Stoel R.]
Tilden, Kelly R. ....'71 '01 C.529 A.B. L.950 J.D. [🄰 Black H.]
Tillson, Kevin J. ....'77 '03 C.37 B.S. L.950 J.D. [🄰 Hunt&Assoc.]
Tindell, Raymond Sidney ....'60 '87 C.472 B.M. L.802 J.D. [R.Tindell]
Tindell, Raymond ....11112 N.E. Halsey, Ste. A
Todd, Dennis F. ....'37 '67 C.628 B.S. L.1066 J.D. Production Parts, Inc.
Todd, Richard W., (BV) ....'53 '79 C.628 B.S. L.1051 J.D. [Bertoni&T.]
Todd, Steven A., (AV) ....'55 '81 C.597 B.A. L.596 J.D. 1021 S.W. 4th Ave.
Toland, Anne C. ....'61 '89 C.813 A.B. L.1065 J.D. Assoc., Legacy Health System
Tom, Michael V. ....'67 '93 C.911 B.A. L.950 J.D. 1000 SW Broadway 200
Tom, Rebecca Biermann ....'67 '95 C.911 B.A. L.950 J.D. [🄰 Ball J.]
Tombleson, David ....'63 '02 C.999 B.A. L.69 J.D. [Tombleson&D.]
Tombleson & Dowell, L.L.C. ....2416 S.W. 5th Avenue, Suite 300
Tomlinson, William M., (AV) ....'48 '74 C.674 B.A. L.629 J.D. [Lindsay,H.N.&W.]
Tompkins, Robin ....'61 '87 C.800 B.A. L.1040 J.D. Portland Gen. Electric
Toncray, Sharon L., (BV) '63 '90
C.683 B.A. L.893 J.D. Labor Rel. Reg. Dir., Providence Health Sys.
Tongue, Thomas Healy, (AV) ....'43 '68 C.629 B.S. L.966 J.D. [Dunn C.A.H.&T.]
Tongue, Thomas M. ....'73 '99 C.880 B.A. L.629 J.D. [🄰 Schwabe,W.&W.]
Tonkin, Edward C., (AV) '54 '79
C&L.911 B.A., J.D. Corp. Coun., Ron Tonkin Chevrolet Co.

Tonkon Torp LLP, (AV)
(Formerly, Tonkon, Torp, Galen, Marmaduke & Booth LLP)
1600 Pioneer Tower, 888 S.W. Fifth Avenue, 97204-2099
Telephone: 503-221-1440 Fax: 503-274-8779
URL: http://www.tonkon.com
Members of Firm: Robert E. Hirshon (Not admitted in OR); Moe M. Tonkon (1905-1984); Frederick H. Torp (1913-2003); David S. Aman; Terry W. Baker; Vicki A. Ballou; Bruce G. Berning; Owen D. Blank; Brian G. Booth; Jeanne M. Chamberlain; Timothy J. Conway; Sherrill A. Corbett; Jeffrey S. Cronn; Justin B. Denton; Morris J. Galen; Ronald L. Greenman; Lynda J. Hartzell; Theodore G. Herzog; Carol Dey Hibbs; Jeffrey H. Keeney; Albert N. Kennedy; Victor J. Kisch; Mark F. LeRoux; Barbee B. Lyon; Don H. Marmaduke; William F. Martson, Jr.; Max M. Miller, Jr.; Michael M. Morgan; Jon W. Nickel; Darcy M. Norville; Ingolf Noto; Turid L. Owren; Thomas P. Palmer; Amy Joseph Pedersen; Edwin C. Perry; Brian J. Posewitz; Brent W. Renison; Shouka D. Rezvani; John H. Rosenfeld; Kurt W. Ruttum; Scott G. Seidman; Daniel H. Skerritt; George C. Spencer; Kenneth D. Stephens; Jon P. Stride; Joseph S. Voboril; Frank J. Weiss; David F. White; Steven M. Wilker; Zachary W.L. Wright. Of Counsel: Christopher M. Bikus; David Copley Forman. Associates: Michael E. Callier; Paul W. Conable; Chandra Emery; Christopher D. Erickson; Michael W. Fletcher; Caroline Harris Crowne; Sonja L. Henning; F. Jackson Lewis; Laura Liebman-Alperson; Michael Millender; Steven D. Olson; Tatiana A. Perry; David J. Petersen; Robyn E. Ridler; Katherine E. Saitas; Ava Schoen; Joshua K. Simko; Christine Uri (Not admitted in OR); Dennis E. Westlind.
Admiralty, Antitrust and Trade Regulation, Business, Communications, Corporate Finance, Creditors' Rights and Bankruptcy, E-Commerce, Emerging Growth, Employee Benefits, Employment and Labor, Energy, Entertainment, Environmental and Natural Resources, Immigration, Intellectual Property, International, Litigation, Media, Mergers and Acquisitions, Nonprofits, Real Estate/Real Property, Securities, Sports, Taxation, Technology, Telecommunications, Utilities, Wealth (Estate) Planning and Administration.
Representative Clients: Americold Corporation; AT&T; CB Commercial Real Estate Croup, Inc.; Congress Financial Corporation; Deloitte & Touche LLP; Greenbrier Companies (The); NIKE, Inc.; Portland General Corp.; Stimson Lumber Co.

See Professional Biographies, PORTLAND, OREGON

Toran, Jana E., (AV) ....'61 '90 C&L.326 B.A., J.D. 4012 Se 17th
Tormala, Alyssa Eve Thirsk ....'76 '01 C.878 B.A. L.813 J.D. [🄰 Miller N.]
Tosswill, Catherine M. ....'65 '97 C.976 B.A. L.705 J.D. [🄰 J.L.Hoffman]
Tourjé, Camille ....'74 '01 C.604 B.A. L.124 J.D. [🄰 Martin,B.T.L.&H.]
Towsley, Bruce W., (BV) ....'25 '56 C.939 B.A. L.596 LL.B. 1500 S.W. 1st Ave.
Tow-Woram, Ping ....'58 '91 C.629 B.S. L.596 J.D. [🄰 Carney,B.H.&M.]
Tracey, Christine ....'54 '01 C.453 B.S.E.E. L.596 J.D. Northwest Lawfirm
Tran, Trinh ....'— '03 C.145 B.A. L.1051 J.D. [🄰 Davis W.T.]
Travis, Catherine S., (AV) ....'— '81 C.881 B.A. L.1051 J.D. [Lane P.]
Traylor, Joe R. ....'70 '96 C.628 B.S. L.950 J.D. 1000 S.W. Bway., Ste. 2000
Traynor, Lana L. ....'66 '93 C.939 B.A. L.1051 J.D. [L.L.Traynor]
Traynor, Lana L., LLC ....317 SW Alder Street, 9th Floor
Tremaine, H. Stewart, (AV) ....'— '47 C.911 B.A. L.976 LL.B. [🄲 Davis W.T.] ‡
Tribe, Deborah Lynn ....'58 '87 C&L.596 B.A., J.D. Law Clk. to Presiding Cir. Ct. J.
Trice, Eric A. ....'72 '99 C&L.629 B.S., J.D. Multnomah County DA Office
Trieu, Jenny L. ....'73 '01 C.104 B.A. L.477 J.D. [🄰 Ater W.]
Trinchero, Mark P. ....'— '88 C.112 B.A. L.1065 J.D. [Davis W.T.]
Trinchero, Paul H. ....'71 '01 C.112 B.S.C. L.596 J.D. [🄰 Grenley,R.E.B.&B.]
Tripi, Joseph A. ....'66 '92 C.690 B.S. L.629 J.D. [🄰 Grenley,R.E.B.&B.]
Triplett, Thomas M., (AV) '40 '65 C.976 A.B. L.813 LL.B.
[Schwabe,W.&W.] (⊙Bend)
Tripp, Dennis F., (AV) ....'52 '82 C.628 B.S. L.809 J.D. [D.F.Tripp]
Tripp, Dennis F., P.C., (AV) ....610 SW Alder Street, Suite 1000
Trompke, Edward H., (AV) ....'52 '84 C.1056 B.S. L.596 J.D. [Jordan S.]
Trow, Michael Edward '53 '87 C.312 B.A. L.629 J.D.
(adm. in HI; not adm. in OR) Off. of Gen. Coun., U.S. Dept. of Agric.
Troy, F.G. (Jamie), II ....'69 '96 C.945 B.A. L.596 J.D. 121 SW Morrision, Ste. 260
Truax, Erin E. ....'76 '03 C.549 B.A. L.1051 J.D. [🄰 Miller N.]
Trubo, Herbert A., (AV) ....'48 '73 C.112 B.A. L.477 J.D. [Sorensen-Jolink,T.W.M.&W.]
Truelsen, Roy Lawrence '53 '87 C.147 B.S. L.770 J.D.
Mgr., Corp. Real Estate, Consolidated Freightways, Inc.
Tsai, Connie ....'78 '05 C.309 B.A. L.893 J.D. [🄰 Miller N.]
Tu, Trung D. ....'73 '00 C.602 B.A. L.1051 J.D. [🄰 McEwen G.]
Tuazon, Rebecca Sexton, (BV) ....'61 '86 C.941 B.A. L.950 J.D. [🄰 D.Heiling&Assoc.]
Tucker, Roslyn L. ....'54 '80 C.1349 B.A. L.107 J.D. 4195 N.E. Alameda
Tucker, Roy W., (AV) ....'52 '80 C.385 B.A. L.107 J.D. [Perkins C.]
Tuenge, Peter O. ....'77 '03 C.285 B.A. L.629 J.D. [🄰 Keating J.B.&H.]
Tujo, John A., (BV) '37 '65 C.670 B.B.A. L.596 LL.B.
825 N.E. Multnomah St., Ste. 925
Turnbull, Thomas R. ....'64 '89 C.678 B.A. L.911 J.D. 2658 S.W. Corona Ave.
Turner, Janice Nystrom ....'64 '90 C.909 B.A. L.950 J.D. [McEwen G.]
Turner, Mark A., (AV) ....'59 '86 C&L.145 A.B., J.D. [Ater W.]
Turner, Robert C. '46 '72 C.112 B.A. L.1067 J.D.
(adm. in DC; not adm. in OR) Dist. Coun., U.S. Army Corps of Engrs.
Turpen, Kjersten H. ....'— '00 C.629 B.A. L.770 J.D. [🄰 Dunn C.A.H.&T.]
Tuthill, Deborah L. ....'48 '77 C.184 B.A. L.1051 J.D. 9617 S.W. 2nd Ave.
Tuttle, Christopher S. ....'70 '99 C.1154 B.S.E.E. L.1218 J.D. [🄰 Kolisch H.] (Pat.)
Tyler, Lee Ogden, (BV) ....'58 '84 C.1056 B.A. L.596 J.D. [L.O.Tyler]
Tyler, Lee Ogden, P.C., (BV) ....1123 SW Yamhill Street
Tylicki, Edward T. ....'67 '97 C.276 B.S.F.S. L.1051 J.D. [🄰 Lindsay,H.N.&W.]
Udvari, Kristin L. ....'74 '99 C.976 B.A. L.596 J.D. [🄰 Ball J.] (⊙Bend)
Ugur, Gulgun ....'— '02 C.1494 B.A. L.1068 J.D. [🄰 Preston G.&E.]
Uhle, William K., (AV) ....'52 '78 C.813 B.A. L.629 J.D. [Thuemmel&U.]
Ukishima, Matthew G. ....'72 '00 C&L.285 B.A., J.D. [🄰 Gilroy]
Underhill, Dayna E. ....'65 '92 C.308 B.A. L.818 J.D. [D.E.Underhill]
Underhill, D.E., Law Office of ....9451 N.W. Fleischner St.
Underwood, Blake E., (BV) ....'60 '85 C.845 B.A. L.596 J.D. [Opton&U.]
Underwood, Lauren M., (AV) ....'40 '68 C.629 B.S. L.596 J.D. [Underwood&N.]
Underwood, Raymond P., (AV) ....'20 '48 C.105 A.B. L.309 J.D. 6236 S.W. Tower Way‡
Underwood & Norwood, (AV) ....621 S.W. Morrison, Suite 1050
Ungar, Steven B., (AV) ....'54 '79 C.910 B.A. L.502 J.D. [Lane P.]
Urban, Jay
(See Lake Oswego)
Uri, Christine '75 '03 C.1331 B.A. L.93
(adm. in WA; not adm. in OR) [🄰 Tonkon T.]
Urrutia, J. Richard, (AV) ....'— '82 L.629 J.D. [Williams,K.&G.P.]
Uyemura, David L. ....'47 '75 C.629 B.A. L.284 J.D. Sr. V.P., Marsh USA Inc.
Vacura, Julie R., (AV) ....'59 '84 C.770 B.S. L.950 J.D. [Larkins V.]
Vail, Bernard F. ....'42 '75 C&L.209 B.A., J.D. Prof. of Law, Northwestern Sch. of Law
Valent, William R. ....'56 '85 C.670 B.A. L.590 J.D. [Forum 5.]
Van Brocklin, Robert D., (AV) ....'53 '87 C&L.629 B.S., J.D. [Stoel R.]
Van Buren, Evans W., Jr., (BV) ....'48 '76 C.939 B.A. L.1051 J.D. 610 S.W. Alder St.
Van Buren, Marybeth ....'54 '80 C.950 B.A. L.629 J.D. Bonneville Power Admin.
Vance, A. Jonathan ....'77 '04 C.101 B.S. L.846 J.D. [🄰 Klarquist S.] (See Pat. Sect.)
Vance, Joseph ....'— '95 C.101 B.S. L.911 J.D. [Davis W.T.]
VanCleave, Richard N., (AV) ....'53 '80 C.628 B.S. L.950 J.D. [Barran L.]
Van Cleve, S. Bradley, (AV) ....'61 '86 C.347 B.A. L.596 J.D. [Davison V.]
Vandall, Donna J. ....'52 '82 C.896 B.A. L.276 J.D. Mental Health Servs. West
Vanden Bos, Robert J, (AV) ....'— '78 C.27 B.A. L.477 J.D. [VandenBos&C.]

Vanden Bos & Chapman, LLP, (AV) BR
Suite 520, The Spalding Building, 319 S.W. Washington Street, 97204-2690
Telephone: 503-241-4869 Fax: 503-241-3731
URL: http://www.vbcattorneys.com
Members of Firm: Robert J Vanden Bos; Ann K. Chapman. Associate: Jeff Payne.
Trial Practice in State and Federal Courts. Bankruptcy, Consumer and Commercial Chapter Eleven (Reorganization), Chapter 13 and Debtor-Creditor Rights.

See Professional Biographies, PORTLAND, OREGON

Vandenberg, John D., (AV) '58 '84
C.674 B.S.E. L.569 J.D. [Klarquist S.] (See Pat. Sect.)
Van Der Weele, Philip S., (AV) ....'59 '84 C.114 B.A. L.477 J.D. [Preston G.&E.]
Vandwettering, Mari Elizabeth '59 '88 C&L.911 B.A., J.D.
(adm. in WA; not adm. in OR) Portland General Electric
Vangelisti, Richard J., (AV) ....'67 '95 C.36 B.A. L.802 J.D. [Vangelisti]
Vangelisti Law Offices PC, (AV) ....9755 SW Barnes Road, Suite 450

Van Hoomissen, Michael F., (AV) '56 '84 C.1070 B.S. L.767 J.D.
Riviera Plaza, Suite 319, 1618 S.W. First Avenue, 97201
Telephone: 503-221-1529 Facsimile: 503-221-6222
Email: mvanhoom@attglobal.net URL: http://www.lawyers.com/vanhoomissen
General Civil and Trial Practice in Oregon and Washington Courts. Litigation, Insurance, Insurance Defense, Aviation and Aerospace, Products Liability, Construction Law, Corporate Law, Commercial Law, Business Law, Real Estate, Family Law, Personal Injury, Wills, Trusts and Estates, Probate, Military Law.

See Professional Biographies, PORTLAND, OREGON

Van Hoomissen, Richard A., (AV) '32 '58 C.670 B.A. L.276 J.D.
1618 S.W. 1st Avenue
VanLeuven, Joseph M., (AV) ....'— '82 C.685 B.A. L.477 J.D. [Davis W.T.]
Van Loh, Sara ....'77 '04 C.629 B.A. L.1066 J.D. [🄰 Bullivant H.B.]
Van Meter, Heather J. ....'— '98 L.950 J.D. [🄰 Williams,K.&G.P.]
Van Nostrand, James M. ....'55 '79 C.351 B.A. L.352 J.D. [Stoel R.] (⊙Seattle, WA)
Van Rysselberghe, Pierre C. '58 '90
C.668 B.A. L.284 J.D. [Kolisch H.] (Pat.) (⊙Palo Alto, CA)
Van Rysselberghe, Todd L., (AV) ....'60 '88 C.629 B.S. L.596 J.D. [Kennedy,W.A.&R.]
VanSpeybroeck, David D. ....'62 '89 C.299 B.A. L.94 J.D. [Bullivant H.B.]
Van Valkenburg, E. Walter, (AV) ....'53 '78 C.911 B.A. L.950 J.D. [Stoel R.]
Van Valkenburg, Margaret M., (AV) ....'57 '83 C.911 B.A. L.629 J.D. [Bullivant H.B.]
Van Walleghem, Tonya ....'— '98 C.02 B.S. L.950 J.D. [🄰 Bullivant H.B.]
VanZanten, Katherine O. ....'72 '97 C.94 B.A. L.284 J.D. [🄰 Schwabe,W.&W.]
Varitz, Robert D., (AV) ....'44 '82 C.878 B.S. L.596 J.D. [R.D.Varitz] (Pat.)
Varitz, Robert D., P.C., (AV) ....2007 SE Grant Street (Pat.)
Varnes, Donald W., (BV) ....'35 '69 C.101 B.S. L.596 J.D. 3020 S.W. Ridge Dr.
Varney, Karen S. ....'72 '01 C.1169 B.A. L.1051 J.D. [🄰 Sather,B.&H.]
Vasquez, Nathan Trumon ....'76 '01 C.112 B.A. L.1051 J.D. Dept. Dist. Atty.
Vaught, Laura E. ....'68 '96 C.769 B.A. L.426 J.D. [🄰 Smith&M.]
Vav Rosky, Dennis R., (AV) ....'43 '68 C.145 L.596 J.D. [VavRosky M.O.]

VavRosky MacColl Olson, P.C., (AV)
555 Umpqua Bank Plaza, One S.W. Columbia, 97258
Telephone: 503-223-2125 Fax: 503-223-1904
URL: http://www.vavrosky.com
Shareholders: Dennis R. Vav Rosky; E. Kimbark MacColl, Jr.; Karli L. Olson; Stephen L. Pfeifer; Thomas P. Busch; David L. Johnstone.
Workers Compensation Defense, Federal Workers Compensation Defense, Employment Law Defense, Longshore and Harbor Workers Compensation Act, Americans with Disabilities Act, Family and Medical Leave Act, Occupational Safety and Health, Appellate Practice.

See Professional Biographies, PORTLAND, OREGON

Vergaretti, Cecelia ....'59 '89 C.705 B.A. L.564 J.D. 620 SW Fifth Avenue‡
Vergun, Lawrence M., LLC '62 '88
C.1375 B.A. L.1068 J.D. 10260 SW Greenburg Rd, Suite 400
Vermilyea, Jeremy T. ....'69 '97 C.17 B.A. L.1194 J.D. [Jordan S.]
Vershum, Mary J. ....'24 '54 L.596 LL.B. 8426 S.E. Stark St.‡
Vetterlein, Eric H. ....'54 '87 C.174 B.A. L.596 J.D. [Duffy K.]
Vial, A. Richard, (BV) ....'54 '81 C.101 B.S. L.950 J.D. [Vial F.]
Vial Fotheringham, LLP, (BV) ....7000 S.W. Varns Street
Vickers, Karen M. ....'66 '91 C.629 B.S. L.950 J.D. [Bullivant H.B.]
Vidas, Daniel F., (AV) ....'42 '77 C&L.339 B.S., J.D. [Dunn C.A.H.&T.]
Viducich, Anthony J. ....'26 '73 C.999 L.596 LL.B. 11409 S.W. Woodlee Heights Ct.
Vieux, Travis Jon ....'71 '99 C.610 B.A. L.596 J.D. 1021 S.W. 4th Ave.
Viewig, Alan R., (BV) ....'45 '76 C.112 B.A. L.1051 J.D. [A.Viewig]
Viewig, Alan, (BV) ....732 S.W. 3rd St., Ste. 302
Vigna, Gary L., (AV) ....'52 '78 C.629 B.S. L.678 J.D. 1618 S.W. 1st Ave., Ste. 403
Vilhauer, Jacob E., Jr., (AV) '40 '64
C.628 B.S. L.629 LL.B. [Chernoff,V.M.&S.] (See Pat. Sect.)
Villa-Smith, Kathryn L., (BV) ....'52 '82 C.556 B.A. L.1051 J.D. [Gevurtz,M.L.&H.]
Virshbo, Eric D. ....'74 '02 C.172 B.A. L.1119 J.D. [🄰 MacMillan,S.&M.]
Viteznik, Peter J., (BV) ....'65 '94 C.629 B.S. L.950 J.D. [Bullivant H.B.]
Vivian, Jean A. '— '83 C.898 B.A. L.585 J.D.
(adm. in ND; not adm. in OR) Sr. Compl. Coun., Harland Financial Solutions, Inc.
Voboril, Joseph S., (AV) ....'48 '73 C.546 B.A. L.477 J.D. [Tonkon T.]

Vogt, Randall, (BV) '50 '77 C.112 A.B. L.950 J.D.
2125 SW Fourth Avenue, Suite 600, 97201
Telephone: 503-228-9858 Fax: 503-222-5405
Email: vogt4me1@comcast.net URL: http://randallvogtlaw.com

(This Listing Continued)

Vogt, Randall (Continued)

Criminal Law, Personal Injury, Sexual Abuse, Driving While intoxicated, Sexual Assault, Drug Crimes, Juvenile Crimes, Parole and Probation, Traffic Violations, Homicide, Civil Litigation.
See Professional Biographies, PORTLAND, OREGON

Volpert, Joan Lisensky, (BV) ... '55 '80 C.231 B.A. L.950 J.D. Legal Dept., U.S. Nat. Bk.
Volpert, Timothy R., (AV) ....'— '81 C.231 B.A. L.950 J.D. [Davis W.T.]
von Bergen, Mark A., (AV) ....'51 '79 C.674 A.B. L.145 J.D. [Holland&K.]
von Ter Stegge, Katharine .... '75 '03 C&L.893 B.A., J.D. Dep. Dist. Atty.
Voorhees, Stephen C., (AV) ....'51 '79 C.629 B.S. L.1051 J.D. [Kilmer,V.&L.]
Vore, Gail P. .... '— '89 C.939 B.A. L.596 J.D. [Ⓐ Dunn C.A.H.&T.]
Voss, Ellen M. .... '— '00 L.950 J.D. [Ⓐ Williams,K.&G.P.]
Voth, Larry I., (BV) ....'49 '77 C.950 B.A. L.596 J.D. 1606 S.E. Glenwood
Vu, Linh T. ....'72 '00 C.950 B.A. L.596 J.D. 1 Sw Columbia St Ste 555
Waage, Shannon K. ....'59 '92 C.629 B.S. L.596 J.D. 111 S.W. Columbia St.‡
Wachsteter, Barton J. .... '69 '96 C.880 B.A. L.1051 J.D. [Ⓐ Mitchell,L.&S.]
Wachter, Carol D. ... '60 '87 C.508 B.S. L.950 J.D. Tax Sr. Mgr., Deloitte & Touche LLP
Wachter, Timothy J., (AV) ....'62 '87 C.906 B.A. L.950 J.D. [Bullivant H.B.]
Wada, Mark R., (AV) ....'53 '78 C.629 B.B.A. L.188 J.D. [Harrang L.G.R.]
Wade, Ronald L., (AV) ....'47 '78 C.1056 B.S. L.596 J.D. [Eves&W.]
Waggoner, James C., (AV) ....'— '74 C.685 B.A. L.629 J.D. [Davis W.T.]
Wagner, George Lowell, (AV) '29 '59 C&L.950 B.A., J.D.
520 SW Yamhill St., Ste. 800
Wagner, Jennifer A. ....'74 '02 C.477 B.A. L.596 J.D. [Ⓐ Stoll S.B.L.&S.]
Wagner, Justin D. ....'74 '03 C.597 B.S. L.112 J.D. [Ⓐ Klarquist S.]
Wagner, Lawrence A. ....'73 '02 C.262 B.A. L.596 J.D. [Ⓐ Stewart S.&G.]
Wagner, Lee S., (BV) ....'45 '84 C.1051 B.A. L.596 J.D. [Forum 5.]
Wah, Linda M. ....'59 '92 C.629 B.A. L.1051 J.D. 825 NE Multnomah, Ste. 1800
Walch, John D. ....'60 '88 C&L.1335 B.S., J.D. [Ⓒ Ater W.]
Waldron, Jay T., (AV) ....'45 '74 C.676 A.B. L.893 J.D. [Schwabe,W.&W.]
Waldum, George R. ....'28 '52 C.964 B.A. L.966 J.D. 1100 S.W. Mitchell St.‡
Walker, Donald C., (BV) ....'17 '47 C&L.629 B.S., LL.B. 2019 Lloyd Ctr.
Walker, Kenneth R., (AV) ....'51 '82 C&L.629 B.S., J.D. [Walker&W.]
Walker, Laura J. ....'53 '79 C.45 B.A. L.276 J.D. [Cable H.B.H.&L.]
Walker, Michael D., (P.C.), (AV) ... '63 '88 C.335 B.A. L.596 J.D. [Samuels Y.K.S.&S.]
Walker, Nelson L., (AV) ....'45 '79 C.506 B.S. L.1051 J.D. 1727 N.W. Hoyt Street
Walker, Stephen S. ....'32 '63 C.1056 B.S. L.596 LL.B. Cir. J.
Walker & Warren, (AV) .... 838 S.W. 1st Ave.
Wall, Bradley R., (BV) ....'54 '81 C.628 B.S. L.596 J.D. [Wall&W.]
Wall, Frank, (AV) ....'46 '73 C.1051 B.A. L.629 J.D. 812 Sw Washington Ste 910
Wall, George J. ....'— '93 C.112 B.S. L.770 J.D. [Welch,B.&G.]
Wall, Marilyn Moylan, (AV) ....'52 '76 C.670 B.A. L.629 J.D. [Wall&W.]
Wall, Mitchell C., (AV) ....'51 '77 C.628 B.S. L.629 J.D. [Wall&W.]
Wall & Wall, P.C., (AV) ....500 N.E. Multnomah Street Suite 700
Wallace, Sarah K. ....'— '00 C.112 B.A. L.1049 J.D. [Ⓐ Ater W.]
Waller, Nan G. ....'54 '79 C.813 B.A. L.629 J.D. Cir.J.
Wallingford, Roger D., (BV) ....'34 '68 L.1051 J.D. 1809 NW Johnson St.
Walseth, Nancy R. ....'53 '78 C.813 B.A. L.1051 J.D. Marine Title NW
Walsh, Denise Turner .....'65 '92 C.112 B.A. L.1065 J.D. 812 S.W. Washington, Ste. 700
Walsh, Jack ....'— '92 C.201 B.S. L.1065 J.D. [Lane P.]
Walters, Christopher M., (AV) ....'61 '86 C.813 A.B. L.1066 J.D. [Ball J.]
Walters, James H. ....'60 '90 C.629 B.A. L.1051 J.D. 310 S.W. 4th Ave. (Pat.)
Walters, Stephen S., (AV) ....'45 '72 C&L.813 B.S., J.D. [Stoel R.]
Walters, William H., (AV) ....'42 '82 C.605 B.A. L.629 J.D. [Ⓒ Miller N.]
Walton, Allyssa J. ....'76 '04 C&L.629 B.A., J.D. [Ⓐ Schwabe,W.&W.]
Walton, Michael K. ....'— '94 C.800 B.A. L.464 J.D. [Cosgrave V.K.]
Wand, Matthew A. ....'75 '00 C.1056 B.A. L.596 J.D. [Ⓐ Stewart S.&G.]
Wang, David C. ....'70 '96 C.1375 B.S. L.188 J.D. [Ⓐ Holland&K.] (Pat.)
Wapnick, Norman, (AV) ....'31 '55 C.102 A.B. L.178 LL.B. [Sussman S.]
Ward, Sharon M. ....'54 '79 C.783 B.A. L.1312 J.D. 1025 N.E. 33rd Ave.
Wardinsky, Shaun M. '58 '96
C.1056 B.S. L.1051 J.D. 6500 S.W. Macadam Ave., Ste. 300
Warfield, Calliste ....'71 '99 C.629 B.A. L.950 J.D. 1000 S.W. Broadway, Ste. 2000
Warner, Jennifer K.T. ....'77 '02 C.878 B.A. L.893 J.D. [Ⓐ Stoel R.]
Warnick, Scott E. '— '00 C.878 B.A. L.494 J.D.
(adm. in UT; not adm. in OR) [Ⓐ Davis W.T.]
Warren, Carlton D., (AV) ....'34 '62 C.1056 L.596 LL.B. [Warren A.]
Warren, David L. '51 '76 C&L.911 B.A., J.D.
(adm. in WA; not adm. in OR) Soc. Sec. Admn.
Warren, Ernest, Jr. ....'60 '89 C.950 B.S. L.36 J.D. [Walker&W.]
Warren, Gwynedd, Ph.D. '— '04 C.477 B.S. L.1066 J.D.
[Klarquist S.] (See Pat. Sect.)
Warren, John B. ....'69 '96 C.628 B.S. L.285 J.D. [Ⓐ Scarborough,M.O.&K.]
Warren Allen, LLP, (AV) ....850 N.E. 122nd Ave.
Waters, Cari ....'77 '03 C.950 B.A. L.549 J.D. [Ⓐ Davis R.E.&X.]
Waters, Sean T. ....'— '00 C.950 B.A. L.629 J.D. [Ⓐ Harrang L.G.R.]
Watkins, Edward C. ....'33 '64 C.517 B.A. L.596 LL.B. 2221 S.W. 1st Ave.‡
Watkins, Rebecca ....'— '04 C.1056 B.S. L.1051 J.D. [Ⓐ Sather,B.&H.]
Watkins, Ulanda L. ....'— '96 C.628 B.S. L.1051 J.D. 838 SW 1st Ave.
Watson, Elizabeth ....'— '94 C.907 B.A. L.629 J.D. [Ⓐ Jaqua&W.] ⊙
Watson, Ronald A., (BV) .... '26 '55 C.024 B.Com. L.950 J.D. 3055 S.W. Cascade Dr.
Watt, Donald I. ....'45 '77 C.1056 B.S. L.596 J.D. 2125 SW Fourth Street, Suite 600
Watts, Anya Danielle '68 '99 C.112 B.A. L.629 J.D.
2928 S.E. Hawthorne Blvd., Ste. 101
Watts, James R., (AV) ....'44 '72 C.629 B.S. L.309 J.D. [Watts&W.]
Watts, John S., (BV) ....'48 '73 C.629 B.A. L.911 J.D. [Watts&W.]
Watts, Peter O. ....'77 '02 C.500 B.A. L.629 J.D. [Ⓐ Jordan S.]
Watts, Roscoe E., (BV) ....'17 '55 C.112 B.S. L.596 LL.B. [Watts&W.]
Watts, Susan E., (AV) ....'52 '77 C&L.629 B.A., J.D. [Kennedy,W.A.&R.]
Watts & Watts, (AV) .... 3434 S.W. Water Ave.
Wax, Steven T., (AV) ....'48 '76 C.165 A.B. L.309 J.D. Fed. Pub. Def.
Waxler, Eric J. ....'69 '99 C.56 B.A. L.596 J.D. Co. Disty. Atty. Off.
Waxler, Sherilyn Holcombe '75 '02 C.685 B.A. L.911 J.D.
1336 E. Burnside St., Ste. 200
Weatherby, Candace H., (AV) ....'42 '85 C.629 B.A. L.596 J.D. [Mitchell,L.&S.]
Weatherhead, Ira R., (BV) ....'50 '78 C.629 B.S. L.1051 J.D. [Ⓒ Draneas&H.]
Weaver, Delbert A., P.C., (AV) ....'31 '56 C&L.629 B.A., LL.B. [D.Weaver]
Weaver, Robert C., Jr., (AV) ....'50 '75 C&L.602 B.A., J.D. [Garvey S.B.]
Weaver, Delbert, P.C., (AV) .... 851 S.W. 6th Ave., Ste. 1350
Webb, Jere M., (AV) ....'44 '69 C.813 A.B. L.145 J.D. [Stoel R.]
Weber, James W. '55 '85
C.1168 B.A. L.1051 J.D. Columbia River Inter-Tribal Fish Comm.
Weber, Stanley E. .... '22 '65 C.629 B.A. L.596 LL.B. 2020 S.W. Salmon St.‡
Webster, Ronald F. ....'68 '01 C.1056 B.A. L.831 J.D. [Ⓐ J.Foote&Assoc.]
Weddell, Margaret F. ....'51 '93 C.502 B.S. L.1051 J.D. [Ⓐ Swanson,T.&C.]
Wei, Li, Law Offices of ....'57 '97 C.999 B.A. L.950 J.D. 7059 SE Powell Boulevard
Weigler, Jerard S., (AV) ....'33 '60 C.165 B.A. L.976 LL.B. [Lindsay,H.N.&W.]
Weil, Joan ....'45 '86 C.347 B.S. L.1051 J.D. 3082 S.W. Fairmount Blvd.
Weil, John W., (AV) ....'51 '80 C.604 B.A. L.950 J.D. [Hooper,E.&W.]
Weil, Richard L., (AV) ....'52 '77 C.976 B.A. L.629 J.D. [Chase&W.]
Weimar, Linda M. ....'54 '97 C.1056 B.S. L.596 J.D. [Ⓐ D'Amore&Assoc.]
Weiner, Adam M. ....'71 '98 C.473 B.S. L.629 J.D. [Ⓐ Zakovics T.&R.]
Weiner, David P., (P.C.), (AV) ....'48 '72 C.154 B.A. L.950 J.D. [Ⓒ Greene&M.]
Weinhouse, Fredric N., (AV) ....'51 '77 C.628 B.S. L.629 J.D. Asst. U.S. Atty.
Weinsoft, Bruce M., (BV) ...'46 '71 C.112 B.A. L.1066 J.D. 815 S.W. 2nd. Ave., Ste. 400
Weirnick, Darren E. '69 '01
C.228 A.B. L.1565 J.D. Staff Atty., Community Develop. Law Ctr.
Weis, Julie A. .... '62 '97 C.69 B.A. L.596 J.D. [Haglund,K.H.&J.]
Weiss, Frank J. ....'70 '95 C.629 B.S. L.1065 J.D. [Tonkon T.]
Weiss, Walter, Jr. ....'70 '01 C.657 B.A. L.950 J.D. [Ⓐ Powers,M.&B.]

Weiss, Jensen, Ellis & Howard
(See Holland & Knight LLP)

Weisser, Herbert D. ......'59 '85 C.800 B.A. L.950 J.D. 5125 Southwest Macadam Avenue
Welch, Brian L., (AV) ....'— '63 C.1042 B.A. L.950 LL.B. [Welch,B.&G.]
Welch, Elizabeth ....'42 '66 C&L.145 B.A., J.D. Cir. J.

Welch, Bruun & Green, Attorneys at Law, (AV)
4380 S.W. Macadam Avenue, Suite 120, 97239
Telephone: 503-221-0870 Fax: 503-221-0515
Email: wbgatty@pcez.com URL: http://www.wbgattylaw.com
Partners of Firm: Brian L. Welch; Larry K. Bruun; Douglas S. Green; Ted M. Lew; George J. Wall; Marybeth Wosko. Associate: Klarissa G. Delehant.
Workers Compensation, Personal Injury, Tort Law, Social Security Disability, Longshore and Harbor Workers Compensation Act Claims, Jones Act Claims.
See Professional Biographies, PORTLAND, OREGON

Wellman, Juliana B., (BV) '48 '82
C.1051 B.S. L.596 J.D. In-House Coun., FLIR Systems, Inc.
Wells, Carolyn E., (AV) ....'51 '84 C.335 B.A. L.596 J.D. 3542 S.W. Alice St.
Wells, J. Douglas '65 '04
C.679 B.S.E.E. L.596 J.D. [Ⓐ Chernoff,V.M.&S.] (See Pat. Sect.)
Wells, Margaret Reinerman ....'69 '95 C.93 B.S. L.1051 J.D. Jud. Clk., Dist. Ct.
Wells, Monica A. ....'78 '03 C.988 B.A. L.629 J.D. [Ⓐ Keating J.B.&H.]
Welsh, Eileen Eakins ....'62 '94 C.1060 B.A. L.596 J.D. CH2M Hill, Inc.
Welty, James N., (CV) ....'61 '89 C.628 B.S. L.629 J.D. Standard Ins. Co.
Weninger, Belle K. '34 '76 C.911 B.A. L.845 J.D.
(adm. in TX; not adm. in OR) 2151 N.W. Johnson St.‡
Wentzien, Mark A. ....'60 '85 C.413 B.A. L.950 J.D. Coun., Bank of America
Werner, Harley R. ....'24 '65 C.629 B.B.A. L.596 LL.B. 6142 S.W. Wilbard St.‡
Werts, J. Stephen, (AV) ....'45 '71 C.911 B.A. L.629 J.D. [Cable H.B.H.&L.]
Werts, Stephen ....'45 '71 C.911 B.A. L.629 J.D. 1001 S.W. Fifth Avenue
Wessel, Madelyn F., (AV) ....'55 '82 C.821 B.A. L.94 J.D. Chf. Dep. City Atty.
Wesson, Frank S. ....'40 '65 C.836 B.A. L.880 J.D. [F.S.Wesson]
Wesson, Frank S., P.C. ....9115 S.W. Oleson Rd., Ste. 201
West, Joseph W., (AV) ....'59 '85 C.950 B.S. L.629 J.D. [Bullivant H.B.]
Westlind, Dennis E. ....'— '01 C.629 B.A. L.477 J.D. [Ⓐ Tonkon T.]
Weston, Cody ....'69 '98 C.309 B.A. L.629 J.D. [Ⓐ Perkins C.]
Westwood, James N., P.C., (AV) ....'44 '74 C.1056 B.A. L.178 J.D. [Stoel R.]
Wetzel, Joseph, (AV) ....'44 '69 C.529 A.B. L.831 J.D. [Wetzel D.&S.]
Wetzel, Michael C. ....'68 '95 C.950 B.S. L.880 J.D. [Ⓐ Sussman S.]

Wetzel DeFrang & Sandor, (AV)
838 S.W. First Avenue Suite 300, 97204
Telephone: 503-220-0299 FAX: 503-225-1322
Email: wdslawyers@aol.com
Members of Firm: Joseph Wetzel; Gary R. DeFrang; Russell A. Sandor. Of Counsel (Retired): Garthe Brown (Retired).
Taxation including Civil and Criminal Tax Litigation, Business Planning and Estate Planning.
See Professional Biographies, PORTLAND, OREGON

Wexler, Amie ....'72 '99 C.966 B.A. L.596 J.D. [Ⓐ Paul&S.]
Whalen, Timothy M. ....'69 '03 C.950 B.S. L.1494 J.D. [Ⓐ Kolisch H.]
Wheatley, William G., (AV) ....'33 '59 C&L.629 B.A., J.D. [Jaqua&W.] ⊙
Wheeler, Brian E. ....'63 '92 C.1071 B.S. L.629 J.D. 4370 N.E. Halsey St.
Wheeler, David H. ....'27 '54 C.813 A.B. L.950 LL.B. 8305 S.W. Carmel Ct.
Wheeler, Nicholas E. ....'— '04 C.628 B.S. L.629 J.D. [Ⓐ Cosgrave V.K.]
Whinston, Arthur L., (AV) '25 '57
C.188 B.C.E. L.569 J.D. [Ⓒ Klarquist S.] (See Pat. Sect.)
Whipple, B. Scott ....'68 '98 C.293 B.A. L.629 J.D. [Ⓐ Schwabe,W.&W.]
Whipple, Stewart M., (AV) '22 '51 C.911 B.A. L.596 J.D.
6501 S.W. Macadam Avenue
White, Bruce M., (AV) ....'50 '76 C.939 B.A. L.596 J.D. [Mitchell,L.&S.]
White, Christen Carlson ....'66 '95 C.112 B.A. L.1066 J.D. [Ball J.]
White, David F. ....'62 '93 C.293 B.A. L.309 J.D. [Tonkon T.]
White, Douglas J., Jr., (AV) ....'34 '58 C.629 B.A. L.950 LL.B. [Schwabe,W.&W.] ‡
White, Phillip A. '64 '02 C.506 B.A. L.508 J.D.
(adm. in NM; not adm. in OR) 333 Sw 1st Ave
White, Van M., III ....'62 '92 C.906 B.A. L.950 J.D. [Samuels Y.K.S.&S.]
Whitehouse, Thomas J. '48 '78 C.645 B.A. L.472 J.D.
(adm. in FL; not adm. in OR) Oregonian Pub. Co.
Whitlow, Mark D., (AV) ....'46 '75 C&L.836 B.S., J.D. [Perkins C.]
Whitney, Susan Z., (AV) ....'44 '78 C.483 B.A. L.999 J.D. [Stewart S.&G.]
Whittemore, Richard J., (AV) ....'56 '82 C.170 B.A. L.1051 J.D. [Bullivant H.B.]
Whitworth, Adrienne W. ....'76 '02 C.950 B.A. L.629 J.D. [Ⓐ Garvey S.B.]
Widder, Susan Jane, (AV) ....'57 '82 C&L.629 B.S., J.D. 1127 NW 24th
Wiener, Norman J., (AV) ....'19 '47 C&L.629 B.S., J.D. [Miller N.] ‡
Wieselman, Jacob (Jack), (BVⓉ) ....'52 '77 C.477 B.A. L.276 J.D. [Winemiller W.]
Wiggins, Karen V., (BV) ....'60 '85 C.628 B.S. L.596 J.D. 7429 S.W. 49th Ct.
Wight, Stephen A. ....'65 '92 C.101 B.S. L.911 J.D. [Klarquist S.] (See Pat. Sect.)
Wigod, Aaron M. ....'75 '02 C.475 B.S. L.1051 J.D. [Ⓐ Greene&M.]
Wihtol, Jeffrey B., (AV) ...'51 '78 C.112 B.A. L.770 J.D. 2121 S.W. Broadway, Suite 150
Wikstrom, Eric J. '71 '97 C.906 B.A. L.378 J.D.
(adm. in KS; not adm. in OR) Sr. Tax Consultant, Deloitte & Touche
Wilcox, Carl E., (BV) '40 '71 C&L.1051 B.S., J.D.
Chmn., Pres. & CEO, Bioject Med. Technologies Inc.
Wilde, Kathleen L. ....'54 '79 C.597 B.A. L.976 J.D. Oregon Advocacy Ctr.
Wilder, LeRoy W. ....'44 '73 C.628 B.S. L.284 J.D. [Haglund,K.H.&J.]
Wiles, David B., (BV) ....'58 '84 C.705 B.A. L.940 J.D. 1000 S.W. Broadway, Ste. 1500
Wilhelm, Richard A. ....'54 '84 C.629 B.S. L.596 J.D. [Ⓐ Birdwell&J.] (See Pat. Sect.)
Wilker, Steven M. ....'— '90 C.659 B.A. L.1068 J.D. [Tonkon T.]
Wilkinson, Jeffrey B., (BV) ....'60 '89 C.1201 B.A. L.950 J.D. [Stewart S.&G.]
Wilkinson, Robert W. ....'69 '99 C.597 B.A. L.629 J.D. [Ⓐ Ball J.]
Willcox-Jones, Peter S. ....'— '99 C.695 B.A. L.629 J.D. [Ⓐ Cosgrave V.K.]

Williams, Billy John .... '56 '90 C.906 B.A. L.950 J.D. Dep. Dist. Atty.
Williams, Brian B. .... '71 '96 C.950 B.S. L.629 J.D. [Hitt H.&M.]
Williams, David H., (AV) ....'— '75 C.393 A.B. L.596 J.D. [Cosgrave V.K.]
Williams, George T. .... '59 '90 C.608 B.A. L.629 J.D. 3661 S.E. Lambert St.
Williams, Karen M., (AV) .... '— '90 C.33 B.A. L.678 J.D. [Lane P.]
Williams, Kenneth A., (AV) ....'50 '80 C&L.629 B.S., J.D. [Black H.]
Williams, Mark B., (AV) '55 '82
C.705 B.A. L.629 J.D. Metropolitan Exposition-Recreation Comm.
Williams, Melinda F. '69 '94 C.1376 B.A. L.16 J.D.
Sr. Compl. Coun., Harland Financial Solutions, Inc.
Williams, Michael D., (AV) .... '46 '74 C.629 B.A. L.1065 J.D. [Williams F.]
Williams, Michael L., (AV) .... '47 '78 C.894 B.A. L.309 J.D. [Williams L.O.C.&P.]
Williams, Richard H., (AV) .... '— '72 C.165 A.B. L.309 J.D. [Lane P.]
Williams, Sharon A., (AV) '60 '85 C.1056 B.S. L.950 J.D.
[Sorensen-Jolink,T.W.M.&W.]
Williams, Susan Howard, (AV) '57 '83
C.862 B.A. L.950 J.D. [Sorensen-Jolink,T.W.M.&W.]
Williams, Thomas R., (AV) .... '26 '51 C&L.813 A.B., LL.B. Dep. City Atty.

Williams Fredrickson, LLC, (AV)
1515 S.W. Fifth, Suite 844, 97201-5447
Telephone: 503-222-9966 Fax: 503-796-1009
Email: info@williamstredrickson.com
Floyd A. Fredrickson (Retired); David R. Williams (1923-2005); John Dudrey; Michael D. Williams.
Admiralty, Eminent Domain, General Business and Business Planning, Corporate, Partnership, Probate, Estate Planning, Wills and Trusts, Real Property, Land Use, Environmental and Hazardous Waste, Insurance and Workers Compensation Law. General Civil and Trial Practice in all State and Federal Courts.
Representative Clients: UNOCAL; Westinghouse Electric Supply Co.
See Professional Biographies, PORTLAND, OREGON

Williams, Kastner & Gibbs PLLC, (AV)
Pioneer Office Tower, 888 SW Fifth Avenue, Suite 600, 97204-2025 ⊙
Telephone: 503-228-7967 Fax: 503-222-7261
Email: info@wkg.com URL: http://www.wkg.com
Members of Firm: Amy J. Carlton; Paul R. Duden; Eric J. Neiman; George S. Pitcher; J. Richard Urrutia. Associates: David C. Campbell; Marc M. Carlton; Thomas A. Ped; Sharon C. Peters; Heather J. Van Meter; Ellen M. Voss. Of Counsel: Stephen R. Frank; Erika J. George; David J. Ryan.
Civil Litigation, Federal Litigation, Trial Practice, Medical Malpractice Defense, Drug and Medical Device Litigation, Products Liability, Professional Liability, Environmental Litigation, Business Law, Mergers and Acquisitions, Real Estate, Corporate Law, Family Law.
Seattle, Washington Office: Telephone: 206-628-6600. Fax: 206-628-6611.
Tacoma, Washington Office: Telephone: 253-593-5620. Fax: 253-593-5625.
See Professional Biographies, PORTLAND, OREGON

Williams Love O'Leary Craine & Powers, P.C., (AV) BR
9755 S.W. Barnes Road, Suite 450, 97225
Telephone: 503-295-2924 Fax: 503-295-3720
Email: info@wdolaw.com URL: http://www.wdolaw.com
Michael L. Williams; Linda C. Love; Leslie W. O'Leary; Diana Craine; Thomas B. Powers;—Brian S. Campf.
Litigation in Product Liability, Lender Liability, Commercial and Franchise Law, Personal Injury, Toxic Tort Litigation, Professional Negligence and Court-Awarded Attorney Fees.
See Professional Biographies, PORTLAND, OREGON

Williams, Zografos & Peck, A Professional Corporation
(See Lake Oswego)

Williamson, Billy L., (AV) '38 '65
C.629 B.A. L.309 LL.B. Prof. of Law, Lewis & Clark Law School
Williamson, Charles R., (AV) .... '44 '68 C.165 B.A. L.818 LL.B. [Kell,A.&R.]
Williamson, Wayne A., (AV) ...... '21 '48 C.629 B.S. L.813 LL.B. [Schwabe,W.&W.] ‡
Willis, Donald Joe, (AV) .... '40 '71 C&L.629 B.S., J.D. [Schwabe,W.&W.] (⊙Bend)
Willner, Don S., (AV) ....'26 '51 C&L.309 A.B., J.D. 1826 N.E. Broadway
Wilson, Daryl Ann '49 '80 C.103 B.A. L.1051 J.D.
Legal Writing Prof., Northwestern Sch. of Law
Wilson, David E., (BV) .... '56 '82 C.1056 B.A. L.950 J.D. [Reinisch,M.H.&W.]
Wilson, David H., Jr., (AV) ....'45 '73 C.674 B.A. L.966 J.D. [Bullard S.J.W.]
Wilson, Janice R. .... '54 '79 C&L.950 B.A., J.D. Cir. J.
Wilson, Joel, (AV) ....'50 '76 C.798 B.A. L.502 J.D. [Bullivant H.B.]
Wilson, Lindsay .... '10 '35 C.628 L.596 LL.B. 1031 S.E. 56th Ave.‡
Wilson, Lyndon A. S., Jr., (AV) .... '39 '67 C.1051 B.S. L.596 J.D. Proj. Dir., Tri-Met
Wilson, Matthew A. '— '92
C.1239 B.S. L.1137 J.D. V.P. & Gen. Coun., Chrome Systems Corp.
Wilson, Paul S. '50 '80 C.685 B.A. L.1051 J.D.
Nat. Res. Prog. Dir., Northwestern Sch. of Law
Winch, Martin T. .... '44 '71 C.674 B.A. L.208 J.D. 19300 Innes Market Rd.
Winemiller, Kristen L., (AV) ....'60 '86 C.118 B.A. L.596 J.D. [Winemiller W.]

Winemiller Wieselman LLP, (AV)
1420 World Trade Center, 121 S.W. Salmon Street, 97204
Telephone: 503-222-2510 Facsimile: 503-227-2103
Email: kriswinemiller@pacificnwlaw.com URL: http://www.lawyers.com/kristenwinemiller
Kristen L. Winemiller; Jacob (Jack) Wieselman.
Criminal Defense, Civil Litigation.
See Professional Biographies, PORTLAND, OREGON

Winfree, Andrew H., (AV) '46 '75
C.628 B.A. L.1051 J.D. 5550 S.W. Macadam Ave., Ste. 220
Winger, Robert K., (AV) ....'48 '73 C&L.629 B.A., J.D. [Dunn C.A.H.&T.]
Winkel, Morton A., (AV) ....'30 '56 C.569 B.A. L.178 LL.B. 1505 S.W. Hall St.
Winkler, James H. ....'50 '78 C.103 A.B. L.1051 J.D. Winkler Develop. Corp.
Winkler, John M. .... '19 '48 C.629 B.S. L.596 LL.B. P.O. Box 14746‡
Winn, Garth A. .... '60 '87 C.877 B.S. L.101 J.D. [Klarquist S.] (See Pat. Sect.)
Winslow, Michael T. .... '54 '81 Stancorp Financial Group
Winters, Eric "Skip" .... '69 '94 C.911 B.A. L.950 J.D. [Bodyfelt M.S.&C.]
Wiscarson, Diane F., (BV) ....'58 '96 C.112 B.A. L.1051 J.D. [D.F.Wiscarson]
Wiscarson, Diane Frost, P.C., (BV) .... 317 SW Alder 9th Fl.
Wise, Michael T., (BV) .... '64 '92 C&L.629 B.S., J.D. [Wise&Assoc.]
Wise & Associates, P.C., (BV) ....806 Southwest Broadway

Wiseman Law Office, P.C.
(See Hillsboro)

Wiser, Ralph E., III
(See Lake Oswego)

Witt, Brian R., (AV) ....'57 '82 C.506 B.S. L.950 J.D. [Farleigh W.]
Wittmayer, John A. ....'46 '73 C.1056 B.S. L.1051 J.D. Cir.J.
Wittrock, John T. .... '53 '83 C.813 B.A. L.629 J.D. [Wittrock&O.]
Wittrock & O'Brien, P.C., (BV) .... 2705 E. Burnside, Suite 212
Wobbrock, Lawrence, (AV) .... '48 '77 C.629 B.S. L.596 J.D. [L.Wobbrock]

Wobbrock, Lawrence, Trial Lawyer P.C., (AV) BR
Tenth Floor Jackson Tower, 806 SW Broadway, 97205
Telephone: 503-228-6600 Fax: 503-222-4787 URL: http://www.lawyers.com/lawrence_wobbrock
URL: http://www.wobbrocklaw.com
Email: lwobbrock@wobbrock.com URL: http://www.wobbrock.com
Lawrence Wobbrock;—Richard A. Lane.
Civil Trial Practice in State and Federal Courts, including Personal Injury, Medical Malpractice, Trade Secret Litigation, Professional Negligence, Products Liability.
See Professional Biographies, PORTLAND, OREGON

Wolf, Robert L., & Associates, (AV) '49 '77 C.912 B.A. L.201 J.D.
1207 S.W. 6th Avenue, 97204
Telephone: 503-241-0992 Fax: 503-228-4529 URL: http://www.wolflaw.net
Email: rwolf8888@att.net URL: http://www.lawyers.com/robertwolf
Personal Injury, Automobile Accidents, Dog Bites, Sexual Abuse, Slip and Fall, Wrongful Death, Legal Malpractice.
See Professional Biographies, PORTLAND, OREGON

Wolfe, Dee J. .... '46 '78 C&L.1051 B.S., J.D. [D.J.Wolfe]
Wolfe, Donald Vincent Sisk '51 '86 C.668 B.A. L.911 J.D.
(adm. in WA; not adm. in OR) Bonneville Power Adm.
Wolfe, Dee J., PC ....818 NW 14th Street
Wolfstone, Jeffrey C., (AV) .... '— '77 C.813 A.B. L.1066 J.D. [Lane P.]
Wolk-Laniewski, Vickie ...... '53 '91 C.628 B.A. L.950 J.D. 520 S.W. Yamhill, Suite 600
Won, Deniece Birdseye .... '45 '92 C.629 B.A. L.1051 J.D. Portland Boundary Comm.
Wong, Francis J. .... '46 '80 C.911 B.A. L.629 J.D. 7931 N.E. Halsey
Wong, Hap Y., (BV) .... '48 '76 C.685 B.A. L.629 J.D. 6803 S.E. 35th Ave.
Wong, Jack C. ....'38 '65 C.629 B.S. L.178 LL.B. 1st Asst. U.S. Atty.
Wong, Jeffrey M., (AV) ....'56 '84 C.685 B.A. L.629 J.D. [Greene&M.]
Wood, Carrie M. ....'77 '04 C.999 B.S. L.950 J.D. [Ⓐ Schwabe,W.&W.]
Wood, Erskine B., (AV) .... '11 '36 C&L.309 A.B., LL.B. 1001 S.W. Fifth Ave.‡
Wood, Marcus, (AV) ....'47 '74 C.880 B.A. L.976 J.D. [Stoel R.]
Wood, Sandra .... '69 '01 C&L.352 B.A., J.D. 8800 S.E. Causey Loop, F304
Wood, Thomas R. ....'61 '93 C.813 B.A. L.178 J.D. [Stoel R.]

Wood Tatum Sanders & Murphy, (AV)
1001 S.W. Fifth Avenue, Suite 1300, 97204-1151
Telephone: 503-224-5430 Facsimile: 503-241-7235
Email: info@woodtatum.com URL: http://www.woodtatum.com
Members of Firm: Robert I. Sanders; John C. Mercer; Craig C. Murphy; Todd A. Zilbert.
General Civil and Trial Practice in all State and Federal Courts. Admiralty/Maritime, Insurance Defense and Estate Planning, Wills and Probate, Trusts and Estates.
Representative Clients: Assuranceforeningen Skuld; Britannia Steam Ship Ins. Assn. Ltd.; Japan Ship Owners' Mutual P & I Assn.; Steamship Mutual Underwriting Assn. Ltd.; United Kingdom Mutual Steam Ship Assurance Assn.
See Professional Biographies, PORTLAND, OREGON

Woodford, Barbara Ann, (BV) '53 '81
C.188 B.S. L.1051 J.D. Liberty Northwest Ins. Corp.
Woodrich, Kenneth B. ....'56 '83 C&L.629 B.S., J.D. [K.B.Woodrich]
Woodrich, Kenneth B., P.C. ....4370 N.E. Halsey
Woods, Lynnia K., (BV) ....'55 '81 C.629 B.S. L.950 J.D. [Ⓒ Yazbeck,C.&H.]
Woods-Eliot, Scot J., Law Office of '67 '00 C.685 B.A. L.1051 J.D.
10565 S.E. 23rd Ave.
Woodward, Peggy Kay ....'55 '80 C.628 B.A. L.629 J.D. Med. Res. Network
Woodworth, Bradley J., (CV) ..... '51 '85 C.604 A.B. L.596 J.D. 1020 Sw Taylor Ste 360
Worthley, Todd R. .... '66 '91 C.629 B.A. L.1194 J.D. 521 S.W. Clay St., Ste. 210
Wosko, Marybeth ....'— '92 C.184 B.A. L.596 J.D. [Welch,B.&G.]
Wray, Deanna L. ....'68 '97 C.576 B.S. L.596 J.D. [Ⓐ Bodyfelt M.S.&C.]
Wren, Geoffrey G., (AV) ....'57 '85 C.893 B.A. L.945 J.D. [Hill&W.]
Wright, Carol B. ....'47 '79 C.112 B.A. L.818 J.D. 1130 S.W. Morrison
Wright, Robin J. ....'57 '86 C.685 B.A. L.178 J.D. [Ⓐ Gevurtz,M.L.&H.]
Wright, Theresa L. '55 '81
C.1331 B.A. L.950 J.D. Clinical Prof., Northwestern Sch. of Law
Wright, Zachary W.L. ....'64 '94 C.882 B.A. L.477 J.D. [Tonkon T.]
Wuepper, Kyle D. ....'72 '00 C.931 B.A. L.629 J.D. [Ⓐ Stoel R.]
Wyatt, Merri Souther ....'48 '78 C.629 B.A. L.950 J.D. Cir. Ct. J.
Wyatt, Wendell, (AV) ....'17 '41 L.629 LL.B. [Schwabe,W.&W.] ‡
Wyers, Jan, (BV) .... '39 '75 C.629 B.A. L.596 J.D. Cir.J.
Wygant, Gerald D., (BV) ....'33 '60 C.629 B.S. L.596 LL.B. 521 SW Clay
Wyman, Ty K. .... '64 '92 C.112 B.A. L.629 J.D. [Ⓒ Dunn C.A.H.&T.]
Wymetalek, Craig, (BV) ....'70 '96 C.629 B.A. L.596 J.D. [Gearing,R.&E.]
Wynn, John M. ....'60 '89 C.602 B.A. L.221 J.D. [McGill,K.&W.]
Wynne, Steven E., (AV) ....'52 '77 C&L.950 B.A., J.D. [Ater W.]
Wyse, Aloha L. .... '44 '80 C.289 B.A. L.1051 J.D. 4309 S.W. Twombly Ave.
Wyse, Scott C., (AV) ....'48 '74 C.659 B.A. L.629 J.D. [Meyer&W.]
Xóchihua, Paul R., (AV) ....'61 '88 C.1051 B.S. L.596 J.D. [Davis R.E.&X.]
Xu, Xin ....'75 '00 C&L.629 B.A., J.D. [Ⓐ Kennedy,W.A.&R.]
Yakimovsky, Yoram ....'49 '95 C.813 Ph.D. L.596 J.D. 2801 N. Gatenbein Ave.
Yamada, Terence J., (AV) .... '50 '75 C.629 B.A. L.596 J.D. [Anderson&Y.]
Yarnall, Rick A., (BVⓉ) '47 '73 C&L.793 B.S., J.D.
(adm. in SD; not adm. in OR) 1300 SW 5th Ave
Yarosh, Steven M. '55 '92 C.1175 B.S. L.597 J.D.
(adm. in IL; not adm. in OR) [Ⓐ Smith F.&E.]
Yates, Michael A., (AV) .... '56 '83 C.381 B.A. L.608 J.D. [Yates,M.&Assoc.]

Yates, Matthews & Associates, P.C., (AV)
One SW Columbia Street, Suite 1800, 97258
Telephone: 503-224-7077 Fax: 503-224-8080
URL: http://www.yatesmatthews.com
Michael A. Yates; Jeffrey S. Matthews;—Brenna A. Tanzosh; Kristin Winnie Eaton. Of Counsel: JoAnn B. Reynolds.
Practice limited to Family Law, including Premarital Agreements, Postnuptial Agreements, Cohabitation Agreements, Domestic Partnerships, Divorce, Separation Agreements, Spousal Support, Child Support, Child Custody and Parenting Time, Post Divorce Modification, Post Divorce Enforcement, Paternity, Third Party Custody, Visitation Rights, Domestic Violence and Name Changes.
See Professional Biographies, PORTLAND, OREGON

Yazbeck, Joseph A., Jr., (AV) .... '48 '74 C.420 B.S. L.861 J.D. [Yazbeck,C.&H.]

Yazbeck, Cloran & Hanson, LLC, (AV)
2750 Wells Fargo Center, 1300 S.W. Fifth Avenue, 97201
Telephone: 503-227-1428 Fax: 503-227-4866 URL: http://www.yazbeckhanson.com
Email: yazbeckhanson.com URL: http://www.lawyers.com/yazbeckhanson
Joseph A. Yazbeck, Jr.; William F. Cloran; Jeffrey K. Hanson;—Heather McNamee; David Hunter Bowser. Of Counsel: Lynnia K. Woods; Robert K. Lau.
Construction, Public Contracts, Surety Bond Claims and Defense, Mechanic's Liens, Information Technology, Commercial, General Business, General Practice, Zoning and Land Use, Wills and Probate, Bankruptcy, Business Enterprises, Real Estate, Commercial Leasing.
See Professional Biographies, PORTLAND, OREGON

Yeats, Elizabeth, (AV) ....'50 '75 C.339 B.A. L.629 J.D. [Seifer,Y.M.&Z.]
Yelnosky, Maryann, (AV) ....'54 '86 C&L.629 B.S., J.D. [Barran L.]
Yimesgen, Michael ....'75 '04 C.112 B.A. L.950 J.D. [Ⓐ Bullivant H.B.]

Yoder, Christian '48 '85 L.037 LL.B.
(adm. in AB; not adm. in OR) Sr. Coun., Enron N. America Corp.
Yoelin, Merritt S., (P.C.), (AV) '40 '66
C.208 B.S.B.A. L.1066 LL.B. [Samuels Y.K.S.&S.]
Yoshida, Stephen P. ... '78 '04 C.670 B.A. L.629 J.D. [⊡ Martin,B.T.L.&H.]
Yoshinaka, Russ K. ... '71 '96 C&L.911 B.A., J.D. [⊡ Davis D.K.]
You, Youlee Yim ... '64 '89 C.914 B.A. L.911 J.D. Dept. of Justice
Youngberg, Leif C. ... '65 '92 C.846 B.B.A. L.560 J.D. 5026 N.E. 21st Avenue
Younger, Laurie M. ... '69 '97 C.629 B.A. L.188 J.D. [⊡ Ater W.]

Yturri Rose, LLP
(See Ontario)

Yu, Chuck ... '59 '91 C.112 B.A. L.629 J.D. 333 S.W. 5th Ave., Ste. 700
Yugler, Richard S., (AV) ... '55 '80 C.823 B.A. L.1051 J.D. [Landye B.B.]

Yunker, Conrad E., P.C.
(See Salem)

Yuska, Joseph E. '53 '79 C.679 B.S. L.1119 J.D.
(adm. in FL; not adm. in OR) Lewis & Clark Coll.

Zabinsky, Zachary, (AV) '54 '80 C.939 B.A. L.629 J.D.
1435 American Bank Building, 621 S.W. Morrison Street, 97205
Telephone: 503-223-8517 Fax: 503-273-8842
Email: zachzabinsky@aol.com
Personal Injury, Housing Discrimination, Social Security Disability.
See Professional Biographies, PORTLAND, OREGON

Zachary, Michael N. ... '56 '84 C.178 B.A. L.309 J.D. [⊡ Klarquist S.] (⊙Seattle, WA)
Zackheim, Ivan S., (BV) '47 '76
C.1154 B.A. L.629 J.D. 5550 S.W. Macadam Ave., Ste. 330
Zakovics, Zigismunds I., (AV) ... '42 '67 C.413 B.S. L.950 J.D. [Zakovics T.&R.]
Zakovics Thompson & Ritchey PC, (AV) ... 101 S.W. Main St., Ste. 1940
Zalutsky, Morton H., (AV) ... '35 '61 C.976 B.A. L.145 J.D. [Zalutsky&K.]
Zalutsky & Klarquist, P.C., (AV) ... 215 S.W. Washington Street, 3rd Floor
Zarosinski, David J., (AV) ... '54 '79 C.628 B.S. L.629 J.D. [Zarosinski&H.]
Zarosinski & Hill LLP, (AV) ... 520 S.W. Sixth Avenue Suite 1200
Zarzana, George J., (CV) ... '43 '78 C.740 B.A. L.426 J.D. 807 N.E. Alberta St.
Zbinden, Jon A., (BV) ... '58 '82 C.1051 B.S. L.596 J.D. [Zbinden&C.]
Zbinden & Curtis, (BV) ... 817 NE Broadway
Zehntbauer, J. David ... '69 '96 C.112 B.A. L.950 J.D. [⊡ Dunn C.A.H.&T.]
Zehren, James A., (AV) ... '48 '85 C.597 B.S. L.1051 J.D. [Stoel R.]
Zeitz, Sanford W., (BV) ... '54 '82 C.184 B.A. L.596 J.D. 8030 N.E. Clackamas St.
Zelenak, Lawrence A. '55 '79 C.770 B.A. L.309 J.D.
(adm. in WA; not adm. in OR)
Asst. Prof., Northwestern Sch. of Law of Lewis and Clark Coll.

Zelko, Katherine M., (AV) '53 '82 C.312 B.A. L.208 J.D.
River Forum, Suite 500, 4380 S.W. Macadam Avenue, 97239-6412
Telephone: 503-223-2321 Facsimile: 503-294-6051
Probate and Estate Planning, Estate, Gift and Fiduciary Income Tax.

Zeuthen, Gregory K., (AV) ... '59 '84 C.1085 B.S. L.1051 J.D. [G.K.Zeuthen]

Zeuthen, Gregory K., Attorney at Law, PC, (AV)
1515 S.W. Fifth Avenue, Suite 808, 97201
Telephone: 503-227-7257 Fax: 503-228-1556
Email: gkz@zlawoffice.com URL: http://www.lawyers.com/zeuthen
Gregory K. Zeuthen.
General Civil and Trial Practice, Plaintiff's Personal Injury, Professional Liability, Products Liability, Medical Malpractice, Lasik Eye Surgery Malpractice, Wrongful Death and Automobile Accidents.
See Professional Biographies, PORTLAND, OREGON

Zilbert, Todd A. ... '60 '88 C.112 A.B. L.1068 J.D. [Wood T.S.&M.]
Zimmer, Gary J., (AV) ... '50 '75 C.251 B.A. L.930 J.D. [Zimmer&B.]
Zimmer & Bunch, LLC, (AV) ... 1 S.W. Columbia Street
Zimmerman, Lin A. ... '45 '75 C.1056 B.A. L.596 J.D. Royal Indemnity Co.
Zipper, Steven M. ... '70 '96 C.477 B.A. L.950 J.D. [⊡ Black H.]
Zipse, Mark L., (AV) '55 '82 C.740 B.S. L.596 J.D.
10260 S.W. Greenburg Rd., Ste. 710
Zittenfield, Lee M. '41 '68
C.1056 B.S. L.596 J.D. Lee Zittenfield Professional Cutlery Sup.
Zollinger, Jay A. ... '67 '97 C.94 B.A. L.1066 J.D. [Perkins C.]
Zotter, James F. ... '43 '69 C.757 A.B. L.309 J.D. Fed. Hwy. Admn.
Zucker, Linda ... '39 '74 C.66 B.A. L.596 J.D. Ref., Environmental Quality Comm.
Zupancic, James D., (AV) ... '— '79 C.101 B.S. L.464 J.D. [Davis W.T.]
Zwerling, Marc, (BV) ... '49 '73 C.685 B.A. L.596 J.D. 1001 S.W. 5th Ave.
Zwierzynski, Steven, (AV) ... '63 '90 C.352 B.B.A. L.596 J.D. [Seifer,Y.M.&Z.]

PORT ORFORD, 1,153, *Curry Co.*

Abbott, Stephen K. ... '40 '69 C.763 A.B. L.1065 J.D. 2110 Jackson Street‡
AuFranc, Richard E. ... '36 '73 C.628 B.S. L.950 J.D. 901 Oregon St.

POST, —, *Crook Co.*

Thompson, Wade R., (AV⊕) '46 '73 C.1060 B.S. L.464 J.D.
(adm. in CA; not adm. in OR) 135808 Shotgun Rd.‡

POWELL BUTTE, 1,059, *Crook Co.*

Steltenpohl, Garth F. ... '27 '54 C.629 B.S. L.596 LL.B. 15620 S.W. Twin Lakes Rd.‡

PRINEVILLE, * 7,356, *Crook Co.*

Borgman, Richard B., (AV) '55 '80 C&L.950 B.S., J.D.
Sr. Exec. V.P. & Gen. Coun., Les Schwab Tire Centers
Borneman, Nancy A., (CV) ... '53 '78 C.628 B.S. L.861 J.D. 545 N.E. 7th St.
Brenneman, Aaron L. ... '72 '99 C.628 B.A. L.950 J.D. Co. Dist. Atty. Off.
Condron, William J. ... '66 '93 C.628 B.A. L.950 J.D. [W.Condron]
Condron, William ... P.O. Box 133
Dutli, Carl M., (BV) ... '47 '74 C.1104 B.S. L.629 J.D. N.E. 7th St.
Eckrem, John P. ... '62 '96 C.1273 B.A. L.629 J.D. 545 N.E. 7th St.
Gibson, David R. '61 '88 C.629 B.S. L.1051 J.D.
Corp. Coun., Les Schwab Tire Centers

Hurley, Lynch & Re, P.C., (AV)
446 NW 3rd Street, Suite 230, 97754 ⊙
Telephone: 541-447-5777 Fax: 541-447-5755
Email: info@hlr-law.com URL: http://www.hlandr.com
Jeffrey M. Wilson.
General Civil and Trial Practice, Business, Corporate, Real Estate and Land Use, Leasing, Insurance Defense, Commercial Litigation, Water Rights Law, Taxation, Intellectual Property, Licensing, Probate and Estate Planning, Health Law, Employment Law.
Representative Clients: David Evans & Associates; Bend Research; Quality Materials, Inc.; Brooks Resources Corporation; Central Oregon Irrigation District; Scottsdale Insurance Co.; USAA; Bend Memorial Clinic.

(This Listing Continued)

Hurley, Lynch & Re, P.C. (Continued)
Bend Office: 747 S.W. Mill View Way, 97702. Telephone: 541-317-5505. Fax: 541-317-5507.
See Professional Biographies, PRINEVILLE, OREGON

Larson, James F., (BV) ... '37 '66 C.1051 B.S. L.950 J.D. 298 Nw 3rd St
McGraw, Noreen K., (AV) ... '32 '55 C&L.629 B.S., J.D. 397 NE Hogan Lane
Minturn, James B., (AV) ... '26 '52 C&L.950 B.A., J.D. 298 W. 3rd St.‡
Parks, Corey J. ... '69 '96 C&L.950 B.S., J.D. Corp. Counsel, Les Schwab Tire Centers
Powers, James W. ... '43 '71 C.637 B.A. L.596 J.D. 200 N. Belknap St.
Rappleyea, Alan A. ... '61 '89 C&L.629 B.A., J.D. Co. Coun.
Thompson, Gary S. ... '45 '72 C.628 B.S. L.950 J.D. Cir. J.
Van Voorhees, James C., (BV) ... '44 '69 C.165 A.B. L.950 J.D. 203 N. Main St.
Williams, Gary L., (BV) ... '51 '84 C.629 B.S. L.950 J.D. Crook Co. Dist. Atty.'s Off.
Wilson, Jeffrey M., (BV) ... '58 '84 C.629 B.S. L.285 J.D. [⊡ Hurley,L.&R.]
York, Daniel A., (CV) ... '45 '85 C.629 B.S. L.950 J.D. 303 E. 3rd St., Ste. 200

RAINIER, 1,674, *Columbia Co.*

Callahan, Cathleen B. ... '54 '00 C.999 B.A. L.950 J.D. [C.B.Callahan]
Callahan, Cathleen B., P.C. ... 69882 Beaverhill Dr
Lucas, Robert A., (BV) ... '38 '65 C.999 L.596 LL.B. P.O. Box 519
Lucas, Ronald Alan ... '65 '92 C.1056 B.S. L.629 J.D. 118 B W. St.

REDMOND, 13,481, *Deschutes Co.*

Brenneman, Delbert J., (BV) ... '50 '76 C.628 B.S. L.629 J.D. [Hoffman,H.&W.]
Bryant, Ronald L., (AV) ... '36 '64 C.678 L.596 J.D. [Bryant,E.&F.]
Bryant, Steven D., (BV) ... '57 '91 C.629 B.S. L.1051 J.D. [Bryant,E.&F.]

Bryant, Emerson & Fitch, (AV)
888 West Evergreen Avenue, P.O. Box 457, 97756-0103
Telephone: 541-548-2151 Fax: 541-548-1895
Email: BEF@redmond-lawyers.com
Ronald L. Bryant; Craig P. Emerson; Edward P. Fitch; Geoffrey J. Gokey; Steven D. Bryant;— Michael R. McLane; John E. Laherty.
Business Law, Corporate, Estate Planning, Personal Injury, Family Law, Insurance, Insurance Defense, Litigation, Municipal Law, Probate, Real Estate, Trusts and Estates, Wills.
Representative Clients: Redmond Public School District; City of Sisters; Eberhard Creamery, Inc.; St. Charles Medical Center; Farm Credit Leasing; Central Oregon Community College; City of Redmond; C Corp.; Sage Builders; Mel Rose Inc.

Bryant, Lovlien & Jarvis, P.C.
(See Bend)

Clark, Stanley E., (CV) ... '41 '67 C.628 B.S. L.1065 J.D. 627 W. Deschutes St.
Duncan, Karen E. ... '52 '92 C.36 B.S. L.1189 J.D. [Oliver&D.]
Emerson, Craig P., (BV) ... '47 '76 C.37 B.A. L.596 J.D. [Bryant,E.&F.]

Farra, Roxanne L., P.C.
(See Bend)

Fendall, Michael R. ... '56 '86 C.1071 B.S. L.596 J.D. [Hoffman,H.&W.]
Fitch, Edward P., (BV) ... '51 '78 C.436 B.A. L.950 J.D. [Bryant,E.&F.]
Folliard, John F., Jr., (AV) ... '48 '74 C&L.596 B.A., J.D. [Hoffman,H.&W.]
Gokey, Geoffrey J., (BV) ... '56 '89 C.1056 B.S. L.596 J.D. [Bryant,E.&F.]
Hart, John E., (AV) ... '46 '74 C.1056 B.S. L.596 J.D. [Hoffman,H.&W.]
Hodgkinson, Martha J., (AV) ... '56 '86 C.628 B.A. L.596 J.D. [Hoffman,H.&W.]
Hoffman, Michael D., (AV) ... '45 '71 C&L.950 B.A., J.D. [Hoffman,H.&W.]
Hoffman, Hart & Wagner, (AV) ... 439 S.E. Umatilla Ave.
Hooper, Ruth J., (AV) ... '53 '77 C.477 B.A. L.629 J.D. [Hoffman,H.&W.]

Hurley, Lynch & Re, P.C.
(See Bend)

Kowolowski, Fred A., (CV) ... '43 '74 C.628 B.S. L.629 J.D. [F.Kowolowski]
Kowolowski, Fred, (CV) ... 1323 S.W. 15th St.
Kraemer, Steven A. ... '56 '88 C.1056 B.S. L.1051 J.D. [Hoffman,H.&W.]
Krause, Thomas Earl '47 '97 C.960 B.S. L.1484 J.D.
(adm. in CA; not adm. in OR) P.O. Box 1471
Laherty, John E. ... '66 '92 C.477 B.A. L.339 J.D. [⊡ Bryant,E.&F.]
Martin, James P., (AV) ... '56 '81 C.229 B.A. L.607 J.D. [Hoffman,H.&W.]
McKelvey, Connie Elkins, (AV) ... '57 '83 C.629 B.S. L.596 J.D. [Hoffman,H.&W.]
McLane, Michael R. ... '— '90 C.628 B.S. L.1051 J.D. [⊡ Bryant,E.&F.]
Mepham, David S., (BV) ... '66 '91 C.911 B.A. L.950 J.D. [Hoffman,H.&W.]
Oliver, Donald E. ... '47 '82 C.629 B.S. L.1148 J.D. [Oliver&D.]
Oliver & Duncan ... 836 SW 12th Street
Olmsted, Mark E., (BV) ... '67 '92 C.906 B.S. L.950 J.D. [Hoffman,H.&W.]
Reese, Dennis S., (AV) ... '50 '79 C&L.950 B.S., J.D. [Hoffman,H.&W.]
Renner, Kenneth D., (AV) ... '39 '69 C&L.629 B.S., J.D. [Hoffman,H.&W.]
Schroer, Janet M., (AV) ... '56 '81 C.97 B.A. L.629 J.D. [Hoffman,H.&W.]
Street, Jeffrey R., (AV) ... '60 '86 C.911 B.A. L.1051 J.D. [Hoffman,H.&W.]
Wagner, Mark H., (AV) ... '46 '73 C.999 B.A. L.477 J.D. [Hoffman,H.&W.]
Welborn, Gordon L., (AV) ... '60 '87 C.1056 B.S. L.596 J.D. 439 S.E. Umatilla Ave.
Wiswall, Michael J. ... '67 '94 C.112 B.A. L.477 J.D. [Hoffman,H.&W.]
Witty, John V., (BV) ... '48 '88 C.330 B.S. L.629 J.D. 145 Se Salmon Ave Ste A

REEDSPORT, 4,378, *Douglas Co.*

Anderson, David R., (BV) ... '45 '72 C&L.378 B.S., J.D. 780 Winchester Ave.
Miller, Stephen H., (BV) ... '44 '69 C.210 B.A. L.851 J.D. [S.H.Miller]
Miller, Stephen H., PC, (BV) ... 320 Fir Ave.

ROGUE RIVER, 1,847, *Jackson Co.*

Heuertz, Loren L. ... '44 '73 C.801 B.A. L.347 J.D. [Heuertz&M.]
Heuertz and Monen, P.C. ... 214 E. Main
Monen, Craig W. ... '48 '75 C.801 B.A. L.546 J.D. [Heuertz&M.]

ROSEBURG, * 20,017, *Douglas Co.*

Aitken, Ronald W., (CV) ... '59 '86 C.310 B.A. L.1355 J.D. [Dole,C.C.M.M.&A.]
Aller, Leeon F., III, (BV) ... '47 '82 C.911 B.A. L.629 J.D. [Aller&M.]
Aller & Morrison, P.C., (BV) ... 223 S.E. Fowler
Anderson, Robert H. ... '23 '51 C.628 B.S. L.950 LL.B. Ret. Dist. J.
Arneson, James A., (BV) ... '45 '77 C.491 B.A. L.1051 J.D. [J.A.Arneson]
Arneson, James A., P.C., (BV) ... 318 S.E. Jackson St.

Arnold Gallagher Saydack Percell Roberts & Potter, P.C.
(See Eugene)

Banta, Jack L., (BV) ... '46 '72 C&L.629 B.S., J.D. Dist. Atty.
Benson, Colin Derek, (CV) ... '68 '98 C.1051 B.A. L.950 J.D. D.A.'s Off., Douglas Cnty.
Bernier, Thomas C., (BV) ... '47 '77 C.475 B.A. L.629 J.D. [⊡ J.A.Arneson]
Brown, Katrina L. ... '69 '97 C.280 B.A. L.629 J.D. Juv. Dept.
Caley, Eldon F., (AV) ... '30 '56 C&L.950 B.A., J.D. [E.F.Caley,II]

Caley, Eldon F., Lawyer, P.C. II, (AV)
326 Rose Street, P.O. Box 2057, 97470
Telephone: 541-672-8877 FAX: 541-672-2740
Email: caley@mcsi.net

(This Listing Continued)

Caley, Eldon F., Lawyer, P.C. II (Continued)

Eldon F. Caley.
Arbitration and Mediation services. General Civil Practice with emphasis on Business or Tort litigation related matters in state court. Personal Injury and other claims for plaintiffs or defense. Legal and Medical Malpractice. School and administrative law, Estate Planning and Litigation.

See Professional Biographies, ROSEBURG, OREGON

Canfield, Michael L. '68 '95 C.1042 B.A. L.1065 J.D. Coun., UMPQUA
Carlson, Gordon G., (AV) '19 '48 C.791 B.S. L.477 J.D. 913 S.E. Main St.‡
Clark, Dan W., (BV) '54 '81 C.906 B.A. L.629 J.D. [Dole,C.C.M.M.&A.]
Coalwell, Bruce R., (BV) '55 '81 C&L.629 B.A., J.D. [Dole,C.C.M.M.&A.]
Cook, Marianna M. '29 '61 C.338 B.S. L.146 J.D.
(adm. in IL; not adm. in OR) 1751 S.W. Fairhill‡
Cook, Nancy E., (CV) '49 '88 C&L.629 B.S., J.D. Asst. Pub. Def.
Cremer, Richard A., (BV) '50 '75 C.1056 B.S. L.596 J.D. [R.A. .P.Cremer]
Cremer, Richard A., PC, (BV) 727 SE Cass Ave Ste 400
Davis, Rebecca '60 '89 C.1051 B.A. L.629 J.D. [[A] J.A.Arneson]
Dole, Donald A., (AV) '27 '51 C&L.629 B.S., LL.B. [Dole,C.C.M.M.&A.] ‡
Dole, Coalwell, Clark, Mountainspring, Mornarich & Aitken, P.C., (BV)
810 S.E. Douglas Avenue
Farrell, James C. '43 '68 C&L.629 B.A., J.D. [J.C.Farrell]
Farrell, James C., P.C. 1243 S.E. Douglas
Felker, Carl M. '12 '42 C.950 L.596 LL.B. P.O. Box 1305‡
Gandy, Harry, Law Offices of, (BV) '49 '79 C.112 B.A. L.284 J.D. 850 S.E. Rose St.
Garrison, Randolph Lee, (BV) '51 '76 C.1051 B.S. L.596 J.D. [R.L.Garrison]
Garrison, Randolph Lee, P.C., (BV) 430 Southeast Main Street
Guerra, Ronald G., (CV) '54 '92 C.999 B.A. L.1187 J.D. 435 Se Kane St
Hill, Gary L., (CV) '46 '74 C.413 B.A. L.950 J.D. P.O. Box 1146
Hockett, Sharon Lee, (CV) '56 '81 C&L.629 B.A., J.D. [S.L.Hockett]
Hockett, Verden L., Jr. '29 '57 C.336 B.S. L.950 LL.B. P.O. Box 986‡
Hockett, Sharon L., (CV) 251 N.E. Garden Vly., Ste. K
Holm, William R., (AVⓉ) '48 '73 C.169 B.A. L.464 J.D. 1380 Whistlers Lane

Hutchinson, Cox, Coons, DuPriest, Orr & Sherlock, P.C.
(See Eugene)

Jaqua & Wheatley, LLC
(See Eugene)

Johnson, Andrew D., (CV) '67 '92 C&L.629 B.A., J.D. [A.D.Johnson]
Johnson, Darryl E. '39 '65 C&L.629 B.S., LL.B. [D.E.Johnson]
Johnson, Roland A., (BV) '47 '74 C.309 A.B. L.629 J.D. [Nilsen,J.&M.]
Johnson, Andrew D., PC, (CV) 840 S.E. Rose St.
Johnson, Darryl E., P.C. 840 S.E. Rose St.
Johnston, Kathryn, (CV) '57 '84 C.65 B.A. L.629 J.D. 850 S.E. Rose St.
Kaser, Stephen W., (BV) '51 '77 C.670 B.A. L.629 J.D. [Lee&K.]
Kelley, Donald S. '21 '50 C&L.629 J.D. P.O. Box 937‡
Kennerly, Clifford W., (BV) '50 '75 C.628 B.S. L.629 J.D. Co. Coun.
Kolberg, Thomas W. '42 '67 C&L.629 B.S., J.D. Cir. J.
Krouse, Lori Lynn '71 '97 C.628 B.A. L.1148 J.D. Dep. Dist. Atty.
Lasswell, Roberta Lee, (CV) '52 '84
C.205 B.A. L.36 J.D. Dist. Atty., Douglas Co. Dist. Atty. Off.
Lasswell, William L. '34 '62 C.950 B.A. L.629 LL.B. Cir. J.
Lee, Charles F., (AV) '48 '74 C.685 B.A. L.629 J.D. [Lee&K.]
Lee and Kaser, P.C., (AV) 880 SE Jackson St.
Long, E. Andrew '77 '03 C.116 B.A. L.950 J.D. [[A] Dole,C.C.M.M.&A.]

Lowry, Robert D., Law Offices of
(See Eugene)

Luoma, George, (AV) '18 '46 C&L.629 B.B.A., J.D. 1012 S.E. Oak St.‡
Madison, Kenneth W., (CV) '53 '82 C.1181 B.S. L.629 J.D. Mun. J.
Marshall, William A., (BV) '54 '80 C.897 B.A. L.950 J.D. Dep. Dist. Atty.
McKinney, Dan G., (AVⓉ) '56 '81
C.1209 B.A. L.464 J.D. [Nilsen,J.&M.] (ⓒRiverside, CA)
McMillin, Jane, (CV) '49 '81 C.375 B.A. L.900 J.D. 1155 S.E. Douglas
Millikan, Robert C. '46 '71 C&L.950 B.A., J.D. Cir. Ct. J.
Mornarich, Jeffrey A., (BV) '67 '93 C.629 B.S. L.950 J.D. [Dole,C.C.M.M.&A.]
Morrison, David, (BV) '49 '75 C.1169 B.A. L.1162 J.D. [Aller&M.]
Mountainspring, Stephen, (BV) '55 '90 C.363 B.S. L.1060 J.D. [Dole,C.C.M.M.&A.]

Muhlheim Boyd
(See Eugene)

Nightingale, Lorraine D. '58 '93 C.909 B.A. L.911 J.D.
(adm. in CA; not adm. in OR) 881 Arcadia Dr.
Nilsen, Peter H., (BV) '47 '72 C.1051 B.S. L.629 J.D. [Nilsen,J.&M.]

Nilsen, Johnson & McKinney, P.C., (AVⓉ)
435 S.E. Kane Street, P.O. Box 1265, 97470
Telephone: 541-673-4451 Fax: 541-673-1202
Email: njm@douglascountylaw.com URL: http://www.douglascountylaw.com
Peter H. Nilsen; Roland A. Johnson; Dan G. McKinney.
General Civil and Trial Practice. Business Transactions, Real Estate, Eminent Domain, Land Use, Mortgages, Insurance, Family Law, Divorce, Conservatorship, Guardianships, Adoption, Child Custody, Child Support, Personal Injury, Automobile Accidents, Wrongful Death, Commercial Banking, Corporate Law, Trusts and Estates, Wills and Probate, Estate Planning, Utility Law.
Representative Clients: United Bancorp; Nationwide Insurance Co.; Commercial Title Co.; Douglas County Lumber Co.; Henry Winery, Inc.

See Professional Biographies, ROSEBURG, OREGON

Packham, Howard Richard '33 '74 C.101 B.A. L.767 J.D. 2145 Melton Rd.‡
Parsons, P.C., (BV) 377 S.E. FowlerSt.
Parsons, Richard E., (BV) '45 '77 C.588 B.A. L.629 J.D. [Parsons]

Peterson Law Offices, PC
(See Portland)

Pollaczek, Peter E., (BV) '47 '73 C.112 B.A. L.1066 J.D. 318 S.E. Jackson St.
Poole, H. Ronald '46 '72 C&L.846 B.A., J.D. Cir. J.
Pugh, Jeffrey L., (BV) '51 '76 C.390 B.A. L.629 J.D. 420 SE Jackson St.
Roberts, Frances Elaine '60 '99 C.112 B.A. L.950 J.D. Douglas Co. Dist. Atty.'s Off.
Robertson, Daniel C. '51 '00 C.1056 B.A. L.629 J.D. [[A] Aller&M.]
Rubenstein, Lori Sue, (CV) '60 '87 C.549 B.A. L.1162 J.D. [L.S.Rubenstein]
Rubenstein, Lori S., L.L.C., (CV) 1032 S.E. Lane St.
Sanders, Don H. '19 '51 C&L.629 LL.B. Ret. Cir. J.
Schiffman, Doyle L. '32 '64 C.101 B.S. L.629 LL.B. 603 S.E. Jackson ST.
Schmerer-Haacke, Susan, (BV) '46 '77 C.643 B.A. L.629 J.D. [[A] J.A.Arneson]
Schwartz, Sharon Lee, (CV) '69 '95
C.198 B.A. L.276 J.D. Reg. Dir., Legal Aid Servs. of Oregon
Seitz, Daniel W., (BV) '47 '74 C.1071 B.S. L.950 J.D. [D.W.Seitz]
Seitz, Joan G. '49 '74 C.1071 B.S. L.950 J.D. Cir. J.
Seitz, Daniel W., PC, (BV) 420 S.E. Jackson St.
Shammel, Wayne A. '67 '92 C.197 A.B. L.309 J.D.
(adm. in CO; not adm. in OR) Gen. Counsel, Cow Creek Umpqua Tribe
Simmons, Ann Marie '70 '98 Douglas Co Courthouse
Smith, Norman J. '47 '72 C.597 B.S. L.950 J.D. AT&T
Smith, Sean M. '73 '97 C&L.629 B.A., J.D. P.O. Box 1233
Spens, Nancy Ellen '61 '89 C&L.629 B.S., J.D. [[A] Dole,C.C.M.M.&A.]
Stults, Robert M. '19 '51 C&L.950 LL.B. 1736 N.W. Beaumont St.‡
Thompson, Eugene M. '63 '93 C&L.502 B.A., J.D. Oregon Legal Servs. Corp.
Tower, Bruce E., (BV) '45 '71 C.623 B.S. L.950 J.D. Pub. Def.
Wales, Diana, (AV) '47 '77 C&L.629 B.S., J.D. [D.Wales]
Wales, Diana, P.C., (AV) 318 S.E. Jackson St.
Walker, Neal, (CV) '42 '76 C.766 B.A. L.629 J.D. 1490 N.W. Valley View Dr.
Washburn, Philip J. '34 '63 C.1056 L.950 LL.B. Mun. J.
Wesenberg, Richard Lee, Jr., (BV) '64 '92 C&L.629 B.S., J.D. Dep. Dist. Atty.
Wiegman, Bruce E. '48 '74 C.46 B.S. L.146 J.D. Co. Health Dept.
Wolf, Sarah J., (CV) '60 '95 C.907 B.A. L.950 J.D. 377 Se Fowler St
Yockim, Ronald S., (BV) '49 '81 C.898 B.A. L.596 J.D. 548 S.E. Jackson St., Ste. 7
Zacher, Theodore D., (BV) '45 '79 C&L.629 B.A., J.D. Chf. Dep. Dist. Atty.
Zuver, Julie A. '56 '93 C&L.629 B.A., J.D. Dist. Atty., Douglas Co. Dist. Atty. Off.

ST. HELENS, * 10,019, *Columbia Co.*

Anderson, Dale L. '48 '74 C.908 B.A. L.950 J.D.
Dep. Dist. Atty., Columbia Co. Dist. Atty. Off.
Atchison, Roy C. '22 '49 C.670 L.596 LL.B. 34876 Sykes Rd.
Atchison, Roy Stephen, (BV) '47 '77 C.629 B.S. L.1051 J.D. Dep. Dist. Atty.
Gordon, Mark A., (BV) '55 '81 C.629 B.S. L.426 J.D. [M.A. .P.Gordon]
Gordon, Mark A., PC, (BV) 1677 St. Helens Street
Grant, Jenefer Stenzel '61 '92 C.1056 B.A. L.273 J.D. 280 S. 1st St.
Huffman, James D., (BV) '49 '75 C.1056 B.S. L.1051 J.D. [O'Hanlon&H.]
Jordan, Jennifer L., (CV) '51 '86 C.629 B.F.A. L.1051 J.D. Dep. Dist. Atty.
Kalberer, Donald L. '32 '60 C&L.629 B.S., LL.B. Cir. J.
Knight, John K. '52 '78 C.906 B.A. L.629 J.D. Co. Coun.
McDonough, Marsha L. '48 '89 C.1056 B.S. L.1051 J.D. 239 South First Street
O'Hanlon, Mary T. '66 '92 C.770 B.S. L.596 J.D. [O'Hanlon&H.]
O'Hanlon & Huffman, (BV) 1905 Columbia Blvd.
Petersen, Agnes M., (AV) '36 '60 C&L.629 B.A., LL.B. [Van Natta&P.]
Reed, Steven B. '49 '72 C.1056 B.S. L.1051 J.D. Cir. J.
Sells, Martin A. '40 '72 C.120 B.A. L.596 J.D. Dist. Atty.
Smith, Berkeley Ashton '47 '75 C.629 B.S. L.285 J.D. Dist. J.
Taylor, Diana M. Shera '— '93 C.766 B.A. L.284 J.D. P.O. Box 232
Vagt, Robt. R. '15 '46 C&L.950 B.A., LL.B. 275 Strand St.‡
Van Natta, George G. '07 '28 L.950 LL.B. 222 S. 1st St.‡
VanNatta, Robert P., (BV) '45 '70 C&L.950 B.A., J.D. [Van Natta&P.]
Van Natta & Petersen, (AV) 222 S. 1st. St.
Williamson, David B., (AV) '25 '54 C.629 B.S. L.596 J.D. [Williamson&W.]
Williamson, David Brian, (BV) '47 '76 C&L.629 B.S., J.D. [Williamson&W.]
Williamson & Williamson, (AV) 230 Columbia Boulevard Post Office Box 656

ST. PAUL, 322, *Marion Co.*

Zorn, Catherine '11 '48 C.477 L.596 LL.B. 8448 Champoeg Rd., N.E.‡

SALEM, * 136,924, *Marion & Polk Cos.*

Abernethy, Pamela L. '51 '80 C.1169 A.B. L.950 J.D. Cir. Ct. J.
Ackerman, Robert M. '51 '76 C.165 B.A. L.309 J.D.
(adm. in CO; not adm. in OR) Dean & Prof. of Law, Willamette Univ.
Adams, Jas Jeffrey, (AV) '49 '76 C.685 B.A. L.1066 J.D. Asst. Atty. Gen.
Adams, Randall J., (BV) '53 '91 C.336 B.S. L.950 J.D. 339 Washington St. S.E.
Addison, C. F. '07 '40 L.950 LL.B. 860 Church St., N.E.‡
Ahmed, James J. '39 '70 C.932 B.A. L.950 J.D. [[A] Ferder,C.&F.]
Aho, Erik C. '56 '87 C.628 B.S. L.1051 J.D.
(adm. in WA; not adm. in OR) Atty., Dep. of Fin. & Corp. Sec.
Aiken, Jane E., (BV) '53 '80 C&L.629 B.S., J.D. 520 State St.
Ainsworth, Alfred, III '62 '91 C&L.378 B.S., J.D. 2364 Twinberry Ave., S.E.
Ainsworth, Todd C., (AV) '53 '79 C.1104 B.A. L.629 J.D. Asst. Atty. Gen.
Albert, John D., (AV) '51 '76 C.1051 B.S. L.629 J.D. [Albert,T.C.&H.]
Albert, Tweet, Connolly & Hanna, (AV) 242 Church Street S.E.
Alessi, Diane L., (BV) '53 '79 C.25 B.A. L.1051 J.D. Chf. Dep. Pub. Def.
Alexander, Carolyn '53 '98 C.629 B.S. L.597 J.D. 1162 Court St. N.E.
Alexander, Douglas C., II, (AV) '56 '83 C.101 B.S. L.950 J.D. [Saalfeld G.]
Alexander, J. Michael, (AV) '46 '75 C.813 B.A. L.950 J.D. [Burt,S.L.A.M.&S.]
Allen, Richard H., (AV) '22 '49 C.878 L.950 LL.B. [Allen,F.&O.]
Allen, Suzzette Carol '61 '94 C.990 B.A. L.911 J.D.
(adm. in WA; not adm. in OR) Oregon State Lottery
Allen, William D. '46 '88 C.1044 B.S. L.1051 J.D. Jud. Clerk, Or. Supm. Ct.
Allen, Fox & Olson, (AV) 100 High St., S.E.
Alway, Richard F., (BV) '50 '77 C.905 B.A. L.950 J.D. [Alway&C.]
Alway & Craig, (BV) P.O. Box 787
Amala, Carl R., (AV) '56 '85 C.446 B.S. L.950 J.D. [Harris,W.&A.]
Ammann, Ken L., (BV) '61 '88 C.906 B.A. L.950 J.D. [Spooner,M.&A.]
Andersen, H. Thomas '51 '77 C.339 B.A. L.629 J.D. Trial Coun., SAIF Corporation
Anderson, Steve, (CV) '14 '42 C&L.950 B.A., LL.B. 3925 Triangle Dr., S.E.
Andrews, Lawrence W., (BV) '57 '87 C.1110 B.A. L.950 J.D. [[A] D.A. .a.L.H.P.Rhoten]
Andrus, Stephanie S., (BV) '67 '92 C&L.950 B.S., J.D. Asst. Atty. Gen.
Anselm, Kevin C. '59 '94 C.670 B.B.A. L.950 J.D. Admin. Law J.
Armitage, Stephen P. '65 '90 C.051 B.A. L.228 J.D. Staff Atty., Supreme Ct. of OR
Armstrong, Rex '50 '77 C.659 B.A. L.629 J.D. Ct. of App. J.
Armstrong, Sean E. '— '01 C.945 B.A. L.1209 J.D. [[A] Garrett,H.R.J.C.&T.]
Arnold, Donald C. '48 '75 C.112 B.A. L.950 J.D. Chf. Coun., Dept. of Jus.
Arritola, Shelly M. '74 '00 C&L.950 B.A., J.D. [[A] Saalfeld G.]
Art, Robert C. '48 '78 C.72 B.A. L.209 J.D.
Prof. of Law, Willamette Univ. Coll. of Law
Ashcroft, Lynn E., (AV) '49 '79 C.101 B.A. L.464 J.D. [Ashcroft W.]
Ashcroft Wiles, LLP, (AV) 1820 Commercial Street SE
Atkinson, Robert M., (AV) '43 '74 C.494 B.A. L.1066 J.D. 1162 Court St Ne
Augustyn, Thomas P. '47 '73 C.963 B.S. L.966 J.D.
(adm. in WI; not adm. in OR) Dept. of Transp.
Babbitt, Michael J. '56 '92 C.172 B.S. L.1065 J.D. 5583 Basil St. N.E.
Babcock, Gary D. '32 '61 C.629 B.S. L.950 LL.B. Pub. Def.
Bailey, Henry J., III '16 '48 C.645 B.A. L.976 J.D.
Prof. of Law, Emeritus, Willamette Univ. Coll. of Law‡
Bailey, Mari, (BV) '54 '90 C&L.950 B.S., J.D. [M.Bailey]
Bailey, Mari, P.C., (BV) 2985 River Rd. S.
Baker, Elizabeth '60 '96 C.740 B.A. L.1051 J.D. P.O. Box 12159
Barber, Richard D., Sr. '28 '55 C.629 B.S. L.950 J.D. Sr. J.
Barker, Carol M. '55 '91 C.939 B.A. L.950 J.D. 4531 Anneka Loop S.E.

Barkin, Thomas G. ....'48 '74 C&L.966 B.A., J.D. Asst. Comm., Pub. Utility Comm.
Barlow, H. William ....'27 '56 C.629 B.S. L.950 LL.B. Sr. Dist. J.
Barlow, Jeffrey N., (CV) '49 '76
C.228 B.A. L.950 J.D. Mgr., Info Tech Projects Off., Jud. Dept.
Bartelt, Alice M., (BV) ..... '47 '81 C.766 B.A. L.1051 J.D. Staff Atty., SAIF Corporation
Barton, Jennelle ....'62 '90 C.1109 B.A. L.1066 J.D. Dep. Pub. Def.
Barton, Jesse Wm., (BV) ....'55 '87 C.629 B.A. L.950 J.D. 161 High St. S.E., Ste. 250
Bartz, Gerald F. ....'21 '55 C.339 B.S. L.950 LL.B. Asst. Atty. Gen.
Bates, David F., (CV) ....'19 '57 C&L.950 B.A., LL.B. 1810 45th Ave., N.E.
Bauer, Keith J., (AV) ....'47 '73 C&L.950 B.A., J.D. [Parks,B.S.&W.]
Belcher, Kathryn M. .... '58 '99 C.635 B.A. L.950 J.D. 1820 Lancaster Dr. N.E.
Benjamin, Joyce Holmes ....'31 '74 C&L.629 A.B., J.D. Assoc. Supt., Dept. of Educ.
Bennett, J. Channing ....'67 '97 C.999 B.A. L.93 J.D. [Garrett,H.R.J.C.&T.]
Bergen, Lowell W. '43 '68 C&L.950 B.S., J.D.
Admin. Law J., Ore. Pub. Utility Comm.‡
Betterton, Ken L., (BV) .... '47 '74 C.629 B.A. L.950 J.D. 875 Union St Rm 208
Bevins, Don C. '58 '84 C.927 B.S. L.36 J.D.
(adm. in IL; not adm. in OR) Reg. Claims Atty., Country Mut. Ins. Co.
Birke, Richard '60 '86 C.861 B.A. L.1202 J.D.
(adm. in MA; not adm. in OR) Asst. Prof. of Law, Willamette Univ.
Bischman, J. Marie .... '60 '89 C.508 B.A. L.629 J.D. [Parks,B.S.&W.]
Bischoff, Susan G., (BV) ....'54 '85 C.628 B.S. L.950 J.D. 1760 Liberty St. S.E.
Bishop, Bruce A. ....'46 '73 C.637 B.A. L.1065 J.D. [Harrang L.G.R.]
Blair, William G., (CV) ....'44 '69 C&L.950 B.A., J.D. Asst. City Atty.
Bloch, Helen Iris ....'53 '81 C.1044 B.A. L.596 J.D. State Pub. Def.
Blunt, David H. ....'25 '62 C.629 B.B.A. L.596 LL.B. P.O. Box 692‡
Bocci, Christopher C., (CV) ....'51 '77 C&L.629 B.A., J.D. 1415 Liberty Street SE
Boenisch, Christian ....'67 '97 C.800 B.A. L.596 J.D. Dept. of Jus.
Bonney, Leslie K., (AV) .... '44 '83 C.66 B.A. L.1051 J.D. 1162 Court St. N.E.
Bonney, Louis S. .... '20 '53 C.950 B.A. L.596 LL.B. 1150 14th St., N.E.‡
Booth, James D., (CV) ....'46 '91 C.136 B.S. L.950 J.D. SAIF Corporation
Bornholdt, Bruce A. .... '60 '94 C.950 B.A. L.117 J.D. Staff Atty., SAIF Corporation
Boss, Frederick M. ....'52 '77 C.112 B.A. L.1049 J.D. Asst. Atty. Gen.
Boss, M. Ann, (BV) ....'53 '84 C&L.326 B.A., J.D. State. Dept. of Jus.
Bostwick, Sarah Moore, (BV) ....'53 '78 C.1062 B.S. L.950 J.D. 825 Liberty St., N.E.
Bourassa, David E. '17 '55 C.628 B.S. L.900 LL.B.
(adm. in KS; not adm. in OR) 1480 Rafael St., N.‡
Boyd, William J. ....'47 '84 C.352 B.S. L.596 J.D. 700 Summer St Ne Ste 300
Bradshaw, Teresa K. .... '60 '85 C.629 B.S. L.767 J.D. Asst. Legal Coun., State Ct. Admr.
Brady, Sean T. .... '75 '00 C.670 B.A. L.950 J.D. 1162 Court St. N.E.
Brand, Malcolm L. ....'35 '65 C&L.950 B.A., J.D. 1122 Natalie Ave. S.‡
Brazeau, Robert James '49 '87 C.1104 B.A. L.950 J.D.
Admin. Law J., Wkrs. Comp. Bd.
Breen, Richard F., Jr. '40 '68 C.197 A.B. L.1294 LL.B.
(adm. in ME; not adm. in OR) Libr. & Prof. of Law, Willamette Univ.
Breithaupt, Henry C., (AV) ....'47 '75 C.668 A.B. L.629 J.D. 1241 State St Ne
Brenton, Craig C. '53 '79 C.602 B.A. L.284 J.D.
(adm. in CA; not adm. in OR) Exec. Asst. Superintendent, State Police
Brewer, David V. ....'51 '77 C.1078 B.A. L.629 J.D. Ct. of App. J.
Brewster, Sydney Eddy ....'49 '92 C.112 A.B. L.950 J.D. Acorn Legal Res., Inc.
Brickey, William E., (AV) ....'37 '67 C.878 B.S. L.950 J.D. Dept. of Jus.
Brickley, Alan K. ....'41 '70 C.1056 L.596 J.D. Key Title Co.
Briggs, Steven M. ....'65 '92 C.197 A.B. L.629 J.D. Dept. of Jus.
Brooks, William J. ....'31 '59 C&L.629 B.S., LL.B. 8915 State St.
Brown, Clarke C. ....'21 '54 C&L.950 B.A., J.D. Ret. Cir. J.

Brown, James M., (AV) '41 '67 C.950 B.A. L.976 LL.B.
117 Commercial Street NE, Suite 207, 97301-3496
Telephone: 503-581-6870
Email: jbrown@enfieldbrown.com
Trials and Appeals in all Courts. Business, Employment, Administrative Law and Arbitration.
See Professional Biographies, SALEM, OREGON

Brown, Lawrence N., (BV) ....'12 '35 C&L.950 B.A., J.D. 3130 Mulberry Dr.
Brown, Michael Duane, (BV) '48 '74 C&L.950 B.A., J.D.
5061 Liberty Road S., Suite 130
Brown, Nancy E. .... '38 '89 C.447 B.A. L.950 J.D. State Conciliator
Bryson, Dean F. ....'10 '34 L.596 Sr. J., Supr. Ct.
Bulkley, Robert D., Jr., (BV) .... '43 '77 C.1051 B.A. L.629 J.D. App. Ct. Staff Atty.
Burgess, John W. .... '41 '65 C&L.424 LL.B. 740 Kingwood Dr., N.W.
Burke, Harold E. '25 '54 C.670 B.A. L.596 LL.B.
Exec. Asst. to Dir., Dept. of Agriculture
Burks, Joel R. ....'76 '01 C.413 B.S. L.950 J.D. 750 Front St. N.E., Ste. 100
Burrows, Michelle R. .... '57 '86 C.1056 B.S. L.596 J.D. 265 State St.
Burt, C. Fredrick, Law Office of, (BV) .... '55 '83 C&L.950 B.A., J.D. 429 Court St. N.E.
Burt, Swanson, Lathen, Alexander, McCann & Smith, P.C., (AV)
Suite 1000, 388 State Street
Bushnell, Andrea L. '56 '88 C.506 B.A. L.596 J.D.
Executive Vice President & General Counsel, Oregon Assoc. of Realtors
Butcher, Sara Louise ....'69 '99 C&L.629 B.A., J.D. 145 Wilson Street S.
Byers, Carl N. ....'36 '64 C.101 B.A. L.1066 LL.B. Tax Ct. J.
Byrnes, Cynthia C., (AV) '58 '90 C.1051 B.A. L.950 J.D.
Asst. Atty. Gen., Dept. of Just.
Call, Christopher Douglas '58 '82 C.941 B.A. L.950 J.D.
Asst. to Pres., Willamette Univ.
Callaghan, John Daniel, (BV) ....'31 '59 C&L.950 B.A., J.D. 437 Mildred Lane S.E.
Cameron, David L. '57 '86 C.453 B.S. L.597 J.D.
(adm. in MA; not adm. in OR) Prof. of Law, Willamette Univ. Col. of Law
Camp, Anna Rachel ....'74 '99 C.473 B.A. L.665 J.D. Oregon Dept. of Justice
Campbell, Larry Craig ....'67 '92 C&L.629 B.S., J.D. Victory Grp., Inc., The
Campbell, Marianne K. ....'48 '81 C.911 B.A. L.950 J.D. P.O. Box 7341
Cannon, Robert C. ....'47 '72 C.629 B.S. L.950 J.D. 1775 32nd Pl., N.E.
Carlile, Stephen D., (BV) ....'48 '90 C.846 B.A. L.950 J.D. 388 State St.
Carlson, David L., (BV) ....'68 '94 C.939 B.A. L.950 J.D. [Pierson,L.C.&G.]
Carlson, Dee Kevin ....'53 '80 C.101 B.A. L.309 J.D. Dept. of Jus.
Carroll, Daniel M. .... '58 '92 C.17 B.A. L.950 J.D. 1320 Capitol Street N.E.
Carroll, Jacob J. ....'74 '03 C.436 B.A. L.823 J.D. Asst. Atty. Gen.
Carson, Wallace P., Jr. ....'34 '62 C.813 A.B. L.950 J.D. Chf. Jus., Supm. Ct.
Carter, Jeff J., (BV) ....'56 '82 C.1071 B.S. L.950 J.D. [J.J.Carter]
Carter, Mary E. ....'77 '05 C.773 B.A. L.629 J.D. [Saalfeld G.]
Carter, Jeff J., P.C., (BV) ....1386 State St.
Case, John H., (BV) .... '71 '97 C.629 B.S. L.628 J.D. [Feibleman&C.]
Casebeer, Christopher J., (BV) .... '59 '84 C.629 B.S. L.950 J.D. [Ferder,C.&F.]
Casey, Daniel J. .... '63 '95 C.112 B.A. L.1051 J.D. 1162 Court St Ne
Castanares, William Thomas '68 '94
C.628 B.S. L.950 J.D. The Prudential Real Estate Professionals

Castle, Thomas .... '47 '74 C.97 B.A. L.607 J.D. Jus. Dept., Trial Div.
Castner, Sarah L., (BV) ....'55 '80 C.941 B.A. L.950 J.D. Asst. Atty. Gen.
Cegla, Kathleen M., (BV) ..... '56 '89 C.489 B.A. L.950 J.D. Asst. Atty. Gen., Appl. Div.
Chatfield, Byron G., (AV) ....'48 '73 C.1056 B.S. L.596 J.D. Asst. Atty. Gen.
Chi, Willard H. ....'72 '97 C.378 B.A. L.1051 J.D. Asst. Atty. Gen.
Chiappetta, Vincent F., (AV) '51 '77 C.453 B.S. L.477 J.D.
(adm. in AZ; not adm. in OR) Assoc. Prof. of Law, Willamette Univ.
Chidester, Robert G. .... '35 '59 C&L.950 B.A., J.D. 1148 Oakhill, S.E.
Christensen, Jean W., (CV) ....'29 '63 C.629 L.950 J.D. P.O. Box 5190
Churchill, Thomas W., (AV) ....'22 '50 C.112 L.950 J.D. [Churchill,L.L.&H.]

Churchill, Leonard, Lodine & Hendrie, LLP, (AV)
605 Center Street N.E., P.O. Box 804, 97308 ⊙
Telephone: 503-585-2255 Telefax: 503-364-8033
Email: legal@churchill-law.com URL: http://www.churchill-law.com
Members of Firm: Thomas W. Churchill; Richard L. Hendrie, Jr.; David H. Leonard; Paul C. Lodine;—Elizabeth E. Howard; Melinda Leaver Roy; Richard E. Slezak.
Agricultural Law, Natural Resource and Environmental Law, Probate, Estate Planning and Administration, Wills, Trusts, Trust Administration, Taxation, Conservatorships, Guardianships, Real Estate and Land Use, Public Lands Law, Water Law, General Civil and Trial Practice, Creditor's Rights, Bankruptcy, Business, Corporate and Commercial Law, Immigration and International Law, Secured Transactions, Criminal Law, Wrongful Death, Personal Injury, Employment Law and Medical Injury.
Reference: First Security Bank.
Lake Oswego, Oregon Office: Two Centerpointe Drive, Suite 580, 97035. Telephone: 503-598-6610.
See Professional Biographies, SALEM, OREGON

Chute, Christine A. '51 '83 C.1084 B.A. L.972 J.D.
Asst. Admr., State Employment Div.
Clark, Edward L., Jr., (AV) ......'23 '50 C.605 B.A. L.629 LL.B. [Clark,L.F.E.L.&C.] ‡

Clark, Lindauer, Fetherston, Edmonds, Lippold & Collier, LLP, (AV)
880 Liberty Street, N.E., P.O. Box 2206, 97308-2206
Telephone: 503-581-1542 Fax: 503-585-3978
Email: contactus@clarklindauer.com
Members of Firm: Edward L. Clark, Jr. (Retired); Ben C. Fetherston, Jr.; James C. Edmonds; Steven M. Lippold; Ryan W. Collier;—Jeffrey A. Trautman. Of Counsel: Eric B. Lindauer.
Trial and Business Practice in State and Federal Courts including Business Litigation, Insurance Law, Agricultural Law, Automobile, Premises Liability, Professional Negligence, including Legal and Medical Malpractice, Product, Toxic Tort and Environmental Liability, Employment Discrimination, Wrongful Discharge and Defamation, Arbitration and Mediation, Business, Real Estate, and Estate Law, Probate.
Representative Clients: North Pacific Insurance Co.; State Farm Insurance Co.; Colonial Penn Insurance Co.; Oregon State Bar Professional Liability Fund; Albertson's Inc.; Fleetwood Enterprises, Inc.; Tillamook County Creamery Association.
See Professional Biographies, SALEM, OREGON

Clarkson, Paige Elaine ....'74 '99 C.112 B.A. L.950 J.D. Marion Co. Dist. Atty. Off.
Clifford, Thomas G. ....'36 '66 C.494 B.A. L.1035 J.D. Legis. Coun.
Clingerman, Aaron E., (CV) .... '70 '98 C.608 B.F.A. L.950 J.D. 456 State St.
Coburn, Catherine P. ....'50 '87 C.1051 B.A. L.596 J.D. 3420 Cherry Avenue NE
Cole, Lois M., (CV) ....'57 '95 C.766 B.A. L.950 J.D. [Ashcroft W.]
Coleman, W. Bradley, (CV) ..... '42 '69 C.1109 B.A. L.950 J.D. [W.B.Coleman&Assoc.]
Coleman, W. Brad, P.C., & Associates, (CV) .... 1467 13th St. S.E.
Collier, Ryan W., (CV) .... '71 '97 C.678 B.A. L.950 J.D. [Clark,L.F.E.L.&C.]
Collins, Howard W., (BV) .... '53 '81 C.1056 B.S. L.950 J.D. 1415 Commercial Street SE
Collins, Loren W., (BV) .... '56 '82 C&L.950 B.A., J.D. Asst. Atty. Gen.
Comstock, Mark B., (AV) ....'54 '81 C.629 B.A. L.950 J.D. [Garrett,H.R.J.C.&T.]
Comstock, Wendy B. .... '55 '81 C.628 B.S. L.950 J.D. Admin. Law J., Employ. Dept.
Condon, Richard W., (BV) ....'51 '78 C.112 B.A. L.950 J.D. [R.Condon]
Condon, Richard, PC, (BV) ....3387 Center St. N.E.
Conley, James H. ....'34 '74 C.763 A.B. L.1068 J.D. Ore. Dept. of Rev.
Conrad, Catherine, (CV) .... '58 '90 C.999 B.S. L.950 J.D. 341 State St.
Conroyd, Cinda M., (AV) ....'52 '84 C.927 M.S. L.950 J.D. [Douglas&C.]
Conroyd, Michael F., (AV) ....'48 '74 C.276 B.S.B.A. L.424 J.D. [Vick&C.]
Cook, Randall W., (AV) ....'62 '88 C.629 B.A. L.50 J.D. [Saalfeld G.]
Cook, William R. ....'56 '82 C.508 B.A. L.596 J.D. Asst. Atty. Gen.
Cooper, Helen L., Law Offices of, (BV) '62 '87
C.628 B.S. L.950 J.D. 475 Cottage St., N.E.
Cordy, Gary M., (AV) ....'51 '78 C&L.629 J.D. Asst. Atty. Gen.
Cotton, Steven R., (AV) ... '49 '79 C.1056 B.A. L.950 J.D. Trial Coun., SAIF Corporation
Cottrell, Kathryn A. .... '73 '00 C.911 B.A. L.596 J.D. Dept. of Jus.-Trial Div.
Cowan, Thomas W., (BV) ....'57 '91 C.1056 B.S. L.950 J.D. Asst. Atty. Gen.
Craig, Jeanean W., (BV) ....'49 '89 C.1181 B.S. L.950 J.D. [Alway&C.]
Creighton, Chas. W., Jr. .... '11 '42 C.152 A.B. L.659 J.D. 1110 Nebraska Ct., N.E.‡
Crider, Lynn-Marie ....'53 '77 C.629 B.S. L.976 J.D. Atty., Oregon AFL-CIO
Cross, Nori J. McCann '50 '78 C.966 B.A. L.1035 J.D.
Educ. Dir., State Ct. Admin. Off.
Crothers, William C., (AV) ....'42 '70 C&L.950 B.A., J.D. [Crothers H.]

Crothers Hansen P.C., (AV)
750 Front Street NE, Suite 100, 97301
Telephone: 503-378-0225 Telecopier: 503-371-2946
URL: http://www.crothers.com
William C. Crothers; Gregory C. Hansen.
Litigation including Business, Commercial, Creditors Rights, Real Property, Personal Injury, Family Law, Conservatorships and Guardianships, Corporate and Partnership Law.
Reference: First Security Bank, Salem, Oregon.
See Professional Biographies, SALEM, OREGON

Crowell, Carl D., Law Office of, (CV) '68 '98
C.1056 B.S. L.950 J.D. 1313 Mill St. S.E. (Pat.)
Crowley, Ruth .... '43 '90 C.668 B.A. L.950 J.D. Hearings Offr., Pub. Utility Comm.
Cumfer, Eric M., (BV) ....'58 '88 C.1111 B.A. L.259 J.D. Dep. Pub. Def.
Cummins, Arthur B., Jr., (BV) '41 '66 C.282 B.A. L.950 J.D.
[Firm of A.B.Cummins,Jr.]
Cummins, A.B., Jr., P.C., The Law Firm of, (BV) .... 180 Church Street SE
Cummins, Goodman, Fish, Denley & Vickers, P.C.
(See Newberg)

Custis, Robert J., (BV) ....'53 '79 C.249 B.S. L.950 J.D. [Kent C.] ⊙
Daines, Rex K. .... '68 '95 C.877 B.A. L.950 J.D. [Olsen,O.&D.]
Dakopolos, Paul A., (BV) ....'59 '85 C.336 B.A. L.950 J.D. [Garrett,H.R.J.C.&T.]
Dale, Alice L. '52 '79 C.629 B.A. L.426 J.D.
Exec. Dir., Oregon Pub. Employees Union, SEIU Local 503
Daniel, M. David '53 '86 C.1181 B.S. L.950 J.D.
Supervising Atty., Willamette Univ. Coll. of Law
Daron, Harold M. .... '29 '56 C&L.629 B.S., LL.B. 1747 Timberline Lane, S.E.‡
Daughtry, Douglas W. ....'42 '70 C&L.629 B.A., J.D. Ref., Wkms. Comp. Bd.
Dawson, Rick ....'62 '86 C&L.950 B.A., J.D. Sr. Asst. Gen. Coun., SAIF Corporation
Degner, David C., (BV) .... '46 '77 C.763 A.B. L.1051 J.D. Pub. Def. Off.
de Looze, Theo. W. ....'23 '50 C&L.145 A.B., J.D. 10256 Oak Dr. S.E.‡
DeLuca, F. Peter .... '46 '75 C.335 B.A. L.950 J.D. Labor Relations Div.

DeMarco, Brian A. ... '55 '90 C.30 B.A. L.1051 J.D. OR Real Estate Agency
DeMartino, David J. ... '37 '65 C.670 B.A. L.596 LL.B. 7162 Darling S.E.
DeMuniz, Paul J. ... '47 '75 C.1056 B.S. L.950 J.D. Appl. Ct. J.
DenHartigh, David L. ... '— '82 C&L.966 B.A., J.D. 1610 12th St., S.E.
Denney, Thomas H. ... '39 '66 C.309 A.B. L.950 J.D. Asst. Atty. Gen.
Dentinger, Tammy M., (BV) ... '68 '94 C&L.950 B.A., J.D. [Garrett,H.R.J.C.&T.]
Dickey, Don A. ... '45 '72 C.629 B.S. L.950 J.D. Cir. J.
Dietz, David H. ... '50 '78 C.628 B.S. L.950 J.D. 1532 Barnes Ave. S.E.
Dingle, Stephen E. ... '59 '84 C.628 B.A. L.629 J.D. Dist. Atty. Off.
Doherty, Stephanie L. ... '76 '02 C.112 B.A. L.950 J.D. [Ⓐ W.W.Lien]
Dorszynski, Robert L., (BV) ... '64 '88 C.999 B.S. L.950 J.D. P.O. Box 3050
Douglas, Bruce E., (BV) ... '41 '70 C.628 B.S. L.950 J.D. [Douglas&C.]
Douglas & Conroyd, P.C., (AV) ... 528 Cottage St. N.E.
Driscoll, Sean M. ... '73 '02 C.174 B.A. L.1051 J.D. [Ⓐ Saalfeld G.]
Dunford, George M., III ... '53 '80 C&L.950 B.S., J.D. 1088 Fernwood Ct. NW
Dunn, Alex C., (CV) ... '73 '99 C.413 B.S. L.950 J.D. [Vick&C.]
Dunn, Brendan C. ... '— '95 C.259 B.A. L.629 J.D. 1162 Court St. N.E.
Dunne, Joseph P. ... '46 '74 C.215 B.S. L.424 J.D. Off. of Atty. Gen.
Durham, Robert D. ... '47 '72 C.940 B.A. L.770 J.D. Supm. Ct. Jus.
Dye, Michael B., (BV) ... '45 '70 456 State St.
Eagan, Alicia Kay ... '63 '98 C.911 B.A. L.508 J.D. Law Clk., Ct. App.
Eager-Vance, Holly A. ... '59 '87 C.882 B.A. L.208 J.D. Asst. Atty. Gen.
Earls, Elizabeth A. ... '66 '92 C.910 B.A. L.950 J.D. [Harrang L.G.R.]
Ebersole, Eugene F., (BV) ... '49 '81 C.1025 B.A. L.596 J.D. Asst. Atty. Gen.
Eder, N. George, (BV) ... '48 '79 C.973 A.B. L.950 J.D. 270 Cottage St., N.E.
Edmonds, James C., (AV) ... '60 '86 C.629 B.A. L.273 J.D. [Clark,L.F.E.L.&C.]
Edmonds, Walter I., Jr. ... '43 '67 C.413 B.A. L.950 J.D. Ct. App. J.
Edwards, Jane ... '42 '71 C.17 B.A. L.629 J.D. 1925 Margaret St., N.W.
Eggert, Christopher J. ... '71 '96 C.628 B.A. L.950 J.D. 4940 Stroll Ct. N.E.
Ehrman, Debra ... '50 '80 C&L.629 B.A., J.D. Trial Coun., SAIF Corporation
Eichelberger, Stephen, (CV) ... '45 '79 C.1051 B.A. L.950 J.D. 915 Lancaster Dr., S.
Elden, Thomas K. ... '40 '66 C.604 B.A. L.813 LL.B. Dept. of Jus.
Elmer, Randy M., (BV) ... '55 '83 C&L.950 B.S., J.D. [Kryger,A.E.&E.]
Elmore, Stephen Henry '52 '87 C.911 B.A. L.838 J.D.
(adm. in TN; not adm. in OR) State Employ. Dept.
Elott, David J. ... '64 '91 C.813 B.A.S. L.309 J.D. Asst. Atty. Gen., Dept. of Jus.
Embick, Marion B., (Mrs.), (BV) ... '25 '63 C.966 A.B. L.950 J.D. 3275 Holiday Dr. S.
Emerick, Hunter B., (AV) ... '57 '82 C&L.950 B.S., J.D. [Saalfeld G.]
Emerson, James L. ... '46 '81 C.549 B.A. L.1051 J.D. Wkrs. Comp. Bd.
English, Laurie Beth ... '52 '88 C.1111 B.A. L.1202 J.D. 775 Winter St. N.E., Apt. 3
Ertsgaard, Duane R. ... '29 '58 C&L.950 B.A., J.D. Ret. Cir. J.
Estes, James P. '74 '01 C.897 B.A. L.950 J.D.
V.P. & Corp. Coun., Sunwest Management, Inc., Legal

Evans, Kathleen A., Attorney at Law, (AV) '57 '82 C.906 B.A. L.950 J.D.
969 - 13th St. SE, 97302
Telephone: 503-588-5670 Fax: 503-588-5673
Email: kathy@kevanslaw.com
Estate Planning, Wealth Transfer and Preservation, Trust Administration, and Probate.
Reference: The Commercial Bank, Salem, Oregon.
See Professional Biographies, SALEM, OREGON

Evans, Roger K., (BV) ... '54 '81 C.629 B.S. L.285 J.D. [O'Neill&E.]
Ewing, Thomas E. ... '45 '84 C.1056 B.A. L.950 J.D. Asst. Atty. Gen., Dept. of Jus.
Eymann, Kathleen P., (CV) ... '52 '79 C&L.629 B.A., J.D. 2250 Eola Dr. N.W.‡
Fabien, Marva Claudette ... '54 '85 C.629 B.A. L.1051 J.D. Oregon Bd. of Parole
Fagan, D. Michael ... '50 '97 C.1377 B.A. L.1051 J.D. Dep. Dist. Atty.
Farmer, Matt ... '46 '71 L.950 J.D. Staff Attorney, Oregon Assoc. of Realtors
Feibleman, Gilbert B., (AV) ... '51 '76 C.629 B.S. L.464 J.D. [Feibleman&C.]
Feibleman & Case P.C., (AV) ... 1815 Commercial St. S.
Feitelson, Ira S., (CV) ... '39 '66 C&L.950 B.A., J.D. 1467 13th St. S.E.
Ferder, Paul M., (AV) ... '46 '72 C.629 B.S. L.1051 J.D. [Ferder,C.&F.]

Ferder, Casebeer & French L.L.P., (AV)
515 High Street, S.E., P.O. Box 843, 97308-0843
Telephone: 503-585-9197 Fax: 503-399-7904
Members of Firm: Paul M. Ferder; Christopher J. Casebeer; Carla M. French. Associate: Jason Edward Thompson. Of Counsel: James J. Ahmed.
Personal Injury, Criminal Law, Family Law, Business, Corporate Law, Appellate Practice.
See Professional Biographies, SALEM, OREGON

Fernety, Michael D., (BV) ... '65 '94 C.112 B.S. L.950 J.D. [Ⓐ Parks,B.S.&W.]
Ferrari, Charles D. ... '58 '87 C.1077 B.A. L.1067 J.D. Dept. of Jus.
Fetherston, Ben C., Jr., (AV) ... '57 '81 C.208 B.A. L.596 J.D. [Clark,L.F.E.L.&C.]
Fetrow, Michael G. ... '50 '85 C.176 B.A. L.629 J.D. Trial Coun., SAIF Corporation
Finch, Monica L. ... '72 '97 C.1369 B.A. L.945 J.D. Pub. Def. Off.
Fisher, Emerson G., (BV) ... '49 '82 C.1097 B.S. L.596 J.D. 2601 25th St. S.E., Ste. 150
Fitch, Ginger ... '67 '98 C.482 B.A. L.93 J.D. Law Clk., Ct. App.
Fjordbeck, Denise G., (BV) ... '56 '82 C&L.629 B.A., J.D. Staff Atty., Dept. of Jus.
Foote, Warren G. ... '52 '77 C&L.629 B.S., J.D. Asst. Atty. Gen.
Foster, Jill F., (BV) ... '69 '94 C.911 B.A. L.950 J.D. 1760 Liberty St., S.E.
Foster, Walter W. ... '20 '51 C.628 B.S. L.950 J.D. 3323 Belvedere N.W.‡
Fowler, David R., (BV) ... '51 '78 C.112 B.A. L.1051 J.D. Trial Coun., SAIF Corporation
Fox, Willard E., (BV) ... '41 '68 C&L.339 A.B., J.D. [Allen,F.&O.]
Freiley, Lisa M. '64 '91 C&L.950 B.S., J.D.
Human Resource Dev. Spec., State Sch. Bd. Assn.
French, Carla M., (BV) ... '53 '94 C.413 B.S. L.950 J.D. [Ferder,C.&F.]
French, Jos. P. ... '29 '54 C.629 B.S. L.950 LL.B. P.O. Box 2167
Fussner, Jonathan H. ... '48 '75 C.309 B.A. L.629 J.D. Asst. Dist. Atty.
Gabliks, Kelly M. ... '59 '88 C.629 B.S. L.36 J.D. Asst. Atty. Gen., Dept. of Jus.
Gage, Gail M., (BV) ... '57 '83 C.637 B.A. L.950 J.D. 1880 Lancaster Drive NE Suite 119

Gage, Kevin C., (AV) '53 '81 C.911 B.A. L.950 J.D.
348 Leslie Street, S.E., P.O. Box 924, 97308-0924
Telephone: 503-399-1355 Fax: 503-399-1353
Email: gagelaw@comcast.net URL: http://www.kevingagelaw.com
Divorce, Family Law, Child Custody, Child Support, Alimony, Marital Property Distribution, Spousal Support, Separation Agreements, Matrimonial Law, Marital Property Law, Equitable Distribution, Domestic Relations, Community Property Law, Domestic Partnerships.
See Professional Biographies, SALEM, OREGON

Gallagher, Thomas J. ... '45 '75 C.190 A.B. L.950 J.D. 1425 Beaumont St. NW
Gangle, Sandra Smith, (BV) ... '43 '80 C.562 B.A. L.950 J.D. [S.S.Gangle]
Gangle, Sandra Smith, P.C., (BV) ... P.O. Box 904

Garrett, Hemann, Robertson, Jennings, Comstock & Trethewey, P.C., (AV)
Willamette Professional Center, 1011 Commercial Street, N.E., P.O. Box 749, 97308-0749
Telephone: 503-581-1501 Telefax: 503-581-5891
URL: http://www.garrettlaw.com

(This Listing Continued)

Garrett, Hemann, Robertson, Jennings, Comstock & Trethewey, P.C. (Continued)
George M. Jennings; Mark B. Comstock; Chess Trethewey; Paul A. Dakopolos; Bruce A. Zagar; John E. Pollino; Tammy M. Dentinger; Kim E. Hoyt; Theresa M. Wade;—Anthony R. Kreitzberg; Tracy A. Prall; J. Channing Bennett; Sean E. Armstrong; Nathan B. Thomas. Of Counsel: John L. Hemann; Steven E. Herron; J. Kevin Shuba.
Bankruptcy and Creditors' Rights, Business and Corporate Law, Civil Litigation, Employment and Labor Law, Estate Planning, Trusts and Probate, Family Law, Government Relations, Insurance and Workers' Compensation Defense, Real Estate Transactions and Development, School Law, Tax Law.
Representative Clients: Boise Cascade Corp.; City of Salem; Coldwell Banker/Mountain West Real Estate; First Interstate Bank; Marion County; Safeco Insurance Co.; Salem/Keizer School District; State Farm Insurance Co.
See Professional Biographies, SALEM, OREGON

Gartlan, Peter, (AV) '52 '87 C.1160 B.A. L.596 J.D.
Chf. Dep. Pub. Def., Pub. Def. Off.
Garza, Keith M., (AV) ... '67 '94 C.36 B.S. L.145 J.D. Supreme Court Bldg, 1163 State St
Gasper, Kym K. ... '50 '95 L.950 J.D. P.O. Box 284
Gatti, Daniel J., (BV) ... '46 '73 C.1181 B.S. L.950 J.D. [Gatti,G.&M.]
Gatti, Richard D., (BV) ... '47 '72 C.1181 B.S. L.950 J.D. [Gatti,G.&M.]
Gatti, Gatti & Maier, (BV) ... 1781 Liberty St., S.E.
Geil, John Clinton, (AV) ... '51 '76 C.605 B.A. L.1051 J.D. 1162 Court Street N.E.
Gemmell, Gayle ... '41 '65 C&L.629 B.A., LL.B. Workmen's Compensation Bd.
Gerber, Roger '42 '83 C.1056 B.A. L.596 J.D.
Hearings Offr., Pub. Utility Comm. of State
Gerner, Jeff, (BV) ... '55 '80 C.335 B.A. L.950 J.D. Trial Coun., SAIF Corporation
Gibb, Ryan Edward, (BV) ... '72 '97 C.635 B.S. L.950 J.D. [R.E.Gibb]
Gibb, Ryan E., (BV) ... 528 Cottage St. N.E.
Gilmore, Heather Opal, (BV) ... '64 '90 C.684 B.A. L.950 J.D. 1855 Fairgrounds Rd. N.E.
Goodwin, Karl ... '— '93 C.1181 B.S. L.950 J.D. 1162 Court St. NE
Gorham, Steven H., (BV) ... '49 '75 C.188 A.B. L.950 J.D. 341 State St.
Gorsuch, Kris Jon, (AV) ... '53 '78 C&L.352 B.A., J.D. [Saalfeld G.]
Gould, Anthony C. ... '61 '96 C.918 B.A. L.629 J.D. Asst. Atty. Gen.
Gragg, Jill B. ... '71 '96 C.112 B.A. L.472 J.D. SAIF Corp.
Graham, Jack H. ... '44 '73 C&L.629 B.S., J.D. Dir., Oregon Corporation Div.
Graham, Kathy T. '47 '72
C.112 A.B. L.1067 J.D. Assoc. Dean, Willamette Univ. Col. of Law
Graham, Paul A., (BV) ... '45 '72 C.112 A.B. L.1067 J.D. Asst. Atty. Gen.
Grainey, Michael W. ... '47 '72 C.285 B.A. L.569 J.D. Dep. Dir., State Dept. of Energy
Grant, Michael W. ... '63 '90 C.608 B.S. L.629 J.D. Admin. Law J., Pub. Utility Comm.
Graves, Dennis J. ... '47 '73 C&L.950 B.A., J.D. Cir. J.
Greene, Alison K. ... '60 '87 C.112 B.A. L.426 J.D. State Wkrs. Comp. Bd.
Greenwald, Wendy L. ... '53 '80 C.610 B.S. L.629 J.D. State Employ. Rel. Bd.
Greer, Tim, (BV) ... '53 '90 C.136 B.S. L.950 J.D. [T.Greer]
Greer, William, Jr. ... '48 '73 C.473 B.A. L.910 J.D. Admin. Law J., Employ. Rel. Bd.
Greer, Tim, P.C., (BV) ... 2842 Cole Rd. S.
Gregg, Tracy L., (BV) ... '68 '95 C.1058 B.B.A. L.911 J.D. [Pierson,L.C.&G.]
Grew, B. Carlton '55 '87 C.309 B.A. L.588 J.D.
Atty., Oregon Pub. Employees Union, SEIU Local 503
Griggs, James C., (AV) ... '49 '75 C&L.950 B.A., J.D. [Saalfeld G.]
Grimms, Linda DeVries, (BV) ... '54 '82 C.112 B.A. L.629 J.D. Asst. Atty. Gen.
Gross, George N., (BV) ... '16 '54 C.629 B.S. L.950 J.D. 388 State St.
Groux, Jonathan ... '68 '98 C.1123 B.A. L.950 J.D. Atty. Gen., Oregon Dept. of Jus.
Gruber, Frank R. ... '46 '77 C.629 B.A. L.950 J.D. 555 Liberty St Se

Gudger, Gregory L.
(See Portland)

Gunn, Marc W., (BV) ... '68 '95 C.101 B.A. L.950 J.D. [Gunn&G.]
Gunn, Robert J., (BV) ... '43 '72 C.101 B.S. L.950 J.D. [Gunn&G.]
Gunn & Gunn, (BV) ... 3635 Liberty Rd. S.
Gutzler, J. Wallace, (AV) ... '28 '57 C&L.950 B.A., J.D. P.O. Box 3006
Haas, Connie Marie ... '51 '78 C.608 B.A. L.851 J.D. Dept. of Jus.
Habekost, Martin C., (BV) ... '63 '90 C.1163 B.A. L.950 J.D. [M.C.Habekost]
Habekost, Martin C., P.C., (BV) ... 1760 Liberty Street SE
Hagedorn, Richard B. '48 '73
C.62 B.S. L.950 J.D. Prof. of Law, Willamette Univ. Col. of Law
Hagemann, Ryan J. ... '72 '01 C.939 B.A. L.629 J.D. Jus. Dept.
Hagen, Leon L. ... '38 '64 C.897 B.S. L.950 LL.B. 6895 Cangon, S.E.
Haggerty-Foster, Jacqueline ... '50 '82 C.906 B.A. L.950 J.D. Dept. of Revenue
Haley, Sam R. '19 '41 L.910 J.D.
(adm. in MO; not adm. in OR) 1590 Fairmount Ave., S.‡
Hall, Jeffrey D., Law Office of ... '75 '00 C&L.629 B.S., J.D. 145 Wilson Street South
Halpern, Michael L., (AVⓉ) ... '49 '75 C.112 B.A. L.1068 J.D. 155 Cottage St Ne
Hamers, James, (BV) ... '53 '79 C.966 B.A. L.950 J.D. 180 Ramsgate St Se
Hamilton, H. Robert ... '44 '69 C&L.950 B.A., J.D. Asst. Atty. Gen.
Hampton, Leslie B. ... '24 '53 C.1056 L.950 J.D. 460 Larry Ave. N.‡
Hanford-Beach, Sharon ... '51 '83 C.939 B.A. L.950 J.D. 4549 Independence Dr. S.E.‡
Hanna, Gordon R., (BV) ... '51 '78 C&L.629 B.S., J.D. 242 Church St. S.E.
Hansen, Gregory C., (AV) ... '64 '89 C.1207 B.A. L.585 J.D. [Crothers H.]
Hansen, Michael J., (BV) ... '47 '77 C.735 B.L. L.950 J.D. 555 Court St Ne
Harbur, Marilyn J., (BV) ... '50 '77 C.942 B.A. L.378 J.D. Asst. Atty. Gen.

Hardman, Christopher R.
(See Portland)

Harrang Long Gary Rudnick P.C., (AV)
333 High Street N.E., Suite 200, P.O. Box 12949, 97309-0949 ⊙
Telephone: 503-371-3330 Fax: 503-371-5336
URL: http://www.harrang.com
Bruce A. Bishop; Elizabeth A. Earls.
General Civil Trial and Appellate Practice in all State and Federal Courts, Governmental and Business Law, Corporate Law, Administrative Law, Financial Services, Securities Law, Creditors Rights, Partnership Law, Real Estate, State and Local Government Law, Environmental Law, Zoning, Planning and Land Use, Estate Planning and Probate, Insurance Law, Civil, Business, Complex and Tort Litigation, Alternative Dispute Resolution, Labor and Employment Law, Employee Benefits, Intellectual Property, Health Law, Nonprofit Law.
Eugene, Oregon Office: 300 East 10th Avenue, Suite 300. Telephone: 541-485-0220. Fax: 541-686-6564.
Portland, Oregon Office: 1001 S.W. 5th Avenue, Suite 1650. Telephone: 503-242-0000. Fax: 503-241-1458.
See Professional Biographies, SALEM, OREGON

Harri, Edward J. '46 '73 C.897 B.A. L.950 J.D.
Asst. Dean, Willamette Univ. Col. of Law
Harris, J. P., II, (AV) ... '47 '73 C.112 B.A. L.950 J.D. [Harris,W.&A.]

Harris, Wyatt & Amala, LLC, (AV)
5778 Commercial Street, S.E., 97306-1213 ⊙
Telephone: 503-378-7744; 800-853-2144 Facsimile: 503-378-1013
URL: http://www.salemattorneys.com
J. P. Harris, II; Gig Wyatt; Carl R. Amala; James B. Rich; James A. Wickwire.
General Civil Practice: General civil trial practice in all state and federal courts. Alternative dispute resolution. General insurance defense practice, automobile accidents, bad faith, fire, coverage, casualty, uninsured and underinsured motorist, trucking liability, premises liability, insurance coverage,

(This Listing Continued)

Harris, Wyatt & Amala, LLC (Continued)

insurance litigation, liquor liability. Criminal Law, Felonies, Misdemeanors, Drug Crimes, Driving While Intoxicated, (DUI). Motor Vehicle Division hearings, Traffic Violations.
Representative Clients: Progressive; Austin Mutual; Leader Insurance; Infinity; Workmen's Auto; Red Shield Insurance Co.; Farm Bureau of Idaho; Lancer Insurance.
West Linn Office: 202 Eight Avenue, PMB No. 35, 97068. Telephone: 503-742-1990. Fax: 503-742-9906.

See Professional Biographies, SALEM, OREGON

Hart, David Anthony '57 '00 C.569 B.S. L.1051 J.D. Dept. of Jus.
Hart, Thomas M. '55 '87 C.63 B.S. L.629 J.D. Cir. J.
Haselton, Rick T. '53 '79 C.813 A.B. L.976 J.D. Assoc. Ct. App. J.
Hassanpour, Dee Anna '— '95 C.69 L.61 (adm. in CA; not adm. in OR) Admin. Law J., Soc. Sec. Admn.
Hassen, Megan Elizabeth '69 '94 C.629 B.S. L.950 J.D. Ct. Mediation
Hayenga, John M. '53 '79 C.1073 B.A. L.950 J.D. 400 High St., S.E.
Hazel, Janice L., (BV) '58 '93 C.1169 B.A. L.336 J.D. [Sherman,S.M.J.&H.]
Heil, Robert M. '27 '55 C&L.950 B.S., LL.B. Williamette Valley Title Co.
Heitsch, Bonnie E. '— '84 C.475 B.S. L.912 J.D. Asst. Atty. Gen.
Heller, Lisa B. '51 '76 C.643 B.A. L.950 J.D. Admr., State Dep. of Rev.
Hellewell, Ronald M., (BV) '50 '83 C.101 B.A. L.950 J.D. [R.M.Hellewell]
Hellewell, Ronald M., P.C., (BV) 2450 Lancaster Dr. N.E.
Heltzel, James G., (AV) '40 '66 C.813 B.S. L.178 J.D. [Heltzel,U.W.Y.R.S.&P.]

Heltzel, Upjohn, Williams, Yandell Roth, Smith & Petersen, P.C., (AV)
Fourth Floor Pioneer Trust Building, P.O. Box 1048, 97308-1048
Telephone: 503-585-4422 Facsimile: 503-370-4302
James G. Heltzel; Donald H. Upjohn; Clark B. Williams; Eric Yandell; David M. Roth; Barbara Jo Smith; Michael C. Petersen; Deborah R. Lush.
Business, Taxation, Estate Planning, Probate and Real Estate Law. Commercial and Tax Litigation, Employee Benefits, Employment Law, Qualified Domestic Relations Order, Creditors Rights and Appeals in all Courts.
Reference: Pioneer Trust Bank, N.A.

See Professional Biographies, SALEM, OREGON

Hemann, John L., (AV) '43 '68 C&L.950 B.A., J.D. [ⓒ Garrett,H.R.J.C.&T.]
Hendrie, Richard L., Jr., (BV) '56 '81 C.629 B.S. L.950 J.D. [Churchill,L.L.&H.] ⊙
Henry, Judy Shipler, (BV) '56 '83 C.629 B.A. L.596 J.D. Dir., App. Settlement Conf. Prog.
Herman, Peter S. '26 '54 C&L.309 A.B., LL.B. 345 Forest Hills Way, N.W.‡
Herron, Steven E. '67 '92 C.1056 B.S. L.1051 J.D. [ⓒ Garrett,H.R.J.C.&T.]
Herzfeld, Marc J. '57 '85 C.378 B.S. L.1051 J.D. Law Clk., Supm. Ct. J.
Hettle, Thaddeus J. '56 '83 C.373 B.A. L.950 J.D. [Hettle&Assoc.]
Hettle & Associates P.O. Box 4110
Heynderickx, David W., (BV) '50 '78 C&L.629 B.A., J.D. Dep. Leg. Coun., Legis. Coun. Comm.
Hicks, Cynthia A., (CV) '59 '97 C.589 B.A. L.629 J.D. Asst. Atty. Gen.
Hicks, David N., Jr. '49 '81 C&L.629 B.S., J.D. Dept. of Jus.
Hicks, Loren D. '19 '49 C&L.950 B.A., LL.B. 3370 Huckleberry Ct. S.‡
Higgins, Peter B., (BV) '34 '59 C&L.93 B.S., J.D. Asst. Atty. Gen.
Hightower, Karen L. '57 '82 C.112 B.A. L.629 J.D. Asst. Leg. Coun., State Ct. Admr. Off.
Hilgemann, David, Law Offices of, (AV) '47 '72 C.590 B.A. L.950 J.D. 530 Center St. N.E., Ste. 700
Hill, Daniel A., (CV) '— '96 C.999 B.S. L.950 J.D. 339 Washington St. S.E.
Hill, James A., Jr. '47 '75 C.475 B.A. L.1119 J.D. State Treas.
Hittle, David W., (AV) '47 '74 C.628 B.S. L.1051 J.D. Suite 1000, 388 State Street
Hohlt, Mark William '55 '80 C&L.950 B.A., J.D. State Div. of Employment
Holland, Michael '48 '80 C&L.950 J.D. Comm. Coll.
Hollander, Joseph W. '52 '85 C.285 B.A. L.629 J.D. Dist. Atty.'s Off.
Holman, Jeannette Kay '51 '82 C.1058 B.A. L.950 J.D. Dep., Legislative Coun. Comm.
Holman, Ralph M. '14 '37 L.596 LL.B. Ret. Supm. Ct. Jus.
Holstedt, R. Brooke, (BV) '48 '79 C.972 B.A. L.629 J.D. P.O. Box 3018
Holstun, Michael A. '48 '80 C.10 B.S. L.1051 J.D. Land Use Bd. of. App.
Holtan, Bruce D. '49 '80 C.966 B.A. L.950 J.D. Admin. Law J., Wkrs. Comp. Bd.
Hoppe, Kyle Bryce '70 '95 C.670 B.A. L.950 J.D. Admin. Law J., Central Hearings Prog.
Hormann, Dale K., (BV) '53 '79 C.350 B.S. L.950 J.D. Asst. Atty. Gen., Jus. Dept.
Howard, Elizabeth E. '75 '01 C.628 B.S. L.596 J.D. [ⓒ Churchill,L.L.&H.]
Howe, Susan G. '63 '88 C.945 B.A. L.477 J.D. Asst. Atty. Gen., OR Dept. of Jus.
Howell, John M. '47 '75 C.908 B.A. L.950 J.D. Ref., Wkrs. Comp. Bd.
Hoyt, Kim E., (BV) '65 '91 C.628 B.A. L.950 J.D. [Garrett,H.R.J.C.&T.]
Hoyt, Mark C., (BV) '65 '92 C.154 B.S. L.950 J.D.
Hulteng, Richard J. '— '81 C.1169 B.A. L.112 J.D. Oregon State Hosp.
Huntsinger, Lester R. '45 '71 C.907 B.A. L.950 J.D. Jus. Dept.-Trial Div./Corrs. Litig.
Hutchings, Robert E. '61 '00 C.629 B.S. L.950 [R.E.Hutchings]
Hutchings, Robert E, P.C. 875 High St. NE
Hutchins, Christina M. '67 '92 C&L.950 B.S., J.D. 1162 Court St Ne
Hyland, Mariann '— '91 C&L.629 B.S., J.D. Oregon Health & Science University
Iparraguirre, Roland H. '— '97 C.629 B.S. L.1051 J.D. State Dept. Jus.
Irvin, John S. '31 '60 C&L.629 B.A., LL.B. Asst. Atty. Gen.
Irving, Janelle, (BV) '56 '80 C.1051 B.A. L.629 J.D. Trial Coun., SAIF Corporation
Isom, Dallas W. '38 '65 C.877 L.878 LL.B. Prof. of Law, Willamette Univ. Col. of Law
Isselmann, John E., Jr. '69 '94 C.800 B.A. L.446 J.D. Vista Strategies
Iverson, Eric F. '51 '79 C.605 B.A. L.1067 J.D. 1162 Court St. N.E.
Jackson, Kathryn E., (BV) '59 '87 C.339 B.S. L.629 J.D. [K.E.Jackson] ⊙
Jackson, Kathryn E., Law Office, (BV) 145 Wilson Street South (⊙Portland)
Jacobson, Marcia J.(Sam) '50 '76 C.629 B.S. L.352 J.D. Instr., Willamette Univ. Col. of Law
Jamieson, Eric William '73 '99 C.906 B.A. L.508 J.D. [Ⓐ Saalfeld G.]
Janet, Bernadette S. '57 '85 C.483 B.A. L.1375 J.D. (adm. in AK; not adm. in OR) Admin. Law J.
Jarman, Bruce E., (AV) '31 '68 C.1051 B.S. L.596 J.D. [Schlegel&J.]
Jenkins, Lori A., (CV) '58 '85 C.475 B.A. L.950 J.D. 1265 Waller St., S.E.
Jennings, George M., (BV) '47 '75 C.911 B.A. L.950 J.D. [Garrett,H.R.J.C.&T.]
Jensen, Timothy T.A., (BV) '44 '80 C.1042 B.A. L.285 J.D. 2490 Alvarado Terr. S.
Johansen, Eric R., (BV) '57 '82 C.1239 B.A. L.950 J.D. Dep. Pub. Def.
Johnnie, Gina Anne, (BV) '61 '87 C&L.950 B.S., J.D. [Sherman,S.M.J.&H.]
Johnson, Dexter A. '61 '89 C.823 B.S. L.982 J.D. Dep. Legis. Coun., OR Legis. Coun. Off.
Johnson, Michael V. '42 '72 C.101 B.S. L.629 J.D. Admin. Law J., Wkrs. Comp. Bd.
Johnson, Wendy J. '72 '98 C.132 B.A. L.950 J.D. Dep. Dir.
Johnson & Sherton, P.C., (AV) 247 Commercial St., N.E., Suite 205 (⊙Portland)
Jones, Gary G., (BV) '33 '64 C.629 B.A. L.596 LL.B. 387 Court Street, Northeast
Jones, Ira W. '26 '58 C&L.950 B.A., LL.B. 2660 E. Nob Hill St., S.E.‡
Jones, Jeffrey M., (BV) '63 '89 C&L.950 B.S., J.D. [J.M.Jones]
Jones, Rod M., (AV) '60 '87 C.629 B.S. L.950 J.D. 387 Court Street NE
Jones, Jeffrey M., PC, (BV) 1840 W. Nob Hill, SE
Jordan, Randall C. '52 '76 C&L.629 B.S., J.D. Asst. Atty. Gen.
Jostad, David R., (BV) '48 '77 C.629 B.S. L.285 J.D. 4185 Brooklake Rd Ne
Juza, Wm. J. '27 '56 C.629 B.B.A. L.950 LL.B. 2590 Sunrise Ave., S.‡
Kamitsuka, P. Rebecca, (CV) '57 '93 C.502 B.S. L.629 J.D. Sr. Asst. Atty. Gen.
Karnes, Keith D. '73 '03 C.101 B.A. L.950 J.D. [Ⓐ Olsen,O.&D.]
Kay, Terrence A. '53 '81 C.629 B.A. L.1051 J.D. [T.Kay]
Kay, Terrence, P.C. 3155 River Road S., Suite 150
Keeling, Gailen L. '30 '55 C.379 A.B. L.900 LL.B. (adm. in KS; not adm. in OR) 1550 Kenard St., N.W.‡
Keenan, Lora E. '64 '95 C.1320 B.A. L.1051 J.D. Staff Atty., Ct. of App.
Kelley, Alison S. '61 '99 C&L.950 B.A., J.D. 494 State St.
Kelley, Ann F. '44 '82 C.1181 B.A. L.950 J.D. Law Clk., Supm. Ct.
Kelley, Norman F. '36 '64 C.413 L.950 J.D. Sr. Asst. Atty. Gen.
Kelly, Timothy P. '49 '87 C.378 B.A. L.900 J.D. (adm. in KS; not adm. in OR) Law Ref. Libr., Willamette Univ. Coll. of Law
Kenagy, David R. '52 '77 C.668 B.A. L.1068 J.D. Assoc. Dean, Willamette Univ. Coll. of Law
Kent Custis, LLP, (AV) 1760 Liberty Street S.E. (⊙Portland)
Kersh, Karol W., (Mr.) '35 '76 C&L.950 B.S., LL.B. P.O. Box 13281‡
Khalsa, Hari Nam S. '52 '77 C.446 B.A. L.724 J.D. State Pub. Def.
Kinkade, Wayne A., (BV) '68 '95 C.628 B.S. L.629 J.D. [Saalfeld G.]
Kirkman, Reymond F. '40 '66 C&L.494 B.A., J.D. (adm. in MN; not adm. in OR) 562 Stagecoach Way Southeast‡
Kistler, Daniel Rives, (AV) '49 '84 C.951 B.A. L.276 J.D. Supm. Ct. J.
Klapstein, Janet A., (AV) '53 '78 C&L.629 B.A., J.D. Asst. Atty. Gen., OR Dept. of Jus.
Kleen, Jerry G. '29 '63 C.950 B.S. L.596 LL.B. 456 State St.
Klosterman, Arthur, (CV) '60 '86 C.628 B.S. L.61 J.D. [Whitehead&K.]
Knapp, Janet C. '49 '81 C.347 B.A. L.345 J.D. P.O. Box 401‡

Knapp, Michael E., (BV) '61 '88 C.1056 B.S. L.950 J.D.
2355 State Street, 97301
Telephone: 503-391-0664 Fax: 503-399-1929
Email: mikeeknapp@aol.com URL: http://www.lawyers.com/mikeeknapp
Business Law, Business Litigation, Construction Law, Contracts, Corporate Law, Collections, Debtor and Creditor, Real Estate, Landlord and Tenant Law.
Representative Clients: ACI Distribution; Eoff Electric Company; Morrow Equipment Company, LLC; The Statesman-Journal Newspaper; Lamar Obie Media Corp. Inc.

See Professional Biographies, SALEM, OREGON

Krasik, Steven L., (BV) '45 '80 C.1049 B.A. L.950 LL.D. 341 State St.
Kreitzberg, Anthony R., (BV) '59 '96 C.94 M.B.A. L.950 J.D. [Ⓐ Garrett,H.R.J.C.&T.]
Kremen, Hattie Bratzel '08 '51 L.596 LL.B. 344 18th St. NE
Krueger, Paul H., (BV) '55 '80 C.506 B.A. L.629 J.D. 1781 Liberty St. S.E.
Kryger, Alexander, Egan & Elmer, P.C., (AV) 355 Miller Street S.E. (⊙Albany)
Kuhns, David Brian, (BV) '61 '86 C.413 B.A. L.950 J.D. [D.B.Kuhns]
Kuhns, David B., Law Offices of, (BV) 835 Liberty St. N.E.
Kulongoski, Theodore R. '40 '70 C&L.502 B.A., J.D. Supm. Ct. J.
Kumley, Lloyd S. '45 '75 C.112 B.A. L.809 J.D. P.O. Box 4153
Kunkle, Jean L., (BV) '56 '83 C.1058 B.A. L.629 J.D. Dep. Dist. Atty.
Kutler, Keith L., (AV) '58 '85 C.685 B.A. L.823 J.D. Asst. Atty. Gen.
Lafky, Elton T., (CV) '30 '59 C&L.950 B.A., LL.B. 429 Court St., N.E.
Lafky, Kevin T., (BV) '59 '85 C.629 B.S. L.911 J.D. 429 Court St. N.E.
Laird, Lucinda E., (BV) '51 '91 C.36 B.S.W. L.950 J.D. P.O. Box 774
LaMont, Kristin, (BV) '59 '94 C.628 B.A. L.950 J.D. [Pierson,L.C.&G.]
Lancaster, Dianne L. '51 '96 C&L.950 B.A., J.D. Asst. Admins., Oreg. Servs. to Children & Families
Larkin, Jerome P. '54 '83 C.597 B.S.J. L.1051 J.D. Appellate Coun., SAIF Corporation
Larson, D. Erik, (BV) '48 '76 C.339 B.S.C.E. L.950 J.D. 100 High St. N.E.
Lathen, Neil F., (AV) '47 '74 C.1051 B.S. L.950 J.D. [Burt,S.L.A.M.&S.]
Lavine, Howard D. '52 '86 C.30 B.A. L.629 J.D. (adm. in MD; not adm. in OR) Communications and Policy Advisor
Lawler, James F., (CV) '72 '98 C&L.823 B.A., J.D. [Ⓐ Spooner,M.&A.]
Lee, Paul A., (BV) '51 '76 C.911 B.A. L.596 J.D. Asst. City Atty.
Lee, Richard D., (BV) '28 '56 C.629 B.B.A. L.950 J.D. 161 High St. S.E.
Leeson, Susan Margaret '46 '82 C&L.950 B.A., J.D. Assoc. Supm. Ct. Jus.
LeFore, Amy '— '04 C.628 B.S. L.950 J.D. [Ⓐ Saalfeld G.]
Leonard, David H., (BV) '46 '73 C.1181 B.S. L.950 J.D. [Churchill,L.L.&H.]
Lewis, Mary Lynn '49 '75 C.597 B.A. L.352 J.D. State Employment Div.
Lewis-Somers, Susan '55 '85 C.112 B.A. L.810 J.D. (adm. in CA; not adm. in OR) Law Ref. Libr., Willamette Univ. Col. of Law
Lien, Wallace W., (BV) '49 '79 C.1181 B.S. L.950 J.D. [W.W.Lien]
Lien, Wallace W., P.C., (BV) 1775 32nd Place, N.E.
Liggett, Dennis B., Attorney at Law '46 '95 C.1335 B.A. L.950 J.D. 2020 Boone Road S.E.
Lillig, David J. '44 '76 C.1056 B.S. L.1051 J.D. Spec. Asst. Atty. Gen., State Accident Ins. Fund
Lindauer, Eric B., (AV) '38 '67 C.628 B.S. L.950 J.D. [ⓒ Clark,L.F.E.L.&C.]
Linde, Hans A. '24 '51 C.685 B.A. L.1066 LL.B. Willamette Univ. Col. of Law
Linden, R. William, Jr. '51 '82 C.686 B.A. L.1209 J.D. State Ct. Adminstr., Ore. Judicial Dept.
Linder, Virginia L. '53 '80 C.1071 B.A. L.950 J.D. Appeals J.
Lindley, Lori Hildenbrand '61 '87 C.950 B.A. L.990 J.D. Asst. Atty. Gen.
Lipetzky, Russell S., (BV) '59 '87 C.112 B.A. L.770 J.D. [R.Lipetzky]
Lipetzky, Russell, (BV) 495 State St., Ste. 410
Lippold, Steven M., (BV) '62 '89 C.911 B.A. L.950 J.D. [Clark,L.F.E.L.&C.]
Lipscomb, Paul J. '48 '75 C.197 A.B. L.94 J.D. Cir. J.
Littlehales, Lewis C. '48 '76 C.950 B.A. L.1051 J.D. Prog. Exec., OR Dept. of Consumer & Bus. Servs., Ins. Div.
Lobo, Anita C. '43 '67 C.66 B.A. L.569 LL.B. Admin. Law J., Central Hearings Panel
Lockwood, Gary E. '35 '60 C&L.950 B.A., J.D. [G.E.Lockwood]
Lockwood, Gary E., P.C. 2270 Dorchester Dr., S.
Lodine, Paul C., (BV) '52 '80 C.939 A.B. L.950 J.D. [Churchill,L.L.&H.]
Loebe, Henry J. '49 '78 C.542 B.A. L.678 J.D. Dep. Dist. Atty.
Logan, Kathryn A. '53 '79 C.684 B.A. L.950 J.D. Hearing Off.
Londahl, Jan P., (AV) '42 '76 C.629 B.A. L.596 J.D. Asst. Atty. Gen.

Lounsbury, Daniel J., (CV) '66 '93 C&L.1335 B.A., J.D.
Jackson Professional Building, 145 Wilson Street South, 97302
Telephone: 503-581-7875 Fax: 503-375-7785
Email: dlounsbury@qwest.net URL: http://www.attorneydan.com
Family Law, Divorce Law, Grandparents Rights, Step Parent Adoptions, Child Custody, Child Support, Spousal Support, Criminal Law, Driving While Intoxicated, Drug Crimes, Felonies, Homicide, Juvenile Law, Misdemeanors, Parole and Probation, Sexual Assault, Traffic Violations, Personal Injury, Automobile Accidents.

See Professional Biographies, SALEM, OREGON

Lowry, Robert D., Law Offices of
(See Eugene)

Lucas, Charles D., (BV) .... '53 '98 C.999 B.S. L.950 J.D. [C.D.Lucas]
Lucas, Judy C., (BV) .... '51 '90 C.575 B.S. L.629 J.D. 1162 Court St. NE
Lucas, Charles D., P.C., (BV) .... 358 Superior Street SE, Suite 101
Lundy, Robt. W. .... '26 '51 C&L.352 B.A., J.D. Dep. Leg. Coun.
Lush, Deborah R. .... '76 '02 C.999 B.A. L.950 J.D. [Heltzel,U.W.Y.R.S.&P.]
Lutz, Dora L., (BV) .... '58 '84 C&L.950 B.A., J.D. 348 Leslie St. S.E.
Luukinen, Charles E., (P.C.), (AV) '47 '75
C.628 B.S. L.950 J.D. 3268 Hidden Valley Dr. N.W.
MacAfee, James J., (BV) .... '54 '79 C.293 B.A. L.950 J.D. [J.J.MacAfee]
MacAfee, James J., P.C., (BV) .... 3000 Market St. N.E., Ste. 325
Mac Donald, Ronald P., (BV) .... '42 '67 C.670 B.B.A. L.950 J.D. 180 Church St., S.E.
MacInnes, Malcolm D. .... '49 '76 C.628 B.A. L.629 J.D. 7014 Fruitland Rd., N.E.‡
Maier, Charles D., (CV) .... '50 '75 C.966 B.B.A. L.950 J.D. [Gatti,G.&M.]
Main, Stephen B. .... '41 '71 C.628 B.S. L.597 J.D. Asst. Atty. Gen.
Malatesta, Adrian Joseph .... '71 '00 C.999 B.A. L.950 J.D. Cascade Employers Assn.
Manary, James D. .... '45 '74 C.413 B.A. L.629 J.D. Dept. of Rev.
Mannix, Kevin L., (BV) .... '49 '74 C&L.893 B.A., J.D. [K.L.Mannix]
Mannix, Kevin L., PC, (BV) .... 2003 State St.
Mansell, Melanie E. .... '59 '89 C.645 B.A. L.950 J.D. 270 Cottage St., N.E.
Marshall, Monte .... '62 '92 C.335 B.A. L.950 J.D. Sr. Staff Atty., Workers Comp. Bd.
Marshall, S. Amanda .... '69 '95 C.629 B.A. L.950 J.D. OR Dept. of Jus., Fam. Law Sect.
Marshall, Ward D. .... '55 '87 C.1056 B.S. L.596 J.D. Asst. Atty. Gen.
Martin, Alan D. .... '44 '00 C.1077 B.A. L.796 J.D. P.O. Box 821
Martinis, Michael J., (BV) .... '52 '77 C.413 B.A. L.950 J.D. 1114 12th St Se
Mason, Renee Bryant, (AV) '53 '82
C.16 B.A. L.596 J.D. Dept. of Human Res., Employ. App. Bd.

Matarazzo, Harris S.
(See Portland)

Mattson, Jeffrey S. .... '51 '77 C&L.629 B.S., J.D. Ore. Dept. of Rev.
Mayer, Kenneth Franklin .... '53 '84 C.1071 B.S. L.950 J.D. Gen. Coun., Key Title Co.
Mazur-Hart, Helen L. .... '47 '83 C.483 B.A. L.950 J.D. Willamette Univ.
McCann, Donald W., (AV) .... '46 '76 C.911 B.A. L.950 J.D. [Burt,S.L.A.M.&S.]
McCann, Todd C., (BV) .... '62 '93 C.267 B.S. L.950 J.D. [T.C.McCann]
McCann, Todd C., P.C., (BV) .... 1795 Commercial Street, S.E.
McClinton, Michael C., (AV) .... '47 '72 C.800 B.A. L.950 J.D. [McClinton&T.]

McClinton & Troutt, (AV)
698 Twelfth Street, S.E., Suite 210, 97301
Telephone: 503-361-3910 Fax: 503-361-3915
Email: mctroutt@quest.net
Michael C. McClinton; Sarah Rhoads Troutt.
Medical Malpractice Defense, Legal Malpractice Defense, Insurance Defense, Products Liability Defense, Employment Law, Commercial Litigation, Environmental Litigation, Media Law.
See Professional Biographies, SALEM, OREGON

McConville, Robert B. .... '33 '64 C.950 B.A. L.629 J.D. Sr. Cir. Ct. J.
McCullough, John P. .... '47 '73 C.1070 B.S. L.1066 J.D. Presiding J., Wkrs. Comp. Bd.,
McDonnell, Mark G., (BV) .... '51 '79 C&L.629 J.D. Dep. Dist. Atty.
McDonough, Michael Lee, (CV) '49 '76 C.1051 B.S. L.950 J.D.
180 Church Street, S.E.
McGavock, Richard M. '38 '74 C.763 B.S. L.1051 J.D.
State Dept. of Bus. & Consumer Servs., Ins. Div.
McGinty, Richard F., (BV) .... '52 '86 C.999 B.S. L.950 J.D. 1820 Lancaster Dr Ne
McGraw, Scott W. .... '56 '82 C.475 B.A. L.950 J.D. P.O. Box 4719
McKeever, Joe G., (BV) .... '45 '73 C.610 B.A. L.608 J.D. Asst. Atty. Gen.
McKinney, William C. .... '33 '66 C&L.950 B.A., J.D. 1015 13th St., S.E.
McMillin, Raymond C., (BV) .... '47 '72 C.335 B.A. L.950 J.D. [Mills&M.]
McMurdo, C. Gregory .... '46 '72 C.628 B.A. L.1051 J.D. Dir. of Govt. Rel.
McNaught, Joseph T., (BV) '51 '78
C.154 B.A. L.629 J.D. Asst. Atty. Gen., OR Dept. of Jus.
Meadowbrook, Paul B. .... '51 '79 C.330 B.A. L.950 J.D. [P.B.Meadowbrook]
Meadowbrook, Paul B., PC .... 285 Liberty St. NE, Ste. 360
Meehan, Terence J. .... '59 '88 C.628 B.S. L.629 J.D. Gen. Couns.
Merrill, Gretchen Gunn .... '64 '87 C.628 B.A. L.629 J.D. Sr. Asst. Atty. Gen.
Mertz, Brady .... '67 '97 C.911 B.A. L.950 J.D. 247 Commercial Street NE, Suite 203
Messoline, Dennis V., (CV) .... '52 '84 C.653 B.A. L.1051 J.D. 2711 12th St., S.E.
Metcalf, Janet A. .... '46 '72 C.174 B.A. L.629 J.D. Asst. Atty. Gen
Milbank, M. Chapin, (AV) .... '33 '60 C.112 B.A. L.950 J.D. P.O. Box 13687
Miller, Mari L. .... '47 '91 C.475 B.S. L.596 J.D. State Dept. of Ins. & Fin.
Miller, Rodney W. .... '30 '59 C&L.352 B.A., LL.B. Cir. J.‡
Millis, A. Edward, (CV) .... '42 '98 L.950 J.D. Marion-Polk Legal Aid Service Inc.
Mills, D. Michael, (BV) .... '42 '72 C.813 B.A. L.950 J.D. [Mills&M.]
Mills & McMillin, (BV) .... 715 Commercial, N.E.
Misner, Robert L. '46 '71
C.767 B.A. L.145 J.D. Prof. of Law, Willamette Univ. Col. of Law
Mitchell, Kristan S. .... '63 '88 C.336 B.A. L.950 J.D. Oregon Sanitary Serv. Institute
Mize, Weisha R. .... '55 '82 C&L.629 B.S., J.D. Hearing Offr. Panel
Moan, Rolf C. .... '65 '92 C.309 A.B. L.276 J.D. Asst. Atty. Gen.
Moffat, Diana L. .... '58 '86 C.112 B.A. L.1051 J.D. Dist. Atty's Off.
Moore, Brian G. .... '76 '04 C.101 B.S. L.950 J.D. [Ⓐ Saalfeld G.]
Moore, Jeffrey G., (BV) .... '70 '98 C&L.101 B.S., J.D. [Saalfeld G.]
Morgan, William W., Law Offices of, (BV) '62 '91
C.101 B.A. L.950 J.D. 525 Glen Creek Road NW, Suite 260
Motley, John B. .... '45 '74 C.112 B.A. L.950 J.D. Trial Coun., SAIF Corporation
Mowery, Bruce L., (BV) .... '47 '73 C.1056 B.S. L.596 J.D. 1212 Court St., N.E.
Moyano, Lucinda D. .... '61 '86 C.679 B.S. L.950 J.D. Asst. Atty. Gen.
Moynahan, Karen Locha '61 '87 C.705 B.A. L.823 J.D.
(adm. in NJ; not adm. in OR) Dep. of Jus.
Much, Joe W., (AV) .... '48 '75 C.950 B.A. L.678 J.D. [Spooner,M.&A.]

Muhlheim Boyd
(See Eugene)

Muir, Robert Warren, (AV) .... '47 '78 C.1111 M.A. L.950 J.D. Asst. Atty. Gen.
Mullen, Gregory H. .... '45 '70 C.628 B.S. L.950 J.D. U.S. Natl. Bk. of Ore.
Muñiz, Michael, Law Offices of, (BV) '52 '78
C.112 B.A. L.1051 J.D. 3000 Market St Ste 529
Munro, John R. .... '45 '75 C.813 B.A. L.629 J.D. Govt. Affs. Coun.
Munsey, Anne Kimiko Fujita .... '66 '99 C.685 B.A. L.629 J.D. Pub. Def. Servs. Off.
Murch, James L., (BV) .... '44 '74 C.222 B.A. L.285 J.D. [Sherman,S.M.J.&H.]
Murray, Dwayne R., (CV) .... '47 '74 C.629 B.B.A. L.596 J.D. [© Olsen,O.&D.]
Myers, A. Carl, (BV) .... '47 '75 C&L.629 B.A., J.D. 1815 Commercial St. S.
Myers, Hardy, (AV) .... '39 '64 C.500 A.B. L.629 LL.B. Atty. Gen.
Myzak, Ioan Terri, (BV) .... '— '82 C&L.950 B.S., J.D. P.O. Box 20416
Nafziger, James A. R. '40 '67 C.966 B.A. L.309 J.D.
(adm. in WI; not adm. in OR)
Thomas B. Stoel Prof. of Law, Willamette Univ. Col. of Law
Nass, James W. .... '49 '74 C.697 B.A. L.950 J.D. App. Coun., Supm. Ct.
Naucler, Mitzi M., (CV) .... '53 '82 C.510 B.A. L.950 J.D. Willamette Univ.
Nedeau, Rochelle .... '51 '79 C.959 B.S. L.950 J.D. Sr. Asst. Atty. Gen.
Nevue, Elizabeth J. .... '54 '89 C.629 B.A. L.950 J.D. Salem Hosp. Social Servs.
Nichols, Marilyn .... '38 '74 C.1104 B.S. L.596 J.D. Admin. Law J., Wkrs. Comp. Bd.
Nielsen, Brian R. .... '71 '98 C&L.950 B.A., J.D. [B.R.Nielsen]
Nielsen, Deryl K., (CV) .... '53 '85 C.999 L.1051 J.D. [D.K.Nielsen]
Nielsen, Patricia, (CV) .... '54 '85 C.413 B.S. L.1051 J.D. [Ⓐ D.K.Nielsen]
Nielsen, Brian R., P.C. .... 687 Court Street Northeast
Nielsen, Deryl K., P.C., (CV) .... P.O. Box 5944
Nisbet-Lance, Thomas .... '58 '90 C.508 B.A. L.950 J.D. 992 Cottage St Ne
Norblad, Albin W. .... '39 '65 C.629 B.S. L.950 J.D. Cir. J.
Nordyke, Robert E., (BV) .... '45 '70 C&L.950 B.A., J.D. 495 State St.
Norman, Stephen .... '71 '97 C.112 B.A. L.950 J.D. HRCentral Corp.
Norris, Scott A. .... '66 '91 C.628 B.A. L.950 J.D. 555 Court St Ne

Norris, Gary G., Law Office of
(See McMinnville)

Northcutt, Raymond E. '29 '72 C.628 B.S. L.596 J.D.
Exec. Secy., Employment App. Bd.
Northrop, James B. .... '57 '84 C&L.629 B.A., J.D. Staff Atty, SAIF Corporation
Obert, Mark Gene .... '70 '96 C.939 B.S. L.950 J.D. [M.G.Obert]
Obert, Mark G., Law Offices of .... 189 Liberty Street N.E.
Ochoa, Joseph V. .... '50 '87 C.1331 B.A. L.596 J.D. Dist. J.

O'Donnell & Clark LLP
(See Portland)

Ogawa, Jenny A. .... '59 '87 C.972 B.S. L.1051 J.D. 2003 State St.
Ogdahl, W. Wallace, (BV) .... '45 '74 C.628 B.S. L.950 J.D. 515 High St. S.E.
Oliver, Elaine B. .... '43 '89 C&L.629 M.S., J.D. 270 Cottage St. NE
Oliver, Robert W. .... '31 '58 C&L.309 A.B., LL.B. 2478 Morning Dove Ct., N.W.‡
Olsen, Eric W., (BV) .... '51 '78 C.101 B.A. L.629 J.D. [Olsen,O.&D.]
Olsen, Kristin E., (BV) .... '57 '88 C.878 B.S. L.950 J.D. 1599 State St.
Olsen, Lars H. .... '65 '91 C&L.950 B.S., J.D. [Olsen,O.&D.]
Olsen, Olsen & Daines, (BV) .... 1599 State Street (©Bellevue, WA)
Olson, Lynda D., (BV) .... '54 '79 C.413 B.A. L.950 J.D. [Allen,F.&O.]
Olsson, David C. .... '62 '91 C&L.37 B.S.B.A., J.D. State Employ. App. Bd.
Onart, Esin .... '74 '00 C.939 B.A. L.1051 J.D. Asst. Atty. Gen.
O'Neill, Timothy B., (BV) .... '46 '75 C.147 B.A. L.950 J.D. [O'Neill&E.]
O'Neill & Evans, (BV) .... 675 Church St., NE
Orlebeke, W. Ronald '34 '66 C&L.950 B.A., J.D.
(adm. in CA; not adm. in OR) 3760 Market St., N.E.‡
Orrio, Bryan J. .... '70 '97 C.1071 B.S. L.950 J.D. Dist. Atty. Off.
Ortega, Darleen R. .... '62 '89 C.635 B.A. L.477 J.D. Ct. App. J.
Osborn, Virgil L. .... '45 '75 C.1071 B.S. L.45 J.D. 4770 Glendale Ave. N.E.
Ositis, Andrew P. .... '44 '74 C.911 B.A. L.1065 J.D. 388 State St.
Paetsch, Erich M. D., (CV) .... '73 '99 C.1051 B.S. L.596 J.D. [Ⓐ Saalfeld G.]
Palladino, Kristen Ellen .... '74 '00 C.911 B.A. L.629 J.D. Asst. Atty. Gen.
Paluska, Michael J., Law Offices of '69 '96
C.670 B.B.A. L.629 J.D. 530 Center St. NE, Ste. 700
Park, Douglas Y.S. .... '65 '94 C.911 B.A. L.629 J.D. Asst. Atty. Gen.
Parks, J. Philip, (AV) .... '44 '70 C&L.950 B.A., J.D. [Parks,B.S.&W.]
Parks, Bauer, Sime & Winkler, (AV) .... 570 Liberty St. S.E., Ste. 200
Pearson, Roger C. .... '53 '80 C.941 B.S. L.950 J.D. Wrks. Comp. Bd.
Penn, Dale W., (AV) .... '49 '76 C.642 B.A. L.629 J.D. Dist. Atty.
Perez-Selsky, Gregorio A. .... '47 '78 C.763 B.A. L.629 J.D. Asst. City Atty.
Perry, James A. .... '36 '65 C.629 B.S. L.596 J.D. [© Saalfeld G.]
Perry, Walter, (AV) .... '49 '77 C.399 B.A. L.94 J.D. Asst. Atty. Gen.
Petersen, Michael C., (BV) .... '69 '95 C.120 B.A. L.950 J.D. [Heltzel,U.W.Y.R.S.&P.]
Petersen, Robert A. .... '42 '71 C.628 B.S. L.1051 J.D. State Dept. of Jus.
Peterson, Edwin J. '30 '57 C&L.629 B.S., LL.B.
Dist. Jurist in Res., Willamette Univ. Col. of Law‡
Peterson, Lee H., (BV) .... '48 '87 C.629 B.S. L.950 J.D. [D.A. .a.L.H.P.Rhoten]
Peterson, Theresa K. .... '58 '89 C.965 B.A. L.477 J.D. P.O. Box 14350

Peterson Law Offices, PC
(See Portland)

Pham, Curt H. .... '— '96 C&L.112 B.S., J.D. Dept. of Jus.
Pickell, R. W. .... '10 '50 C.334 B.S. L.950 LL.B. 515 Washington St. S.‡
Pierson, D. Eugene .... '59 '88 C&L.02 LL.B. [G.Pierson]
Pierson, Dirk L., (BV) .... '65 '94 C.35 B.S. L.950 J.D. [Pierson,L.C.&G.]
Pierson, Gene, P.C. .... 2355 State St.
Pierson, LaMont, Carlson & Gregg, P.C., (BV) .... 1011 Liberty St. S.E.
Pollino, John E., (BV) .... '66 '92 C.678 B.A. L.950 J.D. [Garrett,H.R.J.C.&T.]
Pons, Elaine M. .... '65 '94 C.197 A.B. L.1051 J.D. Jud. Clk., App. Ct.
Potter, Ana .... '72 '01 C.628 B.S. L.596 J.D. [A.Potter]
Potter, Ervin W. .... '17 '51 C&L.950 B.A., J.D. P.O. Box 6035‡
Potter, Ana, P.C. .... 687 Court St. N.E.
Pound, Larry J., (BV) .... '42 '75 C.907 B.A. L.950 J.D. P.O. Box 3050
Prall, Tracy A., (BV) .... '— '95 C.1181 B.S. L.950 J.D. [Ⓐ Garrett,H.R.J.C.&T.]
Prestwich, Travis S., (BV) .... '70 '00 C.101 B.A. L.950 J.D. 388 State Street
Price, George E., (BV) .... '52 '85 C.267 B.A. L.950 J.D. [Price&P.]
Price, Thomas E., (BV) .... '58 '90 [Price&P.]
Price & Price Attorneys, (BV) .... 317 Court St. N.E., Ste. 203
Priest, Alan I. '38 '74 L.1137
(adm. in CA; not adm. in OR) P.O. Box 2312‡
Pritchard, Charles E., (AV) .... '41 '73 C.17 B.A. L.950 J.D. 610 Hawthorne Ave Se #210
Quesseth, Cecil H. .... '17 '46 C&L.950 B.A., LL.B. Hearings Off.‡
Quillinan, Kasia .... '48 '80 C.112 B.A. L.950 J.D. Ref., Workers Comp. Bd.
Quinn, Julene .... '— '85 C.477 B.A. L.904 J.D. Appellate Coun., SAIF Corporation
Rae, Max, (BV) .... '54 '81 C.1056 B.S. L.950 J.D. 1880 Lancaster Dr. N.E., Ste. 113
Ramsay, Raymond M., (BV) .... '48 '73 C.1071 L.950 J.D. [Ramsay&S.]
Ramsay & Stein, P.C., (BV) .... 1395 Liberty Street, S.E., Suite 101
Ramsey, Reynard .... '60 '86 C.705 B.A. L.893 J.D. Econ. Development Dept., 6th Fl.
Rank, Kevin Jay, (BV) .... '63 '91 C.101 B.S. L.950 J.D. 1265 Waller St Se
Raye, Shannon M. .... '78 '03 C&L.93 B.A., J.D. [Ⓐ Saalfeld G.]
Rea, Diane M. .... '61 '87 C.267 B.A. L.990 J.D. State. Bd. of Parole
Reed, Candace A., (BV) .... '51 '82 C.339 B.A. L.629 J.D. 341 State St.
Regnell, Janet K. .... '— '91 C.1056 B.A. L.629 J.D. Dept. of Consumer & Bus. Servs.
Reid, Raymond A., (BV) .... '49 '84 C.774 B.A. L.950 J.D. [Ⓐ D.Hilgemann]
Rennick, Lynne Dorothea .... '48 '98 C&L.629 B.A., J.D. 1162 Court St Ne
Rettkowski, April A. .... '76 '02 C.911 B.A. L.285 J.D. [Ⓐ Saalfeld G.]
Reuling, John A. .... '29 '57 C.94 A.B. L.966 J.D. 4528 Independence Dr., S.E.‡

Reutlinger, Ted W. ....'55 '80 C.413 B.A. L.629 J.D. Sr. Dep. Legis. Coun.
Reynolds, Michael D., (AV) ....'48 '74 C.909 B.A. L.950 J.D. Asst. Atty. Gen.
Rhoades, Jamese Lou, (BV) ....'53 '78 C.906 B.S. L.950 J.D. Cir. J.
Rhoten, David A., (AV) ....'34 '61 C.950 B.S. L.285 LL.B. [D.A. .a.L.H.P.Rhoten]
Rhoten, David A., and Lee H. Peterson, (AV) ....494 State Street, Suite 230
Rich, James B. ....'70 '97 C.549 B.A. L.950 J.D. [Harris,W.&A.]
Richardson, Dean M. '43 '70
C.696 B.A. L.823 J.D. Prof. of Law, Willamette Univ. Sch. of Law
Richardson, Kate Cooper ....'61 '00 C.629 B.A. L.950 J.D. Chf. of Staff
Riggs, R. William ....'38 '68 C.1056 B.S. L.629 J.D. Assoc. Jus., Sup. Ct.
Rinehart, Sarah K., (BV) ....'54 '82 C&L.629 B.S., J.D. 300 Pioneer Trust Building
Ritter, Daniel A., (AV) ....'40 '65 C.767 A.B. L.950 J.D. [D.A.Ritter]

Ritter, Daniel A., P.C., (AV)
Equitable Center, 530 Center Street N.E., Suite 700, 97301-3740
Telephone: 503-585-2236 FAX: 503-585-1006
Email: dritter@danritter.com
Daniel A. Ritter.
Estate Planning, Trusts, Wills and Probate, Federal Estate and Gift Taxation.
See Professional Biographies, SALEM, OREGON

Rives, Carol A. ....'43 '81 C.508 B.A.,M.A. L.1243 J.D. Dept. of Ins.
Robinson, Daniel K. ....'56 '91 C.339 B.S.W. L.596 J.D. Fairview Training Ctr.
Robinson, Wendy Ann, (AV) ....'52 '86 C.685 B.A. L.596 J.D. Asst. Atty. Gen.
Rockett, Helen M., (AV) ....'39 '76 C.623 B.A. L.629 J.D. Justice Bldg., 3rd Flr.‡
Rocklin, Robert B., (AV) '58 '83
C&L.112 A.B., J.D. Asst. Atty. Gen., Dept. of Jus.-App. Div.
Rode, Helle, (AV) ....'54 '80 C.1056 B.A. L.629 J.D. Jus. Dept.
Rogers, Velda H. ....'49 '83 C.1071 B.S. L.950 J.D. 868 Commercial St., N.E.
Ronning, Mark Allen, (CV) ....'65 '95 C.629 B.S. L.950 J.D. [Ⓐ Ashcroft W.]
Rosen, Steven O., (AV) ....'49 '77 C.107 B.S. L.596 J.D. [Rosen] ⊙
Rosen Law Firm, The, (AV) ....512 State Street (⊙Portland)
Rosenblit, Joel L. ....'51 '97 C.393 B.A. L.502 J.D. Lead Atty., SEIU Local 503, OPEU
Rosik, Lynn, (BV) ....'57 '81 C.478 B.A. L.629 J.D. Gen. Coun.
Ross, David Jonathan, (BVⓉ) ....'50 '75 C.861 B.A. L.192 J.D. Asst. City Atty.
Rossman, Kurt C. ....'32 '61 C.1056 L.596 LL.B. Ct. of App. J.
Roth, David M., (BV) ....'61 '92 C.635 B.S. L.950 J.D. [Heltzel,U.W.Y.R.S.&P.]
Roth, Robert T. ....'46 '74 C.262 B.A. L.976 J.D. Asst. Atty. Gen.
Rovics, Caren J. ....'54 '84 C.563 B.A. L.831 J.D. Jus. Dept.
Roy, Matthew Lansing, (CV) ....'68 '94 C.1288 B.S. L.260 J.D. [Vick&C.]
Roy, Melinda Leaver, (BV) ....'68 '94 C.937 B.A. L.260 J.D. [Ⓐ Churchill,L.L.&H.]
Ruff, Erin J. ....'70 '98 C.154 B.A. L.950 J.D. Mediator, Co. Ct.
Runkel, Ross R. '39 '65 C&L.911 B.S., LL.B.
Prof. of Law, Willamette Univ. Sch. of Law
Runner, David ....'55 '84 C&L.950 B.S., J.D. Appellate Coun., SAIF Corporation
Ruona, Mary Q. ....'68 '94 C.309 B.A. L.602 J.D. Jus. Dept.
Russell, Jim G. ....'36 '69 C&L.629 B.S., J.D. Asst. Atty. Gen.
Russell, Kenneth P. ....'60 '85 C.628 B.S. L.596 J.D. Trial Coun., SAIF Corporation
Rutkowski, Mark H. ....'53 '79 C&L.950 B.A., J.D. [Rutkowski]
Rutkowski Law Offices, LLC ....180 Ramsgate Sq. SE, Suite 100
Saalfeld, Robert J., (AV) ....'49 '74 C.767 B.A. L.950 J.D. [Saalfeld G.] ⊙

Saalfeld Griggs PC, (AV)
Park Place, Suite 300, 250 Church Street, SE, P.O. Box 470, 97308 ⊙
Telephone: 503-399-1070 Fax: 503-371-2927
Email: contactus@sglaw.com URL: http://www.sglaw.com
Robert J. Saalfeld; James C. Griggs; Kris Jon Gorsuch; Douglas C. Alexander, II; Hunter B. Emerick; Randall W. Cook; Randall P. Sutton; Mark D. Shipman; Wayne A. Kinkade; Jeffrey G. Moore;—Erich M. D. Paetsch; Shelly M. Arritola; Eric William Jamieson; Caleb A. Williams; April A. Rettkowski; Sean M. Driscoll; Shannon M. Raye; Brian G. Moore; Amy LeFore; Mary E. Carter. Of Counsel: James A. Perry.
Business, Taxation, Intellectual Property, Real Estate and Land Use, Employment, Construction, Banking, Creditors' Rights, Estate Planning and Probate Law, Pension and Profit Sharing, Environmental Law, Labor and Employment, Commercial and Tax Litigation in all Courts.
Bend, Oregon Office: 1001-B SW Disk Drive, Suite 102, 97702-1995. Telephone: 541-322-1822. Fax: 541-322-1823.
See Professional Biographies, SALEM, OREGON

Safford, Susan N. ....'65 '93 C.674 A.B. L.596 J.D. OR Off. of Energy
St. Thomas, Suzanne S., (BV) ....'47 '87 C.1051 B.S. L.336 J.D. [S.S.St.Thomas]
St. Thomas, Suzanne S., P.C., (BV) ....Suite 3, 5778 Commercial St SE
Salinas, Vada A. ....'60 '95 C.623 B.B.A. L.802 J.D. [V.Salinas]
Salinas, Vada, LLC, Law Offices of ....1987 Mockingbird Drive, S.
Sanderson, James A. ....'43 '66 C&L.629 B.S., LL.B. 1266 Crowley Ave. S.E.
Sanderson, Wendy E. ....'69 '98 C.1131 B.A. L.1051 J.D. State Dept. of Jus.
Santos, Daniel P. ....'52 '86 C.1071 B.S. L.950 J.D. Policy Advsr.
Saucy, Paul E., (AV) ....'53 '79 C&L.950 B.A., J.D. 265 State St.
Sayer, Ron L., (BV) ....'62 '91 C.1032 B.A. L.950 J.D. 1781 Liberty St Se
Schanz, Daniel R., (BV) ....'67 '94 C.999 B.S. L.1187 J.D. [Ⓐ Spooner,M.&A.]
Schlegel, Ralph H., (AV) ....'32 '60 C.628 B.S. L.950 J.D. [Schlegel&J.]
Schlegel & Jarman, LLP, (AV) ....544 Ferry St. S.E., Ste. 2
Schnabel-Bray, Mary A., (BV) '57 '93
C.629 B.A. L.950 J.D. Asst. Atty. Gen., OR Dept. of Jus.
Schucht, Larry D. ....'60 '86 C.543 B.S. L.190 J.D. Trial Coun., SAIF Corporation
Schuman, David ....'44 '84 C.813 B.A. L.629 J.D. Appeals Ct. J.
Schweitzer, Margie S. ....'60 '96 C.1181 B.S. L.950 J.D. Jurisnotes.com
Scott, Allen R. ....'43 '73 C.939 A.B. L.950 J.D. 550 Capitol St Ne
Scott, Susan Tracey ....'62 '87 C.112 B.A. L.950 J.D. Dep. Dist. Atty.
Seifert, Henry L. ....'18 '42 C&L.910 B.S., LL.B. Hearings Ref., Wkms. Comp. Bd.
Seymour, Donald C. ....'31 '59 C&L.629 B.A., LL.B. 4270 Alderbrook, S.E.
Shea, Janice Prazma ....'49 '85 C.339 B.S. L.950 J.D. 1163 State St.
Sherman, Kenneth, (AV) ....'17 '46 C.950 L.285 LL.B. [Sherman,S.M.J.&H.] ‡
Sherman, Kenneth, Jr., (AV) ....'46 '74 C.940 B.A. L.285 J.D. [Sherman,S.M.J.&H.]
Sherman, Sherman, Murch, Johnnie & Hazel, L.L.P., (AV)
475 Cottage Street N.E., Suite 120
Sherton, Corinne C., (AV) ....'49 '81 C.145 B.S. L.950 J.D. [Johnson&S.]
Shetterly, Francine S. .....'56 '81 C.339 A.B. L.1051 J.D. App. Staff Atty. OR Ct. of App.
Shine, Christopher J. ....'63 '90 C&L.602 B.B.A., J.D. Employ. App. Bd.
Shipman, Mark D., (BV) ....'60 '93 C.907 B.A. L.950 J.D. [Saalfeld G.]
Shipsey, Steven E. ....'66 '94 C.911 B.A. L.629 J.D. Jud. Clk., Supm. Ct.
Shuba, J. Kevin ....'64 '91 C.911 B.A. L.950 J.D. [Ⓒ Garrett,H.R.J.C.&T.]
Shuba, John Kevin, (BV) ....'64 '91 C.911 B.A. L.950 J.D. Asst. Atty. Gen.
Sieg, Thomas A. ....'54 '84 C.1076 B.S. L.950 J.D. SAIF Corp.
Sime, Billy M., (BV) ....'56 '82 C.628 B.S. L.629 J.D. [Parks,B.S.&W.]
Simons, Christopher J., (BV) '71 '97
C.800 B.A. L.950 J.D. Corp. Coun., May Trucking Co.
Simrin, Andy ....'57 '91 C.112 B.A. L.596 J.D. Dep. Pub. Def.
Sinks, Tahra ....'74 '00 C.950 B.A. L.629 J.D. [Ⓐ Alway&C.]
Slezak, Richard E., (BV) ....'50 '86 C.1201 B.A. L.950 J.D. [Ⓐ Churchill,L.L.&H.]

Sloan, Gordon ....'11 '35 C.378 A.B. L.900 LL.B. Sr. Supm. Ct. Jus.
Sloper, Val D. ....'23 '49 C&L.950 B.A., LL.B. Cir. J.
Smith, Barbara Jo, (BV) ....'68 '95 C.947 A.B. L.910 J.D. [Heltzel,U.W.Y.R.S.&P.]
Smith, Betty .....'47 '78 C.994 B.A. L.629 J.D. Hearings Off., Adult & Fam. Servs. Div.
Smith, Christina M. ....'74 '01 C.945 B.A. L.629 J.D. Pub. Utility Comm.
Smith, Corey B., (BV) ....'55 '82 C.878 B.A. L.950 J.D. 868 Commercial St., N.E.
Smith, Craig A. '47 '82 C.594 B.A. L.950 J.D.
Chief Financial Ofcr., Chemeketa College
Smith, Gregory A., (AV) ....'55 '86 C.591 B.S.N. L.950 J.D. [G.Smith]
Smith, J. Michael, (CV) ....'41 '76 C.1181 B.S. L.678 J.D. 2290 State St.
Smith, Jill ....'73 '00 C.937 B.A. L.950 J.D. 1162 Court St.
Smith, Michael George, (CV) ....'63 '95 C.939 B.A. L.69 J.D. 1781 Liberty St., S.E.
Smith, Susan L. '53 '80
C.685 B.A. L.309 J.D. Prof. of Law, Willamette Univ. Coll. of Law
Smith, Greg, P.C., (AV) ....1781 Liberty Street, S.E.
Smith-Koop, Elaine D., Law Office ....'57 '90 C.999 B.A. L.950 J.D. P.O. Box 247
Snider, Paul R. ....'45 '71 C&L.879 B.A., J.D. Assoc. of Oregon Counties
Snow, Carlton J. '39 '69 C.827 B.A. L.966 J.D.
(adm. in WI; not adm. in OR) Prof. of Law, Willamette Univ. Coll. of Law
Socolofsky, John H. ....'34 '60 C&L.629 B.S., LL.B. Sr. Asst. Atty. Gen.
Sollis, Jack L. ....'26 '52 C&L.629 B.S., LL.B. 2410 Fisher Rd. N.E.‡
Sorensen, Carlotta H. ....'29 '52 C.628 B.S. L.950 LL.B. 830 Clarmount N.W.
Sorensen, Glen V. ....'22 '50 C&L.950 B.A., LL.B. 830 Clarmount N.W.
Spangler, Kirk L. ....'58 '87 C.911 B.S. L.950 J.D. Admin. Law J., Wkrs. Comp. Bd.
Spooner, Ralph C., (AV) ....'46 '73 C.339 B.A. L.46 J.D. [Spooner,M.&A.]

Spooner, Much & Ammann, P.C., (AV)
530 Center Street N.E., Suite 722, 97301-3740
Telephone: 503-378-7777 Fax: 503-588-5899
Email: rspooner@smapc.com URL: http://www.smapc.com
Ralph C. Spooner; Joe W. Much; Ken L. Ammann;—Daniel R. Schanz; James F. Lawler; Melissa J. Ward.
General Civil and Trial Practice in State and Federal Courts. Insurance, Products Liability and Personal Injury Law.
See Professional Biographies, SALEM, OREGON

Staley, Robert W., Jr., (BV) ....'45 '91 C.575 A.B. L.950 J.D. 1075 Hansen Ave., S.
Standen, Jeffrey A. '60 '86
C.276 A.B. L.893 J.D. Prof. of Law, Willamette Univ. Sch. of Law
Stark, William D. ....'44 '89 C.958 B.S. L.950 J.D. 876 Welcome Way, S.E.
Stecker, Carl R., (AV) ....'51 '79 C.184 B.A. L.950 J.D. Chf. Dep. Dist. Atty.
Stein, Debbe, (CV) ....'59 '97 161 High Street S.E.
Stein, Richard C., (BV) ....'50 '75 C&L.950 B.A., J.D. [Ramsay&S.]
Stevens, Leslie S. '65 '94 C.147 B.A. L.1051 J.D.
Asst. City Atty., Salem City Attys. Off.
Stevenson, George B. ....'47 '76 C.1056 B.S. L.950 J.D. City Atty. Off.
Stewart, Jack L., (BV) ....'48 '91 C.112 B.A. L.950 J.D. 247 Commercial Ne Ste 201
Stiteler, David W. '50 '75 C&L.972 B.A., J.D.
(adm. in WY; not adm. in OR) Employ Rel. Bd.
Stonecipher, Jane Ellen ....'52 '77 C.347 A.B. L.813 J.D. Co. Legal Couns.
Storkel, John E., (BV) ....'53 '85 C.999 B.S. L.950 J.D. 1415 Liberty St Se
Stortz, J. William, (BV) ....'24 '49 C&L.950 B.S., LL.B. 1011 Liberty St., S.E.
Striffler, Stephanie L., (AV) '54 '82 C.685 B.A. L.145 J.D.
Special Coun., Atty. Gen. Off.
Sundermier, Paul J., (AV) ....'46 '92 C.705 B.A. L.950 J.D. Sr. Asst. Atty. Gen.
Sushida, Jonathan P. ....'69 '03 C.312 B.A. L.950 J.D. [Ⓐ W.W.Lien]
Sussman, Samuel '31 '59 C.112 B.A. L.800 LL.B.
(adm. in CA; not adm. in OR) P.O. Box 12217‡
Sutton, Randall P., (BV) ....'62 '93 C.763 B.A. L.950 J.D. [Saalfeld G.]
Swaim, Michael E., (BV) ....'43 '72 C.112 B.A. L.1068 J.D. [M.E.Swain]
Swaim, Michael E., P.C., Law Offices of, (BV) ....270 Cottage St., N.E.
Swanson, D. Keith, (AV) ....'43 '69 C.628 B.S. L.950 J.D. [Burt,S.L.A.M.&S.]
Swanson, Kevin K. ....'65 '95 C&L.950 B.S., J.D. 2711 Twelfth St. SE
Swartz, Kevin D. ....'67 '98 C.906 B.A. L.950 J.D. [Ⓐ Olsen,O.&D.]
Swearinger, Eddy R., (BV) ....'42 '72 C.950 B.S. L.596 J.D. 445 Union St. N.E.
Sydlik, BeaLisa ....'52 '81 C.267 B.A. L.1065 J.D. 1163 State Street
Sylwester, Timothy A., (AV) ....'55 '81 C&L.629 B.S., J.D. Asst. Atty. Gen.
Talney, Ronald G., (BV) '36 '66
C.1056 B.A. L.1051 J.D. Marion-Polk Legal Aid Serv., Inc.
Tanner, Jill A. ....'— '88 C.1056 B.S. L.596 J.D. Mag., Tax Ct.
Tatman, David C. ....'53 '81 C.112 B.A. L.629 J.D. Sec., Div. of Finance
Taylor, J. Spencer, Law Offices of, (CV) '67 '96
C.999 B.A. L.950 J.D. 280 Court Street, N.E. Suite 2
Taylor, Margaret Herrmann, (BV) .....'55 '81 C.1056 B.S. L.950 J.D. 1866 Merritt Street
Taylor, Ralph W. ....'23 '50 C&L.950 B.A., LL.B. 1309 Court St. N.E.
Taylor, Suzanne K., (CV) ....'62 '90 C.506 B.S. L.950 J.D. P.O. Box 4428
Taylor, William E., (BVⓉ) ....'48 '75 C&L.383 B.A., J.D. 900 Court St Ne Rm 354
Thayer, Jeffrey Paul ....'73 '98 C.413 B.A. L.1051 J.D. [Ⓐ Gatti,G.&M.]
Thetford, Thomas C., (BV) ....'48 '80 C.309 A.B. L.629 J.D. [T.C.Thetford]
Thetford, Thomas C., PC, (BV) ....242 Church St. S.E.
Thomas, Nathan B. ....'72 '03 C.101 B.S. L.950 J.D. [Ⓐ Garrett,H.R.J.C.&T.]
Thomas, Rita E. '48 '83 C.475 B.A. L.1187 J.D.
(adm. in MI; not adm. in OR) Chief Negotiator State of Ore.
Thomas, Ruth J. ....'50 '76 C.150 B.S. L.861 J.D. Asst. Atty. Gen.
Thompson, Carla D. ....'54 '82 C.1044 B.A. L.823 J.D. 189 Liberty St. NE
Thompson, D. Olcott, (CV) ....'52 '82 C.165 B.A. L.950 J.D. [D.O.Thompson]
Thompson, Jason Edward ....'74 '01 C.1494 B.A. L.950 J.D. [Ⓐ Ferder,C.&F.]
Thompson, Wayne M. ....'30 '58 C&L.950 B.A., LL.B. Mun. J.
Thompson, D. Olcott, P.C., (CV) ....................P.O. Box 1062
Thornton, Robt. Y. ....'10 '37 C.813 B.A. L.273 J.D. Sr. Ct. of Appls. J.
Tiscornia, G. Victor, II ....'64 '89 C.267 B.S. L.950 J.D. 2985 River Road, South
Todd, Jennifer B., (AV) ....'56 '83 C.939 B.A. L.950 J.D. 841 Saginaw St S
Todd, Jerry Michael ....'49 '75 C&L.950 B.A., J.D. 428 Sugarpine Ct. S.E.
Todd, Walter J., Law Office of, (AV) ....'56 '81 C.939 B.A. L.950 J.D. 835 Liberty St NE
Tornquist, Leroy J. ....'40 '65 C&L.597 B.S., J.D. Gen. Coun., Willamette University
Trant, Deborah G. '70 '03 C.670 B.A. L.950 J.D.
Corp. & Trademark Coun., Kettle Foods, Inc.
Trautman, Jeffrey A. ....'77 '04 C.999 B.S. L.950 J.D. [Ⓐ Clark,L.F.E.L.&C.]
Trethewy, Chess, (AV) ....'52 '82 C.37 B.A. L.950 J.D. [Garrett,H.R.J.C.&T.]
Trott, Larry J. ......'57 '90 C.112 B.A. L.1067 J.D. Rules and Policy Analyst, OR Lottery
Troutt, Sarah Rhoads, (BV) ....'67 '95 C.1169 B.A. L.950 J.D. [McClinton&T.]
Turner, David W. ....'56 '82 C.1104 B.A. L.950 J.D. Oregon School Bds. Assn.
Turner, Donald L. '31 '59
C.1051 B.S. L.950 LL.B. Prof. of Law, Willamette Univ. Sch. of Law
Turner, John, (BVⓉ) '48 '78 C.1044 B.S. L.1202 J.D.
(adm. in CT; not adm. in OR) Dist. Atty.
Tuttle, Stephanie J. ....'69 '93 C&L.950 B.A., J.D. Co. Dist. Atty.

Tweedt, Darin E., (BV) ... '67 '92 C.793 B.A. L.950 J.D. Dep. Dist. Atty., Dist. Atty. Off.
Tweet, Stephen T., (AV) .... '52 '78 C.494 B.A. L.950 J.D. [Albert,T.C.&H.]
Twist, Thomas E. .... '35 '71 C.116 A.B. L.770 J.D. Asst. Atty. Gen.
Ulsted, Dennis L. .... '52 '78 C&L.629 B.S., J.D. Trial Coun., SAIF Corporation
Underwood, Suzanne .... '51 '82 C&L.326 B.A., J.D. 1162 Court St Ne
Underwood, Tiffany J. .... '74 '00 C.37 B.A. L.950 J.D. 555 Liberty St Se Rm 205
Unfred, John Michael, (BV) .... '62 '89 C&L.950 B.A., J.D. [J.M.Unfred]
Unfred, John Michael, P.C., (BV) .... 687 Court Street
Unis, Richard L. .... '28 '54 C&L.629 B.S., LL.B. Assoc. Jus., Supm. Ct.
Upite, Daina .... '48 '86 C.1056 B.A. L.596 J.D. 875 Union St Rm 208
Upjohn, Donald H., (BV) .... '42 '70 C.309 B.A. L.1066 J.D. [Heltzel,U.W.Y.R.S.&P.]
Vance, Holly Ann .... '59 '97 C.882 B.A. L.208 J.D. OR Dept. of Jus.
Vande Griend, Douglas K., (BV) .... '54 '79 C.1304 B.A. L.950 J.D. 317 Court N.E.
Vanderbilt, Virginia Ruth .... '48 '86 C.17 B.A. L.950 J.D. Legis. Coun. Comm.
VanderMay, Maureen C. .... '56 '86 C.1169 B.A. L.145 J.D. [VanderMay]
VanderMay, Monty K. .... '66 '92 C.1331 B.A. L.950 J.D. [VanderMay]
VanderMay Law Firm, The .... 388 State St., Ste. 40
Van Eaton, Law Office of .... 350 Mission St., S.E., Ste. 101
Van Eaton, Daniel H. .... '44 '95 [VanEaton]
Van Hoomissen, George A. .... '30 '55 C.670 B.A. L.276 J.D. Assoc. J. Supm. Ct.
Van Valkenburgh, Jefry J., (AV) .... '56 '85 C.629 B.A. L.950 J.D. Asst. Atty. Gen.
Veranth, Amy L. .... '48 '75 C.188 B.A. L.588 J.D. Asst. Atty. Gen.
Vick, James D., (AV) .... '45 '72 C.629 B.S. L.950 J.D. [Vick&C.]

Vick & Conroyd, LLP, (AV) ▣
698 12th Street, S.E., Suite 200, 97301
Telephone: 503-364-8488 Fax: 503-588-3495
Email: info@vickconroydlaw.com URL: http://www.vickconroydlaw.com
James D. Vick; Michael F. Conroyd; Alex C. Dunn; Matthew Lansing Roy.
Language: Spanish.
Personal Injury, Wrongful Death, Medical Malpractice, Automobile Accidents, Slip and Fall, Workers' Compensation, Products Liability.
See Professional Biographies, SALEM, OREGON

Vidgoff, Martin B., (BV) .... '43 '69 C.309 A.B. L.813 J.D. Ct. of App.
Vollmar, Valerie J., (AV) '46 '75 C.629 B.A. L.950 J.D.
Prof. of Law, Willamette Univ.
Wade, Theresa M., (CV) .... '58 '99 C.628 B.S. L.950 J.D. [Garrett,H.R.J.C.&T.]
Wagner, Michael W. .... '53 '96 C.884 B.A. L.1051 J.D. [M.W.Wagner]
Wagner, Michael W., P.C. .... 2711 12th Street SE
Wallace, Eleanor E. .... '61 '92 C.1331 B.A. L.1051 J.D. Staff Atty.
Wallace, James C. .... '49 '82 C.597 B.S.C.E. L.1365 J.D. OR Dept. of Jus.
Wallmark, Gary T., (AV) '53 '78 C.1051 B.S. L.629 J.D.
Trial Coun., SAIF Corporation
Ward, Melissa J. .... '74 '99 C.670 B.A. L.629 J.D. [▣ Spooner,M.&A.]
Warden, John C. .... '23 '53 C&L.966 Ph.B., LL.B. Sr. Assoc. Ct. of Appls. J.
Warren, Edward H. .... '36 '66 C.1056 B.S. L.596 J.D. Ct. of Apps. J.
Warren, Gerald L. .... '53 '81 C&L.950 B.S., J.D. City/County Ins. Servs.
Warren, Roger R., (BV) .... '37 '66 C.1051 B.S. L.596 LL.B. Dept. of Jus., Trial Div.
Washington, Michael R. .... '62 '87 C.1051 B.A. L.950 J.D. Vice Chairman
Weddle, Paul J. .... '50 '96 C.999 B.A. L.950 J.D. 1162 Court St Ne
Weirich, Michael T. .... '55 '82 C.339 B.A. L.629 J.D. Dept. of Jus.
Wenger, Renee G. .....'55 '85 C.999 B.S. L.1051 J.D. Northwest Physicians Mut. Ins. Co.
Wenzel, Karla J. .... '61 '91 C.950 B.A. L.1051 J.D. Portland General Elec. Corp.
West, Greg .... '41 '72 C.550 B.A. L.950 J.D. Cir. J.
Whitehead, Brian R., (CV) .... '56 '83 C.490 B.S. L.950 J.D. [Whitehead&K.]
Whitehead & Klosterman, (CV) .... 1610 12th St., S.E.
Whitford, Trent T., (BV) .... '54 '82 C.911 B.A. L.950 J.D. [Whitford]
Whitford Law Offices LLC, (BV) .... 1819 D St. N.E.
Whitlock, Ian K. .... '57 '83 C.1215 B.A. L.846 J.D. 1162 Court St. N.E.
Whitlock, Richard C., (CV) .... '52 '77 C&L.950 B.A., J.D. Dist. Atty.
Whitman, Richard M., (AV) .... '56 '89 C.860 B.A. L.1066 J.D. 1162 Court St. N.E.
Whitty, Michael O., (BV) .... '39 '68 C&L.629 B.S., J.D. 400 High St., S.E.
Wickwire, James A. .... '54 '80 C.628 B.S. L.464 J.D. [Harris,W.&A.] ⊙
Wiesner, Jeannine Mary, (BV) .... '60 '84 C&L.950 B.A., J.D. Dep. Dist. Atty.
Wight, John M., (AV) .... '43 '67 C&L.846 B.A., LL.B. Shannon Associates, LLC
Wight, R. Alan, (AV) .... '38 '65 C.1085 A.S. L.878 J.D. 1162 COurt Street N.E.
Williams, Caleb A. .... '75 '01 C.635 B.A. L.950 J.D. [▣ Saalfeld G.]
Williams, Clark B., (AV) .... '54 '79 C.911 B.S. L.950 J.D. [Heltzel,U.W.Y.R.S.&P.]
Williams, Mark A. .... '54 '80 C.347 B.S. L.1051 J.D. 1162 Court St Ne
Williamson, Robert C. .... '50 '86 C.629 B.A. L.950 J.D. 960 Broadway Ne
Willis, Wendy Rae .... '66 '94 C.950 B.A. L.276 J.D. Law Clk., Supm. Ct.
Wilson, Charles W. .... '36 '66 C&L.597 B.A., J.D. Legis. Coun. Comm.
Wilson, Deborah A. K., (AV) .... '52 '79 C&L.950 B.A., J.D. Asst. Atty. Gen.
Wilson, John B. .... '51 '78 C&L.950 B.A., J.D. Cir. Ct. J.
Wilson, M. Keith .... '13 '37 C&L.629 B.S., LL.B. 3074 Oakcrest Dr. N.W.‡
Winkler, Robert L., (AV) .... '61 '87 C.988 B.A. L.950 J.D. [Parks,B.S.&W.]
Wise, Michael B. '46 '72 C.976 B.A. L.813 J.D.
(adm. in CA; not adm. in OR) Prof. of Law, Willamette Univ. Sch. of Law
Wiseman, Phillip Tippet, (BV) .... '56 '95 C.911 B.A. L.950 J.D. 1828 Lancaster Dr. N.E.
Wolff, Lyle Robt. .... '19 '48 C.543 B.S. L.309 LL.B. Ret. Cir. J.
Won, Benny, (AV) .... '51 '76 C&L.629 B.S., J.D. Merrill Lynch‡
Wood, Mary Kim, (CV) .... '53 '90 C.556 B.S. L.426 J.D. 687 Court St., Ste. 500
Wood, Timothy M., (CV) .... '45 '73 C.1021 B.A. L.950 J.D. Jus. Dept., Trial Div.
Woodruff, Jennifer E. .... '70 '95 C.550 B.A. L.1194 J.D. Dept. of Jus.
Wootton, John E. .... '70 '01 C.1085 B.A. L.950 J.D. 2003 State St.
Wright, Jennifer L. .. '60 '87 C.821 B.A. L.813 J.D. Wilamette University College of Law
Wyatt, Gig, (BV) .... '54 '85 C.549 B.A. L.950 J.D. [Harris,W.&A.]
Wyckoff, Ralph W. G., Jr. .... '18 '42 C&L.966 B.A., LL.B. P.O. Box 3230‡
Yandell, Eric, (BV) .... '50 '79 C.950 B.A. L.596 J.D. [Heltzel,U.W.Y.R.S.&P.]
Young, Lawrence R., (AV) .... '49 '75 C.813 A.B. L.94 J.D. Asst. Atty. Gen.
Yunker, Conrad E. .... '51 '87 C.508 B.A. L.950 J.D. [C.E.Yunker]

Yunker, Conrad E., P.C.
Suite 25, Sunset Center South, 1193 Royvonne Avenue SE, P.O. Box 101, 97308-0101
Telephone: 503-371-4608 Fax: 503-371-9556
Email: conrad@ceypc.com URL: http://www.lawyers.com/ceypc
Conrad E. Yunker.
Litigation, Appeals, Judicial Review, Regulatory, Licensing, Administrative Government, Insurance Disputes, Probate, Estate Litigation, Business Law, Banking Law, Personal Injury, Automobile Accidents and Injuries, Construction Law, Real Estate, Consumer Law, Libel, Slander and Defamation, Eminent Domain.
See Professional Biographies, SALEM, OREGON

Zagar, Bruce A., (AV) .... '49 '75 C.906 B.A. L.950 J.D. [Garrett,H.R.J.C.&T.]
Zier, Douglas F., (BV) .... '55 '80 C.301 B.A. L.911 J.D. Asst. Atty. Gen.

SANDY, 5,385, *Clackamas Co.*

Bolton, Robert L. '49 '87 C.1222 B.B.A. L.1162 J.D.
(adm. in HI; not adm. in OR) [Bolton&Assoc.]
Bolton & Associates, Inc. .... 17720 Loundree Dr.
Crook, Jeffrey A. .... '51 '78 C.477 B.A. L.767 J.D. 39075 Proctor Blvd., Ste. C
Grider, Mark K., (CV) .... '55 '80 C.473 B.A. L.950 J.D. [M.K.Grider]
Grider, Mark K., P.C., (CV) .... P.O. Box 304
Rieke, Forrest N., (AV) .... '42 '71 C.813 A.B. L.950 J.D. [F.Rieke&Assoc.]
Rieke, Forrest, and Associates, (AV) .... 39120 Proctor Blvd., Ste. 5

SCAPPOOSE, 4,976, *Columbia Co.*

Granath, Lars G., (BV) .... '47 '82 C.629 B.S. L.596 J.D. 50776 Dike Rd. Slip, Ste. 5A
McCray, Joe R., (AVⓉ) '41 '71 C.939 B.A. L.767 J.D.
(adm. in CA; not adm. in OR) [J.R.McCray]
McCray, Joe R., P.C., Law Offices of, (AVⓉ) .... 33470 Chinook Plaza
Sheehan, Michael F. .... '46 '87 C.112 B.S. L.352 J.D. 33126 S.W. Callahan Rd.
Sideras, Nancy, (CV) .... '44 '79 C.629 B.S. L.596 J.D. 26400 N.W. Saint Helens Rd.

SCIO, 695, *Linn Co.*

Daniels, Edward L., Law Office of, (BV) '48 '73 C&L.629 B.S., J.D.
38399 S. Ruby Loop

SEAL ROCK, —, *Lincoln Co.*

Gilbert, Dennis V., (BV) .... '41 '68 C.629 B.A. L.950 J.D. 10563 N.W. Hwy. 101
Smit, Bernardus J. '27 '66 C.999 L.1066 LL.B.
(adm. in CA; not adm. in OR) 5667 N.W. Pacific Coast Hwy.‡

SEASIDE, 5,900, *Clatsop Co.*

Bauske, Donn C., (CV) .... '37 '69 C.1056 L.596 J.D. 1000 S. Holliday Dr.
Campbell, Steven T., (BV) .... '42 '67 C&L.629 B.S., J.D. [Campbell&Assoc.]
Campbell & Associates, (BV) .... 318 Holladay Drive
Dooney, Michael J., (BV) .... '46 '72 C.285 B.A. L.767 J.D. 1111 S. Holladay Dr.
Eiler, Kenneth S., (BV) .... '53 '79 C.198 B.A. L.950 J.D. [K.S.Eiler]
Eiler, Kenneth S., P.C., (BV) .... 322 S. Holladay Dr.
Popkin, Lawrence J. .... '69 '03 C.345 J.D. L.911 LL.M. [▣ Campbell&Assoc.]

SHERIDAN, 3,570, *Yamhill Co.*

Kangas, Dianne E. .... '57 '92 C.413 B.S. L.950 J.D. 6375 Harmony Rd.
Siegel, Mark Ira .... '49 '74 C.1109 B.A. L.1067 J.D. 20950 S.W. Rock Creek Rd.‡

SHERWOOD, 11,791, *Washington Co.*

Babcock, Robert E., (AV) '43 '68
C.821 B.A. L.1119 J.D. 16004 SW Tualatin Sherwood Rd.
Noreen, Kevin C. .... '68 '95 C.1051 B.A. L.1358 J.D. 935 N.W. Meinecke Rd.
Rankin, John A. .... '48 '87 C.911 B.A. L.596 J.D. [J.A.Rankin]
Rankin, John A., L.L.C. .... 26715 S.W. Baker Rd.
Smith, Douglas Dean, (AV) ... '52 '79 C&L.101 B.A., J.D. 15751 S.W. Pleasant Hill Road

SILVERTON, 7,414, *Marion Co.*

Bean, Dennis W., (BV) .... '42 '67 C.670 B.A. L.950 J.D. 302 N. Water St.
Brown, Douglas C., (BV) ...... '50 '76 C.950 B.A. L.678 J.D. 4440 Victor Point Rd., N.E.
Davidson, Jossi KvZ., (BV) .... '49 '77 C.197 B.A. L.950 J.D. [Gracey&D.]
Doyle, Patrick E. .... '64 '95 C.17 B.A. L.950 J.D. 110 N. 2nd
Gracey, Roger W., (BV) .... '45 '72 C.678 B.A. L.950 J.D. [Gracey&D.]
Gracey & Davidson, (BV) .... 104 S. Water St.
Hall, Lawrence J. .... '35 '67 C.139 B.A. L.596 J.D. P.O. Box 785
Hector, Robert B. '47 '76 C.375 B.S. L.734 J.D.
(adm. in CA; not adm. in OR) P.O. Box 1210
Kelley, Donald M., (BV) .... '— '74 C.742 B.A. L.950 110 N. 2nd St.
Little, James F., Attorney at Law .... '61 '87 C.628 B.A. L.950 J.D. 1430 Pine St.
Riveness, Armand L. .... '31 '55 C&L.950 B.A., LL.B. 312 D St.
White, Betty Jo, Law Office of .... '49 '73 C&L.950 B.A., J.D. 107 Rock St.

SISTERS, 959, *Deschutes Co.*

David B. Hydes, P.C., (BV) .... P.O. Box 3500
Goodwin, James O., (AV) .... '25 '50 C&L.629 B.S., LL.B. 317 E. Cascade‡
Hydes, David B., (BV) .... '51 '83 C.1181 B.S. L.629 J.D. [David B.H.]
Massey, James T., (BV) .... '47 '74 C.813 B.A. L.629 J.D. P.O. Box 3500
Nelson, Roger A., (BV) .... '38 '63 C.629 B.S. L.950 J.D. [R.A.Nelson]
Nelson, Roger A., P.C., (BV) .... P.O. Box 2213
Veatch, John C., II .... '20 '48 C&L.629 B.S., J.D. P.O. Box 328‡

SOUTH BEACH, —, *Lincoln Co.*

Knudson, James T., (AV) '28 '53 C&L.336 B.S., LL.B.
(adm. in ID; not adm. in OR) 190 S.E. 127th Dr.‡

SPRINGFIELD, 52,864, *Lane Co.*

Allen, Frederick D., Jr., (BV) .... '18 '57 L.596 LL.B. 6323 B St.

Arnold Gallagher Saydack Percell Roberts & Potter, P.C.
(See Eugene)

Atwood, William C., (BV) .... '52 '94 C&L.629 B.S., J.D. [▣ G.K.Jensen]
Babcock, William A., (BV) .... '11 '36 C.336 A.B. L.477 J.D. 336 N. 6th St.
Becker, Larry E. .... '63 '91 C.339 B.A. L.910 J.D. [▣]
De Puy, Walter A., Jr. .... '58 '83 C.628 B.S. L.678 J.D. 3054 Yolanda Ave.
DeWenter, John C., (BV) .... '44 '73 C.679 B.A. L.276 J.D. [J.C.DeWenter]
DeWenter, John C., P.C., (BV) .... 870 W. Centennial Blvd.

Diment & Walker
(See Eugene)

Franz, Robert E., Jr., (BV) .... '46 '73 C.628 B.S. L.629 J.D. P.O. Box 62
Harms, Edward C., Jr., (AV) .... '24 '49 C&L.629 B.S., J.D. 845 Willacade Ct.‡
Harold, Timothy J., (AV) .... '41 '65 C&L.629 B.S., J.D. [Harold,L.&K.]
Harold, Leahy & Kieran, (AV) .... 223 A Street, Suite D
Hassler, Allison R. '51 '91 C&L.629 M.S., J.D.
Amer. Federation of State, Co. and Mun. Employees
Hatton, Janice E., (CV) .... '65 '91 C.335 B.A. L.629 J.D. [▣ Thorp,P.J.U.&W.]
Hinrichs, Laura, (BVⓉ) .... '34 '79 C.112 B.A. L.809 J.D. P.O. Box 843
Huffman, Kenneth C. .... '74 '00 C.413 B.S. L.629 J.D. 1011 Harlow Rd., Ste 300
Huntsberger, Thomas A., (BV) .... '49 '76 C.309 A.B. L.629 J.D. [T.A.Huntsberger]
Huntsberger, Thomas A., P.C., (BV) .... 870 W. Centennial Blvd.

Jaqua & Wheatley, LLC
(See Eugene)

Jensen, Gary K., (BV) .... '42 '67 C&L.629 B.A., J.D. [G.K.Jensen]
Jensen, Gary K., P.C., (BV) .... 626 B St.

Jessen, Bryce R., (BV) ....'47 '74 C&L.629 B.B.A., J.D. 760 N. 14th St.
Jewett, G. David, (BV) ....'46 '76 C.768 B.A. L.770 J.D. [Thorp,P.J.U.&W.]
Johnson, Dale C., (BV) ....'50 '82 C.494 B.A. L.629 J.D. 1110 North 18th Street, Suite 5
Jordan, Susan Ezzy, (CV) ....'68 '97 C.431 B.S. L.629 J.D. [Harold,L.&K.]
Kieran, Meg E., (BV) ....'48 '89 C.112 B.A. L.629 J.D. [Harold,L.&K.]
Leahy, Joseph J., (AV) ....'43 '70 C.629 B.S. L.602 J.D. [Harold,L.&K.]
LeFever, Lance A. ....'69 '99 C&L.629 B.A., J.D. [Thorp,P.J.U.&W.]
Logan, David M., (BV) ....'41 '67 C.629 B.S. L.950 J.D. P.O. Box 196
Miller, Sarah Susannah, (BV) '42 '77 C.25 B.S. L.596 J.D.
1290 W. Centennial Boulevard
O'Kief, James M., (BV) ....'48 '78 C&L.629 J.D. 1011 Harlow Rd.
O'Neill, Kelly ....'62 '87 C.628 B.S. L.629 J.D. 1950 Yolanda Avenue

Peterson Law Offices, PC
(See Portland)

Petitt, Murray S., (CV) ....'58 '96 C.112 L.629 J.D. [Thorp,P.J.U.&W.]
Purdy, Dwight G., (BV) ....'49 '74 C.629 B.S. L.596 J.D. [Thorp,P.J.U.&W.]
Shimanek, R. Glade ....'30 '57 C.101 B.S. L.629 LL.B. 89800 Hill Rd.‡

Speer, Hoyt, Jones, Feinman, Poppe, Wolf & Griffith, P.C.
(See Eugene)

Thorp, Laurence E., (AV) ....'43 '68 C.628 B.A. L.629 J.D. [Thorp,P.J.U.&W.]
Thorp, Purdy, Jewett, Urness & Wilkinson, P.C., (AV) ....1011 Harlow Rd., Ste. 300
Urness, John C., (AV) ....'56 '83 C.1056 B.S. L.629 J.D. [Thorp,P.J.U.&W.]

Veralrud & Associates, Attorneys, P.C.
(See Eugene)

Wilkinson, Douglas R., (BV) ....'46 '77 C.629 B.S. L.596 J.D. [Thorp,P.J.U.&W.]
Young, Heather A. ....'70 '96 C.216 B.A. L.629 J.D. 1011 Harlow Rd., Ste. 300

STAYTON, 6,816, *Marion Co.*

Bell, Alan J., (CV) ....'38 '68 C.629 B.B.A. L.950 J.D. [A.J.Bell]
Bell, Walter H. ....'10 '34 C&L.950 311 N. 3rd‡
Bell, Alan J., P.C., (CV) ....Bell Bldg.
Duncan, Geo. R., Jr., (BV) ....'28 '55 C&L.950 B.S.L., LL.B. P.O. Box 248
McGehee, James L., (BV) ....'52 '80 C.1181 B.S. L.221 J.D. 1181 W. Washington
Niegel, Jennifer L. ....'73 '99 C&L.629 B.A., J.D. 582 E Washington Street
Summers, Steven R., (BV) ....'48 '74 C.628 B.S. L.629 J.D. [S.R.Summers]
Summers, Steven R., P.C., (BV) ....223 W. Locust St.

SUNRIVER, —, *Deschutes Co.*

Bergmann, L. James, (AV) ....'33 '57 C&L.950 B.A., LL.B. 18160 Cottonwood Rd.‡
Bush, Leo J. '26 '52 C&L.793 B.A., LL.B.
(adm. in SD; not adm. in OR) 20 Siskin Ln.‡
Doud, David H. '21 '71 C.813 B.A. L.770 J.D.
(adm. in CA; not adm. in OR) P.O. Box 3903‡
Padrick, Kevin D., (AV) ....'55 '79 C&L.770 B.S., J.D. P.O. Box 3510
Swenson, Louise, Law Office of, (CV) ....'48 '91 C.1074 B.A. L.770 J.D. P.O. Box 3537
Tout, William E. '33 '60 C&L.813 A.B., LL.B.
(adm. in CA; not adm. in OR) 18160 Cottonwood Rd.
Tuckerman, Jan ....'48 '77 C.679 B.S. L.209 J.D. 18160 Cottonwood Rd.‡

SUTHERLIN, 6,669, *Douglas Co.*

Hendershott, Mark, (CV) ....'45 '72 C.1051 B.S. L.596 J.D. 251 N. Umpqua
Kesner, Michael A. ....'49 '77 C.950 B.A. L.678 J.D. P.O. Box J‡
Lang, Danny R. ....'40 '77 C.597 B.S. L.464 J.D. 140 S State St
Waldier, Lowell J. '14 '38 C&L.494 B.A., J.D.
(adm. in MN; not adm. in OR) 1228 E. 4th Ave.‡

SWEET HOME, 8,016, *Linn Co.*

Adams, Michael E., P.C. ....'71 '00 C.999 B.S. L.950 J.D. [M.E.Adams]
Adams, Michael E., P.C. ....1202 Main Street
Danielson, Robert G. ....'29 '54 C.628 B.S. L.629 LL.B. 1310 Elm St.‡
Engel, Marcy Renee ....'71 '97 C.930 B.A. L.879 J.D. 1019 Main St.
Lewis, William O. ....'37 '66 C.950 L.878 J.D. P.O. Box 868
Snyder, Robert, (CV) ....'50 '77 C&L.972 B.S., J.D. 1275 Main St.
Wittwer, John R. ....'47 '75 C&L.950 B.A., J.D. P.O. Box 447

TIGARD, 41,223, *Washington Co.*

Adams & Uffelman LLP
(See Beaverton)

Anderson, Roger F., (BV) ....'43 '73 C.628 B.S. L.596 J.D. [Anderson&D.]
Anderson & Dittman, LLP, (AV) ....8865 Southwest Center Street
Ben-Zion, Shira, (CVⓉ) '69 '95 C.112 B.A. L.950 J.D.
(adm. in CA; not adm. in OR) 16236 S.W. 103rd Ave.
Berman, John M., (AV) ....'45 '71 C.309 B.A. L.477 J.D. 7175 S.W. Beveland Rd.
Bonciolini, Dennis J. ....'54 '94 C.906 B.S. L.596 J.D. SEH America
Bourgeois, J. Rion, (AV) ....'51 '76 C.276 A.B. L.477 J.D. 7175 Beveland, Suite 210
Braverman, Mark ....'39 '64 C&L.831 B.S., LL.B. P.O. Box 230486
Brislin, Joseph A. '41 '73 C.911 M.S.F. L.629 J.D.
Gen. Coun., TOC Management Servs.
Brown, Franklyn N., (BV) ....'42 '69 C.628 B.S. L.950 J.D. P.O. Box 230087
Charney, Harold S. '35 '63 C.112 B.A. L.800 LL.B.
(adm. in CA; not adm. in OR) 6811 S.W. Firlock Way‡
Chrismer, Charles R. '44 '73 C.845 B.S.M.E. L.36 J.D.
(adm. in CO; not adm. in OR) 16050 S.W. Colony Dr.‡
Christiansen, Kevin T. ....'73 '99 C&L.950 B.A., J.D. [Scott H.]
Cofield, Dorothy Sweet ....'53 '92 C.763 B.A. L.1051 J.D. 8255 S.W. Hunziker Rd
Crnich, Joseph E. '55 '86 C.507 B.S. L.508 J.D.
(adm. in AK; not adm. in OR) 10967 SW Hall Blvd‡
Davis, Karen E. ....'69 '94 C.170 B.A. L.596 J.D. Staff Atty., TOC Management Servs.
Dittman, Derryck H., (AV) ....'43 '68 C.637 B.A. L.950 J.D. [Anderson&D.]
Duffy, Fred B. ....'16 '42 C&L.911 A.B., LL.B. 11415 S.W. 135th‡

Gabin, Sara L., P.C.
(See Lake Oswego)

Gallagher, Douglas L. ....'72 '97 C&L.629 B.A., J.D. [Scott H.] ⊙
Grogan, Thomas J. ....'34 '62 C.768 A.B. L.1066 J.D. 13822 S.W. 12 Oaks Ct.‡
Hampton, Rick Dean '59 '84 C.339 B.A. L.801 J.D.
(adm. in IL; not adm. in OR) NW Food Employers
Hansen, George I. ....'30 '60 C.911 B.A. L.596 LL.B. 11515 S.W. Pacific Hwy.
Hilary, Jerold W., (AV) ....'53 '85 C.629 B.A. L.596 J.D. 9250 S.W. Tigard Street
Hookland, Douglas R., (BV) ....'62 '87 C.147 B.A. L.950 J.D. [Scott H.]
Kirkendall, Valerie I. ....'62 '01 C.1056 B.S. L.1051 J.D. 9250 SW Tigard St.
Kraemer, Teresa M., (BV) '57 '91
C.35 B.S. L.596 J.D. Oregon Alliance of Sr. & Health Servs.

LaVeille, John E. ....'48 '74 C.670 B.A. L.1051 J.D. Pacific N.W. Title of Oregon, Inc.
Lenneberg, Roger A., (AV) '53 '84
C.685 B.A. L.1051 J.D. Corp. Coun., Performance Contracting Group
Luby, Kevin W., (BV) ....'57 '84 C.686 B.S. L.602 J.D. 7360 S.W. Hunziker, Ste. 206
McCaffrey, James F., (BV) ....'29 '62 C.637 L.596 9020 SW Washington Square Road
McClure, Charles J., (BV) ....'35 '65 C.950 B.A. L.276 J.D. 9250 S.W. Tigard Ave.
McKernan, Thomas J. '48 '74 C&L.378 B.A., J.D.
(adm. in MO; not adm. in OR) 11205 S.W. Morgen Ct.‡
Memovich, Robert H. '22 '51 L.508 LL.B.
(adm. in MT; not adm. in OR) 7630 S.W. Cherry St.
Mitchell, Alan L. ....'52 '96 C.473 B.A. L.596 J.D. [Scott H.]
Mohiuddin, Cynthia Ingrid ....'68 '93 C.112 B.A. L.596 J.D. [Westside F.L.]
Monahan, William A. ....'50 '86 C.1200 B.A. L.596 J.D. 13125 S.W. Hall Blvd.
Murphy, Thomas J., (BV) ....'51 '78 C.608 B.A. L.629 J.D. [Scott H.]
Newhouse, David J. '59 '92 C.1307 B.A. L.1194 J.D.
(adm. in VT; not adm. in OR) 7640 S.W. Cedarcrest St.
Oram, Nell A. ....'73 '96 C.629 B.S. L.285 J.D. [J.W.Hilary]
Patterson, Linda S. ....'53 '78 C.1239 B.A. L.1051 J.D. 13630 S.W. Tarleton Ct.
Petticord, Damon J. ....'70 '96 C.472 B.S. L.629 J.D. 7175 S.W. Beveland
Robinson, Melinda C. '64 '94
C&L.878 B.S./B.A., J.D. Staff Atty., TOC Management Servs.
Schwab, Dwight L., (AV) ....'13 '40 C.193 A.B. L.309 J.D. 10100 S.W. Highland Dr.‡
Scott, Michael J., (AV) ....'56 '83 C.637 B.A. L.596 J.D. [Scott H.]

Scott Hookland LLP, (AV)
9185 S.W. Burnham Street, P.O. Box 23414, 97223 ⊙
Telephone: 503-620-4540 Toll Free: 800-334-8986 Fax: 503-620-4315
URL: http://www.scott-hookland.com
Members of Firm: Michael J. Scott; Douglas R. Hookland. Associates: Thomas J. Murphy; Alan L. Mitchell; Douglas L. Gallagher; Kevin T. Christiansen.
Construction, Design, Civil and Trial Practice. Commercial Collections, Business, Real Estate, Mediations, Arbitrations, Creditors Rights.
Eugene, Oregon Office: 423 Lincoln Street, 97401. Telephone: 541 284-5820; 503 754-4700. Fax: 541 284-5821.

See Professional Biographies, TIGARD, OREGON

Shonkwiler, John W., (BV) ....'44 '75 C.347 B.S. L.596 J.D. 13425 S.W. 72nd Ave.
Siegel, Lynne F., (BV) '45 '81
C.339 B.A. L.597 J.D. Gen. Coun., Oregon Education Association
Slominski, Terrance J. ....'47 '81 C.628 B.A. L.596 J.D. 7100 Sw Hampton Ste 129
Spencer, Harry G. ....'18 '50 C.17 L.596 LL.B. 9463 S.W. Lakeside Dr.‡
Toledo, Mark S., (BV) ....'51 '84 C.1193 B.A. L.608 J.D. 6900 S.W. Haines Rd.
Wahl, Jeffrey J. ....'62 '92 C.628 B.S. L.950 J.D. 16301 S.W. Stahl Dr.
Ward, DeLoris B. Narvasa ....'38 '76 C&L.629 B.S., J.D. [Anderson&D.]
Westside Family Law ....13425 S.W. 72nd Avenue
Whitewolf, Celeste ....'49 '88 C.628 B.S. L.1051 J.D. 9770 SW Ventura Ct.
Wise, Kellye T. ....'58 '83 C.1075 L.629 J.D. TOC Management Servs.

TILLAMOOK, * 4,352, *Tillamook Co.*

Albright, Lois A. ....'52 '78 C.966 B.A. L.596 J.D. [Albright&K.]
Albright & Kittell, P.C. ....2308 3rd St.
Costello, Marcus Lee ....'65 '92 C.628 B.S. L.336 J.D. Dep. Dist. Atty.
Ehrlich, James ....'53 '80 C.94 B.A. L.494 J.D. 416 Laurel
Erickson, Brian L. ....'50 '81 C.72 B.A. L.596 J.D. Chf. Dep. Dist. Atty.
Factora, Janelle M. ....'69 '96 C.628 B.S. L.950 J.D. Dep. Dist. Atty.
Gustafson, Bert ....'43 '71 C.350 B.S. L.1049 J.D. Dist. Ct. J.
Hantke, David W. ....'45 '77 C.933 B.A. L.950 J.D. Cir. Ct. J.
Hathaway, John W., (BV) ....'19 '46 C&L.629 B.S., J.D. 306 Main
Kittell, Christopher ....'47 '74 C.1051 B.A. L.276 J.D. [Albright&K.]
Larson, David A. ....'48 '84 C.871 B.S. L.950 J.D. Dep. Dist. Atty.
Nordlander, Nancy A. ....'54 '83 C.413 B.A. L.596 J.D. 2315 1st St.
Porter, William B., (BV) ....'58 '84 C.347 B.A. L.629 J.D. Dist. Atty.
Putman, John R., Law Office of ....'56 '90 C.628 B.S. L.950 J.D. 416 Laurel Avenue
Tuthill, John H., (BV) ....'49 '76 C.429 B.A. L.1051 J.D. 2406 3rd St.
Westmoreland, W. T. ....'42 '78 C.628 B.S. L.596 J.D. [W.T.Westmoreland]
Westmoreland, W. T., P.C. ....2106 4th St

TOLEDO, 3,472, *Lincoln Co.*

Hayden, William H. ....'34 '73 C.629 B.S. L.950 J.D. 747 N.E. Hwy. 20‡
Monson, Ralph G., (BV) ....'40 '68 L.1051 J.D. [R.G.Monson]
Monson, Ralph G., PC, (BV) ....109 1st. St., N.W.
Osterlund, Paul B., (BV) ....'35 '61 C&L.950 B.S., J.D. [P.B.Osterlund]
Osterlund, Paul B., Attorney, P.C., (BV) ....217 S. Main St.
Ruggeri, Jim ....'47 '84 C.813 A.B. L.629 J.D. City Atty.

TOLOVANA PARK, —, *Clatsop Co.*

Schiffman, Ronald P. '45 '71 C.112 A.B. L.1065 J.D.
(adm. in CA; not adm. in OR) P.O. Box 92‡

TROUTDALE, 13,777, *Multnomah Co.*

Troutdale Law Firm, (BV) ....102 W. Historic Columbia River Highway
Urquhart, John R., (BV) ....'43 '74 C.629 B.A. L.1051 J.D. 28408 E. Crown Point Hwy.
Weill, Richard A., (BV) ....'54 '82 C.477 B.G.S. L.1051 J.D. [Troutdale]

TUALATIN, 22,791, *Clackamas & Washington Cos.*

Blair, David M. ....'53 '87 C.1181 B.S. L.1051 J.D. 8875 S.W. Umatilla St.
Braden, Brenda L. ....'40 '80 C.1165 B.A. L.900 J.D. City Atty. Off.
Cardwell, Timothy S. ....'62 '01 C.1056 B.A. L.950 J.D. P.O. Box 2175
Charley, Ellen Rebecca ....'53 '85 C.610 B.S. L.629 J.D. 6401 SW Meridian Way
Ferguson, Ron D., (AV) ....'47 '75 C.628 B.S. L.1051 J.D. 8555 S.W. Tualatin Rd.
Fuchs, Donald C. '71 '98 C.413 B.A. L.950 J.D.
Assistant General Counsel, Legal Anywhere, Inc.
Guay, Kevin H. ....'57 '87 C.907 B.A. L.950 J.D. 11480 S.W. Elmer Ct.‡
Hawkes, Gregory L., (BV) ....'43 '68 C.628 B.S. L.950 J.D. 8555 S.W. Tualatin Rd.
Heninger, John R. ....'60 '88 C.170 B.A. L.352 J.D. U.S. Bancorp
Horgan, Thomas M. ....'58 '86 C.971 B.S.M.E. L.174 J.D. Digimarc Corp. (Pat.)
Kreitzberg, Donna C. ....'62 '92 C.208 B.S.A.C. L.950 J.D. [D.C.Kreitzberg]
Kreitzberg, Donna C., PC ....P.O. Box 3242
Lamberson, Elise S. ....'61 '89 C.674 A.B. L.112 J.D. 4700 S.W. Wichita St.
Martin, Thomas, Jr., (BV) '57 '84 C.1056 B.S. L.950 J.D.
19300 Sw Boones Fy Rd #1B
McDonald, Hugh R. ....'26 '59 C.94 B.S.B.A. L.596 LL.B. 8585 S.W. Sagert St.‡
Morrill, Scott A. ....'61 '91 C.164 B.A. L.1051 J.D. Perry, Morrill, Winegar & Butte
Perlow, Daniel S. ....'61 '91 C&L.629 B.S., J.D. Niku Corp.
Rizzo, Michael J. '59 '85 C.188 B.S. L.477 J.D.
(adm. in NJ; not adm. in OR) Senior Vice President, U.S. Bancorp Leasing & Financial
Schneider, Joseph, (AVⓉ) '32 '63 C.114 A.B. L.477 J.D.
(adm. in HI; not adm. in OR) 21446 S.W. Christensen Ctr.‡

Tharnish, Marcia Graham ....'43 '67 C.375 B.A. L.900 J.D. 4035 Sw Halcyon Road‡
West, Craig O., (BV) ....'50 '76 C.1056 B.S. L.596 J.D. 8555 S.W. Tualatin Rd.
Winegar, Doris C. ....'53 '92 C.1056 B.S. L.596 J.D. P.O. Box 1107
Yoder, Alan D. '71 '99 C.1169 B.A. L.596 J.D.
Labor Coun., Oregon Nurses Association

VALE, * 1,976, *Malheur Co.*

Butler, R. David, II, (CV) ....'61 '89 C.629 B.S. L.596 J.D. [Butler&L.]
Butler, Robert D., (BV) ....'43 '67 C&L.629 B.S., J.D. [Butler&L.]
Butler & Looney, P.C., (BV) ....292 Main St. S.
Carlson, David R., (CV) ....'61 '90 C.670 B.A. L.36 J.D. 449 Washington St., E.
Hutchens, John N., (AV) ....'33 '60 C&L.629 B.S., LL.B. 803 Aldea‡
Looney, H. Clifford, (BV) ....'42 '66 C&L.950 B.S., J.D. [Butler&L.]
Norris, Daniel O., (BV) ....'58 '87 C.1212 B.A. L.336 J.D. Malheur Dist. Atty. Off.
Pratt, J. Burdette ....'50 '76 C.1193 B.B.A. L.336 J.D. Cir. J.
Schroeder, William F., (AV) ....'28 '50 C.145 A.B. L.879 LL.B. [W.F.Schroeder]
Schroeder, William F., P.C., (AV) ....280 A St., East
Skerjanec, Carol DeHaven, (BV) ....'48 '94 C.1104 B.S. L.629 J.D. [W.F.Schroeder]
Stringert, Christian H. ....'73 '00 C&L.629 B.A., J.D. Malheur Co. Dist. Atty.'s Off.
Sullivan, Patricia A. ....'53 '78 C.1051 B.A. L.629 J.D. Cir. Ct. J.
Yraquen, Francisco J. ....'40 '70 C.628 B.S. L.950 J.D. Cir. J.

VENETA, 2,755, *Lane Co.*

VanLeuven, Dean R. ....'33 '69 C&L.629 B.S., J.D. 25034 McCutcheon St.

VIDA, 300, *Lane Co.*

Carpenter, Russell Bruce, (AV⑦) '43 '67 C.813 A.B. L.309 LL.B.
(adm. in CA; not adm. in OR) 47227 Goodpasture Rd.

WALDPORT, 2,050, *Lincoln Co.*

Beckstead, Scott, (CV) '66 '91 C.877 B.S. L.878 J.D.
1310 S.W. Corona Ct. (©Newport)
Dumas, John W. '44 '76 C.911 B.A. L.990 J.D.
(adm. in CA; not adm. in OR) P.O. Box 866‡
Golay, David E. '21 '50 C.675 A.B. L.800 LL.B.
(adm. in CA; not adm. in OR) 3702 Shoreview Loop‡

WALLOWA, 869, *Wallowa Co.*

Johnson, Roland W. ....'45 '70 C.629 B.S. L.911 J.D. Coleman & Chrisman Bldg.

WARREN, 800, *Columbia Co.*

Forbes, Eryn E. ....'61 '88 C.629 B.A. L.596 J.D. 33322 Slaven Rd.

WARRENTON, 4,096, *Clatsop Co.*

Church, Stanley R. ....'09 '60 C.906 L.596 LL.B. Rt. 1‡
Shannon, David S., (BV) ....'40 '67 C.197 A.B. L.911 LL.B. 817 Fifth Ave.

WEDDERBURN, —, *Curry Co.*

Craske, Duane ....'29 '56 C.629 B.S. L.596 LL.B. P.O. Box 258‡

WELCHES, 500, *Clackamas Co.*

Linkous, Gary G. ....'49 '92 C.1056 B.A. L.1051 J.D. [G.G.Linkous]
Linkous, Gary G., PC ....24403 E. Welches Rd #101

WEST LINN, 22,261, *Clackamas Co.*

Amabile, Karen Valerie '53 '94 C.431 B.A. L.1202 J.D.
(adm. in CA; not adm. in OR) 2675 Beacon Hill Dr.
Anicker, John C., Jr., (AV) ....'30 '54 C&L.950 B.A., J.D. 1510 Rosemont Rd.‡
Art, Karen M., (AV) ....'50 '85 C.72 B.A. L.950 J.D. 19702 Suncrest Dr.
Bleifuss, Edward L. ....'48 '78 C.911 B.A. L.950 J.D. 19618 Derby Ct.
Blunck, Lawrence P. ....'56 '84 C&L.101 B.A., J.D. [Blunck&W.]

Blunck & Walhood, LLC
2350 Willamette Falls Drive, 97068-3235
Telephone: 503-656-1654 Fax: 503-650-0603
Email: Larry@bluncklaw.com URL: http://www.blunclaw.com
Lawrence P. Blunck; Kenneth L. Walhood;—Lisa K. Day; Scott D. Preston.
Arbitration, Automobile Accidents, Construction Claims, Contracts, Personal Injury, Insurance.
See Professional Biographies, WEST LINN, OREGON

Daniel, E. Anderson, Attorney at Law, (CV) '60 '86
C.35 B.S. L.1051 J.D. 1919 Willamette Falls Dr.
Dawson, Bryan W. ....'67 '96 C.154 B.A. L.1066 J.D. 5695 Hood St.
Day, Lisa K., (BV) ....'61 '87 C.893 B.A. L.1051 J.D. [Blunck&W.]
Dunbar, Douglas Scott ....'56 '83 C.629 B.S. L.596 J.D. The Dunbar Co.
Dusek, Ronald E., (BV) ....'36 '67 C.945 B.A. L.260 J.D. 2875 Marylhurst Drive
Dziuba, Helen T., Law Office of, (AV) '50 '87
C.957 B.S. L.596 J.D. 24180 S.W. Petes Mountain Rd.
Edwards, Marcy L. ......'54 '83 C.1051 B.A. L.596 J.D. Ste 400, 2875 Sw Marylhurst Dr
Fasano, Louis J. ....'42 '67 C.628 B.S. L.629 J.D. 2455 S.W. Gregory Dr.‡
Feder, Miriam, (AV) ....'55 '80 C.494 B.A. L.596 J.D. 18183 Upper Midhill Dr.
Ferrell-French, Patricia ....'45 '91 C.623 B.A. L.1051 J.D. 1742 Willamette Falls Dr.
Gardner, John Frederick ....'58 '86 C.685 B.A. L.629 J.D. 22308 Skyview Dr.
Gassner, Richard H. '45 '76
C.1056 B.S. L.950 J.D. Mbr., International Business Associates
Goff, Sherrie Kaiser ....'60 '86 C.950 B.S. L.911 J.D. 21790 Willamette Dr.
Harris, Wyatt & Amala, LLC, (AV) ....2020 Eight Avenue (©Salem)
Hutchison, John C., (AV) ....'43 '68 C&L.629 B.S., J.D. [Hutchison&W.]

Hutchison & Walsh, A Professional Corporation, (AV)
21790 Willamette Drive, P.O. Box 648, 97068
Telephone: 503-656-1694 Fax: 503-656-1092
Email: mail@hutchisonetal.com URL: http://www.hutchisonwalsh.com
John C. Hutchison; Michael D. Walsh;—Nicole H. Sakys.
General Civil and Trial Practice. Estate Planning, Probate, Trusts and Estates, Business Law, Contracts, Real Estate, Corporate, Personal Injury, Automobile Accidents, Wrongful Death, Financial Abuse of the Elderly.
See Professional Biographies, WEST LINN, OREGON

La Cesa, Mary M. '64 '90 C.597 B.S. L.990 J.D.
(adm. in CA; not adm. in OR) 2020 8th Ave.
Larson, John K. ....'— '91 C.629 B.S. L.950 J.D. [Larson]
Larson Law Firm, The, P.C. ....1800 Blankenship Rd., Suite 400
Locker, Bryan L. ....'60 '87 C.950 B.A. L.596 J.D. 31070 S.W. Riverlane Dr.
Lohman, Edward F., (CV) ....'56 '86 C.628 B.S. L.1148 J.D. 1579 Burns St.
Mayhew, Amanda L. ....'69 '01 C.1494 B.A. L.1051 J.D. 1919 Willamette Falls Dr.
McKenzie, A. Gregory, (BV) ...'46 '77 C.10 B.A.E. L.1051 J.D. [A.G.McKenzie&Assoc.]
McKenzie, A. Gregory, & Associates, (BV) ....1919 Willamette Falls Dr.
Noble, C. Richard, (AV) ....'46 '70 C&L.477 B.A., J.D. 2875 Marylhurst Dr.
Noble, Richard P., (AV) ....'38 '65 C.1056 L.596 LL.B. [R.P.Noble]
Noble, Richard P., PC, (AV) ....2875 Maryhurst Dr.

O'Hollaren, Paul J. ....'27 '54 L.596 J.D. 2013 Conestoga Ln.‡
Preston, Scott D. ....'71 '02 C.101 B.S. L.596 J.D. [Blunck&W.]
Pynn, Allen B., (CV) ....'36 '65 C.1056 B.S. L.596 LL.B. P.O. Box 528
Sakys, Nicole H. ....'75 '03 C.174 B.A. L.208 J.D. [Hutchison&W.]
Sams, Charles A. ....'28 '65 C.629 B.S. L.950 LL.B. 18845 Parkwood Pl.

Siegel, Timothy E., (BV) '56 '93 C.912 B.S.E.E. L.426 J.D.
1868 Knapps Alley, Suite 206, 97068
Telephone: 503-650-7411; 877-396-7669 Fax: 503-650-9886
Email: tes@intproplaw.com URL: http://www.intproplaw.com
Patent Prosecution, Electrical Patent Prosecution, Electronic Patent Prosecution, Medical Patent Prosecution, Mechanical Devices Prosecution, Trademark Registration Application Preparation and Prosecution.
See Professional Biographies, WEST LINN, OREGON

Thaheld, Johann F. ....'57 '94 C.628 B.S. L.950 J.D. 6477 Sorrel Way
Thompson, Christopher L. ....'49 '75 C.906 B.A. L.1068 J.D. [Larson]
Townsend, Suzanne, (AV) ....'50 '80 C.1056 B.A. L.629 J.D. 6552 Artemis Court
van Bever, Ann ....'48 '84 C.802 B.A. L.436 J.D. 21380 Horton Court
Vestigo, James R. ....'58 '86 C.878 B.A. L.596 J.D. 1800 Blankenship Rd., Ste. 450
Walhood, Kenneth L. ....'66 '94 C.101 B.A. L.336 J.D. [Blunck&W.]
Walsh, Michael D., (AV) ....'42 '73 C.1097 B.A. L.1051 J.D. [Hutchison&W.]
Weege, Don C., (BV) ....'49 '77 C.963 B.S. L.966 J.D. 2260 Hammerle St.
Werst, Dean C., (BV) ....'40 '69 C.625 B.S. L.596 J.D. [Werst&Assoc.]
Werst & Associates, (BV) ....1785 Willamette Falls Drive
Wickwire, James A. ....'54 '80 C.628 B.S. L.464 J.D. [Harris,W.&A.] ⊙
Zeeb, Rodney C., (BV) ....'55 '86 C&L.950 B.S., J.D. 1800 Blankenship Rd., Ste. 310

WHITE CITY, 5,466, *Jackson Co.*

Couch, David Harvey, (BV) '45 '87
C.1071 B.S. L.285 J.D. Gen. Coun., Cascade Wood Products, Inc.

WILSONVILLE, 13,991, *Clackamas Co.*

Abele, Joy D., (AV) ....'41 '71 C.475 B.A. L.1068 J.D. 8455 S.W. Metolius Lane‡
Albright, Warren H. ....'25 '52 C&L.950 B.A., J.D. 28446 S.W. Thunderbird Dr.‡
Bayless, Vicki G., (AV) '55 '82 C.112 B.S. L.596 J.D.
V.P., Real Estate & Gen. Coun., Westwood Develop. Corp.
Burgess Lawson, Yvonne '62 '92 C.685 B.A. L.1051 J.D.
Assoc Gen Cnsl, Mentor Graphics Corporation
Carley, Margaret Murphy '57 '86 C.228 B.S. L.893 J.D.
Dep. Dir. & Legal Coun., Oregon Health Care Association
Carlson, Timothy M. '60 '92 C&L.477 B.S.E., J.D.
Corp. Coun., Dir. Legal Affairs, In Focus Sys., Inc.
Chames, Heidi M. ....'62 '87 C&L.629 B.S., J.D. 29781 Town Center Lp W
Christ, Robt. M. ....'27 '54 C.629 B.A. L.596 LL.B. 31535 S.W. Arbor Glen Loop‡
Dexter, Catherine M. ......'54 '82 C.475 B.A. L.596 J.D. 25260 S.W. Parkway Ave., Ste. C
Driveness, Glen A. ....'49 '79 C.35 B.A. L.508 J.D. Sr. Coun., Mentor Graphics Corp.
Ekman, Donald J. '52 '79 C.911 B.A. L.950 J.D.
V.P. & Gen. Coun., Hollywood Entertainment Corporation
English, Eric O., (AV⑦) .....'58 '85 C&L.846 B.A., J.D. Hollywood Entertainment Corp.
Fanning, David A. ....'61 '88 C.101 B.S. L.1065 J.D. 22409 S.W. Newland Rd. (Pat.)
Freed, Dean M. '58 '83 C&L.629 B.S., J.D.
General Counsel & Secretary, Mentor Graphics Corporation
Gass, Stephen F. ....'63 '94 C.628 B.S. L.112 J.D. 22409 S.W. Newland Rd. (Pat.)
Green, Burl L., (AV) ....'21 '49 C.605 B.A. L.813 LL.B. 7215 Arbor Lake Dr.‡
Griffith, Boulden G. ....'46 '78 C.112 B.S.Chem. L.893 J.D. 26600 S.W. Pkwy.‡
Harris, Philip S. ....'61 '92 C.188 B.S. L.596 J.D. VIP's Industries, Inc.
Hibbard, George L., (AV) .....'12 '36 C&L.629 B.S., J.D. 32140 S.W. Boones Bend Rd.‡
Huss, Lawrence D. '44 '69 C.285 B.B.A. L.508 J.D.
(adm. in CO; not adm. in OR) 32295 S.W. Arbor Lake Dr.
Jacobs, Dale ....'18 '48 L.596 LL.B. 9994 French Prarie Rd.‡
Kroos, Arthur G., III ....'42 '70 C.902 B.A. L.966 J.D. 25599 SW 95th Ave., Ste. F.
Liljegren, John W., (BV) ....'52 '78 C.1106 B.A. L.112 J.D. Westwood Develop. Corp.
Lincoln, Anda ....'79 '04 C.36 B.A. L.1051 J.D. In-House-Coun., Mentor Graphics Corp.
Lopardo, Lawrence '56 '81
C.112 B.S.B.A. L.1066 J.D. Gen. Cnsl., Avamere Health Services, Inc.
Moffet, Susan C., (AV) '45 '87 C.1056 B.S. L.1051 J.D.
25260 S.W. Parkway Ave., Ste. C
Moore, Daniel A., Jr. ....'33 '61 C.602 B.B.A. L.208 LL.B. Ret. Chf. Jus. Supm. Ct.‡
Morten, Robert F. '24 '51 C.674 A.B. L.893 LL.B.
(adm. in NY; not adm. in OR) 32181 S.W. Lake Dr.‡
Ofelt, Jack Cortland, Jr. ....'41 '68 C.1027 B.S. L.596 J.D. 23535 S.W. Gage Rd.‡
Pickerell, Loretta ....'— '78 C.379 b.a. L.174 J.D. 26370 S.W. 45th Dr.
Porter, Mark A. '55 '92 C.30 B.S. L.596 J.D.
Sr. Pat. Coun., Mentor Graphics Corp. (Pat.)
Rodal, Monica B. ....'54 '83 C.1056 B.A. L.1066 J.D. Xerox Corp.
Shiokawa, Masayuki ....'67 '00 C.1051 B.A. L.596 J.D. Xerox Corp.
Sullivan, Thomas J. ....'49 '80 C.477 B.A. L.1051 J.D. P.O. Box 884
Thomson, Karen Duzan '50 '82 C.1056 B.S. L.1051 J.D.
Sr. Coun. & Worldwide Contracts Mgr., Mentor Graphics Corp.
Thrash, Charles E. ...... '42 '84 C.846 B.B.A. L.796 J.D. Hollywood Entertainment Corp.
Wetzel Toepke, Shannon M. '69 '98 C.637 B.A. L.1051 J.D.
Mentor Graphics Corporation
White, Earle V., (AV) ....'16 '49 C.911 B.A. L.596 J.D. 8855 S.W. Holly Lane‡
Yates, Philip ....'50 '77 C.896 B.A. L.575 J.D. [Yates&Y.]
Yates, Vicki Hopman, (AV) ....'52 '77 C.107 B.A. L.823 J.D. [Yates&Y.]
Yates & Yates, (AV) ....30240 Southwest Parkway Avenue, North Suite
Yruegas, Jennifer E. ....'74 '99 C.637 B.S. L.596 J.D. 27700 B. S.W. Pkwy. Ave.

WINCHESTER, 488, *Douglas Co.*

Belveal, Donald N. '24 '70 L.1136 LL.B.
(adm. in CA; not adm. in OR) P.O. Box 31‡

WINSTON, 4,613, *Douglas Co.*

Gallagher & Gaw, P.C., (CV⑦) ....265 S.W. Main St.
Gaw, Patricia D., (CV⑦) ....'37 '83 C.101 B.S. L.678 J.D. [Gallagher&G.]
Shults, Victor S. ....'27 '59 L.596 LL.B. P.O. Box 907‡

WOODBURN, 20,100, *Marion Co.*

Bakken, Albert C. '20 '48 C&L.585 Ph.B., LL.B.
(adm. in ND; not adm. in OR) 1350 Dogwood Dr.‡
Beck, JoAnn K., (BV) ....'40 '91 C.999 B.S. L.950 J.D. [J.K.Beck]
Beck, JoAnn K., PC, (BV) ....330 N. 3rd St.
Cox, James A., (BV) ....'30 '57 C.1071 B.S. L.629 LL.B. 1530 Rainier Road
Engels, David A. ....'46 '74 C&L.336 B.S., J.D. 1492 Umpqua Rd.
Engle, Robert L., (AV) ....'41 '66 C.335 B.A. L.950 J.D. [Engle&S.]
Engle & Schmidtman, (AV) ....610 Glatt Circle Northwood Office Park

Hand, Philip J. ....'45 '75 C.585 B.A. L.221 J.D. 970 N. Cascade Dr.
Hanson, Alan G. ....'66 '97 C.999 B.S. L.950 J.D. 32525 S. Barlow Rd.
Klein, Lucien S., (CV) ....'36 '68 C.939 B.A. L.596 J.D. 970 N. Cascade Dr.
Mowry, Frank W., (BV) ....'25 '62 1331 Princeton Rd.
Pattie, Hugh L. ....'20 '54 C.999 L.596 LL.B. 950 Evergreen Rd., Ste. 107‡
Peterson, P. L. ....'33 '65 C.629 B.B.A. L.596 LL.B. 2261 Country Club Rd.‡
Schmidtman, Kirk A., (BV) ....'51 '76 C.906 B.A. L.950 J.D. [Engle&S.]
Shields, N. Robert, (BV) ....'53 '79 C.293 B.A. L.629 J.D. 270 Montgomery St.
Van Dyke, Daniel J., (BV) ....'47 '74 C.999 B.A. L.1051 J.D. 2215 Country Club Rd.
Zyryanoff, Janice D. ....'48 '79 C.381 B.S.Ed. L.161 J.D. 1155 Young St.

YACHATS, 617, *Lincoln Co.*

Dowsett, Michael G. ....'39 '67 C&L.629 B.S., J.D. 441 N. Hwy 101
Lothrop, David B. ....'56 '94 C.800 B.S.E.E. L.847 J.D. P.O. Box 1089

YAMHILL, 867, *Yamhill Co.*

Skuzeski, Caroline L. ....'58 '87 C.101 B.S. L.878 J.D. 780 E. 2nd St.

PATENT AND TRADEMARK PRACTICE PROFILES SECTION

Legal Professionals Practicing

BEFORE THE

UNITED STATES PATENT AND TRADEMARK OFFICE

NORTH CAROLINA
NORTH DAKOTA, OHIO
OKLAHOMA, OREGON

The listings in this section are, according to information available to the publisher at press time, for those subscribers who are registered to practice Patent Law and for those who practice Trademark Law before the U.S. Patent and Trademark Office and who devote a considerable portion of their time or duties to Patent, Trademark and other related matters. It should be noted that registration is not necessary to practice Trademark Law before the U.S. Patent and Trademark Office.

Firms are not registered with the U.S. Patent and Trademark Office and the listings of such entities are limited to those whose practice includes Patent or Trademark and related matters.

The symbols shown have the same meaning as when used elsewhere in this directory. See page IX for Explanatory Notes and Symbols.

ASHEVILLE, * 68,889, *Buncombe Co.*

Carter, David M., (AV) ... '46 '73 C.929 B.S. L.273 J.D. [Carter S.&M.]
*PRACTICE AREAS: Patent, Trademark and Copyright Law.

Carter Schnedler & Monteith, P.A., (AV)
56 Central Avenue, Suite 101, P.O. Box 2985, 28802
Telephone: 828-252-6225 FAX: 828-252-6316
Email: mail@ashevillepatent.com URL: http://www.ashevillepatent.com
David M. Carter; Steven C. Schnedler; J. Derel Monteith, Jr.
Patents, Trademarks, Copyrights.

See Professional Biographies, ASHEVILLE, NORTH CAROLINA

Monteith, J. Derel, Jr. ... '68 '98 C.472 B.M. L.575 J.D. [Carter S.&M.]
*PRACTICE AREAS: Patents; Trademarks; Copyrights; Unfair Competition.
Schnedler, Steven C., (AV) ... '48 '74 C.475 B.S.E.E. L.213 J.D. [Carter S.&M.]
*PRACTICE AREAS: Patent, Trademark and Copyright Law.

CHAPEL HILL, 48,715, *Durham & Orange Cos.*

Fuierer, Marianne ... '46 '95 C.1381 B.S. L.107 J.D. [Ⓐ Intellectual/ T.L.]
*PRACTICE AREAS: Patents; Trademarks; Copyrights.
Fuierer, Tristan A. ... '68 '03 C.1122 B.S. L.575 J.D. [Ⓐ Intellectual/ T.L.]
*PRACTICE AREAS: Intellectual Property.
Hultquist, Steven J., (BV) ... '49 '80 C.910 B.S.Ch.E. L.262 J.D. [Intellectual/ T.L.]
*PRACTICE AREAS: Patents; Trademarks; Copyrights; Technology Law; Technology Transfers.

Intellectual Property/ Technology Law, (BV)
1414 Raleigh Road, Suite 201, 27517
Mailing Address: P.O. Box 14329, Research Triangle Park, NC 27709
Telephone: 919-419-9350 Fax: 919-419-9354
Email: Info@iptl.com URL: http://www.iptl.com
Steven J. Hultquist. Senior Associate: Marianne Fuierer. Associates: Tristan A. Fuierer.
Intellectual Property, Technology and Biotechnology, Patents, Trademarks, Licensing and Copyright Law.

See Professional Biographies, CHAPEL HILL, NORTH CAROLINA

CHARLOTTE, * 540,828, *Mecklenburg Co.*

Adams, W. Thad, III, (AV) ... '46 '71 C.576 B.S. L.575 J.D. [Adams E.]
*PRACTICE AREAS: Patents; Trademarks; Copyrights; Unfair Competition.

Adams Evans P.A., (AV)
2180 Two Wachovia Center, 301 South Tryon Street, 28282
Telephone: 704-375-9249 Fax: 704-375-0729 URL: http://www.adamsevans.com
URL: http://www.adamspat.com
W. Thad Adams, III;—Stephen S. Ashley, Jr.; Jonathan M. Hines; Brandon C. Trego; Kathryn A. Gromlovits; Seth L. Hudson.
Patent, Trademark, Copyright and Unfair Competition Law.
Representative Clients: Aplix, S.A.; B/E Aerospace, Inc.; Armstrong World Industries, Inc.; Belmont Textile Machinery Co.; BSN Medical, Inc.; Britax Child Safety, Inc.; Nissan Motors; Royal Doulton (UK) Limited.
Reference: Wachovia Bank.

See Professional Biographies, CHARLOTTE, NORTH CAROLINA

Additon, Richard L. ... '66 '96 C.431 B.S. L.893 J.D. [Summa&A.]
*PRACTICE AREAS: Intellectual Property; Patents; Trademarks; Trade Secrets; Chemical Patents.
Allan, Albert P. ... '57 '92 C.472 B.S. L.602 J.D. [Summa&A.]
*PRACTICE AREAS: Patent Litigation; Trademark Litigation; Copyright Litigation; Intellectual Property Litigation; Counterfeiting.

Alston & Bird LLP, (AV) BR
Bank of America Plaza, 101 South Tryon Street, Suite 4000, 28280-4000 ⊙
Telephone: 704-444-1000 Telecopier: 704-444-1111
Email: info@alston.com URL: http://www.alston.com
Members of Firm: Blas P. Arroyo; William M. Atkinson; John J. Barnhardt, III; Michael S. Connor; Jason P. Cooper; Charles B. Elderkin; Guy R. Gosnell; Donald M. Hill, Jr.; Larry C. Jones; Lance A. Lawson; Raymond O. Linker, Jr.; Ernest B. Lipscomb, III; Dickson M. Lupo; Michael D. McCoy; Richard M. McDermott; William Kevin Ransom; Bruce J. Rose; John L. Sullivan, Jr.; George M. Taulbee; Henry B. Ward, III. Of Counsel: Paul B. Bell. Counsel: Samuel G. Layton, Jr. Associates: Timothy Balts; Joseph E. Bracken; Kirk T. Bradley; Gregory J. Carlin; Brian Ellsworth; Christopher J. Gegg; Heather Gregg; Jitendra Malik, Ph.D.; Kevin O'Brien; S. Benjamin Pleune; Keith Roberson; Benjamin F. Sidbury; Andrew T. Spence; Brian J. Teague; Chad Thorson; John Mark Wilson.
Languages: Bangla, Bulgarian, Croatian, French, German, Gujarati, Hindi, Italian, Japanese, Korean, Portuguese, Russian, Spanish, Tamil, Thai, Turkish, Urdu.
Administrative Law, Alternative Dispute Resolution, Antitrust and Trade Regulation, Appellate Practice, Bankruptcy, Banks and Banking, Biotechnology, Business Law, Class Actions, Commercial Real Estate, FCC Licensing, FCC Regulation, Wireless Communications, Complex and Multi-District Litigation, Computers and Software, Constitutional Law, Construction Law, Copyrights, Corporate Ethics, Corporate Governance, Corporate Law, Criminal Law, Debtor and Creditor, Electronic Commerce, Emerging Growth Companies, Employee Benefits, Employment Law, Entertainment Law, ERISA, ERISA Litigation, Energy, Environmental Law, Environmental Litigation, Executive Compensation; Finance, Franchises and Franchising, Government Investigations; Health Care Corporate Law, Health Care Regulation, Immigration Law, Insurance Defense, Intellectual Property, International Finance, International Law, International Taxation, International Trade, Internet Law, Labor Law, Labor and Employment, Land Use, Legislative Practice, Life Sciences, Litigation, Local Taxation, Medical Malpractice, Mergers, Acquisitions and Divestitures, Multimedia Law, Municipal Law, Nonprofit and Charitable Organizations, Occupational Safety and Health, Partnership Law, Patents, Privacy Law, Products Liability, Professional Liability, Public Finance, Public Policy, Real Estate Finance, Regulatory Law, RICO, Securities, Securities Litigation, State Taxation, Taxation, Tax Litigation, Technology and Science, Telecommunications Law, Trademarks, Trusts and Estates, Utility Law, Venture Capital, White Collar Crime, Zoning.
Atlanta, Georgia Office: One Atlantic Center, 1201 West Peachtree Street 30309-3424. Telephone: 404-881-7000. Telecopier: 404-881-7777.
Washington, D.C. Office: 601 Pennsylvania Avenue, N.W., North Building, 10th Floor, 20004-2601. Telephone: 202-756-3300. Telecopier: 202-756-3333.
Raleigh, North Carolina Office (Research Triangle Area): 3201 Beechleaf Court, Suite 600, 27604-1062. Telephone: 919-862-2200. Telecopier: 919-862-2260.
New York, New York Office: 90 Park Avenue, 10016-1387. Telephone: 212-210-9400. Fax: 212-210-9444.
(Liaison Office) Munich, Germany Office: Brienner Strasse 11/V, 80333 Munich. Telephone: (49) (89) 238-0-70. Telecopier: (49) (89) 238-0-7110.

See Professional Biographies, CHARLOTTE, NORTH CAROLINA

Arroyo, Blas P., (AV) ... '56 '81 C.576 B.S. L.902 J.D. [Alston&B.]
*PRACTICE AREAS: Intellectual Property; Patent Litigation; Trademark Litigation; Copyright Litigation; Trade Secrets.
Ashe, Jesse B., III, (CV) ... '63 '98 C.1070 B.S. L.831 J.D. [Summa&A.] (⊙Charlotte)
*PRACTICE AREAS: Patents; Trademarks; Copyrights; Intellectual Property; Intellectual Property Litigation.
Ashley, Stephen S., Jr. ... '71 '97 C.230 B.A. L.356 J.D. [Ⓐ Adams E.]
*PRACTICE AREAS: Patent Prosecution; Patent Litigation.
Atkinson, William M., (AV) ... '58 '88 C.632 B.S. L.1209 J.D. [Alston&B.]
*PRACTICE AREAS: Intellectual Property; Patent Litigation; Trademark Litigation; Copyright Litigation.
Balts, Timothy ... '71 '02 C.628 B.S. L.823 J.D. [Ⓐ Alston&B.]
Barnhardt, John J., III, (AV) ... '45 '72 C.198 B.S. L.893 J.D. [Alston&B.]
*PRACTICE AREAS: Intellectual Property; Patent, Trademark, Copyright and related Litigation; Licensing; Antitrust Law; Trade Regulation.
Bell, Paul B., (AV) ... '22 '48 C&L.896 B.S., J.D. [Ⓒ Alston&B.]
*PRACTICE AREAS: Patents; Trademarks; Copyrights.
Bernard, Christopher L. ... '71 '96 C.477 B.S.E. L.597 J.D. [Dougherty,C.H.&B.]
*PRACTICE AREAS: Patents; Trademarks; Copyrights.
Bracken, Joseph E. ... '75 '04 C.674 B.S.E.E. L.569 J.D. [Ⓐ Alston&B.]
*PRACTICE AREAS: Intellectual Property; Intellectual Property Litigation.
Bradley, Kirk T. ... '74 '99 C.160 B.S. L.790 J.D. [Ⓐ Alston&B.]
Carlin, Gregory J. ... '70 '00 C.665 B.S.M.E. L.273 J.D. [Ⓐ Alston&B.]
Clements, Gregory N. ... '51 '81 C.150 B.S.Ch.E. L.1209 J.D. [Dougherty,C.H.&B.]
*PRACTICE AREAS: Patents; Trademarks; Copyrights; Litigation.
Connor, Michael S., (AV) ... '62 '88 C.871 B.S.M.E. L.575 J.D. [Alston&B.]
*PRACTICE AREAS: Intellectual Property; Patent Litigation; Civil Litigation; Trademark Litigation; Technical Litigation.
Cooper, Jason P., (AV) ... '66 '92 C.679 B.S.M.E. L.347 J.D. [Alston&B.]
*PRACTICE AREAS: Intellectual Property; Mechanical Patent Prosecution; Electro-Mechanical Patents; Patent Infringement; International Patents.
Dougherty, Ralph H., (AV) ... '35 '69 C.171 Met.E. L.229 J.D. [Dougherty,C.H.&B.]
*PRACTICE AREAS: Patents; Trademarks; Copyrights; Trade Secrets.

Dougherty, Clements, Hofer & Bernard, (AV)
1901 Roxborough Road, Suite 300, 28211
Telephone: 704-366-6642 Fax: 704-366-9744 URL: http://www.lawyers.com/dougherty&clements
Email: patlaw@worldpatents.com URL: http://www.worldpatents.com
Members of Firm: Ralph H. Dougherty; Gregory N. Clements; Ronald L. Hofer; Christopher L. Bernard. Associates: Brandon G. Williams (Not admitted in NC).
Intellectual Property Matters including Patent, Trademark, Copyright, Trade Secret, Licensing, Litigation and Computer Law.
Reference: First Commerce Bank.

See Professional Biographies, CHARLOTTE, NORTH CAROLINA

Elderkin, Charles B., (BV) ... '38 '64 C.679 B.S.M.E. L.273 LL.B. [Alston&B.]
*PRACTICE AREAS: Intellectual Property; Patent, Trademark and Copyright, with emphasis in Mechanical Technologies.
Ellsworth, Brian ... '75 '02 C.477 B.S.M.E. L.896 J.D. [Ⓐ Alston&B.]
Gegg, Christopher J. ... '77 '02 C.894 B.A. L.896 J.D. [Ⓐ Alston&B.]
Gosnell, Guy R., (AV) ... '65 '92 C.502 B.S.E.E. L.734 J.D. [Alston&B.]
*PRACTICE AREAS: Intellectual Property; Patents; Electrical Patents; Computer and Software Patents; Patent Prosecution.
Greci, Marcia T. ... '74 '04 C.247 B.S. L.989 J.D. [Ⓐ Summa&A.]
*PRACTICE AREAS: Patents; Trademarks; Copyrights; Chemical Patents; Biochemical Patents.
Gregg, Heather ... '77 '02 C.577 B.S. L.896 J.D. [Ⓐ Alston&B.]
Gromlovits, Kathryn A. ... '76 '04 C.575 B.S. L.790 J.D. [Ⓐ Adams E.]
*PRACTICE AREAS: Trademarks; Patents; Copyrights; Unfair Competition.
Hill, Donald M., Jr. ... '59 '95 C.679 B.S. L.150 J.D. [Alston&B.]
*PRACTICE AREAS: Intellectual Property; Mechanical Intellectual Property.
Hines, Jonathan M. ... '72 '98 C.576 B.S.M.E. L.150 J.D. [Ⓐ Adams E.]
*PRACTICE AREAS: Patents.
Hofer, Ronald L., (AVⓉ) ... '44 '72 C.309 A.B. L.352 J.D. [Dougherty,C.H.&B.]
*PRACTICE AREAS: Patents; Trademarks; Copyrights; Trade Secrets; Litigation.
Hudson, Seth L. ... '75 '02 C.576 B.S. L.692 J.D. [Ⓐ Adams E.]
*PRACTICE AREAS: Patent Prosecution; Patent Litigation.
Johnson, Brian ... '66 '96 C.228 B.S.E.E. L.790 J.D. [Ⓐ Summa&A.] (⊙Charlotte)
*PRACTICE AREAS: Patents; Trademarks.
Jones, Larry C., (AVⓉ) ... '48 '92 C.838 B.S.E.E. L.836 J.D. [Alston&B.]
*PRACTICE AREAS: Trademark Litigation; Copyright Litigation; Intellectual Property Litigation.
Lawson, Lance A. ... '61 '97 C.870 B.S. L.602 J.D. [Alston&B.]
*PRACTICE AREAS: Intellectual Property; Intellectual Property Litigation.
Layton, Samuel G., Jr., (AV) ... '36 '65 C.790 B.S. L.30 J.D. [Ⓒ Alston&B.]
*PRACTICE AREAS: Intellectual Property.
Linker, Raymond O., Jr., (AV) ... '46 '72 C.576 B.S. L.276 J.D. [Alston&B.]
*PRACTICE AREAS: Intellectual Property; Patents; Trademarks; Chemical Patents; International Patents.
Lipscomb, Ernest B., III, (AV) ... '41 '65 C&L.500 B.S., J.D. [Alston&B.]
*PRACTICE AREAS: Intellectual Property; Patents; Trademarks; Copyrights; Licensing.
Lupo, Dickson M., (AV) ... '57 '85 C.576 B.S.M.E. L.896 J.D. [Alston&B.]
*PRACTICE AREAS: Patent Infringement; Electronic Commerce; Trademark Licensing; Patent Licensing; Trademark Infringement.
Malik, Jitendra, Ph.D. ... '74 '04 C.575 B.S. L.896 J.D. [Ⓐ Alston&B.]
*PRACTICE AREAS: Intellectual Property; Intellectual Property Litigation; Products Liability.
McCoy, Michael D., (AV) ... '50 '75 C.339 B.S.E.E. L.146 J.D. [Alston&B.]
*PRACTICE AREAS: Intellectual Property; Computers and Software; Patents; Electronic Commerce; Trademarks.
McDermott, Richard M. ... '69 '94 C&L.436 B.S.E.E., J.D. [Alston&B.]
*PRACTICE AREAS: Intellectual Property; Patents; Trademarks; Copyrights.
O'Brien, Kevin ... '65 '00 C.277 B.S.M.E. L.790 J.D. [Ⓐ Alston&B.]
Pendleton, Melissa B. ... '65 '90 C.576 B.A. L.575 J.D. [Summa&A.]
*PRACTICE AREAS: Intellectual Property; Chemical Intellectual Property; Pharmaceutical Intellectual Property; Chemical Patents; Pharmaceutical Patents.
Pleune, S. Benjamin ... '77 '02 C.966 B.S. L.339 J.D. [Ⓐ Alston&B.]
Ransom, William Kevin ... '70 '97 C&L.838 B.S.E.E., J.D. [Alston&B.]
*PRACTICE AREAS: Intellectual Property; Patents; Electrical Patents; Computer and Software Patents; Trademarks.
Roberson, Keith ... '76 '02 C.160 B.S. L.790 J.D. [Ⓐ Alston&B.]
Rose, Bruce J., (AV) ... '63 '93 C.474 B.S.C.E. L.884 J.D. [Alston&B.]
*PRACTICE AREAS: Intellectual Property; Patent Litigation; Trademark Litigation; Copyright Litigation; Chemical Patent Prosecution.
Sidbury, Benjamin F. ... '76 '01 C.999 B.A. L.823 J.D. [Ⓐ Alston&B.]
Spence, Andrew T. ... '75 '00 C.502 B.S.E.E. L.910 J.D. [Ⓐ Alston&B.]
Sullivan, John L., Jr., (AV) ... '44 '69 C.576 B.S.M.E. L.575 J.D. [Alston&B.]
*PRACTICE AREAS: Intellectual Property Rights; International Patents; Trademarks; Patents; Copyrights.
Summa, Philip, (AV) ... '51 '83 C.282 B.A. L.1228 J.D. [Summa&A.]
*PRACTICE AREAS: Patent; Intellectual Property; Chemistry; Polymers; Semiconductor Technology.

Summa & Allan, P.A., (AV) BR
Ballantyne Corporate Park, 11610 North Community House Road Suite 200, 28277-2162
Telephone: 704-945-6700 Fax: 704-945-6735
Email: phil@psumma.com URL: http://www.psumma.com
Members of Firm: Philip Summa; Albert P. Allan; Richard L. Additon; Jesse B. Ashe III; Melissa B. Pendleton. Associates: Brian Johnson; Marcia T. Greci.
Intellectual Property Law: Patents, Trademarks, Copyrights and Trade Secret Protection. Trials and Appeals in all Federal and State Courts and Proceedings before the United States Patent and Trademark Office.

See Professional Biographies, CHARLOTTE, NORTH CAROLINA

Taulbee, George M., (AV) ... '62 '88 C.886 B.S. L.665 J.D. [Alston&B.]
*PRACTICE AREAS: Intellectual Property; Patents; Trademarks; Copyrights; Licensing.
Teague, Brian J. ... '— '04 C.971 B.S.E.E. L.1509 J.D. [Ⓐ Alston&B.]
*PRACTICE AREAS: Intellectual Property; Electronic Intellectual Property; Computer Technology.
Thorson, Chad ... '73 '05 C.871 B.S. L.184 J.D. [Ⓐ Alston&B.]
*PRACTICE AREAS: Intellectual Property; Electronic Intellectual Property; Patents; Computer and Software Patents; Electronic Patents.
Trego, Brandon C. ... '73 '03 C&L.923 B.S.M.E., J.D. [Ⓐ Adams E.]
*PRACTICE AREAS: Patents.
Ward, Henry B., III ... '70 '96 C.277 B.S.M.E. L.245 J.D. [Alston&B.]
*PRACTICE AREAS: Intellectual Property; Mechanical Intellectual Property; E-Commerce.
Williams, Brandon G. '73 '02 C.846 B.S. L.1363 J.D. (adm. in TX; not adm. in NC) [Ⓐ Dougherty,C.H.&B.]
*PRACTICE AREAS: Intellectual Property; Patents; Trademarks; Copyrights.
Wilson, John Mark ... '72 '98 C.160 B.S.M.E. L.150 J.D. [Ⓐ Alston&B.]

DURHAM, * 187,035, *Durham Co.*

Daly, James, IV, Ph.D. '68 '01 C.1150 B.A. L.421 J.D. (adm. in KY; not adm. in NC) [[A] Jenkins,W.&T.]
*PRACTICE AREAS: Patents; Trademarks; Copyrights.

Hunt, Gregory A. . . . . '69 '96 C.576 B.S.E.E. L.575 J.D. [Jenkins,W.&T.] ⊙
*PRACTICE AREAS: Patents; Trademarks; Copyrights.

Jenkins, Richard E., (AV) . . . . '46 '75 C.576 B.S. L.575 J.D. [Jenkins,W.&T.] ⊙
*PRACTICE AREAS: Patents; Trademarks; Copyrights.

Jenkins, Wilson & Taylor, P.A., (AV) [BB]
University Tower, Suite 1400, 3100 Tower Boulevard, 27707 ⊙
Telephone: 919-493-8000 Fax: 919-419-0383
URL: http://www.jenkinswilsontaylor.com
Richard E. Jenkins; Jeffrey L. Wilson; Arles A. Taylor, Jr.; Gregory A. Hunt;—Bentley J. Olive; E. Eric Mills; Christopher P. Perkins, Ph.D. (Not admitted in NC); James Daly IV, Ph.D. (Not admitted in NC).
Patent, Trademark and Copyright Law.
Representative Clients: Böwe Bell and Howell Mail Co.; Duke University; Freudenberg Spunweb Co.; GlaxoSmithKline, Inc.; Huesker, Inc.; North Carolina State University; Sumitomo Electric Lightwave Corp.; The University of North Carolina at Chapel Hill; Vanderbilt University.
Raleigh, North Carolina Office: NCSU Centennial Campus, Suite 101, Venture II, 920 Main Campus Drive, 27606. Telephone: 919-424-3710. Fax: 919-424-3711.

See Professional Biographies, DURHAM, NORTH CAROLINA

Jones-Richardson, Vedia, (BV) . . . . '56 '83 C.329 B.F.A. L.276 J.D. [[A] Olive&O.]
*PRACTICE AREAS: Business Law; Trademarks; Copyrights; Computer Law.

Mills, E. Eric . . . . '70 '01 C.576 B.S. L.575 J.D. [[A] Jenkins,W.&T.]
*PRACTICE AREAS: Patents; Trademarks; Copyrights.

Olive, B. B., (AV) . . . . '21 '53 C.228 B.S.E.E. L.724 J.D. [Olive&O.]
*PRACTICE AREAS: Patents.

Olive, Bentley J. . . . . '75 '01 C.576 B.S. L.577 J.D. [[A] Jenkins,W.&T.]
*PRACTICE AREAS: Patents; Trademarks; Copyrights.

Olive, Susan Freya, (AV) . . . . '52 '76 C.103 A.B. L.228 J.D. [Olive&O.]
*PRACTICE AREAS: Intellectual Property Law and Related Litigation.

Olive and Olive, P.A., (AV) [BB]
500 Memorial Street, P.O. Box 2049, 27702-2049
Telephone: 919-683-5514 Fax: 919-688-3781 URL: http://www.lawyers.com/oliveandolive
Email: iplaw@oliveandolive.com URL: http://www.oliveandolive.com
B. B. Olive; Susan Freya Olive;—Vedia Jones-Richardson; Joshua L. Price; Andrew T. Prokopetz; Devon E. White.
Intellectual Property, Patent, Trademark, Copyright, Computer and Biotechnology Law and Related Litigation.
Reference: North Carolina Bar Assn.

See Professional Biographies, DURHAM, NORTH CAROLINA

Perkins, Christopher P., Ph.D. '63 '01 C.821 B.A. L.800 J.D. (adm. in CA; not adm. in NC) [[A] Jenkins,W.&T.]
*PRACTICE AREAS: Patents; Trademarks; Copyrights.

Price, Joshua L. . . . . '75 '02 C.628 B.S. L.629 J.D. [[A] Olive&O.]
*PRACTICE AREAS: Patent Prosecution; Patent Litigation; Copyrights; Trademarks.

Prokopetz, Andrew T. . . . . '55 '88 C.693 B.S. L.574 J.D. [[A] Olive&O.]
*PRACTICE AREAS: Patent Prosecution; Patent Drafting; Licensing; Contract Negotiations and Drafting; Intellectual Property.

Taylor, Arles A., Jr. . . . . '68 '94 C.576 B.S.B.A. L.575 J.D. [Jenkins,W.&T.] ⊙
*PRACTICE AREAS: Patents; Trademarks; Copyrights.

White, Devon E. . . . . '— '02 C.953 B.A. L.574 J.D. [[A] Olive&O.]
*PRACTICE AREAS: Intellectual Property.

Wilson, Jeffrey L., (AV) . . . . '65 '90 C.575 B.A. L.1228 J.D. [Jenkins,W.&T.] ⊙
*PRACTICE AREAS: Patents; Trademarks; Copyrights.

GREENSBORO, * 223,891, *Guilford Co.*

Beavers, Walter L., (AV) '38 '72 C.296 B.S. L.836 J.D.
326 South Eugene Street, 27401
Telephone: 336-275-7601 Facsimile: 336-275-2009
Email: wbeavers@bellsouth.net
Practice Limited to Intellectual Property Law including Patent, Trademark, Copyright and Unfair Competition.

See Professional Biographies, GREENSBORO, NORTH CAROLINA

Glasgow, JiNan . . . . '68 '99 C.576 B.S. L.575 J.D. [[C] MacCord M.P.] (⊙Raleigh)
*PRACTICE AREAS: Patents; Trademarks; Copyrights; Patent Licensing.

Jones, R. Kody . . . . '77 '05 C.575 B.S. L.1218 J.D. [[A] MacCord M.P.]
*PRACTICE AREAS: Patents; Copyrights; Trademarks; Unfair Competition; Trade Secrets.

Lester, James L., (AV) . . . . '57 '82 C.453 S.B. L.228 J.D. [MacCord M.P.]
*PRACTICE AREAS: Litigation; Patent Law; Trademark Law; Trade Secret Law.

MacCord, Howard A., Jr., (AV) . . . . '50 '78 C.893 B.A. L.273 J.D. [MacCord M.P.]
*PRACTICE AREAS: Patent Law; Trademark Law; Copyright Law; Trade Secrets Law; Intellectual Property Law.

MacCord Mason PLLC, (AV)
300 North Greene Street, Suite 1600, P.O. Box 2974, 27402 ⊙
Telephone: 336-273-4422 Fax: 336-271-2830
URL: http://www.maccordmason.com
Members of Firm: Edward W. Rilee; Howard A. MacCord, Jr.; William J. Mason (Resident, Wilmington Office); James L. Lester. Associates: Dean Turman; R. Kody Jones. Of Counsel: JiNan Glasgow.
Patent, Trademark, Copyright and Unfair Competition. Trade Secret Practice before all Courts. Intellectual Property Law, Litigation.
Wilmington, North Carolina Office: 1209 Culbreth Drive, Suite 103, 28405. Telephone: 910-256-3557. Fax: 910-256-0523.
Raleigh, North Carolina Office: 510 Glenwood Avenue, Suite 321, 27611. Telephone: 919-664-8624. Fax: 919-664-8625.

See Professional Biographies, GREENSBORO, NORTH CAROLINA

Rilee, Edward W., (AV) . . . . '49 '82 C.886 B.S. L.7 J.D. [MacCord M.P.]
*PRACTICE AREAS: Patent Law; Trademark Law; Copyright Law; Unfair Competition Law; Trade Secrets Law.

Turman, Dean . . . . '69 '01 C.576 B.S. L.312 J.D. [[A] MacCord M.P.]
*PRACTICE AREAS: Patents; Trademarks; Copyrights; Unfair Competition; Trade Secrets.

RALEIGH, * 276,093, *Wake Co.*

Abramson, Jarett K. . . . . '71 '97 C.659 B.A. L.878 J.D. [[A] Myers B.S.&S.]
*PRACTICE AREAS: Patent, Trademark and Copyright; Biotechnology.

Alston & Bird LLP, (AV) [BB]
3201 Beechleaf Court, Suite 600, 27604-1062 ⊙
Telephone: 919-862-2200 Telecopier: 919-862-2260 Cable Address: AMGRAM GA Telex: 54-2 996 Easylink: 62985848
Email: info@alston.com URL: http://www.alston.com
Members of Firm: W. Murray Spruill; Christopher M. Humphrey. Associates: Ryan W. Cagle; Michelle L. Cunningham; Edward R. Ergenzinger, Jr.; Kevin R. Lyn; David M. Saravitz; Leigh W. Thorne.
Languages: Bangla, Bulgarian, Croatian, French, German, Gujarati, Hindi, Italian, Japanese, Korean, Portuguese, Russian, Spanish, Tamil, Thai, Turkish, Urdu.
Administrative Law, Alternative Dispute Resolution, Antitrust and Trade Regulation, Appellate Practice, Bankruptcy, Banks and Banking, Biotechnology, Business Law, Class Actions, Commercial Real Estate, FCC Licensing, FCC Regulation, Wireless Communications, Complex and Multi-District Litigation, Computers and Software, Constitutional Law, Construction Law, Copyrights, Corporate

(This Listing Continued)

Alston & Bird LLP (Continued)
Ethics, Corporate Governance, Corporate Law, Criminal Law, Debtor and Creditor, Electronic Commerce, Emerging Growth Companies, Employee Benefits, Employment Law, Entertainment Law, ERISA, ERISA Litigation, Energy, Environmental Law, Environmental Litigation, Executive Compensation; Finance, Franchises and Franchising, Government Investigations; Health Care Corporate Law, Health Care Regulation, Immigration Law, Insurance Defense, Intellectual Property, International Finance, International Law, International Taxation, International Trade, Internet Law, Labor Law, Labor and Employment, Land Use, Legislative Practice, Life Sciences, Litigation, Local Taxation, Medical Malpractice, Mergers, Acquisitions and Divestitures, Multimedia Law, Municipal Law, Nonprofit and Charitable Organizations, Occupational Safety and Health, Partnership Law, Patents, Privacy Law, Products Liability, Professional Liability, Public Finance, Public Policy, Real Estate Finance, Regulatory Law, RICO, Securities, Securities Litigation, State Taxation, Taxation, Tax Litigation, Technology and Science, Telecommunications Law, Trademarks, Trusts and Estates, Utility Law, Venture Capital, White Collar Crime, Zoning.
Atlanta, Georgia Office: One Atlantic Center, 1201 West Peachtree Street, 30309-3424. Telephone: 404-881-7000. Telecopier: 404-881-7777.
Washington, D.C. Office: 601 Pennsylvania Avenue, N.W., North Building, 10th Floor, 20004-2601. Telephone: 202-756-3300. Telecopier: 202-756-3333.
Charlotte, North Carolina Office: Bank of America Plaza, 101 South Tryon Street, Suite 4000, 28280-4000. Telephone: 704-444-1000. Fax: 704-444-1111.
New York, New York Office: 90 Park Avenue, 10016-1387. Telephone: 212-210-9400. Fax: 212-210-9444.
(Liaison) Munich, Germany Office: Brienner Strasse 11/V, 80333 Munich. Telephone: (49) (89) 238-0-70. Telecopier: (49) (89) 238-0-7110.

See Professional Biographies, RALEIGH, NORTH CAROLINA

Ayers, D. Randal . . . . '63 '94 C&L.893 B.S.E.E., J.D. [Myers B.S.&S.]
*PRACTICE AREAS: Patent, Trademark and Copyright; Litigation.

Beatty, David D., (AV) . . . . '68 '93 C.576 B.S. L.575 J.D. [Myers B.S.&S.]
*PRACTICE AREAS: Patent, Trademark and Copyright.

Bigel, Mitchell S., (AV) . . . . '53 '82 C.563 B.E.E. L.273 J.D. [Myers B.S.&S.]
*PRACTICE AREAS: Patent; Trademark; Copyright; Electrical Intellectual Property; Electronics.

Boddie, Needham J., II . . . . '56 '94 C.228 B.S.M.E. L.896 J.D. [Myers B.S.&S.]
*PRACTICE AREAS: Patent, Trademark and Copyright.

Cagle, Ryan W. . . . . '72 '02 C.619 B.S. L.862 J.D. [[A] Alston&B.]

Cannon, James R. . . . . '60 '91 C.840 B.S. L.228 J.D. [Myers B.S.&S.]
*PRACTICE AREAS: Patent, Trademark and Copyright.

Crouse, Robert N. . . . . '60 '97 C.588 B.S.E.E. L.896 J.D. [Myers B.S.&S.]
*PRACTICE AREAS: Patent, Trademark and Copyright.

Cunningham, Michelle L. . . . . '— '03 C.201 B.S. L.577 J.D. [[A] Alston&B.]

Ergenzinger, Edward R., Jr. . . . . '72 '02 C&L.896 B.A., J.D. [[A] Alston&B.]

Glatz, Robert W., (AV) . . . . '58 '91 C.453 S.B.M.E. L.575 J.D. [Myers B.S.&S.]
*PRACTICE AREAS: Patent, Trademark and Copyright.

Hatfield, Scott C. . . . . '65 '93 C&L.880 B.E., J.D. [Myers B.S.&S.]
*PRACTICE AREAS: Patent, Trademark and Copyright.

Humphrey, Christopher M. . . . . '71 '98 C.576 B.S. L.575 J.D. [Alston&B.]
*PRACTICE AREAS: Intellectual Property; Patents; Chemical Patents; Biotechnology Patents; Mechanical Patents.

Kelley, Laura M. . . . . '74 '00 C.945 B.S. L.228 J.D. [[A] Myers B.S.&S.]
*PRACTICE AREAS: Patents; Intellectual Property; Trademarks.

Lemon, Shawna Cannon . . . . '68 '01 C.968 B.S. L.575 J.D. [[A] Myers B.S.&S.]
*PRACTICE AREAS: Patents; Trademarks; Copyrights.

Lyn, Kevin R. . . . . '66 '98 C.228 B.S.E. L.575 J.D. [[A] Alston&B.]

Magri, Karen A. . . . . '63 '96 C.188 B.S. L.228 J.D. [Myers B.S.&S.]
*PRACTICE AREAS: Patent, Trademark and Copyright; Biotechnology.

Meeks, Robert M. . . . . '59 '95 C.277 B.S.E.E. L.280 J.D. [Myers B.S.&S.]
*PRACTICE AREAS: Patent, Trademark and Copyright.

Miller, Mary L. . . . . '56 '97 C.1111 B.A. L.1059 J.D. [Myers B.S.&S.]
*PRACTICE AREAS: Biotechnology Patents.

Moore, D. Scott . . . . '63 '96 C.339 B.S.E.E. L.146 J.D. [Myers B.S.&S.]
*PRACTICE AREAS: Patent, Trademark and Copyright.

Myers, James D. . . . . '40 '72 C&L.790 B.S.Ch.E., J.D. [Myers B.S.&S.]
*PRACTICE AREAS: Intellectual Property Litigation.

Myers Bigel Sibley & Sajovec, P.A., (AV)
4140 Parklake Avenue, Suite 600, 27612
Telephone: 919-854-1400 Fax: 919-854-1401
Email: mbss@myersbigel.com URL: http://www.myersbigel.com
D. Randal Ayers; David D. Beatty; Mitchell S. Bigel; Needham J. Boddie, II; James R. Cannon; Robert N. Crouse; Robert W. Glatz; Scott C. Hatfield; Dr. Karen A. Magri; Robert M. Meeks; Dr. Mary L. Miller; D. Scott Moore; James D. Myers; Timothy J. O'Sullivan; David K. Purks; Julie H. Richardson; F. Michael Sajovec; Grant J. Scott; Kenneth D. Sibley; Richard P. Vitek;—Jarett K. Abramson; Laura M. Kelley; Dr. Shawna Cannon Lemon; Elizabeth A. Stanek.
Intellectual Property Law: Patents, Trademarks, Copyrights and related Litigation.

See Professional Biographies, RALEIGH, NORTH CAROLINA

O'Sullivan, Timothy J. . . . . '61 '90 C.502 B.S.E.E. L.228 J.D. [Myers B.S.&S.]
*PRACTICE AREAS: Patent, Trademark and Copyright.

Purks, David K. . . . . '63 '94 C.886 B.S. L.734 J.D. [Myers B.S.&S.]
*PRACTICE AREAS: Patents.

Richardson, Julie H. . . . . '59 '95 C.679 B.S.M.E. L.228 J.D. [Myers B.S.&S.]
*PRACTICE AREAS: Patent, Trademark and Copyright.

Sajovec, F. Michael, (AV) . . . . '59 '86 C.119 B.S. L.1003 J.D. [Myers B.S.&S.]
*PRACTICE AREAS: Patent, Trademark and Copyright.

Saravitz, David M. . . . . '— '03 C.645 B.S. L.574 J.D. [[A] Alston&B.]
*PRACTICE AREAS: Intellectual Property; Biotechnology; Biotechnology Patents.

Scott, Grant J. . . . . '62 '91 C.893 B.S.E.E. L.577 J.D. [Myers B.S.&S.]
*PRACTICE AREAS: Patent, Trademark and Copyright.

Sibley, Kenneth D., (AV) . . . . '56 '85 C.1047 B.A. L.228 J.D. [Myers B.S.&S.]
*PRACTICE AREAS: Patent, Trademark and Copyright; Biotechnology; Intellectual Property.

Spruill, W. Murray, (AV) . . . . '54 '92 C.232 B.S. L.273 J.D. [Alston&B.]
*PRACTICE AREAS: Pharmaceutical Intellectual Property; Biotechnology Patents; Intellectual Property Portfolio Management; Intellectual Property Infringement; Intellectual Property Licensing.

Stanek, Elizabeth A. . . . . '75 '00 C.576 B.S. L.575 J.D. [[A] Myers B.S.&S.]
*PRACTICE AREAS: Patent, Trademark and Copyright.

Thorne, Leigh W. . . . . '64 '01 C.188 B.S. L.228 J.D. [[A] Alston&B.]

Vitek, Richard P. . . . . '60 '85 C.813 B.S. L.477 J.D. [Myers B.S.&S.]
*PRACTICE AREAS: Intellectual Property Litigation.

RESEARCH TRIANGLE PARK, —, *Durham Co.*

Barrett, William A. . . . . '66 '97 C.48 B.A. L.896 J.D. [[C] Moore&V.P.]
*PRACTICE AREAS: Intellectual Property.

Chiantera, Dominic J. . . . . '39 '74 C.1046 B.S.E.E. L.1048 J.D. [Moore&V.P.]
*PRACTICE AREAS: Intellectual Property.

Evans, Charles L. . . . . '64 '94 C.576 B.S. L.575 J.D. [[C] Moore&V.P.]
*PRACTICE AREAS: Intellectual Property Law; Computer Law.

Jenkins, Wilson & Taylor, P.A.
(See Durham)

Johnston, Michael G. . . . . '61 '92 C.602 B.S. L.574 J.D. [Moore&V.P.]
*PRACTICE AREAS: Intellectual Property.

Moore, Charles L., Jr. . . . . '52 '87 C&L.836 B.S.E.E., J.D. [Moore&V.P.]
*PRACTICE AREAS: Intellectual Property.

Moore & Van Allen PLLC, (AV) [BB]
430 Davis Drive, Suite 500, P.O. Box 13706, 27709 ⊙
Telephone: 919-286-8000 Fax: 919-286-8199
URL: http://www.mvalaw.com
Resident Members: Dominic J. Chiantera; Michael G. Johnston; Charles L. Moore, Jr.; Steven B. Phillips. Resident Counsel: William A. Barrett; Jerry W. Clark; Jennifer L. Skord; Gregory Stephens. Resident Associates: Charles L. Evans; John E. Slaughter III; Matthew W. Witsil.
Charleston, South Carolina Office: 40 Calhoun Street, Suite 300. Telephone: 843-579-7000. Fax: 843-579-7099.
Charlotte, North Carolina Office: 100 North Tryon Street, Suite 4700. Telephone: 704-331-1000. Fax: 704-331-1159.

See Professional Biographies, RESEARCH TRIANGLE PARK, NORTH CAROLINA

Phillips, Steven B. .... '62 '93 C.659 B.S.E. L.575 J.D. [Moore&V.P.]
*PRACTICE AREAS: Intellectual Property.

Skord, Jennifer L., (BV) .... '48 '80 C.98 B.A. L.209 J.D. [C Moore&V.P.]
*PRACTICE AREAS: Intellectual Property.

Slaughter, John E., III .... '71 '97 C.886 B.A. L.893 J.D. [A Moore&V.P.]
*PRACTICE AREAS: Intellectual Property.

Stephens, Gregory .... '66 '95 C.886 B.S.E.E. L.1292 J.D. [C Moore&V.P.]
*PRACTICE AREAS: Intellectual Property; Patent Prosecution.

Williamson, Dennis J. .... '59 '90 C.339 B.S.G.E. L.209 J.D. [C Moore&V.P.]
*PRACTICE AREAS: Intellectual Property; Patent.

Witsil, Matthew W. .... '65 '99 C.893 B.S. L.228 J.D. [A Moore&V.P.]
*PRACTICE AREAS: Intellectual Property; Patent Law.

WILMINGTON, * 75,838, *New Hanover Co.*

MacCord Mason PLLC, (AV)
1209 Culbreth Drive, Suite 103, 28405 ⊙
Telephone: 910-256-3557 Fax: 910-256-0523
Email: wmason@mmpatent.com URL: http://www.maccordmason.com
William J. Mason (Resident).
Patent, Trademark, Copyright and Unfair Competition. Trade Secret Practice before all Courts. Intellectual Property Law, Litigation.
Greensboro, North Carolina Office: 300 North Greene Street, Suite 1600, P.O. Box 2974. Telephone: 336-273-4422. Fax: 336-271-2830.
Raleigh, North Carolina Office: 510 Glenwood Avenue, Suite 321, 27611. Telephone: 919-664-8624. Fax: 919-664-8625.

See Professional Biographies, WILMINGTON, NORTH CAROLINA

Mason, William J., (BV) .... '40 '68 C.834 B.S. L.273 J.D. [MacCord M.P.]
*PRACTICE AREAS: Patent Law; Trademark Law; Copyright Law; Licensing Law.

AKRON, * 217,074, *Summit Co.*

Bobak, Donald J., (AV) ... '43 '73 C&L.8 B.S., J.D. [Renner,K.G.B.T.&W.]
*PRACTICE AREAS: Intellectual Property Law.

Clark, Robert J. ... '66 '93 C.608 B.S.M.E. L.8 J.D. [Ⓐ Hahn L.&P.]
*PRACTICE AREAS: Patents; Intellectual Property.

Cunniff, John J. ... '62 '99 C.347 B.S. L.7 J.D. [Ⓐ Hahn L.&P.]
*PRACTICE AREAS: Intellectual Property Law; Patent Law; Trademark Law; Copyrights.

Drenski, Tama L. ... '56 '03 C.607 B.A. L.8 J.D. [Ⓐ Renner,K.G.B.T.&W.]
*PRACTICE AREAS: Intellectual Property.

Gaum, R. Eric, (AV) ... '66 '96 C.150 B.S.E.E.T. L.07 J.D. [Hahn L.&P.]
*PRACTICE AREAS: Intellectual Property Litigation; Patents; Trademarks; Copyrights.

Gentilcore, Laura J., (BV) ... '53 '86 C.930 B.A. L.1003 J.D. [Ⓐ Renner,K.G.B.T.&W.]
*PRACTICE AREAS: Intellectual Property Law; Litigation.

Greive, Edward G., (AV) ... '42 '67 C.879 B.S.E.E. L.930 J.D. [Renner,K.G.B.T.&W.]
*PRACTICE AREAS: Intellectual Property Law.

Hahn Loeser & Parks LLP, (AV)
One Gojo Plaza Suite 300, 44311-1076 ⊙
Telephone: 330-864-5550; 1-877-HAHNLAW Facsimile: 330-864-7986
Email: inquiry@hahnlaw.com URL: http://www.hahnlaw.com
Resident Members: R. Eric Gaum; Scott M. Oldham; Mark A. Watkins. Resident Of Counsel: Louis F. Kreek, Jr. Resident Associates: Robert J. Clark; John J. Cunniff; Bret A. Hrivnak; Michael H. Minns; Amanda H. Wilcox.
Business, Corporate and Securities, Litigation, Taxation and Employee Benefits, Estate Planning, Probate, Real Estate, Labor, Creditors Rights, Reorganization and Bankruptcy, Intellectual Property and Technology, Environmental, Patent, Trademark and Copyright Law, Telecommunications Law, Government Relations, Public Utility and Regulatory Law, Health Care, Construction Law.
Reference: Star Bank, Akron, Ohio.
Cleveland, Ohio Office: 3300 BP Tower, 200 Public Square, 44114-2301. Telephone: 216-621-0150. Fax: 216-241-2824.
Columbus, Ohio Office: 65 East State Street, Suite 1400, 43215. Telephone: 614-221-0240. Fax: 614-221-5909.
Naples, Florida Office: 3301 Bonita Beach Road, Suite 308, Bonita Springs, 34134. Telephone: 239-949-6989. Fax: 239-949-6687.

See Professional Biographies, AKRON, OHIO

Hodgkiss, Tim A. ... '73 '03 C.610 B.S.E.E. L.7 J.D. [Ⓐ Renner,K.G.B.T.&W.]
*PRACTICE AREAS: Intellectual Property.

Hrivnak, Bret A. ... '70 '04 C&L.8 B.S., J.D. [Ⓐ Hahn L.&P.]
*PRACTICE AREAS: Intellectual Property; Litigation; Technology Transfers.

Kenner, Phillip L., (AV) ... '35 '65 C.339 B.S. L.8 J.D. [Renner,K.G.B.T.&W.]
*PRACTICE AREAS: Intellectual Property Law.

Kreek, Louis F., Jr. ... '28 '52 C.453 B.S. L.273 J.D. [Ⓒ Hahn L.&P.]
*PRACTICE AREAS: Patents; Technology and Science.

McCue, Shannon V. ... '71 '98 C.608 B.S.M.E. L.8 J.D. [Ⓐ Renner,K.G.B.T.&W.]
*PRACTICE AREAS: Intellectual Property.

Minns, Michael H., (BV) ... '50 '85 C.477 B.S.E. L.1003 J.D. [Ⓐ Hahn L.&P.]
*PRACTICE AREAS: Intellectual Property; Patents.

Morton, Andrew B. ... '62 '93 C.607 B.S.E.E. L.879 J.D. [Renner,K.G.B.T.&W.]
*PRACTICE AREAS: Intellectual Property Law.

Oldham, Scott M., (BV) ... '61 '91 C.171 B.S. L.8 J.D. [Hahn L.&P.]
*PRACTICE AREAS: Patents; Trademarks; Copyrights; Intellectual Property; Technology Licensing.

Reginelli, Arthur M. ... '69 '95 C.363 B.S. L.989 J.D. [Renner,K.G.B.T.&W.]
*PRACTICE AREAS: Intellectual Property Law.

Renner, Kenner, Greive, Bobak, Taylor & Weber, A Legal Professional Association, (AV)
4th Floor, First National Tower, 44308-1456
Telephone: 330-376-1242 Facsimile: 330-376-9646
Email: patlaw@rennerkenner.com URL: http://www.rennerkenner.com
Phillip L. Kenner; Edward G. Greive; Donald J. Bobak; Ray L. Weber; Rodney Lee Skoglund; Andrew B. Morton; Arthur M. Reginelli; Laura J. Gentilcore; Shannon V. McCue; Mark L. Weber; Tama L. Drenski; Tim A. Hodgkiss.
U.S. and Foreign Patent, Trademark and Copyright Law and Licensing. Antitrust and Unfair Competition Law. Litigation.
Reference: Key Bank.

See Professional Biographies, AKRON, OHIO

Skoglund, Rodney Lee ... '65 '91 C.532 B.A. L.8 J.D. [Renner,K.G.B.T.&W.]
*PRACTICE AREAS: Intellectual Property Law.

Watkins, Mark A., (AV) ... '60 '88 C.607 B.S. L.7 J.D. [Hahn L.&P.]
*PRACTICE AREAS: Patents; Trademarks; Licensing; Copyrights; Trade Secrets.

Weber, Mark L. ... '74 '99 C.823 B.S. L.8 J.D. [Ⓐ Renner,K.G.B.T.&W.]
*PRACTICE AREAS: Intellectual Property Law.

Weber, Ray L., (AV) ... '45 '72 C.8 B.S.E.E. L.7 J.D. [Renner,K.G.B.T.&W.]
*PRACTICE AREAS: Intellectual Property Law.

Wilcox, Amanda H. ... '76 '01 C.473 B.S. L.851 J.D. [Ⓐ Hahn L.&P.]
*PRACTICE AREAS: Trademark Law; Patent Law.

CINCINNATI, * 331,285, *Hamilton Co.*

Acheson, Edwin R., Jr., (BV) ... '55 '80 C.502 B.S. L.228 J.D. [Frost B.T.]
*PRACTICE AREAS: Patents; Copyrights; Computer Law; Licensing; Intellectual Property Litigation.

Ahrens, Gregory F., (BV) ... '61 '87 C.846 B.S.Ch.E. L.966 J.D. [Wood,H.&E.]
*PRACTICE AREAS: Intellectual Property; Intellectual Property Litigation; Patent, Trademark and Copyright.

Albainy-Jenei, Stephen R., (BV) ... '64 '95 C.201 B.S. L.150 J.D. [Frost B.T.]
*PRACTICE AREAS: Intellectual Property Law; Patents; Patent Prosecution; Biotechnology; Licensing.

Armstrong, Jody H., (BV) ... '— '92 C.352 B.A. L.209 J.D. [Ⓐ Dinsmore&S.]
*PRACTICE AREAS: Intellectual Property; Trademark Licensing; Trademarks; Copyrights.

Beck, Bradley D. ... '— '88 C.150 B.S.A.E. L.1340 J.D. [Ⓒ Wood,H.&E.]
*PRACTICE AREAS: Patents; Mechanical Patents.

Blatt, P. Andrew ... '66 '98 C.1333 B.S. L.150 J.D. [Ⓐ Wood,H.&E.]
*PRACTICE AREAS: Intellectual Property; Patent, Trademark and Copyright.

Brinkman, David H. ... '61 '94 C.860 B.S.E.E. L.201 J.D. [Wood,H.&E.]
*PRACTICE AREAS: Intellectual Property; Patent, Trademark and Copyright.

Brown, Charles H., III, (BV) ... '57 '87 C.893 B.S.M.E. L.945 J.D. [Dinsmore&S.]
*PRACTICE AREAS: Commercial Litigation; Intellectual Property; Products Liability; Trade Secrets; Unfair Competition.

Burger, Thomas J., (AV) ... '60 '86 C&L.602 B.S.E.E., J.D. [Wood,H.&E.]
*PRACTICE AREAS: Intellectual Property; Patent, Trademark and Copyright.

Calder, Thomas S., (AV) ... '32 '57 C&L.602 A.B., LL.B. [Ⓒ Dinsmore&S.]
*PRACTICE AREAS: General Litigation; Product Liability; Commercial Litigation.

Caldwell, Steven W. '68 '02 C.383 B.S. L.823 J.D.
(adm. in NY; not adm. in OH) [Ⓐ Frost B.T.]

Chambers, J. Robert, (AV) ... '45 '72 C.608 B.Met.E. L.912 J.D. [Wood,H.&E.]
*PRACTICE AREAS: Intellectual Property Litigation; Patent, Trademark and Copyright.

Davidson, Kristi L. ... '71 '97 C.930 B.S. L.201 J.D. [Ⓐ Wood,H.&E.]
*PRACTICE AREAS: Intellectual Property; Patent, Trademark and Copyright.

Dinsmore & Shohl LLP, (AV) BR
255 East Fifth Street, Suite 1900, 45202-4700 ⊙
Telephone: 513-977-8200 FAX: 513-977-8141
Email: info@dinslaw.com URL: http://www.dinslaw.com
Members of Firm: Lynda E. Roesch; Holly D. Kozlowski; Charles H. Brown, III; Martin J. Miller; John V. Harmeyer. Associates: Neal A. Frink; Clayton L. Kuhnell; Geoffrey L. Oberhaus; Jody H. Armstrong; Clare M. Iery. Of Counsel: Thomas S. Calder.

(This Listing Continued)

Dinsmore & Shohl LLP (Continued)

General Practice: Antitrust, Aviation Law, Banking, Bankruptcy, Business Crimes Law, Computers, Construction, Corporations, Creditors' Rights, Drug and Medical Device, Employee Benefits, Environmental, ERISA, Estate Planning, Franchising, Healthcare, Hospitals, Intellectual Property, International, Immigration, Insurance Law, Labor and Employment Law, Litigation, Medical Malpractice Defense, Mergers and Acquisitions, OSHA, Probate, Products Liability, Real Estate, Securities, State and Local Government Law, Taxation, Transportation Law, Trial and Appellate Practice in State and Federal Courts, Trusts, Workers' Compensation, Zoning.
Dayton, Ohio Office: One Dayton Centre, One South Main Street, Suite 1300, 45402. Telephone: 937-449-6400. FAX: 937-449-6405.
Columbus, Ohio Office: 10th Floor, 175 South Third Street, 43215-5134. Telephone: 614-628-6880. FAX: 614-628-6890.
Lexington, Kentucky Office: Lexington Financial Center, 250 West Main Street, Suite 1400, 40507. Telephone: 859-425-1000. FAX: 859-425-1099.
Louisville, Kentucky Office: 1400 PNC Plaza, 500 West Jefferson Street, 40202. Telephone: 502-540-2300. FAX: 502-585-2207.
Pittsburgh, Pennsylvania Office: The Grant Building, 330 Grant Street, Suite 2415, 15219. Telephone: 412-281-5000. FAX: 412-281-5055.
Charleston, West Virginia Office: 900 Lee Street, Huntington Square, Suite 600, 25301. Mailing Address: P.O. Box 11887, 25339. Telephone: 304-357-0900. FAX: 304-357-0919.

See Professional Biographies, CINCINNATI, OHIO

Eby, C. Richard ... '41 '68 C.150 B.S. L.1340 J.D. [Ⓐ Wood,H.&E.]
*PRACTICE AREAS: Intellectual Property; Patent, Trademark and Copyright.

Flynn, Thomas W., (AV) ... '33 '63 C.790 B.S. L.273 J.D. [Ⓒ Wood,H.&E.]
*PRACTICE AREAS: Intellectual Property; Patent, Trademark and Copyright.

Franklin, David E. ... '62 '95 C.378 B.S.E.E. L.734 J.D. [Ⓐ Frost B.T.]
*PRACTICE AREAS: Patent Prosecution; Intellectual Property; Government Contracts; Intellectual Property Infringement; Intellectual Property Licensing.

Frei, Donald F., (AV) ... '38 '65 C.188 B.M.E. L.276 J.D. [Wood,H.&E.]
*PRACTICE AREAS: Intellectual Property; Patent, Trademark and Copyright.

Frink, Neal A. ... '63 '99 C.119 B.S. L.1161 J.D. [Ⓐ Dinsmore&S.]
*PRACTICE AREAS: Environmental Law; Litigation.

Frost Brown Todd LLC, (AV)
2200 PNC Center, 201 East Fifth Street, 45202-4182 ⊙
Telephone: 513-651-6800 Telecopier: 513-651-6981
Email: info@fbtlaw.com URL: http://www.frostbrowntodd.com
Patent, Trademark and Copyright Attorneys Members of Firm: David E. Schmit; Stephen J. Goldstein; Kenneth B. Germain; Edwin R. Acheson, Jr.; Louis K. Ebling; Todd H. Bailey; Stephen E. Gillen. Associates: Ann Gallagher Robinson; Kevin S. Sprecher; Ria Farrell Schalnat. Of Counsel: Gretchen R. Blum; Glenn D. Bellamy.
Columbus, Ohio Office: One Columbus, 10 West Broad Street, 43215-3467. Telephone: 614-464-1211. Telecopier: 614-464-1737.
Middletown, Ohio Office: 300 North Main Street, Suite 200, 45042-1919. Telephone: 513-422-2001. Telecopier: 513-422-3010.
Lexington, Kentucky Office: 250 West Main Street, Suite 2700, 40507-1742. Telephone: 859-231-0000. Telecopier: 859-231-0011.
Louisville, Kentucky Office: 400 West Market Street, 32nd Floor, 40202-3363. Telephone: 502-589-5400. Telecopier: 502-581-1087.
Nashville, Tennessee Office: 424 Church Street, Suite 1600, 37219-2308. Telephone: 615-251-5550. Telecopier: 615-251-5551.
New Albany, Indiana Office: 120 West Spring Street, Suite 400, 47150-3655. Telephone: 812-948-2800. Telecopier: 812-948-7994.

See Professional Biographies, CINCINNATI, OHIO

Goldstein, Steven J., (AV) ... '51 '75 C.453 B.S. L.94 J.D. [Frost B.T.]
*PRACTICE AREAS: Intellectual Property Law; Patents; Trade Secret; International.

Grossman, Kurt L., (AV) ... '55 '81 C.150 B.S.E.E. L.273 J.D. [Wood,H.&E.]
*PRACTICE AREAS: Intellectual Property; Patent, Trademark and Copyright.

Harmeyer, John V. ... '69 '96 C.201 B.S.E.E. L.150 J.D. [Dinsmore&S.]
*PRACTICE AREAS: Intellectual Property; Patents; Computers and Software; Copyrights; Trademarks.

Haupt, Keith R., (AV) ... '63 '92 C.880 B.E. L.608 J.D. [Wood,H.&E.]
*PRACTICE AREAS: Intellectual Property; Patent, Trademark and Copyright.

Humphrey, Thomas W. ... '66 '93 C.453 B.S.E.E. L.309 J.D. [Wood,H.&E.]
*PRACTICE AREAS: Intellectual Property; Patent, Trademark and Copyright.

Iery, Clare M. ... '— '01 C&L.150 B.A., J.D. [Ⓐ Dinsmore&S.]
*PRACTICE AREAS: Intellectual Property; Patents; Trademarks; Copyrights.

Jackson, Randall S., Jr. ... '72 '98 C&L.734 B.A., J.D. [Ⓐ Wood,H.&E.]
*PRACTICE AREAS: Patents; Biochemical Patents; Chemical Patents; Biotechnology Patents; Pharmaceutical Patents.

Jacobs, Wayne L. ... '60 '90 C.839 B.S.M.E. L.421 J.D. [Wood,H.&E.]
*PRACTICE AREAS: Intellectual Property; Patent, Trademark and Copyright.

Jefferies, David E. ... '70 '98 C.231 B.A. L.345 J.D. [Ⓐ Wood,H.&E.]
*PRACTICE AREAS: Intellectual Property; Patent, Trademark and Copyright.

Jordan, Joseph R., (BV) ... '42 '68 C.602 B.S. L.276 J.D. [Ⓐ Wood,H.&E.]
*PRACTICE AREAS: Intellectual Property; Patent, Trademark and Copyright.

Josephic, David J., (AV) ... '35 '66 C.973 B.S.C. L.276 J.D. [Wood,H.&E.]
*PRACTICE AREAS: Intellectual Property; Patent, Trademark and Copyright.

Kipling, James M. ... '— '72 C.150 B.S.M.E. L.276 J.D. [Ⓒ Frost B.T.]
*PRACTICE AREAS: Intellectual Property; Transactions; Licensing; Intellectual Property Protection; Policing Actions.

Kozlowski, Holly D., (AVⓉ) ... '58 '84 C.105 B.S.Ch.E. L.1209 J.D. [Dinsmore&S.]
*PRACTICE AREAS: Intellectual Property.

Kuhnell, Clayton L. ... '75 '01 C&L.150 B.S.Ch.E., J.D. [Ⓐ Dinsmore&S.]
*PRACTICE AREAS: Intellectual Property; Patent Prosecution and Litigation.

Luken, Clement H., Jr., (AV) ... '56 '86 C.973 B.S.Chem. L.1340 J.D. [Wood,H.&E.]
*PRACTICE AREAS: Intellectual Property; Patent, Trademark and Copyright.

Lunn, Gregory J., (AV) ... '55 '78 C.1118 B.A. L.383 J.D. [Wood,H.&E.]
*PRACTICE AREAS: Intellectual Property; Patent, Trademark and Copyright.

Lyman, Beverly A. ... '56 '96 C.999 B.S. L.1015 J.D. [Wood,H.&E.]
*PRACTICE AREAS: Intellectual Property; Patent, Trademark and Copyright.

Miller, Martin J., (AV) ... '63 '91 C.679 B.S. L.851 J.D. [Dinsmore&S.]
*PRACTICE AREAS: Intellectual Property.

Moreno, Victor C. ... '66 '95 C.608 B.S.M.E. L.150 J.D. [Ⓒ Frost B.T.]
*PRACTICE AREAS: Intellectual Property Litigation; Technology and Science.

Oberhaus, Geoffrey L. ... '69 '98 C.215 B.Che.E. L.1292 J.D. [Ⓐ Dinsmore&S.]
*PRACTICE AREAS: Litigation; Intellectual Property; Patents.

Poffenberger, J. Dwight, Jr. ... '64 '94 C.477 B.S.M.E. L.1209 J.D. [Ⓐ Wood,H.&E.]
*PRACTICE AREAS: Intellectual Property; Patent, Trademark and Copyright.

Poffenberger, John D., (AV) ... '34 '61 C.608 B.S.I.E. L.273 LL.B. [Ⓒ Wood,H.&E.]
*PRACTICE AREAS: Intellectual Property; Patent, Trademark and Copyright.

Remaklus, Theodore R. ... '62 '93 C&L.150 B.S.M.E., J.D. [Wood,H.&E.]
*PRACTICE AREAS: Intellectual Property; Intellectual Property Litigation; Patent, Trademark and Copyright.

Robinson, Ann Gallagher ... '62 '94 C.602 B.S. L.1340 J.D. [Frost B.T.]
*PRACTICE AREAS: Intellectual Property Litigation; Patent Prosecution.

Roesch, Lynda E., (AV) ... '53 '79 C.602 B.S. L.851 J.D. [Dinsmore&S.]
*PRACTICE AREAS: Trademark and Unfair Competition Law; Copyright Law; Intellectual Property Law; General Litigation.

Rooney, Kevin G. ... '64 '92 C.150 B.S.M.E. L.273 J.D. [Wood,H.&E.]
*PRACTICE AREAS: Intellectual Property; Patent, Trademark and Copyright.

Schalnat, Ria Farrell ... '71 '99 C.1161 B.S. L.201 J.D. [Ⓐ Frost B.T.]
*PRACTICE AREAS: Patent Prosecution; Patent Litigation; Software Copyright; Software Licensing; Trademark.

Schmit, David E., (AV) . . . . '47 '75 C.150 B.S.E.E. L.1340 J.D. [Frost B.T.]
*PRACTICE AREAS: Intellectual Property Litigation (90%, 12); Intellectual Property Counseling (10%, 75); Patent, Trademark, and Copyright Law; Trade Secrets; Unfair Competition.

Sprecher, Kevin S. . . . . '68 '95 C.679 B.S.I.E. L.879 J.D. [Frost B.T.]
*PRACTICE AREAS: Intellectual Property; Patent Prosecution and Litigation.

Stallard, David S., (AV) . . . . '44 '68 C.275 B.S. L.421 J.D. [Wood,H.&E.]
*PRACTICE AREAS: Intellectual Property; Patent, Trademark and Copyright.

Stinebruner, Scott A. . . . . '68 '93 C.910 B.S.E.E. L.494 J.D. [Wood,H.&E.]
*PRACTICE AREAS: Intellectual Property; Patent, Trademark and Copyright.

Summe, Kurt Andrew, (AV) . . . . '65 '91 C&L.150 B.S., J.D. [Wood,H.&E.]
*PRACTICE AREAS: Intellectual Property; Patent, Trademark and Copyright.

Tittel, Bruce, (AV) . . . . '38 '63 C&L.880 B.A., LL.B. [Wood,H.&E.]
*PRACTICE AREAS: Intellectual Property; Intellectual Property Litigation; Patent, Trademark and Copyright.

Wood, Herron & Evans, L.L.P., (AV) BB
2700 Carew Tower, 45202
Telephone: 513-241-2324 Fax: 513-421-7269
Email: info@whepatent.com URL: http://www.whepatent.com
Members of Firm: Bruce Tittel; Donald F. Frei; David J. Josephic; David S. Stallard; J. Robert Chambers; Gregory J. Lunn; Kurt L. Grossman; Clement H. Luken, Jr.; Thomas J. Burger; Gregory F. Ahrens; Wayne L. Jacobs; Kurt Andrew Summe; Kevin G. Rooney; Keith R. Haupt; Theodore R. Remaklus; Thomas W. Humphrey; Scott A. Stinebruner; David H. Brinkman; Beverly A. Lyman. Senior Associates: Joseph R. Jordan; C. Richard Eby. Associates: J. Dwight Poffenberger, Jr.; Kristi L. Davidson; P. Andrew Blatt; David E. Jefferies; Randall S. Jackson, Jr. Of Counsel: John D. Poffenberger; Thomas W. Flynn; Bradley D. Beck.
Intellectual Property and Related Litigation; Computer Law, Patents, Trademarks and Copyrights.
See Professional Biographies, CINCINNATI, OHIO

CLEVELAND, * 478,403, *Cuyahoga Co.*

Adamo, Kenneth R. . . . . '— '75 C.688 B.S.Ch.E. L.982 J.D. [Jones D.]
*PRACTICE AREAS: Intellectual Property; Patent Litigation; Trademarks; Unfair Competition.

Adams, Thomas W. . . . . '49 '92 C.59 B.A. L.161 J.D. [Renner,O.B.&S.]
*PRACTICE AREAS: Patents; Trademarks; Copyrights; Intellectual Property.

Agozzino, Leozino . . . . '— '85 C.604 B.A. L.608 J.D. [Ⓒ Jones D.]

Amin, Himanshu S. . . . . '65 '95 C.608 B.S.E.E. L.930 J.D. [Amin&T.]

Amin & Turocy, LLP
24th Floor, National City Center, 1900 East 9th Street, 44114
Telephone: 216-696-8730 Fax: 216-696-8731
URL: http://www.thepatentattorneys.com
Partners: Himanshu S. Amin; Gregory Turocy; Jeffrey R. Sadlowski; Deborah Corpus; Jeffrey D. Hale (Not admitted in OH); Eric D. Jorgenson. Associates: Daniel B. Bortnick; James J. Pingor; Vahid Sharifi (Not admitted in OH).
Patents, Patent Prosecution, Trademarks, Trademark Prosecution, Copyrights, Litigation, Intellectual Property.
See Professional Biographies, CLEVELAND, OHIO

Asam, Michael R. . . . . '— '01 C.385 A.B. L.228 J.D. [Ⓐ Jones D.]

Balazs, James A. . . . . '66 '99 C.188 B.S.M.E. L.1003 J.D. [Ⓐ Rankin,H.P.&C.]
*PRACTICE AREAS: Patent Prosecution; Trademark Prosecution.

Bandy, Mark E., (BV) . . . . '62 '91 C.474 B.S.Ch.E. L.1003 J.D. [Fay,S.F.M.&M.]
*PRACTICE AREAS: Patent; Trademark; Copyright; Unfair Competition; Licensing.

Bembenick, Brian G. . . . . '66 '98 C.1062 B.S. L.128 J.D. [Pearne&G.]
*PRACTICE AREAS: Patents; Trademarks; Copyrights.

Biernacki, John V. . . . . '— '95 C&L.215 B.Ch.E., J.D. [Ⓐ Jones D.]

Bodi, Robert F. . . . . '64 '00 C&L.8 B.S., J.D. [Ⓐ Pearne&G.]
*PRACTICE AREAS: Patents; Trademarks; Copyrights; Copyright Litigation.

Boehlefeld, Heidi A. . . . . '61 '90 C&L.930 B.S., J.D. [Renner,O.B.&S.]
*PRACTICE AREAS: Patents; Trademarks; Copyrights; Intellectual Property.

Boisselle, Armand P., (AV) . . . . '31 '65 C.455 B.S.Ed. L.930 J.D. [Renner,O.B.&S.]
*PRACTICE AREAS: Patent; Trademark; Copyright and Intellectual Property.

Bolinger, Brian W. . . . . '77 '02 C.851 B.S. L.930 J.D. [Ⓐ Tarolli,S.C.&T.]
*PRACTICE AREAS: Patents.

Bonner, Chet J. . . . . '66 '02 C.610 B.S. L.989 J.D. [Ⓐ Calfee,H.&G.]
*PRACTICE AREAS: Intellectual Property.

Bortnick, Daniel B. . . . . '60 '00 C.161 B.S.E.E. L.1003 J.D. [Ⓐ Amin&T.]

Brandt, Alan C. . . . . '— '01 C.999 B.S. L.124 J.D. [Ⓐ Calfee,H.&G.]
*PRACTICE AREAS: Intellectual Property; Information Technology; Intellectual Property Licensing.

Briggs, Thomas A. . . . . '— '94 C.8 B.S.Ch.E. L.365 J.D. [Jones D.]
*PRACTICE AREAS: Intellectual Property Rights; Intellectual Property Licensing; Strategic Alliances; Joint Ventures; Technology Contracts.

Bulson, Don W., (AV) . . . . '51 '76 C.610 B.S.M.E. L.608 J.D. [Renner,O.B.&S.]
*PRACTICE AREAS: Patent; Trademark; Copyright and Intellectual Property.

Calfee, Halter & Griswold LLP, (AV) BB
1400 McDonald Investment Center, 800 Superior Avenue, 44114-2688 ⊙
Telephone: 216-622-8200 Telecopier: 216-241-0816 Telex: 980499
URL: http://www.calfee.com
Partners: John S. Cipolla; Tracy Scott Johnson; Tara A. Kastelic; Brian E. Kondas; Leonard L. Lewis; Charles B. Lyon; Sean T. Moorhead; John T. Wiedemann. Associates: Chet J. Bonner; Alan C. Brandt; S. Paige Christopher; Diane Hughes Dobrea; Ryan W. Falk; Kristin J. Frost; Warren M. Haines II; Mark R. Hull; William A. Johnston; Stephen L. McCauley; Nenad Pejic; Billy Carter Raulerson; Kenneth J. Smith. Senior Attorneys: Pamela A. Docherty; Mary E. Golrick; John E. Miller, Jr.; Paul E. Szabo; William E. Zitelli (Not admitted in OH).
Antitrust and Trade Regulation, Banking and Bank Regulation, Bankruptcy and Creditors' Rights, Commercial Business and Finance, General Corporate, Corporate Succession Planning, Employee Benefits, Labor and Employment Relations, Environmental, Estate Planning and Administration, Executive Compensation, Federal Government Contracts and Agency Regulation, Franchise Law, Government Relations and Legislation, Healthcare, Information Technology, Intellectual Property and Technology, International, Litigation, Oil and Gas, Partnerships and Joint Ventures, Public Finance, Public Law, Real Estate, Securities, Tax.
Columbus, Ohio Office: 1100 Fifth Third Center, 21 East State Street. Telephone: 614-621-1500. Fax: 614-621-0010.
See Professional Biographies, CLEVELAND, OHIO

Campbell, Jay R. . . . . '62 '89 C.608 B.S.M.E. L.8 J.D. [Renner,O.B.&S.]
*PRACTICE AREAS: Patent; Trademark; Copyright and Intellectual Property.

Christopher, S. Paige . . . . '68 '95 C.228 B.A. L.365 J.D. [Ⓐ Calfee,H.&G.]
*PRACTICE AREAS: Intellectual Property.

Cipolla, John S., (AV) . . . . '63 '89 C.97 B.S. L.161 J.D. [Calfee,H.&G.]
*PRACTICE AREAS: Intellectual Property.

Clark, Kenneth A. . . . . '58 '86 C.161 B.Met.E. L.1003 J.D. [Rankin,H.P.&C.]
*PRACTICE AREAS: Patent Prosecution; Licensing Agreements; Trademarks.

Cochran, David B. . . . . '— '96 C.339 B.S. L.161 J.D. [Ⓒ Jones D.]

Cooper, Lorri W. . . . . '— '95 C.1048 B.S. L.184 J.D. [Ⓐ Jones D.]

Cornely, John P. . . . . '68 '95 C.363 B.S. L.608 J.D. [Fay,S.F.M.&M.]
*PRACTICE AREAS: Patent Prosecution; Trademark; Copyright; Mechanical, Optical, Electrical and Software Arts.

Corpus, Deborah . . . . *'— '00 C.112 B.S. L.124 J.D. [Amin&T.]*

Corso, Joseph J. . . . . '42 '69 C.610 B.S.Ch.E. L.8 J.D. [Pearne&G.]
*PRACTICE AREAS: Patent; Trademark; Copyright; Trade Secret; Unfair Competition.

Couhig, Stephanie S. . . . . '— '02 C.201 B.S.C.E. L.602 J.D. [Ⓐ Jones D.]

Covell, Calvin G., (AV) . . . . '36 '66 C.477 B.S.M.E. L.276 J.D. [Tarolli,S.C.&T.]
*PRACTICE AREAS: Patent; Trademark.

Daniels, E. Kent, Jr., (AV) . . . . '32 '59 C.923 B.S.M.E. L.273 LL.B. [Ⓒ Fay,S.F.M.&M.]
*PRACTICE AREAS: Patent; Trademark; Unfair Competition; Mechanical and Electrical Arts.

Deioma, David B., (AV) . . . . '40 '65 C.930 B.S.E.S. L.276 J.D. [Pearne&G.]
*PRACTICE AREAS: Patent; Trademark; Copyright; Trade Secret; Unfair Competition.

Del Col, John J. . . . . '63 '98 C.608 B.S.M.E. L.850 J.D. [Ⓐ Renner,O.B.&S.]
*PRACTICE AREAS: Intellectual Property; Patent; Trademark; Copyright.

Digges, Randolph E., III, (BV) . . . . '64 '92 C.608 B.A. L.851 J.D. [Rankin,H.P.&C.]
*PRACTICE AREAS: Patent Prosecution; Patent Litigation; Trademark Prosecution; Trademark Litigation; Copyright Litigation.

Dobrea, Diane Hughes . . . . '64 '94 C&L.124 B.A., J.D. [Ⓐ Calfee,H.&G.]
*PRACTICE AREAS: Intellectual Property; Technology Transfer; Biotechnology Licensing; Biotechnology; Biotechnology Patent Prosecution.

Docherty, Pamela A. . . . . '44 '94 C.903 B.S. L.8 J.D. [Ⓐ Calfee,H.&G.]
*PRACTICE AREAS: Intellectual Property.

Dreher, Joseph D. . . . . '65 '91 C.201 B.E.E. L.930 J.D. [Fay,S.F.M.&M.]
*PRACTICE AREAS: Patent; Trademark; Copyright; Domain Names; Internet Law.

Ducatman, Robert P., (AV) . . . . '— '80 C&L.161 B.A., J.D. [Jones D.]
*PRACTICE AREAS: Intellectual Property; Covenants Not To Compete; Patent Infringement; Trademark Infringement.

DuChez, Neil A., (AV) . . . . '46 '72 C.251 B.Ch.E. L.161 J.D. [Renner,O.B.&S.]
*PRACTICE AREAS: Patent; Trademark; Copyright and Intellectual Property.

Dugan, Matthew P. . . . . '67 '00 C.980 B.E.M.E. L.989 J.D. [Ⓐ Fay,S.F.M.&M.]
*PRACTICE AREAS: Patent and Trademark Prosecution; Mechanical and Electro-Mechanical Arts.

Fafrak, Kenneth W., Jr. . . . . '64 '03 C.161 B.E.E. L.989 J.D. [Ⓐ Renner,O.B.&S.]
*PRACTICE AREAS: Patents; Trademarks; Copyrights; Intellectual Property.

Fagan, Christopher B., (AV) . . . . '37 '65 C.602 B.S.M.E. L.276 J.D. [Ⓒ Fay,S.F.M.&M.]
*PRACTICE AREAS: Patent; Trademark; Copyright; Litigation.

Falk, Ryan W. . . . . '77 '03 C.8 B.S. L.930 J.D. [Ⓐ Calfee,H.&G.]
*PRACTICE AREAS: Intellectual Property; Information Technology.

Fay, Regan J., (AV) . . . . '— '74 C.456 B.S. L.273 J.D. [Jones D.]
*PRACTICE AREAS: Intellectual Property; Patent Litigation; Trademark Litigation.

Fay, Sharpe, Fagan, Minnich & McKee, LLP, (AV) BB
1100 Superior Avenue, Seventh Floor, 44114
Telephone: 216-861-5582 FAX: 216-241-1666
Email: fs@faysharpe.com URL: http://www.faysharpe.com
Members of Firm: Mark E. Bandy; John P. Cornely; Joseph D. Dreher; Jude A. Fry; Steven M. Haas; Michael E. Hudzinski; Richard M. Klein; Thomas E. Kocovsky, Jr.; Sandra M. Koenig; Scott Andrew McCollister; Jay F. Moldovanyi; Philip J. Moy, Jr.; Timothy E. Nauman; Patrick R. Roche; James E. Scarbrough; Ann M. Skerry; Mark S. Svat; Brian E. Turung; Robert V. Vickers. Associates: Matthew P. Dugan; Patrick D. Floyd; Karl William Hauber; Eric M. Highman; Erik J. Overberger†; Sue Ellen Phillips; Robert A. Sidoti; Robert M. Sieg; Scott M. Slaby; Joseph E. Waters†; Jeffrey N. Zahn; Marina V. Zalevsky; John S. Zanghi. Of Counsel: E. Kent Daniels, Jr.; Christopher B. Fagan; James W. McKee; Richard J. Minnich; Thomas E. Young.
Providing a complete range of Domestic and International Intellectual Property Law services including Patents, Trademarks, Copyrights, Trade Secrets, Licensing Matters, Unfair Competition Law and Litigation.
†Member: Cleveland, Ohio State and American Bar Associations; Cleveland Intellectual Property Law Association; American Intellectual Property Law Association.
See Professional Biographies, CLEVELAND, OHIO

Feeling, F. Drexel . . . . '— '95 C.659 B.S. L.608 J.D. [Jones D.]
*PRACTICE AREAS: Intellectual Property Rights; Patent Prosecution; Patent Litigation; International Patent Prosecution; Electrical Patent Prosecution.

Fernengel, Gregory . . . . '75 '03 C.608 B.S. L.124 J.D. [Ⓐ Pearne&G.]
*PRACTICE AREAS: Intellectual Property; Patents; Trademarks; Copyrights; Litigation.

Fishman, Aaron A. . . . . '72 '99 C&L.851 J.D. [Pearne&G.]
*PRACTICE AREAS: Patents; Trademarks; Copyrights.

Fistek, Thomas G. . . . . '76 '04 C.446 B.S.M.E. L.989 J.D. [Ⓐ Renner,O.B.&S.]
*PRACTICE AREAS: Patents; Trademarks; Copyrights; Intellectual Property.

Floyd, Patrick D. . . . . '63 '93 C.150 B.S.E.E. L.851 J.D. [Ⓐ Fay,S.F.M.&M.]
*PRACTICE AREAS: Patents; Trademarks; Copyrights; Electrical and Mechanical Arts.

Franz, Paul E. . . . . '— '99 C.579 B.S.E.E. L.988 J.D. [Ⓐ Jones D.]

Frost, Kristin J. . . . . '72 '01 C.1347 B.S. L.608 J.D. [Ⓐ Calfee,H.&G.]
*PRACTICE AREAS: Intellectual Property.

Fry, Jude A. . . . . '61 '91 C.980 B.E. L.1003 J.D. [Fay,S.F.M.&M.]
*PRACTICE AREAS: Patent; Trademark; Copyright; Litigation; Chemical Arts.

Gagnon, Suzanne B. . . . . '— '00 C.201 B.E.E. L.608 J.D. [Ⓐ Pearne&G.]
*PRACTICE AREAS: Patents; Trademarks; Copyrights.

Galin, M. David . . . . '68 '96 C.277 B.E.E. L.930 J.D. [Renner,O.B.&S.]
*PRACTICE AREAS: Patent; Trademark; Copyright; Intellectual Property.

Garvey, Michael W. . . . . '62 '91 C.602 B.S.E.E. L.945 J.D. [Pearne&G.]
*PRACTICE AREAS: Patents; Trademarks; Prosecution and Appeals; Intellectual Property.

Golrick, Mary E., (BV) . . . . '57 '85 C.161 B.S. L.1003 J.D. [Ⓐ Calfee,H.&G.]
*PRACTICE AREAS: Intellectual Property.

Gordon, Charles B., (AV) . . . . '22 '50 C.674 B.S.E. L.309 LL.B. [Pearne&G.]
*PRACTICE AREAS: Patent; Trademark; Copyright; Trade Secret; Unfair Competition.

Griffith, Calvin P. . . . . '— '88 C&L.608 B.S., J.D. [Jones D.]
*PRACTICE AREAS: Intellectual Property; Patent Infringement; Intellectual Property Licensing.

Haas, Steven M. . . . . '69 '94 C.150 B.S.C.S. L.8 J.D. [Fay,S.F.M.&M.]
*PRACTICE AREAS: Patent and Trademark Prosecution; Litigation; Mechanical and Computer Arts; Fluid Dispensing Systems; Automotive Engine and Drivetrain Systems.

Hackwelder, Scott W. . . . . '— '04 C.228 B.S.E.E. L.823 J.D. [Ⓐ Jones D.]

Haines, Warren M., II . . . . '— '95 C.378 B.S. L.229 J.D. [Ⓐ Calfee,H.&G.]
*PRACTICE AREAS: Intellectual Property.

Hale, Jeffrey D. '65 '97 C.502 B.S.E.E. L.1218 J.D.
(adm. in NY; not adm. in OH) [Amin&T.]

Harris, Christopher P. . . . . '65 '97 C.1109 B.S.E.E. L.1003 J.D. [Tarolli,S.C.&T.]
*PRACTICE AREAS: Patents; Trademarks; Copyrights; Licensing.

Hauber, Karl William . . . . '63 '01 C.161 B.I.E. L.989 J.D. [Ⓐ Fay,S.F.M.&M.]
*PRACTICE AREAS: Patent and Trademark Prosecution; Copyright; Mechanical Arts.

Heinke, Lowell L., (AV) . . . . '32 '60 C.124 B.S. L.273 LL.B. [Ⓒ Pearne&G.]
*PRACTICE AREAS: Intellectual Property; Patents; Trademarks.

Highman, Eric M. . . . . '62 '97 C.161 B.S. L.1003 J.D. [Ⓐ Fay,S.F.M.&M.]
*PRACTICE AREAS: Patent Preparation and Prosecution; Validity Opinions; Microprocessor Electrical Systems; Firmware and Software; Power Systems.

Hill, Stephen A., (AV) . . . . '47 '74 C.453 B.S. L.930 J.D. [Rankin,H.P.&C.] ⊙
*PRACTICE AREAS: Patent, Trademark and Copyright.

Hinton, Jennifer Nock . . . . '66 '98 C.150 B.S.E.E. L.930 J.D. [Ⓐ Watts H.]
*PRACTICE AREAS: Intellectual Property; Patents; Trademarks; Copyrights; Computers and Software.

Hlavka, John R. . . . . '49 '76 C.930 B.S.M.E. L.1003 J.D. [Watts H.]
*PRACTICE AREAS: Intellectual Property; Patents; Trademarks; Copyrights; Litigation.

Hochberg, D. Peter, (AV) . . . . '— '69 C.188 B.M.E. L.276 J.D. [D.P.Hochberg]
*PRACTICE AREAS: Patents; Trademarks; Copyrights; Unfair Competition; Trade Secrets.

Hochberg, D. Peter, Co., L.P.A., (AV)
Baker Building, Sixth Floor, 1940 East Sixth Street, 44114
Telephone: 216-771-3800 Fax: 216-771-3804 1-800-776-8166
Email: dphochberg@aol.com
D. Peter Hochberg;—Katherine R. Vieyra; Sean F. Mellino. Of Counsel: Piero G. Ruffinengo (Not admitted in OH); James A. Rich (Not admitted in OH).
Patent, Trademark, Copyright, Unfair Competition and Trade Secrets Law, Trials.
See Professional Biographies, CLEVELAND, OHIO

Hudak, James A., (AV) '40 '74 C.124 B.S.E.E. L.1003 J.D.
29425 Chagrin Boulevard, Suite 304, 44122-4602
Telephone: 216-292-3900 Fax: 216-292-3930
Email: hudakjames@aol.com

(This Listing Continued)

Hudak, James A. (Continued)

Patent, Trademark, Copyright and Unfair Competition Law.

See Professional Biographies, CLEVELAND, OHIO

Hudzinski, Michael E. . . . .'61 '89 C.161 B.E.E. L.1003 J.D. [Fay,S.F.M.&M.]
*PRACTICE AREAS: Patent; Trademark; Copyright; Electrical and Mechanical Arts.

Hull, Mark R. . . . .'68 '04 C.645 B.S. L.8 J.D. [Ⓐ Calfee,H.&G.]
*PRACTICE AREAS: Intellectual Property.

Jacobs, Christopher B. . . . . '69 '95 C&L.608 B.S.M.E., J.D. [Renner,O.B.&S.]
*PRACTICE AREAS: Patents; Trademarks; Copyrights; Intellectual Property.

Johnson, Mark C. . . . . '74 '00 C.436 B.E. L.124 J.D. [Ⓐ Renner,O.B.&S.]
*PRACTICE AREAS: Patents; Trademarks; Copyrights; Intellectual Property.

Johnson, Tracy Scott . . . .'63 '95 C.871 B.S. L.1338 J.D. [Calfee,H.&G.]
*PRACTICE AREAS: Litigation; Intellectual Property; Intellectual Property Litigation; Intellectual Property Enforcement; Intellectual Property Infringement.

Johnston, William A. . . . . '66 '99 C.645 B.S. L.989 J.D. [Ⓐ Calfee,H.&G.]
*PRACTICE AREAS: Intellectual Property; Patents; Trademark Prosecution.

Jones Day, (AV)
North Point, 901 Lakeside Avenue, 44114-1190 ⊙
Telephone: 216-586-3939 Telecopier: 216-579-0212
Email: counsel@jonesday.com URL: http://www.jonesday.com
Languages: Chinese (Mandarin), French, German, Greek, Hindi, Japanese, Lithuanian, Portuguese and Spanish.
Members of Firm: Kenneth R. Adamo; Thomas A. Briggs; Robert P. Ducatman; Regan J. Fay; F. Drexel Feeling; Calvin P. Griffith; Robert C. Kahrl; Timothy J. O'Hearn; Joseph D. Pollack; Michael W. Vary; James L. Wamsley, III. Of Counsel: David B. Cochran; Richard H. Sayler. Counsel: Leozino Agozzino; Stephen D. Scanlon; H. Duane Switzer. Associates: Michael R. Asam; John V. Biernacki; Lorri W. Cooper; Stephanie S. Couhig; Paul E. Franz; Scott W. Hackwelder; Karl M. Maersch; David M. Maiorana; Isaac A. Molnar; Theodore C. Parsons; Joseph M. Sauer; Jenny L. Sheaffer.
Patent, Trademark and Copyright Law.
In Columbus, Ohio: 325 John H. McConnell Boulevard, Suite 600. Telephone: 614-469-3939. Telecopier: 614-461-4198.
In Atlanta, Georgia: 1420 Peachtree Street, N.E., Suite 800. Telephone: 404-521-3939. Telecopier: 404-581-8330.
In Beijing, China: 3201 China World Tower 1, No. 1 Jianguomenwai Avenue. Telephone: 86-10-5866-1111. Telecopier: 86-10-5866-1122.
In Brussels, Belgium: Boulevard Brand Whitlocklaan 165, 1200 Brussels. Telephone: 32-2-645-14-11. Telecopier: 32-2-645-14-45.
In Chicago, Illinois: 77 West Wacker. Telephone: 312-782-3939. Telecopier: 312-782-8585.
In Dallas, Texas: 2727 North Harwood Street. Telephone: 214-220-3939. Telecopier: 214-969-5100.
In Frankfurt, Germany: Hochhaus am Park, Grüneburgweg 102, 60323 Frankfurt am Main. Telephone: 49-69-9726-3939. Telecopier: 49-69-9726-3993.
In Hong Kong, China: 31st Floor, Edinburgh Tower, The Landmark, 15 Queen's Road, Central. Telephone: 852-2526-6895. Telecopier: 852-2868-5871.
In Houston, Texas: 717 Texas, Suite 3300. Telephone: 832-239-3939. Telecopier: 832-239-3600.
In Irvine, California: 3 Park Plaza, Suite 1100. Telephone: 949-851-3939. Telecopier: 949-553-7539.
In London, England: 21 Tudor Street. Telephone: 44-20-7039-5959. Telecopier: 44-20-7039-5999.
In Los Angeles, California: 555 South Flower Street, Fiftieth Floor. Telephone: 213-489-3939. Telecopier: 213-243-2539.
In Madrid, Spain: Velázquez 51, 4th Floor. Telephone: 34-91-520-39-39. Telecopier: 34-91-520-39-38.
In Menlo Park, California: 2882 Sand Hill Road, Suite 240. Telephone: 650-739-3939. Telecopier: 650-739-3900.
In Milan, Italy: Via Turati, 16/18. Telephone: 39-02-7645-4001. Telecopier: 39-02-7645-4400.
In Moscow, Russia: Smolenskaya Square 3, 9th Floor, 121099 Moscow. Telephone: 7-095-980-6769. Telecopier: 7-095-980-6765.
In Munich, Germany: Prinzregentenstr. 11, 80538 Munich. Telephone: 089-20 60 42-200. Telecopier: 089-20 60 42-293.
In New York, New York: 222 East 41st Street. Telephone: 212-326-3939. Telecopier: 212-755-7306.
In Paris, France: 120, rue du Faubourg Saint-Honoré. Telephone: 33-1-56-59-39-39. Telecopier: 33-1-56-59-39-38.
In Pittsburgh, Pennsylvania: 500 Grant Street, One Mellon Bank Center, 31st Floor. Telephone: 412-391-3939. Telecopier: 412-394-7959.
In San Diego, California: 12750 High Bluff Drive, Suite 300. Telephone: 858-314-1200. Telecopier: 858-314-1150.
In San Francisco, California: 555 California Street, 26th Floor. Telephone: 415-626-3939. Telecopier: 415-875-5700.
In Shanghai, China: 30th Floor, Shanghai Kerry Centre, 1515 Nanjing Road West. Telephone: 86-21-2201-8000. Telecopier: 86-21-5298-6569.
In Singapore, Singapore: 30 Cecil Street, #29-01 Prudential Tower. Telephone: 65 6 538 3939. Telecopier: 65 6 536 3939.
In Sydney, Australia: Australia Square, Level 38, 264-278 George Street. Telephone: 61-2-8272-0500. Telecopier: 61-2-8272-0599.
In Taipei, Taiwan: 6th Floor, 2 Tun Hwa South Road, Section 2. Telephone: (886-2) 2704-6808 or (886-2) 7712-3399. Telecopier: (886-2) 2704-6791.
In Tokyo, Japan: Shiroyama MT Building, 6th Floor, 1-17 Toranomon 4-chome, Minato-ku, Tokyo 105-0001. Telephone: 81-3-3433-3939. Telecopier: 81-3-5401-2725.
In Washington, D.C.: 51 Louisiana Avenue, N.W. Telephone: 202-879-3939. Telecopier: 202-626-1700.

See Professional Biographies, CLEVELAND, OHIO

Jorgenson, Eric D. . . . . '51 '02 C.491 B.A. L.1363 J.D. [Amin&T.]

Kachmarik, Ronald M. . . . .'63 '94 C.8 B.S. L.1003 J.D. [Pearne&G.]
*PRACTICE AREAS: Intellectual Property; Patent; Trademark.

Kahrl, Robert C., (AV) . . . . '— '75 C.674 A.B. L.608 J.D. [Jones D.]
*PRACTICE AREAS: Intellectual Property; Intellectual Property Litigation; Electronic Intellectual Property.

Kastelic, Tara A. . . . . '65 '91 C&L.851 B.S.C.S.E., J.D. [Calfee,H.&G.]
*PRACTICE AREAS: Information Technology; Intellectual Property.

Kinder, Gordon D., (AV) . . . . '48 '77 C&L.930 B.S.M.E., J.D. [Renner,O.B.&S.]
*PRACTICE AREAS: Patent; Trademark; Copyright and Intellectual Property.

Klein, Richard M. . . . . '58 '85 C.608 B.S. L.930 J.D. [Fay,S.F.M.&M.]
*PRACTICE AREAS: Patent Litigation; Patent, Trademark and Copyright Prosecution; Chemical Arts; Biotechnology; Mechanical Arts.

Kocovsky, Thomas E., Jr. . . . . '47 '75 C.188 B.S. L.273 J.D. [Fay,S.F.M.&M.]
*PRACTICE AREAS: Patent; Trademark; Copyright; Electrical Arts.

Koenig, Sandra M. . . . .'60 '87 C.161 B.Ch.E. L.1003 J.D. [Fay,S.F.M.&M.]
*PRACTICE AREAS: Patent; Trademark; Copyright; Litigation.

Kondas, Brian E. . . . .'65 '95 C.477 B.S.E.E. L.1003 J.D. [Calfee,H.&G.]
*PRACTICE AREAS: Intellectual Property.

Korff, Christopher . . . .'66 '03 C.688 B.S. L.124 J.D. [Ⓐ Rankin,H.P.&C.]
*PRACTICE AREAS: Patent Prosecution; Trademark Prosecution.

Lewis, Leonard L. . . . . '54 '84 C.602 B.S.E.E. L.161 J.D. [Calfee,H.&G.]
*PRACTICE AREAS: Intellectual Property.

Lightbody, William S. '50 '77 C.81 B.S. L.569 J.D.
32600 Fairmount Boulevard, Atrium Suite, 100, 44124
Telephone: 216-621-7337 Fax: 216-621-7393
URL: http://www.williamlightbodylaw.com
Litigation, Intellectual Property, Patent, Trademark, Copyright, Unfair Competition, Trade Secrets.

See Professional Biographies, CLEVELAND, OHIO

Ling, Daniel R. . . . .'78 '03 C.477 B.S.C.E. L.124 J.D. [Ⓐ Renner,O.B.&S.]
*PRACTICE AREAS: Patents; Trademarks; Copyrights; Intellectual Property.

Lipcsik, Robert N. . . . .'65 '96 C.930 B.S.M.E. L.989 J.D. [Ⓐ Tarolli,S.C.&T.]
*PRACTICE AREAS: Patents; Trademarks.

Lyon, Charles B., (AV) . . . . '44 '71 C.623 B.S.M.E. L.273 J.D. [Calfee,H.&G.]
*PRACTICE AREAS: Intellectual Property.

Maersch, Karl M. . . . . '— '02 C.679 B.S.M.E. L.365 J.D. [Ⓐ Jones D.]

Maiorana, David M. . . . .'— '99 C.893 B.S. L.904 J.D. [Ⓐ Jones D.]

Manning, Timothy E. . . . .'67 '98 C.363 B.S. L.1003 J.D. [Ⓐ Renner,O.B.&S.]
*PRACTICE AREAS: Patents; Trademarks; Copyrights; Intellectual Property.

McCauley, Stephen L. . . . .'60 '93 C.381 B.S. L.608 J.D. [Ⓐ Calfee,H.&G.]
*PRACTICE AREAS: Intellectual Property.

McCollister, Scott Andrew . . . . '64 '89 C.679 B.S. L.930 J.D. [Fay,S.F.M.&M.]
*PRACTICE AREAS: Patent; Trademark; Copyright; Trade Secrets; Chemical Arts.

McKee, James W., (AV) . . . . '42 '69 C.1229 B.M.E. L.930 J.D. [Ⓒ Fay,S.F.M.&M.]
*PRACTICE AREAS: Patent; Trademark; Copyright; Mechanical Arts.

Mellino, Sean F. . . . .'76 '01 C.216 B.S. L.124 J.D. [Ⓐ D.P.Hochberg]
*PRACTICE AREAS: Patent Law; Trademark Law.

Miller, John E., Jr. . . . . '44 '70 C.679 B.S.Chem.E. L.276 J.D. [Ⓐ Calfee,H.&G.]
*PRACTICE AREAS: Intellectual Property.

Minnich, Richard J., (AV) . . . .'33 '65 C.381 B.S. L.1003 J.D. [Ⓒ Fay,S.F.M.&M.]
*PRACTICE AREAS: Patent; Trademark; Copyright; Licensing and Litigation; International Licensing.

Moldovanyi, Jay F., (AV) . . . .'48 '79 C.930 B.S.M.E. L.608 J.D. [Fay,S.F.M.&M.]
*PRACTICE AREAS: Patent; Trademark; Copyright; Litigation.

Molnar, Isaac A. . . . . '— '99 C&L.608 B.Sc., J.D. [Ⓐ Jones D.]

Moore, James M., (AV) . . . .'48 '88 C.8 B.S.E.E. L.1003 J.D. [Pearne&G.]
*PRACTICE AREAS: Patent; Trademark; Copyright; Trade Secret; Unfair Competition.

Moorhead, Sean T. . . . . '64 '93 C.477 B.S.E. L.608 J.D. [Calfee,H.&G.]
*PRACTICE AREAS: Intellectual Property; Patent Prosecution; Patent Litigation; Trademark; Copyright.

Moy, Philip J., Jr., (BV) . . . .'54 '84 C.197 A.B. L.273 J.D. [Fay,S.F.M.&M.]
*PRACTICE AREAS: Patent; Trademark; Copyright; Licensing; Litigation.

Murphy, Cynthia S. . . . .'60 '88 C.277 B.M.E. L.1003 J.D. [Renner,O.B.&S.]
*PRACTICE AREAS: Intellectual Property; Patent; Trademark and Copyright.

Murtaugh, John P., (AV) . . . . '52 '78 C.602 B.A. L.477 J.D. [Pearne&G.]
*PRACTICE AREAS: Patent; Trademark; Copyright; Trade Secrets; Intellectual Property Litigation.

Nauman, Timothy E. . . . . '58 '83 C.602 B.S.C.E. L.201 J.D. [Fay,S.F.M.&M.]
*PRACTICE AREAS: Patent; Trademark; Copyright; Mechanical and Electro-Mechanical Arts; Preparation and Prosecution.

O'Hearn, Timothy J. . . . . '— '84 C.150 B.S.M.E. L.8 J.D. [Jones D.]
*PRACTICE AREAS: Intellectual Property; Intellectual Property Portfolio Management; Trademarks.

Otto, Donald L., (AV) . . . . '36 '64 C.350 B.S.M.E. L.273 LL.B. [Renner,O.B.&S.]
*PRACTICE AREAS: Patent; Trademark; Copyright and Intellectual Property.

Overberger, Erik J. . . . .'73 '00 C.610 B.S.M.E. L.117 J.D. [Ⓐ Fay,S.F.M.&M.]
*PRACTICE AREAS: Patent; Trademark; Copyright; Mechanical Arts.

Parsons, Theodore C. . . . .'72 '98 C.608 B.S. L.228 J.D. [Ⓐ Jones D.]

Pearne & Gordon LLP, (AV)
1801 East 9th Street Suite 1200, 44114-3108
Telephone: 216-579-1700 Facsimile: 216-579-6073
Email: ip@pearnegordon.com URL: http://www.pearnegordon.com
Members of Firm: Charles B. Gordon; Thomas P. Schiller; David B. Deioma; Joseph J. Corso; Howard G. Shimola; Jeffrey J. Sopko; John P. Murtaugh; James M. Moore; Michael W. Garvey; Richard A. Sharpe; Ronald M. Kachmarik; Paul A. Serbinowski; Brian G. Bembenick; Aaron A. Fishman. Associates: Stephen S. Wentsler; Robert F. Bodi; Suzanne B. Gagnon; Una Schumacher; Steven J. Solomon; Gregory Fernengel. Of Counsel: Lowell L. Heinke; Thaddeus A. Zalenski (Not admitted in OH).
Patent, Trademark, Copyright, Trade Secret, Unfair Competition, and Related Intellectual Property Law.

See Professional Biographies, CLEVELAND, OHIO

Pejic, Nenad . . . . '67 '96 C.608 B.S. L.161 J.D. [Ⓐ Calfee,H.&G.]
*PRACTICE AREAS: Intellectual Property; Electrical Intellectual Property; Electronic Intellectual Property; Intellectual Property Litigation; Intellectual Property Procurement.

Phillips, Sue Ellen . . . .'58 '85 C.610 B.S. L.1003 J.D. [Ⓐ Fay,S.F.M.&M.]
*PRACTICE AREAS: Patent; Trademark; Copyright; Chemical Arts.

Pinchak, George L., Jr., (AV) . . . .'56 '91 C.161 B.I.E. L.1003 J.D. [Watts H.]
*PRACTICE AREAS: Intellectual Property; Patents; Trademarks; Copyrights; Litigation.

Pingor, James J. . . . .'66 '98 C.665 B.S. L.117 J.D. [Ⓐ Amin&T.]

Pitzer, Gary J. . . . . '69 '95 C.608 B.S.E.E. L.472 J.D. [Tarolli,S.C.&T.]
*PRACTICE AREAS: Patents; Trademarks; Trade Secrets; Licensing.

Platt, Jonathan A. . . . .'61 '97 C&L.930 B.S., J.D. [Renner,O.B.&S.]
*PRACTICE AREAS: Patents; Trademarks; Copyrights; Intellectual Property.

Pollack, Joseph D. . . . .'— '84 C.97 B.B.A. L.8 J.D. [Jones D.]
*PRACTICE AREAS: Intellectual Property; Patent Litigation; Trade Secrets.

Porter, Wayne D., Jr., (AV) . . . .'47 '75 C.923 B.S.A.E. L.276 J.D. [Rankin,H.P.&C.]
*PRACTICE AREAS: Patent, Trademark and Copyright; Trade Secret and Unfair Competition; Licensing and Litigation.

Rankin, Hill, Porter & Clark LLP, (AV) BR
925 Euclid Avenue, Suite 700, 44115-1405 ⊙
Telephone: 216-566-9700 Fax: 216-566-9711
Email: info@rankinhill.com URL: http://www.rankinhill.com
Members of Firm: Stephen A. Hill; Wayne D. Porter, Jr.; Kenneth A. Clark; David E. Spaw; Randolph E. Digges, III. Associates: James A. Balazs; Christopher Korff.
Patent, Trademark, Copyright, Unfair Competition Law and Antitrust Law.
Lake County, Ohio Office: 4080 Erie Street, 44094-7836. Telephone: 216-566-9700. Fax: 216-566-9711.

See Professional Biographies, CLEVELAND, OHIO

Raulerson, Billy Carter . . . .'70 '01 C.1111 B.S.C.S. L.201 J.D. [Ⓐ Calfee,H.&G.]
*PRACTICE AREAS: Intellectual Property; Information Technology.

Renner, John W., (AV) . . . .'29 '54 C.81 B.S. L.930 LL.B. [Ⓒ Renner,O.B.&S.]
*PRACTICE AREAS: Patent; Trademark; Copyright and Intellectual Property.

Renner, Otto, Boisselle & Sklar, LLP, (AV) BR
Nineteenth Floor, 1621 Euclid Avenue, 44115-2183
Telephone: 216-621-1113 Fax: 216-621-6165
Email: mailroom@rennerotto.com URL: http://www.rennerotto.com
Members of Firm: Donald L. Otto; Armand P. Boisselle; Warren A. Sklar; Neil A. DuChez; Don W. Bulson; Gordon D. Kinder; Jay R. Campbell; Mark D. Saralino; Cynthia S. Murphy; Christopher B. Jacobs; Jonathan A. Platt; Heidi A. Boehlefeld; Thomas W. Adams; M. David Galin; Todd R. Tucker. Associates: John J. Del Col; Jason A. Worgull; Mark C. Johnson; Kenneth W. Fafrak, Jr.; Daniel R. Ling; Timothy E. Manning; Marisa J. Zink; Thomas G. Fistek; Michele M. Tyrpak. Of Counsel: John W. Renner.
Patent, Trademark, Copyright, Unfair Competition and Related Antitrust Law.

See Professional Biographies, CLEVELAND, OHIO

Rich, James A. '38 '71 C.688 B.S.M.E. L.276 J.D.
(adm. in NY; not adm. in OH) [Ⓒ D.P.Hochberg]
*PRACTICE AREAS: Patents; Trademarks; Trade Secrets; Intellectual Property Agreements.

Roche, Patrick R., (AV) . . . . '52 '78 C.602 B.S.E.E. L.1003 J.D. [Fay,S.F.M.&M.]
*PRACTICE AREAS: Patent; Trademark; Copyright; Electrical Arts.

Ruffinengo, Piero G. '44 '75 C.37 B.S. L.878 J.D.
(adm. in UT; not adm. in OH) [Ⓒ D.P.Hochberg]

Sadlowski, Jeffrey R. . . . .'63 '90 C.192 B.S. L.161 J.D. [Amin&T.]

Saralino, Mark D. . . . . '61 '89 C&L.7 B.S.E.E., J.D. [Renner,O.B.&S.]
*PRACTICE AREAS: Patent; Trademark; Copyright and Intellectual Property.

Sauer, Joseph M. . . . . '— '99 C.923 B.S.E.E. L.229 J.D. [Ⓐ Jones D.]

Sayler, Richard H., (AV) . . . . '— '70 C.197 A.B. L.477 J.D. [Ⓒ Jones D.]
*PRACTICE AREAS: Litigation; Complex Business Litigation; Appellate Practice; Commercial Arbitration.

Scanlon, Stephen D. . . . .'— '85 C.567 B.S. L.150 J.D. [Ⓒ Jones D.]

Scarbrough, James E. . . . .'64 '97 C.645 B.S.M.E. L.930 J.D. [Fay,S.F.M.&M.]
*PRACTICE AREAS: Patent Prosecution; Patent Opinions; Mechanical Arts; Trademark; Copyright.

Schenck, Brett A. . . . . '64 '92 C.679 B.S.E.E. L.879 J.D. [Ⓐ Tarolli,S.C.&T.]
*PRACTICE AREAS: Patents (89%); Trademarks (10%); Copyrights (1%).

Schiller, Thomas P., (AV) .... '34 '60 C.124 B.S. L.930 J.D. [Pearne&G.]
*PRACTICE AREAS: Patent; Trademark; Copyright; Trade Secret; Unfair Competition.
Schultz, Stephen J. .... '50 '77 C.1044 B.S. L.966 J.D. [Watts H.]
*PRACTICE AREAS: Intellectual Property; Patents; Trademarks; Copyrights; Computers and Software.
Schumacher, Una .... '— '02 C.473 L.989 J.D. [[A] Pearne&G.]
*PRACTICE AREAS: Patents; Trademarks; Copyrights.
Serbinowski, Paul A. .... '67 '94 C.24 B.S.C.E. L.1338 J.D. [Pearne&G.]
*PRACTICE AREAS: Intellectual Property; Patents; Trademarks; Copyrights; Chemistry.
Shaheen, Matthew M. .... '68 '97 C&L.8 B.S.M.T., J.D. [Tarolli,S.C.&T.]
*PRACTICE AREAS: Patents; Trademarks.
Sharifi, Vahid '— '00 C.597 M.S. L.424 J.D.
(adm. in IL; not adm. in OH) [[A] Amin&T.]
Sharpe, Richard A., (AV) .... '65 '92 C.631 B.S. L.904 J.D. [Pearne&G.]
*PRACTICE AREAS: Intellectual Property; Patents; Trademarks; Copyrights; Litigation.
Sheaffer, Jenny L. .... '— '98 C.565 B.S. L.823 J.D. [[A] Jones D.]
Shimola, Howard G., (AV) .... '42 '70 C.124 B.S.M.E. L.1003 J.D. [Pearne&G.]
*PRACTICE AREAS: Patent; Trademark; Copyright; Trade Secret; Unfair Competition.
Sidoti, Robert A. .... '71 '98 C.37 B.S.M.E. L.1003 J.D. [[A] Fay,S.F.M.&M.]
*PRACTICE AREAS: Patent; Trademark; Copyright; Litigation; Mechanical Arts.
Sieg, Robert M. .... '69 '05 C.161 B.S. L.1003 J.D. [[A] Fay,S.F.M.&M.]
*PRACTICE AREAS: General Electrical and Mechanical Arts; Medical Imaging; Optoelectronics and Optical Systems; Computer Software; Computer Data Processing.
Skerry, Ann M. .... '56 '97 C.999 B.Sc. L.930 J.D. [Fay,S.F.M.&M.]
*PRACTICE AREAS: Patent Prosecution; Trademarks; Opinions; Sterilization; Carbon Chemistry.
Sklar, Warren A., (AV) .... '44 '71 C.124 B.S.E.E. L.273 J.D. [Renner,O.B.&S.]
*PRACTICE AREAS: Patent; Trademark; Copyright and Intellectual Property.
Slaby, Scott M. .... '73 '03 C.363 B.S. L.1003 J.D. [[A] Fay,S.F.M.&M.]
*PRACTICE AREAS: Patent; Trademark; Copyright; Trade Secrets; Biochemistry.
Smith, Kenneth J. .... '72 '00 C.851 B.S. L.989 J.D. [[A] Calfee,H.&G.]
*PRACTICE AREAS: Intellectual Property.
Solomon, Steven J. .... '75 '03 [[A] Pearne&G.]
*PRACTICE AREAS: Patents; Trademarks; Copyrights; Intellectual Property Litigation.
Sopko, Jeffrey J., (AV) .... '48 '75 C.201 B.T. L.1003 J.D. [Pearne&G.]
*PRACTICE AREAS: Patent; Trademark; Copyright; Trade Secret; Unfair Competition.
Spaw, David E. .... '65 '91 C.161 B.E.E. L.1003 J.D. [Rankin,H.P.&C.]
*PRACTICE AREAS: Patent; Trademark; Copyright.
Sundheim, Robert B., (AV) .... '36 '64 C.971 B.S. L.215 LL.B. [Tarolli,S.C.&T.]
*PRACTICE AREAS: Patent; Trademark.
Sutkus, Richard A. .... '69 '97 C&L.734 B.S., J.D. [Tarolli,S.C.&T.]
*PRACTICE AREAS: Patents; Trademarks.
Svat, Mark S. .... '59 '89 C.161 B.S.E.T. L.989 J.D. [Fay,S.F.M.&M.]
*PRACTICE AREAS: Patent; Trademark; Copyright; Computer Hardware and Software; Internet.
Switzer, H. Duane .... '— '64 C.474 B.S.C.E. L.276 LL.B. [[C] Jones D.]
Szabo, Paul E., (AV) .... '53 '79 C.722 B.A. L.1003 J.D. [[A] Calfee,H.&G.]
*PRACTICE AREAS: Patent; Trademark.
Tarolli, James L. .... '66 '91 C.608 B.S.M.E. L.930 J.D. [Tarolli,S.C.&T.]
*PRACTICE AREAS: Patent; Trademark.
Tarolli, Thomas L., (AV) .... '35 '61 C.665 B.S. L.273 LL.B. [Tarolli,S.C.&T.]
*PRACTICE AREAS: Patent; Trademark.

Tarolli, Sundheim, Covell & Tummino, L.L.P., (AV)
Leader Building, Suite 111, 526 Superior Avenue, 44114
Telephone: 216-621-2234 Telex: 980209 TSC CLV PAT Facsimile: 216-621-4072
Email: tarolli@tarolli.com URL: http://www.tarolli.com
Members of Firm: Thomas L. Tarolli; Robert B. Sundheim; Calvin G. Covell; Barry L. Tummino; James L. Tarolli; Richard S. Wesorick; Richard A. Sutkus; Matthew M. Shaheen; Gary J. Pitzer; Christopher P. Harris. Associates: Robert N. Lipcsik; Brett A. Schenck; Brian W. Bolinger.
Intellectual Property Law including Patent, Trademark, Copyright and Unfair Competition Law.
See Professional Biographies, CLEVELAND, OHIO

Tucker, Todd R. .... '69 '95 C.352 B.S.E. L.200 J.D. [Renner,O.B.&S.]
*PRACTICE AREAS: Patents; Trademarks; Copyrights; Intellectual Property.
Tummino, Barry L., (BV) .... '50 '80 C&L.161 B.E.S., J.D. [Tarolli,S.C.&T.]
*PRACTICE AREAS: Patent.
Turocy, Gregory .... '63 '91 C.608 B.A. L.469 J.D. [Amin&T.]
Turung, Brian E. .... '63 '91 C.326 B.Ch.E. L.734 J.D. [Fay,S.F.M.&M.]
*PRACTICE AREAS: Patent, Trademark and Copyright Prosecution, Licensing and Litigation; Chemical Arts; Electrical and Mechanical Arts.
Tyrpak, Michele M. .... '65 '96 C.161 B.S. L.989 J.D. [[A] Renner,O.B.&S.]
*PRACTICE AREAS: Patents; Trademarks; Copyrights; Intellectual Property.
Vary, Michael W., (AV) .... '— '82 C.363 B.S. L.930 J.D. [Jones D.]
*PRACTICE AREAS: Intellectual Property; Intellectual Property Litigation; Chemical Patents.
Vickers, Robert V., (AV) .... '34 '61 C.999 B.M.E. L.273 J.D. [Fay,S.F.M.&M.]
*PRACTICE AREAS: Trademark; Unfair Competition; Patent and Trademark Prosecution and Litigation.
Vieyra, Katherine R. .... '52 '95 C.691 B.A. L.124 J.D. [[A] D.P.Hochberg]
*PRACTICE AREAS: Intellectual Property; Trademarks.
Wamsley, James L., III, (AV) .... '— '75 C.893 B.S.E.E. L.477 J.D. [Jones D.]
*PRACTICE AREAS: Intellectual Property; Intellectual Property Litigation; Trade Secrets.
Waters, Joseph E. .... '73 '00 C.363 B.S. L.124 J.D. [[A] Fay,S.F.M.&M.]
*PRACTICE AREAS: Patents; Trademarks; Copyrights; Organic Chemistry; Polymers.

Watts Hoffmann Co., L.P.A., (AV)
Diamond Building, 1100 Superior Avenue East Suite 1750, 44114-2518
Telephone: 216-241-6700 Facsimile: 216-241-8151
Blythe D. Watts (1888-1984); Daniel J. Sammon (1934-1991); Thomas E. Fisher (1926-2005); John R. Hlavka; Stephen J. Schultz; George L. Pinchak, Jr.;—Jennifer Nock Hinton; John A. Yirga.
Intellectual Property Law including Patent, Trademark, Copyright and Unfair Competition Law. Trials and Appeals.
See Professional Biographies, CLEVELAND, OHIO

Wentsler, Stephen S. .... '67 '97 C.150 B.S.M.E. L.823 J.D. [[A] Pearne&G.]
*PRACTICE AREAS: Patents; Intellectual Property.
Wesorick, Richard S. .... '66 '95 C.679 B.S.M.E. L.200 J.D. [Tarolli,S.C.&T.]
*PRACTICE AREAS: Patent; Trademark.
Wiedemann, John T., (AV) .... '52 '77 C.150 B.S. L.608 J.D. [Calfee,H.&G.]
*PRACTICE AREAS: Intellectual Property; Patents; Patent Litigation.
Worgull, Jason A. .... '73 '99 C.363 B.S. L.201 J.D. [[A] Renner,O.B.&S.]
*PRACTICE AREAS: Patents; Trademarks; Copyrights; Intellectual Property.
Yirga, John A. .... '69 '03 C.345 B.S. L.1003 J.D. [[A] Watts H.]
*PRACTICE AREAS: Intellectual Property; Patents; Trademarks; Copyrights; Litigation.
Young, Thomas E., (AV) .... '48 '75 C.608 B.S.E.E. L.930 J.D. [[C] Fay,S.F.M.&M.]
*PRACTICE AREAS: Patent; Trademark; Unfair Competition; Electrical and Mechanical Arts.
Zahn, Jeffrey N. .... '62 '04 C.161 B.S. L.1003 J.D. [[A] Fay,S.F.M.&M.]
*PRACTICE AREAS: Patent Preparation, Prosecution and Counseling; General Electrical Arts; Electronic Controls; Robotics; Systems Navigation Guidance Communications.
Zalenski, Thaddeus A., (AV) '36 '66 C.645 B.S. L.276 J.D.
(adm. in PA; not adm. in OH) [[C] Pearne&G.]
*PRACTICE AREAS: Patents; Trademark; Copyright; Trade Secrets; Unfair Competition.
Zalevsky, Marina V. .... '61 '04 C.999 B.S. L.1003 J.D. [[A] Fay,S.F.M.&M.]
*PRACTICE AREAS: Patent Prosecution and Preparation; Medical Imaging Technology; Machine Vision; Optics and Lighting; Power Systems.
Zanghi, John S. .... '65 '95 C.161 B.E.E. L.8 J.D. [[A] Fay,S.F.M.&M.]
*PRACTICE AREAS: Patent; Trademark; Copyright; Licensing; Electrical and Mechanical Arts.
Zink, Marisa J. .... '75 '01 C.124 B.A. L.8 J.D. [[A] Renner,O.B.&S.]
*PRACTICE AREAS: Patents; Trademarks; Copyrights; Intellectual Property.
Zitelli, William E. '41 '86 C.1494 B.S.E. L.228 J.D.
(adm. in PA; not adm. in OH) [[A] Calfee,H.&G.]
*PRACTICE AREAS: Intellectual Property.

COLUMBUS, 711,470, *Delaware, Fairfield & Franklin Cos.*

Baranowski, Edwin M., (AV) .... '47 '72 C.299 B.A. L.893 J.D. [Porter W.M.&A.]
*PRACTICE AREAS: Patents, Trademarks and Copyrights; Litigation; Technology.
Burke, Diane E. .... '73 '98 C&L.896 B.S., J.D. [[A] Mueller&S.]
*PRACTICE AREAS: Intellectual Property Law; Computer Law.

Hahn Loeser & Parks LLP, (AV)
65 East State Street, Suite 1400, 43215 ⊙
Telephone: 614-221-0240 FAX: 614-221-5909/1-877-HAHNLAW
URL: http://www.hahnlaw.com
Resident Members: Arland T. Stein.
Business, Corporate and Securities, Litigation, Taxation and Employee Benefits, Estate Planning, Probate, Real Estate, Labor, Creditors Rights, Reorganization and Bankruptcy, Intellectual Property and Technology, Environmental, Patent, Trademark and Copyright Law, Telecommunications Law, Government Relations, Public Utility and Regulatory Law, Health Care, Construction Law.
References: County Savings Bank; The Fifth Third Bank of Columbus.
Cleveland, Ohio Office: 3300 BP Tower, 200 Public Square, 44114-2301. Telephone: 216-621-0150. Fax: 216-241-2824.
Akron, Ohio Office: One Gojo Plaza, Suite 300, 44311-1076. Telephone: 330-864-5550. Fax: 330-864-7986.
Naples, Florida Office: 3301 Bonita Beach Road, Suite 308, Bonita Springs, 34134. Telephone: 239-949-6989. Fax: 239-949-6687.
See Professional Biographies, COLUMBUS, OHIO

Jacques, Laurie N. .... '58 '90 C.25 B.S. L.608 J.D. [Porter W.M.&A.]
*PRACTICE AREAS: Patent, Trademark and Copyright Law; Intellectual Property Law.
Martin-Jones, Melanie .... '55 '99 C.608 B.S. L.179 J.D. [[A] Porter W.M.&A.]
*PRACTICE AREAS: Intellectual Property; Technology Transfers; Corporate Law.
Mescher, Richard M. .... '60 '93 C.608 B.S.M.E. L.201 J.D. [Porter W.M.&A.]
*PRACTICE AREAS: Patent Prosecution; Intellectual Property Litigation; Intellectual Property Licensing; Trademark Registration; Technology Contracts.
Mueller, Jerry K., Jr., (AV) .... '48 '73 C.124 B.S.Ch.E. L.608 J.D. [Mueller&S.]
*PRACTICE AREAS: Intellectual Property Law; Computer Law.

Mueller and Smith, A Legal Professional Association, (AV)
Mueller-Smith Building, 7700 Rivers Edge Drive, 43235-1355
Telephone: 614-436-0600 Telecopier: 614-436-0057
Email: patents@muellersmith.com URL: http://www.lawyers.com/muellerandsmith
Jerry K. Mueller, Jr.; Gerald L. Smith;—Diane E. Burke.
Intellectual Property Law including Patents, Trademarks, Copyrights, Licensing, Computer Law, Unfair Competition and International Patent Law. Trial and Appellate Practice in all Courts.
Representative Clients: Ashland Chemical Co.; Damon's International; General Electric Superabrasives; Liebert Corp.; OCLC Online Computer Library Center, Inc.; The Edward Orton, Jr. Ceramic Foundation.
See Professional Biographies, COLUMBUS, OHIO

Porter Wright Morris & Arthur LLP, (AV)
41 South High Street, 43215-6194 ⊙
Telephone: 614-227-2000; (800-533-2794) Fax: 614-227-2100
Email: columbus@porterwright.com URL: http://www.porterwright.com
Members of Firm Columbus, Ohio Office: Edwin M. Baranowski; Richard M. Mescher. Associates Columbus, Ohio Office: Joshua Thomas Elliott; Laurie N. Jacques.
General Practice including Patent, Trademark and Copyright Law.
Cincinnati, Ohio Office: 250 E. Fifth Street, Suite 2200, 45202-5117. Telephones: 513-381-4700; (800-582-5813). Fax: 513-421-0991. Internet: cincinnati@porterwright.com.
Cleveland, Ohio Office: 925 Euclid Avenue, Suite 1700, 44115-1483. Telephones: 216-443-9000; (800-824-1980). Fax: 216-443-9011. Internet: cleveland@porterwright.com.
Dayton, Ohio Office: One Dayton Centre, One South Main Street, Suite 1600, 45402-2028. Telephones: 937-449-6810; (800-533-4434). Fax: 937-449-6820. Internet: dayton@porterwright.com.
Naples, Florida Office: 5801 Pelican Bay Boulevard, Suite 300, 34108-2709. Telephones: 239-593-2900; (800-876-7962). Fax: 239-593-2990. Internet: naples@porterwright.com.
Washington, D.C. Office: 1919 Pennsylvania Avenue, N.W., Suite 500, 20006-3434. Telephones: 202-778-3000; (800-456-7962). Fax: 202-778-3063. Internet: washington@porterwright.com.
See Professional Biographies, COLUMBUS, OHIO

Smith, Gerald L., (AV) .... '34 '64 C.608 B.S. L.446 J.D. [Mueller&S.]
*PRACTICE AREAS: Intellectual Property Law; Computer Law.
Stein, Arland T., (AV(T)) .... '38 '65 C.679 B.S. L.893 J.D. [Hahn L.&P.]
*PRACTICE AREAS: Intellectual Property; Litigation; Administrative Law; Appellate Practice; Computer Law.

DAYTON, * 166,179, *Montgomery Co.*

Elleman, Steven J. .... '70 '96 C&L.608 B.S.A.A.E., J.D. [Thompson H.]
*PRACTICE AREAS: Intellectual Property; Patents; Trademarks; Intellectual Property Licensing; Unfair Competition.
Erickson, Douglas E. .... '43 '74 C.453 B.S.A.E. L.629 J.D. [[A] Thompson H.]
*PRACTICE AREAS: Intellectual Property.
Kane, John F. .... '60 '98 C.1208 B.S. L.201 J.D. [[A] Thompson H.]
*PRACTICE AREAS: Intellectual Property; Patent Prosecution; Patent Applications; Patent Infringement; Patent Protection.
Levy, Mark P., (AV) .... '51 '77 C.602 B.S. L.273 J.D. [Thompson H.]
*PRACTICE AREAS: Intellectual Property Law; Unfair Competition Law; Licensing.
Lienesch, Theodore D., (AV) .... '51 '76 C.477 B.S.M.E. L.150 J.D. [Thompson H.]
*PRACTICE AREAS: Intellectual Property Law; Unfair Competition Law; Electronic Commerce.

Standley Law Group LLP
(See Dublin)

Thompson Hine LLP, (AV)
2000 Courthouse Plaza, N.E., P.O. Box 8801, 45401-8801 ⊙
Telephone: 937-443-6600 Fax: 937-443-6635
Email: info@ThompsonHine.com URL: http://www.ThompsonHine.com
Partners: Steven J. Elleman; Mark P. Levy (Group Leader, Intellectual Property); Theodore D. Lienesch. Associates: John F. Kane; Victor J. Wasylyna. Senior Attorneys: Douglas E. Erickson.
Administrative Law, Admiralty and Maritime Law, Agency and Distributorships, Antitrust and Trade Regulation, Aviation and Aerospace, Bankruptcy, Banks and Banking, Biotechnology, Business Law, Business Litigation, Business Regulation, Business Transactions, Closely Held Business Law, Joint Ventures, Class Actions, Commercial Law, Commercial Real Estate, Communications and Media, FCC Regulation, Computers and Software, Construction Law, Contracts, Copyrights, Corporate Law, Corporate Finance, Corporate Litigation, Corporate Tax Controversies, Debtor and Creditor, Employee Benefits, ERISA, Energy, Energy Regulation, Environmental Law, Finance, Commercial Finance, Franchises and Franchising, General Practice, Government, False Claims Act, Qui Tam Litigation, Government Contracts, Health Care, Insurance Coverage, Insurance Regulation, Intellectual Property, International Law, International Trade, Internet Law, Labor and Employment, Life Sciences, Litigation, Complex Litigation, Medicare Fraud and Abuse, Mergers, Acquisitions and Divestitures, Natural Resources, Nonprofit and Charitable Organizations, Occupational Safety and Health, OSHA, Partnership Law, Patents, Probate, Products Liability, Product Safety, Professional Liability, Public Finance, Railroad Law, Real Estate, Regulatory Law, Drug and Medical Device Regulation, Food and Drug Regulation, International Regulatory Law, Regulated Industries, Securities, Initial Public Offerings, Public Offerings, Taxation, Tax Controversies, Toxic Torts, Trade Secrets, Trademarks, Transportation, Trusts and Estates, Unfair Competition, Utility Law, White Collar Crime, Zoning, Planning and Land Use.
Cleveland, Ohio Office: 3900 Key Center, 127 Public Square, 44114-1291. Telephone: 216-566-5500. Fax: 216-566-5800. Email: info@ThompsonHine.com.
Cincinnati, Ohio Office: 312 Walnut Street, 14th Floor, 45202-4089. Telephone: 513-352-6700. Fax: 513-241-4771. Email: info@ThompsonHine.com.
Columbus, Ohio Office: 10 West Broad Street, Suite 700, 43215-3435. Telephone: 614-469-3200. Fax: 614-469-3361. Email: info@ThompsonHine.com.

(This Listing Continued)

Thompson Hine LLP (Continued)

Washington, D.C. Office: 1920 N Street, N.W., Suite 800, 20036-1600. Telephone: 202-331-8800. Fax: 202-331-8330. Email: info@ThompsonHine.com.
New York, N.Y. Office: One Chase Manhattan Plaza, 58th Floor, 10005-1401. Telephone: 212-344-5680. Fax: 212-809-6890. Email: info@ThompsonHine.com.
Brussels, Belgium Office: Avenue Louise 375 - b8, 1050 Brussels, Belgium, Telephone: 011 (32-2) 626-3280. Fax: 011 (32-2) 626-3299. Email: info@ThompsonHine.com.
Atlanta, Georgia Office: Proscenium Center, Suite 1200, 1170 Peachtree Street, 30309-7673. Telephone: 404-541-2900. Fax: 404-541-2905. Email: info@ThompsonHine.com.

See Professional Biographies, DAYTON, OHIO

Wasylyna, Victor J. .... '78 '03 C.608 B.S. L.930 J.D. [A Thompson H.]
*PRACTICE AREAS: Intellectual Property; Patent Prosecution and Litigation; Trademark Prosecution and Litigation; Biotechnology.

DUBLIN, 31,392, *Delaware, Franklin & Union Cos.*

Alig, Wesly A. ....'77 '02 C.49 B.S. L.201 J.D. [A Standley]
*PRACTICE AREAS: Intellectual Property; Patents; Trademarks; Copyrights.
Gayan, Eric M. .... '66 '98 C.980 B.S.M.E. L.117 J.D. [A Standley]
*PRACTICE AREAS: Patents; Trademarks; Copyrights.
Grant, Stephen L., (BV) ....'53 '88 C.608 B.S.Ch.E. L.8 J.D. [A Standley]
*PRACTICE AREAS: Patents; Trademarks; Copyrights.
Kwak, James L. ....'69 '96 C.679 B.S.E.E. L.608 J.D. [Standley]
*PRACTICE AREAS: Patents; Trademarks; Copyrights; Computer Law; Telecommunications.
Norris, Jeffrey C. ....'69 '96 C.679 B.S.E.E. L.201 J.D. [A Standley]
*PRACTICE AREAS: Patents; Copyrights; Trademarks.
Scotney, Cheryl S. ....'54 '98 C.63 B.S. L.117 J.D. [A Standley]
*PRACTICE AREAS: Patents; Trademarks; Copyrights.
Standley, Jeffrey S., (AV) .... '61 '89 C.608 B.S.M.E. L.117 J.D. [Standley]
*PRACTICE AREAS: Intellectual Property Law; Intellectual Property Litigation.

Standley Law Group LLP, (AV)
495 Metro Place South, Suite 210, 43017-5319
Telephone: 614-792-5555 Telecopier: 614-792-5536
Email: lawyers@standleyllp.com URL: http://www.standleyllp.com
Partners of Firm: Jeffrey S. Standley; Carol G. Stovsky; James L. Kwak;—Jeffrey C. Norris; Eric M. Gayan; Cheryl S. Scotney; Stephen L. Grant; Michael R. Stonebrook; Wesly A. Alig. Of Counsel: Michael R. Szolosi, Jr.
Domestic and Foreign Intellectual Property Law, including Patent, Trademark, Copyright, Unfair Competition and Trade Secret Law and related Litigation, Licensing, International Trade Matters, related Antitrust, Computer and other Technology Law.

See Professional Biographies, DUBLIN, OHIO

Stonebrook, Michael R. ....'72 '02 C.8 B.S. L.117 J.D. [A Standley]
*PRACTICE AREAS: Intellectual Property; Intellectual Property Litigation.
Stovsky, Carol G. ....'60 '94 C.477 B.S. L.608 J.D. [Standley]
*PRACTICE AREAS: Intellectual Property Law; Computer Law.
Szolosi, Michael R., Jr. ....'69 '95 C.1229 B.S.M.E. L.201 J.D. [C Standley]
*PRACTICE AREAS: Intellectual Property Litigation; Intellectual Property Licensing; Intellectual Property.

MANSFIELD, * 49,346, *Richland Co.*

Standley Law Group LLP
(See Dublin)

REYNOLDSBURG, 32,069, *Fairfield, Franklin & Licking Cos.*

Foster, Frank H., (AV) .... '40 '66 C&L.608 B.E.E., J.D. [Kremblas,F.P.&P.]
Kremblas, Frank T., (AV) .... '37 '64 C&L.608 B.Ch.E., J.D. [Kremblas,F.P.&P.]

Kremblas, Foster, Phillips & Pollick, (AV)
7632 Slate Ridge Boulevard, 43068-8159
Telephone: 614-575-2100 Fax: 614-575-2149
Email: info@ohiopatent.com URL: http://www.ohiopatent.com

(This Listing Continued)

Kremblas, Foster, Phillips & Pollick (Continued)

Members of Firm: Frank T. Kremblas; Frank H. Foster; Philip J. Pollick (Co., L.P.A.).
Patent, Trademark, Copyright and Intellectual Property Law. Foreign Patent and Trademarks Law. Litigation. Licensing.

See Professional Biographies, REYNOLDSBURG, OHIO

Pollick, Philip J., (Co., L.P.A.) .... '42 '87 C.608 Ph.D. L.117 J.D. [Kremblas,F.P.&P.]

SPRINGFIELD, * 65,358, *Clark Co.*

Standley Law Group LLP
(See Dublin)

TOLEDO, * 313,619, *Lucas Co.*

Dolgorukov, D. Edward, (BVⓉ) .... '44 '72 C&L.912 B.S.I.E., J.D. [Marshall&M.]
*PRACTICE AREAS: Intellectual Property.

Emch, Schaffer, Schaub & Porcello Co., L.P.A., (AV)
One Seagate, Suite 1980, P.O. Box 916, 43697-0916
Telephone: 419-243-1294 Fax: 419-243-8502
URL: http://www.essp-law.com
Mark C. Schaffer; Charles R. Schaub; James F. Porcello, Jr.; Philip M. Rice; Patrick P. Pacella.
Patent, Trademark, Copyright, Licensing, Unfair Competition and Related Litigation.

See Professional Biographies, TOLEDO, OHIO

Evans, Stephen P. .... '72 '98 C.608 B.S.A.A.E. L.851 J.D. [Marshall&M.]
*PRACTICE AREAS: Intellectual Property; Litigation.
Hixon, Mark A. .... '66 '92 C.150 B.S. L.607 J.D. [A Marshall&M.]
*PRACTICE AREAS: Intellectual Property.

Marshall & Melhorn, LLC, (AV)
Four SeaGate, Eighth Floor, 43604
Telephone: 419-249-7100 Facsimile: 419-249-7151 Cable Address: "Patlex Toledo"
Email: attorneys@marshall-melhorn.com URL: http://www.marshall-melhorn.com
Members of Firm: Phillip S. Oberlin; D. Edward Dolgorukov; Donald A. Schurr; Stephen P. Evans; Kenneth J. Mauer. Associates: Mark A. Hixon.
Patent, Trademark and Copyright Law. Litigation.
Counsel For: Acklin Stamping; Advanced Metal Precision Products; Aro Corporation; Auburndale Company, Inc.; Baron Drawn Steel Corp.; Bowling Green State University; Bryan Custom Plastics; Challenger Motor Freight; Children Services Board; Chubb Insurance Company.

See Professional Biographies, TOLEDO, OHIO

Mauer, Kenneth J., (BV) .... '49 '85 C&L.851 B.S., J.D. [Marshall&M.]
*PRACTICE AREAS: Patents; Trademarks; Licensing; Environmental.
Oberlin, Phillip S. .... '33 '59 C.679 B.S. L.273 J.D. [C Marshall&M.]
*PRACTICE AREAS: Patents; Trademarks; Business Law; Licensing.
Pacella, Patrick P. .... '42 '68 C.608 B.S.E.D. L.602 J.D. [Emch,S.S.&P.]
*PRACTICE AREAS: Patent Law; Trademark Law; Copyright Law.
Porcello, James F., Jr., (AV) ....'51 '77 C.679 B.S.E. L.117 J.D. [Emch,S.S.&P.]
*PRACTICE AREAS: Patent; Trademark; Copyright; Litigation; International Practice.
Rice, Philip M. ....'31 '62 C.477 B.S.E. L.851 LL.B. [Emch,S.S.&P.]
*PRACTICE AREAS: Patents; Licensing; Joint Ventures.
Schaffer, Mark C., (AV) .... '42 '69 C&L.608 B.A., J.D. [Emch,S.S.&P.]
*PRACTICE AREAS: Patent; Trademark; Copyright; Unfair Competition Litigation.
Schaub, Charles R., (AV) .... '47 '73 C&L.851 B.S.M.E., J.D. [Emch,S.S.&P.]
*PRACTICE AREAS: Trademarks; Patents; related Business Law and Licensing.
Schurr, Donald A., (BV) .... '63 '89 C.930 B.S. L.851 J.D. [Marshall&M.]
*PRACTICE AREAS: Intellectual Property.

ZANESVILLE, * 25,586, *Muskingum Co.*

Standley Law Group LLP
(See Dublin)

EDMOND, 68,315, *Oklahoma Co.*

Lee, Mary M., (AV) . . . . '51 '83 C.880 B.S.N. L.623 J.D. [M.M.Lee]

Lee, Mary M., P.C., Law Office of, (AV)
1300 E. 9th Street, Suite 4, 73034-5760
Telephone: 405-285-4490 Fax: 405-285-4491
Email: mml@marymlee.com URL: http://www.marymlee.com
Mary M. Lee.
Patents, Trademarks, Copyrights, Trade Secrets, Unfair Competition and Related Licensing and Litigation.

See Professional Biographies, EDMOND, OKLAHOMA

OKLAHOMA CITY, 506,132, *Canadian, Cleveland, Oklahoma & Pottawatomie Cos.*

Brockhaus, Marc A. . . . . '68 '98 C&L.623 B.S., J.D. [Dunlap,C.&R.]
*PRACTICE AREAS: Patent Law; Trademark Law; Copyright Law.

Burdick, Glen M. . . . . '37 '66 C&L.623 B.S., J.D. [A Dunlap,C.&R.]
*PRACTICE AREAS: Patents; Trademarks; Copyrights; Unfair Competition Law; Trade Secret Law.

Codding, Charles A., (AV) . . . . '39 '70 C.612 B.S.E.E. L.616 J.D. [Dunlap,C.&R.]
*PRACTICE AREAS: Patent Law; Trademark Law; Unfair Competition Law; Trade Secrets Law; Antitrust Law.

Dunlap, Jerry J., (AV) . . . . '25 '52 C.623 B.S.M.E. L.862 J.D. [Dunlap,C.&R.]
*PRACTICE AREAS: Patent Law; Trademark Law; Unfair Competition Law; Trade Secrets Law; Antitrust Law.

Dunlap, Codding & Rogers, P.C., (AV)
1601 Northwest Expressway, Suite 1000, 73118
Telephone: 405-607-8600 Fax: 405-607-8686
URL: http://www.okpatents.com
Jerry J. Dunlap; Charles A. Codding; Marc A. Brockhaus; Nicholas D. Rouse; Douglas J. Sorocco. — Glen M. Burdick; Michael Hoyt Smith.
Patent, Trademark, Unfair Competition, Trade Secret, Antitrust and Copyright Practice.

(This Listing Continued)

Dunlap, Codding & Rogers, P.C. (Continued)

Reference: BancFirst, Oklahoma City.

See Professional Biographies, OKLAHOMA CITY, OKLAHOMA

Nelson, Richard, (BV) . . . . '53 '81 C.98 B.S. L.615 J.D. [A Dunlap,C.&R.]
*PRACTICE AREAS: Electronic Technology.

Rouse, Nicholas D. . . . . '64 '90 C&L.623 B.S., J.D. [Dunlap,C.&R.]
*PRACTICE AREAS: Patent Law; Trademark Law; Unfair Competition Law; Trade Secrets Law; Copyright Law.

Smith, Michael Hoyt . . . . '68 '01 C.613 B.S. L.623 J.D. [A Dunlap,C.&R.]
*PRACTICE AREAS: Patents; Trademarks; Copyrights; Trade Secrets.

Sorocco, Douglas J. . . . . '70 '96 C.108 B.S. L.201 J.D. [Dunlap,C.&R.]
*PRACTICE AREAS: Patent; Copyright; Trademark; Antitrust; Intellectual Property Licensing and Litigation.

TULSA, 393,049, *Osage & Tulsa Cos.*

Bennett, Allen . . . . '— '02 C&L.45 B.S., J.D. [Head,J.&K.]
*PRACTICE AREAS: Patents; Trademarks; Copyrights.

Head, James R., (AV) . . . . '28 '57 C.612 B.S.M.E. L.862 LL.B. [Head,J.&K.] ‡
*PRACTICE AREAS: Patents; Trademarks; Copyrights.

Head, Johnson & Kachigian, (AV)
228 West 17th Place, Moore Manor, 74119-4694
Telephone: 918-587-2000; 1-800-627-4323 Telefax: 918-587-5603 URL: http://www.lawyers.com/hjklaw
Email: hjklaw.com URL: http://www.hjklaw.com
James R. Head (Retired); Mark G. Kachigian; Allen Bennett.
Domestic and International Patent, Trademark, Copyright and Intellectual Property Law.

See Professional Biographies, TULSA, OKLAHOMA

Kachigian, Mark G., (AV) . . . . '— '78 C.693 B.S. L.862 J.D. [Head,J.&K.]
*PRACTICE AREAS: Patents; Trademarks; Copyrights.

BEAVERTON, 76,129, *Washington Co.*

Anderson, Vincent H. ....'74 '03 C.101 B.S.E.E. L.950 J.D. [A Blakely,S.T.&Z.]

Blakely, Sokoloff, Taylor & Zafman
A Limited Liability Partnership
1925 NW AmberGlen Parkway, Suite 230, 97006 ⊙
Telephone: 503-439-8778 Facsimile: 503-439-6073
Email: BSTZ_mail@bstz.com URL: http://www.bstz.com
Gregory D. Caldwell; Paul A. Mendonsa;—Mark C. Van Ness (Not admitted in OR); Vincent H. Anderson.
Intellectual Property Law, including Patents, Trademarks, Copyrights, Related Prosecution and Litigation.
Sunnyvale, California Office: 1279 Oakmead Parkway. Telephone: 408-720-8300. Facsimile: 408-720-8383.
Los Angeles, California Office: 7th Floor, 12400 Wilshire Boulevard. Telephone: 310-207-3800. Facsimile: 310-820-5988.
Costa Mesa, California Office: 3200 Park Center Drive, Suite 700. Telephone: 714-557-3800. Facsimile: 714-557-3347.
Denver, Colorado Office: 8055 E. Tufts Avenue, 13th Floor. Telephone: 303-740-1980. Facsimile: 303-740-6962.
Seattle, Washington Office: 601 Union Street, Suite 3000. Telephone: 206-292-8600. Facsimile: 206-292-8606.
San Jose, California Office: 60 S. Market Street, Suite 510. Telephone: 408-947-8200. Facsimile: 408-947-8280.

See Professional Biographies, BEAVERTON, OREGON

Caldwell, Gregory D. ....'63 '95 C.999 B.S. L.770 J.D. [Blakely,S.T.&Z.]
Mendonsa, Paul A..................'71 '97 C.101 B.S.E.E. L.770 J.D. [Blakely,S.T.&Z.]
Van Ness, Mark C. '58 '83 C.174 B.A. L.276 J.D.
(adm. in CO; not adm. in OR) [A Blakely,S.T.&Z.]

PORTLAND, 529,121, *Clackamas, Multnomah & Washington Cos.*

Angello, Paul S., (AV) .... '50 '81 C.659 B.S.E.E. L.800 J.D. [Stoel R.]
*PRACTICE AREAS: Patent Law; Technology Law.

Banner & Witcoff, Ltd.
Established In 1920 - Predecessor Parent
601 SW Second Avenue Suite 1900, 97204 ⊙
Telephone: 503-425-6800 Fax: 503-425-6801
Email: info@bannerwitcoff.com URL: http://www.bannerwitcoff.com
Thomas L. Evans.
Intellectual Property including Procurement of Patents, Trademarks, Copyrights, Trade Secrets, Counseling & Opinions, Unfair Competition, Interferences, Licensing, Antitrust and International Trade Matters. Litigation including Trials and Appeals in Federal and State Courts and International Trade Commission.
Chicago, Illinois Office: Ten South Wacker Drive, Suite 3000. Telephone: 312-463-5000. Facsimile: 312-463-5001.
Washington, D.C. Office: 1001 G Street, N.W., Suite 1100 Telephone: 202-824-3000. Facsimile: 202-824-3001.
Boston, Massachusetts Office: 28 State Street, 28th Floor. Telephone: 617-720-9600. Fax: 617-720-9601.

See Professional Biographies, PORTLAND, OREGON

Bell, Daniel H. '60 '05 C&L.36 B.S., J.D.
(adm. in WA; not adm. in OR) [Klarquist S.]
Birdwell, William A., (AV) ....'46 '73 C.628 B.S.E.E. L.174 J.D. [Birdwell&J.] ⊙
*PRACTICE AREAS: Patent; Trademarks; Trade Secrets; Copyrights; Unfair Competition.

Birdwell & Janke LLP, (AV) BB
1400 Standard Plaza, 1100 S.W. Sixth Avenue, 97204-1221
Telephone: 503-228-1841 Fax: 503-228-2635
Email: portland@birdwelljanke.com URL: http://www.birdwelljanke.com
William A. Birdwell; Garth Janke (Resident). Associates: Richard A. Wilhelm.
Intellectual Property including: Patent, Trademark, Copyright, Trade Secret and Unfair Competition Law, Licensing, Trials in State and Federal Courts, Practice before U.S. Patent and Trademark Office.
Tucson, Arizona Office: 2301 E. Seventh Street, 85719. Telephone: 520-795-1446.

See Professional Biographies, PORTLAND, OREGON

Brooks, Hillary Anne .... '70 '95 C.911 B.A. L.802 J.D. [Marger J.&M.]
*PRACTICE AREAS: Patents; Copyrights; Trademarks; Litigation.
Caldwell, Lisa M. ....'62 '94 C.768 B.S. L.950 J.D. [Klarquist S.]
*PRACTICE AREAS: Patent Prosecution; Trademark Prosecution; Licensing; Chemical Semiconductor Device; Process Patent Prosecution.

Chernoff, Vilhauer, McClung & Stenzel, LLP, (AV) BB
1600 ODS Tower, 601 S.W. Second Avenue, 97204
Telephone: 503-227-5631 Facsimile: 503-228-4373
Email: postmaster@chernofflaw.com URL: http://www.chernofflaw.com
Members of Firm: Jacob E. Vilhauer, Jr.; Dennis E. Stenzel; Charles D. McClung; Donald B. Haslett; J. Peter Staples; William O. Geny; Nancy J. Moriarty; Kevin L. Russell;—Tim A. Long; Kurt A. Rohlfs; Brenna K. Legaard; Susan D. Pitchford; J. Douglas Wells.
Intellectual Property Law and Litigation Relating to Patent, Trademark, Copyright, Trade Secrets, Licensing, Computer Technology. Franchising, Unfair Competition, Trade Dress and False Advertising.
Representative Clients: Bend Research, Inc.; Cascade Corp.; Columbia Sportswear Co.; Gunderson, Inc.; Leatherman Tool Group, Inc.; Pfizer, Inc.; Planar Systems, Inc.; Sharp Laboratories of America, Inc.

See Professional Biographies, PORTLAND, OREGON

Cowger, Graciela Gomez, (BV) ....'66 '97 C.763 B.S.E.E. L.911 J.D. [Marger J.&M.]
*PRACTICE AREAS: Patents; Trademarks; Copyrights; Intellectual Property.
Evans, Thomas L. ....'— '94 C.893 B.S.E.E. L.1209 J.D. [Banner&W.]
*PRACTICE AREAS: Intellectual Property Law; Patents; Patent Prosecution; International Trade; Electronic Intellectual Property Law.
Ferris, Kassim M. ....'68 '96 C.172 B.S.M.E. L.950 J.D. [A Stoel R.]
*PRACTICE AREAS: Intellectual Property; Patents.
Ford, Stephen S.............................'60 '92 C.906 B.S.E.E. L.950 J.D. [Marger J.&M.]
*PRACTICE AREAS: Patents; Trademarks; Copyrights; Intellectual Property; Litigation.
Galbi, Elmer W. '— '61 C.705 B.S. L.276 J.D.
(adm. in NY; not adm. in OR) [C Marger J.&M.]
*PRACTICE AREAS: Intellectual Property (100%).
Geny, William O., (AV) ....'47 '74 C.861 B.S. L.880 J.D. [Chernoff,V.M.&S.]
*PRACTICE AREAS: Copyright Law; Intellectual Property Licensing; Patent Litigation; Computer and Software Patents; Electrical Patents.
Girard, Michael P...............................'68 '94 C.446 B.S. L.893 J.D. [Klarquist S.]
*PRACTICE AREAS: Patent Prosecution; Litigation; Licensing.
Goff, Jared S. ....'72 '99 C&L.101 M.E., J.D. [A Klarquist S.]
*PRACTICE AREAS: Intellectual Property Litigation.
Harding, Tanya M., Ph.D....................'68 '99 C.705 B.S. L.188 J.D. [A Klarquist S.]
*PRACTICE AREAS: Intellectual Property Law; Biotechnology Patent Prosecution and Opinions.
Haslett, Donald B., (AV) ....'45 '77 C.871 B.S. L.188 J.D. [Chernoff,V.M.&S.]
*PRACTICE AREAS: Patents; International Patents; Trademarks; Design Patents; Unfair Competition.
Hayes, Kevin M. ....'74 '01 C.678 B.S. L.628 J.D. [A Klarquist S.]
*PRACTICE AREAS: Patent Prosecution; Trademark Prosecution; Intellectual Property Litigation.
Jakubek, Joseph T. .... '62 '88 C.980 B.E. L.608 J.D. [Klarquist S.]
*PRACTICE AREAS: Patent; Trademark; Copyright; Litigation.
Janke, Garth ....'55 '94 C.112 M.S. L.813 J.D. [Birdwell&J.]
*PRACTICE AREAS: Patent; Trade Secret; Trademark; Copyright; Unfair Competition.

Johnson, Alexander C., Jr., (AV) .....'48 '78 C.152 B.S.E.E. L.101 J.D. [Marger J.&M.]
*PRACTICE AREAS: Patents; Trademarks; Copyrights; Unfair Competition; Trade Secrets.
Joncus, Stephen J. ....'59 '95 C.696 B.S. L.326 J.D. [A Klarquist S.]
*PRACTICE AREAS: Patent Litigation.
Jones, Michael D. .... '50 '97 C.910 A.B. L.596 J.D. [Klarquist S.]
*PRACTICE AREAS: Patent; Trademark; Copyright.
Klarquist, Kenneth S., (AV) .... '21 '50 C.494 B.Ch.E. L.276 J.D. [C Klarquist S.]
*PRACTICE AREAS: Patent, Trademark and Copyright Law; Unfair Competition.

Klarquist Sparkman, LLP, (AV) BB
One World Trade Center, Suite 1600, 121 S.W. Salmon Street, 97204 ⊙
Telephone: 503-226-7391 FAX: 503-228-9446
Email: inquiry@klarquist.com URL: http://www.klarquist.com
Members of Firm: Lisa M. Caldwell; Michael P. Girard; Joseph T. Jakubek; Michael D. Jones; Ramon A. Klitzke, II; Gregory L. Maurer; Dr. William D. Noonan; David P. Petersen; Richard J. Polley; Kyle B. Rinehart; Wayne W. Rupert; Stacey C. Slater; Donald L. Stephens, Jr.; John D. Vandenberg; Stephen A. Wight; Garth A. Winn. Senior Counsel: Kenneth S. Klarquist; James S. Leigh; Arthur L. Whinston. Associates: Jared S. Goff; Tanya M. Harding, Ph.D.; Kevin M. Hayes; Stephen J. Joncus; Richard D. McLeod (Not admitted in OR); A. Jonathan Vance; Gwynedd Warren, Ph.D.
Patent, Trademark, Copyright Law, Trials, Unfair Competition Law.
Clients available upon request.
Reno, Nevada Office: 800 South Meadows Parkway, Suite 700. Telephone: 775-824-0104. Fax: 775-824-0107.
Seattle, Washington Office: Wells Fargo Center, 999 Third Avenue, Suite 4200. Telephone: 206-264-2960.

See Professional Biographies, PORTLAND, OREGON

Klitzke, Ramon A., II, (AV) ....'55 '80 C.790 B.S. L.436 J.D. [Klarquist S.]
*PRACTICE AREAS: Patent Prosecution; Trademark Prosecution; Copyright Law; Litigation and Licensing.
Lee, Hosoon ....'64 '98 C&L.999 B.S., J.D. [Marger J.&M.]
*PRACTICE AREAS: Patents; Intellectual Property; Trademarks; Intellectual Property Licensing; Copyrights.
Legaard, Brenna K................'73 '00 C.1032 B.A. L.124 J.D. [A Chernoff,V.M.&S.]
*PRACTICE AREAS: Intellectual Property; Litigation.
Leigh, James S., (AV) ....'35 '61 C.475 B.S. L.477 J.D. [C Klarquist S.]
*PRACTICE AREAS: Patent, Trademark and Copyright Law; Unfair Competition; Trade Secret Law; Licensing; Litigation.
Long, Tim A. ....'45 '74 C.336 B.S. L.596 J.D. [A Chernoff,V.M.&S.]
*PRACTICE AREAS: Intellectual Property; Patents; Trademarks.
Makuch, Joseph S. ....'65 '95 C.124 B.S.E.E. L.596 J.D. [Marger J.&M.]
*PRACTICE AREAS: Patents; Trademarks; Copyrights; Intellectual Property Litigation.
Marger, Jerome S., (AV) ....'41 '71 C.570 B.S.Ch.E L.7 J.D. [C Marger J.&M.]
*PRACTICE AREAS: Intellectual Property; Patents; Trademarks; Copyrights; Intellectual Property Licensing.

Marger Johnson & McCollom, P.C., (AV) BB
210 S.W. Morrison Street, Suite 400, 97204
Telephone: 503-222-3613 FAX: 503-274-4622
Email: info@techlaw.com URL: http://www.techlaw.com
Alexander C. Johnson, Jr.; Alan T. McCollom; Stephen S. Ford; Scott A. Schaffer; Joseph S. Makuch; Graciela Gomez Cowger; Craig R. Rogers; Julie L. Reed (Not admitted in OR); Ariel S. Rogson; Hosoon Lee; Hillary Anne Brooks. Of Counsel: Jerome S. Marger; Elmer W. Galbi (Not admitted in OR).
Intellectual Property Law, Patents, Trademarks, Copyrights, Computers and Software, Trade Secrets, Licensing Agreements, Nanotechnology, Technology Licensing and Litigation.
Vancouver, Washington Office: 5123 N.E. 94th Avenue, Suite C, 98662. Telephone: 360-260-3613. Fax: 360-695-0271.

See Professional Biographies, PORTLAND, OREGON

Maurer, Gregory L. .... '67 '96 C.1083 B.S. L.893 J.D. [Klarquist S.]
*PRACTICE AREAS: Patent, Trademark and Copyright.
McClung, Charles D., (AV) ..... '39 '75 C.911 B.S.M.E. L.285 J.D. [Chernoff,V.M.&S.]
*PRACTICE AREAS: Patents; Trademarks; False Advertising; Trade Dress; Intellectual Property Licensing.
McCollom, Alan T., (AV) ....'50 '77 C.612 B.S.E.E. L.623 J.D. [Marger J.&M.]
*PRACTICE AREAS: Patent Applications; Computer and Software Patents; Electronic Patents; Semiconductor Technology; Patent Litigation.
McLeod, Richard D. '— '00 C.326 B.S. L.846 J.D.
(adm. in TX; not adm. in OR) [A Klarquist S.]
*PRACTICE AREAS: Intellectual Property Litigation.
Moriarty, Nancy J., (AV) ....'52 '84 C.112 B.S. L.352 J.D. [Chernoff,V.M.&S.]
*PRACTICE AREAS: Trademarks; Trademark Litigation; Intellectual Property Litigation; False Advertising; Copyright.
Noonan, William D. .... '55 '80 C.674 A.B. L.986 J.D. [Klarquist S.]
*PRACTICE AREAS: Patent, Trademark and Copyright Law.
Petersen, David P., (AV) ....'50 '75 C.628 B.S.E.E. L.629 J.D. [Klarquist S.]
*PRACTICE AREAS: Patent, Trademark and Copyright Law; Unfair Competition.
Pitchford, Susan D. .... '71 '96 C&L.285 B.S.,B.A., J.D. [A Chernoff,V.M.&S.]
*PRACTICE AREAS: Intellectual Property; Patents; Trademarks; Copyrights; Litigation.
Polley, Richard J., (AV) ....'48 '75 C&L.950 B.A.Chem., J.D. [Klarquist S.]
*PRACTICE AREAS: Patent, Trademark and Copyright Law; Unfair Competition.
Rafter, John A., Jr. ....'56 '86 C.602 B.S.M.E. L.426 J.D. [Stoel R.]
*PRACTICE AREAS: Intellectual Property.
Reed, Julie L. '66 '95 C.906 B.S.E.E. L.802 J.D.
(adm. in TX; not adm. in OR) [Marger J.&M.]
*PRACTICE AREAS: Intellectual Property; Intellectual Property Portfolio Management; Patents; Electronics; Telecommunications Law.
Rinehart, Kyle B. .... '71 '98 C.378 B.A. L.309 J.D. [Klarquist S.]
*PRACTICE AREAS: Patent Prosecution; Patent Litigation.
Rogers, Craig R. .... '70 '98 C&L.101 B.S.M.E., J.D. [Marger J.&M.]
*PRACTICE AREAS: Intellectual Property; Litigation; Patents; Trademarks; Copyrights.
Rogson, Ariel S. .... '69 '97 C.112 B.S.B.S. L.1067 J.D. [Marger J.&M.]
*PRACTICE AREAS: Patents; Intellectual Property; Trademarks; Copyrights; Trade Secrets.
Rohlfs, Kurt A. .... '67 '97 C.544 B.S. L.1051 J.D. [A Chernoff,V.M.&S.]
*PRACTICE AREAS: Intellectual Property; Patents; Trademarks; Copyrights.
Rupert, Wayne W...........................'63 '89 C.645 B.S. L.273 J.D. [Klarquist S.]
*PRACTICE AREAS: Intellectual Property.
Russell, Kevin L. ....'67 '93 C.906 B.S.E.E. L.950 J.D. [Chernoff,V.M.&S.]
*PRACTICE AREAS: Intellectual Property; Patents; Trademarks; Electronic Intellectual Property; Electrical Patents.
Schaffer, Scott A. .... '67 '94 C.813 B.S. L.623 J.D. [Marger J.&M.]
*PRACTICE AREAS: Patents; Trademarks; Copyrights; Unfair Competition; Intellectual Property.
Slater, Stacey C. .... '61 '90 C.174 B.A. L.629 J.D. [Klarquist S.]
*PRACTICE AREAS: Patent, Trademark and Copyright Law; Unfair Competition.
Staples, J. Peter, (AV) ....'47 '79 C.870 B.S. L.596 J.D. [Chernoff,V.M.&S.]
*PRACTICE AREAS: Intellectual Property Litigation; Trademarks; Patents; Trade Dress; False Advertising.
Stenzel, Dennis E., (AV) ....'42 '72 C.101 B.S. L.273 J.D. [Chernoff,V.M.&S.]
*PRACTICE AREAS: Intellectual Property; Unfair Competition; Litigation; Trademarks; Intellectual Property Licensing.
Stephens, Donald L., Jr. .... '49 '90 C.1109 B.S. L.596 J.D. [Klarquist S.]
*PRACTICE AREAS: Patent, Trademark and Copyright Law; Unfair Competition; Physics; Biotechnology; Chemical and Medical Technologies.

Stoel Rives LLP, (AV) BB
900 S.W. Fifth Avenue Suite 2600, 97204-1268 ⊙
Telephone: 503-224-3380 Facsimile: 503-220-2480 Cable Address: "Lawport"
URL: http://www.stoel.com
Members of Firm: Paul S. Angello; Micah D. Stolowitz. Associate: Kassim M. Ferris. Staff Attorney: James L. Wolfe (Not admitted in OR). Patent Agents: Michael L. Levine; Richard B. Preiss.
General Practice and Litigation in State and Federal Courts. Partnerships, Joint Ventures and Corporate and Securities, Real Estate and Land Use, Federal Taxation, Patent, Trademark and Copyright Law, Commercial, Bankruptcy, Reorganizations and Workouts, Antitrust and Trade Regulation, Hospital and Health Law, Forest Products, Franchise Law, Immigration, Insurance, International Trade and Transactions, Government Law, Media and Advertising Law, Municipal Law and Tax-Exempt Financing, Labor and Employment, Employee Benefits, Construction, Banking, Public Utilities, Trusts and Estates, Mining, Natural Resources, Environmental, State and Local Taxation, International Tax, White Collar Criminal Law.
Counsel for: Attachmate Corporation; Electro Scientific Industries; In Focus Systems, Inc.; Merix, Inc.; PacifiCorp; SLC Technologies, Inc.; Tektronix, Inc.; Traveling Software, Inc.; Ziba Design, Inc.
Seattle, Washington Office: Suite 3600, One Union Square, 600 University. Telephone: 206-624-0900.
Vancouver, Washington Office: Suite 725, 805 Broadway. Telephone: 360-699-5900.
Boise, Idaho Office: Suite 1900, 101 S. Capitol Boulevard. Telephone: 208-389-9000.
Salt Lake City, Utah Office: Suite 1100, One Utah Center, 201 South Main Street. Telephone: 801-328-3131.
San Francisco, California Office: 111 Sutter Street, Suite 700. Telephone: 415-617-8900.
Sacramento, California Office: 770 L Street, Suite 800. Telephone: 916-447-0700.
Tahoe City, California Office: 3000 N. Lake Boulevard, Suite 1, P.O. Box 7336. Telephone: 530-583-2116.
Fresno, California Office: 1233 W. Shaw Avenue, Suite 103. Telephone: 559-228-9900.

See Professional Biographies, PORTLAND, OREGON

Stolowitz, Micah D., (AV) . . . . '54 '81 C.112 B.S.E.E. L.596 J.D. [Stoel R.]
*PRACTICE AREAS: Patent, Trademark and Copyright Law; Licensing Law; Computer Software Law; Internet Law; Trade Secrets Law.

Vance, A. Jonathan . . . .'77 '04 C.101 B.S. L.846 J.D. [A Klarquist S.]
*PRACTICE AREAS: Intellectual Property; Patents.

Vandenberg, John D., (AV) . . . .'58 '84 C.674 B.S.E. L.569 J.D. [Klarquist S.]
*PRACTICE AREAS: Patent Litigation.

Vilhauer, Jacob E., Jr., (AV) . . . .'40 '64 C.628 B.S. L.629 LL.B. [Chernoff,V.M.&S.]
*PRACTICE AREAS: International Patents; International Trademarks; Trade Secrets; Intellectual Property Infringement; Intellectual Property Licensing.

Warren, Gwynedd, Ph.D. . . . . '— '04 C.477 B.S. L.1066 J.D. [Klarquist S.]
*PRACTICE AREAS: Intellectual Property; Intellectual Property Procurement; Intellectual Property Prosecution; Medical Intellectual Property; Pharmaceutical Intellectual Property.

Wells, J. Douglas . . . .'65 '04 C.679 B.S.E.E. L.596 J.D. [A Chernoff,V.M.&S.]
*PRACTICE AREAS: Intellectual Property; Patents; Trademarks; Trade Secrets; Copyrights.

Whinston, Arthur L., (AV) . . . . '25 '57 C.188 B.C.E. L.569 J.D. [C Klarquist S.]
*PRACTICE AREAS: Patent, Trademark and Copyright Law; Unfair Competition.

Wight, Stephen A. . . . .'65 '92 C.101 B.S. L.911 J.D. [Klarquist S.]
*PRACTICE AREAS: Patent, Trademark and Copyright Law; Unfair Competition.

Wilhelm, Richard A. . . . . '54 '84 C.629 B.S. L.596 J.D. [A Birdwell&J.]
*PRACTICE AREAS: Patents; Copyrights; Trademarks; Trade Secrets; Intellectual Property Licensing.

Winn, Garth A. . . . .'60 '87 C.877 B.S. L.101 J.D. [Klarquist S.]
*PRACTICE AREAS: Patent, Trademark and Copyright Law; Unfair Competition.

PROFESSIONAL BIOGRAPHIES SECTION

NORTH CAROLINA
NORTH DAKOTA, OHIO
OKLAHOMA, OREGON

VAN CAMP, MEACHAM & NEWMAN, PLLC

ABERDEEN, NORTH CAROLINA

(See Pinehurst)

General Civil and Criminal Litigation and Appellate Practice in State and Federal Courts. Personal Injury, Commercial, Medical Malpractice, Wrongful Death, Worker's Compensation, Insurance, Land Condemnation, Constitutional and Civil Rights, Family, Corporate, Real Estate, Administrative, Social Security Disability, Construction Law, Labor and Employment, Wills, Estate Planning and Probate Law.

BAKER, JONES, DALY, MURRAY, CARTER & DAUGHTRY, P.A.

Established in 1980

304 WEST SUNSET STREET
P.O. BOX 986
AHOSKIE, NORTH CAROLINA 27910-0986
Telephone: 252-332-2181
Fax: 252-332-8354
Real Estate Fax: 252-209-0046
Email: ahoskie@bjjlawoffices.com

Rocky Mount, North Carolina Office: 140 North Franklin Street, P.O. Box 68. Telephone: 252-442-1977. Facsimile: 252-442-5175.

General Insurance Defense Civil Practice. Trials. Real Estate, Estate Planning, Probate, Business, Personal Injury Defense, Professional Liability, Insurance, Workers Compensation and Collections.

RONALD G. BAKER, born Windsor, North Carolina, January 15, 1949; admitted to bar, 1975, North Carolina. *Education:* University of North Carolina (B.S., 1971; J.D., with honors, 1975). Order of the Coif. Morehead Scholar. Member of Staff, North Carolina Law Review, 1973-1975. Recipient, Chief Justice Walter Clark Award. Hertford County Commissioner, 1984-1988. Member, Hertford County Board of Education, 1998—. *Member:* North Carolina (Member: Executive Council, Young Lawyers Division, 1978-1982; Board of Directors, Litigation Section, 1981-1983) and American Bar Associations; North Carolina State Bar (Councilor, District 6B, 2003—); North Carolina Association of Defense Attorneys (Board of Directors, 1991-1997; President Elect, 1994; President, 1995); Defense Research Institute (North Carolina State Representative, 1998-2000); American Board of Trial Advocates. ***PRACTICE AREAS:*** Insurance Defense; Civil Litigation; Professional Malpractice Defense. ***Email:*** bakerrg@bjjlawoffices.com

ROBERT C. JENKINS (1943-2002)

W. HUGH JONES, JR., born Ahoskie, North Carolina, May 3, 1954; admitted to bar, 1980, North Carolina. *Education:* Davidson College (A.B., cum laude, 1977); University of North Carolina (J.D., 1980). Member, Board of Directors, 1981-1992 and Chairman, 1989-1991, Roanoke-Chowan Area Mental Health Association. Member, Board of Directors, Legal Services of the Coastal Plains, 1981-1986. *Member:* Hertford County and North Carolina Bar Associations; North Carolina State Bar (Councilor, District 6B, 1993-2002); North Carolina Association of Defense Attorneys; Defense Research Institute. ***PRACTICE AREAS:*** Insurance Defense; Civil Litigation; Real Estate; Collections. ***Email:*** joneswh@bjjlawoffices.com

ROSWALD B. DALY, JR., born Charlotte, North Carolina, July 12, 1951; admitted to bar, 1976, North Carolina. *Education:* University of North Carolina (A.B., 1973; J.D., 1976). Member, Board of Directors, Legal Service of the Costal Plains. *Member:* Bertie County, Sixth Judicial District (President, 1984, 1992) and North Carolina Bar Associations; North Carolina State Bar; North Carolina Association of Defense Attorneys; Defense Research Institute. ***PRACTICE AREAS:*** Medical Malpractice Defense; Insurance Defense; General Civil Practice. ***Email:*** dalyrb@bjjlawoffices.com

ERNIE K. MURRAY, born Rocky Mount, North Carolina, June 23, 1952; admitted to bar, 1980, North Carolina and U.S. District Court, Eastern District of North Carolina; 1984, U.S. Court of Appeals, Fourth Circuit and U.S. District Court, Western District of North Carolina; 1985, U.S. Tax Court; 1989, U.S. Supreme Court. *Education:* University of North Carolina (B.A., 1974); Wake Forest University (J.D., 1980). Staff Member, 1978-1979 and Managing Editor, 1979-1980, Wake Forest Law Review. Law Clerk to: Hon. Edward B. Clark, Associate Judge, North Carolina Court of Appeals, 1980-1981; Hon. Joseph Branch, Chief Justice, North Carolina Supreme Court, 1981-1982. *Member:* Defense Research Institute; North Carolina Association of Defense Attorneys (Board of Directors, 1996-1997). (Resident, Rocky Mount Office). ***PRACTICE AREAS:*** Civil Litigation; Appellate Practice. ***Email:*** murrayek@bjjlawoffices.com

ERNEST R. CARTER, JR., born Ahoskie, North Carolina, August 27, 1959; admitted to bar, 1984, North Carolina; 1986, U.S. District Court, Eastern District of North Carolina. *Education:* University of North Carolina (B.S.B.A., 1981); Campbell University (J.D., 1984). Phi Alpha Delta. Business Editor, Campbell Law Review, 1983-1984. Commissioner, Town of Powellsville, 1986—. *Member:* North Carolina Bar Associations; Six-B Judicial District (President, 1997) and North Carolina State Bars. ***PRACTICE AREAS:*** Real Estate; Corporate Law; Business Law; Probate Law. ***Email:*** carterer@bjjlawoffices.com

KEVIN NEIL LEWIS, born September 30, 1965; admitted to bar, 1992, North Carolina. *Education:* Campbell University (B.A., 1987); Norman A. Wiggins School of Law (J.D., 1992). Certified, Superior Court Mediator. *Member:* 6-B Judicial District (President, 1999-2000), North Carolina, North Carolina State and American Bar Associations; North Carolina Association of Defense Attorneys; Defense Research Institute. (Resident, Rocky Mount Office). ***PRACTICE AREAS:*** Insurance Defense; Appellate Practice; Civil Litigation; Real Estate. ***Email:*** lewiskn@bjjlawoffices.com

BRUCE L. DAUGHTRY, born Ahoskie, North Carolina, September 30, 1966; admitted to bar, 1993, North Carolina. *Education:* Campbell University (B.B.A., 1989); Campbell University School of Law (J.D., 1993). Phi Alpha Delta. Federal Society (Treasurer,

(This Listing Continued)

1992). *Member:* Nash County, Seventh Judicial District and North Carolina Bar Associations; North Carolina Association of Defense Attorneys; Defense Research Institute. (Resident, Rocky Mount Office). ***PRACTICE AREAS:*** Insurance Defense. ***Email:*** daughtrybl@bjjlawoffices.com

---

AMY LORRELLE ELLIOTT, born Marietta, Georgia, August 23, 1975; admitted to bar, 2000, North Carolina. *Education:* College of William & Mary (B.A., 1997); Villanova University School of Law (J.D., 2000). Pi Delta Phi, Phi Eta Sigma, Alpha Lambda Delta. Member: Corporate Law Society, 1997-1998; Benjamin Franklin American Inn of Court, 2000; Saint Thomas More Society, 1997-1998; Italian American Law Society, 1999. *Member:* North Carolina and American (Member, Young Lawyers Division) Bar Associations. ***LANGUAGES:*** French. ***PRACTICE AREAS:*** Insurance Defense; Civil Litigation. ***Email:*** elliottal@bjjlawoffices.com

REPRESENTATIVE CLIENTS: North Carolina Farm Bureau Mutual Insurance Co.; Nationwide Mutual Insurance Co.; Great American Insurance Cos.; Travelers Property Casualty Insurance Company; North Carolina League of Municipalities; Orion Auto Insurance Co.; Horace Mann; Auto Owners Insurance; State Farm Insurance Companies; Lawyers Mutual Liability Insurance Company of North Carolina; Travelers Insurance Company; Employers Mutual Insurance Group; Integon Insurance Co.; Allstate Insurance Co.; Crawford and Co.; Universal Insurance Company; Erie Insurance Co.; Millers Mutual Insurance Co.; Claims Control, Inc.; Town of Kelford; A. T. Byrum & Son, Inc.; Commercial Ready Mix Products, Inc.; Harrellsville Metal Works, Inc.; Georgia-Pacific Corp.; Transport Insurance Co.; Rose Brothers Paving Co., Inc.
APPROVED ATTORNEYS FOR: Stewart Title; Chicago Title Insurance; Investors Title Insurance Company; First American Title Insurance Co.
REFERENCES: First Citizens Bank and Trust Co.; RBC Centura Bank; Southern Bank & Trust.

BROWN, BROWN & BROWN, P.L.L.C.

Established in 1878

101 SOUTH SECOND STREET
P.O. DRAWER 400
ALBEMARLE, NORTH CAROLINA 28002
Telephone: 704-982-2141
Telecopier: 704-982-0902
Email: brownlaw28001@ctc.net
URL: http://www.brownbrownandbrown.com

General Civil and Criminal Trial Practice in all State Courts. Business, Insurance, Personal Injury and Wrongful Death, Real Estate, Probate, Estate Administration, Municipal Corporation.

FIRM PROFILE: This firm and its predecessors have been engaged in the active practice of law since 1878.

MEMBERS OF FIRM

JAMES MILTON BROWN (1851-1923)

RICHARD L. BROWN, SR. (1887-1938)

RICHARD L. BROWN, JR. (1910-1998)

CHARLES P. BROWN, born Albemarle, North Carolina, 1942; admitted to bar, 1966, North Carolina. *Education:* University of North Carolina at Chapel Hill (B.S., 1964; J.D., 1966). Phi Delta Phi. John Motley Morehead Scholar. Member: North Carolina Board of Conservation and Development, 1969-1973; North Carolina Criminal Code Commission, 1979-1984; General Alumni Association Board, University of North Carolina, 1996-1999 and 2000-2001. Member, 1992-2005 and President, 2000-2001, University of North Carolina Law Alumni Association. Trustee, North Carolina Lutheran Homes, Inc., 1980-1989. Chairman, Stanly County Board of Education, 1988-1994. Member, Stanly County Economic Development Commission, 2003—. Past President, Stanly County Bar and Twentieth Judicial District Bar. *Member:* American Bar Association; North Carolina Academy of Trial Lawyers. ***PRACTICE AREAS:*** Personal Injury; Civil Litigation; Criminal Litigation; Estate Administration; Municipal Law. ***Email:*** brownlaw28001@ctc.net

G. CRAWFORD RIPPY, III, born Plattsburg, New York, 1956; admitted to bar, 1983, North Carolina and U.S. District Court, Western District of North Carolina; 1985, U.S. Court of Appeals, Fourth Circuit. *Education:* Furman University (B.A., 1977); Cumberland School of Law of Samford University (J.D., 1983). Member, The Henry Upson Sims Moot Court Board. Past President, Stanly County Bar. *Member:* North Carolina Academy of Trial Lawyers. ***PRACTICE AREAS:*** Personal Injury Law; Wrongful Death; Civil Litigation; Real Estate. ***Email:*** brownlaw28001@ctc.net

---

CONNIE E. JOSEY, born Albemarle, North Carolina, 1979; admitted to bar, 2003, North Carolina. *Education:* North Carolina State University (B.S., 2000); University of North Carolina at Chapel Hill (J.D., 2003). Staff Member, 2001-2002 and Executive Editor, 2002-2003, North Carolina Banking Institute Journal. Law Clerk to Hon. Sanford L. Steelman, Jr., Judge, North Carolina Court of Appeals, 2003-2004. *Member:* North Carolina Bar Association (Member, Sections on: Elder Law, Estate Planning and Fiduciary Law). ***PRACTICE AREAS:*** Estate Planning; Estate Administration; Personal Injury; Wrongful Death; Business Planning. ***Email:*** cjoseybrownlaw28001@ctc.net

LEGAL SUPPORT PERSONNEL

Mitzi Morton
Judy H. Miller
Vivian H. Turner
Jill S. Thomas

All members of the firm are members of the Stanly County, 20th Judicial District and North Carolina Bar Associations and the North Carolina State Bar.

REPRESENTATIVE CLIENTS: Aluminum Company of America; Norfolk Southern Railway; Lorch, LLC; Culp Lumber Company, Inc.; Hartsell Funeral Home, Inc.; Albemarle ABC Board; Southeastern Materials, Inc.; Town of Richfield; Village of Misenheimer; Stanly Memorial Hospital, Inc.; Morgan Motor Co.; S & D Construction Company, Inc.

(This Listing Continued)

BROWN, BROWN & BROWN, P.L.L.C., Albemarle—Continued

APPROVED ATTORNEYS FOR: Lawyers Title Insurance Corp.; Chicago Title Insurance Co.; Investors Title Insurance Co.; Ticor Title of North Carolina, Inc.; Piedmont Farm Credit, ACA; Home Savings Bank; Wachovia Bank & Trust Co.; Bank of Stanly; N.C. Department of Transportation.
REFERENCE: Wachovia Bank & Trust Co., Albemarle, N.C.

HARTSELL & WILLIAMS, P.A.

ALBEMARLE, NORTH CAROLINA

(See Concord)

General Civil and Criminal Practice in all Courts. Workers Compensation, Corporation, Insurance, Real Estate, Taxation, Probate Law, Estate Planning, Family Law and Motor Sports (Racing).

THE LAW OFFICES OF HALES & CONAWAY, PLLC

ANGIER, NORTH CAROLINA

(See Clinton)

Family Law, Divorce, Adoption, Custody, Child Support, Premarital Agreements, Separation Agreements, Criminal Defense, Social Security Disability, Collections, Debtor, Creditor, Juvenile Law, Estate Administration and Estate Planning, Civil Litigation, Workers Compensation, Personal Injury, Traffic, DWI.

BENITA WALKER GIBBS

APEX, NORTH CAROLINA

(See Cary)

Residential Real Estate, Commercial Real Estate, Mortgages, Construction Loans, Equity Finance, Reverse Mortgages.

THE LAW OFFICE OF JONATHAN RICHARDSON

APEX, NORTH CAROLINA

(See Cary)

Personal Injury, Real Estate, Closings, Workers Compensation, Injuries, Traffic Violations, Tickets, Wrongful Death.

STAM, FORDHAM & DANCHI, P.A.

Established in 1978

(Successor to Holleman & Stam)

510 WEST WILLIAMS STREET
P.O. BOX 1600
APEX, NORTH CAROLINA 27502
Telephone: 919-362-8873
Fax: 919-387-1171
Email: paulstam@bellsouth.net
URL: http://www.lawyers.com/sfdlaw

General Civil Practice in all State and Federal Courts. Corporation, Real Estate, Probate, Land Condemnation, Municipal Government, Personal Injury and Litigation. Workers Compensation.

FIRM PROFILE: Well established team of lawyers providing personal service ranging from real estate to personal injury.

CARL P. HOLLEMAN (1921-1992)

PAUL STAM, born Princeton, New Jersey, September 5, 1950; admitted to bar, 1975, North Carolina. *Education:* Michigan State University (B.S., with high honors, 1972); University of North Carolina at Chapel Hill (J.D., 1975). Research Assistant for Associate Justice James G. Exum, Jr., North Carolina Supreme Court, 1975-1976. Adjunct Instructor, Campbell University School of Law, 1978. Member, North Carolina House of Representatives, 1989-1990 and 2003-2006. Chairman, North Carolina Juvenile Law Study Commission, 1989-1992. Member, House Select Committee on Non-Profits, 1995-1996. Trustee, Southern Baptist Theological Seminary, 1988-1998. Apex Town Attorney, 1992-1995. *Member:* Wake County and North Carolina Bar Associations; North Carolina State Bar; Christian Legal Society. [Cpl., USMC, 1968-1970]. ***REPORTED CASES:*** Delconte v. North Carolina (home schooling upheld), 313 NC 384 (1985). Local Counsel for Amicus Rutherford Institute; Maready v. Winston-Salem (economic incentives upheld), 342 NC 708 (1996); Amicus for John Locke Foundation; Pulliam v. Smith (custody/change of circumstance homosexuals). Amicus for NC Family Policy Council, 348 NC 616 (1998); Smith Chapel Baptist Church v. Durham (stormwater utility fees) 350 NC 805 (1999); Stam v. State of North Carolina, 302 NC 357 (1981) (county funding of abortion stopped/state abortion funding upheld); Rosie J. v. NC State Department of Human Resources (end of state abortion funding upheld) 347 NC 247 (1997) Amicus Brief for N.C. Right to Life; Manning v. Hunt (parental consent law upheld) 119 F.3rd 254 (4th Cir. 1997). Amicus for NC Right to Life; NC Right to Life v. Bartlett (statutes declared unconstitutional) 163 F3d 705 (4th Cir. 1999) (Local counsel); Stam v. Hunt, 66 NC App 116 (1982); Jackson v. A Woman's Choice - 130 N.C. App. 590 (1998); Covington v. Apex, 108 NC App. 231 (zoning) (1992); Whitman v. Forbes - constructive trust, 55 NC App 706 (1982); Sebrell v. Carter - adverse possession, 105 NC App 322 (1992); Starkey v. Cimarron, 70 NC App 772 (1984) - statute of repose; Strother v. NC Farm Bureau - 90 NC App 734 (1998)-hail coverage; Price v. Price - custody of child by incompetent, 42 NC Ap 66 (1979); Pope v. Easley, 354 NC 544 (judicial appointment statue declared unconstitutional in part) (2001); Batdorff v. State Board of Elections, 150 NC App. 108 (2002) (campaign finance); Dollar v. Town of Cary, 569 S.E.2d 731 (2003) (municipal media campaign to influence election enjoined); In re Stumbo Children, 357 NC 279 (2003) (Local Counsel for Home School Legal Defense). ***PRACTICE AREAS:*** Real Estate Titles and Litigation; Estates Law; Wills and Trusts Law; Municipal Government Law. ***Email:*** paulstam@bellsouth.net

(This Listing Continued)

HENRY C. FORDHAM, JR., born Cleveland, Ohio, November 21, 1954; admitted to bar, 1985, North Carolina. *Education:* University of North Carolina at Chapel Hill (B.A., 1977); Wake Forest University (J.D., magna cum laude, 1985). Research Editor, Wake Forest Law Review, 1984-1985. Author: "The Commerce Power and State Sovereignty: Restriction of National League of Cities v. Usery," 20 Wake Forest Law Review 459, 1984. Law Clerk to Honorable Hiram H. Ward, U.S. District Judge, Middle District of North Carolina, 1985-1988. Apex Town Attorney: 1995-2001; 2003—. *Member:* Wake County and North Carolina Bar Associations; North Carolina State Bar; North Carolina Academy of Trial Lawyers. ***REPORTED CASES:*** Smith Chapel, etal. v. City of Durham, 350 N.C., 805,51 S.E. 2A 874 (1999); Covington v. Apex, 108 NC App. 231 (zoning) (1992); Williamson v. Savage, 104 N.C. App 188, 4085.E.2d 754 (notice of foreclosure) (1991); Sugg v. Field, 139 N.C. App. 160 532 S.E.2d 843 (Fifth Amendment in civil cases) (2000). ***PRACTICE AREAS:*** Condemnation; Municipal Government Law; Personal Injury Law; Wrongful Death Law; Workers Compensation Law; General Litigation. ***Email:*** fordham1000@bellsouth.net

THEODORE S. DANCHI, born Gary, Indiana, July 19, 1950; admitted to bar, 1987, North Carolina and Indiana. *Education:* Valparaiso University (B.S., 1972; J.D., 1987); Purdue University (M.S., 1977). Member, Moot Court. Member of Staff, 1985-1986 and Articles Editor, 1986-1987, Valparaiso University Law Review. Author: Note, "Church Discipline on Trial: Religious Freedom Versus Individual Privacy," Volume 21, Valparaiso University Law Review, 1987. Certified Mediator. *Member:* Wake County and North Carolina Bar Associations; North Carolina State Bar; Indiana State Bar. ***REPORTED CASES:*** Manning v. Hunt (parental consent law upheld) 119 F.3rd 254 (Amicus for NC Right to Life) (4th Cir. 1997); Sugg v. Field, 139 N.C. App. 160 532 S.E.2d 843 (Fifth Amendment in civil cases) (2000). ***PRACTICE AREAS:*** General Litigation; Business and Corporate Law. ***Email:*** tdanchi@bellsouth.net

REPRESENTATIVE CLIENTS: Smith & Smith Surveyors; Surveyors Supply Co.; Apex Sales Co.; Apex Cabinet Co.; Apex Nurseries, Inc.
APPROVED ATTORNEYS FOR: Lawyers Title Insurance Co.; Fidelity National Title Insurance Co.; Security Union Title Insurance Co.; Commonwealth Land Title Insurance Co.
REFERENCE: Crescent State Bank.

FREDERIC E. TOMS & ASSOCIATES, PLLC

APEX, NORTH CAROLINA

(See Cary)

Personal Injury, Medical Malpractice, Creditor, Traffic Violations, Nursing Home Litigation, Automobile Accidents, Wrongful Death.

JEFFREY S. BERMAN

ASHEBORO, NORTH CAROLINA

(Greensboro)

Family Law, Divorce, Child Custody, Alimony, Criminal Law, Traffic Violations, Driving While Intoxicated, Civil Litigation, Personal Injury, Wills and Estates.

BUNCH, ROBINS & STUBBLEFIELD, LLP

117 SUNSET AVENUE
ASHEBORO, NORTH CAROLINA 27203-5607
Telephone: 336-629-2121
Fax: 336-626-5736
Email: asheborolawyers@triad.rr.com

Criminal and Traffic, Family Law, Real Estate, Personal Injury, Mediation, Workers Compensation, Social Security, Civil, Business, Bankruptcy, Wills and Estates.

MEMBERS OF FIRM

W. EDWARD BUNCH, born Asheboro, North Carolina, July 5, 1955; admitted to bar, 1980, North Carolina. *Education:* University of North Carolina (B.A., English, 1976); Wake Forest University (J.D., 1980). *Member:* North Carolina Academy of Trial Lawyers; The Association of Trial Lawyers of America. ***PRACTICE AREAS:*** Criminal Defense; Traffic Violations; Real Estate; Personal Injury; Social Security; Civil Litigation; Business Litigation; Wills; Estate Litigation. ***Email:*** bunched@triad.rr.com

THOMAS D. ROBINS, born Winston-Salem, North Carolina, August 7, 1956; admitted to bar, 1981, North Carolina. *Education:* University of North Carolina (A.B., 1978); Wake Forest University (J.D., 1981). *Member:* North Carolina Bar Association. ***PRACTICE AREAS:*** Family Law; Mediation; Adoptions. ***Email:*** tomrobins@triad.rr.com

JULIE H. STUBBLEFIELD, born Greensboro, North Carolina, May 28, 1968; admitted to bar, 1993, North Carolina. *Education:* Campbell University (B.A., 1990; J.D., 1993). *Member:* North Carolina Bar Association. ***PRACTICE AREAS:*** Family Law; Real Estate; Bankruptcy; Workers Compensation; Social Security Disability. ***Email:*** stubblefield@triad.rr.com

APPROVED ATTORNEYS FOR: Lawyers Title Insurance Corp.; First Title Insurance Co.; Investors Title Insurance Co.; Pilot Title Insurance Co.; U.S. Department of Agriculture; Federal Land Bank of Columbia; Commonwealth Land Title Insurance Co.; Chicago Title Insurance Co.

HEIDI G. CHAPMAN, P.L.L.C.

ASHEBORO, NORTH CAROLINA

(See Chapel Hill)

Workers Compensation, Auto Accidents, Wrongful Death, Personal Injury, Social Security Disability.

DAIL & LINTON

ASHEBORO, NORTH CAROLINA

(See High Point)

Personal Injury, Automobile Accidents, Slip and Fall, Wrongful Death, Family Law, Adoption Law, Child Custody, Child Support, Divorce, Domestic Violence, Criminal Law, Driving While Intoxicated, Drug Crimes, Traffic Violations, Business Litigation, Trial Practice, General Practice, Workers Compensation.

THE DEUTERMAN LAW GROUP, P.A.

ASHEBORO, NORTH CAROLINA

(See Greensboro)

Workers Compensation, Auto Accidents, Social Security Disability, Wrongful Death, Nursing Home Neglect, Slip and Fall, Products Liability.

SCOTT N. DUNN

Established in 1991

162 E. WARD STREET
ASHEBORO, NORTH CAROLINA 27203-5517
Telephone: 336-629-1650
Fax: 336-629-0043
Email: sndunn@earthlink.net
URL: http://www.scottdunnlaw.com

Family Law, Divorce, Child Custody and Support, Juvenile Law, Criminal Law, DWI, Traffic Violations, Social Security Disability.

FIRM PROFILE: Scott N. Dunn is a dedicated, experienced attorney who listens to you, builds a working relationship and works with you through the legal process to achieve your objectives.

SCOTT N. DUNN, born Tarboro, North Carolina, May 13, 1960; admitted to bar, 1990, Florida; 1991, North Carolina. *Education:* Eckerd College (B.A. 1982); Stetson University at St. Petersburg (J.D., 199 0). *Member:* Randolph County, North Carolina and American Bar Associations. ***PRACTICE AREAS:*** Family Law; Divorce; Child Custody; Child Support; Juvenile Law; Criminal Law; Driving While Intoxicated; Traffic Violations; Social Security Disability.

LAW OFFICES OF WILLIAM H. FLOWE, JR.

ASHEBORO, NORTH CAROLINA

(See Liberty)

Real Estate, Closings, Buying and Selling, Wills, Trust and Estates, Estates Planning, Small Business, Limited Liability Companies, Business Enterprises, Family Law, Divorce.

GAVIN, COX, PUGH AND WILHOIT, L.L.P.

Established in 1952

119 WORTH STREET
ASHEBORO, NORTH CAROLINA 27203
Telephone: 336-629-2600
Facsimile: 336-629-4734

General Civil and Criminal Practice, Federal and State Courts. Estate Planning, Personal Injury. Trials, Probate and Real Estate Law. State and Local Government Law, Appellate Practice, Traffic.

W. ED GAVIN, born Sanford, North Carolina, 1921; admitted to bar, 1948, North Carolina. *Education:* Wake Forest University (B.S., 1942; LL.B., 1948). (Retired)

RICHARD L. COX, born Asheboro, North Carolina, May 14, 1954; admitted to bar, 1981, North Carolina. *Education:* Wake Forest University (B.S., 1976); Campbell University (J.D., 1980). Tax Attorney, Randolph County, 1984-1997. Chairman, North Carolina Rural Electrification Authority, 1986-1994. *Member:* North Carolina Bar Association (Member and Legislative Committee Chairman of the Real Property Section Council); North Carolina State Bar. ***PRACTICE AREAS:*** Real Estate; Corporate Law; Estate Planning; Probate Law; Commercial Real Estate; Residential Real Estate; Estate Administration; Traffic Violations. ***Email:*** rcox@gavincox.com

ALAN V. PUGH, born Asheboro, North Carolina, July 10, 1952; admitted to bar, 1976, North Carolina. *Education:* University of North Carolina (A.B., 1973; J.D., 1976). Tax Attorney, Randolph County, 1979-1983. County Attorney, Randolph County, 1994—. Deputy Secretary, North Carolina Department of Administration, 1985. Senior Assistant and Special Counsel to the Governor of North Carolina, 1986-1991. Secretary, North Carolina Department of Crime Control and Public Safety, 1992. General Counsel to the Speaker of N.C. House of Representatives, 1994-1999. Board of Visitors, University of North Carolina at Chapel Hill, 1995-1999. Member, North Carolina Civil Procedure Study Commission, 1998. Member, North Carolina Board of Transportation, 1999. Board of Directors, N.C.

(This Listing Continued)

Institute of Government Foundation, 2001—. *Member:* North Carolina Bar Association; North Carolina State Bar. ***REPORTED CASES:*** Mann Media v. Randolph County 356 NCI (2002); In Re Allred 351 N.C. 1, 1999; Clark v. City of Asheboro, 136 N.C. App. 14 (1999); Johnson v. Burrow, 42 N.C. App. 273 (1979). ***PRACTICE AREAS:*** Administrative Law; Commercial Real Estate; Corporate; Civil Litigation; Estate Planning; Zoning, Planning and Land Use Law; Appellate Practice; Traffic Violations. ***Email:*** apugh@gavincox.com

ROBERT E. WILHOIT, born Pinehurst, North Carolina, February 9, 1953; admitted to bar, 1981, North Carolina. *Education:* Wake Forest University (B.A., 1975); Campbell University (J.D., 1979). Delta Theta Phi. Board Attorney, Randolph County Board of Education, 1995—. City Attorney, Randleman, 1999. City Attorney, Trinity, 2000—. Town Attorney, Ramseur, 1999—. Town Attorney, Seagrove, 2001. Seagrove/Ulah Metropolitan Water District, 2001—. Town Attorney, Staley, 2003. *Member:* North Carolina Bar Association; North Carolina State Bar; North Carolina Council of School Attorneys; North Carolina Association of Municipal Attorney; National School Boards Association (Council of School Attorneys). ***PRACTICE AREAS:*** Education Law; Municipal Law; Corporate Law; Civil Litigation; Traffic Violations; Personal Injury; Estate Administration. ***Email:*** rwilhoit@gavincox.com

REPRESENTATIVE CLIENTS: Randolph County; City of Randleman; City of Trinity; Town of Ramseur; Town of Seagrove; Seagrove/Ulah Metropolitan Water District; Randolph County Board of Education; Randolph Community College; Town of Staley; Pugh Oil Co.; Dan Thomas Pontiac, Inc.; Time-Warner Communications Corp. (Cablevision); First Bank; Hughes Furniture Industries, Inc.; Wayne Thomas Chevrolet, Inc.; Datamark Graphics, Inc.; Automasters of Asheboro, LLC.; Asheboro Nissan, Inc.; Ridge Funeral Home, Inc.; Brubaker and Associates (Real Estate Appraisal); Asheboro Honda-Mazda; Southern Pride Autos, Inc.; Brady Car and Truck Center; David L. Lawson, Jr. Builders and Developers, Inc.; Randolph County Economic Development Corporation; Randolph County Tourism Development Authority; Cross Roads Rest and Retirement Center; Routh Oil Company, Inc.; S.E. Trogdon and Sons (Construction).
APPROVED ATTORNEYS FOR: Investors Title Insurance Company; Chicago Title Insurance Company; Lawyers Title Insurance Company; Farmers Home Administration; Centura Bank; First Union National Bank; Wachovia Mortgage Corp.; First National Bank; Central Carolina Bank; North Central Farm Credit; ACA Branch Bank and Trust Co.; Randolph Bank and Trust Co.

MEGERIAN & WELLS

175 EAST SALISBURY STREET
ASHEBORO, NORTH CAROLINA 27203
Telephone: 336-625-1436
Fax: 336-625-0553
Email: mandwlaw@triad.rr.com

Civil and Criminal Trials in State and Federal Courts. Criminal Defense, Civil Litigation, Family Law.

MEMBERS OF FIRM

JONATHAN L. MEGERIAN, born New York, New York, September 29, 1953; admitted to bar, 1981, North Carolina, U.S. District Court, Western, Eastern and Middle Districts of North Carolina, U.S. Court of Appeals, 4th Circuit and U.S. Supreme Court. *Education:* Fordham University (B.A., 1975); University of Toronto (M.A., 1978); University of North Carolina (J.D., 1981). Phi Beta Kappa. Chairman, Randolph County Board of Elections, 1992-1993. *Member:* North Carolina State Bar (Councilor, 1988-1996); North Carolina Academy of Trial Lawyers (Board of Governors, 2000—). (Board Certified Specialist in Criminal Law, North Carolina State Board of Legal Specialization). ***REPORTED CASES:*** State v. Adams 132 NC App. 819, 513 Se 2d 588 (1999). ***PRACTICE AREAS:*** Criminal Defense; Family Law; Personal Injury; Zoning. ***Email:*** jmegerian@triad.rr.com

FRANKLIN E. WELLS, JR., born Raleigh, North Carolina, January 6, 1960; admitted to bar, 1986, North Carolina, U.S. District Court, Eastern, Middle and Western Districts of North Carolina and U.S. Court of Appeals, 4th Circuit. *Education:* University of North Carolina (A.B., 1982; J.D., 1985). Member, Randolph County Board of Elections, 1988-1992. *Member:* 19B Judicial District Bar (President); North Carolina Bar Association; North Carolina State Bar; North Carolina Academy of Trial Lawyers; National Association of Criminal Defense Lawyers. ***PRACTICE AREAS:*** Civil Litigation; Personal Injury Law; Criminal Defense; Construction Litigation. ***Email:*** fwells@triad.rr.com

REPRESENTATIVE CLIENTS: Randolph Bank and Trust Co.; Shana Knitwear, Inc.; Asheboro Ophthalmology; Handy Sanitary District; Town of Franklinville.
REFERENCE: Randolph Bank and Trust Co.

MORGAN, HERRING, MORGAN, GREEN, ROSENBLUTT & GILL, LLP

ASHEBORO, NORTH CAROLINA

(See High Point)

General Civil and Criminal Trial Practice in all State and Federal Courts. Interstate Commerce, Probate, Real Estate, Corporation and Tax Law. Torts. Traffic Violations and Driving Under the Influence, Personal Injury, Auto Accidents, Wills and Estates, Family Law, Divorce, Custody, Support, Adoption, Workers Compensation, Bankruptcy, Social Security, Employment Discrimination.

THE QUINN LAW FIRM

ASHEBORO, NORTH CAROLINA

(See Greensboro)

Workers Compensation, Personal Injury, Automobile Accidents and Injuries, Employment Discrimination, Immigration.

SCHELL BRAY AYCOCK ABEL & LIVINGSTON P.L.L.C.

ASHEBORO, NORTH CAROLINA

(See Greensboro)

Corporate, Taxation, Securities Regulation, Venture Capital, Real Estate and Real Estate Finance, Mergers and Acquisitions, Health Care, Antitrust and Trade Regulation, Banking, Commercial, Employee Benefits, Estate Planning and Administration.

LAW OFFICE OF MATT A. STOCKDALE, PLLC

ASHEBORO, NORTH CAROLINA

(See Greensboro)

Criminal Law, Traffic Violations, Driving While Intoxicated, Drug Crimes, Parole and Probate, White Collar Crime, Trust and Estates, Estate Planning, Business Law, Child Support.

TUGGLE DUGGINS & MESCHAN, P.A.

ASHEBORO, NORTH CAROLINA

(See Greensboro)

General Civil Practice. Corporation, Tax, Insurance, Banking, Pension and Profit Sharing, Bankruptcy and Creditors' Rights, Trust and Estate, Construction and Real Estate Law. Trials and Appeals in all State and Federal Courts.

DONALD R. VAUGHAN AND ASSOCIATES

ASHEBORO, NORTH CAROLINA

(See Greensboro)

Traffic Violations and Criminal Law.

ADAMS, HENDON, CARSON, CROW & SAENGER, P.A.

Established in 1872

72 PATTON AVENUE
P.O. BOX 2714
ASHEVILLE, NORTH CAROLINA 28802
Telephone: 828-252-7381
Fax: 828-252-5018
URL: http://www.adamsfirm.com

General Civil Trial Practice in State and Federal Courts. Administrative, Corporation, Taxation, Business, Real Estate and Construction Law, Litigation, Wills, Probate, Trusts and Estates, Estate Planning, Contracts, Family Law, Divorce, Child Custody, Child Support.

FIRM PROFILE: Adams, Hendon, Carson, Crow & Saenger, P.A. was founded by Joseph Shepard Adams, who first practiced law in Asheville in 1872. He formed a partnership with his son, John Sneed Adams in 1904. The firm has been in continuous existence since that time, providing comprehensive legal services including all phases of civil litigation, business and corporate law, probate, taxation and real estate.

JUNIUS G. ADAMS, JR. (1908-1991)

GEORGE WARD HENDON, born Asheville, North Carolina, September 16, 1941; admitted to bar, 1967, North Carolina; 1970, U.S. Court of Appeals, Fourth Circuit; 1981, U.S. Supreme Court. *Education:* University of Tennessee (B.S., 1963); University of North Carolina (J.D., 1967). Phi Delta Phi. Member, Fourth Circuit Judicial Conference. Member, IOLTA Board of Trustees 1993-1999, Chairman, 1998-1999. *Member:* Buncombe County (President, 1986-1987), North Carolina and American Bar Associations; The North Carolina State Bar (Member, Disciplinary Hearing Commission, 1983-1989). ***PRACTICE AREAS:*** Litigation. ***Email:*** whendon@adamsfirm.com

PHILIP G. CARSON, born Gastonia, North Carolina, February 7, 1938; admitted to bar, 1967, North Carolina. *Education:* Davidson College and University of North Carolina (B.A., cum laude, 1963); University of North Carolina (J.D., 1967). Phi Delta Phi. Member, Board of Editors, North Carolina Law Review, 1966-1967. Member, 1973-1995 and Chairman, 1984-1988, University of North Carolina Board of Governors. *Member:* Buncombe County (President, 1993-1994; Treasurer, 1968-1969) and North Carolina Bar Associations; The North Carolina State Bar. ***PRACTICE AREAS:*** Business Law; Estates Law; Probate Law; Taxation Law. ***Email:*** pcarson@adamsfirm.com

SAMUEL J. CROW, born Asheville, North Carolina, April 25, 1937; admitted to bar, 1962, North Carolina. *Education:* Emory University (A.B., 1958); Wake Forest University (LL.B., 1962). Phi Delta Phi. *Member:* Buncombe County (President, 1978-1979), North Carolina and American Bar Associations; The North Carolina State Bar (Member, Disciplinary Hearing Commission, 1989-1995); North Carolina Academy of Trial Lawyers; The Association of Trial Lawyers of America. [Capt., JAGC, U.S. Army, 1962-1966]. ***PRACTICE AREAS:*** Civil Litigation; Real Estate Law; Estates Law; Probate Law; Domestic Relations; Divorce; Equitable Distribution. ***Email:*** jcrow@adamsfirm.com

GEORGE W. SAENGER, born New York, N.Y., November 8, 1946; admitted to bar, 1976, North Carolina; 1980, U.S. Court of Appeals, Fourth Circuit; 1985, U.S. Tax Court. *Education:* University of North Carolina (A.B., 1968; J.D., 1976). Phi Delta Phi. *Member:* Buncombe County and North Carolina Bar Associations; The North Carolina State Bar. [Capt., USAF, 1968-1973]. ***PRACTICE AREAS:*** Commercial Litigation; Business Law; Estates Law; Probate Law. ***Email:*** gsaenger@adamsfirm.com

(This Listing Continued)

MARTIN K. REIDINGER, born New Haven, Connecticut, December 18, 1958; admitted to bar, 1984, North Carolina; 1985, U.S. Court of Appeals, Fourth Circuit; 1994, U.S. Supreme Court. *Education:* University of North Carolina at Chapel Hill (B.A., 1981; J.D., with honors, 1984). Order of the Coif. Member, North Carolina Law Review, 1983-1984. *Member:* Buncombe County (President, 2003-2004; Secretary/Treasurer, 1989-1992) and North Carolina Bar Associations; The North Carolina State Bar. ***PRACTICE AREAS:*** Civil Litigation; Appellate Practice; Construction Law; Business Litigation; Municipal Law; Certified Mediator. ***Email:*** mreidinger@adamsfirm.com

GREGORY S. HILDERBRAN, born Conover, North Carolina, December 4, 1963; admitted to bar, 1989, North Carolina. *Education:* University of North Carolina (B.S., 1986); University of Georgia (J.D., magna cum laude, 1989). Order of the Coif. American Inns of Court, 1991-1993. Executive Editor, Georgia Law Review, 1988-1989. *Member:* North Carolina and American Bar Associations; North Carolina State Bar. ***PRACTICE AREAS:*** Business Law; Commercial Real Estate; Estate Planning; Estate Administration; Environmental Law. ***Email:*** ghilderbran@adamsfirm.com

E. THOMISON HOLMAN, born Huntsville, Alabama, November 16, 1966; admitted to bar, 1992, North Carolina; 1997, U.S. Court of Appeals, Fourth Circuit. *Education:* University of North Carolina at Chapel Hill (B.S., 1989); Cumberland School of Law of Samford University (J.D., 1992). Associate Editor, 1991-1992, and Staff Member, 1990-1991, Cumberland Law Review. *Member:* North Carolina Bar Association. ***PRACTICE AREAS:*** Civil Litigation. ***Email:*** tholman@adamsfirm.com

---

SUSAN TAYLOR RASH, born Atlanta, Georgia, June 15, 1961; admitted to bar, 1989, North Carolina and Georgia. *Education:* Clemson University (B.A., summa cum laude, 1982; M.A., 1986); University of Georgia (J.D., cum laude, 1989). Phi Kappa Phi. Recipient, Fulbright Study Grant, 1983-1984. Member, Editorial Board, 1987-1988 and Articles Editor, 1988-1989, Georgia Law Review. *Member:* The North Carolina State Bar. ***PRACTICE AREAS:*** Estate Planning; Estate Administration; Corporate Law; Business Law. ***Email:*** strash@adamsfirm.com

JOY GRAGG McIVER, born Kansas City, Missouri, May 10, 1966; admitted to bar, 1996, North Carolina. *Education:* Georgetown College (B.A., 1988); Appalachian State University (M.A., 1996); University of North Carolina at Chapel Hill (J.D., 1996). North Carolina Law Review Staff, 1994-1995. North Carolina Law Review Note Editor, 1995-1996. Author: "Thunder Basin Coal Company vs. Reich," NC Law Review, Vol. 73, Issue 5, 1995. *Member:* The North Carolina State Bar. ***PRACTICE AREAS:*** Civil Litigation; Family Law; Medical Malpractice; Appellate Practice. ***Email:*** jgragg@adamsfirm.com

DANIEL E. HITCHCOCK, born Akron, Ohio, December 8, 1966; admitted to bar, 1993, Oregon and U.S. District Court, District of Oregon; 2003, North Carolina. *Education:* Denison University (B.A., 1989); Lewis and Clark College (J.D., 1993). Member, Lewis and Clark Environmental Law Review. *Member:* American Bankruptcy Institute. ***PRACTICE AREAS:*** Estate Planning; Business Transactions; Creditors Rights. ***Email:*** dhitchcock@adamsfirm.com

MATTHEW S. ROBERSON, born Asheville, North Carolina, August 3, 1979; admitted to bar, 2004, North Carolina. *Education:* University of North Carolina at Chapel Hill (B.A., 2000); Norman Adrian Wiggins School of Law (J.D., 2004). Phi Beta Kappa. Editor in Chief, Campbell Law Review. Order of Barristers. 25 Campbell Law Review 181 (2003) "Don't Bother Knockin!!! Come On In!" The Constitutionality of Warrantless Searches As a Condition of Probation. *Member:* North Carolina and American Bar Associations. ***PRACTICE AREAS:*** Civil Litigation. ***Email:*** mroberson@adamsfirm.com

ATTORNEYS FOR: Asheville School, Inc.; Asheville-Buncombe Development Corp.; Avondale Mills, Inc.; Anderson Automotive Group; Biltmore Farms, Inc.; Biltmore Parkway Center; Biltmore Plaza Shopping Center; Biltmore Square Mall; Brown & Williamson Tobacco Co.; Carriage Park Development Corp.; Cincinnati Insurance Company (Surety); Citizens Fuel Co.; Fazio Golf Course Designers, Inc.; First Citizens Bank & Trust Co.; General Electric Corp.; General Motors Corp.; Good Neighbors Association of NC; High Hampton, Inc.; McCarroll Construction, Inc.; Morgan Stanley Dean Whitter, Inc.; Price-McNabb Advertising, Inc.; Simon Property Group; St. Luke's Hospital, Inc.; Town of Montreat; 20th Century Heating Co., Inc.; Union Carbide Corp.; USB Financial Services, Inc.; Wade Hampton Golf Course, Inc.; WNC Pallet & Forest Products Co, Inc.
LOCAL COUNSEL FOR: Norfolk Southern Corp.
APPROVED ATTORNEYS FOR: First American Title Insurance Co.; Lawyers Title Insurance Corp.;Old Republic National Title Insurance Co.; Chicago Title Insurance Co.
REFERENCES: First Union National Bank of North Carolina; Bank of America.

WILLIAM E. ANDERSON

Established in 1968

17 NORTH MARKET STREET, SUITE 201
ASHEVILLE, NORTH CAROLINA 28801
Telephone: 828-252-3861
Fax: 828-251-5840

General Criminal Trial Practice in all Courts, Drug Crimes, DWI, Traffic Violations.

WILLIAM E. ANDERSON, born Kalamazoo, Michigan, September 14, 1943; admitted to bar, 1968, North Carolina. *Education:* Presbyterian College (A.B., 1968); University of North Carolina (J.D., 1968). *Member:* North Carolina Bar Association.

BALL, BARDEN & BELL, P.A.

Established in 1986

18-20 NORTH SPRUCE STREET
ASHEVILLE, NORTH CAROLINA 28801
Telephone: 828-252-0682
Fax: 828-252-6774
Email: BalBarBel@aol.com

Mailing Address: P.O. Box 7157, Asheville, NC 28802

Trials and Appeals in State and Federal Courts. Insurance Defense, Workers Compensation, Personal Injury, Commercial Law, Automobile Accidents, Wrongful Death.

(This Listing Continued)

ERVIN L. BALL, JR., born Asheville, North Carolina, March 9, 1945; admitted to bar, 1970, North Carolina; 1971, U.S. District Court, Western District of North Carolina; 1974, U.S. Court of Appeals, Fourth Circuit; 1975, U.S. Supreme Court. *Education:* University of Tennessee at Knoxville (B.S., with honors, 1967; J.D., 1970). Phi Delta Phi. *Member:* North Carolina and American Bar Associations; 28th Judicial District ((President 1994-1995); North Carolina State Bar; North Carolina Association Defense Attorneys (Member, Board of Directors, Pisgah Legal Services, 1995-2000, State Personnel Commission, 1999-2001); The Defense Research Institute. ***PRACTICE AREAS:*** Personal Injury; Insurance Defense; Civil Litigation; Workers Compensation. ***Email:*** ELBALLJR@aol.com

STEPHEN L. BARDEN, III (1945-2005)

THOMAS R. BELL, JR., born Ayer, Massachusetts, April 26, 1947; admitted to bar, 1972, North Carolina; 1975, Alabama; 1980, U.S. Supreme Court. *Education:* University of the South (A.B., 1969); University of North Carolina (J.D., 1972). *Member:* North Carolina and American Bar Associations; Alabama State Bar; 28th Judicial District and North Carolina State Bars; North Carolina Association of Defense Attorneys; Defense Research Institute. ***PRACTICE AREAS:*** Insurance Defense Litigation; Workers Compensation; Civil Litigation; Business Law; Bankruptcy (Creditors) Law. ***Email:*** BELLTJR@aol.com

REPRESENTATIVE CLIENTS: Bituminous Casualty Co.; The Concord Group Insurance Co.; Dependable Insurance Co.; Pennsylvania National Insurance Co.; Maryland Cas. Co.; The Ohio Casualty Group; Pennsylvania National Insurance Co.; The Travelers Insurance Co.; USAA Property & Casualty Insurance Co.; Innsbruck Mall; Ken Wilson Ford, Inc.; Foremost Ins. Co.; Moore's, Inc.; Westgate Shopping Center; Lawyers Mutual Liability Insurance Company of N.C.; Metlife Auto & Home Ins.; Farmers Ins. Group; Zurich U.S.; Colona Insurance Cos.; St. Paul Insurance Cos.; Progressive Insurance Cos.; ORION Auto; Royal & Sun Alliance Insurance Group; Harleysville Insurance Co.; Providence Washington Insur. Co.; Infinity Insurance Co.; Park Ridge Hospital.
REFERENCES: Bank of America; Wachovia Bank.

BEST & BEST PLLC

138 CHARLOTTE STREET, SUITE 200
ASHEVILLE, NORTH CAROLINA 28801
Telephone: 828-255-7772
Fax: 828-255-9232
Email: info@bestpllc.com

Residential, Commercial and Investment Real Estate, Condominium Law, Creditor's Rights, Foreclosures, Estate Administration, Commercial Litigation, Tax Deferred Exchanges, Construction Law.

PETER FARQUHARD BEST, born Asheville, North Carolina, August 26, 1944; admitted to bar, 1969, North Carolina. *Education:* University of the South (B.A., 1966); University of North Carolina (J.D., 1969). *Member:* 28th Judicial District, North Carolina and American Bar Associations; and North Carolina State Bar. ***PRACTICE AREAS:*** Commercial Real Estate; Real Estate Development; Condominium Law; Tax Deferred Exchanges; Estate Administration. ***Email:*** peter@bestpllc.com

SCOTT CAMPBELL BEST, born Asheville, North Carolina, December 14, 1971; admitted to bar, 1999, North Carolina. *Education:* College of William & Mary (B.A., 1994); Cumberland School of Law of Samford University (J.D., 1999). *Member:* Bucombe County (Vice President, Young Lawyers Division, 2002), 28th Judicial District and North Carolina Bar Associations. ***PRACTICE AREAS:*** Commercial Real Estate; Real Estate Investment; Creditors Rights; Foreclosures; Commercial Litigation; Construction Law. ***Email:*** scott@bestpllc.com

JASON M. PELTZ, born Springfield, Missouri, January 30th, 1976; admitted to bar, 2002, North Carolina. *Education:* Washington University in St. Louis (B.A., 1998); Wake Forest University (J.D., 2002). *Member:* North Carolina (Member, Real Property Section) and American Bar Associations; North Carolina State Bar. ***PRACTICE AREAS:*** Residential Real Estate; Commercial Real Estate; Buying and Selling a Home; Foreclosures; Commercial Litigation. ***Email:*** jason@bestpllc.com

BIGGERS & HUNTER, PLLC

79 WOODFIN PLACE, SUITE 211
ASHEVILLE, NORTH CAROLINA 28801
Telephone: 828-258-0576
Fax: 828-258-9857
URL: http://www.lawyers.com/biggers&hunter

Real Estate, Business Law, Wills and Probate, Trusts and Estates, Elder Law, Traffic Violations, Driving While Intoxicated (DWI), Personal Injury, Labor and Employment Law, Wage and Hour Law, Criminal Law, Environmental Law, Real Estate Closings, Real Estate Litigation, Foreclosures, Boundary Disputes, Title Examinations.

WILLIAM T. BIGGERS, born Asheville, North Carolina, November 28, 1946; admitted to bar, 1973, North Carolina and U.S. District Court, Western District of North Carolina; 1974, U.S. Court of Appeals, 4th Circuit, U.S. Tax Court and U.S. Supreme Court. *Education:* Western Carolina University (B.A., 1969); Wake Forest University (J.D., 1973). Phi Alpha Delta. Public Member, North Carolina Board of Pharmacy, 1988-1995. Assistant Secretary to North Carolina Department of Administration, 1974-1976. *Member:* Buncombe County, North Carolina and American Bar Associations; North Carolina State Bar; National Academy of Elder Law Attorneys. [Col. JAG Army Reserve]. ***PRACTICE AREAS:*** Real Estate Litigation; Business Law; Real Estate; Wills; Probate; Trusts and Estates; Real Estate Closings; Elder Law; Traffic Violations; Driving While Intoxicated; Personal Injury. ***Email:*** wtbig@att.net

JOHN C. HUNTER, born Brevard, North Carolina, 1959; admitted to bar, 1985, North Carolina, U.S. District Courts, Western and Eastern Districts of North Carolina and U.S. Court of Appeals, Fourth Circuit. *Education:* Wake Forest University (B.A., 1981; J.D., 1985). Executive Director, Education and Research Consortium of Western Carolinas, Inc., 2001—. Acting President, Blue Ridge Savings Bank, Inc., 1996-1998. Special Counsel, House Select Committee for Personnel Review, North Carolina House of Representatives, 1995-1996. General Counsel, North Carolina Department of Environment, Health and Natural Resources, 1989-1993; Legal Counsel to Governor of North Carolina, 1987-1989. *Member:* North Carolina (Member: Governing Council of Environmental Law Section, 1989-1993; Criminal Law Section; Litigation Section; Administrative Law Section) and American (Member, Sections on: Criminal Law; Litigation) Bar Associations; North Carolina State Bar; North Carolina Academy of Trial Lawyers; National Association of Criminal Defense Lawyers. ***REPORTED CASES:*** Save Our Rivers, Inc. v. Town of Highlands, 341 N.C. 635, 461 S.E.2d 333 (1995); Hodge v. N.C. Department of Transportation, 347 N.C. 602, 499 S.E.2d 187 (1998); Harper v. City of Asheville, 160 N.C. App. 209, 585 S.E. 2d 240 (2003). ***PRACTICE AREAS:*** Administrative Law; Civil Litigation; Labor; Employment Law; Environmental Law; Government Relations; White Collar Crime. ***Email:*** jchesq@bellsouth.net

JEFFREY K. STAHL, born Asheville, North Carolina, November 12, 1976; admitted to bar, 2004, North Carolina. *Education:* Western Carolina University (B.S., 2000); Appalachian School of Law (J.D., 2004). Phi Alpha Delta. Deans List, 2001 and 2004. *Member:* Buncombe County and American Bar Associations; North Carolina State Bar; North Carolina Academy of Trial Lawyers. ***PRACTICE AREAS:*** Real Estate Law; Business Law; Contracts Law; Wills; Trusts and Estates; Traffic Violations; Personal Injury; Driving While Intoxicated. ***Email:*** jstahl@biggersandhunter.com

BLANCHARD, NEWMAN & HAYES

ASHEVILLE, NORTH CAROLINA

(See Hendersonville)

General Civil Litigation, Family Law, Divorce, Criminal in all State and Federal Courts, Traffic, DWI.

BYERS, MARTELLE & WILLIAMS, P.L.L.C.

ASHEVILLE, NORTH CAROLINA

(See Rutherfordton, North Carolina)

General Civil and Criminal Trial Practice in all courts, Family Law, Real Property Law, Elder Law, Wills, Trusts and Estates, Corporate Law, and Municipal Law.

CARTER SCHNEDLER & MONTEITH, P.A.

56 CENTRAL AVENUE, SUITE 101
P.O. BOX 2985
ASHEVILLE, NORTH CAROLINA 28802
Telephone: 828-252-6225
FAX: 828-252-6316
Email: mail@ashevillepatent.com
URL: http://www.ashevillepatent.com

Patents, Trademarks, Copyrights.

DAVID M. CARTER, born Lexington, Kentucky, November 28, 1946; admitted to bar, 1973, Indiana; 1979, North Carolina; registered to practice before U.S. Patent and Trademark Office. *Education:* Western Kentucky (B.S., 1968); George Washington University (J.D., 1972). Examiner, U.S. Patent and Trademark Office, 1968-1972. *Member:* North Carolina State Bar; Carolina Patent, Trademark & Copyright Law Association. ***PRACTICE AREAS:*** Patent, Trademark and Copyright Law. ***Email:*** carter@ashevillepatent.com

STEVEN C. SCHNEDLER, born Middletown, Ohio, August 14, 1948; admitted to bar, 1974, Michigan; 1980, Virginia; 1989, North Carolina; registered to practice before U.S. Patent and Trademark Office. *Education:* Michigan State University (B.S.E.E., 1970); Detroit College of Law (J.D., with honors, 1974); Georgetown University Law Center. *Member:* 28th Judicial District Bar Association; North Carolina State Bar; American Intellectual Property Law Association; Carolina Patent, Trademark and Copyright Law Association. ***PRACTICE AREAS:*** Patent, Trademark and Copyright Law. ***Email:*** schnedler@ashevillepatent.com

J. DEREL MONTEITH, JR., born Charlotte, North Carolina, September 26, 1968; admitted to bar, 1998, North Carolina and U.S. District Court, Western District of North Carolina; 1999, U.S. District Court, Eastern and Middle Districts of North Carolina; registered to practice before the U.S. Patent and Trademark Office. *Education:* University of Miami (B.M., Music Engineering Technology, 1992); University of North Carolina at Chapel Hill (J.D., 1998). Recipient, First Prize, 1997-1998 Nathan Burkan Memorial Competition, University of North Carolina at Chapel Hill. Staff Member, 1996-1997 and Note Editor, 1997-1998, North Carolina Law Review. Co-Author: "The Continuing Saga of Federal Circuit Claim Construction Jurisprudence: Extrinsic Evidence and Other Stories," 8 Federal Circuit B.J. 83 (1999), reprinted in 2000 Intellectual Property Law Review. *Member:* North Carolina State Bar; North Carolina and American (Member, Intellectual Property Section) Bar Associations; Carolina Patent Trademark & Copyright Law Association. ***PRACTICE AREAS:*** Patents; Trademarks; Copyrights; Unfair Competition. ***Email:*** monteith@ashevillepatent.com

CLAXTON LAW FIRM, P.A.

Established in 1995

22 SOUTH PACK SQUARE, SUITE 1200
ASHEVILLE, NORTH CAROLINA 28801
Telephone: 828-253-8818
Fax: 828-253-8812
URL: http://www.claxtonlawfirm.com
Email: doug@claxtonlawfirm.com
URL: http://www.lawyers.com/claxtonlawfirm

Real Estate, Wills, Trusts, Estates, Business.

(This Listing Continued)

CLAXTON LAW FIRM, P.A., Asheville—Continued

DOUGLAS A. CLAXTON, born Heidelberg, West Germany, June 23, 1969; admitted to bar, 1995, North Carolina. *Education:* University of North Carolina at Chapel Hill (B.A., Economics, 1991); Campbell University Norman Adrian Wiggins School of Law (J.D., 1995). *Member:* 28th Judicial District, North Carolina (Member, Real Property Section) and American (Member, Real Property, Probate and Trust Section) Bar Associations; North Carolina State Bar. ***PRACTICE AREAS:*** Real Estate; Residential Real Estate; Commercial Real Estate; Wills. ***Email:*** doug@claxtonlawfirm.com

APPROVED ATTORNEY FOR: Attorneys Title; Commonwealth Title; Fidelity Title; First American Title; Old Republic Title; Chicago Title; Investors Title; Lawyers Title; Southern Title; Stewart Title; Bank of America; Centura Bank; Bank of Asheville; High Street Bank; First Union National Bank; Branch Banking & Trust; NC State Employees' Credit Union; Blue Ridge Savings Bank; Wachovia Bank.

COGBURN, GOOSMANN, BRAZIL & ROSE, P.A.

77 CENTRAL AVENUE, SUITE H
ASHEVILLE, NORTH CAROLINA 28801
Telephone: 828-258-0150
Fax: 828-258-1305
Email: info@cgbrlawfirm.com
URL: http://www.cgbrlawfirm.com
Mailing Address: P.O. Box 7436, Asheville, NC 28802

General Civil Practice before all Courts. Business Torts, Commercial Litigation, Commercial Torts, Commercial Real Estate, Real Estate Acquisition, Contract Litigation, Corporate Litigation, Criminal Law, Drug Crimes, Civil Litigation, Insurance Law, Insurance Defense, Torts, Real Estate, Construction, Eminent Domain, Zoning and Land Use.

MAX O. COGBURN, SR. (1927-2003)

STEVEN DOUGLAS COGBURN, born Asheville, North Carolina, December 13, 1956; admitted to bar, 1982, North Carolina, U.S. District Court, Western District of North Carolina and U.S. Court of Appeals, Fourth Circuit. *Education:* University of North Carolina (A.B., 1979; J.D., 1982). Phi Delta Phi. Research Assistant to the Honorable J. William Copeland, North Carolina Supreme Court, 1982-1983. *Member:* North Carolina Bar Association (Member, Litigation Section); 28th Judicial District and North Carolina State Bars; North Carolina Association of Defense Attorneys; Defense Research Institute. ***PRACTICE AREAS:*** Insurance Law; Civil Litigation; Personal Injury; Wrongful Death. ***Email:*** scogburn@cgbrlawfirm.com

GEORGE F. GOOSMANN, JR., born Asheville, North Carolina, October 4, 1962; admitted to bar, 1988, North Carolina, U.S. District Court, Western District of North Carolina and U.S. Court of Appeals, Fourth Circuit. *Education:* University of North Carolina at Chapel Hill (B.S.B.A., 1985); University of Miami (J.D., 1988). *Member:* North Carolina and American (Member, Real Property Section) Bar Associations; 28th Judicial District (President, Young Lawyers Section, 1990-1991) and North Carolina State Bar. ***PRACTICE AREAS:*** Commercial Real Estate; Residential Real Estate. ***Email:*** ggoosmann@cgbrlawfirm.com

W. O. BRAZIL, III, born New Orleans, Louisiana, January 10, 1964; admitted to bar, 1989, North Carolina and U.S. District Court, Western District of North Carolina. *Education:* Baylor University (B.A., 1986); Wake Forest University School of Law (J.D., 1989). Phi Delta Phi. *Member:* 28th Judicial District and North Carolina State Bar; North Carolina Association of Defense Attorneys; Defense Research Institute; Commissioner, Town of Biltmore Forest. ***PRACTICE AREAS:*** Insurance Defense Law; Criminal Defense; Civil Litigation; Personal Injury; Traffic Violations; Wrongful Death; Driving While Intoxicated. ***Email:*** bbrazil@cgbrlawfirm.com

JOHN R. ROSE, born Goldsboro, North Carolina, July 2, 1962; admitted to bar, 1988, North Carolina. *Education:* University of North Carolina at Chapel Hill (B.S., 1985); Campbell University (J.D., 1988). Membership Editor, Campbell Law Review, 1986-1988. Caselaw Editor, Campbell Law Observer, 1987-1988. *Member:* North Carolina Bar Association (Member, Real Property Section); 28th Judicial District and North Carolina State Bar. (Board Certified Specialist in Real Property Law - Residential Transactions, North Carolina State Board of Legal Specialization). ***PRACTICE AREAS:*** Commercial Real Estate; Residential Real Estate. ***Email:*** jrose@cgbrlawfirm.com

MAX O. COGBURN, JR., born 1951; admitted to bar, 1976, North Carolina. *Education:* University of North Carolina, Chapel Hill (A.B.); Cumberland School of Law of Samford University (J.D.). President, Student Bar Association, 1975-1976. Associate Justice, Moot Court Board, 1975-1976. Member, National Moot Court Team, 1975-1976. With Roberts, Cogburn & Williams, 1976-1980. Assistant U.S. Attorney, Western District of North Carolina, 1980-1992. Lead Attorney, Organized Crime & Drug Enforcement Task Force, 1982-1986, 1988-1991. Chief Assistant U.S. Attorney, Western District of North Carolina, 1986-1988. *Member:* North Carolina Bar Association; North Carolina State and 28th Judicial Bars; North Carolina Academy of Trial Lawyers (Member, Criminal Law Section). ***PRACTICE AREAS:*** Criminal Law; Traffic Violations; Driving While Intoxicated; Drug Crimes; Personal Injury; Automobile Accidents and Injuries; Wrongful Death; Catastrophic Injury; Construction Accidents; Brain Injury; Spinal Injury; Civil Litigation.

WILLIAM KENNON REED, born San Diego, California, April 22, 1971; admitted to bar, 1998, Maryland; 2000, North Carolina and Minnesota. *Education:* State University of New York at Oswego (B.A., 1992); Washington College of Law, American University (J.D., 1995); American University, School of International Services (M.A., 1997). Member, American University Journal of International Law and Policy, 1993-1995; 28th Judicial District. *Member:* North Carolina, Maryland State, Minnesota State and American (Member, Sections on Real Property; Business Law) Bar Associations. ***PRACTICE AREAS:*** Creditors Rights; Foreclosures; Residential Real Estate; Commercial Real Estate; Corporate Law; Business Transactions. ***Email:*** wreed@cgbralwfirm.com

(This Listing Continued)

PHILLIP C. PRICE, born Waynesville, North Carolina, June 28, 1973; admitted to bar, 2001, North Carolina; U.S. District Court, Western District of North Carolina. *Education:* Appalachian State University (B.S., 1996); Campbell University (J.D., 2000). *Member:* North Carolina State Bar; American Bar Association. ***PRACTICE AREAS:*** Commercial Real Estate; Residential Real Estate. ***Email:*** pprice@cgbrlawfirm.com

PATRICIA L. ARCURI, born Goldsboro, North Carolina, August 18, 1950; admitted to bar, 1984, Pennsylvania; 1987, North Carolina; U.S. Court of Appeals, Fourth Circuit and U.S. District Court, Western District of North Carolina. *Education:* College of Charleston, South Carolina (B.A., 1973); Rutgers University Law School, Camden, New Jersey, (J.D., 1984). Associate Editor, 1983-1984, Rutgers Law Journal. 28th Judicial District. *Member:* North Carolina State Bar; North Carolina Association of Defense Attorneys (Certified Mediator). ***PRACTICE AREAS:*** Insurance Defense; Civil Litigation; Personal Injury; Wrongful Death. ***Email:*** parcuri@cgbrlawfirm.com

FRANK J. CONTRIVO, JR., born MacDill AFB, Florida, July 11, 1976; admitted to bar, 2002, North Carolina. *Education:* University of North Carolina, Asheville (B.A., 1998); University of North Carolina at Chapel Hill (J.D., 2002). *Member:* North Carolina Bar Association; North Carolina Association of Defense Attorneys. ***PRACTICE AREAS:*** Civil Litigation. ***Email:*** fcontrivo@cgbrlawfirm.com

REPRESENTATIVE CLIENTS: Allstate Insurance Company; Associated Claims Enterprises; Bank of Asheville; Bi-Lo. Inc.; Buchanan & Sons Realty & Auction Company; Canal Insurance Company; Champion Industries, Inc.; Coldwell Banker Carroll & Kasey Realtors, Inc.; Colonial Freight Systems, Inc.; Employers Reinsurance; ESIS; GMAC Insurance; GEICO Direct; Helmsman Management; IHDS; Investors Title Insurance Company; ISP; Kemper Insurance Company; Nationwide Insurance Companies; North Carolina Farm Bureau; North Carolina League of Municipalities; Northland Insurance Company; Progressive Insurance Company; Ranger Insurance Company; St. Paul Fire & Marine Insurance Company; Selective Insurance Co.; State Employees' Credit Union; State Farm Insurance; Travelers; Tweed Enterprises, Inc.; Valley View Development Company L.L.C.; Westco Claims Management Services, Inc.; Windsor Insurance Group.
APPROVED ATTORNEYS FOR: Asheville Savings Bank; Bank of America; Branch Banking & Trust Company; Blue Ridge Savings Bank; Centura Bank; Chicago Title & Insurance Co.; Clyde Savings Bank; Fidelity National Title Insurance Co.; First American Title Insurance Corporation; First Citizens Bank; Lawyers Title Insurance Corp.; Bank of America Mortgage Corp.; The Title Company of North Carolina, Inc.; Wachovia.

CONSTANGY, BROOKS & SMITH, LLC

80 PEACHTREE ROAD, SUITE 208
ASHEVILLE, NORTH CAROLINA 28803
Telephone: 828-277-5137
Fax: 828-277-5138
URL: http://www.constangy.com

Atlanta, Georgia Office: 230 Peachtree Street, N.W., Suite 2400. Telephone: 404-525-8622. Fax: 404-525-6955.
Austin, Texas Office: 111 Congress Avenue, Fourth Floor. Telephone: 512-391-4989. Fax: 512-391-6821.
Birmingham, Alabama Office: 1901 Sixth Avenue North, Suite 1410. Telephone: 205-252-9321. Fax: 205-323-7674.
Columbia, South Carolina Office: 1301 Gervais Street, Suite 810. Telephone: 803-256-3200. Fax: 803-256-6277.
Fairfax, Virginia Office: 4100 Monument Corner Drive, Suite 520. Telephone: 571-522-6100. Fax: 571-522-6101.
Jacksonville, Florida Office: 200 West Forsyth Street, Suite 1610. Telephone: 904-356-8900. Fax: 904-356-8200.
Kansas City, Missouri Office: 2600 Grand Avenue, Suite 300. Telephone: 816-472-6400. Fax: 816-472-6401.
Macon, Georgia Office: 577 Mulberry Street, Suite 710. Telephone: 478-750-8600. Fax: 478-750-8686.
Nashville, Tennessee Office: Vanderbilt Plaza, Suite 925, 2100 West End Avenue. Telephone: 615-320-5200. Fax: 615-321-5891.
San Antonio, Texas Office: The Forum, 8000 IH 10 West, Suite 600. Telephone: 210-525-7977. Fax: 210-525-7978.
Tampa, Florida Office: 100 North Tampa Street, Suite 3350. Telephone: 813-223-7166. Fax: 813-223-2515.
Winston-Salem, North Carolina Office: 100 North Cherry Street, Suite 300. Telephone: 336-721-1001. Charlotte: 704-344-1040.

Labor Relations, Employment Litigation, Employee Benefits Law, Wage and Hour, OSHA Law, Business Immigration, Affirmative Action.

FIRM PROFILE: Constangy, Brooks & Smith was formed in 1946 to devote its practice exclusively to the representation of management in labor and employment matters. The firm also represents clients in the areas of employee benefits and occupational safety and health. Multinational corporations as well as small local businesses have called upon the firm's experience for over 50 years, many of them retaining the firm's counsel after conducting a nationwide search for the most competent legal representation. Clients are involved in virtually every sector of business and industry, including manufacturing, banking, health care services, insurance, meat and food, retail and transportation.

MEMBER

JONATHAN W. YARBROUGH, born Henderson, North Carolina, July 3, 1967; admitted to bar, 1994, North Carolina; U.S. District Courts, Western, Middle, Eastern Districts of North Carolina; U.S. Court of Appeals, Fourth Circuit; U.S. Supreme Court. *Education:* Wake Forest University (B.A., History, 1989); University of Louisville (J.D., 1994). *Member:* North Carolina Bar. ***PRACTICE AREAS:*** Employment Litigation; Labor and Employment. ***Email:*** jyarbrough@constangy.com

REPRESENTATIVE CLIENTS: Allergy Partners; Asheville Savings Bank; Carolina Day School; Charles Stewart Company; Community Management Corporation; Macon Program for Progress; McDowell Hospital; Mind Your Business, Inc.; Mission Hospitals; PrintPack, Inc.; Renaissance Stone and Biltmore Tile, Inc.; Rich Mount, Inc.; Shogren Industries; The Sway Inn; Trader Construction Company; W.P. Hickman Company; YMCA of Western North Carolina.

ANTHONY ALAN COXIE, PA ATTORNEY AT LAW

BANK OF ASHEVILLE BUILDING, SUITE 203-B
79 WOODFIN PLACE
ASHEVILLE, NORTH CAROLINA 28801
Telephone: 828-252-8808
Fax: 828-252-8188
Email: acoxie@bellsouth.net
URL: http://www.lawyers.com/coxielaw
Mailing Address: P.O. Box 1262, Asheville, NC 28802

Workers Compensation, Employment Law, Wrongful Termination, Personal Injury, Automobile Accidents, Wrongful Death, Slip and Fall, Civil Litigation, General Practice, Health Law, While Collar Crime, Criminal Law, Traffic Violations, DWI, Juvenile Law, Parole and Probation, Administrative Law, Insurance.

ANTHONY ALAN COXIE, born Texas, June 18, 1965; admitted to bar, 2000, North Carolina. *Education:* University of North Carolina at Asheville (B.S., Management, 1997); Wake Forest University School of Law (J.D., 2000). Recipient, North Carolina State Bar Law Student Pro Bono Public Service Award. Captain, Special Services Division, Asheville Fire Department, 1984-1998. *Member:* American Bar Association; North Carolina State Bar; North Carolina Academy of Trial Lawyers. ***PRACTICE AREAS:*** Workers Compensation; Employment Law; Wrongful Termination; Personal Injury; Automobile Accidents and Injuries; Wrongful Death; Slip and Fall; Civil Litigation; General Practice; Health Law; White Collar Crime; Criminal Law; Traffic Violations; Driving While Intoxicated; Juvenile Law; Parole and Probation; Administrative Law; Insurance. ***Email:*** acoxie@bellsouth.net

---

LAW OFFICES OF JOHN S. CURRY

SUITE 515
BB&T BUILDING
ONE WEST PACK SQUARE
ASHEVILLE, NORTH CAROLINA 28802
Telephone: 828-255-8195
Cell: 828-215-4512
Fax: 828-255-8195
Email: jscattorney@bellsouth.net
Mailing Address: P.O. Box 2091, Asheville, NC 28802
Environment Law.

JOHN S. CURRY, admitted to bar, 1970, North Carolina. *Education:* Davidson College (B.A., 1965); University of North Carolina at Chapel Hill (J.D., 1970). Phi Delta Phi. *Member:* North Carolina State Bar; North Carolina and 28th Judicial District Bar Associations. ***PRACTICE AREAS:*** Environmental Law.

ROBERT J. DEUTSCH, P.A.

Established in 1973
75 NORTH MARKET STREET
ASHEVILLE, NORTH CAROLINA 28801
Telephone: 828-251-0600
Fax: 828-251-5508
Email: deutsch@charter.net
URL: http://www.bobdeutschlaw.com

General Civil Trial Practice. Wills and Probate, Business, Family Law, Equitable Distribution, Real Estate, Corporate Law, Zoning, Personal Injury, Products Liability, Wrongful Death, Computer Law.

FIRM PROFILE: Robert J. Deutsch, P.A. has over 30 years experience with complex civil litigation and business transactions. He services all of western North Carolina and is based in Asheville, North Carolina.

ROBERT J. DEUTSCH, born Detroit, Michigan, November 1, 1947; admitted to bar, 1973, North Carolina; 1974, U.S. District Court, Middle and Western Districts of North Carolina; 1980, U.S. Court of Appeals, 4th Circuit; 1981, U.S. Supreme Court. *Education:* University of Michigan (B.A., 1969); Harvard University (J.D., 1972). Phi Beta Kappa. Author: "Legal Implications For Health Systems Agencies," U.S. Department of Health and Human Services, 1975. Chairman: United Jewish Appeal, 1975-1984; Henderson County Zoning Adjustment, 1975-1978; Henderson County Social Services Board, 1979-1984; Henderson County Sheltered Workshop, 1984-1985. President, Western North Carolina Jewish Federation, 1987-1990, 1999—; President, Congregation Beth Israel, 1990-1991; Vice-President, Foursquare Software Corporation, 1982—. Member, Board of Trustees: Warren Wilson College, 1999—; Asheville Art Museum, 1999—. Member, Board of Directors, Definition 6.com. Faculty Member: National Institute of Trial Advocacy, 2003—. Member, National Executive Committee, United Jewish Communities Network, 2005. Attorney, American Camping Association, Southeast District. *Member:* Henderson County, Buncombe County, 28th Judicial District (President Elect, 2005), North Carolina and American Bar Associations; North Carolina State Bar; North Carolina Academy of Trial Lawyers; The Association of Trial Lawyers of America. (Member of Powell & Deutsch). ***LANGUAGES:*** Spanish. ***PRACTICE AREAS:*** Civil Practice; Trial Practice; Wills; Probate; Business Law; Family Law; Equitable Distribution; Real Estate; Corporate Law; Zoning Law; Personal Injury; Products Liability; Wrongful Death; Computer Law. ***Email:*** deutsch@charter.net

LEGAL SUPPORT PERSONNEL

LORETTA P. DRAKE, (Legal Assistant)
CORENE T. CROSBY, (Paralegal)

(This Listing Continued)

REPRESENTATIVE CLIENTS: Blue Star Camps, Inc.; UNI-Comp, Inc.; Parsec Financial Planning, Inc.; Great Smokies Diagnostic Laboratory, Inc.
APPROVED ATTORNEY FOR: Lawyers Title Insurance Corp.; Chicago Title Insurance Corp.; Investors Title Insurance Co.
REFERENCES: RBC Centura Bank; Charles Schwabb & Co.; Parsec Financial Planning, Inc.; Bank of America.

MICHAEL W. DRYE, P.C.

12 1/2 WALL STREET, SUITE C
ASHEVILLE, NORTH CAROLINA 28801
Telephone: 828-258-1384
Fax: 828-258-1871
Email: michaelwdrye@aol.com
URL: http://www.michaeldryelawfirm.com
Family Law, Children, Divorce.

MICHAEL W. DRYE, born Savannah, Georgia, June 14, 1951; admitted to bar, 1976, North Carolina. *Education:* University of North Carolina at Charlotte (B.A., 1973); Wake Forest University (J.D., 1976). Assistant County Attorney, Buncombe County, 1977-1979. Certified Mediator, Equitable Distribution and other Family and Financial Cases. *Member:* Buncombe County, North Carolina and American Bar Associations; North Carolina State Bar; North Carolina Academy of Trial Lawyers. (Board Certified Specialist in Family Law, North Carolina State Board of Legal Specialization). ***PRACTICE AREAS:*** Family Law; Children; Mediation; Divorce; Child Custody; Child Support; Equitable Distribution; Premarital Agreements; Adoption Law.

JACOB C. EHRMANN

68 NORTH MARKET STREET
ASHEVILLE, NORTH CAROLINA 28801
Telephone: 828-582-2768
Fax: 828-255-8693
Email: jacobehrmann@earthlink.net
URL: http://www.jacobehrmann.com
Mailing Address: 825-C Merriman Avenue, Suite 362, Asheville, NC 28804

Domestic Violence, Family Law, Divorce, Child Custody, Child Support, Entertainment Law, Copyrights, Contracts.

JACOB C. EHRMANN, born St. Louis, March 6, 1973; admitted to bar, 2000, North Carolina. *Education:* University of North Carolina at Chapel Hill (B.A., with honors, 1995; J.D., 1999). *Member:* Buncombe County Bar Association; North Carolina State Bar. ***PRACTICE AREAS:*** Domestic Violence; Family Law; Divorce; Child Custody; Child Support; Entertainment Law; Copyrights; Contracts.

ELKINS & ELKINS

ASHEVILLE, NORTH CAROLINA

(See Hendersonville)

Bankruptcy, Real Estate, Residential Real Estate, Buying and Selling a Home, Probate, Corporation, Civil Trial Practice, Out of Court Debt Restructuring.

THE ELMORE LAW FIRM, P.A.

Established in 1947
53 NORTH MARKET STREET
ASHEVILLE, NORTH CAROLINA 28801
Telephone: 828-253-1492
Fax: 828-253-9648
URL: http://www.theelmorelawfirm.com
Email: info@theelmorelawfirm.com
URL: http://www.theelmorelawoffice.com

Catastrophic Injury, Medical Malpractice, Toxic Torts, Pharmaceutical Litigation, Personal Injury, Wrongful Death, Automobile Accidents, Sexual Abuse, Slip and Fall, Construction Accidents, Aviation, Airplane Crashes, Nursing Home Negligence, Products Liability, Birth Trauma, Spinal Injury, Brain Injury, Workers Compensation, Federal Criminal Law and State Criminal Law, Driving While Intoxicated, Drug Crimes, Parole and Probation, Traffic Violations, White Collar Crime, Murder, Social Security Disability.

FIRM PROFILE: Bruce A. Elmore, Sr. established his practice in 1947 and was a member of the N.C. General Assembly while at the University of North Carolina Law School. He received the first million dollar verdict in North Carolina. The firm practices statewide concentrating in medical malpractice, personal injury and wrongful death, product liability, workers' compensation, and federal and state criminal matters.

BRUCE A. ELMORE, born Bryson City, North Carolina, November 1, 1920; admitted to bar, 1947, North Carolina and U.S. District Court, Western District of North Carolina. *Education:* University of North Carolina (A.B., 1941; J.D., 1947). Phi Alpha Delta. Member, North Carolina House of Representatives, 1947-1949. Member, Board of Trustees, 1969-1973 and Chairman of the Board of Trustees, 1973-1975, University of North Carolina at Asheville. *Member:* North Carolina State Bar; The Inner Circle of Advocates; The Association of Trial Lawyers of America; North Carolina Academy of Trial Lawyers (Member, Board of Governors, 1968-1977). ***PRACTICE AREAS:*** Personal Injury; Automobile Accidents and Injuries; Wrongful Death; Medical Malpractice; Product Liability; Federal Criminal Law; State Criminal Law; Driving While Intoxicated; Traffic Violations. ***Email:*** info@theelmorelawfirm.com

BRUCE A. ELMORE, JR., born Asheville, North Carolina, November 1, 1952; admitted to bar, 1976, North Carolina; 1978, U.S. District Court, Western and Middle Dis-

(This Listing Continued)

THE ELMORE LAW FIRM, P.A., Asheville—Continued

tricts of North Carolina. *Education:* University of North Carolina (B.A., 1973; J.D., 1976). *Member:* North Carolina Bar; The Association of Trial Lawyers of America (Sustaining Member); North Carolina Academy of Trial Lawyers (Benefactor); Million Dollar Advocates Forum; North Carolina American Civil Liberties Union (Vice-President, Board of Directors; Legal Committee); National Association of Criminal Defense Lawyers (Member, President's Club). ***REPORTED CASES:*** Cartner vs. Nationwide Mutual Fire Insurance Company, 472 S.E. 2d 389 (N.C. Ct. App), 1996. ***PRACTICE AREAS:*** Medical Malpractice; Personal Injury; Wrongful Death; Nursing Home Negligence; Nursing Home Abuse and Neglect; Product Liability; Federal Criminal Law; State Criminal Law. ***Email:*** bruceelmore@theelmorelawfirm.com

FERIKES & BLEYNAT, PLLC

21 BROAD STREET
ASHEVILLE, NORTH CAROLINA 28801
Telephone: 828-251-1588
Telecopier: 828-251-2214
URL: http://www.lawyers.com/ferikes&bleynat

Business Litigation, Business Torts, Construction Litigation, Appellate Practice, Property Law and Litigation; Personal Injury and Medical Malpractice, Automobile Accidents, Wrongful Death, Brain Injury, Torts, Commercial Liability, Commercial Real Estate Litigation, Construction Defects and Liens, Contract Litigation, Corporate Litigation, Workers Compensation.

JOSEPH A. FERIKES, born Asheville, North Carolina, January 14, 1949; admitted to bar, 1974, Georgia; 1983, North Carolina. *Education:* North Carolina State University (B.A., 1970); University of Alabama (J.D., 1974). Town Attorney: Fletcher, North Carolina, 1991—; Woodfin, North Carolina, 1997—. *Member:* The Association of Trial Lawyers of America; North Carolina Academy of Trial Lawyers. ***LANGUAGES:*** Greek. ***PRACTICE AREAS:*** Personal Injury (20%); Medical Malpractice (20%); Civil Litigation (50%); Municipal Law (10%). ***Email:*** josephferikes@charter.net

EDWARD L. BLEYNAT, JR., born Lexington Park, Maryland, December 31, 1963; admitted to bar, 1989, North Carolina; 1991, Tennessee. *Education:* Clemson University (B.S., magna cum laude, 1986); University of North Carolina (J.D., with honors, 1989). Member, National Moot Court Competition and Holderness Moot Court Bench, 1988-1989. Law Clerk to Hon. James G. Exum Jr., Chief Justice, Supreme Court of North Carolina, 1989-1991. ***REPORTED CASES:*** Mickles vs. Duke Power Company, 342 N.C. 103, 463 S.E.2d 206, 1995; G.P. Publications, Inc. vs. Quebecor Printing-St. Paul, Inc., 125 N.C. App. 424, 481 S.E.2d 674, 1997. ***PRACTICE AREAS:*** Business Litigation; Construction Litigation; Property Litigation; Civil Litigation; Covenants Not To Compete; Quiet Title; Personal Injury; Breach of Contract. ***Email:*** edbleynat@aol.com

SUSAN L. EVANS, born Los Angeles, California; admitted to bar, 2000, North Carolina. *Education:* Queens College (B.A., Communications, 1996); Campbell University (J.D., 2000). Order of Barristers; National Moot Court Team. Law Clerk, Honorable Ralph Walker, North Carolina Court of Appeals, 2000-2001. *Member:* North Carolina Bar (Member, Sections on: Litigation; Real Property; Construction Law) and American Bar Associations; North Carolina Association of Trial Lawyers (Member, Sections on: Consumer Law; Employment Law). ***PRACTICE AREAS:*** Real Estate Litigation; Business Litigation; Construction Litigation; Employment Law; Consumer Law; Civil Litigation. ***Email:*** susanevans@ferikesbleynat.com

THE FRUE LAW FIRM, PLLC

Established in 1984
16 CHURCH STREET
P.O. BOX 7627
ASHEVILLE, NORTH CAROLINA 28802-7627
Telephone: 828-258-0570
Fax: 828-258-0591
Email: law@frue.net

General Civil Practice, Real Estate, Probate, Corporate Law, Business Law.

MEMBERS OF FIRM

WILLIAM C. FRUE, JR., born Pontiac, Michigan, December 29, 1934; admitted to bar, 1960, North Carolina; 1961, U.S. District Court, Western District of North Carolina; 1998, U.S. Court of Appeals, Fourth Circuit. *Education:* Washington & Lee University (A.B., 1956); University of North Carolina (LL.B., 1960). Phi Alpha Delta. Chairman: Planning and Zoning Commission of the City of Asheville, 1978-1986; Board of Trustees, Asheville Policemen's Pension and Disability Fund. *Member:* 28th Judicial District, North Carolina and American (Member, Section on Real Property, Probate and Trust Law) Bar Associations; The North Carolina State Bar; North Carolina College of Advocacy. ***PRACTICE AREAS:*** Real Estate Law; Corporate Law; Wills and Estates; Real Estate Litigation; Boundary Disputes; Commercial Real Estate. ***Email:*** wcfjr.@frue.net

JOHN CALHOUN FRUE, born Asheville, North Carolina, August 27, 1960; admitted to bar, 1986, Georgia, U.S. District Court, Northern District of Georgia and U.S. District Court, Western District of North Carolina; 1987, North Carolina. *Education:* University of North Carolina (A.B., 1983); Walter F. George School of Law, Mercer University (J.D., 1986). *Member:* 28th Judicial District, North Carolina and American Bar Associations; North Carolina State Bar; State Bar of Georgia. ***PRACTICE AREAS:*** Residential Real Estate Law; Criminal Law; DWI; Traffic Offenses; Contract Law. ***Email:*** law@frue.net

REFERENCE: Asheville Savings Bank.

DAVID GANTT LAW OFFICE

Established in 1981
82 CHURCH STREET
ASHEVILLE, NORTH CAROLINA 28801
Telephone: 828-252-2852
Toll Free: 1-800-273-4002
Fax: 828-254-4539
Email: lawyer@davidgantt.com
URL: http://www.davidgantt.com

Insurance Claims, Personal Injury, Automobile, Social Security Claims, Workers' Compensation.

FIRM PROFILE: For over 23 years, David Gantt Law Office has represented accident and disability victims in Western North Carolina. Their law office primarily handles Social Security, Worker's Compensation, Complex Automobile Accidents and Wrongful Death Claims.

DAVID GANTT, born Winston-Salem, North Carolina, October 2, 1956; admitted to bar, 1981, North Carolina and U.S. District Court, Western District of North Carolina; 1984, U.S. Court of Appeals, Fourth Circuit and U.S. District Court, Middle District of North Carolina; 1985, U.S. Supreme Court. *Education:* University of North Carolina at Chapel Hill (B.A. in Economics, 1978); Campbell University (J.D., 1981). Speaker, "Ethics in Worker's Compensation Cases," February 2003; "Intro to Special Security Law," December 2002; "All Star Trial of Sex Harassment Case," February 2001, North Carolina Bar Association; "Interpreting Social Security Language for Beginners," December, 1999, North Carolina Academy of Trial Lawyers; "Social Security Jargon for Beginners," November 1998; "Social Security Language Made Easy," November 1996; "Ethics in Workers' Compensation Cases," January 1996; "Social Security Mistakes," October, 1995; "Ethics in Workers' Compensation Cases," Workers' Compensation, August, 1994; "Ethics from the Plaintiffs' Side," Advanced Workers' Compensation, October 1993; "Trying the Automobile Injury Case in North Carolina," Insurance Law, September, 1991; "Farmer's Right of First Refusal," Consumer Law, April 1991. Author: Woodson Workers Compensation Case, Analysis-NC Academy of Trial Lawyers Magazine, January 1996. Mountain Area Volunteer Lawyer for Pisgah Legal Services (1989 Pro Bono Service Award Nominee). Elected Member, Buncombe County Commission, 1996—. Elected Chairman, Land of Sky Regional Council, 2002-2004. Dean, Peoples Law School, Sponsored by NC Academy of Trial Lawyers. *Member:* 28th Judicial District (Vice President, Young Lawyers Section, Executive Committee, 1992-1995), North Carolina and American Bar Associations; North Carolina Academy of Trial Lawyers; The Association of Trial Lawyers of America; National Association of Social Security Disability Claimants Representatives. ***REPORTED CASES:*** Garren v. PH Gladfelter, 131 NC App. 93, 504 SE2d 810 (1998); Johnson v. Beverly-Hanks, 328 NC 202, 400 SE2d 38 (1991); McMillan v. Mahoney, 99 NC App. 448, 393 SE2d 298 (1990); Branks v. Kern, 83 NC App. 32, 348 SE2d 815 (1986) reversed in 320 NC 621, 359 SE2d 780 (1987); Mehovic v. Ken Wilson Ford, 113 NC App. 559, 439 SE2d 184 (1994); Greenman v. Pony Express, 123 NC App. 136, 472 SE2d 227 (1996); Craig v. Buncombe County Board of Ed, 80 NC App. 683, 343 SE2d 222 (1986); Capps v. Capps, 69 NC App. 775, 318 SE2d 346 (1984). ***PRACTICE AREAS:*** Personal Injury Law; Automobile Accidents; Wrongful Death; Workers Compensation Law; Social Security; Disabilities.

A List of Representative Clients will be furnished upon request.

GRIMES & TEICH

Established in 1979
535 COLLEGE STREET
P.O. BOX 7074
ASHEVILLE, NORTH CAROLINA 28801-2412
Telephone: 800-533-6845; 828-251-0800
Fax: 828-252-4678
URL: http://www.grimesandteich.com
Email: teich@grimesandteich.com
URL: http://www.lawyers.com/grimesandteich

Waynesville Office: 385 N. Haywood Street, 28786. Telephone: 828-452-7888.
Rutherfordton Office: 365 Charlotte Road, 28139. Telephone: 828-286-1033.
Greenville, South Carolina Office: 111 East North Street, 29601. Telephone: 800-533-6845.

Personal Injury, Automobile Accidents, Trucking Accidents, Motorcycle Accidents, Boating Accidents, Brain and Head Injuries, Dog Bites, Products Liability, Catastrophic Injury, Pedestrian Injuries, Slip and Fall Injuries, Workers Compensation, Social Security Law, Social Security Disability, Medical Malpractice, Nursing Home Negligence, Nursing Home Abuse, Wrongful Death, Fire Injuries.

S. JANSON GRIMES, born Greenville, North Carolina, October 3, 1946; admitted to bar, 1972, North Carolina. *Education:* University of North Carolina at Chapel Hill (B.A., 1968; J.D., 1972). *Member:* Buncombe County and North Carolina Bar Associations; North Carolina Academy of Trial Lawyers; National Association of Social Security Claimants' Representatives. ***PRACTICE AREAS:*** Personal Injury; Automobile Accidents and Injuries; Real Estate Law; Workers Compensation Law; Social Security Disability. ***Email:*** grimes@grimesandteich.com

HENRY E. TEICH, born New York, New York, March 17, 1950; admitted to bar, 1978, North Carolina. *Education:* State University of New York at Stony Brook (B.A., 1971); University of South Carolina (Ph.D., Psychology, 1975); University of San Francisco (J.D., 1978). Public Guardian, Buncombe County, 1987—. Member, Workplace Injury Litigation Group. *Member:* Buncombe County Bar Association; North Carolina Academy of Trial Lawyers (Member and Benefactor); The Association of Trial Lawyers of America. (Board Certified Specialist in Workers Compensation, North Carolina State Board of Legal Spe-

(This Listing Continued)

cialization). ***PRACTICE AREAS:*** Personal Injury Law; Automobile Accidents and Injuries; Workers Compensation Law; Guardianship Law. ***Email:*** teich@grimesandteich.com

RUTH C. SMITH, born Greenville, South Carolina, 1972; admitted to bar, 1999, North Carolina. *Education:* University of North Carolina (B.A., 1994; J.D., 1999). *Member:* Buncombe County Bar Association; North Carolina Academy of Trial Lawyers. ***PRACTICE AREAS:*** Personal Injury; Automobile Accidents and Injuries. ***Email:*** ruth.smith@grimesandteich.com

SCOTT M. ANDERSON, born Richmond, Virginia, 1963; admitted to bar, 1989, South Carolina; 1990, North Carolina, U.S. District Court, District of South Carolina and U.S. Court of Appeals, Fourth Circuit; 1993, U.S. District Court, Western District of North Carolina; 1997, U.S. District Court, Middle District of North Carolina. *Education:* University of North Carolina at Chapel Hill (B.A., 1986); University of South Carolina (J.D., 1989). *Member:* The Association of Trial Lawyers of America; South Carolina Trial Lawyers Association; North Carolina Academy of Trial Lawyers; Workplace Injury Litigation Group (Board Member); South Carolina Reflex Sympathetic Dystrophy Association (Board Member). (Also Member, Anderson & Herlong, Greenville, South Carolina). ***PRACTICE AREAS:*** Trial Practice; Workers Compensation; Appellate Practice.

THOMAS W. HENSON, JR., born Chapel Hill, North Carolina, January 15, 1965; admitted to bar, 1989, North Carolina. *Education:* University of North Carolina (B.S.B.A., 1986; J.D., 1989). *Member:* North Carolina State Bar; The Association of Trial Lawyers of America; North Carolina Academy of Trial Lawyers. (Also Member, Henson & Fuerst, Rocky Mount and Raleigh, North Carolina). ***PRACTICE AREAS:*** Nursing Home Abuse and Neglect; Personal Injury; Wrongful Death; Medical Malpractice. ***Email:*** thenson@grimesandteich.com

SARAH LOCKETT, born North Carolina; admitted to bar, 2004, North Carolina. *Education:* College of William & Mary (B.A., International Relations, 2001); University of North Carolina at Chapel Hill School of Law (J.D., 2004). *Member:* North Carolina Academy of Trial Lawyers. ***PRACTICE AREAS:*** Personal Injury; Workers Compensation; Automobile Accidents and Injuries. ***Email:*** lockett@grimesandteich.com

GUM, HILLIER & McCROSKEY, P.A.

Established in 1979

47 N. MARKET STREET
P.O. BOX 3235
ASHEVILLE, NORTH CAROLINA 28802
Telephone: 828-258-3368
Fax: 828-252-6721
Email: info@gumandhillier.com
URL: http://www.gumandhillier.com

Family Law, Bankruptcy, Real Estate, Wills and Corporate Law.

FIRM PROFILE: Gum & Hillier, P.A. was formed in 1979 when David R. Hillier and Howard L. Gum resigned their positions with Van Winkle, Buck, Wall, Starnes, Hyde & Davis, P.A., a well-established Asheville firm. The firm serves primarily individuals in the areas of family law and bankruptcy law. A number of small businesses and institutions are also clients of the firm.

HOWARD L. GUM, born Vandalia, Illinois, June 19, 1951; admitted to bar, 1976, North Carolina and U.S. District Court, Western District of North Carolina. *Education:* Bradley University (B.A., cum laude, 1973); University of Illinois (J.D., 1976). Phi Kappa Phi. Certified Arbitrator, American Academy of Matrimonial Lawyers. Listed in Best Lawyers in America. Member, 1996-2001 and Chair, 1999-2001, North Carolina Board of Legal Specialization. Member, Family Courts Advisory Committee, N.C. Administrative Office of The Courts (2000—). *Member:* North Carolina (Member and Councilor, 1984-1989, 1991-1994, and Chairman, 1986-1987, 1987-1988; Member, Family Law Section; Lawyer Effectiveness and Quality of Life Committee, 1999—) and American (Member, Family Law Section) Bar Associations; 28th Judicial District State Bar (Councilor, 1984-1987) and North Carolina State Bar (Chairman, Family Law Specialization Committee, 1988-1994; Member, Ethics Committee). Fellow, American Academy of Matrimonial Lawyers (President Elect, 2003-2004 and Treasurer, 2000-2001, N.C. Chapter). (Board Certified Specialist in Family Law, North Carolina State Board of Legal Specialization). ***PRACTICE AREAS:*** Family Law (100%). ***Email:*** hgum@gumandhillier.com

DAVID R. HILLIER, born Chicago, Illinois, March 17, 1948; admitted to bar, 1974, North Carolina; 1978, U.S. District Court, Western District of North Carolina. *Education:* University of the South (B.A., cum laude, 1970); Duke University (J.D., 1974). Member, Panel of Trustees, United States Bankruptcy Court, Western District of North Carolina, 1981—. Member, Asheville Civil Service Board, 1981-1983. Member, 1987-1995 and Chairman, 1989-1995, Asheville City Board of Education. Supreme Court Certified Mediator. Past-President, 28th Judicial District Bar Association. *Member:* North Carolina and American Bar Associations; North Carolina State Bar. (Board Certified Specialist in Bankruptcy Law). ***PRACTICE AREAS:*** Bankruptcy Law. ***Email:*** dhillier@gumandhillier.com

PATRICK S. McCROSKEY, born Louisville, Kentucky, February 5, 1970; admitted to bar, 1995, North Carolina. *Education:* Duke University (B.A., 1992); University of North Carolina at Chapel Hill (J.D., 1995). Member, Holderness Moot Court, University of North Carolina at Chapel Hill. Member, Pro Se Litigation Committee and Executive Committee, 28th Judicial District. *Member:* North Carolina State Bar; North Carolina Bar Association (Member: Family Law Section; Family Law Council);. (Board Certified Specialist in Family Law, North Carolina State Board of Legal Specialization). ***PRACTICE AREAS:*** Family Law. ***Email:*** patrick@gumandhillier.com

REPRESENTATIVE CLIENTS: Shoney's Restaurants; Telco Credit Union & Affiliates; Perry Bartsch, Jr. Construction Co.
REFERENCES: Asheville Savings Bank; Wachovia Bank and Trust Co.; Branch Bank & Trust.

HEDRICK EATMAN GARDNER & KINCHELOE, L.L.P.

ASHEVILLE, NORTH CAROLINA

(See Charlotte)

General Civil Litigation and Insurance Defense, Legal and Professional Malpractice, Motor Vehicle Negligence, Premises Liability, Product Liability, Construction, Insurance Coverage Disputes, Arson and Fraud, Employment Law, Trucking and Transportation and Worker's Compensation.

KELLY & ROWE, P.A.

50 MERRIMON AVENUE
ASHEVILLE, NORTH CAROLINA 28801
Telephone: 828-251-9310
FAX: 828-251-9320
Email: kelly_rowe@bellsouth.net
URL: http://www.kellyrowelaw.com

Mailing Address: P.O. Box 2865, Asheville, NC 28802

Asset Protection, Arbitration and Mediation, Automobile Accidents, Banking and Financial Law, Building and Construction Law, Civil Practice in all Federal and State Courts, Commercial Litigation, Condemnation, Contract, Corporate Law, Equitable Distribution, Divorce, Employment, Estate Planning and Administration, Insurance Law, Personal Injury, Products Liability, Medical Malpractice, Negligence, Real Estate Litigation, Eminent Domain, Wrongful Death.

E. GLENN KELLY, born Sanford, North Carolina, January 1, 1938; admitted to bar, 1963, North Carolina. *Education:* University of North Carolina (A.B., 1960); Wake Forest College and University of North Carolina (LL.B., 1963). Delta Theta Phi. Mayor, Town of Biltmore Forest, 1987-1999. Commissioner and Mayor Pro-Tem, Town of Biltmore Forest, 1981-1987. Member, Board of Directors of Metropolitan Sewerage District, 1993—. North Carolina Certified Mediator. *Member:* Buncombe County, North Carolina and American Bar Associations; The North Carolina State Bar (Member, Committee on Medico-Legal Liaison, 1974-1976); North Carolina Academy of Trial Lawyers; The Association of Trial Lawyers of America. ***Email:*** egkelly@bellsouth.net

JAMES GARY ROWE, born Murphy, North Carolina, August 31, 1946; admitted to bar, 1972, North Carolina. *Education:* Clemson University and University of North Carolina (B.A., 1968); University of North Carolina (J.D., 1972). *Member:* Buncombe County, North Carolina and American Bar Associations; 28th Judicial District; North Carolina State Bar; North Carolina Academy of Trial Lawyers. ***Email:*** jgrowekellyrowe@bellsouth.net

LEAKE & SCOTT

501 BB&T BUILDING
ASHEVILLE, NORTH CAROLINA 28801
Telephone: 828-253-3661
Fax: 828-258-8754
Email: leakeandscott@bellsouth.net

Marshall, North Carolina Office: Mashburn Building, P.O. Box 451. Telephone: 828-649-3883.

General Practice and Trial in all Courts. Interstate Commerce, Insurance, Corporation, Real Estate, Governmental, Medical Malpractice, Personal Injury, Taxation Law, Family Law.

FIRM PROFILE: Although the firm's offices are located in Asheville and Marshall, the firm regularly practices in State and Federal Courts in the 20 most western counties in North Carolina.

MEMBERS OF FIRM

A. E. LEAKE (1911-1992)

ROBERT E. HARRELL (1925-2000)

LARRY B. LEAKE, born Asheville, North Carolina, May 19, 1950; admitted to bar, 1974, North Carolina and U.S. District Court, Western District of North Carolina; 1979, U.S. Court of Appeals, Fourth Circuit and U.S. Supreme Court. *Education:* University of North Carolina (B.A., 1972; J.D., 1974). Phi Beta Kappa. Recipient, Order of the Long Leaf Pine, presented by Governor James B. Hunt, 1980, 2000. Attorney, Madison County Board of Commissioners, 1976-1994, 1998—. Attorney, Madison County Board of Education, 1976-1987. Attorney: Town of Hot Springs, 1976-1989, 1991—; Town of Mars Hill, 1994—; Town of Marshall, 1997—. Member: North Carolina State Goals and Policy Board, 1978-1985; North Carolina State Senate, 1979-1981; North Carolina Commission on the Future, 1981-1983. North Carolina State Board of Elections, Member, 1993—; Chairman, 1997—. Board, Blue Ridge Mental Health, Member, 1999-2001. Mars Hill College Board of Advisors, Member, 1992—, Chairman, 2001-2004. *Member:* Buncombe County (Secretary, 1975-1976), North Carolina and American Bar Associations; North Carolina State Bar; North Carolina Association of Defense Attorneys. ***PRACTICE AREAS:*** Civil Defense; Governmental Law; Medical Malpractice; Personal Injury; Wrongful Death. ***Email:*** leakeandscott@bellsouth.net

WARD D. SCOTT, born Buffalo, New York, October 23, 1966; admitted to bar, 1997, North Carolina; 1998, U.S. District Court, Western District of North Carolina. *Education:* University of North Carolina at Asheville (B.A., 1992); University of North Carolina at Chapel Hill (J.D., 1997). *Member:* 28th Judicial District, North Carolina and American Bar Associations; North Carolina Association of Defense Attorneys. ***PRACTICE AREAS:*** Civil Practice; Personal Injury; Criminal; Real Estate; Family Law. ***Email:*** leakeandscott@bellsouth.net

CHRISTOPHER B. REINHARDT, born Chapel Hill, North Carolina, September 22, 1977; admitted to bar, 2003, North Carolina. *Education:* Brevard College (B.A., 1999);

(This Listing Continued)

LEAKE & SCOTT, Asheville—Continued

University of North Carolina at Chapel Hill (J.D., 2003). *Member:* North Carolina State Bar. ***PRACTICE AREAS:*** Family Law; Criminal Law; Personal Injury; Real Estate; Workers Compensation. ***Email:*** leakeandscott@bellsouth.net

REPRESENTATIVE CLIENTS: Academy Life Insurance Co.; American Honda Motor Co.; Bankers & Shippers Insurance Company; Bekins Van Lines Co.; Bruce Dodson and Co.; Burlington Insurance Group; Carolina Power & Light Company; Casualty Insurance Company; Chubb and Son, Inc.; CNA Insurance Co.; Combined Insurance Company of America; Continental Trailways, Inc.; Federated Insurance Co.; Foremost Insurance; French Broad Electric Membership Corp.; Fruehauf Corp.; Guaranty National Insurance Co.; Highlands Insurance Co.; Hot Springs Health Program; Hot Springs Housing Authority; Jefferson Insurance Company of New York; Life and Casualty Insurance Co.; American General Insurance Co.; Madison Housing Authority; Marshall Housing Authority; Maryland Insurance Group; Mission Valley Insurance Co.; Navistar International Corp.; Northland Insurance Co.; Ohio Casualty Insurance Co.; Progressive Insurance Company; Royal Globe Insurance Co.; St. Paul Insurance Co.; Seaboard Underwriters, Inc.; Seibels, Bruce and Co.; Shelby Mutual Insurance Co.; Southern Heritage Insurance Company; Southern Trust Co.; Titan Insurance Company; Transport Acceptance Corp.; United States Fidelity and Guaranty Company; U.S. Aviation Underwriters.
REFERENCE: Branch Banking and Trust, Asheville, North Carolina.

JAMES MICHAEL LLOYD, P.A.

Established in 2000

75 CHURCH STREET
P.O. BOX 948
ASHEVILLE, NORTH CAROLINA 28802
Telephone: 828-350-1765
Fax: 828-350-1766
Email: lloydlaw@att.net
URL: http://www.jameslloydpa.com

Construction Law, Condominium/Homeowner Association Law, Litigation, Corporate and Business Law.

FIRM PROFILE: Since 1993, James M. Lloyd has served commercial and individual clients throughout Western North Carolina. Emphasizing personal service to his clients, James M. Lloyd's firm utilizes state-of-the-art technology to offer its clients the same resources as larger firms. Whether you are in need of someone to represent you at trial or arbitration, or are seeking advice regarding a contract or business transaction, James M. Lloyd will be beside you every step of the way.

Attorney and Counselor at Law

JAMES M. LLOYD, born Hartsville, South Carolina, April 1, 1966; admitted to bar, 1992, North Carolina and U.S. District Court, Middle and Western Districts of North Carolina; 1993, U.S. Court of Appeals, Fourth Circuit. *Education:* University of North Carolina at Chapel Hill (B.S., Business Administration, 1988; J.D., 1992). *Member:* Buncombe County and North Carolina (Member, Advisory Council, Construction Section) Bar Associations. ***REPORTED CASES:*** Woodfield Association, Inc. v. Ackerman, 126 N.C.App. 833, 488 S.E.2d 853 (1997); Ratley Construction Co., Inc. v. Richmond County Board of Education, 125 N.C.App.421, 482 S.E.2d 48 (1997); Vandervoort v. Gateway Mountain Property Owners Association, 114 N.C.App. 655, 442 S.E.2d 350 (1994); Sonopress, Inc. v. Town of Weaverville, 139 N.C.App. 378, 533 S.E.2d 537 (2000). ***PRACTICE AREAS:*** Construction Law; Litigation; Condominium Association Law; Homeowners Association Law; Corporate Law; Business Law; Commercial Law; Professional Liability. ***Email:*** lloydlaw@att.net

REPRESENTATIVE CLIENTS: A-2-Z Plumbing, Inc.; C. Rogers Trucking, Inc; Carolina Cabinets & More; The Cedar Wood Estates Master Association, Inc.; Chamad Warehouses, Inc.; The Cloisters Homeowners Association, Inc.; The Colony Homeowners Association, Inc.; Concrete Walls Unlimited, Inc.; FHC Tile Co.; Hahn Construction; Heywood Crossing Condominium; Independent Ingredients; Meyer Services, Inc.; Morse Properties, Inc.; New Dimensions in Pavement Markings, Inc.; Pioneer Construction; Qualla Electric Company, Inc.; Racquet Club Village Condominiums; Ravenscroft Condominium Association, Inc.; Sheer Comfort Heating & Air Conditioning, Inc.; Southern Classic Stairs, Inc.; Sparkes Construction, Inc.; Sunset Ridge Condominiums; Top Notch Log Homes; Window & Door Specialities, Inc.; Wright's Carpet, Inc.; Yes Builders, Inc.

LONG, PARKER, WARREN & JONES, P.A.

SUITE 600
14 SOUTH PACK SQUARE
P.O. BOX 7216
ASHEVILLE, NORTH CAROLINA 28802
Telephone: 828-258-2296
Fax: 828-253-1073
URL: http://www.longparker.com

General Trial Practice. Civil Litigation, Commercial Litigation, Personal Injury Litigation, Federal Litigation, Eminent Domain, Medical Malpractice, Family Law, Business Litigation.

ROBERT B. LONG, JR., born Greenville, South Carolina, April 17, 1942; admitted to bar, 1965, North Carolina. *Education:* University of North Carolina (A.B., 1963; LL.B., with honors, 1965). Order of the Coif; Phi Delta Phi. Associate Editor, University of North Carolina Law Review, 1964-1965. *Member:* North Carolina and American Bar Associations; 28th Judicial District and The North Carolina State Bars. Fellow, American College of Trial Lawyers. ***PRACTICE AREAS:*** Litigation; Eminent Domain; Commercial Litigation; Personal Injury.

WILLIAM A. PARKER, born Anderson, South Carolina, March 24, 1947; admitted to bar, 1974, North Carolina. *Education:* Wake Forest University (B.A., 1969); University of North Carolina (J.D., with honors, 1974). Omicron Delta Kappa; Order of the Coif. Member, University of North Carolina Law Review, 1973-1974. *Member:* North Carolina Bar Association; 28th Judicial District and North Carolina State Bars; North Carolina Academy of Trial Lawyers. ***PRACTICE AREAS:*** Litigation; Criminal Defense; Personal Injury; Family Law; Divorce.

(This Listing Continued)

STEVE RAY WARREN, born Asheville, North Carolina, October 16, 1957; admitted to bar, 1983, North Carolina. *Education:* Western Carolina University (B.S.B.A., summa cum laude, 1980); University of North Carolina at Chapel Hill (J.D., 1983). Western Carolina University Scholar. Member, Board of Trustees, Western Carolina University. President, Governor's Western Residence Board. Member, North Carolina Journal of International Law and Commercial Regulation, 1980-1981. *Member:* North Carolina Bar Association; 28th Judicial District and North Carolina State Bars; North Carolina Academy of Trial Lawyers. ***PRACTICE AREAS:*** Medical Malpractice; Products Liability; Personal Injury; Civil Litigation. ***Email:*** steve@longparker.com

W. SCOTT JONES, born Shelby, North Carolina, April 28, 1965; admitted to bar, 1991, North Carolina. *Education:* University of North Carolina at Chapel Hill (A.B., with honors, 1987): University of Virginia (J.D., 1991). Clerk, Justice Richard Neely, WVA Supreme Court, 1991-1992. *Member:* North Carolina Bar Association; 28th Judicial District and North Carolina State Bars; The Association of Trial Lawyers of America; North Carolina Academy of Trial Lawyers. ***PRACTICE AREAS:*** Civil Litigation; Commercial Litigation; Personal Injury; Automobile Accidents and Injuries; Eminent Domain; Real Estate Litigation; Indian Law. ***Email:*** scott@longparker.com

PHILIP SCOTT ANDERSON, born Long Island, New York, September 19, 1969; admitted to bar, 1995, North Carolina. *Education:* Georgia Institute of Technology (B.E.E., with highest honors, 1991); University of North Carolina (J.D., 1994). Recipient, Charles S. Mangum Jr. Scholarship, 1991-1994. Author: "Gender Equity: A Football School's Guide To Title IX," Tulane Sports Lawyers Journal, 1995. *Member:* North Carolina Bar Association; North Carolina State Bar; 28th Judicial District Bar; North Carolina Academy of Trial Lawyers. ***PRACTICE AREAS:*** Commercial Litigation; Real Estate Litigation; Contested Wills; Civil Litigation; Personal Injury. ***Email:*** philip@longparker.com

---

RONALD DALE BRONDYKE, born Chicago, Illinois, March 25, 1947; admitted to bar, 1973, North Carolina. *Education:* Olivet College (B.A., 1970); University of North Carolina (J.D., 1973). *Member:* North Carolina and American Bar Associations; 28th Judicial District and North Carolina State Bars. (Board Certified Specialist in Real Property Law-Residential Transactions, North Carolina State Board of Legal Specialization). ***PRACTICE AREAS:*** Real Estate. ***Email:*** ron@longparker.com

ANDREW B. PARKER, born Asheville, North Carolina, February 27, 1977; admitted to bar, 2002, North Carolina. *Education:* Wake Forest University (B.A., with honors, 1999); University of North Carolina at Chapel Hill (J.D., 2002). Member, North Carolina Journal of International Law and Commercial Regulation, 2000-2002. ***PRACTICE AREAS:*** Civil Litigation; Commercial Litigation; Real Estate Litigation. ***Email:*** abp@longparker.com

MARSHALL & ROTH

PROFESSIONAL CORPORATION
90 SOUTHSIDE AVENUE, SUITE 150
ASHEVILLE, NORTH CAROLINA 28801
Telephone: 828-281-2100
Fax: 828-281-2120

Federal and State Court Litigation, Personal Injury, Auto Accidents, Wrongful Death, Medical Malpractice, Civil Litigation, Corporate and Business Transactions, Employment Law, Contract Law, Physician/Patient Confidentiality Matters, Healthcare Litigation, Real Estate Litigation, Real Estate, Probate, Environmental Law, Zoning and Land Use.

CLIFFORD C. MARSHALL, JR., born Birmingham, Alabama, May 28, 1957; admitted to bar, 1982, North Carolina, U.S. District Court, Western District of North Carolina and U.S. Court of Appeals, 4th Circuit. *Education:* University of North Carolina (B.A., 1979; J.D., 1982). Assistant U.S. Attorney, Western District of North Carolina (Chief of Civil Division), 1983-2001. ***PRACTICE AREAS:*** Federal Civil Litigation; Personal Injury; Real Property; Litigation; Business Law. ***Email:*** cmarshall_mr@charter.net

PHILIP J. ROTH, JR., born Madison, Wisconsin, March 2, 1958; admitted to bar, 1992, Wisconsin and Illinois; 1996, North Carolina. *Education:* University of Wisconsin-Madison (B.A., 1981; J.D., 1992). Recipient, American Jurisprudence Award in Constitutional Law, 1991. *Member:* North Carolina Bar Association; North Carolina State Bar; State Bar of Wisconsin; North Carolina Academy of Trial Lawyers. ***PRACTICE AREAS:*** Federal Civil Litigation; Employment Discrimination; Commercial Litigation; Personal Injury; Civil Rights. ***Email:*** proth_mr@charter.net

LYMAN J. GREGORY, born 1967; admitted to bar, 1998, North Carolina. *Education:* Western Carolina University (B.A., 1989); University of North Carolina at Chapel Hill (J.D., 1998). ***PRACTICE AREAS:*** Real Estate; Zoning and Land Use; Probate; Environmental Law; Trusts and Estates. ***Email:*** lgregory_mr@charter.net

McGUIRE, WOOD & BISSETTE, P.A.

DRHUMOR BUILDING
48 PATTON AVENUE
P.O. BOX 3180
ASHEVILLE, NORTH CAROLINA 28802
Telephone: 828-254-8800
Fax: 828-252-2438
Email: mwb@mwbavl.com
URL: http://www.mwbavl.com

General Civil Practice in State and Federal Courts, Bankruptcy (Creditors Representation), Commercial Law, Corporate Law, Construction Law, Condominium Law, Estate Planning, Probate, Health Care, Insurance, Labor and Employment Law, Labor Relations, Litigation, Media, Personal Injury, Product Liability, Wrongful Death, Real Estate, Taxation, Securities Law, Appellate Advocacy, Alternative Dispute Resolution, and Mediation.

(This Listing Continued)

FIRM PROFILE: McGuire, Wood & Bissette, P.A. is the oldest law firm in Asheville, continuously engaged in the practice of law since 1894. The firm engages in a general civil practice, with a focus on the business, financial and litigation needs of its clients. The firm's practice, although tailored to the needs of western North Carolina, enjoys client relationships throughout the United States. Complementing the firm's practice is the continuing involvement of its members in the Asheville community. Most notably, Mr. Wood (1971-1975) and Mr. Bissette (1985-1989) have served as Mayors of Asheville and Mr. Cloninger has served as Vice-Mayor (1999-2001).

W. LOUIS BISSETTE, JR., born Statesville, North Carolina, September 18, 1943; admitted to bar, 1968, North Carolina. *Education:* Wake Forest University (B.A., 1965); University of North Carolina (J.D., 1968); University of Virginia (M.B.A., 1970). Phi Delta Phi. Mayor, City of Asheville, 1985-1989. *Member:* North Carolina (Member: Probate and Fiduciary Law Section and Business Law Section) and American (Member: Tax Section and Business Law Section) Bar Associations. ***PRACTICE AREAS:*** Business Law; Health Law; Estate Planning; Real Estate Development. ***Email:*** lbissette@mwbavl.com

DOUGLAS O. THIGPEN, born Macon, Georgia, November 4, 1951; admitted to bar, 1976, North Carolina. *Education:* University of North Carolina (A.B., 1972; J.D., 1976). *Member:* North Carolina Bar Association (Member, Real Property Section; Member, Real Property Council, 1992-1997). (Board Certified Specialist in Real Property Law, Residential Transactions, Business, Commercial and Industrial Transactions, North Carolina State Board of Legal Specialization). ***PRACTICE AREAS:*** Commercial Real Estate; Residential Real Estate. ***Email:*** dthigpen@mwbavl.com

JOSEPH P. McGUIRE, born Asheville, North Carolina, August 16, 1950; admitted to bar, 1975, North Carolina; 1976, Georgia; 1978, U.S. District Court, Western District of North Carolina; 1980, U.S. Court of Appeals, Fourth Circuit. *Education:* University of North Carolina (B.A., 1972); Harvard Law School (J.D., 1975). Phi Beta Kappa. *Member:* State Bar of Georgia; American Bar Association (Member, Litigation Section); North Carolina Academy of Trial Lawyers. ***PRACTICE AREAS:*** Corporate Litigation; Commercial Litigation; Personal Injury; Medical Malpractice. ***Email:*** jmcguire@mwbavl.com

DORIS PHILLIPS LOOMIS, born Asheville, North Carolina, August 27, 1956; admitted to bar, 1981, North Carolina. *Education:* Davidson College (B.S., 1978); Wake Forest University (J.D., 1981). Commissioner, Town of Biltmore Forest. *Member:* North Carolina (Member, Estate Planning and Fiduciary Law Section) American (Member, Real Property Section) Bar Associations. (Board Certified Specialist in Estate Planning and Probate Law, North Carolina State Board of Legal Specialization). ***PRACTICE AREAS:*** Estate Planning; Probate Law. ***Email:*** dloomis@mwbavl.com

M. CHARLES CLONINGER, born Shelby, North Carolina, December 17, 1955; admitted to bar, 1982, North Carolina; 1984, U.S. District Court, Western District of North Carolina. *Education:* University of North Carolina at Chapel Hill (A.B., 1979; J.D., 1982). Phi Beta Kappa. Asheville City Council, 1995-2001; Vice-Mayor, 1999-2001. Co-Author: "North Carolina Construction Law: Rights and Remedies," Lorman Education Services, 1998. *Member:* North Carolina Bar Association (Member: Litigation Section and Construction Law Section; Construction Law Council, 1993-2000); American Bar Association (Member, Forum on the Construction Industry); North Carolina Academy of Trial Lawyers; The Association of Trial Lawyers of America. ***PRACTICE AREAS:*** Construction Law; Construction Litigation; Commercial Litigation; Personal Injury. ***Email:*** ccloninger@mwbavl.com

THOMAS C. GRELLA, born Bridgeport, Connecticut, 1960; admitted to bar, 1985, North Carolina. *Education:* James Madison University (B.B.A., 1982); Wake Forest University (J.D., 1985). Omicron Delta Kappa. Member, Mortar Board. Recipient: American Jurisprudence Award, Civil Procedure; North Carolina Bar Association Outstanding Young Lawyer Award, 1989-1990. *Member:* North Carolina (Chair, YLD Professionalism Committee, 1988-1990; Chair, YLD Pro Bono Committee, 1991-1993; YLD Division Director, 1990-1992, 1994-1995; Member: Real Property Section; Law Practice Management Section; Business Law Section) and American (Member, House of Delegates, 1993-1995; YLD Division Director, 1996-1997; Chair, YLD Ethics and Professionalism Committee, 1994-1996; YLD Liaison, Standing Committee on Professional Discipline, 1994-1996; YLD Liaison, Law Practice Management Section, 1997-1999; Member, Law Practice Management Section Council, 1999—; Section Chair, 2004-2005; Section Secretary, 2003-2004; Chair, Law Practice Management Section Diversity Committee; Member, Law Practice Management Section Publishing Board, 2000—; Chair, Law Practice Management Section Core Group, 2002-2003; Member, ABA Task Force on the Model Definition of the Practice of Law; Law Practice Management Liaison, Commission on Racial and Ethical Diversity in the Profession, 1999-2002; Member, Real Property and Probate and Trust Section; Member, Section on Natural Resources, Energy and Environmental Law; Member, Section on Business Law) Bar Associations; North Carolina State Bar (Member, Task Force on District Bars); N.C. Christian Legal Society (Member, Advisory Board, 1985-1988). ***PRACTICE AREAS:*** Business; Commercial Real Property; Real Estate Development; Condominium Law; Exempt Securities; Exempt Transactions. ***Email:*** tgrella@mwbavl.com

GRANT B. OSBORNE, born Charlotte, North Carolina, May 31, 1959; admitted to bar, 1986, North Carolina; 1989, U.S. District Court, Western District of North Carolina; 1990, U.S. Court of Appeals, Fourth Circuit. *Education:* Duke University (B.A., 1981); Duke University Law School (J.D., 1985). Author of numerous articles on employment and wage and hour law, Lorman Education Services. Member, Rotary Club of Asheville. *Member:* 28th Judicial District Bar Association (President, Young Lawyers Division, 1993-1994); North Carolina State Bar; North Carolina Bar Association (Member, Sections on: Labor and Employment Law; Litigation); American Bar Association (Member, Sections on: Labor and Employment Law; Litigation). ***PRACTICE AREAS:*** Employment Law; Employment Litigation; Labor Law; Commercial Litigation; Real Estate Litigation. ***Email:*** gosborne@mwbavl.com

T. DOUGLAS WILSON, JR., born Winston-Salem, North Carolina, 1946; admitted to bar, 1973, North Carolina; 1974, Georgia. *Education:* University of North Carolina (A.B., 1968); University of North Carolina Law School (J.D., 1973). Phi Delta Phi (Magister, 1972-1973). Associate Justice Moot Court Board. Co-Author: "North Carolina Construction Law: Rights and Remedies," Lorman Education Services, 1998. Certified Mediator, North Carolina. *Member:* State Bar of Georgia; American Bar Association (Member,

(This Listing Continued)

Antitrust Section); North Carolina Academy of Trial Lawyers; Association of Trial Lawyers of America. ***PRACTICE AREAS:*** Commercial Litigation; Corporate Litigation; Construction Litigation; Personal Injury; Arbitration; Mediation. ***Email:*** tdwilson@mwbavl.com

RICHARD A. KORT, born Charlotte, North Carolina, June 29, 1964; admitted to bar, 1991, North Carolina. *Education:* Emory University (B.B.A., 1987); University of North Carolina (J.D., 1991). Beta Alpha Psi; Beta Gamma Sigma. Certified Public Accountant, North Carolina, 1992. (Board Certified Specialist in Estate Planning and Probate Law, North Carolina State Board of Legal Specialization). ***PRACTICE AREAS:*** Estate Planning; Probate; Business Law. ***Email:*** rkort@mwbavl.com

FREDERICK S. BARBOUR, born Kingsville, Texas, April 2, 1957; admitted to bar, 1984, North Carolina. *Education:* University of North Carolina (B.A., 1979; J.D., 1984). Staff Member, North Carolina Journal of International Law and Commercial Regulation, 1983. *Member:* 28th Judicial District and North Carolina Bar Associations; North Carolina State Bar. ***PRACTICE AREAS:*** Construction Litigation; Commercial Litigation; Personal Injury; Municipal Liability; Estate Litigation; Mediation; Arbitration; Alternative Dispute Resolution.

JOHN N. FLEMING, born Trenton, New Jersey, May 18, 1962; admitted to bar, 1987, Georgia; 1988, Supreme Court of the State of Georgia, Court of Appeals, State of Georgia and U.S. District Court, Northern District of Georgia; 1995, North Carolina. *Education:* The Wharton School, University of Pennsylvania (B.S., 1984); Vanderbilt University (J.D., 1987). Phi Delta Phi. Student Writing Editor, Vanderbilt Journal of Transnational Law, 1986-1987. *Member:* State Bar of Georgia; North Carolina State Bar. ***PRACTICE AREAS:*** Business Law; Health Care Law. ***Email:*** jfleming@mwbavl.com

SUSAN STRAYHORN BARBOUR, born Durham, North Carolina, June 12, 1959; admitted to bar, 1984, North Carolina. *Education:* University of North Carolina (B.A., 1981; J.D., with honors, 1984). Phi Beta Kappa. Member: Order of the Golden Fleece; Order of Barristers. Member: Holderness Moot Court Bench, 1983-1984; Invitational Moot Court Team, 1984. *Member:* 28th Judicial District, North Carolina (Member, Real Property Section) and American Bar Associations; North Carolina State Bar. ***PRACTICE AREAS:*** Commercial Real Estate; Residential Real Estate. ***Email:*** sbarbour@mwbavl.com

---

SARAH SPARBOE THORNBURG, born Pittsburgh, Pennsylvania, April 21, 1969; admitted to bar, 1996, Tennessee; 1997, North Carolina. *Education:* Duke University (A.B., 1990); Wake Forest University School of Law (J.D., 1996). Member, Wake Forest Law Review, 1994-1995. Judicial Clerk for the Honorable Thomas A. Higgins, U.S. District Court, Middle District of Tennessee, 1996-1998. Author: "Must Bar Examiners Accommodate the Disabled on Bar Exams?" 30 Wake Forest L. Rev. 391 (1995). *Member:* 28th Judicial District and North Carolina Bar Associations. ***PRACTICE AREAS:*** Estate Planning; Probate. ***Email:*** sthornburg@mwbavl.com

DOUGLAS J. TATE, born Moses Lake, Washington, March 27, 1963; admitted to bar, 1989, North Carolina. *Education:* University of North Carolina, Chapel Hill (A.B., 1985); Emory University (J.D., 1988). Order of Barristers. Member: Emory University School of Law Moot Court Society, 1984-1985; Moot Court Board of Directors, 1984-1985; Intra-State Moot Court Team, 1985. Qualified Arbitrator, District 10. *Member:* North Carolina Bar Association; North Carolina State Bar; 28th Judicial District Bar of North Carolina. ***PRACTICE AREAS:*** Civil Litigation; Landlord and Tenant Law; Creditors Rights; Insurance Defense. ***Email:*** dtate@mwbavl.com

MARY E. EULER, born Charleston, West Virginia, October 9, 1967; admitted to bar, 1994, Alabama; 1998, North Carolina. *Education:* University of Alabama at Birmingham (B.A., summa cum laude, 1989); Washington and Lee University (J.D., 1994). Omicron Delta Kappa. Recipient, American Jurisprudence Award, Creditor's Rights. *Member:* 28th Judicial District and North Carolina Bar Associations; North Carolina State Bar; Alabama State Bar. [Capt., U.S. Air Force, Judge Advocate, 1994-1999]. ***PRACTICE AREAS:*** Personal Injury; Insurance; Business; Commercial Disputes; Professional Disputes; Construction Matters. ***Email:*** meuler@mwbavl.com

JEFFREY J. OWEN, born Jacksonville, Florida, December 22, 1974; admitted to bar, 2002, North Carolina and U.S. Tax Court. *Education:* Wake Forest University (B.A., History, with honors, 1997; J.D., 2000); University of Denver (LL.M., Taxation, 2001). *Member:* American Bar Association (Member, Tax Section). ***LANGUAGES:*** French. ***PRACTICE AREAS:*** Taxation; Corporate Law. ***Email:*** jowen@mwbavl.com

RENDI MANN-STADT, born Springfield, Massachusetts, November 26, 1955; admitted to bar, 1994, Illinois; 2002, North Carolina. *Education:* Boston College (B.S., magna cum laude, 1977); University of Louisville (M.B.A., cum laude, 1986); University of Illinois (J.D., magna cum laude, 1994). Recipient, Rickert Legal Writing Award. Member and Notes Editor, University of Illinois Law Review. Judicial Clerk to Honorable Benjamin Miller, Illinois Supreme Court, 1994-1996. Author: note, "Limitation of Liability for Interruption of Service for Regulated Telephone Companies: An Outmoded Protection?" 1993 U. Ill. L. Rev. 629. Co-Author: "Negligence Liability in Illinois Schools," Illinois Bar Journal, 1992. *Member:* 28th Judicial District Bar Association; North Carolina State Bar; North Carolina and Illinois State Bar Associations. ***PRACTICE AREAS:*** Employment Law; Telecommunications Law; Commercial Litigation. ***Email:*** rmann-stadt@mwbavl.com

HARRIS M. LIVINGSTAIN, born Charleston, South Carolina, July 28, 1957; admitted to bar, 1985, Pennsylvania (inactive); 1986, District of Columbia (inactive) and U.S. Tax Court; 1992, North Carolina. *Education:* George Washington University (B.A., 1979); Howard University (J.D., 1982); New York University Law School (LL.M., Gen., 1985); Georgetown University Law Center (LL.M., Tax, 1990). Counsel to Aviation Subcommittee of U.S. Senate Committee on Commerce, 1986-1987. Trial Attorney, Tax Division, U.S. Department of Justice, 1989-1992. (Board Certified Specialist in Estate Planning and Probate Law, North Carolina State Board of Legal Specialization). ***PRACTICE AREAS:*** Taxation; Tax Controversies; Estate Planning and Administration. ***Email:*** hlivingstain@mwbavl.com

ADAM H. REYNOLDS, born Nashville, Tennessee; admitted to bar, 2003, North Carolina. *Education:* Vanderbilt University (B.S., magna cum laude, 2000); Washington &

(This Listing Continued)

McGUIRE, WOOD & BISSETTE, P.A., Asheville—Continued

Lee University (J.D., cum laude, 2003). Co-Author: "PCAOB Issues Auditing Standards Regarding Internal Control Over Financial Reporting," Wall Street Lawyers, May 2004. *Member:* North Carolina (Member, Business and Real Property Sections and American Bar Associations. ***PRACTICE AREAS:*** Business Law; Commercial Real Estate. ***Email:*** areynolds@mwbavl.com

CHRISTOPHER B. LYMAN, born New Orleans, Louisiana; admitted to bar, 1993, Georgia; 2002, Colorado; 2004, North Carolina. *Education:* University of Virginia (B.A., 1988); Tulane University (J.D., 1993). Formerly with Kilpatrick Stockton, LLP, Atlanta, Georgia. *Member:* Southwest Colorado and Colorado Bar Associations. ***PRACTICE AREAS:*** Civil Litigation; Construction Law. ***Email:*** clyman@mwbavl.com

OF COUNSEL

RICHARD A. WOOD, JR., born Knoxville, Tennessee, August 18, 1937; admitted to bar, 1962, North Carolina. *Education:* Duke University (A.B., 1959; LL.B., 1962). Delta Theta Phi. Editor-in-Chief, Duke Law Journal, 1961-1962. Mayor, City of Asheville, 1971-1975. *Member, North Carolina Bar Association (Labor Law Section and Law Management Section).* ***PRACTICE AREAS:*** Business Law; Labor Law. ***Email:*** rwood@mwbavl.com

RETIRED

WALTER R. McGUIRE, born Asheville, North Carolina, December 8, 1913; admitted to bar, 1937, North Carolina. *Education:* Asheville City Schools; The Citadel and University of North Carolina (A.B., 1936); University of North Carolina (LL.B., 1937). Member, North Carolina Board of Bar Examiners, 1972-1981.

All Members of the firm are Members of the North Carolina and American Bar Associations and the 28th Judicial District and North Carolina State Bars.

REPRESENTATIVE CLIENTS: Advantage West; Archerd-Bell Investment Group, LLC; Blue Ridge Metals Corporation; Branch Banking and Trust Company; City of Asheville Claims Corporation; Colton Groome & Company (Benefits & Insurance Consultants); The Community Foundation of WNC, Inc.; Daniels Business Services, Inc. (Printing); Dave Steel Co., Inc.; (Steel Fabricating); Emory Electric, Inc.; The Givens Estates, Inc. (Methodist Retirement Community); Grove Arcade Public Market Foundation, Inc.; Hayes & Lunsford Electrical Contractors, Inc.; Home Depot; Interact Systems; Mountain Retreat Association (Presbyterian Assembly); NEC America, Inc.; Progress Energy, Inc.; (formerly Carolina Power & Light Company); Reynolds Mountain Development, LLC; S.B. Coleman Construction Co., Inc.; Sears Roebuck & Co.; Silver-Line Plastics Corporation; Sisters of Mercy Services Corporation; Spaceplan Architecture Interiors & Planning, P.A.; Target Corp.; The Grove Park Inn Resort; Transylvania Community Hospital; Trident Micro Systems, Inc.; US Cellular; Wachovia Bank, N.A.; Wellco Enterprises, Inc.; Western Carolina Industries (WCI); Wilcox Travel Agency, Inc.; W.P. Hickman Company; Zenith Corporation.
APPROVED ATTORNEYS FOR: Asheville Savings Bank; Bank of America, N.A.; Bank of Asheville; First Citizens Bank; Branch Baking and Trust Company; Branch Bank & Trust Mortgage Corp.; Chicago Title Insurance Co.; Clyde Savings Bank; Commonwealth Land Title Insurance Co.; Cunningham & Company; Fidelity National Title Insurance Company; Investors Title Insurance Co.; Lawyers Title Insurance Corp.; Old Republic Title Insurance Co.; Premier Federal Credit Union; Security Union Title Insurance Co.; Stewart Title Insurance Company; Title Company of North Carolina; Wachovia Bank, N.A.; Wachovia Mortgage Co.

THE MOORE LAW FIRM

Established in 1976

ONE OAK PLAZA, SUITE 303
ASHEVILLE, NORTH CAROLINA 28801
Telephone: 828-258-8053
Fax: 828-251-0972
Email: gmoorelaw@charter.net
URL: http://www.georgemoorelawyer.com

Mailing Address: P.O. Box 7602, Asheville, NC 28802

Personal Injury, Medical Malpractice, Family Law, Child Custody, Child Support, Adoptions, Automobile Accidents, Divorce, Equitable Distribution, Workers' Compensation, Labor and Employment, Nursing Home Litigation..

GEORGE W. MOORE, born Siler City, North Carolina, January 5, 1943; admitted to bar, 1971, North Carolina; 1972, U.S. District Court, Western District of North Carolina; 1980, U.S. Court of Appeals, 4th Circuit. *Education:* Wake Forest University (B.A., 1965); University of North Carolina at Chapel Hill (J.D., 1971). *Member:* North Carolina Bar Association; North Carolina State Bar; North Carolina Academy of Trial Lawyers; American Trial Lawyers Association. [1st Lt. U.S. Army, 1966-1968]. ***REPORTED CASES:*** 195 S.E. 2d 40; 195 S.E. 2d 514; 196 S.E. 2d 419; 212 S.E. 2d 410; 518 S.E. 2d 804. ***PRACTICE AREAS:*** Personal Injury; Automobile Accidents and Injuries; Workers Compensation; Medical Malpractice; Products Liability; Employment Discrimination; Nursing Home Negligence. ***Email:*** gmoorelaw@charter.net

JENNIFER WAYLAND MOORE, born Asheville, North Carolina, October 1, 1972; admitted to bar, 1997, North Carolina; 1999, U.S. District Court, Western District of North Carolina; 2001, U.S. Court of Appeals, 4th Circuit. *Education:* Wake Forest University (B.A., 1994; J.D., 1997). Moot Court Board, 1995-1997. Law Clerk, Hon. John C. Martin, North Carolina Court of Appeals. *Member:* North Carolina Bar Association; North Carolina State Bar; North Carolina Academy of Trial Lawyers. ***REPORTED CASES:*** 537 S.E.2d 498. ***PRACTICE AREAS:*** Family Law; Divorce; Alimony; Equitable Distribution; Child Custody; Child Support; Adoptions; Personal Injury; Nursing Home Negligence; Medical Malpractice; Criminal Law; Traffic Violations; Driving While Intoxicated. ***Email:*** jmoorelaw@charter.net

LAW OFFICES OF E.K. MORLEY, PLLC

ASHEVILLE, NORTH CAROLINA

(See Hendersonville)

Contested Wills, Will Contests, Estate Litigation, Decedents Estates, Inheritance, Successions, Trusts and Estates, Surrogates Court Practice, Contested Trusts and Estates, Estate Administration, Estate Settlements, Fiduciary Law, Fiduciary Liability, Fiduciary Litigation, Trust Law, Trust Litigation, Ancillary Probate, Probate Litigation.

MORRIS YORK WILLIAMS SURLES & BARRINGER, L.L.P.

ASHEVILLE, NORTH CAROLINA

(See Charlotte)

Civil, Business and Commercial Litigation. Insurance Defense Litigation, Insurance Coverage and Workers Compensation. Medical and Professional Malpractice Defense. Land Condemnation and Alternative Dispute Resolution Services.

MULLEN HOLLAND & COOPER P.A.

ASHEVILLE, NORTH CAROLINA

(See Gastonia)

General Civil Trial and Appellate Practice, all Federal and State Courts. Banking, Bankruptcy and Reorganization, Construction, Corporate and Commercial, Employment Discrimination, Estate Planning and Administration, Health Care, Insurance, Mergers and Acquisitions, Negligence, Personal Injury, Professional Malpractice, Real Estate, Workers' Compensation.

D. SAMUEL NEILL

ASHEVILLE, NORTH CAROLINA

(See Hendersonville)

Estate Planning, Wills and Probate, Trusts and Estates, Real Estate, Residential Real Estate, Commercial Real Estate, Personal Injury, Business Law and Elder Law.

SCOTT D. NEUMANN

ASHEVILLE, NORTH CAROLINA

(See Brevard)

Family Law, Divorce, Child Custody and Support, Adoptions, Domestic Violence, Visitation Rights, Civil Practice, Criminal Law, Driving While Intoxicated, Traffic Violations, Drug Crimes, Juvenile Crimes, Parole and Probation, White Collar Crime, Real Estate, Buying or Selling a Home, Construction, Commercial Real Estate, Bankruptcy, Business Law, Buying or Selling a Business, Immigration and Naturalization, Visas, Trusts and Estates, Estate Planning, Wills and Probate.

NORTHUP & McCONNELL, PLLC

123 BILTMORE AVENUE
ASHEVILLE, NORTH CAROLINA 28801
Telephone: 828-232-4481
Facsimile: 828-232-4489
URL: http://www.northupmcconnell.com

Medical Malpractice, Professional Malpractice, Personal Injury, Automobile Accidents, Litigation, Products Liability, Employment Law, Commercial Litigation.

ISAAC NOYES NORTHUP, JR., born Asheville, North Carolina, January 15, 1953; admitted to bar, 1980, North Carolina. *Education:* University of North Carolina (A.B., 1975; J.D., 1980). Executive Editor, North Carolina Journal of International Law and Commercial Regulation, 1979-1980. Research Assistant to the Honorable Walter E. Brock and the Honorable Louis B. Meyer, North Carolina Supreme Court, 1980-1981. Member, North Carolina Board of Law Examiners, 1995-2002. *Member:* North Carolina and American Bar Associations; 28th Judicial District and North Carolina State Bars; North Carolina Association of Defense Attorneys (Board Member, 1995-1998); Defense Research Institute. Fellow, American College of Trial Lawyers. ***PRACTICE AREAS:*** Professional Malpractice; Commercial Litigation; Products Liability. ***Email:*** inn@northupmcconnell.com

ELIZABETH ELLEN McCONNELL, born Richmond, Virginia, April 6, 1959; admitted to bar, 1985, Georgia, North Carolina, U.S. District Court, Western District of North Carolina and U.S. Court of Appeals, Fourth Circuit, U.S. Supreme Court. *Education:* St. Mary's College (L.A., 1979); North Carolina State University (B.A., 1981); Wake Forest University (J.D., 1985). Judicial Clerkship to Honorable David B. Sentelle, United States District Court, Western District of North Carolina, 1985-1987. *Member:* North Carolina Bar Association; 28th Judicial District and North Carolina State Bars; North Carolina Association of Defense Attorneys (Board Member, 2000—). ***PRACTICE AREAS:*** Litigation; Products Liability; Employment Law; Commercial Litigation. ***Email:*** eem@northupmcconnell.com

STEVEN WEIR SIZEMORE, born Asheville, North Carolina, June 4, 1965; admitted to bar, 1991, North Carolina and U.S. District Court, Western District of North Carolina. *Education:* Wake Forest University; Western Carolina University (B.S.B.A., with honors, 1988); Campbell University (J.D., 1991). Delta Theta Phi (Vice Dean, 1990-1991). Member, Western Carolina University Mortar Board. Certified Mediator. *Member:* North Carolina State Bar; North Carolina Bar Association (Member, Workers' Compensation Section); 28th Judicial District Bar; North Carolina Association of Defense Attorneys; Southern Association of Workers' Compensation Administrators. ***PRACTICE AREAS:*** Insurance Defense Litigation; Workers Compensation. ***Email:*** sws@northupmcconnell.com

(This Listing Continued)

DERRICK R. BAILEY, born Asheville, North Carolina, March 14, 1957; admitted to bar, 1988, North Carolina; U.S. District Court, Western, Eastern and Middle Districts of North Carolina. *Education:* College of Charleston (B.S., Biology, 1979); Campbell University School of Law (J.D., 1987). Omicron Delta Kappa. President, Campbell Moot Court Association. Assistant Editor, Campbell Law Observer, 1986-1987. *Member:* North Carolina State Bar; 28th Judicial District Bar Association. ***PRACTICE AREAS:*** Professional Malpractice; Workers Compensation; Personal Injury; Social Security Disability; Civil Litigation. ***Email:*** drb@northupmcconnell.com

PATLA, STRAUS, ROBINSON & MOORE, P.A.

Established in 1953

SUITE 300, 29 NORTH MARKET
P.O. BOX 7625
ASHEVILLE, NORTH CAROLINA 28802
Telephone: 828-255-7641
Fax: 828-258-9222
Email: info@psrmlaw.com

Business Organizations, Tax, Planning and Administration of Estates, Employee Benefit Planning, Real Estate, Construction, Health Care, Labor and Employment, Condemnation, General Civil Trial and Appellate Practice before State and Federal Courts and Administrative Agencies.

JOSEPH A. PATLA (1881-1979)

ROBERT J. ROBINSON, born Asheville, North Carolina, November 7, 1936; admitted to bar, 1960, North Carolina. *Education:* Mars Hill College and Wake Forest College (B.A., 1958); Wake Forest College (LL.B., 1960). Phi Delta Phi. Law Clerk, U.S. District Court, 1960-1961. Assistant U.S. Attorney, 1962-1964. President, Buncombe County Bar Association, 1976-1977. Councilor, 28th District, North Carolina State Bar Council, 1983-1991. Trustee, Client Security Fund, 1989-1991; Chairman, 1990-1991; President, 1993-1994, North Carolina State Bar. Trustee, 1997-2003 and Chairman, 2002-2003, North Carolina IOLTA Board. *Member:* American Bar Association (Member, House of Delegates, 1997-2000). ***PRACTICE AREAS:*** Business Organizations; Planning and Administration of Estates.

WILLIAM C. MOORE (Retired, 1987)

STEVEN I. GOLDSTEIN, born New York, N.Y., January 2, 1943; admitted to bar, 1967, North Carolina. *Education:* University of North Carolina (A.B., 1964; J.D., 1967). Phi Delta Phi. Vice President, 28th Judicial District Bar, 1993-1995. Member, Real Estate Specialty Committee of the Board of Legal Specialization, 1993-1999. (Board Certified Specialist in Real Property Law-Residential, Business, Commercial and Industrial Transactions, North Carolina State Board of Legal Specialization). ***PRACTICE AREAS:*** Real Estate; Secured Transactions.

VICTOR W. BUCHANAN, born Albany, Georgia, March 13, 1942; admitted to bar, 1968, North Carolina. *Education:* University of North Carolina (B.A., 1965; J.D., 1968). Phi Alpha Delta. Adjunct Professor, Healthcare Law, University of North Carolina at Asheville, 1976-2001. Law Clerk, North Carolina Court of Appeals, 1968-1969. President, 28th Judicial District Bar, 1992-1993. Chair, North Carolina Conference of Bar Presidents, 1995-1996, Member of Executive Committee, 1992-1997, 2000-2001. Certified Mediator, North Carolina, 1995. ***PRACTICE AREAS:*** Construction; Employment; Mediation.

ROBERT A. FREEMAN, III, born Marion, Virginia, March 27, 1940; admitted to bar, 1969, North Carolina; 1979, U.S. Tax Court. *Education:* Wake Forest University (B.A., 1963; J.D., 1966). Phi Alpha Delta. Estate Tax Attorney, Internal Revenue Service, U.S. Treasury Department, 1967-1975. ***PRACTICE AREAS:*** Planning and Administration of Estates; Tax.

RICHARD S. DANIELS, born Asheville, North Carolina, July 1, 1952; admitted to bar, 1979, North Carolina. *Education:* University of North Carolina (B.A., 1974; J.D., 1979). Morehead Scholar. *Member:* American Bar Association. ***PRACTICE AREAS:*** Litigation; Immigration.

KERRY A. FRIEDMAN, born Asheville, North Carolina, September 28, 1954; admitted to bar, 1980, North Carolina; 1985, U.S. Tax Court. *Education:* University of North Carolina at Chapel Hill (B.A., 1976; J.D., 1980). Phi Eta Sigma; Phi Beta Kappa. Secretary-Treasurer, 28th Judicial District Bar, 1984-1986. President, Legal Services of North Carolina, Inc., 1996; Member, Board of Directors, 1993-1998. ***PRACTICE AREAS:*** Business Organizations; Compensation Planning; Tax.

VIRGINIA P. LITZENBERGER (Retired, 2002)

SHARON TRACEY BARRETT, born Pittsfield, Massachusetts, May 10, 1961; admitted to bar, 1986, North Carolina. *Education:* Boston College (B.A., 1983); Georgetown University (J.D., 1986). *Member:* 28th Judicial District Bar (President, 2002-2003; Secretary-Treasurer, 1998-2001; President, Young Lawyers Section, 1989-1991); North Carolina Academy of Trial Lawyers. ***PRACTICE AREAS:*** Litigation; Real Estate.

MARK C. MARTIN, born Madrid, Spain, May 8, 1965; admitted to bar, 1991, North Carolina. *Education:* University of North Carolina (B.A., 1987); T.C. Williams School of Law, University of Richmond (J.D., 1990). *Member:* North Carolina Academy of Trial Lawyers. ***PRACTICE AREAS:*** Litigation; Real Estate.

CAROL EUBANK, born Covington, Kentucky, November 21, 1949; admitted to bar, 1975, Kentucky; 1976, North Carolina; 1977, U.S. Tax Court. *Education:* University of Kentucky (B.A., 1971; J.D., 1975). Phi Beta Kappa. Member, Kentucky Law Journal, 1973-1975. Law Clerk, Kentucky Supreme Court, 1976. ***PRACTICE AREAS:*** Business Organizations.

EILEEN M. McMINN, born Lynn, Massachusetts, March 24, 1951; admitted to bar, 1990, North Carolina. *Education:* Barnard College (B.A., cum laude, 1973); University of Massachusetts (M.S., 1977); University of Connecticut Law School (J.D., cum laude, 1990). *Member:* American Bar Association. ***PRACTICE AREAS:*** Employment; Benefit Planning.

(This Listing Continued)

DONNA DOUGLAS, born Thomasville, North Carolina, December 15, 1956; admitted to bar, 1984, North Carolina. *Education:* Meredith College (B.S., 1978); North Carolina Central University (J.D., 1984). Phi Delta Phi. Member, North Carolina Central University Law Journal. ***PRACTICE AREAS:*** Business Organizations.

CINDY M. RICE, born Asheville, North Carolina, May 16, 1978; admitted to bar, 2003, North Carolina. *Education:* University of North Carolina at Chapel Hill (B.S., with distinction, 2000; J.D., 2003). ***PRACTICE AREAS:*** Litigation.

OF COUNSEL

KARL H. STRAUS, born Germany, February 7, 1921; admitted to bar, 1951, New York; 1953, North Carolina; 1955, U.S. Tax Court. *Education:* New York University (LL.B., 1950). President, Buncombe County Bar Association, 1970-1971. Member, 1971-1983 and Chairman, 1982-1983, Board of Trustees, University of North Carolina at Asheville. Member, 1984-1992 and Chairman, 1986-1988, Board of Directors, University of North Carolina at Asheville Foundation, Inc. ***LANGUAGES:*** German. ***PRACTICE AREAS:*** Business Organizations; Tax; Planning and Administration of Estates.

All Attorneys are Members of the North Carolina Bar Association, the 28th Judicial District Bar, and The North Carolina State Bar.

COUNSEL FOR: Asheville Board of Alcoholic Control; Asheville Regional Airport Authority; Asheville Waste Paper Co.; Bromley Plastics, Inc.; Cason Companies, Inc.; City of Asheville; Conrad Industries, Inc.; Eliada Homes, Inc.; Giles Chemical Corp.; Grove Park Inn Resort, Inc.; Harry's Cadillac-Pontiac-GMC Truck Co., Inc.; Mars Hill College; Matthews Ford, Inc.; Mills Manufacturing Corp.; Mission Hospitals, Inc.; Plasticard Products, Inc.; Prestige Motors of Asheville, Inc.; Public Interest Projects, Inc.; H. Putsch & Company, an affiliate of H. Putsch & Comp. (Germany); Royal Crown Cola Bottling Co.; Union Transfer and Storage Company, Inc.; Van Wingerden International, Inc.; Western North Carolina Public Radio, Inc.; Woodfin Sanitary Water & Sewer District; YMCA Blue Ridge Assembly, Inc.; YWCA of Asheville, Inc.
LOCAL COUNSEL FOR: Alliance-Carolina Tool & Mold; Norfolk Southern Railway Co.
APPROVED ATTORNEYS FOR: Commonwealth Land Title Insurance Co.; Investors Title Insurance Company; Land America Title Insurance Co.; Lawyers Title Insurance Co.; Stewart Title Guaranty Co.; Fidelity National Title Insurance Co.
REFERENCES: Wachovia Bank, N.A.; Bank of America; High Street Banking Company.

JACK POISSON

Established in 1992

29 NORTH MARKET STREET
THE SEVENTH FLOOR
ASHEVILLE, NORTH CAROLINA 28801-2983
Telephone: 828-252-9889
Toll Free: 800-366-0076
Cell Phone: 828-275-7577
Fax: 828-252-0511
URL: http://www.jackpoisson-law.com
URL: http://www.jackpoissonlaw.com
Email: higherlaw@bellsouth.net
URL: http://www.jpoissonlaw.com

Family Law, Civil Litigation, Personal Injury, Automobile Accidents, Criminal Traffic, Defense, DUI, Divorce, Child Support, Child Custody, Equitable Distribution.

JACK POISSON, born Pleasantville, New York, February 21, 1943; admitted to bar, 1970, North Carolina and U.S. District Court, Eastern District of North Carolina. *Education:* North Carolina State University (B.S., 1965); University of North Carolina at Chapel Hill (J.D., 1970). Phi Delta Phi. *Member:* 28th Judicial District and North Carolina Bar Associations; North Carolina State Bar; North Carolina Academy of Trial Lawyers. ***PRACTICE AREAS:*** Family Law; Child Support; Child Custody; Civil Litigation; Criminal Defense; Divorce.

LAW OFFICES OF SIDNEY POWELL

Established in 1993

1854A HENDERSONVILLE ROAD, SUITE 228
ASHEVILLE, NORTH CAROLINA 28803
Telephone: 828-651-9543
Fax: 828-684-5343
Email: sidneypowell@federalappeals.com

Dallas, Texas Office: 1920 Abrams Parkway, Suite 369, 75214. Telephone: 214-653-3933. Fax: 214-319-2502.

Federal Appeals, Consulting in Complex Federal Litigation.

FIRM PROFILE: Sidney Powell consults in federal trial and appellate cases involving complex litigation. Sidney Powell has served as lead counsel in more than 500 federal appeals resulting in 183 published decisions, in a wide variety of cases.

REPRESENTATIVE CLIENTS: Arthur Anderson, Rosewood Resources; Grob Aerospace; State Farm.

(For biographical data on all personnel, see Professional Biographies, Dallas, Texas)

PRINCE, YOUNGBLOOD & MASSAGEE

ASHEVILLE, NORTH CAROLINA

(See Hendersonville)

General Practice. Probate, Civil Litigation, Commercial, Residential Real Estate, Corporate, Arbitration, Mediation, Healthcare, Employment Law, Family Law, Equitable Distribution, Child Custody, Adoptions.

ROBERTS & STEVENS, P.A.

Established in 1986

BB&T BUILDING
ONE WEST PACK SQUARE, SUITE 1100
P.O. BOX 7647
ASHEVILLE, NORTH CAROLINA 28802
Telephone: 828-252-6600
Facsimile: 828-253-7200
Email: info@roberts-stevens.com
URL: http://www.roberts-stevens.com

General Civil and Trial Practice Before all Courts, Administrative Law, Bankruptcy, Civil Litigation, Construction, Corporation, Education, Employment, Environmental, Health Care, Hospital, Insurance, Estate Planning, Probate, Public Sector, Real Estate, Taxation.

JOHN SHORTER STEVENS, born Asheville, North Carolina, May 30, 1933; admitted to bar, 1961, North Carolina. *Education:* University of North Carolina (A.B., 1956; J.D., 1961). Phi Beta Kappa. Member, House of Representatives, General Assembly, 1969-1976. Member, Board of Trustees, University of North Carolina at Chapel Hill, 1979-1983. Author: "Planning for Death or Retirement for Closely Held Corporations," North Carolina Bar Association, 1978. Author, "What Florida Estate Planners Need to Know About Disposition of North Carolina Real Estate," Florida Bar Association, 1990. Chairman, Asheville Regional Airport Authority, 1980-1988. Chairman, North Carolina Administrative Rules Review Commission, 1986-1990. President, Asheville Area Chamber of Commerce, 1990-1991. Chair, Mission & St. Joseph's Health Systems, Inc., 1995-1998. Chair, University of North Carolina Health Care System, 2001—. *Member:* North Carolina Bar Association (President, 1995-1996); 28th Judicial District and North Carolina State Bars; American Counsel Association; Lawyers Mutual Liability Insurance Company of North Carolina (Board Member, 1981—). ***PRACTICE AREAS:*** Business Law; Corporate Law. ***Email:*** jstevens@roberts-stevens.com

JAMES WALKER WILLIAMS, born Rocky Mount, North Carolina, January 13, 1946; admitted to bar, 1970, North Carolina; U.S. District Court, Western and Middle Districts of North Carolina; 1984, U.S. Court of Appeals, Fourth Circuit. *Education:* University of North Carolina (B.S., 1967; J.D., 1970). Delta Theta Phi (President, Battle Senate, 1969-1970). Listed in: Best Lawyers in America; Best Commercial Lawyers in North Carolina. *Member:* North Carolina (Member, Board of Governors, 1993-1996) and 28th Judicial District (President, 1984-1985) Bar Associations; North Carolina State Bar; North Carolina Association of Defense Attorneys (President, 1991-1992); Defense Research Institute (National Chair, Committee of State and Local Defense Organizations). Fellow: American College of Trial Lawyers. ***PRACTICE AREAS:*** Professional Liability; Products Liability; Commercial Litigation. ***Email:*** jwilliams@roberts-stevens.com

CARL W. LOFTIN, born Asheville, North Carolina, August 20, 1936; admitted to bar, 1961, North Carolina. *Education:* Davidson College (A.B., 1958); University of North Carolina (LL.B., 1961). Phi Delta Phi. Research Assistant, North Carolina Supreme Court, 1961-1962. Chairman, Board of Trustees, University of North Carolina at Asheville, 1980-1982. *Member:* North Carolina Bar Association; 28th Judicial District and North Carolina State Bars. ***PRACTICE AREAS:*** Probate Law; Real Property Law; Government Law. ***Email:*** cloftin@roberts-stevens.com

WALTER L. CURRIE, born Lake City, Florida, October 5, 1940; admitted to bar, 1968, North Carolina; 1972, U.S. District Court, Western District of North Carolina; 1973, U.S. Court of Appeals, Fourth Circuit. *Education:* Duke University (B.A., 1962); University of North Carolina (J.D., 1968). *Member:* North Carolina and American Bar Associations; 28th Judicial District and North Carolina State Bars; Council of School Attorneys of the North Carolina and National School Board Associations; North Carolina-South Carolina Conference of Housing and Redevelopment Attorneys. ***PRACTICE AREAS:*** Education Law; Public Law; Government Law; Construction Law. ***Email:*** wcurrie@roberts-stevens.com

JOHN W. MASON, born Lumberton, North Carolina, October 17, 1944; admitted to bar, 1973, North Carolina. *Education:* Davidson College (B.A., 1967); University of North Carolina (J.D., 1973). Speaker, The Law of Right to Refuse: The Responsibility of the Physician, The Right of the Patient, North Carolina Bar Association Foundation Health and Mental Health Law Seminar, 1983. Member, Board of Directors, Community Foundation of Western North Carolina, 1992-2001. *Member:* North Carolina (Chair, Development Committee, 2002-2005) and American Bar Associations; 28th Judicial District (President, 1998-1999) and The North Carolina State Bars. [1st Lt., U.S. Marine Corps, 1967-1970]. ***PRACTICE AREAS:*** Probate Law; Trust Law; Estate Planning. ***Email:*** jmason@roberts-stevens.com

MARC RUDOW, born New York, New York, November 8, 1953; admitted to bar, 1979, North Carolina. *Education:* New College of the University of South Florida (B.A., 1975); University of North Carolina (J.D., 1979). President, Pisgah Legal Services Board, 1984-1985. President, Mediation Center, 1988-1989. Bankruptcy Trustee, Western District of North Carolina. *Member:* Buncombe County and North Carolina (Member, Bankruptcy Section Council, 1987-1990, 1998-2001) Bar Associations; 28th Judicial District and North Carolina State Bars. ***LANGUAGES:*** French. ***PRACTICE AREAS:*** Real Property Law; Bankruptcy Law. ***Email:*** mrudow@roberts-stevens.com

SHERYL HOWELL WILLIAMS, born Goldsboro, North Carolina, August 8, 1950; admitted to bar, 1980, North Carolina and U.S. District Court, Western District of North Carolina. *Education:* University of North Carolina and Wright State University (B.A., magna cum laude, 1973); University of North Carolina (J.D., 1980). *Member:* North Carolina Bar Association (Secretary, 1983-1985 and Member, 1986-1989, Real Property Section Council and Member, 1988-1991, Residential Task Force and Member, 1989-1990, Land Records Management Task Force); North Carolina State Bar; 28th Judicial District. (Board Certified Specialist in Real Property Law-Residential Transactions). ***PRACTICE AREAS:*** Commercial Real Estate Law; Residential Real Estate Law; Real Estate Development; Condemnation Law. ***Email:*** swilliams@roberts-stevens.com

WILLIAM CLARKE, born Bat Cave, North Carolina, January 30, 1956; admitted to bar, 1982, North Carolina and U.S. District Court, Western and Middle Districts of North Carolina. *Education:* Princeton University (A.B., 1979); University of North Carolina (J.D., 1982). *Member:* North Carolina and American Bar Associations; 28th Judicial District and North Carolina (Council Member, Environmental and Natural Resources Law Section, 1989-1995 and 1999-2002) State Bars. ***LANGUAGES:*** Spanish. ***PRACTICE AREAS:*** Environmental Law and Litigation; Occupational Safety and Health; Condemnation; Brownfields Redevelopment. ***Email:*** bclarke@roberts-stevens.com

VINCENT D. CHILDRESS, JR., born High Point, North Carolina, November 14, 1956; admitted to bar, 1983, North Carolina. *Education:* University of North Carolina (B.A., 1979; J.D., 1983). Phi Eta Sigma; Phi Beta Kappa; Phi Delta Phi. *Member:* North Carolina Bar Association (Member, Sections on: Business Law; Section Council, 1994-1997; Estate Planning and Fiduciary Law, Chairman Related Professionals Committee, 1999-2000); 28th Judicial District (President, Young Lawyers Division, 1986-1987) and North Carolina State Bars. ***PRACTICE AREAS:*** Corporate Law; Trusts and Estates; Health Care Law. ***Email:*** vchildress@roberts-stevens.com

MARJORIE ROWE MANN, born Detroit, Michigan, October 1, 1960; admitted to bar, 1985, North Carolina and U.S. District Court, Western, Middle and Eastern Districts of North Carolina. *Education:* Alma College (B.A., magna cum laude, 1982); Wake Forest University (J.D., 1985). *Member:* Buncombe County, North Carolina and American Bar Associations; 28th Judicial District and North Carolina State Bars; American Bankruptcy Institute; National Association of Bankruptcy Trustees, North Carolina Association of Defense Attorneys. ***PRACTICE AREAS:*** Commercial Litigation; Construction Law; Condemnation; Creditor Bankruptcy; Foreclosures; Collections; Real Estate; Property Law; Bankruptcy Trustees Rights. ***Email:*** mmann@roberts-stevens.com

GREGORY D. HUTCHINS, born Asheville, North Carolina, April 28, 1962; admitted to bar, 1987, North Carolina, U.S. District Court, Western District of North Carolina and U.S. Tax Court. *Education:* Wake Forest University (B.S., Business, 1984); Campbell University (J.D., cum laude, 1987). Kappa Sigma; Delta Theta Phi; Omicron Delta Kappa. George Foster Hankins Scholar. Phillips Scholarship. Member, Campbell Law Review, 1985-1987. Author, Comment, Campbell Law Review 505, Summer 1986. *Member:* 28th Judicial District and North Carolina Bar Associations; North Carolina State Bar (Council Member, Business Law Section, 2002-2005). ***PRACTICE AREAS:*** Corporate Law; Business Transactions; Commercial Real Property; Tax Deferred Exchanges; Taxation; Non-Profit Corporations; Health Care Law. ***Email:*** ghutchins@roberts-stevens.com

JACKSON D. HAMILTON, born Cleveland, Ohio, February 5, 1949; admitted to bar, 1974, California; 1979, U.S. Tax Court; 1987, U.S. Court of Federal Claims; 1989, U.S. Court of Appeals, Sixth and Eleventh Circuits; 1991, North Carolina and U.S. Supreme Court. *Education:* Colgate University (B.A., 1971); University of Pennsylvania (J.D., 1974). Assistant Editor and Editorial Advisory Board, Entertainment Law Reporter, 1979-2005. Adjunct Professor, University of San Diego Law School, Graduate Tax Program, 1981; Golden Gate University, Graduate Tax Program, 1982-1985; University of North Carolina at Asheville (1994). Author: "MCA-Classification of Foreign Entities As Associations or Partnerships," 7 International Tax Journal 292 (1981) and 59 Taxes 303, 1981; "Divorce: Effects of Remarriage on Treatment of Periodic Payments," Points to Remember, 34 The Tax Lawyer 797, 1981; "Internal Revenue Code: Section 385 Sets Stock-or-Debt Rules," 56 California State Bar Journal 278, 1981; "Tax Strategies for Aliens," 7 Los Angeles Lawyer 38, 1984; "Golden Parachutes: Congress Cuts the Ripcord," 85-4 Los Angeles Daily Journal Report 7, 1985; "Using Nuclear Weapons to Kill Mosquitoes: IRS Issues Proposed Partnership Anti-Abuse Regulations", 14 Tax Assessments (1994); "Update: IRS Revises Partnership Anti-Abuse Regulations," 14 Tax Assessments 7 (1995); "Seeking Split Dollars: The IRS Issues Proposed Regulations on Split Dollar Arrangements," 22 Tax Assessments 1 (2003); "What's Happening?" 24 Tax Assessments 10 (2005). Co-Author: "An Investor's Approach to Evaluating a Tax Sheltered Investment," 83-24 Los Angeles Daily Journal, Report 17, 1983; "The Time Value of Money: Section 467 Rental Agreements Under the Tax Reform Act of 1984," 63 Taxes-The Tax Magazine 155, 1985; "Attorneys and the California Athlete Agencies Act: The Toll of the Bill," COMMENT, Hastings College of Law, 1986; "Reallocation of Income and Deductions," Benders Federal Tax Service (1998); "Taxation Section, Gordon and Gordon," Immigration Law and Procedure, Vol. 2 (1989). Consultant, California Senate, Select Committee on Designated and Licensed Sports, 1983-1984. Consultant, California Continuing Education of the Bar, 1983-1984. Board of Advisors, UNC Tax Institute. *Member:* North Carolina (Member and Officer, Tax Section Council) and American Bar Associations (Member, Sections on: Taxation; International Law). ***PRACTICE AREAS:*** Taxation Law; Corporate Law. ***Email:*** jhamilton@roberts-stevens.com

WYATT SHORTER STEVENS, born Asheville, North Carolina, August 7, 1969; admitted to bar, 1994, North Carolina, U.S. District Court, Western and Middle Districts of North Carolina, U.S. Court of Appeals, Fourth Circuit. *Education:* University of North Carolina (B.A., 1991; J.D., 1994). Member, North Carolina Journal of International Law and Commercial Regulation, 1993-1994. *Member:* 28th Judicial District and North Carolina (Member, Litigation Section) Bar Associations; North Carolina State Bar; Defense Research Institute; Association of Ski Defense Attorneys. ***PRACTICE AREAS:*** Insurance Defense Litigation; Personal Injury Litigation; Commercial Litigation; Appeals; Personal Injury. ***Email:*** wstevens@roberts-stevens.com

MARK C. KURDYS, born Toledo, Ohio, August 8, 1956; admitted to bar, 1980, Michigan; 1986, North Carolina, U.S. District Court, Eastern District of Michigan, U.S. District Court, Western, Middle and Eastern Districts of North Carolina and U.S. Court of Appeals, Fourth Circuit. *Education:* University of Michigan (B.G.S., 1977); University of Toledo (J.D., 1980). *Member:* 28th Judicial District and North Carolina Bar Associations; State Bar of Michigan; North Carolina State Bar; North Carolina Association of Defense Attorneys; Defense Research Institute. ***PRACTICE AREAS:*** Medical Liability; Professional Liability; Products Liability; Transportation; Insurance Litigation; Personal Injury; Commercial Litigation; Business Litigation; Appeals. ***Email:*** mkurdys@roberts-stevens.com

JACQUELINE D. GRANT, born Asheville, North Carolina, July 14, 1970; admitted to bar, 1995, North Carolina, U.S. District Court, Western, Middle and Eastern Districts of North Carolina, U.S. Court of Appeals, Fourth Circuit and 28th Judicial District. *Education:* Western Carolina University (B.S., magna cum laude, 1992); University of North Carolina at Chapel Hill (J.D., 1995). Member, Holderness Moot Court. *Member:* North Carolina (Chairperson, Medico-Legal Liaison Committee) and American Bar Associations; North Carolina State Bar; 28th Judicial District Bar; North Carolina Association of

(This Listing Continued)

Defense Attorneys (Member, Board of Directors); North Carolina Association of Women Attorneys; Defense Research Institute; EPPS-Daily-Harrell Law Society. ***PRACTICE AREAS:*** Civil Litigation; Medical Malpractice Defense; Insurance Defense; Employment Law; Personal Injury. ***Email:*** jgrant@roberts-stevens.com

CHRISTOPHER Z. CAMPBELL, born Beaufort, South Carolina, May 11, 1969; admitted to bar, 1996, North Carolina; U.S. District Court, Western District of North Carolina; U.S. Court of Appeals, Fourth Circuit and U.S. Supreme Court. *Education:* University of North Carolina, Chapel Hill (B.A., with honors, 1992; J.D., with honors, 1996). Member, University of North Carolina Law Review, 1994-1995. Author, "Excessive Means: Applying the Eighth Amendment to Civil In REM Forfeitures under United States v. Chandler," 73 NCLR 2284, 1995. President, Student Bar Association, 1995-1996. Member, North Carolina and National School Board Associations. *Member:* North Carolina (Member, Education Law Section; Vice Chairman, 2004-2005; Chairman, 2005-2006; Member, Litigation Law Section) and 28th Judicial District Bar Associations; North Carolina State Bar; North Carolina Council of School Attorneys (Vice President, 2004-2005). ***PRACTICE AREAS:*** Civil Litigation; Education Law; Construction Law. ***Email:*** ccampbell@roberts-stevens.com

SARAH PATTERSON BRISON, born Gastonia, North Carolina, May 20, 1950; admitted to bar, 1983, North Carolina, U.S. District Court, Western and Eastern Districts of North Carolina, U.S. Court of Appeals, Fourth Circuit and U.S. Supreme Court. *Education:* University of North Carolina-Greensboro (B.A., 1972); Campbell University School of Law (J.D., 1983). Phi Alpha Delta; Omicron Delta Kappa. Assistant Justice, Moot Court Board, 1997-1998. Member, Campbell Law Review, 1982-1983. Listed Who's Who Among Students in American Universities and Colleges, 1983. Author: Comment, "North Carolina's 1981 Waste Management Act and Its Impact on Local Governments: The Good, the Bad and the Ugly," Campbell Law Review, Spring, 1983. Member: North Carolina and National School Boards Associations. *Member:* North Carolina Bar Association (Member, Sections on: Construction Law; Education Law; Government and Public Sector Law; and Zoning, Planning and Land Use; Former Member, Council for Construction Law and Government and Public Sector Law Sections); North Carolina State Bar; 28th Judicial District Bar Member, Executive Committee); North Carolina Council of School Attorneys; National School Boards Association Council of School Attorneys. ***PRACTICE AREAS:*** Government; Public Sector Law; Education Law; Land Use; Housing Law; Construction Law. ***Email:*** pbrison@roberts-stevens.com

DAVID L. ENGLISH, born Washington, D.C., January 18, 1967; admitted to bar, 1998, North Carolina. *Education:* Clemson University (B.S., 1989); Cumberland School of Law of Samford University (J.D., 1998). Cordell Hull Teaching Fellow, 1997-1998. Assistant Justice, Cumberland Moot Court Board, 1997-1998. *Member:* 28th Judicial District, and North Carolina Bar Association (Member, Sections on: Business Law; Real Property; Taxation; Health Care Law); North Carolina State Bar. ***PRACTICE AREAS:*** Corporate Law; Real Property; Commercial Litigation. ***Email:*** denglish@roberts-stevens.com

CYNTHIA S. GRADY, born Lima, Ohio, July 19, 1949; admitted to bar, 1987, Texas; 2000, North Carolina; U.S. District Court, Western District of North Carolina, U.S. Court of Appeals, Fourth Circuit and U.S. Supreme Court. *Education:* Ohio State University (B.A., 1971); University of Houston (J.D., cum laude, 1987). *Member:* 28th Judicial District and North Carolina (Member, Education Law Section) Bar Associations; North Carolina State Bar; State Bar of Texas; North Carolina and National School Boards Association; North Carolina Council of School Attorneys; National Council of School Attorneys. ***PRACTICE AREAS:*** Education Law; Real Property; Business Law; Public Housing Law. ***Email:*** cgrady@roberts-stevens.com

F. LACHICOTTE ZEMP, JR., born Camden, South Carolina, October 3, 1960; admitted to bar, 1990, Alaska; 1992, U.S. District Court, District of Alaska; 1994, U.S. Court of Appeals, Ninth Circuit; 2003, North Carolina and U.S. District Court, Western District of North Carolina. *Education:* Davidson College (B.A., 1984); Franklin Pierce Law Center (J.D., 1990). National Finalist, ATLA Trial Competition, 1990. Law Clerk for the Honorable David Brock, Chief Justice of the New Hampshire Supreme Court, 1990-1991. Instructor, Torts and Civil Procedure, University of Alaska, Southeast, 1992-1993. *Member:* Juneau (President, 1994-1995), Alaska, North Carolina and American Bar Associations; North Carolina State Bar; Defense Research Institute. ***PRACTICE AREAS:*** Medical Malpractice; Complex Litigation; Insurance Defense; Products Liability; Professional Malpractice; Construction Law; Municipal Liability. ***Email:*** lzemp@roberts-stevens.com

---

KENNETH R. HUNT, born Marion, Virginia, April 8, 1973; admitted to bar, 1999, North Carolina. *Education:* Mary Washington College (B.A., cum laude, 1995); Wake Forest University (J.D., 1999). Law Clerk, Associate Justice Robert H. Edmunds, Jr., North Carolina Supreme Court, 2001, and North Carolina Court of Appeals, 1999-2000. *Member:* North Carolina State Bar; 28th Judicial District Bar. ***PRACTICE AREAS:*** Insurance Defense; Products Liability; Labor and Employment. ***Email:*** khunt@roberts-stevens.com

DENNIS L. MARTIN, JR., born Temple, Texas, March 19, 1973; admitted to bar, 2001, North Carolina. *Education:* Wofford College (B.A., 1995); Campbell University (J.D., summa cum laude, 2001). Recipient, West Group Outstanding Scholastic Achievement Award, 1998-1999, 2000-2001. Member and Articles Editor, Campbell Law Review. *Member:* North Carolina State Bar; 28th Judicial District (President, Young Lawyers Division). ***PRACTICE AREAS:*** Civil Litigation; Products Liability; Personal Injury; Insurance Litigation; Commercial Litigation. ***Email:*** dmartin@roberts-stevens.com

PETER B. McGUIRE, born Seattle, Washington, November 12, 1973; admitted to bar, 2002, North Carolina and U.S. District Court, Western District of North Carolina. *Education:* Davidson College (B.A., 1996); University of Montana (J.D., with high honors, 2002). Member, National Moot Court Team, 2001; Student Bar Association, 2001-2002. *Member:* North Carolina State Bar; 28th Judicial District Bar Association; North Carolina Association of Defense Attorneys. ***PRACTICE AREAS:*** Litigation; Medical Malpractice Defense; Insurance Defense.

KEVIN P. KOPP, born Asheville, North Carolina, March 20, 1972; admitted to bar, 1998, New Jersey and U.S. District Court, District of New Jersey; 2000, New York and U.S. District Court, Southern and Eastern Districts of New York; 2003, North Carolina and U.S. District Court, Western and Middle Districts of North Carolina; U.S. Court of Appeals, Fourth Circuit. *Education:* Appalachian State University (B.S., 1994); Seton Hall University (J.D., 1998). Member, Seton Hall Constitutional Law Journal, 1996-1998. Author: "Electronic Communications in the Workplace: E-mail Monitoring and the Right of Privacy," Vol. 8, No. 3 Seton-Hall Constitutional Law Journal, 861, 1998. *Member:* North Carolina (Member, Labor and Employment Law Section), New York State, New Jersey State, 29th Judicial District and American (Member, Labor and Employment Section) Bar Associations; North Carolina State Bar; Western North Carolina Human Resources Association. ***PRACTICE AREAS:*** Labor and Employment Law; Employment Litigation. ***Email:*** kkopp@roberts-stevens.com

REBECCA JOHNSTON REINHARDT, born Winston-Salem, North Carolina, November 19, 1974; admitted to bar, 2003, North Carolina. *Education:* Asheville, University of North Carolina (B.S., 1997); University of North Carolina at Chapel Hill (J.D., 2003). Phi Alpha Delta. Member, Holderness Moot Court-Craven Bench. Note & Comment Editor, North Carolina Journal of International Law and Commercial Regulation. *Member:* North Carolina (Member, Sections on: Real Property; Young Lawyers Division)and American (Member, Sections on: Business Law; Real Property; Probate and Trust; Young Lawyers Division) Bar Associations; North Carolina State Bar. ***PRACTICE AREAS:*** Residential Real Estate; Commercial Real Estate; Corporate Law. ***Email:*** rreinhardt@roberts-stevens.com

K. DEAN SHATLEY, II, born Goldsboro, North Carolina, November 12, 1974; admitted to bar, 2003, North Carolina. *Education:* Appalachian State University (B.M., cum laude, 1997); University of North Carolina at Chapel Hill (J.D., 2003). Member, Holderness Moot Court Bench. *Member:* North Carolina State Bar; American Bar Association; National Council of School Attorneys; North Carolina Council of School Attorneys; North Carolina State Personnel Commission. ***PRACTICE AREAS:*** Education Law; Public Sector Employment Law; Copyright Law. ***Email:*** dshatley@roberts-stevens.com

OF COUNSEL

LANDON ROBERTS, born Marshall, North Carolina, December 2, 1921; admitted to bar, 1948, North Carolina. *Education:* University of North Carolina (A.B., 1942; J.D., 1948). Phi Delta Phi. Beta Theta Pi. President, Buncombe County Bar Association, 1961. Member, North Carolina Board of Law Examiners, 1981-1994. *Member:* North Carolina (Member, Board of Governors, 1961-1963; General Practice Hall of Fame, 1994), 28th Judicial District (President, 1979-1980) and American Bar Associations; North Carolina State Bar; Permanent Member, Fourth Circuit Judicial Conference. Fellow: American College of Trial Lawyers (1977). [Lt., USNR, 1942-1946]. ***Email:*** lroberts@roberts-stevens.com

REPRESENTATIVE CLIENTS: Adventist Health System Sunbelt Insurance Corp.; AkzoNobel; Allwin Data Services; American Continental Insurance Co.; Andy Petree Racing; Asheville Board of Realtors, Inc.; Asheville-Buncombe Technical Community College; Asheville Cardiology; Asheville City Board of Education; Asheville Oil Co.; Associated Aviation Underwriters; Auto-Owners Insurance; Bank of America; BASF; Biltmore Estate Wine Company; Bell South; Biltmore House and Gardens; Blue Ridge Paper Products; Bojangles Restaurants, Inc.; The Branigar Organization, Inc.; Branch Banking & Trust Co.; Buncombe County Board of Education; Buncombe County Tax Collector; Burke County Board of Education; Cane Creek Cycling Components; Carolina Day School; Chicago Title Insurance Company; Christ School; Chubb Group of Insurance; CIGNA Group; CNA Insurance Co.; CNI Insurance Co.; Community CarePartners; Crawford & Co.; Constitution State Service Company; Crum & Forster Insurance Company; Daniel Boone Council, Boy Scouts of America; The Doctors Company; Erie Insurance Group; Fidelity & Deposit Company of Maryland; Fishburne International, Inc.; Food Lion, Inc.; General Mills, Inc.; Great American Companies; GEICO; Habitat for Humanity; Handex of the Carolinas; Hanna Development Corporation; Hartford Insurance Group; Haywood Technical Community College; Henderson County Board of Education; Hendersonville Housing Authority; Housing Authority of the City of Asheville; Infinity Insurance Company; John Deere Insurance Co.; Lake Toxaway Co.; Lawyers Title Insurance Corp.; Liberty Mutual Insurance Co.; Lincoln County Board of Education; Litton Industries; Lumber Mutual Insurance Co.; Madison County Board of Education; Manual Woodworkers & Weavers; Medical Mutual Insurance Company of N.C.; Metropolitan Insurance Companies; Metropolitan Sewerage District of Buncombe County; Mission St. Joseph's Health System, Inc.; Montgomery Insurance Company; Mountain Area Hospice; Mountain Housing Opportunities; Mountain Neurological Center; Nappier & Turner Construction Co.; North Carolina School Boards Trust; North Carolina Society of Surveyors; Novant; Octagon Risk Services; OMS National Insurance Company; Pack Place Education, Arts & Science Center, Inc.; Pleasant Cove Adult Care Facility; Polk County; Prime Doc; The Reciprocal Group; Republic Western Insurance Company; Rivendell Woods; St. Paul Fire & Marine Insurance Co.; Scottsdale Insurance Group; SKF, Inc.; Southern Appalachian Highlands Conservancy; Stewart Title Guaranty Company; Thoms Community Care Foundation; TIG Specialty Insurance Solutions; Transylvania County Board of Education; Travelers Insurance Co.; Thoms Rehabilitation Hospital; Union Butterfield Corp.; University of North Carolina at Asheville Foundation; Virginia Reciprocal Insurance Co.; Visiting Health Professionals; Wachovia Bank; Wal-Mart, Inc.; Warren Wilson College; Town of Weaverville; Zurich-American Insurance Group.

RUSSELL & KING, P.A.

17 NORTH MARKET STREET
P.O. BOX 7668
ASHEVILLE, NORTH CAROLINA 28802
Telephone: 910-252-7651
Fax: 910-258-0648

Civil Trials and Appeals in all Courts. Insurance Law, Insurance Defense, Casualty Insurance, General Liability Insurance, Bad Faith, Nursing Home Liability, Medical Negligence, Civil Litigation, Labor and Employment and Workers Compensation Law.

J. WILLIAM RUSSELL, born Cabot, Arkansas, November 19, 1923; admitted to bar, 1950, North Carolina. *Education:* Brevard College and University of North Carolina (B.A., 1948); University of North Carolina (J.D., 1950). Delta Theta Phi. *Member:* North Carolina and American Bar Associations; 28th Judicial District Bar; American Judicature Society; Defense Research Institute; North Carolina Association of Defense Attorneys. ***PRACTICE AREAS:*** Civil Litigation; Labor and Employment; Insurance Defense; Workers Compensation. ***Email:*** jwmrussell@russellkinglaw.com

SANDRA M. KING, born Edgecombe County, North Carolina, September 12, 1945; admitted to bar, 1969, North Carolina; 1972, U.S. District Court, Western District of North Carolina; 1985, U.S. Court of Appeals, Fourth Circuit. *Education:* Peace College (A.A., 1965); University of North Carolina (B.A., 1967; J.D., 1969). *Member:* North Carolina

(This Listing Continued)

RUSSELL & KING, P.A., Asheville—Continued

(Chair, Workers' Compensation Section) and American Bar Associations; 28th Judicial District Bar; Defense Research Institute; North Carolina Association of Defense Attorneys. ***PRACTICE AREAS:*** Civil Litigation; Insurance Defense; Workers Compensation. ***Email:*** sking@russellkinglaw.com

REPRESENTATIVE CLIENTS: *Insurance Companies:* RSKCo.; Allied Claims Administration, Inc.; American International Group; American Modern Home Insurance Co.; Amerisure Cos.; Bituminous Casualty Corp.; Crum & Forster; Electric Insurance Co.; Fireman's Fund; GAB Business Services, Inc.; OneBeacon Insurance; The Horace Mann Insurance Cos.; Indiana Lumbermens Mutual Insurance Co.; GMAC Insurance (Integon); Jefferson Ins. Group; League of Municipalities; National General Insurance Co.; Sentry Insurance; The Travelers; The United States Life Insurance Co.; Zurich; North Carolina League of Municipalities Claims Service.
APPROVED ATTORNEYS FOR: Lawyers Title; SAFECO Title; Asheville Savings Bank; First Federal Savings & Loan; Clyde Savings & Loan.

CATHIE ST. JOHN-RITZEN

188 CHARLOTTE HIGHWAY
P.O. BOX 6318
ASHEVILLE, NORTH CAROLINA 28816-6318
Telephone: 828-255-8813
Fax: 828-255-8823
Email: cathie@asheville-elderlaw.com

Elder Law, Nursing Home Litigation, Probate, Estate Administration, Guardianship, Wills, Trust Law.

CATHIE ST. JOHN-RITZEN, born Oklahoma City, Oklahoma, December 29, 1944; admitted to bar, 2000, North Carolina. *Education:* University of Missouri-Columbia (B.G.S., 1986; J.D., 1998). Phi Beta Kappa. Registered Nurse, Missouri, 1966 (inactive since 2002). Public Administrator, Buncombe County, NC, 2001—. Member, 2000— and President, 2002-2003, 2005-2006, Buncombe County Women's Commission; Member, 2001— and Executive Board Secretary, 2002-2003, Buncombe County Council on Aging Board. Member, Board of Directors and past Secretary, Vanderbilt Apartments, non-profit affordable housing. Mountain Area Volunteer Lawyer, Pisgah Legal Services. Board Member, Aston Park Health Center, 2005—. Member, End-of-Life Care Coalition of Western North Carolina. *Member:* National Academy of Elder Law Attorneys; North Carolina Bar Association (Member, Elder Law Section); North Carolina Association of Women Attorneys; 28th Judicial District Bar of Buncombe County. ***PRACTICE AREAS:*** Elder Law; Nursing Home Litigation; Probate; Estate Administration; Guardianship; Wills; Medicare and Medicaid.

SHUFORD, CAGLE & McCLELLAN, P.A.

Established in 1932
53 ASHELAND AVENUE, SUITE 104
ASHEVILLE, NORTH CAROLINA 28801
Telephone: 828-258-2211
Fax: 828-252-8309
Email: scmlaw@att.net
URL: http://www.lawyers.com/scmlaw
Mailing Address: P.O. Box 1530, Ashville, NC 28802

General Civil Practice. Real Property, Probate Law and Business Law.

FIRM PROFILE: Shuford, Cagle & McClellan, P.A. has been a well established firm since 1932. They are a reliable, client-service oriented firm. The staff here is also knowledgeable and appreciated.

GEORGE H. WRIGHT (1884-1958)

WILLIAM B. CAGLE, born Asheville, North Carolina, December 31, 1937; admitted to bar, 1963, North Carolina. *Education:* Vanderbilt University and University of North Carolina (B.S., 1960); Washington University (J.D., 1963). Phi Delta Phi. Member, Board of Adjustment, Town of Biltmore Forest, 1985-1995. *Member:* Buncombe County and North Carolina Bar Associations; North Carolina State Bar. ***PRACTICE AREAS:*** Wills; Probate; Estate Planning; Real Estate; Buying and Selling a Home; Corporate Law.

THOMAS K. McCLELLAN, born Montgomery, West Virginia, November 5, 1954; admitted to bar, 1979, North Carolina. *Education:* Washington & Lee University (B.A., 1976); Wake Forest University School of Law (J.D., cum laude, 1979). Staff Member, Wake Forest Law Review, 1977-1979. *Member:* North Carolina Bar Association; The North Carolina State Bar. ***PRACTICE AREAS:*** Real Property; Corporate Law; Commercial Law; Probate; Banking Law.

RETIRED OF COUNSEL

JOHN F. SHUFORD, born Asheville, North Carolina, September 19, 1920; admitted to bar, 1944, North Carolina. *Education:* University of North Carolina (A.B., 1941; LBH., 1944). Phi Delta Phi. Member, North Carolina State Senate, 1954-1956. *Member:* North Carolina and American Bar Associations; 28th Judicial District and The North Carolina State Bars. Fellow, American College of Trust and Estate Counsel.

COUNSEL FOR: Biltmore Oil Co.; Asheville Packing Co.; Ice Service, Inc.; Presbyterian Home for Children, Inc.; M.B. Haynes Electric Corp.; Security Union Title Insurance Co.; Asheville Savings Bank.
APPROVED ATTORNEYS FOR: Lawyers Title Insurance Corp.; Chicago Title & Insurance Co.; Wachovia Bank; N.A., Asheville, N.C.; The Title Company of North Carolina, Inc.; Asheville Savings Bank; Clyde Savings & Loan Assn.; Blue Ridge Savings Bank; Security Union Title Insurance Co.; Old Republic Title Co.; Centura Bank.
REFERENCES: Wachovia Bank, N.A., Asheville, North Carolina; Centura Bank, Asheville, N.C.; Asheville Savings Bank, S.S.B.

LAW OFFICES OF GLEN C. SHULTS

14 SOUTH PACK SQUARE
SUITE 360
P.O. BOX 1384
ASHEVILLE, NORTH CAROLINA 28802
Telephone: 828-251-9676
Fax: 828-251-0648
Email: shults.law@worldnet.att.net

Labor and Employment Law, Wrongful Termination, Employer Defense, Employee Rights, Discrimination, Labor Management Relations, Wage and Hour Law, Employee Benefits.

GLEN C. SHULTS, born Newport, Tennessee, December 31, 1955; admitted to bar, 1981, Tennessee; 1989, California; 1998, North Carolina. *Education:* Georgetown University; Cornell University (B.A., 1977); George Washington University (J.D., 1981). Law Clerk to Hon. Richard A. Enslen, U.S. District Court, Western District of Michigan, 1983-1984. Field Attorney, Region 21, National Labor Relations Board, 1984-1990. *Member:* North Carolina Academy of Trial Lawyers; State Bar of California (Member, Labor and Employment Law Section); National Employment Lawyers Association. ***PRACTICE AREAS:*** Labor and Employment; Wrongful Termination; Civil Rights; Civil Litigation.

SIEMENS LAW OFFICE, P.A.

22 SOUTH PACK SQUARE, SUITE 700
ASHEVILLE, NORTH CAROLINA 28801
Telephone: 828-252-5080
Email: jim@wnclaw.com
URL: http://www.wnclaw.com

Family Law, Divorce, Child Custody, Child Support, Domestic Violence, Adoptions, Criminal Law, Traffic Offenses, DWI, Traffic Violations, Personal Injury, Automobile Accidents, Wrongful Death, Medical Malpractice.

A. JAMES SIEMENS, born Russell, Manitoba, January 31, 1967; admitted to bar, 1994, North Carolina. *Education:* University of North Carolina, Chapel Hill (B.A., 1989); Tulane University (J.D., 1993). ***Email:*** jim@wnclaw.com

CURTIS ALAN SLUDER

124 COLLEGE STREET, SUITE 105
ASHEVILLE, NORTH CAROLINA 28801
Telephone: 828-254-9505
Fax: 828-254-9514
Email: curtis@sluderlaw.com
URL: http://www.sluderlawoffice.com

Criminal Law, Traffic Violations, Driving While Intoxicated, Expunction.

CURTIS ALAN SLUDER, born Asheville, North Carolina, March 25, 1968; admitted to bar, 1998, North Carolina. *Education:* University of North Carolina at Asheville (B.A., 1994); University of North Carolina School of Law at Chapel Hill (J.D., 1998). Phi Delta Phi. *Member:* Buncombe County and North Carolina Bar Associations; North Carolina State Bar. ***PRACTICE AREAS:*** Traffic Violations (80%, 2500); Driving While Intoxicated (15%, 300); Criminal Law (5%, 200); Drivers License Suspension; Misdemeanors.

ROGER T. SMITH

70 NORTH MARKET STREET
P.O. BOX 7172
ASHEVILLE, NORTH CAROLINA 28801
Telephone: 828-254-4658
Fax: 828-254-0787
Email: rogertsmithatty@aol.com
URL: http://www.rogertsmithatty.com

Criminal Law, Divorce, Family Law, Child Custody, Child Support, Spousal Support, Palimony, Equitable Distribution, Domestic Violence, Driving While Impaired, Traffic Violations, DMV Hearings, Drug Crimes, Sexual Offenses, Felonies and Misdemeanors, Mediations.

ROGER T. SMITH, born Copiague, New York, April 27, 1954; admitted to bar, 1979, North Carolina and U.S. District Court, Western District of North Carolina. *Education:* University of North Carolina, Chapel Hill (B.A., 1976); Pepperdine University (J.D., 1979). Adjunct Professor, Environmental Law, University of North Carolina at Asheville, 1989-1990. *Member:* North Carolina State Bar; 28th Judicial District Bar Association (President-Elect; Member, Grievance Committee, 1998-2001).

JACK W. STEWART, P.A.

61 NORTH MARKET STREET
P.O. BOX 1920
ASHEVILLE, NORTH CAROLINA 28802
Telephone: 828-253-5673
Fax: 828-253-7100
URL: http://www.ashevillecriminallawyer.com
Email: jack@jackstewartlaw.com
URL: http://www.jackstewartlaw.com

Criminal and Civil Trial Practice in all State and Federal Courts. Criminal Defense, DWI Law, Traffic Citations, Family Law, Divorce, Child Custody, Child Support, Equitable Distribution.

JACK W. STEWART, JR., born Kannapolis, North Carolina, August 28, 1955; admitted to bar, 1981, North Carolina and U.S. District Court, Western District of North Caro-

(This Listing Continued)

lina; 1985, U.S. Court of Appeals, 4th Circuit. *Education:* Appalachian State University (B.A., cum laude, 1977); University of North Carolina (M.A., 1978); Cumberland School of Law of Samford University (J.D., 1981). Member, Moot Court Board. *Member:* Buncombe County, North Carolina and American Bar Associations; North Carolina State Bar; North Carolina Academy of Trial Lawyers; Buncombe County Criminal Defense Lawyers Association; National Association of Criminal Defense Lawyers; Mountain Area Volunteer Lawyers.

STONE & CHRISTY, P.A.

ASHEVILLE, NORTH CAROLINA

(See Black Mountain)

Corporate and Commercial Litigation, Real Estate Litigation, Buying and Selling a Home, Tax Litigation, Fiduciary Litigation, Civil Litigation, Commercial Real Estate, Residential Real Estate, Workers Compensation, Personal Injury, Wrongful Death, Trusts and Estates, Business and Succession Planning, Commercial Collections.

VAN WINKLE, BUCK, WALL, STARNES AND DAVIS, P.A.

Established in 1907

11 NORTH MARKET STREET

P.O. BOX 7376

ASHEVILLE, NORTH CAROLINA 28802-7376

Telephone: 828-258-2991

FAX: 828-255-0255; 257-2767; 257-2773

Email: vw@vwlawfirm.com

URL: http://www.vwlawfirm.com

Hendersonville, North Carolina Office: 422 South Main Street. Telephone: 828-697-6196. Fax: 828-693-3999.

Corporate and Commercial, Tax Litigation, Commercial Real Estate, Business and Succession Planning, Employee Benefits, Intellectual Property, Securities, Banking, Environmental, Construction, Trusts and Estates, Health Care, Civil Litigation, Commercial Litigation, Professional Malpractice, Fiduciary Litigation, Personal Injury, Wrongful Death, Products Liability, Bankruptcy, Creditors Rights, Public Finance, Governmental Regulation.

FIRM PROFILE: Van Winkle is the largest law firm west of Charlotte. While its principal client base is Western North Carolina, the Firm represents clients throughout the State and the Southeast.

Established in 1907, Van Winkle provides prompt services of the highest quality in business and personal matters. The Firm utilizes attorneys with keen minds, real experience, and sound judgment who have demonstrated the ability to solve clients' problems efficiently both in and out of the courtroom.

ROBERTSON WALL (1913-1996)

O. E. STARNES, born Raleigh, North Carolina, May 3, 1924; admitted to bar, 1950, North Carolina. *Education:* Davidson College (B.S., 1947); University of North Carolina (LL.B., 1950). Phi Delta Phi. Corporation Counsel, City of Asheville, North Carolina, 1958-1967. Attorney, Town of Biltmore Forest, 1981—. President, Buncombe County Bar Association, 1972-1973. *Member:* North Carolina Bar Association (Board of Governors, 1963-1966 and 1993-1994; General Practice Hall of Fame, 1992; Chair, Senior Lawyers Division, 1993-1994); 28th Judicial and North Carolina State Bar. Fellow, American College of Trial Lawyers (State Chairman, 1979-1980). ***PRACTICE AREAS:*** General Practice; Municipal Law; Insurance Defense Litigation. ***Email:*** ostarnes@vwlawfirm.com

ROY W. DAVIS, JR., born Marion, North Carolina, January 15, 1930; admitted to bar, 1955, North Carolina. *Education:* Davidson College (B.S., 1952); University of North Carolina (J.D., with honors, 1955). Phi Delta Phi; Order of the Coif. Member, Board of Editors, North Carolina Law Review. *Member:* North Carolina (Chairman, Young Lawyers Division, 1965-1966; Chair, Administration of Justice Task Force, 1999-2002; General Practice Hall of Fame; Member, Litigation Section) and American (Member, House of Delegates, 1988-1992; Sections on: Litigation; Tort and Insurance Practice) Bar Associations; 28th Judicial District (President, 1975-1976) and The North Carolina State (President, 1985-1986; IOLTA Board of Trustees, 1987-1993; Board of Examiners, 2002—) Bars; North Carolina Association of Defense Attorneys. Fellow: American Bar Foundation; American College of Trial Lawyers (State Chair, 1994-1996); International Society of Barristers. ***PRACTICE AREAS:*** Civil Litigation; Professional Liability Litigation; General Practice. ***Email:*** rdavis@vwlawfirm.com

BRIAN F. D. LAVELLE, born Cleveland, Ohio, August 16, 1941; admitted to bar, 1966, North Carolina; 1968, Ohio; 1969, U.S. Tax Court. *Education:* University of Virginia (B.A., 1963); Vanderbilt University (J.D., 1966); New York University (LL.M., in Taxation, 1969). Member: Board of Advisors, UNC Annual Tax Institute, 1981—. Listed, Tax Law, Trusts and Estates, "Best Lawyers in America." *Member:* North Carolina (Member, Board of Governors, 1979-1982; Vice President, 1997-1999) and American Bar Associations; 28th Judicial District and The North Carolina State (Member, Vice-Chairman, 1984-1990 and Chairman, 1990-1991, Estate Planning and Probate Law Specialty Examination Committee) Bars. Fellow, American College of Trust and Estate Counsel (Lecturer, 1982; State Chairman, 1982-1985; Regent, 1984-1990). (Board Certified Specialist in Estate Planning and Probate Law, North Carolina State Board of Legal Specialization). ***PRACTICE AREAS:*** Tax Law; Estate Planning; Estate Administration; Trust Administration. ***Email:*** blavelle@vwlawfirm.com

LARRY S. McDEVITT, born Asheville, North Carolina, June 2, 1942; admitted to bar, 1968, North Carolina; 1973, U.S. Supreme Court. *Education:* University of North Carolina (A.B., 1964; J.D., 1968). Fellow, American College of Trial Lawyers. President, North Carolina Bar Association, 1989-1990. Mayor and Councilman, City of Asheville, 1981-1985. President, 28th Judicial District Bar, 1980-1981. President, University of North Carolina Law School Alumni Association, 1998-1999. State Delegate, ABA House of Delegates, 1996—. North Carolina Board of Specialization (Vice Chair, 1983-1988). Listed, Business and Personal Injury Litigation, "Best Lawyers in America." *Member:* North Carolina (Board of Governors, 1983-1986; 1988-1991) and American (Litigation Section; Standing Committee on Legal Aid and Indigent Defense) Bar Associations; North Carolina Association of Defense Attorneys (Board of Directors, 1983-1985); American Judicature Society; National and Southern Conferences of Bar Presidents; U.S. Fourth Circuit Judicial Conference (Permanent Member). Fellow, American Bar Foundation. ***PRACTICE AREAS:*** Civil Litigation; Business Litigation; Patent Litigation; Products Liability; Business Law. ***Email:*** lmcdevitt@vwlawfirm.com

PHILIP J. SMITH, born Birkenhead, England, March 18, 1946; admitted to bar, 1972, North Carolina. *Education:* Wake Forest University (B.A., 1968); Temple University (J.D., 1972). Listed, Business Litigation, "Best Lawyers in America." *Member:* North Carolina Bar Association (Member, Sections on: Commercial, Banking and Business Law; Litigation; Construction; Health Law; Environmental Law); 28th Judicial District (President, 1995-1996) and The North Carolina State Bars; North Carolina Association of Defense Attorneys; American Health Lawyers Association. ***PRACTICE AREAS:*** Administrative; Banking; Commercial; Construction; Health Litigation; Corporate; Product Liability; Professional Malpractice. ***Email:*** psmith@vwlawfirm.com

BARRY B. KEMPSON, born San Diego, California, April 25, 1943; admitted to bar, 1969, Florida; 1974, North Carolina. *Education:* Florida State University (B.A., 1964); University of Florida (J.D., 1968). Phi Alpha Delta. Secretary, Buncombe County Bar Association, 1977-1978. Listed, Trusts and Estates, "Best Lawyers in America." *Member:* North Carolina (Member, Estate Planning and Fiduciary Law Section, 1977—; Councillor, 1976-1982; 1995-1998; Program Chair, 20th Annual Estate Planning and Fiduciary Law Seminar, 1999. Lecturer: 1981 Probate and Fiduciary Law Seminar, "Grantor Trust Rules-Revisited?"; 1986 Pro Bono Workshop, "Estate Planning for the Elderly Client of Limited Means,") and American Bar Associations; 28th Judicial District and The North Carolina State Bars; The Florida Bar; Land of the Sky Estate Planning Council. Fellow, American College of Trust and Estate Counsel. ***PRACTICE AREAS:*** Estate Planning Law; Estate and Trust Administration. ***Email:*** bkempson@vwlawfirm.com

ALBERT L. SNEED, JR., born October 20, 1943; admitted to bar, 1973, North Carolina. *Education:* University of North Carolina (B.S., Mathematics, 1965); Duke University (J.D., with distinction, 1973). Lecturer, "North Carolina Anti-Deficiency Statute," North Carolina Bar Association, 1985. Listed, Bankruptcy and Creditor-Debtor Rights Law, "Best Lawyers in America." *Member:* North Carolina and American (Member, Section of Corporation, Banking and Business Law) Bar Associations; 28th Judicial District and The North Carolina State Bars. [LCDR, U.S. Navy, 1965-1970]. ***REPORTED CASES:*** Georgia Outdoor v. Waynesville, 900 F2d 783 (4th Cir. 1990); Morris Communications v. City of Asheville, 356 N.C. 103 (2002); Donoho v. City of Asheville, 569 S.E.2d 19 (2002). ***PRACTICE AREAS:*** Corporate Litigation; Commercial Litigation; Administrative Law; Bankruptcy Law; Creditors Rights; Zoning Litigation. ***Email:*** asneed@vwlawfirm.com

ROBERT H. HAGGARD (Board Certified Specialist in Estate Planning and Probate Law, North Carolina State Board of Legal Specialization) (See Hendersonville listing for Biographical Data)

MARLA TUGWELL ADAMS, born Wilson, North Carolina, February 20, 1954; admitted to bar, 1980, North Carolina. *Education:* Meredith College (B.A., magna cum laude, 1976); Wake Forest University (J.D., 1980). Phi Delta Phi. Member, Order of Barristers. *Member:* 28th Judicial District and The North Carolina State Bars; Defense Research Institute. ***PRACTICE AREAS:*** Insurance Law; Tort Law; Civil Litigation. ***Email:*** madams@vwlawfirm.com

JONES PHARR BYRD, born Raleigh, North Carolina, August 13, 1946; admitted to bar, 1971, North Carolina; 1975, U.S. District Court, Western District of North Carolina; 1977, U.S. District Court, Eastern and Middle Districts of North Carolina and U.S. Court of Appeals, Fourth Circuit; 1989, U.S. Supreme Court. *Education:* Wake Forest University (B.A., 1968; J.D., 1971). Phi Delta Phi. Assistant Attorney General, North Carolina Department of Justice, 1971-1974. Member, Panel of Arbitrators, American Arbitration Association (Regular and Construction Panels). Chairperson, Buncombe County Board of Elections, 2001—. *Member:* North Carolina (Member Litigation and Construction Sections) and American Bar Associations; North Carolina State Bar; North Carolina Academy of Trial Lawyers (Board of Governors, 1979-1992; Vice President, 1982-1983); The Association of Trial Lawyers of America; North Carolina Council of School Attorneys (1982-1988, Board Member, 1985-1986). ***PRACTICE AREAS:*** Civil Litigation; Eminent Domain; Construction. ***Email:*** jbyrd@vwlawfirm.com

ALLAN R. TARLETON, born Raleigh, North Carolina, May 1, 1952; admitted to bar, 1980, North Carolina; 1988, U.S. Supreme Court. *Education:* Wake Forest University (B.A., cum laude, 1974; J.D., 1980). *Member:* North Carolina Bar Association (Member, Litigation and Workers Compensation Sections); 28th Judicial District and The North Carolina State Bars; North Carolina Association of Defense Attorneys. (Board Certified Specialist in Worker Compensation Law, North Carolina State Board of Legal Specialization). ***PRACTICE AREAS:*** Medical Malpractice; Workers Compensation Defense; Civil Trial; Appellate Litigation. ***Email:*** atarleton@vwlawfirm.com

LARRY C. HARRIS, JR., born Blowing Rock, North Carolina, February 20, 1953; admitted to bar, 1983, North Carolina. *Education:* University of North Carolina (B.A., 1976); Campbell University (J.D., magna cum laude, 1983). Delta Theta Phi. Member, Editorial Board, Campbell Law Review, 1982-1983. *Member:* North Carolina (Member, Tax and Business Law Section; Councillor, 1997-2000) and American Bar Associations; 28th Judicial District and The North Carolina State Bars. ***PRACTICE AREAS:*** Corporate Planning Law; Commercial Law; Business Law; Banking; Pension and Profit Sharing Law. ***Email:*** lharris@vwlawfirm.com

MICHELLE RIPPON, born Calgary, Alberta, Canada, November 22, 1944; admitted to bar, 1981, North Carolina. *Education:* Dalhousie University (B.A., 1965; B.Ed., 1966); North Carolina State University (M.A., 1976); North Carolina Central University (J.D., 1981). *Member:* North Carolina (General Practice Section, 1987—; Chair, 1992-1993; Board of Governors, 1995-1998) Bar Association; 28th Judicial District and North Carolina State Bar (North Carolina State Bar Quarterly Editorial Board, 1984—; Author, Judicial

(This Listing Continued)

VAN WINKLE, BUCK, WALL, STARNES AND DAVIS, P.A., Asheville—Continued

Biographies). ***REPORTED CASES:*** Branks v. Kern, 68 ALR 4th 817; Pierson v. Buyher, 330 N.C. 182. ***PRACTICE AREAS:*** Employment Law; Appellate Law; Insurance Defense Law; Estate Litigation. ***Email:*** mrippon@vwlawfirm.com

WILLIAM PERRY FISHER, II, born Covington, Kentucky, September 7, 1961; admitted to bar, 1987, North Carolina; U.S. District Court, Western District of North Carolina; U.S. Court of Appeals, Fourth Circuit. *Education:* University of North Carolina (B.A., 1984); Wake Forest University (J.D., 1987). *Member:* North Carolina (Member, Practical Skills Training Committee, 1988-1996, Speakers Bureau 1990-1998, Young Lawyers Division-(Citizenship Education Committee 1993-1994; Special Projects Committee, 1994) and American (Business Law and Litigation Section) Bar Associations; 28th Judicial District (President, 2001-2002, Grievance Committee, 1994-1997) and North Carolina State Bars. ***PRACTICE AREAS:*** Corporate Law; Business Tort and Contract Litigation; ERISA Litigation; Products Liability Law; Warranty Litigation; Condemnation; General Litigation and Criminal Law. ***Email:*** pfisher@vwlawfirm.com

MICHAEL M. THOMPSON (See Hendersonville listing for Biographical Data)

MARK A. PINKSTON, born Waynesville, North Carolina, November 7, 1963; admitted to bar, 1989, North Carolina. *Education:* North Carolina State University (B.S. in Nuclear Engineering, 1986); University of Tennessee (J.D., with highest honors, 1989). Order of the Coif. *Member:* North Carolina (Member, Bankruptcy Section; Executive Council, Bankruptcy Section, 1998-2001) and American Bar Associations; 28th Judicial District; North Carolina State Bar. ***PRACTICE AREAS:*** Commercial Litigation; Bankruptcy; Creditors Rights; Foreclosures; Environmental Law. ***Email:*** mpinkston@vwlawfirm.com

STEPHEN J. GRABENSTEIN, born Buffalo, New York, May 9, 1957; admitted to bar, 1982, Tennessee; 1984, District of Columbia; 1989, U.S. District Court, Middle and Eastern Districts of Tennessee, U.S. Court of Appeals, 6th Circuit; 1992, North Carolina; 1993, U.S. District Court, Western District of North Carolina. *Education:* University of Tennessee (B.A., with high honors, 1979; J.D., 1982). Minority Counsel, U.S. Senate Subcommittee on Intergovernmental Relations, 1984-1985. Legislative Director, U.S. Senator Jim Sasser, 1985-1988. Assistant Attorney General, Tennessee, 1988-1992. ***PRACTICE AREAS:*** Trust and Estates; Wrongful Death; Professional Malpractice; Products Liability; Civil Litigation. ***Email:*** sgrabenstein@vwlawfirm.com

CRAIG D. JUSTUS, born Hendersonville, North Carolina, February 13, 1965; admitted to bar, 1991, North Carolina. *Education:* University of North Carolina (B.A., 1987; J.D., 1991). Masters in Regional Planning Land Use and Environmental Concentration, 1991.*Member:* 28th Judicial District Bar Association; North Carolina Bar Association (Section Member, Environmental Law and Real Estate). ***PRACTICE AREAS:*** Land Use Law; Environmental Law; Real Estate Law. ***Email:*** cjustus@vwlawfirm.com

CYNTHIA W. ELLER, born Dublin, Georgia, August 25, 1951; admitted to bar, 1983, North Carolina; 1985, Illinois; 1991, Tennessee. *Education:* North Carolina State University (B.A., summa cum laude, 1978); University of North Carolina (J.D., 1982). Omicron Delta Epsilon. Former in-house Counsel for McDonald's Corp., Real Estate Department-.*Member:* North Carolina (Member, Real Property Section) Bar Association. (Board Certified Specialist, Real Property Law, Residential Transactions, North Carolina State Board of Legal Specialization). ***PRACTICE AREAS:*** Real Property. ***Email:*** celler@vwlawfirm.com

STEPHEN B. WILLIAMSON, born Evanston, Illinois, September 30, 1963; admitted to bar, 1993, North Carolina, U.S. Court of Appeals, Fourth Circuit and U.S. District Court, Eastern, Middle and Western Districts of North Carolina. *Education:* Sam Houston State University (B.S., 1990); Campbell University School of Law (J.D., 1993). *Member:* North Carolina and American Bar Associations; North Carolina State Bar. ***REPORTED CASES:*** *Christopher's Ariz. Transp. Serv. v. Duncan,* 217 F.3d 838 (4th Cir. 2000), 2000 U.S. App. Lexis 15644 (full-text); *Medical Mut. Ins. Co. v. Mauldin,* 353 N.C. 352, 543 S.E.2d 478 (2001); *Aycock v. Padgett,* 134 N.C. App. 164, 516 S.E.2d 907 (1999); *Lang v. Lang,* 125 N.C. App. 573, 481 S.E.2d 380 (1997); *Biggins v. Blount,* 123 N.C. App. 159, 472 S.E.2d 611 (1996). ***PRACTICE AREAS:*** Civil Litigation; Labor and Employment; Fraud; Complex Commercial Litigation; Professional Malpractice; Asbestos Defense. ***Email:*** swilliamson@vwlawfirm.com

ADAM L. SHEALY (Board Certified Specialist in Estate Planning and Probate Law, North Carolina State Board of Legal Specialization) (See Hendersonville Office for Biographical Data)

JOHN G. KELSO, born Atlanta, Georgia, June 2, 1970; admitted to bar, 1996, North Carolina. *Education:* Davidson College (B.A., cum laude, 1992); University of North Carolina (J.D., with honors, 1996); New York University (LL.M. in Taxation, 1997). Phi Beta Kappa. Publication Editor, North Carolina Law Review. *Member:* 28th Judicial District and North Carolina Bar Associations. (Board Certified Specialist in Estate Planning and Probate Law, North Carolina State Board of Legal Specialization). ***PRACTICE AREAS:*** Tax Law; Estate Planning Law; Probate Law. ***Email:*** jkelso@vwlawfirm.com

DALE A. CURRIDEN, born Bellevue, Washington, June 23, 1969; admitted to bar, 1997, North Carolina and U.S. District Court, Western District of North Carolina; 2001, U.S. Court of Appeals, Fourth Circuit. *Education:* Brigham Young University (B.A., cum laude, 1994); University of North Carolina at Chapel Hill (J.D., with honors, 1997). Holderness Moot Court National Team. *Member:* North Carolina and American Bar Associations. ***LANGUAGES:*** Spanish. ***PRACTICE AREAS:*** General Civil Litigation; Medical Malpractice; Insurance Defense Law; Workers' Compensation Law. ***Email:*** dcurriden@vwlawfirm.com

W. CARLETON METCALF, born Waynesville, North Carolina, January 25, 1972; admitted to bar, 1997, North Carolina and U.S. District Court, Western District of North Carolina; 1998, U.S. District Court, Middle District of North Carolina; 1999, U.S. District Court, Eastern District of North Carolina and U.S. Court of Appeals, Fourth Circuit; 2001, U.S. Court of Appeals, Federal Circuit. *Education:* University of North Carolina at Chapel Hill (B.A., 1994; J.D., 1997). Member: Holderness Moot Court; Order of Barristers. President, University of North Carolina Law Class of 1997. *Member:* North Carolina (Professionalism Committee, 2001-2003; Convention Planning Advisory Committee, 2002-2003) and American (Litigation Section) Bar Associations; 28th Judicial District Bar (Young Lawyers' Division: President, 2001-2002; Vice President/Treasurer, 2000-2001; Judicial District Representative, 1998-2000). ***PRACTICE AREAS:*** Civil Litigation; Business Litigation; Commercial Litigation; Personal Injury; Civil Rights; Governmental Liability; Professional Liability; Insurance Defense. ***Email:*** cmetcalf@vwlawfirm.com

(This Listing Continued)

W. KEVIN McLAUGHLIN, JR., born Washington, North Carolina, June 30, 1971; admitted to bar, 1998, North Carolina. *Education:* University of North Carolina at Chapel Hill (B.A., 1993); Wake Forest University (J.D., 1998). *Member:* North Carolina Bar Association; North Carolina Association of Defense Attorneys; Defense Research Institute (Technology Law Section); Asheville Information Technology Council. ***PRACTICE AREAS:*** Civil Litigation; E-Commerce; Technology Law. ***Email:*** kmclaughlin@vwlawfirm.com

CAROLINE T. KNOX (Resident, Hendersonville Office)

CAROLYN LLOYD COWARD, born Atlanta, Georgia, August 16, 1952; admitted to bar, 1999, North Carolina. *Education:* University of Tennessee (B.S., 1974); University of North Carolina at Chapel Hill (J.D., 1999). Member, American Health Lawyers; North Carolina Hospital Association.*Member:* North Carolina State Bar. ***PRACTICE AREAS:*** Regulatory Law; Health Care Law. ***Email:*** ccoward@vwlawfirm.com

ANNA S. MILLS, born Clyde, North Carolina, October 23, 1970; admitted to bar, 1997, Tennessee; 2001, North Carolina. *Education:* University of North Carolina (B.A. with distinction, 1993; J.D. with honors, 1997). Phi Beta Kappa; Phi Eta Sigma. Articles Editor, North Carolina Journal of International Law and Commercial Regulation, 1996-1997. Author: "Exempt Transactions: Practical Ways to Sell Securities, Nuts and Bolts of Securities Law," 1999, Practicing Law Institute; "Clearing the Air: Environmental Regulation, Dispute Resolution and Domestic Sovereignty Under the World Trade Organization," 22 N.C. J. Int'l. L. & Com. Reg. 241 (1996).*Member:* North Carolina and American Bar Associations. ***PRACTICE AREAS:*** Corporate Law; Securities; Real Estate. ***Email:*** amills@vwlawfirm.com

GUY F. CLERICI, born Beaver Falls, Pennsylvania, February 26, 1959; admitted to bar, 1984, New Jersey and U.S. District Court, District of New Jersey; 1994, North Carolina. *Education:* University of North Carolina at Greensboro (B.S., 1981); Ohio Northern University (J.D., 1984); George Washington University (LL.M., Taxation, 1987). Associate Editor, Ohio Northern University Law Review. ***PRACTICE AREAS:*** Business Law; Taxation Law; Tax Controversies; Estate Planning. ***Email:*** gclerici@vwlawfirm.com

TRACY KREIDER DIEFENBACH, born Philadelphia, Pennsylvania, November 16, 1968; admitted to bar, 1996, Georgia; 1997, U.S. District Court, Northern and Middle Districts of Georgia; 2001, North Carolina; 2002, U.S. District Court, Western District of North Carolina. *Education:* Pennsylvania State University (B.A., 1990); Emory University School of Law (J.D., with distinction, 1996). William H. Agnor Scholar. Recipient, American Jurisprudence Awards for: Legal Research and Writing; Real Property. Member, 1994-1995 and Articles Editor, 1995-1996, Bankruptcy Developments Journal. Dean's Fellow, 1995-1996. *Member:* North Carolina State Bar; State Bar of Georgia; 28th Judicial District Bar; North Carolina Bar Association. ***PRACTICE AREAS:*** Civil Litigation; Bankruptcy; Creditors Rights. ***Email:*** tdiefenbach@vwlawfirm.com

---

ESTHER E. MANHEIMER, born Skyum Bjerge, Denmark, July 24, 1971; admitted to bar, 1998, North Carolina. *Education:* University of Colorado at Boulder (B.A., 1993); University of North Carolina (MPA, 1997; J.D., 1998). *Member:* 28th Judicial District Bar Association; North Carolina State Bar. ***PRACTICE AREAS:*** Civil Litigation. ***Email:*** emanheimer@vwlawfirm.com

WILLIAM JAMES JOHNSON, born Columbia, South Carolina, July 25, 1973; admitted to bar, 2000, South Carolina; 2001, U.S. District Court, District of South Carolina; 2002, North Carolina. *Education:* Wofford College (B.A., 1996); University of South Carolina (J.D., with honors, 2000). Wig and Robe. Member, South Carolina Law Review. Law Clerk to Honorable James R. Barber III, Circuit Court Judge. Author, South Carolina Law Review, Vol. 51. *Member:* Richmond County Bar Association; 28th Judicial District Association. ***LANGUAGES:*** Spanish. ***PRACTICE AREAS:*** Civil Litigation; Regulatory Law. ***Email:*** jjohnson@vwlawfirm.com

VAUGHN S. MONROE, born Fayetteville, North Carolina, December 28, 1976; admitted to bar, 2003, North Carolina. *Education:* East Carolina University (B.S., 1999); North Carolina Central University (J.D., cum laude, 2003). Member, North Carolina Central Law Journal. Member, Moot Court. ***Email:*** vmonroe@vwlawfirm.com

EMILY A. BELCHER REYNOLDS, born May 3, 1978; admitted to bar, 2003, North Carolina. *Education:* Washington & Lee University (B.A., 2000; J.D., 2003). ***PRACTICE AREAS:*** Trusts and Estates. ***Email:*** ereynolds@vwlawfirm.com

Language: Spanish.

REPRESENTATIVE CLIENTS: Asheville Cardiology Associates; Carolina Power & Light Co., a Progress Energy Company; Central Carolina Restaurants, Inc.; Champion Hills Associates; Charles D. Owen Mfg. Co.; Chicago Title Insurance Co.; Chrysler Corp.; Columbia Carolina Corp.;CVS/Revco Drug Centers; EchoStar Communications Companies; E.I. Du Pont de Nemours & Company; First Citizens Bank and Trust Co.; First Union National Bank of North Carolina; Haywood Regional Medical Center; Hedrick Industries Group; High Street Banking Co.; The Hometown Bank; Kenmure Properties, Ltd.; Lawyers Title Insurance Co.; Lowe's Corporation; MCI; McDonald's Corporation; Mission-St. Joseph's Health System, Inc.; Mountain Area Health Education Center; Mountain Energy Corporation; P.H. Glatfelter Company; Public Service Company of N.C. (a SCANA Company); Regional Water Authority of Asheville, Buncombe and Henderson; Steelcase, Inc.; Verizon; Wachovia Bank, N.A.; Westcare Health System; American International Group, Inc.; AXA Corporate Solutions U.S. Insurance Company; CIGNA; CNA Insurance Companies; Federated Insurance; FPIC Insurance Company; Lawyers Mutual Liability Insurance Company of N.C.; Medical Mutual Insurance Co.; Metropolitan Life Insurance Co.; New York Life Insurance Co.; NCMIC Insurance Co.; Prudential Property & Casualty; The Reciprocal Group; St. Paul Insurance Cos.; State Farm Mutual Automobile Insurance Co.

WHITMIRE BEEKER & TOWNSEND

ASHEVILLE, NORTH CAROLINA

(See Hendersonville)

Real Estate - Residential and Commercial, Local Government Law, Land Development, Business and Corporations, Wills and Estates, Bankruptcy, Family Law, Environmental Law, Litigation.

STANLEY D. YOUNG

Established in 1984

68 NORTH MARKET STREET
P.O. BOX 3176
ASHEVILLE, NORTH CAROLINA 28802
Telephone: 828-255-0569
Fax: 828-255-8693

Civil and Criminal Litigation in all State and Federal Courts. Personal Injury, Auto Accidents, Wrongful Death, DWI, Criminal Traffic Offenses, Family Law, Divorce, Child Support and Custody, Adoptions, Equitable Distribution.

STANLEY D. YOUNG, born Asheville, North Carolina, December 4, 1956; admitted to bar, 1984, North Carolina. *Education:* Montreat-Anderson (Assoc. Sci., 1977); University of North Carolina at Asheville; North Carolina Central University (J.D., 1984). Phi Delta Phi. Member, North Carolina Central University Law Journal, 1983-1984. *Member:* North Carolina State Bar; American Bar Association. ***PRACTICE AREAS:*** Criminal Law; Driving While Intoxicated; Traffic Violations; Drugs and Narcotics; Domestic Relations Law; Family Law; Divorce; Child Support; Child Custody; Adoption Law; Equitable Distribution; Domestic Violence.

ROBERT B. ANGLE, JR. ATTORNEY P.A.

BANNER ELK, NORTH CAROLINA

(See Boone)

Real Estate, Wills, Trusts and Estates, Business Law, Traffic Violations.

DAVIS, MURRELLE & LYLES, P.A.

Established in 1981

412 FRONT STREET
P.O. BOX 819
BEAUFORT, NORTH CAROLINA 28516
Telephone: 252-728-4080
Fax: 252-728-3235
Email: dml.law@bizec.rr.com
URL: http://www.lawyers.com/dmlpalaw

Personal Injury, Automobile Accidents, Professional Liability, Products Liability, Arbitration, Premises Liability, Workers' Compensation, Social Security, Business Litigation, Admiralty and Maritime Law.

FIRM PROFILE: Davis, Murrelle & Lyles, P.A. founded in 1981 by Warren J. Davis. In 1991, the firm decided to limit its practice to the above matters.

EDWARD L. MURRELLE, born Greensboro, North Carolina, April 11, 1938; admitted to bar, 1964, North Carolina; 1965, U.S. District Court, Eastern and Middle Districts of North Carolina; 1966, U.S. Court of Appeals, Fourth Circuit. *Education:* Guilford College (A.B., with high honors, 1964); Wake Forest University (J.D., with honors, 1964). Member, Guilford Scholarship Society. Research Assistant, North Carolina Supreme Court, 1964-1965. *Member:* Carteret County, North Carolina (Member, Board of Governors, 1978-1981; Member, Sections on: Litigation; Health; Antitrust) and American (Member, Sections on: Litigation; Antitrust) Bar Associations; North Carolina Academy of Trial Lawyers. ***PRACTICE AREAS:*** Personal Injury Law; Products Liability; Business Litigation. ***Email:*** dml.law@bizec.rr.com

JANET M. LYLES, born Polk County, North Carolina, December 11, 1949; admitted to bar, 1984, North Carolina; 1990, U.S. District Court, Eastern District of North Carolina; 1993, U.S. Court of Appeals, Fourth Circuit. *Education:* University of North Carolina at Chapel Hill (A.B., 1972; J.D., 1984). Phi Beta Kappa. *Member:* Carteret County Bar Association; North Carolina State Bar; North Carolina Academy of Trial Lawyers; Workplace Injury Litigation Group. (Board Certified Specialist in Workers Compensation, North Carolina State Board of Legal Specialization). ***PRACTICE AREAS:*** Workers Compensation; Social Security Law; Personal Injury. ***Email:*** dml.law@bizec.rr.com

---

AMIE M. HUBER, born Reading, Pennsylvania, December 1, 1973; admitted to bar, 2001, North Carolina. *Education:* Catawba College (B.A., 1996); Widener University School of Law (J.D., 1999). Treasurer, Phi Alpha Delta, 1997-1999. First Place Winner: ABA/LSD Negotiation Competition, 1996-1999; ABA/LSD Regional Negotiation Competition, 1998; ABA/LSD National Negotiation Competition, 1999. Member: St. Thomas More Society. Member: Law Student Division, American Bar Association, 1996-1999; Women's Law Caucus, 1996-1999. Intern, Pennsylvania Trial Lawyer's Association, 1998-1999. *Member:* Carteret County Bar Association; North Carolina Academy of Trial Lawyers. ***PRACTICE AREAS:*** Personal Injury; Premises Liability; Products Liability; Wills; Estate Planning. ***Email:*** dml.law@bizec.rr.com

OF COUNSEL

WARREN J. DAVIS, born Fort Worth, Texas, November 6, 1937; admitted to bar, 1965, Virginia and North Carolina; 1966, U.S. District Court, Eastern District of Virginia;

(This Listing Continued)

1971, U.S. Court of Appeals, Fourth Circuit and U.S. Supreme Court; 1973, U.S. District Court, Eastern District of North Carolina. *Education:* Virginia Polytechnic Institute and State University (B.S., 1962); University of Virginia (J.D., 1965). Co-Author and Lecturer: "Persuasion Methods for Settlement Before and During Trial," North Carolina Academy of Trial Lawyers, 1986. Assistant, 1965-1967 and Senior Assistant, 1967-1969, Commonwealth Attorney, Fairfax County. Special Prosecutor, Fairfax County, 1967-1968. Proctor in Admiralty, 1978. Member, Morehead City Navigation and Pilotage Commission, 1986—. *Member:* Carteret County (President, 1978), Virginia (Executive Council, Young Lawyers Section, 1969), North Carolina and American (Executive Council, Young Lawyers Section, 1970-1971) Bar Associations; North Carolina State Bar; North Carolina Academy of Trial Lawyers; U.S. Maritime Law Association; Southeastern Admiralty Law Institute, Inc.; Northern Virginia Young Lawyers (President, 1969-1970). [With U.S. Navy, (Submarine Service) 1957-1959]. ***PRACTICE AREAS:*** Personal Injury Law; Arbitration; Mediation; Civil Trials and Appeals; Admiralty Law; Rezoning Law. ***Email:*** daviswarrenj@mac.com

REPRESENTATIVE CLIENTS: International Longshoreman's Association Local 1807; Cooperative Bank for Savings; Morehead City Export Terminal Inc.; Crow Hill Farms, Inc.; Elite Homes, Inc.; Northland Insurance Co.; Core Sound Waterfowl Museum, Inc.; Carteret Community Sunshine Band.
REFERENCES: First Citizens, Beaufort, NC; Branch Banking & Trust Co., Beaufort, NC; Wachovia Bank & Trust Co., N.A., Beaufort, NC; Cooperative Bank for Savings, Wilmington, NC.

MARGARET ANN GARNER

BEAUFORT, NORTH CAROLINA

(See Morehead City)

Estate Planning, Probate and Estate Administration, Commercial and Residential Real Estate, Corporations, Partnerships and LLCs, Bankruptcy.

MASON & MASON, P.A.

BEAUFORT, NORTH CAROLINA

(See Morehead City)

General Civil Trial Practice. Real Estate Law, Admiralty, Probate, Corporate.

NEWTON LAW FIRM

814 CEDAR STREET (U.S. HIGHWAY 70)
P.O. DRAWER 630
BEAUFORT, NORTH CAROLINA 28516-0630
Telephone: 252-728-4000
Fax: 252-728-3900
Email: info@newtonlaw.com
URL: http://www.newtonlaw.com

Civil Litigation including Personal Injury and Workers' Compensation. Mediation and Arbitration.

J. JEFFERSON NEWTON, born San Diego, California, May 26, 1958; admitted to bar, 1983, North Carolina; 1984, U.S. District Court, Eastern District of North Carolina; 1993, U.S. Court of Appeals, Fourth Circuit. *Education:* Campbell University (B.S., magna cum laude, 1980; J.D., 1983). Phi Alpha Delta. Author and Lecturer: "Handling Admitted Claims-A Guide to Evaluation and Payment of Compensation," Lorman Education Services, 2001; "Unseaworthiness Claims," North Carolina Bar Association, 1990. Co-Author: "Persuasion Methods for Settlement Before and During Trial," North Carolina Academy of Trial Lawyers, 1986. Arbitrator, Third Judicial District. Certified Mediator, North Carolina. Member, Million Dollar Advocates Forum. *Member:* Carteret County, North Carolina (Member, Sections on: Litigation; Workers' Compensation; Dispute Resolution) and American Bar Associations; North Carolina State Bar; North Carolina Academy of Trial Lawyers (Member, Sections on: Auto Torts; Workers' Compensation); Association of Trial Lawyers of America (Sustaining Member). Charter Barrister, Eastern North Carolina Inn of Court. (Certified as a Civil Trial Specialist by the National Board of Trial Advocacy; Board Certified Specialist in Workers Compensation Law, North Carolina State Board of Legal Specialization). ***PRACTICE AREAS:*** Personal Injury; Civil Trials; Workers' Compensation; Mediation and Arbitration. ***Email:*** jeff@newtonlaw.com

---

SUMRELL, SUGG, CARMICHAEL, HICKS & HART, P.A.

BEAUFORT, NORTH CAROLINA

(See New Bern)

General Civil. Trials and Appeals in all Civil Courts. Wills and Estates, Real Estate, Corporate Law, Financial Transactions, Insurance and Negligence, Employment Law, Municipal Law, Law Enforcement Liability Defense, Health Care Law and Intellectual Property.

WALLACE, MORRIS, BARWICK, LANDIS & STROUD, P.A.

BEAUFORT, NORTH CAROLINA

(See Kinston)

General Civil and Trial Practice in all State and Federal Courts. Aviation, Banking, Corporate Law, Insurance, Personal Injury, Probate, Product Liability, Real Estate and Taxation.

WHEATLY, WHEATLY, WEEKS, VALENTINE & LUPTON, P.A.

Established in 1907

710 CEDAR STREET
P.O. BOX 360
BEAUFORT, NORTH CAROLINA 28516
Telephone: 252-728-3158
Fax: 252-728-5282
Email: firm@wwnwpa.com
URL: http://www.wwnwpa.com

General Civil and Criminal Trial Practice. Admiralty, Probate, Corporation and Real Estate Law, Domestic, Family Law, Personal Injury, Criminal, Traffic, DWI, Felonies.

FIRM PROFILE: Wheatly, Wheatly, Weeks, Valentine & Lupton, P.A. was founded in 1907. It is the oldest firm in Carteret County. The firm maintains a general practice with members specializing in different legal areas. The firm encourages continuing professional development and all members participate in continuing legal education seminars, with some partners frequently being speakers.

CLAUD R. WHEATLY, JR., born Beaufort, North Carolina, July 3, 1918; admitted to bar, 1941, North Carolina. *Education:* University of North Carolina (A.B., 1939; LL.B. 1941). Inducted in North Carolina Bar Association General Practice Hall of Fame, June, 1989. *Member:* North Carolina State Bar; North Carolina and American Bar Associations; American Judicature Society; Maritime Law Association of U.S.; Southeast Admiralty Law Institution. Fellow: American College of Trial Lawyers. ***PRACTICE AREAS:*** Civil Litigation; Estate Planning. ***Email:*** cwheatly@wwnwpa.com

CLAUD R. WHEATLY, III, born Morehead City, North Carolina, April 25, 1947; admitted to bar, 1972, North Carolina; 1984, U.S. Supreme Court. *Education:* The Citadel (B.A., 1969); University of South Carolina (J.D., 1972). *Member:* Carteret County and North Carolina Bar Associations; North Carolina State Bar. [1st Lieut., U.S. Army M.P., 1972-1973]. ***PRACTICE AREAS:*** Civil Litigation; Real Estate; Environmental. ***Email:*** rwheatly@wwnwpa.com

STEVENSON L. WEEKS, born Morehead City, North Carolina, August 22, 1952; admitted to bar, 1980, North Carolina; 1983, U.S. Court of Appeals, 4th Circuit; 1984, U.S. Supreme Court. *Education:* University of North Carolina and East Carolina University (B.A., 1975); Campbell University (J.D., 1980). Course Planner, North Carolina Bar Foundation, First and Second Biennial Admiralty Law Seminars. *Member:* Carteret County and North Carolina Bar Association; North Carolina State Bar; South Admiralty Law Institution. ***PRACTICE AREAS:*** Civil Litigation; Personal Injury; Admiralty Law. ***Email:*** sweeks@wwnwpa.com

STEPHEN M. VALENTINE, born Rocky Mount, North Carolina, April 27, 1955; admitted to bar, 1980, North Carolina; 1981, North Carolina Supreme Court and U.S. District Court, Eastern District of North Carolina; 1983, U.S. Court of Military Appeals and U.S. District Court, Western District of Washington, 1998, U.S. District Court, Eastern District of North Carolina. *Education:* University of North Carolina at Chapel Hill (B.S., 1977); Wake Forest University (J.D., 1980). Phi Delta Phi. Member, Moot Court Board. *Member:* Carteret County (President, 1995) and North Carolina Bar Associations; North Carolina State Bar; North Carolina Academy of Trial Lawyers. [Major, Air Force Judge Advocate, 1982-1991]. ***PRACTICE AREAS:*** Domestic; Civil Litigation. ***Email:*** svalentine@wwnwpa.com

JAMES M. LUPTON, born Jacksonville, Florida, January 25, 1965; admitted to bar, 1992, North Carolina; 1998, U.S. District Court, Eastern District of North Carolina; 2001, U.S. Supreme Court. *Education:* Wake Forest University (B.S., 1987); University of North Carolina (J.D., 1992). *Member:* North Carolina State Bar; 3B Judicial District Bar (President, 2002-2003); North Carolina Bar Association (Member, Criminal Justice Section); Carteret County Bar Association; North Carolina Academy of Trial Lawyers. ***PRACTICE AREAS:*** Criminal; Civil Litigation. ***Email:*** jlupton@wwnwpa.com

REFERENCE: First Citizens Bank.

THE LAW OFFICES OF HALES & CONAWAY, PLLC

BENSON, NORTH CAROLINA

(See Clinton)

Family Law, Divorce, Adoption, Custody, Child Support, Premarital Agreements, Separation Agreements, Criminal Defense, Social Security Disability, Collections, Debtor, Creditor, Juvenile Law, Estate Administration and Estate Planning, Civil Litigation, Workers Compensation, Personal Injury, Traffic, DWI.

NARRON, O'HALE & WHITTINGTON, P.A.

Established in 1975

207 EAST MAIN STREET
P.O. BOX 457
BENSON, NORTH CAROLINA 27504
Telephone: 919-894-8565
Fax: 919-894-1198

Smithfield, North Carolina Office: 102 South Third Street, P.O. Box 1567. Telephone: 919-934-6021. Fax: 919-934-6280.

(This Listing Continued)

General Practice. Civil, Criminal Trials and Appeals in State and Federal Courts. DWI, Corporate, Administrative and Real Property Law. Taxation, Probate, Estate Planning and Stock and Asset Acquisitions and Mergers, Personal Injury, Automobile Accidents and Injuries, Wrongful Death, Workers Compensation, Mediation.

O. HAMPTON WHITTINGTON, JR., born Benson, North Carolina, February 25, 1949; admitted to bar, 1975, North Carolina and U.S. District Court, Middle District of North Carolina; 1981, U.S. District Court, Eastern District of North Carolina. *Education:* Davidson College (B.A., 1971); University of North Carolina (J.D., with honors, 1975). Member, Holderness Moot Court Bench, 1974-1975. Assistant District Attorney, Superior Court Division, 11th Judicial District, 1979-1981. Certified Mediator, 1996—. Member, 1984-2002, Chairman, 1997-2002, Johnston County Planning Board. Member, Johnston County Economic Development Commission, 2004— . *Member:* Johnston County (President, 1998), Eleventh Judicial District (President, 2000), North Carolina and American Bar Associations; North Carolina State Bar; North Carolina Academy of Trial Lawyers; The Association of Trial Lawyers of America. ***PRACTICE AREAS:*** Personal Injury Law; Workers Compensation; Wrongful Death; Civil Litigation; Alternative Dispute Resolution. ***Email:*** ohw@nowlaw.com

E. SCOTT TART, born Smithfield, North Carolina, July 27, 1976; admitted to bar, 2001, North Carolina. *Education:* Campbell University (B.A., summa cum laude, 1998); University of North Carolina (J.D., 2001). *Member:* Johnson County (Secretary and Treasurer, 2002), North Carolina, American and Eleventh Judicial District Bar Associations; North Carolina State Bar; North Carolina Academy of Trial Lawyers. ***PRACTICE AREAS:*** Civil Litigation; Criminal Law; Traffic Law; Estate Administration; Real Property; Residential Real Estate; Personal Injury; Workers Compensation; Family Law. ***Email:*** start@nowlaw.com

REPRESENTATIVE CLIENTS: T. E. Johnson Lumber Co., Inc.; E.D. Parker Corporation.
APPROVED ATTORNEYS FOR: Fidelity Title Insurance Corp.; Federal Land Bank of Columbia; Chicago Title Insurance Co.; Investors Title Insurance Co.

(For Complete Biographical data on all Personnel, see Professional Biographies at Smithfield, North Carolina)

STEWART LAW FIRM

BENSON, NORTH CAROLINA

(See Dunn)

Personal Injury, Automobile Accidents, Criminal Law, Traffic Violations, Real Estate, Corporate Law, Family Law, Divorce, Child Custody and Child Support.

BEGLEY LAW FIRM, P.A.

Established in 1985

103 RICHARDSON BOULEVARD
BLACK MOUNTAIN, NORTH CAROLINA 28711
Telephone: 828-669-4000
Fax: 828-669-9619
Email: mike@begleylaw.net

Estate Planning, Estate Administration, Real Estate, Business Law and Non-Profit Administration.

WM. MICHAEL BEGLEY, born Asheville, North Carolina, May 7, 1952; admitted to bar, 1977, North Carolina. *Education:* University of North Carolina at Chapel Hill (B.S.B.A., 1974; J.D., 1977). Morehead Scholar. Mayor, Town of Black Mountain, 1985-1989, 1997—. Director: Community Foundation of SunTrust, Asheville, North Carolina. *Member:* Buncombe County and North Carolina (Director, 1987-1990, Real Property Section State Council; Member, Sections on: Real Property Law; Estates and Fiduciary Law) Bar Associations; North Carolina State Bar. ***PRACTICE AREAS:*** Estate Planning; Estate Administration; Real Estate. ***Email:*** mike@begleylaw.net

REFERENCES: SunTrust; Community Foundation of WNC; Montreat Development Foundation; Black Mountain Community Endowment Fund; Black Mountain Center for the Arts.

STONE & CHRISTY, P.A.

110 N. DOUGHERTY STREET
BLACK MOUNTAIN, NORTH CAROLINA 28711
Telephone: 828-669-7642
Fax: 828-669-5678
URL: http://www.stoneandchristy.com

Corporate and Commercial Litigation, Real Estate Litigation, Buying and Selling a Home, Tax Litigation, Fiduciary Litigation, Civil Litigation, Commercial Real Estate, Residential Real Estate, Workers Compensation, Personal Injury, Wrongful Death, Trusts and Estates, Business and Succession Planning, Commercial Collections.

MEMBERS OF FIRM

RICHARD B. STONE (1925-1998)

WILLIAM H. CHRISTY, born Morganton, North Carolina, March 16, 1956; admitted to bar, 1989, North Carolina. *Education:* Warren Wilson College (B.A., 1979); University of North Carolina at Chapel Hill (M.A.T., 1983); North Carolina Central University (J.D., 1989); University of Florida (LL.M., 1990). *Member:* North Carolina Bar Association (Member, Tax Section); American Bar Association (Member, Real Property and Probate, General Practice Sections). ***PRACTICE AREAS:*** Business Law; Commercial Real Estate; Corporate Law; Probate Administration; Probate Litigation; Real Estate; Real Estate Litigation; Taxation; Trusts and Estates. ***Email:*** bill@stoneandchristy.com

(This Listing Continued)

BRYANT D. WEBSTER, born Durham, North Carolina, October 8, 1969; admitted to bar, 1994, North Carolina; 1995, U.S. District Court, Eastern District of North Carolina; 1996, U.S. District Court, Middle District of North Carolina; 1997, U.S. District Court, Western District of North Carolina. *Education:* University of North Carolina (B.A., 1991; J.D., with honors, 1994). Phi Beta Kappa. *Member:* North Carolina and 28th Judicial District Bar Associations; North Carolina State Bar. ***PRACTICE AREAS:*** Civil Litigation; Boundary Disputes; Easements; Quiet Title; Real Estate Litigation; Right of Way Easements; Contested Trusts and Estates; Construction Liens; Materialmens Liens; Commercial Collections. ***Email:*** bryant@stoneandchristy.com

JAMES M. ELLIS, born Durham, North Carolina, October 11, 1970; admitted to bar, 1996, North Carolina. *Education:* Warren Wilson College (B.A., 1992); University of South Carolina (J.D., 1996). Formerly with William S. Eubanks, PA. ***PRACTICE AREAS:*** Litigation; Workers Compensation; Business Law; Personal Injury; Automobile Accidents and Injuries; Collections; Real Estate; Real Estate Litigation; Estate Administration; Construction Liens. ***Email:*** james@stoneandchristy.com

R. WALTON DAVIS, III, born Fort Rucker, Alabama, September 22, 1956; admitted to bar, 1985, North Carolina. *Education:* University of North Carolina (A.B., 1978); University of Virginia (J.D., 1985); University of Florida (LL.M. in Taxation, 1993). Phi Beta Kappa. *Member:* North Carolina State Bar. (Board Certified Specialist in Estate Planning and Probate Law, North Carolina Board of Legal Specialization). ***PRACTICE AREAS:*** Taxation; Tax Controversies; Estate and Gift Taxation; Estate Administration; Trusts and Estates; Estate Planning; Wills; Probate; Estate Litigation; Contested Wills. ***Email:*** walton@stoneandchristy.com

---

DI SANTI WATSON CAPUA & WILSON

BLOWING ROCK, NORTH CAROLINA

(See Boone)

General Civil Practice and in all State and Federal Courts. Corporation, Real Property, Insurance, Family, Municipal, Personal Injury, Automobile Accidents and Injuries, Estate Planning, Probate, Real Estate Development and Interstate Land Sales.

AUSTIN & COOKE, PLLC

BOLIVIA, NORTH CAROLINA

(See Wilmington)

Estate Planning, Wills, Trusts and Estates, Real Estates, Residential Real Estate, Business Law, Limited Liability Company Law, Family Law, Divorce, Custody, Adoption, Juvenile, Criminal, Tickets, DWI, Contracts.

GODWIN LAW FIRM

BOLIVIA, NORTH CAROLINA

(See Wilmington)

Family Law, Divorce, Property Settlements, Child Custody, Child Support, Adoptions, Alimony, Spousal Support, Personal Injury, Workers Compensation, Social Security Disability, Civil Litigation.

LAW OFFICE OF
PAULINE HANKINS, P.A.

3029 OLD OCEAN HIGHWAY
P.O. BOX 157
BOLIVIA, NORTH CAROLINA 28422
Telephone: 910-253-7400
Fax: 910-253-7403
Email: phankins@2khiway.net

Juvenile Law, Traffic Violations, Divorce, Family Law, Child Custody, Child Support, Spousal Support, Criminal Misdemeanors, Domestic Violence.

PAULINE HANKINS, born New Hanover County, North Carolina, July 19, 1968; admitted to bar, 1994, North Carolina; 1995, U.S. Federal Court, Eastern District of North Carolina. *Education:* North Carolina State University (E.E. 1991); North Carolina Central University (J.D., cum laude, 1994). ***Email:*** phankins@2khiway.net

---

ROBERT B. ANGLE, JR. ATTORNEY P.A.

910 W. KING STREET
BOONE, NORTH CAROLINA 28607
Telephone: 828-265-0016
Fax: 828-265-3651
Email: robangle@charter.net

Real Estate, Wills, Trusts and Estates, Business Law, Traffic Violations.

ROBERT B. ANGLE, JR., born Mt. Airy, North Carolina, March 28, 1956; admitted to bar, 1986, North Carolina. *Education:* University of North Carolina at Chapel Hill (B.A., 1976); Wake Forest University School of Law (J.D., 1986). *Member:* Watauga County and North Carolina Bar Associations. ***PRACTICE AREAS:*** Real Estate; Wills; Trusts and Estates; Business Law; Traffic Violations. ***Email:*** robangle@charter.net

CLEMENT LAW OFFICE

Established in 1972
756 WEST KING STREET
DRAWER 32
BOONE, NORTH CAROLINA 28607
Telephone: 828-264-6411
Fax: 828-264-5424
Email: attorneys@clementlawoffice.com
URL: http://www.clementlawoffice.com

General Civil Practice in all Courts. Real Estate, Civil Litigation, Corporate and Business, Wills and Estates, Public Utilities, Employment, Municipal and Land Use Law, Condemnation and Eminent Domain, Administrative, Regulatory and Governmental Law.

MEMBERS OF FIRM

CHARLES E. CLEMENT, born Valdosta, Georgia, August 4, 1939; admitted to bar, 1964, North Carolina; 1972, U.S. Supreme Court and U.S. District Court, Western Middle and Eastern Districts of North Carolina. *Education:* University of North Carolina at Chapel Hill (B.A., 1961); Wake Forest University (J.D., 1964). Phi Delta Phi. Law Clerk, North Carolina Supreme Court. Trial Attorney, North Carolina Attorney General's Office. Counsel to North Carolina Governor Dan K. Moore. Blowing Rock City Attorney, 1979-1986. Lees-McRae College, Board of Trustees, 1987-1995. Director, North Carolina Crime Commission, 1967-1969; Board of Directors, Avery Health Care System, 1996-2000; Board of Trustees, North Carolina Natural Heritage Trust, 1996—; Advisory Council, Appalachian State University School of Music, 1993—. *Member:* North Carolina (Member, Real Property Council, 1974-1983; Board of Governors, 1999-2002) and American (Member, Sections on: General Practice; Real Property, Probate and Trust Law) Bar Associations; 24th Judicial District (President, 1995) and North Carolina State Bar; North Carolina Academy of Trial Lawyers; North Carolina Association of Municipal Attorneys (President, 1986-1987; Member, Board of Directors, 1983-1987); North Carolina League of Municipalities (Member, Board of Directors, 1986-1988); American Land Development Association (Member, Board of Directors, 1984-1990). ***PRACTICE AREAS:*** Real Estate; Business Law; Civil Litigation; Municipal Law; Zoning, Planning and Land Use; Condemnation. ***Email:*** cclement@clementlawoffice.com

DONALD D. HOWARD, born Wichita, Kansas, November 19, 1944; admitted to bar, 1969, California; 2001, North Carolina. *Education:* University of Kansas (B.A., 1965); Stanford University (LL.B., 1968). *Member:* North Carolina State Bar; North Carolina Bar Association; State Bar of California. [With JAGC, U.S. Naval Reserve, 1969-1972]. ***Email:*** dhoward@clementlawoffice.com

REPRESENTATIVE CLIENTS: Branch Banking & Trust Co.; High Country Bank; Chicago Title Insurance Co.; First American Title Insurance Co.; Downtown Boone Development Association; Avery Health Care System; N.C. Department of Transportation; Wal-Mart; Minor's Printing; Boone Rentals; Beech Mountain Club; Hound Ears Club, Inc.; Hound Ears Property Owners Association; Subway; The St. Paul Property and Liability Insurance; Appalachian State University; Yonahlossee Resort Club; Yonahlossee Property Owners Association; Innkeepers of Boone, Inc.
APPROVED ATTORNEYS FOR: First American Title Insurance Co.; Chicago Title Insurance Co.; Lawyers Title Insurance Co.; Branch Banking & Trust Co.; High Country Bank.
REFERENCES: Branch Banking & Trust Co.; First Union National Bank; First Citizens Bank; First American Title Insurance Co.; Chicago Title Insurance Co.

DI SANTI WATSON CAPUA & WILSON

Established in 1971
642 WEST KING STREET
P.O. BOX 193
BOONE, NORTH CAROLINA 28607-4040
Telephone: 828-264-6126
Telefax: 828-264-7743
URL: http://www.lawyers.com/disantiwatson&capua

Newland, North Carolina Office: 102 Elk Street, 28657. Telephone: 828-733-9273.

General Civil Practice and in all State and Federal Courts. Corporation, Real Property, Insurance, Family, Municipal, Personal Injury, Automobile Accidents and Injuries, Estate Planning, Probate, Real Estate Development and Interstate Land Sales.

FIRM PROFILE: Di Santi Watson Capua & Wilson is a very well established firm since 1971. They have a complete general civil practice in State and Federal Courts. This firm is a very reputable and credible in the Boone Area.

MEMBERS OF FIRM

ANTHONY S. DI SANTI, born Hendersonville, North Carolina, August 25, 1947; admitted to bar, 1975, North Carolina and U.S. District Court, Western, Middle and Eastern Districts of North Carolina; 1979, U.S. Supreme Court; 1980, U.S. Court of Appeals, Fourth Circuit. *Education:* University of North Carolina (B.S., 1971); Wake Forest University (J.D., 1975); North Carolina College of Advocacy; John Alan Appleman's Professional Trial Lawyers Institute, 1979. Phi Delta Phi. Member, Wake Forest Law Review, 1973-1975. Author: Article, "Taxation-Income and Estate Taxes-Claims Against Decedent's Estate," Vol. 10, page 328, June, 1974; selected for reprint in national tax digest. Adjunct Professor, Real Estate Law, Appalachian State University, 1979-1982. Member, Blowing Rock Town Council, 1983-1989. *Member:* Watauga County (President, 1980-1981), North Carolina and American Bar Associations; 24th Judicial District and North Carolina State Bars; North Carolina Academy of Trial Lawyers. [With U.S. Army, 1966-1969. Awarded Silver Star, Purple Heart, Viet Nam, 1968]. (Certified as a Civil Trial Advocate by the National Board of Trial Advocacy). ***PRACTICE AREAS:*** Insurance; Real Estate; Contracts; Wills; Probate; Civil Practice; Corporate Law. ***Email:*** asd@dwc-law.com

DONALD M. WATSON, JR., born Durham, North Carolina, August 11, 1949; admitted to bar, 1974, North Carolina. *Education:* University of North Carolina (B.S., 1971; J.D., 1974). Beta Gamma Sigma. Law Clerk to Judge R.A. Hedrick, North Carolina Court of Appeals, 1974-1975. President, Boone Chamber of Commerce, 1995-1996. Member,

(This Listing Continued)

DI SANTI WATSON CAPUA & WILSON, Boone—Continued

North Carolina College of Advocacy. Boone Town Council, 1995-1996. *Member:* Watauga County (Vice President, 1981-1982; President, 1982-1983), North Carolina (Member: General Practice Committee, 1980-1981, 1981-1982, 1982-1983; General Practice Section Steering Committee, 1984-1985; Real Property Section Council, 1984-1985, 1985-1986, 1986-1987, 1995-1996, 1996-1997; Construction Law Council Section, 1987-1988, 1988-1989, 1991-1995, 1997-1998) and American Bar Associations; 24th Judicial District; North Carolina State Bar. (Also at Newland Office). ***PRACTICE AREAS:*** Real Estate Development. ***Email:*** dwatson@dwc-law.com

ANDREA N. CAPUA, born Miami, Florida, August 30, 1962; admitted to bar, 1988, Florida; 1990, U.S. District Court, Southern District of Florida; 1993, North Carolina. *Education:* Florida State University (A.A., 1983); Florida International University (B.S., 1984); South Texas College of Law (J.D., 1987). Articles Editor, South Texas Law Review, 1986-1987. Author: Kavanaugh & Capua, Trial Preparation, Ch. 8 Nichols on Eminent Domain (Matthew Bender) 1993. Board Member, Watauga County Habitat for Humanity, 1993-1997. Chairman of Board of Trustees, Mountain Pathways Montessori School, 1997-1998. *Member:* Watauga County (Secretary/Treasurer, 1995-1996; Vice-President, 1996-1997; President, 1997-1998) and American Bar Associations; The Florida Bar (Member, Advisory Board, Watauga County Arts Council, 2000—). (Also at Newland Office). ***LANGUAGES:*** Italian, Spanish. ***PRACTICE AREAS:*** Real Estate; Estate Planning; Family Law; Mediation; Business Law; Civil Litigation. ***Email:*** acapua@dwc-law.com

FRANK C. WILSON, III, born Memphis, Tennessee, August 19, 1954; admitted to bar, 1983, Alabama; 2000, North Carolina. *Education:* University of Alabama (B.A., 1979); Cumberland School of Law of Samford University (J.D., 1983). Phi Delta Phi. Associate Municipal Judge, City of Selma, Alabama, 1986-1990. *Member:* Watauga County, North Carolina State and American Bar Associations; Alabama State Bar; Alabama Defense Lawyers Association (Vice President, 1995-1996); Defense Research Institute. (Also at Newland Office). ***PRACTICE AREAS:*** Personal Injury; Automobile Accidents and Injuries; Construction Law; Torts; Litigation; Insurance; Real Estate; Adoption Law. ***Email:*** fcw@dwc-law.com

OF COUNSEL

W. KELLY JOHNSON, born Cincinnati, Ohio, August 23, 1961; admitted to bar, 1986, Ohio and U.S. District Court, Southern District of Ohio; 1990, U.S. Court of Appeals, Sixth Circuit. (Not admitted in North Carolina). *Education:* Indiana University (B.A., 1983); University of Cincinnati (J.D., 1986). *Member:* Cincinnati Bar Association; Greater Cincinnati Criminal Defense Lawyers Association (Secretary/Treasurer, 1994); Ohio Association of Criminal Defense Lawyers. (Also at Newland Office). ***PRACTICE AREAS:*** Criminal Law.

COUNSEL FOR: Boone Industries, Inc.; Boone Mall, Ltd.; Northwestern Regional Housing Authority; Linville Ridge Country Club; Elk River Development Corp.; Log Homes of America, Inc., WJ Office City; High Country Bank.
REPRESENTATIVE CLIENTS: Insurance Company of North America; Fireman's Fund; Shelby Mutual Insurance Co.; Tweetsie Railroad, Inc.; Midwest Mutual Insurance Co.; Piedmont Savings & Loan Assn.; U.S.F. & G. Insurance Co.; Allstate Insurance Co.; First Union National Bank; The Pantry, Inc.; Seibels Bruce Insurance Group; Lloyd's, London; Indiana Lumberman's Insurance Co.; Tenn. Farmers Mutual Insurance Co.; Nationwide Homes, Inc.; Pennsylvania National Insurance Co.; Integon Insurance Co.; Cincinnati Insurance Co.; KM Administrative Services.
APPROVED ATTORNEYS FOR: Lawyers Title Insurance Corp.; Chicago Title Insurance Co.; American Title Insurance Co.; Commonwealth Title Insurance.
REFERENCE: Bank of America, Boone, N.C.

EGGERS, EGGERS, EGGERS & EGGERS

Established in 1950

737 WEST KING STREET
P.O. BOX 248
BOONE, NORTH CAROLINA 28607
Telephone: 828-264-3601
Fax: 828-262-5229
Email: four.eggers@eggers-law.com
URL: http://www.eggers-law.com

Real Estate, General Civil Practice, Domestic Law, Elder Law, Probate, Juvenile Law, Personal Injury, Criminal, Condemnation, Corporate, Commercial, Traffic, Social Security Disability.

MEMBERS OF FIRM

STACY C. EGGERS, JR., born Boone, North Carolina, March 20, 1924; admitted to bar, 1950, North Carolina. *Education:* Appalachian State Teachers College; Wake Forest College; Asheville Law School. Phi Alpha Delta. County Attorney: Watauga County, 1951-1955; 1957-1958; 1990-1999; Secretary, 16th Judicial District of North Carolina, 1955. Bar Councilor, 24th Judicial District, 1984-1991. Town Attorney, Town of Seven Devils. North Carolina General Practice Hall of Fame, 1984-1988. Inducted, General Practice Hall of Fame, 1996. Board Member, Client Security Fund. *Member:* Watauga County (President, 1969-1970), North Carolina and American Bar Associations; 24th Judicial District Bar Association (President, 1974-1975); The North Carolina State Bar; Security Counsel Client. ***PRACTICE AREAS:*** Real Estate; Wills; Corporate Law; Estates; Business Law. ***Email:*** office@eggers-law.com

STACY C. EGGERS, III (1948-1990)

REBECCA EGGERS-GRYDER, born Watauga County, North Carolina, November 14, 1960; admitted to bar, 1986, North Carolina. *Education:* Appalachian State University (B.S., summa cum laude, 1983); Campbell University (J.D., 1986). Phi Kappa Phi; Delta Theta Phi. County Attorney, 1990-1999; County Attorney, Watauga County, 2002-2004; Watauga County Planning Board, 1986-1999. Watauga County Dept of Social Services, 1988-1999. Seven Devils Town Attorney, 2000-2003. *Member:* Watauga County Bar Association (President, 1989-1990), Twenty-Fourth Judicial District (Secretary 1989-1990) and North Carolina Bar Associations; North Carolina State Bar. ***PRACTICE AREAS:*** Family Law; Condemnation; Trial Practice; Juvenile law; Mediation. ***Email:*** becca.eggers@eggers-law.com

(This Listing Continued)

STACY C. EGGERS, IV, born Boone, North Carolina, October 20, 1976; admitted to bar, 2001, North Carolina. *Education:* Appalachian State University (B.A., 1998); Campbell University (J.D, 2001). Author, Comment, Campbell Law Review, Vol. 23, Fall 2000. County Attorney, Watauga County, 2002-2004. Attorney, Watauga County Department of Social Services, 2002-2005. *Member:* Watauga County (President, 2004-2005; Treasurer 2001-2002) and North Carolina Bar Associations; Federalist Society. ***PRACTICE AREAS:*** Criminal Law; Trial Practice; Personal Injury; Social Security Disability; Traffic Violations; Condemnation. ***Email:*** four.eggers@eggers-law.com

REPRESENTATIVE CLIENTS: Centura Bank; NCNB National Bank of North Carolina; First Union National Bank; Federal Land Bank; First Citizens Bank and Trust Co.; BB&T-Branch Banking & Trust; Watauga County, Town of Seven Devils.
APPROVED ATTORNEYS FOR: Lawyers Title Insurance Corp.; Farm Credit Assn.; Jefferson-Pilot Title Insurance Co.; American Title Insurance Co.;
REFERENCES: BB&T-Branch Banking & Trust; First Union National Bank; First Citizens Bank and Trust Co.; Centura Bank.

LAW OFFICES OF E.K. MORLEY, PLLC

BOONE, NORTH CAROLINA

(See Hendersonville)

Contested Wills, Will Contests, Estate Litigation, Decedents Estates, Inheritance, Successions, Trusts and Estates, Surrogates Court Practice, Contested Trusts and Estates, Estate Administration, Estate Settlements, Fiduciary Law, Fiduciary Liability, Fiduciary Litigation, Trust Law, Trust Litigation, Ancillary Probate, Probate Litigation.

JOSEPH W. SEEGERS

BOONE, NORTH CAROLINA

(See Newland)

General Civil and Criminal Trial Practice before all Courts. Criminal Law, Capital Offenses, D.U.I., Traffic Violations, Probate, Estates, Estate Planning, Business and Commercial Law, Negligence Law, Workers Compensation, Municipal Law, Juvenile Law, Family Law, Divorce, Child Custody.

DAVID J. TURLINGTON, III

ATTORNEY AT LAW, PC
756 WEST KING STREET
BOONE, NORTH CAROLINA 28607
Telephone: 828-263-8860
Fax: 828-263-8862
URL: http://www.turlingtonlaw.com
Email: info@turlingtonlaw.com
URL: http://www.lawyers.com/davidjturlington

Family Law, Custody, Divorce, Equitable Distribution, Adoptions, Construction Law, Business Law, Corporate Law, Criminal Law, Traffic, DWI, Drug Offenses.

DAVID J. TURLINGTON, III, born Clinton, North Carolina, November 28, 1958; admitted to bar, 1987, North Carolina. *Education:* East Carolina University (B.A., 1981); North Carolina Central University (J.D., 1985). Phi Delta Phi. Assistant Public Defender, Eighteenth Judicial District, 1988-1990. *Member:* North Carolina State Bar; North Carolina Bar Association (Member, Family Law Section; Construction Section). ***LANGUAGES:*** Spanish. ***PRACTICE AREAS:*** Family Law; Child Custody; Divorce; Equitable Distribution; Adoption Law; Construction Law; Criminal Law; Traffic Violations; Driving While Intoxicated; Drug Crimes; Business Law; Corporate Law.

TURNER & YATES, P.A.

136 NORTH WATER STREET
BOONE, NORTH CAROLINA 28607
Telephone: 828-264-5900
Fax: 828-264-9767
Real Estate Fax: 828-264-5969
URL: http://www.lawyers.com/turnerandyates

Real Estate, Residential and Commercial Real Estate Development, Civil Litigation, Construction Law, Banking Law, Business Law, Corporate Law, Municipal Law, Employment Law, Personal Injury, Wills, Trusts and Estates, Utility Law.

JOHN A. TURNER, born October 3, 1957; admitted to bar, 1983, North Carolina; 1993, Texas (Inactive Status). *Education:* Presbyterian College (B.A., English, Minors in Business Administration and History, summa cum laude, 1980); University of North Carolina (J.D., 1983). CCB and Law Alumni Scholar, 1980-1983. Instructor: Real Estate Law and Business Law, Appalachian State University, 1987-1993. General Counsel, Mission Mortgage of Texas, Inc., 1993-1994. Incorporator and Past President, Blue Ridge (now Watauga County) Habitat for Humanity, Inc. Board of Directors and Past President, OASIS (Opposing Abuse with Shelter, Information and Service), Inc. 1985-1999. Member, Investment and Strategic Planning Committees, Watauga Educational Foundation, Inc., 2004. *Member:* North Carolina Bar Association (Member, Sections on: Real Property, Litigation, Business Law; Member, Real Property Section Council, 2004—); North Carolina Academy of Trial Lawyers; Watauga County Bar Association (President, 1996-1997). ***PRACTICE AREAS:*** Residential Real Estate Law; Commercial Real Estate Law; Real Estate Development; Civil Litigation; Business Law. ***Email:*** jturnerlaw@bellsouth.net

DAVID W. YATES, born Albany, Georgia, March 28, 1962; admitted to bar, 1987, Tennessee and U.S. District Court, Middle District of Tennessee; 1996, North Carolina;

(This Listing Continued)

1989, U.S. Court of Appeals, Sixth Circuit; 1993, U.S. Court of Appeals, District of Columbia Circuit; 2001, U.S. District Court, Western and Middle Districts of North Carolina. *Education:* Appalachian State University (B.A., Advanced Partnership Program, 1983), Temple University (J.D., 1986). Assistant General Counsel, Tennessee Public Service Commission, 1987-1994. Adjunct Professor, Appalachian State University, Labor Relations and Communication Studies, 2000—. Assistant Attorney General, State of Tennessee, 1994-1996. Staff Sub-committee on Law, National Association of Regulatory Utility Commissioners, 1992-1996. *Member:* North Carolina (Member, Sections on: Real Property; Construction Law, Section Council, 2001-2005; Employment Law; Litigation; Business Law) and Tennessee (Member, Sections on Real Property; Litigation) Bar Associations; North Carolina Academy of Trial Lawyers. ***PRACTICE AREAS:*** Civil Litigation; Business Law; Construction Law; Real Estate Law; Real Estate Development; Banking Law; Employment Law; Municipal Law. ***Email:*** davidyates@bellsouth.net

OF COUNSEL

PATRICIA L. WILSON, born Boone, North Carolina, July 26, 1953; admitted to bar, 1989, North Carolina and U.S. District Court, Eastern District of North Carolina. *Education:* University of North Carolina at Chapel Hill (B.A., with honors, 1974); Duke University (J.D., with honors, 1989). *Member:* North Carolina Bar Association (Member, Estate Planning Section, 2004—). ***PRACTICE AREAS:*** Wills; Trust Law; Estate Planning; Probate; Civil Litigation. ***Email:*** twilson@booneattorneys.com

REPRESENTATIVE CLIENTS: Alta Building Systems, Inc.; Branch Bank & Trust; Episcopal Church, Diocese of Western North Carolina; Florida Savings Bank; Mast General Store; Harmony Exchange; Heavenly Mountain Resort; High Country Bank; Northwestern Bank; High Country Conservancy; High Country Home Builders Association; High Country Municipal ABC Board; Maymead, Inc.; New River Building Supply; North Carolina State Employee's Credit Union; Piedmont Federal Savings & Loan; Quality Inn; Town of Boone Board of Adjustment; Watauga Building Supply; Willow Brook Log Homes, Inc.; Wright Brothers Construction, Inc.

APPROVED ATTORNEY FOR: Chicago Title; First American Title; Elk River Club; Hound Ears Club; Investors Title; Lawyers Title; Linville Ridge Golf & Country Club.

BLANCHARD, NEWMAN & HAYES

BREVARD, NORTH CAROLINA

(See Hendersonville)

General Civil Litigation, Family Law, Divorce, Criminal in all State and Federal Courts, Traffic, DWI.

ELKINS & ELKINS

BREVARD, NORTH CAROLINA

(See Hendersonville)

Bankruptcy, Real Estate, Residential Real Estate, Buying and Selling a Home, Probate, Corporation, Civil Trial Practice, Out of Court Debt Restructuring.

MICHAEL C. EUBANKS

52-A WEST MAIN STREET
P.O. BOX 588
BREVARD, NORTH CAROLINA 28712
Telephone: 828-884-7900
Fax: 828-884-7905
Email: insyt@citcom.net

Family Law, Divorce, Child Custody, Equitable Distribution, Personal Injury, Wrongful Death, Automobile Accidents, Business, Estate and Real Property Litigation.

MICHAEL C. EUBANKS, born Grand Junction, Colorado, September 4, 1946; admitted to bar, 1975, Georgia; 1983, South Carolina; 2000, North Carolina; U.S. District Court, Western and Southern Districts of South Carolina; U.S. Court of Appeals, 4th Circuit. *Education:* University of Georgia (A.B., 1968; J.D., 1975). Phi Beta Kappa; Phi Kappa Phi; Phi Alpha Delta. District Attorney, Augusta, GA. Judicial Circuit, 1989-1992. Private practice in Augusta, GA, 1975-1999 and Aiken and Edgefield, SC 1983-1988 and 1993-2000. Private practice in Brevard, NC, 2000—. *Member:* North Carolina State Bar; North Carolina Bar Association; State Bar of Georgia; South Carolina Bar; North Carolina Academy of Trial Lawyers. ***LANGUAGES:*** French.

Languages: French.

FERIKES & BLEYNAT, PLLC

BREVARD, NORTH CAROLINA

(See Asheville)

Business Litigation, Business Torts, Construction Litigation, Appellate Practice, Property Law and Litigation; Personal Injury and Medical Malpractice, Automobile Accidents, Wrongful Death, Brain Injury, Torts, Commercial Liability, Commercial Real Estate Litigation, Construction Defects and Liens, Contract Litigation, Corporate Litigation, Workers Compensation.

WILLIAM L. GARDO, II

BREVARD, NORTH CAROLINA

(See Henderson)

General Civil Trial Practice, Personal Injury, Automobile Accidents, Wrongful Death, Family Law, Divorce, Child Custody, Child Support, Adoptions, Workers Compensation, Criminal Law, Driving While Intoxicated, Traffic Violations, Drug Offenses.

LAW OFFICES OF FRANK B. JACKSON

BREVARD, NORTH CAROLINA

(See Hendersonville)

Civil Litigation in all State and Federal Courts. Domestic Litigation, Divorce, Child Custody, Child Support, Equitable Distribution, Spousal Support, General Civil Practice, Appeals, Probate and Estate Planning.

DONALD E. JORDAN

MCMINN BUILDING
4 WEST MAIN STREET, SUITE 5
BREVARD, NORTH CAROLINA 28712
Telephone: 828-862-8735
Fax: 828-966-9556
Email: jordanlaw@infoave.net

Estate Planning, Trusts and Estates, Wills, Estate Administration, Probate Law, Real Estate Law, Business Law, Corporations.

DONALD E. JORDAN, born Sioux Falls, South Dakota, April 10, 1953; admitted to bar, 1978, Colorado; 1994, North Carolina. *Education:* Colorado State University and University of Denver (B.A., 1974; M.B.A., 1975); University of Colorado (J.D., 1978). Phi Beta Kappa; Beta Gamma Sigma; Order of the Coif. Author: "In-State Preference in Public Contracting: States' Rights versus Economic Sectionalism," University of Colorado Law Review, Vol. 49, p. 205, No. 2, Winter 1978. Co-Author: "Protecting Trust Assets from Tax Liens," Colorado Lawyer, vol. 24, p. 791, No. 4, April 1995. *Member:* North Carolina (Member, Sections on: Estate Planning and Fiduciary Law; Real Property Law) and American (Member, Real Property, Probate and Trust Law Section) Bar Associations. ***PRACTICE AREAS:*** Estate Planning; Trusts and Estates; Wills; Estate Administration; Probate; Real Estate; Business Law; Corporate Law.

SCOTT D. NEUMANN

10 SOUTH BROAD STREET
BREVARD, NORTH CAROLINA 28712
Telephone: 828-884-9899
Fax: 828-862-3334
Email: sneumann@citcom.net
URL: http://www.scottneumannlaw.com

Family Law, Divorce, Child Custody and Support, Adoptions, Domestic Violence, Visitation Rights, Civil Practice, Criminal Law, Driving While Intoxicated, Traffic Violations, Drug Crimes, Juvenile Crimes, Parole and Probation, White Collar Crime, Real Estate, Buying or Selling a Home, Construction, Commercial Real Estate, Bankruptcy, Business Law, Buying or Selling a Business, Immigration and Naturalization, Visas, Trusts and Estates, Estate Planning, Wills and Probate.

SCOTT D. NEUMANN, born Heidelberg, Germany, July 31, 1966; admitted to bar, 1993, Florida; 1994, North Carolina; 1997, U.S. District Court, Western District of North Carolina. *Education:* University of Georgia (B.B.A., 1988); Stetson University College of Law (J.D., cum laude, 1993). Former Assistant District Attorney, McDowell, Polk, Rutherford, Henderson and Transylvania Counties. Former Prudential Insurance Company Property and Casualty Underwriter. Member, Brevard City Council. Former Director, Chamber of Commerce, Heart of Brevard and Healing Place. Past Director, Criminal Justice Partnership Plan. Charter Graduate, Vision of Brevard. *Member:* North Carolina State Bar; The Florida Bar. ***LANGUAGES:*** Spanish.

THE NEUMANN LAW FIRM, PLLC

Established in 1995

46 EAST MAIN STREET
BREVARD, NORTH CAROLINA 28712
Telephone: 828-884-6575
Fax: 828-884-6636
URL: http://www.neumann-law.com
Email: dneumann@citcom.net
URL: http://www.neu-hall-law.com

Business Law, Corporate Law, Business Formation, Business Litigation, Commercial Finance Transactions, Small Business Planning, Family Limited Partnerships, Civil Litigation, Conflict Management Systems, Business Negotiations and Strategic Business Planning, Mediation and Arbitration, Estate Planning, Wills, Trusts, Powers of Attorney, Estate Administration, Probate, Guardianship, Real Estate, Residential and Commercial Real Estate Transactions, IRC 1031 Exchange Planning, Construction Contracts, Transactional Legal Opinions, Tax and Corporate Compliance, Income Tax Planning.

MEMBER OF THE FIRM

DAVID C. NEUMANN, born Shelby, Ohio, July 22, 1940; admitted to bar, 1986, North Carolina. *Education:* United States Military Academy (B.S., 1962); University of Georgia (J.D., cum laude, 1986). Recipient: Bronze Star Medal and 2 Army Commendation Medals. Transylvania County Attorney. Past President, Transylvania Vocational Services. Board of Realtors Attorney, 1990—. Past President and Director, Children's Center. *Member:* 29th Judicial District and American Bar Associations; North Carolina State Bar. [Major, U.S. Army Artillery, 1962-1969]. ***PRACTICE AREAS:*** Real Estate; Estate Planning.

JEANNE P. HALL, born Sumter, South Carolina, January 7, 1959; admitted to bar, 1986, North Carolina; 1989, South Carolina. *Education:* Davidson College (B.A., with honors, 1981); Pace University (J.D., 1986); University of South Carolina (M.A., Taxation,

(This Listing Continued)

THE NEUMANN LAW FIRM, PLLC, Brevard—Continued

1988). Dean's List. Member, Moot Court, American Jurisprudence. Trainer, ADR, 1995-2000. Executive Director, Council for Conflict Resolution, South Carolina. Governor Appointed ADR Ambassador, South Carolina, 2000. Member, South Carolina Commission on ADR. Certified Mediator and Arbitrator, North Carolina and South Carolina. *Member:* North Carolina State Bar; South Carolina Bar (Chair, ADR Section, 1999-2000). ***PRACTICE AREAS:*** Complex Civil Litigation; Business Law; Tax Planning; Appellate Law; Real Estate Law; Estate Planning; Non-Profit Law; Mediation; Arbitration.

PRINCE, YOUNGBLOOD & MASSAGEE

BREVARD, NORTH CAROLINA

(See Hendersonville)

General Practice. Probate, Civil Litigation, Commercial, Residential Real Estate, Corporate, Arbitration, Mediation, Healthcare, Employment Law, Family Law, Equitable Distribution, Child Custody, Adoptions.

RAMSEY & PRATT, P.A.

Established in 1927

LEGAL BUILDING
ONE NORTH GASTON STREET
BREVARD, NORTH CAROLINA 28712
Telephone: 828-884-4113
Telecopier: 828-885-2494
URL: HTTP://WWW.RAMSEY-PRATT.COM

General Practice, State and Federal Courts. Wills and Trusts, Probate and Estates, Estate Planning, Estate Administration, Real Estate, Municipal Law, Administrative Law, Personal Injury, Civil Litigation, Corporate Law, Business Law.

FIRM PROFILE: Ramsey & Pratt, P.A. is a well respected and prestigious law firm established in 1927. The firm is practicing in Transylvania, Henderson and Buncombe counties. The firm is one of the longest standing and well-respected firms in the area.

RALPH H. RAMSEY, JR. (1900-1984)
JOHN K. SMART, JR. (1935-1995)
CECIL J. HILL (1919-2002)

GAYLE E. RAMSEY, born Brevard, North Carolina, August 15, 1938; admitted to bar, 1969, North Carolina. *Education:* Wake Forest University (B.A., magna cum laude, 1960); University of North Carolina (M.A., 1966); Emory University and University of North Carolina (J.D., 1969). Phi Beta Kappa. *Member:* Transylvania County and North Carolina (Member, Sections on: General Practice; Real Property; Council Member, Real Property Section, 1989-1992) Bar Associations; North Carolina State Bar. ***PRACTICE AREAS:*** Real Estate Law; Residential Real Estate; Resorts and Leisure; Real Estate Development; Estate and Probate Law; Corporation Law; General Practice. **Email:** sgore@ramsey-pratt.com

MICHAEL K. PRATT, born Greensboro, North Carolina, February 6, 1956; admitted to bar, 1981, North Carolina. *Education:* University of North Carolina at Greensboro (B.A., 1977); Wake Forest University (J.D., 1981). Phi Alpha Delta. City Attorney for the City of Brevard, 1993—. *Member:* Transylvania County and North Carolina (Member, Sections on: Civil Litigation; Estate Planning and Administration; Elder Care; Municipal Law) Bar Associations; North Carolina State Bar; North Carolina Academy of Trial Lawyers. ***PRACTICE AREAS:*** Estate Planning; Estate Administration; Elder Care; Commercial Law; Corporate Law; Civil Litigation; Business Arbitration; Business Mediation; Municipal Law; General Office Practice. **Email:** mkpratt@ramsey-pratt.com

REPRESENTATIVE CLIENTS: Duke Power Co.; Lake Toxaway Co.; Glen Cannon Country Club; Ridge Haven, Inc.; Brevard College; Gwynn Valley Camp, Inc.; City of Brevard; Citizens Telephone Co.; Sylvan Valley CATV Co.; Eagle's Nest Foundation; Coats North American; Cascade Power Co.; Brevard Housing Authority; Transylvania Partnership, Inc.; Transylvania County Housing Development Corp.; Transylvania County Arts Council, Inc.; Greenwood Development Corporation; Connestee Cove, Inc.; Outdoor Resort of NC, Inc.; Glenn Cannon Property Owners Association Inc.; Morgan Mill Resorts, Inc.; Heart of Brevard, Inc.; Brevard Music Center.
APPROVED ATTORNEYS FOR: Chicago Title Insurance Co.; Commonwealth Land Title Company of North Carolina; Fidelity National Title Insurance Company of New York; Investors Title Insurance Company; Lawyers Title of North Carolina; Stewart Title Guaranty Corp.; Bank of America; United Community Bank; Centura Bank; First Citizens Bank; First Union Home Equity Corp.; Southtrust Bank; Wachovia Bank, N.A.; Wachovia Mortgage Co.; Carolina First Bank; State Employees Credit Union; Bank Atlantic.

BIBERSTEIN & NUNALEE, L.L.P.

Established in 1964

102 SOUTH WALKER STREET
P.O. BOX 428
BURGAW, NORTH CAROLINA 28425-0428
Telephone: 910-259-2175
Fax: 910-259-6823
Email: bnlaw@bellsouth.net

Hampstead, North Carolina Office: 16191 Highway 17. Telephone: 910-270-4347. Fax: 910-270-2293.

General Practice. Trials. Real Estate, Personal Injury, Automobile Accidents, Wrongful Death, Wills, Probate and Estate Planning, Corporate and Commercial Law, Taxation.

RICHARD VON BIBERSTEIN, JR., born Wilmington, North Carolina, December 23, 1935; admitted to bar, 1960, North Carolina; 1961, U.S. Court of Military Appeals; 1965, U.S. District Court, Eastern District of North Carolina; 1967, U.S. Court of Appeals, Fourth Circuit. *Education:* University of North Carolina (B.S., 1958; J.D., with honors, 1960). Phi Beta Kappa; Phi Delta Phi; Order of the Coif. Member, Student Board of Editors, North Carolina Law Review, 1958-1960. *Member:* Pender County, Fifth Judicial District, North Carolina and American Bar Associations; North Carolina State Bar; North Carolina Academy of Trial Lawyers; Defense Research Institute; Association of Defense Trial Attorneys. [Capt., J.A.G.C., U.S.A., active duty, 1960-1963]. ***PRACTICE AREAS:*** Litigation; Real Estate; Commercial; Wills; Trusts and Estates; Administrative Law; Land Use. **Email:** rvbbnlaw@bellsouth.net

(This Listing Continued)

MARK I. NUNALEE, born Burgaw, North Carolina, February 25, 1955; admitted to bar, 1981, North Carolina. *Education:* University of North Carolina at Chapel Hill (B.S., 1977; J.D., 1981). Beta Gamma Sigma. Certified Public Accountant, North Carolina, 1983. *Member:* Pender County and North Carolina Bar Associations; North Carolina State Bar; North Carolina Certified Public Accountant Association. ***PRACTICE AREAS:*** Taxation; Commercial; Corporate Law; Estate Planning; Administrative Law; Traffic Violations. **Email:** minbnlaw@bellsouth.net

COUNSEL FOR: Bank of America; Hedgecock Builders Supply Co.; Pender Memorial Hospital; Pender County Firefighters Assn.; Pender County Rescue Squad; Topsail Realty, Inc.; The Ullman Company, Inc.; Century 21 Action, Inc.
REPRESENTATIVE CLIENTS: Del Laboratories, Inc.; Pres-Tige Label Corp.; Martin-Marietta Corp.; The Nature Conservancy; Phoenix Technology, Ltd.; Robbins Nursery, Inc.; Old Ferry Marina, Inc.; Batts Properties, Inc.; H.W. Williams Lumber Company, Inc.; American Title Insurance Co.; Investors Title Insurance Co.; Century 21 Action, Inc.
APPROVED ATTORNEYS FOR: Lawyers Title Insurance Co.; Security Union Title Insurance Co.; United Title Insurance Co.; Investors Title Insurance Co.; Chicago Title Insurance Co.; The Title Co. of NC, Inc.; Cooperative Savings Bank; Carolina Savings Bank; Peoples Federal Savings Bank; First Union Mortgage Corp.; Wachovia Mortgage Co.; Farmers Home Administration; Bank of America Mortgage Co.; Farm Credit Service; RBC Centura.
REFERENCES: Bank of America; First Citizens Bank & Trust Co.

THE BOYETTE LAW FIRM

BURGAW, NORTH CAROLINA

(See Wilmington)

Family Law, Divorce, Custody, Visitation, Child Support, Adoption, Criminal Law, Traffic, DUI, White Collar Crimes.

CULBRETH LAW FIRM, L.L.P.

BURGAW, NORTH CAROLINA

(See Wilmington)

HALE & HARRELL

107 E. FREMONT
BURGAW, NORTH CAROLINA 28425
Telephone: 910-259-7772
Fax: 910-259-7796

Family Law, Criminal Law, Civil Litigation, Driving While Intoxicated, Traffic Offenses.

FIRM PROFILE: Our firm specializes in criminal defense and family law matters in the trial courts of North Carolina. Our attorneys are respected for their skill and advocacy in the court room. Our firm also handles commercial and residential real estate closings and litigation in Pender and Duplin County.

MEMBERS OF FIRM

CATHERINE HEWLETT-HALE, born Wilmington, North Carolina, June 5, 1957; admitted to bar, 1995, North Carolina. *Education:* University of North Carolina at Wilmington (B.S., magna cum laude, 1979); Campbell University (J.D., 1995). *Member:* North Carolina Academy of Trial Lawyers (Member, Criminal Defense Section). ***PRACTICE AREAS:*** Criminal Defense; Driving While Intoxicated; Traffic Violations. **Email:** chhatty@earthlink.net

R. KENT HARRELL, born Morehead City, North Carolina, August 13, 1970; admitted to bar, 1996, North Carolina. *Education:* University of North Carolina at Charlotte (B.A., 1992); North Carolina Central University(J.D., cum laude, 1996). *Member:* Pender County and North Carolina (Member, Family Law Committee) Bar Associations; North Carolina Academy of Trial Lawyers (Member, Criminal Defense Section). ***SPECIAL AGENCIES:*** Pender County Guardian Ad Litem Attorney Advocate. ***REPORTED CASES:*** In Re Matasich, 149 N.C. App. 975, 563 S.E.2d 309 (2002); Spencer v. Spencer, 156 N.C. App. 1, 575 S.E.2d 780 (2003). ***PRACTICE AREAS:*** Family Law; Criminal Defense; Traffic Violations; Real Estate; Civil Litigation. **Email:** kentharrell@bellsouth.net

MAKO & ASSOCIATES, P.A.

BURGAW, NORTH CAROLINA

(See Wilmington)

Personal Injury, Automobile Accidents, Wrongful Death, Trucking Accidents, Head Trauma, Spinal Cord Injuries, Motorcycle Accidents, Workers Compensation, Mediation and Arbitration, Birth Trauma, Medical Malpractice, Construction Accidents, Nursing Home Negligence, Nursing Home Abuse and Neglect and Dog Bites.

LISA R. BRENMAN

BURLINGTON, NORTH CAROLINA

(See Chapel Hill)

Family Immigration, Business Immigration, Labor Certification, Asylum, Student Visas, Citizenship.

LAW OFFICES OF R. LEE FARMER, P.L.L.C.

BURLINGTON, NORTH CAROLINA

(See Yanceyville)

General Civil and Criminal Practice in all State and Federal Courts. Probate, Real Estate, Personal Injury, Commercial, Construction, Administrative and Corporation Law.

HOLT, LONGEST, WALL & BLAETZ, P.L.L.C.

Established in 1952

407 SOUTH BROAD STREET
P.O. DRAWER 59
BURLINGTON, NORTH CAROLINA 27216
Telephone: 336-227-7461
FAX: 336-227-9716

General Practice in all State and Federal Courts. Trials, Corporation, Insurance, Taxation, Administrative, Real Estate and Probate Law.

FIRM PROFILE: The firm of Holt, Longest, Wall & Blaetz, P.L.L.C. has over 75 combined years of legal experience. The firm has offered continued legal services for over fifty years. The firm offers absolute integrity and the highest quality legal representation, and in so doing has earned Martindale-Hubbell's highest rating for legal ability and ethical conduct. Located in Burlington, the firm extends service to the surrounding areas, and maintains an active presence in community affairs.

W. CLARY HOLT (1913-2003)

FRANK A. LONGEST, JR., born Salisbury, North Carolina, November 2, 1945; admitted to bar, 1971, North Carolina; U.S. District Court Middle District of North Carolina; 1994, U.S. Supreme Court. *Education:* University of North Carolina (B.S. in B.A., 1967; J.D., 1971). Delta Theta Phi. Law Clerk, Chief Judge Walter E. Brock, North Carolina Court of Appeals, 1971-1972. City of Burlington Board of Education, 1989-1996. *Member:* Alamance County (Treasurer, 1983-1995; President, 1996), North Carolina and American (Member, Sections on: Corporation, Banking and Business Law; Taxation) Bar Associations; The North Carolina State Bar. ***PRACTICE AREAS:*** Corporate and Business Law; Business Transactions; Commercial Law; Employment Law; Civil Litigation. **Email:** falatty@netpath.net

N. MADISON WALL, II, born High Point, North Carolina, July 31, 1956; admitted to bar, 1981, North Carolina; 1988, U.S. District Court, Middle District of North Carolina; 1994, U.S. Supreme Court. *Education:* Davidson College (B.A., magna cum laude, 1978); University of North Carolina (J.D., 1981). Phi Beta Kappa; Omicron Delta Epsilon; Phi Delta Phi. *Member:* Alamance County, North Carolina and American Bar Associations; The North Carolina State Bar. ***PRACTICE AREAS:*** Real Estate; Business Law; Civil Litigation; Wills and Estates. **Email:** nmw2law@netpath.net

PETER T. BLAETZ, born Pittsburgh, Pennsylvania, May 24, 1959; admitted to bar, 1985, North Carolina; 1986, U.S. District Court, Middle District of North Carolina. *Education:* Grove City College (B.A., cum laude, 1981); Wake Forest University (J.D., 1985). Delta Mu Delta. *Member:* Alamance County, North Carolina and American Bar Associations; The North Carolina State Bar. (Board Certified Specialist in Estate Planning and Probate Law, North Carolina State Board of Legal Specialization). ***PRACTICE AREAS:*** Wills; Estate Planning and Administration; Business and Corporate Law; Elder Law. ***Email:*** ptbatty@netpath.net

COUNSEL FOR: Bank of America; H.E.A.D.S., Inc.; Alamacle Community College; AT&T Technologies; Piedmont Natural Gas Co.; Lawrence Industries; The Times-News Publishing Co., Inc.; Asheboro Honda; Honda Power Equipment Mfg., Inc.; Sandvik, Inc.; Tarheel Research, LH; Carolina-Koury Hosiery Mills, Inc.; Fairlane, Inc.; Fairystone Fabrics, Inc.; WBAG (Burlington); Goldsboro Automobiles, Inc.; Lynchburg Nissan; Allen's Hatchery; Vil-lane, Inc.; Nypro Carolina, Inc.; The Burlington Insurance Co.; Tarheel Nissan, Inc. (Reidsville, N.C.); United Electric Co. of Ohio, Inc.; Burlington-Lincoln Mercury Sales, Inc.; Nichols Dodge, Inc.; High Point Nissan, Inc.; U.S.F. & G. Co.; Nationwide Insurance Co.; Security Insurance Group; The South Carolina Insurance Co.; Integon; Orion Group; BellSouth PCS; Netpath, Inc.; Sue-Lynn Textiles, Inc.; Carolina Nissan, Inc.; Holt Hosiery Mills, Inc.; Asheboro Nissan; CV Products, Inc.; Motorsports Macking Technology, LLC; Xceldyne Technologies, LLC; Burlington Alamance County Association of Realtors; Burlington Honda.

APPROVED ATTORNEYS: Lawyers Title Insurance Corp.; Chicago Title Insurance Co.; First Title Insurance Co.; The Title Company of North Carolina, Inc.; Investors Title; First American Title Insurance Co.; Fidelity THE Insurance Company.

McENTIRE & DiLELLO

BURLINGTON, NORTH CAROLINA

(See Graham)

Criminal and Traffic, DWI, Municipal, Personal Injury and Estates.

THE QUINN LAW FIRM

BURLINGTON, NORTH CAROLINA

(See Greensboro)

Workers Compensation, Personal Injury, Automobile Accidents and Injuries, Employment Discrimination, Immigration.

SCHELL BRAY AYCOCK ABEL & LIVINGSTON P.L.L.C.

BURLINGTON, NORTH CAROLINA

(See Greensboro)

Corporate, Taxation, Securities Regulation, Venture Capital, Real Estate and Real Estate Finance, Mergers and Acquisitions, Health Care, Antitrust and Trade Regulation, Banking, Commercial, Employee Benefits, Estate Planning and Administration.

STEDMAN LAW FIRM

330 HOLLY HILL LANE
BURLINGTON, NORTH CAROLINA 27215
Telephone: 336-584-6472
Fax: 336-584-6479
Email: cnstedman@triadbiz.rr.com
URL: http://www.stedmanlaw.com

Personal Injury, Workers Compensation Injuries, Commercial & Residential Real Estate, Trusts, Estates & Wills, Business & Corporate Law.

CHARLES NORMAN "CHUCK" STEDMAN, born Moncure, North Carolina, February 22, 1945; admitted to bar, 1971, Tennessee; 1976, North Carolina and U.S. District Court, Middle District of North Carolina. *Education:* University of North Carolina (B.S., 1967); University of Tennessee (J.D., 1970). *Member:* North Carolina State Bar; North Carolina Academy of Trial Lawyers; The Association of Trial Lawyers of America. [With U.S. Marine Corps Reserve, 1967-1972; Corporal, U.S. Coast Guard Reserve, 1972-1973]. ***PRACTICE AREAS:*** Personal Injury; Workers Compensation; Real Estate; Commercial Real Estate; Residential Real Estate; Trusts and Estates; Wills; Business Law; Corporate Law. ***Email:*** cnstedman@triadbiz.rr.com

TUGGLE DUGGINS & MESCHAN, P.A.

BURLINGTON, NORTH CAROLINA

(See Greensboro)

General Civil Practice. Corporation, Tax, Insurance, Banking, Pension and Profit Sharing, Bankruptcy and Creditors' Rights, Trust and Estate, Construction and Real Estate Law. Trials and Appeals in all State and Federal Courts.

STUART N. WATLINGTON

BURLINGTON, NORTH CAROLINA

(See Yanceyville)

General Civil and Criminal Practice in all State and Federal Courts. DWI, Traffic Violations, Personal Injury, Wrongful Death, Probate, Real Estate.

WISHART, NORRIS, HENNINGER & PITTMAN, P.A.

Established in 1976

3120 SOUTH CHURCH STREET
P.O. BOX 1998
BURLINGTON, NORTH CAROLINA 27215-9114
Telephone: 336-584-3388
FAX: 336-584-3994
Email: derek.steed@wnhplaw.com
URL: http://www.wnhplaw.com

Charlotte, North Carolina Office: 6832 Morrison Boulevard. Telephone: 704-364-0010. FAX: 704-365-5945; 704-364-0569.

Mebane, North Carolina Office: 111 East Center Street. Telephone: 919-304-4200. FAX: 919-304-4207.

Arbitration, Appellate Practice, Business Law, Civil Litigation, Commercial and Residential Real Estate, Contracts, Corporate and Commercial Law, Creditor Bankruptcy, Employment Law, Environmental Law, Estate Administration, Estate Planning, Family Law, Federal and State Taxation, Financial Transactions, Franchise Matters, Investments, Joint Ventures and Partnerships, Limited Liability Companies, Mediation, Mergers and Acquisitions, Securities, Succession Planning, Tax Controversy, Wills and Trusts, Zoning, Planning and Land Use, Criminal and Traffic Matters, Elder Law.

FIRM PROFILE: Wishart Norris Henninger & Pittman, P.A. was founded in Burlington, NC, in 1976. The firm has grown from three attorneys to thirty-three attorneys with similar sized offices in both Burlington and Charlotte. The firm also staffs a separate office in Mebane, NC. The firm's growth has been internal rather than by merger.

The firm has built a highly successful practice concentrating on the goals, objectives and needs of closely-held businesses and their owners. Our four core values reflect this concentration. We believe in forging relationships that last with our clients. We believe we must be able to provide the wisdom to reveal optimum solutions for our clients. We encourage a bond of open communication with us and easy access to us for our clients. We are committed to transforming the business of law to meet the needs of business.

We strive to be the firm of choice for entrepreneurs and owners of closely-held businesses who need skilled legal assistance with every aspect of their business, including mergers and acquisitions, succession planning, and estate planning. In addition, the firm handles civil and commercial litigation, commercial and residential real estate transactions, tax controversy, estate administration matters, franchise law matters and family law matters.

(This Listing Continued)

WISHART, NORRIS, HENNINGER & PITTMAN, P.A., Burlington—Continued

ROBERT J. WISHART, born St. Johnsbury, Vermont, February 20, 1944; admitted to bar, 1973, North Carolina; 1974, U.S. District Court, Middle and Eastern Districts of North Carolina and U.S. Court of Appeals, Fourth Circuit. *Education:* Middlebury College (B.A., 1966); University of North Carolina (J.D., with honors, 1973). Order of the Coif. Law Clerk to Judge Eugene A. Gordon, U.S. District Court, Middle District of North Carolina, 1973-1974. *Member:* Alamance County and North Carolina Bar Associations; North Carolina State Bar; North Carolina Association of Defense Attorneys; Defense Research Institute. [Capt., U.S. Army, 1966-1968]. ***PRACTICE AREAS:*** Civil Litigation; Product Liability Law; Municipal Law; Employment Law. ***Email:*** robert.wishart@wnhplaw.com

DORN C. PITTMAN, JR., born Winston-Salem, North Carolina, August 14, 1948; admitted to bar, 1977, North Carolina. *Education:* Wake Forest University (B.B.A., 1971; M.B.A., 1973; J.D., 1977). Certified Public Accountant, North Carolina, 1973. *Member:* North Carolina Bar Association; North Carolina State Bar; North Carolina Association of Certified Public Accountants. ***PRACTICE AREAS:*** Corporate Law; Commercial Transactions; Taxation. ***Email:*** dorn.pittman@wnhplaw.com

WADE HARRISON, born Asheville, North Carolina, May 25, 1954; admitted to bar, 1979, North Carolina. *Education:* University of North Carolina (B.A., 1976; J.D., 1979). Certified Family Law Financial Mediator. Assistant Counsel, Judiciary Subcommittee, U.S. House of Representatives, 1981-1983. Legal Assistant to Congressman Lamar Gudger, 1979-1980. *Member:* North Carolina State Bar; North Carolina Bar Association (Member: Litigation Section Council, 1991-1993; Family Law Section Council, 1993-2000, Ex Officio 2001—; Chair, Alternate Dispute Resolution Committee, 1995-1996; Co-Chair, Legislative Committee, 1997; Administrative Office of the Courts Custody Mediation Advisory Committee; Chair, Long Range Legislative Task Force, 1998-2002; Chair, Family Law Section, 1999-2000); Alternate Dispute Resolution Committee of the North Carolina Judicial Council. Fellow, American Academy of Matrimonial Lawyers. (Board Certified Specialist in Family Law, North Carolina State Board of Legal Specialization). ***PRACTICE AREAS:*** Family Law; Equitable Distribution; Child Custody; Support; Alimony; Adoption. ***Email:*** wade.harrison@wnhplaw.com

BRIAN P. GAVIGAN, born Chicago, Illinois, September 21, 1959; admitted to bar, 1984, Maryland and U.S. Court of the Armed Forces; 1991, North Carolina. *Education:* University of Maryland (B.A., 1981; J.D., 1984). *Member:* North Carolina Bar Association (Member, Health Law Section); North Carolina State Bar; North Carolina Society of Health Care Attorneys (Vice-President, 1996-1997; President, 1997-1998); American Health Lawyers Association. [U.S. Air Force, Judge Advocate, Captain, 1985-1990]. ***PRACTICE AREAS:*** Health Care Law; Employment Law; Commercial Transactions. ***Email:*** brian.gavigan@wnhplaw.com

C. THOMAS STEELE, JR., born Sylva, North Carolina, July 15, 1962; admitted to bar, 1987, North Carolina. *Education:* University of North Carolina at Asheville (B.S., with distinction, 1984); University of North Carolina (J.D., 1987). Phi Alpha Delta. Awarded J. Nelson Young Tax Scholarship. Certified Public Accountant, North Carolina, 2001. Author: "Mandatory Student Fees at Public Universities: Bringing The First Amendment Within the Campus Gate," 13 Journal of College and University Law 353, Spring 1987. Inducted into the James R. and Carolyn B. Davis Society of the University of North Carolina School of Law, 1987. *Member:* Alamance County (Secretary, 1988-1996), North Carolina (Council Treasurer, 2005-2006 and Member, Real Property Section; Chairman, Legislative Committee, 2004-2005) and American Bar Associations; American Land Title Association; North Carolina Land Title Association. (Board Certified Specialist in Real Property Law-Residential, Business, Commercial and Industrial Transactions). ***PRACTICE AREAS:*** Real Estate Law; Trusts and Estates; Estate Planning Law; Foreclosures; Partitions; Residential Real Estate; Commercial Real Estate Transactions; Zoning Law. ***Email:*** tom.steele@wnhplaw.com

PAMELA S. DUFFY, born Weston, Connecticut, June 24, 1967; admitted to bar, 1991, North Carolina. *Education:* Boston University (B.A., with distinction, 1988); Marshall-Wythe School of Law, College of William and Mary (J.D., 1991). *Member:* North Carolina Bar Association; North Carolina State Bar. ***PRACTICE AREAS:*** Civil Litigation; Commercial Litigation; Employment Litigation. ***Email:*** pamela.duffy@wnhplaw.com

JOSEPH J. KALO, IV, born Flint, Michigan, July 2, 1968; admitted to bar, 1994, North Carolina; 1997, South Carolina; U.S. District Court, Eastern, Middle and Western Districts of North Carolina. *Education:* Vanderbilt University (B.A., 1990); University of North Carolina (J.D., 1994). *Member:* North Carolina (Member, Real Property Section) and American (Member, Real Property, Probate and Trust Law Section) Bar Associations; South Carolina Bar (Member, Real Property Practice Section). (Board Certified Specialist in Real Property Law-Residential, Commercial, Business and Industrial Transactions, North Carolina State Board of Legal Specialization). ***LANGUAGES:*** German. ***PRACTICE AREAS:*** Real Estate; Zoning, Planning and Land Use; Real Estate Litigation. ***Email:*** joseph.kalo@wnhplaw.com

DEREK B. STEED, born Albuquerque, New Mexico, July 27, 1972; admitted to bar, 1997, North Carolina. *Education:* West Virginia Wesleyan College (B.A., summa cum laude, 1994); University of North Carolina at Chapel Hill (J.D., 1997). Phi Kappa Phi. Member, Holderness Moot Court. Vice-Chairman, Alamance County Area Chamber of Commerce, 2004-2005. Chairman, Alamance County Sports Development Council, 2004-2005. Volunteer of the Year, Chamber of Commerce, 2003. Director of the Year, Chamber of Commerce, 2004. Member, Board of Directors, Alamance County Meals on Wheels, 1998-2004. *Member:* Alamance County (Member, Board of Directors, 2003-2005), North Carolina (Member, Labor and Employment Law Section) and American (Member, Business Law Section) Bar Associations. ***PRACTICE AREAS:*** Business Law; Corporate Law; Mergers and Acquisitions. ***Email:*** derek.steed@wnhplaw.com

ASSOCIATES

DAWN D. ALLEN, born November 3, 1968; admitted to bar, 2002, North Carolina. *Education:* Elon College (B.A., magna cum laude); North Carolina Central University (J.D., 2002). *Member:* Alamance County and North Carolina Bar Associations; North Carolina State Bar. ***PRACTICE AREAS:*** District Court Litigation; Traffic Offenses; Personal Injury; Criminal Law; Criminal Defense; Driving While Intoxicated; Misdemeanors; Theft; Traffic Violations. ***Email:*** dawn.allen@wnhplaw.com

JILL S. BRITT, born Smithfield, North Carolina, August 17, 1968; admitted to bar, 1993, North Carolina. *Education:* Salem College (B.A., magna cum laude, 1990); University of North Carolina at Chapel Hill (J.D., 1993). *Member:* North Carolina Bar Association (Member, Real Property Section); North Carolina State Bar. ***PRACTICE AREAS:*** Real Property. ***Email:*** jill.britt@wnhplaw.com

HILLARY DAVIS WHITAKER, born Naples, Florida, July 2, 1970; admitted to bar, 1995, North Carolina. *Education:* Davidson College (B.A., 1992); Wake Forest University (J.D., 1995). *Member:* North Carolina State Bar (Member, Family Law Section). ***PRACTICE AREAS:*** Family Law. ***Email:*** hillary.whitaker@wnhplaw.com

CHARLIE D. BROWN, born Smithfield, North Carolina, March 17, 1970; admitted to bar, 1997, North Carolina. *Education:* Wake Forest University (B.A., magna cum laude, 1992; M.B.A., 1997; J.D., 1997). Honor Scholar. Recipient: Charles Babcock Scholarship; A.J. Fletcher Music Scholarship; Excellence in Communication distinction (awarded by department to most outstanding communication major). Business Symposium Editor, Wake Forest Law Review. ***PRACTICE AREAS:*** Estate Planning and Administration; Elder Law; Special Needs Planning; Pooled Trusts; Asset Protection. ***Email:*** charlie@wnhplaw.com

ROBERT C. GILES, II, born Burlington, North Carolina; admitted to bar, 2002, North Carolina. *Education:* University of North Carolina at Chapel Hill (B.M., 1999); North Carolina Central University (J.D., magna cum laude, 2002). ***PRACTICE AREAS:*** Employment Law; Civil Litigation. ***Email:*** robert.giles@wnhplaw.com

NATHAN R. ADAMS, born Winston-Salem, North Carolina, September 22, 1974; admitted to bar, 1999, North Carolina; 2000, South Carolina. *Education:* University of North Carolina at Chapel Hill (B.A., 1995); Wake Forest University (J.D., cum laude, 1999), University of Florida (LL.M., Tax, 2004). Order of the Coif. Member, Wake Forest Law Review. *Member:* North Carolina State Bar; South Carolina Bar. ***PRACTICE AREAS:*** Tax; Business; Estate Planning. ***Email:*** nathan.adams@wnhplaw.com

MOLLY A. ORNDORFF, born Charles Town, West Virigina, 1976; admitted to bar, 2005, North Carolina. *Education:* Elon College (B.A., summa cum laude, 1999); Wake Forest University (J.D., 2005). ***PRACTICE AREAS:*** Business Law; Business Litigation. ***Email:*** molly.orndorff@wnhplaw.com

REPRESENTATIVE CLIENTS: Glen Raven Mills, LLC.; Synthon Pharmaceuticals; Madison River Communications, LLC; Burlington Insurance Group; Town of Elon; W.E. Love & Associates; Burlington Alamance Regional Airport; Sasser Construction; Radiator Specialty Company; First Trust Bank; Z.V. Pate, Inc.; NewDominion Bank; First Charter Bank; Juba Aluminum Products, Inc; Premier Alliance Group, Inc; Overhead Door Company of Charlotte; B & B Contracting, Inc.; Carolina Beer & Beverage Company, LLC; Internetwork Services, Inc; Environmental Drying Services, Inc.; Details, Inc.; Preferred Packagaing, Inc.; Holt Sublimation Printing & Products, Inc.; Perma-Flex Roller Technology; Sound Choice; Marolf Construction, Inc.; The Signature Companies, LLC; Design Strategies, LLC; American Asset Corporation; National Benefits Administrators, Inc; Integraphx, Inc.; Milestone Partners, LLC; Curtin Brothers Contracting; Jenkins Electric Company; Hall Contracting Co., Inc; Slade, Inc; LYF-TYM Building Products Co., Inc.; Choice USA Beverage, Inc.
APPROVED ATTORNEYS FOR: Lawyers Title Insurance Corp.; Chicago Title Insurance Co.; American Title Insurance Co.; Jefferson-Pilot Title Insurance Co.; Investors Title Insurance Co.

(For complete biographical data on other personnel, see Professional Biographies at Charlotte, North Carolina)

JEFFCOAT, PIKE & NAPPIER, LLC

Established in 1994

10150 BEACH DRIVE SW, UNIT 1
P.O. BOX 44000
CALABASH, NORTH CAROLINA 28467
Telephone: 910-579-4050
Telecopier: 910-579-2770
Email: info@jeffcoatlaw.com
URL: http://www.jeffcoatlaw.com

Myrtle Beach, South Carolina Office: 2024 Corporate Centre Drive, Suite 206, 29577. Telephone: 843-626-9000. Telecopier: 843-448-1914. Email: info@jeffcoatlaw.com.

North Myrtle Beach, South Carolina Office: 110 Ye Olde Kings Highway, P.O. Box 4360, 29597-4360. Telephone: 843-249-3581. Telecopier: 843-249-6231. Email: info@jeffcoatlaw.com.

Pawleys Island, South Carolina Office: True Blue Executive Center, 9841 Ocean Highway, Suite D, 29585. Telephone: 843-235-0300. Telecopier: 843-235-2056. Email: info@jeffcoatlaw.com.

Real Estate, Estate Planning and Probate, Construction Law, Corporate/Business Law, Auto Accidents, Personal Injury and Homeowners Association Law, Elder Law, Wrongful Death, Real Estate, Commercial real Estate, Real Estate Development, Residential Real Estate Business Law, Contracts, Construction Law, Leases and Leasing, Trusts and Estates, Probate, Wills, Guardianship and Conservatorship, Personal Injury, Wrongful Death, Collections, Homeowners Association Law, foreclosures, Auto Accidents and Injuries, Estate Planning.

FIRM PROFILE: Jeffcoat, Pike & Nappier, LLC provides a broad array of legal services to business and individual clients. We bring a dedication to quality and effective representation to each of those clients. As a multi-office law firm with a team approach, we are well situated to serve your legal needs. The firm has a long established practice in residential and commercial real estate law, and estate planning and probate law. Our commitment to family law is evident in our success in this area, and we maintain a thriving practice in litigation/personal injury and traffic violation issues. We are also experienced in business law, with issues ranging from business formation to stock transfers. You'll find that our attorneys' experience and depth in their practice areas is second to none. They also possess strong academic credentials, maintain ongoing community ties, and demonstrate the highest level of personal and professional ethics. Our dedication to quality, understanding of the law, trust, and respect are the foundation for a long-standing relationship both with clients and with the community.

(This Listing Continued)

PARTNERS

OTIS ALLEN JEFFCOAT, III (Also at Myrtle Beach, North Myrtle Beach and Pawleys Island, South Carolina Offices)

MARK A. NAPPIER (Also at Myrtle Beach, North Myrtle Beach and Pawleys Island, South Carolina Offices)

ASSOCIATES

AMIE SLOANE (Also at Pawleys Island, Myrtle Beach and North Myrtle Beach Offices)

J. HARRISON RUSHTON (Resident)

LEGAL SUPPORT PERSONNEL

EDIE VIPPERMAN (Real Estate Paralegal)

LAURIE BUTTERWORTH

BARBARA J. STEGMAIER. Email: bstegmaier@jeffcoatlaw.com

(For Complete Biographical Data on all Personnel, see Professional Biographies at Myrtle Beach, South Carolina)

TREST & TWIGG

9580 OCEAN HIGHWAY WEST
CALABASH, NORTH CAROLINA 28467
Telephone: 910-575-7337
Fax: 910-575-7338
Email: TrestTwigg@atmc.net

General Litigation Practice, Probate, Personal Injury, Wrongful Death, Civil Litigation, Criminal Law, Traffic Violations, DWI.

MEMBERS OF FIRM

ROY D. TREST, born Conway, South Carolina, December 21, 1948; admitted to bar, 1977, North Carolina. *Education:* University of North Carolina (B.S., 1970); University of Mississippi (J.D., 1977). Phi Alpha Delta. District Court Judge, 1979-1984. Certified Mediator, North Carolina. *Member:* North Carolina and American Bar Associations; North Carolina State Bar; North Carolina Academy of Trial Lawyers (Board of Governors, 1990-1996); American Trial Lawyers Association. ***PRACTICE AREAS:*** Criminal Law; Civil Litigation; Personal Injury; Automobile Accidents and Injuries; Wrongful Death; Traffic Violations; Driving While Intoxicated. ***Email:*** rtrest@atmc.net

TONIA TREST TWIGG, born Asheville, North Carolina, March 8, 1973; admitted to bar, 2002, North Carolina. *Education:* University of North Carolina at Chapel Hill (B.A., 1995); Meredith College (Paralegal Certification, 1998); North Carolina Central University (J.D., 2002). *Member:* North Carolina and American Bar Associations; North Carolina State Bar; North Carolina Academy of Trial Lawyers; Association of Trial Lawyers of America; North Carolina Association of Women Attorneys; Christian Legal Society. ***PRACTICE AREAS:*** Criminal Law; Civil Litigation; Probate; Traffic Violations; Personal Injury; Automobile Accidents and Injuries. ***Email:*** ttwigg@atmc.net

THE VINCENT LAW FIRM, PC

CAMDEN, NORTH CAROLINA

(See Southern Shores)

Workers Compensation, Personal Injury, Auto Accidents, Social Security Disability, Wrongful Death and Admiralty Longshores.

BLANCHARD, NEWMAN & HAYES

CANDLER, NORTH CAROLINA

(See Hendersonville)

General Civil Litigation, Family Law, Divorce, Criminal in all State and Federal Courts, Traffic, DWI.

LISA R. BRENMAN

CARRBORO, NORTH CAROLINA

(See Carrboro)

Family Immigration, Business Immigration, Labor Certification, Asylum, Student Visas, Citizenship.

THE VIRA LAW FIRM, PA

205 W. MAIN STREET, SUITE 207
CARRBORO, NORTH CAROLINA 27510
Telephone: 919-918-8000
Fax: 919-918-7887
Email: lisa_vira@nc.rr.com
URL: http://www.lisakvira.com

Durham Office: 133 Celeste Circle, 27517. Telephone: 919-918-8000. Fax: 919-918-7887.

Trusts and Estates, Probate, Wills, Real Estate, Taxation, Business Law.

LISA KHIM VIRA, born Mobile, Alabama, March 25, 1970; admitted to bar, 2000, North Carolina and U.S. District Court, Middle District of North Carolina. *Education:* Auburn University (B.S., 1992); North Carolina Central University (J.D., 2000). Ambassador, Chapel Hill-Carrboro Chamber of Commerce. *Member:* Orange County Bar Association; North Carolina State Bar. ***PRACTICE AREAS:*** Trusts and Estates; Probate; Wills; Real Estate; Taxation; Business Law. ***Email:*** lisa_vira@nc.rr.com

MORRIS LAW OFFICE

CARTHAGE, NORTH CAROLINA

(See Whispering Pines)

Criminal Law, Felonies and Misdemeanors, Traffic Violations and Tickets, Trucks, Motorcycles, Driving While Intoxicated, DUI, Animal Law, Equine, Horse Rights and Trusts, Veterans Benefits and Appeals.

HURLEY E. THOMPSON, JR.

Established in 1973
208 MONROE STREET
P.O. BOX 1300
CARTHAGE, NORTH CAROLINA 28327
Telephone: 910-947-5141; 1-800-756-5943
Facsimile: 910-947-2709
Email: hurthom@mindspring.com

Residential Real Property, Foreclosure, Traffic Offenses, Wills, Estates, Personal Injury.

HURLEY E. THOMPSON, JR., born Monroe, North Carolina, September 13, 1946; admitted to bar, 1973, North Carolina. *Education:* University of North Carolina (A.B., 1968; J.D., 1973). Delta Theta Phi. *Member:* Moore County (Secretary, 1977; President-Elect, 1980; President, 1981), 20th Judicial District and North Carolina Bar Associations; North Carolina State Bar. ***PRACTICE AREAS:*** Real Property; Real Estate Finance; Real Estate Foreclosure; Mortgage Finance.

REPRESENTATIVE CLIENTS: Branch Bank & Trust Co.; The Fidelity Bank; Bank of America; Cendant Mobility Financial Services; RBC Centura Bank; First Bank; Farm Credit Service; Wachovia Bank; First National Bank and Trust.
APPROVED ATTORNEY FOR: Lawyers Title Insurance Corp.; Commonwealth Land Title Insurance Co.; First Title Insurance Co.; Investors Title Insurance Co.; St. Paul Title Insurance Corp.; United Title Insurance Co.; Chicago Title Insurance Co.; Consumers Title Co.; First American Title Co.
REFERENCES: The Fidelity Bank, Carthage; First Bank, Southern Pines; Bank of America; Pinehurst Branch Bank & Trust Co., Carthage, N.C.; RBC Centura.

VAN CAMP, MEACHAM & NEWMAN, PLLC

CARTHAGE, NORTH CAROLINA

(See Pinehurst)

General Civil and Criminal Litigation and Appellate Practice in State and Federal Courts. Personal Injury, Commercial, Medical Malpractice, Wrongful Death, Worker's Compensation, Insurance, Land Condemnation, Constitutional and Civil Rights, Family, Corporate, Real Estate, Administrative, Social Security Disability, Construction Law, Labor and Employment, Wills, Estate Planning and Probate Law.

ALEXANDER & DOYLE, P.A.

Established in 1995
523 KEISLER DRIVE, SUITE 102
CARY, NORTH CAROLINA 27511
Telephone: 919-380-1001
Fax: 919-380-4099
Email: info@alexanderdoylelaw.com
URL: http://www.alexander-doylelaw.com

Family Law, Child Custody, Child Support, Spousal Support, Domestic Violence, Adoptions, Termination of Parental Rights, Wills, Trusts and Estates, Probate Law, Criminal Law (Misdemeanors), Traffic Law.

FIRM PROFILE: The firm was established in 1995 by Ann-Margaret Alexander and Andrea Nyren Doyle. Although we practice primarily in the area of family law and adoption, we also represent clients in the areas of wills, estates and trusts, traffic and criminal law. Our clients are important to us. We believe it is important that each client be treated with respect.

ANN-MARGARET ALEXANDER, born Florence, South Carolina, October 8, 1966; admitted to bar, 1995, North Carolina. *Education:* University of South Carolina (B.A., 1988); North Carolina Central University (J.D., cum laude, 1995). *Member:* Wake County (Member, Family Law Section) and North Carolina (Member, Family Law Section) Bar Associations; North Carolina State Bar. ***PRACTICE AREAS:*** Family Law; Custody; Child Support; Spousal Support; Domestic Violence; Adoption Law; Termination of Parental Rights; Wills; Trusts and Estates; Probate; Criminal Law; Misdemeanors; Traffic Violations. ***Email:*** ann-margaret@alexanderdoylelaw.com

ANDREA S. NYREN DOYLE, born St. Cloud, Minnesota, December 26, 1968; admitted to bar, 1995, North Carolina. *Education:* East Carolina University (B.S., 1991); North Carolina Central University (J.D., 1995). *Member:* Wake County and North Carolina (Member, Family Law Section) Bar Associations; North Carolina State Bar. ***PRACTICE AREAS:*** Family Law; Child Custody; Child Support; Spousal Support; Domestic Violence; Adoption Law; Termination of Parental Rights; Wills; Trusts and Estates; Probate; Criminal Law; Misdemeanors; Traffic Violations. ***Email:*** andreadoyle@alexanderdoylelaw.com

ARANEDA LAW FIRM, P.C.

CARY, NORTH CAROLINA

(See Raleigh)

Immigration Law, Business Immigration, Citizenship, Consular Law, Employment Authorizations, Employment Immigration, Employment Visas, Family Immigration Law, Labor Certifications, Permanent Visas, Religious Visas, Visas, Federal Criminal Law, Immigration Defense.

BAILEY & DIXON, L.L.P.

CARY, NORTH CAROLINA

(See Raleigh)

General Civil Trial, Appellate and Administrative Practice. Litigation: Insurance Regulation, Defense of Personal Injury and Professional Malpractice Claims, Commercial Litigation, Including Environmental Law, Employment Law, Insurance Coverage Disputes, Construction, Land Use, Municipal and Police Liability, Products Liability, Drug and Medical Device Liability, Business Torts, and Workers' Compensation. Administrative Law: Public Utilities, Including Electric, Telecommunications, Gas, Transportation, Water and Sewer. Professional and Occupational Licensing, Healthcare, Labor and Employment Law, Business and Corporate Law, Commercial Real Estate, Estate Administration and Taxation.

THE LAW OFFICES OF OMAR BALOCH

CARY, NORTH CAROLINA

(See Raleigh)

Immigration, Traffic Violations, Personal Injury, Small Business and Business Enterprises.

BARRINGER LAW FIRM, LLP

Established in 1986

111 COMMONWEALTH COURT, SUITE 101
P.O. BOX 5566
CARY, NORTH CAROLINA 27511
Telephone: 919-467-6700
Telecopier: 919-481-9190
Email: admin@barringerlaw.com

Corporate and Business, Estate Planning and Administration. Real Estate, Development and Construction Law, Community Associations, Tax.

MEMBERS OF FIRM

BRENT D. BARRINGER, born Quantico, Virginia, April 3, 1959; admitted to bar, 1984, North Carolina; 1985, U.S. District Court, Western, Eastern and Middle Districts of North Carolina and U.S. Court of Appeals, Fourth Circuit; U.S. Tax Court. *Education:* University of North Carolina (B.S., in Business Administration, with Highest Honors, 1981; J.D., 1984). Co-Author: "The 1982 Merger Guidelines: If Too Lenient, Why No Old Style Schlitz or Blue Ribbon?" American Business Law Journal, Vol. 22. Law Clerk, Hon. Eugene A. Gordon, Senior U.S. District Judge, Middle District of North Carolina, 1984-1985. Visiting Lecturer, Business Law, Kenan-Flagler School of Business Administration, University of North Carolina, Chapel Hill, 1987. Chairman, Cary Chamber of Commerce Board of Directors, 1995-1996. Member: Centennial Authority of the RBC Center, 1995—. Charter Board of Directors, Crescent State Bank, 1998—. University of North Carolina System Board of Governors, 2003-2007. *Member:* Wake County and North Carolina Bar Associations; North Carolina State Bar. ***PRACTICE AREAS:*** Corporate and Business; Commercial Real Estate; Residential Development. ***Email:*** brent@barringerlaw.com

TAMARA BARRINGER, born Shelby, North Carolina, December 1, 1958; admitted to bar, 1985, North Carolina and U.S. Tax Court; U.S. District Court, Eastern District of North Carolina. *Education:* University of North Carolina (B.S. in Business Administration, with Highest Honors, 1981; J.D., with honors, 1985). Order of the Coif. Staff Member, University of North Carolina Law Review, 1983-1984. Author: "*Payne v. Cone Mills Corp.:* Should a Doctor's Suspicions Bar a Plaintiff's Meritorious Claim," North Carolina Law Review, Vol. 62. Co-Author: "The Credit Card Fraud Act of 1984: Clarification, or Further Confusion of the Law of Credit Card Fraud?" American Business Law Journal, Vol. 24. Adjunct Professor, Business Law: North Carolina State University, 1989-1993; Meredith College, 1989, 1991, 1995. Visiting Assistant Professor, Kenan-Flagler School of Business Administration, University of North Carolina, Chapel Hill, 1994 and 1996. Member, Carolina Ballet Executive Board, 2003—. Public Member, N.C. House Interim Committee on Child Abuse and Neglect, Foster Care, and Adoption, 2003-2004. *Member:* Wake County and North Carolina Bar Associations (Chairman, Law Practice Management Section, 1997-1998); North Carolina State Bar. ***PRACTICE AREAS:*** Estate Planning; Estate Administration. ***Email:*** tamara@barringerlaw.com

ASSOCIATE

THOMAS J. SCHUETTPELZ, born Janesville, Wisconsin, 1973; admitted to bar, 1998, North Carolina and U.S. District Court, Eastern District of North Carolina. *Education:* Marquette University (B.A., magna cum laude, 1995); Wake Forest University, School of Law (J.D., 1998). Member, Wake Forest Law Review. Deputy Legal Counsel, North Carolina Republican Party, 2002—. *Member:* Wake County and North Carolina Bar Associations. ***PRACTICE AREAS:*** Business Law; Real Estate; Wills; Trust Law. ***Email:*** tom@barringerlaw.com

COUNSEL FOR: MacGregor Development Co.; Smithfield's Chicken 'N Bar-B-Q Companies; Subway Companies; Howarth Family Dental Center; Rufty Homes, Inc.; Data Sign Systems, Inc.; Cary Diagnostic Radiology, P.A.
REFERENCES: Branch Banking & Trust Co.; Crescent State Bank; Central Carolina Bank.

THE BREWER LAW FIRM

CARY, NORTH CAROLINA

(See Raleigh)

Bankruptcy (Debtors and Noninstitutional Creditors), Consumer and Business Bankruptcy.

DEWEY P. BRINKLEY

CARY, NORTH CAROLINA

(See Raleigh)

Criminal Law, Driving While Intoxicated, DWI, Traffic Violations, Drug Crimes, Parole and Probation, Juvenile Crimes, White Collar Crimes.

BROOKS, STEVENS & POPE, P.A.

11000 REGENCY PARKWAY, SUITE 401
P.O. BOX 1870
CARY, NORTH CAROLINA 27512-1870
Telephone: 919-481-9103
Fax: 919-481-9137
URL: http://www.bsp-pa.com

General Civil and Appellate Practice, Employment Law, OSHA, Workers' Compensation, Insurance, Self-Insurance, Municipal and Family Law.

FIRM PROFILE: We serve the entire state of North Carolina including the Wake County area. The firm is listed in Martindale-Hubbell's Register of Preeminent Lawyers.

DAVID VICTOR BROOKS (Retired)

ROBERT H. STEVENS, JR. (Retired)

DANIEL CARTER POPE, JR., born Washington. D.C., April 11,1964; admitted to bar, 1988, North Carolina; 1994, U.S. Supreme Court. *Education:* North Carolina State University (B.A., 1985); University of North Carolina School of Law (J.D., 1988). Clerk, North Carolina Industrial Commission, 1988-1989. Adjunct Faculty, Occupational Safety and Health Educational Resources Center, University of North Carolina at Chapel Hill. ***PRACTICE AREAS:*** Workers' Compensation.

MICHAEL C. SIGMON, born Raleigh, North Carolina, July 8, 1961; admitted to bar, 1986, North Carolina. *Education:* North Carolina State University (B.A., cum laude, 1983); University of North Carolina, School of Law (J.D., 1986). ***PRACTICE AREAS:*** General Civil Practice; Workers' Compensation.

KATHLYN CORBETT HOBBS, born New York, N.Y., February 13, 1962; admitted to bar, 1991, Connecticut; 1992, New York and North Carolina. *Education:* University of New Hampshire (B.A., 1983); Widener University (J.D., 1991). Phi Delta Phi. ***PRACTICE AREAS:*** Workers' Compensation.

ROBERT S. WELCH, born Clarksburg, West Virginia, September 3, 1958; admitted to bar, 1988, North Carolina; 1989, U.S. Court of Military Appeals; 1992, U.S. Supreme Court. *Education:* West Virginia University (B.A., 1981; M.A., 1984); Campbell University (J.D., 1988). Delta Theta Phi. [Lt. JAGC, USNR, 1988-1993]. ***PRACTICE AREAS:*** Workers' Compensation.

JOY H. BREWER, born Fort Lauderdale, Florida, January 23, 1971; admitted to bar, 1996, North Carolina. *Education:* University of North Carolina at Chapel Hill (B.A., 1993); Campbell University (J.D., 1996). Law Clerk to Associate Justice Robert F. Orr, North Carolina Supreme Court, 1996-1998. ***PRACTICE AREAS:*** Workers' Compensation; Appellate Practice.

MATTHEW P. BLAKE, born Chapel Hill, North Carolina, May 21, 1972; admitted to bar, 1998, North Carolina. *Education:* Wake Forest University (B.A., 1994); Campbell University (J.D., 1998). Law Clerk to Judge Donald Smith, North Carolina Court of Appeals, 1998-1999; Judge Bob Edmunds, North Carolina Court of Appeals, 1999. ***PRACTICE AREAS:*** Workers' Compensation.

CATHY H. ELKINS, born Ft. Leonard Wood, Missouri, October 8, 1959; admitted to bar, 1987, North Carolina. *Education:* Coe College (B.A., 1982); University of North Carolina School of Law (J.D., 1987). ***PRACTICE AREAS:*** Workers' Compensation.

BAMBEE B. BLAKE, born Bristol, Tennessee, December 5, 1970; admitted to bar, 1995, North Carolina and U.S. District Court, Eastern District of North Carolina; 1996, South Carolina. *Education:* University of North Carolina at Chapel Hill (B.A., English, 1992); Campbell University (J.D., 1995). ***PRACTICE AREAS:*** Workers' Compensation.

KIMBERLEY A. D'ARRUDA, born Raleigh, North Carolina, November 16, 1972; admitted to bar, 1998, North Carolina; 2003, U.S. District Court, Eastern District of North Carolina. *Education:* University of North Carolina (B.S.B.A., 1995); Campbell University (J.D., magna cum laude, 1998). Law Clerk for Justices Mark D. Martin and George Wainwright, North Carolina Supreme Court, 1998-2000. *Member:* North Carolina State Bar. ***PRACTICE AREAS:*** Workers' Compensation; Appellate Practice; Wills; Trusts and Estates.

LESLIE SUDBURY HAYDEL, born South Bend, Indiana, May 28, 1966; admitted to bar, 1992, North Carolina. *Education:* Xavier University of Louisiana (B.A., cum laude, 1988); Notre Dame University (J.D., 1991). ***PRACTICE AREAS:*** Workers' Compensation.

JOEL J. HARDISON, born Greenville, North Carolina, May 18, 1976; admitted to bar, 2004, North Carolina. *Education:* University of North Carolina at Chapel Hill (B.A., 1999; J.D., 2004). ***PRACTICE AREAS:*** Workers' Compensation. ***Email:*** jhardison@bsp-pa.com

(This Listing Continued)

REBECCA J. LIVERT, born Charlotte, North Carolina, November 8, 1978; admitted to bar, 2005, North Carolina. *Education:* University of North Carolina at Chapel Hill (BA., 2001); Campbell University (J.D., 2005). ***PRACTICE AREAS:*** Workers' Compensation. ***Email:*** blivert@bsp-pa.com

GINNY P. LANIER, born Burlington, North Carolina, September 26, 1976; admitted to bar, 2003, North Carolina. *Education:* Appalachian State University (B.S.B.A., magna cum laude, 1978); Campbell University (J.D., cum laude, 2003). Law Clerk for Justice Robert H. Edmunds, Jr., North Carolina Supreme Court, 2003-2005. ***PRACTICE AREAS:*** Workers' Compensation. ***Email:*** glanier@bsp-pa.com

OF COUNSEL

ARCHIE W. FUTRELL, III, born Leaksville, North Carolina, April 14, 1954; admitted to bar, 1978, North Carolina and U.S. District Court, Eastern District of North Carolina; 1980, U.S. Court of Appeals, Fourth Circuit; 1982, U.S. Claims Court. *Education:* University of North Carolina (A.B., 1976; J.D., 1978). *Member:* Wake County Bar Association (Member, Board of Directors, 1990-1991); North Carolina Academy of Trial Lawyers. ***PRACTICE AREAS:*** Family Law; Business Law; Wills; Trust and Estates.

All attorneys are members of the Tenth Judicial District and North Carolina Bar Associations and North Carolina State Bar.

REPRESENTATIVE CLIENTS: AMR Corp.; GAB Robins; Gallagher Bassett; Gates McDonald; Goodyear Tire & Rubber Co.; International Paper; N.C. Insurance Guaranty Assoc.; Sedgwick CMS; Specialty Risk Services; State Farm Insurance Co.; Tyson; U.S. Airways.

BUMGARDNER & ROSE, P.A.

CARY, NORTH CAROLINA

(See Raleigh)

Family Law, Domestic Relations, Divorce, Premarital Agreement, Separation Agreement, Child Custody, Child Support, Visitation Rights, Mediation, Collaborative Law.

BURNS, DAY & PRESNELL, P.A.

CARY, NORTH CAROLINA

(See Raleigh)

General Practice in State and Federal Courts and Administrative Agencies. Commercial, Construction and Insurance Litigation, Arbitration and Mediation, Public Utilities, Telecommunication, Real Property, Corporate and Probate Law, Bankruptcy and Business Reorganizations.

DAVID R. CHAMBERS

CARY, NORTH CAROLINA

(See Raleigh)

Estate Planning, Wealth Transfer, Asset Protection, Tax Planning, Charitable Giving.

LAW OFFICES OF GREGORY P. CHOCKLETT

CARY, NORTH CAROLINA

(See Raleigh)

Commercial Litigation, Bankruptcy/Creditor, Collections, Contracts, Civil Trials and Appeals, Personal Injury. Medical Malpractice, ERISA, Repossessions, Foreclosures.

CLIFTON & SINGER, L.L.P.

CARY, NORTH CAROLINA

(See Raleigh)

Personal Injury, Medical Malpractice, Wrongful Death, Catastrophic Injury, Residential Real Estate, Commercial Real Estate, Family Law, Divorce, Child Custody, Criminal Law, DWI, Traffic Violations.

COATS & BENNETT, PLLC

1400 CRESCENT GREEN, SUITE 300
CARY, NORTH CAROLINA 27511
Telephone: 919-854-1844
Fax: 919-854-2084
URL: http://www.coatsandbennett.com

Patent, Trademark, Copyright and Unfair Competition Practice before all Courts.

LARRY L. COATS, born Willow Springs, North Carolina, January 29, 1945; admitted to bar, 1971, Pennsylvania; 1973, North Carolina; 1974-1982, U.S. Court of Customs and Patent Appeals; 1982, U.S. Court of Appeals for the Federal Circuit; 1987, U.S. Supreme Court; registered to practice before U.S. Patent and Trademark Office. *Education:* North Carolina State University (B.S., 1967); University of North Carolina (J.D., 1970). *Member:* Wake County, North Carolina and Pennsylvania Bar Associations; North Carolina State Bar; American Intellectual Property Law Association. (Resident). ***PRACTICE AREAS:*** Patents; Trademarks; Copyrights; Litigation. ***Email:*** lcoats@coatsandbennett.com

DAVID E. BENNETT, born Burlington, North Carolina, December 16, 1959; admitted to bar, 1985, North Carolina; registered to practice before U.S. Patent and Trademark Office. *Education:* University of North Carolina at Charlotte, (B.A., 1982); University of North Carolina at Chapel Hill (J.D., 1985). *Member:* Wake County, North Carolina and American Bar Associations; North Carolina State Bar; American Intellectual Property Law Association; Carolina Patent, Trademark and Copyright Law Association. (Resident). ***PRACTICE AREAS:*** Patents; Trademarks; Copyrights; Litigation. ***Email:*** dbennett@coatsandbennett.com

(This Listing Continued)

JOHN R. OWEN, born Dallas, Texas, September 13, 1960; admitted to bar, 1996, North Carolina; registered to practice before U.S. Patent and Trademark Office. *Education:* Duke University (B.S.E., 1983); University of North Carolina (J.D., 1996). Order of the Coif. Member, North Carolina Law Review. (Resident). ***PRACTICE AREAS:*** Patent; Trademark; Copyright; Litigation. ***Email:*** jowen@coatsandbennett.com

DAVID D. KALISH, born Mentor, Ohio, November 13, 1967; admitted to bar, 1997, North Carolina and U.S. District Court, Middle District of North Carolina; registered to practice before U.S. Patent and Trademark Office. *Education:* North Carolina State University (B.S., 1990); Franklin Pierce Law Center (J.D., Masters of Intellectual Property, 1997). *Member:* Greensboro and North Carolina Bar Associations; American Intellectual Property Law Association. ***PRACTICE AREAS:*** Patent; Trademark; Copyright. ***Email:*** dkalish@coatsandbennett.com

ANTHONY J. BILLER, born Grand Rapids, Michigan, February 22, 1968; admitted to bar, 1997, North Carolina. *Education:* Purdue University (B.A., distinguished military graduate, 1990); Campbell University (J.D., magna cum laude, 1997). Managing Editor, Campbell Law Review. Author: "Good Faith Mediation: Improving Efficiency, Cost, and Satisfaction In North Carolina's Pre-Trial Process," Campbell Law Review, Spring 1996. Law Clerk, Hon. William L. Osteen, U.S. District Court, Middle District of North Carolina, 1997-1998. *Member:* North Carolina Bar Association; Federalist Society; Christian Legal Society. [Capt., U.S. Army, 1990-1994]. ***PRACTICE AREAS:*** Litigation. ***Email:*** abiller@coatsandbennett.com

MICHAEL D. MURPHY, born Weirton, West Virginia; admitted to bar, 2004, North Carolina, U.S. District Court, Eastern District of North Carolina and Tenth Judicial District; registered to practice before U.S. Patent and Trademark Office. *Education:* West Virginia Institute of Technology (B.S.E.E., summa cum laude, 1991); North Carolina Central University School of Law (J.D., summa cum laude, 2004). *Member:* North Carolina State and North Carolina Bar Associations; Triangle Intellectual Property Law Association. ***PRACTICE AREAS:*** Patents; Copyright Law; Trademark.

EDWARD H. GREEN, III, born Knoxville, Tennessee, March 6, 1961; admitted to bar, 1999, North Carolina. *Education:* Tennessee Technological University (B.S.E.E., 1985); North Carolina Central University (J.D., summa cum laude, 1999). *Member:* North Carolina State Bar (Member, Intellectual Property Section, 1998-2000); Institute of Electrical and Electronics Engineers; Triangle (North Carolina) Intellectual Property Association. ***PRACTICE AREAS:*** Intellectual Property. ***Email:*** egreen@coatsandbennett.com

ANDREW R. ARANDA, born El Paso, Texas, October 1, 1969; admitted to bar, 2004, North Carolina and U.S. District Court, Eastern District of North Carolina. *Education:* University of Texas at Austin (B.S.M.E., 1992); Southern Methodist University (M.S.E.E., 1998); University of Houston (J.D., 2003). *Member:* North Carolina State Bar. ***PRACTICE AREAS:*** Intellectual Property. ***Email:*** aaranda@coatsandbennett.com

REBECCA CRANDALL, born Picayune, Mississippi, 1978; admitted to bar, 2004, North Carolina. *Education:* Converse College (B.S.B.A., 2001); University of North Carolina at Chapel Hill (J.D., with honors, 2004). Recipient, First Prize, UNC Law Nathan Buchan Memorial Competition, for paper, "Considering Apportionment: Proving Profits in Copyright Infringement Cases." Publication Editor, NC Journal of Law & Technology. Author: "Recent Development: Do Computer Purchasers Need Lemon Aid?" 4 NC Journal of Law & Technology 307 (2003). *Member:* North Carolina State Bar. ***PRACTICE AREAS:*** Litigation. ***Email:*** rcrandall@coatsandbennett.com

LEGAL SUPPORT PERSONNEL

PATENT AGENTS

STEPHEN A. HERRERA, born Trenton, New Jersey, November 9, 1964. *Education:* Rutgers University (B.S.C., with honors, 1996). Member, Triangle Intellectual Property Law Association. [Sgt., U.S. Army, 1982-1986]. ***LANGUAGES:*** German. ***PRACTICE AREAS:*** Patents; Patent Prosecution. ***Email:*** sherrera@coatsandbennett.com

JENNIFER K. STEWART, born Kettering, Ohio, October 7, 1971. *Education:* University of Florida (B.S.E.E., summa cum laude, 1994; M.S.E.E., 1996). Eta Kappa Nu. Member, Society of Photo-Optical Instrumentation Engineers, 1995-1996. ***PRACTICE AREAS:*** Patent Applications; Patent Prosecution. ***Email:*** jstewart@coatsandbennett.com

COLEMAN, GLEDHILL, HARGRAVE & PEEK, P.C.

CARY, NORTH CAROLINA

(See Hillsborough)

General Civil and Criminal Trial Practice in all State and Federal Courts. Litigation, Negligence, Domestic, Real Estate, Corporate, Municipal and Probate Law, Commercial Transactions and Litigation.

PAUL P. CREECH ATTORNEY AT LAW PLLC

CARY, NORTH CAROLINA

(See Raleigh)

Business, Corporate, Tax, Estate Planning, Real Estate, Wills Buying and Selling of Businesses.

THE DALTON LAW FIRM, P.A.

CARY, NORTH CAROLINA

(See Raleigh)

Elder Law, Medicaid Planning, Estate Planning, Asset Protection, Wills, Probate, Trusts, Collaborative Law, Elder Law Mediation.

ADRIAN J. DAVIS
ATTORNEY AT LAW

CARY, NORTH CAROLINA

(See Raleigh)

Family Law, Divorce, Child Custody, Child Support, Collaborative Law.

WAYNE BUCHANAN EADS

CARY, NORTH CAROLINA

(See Raleigh)

Criminal Defense in State and Federal Courts. All Major Crimes, White Collar Crimes, Drug Offenses, Firearms Offenses, Trials and Appeals.

ELLIS & WINTERS LLP

1100 CRESCENT GREEN, SUITE 200
CARY, NORTH CAROLINA 27511-8105
Telephone: 919-865-7000
Facsimile: 919-865-7010
URL: http://www.elliswinters.com

Raleigh, North Carolina Office: P.O. Box 33550, 27636. Telephone: 919-865-7000. Facsimile: 919-865-7010.

Greensboro, North Carolina Office: 100 N. Greene Street, Suite 102, 27401. Telephone: 336-217-4193. Facsimile: 336-217-4198.

Trial and Appellate Practice in all State and Federal Courts. Commercial Litigation, Administrative Litigation, Medical Malpractice, Products Liability, Antitrust, Corporate, Real Estate and Finance.

RICHARD W. ELLIS, born Raleigh, North Carolina, April 20, 1942; admitted to bar, 1969, North Carolina. *Education:* University of North Carolina (A.B., 1964; J.D., with high honors, 1969). Order of the Coif. Associate Editor, North Carolina Law Review, 1968-1969. *Member:* International Association of Defense Counsel; Defense Research Institute; North Carolina Association of Defense Attorneys. Fellow: American College of Trial Lawyers. [U.S. Naval Reserve, Active Duty, 1964-1966]. ***PRACTICE AREAS:*** Products Liability; Civil Litigation; Commercial Litigation; Media Law; Antitrust. ***Email:*** dick_ellis@elliswinters.com

MICHAEL G. WINTERS, born Raleigh, North Carolina, January 6, 1953; admitted to bar, 1978, North Carolina. *Education:* University of North Carolina (B.S., 1975; J.D., 1978). Beta Gamma Sigma. Morehead Scholar. ***PRACTICE AREAS:*** Commercial Real Estate; Real Estate Development. ***Email:*** mike_winters@elliswinters.com

JONATHAN D. SASSER, born Monroe, North Carolina, March 1, 1956; admitted to bar, 1981, North Carolina; 1983, New York. *Education:* University of North Carolina at Chapel Hill (B.A., with honors, Political Science, 1978; J.D., with honors, 1981). Phi Beta Kappa. Morehead Fellow in Law. Morehead Scholar. North Carolina Law Review, 1980-1981. Law Clerk to Hon. Burley B. Mitchell, Jr., Associate Justice, 1982; Hon. J. Frank Huskins, Associate Justice, North Carolina Supreme Court, 1981. *Member:* North Carolina Bar Association (Chair, Constitutional Law Section, 2002-2003). ***PRACTICE AREAS:*** Intellectual Property Litigation; Toxic Torts; Environmental Litigation; Constitutional Law; Commercial Litigation; Securities Litigation. ***Email:*** jon_sasser@elliswinters.com

LESLIE C. O'TOOLE, born Chicago, Illinois, November 14, 1961; admitted to bar, 1986, North Carolina. *Education:* Brown University (A.B., with honors, magna cum laude, 1982); University of North Carolina (J.D., with high honors, 1986). Phi Beta Kappa; Order of the Coif. Morehead Fellow. Research Editor, North Carolina Law Review, 1985-1986. Secretary, Special Olympics World Summer Games, 1999. President, Raleigh Professional Women's Forum, 1988-1989. Board Chair, Special Olympics North Carolina. *Member:* North Carolina Association of Defense Attorneys (Executive Vice President); Defense Research Institute; Federation of Defense and Corporate Counsel. ***PRACTICE AREAS:*** Civil Litigation; Products Liability; Medical Malpractice. ***Email:*** leslie_otoole@elliswinters.com

CHARLES N. ANDERSON, JR., born Raleigh, North Carolina, April 25, 1956; admitted to bar, 1986, North Carolina. *Education:* North Carolina State University (B.A., with honors, 1978); University of North Carolina (J.D., with high honors, 1986). Order of the Coif. Member, North Carolina Law Review, 1984-1985. ***PRACTICE AREAS:*** Corporate; Finance; Real Property. ***Email:*** chuck_anderson@elliswinters.com

PAUL K. SUN, JR., born Toledo, Ohio, May 28, 1957; admitted to bar, 1989, North Carolina. *Education:* Wittenberg University (B.A., magna cum laude, 1979); Vanderbilt University (M.B.A., 1981); Duke University (J.D., with highest honors, 1989). Order of the Coif. Founder's Medalist, Vanderbilt University. Articles Editor, Duke Law Journal, 1988-1989. Clerk to Judge J. Dickson Phillips, Jr., U.S. Court of Appeals, Fourth Circuit, 1989-1990. ***PRACTICE AREAS:*** Civil Litigation; Administrative Litigation; Criminal Litigation; Appellate Practice. ***Email:*** paul_sun@elliswinters.com

MATTHEW W. SAWCHAK, born Washington, D.C., June 3, 1962; admitted to bar, 1989, North Carolina. *Education:* Harvard University (A.B., cum laude, 1984); Duke University (J.D., with honors, 1989; LL.M., 1989). Order of the Coif. Editor-in-Chief, Duke Law Journal, 1988-1989. Clerk to Hon. Clarence Thomas, U.S. Court of Appeals, District of Columbia Circuit, 1990. *Member:* North Carolina Bar Association (Past Chair, Appellate Rules Study Committee; Past Chair, Antitrust and Trade Regulation Section). ***LANGUAGES:*** Russian. ***PRACTICE AREAS:*** Antitrust; Business Litigation; Appellate Practice. ***Email:*** matt_sawchak@elliswinters.com

ANDREW S. CHAMBERLIN, born Rochester, New York, December 18, 1964; admitted to bar, 1990, North Carolina. *Education:* University of Georgia (B.A., 1987; J.D., cum laude, 1990). Member, Georgia Journal of International and Comparative Law, 1989-1990. *Member:* North Carolina and American Bar Associations; Defense Research Institute; International Association of Defense Counsel; North Carolina Association of Defense Attorneys. ***PRACTICE AREAS:*** Products Liability; Civil Litigation; Commercial Litigation; Trade Secrets Litigation. ***Email:*** andrew_chamberlin@elliswinters.com

ALEX J. HAGAN, born Winston-Salem, North Carolina, February 7, 1965; admitted to bar, 1992, North Carolina. *Education:* University of North Carolina (B.A., 1987; J.D., with honors, 1992). Holderness Moot Court. Order of the Barristers. Clerk to Chief Justice James G. Exum, Jr., North Carolina Supreme Court. *Member:* North Carolina and American Bar Associations; North Carolina Association of Defense Attorneys; Defense Research Institute. ***PRACTICE AREAS:*** Civil Litigation; Medical Malpractice; Products Liability. ***Email:*** alex_hagan@elliswinters.com

JULIA F. YOUNGMAN, born Roanoke, Virginia, March 23, 1965; admitted to bar, 1994, North Carolina; 1996, District of Columbia. *Education:* Duke University (B.S., 1987; M.A., Environmental Science, 1994; J.D., with high honors, 1994). Order of the Coif. Managing Editor, Duke Law Journal. Law Clerk, Judge J. Dickson Phillips, Jr., U.S. Court of Appeals, Fourth Circuit, 1994-1995. Certified Mediator. [U.S. Army, 1987-1991, Captain]. ***PRACTICE AREAS:*** Commercial Litigation; Construction Law; First Amendment Law; Appellate Practice; Mediation. ***Email:*** julie_youngman@elliswinters.com

THOMAS D. BLUE, JR., born Charlottesville, Virginia, October 17, 1960; admitted to bar, 1997, North Carolina. *Education:* University of North Carolina at Asheville (B.A., summa cum laude, 1989); University of North Carolina at Chapel Hill (J.D., with honors, 1997). Staff Member, North Carolina Law Review, 1995-1997. ***PRACTICE AREAS:*** Civil Litigation. ***Email:*** tom_blue@elliswinters.com

CURTIS J. SHIPLEY, born Chariton, Iowa, February 21, 1963; admitted to bar, 1990, Illinois; 1991, District of Columbia; 1992, North Carolina. *Education:* Northwestern University (B.S., 1985); University of Iowa (J.D., with high distinction, 1988). Articles Editor, Iowa Law Review, 1987-1988. *Member:* North Carolina State Bar; American Bar Association. ***PRACTICE AREAS:*** Commercial Litigation; Products Liability; Environmental Litigation; Construction Litigation. ***Email:*** curtis_shipley@elliswinters.com

MARY M. DILLON, born Washington, D.C., November 13, 1966; admitted to bar, 1993, North Carolina. *Education:* University of North Carolina (A.B., 1989); University of Virginia (J.D., 1993). Morehead Scholar, University of North Carolina. Executive Editor, Virginia Environmental Law Journal, 1992-1993. ***PRACTICE AREAS:*** Products Liability; Medical Malpractice; Civil Litigation. ***Email:*** mary_dillon@elliswinters.com

ASSOCIATES

SUZANNE COLLINS LAGERHOLM, born Laurinburg, North Carolina, November 15, 1967; admitted to bar, 1999, Pennsylvania; 2004, North Carolina. *Education:* University of North Carolina (B.A., 1994; J.D., 1999). Articles Editor, The North Carolina Journal of International Law and Commercial Regulation, 1998-1999. Former Associate, Buchanan Ingersoll, P.C. Author: In re Jenoptiak AG, 23 NCJILCR 691, Summer 1998. ***PRACTICE AREAS:*** Real Estate; Corporate Law. ***Email:*** suzanne_lagerholm@elliswinters.com

WENDY I. SEXTON, born Toronto, Ontario, Canada, January 17, 1973; admitted to bar, 1999, North Carolina; 2003, U.S. District Court, Eastern District of North Carolina; U.S. Court of Appeals, Fourth Circuit; 2004, U.S. District Court, Western and Middle Districts of North Carolina. *Education:* University of North Carolina at Chapel Hill (B.A., 1995); Wake Forest University School of Law (J.D., 1999). Member, Wake Forest University Law Review, 1997-1999. Member, Wake Forest University Moot Court Board, 1997-1999. *Member:* North Carolina and American Bar Associations; North Carolina Association of Defense Attorneys; Defense Research Institute. ***PRACTICE AREAS:*** Civil Litigation; Products Liability; Professional Malpractice; Antitrust; Commercial Litigation; Appellate Practice. ***Email:*** wendy_sexton@elliswinters.com

GEORGE F. SANDERSON, III, born Carson City, Nevada, June 9, 1973; admitted to bar, 2000, New York; 2001, U.S. District Court, Southern and Eastern Districts of New York; 2004, North Carolina and U.S. District Court, Eastern, Middle and Western Districts of North Carolina. *Education:* Georgetown University (A.B., 1995); New York University (J.D., 1999). Phi Beta Kappa. Law Clerk, Hon. Stephen L. St. John, Eastern District of Virginia Bankruptcy Court, 1999-2000. Author: "Congressional Involvement in Class Action Reform," 2, NYU J. Legis. & Pub. Pol., 315 (1999). ***PRACTICE AREAS:*** Commercial Litigation; Arbitration; Securities Litigation; Antitrust. ***Email:*** george_sanderson@elliswinters.com

DANIELLE ENG ROSE, born Albany, New York, April 13, 1972; admitted to bar, 2000, North Carolina. *Education:* College of William & Mary (B.A., summa cum laude, 1993); Duke University (J.D., with high honors, 2000). Phi Beta Kappa. *Member:* American, North Carolina, and Wake County Bar Associations. ***LANGUAGES:*** Spanish. ***PRACTICE AREAS:*** Business Litigation; Education Law. ***Email:*** danielle_rose@elliswinters.com

THOMAS H. SEGARS, born Wilmington, Delaware, 1975; admitted to bar, 2000, North Carolina; 2001, U.S Court of Appeals, Third Circuit. *Education:* Wake Forest University (B.A., magna cum laude, 1997); University of North Carolina (J.D., with high honors, 2000). Chancellors Scholar. Order of the Coif. Clerk to Judge Jane R. Roth, U.S. Court of Appeals, Third Circuit, 2001-2002. ***PRACTICE AREAS:*** Litigation. ***Email:*** tom_segars@elliswinters.com

BRIAN C. VICK, born Raleigh, North Carolina, April 22, 1972; admitted to bar, 2002, North Carolina. *Education:* Vassar College (B.A., 1994); University of Georgia School of Law (J.D., summa cum laude, 2002). Clerk to Judge Joel F. Dubina, U.S. Court of Appeals, Eleventh Circuit. ***Email:*** brian_vick@elliswinters.com

(This Listing Continued)

STEPHEN C. KEADEY, born Mt. Vernon, Ohio, September 26, 1969; admitted to bar, 2003, North Carolina. *Education:* University of North Carolina at Chapel Hill (A.B., summa cum laude, 1991); North Carolina State University (M.A., 1994); University of North Carolina at Chapel Hill School of Law (J.D., with honors, 2002). Clerk to Judge William Osteen, U.S. District Court, Middle District of North Carolina. ***Email:*** steve_keadey@elliswinters.com

JOHN A. CHILSON, born Wellsboro, Pennsylvania, 1969; admitted to bar, 1999, Michigan; 2003, North Carolina. *Education:* U.S. Naval Academy (B.S., 1991); University of Michigan at Ann Arbor (J.D., cum laude, 1999). Author: "Keeping Clean Waters Clean: Making the Clean Water Act's Antidegradation Policy Work," Vol. 32, University of Michigan Journal of Law Reform. *Member:* North Carolina and American Bar Associations; State Bar of Michigan; Defense Research Institute. [Lt. Commander, U.S. Navy, 1991-2003]. ***PRACTICE AREAS:*** Products Liability; Commercial Litigation; Civil Rights Litigation; Criminal Defense. ***Email:*** john_chilson@elliswinters.com

OF COUNSEL

DONNA K. BLUMBERG, born Lafayette, Louisiana, May 31, 1959; admitted to bar, 1985, North Carolina. *Education:* University of North Carolina (B.A., 1981; J.D., 1985). Order of the Coif. ***PRACTICE AREAS:*** Commercial Real Estate. ***Email:*** donna_blumberg@elliswinters.com

(For complete biographical data on other personnel, see Professional Biographies at Raleigh, North Carolina and Greensboro, North Carolina)

EVERETT, GASKINS, HANCOCK & STEVENS, LLP

CARY, NORTH CAROLINA

(See Raleigh)

Administrative Law, Appellate Practice, Bankruptcy, Business Law, Biotechnology, Commercial Law, Commercial Litigation, Communications and Media Law, Construction Law, Corporate Law, Debtor and Creditor Law, Education Law, First Amendment Law, Franchise Law, Intellectual Property, Insurance Law, International Trade Law, Internet Law, Litigation, Lobbying, Non-Profit Corporations and Charitable Organizations, Parliamentary Law, Tax and Estate Planning, Tax Controversies, Taxation, Toxic Torts, Trade Association Law.

THE FLEXNER LAW FIRM, P.A.

CARY, NORTH CAROLINA

(See Raleigh)

Personal Injury, Products Liability, Medical Malpractice, Automobile Accidents and Injuries, Truck Accidents, Motorcycle Accidents, Workers Compensation, Social Security Disability, Wrongful Death, Civil Litigation, Insurance Litigation, Hospital Negligence, Nursing Home Negligence, Catastrophic Injury.

GAILOR, WALLIS & HUNT, PLLC

CARY, NORTH CAROLINA

(See Raleigh)

Equitable Distribution, Divorce Litigation, Child Custody, Child Support, Hague Convention Proceedings, Domestic Relations Appeals, Divorce Mediation, Arbitration and Adoption, Family Law.

BENITA WALKER GIBBS

209 SOUTH ACADEMY STREET
MAIN LEVEL
CARY, NORTH CAROLINA 27511
Telephone: 919-481-0903
Fax: 919-481-0882
Email: bgibbslaw@hotmail.com
URL: http://www.caryrealestatesclosing.com

Residential Real Estate, Commercial Real Estate, Mortgages, Construction Loans, Equity Finance, Reverse Mortgages.

BENITA WALKER GIBBS, born Burlington, North Carolina, May 6, 1960; admitted to bar, 1990, North Carolina. *Education:* University of North Carolina at Chapel Hill (B.A., 1982); Norman Adrian Wiggins School of Law at Campbell University (J.D., 1990). *Member:* North Carolina Bar Association; North Carolina Academy of Trial Lawyers. ***PRACTICE AREAS:*** Residential Real Estate; Commercial Real Estate; Mortgages; Construction Loans; Equity Finance; Reverse Mortgages.

KYLE S. HALL

CARY, NORTH CAROLINA

(See Raleigh)

Criminal Law, Homicide, Sexual Assault, Drug Crimes, Felonies, Misdemeanors, Driving While Intoxicated, Traffic Violations, Parole and Probation, Personal Injury, Products Liability, Automobile Accidents and Injuries, Wrongful Death, Railroad Accidents.

HAYNSWORTH BALDWIN JOHNSON & GREAVES LLC

CARY, NORTH CAROLINA

(See Ogletree, Deakins, Nash, Smoak & Stewart, P.C., Raleigh)

HEDSPETH LAW FIRM, PLLC

CARY, NORTH CAROLINA

(See Raleigh)

Family Law, Traffic Violations, Criminal Law, Misdemeanors.

HERRING McBENNETT MILLS & FINKELSTEIN, PLLC

CARY, NORTH CAROLINA

(See Raleigh)

Comprehensive Business, Litigation, Real Estate, Domestic and Adoption Practice including, Trial and Appellate Litigation, Administrative, Antitrust, Business Law, Business Crimes, Civil Rights, Commercial, Construction, Corporate, Business Formation, E-Commerce, Employment, Environmental, Estate Planning, Family, Adoption, Equitable Distribution, Divorce, Health Care, Intellectual Property, Negligence, Probate, Products Liability, Real Estate, Toxic Tort, Wills and Trusts Law, Business Ownership Disputes, Disability, Insurance Claims, Wage and Hour, Overtime Disputes, Franchise Disputes, Contracts Disputes, Unfair Trade Practices, Breach of Fiduciary Duty, Partnership Disputes, Non-Compete Covenants, Tortious Interference with Contract, Mergers and Acquisitions, White Collar Criminal Defense, Regulatory Law, Professional Licensing, Eminent Domain and Land Condemnation.

HIGGINS, FRANKSTONE, GRAVES & MORRIS, P.A.

14600 WESTON PARKWAY, SUITE 300
CARY, NORTH CAROLINA 27513-2259
Telephone: 919-968-8880
Fax: 919-678-8885
Email: info@hfgmcary.com
URL: http://www.hfgmlaw.com

Chapel Hill, North Carolina Office: 1414 Raleigh Road, Suite 320. Telephone: 919-968-4717. Fax: 919-929-1415.

Estate Planning, Probate, Corporate, Real Estate, Civil Litigation, Taxation and Business Law.

(For complete biographical data on all personnel, see Professional Biographies at Chapel Hill, NC.)

THE HILBERT LAW FIRM, PLLC

CARY, NORTH CAROLINA

(See Raleigh)

Family Law, Child Custody, Divorce Litigation, Child Support, Domestic Violence, Equitable Distribution, Alimony, Post-Separation Support, Separation Agreements Premarital Agreements, Adoptions, Visition Rights, Divorce.

HOLLOWELL LAW OFFICES, P.A.

CARY, NORTH CAROLINA

(See Cary)

Health Care Law, Administrative Law, Corporate Law, Business Law, Employment, Governmental Estate Planning and Collection.

HOLT YORK McDARRIS & HIGH, LLP

CARY, NORTH CAROLINA

(See Raleigh)

Municipal/Administrative Law, Zoning and Land Use, Real Property, Government Regulations, Condemnation Defense, Corporate Law, Trusts and Estates, Wills and Probate, Alcoholic Beverages, General Trial and Appellate Practice before all State and Federal Courts and Agencies. Legislative Representation before the North Carolina General Assembly.

HOWARD, STALLINGS, FROM & HUTSON, P.A.

CARY, NORTH CAROLINA

(See Raleigh)

General, Civil and Commercial Litigation, Business Law, Commercial Real Estate, Taxation, Employment Law, Computer Law, Estate Planning and Administration, Bankruptcy Law, Loan Structuring and Workouts, Intellectual Property Law, Personal Injury.

BRETT A. HUBBARD

1220 S. E. MAYNARD ROAD, SUITE 203
CARY, NORTH CAROLINA 27511
Telephone: 919-460-6883
Fax: 919-460-8932
Email: hubbard3@bellsouth.net
URL: http://www.bretthubbardlaw.com

Family Law, Separation Agreements, Child Custody, Child Support, Divorce, Bankruptcy, Bankruptcy Chapter 7, Bankruptcy Chapter 13, Wills, Estate Planning, Probate, Estate Administration, Traffic Violations, Criminal Law, Driving While Intoxicated, Real Estate, Employment Law, Small Business Law, Personal Injury.

(This Listing Continued)

BRETT A. HUBBARD, Cary—Continued

BRETT A. HUBBARD, born Junction City, Kansas, August 5, 1954; admitted to bar, 1988, North Carolina; 1989, U.S. District Court, Eastern District of North Carolina. *Education:* University of North Carolina at Chapel Hill (B.A., 1977); Campbell University (J.D., 1988). *Member:* North Carolina Bar Association.

JACKSON LEWIS LLP

1400 CRESCENT GREEN, SUITE 320
CARY, NORTH CAROLINA 27511
Telephone: 919-854-0044
Facsimile: 919-854-0908
URL: http://www.jacksonlewis.com

Other offices located in: Atlanta, GA; Boston, MA; Chicago, IL; Dallas, TX; Greenville, SC; Hartford, CT; Long Island, NY; Los Angeles, CA; Miami, FL; Minneapolis, MN; Morristown, NJ; New York, NY; Orlando, FL; Pittsburgh, PA; Sacramento, CA; San Francisco, CA; Seattle, WA; Stamford, CT; Vienna, VA; White Plains, NY.
Satellite Offices: 127 Dorrance Street, Providence, Rhode Island 02903. Phone: 401-490-3444. Fax: 401-454-8855.
1225 Market Street, Wheeling, West Virginia 26003. Phone: 304-230-1461. Fax: 304-230-1462.
11 Federal Plaza, Suite 300, Youngstown, OH 44503. Phone: 330-746-2324. Fax: 330-746-7023.

Employment, Labor, Benefits, Immigration Law, and Other Related Litigation, On Behalf of Management Exclusively.

PARTNERS

PAUL H. DERRICK, born 1957; admitted to bar, 1989, South Carolina and U.S. Court of Appeals, Fifth Circuit; 1991, Tennessee; 1992, U.S. Court of Appeals, Sixth Circuit; 1997, U.S. Court of Appeals, Fourth Circuit; 2000, North Carolina; U.S. Supreme Court. *Education:* Newberry College (B.A., 1979); University of South Carolina (J.D., 1988). Staff Attorney, National Labor Relations Board, 1988-1990. *Member:* South Carolina Bar; North Carolina State Bar; Defense Research Institute; Society for Human Resource Management. **Email:** derrickp@jacksonlewis.com

RICHARD S. MCATEE, born 1969; admitted to bar, 1995, Pennsylvania and U.S. District Court, Western District of Pennsylvania; U.S. Court of Appeals, Third and Sixth Circuits (Not admitted in North Carolina). *Education:* Cornell University (B.S.I.L.R., 1991); Duquesne University (J.D., magna cum laude, 1995). Author: The ADA and NLRA, Duquesne Law Review, (1994). (Managing Partner, Raleigh-Durham Office). **Email:** mcateer@jacksonlewis.com

JANAK LAW FIRM, P.A.

CARY, NORTH CAROLINA

(See Raleigh)

Bankruptcy, Consumer Bankruptcy, Foreclosures, Real Estate, Buying and Selling, Landlord and Tenant, Business Law, Collections, Creditors Rights.

JORDAN PRICE WALL GRAY JONES & CARLTON

CARY, NORTH CAROLINA

(See Raleigh)

General Practice in all State and Federal Courts. Trials. Banking, Insurance, Health and Hospital Law. Corporate Practice and Administrative Law, Creditors' Rights and Bankruptcy, Insurance Defense. Condominium and Homeowners' Association Law. Estate Planning. Legislative Representation, Commercial Real Estate and Local Government Law.

KIRBY & HOLT, L.L.P.

CARY, NORTH CAROLINA

(See Raleigh)

Personal injury, including medical malpractice, products liability and catastrophic injury, and business torts.

KNOTT, CLARK & BERGER, L.L.P.

CARY, NORTH CAROLINA

(See Raleigh)

General Practice in State and Federal Courts. Medical Malpractice, Nursing Malpractice, Hospital Liability, Plaintiffs Personal Injury, Wrongful Death, Automobile Accidents and Injuries, Commercial Vehicle Liability, Nursing Home Negligence, Workers Compensation, Insurance Bad Faith, Insurance Litigation.

LEDBETTER & TITSWORTH, P.A.

Established in 1999
1135 KILDAIRE FARM ROAD
CARY, NORTH CAROLINA 27511
Telephone: 919-460-9798; Toll Free: 888-222-9656
Fax: 919-460-9631
URL: http://www.ledbetterandtitsworth.com

Workers Compensation, Personal Injury, Automobile Accidents, Trucking Accidents, Medical Malpractice.

(This Listing Continued)

FIRM PROFILE: A Personal Injury Law Firm concentrating on workers' compensation, automobile and trucking accidents, food-borne illnesses, and medical malpractice.

JOEL R. LEDBETTER, born Charlotte, North Carolina, June 26, 1968; admitted to bar, 1994, North Carolina. *Education:* University of North Carolina at Chapel Hill (B.A., 1990); Campbell University (J.D., 1994). ***PRACTICE AREAS:*** Workers Compensation; Wage and Hour Law; Personal Injury; Automobile Accidents and Injuries; Medical Malpractice. **Email:** joel@ledbetterandtitsworth.com

DANIEL B. TITSWORTH, born Hillsboro, Illinois, December 8, 1962; admitted to bar, 1994, North Carolina. *Education:* University of Illinois, Springfield(B.A. Legal Studies, 1990); Campbell University (J.D., 1994). *Member:* Wake County and North Carolina Bar Associations; North Carolina State Bar; North Carolina Academy of Trial Lawyers. ***REPORTED CASES:*** Freeman v. Triangle Grading & Paving, Inc.; Arroyo v. Scotties Professional Window Cleaning. ***PRACTICE AREAS:*** Workers Compensation; Personal Injury; Medical Malpractice. **Email:** dan@ledbetterandtitsworth.com

MANNING & CROUCH

CARY, NORTH CAROLINA

(See Raleigh)

Criminal Trials in State and Federal Courts, Criminal Fraud, Criminal Tax Matters, Grand Jury Investigation, Homicide, Federal Grand Jury, Criminal and Regulatory Investigations, Driving While Intoxicated (DWI), Driving While Impaired, Traffic Violations, Homicide, Sex Crimes, Drug Crimes.

MANNING, FULTON & SKINNER, P.A.

CARY, NORTH CAROLINA

(See Raleigh)

Alternative Dispute Resolution, Appellate; Bankruptcy, Condemnation, Corporate/Business Entities, Corporate Finance, Employee Benefits/ERISA, Employment, Estate/Trust Administration, Estate Planning/Wealth Transfer, Family Law, Franchise, Government Relations, Litigation, Mergers/Acquisitions, Real Property, Sports/Entertainment, Tax Controversies, Tax Planning.

THE LAW OFFICE OF ANDREW McCOPPIN, P.A.

Established in 1995
1320 S.E. MAYNARD ROAD, SUITE 102
CARY, NORTH CAROLINA 27511
Telephone: 919-516-3622
Toll Free: 888-516-3622
Fax: 919-462-8089
URL: http://www.amccoppinlaw.com
Email: andrewmccoppin@nc.rr.com
URL: http://www.andrewmccoppin.com

Mailing Address: P.O. Box 2884, Raleigh, NC 27602

Driving While Intoxicated, Traffic Violations, Violent Crimes, Drug Crimes, White Collar Crimes, Domestic Violence and Federal Criminal Law.

ANDREW McCOPPIN, admitted to bar, 1994, North Carolina and California; 1996, U.S. District Court, Eastern District of North Carolina. *Education:* University of California at Berkeley (B.A., Economics and Rhetoric, 1991); University of California, Hastings College of the Law (J.D., 1994). Panel Attorney, Tenth Judicial District of North Carolina, 1995—; Panel Attorney, Office of the Federal Public Defender, Eastern District of North Carolina, 1999—. Member, Committee on Indigent Appointments, Tenth Judicial District of North Carolina, 2001-2003. Wake County Assistant District Attorney, 1995. Domestic Violence Counselor, 1995. Sentencing Advisor, Wake County Superior Court, 1995. *Member:* North Carolina State Bar; North Carolina Bar Association; State Bar of California; Wake County Academy of Criminal Defense Lawyers. ***PRACTICE AREAS:*** Criminal Law. **Email:** andrewmccoppin@nc.rr.com

MEDIRATTA LAW FIRM

CARY, NORTH CAROLINA

(See Raleigh)

Criminal Law, Driving While Intoxicated, Traffic Violations, Personal Injury, Civil Litigation, Immigration, Automobile Accidents, Juvenile Law.

MILLER & SHEDOR, PLLC

COOPER BUILDING, SUITE 100
315 N. ACADEMY STREET
P.O. BOX 3525
CARY, NORTH CAROLINA 27519-3525
Telephone: 919-462-1640
Fax: 919-462-1641

Criminal Law, Driving While Intoxicated, Juvenile Crimes, Traffic Violations, Bankruptcy, Foreclosures, Family Law, Adoptions, Child Support, Child Custody, Divorce, Visitation Rights, Real Estate, Landlord and Tenant Law, Wills, Probate, Collections, Personal Injury, Automobile Accidents, Slip and Fall, Wrongful Death, Workers Compensation, Discrimination, Sexual Harassment, Wrongful Termination.

(This Listing Continued)

MEMBERS OF THE FIRM

MARTY E. MILLER, born Plymouth, North Carolina, June 10, 1958; admitted to bar, 1995, North Carolina. *Education:* East Carolina University (B.S., Political Science, 1980); Regent University (J.D., 1995). Program Director, WOOW-AM, WRQR-FM, 1979-1985; General Manager, Coastal Plains Imprints, 1985-1988; Account Executive, WGHB-AM, 1988-1989; Athletic Director, Tarboro-Edgecombe Academy, 1989-1990; General Manager, WPNC-AM/WKLX-FM, 1990-1992; Finalist, Burton D. Wechsler First Amendment Moot Court Competition, American University, 1994; Participant, UNC School of Law Moot Court Competition, 1995. *Member:* North Carolina Bar Association; North Carolina Academy of Trial Lawyers; National Association of Consumer Bankruptcy Attorneys; Christian Legal Society. ***REPORTED CASES:*** Phelps v. Spivey, 126 N.C. App. 693, 486 S.E.2d 226 (1997) In Re Hodge, 153 N.C. App. 102, 568 S.E.2d 878 (2002). ***PRACTICE AREAS:*** Bankruptcy (30%); Criminal Law (40%); Domestic Relations (20%); Personal Injury (10%).

PETER R. SHEDOR, born Chicago, Illinois, July 7, 1955; admitted to bar, 1988, North Carolina. *Education:* North Carolina Wesleyan (B.S., 1985); Campbell University School of Law (J.D., 1988). *Member:* North Carolina State Bar; North Carolina Bar Association (Real Property Section, 1999—). [USMC, 1974-1977]. ***PRACTICE AREAS:*** Real Estate; Real Estate Closings; Wills; Small Business Organization. ***Email:*** pete@millerandshedor.com

ASSOCIATE

SOLOMON B. WEINER, born Los Angeles, California, June 15, 1951; admitted to bar, 2002, North Carolina. *Education:* North Carolina State University (B.A., 1998); University of North Carolina at Chapel Hill (J.D., 2002). Phi Beta Kappa. Phi Kappa Phi. Registered Nurse, North Carolina, 1985. *Member:* North Carolina Bar Association; North Carolina Academy of Trial Lawyers. ***PRACTICE AREAS:*** Civil Litigation; Family Law; Employment Law. ***Email:*** sol@millerandshedor.com

---

LAW OFFICES OF CHARLES H. MONTGOMERY

Established in 1993

590 NEW WAVERLY PLACE, SUITE 110
P.O. BOX 1325
CARY, NORTH CAROLINA 27512-1325
Telephone: 919-816-9002
919-816-9003
Email: charles@montylaw.com
URL: http://www.montylaw.com
Mailing Address: P.O. Box 1325, Cary, NC 27512-1325

Family Law, Civil Litigation, Civil Appeals, Mediation, Arbitration, Divorce, Separation Agreements, Child Custody, Spousal Support, Marital Property Distribution, Premarital Agreements.

FIRM PROFILE: The firm is dedicated to the highest level of service and professionalism in handling complex family law matters. Its practice is concentrated in family law, trials, appeals, arbitration and mediation. Charles Montgomery has 30 years experience and is a N.C. Board Certified Specialist in Family Law. He is also a Certified Superior Court Mediator.

CHARLES H. MONTGOMERY, born Spartanburg, South Carolina, January 28, 1949; admitted to bar, 1974, North Carolina and U.S. District Court, Eastern and Middle Districts of North Carolina, 1979, U.S. Supreme Court. *Education:* Duke University (B.A., with distinction, 1971); Vanderbilt University (J.D., 1974). Member, International Moot Court Team and Brief Editor, Moot Court Board, 1973-1974. Listed, "Who's Who In American Law," Marquis (9th Ed.) and "Who's Who In America," Marquis (51st Ed.) Certified Superior Court Mediator. Member, Cary Town Council, 1977-1981, 1983-1987. Wake County Commissioner, 1992. Past-Chair, Public Information Com. and Member, Family Law Council, North Carolina Bar Association, 1994-1997. Director, East Central Community Legal Services, Inc., 1997-2003. President, Family Law Mediation, Inc. Director, Wake County Bar Association, 1999-2001. Director, State Capitol Foundation, 1994—. *Member:* Wake County, North Carolina and American (Member, Family Law Section) Bar Associations; North Carolina State Bar; North Carolina Academy of Trial Lawyers (Chair, Family Law Section, 1996-1998). Board Certified Specialist in Family Law, North Carolina State Board of Legal Specialization. ***REPORTED CASES:*** Francis v. Francis, 612 S.E.2d 141, 2005 N.C. App. LEXIS 647 (N.C. Ct. App., Apr. 5, 2005); Discret. Appeal Den., Francis v. Francis, 2005 N.C. LEXIS 689 (N.C., June 30, 2005). ***PRACTICE AREAS:*** Family Law; Mediation; Arbitration; Civil Appeals.

ASSOCIATE

JEANNE B. FORD, born Fort Clayton, Panama, May 9, 1946; admitted to bar, 1998, North Carolina. *Education:* Sweet Briar College (B.A., 1964); North Carolina Central University (J.D., cum laude, 1998). Associate Editor, Law Review, 1997-1998. *Member:* North Carolina State Bar; North Carolina and American Bar Associations; North Carolina Academy of Trial Lawyers. ***LANGUAGES:*** French. ***REPORTED CASES:*** Francis v. Francis, 612 S.E.2d 141; 2005 N.C. App. LEXIS 647 (N.C. Ct. Ap., April 5, 2005). ***PRACTICE AREAS:*** Family Law. ***Email:*** jeanne@montylaw.com

PATTERSON, DILTHEY, CLAY, BRYSON & ANDERSON, L.L.P.

CARY, NORTH CAROLINA

(See Raleigh)

General Trial and Appellate Practice before all State and Federal Courts. Litigation of Insurance Law, Personal Injury, Medical Malpractice, Legal Malpractice, Workers Compensation and Intentional Torts, Construction Law and Litigation, Products Liability and General Civil and Commercial Litigation.

PINNA JOHNSTON & BURWELL, P.A.

CARY, NORTH CAROLINA

(See Raleigh)

Corporation, Mergers and Acquisitions, Probate, Trusts, Real Estate Law, Taxation and Estate Planning, Wills and Trusts. General Civil Practice in all State and Federal Courts.

RAGSDALE LIGGETT PLLC

CARY, NORTH CAROLINA

(See Raleigh)

General Civil Litigation and Administrative Law in State and Federal Courts and Agencies. Taxation, Estate Planning, Partnership, Landlord and Tenant, Real Estate, Insurance and Reinsurance Law. Corporate, Business, International, Environmental Law. Construction Law, Employment Discrimination and Administrative Hearings and Appeals.

THE LAW OFFICE OF JONATHAN RICHARDSON

1140 KILDAIRE FARM ROAD, SUITE 305
CARY, NORTH CAROLINA 27511
Telephone: 919-469-9904
Fax: 919-469-9905
Email: realestateattorney@earthlink.net
URL: http://www.richardsonlaw-firm.com

Personal Injury, Real Estate, Closings, Workers Compensation, Injuries, Traffic Violations, Tickets, Wrongful Death.

JONATHAN RICHARDSON, born Greensboro, North Carolina, July 4, 1968; admitted to bar, 2004, North Carolina. *Education:* University of North Carolina at Chapel Hill (B.A., Political Science, 1997); University of Dayton (J.D., 2003). *Member:* North Carolina State Bar. ***PRACTICE AREAS:*** Personal Injury; Real Estate; Workers Compensation; Traffic Violations; Wrongful Death.

TRAVIS SASSER

Established in 2000

875 WALNUT STREET, SUITE 342
CARY, NORTH CAROLINA 27511
Telephone: 919-319-7400
Fax: 919-657-7400
URL: http://www.carybankruptcy.com
Email: tsasser@carybankruptcy.com
URL: http://www.lawyers.com/carybankruptcy

Bankruptcy, Consumer Bankruptcy, Commercial Bankruptcy, Foreclosures.

TRAVIS SASSER, born 1974; admitted to bar, 1999, North Carolina. *Education:* North Carolina State University (B.A., 1995); University of Georgia (J.D., 1999). *Member:* North Carolina State Bar; North Carolina Bar Association (Bankruptcy Section); American Bankruptcy Institute; National Association of Consumer Bankruptcy Attorneys. (Board Certified Specialist in Consumer Bankruptcy Law by North Carolina State Board of Legal Specialization); (Board Certified - Consumer Bankruptcy Law - American Board of Certification). ***PRACTICE AREAS:*** Bankruptcy; Consumer Bankruptcy; Commercial Bankruptcy; Foreclosures.

STEPHEN RUSSELL SIMMONS ATTORNEY AND COUNSELLOR AT LAW

CARY, NORTH CAROLINA

(See Raleigh)

Criminal Law, Traffic Violations, Driving While Intoxicated, Speeding Tickets, Driving While License Revoked.

SOKOL McLAMB SCHILAWSKI OLIVER LADD PLLC

CARY, NORTH CAROLINA

(See Raleigh)

Domestic Relations, Civil Litigation, Appellate Practice, Mediation, Arbitration, Family Mediation, Family Arbitration, Collaborative Law, Family Law, Divorce, Child Custody, Equitable Distribution.

STEPHENSON & STEPHENSON, LLP

580 NEW WAVERLY PLACE
SUITE 240
CARY, NORTH CAROLINA 27511
Telephone: 919-858-7008
Fax: 919-858-8414
URL: http://www.stephensonandstephenson.com

Insurance Defense, Construction Litigation, Condemnation, Personal Injury, Health Care Law, Corporate Law, Estate Planning, Estate Administration, Commercial and Residential Real Estate, Foreclosures, Civil Litigation, Collections, Contract Litigation.

MEMBERS OF FIRM

JAMES B. STEPHENSON II, born Burlington, North Carolina, July 26, 1958; admitted to bar, 1984, North Carolina; 1987, U.S. District Court, Eastern District of North Carolina; 1996, U.S. Court of Appeals, Fourth Circuit; 1997, U.S. District Court, Middle District of North Carolina; 2001, U.S. District Court, Western District of North Carolina. *Education:* Elon College (B.A., 1980); Campbell University (J.D., 1984). *Member:* Wake County, North Carolina and American Bar Associations; North Carolina State Bar; North Carolina Association of Defense Attorneys. ***PRACTICE AREAS:*** Insurance Defense; Construction Litigation; Condemnation; Personal Injury; Health Care. ***Email:*** jbs@stephenson-law.com

RICHARD C. STEPHENSON, born Raleigh, North Carolina, September 7, 1964; admitted to bar, 1992, North Carolina; 1995, U.S. Court of Appeals, Fourth Circuit; 1997, U.S. District Court, Eastern District of North Carolina. *Education:* Appalachian State University (B.S.B.A., 1987); Campbell University (J.D., 1992). *Member:* Wake County and North Carolina Bar Associations; North Carolina State Bar; North Carolina Naval Reserve Lawyers Association. [JAGC Lt., U.S. Navy, 1992-1994]. ***PRACTICE AREAS:*** Corporate Law; Estate Planning; Estate Administration; Commercial Real Estate; Residential Real Estate; Foreclosures; Condemnation. ***Email:*** rcs@stephenson-law.com

ASSOCIATES

MARCIA N. SOUTHERLAND, born Raleigh, North Carolina, December 23, 1966; admitted to bar, 1994, North Carolina and U.S. District Court, Eastern District of North Carolina. *Education:* North Carolina State University (B.A., 1989); Campbell University (J.D., cum laude, 1994). *Member:* Wake County, North Carolina and American Bar Associations; North Carolina State Bar. ***PRACTICE AREAS:*** Insurance Defense; Civil Litigation; Commercial Real Estate; Residential Real Estate; Corporate Law; Estate Planning. ***Email:*** mns@stephenson-law.com

PHILIP T. GRAY, born Pittsburgh, Pennsylvania, August 4, 1969; admitted to bar, 1997, North Carolina; 1999, U.S. Court of Appeals, Fourth Circuit and U.S. District Court, Eastern District of North Carolina; 2000, U.S. District Court, Middle District of North Carolina. *Education:* North Carolina State University (B.S., cum laude, 1991); Campbell University (J.D., 1997). *Member:* Wake County, North Carolina and American Bar Associations; North Carolina State Bar; North Carolina Association of Defense Attorneys. ***PRACTICE AREAS:*** Civil Litigation; Construction Litigation; Commercial Litigation; Insurance Defense; Personal Injury. ***Email:*** ptg@stephenson-law.com

DENA WHITE WATERS, born Hertford, North Carolina, November 20, 1974; admitted to bar, 2001, North Carolina and U.S. District Court, Eastern, Middle and Western Districts of North Carolina; 2002, South Carolina. *Education:* Meredith College (B.A., cum laude, 1997); Campbell University (J.D., 2001). *Member:* Wake County and North Carolina Bar Associations; North Carolina State Bar; South Carolina Bar; North Carolina Association of Defense Attorneys. ***PRACTICE AREAS:*** Insurance Defense; Civil Litigation; Collections; Personal Injury; Contract Litigation. ***Email:*** dww@stephenson-law.com

---

STEWART LAW OFFICE, PLLC

201 SHANNON OAKS CIRCLE, SUITE 200
CARY, NORTH CAROLINA 27511
Telephone: 919-654-4583
Fax: 919-654-4584
Email: sstewart@carylawoffice.com
URL: http://www.stewartlawoffice.com

Estate Planning, Trusts, Living Trusts, Trusts and Estates, Wills, Business Law, Contracts, Corporate Law.

STEPHEN P. STEWART, born Florence, South Carolina, July 27, 1966; admitted to bar, 1992, South Carolina and North Carolina. *Education:* University of South Carolina (B.S., Accounting, 1988; J.D., 1991); New York University (LL.M., 1992). Phi Beta Kappa; Beta Gamma Sigma; Phi Alpha Delta. Recipient, American Jurisprudence Award for Torts. Staff Member, South Carolina Law Review, 1989-1991. *Member:* Wake County, North Carolina and American Bar Associations; South Carolina Bar. ***PRACTICE AREAS:*** Estate Planning; Wills; Trust Law; Business Law; Contracts; Corporate Law. ***Email:*** sstewart@carylawoffice.com

---

SULLIVAN & GRACE, P.A.

CARY, NORTH CAROLINA

(See Raleigh)

Family Law, Property Division, Separation Agreements, Child Custody, Child Support, Alimony, Divorce, Adoption, Domestic Violence, Premarital Agreements, Collaborative Family Law, Wills and Probate, Military Pension Division, Arbitration, Mediation and Family Law Appeals.

TENNEY & TENNEY, LLP

CARY, NORTH CAROLINA

(See Raleigh)

Wills, Estates, Probate, Trusts, Living Trusts, Business Law, Corporate Law, Small Business, Intellectual Property, Contracts, Personal Injury, Automobile Accidents, Slip and Fall, Civil Litigation, Real Estate, Residential Real Estate, Real Estate Closings, Family Law.

FREDERIC E. TOMS & ASSOCIATES, PLLC

103-A KILMAYNE DRIVE
CARY, NORTH CAROLINA 27511
Telephone: 919-467-3294
Fax: 919-467-3296
URL: http://www.fredericktomslaw.com

Personal Injury, Medical Malpractice, Creditor, Traffic Violations, Nursing Home Litigation, Automobile Accidents, Wrongful Death.

FREDERIC E. TOMS, born Forest City, North Carolina, April 19, 1941; admitted to bar, 1970, North Carolina; 1973, U.S. District Court, Eastern District of North Carolina; 1978, U.S. District Court, Middle District of North Carolina; 1989, U.S. District Court, Western District of North Carolina. *Education:* University of North Carolina at Chapel Hill (B.A., 1966; J.D., 1970). *Member:* Wake County and North Carolina Bar Associations; Tenth Judicial District Bar; North Carolina State Bar; North Carolina Academy of Trial Lawyers. ***PRACTICE AREAS:*** Commercial Law; Bankruptcy; Personal Injury; Civil Practice. ***Email:*** ftoms@tomslawnc.com

---

DAVID A. BRIDGMAN, born Athens, Georgia, June 7, 1972; admitted to bar, 1998, North Carolina and U.S. District Court, Eastern District of North Carolina; 2000, U.S. District Court, Middle and Western Districts of North Carolina. *Education:* University of North Carolin at Chapel Hill (B.A., 1994); Wake Forest University (J.D., 1998). *Member:* North Carolina State Bar. ***PRACTICE AREAS:*** Plaintiffs Personal Injury; Creditors Rights; Civil Litigation; Construction Law. ***Email:*** dbridgman@tomslawnc.com

ALLEN MILLS, born Louisville, Kentucky, April 24, 1964; admitted to bar, 1989, Minnesota; 1991, Kentucky; 2001, North Carolina. *Education:* Lake Forest College; University of Kentucky (B.A., with distinction, 1986); University of Minnesota (J.D., 1989). ***PRACTICE AREAS:*** Insurance Subrogation. ***Email:*** amills@tomslawnc.com

JOAN W. KURUC, born Fort Benning, Georgia, November 15, 1950; admitted to bar, 1994, Illinois; 2002, North Carolina; 2004, U.S. District Court, Eastern and Middle Districts of North Carolina. *Education:* University of North Carolina (B.A., 1972); Loyola University (J.D., 1994). Phi Beta Kappa. Member, Wagner National Moot Court Team. Legal Instructor, Loyola University Chicago School of Law. Attorney, Cook County. *Member:* Wake County and North Carolina Bar Associations; North Carolina Academy of Trial Lawyers. ***PRACTICE AREAS:*** Personal Injury; Workers Compensation; Civil Litigation. ***Email:*** jkuruc@tomslawnc.com

---

DANIEL T. TOWER, P.A.

CARY, NORTH CAROLINA

(See Raleigh)

Real Estate, Real Estate Development, Real Estate Litigation, Construction Law, Commercial Litigation.

TWIGGS, BESKIND, STRICKLAND & RABENAU, P.A.

CARY, NORTH CAROLINA

(See Raleigh)

Personal Injury, Products Liability, Business Torts, Medical and other Professional Negligence, Federal and State Tort Claims, Environmental Torts, Insurance Bad Faith, Aviation Law and Wrongful Death.

VENTURE COUNSEL

Established in 2005
408 LEGAULT DRIVE
CARY, NORTH CAROLINA 27513
Telephone: 919-463-5500
Fax: 919-463-5600
Email: ken@venture-counsel.com
URL: http://www.venture-counsel.com

Venture Capital, Entrepreneurial Law; Corporate Law; Securities Law; Technology and Science.

FIRM PROFILE: Venture Counsel is a boutique corporate, securities and technology law firm serving entrepreneurs, start-ups and venture-backed companies primarily in the Research Triangle area. We are a highly focused firm, experienced in delivering sophisticated corporate counsel and strategic advice to entrepreneurs and growth companies in a practical manner.

KEN MAREADY, born Wilmington, North Carolina, January 9, 1969; admitted to bar, 1997, North Carolina. *Education:* Wake Forest University (B.A., 1992; J.D., magna cum laude, 1997). Editor-in-Chief, Wake Forest Law Review, 1996-1997; Regional Editor, Newsletter of Venture Capital & Private Equity Committee of the Business Section of the ABA, 2004-present;. *Member:* North Carolina Bar Association and American Bar Asso-

(This Listing Continued)

ciation (Member, Venture Capital and Private Equity Committee, Federal Regulated Securities Committee, Legal Opinions Committee and Health & Biotechnology Committee of Business Section). ***PRACTICE AREAS:*** Venture Capital; Entrepreneurial Business Law; Securities; Corporate Law; Technology and Science. ***Email:*** ken@venture-counsel.com

JEANNE H. WASHBURN

CARY, NORTH CAROLINA

(See Raleigh)

Civil Litigation, Personal Injury, Automobile Accidents and Injuries, Wrongful Death, Medical Malpractice, Workers Compensation.

THE WELLONS LAW FIRM

CARY, NORTH CAROLINA

(See Raleigh)

Corporate Law, Taxation, Employment Law, Family Law, Estate Planning, Estate Administration.

EDWARD V. WILLIAMS ATTORNEY AT LAW

CARY, NORTH CAROLINA

(See Raleigh)

Traffic Violations, Criminal Law, Driving While Intoxicated, Domestic Violence.

COWARD, HICKS & SILER, P.A.

Established in 1951

211 CASHIERS SCHOOL ROAD
P.O. BOX 1918
CASHIERS, NORTH CAROLINA 28717
Telephone: 828-743-2401
Fax: 828-743-2403

Sylva, North Carolina Office: 705 West Main Street, 28779. Telephone: 828-586-2147. Fax: 828-586-2605.

Franklin, North Carolina Office: 43 West Main Street, 28734. Telephone: 828-524-6475. Fax: 828-524-9833.

General Practice in all Courts. Trials, Eminent Domain, Personal Injury and Workers Compensation, Probate, Estate Planning, Real Estate, Corporations, Family Law.

COUNSEL FOR: Cullasaja Club; Highlands Country Club; Fairfield Communities Inc.; Country Club of Sapphire Valley, Inc.; Highlands Falls Country Club, Inc.; Mill Creek Golf Club of Franklin, Inc.; Smoky Mountain Area Mental Health; Zickgrat Enterprises, Inc.; Nantahala Lumber Co.; Golf Properties, Inc.; Franklin Board of Realtors, Inc.; Highland-Cashiers Board of Realtors, Inc.; Signal Ridge Yacht & Country Club; Town of Highlands; Village of Forest Hills; Angel Medical Center.
REPRESENTATIVE CLIENTS: Wachovia Bank and Trust Co.; TransAmerica Title Insurance Co.; Stewart Title Insurance Co.; Fidelity National Title Insurance Co.
APPROVED ATTORNEYS FOR: Lawyers Title Insurance Corp.; Federal Land Bank of Columbia; Farmers Home Administration; Fidelity National Title Insurance Co.; Stewart Title Insurance Co.; National Title Insurance Co.; Safeco Title Insurance Co.; Investors Title Insurance Co.; Title Insurance Company of Minnesota; American Title Insurance Co.; Chicago Title Insurance Co.; TransAmerica Title Insurance Co.; Wachovia Bank and Trust Co.; First Citizens Bank and Trust Co.; Macon Bank, Inc.; Centura Bank; First National Bank of Gainesville d/b/a/ The Mortgage Source; Rabun County Bank.
REFERENCES: First Citizens Bank and Trust Co.; Macon Bank, Inc.; Wachovia Bank and Trust Co.

(For complete biographical data on all personnel, see Professional Biographies at Sylva, North Carolina)

PETER A. PAUL, P.C.

872 U.S. HIGHWAY 64 WEST
P.O. BOX 3049
CASHIERS, NORTH CAROLINA 28717
Telephone: 828-743-5200
Fax: 828-743-5224

Real Estate Law, General Civil Practice, Corporation Law, Business Law, Estate Planning, Wills, Probate, Personal Injury, Automobile Accidents and Injuries.

PETER A. PAUL, born West Palm Beach, Florida, February 10, 1948; admitted to bar, 1982, Florida; 1989, North Carolina. *Education:* Florida State University (B.A., 1972); Cumberland School of Law of Samford University (J.D., 1981). Certified Mediator. *Member:* North Carolina (Member; Real Property Section) and American Bar Associations; 30th Judicial District Bar; The North Carolina State Bar; The Florida Bar. ***PRACTICE AREAS:*** Real Estate Law; Civil Litigation; Construction Litigation; Personal Injury; Automobile Accidents and Injuries.

APPROVED ATTORNEY FOR: American Title Insurance Co.; Chicago Title Insurance Co.; Commonwealth Land Title Insurance Co.; Lawyers Title Insurance Corp.; Stewart Title Guaranty Co.; Fidelity National Title Insurance Co.; Investors Title Insurance Co.; First Title Co.

BAGWELL, HOLT & SMITH, P.A.

Established in 1984

111 CLOISTER COURT, SUITE 200
CHAPEL HILL, NORTH CAROLINA 27517
Telephone: 919-401-0062
Fax: 919-403-0063
Email: info@bhspa.com
URL: http://www.bhspa.com

Commercial and Residential Real Estate, Business, Civil Litigation, Estate Planning, Creditor's Rights, Collections, Workers Compensation, Automobile Accidents, Personal Injury, Wrongful Death, Wills, Probate.

THOMAS R. HOLT, born Lancaster, Pennsylvania, June 23, 1958; admitted to bar, 1990, North Carolina. *Education:* Davis & Elkins College (B.A., 1980); University of North Carolina (J.D., 1990). *Member:* Orange County and North Carolina Bar Associations; North Carolina State Bar. ***PRACTICE AREAS:*** Residential Real Estate. ***Email:*** tholt@bhspa.com

NATHANIEL C. SMITH, born Burlington, North Carolina, May 22, 1961; admitted to bar, 1993, North Carolina. *Education:* University of North Carolina (B.A., 1983; J.D., with honors, 1993). Phi Alpha Delta. *Member:* North Carolina Bar Association; North Carolina State Bar; North Carolina Academy of Trial Lawyers. ***PRACTICE AREAS:*** Civil Litigation; Collections; Workers Compensation; Personal Injury. ***Email:*** nsmith@bhspa.com

---

CHRISTOPHER A. CROWSON, born Asheville, North Carolina, August 7, 1972; admitted to bar, 2004, North Carolina. *Education:* University of North Carolina (B.A., 1994); Campbell University School of Law (J.D., summa cum laude, 2004). Lead Articles Editor, Campbell Law Review, 2003-2004. *Member:* North Carolina Bar Association; North Carolina State Bar. ***PRACTICE AREAS:*** Commercial; Real Estate. ***Email:*** ccrowson@bhspa.com

OF COUNSEL

BETH TILLMAN LOGAN, born Natchez, Mississippi, September 4, 1963; admitted to bar, 1993, North Carolina. *Education:* Vanderbilt University (B.A., magna cum laude, 1985); University of North Carolina (M.A., English, 1988; J.D., with honors, 1993). Phi Beta Kappa. Member, 1991-1992 and Note Editor, 1992-1993, North Carolina Law Review. Author: "Exercising the Right to Die: North Carolina's Amended Natural Death Act and the 1991 Health Care Power of Attorney Act," North Carolina Law Review, Vol. 70. Member: Durham-Orange Estate Planning Council, 1999-2000; Board of Trustees, Chapel Hill Public Library, 1997-2000; Board of Trustees, Chapel Hill Public Library Foundation, 2000-2004. *Member:* North Carolina Bar Association (Member, Estate Planning Section, 1995-2004). ***PRACTICE AREAS:*** Estate Planning; Estate Administration. ***Email:*** leap@aol.com

O. KENNETH BAGWELL, JR., born Atlanta, Georgia, September 24, 1950; admitted to bar, 1979, North Carolina and U.S. District Court, Middle and Eastern Districts of North Carolina. *Education:* University of North Carolina (B.A., with honors, 1972; M.A., 1976; J.D., 1979). *Member:* Orange County (President, 1989) and North Carolina Bar Associations; North Carolina State Bar. ***PRACTICE AREAS:*** Commercial Real Estate; Business Law. ***Email:*** kbagwell@bhspa.com

REPRESENTATIVE CLIENTS: Sun Trust Bank; D.R. Horton, Inc.; KB Home, LLC; VilCom, Inc.; Vision Financial Federal Credit Union.

TRACY HICKS BARLEY & ASSOCIATES, P.A.

CHAPEL HILL, NORTH CAROLINA

(See Durham)

Bankruptcy - Chapters 7 and 13, Family Law, Equitable Distribution, Divorce, Child Custody, Child Support, Estates, Juvenile Law, Incorporations, Personal Injury.

BAYLISS, HUDSON & MERRITT

Established in 1980

BANK OF AMERICA PLAZA, SUITE 31
137 EAST FRANKLIN STREET
P.O. DRAWER 389
CHAPEL HILL, NORTH CAROLINA 27514
Telephone: 919-942-5191
Fax: 919-967-9089
Email: bhmnc@bellsouth.net

General Practice. Trials and Appeals in all State and Federal Courts, Trusts and Estates, Estate Planning, Probate, Wills, Contracts, Corporate, Business Law, Real Estate, Tax, Criminal, Traffic Violations, Driving While Intoxicated.

MEMBERS OF FIRM

MARCUS HUDSON, born Cumberland County, North Carolina, April 21, 1940; admitted to bar, 1965, North Carolina; 1980, U.S. Tax Court. *Education:* Davidson College (A.B., 1962); University of North Carolina (LL.B., 1965). (Board Certified Specialist in Estate Planning and Probate Law, North Carolina State Board of Legal Specialization). ***PRACTICE AREAS:*** Real Estate Law; Estate Planning Law; Taxation Law; Estate Administration; Trust Administration; Wills; Trusts. ***Email:*** mhudsbhm@bellsouth.net

RONALD W. MERRITT, born Durham, North Carolina, February 19, 1953; admitted to bar, 1978, North Carolina; 1983, U.S. District Court, Eastern District of North Carolina;

(This Listing Continued)

BAYLISS, HUDSON & MERRITT, Chapel Hill—Continued

1997, U.S. District Court, Middle District of North Carolina. *Education:* University of North Carolina (A.B., in Economics, 1975; J.D., 1978). ***PRACTICE AREAS:*** Civil Litigation; Family Law; Criminal Law; Driving While Intoxicated; Traffic; Construction Law; Personal Injury. ***Email:*** bhmnc@bellsouth.net

ASSOCIATE

CANDACE A. WEHR, born Chapel Hill, March 13, 1978; admitted to bar, 2003, North Carolina. *Education:* University of North Carolina at Chapel Hill (B.A., 2000); North Carolina Central University (J.D., 2003). ***PRACTICE AREAS:*** Estate Planning; Probate Administration; Individual Taxation; Fiduciary Income Tax; Family Law; Traffic Violations. ***Email:*** cfabhm@bellsouth.net

DONNA E. BENNICK, P.C.

Established in 1993
1829 EAST FRANKLIN STREET
BUILDING 600
CHAPEL HILL, NORTH CAROLINA 27514
Telephone: 919-968-6883
Fax: 919-968-6884
Email: donnabennick@yahoo.com
URL: http://www.donnabennickpc.com

Family Law, Divorce, Separation, Child Custody, Alimony, Property Settlements, Prenuptial Agreements, Certified Guardian Ad Litem and Parent Coordinator, Collaborative Law.

DONNA E. BENNICK, born Concord, North Carolina, April 16, 1959; admitted to bar, 1985, New York; 1991, North Carolina. *Education:* University of North Carolina at Chapel Hill (B.A., with honors, Political Science, 1981; J.D., 1984). Phi Eta Sigma. Honors Thesis, Party Elite Orientations to Merit Selection of Federal District Court Judges, 1981. Certified as a Guardian ad litem in Custody Cases in Orange and Chatham Counties, North Carolina; Certified as a Parent Coordinator in Custody Cases in Orange and Chatham Counties, North Carolina. Co-Author: "Prisoners Rights Project," 1984; Researched and Co-Authored Sections of the North Carolina Inmates Handbook, 1983. Author: "Equitable Distribution: What's Fair," Lorman Educational Services, 2001; "Spousal Support & Maintenance in New York," Lorman Educational Services, 2001. Former Attorney Mentor and Lecturer, In Motion, Inc., New York, New York. Lecturer, The Association of the Bar of the City of New York. Attorney Mentor and Lecturer for the Family Violence Prevention Center of Chapel Hill, North Carolina. *Member:* Orange County Bar Association, North Carolina and New York State Bar Associations; (Member, Sections on: Family Law; Trial Lawyers) Orange County Women's Bar Association; North Carolina Academy of Trial Lawyers; North Carolina Association of Women Attorneys. ***REPORTED CASES:*** Daniels v. Daniels, 243 A.D.2d 254 (1st Dept. 1997); Bartha v. Bartha, 15 A.D.3d 111, 789 N.Y.S.2d 13 (1st Dept. 2005). ***PRACTICE AREAS:*** Family Law; Alimony; Annulment; Cohabitation Agreements; Collaborative Family Law; Divorce; Divorce Taxation; Domestic Relations; Domestic Partnerships; Domestic Violence; Equitable Distribution; Gay and Lesbian Family Law; Interstate Support; Marital Agreements; Marital Property Distribution; Marital Property Law; Marital Property Settlements; Non-Traditional Family Law; Name Changes; Paternity; Post Divorce Modification; Postnuptial Agreements; Premarital Agreements; Qualified Domestic Relations Orders (QDROs); Restraining Orders; Separation Agreements; Spousal Support; Uncontested Divorce. ***Email:*** donnabennick@yahoo.com

LISA R. BRENMAN

BUILDING 600
1829 E. FRANKLIN STREET
CHAPEL HILL, NORTH CAROLINA 27514
Telephone: 919-932-4593
Fax: 919-942-8674
Email: attorney@visas-us.com
URL: http://www.visas-us.com

Family Immigration, Business Immigration, Labor Certification, Asylum, Student Visas, Citizenship.

LISA R. BRENMAN, born Boston, Massachusetts, June 12, 1957; admitted to bar, 1995, Utah; 1998, North Carolina. *Education:* Pennsylvania State University; Rutgers University; Humbolt State University (B.S., Natural Resource Management, 1982); University of Utah (J.D., 1995). Mediator: Landlord/Tenant Disputes; Consumer/Merchant Disputes. *Member:* Utah State Bar; North Carolina and American Bar Associations; American Immigration Lawyers Association. ***LANGUAGES:*** Spanish. ***PRACTICE AREAS:*** Immigration and Naturalization; Family Immigration Law; Business Immigration; Labor Certifications; Asylum; Visas; Citizenship.

BROWN & BUNCH, PLLC

101 NORTH COLUMBIA STREET
CHAPEL HILL, NORTH CAROLINA 27514
Telephone: 919-968-1111
Fax: 919-968-1444

Raleigh, North Carolina Office: 4900 Falls of Neuse Road, Suite 210, Post Office Box 19409. Telephone: 919-878-8060. Fax: 919-878-8062.
Durham, North Carolina Office: 21 West Colony Place, Suite 250, 27705. Telephone: 919-490-9700. Fax: 919-419-9736.

(This Listing Continued)

General Practice in all State and Federal Courts, Administrative Law, Antitrust Litigation, Appeals, Collections, Commercial Litigation, Commercial Transactions, Construction, Corporate Practice, Creditors' Rights, Employment Law, Estates and Trusts, Health Law, Lender Liability Defense, Mediation, Municipal and Land Use Law, Real Estate, State and Federal Taxation, Trade Regulation and Trials.

MEMBERS OF FIRM

CHARLES GORDON BROWN, born Winston-Salem, North Carolina, July 31, 1950; admitted to bar, 1975, Georgia; 1978, North Carolina, U.S. District Court, Eastern, Middle and Western Districts of North Carolina and Northern District of Georgia and U.S. Court of Appeals, Fourth Circuit. *Education:* University of North Carolina (A.B., summa cum laude, 1972); University of Virginia (J.D., 1975). Phi Beta Kappa; Order of the Coif; Phi Delta Phi. Member, Editorial Board, Virginia Law Review, 1974-1975. Assistant Professor of Law, 1978-1981 and Visiting Assistant Professor of Law, 1977-1978, University of North Carolina. Visiting Assistant Professor of Law, University of Texas, 1979. Bar Examination Lecturer, North Carolina Bar Association, 1981-1985. Recipient, Frederick B. McCall Award for Excellence in Teaching, 1980 and 1981. Reporter for N.C. Pattern Jury Instructions Committee, 1979-1981 and 1985-2003. Member, North Carolina State Bar Ethics Committee, 1997-2002. *Member:* Orange County and North Carolina (Member, Antitrust, Real Estate and Business Sections) Bar Associations; North Carolina State Bar; State Bar of Georgia. (Resident). ***PRACTICE AREAS:*** Trade Regulation; Commercial Litigation; Commercial Transactions. ***Email:*** gbrown@brownandbunch.com

WILLIAM W. BUNCH, III, born Edenton, North Carolina, October 18, 1954; admitted to bar, 1980, North Carolina, U.S. District Court, Eastern District of North Carolina and U.S. Court of Appeals, Fourth Circuit. *Education:* University of North Carolina (B.S., 1977; J.D., 1980). Beta Gamma Sigma; Phi Delta Phi. *Member:* Wake County, North Carolina (Member, Real Property Section) and American Bar Associations; North Carolina State Bar. (Resident, Raleigh Office). ***PRACTICE AREAS:*** Commercial Real Estate; Real Estate Development. ***Email:*** bbunch@brownandbunch.net

WILLIAM D. BERNARD, born Minneapolis, Minnesota, May 14, 1956; admitted to bar, 1982, Tennessee and U.S. District Court, Middle District of Tennessee; 1984, North Carolina and U.S. District Court, Eastern and Middle Districts of North Carolina; 1986, U.S. District Court, Western District of North Carolina. *Education:* University of North Carolina (B.A., 1978; M.B.A., 1982; J.D., 1982). *Member:* Orange County, North Carolina (Member, Real Property and Business Law Sections) and American Bar Associations; North Carolina State Bar. (Resident). ***PRACTICE AREAS:*** Commercial Law; Residential and Commercial Real Estate. ***Email:*** wbernard@brownandbunch.com

A. VANN IRVIN, born Shelby, North Carolina, January 14, 1951; admitted to bar, 1982, Tennessee; 1984, Georgia; 1986, North Carolina; 1993, U.S. Tax Court and U.S. Court of Appeals, Fourth and Sixth Circuits. *Education:* College of Albemarle (A.A., 1971); University of North Carolina (B.A., 1973; J.D., 1982). *Member:* Durham County, North Carolina and American Bar Associations; State Bar of Georgia; North Carolina State Bar. (Board Certified Specialist in Estate Planning and Probate Law, North Carolina State Board of Legal Specialization) (Resident, Durham Office). ***PRACTICE AREAS:*** Trusts and Estates; Wills; Business Law; Probate; Taxation; Corporate Law. ***Email:*** vannirvin@aol.com

LEANN NEASE BROWN, born Greensboro, North Carolina, May 7, 1955; admitted to bar, 1984, North Carolina, U.S. District Court, Eastern and Middle Districts of North Carolina, U.S. Court of Appeals, Fourth Circuit and U.S. Tax Court. *Education:* University of North Carolina (B.A., 1977); University of North Carolina School of Medical Allied Health Sciences (M.S., 1981); University of North Carolina School of Law (J.D., 1984). *Member:* Orange County, North Carolina (Member, Sections on: Litigation; Dispute Resolution; Health Law; Chair, 1996-1997, Antitrust and Trade Regulation; Chair, Trial Practice Curriculum Committee, 2002-2005; Member, CLE Committee, 2002—; Zoning, Planning and Land Use, Secretary 2005—) and American Bar Associations; North Carolina State Bar. D.R.C. Certified Mediator, Superior Court Matters and Family Financial Matters, North Carolina. (Resident). ***PRACTICE AREAS:*** Litigation; Zoning, Planning and Land Use; Health Law; Employment Law; Mediation. ***Email:*** lnease@brownandbunch.com

SCOTT D. ZIMMERMAN, born Berea, Ohio, June 1, 1963; admitted to bar, 1989, North Carolina, U.S. District Court, Eastern and Middle Districts of North Carolina and U.S. Court of Appeals, Fourth Circuit. *Education:* University of North Carolina (B.A., 1985; J.D., with honors, 1989). *Member:* Orange County, North Carolina and American Bar Associations; North Carolina State Bar; The Association of Trial Lawyers of America. (Resident). ***PRACTICE AREAS:*** Civil Litigation. ***Email:*** szimmerman@brownandbunch.com

COUNSEL FOR: Bank of America, N.A.; Mellon Bank, N.A.; SunTrust Bank; Chicago Title Insurance Company; Investors Title Insurance Company; Kenan Enterprises, Inc.; Town of Cary; Dycom Industries, Inc; ANSCO & Associates, LLC; Globe Communications, LLC; Hydro Tube Corp.; Fidelity National Title Insurance Company; Horton Enterprises, LLC; Meadowlands Associates; Buckhorn Ridge Associates, LLC; Strategic Properties, LLC; Ford Motor Credit Company; Carolina Hosiery Mills, Inc.
GENERAL COUNSEL FOR: Affordable Care, Inc.; Chapel Hill Internal Medicine, L.L.P.; Crossroads Ford, Inc.; The Educational Foundation, Inc.; Home Health Foundation of Chapel Hill, Inc.; Orange-Person-Chatham Mental Health, Developmental Disabilities and Substance Abuse Authority; Vicious Cycle Software, Inc.; Winston Hotels, Inc. (NYSE); Worden Bros., Inc.; Centrex Properties, Inc.; First Oakland Properties, Inc.
APPROVED ATTORNEYS FOR: Commonwealth Land Title Insurance Co.; Lawyers Title Insurance Co.; First Title Insurance Co.; Investors Title Insurance Co.; Chicago Title Insurance Co.; Title Company of North Carolina, Inc.; Fidelity National Title Insurance Company.
REFERENCES: Centura Bank; Bank of America; SunTrust Bank.

HEIDI G. CHAPMAN, P.L.L.C.

100 EUROPA DRIVE, SUITE 560
CHAPEL HILL, NORTH CAROLINA 27517
Telephone: 919-968-6116
Fax: 919-968-6166
Email: heidi@heidichapmanlaw.com
URL: http://www.lawyers.com/heidichapmanlaw

Workers Compensation, Auto Accidents, Wrongful Death, Personal Injury, Social Security Disability.

(This Listing Continued)

HEIDI G. CHAPMAN, born New York, New York, December 4, 1953; admitted to bar, 1983, North Carolina; 1984, U.S. District Court, Eastern District of North Carolina; 1985, U.S. District Court, Middle District of North Carolina. *Education:* Ludwig-Maximilian Universitat, West Germany; Duke University (B.A., magna cum laude, 1975); University of North Carolina at Chapel Hill (J.D., 1983). *Member:* North Carolina Bar Association; North Carolina State Bar (President, 15B Judicial District Bar, 1990-1991); North Carolina Academy of Trial Lawyers (Secretary, Workers Compensation Law Section, 2004—); The Association of Trial Lawyers of America. ***LANGUAGES:*** German and French.

COLEMAN, GLEDHILL, HARGRAVE & PEEK, P.C.

CHAPEL HILL, NORTH CAROLINA

(See Hillsborough)

General Civil and Criminal Trial Practice in all State and Federal Courts. Litigation, Negligence, Domestic, Real Estate, Corporate, Municipal and Probate Law, Commercial Transactions and Litigation.

EDWARDS & TRENKLE, PLLC

CHAPEL HILL, NORTH CAROLINA

(See Durham)

Criminal Law, Driving While Intoxicated (DWI), Drug Crimes, Felonies, Parole and Probation, Traffic Violations, Personal Injury, Auto Accidents, Dog Bites, Sexual Abuse, Wrongful Death.

EKSTRAND & EKSTRAND, LLP

CHAPEL HILL, NORTH CAROLINA

(See Durham)

Criminal Law, Driving While Intoxicated (DWI), Drug Crimes, Felonies, Misdemeanors, Traffic Violations, Personal Injury, Automobile Accidents, Wrongful Death, Medical Malpractice, Wills, Probate, Commercial Bankruptcy, Contracts, Legal Malpractice, Education.

EPTING & HACKNEY

Established in 1974

410 MARTIN LUTHER KING, JR. BLVD.
P.O. BOX 1329
CHAPEL HILL, NORTH CAROLINA 27514
Telephone: 919-929-0323
Fax: 919-929-3960

General Civil and Criminal Practice, Trials, Family Law, Real Estate, Business and Corporations, Wills, Probate, Estate Planning.

FIRM PROFILE: The firm was founded in 1974, and its members have extensive civil and criminal trial experience and have diverse and lengthy records of public service and service to clients in Orange and Chatham Counties.

MEMBERS OF FIRM

ROBERT EPTING, born High Point, North Carolina, July 18, 1945; admitted to bar, 1970, Ohio; 1972, North Carolina; 1975, U.S. District Court, Eastern, Middle and Western Districts of North Carolina and U.S. Supreme Court; 1980, U.S. Court of Appeals, Fourth Circuit. *Education:* University of North Carolina (A.B., 1967; J.D., 1970). Member, North Carolina Law Review, 1969-1970. Mayor Pro Tem and Council Member, Town of Chapel Hill, 1975-1979. Member, Board of Directors and Secretary-Treasurer, 1976-1979 and General Counsel, 1984—, Orange Water and Sewer Authority. Commissioner, North Carolina Environmental Management Commission, 1992-2002. *Member:* Orange County (President, 1976-1977) and North Carolina Bar Associations; 15-B Judicial District and North Carolina State Bars; North Carolina Academy of Trial Lawyers. ***PRACTICE AREAS:*** Environmental Law; Civil Litigation; Criminal Law; Utilities; Condemnation; Family Law; Aviation Law. **Email:** bobepting@aol.com

JOE HACKNEY, born Siler City, North Carolina, September 23, 1945; admitted to bar, 1970, North Carolina; 1975, U.S. Supreme Court and U.S. District Court, Middle District of North Carolina; 1984, U.S. Court of Appeals, Fourth Circuit. *Education:* North Carolina State University; University of North Carolina (A.B., with honors, 1967); University of North Carolina (J.D., 1970). Research Assistant to the Hon. J. Frank Huskins, Associate Justice, Supreme Court of North Carolina, 1970-1971. Assistant District Attorney, 15th District of North Carolina, 1971-1974. Member, North Carolina House of Representatives, 1981—; Speaker Pro Tempore, 1999-2002; House Democratic Leader, 2003-2004; House Majority Leader, 2005—. Chairman: Committee on Environmental Quality and Natural Resources, Southern Legislative Conference, 1989-1991; Environment Committee, National Conference of State Legislatures, 2000-2001. *Member:* Orange County (President, 1973-1974), North Carolina (Member, Sections on: Family Law; Litigation) and American (Member, Section on: Family Law) Bar Associations; 15-B Judicial District (Vice-President, 1979-1980; President, 1980-1981) and North Carolina State Bars; North Carolina Academy of Trial Lawyers. ***PRACTICE AREAS:*** Civil Litigation; Family Law; Personal Injury; Professional Liability.

ELIZABETH LACKEY JACOBS, born Newport News, Virginia, December 5, 1952; admitted to bar, 1981, North Carolina; 1985, U.S. District Court, Middle District of North Carolina. *Education:* University of South Carolina (B.A., with honors, 1974); University of North Carolina (J.D., 1981). Board Member, 1985-1995, Vice Chairman, 1986 and Chairman, 1987-1989, 1992-1995, Carrboro Planning Board. Board Member: Eno River Association, 1999—, President, 2003—; Orange Community Housing Corporation, 1998-2002. *Member:* Orange County (Vice President, 1987; President, 1988) and North Carolina

(This Listing Continued)

(Member, Section on Real Property) Bar Associations; 15-B Judicial District and North Carolina State Bars. ***PRACTICE AREAS:*** Real Estate; Business; Corporate Law; Development and Zoning; Civil Practice. **Email:** robinjacobs@earthlink.net

KAREN P. DAVIDSON, born Alamance County, North Carolina, June 14, 1950; admitted to bar, 1981, North Carolina. *Education:* Stanford University (B.A., 1972); University of North Carolina at Chapel Hill (M.A., 1977; J.D., 1981). Board of Directors, Chatham County Dispute Settlement Center, 1984-1986. Director, 15B District Bar. Attorney 15B Guardian ad Liten Program, 1995—. *Member:* North Carolina Bar Association; North Carolina State Bar; North Carolina Academy of Trial Lawyers. ***LANGUAGES:*** Russian, French, Spanish, Italian. ***PRACTICE AREAS:*** Criminal; Traffic; Juvenile; Family Law.

STEVE LACKEY, born Charlotte, North Carolina, February 25, 1957; admitted to bar, 1996, North Carolina. *Education:* University of North Carolina at Chapel Hill (B.A., 1980; J.D., 1996); University of Texas (M.A., 1985). Member, Board of Directors, Public School Foundation, 1997-2000. Chair, Triangle United Way Senior Issues Team, 2000—. Co-Chair, Joint Planning Team of Orange County, Advisory Board on Aging and United Way Seniors Team. Volunteer, 15-B Guardian Ad Litem Program, 1993—. *Member:* North Carolina (Member, Sections on: Elder Law; Estate Planning and Fiduciary Law) and American Bar Associations; North Carolina State Bar. ***PRACTICE AREAS:*** Civil Practice; Probate; Estate Planning. **Email:** steve_lackey@excite.com

FERGUSON, STEIN, CHAMBERS, GRESHAM & SUMTER, P.A.

Established in 1964

SUITE 2, 312 WEST FRANKLIN STREET
CHAPEL HILL, NORTH CAROLINA 27516
Telephone: 919-933-5300
Fax: 919-967-4953
Email: astein@fswags.com
Email: wsimpson@law.fswags.com

Charlotte, North Carolina Office: 741 Kenilworth Avenue, Suite 300 Telephone: 704-375-8461. Fax: 704-334-5654.

General Civil, Employment and Labor, Criminal, Trial and Appellate Practice. Specializes in Medical Negligence, Civil Rights, Education and Personal Injury Law.

FIRM PROFILE: Ferguson, Stein, Chambers, Gresham & Sumter, P.A. is a multi-specialty law firm based in Charlotte, North Carolina, which has been in business since 1964. The firm was founded by Julius L. Chambers, who left the firm in 1984 to become Director-Counsel of the NAACP Legal Defense and Educational Fund, Inc. in New York. Currently there are a total of 13 attorneys from diverse backgrounds working in the Charlotte and Chapel Hill offices. The firm has a national and international reputation in school desegregation, employment discrimination, voting rights, general civil rights litigation, and criminal defense. It is also nationally and regionally known for its representation of plaintiffs in personal injury and medical negligence cases, its work in teacher rights and education law, administrative law, workers compensation, and estates, business, corporate and real estate matters. Listed in the Martindale-Hubbell Bar Register of Preeminent Lawyers, the firm encourages professional development and activities: many of its members hold leadership positions in a wide variety of professional organizations and regularly teach academic courses and at trial advocacy and continuing legal education programs.

ADAM STEIN, born New York, N.Y., September 3, 1937; admitted to bar, 1968, District of Columbia and North Carolina. *Education:* Haverford College; Washington Square College; New York University (B.A., 1964); George Washington University (J.D., with honors, 1967). Phi Delta Phi. North Carolina Appellate Defender, 1981-1985. *Member:* Orange County (President, 1975), North Carolina (Member, Appellate Rules Study Committee, 1981—) and American (Member, Section of: Litigation; Criminal Justice; Individual Rights and Responsibilities) Bar Associations; The District of Columbia Bar; 15B District and North Carolina State (Past Councillor) Bars; North Carolina Academy of Trial Lawyers (Vice President, Membership Services, 1989-1990; President-Elect, 1991; President, 1992; Member, Board of Governors, 1988—; Member, Executive Committee, 1989—); The Association of Trial Lawyers of America (Member, Board of Governors, 1993—); North Carolina College of Advocacy; National Association of Criminal Defense Lawyers; National Legal Aid and Defenders Association (Co-Chairman, Defender's Appellate Council, 1983-1984); American Board of Trial Advocates; North State Legal Services, Inc. (Director and President, 1978-1980); Center for Death Penalty Litigation (Member, Board of Directors, 1995-2000); North Carolina Commission on Indigent Defense Services (Chair, 2000—). [With U.S. Army, 1958-1961, 1961-1962]. ***REPORTED CASES:*** Harris v. Miller, 335 N.C. 379, 438 SE.2d 731 (1994); West v. Atkins, 487 US 42 (1988); State v. McCollum & Brown, 321 NC 557, 364 SE.2d 112 (1988); Cotton v. Scotland Neck City Board of Education, (reported with United States v. Scotland Neck), 457 US 484 (1972). ***PRACTICE AREAS:*** Civil Rights Law; Plaintiff's Medical Malpractice; Appellate Practice. **Email:** astein@law.fswags.com

WILLIAM G. SIMPSON, JR., born Plymouth, North Carolina, December 28, 1960; admitted to bar, 1986, North Carolina and U.S. District Court, Eastern and Middle Districts of North Carolina; 1993, Pennsylvania and U.S. District Court, Western District of North Carolina; U.S. Court of Appeals, Fourth Circuit; U.S. Supreme Court. *Education:* University of North Carolina at Chapel Hill (B.A., 1983; J.D., 1986). Author, "The Primary Runoff: Racism's Reprieve," N.C. Law Rev., Vol. 65, No. 2 (1987). Staff Attorney, Legal Directory, ACLU of North Carolina, 1986-1993; Assistant Defender, Defender Association of Philadelphia. *Member:* North Carolina Academy of Trial Lawyers; The Association of Trial Lawyers of America. ***REPORTED CASES:*** Corum v. Univ. of North Carolina, 413 S.E.2d 276 (1992); Harwood v. Johnson, 388S.E.2d 439 (1990); U.S. v, Santoro, 866 F.2d 1538 (4th Cir., 1989). ***PRACTICE AREAS:*** Medical Negligence; Criminal Defense; Civil Rights. **Email:** wsimpson@law.fswags.com

(For complete biographical data on all personnel, see Professional Biographies at Charlotte, North Carolina)

LAW OFFICE OF JOHN C. FITZPATRICK, P.C.

CHAPEL HILL, NORTH CAROLINA

(See Durham)

DWI, Traffic, Criminal, Personal Injury.

FRANKLIN LAW CENTER, PLLC

EXCHANGE WEST AT MEADOWMONT
1414 RALEIGH ROAD, SUITE 290
CHAPEL HILL, NORTH CAROLINA 27517-8834
Telephone: 919-942-0800
Fax: 919-942-0607
Email: sfranklin@franklinlawcenter.com
URL: http://www.franklinlawcenter.com

Pittsboro Office: 60 West Street, P.O. Box 685, 27312. Telephone: 919-942-0800. Fax: 919-942-0607.

Divorce, Alimony, Spousal Support, Separation Agreements, Marital Property Settlements, Equitable Distribution of Assets, Cohabitation Agreements, Community Property Law, Non-Traditional Family Law, Divorce Mediation, Divorce Arbitration, Collaborative Family Law, Adoption, International Family Law, Child Custody, Military Divorce, Military Family Law, Trial Practice in all Courts.

FIRM PROFILE: Serving Orange and Chatham Counties in all family law related matters.

SUSAN R. FRANKLIN, born Willmar, Minnesota, September 7, 1949; admitted to bar, 1979, Illinois and U.S. District Court, Northern District of Illinois; 1981, U.S. Court of Appeals, Seventh Circuit; 1997, North Carolina; 2003, U.S. District Court, Eastern, Western and Middle Districts of North Carolina. *Education:* North Park University (B.A., 1970); Illinois Institute of Technology Chicago-Kent College of Law (J.D., 1979). Current Member, Board of Adjustment, Town of Chapel Hill, 2002—. Mayoral Candidate, Town of Chapel Hill, 1999. Member, Transportation Board, Town of Chapel Hill, 1998-2001. *Member:* North Carolina State Bar; North Carolina Bar Association; North Carolina Academy of Trial Lawyers; American Bar Association; The Association of Trial Lawyers of America. ***Email:*** sfranklin@franklinlawcenter.com

GREGORY HERMAN-GIDDENS
TrustCounsel, P.A.

Established in 1996
205 PROVIDENCE ROAD
CHAPEL HILL, NORTH CAROLINA 27514
Telephone: 919-493-6351
Toll Free: 800-201-0413
Facsimile: 919-493-6355
Email: ghgiddens@trustcounselpa.com
URL: http://www.trustcounselpa.com

Trusts and Estates, Wills, Probate, Taxation, Business Law, Guardianships, Charitable Trusts and Foundations, Elder Law, Estate Planning, Asset Protection.

GREGORY HERMAN-GIDDENS, born Birmingham, Alabama, August 8, 1961; admitted to bar, 1988, North Carolina and U.S. District Court, Middle District of North Carolina; 1992, Florida; 1998, U.S. Supreme Court; 2001, U.S. Tax Court; 2004, Tennessee. *Education:* University of North Carolina (B.A., 1984); Tulane University Law School (J.D., 1988); University of Miami Law School (LL.M., Estate Planning, 1993). Phi Beta Kappa; Psi Chi. Author: "Charitable Remainder Trusts," Taxation for Accountants, Journal, May 1998. Also published in Taxation for Lawyers, July/Aug., 1998. License, Series 6 and 63, National Association of Securities Dealers. *Member:* North Carolina (Member, Sections on: Estate Planning and Fiduciary Law, Taxation, and Elder Law), Tennessee, and American (Member, Sections on: Real Property, Probate and Trust Law and Taxation) Bar Associations; The Florida Bar (Member, Sections on: Real Property, Probate and Trust Law, Taxation, and Elder Law). (Board Certified Specialist in Estate Planning and Probate Law, North Carolina State Bar Board of Legal Specialization). ***PRACTICE AREAS:*** Estate Planning; Probate; Estate and Gift Taxation; Wills; Trust Law; Charitable Trusts and Foundations; Guardianship; Trust Administration; Fiduciary Income Tax; Asset Protection; Family Wealth Transfer; Elder Law.

HIGGINS, FRANKSTONE, GRAVES & MORRIS, P.A.

Established in 1983
THE EXCHANGE WEST AT MEADOWMONT
1414 RALEIGH ROAD, SUITE 320
CHAPEL HILL, NORTH CAROLINA 27517-8834
Telephone: 919-968-4717
Fax: 919-929-1415
URL: http://www.hfgmlaw.com
Mailing Address: P.O. Box 2869, Chapel Hill, NC 27514

Cary, North Carolina Office: 14600 Weston Parkway, Suite 300, 27513-2259. Telephone: 919-678-8880. Fax: 919-678-8885.

Estate Planning, Probate, Corporate, Real Estate, Civil Litigation, Taxation and General Business Law.

FIRM PROFILE: Since the firm's establishment in 1983 by Thomas D. Higgins, III, David R. Frankstone and Wm. Griffin Graves, III, the firm has focused on estate planning, commercial and residential real estate transactions and representation of small businesses. The firm primarily represents individuals and small businesses throughout the counties of Orange, Chatham, Durham and Wake. The firm is dedicated to providing top quality professional service at a reasonable cost.

THOMAS D. HIGGINS, III, born Jamestown, New York, January 26, 1946; admitted to bar, 1971, North Carolina; 1973, U.S. District Court, Middle District of North Carolina; 1979, U.S. Tax Court. *Education:* University of North Carolina (B.A., 1968; J.D., 1971). Phi Delta Phi. *Member:* Orange County and North Carolina (Member, Sections on: Probate and Fiduciary Law; Commercial, Banking and Business Law) Bar Associations; 15-B Judicial District and The North Carolina State Bars. Certified Mediator. ***PRACTICE AREAS:*** Trusts and Estates; Trusts and Estates Taxation; Business Estate Planning; Business Organizations; Commercial Real Estate; Closely Held Corporations; Exchanges. ***Email:*** thiggins@hfgmlaw.com

DAVID R. FRANKSTONE, born San Antonio, Texas, May 2, 1948; admitted to bar, 1975, North Carolina. *Education:* Washington & Lee University (B.S., 1970); University of North Carolina (J.D., with honors, 1975). Staff Member, North Carolina Law Review, 1974-1975. *Member:* Orange County, North Carolina and American (Member, Real Property, Probate and Trust Law Section) Bar Associations; 15-B Judicial District and The North Carolina State Bars. (Board Certified Specialist in Estate Planning and Probate Law, North Carolina State Board of Legal Specialization). ***PRACTICE AREAS:*** Trusts and Estates; Trusts and Estates Taxation; Wills; Family Limited Partnerships; Probate. ***Email:*** dfrankstone@hfgmlaw.com

WM. GRIFFIN GRAVES, III, born Greensboro, North Carolina, March 22, 1950; admitted to bar, 1976, North Carolina. *Education:* University of North Carolina (A.B., 1972); Wake Forest University (J.D., 1976). Phi Delta Phi. *Member:* Orange County and North Carolina Bar Associations; 15-B Judicial District and North Carolina State Bars. (Also at Cary, North Carolina Office). ***PRACTICE AREAS:*** Real Estate; Commercial Real Estate; Wills; Trusts and Estates; Business Law. ***Email:*** wggraves@hfgmlaw.com

DAVID S. MORRIS, born Sanford, North Carolina, August 12, 1946; admitted to bar, 1977, North Carolina. *Education:* University of North Carolina (A.B., 1968; J.D., with honors, 1977); University of Pennsylvania, The Wharton School (M.B.A., 1975). *Member:* Wake County, North Carolina and American Bar Associations; North Carolina State Bar. [Lt., USN, 1968-1973]. (Resident, Cary Office). ***PRACTICE AREAS:*** Business Organizations; Partnership and Corporate Taxation; Commercial Real Estate; Securities; Private Placement. ***Email:*** dmorris@hfgmcary.com

KENNETH L. EAGLE, born Salisbury, North Carolina, June 18, 1949; admitted to bar, 1974, North Carolina. *Education:* University of North Carolina at Chapel Hill (B.A., with honors, 1971; J.D., 1974). Morehead Scholar. *Member:* Wake County, 10th Judicial District and North Carolina Bar Associations; North Carolina State Bar. (Resident, Cary Office). ***PRACTICE AREAS:*** Commercial Real Estate; Business Law; Commercial Leasing. ***Email:*** keagle@hfgmcary.com

---

DAVID J. HART, born Cedar Rapids, Iowa, July 20, 1961; admitted to bar, 1991, North Carolina. *Education:* San Diego State University (B.S., 1983); University of North Carolina (J.D., 1991). Articles Editor, North Carolina Journal of International Law and Commercial Regulation. Certified Public Accountant, Illinois, 1984. *Member:* North Carolina State Bar. ***PRACTICE AREAS:*** Litigation; Corporate Law; Leases and Leasing; Business Law. ***Email:*** dhart@hfgmcary.com

ROBERT KENDRICK RICE, born 1973; admitted to bar, 2002, North Carolina. *Education:* Appalachian State University (B.S., B.A., 1996); University of Miami School of Law (J.D., 2001). ***PRACTICE AREAS:*** Commercial Real Estate; Business Transactions; Automotive Franchises and Dealerships. ***Email:*** rrice@hfgmcary.com

GEOERGE-ANN P. CROCKER, born November 10, 1976; admitted to bar, 2001, North Carolina. *Education:* Peace College (A.A., 1996); University of North Carolina at Chapel Hill (B.A., 1998); Campbell University (J.D., 2001). *Member:* North Carolina and 15-B Judicial District Bar Associations; North Carolina State Bar. ***PRACTICE AREAS:*** Wills; Trusts and Estates; Trusts and Estates Taxation; Business Law; Probate. ***Email:*** gpcrocker@hfgmlaw.com

REPRESENTATIVE CLIENTS: GFD Management, Inc.; Central Carolina Bank & Trust Co., N.A.; Duke Power Co.; PHE, Inc.; Fitch Lumber Co.; Morgan Imports, Inc.; Branch Banking and Trust Co.; A. Klein & Co., Inc.; S & R Realty Partners; Southtrust Bank of North Carolina; Kenan Transport Company; Hendrick Automotive Group; Saturn of Raleigh.
REFERENCES: Central Carolina Bank & Trust Co.; Bank of America; Investors Title Insurance Co.; First Union National Bank; Lawyers Title Insurance Co.; Centura Bank.

HOWARD, STALLINGS, FROM & HUTSON, P.A.

CHAPEL HILL, NORTH CAROLINA

(See Raleigh)

General, Civil and Commercial Litigation, Business Law, Commercial Real Estate, Taxation, Employment Law, Computer Law, Estate Planning and Administration, Bankruptcy Law, Loan Structuring and Workouts, Intellectual Property Law, Personal Injury.

INTELLECTUAL PROPERTY/ TECHNOLOGY LAW

Established in 1992
1414 RALEIGH ROAD, SUITE 201
CHAPEL HILL, NORTH CAROLINA 27517
Telephone: 919-419-9350
Fax: 919-419-9354
Email: Info@iptl.com
URL: http://www.iptl.com
Mailing Address: P.O. Box 14329, Research Triangle Park, NC 27709

(This Listing Continued)

LEWIS, ANDERSON, PHILLIPS, GREENE & HINKLE, PLLC, Chapel Hill—Continued

Staff Member, Journal of International Law and Commercial Regulation. *Member:* North Carolina (Member: Estate Planning & Fiduciary Law and Elder Law Sections), Durham County (President, Young Lawyers Division, 2001-2002) and American (Member, Probate and Property Section) Bar Associations. ***PRACTICE AREAS:*** Estate Planning; Estate Administration; Wills; Probate; Trust Law; Elder Law; Business Law; Real Estate. ***Email:*** anicholson@lapgh.com

CHELLIE MARTIN JOINES, born Edinburgh, Scotland, 1951; admitted to bar, 2004, North Carolina. *Education:* University of North Carolina at Chapel Hill (B.A., 1974); North Carolina Central University Law School (J.D., 2002). *Member:* North Carolina Bar Association. ***PRACTICE AREAS:*** Family Law.

OF COUNSEL

BARBARA D. ANDERSON, born Baltimore, Maryland, March 23, 1936; admitted to bar, 1981, North Carolina. *Education:* Swarthmore College (B.A., 1957); Duke University (J.D., 1980). Chairman, Board of Trustees, The Forest at Duke. *Member:* North Carolina Bar Association. ***PRACTICE AREAS:*** Estate Planning; Estate Administration; Wills; Trust Law.

HERMAN F. GREENE, born Raleigh, North Carolina, 1945; admitted to bar, 1980, New York; 1983, Colorado; 1992, North Carolina. *Education:* University of Florida (B.A., 1966); Stanford University (M.A., 1967); University of Chicago (M. Div., 1969); University of North Carolina (J.D., 1979). Order of the Coif. Research Editor, University of North Carolina Law Review, 1978-1979. Associate, Shearman & Sterling, 1979-1983. Partner, Mayer Brown & Platt, 1983-1990. Director, Office of Public Responsibility, American Express Company, 1990-1991. Partner, Daniels & Daniels, P.A., 1992-2002. *Member:* North Carolina and American Bar Associations. ***PRACTICE AREAS:*** Corporate; Partnerships; International Law; Taxation; Securities; Mergers and Acquisitions; Corporate Finance; Nonprofit Organizations. ***Email:*** hgreene@lapgh.com

LONG & LONG

127 TIMBERHILL PLACE
CHAPEL HILL, NORTH CAROLINA 27514
Telephone: 919-929-0408
Fax: 919-929-6819

Family Law, Custody, Support, Property Division, Mediation, Arbitration, Collaborative Law.

MEMBERS OF FIRM

LUNSFORD LONG, born Cleveland, Ohio, December 26, 1945; admitted to bar, 1972, North Carolina. *Education:* University of North Carolina (A.B., 1967; J.D., with Honors, 1972). Order of the Coif. N.C. Law Review, 1970-1971. Law Clerk to the Hon. J. Frank Huskins, Associate Justice, Supreme Court, 1972-1973. Certified Superior Court Mediator. *Member:* Orange County Bar Association(President, 1981), North Carolina Bar Association (Chairman, Family Law Section, 1988-1989) and American Bar Association; District 15-B (President, 1986) and North Carolina State Bar (Bar Councilor, 1998—). ***PRACTICE AREAS:*** Family Law.

FLORENCE J. LONG, born Philipsburg, Pennsylvania; admitted to bar, 1984, North Carolina. *Education:* University of North Carolina (A.B., 1982; J.D., 1984). Phi Beta Kappa. Registered Nurse, North Carolina, 1973. *Member:* Orange County, North Carolina and American Bar Associations; Judicial District 15-B and North Carolina State Bars.

DANNETTE D. TOTH, born Los Angeles, California, June 19, 1946; admitted to bar, 2003, North Carolina. *Education:* University of California (A.B., 1967; M.B.A., 1979); University of North Carolina (J.D., 2003). *Member:* Orange County, Judicial District 15-B, North Carolina and American Bar Associations; North Carolina State Bar.

MAITLAND & MAITLAND, PLLC

Established in 2002
MAITLAND LAW BUILDING
2 COUCH ROAD
CHAPEL HILL, NORTH CAROLINA 27514
Telephone: 919-265-0800
Fax: 919-960-9554
Email: Info@MaitlandLaw.com
URL: http://www.MaitlandLaw.com

Mailing Address: P.O. Box 2525, Chapel Hill, NC 27515-2525

Real Estate, Closings, Residential, Commercial, Business Law, Entrepreneurial, Partnerships, Small Business, Entrepreneur, Business Formation, Immigration, Naturalization, Citizenship, Permanent Resident, Investor, Teacher Visas, H1B, J1, Visa Petitions, Litigation, Banking, Contracts, Foreclosure, Mortgages, Personal Injury, Traffic Violations, DWI, DUI, Liquor License, Alcohol Permit, Wills, Banking, Collection, Sports, Entertainment Law.

FIRM PROFILE: A law firm centered in Chapel Hill, North Carolina, providing comprehensive legal services to clients in North Carolina and Florida with primary focus on real estate, business and immigration law. Our new building is located in the heart of Franklin Street's "Realtor Row" providing convenience for realtors and clients.

ROBERT N. MAITLAND, II, born Bellflower, California, August 9, 1962; admitted to bar, 1997, Florida; 2002, North Carolina. *Education:* University of California at Los Angeles (B.A., 1984); University of North Carolina at Chapel Hill (J.D., 1997). Phi Eta Sigma. Alumni Scholar, UCLA. Recipient, UNC Law Dearborn Memorial Scholarship. Member, NC Journal of International Law and Commercial Regulation, 1995-1996. Experience: General Counsel, Visiting International Faculty Program, 2001-2002; Associate, McCarthy, Summers, et al, 1997-2001. Vice President, Citibank, 1993-1994. Vice President/Regional Manager, Great Western Bank (nka Washington Mutual) 1987-1993. *Member:* American Immigration Lawyers; North Carolina Academy of Trial Lawyers; American Trial Lawyers; North Carolina and American Bar Associations; The Florida Bar. ***PRACTICE AREAS:*** Real Estate; Business Law; Immigration; Litigation; Banking; Collections; Foreclosures; Visas. ***Email:*** Rob@MaitlandLaw.com

SCOTT MAITLAND, born Bellflower, California, October 12, 1966; admitted to bar, 1997, North Carolina. *Education:* United States Military Academy (B.S., 1988); University of North Carolina at Chapel Hill (J.D., 1995). Kenan Chancellor Scholar and Davis Society Member, UNC Law. Experience: Founder, Top of the Hill Restaurant & Brewery, Chapel Hill, NC, 1996—. Member, Board of Visitors UNC-CH, 2003—. Member, Board of Directors, UNC Educational Foundation, 2003—. President, Chamber of Commerce, Chapel Hill/Carrboro, 2002-2003. Board of Directors, Chapel Hill Downtown Commission, 1996-2002. *Member:* North Carolina Bar Association. [Cpr, Corps of Engineers, United States Army, 1988-1991]. ***PRACTICE AREAS:*** Entrepreneurial Business Law; Real Estate Development; Sports Law; Liquor Licensing. ***Email:*** Scott@MaitlandLaw.com

Language: Spanish.

REPRESENTATIVE CLIENTS: WCHL Radio; The Chapel Hill/Carrboro Chamber of Commerce; Cal-Chem Corp.; Dunkin'Donuts (Durham); The Best Service Co.; Kayye Consulting, Inc.; University Florist; Botamica, LLC; The Laughing Turtle; Design 149.

MANNING & CROUCH

CHAPEL HILL, NORTH CAROLINA

(See Raleigh)

Criminal Trials in State and Federal Courts, Criminal Fraud, Criminal Tax Matters, Grand Jury Investigation, Homicide, Federal Grand Jury, Criminal and Regulatory Investigations, Driving While Intoxicated (DWI), Driving While Impaired, Traffic Violations, Homicide, Sex Crimes, Drug Crimes.

MASSENGALE & OZER

211 NORTH COLUMBIA STREET
CHAPEL HILL, NORTH CAROLINA 27514
Telephone: 919-967-8555
Fax: 919-967-9835
Email: redwood@nc.rr.com
URL: http://www.lawyers.com/massengale&ozer

Criminal Law, Traffic Violations, Driving While Intoxicated (DWI), Felonies, Drug Crimes, Misdemeanors, Sexual Assault, Criminal Appeals, Personal Injury, Motor Vehicle Law, Auto Accidents, Wrongful Death, Wills.

MEMBERS OF FIRM

WILLIAM F.W. MASSENGALE, born Austin, Texas, October 15, 1949; admitted to bar, 1984, North Carolina; 1993, U.S. District Court, Eastern, Middle and Western Districts of North Carolina, U.S. Court of Appeals, Fourth Circuit and U.S. Supreme Court. *Education:* Williams College (A.B., 1971); University of North Carolina (J.D., 1984). Assistant District Attorney, Chapel Hill, North Carolina, 1984-1990. Member, Executive Board of 15B District Bar, 1985-1989. Member, Executive Committee, Orange County Bar, 1985-1989. *Member:* Orange County Bar Association (Member, Executive Committee, 1987-1989); North Carolina Academy of Trial Lawyers. ***PRACTICE AREAS:*** Federal Criminal Law; Criminal Law; Drugs and Narcotics; Driving While Intoxicated; Personal Injury. ***Email:*** redwood@nc.rr.com

MARILYN G. OZER, born Chicago, Illinois, January 31, 1948; admitted to bar, 1991, North Carolina; 1992, U.S. District Court, Eastern, Middle and Western Districts of North Carolina, U.S. Court of Appeals, Fourth Circuit and U.S. Supreme Court. *Education:* Vassar College (A.B., 1969); Columbia University (M.I.A., 1971); University of North Carolina at Chapel Hill (J.D., with honors, 1991). Author: "Amgen Inc. v. United States International Trade Commission: The Living Cell-Product or Process," North Carolina Journal of International Law and Commercial Regulation, Vol. 16, No. 2, Fall, 1991. *Member:* Orange County Bar Association; North Carolina State Bar; National Association of Criminal Defense Lawyers; North Carolina Association of Women Attorneys. ***PRACTICE AREAS:*** Criminal Law; Appellate Practice; Post-Conviction Remedies. ***Email:*** redwood@nc.rr.com

NORTHEN BLUE, L.L.P.

Established in 1986
1414 RALEIGH ROAD
SUITE 435
P.O. BOX 2208
CHAPEL HILL, NORTH CAROLINA 27515-2208
Telephone: 919-968-4441
Facsimile: 919-942-6603
Email: jla@nbfirm.com

Personal Injury, Professional Liability, Trials, Bankruptcy, Business Law, Real Property, Land Use, Family Law, Wills, Estate Planning, Estate Administration, Trusts, Juvenile Law.

FIRM PROFILE: The firm brings outstanding experience and professionalism when addressing a variety of legal matters. The nine members of the firm all contribute using their diverse and extensive legal backgrounds to allow the firm to provide outstanding legal counsel to all client matters. The firm is listed in the Bar Register of Preeminent Lawyers.

(This Listing Continued)

Intellectual Property, Technology and Biotechnology, Patents, Trademarks, Licensing and Copyright Law.

STEVEN J. HULTQUIST, born Sioux City, Iowa, January 29, 1949; admitted to bar, 1980, New York; 1981, California; 1984, Connecticut; 1987, North Carolina; registered to practice before U.S. Patent and Trademark Office. *Education:* Washington University (B.S.Ch.E., 1970; M.S.Ch.E., 1972); Fordham University (J.D., 1979). Sigma Xi, Research Triangle Park Chapter (Secretary 2000-2002). Listed in Who's Who in American Law. Author: "Engineered Proteins as Intellectual Property," Genetic Engineering News, Vol. 7, No. 3, pp. 18-19, March 1987; "The Introduction of Negative Claim Limitations During Ex Parte Prosecutions," JPTOS, March 1991, Vol. 73, No. 3, pp. 218-233; "Patenting Bioinformatics Inventions: Emerging Trends in the United States," Nature Biotechnology, Vol. 20, pp. 743-744, July 2002; "Reach-Through Royalties: The Scope of Research Tool Patents," Journal of the Patent and Trademark Office Society, Vol. 86, No. 4, April 2004. Intellectual Property Editor, North Carolina General Practice Deskbook, 1995—. Adjunct Professor, North Carolina State University, 1995-1997. Principal Speaker, "Jumpstarting Business Relationships with the Western Bio-Pharmaceutical Industry," Shemyakin and Ovchinnikov Institute of Bioorganic Chemistry, Pushchino, Russia, October 2004. Co-Inventor: U.S. Patent 4,936,877, for "Dopant Delivery System for Semiconductor Manufacture," issued June 26, 1990; U.S. Patent 5,543,187, for "Amorphous Metal-Ceramic composite Material," issued August 6, 1996; U.S. Patent 6,070,576, for "Adsorbent-Based Storage and Dispensing System," issued June 6, 2000; U.S. Patent 6,132,492, for "Sorbent-Based Gas Storage and Delivery System for Dispensing High-Purity Gas," issued October 17, 2000; U.S. Patent 6,360,546, for "Fluid Storage and Dispensing System," issued March 26, 2002; U.S. Patent 6,474,076, for "Fluid Storage Storage and Dispensing System," issued November 5, 2002; U.S. Patent 6,764,755, for "Channelized Sorbent Media and Methods of Making Same," issued July 20, 2004. Member, Legal Department: Union Carbide Corp., 1976-1981; Tosco Corporation, 1981-1982; American Cyanamid Company, 1982-1985. *Member:* North Carolina, New York State, Connecticut and American Bar Associations; North Carolina State Bar; State Bar of California; Licensing Executives Society; American Intellectual Property Law Association; Council for Entrepreneurial Development. ***REPORTED CASES:*** Guinn v. Kopf, 96 F.3d 1419 (CAFC 1996). ***PRACTICE AREAS:*** Patents; Trademarks; Copyrights; Technology Law; Technology Transfers; Intellectual Property. ***Email:*** Hultquist@iptl.com

SENIOR ASSOCIATE

MARIANNE FUIERER, born Rochester, New York, July 30, 1946; admitted to bar, 1995, New York and Florida; 2002, North Carolina; registered to practice before U.S. Patent and Trademark Office. *Education:* State University at Brockport (B.S., Chemistry, 1985); University of Rochester (M.S., Toxicology, 1991); State University of New York at Buffalo Law School (J.D., 1995). *Member:* New York State Bar Association; The Florida Bar; North Carolina State Bar; American Chemical Society; American Intellectual Property Law Association; Licensing Executive Society. ***PRACTICE AREAS:*** Patents; Trademarks; Copyrights. ***Email:*** mfuierer@iptl.com

ASSOCIATES

TRISTAN A. FUIERER, born Rochester, New York, 1968; admitted to bar, 2003, North Carolina; registers to practice before U.S. Patent and Trademark Office. *Education:* St. John Fisher College (B.S., 1990); University of North Carolina (J.D., 2003); State University of New York at Buffalo (Ph.D., 1996). *Member:* North Carolina State Bar; American Bar Association. ***PRACTICE AREAS:*** Intellectual Property. ***Email:*** tfuierer@iptl.com

VINCENT K. GUSTAFSON, born Long Beach, California, November 10, 1970; admitted to bar, 1998, California and U.S. District Court, Central District of California (Not admitted in North Carolina). *Education:* University of California, Los Angeles (B.S.M.E., 1993); Loyola Law School, Los Angeles (J.D., 1998). Phi Delta Phi. Professional Engineer, California, 1996. *Member:* American Bar Association; American Intellectual Property Law Association. ***PRACTICE AREAS:*** Patents; Trademarks; Trade Secrets; Copyrights; Intellectual Property. ***Email:*** vgustafson@iptl.com

REPRESENTATIVE CLIENTS: Acme Electric Company; Acroprint Time Recorder Company; Advanced Technology Materials, Inc.; AI Technologies L.L.C.; Align-It Corporation; Alliant Techsystems, Inc.; Allied Technology (Taiwan); American Furnishings International; Ardent Pharmaceuticals, Inc.; Astronics Corporation; Avalanche Snack Group; BioResource International, Inc.; Carolina Ear & Hearing Clinic; CiVenti Chem, Inc.; DAD Inc.; Deutsches Krebsforschungszentrum Stiftung Des Offentlichen Rechts (Germany); Duke University; Elkington & Fife (UK); Ericsson (U.S. and Sweden); ESCO; Excalibur Enterprises; Genetic Concepts L.L.C.; Harmon Labs; HomePerfecT; Huber & Schussler (Germany); Insect Biotechnology, Inc.; Loctite Corporation; Luminescent Systems Incorporated; Marathon Innovations, Inc.; MRCC; MetaSoft Systems, Inc.; Microcell Corporation; Music Emporium; Narda Corporation (Germany); NeoFax PC, Inc.; net32.com, Inc.; Network Power Systems, Inc.; North Carolina SRT, Inc.; NUImage Laboratories, Inc.; OTO-TECH Corporation; Park International (Korea); Phase Biotechnology; Peregrine Semi Conductor Corp.; Point Concept Design; PolyTen Plastics, L.L.C.; Polyzen, Inc.; RTP Pharma, Inc.; R-TEX Equipment & Fabricating, L.L.C.; SmartWay Solutions, Inc.; STC Technologies, Inc.; Tempest Environmental Systems, Inc.; Triangle Biomedical Equipment, Inc.; Triangle Biomedical Sciences, Inc.; UltraCap Technologies (Taiwan); Union Patent Service Center (Taiwan); University of Maryland Biotechnology Institute; University of Maryland at Baltimore.

THE KORNBLUTH LAW FIRM, P.A.

CHAPEL HILL, NORTH CAROLINA

(See Durham)

Personal Injury, Automobile Accidents, Wrongful Death, Workers Compensation, Employment Law, Discrimination, Sexual Harassment, Employee Benefits, Civil Litigation, Criminal, Satellite Litigation, Traffic.

LEVINE & STEWART

Established in 1976

SUITE 202, UNIVERSITY SQUARE
143 WEST FRANKLIN STREET
CHAPEL HILL, NORTH CAROLINA 27516-2517
Telephone: 919-929-0386
Fax: 919-968-4601
Email: info@levineandstewart.com
URL: http://www.levineandstewart.com

Real Estate, Civil, Domestic, Criminal, Corporate and Estate Planning, Personal Injury, Mediation, Arbitration.

FIRM PROFILE: Representing fifty years of solid civil and criminal trial experience the firm is committed to handling all legal matters with expediency at the highest level of professionalism. Residential and commercial real estate.

MEMBERS OF FIRM

MICHAEL D. LEVINE (Retired)

JOHN T. STEWART, born Norfolk, Virginia, June 21, 1946; admitted to bar, 1975, North Carolina, U.S. District Court, Middle and Eastern Districts of North Carolina; 1982, U.S. Supreme Court. *Education:* University of North Carolina at Chapel Hill (B.A., 1968); North Carolina Central University (J.D., 1975). Recipient, Health Law Award, North Carolina Central University, 1975. Author: *The Professional Guide to Estate Planning for Families of Individuals with Developmental Disabilities,* 1987, now in 7th edition; *Estate Planning for Families of Persons with Developmental Disabilities,* now in 4th edition, ARC of North Carolina, Inc. (Volunteer of Year). Certified Mediator. Certified Arbitrator. *Member:* Orange County (President, 1982; Secretary, 1980), North Carolina (Member, Real Estate Section) and American Bar Associations; North Carolina State Bar; North Carolina Academy of Trial Lawyers. ***PRACTICE AREAS:*** Real Estate; Domestic Relations; Disabilities; Civil Mediation; Arbitration; Civil Litigation; Traffic Violations; Wills; Trust Law; Personal Injury; Corporate Law; Business Law. ***Email:*** john@levineandstewart.com

REPRESENTATIVE CLIENTS: Central Carolina Bank and Trust Co.; Association for Retarded Citizens for Housing Development Services, Inc.; ARC of North Carolina, Inc.; NC Subway Group, Inc.; Life Plan Trust, Inc.; Terry/Peterson Residential LLC; The Trails Homeowners Association; Summerfield Crossing Homeowners Association; Cedar Court Unit Association; Couch Automotive Inc.; Cornwallis Hills Homeowners Association; Weatherhill Homeowners Association; Weatherhill Pointe Homeowners Association; Liquid Pleasure Band.

LEWIS, ANDERSON, PHILLIPS, GREENE & HINKLE, PLLC

141 PROVIDENCE ROAD, SUITE 200
CHAPEL HILL, NORTH CAROLINA 27514
Telephone: 919-967-8989
Fax: 919-419-1429
URL: http://www.lapgh.com
Mailing Address: P.O. Drawer 4825, Chapel Hill, NC 27515-4825

Business Law, Commercial Litigation, Family Law, Divorce, Estate Planning and Administration, Probate, Wills, Civil Litigation, Intellectual Property Litigation, Copyright, Trademark, Personal Injury, Real Estate Litigation, Construction, Condemnation, Employment Contracts, Corporate Taxation, Corporate Finance, Partnership Taxation, Mediation, Arbitration, Computer Law.

SUSAN H. LEWIS, born New Orleans, Louisiana, 1945; admitted to bar, 1971, Texas; 1977, North Carolina. *Education:* Randolph-Macon Woman's College (B.A., 1967); University of Texas (J.D., with honors, 1970). Order of the Coif. Editor, Texas Law Review; Law Clerk to Hon. Homer Thornberry, U.S. Court of Appeals for the Fifth Circuit, 1970-1971. Associate, Vinson & Elkins, Houston, Texas, 1971-1974. Assistant Professor of Law, University of North Carolina, 1974-1978. Adjunct Professor, Family Law, University of North Carolina and Duke University Law Schools, 1978-2005. ***LANGUAGES:*** French. ***PRACTICE AREAS:*** Family Law.

J. DICKSON PHILLIPS, III, born Fayetteville, North Carolina, 1954; admitted to bar, 1979, North Carolina, U.S. District Courts, Eastern, Middle and Western Districts of North Carolina and U.S. Court of Appeals, Fourth and Eleventh Circuits. *Education:* Davidson College (A.B., 1975); University of North Carolina at Chapel Hill (J.D., with honors, 1979); Oxford University, Brasenose College (Diploma in Law, 1988). Editor-in-Chief, North Carolina Law Review. Term Professor, Dispute Resolution, University of North Carolina School of Law, 1996-1999. Adjunct Professor of Law, University of North Carolina, 1999—. Attorney Mediator, Duke University Private Adjudication Center, 1996-2002. Partner, Robinson, Bradshaw & Hinson, P.A., Charlotte, North Carolina, 1979-1991. *Member:* North Carolina (Chair, Dispute Resolution Section, 1997-1998) and American (Member, Litigation and Dispute Resolution Sections) Bar Associations. ***PRACTICE AREAS:*** Civil Litigation; Commercial Litigation; Intellectual Property Litigation; Internet and Computer Law; Mediation; Arbitration. ***Email:*** dphillips@lapgh.com

CHRISTINA GOSHAW HINKLE, born Princeton, New Jersey, 1969; admitted to bar, 1993, North Carolina. *Education:* Duke University (B.S., 1990); University of North Carolina (J.D., with high honors, 1993). Order of the Coif. Articles Editor, University of North Carolina Law Review, 1992-1993. Law Clerk, Hon. J. Dickson Phillips, Jr., Fourth Circuit Court of Appeals, 1993-1994. *Member:* North Carolina (Estate Planning and Fiduciary Law, Elder Law and Business Law Sections) and American Bar Associations; Durham/Orange Estate Planning Council. ***PRACTICE AREAS:*** Estate Planning; Estate Administration; Wills; Trust Law; Probate; Business Law; Distribution of Retirement Benefits. ***Email:*** chinkle@lapgh.com

ANTHONY D. NICHOLSON, born Mount Gilead, Ohio, June 23, 1968; admitted to bar, 1998, North Carolina; U.S. District Court, Eastern District of North Carolina. *Education:* University of Cincinnati (B.U.P., 1991); University of North Carolina (J.D., 1998).

(This Listing Continued)

MEMBERS OF FIRM

JOHN A. NORTHEN, born Asheville, North Carolina, April 24, 1950; admitted to bar, 1975, North Carolina; 1976, U.S. District Court, Middle and Eastern Districts of North Carolina; 1981, U.S. Supreme Court; 1987, U.S. Court of Appeals, Fourth Circuit; 1993, U.S. District Court, Western District of North Carolina. *Education:* University of North Carolina (A.B., 1972; J.D., 1975). Member, Panel of Bankruptcy Trustees, Middle District of North Carolina, 1979—. *Member:* Orange County District 15-B and North Carolina (Member, Sections on: Bankruptcy, Bankruptcy Council; Chair Elect, 1991; Chair, 1992) Bar Associations; North Carolina State Bar. (Certified Specialist, Business Bankruptcy Law, American Board of Certification; Board Certified Specialist in Business Bankruptcy Law, North Carolina State Board of Legal Specialization). ***PRACTICE AREAS:*** Bankruptcy Law; Business Law.

J. WILLIAM BLUE, JR., born Pinehurst, North Carolina, August 28, 1950; admitted to bar, 1975, North Carolina; 1976, U.S. District Court, Middle District of North Carolina; 1987, U.S. District Court, Eastern District of North Carolina; 1992, U.S. District Court, Western District of North Carolina; 1994, U.S. Court of Appeals, Federal Circuit. *Education:* University of North Carolina (A.B., 1973; J.D., 1975). Morehead Scholar. Orange County Attorney, 1976-1978. *Member:* Orange County, North Carolina (Member, Committee on Continuing Legal Education, 1982-1988) and American (Member: Litigation Section; Committee on Medicine and Law, 1976-1987) Bar Associations; 15th Judicial District and North Carolina State Bars; North Carolina Academy of Trial Lawyers (Lecturer, 1978—; Education Committee, 1999-2003; Board of Editors, 1996-2000 and 2001-2004). ***PRACTICE AREAS:*** Trial Practice; Personal Injury Law; Professional Liability Law.

DAVID M. ROOKS, III, born Greensboro, North Carolina, September 7, 1949; admitted to bar, 1976, North Carolina; U.S. District Court, Eastern, Middle and Western Districts of North Carolina; U.S. Court of Appeals, Fourth Circuit. *Education:* University of North Carolina (A.B., 1971), Phi Beta Kappa; Duke University (J.D., with distinction, 1976). Adjunct Professor, School of Business, University of North Carolina, 1986. Orange County Attorney, 1976-1978. *Member:* Orange County (Chairman, Litigation Section, 1987-1990) and North Carolina (Member, Sections on: Real Property; Litigation; Land Use) Bar Associations; North Carolina State Bar. ***PRACTICE AREAS:*** Real Property Law; Land Use Regulation; Business Law; Trials.

CHARLES H. THIBAUT, born Chapel Hill, North Carolina, November 5, 1953; admitted to bar, 1981, North Carolina and U.S. District Court, Middle District of North Carolina. *Education:* Guilford College (B.A., 1976); University of London, London, England; North Carolina Central University (J.D., 1981); University of North Carolina. *Member:* Orange County (President, 1986-1987), Judicial District 15-B (President, 1995) and North Carolina (Member, Business Law Section) Bar Associations; North Carolina State Bar. ***LANGUAGES:*** French. ***PRACTICE AREAS:*** Real Property Law; Business Law.

CAROL J. HOLCOMB, born Gadsden, Alabama, June 12, 1949; admitted to bar, 1989, North Carolina. *Education:* Jacksonville State University (B.S., 1970); University of North Carolina (M.S.W., 1980; J.D., 1988). Order of the Valkyries. Attorney, Orange and Chatham County Departments of Social Services. *Member:* Orange County (President, 1997), North Carolina (Member, Section on Family Law); 15 B Judicial District Bar Associations; Chair, Committee to Draft Local Rules for Juvenile Court and Co-Chair, Committee to Draft Local Rules for Deferred Custody Litigation); Center for Cooperative Parenting (Board Member); North Carolina Association of Social Service Attorneys. ***PRACTICE AREAS:*** Family Law; Juvenile Law.

VICKI L. PARROTT, born Greenville, North Carolina, August 26, 1968; admitted to bar, 1998, North Carolina; U.S. District Court, Middle and Eastern Districts of North Carolina. *Education:* University of North Carolina at Chapel Hill (B.A., 1991); Campbell University (J.D., magna cum laude, 1998). Member, Campbell University Law Review. *Member:* North Carolina and American Bar Associations; North Carolina State Bar. ***PRACTICE AREAS:*** Family Law; Bankruptcy; Civil Litigation; Business Law.

ASSOCIATES

EMILY CURTO WEATHERFORD, born Akron, Ohio, December 19, 1973; admitted to bar, 2000, North Carolina and U.S. District Court, Middle and Eastern Districts of North Carolina. *Education:* University of North Carolina at Chapel Hill (B.A., 1996); Campbell University (J.D., 2000). Phi Alpha Delta. *Member:* Orange County, Judicial District 15-B and North Carolina (Member, Bankruptcy Section) Bar Associations; North Carolina State Bar. ***PRACTICE AREAS:*** Civil Litigation; Bankruptcy; Wills; Probate; General Practice.

STEPHANIE OSBORNE-RODGERS, born Covington, Kentucky, May 8, 1967; admitted to bar, 2000, North Carolina and U.S. District Court, Middle and Eastern Districts of North Carolina. *Education:* University of Kentucky (B.A., 1989; M.A., 1991); Wake Forest University (J.D., 2000). Phi Delta Phi. Law Clerk to the Honorable A. Thomas Small, Eastern District of North Carolina, Bankruptcy Court, 2000-2002. Instructor: North Carolina Wesleyan, 2001; North Carolina A & T State University, 2000; Forsyth Technical Community College, 1999. *Member:* Orange County, District 15-B and North Carolina (Member, Bankruptcy Section) Bar Associations. ***PRACTICE AREAS:*** Bankruptcy.

SAMANTHA HYATT CABE, born Sylva, North Carolina, October 8, 1975; admitted to bar, 2002, North Carolina and U.S. District Court, Middle and Eastern Districts of North Carolina; U.S. Court of Appeals, Fourth Circuit. *Education:* Western Carolina University (B.S.B.A., magna cum laude, 1997); University of North Carolina at Chapel Hill (J.D., 2002). Member, University of North Carolina School of Law Holderness Moot Court. *Member:* Orange County, District 15-B and North Carolina Bar Associations; North Carolina Academy of Trial Lawyers. ***PRACTICE AREAS:*** General Practice; Civil Litigation; Business Law; Real Property; Criminal Law.

APPROVED ATTORNEYS FOR: Investors Title Insurance Co.; Jefferson-Pilot Title Insurance Co.; First American Title Insurance Co.; Lawyers Title Insurance Co.; Chicago Title Insurance Co.; Ticor Title Insurance Co.; First Title Insurance Co.; Commonwealth Land Title Insurance Co.; United Title Insurance Co.
REFERENCES: Investors Title Insurance Co.; Lawyers Title Insurance Co.; Chicago Title Insurance Co.; First Union National Bank; First Citizens Bank & Trust Co.; Branch Banking & Trust Co.; Centura Bank; SunTrust Bank; Blackman & Sloop, CPAs; Nelson & Company, CPAs; Balbirer & Coleman, CPA's.

J. KIRK OSBORN

1829 EAST FRANKLIN STREET
600 FRANKLIN SQUARE
CHAPEL HILL, NORTH CAROLINA 27514
Telephone: 919-929-0987
Fax: 919-929-2740
Email: kirkosborn@aol.com
URL: http://www.kirkosborn.com

General Civil and Criminal Litigation in State and Federal Courts. Criminal, Drug Crimes, Driving While Intoxicated (DWI), White Collar Crimes, Homicide, Traffic Violations, Premises Liability, Personal Injury and Nursing Home Litigation, Wrongful Death, Civil Rights.

J. KIRK OSBORN, born Havre, Montana, July 4, 1942; admitted to bar, 1974, North Carolina; 1980, U.S. District Court, Middle and Eastern Districts of North Carolina and U.S. Court of Appeals, Fourth Circuit; 1994, U.S. Supreme Court. *Education:* University of Colorado (B.S., 1965); Colorado State University (M.S., 1967); University of North Carolina (J.D., 1974). Three-Year Letterman, University of Colorado Football. Member of Board of the Fair Trial Initiative. *Member:* Orange County, 15-B Judicial District, North Carolina (Chairman, Criminal Justice Section, 1990-1992; Member Board of Governors, 1992-1995) Bar Associations; The North Carolina State Bar; North Carolina Academy of Trial Lawyers; National Association of Criminal Defense Lawyers. (Board Certified Specialist in Criminal Law including Appellate Practice, North Carolina State Board of Legal Specialization). ***REPORTED CASES:*** State v. Wilson (Little Rascals Defendant) 118 N.C. App.166, 456 SE 2d 870 (1995); State v. Marley 321 NC 415, 364 SE 2d 133 (1988); State v. Parker 315 NC 249, 337 SE 2d 497 (1985).

MICHAEL W. PATRICK

312 WEST FRANKLIN STREET
P.O. BOX 16848
CHAPEL HILL, NORTH CAROLINA 27516-6848
Telephone: 919-960-5848
Fax: 919-967-4953
Email: mpatrick@ncproductslaw.com
URL: http://www.ncproductslaw.com

Mailing Address: P.O. Box 16848, Chapel Hill, NC 27516-6848

Products Liability, Malpractice, Environmental, Toxic Torts, Asbestos, Federal Criminal Law.

MICHAEL W. PATRICK, born Charleston, South Carolina, August 16, 1950; admitted to bar, 1977, North Carolina. *Education:* Duke University (A.B., cum laude, 1972; M.A., in Public Policy Sciences, 1977); University of North Carolina (J.D., with honors, 1977). Staff Member, North Carolina Law Review, 1975-1977. Author: "Golden v. Biscayne Bay Yacht Club: Preventing Discrimination by Private Clubs," 54 North Carolina Law Review 685, 1976; "Toward A Codification of the Law of Evidence in North Carolina," 16 Wake Forest Law Review 669, 1980. Law Clerk to Chief U.S. District Court Judge Eugene A. Gordon, Middle District of North Carolina, 1977-1979. *Member:* The North Carolina State Bar; North Carolina and American Bar Associations; Association of Trial Lawyers of America; North Carolina Academy of Trial Lawyers (Chair, Products Liability Section, 2000-2003). ***PRACTICE AREAS:*** Litigation; Products Liability; Malpractice.

PATTERSON HARKAVY LLP

100 EUROPA DRIVE, SUITE 250
CHAPEL HILL, NORTH CAROLINA 27517
Telephone: 919-942-5200
Toll Free: 800-458-2541
Facsimile: 919-942-5256
URL: http://www.pathlaw.com

Greensboro, North Carolina Office: 101 South Elm Street, P.O. Box 29269, 27429-9269. Telephone: 336-370-4200. Facsimile: 336-274-8490.
Raleigh, North Carolina Office: 414 West Jones Street, P.O. Box 27927, 27611. Telephone: 919-755-1812. Facsimile: 919-755-0124.

Trial, Appellate and Dispute Resolution Practice in all State and Federal Courts. Personal Injury, Wrongful Death, Medical Malpractice, Workers' Compensation, Labor, Employment, Civil Rights, and Criminal.

FIRM PROFILE: The firm is dedicated to providing high quality, energetic advocacy in a few specialized areas of practice: personal injury, wrongful death, medical malpractice, workers' compensation, labor and employment, civil rights, and criminal defense. The firm has extensive experience in complex litigation, class actions, trial and appellate practice, and advocacy before a variety of administrative bodies and the North Carolina General Assembly. Members of the firm regularly provide mediation and arbitration services, teach at law schools, universities and professional education seminars and are active in bar and public interest organizations. The firm has litigated in affiliation with the American Civil Liberties Union, the North Carolina Academy of Trial Lawyers, the NAACP Legal Defense and Education Fund Inc., and local and international unions.

HENRY N. PATTERSON, JR., born Bayside, New York, February 3, 1940; admitted to bar, 1966, North Carolina. *Education:* University of North Carolina (A.B., 1963; LL.B., 1966). Order of the Coif. Law Clerk, the Honorable J. Braxton Craven, Jr., U.S. Court of Appeals, Fourth Circuit, 1966-1967. Attorney, National Labor Relations Board, 1967-1969. ***Email:*** hpatterson@pathlaw.com

LETO COPELEY, born New York, N.Y., June 27, 1954; admitted to bar, 1984, North Carolina. *Education:* Hunter College of the City University of New York (B.A., summa cum laude, 1980); Harvard University (J.D., 1983). Law Clerk, Honorable James B. McMillan, U.S. District Court, Western District of North Carolina, 1983-1984. *Member:* Orange County, North Carolina and American Bar Associations; Association of Trial Lawyers of

(This Listing Continued)

PATTERSON HARKAVY LLP, Chapel Hill—Continued

America; North Carolina Academy of Trial Lawyers (Chair, Workers' Compensation Section); North Carolina Association of Women Attorneys (President, 1998-1999); National Employment Lawyers Association. ***PRACTICE AREAS:*** Workers Compensation; Personal Injury; Civil Rights. ***Email:*** lcopeley@pathlaw.com

VALERIE ALSTON JOHNSON, born Henderson, North Carolina, February 27, 1964; admitted to bar, 1994, North Carolina. *Education:* University of North Carolina at Chapel Hill (B.A., 1987; J.D. with honors, 1994). Member, Moot Court. Adjunct Professor, University of North Carolina School of Law, 2003—. *Member:* Orange County, American and National Bar Associations; North Carolina Association of Black Lawyers; North Carolina Academy of Trial Lawyers (Member, Board of Governors). ***PRACTICE AREAS:*** Workers' Compensation; Employee Benefits; Employment; Social Security; Personal Injury. ***Email:*** vjohnson@pathlaw.com

BURTON CRAIGE (Resident, Raleigh, North Carolina Office)

ANN ELIZABETH GRONINGER (Resident, Raleigh, North Carolina Office)

MICHAEL G. OKUN (Resident, Raleigh, North Carolina Office)

SESSOMS & ROGERS, P.A.

CHAPEL HILL, NORTH CAROLINA

(See Durham)

Collections, Civil Litigation, Commercial Litigation, Banking Law, Consumer Bankruptcy, Traffic Violations.

STARK LAW GROUP, PLLC

Established in 1992

5925 FARRINGTON ROAD, SUITE 200
CHAPEL HILL, NORTH CAROLINA 27517
Telephone: 919-490-5550
Fax: 919-490-5551
Email: tom@starklawgroup.com
URL: http://www.lawyers.com/thomasstark

Construction, Commercial and Corporate Litigation. Personal Injury Litigation, Environmental Law, Computer and Intellectual Property Law, Corporate Acquisitions and Real Property Law, Real Estate Closings, Business Law.

THOMAS H. STARK, born North Carolina, 1955; admitted to bar, 1981, North Carolina; 1983, U.S. District Court, Middle District of North Carolina; 1984, U.S. District Court, Eastern District of North Carolina; 1985, U.S. Court of Appeals, 4th Circuit. *Education:* Duke University (B.A., 1977; J.D., 1981); National Institute for Trial Advocacy at Boulder Advanced Program (1987). *Member:* Durham County, 14th Judicial District, North Carolina (Member, Legislative Committee and Sections On: Construction Law; Real Property; Litigation; Environmental Law) and American (Member, Sections on: Litigation; Real Property, Probate and Trust Law; Natural Resources, Energy, and Environmental Law; Member, Forum Committee on the Construction Industry) Bar Associations; Computer Law Roundtable; Braxton Craven Inn of Court; National Institute for Trial Advocacy, Faculty, Southeast Deposition Program, Southeast Regional Trial Program, 1997. ***Email:*** tom@starklawgroup.com

ASSOCIATES

FIONA VALERIE GINTER, born Huntington, New York, December 1, 1976; admitted to bar, 2002, North Carolina. *Education:* North Carolina State University (B.S., with honors, 1997); Norman A. Wiggins School of Law (J.D., 2002). Order of the Barristers. *Member:* North Carolina Bar Association. ***Email:*** fiona@starklawgroup.com

W. RUSSELL CONGLETON, born Danville, Illinois, February 17, 1957; admitted to bar, 1982, Washington; 2003, North Carolina and U.S. District Court, Middle District of North Carolina. *Education:* Ball State University (B.S., magna cum laude, 1979); Gonzaga University (J.D., 1982). *Member:* Washington State (Member, Young Lawyers Division Judicial Selection Committee, 1985-1987). ***PRACTICE AREAS:*** Civil Litigation. ***Email:*** russ@starklawgroup.com

---

THARRINGTON SMITH

CHAPEL HILL, NORTH CAROLINA

(See Raleigh)

Civil and Criminal Trials and Appeals in all State and Federal Courts, Mediation and Alternative Dispute Resolution, Education Law, Constitutional Law, Employment Law, Family Law, Professional Licensure Proceedings, Personal Injury, Voting Rights, Local Government Law, Construction Contracts and Litigation, Business and Corporate Law, Commercial Litigation, Alcoholic Beverage Control Law, Administrative Law, Tax Litigation, Unfair Competition, Copyright, Legislative and Lobbying, Sports and Entertainment Law.

TWIGGS, BESKIND, STRICKLAND & RABENAU, P.A.

CHAPEL HILL, NORTH CAROLINA

(See Raleigh)

Personal Injury, Products Liability, Business Torts, Medical and other Professional Negligence, Federal and State Tort Claims, Environmental Torts, Insurance Bad Faith, Aviation Law and Wrongful Death.

THE VIRA LAW FIRM, PA

CHAPEL HILL, NORTH CAROLINA

(See Carrboro)

Trusts and Estates, Probate, Wills, Real Estate, Taxation, Business Law.

WINSTON & MAHER

312 W. FRANKLIN STREET
CHAPEL HILL, NORTH CAROLINA 27516
Telephone: 919-929-1043
Fax: 919-967-4953
Email: winstonandmaher.com
URL: http://www.winstonandmaher.com

General Civil, Criminal Trial Practice in all State and Federal Courts, Felonies, Misdemeanors, Drugs and Narcotics, White Collar Crime, Traffic Violations, Driving While Intoxicated.

FIRM PROFILE: Mr. Winston is board Certified Specialist in Criminal Law by the North Carolina State Board Legal Specialization. Mr. Winston and Mr. Maher are listed in the Bar Register Preeminent Lawyers.

MEMBERS OF FIRM

BARRY T. WINSTON, born New York, N.Y., March 3, 1934; admitted to bar, 1961, North Carolina and U.S. District Court, Eastern District of North Carolina; 1964, U.S. District Court, Middle District of North Carolina; 1969, U.S. Court of Appeals, Fourth Circuit; 1972, U.S. Supreme Court; 1992, U.S. District Court, Southern District of Georgia. *Education:* University of North Carolina (A.B., 1958; J.D., 1961). Phi Alpha Delta. Solicitor, Chapel Hill Recorders Court, 1967. Orange County Attorney, 1976-1978. *Member:* Orange County (President, 1970-1971 and 1977-1978), North Carolina and American Bar Associations; 15th Judicial District and North Carolina State Bars; North Carolina Academy of Trial Lawyers; National Association of Criminal Defense Lawyers. [Cpl., U.S.M.C., 1953-1955]. (Board Certified Specialist in Criminal Law, North Carolina State Board of Legal Specialization). ***PRACTICE AREAS:*** Criminal Defense Law; United States Military Criminal Law; Personal Injury. ***Email:*** btw@winstonandmaher.com

THOMAS K. MAHER, born Evanston, Illinois, January 23, 1957; admitted to bar, 1982, Illinois; 1983, U.S. Court of Appeals, 7th Circuit; 1984, U.S. Court of Appeals, 4th Circuit; 1985, North Carolina and U.S. District Court, Eastern District of North Carolina; 1986, U.S. District Court, Middle District of North Carolina; 1987, U.S. Court of Appeals, 9th Circuit; 1988, U.S. Supreme Court; 1990, U.S. Court of Appeals, 11th Circuit. *Education:* Northwestern University (B.A., 1979); University of North Carolina (J.D., with high honors, 1982). Order of the Coif. Articles Editor, University of North Carolina Law Review, 1981-1982. Law Clerk to the Hon. Wilbur F. Pell, Jr., U.S. Court of Appeals, Seventh Circuit, 1982-1984. Adjunct Professor of Law: Duke University School of Law; North Carolina School of Law. Instructor, National Institute of Trial Advocacy. *Member:* North Carolina State Bar; North Carolina Bar Association; North Carolina Academy of Trial Lawyers (Chair, Criminal Law Section, 1998-1999); National Association of Criminal Defense Lawyers. ***PRACTICE AREAS:*** Criminal Defense; Federal Criminal Law; White Collar Crime; Criminal Appeals; Criminal Forfeiture; Civil Trial Practice. ***Email:*** tkmaher@winstonandmaher.com

REFERENCE: Village Bank.

YARBOROUGH LAW OFFICE

P.O. BOX 2635
CHAPEL HILL, NORTH CAROLINA 27515-2635
Telephone: 919-401-5399
Fax: 919-402-9339
Email: jyarborough@jyarborough.com
URL: http://www.lawyers.com/yarboroughlaw

Health Care Law, Hospital Law, Managed Care Contracting and Regulatory Compliance.

JAN E. YARBOROUGH, born 1957; admitted to bar, 1987, North Carolina. *Education:* University of North Carolina at Greensboro (B.S.N., magna cum laude, 1980); Wake Forest University (J.D., magna cum laude, 1987). Research Editor, Wake Forest Law Review, 1986-1987. Registered Nurse, North Carolina, 1980. Adjunct Professor, Health Law, Wake Forest University, 1992. *Member:* North Carolina (Member, Health Law Section; Chair, 1994) and American Bar Associations; American Health Lawyers Association; North Carolina Society of Healthcare Attorneys. ***PRACTICE AREAS:*** Health Care Law; Hospital Law; Managed Care Contracts; Regulatory Law. ***Email:*** jyarborough@jyarborough.com

---

KAREN ZAMAN & ASSOCIATES

CHAPEL HILL, NORTH CAROLINA

(See Charlotte)

Medical Malpractice, Personal Injury, Auto Accidents, Traumatic Brain Injuries, Birth Injuries, Head Injuries, Nursing Home Negligence, Wrongful Death.

ROBERT C. ADAMS

6425 IDLEWILD ROAD, SUITE 212-A
CHARLOTTE, NORTH CAROLINA 28212
Telephone: 704-566-9898
Fax: 704-566-9899
Email: adamslaw@carolina.rr.com
URL: http://www.robertcadamslaw.com

Wills, Living Wills, Trust Law, Trusts and Estates, Estate Planning, Estate Administration, Trust Administration, Probate, Taxation, Tax Law, Income Tax, Business Law, Corporate Law, Business Formation, Incorporation, Contracts Breach of Contract, Contract Litigation.

FIRM PROFILE: This firm handles legal matters in the following practice areas: Wills, Living Wills, Trust Law, Trusts and Estates, Estate Planning, Estate Administration, Trust Administration, Probate, Taxation, Tax Law, Income Tax, Business Law, Corporate Law, Business Formation, Incorporation, Contracts, Breach of Contract, Contract Litigation.

ROBERT C. ADAMS, born High Point, North Carolina, 1961; admitted to bar, 1995, North Carolina and South Carolina; 1997, Florida; U.S. District Court, Western District of North Carolina; U.S. Court of Appeals, 4th Circuit; U.S. District Court, District of South Carolina. *Education:* University of North Carolina at Charlotte (B.A., Math, 1988; B.S., Accounting, 1988; M.Ed., 1991); University of South Carolina (J.D., 1995); Tulane Law School (LL.M., Admiralty, 1996). *Member:* Mecklenburg County, North Carolina and American Bar Associations.

ADAMS EVANS P.A.

Established in 1978

2180 TWO WACHOVIA CENTER
301 SOUTH TRYON STREET
CHARLOTTE, NORTH CAROLINA 28282
Telephone: 704-375-9249
Fax: 704-375-0729
URL: http://www.adamsevans.com
URL: http://www.adamspat.com

Patent, Trademark, Copyright and Unfair Competition Law.

FIRM PROFILE: Adams Evans P.A. specializes solely in intellectual property law, which includes patent, trademark, copyright, trade secrets, unfair competition and internet law. Our practice within this specialty is diverse, including prosecution of patent and trademark applications in the United States Patent and Trademark Office, litigation in Federal and State Courts, domestic and international patent, trademark and copyright licensing and consultation. The firm's clients are located throughout the United States. International clients are located in numerous foreign countries, including Germany, Switzerland, France, United Kingdom, Japan, and Canada. Our clients include companies involved in the design and manufacture of textile machinery and products, filtration equipment, medical products, power transmission equipment, electronic controls, microprocessor-controlled audio and video tape winding and loading equipment, flooring products, fasteners and communications hardware. We also represent advertising agencies, record producers, computer programming specialists, and a large international photographic film processor.

W. THAD ADAMS, III, born Raleigh, North Carolina, July 4, 1946; admitted to bar, 1971, North Carolina and U.S. District Court, Western District of North Carolina; 1976, U.S. District Court, Middle District of North Carolina and U.S. Court of Appeals, Fourth Circuit; 1977, U.S. Supreme Court; 1982, U.S. Court of Appeals for the District of Columbia Circuit; 1984, U.S. Court of Appeals for the Federal Circuit; 1986, U.S. District Court, Eastern District of North Carolina; U.S. Court of Appeals, Second Circuit; registered to practice before U.S. Patent and Trademark Office. *Education:* North Carolina State University (B.S., in Textile Tech., 1968); University of North Carolina (J.D., 1971). Author: "Use of Discovery," North Carolina Rules of Civil Procedure, 1978 Supplement; "Preparation for Trial of Civil Actions," Harrison Co., 1979. Co-Author: "The Continuing Saga of Federal Construction Jurisprudence: Extrinsic Evidence and Other Stories," 8 Federal Circuit B.J. 83 1999, reprinted in 2000 Intellectual Property Law Review. Master, Chief Justice William H. Bobbitt American Inn of Court. *Member:* North Carolina (Member: Intellectual Property Law Section; Sports and Entertainment Law Committee, 1998—) and American Bar Associations; 26th Judicial District and North Carolina State Bars; American Intellectual Property Law Association; Carolina Patent, Trademark & Copyright Law Association; International Trademark Association. ***PRACTICE AREAS:*** Patents; Trademarks; Copyrights; Unfair Competition. ***Email:*** wta@adamspat.com

J. SCOTT EVANS, born Waco, Texas, June 5, 1962; admitted to bar, 1992, Kentucky; 1996, North Carolina and U.S. District Court, Western, Middle and Eastern Districts of North Carolina. *Education:* Baylor University (B.F.A., 1984); University of Louisville School of Law (J.D., cum laude, 1992). Phi Kappa Phi; Phi Alpha Delta. (Vice Justice, 1991-1992). Member, Brandeis Honor Society. President, Moot Court Board, 1991-1992. Member: National Moot Court Team, 1992; Robert F. Wagner Labor Law Moot Court Team, 1991. Co-Author: "Early Retirement Incentive Plans," Eighth Annual Labor and Employment Law Institute (Rothman, 1998). Former Corporate Counsel, Fruit of the Loom. Industry Advisor for the Harmonization of Apparel Labeling Regulations under the NAFTA, 1993-1995. Member, ICANN UDRP Small Drafting Committee, 1999. Member, ICANN Names Council, 2002-2003. Executive Vice President, 2000-2001 and President, 2003-2005, Intellectual Property Constituency. *Member:* Kentucky, North Carolina and American (Member, Intellectual Property Section) Bar Associations; International Trademark Association (Member: Editorial Board Trademark Reporter, 1993-1998; Internet Committee, DNS Subcommittee Chair, 1998-2001; Vice Chair, 2002-2003; Chair, 2004-2005; Board of Directors, 2006). ***PRACTICE AREAS:*** Trademarks; Copyrights; Unfair Competition; Licensing; Internet. ***Email:*** jse@adamspat.com

(This Listing Continued)

STEPHEN S. ASHLEY, JR., born Binghamton, New York, January 12, 1971; admitted to bar, 1997, Mississippi; 2001, North Carolina and U.S. District Court, Western and Middle Districts of North Carolina; registered to practice before U.S. Patent and Trademark Office. *Education:* North Carolina State University (B.A., Chemistry, 1993); Mississippi College School of Law (J.D., 1997). Delta Theta Phi. Barrister, Chief Justice William H. Bobbitt American Inn of Court. *Member:* North Carolina (Member, Intellectual Property Law Section) and American Bar Associations; The Mississippi Bar (Member, Intellectual Property Law Section); Carolina Patent, Trademark and Copyright Law Association; American Chemical Society. ***PRACTICE AREAS:*** Patent Prosecution; Patent Litigation. ***Email:*** ssa@adamspat.com

MATTHEW JACOB LADENHEIM, born Lexington, Virginia, October 25, 1973; admitted to bar, 2000, North Carolina. *Education:* Mary Washington College (B.A., 1996); Dickinson School of Law of the Pennsylvania State University (J.D., 2000). Senior Editor, Dickinson Journal of Environmental Law and Policy, 1999-2000. Judicial Clerk to Hon. Justice Richard B. Sanders, Washington State Supreme Court, 2000-2001. *Member:* North Carolina State Bar (Member, Intellectual Property Section); American Bar Association; International Trademark Association. ***PRACTICE AREAS:*** Trademarks; Copyrights; Unfair Competition. ***Email:*** mjl@adamspat.com

JONATHAN M. HINES, born Cincinnati, Ohio, June 6, 1972; admitted to bar, 1998, North Carolina; 1999, Ohio; 2002, Maine; registered to practice before the U.S. Patent & Trademark Office. *Education:* North Carolina State University (B.S.M.E., 1995); University of Cincinnati (J.D., 1998). *Member:* Ohio State and North Carolina (Member, Intellectual Property Section) Bar Associations. ***PRACTICE AREAS:*** Patents. ***Email:*** jmh@adamspat.com

BRANDON C. TREGO, born Morgantown, West Virginia, June 5, 1973; admitted to bar, 2003, West Virginia and U.S. District Court, Southern District of West Virginia; 2004, North Carolina and U.S. District Court, Western District of North Carolina; registered to practice before U.S. Patent and Trademark Office. *Education:* West Virginia University (B.S.M.E., 1996; M.S.M.E., 1997; J.D., 2003). *Member:* North Carolina State Bar (Member, Intellectual Property Section); West Virginia and American (Committee Member, University Intellectual Property Law Section) Bar Associations. ***PRACTICE AREAS:*** Patents. ***Email:*** bct@adamspat.com

KATHRYN A. GROMLOVITS, born Columbia, South Carolina, August 6, 1976; admitted to bar, 2004, North Carolina; registered to practice before the U.S. Patent and Trademark Office. *Education:* University of North Carolina at Chapel Hill (B.S., Biology, 1998); University of South Carolina (J.D., 2004). Phi Delta Phi (Member, 2002-2004 and Vice-Magister, 2003-2004). Recipient of Roy A. Webster Academic Scholarship; CALI Award Patent Law. Member, Southeastern Environmental Law Journal. *Member:* Mecklenburg County, North Carolina State (Member, Intellectual Property Section) and American Bar Associations; North Carolina Association of Women Attorneys. ***PRACTICE AREAS:*** Trademarks; Patents; Copyrights; Unfair Competition. ***Email:*** kag@adamspat.com

SETH L. HUDSON, born Hamlet, North Carolina, July 8, 1975; admitted to bar, 2002, South Carolina; 2004, North Carolina; registered to practice before U.S. Patent and Trademark Office. *Education:* North Carolina State University (B.S. Mechanical Engineering, 1999; B.A. Chemistry, 1999); University of Richmond (J.D., 2002). Recipient, CALI Award in International Business Transactions. Articles Editor, Richmond Journal of Law and Technology, 2001-2002. *Member:* American Bar Association (Member, Sections on: Intellectual Property, Antitrust); South Carolina Bar (Member, Intellectual Property and Unfair Trade Practices Committee); North Carolina State Bar (Member, Intellectual Property Section); American Intellectual Property Law Association. ***PRACTICE AREAS:*** Patent Prosecution; Patent Litigation. ***Email:*** slh@adamspat.com

REPRESENTATIVE CLIENTS: Aplix, S.A.; Armstrong World Industries, Inc.; B/E Aerospace, Inc.; Belmont Textile Machinery Co.; Carolinas Health Care System; Presbyterian Healthcare System; Conbraco Industries, Inc.; Britax Child Safety, Inc.; Nissan Motors; Internet Services Corporation; Spectrum Marketing, Inc.; John Weiland Homes, Inc.; Lonati S.p.a.; Royal Doulton (UK) Limited; BSN Medical, Inc.; Dr. Th. Boehme KG Chemische Fabrik GmbH & Co.; Spiroflow Systems, Inc.; Jameson, LLC; Cyril Bath Company; Freeman White, Inc.; Tropical Nut & Fruit Co.; Atlantic American Properties, Inc.; Sam Bass Illustration & Design, Inc.

ALSTON & BIRD LLP

Established in 1893

BANK OF AMERICA PLAZA
101 SOUTH TRYON STREET, SUITE 4000
CHARLOTTE, NORTH CAROLINA 28280-4000
Telephone: 704-444-1000
Telecopier: 704-444-1111
Email: info@alston.com
URL: http://www.alston.com

Atlanta, Georgia Office: One Atlantic Center, 1201 West Peachtree Street 30309-3424. Telephone: 404-881-7000. Telecopier: 404-881-7777.

Washington, D.C. Office: 601 Pennsylvania Avenue, N.W., North Building, 10th Floor, 20004-2601. Telephone: 202-756-3300. Telecopier: 202-756-3333.

Raleigh, North Carolina Office (Research Triangle Area): 3201 Beechleaf Court, Suite 600, 27604-1062. Telephone: 919-862-2200. Telecopier: 919-862-2260.

New York, New York Office: 90 Park Avenue, 10016-1387. Telephone: 212-210-9400. Fax: 212-210-9444.

(Liaison Office) Munich, Germany Office: Brienner Strasse 11/V, 80333 Munich. Telephone: (49) (89) 238-0-70. Telecopier: (49) (89) 238-0-7110.

Administrative Law, Alternative Dispute Resolution, Antitrust and Trade Regulation, Appellate Practice, Bankruptcy, Banks and Banking, Biotechnology, Business Law, Class Actions, Commercial Real Estate, FCC Licensing, FCC Regulation, Wireless Communications, Complex and Multi-District Litigation, Computers and Software, Constitutional Law, Construction Law, Copyrights, Corporate Ethics, Corporate Governance, Corporate Law, Criminal Law, Debtor and Creditor, Electronic Commerce, Emerging Growth Companies, Employee Benefits, Employment Law, Entertainment Law, ERISA, ERISA Litigation, Energy, Environmental Law,

(This Listing Continued)

ALSTON & BIRD LLP, Charlotte—Continued

Environmental Litigation, Executive Compensation; Finance, Franchises and Franchising, Government Investigations; Health Care Corporate Law, Health Care Regulation, Immigration Law, Insurance Defense, Intellectual Property, International Finance, International Law, International Taxation, International Trade, Internet Law, Labor Law, Labor and Employment, Land Use, Legislative Practice, Life Sciences, Litigation, Local Taxation, Medical Malpractice, Mergers, Acquisitions and Divestitures, Multimedia Law, Municipal Law, Nonprofit and Charitable Organizations, Occupational Safety and Health, Partnership Law, Patents, Privacy Law, Products Liability, Professional Liability, Public Finance, Public Policy, Real Estate Finance, Regulatory Law, RICO, Securities, Securities Litigation, State Taxation, Taxation, Tax Litigation, Technology and Science, Telecommunications Law, Trademarks, Trusts and Estates, Utility Law, Venture Capital, White Collar Crime, Zoning.

LAW FIRM ALLIANCES/ASSOCIATIONS: **LEX MUNDI**

MEMBERS OF FIRM

BLAS P. ARROYO, born Palatka, Florida, October 30, 1956; admitted to bar, 1981, North Carolina; registered to practice before U.S. Patent and Trademark Office. *Education:* North Carolina State University (B.S., Pulp and Paper Science Technology, with honors, 1978); Washington & Lee University (J.D., 1981). ***LANGUAGES:*** Spanish. ***PRACTICE AREAS:*** Intellectual Property; Patent Litigation; Trademark Litigation; Copyright Litigation; Trade Secrets. ***Email:*** barroyo@alston.com

WILLIAM M. ATKINSON, born Pine Bluff, Arkansas, August 21, 1958; admitted to bar, 1988, Virginia; 1991, North Carolina; registered to practice before U.S. Patent and Trademark Office. *Education:* Ouachita Baptist University (B.S., 1980); Oklahoma State University (M.S., 1983); George Mason University (J.D., 1988). ***PRACTICE AREAS:*** Intellectual Property; Patent Litigation; Trademark Litigation; Copyright Litigation. ***Email:*** watkinson@alston.com

MARTHA GAYLE BARBER, born High Point, North Carolina, October 7, 1953; admitted to bar, 1982, North Carolina. *Education:* Duke University (B.A., 1975); Wake Forest University (J.D., 1981). ***PRACTICE AREAS:*** Intellectual Property; Trademarks; Copyrights; Internet Trademark Law; Internet Law; Electronic Commerce. ***Email:*** mbarber@alston.com

JOHN J. BARNHARDT, III, born Walterboro, South Carolina, October 28, 1945; admitted to bar, 1972, North Carolina; registered to practice before U.S. Patent and Trademark Office. *Education:* Davidson College (B.S., 1967); University of Virginia (J.D., 1972). ***LANGUAGES:*** French. ***PRACTICE AREAS:*** Intellectual Property; Patent, Trademark, Copyright and related Litigation; Licensing; Antitrust Law; Trade Regulation. ***Email:*** jbarnhardt@alston.com

JOHN F. BARON, born Newark, New Jersey, 1962; admitted to bar, 1987, New Jersey; 1989, New York; 1996, North Carolina. *Education:* University of Delaware (B.A., 1984); Seton Hall University (J.D., 1987); New York University (LL.M., Taxation, 1990). ***PRACTICE AREAS:*** Tax Law; International; Mergers and Acquisitions.

MARK T. CALLOWAY, born Winston-Salem, North Carolina, July 22, 1958; admitted to bar, 1983, North Carolina. *Education:* North Carolina State University (B.A., 1980); Campbell University School of Law (J.D., 1983). ***PRACTICE AREAS:*** White Collar Criminal Defense; Internal Investigations; Compliance; Theft of Trade Secrets; Health Care Fraud; Civil Litigation; Environmental Criminal Defense; Computer Crime. ***Email:*** mcalloway@alston.com

MICHAEL S. CONNOR, born Gastonia, North Carolina, September 13, 1962; admitted to bar, 1988, North Carolina; U.S. Court of Appeals, Federal Circuit; U.S. Supreme Court; U.S. Court of Appeals, Fourth Circuit; registered to practice before U.S. Patent and Trademark Office. *Education:* United States Naval Academy; Clemson University (B.S.M.E., cum laude, 1984); University of North Carolina (J.D., 1987). ***PRACTICE AREAS:*** Intellectual Property; Patent Litigation; Civil Litigation; Trademark Litigation; Technical Litigation; Mechanical Patents; Antitrust. ***Email:*** mconnor@alston.com

JASON P. COOPER, born Chipping Norton, England, May 30, 1966; admitted to bar, 1992, North Carolina; registered to practice before U.S. Patent and Trademark Office. *Education:* Purdue University (B.S.M.E., 1988); Indiana University at Bloomington (J.D., cum laude, 1992). ***PRACTICE AREAS:*** Intellectual Property; Mechanical Patent Prosecution; Electro-Mechanical Patents; Patent Infringement; International Patents; Trademarks; Copyrights. ***Email:*** jcooper@alston.com

JAMES A.L. DANIEL, JR., born Princeton, New Jersey, 1967; admitted to bar, 1996, North Carolina. *Education:* Davidson College (B.A., 1989); Wake Forest University (M.B.A., 1995; J.D., 1995). ***PRACTICE AREAS:*** Capital Markets; Finance; Real Estate.

BRIAN M. DAVIS, born Los Banos, California, November 25, 1968; admitted to bar, 1996, Ohio; 1999, North Carolina. *Education:* West Virginia University (B.A., 1990); Washington University (J.D., 1996). ***PRACTICE AREAS:*** Intellectual Property; Trademarks; Copyrights; Internet Intellectual Property.

PAUL S. DONOHUE, born Mineola, New York, 1964; admitted to bar, 1990, New York; 1998, North Carolina. *Education:* College of the Holy Cross (B.A., 1987); St. John's University (J.D., 1990). ***PRACTICE AREAS:*** Capital Markets; Finance; Real Estate.

CHARLES B. ELDERKIN, born Cleveland, Ohio, July 4, 1938; admitted to bar, 1964, Virginia; 1968, New York; 1970, North Carolina; registered to practice before U.S. Patent and Trademark Office. *Education:* Purdue University (B.S.M.E., 1960); George Washington University (LL.B., 1964). ***PRACTICE AREAS:*** Intellectual Property; Patent, Trademark and Copyright, with emphasis in Mechanical Technologies. ***Email:*** celderkin@alston.com

GUY R. GOSNELL, born Kansas City, Missouri, October 29, 1965; admitted to bar, 1992, North Carolina; registered to practice before U.S. Patent and Trademark Office. *Education:* University of Missouri (B.S.E.E., and B.S. Comp. E., summa cum laude, 1988); St. Louis University (J.D., magna cum laude, 1992). ***PRACTICE AREAS:*** Intellectual Property; Patents; Electrical Patents; Computer and Software Patents; Patent Prosecution; Patent Applications; Trademarks; Copyrights. ***Email:*** ggosnell@alston.com

(This Listing Continued)

DONALD M. HILL, JR., born Jacksonville, Florida, February 20, 1959; admitted to bar, 1995, Ohio; 1996, U.S. District Court, Southern District of Ohio; 1998, North Carolina; registered to practice before U.S. Patent and Trademark Office. *Education:* Purdue University (B.S., 1981); University of Cincinnati (J.D., 1995). ***PRACTICE AREAS:*** Intellectual Property; Mechanical Intellectual Property. ***Email:*** dhill@alston.com

H. BRYAN IVES III, born Charlotte, North Carolina, September 13, 1955; admitted to bar, 1980, North Carolina. *Education:* University of North Carolina at Chapel Hill (B.S., with honors, 1977; J.D., with high honors, 1980). ***PRACTICE AREAS:*** Corporate Finance and Securities; Transactional Tax Planning; Venture Capital; Limited Liability Companies; Partnerships. ***Email:*** bives@alston.com

GARY C. IVEY, born Greensboro, North Carolina, November 20, 1955; admitted to bar, 1981, North Carolina. *Education:* University of North Carolina at Chapel Hill (B.S., Business Administration, 1978); Stanford University (J.D., 1981). Phi Beta Kappa. Member, Stanford Law Review. *Member:* North Carolina (Member, Business Section) and American (Member, Business Section) Bar Associations. ***PRACTICE AREAS:*** Securities; Corporate Finance; Mergers and Acquisitions. ***Email:*** givey@alston.com

LARRY C. JONES, born Nashville, Tennessee, July 23, 1948; admitted to bar, 1992, North Carolina; registered to practice before U.S. Patent and Trademark Office. *Education:* University of Tennessee (B.S.E.E., 1970); Memphis State University (J.D., 1979). ***PRACTICE AREAS:*** Trademark Litigation; Copyright Litigation; Intellectual Property Litigation. ***Email:*** lcjones@alston.com

C. MARK KELLY, born Richmond, Virginia, July 28, 1961; admitted to bar, 1986, North Carolina. *Education:* Hampden-Sydney College (B.A., cum laude, 1983); Washington & Lee University (J.D., 1986). ***PRACTICE AREAS:*** Mergers, Acquisitions and Divestitures; Public Offerings; Private Finance; Corporate Law. ***Email:*** mkelly@alston.com

LANCE A. LAWSON, born St. Charles, Missouri, October 27, 1961; admitted to bar, 1997, North Carolina and U.S. District Court, Western District of North Carolina; registered to practice before U.S. Patent and Trademark Office. *Education:* United States Military Academy (B.S., 1984); Stanford University (M.S., 1993); University of Notre Dame (J.D., cum laude, 1996). Recipient: Bronze Star; Meritorious Service Medal, 1992. Member, University of Notre Dame Law Review. Licensed Professional Engineer. Law Clerk, Honorable Robert D. Potter, Senior United States District Court Judge. ***PRACTICE AREAS:*** Intellectual Property; Intellectual Property Litigation.

RAYMOND O. LINKER, JR., born Charlotte, North Carolina, January 18, 1946; admitted to bar, 1972, North Carolina; registered to practice before U.S. Patent and Trademark Office. *Education:* North Carolina State University (B.S., Chem. Eng., 1968); Georgetown University (J.D., 1972). ***PRACTICE AREAS:*** Intellectual Property; Patents; Trademarks; Chemical Patents; International Patents; Mechanical Patents; Patent Licensing. ***Email:*** rlinker@alston.com

ERNEST B. LIPSCOMB, III, born Vicksburg, Mississippi, July 17, 1941; admitted to bar, 1965, Mississippi; 1968, South Carolina; 1978, New York; 1993, North Carolina; registered to practice before U.S. Patent and Trademark Office. *Education:* University of Mississippi (B.S. Chem. Eng., 1963; J.D., 1965); George Washington University (LL.M., 1968). ***PRACTICE AREAS:*** Intellectual Property; Patents; Trademarks; Copyrights; Licensing. ***Email:*** elipscomb@alston.com

DICKSON M. LUPO, born Wilmington, Delaware, May 14, 1957; admitted to bar, 1985, North Carolina; 1998, U.S. Supreme Court; registered to practice before U.S. Patent and Trademark Office. *Education:* North Carolina State University (B.S.M.E., magna cum laude, 1979); Wake Forest University (J.D., 1985). ***PRACTICE AREAS:*** Patent Infringement; Electronic Commerce; Trademark Licensing; Patent Licensing; Trademark Infringement. ***Email:*** dlupo@alston.com

MICHAEL D. McCOY, born Joliet, Illinois, April 8, 1950; admitted to bar, 1975, Illinois; 1983, North Carolina; registered to practice before U.S. Patent and Trademark Office. *Education:* University of Illinois (B.S.E.E., with honors, 1972); Chicago-Kent College of Law (J.D., with honors, 1975). ***PRACTICE AREAS:*** Intellectual Property; Computers and Software; Patents; Electronic Commerce; Trademarks. ***Email:*** mmccoy@alston.com

RICHARD M. McDERMOTT, born Milwaukee, Wisconsin, August 4, 1969; admitted to bar, 1994, Wisconsin and North Carolina; registered to practice before U.S. Patent and Trademark Office. *Education:* Marquette University (B.S.E.E., 1991; J.D., 1994). ***PRACTICE AREAS:*** Intellectual Property; Patents; Trademarks; Copyrights. ***Email:*** rmcdermott@alston.com

CATHERINE AMSPACHER MEEKER, born Fairfield, Connecticut, July 12, 1962; admitted to bar, 1990, Connecticut; 1991, New York and District of Columbia; 1994, Georgia; 1997, North Carolina. *Education:* Boston University (B.S., summa cum laude, 1984); Fairfield University (M.A., 1987); College of William and Mary (J.D., 1990). ***PRACTICE AREAS:*** Corporate Law; Mergers and Acquisitions; Corporate Finance; Capital Markets; Public Offerings. ***Email:*** cmeeker@alston.com

WILLIAM KEVIN RANSOM, born Union City, Tennessee, September 4, 1970; admitted to bar, 1997, North Carolina; registered to practice before U.S. Patent and Trademark Office. *Education:* University of Tennessee (B.S.E.E., in Electrical Eng., 1993; J.D., cum laude, 1997). ***PRACTICE AREAS:*** Intellectual Property; Patents; Electrical Patents; Computer and Software Patents; Trademarks.

BRUCE J. ROSE, born Royal Oak, Michigan, January 13, 1963; admitted to bar, 1993, North Carolina; registered to practice before U.S. Patent and Trademark Office. *Education:* Michigan Technological University (B.S., Chem. Eng., 1985); Villanova University School of Law (J.D., cum laude, 1993). ***PRACTICE AREAS:*** Intellectual Property; Patent Litigation; Trademark Litigation; Copyright Litigation; Chemical Patent Prosecution; Intellectual Property Licensing. ***Email:*** brose@alston.com

CHARLES B. SIMMONS, JR., born Wilmington, North Carolina, March 19, 1961; admitted to bar, 1987, North Carolina. *Education:* Yale University (B.A., summa cum laude, 1984); University of Virginia (J.D., 1987). ***PRACTICE AREAS:*** Mergers and Acquisitions; Venture Capital; Securities; Corporate; Telecommunications. ***Email:*** csimmons@alston.com

JOHN L. SULLIVAN, JR., born Lowell, Massachusetts, April 25, 1944; admitted to bar, 1969, North Carolina; registered to practice before U.S. Patent and Trademark Office.

(This Listing Continued)

Education: North Carolina State University (B.S.M.E., with honors, 1966); University of North Carolina (J.D., 1969). ***PRACTICE AREAS:*** Intellectual Property Rights; International Patents; Trademarks; Patents; Copyrights; Intellectual Property Licensing; Anti-counterfeiting. ***Email:*** jsullivan@alston.com

GEORGE M. TAULBEE, born Cleveland, Ohio, December 13, 1962; admitted to bar, 1988, North Carolina; registered to practice before U.S. Patent and Trademark Office. *Education:* Virginia Polytechnic Institute and State University (B.S., Computer Science, 1984); University of Waterloo, Ontario (M.Math., Computer Science, 1985); University of Pittsburgh (J.D., 1988). ***PRACTICE AREAS:*** Intellectual Property; Patents; Trademarks; Copyrights; Licensing; Piracy; Computer Law; Internet Law; Technology Law; Electronic Commerce; Sports Law; Entertainment Law. ***Email:*** gtaulbee@alston.com

ANNE M. TOMPKINS, born Waynesboro, Virginia, 1962; admitted to bar, 1992, North Carolina. *Education:* University of North Carolina at Charlotte (B.A., 1984); University of North Carolina at Chapel Hill (M.P.A., 1988; J.D., 1992). ***PRACTICE AREAS:*** Litigation; Trial Practice; White Collar Criminal Defense; Corporate Investigations.

HENRY B. WARD, III, born Gainesville, Georgia, July 1, 1970; admitted to bar, 1996, Georgia and North Carolina; registered to practice before U.S. Patent and Trademark Office. *Education:* Georgia Institute of Technology (B.S.M.E., with honors, 1993); Emory University School of Law (J.D., 1996). ***PRACTICE AREAS:*** Intellectual Property; Mechanical Intellectual Property; E-Commerce. ***Email:*** hward@alston.com

OF COUNSEL

PAUL B. BELL, born Charlotte, North Carolina, July 29, 1922; admitted to bar, 1948, North Carolina; 1971, U.S. Supreme Court; registered to practice before U.S. Patent and Trademark Office. *Education:* Wake Forest University (B.S., 1947; J.D., cum laude, 1948). ***PRACTICE AREAS:*** Patents; Trademarks; Copyrights. ***Email:*** pbell@alston.com

COUNSEL

MICHELLE J. COLE, born April 8, 1970; admitted to bar, 1996, New York; 1998, Georgia; 2004, North Carolina. *Education:* Cornell University (B.A., 1992); Vanderbilt University (J.D., 1995). ***LANGUAGES:*** German. ***PRACTICE AREAS:*** Products Liability. ***Email:*** mcole@alston.com

MEREDITH S. JEFFRIES, born Virginia Beach, Virginia, December 19, 1968; admitted to bar, 1994, North Carolina, U.S. District Court, Eastern, Middle and Western Districts of North Carolina and U.S. Court of Appeals, Fourth Circuit. *Education:* University of Virginia (B.A., with honors, 1991; J.D., 1994). ***PRACTICE AREAS:*** Labor and Employment. ***Email:*** mjeffries@alston.com

SAMUEL G. LAYTON, JR., born Union, South Carolina, February 26, 1936; admitted to bar, 1965, North Carolina; 1971, U.S. Supreme Court; registered to practice before U.S. Patent and Trademark Office. *Education:* University of South Carolina (B.S.M.E., 1959); American University (J.D., 1963). ***PRACTICE AREAS:*** Intellectual Property. ***Email:*** slayton@alston.com

LEIGH M. LEVINE, born Stamford, Connecticut, June 27, 1969; admitted to bar, 1995, Georgia; 1998, North Carolina. *Education:* Princeton University (B.A., 1991); Vanderbilt University (J.D., 1995). ***PRACTICE AREAS:*** Commercial Litigation; Wrongful Death; Bodily Injury; Trademarks; Internet Litigation. ***Email:*** llevine@alston.com

LEE R. RIMLER, born Atlanta, Georgia, March 30, 1967; admitted to bar, 1994, Virginia; 1999, North Carolina. *Education:* Virginia Commonwealth University (B.S., Accounting, 1989); Villanova University (M.S., Taxation, 1991); College of William & Mary (J.D., 1994). Certified Public Accountant, Virginia, 1990. *Member:* Virginia State Bar (Member, Trust and Estates Tax Sections, 1994-1998).

ROBERT J. SULLIVAN, born Brooklyn, New York, November 20, 1963; admitted to bar, 1989, New York, New Jersey and Connecticut (Not admitted in North Carolina). *Education:* New York University (B.S., 1984); Brooklyn Law School (J.D., 1988). ***PRACTICE AREAS:*** Corporate Finance; Corporate Workouts; Real Estate Contracts; Mortgage Backed Securities; Construction Law.

THOMAS G. WALKER, admitted to bar, 1990, North Carolina. *Education:* Baylor University (B.A., 1986); Campbell University (J.D., 1990). ***PRACTICE AREAS:*** Government Investigations; Corporate Investigations; White Collar Criminal Defense; Antitrust. ***Email:*** twalker@alston.com

ASSOCIATES

STACY G. ACKERMANN, born Pittsburgh, Pennsylvania, October 21, 1976; admitted to bar, 2001, North Carolina. *Education:* Furman University (B.A., 1998); University of South Carolina (J.D., 2001). ***PRACTICE AREAS:*** Capital Markets; Finance; Secured Finance; Unsecured Finance.

TIMOTHY BALTS, born Minneapolis, MN, February 19, 1971; admitted to bar, 2002, North Carolina; registered to practice before U.S. Patent and Trademark Office. *Education:* Oregon State University (B.S., 1999); Syracuse University (J.D., 2002).

JOSEPH E. BRACKEN, born Columbus, Ohio, 1975; admitted to bar, 2004, North Carolina; registered to practice before U.S. Patent and Trademark Office. *Education:* University of Notre Dame (B.S.E.E., 1997); Princeton University (B.S., 2000); New York University (J.D., 2004). ***PRACTICE AREAS:*** Intellectual Property; Intellectual Property Litigation.

KIRK T. BRADLEY, born Coral Gables, Florida, August 11, 1974; admitted to bar, 1999, North Carolina; registered to practice before U.S. Patent and Trademark Office. *Education:* Clemson University (B.S., Mechanical Engineering, 1996); University of South Carolina (J.D., cum laude, 1999).

NACHAEL L. BRIGHT, born Durham, North Carolina, July 22, 1971; admitted to bar, 2001, North Carolina. *Education:* University of North Carolina at Chapel Hill (B.A., 1998; J.D., 2001). ***PRACTICE AREAS:*** Capital Markets; Finance; Secured Finance; Unsecured Finance; Corporate Law.

(This Listing Continued)

GREGORY J. CARLIN, born September 8, 1970; admitted to bar, 2000, North Carolina; registered to practice before U.S. Patent and Trademark Office. *Education:* University of Pittsburgh (B.S.M.E., 1992; M.S., 1994); George Washington University (J.D., 2000).

MICHAEL T. CECKA, born Minneapolis, Minnesota, June 7, 1974; admitted to bar, 2003, North Carolina. *Education:* St. Bonaventure University (B.A., 1996); Mercer University (J.D., 2003). ***PRACTICE AREAS:*** Capital Markets; Finance; Secured Finance; Unsecured Finance.

GLEN R. DRYSDALE, admitted to bar, 2004, North Carolina and Wisconsin. *Education:* Michigan Technological University (B.S., 1995); University of Wisconsin (J.D., 2004). ***PRACTICE AREAS:*** Intellectual Property; Mechanical Intellectual Property.

BRIAN ELLSWORTH, born Detroit, Michigan, April 7, 1975; admitted to bar, 2002, North Carolina and U.S. District Court, Western District of North Carolina; registered to practice before U.S. Patent and Trademark Office. *Education:* University of Michigan (B.S.M.E., 1997); Wake Forest University (J.D., 2002).

ALEXIS W. FINNISS, born Picayune, Mississippi, March 23, 1978; admitted to bar, 2003, North Carolina and U.S. District Court, Western District of North Carolina; registered to practice before U.S. Patent and Trademark Office. *Education:* University of Georgia (B.S., 2000); Wake Forest University (J.D., 2003).

NICHOLAS F. GALLO, born Lisbon, Ohio, June 17, 1975; admitted to bar, 2001, North Carolina. *Education:* Youngstown State University (B.E., 1998); Boalt Hall School of Law, University of California at Berkeley (J.D., 2001).

CHRISTOPHER J. GEGG, born St. Louis, Missouri, May 2, 1977; admitted to bar, 2002, North Carolina; registered to practice before U.S. Patent and Trademark Office. *Education:* Wabash College (B.A., 1999); Wake Forest University (J.D., 2002).

THEODORE C. GEORGE, born Rochester, New York, December 16, 1972; admitted to bar, 2000, North Carolina. *Education:* University of Georgia (B.S.Ed., 1995); Boston University (J.D., 2000). ***PRACTICE AREAS:*** Finance; Structured Finance; Corporate Law; Secured Finance; Unsecured Finance.

DAVID L. GILDERNEW, born Pittsburgh, Pennsylvania, May 9, 1971; admitted to bar, 1997, Pennsylvania (Not admitted in North Carolina). *Education:* Duquesne University (B.S.B.A., 1993; J.D., 1996). ***PRACTICE AREAS:*** Finance; Structured Finance; Corporate Law; Secured Finance; Unsecured Finance.

HEATHER GREGG, born Rutherfordton, NC, January 17, 1977; admitted to bar, 2002, North Carolina; registered to practice before U.S. Patent and Trademark Office. *Education:* University of North Carolina (B.S., 1999); Wake Forest University (J.D., 2002).

CATHERINE L. HESS, born April 10, 1973; admitted to bar, 2000, North Carolina. *Education:* University of North Carolina at Charlotte (B.S.W., 1995); Case Western Reserve University (J.D., 2000).

HANNAH H. KIM, admitted to bar, 2004, North Carolina. *Education:* University of Tennessee (B.S.B.A., 2001; J.D., 2004). ***LANGUAGES:*** Korean. ***PRACTICE AREAS:*** Mergers and Acquisitions.

TRENT A. KIRK, born Canton, Ohio, April 4, 1976; admitted to bar, 2003, North Carolina. *Education:* Clemson University (B.S., 2000; M.S., 2000); University of South Carolina (J.D., 2003).

JONATHAN E. KUTNER, born New York, N.Y.; admitted to bar, 2004, North Carolina. *Education:* Wake Forest University (B.A., with honors, 1997); Boston University (J.D., 2003). ***PRACTICE AREAS:*** Capital Markets; Finance.

CLAY A. LITTLEFIELD, born Camp Pendleton, California, July 6, 1973; admitted to bar, 1998, Tennessee; 2000, Georgia; 2005, North Carolina. *Education:* Georgia State University (B.A., 1994); University of Mississippi (J.D., 1998); Georgetown University (LL.M., Taxation, 2004). ***PRACTICE AREAS:*** Taxation; Federal Income Tax; Capital Markets.

BETH R. MACDONALD, born Frostburg, Maryland, March 22, 1975; admitted to bar, 2000, North Carolina. *Education:* Frostburg State University (B.A., 1997); Georgetown University (J.D., 2000). ***PRACTICE AREAS:*** Mergers and Acquisitions; Securities; Public Offerings; Corporate Finance.

JITENDRA MALIK, PH.D., born London, England, December 16, 1974; admitted to bar, 2004, North Carolina; registered to practice before U.S. Patent and Trademark Office. *Education:* University of North Carolina at Chapel Hill (B.S., 1995); University of North Carolina at Charlotte (M.S., 1998); University of Cincinnati (M.B.A., 2000; Ph.D., 2002); Wake Forest University (J.D., 2004). ***PRACTICE AREAS:*** Intellectual Property; Intellectual Property Litigation; Products Liability.

ASHLEY B. MENSER, admitted to bar, 2004, North Carolina. *Education:* University of Florida (B.A., 2001); Emory University (J.D., 2004). ***PRACTICE AREAS:*** Finance; Taxation; Nonprofit Organizations Law; Mergers and Acquisitions; Like Kind Exchanges.

MICHAEL G. MOSIER, admitted to bar, 2002, New York; 2004, North Carolina. *Education:* Hamilton College (B.A., 1995); Duke University (J.D., 2001). ***PRACTICE AREAS:*** Intellectual Property; Trademarks; Copyrights; Internet Law.

KEVIN O'BRIEN, born Key West, Florida, June 21, 1965; admitted to bar, 2000, North Carolina; 2001, South Carolina; registered to practice before U.S. Patent and Trademark Office. *Education:* Georgia Institute of Technology (B.S.M.E., with honors, 1987); The Citadel (M.B.A., magna cum laude, 1994); University of South Carolina (J.D., cum laude, 2000).

KATHARINE F. PIERCE, admitted to bar, 2005, North Carolina. *Education:* Duke University (A.B., 2000); University of North Carolina (J.D., 2005). ***PRACTICE AREAS:*** Mergers and Acquisitions.

S. BENJAMIN PLEUNE, born July 7, 1977; admitted to bar, 2002, North Carolina; registered to practice before U.S. Patent and Trademark Office. *Education:* University of Wisconsin (B.S., 1999); University of Illinois (J.D., 2002).

ANNE J. RANDALL, admitted to bar, 2003, North Carolina. *Education:* Wake Forest University (B.A., 1998); Georgetown University (J.D., 2003).

(This Listing Continued)

ALSTON & BIRD LLP, Charlotte—Continued

KEITH ROBERSON, born Little Rock, AR, August 1, 1976; admitted to bar, 2002, North Carolina; registered to practice before U.S. Patent and Trademark Office. *Education:* Clemson University (B.S., 1998); University of South Carolina (J.D., 2002).

BENJAMIN F. SIDBURY, born Charlotte, North Carolina, March 19, 1976; admitted to bar, 2001, North Carolina, U.S. District Court, Eastern, Western and Middle Districts of North Carolina and U.S. Court of Appeals, Fourth and Federal Circuits; 2002, District of Columbia; registered to practice before U.S. Patent and Trademark Office. *Education:* Wingate University (B.A., 1998); Syracuse University (J.D., magna cum laude, 2001).

JASON M. SNEED, born Kansas City, Missouri, 1971; admitted to bar, 1997, Missouri; 1998, Kansas, U.S. District Court, District of Kansas and U.S. Court of Appeals, Tenth Circuit; 2000, North Carolina and U.S. District Court, Western District of Missouri. *Education:* Texas Christian University (B.A., cum laude, 1993); University of Virginia School of Law (J.D., 1997).

JASON J. SOLOMON, born Johnstown, Pennsylvania, November 21, 1974; admitted to bar, 2000, Delaware; 2005, North Carolina. *Education:* University of North Carolina (B.S.B.A., 1997); Washington & Lee University (J.D., 2000). ***PRACTICE AREAS:*** Finance; Capital Markets; Structured Finance; Secured Finance; Unsecured Finance.

ANDREW T. SPENCE, born Tulsa, Oklahoma, April 12, 1975; admitted to bar, 2000, North Carolina; registered to practice before U.S. Patent and Trademark Office. *Education:* University of Missouri (B.S.E.E., 1997); Washington University (J.D., 2000).

R. FLYNT STREAN, admitted to bar, 2004, North Carolina. *Education:* Virginia Polytechnic Institute (B.S., 1993; M.S., 1996); University of Kentucky (J.D., 2004). ***PRACTICE AREAS:*** Intellectual Property; Mechanical Intellectual Property.

BRIAN J. TEAGUE, admitted to bar, 2004, North Carolina; registered to practice before U.S. Patent and Trademark Office. *Education:* Worcester Polytechnic Institute (B.S.E.E., 1987); University of RIchmond (J.D., 2004). ***PRACTICE AREAS:*** Intellectual Property; Electronic Intellectual Property; Computer Technology.

CHAD THORSON, born New Ulm, Minnesota, 1973; admitted to bar, 2005, North Carolina; registered to practice before U.S. Patent and Trademark Office. *Education:* United States Naval Academy (B.S.E.E., 1996); University of Connecticut (J.D., 2005). ***PRACTICE AREAS:*** Intellectual Property; Electronic Intellectual Property; Patents; Computer and Software Patents; Electronic Patents.

CHRISTIAN C. WARPULA, born Tuscumbia, Alabama, May 4, 1973; admitted to bar, 1998, North Carolina and U.S. District Court, Eastern District of North Carolina. *Education:* Harding University (B.S., cum laude, 1995); Wake Forest University (J.D., cum laude, 1998).

JOHN MARK WILSON, born July 19, 1972; admitted to bar, 1998, North Carolina; registered to practice before U.S. Patent and Trademark Office, 1999. *Education:* Clemson University (B.S.M.E., 1995); University of Cincinnati (J.D., 1998).

Languages: Bangla, Bulgarian, Croatian, French, German, Gujarati, Hindi, Italian, Japanese, Korean, Portuguese, Russian, Spanish, Tamil, Thai, Turkish, Urdu.

REPRESENTATIVE CLIENTS: AFLAC, Inc.; AIG; ALCOA; Allegiance Healthcare Corporation; Allied Systems; Altana Inc.; ARCADIS; Arthritis Foundation; Assurant, Inc.; BB&T; Belk Store Services, Inc.; BellSouth Corporation; Bertelsmann AG; GBF Industries, Inc.; BNP Residential Properties, Inc.; The Boeing Company; Boral Industries, Inc.; Borden, Inc.; Bose Corporation; Cable News Network; CGW Southeast Partners & Affiliates; Cingular Wireless LLC; The Community Foundation for Greater Atlanta, Inc.; Delta Air Lines, Inc.; Dimension Data Holdings, Inc.; The Dow Chemical Company; Duke University; Emory University and Emory Healthcare; The Fulton-DeKalb Hospital Authority; Genuine Parts Co. Inc.; Georgia Hospital Association; Georgia-Pacific Corporation; Global Payments, Inc.; Gold Kist Inc.; Goldman, Sachs & Co.; Group Bruxelles Lambert; HealthSouth Corporation; H. Stern Jewelers, Inc.; i:FAO Aktiengesellschaft; IMERYS; Industrial Developments International, Inc. (IDI); INEOS; ING Americas; InterContinental Hotels Group; JDN Realty Corporation; Johns Hopkins University; Knology; Komatsu America Corp.; Lend Lease Real Estate Investments, Inc.; Lowrance Electronics. Inc.; MAG Mutual Insurance Company; Malcolm Pirnie; MANN + HUMMEL Group; Matsushita Electric Corporation of America / Panasonice U.S.A.; MBIA Insurance Corporation; MCNC; Metso Paper, Inc.; Mirant Corporation; Mohawk Industries, Inc.; Municipal Electric Authority of Georgia (MEAG Power); Municipal Gas Authority of Georgia (MGAG); National Association for Stock Car Auto Racing, Inc. (NASCAR); The National Business Coalition on E-Commerce and Privacy; National Industries for the Blind; NDCHealth Corporation; Nokia; Paragon Trade Brands, Inc.; Porcher Industries, S.A.; The Prudential Insurance Company of America; Regions Financial Corporation; Renal Care Group, Inc.; Rexam Corporation; Robert W. Baird & Co.; Rodenstock GmbH; The Rouse Company; Sabre; Saks Incorporated; Shearwater Corporation (nka Nektar Therapeutics); Silhouette Modell; Silicon Valley Bank; Skanska USA Building Inc.; Sonoco Products Company; Southwire Company; Springs Industries, Inc.; SunTrust Banks, Inc.; SunTrust Robinson Humphrey; TAPPI; Turner Broadcasting System, Inc.; Uniden America Corporation; Union Planters Corporation; University of California at Berkeley; University of North Carolina at Charlotte; UnumProvident Corporation; UPS; Verizon Wireless; Visa; Vulcan Materials Company; Wachovia Corporation; Waffle House, Inc.; WebMD Corporation; XL Capital Assurance Inc.

(For complete biographical data on other personnel, see professional biographies at Atlanta, Georgia, Washington, D.C., Raleigh, North Carolina, New York, New York, and Munich, Germany)

ANDRESEN & ASSOCIATES

2319 CRESCENT AVENUE
CHARLOTTE, NORTH CAROLINA 28207
Telephone: 704-377-8881
Fax: 704-377-8880
Email: ken@charlottelawyer.com
URL: http://www.charlottelawyer.com

Business Law, Business Litigation, Contracts, Corporate Law, Criminal Defense, Traffic Violations, DUI, Whit Collar Crimes, Drug Crimes.

KENNETH P. ANDRESEN, born Catskill, New York, January 27, 1950; admitted to bar, 1980, North Carolina, U.S. Court of Appeals, Fourth Circuit, U.S. District Court, Middle and Western Districts of North Carolina, U.S. Tax Court and U.S. Supreme Court. *Education:* St. Lawrence University (B.A., 1972); University of Notre Dame (M.B.A.,

(This Listing Continued)

1975); Wake Forest University (J.D., 1980). Omicron Delta Kappa. Member, Wake Forest Law Review, 1979-1980. Author: Note, "Search and Seizure—Applying the Warrant Requirement to Parolee Searches," 14 Wake Forest Law Review 1203, 1978; Note, "Labor Law—Invoking State Trespass Laws to Enjoin Peaceful Union Picketing," 15 Wake Forest Law Review 288, 1979. Chief Assistant U.S. Attorney, Western District of North Carolina, 1982-1986. *Member:* Charlotte, Mecklenburg County and North Carolina Bar Associations; The North Carolina State Bar; North Carolina Academy of Trial Lawyers. ***PRACTICE AREAS:*** Business Litigation; White Collar Crime. ***Email:*** ken@charlottelawyer.com

LEGAL SUPPORT PERSONNEL

EDWINA W. EUBANKS. *Education:* B.S. Degree, Business Administration; Harvard University Graduate School of Business. Senior Management Agribusiness Executive Education Seminars. (Paralegal)

JOANNA E. WALLE. *Education:* M.A. in Sociology. (Paralegal). ***LANGUAGES:*** Polish.

REPRESENTATIVE CLIENTS: D & D BONDING, Inc.; DeLapp Investigations, Inc.; Zapata Engineering, Inc.; First Financial Services, Inc.; 1st Americard, Inc.; Horizon Energy, Inc.; BAR Investments; David Allen Company; RMA Home Services, Inc.

THOMAS J. ASHCRAFT

SUITE 120, 521 E. MOREHEAD STREET
CHARLOTTE, NORTH CAROLINA 28202-2631
Telephone: 704-333-2300
Fax: 704-333-2352

Litigation in Federal and State Courts.

THOMAS J. ASHCRAFT, born Charlotte, North Carolina, 1951; admitted to bar, 1978, North Carolina. *Education:* University of North Carolina (B.A., 1974); Wake Forest University (J.D., 1978); London School of Economics (LL.M., 1979). Staff Member, Wake Forest Law Review, 1977-1978. Recipient, Judge Edwin M. Stanley Moot Court Award, 1976. Order of the Barristers. United States Attorney, Western District of North Carolina, 1987-1993. Member, Mecklenburg County Board of Elections, 1999-2001, 2002-2003. Court Certified Mediator. Panel Member, American Arbitration Association.

AUGER & AUGER

6425 IDLEWILD ROAD, SUITE 212
CHARLOTTE, NORTH CAROLINA 28212
Telephone: 704-567-7571
Toll Free: 1-800-977-7396
Fax: 704-568-4062
Email: hwa@augerlaw.com
URL: http://www.lawyers.com/augerlaw

Automobile and Truck Accidents, Wrongful Death Claims, Workers' Compensation, Dog Bites, Injuries to Children, Daycare Accidents, Construction Site Accidents, Nursing Home Negligence and Medical Malpractice.

HERBERT W. AUGER, born Bethpage, New York, June 24, 1965; admitted to bar, 1990, Connecticut; 1991, New York; 1994 North Carolina; 1996, Florida; U.S. District Court, Eastern and Southern Districts of New York. *Education:* Long Island University (B.S., 1987); Touro College, Jacob D. Fuchsberg Law Center (J.D., 1990). *Member:* North Carolina and New York State Bar Associations; North Carolina Academy of Trial Lawyers; The Association of Trial Lawyers of America. ***Email:*** hwa@augerlaw.com

ARLENE PATRICIA AUGER, born Bethpage, New York, August 14, 1965; admitted to bar, 1992, Connecticut; 1993, New York; 1994, North Carolina. *Education:* Hofstra University (B.B.A., 1986); Touro College, Jacob D. Fuchsberg Law Center (J.D., 1992). *Member:* Mecklenburg County, North Carolina and New York State Bar Associations. ***Email:*** apa@augerlaw.com

ERIC A. BACH

900 BAXTER STREET, SUITE 109
P.O. BOX 33566
CHARLOTTE, NORTH CAROLINA 28204
Telephone: 704-376-3980
Fax: 704-331-9636
Email: ebach@mindspring.com
URL: http://www.ericbachlaw.com

Criminal Law in State and Federal Courts, Drug Offences, Driving While Impaired, Traffic Violations, Speeding, Assault and Battery, Capital Offenses, Criminal Appeals, Extradition, Felonies, Parole and Probation, Sexual Assault, Personal Injury, Automobile Accidents.

FIRM PROFILE: Mr. Bach has been practicing in Charlotte since 1993.

ERIC A. BACH, born Irving, Texas, December 6, 1966; admitted to bar, 1993, North Carolina and U.S. District Court, Western District of North Carolina; 1996, U.S. Court of Appeals, Fourth Circuit; 1997, U.S. Supreme Court. *Education:* Davidson College (A.B., 1989); University of Richmond (J.D., 1993). *Member:* Mecklenburg, North Carolina and American (Member: Litigation Section; Law Practice Management Section) Bar Associations; National Association of Criminal Defense Lawyers; North Carolina Academy of Trial Lawyers. ***REPORTED CASES:*** U.S. v. Pierce, 4th Circuit 278 F.3d 282; U.S. v. Johnson, 4th Circuit 114 F.3d 435.

BAKER AND BLAKE L.L.P.

106-1 PROVIDENCE ROAD
CHARLOTTE, NORTH CAROLINA 28207
Telephone: 704-332-2959
Fax: 704-332-2357
URL: http://www.bakerblakelaw.com

Personal Injury, Automobile Accidents, Wrongful Death, Nursing Home Abuse, Workers Compensation, Criminal Law, Drug Crimes, DUI/DWI, Traffic Violations, Wills, Estates, Probate, Estate Planning, Estate Administration, Civil Litigation, Business Law, Business Formation, Non-Profit Organization Representation.

TYYAWDI M. BAKER, born Las Vegas, Nevada, March 18, 1973; admitted to bar, 1999, North Carolina; 2001, U.S. District Court, Western District of California. *Education:* Winston-Salem State University (B.A., magna cum laude, 1996); University of North Carolina at Chapel Hill (J.D., 1999). Law Clerk: Chief Justice Henry E. Frye, North Carolina Supreme Court, 1999-2000; Hon. Nancy A. Becket, Nevada Supreme Court, 2000-2001. Volunteer, Big Brothers Big Sisters, Charlotte, North Carolina. Member, Board of Directors, Fellowship Home of Winston-Salem, North Carolina. *Member:* Mecklenburg County and North Carolina Bar Associations; North Carolina State Bar. ***PRACTICE AREAS:*** Personal Injury; Automobile Accidents and Injuries; Wrongful Death; Nursing Home Abuse and Neglect; Workers Compensation; Criminal Law; Drug Crimes; Driving While Intoxicated; Traffic Violations. ***Email:*** baker@bakerandblake.com

ARETHA V. BLAKE, born Charleston, South Carolina, 1978; admitted to bar, 2002, North Carolina and U.S. District Court, Western District of North Carolina; 2003, U.S. District Court, Eastern and Middle Districts of North Carolina. *Education:* Florida State University (B.S., cum laude, 1999); University of Georgia School of Law (J.D., cum laude, 2002). Phi Beta Kappa. Notes Editor, Georgia Law Review, 2001-2002. Member, Junior League of Charlotte. *Member:* Mecklenburg County (Member, Board of Directors; Special Committee on Diversity) and American Bar Associations; North Carolina State Bar; National Bar Association; John S. Leary Bar Association (Co-Vice Chair). ***PRACTICE AREAS:*** Wills; Estates; Probate; Estate Planning; Estate Administration; Civil Litigation; Business Law; Business Formation; Nonprofit and Charitable Organizations. ***Email:*** blake@bakerandblake.com

THE LAW OFFICE OF SALVATORE BALSAMO, P.C.

2100 CRESCENT AVENUE, SUITE 201
CHARLOTTE, NORTH CAROLINA 28207
Telephone: 704-343-2815
Fax: 704-342-3987
Email: sal@salbalsamo.com
URL: http://www.salbalsamo.com

Real Estate, Residential and Commercial Real Estate, Trust and Estates, Estate Planning and Administration, Wills, Probate, Small Business Law.

SALVATORE BALSAMO, born Passaic, New Jersey, November 20, 1968; admitted to bar, 1993, North Carolina; 1998, U.S. District Court, Eastern, Middle and Western Districts of North Carolina. *Education:* Marquette University (B.A., 1990); Wake Forest University (J.D., 1993). *Member:* Mecklenburg County (Member, Real Estate Section) and North Carolina Bar Associations; North Carolina State Bar; Mecklenburg County Young Lawyers. [Capt., U.S. Air Force, 1993-1998]. ***PRACTICE AREAS:*** Real Estate; Residential Real Estate; Commercial Real Estate; Trusts and Estates; Estate Planning; Wills; Small Business Law. ***Email:*** sal@salbalsamo.com

BARNETT & FALLS, P.A.

130 NORTH MCDOWELL STREET, SUITE C
CHARLOTTE, NORTH CAROLINA 28204-2268
Telephone: 704-334-2044
Fax: 704-334-2095
Email: kb@barnettfalls.com
URL: http://www.barnettfalls.com

Trials and Appeals in Federal and State Courts, Criminal Defense, Driving While Intoxicated, Drug Crimes, White Collar Crimes, Felonies, Misdemeanors, Probation Violations, Traffic Violations, Civil Rights Litigation.

KEVIN L. BARNETT, born Durham, North Carolina, September 8, 1958; admitted to bar, 1984, North Carolina; 1990, U.S. District Court, Western District of North Carolina and U.S. Court of Appeals, Fourth Circuit. *Education:* Duke University (B.S., 1980); Mercer University (J.D., 1984). Phi Delta Phi. *Member:* Mecklenburg County and North Carolina Bar Associations; North Carolina State Bar; National Association of Criminal Defense Lawyers. ***PRACTICE AREAS:*** Criminal Defense; Driving While Intoxicated; Traffic Violations. ***Email:*** kb@barnettfalls.com

R. DEKE FALLS, born Albuquerque, New Mexico, October 7, 1970; admitted to bar, 1997, North Carolina and U.S. District Court, Western District of North Carolina; 1999, U.S. Court of Appeals. Fourth Circuit. *Education:* University of North Carolina, Charlotte (B.S., 1993); University of North Carolina, Chapel Hill (J.D., 1997). *Member:* Mecklenburg County and North Carolina Bar Associations; Mecklenburg County Criminal Defense Lawyers Association (Federal Chair); National Association of Criminal Defense Lawyers. ***REPORTED CASES:*** Andrews v. Crump, 144 N.C.App. 68 (2001); U.S. v. Higdon, 15 Fed.Appx. 135, 2001 WL 876847 (4th Cir. 2001); U.S. v. Huntley, 3:98CR10 (acquitted on drug conspiracy charges); U.S. v. Edwards, 5:02CR37 (acquitted on drug conspiracy charges); U.S. v. Liu, 3:02CR233 (acquitted on immigration fraud, bribery charges); U.S. v. Curbelo, 3:99CR109 (acquitted on firearms charges); U.S. v. Valdes, 3:99CR198 (acquitted on interstate prostitution charges); U.S. v. Sigmon, 3:98CR7 (drug conspiracy verdict reversed and charges dismissed); State v. Her, 97CRS20642 (acquitted on murder charges).

(This Listing Continued)

PRACTICE AREAS: Criminal Defense; Civil Rights; Civil Litigation. ***Email:*** deke@barnettfalls.com

A. MARSHALL BASINGER, II

831 EAST MOREHEAD STREET, SUITE 850
CHARLOTTE, NORTH CAROLINA 28202
Telephone: 704-377-2984
Fax: 704-377-4721
Email: marshall@bellsouth.net
Email: ambii@bellsouth.net
URL: http://www.mbasingerlaw.com

Family Law, Separation, Child Custody, Alimony, Equitable Distribution, Divorce, Trial and Appellate Practice, Civil and Domestic Trial Mediator.

FIRM PROFILE: A. Marshall Basinger, II is a sole practitioner now specializing in Domestic Relations, Family Law. He is also a Certified Superior Court and Family Court Mediator.

Mr. Basinger has been active in Church (Deacon, Presbyterian), Civic (1969 Outstanding Young Men Award), and Bar Association (former member, Executive Committee of Local Bar) affairs.

In addition to extensive trial practice, Mr. Basinger has represented parties in numerous appeals to both the North Carolina Court of Appeals and Supreme Courts.

A. MARSHALL BASINGER, II, born Greensboro, North Carolina, August 10, 1939; admitted to bar, 1965, North Carolina and U.S. District Court, Western District of North Carolina. *Education:* University of North Carolina (A.B., 1962; LL.B., 1965). Phi Delta Phi. Certified North Carolina Superior Court Mediator. *Member:* North Carolina Bar Association; 26th Judicial District Bar; North Carolina State Bar (Member, Family Law Section); North Carolina Academy of Trial Lawyers; The Association of Trial Lawyers of America. (Board Certified Specialist in Family Law, North Carolina State Board of Legal Specialization)

BAUCOM, CLAYTOR, BENTON, MORGAN & WOOD, P.A.

Established in 1961
1351 EAST MOREHEAD STREET, SUITE 201
P.O. BOX 35246
CHARLOTTE, NORTH CAROLINA 28235
Telephone: 704-376-6527
Fax: 704-376-6207

General and Trial Practice in all State and Federal Courts. Probate, Real Estate, Condemnation, Labor, Corporation, Commercial, Negligence and Insurance Law.

LLOYD F. BAUCOM, born Marshville, North Carolina, November 12, 1934; admitted to bar, 1961, North Carolina and U.S. District Court, Western District of North Carolina; 1964, U.S. Tax Court. *Education:* Wake Forest University (B.S., 1957; J.D., 1961). Phi Delta Phi. Member, 1990-2000 and Chairman, 2000-2002, Board of Law, Examiners of the State of North Carolina. *Member:* Mecklenburg County (Chairman), North Carolina and American Bar Associations; 26th Judicial District (President, 1987-1988) and North Carolina State Bars. ***PRACTICE AREAS:*** Corporate Law; Probate Law; Real Estate Law; Condemnation. ***Email:*** lbaucom@baucomclaytor.com

WILLIAM M. CLAYTOR, born Nashville, Tennessee, March 31, 1941; admitted to bar, 1969, Tennessee; 1972, North Carolina, U.S. District Court, Western District of North Carolina and U.S. Tax Court. *Education:* University of Memphis (M.A., 1964; J.D., 1969). Delta Theta Phi; Omicron Delta Kappa. *Member:* Mecklenburg County (President, 1996-1997) and 26th Judicial District Bar Associations; North Carolina State Bar. ***PRACTICE AREAS:*** Corporate Law; Elder Law; Estate Planning; Probate Law. ***Email:*** bclaytor@baucomclaytor.com

KENNETH R. BENTON, born Charlotte, North Carolina, March 7, 1949; admitted to bar, 1974, North Carolina and U.S. District Court, Western District of North Carolina. *Education:* Wake Forest University (B.A., 1971; J.D., 1974). *Member:* 26th Judicial District and North Carolina State Bars; North Carolina and American Bar Associations. ***PRACTICE AREAS:*** Real Estate Law; Corporate Law; Probate Law. ***Email:*** kbenton@baucomclaytor.com

REX C. MORGAN, born Raleigh, North Carolina, February 23, 1956; admitted to bar, 1981, North Carolina and U.S. District Court, Western District of North Carolina. *Education:* University of North Carolina (B.A., with high honors, 1978; J.D., 1981). Pi Sigma Alpha. Member: Order of the Barristers; International Moot Court Team; Editorial Board of North Carolina Journal of International Law and Commercial Regulation. Author: "United States v. May May, A Judicial Response to Hovering Narcotic Smugglers," North Carolina Journal of International Law and Commercial Regulations 481, 1980. *Member:* North Carolina and American (Member, Section on Litigation) Bar Associations; North Carolina State Bar; North Carolina Trial Lawyers Association; The Association of Trial Lawyers of America. ***PRACTICE AREAS:*** Business Litigation; Personal Injury Litigation; Insurance Litigation; Estate Litigation; Condemnation. ***Email:*** rmorgan@baucomclaytor.com

JAMES F. WOOD, III, born Charlotte, North Carolina, February 29, 1956; admitted to bar, 1981, North Carolina and U.S. District Court, Western and Middle Districts of North Carolina. *Education:* Davidson College (B.A., 1978); Wake Forest University (J.D., 1981). Phi Delta Phi. *Member:* Mecklenburg County, North Carolina and American Bar Associations; North Carolina State Bar; Defense Research Institute; North Carolina Association of Defense Counsel; North Carolina Insurance Crime Information Exchange. ***PRACTICE AREAS:*** Insurance Defense Law; Civil Litigation; Medical Malpractice; Insurance Fraud. ***Email:*** jwood@baucomclaytor.com

(This Listing Continued)

BAUCOM, CLAYTOR, BENTON, MORGAN & WOOD, P.A., Charlotte—Continued

RICHARD F. KRONK, born Coral Gables, Florida, January 10, 1962; admitted to bar, 1992, Florida; 1993, North Carolina, U.S. District Court, Southern District of Florida and U.S. District Court, Western District of North Carolina. *Education:* University of Florida (B.S., 1984); Nova University (J.D., 1992). Member, Moot Court. *Member:* Mecklenburg County and American Bar Associations; North Carolina State Bar; The Florida Bar; The Association of Trial Lawyers of America. ***PRACTICE AREAS:*** Insurance Litigation; Civil Litigation; Domestic Relations; Criminal Law. ***Email:*** rkronk@baucomclaytor.com

TIMOTHY R. MOORE, born Charlotte, North Carolina, 1971; admitted to bar, 1997, North Carolina and U.S. District Court, Western District of North Carolina. *Education:* University of North Carolina (B.A.); Washington & Lee University (J.D., 1997). Phi Delta Phi.*Member:* Mecklenburg County and North Carolina state Bar Associations. ***PRACTICE AREAS:*** Corporate Law; Probate Law; Estate Planning. ***Email:*** tmoore@baucomclaytor.com

REPRESENTATIVE CLIENTS: Holyoke Mutual Insurance Co.; Grange Insurance Co.; America Security Insurance Co.; Nationwide Mutual Insurance Co.; Canal Insurance Co.; Avis Rent-A-Car; Motorola Communications & Electronics, Inc.; Parnell Martin Cos.; Ranger Insurance Co.; Flanders Filters, Inc.; Metrolina Steel, Inc.; Eldercare Corp.; Dealer Services, Inc.; Associates Commercial Corp.; Yandle-Witherspoon Supply, Inc.; Republic Refrigeration, Inc.; Prestige Farms, Inc.; Tandy Corp.; Grain Dealers Mutual Insurance Co.; Selective Insurance Co.; Indiana Lumberman's Mutual Insurance Co.; Metropolitan Property and Casualty Company; TheEmployers' Association; Simmons Healthcare; Hornets Nest Girl Scout Council; Lake Norman Hospitality. Inc.; Country Suites of Burlington; Super 8 Motel of Mooresville; Campbell-Brown Company, Inc.; Couchell Properties; N.C. Farm Bureau Insurance Co.; The Hartford, Kemper Insurance Co.; Commercial Casualty Insurance Co.; The Seibels Bruce Group; Showmar's Restaurants; Hornwood, Inc.; Gardner Machinery Corp. APPROVED ATTORNEYS FOR: Chicago Title Insurance Co.; Lawyers Title Insurance Corp.; Investors Title Insurance Co.; First American Title Insurance Co.
REFERENCES: First Citizens Bank & Trust Co.; Branch Banking & Trust Co.; Central Carolina Bank; Bank of America.

BELL, DAVIS & PITT, P.A.

Established in 1980
CARILLON BUILDING, SUITE 2160
227 WEST TRADE STREET
CHARLOTTE, NORTH CAROLINA 28202
Telephone: 704-227-0400
Fax: 704-227-0178
URL: http://www.belldavispitt.com

Mailing Address: P.O. Box 21029, Winston-Salem, NC 27120

Winston-Salem, North Carolina Office: Century Plaza, Suite 600, 100 North Cherry Street, 27101. Telephone: 336-722-3700. Fax: 336-748-5890.

General Practice in State and Federal Court Trials. Banking and Commercial Law. Corporation and Labor Law, Federal, State and Local Taxation, Estate Planning, Probate and Real Estate Law.

FIRM PROFILE: Bell, Davis & Pitt, P.A. was founded in 1980. The firm provides a full range of legal services to corporations, individuals and organizations in North Carolina and other states in the southeast.

EDWARD B. DAVIS, born Winston-Salem, North Carolina, May 9, 1972; admitted to bar, 1999, South Carolina; 2001, North Carolina. *Education:* Davidson College (B.A., 1994); University of North Carolina, Chapel Hill (J.D., 1999). Recipient, Pro Bono Certificate of Achievement. *Member:* South Carolina and American Bar Associations. ***PRACTICE AREAS:*** Litigation. ***Email:*** ward.davis@belldavispitt.com

THE LAW OFFICES OF HAROLD J. BENDER

200 NORTH MCDOWELL STREET
CHARLOTTE, NORTH CAROLINA 28204
Telephone: 704-333-2169
Fax: 704-333-0837
Email: hjblaw@bellsouth.net
URL: http://www.hbenderlaw.com

Criminal Law, State and Federal Courts, Drug Crimes, DWI, Assault, Traffic Violations.

FIRM PROFILE: Mr. Bender is Board Certified Specialist in Criminal Law by the North Carolina Board of Legal Specialization.

HAROLD J. BENDER, born Winston-Salem, North Carolina, September 16, 1942; admitted to bar, 1969, North Carolina and U.S. District Court, Western, Middle and Eastern Districts of North Carolina; 1977, U.S. Court of Appeals, Fourth Circuit; 1978, U.S. Supreme Court; 1999, U.S. Court of Appeals, Sixth Circuit. *Education:* Greensboro College (A.B., 1966); University of North Carolina (J.D., 1969). Phi Delta Phi. Chief Assistant United States Attorney, 1977-1981. United States Attorney, Western District of North Carolina, 1981. *Member:* Mecklenburg County, North Carolina and American Bar Associations; North Carolina State Bar; North Carolina Academy of Trial Lawyers; The Association of Trial Lawyers of America; National Association of Criminal Defense Lawyers; National Association of Former United States Attorneys; American Board of Trial Advocates; American Board of Criminal Lawyers; Sports Lawyers Association; National Association of Collegiate Conference Counsel (President). (Board Certified Specialist in Criminal Law, North Carolina Board of Legal Specialization). ***PRACTICE AREAS:*** Criminal Law; Civil Litigation.

KOFI BENTSI-ENCHILL

5222 MONROE ROAD, SUITE 126
CHARLOTTE, NORTH CAROLINA 28205
Telephone: 704-537-8466
Fax: 704-537-1142
Email: kenchill@bellsouth.net
URL: http://www.kofilaw.com

Immigration and Naturalization, Labor Certifications, Citizenship, Visas, Business Visas, Personal Injury, Automobile Accidents, Slip and Fall, Workers Compensation.

KOFI BENTSI-ENCHILL, born Accra, Ghana, January 10, 1962; admitted to bar, 1991, California; 1997, North Carolina; U.S. District Court, Western District of North Carolina. *Education:* University of Massachusetts at Amherst (B.A., 1987); UCLA (J.D., 1990). *Member:* Meckleburg County Bar Association; State Bar of California; North Carolina State Bar; American Immigration Lawyers Association.

HAL BERGER, P.A.

A PROFESSIONAL LAW CORPORATION
5950 FAIRVIEW ROAD, SUITE 808
CHARLOTTE, NORTH CAROLINA 28210
Telephone: 704-553-7614
Facsimile: 704-553-7824
Email: halberger@earthlink.net
URL: http://www.halbergerlaw.com

Real Estate Closings, Residential Real Estate, Commercial Real Estate, Estate Planning, Trusts and Estates, Business Law, Corporate Law.

HAL BERGER, born New York, N.Y., October 30, 1962; admitted to bar, 1998, North Carolina. *Education:* Old Dominion University (B.A., 1986); Thomas M. Cooley Law School (J.D., 1997). Certified Public Accountant. *Member:* Mecklenburg County and North Carolina Bar Associations; Real Property Council. ***PRACTICE AREAS:*** Real Estate Closings; Residential Real Estate; Commercial Real Estate; Estate Planning; Trusts and Estates; Business Law; Corporate Law.

ASSOCIATE

JAIMÉE L. BOND, born Beckley, West Virginia, September 29, 1975; admitted to bar, 2002, North Carolina and U.S. District Court, Western District of North Carolina. *Education:* University of South Alabama (B.A., 1998); Capital University (J.D., 2001). President, 2000-2001, Secretary, 1999-2000, Phi Delta Phi. *Member:* Mecklenburg County and North Carolina State Bar Associations; North Carolina State Bar. ***PRACTICE AREAS:*** Real Estate; Estate Planning; Trusts and Estates; Wills; Probate. ***Email:*** jaimeebond@bellsouth.net

BERNHARDT AND STRAWSER, P.A.

5821 FAIRVIEW ROAD, SUITE 550
CHARLOTTE, NORTH CAROLINA 28209
Telephone: 704-335-0444
Facsimile: 704-335-0551
URL: http://www.bernhardtandstrawser.com

Commercial and Retail Collections, Debtor and Creditor Law, Creditor Rights, Collections.

FIRM PROFILE: The firm's practice is limited to Commercial and Retail Collections, Debtor - Creditor Law. Robert J. Bernhardt has developed a high volume effective debt collection service statewide. His prompt reports and remittances are hallmark of his practice. He is a draftsman of bills enacted by our state legislative to enhance creditor's rights.

ROBERT J. BERNHARDT, born Fort Knox, Kentucky, November 22, 1943; admitted to bar, 1968, North Carolina. *Education:* Indiana University (B.S., 1965); University of Michigan (J.D., 1968). *Member:* North Carolina and American Bar Associations; North Carolina State Bar; Commercial Law League of America. [USAR, 1968-1974]. ***PRACTICE AREAS:*** Commercial and Retail Collections; Debtor-Creditor Law. ***Email:*** rjb@ncsccollections.com

AMY B. STRAWSER, born Charlotte, North Carolina, May 28, 1969; admitted to bar, 1993, North Carolina; 2001, South Carolina. *Education:* Duke University (A.B., 1990); University of North Carolina at Chapel Hill (J.D., with high honors, 1993). Order of the Coif. North Carolina Law Review. ***PRACTICE AREAS:*** Commercial Law; Retail Collections. ***Email:*** abstrawser@ncsccollections.com

CHARLES C. EURIPIDES, born Alexandria, Virginia, July 31, 1961; admitted to bar, 1991, Virginia; 1996, North Carolina. *Education:* University of Virginia (B.A., English, 1983); University of Richmond (J.D., 1987). Member, Old Town North Planning Committee, Alexandria, Virginia, 1990-1993. *Member:* Mecklenburg County, Alexandria, Virginia and North Carolina Bar Associations; Virginia State Bar; North Carolina State Bar. ***LANGUAGES:*** French. ***PRACTICE AREAS:*** Commercial Law; Retail Collections. ***Email:*** cce@ncsccollections.com

TONYA L. URPS, born Welch, West Virginia, December 1, 1967; admitted to bar, 1993, North Carolina. *Education:* West Virginia University (B.A., cum laude, 1990); Wake Forest University (J.D., 1993). *Member:* North Carolina State Bar. ***PRACTICE AREAS:*** Litigation.

BISHOP, CAPITANO & MOSS, P.A.

4521 SHARON ROAD, SUITE 350
CHARLOTTE, NORTH CAROLINA 28211
Telephone: 704-716-1200
Fax: 704-716-1201
URL: http://www.bcandm.com

Business Law, Limited Liability Company Law, Partnerships, Corporate, Contracts, Commercial Litigation, Construction Law, Labor and Employment, Securities Law.

FIRM PROFILE: Bishop, Capitano & Moss, P.A. is a commercial litigation boutique focusing in complex and technical business controversies, including particularly shareholder and partnership disputes, construction claims, employment compensation and noncompete litigation, investment brokerage and securities law, and complex insurance coverage matters.

J. DANIEL BISHOP, born Charlotte, North Carolina, July 1, 1964; admitted to bar, 1990, North Carolina. *Education:* University of North Carolina (B.S., with highest distinction, 1986; J.D., with high honors, 1990). Phi Beta Kappa; Beta Gamma Sigma; Order of the Coif. Member, North Carolina Law Review, 1988-1989. Member, Mecklenburg Board of County Commissioners, 2004—. Listed in, Business North Carolina; "North Carolina Legal Elite, Litigation", 2003-2005. *Member:* Mecklenburg County (Member, Executive Committee, 1994-1997; Fee Arbitration Committee, 1995-1998) and North Carolina Bar Associations. ***PRACTICE AREAS:*** Shareholder Disputes; Partnership Law; Employment Law; Investments Brokerage; Insurance Coverage; Bankruptcy Litigation. ***Email:*** dbishop@bcandm.com

A. TODD CAPITANO, born Atlanta, Georgia, December 6, 1966; admitted to bar, 1994, North Carolina. *Education:* University of North Carolina (B.A., with honors, 1989; J.D., with high honors, 1994). Order of the Coif. John Motley Morehead Scholar. Member, North Carolina Law Review, 1992-1993. *Member:* Mecklenburg County and North Carolina Bar Associations; The Federalist Society. ***PRACTICE AREAS:*** Commercial Litigation; Shareholder Disputes; Partnership Law; Employment Law; Construction Law. ***Email:*** tcapitano@bcandm.com

JOSEPH W. MOSS, JR., born Winston-Salem, North Carolina, May 2, 1966; admitted to bar, 1993, North Carolina and South Carolina. *Education:* Davidson College (B.A., 1988); Wake Forest University (J.D., cum laude, 1993). Omicron Delta Epsilon. Managing Editor, Wake Forest Law Review, 1992-1993. Law Clerk to Honorable N. Carlton Tilley, Jr., U.S. District Judge, Middle District of North Carolina, 1993-1994. *Member:* Mecklenburg County (Member, Board of Directors, 2000-2003), North Carolina (Member, Construction Law Section Council, 2000—) and American (Member, Forum on the Construction Industry; Construction Litigation Committee; House of Delegates, 1999-2001) Bar Associations; South Carolina Bar ((Member, Construction Law Section). ***PRACTICE AREAS:*** Commercial Litigation; Construction Law; Securities Litigation; Shareholder Disputes; Partnership Law; Civil Litigation. ***Email:*** jmoss@bcandm.com

---

RAIZEL ARNHOLT KAHN, born Fayetteville, North Carolina, November 15, 1977; admitted to bar, 2002, North Carolina. *Education:* University of North Carolina at Chapel Hill (B.A., Political Science, 1999; J.D., 2002). Phi Beta Kappa. *Member:* Mecklenburg County and North Carolina Bar Associations. ***PRACTICE AREAS:*** Civil Litigation; Employment Litigation; Shareholder Disputes; Commercial Litigation. ***Email:*** rkahn@bcandm.com

BLAIR CONAWAY BOGRAD & MARTIN, P.A.

CHARLOTTE, NORTH CAROLINA

(See Shumaker, Loop & Kendrick, LLP)

JAMES L. BLANE, PLLC

1057 EAST MOREHEAD STREET
CHARLOTTE, NORTH CAROLINA 28204
Telephone: 704-331-0030
Facsimile: 704-372-1677
Email: JBLANELAW@BELLSOUTH.NET
URL: http://www.james-blanelaw.com

Mailing Address: P.O. Box 31551, Charlotte, NC 28231

Mediation, Creditor Law, Bankruptcy, Business Law, Corporate Law, Contract, Estate and Probate, Real Estate, Civil Litigation.

JAMES L. BLANE, born Roanoke, Virginia, June 23, 1951; admitted to bar, 1976, North Carolina and U.S. District Court, Western District of North Carolina; 1983, U.S. District Court, Middle District of North Carolina; 1992, U.S. Court of Appeals, Fourth Circuit. *Education:* University of North Carolina at Chapel Hill (B.S., 1973); University of Virginia School of Law (J.D., 1976). Beta Gamma Sigma; Phi Delta Phi; The Order of the Old Well. Member, Bankruptcy Section Council, North Carolina Bar Association, 1982. Certified, Superior Court Mediator, 2000—. *Member:* North Carolina (Member, Alternative Dispute Resolution, Bankruptcy, Corporate and Real Estate Sections) and American Bar Associations; Twenty-Sixth Judicial District and North Carolina State Bars; North Carolina Academy of Trial Lawyers. ***PRACTICE AREAS:*** Creditor Bankruptcy; Debtors Rights; Foreclosures; Business Law; Corporate Law; Probate; Estate Planning; Wills; Civil Litigation; Litigation. ***Email:*** jblanelaw@bellsouth.net

REPRESENTATIVE CLIENTS: Beech Mountain Resort, Inc.; Carolina Communities Corp.; R&G Construction Co., Inc.; Rowells, Inc.; Moss Supply Company; Oceanside Village, LLC; Southside, LLC; Preferred Parking Services, Inc.; Charlotte Marble and Granite, Inc.; Horizon CSA, LLC.

APPROVED ATTORNEY FOR: Title Company of North Carolina; Lawyers Title Insurance Corp.; American Title Insurance Corp.; Chicago Title Insurance Corp.; First Title Insurance Co.; Jefferson Pilot Title Insurance Co.; The Title Guarantee Co.; Investors Title Insurance Co.

BLEDSOE & BLEDSOE, P.L.L.C.

Established in 1996
1057 EAST MOREHEAD STREET
P.O. BOX 36779
CHARLOTTE, NORTH CAROLINA 28236-6779
Telephone: 704-372-1676
Fax: 704-372-1677
Email: labjrbled@aol.com
URL: http://www.louisabledsoe.com

General Civil Practice in State and Federal Courts. Litigation, Arbitration and Mediation.

FIRM PROFILE: Bledsoe & Bledsoe, P.L.L.C. was established in 1996.

LOUIS A. BLEDSOE, JR., born Huntsville, Alabama, November 17, 1927; admitted to bar, 1955, North Carolina; 1956, U.S. District Court, Western District of North Carolina and U.S. Court of Appeals, Fourth Circuit and U.S. Tax Court. *Education:* University of North Carolina at Chapel Hill (B.S. in B.A., 1953; LL.B., 1955). Inducted into the North Carolina Bar Association General Practice Hall of Fame, 1995. Member, Panel of Arbitrators, American Arbitration Association, Certified Mediator. Member, Mediation, Inc.*Member:* Mecklenburg County, North Carolina and American Bar Associations; North Carolina State Bar; The Association of Trial Lawyers of America; North Carolina Academy of Trial Lawyers. [Capt., USAFR, 1951-1953]. ***PRACTICE AREAS:*** Business; Trusts and Estates; Taxation; Real Estate; Litigation. ***Email:*** labjrbled@aol.com

---

MARGARET M. BLEDSOE (1966-1996)

BOGLE, ANTHONY & LEACH, P.A.

CHARLOTTE, NORTH CAROLINA

(See Gastonia)

Workers Compensation, Personal Injury, Wrongful Death, Criminal Defense, Traffic Violations, Driving While Intoxicated, Corporate Law, Wills, Trust Law, Family Law/Domestic, Divorce, Child Custody, Child Support.

THE BOLDUC LAW FIRM, PLLC

401 NORTH TRYON STREET, 10TH FLOOR
CHARLOTTE, NORTH CAROLINA 28202
Telephone: 704-998-5188
Fax: 704-998-5704
URL: http://www.bolduclawfirm.com
URL: http://www.bolduclaw.com

NASD Arbitration, Business Litigation, Securities Fraud, Corporate Malfeasance, Mutual Fund Disputes, Wrongful Termination, Banking and Finance Law, and Accounting.

DARRYLL BOLDUC, born Waterville, Maine, April 8, 1960; admitted to bar, 2003, North Carolina. *Education:* Brown University (B.A., 1983); Campbell University (J.D., 2003). V.P. Manager, Foreign Exchange Division, First Union Bank, 1990-1992. Portfolio Manager, Foreign Bonds, Bank of America, 1992-1994; Commodity Trading Advisor, 1995-2000. *Member:* Mecklenberg County Bar Association; North Carolina State Bar; Public Investors Arbitration Bar Association. ***PRACTICE AREAS:*** NASD Arbitration; Business Litigation; Securities Fraud; Corporate Malfeasance; Mutual Funds; Wrongful Termination; Accounting Law.

BOLLINGER & PIEMONTE, PC

Established in 1999
601 E. FIFTH STREET, SUITE 250
CHARLOTTE, NORTH CAROLINA 28202
Telephone: 704-373-1777
Fax: 704-373-1977
URL: http://www.bollingerandpiemonte.com

Workers Compensation, Social Security Disability, Personal Injury, Disability Insurance, General Civil Litigation, Wrongful Death, Railroad Disability.

FIRM PROFILE: We primarily represent individuals who have been injured or are disabled. Bob Bollinger is a State Bar Certified Specialist in Workers' Compensation Law. George Piemonte has a strong background in Social Security and Auto Accident Cases.

BOBBY L. BOLLINGER, JR., born Lincolnton, North Carolina, 1958; admitted to bar, 1988, North Carolina. *Education:* Lenoir-Rhyne College; University of North Carolina-Charlotte (B.A., 1982); Campbell University (J.D., cum laude, 1988). Phi Kappa Phi; Omicron Delta Kappa. Staff Member, 1986-1987 and Business Editor, 1987-1988, Campbell Law Review. Member, National Moot Court Team, 1987. Author: "Warrantless Aerial Surveillance Endorsed - California v. Ciraolo," 9 Campbell Law Review 497, 1987. Author and Speaker: Continuing Legal Education on NC Workers' Compensation, National Business Institute, 1994-1995, 1997-1998 and 2000. Director, 1992-2003 and President, 1995-1999, United Cerebral Palsy of North Carolina, Inc. Member, Governors' Advocacy Council for Persons with Disabilities, 1997—. Director, Easter Seals UCP of North Carolina, Inc., 2004-2005. *Member:* Mecklenburg County and North Carolina Bar Associations; North Carolina Academy of Trial Lawyers. (Board Certified Specialist in Workers' Compensation, North Carolina State Board of Legal Specialization). ***REPORTED CASES:*** Crowder v. Preston Trucking, 161 N.C. App. 181 (2003); Davis v. Trus Joint MacMillan, 148 N.C.App. 248 (2002); Fink v. Fink, 120 N.C. App. 412 (1995); Aycock v. Aycock, 113 N.C. App. 834 (1994); Stancil v. Brock, 108 N.C. App. 745 (1993); Rudisill v. Rudisill, 102

(This Listing Continued)

BOLLINGER & PIEMONTE, PC, Charlotte—Continued

N.C. App. 280 (1991); Watson v. Graf Bae Farm, 99 N.C. App. 210 (1990). ***PRACTICE AREAS:*** Workers Compensation; Personal Injury; Social Security Disability; Civil Litigation. ***Email:*** bbollinger@bplawnc.com

GEORGE C. PIEMONTE, born Oak Park, Illinois, 1959; admitted to bar, 1987, North Carolina and U.S. District Court, Western and Middle Districts of North Carolina. *Education:* University of Florida (B.S., 1982); Nova University (J.D., 1987). Phi Kappa Phi; Golden Key. Life Member, National Registry of Who's Who, Publication Year, 1997. Author: "Property Damage Claims," Mecklenburg County Bar CLE Seminar, Feb. 19, 1993. *Member:* Mecklenburg County, North Carolina and American Bar Associations; The Association of Trial Lawyers of America (NC Workers Comp. Liaison); North Carolina Academy of Trial Lawyers; Mecklenburg County Trial Lawyers Association (Treasurer, 1997-2001); Roscoe Pound Institute; National Organization of Social Security Claimant Representatives. ***REPORTED CASES:*** Onley v. Nationwide Mutual Insurance Company, 456SE2d882, 118 N.C. App 686 (1995); Pomeroy v. Tanner Masonry, 144 N.C. App. _ (2002). ***PRACTICE AREAS:*** Social Security Disability; Railroad Disability; Workers Compensation; Personal Injury. ***Email:*** gpiemonte@bplawnc.com

---

THE BOLSTER LAW FIRM, P.A.

1043 EAST MOREHEAD STREET, SUITE 111
CHARLOTTE, NORTH CAROLINA 28204
Telephone: 704-347-4884
Facsimile: 704-347-1087
Email: jbolster@bolsterlawfirm.com
URL: http://www.bolsterlawfirm.com

Insurance Defense Litigation, Insurance Coverage Disputes and General Civil Litigation.

JEFFREY S. BOLSTER, born Valdosta, Georgia, September 6, 1968; admitted to bar, 1994, North Carolina and U.S. District Court, Western and Middle Districts of North Carolina. *Education:* University of North Carolina (B.A., 1990); Wake Forest University (J.D., 1994). *Member:* North Carolina Bar Association; North Carolina State Bar; North Carolina Association of Defense Attorneys; Defense Research Institute. ***PRACTICE AREAS:*** Insurance Defense; Insurance Coverage; Products Liability; Transportation; Construction Law; Environmental Law; Professional Malpractice. ***Email:*** jbolster@bolsterlawfirm.com

ALEC D. ROGERS, born Houston, Texas, October 31, 1970; admitted to bar, 1996, North Carolina. *Education:* Clemson University (B.A., 1992); Wake Forest University (J.D., 1996). *Member:* North Carolina State Bar. ***PRACTICE AREAS:*** Civil Litigation; Insurance Defense.

AMY FITZGERALD, born Pittsburgh, Pennsylvania, June 19, 1977; admitted to bar, 2002, North Carolina. *Education:* Indiana University of Pennsylvania (B.A., 1999); Pennsylvania State University (J.D., cum laude, 2002). ***PRACTICE AREAS:*** Insurance Defense Litigation. ***Email:*** afitzgerald@bolsterlawfirm.com

REPRESENTATIVE CLIENTS: Auto-Owners Insurance Company; Allstate Insurance Company; Metlife; The St. Paul Travelers; Fed-Ex Freight East, Inc.; Network Adjusters; Nationwide Insurance.

BOOTH HARRINGTON & JOHNS, LLP

CHARLOTTE, NORTH CAROLINA

(See Greensboro)

BRADLEY ARANT ROSE & WHITE LLP

BANK OF AMERICA CORPORATE CENTER
100 N. TRYON STREET
SUITE 2690
CHARLOTTE, NORTH CAROLINA 28202
Telephone: 704-332-8842
Facsimile: 704-332-8858
Email: info@bradleyarant.com
URL: http://www.bradleyarant.com

REVISER OF THE ALABAMA LAW DIGEST FOR THIS DIRECTORY.

Birmingham, Alabama Office: One Federal Place, 1819 5th Avenue North, 35203-2119. Telephone: 205-521-8000. Facsimile: 205-521-8800.
Huntsville, Alabama Office: 200 Clinton Avenue West, Suite 900, 35801. Telephone: 256-517-5100. Facsimile: 256-517-5200.
Montgomery, Alabama Office: Alabama Center for Commerce, 401 Adams Avenue, Suite 780, 36104. Telephone: 334-956-7700. Facsimile: 334-956-7701.
Washington, D.C. Office: 1133 Connecticut Avenue, N.W., 12th Floor, 20036. Telephone: 202-393-7150. Facsimile: 202-347-1684.
Jackson, Mississippi Office: 188 East Capitol Street, Suite 450, 39201. Telephone: 601-948-8000. Facsimile: 601-948-3000.

Alternative Dispute Resolution; Antitrust and Trade Regulation; Appellate Practice; Banking and Financial Services; Bankruptcy; Business Law; Complex and Multi-District Litigation; Compliance; Computers and Software; Construction and Procurement; Corporate Law; Corporate Governance; Energy; Environmental Law; Environmental Litigation; ERISA; ERISA Litigation; Government Contracts; Governmental Affairs; Health Care Fraud; Health Care Law; Intellectual Property; Copyrights; Patents; Trademarks; Trade Secrets; International Law; International Transactions; Labor and Employment; Land Use; Leasing; Life Sciences; Litigation; Media Law; Mergers and Acquisitions; Partnership Law; Private Equity and Investment Funds; Products Liability; Public Finance; Public Utility Law; Real Estate Finance and Development; Real Estate Law; Reorganization Restructuring and Insolvency; Securities;

(This Listing Continued)

Securities Litigation; State and Local Taxation; Tax Exempt Facilities; Tax Litigation; Taxation; Technology and Science; Trusts and Estates; Venture Capital; White Collar Crime; Workouts.

FIRM PROFILE: Bradley Arant's roots can be traced back to the late 1800s and the very early days of the City of Birmingham. Over the years, Bradley Arant has grown along with Birmingham and the rest of the Southeastern United States to a firm of more than 200 lawyers with offices in Birmingham, Huntsville, and Montgomery, Alabama; Jackson, Mississippi; Charlotte, North Carolina; and Washington, D.C.

The firm represents several enterprises listed on national stock exchanges, several banks, including the largest bank holding company in Alabama, and serves as regional counsel for a number of banks and other financial institutions. The many individuals, partnerships, corporations, proprietorships, state and local governments and governmental agencies which are clients of the firm engage in a broad variety of businesses and activities, including accounting, banking, biotechnology, higher education, health care, transportation, petroleum refining, energy production and distribution, construction, government contracting, soft drink bottling, timber, pulp and paper, steel, real estate development, publishing, textile and garment production, manufacturing, materials and aggregate production, coal and mineral mining and distribution, vehicle and equipment leasing, communications, public utilities, and other activities both domestically and internationally.

Firm Activities: All attorneys are members of the American and Alabama Bar Associations. One is a recent past president of the Alabama State Bar; six are Fellows of the American College of Trial Lawyers; six are Fellows of the American College of Tax Counsel; three are members of the American Law Institute; four are Fellows of the American College of Trust and Estate Counsel; two are Fellows of the American College of Construction Lawyers; one is a Fellow of the American College of Bankruptcy; one is a Fellow of the American College of Mortgage Attorneys; three are Fellows of the American College of Bond Counsel; two are Fellows of the College of Labor and Employment Lawyers; and one is a recent past president of the Birmingham Bar Association. Partners are also members of or are affiliated with the National Association of Bond Lawyers, the Alabama Association of School Board Attorneys, the International Association of Defense Counsel, the National Association of Railroad Trial Counsel, the American Association of Real Estate Lawyers, the American and Alabama Law Institutes, the American Association of Tax Counsel, and the International Bar Association. Partners also serve as adjunct faculty at the University of Alabama School of Law and the Cumberland School of Law.

MEMBERS OF FIRM

JOHN D. BOND, III, born Enterprise, Alabama, October 9, 1954; admitted to bar, 1987, Alabama; 1989, District of Columbia; 1990, U.S. Court of Appeals, Fourth, Eleventh and Federal Circuit, U.S. Claims Court; 2004, North Carolina. *Education:* Troy State University (B.S., cum laude, 1980); Cumberland School of Law of Samford University (J.D., 1987). Member, Panel of Arbitrators, American Arbitration Association. *Member:* Birmingham, Federal and American Bar Associations; District of Columbia Bar; Bar Association of the District of Columbia; Alabama State Bar. ***PRACTICE AREAS:*** Construction; Procurement. ***Email:*** jbond@bradleyarant.com

MICHAEL W. KNAPP, born Fairfax, Virginia, July 18, 1970; admitted to bar, 1995, North Carolina; 1997, District of Columbia; 1999, California. *Education:* James Madison University (B.A., 1992); Wake Forest University (J.D., 1995). *Member:* Mecklenburg County, San Diego County and American (Member: Litigation Section; Construction Industry Forum) Bar Associations; North Carolina State Bar; The District of Columbia Bar; State Bar of California. [Lieutenant, United States Navy, Judge Advocate General's Corps, 1995-1998]. ***PRACTICE AREAS:*** Construction Law; Construction Defect. ***Email:*** mknapp@bradleyarant.com

ASSOCIATES

DAVID H. BASHFORD, born Wilmington, North Carolina; admitted to bar, 2002, North Carolina; 2003, Virginia. *Education:* Davidson College (B.A., 1998); University of North Carolina at Chapel Hill (J.D., with honors, 2002). ***PRACTICE AREAS:*** Construction Law. ***Email:*** dbashford@bradleyarant.com

COLIN R. STOCKTON, born Akron, Ohio, August 4, 1974; admitted to bar, 2000, Alabama (Not admitted in North Carolina). *Education:* Wheeling Jesuit University (B.A., magna cum laude, 1997); University of North Carolina School of Law (J.D., honors, 2000). Member, North Carolina Law Review. Phi Delta Phi, Trial Law Academy. *Member:* Alabama State Bar; American Bar Association. ***PRACTICE AREAS:*** Labor and Employment; Products Liability; Transportation. ***Email:*** cstockton@bradleyarant.com

FINANCIAL SERVICE COMPANIES: Aliant Bank; Bank of Alabama; Financial Investors of the South; First Commercial Bank; First National Bank of Jasper; Heritage Bank; Household International, Inc.; New South Federal Savings Bank; Retirement Systems of Alabama; Robertson Banking Company; SOUTHBank; Synovus Financial Corp.; The Bancorporation; The Bank; Traders and Farmers Bank; Wachovia Bank, N.A.
CONSTRUCTION AND ENGINEERING: A.G. Gaston Construction Co., Inc.; Aker Kvaerner Engineering & Construction; BE&K, Inc.; B. L. Harbert International, LLC; Brasfield & Gorrie, LLC; CH2M HILL Companies, Ltd.; Caddell Construction Co., Inc.; Centex Construction Group, Inc.; Chicago Bridge & Iron Company; Clark Construction Group; Hoar Construction LLC; InDyne, Inc.; Insituform Technologies, Inc.; John J. Kirlin, Inc.; Lockwood Greene Engineers, Inc.; Massachusetts Highway Department; McCrory Building Company, Inc.; The AES Corporation; The Robins & Morton Group; Tompkins Builders, Inc.; Wunderlich-Malec Engineering.
EDUCATION: Auburn University; University of Alabama; University of South Alabama.
ENVIRONMENTAL: Alabama Gas Corporation; Chevron Texaco; Energen Corporation; Hanna Steel Corporation; Hunt Refining Co.; Monsanto Company; National Cement Company of Alabama, Inc.; PinnOak Resources LLC; Pneumo-Abex; Rock Wool Manufacturing Company; Russell Corporation; The Valspar Corporation; Vulcan Materials Company.
ENERGY: AES Corp.; Alabama Gas Corporation; Energen Corporation; Tractebel Power, Inc.
FOOD AND BEVERAGE: Associated Grocers of the South, Inc.; Coca-Cola Bottling Company United, Inc.; Shoney's, Inc.; Shop-A-Snack Food Mart, Inc.

(This Listing Continued)

HEALTH CARE: Alacare Home Health Services, Inc.; Alabama Psychiatric Services, P.C.; The Baldwin County Eastern Shore Health Care Authority (Thomas Hospital); The Children's Health System of Alabama; The Colbert County - Northwest Alabama Health Care Authority (Helen Keller Hospital and Red Bay Hospital); DCH Health Care Authority (DCH Regional Medical Center, DCH-Northport Medical Center, and Fayette Medical Center and Nursing Home); DST Systems, Inc.; Gadsden Regional Medical Center; The Heart Center, P.C.; HealthSouth Corporation; Madison Surgery Center; Oncology Specialties, P.C./Comprehensive Cancer Institute; University of Alabama Health Services Foundation, P.C. (The Kirklin Clinic); VIVA Health, Inc.
INSURANCE: AIG Insurance Company; Great American Financial Group; Liberty National Life Insurance Company; MONY Life Insurance Company; Principal Life Insurance Co.; Seaboard/St. Paul Surety Company; State Farm Insurance Company; The Chubb Group; Torchmark Corporation.
MANUFACTURING: Blount Inc.; Bridgestone/Firestone, Inc.; Centex Construction Products, Inc.; Ciba Specialty Chemicals; Cosco; EBSCO Industries, Inc.; Ford Motor Co.; Fruit of the Loom, Inc.; Kenworth Truck Company and Peterbilt; Michelin Tire Corp.; Neptune Technology Group, Inc.; Novartis Corp.; Russell Corporation; The Goodyear Tire & Rubber Co.; ThyssenKrupp Elevator Corporation; U.S. Pipe and Foundry Co.; United Technologies Corporation; WMX Corporation.
MEDIA/PUBLICATIONS/COMMUNICATIONS: EBSCO Industries, Inc.; Randall Publishing Company, Inc.; Southern Progress Corporation; The Huntsville Times; The New York Times Co.; Time Warner Cable.
MINING, MINERALS, NATURAL RESOURCES: Alabama Gas Corporation; Champion International Corp.; Hunt Refining Company; Jim Walter Resources, Inc.; Nelson Brothers, Inc.; Vulcan Materials Company.
REAL ESTATE: Alabama Association of Homebuilders; Colonial Properties Trust; Daniel Realty Corporation; EBSCO Realty; Equity Resources, LLC; Graham & Company; Guilford Capital Corporation; Jim Wilson & Associates, Inc.; Sloss Development Group; Stonegate Realty Company, LLC; The Hays Group; Torchmark Corporation; USX Realty Development.
RETAIL GASOLINE DISTRIBUTION: BP Amoco; Chevron U.S.A., Inc.
TECHNOLOGY AND BIOTECHNOLOGY: BioCryst Pharmaceuticals, Inc.; Bioelastics Research, Ltd.; ComFrame Software Corporation; EVault, Inc.; Galenica Pharmaceuticals; PNP Thearpeutics, Inc.; Regional Nuclear Pharmaceuticals; Southern Applied Technologies, Inc.; Southern BioSystems, Inc.
TELECOMMUNICATIONS: AT&T; Sprint Corporation.
TRADE ASSOCIATIONS: Associated Builders and Contractors, Inc.; Ductile Iron Pipe Research Association.
TRANSPORTATION: Boyd Bros. Transportation, Inc.

REVISER OF THE ALABAMA LAW DIGEST FOR THIS DIRECTORY.

BRADLEY, GUTHERY, TURNER & CURRY

CHARLOTTE, NORTH CAROLINA

(See Horack, Talley, Pharr & Lowndes)

BRANNON STRICKLAND, PLLC

CHARLOTTE, NORTH CAROLINA

(See Raleigh)

Appellate Advocacy, Civil Litigation. Constitutional Law, Criminal Defense, District Court/ Traffic Violations, Divorce, Family Law, Juvenile/DSS, Real Estate.

THE BRAY LAW FIRM, PLLC

Established in 2002

4701 HEDGEMORE DRIVE, SUITE 816
CHARLOTTE, NORTH CAROLINA 28209
Telephone: 704-523-7777
Fax: 704-523-7780
Email: wbray@braylaw.com
URL: http://www.braylaw.com

Business and Litigation Practice including Business Litigation, Contracts, Construction, Employment, Entertainment Law, General Corporate, Incorporation, Intellectual Property, Limited Liability Companies, Mergers and Acquisitions, Partnerships, Products Liability, Professional Liability, Sports Law, Tax, Technology and Emerging Business, and Tort Litigation.

FIRM PROFILE: The Bray Law Firm is dedicated to working with small businesses and individuals throughout North and South Carolina. Primary practice areas include sport and entertainment, construction and business litigation. Please visit our website for more information.

WILLIAM PARKS BRAY, born Athens, Georgia, November 13, 1967; admitted to bar, 1993, South Carolina; 1994, North Carolina. *Education:* Davidson College (B.A., 1989); University of South Carolina (J.D., 1993). Recipient, American Jurisprudence Award, Constitutional Law, 1991. University of South Carolina School of Law Honor Council Representative, 1991-1993. Rock Hill's Favorite Attorney, 1999. Publications and Speaking Engagements: "A Lawyer's Career in Sports," NC Sports & Entertainment Law Newsletter, Vol. 2 Number 1, 2001; "The Seven Commandments of Risk Management," Metrolina Business Council, 2003; "Strengthening Your Contract Drafting Skills in North Carolina," Institute for Paralegal Education, 2003. Previous Employment: Assistant Solicitor, 16th Judicial Circuit of South Carolina (1994-1996); Associate, Morris, York, Williams, Surles & Barringer (1996-1997); Member, Bray & Chiarenza (1997-1999); Managing Director, The Links Golf Group, (1999-2001). *Member:* Mecklenburg County and North Carolina (Member, Technology Committee; Sports and Entertainment Law Section Council) Bar Associations; South Carolina Bar; Association for Corporate Growth. ***PRACTICE AREAS:*** Business Law; Civil Litigation; Contracts; Construction; Entertainment Law; Franchises and Franchising. ***Email:*** wbray@braylaw.com

---

MILTON H. GILBERT, JR, born Fayetteville, North Carolina, June 3, 1971; admitted to bar, 2001, North Carolina; 2003, South Carolina. *Education:* University of North Carolina at Charlotte (B.A., 1993; M.B.A., 1995); University of Akron (J.D., 1995). *Member:* Mecklenburg County and North Carolina (Co-Chair, Young Lawyers Division Peer Mediation Task Force, 2003-2004; Internet Chair, 2004-2005) Bar Associations. ***PRACTICE AREAS:*** Business Litigation; Entertainment Law; Corporate Law. ***Email:*** hgilbert@braylaw.com

(This Listing Continued)

REPRESENTATIVE CLIENTS: Braun Racing; MoRisen Records; Anglerschannel.com; Zobo.tv; Golf Scotland; Golf Podium; Captain Obvious Productions; Calvin Edwards; Chairmen of the Board; Alvacor Construction; Siteworks Construction; Provident Builders.

BRENNAN LAW FIRM, PLLC

CHARLOTTE, NORTH CAROLINA

(See Cornelius)

Employee Benefits, ERISA, Pension and Profit Sharing Plans, Taxation, Tax Planning, Estate and Gift Taxation, Estate Planning, Business Law, Joint Ventures, Limited Liability Law, Partnership Insurance, Nonprofit and Charitable Organizations.

THE BROOKS LAW FIRM, P.C.

401 EAST SECOND STREET, SUITE 101
CHARLOTTE, NORTH CAROLINA 28202
Telephone: 704-332-1618
Fax: 704-332-1624
Cell: 704-488-4343
Email: ABROOKS@THEBROOKSLAWFIRM.COM
URL: http://www.abrookslawfirm.com

Criminal Defense, Driving While Intoxicated, Drug Crimes, Parole and Probation, Misdemeanor and Felony, Traffic Violations, License Reinstatements, Expungements, Name Changes.

ALICIA D. BROOKS, born Fayetteville, North Carolina, June 18, 1966; admitted to bar, 1992, North Carolina. *Education:* University of North Carolina at Chapel Hill (B.S., 1988; J.D., 1991). Assistant District Attorney, Mecklenburg County, 1992-1996. *Member:* Mecklenburg County Bar Association; North Carolina Academy of Trial Lawyers. ***PRACTICE AREAS:*** Criminal Defense; Driving While Intoxicated; Drug Crimes; Parole and Probation; Misdemeanors; Felonies; Traffic Violations; Drivers License Suspension; Name Changes. ***Email:*** ABROOKS@THEBROOKSLAWFIRM.COM

BROOKS LAW OFFICE

5120 MONROE ROAD
CHARLOTTE, NORTH CAROLINA 28205
Telephone: 704-567-5297
Fax: 704-567-5389
Email: lawbrooks@bellsouth.net
URL: http://www.tjbbulldog.com

Medical Malpractice, Wrongful Death, Personal Injury, Automobile Accidents, Slip and Fall, Employment Law, Employment Discrimination, Wrongful Termination, Sexual Harassment, Contracts, Employment Contracts, Sports, Entertainment.

MEMBER

TAMARA W. BROOKS, born Fredericksburg, Virginia, 1966; admitted to bar, 1997, North Carolina and U.S. District Court, Western District of North Carolina. *Education:* James Madison University (B.A., 1988); Mississippi College School of Law (J.D., 1997). *Member:* North Carolina and American Bar Associations; Association of Trial Lawyers of America. ***PRACTICE AREAS:*** Medical Malpractice; Wrongful Death; Personal Injury; Automobile Accidents and Injuries; Slip and Fall; Employment Law; Employment Discrimination; Wrongful Termination; Sexual Harassment; Contracts; Employment Contracts; Sports Law; Entertainment Law. ***Email:*** lawbrooks@bellsouth.net

BROWN, MOORE & ASSOCIATES, PLLC

Established in 1975

200 QUEENS ROAD, SUITE 200
CHARLOTTE, NORTH CAROLINA 28204
Telephone: 704-335-1500
Fax: 704-333-1636
URL: http://www.brownandmoorelaw.com

Catastrophic Injury, Personal Injury, Automobile Accidents, Brain Injury, Spinal Cord Injury, Professional Liability, Wrongful Death, Products Liability, Truck Accidents, Medical Malpractice, Legal Malpractice, Construction Accidents, Nursing Home Negligence and Insurance Law.

R. KENT BROWN, born Charlotte, North Carolina, July 17, 1949; admitted to bar, 1975, North Carolina, U.S. Supreme Court, U.S. Court of Appeals, Fourth Circuit and U.S. District Court, Western District of North Carolina; 1976, U.S. District Court, Middle District of North Carolina. *Education:* University of North Carolina (B.A., in Political Science, 1971); Wake Forest University (J.D., 1974). Phi Delta Phi. *Member:* Mecklenburg County, North Carolina and American Bar Associations; North Carolina State Bar; The Association of Trial Lawyers of America; North Carolina Academy of Trial Lawyers. ***REPORTED CASES:*** Curry v. Baker, 349 N.C. 355, 517 SE2d 890 (1999); Dixon v. CSX Transportation, Inc., 990 F.2d 1440, cert. denied, 510 U.S. 915, 114 Sup. Ct. 305, 126 Law Ed. 2d 252 (1993). ***PRACTICE AREAS:*** Medical Malpractice; Personal Injury; Products Liability. ***Email:*** kbrown@brownmoorelaw.com

JON R. MOORE, born Kansas City, Missouri, March 16, 1976; admitted to bar, 2002, Missouri, North Carolina and U.S. District Court, Western District of North Carolina. *Education:* Northwestern University (B.A., 1997); Georgetown University (J.D., cum laude, 2001). *Member:* Mecklenburg County, North Carolina and American Bar Associations; North Carolina State Bar; The Missouri Bar; The Association of Trial Lawyers of America; North Carolina Academy of Trial Lawyers. ***PRACTICE AREAS:*** Personal Injury; Products Liability. ***Email:*** jmoore@brownmoorelaw.com

(This Listing Continued)

BROWN, MOORE & ASSOCIATES, PLLC, Charlotte—Continued

ASSOCIATE

MARIE C. SHEA, born Buffalo, New York, February 16, 1944; admitted to bar, 1997, New York; 2002, North Carolina. *Education:* D'Youville College (B.S.N., 1965); State University of New York at Buffalo (M.S.N., 1979; J.D., 1996). Registered Nurse License, New York, 1965— North Carolina, 2001—. *Member:* Erie County (Member, Health Care Law Section), Mecklenberg County, New York State and North Carolina Bar Associations; Women Lawyers Association of New York; Association of Trial Lawyers of America; American Association of Legal Nurse Consultants. ***PRACTICE AREAS:*** Medical Malpractice; Nursing Home Abuse and Neglect; Personal Injury; Wrongful Death. ***Email:*** mshea@brownmoorelaw.com

DON H. BUMGARDNER

CHARLOTTE, NORTH CAROLINA

(See Gastonia)

General Civil and Appellate Practice in all State and Federal Courts. Personal Injury, Products Liability, Workers Compensation and Medical Malpractice.

BURRIS, MACMILLAN, PEARCE & BURRIS, PLLC

6857 FAIRVIEW ROAD
CHARLOTTE, NORTH CAROLINA 28210
Telephone: 704-365-2600
Fax: 704-364-2637

General Civil Practice, Real Estate, Residential Real Estate; Commercial Real Estate, Real Estate Litigation, Estate Planning, Administration, Wills and Probate.

ROBERT N. BURRIS, born Monroe, North Carolina, December 21, 1940; admitted to bar, 1970, North Carolina and U.S. District Court, Western District of North Carolina; 1976, U.S. District Court, Middle District of North Carolina; 1972, U.S. Court of International Trade; 1990, South Carolina. *Education:* University of South Carolina (A.B., 1963); University of North Carolina (J.D., 1970). *Member:* Mecklenburg County, North Carolina and American Bar Associations; North Carolina State Bar; North Carolina Trial Lawyers Association. [With U.S. Navy, 1963-1967; CDR, Navy Reserve]. ***PRACTICE AREAS:*** Commercial and Residential Real Estate; Corporate Law; Estate Planning and Administration. ***Email:*** bobburris@bellsouth.net

DOUGLAS P. MACMILLAN, born New York, N.Y., April 25, 1947; admitted to bar, 1972, North Carolina; 1996, South Carolina. *Education:* University of North Carolina (A.B., 1969; J.D., 1972). *Member:* North Carolina Bar Association; 26th Judicial District Bar Association; North Carolina State Bar; South Carolina Bar. ***LANGUAGES:*** French. ***PRACTICE AREAS:*** Commercial and Residential Real Estate; Corporate Law; Estate Planning and Administration. ***Email:*** dpmacm@bellsouth.net

HUGO A. PEARCE, III, born Charleston, South Carolina, July 4, 1945; admitted to bar, 1973, North Carolina; 1974, South Carolina. *Education:* Newberry College (A.B., 1967); University of South Carolina (J.D., 1973). Member, Editorial Board, University of South Carolina Law Review, 1971-1973. Author: Note, "Heirs Property, The Problem, Pitfalls and Possible Solutions," 25 South Carolina Law Review 151, 1973. *Member:* Mecklenburg County, North Carolina and American Bar Associations; The North Carolina State Bar; South Carolina Bar. ***PRACTICE AREAS:*** Civil and Commercial Litigation; Real Estate Law; Business Law. ***Email:*** hugop@bellsouth.net

MARGERY A. BURRIS, born 1967; admitted to bar, 1992, North Carolina. *Education:* Vanderbilt University (B.A.); University of North Carolina at Chapel Hill (J.D.). *Member:* Mecklenburg and North Carolina Bar Associations; North Carolina State Bar. ***PRACTICE AREAS:*** Commercial and Residential Real Estate; Corporate Law; Estate Planning and Administration. ***Email:*** margeryb@bellsouth.net

LAW OFFICES OF BUSH & POWERS

A Partnership of Professional Associations
821 EAST BOULEVARD
CHARLOTTE, NORTH CAROLINA 28203
Telephone: 704-342-4357; 347-0110
704-358-9074 (Espanol)
Fax: 704-347-8840
URL: http://www.CharlotteLegalHelp.com
URL: http://www.bushandpowers.com

Driving While Impaired, Traffic and Criminal Defense, Personal Injury, Bankruptcy, Medical Malpractice, Civil Litigation, Family Law, Immigration.

FIRM PROFILE: A Partnership of Professional Associations providing legal assistance in criminal, traffic and DUI (DWI) law. personal injury, bankruptcy, immigration, civil litigation and family law.

TOM BUSH, born Daytona Beach, Florida, March 16, 1948; admitted to bar, 1973, Florida; 1976, U.S. District Court, Southern District of Florida; 1987, North Carolina and U.S. District Court, Western, Middle and Eastern Districts of North Carolina. *Education:* Florida State University (B.A., 1970); University of Tennessee (J.D., 1973). Delta Theta Phi. Recipient, American Jurisprudence Award for Outstanding Trial Practice. Assistant Public Defender, 1973-1975. Member, Florida House of Representatives, 1978-1980; 1980-1982. City Attorney, Oakland Park, 1983-1985. Vice-Chair, Mecklenburg County Board of Commissioners, 1994-1996. County Commissioner Charlotte, North Carolina, Mecklenburg County, 1994, 1998. Chairman of the Board of Commissioners, 1998. Past Member: National Criminal Defense Lawyers Associations, 1978-1986; North Carolina Academy of Trial Lawyers. *Member:* Broward County and Mecklenburg County Bar Associations; The Florida Bar; North Carolina State Bar (Member, Family Law Section); Mecklenburg County Family Lawyers Association. ***PRACTICE AREAS:*** Personal Injury; Medical Malpractice; Family Law; Divorce; Civil Litigation. ***Email:*** tblaw@aol.com

BILL POWERS, born DeKalb, Illinois, 1965; admitted to bar, 1992, North Carolina, Wisconsin, U.S. District Court, Western District of North Carolina and U.S. District Court, District of Michigan. *Education:* North Carolina State University (B.A., 1988); Campbell University School of Law (J.D., 1992). Delta Theta Phi. Recipient, American Jurisprudence Book Award. Lecturer and Author: DWI Continuing Legal Education. Author: "DWI, The Law & You;" "The Interlock Device - Buck Rogers meets Learned Hand;" "DWIs - How It All Works Knowing the System;" "DWI Ethics - An Intoxicating Survey On What Not To Do." Chair, North Carolina Academy of Trial Lawyers Annual DWI Seminar, 2004. Clerk, Wake County District Attorney's Office. Assistant Public Defender, 1992-1994. *Member:* North Carolina State Bar; Wisconsin State Bar; North Carolina Academy of Trial Lawyers; National Association of Criminal Defense Lawyers; Mecklenburg County Criminal Defense Lawyers Association; Academy Trial Lawyers Association. ***PRACTICE AREAS:*** Traffic Violations; Driving While Impaired; Criminal Defense; Civil Litigation; Immigration Law; Bankruptcy; Personal Injury. ***Email:*** bowties@mindspring.com

Language: Spanish.

THE BUSINESS LAW ADVISORS

1900 SOUTH BOULEVARD, SUITE 304
CHARLOTTE, NORTH CAROLINA 28203
Telephone: 980-297-7900
Fax: 888-463-0097
Email: ddulaney@tbladvisors.com
URL: http://www.tbladvisors.com

Mergers and Acquisitions, Financing, Corporate, Business, Intellectual Property Protection, Contracts, Closely Held Businesses, Limited Liability Company Law, Partnerships, Tax Planning.

FIRM PROFILE: The Business Law Advisors is a boutique law firm that exclusively provides entrepreneurs and middle-market corporate clients with sophisticated in corporate transactions, financing and business law matters.

PARTNERS

DAIN J. DULANEY, JR., born Charlotte, North Carolina, March 14, 1963; admitted to bar, 1989, North Carolina. *Education:* Washington & Lee University (B.A., 1986); Wake Forest University (J.D., 1989). *Member:* North Carolina State Bar. ***PRACTICE AREAS:*** Mergers and Acquisitions; Financing; Corporate. ***Email:*** ddulaney@tbladvisors.com

MICHAEL J. MILLER, born Grosse Pointe, Michigan, September 29, 1967; admitted to bar, 1993, Missouri; 1994, Illinois; 1996, North Carolina. *Education:* University of Michigan (B.A., 1990); Chicago-Kent College of Law (J.D., with honors, 1993). Former General Counsel, Charlotte Based You Centric, Inc. *Member:* Illinois State Bar Association; The Missouri Bar; North Carolina State Bar. ***PRACTICE AREAS:*** Corporate; Employment; Intellectual Property Protection; Mergers and Acquisitions. ***Email:*** mmiller@tbladvisors.com

MICHAEL S. MARR, born Fayetteville, North Carolina, July 31, 1960; admitted to bar, 1986, North Carolina. *Education:* University of North Carolina at Chapel Hill (B.S.B.A., 1982); Campbell University (J.D., 1986); Emory University (LL.M. in Taxation, 1988). *Member:* North Carolina State Bar. ***PRACTICE AREAS:*** Mergers and Acquisitions; Corporate Law; Tax Law. ***Email:*** mmarr@tbladvisors.com

SCOTT S. MEHLER, born Long Beach, California, January 19, 1972; admitted to bar, 1997, California; 2004, North Carolina. *Education:* University of the Pacific (B.A., 1994); McGeorge School of Law (J.D, with honors, 1997). Member, Traynor Honor Society. ***PRACTICE AREAS:*** Corporate Law; Franchise Law; Estate Planning. ***Email:*** smehler@tbladvisors.com

BUTRUS KHOSHBIN WILSON VOGT, LLP

Established in 1997
11520 NORTH COMMUNITY HOUSE ROAD, SUITE 175
CHARLOTTE, NORTH CAROLINA 28277
Telephone: 704-759-0529
Fax: 704-759-0623
URL: http://www.bkwvlaw.com

Dallas, Texas Office: 740 Park Creek Place, 3625 North Hall Street, 75219. Telephone: 214-219-1170. Facsimile: 214-219-1173.

Litigation, Trials and Appeals.

JOHN J. BUTRUS, JR., born Philadelphia, Pennsylvania, March 5, 1961; admitted to bar, 1987, Texas; 1989, Pennsylvania, New Jersey, U.S. District Court, District of New Jersey and U.S. District Court, Northern District of Texas ; 1991, Colorado; 1994, U.S. District Court, Eastern District of Texas; 1996, U.S. District Court, Western District of Texas and U.S. Court of Appeals, Fifth Circuit (Not admitted in North Carolina). *Education:* Hofstra University (B.B.A., 1983); Rutgers University (M.B.A., 1985); Washington University (J.D., 1987). Order of the Barristers. Recipient: Golden Quill Award; Judge Amandus Brackman Moot Court Prize. Winner, Moot Court Competition, Fall, 1986. *Member:* Dallas, Pennsylvania, New Jersey State, Colorado and American Bar Associations; State Bar of Texas; The Association of Trial Lawyers of America. ***PRACTICE AREAS:*** Litigation; Trial Practice; Appellate Practice. ***Email:*** jbutrus@bkwlaw.com

S. A. KHOSHBIN, born January 13, 1965; admitted to bar, 1990, Texas and U.S. District Court, Northern District of Texas; 1992, Illinois and U.S. District Court, Northern District of Illinois; 1996, U.S. District Court, Southern District of Texas; 2000, U.S. District Court, Northern District of New York (Not admitted in North Carolina). *Education:* Macalester College (B.A., cum laude, highest honors, 1987); DePaul University (J.D., 1990).

(This Listing Continued)

Macalester Hill Scholar; Thomas E. Hill Award for Outstanding Work in Philosophy; Dean's Honor Roll; National Achievement Academy Collegiate Award; Highest Honors for thesis, "Perjury and the Lawyer's Conflict of Duty. Member, DePaul University Law Review; Dean's Academic Scholarship. Recipient, American Jurisprudence Award. Member: Access to Excellence Program —; Office of Illinois Attorney General. *Member:* Dallas, Chicago, Illinois and American Bar Associations; State Bar of Texas; Association of Trial Lawyers of America. ***LANGUAGES:*** Farsi. ***PRACTICE AREAS:*** Litigation; Trial Practice; Appellate Practice. ***Email:*** skhoshbin@bkwlaw.com

MICHAEL C. WILSON, born Houston, Texas, January 18, 1966; admitted to bar, 1991, Texas; 1992, U.S. District Court, Northern District of Texas; 1994, U.S. District Court, Southern District of Texas and and U.S. Court of Appeals, Fifth Circuit; 1995, U.S. District Court, Eastern District of Texas; 1997, U.S. District Court, Western District of Texas (Not admitted in North Carolina). *Education:* University of Texas (B.B.A., 1988; J.D., with honors, 1991). *Member:* Dallas Bar Association; State Bar of Texas. ***PRACTICE AREAS:*** Civil Litigation; Trial Practice; Insurance Subrogation. ***Email:*** mwilson@bkwlaw.com

PETER W. VOGT, born Norristown, Pennsylvania, October 6, 1961; admitted to bar, 1989, Pennsylvania and New Jersey; 1995, North Carolina. *Education:* Dickinson College (B.A., 1983); Columbus School of Law, Catholic University of America (J.D., 1989). Staff Member, Catholic University Law Review, 1988-1989. ***PRACTICE AREAS:*** Insurance Subrogation.

MARK W. MORAN, born St. Paul, Minnesota, 1965; admitted to bar, 1993, Texas; 1994, U.S. Court of Appeals, Fifth Circuit and U.S. District Court, Northern, Southern, Eastern and Western Districts of Texas (Not admitted in North Carolina). *Education:* Texas A & M University (B.B.A., 1989); St. Mary's University of San Antonio (J.D., 1993). Phi Delta Phi. Member, Board of Advocates. Articles Editor, St. Mary's Law Journal, 1992-1993. Member, William S. Sessions, American Inns of Court. Law Clerk, U. S. Court of Appeals for the Fifth Circuit, the Honorable Reynaldo Garza, 1993-1994. *Member:* Dallas and American Bar Associations; State Bar of Texas. ***PRACTICE AREAS:*** Commercial Litigation; Appellate Practice; Subrogation. ***Email:*** mmoran@bkwlaw.com

---

JENNIFER DRISCOLL JASPER, born Bryan, Texas, October 19, 1971; admitted to bar, 2000, Texas and U.S. District Court, Northern District of Texas (Not admitted in North Carolina). *Education:* University of Texas at Austin (B.S., 1993); Texas A & M University (M.A., 1995); University of Houston Law Center (J.D., cum laude, 2000). Articles Editor, Houston Journal of International Law, 1999-2000. Founding Editor, Houston Journal of Health Law & Policy, 2000. *Member:* State Bar of Texas. ***PRACTICE AREAS:*** Insurance Subrogation; Medical Malpractice. ***Email:*** jjasper@bkwlaw.com

LAURA L. REED, born Montclair, New Jersey, December 17, 1970; admitted to bar, 1997, Pennsylvania and New Jersey; 1999, North Carolina, U.S. District Court, Eastern District of Pennsylvania and U.S. District Court, Western District of North Carolina. *Education:* Lehigh University (B.A., 1993); Widener University School of Law (J.D., magna cum laude, 1997). Member, Moot Court Honor Society. ***PRACTICE AREAS:*** Insurance Subrogation. ***Email:*** lreed@bkwlaw.com

---

H. MORRIS CADDELL, JR.

CAMERON BROWN BUILDING, SUITE 1210
301 SOUTH MCDOWELL STREET
CHARLOTTE, NORTH CAROLINA 28204
Telephone: 704-333-3700
Fax: 704-373-1308
Email: lawhmc@aol.com
URL: http://www.lawyers.com/lawhmc

Civil Litigation, Family/Domestic Law, Equitable Distribution, Child Custody, Child Support, Alimony, Divorce, Visitation Rights, Commercial Law, Trusts and Estates, Condemnation.

H. MORRIS CADDELL, JR., born Pinehurst, North Carolina, March 24, 1954; admitted to bar, 1979, North Carolina; 1980, District of Columbia and U.S. Court of Appeals for the District of Columbia Circuit. *Education:* University of North Carolina (B.A., 1976); Wake Forest University (J.D., 1979); Georgetown University (LL.M. in Taxation, 1984). Law Clerk to Trial Judge George Willi, U.S. Court of Claims, 1979-1981. *Member:* 26th Judicial District and North Carolina Bar Associations; North Carolina State Bar; District of Columbia Bar. ***PRACTICE AREAS:*** Domestic Relations; Family Law; Commercial Law; Trusts and Estates; Civil Litigation.

CADWALADER, WICKERSHAM & TAFT LLP

227 WEST TRADE STREET
SUITE 2400
CHARLOTTE, NORTH CAROLINA 28202
Telephone: 704-348-5100
Fax: 704-348-5200
Email: cwtinfo@cwt.com
URL: http://www.cadwalader.com

New York, N.Y. Office: One World Financial Center, 10281-0006. Telephone: 212-504-6000. Fax: 212-504-6666.
Washington, D.C. Office: 1201 F Street, N.W., Suite 1100, 20004. Telephone: 202-862-2200. Fax: 202-862-2400.
London, England Office: 265 Strand, WC2R 1BH. Telephone: +44 (0) 20 7170 8700. Fax: +44 (0) 20 7170 8600.

Banks and Banking, Bankruptcy, Capital Markets, Corporate Law, Finance, Litigation, Mergers, Acquisitions and Divestitures, Real Estate, Securities, Securitization and Taxation.

(This Listing Continued)

FIRM PROFILE: As the oldest continuous law practice in the United States, Cadwalader, Wickersham & Taft LLP, founded in downtown New York in 1792, boasts more than 200 years of service to many of the country's and the world's most prestigious institutions. We are proud of our rich history and participation in many of the most significant social, economic and legal issues accompanying the growth of the United States. Our well-established US roots have led us to also become one of the world's most prominent law firms, with influence that has expanded around the globe as we advise clients with interests in Europe, South America and the Pacific Rim. In the process, we have established long-standing relationships with many of the world's premier financial institutions, Fortune 500 companies and other leading corporations, government entities, charitable and health care organizations, and individual private clients.

MEMBERS OF FIRM

JAMES P. CARROLL, born Washington, D.C., August 22, 1952; admitted to bar, 1977, Maryland; 1978, District of Columbia, U.S. District Court for the District of Columbia and U.S. Court of Appeals, District of Columbia Circuit; 1996, North Carolina. *Education:* Georgetown University (B.A., with honors, 1974); Catholic University of America (J.D., with honors, 1977). Adjunct Professor of Law, George Washington University, 1985-1997. *Member:* American Bar Association (Member, Real Estate and Probate Section; Chairman, Real Estate Securitization Committee, 2003-2005). (Also in Washington, D.C. Office). ***PRACTICE AREAS:*** Real Estate Finance; Real Estate Secured Lending; Real Estate Securities. ***Email:*** james.carroll@cwt.com

STEVEN N. COHEN, born Schenectady, New York, September 24, 1953; admitted to bar, 1982, New York; 2003, North Carolina. *Education:* Wesleyan University (B.A., magna cum laude, 1976); New York University (J.D., 1981). Note and Comment Editor, *New York University Law Review,* 1980-1981. Law Clerk, Hon. Max Rosenn, Senior Circuit Judge, U.S. Court of Appeals, Third Circuit, 1981-1982. *Member:* American Bar Association (Member, Section of Business Law). ***LANGUAGES:*** French. ***PRACTICE AREAS:*** Banks and Banking; Secured Transactions; Finance. ***Email:*** steven.cohen@cwt.com

STUART N. GOLDSTEIN, born Rochester, New York, May 26, 1967; admitted to bar, 1992, California; 1996, New York (Not admitted in North Carolina). *Education:* Cornell University (B.S., 1989); Boalt Hall School of Law, University of California (J.D., 1992). ***PRACTICE AREAS:*** Capital Markets; Mortgage Banking. ***Email:*** stuart.goldstein@cwt.com

HENRY A. LABRUN, born Shreveport, Louisiana, April 9, 1965; admitted to bar, 1990, New York; 1996, North Carolina. *Education:* Stanford University (B.A., 1986); Notre Dame Law School (J.D., magna cum laude, 1989). ***PRACTICE AREAS:*** Capital Markets. ***Email:*** henry.labrun@cwt.com

JEFFREY J. LEE, born Seattle, Washington, February 22, 1949; admitted to bar, 1973, New Jersey (Not admitted in North Carolina). *Education:* Boston University (B.A., 1970; J.D., 1973). *Member:* American Bar Association; Mortgage Bankers Association. ***LANGUAGES:*** Chinese. ***PRACTICE AREAS:*** Real Estate Finance; Real Estate Development; Zoning Law. ***Email:*** jeffrey.lee@cwt.com

RICHARD MADDEN, JR., born Fort Lauderdale, Florida, August 12, 1957; admitted to bar, 1983, Florida; 1986, Texas (Not admitted in North Carolina). *Education:* University of Florida (B.S., 1979; J.D., 1983). Member, University of Florida Law Review, 1982-1983. ***PRACTICE AREAS:*** Real Estate. ***Email:*** richard.madden@cwt.com

CHRISTOPHER M. MCDERMOTT, born New Haven, Connecticut, September 1, 1960; admitted to bar, 1987, New York; 1999, North Carolina. *Education:* Williams College (B.A., 1982) Phi Beta Kappa; Duke University School of Law (J.D., 1986). Order of the Coif. *Member:* Association of the Bar of the City of New York; New York State and North Carolina Bar Associations. (Also in New York, N.Y. Office). ***PRACTICE AREAS:*** Commercial Lending; Corporate; Banking. ***Email:*** chris.mcdermott@cwt.com

ROBERT L. UGHETTA, born New York, N.Y., March 23, 1966; admitted to bar, 1994, New York (Not admitted in North Carolina). *Education:* Princeton University (A.B., 1989); Albany Law School of Union University (J.D., cum laude, 1993). ***PRACTICE AREAS:*** Corporate; Structured Finance. ***Email:*** rughetta@cwt.com

SPECIAL COUNSEL

KURT W. BJORKLUND, born St. Paul, Minnesota; admitted to bar, 1990, Texas (inactive); 1992, District of Columbia; 1997, New York (Not admitted in North Carolina). *Education:* Macalester College (B.A., 1978); Harvard Law School (J.D., 1990). ***PRACTICE AREAS:*** Bankruptcy; Corporate Finance. ***Email:*** kurt.bjorklund@cwt.com

JAMES S. HASSAN, born Lima, Ohio, April 2, 1968; admitted to bar, 1994, New York; 1998, North Carolina. *Education:* Vanderbilt University (B.A., summa cum laude, 1990; J.D., 1993). ***PRACTICE AREAS:*** Real Estate Finance. ***Email:*** james.hassan@cwt.com

FRANCISCO J. LINARES, born Cali, Colombia, December 3, 1958; admitted to bar, 1993, New York; 1996, North Carolina. *Education:* United States Military Academy (B.S., 1980); New York University School of Law (J.D., 1992). [U.S. Army, 1980-1989]. ***PRACTICE AREAS:*** Corporate. ***Email:*** francisco.linares@cwt.com

JOHN ROBERT WHITE, born Manchester, Kentucky, 1962; admitted to bar, 1998, New York (Not admitted in North Carolina). *Education:* Union College (B.S., 1984); University of Kentucky (J.D., 1995; M.B.A., 1995); Georgetown University Law Center (LL.M., 2000).

ALEXANDER ZOLFAGHARI, born 1966; admitted to bar, 1993, Pennsylvania; 1998, New York (Not admitted in North Carolina). *Education:* Brandeis University (B.A., magna cum laude, 1989); University of Pennsylvania (J.D., 1992). Phi Beta Kappa. ***LANGUAGES:*** German. ***PRACTICE AREAS:*** Banking and Finance; Acquisition Leveraged Finance; Asset Based Finance; Corporate. ***Email:*** alexander.zolfaghari@cwt.com

SENIOR ATTORNEYS

PATRICK M. MCNEELY, born Newport-News, Virginia, December 20, 1946; admitted to bar, 1973, North Carolina. *Education:* University of North Carolina, Chapel Hill (B.A., 1969; J.D., 1972). Certified North Carolina Superior Court Mediator. Member, Housing Trust Fund Advisory Board to Charlotte City Council. *Member:* North Carolina

(This Listing Continued)

CADWALADER, WICKERSHAM & TAFT LLP, Charlotte—Continued

Bar Association (Real Property Section Council, 1986-1989); North Carolina Land Title Association (President, 1986). ***PRACTICE AREAS:*** Commercial Real Property. ***Email:*** patrick.mcneely@cwt.com

ROBERT W. WATSON, JR., born Wheeling, West Virginia, November 11, 1944; admitted to bar, 1973, Pennsylvania; 1997, North Carolina. *Education:* Virginia Military Institute (B.A., with honors, 1966); University of Virginia (J.D., 1973). *Member:* North Carolina State Bar. [Capt., U.S. Army, 1966-1970]. ***PRACTICE AREAS:*** Real Estate. ***Email:*** robert.watson@cwt.com

ASSOCIATES

JEFFREY W. ALDRICH, JR., born Buffalo, New York, October 8, 1970; admitted to bar, 2002, Ohio (Not admitted in North Carolina). *Education:* Yale University (B.A., 1993); The Ohio State University (M.S., 1999); College of William & Mary (J.D., 2002). *Member:* Ohio State and American (Member: Forum on Sports and Entertainment Law; Business Law Section) Bar Associations. ***PRACTICE AREAS:*** Capital Markets. ***Email:*** jeff.aldrich@cwt.com

MAUREEN CONNOLLY BOLINGER, born Norwood, Massachusetts, 1966; admitted to bar, 1997, Ohio; 1999, New York; 2004, North Carolina. *Education:* University of Massachusetts (B.S., 1989); Cleveland-Marshall College of Law, Cleveland State University (J.D., cum laude, 1997). Managing Editor, Cleveland-Marshall Law Review, 1996-1997. *Member:* Forsyth County, North Carolina and American Bar Associations; North Carolina State Bar. ***PRACTICE AREAS:*** Real Estate. ***Email:*** maureen.bolinger@cwt.com

JOHN D. BRODERICK, III, born Savannah, Georgia, May 28, 1979; (admission pending). *Education:* University of Georgia (A.B.J., 2001); New York University (J.D., 2004). ***PRACTICE AREAS:*** Real Estate. ***Email:*** john.broderick@cwt.com

DAVID S. BURKHOLDER, born Columbus, Ohio, June 28, 1970; admitted to bar, 2000, North Carolina. *Education:* Boston University (B.A., 1992); Case Western Reserve University (J.D., cum laude, 2000). [Captain, U.S. Air Force, 1992-1997]. ***Email:*** dburkhol@cwt.com

ANDERSON DREW CAPERTON, born Roanoke, Virginia, October 13, 1969; admitted to bar, 1997, North Carolina. *Education:* University of Virginia (B.A., 1997); University of North Carolina (J.D., 1997). *Member:* Mecklenburg County Bar Association; North Carolina State Bar. ***PRACTICE AREAS:*** Real Estate Finance; Capital Markets. ***Email:*** acaperto@cwt.com

MARC DANIELS, admitted to bar, 1995, New York (Not admitted in North Carolina). *Education:* Massachusetts Institute of Technology (S.B., 1991); University of Michigan (J.D., 1994). ***PRACTICE AREAS:*** Real Estate. ***Email:*** marc.daniel@cwt.com

JOHN DOMBY, born Columbus, Ohio, August 4, 1979; admitted to bar, 2004, North Carolina. *Education:* University of North Carolina at Chapel Hill (B.A., 2001); University of Virginia (J.D., 2004). ***PRACTICE AREAS:*** Commercial Real Estate. ***Email:*** john.domby@cwt.com

JULIE ANN DURHAM, born Bryan, Ohio, April 17, 1976; admitted to bar, 2000, North Carolina. *Education:* Miami University (B.S., 1997); University of Virginia (J.D., 2000). ***PRACTICE AREAS:*** Real Estate. ***Email:*** julie.durham@cwt.com

DANIEL J. ELLOWITCH, born Livingston, New Jersey, March 1, 1974; admitted to bar, 2002, New Jersey; 2004, New York (Not admitted in North Carolina). *Education:* University of Colorado at Boulder (B.A., 1996); Boston University (J.D., 2001; M.B.A., 2002). ***PRACTICE AREAS:*** Real Estate. ***Email:*** daniel.ellowitch@cwt.com

NICHOLAS R. FINN, born Kansas City, Missouri, March 21, 1978; admitted to bar, 2004, North Carolina. *Education:* Texas Christian University (B.B.A., 2000); Vanderbilt University (J.D., 2004). Journal of Transnational Law; Moot Court. ***LANGUAGES:*** Spanish. ***PRACTICE AREAS:*** Capital Markets. ***Email:*** Nicholas.Finn@cwt.com

KRISTEN FROELICH, admitted to bar, 2003, North Carolina. *Education:* North Dakota State University (B.S., 1999); William and Mary School of Law (J.D., 2003). ***PRACTICE AREAS:*** Banking Law; Finance. ***Email:*** kristen.froelich@cwt.com

BRAD W. FUNK, born Suffern, New York, April 12, 1974; admitted to bar, 2003, North Carolina. *Education:* Union College (B.S., 1996); Wake Forest University (J.D., 2003). Order of Barristers; Order of the Coif. Member, Wake Forest Law Review. ***PRACTICE AREAS:*** Capital Markets. ***Email:*** brad.funk@cwt.com

ANNIE R. GEORGE, born Boston, Massachusetts, July 3, 1972; admitted to bar, 1999, Massachusetts and North Carolina. *Education:* Cornell University (B.S., 1994); Suffolk University Law School (J.D., cum laude, 1999). *Member:* Boston, Massachusetts and American Bar Associations. ***PRACTICE AREAS:*** Real Estate. ***Email:*** annie.george@cwt.com

J. ERIC HOLLAND, born Memphis, Tennessee, December 14, 1979; admitted to bar, 2004, North Carolina. *Education:* George Washington University (B.A., magna cum laude); Vanderbilt University (J.D., 2004). ***LANGUAGES:*** German, French, Portuguese and Spanish. ***PRACTICE AREAS:*** Banking Law; Finance. ***Email:*** eric.holland@cwt.com

DAVID A. IACUZIO, born Boston, Massachusetts, December 2, 1970; admitted to bar, 1997, Massachusetts; 2002, North Carolina. *Education:* Clark University (B.A., 1993); Suffolk University Law School (J.D., cum laude, 1996). Recipient: Best Oral Advocate; Second Best Brief. ***PRACTICE AREAS:*** Real Estate. ***Email:*** diacuzio@cwt.com

STARR S. ILZHOEFER, born Wilmington, North Carolina, August 1, 1977; admitted to bar, 2003, New York (Not admitted in North Carolina). *Education:* University of Washington (B.A., 1998); Boston University (J.D., cum laude, 2002). ***PRACTICE AREAS:*** Banking Law; Finance. ***Email:*** starr.ilzhoefer@cwt.com

(This Listing Continued)

GREGG L. KLINGENBERG, born Fairfax, Virginia, October 5, 1969; admitted to bar, 1999, Colorado (Not admitted in North Carolina). *Education:* Nazareth College (B.A., 1992); University of Denver, College of Law (J.D., 1998). ***PRACTICE AREAS:*** Capital Markets. ***Email:*** gregg.klingenberg@cwt.com

ALEXANDER T. LIN, born Boston, Massachusetts, December 16, 1970; admitted to bar, 1998, New York; 2001, California (inactive); 2005, North Carolina. *Education:* California Institute of Technology (B.S., 1992); Columbia University (J.D., 1997). General Motors Scholar, California Institute of Technology. ***PRACTICE AREAS:*** Financial Restructuring. ***Email:*** alex.lin@cwt.com

BRUCE G. LUNA, II, born Tucson, Arizona, May 28, 1972; admitted to bar, 2001, California; 2004, North Carolina. *Education:* University of Maryland (B.A., 1994); University of Texas at Austin (J.D., 2001). ***LANGUAGES:*** Japanese. ***PRACTICE AREAS:*** Capital Markets. ***Email:*** bruce.luna@cwt.com

DONAL A. LUNA, born Managua, Nicaragua, February 5, 1972; admitted to bar, 2004, North Carolina. *Education:* Cornell University (B.A., 1994); University of Florida (M.S., 1996); Duke University (M.A., 2004; J.D., cum laude, 2004). Lead Editor, Duke University Journal of Comparative and International Law, 2003-2004. *Member:* North Carolina and American Bar Associations. ***LANGUAGES:*** Spanish. ***PRACTICE AREAS:*** Banks and Banking; Secured Transactions; Finance. ***Email:*** donal.luna@cwt.com

PATRICIA J. LUNA, admitted to bar, 2002, California; 2004, North Carolina. *Education:* University of Georgia (B.A., 1998); University of Texas (J.D., 2001). ***PRACTICE AREAS:*** Real Estate. ***Email:*** patricia.luna@cwt.com

GEOFFREY R. MAIBOHM, born Rochester, New York, March 5, 1972; admitted to bar, 1999, North Carolina; 2000, New York. *Education:* State University of New York at Geneseo (B.A., 1994); Syracuse University College of Law (J.D., magna cum laude, 1998). Justinian Honorary Law Society. Syracuse Law Review. ***Email:*** jmaibohm@cwt.com

HOLLY S. MARCILLE, born Gloversville, New York, September 8, 1970; admitted to bar, 1998, New York, Massachusetts and North Carolina. *Education:* State University of New York at Binghamton (B.A., 1992); New York Law School (J.D., magna cum laude, 1977). ***PRACTICE AREAS:*** Corporate; Real Estate Finance. ***Email:*** hmarcill@cwt.com

BRYON J. MULLIGAN, born 1967; admitted to bar, 1998, California; 2000, New York (Not admitted in North Carolina). *Education:* San Diego State University (B.S., 1997); Thomas Jefferson School of Law (J.D., summa cum laude, 1998). ***PRACTICE AREAS:*** Banking; Finance. ***Email:*** bryon.mulligan@cwt.com

JEFFREY NAGLE, born Auburn, New York, June 13, 1976; admitted to bar, 2004, North Carolina. *Education:* State University of New York, Albany (B.A., M.A., 1998); New York University (J.D., 2004). Phi Beta Kappa. ***LANGUAGES:*** Russian. ***PRACTICE AREAS:*** Banking; Finance. ***Email:*** jeffrey.nagle@cwt.com

KATHLEEN PEARSON, born Petersburg, Virginia, March 21, 1963; admitted to bar, 2000, New York; 2002, Louisiana (Not admitted in North Carolina). *Education:* College of William and Mary (B.A., 1996); Pennsylvania State University, Dickinson School of Law (J.D., magna cum laude, 1997). ***PRACTICE AREAS:*** Real Estate. ***Email:*** kathleen.pearson@cwt.com

TIA S. PHILLIPS, admitted to bar, 2001, Georgia (Not admitted in North Carolina). *Education:* University of North Carolina at Chapel Hill (B.A., 1996); University of North Carolina School of Law (J.D., 2001). ***LANGUAGES:*** Spanish. ***PRACTICE AREAS:*** Real Estate. ***Email:*** tia.phillips@cwt.com

MATTHEW H. ROBERTSON, born Akron, Ohio, October 17, 1970; admitted to bar, 1995, New Jersey; 1999, North Carolina. *Education:* University of Delaware (B.A., with honors, 1992); Duke University School of Law (J.D., 1995). Previous Employment: Kilpatrick Stockton LLP. ***PRACTICE AREAS:*** Real Estate Finance; Securitization. ***Email:*** matthew.robertson@cwt.com

CONNIE W. SAWYER, III, born Elizabeth, North Carolina, August 15, 1978; admitted to bar, 2003, North Carolina. *Education:* University of North Carolina at Chapel Hill (B.A., 2000); Columbia University (J.D., 2003). ***PRACTICE AREAS:*** Banking; Finance. ***Email:*** connie.sawyer@cwt.com

HARRY B. SHADOAN, born Somerset, Kentucky, October 7, 1943; admitted to bar, 1969, Maryland; 2003, North Carolina. *Education:* Eastern Kentucky University (B.A., 1965); University of Baltimore (J.D., 1968). *Member:* Mecklenburg County Bar Association; North Carolina State Bar. ***PRACTICE AREAS:*** Real Estate. ***Email:*** harry.shadoan@cwt.com

JOSHUA M. SMITH, admitted to bar, 2002, New York (Not admitted in North Carolina). *Education:* Georgetown University (B.S., cum laude, 1997); University of Michigan Law School (J.D., cum laude, 2001). ***PRACTICE AREAS:*** Banking and Finance. ***Email:*** joshua.smith@cwt.com

RICHARD SPOONER, born Glen Ridge, New Jersey, October 20, 1975; admitted to bar, 2002, North Carolina. *Education:* Wake Forest University (B.S., cum laude, 1997); University of North Carolina at Chapel Hill (J.D., with honors, 2002). Omicron Delta Epsilon; Pi Mu Epsilon. Staff Member, North Carolina Journal of International Law and Commercial Regulation, 2000-2002. *Member:* North Carolina State Bar. ***PRACTICE AREAS:*** Capital Markets. ***Email:*** richard.spooner@cwt.com

VENUS YVETTE SPRINGS, admitted to bar, 2002, North Carolina. *Education:* University of North Carolina at Charlotte (B.S., summa cum laude, 1991); Duke University (J.D., high honors, 2003). *Member:* North Carolina and American Bar Associations. ***LANGUAGES:*** Spanish. ***Email:*** yvette.springs@cwt.com

JOHN A. TEER, born Durham, North Carolina, March 8, 1973; admitted to bar, 2001, North Carolina. *Education:* University of North Carolina at Chapel Hill (B.A., 1995; J.D., with honors, 2001). Staff Member, Law Review, 1998-1999; Editor, Banking Journal, 1999-2000. ***PRACTICE AREAS:*** Capital Markets. ***Email:*** john.teer@cwt.com

EZELL H. UNDERDOWN, born Harvey, Illinois, 1966; admitted to bar, 1998, Ohio (Not admitted in North Carolina). *Education:* University of Michigan (A.B., 1993); Purdue University (M.S., 1995); University of Pennsylvania (J.D., 1998). *Member:* Ohio State Bar Association. ***PRACTICE AREAS:*** Capital Markets. ***Email:*** ezell.underdown@cwt.com

(This Listing Continued)

JIAN WANG, born Changchun, P.R. China, January 29, 1976; admitted to bar, 2003, Delaware and U.S. District Court, District of Delaware; 2004, North Carolina. *Education:* Peking University, Peking, China (B.S., 1997); Johns Hopkins University (M.S., 1999); Duke University (J.D., cum laude, 2002). *Member:* North Carolina State Bar. ***PRACTICE AREAS:*** Capital Markets. ***Email:*** jian.wang@cwt.com

AMY McNUTT WOLTMAN, born Cincinnati, Ohio, May 27, 1973; admitted to bar, 2004, North Carolina. *Education:* Williams College (B.A., 1995); Harvard Law School (J.D., 2004). [Sgt., U.S. Army, 1997-2001]. ***PRACTICE AREAS:*** Capital Markets. ***Email:*** amy.woltman@cwt.com

JOSHUA J. YABLONSKI, born Oswego, New York, May 7, 1972; admitted to bar, 1999, New York; 2000, U.S. District Court, Northern District of New York; 2001, North Carolina. *Education:* State University of New York College at Geneseo (B.A., History and Philosophy); Syracuse University (J.D., 1998). Member, Justinian Honor Society of Syracuse. ***PRACTICE AREAS:*** Capital Markets. ***Email:*** joshua.yablonski@cwt.com

(For data on other personnel, see Professional Biographies at New York City)

CAMPBELL & ASSOCIATES, PLC

Established in 1996

717 EAST BOULEVARD
CHARLOTTE, NORTH CAROLINA 28203
Telephone: 704-333-0885
Fax: 704-372-7718
URL: http://www.campbellandtaylorlaw.com
URL: http://www.lawyers.com/campbellandassoc

Hickory, North Carolina Office: 104 3rd Street. N.E., Suite 400, 28601. Telephone: 828-324-9191. Fax: 828-324-9592.
Gastonia, North Carolina Office: 603 Cox Road, Suite D, 28054. Telephone: 704-866-9191. Fax: 704-830-0104.

Auto Accidents, Personal Injury, Wrongful Death, Head Trauma, Motorcycle Accidents, Spinal Cord Injuries, Civil Litigation, Industrial Accidents, Slip and Fall, Workers Compensation, Medical Malpractice.

MEMBER

CLAIR G. CAMPBELL, born Aberdeen, Maryland, November 27, 1961; admitted to bar, 1985, North Carolina; 1986, South Carolina. *Education:* University of Alabama at Tuscaloosa (B.A., 1982); Cumberland School of Law of Samford University (J.D., 1985). Listed in, Who's Who Among American Lawyers. *Member:* Mecklenburg County and American Bar Associations; North Carolina State Bar; South Carolina Bar; The Association of Trial Lawyers of America; North Carolina Trial Lawyers Association; Mecklenburg Trial Lawyers Association; Million Dollar Advocates Forum. ***PRACTICE AREAS:*** Personal Injury; Workers Compensation. ***Email:*** clair@campbellandtaylor.com

WILLIAM H. CANNON, P.A.

1900 ABBOTT STREET, SUITE 102
CHARLOTTE, NORTH CAROLINA 28203
Telephone: 704-376-7963
Telecopier: 704-335-0921
Email: WCANNONLAW@Aol.com
URL: http://www.wcannonlaw.com

Manteo Office: 207 Queen Elizabeth Avenue, Suite 1, 27954. Telephone: 252-475-1624. Telecopier: 252-475-1625.

Commercial Real Estate, particularly Golf Course and Resort Law. Acquisitions, Dispositions, Development and Lending. Zoning and Land Use.

FIRM PROFILE: Mr. Cannon has been practicing in Charlotte N.C. since 1966. Has been in solo practice since 1991.

WILLIAM H. CANNON, born Winston-Salem, North Carolina, May 25, 1939; admitted to bar, 1966, North Carolina. *Education:* Davidson College (B.A., 1961); University of North Carolina (LL.B., 1966). Phi Delta Phi. Associate Editor, North Carolina Law Review, 1965-1966. *Member:* North Carolina and American Bar Associations; North Carolina State Bar. ***Email:*** WCANNONLAW@aol.com

LEGAL SUPPORT PERSONNEL

ROBIN SHULER (Real Estate Paralegal)

APPROVED ATTORNEY FOR: Lawyers Title Insurance Corp.; Chicago Title Insurance Co.; Commonwealth Land Title Insurance Co.; Stewart Title Guaranty.
REFERENCES: First Citizens Bank, RBC Centera.
REPRESENTATIVE CLIENTS: TGM Realty Consultants; Branch Banking and Trust Company; RBC Centura Bank; MacDonald & Cie.; Bahabri Stores, LLC.; Outer Banks/Kinna Keet Associates, LLC; Camden Square Associates.

MARY V. CARRIGAN

435 EAST MOOREHEAD STREET
CHARLOTTE, NORTH CAROLINA 28202
Telephone: 704-333-8855
Fax: 704-331-0773
URL: http://maryvcarriganlaw.com
URL: http://www.maryvcarrigan.com

Domestic Relations, Family Law, Divorce, Equitable Distribution, Child Custody and Child Support, Alimony, Premarital Agreements.

FIRM PROFILE: Ms. Carrigan is Board Certified in Family Law by the North Carolina State Board.

(This Listing Continued)

MARY V. CARRIGAN, born Grand Rapids, Michigan, July 29, 1945; admitted to bar, 1984, North Carolina. *Education:* Texas Christian University (B.A., 1967); Tulane University (M.S.W., 1971); University of North Carolina (J.D., 1983). Law Clerk to United States Magistrate Barbara H. Delaney, Western District of North Carolina, 1986-1987. *Member:* Mecklenburg County (Member, Family Law Section) and North Carolina (Member, Family Law Section) Bar Associations; State Bar of North Carolina. (Board Certified Specialist in Family Law, North Carolina State Board of Legal Specialization). ***REPORTED CASES:*** Hickory Neighborhood Defense League v. Skinner, 893 F.2d 58 (4th Cir. 1990). 20 Envtl. L. Rep. 20540 (4th Cir. NC 1990).

JAMES H. CARTER

CHARLOTTE, NORTH CAROLINA

(See Matthews)

Construction Law, Personal Injury.

DEBORAH G. CASEY

6525 MORRISON BOULEVARD, SUITE 314
CHARLOTTE, NORTH CAROLINA 28211
Telephone: 704-362-1660
Fax: 704-362-1499
URL: http://www.dgcaseylaw.com
Email: deborah@dgcaseylaw.com
URL: http://www.lawyers.com/deborahcasey

Serious Personal Injury, Medical Malpractice, Auto Accidents, Wrongful Death, Mediation.

FIRM PROFILE: The Law Offices of Deborah G. Casey offers clients the combined medical and legal experience of attorneys and medically trained staff. All potential clients receive in-depth telephone consultation with our registered nurse. Each case is approached in an individualized manner, which allows us to develop complete working knowledge of the client and their objectives. We offer personalized attention, high-level responsiveness and a proven track record from an expert team.

DEBORAH G. CASEY, born Charlotte, North Carolina, October 26, 1954; admitted to bar, 1991, North Carolina. *Education:* Western Carolina University (B.S., medical technology and minor degree in Chemistry, 1976); Cumberland School of Law, Samford University (J.D., 1991). Certified Superior Court Mediator. *Member:* Mecklenburg County Bar Association; North Carolina State Bar; North Carolina Academy of Trial Lawyers; The Association of Trial Lawyers of America. Bobbitt Inns of Court (Barrister). ***PRACTICE AREAS:*** Medical Malpractice; Litigation.

CASSTEVENS, HANNER, GUNTER & RIOPEL, P.A.

Established in 1978

602 EAST MOREHEAD STREET
P.O. BOX 34607
CHARLOTTE, NORTH CAROLINA 28234
Telephone: 704-372-2140
Fax: 704-372-1150
URL: http://www.chgrlaw.com

General Civil, Trial and Appellate Practice for all State and Federal Courts. Personal Injury, Domestic Relations, Family Law, Alimony, Equitable Distribution, Separation Agreements, Child Custody, Divorce, Child Support, Collaborative Law.

NELSON M. CASSTEVENS, JR., born Yadkinville, North Carolina, August 9, 1941; admitted to bar, 1965, North Carolina. *Education:* Catawba College (A.B., 1963); Wake Forest University (LL.B., 1965). Phi Alpha Delta (Vice Justice, 1964). Listed in Best Lawyers in America. *Member:* 26th Judicial District and North Carolina Bar Associations; North Carolina State Bar (Counselor, 1999—). [Capt., U.S. Air Force Reserve]. ***PRACTICE AREAS:*** Domestic Relations; Family Law; Divorce; Civil Litigation. ***Email:*** nmc@chgrlaw.com

ROBERT P. HANNER, II, born Charlotte, North Carolina, January 2, 1944; admitted to bar, 1969, North Carolina; 1970, U.S. Court of Military Appeals. *Education:* The Citadel (B.S.B.A., 1966); Wake Forest University (J.D., 1969). Phi Delta Phi. Chairman, Family Law Section, Mecklenburg County Bar Association, 1992-1993. *Member:* 26th Judicial District, North Carolina and American Bar Associations; North Carolina State Bar; North Carolina Academy of Trial Lawyers; Mecklenburg County Collaborative Family Law Practice Group. [Capt., JAG, U.S. Marine Corps, 1969-1973]. (Board Certified Specialist in Family Law, North Carolina State Board of Legal Specialization). ***PRACTICE AREAS:*** Collaborative Law; Domestic Relations; Family Law; Divorce; Personal Injury; Civil Litigation. ***Email:*** rph@chgrlaw.com

DORIAN H. GUNTER, born Asheville, North Carolina, June 1, 1953; admitted to bar, 1979, North Carolina. *Education:* Wake Forest University (B.A., cum laude, 1975; J.D., 1979). Phi Delta Phi. Member, The Order of Barristers. *Member:* Mecklenburg County Bar Association; North Carolina State Bar; Mecklenburg County Collaborative Family Law Practice Group. ***PRACTICE AREAS:*** Family Law; Collaborative Law; Divorce; Civil Litigation; Child Custody; Child Support. ***Email:*** dhg@chgrlaw.com

MARK D. RIOPEL, born Belton Missouri, November 23, 1966; admitted to bar, 1994, North Carolina. *Education:* Colgate University (B.A., with honors, 1989); Wake Forest University (J.D., 1994). *Member:* Mecklenburg County and North Carolina Bar Associations; North Carolina State Bar; Mecklenburg County Collaborative Family Law Practice Group. ***LANGUAGES:*** Italian. ***PRACTICE AREAS:*** Family Law; Collaborative Law; Personal Injury; Divorce. ***Email:*** markr@chgrlaw.com

(This Listing Continued)

CASSTEVENS, HANNER, GUNTER & RIOPEL, P.A., Charlotte—Continued

---

J. HUNTINGTON WOFFORD, born Columbia, South Carolina, May 2, 1971; admitted to bar, 1996, North Carolina, U.S. District Court, Western District of North Carolina and U.S. Court of Appeals, Fourth Circuit. *Education:* Wofford College (B.A., History and Government, cum laude, 1993); Wake Forest University School of Law (J.D., 1996). Family Financial Mediator. *Member:* Mecklenburg County and North Carolina Bar Associations; North Carolina State Bar. ***PRACTICE AREAS:*** Family Law; General Litigation; Family Financial Mediation. ***Email:*** hwofford@chgrlaw.com

APPROVED ATTORNEYS FOR: Lawyers Title Insurance Corp.; Old Republic Title Company; Fidelity National Title Company; First American Title Co.; Investors Title Company; Stewart Title Company.
REFERENCE: Central Carolina Bank.

CAUDLE & SPEARS, P.A.

Established in 1977

2600 INTERSTATE TOWER
121 WEST TRADE STREET
CHARLOTTE, NORTH CAROLINA 28202
Telephone: 704-377-1200
Telecopier: 704-338-5858
Email: caudlespears@caudlespears.com
URL: http://www.caudlespears.com

General Civil and Trial Practice. Real Estate, Business Associations, Bankruptcy, Personal Injury, Insurance Defense, Probate and Trusts, Taxation, Employee Benefits, Environmental Law; Estate Planning.

FIRM PROFILE: Caudle & Spears, P.A. was formed as a professional corporation in 1977, incorporating a partnership that had been in existence since 1973. The partnership resulted from a division of a prior firm of which Mr. Caudle had been a senior member since 1956.

The firm attorneys come from diverse educational and cultural backgrounds and several states. Each of the various areas of law regularly practiced by the firm is headed by one of the senior members, and each attorney is encouraged to pursue fields of primary and secondary interest. All attorneys are expected to pursue pro bono and community services in addition to professional development. Civil litigation is handled in the various federal and state courts and agencies.

HAROLD C. SPEARS, born Ironton, Ohio, March 15, 1954; admitted to bar, 1979, North Carolina; 1998, South Carolina. *Education:* Duke University (A.B., cum laude, 1976; J.D., with distinction, 1979). *Member:* North Carolina and American Bar Associations; South Carolina Bar; 26th Judicial District and North Carolina State Bars; North Carolina Association of Defense Attorneys; Defense Research Institute. ***PRACTICE AREAS:*** Civil Litigation; Business Litigation; Commercial Litigation; Insurance Law; Construction Law. ***Email:*** hspears@caudlespears.com

L. CAMERON CAUDLE, JR., born Charlotte, North Carolina, July 17, 1960; admitted to bar, 1987, North Carolina. *Education:* Duke University (A.B., 1982); Campbell University (J.D., 1987). *Member:* North Carolina and American Bar Associations; 26th Judicial District and North Carolina State Bars; North Carolina Association of Defense Attorneys. ***PRACTICE AREAS:*** Insurance Defense; Civil Litigation; Real Estate; Business Associations. ***Email:*** ccaudle@caudlespears.com

JEFFREY L. HELMS, born Salisbury, North Carolina, March 5, 1967; admitted to bar, 1993, North Carolina. *Education:* North Carolina State University (B.S., summa cum laude, 1989); University of North Carolina at Chapel Hill (J.D., with high honors, 1993). Phi Delta Phi; Order of the Coif; Staff Member, North Carolina Journal of International Law and Commercial Regulation; Recipient: Ferebee A. Taylor Award, most outstanding graduate in corporate law courses and Investors Title Award. *Member:* 26th Judicial District and North Carolina Bar Associations; North Carolina State Bar. ***PRACTICE AREAS:*** Business Associations; Business Transactions; Tax; Estate Planning; Estate Administration; Commercial Leasing; Employment Law. ***Email:*** jhelms@caudlespears.com

CHRISTOPHER J. LOEBSACK, born Cleveland, Ohio, May 20, 1971; admitted to bar, 1996, North Carolina. *Education:* Clemson University (B.S., summa cum laude, 1993); Duke University (J.D., 1996). *Member:* North Carolina and American Bar Associations; 26th Judicial District and North Carolina State Bar; North Carolina Association of Defense Attorneys; Defense Research Institute. ***PRACTICE AREAS:*** Civil Litigation; Insurance Defense; Landlord-Tenant; Environmental. ***Email:*** cloebsack@caudlespears.com

MICHAEL J. SELLE, born Cincinnati, Ohio, September 17, 1969; admitted to bar, 1994, Georgia and North Carolina. *Education:* University of Georgia (B.A., 1991); Mercer University (J.D., 1994). *Member:* 26th Judicial District and North Carolina Bar Associations; North Carolina State Bar; State Bar of Georgia; North Carolina Association of Defense Attorneys. ***PRACTICE AREAS:*** Insurance Defense; Commercial Litigation. ***Email:*** mselle@caudlespears.com

ERIC ALLEN ROGERS, born Lubbock, Texas, April 6, 1966; admitted to bar, 1992, North Carolina. *Education:* University of Maryland (B.A., 1988); Wake Forest University (J.D., 1991). *Member:* North Carolina Bar Association; North Carolina State Bar. ***PRACTICE AREAS:*** Insurance Defense; Employment Law; Commercial Litigation. ***Email:*** erogers@caudlespears.com

---

C. GRAINGER PIERCE, JR., born Chapel Hill, North Carolina, March 29, 1974; admitted to bar, 2000, North Carolina. *Education:* Duke University (A.B., 1996); University of North Carolina, Chapel Hill (J.D., 1999). Recipient, Judge Heriot Clarkson Award. *Member:* North Carolina State Bar; North Carolina Bar Association; 26 Judicial District Bar; North Carolina Association of Defense Attorneys. ***PRACTICE AREAS:*** Insurance Defense; Commercial Litigation. ***Email:*** gpierce@caudlespears.com

(This Listing Continued)

JOSEPH R. MAREK, born Chicopee, Massachusetts, November 25, 1971; admitted to bar, 2001, North Carolina. *Education:* University of Massachusetts (B.A., 1994); Wake Forest University (J.D., 2001). *Member:* North Carolina State Bar; North Carolina Bar Association; 26 Judicial District Bar. ***PRACTICE AREAS:*** Business Formation; Business Planning; Taxation. ***Email:*** jmarek@caudlespears.com

COUNSEL FOR: Auto-Owners Insurance; Bituminous Casualty Corp.; Baumann Springs A.G.; Boone Sales and Service Co.; Capitol Funds, Inc.; Employers Mutual Casualty Co.; Gainsco Cos.; Great American Ins. Co.; Harris Wholesale, Inc.; Mark Oil Co.; N.C. Farm Bureau Mutual Insurance Co.; Otis Elevator Co.; PFB Construction Co.; Metromont Materials Corp.; Orion Auto; The Ray Roofing Co., Inc.; Royal & Sun Alliance; Royster Development Co.; Royster Transport Co.; The Shuman Co.; S.C. Farm Bureau; Standard Insulation Co.; Toyoda Textile Machinery, Inc.; U.S. Bottlers Machinery Co.; United Technologies Corp.; United Engineering Group, Inc.
APPROVED ATTORNEYS FOR: First American Title Insurance Co.; Investors Title Insurance Co.; Lawyers Title Co.; Stewart Title of the Piedmont; St. Paul Title Insurance Corp.; Chicago Title Insurance Co.; Fidelity National Title Insurance Co.; The Title Company of North Carolina.
REFERENCES: Bank of America; Wachovia Bank.

PETER CHASTAIN & ASSOCIATES, P.A.

CHARLOTTE, NORTH CAROLINA

(See Greensboro)

Real Estate, Commercial Law.

CLAWSON & STAUBES, LLC

Established in 1975

756 TYVOLA ROAD, SUITE 130
CHARLOTTE, NORTH CAROLINA 28217
Telephone: 704-940-9128
Fax: 704-522-9033
Email: rcraig@clawson&staubes.com

Charleston, South Carolina Office: 126 Seven Farms Road, Suite 200, 29492-7595. Telephone: 803-577-2026. Facsimile: 803-722-2867.

Bankruptcy, Commercial Collections, Creditors Rights and Subrogations, Civil Litigation.

SAMUEL R. CLAWSON, born Florence, South Carolina, January 14, 1948; admitted to bar, 1980, South Carolina; 1997, North Carolina. *Education:* Wofford College (B.A., 1970); Campbell University (J.D., cum laude, 1980). Omicron Delta Kappa; Phi Kappa Phi. Articles Editor, Campbell Law Review, 1978-1980. Author: "Public Documents in the Hands of Private Collectors," 1 Campbell Law Review 179, 1979. *Member:* South Carolina Bar; North Carolina State Bar. (Also at Charleston, South Carolina Office). ***PRACTICE AREAS:*** Insurance Law; Civil Litigation. ***Email:*** sclawson@clawsonandstaubes.com

RONNIE F. CRAIG, born Rutherford College, North Carolina, August 2, 1959; admitted to bar, 1986, Arkansas; 1987, U.S. Court of Military Appeals; 1991, South Carolina; 1997, North Carolina. *Education:* St. Andrews Presbyterian College (B.A., 1982); University of Arkansas (J.D., 1986). Phi Delta Phi. Member, University of Arkansas Law Review, 1983. Special Assistant U.S. Attorney, 1990-1991. *Member:* Arkansas Bar Association; South Carolina Bar; North Carolina State Bar. [Lt., JAGC, USNR, 1986-1991]. (Also at Charleston, South Carolina Office). ***PRACTICE AREAS:*** Civil Litigation; Bankruptcy. ***Email:*** rcraig@clawsonandstaubes.com

J. RONALD JONES, JR., born Washington, North Carolina, December 4, 1956; admitted to bar, 1988, North Carolina; 1993, South Carolina. *Education:* University of North Carolina (B.A., 1979); George Washington University (M.A., 1981); Campbell University (J.D., 1988). Omicron Delta Kappa; Delta Theta Phi. Member, Moot Court Board. Member, Editorial Board: Campbell Law Review, 1987-1988; Campbell Law Observer, 1987-1988. Staff Assistant to the Honorable Warren E. Burger, Chief Justice of the United States, 1982-1983. *Member:* South Carolina Bar; North Carolina State Bar. (Certified Specialist, Bankruptcy Law, The Supreme Court of South Carolina) (Also at Charlotte, North Carolina Office). ***PRACTICE AREAS:*** Creditor Rights Law; Creditor Bankruptcy; Commercial Litigation; Collection Law. ***Email:*** rjones@clawsonandstaubes.com

ASSOCIATES

MICHAEL J. KITSON, born Point Pleasant, New Jersey, September 1, 1960; admitted to bar, 1996, North Carolina; U.S. District Court, Western District of North Carolina. *Education:* Rutgers University (B.S., 1984); Widener University School of Law (J.D., 1996). Phi Delta Phi. *Member:* Mecklenburg County and North Carolina Bar Associations; North Carolina State Bar. ***PRACTICE AREAS:*** Insurance; Personal Injury Litigation.

ANDREW J. SANTANIELLO, born Lancaster, Pennsylvania, April 5, 1970; admitted to bar, 1996, North Carolina, U.S. District Court, Western District of North Carolina and U.S. Court of Appeals, Fourth Circuit. *Education:* University of North Carolina at Chapel Hill (B.A., History, 1991); Wake Forest University (J.D., 1996). *Member:* North Carolina State Bar; Meclemburg County and North Carolina Bar Associations; Bar of the Eastern Band of Cherokee Indians; North Carolina Association of Defense Attorneys;. ***PRACTICE AREAS:*** Insurance; Personal Injury; Premises Liability; Products Liability; Municipal Defense. ***Email:*** asantaniello@cgbrlawfirm.com

REPRESENTATIVE CLIENTS: Branch Banking & Trust Co.; Browning Ferris Industries; Brunswick Corporation; Crown Bank of Florida; Ford Motor Credit Company; Integon Insurance; Northland Insurance Company; PYA Monarch; Southern Health Corporation; Unisun Insurance Company; United Carolina Bank; US Food Service; State Farm Insurance Co.; Nationwide Mutual Insurance Co.
REFERENCES: Wachovia Bank of South Carolina, N.A.; NationsBank.

(For Biographical Data on other Firm Personnel see Professional Biographies, Charleston, South Carolina)

CLONTZ & CLONTZ PLLC

Established in 1950
THE JUSTICE BUILDING
225 SOUTH MCDOWELL STREET
CHARLOTTE, NORTH CAROLINA 28204-2294
Telephone: 704-376-0045
Fax: 704-376-2746
URL: http://www.lawyers.com/clontzlegal

Collections, Bankruptcy, Creditor's Rights, Banking, and General Trial and Appellate Practice. Community Law.

FIRM PROFILE: The Clontz & Clontz PLLC firm has built a unique and effective practice for plaintiff debt collection and other debt collection services. The members of the firm are published authors of a variety of books on the subject of debt collection and creditor's rights.

RALPH C. CLONTZ, JR. (1922-2001)

RALPH C. CLONTZ III, born Charlotte, North Carolina, December 8, 1950; admitted to bar, 1976, North Carolina. *Education:* North Carolina State University (B.S., 1973); University of North Carolina (J.D., 1976). Co-Author: *Collection Law for Creditors,* 1987; *Post Judgment Collection Law,* 1988, Professional Education Systems, Inc., Eau Clair, Wisconsin; Collection & Enforcement of Judgments, 1992, 1995, 1998, 2001 (Wake Forest University, School of Law, Winston-Salem, North Carolina. Member, The National Association of Retail Collection Attorneys (NARCA). *Member:* North Carolina (Member: Sections on: Litigation; Law Practice Management; Member, Development Committee, 2003—) and American (Member, Sections on: Litigation; Law Practice Management; Member, Standing Committee on Marketing and Membership Development, Law Practice Management, 2003—) Bar Associations; 26th Judicial District (Member: 1976—; Publicity Committee, 1979-1980); Executive Committee, 1980-1981; Director, Young Lawyers Section, 1980-1982; Judicial District Representative, Young Lawyers Section, 1982-1983) and North Carolina State Bars; North Carolina Academy of Trial Lawyers; National Association of Retail Collection Attorneys. ***PRACTICE AREAS:*** Collections; Civil Litigation; Creditors Rights; Banking. ***Email:*** ralph@clontzlegal.com

---

CLAUDIA L. REISCH, born Norwalk, Connecticut, July 8, 1962; admitted to bar, 1988, New York and U.S. District Court, Eastern and Southern Districts of New York; 1990, Florida and U.S. District Court, Southern and Middle Districts of Florida; 2000, North Carolina. *Education:* Hofstra University (B.A., 1984); St. John's University (J.D., 1987). *Member:* Mecklenburg County, North Carolina and American (Member, Law Practice Management Section) Bar Associations; North Carolina State Bar; National Association of Retail Collection Attorneys. ***PRACTICE AREAS:*** Bankruptcy; Creditors Rights; Collections. ***Email:*** claudia@clontzlegal.com

REPRESENTATIVE CLIENTS: Wachovia National Bank; Bank of America; First Charter.
REFERENCES: Wachovia National Bank; Bank of America.

HOWARD M. COHEN

SUITE 952 JOHNSTON BUILDING
212 SOUTH TRYON STREET
CHARLOTTE, NORTH CAROLINA 28281
Telephone: 704-335-8139
Fax: 704-335-8130
Email: hcohen@bellsouth.net
URL: http://www.lawyers.com/howardcohen

Labor and Employment Law, Personal Injury and Workers Compensation and Civil Litigation before State and Federal Courts and Agencies. Mediation and Arbitration.

HOWARD M. COHEN, born Paterson, New Jersey, November 7, 1950; admitted to bar, 1976, Ohio; 1990, North Carolina. *Education:* George Washington University (B.A., Special Honors, 1972); Cleveland State University (J.D., 1976). Attorney, EPA, Washington, D.C., 1980-1982. Chief Legal Counsel (Acting) and Deputy Chief Legal Counsel, RI Dept. of Environmental Management, 1983-1989. Certified Mediator and Panel Member, American Arbitration Association. ***PRACTICE AREAS:*** Labor and Employment; Personal Injury; Worker's Compensation; Administrative Law.

CONRAD TROSCH & KEMMY, P.A.

CAMERON BROWN BUILDING
301 SOUTH MCDOWELL STREET, SUITE 809
CHARLOTTE, NORTH CAROLINA 28204
Telephone: 704-553-8221
Fax: 704-331-0595
Email: troschbill@ctklawyers.com
URL: http://www.ctklawyers.net

Other Charlotte, North Carolina Office: Park View Building, 5821 Fairview Road, Suite 405, 28209. Telephone: 704-553-8221. Fax: 704-553-7689.

Family Law, Real Estate, Wills, Probate, Estate Planning, Trusts, Business Law, Criminal Law, Divorce, Personal Injury, Wrongful Death.

LOUIS A. TROSCH, born Wheeling, West Virginia, July 9, 1939; admitted to bar, 1965, West Virginia; 1966, North Carolina. *Education:* Bethany College (B.A., 1961); West Virginia University (J.D., 1965). Professor of Business Law, University of North Carolina, Charlotte; Belk College of Business Administration. *Member:* Mecklenburg County and North Carolina Bar Association; North Carolina State Bar. ***PRACTICE AREAS:*** Real Estate Law; Wills; Corporate Law.

(This Listing Continued)

MICHAEL J. KEMMY, born San Antonio, Texas, February 15, 1955; admitted to bar, 1980, Kansas; 1982, Texas; 1987, North Carolina. *Education:* Creighton University (B.S.B.A., 1977); Washburn University of Topeka (J.D., 1979). *Member:* Mecklenburg County (Member, Estate Planning and Probate Section) and North Carolina (Member: Estate Planning and Fiduciary Law; Elder Law and Business Law Sections) Bar Associations; North Carolina State Bar. ***PRACTICE AREAS:*** Probate; Estate Planning; Corporate Law. ***Email:*** mkemmy@ctklawyers.com

WILLIAM CONRAD TROSCH, born Charlotte, North Carolina, September 20, 1968; admitted to bar, 1993, North Carolina and U.S. District Court, Western District of North Carolina. *Education:* University of North Carolina at Chapel Hill (B.A., Mathematics, Economics, with honors, 1990; J.D., with honors, 1993). Member: North Carolina Law Review, 1991-1993; American Inns of Court, William Bobbitt Division, 1998-1999. Author: The Third Generation of Loitering Laws Goes to Court: Do Laws That Criminalize "Loitering With the Intent to Sell Drugs" Pass Constitutional Muster? 71 N.C.L. Rev. 513 (1993). *Member:* 26th Judicial District and North Carolina Bar Associations; North Carolina State Bar; North Carolina Academy of Trial Lawyers; The Association of Trial Lawyers of America. ***PRACTICE AREAS:*** Civil Litigation; Personal Injury; Wrongful Death; Criminal Law; Appellate Practice. ***Email:*** troschbill@ctklawyers.com

MINETTE C. TROSCH, born Chicago, Illinois, November 3, 1942; admitted to bar, 1995, North Carolina. *Education:* DePauw University (B.A., 1964); West Virginia University (M.A., 1984); University of North Carolina at Chapel Hill (J.D., with honors, 1995). Recipient, Advanced Family Law Award. Charlotte City Council as Mayor Pro Tem. Member: National League of Cities Board of Directors; Governor's Urban Transportation Task Force; National Institute of Environmental Health Services Advisory Council. Former CEO, Take-A-Break, Inc. *Member:* North Carolina State Bar; American Bar Association. ***PRACTICE AREAS:*** Domestic Relations; Family Law; Divorce; Child Custody; Collaborative Law. ***Email:*** minettet@ctklawyers.com

KRISTIN L. SMITH, born Charlotte, North Carolina, January 30, 1968; admitted to bar, 1993, North Carolina and U.S. District Court, Western District of North Carolina. *Education:* Duke University (B.A., 1990); University of Georgia (J.D., 1993). Member, Editorial Board, Georgia Journal of International and Comparative Law. Recipient, American Jurisprudence Book Award, Criminal Procedure. *Member:* Mecklenburg County (Young Lawyers Division; Chair, 2000-2001; Past Vice Chair and Secretary; Past Member, Board of Directors; Co-Chair, Family Law Section), North Carolina (Member: Family Law Section; Family Law Council) and American Bar Associations; North Carolina State Bar; 26th Judicial District. ***PRACTICE AREAS:*** Domestic Relations; Civil Litigation; Divorce; Child Custody. ***Email:*** ksmith@ctklawyers.com

---

ANNA D. BAKER, born Fayetteville, North Carolina, January 5, 1978; admitted to bar, 2003, North Carolina. *Education:* Salem College, Winston-Salem, North Carolina (B.A., magna cum laude, English, 2000); University of North Carolina at Chapel Hill School of Law (J.D., 2003). *Member:* Mecklenburg County, Gaston County and North Carolina Bar Associations. ***PRACTICE AREAS:*** Residential Real Estate. ***Email:*** abaker@ctklawyers.com

ERIC C. TROSCH, born Charlotte, North Carolina, February 11, 1974; admitted to bar, 2002, North Carolina and U.S. District Court, Western District of North Carolina. *Education:* University of North Carolina at Chapel Hill (B.A., 1996); Wake Forest University (J.D., 2002). Recipient, North Carolina Chapter, American Academy of Matrimonial Lawyers, Student Advancement of Matrimonial Law Award, 2002. *Member:* 26th Judicial District Bar; North Carolina State Bar. ***LANGUAGES:*** German. ***PRACTICE AREAS:*** Civil Litigation; Divorce; Family Law; Marital Agreements; Equitable Distribution; Domestic Relations; Matrimonial Law. ***Email:*** etrosch@ctklawyers.com

COZEN O'CONNOR

A PROFESSIONAL CORPORATION
ONE FIRST UNION CENTER
SUITE 2100, 301 SOUTH COLLEGE STREET
CHARLOTTE, NORTH CAROLINA 28202
Telephone: 704-376-3400; 800-762-3575
Fax: 704-334-3351
URL: http://www.cozen.com

Dallas, Texas Office: 2300 BankOne Center, 1717 Main Street, 75201. Telephones: 214-462-3000; 800-448-1207. Fax: 214-462-3299.

New York, N.Y. Offices: 45 Broadway Atrium, 16th Floor, 10006. Telephones: 212-509-9400; 800-437-7040. Fax: 212-509-9492. Midtown Office: 909 Third Avenue, 17th Floor, 10022. Telephones: 212-509-9400; 800-437-7040. Fax: 212-207-4938.

Philadelphia, Pennsylvania Office: 1900 Market Street, 19103. Telephones: 215-665-2000; 800-523-2900. Fax: 215-665-2013.

West Conshohocken, Pennsylvania Office: 200 Four Falls Corporate Center, Suite 400, P.O. Box 800, 19428. Telephone: 610-941-5400; 800-379-0695. Fax: 610-941-0711.

San Diego, California Office: Suite 1610, 501 West Broadway, 92101. Telephones: 619-234-1700; 800-782-3366. Fax: 619-234-7831.

Los Angeles, California Office: 777 South Figueroa Street, Suite 2850, 90017. Telephones: 213-892-7900; 800-563-1027. Fax: 213-892-7999.

Seattle, Washington Office: Suite 5200, Washington Mutual Tower, 1201 Third Avenue, 98101. Telephones: 206-340-1000; 800-423-1950. Fax: 206-621-8783.

Newark, New Jersey Office: One Newark Center, Suite 1900, 07102. Telephone: 973-286-1200; 888-200-9521. Fax: 973-242-2121.

Atlanta, Georgia Office: Suite 2200, SunTrust Plaza, 303 Peachtree Street, N.E., 30308. Telephones: 404-572-2000; 800-890-1393. Fax: 404-572-2199.

London, England Office: Fountain House, 130 Fenchurch Street, London EC3M 5DJ. Telephone: 011-44-20-7864-2000. Fax: 011-44-20-7864-2013.

Wilmington, Delaware Office: Chase Manhattan Centre, 1201 North Market Street, Suite 1400, 19801. Telephone: 302-295-2000; 888-207-2440. Fax: 302-295-2013.

(This Listing Continued)

COZEN O'CONNOR, A PROFESSIONAL CORPORATION, Charlotte—Continued

Las Vegas, Nevada Office (Affiliated with the Law Offices of J. Goldberg & D. Grossman): 601 South Rancho, Suite 20, 89106. Telephone: 800-782-3366.
San Francisco, California Office: 425 California Street, Suite 2400, 94104-2203. Telephone: 415-617-6100; 800-818-0165. Fax: 415-617-6101.
Chicago, Illinois Office: 222 South Riverside, Suite 1500, 60606. Telephone: 312-382-3100; 877-992-6036. Fax: 312-382-8910.
Washington, D.C. Office: 1667 K Street, NW, 20006. Telephone: 202-912-4800; 800-540-1355. Fax: 202-912-4830.
Cherry Hill, New Jersey Office: LibertyView, Suite 300, 457 Haddonfield Road, P.O. Box 5459, 08002-2220. Telephone: 856-910-5000; 800-989-0499. Fax: 856-910-5075.
Wichita, Kansas Office: 8415 E. 21st Street, Suite 220, 67206. Telephone: 316-609-3380. Fax: 316-634-3837.
Denver, Colorado Office: 707 17th Street, Suite 3100, 80202. Telephone: 303-292-9080. Fax: 303-292-9650.
Trenton, New Jersey Office: 144-B West State Street, 08608. Telephone: 609-989-8620.
Houston, Texas Office: 1 Houston Center, 1221 McKinney Street, Suite 2900, 77010. Telephone: 800-448-8502; 832-214-3900. Fax: 832-214-3905.
Toronto, Ontario Office: One Queen Street East, Suite 2000, M5C 2W5. Telephone: 416-361-2000. Fax: 416-361-1405.
Santa Fe, New Mexico Office: 125 Lincoln Avenue, Suite 400, 87501. Telephones: 505-820-3346; 866-231-0144. Fax: 505-820-3347.

Advertising Liability/Personal Injury, Alternative Dispute Resolution, Agent/Broker Liability, Antitrust and Unfair Competition, Appellate Practice, Arbitration and Alternative Dispute Resolution, Arson and Fraud, Aviation Litigation, Bad Faith Litigation, Bankruptcy, Insolvency and Restructuring, Business Torts, Cargo Losses, Class Actions, Multi-District Litigation and Other Consolidated Claims, Commercial General Liability, Commercial Litigaion, Construction Law and Litigation, Construction Liability, Corporate and Partnership Law, Corporate Planning, Crisis Management, Cross Border Transactions, Directors' and Officers' Liability, E-Commerce, Internet and Cyber-Peril Insurance, Emerging Business and Venture Capital, Employee Benefits and Executive Compensation, Employment, Labor and Employee Benefits, Environmental Coverage, Environmental Litigation, Estate Planning and Administration, Excess and Surplus Lines, Family Law, Fidelity and Surety, Financial Services, Health Law, Health Care Malpractice, Insurance Corporate and Regulatory Law, Intellectual Property, Intellectual Property Litigation, International Tax and Estate Planning, Labor and Employment, Life, Health and Disability Maritime Law, Medical Device and Drug Litigation, Mergers and Acquisitions, Personal Lines, Privacy Law and Regulation, Private Wealth Services, Products Liability, Professional Liability, Property Insurance, Public and Project Finance, Public Utilities and Energy, Punitive Damages, Real Estate, Real Estate Litigation, Reinsurance, Securities, Securities Litigation and Civil RICO, Security and Premises Liability, Tax, Tax Litigation, Toxic and Other Mass Torts, White Collar Crime.

FIRM PROFILE: Cozen O'Connor is a dynamic, full-service client-oriented firm actively engaged in a diverse business and litigation practice. Headquartered in Philadelphia, Pennsylvania, the firm consists of over 530 lawyers practicing from twenty-four offices in the United States, London and Canada. The firm's practice is divided into four areas: business, business litigation, insurance and intellectual property.

Cozen O'Connor is dedicated to and focused on providing each client with the highest level of legal services rendered in the most efficient and cost-effective manner. Our philosophy acknowledges the paramount importance of each client's interests and we recognize that effective attorney-client relationships not only exist between institutions but with individuals as well. We endeavor to develop trust and confidence through close personal working relationships between our attorneys and the individual representatives of each client. This attention to the specific needs of each client explains our ability to represent a diverse clientele. Our clients range from individuals to corporations, including major utility companies, banks, real estate investment trusts, professional corporations, public companies, domestic insurance companies and foreign insurance syndicates.

FIRM MEMBERS IN CHARLOTTE

PETER F. ASMER, JR., born Columbia, South Carolina, December 4, 1965; admitted to bar, 1991, South Carolina; 1992, North Carolina and U.S. District Court, District of South Carolina; 1993, U.S. District Court, Eastern and Western Districts of North Carolina. *Education:* Wofford College (B.A., magna cum laude, 1988) Phi Beta Kappa; University of South Carolina (J.D., 1991). Order of the Coif; Order of Wig and Robe. Research Editor, 1990-1991 and Editorial Staff Member, 1989-1991, ABA Real Property, Probate and Trust Journal. Student Legal Writing Instructor, University of South Carolina, 1990-1991. *Member:* Mecklenburg County, Federal and American Bar Associations; South Carolina Bar; North Carolina State Bar. ***PRACTICE AREAS:*** Property Subrogation; Construction Litigation; Torts; Products Liability Subrogation; Fire Insurance Subrogation. ***Email:*** pasmer@cozen.com

DOUGLAS BANKS, admitted to bar, 1993, North Carolina and South Carolina; U.S. District Court, District of South Carolina; U.S. District Court, Eastern, Middle and Western Districts of North Carolina. *Education:* Appalachian State University (B.S., 1982); Wake Forest University (J.D., 1993). *Member:* North Carolina Bar Association; South Carolina Bar; National Association of Subrogation Professionals; International Association of Arson Investigators. ***PRACTICE AREAS:*** Insurance Subrogation; Construction Law; Business Litigation; Products Liability. ***Email:*** dbanks@cozen.com

RUSS A. BRINSON, born Kinston, North Carolina, September 11, 1973; admitted to bar, 1999, North Carolina. *Education:* University of North Carolina at Chapel Hill (B.S., 1995); Wake Forest University (J.D., 1998). Phi Alpha Delta. *Member:* North Carolina State Bar (Member, Committee for Small Firms and Solo Practitioners, 2000-2001; Editor, Truebill, Criminal Justice Section Newsletter); Defense Research Institute; North Carolina Academy of Defense Attorneys. ***PRACTICE AREAS:*** Insurance Coverage; Professional Liability; Products Liability; Business Litigation; Commercial Litigation. ***Email:*** rbrinson@cozen.com

(This Listing Continued)

TRACY L. EGGLESTON, born Charlotte, North Carolina, June 12, 1957; admitted to bar, 1982, South Carolina; 1991, North Carolina; 2005, Georgia; U.S. District Court, Western, Eastern and Middle Districts of North Carolina, U.S. District Court, District of South Carolina and U.S. Court of Appeals, Fourth and Fifth Circuits. *Education:* Furman University (B.A., magna cum laude, 1979); University of South Carolina (J.D., 1982). *Member:* North Carolina (Member, Litigation Section) and American (Member, Sections on: Torts; Insurance; Property) Bar Associations; South Carolina Bar; State Bar of Georgia. ***PRACTICE AREAS:*** Commercial Property Insurance; Extra Contractual Insurance Claims; Fire Insurance; General Liability; First and Third Party Insurance; Insurance Bad Faith; Insurance Coverage; Insurance Fraud; Insurance Litigation. ***Email:*** teggleston@cozen.com

B. ELIZABETH GAST, born Fort Myers, Florida, April 15, 1963; admitted to bar, 1992, California; 1997, North Carolina. *Education:* Pasadena City College; University of Colorado at Colorado Springs (B.A., magna cum laude, 1985); Pepperdine University (J.D., cum laude, 1992). Recipient, American Jurisprudence Award, Constitutional Law. Extern to the Honorable William J. Reg, U.S. District Court, Central District of California. *Member:* North Carolina State Bar; State Bar of California (Inactive member). ***PRACTICE AREAS:*** Subrogation; Insurance Litigation. ***Email:*** egast@cozen.com

JOSHUA R. GOODMAN, born New York, N.Y., June 27, 1972; admitted to bar, 1998, Florida; 1999, North Carolina; 2002, U.S. District Court, Western District of Northern Carolina; 2003, U.S. District Court, Eastern District of North Carolina. *Education:* The Citadel (B.A., honors, 1994); Nova Southeastern University (J.D., 1998). *Member:* Mecklenburg County and American Bar Associations; North Carolina State Bar; The Florida Bar. ***PRACTICE AREAS:*** Subrogation; Nonprofit and Charitable Organizations; Litigation. ***Email:*** jrgoodman@cozen.com

T. DAVID HIGGINS, JR., born Charleston, West Virginia, October 2, 1959; admitted to bar, 1987, New Jersey, Pennsylvania, West Virginia, U.S. District Court, Southern District of West Virginia and U.S. Court of Appeals, Fourth Circuit; 1988, U.S. District Court, Eastern District of Pennsylvania; 1992, North Carolina and U.S. District Court, Western District of North Carolina; 1997, U.S. District Court, Eastern District of North Carolina; 1999, U.S. District Court, Middle District of North Carolina. *Education:* West Virginia University (B.S., 1982; J.D., 1987). Student Works Editor, 1986-1987 and Staff Member, 1986, West Virginia University Law Review. *Member:* West Virginia State Bar; New Jersey State Bar Association; North Carolina State Bar; Mecklenburg County Bar Association; The Association of Trial Lawyers of America. ***PRACTICE AREAS:*** General Civil Practice; Labor and Employment; Defective Products Law; Design Professionals; Fire Loss Litigation; General Negligence Trials and Appeals; Litigation; Negligence Law; Premises Liability Law; Products Liability Law (Defective Products); Subrogation Law; Tort; Federal Civil Practice; Fire Insurance Subrogation; Product Liability Subrogation; Warranty Law; Civil Liability. ***Email:*** dhiggins@cozen.com

GARRETT J. McAVOY, born Concord, California, June 3, 1963; admitted to bar, 1993, North Carolina and South Carolina. *Education:* United States Military Academy (B.S., 1985); West Virginia University (J.D., 1993). Member, Moot Court. Jessup Cup Participant. Author, "The Child Witness in Florida," chapter in *Child Trauma: Issues and Research,* Garland Publishing, 1992. [U.S. Army Corps of Engineers, 1985-1990; Capt.]. ***PRACTICE AREAS:*** Insurance Coverage; Insurance Litigation. ***Email:*** gmcavoy@cozen.com

ALBERT S. NALIBOTSKY, born Philadelphia, Pennsylvania, April 29, 1964; admitted to bar, 1991, Maryland; 1992, North Carolina and South Carolina. *Education:* University of Florida (B.S., 1987); Stetson University (J.D., 1990); Vermont Law School (M.S.L., cum laude, 1992). ***PRACTICE AREAS:*** Property Subrogation; Tort Liability. ***Email:*** analibotsky@cozen.com

HUNTER C. QUICK, born Spartanburg, South Carolina, September 20, 1949; admitted to bar, 1981, West Virginia; 1983, Tennessee; 1988, U.S. Court of Appeals, Fourth Circuit; 1989, North Carolina; 1997, U.S. Court of Appeals, Sixth Circuit. *Education:* Wofford College (A.B., 1971); Marshall University (M.A., 1974); West Virginia University (J.D., 1981). Phi Delta Phi. Lead Articles Editor, West Virginia Law Review, 1980-1981. *Member:* Tennessee Bar Association; North Carolina State Bar; West Virginia State Bar. ***PRACTICE AREAS:*** Trial Practice; Civil Litigation; Property Subrogation; Insurance; Entertainment Law. ***Email:*** hquick@cozen.com

PAUL A. REICHS, born Riga, Latvia, January 29, 1942; admitted to bar, 1967, Illinois; 1978, North Carolina. *Education:* Grinnell College (B.A., 1964); University of Illinois (LL.B., 1967). Phi Delta Phi. Member, National Moot Court Team. [Capt., JAG, U.S. Marine Corps, 1968-1971]. ***PRACTICE AREAS:*** Trial Practice; Medical Malpractice Defense; Insurance Coverage. ***Email:*** preichs@cozen.com

KIMBERLY SULLIVAN, born 1964; admitted to bar, 1990, New Jersey and Pennsylvania; 1996, North Carolina; 1997, Florida. *Education:* University of Delaware (B.S., 1987); Rutgers School of Law, Camden (J.D., with honors, 1990). Law Clerk to the Honorable Neil F. Deighan, Jr., New Jersey Superior Court, Appellate Division, 1990-1991. ***PRACTICE AREAS:*** Medical Malpractice Defense; Insurance Litigation and Coverage; Products Liability Defense; Toxic Torts; Appellate Practice. ***Email:*** ksullivan@cozen.com

JOHN W. REIS, born Syracuse, New York, May 24, 1966; admitted to bar, 1992, Florida; 1998, North Carolina; U.S. District Court, Southern, Middle and Northern Districts of Florida; U.S. District Court, Western, Middle and Eastern Districts of North Carolina. *Education:* Duke University (A.B., 1988); University of Miami (J.D., cum laude, 1992). Author: "Measure of Damages in Property Loss Cases: The Road Less Considered," N.C. State Bar Journal Winter 2003 at 12; "Measure of Damages in Property Loss Cases," 76 Fla. Bar J. Oct. 2002, at 32; "Economic Loss Rule: The 'Integrated Part' Approach to the 'Other Property' Exception," Fla. Bar J. July/Aug. 2002, at 42; "Spoliated Evidence: Better Than the Real Thing?" Fla. Bar J. July/Aug. 1997, at 22; "Improper Jury Comment: Gilding the Lustre of the Golden Rule," Fla. Bar J. Jan. 1996, at 60. ***REPORTED CASES:*** Alvarez v. E&A Produce Corp., 708 So.2d 997 (Fla. 3d DCA 1998); Hannah v. Newkirk, 675 So.2d 112 (Fla. 1996); GEICO v. Burns, 672 So.2d 834 (Fla. 3d DCA 1996); Thompson v. State Farm Mutual Ins. Co., 670 So.2d 1070 (Fla. 3d DCA 1996). ***PRACTICE AREAS:*** Subrogation; Business Litigation. ***Email:*** jreis@cozen.com

FIRM ASSOCIATES IN CHARLOTTE

ADAM P. ALTMAN, born Wilmington, Delaware, November 27, 1972; admitted to bar, 1998, North Carolina. *Education:* University of Maryland (B.A., 1994); University of

(This Listing Continued)

North Carolina at Chapel Hill (J.D., 1998). ***REPORTED CASES:*** Charter Oak Fire Insurance Company v. Coleman, 273 F.Supp.2d 903 (W.D. Ky. 2003). ***PRACTICE AREAS:*** Commercial Litigation. ***Email:*** aaltman@cozen.com

MICHAEL DURR, born Utica, New York, November 3, 1969; admitted to bar, 1997, Texas; 2000, North Carolina. *Education:* University of Rochester (B.A., magna cum laude, 1992); University of Houston (J.D., 1996). ***PRACTICE AREAS:*** Civil Litigation.

MEGAN A. LAMMON, born Phoenix, Arizona, June 30, 1974; admitted to bar, 2000, North Carolina. *Education:* Boston College (B.A., 1996); Wake Forest University (J.D., 2000). ***PRACTICE AREAS:*** Subrogation; Civil Litigation. ***Email:*** mlammon@cozen.com

CRANFILL, SUMNER & HARTZOG, L.L.P.

227 WEST TRADE STREET, SUITE 600
P.O. BOX 30787
CHARLOTTE, NORTH CAROLINA 28230
Telephone: 704-332-8300
Fax: 704-332-9994
URL: http://www.cshlaw.com

Raleigh, North Carolina Office: Hillsborough Place, 225 Hillsborough Street, Suite 300, P.O. Box 27808. Telephone: 919-828-5100. Fax: 919-828-2277.
Wilmington, North Carolina Office: 1209 Culbreth Drive, Suite 200, 28405. Telephone: 910-509-9778. Fax: 910-509-9676.

General Trial and Appellate Practice before all State and Federal Courts. Litigation of Insurance Law, Personal Injury, Medical Malpractice, Nursing Home Negligence, Professional Malpractice, Products Liability, Premises Liability, Municipal and Police Liability, Intentional Torts, Commercial Litigation, Worker's Compensation, Employment, Construction and Land Condemnation Law.

MEMBERS OF THE FIRM

SAMUEL H. POOLE, JR., admitted to bar, 1986, North Carolina. *Education:* University of North Carolina at Chapel Hill (B.A., 1982; J.D., 1986).

M. ANDREW AVRAM, admitted to bar, 1990, North Carolina. *Education:* Wake Forest University (B.A., 1982; J.D., 1990).

PATRICK H. FLANAGAN, admitted to bar, 1990, North Carolina. *Education:* St. Lawrence University (B.S., 1987); Wake Forest University (J.D., 1990). [Capt., JAGC, U.S. Army, 1990-1994]

EMERSON M. THOMPSON III, admitted to bar, 1989, North Carolina. *Education:* Wake Forest University (B.A., 1986; J.D., 1989).

NICHOLAS PETER VALAORAS, admitted to bar, 1993, North Carolina. *Education:* Wake Forest University (B.A., 1989; J.D., 1992).

J. SHANNON HARRIS, admitted to bar, 2000, North Carolina. *Education:* University of North Carolina at Chapel Hill (B.A., 1997); University of Miami (J.D., 2000).

LAWRENCE M. BAKER, admitted to bar, 1990, North Carolina. *Education:* Alma College (B.A., 1993); Wake Forest Law School (J.D., 1990).

NICOLE DOLPH VIELE, admitted to bar, 2001, North Carolina. *Education:* University of North Carolina at Charlotte (B.A., 1992); University of North Carolina at Chapel Hill (J.D., 2000).

JEFFREY A. HOWLE, admitted to bar, 1997, North Carolina. *Education:* University of North Carolina at Chapel Hill (B.A., 1992); Florida State University College of Law (J.D., 1997).

TODD ALEXANDER KING, admitted to bar, 2002, North Carolina. *Education:* Wake Forest University (B.S., 1998; J.D., 2002).

ROBERT MARC RUBIN, admitted to bar, 1995, Florida, South Carolina and North Carolina; 1996, U.S. District Court, Eastern District of North Carolina. *Education:* University of South Carolina (B.A., cum laude, 1990); University of Miami (J.D., cum laude, 1994).

JULIE L. KERR, admitted to bar, 2004, North Carolina. *Education:* Campbell University (B.S., 2001); Wake Forest University (J.D., 2004).

VICTORIA A. STREET, admitted to bar, 2004, North Carolina. *Education:* University of North Carolina at Chapel Hill (B.S., 2000; J.D., 2004).

RYAN D. BOLICK, admitted to bar, 1999, North Carolina. *Education:* University of North Carolina at Chapel Hill (B.A., 1994); Campbell University (J.D., 1999). *Member:* North Carolina Bar Association; North Carolina State Bar; North Carolina Association of Defense Attorneys.

HOLLAND L. BARKSDALE, admitted to bar, 2005, North Carolina. *Education:* Duke University (B.A., 2002); University of Miami (J.D., 2005). *Member:* North Carolina State Bar.

BRADLEY P. KLINE, admitted to bar, 2005, North Carolina and U.S. District Court, Western District of North Carolina. *Education:* University of North Carolina at Chapel Hill (B.A., 2001); Wake Forest University (J.D., 2005). *Member:* North Carolina State Bar.

(For complete biographical data on all personnel, see Professional Biographies at Raleigh and Wilmington, North Carolina)

CRANFORD, SCHULTZE AND TOMCHIN, P.A.

2813 COLTSGATE ROAD, SUITE 200
CHARLOTTE, NORTH CAROLINA 28211
Telephone: 704-442-1010
Fax: 704-442-1020
URL: http://www.cstpa.com

General Civil and limited Criminal Trials in all Courts. Residential and Commercial Real Estate Law; General Business Law; Collections and Foreclosures; Debtor and Creditors Rights Law; Bankruptcy; Personal Injury and Wrongful Death Litigation; Estate Planning and Administration.

CHARLES H. CRANFORD, born Albemarle, North Carolina, July 12, 1946; admitted to bar, 1973, North Carolina and U.S. District Court, Western and Eastern Districts of North Carolina; 1980, U.S. Tax Court. *Education:* University of North Carolina (A.B., 1968; J.D., with honors, 1973). Phi Beta Kappa; Phi Eta Sigma; Order of the Coif. Recipient, Judge Walter Clark Award. Member, Editorial Board, North Carolina Law Review, 1972-1973. *Member:* Mecklenburg County Bar Association; North Carolina State Bar. ***PRACTICE AREAS:*** Commercial Real Estate; Residential Real Estate; Commercial Law. ***Email:*** ccranford@cstpa.com

MICHAEL F. SCHULTZE, born Milwaukee, Wisconsin, June 2, 1959; admitted to bar, 1984, North Carolina and U.S. District Court, Middle, Eastern and Western Districts of North Carolina; U.S. Court of Appeals, Fourth Circuit. *Education:* University of North Carolina (B.S., 1981; J.D., 1984). Beta Gamma Sigma; Phi Delta Phi. Member, Holderness Moot Court Bench. *Member:* North Carolina State Bar; North Carolina (Member, Litigation Section) and American Bar Associations; North Carolina Academy of Trial Lawyers. ***PRACTICE AREAS:*** Commercial Litigation; Civil Litigation; Commercial Collections; Personal Injury; Wrongful Death; Bankruptcy; Debtor and Creditor Rights; Criminal Defense Law. ***Email:*** mschultze@cstpa.com

R. GREGORY TOMCHIN, born Bluefield, West Virginia, June 15, 1960; admitted to bar, 1985, West Virginia and U.S. District Court, Southern District of West Virginia; 1988, North Carolina, U.S. District Court, Middle, Eastern and Western Districts of North Carolina and U.S. Court of Appeals, Fourth Circuit. *Education:* Wake Forest University (B.A., Economics, 1982); West Virginia University (J.D., 1985). Phi Delta Phi. Member, Marlyn E. Lugar Trial Association, 1983-1985. *Member:* North Carolina State Bar; West Virginia State Bar. ***PRACTICE AREAS:*** Commercial Law; Commercial Litigation; Foreclosures; Bankruptcy; Residential Real Estate; Business Formation. ***Email:*** gtomchin@cstpa.com

R. MICHAEL ALLEN, born Charlotte, North Carolina, May 28, 1959; admitted to bar, 1984, North Carolina, U.S. District Court, Western and Middle Districts of North Carolina and U.S. Court of Appeals, Fourth Circuit. *Education:* University of North Carolina (B.S., 1981; J.D., 1984). Beta Gamma Sigma. Member, Editorial Board, North Carolina Journal of International Law and Commercial Regulation, 1983-1984. Mecklenburg County Public Administrator, 2003—. *Member:* North Carolina Bar Association; North Carolina State Bar. ***PRACTICE AREAS:*** Estate Administration; Estate Planning; Guardianship; Real Estate. ***Email:*** rmallen@cstpa.com

CULP ELLIOTT & CARPENTER, P.L.L.C.

A Professional Limited Liability Company
4401 BARCLAY DOWNS DRIVE
SUITE 200
CHARLOTTE, NORTH CAROLINA 28209
Telephone: 704-372-6322
Fax: 704-551-5700
URL: http://www.ceandc.com

Federal, State, Local and International Taxation, Real Estate and Commercial Law, International Business Negotiations and Planning, Securities, Partnership and Corporate Law, Employee Benefits, Estate Planning and Tax Litigation and Controversies.

FIRM PROFILE: Culp Elliott & Carpenter, P.L.L.C. was founded in 1982. The firm's practice is highly focused upon U.S. tax, international tax and estate planning, commercial real estate and corporate taxation and commercial tax litigation. The firm serves clients from a local, regional and multi-national client base. The firm frequently contributes tax articles to national tax publications and is very involved in ABA and North Carolina Tax Section committee leadership.

WILLIAM R. CULP, JR., (P.A.), born Gastonia, North Carolina, April 20, 1953; admitted to bar, 1978, North Carolina; 1980, U.S. Tax Court. *Education:* University of North Carolina (B.S., 1975; J.D., 1978); New York University (LL.M., Taxation, 1980). Certified Public Accountant, North Carolina, 1980. Co-Author: "IRS Pronouncements Clarify Status As A Partnership vs. an Association," Journal of Partnership Taxation, Summer, 1989; "Avoiding Cancellation of Debt Income Where the Liability is Disputed," Journal of Taxation, May, 1991; "Owning Assets in Trust Results in Tax and Nontax Benefits," Estate Planning, September/October, 1992; "Ruling on Qualified Sub S Trusts Raises Potential Phantom Gain and Installment Problems," Journal of Taxation, May, 1993; "Valuation Practice in Estate Planning and Litigation," (Clark Boardman Callaghan, 1994); "Outbound L.L.C. Planning Includes Options for China Investment," Journal of International Taxation, July, 1995. Author: "Maximizing the Low Income Housing Credit in Combination with Government Subsidies," Journal of Taxation, September, 1988; "Liquidating Trustee Must File Returns and Pay Tax for Debtors, Supreme Court Says," Journal of Taxation, June, 1992. *Member:* North Carolina State Bar; North Carolina and American (Member: S.C. Department of Revenue Blue Ribbon Advisory Committee, 1996-1997; Legislative Committee, Estate Planning and Probate Law; Sections on: Taxation; Estates and Gift Tax) Bar Associations; North Carolina Association of Certified Public Accountants. (Board Certified Specialist in Estate Planning and Probate Law, North Carolina State Board of Legal Specialization). ***Email:*** wrc@ceclaw.com

W. CURTIS ELLIOTT, JR., born Gastonia, North Carolina, February 1, 1955; admitted to bar, 1980, North Carolina and South Carolina; 1983, U.S. Tax Court; 1984, U.S.

(This Listing Continued)

CULP ELLIOTT & CARPENTER, P.L.L.C., Charlotte—Continued

Claims Court. *Education:* University of South Carolina (B.S., 1977; J.D., 1980); George Washington University National Law Center (LL.M., in Taxation, with highest honors, 1984). Co-Author: "Valuation Practice in Estate Planning and Litigation," (Clark Boardman Callaghan, 1994); "Federal Tax Litigation Involving Leveraged Buyouts," Prentice Hall Tax Ideas, 1987. Author: "Can IRS Trial Attorney Be Barred From Other Years of the Taxpayer?" Journal of Taxation, May, 1991; "Scanlan, Estate Tax Valuations and Subsequent Events," The Valuation Examiner, August/September 1997. Fellow American College of Tax Counsel. Member, Legal Elite Hall of Fame in Trust and Estate Planning, North Carolina Business Magazine, 2004, 2005. *Member:* North Carolina, South Carolina and American (Past Chair, Court Procedure Committee, ABA Tax Section, 1995-1997; Chair, U.S. Tax Court Appointment Committee, 2005—) Bar Associations; North Carolina State Bar. ***PRACTICE AREAS:*** Mergers, Acquisitions and Divestitures (50%); Commercial Real Estate Development (25%); Estate Planning (25%). ***Email:*** wce@ceclaw.com

JOHN JOSEPH CARPENTER, born Rutherfordton, North Carolina, May 11, 1958; admitted to bar, 1984, North Carolina; 1985, U.S. District Court, Western District of North Carolina; 1987, U.S. Tax Court. *Education:* Wake Forest University (B.S., cum laude, 1980; J.D., cum laude, 1984). Certified Public Accountant, North Carolina, 1984. *Member:* Mecklenburg County, North Carolina (Member, Sections of: Business Law; Estate Planning and Fiduciary Law; Real Property and Taxation) and American (Member, Sections of Corporation, Banking and Business Law; Real Property, Probate and Trust Law and Taxation) Bar Associations; North Carolina State Bar; North Carolina Association of Certified Public Accountants; American Institute of Certified Public Accountants. (Board Certified Specialist in Estate Planning and Probate Law, North Carolina State Board of Legal Specialization). ***PRACTICE AREAS:*** Estate and Tax Planning; Business Law; Real Estate; Commercial Transactions. ***Email:*** jjc@ceclaw.com

PAUL M. HATTENHAUER, born Fort Dix, New Jersey, July 4, 1966; admitted to bar, 1991, Wisconsin; 1995, North Carolina; 1998, Florida. *Education:* St. John's University (B.S., summa cum laude, 1988); University of Minnesota (J.D., cum laude, 1991); University of Miami (LL.M., Estate Planning, 1994). Co-Author: "When Will IRS's Invocation of the Reciprocal Trust Doctrine be Upheld by the Courts?" Journal of Taxation, July 1996. Certified Public Accountant, Minnesota, 1988. *Member:* State Bar of Wisconsin; North Carolina State Bar (Member: Tax Section, Estate Planning and Fiduciary Law Section); The Florida Bar. (Board Certified Specialist in Estate Planning and Probate Law, North Carolina State Board of Legal Specialization). ***PRACTICE AREAS:*** Taxation; Business Law; Estate Planning. ***Email:*** pmh@ceclaw.com

CHRISTOPHER E. HANNUM, born Dunkirk, New York, November 24, 1966; admitted to bar, 1992, Florida; 1994, North Carolina. *Education:* Allegheny College (B.A., 1989); University of Florida (J.D., with honors, 1992; LL.M., in Taxation, with honors, 1993). *Member:* Mecklenburg County and American (Member, Tax Section) Bar Associations; North Carolina State Bar (Member, Sections on: Tax; Business Law); The Florida Bar (Member, Tax Section). ***PRACTICE AREAS:*** Estate Planning; Wealth Preservation; Real Estate; Commercial Transactions; Tax Controversy. ***Email:*** ceh@ceclaw.com

MARK LOUIS RICHARDSON, born Greenwood, South Carolina, April 15, 1968; admitted to bar, 1995, South Carolina; 1998, North Carolina. *Education:* University of Virginia (B.S., 1990); University of South Carolina (J.D., 1994); University of Florida (LL.M., in Taxation, 1995). Member, South Carolina Law Review, 1993-1994. Recipient, American Jurisprudence Award for Contracts. *Member:* South Carolina Bar; North Carolina State Bar. (Board Certified Specialist in Estate Planning and Probate Law, North Carolina State Board of Legal Specialization). ***PRACTICE AREAS:*** Taxation. ***Email:*** mlr@ceclaw.com

SENIOR ASSOCIATE

JEFFREY D. BARNES, born Corvallis, Oregon, February 6, 1967; admitted to bar, 1995, North Carolina; 1997, South Carolina. *Education:* Florida State University (B.S., cum laude, 1990); University of North Carolina (J.D., 1995). Articles Editor, University of North Carolina Law Review, 1994-1995. Judicial Law Clerk to the Hon. George R. Hodges, U.S. Bankruptcy Court, Western District of North Carolina, 1995-1996. *Member:* North Carolina State Bar (Member, Sections on: Real Property and Business Law); South Carolina Bar. ***PRACTICE AREAS:*** Real Estate; Commercial Law; Bank Lending; Business Law. ***Email:*** jdb@ceclaw.com

ASSOCIATES

PAUL J. SMITH, born Concord, North Carolina, August 28, 1974; admitted to bar, 1999, North Carolina and U.S. District Court, Middle District of North Carolina. *Education:* East Carolina University (B.S., magna cum laude, 1996); University of North Carolina at Chapel Hill (J.D., 1999). *Member:* Mecklenburg County, Forsyth County and North Carolina Bar Associations. ***PRACTICE AREAS:*** Commercial Real Estate; Banking Law; Business Law; Real Estate Taxation. ***Email:*** pjs@ceclaw.com

HOLLY B. NORVELL, born Pensacola, Florida; admitted to bar, 2002, Texas; 2004, North Carolina. *Education:* University of Texas at Austin (B.B.A., with high honors, 1996; M.P.A., Taxation, 1996; J.D., with honors, 2002). Associate Editor, Texas Review of Law and Politics, 2001-2002. Intern for the Hon. James A. Baker, Supreme Court of Texas, 2001. Certified Public Accountant, Texas, 1996. *Member:* Mecklenburg County (Member, Estate Planning Section) and American (Member, Sections on: Real Property, Probate & Trust Law; Tax) Bar Associations; State Bar of Texas (Member, Real Estate, Probate & Trust Law Section); North Carolina State Bar; Texas Young Lawyers Association; Charlotte Estate Planning Council. ***PRACTICE AREAS:*** Tax Law; Estate Planning. ***Email:*** hbn@ceclaw.com

STANTON P. GELLER, born Columbus, Indiana, 1975; admitted to bar, 2005, North Carolina. *Education:* Queens College of the City University of New York (B.A., 2000), University of Florida (J.D., 2003; LL.M., Taxation, 2004). *Member:* Mecklenburg County and American (Member, Tax Section) Bar Associations; North Carolina State Bar (Member, Tax Section); The Florida Bar (Member, Tax Section). ***Email:*** spg@ceclaw.com

BENJAMIN H. ELLIS, born Bangor, Maine, 1978; admitted to bar, 2005, North Carolina. *Education:* Dartmouth College (B.A., 2001); Wake Forest University (J.D., 2005). Member, Moot Court. *Member:* North Carolina State Bar. ***PRACTICE AREAS:*** Commercial Real Estate; Commercial Law. ***Email:*** bhe@ceclaw.com

CARL L. KING, born Flemington, New Jersey, April 13, 1970; admitted to bar, 1998, Pennsylvania; 1999, New Jersey; 2000, North Carolina; 2002, U.S. Tax Court. *Education:* Wheaton College (B.A., 1992); University of Utah College of Law (J.D., 1998); University of Miami (LL.M., Estate Planning, 1999). Member, Board of Directors, Legal Services for the Elderly, Mecklenburg County. *Member:* American Bar Association (Member, Sections on: Real Property and Probate and Trust). ***PRACTICE AREAS:*** Estate Planning; Individual Taxation; Life Insurance; Closely Held Businesses; Charitable Giving. ***Email:*** clk@ceclaw.com

RICHARD A. PELAK, born Monroe, New York, July 28, 1970; admitted to bar, 1995, North Carolina. *Education:* State University of New York at Binghamton (B.S., 1992); University of North Carolina at Chapel Hill (J.D., 1995). *Member:* North Carolina (Member, Tax Section) and American Bar Associations; North Carolina State Bar; North Carolina Association of Certified Public Accountants. ***PRACTICE AREAS:*** Business Taxation; Individual Taxation; Tax Planning; Tax Controversies. ***Email:*** rap@ceclaw.com

DEBORAH H. KING, born Cincinnati, Ohio; admitted to bar, 2001, Massachusetts; 2003, North Carolina. *Education:* University of New Hampshire (B.A., 1994); Hastings College of the Law at University of California (J.D., 2000); Boston University School of Law (LL.M., Taxation, 2003). Member: Order of the Coif; Thurston Society. Author: "Clara Shortridge Foltz: Angel and Revolutionary," Hastings Women's Law Journal, Volume II, Issue 2. ***PRACTICE AREAS:*** Estate Planning; Taxation; Charitable Giving. ***Email:*** dhk@ceclaw.com

REPRESENTATIVE CLIENTS: References Available Upon Request.

THE CUMMINGS LAW FIRM, P.A.

1230 WEST MOREHEAD, SUITE 404
CHARLOTTE, NORTH CAROLINA 28208-5210
Telephone: 704-376-2853
Fax: 704-376-3334
Email: Cummingslawfirm@aol.com
URL: http://www.thecummingslawfirm.com

Consumer Bankruptcy, Commercial Bankruptcy, Collections, Debtor Rights, Employment Discrimination, Sexual Harassment, Social Security Disability, Federal Workers Compensation, Wrongful Termination, Civil Rights.

SANDRA U. CUMMINGS, born Cleveland, Ohio, December 17, 1951; admitted to bar, 1977, North Carolina. *Education:* Yankton College (B.A., 1971); University of North Carolina at Chapel Hill (J.D., 1975). *Member:* Mecklenburg County and North Carolina Bar Associations; Western District of North Carolina Bar Association (Member, Committees on: Attorney Fee; Bankruptcy Rules); North Carolina State Bar; National Association of Black Lawyers. ***PRACTICE AREAS:*** Consumer Bankruptcy; Commercial Bankruptcy; Collections; Debtors Rights.

HUMPHREY S. CUMMINGS, born 1945; admitted to bar, 1977, North Carolina; U.S. District Court, Western and Middle Districts of North Carolina; U.S. Court of Appeals for the Federal Circuit. *Education:* University of North Carolina, Charlotte (B.A., 1972); University of North Carolina, Chapel Hill (J.D., 1976). Administrative Judge, EEOC, 1991-2000. Senior Trial Attorney, EEOC, 1979-1991. Staff Attorney, Legal Services of Southern Piedmont, 1976-1979. Member, Charlotte Mecklenburg Planning Commission, 1979-1982. Chairman and Member, Mecklenburg County Park and Recreation Commission, 1991-1997. *Member:* North Carolina State Bar Association; Mecklenburg County Bar; The John Leary Bar Association (of Charlotte). ***PRACTICE AREAS:*** Employment Discrimination; Social Security Disability; Civil Rights.

JOHN T. DANIEL

216 N. MCDOWELL STREET, SUITE 208
CHARLOTTE, NORTH CAROLINA 28204-2260
Telephone: 704-333-0900
Fax: 704-333-0993
Email: jtdaniel@bellsouth.net
URL: http://www.lawyers.com/johndaniel

Civil Litigation. Concentration in Business Litigation, Contracts, Construction Claims, Collections, Commercial Litigation, Construction Litigation, Contracts Litigation, Negligence.

JOHN T. DANIEL, born 1954; admitted to bar, 1983, North Carolina, U.S. District Court, Eastern and Western Districts of North Carolina and U.S. Court of Appeals, Fourth Circuit. *Education:* Rhodes College (B.A., with honors, 1976); American University (M.S., 1979; J.D., 1983). Omicron Delta Kappa. Assistant District Attorney, Mecklenburg County, 1983-1985. Court Certified Arbitrator and Mediator. *Member:* Mecklenburg County, North Carolina and American Bar Associations. ***PRACTICE AREAS:*** Business Litigation; Contracts; Construction Claims; Collections.

DAVIES & GRIST, LLP

15720 JOHN J. DELANEY DRIVE, SUITE 445
CHARLOTTE, NORTH CAROLINA 28277
Telephone: 704-731-0600
Fax: 704-731-0606

Other Charlotte Office: 310 Arlington Avenue, 28203. Telephone: 704-376-2059. Fax: 702-335-8161.

Real Estate, Buying and Selling, Zoning, Planning and Land Use, Homeowners Association Law, Family Law, Divorce, Child Custody, Child Support.

(This Listing Continued)

KENNETH T. DAVIES, born Banberg, South Carolina, June 20, 1953; admitted to bar, 1980, North Carolina and U.S. District Court, Western District of North Carolina; 1985, U.S. Court of Appeals, Fourth Circuit. *Education:* University of North Carolina at Chapel Hill (B.A., 1975); Lewis and Clark College (J.D., 1980). *Member:* Mecklenburg, North Carolina and American Bar Associations; North Carolina State Bar; North Carolina Academy of Trial Lawyers. ***PRACTICE AREAS:*** Family Law; Divorce; Real Estate. ***Email:*** ktd@kdavies.com

DANIEL W. GRIST, born Concord, North Carolina, November 15, 1974; admitted to bar, 2002, North Carolina. *Education:* East Carolina University (B.S., 1998); Thomas M. Cooley School of Law (J.D., 2001). *Member:* Mecklenburg County (Member, Real Estate Section), North Carolina and American Bar Associations; North Carolina State Bar. ***PRACTICE AREAS:*** Real Estate. ***Email:*** dgrist@daviesandgrist.com

DEAN & GIBSON, L.L.P.

SUITE 900, CAMERON BROWN BUILDING
301 SOUTH MCDOWELL STREET
CHARLOTTE, NORTH CAROLINA 28204-2686
Telephone: 704-372-2700
Facsimile: 704-372-1804
Email: info@deanandgibson.com
URL: http://www.deanandgibson.com

General Corporate and Insurance Litigation, Products Liability, Professional Malpractice, Construction, First Party, Aviation, Defense and Subrogation, Municipal, Bankruptcy.

FIRM PROFILE: Dean & Gibson, L.L.P. is experienced in handling a wide variety of litigation. Our attorneys provide assistance for numerous insurance carriers, corporate clients and municipalities. We are experienced in all aspects of case handling including case evaluation, coverage analysis, Alternative Dispute Resolution, trials and appeals. The firm is often selected for defense of complex high risk cases. Our size and experience allow for the close relationship required in successfully handling such cases. We also handle routine litigation matters, with the exception of workers compensation.

RODNEY A. DEAN, admitted to bar, 1973, North Carolina. *Education:* Michigan State University (B.A., 1970); University of Michigan (J.D., 1973).

MICHAEL G. GIBSON, admitted to bar, 1979, North Carolina. *Education:* Davidson College (B.A., 1976); Wake Forest University (J.D., 1979).

JOHN WHITELAW ONG, admitted to bar, 1991, Maryland; 1994, District of Columbia; 1997, North Carolina. *Education:* Connecticut College (B.A., 1988); Emory University (J.D., 1991).

SUSAN L. HOFER, admitted to bar, 1988, Maryland; 1990, District of Columbia; 1992, Michigan; 2000, North Carolina. *Education:* Catholic University of America (B.A. Mus., 1981); University of Maryland (J.D., 1988).

ISIDORE T. ZARSADIAS, admitted to bar, 1994, Pennsylvania; 2000, North Carolina. *Education:* Pennsylvania State University (B.S., 1990); University of Akron (J.D., 1994).

ASSOCIATES

COLIN E. SCOTT, admitted to bar, 1997, North Carolina; U.S. District Court, Western, Middle and Eastern Districts of North Carolina. *Education:* Syracuse University (B.A., cum laude, 1990); Loyola University Law School (J.D., 1996). ***LANGUAGES:*** Spanish.

THOMAS G. NANCE, II, admitted to bar, 1997, North Carolina; U.S. District Court, Western, Middle & Eastern Districts. *Education:* East Carolina University (B.A., 1994); Wake Forest University (J.D., 1997).

CHRISTOPHER W. COOK, admitted to bar, 2004, North Carolina and U.S. District Court, Western, Middle and Eastern Districts of North Carolina. *Education:* Messiah College (B.A., 2001); Wake Forest University (J.D., 2004).

AMY E. DRAYTON, admitted to bar, 2004, North Carolina and U.S. District Court, Western, Middle and Eastern District of North Carolina. *Education:* Carson-Newman College (B.A., magna cum laude, 2002); Thomas M. Cooley Law School (J.D., 2004).

OF COUNSEL

BARBARA J. DEAN, admitted to bar, 1973, North Carolina and U.S. District Court, Western District of North Carolina; 1984, U.S. Court of Appeals, Fourth Circuit. *Education:* Denison University (B.A., with honors, 1968); Brown University (M.A.T., 1969); University of Michigan (J.D., 1973).

DECHERT LLP

BANK OF AMERICA CORPORATE CENTER
100 NORTH TRYON STREET, SUITE 4000
CHARLOTTE, NORTH CAROLINA 28202
Telephone: 704.339.3100
Telefax: 704.339.3101
URL: http://www.dechert.com

Philadelphia, Pennsylvania: 4000 Bell Atlantic Tower, 1717 Arch Street, 19103-2793. Telephone: 215.994.4000.
New York, New York: 30 Rockefeller Plaza, 10112. Telephone: 212.698.3500.
Washington, D.C.: 1775 I Street, N.W., 20006-2401. Telephone: 202.261.3300.
Harrisburg, Pennsylvania: Thirty North Third Street, 17101-1603. Telephone: 717.237.2000.
Princeton, New Jersey: Princeton Pike Corporate Center, P.O. Box 5218, 08543-5218. Telephone: 609.620.3200.
Boston, Massachusetts: 200 Clarendon Street, 27th Floor, 02116-5021. Telephone: 617.728.7100.

(This Listing Continued)

Hartford, Connecticut Office: 90 State House Square, 06103-3702. Telephone: 860.524.3999.
Newport Beach, California Office: 4675 MacArthur Court, Suite 1400, 92660-8842. Telephone: 949.442.6000.
San Francisco, California Office: Spear Tower, 1 Market Street, 16th Floor, 94105. Telephone: 415.262.4500.
London, England: 2 Serjeants' Inn, EC4Y 1LT. Telephone: +44.20.7583.5353.
Brussels, Belgium: 13th Floor, Avenue Louise 480, 1050. Telephone: +32.2.535.5411.
Paris, France: 55, avenue Kléber, 75116. Telephone: +33.1.53.65.05.00.
Luxembourg: Brucher & Seimetz in association with Dechert, Avocats a la Cour, 10 rue de Vianden, B.P. 709, L-2017. Telephone: +352.45.62.62.
Frankfurt/Main, Germany Office: Mainzer Landstrasse 16, 60325. Telephone: +49.69.971.68.245.
Palo Alto, California Office: 1117 California Avenue, 94304. Telephone: 650.813.4800. Telefax: 650.813.4848.
Munich, Germany Office: Theresienstrasse 6, 830333. Telephone: +49.0.89.21.21.63.0.

Antitrust, Bankruptcy and Reorganization, Business and Technology, Commercial Litigation, Copyrights, Corporate Finance, Competition, Criminal and Civil Fraud, Defamation, Domestic Taxation, Employee Benefits and Executive Compensation, Employment, Environmental, Estate Planning, Financial Services, First Amendment, Government Affairs, Health Care, Intellectual Property, Information Technology, International Business, International Taxation, International Trade, Investment Management, Labor, Life Sciences, Mass Torts, Media, Mergers and Acquisitions, Patent Law and Litigation, Privacy, Private Equity, Products Liability, Real Estate and Mortgage Finance, Retail, Securities Litigation and Enforcement, Securitization, State and Local Taxation, Tax-Exempt Organizations, Trademarks, Venture Capital, White Collar Litigation.

FIRM PROFILE: Dechert is an international law firm with more than 750 lawyers in 17 offices in the United States, the United Kingdom, and Continental Europe. We provide practical business solutions to diverse clients ranging from small technology companies to the world's largest corporations and financial institutions.

Dechert focuses its strong and deep international resources in four broad areas: corporate and securities, with an emphasis on M&A, private equity and technology transactions; litigation, with an emphasis on antitrust, securities, IP, and mass torts; finance and real estate, particularly mortgage and structured finance; and financial services. We are top-ranked in our core areas and for client satisfaction.

The firm also has practices in corporate, tax, bankruptcy, employment, government regulation, and environmental law.

PARTNERS

TIMOTHY J. BOYCE, born New Haven, Connecticut, 1954; admitted to bar, 1979, Connecticut (Not admitted in North Carolina). *Education:* Georgetown University (B.S.F.S., 1975); University of Pennsylvania (M.B.A., 1979; J.D., 1979). Phi Beta Kappa; Phi Alpha Theta; Phi Sigma Alpha. Editor, University of Pennsylvania Law Review, 1978-79. Author: "Hotel Revenues in Bankruptcy: An Analysis and Analytic Framework," ABA Real Property, Probate and Trust Journal, Fall, 1993; "The Supreme Court and the Death of Durrett," Real Estate Law Journal, Winter, 1995; "Financing Senior Living Facilities," ABA Probate and Property, March/April, 1996; "Collateralizing Nonassignable Contracts, Licenses and Permits: Half a Loaf Is Better Than No Loaf," The Business Lawyer, 1997; "Recent Developments in Credit Tenant Loans," Real Estate Review, Winter, 1997. Lecturer: "Real Estate Finance Potpourri," American Bar Association annual meeting, 1995; "Credit Tenant Loans," Mortgage Bankers Association annual meeting, February, 1996; Collateralizing Nonassignable Contracts, Permits and Licenses," American Bar Association annual meeting, 1996; "The World's Third Annual Mortgage Financing Program," American Bar Association annual meeting, 1997; "Workout Issues With Commercial Loan Securitizations," American Bar Association annual meeting, 1999; "Defeasance: What It Is and How It Works," National CLE Conference, 2001. *Member:* Connecticut and American (Member, Real Property, Probate and Trust Law Section; Vice Chair, Committee on Foreclosure and Related Remedies, 1996-99; Vice Chair, Committee on Mortgage Loan Originations, 2001—) Bar Associations; American College of Real Estate Lawyers. ***PRACTICE AREAS:*** Commercial Real Estate; Commercial Leasing; Lease Finance; Real Estate Finance; Leasing. ***Email:*** timothy.boyce@dechert.com

JAMES R. BRYANT, III, born Charlotte, North Carolina, January 9, 1944; admitted to bar, 1969, North Carolina. *Education:* Davidson College (A.B., 1966); University of North Carolina School of Law (J.D., 1969). Member, Board of Directors, University of North Carolina School of Banking and Law Institute, 1997—. Member, Board of Directors, Mecklenburg Bar Foundation, 1998—. *Member:* North Carolina Bar Association (Member, Real Estate Section and the Corporation, Banking and Business Law Section) and American Bar Associations. [Capt., U.S. Army, 1969-1971]. ***Email:*** james.bryant@dechert.com

JOHN M. TIMPERIO, born 1966; admitted to bar, 1991, Massachusetts; 1998, North Carolina. *Education:* University of Pennsylvania (B.A., 1988); Georgetown University Law Center (J.D., 1991). ***PRACTICE AREAS:*** Finance; Real Estate. ***Email:*** john.timperio@dechert.com

ASSOCIATES

KERRI DeRUYTER, admitted to bar, 2003, New York (Not admitted in North Carolina). *Education:* State University of New York at Binghamton (B.A., 1999); Cornell University (J.D., 2002). ***PRACTICE AREAS:*** Finance; Real Estate. ***Email:*** kerri.deruyter@dechert.com

CHRISTOPHER PAUL DUERDEN, born West Palm Beach, Florida, July 11, 1980; admitted to bar, 2004, North Carolina. *Education:* University of North Carolina at Chapel Hill (B.A., highest distinction honors, Phi Beta Kappa, 2001; J.D., 2004). ***PRACTICE AREAS:*** Business; Finance; Real Estate. ***Email:*** christopher.duerden@dechert.com

(This Listing Continued)

DECHERT LLP, Charlotte—Continued

VICTORIA S. DURHAM, admitted to bar, 1996, Tennessee (Not admitted in North Carolina). *Education:* Furman University (B.A., 1992); University of Tennessee (J.D., 1996). ***PRACTICE AREAS:*** Finance; Real Estate. ***Email:*** victoria.durham@dechert.com

DAVID GRAHAM FINE, born Durham, North Carolina, January 6, 1978; admitted to bar, 2003, North Carolina. *Education:* Yale University (B.A., 2000); Wake Forest University (J.D., 2003). ***PRACTICE AREAS:*** Finance; Real Estate. ***Email:*** david.fine@dechert.com

GERALD F. KEEFE, born Lexington, Kentucky, October 21, 1971; admitted to bar, 2000, New York and District of Columbia; 2002, North Carolina. *Education:* Tulane University (B.A., 1993); George Washington University (J.D., 1998). ***LANGUAGES:*** French. ***PRACTICE AREAS:*** Business; Corporate Law; Corporate Real Estate; Structured Finance; Real Estate. ***Email:*** gerald.keefe@dechert.com

DONALD L. LANCASTER, admitted to bar, 1996, Massachusetts; 1997, New York (Not admitted in North Carolina). *Education:* Trinity College, University of Dublin (B.B.S., 1991); Boston University (J.D., cum laude, 1996: LL.M., banking and finance, 2004). ***PRACTICE AREAS:*** Business. ***Email:*** donald.lancaster@dechert.com

W. TODD STILLERMAN, born Raleigh, North Carolina, August 31, 1971; admitted to bar, 1997, North Carolina. *Education:* Wake Forest University (B.A., 1994); Harvard University Law School (J.D., 1997). ***Email:*** todd.stillerman@dechert.com

COUNSEL

FREDERICK H. SHERLEY, admitted to bar, 1996, New York; 1998, District of Columbia (Not admitted in North Carolina). *Education:* University of Pennsylvania (B.A., 1992); Duke University (J.D., 1995). ***Email:*** frederick.sherely@dechert.com

(Members of the Firm, Counsel, Of Counsel and Associates in Philadelphia, Harrisburg, Pennsylvania; New York, New York; Washington, D.C.; Boston, Massachusetts; Newport Beach, California; Princeton, New Jersey; Hartford, Connecticut; London, England; Brussels, Belgium; Paris, France; Munich, Germany and Luxembourg are listed in the Biographical Section respectively.)

LAW OFFICES OF MICHAEL A. DEMAYO, L.L.P.

741 KENILWORTH (PARK PLAZA), SUITE 100
P.O. BOX 34426
CHARLOTTE, NORTH CAROLINA 28204
Telephone: 704-333-1000
Fax: 704-333-6677
URL: http://www.demayolaw.com
URL: http://www.michaeldemayo.com

Hickory, North Carolina Office: 321 Third Avenue, N.W., 28601. Telephone: 828-345-1111. Fax: 828-345-1112.
Monroe, North Carolina Office: 406 South Sutherland Avenue, 28112. Telephone: 704-291-9200. Fax: 704-291-9292.

Personal Injury, Automobile Accidents, Motorcycle Accidents, Wrongful Death, Brain Injury, Medical Malpractice, Worker's Compensation, Pharmaceutical Litigation, Nursing Home Litigation.

MICHAEL A. DEMAYO, born Silver Spring, Maryland, January 1, 1965; admitted to bar, 1991, North Carolina and U.S. District Court, Western and Middle Districts of North Carolina. *Education:* Wake Forest University (B.A., cum laude, 1987); University of North Carolina (J.D., 1990). Phi Alpha Delta. Moot Court Board, Craven Chairman, 1990. Order of the Barristers. Member, Million Dollar Advocates Forum. *Member:* Mecklenburg County, North Carolina and American Bar Associations; North Carolina State Bar (Member: A.T.L.A. Eagle Club; Brain Injury Foundation); North Carolina Academy of Trial Lawyers (Benefactor); Mecklenburg Trial Lawyers Association (Founding Member); Association of Trial Lawyers of America (Presidents Club; Chairman, Marketing Committee); Bobbitt Inns of Court. (Also at Hickory and Monroe Offices). ***LANGUAGES:*** Spanish. ***PRACTICE AREAS:*** Personal Injury; Wrongful Death; Brain Injury; Medical Malpractice; Workers Compensation; Pharmaceutical Litigation; Nursing Home Litigation. ***Email:*** Michael@DeMayoLaw.com

FRANK F. VOLER, born Novi Sad, Yugoslavia, February 16, 1959; admitted to bar, 1990, North Carolina; 1998, South Carolina. *Education:* United States Naval Academy (B.S.M.E., 1981); University of North Carolina at Chapel Hill (J.D., with honors, 1990); North Carolina Journal of International Law and Commercial Regulation (1989-1990). *Member:* North Carolina, South Carolina and American Bar Associations; North Carolina Academy of Trial Lawyers. [CDR, USNR(ret), Nuclear Trained Submarine Officer, 1981-1986]. ***LANGUAGES:*** Serbo-Croatian. ***PRACTICE AREAS:*** Civil Trials; Civil Appeals; Personal Injury; Wrongful Death; Brain Injury; Medical Malpractice. ***Email:*** Frank@demayolaw.com

---

DEVORE ACTON & STAFFORD, P.A.

831 EAST MOREHEAD STREET, SUITE 245
CHARLOTTE, NORTH CAROLINA 28202-2773
Telephone: 704-377-5242
Facsimile: 704-332-2825
Email: firm@devact.com
URL: http://www.devact.com

General Civil Trial Practice in State and Federal Courts. Personal Injury, Wrongful Death, Automobile Accidents, Workers Compensation, Medical Malpractice, Insurance Bad Faith, Construction Law, Commercial Litigation, Products Liability Litigation.

(This Listing Continued)

FIRM PROFILE: We represent clients throughout North Carolina, but especially Mecklenburg, Catawba, Iredell, Union, Cabarrus, Gaston, Cleveland and Lincoln counties.

In 2004, our firm recovered over ten million dollars ($10,000,000) in settlements and verdicts for our clients. However, our firm also provides consulting and defense representation for physicians, contractors and even other law firms.

Please feel free to submit an email inquiry to one of our attorneys. Depending on the type of case, both hourly and contingency fee contracts are available.

FRED W. DEVORE, III, born Charlotte, North Carolina, May 24, 1953; admitted to bar, 1982, North Carolina; U.S. District Court, Western District of North Carolina; U.S. Court of Appeals, Fourth Circuit; U.S. Supreme Court. *Education:* University of North Carolina (B.A., 1975; M.A., 1977); Wake Forest University (J.D., 1982). Order of the Barristers. *Member:* Mecklenburg County, North Carolina and American Bar Associations; North Carolina State Bar; North Carolina Academy of Trial Lawyers; Bobbitt Inns of Court; The Association of Trial Lawyers of America (Co-Chair, Construction Defects Litigation Group). ***PRACTICE AREAS:*** Personal Injury; Construction Law; Contract; Product Liability; Medical Malpractice; Insurance Bad Faith; ERISA/Insurance Claims; Investment Fraud; Condemnation. ***Email:*** fdevore@devact.com

WILLIAM D. ACTON, JR., born Raleigh, North Carolina, April 11, 1952; admitted to bar, 1977, North Carolina and U.S. District Court, Western District of North Carolina; U.S. Court of Appeals, Fourth Circuit; U.S. Supreme Court. *Education:* North Carolina State University (B.A., 1974); North Carolina Central University (J.D., 1977). *Member:* Mecklenburg County and North Carolina Bar Associations; North Carolina State Bar; North Carolina Academy of Trial Lawyers; The Association of Trial Lawyers of America. (Board Certified Specialist in Workers' Compensation, North Carolina State Board of Legal Specialization). ***PRACTICE AREAS:*** Workers Compensation; Personal Injury. ***Email:*** bacton@devact.com

TROY J. STAFFORD, born Baton Rouge, Louisiana, January 11, 1966; admitted to bar, 1991, North Carolina and U.S. District Court, Western District of North Carolina; U.S. Court of Appeals, Fourth Circuit. *Education:* Louisiana State University (B.A., 1986); Campbell University (J.D., 1991). Delta Theta Phi; Eta Sigma Phi. *Member:* Mecklenburg County, North Carolina and American Bar Associations; North Carolina State Bar; North Carolina Academy of Trial Lawyers; The Association of Trial Lawyers of America; American Inns of Court. ***PRACTICE AREAS:*** Civil Litigation; Medical Malpractice; Personal Injury; Wrongful Death; Contract Litigation; Insurance Litigation; Construction Law. ***Email:*** tstafford@devact.com

REPRESENTATIVE CLIENTS: Beazer Homes; Independence Nissan; John Wieland Homes, Inc.; Piedmont Natural Gas; Portrait Homes.

DICKIE, MCCAMEY & CHILCOTE, P.C.

212 SOUTH TRYON STREET
SUITE 465
CHARLOTTE, NORTH CAROLINA 28281-0007
Telephone: 704-334-1108
Fax: 704-334-1163
URL: http://www.dmclaw.com

Pittsburgh, Pennsylvania Office: Two PPG Place, Suite 400, 15222-5402. Telephone: 412-281-7272. Fax: 412-392-5367.
Camp Hill, Pennsylvania Office: 1200 Camp Hill Bypass, Suite 205, 17011-3700. Telephone: 717-731-4800. Fax: 717-731-4803.
Philadelphia, Pennsylvania Office: Public Ledger Building, Suite 901, 150 South Independence Mall, West, 19106-3409. Telephone: 215-925-2289. Fax: 215-925-0307.
Washington, D.C. Office: 1301 Pennsylvania Avenue, N.W., Suite 1000, 20004-1707. Telephone: 1-888-434-5566.
Haddonfield, New Jersey Office: 30 N. Haddon Avenue, Suite 100, 08033-2429. Telephone: 856-354-0192. Fax: 856-354-8164.
Steubenville, Ohio Office: Dickie, McCamey & Chilcote, A Professional Corporation, 401 Market Street, Suite 401, 43952-2846. Telephone: 740-284-1682. Fax: 740-284-1692.
Wheeling, West Virginia Office: Dickie, McCamey & Chilcote, L.C., 1233 Main Street, Suite 2002, 26003-2839. Telephone: 304-233-1022. Fax: 304-233-1026.

General Practice including Alternative Dispute Resolution; Appellate Advocacy; Antitrust; Asbestos; Bad Faith; Bankruptcy; Business Law; Business Torts; Civil Litigation; Class Actions; Commercial Agreements; Commercial Litigation; Commercial Transactions; Compliance Programs; Construction Law; Contract Disputes; Contract Drafting; Corporate Compliance; Computer Law; Corporate Finance; Corporate Governance; Corporate Law; Corporate Services; Creditors' Rights; Education Law; Employment Law; Environmental Law; Estate Planning and Administration; Estates and Trusts; Family Law; First Amendment/Defamation; Finance Law and Financial Institutions; Food and Beverage; General Liability; Health Law Business; Insurance Defense; Insurance Law and Litigation; Insurance and Risk Management; Intellectual Property; Labor Law; Lender Liability; Licenses; Litigation; Medical Malpractice Defense; Mergers and Acquisitions; Product Liability; Professional Liability; Real Estate Transactions; Securities; Silica; Surety; Technology Law; Technology Transfer; Telecommunications; Toxic Tort; Transportation Law; White Collar Crime; Workers' Compensation.

FIRM PROFILE: Dickie, McCamey & Chilcote is a nationally recognized litigation firm providing comprehensive legal expertise, as well as non-litigation services, in a multitude of practice areas. The firm has grown to include offices in Harrisburg (Camp Hill), Philadelphia, Washington D.C., New Jersey, North Carolina, Ohio and West Virginia to serve industry-leading clients across the country. For more information, please visit www.dmclaw.com.

SHAREHOLDER

THOMAS P. LUTZ, admitted to bar, 1974, Pennsylvania; 2001, New York and North Carolina; 2002, West Virginia; 2003, Ohio and U.S. District Court, Western District of Pennsylvania. *Education:* Lehigh University (B.S., 1968); University of Pittsburgh

(This Listing Continued)

(M.B.A., 1975; J.D., 1974). Certified Public Accountant, Pennsylvania, 1977. *Member:* Allegheny County, North Carolina, Ohio, Pennsylvania (Member, Corporate and Probate and Trust Law Sections) and American Bar Associations; West Virginia State Bar; Estate Planning Counsel of Pittsburgh; Allegheny Tax Society; Pennsylvania Institute of Certified Public Accountants; American Institute of Certified Public Accountants; American College of Trust and Estate Counsel. [1st Lt., Adjutant General Corps, 1968-1971]. (Shareholder-in-Charge) (Also at Pittsburgh, Pennsylvania Office). ***PRACTICE AREAS:*** Estate Litigation; Family Wealth Transfer; Business Planning; Tax Planning; Retirement Planning; Trusts and Estates; Trust Litigation; Shareholders Law; Financing. ***Email:*** TLutz@dmclaw.com

ASSOCIATE

JOHN N. COX, admitted to bar, 1992, Pennsylvania; 1993, West Virginia; 1998, North Carolina; U.S. District Court, Western District of Pennsylvania; U.S. District Court, Eastern, Middle and Western Districts of North Carolina; U.S. District Court, Northern and Southern Districts of West Virginia; U.S. Court of Appeals, District of Columbia, Third and Fourth Circuits; U.S. Supreme Court; registered to practice before U.S. Patent and Trademark Office. *Education:* North Carolina State University (B.S., Chemical Engineering, magna cum laude, 1980); University of Pittsburgh (J.D., cum laude, 1992). Tau Beta Pi. Associate Editor, Journal of Law and Commerce, 1991-1992. *Member:* Mecklenburg County and North Carolina Bar Associations; American Institute of Chemical Engineers; American Society for Testing and Materials. ***PRACTICE AREAS:*** Food Products Liability; Insurance Defense; Toxic Torts; Environmental Law. ***Email:*** JCox@dmclaw.com

(For complete biographical data on personnel at Pittsburgh, Camp Hill and Philadelphia, Pennsylvania; Haddonfield, New Jersey; Charlotte, North Carolina; Steubenville, Ohio; and Wheeling, West Virginia, see Professional Biographies at those locations)

DOUGHERTY, CLEMENTS, HOFER & BERNARD

Established in 1983

1901 ROXBOROUGH ROAD, SUITE 300
CHARLOTTE, NORTH CAROLINA 28211
Telephone: 704-366-6642
Fax: 704-366-9744
URL: http://www.lawyers.com/dougherty&clements
Email: patlaw@worldpatents.com
URL: http://www.worldpatents.com

Intellectual Property Matters including Patent, Trademark, Copyright, Trade Secret, Licensing, Litigation and Computer Law.

FIRM PROFILE: The law firm of Dougherty, Clements, Hofer & Bernard serves companies and individuals seeking to protect, commercialize, transfer, license and profit from intellectual property in North America and throughout the world. We manage the legal processes of patents, trademarks and copyrights and provide counsel in all related matters, including trade secrets and unfair competition.

MEMBERS OF FIRM

RALPH H. DOUGHERTY, born Muskegon, Michigan, March 30, 1935; admitted to bar, 1969, Pennsylvania; 1976, North Carolina; 1988, District of Columbia; U.S. District Court, Western District of Wisconsin; U.S. Supreme Court; registered to practice before U.S. Patent and Trademark Office and Canadian Patent Office. *Education:* Colorado School of Mines (Metallurgical Engineer, 1956); Duquesne University (J.D., 1969). Phi Alpha Delta. Vice President, Optimist International, 1987-1989. *Member:* Mecklenburg County Bar Association; North Carolina State Bar; District of Columbia Bar; American Intellectual Property Law Association; Licensing Executives Society USA/Canada; Carolina Patent, Trademark and Copyright Law Association; Pittsburgh Intellectual Property Law Association; U.S. Bar-Japan Patent Office Liaison Council; The American Group of L'Association Internationale Pour La Protection de Le Propriete Industrielle; American Society for Metals; Society of Mining Engineers. ***PRACTICE AREAS:*** Patents; Trademarks; Copyrights; Trade Secrets. ***Email:*** rdougherty@worldpatents.com

GREGORY N. CLEMENTS, born Owensboro, Kentucky, March 19, 1951; admitted to bar, 1981, Virginia; 1984, Ohio; 1998, North Carolina; U.S. District Court, Western District of North Carolina; U.S. Court of Appeals, Fourth, Fifth, Sixth and Federal Circuits; registered to practice before U.S. Patent and Trademark Office. *Education:* University of Cincinnati (B.S., Chemical Engineering, 1974); George Mason University, School of Law (J.D., 1981). Delta Theta Phi. *Member:* North Carolina State Bar; District of Columbia Bar; American Intellectual Property Law Association; Carolina Patents, Trademark and Copyright Law Association; Licensing Executives Society. ***LANGUAGES:*** German. ***PRACTICE AREAS:*** Patents; Trademarks; Copyrights; Litigation. ***Email:*** gclements@worldpatents.com

RONALD L. HOFER, born Madison, South Dakota, October 1, 1944; admitted to bar, 1972, Iowa and Ohio; 1977, Michigan; U.S. District Court, Eastern District of Michigan; 2000, North Carolina; U.S. District Court, Western District of North Carolina; U.S. Court of Appeals, Sixth Circuit; registered to practice before U.S. Patent and Trademark Office. *Education:* Harvard University (A.B. Chemistry, 1967); University of Iowa (J.D., cum laude, 1972). Phi Alpha Delta. *Member:* State Bar of Michigan; North Carolina and American Bar Associations; Carolina Patent, Trademark and Copyright Law Association; American Intellectual Property Law Association; Lawyer Pilots Bar Association. [Captain, USMCR, 1967-1972]. ***PRACTICE AREAS:*** Patents; Trademarks; Copyrights; Trade Secrets; Litigation; Aviation Law. ***Email:*** rhofer@worldpatents.com

CHRISTOPHER L. BERNARD, born Rochester, New York, February 27, 1971; admitted to bar, 1996, Michigan; 2001, North Carolina; registered to practice before the U.S. Patent and Trademark Office. *Education:* University of Michigan (B.S.E., magna cum laude, Aerospace Engineering, 1993); Northwestern University (J.D., 1996); Arizona State University (Graduate Program, Aeronautical Management Technology). Sigma Gamma Tau. *Member:* State Bar of Michigan; North Carolina State Bar. ***PRACTICE AREAS:*** Patents; Trademarks; Copyrights.

(This Listing Continued)

ASSOCIATES

BRANDON G. WILLIAMS, born Irving, Texas, September 27, 1973; admitted to bar, 2002, Texas; registered to practice before U.S. Patent and Trademark Office (Not admitted in North Carolina). *Education:* University of Texas at Austin (B.S., 1997); Texas Wesleyan University School of Law (J.D., 2002). ***PRACTICE AREAS:*** Intellectual Property; Patents; Trademarks; Copyrights. ***Email:*** bwilliams@worldpatents.com

RUSSELL RACINE, born Spartanburg, South Carolina, July 3, 1971; admitted to bar, 1999, Colorado; 2000, South Carolina (Not admitted in North Carolina). *Education:* Muhlenberg College (B.S., 1993); University of Denver (J.D., 1999). ***PRACTICE AREAS:*** Intellectual Property Litigation. ***Email:*** racine@worldpatents.com

LEGAL SUPPORT PERSONNEL

F. RHETT BROCKINGTON, PH.D., (Patent Agent)

REPRESENTATIVE CLIENTS: Arteva Technologies SARL; Arteva Specialty S.de R.L. de C.V.; Azdel, Inc.; Devant Limited; Drinkard Metalox, Inc.; Fraunhofer-Gesellschaft zur Forderung der angewandten Forshung e. V.; Hapad, Inc.; KoSa; Reeves Brothers Inc.; Midrex Technology Inc.; Mirth, Inc.; Sound Choice; The Bolt Group; Vooner-Flowgard, Inc.; Zia Metallurgical Processes, Inc.; Techint Compagnia Technia Internzionale; General Electric Company; FIA Orthopedics.

DOZIER, MILLER, POLLARD & MURPHY, LLP

Established in 1979

CAMERON BROWN BUILDING
301 SOUTH MCDOWELL STREET, SUITE 700
CHARLOTTE, NORTH CAROLINA 28204
Telephone: 704-372-6373
Fax: 704-347-0674
URL: http://www.lawcharlotte.com

General Civil and Criminal Trial Practice in all State and Federal Courts. Plaintiffs Personal Injury and Wrongful Death, Hazardous Products Liability (Aviation, Motor Vehicles), Medical Malpractice, Domestic Relations, Immigration and Naturalization Law, Business and Corporate Law, Sales and Acquisitions, Banking Litigation, Collections., Bankruptcy, Estate Planning and Probate.

FIRM PROFILE: One of the preeminent law firms in North Carolina, Dozier, Miller, Pollard & Murphy, LLP represents individuals and businesses who have suffered injuries or damages as a result of wrongful acts or omissions. We pride ourselves on our ability to meet and exceed our clients' expectations.

The firm has obtained substantial dollar verdicts and settlements for its clients, including multi-million dollar recoveries in aviation crash, automobile accident, medical malpractice, and patent license infringement cases.

Banks, public and private corporations, merchants and entrepreneurs seek our advice and counsel. Our business attorneys provide solutions to complicated business problems. Our civil litigators give the other side an opportunity to settle, but if they refuse, we take them to court.

Several of our attorneys are former prosecutors and successfully defend our clients when they are accused of violating the law. Our family law, immigration, and estate attorneys have decades of experience and strive to find innovative, effective and practical solutions to our clients' problems.

MEMBERS OF FIRM

W. JOSEPH DOZIER, JR., born Richmond, Virginia, June 11, 1948; admitted to bar, 1973, North Carolina and U.S. District Court, Eastern, Middle and Western Districts of North Carolina. *Education:* Washington & Lee University (B.A., 1970); University of North Carolina (J.D., 1973). Phi Delta Phi. Assistant District Attorney, 26th Judicial District, 1973-1979. Member, 1981-1984 and Chairman, 1983-1984, Mecklenburg County Civil Service Board. *Member:* North Carolina and American Bar Associations; 26th Judicial District (President, Young Lawyers Section, 1980-1981) and North Carolina State Bars; North Carolina Academy of Trial Lawyers; The Association of Trial Lawyers of America. ***PRACTICE AREAS:*** Civil Litigation; Personal Injury; Medical Malpractice; Products Liability. ***Email:*** jdozier@dmpm.com

R. CRAIG MILLER, JR., born Raleigh, North Carolina, June 24, 1948; admitted to bar, 1975, North Carolina and U.S. District Court, Western District of North Carolina. *Education:* Université de Lyon, Lyons, France; University of North Carolina (A.B., 1970; J.D., 1975). *Member:* North Carolina Bar Association; 26th Judicial District and North Carolina State Bars. ***LANGUAGES:*** French. ***PRACTICE AREAS:*** Business and Corporate Law; Business Sales and Acquisitions; Estate Planning; Wills; Estate Administration. ***Email:*** cmiller@dmpm.com

SCOTT T. POLLARD, born Burlington, North Carolina, September 28, 1949; admitted to bar, 1974, North Carolina and U.S. District Court, Western District of North Carolina. *Education:* University of North Carolina (B.S., 1971; J.D., 1974). Phi Beta Kappa; Phi Beta Phi. *Member:* North Carolina Bar Association; 26th Judicial District and North Carolina State Bars; North Carolina Academy of Trial Lawyers. ***PRACTICE AREAS:*** Domestic Relations; Civil Litigation; Personal Injury. ***Email:*** spollard@dmpm.com

GARY L. MURPHY, born Greensboro, North Carolina, March 2, 1948; admitted to bar, 1974, North Carolina; U.S. District Court, Eastern, Middle and Western Districts of North Carolina. *Education:* Washington & Lee University (B.A., 1970); University of North Carolina (J.D., 1974). Research Assistant to the: Honorable Carlisle W. Higgins, Associate Justice, North Carolina Supreme Court, Fall Term, 1974; Honorable James G. Exum, Jr., Associate Justice, North Carolina Supreme Court, Spring Term, 1975. Assistant District Attorney, 26th Judicial District, North Carolina, 1975-1980. *Member:* North Carolina Bar Association (Criminal Justice Section); 26th Judicial District and North Carolina State Bars; North Carolina Academy of Trial Lawyers; National Association of Criminal Defense Lawyers. [With USMC Reserves, 1970-1976]. (Board Certified Specialist in

(This Listing Continued)

DOZIER, MILLER, POLLARD & MURPHY, LLP, Charlotte—Continued

Criminal Law, North Carolina State Board of Legal Specialization). ***PRACTICE AREAS:*** Criminal Litigation (State and Federal Courts); Drug Crimes; White Collar Crimes; Felonies; Misdemeanors; Traffic Violations; Driving While Intoxicated. ***Email:*** gmurphy@dmpm.com

TIMOTHY H. GRAHAM, born Charlotte, North Carolina, September 5, 1961; admitted to bar, 1986, North Carolina and U.S. District Court, Western District of North Carolina; 1987, U.S. Court of Appeals, Fourth Circuit. *Education:* Appalachian State University (B.S., 1983); Campbell University (J.D., cum laude, 1986). Phi Kappa Phi; Omicron Delta Kappa. Member, Order of the Barristers. Notes and Comments Editor, Campbell Law Review, 1986. Recipient: West Hornbook Award, 1985 and 1986; American Jurisprudence Book Award: Property I, Contracts II, Administrative Law, Family Law, Wills and Trusts I, Trial Advocacy, Uniform Commercial Code II. Author: Note, "The Contingent Fee in Domestic Relations Cases-Thompson v. Thompson," 7 Campbell Law Review 427, Summer 1985. *Member:* Mecklenburg County (Member, Family Law Section) North Carolina (Member, Family Law Section) and American Bar Associations; 26th Judicial District and North Carolina State Bars. ***PRACTICE AREAS:*** Civil Litigation; Domestic Relations; Personal Injury. ***Email:*** tgraham@dmpm.com

GEORGE N. MILLER, born Charlotte, North Carolina, July 4, 1960; admitted to bar, 1986, North Carolina and U.S. District Court, Western and Middle Districts of North Carolina. *Education:* University of North Carolina (B.S., 1982); Campbell University (J.D., 1986). *Member:* Mecklenburg County (Member, Board of Directors) and North Carolina (Member Immigration and Nationality Law Committee) Bar Associations; 26th Judicial District and North Carolina State Bars; North Carolina Academy of Trial Lawyers; American Immigration Lawyers Association. (Board Certified Specialist in Immigration and Nationality Law, North Carolina State Board of Legal Specialization). ***PRACTICE AREAS:*** Immigration and Naturalization Law; Criminal Defense. ***Email:*** gmiller@dmpm.com

RICHARD S. GORDON, born Charlotte, North Carolina, October 19, 1945; admitted to bar, 1970, North Carolina; 1971, U.S. Court of Military Appeals; 1973, U.S. District Court, Western District of North Carolina; 1982, U.S. Court of Appeals, Fourth Circuit; 1986, U.S. Supreme Court. *Education:* Wake Forest University (B.A., cum laude, 1967; J.D., 1970). Phi Alpha Delta. Assistant District Attorney, 26th Judicial District, 1974-1982 and 1991-1997. Assistant U.S. Attorney, Western District of North Carolina, 1982. *Member:* North Carolina Bar Association; 26th Judicial District and North Carolina State Bars. [Capt., U.S.M.C., 1970-1974]. ***PRACTICE AREAS:*** Business Litigation; Bankruptcy; Debtor and Creditor; Appellate Practice; White Collar Crime. ***Email:*** rgordon@dmpm.com

THOMAS J. FALISH, born Jersey City, New Jersey, July 21, 1963; admitted to bar, 1989, North Carolina and U.S. District Court, Middle District of North Carolina; 1994, U.S. District Court, Western District of North Carolina. *Education:* University of North Carolina (B.S., 1985); Duke University (J.D., 1989); University of North Carolina at Greensboro (M.B.A., 1996). Phi Beta Kappa; Beta Gamma Sigma. *Member:* North Carolina Bar Association; North Carolina State Bar. ***PRACTICE AREAS:*** Business and Corporate Law; Business Sales and Acquisitions; Estate Planning; Estate Administration. ***Email:*** tfalish@dmpm.com

JOHN C. NIPP, born Doylestown, Pennsylvania, December 21, 1970; admitted to bar, 1996, North Carolina; 2001, U.S. District Court, Western District of North Carolina. *Education:* University of North Carolina at Chapel Hill (B.A., 1993; J.D., with honors, 1996). Phi Alpha Delta; Pi Sigma Alpha. Member, Negotiation Team, Holderness Moot Court. Assistant District Attorney, Eleventh Judicial District of North Carolina, 1996-1998. *Member:* Mecklenburg County, 26th Judicial District, North Carolina and American Bar Associations; North Carolina State Bar; North Carolina Academy of Trial Lawyers; Association of Trial Lawyers of America. ***PRACTICE AREAS:*** Civil Litigation; Negligence; Unfair Competition; Intellectual Property. ***Email:*** jnipp@dmpm.com

ANNE DUNTON LAM, born Elgin, Illinois, September 21, 1976; admitted to bar, 2002, North Carolina and U.S. District Court, Western District of North Carolina. *Education:* Duke University (B.A., cum laude, 1999); University of North Carolina at Chapel Hill School of Law (J.D., 2002). Order of the Barristers. Fellow, Delta Gamma Foundation, 2000-2001, 2001-2002. Member, Negotiation Team, Holderness Moot Court Bench. Recipient, Second Place, National Negotiation Competition, American Bar Association, 2002. Author: "Student Threats and the First Amendment," School Law Bulletin, Spring, 2002. *Member:* Mecklenburg County (Member: Family Law Section; Young Lawyers Division), 26th Judicial District, North Carolina and American Bar Associations; North Carolina State Bar. ***PRACTICE AREAS:*** Domestic Relations; Civil Litigation. ***Email:*** alam@dmpm.com

E. KENNETH COBLE, born Cypress Creek, North Carolina, October 17, 1977; admitted to bar, 2003, North Carolina and U.S. District Court, Western District of North Carolina. *Education:* University of North Carolina at Chapel Hill (B.A., with distinction, 2000; J.D., 2003). Phi Beta Kappa. Member, North Carolina Banking Institute Journal, 2001-2002. *Member:* North Carolina State Bar. ***PRACTICE AREAS:*** Personal Injury; Wrongful Death; Commercial Litigation; Business Litigation. ***Email:*** kcoble@dmpm.com

OF COUNSEL

WILLIAM PATRICK HOBSON, born Dunn, North Carolina, November 14, 1941; admitted to bar, 1971, North Carolina and U.S. District Court, Western District of North Carolina. *Education:* University of North Carolina (A.B., 1964; J.D., 1971). *Member:* North Carolina Bar Association; 26th Judicial District and North Carolina State Bars. [U.S. Army, 1965-1968]. ***PRACTICE AREAS:*** Estate Administration; Probate. ***Email:*** willieph@infionline.net

REPRESENTATIVE CLIENTS: American Community Bank; Aviation Metals, Inc; First Trust Bank; United Sprit, Inc; Loeffler Ketchum Mountjoy; Petro Express, Inc.; Tyler II Construction, Inc.

ELAM & ROUSSEAUX, P.A.

128-A N. MCDOWELL STREET (28204)
P.O. BOX 30457
CHARLOTTE, NORTH CAROLINA 28230
Telephone: 704-343-0000
Facsimile: 704-343-9992
URL: http://www.er-lawfirm.com
Mailing Address: P.O. Box 30457, Charlotte, NC 28230

Medical Malpractice, Nursing Home Abuse and Neglect, Professional Malpractice, Wrongful Death.

FIRM PROFILE: Elam & Rousseaux, P.A., has two Medical Doctors and a Registered Nurse as staff consultants.

WILLIAM H. ELAM, born Charlotte, North Carolina, June 28, 1946; admitted to bar, 1972, North Carolina and U.S. District Court, Eastern, Middle and Western Districts of North Carolina; 1975, U.S. Court of Appeals, 4th Circuit and U.S. Supreme Court. *Education:* East Carolina University (A.B., 1967); University of South Carolina (J.D., 1972). *Member:* Mecklenburg County and American Bar Associations; North Carolina State Bar; North Carolina Academy of Trial Lawyers; The Association of Trial Lawyers of America. (Board Certified, Civil Trial Advocacy, Specialist by the National Board of Trial Advocacy). ***PRACTICE AREAS:*** Medical Malpractice; Nursing Home Abuse and Neglect. ***Email:*** welam@er-lawfirm.com

MICHAEL J. ROUSSEAUX, born Madrid, Spain, 1965; admitted to bar, 1990, North Carolina and U.S. District Court, Eastern and Western Districts of North Carolina; 1993, U.S. Court of Appeals, 4th Circuit. *Education:* Gardner-Webb College (B.S. in Accounting, cum laude, 1987); Campbell University (J.D., 1990). Order of the Barristers. *Member:* North Carolina State Bar; Mecklenburg and North Carolina Bar Associations; North Carolina Academy of Trial Lawyers. ***PRACTICE AREAS:*** Medical Malpractice; Professional Malpractice; Wrongful Death. ***Email:*** mrousseaux@er-lawfirm.com

ELLIOTT LAW FIRM, P.C.

CHARLOTTE, NORTH CAROLINA

(See Huntersville)

Business Law, Limited Liability Company Law, Incorporations, Corporate Law, Mergers and Acquisitions, Tax Law, Real Estate, Construction Law, Trusts and Estates, Asset Protection, Estate Planning, Guardianship, Bankruptcy, Traffic Violations.

ELLZEY & BROOKS, LLC

CHARLOTTE, NORTH CAROLINA

(See Fisher & Phillips LLP)

ERDMAN AND HOCKFIELD, LLP

Established in 1981

2300 EAST SEVENTH STREET, SUITE 100
CHARLOTTE, NORTH CAROLINA 28204-4366
Telephone: 704-333-7800
Fax: 704-343-2886
URL: http://www.lawyers.com/charlotte-nc-law

General Civil Practice. Business Law, Corporate Law, Personal Injury, Family, Marital, Domestic and Matrimonial Law, Commercial Real Estate, Land Use and Zoning. Trial Practice in all State and Federal Courts.

FIRM PROFILE: We are committed to providing our business, domestic and litigation clients with quality legal work through experienced attorneys who are well-known and highly respected in the Charlotte area. Our trial lawyers strive to resolve business and individual disputes whether in the courtroom or through alternative dispute resolution. Our firm size allows efficient, personal attention. Using the latest technology, we provide our clients, large and small, with quality legal services. We are responsive. When seeking legal representation in the Charlotte region, many law firms make us their first referral choice.

DAVID W. ERDMAN, born Camp LeJeune, North Carolina, July 4, 1949; admitted to bar, 1975, North Carolina and U.S. District Court, Western District of North Carolina. *Education:* Duke University (B.S.E., 1971); Georgetown University (J.D., 1975). National President, A.B.A. Law Student Division, 1974-1975. Charlotte City Council At-Large Member, 1999. Member: North Carolina Employment Security Commission, 1978-1982; North Carolina OSHA Review Board, 1982-1985. *Member:* 26th Judicial District and North Carolina State Bars; North Carolina and American Bar Associations; North Carolina Academy of Trial Lawyers; The Association of Trial Lawyers of America. ***PRACTICE AREAS:*** Commercial Litigation; Civil Litigation; Accidents; Personal Injury; Land Use; Zoning Law; Condemnation; Contested Wills; Family; Marital; Domestic; Matrimonial Law. ***Email:*** erdman@charlotte-nc-law.com

STEVEN A. HOCKFIELD, born Durham, North Carolina, July 7, 1945; admitted to bar, 1970, North Carolina and U.S. District Court, Western District of North Carolina. *Education:* University of North Carolina (B.S., 1967; J.D., 1970). Phi Beta Kappa; Beta Gamma Sigma; Phi Alpha Delta. Business North Carolina, 2005 Legal Elite, Business Law. Member, State Banking Commission, 1979-1987. Member, Board of Visitors, University of North Carolina at Chapel Hill, 2003—. *Member:* 26th Judicial District and North Carolina State Bars; North Carolina and American Bar Associations; ABA Forum on Franchising; North Carolina Association of Certified Public Accountants. ***PRACTICE AREAS:*** Business, Commercial and Corporate Law; Contract Law; Litigation; Franchise Law. ***Email:*** hockfield@charlotte-nc-law.com

(This Listing Continued)

ASSOCIATE

LINA E. JAMES, born Kerala, India, July 9, 1971; admitted to bar, 1998, North Carolina. *Education:* University of North Carolina at Chapel Hill (B.A., 1993); Loyola University (J.D., 1997). Moot Court. Co-Chair, Mecklenburg County Bar Lawyer Referral Service, 2004—. Board Member, A Child's Place, 2003—. Faculty Consultant, U.S. Department of Justice National Drug Court Institute, 2002—. Board Member, Centralina Development Corporation, 2000-2001. *Member:* 26th Judicial District and North Carolina State Bars; North Carolina Bar Association; Mecklenburg County Criminal Defense Lawyers Association. ***PRACTICE AREAS:*** Civil Litigation; Personal Injury; Domestic Relations; Criminal Litigation; Contracts; General Practice. ***Email:*** james@charlotte-nc-law.com

REPRESENTATIVE CLIENTS: Childress Klein Properties; Corcoran Properties; Distribution Technology, Inc.; Erwin Capital, Inc.; IFB Transportation Systems, Inc.; Piedmont Distribution Centers; Radiator Specialty Company; Record Storage Systems; The Rosen Group, Inc.; TechnoCom Fine Copiers & Facsimiles; Tribek Properties.
APPROVED ATTORNEYS FOR: First American Title of the Carolinas; Lawyers Title Insurance Corp.
REFERENCE: RBC Centura Bank.

ERWIN AND ELEAZER, P.A.

831 EAST MOREHEAD STREET
840
CHARLOTTE, NORTH CAROLINA 28202
Telephone: 704-369-7900
Facsimile: 704-335-5433
Email: ferwin@eelaw.net
URL: http://www.lawyers.com/eelaw

General Civil Law, Corporate and Commercial Litigation, Construction, Negligence and Personal Injury Litigation, Bankruptcy.

FIRM PROFILE: The firm's principal areas of practice are catastrophic injury, construction, negligence law in litigation, arbitration, mediation and administrative proceedings in all State and Federal Courts. It's lawyers have extensive experience in representing sureties, owners, general contractors, subcontractors and suppliers in construction matters. The firms novel and creative legal theories have been accepted by our Trial and Appellate Courts in precedent setting cases and by our State Legislature as it has enacted bills which the firm has prepared. The lawyers in the firm are frequent speakers at construction trade association conventions, and are popular lecturers for continuing legal education programs sponsored by the Bar.

FENTON T. ERWIN, JR., born Knoxville, Tennessee, July 30, 1941; admitted to bar, 1966, North Carolina. *Education:* East Carolina University (A.B., 1963); University of North Carolina (J.D., 1966). Phi Delta Phi. *Member:* North Carolina (Member, Council, Construction Law Section and Litigation Section) and American Bar Associations; North Carolina State Bar; North Carolina Trial Lawyers Association; The Association of Trial Lawyers of America; North Carolina Counsel for the American Subcontractors Association. ***PRACTICE AREAS:*** Catastrophic Injury; Construction Law; Commercial Law; Negligence; Real Estate Litigation. ***Email:*** ferwin@eelaw.net

L. HOLMES ELEAZER, JR., born New Bern, North Carolina, November 19, 1946; admitted to bar, 1976, North Carolina. *Education:* Davidson College (B.A., 1968); University of South Carolina (M.A., 1971); University of North Carolina (J.D., 1976). Research Assistant, Chief Judge Walter E. Brock, North Carolina Court of Appeals, 1976-1977. *Member:* North Carolina Bar Association (Member, Bankruptcy Section). ***PRACTICE AREAS:*** Bankruptcy; Appellate Practice; Civil Litigation in Commercial and Business Matters. ***Email:*** leleazer@eelaw.net

B. DAVID CARSON, born Charlotte, North Carolina, December 6, 1962; admitted to bar, 1988, North Carolina. *Education:* University of Notre Dame (B.A., cum laude, 1985); University of North Carolina (J.D., 1988). Order of the Coif. Member, Joint Committee Carolinas Association of General Contractors (AGC) & NCBA, 2002-2003. *Member:* Mecklenburg County Bar Association; North Carolina Bar Association (Member, Construction Section, Office - Treasurer 1998-1999, Secretary, 2000-2001); Lien Law Revisions Committee, 2001-2005. ***PRACTICE AREAS:*** Construction Litigation; Commercial Litigation. ***Email:*** bdcarson@eelaw.net

PETER F. MORGAN, born Knoxville, Tennessee, October 11, 1970; admitted to bar, 1995, Virginia; 1998, North Carolina. *Education:* American University (B.A., magna cum laude, 1992); Washington & Lee University (J.D., 1995). Member, National Moot Court Team. *Member:* Mecklenburg County Bar Association; North Carolina State Bar; North Carolina Bar Association (Member, Construction Law Section); North Carolina Academy of Trial Lawyers. ***REPORTED CASES:*** Wayne Bros. Inc. v. North River Ins. Co., 2003 U.S. Dist. Lexis 168 38 (M.D.N.C.) August 20, 2003; Cosentino v. Wales, 160 N.C. App. 511 (2003); Belk v. Cheshire, 159 N.C. App. 325 (2003); Little v. Stognes, 140 N.C. App. 380 (2000). ***PRACTICE AREAS:*** Construction Litigation; Commercial Litigation. ***Email:*** pmorgan@eelaw.net

ESSEX RICHARDS, P.A.

Established in 1976

1701 SOUTH BOULEVARD
CHARLOTTE, NORTH CAROLINA 28203
Telephone: 704-377-4300
Telecopier: 704-372-1357
URL: http://www.essexrichards.com

Business and Personal Matters: including formation and general representation of Business Entities, Estate Planning and Probate, Employment, Labor, Commercial Real Estate, Mergers and Acquisitions, Health Care, Guardianship, Tax.
Litigation Matters: including Personal Injury, Wrongful Death, Condemnation, Employment, Business, Domestic Relations and Equitable Distribution, Constitutional, ERISA, Class Action, Mental Health, Criminal and General Civil.
Arbitration and Mediation.

(This Listing Continued)

EDWARD G. CONNETTE, III, born Nashville, Tennessee, September 23, 1952; admitted to bar, 1977, Connecticut (Inactive); 1978, U.S. District Court, District of Connecticut; 1980, North Carolina and U.S. District Court, Western District of North Carolina; 1981, U.S. District Court, Middle District of North Carolina and U.S. Court of Appeals, Fourth Circuit; 1986, U.S. Supreme Court. *Education:* Davidson College (B.A., 1974); University of North Carolina (J.D., 1977). Member, North Carolina Journal of International Law and Commercial Regulation, 1976-1977. *Member:* North Carolina (Member, Sections on: Labor and Employment Law; Law Office Management); and American Bar Associations; North Carolina State Bar; North Carolina Academy of Trial Lawyers; The Association of Trial Lawyers of America. ***REPORTED CASES:*** Graham vs. Connor, 827 F. 2d 945 (4th Cir. 1988), reversed, 498 U.S. 386 (1989); Gallagher v. Reliance Standard Life Ins. Co., 305 F.3d 264 (4th Cir. 2002); Walker vs. Teamsters Local No. 71, 930 F. 2d 376 (4th Cir. 1991), cert. den. U.S., 116 L.Ed. 2d 654, 112 S. Ct. 636 (1991); Combs vs. Bakker, 886 F. 2d 673 (4th Cir. 1990); Thomas S. vs. Morrow ("Thomas S. I"), 601 F. Supp. 1055 (W.D.N.C. 1984), affirmed 781 F. 2d 367 (4th Cir. 1985), cert. den., 476 U.S. 1124 (1986); Thomas S. vs. Flaherty ("Thomas S. II"), 902 F. 2d 250 (4th Cir. 1990), cert. den. 498 U.S. 951 (1990); MacClements vs. Lafone, 104 N.C. App. 179, 408 S.E. 2d 878 (N.C. App. 1991), rev. den., 330 N.C. 613, 412 S. E2d 87 (1992). ***PRACTICE AREAS:*** Personal Injury; Constitutional Law; ERISA Litigation; Class Actions; Mental Health Law. ***Email:*** econnette@essexrichards.com

KENNETH F. ESSEX, born Morristown, New Jersey, March 9, 1943; admitted to bar, 1970, North Carolina and U.S. Tax Court; U.S. Bankruptcy Court for Western District of North Carolina; U.S. Bankruptcy Court for Eastern District of North Carolina. *Education:* Davidson College (B.A., 1965); University of North Carolina (J.D., 1970). Phi Delta Phi. *Member:* Mecklenburg County, North Carolina (Member, Sections on: Business; Estate Planning and Fiduciary Law; Elder Law) and American (Member, Section on: Business) Bar Associations; North Carolina State Bar; North Carolina Academy of Trial Lawyers; Charlotte Estate Planning Council. [U.S. Army, Active Duty, USARV, 1966-1967]. ***PRACTICE AREAS:*** Business; Mergers and Acquisitions; Estate Planning and Probate; Commercial Real Estate; Business Litigation. ***Email:*** kessex@essexrichards.com

DEBRA L. FOSTER, born Brooklyn, New York, October 16, 1956; admitted to bar, 1982, North Carolina. *Education:* University of North Carolina at Greensboro (B.A., summa cum laude, 1978), Phi Beta Kappa; University of North Carolina (J.D., with honors, 1982). Member: Order of the Coif; National Moot Court Team; North Carolina Law Review. *Member:* Mecklenburg County, North Carolina (Section on: Estate Planning and Fiduciary Law; Chair, 2005-2006) and American (Member, Section on: Probate and Trust Law) Bar Associations; North Carolina State Bar; Charlotte Estate Planning Counsel. Fellow, The American College of Trust and Estate Counsel. (Board Certified Specialist in Estate Planning and Probate Law, North Carolina State Board of Legal Specialization). ***PRACTICE AREAS:*** Estate Planning; Probate; Tax Exempt Organizations. ***Email:*** dfoster@essexrichards.com

G. MILLER JORDAN, born Raleigh, North Carolina, August 11, 1946; admitted to bar, 1972, North Carolina; 1977, U.S. Court of Appeals, Fourth Circuit; 1978, U.S. Supreme Court. *Education:* Wake Forest University (B.A., 1968; J.D., 1971). Phi Delta Phi. CLE Lecturer on Guardianship and Protection of Assets, 1994 and 1996, 2005. *Member:* Mecklenburg County, North Carolina (Former Chairman, UCC and Consumer Credit Committee, Commercial Banking and Business Law Section) and American Bar Associations; North Carolina State Bar; Commercial Law League; North Carolina Academy of Trial Lawyers. ***PRACTICE AREAS:*** Civil Litigation; Business Litigation; Estate Litigation; Probate. ***Email:*** mjordan@essexrichards.com

LISA T. KELLY, born Lexington, North Carolina, September 3, 1958; admitted to bar, 1985, North Carolina. *Education:* Wake Forest University (B.A., 1980; J.D., 1985). *Member:* Mecklenburg County, North Carolina (Member, Sections on: Estate Planning and Fiduciary Law) and American (Member, Sections on: Real Property; Probate and Trust Law) Bar Associations; North Carolina State Bar; Charlotte Estate Planning Council. (Board Certified Specialist in Estate Planning and Probate, North Carolina State Board of Legal Specialization). ***PRACTICE AREAS:*** Estate Planning and Probate. ***Email:*** lkelly@essexrichards.com

LOUIS L. LESESNE, JR., born Dublin, Georgia, June 8, 1945; admitted to bar, 1973, South Carolina and U.S. District Court, District of South Carolina; 1974, U.S. Court of Appeals, Fourth Circuit; 1975, North Carolina; 1976, Supreme Court. *Education:* Davidson College (B.A., 1967); Boston University (J.D., 1973). Certified Mediator, North Carolina Dispute Resolution Commission. *Member:* Mecklenburg and North Carolina (Member, Sections on: Litigation; Labor and Employment Law) Bar Associations; North Carolina State Bar; North Carolina Academy of Trial Lawyers; South Carolina Bar. ***LANGUAGES:*** French. ***REPORTED CASES:*** Jordan v. Civil Service Board, 137 N.C. App. 575, 528 S.E.2d 927 (2000); Price v. City of Charlotte, 93 F.3d 1241 (4th Cir. 1996); McLean v. Mecklenburg County, 116 N.C. App. 431, 448 S.E.2d 137 (1994); Hayes vs. City of Charlotte, 802 F.Supp. 1361 (W.D.N.C. 1992), affd., 10 F.3d 207 (4th Cir. 1993); Nichols vs. ACTWU, 305 S.C. 323, 408 S.E.2d 237 (1991), cert. den., 502 U.S. 1032 (1992); Gordon vs. Kidd, 971 F.2d 1087 (4th Cir. 1992); Gries vs. Zimmer Inc., 742 F.Supp. 1309 (W.D.N.C. 1990), revd., 940 F.2d 652 (4th Cir. 1991), on remand, 795 F.Supp. 1379 (W.D.N.C. 1992); Curl vs. Reavis, 740 F.2d 1323 (4th Cir. 1984), on remand, 608 F.Supp. 1265 (W.D.N.C. 1985); Chisholm vs. U.S. Postal Service, 665 F.2d 482 (4th Cir. 1981), 570 F.Supp. 1044 (W.D.N.C. 1983); Hymes vs. Harnett County Board of Education, 664 F.2d 410 (4th Cir. 1981); Local 2106, International Association of Firefighters, AFL-CIO vs. City of Rock Hill, South Carolina, 660 F.2d 97 (4th Cir. 1981). ***PRACTICE AREAS:*** Employment Law; Labor Law; Constitutional Law; Personal Injury; Arbitration; Mediation. ***Email:*** llesesne@essexrichards.com

T. PATRICK MATUS, II, born Gaffney, South Carolina, February 13, 1947; admitted to bar, 1973, North Carolina. *Education:* University of North Carolina (A.B., 1969; J.D., 1972). Delta Theta Phi. Judge, District Court, 26th Judicial District, State of North Carolina, 1981-1988. *Member:* Mecklenburg County (Member, Section on: Criminal Law) and North Carolina (Member, Section on: Criminal Law) Bar Associations; North Carolina State Bar; The Association of Trial Lawyers of America; National Association of Criminal Defense Lawyers; North Carolina Academy of Trial Lawyers; American Arbitration Association (Member, Panel Arbitrators), Resolute Systems, Inc. and Arbitration Forums.

(This Listing Continued)

ESSEX RICHARDS, P.A., Charlotte—Continued

PRACTICE AREAS: Personal Injury; Wrongful Death; Medical Malpractice; Business Litigation; Criminal Litigation; Civil Litigation; Arbitration; Mediation. ***Email:*** pmatus@essexrichards.com

STEPHEN H. MORRIS, born Charleston, West Virginia, August 25, 1951; admitted to bar, 1976, North Carolina; 1980, U.S. Tax Court. *Education:* University of North Carolina (B.S.B.A., 1973; J.D., 1976). *Member:* Mecklenburg County, North Carolina (Member, Sections on: Taxation; Business; Estate Planning and Fiduciary Law; Real Property Law) and American (Member, Sections on: Taxation; Real Property, Probate and Trust Law; Corporate, Banking and Business Law) Bar Associations; North Carolina State Bar; Charlotte Estate Planning Council. ***PRACTICE AREAS:*** Business; Tax; Estate Planning and Probate; Real Estate. ***Email:*** smorris@essexrichards.com

CHANNING O. RICHARDS, born Washington, D.C., August 9, 1941; admitted to bar, 1966, North Carolina; 1968, U.S. Court of Military Appeals. *Education:* University of North Carolina (A.B., 1963); Duke University (LL.B., 1966). Phi Delta Phi. *Member:* Mecklenburg County, North Carolina and American Bar Associations; North Carolina State Bar; North Carolina Academy of Trial Lawyers. [Commander, JAGC, USNR-R]. ***PRACTICE AREAS:*** Domestic Relations; Equitable Distribution; Condemnation; Arbitration; Mediation. ***Email:*** crichards@essexrichards.com

---

NORRIS A. ADAMS, II, born Columbia, South Carolina, July 22, 1979; admitted to bar, 2004, North Carolina. *Education:* Campbell University (B.A., magna cum laude, 2001); Wake Forest University (J.D., 2004). Clerk, The Honorable Judge Stephen C. St. John, U.S. Bankruptcy Court for the Eastern District of Virginia, 2004-2005. Member: Mecklenburg County, North Carolina (Member, Sections on: Business; Litigation; Sports and Entertainment) and American Bar Associations; North Carolina State Bar. ***PRACTICE AREAS:*** Business; Civil Litigation. ***Email:*** nadams@essexrichards.com

KERRY B. EVERETT

Established in 2005

5120 MONROE ROAD

CHARLOTTE, NORTH CAROLINA 28205

Telephone: 704-567-5297

Fax: 704-567-5389

Email: kbeverett@earthlink.net

URL: http://www.kbeverettlaw.com

Adoptions, Real Estate, Buying or Selling a Home, Buying or Selling a Business, State and Federal Appellate and Civil Practice, Wills and Probate.

FIRM PROFILE: Ms. Everett's practice focuses on adoptions, residential real estate, state and federal appellate practice, and wills and probate. Ms. Everett's practice also includes municipal and environmental matters.

KERRY B. EVERETT, born Birmingham, Alabama, June 11, 1968; admitted to bar, 1999, North Carolina, U.S. District Court, Western District of North Carolina and U.S. Court of Appeals, 4th Circuit. *Education:* University of Alabama (B.A., Communications, cum laude, 1990); Seattle University (J.D., cum laude, 1999). Phi Kappa Phi. Moot Court Board. Editor in Chief, Seattle University Law Review. *Member:* Mecklenburg County Bar Association; North Carolina State Bar. ***PRACTICE AREAS:*** Adoption Law; Real Estate; Real Estate Sales; Buying and Selling of Businesses; Appellate Practice; Civil Practice; Federal Civil Practice; Wills; Probate.

EVERMAN LAW FIRM, PA

6000 FAIRVIEW ROAD

SUITE 1200

CHARLOTTE, NORTH CAROLINA 28210

Telephone: 704-552-3999

Fax: 704-552-3705

URL: http://www.evermanlawfirm.com

Intellectual Property, Trademarks, Patents, Copyrights, Copyrights, Buying or Selling a Home.

GREGORY R. EVERMAN, born Oregon, Ohio, August 9, 1966; admitted to bar, 1999, Ohio; 2001, North Carolina; U.S. District Court, Western District of North Carolina; registered to practice before the U.S. Patent and Trademark Office. *Education:* University of Toledo (B.S.M.E., 1990; J.D., 1998). Phi Tau Sigma Honorary Fraternity. Engineer in Training. Member, Intellectual Property Moot Court. *Member:* Ohio State Bar Association; North Carolina State Bar; Carolina Patent, Trademark and Copyright Law Association. ***PRACTICE AREAS:*** Intellectual Property; Trademarks; Patents; Copyrights; Buying and Selling a Home.

YATES W. FAISON, III

8401 UNIVERSITY EXECUTIVE PARK DRIVE, SUITE 112

CHARLOTTE, NORTH CAROLINA 28262

Telephone: 704-717-0663

Fax: 704-717-0744

Email: faisony@bellsouth.net

Residential and Commercial Real Estate, Mortgages, Real Property Closings.

FIRM PROFILE: Mr. Faison has been practicing in Charlotte since 1973.

YATES W. FAISON, III, born Charlotte, North Carolina, November 24, 1947; admitted to bar, 1972, North Carolina and U.S. District Court, Western District of North Carolina. *Education:* Davidson College (B.A., 1969); University of North Carolina (J.D., 1972).

(This Listing Continued)

Delta Theta Phi. *Member:* North Carolina Bar Association (Member, Real Property Section); North Carolina State Bar. [Captain, U.S. Army Reserve, 1972-1980]

FERGUSON, STEIN, CHAMBERS, GRESHAM & SUMTER, P.A.

Established in 1964

741 KENILWORTH AVENUE, SUITE 300

CHARLOTTE, NORTH CAROLINA 28204-2828

Telephone: 704-375-8461

Fax: 704-334-5654

Email: Fergietwo@aol.com

URL: http://www.fergusonstein.com

Mailing Address: P.O. Box 36486, Charlotte, NC 28236-6486

Chapel Hill, North Carolina Office: Suite 2, 312 West Franklin Street. Telephone: 919-933-5300. Fax: 919-967-4953.

Civil Rights, Employment and Labor, General Civil, Criminal, Plaintiff's Medical Malpractice, Trial and Appellate Practice. Probate and Real Estate Law.

FIRM PROFILE: Ferguson, Stein, Chambers, Gresham & Sumter, P.A. is a multi-specialty law firm based in Charlotte, North Carolina, which has been in business since 1964. The firm was founded by Julius L. Chambers, who left the firm in 1984 to become Director-Counsel of the NAACP Legal Defense and Educational Fund, Inc. in New York and returned to the firm in 2001. Currently there are a total of 14 attorneys from diverse backgrounds working in the Charlotte and Chapel Hill offices. The firm has a national and international reputation in school desegregation, employment discrimination, voting rights, general civil rights litigation, and criminal defense. It is also nationally and regionally known for its representation of plaintiffs in personal injury and medical negligence cases, and its work in teacher rights and education law, administrative law, workers compensation, and estates, business, corporate and real estate matters. Listed in the Martindale-Hubbell Bar Register of Preeminent Lawyers, the firm encourages professional development and activities: many of its members hold leadership positions in a wide variety of professional organizations and regularly teach academic courses and at trial advocacy and continuing legal education programs.

JAMES E. FERGUSON, II, born Asheville, North Carolina, October 10, 1942; admitted to bar, 1967, North Carolina. *Education:* North Carolina Central University (A.B., summa cum laude, 1964) Columbia University (LL.B., 1967). Alpha Kappa Mu Honor Society. Member, Board of Directors, Legal Services of North Carolina, 1983-1989. President, Board of Directors, National Employment Law Project, 1984-1988. Lecturer in Law, Harvard University Law School, 1986-1992. Adjunct Faculty Member, North Carolina Central University School of Law 1981, 1988. *Member:* The North Carolina State Bar (Member, Disciplinary Hearing Commission, 1981-1990); American Bar Association (Co-Chairman, Personal Rights Committee, Litigation Section, 1982); National Bar Association; North Carolina Association of Black Lawyers (President, 1974-1976); North Carolina Academy of Trial Lawyers (Member, Board of Directors, 1984-1992; President, 2001); The Association of Trial Lawyers of America; National Institute of Trial Advocacy (Board Chair, Executive Committee, 1998-2000). Fellow, American College of Trial Lawyers. ***REPORTED CASES:*** Harris v. Miller, 335 N.C. 379, 438 SE2d. 731 (1994); State v. Hunt, 324 N.C. 343, 378 S.E. 2d (1989); McDowell v. Dixon, 858 F.2d 945 (4th in 1988). ***PRACTICE AREAS:*** Plaintiff's Medical Malpractice; Plaintiff's Catastrophic Injury; General Civil Rights Law; Constitutional Law. ***Email:*** James_Ferguson@law.fswags.com

ADAM STEIN (Resident, Chapel Hill Office)

JULIUS LEVONNE CHAMBERS, born Mt. Gilead, North Carolina, October 6, 1936; admitted to bar, 1962, North Carolina; 1987, New York. *Education:* North Carolina Central University (A.B., 1958); University of Michigan, Ann Arbor (M.A., History, 1959); University of North Carolina at Chapel Hill (J.D., 1962); Columbia University School of Law (LL.M., 1963). Order of the Coif; Order of the Golden Fleece. Woodrow Wilson Fellow, University of Michigan. John Hay Whitney Fellow, University of North Carolina at Chappel Hill School of Law. Recipient: Courageous Advocacy Award form the American College of Trial Lawyers; Aetna Voice of Conscience Award; Congressional Black Caucus Foundation's Adam Clayton Powell Award for Legislative and Legal Perfection. Author: "Beyond Affirmative Action," Capital University Law 37.1 (1998): 1-2; Race and Equality: The Still Unfinished Business of the Warren Court," *The Warren Court:* A Retrospective, Ed. Bernard Schwartz, New York, Oxford University Press, 1996: 26-67; "Afterward: Racial Equity and Full Citizenship, The Unfinished Agenda," *African Americans and the Living Constitution,* Eds. John Hope Franklin and Genna Rae McNeil, Washington, D.C.: Smithsonian Institution Press, 1995: 319-325; "Black Americans and the Courts: Has the Clock Been Turned Back Permanently?"*The State of Black America,* 1990, New York: Natural Urban League, Inc. 1990: 9-24; "Adequate Education for All: A Right, An Achievable Goal," Harv. Civil Rights-Civil Liberties Law Review 22.1 (1987):55-74. Adjunct Professor: University of Virginia Law School, 1975-1978; University of Pennsylvania, 1978-1986; Columbia University Law School, 1984-1992; University of Michigan Law School, 1985-1992. Chancellor, North Carolina Central University, 1993-2001. Formerly with, NAACP Legal Defense & Education Fund, New York, NY. *Member:* North Carolina and American (Member, IRR Section) Bar Associations; North Carolina State Bar; American College of Trial Lawyers. ***REPORTED CASES:*** Swann, et al. v. Charlotte-Mecklenburg Board of Education, 402 U.S. 1 (1971); Moody v. Albemarle Paper Corp., 422 U.S. 405 (1975); Thornburg v. Gingles, 478 U.S. 30 (1986). ***PRACTICE AREAS:*** Civil Rights; Education Law; Employment; Housing; Public Accommodation. ***Email:*** jchambers@law.fswags.com

JOHN W. GRESHAM, born Mullins, South Carolina, January 14, 1945; admitted to bar, 1975, North Carolina. *Education:* Davidson College (A.B., 1967); Boston University (J.D., 1974). Omicron Delta Kappa. Member, 1972-1974 and Note and Case Editor, 1973-1974, Boston University Law Review. Author: Comment, "Reemployment Rights: The Veteran and the Vacation Benefit," 53 Boston University Law Review 480, March, 1973. Law Clerk to U.S. District Judge James B. McMillan, 1974-1976. Faculty, Vermont Law School,

(This Listing Continued)

Fall 1992. National Institute of Trial Advocacy (Faculty, 1990—). *Member:* Mecklenburg County (Member, Grievance Committee, 1990-1993, 1998—; Bar Foundation, 1995-2000; President, 2000—), North Carolina (Council Member, Education Law Section, 1987-1991; Appellate Rules Study Committee, 1989-1992) and American Bar Associations; The North Carolina State Bar; North Carolina Academy of Trial Lawyers. ***REPORTED CASES:*** Reed v. United Transportation Union, 488 U.S. 319, 109 S.Ct. 621, 102 L.Ed.2d 665 (1989); Corum v. University of North Carolina, 330 N.C. 761, 413 S.E.2d 276 (1992); Brewer v. Cabarras Plastics, Inc., N.C. App 681, 130 W.C. App 681, 504 S.E.2d 580 (1998). ***PRACTICE AREAS:*** Public Employment Law; Employment Civil Rights Litigation; Education Law; General Civil Litigation; Appellate Practice. ***Email:*** JGresham@law.fswags.com

GERALDINE SUMTER, born Columbia, South Carolina, March 4, 1956; admitted to bar, 1981, South Carolina; 1983, North Carolina. *Education:* Howard University (B.A., summa cum laude, 1978); Duke University (J.D., 1981). Law Clerk to Judge Charles L. Becton, North Carolina Court of Appeals, 1981-1982. Member, Vice Chair, 1993-1996, Chairperson, 1996-1997, IOLTA Board of Trustees. *Member:* Mecklenburg County (Executive Committee, 1989-1992) and North Carolina (Chair, Section Council, Employment Law Section, 1992-1993; Member, Intellectual Property Committee, 1988-1989) Bar Associations; North Carolina State Bar; South Carolina Bar; North Carolina Academy of Trial Lawyers; North Carolina Association of Women Attorneys; North Carolina Association of Black Lawyers (President, 1991-1995; President, Charlotte Chapter, 1988-1990); National Employment Lawyers Association. ***PRACTICE AREAS:*** Civil Rights Litigation; Employment Law. ***Email:*** GSumter@law.fswags.com

HENDERSON HILL, born Brooklyn, N.Y., May 17, 1956; admitted to bar, 1981, District of Columbia; 1991, North Carolina. *Education:* Herbert H. Lehman College of the City University of New York (B.A., 1977); Harvard University (J.D., 1981). Adjunct Associate Professor of Law, University of North Carolina Law School, 1991-1997. Senior Lecturer, Duke University Law School, 1998. Member, Board of Directors, Center for Death Penalty Litigation. *Member:* The District of Columbia Bar; North Carolina Academy of Trial Lawyers (Member: Board of Governors, 1997-1999, 2001—; Executive Committee, 1998-1999). ***PRACTICE AREAS:*** Medical Malpractice; Criminal Trials; Civil Litigation; Civil Rights; Management. ***Email:*** HHill@law.fswags.com

C. MARGARET ERRINGTON, born Yarmouth, Nova Scotia, Canada, September 14, 1954; admitted to bar, 1985, Massachusetts; 1987, North Carolina. *Education:* Wesleyan University (B.A., 1982); Northeastern University (J.D., 1985). Law Clerk to Honorable Herbert P. Wilkins, Massachusetts Supreme Judicial Court, 1985-1986. *Member:* Mecklenburg County (Member, Executive Committee, 1992-1995), North Carolina (Member: Labor and Employment Council, 1992-1994, 1998-2001) and Massachusetts Bar Associations; North Carolina State Bar; North Carolina Association of Women Attorneys; North Carolina Academy of Trial Lawyers; The Association of Trial Lawyers of America. ***PRACTICE AREAS:*** Civil Rights Litigation; General Civil Litigation; Employment Law; Estates. ***Email:*** MErrington@law.fswags.com

STEPHEN LUKE LARGESS, born Newport, Rhode Island, April 20, 1956; admitted to bar, 1990, North Carolina. *Education:* Duke University (B.A., 1979); University of North Carolina (J.D., 1990). *Member:* Mecklenburg County and North Carolina Bar Associations; North Carolina Academy of Trial Lawyers (President, Board of Directors of North Carolina Legal Education Assistance Foundation, 1989-2001). ***LANGUAGES:*** Spanish. ***REPORTED CASES:*** Boring v. Buncombe County Bd of Ed., 136 F3d 364, (4th Cir. 1998); State v. Lineberger 115 N.C. App. 687, 446 SE2d 375 (1994); Belk v. Charlotte Mecklenburg Bd. of Education, 233 F2d. 32 (4th Cir. 2000) (vacated for rehearing en Banc); Craig v. Asheville City Bd. of Ed., 543 SE 2d. 186 (NC App. 2001). ***PRACTICE AREAS:*** General Civil Litigation; Education Law; Employment Law. ***Email:*** LLargess@law.fswags.com

WILLIAM G. SIMPSON, JR. (Resident, Chapel Hill Office)

OF COUNSEL

JONATHAN P. WALLAS, born Charlotte, North Carolina, July 8, 1945; admitted to bar, 1970, North Carolina. *Education:* Duke University (B.A., 1967); Columbia University (J.D., 1970). Member, 1968-1970 and Writing and Research Editor, 1969-1970, Columbia Journal of Law and Social Problems. Law Clerk to U.S. District Court Judge James B. McMillan, 1970-1971. *Member:* Mecklenburg County and North Carolina Bar Associations; The North Carolina State Bar; North Carolina Academy of Trial Lawyers; National Employment Lawyers Association (Member, National Executive Board, 1993-1996). ***REPORTED CASES:*** Anderson v. Bessemer City, 470 U.S. 564; Chisholm v. United States Postal Service, 516 F. Supp. 810, aff'd 665 F.2d 482. ***PRACTICE AREAS:*** Employment Law; Litigation; Torts.

JACOB H. SUSSMAN, admitted to bar, 2003, New York and North Carolina. *Education:* Wesleyan University (B.A., 1997); New York University School of Law (J.D., 2002). Root-Tilden-Kern Public Interest Scholar. Author, Unlimited Innocence: Recognizing an "Actual Innocence" Exception to AEDPA's Statute of Limitations, 27 NYU Rev. L. & Soc. Change 343 (2001-2002); Suspect Choices: Lineup Procedures and the Abdication of Judicial and Prosecutorial Responsibility for Improving the Criminal Justice System, 27 NYU Rev. L. & Soc. Change 507 (2001-2002). Member, Pro Bono Steering Committee, Harvard Civil Rights Project, Charlotte-Mecklenburg Schools System Project, 2005—. *Member:* Mecklenburg County and North Carolina Bar Associations; Mecklenburg County Criminal Defense Lawyers Association (Treasurer, 2003—); National Association of Criminal Defense Lawyers; North Carolina Academy of Trial Lawyers (Membership Chair, Young Lawyers Division, 2004—; Member, Criminal Defense and Civil Rights Sections, 2003—). ***PRACTICE AREAS:*** Criminal Defense; Civil Rights; Education Law. ***Email:*** jsussman@law.fswags.com

BRANDON M. LOFTON, born Philadelphia, Pennsylvania, November 5, 1978; admitted to bar, 2004, North Carolina. *Education:* University of North Carolina at Chapel Hill (B.A., 2001); New York University School of Law (J.D., 2004). Phi Beta Kappa, Highest Honors, 2001. Root-Tilden Kern Scholar, New York University, 2001-2004. Graduation Speaker, New York University, 2004. Member, John S. Leary Bar Political Action Committee. *Member:* Mecklenburg County Bar Association (Member, Diversity Committee).

(This Listing Continued)

PRACTICE AREAS: Business; Nonprofit; Civil Rights Litigation; Employment Discrimination. ***Email:*** blofton@law.fswags.com

---

FISHER & PHILLIPS LLP

Established in 1943

SUITE 2020
227 WEST TRADE STREET
CHARLOTTE, NORTH CAROLINA 28202
Telephone: 704-334-4565
Fax: 704-334-9774
Email: fp@laborlawyers.com
URL: http://www.laborlawyers.com

Atlanta, Georgia Office: 1500 Resurgens Plaza, 945 East Paces Ferry Road, 30326. Telephone: 404-231-1400. Fax: 404-240-4249.
Chicago, Illinois Office: 1000 Marquette Building, 140 South Dearborn Street, 60603. Telephone: 312-346-8061. Fax: 312-346-3179.
Columbia, South Carolina Office: Suite 1400, 1901 Main Street, 29201. Telephone: 803-255-0000. Fax: 803-255-0202.
Dallas, Texas Office: 4343 Thanksgiving Tower, 1601 Elm Street, 75201. Telephone: 214-220-9100. Fax: 214-220-9122.
Fort Lauderdale, Florida Office: Suite 800, 450 East Las Olas Boulevard, 33301. Telephone: 954-525-4800. Fax: 954-525-8739.
Irvine, California Office: Suite 400, 18400 Von Karman Avenue, 92612. Telephone: 949-851-2424. Fax: 949-851-0152.
Kansas City, Missouri Office: Suite 400, 104 West Ninth Street, 64105. Telephone: 816-842-8770. Fax: 816-842-8767.
Las Vegas, Nevada Office: Suite 650, 3993 Howard Hughes Parkway, 89109. Telephone: 702-252-3131. Fax: 702-252-7411.
New Orleans, Louisiana Office: Suite 3710, 201 St. Charles Avenue, 70170. Telephone: 504-522-3303. Fax: 504-529-3850.
Oakland, California Office: City Center, Suite 200, 501 Fourteenth Street, 94612. Telephone: 510-763-4411. Fax: 510-763-4418.
Orlando, Florida Office: 1250 Lincoln Plaza, 300 South Orange Avenue, 32801. Telephone: 407-541-0888. Fax: 407-541-0887.
Portland, Oregon Office: Suite 1600, 1001 S.W. Fifth Avenue, 97204. Telephone: 503-242-4262. Fax: 503-242-4263.
San Diego, California Office: 4225 Executive Square, Suite 950, La Jolla, California, 92037. Telephone: 858-597-9600. Fax: 858-597-9601.
Somerset, New Jersey Office: Corporate Park III, Third Floor, 580 Howard Avenue, 08873. Telephone: 732-560-7100. Fax: 732-560-0788.
Tampa, Florida Office: Suite 2525, 401 East Jackson Street, 33602. Telephone: 813-769-7500. Fax: 813-769-7501.

Labor and Employment, Alternative Dispute Resolution, Arbitration, Business Immigration, Collective Bargaining, Employment Discrimination, Labor Relations, Mergers, Acquisitions and Divestitures, Occupational Safety and Health, Pension and Benefits, Sexual Harassment, Wage and Hour, Whistleblower Litigation, Wrongful Termination.

FIRM PROFILE: *Fisher & Phillips LLP, a national law firm founded in 1943, was one of the first law firms to center its practice on representing employers in labor and employment matters. Now one of the largest in the field, the firm has maintained its commitment to helping employers find innovative legal and practical solutions to their business needs by offering management preventive advice and litigation defense. Working in many areas of employment law, the firm's attorneys offer a wide breadth of expertise covering such traditional subjects as NLRB practice, EEOC, wage and hour, and disability law, as well as business immigration, pension and benefits, education law and occupational safety and health. In addition to defending employers in labor cases, Fisher & Phillips attorneys help their clients to minimize litigation risks through the development of effective contracts, policies and procedures and through training supervisors and administrators in practical compliance strategies and dispute resolution. The firm's integrated communications systems and network of ten offices from coast to coast enable its attorneys to handle matters promptly and efficiently in any state. Its focus on labor law permits the firm to provide cost-effective services to employers ranging from large multi-national companies to small, family-owned businesses. Firm attorneys participate actively in state and local bar associations and in many charitable organizations and public service activities.*

Fisher & Phillips LLP represents employers in a broad range of industries including hospitality, health care, automotive, manufacturing, transportation and logistics, credit unions, banks and financial institutions, private schools, colleges and universities, state and local governments, legal and professional service firms, insurance and related services, and non-profit organizations.

MEMBER OF FIRM

MASON G. ALEXANDER, born Spartanburg, South Carolina, November 25, 1959; admitted to bar, 1985, South Carolina; 1997, North Carolina. *Education:* The University of the South (B.A., 1982); University of South Carolina (J.D., 1985). Delta Theta Phi. Coleman Karesh Scholar; Harry M. Lightsey Scholar. Author: "Master & Servant," South Carolina Jurisprudence. Law Clerk to the Honorable Robert F. Chapman, The United States Court of Appeals for the Fourth Circuit, 1985-1987. *Member:* South Carolina Bar (Chairman, Employment and Labor Law Section, 1997-1998; Member, House of Delegates, 1999-2000). (Certified Specialist, Employment and Labor Law, The Supreme Court of South Carolina). ***PRACTICE AREAS:*** Labor and Employment; Discrimination; Labor and Employment Litigation; Labor Arbitration; Sexual Harassment; Union Avoidance; Union Campaigns; Wrongful Discharge. ***Email:*** malexander@laborlawyers.com

ASSOCIATES

KEVIN JOSEPH DALTON, born Alexandria, Virginia, April 20, 1971; admitted to bar, 1996, Maryland; 1997, North Carolina. *Education:* Wake Forest University (B.A., cum

(This Listing Continued)

FISHER & PHILLIPS LLP, Charlotte—Continued

laude, 1993); University of Baltimore (J.D., cum laude, 1996). University of Baltimore Law Review, 1994-1996. Staff Editor, University of Baltimore Journal of Environmental Law, 1994-1995. Law Clerk to The Honorable J. Norris Byrnes, Circuit Court for Baltimore County, 1995-1996; the Honorable Barbara Kerr Howe, Circuit Court for Baltimore County, 1996-1997. Author: "Gulf War Syndrome: Will the Injuries of Veterans and Their Families Be Redressed?" 25.2 University of Baltimore Law Review. [Captain, Judge Advocate General's Corps., U.S. Army, 1997-2001]. ***PRACTICE AREAS:*** Labor and Employment; Immigration Law; Management Employment Law; Title VII; Unfair Labor Practices (ULP); Union Elections; Wrongful Termination. ***Email:*** kdalton@laborlawyers.com

JAMES MICHAEL HONEYCUTT, born Fayetteville, North Carolina, February 20, 1964; admitted to bar, 2001, Michigan; 2005, North Carolina. *Education:* University of North Carolina (B.A., magna cum laude, 1989); Michigan State University College of Law (J.D., 2001). ***PRACTICE AREAS:*** Labor and Employment; Employment Discrimination; Management-Union Relations; National Labor Relations Board (NLRB); Non-Competition Law; Trade Secrets. ***Email:*** mhoneycutt@laborlawyers.com

KATHERINE R. SHOOK, born Honolulu, Hawaii, October 12, 1975; (admission pending). *Education:* University of Texas, Austin (B.A., high honors, 1998); Wake Forest University (J.D., 2005). ***Email:*** kshook@laborlawyers.com

SHANNON (MISSY) SUMERELL SPAINHOUR, born Charlotte, North Carolina, October 20, 1975; admitted to bar, 2001, North Carolina. *Education:* University of the South (B.A., 1997); Wake Forest University School of Law (J.D., 2001). ***PRACTICE AREAS:*** Labor and Employment; Employment Litigation; Fair Labor Standards Act (FLSA); Family and Medical Leave Act (FMLA); Harassment in the Workplace; National Labor Relations Act (NLRA); Negligent Hiring and Retention. ***Email:*** mspainhour@laborlawyers.com

(For complete biographical data on attorneys in other offices, see Professional Biographies at those locations)

FLETCHER & RHOTON, P.A.

316 EAST WORTHINGTON AVENUE
CHARLOTTE, NORTH CAROLINA 28203
Telephone: 704-334-3400
Facsimile: 704-334-3001
Email: jfletcher@fletcherrhoton.com
URL: http://www.fletcherrhoton.com

Commercial Bankruptcy and Litigation, Motor Vehicle and Leasing Equipment, Foreclosures, Business Law, Buying and Selling Businesses, Limited Liability Company Law, Small Business, Breach of Contracts, Collections, Creditors Rights, Automobile Insurance, Condominium Law, Wills, Estates, Guardianships.

FIRM PROFILE: Fletcher & Rhoton, P.A. is a full service law firm which concentrates its statewide practice on the representation of lenders and creditors in all three Federal Districts, the Federal Bankruptcy Courts, and all the Courts of the State of North Carolina. The firm was organized in 1991 by the owners, John W. Fletcher III, and W. Porter Rhoton III, and has enjoyed a reputation for prompt, effective service to its clients.

JOHN WALTER FLETCHER, III, born Laurinburg, North Carolina, April 21, 1958; admitted to bar, 1988, North Carolina and U.S. District Court, Western, Middle and Eastern Districts of North Carolina; 1994, U.S. Court of Appeals, Fourth Circuit; 1997, U.S. Supreme Court. *Education:* Clemson University (B.S., 1980); Wake Forest University (J.D., 1987). Delta Theta Phi. *Member:* Mecklenburg County and North Carolina Bar Associations; North Carolina State Bar; American Bankruptcy Institute. ***PRACTICE AREAS:*** Vehicle and Equipment Leasing; Commercial Bankruptcy; Commercial Litigation; Foreclosures; Collections; Small Business Law. ***Email:*** jfletcher@fletcherrhoton.com

W. PORTER RHOTON, III, born York, South Carolina, March 15, 1960; admitted to bar, 1987, North Carolina and U.S. District Court, Eastern, Middle and Western Districts of North Carolina. *Education:* Davidson College (B.A., 1982); Wake Forest University (J.D., 1987). *Member:* Mecklenburg County and North Carolina (Member, Bankruptcy, Elder Law, Estate Planning and Fiduciary Law Sections) Bar Associations; North Carolina State Bar; American Bankruptcy Institute. ***PRACTICE AREAS:*** Estate Administration; Guardianship; Creditor Representation; Bankruptcy; Foreclosures; Repossessions; Wills. ***Email:*** prhoton@fletcherrhoton.com

BRYAN W. STONE, born Macon, Georgia, October 23, 1978; admitted to bar, 2004, North Carolina and U.S. District Court, Western, Middle and Eastern Districts of North Carolina. *Education:* University of Georgia (B.B.A., Finance, 2001); Wake Forest University (J.D., 2004). Phi Alpha Delta. Chief Justice, 2003-2004. Editor-in-Chief, The Hearsay Law School Newspaper, 2003-2004. *Member:* Mecklenburg County and North Carolina (Member, Law School Division, President, 2003-2004) Bar Associations; North Carolina State Bar; American Bankruptcy Institute. ***PRACTICE AREAS:*** Business Litigation; Bankruptcy; Foreclosures; Collections; Estates. ***Email:*** bstone@fletcherrhoton.com

REPRESENTATIVE CLIENTS: CitiCapital (formerly the Associates); CitiCapital Commercial Corp.; Citicorp Vendor Finance (Leasing); Branch Banking and Trust Company; Vanderbilt Mortgage and Finance, Inc.; Clayton Homes, Inc.; CMH Homes, Inc.; Marsh & Associates, Inc.; Folger Buick/Kia; Wilmar Leasing, Inc.; Pawnee Leasing, Inc.; Origen Financial L.L.C.; 21st Mortgage Corp.; Central Carolina Bank Leasing.

FOODMAN, HUNTER & KARRES, PLLC

Established in 1998

1001 MOREHEAD SQUARE DRIVE, SUITE 610
CHARLOTTE, NORTH CAROLINA 28203
Telephone: 704-333-3323
Fax: 704-358-1808

Other Charlotte, North Carolina Office: 10710 Sikes Place, Suite 300, 28277. Telephone: 704-849-8649. Fax: 704-849-9278.

Business Law, Commercial and Residential Real Estate, Contracts, Corporate Law, Debt and Equity Finance, E-Commerce, Emerging Growth Companies, Entrepreneurial Business Law, Estate Planning, Franchise Law, Intellectual Property, Land Sales, Land Use Regulation, Limited Liability Companies and Partnerships, Mergers and Acquisitions, Private Equity, Real Estate Development, Real Estate Finance, Real Estate Leasing, Technology Law, Traffic Violations, Trust and Estates, Venture Capital.

MEMBERS

ADAM WILL FOODMAN, born Winner, South Dakota, November 10, 1968; admitted to bar, 1994, North Carolina. *Education:* University of North Carolina at Chapel Hill (B.A., 1991); Mercer University (J.D., 1994). *Member:* Mecklenburg County, North Carolina and American Bar Associations; North Carolina State Bar. ***PRACTICE AREAS:*** Commercial Real Estate; Residential Real Estate; Corporate Law; Limited Liability Company Law; Estate Planning. ***Email:*** awfoodman@fhklaw.com

CATHERINE C. HUNTER, born Raleigh, North Carolina, September 4, 1959; admitted to bar, 1986, North Carolina; 1987, South Carolina. *Education:* Western Carolina University, University of Georgia (B.A.J., 1981); Campbell University (J.D., 1986). *Member:* North Carolina State Bar; South Carolina Bar. ***PRACTICE AREAS:*** Commercial Real Estate; Residential Real Estate. ***Email:*** chunter@fhklaw.com

ANDREW T. KARRES, born Chicago, Illinois, July 30, 1964; admitted to bar, 1993, North Carolina. *Education:* North Carolina State University (B.A., 1987); Ohio Northern University (J.D., 1991). *Member:* Mecklenburg County, North Carolina and American Bar Associations. ***LANGUAGES:*** Greek. ***PRACTICE AREAS:*** Commercial Real Estate; Residential Real Estate; Foreclosures; Estate Planning; Traffic Violations; Driving While Intoxicated. ***Email:*** atkarres@fhklaw.com

BENJAMIN A. YARBROUGH, born Atlanta, Georgia, 1967; admitted to bar, 1994, North Carolina. *Education:* Davidson College (A.B., cum laude, 1989); University of Virginia (J.D., 1994). *Member:* Mecklenburg County and North Carolina Bar Associations; North Carolina State Bar. ***PRACTICE AREAS:*** Mergers and Acquisitions; Corporate Law; Venture Capital; Debt and Equity Finance; Franchise Law; Limited Liability Company Law; Small Business Law; Employment Contracts; Business Planning; Contracts; E-Commerce; Joint Ventures; Intellectual Property; Technology Law. ***Email:*** byarbrough@fhklaw.com

ASSOCIATES

TONI K. GROVE, born Fayetteville, North Carolina, November 8, 1955; admitted to bar, 1993, North Carolina. *Education:* University of North Carolina at Charlotte (B.A., 1977); Campbell University (J.D., 1993). ***LANGUAGES:*** Greek. ***PRACTICE AREAS:*** Commercial Real Estate; Residential Real Estate; Wills; Probate. ***Email:*** tgrove@fhklaw.com

JAMES LARRY "CHIP" BIGGERS, JR., admitted to bar, 1999, Texas; 2001, North Carolina. *Education:* Georgia Institute of Technology (B.S., 1984); University of South Carolina (J.D., 1997). ***LANGUAGES:*** German. ***PRACTICE AREAS:*** Commercial Real Estate; Residential Real Estate; Corporate Law; Business Transactions. ***Email:*** chip@fhklaw.com

ELIZABETH D. MULLIS, born 1961; admitted to bar, 1997, North Carolina. *Education:* Western Carolina University (B.S., 1989); Case Western Reserve University (J.D., 1997). *Member:* Mecklenburg County and North Carolina Bar Associations; North Carolina State Bar. ***PRACTICE AREAS:*** Family Law; Domestic Law; Commercial Real Estate; Residential Real Estate; Wills; Estates; Collections. ***Email:*** emullis@fhklaw.com

LEGAL SUPPORT PERSONNEL

DEBBIE MROZINSKI (Paralegal)
RENEE HODGES (Paralegal)
BARBARA WISLER (Paralegal)
REBECCA GALE (Paralegal)
MAGGIE SMITH (Paralegal)

REPRESENTATIVE CLIENTS: Lewis Homes; Dan Moser Co.; Grubb Properties; Bravo Development Partners, LLC; Lennar Communities of Carolina, Inc.; MDC Homes, Inc.

PATRICK V. FORD, LLC

1401 EAST SEVENTH STREET
CHARLOTTE, NORTH CAROLINA 28204
Telephone: 704-333-3456
Fax: 704-376-9330
Email: ford@lawyer.com
URL: http://www.patrickfordlaw.com

Criminal Law, Assault and Battery, Burglary, Criminal Defense, Criminal Fraud, Domestic Violence, Drivers License Suspension, Driving While Intoxicated, Drug Crimes, Felonies, Misdemeanors, Theft, Traffic Violations, Weapons Charges.

FIRM PROFILE: Former Assistant District Attorney. Free consultations.

PATRICK V. FORD, born Grand Rapids, Michigan, September 3, 1948; admitted to bar, 1975, Michigan; 1981, Missouri; 1999, North Carolina. *Education:* Michigan State

(This Listing Continued)

University (B.A., high honors, Phi Kappa Phi, 1971); Wayne State University (J.D., 1974). Assistant Prosecuting Attorney, Kent County, Michigan, 1975-1980. Attorney, Government Affairs, McDonnell Douglas Corporation, 1981-1990. Assistant District Attorney, Mecklenburg County, North Carolina, 2000-2001. *Member:* Mecklenburg County Bar Association; State Bar of Michigan; The Missouri Bar; North Carolina State Bar; North Carolina Academy of Trial Lawyers. ***LANGUAGES:*** Spanish. ***PRACTICE AREAS:*** Criminal Law; Assault and Battery; Burglary; Criminal Defense; Criminal Fraud; Domestic Violence; Drivers License Suspension; Driving While Intoxicated; Drug Crimes; Felonies; Misdemeanors; Theft; Traffic Violations; Weapons Charges. ***Email:*** ford@lawyer.com

LAW OFFICE OF JULIE H. FOSBINDER

1515 MOCKINGBIRD LANE, SUITE 218
CHARLOTTE, NORTH CAROLINA 28209
Telephone: 704-522-7500
Fax: 704-522-7509
URL: http://www.lawyers.com/jfosbinder

Labor and Employment Law, Employment Discrimination Sexual Harassment, Wrongful Termination, Long Term Disability, Personal Injury.

FIRM PROFILE: The firm areas of practice include all aspects of employment litigation. Ms. Fosbinder was a senior trial attorney with the U.S. Equal Employment Opportunity Commission's Charlotte District Office from 1990-1995, before entering private practice.

JULIE H. FOSBINDER, born Milwaukee, Wisconsin, April 17, 1956; admitted to bar, 1985, New York; 1989, Arizona and U.S. District Court, District of Arizona; 1990, U.S. Court of Appeals, Ninth Circuit; 1992, North Carolina and U.S. District Court, Western District of North Carolina; 1996, U.S. Court of Appeals, Sixth Circuit; 1998, U.S. Court of Appeals, Fourth Circuit. *Education:* Lawrence University (B.A., 1978); New York Law School (J.D., 1983). *Member:* North Carolina Bar Association; National Employment Lawyers Association; The Association of Trial Lawyers of America; North Carolina Academy of Trial Lawyers. ***REPORTED CASES:*** Crowley v. CCair, Inc., 98 Fed Appx 930 (2004); Brewer v. Cabarrus Plastics, 592 S.E.2d 554 (2004); Brewer v. Cabarrus Plastics, 586 S.E.2d 819 (2003); Brewer v. Cabarrus Plastics, 574 S.E.2d 675 (2002); Brewer v. Cabarrus Plastics, 551 S.E.2d 902 (2001); Smith v. First Union National Bank, 202 F.3d 234 (2000); Brewer v. Cabarrus Plastics, 504 S.E.2d 580 (1998); Russell v. Carolina Machine & Associates, Inc., 500 S.E.2d 728 (1998). ***PRACTICE AREAS:*** Discrimination; Labor and Employment.

ASSOCIATE

JOSHUA REED VAN KAMPEN, born Fayetteville, North Carolina, September 2, 1971; admitted to bar, 1998, Illinois; 2004, North Carolina. *Education:* Purdue University (B.A., 1993); University of Illinois (J.D., magna cum laude, 1998). Author: "The Fair Housing Act's Protections of Children," *GP Solo and Small Firm Lawyer,* Volume 15, Number 5, October/November 1998. *Member:* Chicago and Illinois State Bar Associations. ***REPORTED CASES:*** Fantasia Fresh Juice Co., 335 NLRB No. 61; Butera Finer Foods, Inc, 334 NLRB 43 (2001). ***PRACTICE AREAS:*** Labor Relations; Employment Litigation.

GACH LAW FIRM, PLLC

Established in 1990
6000 MONROE ROAD SUITE 350
CHARLOTTE, NORTH CAROLINA 28212
Telephone: 704-531-9355
FAX: 704-531-9354
Email: greg.gach@gachlaw.com
URL: http://www.lawyers.com/gregoryhgach

Corporate, Contract, Corporate Finance, Partnership and Commercial Real Estate. Federal, State and Local Taxation. Sports and Entertainment Law. Motorsports Law and Automobile Dealership Law.

GREGORY H. GACH, born Royal Oak, Michigan, 1959; admitted to bar, 1985, North Carolina and U.S. Tax Court. *Education:* Miami University (B.S., summa cum laude, 1982); The University of Michigan (J.D., cum laude, 1985). Beta Gamma Sigma. *Member:* Mecklenburg County Bar Association; North Carolina State Bar.

BRIAN H. NOLEN, born Carmi, Illinois, August 2, 1976; admitted to bar, 2002, Illinois; 2004, North Carolina. *Education:* Eastern Illinois University (B.S., 1998); John Marshall Law School (J.D., cum laude, 2002). *Member:* North Carolina State Bar. [Enlisted/Commissioned Officer, Army National Guard, 1993-2002]. ***PRACTICE AREAS:*** Corporate Law; Corporate Contracts; Corporate Finance; Partnership Law; Commercial Real Estate; Entertainment Law; Sports Law. ***Email:*** brian.nolen@gachlaw.com

REPRESENTATIVE CLIENTS: Hendrick Automotive Group; Hendrick Motorsports; Beck Imports of the Carolinas; Joe Gibbs Racing; Beck Automotive Group; World Class Automotive Group; National Speed Sport News.
REFERENCES: Branch Banking and Trust Company; Bank of America.

GARFINKEL IMMIGRATION LAW FIRM

6230 FAIRVIEW ROAD, SUITE 105
CHARLOTTE, NORTH CAROLINA 28210
Telephone: 704-442-8000
Fax: 704-442-8080
Email: shg@gilfusa.com
URL: http://www.gilfusa.com

Immigration and Naturalization Law, primarily Employment-Based Immigration.

(This Listing Continued)

FIRM PROFILE: The Garfinkel Immigration Law Firm's primary emphasis is business immigration. We routinely assist companies and individuals throughout the United States in connection with employment-based visa petitions and applications. Will also assist with family based and citizenship matters.

STEVEN H. GARFINKEL, born Belleville, New Jersey, October 25, 1959; admitted to bar, 1984, North Carolina. *Education:* Wake Forest University (B.A., cum laude, 1981; J.D., 1984). Member: Parker, Poe, Adams and Bernstein, 1989-1997. *Member:* Mecklenburg County and North Carolina Bar Associations; American Immigration Lawyers Association, Carolinas Chapter (Chairperson, 1992-1994). (Board Certified Specialist in Immigration Law, North Carolina State Board of Legal Specialization). ***PRACTICE AREAS:*** Immigration and Naturalization; Business Immigration; Citizenship; Consular Law. ***Email:*** shg@gilfusa.com

ASSOCIATES

JENNIFER L. CORY, born Orlando, Florida, May 10, 1969; admitted to bar, 1995, Florida (Not admitted in North Carolina). *Education:* Hollins College (B.A., 1991); Université de Paris-Sorbonne (Certificat Pratique de Langue Français ler Degré, 1991); Chambre de Commerce et d'Industrie de Paris (Certificat Pratique de Français Commerçial et Economique, 1991); Tulane Institute of European Legal Studies (Certificate in European Legal Studies, 1993); Stetson University (J.D., 1994). *Member:* American Immigration Lawyers Association, Central Florida Chapter (Treasurer, 1998; Secretary, 1999). ***LANGUAGES:*** French. ***PRACTICE AREAS:*** Immigration and Naturalization. ***Email:*** jlc@gilfusa.com

SUSAN W. RAMOS, born Smithfield, North Carolina, February 27, 1971; admitted to bar, 1999, Texas; 2000, North Carolina. *Education:* Emory University (B.A., 1993); St. Mary's University (J.D., 1999). *Member:* Mecklenburg County Bar Association; State Bar of Texas; North Carolina State Bar; American Immigration Lawyers Association (Carolinas Chapter). ***LANGUAGES:*** Spanish. ***PRACTICE AREAS:*** Immigration and Naturalization. ***Email:*** swr@gilfusa.com

LEGAL SUPPORT PERSONNEL

BUFFY K. DOVER, born Charlotte, North Carolina, July 1, 1972. *Education:* King's College (Legal Secretarial, 1992). (Legal Assistant). ***Email:*** bkd@gilfusa.com

ALISA DOUGLAS, born Mount Clemens, Michigan, August 3, 1969. *Education:* Saginaw Valley State University (B.A., English, 1993). (Legal Assistant). ***Email:*** amd@gilfusa.com

MARGARET CARR HUGHES, born Boone County, Missouri, May 3, 1972. *Education:* University of Virginia (B.A., 1994); University of Arizona (M.A., 1998). (Legal Assistant). ***Email:*** mch@gilfusa.com

AMY E. HILTON, born Thomasville, North Carolina, June 30, 1973. *Education:* University of North Carolina at Chapel Hill (B.A., 1995). (Legal Assistant). ***LANGUAGES:*** Spanish. ***Email:*** aeh@gilfusa.com

WILLIAM RICHARDSON, born Stokesdale, North Carolina, April 1982. *Education:* Queens University (B.A., 2004). (Legal Assistant)

ANNE GRAY SEMMLER, born New Orleans, Louisiana, July 7, 1956. *Education:* Duke University (B.A., Comparative Literature, 1978). (Legal Assistant). ***LANGUAGES:*** Russian and German. ***Email:*** ags@gilfusa.com

DEBBIE ELIZABETH SIGMON, born Asheville, North Carolina, April 3, 1963. *Education:* University of North Carolina at Charlotte (B.A., English, 1985). (Legal Assistant). ***Email:*** des@gilfusa.com

BETH R. TART, born Durham, North Carolina, June 2, 1960. *Education:* Furman University (B.A., 1983). (Legal Assistant). ***Email:*** brt@gilfusa.com

GARIS LAW FIRM

4929 MONROE ROAD
CHARLOTTE, NORTH CAROLINA 28205
Telephone: 704-536-3336
Fax: 704-536-3316
Email: jeff@garislaw.com
URL: http://www.garislaw.com

Corporate Law, Business Law, Contracts, Collections, Employment, Real Estate, Foreclosure, Trusts and Estates, Wills, Bankruptcy, Debtor and Creditor, Personal Injury, Automobile Accidents, Workers Compensation, Uncontested Divorces, Family Law, Construction, Litigation.

JEFFREY I. GARIS, born New York, N.Y., January 22, 1954; admitted to bar, 1990, New York and Connecticut; 1996, North Carolina; U.S. District Court, Western, Middle and Eastern Districts of North Carolina. *Education:* Polytechnic Institute of New York (B.S.E.E., 1975); Pace University (J.D., 1990). Clerk, Superior Court, Mecklenburg County, North Carolina, 1996. *Member:* Mecklenburg County, New York State, Connecticut and American Bar Associations; North Carolina State Bar. ***LANGUAGES:*** Spanish.

GARLITZ & WILLIAMSON, PLLC

212 SOUTH TRYON STREET
SUITE 930, THE JOHNSTON BUILDING
CHARLOTTE, NORTH CAROLINA 28281
Telephone: 704-372-1282
Fax: 704-372-1621
URL: http://www.lawyers.com/garlitzwilliamson

General Civil Practice in all Courts. Litigation, Appellate Practice, Insurance, Commercial Litigation, Employment Litigation, Transportation, Personal Injury, Creditors Rights, Environmental Litigation, Professional Liability, Governmental Liability, ERISA Litigation, Mediation and Arbitration.

(This Listing Continued)

GARLITZ & WILLIAMSON, PLLC, Charlotte—Continued

FIRM PROFILE: Garlitz & Williamson, PLLC has a general civil litigation practice with particular concentration in the areas of commercial and insurance litigation.

THOMAS D. GARLITZ, born Cumberland, Maryland, May 5, 1953; admitted to bar, 1978, North Carolina, U.S. District Court, Western, Middle and Eastern Districts of North Carolina and U.S. Court of Appeals, Fourth Circuit. *Education:* University of North Carolina (A.B., 1975; J.D., with honors, 1978). Phi Beta Kappa. Research Editor, North Carolina Law Review, 1977-1978. Law Clerk to the Hon. J. Dickson Phillips, Jr., U.S. Court of Appeals, Fourth Circuit, 1978-1979. *Member:* Association of Transportation Practitioners. ***PRACTICE AREAS:*** Appellate Practice; Insurance Litigation; Employment Litigation; Commercial Litigation; Transportation Litigation. ***Email:*** tgarlitz@gwattorneys.com

F. LANE WILLIAMSON, born Charlotte, North Carolina, October 6, 1953; admitted to bar, 1978, North Carolina, U.S. District Court, Western, Middle and Eastern Districts of North Carolina; U.S. Court of Appeals, Fourth Circuit; U.S. Supreme Court. *Education:* New College (B.A., 1975); University of North Carolina at Chapel Hill (J.D., with honors, 1978). Recipient, Henry P. Brandis, Jr. Law Review Award for Best Student Writing. Staff Member, University of North Carolina Law Review, 1976-1978. Certified Mediator. *Member:* North Carolina State Bar Disciplinary Hearing Commission. ***PRACTICE AREAS:*** Commercial Litigation; Insurance Litigation; Creditors Rights; Professional Liability; Personal Injury; Mediation. ***Email:*** lwilliamson@gwattorneys.com

OF COUNSEL

THOMAS ASHE LOCKHART, born Charlotte, North Carolina, April 5, 1928; admitted to bar, 1951, North Carolina, U.S. District Court, Western and Middle Districts of North Carolina, U.S. Court of Appeals, Fourth Circuit and U.S. Supreme Court. *Education:* University of North Carolina (A.B., 1949; J.D., 1951). Phi Delta Phi. Chair, General Practice Section, North Carolina Bar Association, 1989-1991. Permanent Member, Judicial Conference, Fourth Circuit since 1955. *Member:* Federal Bar Association; Association of Life Insurance Counsel; National Association of Railroad Trial Counsel.

All Attorneys are Members of the North Carolina and American Bar Associations and the 26th Judicial District and The North Carolina State Bars.

INSURANCE CLIENTS: Atlantic Mutual Insurance Co.; Allstate Life Insurance Co.; American General Life & Accident Insurance Co.; CNA Insurance Companies; Hartford Accident & Indemnity Co.; Jefferson Pilot Financial Insurance Co.; Metropolitan Life Insurance Co.; Penn Mutual Life Insurance Co.; Phoenix Home Life Insurance Co.; Shelby/Vesta Insurance Cos.; Standard Insurance Co.; Western World Insurance Group.
GENERAL CORPORATE CLIENTS: Environmental Support Services, Inc.; Eurotherm Drives, Inc.; InterCon Building Corp.; United Mortgage Company.
REFERENCES: Bank of America; Branch Banking & Trust Co.

GERDES, MASON & SIMPSON, L.L.P.

Established in 1964
216 NORTH MCDOWELL STREET, SUITE 110
P.O. BOX 30068
CHARLOTTE, NORTH CAROLINA 28230
Telephone: 704-372-3180
Fax: 704-343-2942
Email: gmsl@gmsllaw.com
URL: http://www.gmsllaw.com

General Civil and Criminal Trial Practice before all State and Federal Courts. Personal Injury, Wrongful Death, Social Security Disability, Corporation, Real Estate, Bankruptcy, Domestic Relations, Estate Planning and Probate Law.

MEMBERS OF FIRM

PHILLIP E. GERDES, born Wilmington, North Carolina, August 22, 1938; admitted to bar, 1964, North Carolina. *Education:* University of North Carolina (B.A., 1960; J.D., 1964). Member, Mecklenburg County Board of County Commissioners, 1972-1976. Member, North Carolina Social Services Commission, 1974-1979. *Member:* 26th Judicial District and North Carolina Bar Associations; North Carolina State Bar; North Carolina Academy of Trial Lawyers. ***PRACTICE AREAS:*** Personal Injury; Wrongful Death; Real Estate; Wills; Trusts and Estates. ***Email:*** peg@gmsllaw.com

JAMES L. MASON, JR., born Charlotte, North Carolina, February 16, 1945; admitted to bar, 1972, North Carolina. *Education:* Davidson College (B.A., 1967); University of North Carolina (J.D., 1972). *Member:* 26th Judicial District and North Carolina Bar Associations; North Carolina State Bar; North Carolina Academy of Trial Lawyers. [1st Lt. U.S. Army, 1967-1969]. ***PRACTICE AREAS:*** Domestic Relations; Corporate Law; Personal Injury; Wills; Trusts and Estates. ***Email:*** jm@gmsllaw.com

DAVID T. SIMPSON, JR., born Charlotte, North Carolina, May 14, 1959; admitted to bar, 1984, North Carolina and U.S. District Court, Western District of North Carolina; 1992, U.S. Court of Appeals, Fourth Circuit. *Education:* University of North Carolina at Chapel Hill (B.S., 1981; J.D., 1984). Beta Gamma Sigma. Author: "Involuntary Civil Commitment: The Dangerousness Standard and Its Problems," University of North Carolina Law Review, Vol. 63, Issue 1, 1984. *Member:* 26th Judicial District and North Carolina Bar Associations; North Carolina State Bar; North Carolina Academy of Trial Lawyers; National Organization of Social Security Claimant's Representatives. ***PRACTICE AREAS:*** Collections; Social Security Disability; Personal Injury; Bankruptcy. ***Email:*** dts@gmsllaw.com

BENJAMIN D. WILLIAMS, born Charlotte, North Carolina, January 12, 1978; admitted to bar, 2003, North Carolina and U.S. District Court, Western District of North Carolina; 2004, U.S. District Curt, Eastern District of North Carolina. *Education:* University of North Carolina at Chapel Hill (B.A., 2000; J.D., 2003). *Member:* North Carolina State Bar. ***PRACTICE AREAS:*** Collections; Personal Injury; Social Security Disability; Litigation. ***Email:*** bdw@gmsllaw.com

(This Listing Continued)

REPRESENTATIVE CLIENTS: First Charter National Bank; First-Citizens Bank and Trust Co.; Trinity Bank, American Community Bank; Charlotte Gift and Jewelry Show, Inc.; Mecklenburg Printing, Inc.; Griffin Management Services, Inc.; First Charter Insurance Services, Inc.; Carolina Concrete, Inc.; Griffin Motor Company; Benderson Development Company; County Electric Supply Company, Ltd.
APPROVED ATTORNEYS FOR: Lawyers Title Insurance Corp.; First Title Insurance Co.; Stewart Title Insurance Co.; Farmers Home Administration; Chicago Title Insurance; Commonwealth Title Insurance; Investors Title Insurance Co.
REFERENCE: First Trust Bank.

DONALD S. GILLESPIE, JR.

122 NORTH MCDOWELL STREET
CHARLOTTE, NORTH CAROLINA 28204
Telephone: 704-375-8750
Fax: 704-375-8759
Email: Donald-Gillespie@hbm-attys.com

General Civil and Trial Practice in all Courts, Family Law, Real Property, Guardianships, Decedent's Estates and Probate.

DONALD S. GILLESPIE, JR., born East Orange, New Jersey, August 29, 1945; admitted to bar, 1971, North Carolina and U.S. District Court, Western District of North Carolina; 1973, U.S. Court of Appeals, Fourth Circuit; 1978, U.S. Supreme Court; 1980, U.S. District Court, Middle and Eastern Districts of North Carolina. *Education:* Davidson College (B.A., 1967); University of North Carolina (J.D., 1970). *Member:* North Carolina and American Bar Associations; North Carolina State Bar; North Carolina Academy of Trial Lawyers.

REFERENCES: Bank of America; First Trust Bank; Wachovia Bank; The Scottish Bank.

GOLDING HOLDEN & POPE, L.L.P.

3325 SPRINGBANK LANE, SUITE 304
CHARLOTTE, NORTH CAROLINA 28226
Telephone: 704-374-1600
Fax: 704-759-8966

General Insurance and Civil Defense Practice in State and Federal Courts, Professional Malpractice, Fire, Casualty and Life Insurance, Surety Practice, Workers Compensation, Construction, Premises and Products Liability.

MEMBERS OF FIRM

JOHN G. GOLDING, born 1928; admitted to bar, 1953, North Carolina; U.S. District Court, Western District of North Carolina. *Education:* Williams College (B.A., 1950); University of North Carolina (J.D., 1953). Editor-in-Chief, North Carolina Law Review, 1953. Listed in The Best Lawyers in America, (White/Woodward). *Member:* American College of Trial Lawyers; North Carolina State Bar; North Carolina Bar Association; Mecklenburg County Bar Association (President, 1975-1976); Association of Insurance Attorneys; North Carolina Association of Defense Attorneys (President, 1983-1984); Defense Research Institute.

C. BYRON HOLDEN, born 1950; admitted to bar, 1975, North Carolina; U.S. District Court, Eastern, Western and Middle Districts of North Carolina; U.S. Court of Appeals, Fourth Circuit. *Education:* Yale University (B.A., 1972); Wake Forest University (J.D., 1975). Board of Editors, Wake Forest Law Review. *Member:* North Carolina State Bar; North Carolina Bar Association; Mecklenburg County Bar Association; North Carolina Association of Defense Attorneys; North Carolina Chapter, International Association of Arson Investigators; Defense Research Institute; North Carolina Insurance Crime Information Exchange; North Carolina Chapter, International Association of Special Investigative Units.

JAMES W. POPE, born 1952; admitted to bar, 1981, North Carolina and South Carolina; U.S. District Court, Western and Middle Districts of North Carolina. *Education:* University of North Carolina at Chapel Hill (B.A., 1977); University of South Carolina (J.D., 1981). Member, South Carolina Law Review, 1979-1981. *Member:* North Carolina Bar Association; Mecklenburg County Bar Association; North Carolina State Bar; South Carolina Bar; North Carolina Association of Defence Attorneys; Defense Research Institute; North Carolina Insurance Crime Information Exchange. [With U.S. Army, 1972-1974]

ASSOCIATES

ROBERT J. AYLWARD, born 1961; admitted to bar, 1993, North Carolina and New York; U.S. District Court, Western and Middle Districts of North Carolina. *Education:* State University of New York, Oneonta (B.A., 1983); Webster University (M.A., 1986); Jacob D. Fuchsberg Law School, Touro College (J.D., 1992). Recipient, American Jurisprudence Award, Trial Practice. *Member:* Mecklenburg County Bar Association; North Carolina State Bar; New York State Bar Association; North Carolina Association of Defense Attorneys; North Carolina Chapter, International Association of Arson Investigators; North Carolina Insurance Crime Information Exchange. [United States Air Force, 1983-1987]

ELIZABETH SPRENGER, born 1975; admitted to bar, 2001, North Carolina; U.S. District Court, Western District of North Carolina. *Education:* Wake Forest University (B.A., 1998); Columbus School of Law of The Catholic University of America (J.D., 2001). Managing Editor, Journal of Contemporary Health Law and Policy. Author: "The Family and Medical Leave Act—Well Meaning Legislation Meets the Strong Arm of the Constitution of the United States," 17 J. Contemp. Health L. & Pol'y 349 (2000). *Member:* North Carolina State Bar; Mecklenburg County Bar Association; North Carolina Association of Defense Attorneys; North Carolina Insurance Crime Information Exchange.

J. SCOTT BAYNE, born Genoa, Nebraska, September 6, 1963; admitted to bar, 1988, Iowa; 2000, North Carolina. *Education:* Nebraska Wesleyan University (B.A., 1985); University of Nebraska at Lincoln (J.D., with distinction, 1988). Phi Delta Phi. Member, National College of Advocates, 1990. *Member:* American Bar Association; North Carolina

(This Listing Continued)

State Bar; Mecklenburg County Bar Association. ***PRACTICE AREAS:*** Litigation; Personal Injury; Medical Malpractice; Automobile Accidents; Slip and Fall; Wrongful Death; Workers Compensation.

REPRESENTATIVE CLIENTS: Allstate Insurance Company; AIG; Amerisure Companies; AMICA Mutual Insurance Company; Atlantic Companies; Auto-Owners Insurance Company; Builders Mutual Insurance Company; Carolinas Medical Center/Healthcare; Cincinnati Insurance Companies; CNA Insurance; Chubb Group; Farmers Insurance Group; Freightliner Corporation; Gallagher Bassett Services, Inc.; GMAC; MAG Mutual Insurance; Montgomery Mutual Insurance Company; Nationwide Mutual Insurance Company; North Carolina Farm Bureau; North Carolina Insurance Guaranty Assoc.; Preferred Mutual Fire Insurance Company; Reciprocal Group; Roadway Express, Inc.; Selective Insurance Company; State Auto Group; State Farm Insurance Companies; The Doctor's Company; Transport Insurance Company.

PAUL M. GOODSON

MIDTOWN PLAZA, SUITE 425
1300 BAXTER STREET
P.O. BOX 35341
CHARLOTTE, NORTH CAROLINA 28235
Telephone: 704-331-8014
Toll Free 1-866-NC HURT 1 (866-624-8781)
Fax: 704-331-8017
URL: http://www.lawyers.com/goodson
Email: potentialclient@pgoodsonlaw.com
URL: http://www.pgoodson.com

Durham, North Carolina Office: 3101 Guess Road, F-106, 27705. Telephone: 919-471-5000; 877-298-3634.
Raleigh, North Carolina Office: 422 St. Mary's Street, Suite 1, 27605. Telephone: 919-834-6360; 877-298-3634.

Civil Litigation, Personal Injury, Auto Accidents, Slip & Fall, Social Security Disability, Wrongful Death and Workers Compensation, Class Action, Pharmaceutical Class Action.

PAUL M. GOODSON, born Charlotte, North Carolina, August 14, 1968; admitted to bar, 1995, North Carolina; 1996, U.S. Court of Appeals, Fourth Circuit; 2000, South Carolina. *Education:* University of North Carolina, Chapel Hill (B.S., 1990); Wake Forest University (J.D., 1995). Former Insurance Defense Attorney. *Member:* Mecklenburg County Bar Association; North Carolina State Bar; South Carolina State Bar, National Organization of Social Security Claimants Representatives; North Carolina Academy of Trial Lawyers. ***PRACTICE AREAS:*** Civil Litigation; Personal Injury; Automobile Accidents; Slip and Fall; Social Security Disability; Wrongful Death; Workers' Compensation; Mass Torts; Class Actions - Pharmaceutical.

ASSOCIATE

WILLIAM J. GARRITY, born Evanston, Illinois, January 22, 1960; admitted to bar, 1985, North Carolina. *Education:* Washington & Lee University (B.S., 1982); Wake Forest University (J.D., 1985). *Member:* Mecklenburg County and North Carolina Bar Association; North Carolina Academy of Trial Lawyers. ***PRACTICE AREAS:*** Workers' Compensation.

ALAN GORDON IMMIGRATION LAW

Established in 1982

1018 EAST BOULEVARD, SUITE 7
CHARLOTTE, NORTH CAROLINA 28203
Telephone: 704-332-2555
Fax: 704-377-1172
Email: asgordon@greencards.com
URL: http://www.greencards.com

Concentrating in Immigration Law including Employment Visas, Visas for Healthcare Professionals, Investor Visas, Consular Processing, Citizenship Law, Employment Verification (Form I-9) Law, Due Diligence during Mergers and Acquisitions; and Immigration and Citizenship Matters for Foreign Nationals, and their families.

FIRM PROFILE: Alan Gordon Immigration Law is committed to providing its clients with superior professional legal services in the area of Immigration Law. With 27 years of experience, Mr. Gordon is a Board Certified Immigration Specialist and is past President of the American Immigration Lawyers Association (AILA), Carolinas Chapter.

MEMBER OF FIRM

ALAN GORDON, admitted to bar, 1977, North Carolina; 1978, Florida. *Education:* Pennsylvania State University (B.A., with distinction, 1974); University of Miami (J.D., 1977). Speaker, numerous seminars for: North Carolina and South Carolina Bar Associations; Metrolina World Trade Association; The Society for Human Resource Management; The National Association of Public Sector Equal Opportunity Officers; The Employers Association; Latin America Chamber of Commerce Charlotte, 2004; The American Immigration Lawyers Association. Listed in, The Best Lawyers in America, 1992-2004. Recognized as, Best Immigration Attorney, Charlotte Magazine, August 1991-2003. Awarded Latin American Excelente Award for Non-Latin Person Most Supportive of the Latino Community, La Noticia, 2002. *Member:* Mecklenburg Bar Association; North Carolina State Bar (Past Chair, Committee on Immigration and Naturalization Law, 1994-1999; Founding Chair, Committee on Certification of Immigration Law as a Specialty in North Carolina, 1994-1999); North Carolina Bar Association; The Florida Bar; American Immigration Lawyers Association (Co-Chair, Economics of Law Practice Committee, 1989-1990; Chair and Past President, Carolinas Chapter, 1981-1982.). (Board Certified Specialist in Immigration, North Carolina State Board of Legal Specialization). ***LANGUAGES:*** Spanish. ***REPORTED CASES:*** Manwani v. INS, 736 F. Supp. 1367 (W.D.N.C. 1990).

(This Listing Continued)

ASSOCIATE

MIGUEL MANNA, born Caracas, Venezuela, September 8, 1974; admitted to bar, 2004, Texas. *Education:* University of North Carolina at Charlotte (B.A., 1998); St. Mary's University of San Antonio (J.D., 2004). Pro Bono Achievement Award, Clinical Student of the Year. *Member:* State Bar of Texas. ***LANGUAGES:*** Spanish. ***PRACTICE AREAS:*** Immigration Law. ***Email:*** mmanna@greencards.com

Languages: Spanish.

GORMAN & DITTNER

13925 BALLANTYNE CORPORATE PLACE, SUITE 200
CHARLOTTE, NORTH CAROLINA 28277
Telephone: 704-544-2500
Facsimile: 704-544-2596
URL: http://www.gormlaw.com

Trusts and Estates, Asset Protection, Estate Planning, Wills and Probate, Real Estate, Buying or Selling, Commercial Leasing, Construction, Corporate, Business Law, Franchises, Limited Liability Companies, Partnership, Contracts, Lawsuits, Mergers, Personal Injury, Automobile Accidents, Criminal Law, Shopping Center Development.

THOMAS J. GORMAN, born Rockville Centre, New York, May 16, 1960; admitted to bar, 1985, Texas and U.S. District Court, Northern District of Texas; 1987, North Carolina and U.S. District Court, Western District of North Carolina. *Education:* Boston College (B.A., Economics and English, magna cum laude, 1982); Duke University School of Law (J.D., 1985). Author and Lecturer: "Mastering Real Estate Titles in North Carolina," National Business Institute, 1995. Instructor, Real Estate Law, Institute of Financial Education, 1996. *Member:* Mecklenburg County and North Carolina (Member, Sections on: Real Property; Trusts and Estates) Bar Associations. ***PRACTICE AREAS:*** Commercial Real Estate; Corporate Law; Commercial Law; Wills; Trust Planning; Estate Planning; Probate.

DEREK E. DITTNER, born Washington, D.C., September 17, 1968; admitted to bar, 1995, North Carolina; 1998, South Carolina. *Education:* Clemson University (B.S., 1990); University of Baltimore (J.D., 1995). Staff Editor, Journal of Environmental Law. *Member:* Mecklenburg County Bar Association. ***PRACTICE AREAS:*** Residential Real Estate; Commercial Real Estate; Foreclosures; Corporate Law; Wills; Probate.

ASSOCIATES

DAVID GILARDI, admitted to bar, 1985, Massachusetts; 1988, U.S. District Court, Eastern District of Massachusetts; 1989, U.S. Court of Appeals, First Circuit; 2004, North Carolina. *Education:* Merrimack College (B.S. Business Administration, cum laude, 1981); Quinnipiac University School of Law (J.D., 1985). Men of Merrimack Award for Academic Excellence. Complex Entity Control Auditor, U.S. Department of the Treasury, Internal Revenue Service, 1986-1987, Law Office of David Gilardi, Gloucester, Massachusetts, 1987-1984. Essex County, Mass. Public Defender, 1995-2003. Attorney, Gorman & Dittner, P.A., June, 2005—. *Member:* Mecklenburg County Bar; North Carolina Bar Association. ***PRACTICE AREAS:*** Civil Litigation; Business Litigation; Commercial Litigation; Personal Injury; Automobile Accidents and Injuries; Domestic Relations; Criminal Law; Real Estate; Corporate Law; Foreclosures; Wills; Estate Administration.

JESSICA E. THURBEE, admitted to bar, 1997, North Carolina; 1999, South Carolina. *Education:* Davidson College (B.A., Psychology, 1992); Ohio Northern University (J.D., 1996). Staff Editor, Pharmacy Law Journal. Attorney, Professional Settlement Services, Charlotte, North Carolina 1998-1999; Attorney, Likens, Blomquist & Rank, P.A., Charlotte, North Carolina, 1999; Attorney, Sellers, Hinshaw, Ayers, Dortch & Lyons, P.A., Charlotte, North Carolina 2000-2005; Attorney, Gorman & Dittner, P.A., July 2005—. *Member:* Mecklenburg County Bar; North Carolina Bar Association. ***PRACTICE AREAS:*** Residential Real Estate; Commercial Real Estate; Homeowners Association Law; Foreclosures; Corporate Law; Commercial Law; Wills; Estate Planning; Estate Administration.

MARY LEE E. MROCHEK, admitted to bar, 1998, North Carolina; 1999, Alabama. *Education:* University of Alabama (B.A., English minors in Finance and Spanish, cum laude, 1995); Washington & Lee University School of Law (J.D., 1998). Alpha Delta Pi Sorority. Articles Staff, Environmental Law Digest. Attorney, Wainwright and Pope, Birmingham, Alabama, 1998-1999; Staff Attorney, J.A. Jones, Inc., Construction and Environmental Litigation Projects, and Corporate Transactional Work, 1999-2004; Attorney, Gorman & Dittner, P.A. 2005—. *Member:* Mecklenburg County Bar: North Carolina Bar Association. ***PRACTICE AREAS:*** Residential Real Estate; Commercial Real Estate; Corporate Law; Commercial Law; Wills; Trust Law. ***Email:*** mmrochek@jajones.com

GORMAN LAW FIRM

EL CENTRO HISPANO

Established in 1994

3410 CENTRAL AVENUE
CHARLOTTE, NORTH CAROLINA 28205
Telephone: 704-537-1400
Toll Free: 1-888-523-6876
Fax: 704-537-3727
URL: http://www.elcentrohispano.com
URL: http://www.lawyers.com/ruthgorman

Immigration and Naturalization, Business Immigration, Citizenship, Employment Authorizations, Employment Immigration, Employment Visas, Family Immigration, Labor Certificates, Visas, General Business Practice, Contracts, Corporations, International Law, Criminal Law, Misdemeanors.

FIRM PROFILE: Foreign Associated Professionals licensed and trained in Latin America (Peru, Venezuela, Mexico, Columbia & Costa Rica).

(This Listing Continued)

GORMAN LAW FIRM, EL CENTRO HISPANO, Charlotte—Continued

Our professional staff of accountants and lawyers uniquely equip us to provide a full service to both businesses and individuals with interests in Latin America - be it matters pertaining to immigration, business contracts or taxes. Our financial and legal professionals are bilingual and trained in both Latin American and U.S. Universities in their respective fields of expertise. We have assisted both employers and employees in facilitating employment in the U.S. along with assisting them in the development of their companies.

The firm is a member of the American Immigration Lawyers Association.

RUTH GORMAN-VEGA, born Managua, Nicaragua, September 28, 1965; admitted to bar, 1994, North Carolina. *Education:* Baylor University (B.B.A., 1988); Pepperdine University (J.D., 1990). Successful candidate of CPA exam, VA. KPMG Peat Marwick. *Member:* North Carolina Bar Association; American Immigration Lawyers Association. ***LANGUAGES:*** Spanish. ***PRACTICE AREAS:*** Immigration and Naturalization; Citizenship; Business Law; Construction Law; Criminal Law.

Language: Spanish.

REPRESENTATIVE CLIENTS: Bank of America; Wachovia.

GRIER FURR & CRISP

Established in 1984

101 NORTH TRYON STREET, SUITE 1240
CHARLOTTE, NORTH CAROLINA 28246
Telephone: 704-375-3720
FAX: 704-332-0215
URL: http://www.grierlaw.com

General Civil Trial and Business Practice. Business, Bankruptcy, Corporations, Municipal, Real Estate and Land Use Regulation, Trusts, Wills, and Estates.

MEMBERS OF FIRM

JOSEPH W. GRIER, III, born Charlotte, North Carolina, April 8, 1951; admitted to bar, 1977, North Carolina and U.S. District Court, Western District of North Carolina; 1979, U.S. Court of Appeals, Fourth Circuit; 1988, U.S. District Court, Middle District of North Carolina. *Education:* University of North Carolina of Chapel Hill (B.A., 1973; J.D., 1977). Member, Order of the Grail. Member, American Law Institute. *Member:* North Carolina State Bar. (Board Certified Specialist in Bankruptcy Law, North Carolina State Board of Legal Specialization). ***PRACTICE AREAS:*** Business; Bankruptcy; Business Law; Commercial Real Estate; Debtor and Creditor. ***Email:*** jgrier@grierlaw.com

J. CAMERON FURR, JR., born Monroe, North Carolina, June 21, 1964; admitted to bar, 1989, North Carolina and U.S. District Court, Western District of North Carolina; 1991, U.S. Court of Appeals, Fourth Circuit. *Education:* University of North Carolina (B.A., 1986; J.D., 1989). Phi Delta Phi. Note and Comment Editor, North Carolina Law Review, 1988-1989. Author: "*Whitley v. Columbia Lumber Manufacturing Co.*: Abolishing the Exclusive Remedy Requirement for the Scheduled Injuries Section of the North Carolina Workers' Compensation Act," 66 North Carolina Law Review 1366 (1988). *Member:* North Carolina State Bar. ***PRACTICE AREAS:*** Business Law; Contracts; Corporate Law; Partnership Law; Zoning, Planning and Land Use. ***Email:*** cfurr@grierlaw.com

C. MICHAEL CRISP, born Gastonia, North Carolina, March 27, 1973; admitted to bar, 1998, North Carolina and U.S. District Court, Western District of North Carolina. *Education:* University of North Carolina at Chapel Hill (B.S., with distinction, 1995; J.D., 1998). Order of the Grail (Vice President); Order of the Golden Fleece; Phi Delta Phi. Member, North Carolina Journal of International Law and Commercial Regulation, 1996-1998. *Member:* North Carolina State Bar. ***PRACTICE AREAS:*** Estate Planning; Probate; Corporate Law; Contracts; Business Law. ***Email:*** mcrisp@grierlaw.com

ASSOCIATES

ALAN M. PRESEL, born Providence, Rhode Island, July 26, 1972; admitted to bar, 1997, North Carolina and U.S. District Court, Western and Eastern Districts of North Carolina. *Education:* Tufts University (B.S., summa cum laude, 1994); University of North Carolina at Chapel Hill (J.D., with honors, 1997). Phi Beta Kappa; Phi Delta Phi. Staff Member, North Carolina Law Review, 1995-1996. Publications Editor, North Carolina Banking Institute, 1996-1997. *Member:* North Carolina State Bar. ***PRACTICE AREAS:*** Business Law; Contracts; Corporate Law; Civil Litigation. ***Email:*** apresel@grierlaw.com

A. COTTEN WRIGHT, born Jacksonville, Florida, September 29, 1951; admitted to bar, 2001, North Carolina. *Education:* Jacksonville University (B.A., 1973); University of North Carolina at Chapel Hill (J.D., 2001). Member, North Carolina Journal of International Law & Commercial Regulation, 1999-2001. Law Clerk to the Honorable George R. Hodges, U.S. Bankruptcy Court, Western District of North Carolina, 2001-2002. ***PRACTICE AREAS:*** Bankruptcy. ***Email:*** cwright@grierlaw.com

OF COUNSEL

JOSEPH W. GRIER, JR., born Charlotte, North Carolina, August 5, 1915; admitted to bar, 1940, North Carolina; 1947, U.S. Supreme Court; 1952, U.S. Court of Appeals, Fourth Circuit. *Education:* University of North Carolina at Chapel Hill (A.B., 1937); Harvard Law School (LL.B., 1940). Member, Grier, Parker, Poe, Thompson, Bernstein, Gage and Preston, 1946-1983. Member, Fourth Circuit Judicial Conference, 1953—. *Member:* The North Carolina State Bar; American Law Institute. Fellow, American Bar Foundation. ***PRACTICE AREAS:*** Eminent Domain; Intellectual Property; Municipal Law; Religious Institutions; Trusts and Estates. ***Email:*** jgrierjr@grierlaw.com

REPRESENTATIVE CLIENTS: Audio/Video Systems; Auditorium-Coliseum-Convention Center Authority; Hagaman Animal Hospital, Inc.; Mary Ruth Robinson Educational Trust; Nisbet Oil Co.; Pyramid Motor Company; Rhodes & Beal Oil Co.; Triangle Leasing, Inc.

(This Listing Continued)

APPROVED ATTORNEYS FOR: Lawyers Title Insurance Corp.; Associates Commercial Corp.
REFERENCE: Bank of America.

GUTHRIE, DAVIS, HENDERSON & STATON, P.L.L.C.

Established in 1992

719 EAST BOULEVARD
CHARLOTTE, NORTH CAROLINA 28203
Telephone: 704-372-5600; 375-1431; 332-6141
Fax: 704-372-4601
Email: firm@gdhs.com
URL: http://www.firm@gdhs.com

Trial Practice in State and Federal Court. Litigation of Personal Injury, Premises Liability, Products Liability, and Criminal Law, General Civil Practice, Business Representation, Commercial Real Estate, Taxation, Estate Planning, Corporate and Securities Law, Zoning and Land Use, Creditor's Rights, Bankruptcy (creditors), Alcoholic Beverage Control, Media, Communications, Libel, Defamation, Banking, Probate and Construction.

MEMBERS OF FIRM

DENNIS L. GUTHRIE, born St. Louis, Missouri, August 21, 1944; admitted to bar, 1969, North Carolina. *Education:* Wofford College (A.B., 1966); Mercer University (J.D., 1969). Phi Alpha Delta (Vice-Justice, District XVI, 1968-1969). Assistant District Attorney, Mecklenburg County, 1971-1974. *Member:* 26th Judicial District, North Carolina and American (Member, Sections on: General Practice; Litigation) Bar Associations; North Carolina State Bar; The Association of Trial Lawyers of America. [(Captain, U.S. Army 1969-1971)]. ***PRACTICE AREAS:*** Commercial Litigation; Creditor's Rights; Bankruptcy; Administrative; Alcoholic Beverage Control. ***Email:*** dlguthrie@gdhs.com

K. NEAL DAVIS, born Goldsboro, North Carolina, September 28, 1948; admitted to bar, 1973, North Carolina. *Education:* Western Carolina University (B.S. in Business Administration, 1970); Cumberland School of Law of Samford University (J.D., 1973). Delta Theta Phi. Assistant District Attorney, Mecklenburg County, 1973-1979. *Member:* 26th Judicial District, North Carolina and American (Member, Sections on: General Practice, Litigation, Tort and Insurance Practice) Bar Associations; North Carolina State Bar; North Carolina Association of Defense Attorneys; Defense Research Institute. ***PRACTICE AREAS:*** Civil Litigation; Premises Liability; Products Liability; Personal Injury Litigation. ***Email:*** kndavis@gdhs.com

ROBERT E. HENDERSON, born Charlotte, North Carolina, March 1, 1954; admitted to bar, 1979, North Carolina. *Education:* Duke University (B.A., magna cum laude, 1976; J.D., 1979). *Member:* Mecklenburg County (President, 2001-2002), North Carolina and American (Member, Sections on: Real Property, Probate and Trust Law) Bar Associations; North Carolina State Bar. ***PRACTICE AREAS:*** Business Representation; Real Estate; Zoning and Land Use; Litigation. ***Email:*** rehenderson@gdhs.com

KEVIN W. TYDINGS, born Fairfax, Virginia, April 4, 1967; admitted to bar, 1992, Virginia; 1995, North Carolina. *Education:* University of Virginia (B.A., 1989); University of Richmond (J.D., 1992). Recipient, American Jurisprudence Award in Remedies. *Member:* Mecklenburg County, 26th Judicial District and North Carolina Bar Associations; North Carolina State Bar; Virginia State Bar. ***PRACTICE AREAS:*** Commercial Real Estate; Commercial Transactions; Corporate Law; Business Formation; Business Planning; Commercial Litigation. ***Email:*** ktydings@gdhs.com

RETIRED MEMBER

JOHN S. STATON, born Philadelphia, Pennsylvania, November 15, 1953; admitted to bar, 1980, North Carolina. *Education:* Duke University (B.A., 1976); Wake Forest University (J.D., 1980). Phi Delta Phi. Assistant District Attorney, Mecklenburg County, 1982-1987. *Member:* 26th Judicial District, North Carolina and American (Member, Sections on: Litigation and General Practice) Bar Associations; North Carolina State Bar; North Carolina Association of Defense Attorneys; Defense Research Institute. (Retired). ***PRACTICE AREAS:*** Premises Liability; Construction Litigation; Products Liability; Personal Injury Litigation; Criminal Law.

ASSOCIATE

BENJAMIN R. HARDWICK, born Winston-Salem, North Carolina, March 5, 1972; admitted to bar, 1997, North Carolina and U.S. District Court, Eastern, Middle and Western Districts of North Carolina. *Education:* University of North Carolina at Chapel Hill (B.A., 1994); Wake Forest University, School of Law (J.D., 1997). Phi Beta Kappa, Phi Delta Phi. *Member:* 26th Judicial District, North Carolina and American Bar Associations; North Carolina State Bar; North Carolina Association of Defense Attorneys. ***PRACTICE AREAS:*** Premises Liability; Products Liability; Personal Injury; Construction; Workers Compensation. ***Email:*** bhardwick@gdhs.com

OF COUNSEL

JOHN H. HASTY, born Charlotte, North Carolina, December 4, 1935; admitted to bar, 1960, North Carolina. *Education:* Wake Forest University (B.A., 1957; LL.B., 1960). Phi Delta Phi. Assistant District Attorney, 26th Judicial District, 1961-1966. *Member:* Mecklenburg County, North Carolina and American Bar Associations; North Carolina State Bar. ***PRACTICE AREAS:*** Media; Communications; Defense Litigation; First Amendment; Libel; Real Estate Zoning. ***Email:*** jhhasty@gdhs.com

JAMES D. MONTEITH, born Bushnell, North Carolina, February 22, 1931; admitted to bar, 1960, North Carolina; 1984, U.S. Tax Court. *Education:* University of North Carolina (A.B., 1957); Harvard University (LL.B., 1960). Phi Beta Kappa; Phi Eta Sigma. Member, American Law Institute. Permanent Member, Federal Judicial Conference for the Fourth Circuit. *Member:* Mecklenburg County, North Carolina and American Bar Associations; North Carolina State Bar. ***PRACTICE AREAS:*** Corporate and Banking Law; Taxation; Commercial Real Estate; Estate Planning. ***Email:*** jdmonteith@gdhs.com

(This Listing Continued)

WILLIAM J. WAGGONER, born Salisbury, North Carolina, October 13, 1928; admitted to bar, 1954, North Carolina. *Education:* Catawba College; University of North Carolina (A.B., 1951; LL.B., 1954). Assistant United States Attorney, Western District of North Carolina, 1957-1959. Chairman, Charlotte Zoning Board of Adjustment, 1970-1972. Member, North Carolina State Board of Elections, 1973-1977. Listed in Who's Who in American Law. *Member:* Mecklenburg County, North Carolina and American Bar Associations; North Carolina State Bar. ***PRACTICE AREAS:*** Business Law; Tax; Estate Planning; Construction. ***Email:*** wjwaggoner@gdhs.com

S. DEAN HAMRICK, born Shelby, North Carolina, September 12, 1928; admitted to bar, 1952, North Carolina. *Education:* Wake Forest University (B.S., 1949); University of North Carolina (J.D., with honors, 1952). Phi Delta Phi (Province President, 1964-1970). Member, Editorial Staff, North Carolina Law Review, 1950-1952. Permanent Member, Federal Judicial Conference for the Fourth Circuit. *Member:* Mecklenburg County (President, 1977-1978), North Carolina and American Bar Associations; North Carolina State Bar (Council Member, 1980-1986). Fellow, American Bar Foundation. ***PRACTICE AREAS:*** Civil Litigation; Fidelity & Surety Law; Insurance; Workers Compensation Law; Creditor's Rights Law. ***Email:*** sdhamrick@gdhs.com

KIMBERLY R. MATTHEWS, born Richmond, Virginia, December 25, 1966; admitted to bar, 1992, North Carolina. *Education:* Davidson College (B.A., 1989); Wake Forest University (J.D., 1992). *Member:* 26th Judicial District and North Carolina Bar Associations; North Carolina State Bar; North Carolina Association of Defense Attorneys; Defense Research Institute. ***PRACTICE AREAS:*** Premises Liability; Civil Litigation. ***Email:*** kmatthews@gdhs.com

REPRESENTATIVE CLIENTS: Aramark, Inc.; Blalock Realty; Carolina Industrial Equipment; Chrysler Credit Corp.; Claude Smith Enterprise, Inc.; Club Corp of America, Inc.; Cox Enterprises, Inc.; Creative Loafing Publishing; Crown Castle USA, Inc.; Empire Distributors of North Carolina, Inc.; The F.A. Bartlett Tree Expert Co.; The FWA Group; Federal Insurance Co.; Firemen's Insurance Co.; First Carolina Investors; First Scotland Financial Corp.; Hooters, Inc.; Hughes Supply, Inc.; Huntington Management, Co.; Lowe's Companies, Inc.; Michael M. King & Associates, Inc.; National Golf Club; National Golf Corp.; Pep Boys - Manny, Moe & Jack; Piedmont Natural Gas Co.; Peterbilt of Knoxville, Inc.; Rare Hospitality, Inc.; Ruth's Salads Cos.; SPC Food Service, Benz, Inc.; Specialty Risk Services (SRS); SouthTrust Mortgage Corp.; Starbucks Corp.; Time Oil Corp.; T.L. Harrell's Construction Co.; Tri-City, Inc.; Union Carbide Corp.; W.A. Brown & Son, Inc.; Wal-Mart Stores, Inc.; WAXN-TV; WSOC Television, Inc.
APPROVED ATTORNEYS FOR: Chicago Title Insurance Co.; Commonwealth Land Title Insurance Co.; Lawyers Title Insurance Corp.; First American Title Insurance Co., LLC; Jefferson Pilot Insurance Co.; Stewart Title of the Piedmont; Ticor Title Insurance Co.; Fidelity National Title Insurance Company of Pennsylvania.

THE HAMEL LAW FIRM, P.A.

WOODFIELD CORPORATE CENTER, SUITE 208
8008 CORPORATE CENTER DRIVE
CHARLOTTE, NORTH CAROLINA 28226
Telephone: 704-542-1648
Telecopier: 704-542-8616
Email: thehamellawfirm.com
URL: http://www.lawyers.com/hamellawfirm

General Practice, Civil Litigation, Commercial Law, Business Law, Corporate Law, Immigration Law, Personal Injury, Estate Planning, Trust Law, Probate, Insurance, Real Estate.

REGINALD S. HAMEL, born Burlington, Vermont, June 7, 1933; admitted to bar, 1962, North Carolina, U.S. District Court, Eastern, Middle and Western Districts of North Carolina and U.S. Court of Appeals, Fourth Circuit. *Education:* University of North Carolina and Duke University (A.B., 1954); George Washington University and Wake Forest University (J.D., 1962). Research Assistant to Justice Carlisle W. Higgins, North Carolina Supreme Court, 1962-1963. *Member:* Mecklenburg County (Former Member, Executive Committee; Former Chairman, Grievance and Ethics, Law Day, and Public Information Committees; Former Member, Professionalism and Long Range Planning Committees), North Carolina (Member, Sections on: Business; Estate Planning; Litigation; Real Property) and American (Member, Sections on: Business; Litigation; Real Property, Probate and Trust) Bar Associations; North Carolina State Bar; The Association of Trial Lawyers of America; American Immigration Lawyers Association. ***LANGUAGES:*** Vietnamese. ***PRACTICE AREAS:*** Business Law; Commercial Litigation; Corporate Law; Estate Planning; Commercial Real Estate; Commercial Leasing; Immigration Law; Franchise Law; Securities. ***Email:*** rshamel@thehamellawfirm.com

WILLIAM F. HAMEL, born Burlington, Vermont, August 8, 1939; admitted to bar, 1969, North Carolina; U.S. District Court, Western and Middle Districts of North Carolina. *Education:* Belmont University (B.S., 1962); University of Memphis (J.D., 1969). Phi Delta Phi (Magistrate, 1969). Certified Mediator. *Member:* Mecklenburg County (Member: Grievance and Ethics Committee, 1985-1988; Public Information and Education Committee, 1990-1992; Fee Arbitration Committee, 1991-1994; North Carolina Public Information and Education Committee, 1991-1994; Authorized Practice of Law Committee, 1997—, Chairman, 1997-2000), North Carolina and American (Member: Negligence and Compensation Law Section; Commercial Transactions Committee; Intellectual Property Law Committee; Litigation Section; Lawyer Effective and Quality of Life Committee) Bar Associations; North Carolina State Bar; 26th Judicial District; North Carolina Academy of Trial Lawyers; Conference on Personal Finance Law. ***PRACTICE AREAS:*** Civil Litigation; Commercial Litigation; Administrative Law; Corporate Law; Business Law; Personal Injury; Real Estate; Workers Compensation; Estate Planning; Estate Administration; Insurance. ***Email:*** billhamel@thehamellawfirm.com

PAUL G. WAMSLEY, born Atlanta, Georgia, May 10, 1962; admitted to bar, 1990, North Carolina and U.S. District Court, Western District of North Carolina. *Education:* The Catholic University of America (B.A., 1985); University of Dayton School of Law (J.D., 1990). *Member:* Mecklenburg County and North Carolina Bar Associations. ***PRACTICE AREAS:*** Civil Litigation; Corporate; Commercial; Personal Injury. ***Email:*** pgwamsley@thehamellawfirm.com

HAMILTON FAY MOON STEPHENS STEELE & MARTIN, PLLC

201 SOUTH COLLEGE STREET, SUITE 2020
CHARLOTTE, NORTH CAROLINA 28244-2020
Telephone: 704-344-1117
Facsimile: 704-344-1483
URL: http://www.lawHFM.com

Litigation, including Civil, Trial and Appellate Practice in all State and Federal Courts in North Carolina, and all Areas of Law, including Construction, Debtor/Creditor, Environmental, General Business, Intellectual Property, Labor and Employment, Land Use, Securities, Telecommunications, and Unfair Competition. Alternative Dispute Resolution, Arbitration and Mediation. Probate and Trusts and Estates, Business Litigation.

T. JONATHAN ADAMS, born Shelbyville, Kentucky, August 2, 1963; admitted to bar, 1995, North Carolina; 1996, U.S. District Court, Western District of North Carolina. *Education:* University of Kentucky (B.B.A., 1985); Duke University (M.Div., 1990); University of North Carolina (J.D., with honors, 1995). Note Editor, North Carolina Law Review, 1994-1995. Judicial Clerk to the Honorable John C. Martin, North Carolina Court of Appeals, 1995-1996. ***PRACTICE AREAS:*** Debtor/Creditor Law; Commercial Litigation; Appellate; Civil Litigation. ***Email:*** jadams@lawHFM.com

RICHARD E. FAY, born 1956; admitted to bar, 1981, Virginia; 1987, North Carolina; U.S. Supreme Court. *Education:* Davidson College (A.B., cum laude, 1978); University of Virginia (M.A., cum laude, 1981; J.D., 1981). Phi Delta Phi. Certified Mediator, North Carolina State and Federal Courts. *Member:* Mecklenburg County, North Carolina (CLE Chairman, Environmental and Natural Resources Law Section), Virginia, Federal and American (Chairman, Hazardous Waste Committee; Member: Natural Resources, Energy and Environmental Section; Litigation Section) Bar Associations. ***PRACTICE AREAS:*** Environmental; Telecommunications; Litigation. ***Email:*** rfay@lawHFM.com

MEG D. GOLDSTEIN, born 1954; admitted to bar, 1979, North Carolina; 1980, Georgia. *Education:* Washington University (B.A., 1976); University of North Carolina (J.D., 1979); New York University (LL.M., in Taxation, 1980). Author and Co-Editor, North Carolina Estate Administration Manual, 1984. *Member:* Mecklenburg County and North Carolina Bar Associations; State Bar of Georgia. ***PRACTICE AREAS:*** Charitable Organizations; Probate; Trusts and Estates. ***Email:*** mgoldstein@lawHFM.com

DAVID B. HAMILTON, born 1952; admitted to bar, 1977, North Carolina. *Education:* Georgetown University (B.S.F.S., magna cum laude, 1974); University of North Carolina (J.D., with honors, 1977). Phi Beta Kappa; Order of the Coif. Certified Mediator, North Carolina State and Federal Courts. Member: Panel of Arbitrators and Mediators, American Arbitration Association. *Member:* Mecklenburg County, North Carolina and American Bar Associations; The Arbitration Group. ***PRACTICE AREAS:*** Construction Litigation; Commercial Litigation; Civil Litigation; Mediation; Arbitration. ***Email:*** dhamilton@lawHFM.com

MARGARET BEHRINGER MALONEY, born 1959; admitted to bar, 1986, North Carolina. *Education:* Northwestern University (B.A., 1982), Duke University (J.D., 1985). Phi Beta Kappa. *Member:* Mecklenburg County, North Carolina and American (Member, Litigation and Employment Law Sections) Bar Associations. ***PRACTICE AREAS:*** Labor and Employment; Litigation. ***Email:*** mmaloney@lawHFM.com

BENTFORD E. MARTIN, born 1953; admitted to bar, 1978, North Carolina; U.S. Court of Appeals, Fourth Circuit; U.S. Supreme Court. *Education:* Wake Forest University (B.A., magna cum laude, 1975); University of North Carolina (J.D., with honors, 1978). Phi Alpha Theta; Phi Beta Kappa. North Carolina Law Review. *Member:* North Carolina and American Bar Associations; North Carolina State Bar. ***PRACTICE AREAS:*** Commercial Litigation; Construction Law. ***Email:*** bmartin@lawHFM.com

KEITH J. MERRITT, born 1965; admitted to bar, 1990, North Carolina; 1993, Texas. *Education:* University of North Carolina at Chapel Hill (B.A., with distinction, 1987; J.D., with honors, 1990). Member, North Carolina Journal of International Law and Commercial Regulation. *Member:* Mecklenburg County, North Carolina (Member, Litigation and Antitrust Sections) and American (Member: Litigation and Antitrust Sections; Natural Resources Section) Bar Associations. ***PRACTICE AREAS:*** Commercial Litigation; Petroleum Marketing; Litigation; Land Use Litigation. ***Email:*** kmerritt@lawHFM.com

TRAVIS W. MOON, born Berkeley, California, August 14, 1945; admitted to bar, 1971, North Carolina. *Education:* University of the South (B.A., 1967); University of North Carolina (J.D., 1971). Member, Board of Editors, North Carolina Law Review, 1970-1971. *Member:* Mecklenburg County, North Carolina (Member, Bankruptcy Section Council, 1982-1985) and American Bar Associations; The North Carolina State Bar; North Carolina Academy of Trial Lawyers. ***PRACTICE AREAS:*** Bankruptcy Law; Commercial Litigation; Real Estate. ***Email:*** tmoon@lawHFM.com

DAVID G. REDDING, born 1963; admitted to bar, 1997, North Carolina. *Education:* Boston College (B.A., cum laude, 1985); Wake Forest University (J.D., 1997). ***PRACTICE AREAS:*** Construction Litigation; Commercial Litigation. ***Email:*** dredding@lawHFM.com

JACKSON N. STEELE, born 1949; admitted to bar, 1975, North Carolina. *Education:* Davidson College (B.A., 1971); Vanderbilt University (J.D., 1975). Order of the Coif. Associate Editor, Vanderbilt Law Review, 1974-1975. Certified Mediator: North Carolina State and Federal Courts; Panel of Arbitrators and Mediators, American Arbitration Association. *Member:* Mecklenburg County (Chairman, ADR Section, 1999-2001) and North Carolina (Chairman, Litigation Section, 1987-1988) Bar Associations. ***PRACTICE AREAS:*** Commercial Litigation; Construction Litigation; Mediation; Arbitration. ***Email:*** jsteele@lawHFM.com

ROBERT C. STEPHENS, born Charlotte, North Carolina, August 18, 1945; admitted to bar, 1970, North Carolina; 1973, U.S. Court of Appeals, Fourth Circuit and U.S Supreme Court. *Education:* Wake Forest University (B.A., 1967; J.D., 1970). Phi Delta Phi. Editor in Chief, Wake Forest Law Review, 1969-1970. Member, Commercial and Construction Panel of Arbitrators, American Arbitration Association. Selected by Business North Carolina Magazine as One of the Elite Construction Lawyers in the State of North Carolina. CLE

(This Listing Continued)

HAMILTON FAY MOON STEPHENS STEELE & MARTIN, PLLC, Charlotte—Continued

Lecturer on Construction Law Issues. *Member:* Mecklenburg County Bar Association (Member and President, Board of Directors). [1st Lt., USAR, Active Duty, 1970-1972]. ***PRACTICE AREAS:*** Commercial Litigation; Construction Litigation; Arbitration; Real Estate Litigation; Appellate Practice. ***Email:*** bstephens@lawHFM.com

GEORGE W. SISTRUNK, III, born 1973; admitted to bar, 1998, North Carolina. *Education:* College of William and Mary (B.A., 1995); Wake Forest University (J.D., 1998). Phi Delta Phi. Member, Moot Court Board. Member, Wake Forest University Law Review. Author: 32 Wake Forest Law Review 1021 (Fall 1997). ***PRACTICE AREAS:*** Real Estate; Real Estate Litigation; Commercial Litigation; Land Use. ***Email:*** gsistrunk@lawHFM.com

ALLEN L. WEST, born New York, New York,; admitted to bar, 1998, North Carolina and South Carolina. *Education:* University of South Carolina (B.A., 1991; J.D., 1998). Publications Editor, University of South Carolina Law Review. Member, Society of Wig and Robe. *Member:* Mecklenburg County, North Carolina and American Bar Associations; South Carolina Bar; William H. Bobbitt, American Inn of Court. [Corporal, USMC Active Duty, 1982-1986]. ***PRACTICE AREAS:*** Commercial Litigation; Construction Litigation; Bankruptcy Litigation; Real Estate Litigation. ***Email:*** awest@lawHFM.com

---

ADRIANNE HUFFMAN COLGATE, born North Wilkesboro, North Carolina; admitted to bar, 2003, New York, North Carolina and U.S. District Court, Western District of North Carolina. *Education:* University of North Carolina (B.A., 1998; J.D., 2001). Morehead Scholar. Comment Editor, North Carolina Law Review. Formerly with: Pillsbury Winthrop LLP; Moore & Van Allen PLLC. *Member:* Mecklenburg County and North Carolina Bar Associations. ***PRACTICE AREAS:*** Bankruptcy Law; Commercial Litigation; Construction Litigation. ***Email:*** ahuffman@lawHFM.com

KEVIN M. PROFIT, born Ann Arbor, Michigan, April 24, 1975; admitted to bar, 2002, Delaware; 2003, North Carolina. *Education:* University of Michigan (B.A., 1997); University of Pittsburgh (J.D., 2001). Formerly with Young Conaway Stargatt & Taylor, LLP. *Member:* Delaware, North Carolina and American Bar Associations; American Bankruptcy Institute. ***PRACTICE AREAS:*** Corporate Bankruptcy; Creditors Rights. ***Email:*** kprofit@lawHFM.com

MARK R. KUTNY, born Albuquerque, New Mexico, 1975; admitted to bar, 2000, North Carolina. *Education:* Dartmouth College (B.A., cum laude, 1997); University of Virginia (J.D., 2000). Phi Delta Phi. Articles Editor, Virginia Tax Review. *Member:* Mecklenburg County, North Carolina State and American Bar Associations. ***PRACTICE AREAS:*** Commercial Litigation; Construction Litigation; Civil Litigation; Environmental Litigation. ***Email:*** mkutny@lawHFM.com

ROXANNE MATTHEWS LUCY, born Wolfeboro, New Hampshire, April 5, 1975; admitted to bar, 2001, New Hampshire (inactive); 2002, Massachusetts and Maine (inactive); 2004, North Carolina. *Education:* Middlebury College (B.A., 1996); Boston College Law School (J.D., 2001). Member: Board of Student Advisors; Commentary Editor, Boston College Intellectual Property and Technology Forum. *Member:* Mecklenburg County, North Carolina and American Bar Associations. ***PRACTICE AREAS:*** Environmental Law; Employment Law; Commercial Litigation. ***Email:*** rlucy@lawHFM.com

ERIK M. ROSENWOOD, born 1974; admitted to bar, 2001, North Carolina. *Education:* Whitman College (B.A., 1996); University of St. Andrews (M. LITT., 1998); Washington and Lee University (J.D., cum laude, 2001). ***PRACTICE AREAS:*** Commercial Law; Litigation; Construction Litigation; Criminal Defense. ***Email:*** erosenwood@lawHFM.com

---

HAMMER, ASHBURG & HANF, P.C.

Established in 2001

3125 SPRINGBANK LANE
SUITE G
CHARLOTTE, NORTH CAROLINA 28226
Telephone: 704-927-0400
Fax: 704-927-0485
Email: bhammer@hammerpatent.com
URL: http://www.hammerpatent.com

Patent, Trademark, Copyright, Trade Secret, Unfair Competition, Intellectual Property, Antitrust Law.

FIRM PROFILE: Hammer, Ashburg & Hanf, P.C. is a law firm that concentrates its practice in the area of Intellectual Property Law, including Patents, Trademarks, Copyrights, Trade Secrets, and related Antitrust matters. The firm provides full service in the IP area including patent procurement, enforcement, and portfolio management; trademark procurement, enforcement, and portfolio management; copyright procurement, enforcement, and portfolio management; and trade secret maintenance and enforcement. The firm assists clients in shaping decisions in these important areas that are the foundation of new business development, which includes assistance in determination of IP needs and strategies to obtain and protect them.

ROBERT H. HAMMER, III, born Bellefonte, Pennsylvania, June 5, 1955; admitted to bar, 1985, Pennsylvania; 2000, North Carolina; registered to practice before U.S. Patent and Trademark Office. *Education:* Rensselaer Polytechnic Institute (B.S.Ch.E., 1977); Drexel University (M.B.A., 1982); Temple University (J.D., 1984). *Member:* Mecklenburg County, Pennsylvania, North Carolina and American Bar Associations; Carolina Patent and Trademark Law Association; American Intellectual Property Law Association; American Institute of Chemical Engineers. ***Email:*** bhammer@hammerpatent.com

SCOTT E. HANF, born Cleveland, Ohio, August 20, 1961; admitted to bar, 1994, North Carolina; registered to practice before U.S. Patent and Trademark Office. *Education:* Baldwin-Wallace College (B.S., Chemistry, summa cum laude, 1983); Cleveland-Marshall College of Law (J.D., 1992). *Member:* Mecklenburg County and North Carolina Bar Associations; Carolina Patent and Trademark Law Association; American Intellectual Property Law Association; American Chemical Society. ***PRACTICE AREAS:*** Patents; Trademarks; Copyrights; Trade Secrets. ***Email:*** scotthanf@hammerpatent.com

RAY ASHBURG, born Mashad, Iran, January 14, 1971; admitted to bar, 2003, North Carolina; registered to practice before U.S. Patent and Trademark Office. *Education:* University of North Carolina at Charlotte (B.S., Biology, cum laude, 1998); Wake Forest University (J.D., 2003). *Member:* Mecklenburg County, North Carolina and American Bar Associations; Carolina Patent and Trademark Law Association; American Intellectual Property Law Association. ***PRACTICE AREAS:*** Patents; Trademarks; Copyrights; Trade Secrets. ***Email:*** rayashburg@hammerpatent.com

---

JAMES C. HARDIN III, PLLC

6201 FAIRVIEW ROAD, SUITE 200
CHARLOTTE, NORTH CAROLINA 28210
Telephone: 704-944-4286
Fax: 704-552-6332
Email: jhardin@jimhardinlaw.com
URL: http://www.jimchardinlaw.com

Rock Hill, South Carolina Office: 113 East Main Street, Suite 330, 29730. Telephone: 803-329-7601. Fax: 803-329-8121

Estate Planning, Wills and Probate, Trust Law, Elder Law, Tax Planning, Asset Protection, Guardianship, IRS Audits.

FIRM PROFILE: Planned estate for a North Carolina real estate developer with assets aggregating $50 million, including the establishment of multi-generational trusts. Assisting in administration of estate with business assets in excess of $100 million in several states. Administration of the estate of a deceased South Carolina resident with gross assets totaling $80 million, including establishing a blockage discount for estate tax purposes, negotiating a sale of some of the decedent's shares back to the issuing company for purposes of raising funds necessary to pay the estate tax, and negotiating the Family Settlement Agreement. Engaged by a Duke University of Durham, North Carolina to revise its charitable giving forms. Established private foundations and prepared charitable lead trusts as well as charitable remainder trusts. Established family limited partnerships and limited liability companies for purposes of intergenerational wealth transfers in estate planning. Assisted clients in planning and implementing open space easements on real estate for income and transfer tax savings. Served as expert witness on approximately ten estate tax and trust cases.

JAMES C. HARDIN III, born Rock Hill, South Carolina; admitted to bar, 1974, South Carolina; 1989, North Carolina. *Education:* Wofford College (A.B., magna cum laude, 1969); University of Virginia (M.A., 1970); Duke University (J.D., with distinction, 1974). Phi Beta Kappa. Listed in: Best Lawyers in America, Trusts and Estates, 1991-2006; Business North Carolina Magazine, 2005 Legal Elite. Fellow, American College of Trust and Estate Counsel, 1986—. South Carolina State Chair, 2001-2006. Instructor, Winthrop University, 1979-1990. Speaker: The South Carolina Trust Code, South Carolina Bar Seminar, June 2005; "The Section 643 Regulations," and "The North Carolina Trust Code," North Carolina Bar Association Seminar, July 2005; "Hot Topics: The New North Carolina Principal and Income Act," North Carolina Bar Association Seminar, September 2004; "Charitable Giving Techniques," South Carolina Association of Planned Giving Administrators, February 2004; "Mapping the Plan," Estate Planning in South Carolina, Vol. II, Chapter 3 (ed. Albert C. Todd III; South Carolina Bar 2002); "Advanced Post-Mortem Estate Planning," North Carolina Bar Foundation, Estate Planning Section Annual Meeting, July 2001; "The New Prudent Investor Act," South Carolina Lawyer, Fall 2003; "Transfer of Real Estate at Death-Do Probate Code Changes Resolve the Issue?" South Carolina Lawyer, January 2001. Member: Charlotte Estate Planning Council; Charlotte Estate Planning Luncheon Group. Board Member, Secretary, 1988—, York County Community Foundation. Board Chairman, Piedmont Medical Center, Rock Hill, S.C., 1996; Board Chairman, Rock Hill Economic Development Corporation, 1998-2000. Board Member, Secretary, 1988—, South Carolina United Methodist Foundation. *Member:* North Carolina Bar Association (Member: Estate Planning and Fiduciary Law Section; Council Member, Legislative Committee and Uniform Trust and Code Committee); South Carolina Bar (Member, Probate; Estate Planning and Trust Section; Chairman, 1981, 1991, 2005; Chair, Legislative Committee, 2001; Chair Uniform Trust Code Study Committee, 2003-2005). (Board Certified Specialist in Estate Planning and Probate Law, North Carolina State Board of Legal Specialization); (Certified Specialist, Estate Planning and Probate Law, The Supreme Court of South Carolina). ***PRACTICE AREAS:*** Estate Planning; Wills; Probate; Trust Law; Elder Law; Tax Planning; Asset Protection; Guardianship; Tax Audits.

JAMES M. HARRINGTON, P.A.

P.O. BOX 481095
CHARLOTTE, NORTH CAROLINA 28269
Telephone: 704-625-0282
Fax: 704-625-0284
Email: jim@jimharrington.net
URL: http://www.lawyers.com/jimharrington

Patent Law, Patent Applications, Patent Litigation, Patent Licensing, Trademark Registration, Trademark Litigation, Copyright Litigation, Intellectual Property, Internet Law, E-Commerce, Licensing Agreements, Domain Name Disputes, Trade Secrets, Slander, Libel, Defamation, and Invasion of Privacy.

JAMES M. HARRINGTON, born October 15, 1975; admitted to bar, 2001, North Carolina and U.S. District Court, Western District of North Carolina; registered before the U.S. Patent and Trademark Office. *Education:* University of Arkansas (B.A., Physics, 1998); Georgetown University (J.D., 2001). *Member:* Mecklenburg County Bar Association; North Carolina State Bar. ***PRACTICE AREAS:*** Patent Applications; Patent Litiga-

(This Listing Continued)

tion; Patent Licensing; Trademark Registration; Trademark Litigation; Copyright Litigation; Intellectual Property; Patents; Internet Law; E-Commerce; Domain Name Infringement; Trade Secrets; Libel and Slander; Defamation. **Email:** jim@jimharrington.net

HAYNSWORTH BALDWIN JOHNSON & GREAVES LLC

CHARLOTTE, NORTH CAROLINA

(See Ogletree, Deakins, Nash, Smoak & Stewart, P.C.)

C. WAYNE HEASLEY

MERCHANDISE MART OFFICE BUILDING
800 BRIAR CREEK ROAD, SUITE DD-518
CHARLOTTE, NORTH CAROLINA 28205
Telephone: 704-338-1322
Fax: 704-338-1338
URL: http://www.cwayneleasleylaw.com

Family Law, Divorce, Alimony, Equitable Distribution, Expungements, Child Support, Child Custody, Visitation Rights, Criminal, Driving While Intoxicated (DWI), Traffic Violations.

FIRM PROFILE: Mr. Heasley is a Former District Court Judge.

C. WAYNE HEASLEY, admitted to bar, 1983, Florida; 1984, North Carolina. *Education:* Central Connecticut State College (B.S., 1968); University of Tennessee (M.S., counseling and guidance, 1970); Oklahoma State University (M.S., adult/juvenile corrections, 1978); Washburn University of Topeka (J.D., 1980). Co-Author: "Improving Juvenile Justice," Human Science Press, 1981. District Court Judge, Mecklenburg County, North Carolina (1994-1998).

HEDRICK EATMAN GARDNER & KINCHELOE, L.L.P.

Established in 1956
6000 FAIRVIEW ROAD, SUITE 1000
CHARLOTTE, NORTH CAROLINA 28210
Telephone: 704-366-1101
Fax: 704-366-6181
URL: http://www.hedrickeatman.com
Mailing Address: P.O. Box 30397, Charlotte, NC 28230

Raleigh, North Carolina Office: 4011 Westchase Boulevard, Suite 300, 27607. Telephone: 919-832-9424. Fax: 919-832-9425.

Wilmington, North Carolina Office: 1508 Military Cutoff Road, Suite 202, 28403. Telephone: 910-509-9664. Fax: 910-509-9630.

Columbia, South Carolina Office: 1201 Main Street, Suite 1200, 29201. Mailing Address: P.O. Box 11267, 29211. Telephone: 803-727-1200. Fax: 803-727-1259.

General Civil Litigation and Insurance Defense, Legal and Professional Malpractice, Motor Vehicle Negligence, Premises Liability, Product Liability, Construction, Insurance Coverage Disputes, Arson and Fraud, Employment Law, Trucking and Transportation and Worker's Compensation.

FIRM PROFILE: Hedrick Eatman Gardner & Kincheloe, L.L.P. is a full-service litigation defense firm which serves insurance and business clients. Founded in North Carolina in 1956, the firm's four offices allow us to provide cost-effective representation throughout North and South Carolina. Our attorneys have superior litigation and dispute resolution skills. We zealously represent our loyal client base, while maintaining a high degree of ethics and professionalism. Client satisfaction is a priority, which is how we preserve long-term relationships. We strive for continued growth while maintaining our solid reputation before the bench and the Bar, our focus on client service, and qualifty of life for our attorneys and staff.

PARTNERS

PHILIP R. HEDRICK (1919-1999)

EDWARD L. EATMAN, JR., admitted to bar, 1969, North Carolina, U.S. District Court, Western, Middle and Eastern Districts of North Carolina and U.S. Court of Appeals, Fourth Circuit. *Education:* University of North Carolina at Chapel Hill (A.B., 1966; J.D., 1969). **PRACTICE AREAS:** Civil Litigation; Public Entities; Municipalities; Workers Compensation. **Email:** eeatman@hedrickeatman.com

JOHN A. GARDNER, III, admitted to bar, 1974, North Carolina, U.S. District Court, Western, Middle and Eastern Districts of North Carolina and U.S. Court of Appeals, Fourth Circuit. *Education:* North Carolina State University (B.S., 1969); University of North Carolina at Chapel Hill (J.D., 1974). **PRACTICE AREAS:** Civil Litigation; Construction Litigation; Medical Malpractice Defense; Occupational Disease; Products Liability Defense; Workers Compensation Defense. **Email:** jgardner@hedrickeatman.com

HATCHER B. KINCHELOE, admitted to bar, 1975, North Carolina, U.S. District Court, Western, Middle and Eastern Districts of North Carolina and U.S. Court of Appeals, Fourth Circuit. *Education:* University of North Carolina at Chapel Hill (A.B., 1971; J.D., 1975). **PRACTICE AREAS:** Civil Litigation; Occupational Disease; Construction Litigation; Nursing Home Malpractice; Toxic Tort Defense; Workers Compensation. **Email:** hkincheloe@hedrickeatman.com

MEL J. GAROFALO, admitted to bar, 1978, North Carolina, U.S. District Court, Western, Middle and Eastern Districts of North Carolina and U.S. Court of Appeals, Fourth Circuit. *Education:* University of Dayton (B.A., 1975); Wake Forest University (J.D., 1978). **PRACTICE AREAS:** Civil Litigation; Complex Litigation; Motor Vehicle Negligence; Products Liability Defense; Professional Malpractice; Workers Compensation. **Email:** mgarofalo@hedrickeatman.com

THOMAS W. PAGE, admitted to bar, 1990, North Carolina; 1992, U.S. District Court, Western, Eastern and Middle Districts of North Carolina. *Education:* University of Kentucky (B.B.A., 1986); University of Louisville (J.D., 1989). **PRACTICE AREAS:** Civil Litigation; Nursing Home Malpractice; Premises Liability; Workers Compensation. **Email:** tpage@hedrickeatman.com

L. KRISTIN KING, admitted to bar, 1991, North Carolina and U.S. District Court, Western and Middle Districts of North Carolina. *Education:* University of North Carolina at Charlotte (B.S., magna cum laude, 1987); University of North Carolina at Chapel Hill (J.D., 1990). **PRACTICE AREAS:** Civil Litigation; Motor Vehicle Negligence; Professional Malpractice; Trucking Law; Transportation; Workers Compensation. **Email:** kking@hedrickeatman.com

PAUL C. LAWRENCE, admitted to bar, 1986, Pennsylvania and New Jersey; 1988, U.S. District Court, Eastern District of Pennsylvania; 1992, U.S. District Court, Middle District of Pennsylvania; 1994, North Carolina; 1995, U.S. District Court, Western, Middle and Eastern Districts of North Carolina; 1996, U.S. Court of Appeals, Fourth Circuit. *Education:* University of Scranton (B.S., 1982); Villanova University (J.D., 1985). **PRACTICE AREAS:** Arson and Insurance Fraud; Civil Litigation; Employment Law; Premises Liability; Workers Compensation. **Email:** plawrence@hedrickeatman.com

ALLEN C. SMITH, admitted to bar, 1992, North Carolina, U.S. District Court, Western, Middle and Eastern Districts of North Carolina and U.S. Court of Appeals, Fourth Circuit. *Education:* Davidson College (B.A., 1988); Cambridge University, England; University of North Carolina at Chapel Hill (J.D., with honors, 1992). **PRACTICE AREAS:** Civil Litigation; Commercial Litigation; Construction Law; Premises Liability; Products Liability; Trucking Litigation; Workers Compensation. **Email:** asmith@hedrickeatman.com

JEFFREY A. DOYLE, admitted to bar, 1993, North Carolina and U.S. District Court, Western and Eastern Districts of North Carolina. *Education:* University of North Carolina at Chapel Hill (B.A., 1990; J.D., with honors, 1993). (Resident, Raleigh Office). **PRACTICE AREAS:** Civil Litigation; Construction Litigation; Motor Vehicle Negligence; Nursing Home Malpractice; Premises Liability; Products Liability Defense; Toxic Tort Defense; Workers Compensation. **Email:** jdoyle@hedrickeatman.com

JEFFREY A. KADIS, admitted to bar, 1994, North Carolina and U.S. District Court, Western, Middle and Eastern Districts of North Carolina. *Education:* University of North Carolina at Chapel Hill (B.S., 1989); Wake Forest University (J.D., 1994). **PRACTICE AREAS:** Civil Litigation; Occupational Disease; Workers Compensation Defense. **Email:** jkadis@hedrickeatman.com

JENNIFER I. MITCHELL, admitted to bar, 1992, North Carolina. *Education:* Davidson College (B.A., 1989); Wake Forest University (J.D., cum laude, 1992). **PRACTICE AREAS:** Appellate Practice; Civil Litigation; Insurance Coverage Disputes; Workers Compensation Defense. **Email:** jmitchell@hedrickeatman.com

ERICA B. LEWIS, admitted to bar, 1995, North Carolina and U.S. District Court, Western and Eastern Districts of North Carolina. *Education:* University of California, Davis (B.A., with honors, 1991); Wake Forest University (J.D., 1995). (Resident, Wilmington Office). **PRACTICE AREAS:** Appellate Advocacy; Arson and Insurance Fraud; Civil Litigation; Construction Law; Workers Compensation Defense. **Email:** elewis@hedrickeatman.com

JEFFREY H. BLACKWELL, admitted to bar, 1986, North Carolina; 1990, U.S. District Court, Eastern, Middle and Western Districts of North Carolina. *Education:* University of North Carolina at Chapel Hill (B.S., with honors, 1981; J.D., 1986). (Resident, Wilmington Office). **PRACTICE AREAS:** Civil Litigation; Motor Vehicle Negligence; Public Entities; Public Municipal Law; Toxic Tort Defense. **Email:** jblackwell@hedrickeatman.com

SHELLEY W. COLEMAN, admitted to bar, 1996, North Carolina, U.S. District Court, Western and Eastern Districts of North Carolina and U.S. Court of Appeals, Fourth Circuit. *Education:* University of Alabama (B.A., cum laude, 1991); Washington & Lee University (J.D., 1995). **PRACTICE AREAS:** Appellate Advocacy; Civil Litigation; Complex Litigation; Products Liability Defense; Workers Compensation Defense. **Email:** scoleman@hedrickeatman.com

THOMAS M. MORROW, admitted to bar, 1997, North Carolina and U.S. District Court, Eastern District of North Carolina. *Education:* University of Virginia (B.S., 1991); Wake Forest University (J.D., 1997). (Resident, Raleigh Office). **PRACTICE AREAS:** Civil Litigation; Motor Vehicle Negligence; Premises Liability; Trucking Litigation; Transportation; Workers Compensation. **Email:** tmorrow@hedrickeatman.com

DONALD J. VICINI, admitted to bar, 1991, Texas and U.S. District Court, Northern, Southern, Eastern and Western Districts of Texas; 2003, North Carolina. *Education:* Michigan State University (B.A., 1980); South Texas College of Law (J.D., 1990). **PRACTICE AREAS:** Civil Litigation; Medical Malpractice; Transportation; Employment; Alternative Dispute Resolution. **Email:** dvicini@hedrickeatman.com

NEIL P. ANDREWS, admitted to bar, 1995, North Carolina and U.S. District Court, Western and Middle Districts of North Carolina. *Education:* University of Connecticut (B.S., 1992); Western New England College (J.D., 1995). **PRACTICE AREAS:** Civil Litigation; Workers Compensation. **Email:** nandrews@hedrickeatman.com

EDWIN P. MARTIN, JR., admitted to bar, 1991, South Carolina; 1992, U.S. District Court, District of South Carolina and U.S. Court of Appeals, Fourth Circuit; 1995, U.S. Supreme Court. *Education:* The Citadel (B.S., 1984); University of South Carolina (J.D., 1991). (Resident, Columbia, South Carolina Office). **PRACTICE AREAS:** Workers Compensation. **Email:** edwinmartin@hedrickeatman.com

R. DANIEL ADDISON, admitted to bar, 1994, South Carolina; 1995, U.S. District Court, District of South Carolina. *Education:* Clemson University (B.A., 1987); University of South Carolina (J.D., 1994). (Resident, Columbia, South Carolina Office). **PRACTICE AREAS:** Workers Compensation. **Email:** daddison@hedrickeatman.com

(This Listing Continued)

HEDRICK EATMAN GARDNER & KINCHELOE, L.L.P., Charlotte—Continued

OF COUNSEL

MARK A. MICHAEL, admitted to bar, 1975, North Carolina, U.S. District Court, Western, Middle and Eastern Districts of North Carolina, U.S. Court of Appeals, Fourth Circuit and U.S. Supreme Court. *Education:* Providence College (B.S., 1969); Duke University (J.D., 1975). (Certified as a Civil Trial Advocacy Specialist by the National Board of Trial Advocacy). ***PRACTICE AREAS:*** Insurance Coverage; Complex Litigation. ***Email:*** mmichael@hedrickeatman.com

ASSOCIATES

Elizabeth A. Martineau
Jessica C. Smythe (Resident, Raleigh Office)
Melissa L. McDonald
Kimberly P. Reaves
Sharon E. Dent
C. J. Childers
Erin Dancy Eveson (Resident, Raleigh Office)
Matthew D. Glidewell
Jennifer S. Jerzak (Resident, Raleigh Office)
Shannon Metcalf
Harmony Whalen Taylor
Hope Fisher Smelcer
W. James Flynn
Heidi L. Maske
Tracie H. Brisson (Resident, Wilmington Office)
Tonya D. Davis (Resident, Raleigh Office)
Jennifer Vega Ruiz (Resident, Raleigh Office)
Michael Duane Jones
Jeremy T. Canipe
Heather Teale Twiddy
Michelle V. Crawford
Andrew S. Culicerto
Barry C. Jennings (Resident, Raleigh Office)
Joel K. Turner
Adam E. Whitten
Meredith T. Everhart (Resident, Wilmington Office)
Bettina Mumme (Resident, Raleigh Office)
Luke Sbarra
Dalton G. Blair
Ryan W. Keevan
Samuel E. Barker
Taurus E. Becton
Brendan G. Dillashaw
William B. Dulaney (Resident, Wilmington Office)
Erika D. Taylor (Resident, Raleigh Office)
J. Douglas Grimes
Edward A. Sweeney
Vachelle D. Willis
Benton L. Toups (Resident, Wilmington Office)
Stacy M. Race (Resident, Raleigh Office)
Jennifer S. Anderson
Leah L. Rudd
Jennifer P. Pulley
M. Kathleen Short
Deepa Tungare
J. Philip Murphy (Resident, Columbia, South Carolina Office)
Dana C. Moody (Resident, Raleigh Office)
Keri A. Rose (Resident, Columbia, South Carolina Office)
Susan J. VanDerweert (Resident, Raleigh Office)
Joseph S. Murray IV
Marc A. Metcalf
Megan V. Johnson

REPRESENTATIVE CLIENTS: Ace-USA; Food Lion; Great American Insurance Co.; PMA Group; St. Paul Travelers Insurance Co.; Waffle House.
REFERENCE: Bank of America.

HEFFERON & HEFFERON

CAMERON BROWN BUILDING
301 SOUTH MCDOWELL STREET, SUITE 130
CHARLOTTE, NORTH CAROLINA 28204
Telephone: 704-376-3700
888-200-7977
Fax: 704-376-6090
URL: http://www.hefferonlaw.com
Email: firm@hefferonlaw.com
URL: http://www.hefferonandhefferon.com

Catastrophic Injury, Wrongful Death, Products Liability, Inadequate Security, Insurance Claims, Business Torts, Truck Accidents, Medical Malpractice, Legal Malpractice, Construction Accidents, Automobile Accidents, Nursing Home Negligence, Commercial Litigation.

FIRM PROFILE: Thomas and Paul Hefferon have extensive experience in plaintiff's personal injury litigation in the North Carolina Courts. They have appeared for their clients throughout the state at every court level, and have had considerable success with most areas of personal injury law. The firm believes in moving cases through the claims and litigation process as quickly and efficiently as possible while making every effort to maximize the client's recovery. Their prime directive is to treat the client fairly. Most of the firm's serious injury cases are referred by other lawyers. The firm is flexible in all arrangements with associating and referring attorneys.

THOMAS J. HEFFERON, born Lincolnton, North Carolina, January 10, 1952; admitted to bar, 1981, North Carolina. *Education:* University of North Carolina at Charlotte (B.A., 1978); University of North Carolina at Chapel Hill (J.D., 1981). Member, North Carolina Law Review, 1980-1981. Certified Mediator. *Member:* Mecklenburg County, 26th Judicial District and North Carolina Bar Associations; North Carolina State Bar; North Carolina Academy of Trial Lawyers; The Association of Trial Lawyers of America. ***PRACTICE AREAS:*** Litigation; Mediation. ***Email:*** tom@hefferonlaw.com

PAUL HEFFERON, born Lincolnton, North Carolina, April 20, 1954; admitted to bar, 1983, North Carolina. *Education:* University of North Carolina at Charlotte (B.A., 1980); University of North Carolina at Chapel Hill (J.D., 1982). *Member:* Mecklenburg County and North Carolina Bar Associations; North Carolina State Bar; North Carolina Academy of Trial Lawyers; Association of Trial Lawyers of America. ***PRACTICE AREAS:*** Litigation; Mediation. ***Email:*** paul@hefferonlaw.com

HELMS, HENDERSON & ASSOCIATES, P.A.

Established in 1999
SUITE 340, MOREHEAD PLACE
521 EAST MOREHEAD STREET
CHARLOTTE, NORTH CAROLINA 28202
Telephone: 704-372-4884
Fax: 704-332-0585
Email: nreid@helmshenderson.com
URL: http://www.lawyers.com/helmshenderson

General, Civil and Criminal Trial Practice in State and Federal Courts and Agencies, Corporation, Real Estate, Probate, Insurance, Bankruptcy, Commercial, Personal Injury, Collections and Tax.

FIRM PROFILE: Helms, Henderson & Associates, P.A. has a broad general practice encompassing, but not limited to, real estate law including commercial and residential sales, leases, development, construction, liens, and foreclosures; business law including corporations, partnerships, employment agreements, tax advice, acquisitions and mergers; litigation including contracts, bankruptcies, collections, personal injury, and workers' compensation; and estate planning law including wills, trusts, probate, administration of estates, and tax advice.

H. PARKS HELMS, born Charlotte, North Carolina, November 5, 1935; admitted to bar, 1961, North Carolina; 1963, U.S. District Court, Western District of North Carolina; 1967, U.S. Court of Appeals, Fourth Circuit; 1983, U.S. District Court, Northern District of Georgia; 1984, U.S. District Court, Eastern District of North Carolina; 1989, U.S. Supreme Court. *Education:* University of North Carolina (B.A., 1959; J.D., 1961). Delta Theta Phi. Member, North Carolina House of Representatives, 1974-1984. Chairman, Mecklenburg County Board of Commissioners, 1992—. Chairman, North Carolina Courts Commission, 1980-1986. Member, Commission for the Future of Justice and the Courts in North Carolina, 1994-1996. *Member:* North Carolina (Vice President, 1991-1993) and American Bar Associations; North Carolina State Bar; 26th Judicial District; North Carolina Academy of Trial Lawyers. ***PRACTICE AREAS:*** Corporate Law; Real Estate Law; Estate Planning; Administration; Personal Injury Law; Civil Litigation; Commercial Litigation; Government Relations. ***Email:*** phelms@helmshenderson.com

DAVID L. HENDERSON, born Charlotte, North Carolina, September 18, 1950; admitted to bar, 1977, North Carolina. *Education:* North Carolina State University (B.A., 1973); Cumberland School of Law of Samford University (J.D., 1977). Phi Alpha Delta. *Member:* North Carolina and American Bar Associations; North Carolina State Bar. ***PRACTICE AREAS:*** Corporate Law; Business Law; Real Estate Law; Estate Planning and Probate. ***Email:*** dhenderson@helmshenderson.com

CHARLES J. HENDERSON (1920-1999)

HELMS MULLISS & WICKER, PLLC

Established in 1922
201 NORTH TRYON STREET
P.O. BOX 31247 (28231)
CHARLOTTE, NORTH CAROLINA 28202
Telephone: 704-343-2000
Fax: 704-343-2300.
Telex: 572460
URL: http://www.hmw.com

Raleigh, North Carolina Office: 2600 Two Hannover Square (27601), P.O. Box 27507 (27611). Telephone: 919-755-6600. Fax: 919-755-6699.
Wilmington, North Carolina Office: 127 Grace Street (28401), P.O. Box 599 (28402). Telephone: 910-254-3800. Fax: 910-254-3900.

Banking, Finance, Corporate, Government Relations, Business Litigation, Tax, Securities, Real Property and Finance, Labor and Employment (Management) Law, Employee Benefits, International, Technology, Insurance Coverage, Media, Commercial Bankruptcy, Environmental, Public Finance, ERISA, Estate Planning and Administration, Education, Venture Capital, Intellectual Property.

WILLIAM F. MULLISS (1911-1987)
FRED B. HELMS (1896-1998)

MEMBERS OF FIRM

STEPHEN DAVID ALLRED, born Alexandria, Virginia, October 26, 1963; admitted to bar, 1992, North Carolina. *Education:* St. Johns College (B.A., 1986); University of Virginia (J.D., 1992). Member, Editorial Board, Virginia Law Review, 1991-1992. ***PRACTICE AREAS:*** Civil Litigation; Insurance Coverage; Commercial Litigation. ***Email:*** Stephen.Allred@hmw.com

CORBY COCHRAN ANDERSON, born Roanoke, Virginia, December 30, 1954; admitted to bar, 1994, North Carolina. *Education:* College of William & Mary (B.A., magna cum laude, 1976); University of Virginia (J.D., 1994). Member, Editorial Board, Virginia Journal of International Law, 1993-1994. Dillard Legal Writing Fellow, 1992-1993. Clerk to Honorable Eric G. Bruggink, U.S. Court of Federal Claims, 1994-1995. ***PRACTICE AREAS:*** Media; Appellate; Civil Litigation; Intellectual Property. ***Email:*** Corby.Anderson@hmw.com

(This Listing Continued)

BRIAN D. BARGER, born Roanoke, Virginia, June 9, 1965; admitted to bar, 1990, North Carolina. *Education:* University of Virginia (B.A., with honors, 1987; J.D., with honors, 1990). Phi Beta Kappa; Order of the Coif; Phi Sigma Alpha. Recipient, Earle K. Shawe Labor Relations Award. ***LANGUAGES:*** German. ***PRACTICE AREAS:*** Labor and Employment (Management); Education; Commercial Litigation. ***Email:*** Brian.Barger@hmw.com

IRVING M. BRENNER, born Montgomery, Alabama, July 2, 1960; admitted to bar, 1986, Pennsylvania; 1988, North Carolina. *Education:* University of Virginia (B.S., 1982; J.D., 1986). Order of the Coif. Member, Editorial Board, Virginia Law Review, 1985-1986. Clerk to Honorable Edward N. Cahn, U.S. District Court, Eastern District of Pennsylvania, 1986-1987. ***PRACTICE AREAS:*** Commercial Litigation; Intellectual Property. ***Email:*** Irving.Brenner@hmw.com

JONATHAN E. BUCHAN, JR., born Mullins, South Carolina, September 1, 1950; admitted to bar, 1978, North Carolina. *Education:* Princeton University (A.B., magna cum laude, 1972); Duke University (J.D., 1978). ***PRACTICE AREAS:*** Media; Intellectual Property; Commercial Litigation. ***Email:*** Jon.Buchan@hmw.com

C. TODD BURBANK, born Falls Church, Virginia, August 29, 1970; admitted to bar, 1998, Florida; 2001, North Carolina. *Education:* University of North Carolina at Chapel Hill (B.A., 1992); University of Florida (J.D., with honors, 1997). Notes and Comments Editor and Associate Management Editor, Florida Law Review. Legal Research and Writing Teaching Fellowship, Spring 1997; Appellate Advocacy Teaching Fellowship, Fall 1997. *Member:* Orange County, North Carolina and American Bar Associations; The Florida Bar. ***PRACTICE AREAS:*** Commercial Real Estate. ***Email:*** Todd.Burbank@hmw.com

BOYD C. CAMPBELL, JR., born Abingdon, Virginia, December 1, 1941; admitted to bar, 1966, Virginia and North Carolina; 1983, Florida. *Education:* Davidson College (A.B., 1963); University of Virginia (J.D., 1966). [U.S. Army, Military Intelligence, 1966-1968]. ***PRACTICE AREAS:*** Corporate; Mergers and Acquisitions; Financial Institutions Law; Securities; International Law. ***Email:*** Boyd.Campbell@hmw.com

REBECCA S. CHAFFIN, born Salem, Ohio, 1964; admitted to bar, 1989, California; 1991, Virginia; 1994, Ohio; 1997, North Carolina. *Education:* Duke University (B.A., 1986); University of Virginia (J.D., 1989). Member, University of Virginia Law Review, 1988-1989. ***PRACTICE AREAS:*** Corporate Finance; Tax-Exempt Finance. ***Email:*** Rebecca.Chaffin@hmw.com

JOHN H. COBB, born Charlotte, North Carolina, December 31, 1962; admitted to bar, 1989, North Carolina. *Education:* Davidson College (B.A., magna cum laude, 1985); University of Virginia (J.D., 1989). Phi Beta Kappa; Omicron Delta Kappa. Editor, Virginia Law Review. Law Clerk, The Honorable John D. Butzner, Jr., United States Court of Appeals for the Fourth Circuit, 1989-1990. Counsel, United States Senate Permanent Subcommittee on Investigations, 1995-1996. Counsel and Staff Director, Special Investigation, United States Senate Committee on Governmental Affairs, 1997-1998. Permanent Member, Fourth Circuit Judicial Conference. ***PRACTICE AREAS:*** Litigation. ***Email:*** Jack.Cobb@hmw.com

STEPHEN L. CORDELL, born Asheville, North Carolina, April 26, 1957; admitted to bar, 1983, North Carolina; 1985, U.S. Tax Court; 1990, U.S. Court of Appeals, Eleventh Circuit. *Education:* North Carolina State University (B.A., cum laude, 1979); Wake Forest University (J.D., 1982); University of Florida (LL.M., Taxation, 1983). Phi Delta Phi (Treasurer, 1982). Attorney-Advisor to Judge Edna G. Parker, U.S. Tax Court, 1983-1985. ***PRACTICE AREAS:*** Public Finance; Taxation. ***Email:*** Steve.Cordell@hmw.com

PETER J. COVINGTON, born Brookline, Massachusetts, March 9, 1953; admitted to bar, 1980, North Carolina. *Education:* University of Virginia; University of North Carolina (B.A., 1975); Tulane University (J.D., cum laude, 1980). Member and Associate Editor, Tulane Law Review, 1978-1980. ***PRACTICE AREAS:*** Commercial; Business; Securities Litigation; Banking Litigation. ***Email:*** Peter.Covington@hmw.com

ROBERT W. CRAMER, born Monticello, Indiana, November 10, 1957; admitted to bar, 1984, North Carolina. *Education:* University of North Carolina (A.B., 1980; M.B.A., 1984; J.D., 1984). Phi Beta Kappa. Morehead Scholar. ***PRACTICE AREAS:*** Debt Finance; Corporate Finance; Corporate. ***Email:*** Bob.Cramer@hmw.com

JAMES H. CULBRETH, JR., born Durham, North Carolina, November 12, 1953; admitted to bar, 1981, District of Columbia; 1982, Virginia; 1984, North Carolina. *Education:* Wake Forest University (B.A., 1977); George Washington University (J.D., 1980). ***PRACTICE AREAS:*** Employee Benefits; Executive Compensation; Corporate; Tax Law. ***Email:*** Jim.Culbreth@hmw.com

KATHLEEN H. DOOLEY, born Orange, New Jersey, December 20, 1959; admitted to bar, 1988, New Jersey and Pennsylvania; 2002, North Carolina; U.S. Court of Appeals, Third Circuit; U.S. District Court, Western District of North Carolina; U.S. District Court, District of New Jersey; U.S. District Court, Northern, Eastern and Southern Districts of New York; U.S. District Court, Eastern District of Michigan. *Education:* Seton Hall University (B.A., 1981); Seton Hall School of Law (J.D., cum laude, 1988). Articles Editor, Seton Hall Law Review. Law Clerk, The Honorable Melvin P. Antell, Presiding Judge Superior Court of New Jersey, Appellate Division. ***PRACTICE AREAS:*** Litigation; Insurance Coverage. ***Email:*** kathleen.dooley@hmw.com

DOUGLAS W. EY, JR., born Huntington, West Virginia, August 29, 1955; admitted to bar, 1979, North Carolina. *Education:* Davidson College (A.B., cum laude, 1976); Vanderbilt University (J.D., 1979). Phi Beta Kappa. Special Projects Editor, Vanderbilt Law Review, 1978-1979. ***PRACTICE AREAS:*** Technology; Intellectual Property Litigation; Commercial Litigation. ***Email:*** Doug.Ey@hmw.com

ELIZABETH WHITENER GOODE, born Winston-Salem, North Carolina, June 11, 1960; admitted to bar, 1985, North Carolina. *Education:* University of North Carolina (B.A., 1982); Columbia University (J.D., 1985). Phi Beta Kappa. Harlan Fiske Stone Scholar. ***PRACTICE AREAS:*** Real Property; Corporate and Real Estate Finance. ***Email:*** Beth.Goode@hmw.com

JAMES H. GUTERMAN, born Ridgewood, New Jersey, October 21, 1952; admitted to bar, 1978, North Carolina; 1983, Florida. *Education:* Vassar College (A.B., with honors, 1974); University of North Carolina (J.D., with honors, 1978). Order of the Coif. Editor-in-Chief, North Carolina Law Review, 1977-1978. Clerk to Honorable James B. McMillan, U.S. District Court, Western District of North Carolina, 1978-1979. ***PRACTICE AREAS:*** Corporate Finance; Sports Law; Antitrust and Trade Regulation; Banking. ***Email:*** Jim.Guterman@hmw.com

J. RICHARD HAZLETT, born Fort Campbell, Kentucky, April 30, 1955; admitted to bar, 1980, North Carolina. *Education:* Wake Forest University (B.A., cum laude, 1977); University of North Carolina (J.D., with honors, 1980). Member, North Carolina Law Review. ***PRACTICE AREAS:*** Corporate; Finance; Securities Regulation; Tax-Exempt Finance; International Law. ***Email:*** Rick.Hazlett@hmw.com

BENNE C. HUTSON, born Southgate, Michigan, August 21, 1957; admitted to bar, 1982, Ohio; 1986, North Carolina. *Education:* Hillsdale College (B.A., summa cum laude, 1979); Harvard University (J.D., cum laude, 1982). Omicron Delta Kappa. ***PRACTICE AREAS:*** Environmental Law. ***Email:*** Benne.Hutson@hmw.com

BRADLEY R. KUTROW, born West Point, Mississippi, August 13, 1959; admitted to bar, 1986, North Carolina; 1990, District of Columbia. *Education:* University of North Carolina (A.B., 1981); University of Virginia (J.D., 1986). Omicron Delta Kappa. Clerk to Honorable Joseph Young, U.S. District Court, District of Maryland, 1986-1987. Member, Fourth Circuit Judicial Conference. ***PRACTICE AREAS:*** Commercial Litigation; Business Tort Litigation; Securities Litigation; Products Liability; Media Law; Appellate Practice; Intellectual Property. ***Email:*** Brad.Kutrow@hmw.com

HARRISON L. MARSHALL, JR., born Greenville, South Carolina, July 27, 1957; admitted to bar, 1982, North Carolina. *Education:* Davidson College (A.B., cum laude, 1979); Vanderbilt University (J.D., 1982). Phi Beta Kappa; Order of the Coif. Managing Editor, Vanderbilt Law Review, 1981-1982. [Capt., JAGC, U.S. Army, 1982-1986]. ***PRACTICE AREAS:*** Corporate; Mergers and Acquisitions; Education; Venture Capital. ***Email:*** Harrison.Marshall@hmw.com

WILLIAM C. MAYBERRY, born Lynchburg, Virginia, November 16, 1966; admitted to bar, 1991, Virginia; 1994, North Carolina; U.S. Bankruptcy Court; U.S. District Court, Eastern, Middle and Western Districts of North Carolina; U.S. District Court, Western District of Virginia; U.S. Court of Appeals, Federal and Fourth Circuits. *Education:* Duke University (A.B., 1988); Washington & Lee University (J.D., cum laude, 1991). Burks Scholar. Clerk to the Honorable Robert D. Potter, U.S. District Court, Western District of North Carolina, 1991-1993 and the Honorable Marvin R. Wooten, U.S. Bankruptcy Court, Western District of North Carolina, 1993-1994. *Member:* North Carolina and American (Member, Antitrust, Intellectual Property and Litigation Sections) Bar Associations; American Intellectual Property Law Association; Carolinas Patent Trademark and Copyright Law Association. ***PRACTICE AREAS:*** Bankruptcy; Commercial Litigation; Intellectual Property. ***Email:*** Bil.Mayberry@hmw.com

JOHN G. McDONALD, born Watertown, New York, June 4, 1966; admitted to bar, 1993, New York; 1997, North Carolina. *Education:* Le Moyne College (B.S., 1988); Syracuse University (J.D., 1992). Editor-in-Chief, Syracuse Law Review, 1991-1992. *Member:* North Carolina and American (Member, Labor and Employment Law Section) Bar Associations. ***PRACTICE AREAS:*** Labor and Employment. ***Email:*** John.Mcdonald@hmw.com

E. GRAHAM McGOOGAN, JR., born Wadesboro, North Carolina, August 15, 1949; admitted to bar, 1974, North Carolina. *Education:* Davidson College (B.A., cum laude, 1971); University of North Carolina (J.D., with honors, 1974). Phi Beta Kappa; Order of the Coif. Member, North Carolina Law Review, 1973-1974. *Member:* North Carolina Association of Certified Public Accountants; American Institute of Certified Public Accountants. (Board Certified Specialist in Estate Planning and Probate Law, North Carolina State Board of Legal Specialization). ***PRACTICE AREAS:*** Taxation; Estate Planning and Probate. ***Email:*** Graham.Mcgoogan@hmw.com

JAMES G. MIDDLEBROOKS, born Atlanta, Georgia, July 13, 1958; admitted to bar, 1983, District of Columbia; 1984, Georgia; 1986, North Carolina. *Education:* Emory University (B.A., 1978); University of Georgia (J.D., summa cum laude, 1982). Order of the Coif. Editor-in-Chief, Georgia Law Review, 1981-1982. Clerk to Honorable Phyllis A. Kravitch, U.S. Court of Appeals, Eleventh Circuit, 1982-1983. ***PRACTICE AREAS:*** Civil Litigation; Education; White Collar Crime. ***Email:*** Gil.Middlebrooks@hmw.com

ROBERT A. MUCKENFUSS, born 1971; admitted to bar, 1997, South Carolina; 2001, North Carolina. *Education:* University of Virginia (B.A., 1993); University of South Carolina (J.D., 1997). Order of Wig and Robe. Law Clerk to Associate Justice Jean H. Toal, Supreme Court of South Carolina, 1997-1999. ***PRACTICE AREAS:*** Appellate Practice; Complex Commercial Litigation; Intellectual Property; Sports Law; White Collar Crime; Government Investigations.

CHRISTOPHER S. M. NESBIT, born Charlottesville, Virginia, November 19, 1963; admitted to bar, 1991, Georgia; 1993, North Carolina. *Education:* University of Virginia (B.A., 1986); University of North Carolina (J.D., with honors, 1991). Articles Editor, North Carolina Law Review, 1990-1991. ***PRACTICE AREAS:*** Corporate; Emerging Business; Technology Law; Mergers and Acquisitions; Venture Capital; Intellectual Property. ***Email:*** Chris.Nesbit@hmw.com

KATHY L. PILKINGTON, born Gastonia, North Carolina, February 23, 1951; admitted to bar, 1989, North Carolina. *Education:* University of North Carolina (B.S., magna cum laude, 1973; M.P.H., 1976; J.D., with high honors, 1989). Order of the Coif. Member, North Carolina Law Review, 1987-1988. ***PRACTICE AREAS:*** Real Property; Real Estate Finance. ***Email:*** Kathy.Pilkington@hmw.com

WILLIAM F. POTTS, JR., born Niagara Falls, New York, March 10, 1953; admitted to bar, 1978, North Carolina. *Education:* University of Virginia (B.A., with distinction, 1975); University of North Carolina (J.D., 1978). Board of Editors, North Carolina Journal of International Law and Commercial Regulation, 1977-1978. *Member:* Mecklenburg County, North Carolina and American (Member, Business Law and Real Property Sections) Bar Associations. ***PRACTICE AREAS:*** Commercial Lending; Commercial Real Estate; Secured Transactions; Bankruptcy Law. ***Email:*** Rich.Potts@hmw.com

ROBERT H. PRYOR, born Hendersonville, North Carolina, August 19, 1957; admitted to bar, 1982, North Carolina. *Education:* Wake Forest University (B.A., cum laude,

(This Listing Continued)

HELMS MULLISS & WICKER, PLLC, Charlotte—Continued

1979; J.D., magna cum laude, 1982). Member, Wake Forest Law Review, 1981-1982. ***PRACTICE AREAS:*** Commercial Litigation; Bankruptcy; Creditors Rights. ***Email:*** Bob.Pryor@hmw.com

MANLEY W. ROBERTS, born Durham, North Carolina, February 26, 1958; admitted to bar, 1984, Georgia; 1985, District of Columbia; 1993, North Carolina. *Education:* University of North Carolina (A.B., 1980); Yale University (J.D., 1983). Phi Beta Kappa. Morehead Scholar. Editor, Yale Law Journal, 1982-1983. Clerk to Honorable Irving Goldberg, U.S. Court of Appeals, Fifth Circuit, 1983-1984. ***LANGUAGES:*** French. ***PRACTICE AREAS:*** Debt Finance; Asset Based Finance; Leasing; General Corporate; International Law. ***Email:*** Manley.Roberts@hmw.com

P. CHRISTIAN SCHEURER, born Murphysboro, Illinois, June 13, 1967; admitted to bar, 1992, Tennessee; 1993, District of Columbia; 2000, North Carolina. *Education:* University of Tennessee at Knoxville (B.S., magna cum laude, 1989; J.D., 1992). Moot Court Board. Editorial Board, Tennessee Law Review. ***PRACTICE AREAS:*** Corporate Law; Mergers and Acquisitions; Securities Regulation; Venture Capital.

L. D. SIMMONS, II, born Clarksburg, West Virginia, May 23, 1959; admitted to bar, 1984, North Carolina. *Education:* Davidson College (A.B., 1981); Vanderbilt University (J.D., 1984). Student Writing Editor, Vanderbilt Law Review, 1983-1984. ***PRACTICE AREAS:*** Insurance Coverage; Insurance Litigation; Commercial Litigation; Civil Litigation. ***Email:*** L.D.Simmons@hmw.com

ROBERT W. SIMMONS, admitted to bar, 1984, Texas (inactive); 1986, North Carolina. *Education:* University of North Carolina at Chapel Hill (A.B., 1980) Phi Beta Kappa; University of Virginia (J.D., 1983). Morehead Scholar, University of North Carolina at Chapel Hill. *Member:* Mecklenburg County, North Carolina (Member, Real Property Section) and American (Member, Sections on: Real Property; Probate and Trust) Bar Associations. ***PRACTICE AREAS:*** Real Estate. ***Email:*** Bob.Simmons@hmw.com

WILLIAM DeVANE TIDWELL, born Charlotte, North Carolina, December 25, 1971; admitted to bar, 1997, North Carolina. *Education:* Davidson College (B.A., 1994); University of North Carolina, Chapel Hill (J.D., 1997). *Member:* Mecklenburg County, North Carolina and American Bar Associations. ***PRACTICE AREAS:*** Debt Finance; General Corporate; Private Placement; Securities; Mergers and Acquisitions. ***Email:*** Devane.Tidwell@hmw.com

SCOTT P. VAUGHN, born Winston-Salem, North Carolina, March 27, 1961; admitted to bar, 1986, North Carolina. *Education:* University of North Carolina (B.S., 1983; J.D., with honors, 1986). ***PRACTICE AREAS:*** Bankruptcy Law; Creditors Rights; Corporate Finance. ***Email:*** Scott.Vaughn@hmw.com

RICHARD W. VIOLA, born New Haven, Connecticut, May 1, 1968; admitted to bar, 1994, New York; 1999, North Carolina. *Education:* Villanova University (B.S., cum laude, 1990); St. John's University (J.D., magna cum laude, 1993). Beta Gamma Sigma Honor Society. Member, St. John's Law Review; Associate Managing Editor, American Bankruptcy Institute Law Review. ***PRACTICE AREAS:*** Securities Regulation; Corporate; Mergers and Acquisitions. ***Email:*** Rick.Viola@hmw.com

H. LANDIS WADE, JR., born Chapel Hill, North Carolina, September 10, 1957; admitted to bar, 1983, North Carolina. *Education:* Davidson College (A.B., 1979); Wake Forest University (J.D., 1983). Member, Wake Forest Law Review, 1981-1983. Certified: Arbitrator and Mediator. ***PRACTICE AREAS:*** Employment Litigation; Product Litigation; Real Estate Brokerage Litigation; Commercial Litigation; Dispute Resolution. ***Email:*** Landis.Wade@hmw.com

W. KENT WALKER, born Charlotte, North Carolina, January 1, 1968; admitted to bar, 1994, Georgia; 1995, Florida; U.S. District Court, Northern District of Georgia and Southern District of Florida; U.S. Court of Appeals, Eleventh Circuit; 1997, North Carolina. *Education:* University of North Carolina at Chapel Hill (B.S.B.A., with highest distinction, 1990); Harvard University (J.D., cum laude, 1993). Phi Beta Kappa. Morehead Scholar. Comments Editor, Harvard International Law Journal, 1992-1993. Law Clerk to the Hon. Stanley F. Birch, Jr., U.S. Court of Appeals, Eleventh Circuit, 1993-1994. *Member:* American Bar Association. ***PRACTICE AREAS:*** Finance.

JOHN B. YORKE, born Rock Hill, South Carolina, August 5, 1954; admitted to bar, 1979, North Carolina; 1987, South Carolina. *Education:* Wofford College (B.A., magna cum laude, 1976); Wake Forest University (J.D., 1979). Phi Beta Kappa. President, North Carolina Chapter of American Corporate Counsel Association, 1997. Former General Counsel: WorldWay Corporation; Integon Corporation. *Member:* North Carolina (Chair, Corporate Counsel Section, 1992) and American Bar Associations; North Carolina State Bar; South Carolina Bar. ***PRACTICE AREAS:*** Corporate Law; Mergers and Acquisitions; Private Equity; Insurance Regulation; Transportation; Franchise Law. ***Email:*** john.yorke@hmw.com

OF COUNSEL

E. OSBORNE AYSCUE, JR., born Monroe, North Carolina, May 21, 1933; admitted to bar, 1960, North Carolina. *Education:* Phillips Academy, Andover, Massachusetts (cum laude, 1951); University of North Carolina (A.B., 1954; J.D., with honors, 1960). Phi Beta Kappa; Order of the Coif. Editor-in-Chief, North Carolina Law Review, 1959-1960. Member: Supreme Court Historical Society (Trustee, 1999—); Permanent Member, Fourth Circuit Judicial Conference. Life Patron, American Bar Foundation. Fellow, American College of Trial Lawyers (President, 1998-1999). *Member:* Mecklenburg County (President, 1980-1981), North Carolina (President, 1984-1985) and American (Member: House of Delegates, 1991-1995; Standing Committee on Federal Judiciary, 2001—) Bar Associations. [U.S. Naval Reserve, Active Duty, 1955-1957]. ***PRACTICE AREAS:*** Civil Litigation; Media; Antitrust Law. ***Email:*** Ozzie.Ayscue@hmw.com

HERBERT H. BROWNE, JR., born Macon, Georgia, March 20, 1933; admitted to bar, 1958, North Carolina. *Education:* University of North Carolina (A.B., 1955); Harvard University (LL.B., 1958). Phi Beta Kappa. Fellow: American College of Trust and Estate Counsel. [U.S. Army Reserve, Active Duty, 1959]. (Board Certified Specialist in Estate Planning and Probate Law, North Carolina State Board of Legal Specialization). ***PRACTICE AREAS:*** Estate Planning; Estate Administration; Tax Exempt Organizations; Corporate. ***Email:*** Herb.Browne@hmw.com

(This Listing Continued)

LARRY J. DAGENHART, born Taylorsville, North Carolina, July 20, 1932; admitted to bar, 1958, North Carolina. *Education:* Davidson College (B.S., cum laude, 1953); New York University (LL.B., cum laude, 1958). Phi Beta Kappa; Omicron Delta Kappa. Root-Tilden Scholar. Comment Editor, New York University Law Review, 1957-1958. Fellow: American Law Institute; American Bar Foundation. *Member:* Mecklenburg County Bar Association (President, 1974-1975). [U.S. Army, Active Duty, 1954-1956]. ***PRACTICE AREAS:*** Corporate; Securities Regulation; Mergers and Acquisitions; Education; International Law. ***Email:*** Larry.Dagenhart@hmw.com

ANN TERRELL DORSETT, born Ridgewood, New Jersey, March 30, 1960; admitted to bar, 1989, Virginia; 1998, North Carolina. *Education:* University of North Carolina-Chapel Hill (A.B., 1982; J.D., 1989). *Member:* Virginia, North Carolina and American Bar Associations. ***REPORTED CASES:*** Fireman's Fund Ins. Co. v. Acc Chemical Co., et al, 538 N.W. 2nd 259 (Iowa, 1995). ***PRACTICE AREAS:*** Insurance Coverage; Insurance Litigation. ***Email:*** ann.dorsett@hmw.com

JULIA KATE HARRIS HATCHER, born 1970; admitted to bar, 1995, North Carolina and South Carolina. *Education:* University of Virginia (B.A., 1992); Wake Forest University (J.D., 1995). Member, Metrolina Entrepreneurial Council. ***PRACTICE AREAS:*** Corporate; E-Business and the Internet; Intellectual Property; Mergers and Acquisitions; Technology and Intellectual Property.

ANNE TEAM KELLY, born Lexington, North Carolina, February 25, 1962; admitted to bar, 1987, North Carolina. *Education:* University of North Carolina (B.S., 1984; J.D., with honors, 1987). Order of the Coif. Research Editor, University of North Carolina Law Review, 1986-1987. ***PRACTICE AREAS:*** Corporate Finance; Securities Regulation; Mergers and Acquisitions. ***Email:*** Anne.Kelly@hmw.com

R. MALLOY McKEITHEN, born Winston-Salem, North Carolina, October 31, 1939; admitted to bar, 1966, North Carolina. *Education:* Davidson College (A.B., 1961); University of North Carolina (J.D., with honors, 1966). Order of the Coif. Member, North Carolina Law Review, 1964-1966. [U.S. Army Reserve, Active Duty, 1961-1963]. ***PRACTICE AREAS:*** Corporate; Finance; Real Property; International Law. ***Email:*** Loy.Mckeithen@hmw.com

THOMAS W. MURRELL, III, born Richmond, Virginia, November 28, 1948; admitted to bar, 1974, Pennsylvania; 1997, North Carolina. *Education:* Yale University (B.A., cum laude, 1971); University of Virginia (J.D., 1974). *Member:* Pennsylvania and North Carolina Bar Associations; American Health Lawyers Association; Pennsylvania Health Care Association. ***PRACTICE AREAS:*** Commercial Litigation; Health Care Litigation; Estate Litigation. ***Email:*** Tom.Murrell@hmw.com

CATHERINE E. THOMPSON, born Fayetteville, North Carolina, October 21, 1954; admitted to bar, 1980, North Carolina. *Education:* Duke University (B.A., summa cum laude, 1976); Yale Law School (J.D., 1980). Phi Beta Kappa. Clerk to Honorable Sam J. Ervin, III, U.S. Court of Appeals, Fourth Circuit, 1980-1981. Permanent Member, Fourth Circuit Judicial Conference. President, Mecklenburg County Bar, 1991-1992. ***PRACTICE AREAS:*** Civil Litigation; Labor and Employment (Management). ***Email:*** Cathy.Thompson@hmw.com

ASSOCIATES

A. Carter Arey
R. Christian Brose (Not admitted in NC)
Jack William Campbell IV
David M. Chromy
Elizabeth Chase Coale
Richard Horace Conner, III
Jason Doughton Evans
Stephanie K. Briggs Evans
Sheldon M. Francis
Grant D. Goldenberg
Jill Crawley Griset
Matthew Hoefling
James S. Humphrey
Mark Weston Johnson
J. Trevor Johnston
Brian A. Kahn
Melissa M. Kidd
Gregory R. Kilpatrick
Mark W. Kinghorn
C. Andrew Konia
Kevin Landmesser
Amy Rickner Langdon
Tony Lauro
Jennifer Rouse Leahy
Marcus S. Lee
Julianna P. Lowe
Ingrid McClintock
Kevin A. McGinnis
Robynn E. Moraites
Paul M. Navarro
Lowndes C. Quinlan
Amanda K. Short
Tracy E. Strickland
Benjamin R. Thomas
Clay B. Tousey III
Mayleng F. Watson
Mary Lindsay Weatherly
Danielle E. Webb
Brett G. Weber
H. Ramsey White III
Amy R. Worley

Attorneys in the Charlotte Office Are Members of: Mecklenburg County, North Carolina Bar Associations and North Carolina State Bar.

REPRESENTATIVE CLIENTS: Bank of America; Branch Banking and Trust Co.; Digital Optics; Kitty Hawk Capital; Royal & SunAlliance; Compass Group USA, Inc.; Harris Teeter; Johnson & Wales University; The Charlotte Observer; First Charter Corporation; Continental Tire; Central Carolina Bank.

(For biographical data on other personnel, see Professional Biographies at Raleigh and Wilmington, North Carolina)

THOMAS B. HENSON

6100 FAIRVIEW ROAD, SUITE 650
CHARLOTTE, NORTH CAROLINA 28210
Telephone: 704-643-4148
Fax: 704-643-4482
Email: tom.henson@mailsouth.net
URL: http://www.lawyers.com/thomasbhenson

Mergers and Acquisitions, Corporate Law, Executive Compensation.

THOMAS B. HENSON, born Lawrenceburg, Tennessee, 1955; admitted to bar, 1980, North Carolina. *Education:* Vanderbilt University (B.A., magna cum laude, 1977); Washington & Lee University (J.D., summa cum laude, 1980). Omicron Delta Kappa; Order of the Coif. Recipient, John W. Davis Award. Editor-in-Chief, Washington & Lee Law Review, 1979-80. *Member:* North Carolina and American Bar Associations; North Carolina State Bar. ***PRACTICE AREAS:*** Mergers and Acquisitions; Corporate; Executive Compensation.

JOHN E. HODGE, JR.

6725-D FAIRVIEW ROAD
CHARLOTTE, NORTH CAROLINA 28210
Telephone: 704-442-9422
Telecopier: 704-442-1033
Email: hodgelaw@jehodgelaw.com
URL: http://www.lawyers.com/johnehodgelaw

General and Civil Trial, Civil Appeals, Commercial Litigation, Contracts, Collection, Business Litigation, Insurance Litigation, Complex Litigation, Real Estate Litigation, Construction Defects, Unfair Trade Practice, Fraud.

JOHN E. HODGE, JR., born Charlotte, North Carolina, December 3, 1944; admitted to bar, 1972, North Carolina and U.S. District Court, Middle and Western Districts of North Carolina; U.S. Court of Appeals, Fourth Circuit. *Education:* University of North Carolina (B.S., 1967; J.D., with honors, 1972). Beta Gamma Sigma; Order of the Coif. Managing Editor, Editorial Board, North Carolina Law Review, 1971-1972. Author: "Products Liability: The State of the Law in North Carolina," 8 Wake Forest Law Review 481, 1972. *Member:* North Carolina and American Bar Associations; The North Carolina State Bar; North Carolina Academy of Trial Lawyers.

THE HONNOLD LAW FIRM, P.A.

6000 FAIRVIEW ROAD, SUITE 1200
CHARLOTTE, NORTH CAROLINA 28210
Telephone: 704-552-3707
Email: bhonnold@honnoldlaw.com

Family Law, Domestic Relations, Civil Litigation, Separation Agreements, Divorce, Child Custody, Child Support, Alimony, Post Separation Support, Property Division, Domestic Violence, Premarital Agreements.

FIRM PROFILE: The Honnold Law Firm concentrates on providing quality legal services in the area of Family/Domestic Law, Civil Litigation, Separation and Divorce, Child Custody and Support, Alimony and Post Separation Support, Property Division, Domestic Violence and Premarital Agreements.

BRADLEY B. HONNOLD, born Anderson, Indiana, December 22, 1961; admitted to bar, 1995, New Jersey; 1996, North Carolina; U.S. District Court, Western and Middle Districts of North Carolina; U.S. Court of Appeals, Fourth Circuit. *Education:* Clarkson University (B.S.E.M., 1984); Syracuse University (J.D., magna cum laude, 1995). *Member:* Mecklenburg County (Family Law and Litigation Sections), North Carolina and American Bar Associations. ***PRACTICE AREAS:*** Family Law; Domestic Relations; Civil Litigation; Separation Agreements; Divorce; Child Custody; Child Support; Alimony; Post Separation Support; Property Division; Domestic Violence; Premarital Agreements. ***Email:*** bhonnold@honnoldlaw.com

HORACK, TALLEY, PHARR & LOWNDES

A PROFESSIONAL ASSOCIATION

Established in 1932

2600 ONE WACHOVIA CENTER
301 SOUTH COLLEGE STREET
CHARLOTTE, NORTH CAROLINA 28202-6038
Telephone: 704-377-2500
Fax: 704-372-2619
URL: http://www.horacktalley.com

Other Charlotte, North Carolina Office: 4701 Hedgemore Drive, Suite 812, 28209. Telephone: 704-522-1575. Fax: 704-522-1736.

General Trial and Appellate Practice in all State and Federal Courts, Family Law, Business and Corporate Law for Small and Closely Held Businesses, Taxation, Securities, Commercial and Residential Real Estate Development, Administrative Law, Creditors Rights and Bankruptcy, Real Estate Title Disputes, Homebuilders, Personal and Business Asset Preservation, Estate Administration, Governments and Municipalities, Employer's Rights, Construction Litigation.

FIRM PROFILE: Horack, Talley, Pharr & Lowndes was founded in 1932 and provides a range of specialized legal services to businesses and individuals. The firm concentrates on serving commercial and residential developers; commercial litigation and creditors' rights; the title insurance industry; homebuilders and governmental entities. It also assists individuals with wealth transfers, asset preservation, estate administration, and divorce and other family law issues.

PAUL R. ERVIN (1908-1970)

RAY W. BRADLEY, JR. (1922-2000)

JAMES M. TALLEY, JR., born Durham, North Carolina, April 7, 1937; admitted to bar, 1964, North Carolina. *Education:* University of North Carolina (B.S., 1959; J.D., with honors, 1964). Order of the Coif. Member, Board of Editors, North Carolina Law Review, 1963-1964. Member, Board of Directors, 1976-1982 and President, 1978-1982, Legal Services of North Carolina Inc. Member, Board of Directors, 1974-1982 and President, 1977-1980, Board of Directors, Legal Services of Southern Piedmont, Inc. Member, Board of Directors, North Carolina Prisoners Legal Services, Inc., 1978-1981. Member, Board of Governors, 1983-1986 and President, 1994-1995, North Carolina Bar Association. President, Southern Conference of Bar Presidents, 1995-1996. Member, Board of Trustees, University of North Carolina School of Law Alumni Association, 2001—. Member, Board of Trustees, North Carolina State Bar Plan for Interest on Lawyers Trust Accounts, 2002—. Fellow, American Bar Foundation. [Captain, USNR (Retired)]. ***PRACTICE AREAS:*** Business Law; Securities; Commercial Real Estate; Real Estate Development; Real Estate Finance. ***Email:*** JTalley@HorackTalley.com

HENRY N. PHARR, II, born Charlotte, North Carolina, January 28, 1939; admitted to bar, 1964, North Carolina. *Education:* Davidson College (A.B., 1961); University of North Carolina (J.D., 1964). ***PRACTICE AREAS:*** Commercial Real Estate; Real Estate Development; Commercial Real Estate Finance; Government Relations. ***Email:*** HPharr2@HorackTalley.com

WILLIAM S. LOWNDES, born Washington, D.C., January 27, 1932; admitted to bar, 1966, North Carolina. *Education:* Duke University (A.B., 1954); University of North Carolina (J.D., with honors, 1966). Order of the Coif. Member, Board of Editors, North Carolina Law Review, 1965-1966. (Retired). ***PRACTICE AREAS:*** Corporations; Estate and Gift Taxation; Trusts and Estates. ***Email:*** BLowndes@HorackTalley.com

THOMAS R. CANNON, born Durham, North Carolina, May 22, 1940; admitted to bar, 1965, North Carolina. *Education:* University of North Carolina (A.B., 1962; LL.B., 1965). Phi Delta Phi. Morehead Scholar. Chairman, Family Law Section, North Carolina Bar Association, 1982-1983. Member, North Carolina State Bar Board of Legal Specialization Family Law Certification Committee, 1988-1994. Fellow, American Academy of Matrimonial Lawyers (Certified Arbitrator). [Lt. Cmdr., USNR, Ret.]. (Board Certified Specialist in Family Law, North Carolina State Bar, Board of Legal Specialization). ***PRACTICE AREAS:*** Family Law; Litigation. ***Email:*** TCannon@HorackTalley.com

NEIL C. WILLIAMS, born Charlotte, North Carolina, October 18, 1941; admitted to bar, 1966, North Carolina. *Education:* Duke University (A.B., 1963; LL.B., 1966). Omicron Delta Kappa; Phi Delta Phi. Member, Charlotte City Council, 1973-1977. [Capt., JAGC, U.S.N.R. (Retired)]. ***PRACTICE AREAS:*** Civil Litigation; Insurance; Land Use; Government Relations; Administrative Law. ***Email:*** NWilliams@HorackTalley.com

PAUL H. EFIRD, III, born Charlotte, North Carolina, 1944; admitted to bar, 1969, North Carolina. *Education:* Davidson College (B.A., 1966); University of North Carolina (J.D., 1969). *Member:* Mecklenburg County and North Carolina Bar Associations. (Also at Hedgemore Drive Office). ***PRACTICE AREAS:*** Residential Real Estate. ***Email:*** wefird@horacktalley.com

G. ROBERT TURNER, III, born Wilmington, Delaware, May 8, 1944; admitted to bar, 1969, North Carolina. *Education:* Duke University (B.A., 1966); University of North Carolina (J.D., 1969). Former Member, Executive Committee, Mecklenburg County Bar Association. ***PRACTICE AREAS:*** Commercial Real Estate; Real Estate Development; Real Estate Finance; Banking Law; Creditors Rights; Bankruptcy; Foreclosures. ***Email:*** BTurner@HorackTalley.com

CLAYTON S. CURRY, JR., born Charlotte, North Carolina, August 30, 1948; admitted to bar, 1972, North Carolina. *Education:* University of North Carolina (B.S., 1970); University of Tennessee (J.D., 1972). ***PRACTICE AREAS:*** Commercial Real Estate; Residential Real Estate; Real Estate Development; Banking Law; Financial Law; Corporate Law; Partnership Law. ***Email:*** SCurry@HorackTalley.com

TATE K. STERRETT, born Charlottesville, Virginia, December 6, 1946; admitted to bar, 1973, North Carolina. *Education:* Davidson College (B.A., 1969); University of Virginia (J.D., 1972). Certified Mediator. (Board Certified Specialist in Family Law, North Carolina State Board of Legal Specialization). ***PRACTICE AREAS:*** Family Law; Civil Litigation; Mediation. ***Email:*** TSterrett@HorackTalley.com

SUSAN CHRISTMAN, born Wichita, Kansas, January 22, 1951; admitted to bar, 1976, North Carolina. *Education:* University of Arkansas (B.A., 1973); Vanderbilt University (J.D., 1976). Phi Beta Kappa. ***PRACTICE AREAS:*** Corporate Law; Partnership Law; Commercial Real Estate; Securities. ***Email:*** SChristman@HorackTalley.com

STEPHEN L. SMITH, born Charleston, South Carolina, April 19, 1952; admitted to bar, 1976, North Carolina. *Education:* University of North Carolina (A.B., 1973); University of Virginia (J.D., 1976). Phi Beta Kappa. Order of the Coif. ***PRACTICE AREAS:*** Asset Protection; Equity Planning; Real Estate Tax Appeals; Real Estate Planning. ***Email:*** SSmith@HorackTalley.com

ELIZABETH T. HODGES, born High Point, North Carolina, March 2, 1954; admitted to bar, 1979, North Carolina; U.S. District Court, Western District of North Carolina. *Education:* University of North Carolina (A.B., cum laude, 1975; J.D., 1979). Phi Alpha Delta. Managing Editor, North Carolina Journal of International Law and Commercial Regulation, 1977-1979. *Member:* Mecklenburg County, North Carolina (Member: Family Law Section; Family Law Council) and American Bar Associations; The North Carolina State Bar; North Carolina Academy of Trial Lawyers. (Board Certified Specialist in Family Law, North Carolina State Bar, Board of Legal Specialization). ***PRACTICE AREAS:*** Family Law; Litigation. ***Email:*** BHodges@HorackTalley.com

(This Listing Continued)

HORACK, TALLEY, PHARR & LOWNDES, A PROFESSIONAL ASSOCIATION, Charlotte—Continued

H. DAVID POWELL, born Winston-Salem, North Carolina, July 31, 1959; admitted to bar, 1985, North Carolina. *Education:* University of North Carolina (B.S., 1981); Wake Forest University (J.D., 1985). ***PRACTICE AREAS:*** Real Estate; Banking Law; Finance; Corporate Law; Partnership Law. ***Email:*** DPowell@HorackTalley.com

ROBERT B. McNEILL, born Chapel Hill, North Carolina, June 5, 1960; admitted to bar, 1985, North Carolina. *Education:* University of North Carolina (B.S.B.A., 1982; J.D., 1985). ***PRACTICE AREAS:*** Title Insurance Litigation; Real Estate Litigation; Construction Litigation; Arbitration; Mediation. ***Email:*** RMcNeill@HorackTalley.com

CHERYL D. STEELE, born South Boston, Virginia, February 14, 1961; admitted to bar, 1987, North Carolina. *Education:* Meredith College (B.S., magna cum laude, 1983); University of North Carolina at Chapel Hill (J.D., 1987). ***PRACTICE AREAS:*** Commercial Real Estate; Real Estate Development; Banking Law; Finance Law. ***Email:*** CSteele@HorackTalley.com

MICHAEL S. HUNTER, born Charlotte, North Carolina, May 14, 1962; admitted to bar, 1987, North Carolina, U.S. District Court, Western, Middle and Eastern Districts of North Carolina and U.S. Court of Appeals, Fourth Circuit. *Education:* University of North Carolina-Chapel Hill (B.S., 1984); Harvard University; Wake Forest University (J.D., 1987). Co-Author: "How to Get Results in the Collection of Delinquent Debts in North Carolina," 1996, National Business Institute, Inc., Eau Claire, Wisconsin. Member, American Bankruptcy Institute. Attorney for Mecklenburg Sheriffs Office. *Member:* Mecklenburg County, North Carolina and American Bar Associations; North Carolina State Bar. ***PRACTICE AREAS:*** Bankruptcy; Creditors Rights; Collections; Secured Transactions; Commercial Litigation; Real Estate; Community Association Law; Condominium Association Law. ***Email:*** MHunter@HorackTalley.com

HENRY N. PHARR, III, born Charlotte, North Carolina, January 11, 1966; admitted to bar, 1993, North Carolina; U.S. District Court, Western, Middle and Eastern Districts of North Carolina. *Education:* University of North Carolina (B.A., 1988; J.D., 1993). Morehead Scholar. *Member:* North Carolina and American Bar Associations; North Carolina State Bar. ***PRACTICE AREAS:*** Civil Litigation; Commercial Litigation; Real Property; Land Use; Municipal Law. ***Email:*** HPharr3@HorackTalley.com

GENA GRAHAM MORRIS, born Charlotte, North Carolina, March, 8, 1965; admitted to bar, 1992, North Carolina. *Education:* University of North Carolina (B.A., 1987); Campbell University (J.D., 1992). *Member:* Mecklenburg County and North Carolina Bar Associations; North Carolina Bar Family Law Council; North Carolina State Bar. (Board Certified Specialist in Family Law, North Carolina State Board of Legal Specialization). ***PRACTICE AREAS:*** Family Law; Litigation. ***Email:*** GMorris@HorackTalley.com

KRISTIN DECKER OGBURN, born Annapolis, Maryland, July 1, 1967; admitted to bar, 1994, North Carolina and South Carolina; 1996, District of Columbia, U.S. District Court, Western, Middle and Eastern Districts of North Carolina and U.S. District Court, District of South Carolina. *Education:* University of Virginia (B.A., 1989); Wake Forest University (J.D., 1993). *Member:* Mecklenburg County (Member, Board of Directors, 2004-2007), North Carolina (Member, Bankruptcy Section Council, 2003-2006) and American Bar Associations. ***LANGUAGES:*** Spanish. ***PRACTICE AREAS:*** Bankruptcy; Creditors Rights. ***Email:*** KOgburn@HorackTalley.com

WILLIAM B. HAMEL, SR., born Nashville, Tennessee, June 18, 1965; admitted to bar, 1990, North Carolina and U.S. District Court, Western District of North Carolina; U.S. Court of Appeals, Fourth and Federal Circuits. *Education:* Wake Forest University (B.A., 1987); Campbell University (J.D., 1990). ***PRACTICE AREAS:*** Civil Litigation; Corporate Law; Estate Planning; Real Estate; Community Association Law. ***Email:*** BHamel@HorackTalley.com

ROBERT S. BLAIR, JR., born New York, N.Y., May 1, 1965; admitted to bar, 1991, North Carolina. *Education:* Wofford College (B.A., 1987); Wake Forest University (J.D., 1990). *Member:* Mecklenburg County (Co-Chairman, Family Law Section), North Carolina (Member, Family Law Section) and American Bar Associations; North Carolina State Bar; North Carolina Academy of Trial Lawyers. (Board Certified Specialist in Family Law, North Carolina State Board of Legal Specialization). ***PRACTICE AREAS:*** Civil Litigation; Domestic Relations; Equitable Distribution. ***Email:*** rblair@horacktalley.com

ZIPPORAH MARIE BASILE EDWARDS, born Cleveland, Ohio, August 4, 1969; admitted to bar, 1994, North Carolina; 1995, U.S. Court of Appeals, Fourth Circuit. *Education:* Wake Forest University (B.A., cum laude, 1991; J.D., cum laude, 1994). Member, Editorial Staff, Wake Forest University Law Review. *Member:* Mecklenburg County and North Carolina (Member, Real Property Litigation Section) Bar Associations. ***PRACTICE AREAS:*** Commercial Litigation; Title Insurance Litigation. ***Email:*** ZEdwards@HorackTalley.com

D. CHRISTOPHER OSBORN, born Charlotte, North Carolina, January 24, 1970; admitted to bar, 1995, North Carolina. *Education:* University of North Carolina (B.A., with highest distinction, 1992); University of Virginia (J.D., 1995). Phi Beta Kappa. James M. Johnston Scholar. Hardy Cross Dillard Scholar. Member, Editorial Board, Virginia Law Review, 1993-1994; Articles Review Board, 1994-1995. Law Clerk, Hon. Carl Horn, III, Chief U.S. Magistrate Judge, Western District of North Carolina, 1997-1999. Co-author: with Carl Horn and Donald Caldwell, "Law for Physicians: An Overview of Medical Legal Issues," AMA Press, 1999; with Jill Rose, "FACE-ial Neutrality: A Free Speech Challenge To The Freedom of Access To Clinic Entrances Act," 81 Va. L. Rev. 1501, 1995. *Member:* Mecklenburg County and North Carolina (Member, Sections on: Construction Law; Employment Law) Bar Associations. ***PRACTICE AREAS:*** Employment Law; Commercial Litigation; Construction Litigation; Real Estate Litigation. ***Email:*** COsborn@HorackTalley.com

LOUISE F. HARMON, born Honolulu, Hawaii, September 14, 1971; admitted to bar, 1996, North Carolina. *Education:* Clemson University (B.A., 1993); Wake Forest University (J.D., 1996). *Member:* Mecklenburg County (Member, Real Property Section) and North Carolina (Member, Real Property Section) Bar Associations. ***PRACTICE AREAS:*** Residential Real Estate; Commercial Real Estate; Real Estate Finance. ***Email:*** LFisher@HorackTalley.com

(This Listing Continued)

JOHN W. BOWERS, born Charlotte, North Carolina, April 1, 1971; admitted to bar, 1997, North Carolina; 1998, U.S. District Court, Western District of North Carolina. *Education:* University of North Carolina at Chapel Hill (B.A., 1993; J.D., with honors, 1997). Phi Beta Kappa; Phi Alpha Delta, 1994-1997. Member, North Carolina Law Review, 1995-1996. Law Clerk, Hon. John W. Webb. Associate Justice, North Carolina Supreme Court, 1997-1998. *Member:* Mecklenburg County, North Carolina (Member, Sections on: Litigation; Constitutional Law) and American Bar Associations; North Carolina State Bar. ***PRACTICE AREAS:*** Business Law; Corporate Law; Civil Litigation; Appellate Practice; Real Estate Litigation; Commercial Litigation; Construction Litigation; Appellate Advocacy. ***Email:*** jbowers@horacktalley.com

KATHRYN MITCHELL KELLING, born Durham, North Carolina, October 22, 1972; admitted to bar, 1998, North Carolina. *Education:* Harvard University (B.A., cum laude, 1995); Wake Forest University (J.D., 1998). *Member:* Mecklenburg County and North Carolina (Member, Family Law Section) Bar Associations; Mecklenburg County Young Lawyers Section (Board of Directors). (Board Certified Specialist in Family Law, North Carolina State Board of Legal Specialization). ***PRACTICE AREAS:*** Family Law; Litigation. ***Email:*** MKelling@HorackTalley.com

KARY C. WATSON, born Silver Spring, Maryland, October 16, 1974; admitted to bar, 2001, North Carolina. *Education:* University of North Carolina at Chapel Hill (B.A., 1996); Bowling Green State University (M.A., 1998); Wake Forest University (J.D., 2001). *Member:* Mecklenburg County (Member, Family Law Section) and North Carolina (Member, Family Law Section) Bar Associations. ***PRACTICE AREAS:*** Family Law. ***Email:*** KWatson@HorackTalley.com

ROBYN M. SAYE, born Yonkers, New York, April 10, 1977; admitted to bar, 2002, North Carolina. *Education:* Duke University (A.B., 1999); University of North Carolina (J.D., 2002). Article and Notes Editor, North Carolina Banking Institute Law Journal, 2001-2002. Author, "Eyeing The Future: Surviving the Criticism of Biometrics Authentication," North Carolina Banking Institute vol. 5 Spring, 2001. *Member:* Mecklenburg County, North Carolina and American Bar Associations. ***PRACTICE AREAS:*** Civil Litigation. ***Email:*** rsaye@horacktalley.com

JONATHAN CHARLES WINDHAM, born Gastonia, North Carolina, June 23, 1975; admitted to bar, 2003, North Carolina. *Education:* University of North Carolina at Chapel Hill (B.S.B.A., 1998; M.A., Accounting, 1999; J.D., 2002). Articles and Notes Editor, North Carolina Banking Institute Law Journal, 2001-2002. Author: "The Search for Clarity in the Accounting for Loan-Loss Reserves: Earnings Management vs. Safety and Soundness," North Carolina Banking Institute, Vol. 5, Spring 2001. *Member:* Mecklenburg County, North Carolina and American Bar Associations. ***PRACTICE AREAS:*** Wills; Trusts and Estates; Estate Planning; Taxation; Business Law. ***Email:*** jwindham@horacktalley.com

COLLIN W. BROWN, born Atlanta, Georgia, January 27, 1977; admitted to bar, 2003, North Carolina. *Education:* University of Mississippi (B.A., 1999); Wake Forest University (J.D., 2003). Senior Notes and Comments Editor, Wake Forest Law Review, 2002-2003. ***PRACTICE AREAS:*** Land Use; Zoning Law; Commercial Real Estate. ***Email:*** cbrown@horacktalley.com

KATHERINE M. LeBAR, born Cleveland, Ohio, May 17, 1973; admitted to bar, 2003, North Carolina. *Education:* University of Chicago (A.B., 1995); Washington University (J.D., 2003). *Member:* North Carolina, North Carolina State and American Bar Associations. ***PRACTICE AREAS:*** Commercial Real Estate; Real Estate Development; Residential Real Estate; Banking Law; Finance Law. ***Email:*** klebar@horacktalley.com

PHILLIP E. LEWIS, born Jefferson, North Carolina, August 19, 1971; admitted to bar, 2001, North Carolina. *Education:* University of North Carolina at Chapel Hill (B.A., 1993); Campbell University (J.D., cum laude, 2001). Editor-in-Chief, Campbell Law Review. (Also at Hedgemore Drive Office). ***PRACTICE AREAS:*** Corporate Commercial Law; Commercial Real Estate; Residential Real Estate. ***Email:*** plewis@horacktalley.com

DAVID L. EDWARDS, born Atlanta, Georgia, September 8, 1969; admitted to bar, 2002, North Carolina. *Education:* Wake Forest University (B.A., 1992; J.D., 2002). *Member:* North Carolina State Bar. ***PRACTICE AREAS:*** Litigation; Bankruptcy. ***Email:*** dedwards@horacktalley.com

HEATHER E. LEWIS, born Mount Airy, North Carolina, May 27, 1976; admitted to bar, 2004, North Carolina. *Education:* Wake Forest University (B.S., cum laude, 1999; M.S., 1999; J.D., 2004). *Member:* North Carolina State Bar. ***PRACTICE AREAS:*** Creditors Rights; Commercial Litigation; Commercial Real Estate. ***Email:*** hsawyers@horacktalley.com

AMY E. BUTTERWORTH, born Knoxville, Tennessee, July 13, 1978; admitted to bar, 2004, North Carolina. *Education:* University of Maryland (B.A., 2001); Wake Forest University (J.D., 2004). *Member:* North Carolina State Bar. ***PRACTICE AREAS:*** Family Law. ***Email:*** abutterworth@horacktalley.com

JOHN T. MAHERAS, born Charlotte, North Carolina, December 23, 1968; admitted to bar, 1994, North Carolina. *Education:* Davidson College (B.A., Economics, second honors, 1991); University of North Carolina, Chapel Hill (J.D., with honors, 1994). Articles Editor, North Carolina Journal of International Law and Commercial Regulation, 1993-1994. ***LANGUAGES:*** Greek. ***PRACTICE AREAS:*** Commercial Real Estate; Residential Real Estate; Commercial Lending; Banking Transactions.

OF COUNSEL

RUSSELL J. SCHWARTZ, born Pittsburgh, Pennsylvania, November 24, 1958; admitted to bar, 1982, North Carolina and South Carolina. *Education:* University of South Carolina (B.A., magna cum laude, 1979); Duke University (J.D., 1982). Phi Beta Kappa. ***PRACTICE AREAS:*** Communications Law; Intellectual Property; Land Use; Government Relations; Employment Law. ***Email:*** RSchwartz@HorackTalley.com

RETIRED

BENJ. S. HORACK, born Iowa City, Iowa, October 3, 1917; admitted to bar, 1941, North Carolina. *Education:* Duke University (A.B., 1939; LL.B., 1941). Phi Beta Kappa; Order of the Coif. Editor-in-Chief, Duke Law Journal, 1940-1941. Member, Charlotte School Board, 1954-1962. (Retired). ***Email:*** BHorack@HorackTalley.com

(This Listing Continued)

PAUL B. GUTHERY, JR., born Charlotte, North Carolina, August 5, 1929; admitted to bar, 1956, North Carolina; 1959, U.S. Court of Appeals, Fourth Circuit. *Education:* Davidson College (B.S., 1951); University of North Carolina (J.D., with honors, 1956). Member, Board of Editors, North Carolina Law Review, 1954-1955. (Retired)

All Attorneys are Members of the Mecklenburg County, North Carolina and American Bar Associations; North Carolina State Bar.

REPRESENTATIVE CLIENTS: Allied Domecz Quick Service Restaurants (Dunkin Donuts); American General Finance; American Honda Finance Co.; Bahakel Communications; Branch Banking and Trust Co.; Central Carolina Bank; Chicago Title Insurance Co.; Childress Klein Properties; City of Charlotte; Collett & Associates; Dahlem Realty Co.; Easlan Capital of Charlotte; Edens & Avant; eResources Capital Group; Fidelity Bank; Fidelity National Title Insurance Co.; First Charter Bank; First Trust Bank; Ford Motor Credit Co.; G.E. Capital; Grubb Properties; Harvest Corporate Services; High Associates; Hospitality Advisors Corp.; Hospitality Group; The Inspirational Network, Inc.; Investors Title Insurance Company; Kahn Properties; Kirco Realty Services Group; Lawyers Title Insurance Company; Life Insurance Company of Baltimore; Bank of America; Lions Services Inc.; Old Republic Title Insurance Co.; Panos/Smith Hotel Group; Principal Mutual Life Insurance Co.; Pulte Home Corporation; RBC Centura Bank; Ryder Systems, Inc.; Shenandoah Life Insurance Co.; The Shopping Center Group; Shoreline Management; SouthTrust Bank; Stanley Tool Co.; Town of Pineville; Vulcan Materials Co.; WCCB-TV; Wachovia Bank; Weekley Homes, L.P.; Weingarten Realty; Withrow Capital, Inc.
REFERENCE: Wachovia Bank.

HULL & CHANDLER, P.A.

521 EAST MOREHEAD STREET, SUITE 101
CHARLOTTE, NORTH CAROLINA 28202
Telephone: 704-375-8488
Fax: 704-375-8487
URL: http://www.lawyercarolina.com
Email: nmhull@lawyercarolina.com
URL: http://www.nathanhulllaw.com

Business Law, Limited Liability Law Companies, Corporate Law, Partnership Law, Joint Ventures, Licensing Agreements, Mergers and Acquisitions, Contracts, Non Profit and Charitable Organizations, Lawsuits, Commercial Litigation, Transactions, Collections, Franchise Law, Tax Law, Estate Planning, Trusts and Estates, Wills, Probate, Intellectual Property, Patents, Copyrights, Trademarks, Personal Injury, Automobile Accidents, Automobile Insurance, Dog Bites, Construction Accidents and Workers Compensation.

SHAREHOLDERS

NATHAN M. HULL, born Denver, Colorado, September 24, 1973; admitted to bar, 1999, North Carolina and U.S. District Court, Western District of North Carolina. *Education:* De Pauw University (B.A., 1995); Wake Forest University School of Law (J.D., 1999). Academic All American (1992-95). Classes/Seminars Taught: *Practical Estate Planning After the Estate Tax Changes of 2001,* Financial Planning Association of Charlotte, October 16, 2001 and National Association of Insurance and Financial Advisors, March 19, 2001; *Choosing the Form of Your Business,* Central Piedmont Community College, 2000—; CLEs Taught: *Drafting Wills and Trusts in North Carolina,* September 24, 2002. *Member:* Mecklenburg County, North Carolina and American Bar Associations. ***PRACTICE AREAS:*** Corporations; Limited Liability Company Law; Charitable Giving; Estate Planning; Mergers and Acquisitions; Transactions; Tax Law; Employment Law; Intellectual Property; Security Interests. ***Email:*** nmhull@lawyercarolina.com

R. MICHAEL CHANDLER, born Danville, Virginia, December 17, 1972; admitted to bar, 1999, North Carolina and U.S. District Court, Western District of North Carolina. *Education:* Elon College (B.S., 1995); Wake Forest University School of Law (J.D., 1999). Member, Moot Court Board, Pace Environmental Law Team, 1999. *Member:* Mecklenburg County and North Carolina State Bar Associations; North Carolina State Bar; North Carolina Academy of Trial Lawyers. ***REPORTED CASES:*** Stilwell v. Gust v. Stilwell, 557 S.E.2d 627 (NC App 2001). ***PRACTICE AREAS:*** Civil Litigation; Personal Injury; Business Litigation; Collections; Wrongful Death. ***Email:*** mchandler@lawyercarolina.com

ASSOCIATE

CHRISTOPHER S. SHUMATE, born Gastonia, North Carolina, July 5, 1978; admitted to bar, 2003, North Carolina; 2004, South Carolina. *Education:* University of South Carolina (B.A., 2000; J.D., 2003). ***PRACTICE AREAS:*** Plaintiffs Personal Injury (30%); Workers Compensation (20%); Commercial Vehicle Liability (10%); Motorcycle Accidents (10%); Civil Litigation (10%); Business Litigation (10%); Catastrophic Injury (5%); Wrongful Death (5%). ***Email:*** cshumate@lawyercarolina.com

Language: Spanish.

REPRESENTATIVE CLIENTS: A.M.E. Zion Church, Inc.; AddLogos, LLC.; American Products Distributors, Inc.; Animal Care Clinic of Concord, P.A.; Financial Planning Association of Charlotte; Greenfield Construction, Inc.; Hickory Adult Medicine and Kidney Specialists, P.A.; Integrated Visual Systems, Inc.; Lyf-Tym Building Products Co., Inc.; Piedmont Endocrinology, P.A.; South Trust Bank; The Center for Safety Development, Inc.; The Mighty Dollar, LLC; Triad Clinical Laboratories, Inc.; World Wide Capital Funding, LLC.

HUNTON & WILLIAMS LLP

BANK OF AMERICA PLAZA
SUITE 3500
101 SOUTH TRYON STREET
CHARLOTTE, NORTH CAROLINA 28280
Telephone: 704-378-4700
Fax: 704-378-4890
URL: http://www.hunton.com

Washington, D.C. Office: 1900 K Street, N.W., 20006-1109. Telephone: 202-955-1500. Fax: 202-778-2201.
Miami, Florida Office: 1111 Brickell Avenue, Suite 2500, 33131. Telephone: 305-810-2500. Fax: 305-810-2460.

(This Listing Continued)

Atlanta, Georgia Office: Bank of America Plaza, 600 Peachtree Street, N.E., Suite 4100, 30308-2216. Telephone: 404-888-4000. Fax: 404-888-4190 and Georgia-Hill Office: Southside Legal Center, 250 Georgia Avenue, S.E., Suite 211, 30312. Telephone: 404-688-5512; 404-688-5513.
New York, New York Office: 200 Park Avenue, 43rd Floor, 10166-0136. Telephone: 212-309-1000. Fax: 212-309-1100.
Raleigh, North Carolina Office: One Bank of America Plaza, 421 Fayetteville Street Mall, Suite 1400, 27601. Telephone: 919-899-3000. Fax: 919-833-6352.
Knoxville, Tennessee Office: 2000 Riverview Tower, 900 South Gay Street, 37902. Telephone: 865-549-7700. Fax: 865-549-7704.
Dallas, Texas Office: Energy Plaza, 30th Floor, 1601 Bryan Street, 75201-3402. Telephone: 214-979-3000. Fax: 214-880-0011.
Richmond, Virginia Office: Riverfront Plaza, East Tower, 951 East Byrd Street, 23219-4074. Telephone: 804-788-8200. Fax: 804-788-8218; 804-788-8219 and Church Hill Office: 2300 East Marshall Street, 23223. Telephone: 804-775-2248.
McLean, Virginia Office: 1751 Pinnacle Drive, Suite 1700, Tysons Corner, 22102. Telephone: 703-714-7400. Fax: 703-714-7410.
Norfolk, Virginia Office: 500 East Main Street, Suite 1000, 23510-3889. Telephone: 757-640-5300. Fax: 757-625-7720.
Brussels, Belgium Office: Ave Louise 326, B6, 1050 Brussels, Belgium. Telephone: +32 0-2-643-5800. Fax: +32 0-2-643-5822.
Bangkok, Thailand Office: 34/F Abdulrahim Place, 990 Rama IV Road, Bangkok, Thailand, 1050. Telephone: +011 662 636-2366. Fax: +011 662 636-2377.
London, England Office: Fleetway House, 25 Farringdon Street, London EC4A 4AB, England. Telephone: +44 (0)20 7246 5700. Fax: +44 (0)20 7246 5772.
Singapore, Singapore Office: 6 Battery Road, #24-01, Singapore, 049909. Telephone: +65 6534-5608. Fax: +65 6534-5532.
Beijing, China Office: 517-520 South Office Tower, Beijing Kerry Centre, No. 1 Guanghua Road, Chaoyang District, Beijing, PRC 100020, China. Telephone: +86 10 5863 7500. Fax: +86 10 5863 7591.

General Practice. Administrative/Regulatory Law, Admiralty, Antitrust, Unfair Trade Practices, Bankruptcy, Business, Corporation, Environmental, Insurance, International, Labor, Municipal Bond and Finance Law, Non-Criminal Trials and Appeals, Real Property, Condemnation, Securities Regulation, Taxation, Trademarks, Copyright, Utilities, Probate and Estate Planning.

FIRM PROFILE: Hunton & Williams provides legal counsel to corporations, financial institutions, governments and individuals as well as a broad array of other entities. Founded in 1901, Hunton & Williams is a US law firm with a significant international presence. More than 850 attorneys in 16 offices have served clients in over 100 countries around the world.

PARTNERS

HAYWOOD A. BARNES, born Wilson, North Carolina, October 3, 1964; admitted to bar, 1994, North Carolina. *Education:* University of North Carolina at Wilmington (B.S., Finance, 1987); Wake Forest University (J.D., 1994; M.B.A., 1994). Recipient, E. McGruder Faris Memorial Award for High Standards of Character, Leadership and Scholarship, Wake Forest University School of Law, 1994. Member, 1992-1993 and Symposium Editor, 1993-1994, Wake Forest Law Review. *Member:* Association of Commercial Finance Attorneys; Turnaround Management Association. ***PRACTICE AREAS:*** Banking; Commercial Finance; Insolvency; Workouts; Bankruptcy. ***Email:*** hbarnes@hunton.com

A. TODD BROWN, born Chester, South Carolina, August 12, 1960; admitted to bar, 1986, North Carolina. *Education:* University of South Carolina (B.S., 1982; J.D., 1986). Member, Society of Wig and Robe. Student Works Editor, South Carolina Law Review, 1985-1986. Legal Writing Instructor, University of South Carolina School of Law, 1985-1986. Member: Litigation and Labor and Employment Sections of American Bar Association; Litigation and Labor and Employment Sections of North Carolina Bar Association. Chair, Business Torts Committee, Tort and Insurance Practice Section, American Bar Association, 1998-1999. *Member:* National Bar Association; Defense Research Institute. ***PRACTICE AREAS:*** Commercial Litigation; Labor and Employment. ***Email:*** tbrown@hunton.com

JOSEPH B. BUONANNO, born Killeen, Texas, April 3, 1963; admitted to bar, 1990, New York; 1991, District of Columbia (Not admitted in North Carolina). *Education:* Eastman School of Music, University of Rochester (B.M., 1985); Cornell University (M.B.A., 1988; J.D., 1989). Author, Publications, Bank Insurance: *The Moving Frontier Between Banking and Insurance,* 1992; *Protections for Depositors and Other Consumers of United States Banking Services,* 1991. *Member:* Association of the Bar of the City of New York; The District of Columbia Bar; New York State and American Bar Associations. ***PRACTICE AREAS:*** Mortgage Securitization; Corporate Law; Securitization; Finance; Structured Finance; Insurance Guaranty Association Law; Real Estate Finance. ***Email:*** jbuonanno@hunton.com

T. THOMAS COTTINGHAM, III, born Fayetteville, North Carolina, July 17, 1947; admitted to bar, 1976, Alabama; 1989, North Carolina. *Education:* Davidson College (A.B., 1969); Cornell University (J.D., cum laude, 1976). Co-Chair, Expert Witness Committee, Litigation Section, American Bar Association, 2003—; Co-Director, Division IV Procedural, Litigation Section, American Bar Association, 2002-2003; Co-Chair, Trial Evidence Committee, Litigation Section, American Bar Association, 1999-2002; Co-Chair, Southeast Region, Business Torts Committee, Litigation Section, American Bar Association, 1996-1999; Alabama State Bar Examiner, 1989-1993; Litigation Section, North Carolina Bar Association; Mecklenburg County Bar Association and Birmingham Bar Association; Alabama State Bar, Instructor, National Institute of Trial Advocacy; Defense Research Institute; Chair, Legal and Personnel Committee, Board of Directors, Alabama Symphony Association 1996-1998. [Captain, U.S. Army, 1969-1973]. ***PRACTICE AREAS:*** Litigation; International Law; Labor and Employment. ***Email:*** tcottingham@hunton.com

FRANK E. EMORY, JR., born Wilson, North Carolina, 1957; admitted to bar, 1982, North Carolina; U.S. District Court, Eastern, Western and Middle Districts of North Carolina; U.S. Court of Appeals, Fourth Circuit; U.S. Court of Appeals for the Federal Circuit; U.S. Supreme Court. *Education:* Duke University (A.B., cum laude, 1979); University of North Carolina (J.D., 1982). Angier B. Duke Scholar. John Motley Morehead Law Fellow.

(This Listing Continued)

HUNTON & WILLIAMS LLP, Charlotte—Continued

Recipient, Schley Lyons Leadership Award, Leadership Charlotte, 1991. Law Clerk to The Hon. Charles L. Becton, North Carolina Court of Appeals, 1982. Member, Board of Trustees and Member, Executive Committee, Duke University. Vice-Chair, Board of Directors, North Carolina Blumenthal Performing Arts Center. Board of Directors, Duke University Health System, Inc.; North Carolina Board of Transportation, 1993-2001. Chairman, Board of Directors, Charlotte-Mecklenburg Urban League, 1991-1993. Chair, Charlotte-Mecklenburg Planning Commission, 1987-1991Certified Instructor, National Institute of Trial Advocacy. *Member:* Mecklenburg County (President, 2002-2003) and American (Co-Chair, Trial Evidence Committee, Litigation Section) Bar Associations; North Carolina State Bar (Vice Chair, Disciplinary Hearing Commission, 1995-1996); North Carolina Association of Black Lawyers; American Law Institute. ***PRACTICE AREAS:*** Complex Commercial Litigation; Intellectual Property Litigation; Consumer Lending Claims; Medical Negligence Claims. ***Email:*** femory@hunton.com

ANDREW A. GERBER, born Baltimore, Maryland, February 3, 1967; admitted to bar, 1993, Maryland; 1999, North Carolina. *Education:* University of Maryland (B.S., Business Administration, 1989; J.D., with honors, 1993). Order of the Coif. ***PRACTICE AREAS:*** Securities; Capital Markets; Real Estate Investment Trusts; Mergers and Acquisitions; Project Finance; Corporate Law. ***Email:*** agerber@hunton.com

ROBERT J. HAHN, admitted to bar, 1985, New York; 1995, North Carolina. *Education:* St. John's University (B.A., 1979; J.D., 1984). ***PRACTICE AREAS:*** Securitization; Financial Services. ***Email:*** rhahn@hunton.com

MICHAEL C. KERRIGAN, born Phoenix, Arizona, June 4, 1971; admitted to bar, 1996, Virginia; 2002, North Carolina. *Education:* University of Virginia (B.A., 1993; J.D., 1996). Phi Beta Kappa. Member, Raven Society. *Member:* Mecklenburg County and North Carolina Bar Associations; Loan Syndications and Trading Association. ***PRACTICE AREAS:*** Banking Law; Finance; Bankruptcy; Creditors Rights; Debt Finance; Debt Trading. ***Email:*** Mkerrigan@hunton.com

WOOD W. LAY, born Oklahoma City, Oklahoma, November 25, 1965; admitted to bar, 1991, Virginia; 1998, North Carolina. *Education:* University of Virginia (B.A., 1988); Washington & Lee University (J.D., 1991). Omicron Delta Kappa; Order of the Coif; Editor-in-Chief, Washington & Lee Law Review, 1990-1991. Law Clerk to Hon. Walter E. Hoffman, U.S. District Court, Eastern District of Virginia, 1991-1992. ***PRACTICE AREAS:*** Labor and Employment; Commercial Litigation. ***Email:*** wlay@hunton.com

NASH E. LONG, III, born Dallas, Texas, April 8, 1971; admitted to bar, 1997, North Carolina; 1999, South Carolina. *Education:* Southern Methodist University (B.S., 1993; B.A., magna cum laude, 1993); Harvard University (J.D., magna cum laude, 1997). Phi Beta Kappa. *Member:* North Carolina (Member, Sections on: Litigation; Construction Law) and American (Member, Litigation Section) Bar Associations; South Carolina Bar. ***PRACTICE AREAS:*** Appellate Practice; Commercial Litigation; Energy; Environmental Litigation; Financial Institutions Litigation; Intellectual Property Litigation; Construction Litigation. ***Email:*** nlong@hunton.com

CHARLES R. MONROE, JR., born Chapel Hill, North Carolina, November 7, 1958; admitted to bar, 1989, Virginia; 1991, District of Columbia; 1993, North Carolina. *Education:* University of North Carolina (B.S., 1981); George Washington University (J.D., with highest honors, 1989). Order of the Coif. Member, George Washington University Law Review. Certified Public Accountant: North Carolina, 1985; Virginia, 1991. Member, Federal Regulation of Securities Committee, American Bar Association. ***PRACTICE AREAS:*** Capital Markets; Mergers and Acquisitions; General Corporate. ***Email:*** cmonroe@hunton.com

FRANK J. MURPHY, JR., born New York, N.Y., May 20, 1947; admitted to bar, 1975, New Jersey; 1979, New York; 1983, North Carolina. *Education:* St Peter's College (B.S., 1969); New York University (M.B.A., 1971); Fordham University (J.D., 1975). Law Clerk to Justice Mark A. Sullivan, Supreme Court of New Jersey, 1975-1976. Associate Counsel, BankAmerica Corporation, 1979-1982. Attorney, Metropolitan Life Insurance Company, Real Estate Investments, 1978-1979. Associate, Riker Danzig Scherer & Debevoise, 1976-1978. *Member:* American Bar Association; North Carolina Bar Association; Mecklenburg County Bar Association. ***Email:*** fmurphy@hunton.com

MICHAEL NEDZBALA, born Washington, D. C., February 2, 1962; admitted to bar, 1987, Virginia; 1996, North Carolina. *Education:* University of Virginia (B.A., 1984); University of North Carolina (J.D., 1987). *Member:* Mecklenburg County, North Carolina State and Virginia State Bar Associations. ***PRACTICE AREAS:*** Capital Markets; Securitization; Real Estate Finance. ***Email:*** mnedzbala@hunton.com

ASSOCIATES

MARCUS L. ANDERSON, born Los Angeles, California, October 30, 1978; admitted to bar, 2004, North Carolina. *Education:* University of Texas at Austin (B.A., 2001); Wake Forest University School of Law (J.D., 2004); Boston University, Morin Center for Banking and Financial Law (LL.M., 2005). *Member:* Mecklenburg County Bar Association. ***LANGUAGES:*** Swedish. ***PRACTICE AREAS:*** Asset Securitization. ***Email:*** manderson@hunton.com

JOSEPH K. BARNETTE, admitted to bar, 2003, North Carolina. *Education:* University of North Carolina at Chapel Hill (B.S.B.A., 2000); Harvard Law School (J.D, cum laude, 2003). ***PRACTICE AREAS:*** Finance. ***Email:*** jbarnette@hunton.com

MELINDA R. BERES, born Chicago, Illinois; admitted to bar, 1999, South Carolina; 2002, New York; 2005, North Carolina. *Education:* Presbyterian College (B.A., 1995); University of Sussex (LL.M., 1997); University of South Carolina (J.D., 1999). ***LANGUAGES:*** German and Spanish. ***PRACTICE AREAS:*** Securities; Mergers, Acquisitions and Divestitures. ***Email:*** mberes@hunton.com

DANIEL JOSEV BREWER, born Ann Arbor, Michigan, January 7, 1975; admitted to bar, 2001, South Carolina; 2003, North Carolina and U.S. District Court, District of South Carolina; 2004, U.S. District Court, District of North Carolina. *Education:* Furman University (B.A., 1997); University of South Carolina (J.D., cum laude, 2001). Order of the Coif; Wig and Robe. Compleat Lawyer Award Recipient; Claude Sapp Award Recipient. Articles Editor, South Carolina Law Review. Member, National Moot Court Team. Law Clerk to Hon. P. Michael Duffy, U.S. District Court Judge, District of South Carolina. *Member:* South Carolina Bar; North Carolina State Bar; North Carolina Young Alumni Association; Furman University Young Alumni Council. ***PRACTICE AREAS:*** Civil Litigation; Labor and Employment. ***Email:*** jbrewer@hunton.com

(This Listing Continued)

K. STACIE CORBETT, born Charlotte, North Carolina, February 11, 1977; admitted to bar, 2002, North Carolina. *Education:* University of North Carolina at Chapel Hill (B.A., with distinction, 1999); University of Virginia (J.D., 2002). *Member:* North Carolina Bar Association. ***PRACTICE AREAS:*** Litigation. ***Email:*** scorbett@hunton.com

PATRICK V. FIEL, JR., born Portsmouth, Virginia; admitted to bar, 2004, Tennessee; 2005, U.S. District Court, Eastern District of Tennessee (Not admitted in North Carolina). *Education:* College of William & Mary (B.S., 1997); University of Tennessee College of Law (J.D., 2004). Editor-in-Chief, Tennessee Journal of Business Law. Dean's Citation. ***PRACTICE AREAS:*** Asset Securitization. ***Email:*** pfiel@hunton.com

MELANIE FITZGERALD, born Chattanooga, Tennessee, April 23, 1973; admitted to bar, 2002, North Carolina. *Education:* Bryn Mawr College (1991-1993); University of Tennessee (B.A., Political Science, 1999); University of South Carolina (J.D., magna cum laude, 2002). *Member:* Mecklenburg County Bar Association; North Carolina State Bar; American Bar Association; Loan Syndications and Trading Association. ***PRACTICE AREAS:*** Corporate Finance; Creditors Rights; Distressed Debt Trading; Bankruptcy; Secured Lending. ***Email:*** mfitzgerald@hunton.com

ANTHONY FOXX, born Charlotte, North Carolina, April 30, 1971; admitted to bar, 1997, North Carolina. *Education:* Davidson College (A.B., History, 1993); New York University (J.D., 1996). Root-Tilden-Snow Scholar. Law Clerk to the Hon. Nathaniel R. Jones, U.S. Court of Appeals, Sixth Circuit. Trial Attorney, U.S. Department of Justice, Civil Rights Division, 1998-1999. Democratic Counsel, Subcommittee on the Constitution, 1999-2001 and Subcommittee on Commercial and Administrative Law, 2001, U.S. House Judiciary Committee. *Member:* Mecklenburg County and North Carolina (Member, Sections on: Business Law; Litigation) Bar Associations. ***PRACTICE AREAS:*** Commercial Litigation.

MICHAEL J. GENAY, born Atlantic City, New Jersey, 1965; admitted to bar, 2001, North Carolina. *Education:* Palm Beach Atlantic College (B.S., 1995); University of Virginia (J.D., 2001). *Member:* North Carolina State Bar. ***PRACTICE AREAS:*** Asset Based Finance; Commercial Finance; Structured Finance. ***Email:*** mgenay@hunton.com

ANDREW M. JOHNSON, born 1974; admitted to bar, 1999, North Carolina. *Education:* Miami University (B.A., 1996); University of Virginia (J.D., 1999). ***PRACTICE AREAS:*** Capital Markets; Securitization. ***Email:*** ajohnson@hunton.com

HYUN "JONATHAN" S. KIM, born 1974; admitted to bar, 2004, North Carolina. *Education:* North Carolina State University (B.A., Political Science, 1997); Wake Forest University (J.D., 2004; M.B.A., 2004). *Member:* Mecklenburg County and North Carolina Bar Associations; North Carolina State Bar. ***LANGUAGES:*** Korean and Spanish. ***PRACTICE AREAS:*** Asset Securitization. ***Email:*** jkim@hunton.com

STEPHEN D. LEASURE, born Fredericksburg, Virginia, February 12, 1971; admitted to bar, 2000, North Carolina. *Education:* University of Virginia (B.S., with distinction, 1993; J.D., 2000). *Member:* Mecklenburg County and North Carolina Bar Associations. ***PRACTICE AREAS:*** Securities (40%); Capital Markets (40%); Corporate (10%); Mergers, Acquisitions and Divestitures (10%). ***Email:*** sleasure@hunton.com

BRENT A. ROSSER, born February 28, 1977; admitted to bar, 2002, North Carolina. *Education:* Furman University (B.A., 1999); Case Western Reserve University (J.D., cum laude, 2002). *Member:* North Carolina and American Bar Associations. ***PRACTICE AREAS:*** Commercial Litigation; Complex Litigation. ***Email:*** brosser@hunton.com

WENDY L. SPANBAUER, born Hendersonville, North Carolina, January 3, 1971; admitted to bar, 1998, North Carolina. *Education:* Duke University (B.A., Public Policy Studies, 1993); University of North Carolina (J.D., with honors, 1998). Staff Member, North Carolina Journal of International Law and Commercial Regulation, 1996-1998. Law Clerk, Honorable I. Beverly Lake, Jr., North Carolina Supreme Court, 1996. *Member:* North Carolina Bar Association; North Carolina State Bar. ***PRACTICE AREAS:*** Banking; Commercial Finance. ***Email:*** wspanbauer@hunton.com

CRAIG W. WALKER, admitted to bar, 2004, Virginia (inactive); 2005, North Carolina. *Education:* Duke University (A.B., cum laude, 2000); University of Virginia (J.D., 2004). ***PRACTICE AREAS:*** Securitization. ***Email:*** cwalker@hunton.com

K. CAMERON WALTON, born Conway, South Carolina; admitted to bar, 1999, North Carolina. *Education:* Queens College (B.A., 1996); University of North Carolina School of Law (J.D., 1999). ***Email:*** cwalton@hunton.com

VALERIE B. WRIGHT, born Merrillville, Indiana, March 3, 1978; admitted to bar, 2003, Illinois and U.S. District Court, Northern District of Illinois; 2004, North Carolina and U.S. District Court for the Western District of North Carolina. *Education:* Northwestern University (B.S. in Journalism, cum laude, 2000); University of Chicago Law School (J.D., with honors, 2003). Order of the Coif. *Member:* Chicago, North Carolina and Illinois State Bar Associations. ***PRACTICE AREAS:*** Litigation (100%). ***Email:*** vwright@hunton.com

JACQUELINE M. YOUNT, born Indianapolis, Indiana, 1974; admitted to bar, 2001, North Carolina; U.S. District Court, Western and Middle Districts of North Carolina. *Education:* Duke University (B.A., magna cum laude, 1997); University of Virginia (J.D., 2000). Member, Virginia Law Review, 1998-2000. Member, Employment Law Clinic, 1999-2000. *Member:* Mecklenburg County; North Carolina and American Bar Associations. ***LANGUAGES:*** Spanish. ***PRACTICE AREAS:*** Labor and Employment; Litigation. ***Email:*** jyount@hunton.com

Most lawyers are admitted in North Carolina and are members of the North Carolina State Bar and the Mecklenburg County, North Carolina and American Bar Associations.

(For complete biographical data on other personnel, see Professional Biographies at other locations)

THE JACKSON LAW FIRM, PLLC

6201 FAIRVIEW ROAD, SUITE 200
CHARLOTTE, NORTH CAROLINA 28210
Telephone: 704-944-3151
Fax: 704-944-3164
Email: EdJackson@carolina.rr.com
URL: http://www.thejacksonlawfirm.com

Business Law, Limited Liability, Trusts and Estates, Company Law, Contracts, Estate Planning, Tax-Estate and Gift, Asset Protection, Tax Planning, Wills and Probate.

EDWARD K. JACKSON, born Longmont, Colorado, March 24, 1957; admitted to bar, 1982, Texas; 1993, North Carolina. *Education:* Wofford College (B.A., 1979); University of Alabama (J.D., 1982). *Member:* Mecklenburg County (Section: Estate Planning), North Carolina and American Bar (Member, Business Law Section) Associations; North Carolina State Bar. ***Email:*** EdJackson@carolina.rr.com

LEGAL SUPPORT PERSONNEL

ERIN BRIER, (Legal Assistant)

THE JACKSON LAW GROUP, PLLC

831 EAST MOREHEAD STREET, SUITE 550
CHARLOTTE, NORTH CAROLINA 28202
Telephone: 704-377-6680
Toll Free: 866-377-6680
Fax: 704-337-6690
URL: http://www.thejacksonlawgroup.com

Personal Injury, Products Liability, Construction Defects, Class Actions, Consumer Fraud, Environmental, Toxic Torts, Pharmaceutical Litigation, Professional Negligence, Business Torts, FELA.

GARY W. JACKSON, born Center, Texas, November 9, 1954; admitted to bar, 1979, California; 1985, New York; 1987, North Carolina. *Education:* Duke University (A.B., magna cum laude, 1976; J.D., 1979). Staff Member, 1977-1978 and Editorial Board Member, 1978-1979, Duke Law Journal. Law Clerk to U.S. District Judge Robert P. Aguilar, Northern District of California, 1980-1981. Visiting Researcher, Harvard Law School, 1984-1985. Senior Lecturing Fellow, Duke University School of Law, 2002—. *Member:* North Carolina Bar Association (Chair, Litigation Section, 2002-2003); North Carolina Academy of Trial Lawyers (President's Club; Chair, Consumer Areas of Practice Litigation Group); The Association of Trial Lawyers of America (President's Club; Co-Chair, Construction Defects Litigation Group; Member, Public Affairs Committee). ***PRACTICE AREAS:*** Construction Defects; Class Actions; Consumer Fraud; Products Liability; Environmental; Toxic Torts; Professional Negligence. ***Email:*** gjackson@thejacksonlawgroup.com

KURT F. HAUSLER, born Raleigh, North Carolina, November 17, 1964; admitted to bar, 1995, North Carolina. *Education:* University of North Carolina at Chapel Hill (B.S.B.A., 1987); Campbell University (J.D., cum laude, 1995). Articles Editor, Campbell University Law Review, 1994-1995. *Member:* North Carolina Bar Association (Member, Sections on: Construction Law, Litigation); North Carolina Academy of Trial Lawyers; The Association of Trial Lawyers of America. ***PRACTICE AREAS:*** Construction Defects; Construction Litigation; Products Liability; Commercial Litigation; Catastrophic Injury; Consumer Class Actions. ***Email:*** khausler@thejacksonlawgroup.com

OF COUNSEL

MONA LISA WALLACE, born Salisbury, North Carolina, November 14, 1954; admitted to bar, 1979, North Carolina; 1980, U.S. District Court, Western District of North Carolina; 1984, U.S. District Court, Middle District of North Carolina; 1991, U.S. Court of Appeals, Fourth Circuit; 1998, U.S. Supreme Court; 1999, South Carolina. *Education:* University of North Carolina, Chapel Hill (B.A., 1976); Wake Forest University (J.D., 1979). *Member:* North Carolina State Bar; American Bar Association; North Carolina Academy of Trial Lawyers. (Also Member, Wallace and Graham, P.A.). ***PRACTICE AREAS:*** Toxic Torts; Workers Compensation; Personal Injury; Asbestos Litigation. ***Email:*** mwallace@wallacegraham.com

WILLIAM M. GRAHAM, born Concord, North Carolina, October 25, 1960; admitted to bar, 1991, North Carolina. *Education:* Catawba College (B.A., 1983); Antioch, School of Law (J.D., 1987). Phi Delta Phi. Former Assistant District Attorney for Judicial District 19A, 1991-1993. *Member:* North Carolina State Bar; American Bar Association. (Also Member, Wallace and Graham, P.A.). ***PRACTICE AREAS:*** Workers' Compensation; Asbestos Litigation; Pharmaceutical Litigation. ***Email:*** bgraham@wallacegraham.com

BRUCE L. JAMES

CHARLOTTE, NORTH CAROLINA

(See Huntersville)

Estate Planning, Asset Protection, Estate Litigation, Tax, Wills and Probate, Non Profit and Charitable Organizations, Business Law, Corporate Law, Collections, Eminent Domain, Employee Benefits, Civil Litigation, Taxation.

JAMES, McELROY & DIEHL, P.A.

Established in 1959

600 SOUTH COLLEGE STREET, SUITE 3000
CHARLOTTE, NORTH CAROLINA 28202
Telephone: 704-372-9870; 800-247-9870
Fax: 704-333-5508
URL: http://www.jmdlaw.com

Civil Litigation, Appellate Practice, Family Law, Real Estate, Corporate Law, Professional Liability, Personal Injury, Criminal Law, Estate Planning, Estate Administration, Products Liability, Taxation, Securities, Environmental Law, Commercial Law.

FIRM PROFILE: James, McElroy & Diehl, P.A. was established in 1959. It is a firm of dedicated lawyers who give highly professional, intensely personal service to our clients. The firm serves a wide variety of individual and corporate clients in a broad spectrum of practice areas.

J. MITCHELL ABERMAN, born Rock Hill, South Carolina, December 26, 1956; admitted to bar, 1984, North Carolina and South Carolina. *Education:* University of Virginia (B.S., with distinction, 1980; J.D., 1984); Edinburgh University; University of South Carolina (M.B.A., 1983). Author: "Partnerships and Joint Ventures," South Carolina Jurisprudence Series. Instructor, Legal Research and Writing, University of Virginia, 1983-1984. Member, North Carolina Business Court Rules Advisory Committee. *Member:* North Carolina and American (Member, Sections on: Antitrust Law and Science and Technology) Bar Associations; South Carolina Bar; North Carolina State Bars. ***PRACTICE AREAS:*** Computer Law; Corporate Law; Finance; Complex Litigation. ***Email:*** maberman@jmdlaw.com

JOHN S. ARROWOOD, born Burnsville, North Carolina, November 4, 1956; admitted to bar, 1982, North Carolina. *Education:* Catawba College (B.A., magna cum laude, 1979); University of North Carolina (J.D., 1982). Phi Delta Phi (Exchequer, 1981-1982). Research Assistant, Judge Gerald S. Arnold, 1985-1986, North Carolina Court of Appeals. Member: North Carolina Banking Commission, 1995—; North Carolina Rules Review Commission, 1998—. *Member:* North Carolina (Member, Litigation Section; Co-Chairman, Appellate Survey Committee, 1987-1988, Chairman, Scholarship Committee, 1988-1989 and Division Director, 1989-1990, Chairman, Special Projects Committee, 1990-1992; Young Lawyers Division) and American Bar Association; 26th Judicial District and North Carolina State Bars. ***PRACTICE AREAS:*** Litigation. ***Email:*** jarrowood@jmdlaw.com

CATHERINE ALLEN BARNES, born Danvers, Massachusetts, October 7, 1962; admitted to bar, 1995, North Carolina. *Education:* Salem State College (B.A., summa cum laude, 1990); University of North Carolina (J.D., 1995). *Member:* Mecklenburg County, North Carolina and American Bar Associations; North Carolina State Bar. ***PRACTICE AREAS:*** Corporate Law; Real Estate. ***Email:*** cbarnes@jmdlaw.com

JOHN W. BEDDOW, born Washington, D.C., April 8, 1952; admitted to bar, 1977, North Carolina. *Education:* University of North Carolina (B.S., 1974; J.D., 1977). Phi Eta Sigma; Phi Beta Kappa. *Member:* North Carolina and American Bar Associations; North Carolina State Bar. ***PRACTICE AREAS:*** Real Estate; Corporate Law; Business Law; Estate Planning; Estate Administration; Taxation. ***Email:*** jbeddow@jmdlaw.com

SARAH M. BRADY, born Norfolk, Virginia, June 1, 1978; admitted to bar, 2004, North Carolina. *Education:* University of North Carolina at Chapel Hill (B.A., 2000); Cornell University Law School (J.D., 2004). *Member:* North Carolina State Bar. ***PRACTICE AREAS:*** Family Law. ***Email:*** sbrady@jmdlaw.com

JOHN ROBERT BURIC, born Berkeley, California, March 26, 1964; admitted to bar, 1996, North Carolina. *Education:* North Carolina State University (B.S.C.E., cum laude, 1992); Boston University (J.D., 1995). *Member:* Mecklenburg County and North Carolina Bar Associations; North Carolina State Bar. [U.S. Navy, 1982-1988, E5]. ***PRACTICE AREAS:*** Civil Litigation; Construction Litigation; Personal Injury; Wrongful Death. ***Email:*** jburic@jmdlaw.com

WILLIAM K. DIEHL, JR., born Norfolk, Virginia, October 4, 1944; admitted to bar, 1969, Virginia and North Carolina. *Education:* University of North Carolina (A.B., 1966); University of Virginia (LL.B., 1969). *Member:* Mecklenburg County, North Carolina, Virginia and American (Member, Section on Family Law) Bar Associations; American Board of Trial Advocates; American Academy of Matrimonial Lawyers. ***PRACTICE AREAS:*** Civil Litigation; Appellate Practice; Criminal Law; Family Law; Professional Liability; Securities Litigation.

RICHARD A. ELKINS, born Martinsville, Virginia, March 7, 1951; admitted to bar, 1976, North Carolina; 1977, U.S. District Court, Western District of North Carolina. *Education:* University of North Carolina at Chapel Hill (B.A., with honors, 1973; J.D., 1976). John Motley Morehead Scholar. District Court Judge, 26th Judicial District of North Carolina, 1984-1992. *Member:* North Carolina Bar Association; 26th Judicial District (Member, Executive Committee, 1983-1984) and North Carolina State Bars. ***PRACTICE AREAS:*** Family Law; Civil Litigation. ***Email:*** relkins@jmdlaw.com

JONATHAN D. FEIT, born New York, New York, March 25, 1974; admitted to bar, 2001, North Carolina. *Education:* Auburn University (B.A., 1996); University of Tennessee College of Law (J.D., 2001). Phi Alpha Delta. *Member:* North Carolina and American Bar Associations; The Association of Trial Lawyers of America. ***PRACTICE AREAS:*** Family Law; Civil Litigation. ***Email:*** jfeit@jmdlaw.com

RICHARD B. FENNELL, born Sewickley, Pennsylvania, March 24, 1963; admitted to bar, 1990, North Carolina. *Education:* University of North Carolina at Chapel Hill (A.B., with highest distinction, 1986; J.D., 1990). Phi Beta Kappa. Law Clerk to Hon. Hugh A. Wells, North Carolina Court of Appeals, 1990-1991. *Member:* North Carolina Bar Association; North Carolina Academy of Trial Lawyers. ***PRACTICE AREAS:*** Civil Litigation; Criminal Law. ***Email:*** rfennell@jmdlaw.com

JARED E. GARDNER, born October 19, 1970; admitted to bar, 1999, California; 2002, North Carolina. *Education:* San Diego State University (B.S., summa cum laude,

(This Listing Continued)

JAMES, McELROY & DIEHL, P.A., Charlotte—Continued

1996); Boalt Hall School of Law, University of California (J.D., 1999). ***PRACTICE AREAS:*** Employment Litigation; Commercial Litigation. ***Email:*** jgardner@jmdlaw.com

GARY S. HEMRIC, born Greensboro, North Carolina, May 1, 1948; admitted to bar, 1974, North Carolina. *Education:* Davidson College (B.A., 1970); University of North Carolina (J.D., 1974). *Member:* North Carolina and American (Member, Litigation Section) Bar Associations; Twenty-Sixth Judicial District and The North Carolina State Bars; North Carolina Academy of Trial Lawyers; The Association of Trial Lawyers of America. North Carolina Certified Mediator. ***PRACTICE AREAS:*** Civil Litigation; Personal Injury; Wrongful Death; Professional Liability. ***Email:*** ghemric@jmdlaw.com

LAWRENCE W. HEWITT, born Washington, D.C., March 21, 1944; admitted to bar, 1969, North Carolina. *Education:* Wake Forest University (B.A., 1966; J.D., 1969). Phi Delta Phi. *Member:* Mecklenburg County (Member, Ethics Committee, 1982-1985) and North Carolina Bar Associations; North Carolina State Bar; North Carolina Trial Lawyers Association; The Association of Trial Lawyers of America. [1st Lt., U.S. Army, Armor, 1969-1971]. ***PRACTICE AREAS:*** Civil Litigation; Criminal Law; Family Law.

EDWARD T. HINSON, JR., born Rock Hill, South Carolina, October 30, 1952; admitted to bar, 1977, North Carolina. *Education:* Wofford College (B.A., summa cum laude, 1974); Duke University (J.D., 1977). Phi Beta Kappa. Assistant District Attorney, 26th Judicial District, 1977-1981. *Member:* Mecklenburg County (Chairman, Criminal Justice Section, 1991; Member, Executive Committee, 1991-1995), North Carolina and American Bar Associations; North Carolina State Bar; American Board of Trial Advocates; North Carolina Academy of Trial Lawyers; Association of Trial Lawyers of America. ***PRACTICE AREAS:*** Civil Litigation; Criminal Law. ***Email:*** ehinson@jmdlaw.com

KATHERINE S. HOLLIDAY, born Brevard, North Carolina, June 25, 1948; admitted to bar, 1980, North Carolina. *Education:* Wake Forest University (B.A., 1970); University of North Carolina at Charlotte (M.Ed., 1973); Duke University (J.D., 1980). Member, Order of the Coif. Law Clerk to U.S. District Court Judge James B. McMillan, 1980-1981. Board of Directors, 1993—, Treasurer, 1995, Secretary, 1996-1997 and President, 2001-2003, National Association of Counsel for Children. *Member:* North Carolina (Chair, Juvenile Justice and Children's Rights Section, 1997-1998), 26th Judicial District (Member, Grievance Committee, 1995— and Chair, 1997-1998) and American (Outstanding Child Advocate, 1990) Bar Associations; North Carolina State Bar. ***PRACTICE AREAS:*** Family Law; Juvenile Law; Civil Litigation. ***Email:*** kholliday@jmdlaw.com

ADAM L. HORNER, born Ann Arbor, Michigan, December 17, 1978; admitted to bar, 2004, North Carolina. *Education:* University of North Carolina at Chapel Hill (B.A., 2001); Campbell University (J.D., 2004). *Member:* North Carolina State Bar. ***PRACTICE AREAS:*** Civil Litigation. ***Email:*** ahorner@jmdlaw.com

DAVID M. KERN, born Winchester, Virginia, December 19, 1952; admitted to bar, 1978, North Carolina. *Education:* University of North Carolina (A.B., 1975); University of Virginia (J.D., 1978). Phi Beta Kappa. John Motley Morehead Scholar. *Member:* North Carolina and American Bar Associations; 26th Judicial District and The North Carolina State Bars; North Carolina Academy of Trial Lawyers. (Board Certified Specialist in Family Law, North Carolina State Board of Legal Specialization). ***PRACTICE AREAS:*** Family Law; Civil Litigation. ***Email:*** dkern@jmdlaw.com

IRENE P. KING, born Fort Wayne, Indiana, January 14, 1979; admitted to bar, 2004, North Carolina. *Education:* Miami University (B.A., Political Science, Vocal Music Performance minor, 2000); University of North Carolina at Chapel Hill (J.D., 2004). Author: Note, "Are Foreign Sovereigns Entitled to Constitutional Due Process? The Ninth Circuit's Analysis of Personal Jurisdiction In Altmann v. Republic of Austria," Journal of International Law and Commercial Regulation 389, Winter 2003. *Member:* North Carolina State Bar. ***PRACTICE AREAS:*** Civil Litigation; Family Law. ***Email:*** iking@jmdlaw.com

G. RUSSELL KORNEGAY, III, born Chapel Hill, North Carolina, September 29, 1959; admitted to bar, 1984, North Carolina. *Education:* University of North Carolina (B.S., 1981); Campbell University (J.D., 1984). Phi Alpha Delta. *Member:* North Carolina and American Bar Associations; North Carolina State Bar; North Carolina Academy of Trial Lawyers. ***PRACTICE AREAS:*** Family Law; Civil Litigation. ***Email:*** rkornegay@jmdlaw.com

JEFFREY A. LONG, born October 4, 1970; admitted to bar, 2002, North Carolina. *Education:* North Carolina State University (B.A., Business, Communication, 1993); University of South Carolina (J.D., 2002). ***PRACTICE AREAS:*** Commercial Litigation; Civil Litigation. ***Email:*** jefflong@jmdlaw.com

PENDER R. McELROY, born Asheville, North Carolina, December 25, 1940; admitted to bar, 1968, North Carolina. *Education:* University of North Carolina (B.S., 1962; J.D., 1968). Member of Staff, North Carolina Law Review, 1966-1968. Research Assistant to Justice William H. Bobbitt of North Carolina Supreme Court, 1968-1969. Panel of Arbitrators, American Arbitration Association. *Member:* Mecklenburg County (Chairman, Young Lawyers Section, 1973-1974; Member, Executive Committee, 1991-1996; President, 1994-1995), North Carolina and American Bar Associations; The North Carolina State Bar. ***PRACTICE AREAS:*** Corporate Law; Commercial Law; Real Estate. ***Email:*** pmcelroy@jmdlaw.com

FRED B. MONROE, born Charlottesville, Virginia, July 26, 1968; admitted to bar, 1996, North Carolina; 1997, Georgia. *Education:* University of North Carolina at Chapel Hill (A.B., 1991); Mercer University (J.D., 1996). Member, Mercer Law Review, 1995-1996. Law Clerk to the Honorable Gerald S. Arnold, Chief Judge, North Carolina Court of Appeals. *Member:* Mecklenburg County, North Carolina and American Bar Associations; State Bar of North Carolina; State Bar of Georgia. ***PRACTICE AREAS:*** Litigation. ***Email:*** fmonroe@jmdlaw.com

PRESTON O. ODOM, III, born Cocoa Beach, Florida, December 30, 1971; admitted to bar, 1997, Florida; 2000 North Carolina. *Education:* Florida State University (B.A., History, 1993; J.D., high honors, 1997). Order of the Coif. *Member:* The Florida Bar; North Carolina State Bar. [Cadet, U.S. Air Force Academy, 1989-1990]. ***PRACTICE AREAS:*** Appellate Practice; Civil Litigation; Criminal Law; Employment Law; Bankruptcy. ***Email:*** podom@jmdlaw.com

(This Listing Continued)

ADAM L. ROSS, born East Islip, New York, March 4, 1978; admitted to bar, 2003, North Carolina and U.S. District Court, Western District of North Carolina. *Education:* University of North Carolina at Chapel Hill (B.A., Psychology, with distinction, 2000); University of North Carolina School of Law (J.D., 2003). Member, Golden Key Honor Society. *Member:* North Carolina Bar Association. ***PRACTICE AREAS:*** Civil Litigation; Criminal Litigation. ***Email:*** aross@jmdlaw.com

ROBERT H. SHEPPARD, born Norfolk, Virginia, March 9, 1948; admitted to bar, 1979, North Carolina. *Education:* University of Virginia (B.A., 1970); St. Mary's University of San Antonio (J.D., with distinction, 1979). Senior Associate Editor, St. Mary's Law Journal, 1978-1979. *Member:* North Carolina and American Bar Associations; 26th Judicial District and North Carolina State Bars. ***PRACTICE AREAS:*** Real Estate; Corporate Law. ***Email:*** bsheppard@jmdlaw.com

BRUCE M. SIMPSON, born Union County, North Carolina, November 15, 1952; admitted to bar, 1978, North Carolina and U.S. District Court, Western District of North Carolina; 1985, U.S. Court of Appeals, Fourth Circuit. *Education:* Davidson College (A.B., 1975); University of North Carolina (J.D., with honors, 1978). Member, North Carolina Law Review, 1976-1977. Order of the Coif. ***PRACTICE AREAS:*** Civil Litigation. ***Email:*** bsimpson@jmdlaw.com

PATRA SINNER, born Manning, South Carolina, October 2, 1973; admitted to bar, 2003, North Carolina. *Education:* University of South Carolina (B.S., Administration, magna cum laude, 1995; J.D., 2003). *Member:* Mecklenburg County and North Carolina Bar Associations. ***PRACTICE AREAS:*** Family Law; Criminal Defense; Entertainment Law. ***Email:*** psinner@jmdlaw.com

CHARLES MALCOLM VISER, born Charlotte, North Carolina; admitted to bar, 2000, North Carolina and U.S. District Court, Western District of North Carolina; 2004, U.S. Court of Appeals, Fourth Circuit. *Education:* Hampden-Sydney College (B.A., Economics/Spanish, 1994); Campbell University School of Law (J.D., 2000). President, Student Bar Association. *Member:* Mecklenburg County, North Carolina and American Bar Associations; North Carolina State Bar; North Carolina Academy of Trial Lawyers. ***PRACTICE AREAS:*** Civil Litigation; Criminal Law. ***Email:*** cviser@jmdlaw.com

M. NEYA WARREN, born Clinton, North Carolina, January 4, 1975; admitted to bar, 2002, North Carolina. *Education:* University of North Carolina at Chapel Hill (B.A., 1998); Campbell University (J.D., 2002). ***PRACTICE AREAS:*** Family Law. ***Email:*** nwarren@jmdlaw.com

RICHARD S. WRIGHT, born Winston-Salem, North Carolina, March 23, 1971; admitted to bar, 1997, North Carolina. *Education:* Wake Forest University (B.A., 1993, J.D., 1997). Research Editor, Wake Forest Law Review. Law Clerk, U.S. Bankruptcy Court, Hon. J. Craig Whitley, 2000-2001. Author, "A Half-Hearted Attempt at Regulatory Reform in the Law Use Context: The Proposed North Carolina Property Rights Act," 31 Wake Forest L Rev. 809. *Member:* North Carolina State Bar. ***PRACTICE AREAS:*** Civil Litigation; Bankruptcy. ***Email:*** rwright@jmdlaw.com

OF COUNSEL

MARY KAY BAYNARD, born Raleigh, North Carolina, February 17, 1961; admitted to bar, 1986, North Carolina. *Education:* University of North Carolina at Chapel Hill (B.A., 1983; J.D., 1986). Phi Beta Kappa; Phi Delta Phi (Secretary, 1985-1986). Research Assistant to Judge Robert F. Orr, 1986-1987 and to Judge Jack L. Cozort, 1987-1988, North Carolina Court of Appeals. *Member:* Mecklenburg County, North Carolina and American Bar Associations; 26th Judicial District and North Carolina State Bars. ***PRACTICE AREAS:*** Estate Planning; Estate Administration; Real Estate. ***Email:*** mbaynard@jmdlaw.com

HENRY JAMES, JR., born Portland, Oregon, August 5, 1930; admitted to bar, 1957, North Carolina. *Education:* Williams College (A.B., 1952); University of Virginia (J.D., 1957). Sigma Nu Phi (Vice President, 1956-1957). Instructor, Law and Accounting, University of Virginia Law School, 1956. Member, North Carolina Cemetery Commission, 1975-1979. *Member:* North Carolina and American Bar Associations; 26th Judicial District and The North Carolina State Bars. ***PRACTICE AREAS:*** Securities Regulation; Franchise Law; Corporate Law.

B FREDERICK WILLIAMS, born Charlotte, North Carolina, July 20, 1944; admitted to bar, 1978, District of Columbia; 1989, North Carolina. *Education:* Duke University (A.B., 1965); Catholic University (J.D., 1978). Member, American Economics Association, various dates, 1966-1984. Author: "Federal Money Laundering," Lexis Pub., 1999. Professor, Computer and IP Law, University of North Carolina at Charlotte, 2001—. Deputy Assistant Director, Federal Trade Commission, 1982-1985. Deputy Criminal Chief, USAO-WDNC, 2002-2004. ***Email:*** fwilliams@jmdlaw.com

REPRESENTATIVE CLIENTS: Burke Mills, Inc.; Centura Bank; Crescent Resources, LLC; Charlotte Motor Speedway, Inc.; Cottinghan-Chalk & Associates, Inc.; First Indiana Bank, N.A.; Goodwill Industries of Southern Piedmont, Inc.; HLM Design, Inc.; Interstate/Johnson Lane, Inc.; MECA Real Estate Services, L.L.C.; Office Environments, Inc.; Quality Sprinkler Co., Inc.; C.F. Sauer Co.; Simonini Builders, Inc.; Software Design and Development, Inc.; Spectator Sports Services, Inc.; Speedway Motorsports, Inc.; Sunbelt Corp.; Sunrise Apparel, Inc.; Superior Construction Corporation; Swisher International, Inc.; Town and Country Ford, Inc.; Wachovia Bank, N.A.
APPROVED ATTORNEYS FOR: Chicago Title Insurance Co.; Commonwealth Land Title Insurance Co.; Fidelity National Title Insurance Co.; First Title Insurance Co.; Jefferson-Pilot Title Insurance Co.; Lawyers Title Insurance Corp.; Stewart Title Guaranty Corp.
REFERENCE: Wachovia Bank, N.A.

LAW OFFICES OF
LISA F. JARVIS, SC, PC

7825 BALLANTYNE COMMONS PARKWAY, SUITE 230
CHARLOTTE, NORTH CAROLINA 28277
Telephone: 704-544-6303
Fax: 866-209-3745

Rock Hill, South Carolina Office: 1373 Ebenezer Road, 29732. Telephone: 803-980-2765. Fax: 803-980-2796.

(This Listing Continued)

Real Estate, Wills, Probate, Business Law, Corporate Law.

LISA F. JARVIS, born Greenville, Tennessee, August 11, 1963; admitted to bar, 1988, Tennessee; 1991, North Carolina. *Education:* University of North Carolina/Asheville (B.A., 1985); University of Tennessee at Knoxville (J.D., 1988). *Member:* Mecklenburg County and American Bar Associations; North Carolina State Bar. ***PRACTICE AREAS:*** Real Estate Law.

JERRY W. JERNIGAN, P.A.

1801 EAST BOULEVARD
CHARLOTTE, NORTH CAROLINA 28203
Telephone: 704-375-1008
Mobile: 704-458-6400
Fax: 704-375-3240
Email: jerry@jerrywjernigan.com
URL: http://www.jerrywjernigan.com

Business Law, Commercial Lending, Employment Law, Entertainment Law, Estate Planning, Estate Administration, International Law, Leases, Licensing, Mergers and Acquisitions, Private Placements.

JERRY W. JERNIGAN, born Greensboro, North Carolina, 1946; admitted to bar, 1974, North Carolina. *Education:* Duke University (B.A., 1968; J.D., 1974). Member, Editorial Board, Duke Law Journal, 1972-1974. *Member:* North Carolina State Bar. [LTJG, U.S. Navy, 1968-1971]. ***PRACTICE AREAS:*** Business Law; Estate Planning; Estate Administration. ***Email:*** jerry@jerrywjernigan.com

JOHNSTON, ALLISON & HORD, P.A.

Established in 1922
610 EAST MOREHEAD STREET
P.O. BOX 36469
CHARLOTTE, NORTH CAROLINA 28236
Telephone: 704-332-1181
Fax: 704-376-1628
Email: jahlaw.com
URL: http://www.jahlaw.com

Administrative, Banking and Finance, Business, Bankruptcy, Commercial, Construction, Corporate Law and Business Planning, Creditors' Rights and Collections, Employee Benefit Plans, Employment Discrimination, Estate and Trust, Estate Planning and Administration, Health Care, Litigation, International Transactions, Mediation, Mergers and Acquisitions, OSHA, Real Estate Development and Zoning, Taxation, Trial and Appellate Practice in State and Federal Courts.

FIRM PROFILE: Johnston, Allison & Hord, P.A., founded in 1922, is one of Charlotte's oldest and most respected law firms. The firm offers the expertise of a large firm with the personal touch of a small firm. Its goal is to meet the individual needs of each client while providing the highest quality legal services. The firm has a general civil practice with an emphasis in Health Care, Estate Planning, Taxation, Closely Held Corporations and Construction and Commercial Real Estate Development.

Johnston, Allison & Hord, P.A. is the exclusive Charlotte, North Carolina member of Meritas, the world's largest affiliation of mid-sized independent commercial litigation and business law firms. The network comprises over 200 firms in nearly 70 countries on six continents, with members in more than 250 cities, including every major business center worldwide. Through this affiliation, we are able to locate and engage specialists in all areas of the law throughout the world to handle the specific legal needs or our clients.

CLAUDE A. COCHRAN (1884-1958)
FRANK A. McCLENEGHAN (1901-1970)
F. THOMAS MILLER, JR. (1917-1985)

H. MORRISON JOHNSTON, JR., born Charlotte, North Carolina, November 12, 1937; admitted to bar, 1962, North Carolina. *Education:* University of North Carolina (A.B., 1960; LL.B., with honors, 1962). Phi Delta Phi; Order of the Coif. Member, Board of Editors, 1960-1961 and Business Manager, 1961-1962, North Carolina Law Review. Attorney, Chief Counsel's Office, Internal Revenue Service, 1962-1966. ***PRACTICE AREAS:*** Taxation; Mergers and Acquisitions; Corporate Law. ***Email:*** mjohnston@jahlaw.com

JAMES W. ALLISON, born Charlotte, North Carolina, April 27, 1944; admitted to bar, 1969, North Carolina. *Education:* Davidson College (A.B., 1966); University of North Carolina (J.D., 1969). Author: "Informed Consent - A Community Perspective Public Research Forum"; "Taking Charge - Innovative Strategies in Managed Care"; "Managed Care Happens - Legislative Update." *Member:* American Academy of Hospital Attorneys; North Carolina Society of Health Care Attorneys; National Health Lawyers Association (Former Board Member). [Capt., U.S. Army, Vietnam, 1971]. ***PRACTICE AREAS:*** Health Care; Health Care Fraud; Construction Law; Corporate Law; Real Property. ***Email:*** jallison@jahlaw.com

ROBERT C. HORD, JR., born Charlotte, North Carolina, September 26, 1940; admitted to bar, 1965, North Carolina. *Education:* Davidson College (A.B., 1962); University of North Carolina (LL.B., 1965). Phi Delta Phi; Scabbard & Blade. *Member:* American Judicature Society. [Capt., U.S. Army, active duty, 1965-1967; USAR, 1967-1973]. ***PRACTICE AREAS:*** Commercial Real Estate Development; Secured Lending; Corporate Law; Estate Administration. ***Email:*** rhord@jahlaw.com

RAY S. FARRIS, born 1940; admitted to bar, 1967, North Carolina. *Education:* University of North Carolina (A.B., 1962; J.D., 1967). Trustee, 1989-1996 and Chairman, 1995-1996, North Carolina State Bar IOLTA Plan. Member, Board of Governors of University of North Carolina; Chair, Charlotte Mecklenburg Community Foundation. *Member:* Mecklenburg County (President, 1984-1985), North Carolina and American Bar Associations. Fellow: American College of Trust and Estate Counsel; Fellow: American Bar Foundation. ***PRACTICE AREAS:*** Estate Planning and Estate Administration; Probate; Shareholder and Fiduciary Litigation; Corporate. ***Email:*** rfarris@jahlaw.com

ROBERT L. BURCHETTE, born New Bern, North Carolina, July 5, 1949; admitted to bar, 1976, North Carolina; U.S. Court of Appeals, Fourth Circuit; U.S. Claims Court; U.S. District Court, Western, Middle and Eastern Districts of North Carolina. *Education:* Guilford College (B.A., 1971); Wake Forest University (J.D., 1976). Staff Member, Wake Forest University Law Review, 1975-1976. Author, "Construction Claims" and "Insurance", The North Carolina Bar Association's Construction Law Deskbook, 1997-2000. Master, Justice William Bobbitt Inn of Court, 1987-1988. Member, North Carolina Courts Commissioner, 1995-1997. Member, Panel of Arbitrators, American Arbitration Association. Certified Mediator, in North Carolina. Member, American Bar Association's Forum On The Construction Industry, Member Division 7 Steering Committee Liens, Bonds and Insurance. Member, Citizens Design Committee, The Charlotte Coliseum. *Member:* North Carolina State Bar (Councilman, Construction Section, 1989-1992; Editor, Change Order, 1991-1993); American Bar Association; American Academy of Trial Lawyers; North Carolina Academy of Trial Lawyers. ***PRACTICE AREAS:*** Commercial Litigation; Personal Injury; Civil Litigation; Insurance Litigation; Construction Litigation; Construction Mediation; Construction; Litigation; Arbitration; Mediation. ***Email:*** rburchette@jahlaw.com

PAUL A. KOHUT, born Chicago, Illinois, February 14, 1958; admitted to bar, 1983, North Carolina. *Education:* University of California at Irvine (B.A., 1980); Wake Forest University (J.D., cum laude, 1983). Adjunct Lecturer, Winthrop University School of Business Administration, 1994-1998. Instructor, Credit Union National Association, Inc., Fall 1989. *Member:* North Carolina Bar Association (Member, Estate Planning and Fiduciary Law Section; Estate Administration Manual Committee, 1995—). ***PRACTICE AREAS:*** Estate Planning; Estate Administration; Corporate Law; Creditor's Rights. ***Email:*** pkohut@jahlaw.com

JOHN A. MORRICE, born Lombard, Illinois, January 8, 1958; admitted to bar, 1983, North Carolina and U.S. District Court, Western District of North Carolina. *Education:* Wake Forest University (B.A., 1980; J.D., cum laude, 1983). Staff Member, Wake Forest Law Review, 1981-1983. Member, Board of Directors, Meritas Law Firms Worldwide, 2003-2006. *Member:* North Carolina Society of Health Care Attorneys; Southern Employee Benefits Conference. ***PRACTICE AREAS:*** Employee Benefits; Tax Exempt Organizations; Commercial Real Estate; Mergers and Acquisitions. ***Email:*** jmorrice@jahlaw.com

J. DARRELL SHEALY, born Greenville, South Carolina, March 21, 1955; admitted to bar, 1983, North Carolina. *Education:* University of North Carolina (B.S., 1977; M.B.A., 1982; J.D., 1982). Certified Public Accountant, North Carolina, 1987. Board of Advisors, University of North Carolina at Chapel Hill Tax Institute. *Member:* Mecklenburg County and North Carolina (Member, Estate Planning and Fiduciary Law Section) Bar Associations; American Institute of Certified Public Accountants. ***PRACTICE AREAS:*** Estate Planning; Estate Administration; Taxation. ***Email:*** dshealy@jahlaw.com

GREG C. AHLUM, born Abington, Pennsylvania, October 17, 1962; admitted to bar, 1987, North Carolina and U.S. District Court, Western, Middle and Eastern Districts of North Carolina. *Education:* Wake Forest University (B.S., cum laude, 1984; J.D., cum laude, 1987). Notes and Comments Editor, Wake Forest Law Review, 1985-1987. Co-Author: "Construction Law," Lorman Education Services, 1994, 1997, 1999; "Occupation Safety and Health Act of North Carolina," Construction Law Deskbook, 1997. ***PRACTICE AREAS:*** Construction Law; Commercial Litigation; Civil Litigation; Arbitration; OSHA. ***Email:*** gahlum@jahlaw.com

PATRICK E. KELLY, born Frankfurt, West Germany, February 4, 1959; admitted to bar, 1989, North Carolina, U.S. District Court, Western District of North Carolina and U.S. Court of Appeals, Fourth Circuit. *Education:* United States Military Academy (B.S., 1981); University of North Carolina (J.D., 1989). Notes and Comments Editor, North Carolina Journal of International Law and Commercial Regulation, 1988-1989. [Capt., U.S. Army, 1981-1986]. ***PRACTICE AREAS:*** Health Care; Employment Law; Corporate Law; Civil Litigation. ***Email:*** pkelly@jahlaw.com

STEPHEN P. GENNETT, II, born Louisville, Kentucky, May 25, 1965; admitted to bar, 1991, North Carolina and U.S. District Court, Western District of North Carolina. *Education:* Georgetown University (B.S., Foreign Service, magna cum laude, 1988); Sophia University, Tokyo, Japan; University of North Carolina (J.D., 1991). Phi Alpha Theta. Recipient, Japan-America Society of Washington U Alexis Johnson Scholarship. ***LANGUAGES:*** Japanese and French. ***PRACTICE AREAS:*** Corporate Law; Commercial Real Estate; Local Government Law; Zoning Law; Insurance; Regulation. ***Email:*** sgennett@jahlaw.com

JOHN R. BUBEN, JR., born Buffalo, New York, December 18, 1965; admitted to bar, 1991, North Carolina and U.S. District Court, Western District of North Carolina. *Education:* University of Florida (B.S., Finance, with honors, 1988); Florida State University (J.D., with high honors, 1991). *Member:* North Carolina and American Bar Associations; National Association of Stock Plan Professionals. ***PRACTICE AREAS:*** Commercial Real Estate; Lender Law; Corporate Taxation; Securities; Sports Law. ***Email:*** jbuben@jahlaw.com

ALICE K. MOORE, born Clarkton, North Carolina, November 18, 1964; admitted to bar, 1992, North Carolina and U.S. District Court, Western and Middle Districts of North Carolina. *Education:* Wake Forest University (B.A., 1987; J.D., 1992). Chief Justice, Wake Forest Moot Court Board, 1991-1992. Member: Moot Court Board, 1990-1992; Jessup International Law Team, Southeastern Competition Winners, 1992. ***PRACTICE AREAS:*** Employment Discrimination; Employer Rights; Health Care; Corporate Law. ***Email:*** amoore@jahlaw.com

GARY J. WELCH, born Louisville, Kentucky, April 19, 1969; admitted to bar, 1994, North Carolina, U.S. District Court, Western and Middle Districts of North Carolina and U.S. Court of Appeals, Fourth Circuit. *Education:* University of North Carolina (B.S., Business Administration, with distinction, 1991; J.D., 1994). Phi Beta Kappa; Beta Gamma Sigma; Christian Legal Society; Moot Court Board, 1992-1994. Co-Author: "Construction Claims," Construction Law Deskbook, 1997, 1999 and 2003; "Rule 53: The Use of Special

(This Listing Continued)

JOHNSTON, ALLISON & HORD, P.A., Charlotte—Continued

Masters in Construction Litigation," Wiley Construction Law Update, 1999. *Member:* North Carolina Bar Association. ***PRACTICE AREAS:*** Construction Litigation; Arbitration; Commercial Litigation; Employment Law. ***Email:*** gwelch@jahlaw.com

WANDA C. TOWNSEND, born Charlotte, North Carolina. September 3, 1964; admitted to bar, 1991, North Carolina. *Education:* University of North Carolina-Chapel Hill (B.A., 1987; J.D., with honors, 1991). Member, The North Carolina Journal of International Law and Commercial Regulations, 1990-1991. ***PRACTICE AREAS:*** Corporate Law; Commercial Real Estate; Health Care Law; Banking Law. ***Email:*** wtownsend@jahlaw.com

BRIAN J. SCHOECK, born Detroit, Michigan, April 4, 1966; admitted to bar, 1997, North Carolina. *Education:* University of Florida (B.S., Finance, with high honors, 1988; M.B.A., Real Estate, with high honors, 1990; J.D., with high honors, 1997). Order of the Coif. Editor, Florida Law Review, 1996-1997. ***PRACTICE AREAS:*** Commercial Real Estate; Corporate Law; Limited Liability Company Law; Lender Finance; Corporate Taxation; Securities. ***Email:*** bschoeck@jahlaw.com

MICHAEL L. WILSON, born Richmond, Virginia, October 3, 1969; admitted to bar, 1996, North Carolina; U.S. District Court, Western, Middle and Eastern Districts of North Carolina. *Education:* University of North Carolina at Charlotte (B.A., 1993); University of North Carolina at Chapel Hill (J.D., 1996). Order of the Barristers. Chief Justice, Moot Court, 1995-1996. Member, Invitational Appellate Advocacy Team. Recipient: Moot Court James William Morrow Award, 1996; UNC-Law Davis Society Award, 1996. Co-Author: "Construction Law: Can this job be saved?," Lorman Educational Services, 1999; "North Carolina Construction Law," Lorman Educations Services, 2000; North Carolina Construction Law Desk Book, 2003. Co-Contributor: "Design/Build and the Law," NC AIA and AGC, 1999. ***PRACTICE AREAS:*** Commercial Litigation; Civil Litigation; Construction Litigation; Construction Arbitration; Federal and State Criminal Law. ***Email:*** mwilson@jahlaw.com

KENNETH T. LAUTENSCHLAGER, born Montgomery, Alabama, January 21, 1971; admitted to bar, 1996, North Carolina. *Education:* Queens College (B.A., summa cum laude, 1993); University of North Carolina at Chapel Hill (J.D., with honors, 1996). Phi Delta Phi. Order of the Barristers. Member, National Moot Court Team. Co-Author, "North Carolina Construction Law," Lorman Education Services, 2000; "North Carolina Construction Law Deskbook: Insurance Issued in Construction," North Carolina Bar Association Foundation, 2000. ***PRACTICE AREAS:*** Commercial Litigation; Construction Litigation; Civil Litigation; Construction Arbitration. ***Email:*** klauten@jahlaw.com

---

MARTIN L. WHITE, born Atlanta, Georgia, September 27, 1971; admitted to bar, 1996, North Carolina. *Education:* Gardner-Webb University (B.A., summa cum laude, 1993); University of North Carolina, Chapel Hill (J.D., with honors, 1996). Alpha Chi; Phi Delta Phi. Member, Holderness Moot Court. Winner, Invitational Team Competition. Finalist, Tulane National Moot Court Sports Law Competition. Recipient: Withrow Political Science Award; Huggins Most Outstanding Male Graduate Medal.*Member:* Mecklenburg County and North Carolina Bar Associations. [U.S. Navy, JAGC, 1996-2000, Lieutenant]. (Resident). ***PRACTICE AREAS:*** Arbitration; Civil Litigation; Commercial Litigation; Construction Law; Criminal Law; Workers Compensation; Personal Injury. ***Email:*** mwhite@jahlaw.com

N. LUCILLE SILER, born London, England, July 6, 1969; admitted to bar, 1997, North Carolina. *Education:* North Carolina School of Science and Mathematics (1987); Davidson College (B.S., 1991); University of North Carolina (J.D., 1997). Phi Alpha Delta. *Member:* Mecklenburg County (Member, Board of Directors, 1999—) and North Carolina Bar Associations. ***PRACTICE AREAS:*** Estate Planning; Estate Administration; Employee Benefits; Corporate Law. ***Email:*** lsiler@jahlaw.com

JOE FRANKLIN TEAGUE, JR., born Hickory, North Carolina, September 5, 1969; admitted to bar, 1998, North Carolina. *Education:* Lenoir-Rhyne College (A.B., magna cum laude, 1991); University of North Carolina (J.D., 1998). Certified Public Accountant, North Carolina, 1993. Member: North Carolina Association of Certified Public Accountants; American Institute of Certified Public Accountants. ***PRACTICE AREAS:*** Taxation; Business; Corporate; Partnership; Limited Liability Company; Estate Planning. ***Email:*** jteague@jahlaw.com

ROBERT G. LINDAUER, JR., born Cocoa Beach, Florida, May 10, 1970; admitted to bar, 2000, North Carolina. *Education:* Queens College (B.A., magna cum laude, 1992); University of North Carolina (J.D., 2000). Publication Editor, North Carolina Law Review, 1999-2000. Author, "State v. Pearson and State v. McClendon: Determining Reasonable, Articulable Suspicion from the Totality of the Circumstances in North Carolina," 78 N.C. L. Rev. 831 (2000). *Member:* Mecklenburg County, North Carolina and American Bar Associations; North Carolina State Bar; UNC-Law Davis Society, 2000. ***PRACTICE AREAS:*** Commercial Real Estate; Corporate; Transactional. ***Email:*** rlindauer@jahlaw.com

JENNIFER M. PATTERSON, born Miami, Florida, August 30, 1969; admitted to bar, 2000, North Carolina. *Education:* University of North Carolina (B.A., with honors, 1991; M.P.A., 1993); Wake Forest University (J.D., magna cum laude, 2000). Phi Beta Kappa. Omicron Delta Epsilon. A.J. Fletcher Law Scholar. Member: Order of the Coif; Order of the Barristers; Moot Court Board, 1998-2000; Philip C. Jessup International Law Moot Court Team. Recipient, I. Beverly Lake Award. Wake Forest Law Review, 1998-2000; Articles Editor, 1999-2000. Law Clerk, Honorable Richard L. Voorhees, U.S. District Court, Western District of North Carolina, 2000-2001. Author: "Chamberlain v. Thames: Will a New Rule of Appellate Procedure Help Resolve an Old Controversy," 34 Wake Forest L.R. 1227 (1999). *Member:* North Carolina and American Bar Associations. ***PRACTICE AREAS:*** Health Care; Corporate Law; Commercial Litigation. ***Email:*** jpatterson@jahlaw.com

CAMERON T. WARE, born Kings Mountain, North Carolina, April 18, 1975; admitted to bar, 2000, North Carolina. *Education:* University of North Carolina at Charlotte (B.A., cum laude, 1997); University of North Carolina at Chapel Hill (J.D., 2000). *Member:* North Carolina and American Bar Associations. ***PRACTICE AREAS:*** Commercial Real Estate. ***Email:*** tware@jahlaw.com

DAVID A. BOHM, born Osborne, Kansas, August 3, 1972; admitted to bar, 1998, Kansas; 1999, North Carolina. *Education:* Washburn University of Topeka (B.A., Political Science, magna cum laude, 1995; J.D., 1998); Loyola University Chicago School of Law (LL.M., Health Law, 2000). *Member:* Mecklenburg County, North Carolina (Health Law Section) and American (Health Law Section) Bar Associations; North Carolina State Bar; North Carolina Society of Healthcare Attorneys; American Health Lawyers Association. ***PRACTICE AREAS:*** Health Care; Corporate Law; Civil Litigation. ***Email:*** dbohm@jahlaw.com

LAURA PLEICONES, born Fort Rucker, Alabama, September 21, 1972; admitted to bar, 2000, South Carolina; 2001, North Carolina. *Education:* University of Georgia (A.B., 1994); University of South Carolina (M.A., 1999; J.D., cum laude, 2000). Member, Order of the Wig and Robe. Recipient, Victor A. Michalewitz Award for Excellence in Legal Writing; Editor's Award for Outstanding Service and Extraordinary Commitment; Roy Webster Scholarship. University of South Carolina Law Review, 1998-2000; Associate Editor, Chief, 1999-2000. Author: Note, Passing the Essence Test: Health Care Providers Escape Strict Liability for Medical Devices, 50 S.C.L. REV. 451 (1999). Co-Author: "New Regime for the Total Return Trust: The 2001 South Carolina Uniform Principal and Income Act," South Carolina Lawyer, July/August 2002. *Member:* North Carolina and American Bar Associations; South Carolina Bar. ***PRACTICE AREAS:*** Estate Planning; Estate Administration; Corporate Law. ***Email:*** lpleicones@jahlaw.com

ASHLEY DAVIDSON TISON, born Carmel, Indiana, June 25, 1975; admitted to bar, 2000, North Carolina; 2001, South Carolina. *Education:* University of North Carolina at Charlotte (B.S.B.A., 1997); University of North Carolina at Chapel Hill (J.D., 2000). *Member:* North Carolina State Bar; South Carolina Bar. ***PRACTICE AREAS:*** Commercial Real Estate; Corporate Law; Mergers and Acquisitions; Sports Law; Entertainment Law.

J. NICHOLAS KENDALL, born Albemarle, North Carolina, August 18, 1978; admitted to bar, 2003, North Carolina. *Education:* University of North Carolina at Charlotte (B.A., Political, summa cum laude, 2000, B.S., Accounting, summa cum laude, 2000); University of North Carolina at Chapel Hill (J.D., with high honors, 2003). Author: Israeli Counter-Terrorism: "Targeted Killings," Under International Law, 80 N.C.L. Rev. 1069 (2002). ***PRACTICE AREAS:*** Corporate Law; Commercial Real Estate.

JOHN C. LINDLEY, III, born Richmond, Virginia, January 31, 1977; admitted to bar, 2003, North Carolina. *Education:* University of North Carolina at Chapel Hill (B.A., 1999; J.D., 2003). Staff Member, Law Review. *Member:* Meek County, North Carolina and American Bar Associations. ***PRACTICE AREAS:*** Litigation. ***Email:*** tlindley@jahlaw.com

WILLIAM C. ISENHOUR, born Charlotte, North Carolina; admitted to bar, 2003, North Carolina; 2004, South Carolina. *Education:* Davidson College (B.A., with honors, cum laude, History, 2000); University of North Carolina School of Law (J.D., 2003). Phi Beta Kappa. *Member:* Mecklenberg County (Member, Real Property Council), North Carolina and American Bar Associations; South Carolina Bar. ***PRACTICE AREAS:*** Commercial Transactions; Lender Law; Acquisitions; Dispositions; Leasing; Commercial Real Estate. ***Email:*** wisenhour@jahlaw.com

OF COUNSEL

LELIA M. ALEXANDER, (MISS) (1911-1991)

B. IRVIN BOYLE, born Augusta, Georgia, March 13, 1912; admitted to bar, 1936, North Carolina. *Education:* University of North Carolina (A.B., 1934; LL.B., 1936). Phi Delta Phi. Editor, University of North Carolina Law Review, 1935. *Member:* Mecklenburg County Bar Association (President, 1951); American Judicature Society; North Carolina Association of Defense Counsel. [Lt. Comdr., U.S.N.R., active duty, 1942-1945]. ***PRACTICE AREAS:*** Administrative Law; Corporate Law.

All Attorneys are Members of the Mecklenburg County, North Carolina and American Bar Associations, U.S. District Court, Western District of North Carolina and the North Carolina State Bar.

ATTORNEYS FOR: Alemite; Alex Lee; American Truetzschler; Americas Homeplace; Ayrsley Retail Development Group; BB&T; Baucom's Nursery; Beacon Development; Beazer Homes Corp.; Bradford OBGYN; Carolina Petroleum; Carolinas Associated General Contractors; Charlotte Eye, Ear, Nose & Throat Associates; Commonwealth Title; Crowder Construction Co.; Dienst Custom Homes; Eastern Federal Corp.; Eastern Seaboard Packaging; Federal Express; Fidelity National Title; Forms and Supply; Gambro Health Care; Hickory Construction Co.; JDH Capital, LLC; John Boyle & Company; Jones and DeBonis Co.; Kewaunee Scientific; Lawyers Title; MarkPiercePoole Properties; MEDIC; Merchant Distributors; Morrison Plantation; Murata of America; National Association of Hosiery Manufacturers; NewDominion Bank; NorthEast Medical Center; Novant Health; Old Republic Title; J.N. Pease & Co. (Architects); Petro Express; Pharr Yarns; Presbyterian Hospital; RBC Centura Bank; Regions Bank; Rodgers Builders; SAFECO Ins.; F.N. Thompson, Co.; Tuscan Development; Wachovia Bank; Watauga Medical Center; Wilkie Construction Company.
APPROVED ATTORNEYS FOR: All major Title Insurance Companies.
REFERENCES: Centura Bank; Wachovia Bank; SouthTrust Bank.

(This Listing Continued)

GREG JONES & ASSOCIATES, P.A.

CHARLOTTE, NORTH CAROLINA

(See Wilmington)

Personal Injury, Automobile Accidents, Brain Injury, Motorcycle Accidents, Wrongful Death, Medical Malpractice, Spinal Cord Injuries, Drug and Medical Device Litigation, Pharmacists Liability, Head Injuries, Products Liability, Medical and Nursing Home Negligence, Workers Compensation, Toxic Torts, Nursing Home Abuse, Stock Fraud.

JONES, HEWSON & WOOLARD

831 E. MOREHEAD STREET
SUITE 560
CHARLOTTE, NORTH CAROLINA 28202
Telephone: 704-372-6541
FAX: 704-331-9068

General Civil Litigation, Insurance Defense, Automobile Negligence, Premises Liability, Product Liability, Professional Liability, Workers' Compensation.

MEMBERS OF FIRM

HUNTER M. JONES (1902-1996)

HARRY C. HEWSON (1922-1999)

ROBERT GILROY SPRATT, III, born Charlotte, North Carolina, September 26, 1948; admitted to bar, 1973, North Carolina. *Education:* University of North Carolina (A.B., 1970; J.D., 1973). Phi Beta Kappa; John M. Morehead Scholar. *Member:* Twenty-Sixth Judicial District Bar; North Carolina State Bar; North Carolina Bar Association; Mecklenburg County Bar Association; Defense Research Institute. ***PRACTICE AREAS:*** General Civil Litigation; Insurance Defense; Workers Compensation. ***Email:*** rspratt@jhandw.com

LAWRENCE J. GOLDMAN, born Philadelphia, Pennsylvania, April 5, 1961; admitted to bar, 1988, Louisiana; 1992, North Carolina. *Education:* Tulane University (1979-1980); Louisiana State University at Shreveport (B.S., 1985); Louisiana State University (J.D., 1988). *Member:* Louisiana State Bar Association; Twenty-Sixth Judicial District Bar; North Carolina State Bar; North Carolina Bar Association; Mecklenburg County Bar Association; National Association of Railroad Trial Counsel; American Bar Association. ***PRACTICE AREAS:*** General Civil Litigation; Insurance Defense; Construction Litigation; Workers Compensation. ***Email:*** lgoldman@jhandw.com

WILLIAM L. WOOLARD (1931-2005)

REPRESENTATIVE CLIENTS: Norfolk Southern Corp.; Norfolk Southern Railway Co. (Assistant Division Counsel); Cincinnati Insurance Co.; CNA Insurance; Zurich U.S. Insurance Co.; The Hartford; Crum & Forster; City of Charlotte.

MATTHEW R. JOYNER, PLLC

708 EAST BOULEVARD, SUITE 300
CHARLOTTE, NORTH CAROLINA 28203
Telephone: 704-295-0226
Fax: 704-295-0228
Email: mrjesq@prodigy.net
URL: http://www.mattjoyner.net

General Counsel and Administration Services, Business Law, Contracts, Commercial, Employment Law, Mergers and Acquisitions.

MATTHEW R. JOYNER, born Durham, North Carolina, March 24, 1959; admitted to bar, 1985, North Carolina; U.S. District Court, Western, Middle and Eastern Districts of North Carolina and U.S. Court of Appeals, Fourth Circuit. *Education:* Dartmouth College (A.B., magna cum laude, 1981); University of Pennsylvania (J.D., 1984). Phi Beta Kappa. Editor, University of Pennsylvania Law Review, 1983-1984. Law Clerk to Hon. J. Dickson Phillips, Jr., U.S. Court of Appeals, Fourth Circuit, 1984-1985. *Member:* Mecklenburg County, North Carolina and American Bar Associations; The North Carolina State Bar.

JUSTICE, EVE & EDWARDS, P.A.

1801 EAST BOULEVARD
CHARLOTTE, NORTH CAROLINA 28203
Telephone: 704-333-5176
Fax: 704-333-5443
URL: http://www.lawyers.com/jee

Civil Trials in State Courts. Construction, Eminent Domain, Land Condemnation, Family Law, Equitable Distribution, Alimony, Divorce, Workers Compensation, Personal Injury.

JAMES F. JUSTICE (1922-1998)

R. MICHAEL EVE, JR., born Charlotte, North Carolina, April 26, 1953; admitted to bar, 1978, Alabama; 1979, North Carolina. *Education:* University of North Carolina (B.A., with honors, 1975); Cumberland School of Law of Samford University (J.D., cum laude, 1978). Order of the Old Well. Editor-in-Chief, Cumberland Law Review, 1977-1978. Law Clerk, Supreme Court of Alabama, 1978-1979. *Member:* North Carolina Bar Association; 26th Judicial District (Member, Board of Directors, Executive Committee, 1997-2000) and North Carolina State Bars; Alabama State Bar; North Carolina Academy of Trial Lawyers. ***REPORTED CASES:*** Beam v. Beam, 92 N.C. App. 509, 374 S.E.2d 636 (1988); Heath v. Craighill, 97 N.C. App. 236, 388 S.E.2d 178 (1990); Principal Mutual Life Insurance Co. v. Burnup & Sims, Inc., 114 N.C. App. 494, 442 S.E.2d 85 (1994). ***PRACTICE AREAS:*** Civil Litigation; Family Law; Personal Injury Law; Condemnation. ***Email:*** RMEve@AOL.COM

DAVID L. EDWARDS, born Charlotte, North Carolina, June 16, 1955; admitted to bar, 1990, North Carolina. *Education:* University of North Carolina at Charlotte (B.S., 1986); Cumberland School of Law of Samford University (J.D., 1989). Associate Editor, American Journal of Trial Advocacy, 1988-1989. *Member:* North Carolina Bar Association; 26th Judicial District and North Carolina State Bars; North Carolina Academy of Trial Lawyers. ***REPORTED CASES:*** Newland v. Newland, 129 N.C. App. 418, 498 S.E.2d 855 (1998); Schmidt v. Breeden, Owens and Charlotte-Mecklenburg Bd. of Educ., 134 N.C. App. 248 (1999). ***PRACTICE AREAS:*** Personal Injury Law; Construction Law. ***Email:*** davemanedwards@outdrs.net

(This Listing Continued)

REPRESENTATIVE CLIENTS: Bealer Wholesale; BB&T Leasing Corp.; Carolina Builders Corp.; Draw Enterprises, Inc.; Mechanical Supply Co.; Service Thread Co.; Stock Building Supply; Superior Tile; Marble & Terrazzo Co.
REFERENCE: Bank of America.

KATTEN MUCHIN ROSENMAN LLP

A Partnership including Professional Corporations
401 SOUTH TRYON STREET, SUITE 2600
CHARLOTTE, NORTH CAROLINA 28202-1935
Telephone: 704-444-2000
Fax: 704-444-2050
URL: http://www.kattenlaw.com

Chicago, Illinois Office: 525 West Monroe Street, Suite 1600, 60661-3693. Telephone: 312-902-5200. Fax: 312-902-1061.
New York, New York Office: 575 Madison Avenue, 10022-2585. Telephone: 212-940-8800. Fax: 212-940-8776.
Los Angeles, California Office: 2029 Century Park East, Suite 2600, 90067-3012. Telephone: 310-788-4400. Fax: 310-788-4471.
Washington, D.C. Office: 1025 Thomas Jefferson Street, N.W., East Lobby, Suite 700, 20007-5201. Telephone: 202-625-3500. Fax: 202-298-7570.
Palo Alto, California Office: 260 Sheridan Avenue, Suite 450, 94306-2047. Telephone: 650-330-3652. Fax: 650-321-4746.
Irving, Texas Office: 5215 N. O'Connor Boulevard, Suite 200, 75039-3732. Telephone: 972-868-9058. Fax: 972-868-9068.

Advertising, Anti-Fraud Counseling and Litigation, Antitrust, Apparel and Fashion, Aviation, Bankruptcy, Reorganization and Creditors' Rights, Corporate and Securities, Corporate Governance, Customs and International Trade, Employee Benefits and Executive Compensation, Entertainment and Media, Entertainment and Media Finance, Entertainment and Media Litigation, Environmental, FCC and Telecommunications, Finance and Structured Finance, Financial Institutions, Financial Markets and Products, Financial Services, Health Care, Health Care Compliance, Health Care Insolvency, Health Information and HIPAA Compliance, Hotel and Hospitality, Intellectual Property, Intellectual Property Litigation, Investment Management, Labor and Employment, Licensing and Distribution, Life Sciences, Litigation and Dispute Resolution, Matrimonial and Family Law, Mergers and Acquisitions, Music Law, Private Client Services, Private Equity, Public Finance, Publishing, Real Estate, Real Estate Development, Real Estate Finance, Real Estate Litigation, Real Estate Taxation, Securities, Securities Litigation, Shopping Center and Retail Law, Sports Law and Sports Facilities, Tax Planning and Litigation, Taxation of Financial Products, Technology, Trusts and Estates, White Collar Criminal and Civil Litigation.

FIRM PROFILE: Katten Muchin Rosenman LLP is a national, full-service law firm with offices in the nation's largest centers of business, government, finance and technology. Our 600 attorneys in more than 50 practice areas provide timely and cost-effective counsel to clients in numerous industries. We are business advisors and advocates for a wide range of public and private companies, from entrepreneurial, emerging-growth, and middle market firms to global Fortune 100 corporations, as well as government entities and major universities, museums and other charitable and cultural organizations.

Based on a survey of corporate counsel at Fortune 1000 companies, we have been placed on BTI Consulting Client Service A Team. Our leading practices and attorneys have been recognized in Chambers & Partners Guides, Who's Who Legal, Leading Lawyers Network, Corporate Counsel, and the Expert Guides published by Euromoney Institutional Investor PLC. In addition, Corporate Board Member has recognized the Firm based on its survey of CEOs and directors of major public companies.

Katten Muchin ZavisRosenman & Colin

PARTNERS

RICHARD L. FARLEY, born Columbia, South Carolina, March 18, 1957; admitted to bar, 1987, North Carolina and U.S. District Court, Western District of North Carolina; 1988, U.S. Court of Appeals, 4th Circuit; 1993, U.S. District Court, Eastern District of North Carolina; 1995, U.S. District Court, Middle District of North Carolina. *Education:* University of South Carolina (B.A., cum laude, 1978); University of North Carolina (J.D., cum laude, 1987). Order of the Coif. Staff Member, University of North Carolina Law Review, 1985-1986. Member, University of North Carolina Law School Charlotte Regional Alumni Council. Pro Bono Attorney, Legal Services for the Elderly, 1990-2000. *Member:* Mecklenburg County, North Carolina and American Bar Associations; North Carolina State Bar; North Carolina Association of Defense Attorneys; Defense Research Institute. ***LANGUAGES:*** French. ***REPORTED CASES:*** Lockwood v. Porter, 98 N.C. App. 410, 390 S.E. 2d 742 (1990); Evans v. Full Circle Productions, 443 S.E.2d 108 (N.C. App., 1994); Beaver v. City of Salisbury, 502 S.E.2d 885 (N.C. App., 1998); review dismissed 514 S.E.2d 89 (N.C., 1999). ***PRACTICE AREAS:*** Commercial Litigation; Insurance Coverage; Contractors Liability; Software Licensing; Employment Contracts; Employment Covenants; Motor Sports Law. ***Email:*** richard.farley@kattenlaw.com

FRED A. HICKS, born Richmond, Virginia, 1942; admitted to bar, 1968, North Carolina. *Education:* University of North Carolina (A.B., 1965; J.D., 1968). Law Clerk to Honorable James B. McMillan, Judge, U.S. District Court for the Western District of North Carolina, 1968-1970. Permanent Member, U.S. Fourth Circuit Judicial Conference, 1984. Recipient, Distinguished Service Award, North Carolina Bar Association, 1995. *Member:* North Carolina (Member, Family Law Section Council, 1983-1986; Family Law Curriculum Committee, 1987—; Chairman, 1992-1993; Family Law CLE Committee, 1992-1995; Chairman, Long Range Planning Committee, 1991-1993, Chairman) and American (Member, Family Law Section) Bar Associations; North Carolina State Bar. Fellow, American Academy of Matrimonial Lawyers (President, North Carolina Chapter, 1997—). (Board Certified Specialist in Family Law, North Carolina State Board of Legal Specialization). ***PRACTICE AREAS:*** Family Law. ***Email:*** fred.hicks@kattenlaw.com

DANIEL S. HUFFENUS, admitted to bar, 1994, New Jersey; 1995, New York; 1997, North Carolina. *Education:* Lafayette College (B.A., 1986); Columbia University (M.S.,

(This Listing Continued)

KATTEN MUCHIN ROSENMAN LLP, Charlotte—Continued

1988); New York University (J.D., 1994). *Member:* Mecklenburg County, North Carolina and American Bar Associations. ***PRACTICE AREAS:*** Real Estate; Real Estate Finance; Finance; Structured Finance. ***Email:*** dan.huffenus@kattenlaw.com

WILLIAM P. McMILLAN, born Roanoke Rapids, North Carolina, March 22, 1960; admitted to bar, 1985, Texas; 1994, North Carolina. *Education:* University of Virginia (B.A., with highest distinction, 1982); Duke University School of Law (J.D., with high honors, 1985). Phi Beta Kappa. Member, Editorial Board, Duke Law Journal. ***PRACTICE AREAS:*** Commercial Finance; Commercial Real Estate; Bankruptcy, Reorganization and Creditors' Rights. ***Email:*** william.mcmillan@kattenlaw.com

BRADLEY E. PEARCE, born 1960; admitted to bar, 1991, North Carolina; U.S. Court of Appeals, Fourth and Eleventh Circuits. *Education:* University of Tennessee, Knoxville (B.A., summa cum laude, 1982); Harvard University (J.D., cum laude, 1991). *Member:* American Bar Association; American Bankruptcy Institute. (Board Certified Specialist in Bankruptcy Law, North Carolina State Board of Legal Specialization). ***PRACTICE AREAS:*** Bankruptcy; Bankruptcy Reorganization; Creditors Rights; Finance; Financial Institutions Law. ***Email:*** brad.pearce@kattenlaw.com

PETER J. SHEA, born Philadelphia, Pennsylvania, 1960; admitted to bar, 1988, Pennsylvania; 1991, District of Columbia; 1994, North Carolina. *Education:* College of William & Mary (B.A., 1982); University of Pennsylvania Law School (J.D., 1988). Former Staff Attorney, U.S. Securities and Exchange Commission, Division of Enforcement. ***PRACTICE AREAS:*** Financial Services Law; Corporate Law; Securities; Corporate Governance; Investment Management; Private Equity. ***Email:*** peter.shea@kattenlaw.com

WILLIAM L. SITTON, JR., born Hickory, North Carolina, February 17, 1953; admitted to bar, 1978, North Carolina and U.S. District Court, Western District of North Carolina; 1999, U.S. District Court, Middle District of North Carolina. *Education:* University of North Carolina (A.B., with honors, 1975; J.D., 1978). Phi Beta Kappa; Order of Barristers. Master of The Bench, 1990— and Secretary Treasurer, 1990-1995, American Inn of Court. Faculty, NCATL Trial Advocacy Clinic, 1986. Co-Author: *Professional Negligence Manual,* 1987. Editor and Author: *North Carolina Manual of Complaints,* Vol. I, 1986; Vol. II, 1990. *Member:* Mecklenburg County and North Carolina Bar Associations; North Carolina State Bar; North Carolina Academy of Trial Lawyers (Member, Board of Governors, 1986-1988; Vice President, 1987-1988); The Association of Trial Lawyers of America. ***REPORTED CASES:*** United States v. Anderson, 611 F. 2d 504; Bowman v. United States, 820 F. 2d 716; Dillon v. Consolidated Delivery, 43 N.C. App. 395, 258 S.E. 2d 829; Equitable Leasing v. Myers, 46 N.C. App. 162, 265 S.E. 2d 240; Lowe v. Tarble, 312 N.C. 467, 323 S.E. 2d 19; Lormic v. North American, 95 N.C. App. 705, 383 S.E. 2d 694; Virmani v. Presbyterian, 127 N.C.App. 71, 488 S.E.2d 284. ***PRACTICE AREAS:*** Personal Injury; Professional Negligence; Civil Litigation. ***Email:*** william.sitton@kattenlaw.com

ROBERT B. TUCKER, JR., born Shreveport, Louisiana, July 12, 1943; admitted to bar, 1972, North Carolina and U.S. District Court, Western District of North Carolina. *Education:* North Carolina State University (B.S.E.E., 1966); University of North Carolina School of Law (J.D., with high honors, 1972). Order of the Coif. Editor-in-Chief, North Carolina Law Review, 1971-1972. *Member:* Mecklenburg County, North Carolina and American Bar Associations; North Carolina State Bar. ***PRACTICE AREAS:*** Contracts; Corporate Law; Securities. ***Email:*** robert.tucker@kattenlaw.com

DAVID R. VINES, born 1966; admitted to bar, 1994, North Carolina. *Education:* Northeast Louisiana University (B.B.A., cum laude, 1988); University of North Carolina (J.D., with honors, 1994). Certified Public Accountant, North Carolina, 1992. Member, North Carolina Association of Certified Public Accountants. *Member:* North Carolina (Member, Sections on: Estate Planning and Fiduciary Law; Taxation Law; Business Law) and American (Member, Sections on: Real Property, Probate and Trust Law; Taxation Law; Business Law) Bar Associations; Charlotte Estate Planning Council. (Board Certified Specialist in Estate Planning and Probate Law, North Carolina State Board of Legal Specialization). ***PRACTICE AREAS:*** Trusts and Estates; Tax Planning; Tax Litigation; Private Client Services; Joint Ventures; Strategic Alliances; Partnerships. ***Email:*** david.vines@kattenlaw.com

A. VICTOR WRAY, born Shelby, North Carolina, January 6, 1943; admitted to bar, 1968, North Carolina. *Education:* Duke University (A.B., 1965); University of North Carolina at Chapel Hill (J.D., with honors, 1968). Phi Alpha Delta; Order of the Coif. Associate Editor, North Carolina Law Review, 1967-1968. Member: Charlotte Estate Planning Council, 1978—; Charlotte Pension Forum, 1980—. *Member:* North Carolina (Member, Taxation, Estate Planning and Fiduciary Law Practice Management Section, 1996—; Council Member, 1996-1999 and Chair, 2000-2001, Law Practice Management Section; Member, Technology Committee) and American (Member, Sections on: Taxation; Real Property and Probate; Business Law) Bar Associations. ***LANGUAGES:*** Spanish and German. ***PRACTICE AREAS:*** International; Corporate; Taxation; Employee Benefits; Estate Planning; Mergers and Acquisitions. ***Email:*** victor.wray@kattenlaw.com

ASSOCIATES

TERRA K. ATKINSON, born 1977; admitted to bar, 2002, North Carolina. *Education:* Rollins College (B.A., magna cum laude, 1999); University of Virginia School of Law (J.D., 2002). ***PRACTICE AREAS:*** Litigation; Alternative Dispute Resolution. ***Email:*** terra.atkinson@kattenlaw.com

ABBIE G. BAYNES, born Greensboro, North Carolina; admitted to bar, 1991, Maryland; 1992, District of Columbia; 2000, New York (Not admitted in North Carolina). *Education:* Duke University (A.B., cum laude, 1985); George Washington University (J.D., 1991; M.B.A., 1994). Member, Board of Directors, George Washington University Law Alumni Association, 2000-2004. *Member:* The Association of the Bar of the City of New York (Member, Telecommunications Committee, 1997-2003); Charlotte Women's Bar. ***PRACTICE AREAS:*** Corporate Transactions; Real Estate. ***Email:*** abbie.baynes@kattenlaw.com

JEFFREY C. GRADY, admitted to bar, 2004, North Carolina. *Education:* University of Washington (B.A. in Political Science, 1993); Wake Forest University (J.D., cum laude, 2004). Order of the Coif. Staff Member, Wake Forest University Law Review. ***PRACTICE AREAS:*** Litigation; Dispute Resolution. ***Email:*** jeffrey.grady@kattenlaw.com

(This Listing Continued)

CHRISTOPHER A. HICKS, born Charlotte, North Carolina, August 13, 1969; admitted to bar, 1999, North Carolina. *Education:* University of North Carolina, Chapel Hill (B.A., 1991); Appalachian State University (M.A., 1996); Wake Forest University (J.D., 1999). Wake Forest Moot Court Board and Trial Bar. ***PRACTICE AREAS:*** Litigation and Dispute Resolution. ***Email:*** christopher.hicks@kattenlaw.com

REBECCA J. HORTON, born Lancaster, South Carolina, November 12, 1973; admitted to bar, 1999, South Carolina; 2000, North Carolina. *Education:* Furman University (B.A., 1996); University of South Carolina (J.D., 1999). Order of the Wig and Robe. ***PRACTICE AREAS:*** Taxation; Real Estate; Real Estate Finance. ***Email:*** rebecca.horton@kattenlaw.com

BARRETT C. MALLOS, admitted to bar, 2004, North Carolina. *Education:* Davidson College (B.A., 2000); University of North Carolina at Chapel Hill School of Law (J.D., 2004). ***PRACTICE AREAS:*** Real Estate. ***Email:*** barrett.mallos@kattenlaw.com

CHARLES A. PETTIGREW, admitted to bar, 2004, North Carolina. *Education:* University of North Carolina at Chapel Hill (B.A., 1998; J.D., with honors, 2004). ***PRACTICE AREAS:*** Real Estate. ***Email:*** charles.pettigrew@kattenlaw.com

G. LAURENCE PLAISTED, born Iowa City, Iowa, June 18, 1971; admitted to bar, 1996, Kansas and U.S. District Court, District of Kansas; 1998, District of Columbia; 2003, North Carolina and U.S. District Court, Western District of North Carolina. *Education:* University of Kansas (B.S., 1993); University of Kansas School of Law (J.D., 1996); Georgetown University Law Center (LL.M., 1997). ***PRACTICE AREAS:*** Corporate; Securities. ***Email:*** larry.plaisted@kattenlaw.com

NINA SHOR, born Neuss, Germany, January 14, 1960; admitted to bar, 1986, New York; 1988, District of Columbia; 1998, Maryland; 2004, North Carolina. *Education:* University of Toronto (B.A., with distinction, 1982); New York Law School (J.D., cum laude, 1985). Member, NYLS Journal of International and Comparative Law. Instructor, Banking Law, American Banker's Institute, 1995-2002. *Member:* District of Columbia Bar; Maryland State Bar Association; Women's Bar Association. ***LANGUAGES:*** Greek. ***PRACTICE AREAS:*** Real Estate. ***Email:*** nina.shor@kattenlaw.com

AMY SIMPSON, born January 9, 1970; admitted to bar, 1996, North Carolina. *Education:* Duke University (B.A., cum laude, 1992); University of North Carolina at Chapel Hill (J.D., with honors, 1996); Kenan-Flager School of Business (M.B.A., 1996). ***PRACTICE AREAS:*** Employment Litigation; Matrimonial Litigation; Private Client Services. ***Email:*** amy.simpson@kattenlaw.com

JENNIFER M. STOKLEY, born Saginaw, Michigan, July 30, 1969; admitted to bar, 1995, North Dakota; 1997, Colorado; 2002, North Carolina. *Education:* Huntingdon College (B.A., 1991); University of North Dakota School of Law (J.D., with distinction, 1995). Member, Intraschool Moot Court Competition. Editor-in-chief, North Dakota Law Review. Law Clerk, Hon. Chief Judge, Rodney S. Webb, U.S. District Court, District of North Dakota, 1995-1997. Author: "Withholding or Withdrawing Medical Care From Premature Infants: Who Should Decide, and How?" 70 N.D. L. Rev. 1. *Member:* El Paso, Colorado and American Bar Associations. ***PRACTICE AREAS:*** Real Estate; Real Estate Finance; Real Estate Litigation; Anti-Fraud Counseling and Litigation; Financial Institutions. ***Email:*** jennifer.stokley@kattenlaw.com

SUSAN M. WALKER, admitted to bar, 2000, Georgia; 2002, North Carolina. *Education:* Mary Washington College (B.A., 1997); Harvard Law School (J.D., 2000). *Member:* North Carolina Bar Association; State Bar of Georgia. ***PRACTICE AREAS:*** Real Estate; Real Estate Finance. ***Email:*** susan.walker@kattenlaw.com

SPECIAL COUNSEL

RUSSELL M. BLACK, born Knoxville, Tennessee, March 24, 1962; admitted to bar, 1988, North Carolina; U.S. District Court, Western District of North Carolina. *Education:* University of Tennessee (B.S., with honors, 1985); Vanderbilt University (J.D., 1988). Phi Alpha Delta (Treasurer, 1987-1988). *Member:* Mecklenburg County and North Carolina Bar Associations; North Carolina State Bar. ***PRACTICE AREAS:*** Labor and Employment; Corporate; Licensing and Distribution; Mergers and Acquisitions. ***Email:*** russell.black@kattenlaw.com

CHARLES D. LANSDEN, born Memphis, Tennessee, October 10, 1960; admitted to bar, 1987, North Carolina; 1992, U.S. District Court, Western District of North Carolina. *Education:* University of North Carolina at Chapel Hill (B.A., 1983; J.D., with honors, 1987); University of South Carolina (Master of International Business Studies, 1997). Phi Beta Kappa; Beta Gamma Sigma. [JAG, U.S. Air Force, 1987-1992.]. ***LANGUAGES:*** German. ***PRACTICE AREAS:*** Real Estate; Real Estate Finance. ***Email:*** charles.lansden@kattenlaw.com

CARLTON A. SHANNON, JR., born Elizabeth City, North Carolina, May 16, 1960; admitted to bar, 1985, North Carolina. *Education:* University of North Carolina (B.A., with honors, 1982; J.D., with honors, 1985). Order of the Grail; Order of the Coif. Staff Member, North Carolina Law Review, 1984-1985. *Member:* Mecklenburg County and North Carolina Bar Associations; North Carolina State Bar. ***PRACTICE AREAS:*** Real Estate Law; Landlord/Tenant Law; Commercial Law; Corporate Law. ***Email:*** carlton.shannon@kattenlaw.com

OF COUNSEL

WILLIAM E. UNDERWOOD, JR., born Asheville, North Carolina, October 5, 1937; admitted to bar, 1964, North Carolina. *Education:* University of North Carolina at Chapel Hill (A.B., 1960; J.D., with honors, 1964). Phi Delta Phi. Member, Order of the Coif. Member, Board of Editors, 1962-1963 and Associate Editor, 1963-1964, North Carolina Law Review. *Member:* Mecklenburg County, North Carolina and American Bar Associations; North Carolina State Bar. ***REPORTED CASES:*** Long v. City of Charlotte, 306 N.C.187, 293 S.E.2d 101; Steel Creek Community Assoc. v. U.S. Dept of Transportation, 435 F. Supp. 196. ***PRACTICE AREAS:*** Corporate and Securities; Environmental Services; Litigation and Dispute Resolution; Public Finance; Trusts and Estates. ***Email:*** bill.underwood@kattenlaw.com

All attorneys are members of: The Mecklenburg County Bar, the North Carolina State Bar and the North Carolina and American Bar Associations.

GARY KEITH, P.A.

1230 WEST MOREHEAD STREET, SUITE 410
CHARLOTTE, NORTH CAROLINA 28208
Telephone: 704-333-4411
Fax: 704-333-2555
URL: http://www.garykeithpa.com
Email: garykeithpa@hotmail.com
URL: http://www.lawyers.com/garykeithpa

Personal Injury, Wrongful Death, Automobile Accidents and Injuries, Motorcycle Accidents, Trucking Accidents, Head Injury, Spinal Injury.

GARY KEITH, born Charlotte, North Carolina, September 8, 1962; admitted to bar, 1991, North Carolina. *Education:* St. Andrews Presbyterian College (B.A., 1985); University of South Carolina (J.D., 1991). *Member:* Mecklenburg County, North Carolina and American Bar Associations; North Carolina State Bar; North Carolina Academy of Trial Lawyers; South Carolina Academy of Trial Lawyers. ***PRACTICE AREAS:*** Personal Injury; Wrongful Death; Automobile Accidents and Injuries; Motorcycle Accidents; Head Injury; Spinal Injury.

KELLAM & PETTIT, P.A.

Established in 1998

2701 COLTSGATE ROAD, SUITE 300
CHARLOTTE, NORTH CAROLINA 28211
Telephone: 704-442-9500
Telecopier: 704-442-8595
URL: http://kellampettit.com
URL: http://www.lawyers.com/kellam&pettit

Corporation, Bankruptcy, Creditors Rights, Foreclosure, Collections, Commercial Law. State and Federal Trial Practice.

FIRM PROFILE: Kellam & Pettit, P.A., is a law firm specializing in the resolution of debtor/creditor problems. This includes representation of parties at all stages including initial work-out efforts, bankruptcy proceedings, civil litigation, collection actions and foreclosure proceedings. The firm's collective bankruptcy experience ranges from debtor counseling to creditor representation.

W. J. KELLAM, JR., born Greensboro, North Carolina, December 21, 1937; admitted to bar, 1963, North Carolina. *Education:* University of North Carolina (A.B., 1960; LL.B., 1963). Attorney, Law Department, Seaboard Coast Line Railroad Company, 1963-1968. *Member:* 26th Judicial District Bar; North Carolina Bar Association; North Carolina State Bar. ***PRACTICE AREAS:*** Banking; Foreclosure; Real Estate.

WILLIAM WALT PETTIT, born Charlotte, North Carolina, August 26, 1955; admitted to bar, 1980, Georgia and North Carolina. *Education:* North Carolina State University (B.A., with honors, in Business Management, 1977); Mercer University (J.D., 1980). Phi Delta Phi. Member: Order of the Barristers; Moot Court Board. *Member:* 26th Judicial District Bar; State Bar of Georgia; North Carolina State Bar; North Carolina and American (Member, Section on Corporation, Banking and Business Law) Bar Associations. ***PRACTICE AREAS:*** Business; Foreclosure; Bankruptcy; Collections; Creditors Rights.

MICHAEL BARRY STEIN, born Queens, New York, May 25, 1970; admitted to bar, 1995, North Carolina. *Education:* University of North Carolina (B.A., 1992); Wake Forest University (J.D., 1995). Phi Alpha Delta. *Member:* Mecklenburg County and North Carolina Bar Associations; North Carolina State Bar. ***PRACTICE AREAS:*** Bankruptcy; Foreclosure; Collections.

ASSOCIATES

MATTHEW THOR McKEE, born Shelby, North Carolina, February 26, 1967; admitted to bar, 2002, North Carolina. *Education:* Western Carolina University (B.S., 1989); Mercer University School of Law (J.D., 2001). Phi Delta Phi. Member: William Augustus Bootle Inn of Court; Environmental Law Society. *Member:* Mecklenburg County, North Carolina (Member, Bankruptcy Law Section) and American Bar Associations; American Bankruptcy Institute. ***PRACTICE AREAS:*** Bankruptcy; Foreclosures; Collections.

W. CHRIS PARNELL, born Charlotte, North Carolina, March 28, 1949; admitted to bar, 1975, North Carolina. *Education:* University of North Carolina at Chapel Hill (B.A., 1971); Cumberland School of Law (J.D., 1975). *Member:* Mecklenburg County and North Carolina Bar Associations. ***PRACTICE AREAS:*** Real Property; Commercial Real Estate; Residential Real Estate; Business Law. ***Email:*** cparnell@kellampettit.com

CHARLENE A. FRAVEL, born Plymouth, Pennsylvania, May 18, 1973; admitted to bar, 1998, Pennsylvania; 2004, South Carolina; 2005, North Carolina. *Education:* Susquehanna University (B.A., cum laude, Political Science, 1995); Widener University School of Law (J.D., 1998). Pi Gamma Mu (Vice President, 1994); Social Science Honor Society. Recipient: Faculty Award for Academics; Faculty Award for 2nd Best Brief in 1st year class; Certificate of Achievement in Legal Methods/Advocacy. *Member:* Snyder County, Mecklenburg County, Pennsylvania, (Member, Client and Community Relations Committee, 1999-2002; Zone Chair, Young Lawyers Division, 1999-2002; Chair, Website Subcommittee, 1999-2003) and North Carolina Bar Associations; Women's Bar Association of Snyder and Union Counties. ***PRACTICE AREAS:*** Residential Real Estate Closings; Commercial Real Estate Closings; Foreclosures; Evictions. ***Email:*** charlenef@kellampettit.com

REPRESENTATIVE CLIENTS: Park Meridian Bank; Eagle Industries, Inc.; Chase Manhattan Mortgage Co.; Glendale Federal Bank; First Charter National Bank; Branch Banking and Trust Company; Aerospace Corp.; G.E. Capitol Mortgage Services, Inc.; Northwest Mortgage Services, Inc.; Northwest Legal Services, P.A.; TransAmerica Financial Services; Cabarrus Bank of North Carolina; Central Carolina Bank and Trust Co.; SouthTrust Bank, N.A.
APPROVED ATTORNEYS FOR: Chicago Title Corp.; First Title Insurance Co.; American Title Co.
REFERENCES: Cabarrus Bank of North Carolina; First Charter National Bank.

KENNEDY COVINGTON LOBDELL & HICKMAN, L.L.P.

Established in 1957

HEARST TOWER
214 NORTH TRYON STREET, 47TH FLOOR
CHARLOTTE, NORTH CAROLINA 28202
Telephone: 704-331-7400
Fax: 704-331-7598
URL: http://www.kennedycovington.com

Raleigh, North Carolina Office: 434 Fayetteville Street Mall, 19th Floor, P.O. Box 1070, 27602-1070. Telephone: 919-743-7300. Fax: 919-743-7358.
Research Triangle Park, North Carolina Office: P.O. Box 14210, Research Triangle Park, 27709-4210, 2801 Slater Road, Suite 120, Morrisville, 27560. Telephone: 919-466-1190. Fax: 919-831-7040.
Columbia, South Carolina Office: NBSC Building, Suite 850, 1122 Lady Street, 29201. Telephone: 803-251-2300. Fax: 803-251-2315.
Rock Hill, South Carolina Office: 140 East Main Street, Suite 220, P.O. Box 11429, 29731-1429. Telephone: 803-329-7600. Fax: 803-329-7677.

Administrative Law, Alternative Dispute Resolution, Antitrust and Trade Regulation, Bankruptcy, Banks and Banking, Business Law, Commercial Law, Commercial Real Estate Development, Construction Law, Corporate Law, Debt and Equity Finance, Emerging Growth Companies, Employee Benefits, Employment Law, Entrepreneurial Business Law, Environmental Law, Family Law, Finance, Governmental, Health Care, Immigration and Naturalization, Intellectual Property, International Law, Labor and Employment, Land Sales, Land Use Regulation, Limited Liability Companies and Partnerships, Litigation, Medical Malpractice, Mergers, Acquisitions and Divestitures, Non-Profit and Charitable Organizations, Patents, Private Equity, Products Liability, Professional Liability, Public Utility Law, Real Estate Development, Real Estate Leasing, Real Estate Finance, Securities, Taxation, Technology Law, Trademarks, Trial Practice, Trusts and Estates, Utility Law, Venture Capital, Zoning, Planning and Land Use.

FIRM PROFILE: Kennedy Covington Lobdell & Hickman, L.L.P. is one of the largest full service law firms in the Carolinas, with offices in Charlotte, Columbia, Raleigh, Research Triangle Park and Rock Hill. Our lawyers bring a depth of experience and a knowledge of the law to bear in solving problems and leveraging opportunities for clients in varied industries such as banking, real estate, technology and manufacturing. At Kennedy Covington, we give more than a legal opinion; we provide a business perspective.

PARTNERS

FRANK H. KENNEDY (1893-1975)

HUGH L. LOBDELL (1908-1982)

WILLIAM T. COVINGTON, JR. (1907-2001)

JOHN D. ALLISON, admitted to bar, 1992, Georgia; 1993, District of Columbia; 1995, North Carolina. *Education:* Davidson College (B.A., cum laude, 1988); Emory University (J.D., with distinction, 1991). ***PRACTICE AREAS:*** Mergers and Acquisitions; Corporate Law; Business Law; International Contracts; International Joint Ventures; Debt and Equity Finance. ***Email:*** jallison@kennedycovington.com

STANFORD D. BAIRD (Resident, Raleigh, North Carolina Office)

DAVID L. BATTY, admitted to bar, 1991, Maryland (inactive); 1996, North Carolina. *Education:* George Washington University (B.A., cum laude, 1988); Boston College (J.D., cum laude, 1991). ***PRACTICE AREAS:*** Banking Law; Debt Finance; Business Law. ***Email:*** dbatty@kennedycovington.com

F. DANIEL BELL, III (Resident, Raleigh, North Carolina Office)

J. MICHAEL BOOE, admitted to bar, 1971, North Carolina. *Education:* Davidson College (B.A., 1967); University of North Carolina (J.D., 1971). ***PRACTICE AREAS:*** Bankruptcy; Out of Court Debt Restructuring; Pre-Bankruptcy Workouts; Debt Finance. ***Email:*** mbooe@kennedycovington.com

KEN R. BRAMLETT, JR., admitted to bar, 1984, North Carolina. *Education:* Wake Forest University (B.S., Philosophy, 1981); University of North Carolina (J.D., 1984). ***PRACTICE AREAS:*** Corporate Law; Mergers and Acquisitions; Securities; Private Equity; Mezzanine Finance. ***Email:*** kbramlett@kennedycovington.com

CURTIS C. BREWER, IV (Resident, Raleigh, North Carolina Office)

WILLIAM J. BRIAN (Raleigh and Research Triangle Park, North Carolina Offices)

JEFFERSON W. BROWN, admitted to bar, 1984, North Carolina. *Education:* University of North Carolina (B.S., 1981); Vanderbilt University (J.D., 1984). Phi Beta Kappa. ***PRACTICE AREAS:*** Real Estate Finance; Real Estate Development; Land Use Regulation; Zoning Law; Governmental Law. ***Email:*** jbrown@kennedycovington.com

ERIC L. BURK, admitted to bar, 1997, West Virginia; 1999, North Carolina. *Education:* Clemson University (B.S., 1991); West Virginia University College of Law (J.D., 1997). ***PRACTICE AREAS:*** Finance; Banks and Banking; Business Law. ***Email:*** eburk@kennedycovington.com

MARK R. BUSCH, admitted to bar, 1995, North Carolina. *Education:* University of California at Berkeley (B.A., with high distinction, 1992); Duke University (J.D., with honors, 1995). ***PRACTICE AREAS:*** Business Law; Corporate Law; Debt and Equity Finance; Mergers and Acquisitions; Securities; Venture Capital. ***Email:*** mbusch@kennedycovington.com

AMIE F. CARMACK (Resident, Raleigh, North Carolina Office)

JOHN H. CARMICHAEL, admitted to bar, 1993, North Carolina. *Education:* University of North Carolina (B.A., 1985; J.D., with honors, 1993). ***PRACTICE AREAS:*** Commercial Real Estate; Zoning, Planning and Land Use; Land Use Litigation. ***Email:*** jcarmichael@kennedycovington.com

(This Listing Continued)

KENNEDY COVINGTON LOBDELL & HICKMAN, L.L.P., Charlotte—Continued

BEVERLY A. CARROLL, admitted to bar, 1981, South Carolina; 2003, North Carolina. *Education:* Winthrop College (B.A., 1974); University of South Carolina (J.D., 1981). ***PRACTICE AREAS:*** Employment Law; Health Law; Civil Practice. ***Email:*** bcarroll@kennedycovington.com

KENT F. CHRISTISON (Resident, Raleigh, North Carolina Office)

G. LEE CORY, JR., admitted to bar, 1993, North Carolina. *Education:* University of North Carolina (B.A., with distinction, 1989); University of Virginia (J.D., 1993). ***PRACTICE AREAS:*** Commercial Real Estate Development; Real Estate Leasing; Shopping Center Development; Real Estate Finance. ***Email:*** lcory@kennedycovington.com

GEORGE C. COVINGTON, admitted to bar, 1984, North Carolina; 1986, South Carolina. *Education:* Davidson College (A.B., 1975); University of North Carolina (J.D., with honors, 1984). ***PRACTICE AREAS:*** Securities Litigation; Securities Fraud Class Actions; Shareholder Derivative Actions; Securities Arbitration. ***Email:*** gcovington@kennedycovington.com

DAVID SCOTT COWARD (Resident, Raleigh, North Carolina Office)

JOHN H. CULVER III, admitted to bar, 1985, Maryland; 1991, North Carolina. *Education:* University of Virginia (B.A., with high honors, 1981); University of Maryland (J.D., with honors, 1984). ***PRACTICE AREAS:*** Litigation; Federal Litigation; Lender Liability; Class Action Defense; Complex Litigation; Commercial Bankruptcy. ***Email:*** jculver@kennedycovington.com

CHARLES O. DUBOSE, admitted to bar, 1968, North Carolina. *Education:* Davidson College (A.B., 1965); University of North Carolina (J.D., 1968). (Co-Managing Partner). ***PRACTICE AREAS:*** Real Estate Acquisitions; Real Estate Development; Condominium Development; Common Interest Community Law; Planned Unit Development Law; Residential Real Estate Development. ***Email:*** bdubose@kennedycovington.com

JAMES E. EARLE, admitted to bar, 1991, North Carolina. *Education:* Davidson College (B.A., First Honor, magna cum laude, 1988); Stanford University (J.D., with distinction, 1991). ***PRACTICE AREAS:*** Employee Benefits; Executive Compensation. ***Email:*** jearle@kennedycovington.com

BRIAN P. EVANS, admitted to bar, 1975, North Carolina. *Education:* Davidson College (B.A., cum laude, 1972); University of North Carolina (J.D., 1975). ***PRACTICE AREAS:*** Real Estate Acquisitions; Real Estate Finance; Condominium Law. ***Email:*** bevans@kennedycovington.com

B. D. FARMER, III, admitted to bar, 1968, North Carolina. *Education:* Yale University (B.A., 1965); University of Virginia (LL.B., 1968). ***PRACTICE AREAS:*** Real Estate Development; Real Estate Leasing. ***Email:*** bfarmer@kennedycovington.com

WALTER D. FISHER, JR., admitted to bar, 1986, North Carolina; 1988, South Carolina. *Education:* Clemson University (B.A., summa cum laude, 1983); University of North Carolina (J.D., with high honors, 1986). ***PRACTICE AREAS:*** Real Estate Development; Real Estate Leasing; Real Estate Finance; Commercial Real Estate; Real Estate; Leases and Leasing. ***Email:*** wfisher@kennedycovington.com

DAVID A. FRANCHINA, admitted to bar, 1988, New York (inactive); 1989, District of Columbia (inactive); 1995, North Carolina. *Education:* Johns Hopkins University (B.A., with honors, 1984); Fordham University (J.D., cum laude, 1987). ***PRACTICE AREAS:*** Environmental Law; Environmental Compliance; Environmental Regulation; Environmental Permitting; Environmental Real Estate; Water Quality; Wetlands Protection; Wetlands Regulation. ***Email:*** dfranchina@kennedycovington.com

T. RICHARD GIOVANNELLI, admitted to bar, 1996, North Carolina. *Education:* University of Virginia (B.A., 1990); College of William and Mary, Marshall Wythe School of Law (J.D., 1996). ***PRACTICE AREAS:*** Debt and Equity Finance; Mergers and Acquisitions; Venture Capital; Corporate Law; Emerging Business Law; Business Law. ***Email:*** rgiovannelli@kennedycovington.com

GLEN B. HARDYMON, admitted to bar, 1963, North Carolina. *Education:* Duke University (A.B., 1960); University of North Carolina (LL.B., with high honors, 1963). ***PRACTICE AREAS:*** Commercial Real Estate Development; Commercial Real Estate Investment; Real Estate Joint Ventures; Real Estate Restructuring; Public-Private Partnerships; Art Law. ***Email:*** ghardymon@kennedycovington.com

WILLIAM N. HARRIS, admitted to bar, 1989, North Carolina. *Education:* University of North Carolina (B.A., with honors, 1984); University of Virginia (J.D., 1989). ***PRACTICE AREAS:*** Commercial Real Estate Development; Real Estate Finance; Shopping Center Development. ***Email:*** wharris@kennedycovington.com

MICHAEL S. HAWLEY, admitted to bar, 1980, Florida; 1983, North Carolina. *Education:* University of Florida (B.S.B.A., 1971; J.D., 1980; LL.M., in Taxation, 1981). ***PRACTICE AREAS:*** Business Law; Corporate Law; International Law; Health Law; Emerging Business Law. ***Email:*** mhawley@kennedycovington.com

J. PATRICK HAYDEN, admitted to bar, 1995, New York; 1998, North Carolina. *Education:* University of North Carolina (B.A., with honors, 1990); Columbia University (J.D., 1994). ***PRACTICE AREAS:*** Real Estate Finance; Securitization; Business Law. ***Email:*** phayden@kennedycovington.com

JAMES T. HEDRICK, JR., admitted to bar, 1994, North Carolina. *Education:* University of North Carolina (A.B., with highest honors and highest distinction, 1991); Duke University (J.D., 1994). ***PRACTICE AREAS:*** Business Law; Banking Law; Debtor and Creditor; Debt Finance; Secured Finance. ***Email:*** jhedrick@kennedycovington.com

SARA W. HIGGINS, admitted to bar, 1995, North Carolina. *Education:* Duke University (A.B., cum laude, 1990); University of North Carolina (J.D., with high honors, 1995). ***PRACTICE AREAS:*** Civil Litigation; Business Litigation; Employee Benefits Litigation; Securities Litigation; Appellate Practice. ***Email:*** shiggins@kennedycovington.com

JAMES H. HODGES, admitted to bar, 1982, South Carolina. *Education:* University of South Carolina (B.A., cum laude, 1979; J.D., 1982). Governor of South Carolina, 1998-2002. (Resident, Columbia, South Carolina Office). ***PRACTICE AREAS:*** Government Relations; Emerging Business; Venture Capital; International Law. ***Email:*** jhodges@kennedycovington.com

A. LEE HOGEWOOD III (Resident Raleigh, North Carolina Office)

CORY HOHNBAUM, admitted to bar, 1990, North Carolina. *Education:* Westminster College (B.A., cum laude, 1987); Vanderbilt University (J.D., 1990). ***PRACTICE AREAS:*** Litigation. ***Email:*** chohnbaum@kennedycovington.com

C. CORLEY HOLT, admitted to bar, 1990, North Carolina; 1991, District of Columbia. *Education:* Duke University (B.S., magna cum laude, 1986); Yale University (J.D., 1990). ***PRACTICE AREAS:*** Commercial Loans; Commercial Real Estate Finance; Debt Finance; Mortgage Banking and Finance; Secured Transactions; Uniform Commercial Code; Warehousing. ***Email:*** cholt@kennedycovington.com

WAYNE P. HUCKEL, admitted to bar, 1972, North Carolina. *Education:* Davidson College (A.B., 1969); New York University (J.D., 1972). ***PRACTICE AREAS:*** Commercial Litigation; Construction Law; Insurance Agents and Brokers Errors and Omissions; Agents and Brokers Liability; Real Estate; Brokers Malpractice Defense; Alternative Dispute Resolution. ***Email:*** whuckel@kennedycovington.com

SUSAN SERAD JACKSON, admitted to bar, 1997, North Carolina and South Carolina. *Education:* Clemson University (B.S., 1994); Wake Forest University (J.D., 1997). ***PRACTICE AREAS:*** Intellectual Property; Patents; Trademarks; Copyrights; Patent Licensing; Trademark Licensing; Software Licensing. ***Email:*** sjackson@kennedycovington.com

F. FINCHER JARRELL, admitted to bar, 1971, North Carolina. *Education:* University of North Carolina (A.B., 1967; J.D., with honors, 1971). ***PRACTICE AREAS:*** Products Liability Defense; Insurance Litigation. ***Email:*** fjarrell@kennedycovington.com

CLIFFORD R. JARRETT, admitted to bar, 1991, North Carolina. *Education:* Guilford College (A.B., with high honors, 1988); Washington & Lee University (J.D., cum laude, 1991). ***PRACTICE AREAS:*** Intellectual Property Litigation; Commercial Litigation. ***Email:*** cjarrett@kennedycovington.com

BRADLEY H. JOHNSON, admitted to bar, 1995, South Carolina; 1997, North Carolina. *Education:* Clemson University (B.S., 1992); University of South Carolina (J.D., 1995). ***PRACTICE AREAS:*** Debt Finance; Securitization; Business Law.

MARY BETH JOHNSTON (Resident, Research Triangle Park, North Carolina Office)

DAVID H. JONES, admitted to bar, 1980, North Carolina. *Education:* Austin Peay State University (B.S., summa cum laude, 1977); Wake Forest University (J.D., magna cum laude, 1980). ***PRACTICE AREAS:*** Real Estate Acquisitions; Real Estate Development; Real Estate Finance; Real Estate Investment; Real Estate Joint Ventures; Commercial Mortgages; Partnership Law; Limited Liability Company Law. ***Email:*** djones@kennedycovington.com

SEAN M. JONES, admitted to bar, 1990, New York; 1994, North Carolina. *Education:* University of Tennessee (B.A., with high honors, 1986; J.D., with honors, 1989). ***PRACTICE AREAS:*** Securities; Mergers and Acquisitions; Corporate Law; Business Law. ***Email:*** sjones@kennedycovington.com

WARREN P. KEAN, admitted to bar, 1985, Louisiana; 1989, New York; 1993, North Carolina. *Education:* Washington and Lee University (B.A., cum laude, 1981); Louisiana State University (J.D., 1985); New York University (LL.M., in Taxation, 1987); Georgetown University (LL.M., Securities Regulation, with distinction, 1992). ***PRACTICE AREAS:*** Limited Liability Companies; Partnership and Business Entities; Corporate Law; Mergers and Acquisitions; Taxation. ***Email:*** wkean@kennedycovington.com

JOSEPH B. C. KLUTTZ, admitted to bar, 1977, North Carolina. *Education:* Princeton University (B.A., cum laude, 1973); University of Virginia (J.D., 1977). ***PRACTICE AREAS:*** Debt Finance; Debt Restructuring; Financial Restructuring; Bankruptcy; Banking Law; Business Law. ***Email:*** jkluttz@kennedycovington.com

RAYMOND S. KOLOSKI, admitted to bar, 1995, New York; 1999, North Carolina. *Education:* Dickinson College Center for European Studies, Bologna, Italy, 1984-1985; Tulane University (B.A., International Relations, 1986); Case Western Reserve University (J.D., 1994). ***PRACTICE AREAS:*** Banking and Finance; Financial Restructuring. ***Email:*** rkoloski@kennedycovington.com

WILLIAM C. LIVINGSTON, admitted to bar, 1974, North Carolina. *Education:* University of North Carolina (A.B., 1970; J.D., with high honors, 1974). ***PRACTICE AREAS:*** Commercial Litigation; Labor and Employment; Employment Law. ***Email:*** blivingston@kennedycovington.com

FELICIA WASHINGTON MAUNEY, admitted to bar, 1990, North Carolina. *Education:* University of North Carolina, Chapel Hill (B.A., 1987); University of Virginia (J.D., 1990). ***PRACTICE AREAS:*** Employment Law; Immigration Law; Labor and Employment Law; Labor and Employment. ***Email:*** fmauney@kennedycovington.com

STEPHEN R. McCRAE, JR. (Resident, Rock Hill, South Carolina Office)

PETER McLEAN III, admitted to bar, 1981, North Carolina. *Education:* Dartmouth College (A.B., 1971); Wake Forest University (J.D., cum laude, 1981). ***PRACTICE AREAS:*** Commercial Real Estate Development; Real Estate Leasing; Commercial Real Estate Finance; Shopping Center Development; Commercial Real Estate Acquisitions; Commercial Real Estate Sales. ***Email:*** pmclean@kennedycovington.com

PATRICIA T. MEADOR (Resident, Research Triangle Park, North Carolina Office)

KIRAN H. MEHTA, admitted to bar, 1983, North Carolina. *Education:* Cornell University (A.B., magna cum laude, 1978); Harvard University (J.D., cum laude, 1981). ***PRACTICE AREAS:*** Business Litigation; Complex and Multi-District Litigation; Construction Law; Environmental Litigation; Zoning, Planning and Land Use Litigation; Real Estate Litigation; Toxic Torts. ***Email:*** kmehta@kennedycovington.com

ROY H. MICHAUX, JR., admitted to bar, 1965, North Carolina. *Education:* University of North Carolina (B.S., 1962; LL.B., 1965). ***PRACTICE AREAS:*** Civil Litigation; Construction Arbitration and Litigation; Condemnation; Environmental Law; Land Use Litigation; Real Estate Litigation. ***Email:*** rmichaux@kennedycovington.com

(This Listing Continued)

LEE WEST MOVIUS, admitted to bar, 1973, North Carolina. *Education:* Harvard University (A.B., cum laude, 1969); University of Chicago (M.A., 1970; J.D., 1973). ***PRACTICE AREAS:*** ERISA; Employee Stock Ownership Plans; Employee Compensation; Employee Benefits. ***Email:*** lmovius@kennedycovington.com

RAYMOND E. OWENS, JR., admitted to bar, 1978, North Carolina. *Education:* Davidson College; University of North Carolina (A.B., with highest honors, 1975; J.D., 1978). ***PRACTICE AREAS:*** Civil Litigation; Commercial Litigation; Products Liability; Criminal Litigation; Personal Injury; Insurance Litigation. ***Email:*** rowens@kennedycovington.com

BAILEY PATRICK, JR., admitted to bar, 1960, North Carolina. *Education:* University of North Carolina (B.S., 1957; J.D., with honors, 1960). ***PRACTICE AREAS:*** Corporate Law; Estate Planning; Zoning, Planning and Land Use; Government Relations. ***Email:*** bpatrick@kennedycovington.com

ALAN H. PETERSON (Resident, Raleigh, North Carolina Office)

E. ALLEN PRICHARD, admitted to bar, 1975, North Carolina. *Education:* University of North Carolina (B.A., 1971); Georgetown University (J.D., 1974). ***PRACTICE AREAS:*** Commercial Real Estate Development and Financing; Banking; Federal and State Land Sales Regulation. ***Email:*** aprichard@kennedycovington.com

EUGENE C. PRIDGEN, admitted to bar, 1978, North Carolina. *Education:* North Carolina State University (B.S., 1969); Wake Forest University (M.B.A., with distinction, 1975; J.D., magna cum laude, 1978). ***PRACTICE AREAS:*** Business Law; Mergers and Acquisitions; Corporate Law. ***Email:*** gpridgen@kennedycovington.com

J. NORFLEET PRUDEN III, admitted to bar, 1973, North Carolina. *Education:* University of North Carolina (A.B., 1970); University of Virginia (J.D., 1973). ***PRACTICE AREAS:*** Business Law; Corporate Law; Debt and Equity Finance; Securities; Mergers and Acquisitions. ***Email:*** npruden@kennedycovington.com

GARY S. QUALLS (Resident, Research Triangle Park, North Carolina Office)

LACY H. REAVES (Resident, Raleigh, North Carolina Office)

STEPHEN K. RHYNE, admitted to bar, 1977, North Carolina. *Education:* United States Military Academy (B.S., 1969); George Washington University (J.D., with high honors, 1977). ***PRACTICE AREAS:*** Business Law; Mergers and Acquisitions; Corporate Law; Private Equity; Mezzanine Finance. ***Email:*** srhyne@kennedycovington.com

ALICE CARMICHAEL RICHEY, admitted to bar, 1986, North Carolina. *Education:* Amherst College (1977-1979); University of North Carolina (B.A., with highest honors, 1982; J.D., with honors, 1986). ***PRACTICE AREAS:*** Litigation; Intellectual Property Infringement; Intellectual Property Litigation; Trademark Infringement; Unfair Competition; Copyright Litigation. ***Email:*** arichey@kennedycovington.com

MICHAEL E. ROBBE, admitted to bar, 1995, North Carolina. *Education:* Miami University (B.S., cum laude, 1992); Vanderbilt University (J.D., 1995). ***PRACTICE AREAS:*** Commercial Real Estate Development; Real Estate Leasing; Shopping Center Development. ***Email:*** mrobbe@kennedycovington.com

JOHN L. SARRATT (Resident, Raleigh, North Carolina Office)

KARL S. SAWYER, JR., admitted to bar, 1977, North Carolina. *Education:* North Carolina State University (B.S., in Textile Technology, with high honors, 1974); Wake Forest University (J.D., 1977). ***PRACTICE AREAS:*** Intellectual Property; Patents; Trademarks; Copyrights; Unfair Competition; Litigation; Business Law. ***Email:*** ksawyer@kennedycovington.com

WILLIAM G. SCOGGIN (Resident, Raleigh, North Carolina Office)

RALEIGH A. SHOEMAKER, admitted to bar, 1970, North Carolina. *Education:* Duke University (A.B., magna cum laude, 1967); University of North Carolina (J.D., with high honors, 1970). ***PRACTICE AREAS:*** Employee Benefits; Executive Compensation; Taxation; Estate Planning; Corporate Law. ***Email:*** rshoemaker@kennedycovington.com

RUSSELL F. SIZEMORE, admitted to bar, 1996, North Carolina. *Education:* Amherst College (A.B., summa cum laude, 1977); Yale Divinity School (M.A.R., 1980); Harvard University (A.M., 1983; Ph.D., with highest honors, 1987); Yale Law School (J.D., 1996). ***PRACTICE AREAS:*** Employment Law; Employment Litigation; Civil Litigation; Trial Practice; Personnel Policies; Employment Discrimination. ***Email:*** rsizemore@kennedycovington.com

A. ZACHARY SMITH III, admitted to bar, 1966, North Carolina. *Education:* Davidson College (A.B., 1963); University of Virginia (LL.B., 1966). ***PRACTICE AREAS:*** Securities; Mergers and Acquisitions; Nonprofit and Charitable Organizations; Art Law. ***Email:*** zsmith@kennedycovington.com

PAUL A. STEFFENS, admitted to bar, 1996, North Carolina. *Education:* Duke University (B.S.E., magna cum laude, 1990); University of North Carolina (J.D., with honors, 1996). ***PRACTICE AREAS:*** Corporate Law; Mergers and Acquisitions; Investment Partnerships; Technology Licensing. ***Email:*** psteffens@kennedycovington.com

RICHARD D. STEPHENS, admitted to bar, 1970, North Carolina. *Education:* University of North Carolina (A.B., 1967); Columbia University (J.D., 1970). ***PRACTICE AREAS:*** Family Law. ***Email:*** rstephens@kclh.com

KEVIN P. STICHTER, admitted to bar, 1993, Colorado; 1998, North Carolina. *Education:* Brown University (A.B., 1987); Vanderbilt University Law School (J.D. 1991). ***PRACTICE AREAS:*** Business Law; Mergers and Acquisitions; Debt and Equity Finance; Venture Capital; Securities; Corporate Law. ***Email:*** kstichter@kennedycovington.com

MICHAEL R. THORNTON (Resident, Raleigh, North Carolina Office)

MAYNARD E. TIPPS, admitted to bar, 1971, Tennessee, 1972, North Carolina. *Education:* University of Tennessee (B.S., 1968); Vanderbilt University (J.D., 1971). ***PRACTICE AREAS:*** Real Estate Development; Real Estate Acquisitions; Real Estate Finance; Real Estate Leasing; Mineral Leasing. ***Email:*** mtipps@kennedycovington.com

MICHAEL A. TOBIN, admitted to bar, 1997, North Carolina. *Education:* United States Naval Academy (B.S., with distinction, 1987); Georgetown University (M.A., 1988); Wake Forest University (J.D., magna cum laude, valedictorian, 1997). ***PRACTICE AREAS:*** Intellectual Property; Patents; Trademarks; Copyrights; Internet Law; Electronic Commerce; Computer Law. ***Email:*** mtobin@kennedycovington.com

(This Listing Continued)

MARY TURK-MEENA, admitted to bar, 1979, Pennsylvania; 1986, New York; 1989, Ohio and North Carolina. *Education:* Baldwin-Wallace College Conservatory of Music (B.M., with honors, 1974); Temple University (J.D., 1979). ***PRACTICE AREAS:*** Employee Benefits. ***Email:*** mturkmeena@kennedycovington.com

CAROL A. JONES VAN BUREN, admitted to bar, 1991, North Carolina. *Education:* Wake Forest University (B.S., summa cum laude, Physics, 1988; J.D., 1991). ***PRACTICE AREAS:*** Environmental Law; Environmental Compliance; Environmental Regulation; Real Estate Development; Administrative Law. ***Email:*** cvanburen@kennedycovington.com

MICHEL P. VANESSE, admitted to bar, 1995, Illinois (Not admitted in North Carolina). *Education:* Universite Libre de Bruxelles, Brussels, Belgium (J.D., with high honors, 1988; LL.M., Economic Law, with high honors, 1989); University of Chicago (LL.M., 1991; J.D., 1995). ***PRACTICE AREAS:*** Employee Benefits; ERISA. ***Email:*** mvanesse@kennedycovington.com

DEAN A. WARREN, admitted to bar, 1985, North Carolina. *Education:* University of North Carolina (B.S., 1981; J.D., 1985). ***PRACTICE AREAS:*** Business Law; Debt and Equity Finance; Financial Restructuring; Banking Law. ***Email:*** dwarren@kennedycovington.com

AMY PRITCHARD WILLIAMS, admitted to bar, 1992, North Carolina. *Education:* University of North Carolina (B.A., with distinction, 1989); University of Virginia (J.D., 1992). ***PRACTICE AREAS:*** Civil Litigation; Bankruptcy. ***Email:*** awilliams@kennedycovington.com

J. MICHAEL WILSON, admitted to bar, 1990, North Carolina. *Education:* University of North Carolina at Chapel Hill (B.S.B.A., 1985; J.D., 1990). ***PRACTICE AREAS:*** Taxation; Mergers and Acquisitions; Joint Ventures; Business Law. ***Email:*** mwilson@kennedycovington.com

ROBERT B. WOMBLE (Resident, Raleigh, North Carolina Office)

SCOTT YARBROUGH, admitted to bar, 1996, New York (Not admitted in North Carolina). *Education:* University of Texas at Austin (B.A., with university high honors, 1992); New York University (J.D., 1995). ***PRACTICE AREAS:*** Banks and Banking. ***Email:*** syarbrough@kennedycovington.com

OF COUNSEL

HENRY W. FLINT, admitted to bar, 1980, North Carolina. *Education:* University of Virginia (B.A., cum laude, 1976; M.B.A., 1980; J.D., 1980).

J. DONNELL LASSITER, admitted to bar, 1963, North Carolina. *Education:* University of North Carolina (A.B., 1959; J.D., with honors, 1963). ***PRACTICE AREAS:*** Commercial Real Estate; Debt Finance; Banking Law; Business Law. ***Email:*** dlassiter@kennedycovington.com

JOHN M. MURCHISON, JR., admitted to bar, 1971, New York; 1973, North Carolina. *Education:* Davidson College (A.B., 1961); University of North Carolina (J.D., with honors, 1970). ***PRACTICE AREAS:*** Antitrust; Trade Regulation; Commercial Law; International Law; Business Law. ***Email:*** jmurchison@kennedycovington.com

FRANCIS M. PINCKNEY, admitted to bar, 1965, North Carolina. *Education:* University of South Carolina (B.S. in Mechanical Engineering, 1957); George Washington University (J.D., with honors, 1963). ***PRACTICE AREAS:*** Intellectual Property; Litigation; Business Law. ***Email:*** fpinckney@kennedycovington.com

DALBERT U. SHEFTE, admitted to bar, 1952, Illinois; 1960, North Carolina. *Education:* Northwestern University (B.S. in Mechanical Engineering, 1949; J.D., 1952). ***PRACTICE AREAS:*** Intellectual Property; Litigation; Business Law. ***Email:*** dshefte@kennedycovington.com

CHARLES V. TOMPKINS, JR., admitted to bar, 1961, North Carolina. *Education:* University of North Carolina (A.B., 1958); Harvard University (LL.B., 1961). ***PRACTICE AREAS:*** Mediation; Commercial Litigation; Products Liability Defense; Medical Malpractice Claims; Law Enforcement Officers Defense. ***Email:*** ctompkins@kennedycovington.com

CLARENCE W. WALKER, admitted to bar, 1955, North Carolina; 1956, New York. *Education:* Duke University (A.B., 1953; LL.B., 1955). ***PRACTICE AREAS:*** Business Law; Corporate Law; Utility Law; Securities Law; Alternative Dispute Resolution. ***Email:*** cwalker@kennedycovington.com

SPECIAL COUNSEL

JACQUELINE C. BARES, admitted to bar, 1990, Illinois; 2001, District of Columbia; 2005, North Carolina. *Education:* Marquette University (B.A., 1970); Northwestern University (J.D., cum laude, 1990). Order of the Coif. *Member:* American Bar Association; Bar Association of Circuit Court of Appeals of the District of Columbia. ***PRACTICE AREAS:*** Corporate; International Law. ***Email:*** jbares@kennedycovington.com

LAWRENCE E. BEHNING, admitted to bar, 1992, New York and New Jersey; 1997, North Carolina. *Education:* Susquehanna University (B.S., 1975); Seton Hall University (M.B.A., 1982; J.D., 1991). ***PRACTICE AREAS:*** Debt Restructuring; Debt Finance; Financial Restructuring; Workouts; Business Law. ***Email:*** lbehning@kennedycovington.com

ERIC M. BRAUN (Resident, Research Triangle Park and Raleigh, North Carolina Offices)

JO ANN BRIGHTON, admitted to bar, 1989, Pennsylvania and New Jersey; 1993, New Hampshire; 2004, North Carolina. *Education:* University of Delaware (B.S., 1986); New York Law School (J.D., magna cum laude, 1989). Editor, New York Law School Law Review. Extensive publications for ABI Journal, Bankruptcy Law Review, Commercial Law Journal and others. *Member:* American Bankruptcy Institute; International Womens

(This Listing Continued)

KENNEDY COVINGTON LOBDELL & HICKMAN, L.L.P., Charlotte—Continued

Insolvency and Restructuring Association. ***PRACTICE AREAS:*** Debt Finance; Debt Restructuring; Financial Restructuring; Bankruptcy; Banking Law. ***Email:*** jbrighton@kennedycovington.com

RICHARD K. BROWN, admitted to bar, 1987, Connecticut; 1996, New York; 2002, North Carolina. *Education:* University of Vermont (B.S., 1978); Quinnipiac University/University of Bridgeport (J.D., magna cum laude, 1987). ***PRACTICE AREAS:*** Debt Finance; Loan Restructuring; Loan Workouts; Asset Based Lending; Factoring; Syndication. ***Email:*** rbrown@kennedycovington.com

PATRICK L. BYKER (Raleigh and Research Triangle Park, North Carolina Offices)

LESLEE K. DAUGHERTY, admitted to bar, 1988, North Carolina. *Education:* University of North Carolina (B.S., 1979; M.S., 1981; J.D., with honors, 1988). ***PRACTICE AREAS:*** Estate Planning; Estates. ***Email:*** ldaugherty@kennedycovington.com

BRETT T. HANNA (Resident, Raleigh, North Carolina Office)

THOMAS I. LYON, admitted to bar, 1998, North Carolina. *Education:* University of North Carolina (B.S.B.A., with distinction, 1995); University of Kentucky (J.D., cum laude, 1998). Beta Gamma Sigma; Order of the Coif. Associate Editor, Kentucky Law Journal. (Resident, Raleigh, North Carolina Office). ***PRACTICE AREAS:*** Corporate Law; Entrepreneurial Business; Mergers and Acquisitions; Private Equity; Venture Capital.

JOHN E. (JACK) MARKHAM, JR. (Raleigh and Research Triangle Park, North Carolina Offices)

JEANNE A. PEARSON, admitted to bar, 1996, South Carolina and North Carolina. *Education:* Clemson University (B.A., History, 1993); University of Tulsa (J.D., 1996). ***PRACTICE AREAS:*** Environmental; Real Estate Development; Real Estate Finance. ***Email:*** jpearson@kennedycovington.com

CAROLYN GILMER SHAW, admitted to bar, 1977, North Carolina. *Education:* Mary Baldwin College (B.A., 1960); Johns Hopkins University (M.L.A., 1968); University of North Carolina (J.D., 1977). ***PRACTICE AREAS:*** Estate Planning; Estates; Corporate Law. ***Email:*** cshaw@kennedycovington.com

NEAL B. WOLGIN (Resident, Raleigh, North Carolina Office)

RETIRED

William F. Drew, Jr. ***Henry C. Lomax***
Marcus T. Hickman ***Edgar Love III***
Ross J. Smyth

ASSOCIATES

ANN M. ANDERSON (Resident, Raleigh, North Carolina Office)

KATHERINE R. ANNAS, admitted to bar, 2003, North Carolina. *Education:* Wofford College (B.A., summa cum laude, 2000); University of North Carolina (J.D., with honors, 2003). ***PRACTICE AREAS:*** Real Estate Development; Real Estate Finance. ***Email:*** kannas@kennedycovington.com

ABRAHAM M. ASHTON, admitted to bar, 2005, North Carolina. *Education:* Shepherd College (B.S., magna cum laude, 1999); West Virginia University (J.D., 2005). Executive Publications Editor, West Virginia Law Review, 2003-2005. ***PRACTICE AREAS:*** Real Estate; Real Estate Development. ***Email:*** aashton@kennedycovington.com

MYRA T. ASKINS-SULLIVAN, admitted to bar, 1994, North Carolina. *Education:* University of Tennessee at Knoxville (B.S., with highest honors, Industrial Engineer, 1985); Wake Forest University (J.D., 1994). ***PRACTICE AREAS:*** Intellectual Property; Software Licensing; Copyrights; Trademarks. ***Email:*** maskins@kennedycovington.com

EDWIN L. BARNES, JR., admitted to bar, 2000, South Carolina; 2001, North Carolina. *Education:* Washington & Lee University (B.S., magna cum laude, 1986); University of South Carolina (J.D., cum laude, 2000). ***PRACTICE AREAS:*** Business Law; Corporate Law; Debt and Equity Finance; Mergers and Acquisitions; Commercial Contracts. ***Email:*** ebarnes@kennedycovington.com

JASON L. BARRON (Resident, Raleigh, North Carolina Office)

PETER S. BARWICK, admitted to bar, 2001, North Carolina. *Education:* Amherst College (B.A., magna cum laude, 1992); Yale Divinity School (M.A.R., cum laude, 1995); Duke University (J.D., 2001). ***PRACTICE AREAS:*** Securitization; Debt Finance; Business Law. ***Email:*** pbarwick@kennedycovington.com

GINA LOUISE BERTOLINI (Resident, Research Triangle Park, North Carolina Office)

WHITNEY G. BOUKNIGHT, admitted to bar, 2004, North Carolina. *Education:* Furman University (B.A., History and Political Science, magna cum laude, 2001); Washington & Lee University (J.D., 2004). Staff Writer, Washington and Lee Law Review. ***PRACTICE AREAS:*** Corporate. ***Email:*** wbouknight@kennedycovington.com

CAROLINE BROWN, admitted to bar, 2005, North Carolina. *Education:* Clemson University (B.S., magna cum laude, 2001); University of South Carolina (J.D., 2005; M.B.A., 2005). ***PRACTICE AREAS:*** Corporate Law. ***Email:*** cbrown@kennedycovington.com

AMELIA Y. BURNETTE, admitted to bar, 2005, North Carolina. *Education:* University of North Carolina, Asheville (B.A., cum laude, 1999); University of North Carolina (J.D., 2005). ***PRACTICE AREAS:*** Litigation; Civil Litigation. ***Email:*** aburnette@kennedycovington.com

JOHN H. CAPITANO, admitted to bar, 1995, North Carolina. *Education:* Davidson College (B.A., 1991); Campbell University (J.D., magna cum laude, 1995). ***PRACTICE AREAS:*** Real Estate Litigation; Creditors Rights; Civil Litigation. ***Email:*** jcapitano@kennedycovington.com

(This Listing Continued)

ROBERT ALLEN CLARY, II, admitted to bar, 2005, North Carolina. *Education:* Appalachian State University (B.A 2000); University of Miami (J.D., magna cum laude, 2003); New York University (LL.M., in Taxation, 2004). ***PRACTICE AREAS:*** Limited Liability Companies and Partnerships; Taxation.

BRIAN C. COX, admitted to bar, 1999, North Carolina. *Education:* Duke University (A.B., cum laude, 1991; M.A.T., 1992); University of Virginia School of Law (J.D., 1998). ***PRACTICE AREAS:*** Securitization; Business Law. ***Email:*** bcox@kennedycovington.com

MARIE GIBBS COX, admitted to bar, 1996, Texas; 1999, North Carolina. *Education:* University of North Carolina (B.A., with distinction and highest honors, 1992); University of Virginia (J.D., 1996). ***PRACTICE AREAS:*** Commercial Litigation. ***Email:*** mcox@kennedycovington.com

COLLEEN M. CROWLEY (Resident, Research Triangle Park, North Carolina Office)

ABIGAIL LOFTUS DeBLASIS, admitted to bar, 2004, North Carolina. *Education:* Miami University (B.S., Business, magna cum laude, 2001); Wake Forest University (J.D., 2004). Order of the Coif. Editor in Chief, Wake Forest Law Review, 2003-2004. ***PRACTICE AREAS:*** Banking and Finance. ***Email:*** adeblasis@kennedycovington.com

CHRISTINE DeMAERE, admitted to bar, 2005, North Carolina. *Education:* North Carolina State University (B.A., summa cum laude, 2002); Florida State University (J.D., 2005). ***PRACTICE AREAS:*** Corporate Law. ***Email:*** cdemaere@kennedycovington.com

MICHAEL J. DENNY, admitted to bar, 2002, North Carolina. *Education:* Clemson University (B.S., Accounting, 1992); Indiana University School of Law - Bloomington (J.D., cum laude, 2002). ***PRACTICE AREAS:*** Corporate Law; Securities; Mergers, Acquisitions and Divestitures; Debt and Equity Finance; Business Law. ***Email:*** mdenny@kennedycovington.com

BRETT A. DURHAM, admitted to bar, 2000, North Carolina. *Education:* University of Richmond (B.S., magna cum laude, 1996); University of Virginia (J.D., 2000). ***PRACTICE AREAS:*** Business Law; Corporate Law; Mergers and Acquisitions; Debt and Equity Finance; Venture Capital. ***Email:*** bdurham@kennedycovington.com

JAMES EWING (Resident, Raleigh, North Carolina Office)

FREDERICK W. FAIRCLOTH, IV, admitted to bar, 2003, North Carolina and South Carolina. *Education:* Clemson University (B.S., Accounting, cum laude, 2000); University of South Carolina (J.D., cum laude, 2003); University of Florida (LL.M., Taxation, 2004). Member, South Carolina Law Review. Recipient, Arthur B. Custy Tax Award. ***PRACTICE AREAS:*** Investment Funds; Taxation. ***Email:*** ffaircloth@kennedycovington.com

BRIAN FORK (Resident, Raleigh, North Carolina Office)

STEPHANIE FULCHER, admitted to bar, 2005, North Carolina. *Education:* University of North Carolina (B.A., Journalism, 1995); Wake Forest University (J.D., 2005). Member, Wake Forest University Law Review. ***PRACTICE AREAS:*** Financial Law; Banks and Banking. ***Email:*** sfulcher@kennedycovington.com

JOHN GARDNER, admitted to bar, 2004, North Carolina. *Education:* University of North Carolina (B.A., 2000); Wake Forest University (J.D., 2004). ***PRACTICE AREAS:*** Bankruptcy; Workouts. ***Email:*** jgardner@kennedycovington.com

JON GOLDBERG, admitted to bar, 2005, North Carolina. *Education:* University of North Carolina (B.A., 1995; J.D., 2005). ***PRACTICE AREAS:*** Real Estate; Real Estate Development. ***Email:*** jgoldberg@kennedycovington.com

MARC GUSTAFSON, admitted to bar, 2002, Georgia (Not admitted in North Carolina). *Education:* University of North Carolina (A.B, 1997); Indiana University (J.D., 2001). ***PRACTICE AREAS:*** Litigation. ***Email:*** mgustafson@kennedycovington.com

ANDREW M. HABENICHT, admitted to bar, 2004, North Carolina. *Education:* Hampden-Sydney College (B.A., English, cum laude, 1999); George Mason University (J.D., cum laude, 2004). Omicron Delta Kappa. Senior Articles Editor, George Mason Law Review, 2003-2004. ***PRACTICE AREAS:*** Employment Law; Litigation. ***Email:*** ahabenicht@kennedycovington.com

GRAYSON S. HALE (Resident, Raleigh, North Carolina Office)

DAVID R. HIGGINS, admitted to bar, 2004, North Carolina. *Education:* North Carolina State University (B.S., Biochemistry, summa cum laude, 1999; B.A., Chemistry, summa cum laude, 1999); Wake Forest University (J.D., 2004). Phi Beta Kappa. Executive Editor, Wake Forest Law Review, 2003-2004. ***PRACTICE AREAS:*** Intellectual Property. ***Email:*** dhiggins@kennedycovington.com

R. GATES HINDS, admitted to bar, 2002, North Carolina. *Education:* Duke University (B.A., 1993); University of Alabama School of Law (J.D., 2002). ***PRACTICE AREAS:*** Corporate Law. ***Email:*** ghinds@kennedycovington.com

BRIAN D. HOLOFCHAK, admitted to bar, 2002, North Carolina. *Education:* University of North Carolina (B.A., 1996); North Carolina State University (M.A., 1999); University of Mississippi School of Law (J.D., magna cum laude, 2002). ***PRACTICE AREAS:*** Real Estate Development; Real Estate Leasing. ***Email:*** bholofchak@kennedycovington.com

SETON BLAKE HUNT, admitted to bar, 1999, Oregon; 2001, California; 2005, North Carolina. *Education:* University of California at Berkeley (B.A., 1995); University of California at Los Angeles (J.D., 1999). Recipient, American Jurisprudence Award. ***PRACTICE AREAS:*** Real Estate Litigation; Litigation. ***Email:*** shunt@kennedycovington.com

WILLIAM O. HUTCHINSON, admitted to bar, 2004, Alabama and North Carolina. *Education:* Washington & Lee University (B.S., Management, 1996; J.D., 1999). ***PRACTICE AREAS:*** Financial Services Litigation. ***Email:*** whutchinson@kennedycovington.com

DAVID N. JONSON (Member, Raleigh, North Carolina Office)

TED KAPLAN, admitted to bar, 2005, North Carolina. *Education:* Davidson College (B.A., 1998); University of North Carolina (J.D., 2005; M.P.A., Government, 2005). ***PRACTICE AREAS:*** Real Estate Litigation. ***Email:*** tkaplan@kennedycovington.com

(This Listing Continued)

MICHAEL F. KING (Resident, Raleigh, North Carolina Office)

CHRISTOPHER C. LAM, admitted to bar, 2002, North Carolina. *Education:* Duke University (B.A., cum laude, 1998); University of North Carolina School of Law (J.D., 2002). ***PRACTICE AREAS:*** Commercial Litigation. ***Email:*** clam@kennedycovington.com

DAVID R. LAPP, admitted to bar, 2000, North Carolina. *Education:* James Madison University (B.S., summa cum laude, 1997); College of William & Mary (J.D., 2000). ***PRACTICE AREAS:*** Business Law; Syndicated Loans; Securitization; Corporate Law; Mergers and Acquisitions; Securities. ***Email:*** dlapp@kennedycovington.com

ALLYSON BRYANT LAVINS, admitted to bar, 2005, North Carolina. *Education:* Dartmouth College (B.A., magna cum laude, 2002); Boston College (J.D., 2005). ***PRACTICE AREAS:*** Employment Benefits; ERISA. ***Email:*** alavins@kennedycovington.com

RENÉ J. LEBLANC-ALLMAN, admitted to bar, 2000, North Carolina. *Education:* University of South Carolina (B.A., magna cum laude, 1995; J.D., magna cum laude, 1999). ***PRACTICE AREAS:*** Debt Finance; Banking Law; Corporate Law; Business Law. ***Email:*** rleblanc-allman@kennedycovington.com

ANNE S. LEGGETT, born Baltimore, Maryland, September 18, 1956; admitted to bar, 1983, New York; 2004, North Carolina. *Education:* Duke University (B.A., History, summa cum laude, 1978); Columbia University (J.D., 1982). ***PRACTICE AREAS:*** Banking; Finance. ***Email:*** aleggett@kennedycovington.com

TRACEY MITCHELL LEROY, admitted to bar, 2001, North Carolina. *Education:* Beloit College (B.A., 1997); University of South Carolina (M.I.B.S., 2001; J.D., 2001). ***PRACTICE AREAS:*** Business Law; Corporate Law; Emerging Business Law; International. ***Email:*** tleroy@kennedycovington.com

WILLIAM B. MACURDA, admitted to bar, 1997, North Carolina. *Education:* Wheaton College (B.A., 1991); Case-Western Reserve University (J.D., 1997). ***PRACTICE AREAS:*** Securitization; Debt Finance; Real Estate Finance; Business Law. ***Email:*** bmacurda@kennedycovington.com

DONALD E. MARTIN, admitted to bar, 1998, Kentucky; 2001, North Carolina. *Education:* Transylvania University (B.A., summa cum laude, 1993); University of Kentucky (J.D., cum laude, 1998). ***PRACTICE AREAS:*** Commercial Real Estate; Real Estate Development; Real Estate Leasing; Corporate Law; Business Law. ***Email:*** dmartin@kennedycovington.com

STEPHANIE E. MASCIA, admitted to bar, 1999, Virginia and North Carolina; 2002, Massachusetts. *Education:* The College of William and Mary (B.A., Psychology, 1994); Wake Forest University (J.D., magna cum laude, 1998). Order of the Coif. Member, Moot Court, 1996-1998. Golden Key National Honor Society. Member, Wake Forest Law Review. ***PRACTICE AREAS:*** Employment Law; Litigation. ***Email:*** smascia@kennedycovington.com

CHRISTOPHER D. MCCOY, admitted to bar, 2001, North Carolina. *Education:* University of North Carolina at Chapel Hill (A.B., 1994); University of Richmond (J.D., 2001). ***PRACTICE AREAS:*** Real Estate Development; Real Estate Finance; Government Relations. ***Email:*** cmccoy@kennedycovington.com

KATHERINE STUKES MCKENZIE (Resident, Raleigh, North Carolina Office)

SHAWN A. MCMILLAN (Resident, Research Triangle Park, North Carolina Office)

CAROLYN FIXEL MERRITT (Resident, Research Triangle Park, North Carolina Office)

CHARLOTTE MITCHELL (Resident, Raleigh, North Carolina Office)

JARED D. MOBLEY, admitted to bar, 1998, South Carolina; 2000, North Carolina. *Education:* University of South Carolina (B.S., 1995; J.D., 1998); New York University (LL.M. in Taxation, 1999). ***PRACTICE AREAS:*** Taxation; Business Law. ***Email:*** jmobley@kennedycovington.com

CANDICE M. MURPHY-FARMER (Resident, Research Triangle Park, North Carolina Office)

ERIKA OLSON, admitted to bar, 2005, North Carolina. *Education:* Boston College (B.A., 2000); Wake Forest University (J.D., 2005). ***PRACTICE AREAS:*** Litigation. ***Email:*** eolson@kennedycovington.com

DANIEL J. PALMIERI (Resident, Raleigh, North Carolina Office)

JONATHAN B. POLKING, admitted to bar, 2005, North Carolina. *Education:* University of Notre Dame (B.B.A., Finance and Business Economics & Computer Applications, 1999; J.D., 2004). ***PRACTICE AREAS:*** Structured Finance. ***Email:*** jpolking@kennedycovington.com

SAMUEL T. REAVES, admitted to bar, 1998, Alabama; 2000, North Carolina. *Education:* University of Alabama (B.A., magna cum laude, 1994; J.D., magna cum laude, 1998). ***PRACTICE AREAS:*** Real Estate Litigation; Land Use and Zoning Litigation; Construction Litigation; Business and Corporate Litigation. ***Email:*** sreaves@kennedycovington.com

RUSSELL M. REED, born Starkville, Mississippi; admitted to bar, 1995, North Carolina. *Education:* University of Mississippi (B.A., Accountancy, cum laude, 1991); Wake Forest University (J.D., 1995). Member, Queens College Estate Planners Day Steering Committee. *Member:* Mecklenburg County (Chairman, Estate Planning Section) and North Carolina (Member: Estate Planning and Fiduciary Law Section; CLE Committee, Estate Section; Business Law Curriculum Committee) Bar Associations; North Carolina State Bar. ***PRACTICE AREAS:*** Estate Planning; Estate Administration; Business Succession Planning; Charitable Planning; Tax Planning. ***Email:*** rreed@kennedycovington.com

ALLYN BURCHFIELD RHODES, admitted to bar, 2003, North Carolina. *Education:* Mississippi State University (B.S. 1998); Tulane Law School (J.D. 2003). ***PRACTICE AREAS:*** Intellectual Property. ***Email:*** arhodes@kennedycovington.com

(This Listing Continued)

PATRICK L. RIDINGER, admitted to bar, 1998, North Carolina and South Carolina. *Education:* Wofford College (B.S., magna cum laude, 1995); University of South Carolina (J.D., cum laude, 1998). ***PRACTICE AREAS:*** Commercial Real Estate Development; Real Estate Leasing. ***Email:*** pridinger@kennedycovington.com

THOMAS D. RIVERS, admitted to bar, 2005, North Carolina. *Education:* Rhodes College (B.A., cum laude, 2001); Vanderbilt University (J.D., 2005). ***PRACTICE AREAS:*** Real Estate; Real Estate Development. ***Email:*** trivers@kennedycovington.com

KIMBERLY RAYMER ROBERTSON, admitted to bar, 1988, North Carolina. *Education:* University of North Carolina (B.S., 1984; J.D., 1988). ***PRACTICE AREAS:*** Family Law. ***Email:*** krobertson@kennedycovington.com

ALLISON G. RUNGE, admitted to bar, 2001, North Carolina. *Education:* Davidson College (B.A., 1997); University of South Carolina (J.D., 2001). ***PRACTICE AREAS:*** Family Law; Litigation. ***Email:*** arunge@kennedycovington.com

CECILIA E. RUTHERFORD, admitted to bar, 2000, New York (Not admitted in North Carolina). *Education:* Carleton College (B.A., 1993); Boston University (J.D., 2000). ***PRACTICE AREAS:*** Structured Finance. ***Email:*** crutherford@kennedycovington.com

MATTHEW G. ST. AMAND, admitted to bar, 2000, Florida and Connecticut (Not admitted in North Carolina). *Education:* Mary Washington College (B.A., 1995); University of North Carolina (M.R.P., 1997; J.D., 2000). ***PRACTICE AREAS:*** Real Estate Development; Real Estate Finance. ***Email:*** mstamand@kennedycovington.com

CRAIGIE D. SANDERS (Raleigh and Research Triangle Park, North Carolina Offices)

ADAM SMITH, admitted to bar, 2005, North Carolina. *Education:* Brigham Young University (B.A., 2001); Washington and Lee University (J.D., 2005). ***PRACTICE AREAS:*** Finance; Structured Finance. ***Email:*** asmith@kennedycovington.com

VIRGINIA LEGGETT STEVENSON, admitted to bar, 1996, New Jersey; 1999, North Carolina and District of Columbia. *Education:* College of William and Mary (B.A., History, with honors, and Philosophy, 1993); Washington and Lee University (J.D., 1996); New York University (LL.M. in Taxation, 1998). Managing Editor, Environmental Law Digest. ***PRACTICE AREAS:*** Structured Finance. ***Email:*** vstevenson@kennedycovington.com

MARK V. THIGPEN, admitted to bar, 1999, North Carolina. *Education:* Hampden-Sydney College (B.S., 1993); University of South Carolina (J.D., 1999). ***PRACTICE AREAS:*** Real Estate Development; Real Estate Leasing. ***Email:*** mthigpen@kennedycovington.com

MICHAEL F. TOMLINSON, admitted to bar, 2000, New York; 2005, North Carolina. *Education:* Cornell University (B.A., Economics, 1996); University of Pennsylvania (J.D., 1999). ***PRACTICE AREAS:*** Real Estate Development; Real Estate Leasing. ***Email:*** mtomlinson@kennedycovington.com

J. GARRETT VAN OSDELL, admitted to bar, 1999, California; 2004, North Carolina. *Education:* University of Florida (B.A., with honors, 1993); University of South Carolina (J.D., cum laude, 1998); University of South Carolina, Moore School of Business (M.I.B.S., 1999). ***PRACTICE AREAS:*** Corporate Law; Mergers, Acquisitions and Divestitures; Private Equity; Mezzanine Finance. ***Email:*** gvanosdell@kennedycovington.com

RUBEN M. VELIZ, admitted to bar, 2001, North Carolina. *Education:* Georgetown University (B.A., 1998); New York University (J.D., 2001). ***PRACTICE AREAS:*** Business Law; Debt Finance. ***Email:*** rveliz@kennedycovington.com

DAVID E. WAGNER (Resident, Raleigh, North Carolina Office)

ALEXANDER F. WATSON, admitted to bar, 2001, North Carolina. *Education:* Clemson University (B.S., 1998); University of North Carolina (J.D., 2001). ***PRACTICE AREAS:*** Business Law; Corporate Law; Mergers and Acquisitions. ***Email:*** awatson@kennedycovington.com

MARGARET ROSE WESTBROOK (Resident, Raleigh, North Carolina Office)

SUZANNE CRESS WILLIAMS, admitted to bar, 2003, North Carolina. *Education:* University of North Carolina (B.A., 1999); University of Richmond School of Law (J.D., 2003). ***PRACTICE AREAS:*** Business Law; Debt Finance. ***Email:*** swilliams@kennedycovington.com

EVAN N. WOLKOFSKY, admitted to bar, 1998, North Carolina. *Education:* Pennsylvania State University (B.S., 1995); Wake Forest University (J.D., 1998). ***PRACTICE AREAS:*** Debt and Equity Finance; Banking Law; Business Law; Commercial Law; Corporate Law; Debtor and Creditor; Contracts. ***Email:*** ewolkofsky@kennedycovington.com

JULIANNE G. WOOD, admitted to bar, 2004, North Carolina. *Education:* North Carolina State University (B.A., Mass Communication, summa cum laude, 1999); University of North Carolina (J.D., with honors, 2004). North Carolina Journal of International Law & Commercial Regulation, Note & Comment Editor, Phi Beta Kappa. ***PRACTICE AREAS:*** Real Estate Development; Real Estate Leasing. ***Email:*** jwood@kennedycovington.com

JAMES D. WRIGHT, admitted to bar, 1997, Georgia; 2000, North Carolina. *Education:* North Carolina State University (B.S., Electrical Engineering, cum laude, 1988); University of North Carolina School of Law (J.D., 1997). ***PRACTICE AREAS:*** Intellectual Property; Patents; Trademarks; Internet Law; Copyrights; Litigation; Business Law. ***Email:*** jwright@kennedycovington.com

JAMES R. WYCHE, admitted to bar, 2003, North Carolina. *Education:* Clemson University (B.S., magna cum laude, 2000); Duke University School of Law (J.D., cum laude, 2003). ***PRACTICE AREAS:*** Corporate Law; Securities; Mergers, Acquisitions and Divestitures; Debt and Equity Finance; Business Law. ***Email:*** jwyche@kennedycovington.com

C. ALLEN YORK (Resident, Raleigh, North Carolina Office)

All Attorneys are Members of the North Carolina and American Bar Associations with the exception of Stephen R. McCrae, Jr., who is a Member of the South Carolina Bar Association.

(This Listing Continued)

KENNEDY COVINGTON LOBDELL & HICKMAN, L.L.P., Charlotte—Continued

REPRESENTATIVE CLIENTS: Academy Funds; American Asset Corporation; American Tower Corporation; Arvida Mid-Atlantic Homes, Inc.; Bank of America Corporation and Subsidiaries; Beacon Industrial Group; Blue Point Capital Partners; Cape Fear Valley Health System; Carolinas Healthcare System; Carousel Capital Partners; Charlotte Pipe and Foundry Company; CIT Group, Inc., The; City of Charlotte; Clariant Corporation; Coca-Cola Bottling Co. Consolidated; Collett & Associates; Comporium Communications; Corning Cable Systems LLC; Crescent Resources, LLC; Cresset Capital Partners; Crosland, Inc.; CSX World Terminals LLC; Duke Energy Corporation and Subsidiaries; Duke/Fluor Daniel ; EnPro Industries, Inc.; Essent Healthcare ; Fluor Corporation; Framatome ANP, Inc.; Glenayre Technologies, Inc.; Hickory Springs Manufacturing Company; Laird Group, PLC, The; Lance, Inc.; LaSalle Bank National Association; Lehman Brothers; LendingTree, Inc. ; Lincoln Harris LLC; MCI ; McRae Industries, Inc.; Microsoft Corporation; Miller Orthopaedic Clinic; Mills Corporation, The; National Housing Development Corporation; North Carolina State University; Novozymes; Oakwood Homes Corporation; Paramount's Carowinds; Pfizer, Inc.; Piedmont Natural Gas Company, Inc.; Porvair plc and Subsidiaries; Principal Financial Group/ Principal Real Estate Investors; Salomon Smith Barney Inc.; Sealed Air Corporation; Selee Corporation; Setra of North America, Inc.; Shurgard/Morningstar Storage Centers, LLC; Simpson Performance Products, Inc.; Soliant LLC; Spectrum Properties; Springs Company and Subsidiaries, The; St. Paul Fire & Marine Insurance Co., The; Summit Properties, Inc.; SVI America Corporation; Third Wave Technologies, Inc.; Trammell Crow Company; UBS PaineWebber Inc.; Wachovia Corporation and Subsidiaries; Wake Forest University Health Sciences; Wells Fargo Bank Minnesota, National Association; ZF Meritor LLC.

KILPATRICK STOCKTON LLP

SUITE 2500, 214 NORTH TRYON STREET
CHARLOTTE, NORTH CAROLINA 28202
Telephone: 704-338-5000
Facsimile: 704-338-5125
Email: info@KilpatrickStockton.com
URL: http://www.KilpatrickStockton.com

Atlanta, Georgia Office: Suite 2800, 1100 Peachtree Street. Telephone: 404-815-6500. Facsimile: 404-815-6555. Telex: 54-2307.
Augusta, Georgia Office: 699 Broad Street, Suite 1400, 30903-2043. Telephone: 706-724-2622. Facsimile: 706-722-0219.
London, England Office: 39th Floor, One Canada Square, London E145 NZ. Telephone: 44 (0)20 7154 6000. Facsimile: 44 (0)20 7154 6100.
New York, New York Office: 805 Third Avenue, 20th Floor, 10022. Telephone: 212-912-3527.
Raleigh, North Carolina Office: Suite 400, 3737 Glenwood Avenue, 27612. Telephone: 919-420-1700. Facsimile: 919-420-1800.
Stockholm, Sweden Office: Box 5421, SE-114 84. Telephone: 46-8-505-646-00. Facsimile: 46-8-505-646-99.
Washington, D.C. Office: Suite 900, 607 14th Street, N.W., 20005-2018. Telephone: 202-508-5800. Facsimile: 202-508-5858.
Winston-Salem, North Carolina Office: 1001 West Fourth Street, 27101-2400. Telephone: 336-607-7300. Facsimile: 336-607-7500.

Civil Trial and Appellate Practice in all State and Federal Courts, Federal State and Local Taxation, Probate, Trust and Estate Planning, Real Estate, Environmental, Corporate, Corporate Reorganization, Securities, Banking Commercial, Antitrust, Labor, Employment, Administrative, Bankruptcy, Construction, Healthcare, Intellectual Property, Professional Malpractice, Products Liability and Negligence Law, Domestic Law and Equitable Distribution, Employee Benefits and Executive Compensation, Entrepreneurial Development, Franchising, Insurance Defense, Sports and Entertainment, State Agency and Lobbying Practice.

FIRM PROFILE: Kilpatrick Stockton LLP is a full-service international law firm with more than 470 attorneys in nine offices across the globe: Atlanta and Augusta, GA; Charlotte, Raleigh and Winston-Salem, NC; New York, NY; Washington, DC; London, England; and Stockholm, Sweden. Kilpatrick Stockton's delivery of innovative business solutions provides results-oriented counsel for corporations, from the challenging demands of financial transactions and securities to the disciplines of intellectual property management. Collaboration among Kilpatrick Stockton's corporate, tax, employment and employee benefit attorneys provides knowledgeable and proactive guidance for companies at every stage of the business life cycle.

MEMBERS OF FIRM

JOHN T. ALLRED, admitted to bar, 1959, North Carolina. *Education:* University of North Carolina (B.S., 1951; J.D., with honors, 1959). (Resident). ***PRACTICE AREAS:*** Litigation; Commercial Litigation. ***Email:*** JAllred@KilpatrickStockton.com

SUSAN HAGER COOPER, admitted to bar, 1993, North Carolina. *Education:* University of North Carolina at Chapel Hill (B.A., Political Science, 1990; J.D., with honors, 1993). ***PRACTICE AREAS:*** Environmental Law; Litigation. ***Email:*** SCooper@KilpatrickStockton.com

DEBORAH L. FLETCHER, admitted to bar, 1982, Virginia; 1993, North Carolina. *Education:* Virginia Commonwealth University (B.A., 1979); University of Richmond (J.D., 1982). Associate Editor, University of Richmond Law Review. Author, "Bankruptcy - A Survival Guide for Lenders"; "Partnerships, Chapter 11 Theory and Practice"; "Executory Contracts, Norton Bankruptcy Law and Practice". *Member:* Virginia State Bar (Member, Board of Governors, 1990-1998; Director, National, 1994-1998, President, Carolinas Chapter, 1994-1998 and Director, Carolinas Chapter, 1994—, Executive Council, Section of Business Law, Bankruptcy Section); Turnaround Management Association; American Bankruptcy Institute. ***PRACTICE AREAS:*** Bankruptcy Litigation; Creditor's Rights; Commercial Law. ***Email:*** DeFletcher@KilpatrickStockton.com

G. SCOTT HUMPHREY, admitted to bar, 1989, North Carolina; 1990, South Carolina; U.S. Court of Appeals, Fourth Circuit; U.S. District Court, Eastern Western and Middle Districts of North Carolina; U.S.District Court, District of South Carolina. *Education:* University of North Carolina at Chapel Hill (B.A., 1986); Wake Forest University (J.D., 1989). ***PRACTICE AREAS:*** Labor and Employment.

(This Listing Continued)

E. LYNWOOD MALLARD, admitted to bar, 1965, North Carolina. *Education:* Davidson College (A.B., 1962); University of North Carolina (J.D., 1965). (Resident). ***PRACTICE AREAS:*** Business Transactions; Mergers and Acquisitions. ***Email:*** EMallard@KilpatrickStockton.com

JONATHAN J. NUGENT, admitted to bar, 1996, North Carolina. *Education:* University College, Dublin (B.C.L., with honors, 1989); Honorable Society of Kings Inn (B.L., with honors, 1991); University of North Carolina (J.D., 1996). ***PRACTICE AREAS:*** Real Estate; Real Estate Finance; Immigration; International Trade. ***Email:*** JNugent@KilpatrickStockton.com

MARK C. PRYBYLSKI, admitted to bar, 1994, New York; 1996, North Carolina. *Education:* St. Lawrence University (B.A., 1989); University of Virginia (J.D., 1993). ***PRACTICE AREAS:*** Corporate; Mergers and Acquisitions. ***Email:*** MPrybylski@KilpatrickStockton.com

JOHN NICHOLAS SUHR, JR., admitted to bar, 1992, Virginia; 1993, District of Columbia; 1996, North Carolina. *Education:* University of Virginia (B.A., 1988); American University, Washington College of Law (J.D., magna cum laude, 1992). ***PRACTICE AREAS:*** Commercial Real Estate; Secured Lending; Loans; Commercial Leasing; Mortgage Backed Securities. ***Email:*** JSuhr@KilpatrickStockton.com

DAVID B. WHELPLEY, JR., admitted to bar, 1989, Georgia and North Carolina. *Education:* Clemson University (B.S., cum laude, 1986); Emory University (J.D., with distinction, 1989). (Resident). ***PRACTICE AREAS:*** Corporate; Mergers; Acquisitions; Finance. ***Email:*** DWhelpley@KilpatrickStockton.com

NOELLE E. WOOTEN, admitted to bar, 1992, North Carolina. *Education:* Virginia Polytechnic Institute and State University (B.A. in Chemistry, magna cum laude, 1988); University of Virginia (J.D., 1992). (Resident). ***PRACTICE AREAS:*** Environmental; Litigation. ***Email:*** NWooten@KilpatrickStockton.com

ELIZABETH G. WREN, admitted to bar, 1980, North Carolina and U.S. District Court, Western District of North Carolina. *Education:* Emory University (B.A., 1975); University of North Carolina (M.S.L.S., 1976; J.D., with honors, 1980). (Resident). ***PRACTICE AREAS:*** Securities Regulation Law; Corporate Law. ***Email:*** BWren@KilpatrickStockton.com

RESIDENT COUNSEL

MARION A. COWELL, JR., admitted to bar, 1964, North Carolina. *Education:* University of North Carolina (B.S., 1958; LL. B., 1964). ***PRACTICE AREAS:*** Corporate; Corporate Governance; Banking Matters. ***Email:*** MCowell@KilpatrickStockton.com

J. KEITH JONES, admitted to bar, 1997, North Carolina and South Carolina. *Education:* Queens College (B.A., 1993); Wake Forest University (J.D., 1997). *Member:* North Carolina Bar Association; South Carolina Bar.

RESIDENT ASSOCIATES

VIRGINIA L. BAILEY, admitted to bar, 2003, North Carolina. *Education:* University of the South (B.A. in Art History, cum laude, 1998); University of South Carolina (M.A. in Art History, 2001); Wake Forest University (J.D., 2003). ***LANGUAGES:*** German. ***PRACTICE AREAS:*** Capital Markets. ***Email:*** GBailey@KilpatrickStockton.com

AYANNA BARROW, admitted to bar, 2002, New York; 2005, North Carolina. *Education:* Duke University (A.B., 1994); Georgetown University Law Center (J.D., 2001). ***PRACTICE AREAS:*** Mergers and Acquisitions. ***Email:*** ABarrow@KilpatrickStockton.com

NICOLE BROVET CANTU, admitted to bar, 2000, North Carolina. *Education:* University of Arizona (B.A., 1995); University of Michigan (J.D., 2000). ***PRACTICE AREAS:*** Commercial Real Estate; Finance. ***Email:*** NCantu@KilpatrickStockton.com

DAVID L. CHEATWOOD, admitted to bar, 2004, North Carolina. *Education:* University of North Carolina at Chapel Hill (B.S., 2001; J.D., 2004). ***PRACTICE AREAS:*** Corporate Law.

MATTHEW W. FINNISS, admitted to bar, 2001, North Carolina and U.S. District Court, Western District of North Carolina. *Education:* University of Rochester (B.A., cum laude, 1998); Wake Forest University (J.D., 2001). ***LANGUAGES:*** French.

D. SHANE GUNTER, admitted to bar, 2000, Delaware (Not admitted in North Carolina). *Education:* Gardner-Webb University (B.S., magna cum laude, 1996); The Dickinson School of Law of the Pennsylvania State University (J.D., 1999).

SARAH R. HAMILTON, admitted to bar, 2004, Florida (Not admitted in North Carolina). *Education:* Florida State University (B.S., Multi National Business Marketing, cum laude, 2000; M.B.A.; J.D., 2003).

JILL KLEMENTS, admitted to bar, 2002, New York; 2005, North Carolina. *Education:* University of Maryland, College Park (B.A., 1998); George Washington University (J.D., 2001). ***PRACTICE AREAS:*** Real Estate Finance; Finance; Corporate. ***Email:*** JKlements@KilpatrickStockton.com

PAUL J. McNAMARA, admitted to bar, 2003, North Carolina. *Education:* University of North Carolina (B.A., Business Administration, 2000); Wake Forest University School of Law (J.D., 2003). ***PRACTICE AREAS:*** Real Estate.

JOHN W. OAKES, admitted to bar, 2000, North Carolina. *Education:* University of North Carolina, Asheville (B.A., 1996); Michigan State University College of Law (J.D., 2000). ***PRACTICE AREAS:*** Real Estate; Wills; Trust Law; Corporate Law.

SETH E. STRICKLAND, (admission pending). *Education:* Duke University (B.S., B.A., 2002); University of North Carolina School of Law (J.D., with honors, 2005). ***PRACTICE AREAS:*** Commercial Real Estate; Finance.

JAMES M. TUCKER, admitted to bar, 1999, North Carolina. *Education:* University of Florida (B.A., Political Science, with highest honors, 1996); University of Iowa (J.D., with high honors, 1999). ***PRACTICE AREAS:*** Commercial Real Estate Finance; Secured Lending; Real Estate Development. ***Email:*** JTucker@KilpatrickStockton.com

(For complete biographical data on all personnel, see Professional Biographies at Atlanta and Augusta, Georgia; Washington, D.C.; Raleigh and Winston Salem, North Carolina; Stockholm, Sweden and London, England).

THE KING LAW FIRM PLLC

CHARLOTTE, NORTH CAROLINA

(See Huntersville)

Bankruptcy, Domestic, Family, Wills, Trusts, Criminal.

KLEIN & FREEMAN, PLLC

4521 SHARON ROAD, SUITE 150
P.O. BOX 221648
CHARLOTTE, NORTH CAROLINA 28222-1648
Telephone: 704-442-0660
Facsimile: 704-364-2295
URL: http://www.kleinfreeman.com

General Civil Trial Practice in all State and Federal Courts, Professional Liability and Personal Injury Law, Commercial Litigation, Products Liability, Wrongful Death, Head Injury.

JAMES P. CREWS (1933-1999)

PARTNERS

PAUL I. KLEIN, born Newark, New Jersey, September 30, 1948; admitted to bar, 1975, New York; 1985, New Jersey; 1992, North Carolina. *Education:* Rutgers University (A.B., 1970); St. John's University (J.D., 1974). *Member:* North Carolina (Member, Sections on: Litigation, Health Care), New York State (Member, Section on: Insurance, Negligence and Compensation Law), New Jersey State and American (Member, Sections on: Health Law and Litigation) Bar Associations; North Carolina State Bar; North Carolina Society of Health Care Attorneys; North Carolina Association of Defense Attorneys; Association of Trial Lawyers of America; North Carolina Academy of Trial Lawyers. ***PRACTICE AREAS:*** Professional Liability; Wrongful Death; Head Injury; Federal and State Civil Litigation. ***Email:*** paulklein@kleinfreeman.com

KATHERINE FREEMAN, born Chicago, Illinois, May 24, 1959; admitted to bar, 1985, Indiana; 1995, Arizona; 2000, North Carolina. *Education:* University of Iowa (B.A., 1982); Valparaiso University (J.D., 1985). Merit Scholar and Criminal Practice Honors, Valparaiso University. Pro bono appellate advocate for North Carolina Guardian ad Litem. *Member:* North Carolina State Bar; North Carolina Bar Association; State Bar of Arizona; Association of Trial Lawyers of America. ***PRACTICE AREAS:*** Civil Litigation; Professional Liability; Wrongful Death; Medical Malpractice; Products Liability. ***Email:*** katefreeman@kleinfreeman.com

ASSOCIATE

MINDY B. NEWMAN, admitted to bar, 2003, North Carolina and U.S. District Court, Middle and Western Districts of North Carolina. *Education:* Rutgers University (B.S., 1991); Campbell University School of Law (J.D., 2002). *Member:* Mecklenburg County Bar Association; North Carolina State Bar; North Carolina Academy of Trial Lawyers. ***PRACTICE AREAS:*** Personal Injury; Medical Malpractice. ***Email:*** mindynewman@kleinfreeman.com

KNOX BROTHERTON KNOX & GODFREY

817 E. TRADE STREET
CHARLOTTE, NORTH CAROLINA 28230
Telephone: 704-372-1360
Fax: 704-372-7402
Email: eknox@knoxlawcenter.com
URL: http://www.knoxlawcenter.com

Cornelius, North Carolina Office: 104 Torrence Commons. Telephone: 704-892-0199.

General Trial Practice including Criminal, Civil, Personal Injury, Medical Malpractice, Worker Compensation, Corporate and Criminal Litigation, Condemnation, Construction Law, Domestic and Traffic Offenses.

MEMBERS OF FIRM

H. EDWARD KNOX, born Davidson, North Carolina, January 22, 1937; admitted to bar, 1963, North Carolina, U.S. District Court, Western District of North Carolina and U.S. Supreme Court; 1981, U.S. Court of Appeals, Fourth Circuit. *Education:* University of North Carolina State College (B.S., 1960); Wake Forest University School of Law (J.D., 1963). Phi Alpha Delta. Babcock Scholar. President, North Carolina State Student Body, Wake Forest Law Review, 1960. Recipient: Outstanding Alumnus, Wake Forest University, 1982; Outstanding Alumnus N.C. State, 1970; Distinguished Service Award Mecklenburg County, 1968; Outstanding Young Man of America, 1969. President, Student Bar Association, Wake Forest Law School, 1962. Member, North Carolina General Assembly, 1971-1974. Chairman, North Carolina Advisory Budget Commission, 1977-1981. Mayor, City of Charlotte, 1979-1983. *Member:* North Carolina and American Bar Associations; 26th Judicial District Bar; North Carolina Academy of Trial Lawyers. (Board Certified Civil Trial Advocacy Specialist by the National Board of Trial Advocacy). ***PRACTICE AREAS:*** Personal Injury; Automobile Accidents; Wrongful Death; Workers Compensation; Medical Malpractice; Legal Malpractice; Litigation. ***Email:*** eknox@knoxlawcenter.com

ALLEN C. BROTHERTON, born Gastonia, North Carolina, April 30, 1960; admitted to bar, 1985, North Carolina, U.S. District Court, Eastern, Middle and Western Districts of North Carolina and U.S. Court of Appeals, Fourth Circuit. *Education:* University of North Carolina (B.A., Political Science, 1982; J.D., 1985). Phi Eta Sigma Honor Society. Morehead Scholar. *Member:* 26th Judicial District, North Carolina and American Bar Associations; North Carolina Academy of Trial Lawyers; Mecklenburg County Criminal Defense Lawyers Association. ***PRACTICE AREAS:*** Personal Injury; Automobile Accidents; Criminal Law; Traffic Violations; Theft; Federal Law; State Government Law; Driving While Intoxicated; Litigation. ***Email:*** abrotherton@knoxlawcenter.com

(This Listing Continued)

FRANCES S. KNOX, born Cabarrus, North Carolina, August 12, 1946; admitted to bar, 1991, North Carolina; 1992, U.S. District Court, Western, Middle and Eastern Districts of North Carolina; 1996, U.S. Supreme Court. *Education:* University of North Carolina-Charlotte (B.A., summa cum laude, 1979); Wake Forest Law School (J.D., 1991). Recipient, American Jurisprudence Award, Trial Practice and Torts. *Member:* Mecklenburg County and American Bar Associations; North Carolina State Bar; North Carolina Academy of Trial Lawyers (Member, Torts Section). ***PRACTICE AREAS:*** Personal Injury; Medical Malpractice; Automobile Accidents and Injuries; Wrongful Death; Nursing Home Negligence; Workers Compensation.

LISA G. GODFREY, born Baltimore, Maryland, July 1, 1956; admitted to bar, 1981, Illinois and U.S. Claims Court; 1982, North Carolina; U.S. District Court, Western and Middle Districts of North Carolina and U.S. Court of Appeals, Fourth Circuit. *Education:* University of Maryland (B.S., cum laude, with honors, 1977); Catholic University of America Columbus School of Law (J.D., cum laude, 1980). Law Clerk, U.S. Court of Claims, 1980-1981. *Member:* Mecklenburg County Bar Association; North Carolina State Bar; North Carolina Academy of Trial Lawyers. ***PRACTICE AREAS:*** Construction Litigation; Employment Law; Business Litigation; Corporate Law; Personal Injury; Medical Malpractice; Insurance Law. ***Email:*** lgodfrey@knoxlawcenter.com

PETER E. McARDLE, born Kingston, New York, 1969; admitted to bar, 1995, North Carolina and U.S. District Court, Western District of North Carolina. *Education:* University of North Carolina, Chapel Hill (B.A., Political Science, 1991); Campbell University Norman Adrian Wiggins School of Law (J.D., 1995). Member, Order of the Barristers. Member, Prince Evidence National Moot Court Team, 1995. *Member:* Mecklenburg County (Member, Family Law Section) and North Carolina Bar Associations; North Carolina Academy of Trial Lawyers. ***PRACTICE AREAS:*** Family Law; Separation Agreements; Equitable Distribution; Child Custody; Domestic Violence; Traffic Violations; Driving While Intoxicated; Civil Litigation. ***Email:*** pmcardle@knoxlawcenter.com

KARA F. McIVOR, born Lexington, Kentucky, May 22, 1971; admitted to bar, 1998, North Carolina; 2000, U.S. District Court, Western and Middle Districts of North Carolina. *Education:* Vanderbilt University (B.A., cum laude, 1993); Washington & Lee University (J.D., 1997). Finalist, Regional Negotiations Competition. Morton C. Johnson Scholar. Published Work: Medical Entitlement and Liens on Tort Recoveries, NCATL, Oct., 2002. Adjunct Professor, Paralegal Program, Workers Compensation Central Piedmont Community College. *Member:* American Bar Association. ***PRACTICE AREAS:*** Workers Compensation; Civil Litigation; Personal Injury. ***Email:*** kmcivor@knowlawcenter.com

CHARLES ASHLEY LAMM, born Charlotte, North Carolina, October 1, 1972; admitted to bar, 2002, North Carolina. *Education:* North Carolina State University (B.S., 1995); Campbell University Norman Adrian Wiggins School of Law (J.D., 2002). Director of Youth Ministries, Benson Memorial United Methodist Church. *Member:* Mecklenburg County Bar Association; North Carolina State Bar; North Carolina Academy of Trial Lawyers. ***PRACTICE AREAS:*** Estate Administration; Family Law; Divorce; Child Custody; Civil Litigation.

REPRESENTATIVE CLIENTS: Beck Mercedes; Century 21 of the Carolinas; Magla Products; United States Tire Disposal.

SANDRA L. KNOX, P.C.

CHARLOTTE, NORTH CAROLINA

(See Cornelius)

Commercial and Residential Real Estate, Condominium Law, Wills, Probate, Estate Planning, Trust, Small Business, Partnership.

ALAN R. KRUSCH, P.A.

5950 FAIRVIEW ROAD, SUITE 808
CHARLOTTE, NORTH CAROLINA 28210
Telephone: 704-556-0707
Fax: 704-553-7824
Email: kruschlaw@earthlink.net
URL: http://www.akruschlaw.com

Family Law, Domestic Relations, Divorce, Child Custody, Child Support, Equitable Distribution, Alimony, Post Separation Support.

FIRM PROFILE: Mr. Krusch is a Board Certified Specialist in Family Law by the North Carolina State Board of Legal Specialization.

ALAN R. KRUSCH, born Newark, New Jersey, April 17, 1952; admitted to bar, 1977, North Carolina. *Education:* Rutgers University (B.A., in Sociology, 1974); University of Miami (J.D., 1977). Phi Alpha Delta. Certified Superior Court Mediator. *Member:* North Carolina and American Bar Associations; North Carolina State Bar. (Board Certified Specialist in Family Law, North Carolina State Board of Legal Specialization). ***PRACTICE AREAS:*** Family Law; Collaborative Family Law; -. ***Email:*** alan.krusch@kruschlaw.com

LEIGH BALLENGER SELLERS, born Spartanburg, South Carolina, December 28, 1963; admitted to bar, 1990, South Carolina; 1993, U.S. District Court, District of South Carolina; 1996, North Carolina; 2004, U.S. District Court, Middle District of North Carolina. *Education:* Vanderbilt University (B.A., 1986); University of South Carolina (J.D., 1990); Ann Arbor Center for Mediation, Ann Arbor, Michigan (Domestic Mediation Certification). Classes/seminars taught at Southern and North Carolina Continuing Legal Education seminars; Legal Research, Midlands Technical College, West Columbia, South Carolina. Formerly, Attorney, South Carolina Supreme Court. Member: Junior League of Charlotte; Sardis Presbyterian Church. *Member:* Mecklenburg County, North Carolina and American Bar Associations; South Carolina Bar. ***PRACTICE AREAS:*** Family Law; Domestic Relations; Collaborative Family Law; Mediation. ***Email:*** Leigh.Sellers@kruschlaw.com

COREY A. LAWRENCE, P.A.

CAMERON BROWN BUILDING
301 SOUTH MCDOWELL STREET, SUITE 305
CHARLOTTE, NORTH CAROLINA 28204
Telephone: 704-342-1444
Fax: 704-372-4477
Email: lawrence4law@juno.com
URL: http://www.lawyers.com/coreylawrence

Criminal Law, Federal and State, Traffic Law, DWI, Drug Crimes, Felonies, Sexual Assault, Family Law, Personal Injury.

COREY A. LAWRENCE, born Queens, New York, November 27, 1968; admitted to bar, 1997, North Carolina. *Education:* Howard University (B.B.A., 1990); Emory University (J.D., 1995). Assistant Public Defender, Mecklenburg County, 1997-2000. *Member:* Mecklenburg County Bar Association (Member, Section: Criminal Law); North Carolina State Bar; North Carolina Academy of Trial Lawyers. ***PRACTICE AREAS:*** Criminal Law; Family Law; Wills; Estate Planning. ***Email:*** lawrence4law@juno.com

CINDY PAULEY LEONE

Established in 1982
SUITE 1106 CAMERON BROWN BUILDING
301 SOUTH MCDOWELL STREET
P.O. BOX 34546
CHARLOTTE, NORTH CAROLINA 28204
Telephone: 704-332-5297
Fax: 704-372-5001
URL: http://www.cynthiapauleyleone.com

Practice limited to Family/Domestic Law. Equitable Distribution, Divorce, Child Custody, Child Support, Alimony and Separation Agreements.

FIRM PROFILE: Ms. Leone is certified as a specialist in Family Law by the North Carolina State Bar Board of Legal Specialization. She has been certified since 1989.

CINDY PAULEY LEONE, born Charleston, West Virginia, March 31, 1952; admitted to bar, 1980, North Carolina. *Education:* Duke University (B.A., cum laude, 1974); Wake Forest University (J.D., 1980). Recipient, American Jurisprudence Award in Property Publication. Notes and Comments Editor, Wake Forest Law Review, 1979-1980. Chairman, Mecklenburg County Family Law Section, 1993-1996. Co-Chair, Mecklenburg County Family Law Section, 2001-2004. *Member:* North Carolina and American Bar Associations (Member, Family Law Section). (Board Certified Specialist in Family Law, North Carolina State Board of Legal Specialization)

REFERENCE: Bank of Granite.

MATTHEW J. LESTER, PLLC

6100 FAIRVIEW ROAD, SUITE 1200
CHARLOTTE, NORTH CAROLINA 28210
Telephone: 704-556-1101
Fax: 704-556-1044
Email: m_j_lester@hotmail.com
URL: http://www.mjlesterlaw.com

Residential Real Estate, Commercial Real Estate, Mortgages, Trusts and Estates, Estate Planning, Wills, Probate, Business Law, Corporate Law, Limited Liability Companies, Contracts.

FIRM PROFILE: Mr. Lester is Licensed in North Carolina and South Carolina.

MATTHEW J. LESTER, born Toledo, Ohio, April 9, 1973; admitted to bar, 2000, North Carolina; 2001, South Carolina. *Education:* University of North Carolina at Chapel Hill (B.S.B.A., 1997); University of South Carolina (J.D., 2000). Member, University of South Carolina Environmental Law Journal. *Member:* Mecklenburg County Bar Association; North Carolina State Bar; South Carolina Bar.

ERIC D. LEVINE

SUITE 602 CAMERON-BROWN BUILDING
301 SOUTH MCDOWELL STREET
CHARLOTTE, NORTH CAROLINA 28204
Telephone: 704-372-2800
FAX: 704-372-6337
Email: ericlevine@cs.com
URL: http://www.lawyers.com/ericdlevine

Civil Trial Practice, Personal Injury, Family, Domestic, Child Custody, Real Estate, Corporations, Business, Landlord Tenant Law.

ERIC D. LEVINE, born Charlotte, North Carolina, September 19, 1957; admitted to bar, 1983, Illinois and U.S. District Court, Northern District of Illinois; 1986, North Carolina; 1995, U.S. District Court, Western District of North Carolina. *Education:* University of Illinois (B.A., 1979); University of Tulsa (J.D., 1983). Phi Alpha Delta. *Member:* Mecklenburg County and American Bar Associations; North Carolina State Bar. ***PRACTICE AREAS:*** Litigation; Real Estate-Residential Law; Real Estate-Commercial Law; Family Law; Corporations; Business Law; Landlord and Tenant Law.

LEWIS & ROBERTS, P.L.L.C.

128 SOUTH TRYON STREET, SUITE 1100
CHARLOTTE, NORTH CAROLINA 28202-5012
Telephone: 704-347-8990
Facsimile: 704-347-8929
URL: http://www.lewis-roberts.com

Raleigh Office: 1305 Navaho Drive, Suite 400. Telephone: 919-981-0191. Facsimile: 919-981-0199.

Workers' Compensation Law, Commercial Litigation, Construction Law, Surety Law, Civil Trial Practice.

GARY VANCE MAUNEY, born Tampa, Florida, May 14, 1965; admitted to bar, 1995, North Carolina. *Education:* North Carolina State University (B.A., Business Management; B.A., Economics, 1988); American University, Washington College of Law (J.D., 1995). Paul J. Sedgewick Scholar, American University, Washington College of Law. Law Clerk to the Honorable: Jack Cozort and Donald L. Smith, North Carolina Court of Appeals, 1995-1997. *Member:* North Carolina (Newsletter Committee Chairperson for the Litigation Section, 2003-2004; Chair, Disaster Legal Services Committee, 1997-1998) and American Bar (Member, Sections on: Business Law, Litigation, Tort and Insurance Law) Associations; Mecklenburg and American Trial Lawyers Association (Member, Professional Negligence Section); North Carolina Academy of Trial Lawyers. Joseph Brown Inn of Court. ***PRACTICE AREAS:*** Complex Civil Litigation; Catastrophic Injury; Personal Injury; Professional Malpractice; Nursing Home Negligence; Products Liability; Aviation Litigation; Business Torts; Class Actions; Tax Shelters. ***Email:*** garymauney@lewis-roberts.com

PAUL R. DICKINSON, JR., born Suffolk, Virginia, April 3, 1960; admitted to bar, 1990, Texas; 1993, North Carolina. *Education:* University of South Florida (B.A., 1986); South Texas College of Law (J.D., 1990). *Member:* North Carolina Bar Associations (Member, Sections on: Litigation, Professional Negligence); North Carolina Academy of Trial Lawyers; The Association of Trial Lawyers of America (Member, Professional Negligence Section). ***PRACTICE AREAS:*** Construction Defects; Stucco Litigation; Truck Accidents; Nursing Home Abuse and Neglect; Nursing Negligence; Medical Malpractice; Construction Litigation; Construction Products Liability; Products Liability; Catastrophic Injury; Birth Trauma; Obstetric Malpractice. ***Email:*** pauldickinson@lewis-roberts.com

REPRESENTATIVE CLIENTS: Collins & Aikman Corp.; Springs Industries; Great American Insurance Co.; Builders Mutual Ins. Co.; J.M. Thompson Const. Co., Inc.; St. Paul Fire & Marine Ins. Co.; RSKCo.; Kemper Insurance Companies; Zenith Insurance Co.; Key Risk Management Services; Hewitt, Coleman & Associates, Inc.; Southern States Insurance Exchange; Overnite Transportation; RPC Contracting, Inc.; Eaton Corp.; Central Insurance Companies; J.W. Grand Const. Co.; Travelers Insurance Co.; Smithfield Foods; The Lundy Packing Co.; Glaxo-Wellcome, Inc.; NACCO Materials Handling Group, Inc.; Zurich US Inc.; ITT-Hartford; Erie Insurance Group; Food Lion; Discovery Insurance; Crawford and Co.; City of Durham; Carolina Holding, Inc.; Abbott Laboratories; Dupont; Carolina Builders Corp.; Forestry Mutual Insurance Co.; Pella Corp.; Blue Rhino Corp.; NC Association of Home Inspectors; Royal & Sunalliance Insurance Co..

(For complete biographical data on all personnel, see Professional Biographies at Raleigh, North Carolina)

JACK G. LEZMAN, P.A.

4801 E. INDEPENDENCE BOULEVARD
SUITE 616
CHARLOTTE, NORTH CAROLINA 28212
Telephone: 704-536-7669
Toll Free: 888-693-7669
Fax: 704-536-0179
URL: http://www.lawyers.com/jlezman
Email: jlezman@dasia.net
URL: http://www.jlezman.com

Consumer Bankruptcy, Bankruptcy, Debtor Rights, Personal Injury, Auto Accidents, Workers Compensation and Social Security Disability Law.

JACK G. LEZMAN, born Grand Rapids, Michigan, June 14, 1970; admitted to bar, 1995, North Carolina. *Education:* Michigan State University (B.A., 1992); University of Dayton (J.D., 1995). *Member:* Mecklenburg County Bar Association; North Carolina State Bar; National Association of Consumer Bankruptcy Attorneys. ***PRACTICE AREAS:*** Consumer Bankruptcy; Bankruptcy; Debtors Rights; Personal Injury; Automobile Accidents and Injuries; Workers Compensation; Social Security Disability.

LITTLER MENDELSON

A PROFESSIONAL CORPORATION
Established in 1942
BANK OF AMERICA CORPORATE CENTER
100 NORTH TRYON STREET, SUITE 4150
CHARLOTTE, NORTH CAROLINA 28202
Telephone: 704-972-7000
Facsimile: 704-333-4005
Email: info@littler.com
URL: http://www.littler.com

Offices located in: Phoenix, Arizona; California -- Fresno, Los Angeles, Sacramento, San Diego, San Francisco, San Jose, Santa Maria, Stockton and Walnut Creek; Denver, Colorado; Washington, D.C.; Miami, Florida; Atlanta, Georgia; Chicago, Illinois; Boston, Massachusetts; Minneapolis, Minnesota; Reno and Las Vegas, Nevada; Newark, New Jersey; New York, New York; Columbus, Ohio; Philadelphia and Pittsburgh, Pennsylvania; Dallas and Houston, Texas; Seattle, Washington.

(This Listing Continued)

Employment and Labor Law; Affirmative Action; Age Discrimination in Employment Civil Service; Collective Bargaining; Confidentiality Agreements; Covenants Not To Compete; Employee Drug Testing; Employee Privacy; Employer Liability; Employment Arbitration; Employment Breach of Contract; Employment Civil Rights; Employment Class Actions; Employment Discrimination; Employment Litigation; Equal Employment Opportunity Law; Fair Labor Standards; Family and Medical Leave Act; Harassment; Labor Relations; Labor Strikes; National Labor Relations Act; Noncompete Litigation; Noncompetition and Non-Solicitation Agreements; Personnel Policies; Prevailing Wage Litigation; Reductions in Force; Restrictive Covenants; Sexual Harassment; Title VII Discrimination; Unfair Labor Practices; Union Contract Negotiations; Union Elections; Union Organization; Wage and Hour Law; WARN Act; Whistleblower Litigation; Workplace Violence; Wrongful Termination; Wrongful Termination Defense.

FIRM PROFILE: Littler Mendelson, a Professional Corporation, is the largest law firm in the United States engaged exclusively in the practice of employment and labor law. The firm has 400 attorneys in 28 offices nationwide who represent and advise management in all major subspecialties of employment and labor law including wrongful termination; sex, race, and age discrimination; wage and hour law; NLRB cases and collective bargaining; workers' compensation; unemployment benefits; workplace violence; substance abuse; employee privacy rights; occupational safety and health; the ADA; FMLA; ERISA; employee benefits; tax issues and immigration.

MARYLIN E. CULP, admitted to bar, 1986, Florida, U.S. District Court, Middle District of Florida and U.S. Court of Appeals, 11th Circuit; 1999, North Carolina. *Education:* University of Iowa (B.A., cum laude, 1970); University of Kansas; University of South Florida; Stetson University College of Law (J.D., with distinction, 1985). Phi Beta Kappa; Pi Lambda Theta. (Resident)

CORIE D. PAULING, born Detroit, Michigan, February 1, 1971; admitted to bar, 1998, North Carolina. *Education:* University of Michigan (B.Sc., 1993); Northwestern University School of Law (J.D., 1997). *Member:* North Carolina State Bar; North Carolina Academy of Trial Lawyers; North Carolina Association of Black Lawyers; Orange County Domestic Violence Task Force; John Leary Bar Foundation. ***PRACTICE AREAS:*** Labor and Employment. ***Email:*** cpauling@littler.com

L. STANFORD SHERRILL, JR., born Rocky Mount, North Carolina, July 5, 1971; admitted to bar, 1995, Georgia; 2004, North Carolina. *Education:* University of North Carolina, Charlotte (B.A., 1992); University of North Carolina, Chapel Hill (J.D., with honors, 1995). Order of the Coif. Staff Member, North Carolina Law Review, 1993-1994. Author: *Limited Liability Company Act,* 72 N.C.L. Rev. 1654 (1994). *Member:* State Bar of Georgia. (Also at Atlanta, Georgia Office). ***PRACTICE AREAS:*** Labor and Employment. ***Email:*** ssherrill@littler.com

J. RENÉ TOADVINE, admitted to bar, 1993, Kentucky; 1996, District of Columbia; 1998, North Carolina. *Education:* Northern Kentucky University (B.S., 1984); Indiana University at Bloomington (J.D., magna cum laude, 1993). ***PRACTICE AREAS:*** Employee Benefits; ERISA; Executive Compensation. ***Email:*** rtoadvine@littler.com

NICOLE E. BOURGET, admitted to bar, 2000, North Carolina. *Education:* College of William & Mary (B.A., 1996); University of Virginia (J.D., 2000).

ANGELA B. CUMMINGS, admitted to bar, 1999, North Carolina. *Education:* University of North Carolina (B.A., with distinction, 1994; J.D., with honors, 1999). Phi Beta Kappa. Note and Comment Editor, North Carolina Journal of International Law and Commercial Regulation, 1998-1999. *Member:* American Bar Association (Labor and Employment Law Division, 1998—),.

JASON McCONNELL, admitted to bar, 2000, North Carolina. *Education:* University of North Carolina (B.A., 1994); Loyola University (J.D., 2000).

AARON MENSER, admitted to bar, 2004, North Carolina. *Education:* Elon College (B.A., 2001); Emory University School of Law (J.D., 2004).

JERRY H. WALTERS, JR., born Charlotte, North Carolina, October 24, 1970; admitted to bar, 1996, North Carolina; 2005, Georgia; U.S. District Court, Western, Middle and Eastern Districts of North Carolina; U.S. District Court, Northern and Middle Districts of Georgia; U.S. Courts of Appeals, Fourth, Eighth and Eleventh Circuits; U.S. Supreme Court. *Education:* University of North Carolina (B.A., with distinction, 1993); Campbell University (J.D., cum laude, 1996). Law Clerk to the Hon. Richard L. Voorhees, Chief Judge, United States District Court for the Western District of North Carolina, 1996-1997.

(For biographical data on personnel at other locations, see Professional Biographies at those cities)

MANN BRACKEN, LLC

Established in 1962

227 WEST TRADE STREET, SUITE 1610, CARILLON
CHARLOTTE, NORTH CAROLINA 28202

Telephone: 678-801-2352
Facsimile: 678-801-2355
Email: cbracken@mannbracken.com
URL: http://www.mannbracken.com

Vienna, Virginia Office: 1953 Gallows Road, Suite 240, 22182. Telephone: 703-245-0580. Facsimile: 703-288-4070.
Nashville, Tennessee Office: 209 10th Avenue South, Suite 542, Cummins Station, 37203. Telephone: 678-801-2352. Fax: 678-801-2355.
Atlanta, Georgia Office: One Paces West, Suite 1400, 30339. Telephone: 678-801-2352. Fax: 678-801-2355.

Creditors Rights, Arbitration.

(This Listing Continued)

FIRM PROFILE: Mann Bracken, LLC is a successor to the partnership that was formed September 1, 1962 as Maley and Crowe, as well as being the successor to the Washington, D.C. firm of McNeily & Rosenfeld. Since its inception, Mann Bracken, LLC attorneys have carried on a tradition of leadership in the representation of creditors that has spanned over forty years of continuous and dedicated practice.

Throughout its existence the firm has specialized in representing creditors in all phases of credit related matters. Mann Bracken is recognized for its representation of creditors in Arbitration proceeding, as well as in litigation.

APPROVED ATTORNEYS FOR: American Title Insurance Co.
REFERENCE: Wachovia Bank of Georgia, N.A.

(For complete biographical data on all personnel, see Professional Biographies at Atlanta, Georgia)

MARSH LAW FIRM

828 EAST BOULEVARD
CHARLOTTE, NORTH CAROLINA 28203

Telephone: 704-372-1112
Fax: 704-372-0133
Email: rmarsh@marshlawfirm.com

Taxation, Estate Planning, International Business Law, Business Planning.

FIRM PROFILE: Marsh Law Firm represents investors and entrepreneurs in wealth enhancement, management and transfer, including tax-advantaged business and real property transactions, domestic and international, and asset and privacy protection.

RICHARD E. MARSH, JR., admitted to bar, 1981, North Carolina, U.S. District Court, Western District of North Carolina and U.S. Tax Court; 1984, Florida; 1999, South Carolina. *Education:* Bucknell University (B.A., 1977); University of North Carolina at Chapel Hill (J.D., 1981; M.B.A., 1981); Georgetown University (LL.M., Taxation, 1985). Certified Public Accountant, North Carolina, 1982. ***PRACTICE AREAS:*** Taxation; Estate Planning; International Business Law; Business Planning.

JAMES E. MARTIN, JR.

122 NORTH MCDOWELL STREET
P.O. BOX 36331
CHARLOTTE, NORTH CAROLINA 28236

Telephone: 704-333-4711
Fax: 704-333-2884
Email: jem@hbm-attys.com

Estate Planning, Wills, Trusts, Probate, Corporate and Real Estate Law.

JAMES E. MARTIN, JR., born Charlotte, North Carolina, November 22, 1934; admitted to bar, 1964, North Carolina. *Education:* University of North Carolina at Chapel Hill (A.B., 1957; J.D., 1964). Phi Delta Phi. *Member:* Mecklenburg County and North Carolina Bar Associations.

REPRESENTATIVE CLIENTS AND REFERENCES: Upon Request.

MAYER, BROWN, ROWE & MAW LLP

Established in 1881

214 N. TRYON STREET, SUITE 3800
CHARLOTTE, NORTH CAROLINA 28202

Telephone: 704-444-3500
Fax: 704-377-2033
URL: http://www.mayerbrownrowe.com

Brussels, Belgium Office: Square de Meeûs 35, B-1000. Telephone: +011-32 2 502 55 17. Facsimile: + 011-32 2 502 54 21.
Chicago, Illinois Office: 71 S. Wacker, 60606-4637. Telephone: (312) 782-0600. Facsimile: (312) 701-7711. Telex: 190404. Cable Address: LEMAY.
Cologne, Germany Office: Kaiser-Wilhelm-Ring 27-29, 50672. Telephone: +49-221-5771-100. Facsimile: +49-221-5771-199.
Frankfurt am Main, Germany Office: Bockenheimer Landstraße 98-100, D-60323. Telephone: 011-49-69 79 41-0. Facsimile: 011-49-69 79 41-100.
Houston, Texas Office: 700 Louisiana Street, Suite 3600, 77002-2730. Telephone: (713) 221-1651. Facsimile: (713) 224-6410. Telex: 775809. Cable: LEMAYHOU.
London, England Office: 11 Pilgrim Street, London EC4V 6RW. Telephone: 011-44-207-248-4282. Facsimile: 011-44-207-248-2009.
Los Angeles, California Office: 350 South Grand Avenue, 25th Floor, 90071-1503. Telephone: (213) 229-9500. Facsimile: (213) 625-0248. Telex: 188089. Cable: LEMAYLA.
New York, New York Office: 1675 Broadway, 10019-5820. Telephone: (212) 506-2500. Facsimile: (212) 262-1910. Telex: 701842. Cable: LEMAYEN.
Palo Alto, California Office: Two Palo Alto Square, Suite 300, 94306. Telephone: (650) 331-2000. Facsimile: (650) 331-2060.
Paris, France Office: 41 Avenue Hoche, 75008. Telephone: 011-33-1-53-53-43-43. Facsimile: 011-33-1-53-96-03-83.
Washington, D.C. Office: 1909 K Street, N.W., 20006-1101. Telephone: (202) 263-3000. Facsimile: (202) 263-3300. Telex: 892603. Cable: LEMAYDC.
Representative Offices:
Beijing, People's Republic of China: 7-1-31, Qijayuanr, 9 Jianguomen Wai Avenue, Chaoyang District, 100600. Telephone: 011-86-10-85322221. Facsimile: 011-86-10-85322156.
Shanghai, People's Republic of China: 2805 Plaza 66, 1266 Nanjing Road West. Telephone: 011-86-21-6288-1250. Facsimile: 011-86-21-6288-1255.

(This Listing Continued)

MAYER, BROWN, ROWE & MAW LLP, Charlotte—Continued

Mexico City, Mexico, D.F., Independent Mexico Correspondent: Jáuregui, Navarrete, Nader y Rojas, S.C., Abogados Torre Arcos, Paseo de los Tamarindos No. 400-B. Col. Bosques de las Lomas, 05120. Telephone: 011-5255-5-267-45-00. Facsimile: 011-5255-5-267-45-98.

Antitrust, Appellate, Asia, Bankruptcy, Biotech, Pharma & Life Science, Chemicals, Collateralized Debt Obligation, Company Secretarial, Construction & Engineering, Corporate & Securities, Corporate Governance, Derivatives, E-commerce, Emerging Companies, Employee Benefits & Executive Compensation, Employee Share Incentives, Employment & Labour, Energy, Environment, Finance, Financial Services, Global Trade, Government, Government Contracts, Health Care, Information Technology, Insurance & Reinsurance, Intellectual Property, International Arbitration, Investment Management, Latin America, Legislative, Litigation & Dispute Resolution, Natural Resources, Outsourcing, Pensions, PPP/PFI & Infrastructure, Private Equity, Private Investment Fund, Pro Bono, Professional Practices, Project Finance, Property Rights, Public Law, Rail, Real Estate, Regulated Industries, Restructuring & Insolvency, Securitisation, Tax Controversy & Transfer Pricing, Tax Transactions & Consulting, Telecommunications & Media, Venture & Technology, Wealth Management.

MEMBERS OF FIRM

RODNEY E. ALEXANDER, born Atlanta, Georgia, March 21, 1960; admitted to bar, 1988, Texas; 1996, North Carolina. *Education:* Sam Houston State University (B.S.P.S., cum laude, 1984); University of Houston (J.D., cum laude, 1988). Order of the Coif; Order of the Barons. Associate Editor, Houston Law Review, 1988; Assistant District Attorney, Mecklenburg County, North Carolina, 1998-2000. ***REPORTED CASES:*** United States v. Pennington, 20 F.3d 593 (5th Cir. 1994). ***PRACTICE AREAS:*** Complex Commercial Litigation; Insurance and Reinsurance Litigation; Trade Secrets; Intellectual Property Litigation. ***Email:*** ralexander@mayerbrownrowe.com

JONATHAN A. BARRETT, born Durham, North Carolina, September 14, 1949; admitted to bar, 1978, North Carolina. *Education:* University of North Carolina at Chapel Hill (B.A., 1972; J.D., with honors, 1978). Phi Beta Kappa. Business Manager, North Carolina Law Review, 1977-1978. [Lt. USNR, 1972-1975]. ***PRACTICE AREAS:*** Business Law; Corporate Law; Mergers, Acquisitions and Divestitures. ***Email:*** jbarrett@mayerbrownrowe.com

KENNETH D. BELL, admitted to bar, 1983, North Carolina. *Education:* Wake Forest University (B.A., 1980; J.D., 1983). First Assistant United States Attorney, 1993-2003 and Assistant United States Attorney, 1983-1988 and 1990-2003, U.S District Court, Western District of North Carolina. Republican Nominee, United States House of Representatives, 5th Congressional District of North Carolina, 1990. ***REPORTED CASES:*** U.S. v. Bowe, 309 F.3d 234 (4th Cir. 2002); U.S. v. Bowe, 257 F.3d 336 (4th Cir. 2001); U.S. v. Brown, 155 F.3d 431 (4th Cir. 1998); U.S. v. McHan, 101 F.3d 1027 (4th Cir. 1996); U.S. v. Cheek, 94 F.3d 136 (4th Cir. 1996); U.S. v. Mackins, 32 F.3d 134 (4th Cir. 1994); U.S. v. McManus, 23 F.3d 878 (4th Cir. 1994); U.S. v. Brown, 856 F.2d 710 (4th Cir. 1988). ***PRACTICE AREAS:*** Litigation; Criminal Law. ***Email:*** kbell@mayerbrownrowe.com

FRANCIS J. BLANCHFIELD, JR., born Chicago, Illinois, September 19, 1945; admitted to bar, 1970, New Jersey; 1974, New York; 1976, Georgia; 1981, North Carolina. *Education:* College of the Holy Cross (A.B., 1967); New York University (J.D., 1970; LL.M., in Taxation, 1974). Recipient: Vanderbilt Medal; Root-Tilden Scholarship. Law Secretary to Judge Samuel Allcorn, Jr., Chancery Division, New Jersey Superior Court, 1970-1971. Special Assistant to Assistant Attorney General, 1977-1979, Deputy Assistant Attorney General, Tax Division, U.S. Department of Justice, 1979-1980. Recipient, The Attorney General's Medal, 1980. Fellow, American College of Tax Counsel. [1st Lt., U.S. Army, 1971-1973]. ***Email:*** fblanchfield@mayerbrownrowe.com

CHRISTOPHER J. BRADY, born Asheville, North Carolina, June 16, 1961; admitted to bar, 1993, North Carolina. *Education:* University of North Carolina at Charlotte (B.S., cum laude, 1983); University of North Carolina at Chapel Hill (J.D., with high honors, 1993). Member, Order of the Coif. Recipient, Chief Justice Walter Clark Award. ***Email:*** cbrady@mayerbrownrowe.com

HAYDEN D. BROWN, born Cleveland, Ohio, June 30, 1958; admitted to bar, 1984, Colorado; 1988, North Carolina. *Education:* University of Colorado at Boulder (B.A., cum laude, 1980); Northwestern School of Law of Lewis and Clark College (J.D., 1984); University of Denver (LL.M., in Taxation, 1986). *Member:* American Bar Association (Member: Section of Taxation; Committee on Banking and Savings Institutions; Chairman, 2001-2003). ***Email:*** haydenbrown@mayerbrownrowe.com

JEFFREY P. CANTRELL, born August 11, 1961; admitted to bar, 1988, Georgia; 1989, New York; 1999, North Carolina. *Education:* Florida State University (B.A., magna cum laude, 1983); University of Florida College of Law (J.D., with honors, 1988); New York University (LL.M. in Taxation, 1989). ***PRACTICE AREAS:*** Taxation. ***Email:*** jcantrell@mayerbrownrowe.com

ROBERT B. CORDLE, born Apex, North Carolina, March 14, 1941; admitted to bar, 1966, North Carolina. *Education:* Davidson College (A.B., with honors, 1963); New York University (LL.B., cum laude, 1966). Omicron Delta Kappa. Order of the Coif. Root-Tilden Scholar. Member, New York University Law Review, 1964-1965. Advocate, American Board of Trial Advocates (President, North Carolina Chapter, 1991-1995). Fellow, American College of Trial Lawyers. [Captain, U.S. Army, Active Duty, 1966-1968]. ***Email:*** rcordle@mayerbrownrowe.com

ROBERT T. DUFFY, born Columbus, Ohio, December 12, 1945; admitted to bar, 1971, Ohio (inactive); 1972, U.S. District Court, Southern District of Ohio; 1975, U.S. Court of Appeals, Second and Eighth Circuits; 1976, U.S. Court of Appeals, Ninth Circuit; 1977, U.S. Court of Appeals, Seventh Circuit; 1978, U.S. Supreme Court, U.S. Court of Appeals, Fourth and Tenth Circuits and U.S. Court of Appeals for the District of Columbia Circuit; 1979, U.S. Court of Appeals, First Circuit; 1981, U.S. Court of Appeals, Fifth and Eleventh Circuits; 1983, U.S. Tax Court and U.S. Court of Federal Claims; 1990, North Carolina and U.S. District Court, Middle District of North Carolina; 1993, U.S. District Court, Western District of North Carolina. *Education:* Wright State University (B.A., 1968); Harvard Law School (J.D., 1971). Author: "Awards of Costs to Taxpayers: A Reform Proposal for Section 7430," 48 Tax Lawyer 937 (1995). Attorney, U.S. Department of Justice, Tax Division, 1974-1983. Recipient, Tax Division's Outstanding Attorney Award, 1977 and 1982. *Member:* Mecklenburg County (Trustee, 1999-2002; Chair, Tax Section, 1998-1999; Chair, Continuing Legal Education Committee, 1997-1999) and American (Chair, Committee on Court Procedure and Practice, Tax Section, 2001-2003) Bar Associations. Fellow, American College of Tax Counsel. ***PRACTICE AREAS:*** Tax Controversies. ***Email:*** robertduffy@mayerbrownrowe.com

RON D. FRANKLIN, born New York, N.Y., June 26, 1965; admitted to bar, 1994, New York and New Jersey (Not admitted in North Carolina). *Education:* Occidental College (A.B., cum laude, 1987); Columbia Business School (M.B.A., 1990); University of Michigan Law School (J.D., 1993). Phi Delta Phi. ***LANGUAGES:*** Russian. ***PRACTICE AREAS:*** Finance; Corporate. ***Email:*** rfranklin@mayerbrownrowe.com

C. WELLS HALL III, born 1947; admitted to bar, 1973, North Carolina; 1987, South Carolina. *Education:* North Carolina State University (B.S., with honors, 1970); Duke University (J.D., 1973). *Member:* North Carolina Bar Association (Chairman, Young Lawyers Division, 1984-1985; Chairman, Taxation Section, 1986-1988; Member, Board of Governors, 1989-1992). Fellow, American College of Trust and Estate Counsel (Regent, 2000-2005). Fellow, American College of Tax Counsel. ***PRACTICE AREAS:*** Tax Transactions; Corporate and Business Planning; Estate Planning. ***Email:*** whall@mayerbrownrowe.com

CHRISTOPHER C. KUPEC, born 1953; admitted to bar, 1980, North Carolina. *Education:* University of North Carolina (B.A., 1975; J.D., 1980). ***PRACTICE AREAS:*** Banking Law; Finance. ***Email:*** ckupec@mayerbrownrowe.com

MARY K. MANDEVILLE, born St. Paul, Minnesota, February 6, 1963; admitted to bar, 1988, North Carolina. *Education:* University of South Carolina (B.S., magna cum laude, 1985); Duke University (J.D., with honors, 1988). Phi Beta Kappa. ***PRACTICE AREAS:*** Commercial Litigation. ***Email:*** mmandeville@mayerbrownrowe.com

KRISTIN PERNOLL MANZANO, born Honolulu, Hawaii, December 6, 1965; admitted to bar, 1992, Georgia; 1993, New York; 1995, U.S. District Court, Southern and Eastern Districts of New York; 1998, North Carolina. *Education:* Southern Methodist University (B.A., 1988); Tulane University Law School (J.D., cum laude, 1992). ***LANGUAGES:*** French. ***Email:*** kmanzano@mayerbrownrowe.com

KATHLEEN A. McGILL, admitted to bar, 1986, New York and District of Columbia; 1996, North Carolina. *Education:* University of Colorado (B.A., 1978); Georgetown University Law Center (J.D., 1985); The Edmund Walsh School of Foreign Service, Georgetown University (M.S.F.S., 1985). ***LANGUAGES:*** Spanish. ***PRACTICE AREAS:*** Banking Law; Finance. ***Email:*** mmcgill@mayerbrownrowe.com

ROBERT L. MENDENHALL, born Greensboro, North Carolina, July 15, 1954; admitted to bar, 1983, North Carolina; 1993, U.S. Tax Court. *Education:* Davidson College (A.B., 1976); University of North Carolina at Chapel Hill (J.D., 1983; M.B.A., 1983). Business Manager, 1982-1983, North Carolina Law Review. ***Email:*** rmendenhall@mayerbrownrowe.com

JAY PARRY MONGE, born New York, N.Y., March 15, 1943; admitted to bar, 1969, Illinois; 1981, New York; 2003, North Carolina. *Education:* Harvard University (A.B., cum laude, 1966); University of Virginia (LL.B., 1969). Contributing Author: "Advising Illinois Financial Institutions," Illinois Institute of Continuing Legal Education, I.I.C.L.E., 1974, 1978, 1981, 1984, 1987, 1993, 1997, 2002. ***PRACTICE AREAS:*** Finance and Investments; Mergers and Acquisitions; Divestitures. ***Email:*** jmonge@mayerbrownrowe.com

KEITH F. OBERKFELL, born St. Louis, Missouri, March 19, 1968; admitted to bar, 1993, Illinois; 2000, North Carolina. *Education:* University of Virginia (B.A., with highest distinction, 1990); Harvard Law School (J.D., cum laude, 1993). Phi Beta Kappa. ***PRACTICE AREAS:*** Structured Finance. ***Email:*** koberkfell@mayerbrownrowe.com

ASSOCIATES

THAIS M. ALEXANDER, born Worcester, Massachusetts, August 22, 1974; admitted to bar, 2002, New York (Not admitted in North Carolina). *Education:* Canisius College (B.A., magna cum laude, 1996); State University of New York at Buffalo (M.B.A., 2001; J.D., 2001). ***PRACTICE AREAS:*** Banking and Finance. ***Email:*** talexander@mayerbrownrowe.com

SUZANNE V. ALWAN, born Laguna Beach, California, 1965; admitted to bar, 1999, New York; 2004, Georgia (Not admitted in North Carolina). *Education:* Arizona State University (B.A., summa cum laude, 1993); Duke University School of Law (J.D., 1998). ***PRACTICE AREAS:*** Banking; Finance. ***Email:*** salwan@mayerbrownrowe.com

CHRISTY-ANNE V. BETLER, admitted to bar, 2001, Massachusetts; 2003, North Carolina. *Education:* University of Virginia (B.A., 1997), University of North Carolina at Chapel Hill (J.D., 2001). *Member:* North Carolina State Bar; North Carolina Bar Association. ***PRACTICE AREAS:*** Banking; Finance. ***Email:*** cbetler@mayerbrownrowe.com

CHRISTINE D. CAGNINA, admitted to bar, 1995, Illinois (Not admitted in North Carolina). *Education:* University of Arizona (B.S., 1992); Northwestern University School of Law (J.D., 1995); DePaul University College of Law (LL.M., 2001). ***PRACTICE AREAS:*** Tax Law. ***Email:*** ccagnina@mayerbrownrowe.com

ERIC H. COTTRELL, born Frankfort, Kentucky, September 20, 1970; admitted to bar, 1995, North Carolina; 2001, U.S. District Court, Western District of North Carolina; 2003, U.S. District Court, Eastern and Middle Districts of North Carolina. *Education:* Wake Forest University (B.A., History, cum laude, 1992); University of North Carolina at Chapel Hill School of Law (J.D., with honors, 1995). Law Clerk to The Honorable Judge William T. Prince, U.S. Magistrate, Norfolk, VA., 1995-1996. Author: Casenote: "Civil Rights Plaintiffs, Clogged Courts, and the Federal Rules of Civil Procedure: The Supreme Court Takes a Look at Heightened Pleading Standards in Leatherman v. Tarrant County," 72 North Carolina Law Review, No. 4, May 1994; "There's Too Much Confusion Here, and I Can't Get No Relief: Alcoholic Employees and the Federal Rehabilitation Act in Little v. F.B.I.," 72 North Carolina Law Review, No. 6, October 1994. Assistant District Attorney, Charlotte, N.C., 1996-2000. ***PRACTICE AREAS:*** Litigation. ***Email:*** ecottrell@mayerbrownrowe.com

BRIAN S. CROMWELL, born Bronx, New York, June 21, 1964; admitted to bar, 1996, North Carolina; 2000, U.S. District Court, Western District of North Carolina. *Edu-*

(This Listing Continued)

cation: Fairleigh Dickinson University (B.S., 1987); Fordham University School of Law (J.D., 1995). ***PRACTICE AREAS:*** Litigation. ***Email:*** bcromwell@mayerbrownrowe.com

J. BENJAMIN EARTHMAN, born March 28, 1976; admitted to bar, 2002, New York; 2004, Tennessee (Not admitted in North Carolina). *Education:* Christian Brothers University (B.A., cum laude, 1998); University of Memphis, Cecil C. Humphreys School of Law (J.D., cum laude, 2001). *Member:* American Bar Association; New York State Bar Association; Tennessee Bar Association. ***PRACTICE AREAS:*** Banking and Finance. ***Email:*** bearthman@mayerbrownrowe.com

CAROLYN R. GEORGIADE, born Durham, North Carolina, August 29, 1975; admitted to bar, 2003, North Carolina. *Education:* Rhodes College (B.A., 1998); Duke University (J.D., 2003). ***PRACTICE AREAS:*** Litigation. ***Email:*** crgeorgiade@mayerbrownrowe.com

JENNIFER T. HA, admitted to bar, 2002, New York (Not admitted in North Carolina). *Education:* University of California, Los Angeles (B.S., cum laude, 1994); California State University, Los Angeles (M.S., 1997); University of California, Berkeley School of Law (J.D., 2000). ***PRACTICE AREAS:*** Finance. ***Email:*** jha@mayerbrownrowe.com

FRED W. HARTMAN, born Lewistown, Pennsylvania, December 22, 1973; admitted to bar, 1999, Pennsylvania (Not admitted in North Carolina). *Education:* Pennsylvania State University (B.A., 1996); University of Pittsburgh School of Law (J.D., 1999); Georgetown University (LL.M., with distinction, 2002). ***PRACTICE AREAS:*** Tax Transactions. ***Email:*** fhartman@mayerbrownrowe.com

W.C. TURNER HERBERT, born Dallas, Texas, June 25, 1976; admitted to bar, 2004, North Carolina, U.S. Court of Appeals, Seventh Circuit and U.S. District Court, Western District of North Carolina; 2005, U.S. District Court, Eastern District of North Carolina. *Education:* Davidson College (B.A., Honors in Classics, 1998); University of St. Andrews (M.Litt., Classical Greek Language, 2000); University of North Carolina (J.D., 2004). Author: "Let's Be Reasonable: Rethinking the Prohibition Against Noncompete Clauses in Employment Contracts Between Attorneys in North Carolina," 82 N.C.L. Rev. 249 (2003); "Off the Beaten Path: An Analysis of the Supreme Court's Surprising Decision in Mickens v. Taylor," 81 N.C.L. Rev. 1268 (2003). ***PRACTICE AREAS:*** Litigation. ***Email:*** therbert@mayerbrownrowe.com

JACK M. KNIGHT, JR., admitted to bar, 1994, North Carolina, U.S. District Court, Western, Middle and Eastern Districts of North Carolina and U.S. Court of Appeals, Fourth Circuit. *Education:* University of North Carolina at Chapel Hill (B.A., 1990); Washington College of Law, American University (J.D., cum laude, 1994). Jody Akers Scholar. ***PRACTICE AREAS:*** Litigation; White Collar Fraud; Internal Investigations. ***Email:*** jknight@mayerbrownrowe.com

JENNIFER D. LAWRENCE, born July 7, 1974; admitted to bar, 2003, New York (Not admitted in North Carolina). *Education:* Boston College (B.A., 1996); New York University School of Law (J.D., 2002). ***PRACTICE AREAS:*** Corporate and Securities. ***Email:*** jlawrence@mayerbrownrowe.com

MICHAEL C. MASCIA, born Terrytown, New York, December 24, 1971; admitted to bar, 1998, North Carolina; 2003, Massachusetts. *Education:* University of North Carolina (B.A., 1994; J.D., 1998); Massachusetts Institute of Technology, Sloan School of Management (M.B.A., 2003). ***PRACTICE AREAS:*** Banking; Finance. ***Email:*** mmascia@mayerbrownrowe.com

THOMAS D. RICKS, admitted to bar, 2002, North Carolina. *Education:* Wake Forest University (B.S., 1996; J.D., magna cum laude, 2002). ***PRACTICE AREAS:*** Corporate; Securities. ***Email:*** tdricks@mayerbrownrowe.com

DANIEL L. TEDRICK, born Atlanta, Georgia, July 15, 1975; admitted to bar, 2000, North Carolina. *Education:* Davidson College (B.A., 1997); Wake Forest University (J.D., 2000). Member, Editorial Staff, Wake Forest Law Review, 1999-2000. ***PRACTICE AREAS:*** Litigation. ***Email:*** dltedrick@mayerbrownrowe.com

MARGARET J. THOMPSON, admitted to bar, 2002, Illinois; 2005, North Carolina. *Education:* Duke University (B.A., magna cum laude, 1999); Vanderbilt University Law School (J.D., 2002). ***LANGUAGES:*** Spanish, Italian. ***PRACTICE AREAS:*** Banking and Finance. ***Email:*** mjthompson@mayerbrownrowe.com

McANGUS GOUDELOCK & COURIE, P.L.L.C.

6302 FAIRVIEW ROAD, SUITE 700
P.O. BOX 30307
CHARLOTTE, NORTH CAROLINA 28230
Telephone: 704-643-6303
Telecopier: 704-643-2376
Email: mgc@mgclaw.com
URL: http://www.mgclaw.com

Columbia, South Carolina Office: 700 Gervais Street, Suite 300, P.O. Box 12519, Capitol Station, 29211-2519. Telephone: 803-779-2300. Telecopier: 803-748-0526.
Charleston, South Carolina Office: 78 Wentworth Street, Suite 200, P.O. Box 877, 29402. Telephone: 843-534-0101. Telecopier: 843-534-0605.
Greenville, South Carolina Office: 420 Park Avenue, Suite 301, P.O. Box 2980, 29602. Telephone: 864-239-4000. Telecopier: 864-242-3199.

General Civil Litigation Practice, Administrative, Insurance Defense, Workers Compensation, Employment Law, Bankruptcy, Banking and Consumer Law; Government, Construction, Product Liability, Premises Liability, Environmental, Commercial Law, Health Care, Administration and Litigation.

REPRESENTATIVE CLIENTS: ACE USA/ESIS; AIG Insurance Companies; American Express; Auto-Owners Insurance Company; Bridgestone; Broadspire Services, Inc.; CNA Insurance Companies; Companion Property and Casualty Insurance Company; Crawford & Co.; GAB Robins North America; Gallagher Bassett Services; Gold Kist, Inc.; The Hartford; J.B. Hunt Transport, Inc.; Michelin; Palmetto Hospital Trust; Royal & SunAlliance; Safeco Insurance Company; Wachovia.

(For Additional Biographical data on other personnel, see professional biographies at Columbia, South Carolina, and Charleston, South Carolina)

McGUIREWOODS LLP

BANK OF AMERICA CORPORATE CENTER
100 NORTH TRYON STREET, SUITE 2900
CHARLOTTE, NORTH CAROLINA 28202-4011
Telephone: 704-373-8999
Fax: 704-373-8935
Email: info@mcguirewoods.com
URL: http://www.mcguirewoods.com

REVISER OF THE VIRGINIA LAW DIGEST FOR THIS DIRECTORY.

Atlanta, Georgia Office: The Proscenium, 1170 Peachtree Street, N.E., Suite 2100, 30309-7649. Telephone: 404-443-5500. Fax: 404-443-5599.
Baltimore, Maryland Office: 7 Saint Paul Street, Suite 1000, 21202-1671. Telephone: 410-659-4400. Fax: 410-659-4599.
Charlottesville, Virginia Office: Court Square Building, 310 Fourth Street N.E., Suite 300, P.O. Box 1288, 22902-1288. Telephone: 434-977-2500. Fax: 434-980-2222.
Chicago, Illinois Office: 77 West Wacker Drive, Suite 4100, 60601-1815. Telephone: 312-849-8100. Fax: 312-849-3690.
Jacksonville, Florida Office: Bank of America Tower, 50 North Laura Street, Suite 3300, 32202-3661. Telephone: 904-798-3200. Fax: 904-798-3207.
Los Angeles, California Office: 11601 Wilshire Boulevard, 90025. Telephone: 310-575-1848.
McLean, (Tysons Corner) Virginia Office: 1750 Tysons Boulevard, Suite 1800, 22102-4215. Telephone: 703-712-5000. Fax: 703-712-5050.
New York, New York Office: 1345 Avenue of the Americas, 10105-0106. Telephone: 212-548-2100. Fax: 212-548-2150.
Norfolk, Virginia Office: World Trade Center, 101 West Main Street, Suite 9000, 23510-1655. Telephone: 757-640-3700. Fax: 757-640-3701.
Pittsburgh, Pennsylvania Office: Dominion Tower, 23rd Floor, 625 Liberty Avenue, 15222-3142. Telephone: 412-667-6000. Fax: 412-667-6050.
Richmond, Virginia Office: One James Center, 901 East Cary Street, 23219-4030. Telephone: 804-775-1000. Fax: 804-775-1061.
Washington, D.C. Office: Washington Square, 1050 Connecticut Avenue, N.W., Suite 1200, 20036-5317. Telephone: 202-857-1700. Fax: 202-857-1737.
Almaty, Republic of Kazakhstan Office: McGuireWoods Kazakhstan LLP, 41B, Kazibek Bi Street, 5th Floor, 480100. Telephone: +7-3272-596-100. Fax: +7-3272-596-116.
Brussels, Belgium Office: Avenue Louise 250, bte 64, 1050. Telephone: +32-(0)2-629-42-11. Fax: +32 (0)2 629 42 22.

Accountants Liability, Administrative Law, Advertising Law, Affordable Housing, Alternative Dispute Resolution, Americans with Disabilities Act, Antitrust, Appellate Practice, Asbestos Litigation, Asset Based Finance, Automotive Products Liability, Bankruptcy, Banks and Banking, Business Acquisitions, Business Divestitures, Business Law, Business Litigation, Buying and Selling of Businesses, Capital Markets, Charitable Giving, Class Actions, Coal Mining, Cogeneration; College and University Law, Commercial Litigation, Commercial Real Estate, Communications and Media, Complex Commercial Litigation, Computer Contracts, Confidentiality Agreements, Construction Equipment Liability, Construction Litigation, Consumer Finance, Content Licensing, Contracts, Copyright Licensing, Corporate Control Contests, Corporate Finance, Corporate Governance, Corporate Investigations, Corporate Law, Corporate Reorganization, Covenants Not to Compete, Creditors Rights, Criminal Taxation, Digital Signatures, Domain Name Infringement, Domain Names, Drug and Medical Device Defense, Drug and Medical Device Litigation, E-Commerce, Education Law, Electric Utilities, Emerging Growth Companies, Employee Benefits, Employee Benefits Litigation, Employment Breach of Contract, Employment Contracts, Employment Discrimination, Energy, Energy Acquisitions, Energy Project Development, Energy Regulation, Entertainment Law, Environmental Administrative Law, Environmental Compliance, Environmental Land Use, Environmental Law, Environmental Litigation, Environmental Real Estate, ERISA, Executive Compensation, False Advertising, Family Business Law, Fiduciary Litigation, Finance, First Amendment Law, Franchises and Franchising, Gas Utilities, Government Investigations, Government Relations, Health Care, High Technology Contracts, Hospital Administration, Hospital Law, Hostile Takeovers, Immigration Law, Independent Power, Insurance Litigation, Intellectual Property, Intellectual Property Licensing, Intellectual Property Litigation, Intellectual Property Portfolio Management, Intellectual Property Procurement, Intellectual Property Rights, International Arbitration, International Mergers and Acquisitions, International Taxation, International Trade, Internet Licensing, Joint Venture Litigation, Joint Ventures, Labor and Employment, Labor Relations, Land Use, Latex Allergy Litigation, Lead Poisoning, Leasing, Legal Ethics and Professional Responsibility, Leveraged Buyouts, Litigation, Litigation Management, Lobbying, Local Taxation, Marketing Law, Media Law, Merger Reorganization, Mergers and Acquisitions Finance, Mergers, Acquisitions and Divestitures, Motorcycle Products Liability, Municipal Law, Music Law, Natural Gas, North American Energy Trade, Oil and Gas Law, Partnership Law, Partnership Litigation, Partnership Taxation, Patent Litigation, Patent Prosecution, Patents, Petroleum Trading, Products Liability, Products Liability Insurance Coverage, Project Finance, Promotion Law, Proprietary Rights, Proxy Contests, Public Finance, Public Utility Law, Railroad Law, Real Estate, Real Estate Acquisitions, Real Estate Development, Real Estate Investment Trusts, Real Estate Leasing, Regulatory Law, Resorts and Leisure, Securities, Securities Litigation, Securities Regulation, Securitization, Software Copyright, Software Licensing, Software Protection, Spin-Offs, Sponsorship Law, Sports Law, Sports Licensing, Sports Marketing Law, State Taxation, Structured Finance, Sweepstakes, Takeovers, Tax Audits, Tax Credits, Tax Exempt Organizations, Tax Litigation, Taxation, Technology Licensing, Telephone Utility Regulation, Toxic Tort Class Actions, Toxic Torts, Trade Regulation, Trade Secrets, Trademark Registration, Trademarks, Transportation, Trusts and Estates, Trusts and Estates Taxation, Union Labor Law, Utility Law, Utility Regulation, Vaccine Injury, Web Site Development, White Collar Crime, Wrongful Termination.

FIRM PROFILE: Whether assisting a Fortune 50 giant or a small start-up, our focus is on building relationships that drive results. Our clients' businesses and industries are as important to us today as they were when we began in 1834, proven by the fact that many of our client relationships have lasted for decades. With lawyers working from 15 strategically located offices worldwide, McGuireWoods uses client focused teams to serve public, private, government and nonprofit clients from such industries as automotive, banking and financial services,

(This Listing Continued)

McGuireWOODS LLP, Charlotte—Continued

chemicals, energy resources, food processing, general manufacturing, government, health care, insurance, real estate, retailing, sports and entertainment, technology and telecom, and transportation.

PARTNERS

THOMAS E. CABANISS, born Farmville, Virginia, 1949; admitted to bar, 1975, Virginia, U.S. Court of Appeals, Fourth Circuit and U.S. Bankruptcy Court; 1979, U.S. Supreme Court; 1998, North Carolina. *Education:* North Carolina State University (B.S., 1972); University of Virginia School of Law (J.D., 1975). Phi Kappa Phi; Tau Beta Phi. ***PRACTICE AREAS:*** Finance; Corporate; Creditors Rights; Bankruptcy. ***Email:*** tcabaniss@mcguirewoods.com

KIMBERLY Q. CACHERIS, born Grosse Pointe, Michigan, 1968; admitted to bar, 1993, North Carolina and U.S. District Court, Western District of North Carolina; 1994, U.S. District Court, Eastern and Middle Districts of North Carolina; 2000, U.S. Court of Appeals, Fourth Circuit. *Education:* University of Michigan (B.A., 1990); Wake Forest University (J.D., 1993). ***PRACTICE AREAS:*** Labor and Employment; Employment Discrimination; Wrongful Termination; Noncompete Litigation; Workers Compensation. ***Email:*** kcacheris@mcguirewoods.com

JEFFREY R. CAPWELL, born Binghamton, New York, 1963; admitted to bar, 1990, New York and District of Columbia; 1993, Virginia; 2002, North Carolina. *Education:* Dartmouth College (A.B., 1986); Syracuse University (J.D., 1989). Order of the Coif. Editor in Chief, Syracuse Law Review, 1988-1989. Recipient, Terry R. Alexander Award, North Carolina Association of Public Accountants, 2003. Faculty Member, Southeastern Trust School.*Member:* American Bar Association (Member, Taxation Section); Southern Employee Benefits Conference. ***PRACTICE AREAS:*** Employee Benefits; Executive Compensation; Tax Controversies; Nonprofit and Charitable Organizations. ***Email:*** jcapwell@mcguirewoods.com

W. T. CRANFILL, JR., born Winston-Salem, North Carolina, 1941; admitted to bar, 1968, North Carolina; 1970, U.S. Court of Military Appeals; 1975, U.S. Court of Appeals, Fourth Circuit and U.S. District Court, Western and Middle Districts of North Carolina; 1980, U.S. Supreme Court; 1983, U.S. Court of Appeals for the District of Columbia and U.S. Court of Appeals, Eleventh Circuit; 1985, U.S. Court of Appeals, Sixth Circuit and U.S. District Court, Eastern District of North Carolina. *Education:* Wake Forest University (B.A., 1965; J.D., 1968); University of Arkansas (M.S., 1974). Phi Delta Phi. [LCDR, JAGC, USNR, 1968-1974]. ***PRACTICE AREAS:*** Employment Discrimination; Labor Management Relations; Wrongful Termination; Government Compliance; Noncompete Litigation. ***Email:*** wcranfill@mcguirewoods.com

JOHN C. FENNEBRESQUE, born Oyster Bay, New York, 1947; admitted to bar, 1973, North Carolina. *Education:* The Choate School (1965); University of North Carolina at Chapel Hill (B.A., 1970); Vanderbilt University Law School (J.D., 1973). Member, Vanderbilt Law Review, 1972-1973. Founding Partner, Fennebresque, Clark, Swindell & Hay. ***PRACTICE AREAS:*** Corporate; Banking. ***Email:*** jfennebresque@mcguirewoods.com

PATRICIA F. HOSMER, born Falls Church, Virginia, 1969; admitted to bar, 1994, North Carolina and South Carolina. *Education:* Yale University (B.A., 1991); University of North Carolina at Chapel Hill School of Law (J.D., 1994). ***PRACTICE AREAS:*** Equipment Finance and Leasing; Leveraged Leasing; Project Finance; Aircraft Finance and Leasing; Aircraft Sales; Structured Finance; Secured Transactions; Corporate Transactions. ***Email:*** phosmer@mcguirewoods.com

BRENTON D. JEFFCOAT, born Cayce, South Carolina, 1947; admitted to bar, 1974, South Carolina; 1975, U.S. District Court, District of South Carolina; 1977, U.S. Court of Appeals, Fourth Circuit; 2001, North Carolina; 2005, Georgia. *Education:* University of South Carolina (B.A., 1971; J.D., 1974). Partner, Parker Poe Adams & Bernstein LLP, 1999-2003. Shareholder/Member, Sinkler & Boyd P.A., 1995-1998. Partner, Nelson Mullins Riley & Scarborough LLP, 1987-1995. Shareholder/Member, McNair Law Firm P.A., 1974-1987. ***PRACTICE AREAS:*** Public Finance; Local Government. ***Email:*** bjeffcoat@mcguirewoods.com

RICHARD F. KANE, born Wareham, Massachusetts, 1944; admitted to bar, 1973, North Carolina; 1974, U.S. Court of Appeals, Fourth Circuit and U.S. District Court, Western District of North Carolina; 1980, U.S. Supreme Court; 1985, U.S. Court of Appeals, Sixth and Eleventh Circuits; 1988, U.S. District Court, Middle District of North Carolina; 1995, U.S. Court of Appeals, Fifth Circuit; 1998, U.S. District Court, Eastern District of North Carolina. *Education:* Boston College (B.S., 1967); University of Florida (J.D., 1973). Phi Delta Phi. Assistant and Associate Attorney General, North Carolina Department of Justice, 1973-1976. Administrative Law Judge, Safety and Health Review Board of North Carolina, 1985-1988. [Lt., (jg), U.S. Navy, 1967-1970]. ***PRACTICE AREAS:*** Labor and Employment; Affirmative Action; Title VII; ADEA; Management Collective Bargaining and Organizing Activity; Class Action Defense; Occupational Safety and Health. ***Email:*** rkane@mcguirewoods.com

WADE M. KENNEDY, born Berkeley, California, 1963; admitted to bar, 1989, Illinois; 1994, North Carolina. *Education:* St. Lawrence University (B.A., 1986); University of Michigan Law School (J.D., 1989). ***PRACTICE AREAS:*** Banks and Banking; Finance. ***Email:*** wkennedy@mcguirewoods.com

C. RALPH KINSEY, JR., born Charlotte, North Carolina, 1942; admitted to bar, 1967, North Carolina; U.S. Tax Court; U.S. District Court, Western, Middle and Eastern Districts of North Carolina; U.S. Court of Appeals, Fourth Circuit; U.S. Supreme Court. *Education:* East Carolina University (B.A., 1964); University of North Carolina (J.D., 1967). Phi Delta Phi; Order of the Coif. Business Manager and Member, Board of Editors, North Carolina Law Review, 1966-1967. Member, Board of Governors, University of North Carolina, 1995-1999. Member, Board of Trustees, 1979-1987 and Chair, 1985-1987, East Carolina University. ***PRACTICE AREAS:*** Complex Commercial Litigation; Fiduciary Litigation; Legal Ethics; Legal Malpractice; Litigation Management; Insurance Coverage Litigation; Government Relations. ***Email:*** rkinsey@mcguirewoods.com

(This Listing Continued)

KEITH M. KORENCHUK, born Lyons, Illinois, 1953; admitted to bar, 1982, North Carolina. *Education:* Duke University (B.A., 1975); University of Virginia (J.D., 1978); Harvard University (M.P.H., 1982). ***PRACTICE AREAS:*** Corporate Governance; Emerging Growth; Technology; Mergers and Acquisitions; Joint Ventures; Regulatory; Health Care Financial Services; Health Care Regulation; Health Care Corporate Services; Health Care Technology. ***Email:*** kkorenchuk@mcguirewoods.com

J. MARK LANGDON, born Raleigh, North Carolina, 1965; admitted to bar, 1992, North Carolina and U.S. District Court, Eastern District of North Carolina; 1995, U.S. District Court, Middle and Western Districts of North Carolina. *Education:* University of Virginia (B.A., 1987); Florida State University (J.D., 1992). ***PRACTICE AREAS:*** Complex Commercial Litigation; Construction Litigation; Tort Litigation; Toxic Tort Litigation; Zoning, Planning and Land Use Litigation. ***Email:*** mlangdon@mcguirewoods.com

JOSIAH C. T. LUCAS, born Charlotte, North Carolina, 1963; admitted to bar, 1988, North Carolina. *Education:* University of North Carolina (B.A., 1985); Duke University School of Law (J.D., 1988). Partner, Parker Poe Adams & Bernstein L.L.P., 1996-2003. ***PRACTICE AREAS:*** Banking; Public Finance. ***Email:*** jlucas@mcguirewoods.com

JOHN O. POLLARD, born American Falls, Idaho, 1937; admitted to bar, 1973, North Carolina and U.S. District Court, Western District of North Carolina; 1974, U.S. Court of Appeals, Fourth Circuit and U.S. District Court, Eastern and Middle Districts of North Carolina; 1979, U.S. Court of Appeals for the District of Columbia; 1980, U.S. Supreme Court; 1987, U.S. Court of Appeals, Eleventh Circuit; 1990, U.S. Court of Appeals, Sixth and Seventh Circuits. *Education:* American University School of International Service (B.A., 1964); University of North Carolina at Chapel Hill (J.D., 1973). Pi Sigma Alpha. [SGT., USMC, 1955-1960]. ***PRACTICE AREAS:*** Employment Discrimination; Labor Management Relations; Noncompete Litigation; Wrongful Termination. ***Email:*** jpollard@mcguirewoods.com

PAUL G. PORTER, born St. Louis, Missouri; admitted to bar, 1989, Missouri; 1991, Kansas; 1994, North Carolina. *Education:* University of Arkansas (B.S.B.A., 1986); University of Notre Dame (J.D., 1989). ***PRACTICE AREAS:*** Mergers and Acquisitions; Corporate Transactional; Joint Venture. ***Email:*** pporter@mcguirewoods.com

MARVIN L. ROGERS, born Charleston, South Carolina, 1960; admitted to bar, 1986, Texas; 1993, North Carolina. *Education:* Davidson College (B.S., 1982); University of South Carolina Law School (J.D., 1986). ***PRACTICE AREAS:*** Banking; Energy; Real Estate. ***Email:*** mrogers@mcguirewoods.com

JASON H. SCOTT, born East Cleveland, Ohio, 1971; admitted to bar, 1996, New York; 1998, West Virginia; 2002, North Carolina. *Education:* Cornell University (B.A., 1993); West Virginia College of Law (J.D., 1996); Georgetown University Law Center (LL.M., 1999). ***PRACTICE AREAS:*** Securities; Corporate Finance; Emerging Growth Companies; Securities Litigation. ***Email:*** jscott@mcguirewoods.com

JAMES C. SMITH, born Norfolk, Virginia, 1946; admitted to bar, 1976, New York; 1978, North Carolina; U.S. Supreme Court; U.S. Court of Appeals, Second and Fourth Circuits; U.S. District Court, Western, Middle and Eastern Districts of North Carolina; U.S. District Court, Southern and Eastern Districts of New York. *Education:* Dartmouth College (A.B., 1968); Vanderbilt Law School (J.D., 1975). Partner, Moore & Van Allen, 1984-1988; Rayburn Moon & Smith, 1988-2000. [Lt., U.S. Army Infantry, 1970-1971]. ***PRACTICE AREAS:*** Complex Commercial Litigation; Intellectual Property; Securities Litigation; Non-Compete Litigation; Fiduciary Litigation; Insurance Coverage Litigation. ***Email:*** jcsmith@mcguirewoods.com

BRUCE M. STEEN, born Manhasset, New York, 1961; admitted to bar, 1990, Virginia; 1992, District of Columbia; 2002, North Carolina. *Education:* Michigan State University (B.A., 1983); University of Virginia (J.D., 1988; M.A., 1989). Order of the Coif; Raven Society. Articles Development Editor, University of Virginia Law Review, 1987-1988. Law Clerk to Hon. J. Harvie Wilkinson III, U.S. Court of Appeals, Fourth Circuit, 1988-1989. Adjunct Professor, University of Virginia School of Law (2000—). ***PRACTICE AREAS:*** Civil Practice; Constitutional Law; Defamation; ERISA; Employment Discrimination; Labor and Employment. ***Email:*** bsteen@mcguirewoods.com

THOMAS E. TAYLOR, born Jersey City, New Jersey, 1946; admitted to bar, 1972, New York; 1975, U.S. District Court, Southern and Eastern Districts of New York and U.S. Court of Appeals, Second Circuit; 1978, U.S. Tax Court and U.S. Supreme Court; 1989, Connecticut; 2000, North Carolina. *Education:* University of Pennsylvania (B.A., 1968); Harvard University (J.D., 1971); New York University School of Law (LL.M., Taxation, 1978); University of Connecticut (M.B.A., 1996). ***LANGUAGES:*** French. ***PRACTICE AREAS:*** Business Acquisitions; Business Reorganizations; Business Divestitures; Partnership Law; Joint Ventures; Equipment Leasing; State Taxation; Local Taxation. ***Email:*** tetaylor@mcguirewoods.com

OF COUNSEL

B. BERNARD BURNS, JR., born Greenwood, South Carolina, 1948; admitted to bar, 1973, North Carolina. *Education:* Furman University (B.A., 1970); Duke University (J.D., 1973). Vice President and Associate General Counsel, 1989-1993, Senior Vice President and General Counsel, 1993-1997, President, Building Products Segment, 1996-1997, President, Door Products Division, 1997-1998, President, Specialty Engineered Products Segment, 1998-1999, Executive Vice President and Chief Administrative Officer, 2000 and President, Test Instrumentation Segment, 2000-2001, United Dominion Industries. Interim CEO, Siegel-Robert, Inc., 2002-2003. [Ret. Capt., U.S. Army Reserve, 1978]. ***PRACTICE AREAS:*** Corporate Finance; Mergers and Acquisitions; Securities. ***Email:*** bburns@mcguirewoods.com

ASSOCIATES

STEVEN T. ACKERMANN, born Belleville, Illinois; admitted to bar, 2002, North Carolina and U.S. District Court, Western, Middle and Eastern Districts of North Carolina. *Education:* Southern Illinois University (B.S., 1998); Indiana University (J.D., 2002). ***PRACTICE AREAS:*** Employee Benefits; Employment Discrimination; Executive Compensation Litigation; Government Compliance; Labor Relations; Covenants Not To Compete; Wrongful Termination; Workers Compensation. ***Email:*** sackermann@mcguirewoods.com

(This Listing Continued)

MARGARET N. BOYLE, born Greensburg, Pennsylvania, 1978; admitted to bar, 2004, North Carolina. *Education:* University of Pittsburgh (B.A., 2000); University of Richmond (J.D., 2004). ***PRACTICE AREAS:*** Commercial Litigation. ***Email:*** mboyle@mcguirewoods.com

ROBERT A. COX, JR., born Jackson, Mississippi, 1969; admitted to bar, 1995, North Carolina; 1996, U.S. District Court, Eastern District of North Carolina and U.S. Court of Appeals, Fourth Circuit; 1998, U.S. District Court, Western District of North Carolina; 2000, U.S. District Court, Middle District of North Carolina. *Education:* University of North Carolina-Chapel Hill (B.A., 1992); Wake Forest University (J.D., 1995). Law Clerk, The Honorable J. Craig Whitley, U.S. Bankruptcy Court, Western District of North Carolina, 1997-1998. ***PRACTICE AREAS:*** Bankruptcy; Bankruptcy Chapter 11; Creditors Rights; Loan Workouts. ***Email:*** rcox@mcguirewoods.com

MATTHEW J. DAVIS, born New York, N.Y., 1973; admitted to bar, 1998, North Carolina. *Education:* University of Michigan (B.A., 1995); University of Virginia School of Law (J.D., 1998). ***PRACTICE AREAS:*** Public Finance. ***Email:*** mdavis@mcguirewoods.com

SUSAN PYLE DION, born Pittsburgh, Pennsylvania; admitted to bar, 2001, North Carolina, U.S. District Court, Western, Eastern and Middle Districts of North Carolina and U.S. Court of Appeals, Fourth Circuit. *Education:* North Carolina State University (B.A., 1998); Wake Forest University (J.D., 2001). ***PRACTICE AREAS:*** Employee Benefits; Executive Compensation Litigation; Employment Discrimination; Government Law; Labor Relations; Management Labor Law; Noncompete Litigation. ***Email:*** sdion@mcguirewoods.com

WALTER T. DONALDSON, III, born Baton Rouge, Louisiana, 1977; admitted to bar, 2003, North Carolina. *Education:* North Carolina State University (B.A., 1999); Villanova University, College of Commerce and Finance (M.B.A., 2003); Villanova University School of Law (J.D., 2003). ***LANGUAGES:*** Danish. ***PRACTICE AREAS:*** Banking; Public Finance. ***Email:*** wdonaldson@mcguirewoods.com

JONATHAN HARLAN EDGAR, born Arlington, Virginia, 1974; admitted to bar, 2000, Virginia; 2002, District of Columbia; 2004, U.S. District Court for the District of Columbia; 2005, North Carolina and U.S. District Court, Western District of North Carolina. *Education:* Princeton University (B.A., 1997); George Washington University (J.D., 2000). ***PRACTICE AREAS:*** Complex Commercial Litigation; Fiduciary Litigation; Litigation Management; Partnerships; Joint Ventures. ***Email:*** jedgar@mcguirewoods.com

ALLYSON GRAINGER, born Inglewood, California, 1972; admitted to bar, 1997, North Carolina. *Education:* Arizona State University (B.S., 1994); Duke University (J.D., 1997). ***PRACTICE AREAS:*** Banking Law. ***Email:*** agrainger@mcguirewoods.com

MICHAEL C. GRIFFIN, born Birmingham, Alabama, 1969; admitted to bar, 2000, Virginia; 2001, District of Columbia; 2004, North Carolina. *Education:* The Citadel (B.A., 1991); George Washington University (J.D., 2000). Phi Kappa Phi. [2nd Lt. Capt., U.S.M.C., 1991-1997; Major, U.S.M.C.R., 1997—]. ***Email:*** mgriffin@mcguirewoods.com

JAMES EDWARD HICKMON, born Charlotte, North Carolina; admitted to bar, 2001, Virginia, U.S. District Court, Eastern and Western Districts of Virginia and U.S. Bankruptcy Court, Eastern District of Virginia; 2002, U.S. Tax Court; 2004, North Carolina. *Education:* University of North Carolina, Wilmington (B.S.B.A., 1992); East Carolina University (M.B.A., 1996); Wake Forest University (J.D., 2001). Author: "Sarbanes-Oxley Produces Complex Blackout Notice Requirements and Imposes Personal Civil Liability for Plan Administrators," Tax Management Compensation Planning Journal, July 2003; "Current Considerations in Adopting New Employee Benefit Plan Claims Procedures," Tax Management Compensation Planning Journal, May 2002. Associate, Williams Mullen, 2001-2003; Vice President, First Citizens Bank & Trust Company of North Carolina, 1995-1998; Trust Officer, Wachovia Corporation, 1993-1995; Certified Financial Planner, 1996. ***PRACTICE AREAS:*** Employee Benefits; Executive Compensation; Executive Compensation Litigation. ***Email:*** jhickmon@mcguirewoods.com

MELISSA M. KEMMER, born San Pedro, California, 1969; admitted to bar, 1997, Texas; 1998, North Carolina. *Education:* California State Polytechnic University (B.A., 1992); Tulane University (J.D., 1997). Order of the Barristers. ***PRACTICE AREAS:*** Complex Commercial Litigation; Torts; Workers Compensation. ***Email:*** mkemmer@mcguirewoods.com

AARON J. LONGO, born Oil City, Pennsylvania, 1975; admitted to bar, 2003, Virginia; 2005, North Carolina. *Education:* Georgetown University (B.A., 1997); University of Massachusetts-Amherst (M.Ed., 1998); University of Virginia Law School (J.D., 2003). ***PRACTICE AREAS:*** Employment Discrimination; Government Compliance; Labor-Management Relations; Non-Compete Litigation; Wrongful Discharge. ***Email:*** alongo@mcguirewoods.com

STEPHEN C. MATHENY, born Pittsburgh, Pennsylvania; admitted to bar, 1999, Illinois and U.S. District Court, Northern District of Illinois (Not admitted in North Carolina). *Education:* University of Colorado (B.S., 1990); DePaul University College of Law (J.D., 1998). Editor in Chief, Business Law Journal, 1997-1998. ***PRACTICE AREAS:*** Commercial Lending Law; Corporate Law. ***Email:*** smatheny@mcguirewoods.com

STACI E. ROSCHE, born Wilkesboro, North Carolina; admitted to bar, 2000, New York; 2002, North Carolina. *Education:* University of North Carolina at Chapel Hill (B.A., 1991); Fordham University (J.D., 1998). ***PRACTICE AREAS:*** Banking Law; Corporate Finance; Securities. ***Email:*** srosche@mcguirewoods.com

MIRANDA M. ZOLOT, born Atlanta, Georgia, 1975; admitted to bar, 1998, New Jersey and U.S. District Court, District of New Jersey; 1999, New York and U.S. District Court, Southern and Eastern Districts of New York (Not admitted in North Carolina). *Education:* Boston University (B.A., 1995); Duke University (J.D., 1998). ***PRACTICE AREAS:*** Employee Benefits; Executive Compensation Litigation; Employee Discrimination; Government Compliance; Labor Relations; Noncompete Litigation; Wrongful Discharge. ***Email:*** mzolot@mcguirewoods.com

REVISER OF THE VIRGINIA LAW DIGEST FOR THIS DIRECTORY.

THE McINTOSH LAW FIRM, P.C.

CHARLOTTE, NORTH CAROLINA

(See Davidson)

Adoptions, Appeals, Bankruptcy, Business Law, Civil Litigation, Commercial and Consumer Collections, Commercial and Residential Real Estate, Corporate Law, Foreclosures, Insurance Subrogation, Estate Administration, Family Law, Personal Injury, Wrongful Death, Wills, Workers Compensation, Planning and Land Use.

McKAIG & McCUTCHEON, P.A.

Established in 1970

219 GREENWICH ROAD
CHARLOTTE, NORTH CAROLINA 28211
Telephone: 704-365-0390
Fax: 704-365-0652
URL: http://www.mckaigandmccutcheonlaw.com

Business Law, Buying and Selling of Businesses, Limited Liability Law, Family Business, Partnership Law, Corporate Law, Business Litigation, Collections, Contracts, Estate Planning, Trusts and Estates, Real Estate, Condominium Law, Landlord and Tenant Law, Wills and Probate.

A. STUART McKAIG, III, born Toledo, Ohio, January 23, 1945; admitted to bar, 1974, North Carolina and U.S. District Court, Western District of North Carolina. *Education:* Duke University (A.B., 1967); Vanderbilt University (J.D., 1973). Patrick Wilson Merit Scholar. *Member:* North Carolina and American Bar Associations; North Carolina State Bar; North Carolina Academy of Trial Lawyers. [Lt., U.S. Navy, 1967-1971]. ***PRACTICE AREAS:*** Business Law; Litigation; Estate Planning. ***Email:*** smckaig@bellsouth.net

R. SCOTT McCUTCHEON, born Akron, Ohio, August 25, 1946; admitted to bar, 1972, Ohio; 1973, North Carolina. *Education:* The Ohio State University (B.A., 1969); University of Akron (J.D., 1972). *Member:* North Carolina and American Bar Associations; North Carolina State Bar. ***PRACTICE AREAS:*** Commercial Real Estate; Residential Real Estate; Land Use Law. ***Email:*** scotmcc@bellsouth.net

HEATHER McKAIG TILLMAN, born Nashville, Tennessee, March 17, 1972; admitted to bar, 1996, North Carolina. *Education:* Duke University (A.B., 1993); University of Richmond (J.D., 1995). Assistant District Attorney, 26th Judicial District, 1996-2002. *Member:* North Carolina State Bar; North Carolina Bar Association; North Carolina Academy of Trial Lawyers. ***PRACTICE AREAS:*** Litigation. ***Email:*** hmtillman@bellsouth.net

REPRESENTATIVE CLIENTS: Rea Brothers, Inc.; P.C. Godfrey, Inc.; Welders Supply; D & L Appliance Parts Co., Inc.; Frye Electric Company; Charlotte Scale Company, Inc.; Adkins Truck Equipment Co.; Southern Cabinet Company; Multi-Shifter, Inc.; Vantage Lincoln-Mercury, Inc.; Sales Performance International, Inc.; Providence Day School; Elm Land Company.

McMILLAN & TERRY, P.A.

6101 CARNEGIE BOULEVARD, SUITE 310
CHARLOTTE, NORTH CAROLINA 28209
Telephone: 704-552-9997
Facsimile: 704-552-0540
Email: mailbox@mcmillan-terry.com
URL: http://www.lawyers.com/mcmillanandterry

Residential and Commercial Real Estate, Corporate, Estate Planning.

RALPH R. McMILLAN, born Charlotte, North Carolina, May 30, 1949; admitted to bar, 1977, North Carolina. *Education:* Wofford College (A.B., cum laude, 1971); University of North Carolina (J.D., 1977). *Member:* Mecklenburg County and North Carolina Bar Associations; The North Carolina State Bar. ***PRACTICE AREAS:*** Residential Real Estate; Commercial Real Estate; Corporate Law; Estate Planning. ***Email:*** rmcmillan@mcmillan-terry.com

DANIEL A. TERRY, born Charlotte, North Carolina, July 4, 1962; admitted to bar, 1989, North Carolina. *Education:* Hampden-Sydney College (B.A., cum laude, 1986); Wake Forest University (J.D., 1989). Omicron Delta Epsilon; Phi Beta Kappa; Phi Delta Phi. *Member:* Mecklenburg County and North Carolina Bar Associations; North Carolina State Bar. ***PRACTICE AREAS:*** Residential Real Estate; Commercial Real Estate; Corporate Law. ***Email:*** dterry@mcmillan-terry.com

BRAD ALLEN BAILEY, born Hanford, California, December 21, 1964; admitted to bar, 2000, North Carolina. *Education:* University of North Carolina at Chapel Hill (B.A., 1987); Widener University School of Law (J.D., 1998). Phi Delta Phi. *Member:* Mecklenburg County and North Carolina Bar Associations; North Carolina State Bar. ***PRACTICE AREAS:*** Residential Real Estate; Commercial Real Estate; Corporate Law. ***Email:*** bbailey@mcmillan-terry.com

MICHELLE S. CRABTREE, born Stillwater, Oklahoma, November 9, 1966; admitted to bar, 1992, North Carolina; 1993, South Carolina. *Education:* West Virginia University (B.S.B.A., 1989; J.D., 1992). *Member:* Mecklenburg County and North Carolina State Bar Associations; South Carolina Bar. ***PRACTICE AREAS:*** Residential Real Estate; Commercial Real Estate; Corporate Law. ***Email:*** mcrabtree@mcmillan-terry.com

CHRISTOPHER JAY ALBEE, born Philadelphia, Pennsylvania, April 27, 1966; admitted to bar, 2000, North Carolina. *Education:* Virginia Polytechnic Institute and State University (B.A., 1989); North Carolina Central University (J.D., 2000). *Member:* Mecklenburg County and North Carolina Bar Associations; North Carolina State Bar. ***PRAC-***

(This Listing Continued)

McMILLAN & TERRY, P.A., Charlotte—Continued

TICE AREAS: Residential Real Estate; Commercial Real Estate; Corporate Law. **Email:** calbee@mcmillan-terry.com

McNAIR LAW FIRM, P.A.

TWO WACHOVIA CENTER
301 SOUTH TRYON STREET, SUITE 1615
CHARLOTTE, NORTH CAROLINA 28282
Telephone: 704-347-1170
Facsimile: 704-347-4467
Email: cfort@mcnair.net
URL: http://www.mcnair.net

Columbia, South Carolina Office: 1301 Gervais Street, P.O. Box 11390, 29211. Telephone: 803-799-9800. Facsimile: 803-799-9804.
Anderson, South Carolina Office: 500 South McDuffie Street, P.O. Box 4086, 29621. Telephone: 864-226-1688. Facsimile: 864-225-6456.
Bluffton, South Carolina Office: 5 Belfair Village Drive, 29910-2605. Telephone: 843-815-2171. Facsimile: 843-815-5991.
Charleston, South Carolina Office: 100 Calhoun Street, Suite 400, 29401. Telephone: 843-723-7831. Facsimile: 843-722-3227.
Georgetown, South Carolina Office: 121 Screven Street, P.O. Drawer 418, 29442. Telephone: 843-546-6102. Facsimile: 843-546-0096.
Greenville, South Carolina Office: Bank of America Plaza, 7 North Laurens Street-Suite 600, P.O. Box 447. 29602. Telephone: 864-271-4940. Facsimile: 864-233-0423; 864-271-4015.
Hilton Head Island, South Carolina Office: Shelter Cove Executive Park, 23-B Shelter Cove Lane, Suite 400, P.O. Drawer 3, 29938-0003. Telephone: 843-785-2171. Facsimile: 843-686-5991.
Myrtle Beach, South Carolina Office: Founders Centre, 2411 Oak Street, Suite 206, 29577. Telephone: 843-444-1107. Facsimile: 843-444-4729.
Raleigh, North Carolina Office: Landmark Center, Suite 500, 4601 Six Forks Road, 27609. Telephone: 919-786-4061. Fax: 919-786-4076.

Administrative, Admiralty, Antitrust, Banking, Bankruptcy, Civil and Criminal Practice in all State and Federal Courts of Record, Corporate, Environmental, ERISA, Estate Planning, Health Care, Intellectual Property, Immigration, International, Interstate Land Sales, Labor and Employment Relations, Legislative/Governmental (National and State), Mergers and Acquisitions, Municipal Finance, Probate, Real Estate, Regulatory, Securities, Tax, Telecommunications, and Utility Law.

ANDREW W. LAX, admitted to bar, 1985, North Carolina, U.S. District Court, Western District of North Carolina; 1988, U.S. District Court, Middle District of North Carolina and U.S. Court of Appeals, Fourth Circuit; 2003, U.S. Supreme Court. *Education:* College of William & Mary (B.A., 1977); Wake Forest University (J.D., 1985). Member, Moot Court Board. Certified Mediator, North Carolina. *Member:* North Carolina Bar Association; North Carolina Association of Defense Attorneys. ***REPORTED CASES:*** Raritan River Steel Co. v. Cherry, Bekaert & Holland, 322 N.C. 200, 367 S.E.2d 609, 1988; Di Donato v. Wortman, 320 N.C. 423, 358 S.E.2d 489, 1987; Desmond v. City of Charlotte, 142 N.C. App. 590, 544 S.E.2d 269, 2001; Gibson v. Lambeth, 86 N.C. App. 264, 357 S.E.2d 404, 1987. ***PRACTICE AREAS:*** Civil Litigation; Insurance Law; Construction Law. ***Email:*** alax@mcnair.net

SHERRI L. McGIRT, admitted to bar, 1974, North Carolina and U.S. District Court, Middle District of North Carolina; 1979, U.S. District Court, Western District of North Carolina; 1982, U.S. Tax Court. *Education:* University of North Carolina (A.B., 1971; J.D., 1974). Dean's List. Attorney: Internal Revenue Service, 1974-1979; Touche Ross & Company, 1979-1981. Member, Planning Committee Board of Advisors, University of North Carolina J. Nelson Young Tax Institute, 1981—. Certified Public Accountant North Carolina, 1983. *Member:* Mecklenburg County (Chairman, Legal Service for the Elderly, 1982-1985; Chairman, Lawyers Referral Service, 1987-1989; Executive Committee, 1987-1990; Chairman, Estate Planning, Probate and Fiduciary Section, 1999-2000), North Carolina (Member, Sections on: Taxation; Probate and Fiduciary; Business; Member, Quality of Life Task Force, 1989-1991) and American (Member: Sections on: Taxation; Real Property, Probate and Trust Law) Bar Associations; North Carolina State Bar; North Carolina Association of Certified Public Accountants; American Institute of Certified Public Accountants. ***PRACTICE AREAS:*** Estate Planning; Tax; Business. ***Email:*** smcgirt@mcnair.net

ALLAN W. SINGER, admitted to bar, 1969, North Carolina and U.S. Court of Military Appeals; 1973, Massachusetts. *Education:* Dartmouth College (A.B., 1966); Duke University (J.D., 1969). *Member:* American Bar Association (Member, Section on Corporate, Banking and Business Law). [Capt., JAGC, U.S. Army, 1969-1973]. ***PRACTICE AREAS:*** Corporate; Civil Litigation. ***Email:*** asinger@mcnair.net

SPECIAL COUNSEL

CHASE B. SAUNDERS, admitted to bar, 1972, North Carolina, U.S. District Court, Western District of North Carolina. *Education:* University of North Carolina at Chapel Hill (A.B., 1969; J.D., 1972); Central Piedmont Community College (A.A., in Acct., 1980). Author: "The Evidence Navigator," electronic Format, The Raleigh Computer Company, 1996. Adjunct Professor, Business Law, Central Piedmont Community College, 1977-1978. Assistant District Attorney, 26th N.C. Judicial District, 1972-1976. District Court Judge, 26th N.C. Judicial District, 1976-1982. Superior Court Judge, 26th N.C. Judicial District, 1982-1997. Chief District Court Judge, 1977-1982. Senior Resident Superior Judge, 1994-1997. Emergency Superior Court Judge, 1997-1999. ADR and AAA Certified Mediator. Commercial Arbitrator. NASD Arbitrator and Mediator. *Member:* Mecklenburg County Bar (Member, Dispute Resolution, Litigation and Domestic Sections) and North Carolina State Bar; Justice Bobbitt Inn (President). ***PRACTICE AREAS:*** Civil Litigation; Business; Technology; Construction; Employment; Equitable Distribution. ***Email:*** csaunders@mcnair.net

(This Listing Continued)

MARNA M. ALBANESE, admitted to bar, 1998, New Jersey and California; 2000, North Carolina; 2001, U.S. District Court, Western District of North Carolina. *Education:* Mary Washington College (B.A., 1993); New York Law School (J.D., 1997). Member, New York Law School Moot Court Association. ***PRACTICE AREAS:*** Litigation. ***Email:*** malbanese@mcnair.net

CHARITY BABINGTON FALLS, admitted to bar, 2003, North Carolina. *Education:* University of North Carolina at Charlotte (B.A., magna cum laude, 1998); University of San Diego (J.D., 2003, LL.M., Taxation, 2003). Recipient, Graduate Law Merit Scholarship for Taxation, 2003. Law Clerk to Chief United States District Court Judge Graham Mullen, Western District of North Carolina. *Member:* North Carolina Association of Women Attorneys. ***PRACTICE AREAS:*** Taxation; Trusts and Estates Planning; Business Law. ***Email:*** cfalls@mcnair.net

REPRESENTATIVE CLIENTS: Bank of America; Brunswick County, North Carolina; Colonial Life & Accident Insurance Company; Food Lion, Inc.; Fuji Photo Film, Inc.; Georgetown Steel Corp.; Georgia-Pacific Corporation; International Paper; McDevitt & Street Co.; Milliken & Co.; Norfolk Southern Corporation; Palmetto Health Alliance; Palmetto Seed Capital Corporation; Piedmont Municipal Power Agency; Pirelli Cable Corporation; Safety-Kleen Corp.; SCANA Corporation; Showa Denko Carbon, Inc.; South Carolina Electric & Gas Company; South Carolina State Ports Authority; Union Camp Corporation; UNISYS Corporation; Westinghouse Electric Corporation.

(For complete biographical data on Columbia, Anderson, Bluffton, Charleston, Georgetown, Greenville, Hilton Head Island and Myrtle Beach, South Carolina and Raleigh, North Carolina personnel, see Professional Biographies of those cities)

THOMAS A. McNEELY

1011 EAST MOREHEAD STREET, SUITE 300
CHARLOTTE, NORTH CAROLINA 28204
Telephone: 704-376-6114
Fax: 704-332-2716
Email: tam@tmcneelylaw.com
URL: http://www.lawyers.com/thomasmcneelylaw

Catastrophic Injury, Professional Liability, Wrongful Death, Products Liability, Inadequate Security, Bad Faith, Insurance Claims.

THOMAS A. McNEELY, born Thomasville, North Carolina, October 28, 1940; admitted to bar, 1970, North Carolina. *Education:* University of South Carolina (A.B., 1962); University of North Carolina (J.D., 1970). Staff Member, North Carolina Law Review, 1969. *Member:* North Carolina and American Bar Associations; 26th Judicial District and North Carolina State Bars; North Carolina Academy of Trial Lawyers; The Association of Trial Lawyers of America. ***PRACTICE AREAS:*** Catastrophic Injury; Professional Liability; Wrongful Death; Products Liability; Inadequate Security; Bad Faith; Insurance Claims; Business Torts.

AARON E. MICHEL

Established in 1992
3736 SURRY RIDGE COURT
CHARLOTTE, NORTH CAROLINA 28210-6921
Telephone: 704-451-8351
Fax: 704-643-1004
Email: mail@aaronmichel.com
URL: http://www.aaronmichel.com

Litigation: Federal and State Practice.

AARON E. MICHEL, admitted to bar, 1981, Ohio; 1982, Pennsylvania; 1990, North Carolina and U.S. District Court, Western District of North Carolina. *Education:* Ohio State University (B.S., 1978); Capital University (J.D., 1981).

MILLER & HALL, P.A.

216 N. MCDOWELL STREET, SUITE 106
CHARLOTTE, NORTH CAROLINA 28204
Telephone: 704-375-8007
Fax: 704-375-1374
URL: http://www.millerandhallpa.com
Mailing Address: P.O. Box 36957, Charlotte, NC 28236-6957

General Civil Trial Practice, Real Estate, Corporate, Wills, Trust, Probate, Estate Planning and Collection Law.

LESLIE H. MILLER, born Charlotte, North Carolina, March 2, 1954; admitted to bar, 1979, North Carolina. *Education:* East Carolina University (B.A., 1976); University of Richmond (J.D., 1979). ***PRACTICE AREAS:*** Real Estate; Corporate; Probate; Collection. ***Email:*** lhmiller@bellsouth.net

DANA C. HALL, born Charlotte, North Carolina, June 27, 1956; admitted to bar, 1982, North Carolina. *Education:* University of North Carolina at Chapel Hill (B.A., 1978); Campbell University (J.D., 1982). ***PRACTICE AREAS:*** Real Estate; Probate; Corporate. ***Email:*** danahall@bellsouth.net

JOE T. MILLSAPS

Established in 1961

404 CHARLOTTE NATIONAL BUILDING
428 EAST FOURTH STREET
CHARLOTTE, NORTH CAROLINA 28202
Telephone: 704-358-8524
Fax: 704-358-8405; Toll Free: 800-500-8524
Email: attyjtm@bellsouth.net
URL: http://www.lawyers.com/joemillsapslaw

Civil Trial Practice, Negligence, Personal Injury, Wills and Probate, Trusts, Estates, Estate Planning and Administration.

JOE T. MILLSAPS, born Mooresville, North Carolina, October 3, 1934; admitted to bar, 1961, North Carolina; 1967, U.S. District Court, Western District of North Carolina; 1974, U.S. Court of Appeals for the Fourth Circuit; 1977, U.S. Supreme Court; 1994, U.S. District Court, Middle District of North Carolina. *Education:* Wake Forest University (B.A., 1957; LL.B., 1961). Phi Delta Phi. *Member:* Mecklenburg County and North Carolina (Member, Public Information Committee, 1980-1990; Chairman, 1987-1990) Bar Associations; The North Carolina State Bar (N.C. Lawyer Referral Committee, 2003—); The Association of Trial Lawyers of America; North Carolina Academy of Trial Lawyers. [Capt., USAR, 1955-1965]

REPRESENTATIVE CLIENTS: A & E Blueprint and Supply, Inc.; Austin, Falls & Chandler, CPA's; Barger Construction Co., Inc.; Duncan-Parnell; Fletcher-Butler Corporation (Florida); Fletcher Nursery, Inc. (Florida); Forms & Supply, Inc.; Ralston Purina Co.; Swofford Associates, Inc.; James R. Tice & Co.
APPROVED ATTORNEY FOR: First American Title Insurance Co.; Chicago Title Insurance Co.; Lawyers Title Insurance Corp.; Investors Title Insurance Co.
REFERENCE: Central Carolina Bank and Trust Company.

MITCHELL, RALLINGS & TISSUE, PLLC

Established in 1983

1800 CARILLON
227 WEST TRADE STREET
CHARLOTTE, NORTH CAROLINA 28202
Telephone: 704-376-6574
FAX: 704-342-1531

General Civil and Trial Practice in all State and Federal Courts. Bankruptcy, Real Estate, Commercial Law, Corporate, Negligence, Banking, Business Law, Construction Law, Debtor and Creditor, Employment.

MEMBERS OF FIRM

RICHARD M. MITCHELL, born Richmond, Virginia, June 22, 1940; admitted to bar, 1972, North Carolina and U.S. District Court, Western District of North Carolina; 1974, U.S. Court of Appeals, 4th Circuit; 1978, U.S. District Court, Eastern District of North Carolina. *Education:* Wingate College; University of North Carolina-Charlotte (B.A., 1969); University of North Carolina (J.D., 1972). Delta Theta Phi. Member, Panel of Arbitrators, American Arbitration Association. *Member:* North Carolina, Federal and American Bar Associations; North Carolina State Bar; North Carolina Trial Lawyers Association; Commercial Law League of America; American Bankruptcy Institute; National Association of Bankruptcy Trustees. (Board Certified Specialist in Bankruptcy Law, North Carolina State Board of Legal Specialization). ***PRACTICE AREAS:*** Bankruptcy. ***Email:*** rmitchell@mrsmt.com

THOMAS B. RALLINGS, JR., born Charlotte, North Carolina, September 2, 1952; admitted to bar, 1977, North Carolina and U.S. District Court, Western District of North Carolina; 1985, U.S. Court of Appeals, 4th Circuit. *Education:* University of North Carolina (B.S., 1974; J.D., 1977). Phi Delta Phi; Beta Gamma Sigma. *Member:* North Carolina and American (Member: Forum Committee on the Construction Industry; Section of Corporation, Banking and Business Law) Bar Associations; North Carolina State Bar; North Carolina Academy of Trial Lawyers; Commercial Law League of America; The Association of Trial Lawyers of America. ***PRACTICE AREAS:*** Commercial Law; Civil Litigation. ***Email:*** trallings@mrsmt.com

JOSEPH N. TISSUE, born Meyersdale, Pennsylvania, May 28, 1954; admitted to bar, 1980, Pennsylvania; 1982, North Carolina. *Education:* University of Pennsylvania (B.A., 1976); University of Pittsburgh (J.D., 1980). Order of Barristers. Law Clerk to the Honorable Norman A. Shaulis, Pennsylvania Court of Common Pleas, 1980-1981. *Member:* Mecklenburg County (Member, Real Estate Section) and North Carolina (Member, Real Estate and Business Sections) Bar Associations; North Carolina State Bar. ***PRACTICE AREAS:*** Commercial Real Estate Law; Real Estate Finance Law; Closely Held Businesses. ***Email:*** joetissue@mrsmt.com

ASSOCIATES

JAMES L. FRETWELL, born Albany, New York, March 7, 1957; admitted to bar, 1982, North Carolina and U.S. District Court, Western District of North Carolina; 1985, U.S. Court of Appeals, 4th Circuit. *Education:* Wesleyan University (B.A., 1979); Syracuse University (J.D., 1982). *Member:* North Carolina and American Bar Associations. ***PRACTICE AREAS:*** Commercial Law; Civil Litigation. ***Email:*** jfretwell@mrsmt.com

HEATHER W. CULP, born Killeen, Texas, March 1, 1973; admitted to bar, 1997, Kentucky; 1998, U.S. District Court, Eastern District of Kentucky; 2000, U.S. District Court, Western District of Kentucky; 2002, North Carolina and U.S. District Court, Western District of North Carolina. *Education:* Miami University of Ohio (B.A., cum laude, 1994); University of Kentucky (J.D., 1997). *Member:* North Carolina and Kentucky Bar Associations. ***PRACTICE AREAS:*** Litigation; Construction Law; Bankruptcy. ***Email:*** hculp@mrsmt.com

CHRISTOPHER J. CULP, admitted to bar, 1986, North Carolina; U.S. District Court, Western District of North Carolina; 1990, Georgia; U.S. District Court, Northern District of Georgia; 1998, U.S. District Court, Middle and Eastern Districts of North Carolina. *Education:* Davidson College (A.B., 1983); University of North Carolina (J.D., 1986). Phi Eta Sigma; Phi Delta Phi. *Member:* Mecklenburg County and North Carolina Bar Associations; State North Carolina State Bar; State Bar of Georgia; North Carolina Association of Defense Attorneys. ***PRACTICE AREAS:*** Bankruptcy; Litigation; Products Liability; Insurance Defense; Construction Law. ***Email:*** cculp@mrsmt.com

REPRESENTATIVE CLIENTS: Bonitz Contracting Co.; Dyke Industries, Inc.; Edgcomb Metals; Titan Building Products, Inc.; H & S Lumber Co.; L & W Supply; McClure Lumber Co.; Central Carolina Bank; United Scrap, Inc.; Twin Lakes Business Park; RNS International, Inc.; Smart Products, Inc.; Charlotte Paint Co.; Willow Branch Landscaping; ; McClancy Seasoning Co.; Carolina Builders Corporation; Gentek Building Products, Inc.; Inotexx Corp.; Hughes Supply; Sunbelt Rentals, Inc.; Fire Thorne Country Club.
APPROVED ATTORNEYS FOR: Lawyers Title Insurance Corp.; Commonwealth Land Title Insurance Co.; Jefferson Pilot Title Insurance Co.; St. Paul Title Insurance Co.; Investors Title Insurance Co.; Meridian Title Insurance Co.; Chicago Title Insurance Co.; Fidelity National Title Insurance Company; American National Insurance Company; Fidelity National Title Insurance Company.
REFERENCES: Central Carolina Bank; Bank of Mecklenburg.

CHARLES G. MONNETT III & ASSOCIATES

Established in 1983

200 QUEENS ROAD, SUITE 300
CHARLOTTE, NORTH CAROLINA 28204
Telephone: 704-376-1911
Fax: 704-376-1921
Email: cmonnett@carolinalaw.com
URL: http://www.carolinalaw.com

Mailing Address: P.O. Box 37206, Charlotte, NC 28237

Catastrophic Injury, Personal Injury, Brain Injury, Medical Malpractice, Birth Trauma, Spinal Cord Injury, Professional Liability, Wrongful Death, Products Liability, Inadequate Security, Insurance Bad Faith, Insurance Claims and Business Torts, Truck Accidents, Legal Malpractice, Construction Accidents, Automobile Accidents and Injuries, Nursing Home Negligence and Insurance Law.

FIRM PROFILE: Charles G. Monnett III & Associates have extensive trial and appellate experience in both State and Federal Courts.

CHARLES G. MONNETT, III, born Greensboro, North Carolina, June 9, 1957; admitted to bar, 1983, North Carolina and U.S. District Court, Western District of North Carolina; 1989, U.S. Court of Appeals, Fourth Circuit; 1991, U.S. Supreme Court. *Education:* Appalachian State University (B.A., 1980); University of North Carolina (J.D., 1983). Past President, Mecklenburg County Trial Lawyers Association. Member: Board of Governors, North Carolina Academy of Trial Lawyers; Board of Directors, Brain Injury Association of North Carolina. Current Chair, ATLA Traumatic Brain Injury Litigation Group; Past Treasurer, ATLA Traumatic Brain Injury Litigation Group. North Carolina Governor's Advisory Counsel on Traumatic Brain Injury. Fellow, Roscoe Pound Foundation. Member, Melvin Belli Society. Member, Birth Trauma Litigation Group. Southern Trial Lawyers Association;. *Member:* American Bar Association; North Carolina State Bar Association; Association of Trial Lawyers of America (President's Club,); North Carolina Academy of Trial Lawyers (President's Club); Mecklenburg County Trial Lawyers Association. ***PRACTICE AREAS:*** Personal Injury; Medical Negligence; Brain Injury; Birth Trauma; Wrongful Death; Automobile Accidents and Injuries; Medical Malpractice; Catastrophic Injury; Neurolaw; Motorcycle Accidents; Workers Compensation; Pedestrian Injuries; Plaintiffs Personal Injury; Spinal Injury; Third Party Wrongful Death; Boating Accidents; Obstetric Malpractice; Pediatric Malpractice; Gynecology Malpractice; Head Injury; Electrical Injury.

OF COUNSEL

CRAIG O. ASBILL, born Asheboro, North Carolina, February 26, 1974; admitted to bar, 2000, North Carolina; 2002, South Carolina and U.S. District Court, Western District of North Carolina. *Education:* North Carolina State University (B.A., 1996); Mercer University (J.D., 2000). *Member:* Mecklenburg County Bar Association; North Carolina State Bar; South Carolina Bar; North Carolina Academy of Trial Lawyers; South Carolina Trial Lawyers Association; The Association of Trial Lawyers of America; Mecklenburg Trial Lawyers Association. ***PRACTICE AREAS:*** Personal Injury; Workers Compensation. ***Email:*** casbill@carolinalaw.com

MOORE & VAN ALLEN PLLC

100 NORTH TRYON STREET, SUITE 4700
CHARLOTTE, NORTH CAROLINA 28202-4003
Telephone: 704-331-1000
Fax: 704-331-1159
URL: http://www.mvalaw.com

Charleston, South Carolina Office: 40 Calhoun Street, Suite 300. Telephone: 843-579-7000. Fax: 843-579-7099.
Research Triangle Park, North Carolina Office: 430 Davis Drive, Suite 500, P.O. Box 13706. Telephone: 919-286-8000. Fax: 919-286-8199.

Admiralty, Banking, Bankruptcy, Commercial Finance, Conduit Lending, Construction, Corporate, Distressed Debt Trading, Employee Benefits, Employment, Energy, Environmental, ERISA, Estate Planning and Administration, Government Contracts, Health Care, Immigration, Information Technology and E-Commerce, Insurance, Intellectual Property, International, Leasing, Litigation, Lobbying and Legislative Representation, Patent and Copyright, Real Estate, Securities, Surety, Taxation, Tax Incentives, Trusts, Utilities and Venture Capital.

FIRM PROFILE: Moore & Van Allen, PLLC is one of the largest and fastest-growing law firms in the Southeast, with approximately 250 attorneys engaged in a general business, banking, and litigation practice.

(This Listing Continued)

MOORE & VAN ALLEN PLLC, Charlotte—Continued

RESIDENT MEMBERS

W. MILLER ABERNETHY, JR., born 1961; admitted to bar, 1987, North Carolina. *Education:* University of North Carolina (B.A., 1984); Harvard University (J.D., 1987). Phi Beta Kappa. ***PRACTICE AREAS:*** Leasing; Banking; Corporate. ***Email:*** millerabernethy@mvalaw.com

A. MARK ADCOCK, born 1957; admitted to bar, 1983, North Carolina. *Education:* Wake Forest University (B.A., 1980); University of North Carolina (J.D., with honors, 1983). Order of the Coif. Articles Editor, North Carolina Law Review, 1982-1983. ***PRACTICE AREAS:*** Commercial; Corporate; Consumer Credit; Banking; Real Estate Finance; Workouts. ***Email:*** markadcock@mvalaw.com

LOU M. AGOSTO, born 1967; admitted to bar, 1997, Colorado; 2001, North Carolina. *Education:* University of North Carolina, Chapel Hill (B.S., with distinction, 1990; M.A., 1991); Vanderbilt University (J.D., 1997). Associate Notes Editor, Vanderbilt Law Review. ***PRACTICE AREAS:*** Bankruptcy; Litigation. ***Email:*** louagosto@mvalaw.com

JAMES E. AKERS, born 1971; admitted to bar, 1997, Texas; 2000, North Carolina. *Education:* Vanderbilt University (B.A., 1993); Texas Tech University (J.D., 1997). Comment Editor, Texas Tech Law Review. Editorial Board, Texas Bank Lawyer. ***PRACTICE AREAS:*** Banking. ***Email:*** jayakers@mvalaw.com

H. HEATH ALEXANDER, born 1954; admitted to bar, 1979, North Carolina; 1987, South Carolina. *Education:* University of North Carolina (B.S., 1976; J.D., with honors, 1979). Phi Beta Kappa. Order of the Coif. Jackson Scholar. Board of Editors, North Carolina Law Review, 1978-1979. ***PRACTICE AREAS:*** Corporate; Partnership; Limited Liability Company Law; Tax. ***Email:*** heathalexander@mvalaw.com

SCOTT K. AMES, born 1953; admitted to bar, 1993, Arizona; 1999, South Carolina (Not admitted in North Carolina). *Education:* Arizona State University (B.S., 1979; M.S., 1989); Lewis & Clark University, Northwestern School of Law (J.D., 1993). ***PRACTICE AREAS:*** Litigation; Environmental. ***Email:*** scottames@mvalaw.com

BRIAN THOMAS ATKINSON, born 1965; admitted to bar, 1992, North Carolina. *Education:* University of North Carolina at Charlotte (B.S., cum laude, 1987); University of North Carolina at Chapel Hill (J.D., 1992). North Carolina Law Review, 1991-1992. Certified Public Accountant, North Carolina, 1992. ***PRACTICE AREAS:*** Corporate; Securities. ***Email:*** btatkinson@mvalaw.com

ROBERT V. BAKER, born 1954; admitted to bar, 1982, Mississippi; 1984, North Carolina. *Education:* Mississippi College (B.S., 1976) University of Mississippi School of Law (J.D., with honors, 1982); New York University School of Law (LL.M., 1984). Business Manager, University of Mississippi Law Journal. Certified Public Accountant: Mississippi, 1978; North Carolina, 1984. ***PRACTICE AREAS:*** Corporate; Leasing; Taxation. ***Email:*** bobbaker@mvalaw.com

W. DOAK BARNHARDT, born 1957; admitted to bar, 1984, North Carolina. *Education:* Wake Forest University (B.A., 1980); University of North Carolina (M.B.A., 1984; J.D., 1984). ***PRACTICE AREAS:*** Banking; Corporate. ***Email:*** doakbarnhardt@mvalaw.com

JOHN E. BELTZ, born 1964; admitted to bar, 1991, Florida, Connecticut, New Jersey and New York; 1998, North Carolina. *Education:* Lehigh University (B.S., 1987); Cornell University (J.D., 1990); New York University (LL.M. in Taxation, 1991). ***PRACTICE AREAS:*** Corporate; Securities. ***Email:*** johnbeltz@mvalaw.com

EDWARD S. BOOHER, JR., born 1951; admitted to bar, 1982, District of Columbia; 1997, North Carolina. *Education:* Wake Forest University (B.A., 1973; J.D., 1982); Trinity University (M.S., 1978). ***PRACTICE AREAS:*** Real Estate Finance; Securitization; Conduit Lending. ***Email:*** eddiebooher@mvalaw.com

CAROL EWALD BOWEN, born 1957; admitted to bar, 1985, Massachusetts; 1987, New Jersey; 1997, North Carolina. *Education:* Duke University (A.B., 1979); Vanderbilt University (J.D., 1984). ***PRACTICE AREAS:*** Health Care. ***Email:*** carolbowen@mvalaw.com

ROBERT C. BOWERS, born 1971; admitted to bar, 1996, North Carolina. *Education:* Davidson College (A.B., magna cum laude, 1993); Duke University (J.D., magna cum laude, 1996). ***PRACTICE AREAS:*** Litigation. ***Email:*** robertbowers@mvalaw.com

R. ALEXANDER BURROUGHS, born 1969; admitted to bar, 1994, North Carolina. *Education:* Emory University (B.A., summa cum laude, 1991); Temple University (J.D., 1994). ***PRACTICE AREAS:*** Commercial Real Estate; Business Law. ***Email:*** alexburroughs@mvalaw.com

TODD A. CARAWAY, born 1962; admitted to bar, 1993, Michigan; 1998, North Carolina. *Education:* University of Wisconsin-Madison (B.B.A., 1984); University of South Florida (M.B.A., 1989); University of Pittsburgh (J.D., 1992). Notes and Comments Editor, University of Pittsburgh Journal of Law and Commerce, 1991-1992. ***PRACTICE AREAS:*** Banking. ***Email:*** toddcaraway@mvalaw.com

MARK E. CARPENTER, born 1960; admitted to bar, 1985, North Carolina. *Education:* University of North Carolina (A.B., 1982); University of Virginia (J.D., 1985). Phi Beta Kappa. ***PRACTICE AREAS:*** Banking; Project Finance; Corporate; Real Estate; Conduit Lending. ***Email:*** markcarpenter@mvalaw.com

BRIAN K. CARY, born 1962; admitted to bar, 1993, Virginia; 2002, North Carolina. *Education:* University of North Carolina at Chapel Hill (B.A., 1983); University of Richmond (J.D., cum laude, 1993). Member, University of Richmond Law Review. ***PRACTICE AREAS:*** Commercial Real Estate. ***Email:*** briancary@mvalaw.com

ALAN J. CHADD, born 1969; admitted to bar, 1997, Texas; 1999, North Carolina. *Education:* Duke University (B.A., cum laude, 1991; M.B.A., 1997; J.D., 1997). ***PRACTICE AREAS:*** Banking. ***Email:*** alanchadd@mvalaw.com

JOHN S. CHINUNTDET, born 1966; admitted to bar, 1992, Texas; 2002, North Carolina. *Education:* Wake Forest University (B.A., 1988); Southern Methodist University (J.D., 1991). Chairman and President, Association for Corporate Growth-Carolinas, 2003-2004. Member, Wake Forest University Alumni Council. Fellow, American College of Investment Counsel. ***PRACTICE AREAS:*** Mezzanine Finance; Private Equity. ***Email:*** johnchinuntdet@mvalaw.com

BERNARD B. CLARK, born 1947; admitted to bar, 1972, North Carolina. *Education:* University of South Carolina (B.A., cum laude, 1969); Duke University (J.D., 1972). Phi Beta Kappa. Certified Public Accountant. ***PRACTICE AREAS:*** Taxation. ***Email:*** bernardclark@mvalaw.com

DUMONT CLARKE, IV, born 1952; admitted to bar, 1978, North Carolina; 1980, New York. *Education:* Vassar College (B.A., 1974); University of North Carolina (J.D., with honors, 1978). Board of Editors, North Carolina Law Review, 1977-1978. Law Clerk to Hon. Walter E. Brock, North Carolina Supreme Court, 1978-1979. Member, Mecklenburg County Board of Commissioners, 2001-2002. ***PRACTICE AREAS:*** Corporate and Securities; Municipal Finance. ***Email:*** dumontclarke@mvalaw.com

DANIEL G. CLODFELTER, born 1950; admitted to bar, 1977, North Carolina. *Education:* Davidson College (B.A., cum laude, 1972); Corpus Christi College, Oxford University, Oxford, England (B.A., 1974); Yale University (J.D., 1977). Phi Beta Kappa. Rhodes Scholar. Law Clerk to Hon. James B. McMillan, United States District Court, Western District of North Carolina, 1977. Member, 1984-1987 and Chairman, 1986-1987, Charlotte-Mecklenburg Planning Commission. Charlotte City Council, 1987-1993. North Carolina State Senate, 1999—. ***PRACTICE AREAS:*** Bankruptcy; Workouts; Antitrust; Unfair Trade Practices. ***Email:*** danclodfelter@mvalaw.com

KENNETH S. COE, born 1950; admitted to bar, 1976, North Carolina. *Education:* University of North Carolina (A.B., 1972); Duke University (J.D., 1976). Phi Beta Kappa. Morehead Scholar. Panel of Arbitrators, American Arbitration Association. ***PRACTICE AREAS:*** Corporate; Real Estate; Estate Planning; Taxation. ***Email:*** kencoe@mvalaw.com

TIMOTHY W. CORRIGAN, born 1968; admitted to bar, 1994, North Carolina. *Education:* Indiana University, Bloomington (B.S., 1990); University of North Carolina (J.D., 1994). ***PRACTICE AREAS:*** Banking. ***Email:*** timcorrigan@mvalaw.com

JEFFREY J. DAVIS, born 1947; admitted to bar, 1975, North Carolina. *Education:* University of Illinois (B.S., with honors, 1972; J.D., with honors, 1975). Order of the Coif. Articles Editor, University of Illinois Law Forum, 1974-1975. Law Clerk to Hon. James B. McMillan, United States District Court, Western District of North Carolina, 1975-1976. Fellow, American College of Trial Lawyers. Panel of Arbitrators, American Arbitration Association. ***PRACTICE AREAS:*** Commercial Litigation; Securities Litigation; Arbitration; Construction Litigation. ***Email:*** jeffdavis@mvalaw.com

ERNEST S. (MIKE) DeLANEY III, born 1948; admitted to bar, 1973, North Carolina. *Education:* Duke University (B.A., 1970); University of North Carolina (J.D., with honors, 1973). Order of the Coif. Associate Editor, *North Carolina Law Review,* 1972-1973. ***PRACTICE AREAS:*** Corporate; Business; Corporate Finance; Environmental. ***Email:*** mikedelaney@mvalaw.com

MIRIAM ANN DIXON, born 1962; admitted to bar, 1987, North Carolina. *Education:* Duke University (A.B., magna cum laude, 1984); Harvard University (J.D., 1987). Phi Beta Kappa. ***PRACTICE AREAS:*** Commercial Real Estate. ***Email:*** miriamdixon@mvalaw.com

J. THOMAS DUNN, JR., born 1943; admitted to bar, 1968, North Carolina. *Education:* Belmont Abbey College (A.B., 1965); University of North Carolina (J.D., 1968). ***PRACTICE AREAS:*** Financial Services; Insolvency. ***Email:*** tomdunn@mvalaw.com

BRYAN P. DURRETT, born 1959; admitted to bar, 1996, Colorado; 1998, North Carolina. *Education:* Duke University (B.A., 1981); University of Pittsburgh School of Law (J.D., cum laude, 1993); University of Miami School of Law (LL.M., Real Property Development, 1996). Order of the Coif. ***PRACTICE AREAS:*** Commercial Real Estate. ***Email:*** bryandurett@mvalaw.com

DAVID L. EADES, born 1960; admitted to bar, 1986, North Carolina. *Education:* Rhodes College (B.A., with honors, 1982); Vanderbilt University (J.D., 1986). Phi Beta Kappa. Vanderbilt Law Review, 1984-1986. ***PRACTICE AREAS:*** Bankruptcy; Workouts. ***Email:*** davideades@mvalaw.com

JOSEPH A. FERNANDEZ, born 1972; admitted to bar, 1997, North Carolina. *Education:* University of North Carolina at Chapel Hill (B.A., 1994); Wake Forest University (J.D., 1997). ***PRACTICE AREAS:*** Corporate Law; Energy; Mergers and Acquisitions. ***Email:*** joefernandez@mvalaw.com

ANA M. FLYNN, born 1948; admitted to bar, 1993, Illinois; 2001, North Carolina. *Education:* Smith College (B.A., cum laude, 1971); Chicago-Kent College of Law (J.D., with high honors, 1993). Phi Beta Kappa. Order of the Coif. Executive Articles Editor, Chicago-Kent Law Review, 1992-1993. ***PRACTICE AREAS:*** Employee Benefits; ERISA. ***Email:*** anaflynn@mvalaw.com

WILLIAM H. FULLER, III, born 1966; admitted to bar, 1993, North Carolina. *Education:* University of North Carolina (B.A., with honors, 1989) Morehead Scholar. University of Virginia (J.D., 1993). Notes Editor and Article Review Board of Journal of Law and Politics. ***PRACTICE AREAS:*** Banking; Corporate. ***Email:*** billfuller@mvalaw.com

RICHARD C. GASKINS, JR., born 1958; admitted to bar, 1984, North Carolina. *Education:* Duke University (B.S.M.E., summa cum laude, 1980); Harvard University (J.D., cum laude, 1984). Tau Beta Pi. Managing Editor, Harvard Environmental Law Review, 1983. Member, Legislative and Legal Issues Committee, North Carolina Governor's Waste Management Board, 1988-1990. Member, ASTM Environmental Assessment Committee. Past Chair, Environmental Risk Management Committee. Past Chair, Pollution Prevention & Global Sustainability Subcommittee. *Member:* Mecklenburg County (Grievance Committee, 1998-2000), North Carolina (Member, Environmental Planning Committee; Past Chairman, Environmental and Natural Resources Law Section) and American (Vice Chair: Environmental Litigation Committee; Toxic Torts Committee) Bar Associations; North Carolina Bar Foundation (Continuing Legal Education Committee, 1990—). ***PRACTICE AREAS:*** Litigation; Environmental. ***Email:*** rickgaskins@mvalaw.com

JOHN T. GATHINGS, JR., born 1965; admitted to bar, 1990, South Carolina; 1991, North Carolina. *Education:* Davidson College (A.B., 1987); Cumberland School of Law (J.D., summa cum laude, 1990). Editor in Chief, Cumberland Law Review, 1989-1990. Law

(This Listing Continued)

Clerk to Hon. Donald Russell, United States Court of Appeals, Fourth Circuit, 1990-1991. ***PRACTICE AREAS:*** Corporate; Mergers and Acquisitions. ***Email:*** johngathings@mvalaw.com

M. BRYANT GATRELL, born 1970; admitted to bar, 1997, North Carolina. *Education:* University of Missouri (B.A., summa cum laude, 1993); University of Michigan (J.D., cum laude, 1996). Phi Beta Kappa. ***PRACTICE AREAS:*** Banking. ***Email:*** bryantgatrell@mvalaw.com

DOUGLAS R. GHIDINA, born 1962; admitted to bar, 1987, North Carolina. *Education:* Illinois Wesleyan University (B.A., magna cum laude, 1984); University of Michigan (J.D., 1987). ***PRACTICE AREAS:*** Bankruptcy; Commercial Litigation. ***Email:*** dougghidina@mvalaw.com

JEFFREY W. GLENNEY, born 1963; admitted to bar, 1989, Texas; 1994, North Carolina. *Education:* Duke University (B.A., 1986); University of Southern California (J.D., 1989). Legal Writing Instructor, University of Southern California Law Review. ***PRACTICE AREAS:*** Commercial Real Estate; Banking. ***Email:*** jeffglenney@mvalaw.com

JEREMY H. GODWIN, born 1971; admitted to bar, 1996, North Carolina and South Carolina. *Education:* Davidson College (B.A., 1992); Wake Forest University (M.B.A., 1996; J.D., 1996). Member, Moot Court Board, 1993-1996. ***PRACTICE AREAS:*** Corporate; Business; Information Technology. ***Email:*** jeremygodwin@mvalaw.com

THOMAS E. GRAHAM, born 1957; admitted to bar, 1984, North Carolina. *Education:* Ohio State University (B.S./B.A., summa cum laude, 1980); George Washington University (J.D., with honors, 1984). ***PRACTICE AREAS:*** Intellectual Property; Information Technology; E-Commerce. ***Email:*** thomgraham@mvalaw.com

STEPHEN M. HADER, born 1962; admitted to bar, 1987, New Jersey; 1988, New York; 1998, North Carolina. *Education:* State University of New York (B.A., cum laude, 1984); Rutgers University (J.D., 1987). *Member:* American Immigration Lawyers Association. ***PRACTICE AREAS:*** International; Corporate. ***Email:*** stevehader@mvalaw.com

GEORGE V. HANNA III, born 1943; admitted to bar, 1968, North Carolina. *Education:* University of North Carolina (A.B., 1965; J.D., 1968). Board of Editors, North Carolina Law Review, 1967. Law Clerk to Hon. Joseph Branch, Chief Justice, North Carolina Supreme Court, 1968-1969. Panel of Arbitrators, American Arbitration Association. ***PRACTICE AREAS:*** Commercial Litigation and Arbitration; Construction; Banking Litigation; Environmental. ***Email:*** georgehanna@mvalaw.com

HOLLIE H. HART, born 1972; admitted to bar, 1997, North Carolina. *Education:* University of Virginia (B.A., 1994); Duke University (J.D., 1997). ***PRACTICE AREAS:*** Real Estate. ***Email:*** holliehart@mvalaw.com

W. B. HAWFIELD, JR., born 1947; admitted to bar, 1972, North Carolina. *Education:* University of North Carolina (A.B., 1969); Stanford University (J.D., 1972). Phi Beta Kappa. Morehead Scholar. Chairman, Bankruptcy Section, North Carolina Bar Association, 1981-1982. ***PRACTICE AREAS:*** Bankruptcy; Workouts; Corporate. ***Email:*** benhawfield@mvalaw.com

STEPHEN D. HOPE, born 1947; admitted to bar, 1974, New York; 1977, North Carolina. *Education:* University of North Carolina (A.B., 1969); Columbia University (J.D., 1973). Harlan Fiske Stone Scholar. Board of Editors, Columbia Law Review, 1971-1973. ***PRACTICE AREAS:*** Corporate Finance; Corporate; Energy; Mergers and Acquisitions. ***Email:*** stevehope@mvalaw.com

MARK R. A. HORN, born 1971; admitted to bar, 1997, North Carolina. *Education:* University of North Carolina (B.A., with distinction, 1994); University of Virginia (J.D., 1997). Phi Beta Kappa. Phi Delta Phi. Articles Review Board, Virginia Environmental Law Journal. Member, Charlotte Estate Planning Council. (Board Certified Specialist in Estate Planning and Probate Law, North Carolina State Board of Legal Specialization). ***PRACTICE AREAS:*** Trusts and Estates; Taxation; Probate. ***Email:*** markhorn@mvalaw.com

JAMES W. HOVIS, born 1954; admitted to bar, 1980, North Carolina. *Education:* University of North Carolina (B.S., 1976; J.D., with high honors, 1980). Phi Beta Kappa. Order of the Coif. Managing Editor, North Carolina Law Review, 1979-1980. ***PRACTICE AREAS:*** Banking; Corporate. ***Email:*** jimhovis@mvalaw.com

JAMES H. JEFFRIES, IV, born 1958; admitted to bar, 1988, North Carolina, U.S. Court of Appeals, Fourth and District of Columbia Circuits and U.S. Court of Federal Claims. *Education:* Duke University (B.A., cum laude, 1980); University of North Carolina at Chapel Hill (J.D., with honors, 1988). Order of the Coif. Articles Editor, North Carolina Law Review, 1987-1988. *Member:* Energy Bar Association. [Lieutenant Colonel, U.S. Marine Corps Reserve]. ***PRACTICE AREAS:*** Business Litigation; Telecommunications Law; Utility Regulation. ***Email:*** jamesjeffries@mvalaw.com

DANIEL L. JOHNSON, JR., born 1960; admitted to bar, 1985, North Carolina. *Education:* University of North Carolina (B.S.B.A., 1981; J.D., with high honors, 1985). Order of the Coif. Research Editor, North Carolina Law Review. ***PRACTICE AREAS:*** Employee Benefits; ERISA. ***Email:*** dannyjohnson@mvalaw.com

LEA STROMIRE JOHNSON, born 1960; admitted to bar, 1985, North Carolina. *Education:* The Centre College of Kentucky (B.A., summa cum laude, 1982); Vanderbilt University (J.D., 1985). Phi Beta Kappa. Order of the Coif. Associate Editor, Vanderbilt Law Review, 1984-1985. ***PRACTICE AREAS:*** Banking; Corporate. ***Email:*** leajohnson@mvalaw.com

ROBERT I. KENNY, born 1965; admitted to bar, 1991, Illinois; 1996, North Carolina. *Education:* University of Illinois (B.A., 1987; J.D., 1991). ***PRACTICE AREAS:*** Leasing; Banking. ***Email:*** robkenny@mvalaw.com

KENNETH P. KERR, born 1964; admitted to bar, 1990, Pennsylvania; 1992, Florida; 1997, North Carolina. *Education:* Indiana University of Pennsylvania (B.A., summa cum laude, 1987); The Dickinson School of Law of the Pennsylvania State University (J.D., 1990). ***PRACTICE AREAS:*** Banking; Real Estate; Commercial Litigation. ***Email:*** kenkerr@mvalaw.com

(This Listing Continued)

ANTHONY T. LATHROP, born 1961; admitted to bar, 1988, North Carolina. *Education:* University of North Carolina at Chapel Hill (B.A., 1983; J.D., 1988). Order of Barristers. Member, Holderness Moot Court. Recipient, James W. Morrow Award. ***PRACTICE AREAS:*** Litigation. ***Email:*** tonylathrop@mvalaw.com

SANDRA M. LAZORCHECK, born 1971; admitted to bar, 1997, New Jersey; 1998, New York; 1999, North Carolina. *Education:* Syracuse University (B.A./B.S., cum laude, 1993); New York Law School (J.D., magna cum laude, 1997). Articles Editor, New York Law School Law Review. ***PRACTICE AREAS:*** Banking. ***Email:*** sandralazorcheck@mvalaw.com

HAL A. LEVINSON, born 1956; admitted to bar, 1982, North Carolina. *Education:* University of North Carolina (A.B., with honors, 1978); University of Michigan (J.D., 1981). Phi Beta Kappa. Law Clerk to Hon. James B. McMillan, United States District Court, Western District of North Carolina, 1981-1982. ***PRACTICE AREAS:*** Mergers and Acquisitions; Corporate; Finance. ***Email:*** hallevinson@mvalaw.com

DAVID T. LEWIS, born 1965; admitted to bar, 1993, Alabama and Mississippi; 1997, Virginia; 2000, North Carolina. *Education:* University of Richmond (B.S., 1988); Cumberland School of Law of Samford University (J.D., magna cum laude, 1992); University of Alabama (LL.M., Taxation, 1996). Law Clerk to the Hon. Robert R. Merhige, Jr., U.S. District Judge, Eastern District of Virginia, 1992-1993. [1st Lt., U.S. Marine Corps Reserve, 1986-1992]. ***PRACTICE AREAS:*** Taxation; Trusts and Estates. ***Email:*** davidlewis@mvalaw.com

B. PALMER McARTHUR, JR., born 1954; admitted to bar, 1982, North Carolina. *Education:* University of Virginia (B.S., 1977); University of Texas (J.D., with honors, 1982). Order of the Coif. Certified Public Accountant. ***PRACTICE AREAS:*** Business Law; Taxation; Commercial Real Estate. ***Email:*** palmermcarthur@mvalaw.com

NEILL G. McBRYDE, born 1944; admitted to bar, 1969, North Carolina; 1972, Georgia. *Education:* Davidson College (A.B., cum laude, 1966); University of North Carolina (J.D., with high honors, 1969). Omicron Delta Kappa. Order of the Coif. Phi Beta Kappa. Morehead Fellow in Law. Editor-in-Chief, North Carolina Law Review, 1968-1969. Chairman, Estate Planning and Fiduciary Law Section, North Carolina Bar Association, 1983-1984. President, 2000-2001, Fellow and Regent, American College of Trust and Estate Counsel. Fellow, American College of Tax Counsel. Board Certified Specialist in Estate Planning and Probate Law. ***PRACTICE AREAS:*** Taxation; Estate and Business Planning; Estate Administration; Mergers and Acquisitions. ***Email:*** neillmcbryde@mvalaw.com

KARIN M. McGINNIS, born 1967; admitted to bar, 1992, North Carolina. *Education:* East Carolina University (B.A., English, 1989); University of North Carolina (J.D., with high honors, 1992). Order of the Coif. Senior Staff, North Carolina Law Review. ***PRACTICE AREAS:*** Litigation; Employment; Entertainment. ***Email:*** karinmcginnis@mvalaw.com

PETER J. McGRATH, JR., born 1961; admitted to bar, 1986, North Carolina. *Education:* Yale University (B.A., 1983); University of North Carolina (J.D., with honors, 1986). North Carolina Law Review, 1984-1985. ***PRACTICE AREAS:*** Environmental; Litigation. ***Email:*** petermcgrath@mvalaw.com

JOHN V. McINTOSH, born 1954; admitted to bar, 1979, North Carolina. *Education:* University of North Carolina (B.A., summa cum laude, 1976; J.D., 1979). Phi Beta Kappa. ***PRACTICE AREAS:*** Corporate; Mergers and Acquisitions; International. ***Email:*** johnmcintosh@mvalaw.com

C. WAYNE McKINZIE, born 1967; admitted to bar, 1993, California; 1995, North Carolina. *Education:* Princeton University (B.A., 1989); University of Virginia (J.D., 1993). Executive Editor, Virginia Environmental Law Journal, 1992-1993. Extern to Hon. Laughlin E. Waters, United States District Court, Central District of California, 1991. ***PRACTICE AREAS:*** Banking; Corporate; Securities. ***Email:*** waynemckinzie@mvalaw.com

JAMES P. McLOUGHLIN, JR., born 1956; admitted to bar, 1984, New York; 1986, North Carolina. *Education:* Holy Cross (B.A., cum laude, 1978); Duke University (J.D., 1982). Phi Beta Kappa. Order of the Coif. Articles Editor, Duke Law Journal, 1981-1982. Law Clerk to Hon. Eugene A. Gordon, United States District Court, Middle District of North Carolina, 1982-1983. ***PRACTICE AREAS:*** Securities Litigation and Arbitration; General Litigation; Arbitration. ***Email:*** jimmcloughlin@mvalaw.com

THOMAS L. MITCHELL, born 1964; admitted to bar, 1993, North Carolina. *Education:* University of Illinois (B.S., with honors, 1986); Washington & Lee University (J.D., cum laude, 1993). ***PRACTICE AREAS:*** Banking; Corporate. ***Email:*** tommitchell@mvalaw.com

WILLIAM H. MOORE, JR., born 1957; admitted to bar, 1983, North Carolina and South Carolina. *Education:* University of South Carolina (B.S., magna cum laude, 1980; J.D., 1983). Phi Beta Kappa. ***PRACTICE AREAS:*** Federal and State Taxation; Tax Incentives. ***Email:*** billymoore@mvalaw.com

THOMAS S. MULLIKIN, born 1960; admitted to bar, 1986, South Carolina (Not admitted in North Carolina). *Education:* University of South Carolina (B.A., cum laude, 1982; J.D., 1986). Phi Beta Kappa. ***PRACTICE AREAS:*** Environmental; Litigation. ***Email:*** tommullikin@mvalaw.com

GREGORY J. MURPHY, born 1964; admitted to bar, 1989, North Carolina. *Education:* Canisius College (B.A., summa cum laude, 1986); University of Michigan (J.D., cum laude, 1988). Law Clerk to Hon. James B. McMillan, United States District Court, Western District of North Carolina, 1989-1990. ***PRACTICE AREAS:*** Commercial Litigation; Construction Litigation; Banking Litigation. ***Email:*** gregmurphy@mvalaw.com

PAUL G. MURPHY, born 1964; admitted to bar, 1992, New York; 1997, North Carolina. *Education:* University of Virginia (B.S., 1986); University of North Carolina (J.D., 1989). ***PRACTICE AREAS:*** Financial Services. ***Email:*** paulmurphy@mvalaw.com

THOMAS D. MYRICK, born 1954; admitted to bar, 1984, North Carolina. *Education:* University of North Carolina (B.S.B.A., 1978; J.D., 1983). ***PRACTICE AREAS:*** Litigation. ***Email:*** tommyrick@mvalaw.com

(This Listing Continued)

MOORE & VAN ALLEN PLLC, Charlotte—Continued

J. CHRISTOPHER OATES, born 1954; admitted to bar, 1984, North Carolina. *Education:* Williams College (A.B., cum laude, 1976); University of North Carolina (J.D., 1984). ***PRACTICE AREAS:*** Commercial Real Estate; Land Use Law. ***Email:*** chrisoates@mvalaw.com

THOMAS C. O'BANNON, born 1960; admitted to bar, 1988, Texas; 1993, North Carolina. *Education:* University of Oklahoma (B.B.A., with highest honors, 1982); University of Texas (M.B.A., 1984; J.D., with honors, 1987). ***PRACTICE AREAS:*** Banking; Corporate. ***Email:*** tomobannon@mvalaw.com

EDWARD K. ODEN, born 1961; admitted to bar, 1986, Texas; 1997, North Carolina. *Education:* Southern Methodist University (B.A., 1983); Washington & Lee University (J.D., 1986). ***PRACTICE AREAS:*** Real Estate; Banking; Conduit Lending. ***Email:*** edoden@mvalaw.com

THOMAS H. O'DONNELL, JR., born 1969; admitted to bar, 1997, New York; 1999, North Carolina. *Education:* Seton Hall University (B.A., 1992); Vermont Law School (J.D., cum laude, 1996). ***PRACTICE AREAS:*** Business; Energy. ***Email:*** tomodonnell@mvalaw.com

KURT T. OOSTERHOUSE, born 1968; admitted to bar, 1993, Wisconsin; 1999, North Carolina. *Education:* Hope College (B.A., cum laude, 1990); University of Minnesota (J.D., cum laude, 1993). ***PRACTICE AREAS:*** Banking; Leasing; Commercial. ***Email:*** kurtoosterhouse@mvalaw.com

T. RANDOLPH PERKINS, born 1955; admitted to bar, 1982, New York; 1983, North Carolina. *Education:* University of North Carolina (A.B., 1977); Yale University (J.D., 1981). Phi Beta Kappa. ***PRACTICE AREAS:*** Corporate; Energy; Banking. ***Email:*** randyperkins@mvalaw.com

RANDEL E. PHILLIPS, born 1947; admitted to bar, 1980, North Carolina. *Education:* Davidson College (B.A., cum laude, 1969); Wadham College, Oxford University, Oxford, England (B.A., 1971); Harvard University (J.D., magna cum laude, 1979). Phi Beta Kappa. Rhodes Scholar. Board of Editors, Harvard Law Review, 1977-1979. Law Clerk to Hon. James B. McMillan, United States District Court, Western District of North Carolina, 1979-1980. Management Chair, ABA Committee on State Labor Law Developments, 1991-1994. ***PRACTICE AREAS:*** Employment; Litigation. ***Email:*** randyphillips@mvalaw.com

M. MATTHEW PLYLER, born 1971; admitted to bar, 1996, North Carolina. *Education:* University of North Carolina (B.S., with distinction, 1993; J.D., with honors, 1996). North Carolina Journal of International Law and Commercial Regulation. ***PRACTICE AREAS:*** Banking. ***Email:*** mattplyler@mvalaw.com

ALAN W. POPE, born 1966; admitted to bar, 1994, North Carolina and South Carolina. *Education:* Clemson University (B.S., summa cum laude, 1989); Northwestern University (M.S., 1992); Emory University (J.D., First honor graduate, 1994). Order of the Coif. Law Clerk to Hon. Henry Politz, United States Court of Appeals for the Fifth Circuit, 1994-1995. ***PRACTICE AREAS:*** Bankruptcy; Workouts. ***Email:*** alanpope@mvalaw.com

STEPHEN G. PORTER, JR., born 1970; admitted to bar, 1996, North Carolina. *Education:* University of North Carolina (B.A., 1993; J.D. with honors, 1996). ***PRACTICE AREAS:*** Banking. ***Email:*** winporter@mvalaw.com

DAVID J. QUATTLEBAUM, born 1960; admitted to bar, 1986, North Carolina. *Education:* Dartmouth College (A.B., 1983); Duke University (J.D., magna cum laude, 1986). Order of the Coif. Duke Law Journal, 1985-1986. ***PRACTICE AREAS:*** Banking; Acquisition Finance. ***Email:*** davidquattlebaum@mvalaw.com

ERNEST W. REIGEL, born 1957; admitted to bar, 1983, North Carolina. *Education:* Davidson College (A.B., 1980); College of William and Mary (J.D., 1983). Society of International Business Fellows; International Bar Association; North Carolina Medical Care Commission. ***PRACTICE AREAS:*** Corporate; International; Immigration; Customs; Trade Regulation. ***Email:*** erniereigel@mvalaw.com

SKOTTOWE W. SMITH, JR., born 1969; admitted to bar, 1994, North Carolina. *Education:* Wake Forest University (B.S., with honors, 1991; J.D., with honors, 1994). ***PRACTICE AREAS:*** Commercial Real Estate. ***Email:*** skottsmith@mvalaw.com

RYAN M. SMITH, born 1971; admitted to bar, 1996, North Carolina. *Education:* University of North Carolina (B.A., with distinction, 1993; J.D., 1996). Phi Beta Kappa. Order of the Barristers. Member, Holderness Moot Court. ***PRACTICE AREAS:*** Mezzanine Finance; Private Equity; Corporate. ***Email:*** ryansmith@mvalaw.com

BARNEY STEWART, III, born 1938; admitted to bar, 1967, Oklahoma; 1971, North Carolina. *Education:* Yale University (B.A., 1960); University of Oklahoma (J.D., 1967). Case Editor, Oklahoma Law Review, 1966-1967. Chairman, Securities Regulation Committee, 1981-1985; Vice-Chairman, 1985-1987, Business Law Section, North Carolina Bar Association. ***PRACTICE AREAS:*** Securities; Corporate; Corporate Finance. ***Email:*** barneystewart@mvalaw.com

SCOTT D. SYFERT, born 1969; admitted to bar, 1997, North Carolina. *Education:* The London School of Economics (G.C., 1990); University of North Carolina (B.A., with honors, 1991; J.D., with honors, 1997); University of Virginia, Foreign Affairs (M.A., with honors, 1997). *Member:* American Immigration Lawyers Association. ***PRACTICE AREAS:*** International; Corporate. ***Email:*** scottsyfert@mvalaw.com

BETH A. TURNER, born 1968; admitted to bar, 1996, North Carolina. *Education:* Salisbury State University (B.S., 1992); Temple University (J.D., 1996; LL.M., Taxation, 1997). ***PRACTICE AREAS:*** Estate Planning; Taxation. ***Email:*** bethturner@mvalaw.com

SCOTT M. TYLER, born 1970; admitted to bar, 1996, North Carolina and South Carolina; 1997, New York. *Education:* Hamilton College (B.A., magna cum laude, 1992); Duke University (J.D., 1995). Phi Beta Kappa. Editorial Board, Duke Law Journal. Law Clerk to Hon. Thomas J. McAvoy, United States District Court, Northern District of New York, 1995-1996. ***PRACTICE AREAS:*** Litigation. ***Email:*** scotttyler@mvalaw.com

(This Listing Continued)

DAVID S. WALLS, born 1959; admitted to bar, 1984, North Carolina. *Education:* Davidson College (B.A., magna cum laude, 1981); Harvard University (J.D., magna cum laude, 1984). Phi Beta Kappa. ***PRACTICE AREAS:*** Bankruptcy; Workouts; Banking; Corporate. ***Email:*** davidwalls@mvalaw.com

VICTORIA S. WINDELL, born 1967; admitted to bar, 1993, North Carolina. *Education:* Wake Forest University (B.S., cum laude, 1989); Campbell University (J.D., cum laude, 1993). ***PRACTICE AREAS:*** Estate Planning. ***Email:*** vickywindell@mvalaw.com

MICHAEL E. ZELLER, born 1967; admitted to bar, 1993, New York; 1996, North Carolina. *Education:* Union College (B.A., 1989); Temple University (J.D., 1992); University of Hamburg (LL.M., magna cum laude, 1994). ***LANGUAGES:*** German and Spanish. ***PRACTICE AREAS:*** Corporate; International; Immigration; Mergers and Acquisitions. ***Email:*** mikezeller@mvalaw.com

RESIDENT OF COUNSEL

JAY S. BILAS, born 1963; admitted to bar, 1992, North Carolina. *Education:* Duke University (A.B., 1986; J.D., 1992). ***PRACTICE AREAS:*** Litigation. ***Email:*** jaybilas@mvalaw.com

HARRY J. GRIM, born 1930; admitted to bar, 1959, North Carolina. *Education:* Washington & Lee University (A.B., 1952; LL.B., 1954). General Counsel, NationsBank-Texas, 1988-1993. ***PRACTICE AREAS:*** Corporate; Banking. ***Email:*** harrygrim@mvalaw.com

ROBERT W. KING, JR., born 1930; admitted to bar, 1959, North Carolina and U.S. Court of Appeals, 4th and 6th Circuits. *Education:* Hampden-Sydney College (B.S., 1952); University of North Carolina (J.D., with honors, 1959). Order of the Coif; Phi Beta Kappa; Phi Delta Phi. Associate Editor, North Carolina Law Review, 1958-1959. Moore & Van Allen, 1959-1988; Senior Vice President and General Counsel, Carolinas Healthcare System, 1988-1999. President, Mecklenburg County Bar, 1979-1980. Member, Hampden-Sydney College Board of Trustees, 1979-1996; 1999—. President, University of North Carolina Law Alumni Association, 1988-1989. Chairman, YMCA of Greater Charlotte, 1990-1992. *Member:* American Health Lawyers Association. [LCDR, USNR, Active Duty, 1952-1956]. ***PRACTICE AREAS:*** Business; Health Care. ***Email:*** bobking@mvalaw.com

KIMBERLY S. KIRK, admitted to bar, 1994, North Carolina. *Education:* Davidson College (A.B., magna cum laude, 1991); Vanderbilt University (J.D., 1994). Order of the Coif. Member, Vanderbilt Journal of Transnational Law. ***PRACTICE AREAS:*** Health Care.

T. EDMUND RAST, born 1947; admitted to bar, 1974, Ohio; 1979, North Carolina. *Education:* Yale University (B.A., 1969); University of Pennsylvania (J.D., 1974). ***PRACTICE AREAS:*** Commercial Real Estate. ***Email:*** tedrast@mvalaw.com

WILLIAM K. VAN ALLEN, born 1914; admitted to bar, 1938, New York; 1939, District of Columbia; 1951, North Carolina. *Education:* Hamilton College (B.A., 1935); Harvard University (LL.B., 1938). Phi Beta Kappa. Permanent Member, Federal Judicial Conference for the Fourth Circuit. ***Email:*** billvanallen@mvalaw.com

RESIDENT COUNSEL

KRISTEN NESS AYERS, born 1973; admitted to bar, 2000, North Carolina. *Education:* Duke University (B.A., 1996); University of South Carolina (J.D., 2000). Chairman, Charlotte Sister Cities. Board of Directors, Carolina International School. Coral Advisory Panel, South Atlantic Fishery Management Council. *Member:* American Immigration Lawyers Association. ***LANGUAGES:*** French (read). ***PRACTICE AREAS:*** Business Law; International Law; Immigration Law. ***Email:*** kristenayers@mvalaw.com

MELISSA G. BURNS, born 1963; admitted to bar, 1990, Missouri; 1993, North Carolina. *Education:* Vanderbilt University (B.A., cum laude, 1985); Washington University (J.D., 1990). Omicron Delta Kappa. ***PRACTICE AREAS:*** Financial Services Law. ***Email:*** melissaburns@mvalaw.com

MICHAEL T. CRONIN, born 1971; admitted to bar, 1996, Ohio; 2000, North Carolina. *Education:* The Ohio State University (B.A., with honors, 1993); Case Western Reserve University (J.D., cum laude, 1996). ***PRACTICE AREAS:*** Business Law; Financial Services Law; Taxation. ***Email:*** michaelcronin@mvalaw.com

KAREN A. DEAN, born 1957; admitted to bar, 1995, New Jersey and Pennsylvania; 1998, North Carolina. *Education:* Susquehanna University (B.A., cum laude, 1979); Rutgers University (J.D., 1995). ***PRACTICE AREAS:*** Banking; Conduit Lending. ***Email:*** karendean@mvalaw.com

TIMOTHY W. GILBERT, admitted to bar, 1981, North Carolina. *Education:* Wake Forest University (B.A., cum laude, 1978; J.D., 1981). ***PRACTICE AREAS:*** Financial Services Law. ***Email:*** timgilbert@mvalaw.com

TANYA D. GREELEY, born 1973; admitted to bar, 1999, North Carolina. *Education:* Pennsylvania State University (B.S., 1995); University of Maryland (J.D., 1999). Associate Editor, The Business Lawyer. ***PRACTICE AREAS:*** Business. ***Email:*** tanyagreeley@mvalaw.com

LAWRENCE P. LEVINE, born 1952; admitted to bar, 1977, Pennsylvania and New Jersey; 1988, Florida; 1989, New York; 2003, North Carolina. *Education:* University of Pennsylvania (B.A., 1974); Case Western Reserve University (J.D., 1977). *Member:* Dade County and American Bar Associations; The Florida Bar; American Corporate Counsel Association. (Senior Division Counsel). ***PRACTICE AREAS:*** Employment; Litigation. ***Email:*** larrylevine@mvalaw.com

DAVID L. RALLS, born 1948; admitted to bar, 1975, California; 1978, North Carolina; 1990, Florida. *Education:* University of California, Berkeley (B.A., 1971); University of San Francisco (J.D., 1974). ***PRACTICE AREAS:*** Banking. ***Email:*** davidralls@mvalaw.com

RICHARD S. SWEET, born 1941; admitted to bar, 1969, District of Columbia (Not admitted in North Carolina). *Education:* Lehigh University (B.A., with honors, 1963); University of Virginia (J.D., 1966); Georgetown University (LL.M., 1975). ***PRACTICE AREAS:*** Federal Taxation; International Taxation. ***Email:*** dicksweet@mvalaw.com

(This Listing Continued)

ANN P. WEST, born 1961; admitted to bar, 1991, North Carolina. *Education:* Wake Forest University (B.A., cum laude, 1983; J.D., cum laude, 1991). ***PRACTICE AREAS:*** Business; Employee Benefits. ***Email:*** annwest@mvalaw.com

WILLIAM A. WHITE, born 1945; admitted to bar, 1972, Pennsylvania; 1975, District of Columbia; 1995, North Carolina; 1997, South Carolina. *Education:* University of Wisconsin (B.A., 1967; J.D., 1971). Order of the Coif. Note and Comment Editor, Wisconsin Law Review, 1970. Enforcement Counsel for Superfund Enforcement, U.S. Environmental Protection Agency, Washington, D.C., 1991-1994. ***PRACTICE AREAS:*** Environmental; Litigation. ***Email:*** billwhite@mvalaw.com

RESIDENT ASSOCIATES

ADAM E. ABERRA, born 1977; admitted to bar, 2002, North Carolina. *Education:* University of North Carolina at Chapel Hill (B.A., 1999; J.D., 2002). ***PRACTICE AREAS:*** Financial Services Law. ***Email:*** adamaberra@mvalaw.com

KEVIN M. BARNES, born 1972; admitted to bar, 2004, North Carolina. *Education:* United States Air Force Academy (B.S., Military Distinction, 1994); College of William and Mary (M.B.A., 2003; J.D., 2003). ***PRACTICE AREAS:*** Business. ***Email:*** kevinbarnes@mvalaw.com

EVAN M. BASS, born 1979; admitted to bar, 2005, North Carolina. *Education:* Illinois Wesleyan University (B.S., 2002); Wake Forest University (J.D., 2005). ***PRACTICE AREAS:*** Commercial Real Estate.

JASON E. BENNETT, born 1974; admitted to bar, 2004, North Carolina. *Education:* North Carolina State University (B.S.M.E., summa cum laude, 1997); University of Texas (J.D., 2004). ***Email:*** jasonbennett@mvalaw.com

DOUGLAS W. BENSON, born 1974; admitted to bar, 2000, North Carolina. *Education:* University of Rochester (B.A., cum laude, 1997); Duke University (J.D., cum laude, 2000). Editor-in-Chief, Duke Journal of Gender Law and Policy, 1999-2000. ***PRACTICE AREAS:*** Trusts and Estates. ***Email:*** dougbenson@mvalaw.com

MELINDA S. BLUNDELL, born 1977; admitted to bar, 2002, North Carolina. *Education:* Oklahoma State University (B.S., summa cum laude, 1999); University of Virginia (J.D., 2002). Executive Editor, Virginia Tax Review, 2001-2002. ***PRACTICE AREAS:*** Business Law. ***Email:*** melindablundell@mvalaw.com

JONATHAN D. BRODHAG, born 1979; admitted to bar, 2005, North Carolina. *Education:* University of North Carolina (B.S., 2001; B.A., 2001); University of Michigan (M.S.I., 2005; J.D., 2005). ***PRACTICE AREAS:*** Financial Services.

TABER C. BRUNER, born 1972; admitted to bar, 2002, North Carolina. *Education:* University of South Carolina (B.A., 1996; J.D., cum laude, 2002). Member, Moot Court National Competition Team. Law Clerk, South Carolina Senate Judiciary Committee. Articles Editor, ABA Real Property Probate & Trust Journal. ***PRACTICE AREAS:*** Financial Services Law. ***Email:*** taberbruner@mvalaw.com

CHRISTOPHER T. BUCHANAN, born 1971; admitted to bar, 1998, North Carolina. *Education:* Rhodes College (B.A., 1993); Wake Forest University (J.D., cum laude, 1998). Order of the Coif. Articles Editor, Wake Forest Law Review. ***PRACTICE AREAS:*** Banking. ***Email:*** chrisbuchanan@mvalaw.com

MICHAEL T. CHAMPION, born 1973; admitted to bar, 2004, North Carolina. *Education:* University of North Carolina - Charlotte (B.A., 1996; M.A., 1999); University of North Carolina at Chapel Hill (J.D., 2004). Executive Editor, North Carolina Journal of International Law and Commercial Regulation. Editor-in-Chief, Environmental Law Symposium, University of North Carolina Law. ***PRACTICE AREAS:*** Environmental; Litigation; Business. ***Email:*** mikechampion@mvalaw.com

ANDREA C. CHOMAKOS, born 1971; admitted to bar, 1997, Michigan; 2001, North Carolina. *Education:* University of Michigan (B.A., 1993); University of Detroit Mercy School of Law (J.D., summa cum laude, 1997); New York University School of Law (LL.M., 2001). ***PRACTICE AREAS:*** Trusts and Estates; Wealth Transfer. ***Email:*** andreachomakos@mvalaw.com

RACHEL WORLDS COYNE, born 1972; admitted to bar, 1999, North Carolina; 2003, California. *Education:* Davidson College (B.A., 1995); Wake Forest University (J.D., 1999). ***PRACTICE AREAS:*** Business. ***Email:*** rachelcoyne@mvalaw.com

HILLARY B. CRABTREE, born 1969; admitted to bar, 1999, North Carolina. *Education:* Davidson College (B.A., 1992); University of North Carolina (J.D., 1999). Law Clerk to Hon. A. Thomas Small, United States Bankruptcy Court for the Eastern District of North Carolina. ***PRACTICE AREAS:*** Bankruptcy and Restructuring. ***Email:*** hillarycrabtree@mvalaw.com

RANDALL T. DINGLE, born 1977; admitted to bar, 2002, North Carolina. *Education:* Kent State University (B.B.A., summa cum laude, 1999); Duke University (J.D., 2002). ***PRACTICE AREAS:*** Bankruptcy; Bankruptcy Reorganization. ***Email:*** randalldingle@mvalaw.com

JOHN R. EVANS, born 1973; admitted to bar, 1999, North Carolina. *Education:* Duke University (B.A., 1995); Northwestern University (J.D., 1999). ***PRACTICE AREAS:*** Business. ***Email:*** johnevans@mvalaw.com

EDGAR B. FISHER III, born 1969; admitted to bar, 1998, North Carolina. *Education:* University of North Carolina (B.A., 1991; J.D., 1998; M.B.A., 1998). ***PRACTICE AREAS:*** Corporate. ***Email:*** beaufisher@mvalaw.com

ROBERT A. FISHER, born 1967; admitted to bar, 2001, North Carolina. *Education:* Texas Tech University (B.B.A., 1998; M.S., 1998); College of William and Mary (J.D., 2001). ***PRACTICE AREAS:*** Corporate Tax. ***Email:*** robfisher@mvalaw.com

ERIN L. FITZGERALD, born 1978; admitted to bar, 2004, North Carolina. *Education:* Davidson College (B.A., 2000); University of South Carolina (I.M.B.A., 2004; J.D., 2004). ***PRACTICE AREAS:*** Financial Services. ***Email:*** erinfitzgerald@mvalaw.com

NICOLE L. GARDNER, born 1972; admitted to bar, 1999, California and U.S. District Court, Northern District of California; 2000, U.S. Court of Appeals, Ninth Circuit; 2002, North Carolina; 2004, South Carolina. *Education:* Pennsylvania State University (B.A., 1994); University of California, Boalt Hall School of Law (J.D., 1999). Phi Beta Kappa. Moot Court Board. Fulbright Scholar. ***PRACTICE AREAS:*** Labor and Employment. ***Email:*** nicolegardner@mvalaw.com

LAWRENCE P. GRAYSON II, born 1969; admitted to bar, 2000, Illinois; 2002, North Carolina. *Education:* University of Maryland (B.A., 1992); Northwestern University (M.A., 1993; J.D., 2000). ***PRACTICE AREAS:*** Litigation; Construction and Surety Law. ***Email:*** larrygrayson@mvalaw.com

BETH YOUNT GRIMES, born 1972; admitted to bar, 1999, North Carolina. *Education:* Appalachian State University (B.A., magna cum laude, 1995); University of North Carolina (J.D., swith honors, 1999). Staff Member, North Carolina Law Review. ***PRACTICE AREAS:*** Employment; Employee Benefits. ***Email:*** bethyountgrimes@mvalaw.com

STEPHEN E. GRUENDEL, born 1972; admitted to bar, 1998, Massachusetts; 1999, North Carolina and Connecticut. *Education:* Yale University (B.A., 1994); Boston College (J.D., summa cum laude, 1998). Order of the Coif. Member, Editorial Board, Boston College Law Review. ***PRACTICE AREAS:*** Insolvency. ***Email:*** stephengruendel@mvalaw.com

ALTON LARUE GWALTNEY, III, born 1968; admitted to bar, 1993, Virginia; 2003, North Carolina. *Education:* Hampden-Sydney College (B.A., cum laude, 1990); University of Richmond (J.D., 1993). ***PRACTICE AREAS:*** Litigation. ***Email:*** larrygwaltney@mvalaw.com

JAMES W. HALDIN, born 1974; admitted to bar, 2000, North Carolina. *Education:* University of Florida (B.A., magna cum laude, 1996); Washington & Lee University (J.D., cum laude, 2000). Senior Articles Editor, Washington & Lee Law Review. ***PRACTICE AREAS:*** Litigation. ***Email:*** jamiehaldin@mvalaw.com

CHARLES J. HARRIS, born 1976; admitted to bar, 2002, North Carolina. *Education:* University of North Carolina (B.A., 1998); University of Virginia (J.D., 2002). Morehead Scholar. Student Attorney General. Editor: Virginia Tax Review; Journal of Law & Politics. ***PRACTICE AREAS:*** Financial Services. ***Email:*** charlieharris@mvalaw.com

MICHAEL P. HEBERT, born 1976; admitted to bar, 2002, Massachusetts; 2005, North Carolina. *Education:* Northeastern University (B.A., summa cum laude, 1998); Wake Forest University (J.D., 2001). ***PRACTICE AREAS:*** Commercial Real Estate. ***Email:*** michaelhebert@mvalaw.com

BRIAN S. HESLIN, born 1970; admitted to bar, 1997, Virginia; 2005, North Carolina. *Education:* University of Southern California (B.A., 1992); George Mason University (J.D., 1997). Student President, George Mason Inn of Court. Editor, George Mason Law Review. [U.S. Army Reserves, Defense Appellate Division]. ***PRACTICE AREAS:*** Litigation; Environmental; Regulatory Law; Legislative Law. ***Email:*** brianheslin@mvalaw.com

L. CAROLINE HUBBELL, born 1977; admitted to bar, 2004, North Carolina. *Education:* Davidson College (B.A., 1999); Boston College (J.D., cum laude, 2004). ***PRACTICE AREAS:*** Bankruptcy and Restructuring. ***Email:*** carolinehubbell@mvalaw.com

JASON P. HUFF, born 1968; admitted to bar, 1999, North Carolina. *Education:* William & Mary (B.A., 1991); Wake Forest University (J.D., 1999). ***PRACTICE AREAS:*** Financial Services. ***Email:*** jasonhuff@mvalaw.com

N. RENEE HUGHES, born 1969; admitted to bar, 2002, North Carolina. *Education:* Wake Forest University (B.S., 1991); North Carolina Central University (J.D., summa cum laude, 2002). Executive Editor, North Carolina Central University Law Journal, 2001-2002. ***PRACTICE AREAS:*** Litigation. ***Email:*** reneehughes@mvalaw.com

WILLIAM W. JETTON, born 1967; admitted to bar, 1995, North Carolina. *Education:* Furman University (B.A., magna cum laude, 1990); University of Virginia (J.D., 1995). Phi Beta Kappa. Editorial Board, Virginia Journal of International Law. Law Clerk to Hon. William W. Wilkins, Jr., Circuit Judge, U.S. Court of Appeals for the Fourth Circuit, 1995-1996. ***PRACTICE AREAS:*** Financial Services Law; Corporate Law; Telecommunications. ***Email:*** willjetton@mvalaw.com

CHRISTOPHER J.C. JONES, born 1972; admitted to bar, 1997, Virginia; 1999, North Carolina. *Education:* University of Virginia (B.A., 1994); Nova Southeastern University (J.D., magna cum laude, 1997); Georgetown University (LL.M., 1998). Phi Delta Phi. Member, Journal of International and Comparative Law. ***PRACTICE AREAS:*** Trusts and Estates; Taxation. ***Email:*** chrisjones@mvalaw.com

DIANA B. JONES, born 1973; admitted to bar, 1998, North Carolina. *Education:* University of North Carolina (B.A., 1995; J.D., 1998). Law Clerk to the Honorable Robert F. Orr, North Carolina Supreme Court, 1998-2000. ***PRACTICE AREAS:*** Business. ***Email:*** dianajones@mvalaw.com

McHENRY J. KANE, born 1976; admitted to bar, 2002, South Carolina; 2004, North Carolina. *Education:* Wake Forest University (B.A., 1997); University of South Carolina (J.D., 2002; M.I.B.S., 2002). ***PRACTICE AREAS:*** Business Law. ***Email:*** mchenrykane@mvalaw.com

AMY R. KING, born 1974; admitted to bar, 2002, North Carolina. *Education:* University of Richmond (B.S.B.A., cum laude, 1996); Washington & Lee University (J.D., 2002). ***PRACTICE AREAS:*** Financial Services Law. ***Email:*** amyking@mvalaw.com

JEFFREY B. KING, born 1971; admitted to bar, 1996, Texas; 2002, Illinois; 2004, North Carolina. *Education:* Southern Illinois University (B.A., Valedictorian, 1993); University of Houston (J.D., 1996). Managing Editor, University of Houston Law Review. ***PRACTICE AREAS:*** Commercial Real Estate. ***Email:*** jeffking@mvalaw.com

ROSALIND L. LANE, born 1970; admitted to bar, 2001, North Carolina. *Education:* University of Missouri (B.S.B.A., 1992; M.P.A., 1994); Duke University (J.D., 2000). ***PRACTICE AREAS:*** Business. ***Email:*** rosalindlane@mvalaw.com

JAMES R. LANGDON, born 1970; admitted to bar, 1996, North Carolina. *Education:* University of California-Santa Barbara (B.A., 1992); Wake Forest University (J.D., cum laude, 1996). Law Clerk to Hon. William L. Stocks, Chief Judge, U.S. Bankruptcy Court, Middle District, North Carolina. ***PRACTICE AREAS:*** Bankruptcy; Insolvency. ***Email:*** jimlangdon@mvalaw.com

(This Listing Continued)

MOORE & VAN ALLEN PLLC, Charlotte—Continued

KERRY M. F. LINDAUER, born 1974; admitted to bar, 2000, North Carolina. *Education:* University of South Carolina (B.S., magna cum laude, 1996); University of North Carolina (J.D., 2000). Phi Beta Kappa. Member, Board of Editors, Banking Institute Journal, University of North Carolina School of Law. ***PRACTICE AREAS:*** Business; Taxation. ***Email:*** kerryfraas@mvalaw.com

RONALD S. LOVELACE, born 1978; admitted to bar, 2002, North Carolina. *Education:* University of North Carolina at Chapel Hill (B.S.B.A., with highest distinction, 1999; J.D., 2002). ***PRACTICE AREAS:*** Financial Services Law. ***Email:*** ronlovelace@mvalaw.com

CHRISTOPHER B. MAJOR, born 1978; admitted to bar, 2003, North Carolina; 2004, South Carolina. *Education:* University of South Carolina (B.A., magna cum laude, 2000; J.D., magna cum laude, 2003). Phi Beta Kappa. Order of the Coif. Wig & Robe. Member, South Carolina Law Review. Law Clerk for the Honorable G. Ross Anderson, Jr., U.S. District Judge for the District of South Carolina. ***PRACTICE AREAS:*** Litigation. ***Email:*** christophermajor@mvalaw.com

MELODY Y. MALONE, admitted to bar, 1997, North Carolina. *Education:* University of North Carolina (B.A., with honors and distinction, 1994; J.D., 1997). ***PRACTICE AREAS:*** Business Law. ***Email:*** melodymalone@mvalaw.com

KERRI L. MAST, born 1976; admitted to bar, 2003, North Carolina. *Education:* Wake Forest University (B.A., cum laude, with honors, 1999); Emory University (J.D., with honors, 2003). Managing Editor, Emory International Law Review. ***PRACTICE AREAS:*** Trusts and Estates. ***Email:*** kerrimast@mvalaw.com

VALECIA M. McDOWELL, born 1973; admitted to bar, 1998, North Carolina. *Education:* Duke University (A.B., cum laude, 1995; J.D., 1998). ***PRACTICE AREAS:*** Litigation. ***Email:*** valeciamcdowell@mvalaw.com

CAROLYN P. MEADE, born 1972; admitted to bar, 2001, North Carolina. *Education:* University of Virginia (B.A., 1994; J.D., 2001). Phi Beta Kappa. Editorial Board, 1999-2000, Business Manager, 2000-2001, Virginia Law Review. ***PRACTICE AREAS:*** Business. ***Email:*** carolynmeade@mvalaw.com

BRIAN D. MESIBOV, born 1972; admitted to bar, 1998, North Carolina. *Education:* Stanford University (A.B., 1994); Boalt Hall School of Law, University of California, Berkeley (J.D., 1998). Phi Beta Kappa; Order of the Coif. ***PRACTICE AREAS:*** Business Law; Information Technology. ***Email:*** brianmesibov@mvalaw.com

WILLIAM R. MORTON, born 1976; admitted to bar, 2005, North Carolina. *Education:* University of North Carolina (B.A., 1998); University of Georgia (J.D., 2005). ***PRACTICE AREAS:*** Trusts and Estates. ***Email:*** billymorton@mvalaw.com

KEITH A. MROCHEK, born 1973; admitted to bar, 1999, North Carolina. *Education:* Grove City College (B.A., 1995); Washington & Lee University (J.D., cum laude, 1998). Staff Member, Washington & Lee University Law Review. Law Clerk to Sen. District Judge Robert B. Propst, 1998-1999. ***PRACTICE AREAS:*** Financial Services. ***Email:*** keithmrochek@mvalaw.com

TODD H. MULDREW, born 1974; admitted to bar, 2004, North Carolina. *Education:* University of Tennessee (B.A., 1998; M.S., 2001); College of William and Mary (J.D., 2004). ***PRACTICE AREAS:*** Environmental Law; Governmental; Regulatory and Legislative. ***Email:*** toddmuldrew@mvalaw.com

JONATHAN K. MURRAY, born 1973; admitted to bar, 2000, North Carolina. *Education:* Hampton University (B.A., with honors, 1995); Wake Forest University (J.D., 2000). ***PRACTICE AREAS:*** Financial Services Law. ***Email:*** jonathanmurray@mvalaw.com

MARK A. NEBRIG, born 1969; admitted to bar, 2002, North Carolina. *Education:* University of North Carolina at Chapel Hill (B.A., 1991); Temple University (J.D., magna cum laude, 2002). ***PRACTICE AREAS:*** Litigation. ***Email:*** marknebrig@mvalaw.com

ANDREW L. NESBITT, born 1977; admitted to bar, 2002, North Carolina. *Education:* University of North Carolina (B.A., 1999; J.D., 2002). ***PRACTICE AREAS:*** Trusts and Estates; Taxation. ***Email:*** andrewnesbitt@mvalaw.com

LINDSAY M. PEED, born 1976; admitted to bar, 2003, Virginia; 2004, North Carolina; U.S. District Court, Western District of North Carolina. *Education:* University of Virginia (B.A., 1998); Washington & Lee University (J.D., 2002). Executive Officer, Moot Court Board. *Member:* Mecklenburg County, Virginia and American Bar Associations; Virginia State Bar; North Carolina State Bar; Virginia Trial Lawyers Association; North Carolina Association of Defense Attorneys; North Carolina Insurance Crime Information Exchange. ***PRACTICE AREAS:*** Litigation. ***Email:*** lindsaypeed@mvalaw.com

CHRISTIAN L. POLKING, born 1972; admitted to bar, 2004, North Carolina. *Education:* The Catholic University of America (B.A., 1995); University of North Carolina (J.D., 2004). First Amendment Law Review, Managing Editor 2003-2004, Staff Writer 2002-2003. ***PRACTICE AREAS:*** Financial Services. ***Email:*** christianpolking@mvalaw.com

JARED W. POPLIN, born 1977; admitted to bar, 2002, North Carolina. *Education:* Samford University (B.A., summa cum laude, 1999); University of North Carolina at Chapel Hill (J.D., with honors, 2002). Member, North Carolina Law Review. ***PRACTICE AREAS:*** Business Law. ***Email:*** jaredpoplin@mvalaw.com

JUSTIN M. RIESS, born 1974; admitted to bar, 2001, North Carolina. *Education:* Vanderbilt University (B.S., 1996; J.D., 2001). ***PRACTICE AREAS:*** Financial Services; Corporate. ***Email:*** justinriess@mvalaw.com

ROBERT N. RUST IV, born 1978; admitted to bar, 2005, North Carolina. *Education:* University of the South (B.A., 2000); Vanderbilt University (J.D., 2003). ***PRACTICE AREAS:*** Mergers and Acquisitions; Business. ***Email:*** robertrust@mvalaw.com

JOHN C. SAYDLOWSKI, born 1971; admitted to bar, 1997, North Carolina and South Carolina. *Education:* Wake Forest University (B.A., cum laude, 1993; J.D., 1996); Vermont Law School (M.S.E.L., cum laude, 1997). ***PRACTICE AREAS:*** Business; Environmental. ***Email:*** johnsaydlowski@mvalaw.com

(This Listing Continued)

NANCY F. SMITH, born 1973; admitted to bar, 1998, North Carolina. *Education:* University of North Carolina (B.A., 1995; J.D., 1998). ***PRACTICE AREAS:*** Business; Environmental. ***Email:*** nancysmith@mvalaw.com

ROBERT R. SMITH, II, born 1973; admitted to bar, 2001, South Carolina (Not admitted in North Carolina). *Education:* University of South Carolina (B.A., 1996; J.D., 2001). Law Clerk to the Hon. Larry R. Patterson, Circuit Judge, 13th Judicial Circuit. Member, Board of Visitors, University of South Carolina. *Member:* South Carolina Bar. ***PRACTICE AREAS:*** Regulatory Law; Legislative Practice; Business Law. ***Email:*** robsmith@mvalaw.com

NOELLE HICKS SPROUL, born 1976; admitted to bar, 2003, North Carolina. *Education:* Vanderbilt University (B.S., cum laude, 1998); University of Richmond (J.D., cum laude, 2003). Manuscripts Editor, Law Review. ***PRACTICE AREAS:*** Financial Services. ***Email:*** noellesproul@mvalaw.com

ALYSON R. SPURLOCK, born 1979; admitted to bar, 2004, North Carolina. *Education:* University of Kentucky (B.S., summa cum laude, 2001); Wake Forest University (J.D., cum laude, 2004). Order of the Coif. Executive Editor, Wake Forest Law Review, 2003-2004. ***PRACTICE AREAS:*** Financial Services. ***Email:*** alysonspurlock@mvalaw.com

MARANDA W. STEVENS, born 1978; admitted to bar, 2003, North Carolina. *Education:* Duke University (A.B., magna cum laude, 2000; J.D., 2003). ***PRACTICE AREAS:*** Litigation. ***Email:*** marandastevens@mvalaw.com

WESLEY D. THORNTON, born 1977; admitted to bar, 2004, North Carolina. *Education:* Davidson College (B.A., 1999); University of South Carolina (J.D., 2003). ***PRACTICE AREAS:*** Business. ***Email:*** westhornton@mvalaw.com

BRADLEY T. VAN HOY, born 1975; admitted to bar, 2000, North Carolina. *Education:* University of North Carolina (B.A., 1997; J.D., with honors, 2000). Phi Beta Kappa. Staff, University of North Carolina Journal of International Law. ***PRACTICE AREAS:*** Trusts and Estates. ***Email:*** bradvanhoy@mvalaw.com

SUZANNE WENTZEL, born 1971; admitted to bar, 1996, Ohio; 1998, U.S. District Court, Northern District of Ohio; 2003, North Carolina. *Education:* Miami University (B.A., 1993); University of Akron (J.D., magna cum laude, 1996). Law Clerk to the Hon. Marilyn Shea-Storum, U.S. Bankruptcy Court, Northern District of Ohio, 1996-1998. *Member:* International Council of Shopping Centers. ***PRACTICE AREAS:*** Commercial Real Estate. ***Email:*** suzannewentzel@mvalaw.com

McNEILL Y. WESTER, born 1974; admitted to bar, 2002, North Carolina. *Education:* University of North Carolina at Chapel Hill (B.A., 1997; J.D., 2002). Articles and Notes Editor, North Carolina Banking Institute Journal, 2001-2002. ***PRACTICE AREAS:*** Litigation. ***Email:*** mcneillwester@mvalaw.com

LEGAL SUPPORT PERSONNEL

JOSH S. MEEKS. Email: joshmeeks@mvalaw.com

WILLIAM L. FERGUSON, (Director of Information Services). ***Email:*** williamferguson@mvalaw.com

MATTHEW F. GILLESPIE, (Executive Director). ***Email:*** matthewgillespie@mvalaw.com

CHARIS R. WILSON, (Marketing Manager). ***Email:*** chariswilson@mvalaw.com

LISA W. McGUIRE, (Controller). ***Email:*** lisamcguire@mvalaw.com

PATTI J. OSWALD, (Director of Human Resources). ***Email:*** pattioswald@mvalaw.com

REPRESENTATIVE CLIENTS: Client references furnished upon request.

MORRIS, MANNING & MARTIN, LLP

201 SOUTH COLLEGE STREET, SUITE 2300
CHARLOTTE, NORTH CAROLINA 28244
Telephone: 704-554-7070
Fax: 704-554-5050
URL: http://www.mmmlaw.com

Other State Office Address:
Charlotte, NC Office: 10150 Mallard Creek Drive, Suite 105, 28262. Telephone: 704-369-7012. Fax: 704-369-7071.
Durham, NC Office: 1000 Park 40 Plaza, Suite 300. Telephone: 704-369-7012. Fax: 704-369-7071.
Washington, D.C. Office: City Center Building, 1401 H Street, N.W., Suite 760, 20005. Telephone: 202-408-5153. Fax: 202-408-5146.
Princeton, NJ Office: 601 Ewing Street, Suite C-8, 08540. Telephone: 609-430-1414. Fax: 609-430-1411.
Georgia Office Addresses:
Atlanta (Buckhead) Office: 1600 Atlanta Financial Center, 3343 Peachtree Road, N.E., Atlanta, GA 30326. Telephone: 404-233-7000.
Peachtree Dunwoody Office: 5775-C Peachtree Dunwoody Road, Suite 150, Atlanta, GA 30342. Telephone: 404-255-6900. Fax: 404-843-2317.
Cumming Office: 307 Atlanta Highway, Cumming, GA 30040. Telephone: 770-781-3000. Fax: 770-781-3007.
Duluth Office: 2180 Satellite Boulevard, Suite 180, Duluth, GA 30097. Telephone: 678-987-2800. Fax: 678-417-0056.
Alpharetta Office: 5780 Windward Parkway, Suite 225, Alpharetta, GA 30005. Telephone: 770-781-3000. Fax: 770-781-3007.

Benefits and Compensation, Commercial Lending, Construction, Corporate, Corporate Technology, Creditor's Rights and Bankruptcy, Emerging Companies, Employment, Environmental, Healthcare, Hospitality, Insurance and Reinsurance, Insurance and Reinsurance Dispute Resolution, Intellectual Property, International, Life Sciences, Litigation, Medical Device, Mergers and Acquisitions, Privacy and Security, Products Liability and Toxic Torts, Real Estate Capital Markets, Real Estate Development and Finance, Residential Real Estate, Securities, Taxation, Technology, Technology Litigation, Telecommunications, Wealth Planning.

(This Listing Continued)

FIRM PROFILE: Morris, Manning & Martin, LLP, is a leading law firm in the banking, environmental, healthcare, insurance, real estate and technology industries. As industry leaders, we take pride in participating in trade associations, speaking at conferences, and helping our clients network within these business communities. We understand that a good attorney is more than just a legal expert; he or she also is an ally in helping clients build their companies and become successes in their own industries.

LAW FIRM ALLIANCES/ASSOCIATIONS: **LAWYERS ASSOCIATED WORLDWIDE (L.A.W.)**

MEMBERS OF FIRM

LYNN F. CHANDLER, born March 9, 1955; admitted to bar, 1988, Arizona; 1996, North Carolina; 2004, South Carolina. *Education:* University of North Carolina (B.S.B.A., 1976); University of Nebraska (M.B.A., 1982); Creighton University (J.D., summa cum laude, 1988). *Member:* American Bar Association (Member, Tax Section and Real Property, Probate and Trust Law Section); State Bar of Arizona; North Carolina State Bar; South Carolina Bar; North Carolina Bar Association (Council Member: Estate Planning and Fiduciary Law Section; Tax Section); Charlotte Estate Planning Council. (Board Certified Specialist in Estate Planning and Probate Law, North Carolina State Board of Legal Specialization). ***PRACTICE AREAS:*** Tax; Wealth Planning. ***Email:*** lchandler@mmmlaw.com

RICHARD N. DRAKE, born Albuquerque, New Mexico, January 12, 1961; admitted to bar, 1986, Ohio; 1998, North Carolina. *Education:* Duke University (A.B., magna cum laude, 1983). Phi Beta Kappa, John Wesley Jones Scholar; The University of Michigan Law School (J.D., 1986). Past Chair, Business Law Section, Mecklenburg County Bar Association (July 2002-June 2003). Advisory Board Member, The Entrepreneurship Institute, Charlotte Chapter, 2000—. Listed in Who's Who in American Law, 1989—. Trustee, Board of Trustees, The Charlotte Repertory Theatre, 2004—. *Member:* Mecklenburg County (Past Chair, Business Law Section), North Carolina (Member, Business Law Section) and American (Member, Sections on: Business Law; Science & Technology) Bar Associations; North Carolina State Bar. ***PRACTICE AREAS:*** Corporate Law; Mergers and Acquisitions; Financial Services Law; Securities Law. ***Email:*** rdrake@mmmlaw.com

JOHN H. NORTHEY III, born Lumberton, North Carolina, October 11, 1949; admitted to bar, 1975, North Carolina. *Education:* University of North Carolina (A.B., with highest honors, 1971); Cornell University (J.D., magna cum laude, 1975). Phi Beta Kappa; Omicron Delta Epsilon; Phi Kappa Phi. Member, Board of Editors, Cornell Law Review, 1974-1975. *Member:* Mecklenburg County, North Carolina and American Bar Associations; North Carolina State Bar. (Resident). ***PRACTICE AREAS:*** Corporate; Mergers and Acquisitions; Securities; Financial Institutions Law; Technology Law; Commercial Real Estate; Environmental Law. ***Email:*** jnorthey@mmmlaw.com

ASSOCIATES

JANICE L. DAVIES, born Lima, Pennsylvania, April 9, 1966; admitted to bar, 1999, North Carolina; 2001, South Carolina and District of Columbia. *Education:* Pfeiffer College (B.S., cum laude, 1993); Campbell University (J.D., 1999); University of Miami (LL.M., Estate Planning, 2000). Member, Campbell University Law Review. *Member:* Mecklenburg County, North Carolina (Member, Estate Planning; Fiduciary Law and Tax Law Sections) and American (Member, Real Property, Probate and Trust Law Section) Bar Associations; Charlotte Estate Planning Council. ***PRACTICE AREAS:*** Estate Planning; Trusts and Estates; Taxation. ***Email:*** jdavies@mmmlaw.com

GIDEON C. MOORE, born Columbia, South Carolina, August 30, 1975; admitted to bar, 2002, New York; 2005, North Carolina. *Education:* University of North Carolina at Chapel Hill (B.A., with honors, 1998); Duke University (J.D., 2001). Member, Federalist Society, 1999. Editor-in-Chief, Duke Law and Technology Review. *Member:* North Carolina State Bar. ***PRACTICE AREAS:*** Corporate Law; Securities; Mergers and Acquisitions; Emerging Growth Companies; Corporate Technology. ***Email:*** gmoore@mmmlaw.com

OF COUNSEL

JOSEPH WARREN III, born Chicago, Illinois, June 23, 1939; admitted to bar, 1965, North Carolina. *Education:* Duke University (A.B., 1961; LL.B., 1965); New York University (LL.M., in Taxation, 1968). Phi Delta Phi. Member, North Carolina Association of Certified Public Accountants, 1967-1983. *Member:* Mecklenburg County and North Carolina Bar Associations; North Carolina State Bar. ***REPORTED CASES:*** Glen Raven Mills, Inc. v. Commissioner 59 T.C. 1 (1972). ***PRACTICE AREAS:*** Corporate; Taxation; Mergers and Acquisitions; Wealth Planning. ***Email:*** jwarren@mmmlaw.com

---

MORRIS, MANNING & MARTIN, LLP

A Limited Liability Partnership

Established in 1976

10150 MALLARD CREEK DRIVE
SUITE 105
CHARLOTTE, NORTH CAROLINA 28262
Telephone: 704-369-7012
Fax: 704-369-7071
URL: http://www.mmmlaw.com

Other State Office Addresses:
Charlotte, NC Office: 201 South College Street, Suite 2300, 28244. Telephone: 704-554-7070. Fax: 704-556-5050.
Durham, NC Office: 1000 Park 40 Plaza, Suite 300. Telephone: 704-369-7012. Fax: 704-369-7071.
Washington, D.C. Office: City Center Building, 1401 H Street, N.W., Suite 760, 20005. Telephone: 202-408-5153. Fax: 202-408-5146.
Princeton, NJ Office: 601 Ewing Street, Suite C-8, 08540. Telephone: 609-430-1414. Fax: 609-430-1411.

(This Listing Continued)

Other Georgia Office Addresses:
Atlanta (Buckhead) Office: 1600 Atlanta Financial Center, 3343 Peachtree Road, N.E., Atlanta, GA 30326. Telephone: 404-233-7000.
Peachtree Dunwoody Office: 5775-C Peachtree Dunwoody Road, Suite 150, Atlanta, GA 30342. Telephone: 404-255-6900. Fax: 404-843-2317.
Duluth Office: 2180 Satellite Boulevard, Suite 180, Duluth, GA 30097. Telephone: 678-987-2800. Fax: 678-417-0056.
Cumming Office: 307 Atlanta Highway, Cumming, GA 30040. Telephone: 770-781-3000. Fax: 770-781-3007.
Alpharetta Office: 5780 Windward Parkway, Suite 225, Alpharetta, GA 30005. Telephone: 770-781-3000. Fax: 770-781-3007.

Benefits and Compensation, Commercial Lending, Construction, Corporate, Corporate Technology, Creditor's Rights and Bankruptcy, Emerging Companies, Employment, Environmental, Healthcare, Hospitality, Insurance and Reinsurance, Insurance and Reinsurance Dispute Resolution, Intellectual Property, International, Life Sciences, Litigation, Medical Device, Mergers and Acquisitions, Privacy and Security, Products Liability and Toxic Torts, Real Estate Capital Markets, Real Estate Development and Finance, Residential Real Estate, Securities, Taxation, Technology, Technology Litigation, Telecommunications, Wealth Planning.

FIRM PROFILE: Morris, Manning & Martin, LLP's Charlotte office represent buyers, sellers, agents and lenders in the Atlanta and national markets, as well as some of the region's top real estate developers. Our practice encompasses all areas and types of real estate transactions, including real estate loan closings, construction loan closings, buyer and seller representation, contract reviews, title insurance and the formation of subdivisions and condominiums.

LAW FIRM ALLIANCES/ASSOCIATIONS: **LAWYERS ASSOCIATED WORLDWIDE (L.A.W.)**

ASSOCIATE

DEBORAH S. AZZARITI, born Fort Rucker, Alabama, March 5, 1972; admitted to bar, 1997, Georgia (Not admitted in North Carolina). *Education:* Wake Forest University (B.A., magna cum laude, 1994); Emory University School of Law (J.D., 1997). *Member:* State Bar of Georgia. ***PRACTICE AREAS:*** Residential Real Estate. ***Email:*** dazzariti@mmmlaw.com

---

MORRIS YORK WILLIAMS SURLES & BARRINGER, L.L.P.

Established in 1994

525 NORTH TRYON STREET, SUITE 1400
CHARLOTTE, NORTH CAROLINA 28202
Telephone: 704-375-4480
Facsimile: 704-375-6895
Email: firm@morrisyork.com
URL: http://www.morrisyork.com

Civil, Business and Commercial Litigation. Insurance Defense Litigation, Insurance Coverage and Workers Compensation. Medical and Professional Malpractice Defense. Land Condemnation and Alternative Dispute Resolution Services.

JOHN F. MORRIS, born Orange, New Jersey, October 14, 1956; admitted to bar, 1981, North Carolina. *Education:* Duke University (A.B., cum laude, 1978); University of North Carolina (J.D., 1981). Staff Member, North Carolina Law Review, 1980-1981. *Member:* Mecklenburg County, North Carolina and American Bar Associations; North Carolina Association of Defense Attorneys. ***PRACTICE AREAS:*** Insurance Defense; Workers Compensation Defense. ***Email:*** jmorris@morrisyork.com

GREGORY C. YORK, born Charlotte, North Carolina, March 4, 1956; admitted to bar, 1981, North Carolina. *Education:* University of North Carolina (B.A., with honors, 1978; J.D., 1981). Phi Delta Phi (Historian, 1981). *Member:* Mecklenburg County and North Carolina Bar Associations; North Carolina State Bar; North Carolina Association of Defense Attorneys. ***PRACTICE AREAS:*** Insurance Defense; Business Litigation; Commercial Litigation. ***Email:*** gyork@morrisyork.com

THOMAS E. WILLIAMS, born Charlotte, North Carolina, April 29, 1957; admitted to bar, 1982, North Carolina. *Education:* Appalachian State University (B.A., 1979); Wake Forest University (J.D., 1982). Justice, Moot Court Board, 1981-1982. Recipient, American Jurisprudence Award in Remedies, 1982. *Member:* North Carolina Bar Association; North Carolina State Bar. ***PRACTICE AREAS:*** Insurance Defense; Workers Compensation Defense. ***Email:*** twilliams@morrisyork.com

MARTHA W. SURLES, born Greensboro, North Carolina, April 12, 1957; admitted to bar, 1982, North Carolina and U.S. District Court, Western District of North Carolina. *Education:* University of North Carolina (B.A., 1979; J.D., with honors, 1982). Phi Delta Phi. Member: Order of the Barristers; National Moot Court Team. *Member:* Mecklenburg County and North Carolina Bar Associations; North Carolina State Bar; North Carolina Association of Defense Attorneys. ***PRACTICE AREAS:*** Insurance Defense; Workers Compensation Defense. ***Email:*** msurles@morrisyork.com

JOHN P. BARRINGER, born Concord, North Carolina, April 13, 1959; admitted to bar, 1986, California and U.S. District Court, Northern District of California; 1989, North Carolina. *Education:* University of North Carolina-Charlotte (B.S., in History, cum laude, 1983); Brigham Young University (J.D., 1986). Phi Alpha Delta. Member: Moot Court Team; The Order of Barristers. *Member:* Contra Costa County, Mecklenburg County and North Carolina Bar Associations; State Bar of California; North Carolina State Bar. ***PRACTICE AREAS:*** Insurance Defense; Insurance Coverage. ***Email:*** jbarringer@morrisyork.com

ROBERT GREGORY LEWIS, born Asheville, North Carolina, February 15, 1964; admitted to bar, 1990, North Carolina. *Education:* University of North Carolina at Chapel Hill (B.S., 1986); North Carolina Central University (J.D., 1990). Phi Delta Phi (Member, 1987-1989 and President, Turner Inn, 1989-1990). Law Clerk to the Honorable R.A. Hedrick, Chief Judge, North Carolina Court of Appeals, 1990-1991. *Member:* Mecklenburg

(This Listing Continued)

MORRIS YORK WILLIAMS SURLES & BARRINGER, L.L.P., Charlotte—Continued

County, North Carolina (Member, Group Insurance Committee) and American Bar Associations; North Carolina State Bar; North Carolina Association of Defense Attorneys. ***PRACTICE AREAS:*** Civil Litigation; Insurance Defense. ***Email:*** glewis@morrisyork.com

MICHELLE SAIN LANGDON, born Morganton, North Carolina, August 23, 1965; admitted to bar, 1990, North Carolina. *Education:* University of North Carolina-Chapel Hill (B.A., 1987; J.D., with honors, 1990). Phi Beta Kappa; Phi Eta Sigma. Member, Holderness Moot Court, 1989-1990. Recipient, American Jurisprudence Award for Contracts. *Member:* North Carolina State Bar; North Carolina Association of Defense Attorneys. ***PRACTICE AREAS:*** Insurance Defense; Workers Compensation Defense. ***Email:*** msain@morrisyork.com

SUSAN HUNT BRIGGS, born Madrid, Spain, December 11, 1968; admitted to bar, 1994, North Carolina and U.S. District Court, Eastern District of North Carolina. *Education:* University of North Carolina at Chapel Hill (B.A., 1991; J.D., 1994). Phi Alpha Delta. *Member:* North Carolina State Bar. ***PRACTICE AREAS:*** Civil Litigation; Workers Compensation Defense; Native American Law. ***Email:*** sbriggs@morrisyork.com

L. STEPHEN KUSHNER, born Fayetteville, North Carolina, April 28, 1974; admitted to bar, 1998, North Carolina. *Education:* Duke University (B.A., cum laude, 1995); University of North Carolina (J.D., 1998). *Member:* North Carolina Bar Association. ***PRACTICE AREAS:*** Civil Litigation; Insurance Defense; Workers Compensation Defense. ***Email:*** skushner@morrisyork.com

---

KEITH B. NICHOLS, born New Hyde Park. New York, March 20, 1975; admitted to bar, 2000, North Carolina. *Education:* Vanderbilt University (B.A., 1997); University of Miami (J.D., 2000). Member: Negotiation Team; Mediation Advocacy Team. *Member:* Mecklenburg County and North Carolina Bar Associations; North Carolina State Bar; North Carolina Association of Defense Attorneys. ***PRACTICE AREAS:*** Workers Compensation; Insurance Defense. ***Email:*** knichols@morrisyork.com

KIMBERLY A. GOSSAGE, born Wytheville, Virginia, April 24, 1964; admitted to bar, 1998, North Carolina and U.S. District Court, Western, Middle and Eastern Districts of North Carolina. *Education:* University of North Carolina at Charlotte (B.A., magna cum laude, 1995); Wake Forest University (J.D., 1998). Member: Moot Court Board, 1995-1998; National Moot Court Team, 1997-1998. Formerly with: Dean & Gibson; Cranfill, Sumner & Hartzog, LLP.*Member:* Mecklenburg County and North Carolina Bar Associations; Defense Research Institute. ***PRACTICE AREAS:*** Insurance Defense; Civil Litigation. ***Email:*** kgossage@morrisyork.com

ROBERTA S. SPERRY, born Hollywood, Florida, May 4, 1974; admitted to bar, 1999, North Carolina. *Education:* Davidson College (B.A., 1996); University of North Carolina at Chapel Hill (J.D., 1999). Phi Alpha Delta. *Member:* North Carolina Bar Association; North Carolina State Bar; North Carolina Association of Defense Attorneys. ***PRACTICE AREAS:*** Workers Compensation; Civil Liability. ***Email:*** rsperry@morrisyork.com

JOCELYN FERGUSON, born Charlotte, North Carolina, February 12, 1978; admitted to bar, 2003, North Carolina. *Education:* University of Florida (B.S.B.A., 1999); University of North Carolina at Chapel Hill (J.D., 2003). *Member:* North Carolina State Bar; North Carolina Association of Defense Attorneys. ***PRACTICE AREAS:*** Workers Compensation Defense; Insurance Defense. ***Email:*** jferguson@morrisyork.com

HEATHER GRAHAM CONNOR, born Baton Rouge, Louisiana, August 27, 1973; admitted to bar, 1998, Louisiana, U.S. District Court, Eastern, Western and Middle Districts of Louisiana and U.S. Court of Appeals, Fifth Circuit; 2001, North Carolina. *Education:* Louisiana State University (B.A., 1995); Tulane University (J.D., cum laude, 1998). *Member:* Gaston County, Louisiana State and American Bar Associations; North Carolina State Bar; North Carolina Association of Defense Attorneys. ***Email:*** hconnor@morrisyork.com

CHRISTOPHER B. RAWLS, born Whiteville, North Carolina, May 5, 1979; admitted to bar, 2004, North Carolina. *Education:* North Carolina State University (B.S., 2001); University of North Carolina at Chapel Hill (J.D., 2004). *Member:* North Carolina State Bar. ***PRACTICE AREAS:*** Workers Compensation Defense; Civil Litigation. ***Email:*** crawls@morrisyork.com

ROBYN M. LACY, born Morgantown, West Virginia, October 28, 1973; admitted to bar, 2000, North Carolina. *Education:* West Virginia University (B.S.J., 1995; J.D., 2000). *Member:* Mecklenburg County Bar Association; North Carolina State Bar. ***PRACTICE AREAS:*** Insurance Defense; Workers Compensation Defense. ***Email:*** rlacy@morrisyork.com

DEAN P. LOVEN, born Newton, Indiana, May 22, 1956; admitted to bar, 1996, North Carolina. *Education:* University of Iowa (Ph.D., 1981); University of North Carolina (J.D., 1996). *Member:* North Carolina State Bar; North Carolina Association of Defense Attorneys. ***PRACTICE AREAS:*** Workers Compensation Defense; Insurance Defense. ***Email:*** dloven@morrisyork.com

MARK B. CANEPA, born San Francisco, California, January 26, 1959; admitted to bar, 1989, California, New Mexico, U.S. District Court, District of New Mexico and Northern District of California and U.S. Court of Appeals, Ninth and Tenth Circuits; 2004, North Carolina; 2005, South Carolina. *Education:* San Francisco State University (B.A., History, magna cum laude, 1985; B.A., Journalism, magna cum laude, 1986); Hastings College of the Law, University of California (J.D, 1988). *Member:* North Carolina Bar Association; State Bar of California; North Carolina Association of Defense Attorneys. ***PRACTICE AREAS:*** Medical Malpractice Defense; Insurance Defense. ***Email:*** mcanepa@morrisyork.com

REPRESENTATIVE CLIENTS: Brentwood Services; Cape Fear Valley Medical Center; Travelers; Allstate; Amerisure; City of Charlotte; Companion; Crawford & Co.; Eaton Corp.; Fireman's Fund; Geico Ins.; Freightliner, Inc.; Harleysville; Hartford; J.B. Hunt; Jefferson-Pilot; John Deere Co.; Kemper; Key Risk; Liberty Mutual; MetLife; Montgomery Ins.; Nautilus; Peerless; Protective; Royal and SunAlliance; Sedgwick; Sentry Ins.; Southern Guaranty; State Farm; Transamerica (TIG) Trigon; Wausau; Winn-Dixie; Zenith Insurance Co.; Carolinas Medical Center; Cambridge; American International Group (AIG); State Auto Ins. Co.

(This Listing Continued)

LAW OFFICES OF DALE S. MORRISON

1043 EAST MOREHEAD STREET, SUITE 200
CHARLOTTE, NORTH CAROLINA 28204
Telephone: 704-375-6788
Fax: 704-335-0853
URL: http://www.morrisonfiorella.com
Email: dsm@dalesmorrisonlaw.com
URL: http://www.dalemorrisonlaw.com

Business Enterprises, Contracts, Corporate, Complex Civil Litigation, Estate Litigation, Personal Injury, Products Liability, White Collar Crime.

DALE S. MORRISON, born Staunton, Virginia, October 20, 1946; admitted to bar, 1978, North Carolina, U.S. District Courts, Western, Middle and Eastern Districts of North Carolina, U.S. Tax Court, U.S. Court of Appeals, 4th Circuit, and U.S. Supreme Court. *Education:* Elon College (A.B., 1968); University of Virginia (J.D., 1978). *Member:* Mecklenburg County (Member, Civil Law Section) and North Carolina (Member, Sections on: Business and Litigation) Bar Associations; Master, William Bobbitt American Inns of Court. [Captain, U.S. Army, 1968-1975]. ***REPORTED CASES:*** U.S. v. Chambers, 985 F.2d 1263 (4th Cir. 1993); State v. Ward, 487 S.E.2d 798, 127 N.C.App. 115 (1997); H.McBride Realty, Inc. v. Myers, 380 S.E.2d 586 94 N.C.App. 511 (1989); Helms v. Church's Fried Chicken, Inc., 344 S.E.2d 349, 81 N.C.App. 427 (1986).

MULLEN HOLLAND & COOPER P.A.

CHARLOTTE, NORTH CAROLINA
(See Gastonia)

General Civil Trial and Appellate Practice, all Federal and State Courts. Banking, Bankruptcy and Reorganization, Construction, Corporate and Commercial, Employment Discrimination, Estate Planning and Administration, Health Care, Insurance, Mergers and Acquisitions, Negligence, Personal Injury, Professional Malpractice, Real Estate, Workers' Compensation.

NELSON MULLINS RILEY & SCARBOROUGH LLP

BANK OF AMERICA CORPORATE CENTER, SUITE 2400
100 NORTH TRYON STREET
CHARLOTTE, NORTH CAROLINA 28202-4007
Telephone: 704-417-3000
Telecopy: 704-377-4814
URL: http://www.nelsonmullins.com

Atlanta, Georgia Office: 999 Peachtree Street, N.E., Suite 1400, 30309-3964, P.O. Box 77707, 30357-0707. Telephone: 404-817-6000. Telecopy: 404-817-6050.
Charleston, South Carolina Office: Liberty Center, Suite 600, 151 Meeting Street, 29401-2239. P.O. Box 1806, 29402-1806. Telephone: 843-853-5200. Telecopy: 843-722-8700.
Columbia, South Carolina Office: Meridian, 17th Floor, 1320 Main Street, 29201, P.O. Box 11070, 29211-1070. Telephone: 803-799-2000. Telecopy: 803-256-7500.
Greenville, South Carolina Office: Poinsett Plaza, 104 South Main Street, Suite 900, 29601. P.O. Box 10084, 29603-0084. Telephone: 864-250-2300. Telecopy: 864-232-2925.
Myrtle Beach, South Carolina Office: Founders Centre, Suite 301, 2411 North Oak Street, 29577-3165. P.O. Box 3939, 29578-3939. Telephone: 843-448-3500. Telecopy: 843-448-3437.
Raleigh, North Carolina Office: GlenLake One, Suite 200, 4140 Parklake Avenue, 27612. Telephone: 919-877-3800. Telecopy: 919-877-3799.
Washington, D.C. Office: 101 Constitution Avenue, NW, Suite 900, 20001. Telephone: 202-712-2800. Fax: 202-712-2860.
Winston-Salem, North Carolina Office: The Knollwood, 380 Knollwood Street, Suite 530, 27103. Telephone: 336-774-3300. Fax: 336-774-3299.

Business Litigation, Corporate, Government Relations and Administrative Law, Health Care, Labor and Employment Litigation, Product Liability, Securities Litigation, Taxation, Technology, Telecommunications, Utility Regulation.

PARTNERS

KURT E. LINDQUIST, II, admitted to bar, 1983, North Carolina; U.S. District Court, Eastern, Middle and Western Districts of North Carolina; U.S. Tax Court; U.S. Court of Appeals, Fourth Circuit; U.S. Supreme Court. *Education:* Duke University (A.B., cum laude, 1980); Wake Forest University (J.D., 1983). *Member:* North Carolina Bar Association. ***PRACTICE AREAS:*** Complex Commercial Litigation. ***Email:*** kurt.lindquist@nelsonmullins.com

PAUL J. OSOWSKI, born St. Paul, Minnesota, March 28, 1968; admitted to bar, 1996, North Carolina; U.S. District Court, Western, Middle and Eastern Districts of North Carolina; U.S. Court of Apeals, Fourth Circuit. *Education:* Wake Forest University (B.S., 1990); Campbell University (J.D., cum laude, 1996). Order of the Barristers. Member, National Moot Court Team. Editor, Campbell Law Review, 1994-1996. Author: "Underinsured Motorist Coverage: North Carolina's Multiple Claimant Wrinkle-Ray v. Atlantic Casualty Insurance Co.", 17 Campbell Law Review 147, 1995. *Member:* North Carolina State Bar; North Carolina Bar Association; Mecklenburg County Bar Association; American Bar Association; North Carolina Association of Defense Attorneys; Defense Research Institute. ***PRACTICE AREAS:*** Products Liability; Premises Liability; Professional Negligence; Insurance Defense; Workers Compensation; Commercial Litigation; Aviation Law. ***Email:*** paul.osowski@nelsonmullins.com

FRANCIS C. PRAY, JR., born Perth Amboy, New Jersey, December 5, 1964; admitted to bar, 1989, New Jersey; 1990, New York; 1992, District of Columbia; 2001, North Caro-

(This Listing Continued)

lina. *Education:* University of Virginia (B.A., 1986; J.D., 1989). Phi Delta Phi. Author: "Debt Financing for Technology Companies," New Jersey Financing Manual, May 1998. *Member:* North Carolina and American Bar Associations. ***PRACTICE AREAS:*** Banks and Banking; Finance; Real Estate; Business Law. ***Email:*** frank.pray@nelsonmullins.com

LAWRENCE J. SCOTT, born Miami, Florida, January 11, 1959; admitted to bar, 1984, South Carolina; 1985, North Carolina. *Education:* Furman University (B.A., cum laude, 1981); University of South Carolina (J.D., 1984). Order of the Wig and Robe. Order of the Coif. Arthur B. Custy Tax Award, 1984. University of South Carolina Law Review. Certified Public Accountant, North Carolina, 1986. *Member:* American Health Lawyers Association; American Institute of Certified Public Accountants. ***PRACTICE AREAS:*** Business Law; Corporation; Health Care; Mergers and Acquisitions; Taxation. ***Email:*** larry.scott@nelsonmullins.com

TRACY E. TOMLIN, born Bethesda, Maryland, October 27, 1955; admitted to bar, 1985, Florida; 1999, North Carolina; U.S. District Court, Southern and Middle Districts of Florida; U.S. District Court, Western, Middle and Eastern Districts of North Carolina; U.S. Court of Appeals, Fourth, Third, Eleventh, Sixth and Federal Circuits. *Education:* Duke University (B.S., 1977); Old Dominion University (M.S., 1980); University of Miami (J.D., cum laude, 1984). Member, Order of Barristers. Vice President, Moot Court Board, 1983-1984. Member, National Moot Court Team, 1982. *Member:* North Carolina and American (Litigation Section) Bar Associations; The Florida Bar; Southeast Admiralty Law Institute. ***PRACTICE AREAS:*** Business Litigation; Insurance Litigation; Admiralty Law; Products Liability. ***Email:*** tracy.tomlin@nelsonmullins.com

MARK VASCO, born Newark, New Jersey, March 11, 1968; admitted to bar, 1994, New York and U.S. District Court, Southern and Eastern Districts of New York; 1996, U.S. Court of Appeals, Second Circuit; 1999, North Carolina and U.S. District Court, Western District of North Carolina; 2001, U.S. Court of Appeals, Fourth Circuit; U.S. District Court, Eastern and Middle Districts of North Carolina. *Education:* Syracuse University (B.A. in Political Science, magna cum laude, 1990); University of North Carolina at Chapel Hill (J.D., with honors, 1993). Phi Beta Kappa. Member, Federal Bar Council, 1995-2003. *Member:* Mecklenburg County, New York State, North Carolina and American Bar Associations. ***PRACTICE AREAS:*** Complex Commercial Litigation; Class Action Litigation; Consumer Financial Services Litigation. ***Email:*** mark.vasco@nelsonmullins.com

RABOTEAU T. WILDER, JR., born Wilmington, North Carolina, April 1, 1948; admitted to bar, 1973, North Carolina and U.S. District Court, Middle and Western Districts of North Carolina; 1974, U.S. Tax Court; 1975, U.S. Court of Appeals, Fourth Circuit; 1993, U.S. Supreme Court and U.S. Court of Appeals for the Eleventh and Federal Circuits. *Education:* Wake Forest University (B.A., magna cum laude, 1970); Duke University (J.D., 1973). Phi Beta Kappa. Assistant U.S. Attorney, Western District of North Carolina, 1974-1976. Listed in The Best Lawyers in America, 2003-2006 editions. *Member:* North Carolina Bar Association; American Board of Trial Advocacy (President, North Carolina Chapter, 1996-1997); Fourth Circuit Judicial Conference. ***PRACTICE AREAS:*** Health Care; Business Litigation; Products Liability; Employment Litigation. ***Email:*** rob.wilder@nelsonmullins.com

FRED M. WOOD, JR., born St. Louis, Missouri, December 13, 1963; admitted to bar, 1991, North Carolina and U.S. District Court, Eastern, Western and Middle Districts of North Carolina; 1993, U.S. Court of Appeals, Fourth Circuit. *Education:* University of North Carolina at Chapel Hill (B.A., Biology, 1986); Wake Forest University (J.D., 1991; M.B.A., 1991). Phi Delta Phi. Recipient, American Jurisprudence Award in Trial Advocacy, 1991. Author, "North Carolina Law of Design Professionals," North Carolina Continuing Legal Education Seminar, 1997. Member, Litigation Section, American Bar Association. *Member:* Wake County, Mecklenburg County (Member, Litigation Section) and North Carolina (Member, Litigation Section) Bar Associations; North Carolina State Bar; Defense Research Institute (Member, Commercial Litigation Section). ***PRACTICE AREAS:*** Complex Commercial Litigation; Business Litigation; Construction Litigation; Products Liability; Class Actions. ***Email:*** fred.wood@nelsonmullins.com

ASSOCIATES

VIRGINIA "GINGER" THEIS DALY, admitted to bar, 1999, Ohio; 2000, District of Columbia (Not admitted in North Carolina). *Education:* University of Virginia (B.A., 1996); George Washington University (J.D., 1999). ***PRACTICE AREAS:*** Litigation. ***Email:*** ginger.daly@nelsonmullins.com

NATHAN C. FULLER, born April 19, 1972; admitted to bar, 1998, North Carolina and South Carolina. *Education:* The Ohio State University (B.S.B.A., 1994); University of South Carolina School of Law (J.D., 1998). *Member:* Mecklenburg County and North Carolina Bar Associations; North Carolina State Bar; South Carolina Bar. ***PRACTICE AREAS:*** Finance; Corporate; Real Estate. ***Email:*** nathan.fuller@nelsonmullins.com

KEVIN J. HEISER, born Charlottesville, Virginia, January 24, 1972; admitted to bar, 1998, South Carolina; 2003, North Carolina. *Education:* James Madison University (B.S., 1994); University of South Carolina School of Law (J.D., 1998). Recipient, American Bankruptcy Institute Medal of Excellence for South Carolina, 1998. Law Clerk to the Honorable John S. Dalis, Chief U.S. Bankruptcy Judge for the Southern District of Georgia, 1998-1999. *Member:* American Bankruptcy Institute. ***PRACTICE AREAS:*** Bankruptcy; Creditors Rights; Commercial Litigation. ***Email:*** kevin.heiser@nelsonmullins.com

THOMAS G. HOOPER, born Charlotte, North Carolina, April 22, 1972; admitted to bar, 1998, North Carolina and U.S. District Court, Middle District of North Carolina; 1999, U.S. District Court, Eastern District of North Carolina; 2000, U.S. District Court, Western District of North Carolina; 2002, U.S. Court of Appeals, Fourth Circuit. *Education:* Davidson College (A.B., 1994); University of North Carolina at Chapel Hill (J.D., with honors, 1998). Articles Editor, North Carolina Law Review, 1997-1998. *Member:* North Carolina and American Bar Associations. ***PRACTICE AREAS:*** Commercial Litigation; Consumer Financial Services Litigation; Real Estate Litigation; Business Torts. ***Email:*** tom.hooper@nelsonmullins.com

CHRISTINA M. K. JACUZZO, born Chautauqua, New York, October 13, 1967; admitted to bar, 2000, North Carolina. *Education:* University of South Carolina (B.S., Business Administration, with honors, 1992; J.D., 1999). Order of Wig and Robe. Captain Debate Team. President Communications and Debate Association, 1990-1992. Recipient: CALI Award for Interviewing, Counseling, and Negotiation; John Belton O'Neall Scholarship, 1996-1999. Editorial Staff ABA Real Property, Probate and Trust Journal. *Member:* Mecklenburg County, North Carolina (Member: Business Section; Young Lawyers Division) and American (Member, Business Section) Bar Associations. ***LANGUAGES:*** Spanish. ***PRACTICE AREAS:*** Financial Institutions; Corporate Law; Telecommunications Law; Corporate Tax. ***Email:*** christina.jacuzzo@nelsonmullins.com

C. MARSHALL LINDSAY, born 1972; admitted to bar, 1998, North Carolina; 1999, South Carolina. *Education:* University of North Carolina at Chapel Hill (B.A., 1994); University of South Carolina (J.D., 1998). Member, Moot Court Bar. *Member:* Mecklenburg County and North Carolina Bar Associations; North Carolina State Bar; South Carolina Bar. ***PRACTICE AREAS:*** Complex Commercial Litigation; Construction Litigation; Products Liability. ***Email:*** marshall.lindsay@nelsonmullins.com

VALERIE PAIGE MAHONEY, born Milwaukee, Wisconsin, May 3, 1963; admitted to bar, 2001, New York; 2002, North Carolina. *Education:* University of Pennsylvania, Wharton School of Business (B.S.Ec., 1983); University of North Carolina-Chapel Hill (M.B.A., 1986); Benjamin N. Cardozo School of Law, Yeshiva University (J.D., 2000). Order of the Coif. Editor-in-Chief, Cardozo Law Review. Author: Student Note, "Environmental Justice," Cardozo Law Review. Formerly with Thelen Reid & Priest. *Member:* State Bar of North Carolina; New York State and American Bar Associations. ***PRACTICE AREAS:*** Corporate Transactions; Taxation. ***Email:*** valerie.mahoney@nelsonmullins.com

JULIE R. MUELLER, admitted to bar, 2001, North Carolina. *Education:* University of North Carolina at Chapel Hill (B.A., 1997); Norman Adrian Wiggins School of Law, Campbell University (J.D., 2001). *Member:* Mecklenburg County (Member, Young Lawyers Division) and North Carolina Bar Associations; Defense Research Institute. ***PRACTICE AREAS:*** Litigation. ***Email:*** julie.mueller@nelsonmullins.com

CHRISTOPHER M. OLDS, born Newport, Rhode Island, 1971; admitted to bar, 2002, North Carolina; U.S. District Court, Eastern, Western and Middle Districts of North Carolina. *Education:* Virginia Polytechnic Institute and State University (B.S.Ch.E., 1994); University of South Carolina (J.D., 2002). Former Member, Order of the Wig and Robe. Former Member, Editorial Board, South Carolina Law Review. Former Environmental Engineer, North Carolina Department of Environmental and Natural Resources and the U.S. Army Chemical and Biological Defense Command. *Member:* North Carolina Bar Association; Defense Research Institute. ***PRACTICE AREAS:*** Corporate Litigation; Environmental Litigation; Natural Resources Litigation. ***Email:*** chris.olds@nelsonmullins.com

POLLYBETH PROCTOR, born Richmond, Virginia, December 17, 1976; admitted to bar, 2003, North Carolina; 2004, South Carolina; U.S. District Court, Western, Middle and Eastern Districts of North Carolina; U.S. Court of Appeals, Fourth Circuit. *Education:* Davidson College (B.A., 1999); University of Georgia (J.D., cum laude, 2003). Member, Editorial Board, 2001-2002 and Executive Notes Editor, 2002-2003, Georgia Journal of International and Comparative Law. Author: "Procreating from Prison: Evaluating British Prisoners' Rights to Artificially Inseminate Their Wives Under the United Kingdom's New Human Rights Act and the 2001 Mellor Case," Georgia Journal of International and Comparative Law, Winter 2003; "Determining Reasonable Accomodation Under the ADA: Understanding Employers' and Employees' Rights and Responsibilities During the Interactive Process," Southwestern Law Review, 2003; "Toward Mythos and Mythology: Applying a Feminist Critique to Legal Education to Effectuate a Socialization of Both Sexes in Law School Classrooms," Cardozo Women's Law Journal, 2004. *Member:* North Carolina State Bar; South Carolina Bar; Mecklenburg County, North Carolina and American Bar Associations; Defense Research Institute. ***LANGUAGES:*** French. ***PRACTICE AREAS:*** Commercial Litigation; Business Litigation; Franchise Litigation; Product Liability. ***Email:*** pollybeth.proctor@nelsonmullins.com

CAROLINE H. "CARRIE" RYAN, born Greenville, South Carolina, January 15, 1978; admitted to bar, 2005, North Carolina. *Education:* Williams College (B.A. in English, with honors, 2000); Duke University School of Law (J.D., with honors, 2005). Managing Editor, The Devil's Advocate, Duke University School of Law. Representative, Graduate and Professional Student Council, Duke University School of Law. *Member:* North Carolina Bar Association. ***PRACTICE AREAS:*** Litigation; Business Litigation. ***Email:*** carrie.ryan@nelsonmullins.com

EVAN M. SAUDA, born Charlotte, North Carolina, 1979; admitted to bar, 2004, North Carolina and U.S. District Court, Western District of North Carolina; U.S. District Court, Eastern and Middle Districts of North Carolina. *Education:* University of North Carolina at Chapel Hill (B.A., 2001); Washington & Lee University (J.D., 2004). Member, Moot Court Board. Semifinalist, 23rd Annual John W. Davis Moot Court Competition. *Member:* Mecklenburg County, North Carolina Bar Association; North Carolina State Bar; Defense Research Institute. ***PRACTICE AREAS:*** Litigation. ***Email:*** evan.sauda@nelsonmullins.com

ERIK A. SCHWANZ, born Menominee, Michigan, April 3, 1973; admitted to bar, 1998, North Carolina; 1999, South Carolina; U.S. District Court, Western, Middle and Eastern Districts of North Carolina; U.S. Court of Appeals, Fourth Circuit. *Education:* Wake Forest University (B.A., cum laude, 1995; J.D., 1998). *Member:* Mecklenburg County Bar Association; North Carolina Association of Defense Attorneys; Defense Research Institute. ***PRACTICE AREAS:*** Products Liability; Commercial Litigation; Employment Litigation; Premises Liability; Insurance. ***Email:*** erik.schwanz@nelsonmullins.com

WILLIAM M. STARR, born Albany, New York, February 23, 1978; admitted to bar, 2003, North Carolina and U.S. District Court, Eastern and Middle Districts of North Carolina. *Education:* State University of New York College at Geneseo (B.A., summa cum laude, 2000); University of North Carolina at Chapel Hill (J.D., with honors, 2003). Recipient: 2000 Gressman-Pollit Appelate Advocacy Award. Member 2000 Moot Court Tournament Championship Team. Senior Staff Member, North Carolina Journal of International Law and Commercial Regulation. Chief Investigator of Law School's Attorney General Office. *Member:* Mecklenburg Bar Association; North Carolina State Bar. ***PRACTICE AREAS:*** Products Liability; Premises Liability; Business Litigation. ***Email:*** bill.starr@nelsonmullins.com

KERRY L. TRAYNUM, admitted to bar, 2004, North Carolina. *Education:* Gardner-Webb University (B.A., 1997); University of North Carolina School of Law (J.D., 2004).

(This Listing Continued)

NELSON MULLINS RILEY & SCARBOROUGH LLP, Charlotte—Continued

Order of the Coif. Member, First Amendment Law Review. *Member:* Mecklenburg County, North Carolina and American Bar Associations; North Carolina State Bar. ***PRACTICE AREAS:*** Business Litigation. ***Email:*** kerry.traynum@nelsonmullins.com

CLARK C. WALTON, born 1978; admitted to bar, 2005, North Carolina. *Education:* University of North Carolina at Chapel Hill (B.S. in Mathematical Sciences, 1999); Georgetown University Law Center (J.D., 2005). Former White House intern to the Vice President's Homeland Security Assistant, 2003. Former intelligence officer for the Central Intelligence Agency, 2000-2005. Completed the Federal Bureau of Investigation's Honors Internship Program, 1999. Two-term Law Student Division Delegate to the ABA House of Delegates, 2003-2005. Former contributor, ABA Student Lawyer magazine. Director of public relations, Georgetown Student Bar Association. *Member:* North Carolina Bar Association. ***PRACTICE AREAS:*** Commercial Litigation; Litigation; Products Liability. ***Email:*** clark.walton@nelsonmullins.com

MEGAN K. WATKINS, admitted to bar, 2002, Georgia; 2005, North Carolina. *Education:* University of Georgia (B.A., 1999; J.D., 2002). ***PRACTICE AREAS:*** Litigation. ***Email:*** megan.watkins@nelsonmullins.com

All attorneys are members of the American Bar Association.

(For biographical data on Atlanta, Georgia, Charleston, South Carolina, Columbia, South Carolina, Greenville, South Carolina, Myrtle Beach, South Carolina, Raleigh, North Carolina, Washington, D.C. and Winston-Salem, North Carolina, see Professional Biographies of those cities)

NEWITT & BRUNY

Established in 1925

SUITE 104, 417 EAST BOULEVARD

CHARLOTTE, NORTH CAROLINA 28203

Telephone: 704-372-6181
Facsimile: 704-377-0535
Email: NEWITTBRU@CS.COM

Business, Construction and Commercial, Civil Litigation, Mergers, Acquisitions and Divestitures, Commercial Real Estate, Collections.

MEMBERS OF FIRM

JOHN G. NEWITT, SR. (1897-1973)

JOHN G. NEWITT, JR., born Charlotte, North Carolina, 1941; admitted to bar, 1965, North Carolina. *Education:* Wake Forest University (B.A., 1963; J.D., 1965); University of Virginia (1965-1968); Central Piedmont Community College (C.B.A., Business Management, 2001). Writer, Wake Forest Law Review (1965). Chairman, Board of Zoning Adjustment, 1972-1976. Lecturer, Legal Responsibilities of Boards of Directors, United Way Volunteer Leadership Development Program, 1986-1990. *Member:* 26th Judicial District and North Carolina Bar Associations; North Carolina State Bar. [Capt., US Army, JAGC, active duty, 1965-1968]

ROGER H. BRUNY, born Monroe, Wisconsin, 1942; admitted to bar, 1968, Illinois; 1973, North Carolina. *Education:* University of Chicago (B.S., 1965; J.D., 1968). Staff Counsel, Lake Michigan and Adjoining Land Study Commission, 1970-1971. *Member:* 26th Judicial District; North Carolina State Bar.

NEXSEN PRUET ADAMS KLEEMEIER, PLLC

Established in 1945

201 SOUTH TRYON STREET
SUITE 1200

CHARLOTTE, NORTH CAROLINA 28202

Telephone: 704-339-0304
Facsimile: 704-338-5377
URL: http://www.npaklaw.com

Acquisitions, Administrative Law, Alternative Dispute Resolution, Antitrust Law, Appellate Practice, Arbitration, Bankruptcy Law, Business Law, Collections Law, Construction Law, Commercial Law, Commercial Real Estate, Computers, Contracts, Copyrights, Corporate Law, Creditor-Debtor Rights, Disabilities, Domestic Relations Law, Economic Development Law, Education Law, Election, Eminent Domain Employee Benefits Law, Employment Law, Environmental Law, Estate Planning, Family Law, Fidelity Law, Finance Law, Governmental Representation, Health Care Law, Hospital Law, Immigration Law, Insurance Law, Insurance Defense, Intellectual Property Law, International Law, Internet Law, Investments, Labor Law, Land Use, Leasing Law, Litigation, Maritime Law, Mediation, Mergers, Naturalization Law, Partnership Law, Patents, Personal Injury, Probate, Products Liability Law, Professional Liability, Public Contracts, Public Finance, Real Estate Law, Real Estate Planning, Regulatory Law, Securities, Surety Law, Taxation Law, Technology Law, Torts, Trade Regulation, Trade Secrets, Trademarks, Transportation, Trusts, Utility Law, Wills, Workers' Compensation and Zoning Law.

FIRM PROFILE: Nexsen Pruet Adams Kleemeier is the Carolinas Law Firm. With 7 offices in North and South Carolina, Nexsen Pruet Adams Kleemeier attorneys can, and do, handle a broad range of legal needs for those doing business in the Carolinas. Our attorneys are licensed to practice in state and federal courts and before the U.S. Patent and Trademark Office. The firm's website is www.npaklaw.com.

LAW FIRM ALLIANCES/ASSOCIATIONS: ***LAWORLD:*** *http://www.LaWorld.com.*

WILLIAM J. ADAMS, JR. (1908-1993)

WILBURN BREWER, JR. (1939-2003)

C. ALVIN BROWN (1940-1978)

PAUL A. COOPER (1889-1956)

DANIEL W. FOUTS (1932-2003)

FRANK B. GARY (1900-1971)

JOHN A. KLEEMEIER, JR. (1911-1973)

ELIZABETH DUNN WHITE (1954-1995)

MEMBERS OF FIRM

PATRICK F. BROWN, admitted to bar, 1987, Maryland, District of Columbia and North Carolina. *Education:* Western State College of Colorado (B.A., 1978); The Catholic University of America (J.D., 1987). Associate Editor, Catholic University of America Law Review. ***PRACTICE AREAS:*** Commercial Finance; Commercial Real Estate; Corporate Finance; Corporate Law; Public Finance. ***Email:*** PBrown@nexsepruet.com

DAVID REES CANNON, admitted to bar, 1977, North Carolina and U.S. Tax Court. *Education:* Furman University (B.A., 1970); University of South Carolina (J.D., 1977). *Member:* Mecklenburg County and North Carolina Bar Associations; North Carolina State Bar (Member, Real Estate Section and Business Law Section). [LTJG, U.S. Navy, 1970-1973]. ***PRACTICE AREAS:*** Commercial Leasing; Real Estate; Corporate; Mergers and Acquisitions; Liquor Licensing; Beverage Alcohol Law. ***Email:*** DCannon@nexsenpruet.com

DAVID W. GOSSETT (Resident, Greenville, SC Office)

J. HAYDEN HARRELL, admitted to bar, 1985, North Carolina. *Education:* Wake Forest University (B.A., cum laude, 1982; J.D., 1985). ***PRACTICE AREAS:*** Commercial Real Estate; Construction Finance; Commercial Finance; Structured Finance. ***Email:*** HHarrell@nexsenpruet.com

ROBERT H. HULL, JR., admitted to bar, 1980, North Carolina. *Education:* University of North Carolina at Charlotte (B.A., 1976); Wake Forest University (J.D., 1980). ***PRACTICE AREAS:*** Business Law; Commercial Transactions; Commercial Real Estate; Corporate Law; Real Estate Secured Lending. ***Email:*** RHull@nexsenpruet.com

MARCUS A. MANOS (Resident, Columbia, SC Office)

JOSEPH D. McCULLOUGH, admitted to bar, 1983, North Carolina. *Education:* Wake Forest University (B.A., magna cum laude, 1980; J.D., cum laude, 1983). Phi Beta Kappa. Member, Editorial Staff, Wake Forest Law Review, 1982-1983. ***PRACTICE AREAS:*** Commercial Real Estate; Banking Law; Finance; Corporate Law; Partnership Law. ***Email:*** JMccullough@nexsenpruet.com

SEAN M. PHELAN, admitted to bar, 1992, North Carolina. *Education:* University of North Carolina at Chapel Hill (B.A., with highest honors, 1988; J.D., 1992; M.B.A., 1992). Phi Beta Kappa. Recipient, Morehead Scholarship. Articles Editor, N.C. Journal of International Law and Commercial Regulation. *Member:* 26th Judicial District and North Carolina Bar Associations. ***PRACTICE AREAS:*** Commercial Real Estate; Business Associations; Workers Compensation. ***Email:*** SPhelan@nexsenpruet.com

JAMES H. PULLIAM, admitted to bar, 1989, North Carolina; 1998, South Carolina; U.S. District Court, Western, Middle and Eastern Districts of North Carolina; U.S. Court of Appeals, Fourth Circuit. *Education:* University of Kentucky (B.A., 1985; J.D., 1989). *Member:* North Carolina State Bar (Member, Sections on: Bankruptcy; Construction Law); South Carolina Bar; American Bankruptcy Institute. ***PRACTICE AREAS:*** Bankruptcy; Banking Litigation; Construction Litigation; Commercial Litigation; Arbitration. ***Email:*** JPulliam@nexsenpruet.com

MATTHEW B. ROBERTS (Resident, Columbia, SC Office)

PETER A. SANTOS, admitted to bar, 1989, Pennsylvania; 2004, North Carolina. *Education:* Duquesne University (B.A., 1985; J.D., 1989). Order of Barristers. Member, Duquesne Law Review. ***PRACTICE AREAS:*** Commercial Litigation; Business Law; Bankruptcy; Products Liability Litigation; Toxic Torts. ***Email:*** psantos@nexsenpruet.com

MARGUERITE SMITH WILLIS (Resident, Columbia, SC Office)

RICHARD W. WILSON, admitted to bar, 1974, North Carolina. *Education:* University of North Carolina (B.A., 1970; J.D., 1974). Phi Beta Kappa; Phi Delta Phi. *Member:* North Carolina (Past Chair, Construction Law Section) and American (Member, Forum on the Construction Industry) Bar Associations; 26th Judicial District and North Carolina State Bars. ***PRACTICE AREAS:*** Construction Law and Litigation; Commercial Litigation; Creditor Rights; Bankruptcy; Real Estate Foreclosure; Receiverships. ***Email:*** RWilson@nexsenpruet.com

ASSOCIATES

LAURIE A. BECKER (Resident, Columbia, SC Office)

CHRISTIE S. MATTHEWS, admitted to bar, 2000, North Carolina. *Education:* North Carolina Central University (B.A., 1997); Yale University (J.D., 2000). Valedictorian. Moot Court Board Member. Member, Editorial Board, Yale Law and Policy Review. Professor: Central Piedmont Community College, 2004; Strayer University, 2004—; University of Phoenix, 2004—. ***PRACTICE AREAS:*** Litigation. ***Email:*** CMatthews@nexsenpruet.com

NIKOLE SETZLER MERGO (Resident, Columbia, SC Office)

LACEY M. MOORE, admitted to bar, 2003, North Carolina and U.S. District Court, Western District of North Carolina; 2004, Mississippi, U.S. District Court, Northern and Southern Districts of Mississippi and U.S. Court of Appeals, Fifth Circuit. *Education:* University of Georgia (B.A., 1999); Samford University (J.D., 2002). The American Journal of Trial Advocacy. *Member:* North Carolina State Bar. ***PRACTICE AREAS:*** Commercial Litigation; Toxic Tort Litigation; Bankruptcy/Workout; Consumer Litigation. ***Email:*** lmoore@nexsenpruet.com

ANDREA B. RICKS, admitted to bar, 2002, North Carolina. *Education:* University of North Carolina at Chapel Hill (B.A., 1992); Wake Forest University School of Law (J.D., cum laude, 2002). Order of the Coif. Scholastic Honors Graduate. *Member:* North Carolina State Bar. ***PRACTICE AREAS:*** Real Estate. ***Email:*** aricks@nexsenpruet.com

(This Listing Continued)

PATRICK D. SARSFIELD II, admitted to bar, 1993, North Carolina and U.S. District Court, Middle and Western Districts of North Carolina. *Education:* University of North Carolina at Chapel Hill (B.A., 1989; J.D., 1993). Member, North Carolina School of Law Holderness Moot Court Team. *Member:* North Carolina State Bar. ***PRACTICE AREAS:*** Commercial Litigation; Creditors Rights; Real Property Litigation; Insurance Law; Labor and Employment. ***Email:*** PSarsfield@nexsenpruet.com

MELINDA FOX STALEY, admitted to bar, 1999, South Carolina; 2001, North Carolina. *Education:* Michigan State University (B.A., 1992); Thomas M. Cooley Law School (J.D., magna cum laude, 1999); New York University School of Law (LL.M., Tax, 2000). Law Review. *Member:* South Carolina Bar; North Carolina State Bar. ***PRACTICE AREAS:*** Health Care; Taxation; Corporate Law. ***Email:*** MStaley@nexsenpruet.com

THE NICKERSON LAW FIRM

200 N. MCDOWELL STREET
CHARLOTTE, NORTH CAROLINA 28204
Telephone: 704-370-7741
Fax: 704-370-0447
URL: http://www.nickersonlawfirm.com

Criminal, Drugs, Fraud, Burglary, Appeals, Traffic, Speeding, Forfeiture, Felonies, Federal Criminal, Forgery, Homicide, Murder, Search and Seizures.

JOHN NICKERSON, born Greenville, South Carolina, May 30, 1968; admitted to bar, 1999, North Carolina. *Education:* College of Charleston (Polical Science, 1991); Campbell Law School (J.D., 1999). *Member:* North Carolina BarAssociation; American Trial Lawyers Association; National Association of Criminal Defense Lawyers. ***PRACTICE AREAS:*** Criminal; Drug Crimes; Fraud; Burglary; Appellate Practice; Traffic Violations; Felonies; Federal Criminal Law; Forgery; Driving While Intoxicated; Sex Crimes; Theft; Search and Seizure; Weapons Charges.

THE ODOM FIRM, PLLC

Established in 2000

1109 GREENWOOD CLIFF
CHARLOTTE, NORTH CAROLINA 28204
Telephone: 704-377-7333
Fax: 704-377-5747
Email: theodomfirm@mecklaw.com
URL: http://www.mecklaw.com

Raleigh, North Carolina Office: 1046 Washington Street, 27605.

Civil Litigation, Condemnation, Personal Injury, Legal Malpractice, Products Liability, Construction Law, Environmental Law, Disability Law, Guardianship, Competency Proceedings, Employment Law, Zoning and Land Use.

T. LaFONTINE ODOM, SR., born Rocky Mount, North Carolina, April 18, 1938; admitted to bar, 1962, North Carolina. *Education:* University of North Carolina (A.B., 1960; LL.B., 1962). Phi Alpha Delta. Research Assistant with North Carolina Supreme Court, 1962-1963. Assistant City Attorney, 1963-1964. Member, 1980-1986, Vice Chairman, 1980-1982 and Chairman, 1982-1984, Mecklenburg County Board of Commissioners. Member, North Carolina Senate, 1989-2002. *Member:* North Carolina and American Bar Associations; The Association of Trial Lawyers of America; North Carolina Academy of Trial Lawyers. ***SPECIAL AGENCIES:*** Board of Commissioners of Carolinas Healthcare Systems. ***REPORTED CASES:*** Long v. City of Charlotte, 306 N.C. 187, 293 S.E. 2d 101 (1982); Northwestern Fin. Group, Inc. v. County of Gaston, 329 N.C. 180, 405 S.E. 2d 138 (1991); Department of Transportation v. Elm Land, 163 N.C. App. 257, 593 S.E.2d 131 cert. denied, 358 N.C. 542, 599 S.E. 2d 42 (2004). ***PRACTICE AREAS:*** Contracts; Business Law; Environmental Law; Personal Injury Civil Litigation; Condemnation; Administrative Law. ***Email:*** fountainodom@mecklaw.com

THOMAS L. ODOM, JR., born Chapel Hill, North Carolina, September 4, 1961; admitted to bar, 1988, North Carolina. *Education:* University of North Carolina at Chapel Hill (B.A., 1983); Wake Forest University (J.D., 1987). Litigator, condemnation cases against the North Carolina Department of Transportation and the city of Charlotte before judges and juries in the trial court, the North Carolina Court of Appeals and the North Carolina Supreme Court. *Member:* North Carolina Bar Association; North Carolina Academy of Trial Lawyers. ***REPORTED CASES:*** Fraser v. Littlejohn, 96 N.C. App. 377, 386 S.E. 2d 230 (1989); Fraser v. Littlejohn, 96 N.C. App. 388, 386 S.E. 2d 237 (1989); Northwestern Fin. Group, Inc. v. County of Gaston, 329 N.C. 180, 405 S.E. 2d 138 (1991); Kern v. Creative Entertainment, Inc., 130 N.C. App. 611, 506 S.E. 2d 492 (1998); Department of Transportation v. Elm Land, 163 N.C. App. 257, 599 S.E. 2d 42, cert.denied, 358 N.C. 542, 593 S.E.2d 131 (2004). ***PRACTICE AREAS:*** Civil Trial Law; Real Estate; Condemnation; Professional Negligence; Professional Malpractice; Appellate Law; Criminal Defense. ***Email:*** tommyodom@mecklaw.com

MARTHA C. ODOM, born Lumberton, North Carolina, July 29, 1966; admitted to bar, 1993, South Carolina (Inactive); 1994, North Carolina; U.S. District Court, Western District of North Carolina. *Education:* Guilford College (B.S., 1988); University of South Carolina (J.D., 1993). Phi Delta Phi. Member, South Carolina Environmental Law Journal, 1992-1993. *Member:* North Carolina Bar Association (Member, North Carolina General Practice, Solo and Small Firm Section; Section Chairperson, 2002-2003). ***REPORTED CASES:*** Crowley v. CC Air, Inc., 98 Fed. Appx. 930, 2004 WL 1000344 (4th Cir. 2004). ***PRACTICE AREAS:*** Disability Law; Guardianship; Competency Proceedings; Employment Law. ***Email:*** marthaodom@mecklaw.com

OGLETREE, DEAKINS, NASH, SMOAK & STEWART, P.C.

Established in 1972

400 WEST TRADE STREET
CHARLOTTE, NORTH CAROLINA 28202-1627
Telephone: 704-342-2588
Facsimile: 704-342-4379
Email: clientservices@ogletreedeakins.com
URL: http://www.ogletreedeakins.com

Atlanta, Georgia Office: 600 Peachtree Street, N.E., Suite 2100. Telephone: 404-881-1300.
Austin, Texas Office: 301 Congress Avenue, Suite 1250. Telephone: 512-344-4700.
Birmingham, Alabama Office: One Federal Place, Suite 1000, 1819 Fifth Avenue North. Telephone: 205-328-1900.
Charleston, South Carolina Office: 134 Meeting Street, Suite 160, P.O. Box 1808. Telephone: 843-853-1300.
Chicago, Illinois Office: Twenty-Fifth Floor, Two First National Plaza, 20 South Clark Street. Telephone: 312-558-1220.
Columbia, South Carolina Office: 1320 Main Street, Suite 600. Telephone: 803-252-1300.
Dallas, Texas Office: 700 Preston Commons, 8117 Preston Road. Telephone: 214-987-3800.
Greensboro, North Carolina Office: 2725 Horse Pen Creek Road, Suite 101. Telephone: 336-375-9737.
Greenville, South Carolina Office: The Ogletree Building, 300 North Main Street, P.O. Box 2757. Telephone: 864-271-1300.
Houston, Texas Office: One Allen Center, 500 Dallas Street, Suite 3000. Telephone: 713-655-0855.
Kansas City, Missouri Office: 4717 Grand Avenue, Suite 300. Telephone: 816-471-1301.
Los Angeles, California Office: 633 West Fifth Street, Suite 5300. Telephone: 213-239-9800.
Indianapolis, Indiana Office: Suite 4600, 111 Monument Circle. Telephone: 317-916-1300.
Miami, Florida Office: 80 S.W. 8th Street, Suite 1830. Telephone: 305-374-0506.
Morristown, New Jersey Office: 10 Madison Avenue, Suite 402. Telephone: 973-656-1600.
Nashville, Tennessee Office: SunTrust Center, Suite 800, 424 Church Street. Telephone: 615-254-1900.
Phoenix, Arizona Office: 2415 East Camelback Road, Suite 800. Telephone: 602-778-3700.
Raleigh, North Carolina Office: 2301 Sugar Bush Road, Suite 600, P.O. Box 31608. Telephone: 919-787-9700.
San Antonio, Texas Office: 2600 Weston Centre, 112 East Pecan Street. Telephone: 210-354-1300.
St. Thomas, U.S. Virgin Islands Office: The Tunick Building, 1336 Beltjen Road, Suite 202. Telephone: 340-714-1235.
Tampa, Florida Office: 100 North Tampa Street, Suite 3600. Telephone: 813-289-1247.
Washington, D.C. Office: Fifth Floor, 2400 N Street, N.W. Telephone: 202-887-0855.

Labor Relations, Employment Litigation, Workers' Compensation. Civil Litigation in all State and Federal Courts and Administrative Agencies.

JAMES B. SPEARS, JR., born Auburn, Alabama, March 16, 1948; admitted to bar, 1973, North Carolina; 1974, South Carolina, U.S. Supreme Court, U.S. Court of Appeals, Fourth, Fifth, Eleventh and District of Columbia Circuits, U.S. District Court, Western, Middle and Eastern Districts of North Carolina; U.S. District Court, District of South Carolina. *Education:* Wake Forest University (B.S., 1970; J.D., 1973). Phi Delta Phi. Editor, Wake Forest Law Review, 1973. Member, South Carolina Commission on Continuing Lawyer Competence, 1980-1984. Listed in Business North Carolina's Legal Elite, The Best Lawyers in America, and The International Who's Who of Management Labour and Employment Lawyers. *Member:* Mecklenburg, Wake County, North Carolina and American Bar Associations. [U.S. Army, Military Police Officer]. (Certified Specialist, Employment and Labor Law, South Carolina Supreme Court). ***REPORTED CASES:*** Gilmer v. Interstate Johnson/Lane Corp., 500 U.S. 20 (1991); O'Connor v. Consol. Coin Caterers Corp., 517 U.S. 308 (1996). ***PRACTICE AREAS:*** Employment and Labor Law; Employer Rights; Management Labor Law; Wrongful Termination Defense; U.S. Supreme Court Litigation. ***Email:*** jim.spears@ogletreedeakins.com

ROBERT S. PHIFER, born Charlotte, North Carolina, September 22, 1952; admitted to bar, 1977, South Carolina and U.S. District Court, District of South Carolina; 1986, U.S. Court of Appeals, Eleventh Circuit; 1987, North Carolina and U.S. District Court, Western, Eastern and Middle Districts of North Carolina; 1989, U.S. Court of Appeals, Fourth Circuit; 1990, U.S. Supreme Court. *Education:* University of South Carolina (B.A., 1973; J.D., 1977). Member, 1975-1977 and Executive Editor, 1976-1977, South Carolina Law Review. Member, Society of Wig and Robe (University of South Carolina School of Law). Instructor, Legal Writing, University of South Carolina School of Law, 1976-1977. Author: Note, "The Class Action Device in Title VII Civil Suits," 28 South Carolina Law Review 639, 1977; "Employee Arbitration Agreements Can Control the Risk of Litigation," Business North Carolina, at 72, August 2001. Co-Author: *COBRA Compliance Manual,* Haynsworth Baldwin Johnson & Greaves LLC, 2003. Leadership Charlotte, Class XIX (1998). Member, Haynsworth Baldwin Johnson & Greaves LLC, 1982-2004. Associate, Haynsworth, Baldwin, Johnson & Greaves LLC, 1977-1982. *Member:* Mecklenburg County and North Carolina (Member, Labor and Employment Law Section) Bar Associations; North Carolina State Bar; South Carolina Bar (Member, Labor and Employment Law Section); American Bar Association (Member, Labor and Employment Law Section and Employee Benefits Committee); National Retail Federation Committee on Employment Law (Associate Member); Society for Human Resources Management; Charlotte Area Society for Human Resources Management; Charlotte Chamber of Commerce (Associate Member, Manufacturers Business Alliance); Rotary Club of Charlotte, North Carolina. ***REPORTED CASES:*** Gilmer v. Interstate Johnson/Lane Corp., 500 U.S. 20 (1991); Harrison v. Edison Brothers Apparel Stores, 151F.3d 176 (4th Cir. 1998); Ard v. Southwest Forest Industries, 849 F.2d

(This Listing Continued)

OGLETREE, DEAKINS, NASH, SMOAK & STEWART, P.C., Charlotte—Continued

517 (11th Cir. 1988); Barnes v. Southwest Forest Industries, 814 F.2d 607 (11th Cir. 1987). ***PRACTICE AREAS:*** Employment Related Litigation; Employment Discrimination; Employee Benefits Litigation; Affirmative Action; Family and Medical Leave Act; Americans with Disabilities Act; Military Leave; Employee Benefits Claims; Employment Contracts; Arbitration Agreements; COBRA; Severance Agreements; Noncompetition Agreements. ***Email:*** bob.phifer@ogletreedeakins.com

STEPHEN D. DELLINGER, born Charlotte, North Carolina, February 9, 1964; admitted to bar, 1989, North Carolina and U.S. District Court, Western District of North Carolina; 1991, U.S. District Court, Middle District of North Carolina; 1993, U.S. District Court, Eastern District of North Carolina; 1994, U.S. Court of Appeals, Fourth, Eighth and Eleventh Circuits and U.S. Supreme Court. *Education:* Appalachian State University (B.A., cum laude, 1986); Wake Forest School of Law (J.D., 1989). Phi Alpha Delta. *Member:* Mecklenburg County (Member, Young Lawyers Division) Bar Association; North Carolina State Bar (Labor Section). ***PRACTICE AREAS:*** Employment Discrimination; Employment Law; Employment Litigation. ***Email:*** steve.dellinger@ogletreedeakins.com

JOHN D. COLE, born Dover-Foxcroft, Maine, April 15, 1962; admitted to bar, 1991, Georgia and South Carolina; 1995, North Carolina. *Education:* Washington & Lee University (B.A., magna cum laude, 1984); University of Georgia (J.D., 1991). Omicron Delta Kappa. *Member:* State Bar of Georgia; South Carolina Bar; North Carolina State Bar. [Officer, U.S. Army, 1984-1988]. ***PRACTICE AREAS:*** Employment Discrimination; Employment Litigation; National Labor Relations Act; Unfair Labor Practices; Union Elections. ***Email:*** john.cole@ogletreedeakins.com

---

KELLY S. HUGHES, admitted to bar, 2003, Florida, U.S. Court of Appeals, Eleventh Circuit and U.S. District Court, Southern District of Florida; 2004, U.S. District Court, Middle and Northern Districts of Florida; 2005, North Carolina and U.S. District Court, Western, Eastern and Middle Districts of North Carolina. *Education:* Vanderbilt University (B.M., cum laude, 1999); University of Miami School of Law (J.D., magna cum laude, 2003). Dean's List (Fall 2000, Spring 2001, Fall 2001, Spring 2002, Fall 2002). Order of the Coif. Member, University of Miami Law Review (2001-2003). McDougall Scholar (2001-2002, 2002-2003). Awarded Dean's Merit Scholarship (2002-2002, 2002-2003). Awarded Dean's Certificate of Achievement - Property (Fall 2000). Winner of First-Year Moot Court Competition (Spring 2001). ***PRACTICE AREAS:*** Labor and Employment. ***Email:*** kelly.hughes@ogletreedeakins.com

BENJAMIN R. HOLLAND, born Wooster, Ohio; admitted to bar, 2002, North Carolina and U.S. District Court, Western, Eastern and Middle Districts of North Carolina. *Education:* Kenyon College (B.A., 1999); Case Western Reserve University School of Law (J.D., 2002). ***PRACTICE AREAS:*** Labor and Employment. ***Email:*** ben.holland@ogletreedeakins.com

JEREMY A. STEPHENSON, born Chicago, Illinois; admitted to bar, 1999, Illinois; U.S. District Court, Northern District of Illinois (Not admitted in North Carolina). *Education:* University of Virginia (B.A., 1995); Loyola University, Chicago (J.D., 1999). Member, Law Journal. Editor-in-Chief, Loyola Consumer Law Review. Member, Jefferson Literary Society. *Member:* American Bar Association. ***PRACTICE AREAS:*** Labor and Employment. ***Email:*** jeremy.stephenson@ogletreedeakins.com

REPRESENTATIVE CLIENTS: Alamance Regional Medical Center; Allegheny Technologies Inc.; American Express Company; Baxter Corporation; BFI (Browning-Ferris Industries); Belk Stores Services, Inc.; Cameron M. Harris & Co.; Charlotte Pipe and Foundry Company; Chubb Group of Insurance Companies; Cleveland Regional Medical Center; Coca-Cola Bottling Co. Consolidated; Compass Group USA, Inc.; Conbraco Industries, Inc.; Cone Mills Corporation; Cooper Industries, Inc.; Curtiss Wright Corporation; Dillard's, Inc.; Drexel Heritage Furnishings, Inc.; Family Dollar Stores, Inc.; Fluor Daniel, Inc.; Fresenius Medical Care North America; Gaston Memorial Hospital; Gerdau AmeriSteel Corporation; Harris Teeter Inc.; Hendrick Automotive Group; Henkel Corporation; Hickory Springs Manufacturing Co.; Hitachi Metals North Carolina, Ltd.; Iredell County; Jockey International, Inc.; Jordan Graphics Corporation; The Kroger Co.; Mitsubishi Semiconductor America, Inc.; B.C. Moore & Sons, Inc.; National Starch & Chemical Co.; NorthEast Medical Center; Nucor Corporation; J.C. Penney Company, Inc.; Perdue Farms Incorporated; PYA/Monarch, Inc.; Radio Shack/ Tandy Corporation; Rockwell International; Rowan Regional Medical Center; Sears, Roebuck & Co.; Southeastern Freight Lines; Stonecutter Mills Corporation; Target Stores, Inc.; The Timken Company; Travelers Insurance Co.; Tyson Foods, Inc.; United Carolina Bank; Valmet Paper Machinery; Wampler-Longacre, Inc.; Wellman, Inc.; W.W. Grainger, Inc.

ORBOCK RUARK & DILLARD, PC

CHARLOTTE, NORTH CAROLINA

(See Winston Salem)

Workers Compensation, Personal Injury Defense.

ORSBON & FENNINGER LLP

4201 CONGRESS STREET
SUITE 110
CHARLOTTE, NORTH CAROLINA 28209
Telephone: 704-556-9600
Fax: 704-556-9601
Email: oandflaw.com
URL: http://www.orsbonandfenninger.com

Estate Planning, Probate, Trusts and Estates, Taxation, Business Law.

FIRM PROFILE: Both Partners are Board Certified Specialists in Estate Planning and Probate Law.

R. ANTHONY ORSBON, born Wilkes County, North Carolina, 1947; admitted to bar, 1972, North Carolina. *Education:* Davidson College (B.A., 1969); Vanderbilt University (J.D., 1972). Patrick Wilson Scholar. Member, Vanderbilt Law Review. President, Charlotte Estate Planning Council. (Board Certified Specialist in Estate Planning and Probate Law, North Carolina State Board of Legal Specialization). ***PRACTICE AREAS:*** Estate Planning; Estate Administration; Trust Law; Tax Law. ***Email:*** torsbon@oandflaw.com

(This Listing Continued)

CYNTHIA T. FENNINGER, born Charlotte, North Carolina, July 15, 1967; admitted to bar, 1993, North Carolina. *Education:* University of North Carolina at Chapel Hill (B.A., with honors, 1989; J.D., with honors, 1993). Order of the Coif; Phi Beta Kappa. North Carolina Law Review. (Board Certified Specialist in Estate Planning and Probate Law, North Carolina State Board of Legal Specialization). ***PRACTICE AREAS:*** Estate Planning; Estate Administration; Trusts. ***Email:*** cfenninger@oandflaw.com

---

LAW OFFICE OF ANNEMARIE PANTAZIS

1419 E. 7TH STREET
CHARLOTTE, NORTH CAROLINA 28204
Telephone: 704-342-2243
Fax: 704-342-3266
Email: pantazisa@carolina.rr.com
URL: http://www.pantazislaw.com

Mailing Address: P.O. Box 34278, Charlotte, NC 28234

Workers' Compensation, Personal Injury, Traffic Violations.

ANNEMARIE PANTAZIS, born Washington, D.C., September 12, 1973; admitted to bar, 1999, North Carolina and U.S. District Court, Western District of North Carolina; 2002, U.S. Court of Appeals, Fourth Circuit. *Education:* College of William & Mary (B.A., Government, 1994); Wake Forest University (J.D., 1999). Member, 1997-1999 and Editorial Staff Member, 1998-1999, Wake Forest Law Review. Member, 1997-1999 and Chief Justice, 1998-1999, Wake Forest Moot Court Board. Author: "Zeran v. America Online, Inc.: Insulating Service Providers from Defamation Liability", 34 Wake Forest L. Rev. 531 (1999); *Workers Compensation Law Update,* Chapter 5, General Practice Handbook 2003; *Employment Covered and Defenses,* Chapter 4, Workers' Compensation 2003, November 2003. Speaker, Workers' Compensation, Wake Forest Continuing Legal Education Series, 2002-2003.*Member:* North Carolina State Bar; North Carolina Bar Association (Member, Workers Compensation Section); North Carolina Association of Trial Attorneys (Member, Workers Compensation Section); Workplace Injury Litigation Group. ***PRACTICE AREAS:*** Personal Injury; Traffic Violations; Workers Compensation.

PARHAM, HELMS, HARRIS, BLYTHE & MORTON

6100 FAIRVIEW ROAD, SUITE 1200
CHARLOTTE, NORTH CAROLINA 28210
Telephone: 704-556-1101
Fax: 704-556-1044
Email: phhbmlaw@aol.com

General Civil Practice. Probate, Real Estate, Foreclosures, Corporation, Banking and Bankruptcy Law.

MEMBERS OF FIRM

LEWIS H. PARHAM, JR., born Wilson, North Carolina, November 5, 1932; admitted to bar, 1957, North Carolina. *Education:* University of North Carolina (B.S., 1954; J.D., with honors, 1957); Georgetown University (LL.M., 1960). Phi Delta Phi. Member, Board of Editors, North Carolina Law Review, 1956-1957. *Member:* The North Carolina State Bar; North Carolina, Federal and American Bar Associations. ***PRACTICE AREAS:*** Real Estate Development; Commercial.

NEAL G. HELMS, born Monroe, North Carolina, October 30, 1934; admitted to bar, 1963, North Carolina. *Education:* University of North Carolina (LL.B., 1963). Delta Theta Phi. *Member:* North Carolina Bar Association; 26th Judicial District and The North Carolina State Bars. ***PRACTICE AREAS:*** Real Estate; Real Estate Development. ***Email:*** nhelms@phhbm.com

RALPH C. HARRIS, JR., born Hamlet, North Carolina, March 18, 1944; admitted to bar, 1969, North Carolina. *Education:* University of North Carolina (B.S., 1966; J.D., 1969). Phi Alpha Delta (Secretary, 1968-1969). *Member:* 26th Judicial District and North Carolina State Bars; American Bar Association. ***PRACTICE AREAS:*** Real Estate; Real Estate Development. ***Email:*** rcharrisjr@phhbm.com

ROBERT B. BLYTHE, born Charlotte, North Carolina, March 27, 1935; admitted to bar, 1961, North Carolina. *Education:* Davidson College (A.B., 1957); University of North Carolina (LL.B., 1961). Phi Delta Phi. Member, Student Board of Editors, North Carolina Law Review, 1960-1961. *Member:* North Carolina and American Bar Associations. ***PRACTICE AREAS:*** Real Property Law; Municipal Law; Wills Law; Estates Law. ***Email:*** rblythe@phhbm.com

JAMES H. MORTON, born Danville, Virginia, April 4, 1935; admitted to bar, 1966, North Carolina. *Education:* North Carolina State University; University of North Carolina (LL.B., 1964). Delta Theta Phi. *Member:* North Carolina (Member, Bankruptcy Section) and American Bar Associations; 26th Judicial District and North Carolina State Bars. [Ret. Lt Col, U.S. Air Force Reserve]. ***PRACTICE AREAS:*** Bankruptcy Law; Creditors Rights Law; Banking Law. ***Email:*** jmorton@phhbm.com

OF COUNSEL

JOHN L. HAZLEHURST, born Chapel Hill, North Carolina, January 8, 1956; admitted to bar, 1980, North Carolina. *Education:* University of North Carolina at Chapel Hill (B.A., 1977); Yale University (J.D., 1980). Phi Beta Kappa. ***PRACTICE AREAS:*** Corporate; Commercial. ***Email:*** JohnHazlehurst@mindspring.com

REPRESENTATIVE CLIENTS: The McAlpine Group; Medical Specialties, Inc.; Branch Banking & Trust Co.; First Charter National Bank; Portrait Homes Construction Co.; General Motors Acceptance Corp.; Consolidated Freightways Corp.; Freightliner Corp.; Town of Hunterville; Town of Matthews Board of Adjustment; Old Republic Surety Co.; Beazer Homes Corp.; Homebuilders Association of Charlotte; Bank of America.

(This Listing Continued)

APPROVED ATTORNEYS FOR: Lawyers Title Insurance Corp; Chicago Title Insurance Co.; Commonwealth Land Title Insurance Co.; First American Title Insurance Co.; Investors Title Insurance Co.

JOHN J. PARKER, III

212 SOUTH TRYON STREET, SUITE 1660
CHARLOTTE, NORTH CAROLINA 28281
Telephone: 704-375-2100
Fax: 704-375-8770
Email: jparker@jjparkeriii.com
URL: http://www.lawyers.com/jjparkeriii

General Civil Litigation including Business, Commercial, Contract, Employment and Real Estate Litigation.

JOHN J. PARKER, III, born Charlotte, North Carolina, 1951; admitted to bar, 1976, North Carolina; 1980, U.S. Court of Appeals, Fourth Circuit and U.S. Supreme Court. *Education:* University of North Carolina (B.A., 1973); Wake Forest University (J.D., 1976). Certified Mediator. *Member:* Mecklenburg County, North Carolina and American Bar Associations; North Carolina State Bar; Fourth Circuit Judicial Conference.

PARKER, POE, ADAMS & BERNSTEIN L.L.P.

Established in 1884

THREE WACHOVIA CENTER
401 SOUTH TRYON STREET, SUITE 3000
CHARLOTTE, NORTH CAROLINA 28202
Telephone: 704-372-9000
Facsimile: 704-334-4706
Email: info@parkerpoe.com
URL: http://www.parkerpoe.com

Raleigh, North Carolina Office: Wachovia Capitol Center, 150 Fayetteville Street Mall, Suite 1400, P.O. Box 389, 27602-0389. Telephone: 919-828-0564. Facsimile: 919-834-4564.

Columbia, South Carolina Office: 1201 Main Street, Suite 1450, 29201. Telephone: 803-255-8000. Facsimile: 803-255-8017.

Spartanburg, South Carolina Office: 101 W. St. John Street, Suite 203, 29306. Telephone: 803-591-2030. Facsimile: 803-591-2050.

Charleston, South Carolina Office: 200 Meeting Street, Suite 301, 29401. Telephone: 843-727-2650. Facsimile: 843-727-2680.

Administrative and Regulatory, Antitrust and Trade Regulation, Arbitration, Banking, Bankruptcy, Insolvency and Reorganization, Biotechnology, Capital Markets, Computer, Construction, Copyright, Corporate, Corporate Finance, Education, Employee Benefits and Compensation Plans, Employment, Environmental, Estate Planning and Administration, Governmental Contracts and Procurement, Governmental Relations, Health Care, Immigration, Insurance, Intellectual Property, International Trade and Investment, Joint Ventures, Lending and Finance, Limited Liability Companies and Partnerships, Litigation, Malpractice Defense, Mergers and Acquisitions, Municipal, Products Liability, Project Development, Project Finance, Public Finance, Commercial Real Estate, Securities, Tax Exempt Organizations, Taxation, Technology Management and Licensing, Telecommunications, Trademark, Transportation, Utilities Regulation, Zoning.

FIRM PROFILE: Parker, Poe, Adams & Bernstein L.L.P. is one of the oldest and largest firms in the Carolinas. From our Raleigh, Charlotte, Charleston, Spartanburg and Columbia offices we serve a region recognized as an emerging center for business and industry. For information contact Allison L. Karp, Development Director, 704-372-9000.

PARTNERS

MICHAEL G. ADAMS, born Minneapolis, Minnesota, 1962; admitted to bar, 1989, North Carolina; U.S. District Court, Western, Middle and Eastern Districts of North Carolina and U.S. Court of Appeals, 4th, 6th and 7th Circuits. *Education:* University of Virginia (B.A., 1984); University of Texas (J.D., with honors, 1989). ***PRACTICE AREAS:*** Commercial Litigation; Bankruptcy. ***Email:*** mikeadams@parkerpoe.com

DAVID NEAL ALLEN, born Charlotte, North Carolina, 1955; admitted to bar, 1980, North Carolina. *Education:* University of North Carolina at Chapel Hill (A.B., 1977; J.D., 1980). *Member:* North Carolina Association of Defense Attorneys (Member, Board of Directors, 1998-2000, 2005—); Defense Research Institute; Federation of Defense and Corporate Counsel; International Association of Defense Counsel. ***PRACTICE AREAS:*** Mass Tort; Toxic Exposure; Professional Malpractice; Insurance Coverage. ***Email:*** davidallen@parkerpoe.com

JOHN H. BEYER, born Milwaukee, Wisconsin, April 9, 1970; admitted to bar, 1997, North Carolina and U.S. District Court, Western District of North Carolina. *Education:* Davidson College (B.A., 1992) University of North Carolina at Chapel Hill (J.D., 1997). *Member:* North Carolina and American Bar Associations; North Carolina State Bar; North Carolina Association of Defense Attorneys. ***PRACTICE AREAS:*** Civil Litigation; Defense Litigation; Trial Practice; Medical Malpractice Defense. ***Email:*** johnbeyer@parkerpoe.com

JAMES N. BRENNAN IV, born Heidelberg, West Germany, 1958; admitted to bar, 1986, Illinois; 1990, Virginia; 1996, North Carolina. *Education:* Randolph-Macon College (B.S., 1980); DePaul University (J.D., 1986). *Member:* North Carolina and American Bar Associations; Virginia State Bar; National Association of Bond Lawyers. ***PRACTICE AREAS:*** Public Finance; Capital Markets; Banking; Taxation. ***Email:*** jimbrennan@parkerpoe.com

P. NEAL COOK, born Marion, North Carolina, 1969; admitted to bar, 1995, North Carolina. *Education:* University of North Carolina at Chapel Hill (B.A., 1991); Wake Forest University (J.D., 1995). *Member:* North Carolina and American (Member, Business Law Section) Bar Association; North Carolina State Bar. ***PRACTICE AREAS:*** Capital Markets; Real Estate Finance. ***Email:*** nealcook@parkerpoe.com

HARVEY L. COSPER, JR., born Atlanta, Georgia, 1948; admitted to bar, 1975, North Carolina. *Education:* University of North Carolina at Chapel Hill (B.A., 1970); Wake Forest University (J.D., 1975). Listed in Best Lawyers in America, Litigation, 1999-2004. Member, Select Drafting Committee, North Carolina Board of Law Examiners, 1999. *Member:* North Carolina Association of Defense Attorneys (Member, Board of Directors, 1999-2001; Secretary, 2002-2004). [U.S. Army Reserves, 1970-1976]. ***PRACTICE AREAS:*** Professional Malpractice Law; Tort Defense; Products Liability Litigation. ***Email:*** harveycosper@parkerpoe.com

JONATHAN M. CROTTY, born Gainesville, Florida, 1963; admitted to bar, 1988, North Carolina. *Education:* Duke University (B.A., magna cum laude, 1985; J.D., with high honors, 1988). Named to Business North Carolina's Legal Elite, Employment Specialty, 2004 and 2005. ***PRACTICE AREAS:*** Employment Law; Transportation Law; Liquor Licensing. ***Email:*** jonathancrotty@parkerpoe.com

ALAN G. DEXTER, born Salem, Massachusetts, 1960; admitted to bar, 1985, North Carolina. *Education:* Cornell University (B.A., with distinction, 1982); Duke University (J.D., with honors, 1985). Phi Beta Kappa. Past Chair, Mecklenburg County Board of Tax Equalization and Review. *Member:* Mecklenburg County Bar Association (Past Chair, Real Property Section). ***PRACTICE AREAS:*** Real Estate; Commercial Development; Banking. ***Email:*** alandexter@parkerpoe.com

WOODARD E. FARMER, JR., born Asheville, North Carolina, 1948; admitted to bar, 1973, North Carolina. *Education:* Tulane University (B.A., 1970); Vanderbilt University (J.D., 1973). ***PRACTICE AREAS:*** Real Estate; Commercial Development; Capital Markets; Lender Representation. ***Email:*** woodyfarmer@parkerpoe.com

WILLIAM P. FARTHING, JR., born Lenoir, North Carolina, 1948; admitted to bar, 1974, North Carolina. *Education:* University of North Carolina at Chapel Hill (A.B., 1970; J.D., with honors, 1974). John Motley Morehead Scholar. Member, University of North Carolina Law Review, 1973-1974. Associate Justice, Holderness Moot Court Bench, 1973-1974. *Member:* North Carolina State Bar. ***PRACTICE AREAS:*** Employment Law; College and University Law. ***Email:*** billfarthing@parkerpoe.com

KIAH T. FORD, IV, born Charlottesville, Virginia, 1969; admitted to bar, 1994, North Carolina. *Education:* University of Virginia (B.A., 1991); Washington and Lee University (J.D., cum laude, 1994). Member, Mecklenburg County Bar Leadership Institute, Class of 2004. *Member:* Mecklenburg County Bar; North Carolina State Bar (Member, Bankruptcy Section); American Bar Association (Member, Bankruptcy Section); American Bankruptcy Institute. ***PRACTICE AREAS:*** Bankruptcy; Debtor and Creditor; Commercial Litigation. ***Email:*** chipford@parkerpoe.com

ANTHONY FOX, born Charlotte, North Carolina, 1955; admitted to bar, 1983, North Carolina. *Education:* North Carolina Agricultural & Technical State University (B.A., cum laude, 1977); University of North Carolina at Chapel Hill (M.P.A., 1982); North Carolina Central University (J.D., 1982). Former Secretary, Mecklenburg County Bar Association. Senior Assistant City Attorney, City of Charlotte, 1988-1994. Member, Board of Directors, Municipal Attorneys' of Central Carolinas Association. Chair, Board of Trustees, United Way, 2002. Board of Directors: Mecklenburg Bar Foundation; Charlotte Chamber of Commerce; Charlotte City Partners and Charlotte Coliseum Convention Center Authority. ***PRACTICE AREAS:*** Municipal Law; Government Relations; Government Contracts. ***Email:*** anthonyfox@parkerpoe.com

JOHN W. FRANCISCO, born San Jose, California, 1968; admitted to bar, 1993, North Carolina. *Education:* University of Virginia (B.A., 1990); Washington & Lee University (J.D., cum laude, 1993). ***PRACTICE AREAS:*** Energy; Property Law; Tort. ***Email:*** johnfrancisco@parkerpoe.com

JAMES N. GREENE III, born Salisbury, North Carolina, August 8, 1971; admitted to bar, 1999, North Carolina and U.S. District Court, Western District of North Carolina; 2004, U.S. Tax Court. *Education:* University of North Carolina at Charlotte (B.S., magna cum laude, 1993); University of North Carolina at Chapel Hill (J.D. with honors, 1999). Recipient, J. Nelson Young Tax Scholarship. Certified Public Accountant, North Carolina, 1993. Speaker, "Drafting LLC and LLP Agreements in North Carolina," North Carolina Continuing Legal Education Seminar, 2004. Member, Board of Governors, University of North Carolina at Charlotte Alumni Association, 2000-2004. *Member:* North Carolina State Bar; North Carolina (Member, Tax Section) and American (Member, Tax Section) Bar Associations. ***PRACTICE AREAS:*** Federal Income Tax; Limited Liability Companies; Partnership Taxation; Like Kind Exchanges; Low Income Housing Tax Credits. ***Email:*** jimmygreene@parkerpoe.com

THOMAS N. GRIFFIN III, born Munich, Germany, 1958; admitted to bar, 1983, Virginia; 1988, District of Columbia; 1989, North Carolina. *Education:* Wake Forest University (B.A., magna cum laude, 1980); University of Virginia (J.D., 1983). Phi Beta Kappa. Captain, U.S. Army Corps of Engineers, Honors Attorney, Environmental Law and Regulatory Programs, 1983-1987. Listed in Best Lawyers in America, Environmental Law. Named to Business North Carolina's Legal Elite, Environmental Specialty. ***PRACTICE AREAS:*** Environmental; Environmental Litigation. ***Email:*** tomgriffin@parkerpoe.com

JOHN E. GRUPP, born Garden City, New York, 1970; admitted to bar, 1995, North Carolina. *Education:* Duke University (B.S.E., magna cum laude, 1992); University of Virginia (J.D., 1995). Phi Beta Kappa; Tau Beta Pi. ***PRACTICE AREAS:*** Professional Malpractice; Products Liability; Tort Defense. ***Email:*** johngrupp@parkerpoe.com

ALBERT E. GUARNIERI, born Warren, Ohio, 1960; admitted to bar, 1986, North Carolina. *Education:* University of Michigan (B.A., 1982); University of Virginia (J.D., 1986). *Member:* North Carolina Bar Association (Chair, International Law and Practice Section, 2000-2001). ***LANGUAGES:*** German. ***PRACTICE AREAS:*** International; Mergers and Acquisitions; Industrial Development. ***Email:*** alguarnieri@parkerpoe.com

JOHN R. HAIRR III, born Raleigh, North Carolina, 1965; admitted to bar, 1990, North Carolina. *Education:* University of North Carolina at Chapel Hill (B.A., with honors, 1987); Duke University (J.D., with honors, 1990). Phi Beta Kappa. *Member:* North Caro-

(This Listing Continued)

(This Listing Continued)

PARKER, POE, ADAMS & BERNSTEIN L.L.P., Charlotte—Continued

lina and American Bar Associations. ***PRACTICE AREAS:*** Mergers, Acquisitions and Divestitures; Securities; Joint Ventures; Corporate Law; Commercial Law. ***Email:*** johnhairr@parkerpoe.com

IRVIN W. HANKINS III, born Charlotte, North Carolina, 1946; admitted to bar, 1975, North Carolina. *Education:* University of North Carolina at Chapel Hill (A.B., 1968; J.D., with honors, 1975). Order of the Coif. Administrative Editor, N.C. Law Review, 1974-1975. Vice President, North Carolina State Bar 2006. Past Chair, North Carolina State Bar Council Ethics Committee, 2002-2003. General Counsel, Charlotte Chamber of Commerce, 2002-2003. President, UNC Law Alumni. Member, Queens University of Charlotte Board of Trustees. Listed in the 2005-2006 edition of Best Lawyers in America, Business Litigation. Named to Business North Carolina's Legal Elite, Litigation Specialty. Managing Partner, 1986-2002. *Member:* North Carolina Association of Defense Attorneys. [Lt., USN, 1968-1972]. (General Counsel). ***PRACTICE AREAS:*** Utility Law; Insurance Coverage; Products Liability; Professional Malpractice. ***Email:*** iwhankins@parkerpoe.com

R. DOUGLAS HARMON, born Newton, Mississippi, 1958; admitted to bar, 1983, North Carolina. *Education:* Tulane University (B.A., summa cum laude, 1980); Duke University (J.D., 1983). Phi Beta Kappa. ***PRACTICE AREAS:*** Securities; Corporate Finance; Mergers and Acquisitions. ***Email:*** dougharmon@parkerpoe.com

JOSEPHINE H. HICKS, born Lancaster, South Carolina, 1961; admitted to bar, 1986, North Carolina. *Education:* University of the South (B.A., summa cum laude, with honors in History, 1983); Vanderbilt University (J.D., 1986). Phi Beta Kappa; Order of the Coif. Senior Student Writing Editor, Vanderbilt Law Review, 1985-1986. Law Clerk to the Hon. Harry W. Wellford, U.S. Court of Appeals, Sixth Circuit, 1986-1987. ***PRACTICE AREAS:*** Insurance Coverage; Tort Defense. ***Email:*** josephinehicks@parkerpoe.com

WILLIAM L. HIRATA, born New Haven, Connecticut, 1957; admitted to bar, 1986, South Carolina; 1990, Maryland; 2000, North Carolina. *Education:* Princeton University (A.B., 1982); University of South Carolina (M.B.A., 1985; J.D., 1986). *Member:* National Association of Bond Lawyers (Member, Attorney's Workshop Steering Committee, 1998-2000). ***PRACTICE AREAS:*** Public Finance; Capital Markets; Banking. ***Email:*** billhirata@parkerpoe.com

ASHLEY L. HOGEWOOD, JR., born Charlotte, North Carolina, 1940; admitted to bar, 1963, North Carolina. *Education:* Wake Forest University (B.A., 1961; J.D., 1963). Listed in Best Lawyers in America, Real Estate Law. Former Chairman and Vice Chair, Charlotte-Mecklenburg Board of Education. Former Trustee of Central Piedmont Community College. [Staff Sgt., U.S. Army Reserve, 1963-1969]. ***PRACTICE AREAS:*** Real Estate; Commercial Development; Public Finance. ***Email:*** ashleyhogewood@parkerpoe.com

HAROLD D. "CHIP" HOLMES, JR., born 1968; admitted to bar, 1993, North Carolina. *Education:* University of North Carolina at Chapel Hill (B.A., 1990); Wake Forest University (J.D., 1993). Certified Superior Court Mediator. *Member:* North Carolina and American Bar Associations; North Carolina Association of Defense Attorneys. ***PRACTICE AREAS:*** Physicians; Tort Defense; Products Liability Litigation; Civil Litigation; Insurance. ***Email:*** chipholmes@parkerpoe.com

JOY M. HORD, born Murfreesboro, Tennessee, 1970; admitted to bar, 1995, North Carolina. *Education:* Davidson College (A.B., 1992); Vanderbilt University (J.D., 1995). *Member:* North Carolina (Member, Sections on: Business Law; Health Law) and American (Member, Sections on: Business Law; Health Law) Bar Associations; American Health Lawyers Association; North Carolina Society of Healthcare Attorneys. ***PRACTICE AREAS:*** Health Care; Corporate Law; Mergers and Acquisitions. ***Email:*** joyhord@parkerpoe.com

STEPHEN R. HUNTING, born Charlotte, North Carolina, 1959; admitted to bar, 1984, North Carolina. *Education:* University of North Carolina at Chapel Hill (B.A., 1981; J.D., with honors, 1984). Former Associate General Counsel, Duke Energy Corporation. ***PRACTICE AREAS:*** Computers and Software; Commercial Law; Corporate Law; Mergers, Acquisitions and Divestitures. ***Email:*** stevehunting@parkerpoe.com

MAX EDWARD JUSTICE, born Hendersonville, North Carolina, 1945; admitted to bar, 1970, North Carolina. *Education:* University of North Carolina at Chapel Hill (A.B., 1967); Wake Forest University (J.D., cum laude, 1970). Listed in Best Lawyers in America, Environmental Law. ***PRACTICE AREAS:*** Environmental; Environmental Litigation. ***Email:*** maxjustice@parkerpoe.com

CHARLES B. LEE, JR., born Comanche County, Oklahoma, 1957; admitted to bar, 1983, Texas; 1987, North Carolina. *Education:* Duke University (B.A., magna cum laude, 1979); University of Virginia (J.D., 1983). ***PRACTICE AREAS:*** Capital Markets; Banking; Real Estate. ***Email:*** chucklee@parkerpoe.com

SCOTT E. LEO, born Binghamton, New York, April 25, 1968; admitted to bar, 1997, North Carolina. *Education:* North Carolina State University (B.A., cum laude, 1990); University of North Carolina at Chapel Hill (M.P.A., 1993; J.D., with honors, 1997). ***PRACTICE AREAS:*** Public Finance; Capital Markets; Banking Law. ***Email:*** scottleo@parkerpoe.com

BRANDON K. LEWISOHN, born New York, N.Y., May 6, 1970; admitted to bar, 1997, North Carolina; 1998, South Carolina. *Education:* University of Richmond (B.A., 1992); Wake Forest University (J.D., 1997). Member, Editorial Staff, Wake Forest Law Review. ***PRACTICE AREAS:*** Public Finance; Banking Law; Capital Markets. ***Email:*** brandonlewisohn@parkerpoe.com

FRED T. LOWRANCE, born Sumter, South Carolina, 1947; admitted to bar, 1972, North Carolina. *Education:* Davidson College (A.B., 1969); University of Virginia (J.D., 1972). Member, American Arbitration Association National Panel of Arbitrators. *Member:* North Carolina (Member, Construction Section) and American (Member: Construction Law Forum; Litigation Section) Bar Associations. ***PRACTICE AREAS:*** Construction; Commercial Litigation; Securities Litigation. ***Email:*** fredlowrance@parkerpoe.com

(This Listing Continued)

CRAIG T. LYNCH, born Miami, Florida, 1959; admitted to bar, 1986, North Carolina. *Education:* Florida State University (B.S., summa cum laude, 1981) Valedictorian; University of North Carolina at Chapel Hill (J.D., 1986). ***PRACTICE AREAS:*** Real Estate; Commercial Development. ***Email:*** craiglynch@parkerpoe.com

HELOISE C. MERRILL, born Birmingham, Alabama, 1950; admitted to bar, 1977, North Carolina. *Education:* Duke University (B.A., magna cum laude, 1971; J.D., with distinction, 1977). Editor in Chief, The Duke Legal Research Program, 1976-1977. Student Editorial Assistant, Law and Contemporary Problems, Duke University, 1975. *Member:* National Association of Stock Plan Professionals; ESOP Association. ***PRACTICE AREAS:*** Employee Benefits; Executive Compensation. ***Email:*** heloisemerrill@parkerpoe.com

BRENT M. MILGROM, JR., born Chapel Hill, North Carolina, 1967; admitted to bar, 1992, North Carolina; 1994, South Carolina. *Education:* University of North Carolina (B.A., with honors and distinction, 1989); University of Virginia (J.D., 1992). Phi Beta Kappa. ***PRACTICE AREAS:*** Commercial Real Estate Development; Commercial Real Estate Finance; Leasing. ***Email:*** brentmilgrom@parkerpoe.com

CHARLOTTE L. OFFERDAHL, born Plainfield, New Jersey, 1952; admitted to bar, 1988, North Carolina. *Education:* Lehigh University (B.A., 1975); The London School of Economics (M.Sc.Econ., 1976); University of North Carolina at Chapel Hill (J.D., with honors, 1988). *Member:* Mecklenburg County, North Carolina (Member, Tax Section) and American (Member, Tax Section) Bar Associations. ***PRACTICE AREAS:*** Employee Benefits; Executive Compensation; ERISA. ***Email:*** charlotteofferdahl@parkerpoe.com

W. EDWARD POE, JR., born Boston, Massachusetts, 1949; admitted to bar, 1974, North Carolina, U.S. District Court, Western District of North Carolinea; 1976, U.S. District Court, Middle District of North Carolina. *Education:* Wake Forest University (B.A., 1971; J.D., 1974); Harvard University (Advanced Management Program, 1994). Former Deputy General Counsel, Duke Energy Corporation. Former Chair, Corporate Counsel Section, North Carolina Bar Association. Former Member, Board of Governors of the North Carolina Bar Association. Listed in the Best Lawyers in America, Public Utility Law. *Member:* North Carolina and American Bar Associations; North Carolina Association of Defense Attorneys. [U.S. Army Reserve, 1970-1976]. ***PRACTICE AREAS:*** Energy; Utility Law; Tort Defense. ***Email:*** eddiepoe@parkerpoe.com

J. WILLIAM PORTER, born Shelby, North Carolina, 1951; admitted to bar, 1977, North Carolina. *Education:* University of North Carolina at Chapel Hill (A.B., 1974; J.D., with honors, 1977). Listed in the Best Lawyers in America, Bankruptcy and Creditor-Debtor Rights Law. *Member:* Mecklenburg County and North Carolina Bar Associations; North Carolina State Bar. ***PRACTICE AREAS:*** Bankruptcy Reorganization; Creditors Rights. ***Email:*** billporter@parkerpoe.com

GEORGE H. PRETTY II, born Ardmore, Oklahoma, 1951; admitted to bar, 1977, South Carolina; 1989, North Carolina. *Education:* Duke University (B.A., 1973); University of South Carolina (J.D., 1977); Emory University (LL.M., Taxation, 1985). ***PRACTICE AREAS:*** Mergers and Acquisitions; Industrial Development; Corporate Commercial Law; International Trade; Tax Law. ***Email:*** georgepretty@parkerpoe.com

WILLIAM L. RIKARD, JR., born Canton, North Carolina, 1945; admitted to bar, 1970, North Carolina. *Education:* Davidson College (B.A., 1967); Vanderbilt University (J.D., 1970). Recipient: Alumni Service Award, Davidson College; John W. Kuykendall Award for Community Service, Davidson College; James P. Hendrix Award, Davidson College. Listed in: Best Lawyers in America, Business Litigation, since 1993-1994. Chambers USA, Business Litigation, 2004 and 2005 edition; Recognized as one of the "Legal Elite" in litigation by Business North Carolina Magazine. Patrick Wilson Merit Scholar, Vanderbilt University School of Law. Vanderbilt Law School National Council, 2002-2005. Former Chairman and Vice Chair, Charlotte Mecklenburg Board of Education, 1988-1995. Author: "Damages in Commercial Cases," North Carolina Association of Defense Attorneys', Summer Meeting, June 13, 2003; "Fair Competition: Probing the Outer Limits," Current Issues for Business Lawyers and Corporate Counsel Seminar sponsored by the North Carolina Bar Foundation, February 20, 2004; "Legal and Practical Implications of Electronic Discovery," American Bar Association Section of Litigation Seminar, March 8, 2004; "All's Fair in Love & War? Hiring Competitors' Key Employees and Stealing Trade Secrets," American Bar Association Section of Litigation Conference, May 6, 2004. *Member:* Mecklenburg County, North Carolina and American (Member, Business Torts Committee) Bar Associations. [1st Lt., U.S. Army Adjutant General Corps, 1970-1972]. ***PRACTICE AREAS:*** Complex Civil Litigation; Antitrust and Trade Regulation; Business Torts; Trade Secrets. ***Email:*** williamrikard@parkerpoe.com

RICHARD K. SCHELL, born Greensboro, North Carolina, 1959; admitted to bar, 1985, North Carolina. *Education:* University of North Carolina at Chapel Hill (B.A., 1981; M.B.A., 1985; J.D., 1985). Phi Beta Kappa. ***PRACTICE AREAS:*** Mergers and Acquisitions; Joint Ventures; Corporate Finance. ***Email:*** richschell@parkerpoe.com

ROY L. SMART III, born Atlanta, Georgia, 1953; admitted to bar, 1980, New York; 1983, North Carolina. *Education:* Harvard University (B.A., magna cum laude, 1976); University of Virginia (J.D., 1979). Member, North Carolina Bar Association Business Law Section Council. Member, North Carolina Commission on Business Laws and the Economy. Listed in the Best Lawyers in America, Corporate, M&A, and Securities Law. ***PRACTICE AREAS:*** Mergers and Acquisitions; Corporate Finance; Commercial Law. ***Email:*** skipsmart@parkerpoe.com

FRED C. THOMPSON, JR., born Lincolnton, North Carolina, 1942; admitted to bar, 1974, North Carolina. *Education:* University of North Carolina at Chapel Hill (A.B., 1965; J.D., with honors, 1973). [Lt., USN, 1965-1971]. ***PRACTICE AREAS:*** Mergers and Acquisitions; Corporate Finance; International; Commercial Contracts. ***Email:*** fredthompson@parkerpoe.com

DONALD P. UBELL, born Rome, New York, 1945; admitted to bar, 1970, Michigan; 1984, Georgia; 1993, North Carolina. *Education:* University of North Carolina at Chapel Hill (A.B., 1967); University of Michigan (J.D., 1969). Phi Beta Kappa. Former Commissioner, Michigan Supreme Court. Former Judicial Fellow, U.S. Supreme Court. Listed in the Best Lawyers in America, Public Finance Law. *Member:* American Bar Association

(This Listing Continued)

(Member, Standing Committee on Continuing Legal Education); National Association of Bond Lawyers. ***PRACTICE AREAS:*** Capital Markets. ***Email:*** donubell@parkerpoe.com

S. ROGERS WARNER, JR., born Raleigh, North Carolina, 1964; admitted to bar, 1991, North Carolina. *Education:* University of North Carolina at Chapel Hill (B.A., 1987; J.D., 1991). *Member:* North Carolina Bar Association (Member, Sections on: Business Law; Health Law). ***PRACTICE AREAS:*** Health Care; Mergers and Acquisitions; Joint Ventures. ***Email:*** rogerswarner@parkerpoe.com

STEVEN D. WEBER, born Colorado Springs, Colorado, 1969; admitted to bar, 1993, North Carolina; 1999, South Carolina. *Education:* Spring Hill College (B.A., summa cum laude, 1990); McGeorge School of Law, University of the Pacific (J.D., with great distinction, 1993). Chairman: Mecklenburg County Environmental Protection Commission; Mecklenburg County Air Quality Commission. ***PRACTICE AREAS:*** Environmental; Administrative; Class Actions. ***Email:*** steveweber@parkerpoe.com

KEITH M. WEDDINGTON, born Charlotte, North Carolina, 1961; admitted to bar, 1987, North Carolina. *Education:* University of North Carolina at Chapel Hill (B.A., 1984; J.D., with honors, 1987). Phi Beta Kappa. Listed in America's Leading Lawyers for Business, Chambers USA. *Member:* North Carolina (Member, Sections on: Labor and Employment Law; Litigation) and American (Member, Sections on: Labor and Employment Law; Litigation) Bar Associations; Employment Law Alliance (North Carolina Representative). (Employment and Employee Benefits Practice Group Leader). ***PRACTICE AREAS:*** Employment Law; Employment Litigation; ERISA Litigation. ***Email:*** keithweddington@parkerpoe.com

EDWARD W. WELLMAN, JR., born New York, N.Y., 1945; admitted to bar, 1973, New York; 1977, Connecticut; 1997, North Carolina. *Education:* Yale University (B.A., 1967); University of Bordeaux, France (Fulbright Scholar); University of Virginia (J.D., 1972). ***PRACTICE AREAS:*** Mergers and Acquisitions; Securities; Corporate Finance. ***Email:*** wardwellman@parkerpoe.com

ERIC D. WELSH, born Torrance, California, 1962; admitted to bar, 1988, New York; 2000, North Carolina; U.S. District Court, Southern and Eastern Districts of New York; U.S. District Court, Western, Middle and Eastern Districts of North Carolina. *Education:* Duke University (A.B., cum laude, 1984; J.D., with honors, 1987). *Member:* North Carolina Bar Association (Antitrust and Trade Regulation Section); American Bar Association (Committee on Business Torts Litigation). ***PRACTICE AREAS:*** Trade Secrets; Unfair Competition; Fraud and Deceit; Commercial Litigation; Intellectual Property; Antitrust and Trade Regulation; Civil RICO. ***Email:*** ericwelsh@parkerpoe.com

A. GRANT WHITNEY, JR., born Charlotte, North Carolina, 1954; admitted to bar, 1979, North Carolina. *Education:* Davidson College; Wake Forest University (B.A., cum laude, 1976; J.D., 1979). ***PRACTICE AREAS:*** Real Estate; Commercial Development; Title Insurance Matters. ***Email:*** grantwhitney@parkerpoe.com

STACY K. WOOD, born Rochester, New York, 1966; admitted to bar, 1991, Pennsylvania; 1995, North Carolina and South Carolina. *Education:* University of North Carolina at Chapel Hill (B.S., with honors, 1988); University of Pennsylvania (J.D., cum laude, 1991). Phi Beta Kappa. *Member:* North Carolina and American (Member, Labor and Employment Law Section) Bar Associations; South Carolina Bar; Employment Law Alliance (North Carolina Representative). ***PRACTICE AREAS:*** Employment; Colleges and Universities; ERISA Litigation. ***Email:*** stacywood@parkerpoe.com

W. SAMUEL WOODARD, born Greensboro, North Carolina, 1944; admitted to bar, 1969, North Carolina. *Education:* University of North Carolina at Chapel Hill (B.S., with honors, 1966; J.D., 1969). Listed in the Best Lawyers in America, Real Estate Law. ***PRACTICE AREAS:*** Banking; Capital Markets; Real Estate. ***Email:*** samwoodard@parkerpoe.com

OF COUNSEL

MICHAEL A. ALMOND, born Pilot Mountain, North Carolina, January 24, 1949; admitted to bar, 1975, North Carolina. *Education:* University of North Carolina (B.A., with highest honors, 1971); University of North Carolina School of Law (J.D., with honors, 1975). Phi Beta Kappa; Order of the Coif. University of North Carolina Law Review. Morehead Scholar. Fulbright Fellow, University of Mannheim, Germany. Recipient, Knight's Cross of the Order of Merit of the Federal Republic of Germany. Member, American Arbitration Association National Roster of Neutrals (Commercial, including Large, Complex Commercial Disputes). ***LANGUAGES:*** German. ***PRACTICE AREAS:*** International Business; Economic Development. ***Email:*** malmond@parkerpoe.com

MARK R. BERNSTEIN, born York, Pennsylvania, 1930; admitted to bar, 1957, North Carolina. *Education:* University of Pennsylvania (A.B., magna cum laude, 1952); Yale University (LL.B., 1957). Past President, Mecklenburg County Bar. Fellow, American Bar Foundation. *Member:* American Bar Association. [1st Lt., Inf, U.S.Army,1952-1954]. ***PRACTICE AREAS:*** Mergers and Acquisitions; Commercial Contracts; Venture Capital. ***Email:*** markbernstein@parkerpoe.com

GASTON H. GAGE, born Charlotte, North Carolina, 1930; admitted to bar, 1958, North Carolina. *Education:* Duke University (B.A., 1953); University of North Carolina at Chapel Hill (LL.B., 1958). ***PRACTICE AREAS:*** Commercial Litigation. ***Email:*** gastongage@parkerpoe.com

FRANCIS I. PARKER, born Charlotte, North Carolina, 1923; admitted to bar, 1949, North Carolina. *Education:* University of North Carolina at Chapel Hill (A .B., 1945; LL.B., 1949). Former Chairman and Emeritus, North Carolina Board of Law Examiners. Former Associate Justice, Supreme Court of North Carolina. Past President, Mecklenburg County Bar Association. *Member:* American Law Institute. Fellow, American Bar Foundation. ***PRACTICE AREAS:*** Real Estate; Commercial Development. ***Email:*** francisparker@parkerpoe.com

JAMES Y. PRESTON, born Atlanta, Georgia, 1937; admitted to bar, 1961, North Carolina. *Education:* University of North Carolina at Chapel Hill (A.B., 1958; J.D., with high honors, 1961). Phi Beta Kappa. Past President, North Carolina State Bar. Member, American Law Institute. Fellow, American Bar Foundation. ***PRACTICE AREAS:*** Estate and Succession Planning; Estate Administration. ***Email:*** jimpreston@parkerpoe.com

(This Listing Continued)

MICHAEL W. TAYLOR, born Little Rock, Arkansas,1947; admitted to bar, 1978, North Carolina. *Education:* University of North Carolina at Chapel Hill (B.A., with honors 1969; J.D., 1978); Harvard University (M.A., 1972; Ph.D., 1975). Judicial Clerk: North Carolina Court of Appeals, 1978-1979; County Attorney, 1994-1998; Airport Attorney, 1996-2000. Area Mental Health Authority Attorney, 1983—. Parliamentarian, North Carolina Baptist State Convention, 1986-1990. Town Attorney: Town of New London, 2000—; Town of Stanfield, 2003—. [LT. JG, U.S. Navy Reserve, 1969-1971]. ***PRACTICE AREAS:*** Municipal Law; Health Care; Financial Law; Mental Health Law. ***Email:*** miketaylor@parkerpoe.com

SYDNOR THOMPSON, born Baltimore, Maryland, 1924; admitted to bar, 1952, New York; 1956, North Carolina. *Education:* St. Andrews University, Scotland; Syracuse University (B.A., cum laude, 1947); Harvard University (LL.B., cum laude, 1950); Manchester University; London University. Fulbright Scholar. Former Judge, N.C. Court of Appeals. Past President, Mecklenburg County Bar Association. Certified Mediator. Certified Arbitrator. Chair, Ethics and Professionalism Committee, Dispute Resolution Section Council, North Carolina Bar Association. ***PRACTICE AREAS:*** Commercial Litigation; Mediation; Arbitration. ***Email:*** sydnorthompson@parkerpoe.com

SPECIAL COUNSEL

DAVID W. BROWN JR., born Knoxville, Tennessee, May 16, 1966; admitted to bar, 1991, North Carolina. *Education:* University of North Carolina at Chapel Hill (A.B., with distinction, 1988); Vanderbilt University School of Law (J.D., 1991). Phi Beta Kappa. President, Vanderbilt Law School Honor Council. ***PRACTICE AREAS:*** Commercial Real Estate Development; Commercial Real Estate Leasing; Commercial Real Estate Lending. ***Email:*** davidbrown@parkerpoe.com

ROBERT P. BRYAN III, born Raleigh, North Carolina, June 4, 1971; admitted to bar, 1998, North Carolina. *Education:* University of North Carolina at Chapel Hill (B.A., with distinction, 1993); Duke University (J.D., with honors, 1998); Pontificia Universidad Catolica de Chile. Phi Eta Sigma; Golden Key. *Member:* Mecklenburg County and North Carolina Bar Associations; North Carolina State Bar. ***LANGUAGES:*** Spanish. ***PRACTICE AREAS:*** Commercial Real Estate; Corporate Law. ***Email:*** robbryan@parkerpoe.com

JAMES C. DAVIS, JR., born Lakenheath, U.K., April 13, 1970; admitted to bar, 1997, California; 1999, North Carolina. *Education:* Wake Forest University (B.A., magna cum laude, 1992); Duke University (J.D., 1997). Phi Beta Kappa. Staff Editor, Law and Contemporary Problems, Duke University, 1996-1997. ***PRACTICE AREAS:*** Capital Markets; Finance. ***Email:*** jamesdavis@parkerpoe.com

DEBORAH L. EDNEY, born Sussex, England, October 29, 1967; admitted to bar, 1997, North Carolina. *Education:* Louisiana Tech University (B.A., magna cum laude, 1991; B.S., magna cum laude, 1991); University of North Carolina at Chapel Hill (J.D., with honors, 1997). *Member:* Mecklenburg County, North Carolina and American (Member, Sections on: Antitrust; Litigation) Bar Associations; Inns of Court. ***PRACTICE AREAS:*** Business Torts; Antitrust. ***Email:*** debbieedney@parkerpoe.com

NANCY LYNNE OLAH, born Cleveland, Ohio, 1955; admitted to bar, 1979, Ohio; 1983, North Carolina; 1985, South Carolina. *Education:* Oberlin College (B.A., 1976); University of Michigan (J.D., cum laude, 1978). Member, CREW Network. President, CREW Charlotte, 2005.*Member:* Mecklenburg County, York County, North Carolina and American Bar Associations; North Carolina State Bar; South Carolina Bar. ***PRACTICE AREAS:*** Commercial Real Estate; Commercial Development; Leases and Leasing; Land Sales. ***Email:*** nancyolah@parkerpoe.com

REGINA WHEELER SWINEA, born Athens, Georgia, 1961; admitted to bar, 1986, North Carolina. *Education:* University of North Carolina at Chapel Hill (B.A., with honors, 1983; J.D., 1986). Law Clerk to the Hon. Harry W. Wellford, U.S. Court of Appeals, Sixth Circuit, 1987-1988. ***PRACTICE AREAS:*** Civil Litigation; Professional Malpractice. ***Email:*** reginaswinea@parkerpoe.com

SENIOR COUNSEL

ROSE MARIE WEBER, born St. Louis, Missouri, January 27; admitted to bar, 1994, Maryland; 2005, North Carolina. *Education:* Southern Illinois University (B.A., 1973); Johns Hopkins University Evening College (M.S., 1981); University of Baltimore School (J.D., cum laude, 1994; LL.M., in Taxation, 1995). Recipient, Office of Chief Counsel Hammer Award, 1999; Office of Chief Counsel Special Act Award, 1999, 2000, 2002 and 2003. Attorney-Advisor to: Honorable Howard A. Dawson, Jr., U.S. Tax Court, 1995-1997; Internal Revenue Service, Office of Chief Counsel, 1997-2004. *Member:* North Carolina State and American Bar Associations; National Association of Bond Laywers. ***PRACTICE AREAS:*** Taxation. ***Email:*** roseweber@parkerpoe.com

ASSOCIATES

JASON R. BENTON, born Charlotte, North Carolina, March 10, 1976; admitted to bar, 2001, North Carolina; 2004, U.S. District Court, Western District of North Carolina. *Education:* Wake Forest University (B.A., cum laude, 1998; J.D., 2001). Order of Barristers. Listed in Who's Who in American Law, 2005-2006. *Member:* Mecklenburg County, North Carolina (Member, Litigation Section) and American (Member, Torts, Trial and Insurance Section) Bar Associations; North Carolina State Bar; North Carolina Association of Defense Attorneys. ***PRACTICE AREAS:*** Litigation; Personal Injury Defense; Professional Liability; Premises Liability; Insurance Coverage. ***Email:*** jasonbenton@parkerpoe.com

KIMBERLY A. BETZ, born Gainesville, Florida, January 1, 1971; admitted to bar, 1999, North Carolina. *Education:* Wake Forest University (B.S., cum laude, 1993); University of North Carolina at Chapel Hill (J.D., with honors, 1999). Notes and Comments Editor, North Carolina Law Review, 1998-1999. *Member:* Mecklenburg County, North Carolina and American Bar Associations. ***PRACTICE AREAS:*** Mergers and Acquisitions; Commercial Law; Information Technology. ***Email:*** kimbetz@parkerpoe.com

(This Listing Continued)

PARKER, POE, ADAMS & BERNSTEIN L.L.P., Charlotte—Continued

WILLIAM B. CANNON, born New Bern, North Carolina, April 13, 1980; admitted to bar, 2005, North Carolina. *Education:* Davidson College (B.S., 2002); University of North Carolina at Chapel Hill (J.D., cum laude, 2005). ***PRACTICE AREAS:*** Torts; Insurance. ***Email:*** willcannon@parkerpoe.com

AMANDA HARMON COOLEY, born Flagstaff, Arizona, August 7, 1978; admitted to bar, 2003, North Carolina. *Education:* University of North Carolina at Chapel Hill (B.A., with highest honors, 2000); University of North Carolina (J.D., with honors, May 2003). ***PRACTICE AREAS:*** Antitrust; Business Torts. ***Email:*** amandacooley@parkerpoe.com

JONATHAN W. DION, born Biddeford, Maine, June 11, 1973; admitted to bar, 1999, North Carolina. *Education:* University of New Hampshire (B.A., magna cum laude, 1995) Wake Forest University (J.D., cum laude, 1999). Phi Beta Kappa. Order of the Coif. Member, Wake Forest Law Review. Member, International Council of Shopping Centers. ***PRACTICE AREAS:*** Real Estate; Commercial Real Estate Development. ***Email:*** jonathandion@parkerpoe.com

ALLISON B. EDGAR, born November 17, 1976; admitted to bar, 2001, Virginia; 2002, District of Columbia; 2005, North Carolina. *Education:* University of Virginia (B.A., 1998; J.D., 2001). ***PRACTICE AREAS:*** Environmental; Litigation. ***Email:*** allisonedgar@parkerpoe.com

WILLIAM L. ESSER, IV, born Lake Worth, Florida; admitted to bar, 1999, Florida and U.S. Court of Appeals, Tenth Circuit; 2000, North Carolina, U.S. District Court, Western, Middle and Eastern Districts of North Carolina and U.S. Court of Appeals, Fourth and Eleventh Circuits. *Education:* Belmont Abbey College (B.A., summa cum laude, 1995); University of Notre Dame (J.D., magna cum laude, 1999). *Member:* Mecklenburg County and North Carolina Bar Associations; The Florida Bar; American Bankruptcy Institute. ***PRACTICE AREAS:*** Bankruptcy; Commercial Litigation; Real Estate Foreclosure; Franchise Litigation; Receiverships; Litigation. ***Email:*** willesser@parkerpoe.com

JAMI JACKSON FARRIS, born Raleigh, North Carolina, September 17, 1971; admitted to bar, 1999, North Carolina, U.S. District Court, Western District of North Carolina and U.S. Court of Federal Claims; 2001, U.S. District Court, Middle District of North Carolina and U.S. Court of Appeals, Seventh Circuit; 2002, U.S. District Court, Eastern District of North Carolina. *Education:* College of William & Mary (B.A., 1993); University of North Carolina at Chapel Hill (J.D., with honors, 1999). Member, James E. and Carolyn B. Davis Society, 1999. Articles Editor, North Carolina Journal of International Law and Commercial Regulation, 1998-1999. Author, "The Legality of Assassination of Independent Terrorist Leaders: An Examination of National and International Implications," N.C. J. Int'l L. & Com. Reg. (1999). *Member:* Mecklenburg County, North Carolina and American (Member: Litigation Section; Young Lawyers Division) Bar Associations; North Carolina State Bar. ***PRACTICE AREAS:*** Litigation; Commercial Law. ***Email:*** jamifarris@parkerpoe.com

CHRISTOPHER J. FERNANDEZ, born Tampa, Florida, December 11, 1968; admitted to bar, 2001, North Carolina. *Education:* University of Texas at Austin (B.S., 1990); Washington & Lee University (J.D., cum laude, 2001). Executive Editor, Washington & Lee Law Review. Author: Washington & Lee Law Review, Vol. 58-2. [Lieutenant, U.S. Navy, 1990-1994]. ***PRACTICE AREAS:*** Bankruptcy Reorganization; Creditors Rights. ***Email:*** chrisfernandez@parkerpoe.com

CARRIE S. FISHER, born Palm Beach, Florida, September 27, 1975; admitted to bar, 2001, North Carolina. *Education:* Birmingham Southern College (B.A., 1998); Wake Forest University (J.D., 2001). *Member:* North Carolina State Bar. ***PRACTICE AREAS:*** Business Law; Commercial Law; Corporate Law. ***Email:*** carriefisher@parkerpoe.com

W. LEWIS GLENN, III, born Monterey, California, January 10, 1968; admitted to bar, 1998, North Carolina and U.S. District Court, Western District of North Carolina; 2004, U.S. District Court, Middle District of North Carolina. *Education:* United States Naval Academy (B.S., 1990) College of William & Mary (J.D., 1998). Order of the Coif. Co-Author: "Trigger of Coverage for Latent Damages Claims: The Last Vestiges of the Manifestation Theory," Journal of Insurance Coverage, Vol. 3, No.3, 2000. *Member:* Mecklenburg County, North Carolina and American (Member, Sections on: Tort, Trial and Insurance Practice; Litigation) Bar Associations. [Lieutenant, U.S. Navy, 1990-1995]. ***PRACTICE AREAS:*** Litigation; Real Estate Litigation; Professional Liability; Tort Defense; Toxic Tort Defense; Products Liability Defense; Insurance Coverage. ***Email:*** lewglenn@parkerpoe.com

KEVIN B. GOTTEHRER, born Lincoln, Massachusetts, March 3, 1975; admitted to bar, 2001, North Carolina. *Education:* Brown University (B.A., 1998); Boston University (J.D., 2001). *Member:* North Carolina State Bar. ***PRACTICE AREAS:*** Mergers and Acquisitions. ***Email:*** kevingottehrer@parkerpoe.com

KENNETH R. HARRIS, JR., born Charlotte, North Carolina, January 20, 1972; admitted to bar, 2002, North Carolina; 2003, U.S. District Court, Middle District of North Carolina. *Education:* Duke University (B.A., 1994; J.D., cum laude, 2002). *Member:* Mecklenburg County, North Carolina (Member: Litigation Section; Law School Liaison Committee; Young Lawyers Executive Committee) and American (Member, Litigation Section) Bar Associations. ***PRACTICE AREAS:*** Commercial Contracts (95%). ***Email:*** kenharris@parkerpoe.com

MARY ELIZABETH HOLSENBECK, born Winston-Salem, North Carolina, January 23, 1980; admitted to bar, 2005, North Carolina. *Education:* University of North Carolina at Chapel Hill (B.A., 2002; J.D., 2005). Phi Beta Kappa. ***PRACTICE AREAS:*** Employment Law. ***Email:*** maryholsenbeck@parkerpoe.com

P. MICHAEL JUBY, born Raleigh, North Carolina, November 6, 1978; admitted to bar, 2005, North Carolina. *Education:* North Carolina State University (B.S., 2000); University of North Carolina at Chapel Hill (J.D., 2005). Park Scholar. Author: "Tax Increment Financing in North Carolina: The Myth of the Countermajoritarian Difficulty," 83 N.C. L. Rev. 1526 (2005). ***PRACTICE AREAS:*** Public Finance; Banking Law. ***Email:*** michaeljuby@parkerpoe.com

(This Listing Continued)

LORI R. KEETON, born Jackson, Mississippi, June 22, 1973; admitted to bar, 1998, North Carolina. *Education:* Stetson University (B.A., summa cum laude, 1995); University of Florida (J.D., with honors, 1998). Phi Beta Kappa; Order of the Coif. Recipient, Book Awards in: Media Law; Sales; Women in the Law. Notes and Comments Senior Editor, Florida Law Review, 1995. Author, Note, "What is Really Rotten in the Food Lion Case: Chilling the Media's Unethical Newsgathering Techniques," 49 Florida Law Review 111, Spring 1998. *Member:* North Carolina Bar Association (Member, Litigation Section); North Carolina Assocation of Defense Attorneys; Carolina Assocation of Defense Attorneys. ***PRACTICE AREAS:*** Property Damage; Personal Injury; Torts; Professional Malpractice; Insurance Coverage. ***Email:*** lorikeeton@parkerpoe.com

LEIGH A. KITE, born Asheboro, North Carolina, October 2, 1979; admitted to bar, 2005, North Carolina. *Education:* University of North Carolina at Chapel Hill (B.A., with honors, 2002); Washington & Lee University (J.D., 2005). Omicron Delta Kappa; Phi Delta Phi. Managing Editor, Washington & Lee Law Review. Author, "Red Flagging Civil Liberties & Due Process Rights of Airline Passengers: Will a Revised CAPPS II System Meet the Constitutional Challenge?" 61 Washington & Lee Law Review 1385, 2004. ***PRACTICE AREAS:*** Litigation; Medical Malpractice; Torts; Insurance Defense. ***Email:*** leighkite@parkerpoe.com

ASHLEY M. LONG, born Columbia, South Carolina, April 23, 1980; admitted to bar, 2005, North Carolina. *Education:* Clemson University (B.S., summa cum laude, 2002); Wake Forest University (J.D., cum laude, 2005). Order of the Coif. Member, Wake Forest Law Review, 2003-2005. ***PRACTICE AREAS:*** Commercial Litigation. ***Email:*** ashleylong@parkerpoe.com

GARY T. McDERMOTT, born Watertown, New York, August 21, 1975; admitted to bar, 2005, North Carolina. *Education:* State University of New York at Oswego (B.A., magna cum laude, 1998); University of Georgia (J.D., magna cum laude, 2005). Phi Kappa Phi; Pi Sigma Alpha; Omicron Delta Kappa; Order of the Coif. Recipient, Paideia Award. Member, University of Georgia Journal of Intellectual Property. ***PRACTICE AREAS:*** Commercial Real Estate Development; Real Estate. ***Email:*** garymcdermott@parkerpoe.com

KRISTIN R. POOLOS, born Mountain View, California; admitted to bar, 2003, North Carolina. *Education:* Duke University (B.A., cum laude, 2000); Harvard Law School (J.D., 2003). *Member:* Mecklenburg County and American Bar Associations; North Carolina State Bar. ***PRACTICE AREAS:*** Antitrust and Trade Regulation. ***Email:*** kristinpoolos@parkerpoe.com

THOMAS M. QUIRK, born Fairfax, Virginia, October 4, 1970; admitted to bar, 1998, North Carolina. *Education:* University of Virginia (B.A., 1992); Wake Forest University (J.D., 1998). Notes and Comments Editor, Wake Forest Law Review. ***PRACTICE AREAS:*** Real Estate; Commercial Real Estate Development. ***Email:*** tomquirk@parkerpoe.com

RICHARD J. RIVERA, born Goldsboro, North Carolina, 1972; admitted to bar, 1997, North Carolina. *Education:* Davidson College (B.A., cum laude, 1994); Wake Forest University (J.D., 1997). *Member:* Mecklenburg County, North Carolina and American (Member, Litigation Section) Bar Associations; North Carolina Association of Defense Attorneys. [Captain, U.S. Army, Judge Advocate General's Corps, 1997-2002]. ***PRACTICE AREAS:*** Medical Malpractice; Tort Defense. ***Email:*** richardrivera@parkerpoe.com

ADAM C. SHEARER, born Binghamton, New York, May 20, 1975; admitted to bar, 2002, North Carolina and U.S. District Court, Western District of North Carolina; 2005, U.S. District Court, Middle District of North Carolina. *Education:* North Carolina State University (B.A., cum laude, 1997); Wake Forest University (J.D., 2002). *Member:* Mecklenburg County, North Carolina and American Bar Associations; North Carolina State Bar; Defense Research Institute; North Carolina Association of Defense Attorneys. ***PRACTICE AREAS:*** Litigation; Medical Malpractice; Torts; Insurance Defense. ***Email:*** adamshearer@parkerpoe.com

SHANNON N. STOKES, born Mankato, Minnesota, December 1, 1977; admitted to bar, 2004, North Carolina. *Education:* Texas Tech University (B.A., magna cum laude, 2000); University of Minnesota (J.D., cum laude, 2003). *Member:* North Carolina State Bar; American Bar Association. ***PRACTICE AREAS:*** Commercial Contracts; International Law; Business Acquisitions; Mergers and Acquisitions. ***Email:*** shannonstokes@parkerpoe.com

BENJAMIN R. SULLIVAN, JR., born Seneca, South Carolina, March 15, 1977; admitted to bar, 2002, South Carolina; 2005, North Carolina. *Education:* University of Richmond (B.S., summa cum laude, 1999) Harvard University (J.D., cum laude, 2002). Phi Beta Kappa. *Member:* North Carolina and American Bar Associations. ***PRACTICE AREAS:*** Municipal Law; Litigation; Local Government Law. ***Email:*** bobbysullivan@parkerpoe.com

F. SCOTT THOMAS, born Richmond, Virginia, October 24, 1971; admitted to bar, 1999, North Carolina and U.S. District Court, Middle District of North Carolina. *Education:* Woodberry Forest School; University of North Carolina at Chapel Hill (B.A., Anthropology, 1995); Cumberland School of Law at Samford University (J.D., 1999). Co-Author: "A Refresher Course on Letters of Intent, Other Deal Papers," Triangle Business Journal, June 27, 2003; "Federal Regulation of Biotechnology: The Continuing Balance," 44 Jurimetrics, The Journal of Law, Science & Technology 283, Arizona State University College of Law/ABA, Spring 2004. *Member:* North Carolina (Member, Business Law Section) and American (Member, Business Law Section) Bar Associations. ***PRACTICE AREAS:*** Securities; Corporate Law; Finance; Investment Management; Investment Regulation; Biotechnology. ***Email:*** scottthomas@parkerpoe.com

KENDRA W. THORNTON, born Anderson, South Carolina, 1977; admitted to bar, 2004, North Carolina. *Education:* Clemson University (B.A., 1999; M.H.R.D., 2000); University of South Carolina (J.D., 2003). *Member:* North Carolina (Member, Labor and Employment Law Section) and American (Member, Labor and Employment Law Section) Bar Associations. ***PRACTICE AREAS:*** Employment Law. ***Email:*** kendrathornton@parkerpoe.com

KRISTI K. WALTERS, born Houston, Texas; admitted to bar, 1999, North Carolina and U.S. District Court, Western District of North Carolina; 2001, U.S. District Court, Eastern and Middle Districts of North Carolina and U.S. Court of Appeals, 4th Circuit. *Education-*

(This Listing Continued)

tion: Davidson College (B.A., cum laude, 1991); University of North Carolina at Chapel Hill (J.D., with honors, 1999). *Member:* North Carolina and American Bar Associations; National Association of College and University Attorneys; Employment Law Alliance (North Carolina Representative). ***PRACTICE AREAS:*** Labor and Employment; Education Law. ***Email:*** kristiwalters@parkerpoe.com

AMY L. WALTON, born 1974; admitted to bar, 2001, Rhode Island; 2003, North Carolina. *Education:* Brown University (B.A., with honors, 1997) Washington and Lee University School of Law (J.D., 2001). ***PRACTICE AREAS:*** Real Estate. ***Email:*** amywalton@parkerpoe.com

JASON P. WALTON, born Mobile, Alabama, April 1, 1975; admitted to bar, 2001, Rhode Island; 2002, Masschusetts and North Carolina. *Education:* Spring Hill College (B.A., summa cum laude, 1997; M.B.A., summa cum laude, 1998); Washington & Lee University (J.D., cum laude, 2001); New York University (LL.M., 2002). *Member:* North Carolina (Member, Tax Section), Massachusetts, Rhode Island and American (Member, Tax Section) Bar Associations. ***PRACTICE AREAS:*** Taxation; Business Law; Partnership Law. ***Email:*** jasonwalton@parkerpoe.com

L. KENT WORKMAN, born Okinawa, Japan, May 21, 1969; admitted to bar, 2000, New York; 2001, District of Columbia; 2005, North Carolina. *Education:* The Citadel (B.S.E.E., 1991); University of Virginia School of Law (J.D., 1999). [U.S. Naval Officer, 1991-1996]. ***PRACTICE AREAS:*** Mergers and Acquisitions; Venture Capital; Corporate Finance. ***Email:*** kentworkman@parkerpoe.com

REPRESENTATIVE CLIENTS: Accor Hotels; Association for Home and Hospice Care of North Carolina; Atlantic Partners, LLC; Attorneys Liability Protection Society; Asahi Glass America; Ashtead Group plc; Aston Properties; AVX; Bank of America, N.A.; Barnhardt Manufacturing Co.; Bauer International Inc.; Blackbaud, Inc.; Board of Governors of the University of North Carolina; Bombardier Capital Inc.; BP, Inc.; Burroughs & Chapin Company, Inc.; Brunswick County; Cardinal Health, Inc.; Carolina Federal Savings Bank; Charlotte Mecklenburg Hospital Authority; Childress Klein Properties; City of Charlotte; City of Durham; City of Winston-Salem; Coen Capital, Inc.; Collins & Aikman; Conseco, Inc.; Consulting Engineers Council; Crescent Resources; DAK Americas; Domnick Hunter; Duke Energy; DukeNet Communication; DyStar LP; Family Dollar Stores; First State Management; Fluor Corporation; Freightliner Corporation; Freudenberg Group; Gaston Memorial Hospital; Genpharm; Gibbs International; Golf Trust of America, L.P.; Great Harvest Franchising; Hilton Hotels Corporation; Horace Mann Insurance; Hospitality Management Group, Inc.; Invista S.a.r.l., John Wieland Homes; Johnson C. Smith University; Kiawah Resort Associates, L.P.; Klerk's Plastic Products Manufacturing, Inc.; Laboratory Corporation of America Holdings; Legg Mason; Lowe's Motor Speedway; MAG Mutual Insurance; Media General, Inc.; Merit Group; National Spinning Co.; National Welders Supply Co.; Nextel Communications; NGK Ceramics USA; NICCA, USA; North Carolina Biotechnology Center; North Carolina State University; N. Schlumberger USA; Nucor Corporation; Osram Sylvania; Otto Industries; Pergo; Progress Energy; Rack Room Shoes; Reeves Brothers; Robinson-Humphrey; Roper St. Francis HealthCare; Self Regional HealthCare; SGL Carbon Group; Sonic Automotive; South Carolina Federal Credit Union; Speedway Motorsports; St. Paul Travelers; Suburban Propane; Sunbelt Rentals, Inc. ; Sun Microsystems; Tanner Companies; The Crosland Group; Trammell Crow Companies; Triangle Transit Authority; U-Haul International, Inc.; University Medical Associates; University of North Carolina; Union County North Carolina; Wachovia; Wood Partners.

(For biographical data on other personnel, see Professional Biographies at Raleigh, North Carolina, Charleston, South Carolina, Columbia, South Carolina and Spartanburg, South Carolina)

PARKS, CHESIN & WALBERT, P.C.

521 EAST MOREHEAD STREET, SUITE 120
CHARLOTTE, NORTH CAROLINA 28202
Telephone: 704-377-2770
Facsimile: 704-377-2703
Email: firm@pcwlawfirm.com
URL: http://www.pcwlawfirm.com

Atlanta, Georgia Office: 26th Floor, 75 Fourteenth Street. 30309. Telephone: 404-873-8000. Facsimile: 404-873-8050.

General Civil, Trial and Appellate Practice in all State and Federal Courts and Administrative Agencies. Antitrust, Arbitration, Bankruptcy, Commercial, Constitutional, Construction, Corporate, Employment Discrimination, Environmental, Family, Health Care, Labor, Professional Liability, Insurance, Intellectual Properties, Libel and Slander, Malpractice, Negligence, Personal Injury, Probate, Products Liability and Voting Rights.

KEVIN V. PARSONS, born Ontario, California, December 18, 1964; admitted to bar, 1992, North Carolina and U.S. District Court, Western District of North Carolina; 1995, U.S. Court of Appeals, Fourth Circuit; 1998, U.S. District Court, Middle and Eastern Districts of North Carolina; 2002, Georgia. *Education:* University of Nebraska (B.A., 1987); University of Notre Dame Law School (J.D., 1992). Editor in Chief, Journal of Legislation, 1992. Law Clerk to Hon. Robert D. Potter, U.S. District Court Judge, Western District of North Carolina, 1992-1994. Member, Fourth Circuit Judicial Conference. *Member:* North Carolina State Bar; North Carolina Bar Association; National Lawyers Association; Federalist Society. (Resident). ***PRACTICE AREAS:*** Litigation; Labor and Employment; Constitutional Law.

ASSOCIATE

JANET J. HIGLEY, born Atlanta, Georgia, September 21, 1972; admitted to bar, 2001, North Carolina. *Education:* University of Virginia (B.A., with distinction, 1996; M.T., 1996); Wake Forest University (J.D., cum laude, 2001). Order of the Coif. Executive Member, Wake Forest Moot Court Board. Member, Wake Forest Law Review. ***PRACTICE AREAS:*** Labor and Employment; Litigation; Constitutional Law. ***Email:*** jhigley@pcwlawfirm.com

REPRESENTATIVE CLIENT: Northeast Medical Center; Dai Nippon; IMS America Corp.; Morton Custom Plastics; United Mortgage and Loan Investment, Corp.; Southeast Anesthesiology Consultants, PA; United Construction; H.B. Rowe & Co.; Nations Fence, Inc.
REFERENCE: SunTrust Bank.

(For complete Biographical Data on all Personnel, see Professional Biographies at Atlanta, Georgia)

PAUL L. PAWLOWSKI

Established in 1972

1001 ELIZABETH AVENUE, SUITE 2-A
CHARLOTTE, NORTH CAROLINA 28204
Telephone: 704-333-0312
Fax: 704-333-0313
Email: pawlowskilaw@yahoo.com
URL: http://www.paulpawlowskilaw.com

Family Law, Child Custody, Child Support, Divorce, Equitable Distribution, Domestic Violence, Collaborative Law, Criminal Law, Traffic Violations, Driving While Impaired, Personal Injury, Automobile Accidents and Injuries, Wrongful Death.

FIRM PROFILE: Paul L. Pawlowski has practiced law in the greater Charlotte area since 1972, having a trial practice mainly in Mecklenberg County courts in the areas of family law, criminal law and civil litigation (including personal injury).

PAUL L. PAWLOWSKI, born Milwaukee, Wisconsin, 1944; admitted to bar, 1972, North Carolina. *Education:* University of Wisconsin-Milwaukee (B.S., 1966); University of North Carolina (J.D., 1972). *Member:* Mecklenburg County Bar Association (Member, Family Law Section); North Carolina State Bar; Mecklenburg County Criminal Defense Association. [Lt., U.S. Army, 1966-1969 (Vietnam Veteran, 1968-1969)]. ***PRACTICE AREAS:*** Family Law; Child Custody; Support; Divorce; Equitable Distribution; Domestic Violence; Collaborative Law; Criminal Law; Traffic Violations; Driving While Intoxicated; Personal Injury; Automobile Accidents and Injuries; Wrongful Death.

RICHARD A. PENISTON & ASSOCIATES, P.A.

1901 CENTRAL AVENUE
CHARLOTTE, NORTH CAROLINA 28205
Telephone: 704-373-0203; 800-279-2889
Facsimile: 704-373-2858
URL: http://www.lawyers.com/rpenistonlaw

Raleigh, North Carolina Office: 811 W. Morgan Street, 27603. Telephone: 919-834-2889. Facsimile: 919-834-1533.

Monroe, North Carolina Office: 211 Lancaster Avenue, 28112. Telephone: 704-225-8700. Facsimile: 704-238-0317.

Personal Injury, Automobile Accidents, Workers Compensation, Wrongful Death, Medical Malpractice, Social Security Disability, Criminal Law, Traffic, DWI, Wills and Estates, Business Law, General Practice.

FIRM PROFILE: The firm offers general legal services with particular emphasis on personal injury, wrongful death, and workers compensation as well as business entities and litigation, criminal, traffic and DWI, and wills and estates. The firm welcomes telephone or internet inquiries concerning new matters.

RICHARD A. PENISTON, born New Brunswick, New Jersey, December 11, 1949; admitted to bar, 1977, North Carolina and U.S. District Court, Western District of North Carolina. *Education:* University of North Carolina at Charlotte (B.A., 1974) University of North Carolina at Chapel Hill (J.D., 1977). *Member:* Mecklenburg County Bar Association; North Carolina State Bar. ***PRACTICE AREAS:*** Personal Injury Law; Workers Compensation; Business Law; Wills; Trust Law; General Practice. ***Email:*** penistonr@raplaw.com

DAVID A. MANZI, born Patuxent River, Maryland, May 6, 1950; admitted to bar, 1990, California; 1996, North Carolina. *Education:* Quinnipiac College (B.S., 1972); University of New Haven (M.S., 1978); University of San Diego (J.D., 1990). *Member:* Mecklenburg County and American Bar Associations; North Carolina State Bar; The Association of Trial Lawyers of America. ***PRACTICE AREAS:*** Medical Malpractice; Personal Injury. ***Email:*** manzid@raplaw.com

ADAM M. SEIFER, born Chicago, Illinois, October 29, 1974; admitted to bar, 2000, North Carolina and U.S. District Court, Western District of North Carolina. *Education:* Tufts University (B.A., magna cum laude, 1996); University of Illinois (M.B.A., 2000; J.D., cum laude, 2000). *Member:* Mecklenburg County Bar Association; North Carolina State Bar. ***LANGUAGES:*** French and Spanish. ***PRACTICE AREAS:*** Criminal Law; Personal Injury; Workers Compensation. ***Email:*** seifera@raplaw.com

W. FRANK PORTER P.A.

8625 CROWN CRESCENT COURT, SUITE 110
CHARLOTTE, NORTH CAROLINA 28227
Telephone: 704-708-5176
Fax: 704-845-9629
Email: frankporter@wfrankporter.com
URL: http://www.frankporterlaw.com

Commercial Law, Commercial Litigation, Creditors Rights.

W. FRANK PORTER, born Wilkes County, North Carolina, June 29, 1962; admitted to bar, 1990, North Carolina and South Carolina; U.S. District Court, Western and Middle Districts of North Carolina. *Education:* Mars Hill College, Wake Forest University (B.A., 1984); Campbell University (J.D., 1989). *Member:* Mecklenburg County and North Carolina Bar Associations; North Carolina State Bar; South Carolina Bar; North Carolina Academy of Trial Lawyers; Commercial Law League of America. ***PRACTICE AREAS:*** Commercial Law; Commercial Litigation; Creditors Rights.

(This Listing Continued)

W. FRANK PORTER P.A., Charlotte—Continued

BENJAMIN D. SCHWARTZ, born Livingston, New Jersey, 1973; admitted to bar, 1999, New Jersey; 2001, North Carolina; 2005, Georgia. *Education:* Rutgers University (B.S., 1996); Wake Forest University (J.D., 1999). *Mecklenburg County and North Carolina Bar Associations; State Bar of Georgia.* **PRACTICE AREAS:** Commercial Law; Commercial Litigation; Creditors Rights; Insurance Defense Litigation. **Email:** bschwartz@frankporter.com

ANDREW N. BERNARDINI, born Syracuse, New York, November 14, 1974; admitted to bar, 2000, North Carolina. *Education:* State University of New York at Plattsburgh (B.A., 1996); Albany Law School of Union University (J.D., 2000). *Member:* Mecklenburg and North Carolina Bar Associations. **PRACTICE AREAS:** Commercial Law; Commercial Litigation; Creditors Rights; Insurance Defense Litigation. **Email:** abernardini@wfrankporter.com

BRIAN S. RUDOLPH, born Covington, Kentucky, 1971; admitted to bar, 1999, North Carolina. *Education:* Northern Kentucky University (B.A., cum laude, 1994); Salmon P. Chase College of Law (J.D., 1999). *Member:* Mecklenburg and North Carolina Bar Associations. **PRACTICE AREAS:** Commercial Law; Commercial Litigation; Creditors Rights; Insurance Defense Litigation. **Email:** brudolph@wfrankporter.com

ROBERT D. POTTER, JR.

Established in 1994

5821 FAIRVIEW ROAD, SUITE 207
CHARLOTTE, NORTH CAROLINA 28209
Telephone: 704-552-7742
Fax: 704-552-9287
URL: http://www.lawyers.com/robertdpotter

Aviation Law, General Practice, Commercial Litigation, Construction Law, Contracts, Qui Tam Litigation.

FIRM PROFILE: The firm offers general legal services with particular emphasis on aviation law, civil litigation involving construction disputes, aviation and qui tam/whistleblower litigation. The firm does not accept new clients based solely on Internet contact.

ROBERT D. POTTER, JR., born Charlotte, North Carolina, 1957; admitted to bar, 1990, North Carolina and U.S. District Court, Western District of North Carolina; 1991, U.S. Court of Appeals, 4th Circuit; 1993, U.S. District Court, Eastern District of North Carolina; 1994, U.S. District Court, Middle District of North Carolina and U.S. Supreme Court. *Education:* U.S. Naval Academy (B.S., 1979); L'Université de Aix-Marseille III, Aix-en-Provence, France, Diplôme de Langue, Litterature et Civilisation, Niveau Deux, Mention Bien 1987; Wake Forest University (J.D., cum laude, 1990). Member, Wake Forest University Law Review. Author: Note: The Regulation of Telephone Pornography, 24 Wake Forest L.R. 433 (1989). Assistant U.S. Attorney, Eastern District of North Carolina, 1990-1994. Member, Fourth Circuit Judicial Conference. *Member:* Mecklenburg County Bar Association; North Carolina State Bar. [U.S. Navy, Lieutenant (Naval Aviator), 1975-1986]. **LANGUAGES:** French. **REPORTED CASES:** Hyde v. Anderson, 580 S.E.2d 424 (N.C. App. 2003); Sherwin-Williams Co. v. ASBN, Inc., 594 S.E.2d 135 (N.C. App. 2004). **PRACTICE AREAS:** General Practice; Commercial Litigation; Aviation Law; Construction Law; Contracts; Qui Tam Litigation.

LEGAL SUPPORT PERSONNEL

SALLY MORRIS, born Lancaster, Pennsylvania, 1966. *Education:* Central Pennsylvania Business School (A.B., 1986). Former President, Shenandoah Valley Paralegal Association. (Paralegal)

Language: French.

REPRESENTATIVE CLIENTS: The SMTC Manufacturing Corporation; Republic Electric Co., Inc.

POYNER & SPRUILL LLP

ONE WACHOVIA CENTER
301 SOUTH COLLEGE STREET
SUITE 2300
CHARLOTTE, NORTH CAROLINA 28202
Telephone: 704-342-5250
Telecopier: 704-342-5264
URL: http://www.poynerspruill.com

Raleigh, North Carolina Office: 3600 Glenwood Avenue, P.O. Box 10096, 27605-0096. Telephone: 919-783-6400. Telecopier: 919-783-1075.

Rocky Mount, North Carolina Office: 130 S. Franklin Street, P.O. Box 353, 27802-0353. Telephone: 252-446-2341. Telecopier: 252-972-7045.

Southern Pines, North Carolina Office: 135 West New Hampshire Avenue, 28388-0371. Telephone: 910-692-6866. Telecopier: 910-695-3036.

Comprehensive business and litigation practice including: Appellate, Arbitration, Banking, Bankruptcy/Creditors' Rights, Complex Business Litigation, Construction, Credit and Financial Services, Eminent Domain/Condemnation, Employment Benefits, Employment Practices, Entertainment Law, Environmental, Estate, Exempt Organizations, General Corporate, Governmental Relations, Health Care, Intellectual Property Law, International, Land Use and Zoning, Limited Liability Companies, Local Government, Mediation, Partnerships, Personal and Financial Planning, Probate, Product Liability, Professional Liability, Railroad, Real Estate, Regulatory and Municipal, Securities, Sports Law, Tax, Technology and Emerging Business, Tort Litigation and Insurance Defense, Transactional including Mergers and Acquisitions, Transportation, Utilities, White Collar Criminal Defense.

(This Listing Continued)

MEMBERS

C. MARCUS HARRIS, born Orange, New Jersey, July 5, 1943; admitted to bar, 1972, North Carolina. *Education:* Duke University (A.B., 1965; J.D., with honors, 1972); University of Arizona (M.A., Economics, 1966). **PRACTICE AREAS:** Employee Benefits Law; Corporate Law; Health Care Law. **Email:** cmharris@poynerspruill.com

LEE A. SPINKS, born Asheboro, North Carolina, December 30, 1955; admitted to bar, 1980, North Carolina. *Education:* Furman University (B.A., cum laude, 1977); University of North Carolina (J.D., 1980). **PRACTICE AREAS:** Health Care (35%); Business Law (35%); Business Litigation (30%). **Email:** lspinks@poynerspruill.com

DOUGLAS M. MARTIN, born Asheville, North Carolina, September 20, 1948; admitted to bar, 1974, North Carolina. *Education:* Emory University (B.A., 1970); University of North Carolina (J.D., 1974). **PRACTICE AREAS:** Litigation. **Email:** dmartin@poynerspruill.com

TIMOTHY W. GRIFFIN, born Raleigh, North Carolina, June 23, 1954; admitted to bar, 1980, North Carolina. *Education:* University of North Carolina-Chapel Hill (B.A., 1976; J.D., 1980). **PRACTICE AREAS:** Finance; Creditors Rights; Workouts; Real Estate. **Email:** twgriffin@poynerspruill.com

JUDY D. THOMPSON, born St. Augustine, Florida, March 26, 1947; admitted to bar, 1985, Texas; 1988, North Carolina. *Education:* University of Florida (B.A., 1969); Florida State University (M.S., cum laude, 1973); University of Houston Law Center (J.D., cum laude, 1985). **PRACTICE AREAS:** Bankruptcy and Creditors; Workouts; Commercial Litigation. **Email:** jdthompson@poynerspruill.com

TERRY RICHARD KANE, born Brookings, South Dakota, March 11, 1947; admitted to bar, 1980, Tennessee; 1990, North Carolina; 1992, U.S. Supreme Court. *Education:* Duke University (A.B., 1970; LL.M., 1986); Boston University (M.A., 1978); Vanderbilt University (J.D., 1980). Certified Mediator, North Carolina, 1997. [U.S. Marine Corps, 1970-1990, Lt. Colonel]. **PRACTICE AREAS:** Environmental Law and Litigation; Professional Liability; Civil Litigation. **Email:** trkane@poynerspruill.com

E. FITZGERALD PARNELL, III, born Asheville, North Carolina, May 30, 1947; admitted to bar, 1973, North Carolina; 1981, U.S. Supreme Court. *Education:* North Carolina State University (B.S. in Engineering, 1969); University of North Carolina (J.D., 1973). President, The North Carolina State Bar, 2001-2002. **PRACTICE AREAS:** Professional Malpractice Defense; White Collar Criminal Defense; Civil Litigation; Federal Appellate Practice. **Email:** parnell@poynerspruill.com

NANCY C. BROWER, born Lake Charles, Louisiana, December 23, 1962; admitted to bar, 1989, North Carolina. *Education:* Louisiana Tech University (B.S., magna cum laude, 1983); University of North Carolina (J.D., 1989). **PRACTICE AREAS:** Employee Benefits. **Email:** ncbrower@poynerspruill.com

P. MARSHALL YODER, born Newton, Kansas, April 24, 1958; admitted to bar, 1987, North Carolina. *Education:* University of North Carolina (B.A., 1980); Campbell University (J.D., cum laude, 1987). **PRACTICE AREAS:** Construction Law; Business Litigation; Insurance Fraud Litigation; Zoning, Planning and Land Use. **Email:** pmyoder@poynerspruill.com

THOMAS D. EATMAN, JR., born Wilson, North Carolina, September 10, 1958; admitted to bar, 1983, North Carolina. *Education:* University of North Carolina at Chapel Hill (B.A., 1980; J.D., 1983). **PRACTICE AREAS:** Banking Law; Commercial Real Estate Law. **Email:** tdeatman@poynerspruill.com

CYNTHIA L. VAN HORNE, born Evanston. Illinois, May 6, 1959; admitted to bar, 1991, North Carolina. *Education:* University of Montana; University of North Carolina-Charlotte (B.A., magna cum laude, 1982); University of North Carolina-Chapel Hill (J.D., 1991). **PRACTICE AREAS:** Business Litigation; Securities Litigation. **Email:** cvanhorne@poynerspruill.com

CONSTANCE L. YOUNG, born Tulsa, Oklahoma, September 5, 1952; admitted to bar, 1988, North Carolina; 1990, Oklahoma. *Education:* Oklahoma State University (B.A., 1983); University of Tulsa (J.D., with honors, 1988). **PRACTICE AREAS:** Corporate Law; Business Litigation; Shareholder Disputes; Creditors Rights. **Email:** clyoung@poynerspruill.com

FRANK L. BRYANT, born Charlotte, North Carolina, May 6, 1947; admitted to bar, 1972, North Carolina. *Education:* University of North Carolina (B.A., 1969; J.D., 1972). **PRACTICE AREAS:** Business Law; Corporate Law; Commercial Real Estate. **Email:** fbryant@poynerspruill.com

DAVID L. TERRY, born Hickory, North Carolina, May 3, 1958; admitted to bar, 1983, North Carolina and U.S. Supreme Court. *Education:* Wake Forest University (B.S., cum laude, 1980; J.D., 1983). **PRACTICE AREAS:** Labor Management Relations; Health Care; Employment Discrimination. **Email:** dterry@poynerspruill.com

PATRICK J. FOGARTY, born New York, New York, December 4, 1960; admitted to bar, 1986, Massachusetts; 1987, New York; 1989, District of Columbia; 1991, U.S. Supreme Court; 1999, North Carolina. *Education:* Cornell University (B.A., 1983); Fordham University School of Law (J.D., 1986). **PRACTICE AREAS:** Civil Litigation; Insurance; Professional Malpractice; Products Liability. **Email:** pfogarty@poynerspruill.com

SHELIA JUNE COX, born Carthage, Missouri, July 13, 1969; admitted to bar, 1994, North Carolina; 1996, Texas. *Education:* Stetson University (B.A., magna cum laude, 1991); Wake Forest University School of Law (J.D., 1994). **PRACTICE AREAS:** Real Estate; Financial Services. **Email:** scox@poynerspruill.com

WILLIAM T. BELCHER, born Bluefield, West Virginia, 1950; admitted to bar, 1975, West Virginia; 2002, North Carolina. *Education:* Concord College (B.S., cum laude, 1972); West Virginia University (J.D., 1975); University of Miami (LL.M. in Taxation, 1978). Adjunct Professor, Estate Planning Law, West Virginia University College of Law. Fellow, The American College of Trust and Estate Counsel. **PRACTICE AREAS:** Estate Planning; Taxation. **Email:** wbelcher@poynerspruill.com

PARMELE PRICE CALAME, born Sanford, North Carolina, March 5, 1970; admitted to bar, 1995, North Carolina and South Carolina. *Education:* The University of the

(This Listing Continued)

South, Sewanee, Tennessee (B.A., 1992); University of South Carolina (J.D., 1995). ***PRACTICE AREAS:*** Employment Law; Civil Litigation. ***Email:*** pcalame@poynerspruill.com

ANNA SHEDDEN GORMAN, born Chapel Hill, North Carolina, September 22, 1967; admitted to bar, 1994, North Carolina. *Education:* University of North Carolina at Chapel Hill (B.S., 1989); Campbell University (J.D., 1994). ***PRACTICE AREAS:*** Bankruptcy; Commercial; Creditors Rights. ***Email:*** agorman@poynerspruill.com

THOMAS L. OGBURN, III, born Winston-Salem, North Carolina, September 15, 1969; admitted to bar, 1996, North Carolina and South Carolina. *Education:* University of North Carolina, Chapel Hill (B.A., 1992); Wake Forest University (M.B.A., 1996; J.D., 1996). ***PRACTICE AREAS:*** Business Litigation; Construction Law. ***Email:*** togburn@poynerspruill.com

STEPHEN ANDREW JURS, born Longmont, Colorado, May 3, 1970; admitted to bar, 1994, North Carolina; 1996, South Carolina and U.S. Supreme Court. *Education:* Duke University (B.A., 1991); Emory University (J.D., 1994). (Board Certified Specialist in Consumer Bankruptcy Law and Business Bankruptcy Law, North Carolina State Board of Legal Specialization). ***PRACTICE AREAS:*** Bankruptcy; Creditors Rights. ***Email:*** sajurs@poynerspruill.com

DIANE P. FURR, born 1957; admitted to bar, 1982, North Carolina; 1994, South Carolina. *Education:* Meredith College (B.A., cum laude, 1979); Wake Forest University (J.D., 1982). ***PRACTICE AREAS:*** Bankruptcy; Creditors Rights; Banking; Commercial Law. ***Email:*** dfurr@poynerspruill.com

PEGGY HOWARD HEY, born Geneva, New York, August 29, 1970; admitted to bar, 1996, New York; 1997, North Carolina. *Education:* Nazareth College of Rochester (B.A., 1992); Syracuse University (J.D., 1995). ***PRACTICE AREAS:*** Commercial Real Estate; Financial Services. ***Email:*** phey@poynerspruill.com

EUGENE S. GRIGGS, born Concord, North Carolina, August 15, 1961; admitted to bar, 1987, North Carolina. *Education:* Davidson College (A.B., magna cum laude, 1983) Phi Beta Kappa; University of North Carolina (J.D., with honors, 1987). ***PRACTICE AREAS:*** Employee Benefits; Taxation; Corporate Law. ***Email:*** ggriggs@poynerspruill.com

RESIDENT ASSOCIATES

JOSHUA BLAKE DURHAM, born Burlington, North Carolina, October 15, 1971; admitted to bar, 1998, North Carolina. *Education:* North Carolina State University (B.A., 1994); Campbell Law School (J.D., summa cum laude, 1998). ***PRACTICE AREAS:*** Commercial Litigation; Construction Law. ***Email:*** jdurham@poynerspruill.com

REBECCA B. WOFFORD, born Huntington, West Virginia, September 27, 1972; admitted to bar, 1997, North Carolina. *Education:* Randolph Macon Woman's College (B.S., 1994); Wake Forest University (J.D., 1997). ***PRACTICE AREAS:*** Business Litigation; Tort Litigation; Commercial Litigation. ***Email:*** rebeccaw@poynerspruill.com

COURTAULD McBRYDE YOUNG, born Atlanta, Georgia, August 30, 1973; admitted to bar, 2001, North Carolina. *Education:* Davidson College (B.A., 1996); Wake Forest University (J.D., 2001). ***PRACTICE AREAS:*** Litigation. ***Email:*** cyoung@poynerspruill.com

DEBORAH M. TYSON, born Rocky Mount, North Carolina, December, 28, 1975; admitted to bar, 2001, North Carolina. *Education:* Wake Forest University (B.A., 1998; J.D., 2001). ***PRACTICE AREAS:*** Bankruptcy. ***Email:*** dtyson@poynerspruill.com

W. MARK GRIFFITH, born Burlington, North Carolina, January 16, 1971; admitted to bar, 1996, North Carolina. *Education:* University of North Carolina, Chapel Hill (B.A., 1993; J.D., 1996). ***PRACTICE AREAS:*** Corporate; Securities; Business Litigation. ***Email:*** mgriffith@poynerspruill.com

WILLIAM C. PARISE, born Brooklyn, New York, June 30, 1969; admitted to bar, 2001, North Carolina. *Education:* State University of New York at Binghamton (B.A., cum laude, 1990); University of North Carolina at Chapel Hill (M.Ed., 1992); Duke University (M.Div., magna cum laude, 1996); University of Virginia (J.D., 2001). ***PRACTICE AREAS:*** Commercial Real Estate; Financial Services Law. ***Email:*** wparise@poynerspruill.com

JASON BURKE JAMES, born High Point, North Carolina, April 9, 1974; admitted to bar, 2001, North Carolina. *Education:* Wake Forest University (B.A., 1996); Campbell University (J.D., 2001). ***PRACTICE AREAS:*** Litigation; Construction Law. ***Email:*** jjames@poynerspruill.com

MICHELLE C. HUNT, admitted to bar, 2001, California; 2005, North Carolina. *Education:* Stanford University (B.A., 1998); University of San Francisco (J.D., 2001). ***PRACTICE AREAS:*** Litigation; Employment Litigation; Regulatory Law. ***Email:*** mhunt@poynerspruill.com

THOMAS M. ASMAR, born Chicago, Illinios, October 23, 1974; admitted to bar, 2001, Illinois (Not admitted in North Carolina). *Education:* University of Illinois (B.S., with honors, 1996; J.D., magna cum laude, 2001). Certified Public Accountant. ***PRACTICE AREAS:*** Employee Benefits. ***Email:*** tasmar@poynerspruill.com

BRYAN A. HAYLES, born Dallas, Texas, June 2, 1977; admitted to bar, 2005, North Carolina. *Education:* North Carolina State University (B.S., 1999); Wake Forest University (J.D., 2005). ***PRACTICE AREAS:*** Litigation. ***Email:*** bhayles@poynerspruill.com

RESIDENT OF COUNSEL

MARK B. EDWARDS, born Asheville, North Carolina, November 14, 1939; admitted to bar, 1963, North Carolina. *Education:* Duke University (A.B., 1961; J.D., 1963). ***PRACTICE AREAS:*** Estate Planning Law (40%); Probate Law (40%); Taxation Law (20%). ***Email:*** mbe1939@bellsouth.net

DAVID E. JOHNSTON, born Chicago, Illinois, November 10, 1948; admitted to bar, 1974, North Carolina. *Education:* Kenyon College (B.A., cum laude, 1971); Indiana University School of Law (J.D., 1974). ***PRACTICE AREAS:*** Corporate; Securities. ***Email:*** djohnston@poynerspruill.com

(This Listing Continued)

JASON T. SHERWOOD, born Oneonta, New York, February 14, 1968; admitted to bar, 1993, Massachusetts; 2005, North Carolina. *Education:* Boston College (B.A., summa cum laude, 1990); Harvard University (J.D., 1993). ***PRACTICE AREAS:*** Litigation. ***Email:*** jsherwood@poynerspruill.com

All Attorneys are Members of The North Carolina State Bar and North Carolina Bar Association and Members of their County Bar Associations.

REPRESENTATIVE CLIENTS: American Airlines; Alliance One International; BB&T; Boddie-Noell Enterprises, Inc.; The Body Shop, Inc.; Browning-Ferris Industries; CSX Transportations, Inc.; Data General Corp.; Electricities of North Carolina, Inc.; Farm Bureau Mutual Insurance Co.; Food Lion, Inc.; General Electric Capital Corp.; General Electric Company; General Electric Mortgage Insurance Company; General Motors, Inc.; Granutec, Inc.; Guardian Corporation, Inc.; H&R Block, Inc.; Investors Holding Company (Golden Corral and affiliates); LSB Bancshares, Inc.; Martin Marietta Materials; Mitsubishi Semiconductor America, Inc.; Nomaco, Inc.; N.C. Eastern Municipal Power Agency; North Carolina Enterprise Corporation; N.C. Housing Finance Agency; North Carolina Municipal Power Agency; Pepsico, Inc.; PF Properties; Pitt County Memorial Hospital; Premium Standard Farms, Inc.; Purdue Pharmaceuticals, L.P.; RBC Centura Banks, Inc.; Research Triangle Foundation; Richardson Sports (Carolina Panthers); Roses Stores, Inc.; R.J. Reynolds Tobacco Co.; Schwarz Biosciences, Inc.; Semi-Conductor Research Corp.; T.A. Loving Company; WakeMed.

(For additional Personnel and Biographical data see listings at Raleigh, Rocky Mount and Southern Pines)

PRICE, SMITH, HARGETT, PETHO & ANDERSON

A Partnership including a Professional Corporation

Established in 1979

1430 ELIZABETH AVENUE

CHARLOTTE, NORTH CAROLINA 28204

Telephone: 704-372-2160

800-737-2160

Facsimile: 704-372-6516

Email: priceatty@aol.com

URL: http://www.pshpanda.com

Forest City, North Carolina Office: 552 Oak Street, 28043. Telephone: 828-248-1448. Fax: 828-248-4405.

Plaintiffs Catastrophic Personal Injury, Medical Malpractice, Brain Injury, Wrongful Death, Workers Compensation, Insurance Litigation for Plaintiff, Motor Vehicle Accidents .

FIRM PROFILE: Price, Smith, Hargett, Petho & Anderson was established in 1979. The firm holds the highest rating attainable by Martindale-Hubbell. The firm has grown to its current complement of five attorneys and fifteen support personnel. Throughout its history the attorneys have limited their practice to the representation of plaintiffs in personal injury claims, and other types of insurance matters. Firm members are presently involved in a wide range of activities, including serving as presenters in continuing legal education and serving on Mecklenburg County Bar Committees. The firm consistently handles a high volume of litigation with a team approach which is calculated to involve all the attorneys in every aspect of the practice, as well as providing the clients with consistent professional representation from the case's beginning to its end.

LARRY E. PRICE, (P.A.), born Rockingham, North Carolina, June 11, 1942; admitted to bar, 1972, North Carolina and U.S. District Court, Western District of North Carolina; U.S. Supreme Court. *Education:* Wingate College (A.A., 1962); St. Andrews College (B.S., 1964); Wake Forest University (J.D., 1972). Phi Alpha Delta. Member: National Campaign Committee, Wake Forest University, School of Law, 1999—; Law Board of Visitors, Wake Forest University, School of Law, 1997—; Law Alumni Council, Wake Forest University, School of Law, 1993-1996; Board of Directors, the Wingate University Foundation, Inc., 1993-1998; Chairman, 1995 and 1996; Board of Trustees, Wingate University, 2002-2004. *Member:* North Carolina and American Bar Associations; North Carolina State Bar; North Carolina Academy of Trial Lawyers; The Association of Trial Lawyers of America; New York State Trial Lawyers Association; Million Dollar Advocates Forum. ***PRACTICE AREAS:*** Plaintiffs Personal Injury; Wrongful Death; Medical Malpractice; Insurance (Plaintiff) Litigation. ***Email:*** priceatty@aol.com

WM. BENJAMIN SMITH, born Rocky Mount, North Carolina, February 9, 1950; admitted to bar, 1979, North Carolina and U.S. District Court, Western District of North Carolina; U.S. Court of Appeals, Fourth Circuit. *Education:* University of North Carolina at Chapel Hill (B.A., 1976; J.D., 1979). Voted Legal Elite, Litigation-Business North Carolina Magazine. Certified, Civil Trial Lawyer, National Board of Trial Advocacy. *Member:* Mecklenburg County and American Bar Associations; North Carolina State Bar; Mecklenburg County Trial Lawyers Association (Past President); North Carolina Academy of Trial Lawyers; The Association of Trial Lawyers of America; Master, Bobbitt Chapter, American Inns of Court; Million Dollar Advocates Forum. ***PRACTICE AREAS:*** Medical Malpractice; Plaintiffs Personal Injury; Workers Compensation; Wrongful Death; Insurance (Plaintiff) Litigation. ***Email:*** benlaw68@hotmail.com

JEFFREY B. HARGETT, born Charlotte, North Carolina, October 5, 1964; admitted to bar, 1990, North Carolina and U.S. District Court, Western District of North Carolina. *Education:* University of North Carolina at Chapel Hill (B.A., with honors, 1987; J.D., 1990). Phi Delta Phi. Author: "Defining the Unauthorized Practice of Law"; "Judicial Selection Methods and Judicial Politics in North Carolina and South Carolina." Member, Board of Directors, Nevins Center, 2000-2003. *Member:* Mecklenburg County (Authorized Practice Committee, 1995-2003), North Carolina and American Bar Associations; North Carolina Academy of Trial Lawyers (Vice Chair, 2001-2002 and Chair, 2002-2003, Hispanic-Latino Issues Division); Mecklenberg County Trial Lawyers Association. ***LANGUAGES:*** Spanish. ***PRACTICE AREAS:*** Plaintiffs Personal Injury; Workers Compensation; Motor Vehicle Accidents and Injuries; Wrongful Death; Medical Malpractice. ***Email:*** hargettfamily@msn.com

DOUGLAS A. PETHO, born Cleveland, Ohio, April 26, 1966; admitted to bar, 1991, North Carolina and U.S. District Court, Western District of North Carolina. *Education:* North Carolina State University; University of North Carolina at Chapel Hill (B.S., 1988;

(This Listing Continued)

PRICE, SMITH, HARGETT, PETHO & ANDERSON, Charlotte—Continued

J.D., 1991). Phi Sigma Alpha. Assistant District Attorney, 1991-1993. *Member:* Mecklenburg County, North Carolina and American Bar Associations; North Carolina Academy of Trial Lawyers; The Association of Trial Lawyers of America. ***PRACTICE AREAS:*** Medical Malpractice; Plaintiffs Personal Injury; Workers Compensation; Wrongful Death; Products Liability. ***Email:*** DougPetho@aol.com

RICHARD LEE ANDERSON, born Charlotte, North Carolina, July 2, 1968; admitted to bar, 1993, North Carolina and U.S. District Court, Western and Middle Districts of North Carolina. *Education:* University of North Carolina at Chapel Hill (B.A., 1990); Wake Forest University (J.D., 1993). *Member:* Mecklenburg County, North Carolina and American Bar Associations; North Carolina Academy of Trial Lawyers; Mecklenburg County Trial Lawyers Association; Brain Injury Association of North Carolina; Million Dollar Advocates Forum. ***PRACTICE AREAS:*** Catastrophic Personal Injury; Medical Malpractice; Workers Compensation; Wrongful Death. ***Email:*** rlanderson@carolina.rr.com

RONNIE A. PRUETT

744 TYVOLA ROAD, SUITE C
CHARLOTTE, NORTH CAROLINA 28217
Telephone: 704-523-6020
Fax: 704-527-7711
Email: pruett@sprintmail.com

Immigration, International Trade, U.S. Customs and Antitrust Law.

RONNIE A. PRUETT, born Mount Airy, North Carolina, April 26, 1938; admitted to bar, 1966, North Carolina; 1988, U.S. Court of International Trade. *Education:* University of North Carolina (A.B., 1960); Columbia University (LL.B., 1966). Fulbright Scholar, National University of Buenos Aires, Argentina, 1960-1961. Pi Sigma Alpha. Member, Amphoterothen Society. Attorney, Cannon Mills Company, Legal Department, 1966-1977. Clerk, Womble, Carlyle, Sandridge & Rice, Winston-Salem, North Carolina, Summer 1964 and 1965. Participating Draftsman, Antitrust Law Developments, American Bar Association, 1975. General Counsel, Charlotte Foreign Trade Zone, Inc., 1979-2004. President, Cabarrus County Bar Association, 1982-1983. President, Downtown Charlotte Rotary Club, 1998-1999. President, Charlotte Area Rotary Council, 1999-2000. President, Charlotte World Trade Association, 1981-1982. President, North Carolina World Trade Association, 1983-1984. *Member:* Mecklenburg County Bar Association; North Carolina State Bar; Customs and International Trade Bar Association; American Immigration Lawyers Association. ***LANGUAGES:*** Spanish and Portuguese.

RAGAN & RAGAN PLLC

CHARLOTTE, NORTH CAROLINA

(See Gastonia)

Personal Injury, Workers Compensation, Medical Malpractice, Wrongful Death, Automobile Accidents, Products Liability.

RAWLS, DICKINSON & SCHEER, P.A.

1011 EAST MOREHEAD STREET
SUITE 300
CHARLOTTE, NORTH CAROLINA 28204
Telephone: 704-376-3200
Facsimile: 704-332-2716
URL: http://www.rdslaw.com
URL: http://www.rawlsdickinsonandscheer.com

General Civil and Criminal Trial Practice in State and Federal Courts. Appellate Practice, Criminal Law, Driving While Intoxicated (DWI), Drug Crimes, Parole and Probation, Traffic Violations, White Collar Crimes, Personal Injury, Wrongful Death, Automobile Accidents, Products Liability, Medical Malpractice, Consumer Law.

EBEN T. RAWLS III, born Winston-Salem, North Carolina, August 31, 1949; admitted to bar, 1978, North Carolina; U.S. Supreme Court. *Education:* Duke University (B.A., cum laude, 1972); University of North Carolina (J.D., 1978). Member: Order of Barristers. Recipient, Lewis F. Powell Medal for Excellence in Oral Advocacy. Master, Bobbitt Inn of Court. *Member:* 26th Judicial District and North Carolina State Bars; North Carolina and American Bar Associations; North Carolina Academy of Trial Lawyers; National Association of Criminal Defense Lawyers. (Board Certified Specialist in Criminal Law, North Carolina State Board of Legal Specialization). ***PRACTICE AREAS:*** State and Federal Criminal Defense and Appeals; DWI Defense; Traffic Law; Criminal Conspiracy; Bank Fraud; Mail Fraud; White Collar Crime; Grand Jury Practice. ***Email:*** erawls@rdslaw.com

THOMAS W. DICKINSON, born Richmond, Virginia, September 15, 1949; admitted to bar, 1975, North Carolina. *Education:* University of North Carolina (B.A., 1971; J.D., 1975). *Member:* 26th Judicial District and North Carolina State Bars; North Carolina Bar Association; North Carolina Academy of Trial Lawyers; American Trial Lawyers Association. ***PRACTICE AREAS:*** Personal Injury; Civil Litigation; Wrongful Death; Consumer Law. ***Email:*** tomdickinson@perigee.net

ANTHONY G. SCHEER, born Syracuse, New York, October 29, 1957; admitted to bar, 1992, North Carolina. *Education:* Duke University (B.A., 1979); University of North Carolina, Chapel Hill, (J.D., 1992). Law Review, University North Carolina. Assistant District Attorney, Charlotte, North Carolina, 1993-1997. Law Clerk, United States District Court, Eastern District of Virginia, 1992-1993. Author, "Fourth Amendment Implications of Private Citizen Actions," 69 N.C. L. Rev. 1449 (1991). *Member:* North Carolina State Bar; American Bar Association; North Carolina Academy of Trial Lawyers; National Association of Criminal Defense Lawyers. ***PRACTICE AREAS:*** Federal Criminal Law; State Criminal Law; Whistleblower Litigation. ***Email:*** tscheer@rdslaw.com

(This Listing Continued)

SHEENA M. WEST, born Naples, Florida, August 16, 1972; admitted to bar, 1998, North Carolina; 2003, U.S. District Court, Western District of North Carolina. *Education:* University of North Carolina at Asheville (B.A., 1994); North Carolina Central University (J.D., 1998). *Member:* North Carolina State Bar; 26th Judicial Bar; North Carolina Academy of Trial Lawyers. ***Email:*** swest@rdslaw.com

AMANDA A. MINGO, admitted to bar, 1997, North Carolina. *Education:* University of North Carolina, Asheville (B.A., 1992); North Carolina State University School of Law (J.D., 1997). ***PRACTICE AREAS:*** Criminal Law.

RAYBURN COOPER & DURHAM, P.A.

THE CARILLON
227 WEST TRADE STREET, SUITE 1200
CHARLOTTE, NORTH CAROLINA 28202-1675
Telephone: 704-334-0891
Fax: 704-377-1897; 704-377-0395
Email: info@rcdlaw.net
URL: http://www.rcdlaw.net

General Civil Practice including Corporate, Business Organizations, Securities and Business Bankruptcy. Trial and Appellate Practice in all State and Federal Courts.

FIRM PROFILE: Rayburn Cooper & Durham, P.A. represents individuals and business entities in sophisticated matters that require creative and unique applications and solutions. We also represent entrepreneurs in a wide variety of business activities. Attorneys have significant experience in the areas of business organizations, business restructuring and bankruptcy, employment law, merger and acquisitions, and securities regulation. Trial practice expertise is in the areas of civil and commercial, employment law, and securities litigation.

C. RICHARD RAYBURN, JR., born Columbia, Tennessee, March 27, 1947; admitted to bar, 1974, North Carolina, U.S. Tax Court; U.S. District Court, Middle and Eastern Districts of North Carolina and U.S. Court of Appeals, Fourth Circuit. *Education:* University of Tennessee (B.S., with honors, 1969); Duke University (J.D., 1974). Omicron Delta Kappa; Order of the Coif; Sigma Pi Sigma; Phi Delta Phi. Research and Managing Editor, Duke Law Journal, 1973-1974. *Member:* Mecklenburg County, North Carolina (Member, Bankruptcy Section Council, 1993-1996) and American Bar Associations; The North Carolina State Bar. ***PRACTICE AREAS:*** Banking Law; Business Law; Business Litigation; Finance; Business Bankruptcy Law; Corporate Law; Securities; Mergers and Acquisitions. ***Email:*** rrayburn@rcdlaw.net

W. SCOTT COOPER, born Medford, Massachusetts, January 22, 1952; admitted to bar, 1977, Virginia; 1983, North Carolina. *Education:* Duke University (B.A., 1974); Marshall-Wythe School of Law, College of William & Mary (J.D., 1977). Attorney, Division of Investment Management, Securities and Exchange Commission, 1978-1979. Attorney, 1979-1981 and Special Counsel, 1981-1982, Office of Disclosure Policy, Division of Corporation Finance, Securities and Exchange Commission. *Member:* Mecklenburg County, North Carolina (Chairman, Securities Regulation Committee, 1993-1995) and American (Member, Federal Regulation of Securities Committee) Bar Associations; The North Carolina State Bar; Virginia State Bar. ***PRACTICE AREAS:*** Business Organization; Corporate Law; Securities; Mergers and Acquisitions. ***Email:*** scooper@rcdlaw.net

ALBERT F. DURHAM, born Charlotte, North Carolina, May 15, 1947; admitted to bar, 1975, North Carolina; 1979, U.S. Supreme Court. *Education:* University of North Carolina (B.A., 1970; J.D., 1975). *Member:* Mecklenburg County, North Carolina (Bankruptcy Council and Chairman, Bankruptcy Section, 1990-1991) and American Bar Associations; North Carolina State Bar; American Bankruptcy Institute. (Board Certified Specialist in Bankruptcy, North Carolina State Board of Legal Specialization)(Certified in Business Bankruptcy Law by the American Board of Certification). ***PRACTICE AREAS:*** Bankruptcy; Commercial Law; Business Workouts. ***Email:*** adurham@rcdlaw.net

PAUL R. BAYNARD, born Greensboro, North Carolina, April 15, 1961; admitted to bar, 1988, Georgia and North Carolina, U.S. District Court, Western, Middle and Eastern Districts of North Carolina, U.S. District Court, Northern District of Georgia and U.S. Court of Appeals, Fourth and Eleventh Circuits. *Education:* Davidson College (B.A., 1983); University of North Carolina (M.B.A., 1988; J.D., 1988). Phi Delta Phi. Holderness Moot Court Bench, University of North Carolina School of Law, 1987-1988. *Member:* Mecklenburg County, North Carolina and American Bar Associations; The North Carolina State Bar; State Bar of Georgia. ***PRACTICE AREAS:*** Bankruptcy; Civil Litigation; Business Workouts; Business Law; Commercial Law. ***Email:*** pbaynard@rcdlaw.net

JAMES B. GATEHOUSE, born Oak Hill, West Virginia, June 14, 1966; admitted to bar, 1992, New York, West Virginia and U.S. District Court, Southern and Eastern Districts of New York; 1996, North Carolina; U.S. District Court, Eastern, Middle and Western Districts of North Carolina; U.S. Court of Appeals, Fourth Circuit and U.S. Supreme Court. *Education:* West Virginia University (B.A., summa cum laude, 1988); University of Virginia (J.D., 1991). *Member:* Mecklenburg County, North Carolina and American Bar Associations; North Carolina State Bar; West Virginia State Bar. American Inns of Court. ***PRACTICE AREAS:*** Corporate; Securities; Business Litigation; General Civil Litigation; Antitrust; Bankruptcy; Construction; Real Estate Disputes; Technology; Products Liability; Personal Injury; White Collar Crime. ***Email:*** bgatehouse@rcdlaw.net

G. KIRKLAND HARDYMON, born Charlotte, North Carolina, April 7, 1964; admitted to bar, 1992, North Carolina and U.S. District Court, Middle District of North Carolina; 1993, U.S. District Court, Western District of North Carolina. *Education:* Appalachian State University (B.S.B.A., 1986); Wake Forest University (J.D., cum laude, 1992). Member, Wake Forest Law Review, 1990-1992. Law Clerk to the Honorable Frank W. Bullock, Jr., Chief Judge, U.S. District Court, Middle District of North Carolina, 1992-1993. *Member:* Mecklenburg County, North Carolina and American Bar Associations; The North Carolina State Bar. ***PRACTICE AREAS:*** Commercial Litigation; Bankruptcy Law; Civil Litigation. ***Email:*** khardymon@rcdlaw.net

(This Listing Continued)

PATRICIA B. EDMONDSON, born Boise, Idaho, September 22, 1942; admitted to bar, 1985, North Carolina and U.S. District Court, Western District of North Carolina. *Education:* Midwestern University (B.A., summa cum laude, 1964); Duke University (Ph.D., 1967); Wake Forest University (J.D., cum laude, 1985). *Member:* Mecklenburg County, North Carolina and American Bar Associations; The North Carolina State Bar. ***PRACTICE AREAS:*** Bankruptcy Law; Corporate Law; Commercial Law. ***Email:*** pedmondson@rcdlaw.net

ASSOCIATES

DAVID S. MELIN, born Milwaukee, Wisconsin, February 2, 1975; admitted to bar, 2000, North Carolina and U.S. District Court, Western District of North Carolina. *Education:* University of Wisconsin-Madison (B.A., with honors, 1997); University of North Carolina at Chapel Hill (J.D., 2000). Phi Beta Kappa; Phi Delta Phi; Order of Barristers. Member, Holderness Moot Court National Team, University of North Carolina, 1999-2000. *Member:* Mecklenburg County, North Carolina and American Bar Associations; North Carolina State Bar. ***PRACTICE AREAS:*** Civil Litigation; Commercial Litigation. ***Email:*** dmelin@rcdlaw.net

JOHN R. MILLER, JR., born Hampton, Virginia, December 22, 1975; admitted to bar, 2002, North Carolina and U.S. District Court, Eastern, Middle and Western Districts of North Carolina. *Education:* University of Virginia (B.A., 1997); Wake Forest University School of Law (J.D., 2002). Member, 1999-2002 and Chief Justice, 2001-2002, Phi Alpha Delta. Author, "Does E-Commerce Spell the End of Geography-Based Trademark Analysis?" 2002 Wake Forest Intell. Prop. L.J. 8, Posted May 10, 2002. ***PRACTICE AREAS:*** Bankruptcy; Business Law; Commercial Law. ***Email:*** jmiller@rcdlaw.net

ROSS R. FULTON, born Portland, Maine; admitted to bar, 2003, North Carolina and U.S. District Court, Eastern, Middle and Western Districts of North Carolina. *Education:* State University of New York College at Geneseo (B.A., 2000) Dean's List; College of William & Mary (J.D., 2002). Pi Sigma Alpha. Member, William & Mary Moot Court Team, 2002-2003. *Member:* Mecklenburg, North Carolina and American Bar Association; The North Carolina State Bar. ***PRACTICE AREAS:*** Commercial Litigation; Bankruptcy. ***Email:*** rfulton@rcdlaw.net

TASHA LEIGH WINEBARGER, born Elkin, North Carolina, January 4, 1979; admitted to bar, 2004, North Carolina and U.S. District Court, Western District of North Carolina. *Education:* Duke University (B.S., 2001); University of North Carolina at Chapel Hill (J.D., 2004). Member: Holderness Moot Court Bench; Banking Institute Journal. *Member:* Mecklenburg County, North Carolina and American Bar Associations; The North Carolina State Bar. ***PRACTICE AREAS.*** Business Organization; Business Transactions. ***Email:*** twinebarger@rcdlaw.net

SHAWNA R. GARRETT, born St. Louis, Missouri; admitted to bar, 2004, North Carolina and U.S. District Court, Western District of North Carolina. *Education:* Western Carolina University (B.S., summa cum laude, 1999); University of North Carolina at Chapel Hill School of Law (J.D., with honors, 2004). *Member:* Mecklenburg County, North Carolina and American Bar Associations; The North Carolina State Bar. ***PRACTICE AREAS:*** Business Organization; Business Transactions. ***Email:*** sgarrett@rcdlaw.net

SHELLEY K. ABEL, born 1980; admitted to bar, 2005, North Carolina and U.S. District Court, Western District of North Carolina. *Education:* University of North Carolina at Chapel Hill (A.B., 2002; J.D., 2005). *Member:* Mecklenburg County, North Carolina and American Bar Associations; North Carolina State Bar.

PETER T. REYNOLDS, born Indianapolis, Indiana, 1979; admitted to bar, 2005, North Carolina and U.S. District Court, Western District of North Carolina. *Education:* Northwestern University (B.A., 2002); University of North Carolina at Chapel Hill (J.D., 2005). *Member:* Mecklenburg County, North Carolina and American Bar Associations; North Carolina State Bar.

REPRESENTATIVE CLIENTS: The Dickerson Group, Inc.; First Tryon Securities, LLC; Forshaw Industries, Inc.; Mack Truck Sales of Charlotte, Inc.; Parks & Company, LLC; Pumps, Parts and Service, Inc.; Tweetsie Railroad, Inc.; William Ives Consulting; The Elevator Channel, Inc.

JERRY ALAN REESE, P.C.

Established in 1995

411 LANSDOWNE ROAD
P.O. BOX 32066
CHARLOTTE, NORTH CAROLINA 28270
Telephone: 704-347-1044
Telecopier: 704-347-1045
Email: jreese@tryonlg.com
URL: http://www.tryonlegalgroup.com

Residential and Commercial Real Estate, Commercial and Real Estate Lending and Business Law.

FIRM PROFILE: Our firm is a group of dedicated professionals with substantial experience in the representation of parties in commercial real estate, real estate lending and general business transactions. Through the use of state-of-the-art technology and the limitation of our practice to our chosen fields of concentration, we are able to provide our builder, developer, investor and financial institution clients with personal attention and quality service, thus fulfilling our firm slogan "In Pursuit of Professional Excellence with a Personal Touch".

JERRY ALAN REESE, born Hickory, North Carolina, January 24, 1952; admitted to bar, 1977, North Carolina. *Education:* University of North Carolina (A.B., with highest honors, 1974; J.D., with honors, 1977). Phi Eta Sigma; Phi Beta Kappa; Order of the Coif. Note and Comment Editor, North Carolina Law Review, 1976-1977. Board Certified in Real Property Law, Business, Commercial and Industrial Transaction, November, 1995. *Member:* North Carolina (Member, Real Property Section) and American Bar Associations; North Carolina State Bar. ***REPORTED CASES:*** Van Every v. McGuire, 125 N.C. App. 578, 481 S.E.2d 377 (1997), affirmed as modified, 348 N.C. 58, 497 S.E.2d 689 (1998); Harry v. Mecklenburg County, et al., 200 W.L. 4755 (COA99-476)(N.C. App. 1999). ***PRACTICE AREAS:*** Residential Real Estate; Commercial Real Estate; Commercial Loans; Business Law. ***Email:*** jreese@tryonlg.com

LEGAL SUPPORT PERSONNEL

PATRICIA G. DAVIES, born North Bend, Oregon, October 27, 1952. *Education:* Central Piedmont Community College (Paralegal Degree); Merritt Davis Business College (Legal Secretarial); Southwestern Community College. (Paralegal). ***Email:*** pdavies@tryonlg.com

REPRESENTATIVE CLIENTS: Americh Corporation; Kruss, U.S.A.; Lawyers Title Insurance; Matthews Management, Inc.; Cytosol Ophthalmics, Inc.; Palisades Properties, Inc.; Presspart Inc.; Seaboard Realty Company; Tropical Nut & Fruit Corp.; Yamada Dobby, Inc.; Winn-Dixie Charlotte, Inc.; Broad Street Partners; Crocker Realty Trust, PL; Highland Mortgage Company.

THE ROBERTS LAW FIRM, P.A.

CHARLOTTE, NORTH CAROLINA

(See Gastonia)

Trial Practice. Personal Injury, Workers Compensation, Social Security Disability, Medical Malpractice, Nursing home Litigation, Products Liability and Wrongful Death.

MARCOS ROBERTS, P.A.

728 CENTRAL AVENUE
CHARLOTTE, NORTH CAROLINA 28204
Telephone: 704-335-7272
Espanol: 704-333-3676
Fax: 704-335-7277
URL: http://www.marcosroberts.com

State and Federal Criminal Defense, Driving While Intoxicated (DWI), Drug Crimes, Felonies, Misdemeanors, Assault, Rape, Traffic Violations, White Collar Crimes.

MARCOS ROBERTS, born 1957; admitted to bar, 1997, North Carolina. *Education:* University of North Carolina (Political Science, 1984); Washington College of Law, American University (J.D., 1997). *Member:* Mecklenburg County Bar; National Association of Criminal Defense Attorneys; Association of Trial Lawyers of America; Federal Bar Association.

Language: Spanish.

RICHARD L. ROBERTSON & ASSOCIATES, P.A.

2730 EAST HARRIS BOULEVARD
SUITE 101
CHARLOTTE, NORTH CAROLINA 28213-4108
Telephone: 704-597-5774
Facsimile: 704-599-5603
URL: http://www.rlrobertson.com
Email: rlrobertson@rlrobertson.com
URL: http://www.rlrobertsonpa.com

General Civil Trial and Business Practice, Commercial Litigation, Insurance Defense, Personal Injury, Bankruptcy, Commercial Real Estate, Estate Planning, Estate Administration, Collections and Corporations.

MEMBER OF FIRM

RICHARD L. ROBERTSON, born High Point, North Carolina, April 24, 1952; admitted to bar, 1977, North Carolina and U.S. District Court, Middle and Western Districts of North Carolina; 1992, U.S. Court of Appeals, Fourth Circuit. *Education:* University of North Carolina (B.A., with honors, 1974; J.D., 1977). Recipient: U.S. Department of Justice Director's Award for Superior Performance as an Assistant U.S. Attorney, 1989. Assistant U.S. Attorney, Middle District of North Carolina, 1982-1990. *Member:* Mecklenburg County, North Carolina (Member, Sections on: Litigation; Bankruptcy Law); and American Bar Associations; North Carolina State Bar; North Carolina Association of Defense Attorneys; Defense Research Institute, Inc. ***PRACTICE AREAS:*** Insurance Defense; Litigation; Business Law. ***Email:*** rlrobertson@rlrobertson.com

KAREN R. FEEKEN, born Hastings, Nebraska, August 27, 1977; admitted to bar, 2003, North Carolina. *Education:* Doane College (B.A., 2000); University of Missouri at Columbia, School of Law (J.D., 2003). *Member:* North Carolina State Bar. ***PRACTICE AREAS:*** Collections; Estate Planning; Business Law.

SUSANNE M. ROBICSEK

1701 SCOTT AVENUE
CHARLOTTE, NORTH CAROLINA 28203
Telephone: 704-377-0776
Fax: 704-377-0775
URL: http://www.robicsek.com
URL: http://www.lawyers.com/robicseklaw

Bankruptcy Law, Consumer, Bankruptcy, Commercial Bankruptcy, Foreclosures.

FIRM PROFILE: Concentrating in Bankruptcy Law since 1988.

SUSANNE M. ROBICSEK, born Charlotte, North Carolina, June 13, 1960; admitted to bar, 1987, North Carolina. *Education:* North Carolina State University (B.E.D., in Architecture, 1982); Wake Forest University (J.D., 1987). Law Clerk to the Honorable Rufus

(This Listing Continued)

SUSANNE M. ROBICSEK, Charlotte—Continued

W. Reynolds, United States Bankruptcy Judge, Middle District of North Carolina, 1988. *Member:* North Carolina State Bar; National Association of Consumer Bankruptcy Attorneys. ***LANGUAGES:*** Hungarian.

ROBERT NELSON ROBINSON

P.O. BOX 220104
CHARLOTTE, NORTH CAROLINA 28222
Telephone: 704-332-4833
URL: http://www.lawyers.com/robertnelsonrobinson

General and Trial Practice before State and Federal Courts. Corporation, Probate, Real Estate, Bankruptcy and Reorganization Law.

ROBERT NELSON ROBINSON, born Atlanta, Georgia; admitted to bar, 1955, North Carolina. *Education:* Emory University (B.A., 1949); Emory University and University of Virginia (LL.B., 1954). Phi Delta Phi. Member, Business Board of Editors, University of Virginia Law Review, 1953-1954. Lecturer, Practical Skills Course, North Carolina Bar Foundation, 1963-1968. Judge Pro Tem, Mecklenburg County Recorders Court, 1959-1960 and 1963. Assistant State Solicitor, 14-A Solicitorial District of North Carolina, 1960-1962. Member, Special Committee appointed by U.S. District Court for the Western District of North Carolina for Drafting of Local Federal Rules of Civil and Criminal Procedure, 1965. Special Counsel to Mayor of Charlotte, 1979-1983. *Member:* Mecklenburg County and North Carolina (Member and Treasurer, Bankruptcy Section, 1979-1981) Bar Associations; The North Carolina State Bar.

APPROVED ATTORNEY FOR: Lawyers Title Insurance Corp.; Commonwealth Land Title Insurance Co.; Chicago Title Insurance Co.; The Title Insurance Company of Minnesota. REFERENCE: Bank of America.

ROBINSON, BRADSHAW & HINSON, P.A.

Established in 1960

101 NORTH TRYON STREET, SUITE 1900
CHARLOTTE, NORTH CAROLINA 28246-1900
Telephone: 704-377-2536
Fax: 704-378-4000
Email: ylevine@rbh.com
URL: http://www.rbh.com

Rock Hill, South Carolina Office: 140 East Main Street, Suite 420, Post Office Drawer 12070. Telephone: 803-325-2900. FAX: 803-325-2929.

Antitrust and Trade Regulation, Banking and Finance, Bankruptcy, Business Law, Civil and Commercial Litigation, Class Action Litigation, Construction, Corporate and Commercial Law, Criminal Matters, E-Commerce, Employee Benefits, Employment and Labor Law, Energy Law, Environmental Law, Federal and State Taxation, Health Care, Insurance Coverage, Intellectual Property and Technology, International Law, Mergers and Acquisitions, Not-for-Profit Organizations and Foundations, Public Finance, Real Estate, Securities Regulation and Litigation, Sports and Entertainment Law, Tort and Product Liability Litigation, Trusts and Estates, and Venture Capital and Private Equity.

FIRM PROFILE: Robinson, Bradshaw & Hinson, P.A. is a business law firm specializing in complex corporate transactions and litigation. For over forty years, the firm has consistently provided innovative solutions to its clients' business needs from both a legal and practical perspective. The firm serves as counsel to public and closely-held corporations operating in domestic and foreign markets; limited liability companies; limited and general partnerships; individuals; municipal, county and state agencies; public utilities; health care institutions; financial institutions and tax-exempt organizations.

LAW FIRM ALLIANCES/ASSOCIATIONS: **SOUTHERN LAW NETWORK**

SHAREHOLDERS

RUSSELL M. ROBINSON II, admitted to bar, 1956, North Carolina. *Education:* Princeton University; Duke University (LL.B., 1956). Phi Beta Kappa; Delta Theta Phi; Order of the Coif. Editor-in-Chief, *Duke Law Journal,* 1955-56. Author: *Robinson on North Carolina Corporation Law,* The Michie Company, 6th Edition, 2000. Trustee, The Duke Endowment, 1987—. Chairman, Business Corporation Act Drafting Committee of General Statutes Commission, 1968-73; 1985-90. Chairman, Board of Trustees, University of North Carolina at Charlotte. ***PRACTICE AREAS:*** Corporate; Commercial; Securities; Charitable Trusts and Foundations. ***Email:*** rrobinson@rbh.com

ROBIN L. HINSON, admitted to bar, 1958, North Carolina. *Education:* Davidson College (B.S., 1953); University of North Carolina (J.D., 1958). Phi Beta Kappa; Order of the Coif. Editor-in-Chief, *North Carolina Law Review,* 1957-58. Assistant Professor, 1958-61 and Assistant Dean, 1959-61, University of North Carolina School of Law. Member: North Carolina General Statutes Commission, 1961-66; State Constitution Study Commission, 1967-68. Associate General Counsel, Carolina Power & Light Co., 1969-70. Vice President and General Counsel, Hanes Corp., 1970-73. Senior Vice President and General Counsel, First Union Corp., 1973-78. Fellow, American Bar Foundation. [Lt., USNR; active duty, 1953-55]. ***PRACTICE AREAS:*** Banking; Finance; Mergers and Acquisitions; Corporate; Commercial Law. ***Email:*** rhinson@rbh.com

ROBERT C. SINK, admitted to bar, 1965, North Carolina. *Education:* Duke University (A.B., 1959; LL.B., 1965). Phi Beta Kappa; Order of the Coif. Associate Editor, *Duke Law Journal,* 1964-65. Member, Board of Trustees, 1985-90 and Chairman, 1988-90, Public Library of Charlotte and Mecklenburg County. Board of Directors, Museum of the New South, 1991-97 and Chairman, 1996-97. *Member:* Mecklenburg County (President, 1986-87), North Carolina State Bar (Councelor, 1988-96; President-Elect, 1997-98; President, 1998—). [Lt., USNR; active duty, 1959-62]. ***PRACTICE AREAS:*** Construction; Real Estate. ***Email:*** rsink@rbh.com

(This Listing Continued)

A. WARD McKEITHEN, admitted to bar, 1963, North Carolina. *Education:* Davidson College (A.B., 1960); Duke University (LL.B., 1963). Omicron Delta Kappa; Phi Delta Phi; Order of the Coif. Associate Editor, *Duke Law Journal,* 1962-63. Member, Charlotte-Mecklenburg Board of Education, 1976-88. Member, Board of Trustees, Queens College, 1974—. *Member:* Mecklenburg County Bar Association (President, 1993-94). Fellow: American College of Trial Lawyers. [1st Lt., USAR; active duty, 1964-65]. ***PRACTICE AREAS:*** Commercial Litigation; Intellectual Property Litigation; Trade Practice Litigation. ***Email:*** wmckeithen@rbh.com

GRAHAM D. HOLDING, JR., admitted to bar, 1964, North Carolina. *Education:* University of North Carolina (A.B., 1958); University of Virginia (LL.B., 1964). Phi Beta Kappa; Order of the Coif. Associate Editor, *Virginia Law Review,* 1963-64. Fellow, American College of Trust and Estate Counsel. [USA active duty, 1958-1961]. (Board Certified Specialist in Estate Planning and Probate Law, North Carolina State Board of Legal Specialization). ***PRACTICE AREAS:*** Estate Planning; Estate Administration; Taxation. ***Email:*** gholding@rbh.com

RICHARD A. VINROOT, admitted to bar, 1966, North Carolina. *Education:* University of North Carolina (B.S., 1963; LL.B., 1966). Phi Delta Phi. John Motley Morehead Scholar. Member, Charlotte City Council, 1983-91. Mayor of Charlotte, 1991-95. [USA; active duty, 1967-68]. ***PRACTICE AREAS:*** Commercial Litigation; Employment Discrimination; Labor Law; Construction Litigation. ***Email:*** rvinroot@rbh.com

CLAUDE Q. FREEMAN, JR., admitted to bar, 1968, North Carolina. *Education:* University of North Carolina (A.B., 1965; J.D., 1968). Law Clerk to The Hon. J. Braxton Craven, United States Court of Appeals, Fourth Circuit, 1968-69. *Member:* Mecklenburg County Bar Association (Chairman, Real Property Section, 1991-93). ***PRACTICE AREAS:*** Commercial Real Estate. ***Email:*** cfreeman@rbh.com

JOHN R. WESTER, admitted to bar, 1972, North Carolina. *Education:* University of North Carolina (A.B., 1968); Duke University (J.D., with high honors, 1972). Order of the Coif. John Motley Morehead Scholar. Note and Comment Editor, *Duke Law Journal,* 1971-72. Fellow, American College of Trial Lawyers. ***PRACTICE AREAS:*** Trial Practice; Appellate Practice; Complex Litigation; Class Actions. ***Email:*** jwester@rbh.com

MARTIN L. BRACKETT, JR., admitted to bar, 1972, North Carolina. *Education:* Davidson College (B.A., 1969); University of North Carolina (J.D., 1972). *Member:* North Carolina Academy of Trial Lawyers (Member, Board of Governors, 1980-86; 1988-95; Vice-President, 1984-86); The Association of Trial Lawyers of America; American Inns of Court. Fellow: American College of Trial Lawyers. ***PRACTICE AREAS:*** Negligence Litigation; Criminal Litigation. ***Email:*** mbrackett@rbh.com

JOHN R. MILLER, admitted to bar, 1975, North Carolina. *Education:* Duke University (A.B., 1968; J.D., with distinction, 1975). Pi Mu Epsilon; Sigma Pi Sigma; Order of the Coif. Angier B. Duke Scholar. Editorial Assistant, *Law and Contemporary Problems,* 1973. Article Editor, *Duke Law Journal,* 1974-75. National Panel of Arbitrators, American Arbitration Association, 1986—. [Lt., USNR; active duty, 1969-72]. ***PRACTICE AREAS:*** Corporate; Securities; Mergers and Acquisitions; Finance; Construction. ***Email:*** jmiller@rbh.com

ROBERT S. LILIEN, admitted to bar, 1975, North Carolina, U.S. District Court, Western and Middle Districts of North Carolina and U.S. Tax Court. *Education:* Duke University (A.B., 1969); University of North Carolina at Chapel Hill (J.D., with honors, 1975). Order of the Coif. Articles Editor, North Carolina Law Review, 1974-1975. American Institute of Certified Public Accountants. Vice President and Tax Counsel, Duke Power, 1993-1997. General Counsel, Corporate and Energy Services, Duke Energy Corporation, 1997-1999. Senior Vice President, Duke Energy Corporation and President Duke Ventures, 1999-2002. Chairman and CEO, Crescent Resources, 1998-2002. Certified Public Accountant, North Carolina. [1st Lt., U.S. Army and Army Reserve, 1969-1975]. ***PRACTICE AREAS:*** Corporate Law; Real Estate; Mergers and Acquisitions; Taxation; Venture Capital; Private Equity. ***Email:*** rlilien@rbh.com

PETER C. BUCK, admitted to bar, 1976, North Carolina. *Education:* Duke University (A.B., 1969; J.D., 1976). Order of the Coif. Editor-in-Chief, *Duke Law Journal,* 1975-76. Deputy General Counsel, Duke Energy Corporation, 1996-1998. ***PRACTICE AREAS:*** Corporate; Banking and Finance; Mergers and Acquisitions; Energy. ***Email:*** pbuck@rbh.com

ROBERT M. BRYAN, admitted to bar, 1976, Ohio; 1978, North Carolina. *Education:* University of Virginia (A.B., 1971; J.D., 1976). Order of the Coif. Member, Editorial Board, *Virginia Law Review,* 1974-76. ***PRACTICE AREAS:*** Corporate Law; Intellectual Property Law; Technology Law. ***Email:*** bbryan@rbh.com

CHRISTY EVE REID, admitted to bar, 1976, North Carolina. *Education:* Smith College (B.A., 1973) Phi Beta Kappa; University of North Carolina (J.D., with honors, 1976). Note and Comment Editor, *North Carolina Law Review,* 1975-76. Law Clerk to The Hon. J. William Copeland, North Carolina Supreme Court, 1976-77. *Member:* North Carolina Bar Association (Member, Board of Governors, 1996-99; Chair, Estate Planning and Fiduciary Law Section, 1995-96); North Carolina State Bar (Member, Board of Legal Specialization, 1997-00); Charlotte Estate Planning Council (Member, Executive Committee, 1994-01). Fellow, American College of Trust and Estate Counsel. (Board Certified Specialist in Estate Planning and Probate Law, North Carolina State Board of Legal Specialization). ***PRACTICE AREAS:*** Trusts and Estates; Taxation. ***Email:*** creid@rbh.com

ROBERT G. GRIFFIN, admitted to bar, 1978, North Carolina. *Education:* University of North Carolina (A.B., with honors, 1975; J.D., with honors, 1978). Phi Beta Kappa; Order of the Coif. John Motley Morehead Scholar. Staff Member, *North Carolina Law Review,* 1976-77. John Motley Morehead Law Fellow. ***PRACTICE AREAS:*** Mergers and Acquisitions; Commercial Lending; Executive Compensation; Corporate. ***Email:*** rgriffin@rbh.com

EDWIN F. LUCAS III, admitted to bar, 1978, North Carolina. *Education:* University of North Carolina (A.B., 1972); University of Virginia (J.D., 1978). Phi Beta Kappa. John Motley Morehead Scholar. ***PRACTICE AREAS:*** Public Finance. ***Email:*** elucas@rbh.com

EVERETT J. BOWMAN, admitted to bar, 1979, Georgia; 1980, North Carolina. *Education:* Harvard University (A.B., summa cum laude, 1975; J.D., cum laude, 1979); Henry Fellow, Christ's College, Cambridge University, Cambridge, England, 1975-76. Phi Beta

(This Listing Continued)

Kappa. Law Clerk to The Hon. Gerald B. Tjoflat, United States Court of Appeals for the Fifth Circuit, 1979-80. Chair, Antitrust and Trade Regulation Law Section, North Carolina Bar Association, 1994-95. **PRACTICE AREAS:** Antitrust Litigation; Commercial Litigation; Health Care. **Email:** ebowman@rbh.com

CHARLES E. JOHNSON, admitted to bar, 1981, North Carolina. *Education:* Wake Forest University (B.A., summa cum laude, 1977); Harvard Law School (J.D., 1980). Phi Beta Kappa. Carswell Scholar. Member, Harvard Civil Rights-Civil Liberties Law Review, 1978-80. Law Clerk to The Honorable James B. McMillan of the United States District Court for the Western District of North Carolina, 1980-81. Member, Employment Law Specialty Committee, Board of Legal Specialization of the North Carolina State Bar. **PRACTICE AREAS:** Labor and Employment; Civil Litigation. **Email:** cejohnson@rbh.com

HAYNES P. LEA, admitted to bar, 1982, North Carolina. *Education:* University of North Carolina (B.A., 1977; M.B.A. and J.D., with honors, 1982). Order of the Coif. *University of North Carolina Law Review,* 1981-82. Business Manager, 1980-81 and Articles Editor, 1981-82, *North Carolina Journal of International Law and Commercial Regulation.* Certified Public Accountant, North Carolina, 1983. Member, Board of Advisors, UNC Tax Institute, 1993-95. **PRACTICE AREAS:** Corporate; Banking and Capital Markets; Venture Capital and Private Equity; Taxation. **Email:** hlea@rbh.com

CAROLINE WANNAMAKER SINK, admitted to bar, 1982, North Carolina. *Education:* Salem College (B.A., 1979); Washington and Lee University (J.D., cum laude, 1982). Order of the Coif. Note and Comment Editor, *Washington and Lee Law Review,* 1981-82. **PRACTICE AREAS:** Commercial Real Estate; Commercial Lending; Public Finance. **Email:** csink@rbh.com

HENRY H. RALSTON, admitted to bar, 1983, North Carolina. *Education:* University of North Carolina (B.A., with honors, 1980; J.D., with honors, 1983). Phi Eta Sigma; Phi Beta Kappa; Order of the Coif. *North Carolina Law Review,* 1981-82. **PRACTICE AREAS:** Corporate; Mergers and Acquisitions; Banking; Securities. **Email:** hralston@rbh.com

HERMAN SPENCE III, admitted to bar, 1982, North Carolina. *Education:* University of North Carolina (B.S., with honors, 1979; J.D., with high honors, 1982). Phi Beta Kappa; Beta Gamma Sigma; Order of the Coif. John Motley Morehead Law Fellow. Articles Editor, *North Carolina Law Review,* 1981-82. Law Clerk to The Hon. Edward A. Tamm, United States Court of Appeals, District of Columbia, 1982-83. **PRACTICE AREAS:** Taxation; Partnership; Tax Controversies. **Email:** hspence@rbh.com

BRENT A. TORSTRICK, admitted to bar, 1983, North Carolina. *Education:* Duke University (A.B., summa cum laude, 1980); University of Virginia (J.D., 1983). Phi Beta Kappa; Order of the Coif. Member, Editorial Board, *Virginia Law Review,* 1981-83. *Member:* North Carolina State Bar (Member, Real Property Specialization Committee, 1995—). (Board Certified Specialist in Real Property Law - Business, Commercial and Industrial Transactions, North Carolina State Board of Legal Specialization). **PRACTICE AREAS:** Commercial Real Estate; Commercial Lending; Shopping Center Development. **Email:** btorstrick@rbh.com

MARK W. MERRITT, admitted to bar, 1984, North Carolina. *Education:* University of North Carolina (B.A., 1979); University of Virginia (J.D., 1982). Phi Eta Sigma; Phi Beta Kappa; Order of the Coif. John Motley Morehead Scholar. Editor-in-Chief, *Virginia Law Review,* 1981-82. Law Clerk to The Hon. John Minor Wisdom, United States Court of Appeals for the Fifth Circuit, 1982-83. *Member:* Mecklenburg County Bar Association (Treasurer, 1996-98). Fellow, American College of Trial Lawyers. **PRACTICE AREAS:** Antitrust; Complex Litigation; Securities Litigation. **Email:** mmerritt@rbh.com

GARLAND S. CASSADA, admitted to bar, 1984, North Carolina. *Education:* University of Virginia (B.A., with distinction, 1980; J.D., 1984). Moot Court Board, 1983-84. **PRACTICE AREAS:** Commercial Litigation; Business Litigation; Bankruptcy. **Email:** gcassada@rbh.com

ROBERT W. FULLER, admitted to bar, 1983, North Carolina. *Education:* University of North Carolina (B.S., 1980); Duke University (J.D., with highest honors, 1983). Phi Beta Kappa; Beta Gamma Sigma; Order of the Coif. Editor-in-Chief, *Duke Law Journal,* 1982-83. Law Clerk to The Hon. James C. Hill, United States Court of Appeals for the Eleventh Circuit, 1983-84. **PRACTICE AREAS:** Business Litigation; Construction Litigation. **Email:** rfuller@rbh.com

KENT J. McCREADY, admitted to bar, 1984, North Carolina. *Education:* University of Delaware (B.A., 1980); University of North Carolina (J.D., with high honors, 1984). Order of the Coif. Editor-in-Chief, *North Carolina Law Review,* 1983-84. **PRACTICE AREAS:** Mergers and Acquisitions; Structured Banking and Finance; Corporate. **Email:** kmccready@rbh.com

DAVID C. WRIGHT III, admitted to bar, 1983, North Carolina. *Education:* University of North Carolina (B.A., with highest honors, 1980); University of Virginia (J.D., 1983). Phi Eta Sigma; Phi Beta Kappa; Order of the Coif. John Motley Morehead Scholar. Member, Editorial Board, 1981-82 and Executive Editor, 1982-83, *Virginia Law Review.* Law Clerk to The Hon. J. Dickson Phillips, Jr., United States Court of Appeals for the Fourth Circuit, 1983-84. **PRACTICE AREAS:** Employment Litigation; Commercial Litigation; Class Action Litigation; Product Liability. **Email:** dwright@rbh.com

LOUIS A. BLEDSOE III, admitted to bar, 1985, North Carolina. *Education:* University of North Carolina (A.B., 1981); Harvard University (J.D., cum laude, 1984). Phi Beta Kappa. John Motley Morehead Scholar. Law Clerk to The Hon. Sam J. Ervin III, United States Court of Appeals for the Fourth Circuit, 1984-85. **PRACTICE AREAS:** Employment Counseling; Employment Litigation; Business Litigation. **Email:** lbledsoe@rbh.com

CHRISTOPHER W. LOEB, admitted to bar, 1984, North Carolina. *Education:* Davidson College (B.A., magna cum laude, 1979); Duke University (J.D., with highest honors, 1984). Phi Beta Kappa. Order of the Coif. Note and Comment Editor, *Duke Law Journal,* 1983-84. Law Clerk to The Hon. J. Dickson Phillips, Jr., United States Court of Appeals for the Fourth Circuit, 1984-85. **PRACTICE AREAS:** Commercial Real Estate; Environmental. **Email:** cloeb@rbh.com

D. BLAINE SANDERS, admitted to bar, 1984, North Carolina. *Education:* Davidson College (A.B., magna cum laude, 1981); Vanderbilt University (J.D., 1984). Phi Beta Kappa. Member, Vanderbilt Law Review. Law Clerk to The Honorable Edward Rafeedie,

(This Listing Continued)

United States District Court for the Central District of California, 1984-1985. Formerly Associate General Counsel with United Dominion Industries, 1998-2001. **PRACTICE AREAS:** Civil and Commercial Litigation; Intellectual Property; Sports and Entertainment.

RICHARD W. GIBSON, JR., admitted to bar, 1983, North Carolina. *Education:* University of North Carolina (B.A., 1980; J.D., with honors, 1983). Phi Eta Sigma; Phi Beta Kappa. Staff Member, 1981-82 and Business Manager, 1982-83, *North Carolina Journal of International Law and Commercial Regulation.* . **PRACTICE AREAS:** Employee Compensation; Employee Benefits; ERISA. **Email:** rgibson@rbh.com

STOKELY G. CALDWELL, JR., admitted to bar, 1986, North Carolina. *Education:* Hampden-Sydney College (B.A., 1978); Washington and Lee University (J.D., summa cum laude, 1986). Omicron Delta Kappa; Order of the Coif. Recipient, John W. Davis Award. Note and Comment Editor, *Washington and Lee Law Review,* 1985-86. **PRACTICE AREAS:** Corporate; Banking and Capital Markets; Mergers and Acquisitions; Sports Licensing. **Email:** scaldwell@rbh.com

STEPHEN M. LYNCH, admitted to bar, 1986, North Carolina. *Education:* Alfred University (B.S., summa cum laude, 1982; M.S., 1983); Duke University (J.D., with high honors, 1986). Order of the Coif. Editor-in-Chief, *Duke Law Journal,* 1985-86. **PRACTICE AREAS:** Securities; Mergers and Acquisitions; Venture Capital; Corporate. **Email:** slynch@rbh.com

R. STEVEN DeGEORGE, admitted to bar, 1986, Ohio and Wisconsin; 1994, North Carolina. *Education:* University of Wisconsin (B.A., with high honors, 1982; J.D., with honors, 1985). Member, Board of Advisors, *Chemical Waste Litigation Reporter.* . **PRACTICE AREAS:** Environmental Litigation and Counseling; Commercial Litigation. **Email:** sdegeorge@rbh.com

JANE S. RATTEREE, admitted to bar, 1986, North Carolina. *Education:* Davidson College (A.B., magna cum laude, 1980); University of North Carolina (J.D., with honors, 1986). Phi Eta Sigma; Phi Beta Kappa; Order of the Coif. Articles Editor, *North Carolina Law Review,* 1985-86. Law Clerk to The Hon. Sam J. Ervin, III, United States Court of Appeals for the Fourth Circuit, 1986-87. **PRACTICE AREAS:** Commercial Real Estate; Commercial Lending; Financial Institutions Law. **Email:** jratteree@rbh.com

ROBERT E. HARRINGTON, admitted to bar, 1989, Louisiana and District of Columbia; 1999, North Carolina. *Education:* Duke University (A.B., magna cum laude, 1984; J.D., with high honors, 1987). Angier B. Duke Memorial Scholar. Member, 1985-1987, and Notes Editor, 1986-1987, *Alaska Law Review.* Law Clerk to the Hon. Martin L.C. Feldman, Judge, U.S. District Court, Eastern District of Louisiana, 1987-1988. **PRACTICE AREAS:** Commercial and Civil Litigation; Class Action Litigation. **Email:** rharrington@rbh.com

JULIE ZYDRON GRIGGS, born Portsmouth, Virginia, 1962; admitted to bar, 1987, North Carolina; 1988, Virginia. *Education:* College of William & Mary (B.A., 1984); University of Virginia (J.D., 1987). Phi Beta Kappa. Fellow, American College of Trust and Estate Counsel. (Board Certified Specialist in Estate Planning and Probate Law, North Carolina State Board of Legal Specialization). **PRACTICE AREAS:** Trusts and Estates; Federal Taxation; State Taxation. **Email:** jgriggs@rbh.com

BENJAMIN W. BALDWIN, admitted to bar, 1988, North Carolina. *Education:* University of North Carolina (B.A., 1984; J.D., with honors, 1988). Phi Eta Sigma; Phi Beta Kappa; Order of the Coif. Note and Comment Editor, *North Carolina Law Review,* 1987-88. **PRACTICE AREAS:** Corporate; Banking and Capital Markets; Mergers and Acquisitions. **Email:** bbaldwin@rbh.com

JOHN B. GARVER, III, admitted to bar, 1983, North Carolina. *Education:* United States Military Academy (B.S., 1975); Duke University (J.D., with honors, 1983); Judge Advocate General's School (LL.M., with honors, 1987). Assistant Professor of Law and Chief of Communications Branch and Writing Office, JAG School, 1987-89. [Lieutenant Colonel, USAR; active duty, 1975-1989]. **PRACTICE AREAS:** Public Finance; Corporate; Banking and Capital Markets. **Email:** jgarver@rbh.com

EDWARD F. HENNESSEY, IV, admitted to bar, 1988, North Carolina. *Education:* Dartmouth College (A.B., cum laude, 1984); Cornell University (J.D., cum laude, 1988). Note Editor, *Cornell International Law Journal,* 1987-1988. Law Clerk to The Hon. Sam J. Ervin, III, United States Court of Appeals for the Fourth Circuit, 1988-89. **PRACTICE AREAS:** Employment Litigation; Construction Litigation; Commercial Litigation. **Email:** thennessey@rbh.com

RICHARD L. MACK, admitted to bar, 1989, North Carolina. *Education:* University of North Carolina (B.A., 1985); University of Virginia (J.D., 1989). Phi Beta Kappa; Order of the Coif. Managing Editor, *Virginia Tax Review,* 1988-1989. Member, Editorial Board, *Virginia Law Review,* 1988-1989. **PRACTICE AREAS:** Corporate; Banking and Finance; Mergers and Acquisitions. **Email:** rmack@rbh.com

ALLEN K. ROBERTSON, admitted to bar, 1988, North Carolina. *Education:* University of North Carolina (B.A., with highest honors, 1985); Harvard University (J.D., magna cum laude, 1988). Phi Beta Kappa. John Motley Morehead Scholar; Harry S. Truman Scholar. Law Clerk to The Hon. James B. McMillan, United States District Court for the Western District of North Carolina, 1988-89. **PRACTICE AREAS:** Public Finance; Banking and Finance; Bankruptcy. **Email:** arobertson@rbh.com

STUART H. JOHNSON, admitted to bar, 1989, North Carolina. *Education:* Carleton College (B.A., 1973); Boston University (M.A., 1976; Ph.D., 1980) University Fellow; University of North Carolina (J.D., with high honors, 1989). Order of the Coif. Member, 1987-88 and Editor-in-Chief, 1988-89, *North Carolina Law Review.* Instructor, Massachusetts Institute of Technology, 1978-80. Visiting Assistant Professor, Connecticut College, 1982-84. **PRACTICE AREAS:** Corporate; Energy; Mergers and Acquisitions. **Email:** sjohnson@rbh.com

KAREN A. GLEDHILL, admitted to bar, 1988, Massachusetts; 1991, North Carolina; 1992, South Carolina. *Education:* University of South Carolina (B.A., magna cum laude, 1980; M.B.A., 1984); Columbia University (J.D., 1988). *Columbia Law Review,* 1986-87. **PRACTICE AREAS:** Health Care; Corporate; Mergers and Acquisitions. **Email:** kgledhill@rbh.com

(This Listing Continued)

ROBINSON, BRADSHAW & HINSON, P.A., Charlotte—Continued

ALLAIN C. ANDRY, IV, admitted to bar, 1986, Minnesota; 1987, North Carolina. *Education:* Duke University (A.B., summa cum laude, 1982); Stanford University (J.D., with honors, 1986). Phi Beta Kappa; Order of the Coif. ***PRACTICE AREAS:*** Corporate; Banking and Capital Markets; Mergers and Acquisitions; Energy. ***Email:*** aandry@rbh.com

PATRICK S. BRYANT, admitted to bar, 1990, Georgia; 1992, North Carolina. *Education:* Vanderbilt University (B.A., summa cum laude, 1985; J.D., 1989). Order of the Coif. Articles Editor, *Vanderbilt Law Review,* 1988-89. Law Clerk to The Hon. Kenneth F. Ripple, U.S. Court of Appeals for the Seventh Circuit, 1989-90. ***PRACTICE AREAS:*** Securities; Mergers and Acquisitions; Corporate. ***Email:*** pbryant@rbh.com

DAVID W. DABBS, admitted to bar, 1990, North Carolina. *Education:* Wake Forest University (B.S., magna cum laude, 1984); Duke University (J.D., with highest honors, 1990). Phi Beta Kappa; Order of the Coif. Editorial Staff, *Law and Contemporary Problems.* Certified Public Accountant, North Carolina, 1986. ***PRACTICE AREAS:*** Corporate; Securities; Mergers and Acquisitions. ***Email:*** ddabbs@rbh.com

JULIE C. CHIU, admitted to bar, 1989, California; 1994, North Carolina. *Education:* University of North Carolina (B.A., with highest honors, 1984); Harvard University (J.D., cum laude, 1988); University of Stockholm (Diploma in Post-Graduate Legal Studies, with distinction, 1989). Phi Beta Kappa. Fulbright Scholar. ***PRACTICE AREAS:*** Commercial Real Estate. ***Email:*** jchiu@rbh.com

DAVID M. SCHILLI, admitted to bar, 1988, Missouri; 1991, North Carolina. *Education:* Furman University (B.A., cum laude, 1985); Washington and Lee University (J.D., magna cum laude, 1988). Order of the Coif. Executive Editor, *Washington and Lee Law Review,* 1987-88. Law Clerk to The Honorable Robert D. Potter, U.S. District Court for the Western District of North Carolina, 1988-90. Law Clerk to The Hon. George R. Hodges, U.S. Bankruptcy Court for the Western District of North Carolina, 1990-91. ***PRACTICE AREAS:*** Bankruptcy; Workouts; Commercial Litigation. ***Email:*** dschilli@rbh.com

WILLIAM W. TOOLE, admitted to bar, 1989, North Carolina; 1990, Maryland; 1992, Virginia. *Education:* Haverford College (B.A., 1982); Wake Forest University (J.D., 1989; M.B.A., with distinction, 1989). Law Clerk to The Hon. Louis B. Meyer, North Carolina Supreme Court, 1989-90. ***PRACTICE AREAS:*** Environmental Litigation; Environmental Counseling. ***Email:*** wtoole@rbh.com

ROBERT S. McLEAN, admitted to bar, 1991, Georgia; 1994, North Carolina. *Education:* Davidson College (B.A., 1986); University of North Carolina (M.B.A., 1991; J.D., with honors, 1991). Omicron Delta Epsilon; Omicron Delta Kappa; Order of the Coif. *North Carolina Law Review,* 1988-91. ***PRACTICE AREAS:*** Corporate; Mergers and Acquisitions; Intellectual Property. ***Email:*** rmclean@rbh.com

S. GRAHAM ROBINSON, admitted to bar, 1993, North Carolina. *Education:* University of North Carolina (B.A., with highest honors, 1989; J.D., with honors, 1993). Order of the Coif. *North Carolina Law Review,* 1991-92. ***PRACTICE AREAS:*** Mergers and Acquisitions; Banking and Capital Markets; Corporate. ***Email:*** grobinson@rbh.com

JULIAN H. WRIGHT, JR., admitted to bar, 1992, North Carolina. *Education:* Davidson College (A.B., magna cum laude, 1987); Vanderbilt University (J.D. and M.Div., 1992). Phi Beta Kappa; Omicron Delta Kappa; Order of the Coif. Divinity School Founders Medal. Patrick Wilson Scholar. Editor-in-Chief, *Vanderbilt Law Review,* 1989-90. Law Clerk to The Hon. J. Harvie Wilkinson III, U.S. Court of Appeals for the Fourth Circuit, 1992-93. ***PRACTICE AREAS:*** Employment Litigation; Civil Litigation; Commercial Litigation. ***Email:*** jwright@rbh.com

STEPHAN J. WILLEN, admitted to bar, 1991, New Jersey; 1992, Virginia; 1997, North Carolina. *Education:* University of Michigan (B.A., 1988); Duke University (J.D., 1991). ***PRACTICE AREAS:*** Banking and Capital Markets; Mergers and Acquisitions; Corporate. ***Email:*** swillen@rbh.com

MATTHEW S. CHURCHILL, admitted to bar, 1994, New York; 1997, North Carolina. *Education:* Duke University (A.B., magna cum laude, 1988) Phi Beta Kappa; Stanford University (J.D., 1993). *Stanford Law Review,* 1991-93. ***PRACTICE AREAS:*** Corporate; Mergers and Acquisitions; Banking and Capital Markets; Securities. ***Email:*** mchurchill@rbh.com

JOHN M. HERRING, admitted to bar, 1994, North Carolina. *Education:* University of North Carolina (B.S., 1991; J.D., with honors, 1994). Order of the Coif. *North Carolina Law Review,* 1992-93. ***PRACTICE AREAS:*** Corporate; Mergers and Acquisitions; Securities; Banking and Capital Markets; Venture Capital and Private Equity. ***Email:*** jherring@rbh.com

LAWRENCE C. MOORE, III, admitted to bar, 1995, North Carolina. *Education:* Duke University (B.A., summa cum laude, 1990); Harvard University (J.D., magna cum laude, 1993). Phi Eta Sigma; Phi Beta Kappa. Editor, *Harvard Law Review,* 1992-93. Law Clerk to The Hon. Ed Carnes, U.S. Court of Appeals for the Eleventh Circuit, 1993-94. ***PRACTICE AREAS:*** Antitrust and Trade Regulation; Intellectual Property and Technology; Civil and Commercial Litigation. ***Email:*** lmoore@rbh.com

THOMAS P. HOLDERNESS, admitted to bar, 1990, North Carolina. *Education:* University of North Carolina (B.S., 1986; J.D., with honors, 1990). Order of the Coif. Moot Court Board, 1989-90. ***PRACTICE AREAS:*** Civil Litigation; Commercial Litigation; Construction Law; Fiduciary Litigation. ***Email:*** tholderness@rbh.com

DOUGLAS M. JARRELL, admitted to bar, 1994, North Carolina. *Education:* University of North Carolina (B.A., with distinction, 1991; J.D., with high honors, 1994). Phi Beta Kappa; Order of the Coif. Articles Editor, *North Carolina Law Review,* 1993-94. Law Clerk to The Hon. Ed Carnes, U.S. Court of Appeals for the Eleventh Circuit, 1994-95. ***PRACTICE AREAS:*** Commercial Litigation; Employment Litigation. ***Email:*** djarrell@rbh.com

AMY K. JOHNSON, admitted to bar, 1994, North Carolina. *Education:* University of Michigan (B.A., with high distinction, 1991) Beta Gamma Sigma; University of North Carolina (J.D., with highest honors, 1994). Order of the Coif. Davis Society. Editor-in-Chief, *North Carolina Law Review,* 1993-94. Law Clerk to the Hon. J. Dickson Phillips, Jr., United States Court of Appeals for the Fourth Circuit, 1994-95. ***PRACTICE AREAS:*** Public Finance. ***Email:*** ajohnson@rbh.com

LAURA C. SMITH, admitted to bar, 1995, North Carolina. *Education:* University of North Carolina (A.B., Political Science and International Studies, with honors and highest distinction, 1992) Phi Beta Kappa; Yale University (J.D., 1995). ***PRACTICE AREAS:*** Corporate; Banking and Capital Markets; Securities. ***Email:*** lsmith@rbh.com

ALICE PINCKNEY ADAMS, admitted to bar, 1997, North Carolina. *Education:* University of Tennessee (B.A., summa cum laude, 1993; J.D., summa cum laude, 1997). Phi Beta Kappa; Order of the Coif; Moot Court Board, 1996-97. ***PRACTICE AREAS:*** Banking and Finance; Public Finance. ***Email:*** aadams@rbh.com

DAVID J. CLARK, admitted to bar, 1977, Georgia; 1982, New Hampshire; 1988, Pennsylvania; 2000, North Carolina. *Education:* Dartmouth University (B.A., 1973); University of Texas (J.D., 1977). ***PRACTICE AREAS:*** Construction; Corporate; Intellectual Property and Technology; International. ***Email:*** dclark@rbh.com

JEFFREY C. HART, admitted to bar, 1997, North Carolina. *Education:* Davidson College (B.A., with honors, cum laude, 1994), Ken Kelley Scholar, Phi Beta Kappa; Duke University (J.D., 1997). ***PRACTICE AREAS:*** Venture Capital and Private Equity; Mergers and Acquisitions; Corporate. ***Email:*** jhart@rbh.com

JEFFREY A. HENSON, admitted to bar, 1992, North Carolina. *Education:* United States Naval Academy (B.S., 1985); Duke University (J.D., with honors, 1992). Order of the Coif. Managing Editor, *Duke Law Journal,* 1991-92. ***PRACTICE AREAS:*** Corporate; Banking and Capital Markets. ***Email:*** jhenson@rbh.com

RICHARD S. STARLING, admitted to bar, 1996, North Carolina. *Education:* University of Virginia (B.A., with distinction, 1993; J.D., 1996). Phi Beta Kappa. Jefferson Scholar. Order of the Coif. Editorial Board, *Virginia Law Review,* 1994-96. Law Clerk to The Hon. Richard E. Williams, United States District Court for the Eastern District of Virginia, 1996-97. ***PRACTICE AREAS:*** Mergers and Acquisitions; Corporate and Commercial Law; Venture Capital and Private Equity. ***Email:*** rstarling@rbh.com

KRISTA R. BOWEN, admitted to bar, 1998, North Carolina. *Education:* West Virginia University (B.S.B.Ad., summa cum laude, 1994); Washington & Lee University (J.D., summa cum laude, 1997). Phi Beta Kappa. Recipient, John W. Davis Award. Lead Articles Editor, *Washington & Lee Law Review.* Law Clerk to the Hon. H. Emory Widener, Jr., United States Court of Appeals for the Fourth Circuit, 1997-98. ***PRACTICE AREAS:*** Banking and Capital Markets; Corporate; Securities. ***Email:*** kbowen@rbh.com

THOMAS J. MOLONY, admitted to bar, 1998, North Carolina. *Education:* Washington and Lee University (B.S., summa cum laude, 1993; J.D., summa cum laude, 1998). Phi Beta Kappa; Order of the Coif. Managing Editor, *Washington and Lee Law Review,* 1997-98. ***PRACTICE AREAS:*** Banking and Capital Markets; Bankruptcy; Corporate. ***Email:*** tmolony@rbh.com

STEVEN D. NEWMARK, admitted to bar, 1996, North Carolina. *Education:* College of William and Mary (B.A., magna cum laude, 1993); University of Virginia (J.D., 1996). Order of the Coif. Editorial Board Member, *Virginia Law Review, Virginia Tax Review.* Law Clerk to the Hon. W. Earl Britt, United States District Court for the Eastern District of North Carolina, 1996-1997. Law Clerk to the Hon. J. Dickson Phillips, Jr., United States Court of Appeals for the Fourth Circuit, 1997-98. ***PRACTICE AREAS:*** Corporate; Intellectual Property and Technology; Mergers and Acquisitions; Venture Capital and Private Equity. ***Email:*** snewmark@rbh.com

W. SCOTT DOVE, admitted to bar, 1999, New York; 2000, North Carolina. *Education:* Wake Forest University (B.A., summa cum laude, 1993); New York University School of Law (J.D., cum laude, 1997). Phi Beta Kappa. [Sgt., U.S. Army, 1986-1989]. ***PRACTICE AREAS:*** Corporate; Mergers and Acquisitions; Banking and Capital Markets. ***Email:*** sdove@rbh.com

TILMAN THOMAS GATES, admitted to bar, 1998, Maryland; 2000, North Carolina. *Education:* Duke University (A.B., cum laude, 1992; J.D., cum laude, 1998); Johns Hopkins University (M.S. in Real Estate, 1996). Special Editor, Harvard Journal of Law and Public Policy, 1997-1998. ***LANGUAGES:*** Spanish. ***PRACTICE AREAS:*** Real Estate. ***Email:*** tgates@rbh.com

KELLY LUONGO LOVING, admitted to bar, 1998, Georgia; 2000, North Carolina. *Education:* Duke University (B.A., 1993); University of Virginia (J.D., 1998). [Lt. JG., U.S. Navy, 1993-1995]. ***PRACTICE AREAS:*** Mergers and Acquisitions; Corporate; Banking and Capital Markets; Securities. ***Email:*** kloving@rbh.com

ASSOCIATES

SUSAN I. McCRORY, admitted to bar, 1981, Mississippi; 1985, North Carolina. *Education:* University of Mississippi (B.A., 1978; J.D., with honors, 1981). Comment Editor, *Mississippi Law Journal,* 1980-81. ***PRACTICE AREAS:*** Tax; Trusts; Estate Planning. ***Email:*** smccrory@rbh.com

ARTHUR E. MOREHEAD, IV, admitted to bar, 1996, South Carolina; 2001, North Carolina. *Education:* Davidson College (B.A., 1993); University of South Carolina (J.D., 1996); University of Miami (LL.M. in Estate Planning, 2000). ***PRACTICE AREAS:*** Trusts and Estates; Federal Taxation; State Taxation. ***Email:*** amorehead@rbh.com

DANIEL F. BASNIGHT, admitted to bar, 1998, Virginia; 1999, North Carolina. *Education:* University of Virginia (B.A., 1975; J.D., 1998); Virginia Tech (M.B.A., 1979); Old Dominion University (M.A. in International Studies, 1990). Order of the Coif. Dillard Fellow. ***PRACTICE AREAS:*** Litigation. ***Email:*** dbasnight@rbh.com

CARL R. BOEHM, admitted to bar, 1999, North Carolina. *Education:* Anderson University (B.A., 1981); Southern Methodist University (M.B.A., 1988); Duke University (J.D., 1999). Article Editor, *Duke Law Journal,* 1998-1999. Certified Public Accountant, Texas, 1983. ***PRACTICE AREAS:*** Employee Benefits; Corporate; Commercial Law. ***Email:*** cboehm@rbh.com

ANTHONY S. KETRON, admitted to bar, 1999, North Carolina and U.S. District Court, Western District of North Carolina. *Education:* United States Military Academy (B.S., 1988); University of Virginia (J.D., 1998). Order of the Coif. Dillard Scholar. Man-

(This Listing Continued)

aging Editor, Journal of Law and Politics. *Member:* North Carolina and American Bar Associations. [Capt., USAR, 1988—]. ***PRACTICE AREAS:*** Civil and Commercial Litigation; Bankruptcy; Class Action Litigation. ***Email:*** aketron@rbh.com

WILLIAM K. PACKARD, admitted to bar, 1999, North Carolina. *Education:* Duke University (A.B., 1995); University of North Carolina (J.D., with high honors, 1999). Order of the Coif. Articles Editor, North Carolina Law Review. ***PRACTICE AREAS:*** Real Estate; Bankruptcy. ***Email:*** wpackard@rbh.com

DIANNE CHIPPS BAILEY, admitted to bar, 1996, California; 2000, New York; 2001, North Carolina. *Education:* University of California, Berkeley (B.A., high honors, 1992); Georgetown University (J.D., cum laude, 1995). Adjunct Professor, Georgetown University Law Center, 1997-1998. ***PRACTICE AREAS:*** Corporate; Non Profit Organizations; Banking and Capital Markets; Venture Capital and Private Equity. ***Email:*** dbailey@rbh.com

KATHERINE GORDON MAYNARD, admitted to bar, 1999, North Carolina; 2000, Kentucky. *Education:* Wake Forest University (B.A., 1995); University of Louisville Louis D. Brandeis School of Law (J.D., 2000). Member, Brandeis Society. Senior Editor, Brandeis Law Journal. ***PRACTICE AREAS:*** Civil and Commerical Litigation; Securities Litigation. ***Email:*** kmaynard@rbh.com

SCOTT W. GAYLORD, admitted to bar, 1999, North Carolina. *Education:* Colgate University (B.A., 1990); University of North Carolina at Chapel Hill (M.A., 1993; Ph.D., 1996); University of Notre Dame (J.D., 1999). Phi Beta Kappa. Williams Fellowship; Kiley Fellow. Book Review Editor, Notre Dame Law Review, 1998-1999. Recipient, Students Undergraduate Teaching Award. Law Clerk to the Honorable Edith H. Jones, Fifth Circuit. ***PRACTICE AREAS:*** Civil and Commercial Litigation; Bankruptcy; Construction. ***Email:*** sgaylord@rbh.com

CHARLES R. LEWIS, admitted to bar, 1999, North Carolina and U.S. District Court, Eastern District of North Carolina; 2001, U.S. District Court, Western District of North Carolina. *Education:* North Carolina State University (B.S.A.E., 1987; M.S.M.E., 1990); University of North Carolina at Chapel Hill (J.D., with high honors, 1999). Member, Order of the Coif. Member, North Carolina Law Review. ***PRACTICE AREAS:*** Banking and Capital Markets; Corporate; Mergers and Acquisitions. ***Email:*** clewis@rbh.com

BLAKE W. THOMAS, admitted to bar, 2000, North Carolina. *Education:* Williams College (B.A., 1997); Harvard University (J.D., cum laude, 2000). Phi Beta Kappa. ***PRACTICE AREAS:*** Commercial Litigation; Antitrust; Environmental. ***Email:*** bthomas@rbh.com

ANGELIQUE R. VINCENT, admitted to bar, 2000, North Carolina. *Education:* Duke University (B.A., summa cum laude, 1997); Harvard University (J.D., 2000). ***PRACTICE AREAS:*** Civil Litigation; Commercial Litigation; Employment and Labor. ***Email:*** avincent@rbh.com

DEBRA B. BINGHAM, admitted to bar, 2000, North Carolina. *Education:* University of North Carolina (B.A., 1997); Wake Forest University (J.D., cum laude, 2000). Order of the Coif. Executive Board Member, Wake Forest Moot Court Board, 1998-2000. Senior Articles Editor, Wake Forest Law Review, 1999-2000. Law Clerk to The Honorable William L. Osteen, Sr., United States District Court for the Middle District of North Carolina, 2000-2001. ***PRACTICE AREAS:*** Civil and Commercial Litigation; Employment. ***Email:*** dbingham@rbh.com

JAMES H. BINGHAM, JR., admitted to bar, 2000, North Carolina. *Education:* Harvard University (A.B., magna cum laude, 1996); Duke University (J.D., cum laude, 2000). Law Clerk to The Honorable N. Carlton Tilley, Jr., Chief Judge, Middle District of North Carolina, 2000-2001. ***PRACTICE AREAS:*** Civil and Commercial Litigation; Employment. ***Email:*** jbingham@rbh.com

LAURA CONSIDINE BUDZICHOWSKI, admitted to bar, 2002, North Carolina. *Education:* University of Notre Dame (B.A., magna cum laude, 1995); University of Portland (M.A.T., 1997); University of Michigan (J.D., cum laude, 2001). Phi Beta Kappa. Associate Editor, Michigan Journal of Law Reform, 2000-2001. ***LANGUAGES:*** Spanish. ***PRACTICE AREAS:*** Corporate and Commercial Law. ***Email:*** lbudzichowski@rbh.com

MARK O. HENRY, admitted to bar, 2000, North Carolina; 2001, District of Columbia. *Education:* The Ohio State University (B.S.B.A., summa cum laude, 1994); University of North Carolina at Chapel Hill (J.D., with honors, 2000). Order of the Coif. Certified Public Accountant; Certified Management Accountant. ***PRACTICE AREAS:*** Corporate; Banking and Capital Markets; Mergers and Acquisitions; Securities. ***Email:*** mhenry@rbh.com

RICHARD C. DUNN, admitted to bar, 2002, North Carolina. *Education:* Duke University (B.A., magna cum laude, 1995); William & Mary School of Law (J.D., 2002). Order of the Coif. Member, William & Mary Law Review, 2001-2002. ***PRACTICE AREAS:*** Corporate and Commercial Law; Banking and Capital Markets; Intellectual Property. ***Email:*** rdunn@rbh.com

B. CHAD EWING, admitted to bar, 2002, North Carolina. *Education:* Furman University (B.A., magna cum laude, 1988); University of Virginia (J.D., 2001). Order of the Coif. Dillard Fellow. Executive Editor, Journal of Law & Politcs, 2000-2001. Law Clerk to The Honorable B. Avant Edenfield, US District Court Judge, South District of Georgia, 2001-2002. ***PRACTICE AREAS:*** Civil and Commerical Litigation. ***Email:*** cewing@rbh.com

LINDA KONERDING MONTGOMERY, admitted to bar, 2002, North Carolina. *Education:* Georgetown University (A.B., summa cum laude, 1990); University of Virginia (J.D., 2002). Phi Beta Kappa. Research and Projects Editor, Virginia Journal of International Law, 2001-2002. ***PRACTICE AREAS:*** Corporate and Commercial Law; Health Care. ***Email:*** lmontgomery@rbh.com

JONATHAN C. KRISKO, admitted to bar, 2002, North Carolina. *Education:* Duke University (B.A., 1995); University of North Carolina at Chapel Hill (J.D., with high honors, 2002). Order of the Coif. Editor-in-Chief, North Carolina Law Review, 2001-2002. Law Clerk to the Hon. Karen LeCraft Henderson, U.S. Court of Appeals, District of Columbia Circuit, 2002-2003. ***PRACTICE AREAS:*** Civil and Commercial Litigation. ***Email:*** jkrisko@rbh.com

KRISTOFFER B. SHEPARD, admitted to bar, 2003, North Carolina. *Education:* University of North Carolina at Chapel Hill (B.A., 1995); Emory University (M.A., 1999; Ph.D., 2001); University of Virginia (J.D., 2003). Phi Beta Kappa. Member, Editorial Board, Virginia Tax Review, 2002-2003. ***PRACTICE AREAS:*** Corporate and Commercial Law. ***Email:*** kshepard@rbh.com

ANDREW W.J. TARR, admitted to bar, 2003, North Carolina. *Education:* University of North Carolina at Chapel Hill (B.A., 2000; J.D., with honors, 2003). Order of the Coif. Executive Comments Editor, North Carolina Law Review, 2002-2003. ***PRACTICE AREAS:*** Civil and Commercial Litigation; Bankruptcy. ***Email:*** atarr@rbh.com

ERIN G. PALMER, admitted to bar, 2004, North Carolina. *Education:* Northwestern University (B.A., 1996); University of North Carolina at Chapel Hill (J.D., with honors, 2004). ***Email:*** epalmer@rbh.com

JENNIFER FISHER REVELLE, admitted to bar, 2004, North Carolina. *Education:* Washington & Lee University (B.A., summa cum laude, 2000); Yale University (J.D., 2002). Phi Beta Kappa. ***Email:*** jrevelle@rbh.com

JON R. JORDAN, admitted to bar, 2004, North Carolina. *Education:* Wake Forest University (B.A., summa cum laude, 2001; J.D., cum laude, 2004). Phi Beta Kappa. Member, Wake Forest Law Review, 2002-2003. ***Email:*** jjordan@rbh.com

HEIDI E. ROYAL, admitted to bar, 2004, North Carolina. *Education:* Rhodes College (B.S., 2001); University of Georgia (J.D., summa cum laude, 2004). Phi Beta Kappa. Notes Editor, Georgia Law Review, 2003-2004. ***Email:*** hroyal@rbh.com

JAYNE C. HUNTER, admitted to bar, 1990, North Carolina. *Education:* University of North Carolina (B.A., 1986; J.D., 1989). *Member:* North Carolina and American (Member, International Property Law Section) Bar Associations. ***PRACTICE AREAS:*** Intellectual Property; Technology Law; Corporate Law. ***Email:*** jhunter@rbh.com

OF COUNSEL

ROBERT W. BRADSHAW, JR., admitted to bar, 1957, North Carolina. *Education:* Duke University (A.B., 1954; LL.B., 1957). Phi Beta Kappa; Omicron Delta Kappa; Delta Theta Phi; Order of the Coif. Editor-in-Chief, *Duke Law Journal,* 1956-57. ***PRACTICE AREAS:*** Estate Planning; Corporate; Commercial; Land Use Planning; Nonprofit Organizations Law. ***Email:*** rbradshaw@rbh.com

JOHN M. CONLEY, admitted to bar, 1977, Massachusetts; 1980, California; 1984, North Carolina. *Education:* Harvard College (A.B., 1971); Duke University (J.D., 1977; Ph.D., Anthropology, 1980). Phi Beta Kappa; Order of the Coif. Editor-in-Chief, *Duke Law Journal,* 1976-77. Visiting Professor, Boston College, 1981-82. Associate Professor, 1983-87, Professor of Law, 1987-93, Kenan Professor of Law, 1993—, University of North Carolina. ***PRACTICE AREAS:*** Litigation; Intellectual Property. ***Email:*** jconley@rbh.com

GUNDARS APERANS, admitted to bar, 1972, New York (Not admitted in North Carolina). *Education:* Dartmouth College (A.B., 1966); Columbia University (M.B.A., 1968); University of Virginia (J.D., 1971). ***PRACTICE AREAS:*** Public Finance. ***Email:*** gaperans@rbh.com

ROBERT W. ALLEN, admitted to bar, 1985, North Carolina. *Education:* University of North Carolina (A.B., 1981; J.D., 1985). Phi Delta Phi. ***PRACTICE AREAS:*** Real Estate Law. ***Email:*** rallen@rbh.com

THOMAS E. McNEILL, admitted to bar, 1988, North Carolina. *Education:* University of North Carolina at Chapel Hill (B.S.B.A., 1985); Wake Forest University (J.D., 1988). Recipient, American Jurisprudence Award in Property II. ***PRACTICE AREAS:*** Real Estate. ***Email:*** tmcneill@rbh.com

CARL E. JOHNSON, JR., admitted to bar, 1968, North Carolina. *Education:* Oberlin College (A.B., 1964); Duke University (J.D., 1968). Editorial Assistant, *Law and Contemporary Problems,* 1967-68. ***PRACTICE AREAS:*** Employee Compensation; Employee Benefits; ERISA. ***Email:*** cjohnson@rbh.com

REPRESENTATIVE CLIENTS: aaiPharma; Allied Capital Corporation; American Wholesale Insurance Group; Blue Cross Blue Shield of North Carolina; Bovis Lend Lease; Caraustar Industries, Inc.; Carolina Panthers Corporation; The Charlotte-Mecklenburg Hospital Authority; CommScope, Inc.; Culp, Inc.; Duke Energy Corporation; EnPro Industries, Inc.; Faison & Associates, Inc.; Goodrich Corporation; Jeff Gordon Inc.; Martin Marietta Materials, Inc.; Mecklenburg County; National Gypsum Company; Parish Capital Advisors, LLC; PCA International, Inc.; Springs Industries, Inc.; SPX Corporation; Stork Screens America, Inc.; The Cato Corporation; Wachovia.

ROBINSON LAW OFFICE

1125 EAST MOREHEAD STREET, SUITE 207
CHARLOTTE, NORTH CAROLINA 28204
Telephone: 704-373-0077
Fax: 704-332-1261
URL: http://www.jnrobinsonlaw.com
Email: jnrlaw@bellsouth.net
URL: http://www.jnrobinsonlawfirm.com

Civil Practice, Appellate Practice, Commercial Litigation, Complex Litigation, Business Litigation, Products Liability, Estate Litigation, Trust Litigation, Personal Injury, Construction Litigation, Professional Liability, Banking Litigation, Insurance Litigation, Federal Indian Law.

FIRM PROFILE: Robinson Law Office is a trial law firm engaged in handling serious, significant cases for individuals and businesses seriously injured or wronged. These cases include wrongful death, brain injury, spinal cord injury and other such serious or catastrophic injuries, as well as cases such as products liability, premises liability, will contest (caveat), trust suit, business litigation or other complex litigation.

J. NEIL ROBINSON, born 1958; admitted to bar, 1983, North Carolina. *Education:* University of North Carolina (B.A., with highest honors, 1980; J.D., 1983). Phi Eta Sigma; Phi Beta Kappa. Kenan Scholar; Johnston Scholar. Editor, North Carolina Law Review, 1982-1983. *Member:* North Carolina Bar Association (Member, Litigation Council Section); North Carolina Academy of Trial Lawyers; North Carolina Trial Lawyers Associa-

(This Listing Continued)

ROBINSON LAW OFFICE, Charlotte—Continued

tion; Association of Trial Lawyers of America; Million Dollar Advocates Forum. ***PRACTICE AREAS:*** Civil Litigation; Commercial Litigation; Estate Litigation; Product Liability Litigation; Wrongful Death; Personal Injury. ***Email:*** jnrlaw@bellsouth.net

LEGAL SUPPORT PERSONNEL

FRAN THRESHER, (Contract Paralegal)

REPRESENTATIVE CLIENTS: Aerial Devices, Inc; Bishop Brick and Construction Co.; Broad River Ventures; Cambridge Investments, Ltd.; D.A. Beam Enterprises, Ltd.; Information Technology Co.; The Learning Curve, Inc.; Safety Test and Equipment Co.; TRAVMED USA, Inc.; Wood/Chuck Chipper Corporation; Zulu Capital Corporation.

LAW OFFICES OF J. NEAL RODGERS, PLLC

(Formerly, Tim L. Harris and Associates).

4000 TUCKASEEGEE ROAD
CHARLOTTE, NORTH CAROLINA 28208
Telephone: 704-392-4111
Fax: 704-391-1905
Email: neal@jnrodgerslaw.com

Gastonia, North Carolina Office: 616 Cox Road. P.O. Box 249. Telephone: 704-864-3409. Fax: 704-853-1040.

Concord, North Carolina Office: 435 Church Street. Telephone: 704-795-9317. Fax: 704-795-5738

Personal Injury, Wrongful Death, Automobile Accidents, Medical Malpractice, Jail Injury Cases, Employment Law, Civil Rights.

J. NEAL RODGERS, born Tulsa, Oklahoma, May 17, 1953; admitted to bar, 1993, Texas; 1994, North Carolina, U.S. District Court, Western, Eastern and Middle Districts of North Carolina and U.S. Court of Appeals, 4th Circuit. *Education:* Ouachita Baptist University (B.A., 1976); Southwestern Baptist Theological Seminary (M.Div., 1980); Baylor University (PhD, 1985); University of Houston (J.D., 1993). *Member:* North Carolina State Bar; State Bar of Texas. (Resident). ***PRACTICE AREAS:*** Personal Injury; Section 1983; Medical Malpractice. ***Email:*** neal@jnrodgerslaw.com

VICKI BROWN ROWAN

1515 MOCKINGBIRD LANE, SUITE 400
CHARLOTTE, NORTH CAROLINA 28209
Telephone: 704-525-4110
Fax: 704-525-4301
Email: VBRowan@bellsouth.net
URL: http://www.vickibrowan.com

Concentrating in Employment Law, and General Civil Litigation in State and Federal Courts. Employment Discrimination, Sexual Harassment, Wage and Hours, Fair Labor Standards, Non-Compete Disputes, Family and Medical Leave, Severance Agreements, Americans with Disabilities Act, Wrongful Termination.

FIRM PROFILE: Vicki B. Rowan has practiced in Charlotte, NC since 1987. She established a sole practice in 1991, concentrating in the representation of employees in employment discrimination, sex harassment, FMLA, wage & hour, fair labor standards and non-compete disputes.

VICKI BROWN ROWAN, born Sumter, South Carolina, February 8, 1948; admitted to bar, 1987, North Carolina and U.S. District Court, Western District of North Carolina; 1989, U.S. Court of Appeals, Fourth Circuit; 1993, U.S. District Court, Middle District of North Carolina. *Education:* Tennessee Technological University (B.S., with high distinction, 1971); East Carolina University (M.S., with honors, 1978); University of Texas (J.D., with honors, 1987). Phi Alpha Delta. Member, Order of Barristers. *Member:* Mecklenburg County, North Carolina and American (Member, Employment Section) Bar Associations; North Carolina Academy of Trial Lawyers; North Carolina Association of Women Attorneys; National Employment Lawyers Association (NELA).

RUFF, BOND, COBB, WADE & BETHUNE, L.L.P.

Established in 1918

THE ADDISON BUILDING
831 EAST MOREHEAD STREET, SUITE 860
CHARLOTTE, NORTH CAROLINA 28202
Telephone: 704-377-1634
FAX: 704-342-3308

General Civil and Trial Practice.

MEMBERS OF FIRM

THOMAS C. RUFF, born Naxera, Virginia, July 16, 1919; admitted to bar, 1948, North Carolina. *Education:* Hampden-Sydney College (B.A., 1941); University of Virginia (LL.B., 1948). County Attorney, Mecklenburg County, 1960-1978. *Member:* Mecklenburg County and North Carolina Bar Associations; North Carolina State Bar. ***PRACTICE AREAS:*** Residential and Commercial Real Estate Law; Municipal Law.

LYN BOND, JR., born Tarboro, North Carolina, October 14, 1927; admitted to bar, 1954, North Carolina. *Education:* University of North Carolina (A.B., 1950; J.D., 1953). Phi Delta Phi. *Member:* Mecklenburg County, North Carolina and American Bar Associations; North Carolina State Bar. ***PRACTICE AREAS:*** Real Estate Law; Taxation Law; Estates Law; Trusts Law.

JAMES O. COBB, born Durham, North Carolina, February 28, 1927; admitted to bar, 1955, North Carolina. *Education:* The McCallie School; Davidson College (B.S., 1950); University of North Carolina (LL.B., 1955). Phi Alpha Delta. *Member:* Mecklenburg County (President, 1972-1973), North Carolina and American Bar Associations; North Carolina State Bar; Federal Judicial Conference For The Fourth Circuit (Permanent Member). ***PRACTICE AREAS:*** Civil Litigation. ***Email:*** jcobb@rbcwb.com

HAMLIN L. WADE, born Greensboro, North Carolina, February 26, 1930; admitted to bar, 1957, North Carolina; 1959, U.S. District Court, Western District of North Carolina. *Education:* Davidson College (B.S., 1952); University of North Carolina (J.D., with honors, 1957). Delta Theta Phi. Member, Board of Editors, North Carolina Law Review, 1955-1957. Research Assistant for Chief Justice J. Wallace Winborne, North Carolina Supreme Court, 1957-1958. *Member:* Mecklenburg County (President, 1982-1983), North Carolina and American Bar Associations; North Carolina State Bar. ***PRACTICE AREAS:*** Civil Litigation; Ad Valorem Taxation Law; Residential Real Estate; Commercial Real Estate. ***Email:*** hwade@rbcwb.com

MARVIN A. BETHUNE, born Charlotte, North Carolina, March 6, 1948; admitted to bar, 1973, North Carolina. *Education:* Davidson College (B.A., 1970); University of North Carolina (J.D., with honors, 1973). Order of the Coif. Member, The Order of Barristers. Staff Member, North Carolina Law Review, 1972-1973. Research Assistant for Associate Justice J. Frank Huskins, North Carolina Supreme Court, 1973-1974. County Attorney, Mecklenburg County, 1978—. *Member:* Mecklenburg County, North Carolina and American Bar Associations; North Carolina State Bar; North Carolina Association of County Attorneys (President, 1991-1992). ***PRACTICE AREAS:*** Local Government Law; Commercial Real Estate Law. ***Email:*** mbethune@rbcwb.com

ROBERT S. ADDEN, JR., born Charleston, South Carolina, May 25, 1957; admitted to bar, 1982, North Carolina. *Education:* The Citadel (B.S., with honors, 1979); University of North Carolina (J.D., with honors, 1982). Phi Kappa Phi. Member, The Order of Barristers. *Member:* Mecklenburg County, North Carolina and American Bar Associations; North Carolina State Bar. ***PRACTICE AREAS:*** Civil Litigation. ***Email:*** radden@rbcwb.com

JAMES D. DuPUY, born Charlotte, North Carolina, September 5, 1973; admitted to bar, 1999, North Carolina. *Education:* Davidson College (B.A., 1996); University of North Carolina (J.D., 1999). Staff Member, N.C.J. Int'l L. & Comm. Reg. *Member:* American Bar Association; MLB. ***PRACTICE AREAS:*** Local Government Law; Civil Litigation. ***Email:*** jdupuy@rbcwb.com

GENERAL COUNSEL FOR: Board of Commissioners of Mecklenburg County; Charlotte Merchants Foundation, Inc.; Crown Memorial Park; Express Properties, LLC; The Howey Co.; Howey Construction & Development; Laureldale Co., Inc.; Mecklenburg County ABC Board; New Millennium Digital, LLC; Vinson Enterprises; Vinson Realty Co.
ATTORNEYS FOR: Delhaize America, Inc.; Duke Power Company; New York Life Insurance Co.; Texaco Inc.; Vinson Realty Co.
LOCAL COUNSEL FOR: American Title Insurance Co.; Commercial Standard Insurance Co.; Chicago Title Insurance Co.; Lawyers Title Insurance Corp.; Minnesota Title Insurance Co.; Jefferson-Pilot Title Insurance Co.; The Title Guaranty Co.
REFERENCE: Wachovia Bank, N.A.

(This Listing Continued)

THOMAS C. RUFF, JR. & ASSOCIATES

201 MCCULLOUGH DRIVE, SUITE 130
CHARLOTTE, NORTH CAROLINA 28262
Telephone: 704-549-9200
Facsimile: 704-549-0970
Email: truff@rufflaw.com
URL: http://www.trufflaw.com

Real Estate, Commercial Real Estate, Condominium Law, Mortgages, Trust and Estates, Estate Planning, Wills, Probate, Zoning, Planning and Land Use, Business Law, Buying and Selling of Businesses, Limited Liability Company Law, Partnership Law, Contracts, Corporate Law, Elder Law, Health Care Law, Medicare and Medicaid.

THOMAS C. RUFF, born Charlotte, North Carolina, October 20, 1948; admitted to bar, 1974, North Carolina and U.S. District Court, Western District of North Carolina; 1976, U.S. Court of Appeals, Fourth Circuit. *Education:* University of North Carolina (A.B., 1970; J.D., 1974). *Member:* Mecklenburg County and North Carolina Bar Associations; North Carolina State Bar.

THE SASSER LAW FIRM

1011 EAST MOREHEAD STREET
SUITE 350
CHARLOTTE, NORTH CAROLINA 28204
Telephone: 704-342-4200
800-669-9529
Fax: 704-342-0798

Litigation, Personal Injury, Products Liability, Serious Injury, Class Action Litigation, Complex Litigation, Medical Negligence, Business, Workers Compensation, Social Security Disability and Employment Law.

CHARLES McBRAYER SASSER, born Morganton, North Carolina, November 3, 1953; admitted to bar, 1981, North Carolina; 1982, U.S. District Court, Eastern, Middle and Western Districts of North Carolina; U.S. Court of Appeals, Fourth Circuit; 1985, U.S. Supreme Court. *Education:* University of North Carolina (B.S., with honors, 1978; J.D., 1981). Co-Author with Michael Weinberger: "North Carolina Products Liability," The Harrison Company, Supplement, 1997. Member, 1994-1995 and President, 1992-1993, National Association of Social Security Representatives. *Member:* Mecklenburg County, North Carolina Bar and American Bar Associations; North Carolina Academy of Trial Lawyers; Association of Trial Lawyers of America. ***PRACTICE AREAS:*** Civil Litigation; Products Liability; Torts; ERISA; Insurance; Workers Compensation. ***Email:*** msasser@sasserlawoffice.com

(This Listing Continued)

ASSOCIATES

MARGARET B. DeVRIES, born Newton, New Jersey, January 2, 1946; admitted to bar, 1997, North Carolina. *Education:* Eckerd College (B.A., 1966); University of North Carolina (J.D., 1997). *Member:* North Carolina State Bar; National Association of Social Security Representatives; North Carolina Association of Women Attorneys. ***PRACTICE AREAS:*** Social Security Disability; Workers Compensation. ***Email:*** mbdevries@sasserlawoffice.com

HEATHER R. HANES, born Lexington, North Carolina, October 26, 1971; admitted to bar, 1999, North Carolina. *Education:* Wake Forest University (B.A., magna cum laude, 1995; J.D., 1999). Wake Forest Law Review, 1997-1999. ***PRACTICE AREAS:*** Health Law; Hospital Law; Insurance Law.

OF COUNSEL

J. DAVID TOLBERT, born Hendersonville, North Carolina, March 4, 1956; admitted to bar, 1982, North Carolina. *Education:* Furman University (B.A., magna cum laude, 1979); University of North Carolina (J.D., 1982); University of Nottingham, England (LL.M., with distinction, 1990). Holderness Moot Court Bench, 1981-1982. *Member:* North Carolina Bar Association; North Carolina State Bar.

MICHAEL WEINBERGER, born Brooklyn, New York, 1954; admitted to bar, 1979, New York, U.S. Court of Appeals, Second Circuit and U.S. District Court, Southern and Eastern Districts of New York; 1993, North Carolina. *Education:* Brooklyn College (B.A., 1975); Brooklyn Law School (J.D., 1978). Co-Author with Charles Sasser: "North Carolina Products Liability," The Harrison Company, 1995. Member, Board of Editors, The Corporation Law Review, 1982-1986. Chairman, Products Liability Committee, New York State Trial Lawyers Association, 1986—. (Also practicing Individually, New York, N.Y.). ***PRACTICE AREAS:*** Products Liability Law; Commercial Law.

THE SCHATTENFIELD LAW FIRM, PLLC

6000 FAIRVIEW ROAD, SUITE 1200
CHARLOTTE, NORTH CAROLINA 28210
Telephone: 704-552-4004
Cell: 704-293-1405
Fax: 704-552-4005

Trust and Estates, Estate Planning, Asset Protection, Estate and Trust Administration, Fiduciary Law, Business, Family Business, Limited Liability, Wills and Probate, Taxation.

SCOTT W. SCHATTENFIELD, born Washington, D.C., 1958; admitted to bar, 1988, Maryland; 1990, District of Columbia; 1995, North Carolina. *Education:* University of Maryland (B.A., 1983); George Washington University (J.D., with high honors, 1988). Order of the Coif. Former Partner, Moore & Van Allen. Former Partner, Kennedy Covington. Former Director of Private Client Services, Arthur Andersen, North and South Carolina. Chairman, Estate Planning and Fiduciary Law Section, Mecklenburg County Bar Association, 2000-2001. ***Email:*** scott@schattenfield.com

SCHWARTZ LAW FIRM, P.C.

SOUTH PARK TOWERS
6100 FAIRVIEW ROAD, SUITE 530
CHARLOTTE, NORTH CAROLINA 28210
Telephone: 704-552-1889
Fax: 704-552-1866
URL: http://www.schwartz-iplaw.com
Email: jjs@schwartz-iplaw.com
URL: http://www.schwartz-ip.com

Patents, Trademarks, Copyrights, Intellectual Property.

FIRM PROFILE: Schwartz Law Firm, P.C. specializes in serving the legal needs of business owners, entrepreneurs, and inventors by protecting its clients' inventions and designs, trademarks, copyrights, and trade secrets.

JEFFREY J. SCHWARTZ, born Anderson, South Carolina, July 11, 1966; admitted to bar, 1992, North Carolina and U.S. District Court, Western District of North Carolina; 1994, U.S. Court of Appeals, Federal Circuit; registered to practice before the U.S. Patent and Trademark Office. *Education:* Clemson University (B.S. Civil Engineering, 1989); University of South Carolina School of Law (J.D., 1992). *Member:* North Carolina and American Bar Associations (Member, Intellectual Property Law Sections); Carolina Patent, Trademark & Copyright Law Association; American Intellectual Property Law Association; Federal Circuit Bar Association; American Society of Civil Engineers. ***PRACTICE AREAS:*** Patents; Trademarks; Copyrights; Unfair Competition.

SELLERS, HINSHAW, AYERS, DORTCH & LYONS, P.A.

Established in 1986
SUITE 410 CAMERON-BROWN BUILDING
301 SOUTH MCDOWELL STREET
CHARLOTTE, NORTH CAROLINA 28204-2686
Telephone: 704-377-5050
Fax: 704-339-0172
URL: http://www.lawyers.com/shadl

Arbitration, Bankruptcy, Civil Litigation in all State, Federal and Tax Courts, Commercial Real Estate, Community Associations, Condemnation, Construction, Corporate and Commercial Law, Corporate and Municipal Finance, Employment, Foreclosures, Personal Injury, Estate Planning and Probate, Taxation, UCC and Workers' Compensation.

(This Listing Continued)

JOHN F. AYERS III, born New Bern, North Carolina, January 8, 1960; admitted to bar, 1986, North Carolina and U.S. Court of Appeals, Fourth Circuit. *Education:* University of North Carolina (B.S., 1982); Campbell University (J.D., 1986). *Member:* North Carolina Academy of Trial Lawyers. ***PRACTICE AREAS:*** Workers Compensation; Brain Injury; Personal Injury; Commercial Collections; Community Association Law. ***Email:*** jfayers@shadl.com

ROBERT C. DORTCH, JR., born Knoxville, Tennessee, July 4, 1958; admitted to bar, 1983, North Carolina and U.S. Court of Appeals, Fourth Circuit. *Education:* Wake Forest University (B.S. and B.A., 1980); Campbell University (J.D., cum laude, 1983). Phi Alpha Theta; Omicron Delta Kappa. Candidate Member, 1980-1981, Staff Member, 1981-1982 and Editor in Chief, 1982-1983, Campbell Law Review. Law Clerk to Hon. Russell A. Eliason, U.S. Magistrate Judge, Middle District of North Carolina, 1983-1984. ***PRACTICE AREAS:*** Construction Law; Unfair Trade; Commercial Litigation; Employment Law; Covenants Not To Compete. ***Email:*** rcdortch@shadl.com

MARK D. GOTT, born Elyria, Ohio, August 22, 1968; admitted to bar, 1995, North Carolina; U.S. District Court, Western District of North Carolina; 1998, Alabama and U.S. Court of Appeals, 4th Circuit. *Education:* Liberty University (B.S., Political Science, magna cum laude, 1990); Regent University School of Law (J.D., 1994). *Member:* Mecklenburg County Bar Association; North Carolina State Bar. ***PRACTICE AREAS:*** Civil Litigation; Misdemeanor Criminal Defense; Business Law; Collections; Estate Planning; Foreclosures; Guardianship; Incompetency Proceedings. ***Email:*** mdgott@shadl.com

GARL EDWARD (EDDIE) HINSHAW, JR., born Winston-Salem, North Carolina, February 12, 1955; admitted to bar, 1983, North Carolina; 1986, U.S. Tax Court; 1987, U.S. Claims Court; 1991, U.S. Court of Appeals, Fourth Circuit. *Education:* Appalachian State University (B.S.B.A., cum laude, 1977); Wake Forest University (J.D., 1983). Member, Wake Forest Law Review, 1982-1983. Member, North Carolina Bar Tax Section Council, 1993-1995. *Member:* North Carolina Association of Certified Public Accountants; American Institute of Certified Public Accountants; Mecklenburg County Tax Section. ***PRACTICE AREAS:*** Business Law; Corporate Law; Tax Law; Estate and Gift Taxation; Probate Administration. ***Email:*** gehinshaw@shadl.com

T. PATRICK JENKINS, born Canton, Pennsylvania, February 11, 1955; admitted to bar, 1980, Rhode Island; 1983, North Carolina. *Education:* Dickinson College (B.A., magna cum laude, 1977); Duke University (J.D., 1980). *Member:* North Carolina Bar Association. ***PRACTICE AREAS:*** Estate Planning; Probate; Business Planning; Closely Held Business Law; Taxation. ***Email:*** tpjenkins@shadl.com

CHARLES E. (ED) LYONS II, born Rutherfordton, North Carolina, August 9, 1960; admitted to bar, 1985, North Carolina and U.S. Court of Appeals, Fourth Circuit; 1995, South Carolina. *Education:* Oral Roberts University (B.A., 1982); Wake Forest University (J.D., 1985). Assistant United States Attorney, 1985-1989. President, Wake Forest Federalist Society, 1984-1985. Treasurer, Iredell County Republican Party. ***PRACTICE AREAS:*** Bankruptcy; Collections; Debtor and Creditor; Construction Law; Community Association Law. ***Email:*** celyons@shadl.com

MICHELLE PRICE MASSINGALE, born Slippery Rock, Pennsylvania, October 28, 1970; admitted to bar, 1994, West Virginia and U.S. District Court, Southern District of West Virginia, U.S. Court of Appeals, Fourth Circuit; 1998, U.S. District Court, Northern District of West Virginia; 2000, North Carolina and U.S. District Court, Western and Eastern Districts of North Carolina. *Education:* West Virginia University (B.A., magna cum laude, 1991; J.D., 1994). Phi Beta Kappa; Golden Key; Order of the Coif; Articles Editor, West Virginia Law Review, 1993-1994. ***PRACTICE AREAS:*** Commercial Litigation; Employment Law. ***Email:*** mpmassingale@shadl.com

TIMOTHY G. SELLERS, born Goldsboro, North Carolina, November 24, 1954; admitted to bar, 1980, North Carolina; 1988, U.S. Court of Appeals, Fourth Circuit; 1995, South Carolina. *Education:* Davidson College (B.A., 1977); University of North Carolina (J.D., with honors, 1980). Order of the Barristers. Certified Christian Conciliator. Member, Charlotte City Council, 1995-1999. *Member:* North Carolina Bar Association (Member, Committees on: Construction Liens; Foreclosure; Planned Community Legislation); North Carolina Academy of Trial Lawyers. ***PRACTICE AREAS:*** Alternative Dispute Resolution; Commercial Law; Condemnation; Litigation; Foreclosures; Community Association Law. ***Email:*** tgsellers@shadl.com

ROBERT A. WHITLOW, born Chattanooga, Tennessee, June 5, 1954; admitted to bar, 1979, Georgia; 1999, North Carolina; U.S. District Court, Northern District of Georgia and Western District of North Carolina; U.S. Court of Appeals, 11th Circuit. *Education:* Furman University (B.A., magna cum laude, 1976); University of Georgia (J.D., cum laude, 1979). Phi Beta Kappa. Member, University of Georgia Law Review, 1978-1979. Author: "The List;" "The Trial;" "The Sacrifice;" "Life Support," "Life Everlasting," Westbow Publishing. Certified Mediator. Certified Christian Conciliator. *Member:* State Bar of Georgia; North Carolina State Bar; North Carolina Academy of Trial Lawyers; Christian Legal Society. ***PRACTICE AREAS:*** Workers Compensation Law; Social Security Law; Alternative Dispute Resolution. ***Email:*** rawhitlow@shadl.com

REPRESENTATIVE CLIENTS: All-Interior Supply, Inc.; Bank of America; Besco Electrical Contractors, Inc.; Blue Max Trucking, Inc.; Bryant Electric Supply, Inc.; Concrete Supply Company; Consolidated Diesel Company; Cummins, Inc.; Edgewater Technologies; Genuine Parts Corporation; Global Medical Imaging, LLC; Hudson Brothers Trailer Manufacturing, Inc.; ITW Packaging Brands; Jim Walter Homes, Inc.; Metrolina Credit Company; Metrolina Wall & Ceiling Assoc.; N.C. Ventures; Patrick Yarn Mill, Inc.; Rea Contracting, LLC; Southern Concrete Materials; Strapex Corporation; Transamerica Commercial Finance Corp.; Walter Mortgage Co.

MARK E. SHELLEY

CHARLOTTE, NORTH CAROLINA

(See Concord)

Tax, IRS Audits, Property Tax, Tax Planning, Trust and Estates, Asset Protection, Estate Planning, Wills and Probate.

SHUFORD, HUNTER & BROWN, P.A.

Established in 1992

301 SOUTH MCDOWELL STREET, SUITE 1012
CHARLOTTE, NORTH CAROLINA 28204
Telephone: 704-377-0280
Fax: 704-377-8666
Email: katelliott@shblawyers.com
URL: http://www.shblawyers.com

General Practice in State and Federal Courts.

FIRM PROFILE: Founded in 1992, Shuford, Hunter & Brown, P.A. is a small firm with an expertise in debtor-creditor matters and real estate. Our three attorneys advise a wide range of clients from individuals dealing with personal legal matters to businesses seeking representation on an extensive variety of issues. We are regularly referred individuals and small businesses by large law firms, as well as clients and former clients.

We frequently represent a diverse clientele of individuals, debtors, trustees, unsecured creditors' committees, and creditors in the federal bankruptcy court in the Western District of North Carolina. We have routinely represented clients in litigation involving relief from stay, preferences, lien avoidance, secured transactions, fraudulent transfers and setoffs in the bankruptcy court.

We also represent clients in collections, workouts, deficiency and guaranty defense, landlord-tenant matters, receiverships, and other commercial litigation disputes, and other matters in state court.

We also advise individuals and small businesses in real estate transactions, estate plans, small business formation and general corporate law.

We believe in helping our clients reach practical solutions to their problems in a professional, levelheaded manner.

A. BURTON SHUFORD, born Charlotte, North Carolina, September 18, 1956; admitted to bar, 1981, North Carolina and U.S. District Court, Western District of North Carolina; 1988, U.S. District Court, Middle District of North Carolina; 1990 U.S. District Court, Eastern District of North Carolina; 1993, U.S. Court of Appeals, Fourth Circuit. *Education:* Wake Forest University (B.A., cum laude, 1978); University of North Carolina (J.D., 1981). *Member:* North Carolina State Bar ; North Carolina Bar Association (Member, Council of Bankruptcy Section, 1993-1996); 26th Judicial District; National Association of Bankruptcy Trustees, 1990—; Panel Trustee for Chapter 7 Bankruptcy Cases. ***PRACTICE AREAS:*** Commercial and Consumer Bankruptcy; Consumer Credit; Consumer Fraud; Consumer Protection; Debtor and Creditor Collections; Debtor and Creditor Rights. ***Email:*** burtshuford@shblawyers.com

G. MARTIN HUNTER, born Aiken, South Carolina, January 11, 1959; admitted to bar, 1986, North Carolina and U.S. District Court, Western District of North Carolina; 1989, U.S. District Court, Middle District of North Carolina; 1990, South Carolina (inactive); 1993, U.S. Court of Appeals, Fourth Circuit. *Education:* Davidson College (A.B., 1980); Wake Forest University (J.D., 1986). Law Clerk to the Honorable George R. Hodges, U.S. Bankruptcy Judge, Western District of North Carolina, 1987-1989. Certified, Superior Court Mediator. Member, Panel of Arbitrators, District Court, 26th Judicial District, 1996—. *Member:* North Carolina State Bar; South Carolina Bar; North Carolina Bar Association (Council Member, Bankruptcy Section, 1997-2000); 26th Judicial District. (Board Certified Specialist in Business and Consumer Bankruptcy Law, North Carolina State Bar Board of Legal Specialization). ***PRACTICE AREAS:*** Commercial and Consumer Bankruptcy; Foreclosures; Consumer Law; Debtor and Creditor Collections; Debtor and Creditor Rights. ***Email:*** martinhunter@shblawyers.com

THOMAS DANIEL BROWN, born Baltimore, Maryland, May 21, 1959; admitted to bar, 1985, North Carolina and U.S. District Court, Western District of North Carolina; 1986, U.S. Tax Court and U.S. Court of Appeals, Fourth Circuit; 1995, U.S. Supreme Court. *Education:* Wofford College (B.A. magna cum laude, 1981); George Washington University (J.D., 1984). George Washington University National Law Center Trustees' Scholar. Member, Southern Conference Sport Media Association. *Member:* North Carolina State Bar; North Carolina Bar Association (Member, Real Estate Section; Council of General Practice Section, 1993-1996); 26th Judicial District;. ***PRACTICE AREAS:*** Business Law; Construction Law; General Practice; Real Estate; Trusts and Estates; Wills; Probate. ***Email:*** tombrown@shblawyers.com

REPRESENTATIVE CLIENTS: Anderson & Anderson, Inc.; Brown & Glenn Realty Co., Inc.; Charlotte Eastland Mall, LLC; Hi Q Photolith Corporation; First Centrum; Hall's Park Road Firestone; Boyles Distinctive Furniture, Inc.; Martin & Harrill, Inc.; Universal Drywall, Inc.; Lomax Tile & Marble, Inc.; TCF Financial.
APPROVED ATTORNEYS FOR: Stewart Title Guaranty Co.; First Title Insurance Co.; Lawyers Title Insurance Co.; Investors Title Insurance Co.; Security Union Title Insurance Co.; First American Title Insurance Co.
REFERENCES: Bank of America (Bankruptcy Trustee Cases).

SHUMAKER, LOOP & KENDRICK, LLP

128 SOUTH TRYON STREET
SUITE 1800
CHARLOTTE, NORTH CAROLINA 28202
Telephone: 704-375-0057
Fax: 704-332-1197
URL: http://www.slk-law.com

Toledo, Ohio Office: North Courthouse Square, 1000 Jackson, 43624-1573. Telephone: 419-241-9000. Fax: 419-241-6894.
Tampa, Florida Office: 101 East Kennedy Boulevard, Suite 2800, 33602-5151. Telephone: 813-229-7600. Fax: 813-229-1660.
Columbus, Ohio Office: Huntington Center, 41 South High Street, Suite 2400, 43215. Telephone: 614-463-9441. Fax: 614-463-1108.

Administrative Law; Advertising and Marketing; Agency and Distributorships; Agricultural Law; Alternative Dispute Resolution; Antitrust and Trade Regulation; Appellate Practice; Bankruptcy; Banks and Banking; Business Law; Business Crimes; Business Torts; Civil Rights; Commercial Law; Commercial Litigation; Commercial Real Estate; Communications and Media; Complex and Multi-District Litigation; Computers and Software; Construction Law; Contracts; Copyrights; Corporate Law; Federal Criminal Law; Debtor and Creditor; Domestic Relations; Education Law; Employee Benefits; Entertainment Law; Environmental Law; Fidelity and Surety; Finance; Franchises and Franchising; Health Care; Hospital Law; Immigration and Naturalization; Intellectual Property; International Law; Labor and Employment; Leases and Leasing; Litigation; Media Law; Medicare and Medicaid; Mergers, Acquisitions and Divestitures; Nonprofit and Charitable Organizations; Patent Litigation; Personal Injury; Probate; Products Liability; Professional Liability; Public Finance; Real Estate; Securities; Sports Law; Taxation; Torts; Trade Secrets; Trademarks; Trusts and Estates; Unfair Competition; Wills; Zoning, Planning and Land Use.

FIRM PROFILE: Shumaker, Loop & Kendrick, LLP is a full service law firm whose practice includes civil litigation, corporate, tax, securities, banking and commercial law, creditors' rights, real property, employment relations, employee benefits, estate planning and probate, health, domestic relations, environmental, immigration and administrative law. Our practice areas are organized into the following departments: litigation, corporate, health law, real estate, trusts and estates, taxation, employment law, environmental law and intellectual property. The firm is located in four cities -- Toledo and Columbus, Ohio, Charlotte, North Carolina, and Tampa, Florida.

We represent a wide variety of business, institutional, governmental and individual clients including manufacturers, banks and other financial institutions, insurance companies, contractors, broadcasters, accounting firms, real estate developers and brokers, public utilities, transportation companies, health care providers, trade associations and various public bodies and agencies.

LAW FIRM ALLIANCES/ASSOCIATIONS: ***TOLEDO CONFERENCE GROUP***

RESIDENT PARTNERS

PETER C. ANDERSON, born Montclair, New Jersey, September 10, 1963; admitted to bar, 1992, North Carolina; 1993, District of Columbia. *Education:* Rutgers University (B.S., summa cum laude, 1986); University of Virginia (J.D., 1991). Trial Attorney, U.S. Department of Justice, Environmental Crimes Section, 1992-1994. Assistant U.S. Attorney, Western District of North Carolina. Judicial Law Clerk, Hon. Graham C. Mullen, U.S. District Court, Western District of North Carolina, 1991-1992. Certified Arbitrator and Mediator, Commercial Litigation and Environmental Law. ***PRACTICE AREAS:*** Commercial Litigation; Business Crimes; Environmental Law; Preventive Law; Federal Criminal Law. ***Email:*** panderson@slk-law.com

PHILIP S. CHUBB, born Key West, Florida, October 22, 1956; admitted to bar, 1982, Ohio; 1989, North Carolina. *Education:* Miami University (A.B., cum laude, 1979); University of Toledo (J.D., magna cum laude, 1982). Phi Beta Kappa; Phi Alpha Theta; Phi Kappa Phi. *Member:* Ohio State and American (Member, Sections on: Business Law; Taxation) Bar Associations; 26th Judicial District and North Carolina State Bars. ***PRACTICE AREAS:*** Business Law; Mergers, Acquisitions and Divestitures; Securities Law. ***Email:*** pchubb@slk-law.com

DAVID HARRIS CONAWAY, born Augusta, Georgia, May 26, 1958; admitted to bar, 1983, North Carolina. *Education:* University of North Carolina (B.A., 1979); University of Alabama (J.D., 1982). Editor: Alabama Law Review, 1980-1982; American Journal of Tax Policy, 1981-1982. *Member:* North Carolina and American (Vice Chairman, Corporation, Business and Banking Law Committee, Young Lawyers Division, 1984-1985) Bar Associations; North Carolina State Bar; American Bankruptcy Institute. ***PRACTICE AREAS:*** Bankruptcy; Commercial Law; Business Law. ***Email:*** dconaway@slk-law.com

DAVID M. GROGAN, born Daytona Beach, Florida, December 15, 1949; admitted to bar, 1984, Oregon; 1992, Georgia; 1993, North Carolina. *Education:* Florida State University (B.S., magna cum laude, 1971); Duke University (J.D., with honors, 1984). *Member:* North Carolina State Bar; North Carolina Bar Association; American Bankruptcy Institute. ***PRACTICE AREAS:*** Commercial Bankruptcy; Insolvency; Business Reorganization. ***Email:*** dgrogan@slk-law.com

DANIEL R. HANSEN, born Milwaukee, Wisconsin, October 3, 1967; admitted to bar, 1995, Ohio; 1996, Michigan; 1998, North Carolina. *Education:* Bowling Green State University (B.A., 1990); Case Western Reserve School of Law (J.D., 1995). Phi Beta Kappa; Phi Delta Phi (Secretary, 1994-1995). Order of the Coif. Case Western Reserve of Law Review. *Member:* Mecklenburg County, North Carolina and American Bar Associations; North Carolina State Bar. ***PRACTICE AREAS:*** Commercial Litigation; Shareholder Disputes; Construction Law; Local Government Law. ***Email:*** dhansen@slk-law.com

MOSES LUSKI, born Havana, Cuba, May 23, 1953; admitted to bar, 1978, North Carolina. *Education:* Columbia University (B.A., 1975); University of North Carolina (J.D., 1978). Staff Member, North Carolina Law Review, 1976-1978. Research Assistant to Justice J. Frank Huskins, North Carolina Supreme Court, 1978-1980. *Member:* Mecklenburg County Bar Association; North Carolina State Bar. ***LANGUAGES:*** Spanish. ***PRACTICE AREAS:*** Real Estate Law; Commercial Real Estate; Commercial Real Estate Finance; Leases and Leasing; Landlord and Tenant Law. ***Email:*** mluski@slk-law.com

WILLIAM H. McNAIR, born Winston-Salem, North Carolina, March 7, 1934; admitted to bar, 1961, North Carolina. *Education:* Davidson College (B.S., 1956); University of North Carolina (J.D., with honors, 1961). Delta Theta Phi; Order of the Coif. Associate Editor, North Carolina Law Review, 1960-1961. *Member:* Mecklenburg County and North Carolina Bar Associations; North Carolina State Bar. ***PRACTICE AREAS:*** Trusts and Estates; Tax Planning; Estate and Gift Taxation; Corporate Formation; Wills; Trust Law. ***Email:*** wmcnair@slk-law.com

SCOTT M. STEVENSON, born Houston, Texas, July 25, 1954; admitted to bar, 1979, North Carolina; U.S. Supreme Court; U.S. Court of Appeals, Fourth Circuit; U.S. District Court, Eastern and Western Districts. *Education:* Washington & Lee University (B.A., 1976); Wake Forest University (J.D., 1979). *Member:* Mecklenburg County, North Carolina

(This Listing Continued)

and American Bar Associations; North Carolina State Bar; Defense Research Institute; North Carolina Association of Defense Attorneys. ***LANGUAGES:*** Spanish and Norwegian. ***PRACTICE AREAS:*** Medical Malpractice. ***Email:*** sstevenson@slk-law.com

WILLIAM H. STURGES, born Brazil, Indiana, July 24, 1953; admitted to bar, 1978, North Carolina. *Education:* Washington & Lee University (B.A., cum laude, 1975); Wake Forest University (J.D., cum laude, 1978). Recipient, Algernon Sidney Sullivan Award. Staff Member, Wake Forest Law Review, 1976-1978. Research Assistant to Chief Justice Susie Sharp, North Carolina Supreme Court, 1978-1979. Faculty Member, various programs, National Institute of Trial Advocacy. Member, 1996-2002 and Chair, 2000-2002, Charlotte Zoning Board of Adjustment. *Member:* North Carolina (Council Member, 1994-2001 and Chair, 1999-2000; Member, Sections on: Labor and Employment Law; Litigation; Environmental Law) and American (Member, Sections on: Labor and Employment Law; Litigation; Tort and Insurance Practice) Bar Associations. ***PRACTICE AREAS:*** Labor and Employment Law; Commercial Litigation; Fidelity and Surety; Zoning and Land Use. ***Email:*** wsturges@slk-law.com

FREDERICK M. THURMAN, JR., born Marietta, Georgia, May 3, 1970; admitted to bar, 1995, Alabama; 1999, North Carolina. *Education:* Clemson University (B.S., magna cum laude, 1992); Cumberland School of Law of Samford University (J.D., 1995). Phi Kappa Phi; Omicron Delta Kappa; Tau Beta Pi. Cordell Hull Teaching Fellow, 1993-1994. Article Editor, Cumberland Law Review, 1994-1995. *Member:* North Carolina and American Bar Associations; Alabama State Bar; North Carolina State Bar. ***PRACTICE AREAS:*** Labor and Employment; Litigation. ***Email:*** fthurman@slk-law.com

RESIDENT ASSOCIATES

WILLIAM C. BUNTING, JR., born Garner, North Carolina, April 17, 1975; admitted to bar, 2001, North Carolina. *Education:* Appalachian State University (B.S., summa cum laude, 1997); University of North Carolina at Chapel Hill (J.D., 2001). Associate Editor, North Carolina Journal of Law and Technology, 2000-2001. *Member:* Mecklenburg County, North Carolina and American Bar Associations; North Carolina State Bar. ***PRACTICE AREAS:*** Commercial Litigation; Federal Criminal Law; Business Crimes; Landlord and Tenant Law. ***Email:*** wbunting@slk-law.com

C. CHRISTOPHER CLARK, born Roanoke, Virginia, March 10, 1971; admitted to bar, 2001, North Carolina. *Education:* Radford University (B.M., 1998); University of North Carolina (J.D., 2001). Associate Editor, North Carolina Journal of Law and Technology, 2000-2001. ***PRACTICE AREAS:*** Corporate Law; Business Transactions; Entertainment Law; Intellectual Property; Internet Law. ***Email:*** cclark@slk-law.com

MATTHEW J. GINSBURG, born November 10, 1971; admitted to bar, 1998, Massachusetts; 2002, North Carolina. *Education:* Emory University (B.A., 1994); Boston College Law School (J.D., 1998). Member, National Slavic Honor Society, 1993-1994. *Member:* Boston, Massachusetts and American Bar Associations; North Carolina State Bar. ***LANGUAGES:*** Russian. ***PRACTICE AREAS:*** Commercial Litigation; Construction Litigation; Bankruptcy Litigation; Employment Litigation. ***Email:*** mginsburg@slk-law.com

JOHN D. KOCHER, born Harrisburg, Pennsylvania, February 25, 1968; admitted to bar, 1993, New Jersey and U.S. District Court, District of New Jersey; 1994, Pennsylvania; 2000, North Carolina and U.S. District Court, Western District of North Carolina; 2001, U.S. District Court, Middle and Western Districts of North Carolina. *Education:* Pennsylvania State University (B.A., History, cum laude, 1990); Dickinson School of Law of the Pennsylvania State University (J.D., cum laude, 1993). Member: Woolack Society; The Federalist Society. *Member:* Bergen County, Mecklenburg County, North Carolina, New Jersey State and Pennsylvania Bar Associations; North Carolina State Bar; Morris Pashman Inns of Court. ***PRACTICE AREAS:*** Medical Malpractice Litigation; Insurance Defense Litigation. ***Email:*** jkocher@slk-law.com

KATHLEEN K. LUCCHESI, born Anderson, Indiana, September 20, 1968; admitted to bar, 1997, North Carolina. *Education:* University of Indianapolis (B.S., cum laude, 1990); University of Mississippi (J.D., cum laude, 1997). Runner-Up, Ole Miss Moot Court Oral Advocacy Competition, Fall 1995. First Place, Feature Division, Indiana Associated Press Television Award, 1992. Author, "The Pros Don't Always Get Three Strikes: How Gambling Shaped the Supervisory Powers Governing Professional Sports," Gaming Law Review, Winter 1997. Instructor, Queens University Forensic Medicine Course, North Carolina Statutory Law Section, Fall 2002 and Spring 2003. Assistant District Attorney, Mecklenburg County, Charlotte, North Carolina, 1997-2003. *Member:* Mecklenburg County, North Carolina and American Bar Associations; North Carolina State Bar; North Carolina Association of Defense Attorneys; Defense Research Institute. ***PRACTICE AREAS:*** Litigation; Medical Malpractice. ***Email:*** klucchesi@slk-law.com

PATRICIA WILSON MAGEE, born Charlotte, North Carolina, January 8, 1978; admitted to bar, 2003, North Carolina. *Education:* University of North Carolina at Chapel Hill (B.A., 2000); Campbell University (J.D., 2003). Phi Alpha Delta (Chief Justice, Iredell Chapter, 2002-2003); Order of the Old Kivett. Law Clerk to the Hon. John M. Tyson, North Carolina Court of Appeals, 2003-2005. *Member:* Mecklenburg County, North Carolina and American Bar Associations; North Carolina State Bar. ***PRACTICE AREAS:*** Civil Litigation. ***Email:*** tmagee@slk-law.com

DAVID A. MATTHEWS, born Long Beach, California, 1968; admitted to bar, 1998, California; 2002, North Carolina. *Education:* Azusa Pacific University (B.A., cum laude, 1995); McGeorge School of Law (J.D., with distinction, 1998). Member, Traynor Honor Society. *Member:* Mecklenburg County, North Carolina and Amercian Bar Associations; State Bar of California; American Bankruptcy Institute. ***PRACTICE AREAS:*** Bankruptcy; Creditors Rights; Commercial Litigation. ***Email:*** dmatthews@slk-law.com

STEVEN A. MECKLER, born Akron, Ohio, December 30, 1970; admitted to bar, 1999, North Carolina and U.S. District Court, Eastern, Middle and Western Districts of North Carolina; 2000, South Carolina and U.S. District Court, District of South Carolina. *Education:* Kent State University (B.A., 1993); Case Western Reserve University (J.D., cum laude, 1999). Member, State Liason, DRI Medical Liability and Health Care Law Committee. *Member:* Mecklenburg County (Member, Professionalism Committee, 2002—; Chair, Education Committee, 2002— and Member, Board of Directors, 2003—, Young Lawyers Division), North Carolina (Appointed Member, Bench/Bar Liason Com-

(This Listing Continued)

mittee, 2002—; Vice-Chairman, Litigation CLE Committee, 2003-2004) and American Bar Associations; North Carolina State Bar; South Carolina Bar; North Carolina Association of Defense Attorneys; Defense Research Institute. ***PRACTICE AREAS:*** Complex Commercial Litigation; Products Liability; Medical Malpractice; Catastrophic Injury; Personal Injury; Federal Court Litigation. ***Email:*** smeckler@slk-law.com

JOSEPH J. SANTANIELLO, born Jamaica, New York, April 21, 1972; admitted to bar, 1997, North Carolina. *Education:* University of North Carolina (B.A., 1994; J.D., 1997). Phi Delta Phi. *Member:* North Carolina and American Bar Associations; North Carolina State Bar. ***LANGUAGES:*** Spanish. ***PRACTICE AREAS:*** Business Law; Commercial Law; Bankruptcy. ***Email:*** jsantaniello@slk-law.com

KAREN H. STILES, born Mooresville, North Carolina, February 16, 1972; admitted to bar, 2002, North Carolina. *Education:* Peace College (A.A., 1992); University of North Carolina at Chapel Hill (B.A., 1994); Meredith College (Paralegal Certification, 1994); Norman A. Wiggins, School of Law (J.D., 2002). *Member:* Mecklenburg County and North Carolina Bar Associations; North Carolina State Bar; North Carolina Association of Defense Attorneys; Defense Research Institute. ***PRACTICE AREAS:*** Medical Malpractice. ***Email:*** kstiles@slk-law.com

ROBERT ERNEST SUMNER, IV, born Columbia, South Carolina, May 9, 1977; admitted to bar, 2002, North Carolina and U.S. District Court, Western District of North Carolina; 2003, South Carolina. *Education:* University of North Carolina at Chapel Hill (B.A., English, 1999); University of South Carolina (J.D., 2002). *Member:* Mecklenburg County and North Carolina Bar Associations; North Carolina State Bar; South Carolina Bar; Noarth Carolina Association of Defense Attorneys; Defense Research Institute. ***PRACTICE AREAS:*** Medical Malpractice. ***Email:*** rsumner@slk-law.com

S. FREDERICK WINIKER, III, born Charlotte, North Carolina, November 21, 1966; admitted to bar, 1995, North Carolina; 1999, U.S. District Court, Eastern District of Washington and U.S. Court Appeals, Ninth Circuit. *Education:* Wake Forest University (B.A., 1989); Gonzaga University (J.D., cum laude, 1995). *Member:* Mecklenburg and North Carolina Bar Associations. [1st Lt., U.S. Army, 1989-1992]. ***LANGUAGES:*** German. ***REPORTED CASES:*** United States v. Kafka, 222 F.3d 1129, (9th Cir. 2000). ***PRACTICE AREAS:*** Commercial Litigation; Medical Malpractice. ***Email:*** rwiniker@slk-law.com

REPRESENTATIVE CLIENTS: AVAILABLE UPON REQUEST.

(For complete biographical data on all personnel, see Professional Biographies at Toledo, Ohio)

LAW OFFICE OF TIMOTHY D. SMITH

122 NORTH MCDOWELL STREET
CHARLOTTE, NORTH CAROLINA 28204
Telephone: 704-334-9909
Fax: 704-714-1451
Email: timsmith8615@hotmail.com
URL: http://www.timsmithlawfirm.com

Immigration Law, Criminal Law, Driving While Intoxicated (DWI), Drug Crimes, Traffic Violations, Family Law/Divorce.

TIMOTHY D. SMITH, born Charlotte, North Carolina, September 21, 1967; admitted to bar, 1993, California; 2001, North Carolina. *Education:* University of North Carolina at Chapel Hill (B.A., 1989); California Western School of Law (J.D., 1993). *Member:* Mecklenburg County and North Carolina Bar Associations.

SMITH AND CHRISTENSEN, L.L.P.

ONE FAIRVIEW CENTER
6302 FAIRVIEW ROAD, SUITE 309
CHARLOTTE, NORTH CAROLINA 28210-2226
Telephone: 704-522-1616
Fax: 704-522-7111
Email: attorneys@smithchrist.com
URL: http://www.smithchrist.com
Labor and Employment, Corporate Transactions.

MEMBERS OF FIRM

W. BRITTON SMITH, JR., born Wilson, North Carolina, October 6, 1942; admitted to bar, 1967, North Carolina; 1972, U.S. District Court, Eastern, Middle and Western Districts of North Carolina; 1973, U.S. Court of Appeals, Fourth Circuit and U.S. Supreme Court. *Education:* University of North Carolina (B.S., 1965; J.D., 1967). Phi Alpha Delta (President, 1967). Attorney, National Labor Relations Board, 1967-1972. *Member:* Mecklenburg County and North Carolina Bar Associations; North Carolina State Bar. ***PRACTICE AREAS:*** Management Labor Law; Corporate Law.

AARON M. CHRISTENSEN, born Lincoln, Nebraska, October 19, 1967; admitted to bar, 1993, South Carolina and U.S. District Court, District of South Carolina; 1995, North Carolina and U.S. District Court, Western, Middle and Eastern Districts of North Carolina; U.S. Court of Appeals, Fourth Circuit; 2002, U.S. Court of Appeals, Eleventh Circuit. *Education:* Wake Forest University (B.A., magna cum laude, 1990); University of Virginia (J.D., 1993). Phi Beta Kappa; Omicron Delta Kappa; Omicron Delta Epsilon. Officer, Moot Court Board, University of Virginia. Certified Mediator, North Carolina Bar Association, 2003. *Member:* Mecklenburg County and North Carolina Bar Associations; North Carolina State Bar; South Carolina Bar. ***PRACTICE AREAS:*** Management Labor Law; Employment Law; Employee Benefits; Corporate Law.

REPRESENTATIVE CLIENTS: Conitex-Sonoco, U.S.A., Inc.; Papertech Corp.; Electric and Telephone Cooperatives; Commercial Credit Co.; Chem-Way Corporation; General Transport Systems, Inc.; Griffin 88 Stores, Inc.; Solite Corporation; Patterson & Wilder Construction Co., Inc.; City and County Governments; Sola Optical, Inc.; Elizabeth Carbide Die Co. Inc.

SMITH, COOKSEY & VICKSTROM, PLLC

6060 J.A. JONES DRIVE, SUITE 208
CHARLOTTE, NORTH CAROLINA 28287
Telephone: 704-557-9929
Fax: 704-557-9932
URL: http://www.scvlawfirm.com

Litigation, Corporate Counseling, Contract Drafting and Negotiation, Dispute Prevention, Alternative Dispute Resolution, Construction Litigation, Federal Procurement Litigation, State Procurement Litigation, Business Formation, Corporate Transactions, Manufacturing and Service Issues.

FIRM PROFILE: Smith, Cooksey & Vickstrom, PLLC seeks to provide clients with high quality legal service that is thorough, efficient, responsive and cost effective. Our goal is to help clients to avoid disputes if possible, document disputes when they arise, and to resolve disputes in the most efficient manner. We strive to apply common sense, hard work, creativity and a practical approach to legal issues.

STEVEN L. SMITH, born Cleveland, Ohio, October 3, 1968; admitted to bar, 1994, Georgia; 2000, North Carolina. *Education:* University of Richmond (B.A., summa cum laude, 1991); University of Georgia (J.D., 1994). *Member:* Mecklenburg County and American Bar Associations; State Bar of Georgia; State Bar of North Carolina (Construction Law Section). [Capt., U.S. Army, JAG Corps 1994-1998]. ***PRACTICE AREAS:*** Construction Litigation; Government Contracts; Alternative Dispute Resolution. ***Email:*** ssmith@scv-law.com

NEIL C. COOKSEY, born Boardman, Ohio, July 25, 1961; admitted to bar, 1986, North Carolina. *Education:* Davidson College (A.B., cum laude, 1983); Youngstown State University, 1979-1980; The University of Michigan Law School (J.D., 1986). Associate Editor, Michigan Yearbook of International Legal Studies, 1985-1986. *Member:* Mecklenburg County and North Carolina Bar Associations. ***PRACTICE AREAS:*** Construction; Government Contracts; Corporate. ***Email:*** ncooksey@scv-law.com

DWANE E. VICKSTROM, born Miami, Florida, November 23, 1946; admitted to bar, 1977, Nebraska; 1997, North Carolina. *Education:* University of Nebraska at Lincoln (B.S., Civil Engineering, 1970; J.D., 1977). Registered Professional Engineer, Nebraska. *Member:* Mecklenburg County, Nebraska State and North Carolina Bar Associations. ***PRACTICE AREAS:*** Construction; Government Contracts; Corporate; Manufacturing. ***Email:*** dvickstrom@scv-law.com

SMITH, CURRIE & HANCOCK LLP

SUITE 301
1023 WEST MOREHEAD STREET
CHARLOTTE, NORTH CAROLINA 28208
Telephone: 704-334-3459
Telecopier: 704-334-7850
URL: http://www.smithcurrie.com

Atlanta, Georgia Office: 2600 Harris Tower-Peachtree Center, 233 Peachtree Street, N.E. Telephone: 404-521-3800. Fax: 404-688-0671.
Tallahassee, Florida Office: 1004 DeSoto Park Drive, P.O. Box 589. Telephone: 850-878-3700. Fax: 850-656-0329.
Fort Lauderdale, Florida Office: Suit 620, One East Broward Boulevard. Telephone: 954-761-8700. Fax: 954-524-6927.

Construction, Government Contracts, Surety, Commercial, Environmental, International and related Mediations, Arbitration, Labor and Litigation.

FIRM PROFILE: The firm was established in 1965 and is one of the largest law firms in the United States concentrating in Construction Law and Government Contracts, as well as handling Commercial Matters, Litigation, Arbitration and Mediation. Clients include multinational and Fortune 500 Companies and Trade Associations.

PARTNERS OF THE FIRM

ROLLY L. CHAMBERS, born Aurora, Illinois, February 9, 1953; admitted to bar, 1984, North Carolina. *Education:* University of North Carolina (A.B., with honors, 1975); College of William & Mary (J.D., 1984). Morehead Scholar. Executive Editor, William & Mary Law Review, 1983-1984. Contributing Author, Common Sense Construction Law, 3rd ed. John Wiley & Sons, Inc. 2004. Contributing Author, Alternative Clauses to Standard Construction Contracts, "Contractors' Amending AGC Document No. 650-1998," Aspen Publishers, Supp. 2002. Author: "Hidden Contract Pitfalls, Part 1: Implied Contractual Obligations," CFMA Building Profits Magazine, January/February, 2002. Speaker, "AIA Contracts in North Carolina," Lorman Education Services Seminar, 2004. Speaker, "Practical Construction Project Documentation for Project Site Managers," Carolinas AGC Seminar, 2004. *Member:* North Carolina Bar Association (Member, Construction Law Section; Litigation Section) and American Bar Association (Member, Construction Industry Forum; Member, Sections on: Science and Technology Law; Litigation). [Lieutenant, U.S. Naval Reserve, Active Duty, 1976-1981]. ***PRACTICE AREAS:*** Construction; Government Contracts; Civil Litigation. ***Email:*** rlchambers@smithcurrie.com

ROBERT J. GREENE, JR., born Elmira, New York, April 15, 1946; admitted to bar, 1979, North Carolina and U.S. District Court, Eastern, Western and Middle Districts of North Carolina. *Education:* University of Utah (B.A., cum laude, 1973; J.D., 1978). Certified Mediator, North Carolina Superior Court. Former Member, National Panel of Arbitrators, American Arbitration Association. Founding Member, The Arbitration Group of the Carolinas. *Member:* North Carolina (Member, Sections on: Construction Law; Litigation) and American (Member: Construction Industry Forum, 1982—; Sections on: Litigation) Bar Associations; North Carolina State Bar. [1st Lieut., U.S. Army Chemical Corps, 1969-1972]. ***PRACTICE AREAS:*** Construction Law. ***Email:*** rjgreene@smithcurrie.com

STEELE B. ("AL") WINDLE, III, born Charlotte, North Carolina, May 24, 1956; admitted to bar, 1981, North Carolina and Georgia. *Education:* University of Virginia (B.S., 1978); Wake Forest University School of Law (J.D., 1981). Member, Order of the Barristers. Co-Author: North Carolina Construction Law, Lorman Education Services. Author: Construction Management/Design-Build in North Carolina, Lorman Education Systems; The Use of Special Masters in Construction Litigation, Wiley, Update, 1999; Contracting with Public Entities in North Carolina, Lorman Education Systems: Working With The AIA Contracts, Lorman Education Systems; Handling Change Orders & Change Order Disputes, Lorman Education Systems; Construction Claims, Lorman Education Systems. *Member:* North Carolina State Bar (Member: Construction Section; Director 1990-1992, 1996-1998); State Bar of Georgia; American Arbitration Association (Member, Construction Litigation and Mediation Panels). ***PRACTICE AREAS:*** Construction Litigation; Arbitration; Mediation; Civil Litigation. ***Email:*** sbwindle@smithcurrie.com

OF COUNSEL

HARRY R. BIVENS, born Memphis, Tennessee, July 21, 1954; admitted to bar, 1990, California, U.S. District Court, Northern District of California and U.S. Court of Appeals, 9th Circuit; 1992, U.S. District Court, Eastern District of California; 1997, North Carolina; 1998, U.S. District Court, Eastern District of North Carolina; 1999, U.S. District Court, Western and Middle Districts of North Carolina. *Education:* University of Tennessee (B.S.C.E., 1976); University of the Pacific, McGeorge School of Law (J.D., with highest honors, 1990). Order of the Coif. Member: Traynor Honor Society; International Moot Court Honor Society. Registered Professional Civil Engineer, California.*Member:* North Carolina and American (Member, Construction Forum) Bar Associations. ***PRACTICE AREAS:*** Construction Litigation. ***Email:*** hrbivens@smithcurrie.com

ASSOCIATES

MATTHEW E. COX, born Radford, Virginia, November 14, 1971; admitted to bar, 1999, South Carolina; 2000, U.S. District Court, District of South Carolina; 2004, U.S. Court of Appeals, Fourth Circuit (Not admitted in North Carolina). *Education:* Brigham Young University (B.S., 1996); University of South Carolina (J.D., 1999). Mu Sigma Rho (Brigham Young University). Recipient, 1999, SCTLA Mock Trial Competition, 1st Place. *Member:* Spartanburg County and American Bar Associations; South Carolina Bar. ***LANGUAGES:*** Dutch. ***PRACTICE AREAS:*** Business Law; Construction Law; Civil Litigation.

GREGORY L. SHELTON, born Tallahassee, Florida, 1969; admitted to bar, 1995, Florida; 1996, U.S. District Court, Northern District of Florida; 1997, U.S. District Court, Middle and Southern Districts of Florida; 1998, North Carolina; 2001, U.S. District Court, Western District of North Carolina; 2003, U.S. District Court, Eastern District of North Carolina; 2004, U.S. District Court, Middle District of North Carolina. *Education:* Florida State University (B.S., Finance, 1991); Florida State University College of Law (J.D., with honors, 1995). Member, Florida State University Law Review, 1992-1995. Executive Editor, Florida State University Law Review, 1994-1995. Commissioner, Mountain Island Lake Marine Commission, 2004-2007. Judicial Externship for the U.S. District Court, Northern District of Florida, 1995. *Member:* Mecklenburg County and American Bar Associations; The Florida Bar; North Carolina State Bar; Forum on the Construction Industry. (Board Certified Construction Law Lawyer, Florida Bar Board of Legal Specialization and Education). ***PRACTICE AREAS:*** Construction Litigation (80%); Surety Law (15%); Civil Litigation (5%). ***Email:*** glshelton@smithcurrie.com

CLIENTS: American Bridge Company; APAC, Inc.; American International Group; Travelers Property Casualty Corp.; St. Paul Fire and Marine Insurance Company; Condottee America; Hubbard Construction Company; Prinee Contracting Co., Inc.; Durocher Dock & Dredge, Inc.; Russell Engineering, Inc.; Bergeron Land Development, Inc.

(For biographical data on other personnel, see Professional Biographies at other locations)

SMITH DEBNAM NARRON WYCHE SAINTSING & MYERS, L.L.P.

Established in 1972
4201 CONGRESS STREET, SUITE 460
CHARLOTTE, NORTH CAROLINA 28209
Telephone: 704-643-3220
Facsimile: 704-643-3898
Email: mail@smithdebnamlaw.com
URL: http://www.smithdebnamlaw.com

Raleigh, North Carolina Office: 4601 Six Forks Road, Suite 400, 27609. Telephone: 919-250-2000. Fax: 919-250-2211.

General and Appellate Practice in all State and Federal Courts. Corporation, Bankruptcy, Non-Judicial Workouts and Reorganizations, Corporate Reorganization, Construction, Equipment Leasing and Finance, Estate Planning and Administration, Commercial and Retail Collections and Litigation. Administrative and Regulatory, Government Contracts and Procurement, Health Care, Land Use and Zoning, Limited Liability Companies and Partnerships, Public Finance, Residential and Commercial Real Estate, Family Law and Equitable Distribution, Telecommunications, Plaintiff's Personal Injury.

FIRM PROFILE: The firm began in 1972 when Fred J. Smith, Jr. joined with Thurston Debnam and two other attorneys to form a partnership in Raleigh. During the quarter century since its founding, the firm has expanded to become one of the largest law firms in the Triangle area.

JOHN B. HONEYCUTT, JR., born September 14, 1950; admitted to bar, 1978, Louisiana, U.S. District Court, Western District of Louisiana and U.S. Court of Appeals, Fifth Circuit; 1981, U.S. Court of Appeals, Eleventh Circuit; 1988, U.S. Court of Federal Claims; 1990, U.S. Supreme Court; 1992, North Carolina and South Carolina; 1994, U.S. District Court, Eastern, Middle and Western Districts of North Carolina and U.S. Court of Appeals, Fourth Circuit; 1996, U.S. District Court, District of South Carolina. *Education:* University of Louisiana (B.A., 1972); Loyola University, New Orleans (J.D., 1978). Certified Circuit Court Arbitrator, South Carolina. ***PRACTICE AREAS:*** Banking Law; Commercial Contracts; Commercial Litigation; Construction Law.

(This Listing Continued)

HEATHER N. JOHNSON, born Wooster, Ohio, December 30, 1976; admitted to bar, 2002, North Carolina and U.S. District Court, Western District of North Carolina. *Education:* Ohio University (B.A., 1999); University of Pittsburgh School of Law (J.D., 2002). *Member:* Mecklenburg County Bar Association; North Carolina State Bar. ***PRACTICE AREAS:*** Business Transactions; Business Organization; Corporate Law; Litigation.

REPRESENTATIVE CLIENTS: CitiCapital Relocation; Ford Motor Credit Co.; Carolina Builders Corp.; General Electric Capital Corp.; Advanta Leasing Corp.; N.B. Handy Co.; Oakwood Acceptance Corp.; Bank One; Chrysler Credit; Toyota Motor Credit/Lexus Financial Services; Duke University Federal Credit Union; NC Credit Union Network; United Rentals, Inc.; Citibank, N.A.; Wells Fargo Financial Leasing, Inc.; Oberlin Capital, L.P.
APPROVED ATTORNEYS FOR: Fidelity National Title; Lawyers Title Insurance Corp.; Commonwealth Land Title Insurance Co.; Chicago Title Insurance Co.; Investors Title Insurance Co.; First American Title Insurance Co.; Stewart Title Guaranty Co.
REFERENCE: Centura Bank.

(For complete biographical data on other personnel, see professional biographies at Raleigh, North Carolina)

SMITH LAW FIRM, P.C.

Established in 2004

5950 FAIRVIEW ROAD, SUITE 710
CHARLOTTE, NORTH CAROLINA 28210
Telephone: 704-643-6650
Telecopier: 704-643-6651
Email: jsmith@smithlawfirm.biz
URL: http://www.smith-lawfirm.net

Employment Law, Workers' Compensation, Litigation, Mediation.

FIRM PROFILE: John Brem Smith (Jack) founded to provide efficient and effective representation and counseling for clients, both employers and employees, in all areas of employment law.

JOHN BREM SMITH, born 1961; admitted to bar, 1986, North Carolina; U.S. District Court, Western, Middle and Eastern Districts of North Carolina; U.S. Court of Appeals, Fourth Circuit. *Education:* Davidson College (A.B., 1983); Wake Forest University (J.D., 1986). Phi Delta Phi. Certified Mediator and Arbitrator. Finalist: Stanley Cup Moot Court Competition, 1984; National Moot Court Competition, 1985. Author: "Statutory Modifications," North Carolina Tort Practice Handbook, Wake Forest Continuing Legal Education, 1985; "Americans With Disabilities Act & Workers' Compensation Claims" and "Repetitive Motion Disorder Claims-Prevention, Handling & Defending," Workers' Compensation in North Carolina, Lorman Business Center, Inc., 1991; "The Interplay Between Worker's Compensation and Other Disability Laws," North Carolina Association of Defense Attorneys, 1997; "Employment Law for the Workers' Compensation Practitioner," North Carolina Bar Foundation, 1998; "Departing Employee Issues," North Carolina Association of Defense Attorneys, 2002. *Member:* The Mecklenburg County and North Carolina Bar Associations; North Carolina State Bar. ***PRACTICE AREAS:*** Employment Law; Workers Compensation; Litigation; Mediation; Arbitration. ***Email:*** jsmith@smithlawfirm.biz

LEGAL SUPPORT PERSONNEL

ABNEY HUDNALL, (Paralegal)

REPRESENTATIVE CLIENTS: Shuford Mills Inc.; Shurtape Technologies, Inc.; Cooper Tools; PSNC Energy; City of Charlotte; Mecklenburg County; Cabarrus County; Rowan County; CT Group; Lake Norman Charter School.

SPERRY & TYSON, PLLC

CHARLOTTE, NORTH CAROLINA

(See Matthews)

Real Estate, Residential Real Estate, Commercial Real Estate, Mortgages, Trusts and Estates, Estate Planning, Business Law, Partnerships, Contracts, Collections, Corporate, Taxation, Bankruptcy.

STILES BYRUM & HORNE, L.L.P.

Established in 1999

THE ARLINGTON, SUITE 650
325 ARLINGTON AVENUE
CHARLOTTE, NORTH CAROLINA 28203
Telephone: 704-332-2830
Facsimile: 704-332-3281
Email: kvalentine@sbhlaw.net
Email: sbh@sbhlaw.net
URL: http://www.sbh-lawfirm.com

General Civil Practice. Employment, Workers Compensation and Insurance Law. Trials, State and Federal Courts.

FIRM PROFILE: The law firm of Stiles Byrum & Horne, L.L.P., in Charlotte, North Carolina, concentrates in civil litigation, primarily insurance defense, with particular expertise in the following areas: trucking and motor vehicle liability, products liability, property and casualty claims, construction claims, and workers' compensation.

NED A. STILES, born Maysville, Kentucky, July 21, 1952; admitted to bar, 1979, North Carolina; U.S. District Court, Western, Middle and Eastern Districts of North Carolina; U.S. Court of Appeals, Fourth Circuit. *Education:* University of North Carolina (B.S., 1974); Wake Forest University (J.D., 1979). Phi Delta Phi. Associate Justice, Wake Forest Moot Court Board. *Member:* North Carolina Bar Association; North Carolina State Bar; North Carolina Association of Defense Attorneys; Defense Research Institute; National Association of Defense Attorneys; Trucking Industry Defense Association(TIDA). ***PRACTICE AREAS:*** Civil Defense Practice; Trucking; Construction; Insurance; General Liability Litigation. ***Email:*** nstiles@sbhlaw.net

(This Listing Continued)

HENRY C. BYRUM, JR., born Monroe, North Carolina, July 17, 1953; admitted to bar, 1981, Georgia and North Carolina. *Education:* Wingate College (A.A., with honors, 1973); University of North Carolina at Charlotte (B.A., with honors, 1975); Auburn University (M.A., 1977); Mercer University (J.D., cum laude, 1981). Phi Theta Kappa; Pi Sigma Alpha. Listed, Best Lawyers in America. *Member:* North Carolina Bar Association-(Chair, Workers' Compensation Section); North Carolina State Bar; State Bar of Georgia; North Carolina Association of Defense Attorneys. ***PRACTICE AREAS:*** General Civil Practice; Employment; Workers Compensation Law. ***Email:*** hbyrum@sbhlaw.net

TERRY D. HORNE, born Wadesboro, North Carolina, July 6, 1959; admitted to bar, 1985, North Carolina. *Education:* University of North Carolina at Chapel Hill (B.A., 1981); Wake Forest University (J.D., 1985). Member, Order of Barristers. Associate Justice, Wake Forest Moot Court Board. Recipient, Moot Court Award. *Member:* North Carolina and American Bar Associations; North Carolina State Bar; North Carolina Association of Defense Attorneys; Defense Research Institute. ***PRACTICE AREAS:*** Civil Practice; Municipal and Police Liability; General Liability and Insurance Litigation; Workers Compensation. ***Email:*** thorne@sbhlaw.net

D. LANE MATTHEWS, born Charlotte, North Carolina, December 17, 1965; admitted to bar, 1992, North Carolina. *Education:* University of North Carolina at Chapel Hill (B.A., 1988); University of Tennessee (J.D., 1992). Staff Member, Tennessee Law Review. Order of the Barristers, Member, Tennessee Moot Court Board; National Moot Court Team. *Member:* North Carolina State Bar; North Carolina Bar Association; North Carolina Association of Defense Attorneys; Defense Research Institute. ***PRACTICE AREAS:*** Civil Practice; Construction Law; Insurance Liability; Litigation; Workers Compensation. ***Email:*** lmatthews@sbhlaw.net

MARK O. CROWTHER, born Worcester, Massachusetts, July 18, 1966; admitted to bar, 1993, North Carolina. *Education:* Davidson College (B.A., 1988); Campbell University (J.D., cum laude, 1993). Order of Barristers. Member: Moot Court Board; National Moot Court Team. *Member:* North Carolina Bar Association; North Carolina State Bar; North Carolina Association of Defense Attorneys. ***PRACTICE AREAS:*** General Civil Practice; Workers Compensation. ***Email:*** mcrowther@sbhlaw.net

BRIAYN G. SMITH, born Charlotte, North Carolina, 1979; admitted to bar, 2004, North Carolina. *Education:* University of North Carolina (B.A., Communications, 2001); Wake Forest University (J.D., 2004). Member: Order of Omega; Communications Honor Society; Student Bar Association. *Member:* North Carolina Bar Association; North Carolina Association of Defense Attorneys. ***LANGUAGES:*** Spanish. ***PRACTICE AREAS:*** Workers Compensation; Civil Litigation. ***Email:*** bsmith@sbhlaw.net

SARAH B. SPISICH, born Warren, Michigan, 1980; admitted to bar, 2005, North Carolina. *Education:* Washington & Lee University (B.A., cum laude, 2002); Wake Forest University (J.D., 2005). Phi Alpha Delta; Order of the Barristers. Member, Moot Court Board. Author, "The Aftermath of Davila: Are Healthcare Enrollees Now in a Sinking Ship Without a Paddle?" The Health Lawyer, Vol. 17, Issue 4, 2005. *Member:* North Carolina and American Bar Associations; North Carolina State Bar; North Carolina Association of Defense Attorneys. ***Email:*** sspisich@sbhlaw.net

REPRESENTATIVE CLIENTS: AIG Claim Services, Inc.; Freightliner Corp.; Crete Transporation; PPG Industries; Cincinnati Insurance Cos.; Penn National Ins. Co.; Zuirch-American Ins. Co.; Central Mutual Ins. Cos.; FedEx Companies; State Farm Mutual Insurance Cos.; OneBeacon Insurance; Amerisure Insurance Co.; Carolina Casualty Ins. Co.; SAFECO; N.C. League of Municipalities.

STOTT, HOLLOWELL, PALMER & WINDHAM, L.L.P.

CHARLOTTE, NORTH CAROLINA

(See Gastonia)

General Civil and Trial Practice in all Courts. Corporation, Real Estate, Estate Planning and Probate, Insurance, Commercial Law, Municipal Law, Worker Compensation, Bankruptcy, Labor and Employment Law.

LAW OFFICE OF DAVID H. STRICKLAND, PLLC

1409 EAST BOULEVARD, SUITE 117
CHARLOTTE, NORTH CAROLINA 28220
Telephone: 704-373-6077
Fax: 704-373-6306
URL: http://www.davidstricklandlaw.com

Criminal Law, Driving While Intoxicated (DWI), Juvenile Crimes, Parole and Probation, Traffic Violations, Speeding, Felonies, Automobile Accidents, Medical Malpractice, Slip and Fall, Construction.

DAVID H. STRICKLAND, born Winston-Salem, North Carolina, October 8, 1976; admitted to bar, 2002, North Carolina. *Education:* Wake Forest University (B.A., 1999); Campbell University (J.D., 2002). *Member:* Mecklenburg County and North Carolina Bar Associations; North Carolina State Bar. ***Email:*** davidstrickland@carolina.rr.com

SUMMA & ALLAN, P.A.

Established in 1997

BALLANTYNE CORPORATE PARK
11610 NORTH COMMUNITY HOUSE ROAD
SUITE 200
CHARLOTTE, NORTH CAROLINA 28277-2162
Telephone: 704-945-6700
Fax: 704-945-6735
Email: phil@psumma.com
URL: http://www.psumma.com

Intellectual Property Law: Patents, Trademarks, Copyrights and Trade Secret Protection. Trials and Appeals in all Federal and State Courts and Proceedings before the United States Patent and Trademark Office.

FIRM PROFILE: Summa & Allan, P.A. is a rapidly growing law firm dedicated exclusively to the practice of intellectual property law. The majority of the firm's work involves securing patent and trademark protection for clients throughout the world, and the protection of those rights in trial and appellate courts, and in proceedings in the United States Patent and Trademark Office, the European Patent Office, and other patent offices worldwide. In addition, the firm renders patent and trademark opinions; prepares and negotiates patent, trademark, and other intellectual property licenses; and maintains issued patents and trademark registrations. All of our attorneys are members of the American Bar Association, the American Intellectual Property Law Association, the State Bar of North Carolina, the North Carolina Bar Association, and the Carolina Patent, Trademark and Copyright Law Association. All of our attorneys have a technical undergraduate degree, and all are registered to practice or preparing to practice before the United States Patent and Trademark Office.

MEMBERS OF FIRM

PHILIP SUMMA, born Philadelphia, Pennsylvania, October 1, 1951; admitted to bar, 1983, North Carolina; 1986, U.S. Supreme Court; 1987, U.S. Court of Appeals for the Federal Circuit; registered to practice before U.S. Patent and Trademark Office. *Education:* Gettysburg College (B.A., Chem., 1973); North Carolina State University (M.S., Chem., 1975); Campbell University (J.D., 1983). Member, Fourth Circuit Judicial Conference; American Chemical Society; Licensing Executives Society. Author: "A New Test For Trademark Dilution - Why North Carolina Should Adopt Section 12 of the Model State Trademark Bill," Campbell Law Review, Fall, 1982. Member, Business North Carolina's "Legal Elite," 2002, 2003 and 2004. *Member:* North Carolina State Bar; North Carolina-(Past Chairman, Intellectual Property Law Section) and American(Member, Intellectual Property Law Section) Bar Associations; Carolina Patent, Trademark and Copyright Law Association; American Intellectual Property Law Association. ***PRACTICE AREAS:*** Patent; Intellectual Property; Chemistry; Polymers; Semiconductor Technology. ***Email:*** phil@psumma.com

ALBERT P. ALLAN, born Raleigh, North Carolina, May 16, 1957; admitted to bar, 1992, North Carolina; 1994, U.S. Court of Appeals for the Federal Circuit; registered to practice before U.S. Patent and Trademark Office. *Education:* University of Miami (B.S., Arch.E., 1979); Air Force Institute of Technology (M.S., 1980); Arizona State University (M.B.A., 1984); University of Notre Dame (J.D., cum laude, 1992). Law Clerk to the Hon. Graham C. Mullen, United States District Court, Western District of North Carolina, 1992-1994. *Member:* North Carolina State Bar; North Carolina and American Bar Associations (Member, Sections on: Intellectual Property Law, Litigation, Law Practice Management); Carolina Patent, Trademark and Copyright Law Association (Second Vice-President, 1999-2000); American Intellectual Property Law Association. [Captain, United States Air Force, 1979-1984]. ***PRACTICE AREAS:*** Patent Litigation; Trademark Litigation; Copyright Litigation; Intellectual Property Litigation; Counterfeiting. ***Email:*** aallan@psumma.com

RICHARD L. ADDITON, born Augusta, Maine, July 24, 1966; admitted to bar, 1996, Florida; 1997, Virginia; 1998, North Carolina; registered to practice before U.S. Patent and Trademark Office. *Education:* University of Maine (B.S., with highest distinction, Chem.E., 1989); University of Virginia (J.D., 1996). *Member:* North Carolina State Bar; The Florida Bar; Virginia State Bar; American Bar Association; Carolina Patent, Trademark and Copyright Law Association. ***PRACTICE AREAS:*** Intellectual Property; Patents; Trademarks; Trade Secrets; Chemical Patents; Mechanical Patents; Semiconductor Patents; Computer and Software Patents; International Patents. ***Email:*** additon@psumma.com

JESSE B. ASHE III, born Charlotte, North Carolina, October 30, 1963; admitted to bar, 1998, North Carolina; registered to practice before U.S. Patent and Trademark Office. *Education:* United States Air Force Academy (B.S., Int'l.Aff., 1986); Temple University School of Law (J.D., 1996). Editor-in-Chief, Temple International and Comparative Law Journal, 1995-1996. Author: "Space Station Alpha," Temple Int'l. and Comp. L. J., Vol. 9, No. 2, Fall, 1995. White House Aide to President George Bush, 1989-1990. *Member:* North Carolina and American Bar Associations (Member, Intellectual Property Law Section); North Carolina State Bar; American Intellectual Property Law Association; International Trademark Association; Carolina Patent, Trademark and Copyright Law Association. [Captain, U.S. Air Force, 1986-1991]. ***PRACTICE AREAS:*** Patents; Trademarks; Copyrights; Intellectual Property; Intellectual Property Litigation; Mechanical Patents; Licensing. ***Email:*** jbashe@psumma.com

MELISSA B. PENDLETON, born Winston-Salem, North Carolina, February 12, 1965; admitted to bar, 1990, North Carolina; registered to practice before U.S. Patent and Trademark Office. *Education:* North Carolina State University (B.A., summa cum laude, 1987); University of North Carolina (J.D., 1990). *Member:* Mecklenburg County and North Carolina (Section Council, Intellectual Property Section) Bar Associations; American Intellectual Property Law Association; Carolina Patent, Trademark and Copyright Law Association. ***PRACTICE AREAS:*** Intellectual Property; Chemical Intellectual Property; Pharmaceutical Intellectual Property; Chemical Patents; Pharmaceutical Patents; Biotechnology Patents; Trademarks. ***Email:*** mpendleton@psumma.com

(This Listing Continued)

ASSOCIATES

BRIAN JOHNSON, born Mullins, South Carolina, June 20, 1966; admitted to bar, 1996, South Carolina; 2001, North Carolina; registered to practice before U.S. Patent and Trademark Office. *Education:* Duke University (B.S.E.E., 1988); University of South Carolina (J.D., 1995). J.A. Jones Memorial Scholar, Duke University. Teaching Assistant, Legal Writing, University of South Carolina Law, 1994-1995. *Member:* North Carolina Bar Association; South Carolina Bar; Patent Law Associates. ***PRACTICE AREAS:*** Patents; Trademarks. ***Email:*** rbjohnson@psumma.com

MARCIA T. GRECI, born Panama City, Florida, May 7, 1974; admitted to bar, 2004, North Carolina; registered to practice before U.S. Patent and Trademark Office. *Education:* Erskine College (B.S., 1996); University of Southern California, (Ph.D., Organic Chemistry, 2000); Cleveland-Marshall College of Law (J.D., cum laude, 2003). Member, American Chemical Society, 1993. Excellence in Research and Teaching, Cleveland Marshall College of Law. *Member:* American Bar Association; Carolina Patent, Trademark, and Copyright Law Association; American Intellectual Property Law Association. ***PRACTICE AREAS:*** Patents; Trademarks; Copyrights; Chemical Patents; Biochemical Patents. ***Email:*** mgreci@psumma.com

PATENT AGENT

JAMES CORBITT, born Rosebud, Texas. *Education:* Texas A & M University (Gene., 1992); University of Texas Health Science Center (Ph.D., Phrm., 2000). Member, Association of University Technology Managers. ***Email:*** jcorbitt@psumma.com

REPRESENTATIVE CLIENTS: Acme McCrary, Corporation; Air T. Inc.; Akima Corporation; Cadmus Communications Corp.; Caraustar Industries, Inc.; CEM Corporation; Consolidated Theaters; Cree, Inc.; SYMYX, Inc.; Environmental Protection Agency (EPA); Jeff Gordon, Inc.; J.L. Powell & Co. Inc.; Lifestyles Furnishing International Limited; Milk Specialties Co.; Rexam, Inc.; Röching Engineered Plastics; TeamVest Retirement Plan Service, Inc.; Wellman, Inc.; Roush Racing; InteliCoat Technologies; Canal Industries; LeadFirst & Associates, Inc.

THE LAW OFFICES OF GARY W. SWINDELL

227 WEST TRADE STREET, SUITE 2030
CHARLOTTE, NORTH CAROLINA 28202
Telephone: 704-376-1390
Fax: 704-376-1391
Email: gary@swindelllaw.com
URL: http://www.lawyers.com/swindelllaw

Commercial Real Estate, Commercial Leasing, Zoning Planning and Land Use, Corporate, Capital Markets.

GARY W. SWINDELL, born Woodbury, New Jersey, March 13, 1954; admitted to bar, 1979, Virginia and District of Columbia; 1986, North Carolina; U.S. Supreme Court. *Education:* University of Delaware (B.A., with distinction and high honors, 1976); Georgetown University Law Center (J.D., 1979). Founding Partner, Fennebresque, Clark, Swindell & Hay. ***PRACTICE AREAS:*** Capital Markets; Real Estate; Land Use; Leasing.

ASSOCIATE

KENT D. JONES, born Charlotte, North Carolina, November 18, 1968; admitted to bar, 1995, Alabama; 1996, North Carolina. *Education:* University of The South (B.A., 1991); Cumberland School of Law of Samford University (J.D., magna cum laude, 1995). Casenote Editor, Cumberland Law Review, 1994-1995. *Member:* Mecklenburg County, North Carolina and American Bar Associations; Alabama State Bar. ***PRACTICE AREAS:*** Real Estate Development; Real Estate Leasing; Real Estate Finance; Corporate. ***Email:*** kent@swindelllaw.com

ANDREW D. TAYLOR, JR. & ASSOCIATES

Established in 1976

THE ARNOLD PALMER CORPORATE CENTER
CALCUTTA CONDOMINIUMS ON THE LAKES
3701 LATROBE DRIVE, SUITE 130
P.O. BOX 221255
CHARLOTTE, NORTH CAROLINA 28222-1255
Telephone: 704-366-6210
Telecopier: 704-366-4654
Email: adtaylor@vnet.net
URL: http://www.lawyers.com/taylor&associates

General, Civil Trial and Appellate Practice in all State and Federal Courts. Commercial, Corporate, Real Estate, Probate, Wills and Trusts, Domestic Relations, Family Law, Child Custody, Child Support, Divorce, Personal Injury, Auto Accidents, Slip and Fall, Wrongful Death, Credit Union, Collections, Product Liability, Business Law, Partnership.

FIRM PROFILE: The firm is a general practice firm with more than 30 years experience in the representation of both plaintiffs and defendants in State, Federal and Appellate Civil Litigation, Business Transactions, Contracts, Collections, Negotiations, Settlements, Family Law, Personal Injury, Real Estate, Product Liability, Estate Planning and Administration, Wills and Trusts. The firm was founded by Andrew D. Taylor, Jr., a Charlotte, NC native, who has been licensed to practice law since 1969 and who has practiced continuously in Charlotte, NC since his return from military service in Vietnam in 1971. The firm is committed to excellence and to providing only the highest quality legal services through its staff and extended support network and consulting experts.

ANDREW D. TAYLOR, JR., born Boca Raton, Florida, August 22, 1944; admitted to bar, 1969, North Carolina; 1971, U.S. District Court, Western District of North Carolina;

(This Listing Continued)

1974, U.S. Court of Appeals, Fourth Circuit; U.S. Court of Appeals for the Federal Circuit. *Education:* Wake Forest University (B.A., 1966); University of North Carolina (J.D., 1969). Legal Officer, U.S. Army Medical Service Corp, 1969-1971. *Member:* North Carolina and American Bar Associations; 26th Judicial District and North Carolina State Bars; North Carolina Academy of Trial Lawyers. ***PRACTICE AREAS:*** Civil Litigation; Collection Law; Family Law; Product Liability; Wills; Trust Law.

ASSOCIATE

MELISSA D. WRIGHT, born Brookhaven, New York, August 26, 1974; admitted to bar, 2003, North Carolina. *Education:* Pfeiffer University (B.A., 1999); Cumberland School of Law (J.D., 2003). Phi Alpha Delta (Vice Justice, 2000-2003). Associate Justice, Moot Court Board, 2003. *Member:* North Carolina and American Bar Associations. ***PRACTICE AREAS:*** Civil Litigation; Collections; Family Law. ***Email:*** adtcoll@vnet.net

REPRESENTATIVE CLIENTS: Michael Weinig, AG of Germany; McGowan Painting Contractors, Inc.; Charlotte Surgical Group, P.A.; Calcutta Condominium Associates, Inc.; Knauff Insurance, Inc.; C.I.T. Financial Services Corp.; Andrews Federal Credit Union; Nationwide Mutual Insurance Co.; Eastern Financial Florida Credit Union; Massachusetts Federal Credit Union; Claim Management, Inc.; Northland Insurance Companies; Selective Insurance Co.; USAA Insurance Company; Bankers & Shippers Insurance Co.; Allstate Insurance Company; GreCon Dimter, Inc.; Binswanger Glass Co.; Hobbs & Crossley, P.A.; CISTECH Inc.; Imperial Business Credit, Inc.; Machinery Finance Group, Inc.; Apperson Properties, Inc.; RAIMANN USA/Interholz Gmbtt; The Leasing Company; Michael Weinig, Inc.
APPROVED ATTORNEY FOR: Lawyers Title Insurance Corp.; Pioneer National Title Insurance Co.; First Title Insurance Co.; Investors Title Insurance Co.; Jefferson-Pilot Title Insurance Co.; AMI Title Insurance Co.; Commonwealth Land Title Insurance Co.; St. Paul Title Insurance Corp.; Lawyers Title of North Carolina, Inc.; Chicago Title Insurance Co.

TAYLOR, PENRY, RASH & RIEMANN, PLLC

Established in 2001

2359 PERIMETER POINTE PARKWAY, SUITE 360
CHARLOTTE, NORTH CAROLINA 28208
Telephone: 704-424-2900
Fax: 704-424-2999
URL: http://www.tprr.com

Raleigh, North Carolina Office: 510 Glenwood Avenue, Suite 319, 27603. Telephone: 919-833-9449. Fax: 919-833-9448.

Construction Law, Construction Litigation, Commercial Litigation, Securities Litigation, Mediation, Arbitration, Intellectual Property Litigation, Insurance Coverage Litigation, Government Relations and Administrative Litigation.

JOHN B. TAYLOR, born Danville, Virginia, October 4, 1937; admitted to bar, 1965, North Carolina. *Education:* North Carolina State University (B.S., Geological Engineering, 1960); University of North Carolina at Chapel Hill (LL.B., 1965). Phi Delta Phi. Author: "North Carolina Construction Law," Professional Education Systems, Inc.; "Construction Law," and "North Carolina Building and Highway Construction Law," Carolinas AGC, Inc. Co-Author: "Construction Management/Design-Build in North Carolina," and "Construction Law For Attorneys in North Carolina," Lorman Education Services, Inc. Member, American Arbitration Association, and its Construction Advisory Council. *Member:* North Carolina (Member, Construction Law Section) and American (Member, Construction Law Section) Bar Associations. [Capt., U.S. Army, 1960-1962]. ***PRACTICE AREAS:*** Construction Law; Mediation; Arbitration and Litigation.

EUGENE F. RASH, born Jefferson, North Carolina, January 24, 1962; admitted to bar, 1995, North Carolina and South Carolina. *Education:* North Carolina State University (B.S., in Civil Engineering, 1985); Wake Forest University (J.D., 1995). Chi Epsilon. National Civil Engineering Honor Society. Member, Wake Forest National Trial Team, 1994, 1995. Brown Scholar. Recipient: American Jurisprudence Awards in Civil Procedure I & II; Corpus Juris Secundum Award in Civil Procedure; Book Awards, Sales, Trial Practice. *Member:* North Carolina and American Bar Associations; South Carolina Bar; American Society of Civil Engineers. ***PRACTICE AREAS:*** Construction Litigation; Commercial Litigation. ***Email:*** gene.rash@tprr.com

TEMPLE LAW FIRM, PLLC

CHARLOTTE, NORTH CAROLINA

(See Raleigh)

Pharmaceutical and Defective Medical Devices (Fen-hen, Vioxx, Celebrex & Bextra), Environmental and Toxic Torts, Personal Injury, Products Liability, Wrongful Death, Civil Litigation.

SUSAN V. THOMAS

CHARLOTTE, NORTH CAROLINA

(See Cornelius)

Family Law, Domestic Relations, Premarital Agreements, Child Custody, Child Support, Visitation Rights, Alimony, Divorce, Settlements, Paternity, Name Changes.

TIN FULTON GREENE & OWEN, PLLC

212 SOUTH TRYON STREET
SUITE 1200
CHARLOTTE, NORTH CAROLINA 28281
Telephone: 704-338-1220
Fax: 704-338-1312
URL: http://www.tfgolawfirm.com

Immigration, Criminal Defense Trial and Appellate Practice, Drug Crimes, Felonies, Misdemeanors, White Collar Crime, Criminal Conspiracy.

(This Listing Continued)

MEMBERS OF FIRM

NOELL P. TIN, born Columbus, Ohio, August 9, 1968; admitted to bar, 1994, North Carolina and U.S. District Court, Western District of North Carolina; 1995, U.S. District Court, Middle District of North Carolina; 1996, U.S. Court of Appeals, Fourth Circuit; 2000, U.S. Supreme Court; 2001, U.S. District Court, Eastern District of North Carolina. *Education:* Miami University (B.A., Political Science, 1990); Northeastern University School of Law (J.D., 1993). *Member:* North Carolina Academy of Trial Lawyers; National Association of Criminal Defense Lawyers. ***REPORTED CASES:*** Thompson v. Three Guys Furniture Co., 469 S.E.2d 583 (N.C. App. 1996); United States v.Sampson, 140 F.3d 585 (4th Cir. 1998); United States v. Rhynes, 196 F.3d 207 (4th Cir. 1999); United States v. Brown, 202 F.3d 691 (4th Cir. 2000); United States v. Promise, 255 F.3d 150 (4th Cir. 2001) (en banc); State v. Nance, 149 N.C.App.734, 562 S.E.2d 557 (2002). ***PRACTICE AREAS:*** Criminal Defense; Trial Practice; Appellate Practice. ***Email:*** ntin@tfgolaw.com

SHIRLEY L. FULTON, admitted to bar, 1981, North Carolina. *Education:* North Carolina Agricultural & Technical State University (B.S., 1977); Duke University School of Law (J.D., 1980); Queens University, Mccoll School of Business (M.B.A., 1988). Former Senior Resident, Superior Court Judge, 26th Judicial District. Member, Board of Trustees: Evergreen Fund Board; Charlotte-Mecklenburg Public Schools Foundation. Chair, Board of Trustees, Charlotte Law School. Co-Chair, United Agenda for Children in Mecklenburg County. *Member:* Mecklenburg County Bar Association (President). ***PRACTICE AREAS:*** Contracts; Business Law; Real Estate; Successions; Litigation. ***Email:*** sfulton@tfgolaw.com

CHRISTOPHER E. GREENE, born Houlton, Maine, April 5, 1968; admitted to bar, 1998, North Carolina. *Education:* University of North Carolina at Charlotte (B.A., Political Science, cum laude, 1995); University of Miami (J.D., cum laude, 1998). *Member:* North Carolina and American Bar Associations; American Immigration Lawyers Association; National Immigration Project. ***PRACTICE AREAS:*** Visas; Labor Certifications; Employment Visas; Family Immigration Law; Deportation; Immigration and Naturalization. ***Email:*** cgreene@tfgolaw.com

C. MELISSA OWEN, born Pittsburgh, Pennsylvania, September 17, 1974; admitted to bar, 1999, Pennsylvania and U.S. District Court, Western District of Pennsylvania; 2002, North Carolina and U.S. District Court, Western District of North Carolina. *Education:* Miami University (B.A., English, 1996); Duquesne University School of Law (J.D., 1999). *Member:* National Association of Criminal Defense Lawyers; North Carolina Academy of Trial Lawyers; Mecklenburg County Bar Association; American Inns of Court (Board Member, 1999-2002). ***PRACTICE AREAS:*** Criminal Law; Criminal Appeals. ***Email:*** cmowen@tfgolaw.com

OF COUNSEL

RONALD L. GIBSON, born Winnsboro, South Carolina, November 28, 1951; admitted to bar, 1978, North Carolina, U.S. District Court, Western, Middle and Eastern Districts of North Carolina and U.S. Court of Appeals, Fourth Circuit. *Education:* Davidson College (A.B., 1974); University of North Carolina (J.D., 1978). Recipient, Thomas J. Watson Fellowship. Law Clerk to U.S. District Judge James B. McMillan, 1978-1979. *Member:* North Carolina State Bar (Councilor); North Carolina Bar Association. ***PRACTICE AREAS:*** Business Law. ***Email:*** rgibson@murphychapman.com

MATTHEW G. PRUDEN, born Charlotte, North Carolina, September 7, 1975.; admitted to bar, 2004, North Carolina. *Education:* Guillford College (B.S. Justice and Policy Studies 1998); Wake Forest University School of Law (J.D. 2004). *Member:* North Carolina Bar Association; National Association of Criminal Defense Lawyers; North Carolina Academy of Trial Lawyers. ***PRACTICE AREAS:*** Criminal Law; Felonies; Federal Criminal Law.

BETHELEHEM FELEKE, born Addis-Ababa, Ethiopia, October 4, 1968; admitted to bar, 1999, Maryland (Not admitted in North Carolina). *Education:* Université de Reims, France (Maîtrise de Droit des Affaires, 1992); Regent University School of Law (J.D., 1997). *Member:* Maryland State Bar Association, Inc.; American Immigration Lawyers Association. ***LANGUAGES:*** Amharic and French. ***PRACTICE AREAS:*** Immigration Law; Business Immigration; Family Immigration Law. ***Email:*** bfeleke@tfgolaw.com

PETER J. UNDERHILL

4701 HEDGEMORE DRIVE, SUITE 740
CHARLOTTE, NORTH CAROLINA 28209
Telephone: 704-561-0090
Fax: 704-561-0905
Email: punderhill@carolina.rr.com
URL: http://www.underhill-law.com

Consumer Bankruptcy, Bankruptcy Law, Foreclosures, Debtor and Creditor, Collections, Creditor Rights, Residential Real Estate, Mortgages, Business Law, Limited Liability Law, Wills and Probate.

PETER J. UNDERHILL, born New Orleans, Louisiana, January 21, 1946; admitted to bar, 1974, North Carolina. *Education:* University of North Carolina at Chapel Hill (B.S., 1968; J.D., 1974). *Member:* Mecklenburg County Bar Association; North Carolina State Bar (Member, Sections on: Real Property; Bankruptcy); National Association of Consumer Bankruptcy Attorneys.

ESTATE & ELDER LAW FIRM OF VANDIVER & BRYAN

CHARLOTTE, NORTH CAROLINA

(See Cornelius)

Elder Law, Estate Planning, Estate and Trust Administration, Medicaid Planning and Application, Wills, Trusts and Estates, Advance Directives, Taxation, Probate, Guardianship, Incompetency Proceedings, Medicare, Special Needs Trusts, Disability Law, Social Security, Veter-

(This Listing Continued)

ESTATE & ELDER LAW FIRM OF VANDIVER & BRYAN, Charlotte—Continued

an's Benefits, Long Term Care Planning, Estate Planning for the Disabled, Estate Planning for the Elderly, Business Law, Corporate Law, Business Succession Planning, Family Limited Partnerships, Limited Liability Company Law, Commercial and Contracts.

VAN HOY, REUTLINGER, ADAMS & DUNN

737 EAST BOULEVARD
CHARLOTTE, NORTH CAROLINA 28203
Telephone: 704-375-6022
Fax: 704-375-6024
URL: http://www.lawyers.com/vradlawfirm

Labor Relations, Employment Discrimination, Employment Litigation, Employer Rights and Management Employment Law, OSHA and Wage and Hour (Employers only). Business Law, Health Law representing Health Care Providers.

MEMBERS OF FIRM

PHILIP M. VAN HOY, born Washington, D.C., November 8, 1947; admitted to bar, 1973, North Carolina; 1974, U.S. Court of Appeals, Fourth Circuit; 1978, U.S. Supreme Court. *Education:* Duke University (A.B., 1970); University of North Carolina (J.D., 1973). Member: North Carolina OSHA Review Board, 1985-1992; Mecklenburg County Personnel Commission, 1985-1993; Duke University Athletics Council, 1999-2002. Listed in: The Best Lawyers in America, 2001—; Outstanding Lawyers of America, 2003; Chambers USA America's Leading Business Lawyers, 2003-2004; Named the Top Employment Lawyer in North Carolina, Business North Carolina Magazine, 2002; Business North Carolina Legal Elite Hall of Fame, 2003. Charter Member, Civil Justice Reform Act Committee, Western District of North Carolina. *Member:* Mecklenburg County and North Carolina (Councilor, Labor and Employment Law Section, 1983-1988; Co-Chairman, EEOC Liaison Committee, 1983-1992) Bar Associations; Fourth Circuit Judicial Conference (Permanent Member); North Carolina State Bar. [1st Lt., U.S. Army Reserve, 1973-1981]. ***PRACTICE AREAS:*** Labor and Employment Law representing Employers; Employment Discrimination; Employment Litigation; OSHA; Wage and Hour; Employment Contracts. **Email:** pvanhoy-vrad@carolina.rr.com

CRAIG A. REUTLINGER, born Providence, Rhode Island, December 10, 1947; admitted to bar, 1973, Florida and U.S. Court of Military Appeals; 1977, U.S Supreme Court; 1979, North Carolina; 1994, U.S. Court of Appeals, Fourth Circuit. *Education:* Florida State University (B.A., 1970; J.D., 1972). Chief Legal Counsel, Carolinas HealthCare System, 1978-1988. *Member:* North Carolina Bar Association (Chairman, Health Law Section, 1989-1990); American Health Lawyers Association; Fourth Circuit Judicial Conference (Permanent Member). [U.S. Air Force Judge Advocate, 1973-1978]. ***PRACTICE AREAS:*** Labor and Employment Law representing Employers; Business Law; Health Care. **Email:** cbrooks-vrad@carolina.rr.com

G. BRYAN ADAMS, III, born Charlotte, North Carolina, September 11, 1965; admitted to bar, 1990, North Carolina and U.S. District Court, Western, Middle and Eastern Districts of North Carolina; 1995, U.S. Court of Appeals, Fourth Circuit; U.S. Supreme Court. *Education:* Wofford College (B.A., cum laude, 1987); Wake Forest University (J.D., 1990). Phi Delta Phi. *Member:* Mecklenburg County and North Carolina (Member, Sections on: Labor and Employment; Litigation) Bar Associations; North Carolina Association of Defense Attorneys. ***PRACTICE AREAS:*** Labor and Employment Law representing Employers; Employment Discrimination; Employment Litigation. **Email:** badams-vrad@carolina.rr.com

STEPHEN J. DUNN, born Abilene, Texas, January 17, 1973; admitted to bar, 1998, North Carolina and U.S. District Court, Western, Middle and Eastern Districts of North Carolina; U.S. Court of Appeals, Fourth Circuit. *Education:* Duke University (B.A., 1995); University of North Carolina (J.D., 1998). *Member:* Mecklenburg County Bar Association (Civil Litigation Section); North Carolina State Bar. ***PRACTICE AREAS:*** Employment Law representing Employers; Discrimination; Wage and Hour; Non-Competition Agreements; Contracts; Health Care. **Email:** sdunn-vrad@carolina.rr.com

REPRESENTATIVE CLIENTS: AAA Carolinas Motor Club; Bealer Wholesale, Inc.; Bonsal American; Bradco Supply Corp.; Bryant Supply Co.; Cape Fear Valley Health System; Cato Corp.; Central Piedmont Community College; Charlotte's Finest Produce; Charlotte Plastic Surgery; City of Charlotte; City of Fayetteville, North Carolina; City of Gastonia, North Carolina; Corporate Health International; Crowder Construction Co.; David Weekley Homes; Duke Energy Corp.; The Employers' Association; Evernham Motorsports; Freeman White Architects; Gaston Anesthesia Associates; Geoscience Group, Inc.; Heart Group of the Carolinas; Highland Mills, Inc.; IndianHead Industries, Inc.; Mecklenburg County, North Carolina; Mecklenburg County ABC Board; Medical Review of North Carolina; Meridian Laboratory Corp.; National Gypsum Company; National Welders Supply Co.; New Horizons Computer Learning Centers; New York Life Insurance Co.; Pelton & Crane Company; Pfeiffer University; The Park Hotel; Ryan Homes; Salvation Army of NC and SC; Southeast Renal Associates; Verbatim Corp.

VANN LAW FIRM, P.A.

CHARLOTTE, NORTH CAROLINA
(See Matthews)

Business Law, Corporate, Limited Liability Companies, Small Business, Contracts, Collections, Creditor Rights, Employment, Discrimination, Driving While Intoxicated, Traffic Violations and Wrongful Termination Law.

JAMES S. WALKER

6109 ROSECREST DRIVE
P.O. BOX 240057
CHARLOTTE, NORTH CAROLINA 28224-0057
Telephone: 704-552-7276
Fax: 704-552-5324
Email: js-walker@mindspring.com

Workers Compensation, Workers Compensation Mediation.

FIRM PROFILE: Seventeen years of trial experience limited exclusively to workers compensation cases. Over 1,200 workers compensation mediations.

JAMES S. WALKER, born Charlotte, North Carolina, December 9, 1957; admitted to bar, 1988, North Carolina, U.S. District Court, Eastern and Middle Districts of North Carolina, U.S. Court of Appeals, Fourth Circuit and U.S. Supreme Court. *Education:* North Carolina State University (B.A., 1982); North Carolina Central University (J.D., summa cum laude, 1988). Staff Member, North Carolina Central Law Journal. Certified Mediator. *Member:* North Carolina Bar Association. ***REPORTED CASES:*** Melton vs. City of Rocky Mount, 118 N.C.App. 249 (1995); Higgins vs. Powell Builders, 132 N.C.App. 720 (1999). ***PRACTICE AREAS:*** Workers Compensation; Mediation.

WALLACE, PITTMAN & WEBB, PLLC

2101 REXFORD ROAD, SUITE 100E
CHARLOTTE, NORTH CAROLINA 28211
Telephone: 704-365-5566
Facsimile: 704-364-9698; 365-6735

Commercial and Residential Real Estate, Real Estate Development, Condominium Law.

FIRM PROFILE: Wallace, Pittman & Webb, PLLC is a law firm specializing in all aspects of real property transactions. The firm represents commercial developers, lenders, landlords and tenants, single and multifamily residential developers, builders, purchasers and sellers of new and existing homes, including relocation representation.

JAMES G. WALLACE, born Charlotte, North Carolina, July 29, 1949; admitted to bar, 1975, North Carolina. *Education:* University of North Carolina (B.S., 1971); Wake Forest University (J.D., 1975). Phi Delta Phi. *Member:* Mecklenburg County, 26th Judicial District and North Carolina Bar Associations; North Carolina State Bar. ***PRACTICE AREAS:*** Commercial Real Estate; Residential Real Estate; Real Estate Development. **Email:** jwallace@wppw.net

BRYAN W. PITTMAN, born Charlotte, North Carolina, November 22, 1946; admitted to bar, 1973, North Carolina. *Education:* Davidson College (A.B., 1969); University of North Carolina (J.D., 1973). *Member:* Mecklenburg County, 26th Judicial District and North Carolina Bar Associations; North Carolina State Bar. ***PRACTICE AREAS:*** Residential Real Estate; Real Estate Development.

LESLIE MILLER WEBB, born Charlotte, North Carolina, March 11, 1959; admitted to bar, 1985, North Carolina. *Education:* Davidson College (A.B., 1980); Wake Forest University (M.B.A., 1984); Wake Forest University (J.D., 1984). *Member:* Mecklenburg County, 26th Judicial District and North Carolina Bar Associations; North Carolina State Bar. (Board Certified Specialist in Residential, Business, Commercial and Industrial Transactions, North Carolina State Board of Legal Specialization). ***PRACTICE AREAS:*** Commercial Real Estate; Residential Real Estate; Real Estate Development. **Email:** lwebb@wppw.net

REPRESENTATIVE CLIENTS: Bank of America, N.A.; Centex Homes; KB Home Charlotte LLC; Levine Properties; Lillian Floyd Homes, Inc.; ReloAction; Robert C. Rhein Interests, Inc.; The Ryland Group, Inc.; Saussy Burbank, Inc.; St. Lawrence Homes, Inc.; Turnberry Homes, Inc.; WKB Charlotte, Inc.; Waters Incorporated of Charlotte.
APPROVED ATTORNEYS FOR: Chicaco Title Insurance Corporation; Colonial Title Company; Commonwealth Land Title Company of North Carolina; Fidelity National Title Insurance; First American Title of the Carolinas; Investors Title Insurance Company; Lawyers Title Insurance Corporation; Stewart Title Company; The Title Company of North Carolina.

WARREN & KALLIANOS

301 SOUTH MCDOWELL STREET, SUITE 130
CHARLOTTE, NORTH CAROLINA 28204
Telephone: 704-377-7777
Fax: 704-376-6090
Email: warkal@bellsouth.net
URL: http://www.attorneysfortheinjured.net

Plaintiff's Personal Injury, Litigation, Medical Malpractice, Nursing Home Neglect, Business Torts.

MEMBERS OF FIRM

C. JEFF WARREN, born Washington, D.C., March 24, 1958; admitted to bar, 1991, North Carolina; U.S. District Court, Western District of North Carolina. *Education:* Towson State University (B.S., magna cum laude, 1980); University of North Carolina at Chapel Hill (J.D., with honors, 1991). Order of the Coif. Member, North Carolina Journal of International Law and Commercial Regulation, 1989-1990. *Member:* Mecklenburg County, 26th Judicial District, North Carolina and American Bar Associations; North Carolina State Bar; North Carolina Academy of Trial Lawyers; The Association of Trial Lawyers of America; National Academy of Elder Law Attorneys, Inc.; Million Dollar Advocates Forum. [Captain, U.S. Air Force, 1982-1987]. ***REPORTED CASES:*** Teresa E. Vera v. Five Crow Promotions, Inc., et al, 130 N.C.App. 645, 503 S.E.2d 692 (1998); John Belton v. Barnhardt Manufacturing Co., 126 N.C. App. 654 487 S.E.2d 589 (1997). ***PRACTICE AREAS:*** Personal Injury; Medical Malpractice; Nursing Home Negligence; Business Litigation.

(This Listing Continued)

CHRIS M. KALLIANOS, born Durham, North Carolina, January 16, 1962; admitted to bar, 1987, North Carolina; U.S. District Court, Western District of North Carolina; 1989, U.S. District Court, Middle District of North Carolina; U.S. District Court, Eastern District of North Carolina; 1992, U.S. Claims Court. *Education:* University of North Carolina at Chapel Hill (B.A., 1984; J.D., with honors, 1987). Phi Beta Kappa. Member, Phi Delta Phi, 1985-1987. Staff Member, 1985-1986 and Note and Comment Editor, 1986-1987, North Carolina Law Review. Author: Note, "Bad Faith Refusal to Pay First Party Insurance Claims: A Growing Recognition of Extra-Contract Damages," 1986; Note, "Psychiatrists' Liability to Third Parties for Harmful Acts Committed by Dangerous Patients," North Carolina Law Review, Volume 64, 1985-1986. *Member:* Mecklenburg County and North Carolina (Litigation Section, 1987—) Bar Associations; North Carolina Academy of Trial Lawyers; The Association of Trial Lawyers of America; National Academy of Elder Law Attorneys, Inc.; Million Dollar Advocates Forum. ***REPORTED CASES:*** Herdlein Tech., Inc. v. Century Contractors, 147 F.R.D. 103 (1993). ***PRACTICE AREAS:*** Personal Injury; Medical Malpractice; Nursing Home Negligence; Business Litigation.

WATSON LAW FIRM, PLLC

212 SOUTH TRYON STREET, SUITE 480
CHARLOTTE, NORTH CAROLINA 28281
Telephone: 704-333-4663
Fax: 704-333-7727
Email: cdwatson@watsonlawpllc.com
URL: http://www.cdwatsonlaw.com

Personal Injury, Automobile Accidents, Slip and Fall, Wrongful Death, Business Law, Joint Ventures, Limited Liability Company Law, Contracts, Criminal Law, Driving While Intoxicated, DWI, Traffic Violations.

CARLOS D. WATSON, born Charlotte, North Carolina, August 17, 1970; admitted to bar, 2002, North Carolina and U.S. District Court, Western District of North Carolina. *Education:* North Carolina Central University (B.A., 1994); University of North Carolina, Greensboro (M.A., 1998); Ohio Northern University College of Law (J.D., 2001). *Member:* Mecklenburg County, North Carolina and American Bar Associations; North Carolina State Bar; National Bar Association; North Carolina Academy of Trial Lawyers.

LAW OFFICE OF ANNA N. WESTMORELAND

5120 MONROE ROAD
CHARLOTTE, NORTH CAROLINA 28205
Telephone: 704-567-5297
Fax: 704-567-5389
Email: anw@westmorelandlawfirm.com
URL: http://www.westmorelandlawfirm.com

Family Law, Divorce, Child Support, Employment Law, Employment Contracts, Wrongful Termination, Severance, Employment Benefits, Bankruptcy, Wills, Probate, Trusts and Estates.

ANNA N. WESTMORELAND, born Brooklyn, New York; admitted to bar, 2004, North Carolina. *Education:* University of North Carolina at Charlotte (B.A., cum laude, with honors in Political Science, 2000); New England School of Law (J.D., 2004). ***PRACTICE AREAS:*** Family Law; Divorce; Child Support; Employment Law; Employment Contracts; Wrongful Termination; Employee Benefits; Bankruptcy; Wills; Probate; Trusts and Estates.

LEGAL SUPPORT PERSONNEL

MIKE SWINDELL. *Education:* Winthrop University (BA in Philosophy, minor in Human Resource Management).

WHITESIDES & WALKER, L.L.P.

212 SOUTH TRYON STREET, SUITE 980
CHARLOTTE, NORTH CAROLINA 28281
Telephone: 704-376-6455
Fax: 704-332-5010
URL: http://www.whitesideswalker.com

General Civil and Criminal Litigation, Appellate Practice, Personal Injury, Wrongful Death, Automobile Accidents and Injuries, Trucking and Transportation Defense, Asset Forfeiture, Insurance Defense, Sports Law, Entertainment Law, Employment, Violations, Collections, Environmental Law, Family Law, Domestic Relations, Divorce, Child Custody, Child Support, Traffic Violations.

MEMBERS OF THE FIRM

H. MONROE WHITESIDES, JR., born Gastonia, North Carolina, April 3, 1959; admitted to bar, 1985, North Carolina. *Education:* Wofford College (B.A., 1981); Campbell University (J.D., 1984). Phi Alpha Delta. Article: "Motions Practice and Trial of a Clear Water Act Case," The Champion, July 1994. Assistant District Attorney, 26th Judicial District, 1985-1990. *Member:* North Carolina State Bar; North Carolina Bar Association; Transportation Lawyers Association; Trucking Industry Defense Association; National Association Criminal Defense Attorneys. (Board Certified Specialist, Federal and State Criminal Law). ***PRACTICE AREAS:*** Federal Criminal Law; Criminal Law; Asset Forfeiture; Transportation; Trucking Law; Entertainment Law; Sports Law; Environmental Law; Business Litigation. ***Email:*** hmwhitesides@whitesideswalker.com

NANCY E. WALKER, born Charlotte, North Carolina, January 7, 1962; admitted to bar, 1988, North Carolina. *Education:* Wake Forest University (B.A., 1984; J.D., 1988). Business Editor, Wake Forest Law Review, 1987-1988. *Member:* Mecklenburg County, North Carolina and American Bar Associations; 26th Judicial District and North Carolina State Bars; North Carolina Association of Women Attorneys. ***PRACTICE AREAS:*** Civil Litigation; Personal Injury; Wrongful Death; Automobile Accidents and Injuries; Traffic Violations; Insurance Defense; Trucking Defense; Business Litigation; Appellate Practice. ***Email:*** nwalker@whitesideswalker.com

JULIE CURRAN GEROCK, born Melrose, Massachusetts, March 30, 1972; admitted to bar, 1999, North Carolina. *Education:* University of Miami (B.A., 1994); Boston College (J.D., 1998). President, Boston College Environmental Law Society, 1997-1998; Co-professor of undergraduate environmental law, Boston College, Spring 1998. *Member:* Mecklenburg County, North Carolina and American (Member, Family Law Section) Bar Associations; North Carolina State Bar. ***PRACTICE AREAS:*** Family Law; Domestic Relations; Divorce; Child Custody; Child Support; Civil Litigation; Business Litigation. ***Email:*** jcgerock@whitesideswalker.com

ASSOCIATE

MICHAEL B. KEMPER, born Roanoke, Virginia, March 29, 1973; admitted to bar, 2002, North Carolina. *Education:* University of the South (B.A., 1995); University of Richmond, T.C. Williams School of Law (J.D., 2001). *Member:* Mecklenburg County and North Carolina Bar Associations; North Carolina State Bar. ***PRACTICE AREAS:*** Civil Litigation; Family Law; Child Custody; Child Support; Collections; Business Litigation. ***Email:*** mkemper@whitesideswalker.com

REPRESENTATIVE CLIENTS: Carolina Panthers; Trans World Airlines; Daimler-Chrysler; Freightliner U.S.A.; Burlington Insurance Group; First Financial Insurance Co.; Swift Transportation Co.; Norfold-Southern Railway; Roadway Express, Inc.; CSX Railway; Classic Arms, Inc.; InterCity Lines, Inc.; Lake Norman Leasing Inc.; Lake Norman Logistics, Inc.; Remodeling Specialities; Wachovia Bank, N.A.; debis Financial Services; CLT Air Freight Carrier, L.L.C.; Duvall Investment Group; Branch Banking and Trust; Mercedes Benz Credit; FasTruck; The Art Bar, Inc.; Two Moon Dog, Inc.; Charlotte Entertainment Enterprises, Inc.

ROY H. WIGGINS

122 NORTH MCDOWELL STREET
CHARLOTTE, NORTH CAROLINA 28204
Telephone: 704-332-6500
Fax: 704-332-6258
Email: rhwiggins@hbm-attys.com
URL: http://www.lawyers.com/royhwiggins
Mailing Address: P.O. Box 36291, Charlotte, NC 28236-6291

Criminal Defense in all State and Federal Courts. Driving While Intoxicated, (DWI), Assault, Drug Crimes, Traffic Violations, Personal Injury, Automobile Accidents, Wrongful Death, Workers Compensation and Commercial Litigation Lawsuits.

ROY H. WIGGINS, born Henderson, North Carolina, September 6, 1961; admitted to bar, 1990, North Carolina, U.S. District Court, Middle and Western Districts of North Carolina and U.S. Court of Appeals, Fourth Circuit. *Education:* East Carolina University (B.S., 1984); Campbell University (J.D., cum laude, 1990). Phi Kappa Phi. Assistant District Attorney, 1992-1995. *Member:* North Carolina State Bar; Association of Trial Lawyers of America; North Carolina Academy of Trial Lawyers; Mecklenburg County Criminal Lawyers; National Association of Criminal Defense Lawyers.

REPRESENTATIVE CLIENTS: North Carolina Home Inspections LLC.

STATEN L. WILCOX, P.A.

Established in 1978

1208 S. TRYON STREET
CHARLOTTE, NORTH CAROLINA 28203
Telephone: 704-342-2266
Fax: 704-342-9856
Email: rexatty@aol.com
URL: http://www.statenwilcoxpa.com

Securities Arbitration Litigation, NASD Arbitration, Personal Injury, Automobile Accidents, Wrongful Death.

STATEN L. WILCOX, JR., born Germany, December 13, 1946; admitted to bar, 1978, North Carolina. *Education:* University of North Carolina at Chapel Hill (B.A., 1969); Wake Forest University (J.D., 1978). Vice President, Wake Forest University Student Bar Association (1978). Examiner, Board of Chiropractors, State of North Carolina. *Member:* Mecklenburg County and North Carolina Bar Associations; North Carolina State Bar; North Carolina Academy of Trial Lawyers; The Association of Trial Lawyers of America; Private Investor Arbitration Bar Association (PIABA).

WILSON & BOS

Established in 1994

521 EAST MOREHEAD STREET, SUITE 510
CHARLOTTE, NORTH CAROLINA 28202
Telephone: 704-376-2225
Fax: 704-376-0703
URL: http://www.wilsboslaw.com
Email: hhwilson@wilsonbos.com
URL: http://www.wilsonbos.com

General Civil and Commercial Litigation in all State and Federal Courts. Labor and Employment, Employment Discrimination, Wrongful Termination, Discrimination, Construction Law, Product Liability, Landlord and Tenant Law.

MEMBERS OF FIRM

HENRY HALL WILSON, III, born Monroe, North Carolina, June 25, 1951; admitted to bar, 1978, North Carolina. *Education:* Harvard University (B.A., cum laude, 1973);

(This Listing Continued)

WILSON & BOS, Charlotte—Continued

Duke University (J.D., 1978). Member, Board of Ethics for the State of North Carolina, 1984-1986. Member, U.S. Selective Service System Local Board, 1982-1983. Member, U.S. Selective Service Appeals Board, 1983-2004. Member, Board of Directors: Goodwill Industries of the Southern Piedmont, Inc., 1988-1990; Member, Board of Directors, Programs for Accessible Living, 1988-1995, President, 1992. Volunteer Lawyer Program, 1998; Public Speaking to Business Groups on Legal Topics (groups including: engineers, building managers, painters, medical office managers, dry-cleaners, home builders, electrical contractors, travel agents, etc.), and litigation regarding Real Estate; litigation involving Breach of Contract, Unfair Trade Practice, Fraud, 1999—. Public Speaking to Small Business Owners (Through CPCC) on a regular basis. *Member:* North Carolina and 26th Judicial District Bar Associations; North Carolina State Bar. ***PRACTICE AREAS:*** Commercial Litigation; Construction Litigation; Real Estate Litigation; Landlord and Tenant Litigation; Estate Litigation; Lender Litigation; Employment Litigation; Corporate Law. **Email:** hhwilson@wilsonbos.com

GERARD ALFORD BOS, born Niagara Falls, New York, October 20, 1950; admitted to bar, 1976, Louisiana; 1977, North Carolina. *Education:* Washington College (B.A., 1973); Tulane University (J.D., 1976). Member, Board of Editors, 1975 and Articles Editor, 1975-1976, Tulane Law Review. *Member:* Louisiana State, North Carolina and 26th Judicial District Bar Associations; North Carolina State Bar. ***PRACTICE AREAS:*** Commercial Litigation; Employment Litigation. **Email:** gabos@wilsonbos.com

REPRESENTATIVE CLIENTS: Available upon request.

WILSON & ISEMAN, L.L.P.

Established in 1992

435 E. MOREHEAD STREET
CHARLOTTE, NORTH CAROLINA 28202
Telephone: 704-331-9585
Fax: 704-331-0773

Winston-Salem Office: 110 Oakwood Drive, Suite 400, 27103. Telephone: 336-631-8866. Fax: 336-631-9770. URL: http://www.wilsonandiseman.com.

General Civil Practice, including Civil Trial and Appellate Work in all State and Federal Courts, Administrative, Aviation, Commercial, Construction, Corporate, Employee Benefits and Executive Compensation, Employment, Criminal, Federal, State and Local Taxation, Insurance Defense, Personal Injury, Probate, Wills, Trusts and Estate Planning, Products Liability and Negligence Law, Professional Malpractice and Real Estate.

FIRM PROFILE: Wilson & Iseman was established in April 1992 by four attorneys formerly with a large local law firm. G. Gray Wilson has been practicing for over twenty-eight years in the area of insurance defense litigation, with concentration in the specialties of professional malpractice and product liability defense. His partner, James M. Iseman, Jr., has been in practice for twenty-seven years and is a business and tax specialist who also practices in the areas of probate and estate work and corporate planning. Tamura D. Coffey joined the firm in 1994 and became a partner in January 2000. S. Ranchor Harris, III, a partner, joined the firm in 1998 and became a partner in January 2001. Linda L. Helms, a partner, joined the firm in 1999 and became a partner in January 2002. Kevin B. Cartledge, joined the firm in 1998 and became a partner in 2004. Associate Maria C. Papoulias joined the firm in 2001, associate J. Chad Bomar joined the firm in 2002, associate David M. Fothergill joined the firm in 2003 and associate Edward T. Shipley III joined the firm in 2004.

(for complete biographical data on all personnel see Professional Biographies at Winston-Salem)

WISHART, NORRIS, HENNINGER & PITTMAN, P.A.

Established in 1976

6832 MORRISON BOULEVARD
CHARLOTTE, NORTH CAROLINA 28211
Telephone: 704-364-0010
FAX: 704-364-0569; 704-365-5945
Email: gary.smith@wnhplaw.com
URL: http://www.wnhplaw.com

Burlington, North Carolina Office: 3120 South Church Street, P.O. Box 1998. Telephone: 336-584-3388. FAX: 336-584-3994.

Mebane, North Carolina Office: 111 East Center Street. Telephone: 919-304-4200. FAX: 919-304-4207.

Arbitration, Appellate Practice, Business Law, Civil Litigation, Commercial and Residential Real Estate, Contracts, Corporate and Commercial Law, Creditor Bankruptcy, Employment Law, Environmental Law, Estate Administration, Estate Planning, Family Law, Federal and State Taxation, Financial Transactions, Franchise Matters, Investments, Joint Ventures and Partnerships, Limited Liability Companies, Mediation, Mergers and Acquisitions, Securities, Succession Planning, Tax Controversy, Wills and Trusts, Zoning, Planning and Land Use, Criminal and Traffic Matters, Elder Law.

FIRM PROFILE: Wishart Norris Henninger & Pittman, P.A. was founded in Burlington, NC, in 1976. The firm has grown from three attorneys to thirty-three attorneys with similar sized offices in both Burlington and Charlotte. The firm also staffs a separate office in Mebane, NC. The firm's growth has been internal rather than by merger.

The firm has built a highly successful practice concentrating on the goals, objectives and needs of closely-held businesses and their owners. Our four core values reflect this concentration. We believe in forging relationships that last with our clients. We believe we must be able to provide the wisdom to reveal optimum solutions for our clients. We encourage a bond of open communication with us and easy access to us for our clients. We are committed to transforming the business of law to meet the needs of business.

(This Listing Continued)

We strive to be the firm of choice for entrepreneurs and owners of closely-held businesses who need skilled legal assistance with every aspect of their business, including mergers and acquisitions, succession planning, and estate planning. In addition, the firm handles civil and commercial litigation, commercial and residential real estate transactions, tax controversy, estate administration matters, franchise law matters and family law matters.

ROBERT B. NORRIS, born Charlotte, North Carolina, January 1, 1950; admitted to bar, 1976, North Carolina. *Education:* Davidson College (A.B., cum laude, 1972); University of North Carolina (M.B.A., 1976; J.D., 1976). Phi Beta Kappa; Omicron Delta Kappa; Omicron Delta Epsilon; Beta Gamma Sigma; Order of the Coif. *Member:* Alamance County, North Carolina and American Bar Associations; North Carolina State Bar. ***PRACTICE AREAS:*** Business Law; Mergers and Acquisitions; Succession Planning. **Email:** robert.norris@wnhplaw.com

JOSEPH B. HENNINGER, JR., born Charlotte, North Carolina, April 1, 1950; admitted to bar, 1979, North Carolina; 1989, U.S Tax Court. *Education:* University of North Carolina (B.A., Economics, 1972); Seattle University School of Law (J.D., 1978). Omicron Delta Epsilon. Morehead Scholar. Member, National Academy of Elder Law. *Member:* Mecklenburg County, North Carolina and American Bar Associations; North Carolina State Bar (Member, Charlotte Estate Plan Council). (Board Certified Specialist in Estate Planning and Probate Law, North Carolina State Board of Legal Specialization). ***PRACTICE AREAS:*** Estate Planning (100%, 5000); Estate and Gift Tax; Estate Administration. **Email:** josh.henninger@wnhplaw.com

GREGORY L. KUNKLEMAN, born Charlotte, North Carolina, September 28, 1955; admitted to bar, 1980, North Carolina and U.S. District Court, Western District of North Carolina. *Education:* Davidson College (B.S., 1977); University of North Carolina (J.D., 1980). Phi Alpha Delta (Treasurer, 1979-1980). Licensed Real Estate Broker, North Carolina, 1976. *Member:* 26th Judicial District, North Carolina and American Bar Associations; North Carolina State Bar; North Carolina Academy of Trial Lawyers. ***PRACTICE AREAS:*** Real Estate. **Email:** greg.kunkleman@wnhplaw.com

STEVE C. HOROWITZ, born Bronx, New York, May 22, 1940; admitted to bar, 1965, Florida; 1967, U.S. Tax Court; 1968, North Carolina. *Education:* University of Florida (B.S.B.A., Accounting, 1962; J.D., 1965); New York University (LL.M., in Taxation, 1966). Phi Alpha Delta. Author: "Negotiating Strategies for Effectively Settling Civil Tax Controversies with the IRS," Taxation for Accountants, April, 1979. Trial Attorney, Office of the Chief Counsel, IRS, 1967-1972. Frequent Lecturer: NC Association of CPA and other States' CPA societies; North Carolina Bar Association. Board/Executive Committee Member, UNC Tax Institute. *Member:* North Carolina (Chairman, Tax Section, 1989—; President; Member, Southeastern Region Tax Liaison Committee, 1995—) and American (Member: Section of Taxation; Committee on Administrative Practice, 1979—) Bar Associations; The Florida Bar; North Carolina State Bar. American College of Tax Counsel. ***PRACTICE AREAS:*** Taxation; Tax Controversies; Corporate Law; Estate Planning; Administrative. **Email:** steve.horowitz@wnhplaw.com

JUNE K. ALLISON, born Asheville, North Carolina, July 16, 1954; admitted to bar, 1981, North Carolina. *Education:* University of North Carolina (B.A., 1976; M.B.A., 1981; J.D., 1981). Phi Beta Kappa; Order of the Coif. *Member:* Mecklenburg County, North Carolina and American Bar Associations; North Carolina State Bar. ***PRACTICE AREAS:*** Corporate Law; Commercial Transactions; Appellate Practice; Creditor Bankruptcy. **Email:** june.allison@wnhplaw.com

GARTH K. DUNKLIN, born El Dorado, Arkansas, December 3, 1962; admitted to bar, 1988, North Carolina. *Education:* University of North Carolina (B.A., 1985) Morehead Scholar; Phi Beta Kappa; University of North Carolina (J.D., 1988). North Carolina Real Estate Commission Certified Continuing Education and Prelicensing Instructor. Certified Commercial Investment Member (CCIM), Commercial Investment Real Estate Institute. *Member:* North Carolina (Member, Real Property Section) and American Bar Associations. (Board Certified Specialist in Real Property Law - Residential, Commercial, Business and Industrial Transactions, North Carolina State Bar Board of Legal Specialization). ***PRACTICE AREAS:*** Commercial Real Property; Administrative Law. **Email:** garth.dunklin@wnhplaw.com

WILLIAM A. NAVARRO, born Brockton, Massachusetts, November 10, 1961; admitted to bar, 1987, Massachusetts; 1995, North Carolina. *Education:* Northeastern University (B.S., 1984); Boston College (J.D., 1987). *Member:* North Carolina Bar Association; North Carolina State Bar. ***PRACTICE AREAS:*** Business Litigation; Commercial Litigation. **Email:** bill.navarro@wnhplaw.com

DAVID C. BOGGS, born Landstuhl, Germany, January 19, 1953; admitted to bar, 1978, North Carolina and U.S. District Court, Western District of North Carolina; U.S. Court of Appeals, Fourth Circuit. *Education:* Davidson College (B.A., cum laude, 1975); Wake Forest University (J.D., 1978). Phi Delta Phi. *Member:* North Carolina State Bar; North Carolina Bar Association. ***PRACTICE AREAS:*** Business, Commercial and Corporate Law; Franchise Law; Contract Law; Civil Litigation; Real Property. **Email:** david.boggs@wnhplaw.com

GARY W. SMITH, born Memphis, Tennessee, March 10, 1973; admitted to bar, 1998, North Carolina; 2003, U.S. District Court, Western District of North Carolina and U.S. Supreme Court. *Education:* University of Mississippi (B.A., summa cum laude, 1995); University of North Carolina (J.D., with honors, 1998). Phi Kappa Phi; Omicron Delta Kappa; Order of Barristers; Holderness Moot Court. Member: American Institute of Aeronautics and Astronautics; North Carolina Bankers Association; Wishart, Norris, Henninger & Pittman Charitable Foundation, Inc.- Mecklenburg Division President; The Fund for American Studies Alumni Council; 1994 Bryce Harlow Institute on Business and Government Affairs Graduate. *Member:* Mecklenburg County, North Carolina and American Bar Associations; North Carolina State Bar; Mecklenburg County Bar. ***PRACTICE AREAS:*** Business Law; Commercial Transactions; Business Associations Law; Business Development; Business Dissolutions; Business Enterprises; Business Formation; Business Estate Planning; Business Organization; Business Planning; Business Regulation; Business Succession Planning; Business Successions; Business Taxation; Business Start-Ups; Business Reorganization; Business Transactions; Business Transfers; Buy-Sell Agreements; Buying and Selling of Businesses; Closely Held Business Law; Closely Held Business Taxation; Entrepreneurial Business Law; Family Business Law; Family Business Successions; Joint Ventures;

(This Listing Continued)

Limited Liability Company Law; Pass-Through Entities; Private Business Law; Professional Practices; Small Business Law; Strategic Alliances; Contracts; Corporate Law; Closely Held Corporations; Corporate Contracts; Corporate Commercial Law; Corporate Control Contests; Corporate Dissolutions; Corporate Formation; Corporate Governance; Corporate Fiduciary Law; Corporate Income Tax; Corporate Organization; Corporate Partnerships; Corporate Planning; Corporate Reorganization; Corporate Successions; Corporate Tax Planning; Corporate Taxation; Family Corporations; Incorporation; S Corporations; Small Business Corporations; Franchises and Franchising; Mergers, Acquisitions and Divestitures; Business Acquisitions; Business Divestitures; Leveraged Acquisitions; Leveraged Buyouts; Merger Reorganization; Mergers and Acquisitions; Mergers and Acquisitions Finance; Spin-Offs; Partnership Taxation. **Email:** gary.smith@wnhplaw.com

ASSOCIATES

MEGAN SADLER, admitted to bar, 2005, North Carolina. *Education:* West Virginia University (B.A., summa cum laude, 1999); University of Charleston (M.S., Environmental Studies, 2001); Wake Forest University (J.D., cum laude, 2004). Order of the Coif. Staff Editor, 2002-2003 and Research Editor, 2003-2004, Wake Forest University Law Review. Law Clerk to Associate Justice Edward Brady, North Carolina Supreme Court, 2004-2005. **Email:** megan.sadler@wnhplaw.com

RICHARD A. BIGGER, JR., born Charlotte, North Carolina, March 4, 1937; admitted to bar, 1964, North Carolina. *Education:* Princeton University (A.B., 1959); University of Virginia (LL.B., 1964). Phi Alpha Delta. *Member:* North Carolina Bar Association (Chairman, Estate Planning and Fiduciary Law Section, 1991-1992); North Carolina State Bar. Fellow, American College of Trust and Estate Counsel. (Board Certified Specialist in Estate Planning and Probate Law, North Carolina State Board of Legal Specialization). ***PRACTICE AREAS:*** Estate Planning and Administration; Corporate Law. **Email:** randy.bigger@wnhplaw.com

BARBARA HOWIE LEMBO, born Detroit, Michigan, October 3, 1949; admitted to bar, 1976, Indiana; 1977, North Carolina; 1991, Florida. *Education:* St. Olaf College (B.A., 1971); Indiana University (M.L.S., 1972; J.D., 1976). Instructor: Real Property and Title Abstracting; Legal Research, Central Piedmont Community College, 1994-2002. *Member:* North Carolina Bar Association (Member, Real Property Section Council, 1985-1988); The Florida Bar. ***PRACTICE AREAS:*** Real Property. **Email:** barbara.lembo@wnhplaw.com

SAMUEL ERIC BASS, born Raleigh, North Carolina, May 30, 1970; admitted to bar, 2002, North Carolina. *Education:* University of North Texas (B.B.A., 1993); Queens University (M.B.A., 1998); Wake Forest University (J.D., 2002). Member, Moot Court Board, Wake Forest University. ***PRACTICE AREAS:*** Business Law. **Email:** eric.bass@wnhplaw.com

STEVEN B. OCKERMAN, born August 5, 1960; admitted to bar, 1992, Missouri; 2002, North Carolina. *Education:* United States Naval Academy (B.S., 1983); Washington University (J.D., 1991). *Member:* Mecklenburg County and North Carolina Bar Associations. [U.S. Marine Corps, 1983-2003]. ***PRACTICE AREAS:*** Family Law. **Email:** steve.ockerman@wnhplaw.com

DANICA L. LITTLE, born Tampa, Florida, May 4, 1973; admitted to bar, 2004, North Carolina. *Education:* University of South Florida (B.A., 1999; M.A., 2001); Florida State University (J.D., magna cum laude, 2004). Order of the Coif; Phi Detla Phi; Golden Key Honor Society. Recipient: Book Award, Torts 2001; Book Award, Sales and Leases, 2003; Article and Notes Editor of the Year Journal of Transnational Law and Policy, 2003-2004. Member: Journal of Transnational Law and Policy, 2001-2004; Women's Law Symposium, 2001-2004. Certified Public Accountant, Florida, 2002. Certified Public Accountant, North Carolina, 2005. Member: American Institute of Certified Public Accountants. Member: North Carolina Association of Certified Public Accountants. Member: Institute of Management Accountants, 2000-2005. *Member:* Mecklenburg County and North Carolina Bar Associations. ***PRACTICE AREAS:*** Estate Planning; Taxation; Asset Protection; Commercial. **Email:** danica.little@wnhplaw.com

ANDREW M. McCULLOUGH, born Charlotte, North Carolina, January 18, 1979; admitted to bar, 2004, North Carolina. *Education:* University of North Carolina at Chapel Hill (B.A. magna cum laude, 2001; J.D. 2004). ***PRACTICE AREAS:*** Commercial Real Estate; Business Transactions; Tax. **Email:** andrew.mccullough@wnhplaw.com

GILBERT (TREY) BAKER, born Clinton, Iowa, September 23, 1977; admitted to bar, 2005, North Carolina. *Education:* University of Iowa (B.S., with high distinction, 2001; B.B.A., 2001); College of William & Mary (J.D., 2005). Phi Beta Kappa; Phi Delta Phi (Treasurer, 2002-2005). Member, Golden Key. Member, College of William & Mary Law Review. *Member:* North Carolina State Bar. ***PRACTICE AREAS:*** Business Law (100%). **Email:** trey.baker@wnhplaw.com

OF COUNSEL

GEORGE J. MILLER, born Charlotte, North Carolina, December 1, 1926; admitted to bar, 1953, North Carolina; 1954, U.S. District Court, Western District of North Carolina; 1965, U.S. Court of Appeals, Fourth Circuit; 1978, U.S. Supreme Court. *Education:* University of North Carolina (B.S., 1950; LL.B., 1953). Phi Alpha Delta. Prosecuting Attorney, City of Charlotte Criminal Court, 1957-1961. *Member:* Mecklenburg County, North Carolina and American (Member, House of Delegates, 1978-1982) Bar Associations; North Carolina State Bar (Councillor, 1968-1978; Chairman, Grievance Committee, 1973-1975, President, 1976-1977). [U.S. Army Infantry, 1944-1946]. ***LANGUAGES:*** Greek. ***PRACTICE AREAS:*** General Practice. **Email:** george.miller@wnhplaw.com

REPRESENTATIVE CLIENTS: Radiator Specialty Company; First Trust Bank; Z. V. Pate, Inc.; NewDominion Bank; First Charter Bank; Juba Aluminum Products, Inc.; Premier Alliance Group, Inc.; Overhead Door Company of Charlotte; B & B Contracting, Inc.; Carolina Beer and Beverage Company, LLC; Internetwork Services Inc.; Environmental Drying Services, Inc.; Details, Inc; Preferred Packaging, Inc.; Holt Sublimation Printing & Products, Inc.; Perma-Flex Roller Technology; Sound Choice; Marolf Construction, Inc.; The Signature Companies, LLC; Design Stragies, LLC; American Asset Corporation; National Benefit Administrators, Inc.; Integraphx, Inc.; Milestone Partners, LLC; Glen Raven, Mills, LLC.; Curtin Brothers Contracting; Jenkins Electric Company; Hall Contracting Co., Inc; Slade, Inc.; LYF-TYM Building Products Co., Inc.; Choice USA Beverage, Inc..; Synthon Pharmaceuticals, LTD; Madison River Communications, LLC; Burlington Insurance Group; Town of Elon; W.E. Love & Associates; Burlington Alamance Regional Airport; Sasser Construction.

(This Listing Continued)

APPROVED ATTORNEYS FOR: Lawyers Title Insurance Corp.; Chicago Title Insurance Co.; American Title Insurance Co.; Jefferson-Pilot Title Insurance Co.; Investors Title Insurance Co.

(For complete biographical data on other personnel, see Professional Biographies at Burlington, North Carolina)

WOMBLE CARLYLE SANDRIDGE & RICE

A Professional Limited Liability Company

3500 ONE WACHOVIA CENTER
301 SOUTH COLLEGE STREET
CHARLOTTE, NORTH CAROLINA 28202-6025
Telephone: 704-331-4900
Fax: 704-331-4955
Email: lawyers@wcsr.com
URL: http://www.wcsr.com

REVISER OF THE NORTH CAROLINA LAW DIGEST FOR THIS DIRECTORY.

Winston-Salem, North Carolina Office: One West Fourth Street, 27101. Telephone: 336-721-3600. Fax: 336-721-3660.
Raleigh, North Carolina Office: 2100 First Union Capitol Center, 150 Fayetteville Street Mall, P.O. Box 831. Telephone: 919-755-2100. Fax: 919-755-2150.
Research Triangle Park, North Carolina Office: 2530 Meridian Parkway, Suite 400 (Durham), 27713, P.O. Box 13069, Research Triangle Park, 27709. Telephone: 919-484-2300. Fax: 919-484-2340.
Greensboro, North Carolina Office: 300 North Greene Street. Telephone: 336-574-8030. Fax: 336-574-4520.
Atlanta, Georgia Office: One Atlantic Center, 1201 West Peachtree Street, Suite 3500. Telephone: 404-872-7000. Fax: 404-888-7490.
Other Atlanta, Georgia Office: Suite 404, 2296 Henderson Mill Road, N.E. Telephone: 770-492-9030. Fax: 770-492-9609.
Washington, D.C. Office: Suite 700, 1401 Eye Street. Telephone: 202-857-4400. Fax: 202-467-6910.
Greenville, South Carolina Office: 700 Poinsett Plaza, 104 South Main Street, P.O. Box 10208. Telephone: 864-255-5400. Fax: 864-255-5440.
Tysons Corner, Virginia Office: 8065 Leesburg Pike, Fourth Floor. Telephone: 703-790-3310. Fax: 703-790-2623.

General Civil Practice, Trial and Appellate Litigation. Administrative, Antitrust, Aviation, Banking, Bankruptcy and Creditor's Rights, Bond Financing, Civil Rights, Commercial, Construction, Consumer Lending, Corporate, E-Commerce, Employee Benefits, Environmental, Estate Planning, Family, Government Relations, Health Care, Insurance, Intellectual Property, International, Labor and Employment, Municipal, Negligence, Probate, Product Liability, Real Estate, Retirement Plans, Securities, Taxation, Toxic Tort, Wills and Trusts Law.

FIRM PROFILE: Womble Carlyle Sandridge & Rice, PLLC, which traces its history to 1876, is a full-service law firm that delivers sophisticated and innovative legal services to a wide spectrum of business clients in industries that include information technology, health care, manufacturing, telecommunications and financial services. The Firm also represents a variety of governmental units and agencies.

Womble Carlyle's mission is to provide value to clients by combining professional skill, technology and a thorough understanding of clients' needs to deliver high quality, cost-effective and responsive service. The firm is comprised of approximately 470 lawyers and 838 staff members operating from offices in Atlanta, GA; Greenville, SC; Charlotte, Winston-Salem, Research Triangle Park, Raleigh and Greensboro, NC; Tysons Corner, VA and Washington, DC.

The Firm considers technology and the benefits it offers an integral part of the legal services it provides. All of the Firm's offices are linked for full communications by telephone, fax, electronic mail and video conference over a wide area network. The Firm takes full advantage of its sophisticated computer technology for support in large-case litigation, as well as management of complex transactions. The Director of Technology is responsible for implementing existing systems, and in some instances, developing new software applications to meet specific client needs. The firm-wide communications and computer network permit the Firm to allocate resources from all offices, as needed, as well as to establish direct, secure links with clients and their legal departments, thus enhancing the responsiveness and efficiency of the Firm's lawyers.

The lawyers of Womble Carlyle have traditionally been active in community affairs, in Bar and other professional activities, and in state government. Many lawyers assume leading roles in civic and professional organizations, and several have served the government in elected or appointed positions.

LAW FIRM ALLIANCES/ASSOCIATIONS: ***TOLEDO CONFERENCE GROUP***
LEX MUNDI

RESIDENT MEMBERS

GARZA BALDWIN, III, born Sullivan, Indiana, January 12, 1951; admitted to bar, 1978, North Carolina. *Education:* University of North Carolina (B.A., 1973); Wake Forest University (J.D., 1978). Staff Member, 1976-1977 and Managing Editor, 1977-1978, Wake Forest Law Review. Listed in The Best Lawyers in America. *Member:* North Carolina (Chairman: Securities Regulation Committee, 1989-1991; Member, Business Law Section Council, 1992-1995) and American Bar Associations. ***PRACTICE AREAS:*** Securities Regulation Law; Corporate Law. **Email:** gbaldwin@wcsr.com

TIMOTHY G. BARBER, born Elgin, Illinois, May 26, 1955; admitted to bar, 1985, North Carolina; U.S. District Court, Eastern, Middle and Western Districts of North Carolina; U.S. Supreme Court; U.S. Court of Appeals, Fourth Circuit; U.S. Court of Appeals, Federal Circuit. *Education:* Kenyon College (B.A., 1977); Wake Forest University (J.D., cum laude, 1985). Editor-in-Chief, Wake Forest Law Review, 1984-1985. Arbitrator,

(This Listing Continued)

WOMBLE CARLYLE SANDRIDGE & RICE, Charlotte—Continued

American Arbitration Association. *Member:* North Carolina and American (Member, Construction Law and Litigation Sections) Bar Associations. (Practice Group Leader, Business Litigation). ***PRACTICE AREAS:*** Litigation. ***Email:*** tim.barber@wcsr.com

G. MICHAEL BARNHILL, born Rocky Mount, North Carolina, July 16, 1956; admitted to bar, 1981, North Carolina; U.S. District Court, Western, Middle and Eastern Districts of North Carolina; U.S. Court of Appeals, Fourth Circuit; U.S. Supreme Court. *Education:* Davidson College (B.A., cum laude, 1978); Wake Forest University (J.D., 1981). Member, Moot Court. Law Clerk to Chief Judge Woodrow W. Jones, Western District of North Carolina, 1981-1983. *Member:* Mecklenburg County, North Carolina and American Bar Associations; North Carolina Association of Defense Attorneys. (Managing Member, Charlotte Office). ***PRACTICE AREAS:*** Business Litigation; Insurance Defense Law; Public Officer Defense; Civil Rights Defense; ERISA. ***Email:*** mbarnhill@wcsr.com

GARY D. CHAMBLEE, born Raleigh, North Carolina, January 17, 1952; admitted to bar, 1978, North Carolina. *Education:* University of North Carolina at Chapel Hill (A.B., 1973; J.D., with honors, 1978). Phi Beta Kappa; Order of the Coif. Member, North Carolina Law Review, 1977-1978. Law Clerk to Hon. Susie Sharp, Chief Justice, North Carolina Supreme Court, 1978-1979. *Member:* Mecklenburg County and North Carolina Bar Associations. ***PRACTICE AREAS:*** Commercial Real Estate; Commercial Finance; Real Estate Partnerships. ***Email:*** gchamblee@wcsr.com

THEODORE F. CLAYPOOLE, born Dayton, OH, March 15, 1963; admitted to bar, 1988, Ohio; 2000, North Carolina. *Education:* Duke University (A.B., cum laude, 1985); Ohio State University (J.D., 1988). Corporate Counsel, CompuServe Incorporated. *Member:* Ohio State and American Bar Associations. (Assistant General Counsel). ***PRACTICE AREAS:*** Technology and Commerce. ***Email:*** tclaypoole@wcsr.com

JOE B. COGDELL, JR., born Duncan, Oklahoma, May 6, 1953; admitted to bar, 1978, Arkansas; 1979, Oklahoma, U.S. Tax Court and U.S. Claims Court; 1980, U.S. District Court, Western District of Oklahoma; 1981, U.S. Supreme Court; 1989, North Carolina. *Education:* University of Arkansas (B.A., 1975; J.D., 1977); Southern Methodist University (LL.M. in Taxation, 1979). Blue Key. Author: "Practice Before the IRS and Circular 230," Tax Management, Inc., BNA Tax Management Portfolio 620, 1997; "Introduction to North Carolina Individual Income Taxation," North Carolina State and Local Taxes, Research Institute of America, 1991; Contributing Author to Tax Ideas, Warren Gorham & Lamont. Adjunct Professor of Law, Oklahoma City University School of Law, 1982-1988. *Member:* Arkansas, Oklahoma, North Carolina and American (Member: Business Law and Taxation Sections; Corporate Tax Committee) Bar Associations. ***PRACTICE AREAS:*** Corporate Law; Mergers and Acquisitions Law; Tax Law. ***Email:*** jcogdell@wcsr.com

CORNELIUS W. COGHILL, III, born Fort Benning, Georgia, May 16, 1951; admitted to bar, 1978, North Carolina. *Education:* Davidson College (A.B., cum laude, 1973); University of Virginia (M.A., 1974); University of North Carolina (J.D., 1978). Phi Beta Kappa. Member, North Carolina Law Review, 1977-1978. *Member:* Mecklenburg County, North Carolina (Council Member, 1989-1994 and Chairman, 1992-1993, Estate Planning and Fiduciary Law Section) and American (Member, Real Property, Probate and Trust Section) Bar Associations. Fellow, American College of Trust and Estate Counsel. ***PRACTICE AREAS:*** Estate Planning Law; Probate Law; Trusts and Estates; Exempt Organizations. ***Email:*** ncoghill@wcsr.com

JIM D. COOLEY, born Spartanburg, South Carolina, December 4, 1946; admitted to bar, 1973, North Carolina; U.S. District Court, Eastern, Middle and Western District Courts, District of North Carolina; U.S. Court of Appeals, Fourth Circuit; U.S. Supreme Court. *Education:* Davidson College (B.A., cum laude, 1969); Union Theological Seminary; University of North Carolina (J.D., with honors, 1973). Phi Beta Kappa. Member, North Carolina Law Review, 1972-1973. Member, Select Drafting Committee of North Carolina Board of Bar Examiners, 1986-1993. Member, Board of Directors: Legal Aid Society of Northwest North Carolina, 1983-1987; Legal Services of the Southern Piedmont, 2001—. Firm Management Committee, 1990-1998. Practice Group Leader, Business Litigation, 1996-1998. *Member:* Mecklenburg County; North Carolina (Member, Sections on: Litigation; Constitutional Law, Chair, Large Law Firm Committee, 1997-1998); and American (Member, Sections on: Litigation; Business Law) Bar Associations; Center for Public Resources (Member, Construction Arbitration Study Committee). ***REPORTED CASES:*** Moore v. Wykle, 107 N.C. App. 120, 419 S.E. 2d 176 (1992); Hartsell v. Duplex Products, et al., 123 F.3d 766; Hayes, et al. v. City of Charlotte, 10 F.3d 207 (4th Cir. 1993), Civil Action No. C-C-91-0158-P (4th Cir. 1994); Boring v. Buncombe County Board of Education, 136 F.3d 364 (4th Cir.1998), cert.denied, 525 U.S. 813, 199 S.Ct.47, 142 L.Ed.2d 36 (1998); Dabbs v. Amos, 70 F.3d 1261 date (4th Cir. 1995); Friedland v. Snider, et al., Case No. 97 CVS 7174, Mecklenburg Superior Court 2001 and Friedland v. City of Charlotte, et al., Case No 3:98 CV 122-MU, W.D.N.C. 2002; Gersing v Hound Ears Club Limited Partnership, Case No. 01 CVS 777, Watauga Superior Court 2003. ***PRACTICE AREAS:*** Business Litigation (including Class Actions and Multidistrict Litigation); Internal Corporate Investigations; Unfair Competition; Constitutional Rights Litigation. ***Email:*** jcooley@wcsr.com

JAMES P. COONEY III, born San Francisco, California, October 26, 1957; admitted to bar, 1984, North Carolina. *Education:* Duke University (A.B., summa cum laude, 1979); University of Virginia (J.D., 1982). Phi Beta Kappa; Phi Eta Sigma; Order of the Coif. Research & Projects Editor, Virginia Law Review, 1981-1982. Law Clerk to Hon. John D. Butzner, Jr., U.S. Court of Appeals, Fourth Circuit, 1982-1983. Member, General Assembly Task Force on the Rules of Civil Procedure, 1997-1998. Permanent Member, Fourth Circuit Judicial Conference. Chair, Mecklenburg County Civil Courts Committee, 1993-1998. *Member:* North Carolina Association of Defense Attorneys (Board of Directors, 1992-1998; President, 1996-1997); American College of Trial Lawyers. ***REPORTED CASES:*** Davis v. Burlington Indus., 966 F.2d 890 (4th Cir. 1992) (ERISA suit; opinion upheld summary judgment finding ERISA violation). ***PRACTICE AREAS:*** Medical Malpractice Defense; Criminal Defense; Commercial Litigation; Appellate Practice; Litigation.

JAMES E. DANIEL, born Danville, Virginia, December 27, 1955; admitted to bar, 1982, North Carolina. *Education:* University of North Carolina (B.S., 1978); Emory University (M.B.A., 1979; J.D., with distinction, 1982). Phi Beta Kappa; Beta Gamma Sigma; Phi Eta Sigma; Order of the Coif. Staff Member, 1980-1981 and Member, Editorial Board,

(This Listing Continued)

1981-1982, Emory Law Journal. *Member:* North Carolina and American (Member: Employee Benefits Committees, Tax Section and Business Law Section) Bar Associations; Southern Employee Benefits Conference and Charlotte Pension Forum. ***PRACTICE AREAS:*** ERISA; Employee Benefits and Executive Compensation Law. ***Email:*** jdaniel@wcsr.com

BRADFORD A. DE VORE, born Detroit, Michigan, March 22, 1960; admitted to bar, 1986, North Carolina. *Education:* Michigan State University (B.A., 1983); University of South Carolina (J.D., 1986). Member: Society of Wig and Robe; International Moot Court Team. Member: North Carolina Groundwater Professionals; International Society for Environmental Epidemiology; International Society for Exposure Analysis. *Member:* North Carolina and American Bar Associations; District of Columbia Bar; Society of Environmental Toxicology and Chemistry. ***PRACTICE AREAS:*** Products Liability; Environmental; Toxic Torts; Litigation. ***Email:*** bdevore@wcsr.com

ROBERT M. DONLON, born Albany, New York, September 19, 1957; admitted to bar, 1983, New York; 1997, North Carolina. *Education:* Boston College (B.A., 1979); Albany Law School (J.D., 1982). Listed in: "Best Lawyers in America," 1993—; "Charlotte's Best." *Member:* North Carolina and American Bar Associations. ***PRACTICE AREAS:*** Corporate; Securities. ***Email:*** bdonlon@wcsr.com

J. CARLTON FLEMING, born Kinston, North Carolina, 1928; admitted to bar, 1951, North Carolina. *Education:* Duke University (A.B., 1949; J.D., 1951); George Washington University (LL.M., 1953). Order of the Coif; Omicron Delta Kappa; Delta Theta Phi. Listed in The Best Lawyers in America, Corporate Law Section. Associate Editor, Duke Law Journal, 1950-1951. President, 1978-1979 and Chairman, 1979-1980, Southern Federal Tax Institute. U.S. Circuit Judge Nominating Commission (4th Cir.), 1977-1979. *Member:* North Carolina (Member, Board of Governors, 1960-1961; 1969-1972) and American (State Chairman, Junior Bar Conference, 1960-1961) Bar Associations; U.S. Fourth Circuit Judicial Conference (Permanent Member). Fellow, American Bar Foundation. [Lieut., U.S. Naval Reserve, active duty, 1951-1953]. ***PRACTICE AREAS:*** Corporate Law; Taxation Law; Construction Law. ***Email:*** cfleming@wcsr.com

W. CLARK GOODMAN, born December 29, 1967; admitted to bar, 1993, North Carolina and U.S. District Court, Western and Middle Districts of North Carolina; U.S. Court of Appeals, Fourth Circuit. *Education:* Duke University (A.B., magna cum laude, 1990); Harvard University (J.D., cum laude, 1993). Phi Beta Kappa. *Member:* Mecklenburg County, North Carolina (Member, Young Lawyers Division, Litigation Section) and American Bar Associations. ***LANGUAGES:*** Spanish. ***PRACTICE AREAS:*** Litigation-Insurance/Public Official Defense; Environmental Law; Toxic Torts. ***Email:*** cgoodman@wcsr.com

DEBBIE WESTON HARDEN, born Kinston, North Carolina, April 16, 1957; admitted to bar, 1982, Georgia and North Carolina. *Education:* University of North Carolina at Chapel Hill (B.A., with honors, 1979; J.D., with honors, 1982). Phi Delta Phi. John Motley Morehead Scholar. Member, Holderness Moot Court Bench, 1980-1982. Staff Member, University of North Carolina Law Review, 1981-1982. *Member:* Mecklenburg County, North Carolina and American Bar Associations; State Bar of Georgia. ***PRACTICE AREAS:*** Business Litigation; Fiduciary Law; ERISA. ***Email:*** dharden@wcsr.com

JEFFREY S. HAY, born Brunswick, Maine, September 20, 1960; admitted to bar, 1983, North Carolina; 1986, Massachusetts. *Education:* Erskine College (B.A., summa cum laude, 1980); University of South Carolina (J.D., magna cum laude, 1983). Order of the Coif. Member: Charlotte/Douglas International Airport Advisory Committee. *Member:* Massachusetts Bar Association. ***PRACTICE AREAS:*** Corporate; Securities. ***Email:*** jhay@wcsr.com

MARK P. HENRIQUES, born Jacksonville, Florida, December 10, 1964; admitted to bar, 1992, North Carolina; U.S. District Court, Eastern, Middle and Western District Court; U.S. Court of Appeals, Fourth Circuit; U.S. Supreme Court. *Education:* University of Virginia (B.A., with highest distinction, 1987; J.D., 1990). Phi Beta Kappa; Order of the Coif; Omicron Delta Epsilon. Member: Moot Court Board, Rules Committee. Editorial Board, Virginia Law Review. Law Clerk to Honorable Richard L. Williams, U.S. District Court, Eastern District of Virginia, 1990-1991. Author: "Desuetude and Declaratory Judgment: A New Attack on Obsolete Laws," Virginia Law Review, August 1990. Fourth Circuit Review Advisory Board, Commercial Law, 2000—. President and Chairman, Board Legal Services for the Elderly. Co-Chair, United Way Older Adult Wellness Council. Member, Board of Trustees, North Carolina Museum of History. Member, Advisory Board, Fourth Circuit Review. *Member:* Mecklenburg County; North Carolina Bar Association (Member, Litigation Section); American Bar Association (Member, Sections on: Litigation; Construction); North Carolina Council of School Attorneys. ***REPORTED CASES:*** A.H. Beck Foundation Co., Inc. v. Jones Bros. Inc., 603 S.E. 2d 819 (N.C. App. 2004); Richardson v. Cabarrus County Board of Education, 111 Fed.Appx. 173 (2004); Redless/SCS, Inc. v. Pieper, 153 N.C. App. 421, 571 S.E.2d 8 (N.C. App. 2002); Hartsell v. Duplex Products, Inc., 123 F.3d 766 (4th Cir. 1997); Dabbs v. Amos, 70 F.3d 1261 (4th Cir. 1995); Glenn III by and through Glen II v. Charlotte-Mecklenburg School Bd. of Educ., 903 F. Supp. 918 (W.D.N.C. 1995); Mack v. Reddick, 47 F.3d 1165 (4th Cir. 1995); White v. Leonhardt, 46 F.3d 1130 (4th Cir. 1995). ***PRACTICE AREAS:*** Business Litigation; Construction Litigation; Education. ***Email:*** mhenriques@wcsr.com

BOBBY D. HINSON, born Lancaster, South Carolina, March 14, 1962; admitted to bar, 1987, North Carolina; 1989, South Carolina. *Education:* Duke University (A.B., magna cum laude, 1984); University of Virginia School of Law (J.D., 1987). *Member:* Mecklenburg County and North Carolina Bar Associations; North Carolina State Bar (Member, Real Property Section); South Carolina Bar (Member, Real Property Section). ***PRACTICE AREAS:*** Commercial Real Estate; Finance and Development; Foreclosure; Leasing. ***Email:*** bhinson@wcsr.com

MARK J. HOROSCHAK, born Philadelphia, Pennsylvania, November 15, 1951; admitted to bar, 1977, Michigan and U.S. District Court, Eastern District of Michigan; 1980, Virginia; 1981, U.S. Court of Appeals, Fourth Circuit; 1983, U.S. District Court, Eastern District of Virginia; 1996, North Carolina and U.S. District Court, Western District of North Carolina. *Education:* American University (B.A., 1973); College of William and Mary (J.D., 1976). Phi Kappa Phi; Pi Sigma Alpha. Articles Editor, William & Mary Law Review, 1975-1976. Author: "Antitrust Guidance for Health Care Providers Enters a New Phase," Antitrust Magazine at 28 (Fall 1996); "New Market for Hospital Mergers," Legal Times,

(This Listing Continued)

March 4, 1996, at S25; "Antitrust Developments in Evolving Health Care Markets," ABA Section of Antitrust Law (1996) (contributing author); "Antitrust Perspectives on Joint Ventures Among Health Care Providers," 6 ABA Antitrust Health Care Chron. 2 (1992); "Medical Staff Privileges and the Antitrust Laws: A View from the Federal Trade Commission," 6 Medical Staff Counselor 17 (1992). Attorney-Advisor for the Chairman, Federal Trade Commission (1987-1988). Assistant General Counsel, Federal Trade Commission, 1988-1989. Assistant Director, Bureau of Competition, Federal Trade Commission, 1989-1995. *Member:* North Carolina (Council Member, Antitrust and Trade Regulation Section, 1996—) and American (Vice-Chair, Health Care Committee, ABA Antitrust Section, 1995-1996) Bar Associations; National Health Lawyers Association. ***PRACTICE AREAS:*** Antitrust; Health Care; Trade Regulation. ***Email:*** mhoroschak@wcsr.com

CYRUS M. JOHNSON, JR., born Henderson, North Carolina, April 26, 1954; admitted to bar, 1982, North Carolina. *Education:* University of North Carolina (B.A., with highest honors in Chem. and Pol. Sci., 1976; M.B.A. and J.D., with honors, 1982). Notes and Comments Editor, North Carolina Journal International Law and Com. Reg., 1981-1982. Member, Jessup Cup International Moot Court Team, 1980-1981. Member, Holderness Moot Court Bench, 1981-1982. Author: North Carolina Limited Liability Company, Forms and Practice Manual, 1996. *Member:* Mecklenburg County, North Carolina (Business Section) and American (Business Law Section, Partnership Committee and Small Business Committee) Bar Associations. ***PRACTICE AREAS:*** Corporate Law; Partnership Law; Limited Liability Company; Securities Law. ***Email:*** cjohnson@wcsr.com

JANE JEFFRIES JONES, born Beckley, West Virginia, April 12, 1960; admitted to bar, 1986, North Carolina. *Education:* Wake Forest University (B.A., cum laude, 1982); Wake Forest University School of Law (J.D., 1986). Member: Order of the Barrister; National Moot Court Team; Jessup International Moot Court Team. *Member:* Mecklenburg County and North Carolina Bar Associations; North Carolina State Bar. ***PRACTICE AREAS:*** Securities; Corporate; Employee Benefits. ***Email:*** jjeffries@wcsr.com

DONALD C. LAMPE, admitted to bar, 1982, Texas; 1986, North Carolina. *Education:* Massachusetts Institute of Technology (B.S., 1978); Duke University (J.D., 1982). Author: "ECOA and Spousal Guaranties," N.C. Lawyers Weekly, June 1992; "Loan Commitments: Five Steps Will Avoid Litigation," N.C. Lawyers Weekly, December 1992; "Consumer Credit Law Update," NCBA Real Property Section Newsletter, September 1994; "Sub-Prime Primer," NCBA Real Property Section Newsletter, December 1996; "Regulation of Mortgage Brokers and Mortgage Bankers in North Carolina," NCBA Real Property Section Newsletter, January 1998; "Dealer Finance," Notes Bearing Interest (NCBA Business Law Section Newsletter), May 1999; "N.C. Residential Lending Overhaul Becomes Law," NCBA Real Property Section Newsletter, November 1999; "New State Predatory Lending Law: Legislative Developments in Consumer Credit," Notes Bearing Interest (NCBA Business Law Section Newsletter), January 2000; "Predatory Lending: Analysis and Perspective," BNA Banking Law Report, April 30, 2001; "An Overview of the Uniform Electronic Transactions Act and Federal ESIGN Law," The Conference on Consumer Finance Law Quarterly Report, Spring/Summer/Fall 2001; "The North Carolina Predatory Lending Usury Statute," The Conference on Consumer Finance Law Quarterly Report, Winter 2001; "Georgia Fair Lending Act Compliance Toolkit," Georgia Bankers Association, August 2002; "Predatory Lending: Federal Legislation, State Law and Preemption," The Conference on Consumer Finance Law Quarterly Report, Winter 2002 (upcoming); Rohner and Miller, Truth in Lending, Update to Section 6.09 (High-Cost Mortgage Loans), 2002 supplement (scheduled). *Member:* American Bar Association (Chair: Access to Services Subcommittee; Consumer Financial Services Committee; Predatory Lending Task Force); North Carolina Bar Association (Member: CLE Committee, 1999—; Real Property Section Council, 1997-2000; Real Property Section Executive Committee, Treasurer, 2000-2001; Real Property Curriculum Committee, 1998-1999; Business Law Section, 1999—. (Also at Greensboro, North Carolina Office). ***PRACTICE AREAS:*** Capital Markets; Banking; Consumer Practice; Regulatory Practice. ***Email:*** dlampe@wcsr.com

JAMES E. LILLY, born Birmingham, Alabama, August 5, 1960; admitted to bar, 1985, North Carolina; 1991, Georgia. *Education:* Birmingham-Southern College (B.A., summa cum laude, 1982); Duke University (J.D., with high honors, 1985). *Member:* State Bar of Georgia (Member: Corporate and Banking Law Section; Uniform Commercial Code Committee); American Bar Association. ***PRACTICE AREAS:*** Corporate Finance; Banking Law; Tax-Exempt Financings; Capital Markets. ***Email:*** jlilly@wcsr.com

SCOTT D. MacLATCHIE, born Santa Monica, California, September 9, 1957; admitted to bar, 1984, California; 1985, Nebraska; 1996, North Carolina. *Education:* University of Southern California (B.S., cum laude, 1979); Loyola Marymount University (J.D., 1984). Phi Alpha Delta (Marshall, 1982-1983). Associate Justice, Scott Moot Court Honors Board, 1983-1984. *Member:* Federal Bar Association; American Board of Trial Advocates; International Association of Chiefs of Police (Member, Legal Officers Section); Defense Research Institute. ***REPORTED CASES:*** Mendoza v. Block, 27 F.3d 1357 (9th Cir. 1994); Alexander v. County of Los Angeles, 64 F.3d 1315 (9th Cir. 1995); Gabbert v. Conn, 131 F.3d 793 (9th Cir. 1997); County of Los Angeles v. Superior Court (Peters), 80 Cal.Rptr.2d 860 (1998); Valentin v. County of Los Angeles, 92 Cal.Rptr.2d 668 (2000); Streit v. County of Los Angeles, 236 F.3d 552 (9th Cir. 2001). ***PRACTICE AREAS:*** Police Misconduct; Civil Rights; Municipal Law; Appellate Practice. ***Email:*** smaclatchie@wcsr.com

RICHARD E. MORTON, born Columbia, South Carolina, April 9, 1957; admitted to bar, 1990, North Carolina; 1991, South Carolina. *Education:* Guilford College (B.S., 1980); University of South Carolina (J.D., 1990). ***PRACTICE AREAS:*** Environmental; Toxic Torts. ***Email:*** rmorton@wcsr.com

WILLIAM RUFFIN PEARCE, JR., born Charlotte, North Carolina, March 27, 1969; admitted to bar, 1996, North Carolina; 1997, South Carolina; U.S. District Court, Western District of North Carolina. *Education:* Wake Forest University (B.S., cum laude, 1992; J.D., 1996; M.B.A., 1996). *Member:* North Carolina State Bar; South Carolina Bar. ***PRACTICE AREAS:*** Commercial Real Estate; Commercial Real Estate Finance; Commercial Real Estate Development; Leasing. ***Email:*** rpearce@wcsr.com

RICHARD L. RAINEY, born Chester, Pennsylvania, October 23, 1962; admitted to bar, 1987, North Carolina and U.S. District Court, Eastern, Middle and Western Districts of North Carolina; U.S. District Court, Eastern District of Michigan and District of Colorado; U.S. Court of Appeals, Fourth Circuit. *Education:* University of Delaware (B.A., summa cum laude, 1984); University of North Carolina (J.D., 1987). Order of the Coif. Co-Editor,

(This Listing Continued)

North Carolina Employment Law Letter. *Member:* Mecklenburg County, North Carolina and American (Labor and Employment Sections) Bar Association. ***REPORTED CASES:*** Hatton v. Thomasville Furniture Industries, 2001 WL 52679 (4th Cir. 2001); Woody v. Walters, 54 F.Supp.2d 574 (W.D.N.C. 1999); Dewitt v. Mecklenburg County, 73 F.Supp.2d 589 (W.D.N.C. 1999); Wilson v. McDaniel and Winston-Salem/Forsyth County Schools, 54 FEP Cases 1499 (M.D.N.C. 1991), affirmed 935 F.2d 1289 (4th Cir. 1991); Richardson v. Cabarrus County Board of Education, 151 F.3d 1030, 1948 WL 371999 (4th Cir. 1998); Morrocco v. Goodwill Industries, 61 FEP Cases 1547 (M.D.N.C. 1993); Glenn v. Baluss, 884 F.2d 1388, 1989 WL 100559 (4th Cir. 1989). ***PRACTICE AREAS:*** Labor and Employment Law. ***Email:*** rrainey@wcsr.com

WILLIAM C. RAPER, born Asheville, North Carolina, August 17, 1946; admitted to bar, 1972, North Carolina; 1977, U.S. Supreme Court. *Education:* University of North Carolina (A.B., 1968); Vanderbilt University (J.D., 1972). Editor, Vanderbilt Law Review, 1971-1972. Listed in The Best Lawyers in America, Business Litigation. Assistant, Senator Sam J. Ervin, Jr., U.S. Senate Subcommittee on Constitutional Rights, 1970. Law Clerk, Judge J. Braxton Craven, Jr., U.S. Court of Appeals for the Fourth Circuit, 1972-1973. *Member:* Mecklenburg County (Fee Dispute Arbitration Committee), Forsyth County, North Carolina and American (Member, Litigation Section) Bar Associations; North Carolina Association of Defense Attorneys; CPR Institute for Dispute Resolution (Member, Securities Litigation Committee, Law Firm Alternative Dispute Resolution Committee). ***PRACTICE AREAS:*** Litigation; Professional Malpractice; Commercial and Complex Litigation. ***Email:*** braper@wcsr.com

J. ALEXANDER SALISBURY, born Charlotte, North Carolina, November 16, 1952; admitted to bar, 1980, District of Columbia; 1981, U.S. Court of Appeals, District of Columbia Circuit; 1987, North Carolina. *Education:* University of Virginia (B.A., with distinction, 1975); University of Michigan (M.A., 1977); University of North Carolina (J.D., 1980). Staff Member, 1978-1979 and Business Manager, 1979-1980, North Carolina Law Review. *Member:* Mecklenburg County, North Carolina and American (Member, Business Law Section, Committee on Negotiated Acquisitions) Bar Associations. ***PRACTICE AREAS:*** Corporate Law; Mergers and Acquisitions; Public Utilities. ***Email:*** asalisbury@wcsr.com

PATRICIA SNYDER, born Cocoa Beach, Florida, November 13, 1963; admitted to bar, 1995, Georgia; 2003, North Carolina. *Education:* Georgia State University (B.S., magna cum laude, 1992); Emory University (J.D., with distinction, 1995). Phi Kappa Phi; Golden Key. Author: "From Feudal to Modern: The Evolution of Real Estate Finance in Russia," Emory International Law Review, Fall, 1994. *Member:* State Bar of Georgia (Member, Corporate and Banking Law Section); American Bar Association (Member, Business Law Section). ***PRACTICE AREAS:*** Corporate Finance; Banking Law; Tax-Exempt Financings; Capital Markets; Loan Syndications; Derivatives; Municipal Finance. ***Email:*** tsnyder@wcsr.com

WILLIAM R. WHITEHURST, born December 19, 1956; admitted to bar, 1982, Georgia; 1984, North Carolina; U.S. District Court, Northern District of Georgia and U.S. Court of Appeals, 11th and 5th Circuits. *Education:* Wake Forest University (B.A., cum laude, 1978); University of North Carolina (M.B.A., 1982; J.D., with honors, 1982). Order of the Coif; Beta Gamma Sigma. Member, North Carolina Law Review, 1981-1982. *Member:* Forsyth County, North Carolina and American Bar Associations; State Bar of Georgia. (Also at Winston-Salem, North Carolina Office). ***PRACTICE AREAS:*** Executive Compensation Law; Employee Benefits Law. ***Email:*** wwhitehurst@wcsr.com

RESIDENT ASSOCIATES

BRANDY D. BERRY, born Hickory, North Carolina, September 16, 1975; admitted to bar, 2001, South Carolina; 2002, North Carolina. *Education:* Campbell University (B.A., 1997); University of South Carolina (M.I.B.S., 2001; J.D., 2001). Dean's List; Order of Wig and Robe. Recipient: James R. Petigru Complete Lawyer Award; Real Estate/Domestic Relations, Susan McCrany Scholarship. ***LANGUAGES:*** French. ***PRACTICE AREAS:*** Corporate; Securities. ***Email:*** bberry@wcsr.com

STUART A. BROCK, born Whiteville, North Carolina, October 26, 1967; admitted to bar, 2000, North Carolina. *Education:* Wake Forest University (B.S., Biology, cum laude, 1990); Bowman Gray School of Medicine, Wake Forest University (Clinical Studies, 1992); North Carolina Central University School of Law (J.D., cum laude, 2000). CCM Certified Case Manager, 1995; Certification of Insurance Rehabilitation Specialists Commission. Managed Care Consultant, Winston-Salem, NC, 1994-2000; Case Manager, QualChoice of North Carolina, Inc., Winston-Salem, NC, 1995-1997; Case Management Specialist, MedCost, Inc., Winston-Salem, NC, 1994-1995; Manager ACS Medical Services, ACS Group, Inc., Winston-Salem, NC, 1992-1994. *Member:* Forsyth County and North Carolina (Member, Sections on: Litigation; Labor and Employment; Health Law) Bar Associations; Forsyth County Young Lawyers' Association; Case Management Society of America (North Carolina Chapter); American Society of Law, Medicine & Ethics; Health Insurance Association of America. (Also at Charlotte, North Carolina Office). ***PRACTICE AREAS:*** Labor and Employment; Pharmaceutical Patent Prosecution; Workers Compensation; Governmental Litigation; Tort Litigation. ***Email:*** sbrock@wcsr.com

MEREDITH P. BURBANK, born Anaheim, California, January 30, 1975; admitted to bar, 1999, North Carolina. *Education:* University of North Carolina (B.A., with distinction, 1995); University of Virginia (J.D., 1999). Phi Beta Kappa. Virginia Journal of Social Policy and the Law, Articles Review Board. *Member:* Mecklenburg County (Member, Pro Bono Committee), North Carolina and American Bar Associations. ***PRACTICE AREAS:*** Corporate Law; Securities. ***Email:*** mpaul@wcsr.com

ERIN E. BURKE, born Pittsburgh, Pennsylvania, October 8, 1970; admitted to bar, 1995, Pennsylvania; 1997, North Carolina; U.S. District Court, Western District of Pennsylvania; U.S. District Court, Eastern, Middle and Western Districts of North Carolina. *Education:* Pennsylvania State University (B.A., 1992); University of Notre Dame Law School (J.D., 1995). Member and Notes Editor, Journal of College & University Law, Notre Dame Legal Aid Clinic. Associate, Eckert Seamans Cherin & Mellott, LLC, Pittsburgh, PA, September 1995 - June 1998. Associate, McGuireWoods, LLP, Charlotte, NC, June 1998 - June 2002. *Member:* Mecklenburg County and North Carolina Bar Associations; American Inns of Court. ***PRACTICE AREAS:*** Business Litigation. ***Email:*** eburke@wcsr.com

(This Listing Continued)

WOMBLE CARLYLE SANDRIDGE & RICE, Charlotte—Continued

TRICIA MORVAN DERR, born Baton Rouge, Louisiana, August 2, 1972; admitted to bar, 1997, North Carolina. *Education:* University of North Carolina at Chapel Hill (B.A., 1994; J.D., 1997). Holderness Moot Court; Order of the Barristers. *Member:* Mecklenburg County Bar Association; North Carolina State Bar; International Association of Arson Investigators (Member, North Carolina Chapter); North Carolina Insurance Crime Information Exchange. ***PRACTICE AREAS:*** Medical Malpractice Defense; Civil Litigation; Civil Appeals; Criminal Defense; Commercial Litigation; Appellate Practice; Litigation.

STANLEY B. GREEN, born Macon, Georgia, February 28, 1970; admitted to bar, 1998, North Carolina. *Education:* University of North Carolina at Chapel Hill (B.A., 1993); Vermont Law School (M.S. in Environmental Law, magna cum laude, 1998; J.D., magna cum laude, 1998). Note Editor, Vermont Law Review. *Member:* North Carolina Bar Association. (Also at Winston-Salem, North Carolina Office). ***PRACTICE AREAS:*** Environmental; Toxic Tort. ***Email:*** sgreen@wcsr.com

DONNA L. HARGROVE, born Paris, Tennessee, July 3, 1968; admitted to bar, 1998, North Carolina. *Education:* University of Tennessee (B.S.N., 1990); University of South Carolina (J.D., 1998). Order of Wig and Robe. Member, South Carolina Law Review. Registered Nurse: Tennessee and Georgia, 1990; South Carolina, 1992. Author: Donna L. Casto, Note, "Whitner v. South Carolina: Prosecution for Child Abuse Extends in the Womb," 48 S.C.L. Rev. 657 (1997). *Member:* North Carolina Bar Association. ***PRACTICE AREAS:*** Corporate; Securities. ***Email:*** dhargrove@wcsr.com

MATTHEW B. HOMAN, born La Jolla, California, March 11, 1972; admitted to bar, 2001, North Carolina. *Education:* University of Virginia (B.A., 1994); Wake Forest University School of Law (J.D., cum laude, 2001). Order of the Coif. Member, Wake Forest Law Review. ***PRACTICE AREAS:*** Corporate Law; Securities. ***Email:*** mhoman@wcsr.com

SETH HUFFSTETLER, born Morganton, North Carolina, 1977; admitted to bar, 2003, North Carolina. *Education:* Duke University (B.A., 1998; J.D., 2003). ***PRACTICE AREAS:*** Corporate Law; Securities. ***Email:*** shuffstetler@wcsr.com

SARA R. LINCOLN, born Rochester, New York, August 24, 1968; admitted to bar, 1993, Ohio; 1996, North Carolina. *Education:* Wheaton College (B.A., 1990); University of Akron (J.D., 1993). ***PRACTICE AREAS:*** Medical Malpractice Defense; Civil Litigation; Civil Appeals.

RACHEL N. LOKKEN, born Cambridge, Massachusetts, April 1, 1971; admitted to bar, 1997, Illinois; 2004, North Carolina. *Education:* Oberlin College (B.A., 1993); University of Michigan Law School (J.D., 1997). Co-author: "Fresh Approaches to Firm Recruitment and Retention," The National Law Journal, July 31, 2000. *Member:* Winston-Salem and American Bar Associations; Forsyth County Young Lawyers Association. ***PRACTICE AREAS:*** Business Litigation; Corporate Governance; Pro Bono; Entertainment Law. ***Email:*** rlokken@wcsr.com

MEREDITH McKEE, born Portland, Oregon, March 30, 1977; admitted to bar, 2002, California; U.S. District Court, Central District of California and U.S. Court of Appeals, Ninth Circuit (Not admitted in North Carolina). *Education:* Northwestern University (B.S., Journalism and International Studies, magna cum laude, 1999); Harvard Law School (J.D., cum laude, 2002). Kappa Tau Alpha. Editor-in-Chief, Harvard Law RECORD, 2001-2002. Associate, O'Melveny & Myers, Los Angeles and Century City, California, 2002-2004. *Member:* State Bar of California. ***PRACTICE AREAS:*** Business Litigation. ***Email:*** mmckee@wcsr.com

K. MATTHEW MILLER, born Charlotte, North Carolina, June 2, 1975; admitted to bar, 2001, North Carolina. *Education:* Davidson College (B.A., 1997); Tulane University (J.D., 2001). ***PRACTICE AREAS:*** Business Litigation. ***Email:*** mmiller2@wcsr.com

DAWN T. MISTRETTA, born Jefferson, Louisiana, February 3, 1973; admitted to bar, 2003, North Carolina and U.S. District Court, Western and Middle Districts of North Carolina. *Education:* Louisiana State University (B.A., 1996); Campbell University (J.D., 2003). ***PRACTICE AREAS:*** Environmental. ***Email:*** dmistretta@wcsr.com

ROSS H. PARR, born Lansing, Michigan, 1972; admitted to bar, 1999, Pennsylvania; 2001, District of Columbia; 2004, North Carolina. *Education:* Michigan State University (B.A., with honors, 1994); College of William & Mary (J.D., 1999). Member, Moot Court. Member: Mortar Board National Honor Society; Golden Key National Honor Society. Recipient, Thomas Jefferson Prize. Article Editor, Bill of Rights Journal, 1998-1999. Author: "Suspicionless Drug Testing and Chandler v. Miller, Is the Supreme Court Making the Right Decisions?" 7 William & Mary Bill of Rights Journal 241, 1998. *Member:* American Bar Association (Member, Business Law Section, Committee on Federal Regulation of Securities and Corporate Governance Committee); North Carolina Bar Association (Member, Business Law Section); Mecklenburg County Bar Association; District of Columbia Bar; Pennsylvania Bar Association. ***PRACTICE AREAS:*** Federal Securities; Corporate; Corporate Governance.

SEAN F. PERRIN, born Worcester, Massachusetts, 1970; admitted to bar, 1995, North Carolina. *Education:* James Madison University (B.A., 1992); University of North Carolina at Chapel Hill (J.D., 1995). *Member:* North Carolina State Bar. ***PRACTICE AREAS:*** Insurance; Governmental Tort Litigation. ***Email:*** sperrin@wcsr.com

ROBERT JOHN PHOCAS, born Amityville, New York, January 5, 1970; admitted to bar, 1998, North Carolina; 1999, District of Columbia; 2001, Massachusetts; U.S. District Court, District of North Carolina, U.S. District Court, District of Columbia and U.S. District Court, District of Massachusetts. *Education:* Vassar College (B.A., 1991); Duke University (J.D., 1998; M.E.M., 1998). Member, Duke University Moot Court Board. Teaching Assistant, Legal Research and Writing. Member, Dean's Advisory Council, Duke University. Enforcement Counsel, U.S. Environmental Protection Agency, Region I, Boston, MA, 2001-2004. Associate: Hale and Dorr, LLP, Boston, MA, 2000-2001; Beveridge & Diamond, PC, Washington, DC, 1998-1999. *Member:* Massachusetts Bar Association; North Carolina State Bar; The District of Columbia Bar. ***PRACTICE AREAS:*** Environmental Law; Toxic Torts. ***Email:*** rphocas@wcsr.com

O. AKOMEN POKU-KANKAM, born Accra, Ghana, September 6, 1974; admitted to bar, 2000, Michigan; 2003, North Carolina. *Education:* University of Michigan (B.A., African and African American Studies, 1996; J.D., 1999). Associate: Cadwalader, Wickersham & Taft LLP, Charlotte, NC, 2001-2003; Dickinson Wright PLLC, Detroit, Michigan, 1999-2001. Member, 2003— and Treasurer, 2004—, Charlotte Emergency Housing. *Member:* Mecklenburg County and North Carolina Bar Associations; North Carolina State Bar; State Bar of Michigan. ***PRACTICE AREAS:*** Real Estate Development. ***Email:*** apokukankam@wcsr.com

PHILIP S. RUNKEL, born Dayton, Ohio, May 3, 1964; admitted to bar, 1995, New York and U.S. District Court, Western District of New York; 1999, North Carolina. *Education:* University of Virginia (B.A., 1986); College of William & Mary, Marshall Wythe School of Law (J.D., 1994). Member, William & Mary Law Review. Author: William & Mary Law Review, Vol. 35, Spring 1993; "Environmental Compliance & Litigation Strategy," February 1996. *Member:* New York State and American Bar Associations; North Carolina State Bar. ***PRACTICE AREAS:*** Real Estate. ***Email:*** prunkel@wcsr.com

DAVID B. SAYE, born Lancaster, Pennsylvania, June 9, 1976; admitted to bar, 2002, North Carolina. *Education:* Duke University (A.B., cum laude, 1998); Wake Forest University (J.D., 2002). Member, Wake Forest University Law Review. ***PRACTICE AREAS:*** Commercial Real Estate; Real Estate Finance; Real Estate Development. ***Email:*** dsaye@wcsr.com

JASON E. SITO, born Charlotte, North Carolina, January 16, 1977; admitted to bar, 2003, Virginia (Not admitted in North Carolina). *Education:* University of North Carolina (B.A., 1999); University of Virginia School of Law (J.D., 2003). ***PRACTICE AREAS:*** Capital Markets. ***Email:*** jsito@wcsr.com

JOLIE AMIE TENHOLDER, born St. Louis, Missouri, June 4, 1975; admitted to bar, 2000, North Carolina. *Education:* Truman State University (B.A., Business Administration, summa cum laude, 1997; B.S., Accounting, 1997); Wake Forest University (J.D., 2000). Alpha Phi; Delta Sigma Pi. Recipient: Corpus Juris Secundum Award for Scholastic Excellence; CALI Excellence for the Future Award. Associate, McGuire Woods LLP, Charlotte, NC, 2000-2004. *Member:* Mecklenburg County and American Bar Associations; North Carolina State Bar. ***PRACTICE AREAS:*** Capital Markets; Loan Syndication; Corporate Finance.

BRYAN L. TYSON, admitted to bar, 1996, Georgia; 2003, Texas; 2004, North Carolina. *Education:* University of North Carolina, Chapel Hill (B.A., Political Science, with honors, 1993; J.D., with honors, 1996); Georgetown University Law Center (LL.M. in Taxation with Distinction Certificate in Employee Benefits, 2002). Author: "Under Lock and Key (and Covenant): Practical Aspects to Protecting Your Clients with Restrictive Employment Covenants," Ga. Bar J., Volume 7, Number 1, August 2001; "Is the Merger of Participant—Directed 401(k) Plans Subject to ERISA's Fiduciary Duties?: An Analysis of the Franklin v. First Union Litigation and Its Aftermath," 105 West Virginia Law Review, 2003. ***PRACTICE AREAS:*** Employee Benefits; Executive Compensation; ERISA. ***Email:*** btyson@wcsr.com

STEVEN WILLIAMS ("WILL") WALKER, born Burlington, North Carolina, September 6, 1974; admitted to bar, 2000, North Carolina. *Education:* Wake Forest University (B.A., 1996); Duke University (M.B.A.; J.D., 2000). ***PRACTICE AREAS:*** Corporate; Securities. ***Email:*** swalker@wcsr.com

JAMES B. YOUNG, JR., born Sylva, North Carolina, December 8, 1974; admitted to bar, 2001, North Carolina and U.S. District Court, Western District of North Carolina. *Education:* University of Florida (B.S., 1996; M.B.A., 2000; J.D., 2001). *Member:* North Carolina Bar Association. ***PRACTICE AREAS:*** Corporate; Securities. ***Email:*** brit.young@wcsr.com

ERIC M.D. ZION, born Mission Viejo, California, December 17, 1975; admitted to bar, 2001, Georgia; 2002, North Carolina; U.S. Court of Appeals, Fourth and Eleventh Circuits, U.S. District Court, Northern and Middle Districts of Georgia and Western, Middle and Eastern Districts of North Carolina and Georgia and North Carolina Trial and Appellate Courts. *Education:* North Carolina State University (B.A., cum laude, 1998); Indiana University, Bloomington (J.D., magna cum laude, Order of the Coif, 2001). Author: "Protecting the E-Marketplace of Ideas by Protecting Employers: Immunity for Employers Under Section 230 of the Communications Decency Act," 54 F.C.L.J. 493 (2002); Author: "Overcoming Adversity: Distinguishing Retaliation From General Prohibitions Under Federal Employment Discrimination Law," 76 IND. L.J. 191 (2001). Judicial Clerkship: Intern, Hon. John D. Tinder, U.S. District Court, Southern District of Indiana, Indianapolis, Indiana, 2001. Prior Legal Experience: Enforcement Intern, U.S. EEOC, Raleigh, North Carolina, 1997; Legal Intern, U.S. EEOC, Charlotte, North Carolina, 1999; Associate, Fisher & Phillips LLP, Atlanta, GA, 2001-2004. *Member:* Atlanta, North Carolina and American Bar Associations. ***PRACTICE AREAS:*** Labor and Employment; Federal Litigation; State Litigation; Administrative Investigations. ***Email:*** ezion@wcsr.com

SENIOR COUNSEL

JOHN N. HUNTER, born Greensboro, North Carolina, October 31, 1965; admitted to bar, 1993, North Carolina. *Education:* Duke University (A.B., 1988); University of North Carolina, Chapel Hill (J.D., 1993). Member, International Law Journal. *Member:* North Carolina Bar Association; North Carolina International Law Council. ***LANGUAGES:*** Japanese. ***SPECIAL AGENCIES:*** North Carolina and South Carolina Economic Development Associations. ***PRACTICE AREAS:*** Economic Development; Corporate; Finance; Real Estate. ***Email:*** jhunter@wcsr.com

KATHERINE THOMPSON LANGE, born Fayetteville, North Carolina, September 12, 1963; admitted to bar, 1991, North Carolina. *Education:* University of North Carolina (B.S., 1986); Phi Beta Kappa, Wake Forest University (J.D., magna cum laude, 1991). Moot Court. Member, Wake Forest Law Review. *Member:* Mecklenburg County, North Carolina (Member, Civic Literacy Committee, 1995-1996) and American Bar Associations. ***REPORTED CASES:*** Knight Publishing Company v. Chase Manhattan Bank, N.C. App., 479 SE2d 478 (1997). ***PRACTICE AREAS:*** Commercial Litigation; ERISA Litigation. ***Email:*** klange@wcsr.com

RESIDENT OF COUNSEL

BRUCE A. BUCKLEY, born Washington, D.C., March 17, 1955; admitted to bar, 1981, North Carolina. *Education:* University of North Carolina (A.B., 1977; J.D., 1981).

(This Listing Continued)

Phi Beta Kappa. *Member:* Mecklenburg County (Member, Real Property Section), North Carolina (Member, Real Property Section) and American (Member, Real Property, Probate and Trust Section) Bar Associations. ***PRACTICE AREAS:*** Commercial Real Estate. ***Email:*** bbuckley@wcsr.com

ELIZABETH C. COSS, born Durham, North Carolina, January 30, 1965; admitted to bar, 1990, North Carolina. *Education:* University of North Carolina (B.S., Business Administrative, 1987); Wake Forest University (J.D., cum laude, 1990). Co-Author: Supplement to the North Carolina Probate Handbook, 1996 and 1997. *Member:* Mecklenburg, North Carolina (Member, Elder Law and Estate Planning and Fiduciary Law Sections) and American Bar Associations. ***PRACTICE AREAS:*** Estate Administration Law; Estate Planning Law. ***Email:*** ecoss@wcsr.com

KENNETH B. OETTINGER, JR., born Chapel Hill, North Carolina, April 14, 1966; admitted to bar, 1993, North Carolina; 1994, U.S. District Court, Western District of North Carolina. *Education:* University of North Carolina (B.A., 1989; J.D., with honors, 1993). Pi Sigma Alpha Honor Society. Member: Order of Barristers; Holderness Moot Court Invitational Team. *Member:* Mecklenburg County and American Bar Associations; North Carolina State Bar. ***PRACTICE AREAS:*** Bankruptcy; Creditors' Rights. ***Email:*** koettinger@wcsr.com

LORI REESE PATTON, born May 7, 1968; admitted to bar, 1993, Georgia; 1994, South Carolina; 2003, North Carolina. *Education:* Wesleyan College (B.A., 1990); Mercer University (J.D., 1993). ***PRACTICE AREAS:*** Business Litigation; Government Relations. ***Email:*** lpatton@wcsr.com

JOYCE E. PLYLER, admitted to bar, 1984, District of Columbia; 1996, North Carolina. *Education:* Winthrop College (B.A., cum laude, 1980); Emory University (J.D., 1983). Associate Managing Editor, Emory Law Journal. Author: "Building Web Site Brings Many Legal Considerations," The Charlotte Business Journal, February 18, 2000; "Consumer Privacy in the United States and European Union," Consumer Protection Update, A.B.A. Section of Antitrust Law, Fall, 1999. *Member:* Mecklenburg County and American (Member, Antitrust Section) Bar Associations. ***PRACTICE AREAS:*** Advertising and Marketing Law; Internet Law; Trade Practices. ***Email:*** jplyler@wcsr.com

THOMAS A. PRICE, born Augusta, Georgia, May 14, 1971; admitted to bar, 1998, North Carolina. *Education:* Davidson College (B.A., 1993); Wake Forest University (J.D., 1998). Member, Moot Court. ***PRACTICE AREAS:*** Corporate; Securities. ***Email:*** tprice@wcsr.com

JOHN W. SPRINGER, born Montgomery, Alabama, October 20, 1953; admitted to bar, 1978, Georgia; 2005, North Carolina. *Education:* University of Virginia (B.A., 1975); University of Alabama School of Law (J.D., 1978); New York University (LL.M., Taxation, 1981). *Member:* Columbus and American (Member, Antitrust Law, Forum Committee on the Construction Industry Public Contract Law and Taxation Committees) Bar Associations; State Bar of Georgia (Member of Alternative Dispute, Corporate Counsel, and General Practice and Trial Committees); North Carolina State Bar. ***PRACTICE AREAS:*** Construction Law; Government Contracts; Litigation Risk Management. ***Email:*** jwspringer@wcsr.com

TODD C. TAYLOR, born Murray, Kentucky, May 17, 1971; admitted to bar, 1995, North Carolina. *Education:* North Carolina State University (B.A., 1992); University of North Carolina at Chapel Hill (J.D., with honors, 1995). Articles Editor, North Carolina International Law Journal, 1994-1995. *Member:* North Carolina Bar Association. ***PRACTICE AREAS:*** Corporate; Securities. ***Email:*** ttaylor@wcsr.com

JAMES A. WITHERSPOON, born Charleston, West Virginia, January 28, 1964; admitted to bar, 1995, Georgia; 1999, North Carolina; registered to practice before U.S. Patent and Trademark Office. *Education:* North Carolina State University (B.S., Mechanical Engineering, 1987); Georgia State University College of Law (J.D., 1995). North Carolina Engineer in Training Certificate, 1987. Member, American Society of Mechanical Engineers Working Group on Nuclear Power Plant Codes and Standards for Pumps and Valves, 1990-1992. Member, Board of the Carolina Patent, Trademark and Copyright Association. *Member:* State Bar of Georgia; Carolina Patent, Trademark and Copyright Law Association (Board Member). ***PRACTICE AREAS:*** Patent Preparation and Prosecution; Patent-Related Opinions; Trademark Preparation and Prosecution. ***Email:*** jwitherspoon@wcsr.com

LEGAL SUPPORT PERSONNEL

Terry Michael Wiley (Executive Director)
Susan DeVore (Office Administrator - Atlanta)
Keith Tedrow (Office Administrator - Winston-Salem)
John E. Turlington (Office Administrator - Research Triangle Park and Raleigh)
Cheri Edwards (Office Administrator - Tysons Corner, VA)
Patricia A. Kight (Director of Human Resources)
Charles R. Allison, III (Office Administrator - Charlotte)
John T. Boyer (Office Administrator - Washington, DC)
Hails Foster (Director of Finance and Systems)
Mark Whitley (Director, Strategic Planning and Marketing)
Julie D. Beavers (Professional Development/Recruiting Administrator - Research Triangle Park and Raleigh)
Cynthia K. Pruitt (Professional Development/Recruiting Administrator - Winston-Salem and Greensboro)
Kristin F. Carretta (Director of Professional Development and Recruiting)
Elizabeth P. Keasler (Professional Development/Recruiting Administrator - Charlotte and Greenville, SC)
Stacy H. Stephens (Professional Development/Recruiting Administrator - Atlanta)
Barbara Fountain (Office Manager - Greenville)
Melissa B. Weaver (Office Manager/Billing Coordinator - Greensboro)

GENERAL COUNSEL FOR: Brenner Companies; Charles & Colvard, Ltd.; Inmar Enterprises, Inc.; NC Biosciences Industry Organization; Piedmont Federal Savings & Loan Assn.; RF Micro Devices, Inc.; Venture First Associates.
REPRESENTATIVE CLIENTS: ALLTEL Corp.; Ardent Health Services; Bank of America; BB&T Corporation; Blue Point Capital Partners; Boulevard CENTRO; Cabarrus County Board of Education; Carolinas Healthcare System; Carolina Mills, Inc.; Charles & Colvard, Ltd.; Childress Klein Properties, Inc.; City of Charlotte, North Carolina; The Crosland Group, Inc.; Duke Energy; Enterprise Leasing Company - Southeast; Enterprise Rent-A-Car Company; Exxon Mobil; First Colony; First Horizon Corporate Financial; Frontier Capital, LLC; Grubb

(This Listing Continued)

Properties; The Harris Group; Hartford Insurance; HCA; Inmar Enterprises, Inc.; Jefferson-Pilot Life Insurance Company; Magneti Marelli USA, Inc.; Mecklenburg County; Medical Mutual Insurance; North Carolina Association of County Commissioners; Novant Health, Inc.; Peak 10, Inc.; Regions Bank; Republic Services; RF Micro Devices, Inc.; Rusty Wallace, Inc.; Sedgwick James; Spectrum Properties; The Travelers Insurance Companies; Turkington Industries Limited; Wachovia Bank, N.A.; Washington Mutual; Zemex Industrial Minerals.

REVISER OF THE NORTH CAROLINA LAW DIGEST FOR THIS DIRECTORY.

(For Biographical Data on other Personnel, see Professional Biographies at Raleigh, Winston-Salem, Research Triangle Park, North Carolina, Atlanta, Georgia, Washington, D.C., Greenville, South Carolina and Tysons Corner, Virginia)

WYATT & BLAKE, L.L.P.

Established in 1986

435 EAST MOREHEAD STREET
CHARLOTTE, NORTH CAROLINA 28202-2609
Telephone: 704-331-0767
Fax: 704-331-0773
URL: http://www.wyattandblakelaw.com
Email: jfw@wyattlaw.net
URL: http://www.wyattandblake.com

Criminal and Civil Trial Practice in all State and Federal Courts.

JAMES F. WYATT, III, born March 19, 1958; admitted to bar, 1982, Georgia, U.S. District Court, Northern District of Georgia and U.S. Court of Appeals, 11th Circuit; 1986, North Carolina, U.S. District Court, Eastern Middle and Western Districts of North Carolina and U.S. Court of Appeals, 4th Circuit. *Education:* Vanderbilt University (B.S., Salutatorian, summa cum laude, 1978); Duke University (J.D., 1982). Executive Editor, Duke Law Journal. Member, Moot Court Board, 1981-1982. Law Clerk for United States District Court Judge Harold L. Murphy, 1982-1984. Associate with Bobby Lee Cook, Sr., Cook & Palmour, Summerville, Georgia, 1984-1986. Listed in: The Best Lawyers in America, 1994—; The Best Lawyers in Charlotte, 1999—; The Legal Elite, 2003—; Business North Carolina's Legal Elite: Top Criminal Defense Lawyer, 2004. Representative Articles: "Filing A Civil Rights Action As Part Of An Aggressive Criminal Defense," The Champion, vol. XVI, No. 6 at 14-18, July 1992; "Preserving The Record For Appeal," Trial, vol. 29, No. 3 at 58-62, March 1993; "Health Care Fraud," Trial Briefs, at 10-12, Spring 1997. *Member:* North Carolina State Bar; National Association of Criminal Defense Lawyers; North Carolina Academy of Trial Lawyers (Member, Board of Governors, 1996-1999; President, Criminal Law Section, 1994-1995). ***PRACTICE AREAS:*** Civil and Criminal Trial Practice.

ROBERT A. BLAKE, JR., born Tucson, Arizona, February 18, 1969; admitted to bar, 1994, North Carolina and U.S. District Court, Western District of North Carolina; U.S. Court of Appeals, Tenth Circuit and U.S. Court of Appeals, Fourth Circuit. *Education:* University of North Carolina at Chapel Hill (B.S., 1991); Wake Forest University (J.D., cum laude, 1994). Editorial Board Member, Wake Forest Law Review. Law Clerk for United States Circuit Judge Wade Brorby, Tenth Circuit Court of Appeals, 1996-1997; Law Clerk for United States District Judge Graham C. Mullen, Western District of North Carolina, 1994-1996. Author, "A Step Toward a Colorblind Society," 29 Wake Forest Law Review 937 (1994). *Member:* Mecklenburg County and North Carolina Bar Associations; North Carolina Academy of Trial Lawyers. ***PRACTICE AREAS:*** Civil and Criminal Trial Practice. ***Email:*** rblake@wyattlaw.net

LAURA L. YAEGER

401 NORTH TRYON STREET, 10TH FLOOR
CHARLOTTE, NORTH CAROLINA 28202-2108
Telephone: 704-358-4984
Facsimile: 704-334-1785
Email: laura@lyaeger.com
URL: http://www.lyaegerlaw.com

Business, Family Business, Limited Liability, Corporate Law, Trust and Estates, Estate Planning, Wills and Probate, Taxation.

FIRM PROFILE: Ms. Yaeger has been in private practice since 1977.

LAURA L. YAEGER, born Des Moines, Iowa, May 7, 1952; admitted to bar, 1977, North Carolina. *Education:* University of North Carolina at Chapel Hill (B.A., 1974; J.D., 1977). Certified Public Accountant, North Carolina, 1983. *Member:* 26th Judicial District and North Carolina State Bars. ***PRACTICE AREAS:*** Business; Family Business Law; Limited Liability Company Law; Corporate Law; Trusts and Estates; Estate Planning; Wills; Probate; Taxation.

KAREN ZAMAN & ASSOCIATES

Established in 1981

P.O. BOX 16577
CHARLOTTE, NORTH CAROLINA 28209
Telephone: Toll Free: 866-960-8662
Fax: Toll Free: 866-960-8664
URL: http://www.karenzamanandassoc.com

Medical Malpractice, Personal Injury, Auto Accidents, Traumatic Brain Injuries, Birth Injuries, Head Injuries, Nursing Home Negligence, Wrongful Death.

KAREN ZAMAN, born Cleveland, Ohio, May 3, 1951; admitted to bar, 1979, North Carolina; 1981, U.S. District Court, Western District of North Carolina; 1982, U.S. Court of Appeals, Fourth Circuit; 1983, U.S. Supreme Court; 2003, U.S. District Court, Middle District of North Carolina. *Education:* Duke University (B.A., 1973); University of North Carolina (J.D., 1979). Recipient, Angier B. Duke Scholar. *Member:* Mecklenburg County Bar Association; North Carolina State Bar; The Association of Trial Lawyers of America;

(This Listing Continued)

KAREN ZAMAN & ASSOCIATES, Charlotte—Continued

North Carolina Academy of Trial Lawyers; North Carolina Association of Women Attorneys; National Association of Elder Law Attorneys.

A. MELTON BLACK, JR.
ATTORNEY AT LAW, PA

Established in 2003

201 NORTH CHERRY STREET
P.O. BOX 459
CHERRYVILLE, NORTH CAROLINA 28021
Telephone: 704-435-0753
Fax: 704-435-8181
Email: mel@melblack.us
URL: http://www.melblack.us

Administrative Law, Licensing Law, Real Estate.

MEL BLACK, born Erwin, North Carolina, September 22, 1964; admitted to bar, 1998, North Carolina; 2001, District of Columbia. *Education:* Winthrop College (M.Ed., 1985); Appalachian State University (Ed.S., 1988); North Carolina Central University (J.D., cum laude, 1998). Member, North Carolina Central University Law Journal, 1997-1998. Co-Author: with Hagan, *Instructors Manual for North Carolina Real Estate for Brokers and Salesmen,* Fourth Edition, Prentice Hall, 1995. Officer, North Carolina Real Estate Commission, 1992-1995. Executive Director, North Carolina Appraisal Board, 1995-2003. Member, Board of Directors, Council on Licensure, Enforcement, and Regulation, 1995-2000. President, Association of Appraiser Regulatory Officials, 2001-2002. Member, The Appraisal Foundation's State Regulator Advisory Group, 2002-2003. Member, The Appraisal Foundation Advisory Council, 2002-2003*Member:* Gaston County Bar Association; North Carolina State Bar; District of Columbia Bar. ***Email:*** mblack@blackandblacklaw.com

HUFFSTETLER LAW OFFICES

106 NORTH CHERRY STREET
CHERRYVILLE, NORTH CAROLINA 28021-2903
Telephone: 704-435-4907; 800-259-9552
Fax: 704-435-1275
Email: huffstetler@lawyers.com
URL: http://www.lawyers.com/huffstetler

General Practice, Real Estate, Loan Closings, Estates, Wills, Criminal Law, Traffic, Uncontested Divorce, Separation Agreements, Business Law.

PALMER E. HUFFSTETLER, JR., born Gastonia, North Carolina, February 13, 1962; admitted to bar, 1987, North Carolina. *Education:* Wake Forest University (B.A., cum laude, 1984; J.D., 1987). City Attorney, Cherryville, North Carolina, 1991—. *Member:* Gaston County and North Carolina (Member, Real Property Section) Bar Associations; North Carolina Association of Municipal Attorneys. ***Email:*** huffstetler@carolina.rr.com

THE LAW OFFICES OF
HALES & CONAWAY, PLLC

490 HIGHWAY 42 WEST
P.O. BOX 1025
CLAYTON, NORTH CAROLINA 27528
Telephone: 919-359-3093
Toll Free: 1-877-359-3093
Fax: 919-359-3095
URL: http://www.halesandconawaylaw.com

Clinton, North Carolina Office: 100 Fayetteville Street, Suite 103, 28328. Telephone: 919-359-3093. Toll Free: 877-359-3093.

Family Law, Divorce, Adoption, Custody, Child Support, Premarital Agreements, Separation Agreements, Criminal Defense, Social Security Disability, Collections, Debtor, Creditor, Juvenile Law, Estate Administration and Estate Planning, Civil Litigation, Workers Compensation, Personal Injury, Traffic, DWI.

MELISSA IVERSEN HALES, admitted to bar, 2004, North Carolina. *Education:* Duke University (B.A., 2000); Norman A. Wiggins School of Law, Campbell University (J.D., 2004). ***PRACTICE AREAS:*** Family Law; Criminal Defense; Social Security Disability; Collections; Juvenile Law. ***Email:*** mhales@halesandconawaylaw.com

AMY CONAWAY, admitted to bar, 2004, North Carolina. *Education:* University of Dayton (B.A., 2001); Campbell University (J.D., 2004). ***PRACTICE AREAS:*** Family Law; Estate Administration; Estate Planning; Civil Litigation; Traffic Violations; DWI; Criminal Law; Juvenile Law. ***Email:*** aconaway@halesandconawaylaw.com

LAW OFFICE OF ROBERT S. PLEASANT

224 WEST MAIN STREET
CLAYTON, NORTH CAROLINA 27520
Telephone: 919-550-5677
Fax: 919-550-7677
Email: robert.pleasant@earthlink.net
URL: http://www.rpleasantlaw.com
Mailing Address: P.O. Box 1191, Clayton, NC 27528
(This Listing Continued)

Personal Injury, Wrongful Death, Auto Accidents, Workers Compensation, Criminal, DWI, Traffic Offenses, Family Law, Divorce, Child Custody.

ROBERT S. PLEASANT, born Fort Belvoir, Virginia, February 13, 1969; admitted to bar, 1994, North Carolina. *Education:* University of North Carolina at Chapel Hill (B.A., 1991; J.D., 1994). Phi Delta Phi. *Member:* North Carolina State Bar; North Carolina Bar Association; North Carolina Trial Lawyers Association. ***PRACTICE AREAS:*** Personal Injury; Wrongful Death; Automobile Accidents; Workers Compensation; Criminal Law; Driving While Intoxicated; Traffic Violations; Family Law; Divorce; Child Custody.

STEWART LAW OFFICE, PLLC

CLAYTON, NORTH CAROLINA

(See Cary)

Estate Planning, Trusts, Living Trusts, Trusts and Estates, Wills, Business Law, Contracts, Corporate Law.

ALLEN R. TEW, P.A.

Established in 1987

202 SOUTH LOMBARD STREET
P.O. BOX 145
CLAYTON, NORTH CAROLINA 27528
Telephone: 919-553-6142; 553-2143
Fax: 919-553-8742
Email: allen@atewlawfirm.com
URL: http://www.lawyers.com/allentewpa

General and Trial Practice in all State and Federal Courts, Civil Litigation, Personal Injury Law, Automobile Accidents, Wrongful Death, Domestic Relations and Real Estate, Construction Litigation, Mediation.

FIRM PROFILE: Allen R. Tew, P.A. was founded in 1987. Allen Tew formerly practiced law with George B. Mast in the firm of Mast, Tew, Morris and Mast in the Clayton, North Carolina office from 1971 until 1987 when the firm of Allen R. Tew, P.A. was established.

ALLEN R. TEW, born Raleigh, North Carolina, May 5, 1944; admitted to bar, 1971, North Carolina and South Carolina; 1974, U.S. District Court, Eastern District of North Carolina; 1980, U.S. Court of Appeals, Fourth Circuit. *Education:* University of North Carolina (A.B., 1966); University of South Carolina (J.D., 1971); Duke Private Adjudication Center Mediation Course (2001). Phi Alpha Delta. Member, Board of Editors, South Carolina Law Review, 1970-1971. Certified Superior Court Mediator. Author: "Domestic Relations, 1969 Survey of South Carolina Law," 21 South Carolina Law Review 561. Teaching Assistant, University of South Carolina School of Law, 1970-1971. *Member:* Johnston County, North Carolina (Member, Alternative Dispute Resolution Committee, 1986-1993; Chairman, Summary Jury Trial Subcommittee, 1990-1992), and American Bar Associations; North Carolina State Bar; South Carolina Bar; North Carolina Academy of Trial Lawyers. ***REPORTED CASES:*** Ray v. Atlantic Casualty Insurance Co., 112 N.C. App. 259 435 S.E. 2d80. ***PRACTICE AREAS:*** Civil Practice; Commercial Litigation; Construction Law; Eminent Domain; Family Law; General Practice; Land Use; Medical Malpractice; Personal Injury; Real Estate; Municipal Law; Zoning Law. ***Email:*** allen@atewlawfirm.com

APPROVED ATTORNEY FOR: Title Company of North Carolina; Commonwealth Title Company.
REPRESENTATIVE CLIENTS: Carolina Packers, Inc.; Innovative Design; First Citizens Bank & Trust Co.; Walthom Group.
REFERENCES: First Citizens Bank & Trust Co.; Four Oaks Bank and Trust Company.

NORMAN L. SLOAN

3550 CLEMMONS ROAD, SUITE 110
CLEMMONS, NORTH CAROLINA 27012
Telephone: 336-748-0008
Fax: 336-766-0903
Email: nlsloanlaw@aol.com
URL: http://www.nsloan.com

General and Complex Litigation, Franchise Law and Franchising, Corporate Law, Business Law, Commercial Law, Personal Injury, Trademarks, Copyrights, Intellectual Property Law, Entertainment Law, Unfair Trade Practice Law, and Bankruptcy.

NORMAN L. SLOAN, born Winston-Salem, North Carolina, October 30, 1947; admitted to bar, 1972, North Carolina; 1975, U.S. District Court, Eastern, Western and Middle Districts of North Carolina; 1976, U.S. Tax Court and U.S. Supreme Court. *Education:* University of North Carolina (A.B., 1969); Wake Forest University (J.D., 1972). Phi Delta Phi. Department of Justice, Assistant Attorney General, North Carolina, 1973-1975. Vice-President and General Counsel, Specialty Retail Concepts, Inc., 1988-1990. *Member:* Forsyth County, North Carolina and American Bar Associations; North Carolina State Bar.

REPRESENTATIVE CLIENTS: Leonard Aluminum Utility Buildings, Inc.; Doctor's Associates Inc.; Subway Restaurants, Inc.; Meridian Aerospace Group, Ltd.; Longhorn Finance, LLC; Slick Enterprises; Bagel Station, Inc.; MRV International, LLC; Silver Tread, Inc.; Lydall, Inc.
REFERENCES: Branch Bank & Trust; Wachovia Bank & Trust.

WILLIAM E. CLARK

CLINTON, NORTH CAROLINA

(See Fayetteville)

General Civil Practice. Wills, Estate Planning and Probate. Corporate and Business Law. Real Estate Closings and Development.

DAVID AND ASSOCIATES, PLLC

610 BEAMAN STREET
CLINTON, NORTH CAROLINA 28328
Telephone: 910-592-8400
Toll Free: 1-800-856-9927
Email: aeverhart@davidandassociates.com
URL: http://www.wilmingtonpiattorneys.com

Jacksonville, North Carolina Office: 405-B Western Boulevard. 28546. Telephone: 910-219-4878.
Supply, North Carolina Office: Highway 17. 28462. Telephone: 910-754-8465.
Wallace, North Carolina Office: 107 North Norwood Street. 28466. Telephone: 910-285-8777.
Wilmington, North Carolina Office: 1516 Dawson Street. 28401. Telephone: 910-251-8088.
Winston-Salem, North Carolina Office: 1100-A South Stratford Road. 27103. Telephone: 336-354-1040.
Greensboro, North Carolina Office: 529 College Road. Suite G. 27410. Telephone: 336-354-1040.

Personal Injury, Medical Malpractice, Wrongful Death, Products Liability, Workers Compensation, Aviation, Airplane Crashes, Negligence, Class Actions, Maritime Accidents, Boating Accidents, Bicycle Accidents, Motorcycle Accidents, Truck Accidents, School Bus Accidents, Railroad Accidents, Dog Bites, Slip and Fall, Birth Trauma, Brain Injury, Spinal Injury, Head Injury, Catastrophic Injury, Vehicular Homicide, Personal Injury Mediation, Products Liability, Drug and Medical Device Litigation, Product Defects, Automobile Liability, Motorcycle Products Liability, Amusement Park Liability, Hotel Liability, Marina Liability, Sports Injury.

(For complete biographical data on all personnel, see Professional Biographies, Wilmington, North Carolina)

THE LAW OFFICES OF HALES & CONAWAY, PLLC

CLINTON, NORTH CAROLINA
(See Clinton)

Family Law, Divorce, Adoption, Custody, Child Support, Premarital Agreements, Separation Agreements, Criminal Defense, Social Security Disability, Collections, Debtor, Creditor, Juvenile Law, Estate Administration and Estate Planning, Civil Litigation, Workers Compensation, Personal Injury, Traffic, DWI.

HOLLAND, POOLE, HOLLAND & SANDERSON, P.A.

Established in 1948
212 WEST MAIN STREET
P.O. BOX 1046
CLINTON, NORTH CAROLINA 28328
Telephone: 910-592-5751
Fax: 910-592-7127
Email: rmholland@intrstar.net
URL: http://www.attorneyshphs.com

General Civil and Criminal Practice. Trials in all State Courts. Negligence, Probate, Real Estate, Contract and Insurance Law, Domestic Relations, Traffic Violations, DWI, Personal Injury, Workers Compensation, Social Security Disability.

FIRM PROFILE: Holland, Poole & Holland, P.A. was founded in 1948 by R. Maurice Holland. The firm serves clients as a general practice with individual lawyers practicing in specific areas of law throughout Sampson County.

R. MAURICE HOLLAND (1922-1996)

BILLIE L. POOLE, born Pinehurst, North Carolina, May 20, 1936; admitted to bar, 1965, North Carolina. *Education:* Wake Forest College (B.S., 1958; J.D., 1965). Phi Alpha Delta. Member, North Carolina Board of Law Examiners, 1990-1998. *Member:* Sampson County, North Carolina and American Bar Associations; Fourth Judicial District and The North Carolina State Bars; North Carolina Academy of Trial Lawyers. ***PRACTICE AREAS:*** Corporate; Business Law; Personal Injury; Civil Litigation; Estates; Municipal Law. **Email:** blpoole@intrstar.net

ROSCOE "ROSS" M. HOLLAND, JR., born Clinton, North Carolina, January 28, 1955; admitted to bar, 1981, North Carolina. *Education:* University of North Carolina (B.A., 1977); Campbell University (J.D., 1981). Phi Alpha Delta. *Member:* Sampson County, North Carolina and American Bar Associations; Fourth Judicial District and North Carolina State Bars; North Carolina Academy of Trial Lawyers. (Board Certified Specialist in Criminal Law, North Carolina State Board of Legal Specialization). ***PRACTICE AREAS:*** Criminal Law/Traffic Offenses; Family Law; Divorce Law. **Email:** rmholland@intrstar.net

HEBERN "SANDY" W. SANDERSON, JR., born Fayetteville, North Carolina, September 6, 1966; admitted to bar, 1992, North Carolina. *Education:* North Carolina State University (B.A., 1989); Campbell University (J.D., cum laude, 1992). Phi Kappa Phi. Member, Editorial Board, Campbell Law Review. Staff Member, Campbell Law Observer. Recipient, American Jurisprudence Award in Trial Advocacy and Civil Procedure. *Member:* Sampson County (President, 2001-2002) and North Carolina Bar Associations; North Carolina State Bar; North Carolina Academy of Trial Lawyers. ***PRACTICE AREAS:*** Workers Compensation; Social Security Disability; Personal Injury; Wrongful Death. **Email:** hwsjr@intrstar.net

REPRESENTATIVE CLIENTS: First-Citizens Bank & Trust Co.; Plastic Tubing, Inc.; Star Telephone Membership Corp.; Branch Banking and Trust Company; Town of Roseboro; Town of Salemburg.

(This Listing Continued)

APPROVED ATTORNEYS FOR: Lawyers Title Insurance Corp.; Cape Fear Farm Service; First Title Insurance Co.; consumers Title Company; Investors Title Company.

JOHNSON, PARSONS & HOBSON, P.L.L.C.

500 COLLEGE STREET
P.O. DRAWER 1049
CLINTON, NORTH CAROLINA 28329-4012
Telephone: 910-592-7066
Fax: 910-592-9144
URL: http://www.johnsonandparsons.com
URL: http://www.lawyers.com/johnson&parsons

General Civil and Criminal Practice. Trials in all State and Federal Courts. Negligence, Workers Compensation, Insurance and Personal Injury Law.

DALE P. JOHNSON, born Elizabethtown, North Carolina, July 20, 1943; admitted to bar, 1968, North Carolina; U.S. District Court, Eastern District of North Carolina; U.S. Court of Appeals, Fourth Circuit. *Education:* University of North Carolina (A.B., 1965; J.D., 1968). Delta Theta Phi. Member, Holderness Moot Court Bench, 1967. Author: "The Elements of Proof and Procedure," North Carolina Department of Justice, 1972. Visiting Professor of Law, Motor Vehicle Law, Campbell University School of Law, 1982—. City Attorney, City of Clinton, North Carolina, 2001—. Assistant District Attorney, 1968-1972. Statewide Special Prosecutor. Legal Advisor, State Bureau of Investigation. Member: North Carolina Criminal Code Commission, 1969-1973; North Carolina Fair Sentencing Commission, 1979-1981. North Carolina Assistant Attorney General, 1972-1973. County Attorney, Sampson County, 1975-1978. Asst. Attorney General, State-wide Prosecutor, Legal Advisor to North Carolina State Bureau of Investigation. Attorney, Sampson Memorial Hospital, 1973-1998. North Carolina General Statutes Commission, 1982. Member, Board of Trustees, UNC Law Alumni Association, 2000—. *Member:* Sampson County, Fourth Judicial District and North Carolina Bar Associations; The North Carolina State Bar; North Carolina Academy of Trial Lawyers (Member, Board of Directors, 1981-1987); The Association of Trial Lawyers of America. ***PRACTICE AREAS:*** Personal Injury; Wrongful Death; Workers Compensation; Products Liability; Insurance.

W. DOUGLAS PARSONS, born Clinton, North Carolina, October 7, 1950; admitted to bar, 1975, North Carolina, U.S. District Court, Eastern District of North Carolina; U.S. District Court, Middle and Western Districts of North Carolina; U.S. Supreme Court; U.S. Court of Appeals, Fourth Circuit. *Education:* University of North Carolina (A.B., 1972); Wake Forest University (J.D., 1975). Phi Delta Phi. Listed in the Best Lawyers in America, 1993—. Lecturer: Manuscripts on Criminal Law and Trial of Criminal Cases, North Carolina Academy of Trial Lawyers; Wake Forest School of Law; University of North Carolina School of Law; North Carolina Bar Association; Eastern District Federal Defenders Conference; North Carolina Public Defenders Conference; North Carolina District Attorneys Conference. Assistant District Attorney, Fourth Judicial District, 1975-1978. Assistant United States Attorney, Criminal Division, Eastern District of North Carolina, 1978-1979. City Attorney, Town of Newton Grove, 1980-1988. Member, North Carolina Criminal Justice Education and Training Standards Commission, 1985-1989. Member, North Carolina Courts Commission, 1993-2001. *Member:* Sampson County (President, 1984), North Carolina and American Bar Associations; Fourth Judicial District (Vice President, 1985; President, 1986) and North Carolina State Bar (Member, Criminal Justice Section; Counsel Member, 1981-1984, 1999-2002; Member, Criminal Law Specialization Committee, 1991-1999; Chairman, 1995-1999); North Carolina Academy of Trial Lawyers (Member, Board of Governors, 1987-1997; Legislative Chair, Criminal Law Section; Vice-President of Legislation, 1989-1991); National Association of Criminal Defense Lawyers. (Board Certified Specialist in State Criminal Law and Federal Criminal Law, North Carolina State Board of Legal Specialization). ***PRACTICE AREAS:*** State Criminal Law; Federal Criminal Law.

DAVID H. HOBSON, born Lumberton, North Carolina, April 25, 1970; admitted to bar, 1995, North Carolina. *Education:* North Carolina State University (B.A., 1992); Campbell University (J.D., 1995). Membership Editor, "Campbell Law Review," N.C. Superior Court Pattern Jury Instructions Committee-Criminal Subcommittee, 1993-1995. *Member:* Fourth Judicial Bar Association(Chairman, Bar Candidate Committee); North Carolina State Bar; North Carolina Academy of Trial Lawyers; National Association of Criminal Defense Lawyers. ***PRACTICE AREAS:*** Criminal Law; Motor Vehicle Law.

REFERENCE: Branch Banking & Trust Co.

THE KIRBY LAW FIRM

118 LISBON STREET
P.O. BOX 1250
CLINTON, NORTH CAROLINA 28329-1250
Telephone: 910-592-4481
Facsimile: 910-596-0159
Email: kirbylaw@earthlink.net
URL: http://www.kirbylawfirm.com

Personal Injury, Workers Compensation, Criminal Defense, Domestic Relations.

MEMBER

ALBERT D. KIRBY, JR., born Clinton, North Carolina, March 31, 1958; admitted to bar, 1987, North Carolina and U.S. District Court, Eastern District of North Carolina. *Education:* Wake Forest University (B.A., 1980); Campbell University (J.D., 1986). President, Sampson County Bar Association, 1999. Member: North Carolina Bar Association, 1987; North Carolina Academy of Trial Lawyers, 1988. Assistant District Attorney, 12th and 3rd Prosecutorial Districts. Associate Professor of Criminal Justice, East Carolina University. *Member:* North Carolina State Bar; Association of Trial Lawyers of America; North Carolina Association of Black Lawyers. ***PRACTICE AREAS:*** Personal Injury; Workers Compensation; Criminal Defense; Domestic Relations; Social Security Disability; Bankruptcy. **Email:** kirbylaw@earthlink.net

CHRISTINA RIVENBARK & ASSOCIATES

603A NORTHEAST BOULEVARD
CLINTON, NORTH CAROLINA 28328
Telephone: 1-800-777-5159

Wilmington, North Carolina Office: 4009 Oleander Drive, 28403. Telephone: 1-800-806-8896.
Garner, North Carolina Office: 5533 NC Highway 42 West, 27529. Telephone: 1-800-561-9221.

Personal Injury, Automobile Accidents, Workers Compensation, Wrongful Death, Medical Malpractice, Slip and Fall, Criminal Law, Driving While Intoxicated, Traffic Violations, Drug Offenses, Misdemeanors, Felonies, Sexual Assaults, Assaults, Burglary, Motorcycle Accidents, Head Injuries.

(For Complete Biographical Data on Personnel, see Professional Biography at Wilmington, North Carolina)

BENJAMIN R. WARRICK

Established in 1967
609 COLLEGE STREET
P.O. BOX 1216
CLINTON, NORTH CAROLINA 28328
Telephone: 910-590-2900
Fax: 910-590-2555
Email: bwarrick.01@earthlink.net*

General Civil Practice. Trials in all State Courts. Family, Juvenile Law, Probate, Real Estate and Corporation Law.

FIRM PROFILE: Benjamin R. Warrick serves clients with over thirty years of experience throughout Sampson and Duplin Counties. The firm is listed in the Bar Register of Preeminent Lawyers in the area of family and domestic law.

BENJAMIN R. WARRICK, born Smithfield, North Carolina, July 3, 1936; admitted to bar, 1967, North Carolina. *Education:* University of North Carolina at Chapel Hill (A.B., 1964; J.D., 1967). Phi Alpha Delta. *Member:* Sampson County, North Carolina and American Bar Associations; North Carolina State Bar; North Carolina Academy of Trial Lawyers. ***SPECIAL AGENCIES:*** Sampson County DSS. ***PRACTICE AREAS:*** Family Law; Real Estate; Trusts and Estates; Wills; Probate.

ASSOCIATE

CORINNE A. RAILEY, born Cedar Rapids, Iowa, May 16, 1969; admitted to bar, 1998, North Carolina. *Education:* University of Iowa (B.A., 1995; J.D., 1998). National Moot Court Team. *Member:* Sampson County Bar Association; North Carolina State Bar. ***SPECIAL AGENCIES:*** Sampson County DSS; CSRU. ***PRACTICE AREAS:*** Family Law; Juvenile Law. **Email:** crailey99@earthlink.net

REPRESENTATIVE CLIENTS: Sampson County Department of Social Services; Sampson County Child Support Office; Branch Banking & Trust Co.; The Big Blue Store of Clinton, Inc.
APPROVED ATTORNEYS FOR: Federal Land Bank of Columbia, South Carolina; Lawyers Title Insurance Corp.; First Title Insurance Co.; A.M.I. Title Insurance Co.; First American Federal; Branch Banking & Trust Co.; Investors Title Insurance Co.
REFERENCE: Branch Banking & Trust Co.

WHELESS & WHELESS, PLLC

402 MAIN STREET
COLUMBIA, NORTH CAROLINA 27925
Telephone: 252-796-5500
Fax: 252-796-1154
URL: http://www.whelesslawfirm.com

Manteo, North Carolina Office: 101 South Virginia Dare Road, P.O. Box 500, 27954. Telephone: 252-473-5500. Fax: 252-473-1154.

Traffic Violations, General Practice. Real Estate, Driving While Intoxicated, Civil Litigation, County Government Law, Insurance Defense, Real Estate Development, Residential Real Estate Development, Waterfront Development, Zoning Law, Ship Documentation and Ship Finance and Family Law.

FIRM PROFILE: Wheless & Wheless, PLLC is a general practice law firm with attorneys licensed to practice in state and federal courts. The father/son team strives to provide prompt, personalized service and each is active in professional associations and civic affairs. Located in Manteo, the county seat of Dare County, Wheless & Wheless, PLLC handles a variety of matters throughout Dare, Currituck, Hyde and Tyrrell Counties.

REPRESENTATIVE CLIENTS: R.D. Sawyer Motor Co., Inc.; Midgett Realty, Inc.; Dare County Tourism Board; Roanoke Properties Limited Partnership; Pirate's Cove Subdivision; Oregon Inlet Charter Captains Association, Town of Columbia; The Albemarle Commission.
APPROVED ATTORNEYS FOR: Lawyers Title Insurance Co.; Title Company of North Carolina; Commonwealth Land Title Insurance Co.; Investors' Title Insurance Co.; United Title Insurance Co.; Old Republic Title Insurance Company; Chicago title Insurance Company.

(For complete biographical data on all personnel, see Professional Biographies at Manteo)

BLANCHARD, NEWMAN & HAYES

COLUMBUS, NORTH CAROLINA

(See Hendersonville)

General Civil Litigation, Family Law, Divorce, Criminal in all State and Federal Courts, Traffic, DWI.

R. ANDERSON HAYNES

COLUMBUS, NORTH CAROLINA

(See Tryon)

Estate Planning, Elder Law, Estate Administration, Probate, Real Estate, Corporate Law.

JOHN A. BASINGER
ATTORNEY AT LAW

CONCORD, NORTH CAROLINA

(See Salisbury)

Criminal Law, Felonies, Misdemeanors, Drug Crimes, Driving While Intoxicated, DUI, Juvenile Criminal Law, Family Law, Divorce, Child Custody, Child Support, Adoption Law, Domestic Violence, Visitation Rights, Premarital Agreements, Personal Injury, White Collar Crime, Parole and Probation.

BLACK, ROGERS, RUTH, & GROSSMAN, P.L.L.C.

47 UNION STREET NORTH
P.O. BOX 770
CONCORD, NORTH CAROLINA 28026-0770
Telephone: 704-788-3900
Fax: 704-782-6288

Personal Injury, Automobile Accidents, Dog Bites, Slip and Fall, Wrongful Death, Social Security Disability, Criminal Law, Driving While Intoxicated (DWI), Drug Crimes, Traffic Violations, Family Law, Adoptions, Child Support, Child Custody, Divorce, Real Estate, Eminent Domain, Landlord Tenant, Business, Corporate, Limited Liability, Trust and Estates, Estate Planning, Wills and Probate.

MEMBERS OF FIRM

DAVID H. BLACK, born Greensboro, North Carolina, December 3, 1955; admitted to bar, 1981, North Carolina. *Education:* University of North Carolina (B.S., 1978; J.D., 1981). President, District 19-A Bar, 1993-1997. *Member:* Cabarrus County (President, 1997) Bar Association; North Carolina State Bar. ***PRACTICE AREAS:*** Civil Litigation; Criminal Law; Contracts; Corporate Law. **Email:** dhblack@carolina.rr.com

WILLIAM F. ROGERS, JR., born Blount County, Tennessee, October 6, 1954; admitted to bar, 1979, Tennessee; 1980, North Carolina. *Education:* University of Tennessee (B.S., 1976; J.D., 1979). *Member:* North Carolina State Bar. ***PRACTICE AREAS:*** Domestic Relations; Family Law; Social Security Disability. **Email:** bfrogers@carolina.rr.com

HILTON L. RUTH, III, born Charlotte, North Carolina, October 12, 1957; admitted to bar, 1983, North Carolina. *Education:* Davidson College (B.A., 1980); Campbell University (J.D., 1983). *Member:* North Carolina State Bar; American Bar Association. ***PRACTICE AREAS:*** Residential Real Estate; Commercial Real Estate; Estate Planning. **Email:** tlruth@carolina.rr.com

STEVEN A. GROSSMAN, born Baltimore, Maryland, February 22, 1952; admitted to bar, 1977, North Carolina. *Education:* Wake Forest University (B.A., 1974; J.D., 1977). *Member:* North Carolina Bar Association; North Carolina State Bar. ***PRACTICE AREAS:*** Criminal Law; Traffic Violations; Domestic Relations; Collections. **Email:** sagrossman@carolina.rr.com

AIMEE E. CAIN, born Concord, North Carolina, July 18, 1964; admitted to bar, 1997, California; 1998, New York; 2001, New Hampshire; 2004, North Carolina. *Education:* University of California at Los Angeles (B.A., 1993); Loyola Law School (J.D., 1997). Member, Loyola Entertainment Law Journal, 1995-1997. Certified Supierior Court Mediator. Certified Family Finanical Mediator. ***PRACTICE AREAS:*** Family Law; Divorce; Civil Litigation. **Email:** acain@accainlaw.com

BLANTON LAW FIRM, P.A.

CONCORD, NORTH CAROLINA

(See Salisbury)

Family Law, Divorce, Collaborative Law, Child Custody, Child Support, Spousal Support, Criminal Law, Driving While Intoxicated (DWI), Drug Crimes, Felonies, Parole and Probation, Misdemeanors, Traffic Violations, Wrongful Death, Personal Injury, Real Estate, Civil Litigation, Contracts, Family Financial Mediation.

THE BOLDUC LAW FIRM, PLLC

CONCORD, NORTH CAROLINA

(See Charlotte)

NASD Arbitration, Business Litigation, Securities Fraud, Corporate Malfeasance, Mutual Fund Disputes, Wrongful Termination, Banking and Finance Law, and Accounting.

CLONINGER LAW OFFICE

CONCORD, NORTH CAROLINA

(See Mount Pleasant)

Criminal, Traffic, Driving While Intoxicated, Family Law, Custody, Divorce, Child Support, Visitation Rights, Wills and Probate.

CONRAD TROSCH & KEMMY, P.A.

CONCORD, NORTH CAROLINA

(See Charlotte)

Family Law, Real Estate, Wills, Probate, Estate Planning, Trusts, Business Law, Criminal Law, Divorce, Personal Injury, Wrongful Death.

AMY S. DAVIS

235 CABARRAS AVENUE EAST
CONCORD, NORTH CAROLINA 28025
Telephone: 704-784-9440
Fax: 704-721-5175
URL: http://www.amysdavislaw.com
Mailing Address: P.O. Box 1394, Concord, NC 28026

Personal Bankruptcy, Business Bankruptcy, Foreclosures, Adoptions, Child Custody, Child Support.

AMY S. DAVIS, born Pottsville, Pennsylvania, December 6,1968; admitted to bar, 1996, North Carolina. *Education:* Oral Roberts University (B.S., 1991); Regent University (M.A., Public Policy, 1995; J.D., 1995). Governor Fellow, Inns of Court, 1994. *Member:* North Carolina State Bar. ***PRACTICE AREAS:*** Personal Bankruptcy; Business Bankruptcy; Foreclosures; Adoption Law; Child Custody; Child Support.

ELLIOTT LAW FIRM, P.C.

CONCORD, NORTH CAROLINA

(See Huntersville)

Business Law, Limited Liability Company Law, Incorporations, Corporate Law, Mergers and Acquisitions, Tax Law, Real Estate, Construction Law, Trusts and Estates, Asset Protection, Estate Planning, Guardianship, Bankruptcy, Traffic Violations.

GACH LAW FIRM, PLLC

CONCORD, NORTH CAROLINA

(See Charlotte)

HARTSELL & WILLIAMS, P.A.

Established in 1896
71 MCCACHERN BOULEVARD, S.E.
P.O. BOX 368
CONCORD, NORTH CAROLINA 28025
Telephone: 704-786-5161
Facsimile: 704-788-8058
Email: hwpalaw@hwpalaw.com
URL: http://www.hwpalaw.com

Kannapolis, North Carolina Office: 708 McLain Road, P.O. Box 2, 28082. Telephone: 704-932-3157. Facsimile: 704-932-9597.

General Civil and Criminal Practice in all Courts. Workers Compensation, Corporation, Insurance, Real Estate, Taxation, Probate Law, Estate Planning, Family Law and Motor Sports (Racing).

FIRM PROFILE: Established in 1896, Hartsell & Williams, P.A. is a regional firm with a small-town personality, providing excellence in legal services to individuals and businesses. The firm has achieved and maintained Martindale-Hubbell's highest rating for legal ability and ethical conduct and is committed to providing quality, cost-effective representation, reflecting the highest diligence and integrity. The attorneys of Hartsell & Williams, P.A. focus on civil and criminal litigation, estate planning, probate, administrative, government, banking, motor sports (racing), corporate law and real estate transactions of all types.

LUTHER T. HARTSELL (1870-1961)
LUTHER T. HARTSELL, JR. (1902-1961)
JOHN HUGH WILLIAMS (1913-1995)
JOHN SHARPE HARTSELL (1907-2004)

FLETCHER L. HARTSELL, JR., born Concord, North Carolina, February 15, 1947; admitted to bar, 1972, North Carolina. *Education:* Davidson College (A.B., 1969); University of North Carolina (J.D., 1972). Contributor, "Adversary Presentation and Bias in Legal Decisionmaking," Harvard Law Review, December, 1972. Cabarrus County Attorney, 1985—. Member, N.C. Senate, 1991—. *Member:* Cabarrus County (President, 1987-1988), North Carolina and American Bar Associations; 19-A Judicial District (President, 1985-1986) and The North Carolina State Bars; North Carolina Council of School Attorneys; National Council of School Attorneys; National Institute of Municipal Legal Officers. ***PRACTICE AREAS:*** Administrative and Governmental Law; Civil Litigation; Environmental Law; Probate and Estate Planning. ***Email:*** fhartsell@hwpalaw.com

SAMUEL F. DAVIS, JR., born Concord, North Carolina, October 16, 1947; admitted to bar, 1972, North Carolina. *Education:* Davidson College (A.B., 1969); University of North Carolina (J.D., 1972). Chairman, Concord City School Board, 1981-1983; Vice-Chairman, Cabarrus County School Board, 1983-1990. General Counsel, Cabarrus Regional Chamber of Commerce. Member, North Carolina State Bar Councilor, District 19A. *Member:* Cabarrus County (President, 1989-1990), North Carolina and American Bar Associations; 19-A Judicial District (President, 1987-1988) and North Carolina State Bars. ***PRACTICE AREAS:*** Corporate; Commercial Real Estate; Estate Planning. ***Email:*** sdavis@hwpalaw.com

(This Listing Continued)

HERBERT J. WHITE, SR., born Jacksonville, Florida, June 17, 1964; admitted to bar, 1991, North Carolina. *Education:* Guilford College (B.S., 1986); Campbell University (J.D., 1991). Assistant District Attorney, Drug Prosecution Team, Mecklenburg County, 1991-1994. *Member:* Cabarrus County and 19-A Judicial District Bar Associations; North Carolina State Bar; North Carolina Academy of Trial Lawyers. ***PRACTICE AREAS:*** Criminal Law; Civil Litigation; Workers Compensation; Personal Injury. ***Email:*** jaywhite@hwpalaw.com

DAVID C. WILLIAMS, born Concord, North Carolina, October 14, 1968; admitted to bar, 1995, North Carolina. *Education:* Duke University (A.B., 1991); Campbell University (J.D., 1995). *Member:* Cabarrus County (Secretary and Treasurer, 1997-2000), North Carolina and American Bar Associations; North Carolina State Bar. ***PRACTICE AREAS:*** Civil Litigation; Commercial Real Estate; Residential Real Estate; Foreclosures; Tax Collection. ***Email:*** dwilliams@hwpalaw.com

K. TODD PHILLIPS, born Raleigh, North Carolina, March 8, 1962; admitted to bar, 1986, Georgia; 1987, North Carolina. *Education:* Gardner-Webb University (B.A., magna cum laude, 1983); University of North Carolina (J.D., 1986). Alpha Chi; Phi Alpha Delta. *Member:* Cabarrus County, North Carolina and American Bar Associations. ***PRACTICE AREAS:*** Bankruptcy Law; Creditors Rights Law; Commercial Law; Business Law. ***Email:*** tphillips@hwpalaw.com

ASSOCIATE

KARLA G. EAVES, born Charlotte, North Carolina, June 21, 1972; admitted to bar, 2003, North Carolina. *Education:* Davidson College (B.A., 1994); University of Richmond (J.D., 2003). *Member:* Cabaccus County and North Carolina Bar Associations; North Carolina State Bar Association. ***PRACTICE AREAS:*** Civil Litigation; Domestic Law; Criminal Law. ***Email:*** keaves@hwpalaw.com

OF COUNSEL

JOHN R. BOGER, JR., born Concord, North Carolina, April 2, 1929; admitted to bar, 1952, North Carolina. *Education:* Duke University (A.B., 1950); Duke University School of Law (LL.B., 1952). Member, Editorial Board, Duke Bar Journal, 1951-1952. Member: North Carolina House of Representatives, 1961-1962; North Carolina Senate, 1967-1970. *Member:* Cabarrus County and North Carolina Bar Associations; North Carolina State Bar. ***PRACTICE AREAS:*** Real Estate; Probate; Wills; Estates.

RETIRED

J. MAXTON ELLIOTT (Retired)

Languages: English and Spanish.

GENERAL COUNSEL: Cabarrus Regional Chamber of Commerce; NorthEast Medical Center; Cabarrus Health Alliance (Public Health Authority of Cabarrus County); Water and Sewer Authority of Cabarrus County, North Carolina; Hall-Storey Inc. (Carolina Mall).
REPRESENTATIVE CLIENTS: First Charter National Bank; Wachovia Bank; CTC Communications; Duke Energy Co.; Cabarrus County Board of Education; The Mills Corporation (Concord Mills Mall); The Shoe Show, Inc.; Schrader Racing, Inc.; Wallace Racing, Inc.; Camp & Associates, Inc.; Rickey Craven Racing, Inc.; Bodine Racing, Inc.; Fitz-Bradshaw Racing, Inc.; Habitat for Humanity Cabarrus County, Inc.; Board of County Commissioners, Cabarrus County; Sparks Chrysler-Plymouth-Jeep, Inc.; Hilbish (Ford) Motor Co.; Ben Mynatt Chevrolet-Cadillac-GMC, Inc.; Beasley-Cross Chevrolet; E.L. Morrison Lumber Co., Inc.; R.S. Braswell Co.; Propst Construction Co.; Public Service Company of North Carolina; Norfolk & Southern Railway; Lawyers Mutual Liability Company of North Carolina; Allstate Insurance Co.; Nationwide Insurance Co.; Integon Insurance Co.; South Carolina Insurance Companies; Moss & Moore, Inc.; Gullege Building Supply; Sundrop Bottling Co. of Concord; State Employees' Credit Union; Piedmont Natural Gas Corp.
APPROVED ATTORNEYS FOR: AMI Title Insurance Co.; Pioneer Title Insurance Co.; First Title Insurance Co.; St. Paul Title Insurance Co.; Chicago Title Insurance Co.; Lawyers Title Insurance Corp.; Investors Title Insurance Co.; First American Title Co.; State Land Title Co.; The Title Company of North Carolina; Statewide Title Insurance Co.

THE LAW OFFICE OF RANDELL F. HASTINGS

77 MCCACHERN BOULEVARD S.E.
CONCORD, NORTH CAROLINA 28025
Telephone: 704-786-4567
Fax: 704-786-2664
Email: rfhastings@aol.com
URL: http://www.rhastingslaw.com
Mailing Address: P.O. Box 666, Concord, NC 28026-0666

Family Law, Divorce, Child Custody, Child Support, Visitation Rights, Domestic Violence, Personal injury, Automobile Accidents, Wrongful Death, Civil Litigation.

RANDELL F. HASTINGS, born Concord, North Carolina, July 30, 1953; admitted to bar, 1978, North Carolina and U.S. District Court, Middle District of North Carolina; 1980, U.S. Court of Appeals, Fourth Circuit. *Education:* Davidson College (A.B., 1975); University of North Carolina (J.D., 1978). *Member:* Cabarrus County and North Carolina Bar Associations; North Carolina State Bar. ***PRACTICE AREAS:*** Domestic Relations; Family Law; Civil Litigation; Personal Injury.

HELMS, HENDERSON & ASSOCIATES, P.A.

CONCORD, NORTH CAROLINA

(See Charlotte)

General, Civil and Criminal Trial Practice in State and Federal Courts and Agencies, Corporation, Real Estate, Probate, Insurance, Bankruptcy, Commercial, Personal Injury, Collections and Tax.

JAMES C. JOHNSON, JR.
ATTORNEY AT LAW

400 CHURCH STREET, NORTH
CONCORD, NORTH CAROLINA 28025
Telephone: 704-784-8404
Fax: 704-784-8714
Email: jjohnson01@vnet.net
URL: http://www.lawyers.com/jamescjohnson

Criminal Law, DWI, Drug Crimes, Felonies, Homicide, Misdemeanors, Parole, Traffic Violations.

JAMES C. JOHNSON, JR., born Greensboro, North Carolina, June 5, 1935; admitted to bar, 1962, North Carolina. *Education:* Spartanburg Junior College and East Tennessee State University (B.A., 1958); Wake Forest University (LL.B., 1962). Phi Delta Phi. Law Clerk to Hon. Edwin M. Stanley, Chief District Judge for the Middle District of North Carolina, 1962-1963. Guest Lecturer in Criminal Law at Wake Forrest Law School. Judge, Domestic and Juvenile Court, Cabarrus County, North Carolina, 1963-1967. Member, National Council of Juvenile Court Judges, 1963-1968. President, North Carolina Domestic and Juvenile Court Judges Association, 1964-1967. County Attorney, Cabarrus County, 1967-1970. Member, North Carolina House of Representatives, 1967-1970. North Carolina State Senate, 1984-1990. *Member:* Cabarrus County Bar Association; North Carolina State Bar; North Carolina Academy of Trial Lawyers. [With National Guard, 30th Division, 1953-1962]

THE KING LAW FIRM PLLC

CONCORD, NORTH CAROLINA

(See Huntersville)

Bankruptcy, Domestic, Family, Wills, Trusts, Criminal.

KLUTTZ, REAMER, HAYES, RANDOLPH & ADKINS, L.L.P.

CONCORD, NORTH CAROLINA

(See Salisbury)

General Civil Practice. Trials. Employment Law, Corporation, Taxation, Real Estate, Estate Planning, Probate and Trusts, Traffic, Criminal Law, Mediation, Personal Injury, Driving While Impaired, Workers Compensation.

KOONTZ, HAWKINS, NIXON & MILLER

Established in 1971
2 CHURCH STREET, S.E.
P.O. BOX 744
CONCORD, NORTH CAROLINA 28026-0744
Telephone: 704-786-3145
Fax: 704-782-4314
Email: khnlaw@vnet.net
URL: http://www.concordnclaw.com

Civil Trial Practice, Criminal Trial Practice, Driving While Intoxicated, Drug Crimes, Juvenile Crimes, Parole and Probation, Traffic Violations, White Collar Crimes, Personal Injury, Automobile Accidents, Wrongful Death, Social Security Disability, Workers Compensation, Family Law, Divorce, Domestic Violence, Child Support, Child Custody.

MEMBERS OF FIRM

K. MICHAEL KOONTZ, born Mooresville, North Carolina, February 22, 1936; admitted to bar, 1965, North Carolina. *Education:* Lenoir-Rhyne College; Wake Forest College (LL.B., 1964). Phi Delta Phi. *Member:* Cabarrus County, North Carolina and American Bar Associations; North Carolina State Bar; North Carolina Academy of Trial Lawyers. ***PRACTICE AREAS:*** Personal Injury; Social Security Disability.

TIMOTHY M. HAWKINS, born Charlottesville, Virginia, August 6, 1948; admitted to bar, 1973, North Carolina. *Education:* University of North Carolina at Chapel Hill (B.A., 1970; J.D., 1973). Assistant District Attorney, 19th Judicial District, 1973-1977. *Member:* Cabarrus County, North Carolina and American Bar Associations; North Carolina Academy of Trial Lawyers; National Association of Criminal Defense Lawyers. ***PRACTICE AREAS:*** Criminal and Traffic Cases.

M. WAYNE NIXON, JR., born Concord, North Carolina, April 22, 1951; admitted to bar, 1977, North Carolina. *Education:* University of North Carolina (B.A., 1973); North Carolina State University (B.S., 1974); Wake Forest University (J.D., 1977). Phi Alpha Delta. Assistant District Attorney, 19th Judicial District, 1978-1981. *Member:* Cabarrus County, 19-A Judicial District (Secretary-Treasurer, 1985—; Vice President, 1989) and North Carolina State Bar Associations; North Carolina Academy of Trial Lawyers. ***LANGUAGES:*** Spanish. ***PRACTICE AREAS:*** Criminal Law; Traffic.

DUANE S. MILLER, born Concord, North Carolina, July 6, 1966; admitted to bar, 1991, North Carolina. *Education:* University of North Carolina at Charlotte (B.S., cum laude, 1988); University of North Carolina at Chapel Hill (J.D., 1991). *Member:* Cabarrus County, North Carolina and American Bar Associations. ***PRACTICE AREAS:*** Personal Injury; Civil; Criminal; Traffic Violations; Family Law.

MILLS LAW, P.A.

45 CHURCH STREET, S.E.
CONCORD, NORTH CAROLINA 28026-0528
Telephone: 704-782-3315
Fax: 704-782-0436
URL: http://www.millslawfirmpa.com

Mailing Address: P.O. Box 528, Concord, NC 28026-0528

Trusts and Estates, Asset Protection, Estate Planning, Probate, Taxation, Corporate Law, Real Estate.

FIRM PROFILE: Mr. Mills is a Board Certified Specialist in Estate Planning and Probate Law.

WILLIAM L. MILLS, III, born Concord, North Carolina, July 20, 1954; admitted to bar, 1980, North Carolina. *Education:* University of North Carolina at Chapel Hill (A.B., 1977); Wake Forest University (J.D., 1980). Phi Alpha Delta. Member: The Order of Barristers; Moot Court Board. Member, Wake Forest Law Review, 1978-1980. *Member:* Cabarrus County, 19-A Judicial District, North Carolina (Young Lawyer Division District Representative, 1980-1983) and American Bar Associations. (Board Certified Specialist in Estate Planning and Probate Law, North Carolina State Board of Legal Specialization)

THE LAW OFFICE OF JOHN R. NANCE, P.A.

5 CABARRUS AVENUE WEST
P.O. BOX 1149
CONCORD, NORTH CAROLINA 28025
Telephone: 704-782-9138
Fax: 704-782-4767
Email: lawyernance@vnet.net
URL: http://www.jnancelaw.com

Criminal Defense, Driving While Impaired, Traffic Violations, Juvenile Law, Custody Agreements and Child Support, Guardianship, Incompetency Proceedings, Wills, Powers of Attorney, Adoptions, Family Law.

JOHN R. NANCE, born Hill Air Force Base, Utah, 1955; admitted to bar, 1992, Virginia, U.S. District Court, Eastern District of Virginia and U.S. Court of Appeals, Fourth Circuit; 1993, Maryland and U.S. District Court, District of Maryland; 1997, North Carolina and U.S. District Court, Middle District of North Carolina; 1998, U.S. Supreme Court. *Education:* Oklahoma State University (B.S., 1977); Webster University (M.A., 1987); Regent University (J.D., 1991). *Member:* Cabarrus County and North Carolina Bar Associations; North Carolina State Bar. ***PRACTICE AREAS:*** Juvenile Law; Child Support; Traffic Violations; Guardianship; Incompetency Proceedings; Driving While Intoxicated; Wills; Adoption Law; Family Law; Criminal Defense; Felonies; Misdemeanors.

THE NICKERSON LAW FIRM

CONCORD, NORTH CAROLINA

(See Charlotte)

Criminal, Drugs, Fraud, Burglary, Appeals, Traffic, Speeding, Forfeiture, Felonies, Federal Criminal, Forgery, Homicide, Murder, Search and Seizures.

PATTERSON AND ADAMS PLLC

433 CHURCH STREET NORTH
CONCORD, NORTH CAROLINA 28025
Telephone: 704-795-4317
Fax: 704-795-5738
URL: http://www.patterson-adams.com
URL: http://www.pattersonadamslawoffice.com

Gastonia, North Carolina Office: 1305 East Garrison Boulevard, 28054. Telephone: 704-867-1955. Fax: 704-853-1875.
Salisbury, North Carolina Office: 710 North Main Street, 28144. Telephone: 704-795-4317.

Personal Injury, Automobile Accidents, Wrongful Deaths, Workers Compensation, Medical Malpractice.

SCOTT M. ADAMS, born Takoma Park, Maryland, July 3, 1971; admitted to bar, 1997, North Carolina and U.S. District Court, Western District of North Carolina. *Education:* College of William and Mary (B.A., 1992); Wake Forest University (J.D., 1997). Member, Moot Court Board, Trial Bar. *Member:* Cabarrus County Bar Association; North Carolina State Bar; North Carolina Association of Trial Lawyers. ***PRACTICE AREAS:*** Personal Injury; Automobile Accidents and Injuries; Wrongful Death; Workers Compensation; Medical Malpractice. **Email:** scott@patterson-adams.com

BRENT A. PATTERSON, born Baton Rouge, Louisiana, April 25, 1967; admitted to bar, 1992, North Carolina and U.S. District Court, Western, Eastern and Middle Districts of North Carolina; 1999, South Carolina. *Education:* Louisiana State University (B.A., 1989); Wake Forest University (J.D., 1992). President, 27-D Judicial District, 2005. *Member:* Gaston County Bar Association (President, 2005); North Carolina State Bar; South Carolina Bar. ***PRACTICE AREAS:*** Personal Injury; Wrongful Death; Workers Compensation; Automobile Accidents and Injuries; Medical Malpractice. **Email:** brent@patterson-adams.com

R. WAYNE PICKETT

20 CABARRUS AVENUE EAST
CONCORD, NORTH CAROLINA 28025
Telephone: 704-786-5115
Fax: 704-786-5116
Email: rwaynepickett@ctc.net
URL: http://www.rwaynepickett.com

Criminal Law, Driving While Intoxicated, Drug Crimes, Felonies, Homicide, Misdemeanors, Parole, Assault, Traffic Violations.

FIRM PROFILE: Mr. Pickett was an Assistant District Attorney, Cabarrus County for 14 years.

R. WAYNE PICKETT, born Lexington, North Carolina, June 19, 1946; admitted to bar, 1974, North Carolina. *Education:* University of North Carolina (A.B., 1971; J.D., 1974). Assistant District Attorney, Cabarrus County, 1989-2003. *Member:* Cabarrus County Bar Association; North Carolina State Bar. [United States Army, 1964-1967]

MARK E. SHELLEY

115 CHURCH STREET NORTH
P.O. BOX 683
CONCORD, NORTH CAROLINA 28026
Telephone: 704-782-8282
Facsimile: 704-782-8285
Email: MarkShelley@ctc.net
URL: http://www.shelleylaw.com

Tax, IRS Audits, Property Tax, Tax Planning, Trust and Estates, Asset Protection, Estate Planning, Wills and Probate.

MARK E. SHELLEY, born Hamlet, North Carolina, October 21, 1956; admitted to bar, 1983, North Carolina; 1988, U.S. Tax Court; 1993, U.S. Supreme Court. *Education:* Davidson College (A.B., 1979); Wake Forest University (J.D., 1983); University of Florida (LL.M., Taxation, 1984). *Member:* Cabarrus County and North Carolina Bar Associations; North Carolina State Bar; American Institute of Certified Public Accountants. ***PRACTICE AREAS:*** Taxation; IRS Audits; Property Tax; Tax Planning; Trusts and Estates; Asset Protection; Wills; Probate.

DOUGLAS A. SMITH

CONCORD, NORTH CAROLINA

(See Salisbury)

Criminal Law, Felonies, Misdemeanors, Family Law, Divorce, Child Custody, Child Support, Separation, Traffic Violations, Driving While Intoxicated, Construction Law, Children, Child Abuse and Neglect, Child Care, Grandparents Custody, Grandparents Visitation Rights, Juvenile Criminal Law, Step Parent Adoptions, Criminal Defense, Drivers License Suspension, Theft, Weapons Charges, Drug Crimes, Alimony, Domestic Violence, Equitable Distribution, Military Divorce, Name Changes, Paternity, Qualified Domestic Relations Orders, Separation Agreements, Spousal Support, Uncontested Divorce, Guardianship and Conservatorship, Guardian Ad Litem, Incompetency Proceedings, Personal Injury, Accidents, Automobile Accidents and Injuries, Motor Vehicle Accidents and Injuries, Pedestrian Injuries.

LAW OFFICE OF TIMOTHY D. SMITH

CONCORD, NORTH CAROLINA

(See Charlotte)

Immigration Law, Criminal Law, Driving While Intoxicated (DWI), Drug Crimes, Traffic Violations, Family Law/Divorce.

WOODSON, SAYERS, LAWTHER, SHORT, PARROTT & WALKER, LLP

CONCORD, NORTH CAROLINA

(See Salisbury)

General Practice. Trials in all State and Federal Courts. Estate Planning, Probate and Taxation, Corporate, Municipal and Real Estate Law. Criminal, Family and Domestic Relations Law. Personal Injury.

THE BARONE LAW FIRM, P.A.

9735 CALDWELL COMMONS CIRCLE
SUITE 100
CORNELIUS, NORTH CAROLINA 28031
Telephone: 704-895-2792
Fax: 704-895-2793
Email: cbarone@baronelawfirm.com
URL: http://www.baronefirm.com

Real Estate, Buying and Selling a Home, Construction, Landlord and Tenant, Zoning Planning and Land Use, Business Law, Corporate, Limited Liability Companies, Partnerships, Trusts and Estates, Asset Protection, Estate Planning, Bankruptcy, Foreclosures, Personal Injury, Automobile Accidents, Dog Bites, Wrongful Death, Criminal Law, Traffic Violations, Driving While Intoxicated, Parole and Probation, Federal Criminal Law, Collections, Contracts, Intellectual Property.

(This Listing Continued)

CHARLES F. BARONE, born Buffalo, New York, February 23, 1959; admitted to bar, 1987, California; 1991, North Carolina; U.S. District Court, Western and Middle Districts of North Carolina; U.S. District Court, Central District of California. *Education:* State University of New York at Buffalo (B.A., 1983); Thomas M. Cooley Law School (J.D., 1987). Licensed Real Estate Broker. Member: North Carolina Real Estate Commission; National Association of Realtors; Charlotte Regional Realtor Association. *Member:* Mecklenburg County, North Carolina and American Bar Associations; North Carolina State Bar; State Bar of California; Academy of Trial Lawyers of America; Academy of Trial Lawyers of North Carolina; American Arbitration Association; National Association of Consumer Bankruptcy Attorneys. ***Email:*** cbarone@baronelawfirm.com

THE BOLDUC LAW FIRM, PLLC

CORNELIUS, NORTH CAROLINA

(See Charlotte)

NASD Arbitration, Business Litigation, Securities Fraud, Corporate Malfeasance, Mutual Fund Disputes, Wrongful Termination, Banking and Finance Law, and Accounting.

BRENNAN LAW FIRM, PLLC

17115 KENTON DRIVE, SUITE 204A
CORNELIUS, NORTH CAROLINA 28031
Telephone: 704-876-6441
Fax: 704-896-6449

Employee Benefits, ERISA, Pension and Profit Sharing Plans, Taxation, Tax Planning, Estate and Gift Taxation, Estate Planning, Business Law, Joint Ventures, Limited Liability Law, Partnership Insurance, Nonprofit and Charitable Organizations.

MARTIN M. BRENNAN, JR., born Brisbin, Pennsylvania, February 12, 1960; admitted to bar, 1987, North Carolina; 1988, U.S. District Court, Eastern District of North Carolina; 1989, U.S. Tax Court; 1991, Virginia and U.S. District Court, Eastern District of Virginia. *Education:* Pennsylvania State University (B.S., 1982); Duquesne University (J.D., 1986). Certified Public Accountant, North Carolina, 1988. Certified Employee Benefits Specialist, 1996. *Member:* Mecklenburg County, North Carolina and American Bar Associations; American Institute of Certified Public Accountants; International Society of Certified Employee Benefit Specialists. ***PRACTICE AREAS:*** ERISA; Employee Benefits; Estate and Gift Taxation; Tax Law.

RAY A. HAYES II P.A.

19425-E LIVERPOOL PARKWAY
CORNELIUS, NORTH CAROLINA 28031
Telephone: 704-987-3807
Fax: 704-987-3808
http://www.ncattorneyatlawfirm.com
Email: rayhayes2@aol.com
URL: http://www.ncattorneyatlaw.com

Business Transactions, Business Litigation, Corporate Law, Business Planning, Buying or Selling a Business, Securities, Contracts, Trusts and Estates, Wills and Probate, Bankruptcy, Consumer Bankruptcy, Traffic Violations.

RAY HAYES, born Bellflower, California, June 12, 1977; admitted to bar, 2004, North Carolina; 2005, U.S. District Court, Western District of North Carolina. *Education:* University of North Carolina at Chapel Hill (B.A., 1999); New York Law School (J.D., 2002). UNC Dean's List and current member of the General Alumni Association; Senator of Law School Student Bar Association; Articles Editor of NYLS Journal of Human Rights. *Member:* North Carolina State Bar; North Carolina Bar Association; Mecklenburg County Bar Association. ***PRACTICE AREAS:*** Business Transactions; Business Litigation; Corporate Law; Business Planning; Buying and Selling of Businesses; Securities; Contracts; Trusts and Estates; Wills; Probate; Bankruptcy; Consumer Bankruptcy; Traffic Violations. ***Email:*** rayhayes2@aol.com

SANDRA L. KNOX, P.C.

LAKESIDE PROFESSIONAL BUILDING
19453 WEST CATAWBA AVENUE, SUITE E
P.O. BOX 756
CORNELIUS, NORTH CAROLINA 28031
Telephone: 704-892-1636
Fax: 704-892-6910
Email: sknoxlaw@aol.com
URL: http://www.lawyers.com/sknoxlaw

Commercial and Residential Real Estate, Condominium Law, Wills, Probate, Estate Planning, Trust, Small Business, Partnership.

FIRM PROFILE: Our firm provides high quality legal representation to clients throughout the following counties, Cabarrus, Catawba, Iredell, Lincoln, Mecklenburg, Rowan and Union.

SANDRA L. KNOX, born Charlotte, North Carolina, February 19, 1967; admitted to bar, 1997 North Carolina and U.S. District Court, Western District of North Carolina. *Education:* Davidson College (A.B., 1989); George Mason University School of Law (J.D., 1996). *Member:* Mecklenburg County and North Carolina (Member, Real Property and Estate Planning Sections) Bar Associations. ***PRACTICE AREAS:*** Commercial Real Estate; Residential Real Estate; Condominium Law; Wills; Probate; Estate Planning; Trust Law; Small Business Law; Partnership Law.

THE LAW OFFICES OF MICHAEL V. MATTHEWS, P.C.

19300 STATESVILLE ROAD, SUITE 300
CORNELIUS, NORTH CAROLINA 28031
Telephone: 704-655-8786
Fax: 704-655-8796
Email: mvmlaw@mindspring.com
URL: http://www.mvmlaw.com

Labor and Employment, Employment Litigation, Employment Rights, Employment Contracts, Employment Discrimination, Family and Medical Leave Act, Sexual Harassment, Wage and Hour Law, Non-Competition/Non-Solicitation Agreements.

FIRM PROFILE: Mr. Matthews represents employers and management level executives in employment relations litigating and counseling.

MICHAEL V. MATTHEWS, born Kernersville, North Carolina, October 21, 1958; admitted to bar, 1986, Maryland; 1989, North Carolina. *Education:* University of North Carolina at Chapel Hill (B.S., Industrial Relations; B.S., Psychology, 1981); Wake Forest University (J.D., 1986). *Member:* Mecklenburg County, Maryland State and North Carolina (Member, Labor and Employment Section) Bar Associations; North Carolina State Bar.

SINGLETARY LAW FIRM, PLLC

19109 WEST CATAWBA AVENUE, SUITE 200
CORNELIUS, NORTH CAROLINA 28031
Telephone: 704-895-4449
Toll Free: 866-895-LAW1
Fax: 704-895-1170
Email: jdsingletary@singletarylawfirm.com
URL: http://www.singletarylawfirm.com

Immigration, Sports and Entertainment, Business Law, Business Formation, Buying and Selling a Business.

FIRM PROFILE: General Practice with Focus in Immigration, Business, Sports, Entertainment and Leisure. Practice areas converge when artists want start up labels and foreign business executives form new USA affiliates.

Spanish and French Interpreters by appointment.

MEMBER OF FIRM

JOCELYN DAVIS SINGLETARY, born Miami, Florida, May 20, 1950; admitted to bar, 2000, North Carolina and U.S. District Court, Western and Middle Districts of North Carolina. *Education:* Roosevelt University (B.A., 1972); Cecil C. Humphreys School of Law, University of Memphis (J.D., 1997). Member: eWomen Network; Lake Norman and Lincoln County Chambers; Planning Board, Town of Cornelius. *Member:* Mecklenburg County Bar Association; North Carolina State Bar; John S. Leary Bar Association; Immigration Lawyers Association. ***PRACTICE AREAS:*** Business Law; Deportation; Visas; Entertainment Law; Sports Law; Immigration Law. ***Email:*** jdsingletary@singletarylawfirm.com

---

SUSAN V. THOMAS

19453 WEST CATAWBA AVENUE, SUITE E
CORNELIUS, NORTH CAROLINA 28031
Telephone: 704-896-7570
Facsimile: 704-892-6910
Email: susanvthomas1@aol.com
URL: http://www.susanvthomas.com

Family Law, Domestic Relations, Premarital Agreements, Child Custody, Child Support, Visitation Rights, Alimony, Divorce, Settlements, Paternity, Name Changes.

SUSAN V. THOMAS, born Charlotte, North Carolina, February 22, 1961; admitted to bar, 1986, North Carolina. *Education:* University of North Carolina at Chapel Hill (B.A., 1983); American University (J.D., 1986). *Member:* Mecklenburg County (Member, Family Law Section) and North Carolina (Member, Family Law Section) Bar Associations; The District of Columbia Bar.

ESTATE & ELDER LAW FIRM OF VANDIVER & BRYAN

Established in 1999
18809 WEST CATAWBA AVENUE, SUITE 102
CORNELIUS, NORTH CAROLINA 28031
Telephone: 704-892-9355
Facsimile: 704-892-9309
Email: chbryan@vbfirm.com
URL: http://www.nclaw1.com

Elder Law, Estate Planning, Estate and Trust Administration, Medicaid Planning and Application, Wills, Trusts and Estates, Advance Directives, Taxation, Probate, Guardianship, Incompetency Proceedings, Medicare, Special Needs Trusts, Disability Law, Social Security, Veteran's Benefits, Long Term Care Planning, Estate Planning for the Disabled, Estate Planning for the Elderly, Business Law, Corporate Law, Business Succession Planning, Family Limited Partnerships, Limited Liability Company Law, Commercial and Contracts.

(This Listing Continued)

FIRM PROFILE: Estate & Elder Law Firm of Vandiver & Bryan, PLLC was founded in 1999 by Callan H. Bryan and Nicole Vandiver, former classmates and graduates of Norman A. Wiggins School of Law at Campbell University. The firm serves individuals, families and businesses in the areas of estate planning, estate administration, elder law and business law. The firm's attorneys are active members of the National Academy of Elder Law Attorneys (NAELA) and present and participate in continuing legal education seminars and community educational workshops in their respective areas.

NICOLE VANDIVER BRYAN, born Charlotte, North Carolina, March 12, 1974; admitted to bar, 1999, North Carolina and U.S. District Court, Western District of North Carolina. *Education:* University of North Carolina (B.A. Political Science, 1996); Campbell University (J.D., 1999). The Order of the Barristers; Omicron Delta Kappa. Editor-in-Chief, Campbell Law Observer, 1998-1999. Member, National Trial Team. Editor, Elder Law Newsletter of the North Carolina Bar Association. *Member:* Mecklenburg County (Member, Estate Planning and Probate Section) and North Carolina (Member, Estate Planning, Fiduciary Law and Elder Law Section; Member, Law & Aging Task Force Committee, Young Lawyers Committee; Member, Executive Council, Elder Law Section) Bar Associations; National Academy of Elder Law Attorneys (Member, Affinity Committee); Christian Legal Society; North Carolina Legal Education Assistance Foundation (Member, Board of Directors). ***PRACTICE AREAS:*** Elder Law; Estate Planning; Estate Administration; Trust Administration; Medicaid Planning and Application; Wills; Trusts and Estates; Advance Directives; Taxation; Probate; Guardianship; Incompetency Proceedings; Medicare and Medicaid; Special Needs Trusts; Disabilities; Social Security; Veteran's Benefits; Long Term Care; Business Succession Planning; Family Limited Partnerships; Estate Planning for the Disabled; Estate Planning for the Elderly. ***Email:*** nvbryan@vbfirm.com

CALLAN H. BRYAN, born Fayetteville, North Carolina, March 8, 1972; admitted to bar, 1999, North Carolina and U.S. District Court, Western District of North Carolina. *Education:* Appalachian State University (B.A. Psychology and Political Science, 1994); Campbell University (J.D., 1999). The Order of Old Kivett. Member, National Moot Court Team. Member: North Mecklenburg Rotary; Leadership Lake Norman. *Member:* North Carolina Bar Association (Member, Business Law and Elder Law Sections); National Academy of Elder Law Attorneys. ***PRACTICE AREAS:*** Business Law; Corporate Law; Business Succession Planning; Limited Liability Company Law; Contracts; Buy-Sell Agreements; Elder Law; Estate Planning; Wills; Trusts and Estates; Advance Directives; Long Term Care; Estate Planning for the Elderly. ***Email:*** chbryan@vbfirm.com

---

G. PATTESON WILLIAMS

19700-J WEST CATAWBA AVENUE
P.O. BOX 2009
CORNELIUS, NORTH CAROLINA 28031
Telephone: 704-892-0474
Fax: 704-892-0494
Email: attygpw@adelphia.net

Real Estate, Residential Real Estate, Commercial Real Estate, Wills, Estates, Estate Administration, Business, Corporate, Automobile Accidents, Personal Injury.

PATTESON (PAT) WILLIAMS, born Chapel Hill, North Carolina, March 17, 1957; admitted to bar, 1986, North Carolina. *Education:* University of North Carolina at Chapel Hill (B.A., 1980); Wake Forest University (M.B.A., 1986; J.D., 1986). *Member:* Mecklenburg County (Member, Real Property Section) and North Carolina Bar Associations. ***PRACTICE AREAS:*** Real Estate; Residential Real Estate; Commercial Real Estate; Wills; Estates; Estate Administration; Business; Corporate; Automobile Accidents; Personal Injury. ***Email:*** attypgw@adelphia.net

---

RONALD E. DEVEAU, P.C.

CURRITUCK, NORTH CAROLINA

(See Nags Head)

General Civil and Trial Practice in State and Federal Courts, Personal Injury and Negligence, Workers Compensation, Family Law, Business Torts, Estates.

THE VINCENT LAW FIRM, PC

CURRITUCK, NORTH CAROLINA

(See Southern Shores)

Workers Compensation, Personal Injury, Auto Accidents, Social Security Disability, Wrongful Death and Admiralty Longshores.

PENNIE M. THROWER

Established in 2004
140 WEST TRADE STREET
P.O. BOX 459
DALLAS, NORTH CAROLINA 28034
Telephone: 704-922-6739
Fax: 704-922-0650
Email: Pennie@penniethrowerlaw.com
URL: http://www.penniethrowerlaw.com

Residence Real Estate, Traffic Offenses, Wills, Powers of Attorney, Living Wills, Incorporations.

FIRM PROFILE: Sole Practitioner, General Practice in Dallas, North Carolina.

PENNIE M. THROWER, born New Orleans, Louisiana; admitted to bar, 1996, North Carolina; 1999, Massachusetts. *Education:* University of North Carolina at Greensboro (B.A., Psychology, magna cum laude, 1987); Campbell University School of Law (J.D.,

(This Listing Continued)

1996). Licensed North Carolina 1996. Licensed Massachusetts 1999. Gaston County Assistant District Attorney 2000-2003. Sole Practitioner in Dallas, NC 2004 —. Member First United Methodist Church, Gastonia, NC. Community involvement in Gaston County Museum, Junior League of Gaston County, United Way of Gaston County, Dallas NC Optimist Club. *Member:* North Carolina State Bar; Gaston County, North Carolina Bar and Massachusetts State Bar Associations. ***PRACTICE AREAS:*** Residential Real Estate; Traffic Violations; Misdemeanors; Incorporation; Wills; Living Wills; Name Changes; Powers of Attorney.

HARTSELL & WILLIAMS, P.A.

DAVIDSON, NORTH CAROLINA

(See Concord)

General Civil and Criminal Practice in all Courts. Workers Compensation, Corporation, Insurance, Real Estate, Taxation, Probate Law, Estate Planning, Family Law and Motor Sports (Racing).

RAY A. HAYES II P.A.

DAVIDSON, NORTH CAROLINA

(See Cornelius)

Business Transactions, Business Litigation, Corporate Law, Business Planning, Buying or Selling a Business, Securities, Contracts, Trusts and Estates, Wills and Probate, Bankruptcy, Consumer Bankruptcy, Traffic Violations.

HORACK, TALLEY, PHARR & LOWNDES

A PROFESSIONAL ASSOCIATION

DAVIDSON, NORTH CAROLINA

(See Charlotte)

General Trial and Appellate Practice in all State and Federal Courts, Family Law, Business and Corporate Law for Small and Closely Held Businesses, Taxation, Securities, Commercial and Residential Real Estate Development, Administrative Law, Creditors Rights and Bankruptcy, Real Estate Title Disputes, Homebuilders, Personal and Business Asset Preservation, Estate Administration, Governments and Municipalities, Employer's Rights, Construction Litigation.

SUSAN K. IRVIN

P.O. BOX 2376

DAVIDSON, NORTH CAROLINA 28036

Telephone: 704-896-0820
Fax: 704-896-0875
Email: susan@skirvinlaw.com
URL: http://www.skirvinlaw.com

Commercial Real Estate Development, Zoning, Planning and Land Use Law.

FIRM PROFILE: Commercial Real Estate Development, Acquisitions and Sales, Zoning, Planning and Land Use Law. Clients consists of Commercial Real Estate Developers, Financial Institutions, Individuals and Entities with Real Estate Holdings.

SUSAN K. IRVIN, admitted to bar, 1984, Texas; 1989, District of Columbia; 1994, New York; 1995, North Carolina. *Education:* Duke University (B.A., 1979); University of Texas (J.D., 1983). ***PRACTICE AREAS:*** Commercial Real Estate Development; Zoning, Planning and Land Use Law.

RICHARD J. KLINE

230 SOUTH MAIN STREET
P.O. BOX 1508

DAVIDSON, NORTH CAROLINA 28036

Telephone: 704-892-8823
Fax: 704-892-8683
Email: rjkline@bellsouth.net
URL: http://www.lawyers.com/rjkline

Commercial Real Estate, Real Estate Lending, Municipal Law, Zoning and Land Use.

RICHARD J. KLINE, born Akron, Ohio, July 31, 1947; admitted to bar, 1972, Ohio (inactive); 1974, North Carolina. *Education:* The Ohio State University (B.S.B.A., 1969); Akron University Law School (J.D., 1972). Associate Editor, Akron Law Review, 1971-1972. Davidson Town Attorney, 1976—. *Member:* North Carolina, Ohio State (inactive) and American Bar Associations; North Carolina State Bar.

THE McINTOSH LAW FIRM, P.C.

Established in 1997

THE DAVIDSON COTTON MILL
P.O. BOX 2270

DAVIDSON, NORTH CAROLINA 28036

Telephone: 704-892-1699
Telecopier: 704-892-8664
Email: bob@mcintoshlawfirm.com
URL: http://www.mcintoshlawfirm.com

Adoptions, Appeals, Bankruptcy, Business Law, Civil Litigation, Commercial and Consumer Collections, Commercial and Residential Real Estate, Corporate Law, Foreclosures, Insurance Subrogation, Estate Administration, Family Law, Personal Injury, Wrongful Death, Wills, Workers Compensation, Planning and Land Use.

(This Listing Continued)

ROBERT G. McINTOSH, born Mooresville, North Carolina, April 2, 1962; admitted to bar, 1987, North Carolina; 1988, U.S. District Court, Eastern District of North Carolina; 1990, U.S. District Court, Western District of North Carolina. *Education:* University of North Carolina (B.S., 1984; J.D., 1987). Certified Mediator, North Carolina Dispute Resolution Commission. *Member:* Mecklenburg County and North Carolina Bar Associations; North Carolina State Bar; North Carolina Academy of Trial Lawyers; National Association of Retail Collection Attorneys; Commercial Law League of America. ***PRACTICE AREAS:*** Collections; Personal Injury; Civil Litigation; Workers Compensation. ***Email:*** bob@mcintoshlawfirm.com

ROBERT EDWARD WICK, III, born Bristol, Tennessee, August 14, 1972; admitted to bar, 1999, North Carolina and U.S. District Court, Western District of North Carolina. *Education:* The Citadel (B.A., 1995); Cumberland School of Law of Samford University (J.D., 1999). Phi Alpha Delta. *Member:* 26th Judicial District and American Bar Associations; North Carolina State Bar (Member, Family Law Section); North Carolina Academy of Trial Lawyers. ***PRACTICE AREAS:*** Corporate Law; Family Law; Business Law; Collections; Civil Litigation. ***Email:*** rob@mcintoshlawfirm.com

PROSSER D. CARNEGIE, born Davidson, North Carolina, January 31, 1951; admitted to bar, 1977, Virginia, U.S. Court of Appeals, 4th Circuit and U.S. District Court, Western District of Virginia; 1979, North Carolina; U.S. Supreme Court. *Education:* Davidson College (B.A., 1973); University of Richmond (J.D., 1977). Phi Delta Phi. Commissioner, Town of Davidson, 1983-1997. *Member:* Mecklenburg County, 26th Judicial District and North Carolina Bar Associations; North Carolina State Bar. ***PRACTICE AREAS:*** Litigation; Real Estate; Corporate; Contracts. ***Email:*** sandy@mcintoshlawfirm.com

AMANDA L. SHUE, born Charlotte, North Carolina, August 17, 1970; admitted to bar, 2000, North Carolina. *Education:* University of North Carolina at Charlotte (B.A., 1992); Campbell University (J.D., 2000). Delta Theta Phi. *Member:* North Carolina Bar and American Bar Associations; 26th Judicial District Bar Association; North Carolina State Bar; North Carolina Academy of Trial Lawyers. ***PRACTICE AREAS:*** Estate Planning; Estate Probate and Administration; Collections; Civil Litigation. ***Email:*** amy@mcintoshlawfirm.com

JENNIFER SUSAN AHLERS, born Suffern, New York, February 8, 1968; admitted to bar, 1996, North Carolina. *Education:* University of North Carolina at Wilmington (B.A., 1990); Campbell University (J.D., 1996). Phi Alpha Delta. Member: Moot Court Board, 1994-1996; Safran Moot Court Award, Campbell Law Observer, 1995-1996. *Member:* Mecklenburg County and American Bar Associations; North Carolina Bar. ***PRACTICE AREAS:*** Insurance Subrogation; Commercial Collections; Litigation; Product Liability; Personal Injury. ***Email:*** jennifer@mcintoshlawfirm.com

WILLIAM LEWIS ELLISON, JR., born Beaufort, North Carolina, November 23, 1970; admitted to bar, 1996, South Carolina and U.S. District Court, District of South Carolina; 1997, North Carolina. *Education:* Campbell University (M.A., 1993; J.D., 1996). *Member:* South Carolina Bar; North Carolina State Bar. (Also at Charlotte, North Carolina Office). ***PRACTICE AREAS:*** Bankruptcy; Commercial Law; Insurance Defense; Workers Compensation. ***Email:*** bill@mcintoshlawfirm.com

BETH B. CARTER, born Punxsutawney, Pennsylvania, July 28, 1965; admitted to bar, 1995, Pennsylvania; 1997, North Carolina; U.S. District Court, Western District of North Carolina; 2000, Eastern and Middle Districts of North Carolina. *Education:* Villanova University (B.S., Biology, 1987); Widener University Law School (J.D., 1997). ***PRACTICE AREAS:*** Bankruptcy; Real Estate. ***Email:*** beth@mcintoshlawfirm.com

OF COUNSEL

JAMES C. FULLER, born Salisbury, North Carolina, July 19, 1942; admitted to bar, 1971, North Carolina; 1974, U.S Court of Appeals, Fourth Circuit; 1977, U.S. Supreme Court. *Education:* Davidson College (B.A., 1965); University of North Carolina (J.D., 1971). Recipient: Chief Justice Walter Clark Award, North Carolina Academy of Trial Lawyers, 1995; Lawyer of the Year Award, North Carolina Association of Black Lawyers, 1998. Law Clerk to Susie M. Sharp, Chief Justice of the North Carolina Supreme Court, 1971-1972. Judge, North Carolina Court of Appeals, 2000. Listed, Best Lawyers In America, 1984-2004. Adjunct Professor of Trial Advocacy, University of North Carolina School of Law, 1983-2004. Adjunct Professor of Trial Advocacy, Duke University School of Law, 1989-2004. Adjunct Professor, Civil Rights, North Carolina Central University School of Law, 1983-1988. Instructor, National Institute of Trial Advocacy, 1979-2001 in U.S. and South Africa. Author: "Coastal Land Use Development: A Proposal for Cumulative Area-Wide Zoning," 49 North Carolina Law Review 866, 1971. *Member:* Mecklenburg County, Wake County and North Carolina (Member, Board of Governors; Chair, Commission on Race Relations) Bar Associations; North Carolina State Bar; North Carolina Academy of Trial Lawyers (President, 1989-1990; Vice President, Legislation, 1987-1988; Vice President, Public Service, 1986-1987; Chair, Victims Rights Committee, 1985-1986); The Association of Trial Lawyers of America; International Society of Barristers; American Board of Trial Advocates (President, Eastern North Carolina Chapter, 1997-1999); Chief Justice Sharp Inn of Court (President, 1996-1997); American College of Trial Lawyers (Member, State Committee). ***PRACTICE AREAS:*** Civil Litigation; Personal Injury; Wrongful Death; Medical Malpractice; Products Liability; Condemnation Litigation; Arbitration; Mediation. ***Email:*** jimfuller@mcintoshlawfirm.com

REPRESENTATIVE CLIENTS: The Charlotte-Mecklenburg Hospital Authority; 2K Com, Inc.; Bubba's Barbecue, Inc.; Erie Insurance Group; United Mortgage & Loan Investment Corporation; Drive Financial; United Federal Credit Union; Raceports Distribution, Inc.; Oasis Shriners.

G. PATTESON WILLIAMS

DAVIDSON, NORTH CAROLINA

(See Cornelius)

Real Estate, Residential Real Estate, Commercial Real Estate, Wills, Estates, Estate Administration, Business, Corporate, Automobile Accidents, Personal Injury.

KENNEDY & WULFHORST, P.A.

3758 HIGHWAY 16 NORTH
DENVER, NORTH CAROLINA 28037
Telephone: 704-483-3415
Telecopier: 704-483-9755
URL: http://www.kennedyandwulfhorst.com
URL: http://www.kandwlaw.com

Residential and Commercial Real Estate, Corporate and Business Law, Wills, Probate, Estate Planning, Domestic and Family Law, Criminal Law, Traffic, Juvenile, Divorce, Collections.

FIRM PROFILE: Mr. Wulfhorst joined Mr. Kennedy in 2000 to form Kennedy & Wulfhorst, P.A. (formerly Kennedy & Black, P.A.).

D. TODD WULFHORST, born Columbus, Indiana, July 3, 1967; admitted to bar, 1992, North Carolina and U.S. District Court, Western District of North Carolina. *Education:* Pennsylvania State University (B.S.M.E., 1989); University of North Carolina at Chapel Hill (J.D., 1992). *Member:* Lincoln County and North Carolina Bar Associations; North Carolina Academy of Trial Lawyers. ***PRACTICE AREAS:*** Real Estate; Corporate Law; Business Law; Estate Planning; Probate; Domestic Relations; Criminal Law. ***Email:*** dtw@kandwlaw.com

---

PETER C. CAPECE, born Staten Island, New York, April 28, 1976; admitted to bar, 2002, North Carolina. *Education:* Catawba College (B.A., 1998); North Carolina Central University (J.D., 2002). *Member:* Lincoln County and North Carolina Bar Associations; North Carolina Academy of Trial Lawyers. ***PRACTICE AREAS:*** Traffic Violations; Juvenile Law; Real Estate; Collections. ***Email:*** pcc@kandwlaw.com

OF COUNSEL

RICHARD L. KENNEDY, born Fitzgerald, Georgia, March 14, 1932; admitted to bar, 1956, North Carolina; 1963, U.S. District Court, Western District of North Carolina 1969, U.S. Court of Appeals, Fourth Circuit. *Education:* Wake Forest University (B.B.A., 1953; LL.B., 1955). *Member:* Lincoln County and North Carolina Bar Associations; North Carolina State Bar; North Carolina Academy of Trial Lawyers. ***Email:*** rlk@kandwlaw.com

KAREN J. ADAMS

124 WEST KAPP STREET
P.O. BOX 1271
DOBSON, NORTH CAROLINA 27017
Telephone: 336-356-4900
Fax: 336-356-2900
Email: kjadams@surry.net
URL: http://www.karenadamslaw.com

Criminal Law, Divorce, Speeding Tickets, DUI, DWI.

KAREN J. ADAMS, born Mount Airy, North Carolina, February 21, 1970; admitted to bar, 1997, North Carolina. *Education:* University of North Carolina, Charlotte (B.S., 1992); North Carolina Central University (J.D., 1997). *Member:* North Carolina State Bar Association; North Academy Trial Lawyers. ***PRACTICE AREAS:*** Criminal Law; Divorce; Driving While Intoxicated.

ROYSTER AND ROYSTER

DOBSON, NORTH CAROLINA

(See Mount Airy)

General Civil and Criminal Trial Practice. DWI, Traffic Offenses, Felonies. Personal Injury, Automobile Accidents, Wrongful Death, Real Estate Law, Trusts and Estates, Wills and Probate, Probate Law and Workers Compensation.

W. DAVID WHITE, P.A.

Established in 1980
220 WEST KAPP STREET
P.O. BOX 1061
DOBSON, NORTH CAROLINA 27017
Telephone: 336-386-8225
Fax: 336-386-8227
Email: wileywhite51@hotmail.com
URL: http://www.wdavidwhitelaw.com

Civil, Criminal, Family, Alimony, Cohabitation Agreements, Divorce, Divorce Mediation, Domestic Partnerships, Domestic Relations, Domestic Torts, Domestic Violence, Equitable Distribution, Family Arbitration, Family Mediation, Name Changes, Non Traditional Family Law, Paternity, Post Divorce Modification, Postnuptial Agreements, Premarital Agreements, Qualified Domestic Relations Orders, Restraining Orders, Separation Agreements, Spousal Support, Personal Injury, Personal Injury Mediation, Plaintiffs Personal Injury, Accidents, Auto Accidents, Automobile Negligence, School Bus Accidents, Bodily Injury, Brain Injury, Catastrophic Injury, Head Injury, Spinal Injury, Tourist Injuries, Motor Vehicle Accidents and Injuries, Motorcycle Accidents, Wrongful Death, DWI, Speeding Tickets, Traffic Violations.

W. DAVID WHITE, born Winston Salem, North Carolina, January 28, 1951; admitted to bar, 1980, North Carolina. *Education:* Western Carolina University (B.S.B.A, 1977); Campbell University (J.D., 1980). Certified Family Financial Mediator. Certified Superior Court Mediator. *Member:* North Carolina and American Bar Associations; North Carolina State Bar; American Academy of Trial Lawyers; North Carolina Academy of Trial Lawyers;

(This Listing Continued)

National Academy of Criminal Defense Lawyers. [Sgt., U.S. Army, 1970-1973]. ***Email:*** wileywhite51@hotmail.com

HORNTHAL, RILEY, ELLIS & MALAND, L.L.P.

DUCK, NORTH CAROLINA

(See Elizabeth City)

General Trial and Appellate Practice in all Courts. Personal Injury, Products Liability, Professional Malpractice, Corporate, Tax, Bankruptcy, Employment, Education, Criminal, Insurance, Construction, Real Estate, Environmental, Elder, Local Government, Wills and Trusts, Probate and Admiralty Law.

CHARLENE EDWARDS LAW OFFICE

DUNN, NORTH CAROLINA

(See Lillington)

Family Law, Divorce, Domestic Relations, Personal Injury, Automobile Accidents, Wrongful Death, Construction Accidents, Criminal Law, Workers Compensation, Social Security Disability, Traffic Law.

HARDISON & LEONE, L.L.P.

Established in 1997
212 S. WILSON AVENUE
P.O. BOX 759
DUNN, NORTH CAROLINA 28335-0759
Telephone: 910-892-1181; Toll-Free 1-888-892-1181
Fax: 910-892-7874
URL: http://www.hardisonandleone.com

Personal Injury, Auto and Trucking Accidents, Pedestrian Accidents, Catastrophic Injury, Medical Malpractice, Workers' Compensation, Social Security Disability, Nursing Home Negligence, Security Investment Fraud, Inadequate Security Claims, Premises Liability, Mass Torts, Drug Liability Claims, Employment Law, Appellate Practice.

(For complete information on all personnel, see Professional Biographies at Raleigh, North Carolina)

HAYES, WILLIAMS, TURNER & DAUGHTRY, P.A.

Established in 1969
804 WEST BROAD STREET
DUNN, NORTH CAROLINA 28334
Telephone: 910-892-2178
Fax: 910-891-1198
Email: ghayes@harnettlaw.com
Email: hwilliams@harnettlaw.com
Email: pdaughtry@harnettlaw.com
Email: dturner@harnettlaw.com
URL: http://www.harnettlaw.com

General Criminal and Civil Practice. Personal Injury, Traffic Court, Real Estate, Probate, Juvenile, Family and Corporation Law. Trials in all Courts.

FIRM PROFILE: The firm of Hayes, Williams, Turner & Daughtry, P.A., originally Stewart & Hayes P.A., was formed in 1969 by D.K. Stewart and Gerald W. Hayes. Jr. Heather Hayes Williams joined the firm in 1994, Doug Turner joined in 1997, and Parrish Hayes Daughtry became a member in 2000.

The firm concentrates on personal injury, automobile accidents, criminal law, motor vehicle law, real estate, divorce, family law, civil litigation, business practice, juvenile law, wills and estates. All initial conferences are without charge with the exception of domestic consultations. All personal injury cases are handled on a contingent fee basis, without cost to the client unless recovery is made.

GERALD W. HAYES, JR., born Harnett County, North Carolina, November 6, 1943; admitted to bar, 1969, North Carolina. *Education:* University of North Carolina (A.B., 1966); Wake Forest University (J.D., 1969). Phi Alpha Delta. Member, 1978-1990 and Chairman, 1984-1990, Harnett County Board of Education. Member, Judicial Council of North Carolina, 1977-1981. Director: New Century Bank of Dunn, N.C.; New Century BankCorp. *Member:* Harnett County Bar Association (President, 1982); North Carolina State Bar; North Carolina Academy of Trial Lawyers. ***PRACTICE AREAS:*** Criminal Law; Traffic Law; Personal Injury Law; Decedents Estates. ***Email:*** ghayes@harnettlaw.com

HEATHER HAYES WILLIAMS, born Winston Salem, North Carolina, August 11, 1969; admitted to bar, 1994, North Carolina. *Education:* University of North Carolina at Chapel Hill (B.S.P.H., 1991); Campbell University (J.D., 1994). Phi Alpha Delta. *Member:* Harnett County (President, 1999) and American Bar Associations; North Carolina State Bar (Secretary, 1997, N.C. Family Law Council); North Carolina Academy of Trial Lawyers. ***SPECIAL AGENCIES:*** Governor's Crime Commission Through the Violence Against Women Committee; Juvenile Crime Prevention Council. Board of Trustees, Betsy Johnson Regional Hospital. ***PRACTICE AREAS:*** Family Law; Personal Injury Law; Civil Litigation. ***Email:*** hwilliams@harnettlaw.com

DOUGLAS EUGENE TURNER, JR., born Cabarrus County, North Carolina, November 13, 1971; admitted to bar, 1997, North Carolina. *Education:* Wingate University (B.A., 1994); Campbell University (J.D., 1997). *Member:* Harnett County, North Carolina and American Bar Associations; North Carolina State Bar; North Carolina Academy of Trial Lawyers. ***PRACTICE AREAS:*** Criminal Law; Family Law; Personal Injury; Traffic Violations; Civil Litigation; Municipal Law. ***Email:*** dturner@harnettlaw.com

(This Listing Continued)

PARRISH HAYES DAUGHTRY, born Raleigh, North Carolina, February 24, 1975; admitted to bar, 2000, North Carolina. *Education:* University of North Carolina at Chapel Hill (B.S., 1997); Campbell University (J.D., 2000). Phi Alpha Delta. *Member:* Harnett County (President, 2003), North Carolina and American Bar Associations; North Carolina Academy of Trial Lawyers. ***SPECIAL AGENCIES:*** Harnett County Business Education Partnership Member; Alternative Harnett County IVD Agency Attorney. ***PRACTICE AREAS:*** Criminal Law; Family Law; Personal Injury Law; Wills and Estate Law; Juvenile Law. ***Email:*** pdaughtry@harnettlaw.com

REPRESENTATIVE CLIENTS: Amerigas Propane/Petrolane; Warren Oil Co.; Godwin Manufacturing, Inc.; Time Warner Cablevision; Police Benevolent Assn.; Quail Run Homes, Inc.; Cape Fear Quail Unlimited, Inc.; Alternate Harnett County IVD Child Support Enforcement Agency; New Century Bank Corp.; New Century Bank of Dunn.
APPROVED ATTORNEYS FOR: Lawyers Title Insurance Corp.; Investors Title Insurance Co.; Farmers Home Administration; Federal Land Bank of Columbia.
REFERENCES: New Century Bank; Central Carolina Bank.

STEWART LAW FIRM

111 COMMERCE DRIVE
DUNN, NORTH CAROLINA 28334
Telephone: 910-892-4970
Fax: 910-892-4976
URL: http://www.stewartlawfirmnc.com
URL: stewartlaw-firm.com
Email: stewartlaw@dockport.net
URL: http://www.stewartlawfirm.com

Personal Injury, Automobile Accidents, Criminal Law, Traffic Violations, Real Estate, Corporate Law, Family Law, Divorce, Child Custody and Child Support.

MEMBERS OF FIRM

VERNON K. STEWART, born Dunn, North Carolina, August 5, 1960; admitted to bar, 1986, North Carolina. *Education:* Campbell University (B.B.A., 1982); Campbell University School of Law (J.D., 1986). Phi Alpha Delta. *Member:* North Carolina Bar Association (Criminal Law Section, Family Law Section and Personal Injury Section); North Carolina Academy of Trial Lawyers. ***PRACTICE AREAS:*** Personal Injury; Criminal Law; Real Estate; Municipal Law; Trial Practice; Corporate Law; Domestic Relations; Civil Litigation. ***Email:*** stewartvernon@yahoo.com

CARON H. STEWART, born Rockingham, North Carolina, November 13, 1961; admitted to bar, 1986, North Carolina. *Education:* East Carolina University (B.S., 1983); Campbell University School of Law (J.D., 1986). Phi Alpha Delta. Assistant District Attorney, 1987-1995 and Part-Time/Temporary Assistant District Attorney, 1998, 1999 and 2000, Harnett, Johnston and Lee Counties. *Member:* North Carolina Bar Association; North Carolina State Bar; North Carolina Academy of Trial Lawyers. ***PRACTICE AREAS:*** Social Security; Criminal Law; Traffic Violations; Administrative Law; Personal Injury; Probate; Real Estate.

ASSOCIATE

CHRISTOPHER D. MUNZ, born Pinehurst, North Carolina, March 24, 1976; admitted to bar, 2001, North Carolina. *Education:* University of North Carolina at Chapel Hill (B.A., 1998); Campbell University School of Law (J.D., 2001). ***PRACTICE AREAS:*** Traffic Violations; Criminal Law; Personal Injury; Family Law. ***Email:*** stewartlaw@dockport.net

BAGWELL, HOLT & SMITH, P.A.

DURHAM, NORTH CAROLINA

(See Chapel Hill)

Commercial and Residential Real Estate, Business, Civil Litigation, Estate Planning, Creditor's Rights, Collections, Workers Compensation, Automobile Accidents, Personal Injury, Wrongful Death, Wills, Probate.

THE LAW OFFICES OF OMAR BALOCH

DURHAM, NORTH CAROLINA

(See Raleigh)

Immigration, Traffic Violations, Personal Injury, Small Business and Business Enterprises.

TRACY HICKS BARLEY & ASSOCIATES, P.A.

Established in 1996

413 E. CHAPEL HILL STREET
SUITE 112
DURHAM, NORTH CAROLINA 27702
Telephone: 919-956-9440
Fax: 919-956-9443
Email: thbarley@nc.rr.com
URL: http://www.tracybarleylaw.com

Bankruptcy - Chapters 7 and 13, Family Law, Equitable Distribution, Divorce, Child Custody, Child Support, Estates, Juvenile Law, Incorporations, Personal Injury.

TRACY HICKS BARLEY, born Roanoke Rapids, North Carolina; admitted to bar, 1993, North Carolina; 1994, U.S. District Court, Eastern and Middle Districts of North Carolina; U.S. Court of Appeals, Fourth Circuit and U.S. Supreme Court. *Education:* Win-

(This Listing Continued)

ston-Salem State University (B.A., 1983); North Carolina Central University (J.D., 1993). ***PRACTICE AREAS:*** Bankruptcy Chapter 7; Bankruptcy Chapter 13; Family Law; Equitable Distribution; Divorce; Child Custody; Child Support; Juvenile Law; Personal Injury; Estate Administration; Incorporation; Adoption Law. ***Email:*** thbarley@nc.rr.com

BECTON, SLIFKIN & BELL, P.A.

DURHAM, NORTH CAROLINA

(See Raleigh)

Personal Injury and Wrongful Death, Vehicle Collisions, Medical Malpractice and Product Liability.

DONNA E. BENNICK, P.C.

DURHAM, NORTH CAROLINA

(See Chapel Hill)

Family Law, Divorce, Separation, Child Custody, Alimony, Property Settlements, Prenuptial Agreements, Certified Guardian Ad Litem and Parent Coordinator, Collaborative Law.

BENTLEY LAW OFFICES, P.A.

Established in 1981

SUITE 501 SOUTHBANK BUILDING
400 WEST MAIN STREET
P.O. BOX 52089
DURHAM, NORTH CAROLINA 27717-2089
Telephone: 919-682-3700
Fax: 919-419-1847
URL: http://www.lawyers.com/bentleylawoffices
Email: cbentley@bentleylawfirm.com
URL: http://www.bentleylawfirm.com

Medical Malpractice Law, Wrongful Death, Personal Injury, Consumer Fraud, Predatory Lending and Unfair and Deceptive Trade Practices, Commercial Litigation, Products Liability, Truck Accidents, Premises Liability and Inadequate Security.

FIRM PROFILE: Charles A. Bentley, Jr. has been a trial lawyer for over 33 years. He maintains a civil litigation practice with an emphasis on medical malpractice and inadequate security. Mr. Bentley practiced law in Mobile, Alabama from 1971-1973 with the firm of Johnstone, Adams, May, Howard & Hill. From 1974-1981, Mr. Bentley practiced with the North Central Legal Assistance Program in Durham, serving as Senior Staff Attorney, Managing Attorney and Executive Director. From 1982-1990, Mr. Bentley was a founding partner in the firms of Glenn & Bentley, P.A. and Glenn, Bentley, Mills & Fisher, P.A. in Durham, where he concentrated his practice in plaintiff's civil litigation. Since 1991, Mr. Bentley has concentrated his practice in the areas of medical negligence, commercial litigation and products liability.

CHARLES A. BENTLEY, JR., born Louisville, Kentucky, January 27, 1946; admitted to bar, 1971, Alabama; 1974, North Carolina, U.S. District Court, Middle and Eastern Districts of North Carolina and U.S. Court of Appeals, Fourth Circuit; U.S. District Court, Southern District of Alabama; U.S. Court of Appeals, Eleventh Circuit. *Education:* Auburn University (B.A., 1968); University of Virginia (J.D., 1971). Adjunct, Assistant Professor of Law, Duke University School of Law, 1976-1978. Faculty, National Institute for Trial Advocacy, 1988-1998, 2005. Lecturer: Continuing Legal Education Programs: American Bar Association Section of Litigation; North Carolina Academy of Trial Lawyers; North Carolina Bar Association; Professional Education Seminars, Inc. Certified Mediator, Administrative Office of the Courts. Vice-President, Financial Protection Law Center, 2001— .*Member:* North Carolina Bar Association (Member, Health Law and Litigation Sections); North Carolina State Bar; Alabama State Bar; North Carolina Academy of Trial Lawyers (Trustee, Political Action Committee, 1989-1991; Professional Negligence Section); The Association of Trial Lawyers of America (Member: Breast Cancer Litigation Group; HMO Litigation Group; Inadequate Security Litigation Group; Professional Negligence Section); American Board of Trial Advocates, Eastern North Carolina Chapter; National Crime Victim Bar Association. [U.S. Army, Judge Advocate General's Office, Fifth Army H.Q., 1972; Captain, Medical Services Corps, U.S. Army Reserves, 1972-1978]. (Board Certified Civil Trial Advocate, National Board of Trial Advocacy). ***REPORTED CASES:*** Wrenn v. Byrd, 120 N.C.App. 761, 464 S.E.2d 89 (1995), cert. den. 342 N.C. 666, 467 S.E.2d 738 (1996); Custom Molders, Inc. v. Roper Corp., 101 N.C.App. 606, 401 S.E.2d 96 (1991), aff'd. 330 N.C. 191, 410 S.E.2d 55 (1991); Custom Molders v. American Yard Products, Inc., 342 N.C. 133, 463 S.E.2d 199 (1995). ***PRACTICE AREAS:*** Medical Malpractice Law; Wrongful Death; Personal Injury; Consumer Fraud; Deceptive Trade Practices; Commercial Litigation; Products Liability; Truck Accidents; Premises Liability. ***Email:*** cbentley@bentleylawfirm.com

BRADY, NORDGREN, KLYM & MORTON, PLLC

DURHAM, NORTH CAROLINA

(See Raleigh)

Trusts and Estates, Estate Planning, Estate Litigation, Personal Injury, Civil Litigation, Commercial Litigation, Wills, Probate, Corporate Law, Business Law, Taxation, Elder Law.

LISA R. BRENMAN

DURHAM, NORTH CAROLINA

(See Carrboro)

Family Immigration, Business Immigration, Labor Certification, Asylum, Student Visas, Citizenship.

BROCK, PAYNE & MEECE, P.A.

Established in 2001

3130 HOPE VALLEY ROAD

DURHAM, NORTH CAROLINA 27707

Telephone: 919-401-5913
Fax: 919-419-1018
Email: paul.brock@verizon.net

General Practice, Family Law, Child Custody, Child Support, Divorce, Alimony, Separation Agreements, Spousal Support, Equitable Distribution, Misdemeanors, Traffic, Personal Injury, Contracts, Mediation, Civil Litigation, Wills, Real Estate.

PAUL B. BROCK, born Chapel Hill, North Carolina, May 22, 1966; admitted to bar, 1992, North Carolina. *Education:* University of North Carolina at Chapel Hill (B.S.B.A., 1988; J.D., 1992). Certified Family Law Mediator. *Member:* Durham County Bar Association; North Carolina State Bar. ***PRACTICE AREAS:*** Family Law; Civil Litigation; Mediation; Traffic Violations. **Email:** paul.brock@verizon.net

BARRI HILTON PAYNE, born High Point, North Carolina, July 30, 1970; admitted to bar, 1999, North Carolina. *Education:* University of North Carolina at Charlotte (B.A., 1992); University of North Carolina at Chapel Hill (J.D., 1999). Member: The Order of Barristers, Moot Court Board. *Member:* Durham County and North Carolina Bar Associations; North Carolina State Bar. ***PRACTICE AREAS:*** Family Law; Wills. **Email:** barri.payne@verizon.net

DARIN P. MEECE, born Lexington, Kentucky, December 12, 1970; admitted to bar, 1995, North Carolina; 1996, U.S. District Court, Middle District of North Carolina. *Education:* University of North Carolina at Charlotte (B.A., 1991); University of North Carolina (J.D., 1995). *Member:* Durham County and North Carolina Bar Associations; North Carolina State Bar. ***PRACTICE AREAS:*** Wills and Estates; Real Estate.

BROWN & BUNCH, PLLC

21 WEST COLONY PLACE, SUITE 250

DURHAM, NORTH CAROLINA 27705

Telephone: 919-490-9700
Fax: 919-419-9736

Chapel Hill, North Carolina Office: 101 North Columbia Street, 27514. Telephone: 919-968-1111. Fax: 919-968-1444.
Raleigh, North Carolina Office: 4900 Falls of Neuse Road, Suite 210, Post Office Box 19409. Telephone: 919-878-8060. Fax: 919-878-8062.

A. VANN IRVIN, born Shelby, North Carolina, January 14, 1951; admitted to bar, 1982, Tennessee; 1984, Georgia; 1986, North Carolina; 1993, U.S. Tax Court and U.S. Court of Appeals, Fourth and Sixth Circuits. *Education:* College of Albemarle (A.A., 1971); University of North Carolina (B.A., 1973; J.D., 1982). *Member:* Durham County, North Carolina and American Bar Associations; State Bar of Georgia; North Carolina State Bar. (Board Certified Specialist in Estate Planning and Probate Law, North Carolina State Board of Legal Specialization) (Resident). ***PRACTICE AREAS:*** Trusts and Estates; Wills; Business Law; Probate; Taxation; Corporate Law. **Email:** vannirvin@aol.com

(For complete biographical data on all personnel, practice areas and representative clients, see Professional Biographies at Chapel Hill, North Carolina and Raleigh, North Carolina)

BROWNE, FLEBOTTE, WILSON & WEBB, PLLC

Established in 1982

MERIDIAN BUSINESS CAMPUS
2525 MERIDIAN PARKWAY, SUITE 300
P.O. BOX 2247

DURHAM, NORTH CAROLINA 27702

Telephone: 919-688-7393
919-688-1580
Toll Free: 800-556-8404
Facsimile: 919-683-6323
Email: bfwh@browneflebotte.com
URL: http://www.browneflebotte.com

Creedmoor, North Carolina Office: 506 North Main Street, P.O. Box 886, 27522. Telephone: 919-528-3061. Fax: 919-528-3505.
Greensboro, North Carolina Office: 503 West McGee Street, 27401. Telephone: 336-273-4480. Fax: 336-273-4362.
Charlotte, North Carolina Office: Cameron Brown Building, 301 South McDowell Street, Suite 1201, 28204. Telephone: 704-370-7771. Fax: 704-370-7798.
Fayetteville, North Carolina Office: Systel Building, 225 Green Street, Suite 204, 28301. Telephone: 910-323-3435. Fax: 910-323-2645.

General Civil and Criminal Trial Practice in State and Federal Courts. Personal Injury Litigation, Wrongful Death, Workers Compensation, Bankruptcy, Employment Law, Appellate Practice, Construction Law, Real Estate, Domestic Relations, Traffic Violations, Corporate Law, Labor Law.

FIRM PROFILE: The firm was established in 1982 by T. Marcus Browne III and Daniel R. Flebotte, and is well known in the area as a full service law firm able to satisfy your legal needs. The firm has over 40 attorneys practicing in it's five locations.

T. MARCUS BROWNE, III, born Mount Airy, North Carolina, February 19, 1951; admitted to bar, 1980, North Carolina; 1981, U.S. District Court, Middle District of North Carolina; 1990, U.S. District Court, Western District of North Carolina; 1991, U.S. District Court, Eastern District of North Carolina; 1999, U.S. Court of Appeals, Fourth Circuit. *Education:* East Carolina University (B.A., 1973); North Carolina Central University (J.D., 1979). Phi Delta Phi. Recipient, N.C. Governor's Community Service Award, 1994. Instructor, Durham Technical Community College Paralegal School, 1985-1987. *Member:* Durham County (Member, Board of Directors, 1987) and Granville County (Treasurer, 1992) Bar Associations; U.S. Supreme Court Bar Association; Durham County Association of Criminal Defense Attorneys (President, 1987-1988). ***PRACTICE AREAS:*** Real Estate; Domestic Relations; Criminal Law; Civil Litigation.

DANIEL R. FLEBOTTE, born Ludlow, Massachusetts, January 21, 1952; admitted to bar, 1980, North Carolina; 1981, U.S. District Court, Middle, Eastern and Western Districts of North Carolina. *Education:* Duke University (B.A., magna cum laude, 1977); Washington University (J.D., 1980). Winner, Moot Court Competition. National Finalist, Moot Court Competition. North Carolina Supreme Court Certified Mediator. ***PRACTICE AREAS:*** Trial Practice; Civil Appeals; Real Estate; Construction Law; Business Law. **Email:** drflaw@aol.com

JOSEPH M. WILSON, JR., born Columbia, South Carolina, February 25, 1961; admitted to bar, 1991, North Carolina; 1996, U.S. District Court, Eastern, Western and Middle Districts of North Carolina; 1998, U.S. Court of Appeals, 4th Circuit. *Education:* University of South Carolina (B.A., 1983); North Carolina Central University (J.D., 1988). Phi Delta Phi. *Member:* North Carolina and American Bar Associations; North Carolina Academy of Trial Lawyers. ***PRACTICE AREAS:*** Criminal Law; Civil Litigation; Bankruptcy. **Email:** jwilson@browneflebotte.com

JOY RHYNE WEBB, born Hickory, North Carolina, November 25, 1969; admitted to bar, 1995, North Carolina; 1996, U.S. District Court, Western District of North Carolina; 1997, U.S. District Court, Eastern and Middle Districts of North Carolina. *Education:* University of North Carolina at Chapel Hill (B.A., with distinction, 1992; J.D., with honors, 1995). Note & Comment Editor, North Carolina Journal of International Law & Commercial Regulation, 1994-1995. *Member:* 14th Judicial District and North Carolina Bar Associations. ***PRACTICE AREAS:*** Employment Law; Personal Injury; Civil Litigation. **Email:** jwebb@browneflebotte.com

ROBERT E. WHITFIELD, born Durham, North Carolina, April 3, 1947; admitted to bar, 1978, North Carolina; 1991, Tennessee. *Education:* East Carolina University (B.A., 1969); North Carolina Central University (J.D., 1978). Member, National Association of Consumer Bankruptcy Attorneys, 1998-1999. [Sgt., U.S. Air Force, 1969-1973]. ***PRACTICE AREAS:*** Bankruptcy; Consumer Law; Personal Injury. **Email:** rwhitfield@browneflebotte.com

BROWNLEE LAW FIRM

DURHAM, NORTH CAROLINA

(See Raleigh)

Residential and Commercial Real Estate, Landlord-Tenant Law, Business Law, Contracts, Debtor and Creditor, Commercial Leasing, Mechanics Liens.

BRYANT, PATTERSON, COVINGTON IDOL & LEWIS, P.A.

Established in 1895

103 WEST MAIN STREET
KRESS BUILDING, MEZZANINE FLOOR
P.O. BOX 341

DURHAM, NORTH CAROLINA 27702

Telephone: 919-688-6341
Fax: 919-688-6343
URL: http://www.bpcilaw.com

Trial and Appeals in all State and Federal Courts, Personal Injury, Insurance, Medical and Legal Malpractice, Commercial Litigation, Workers Compensation, Corporation Law, Banking, Estate Planning and Administration, Taxation, Criminal and Traffic.

FIRM PROFILE: Since the firm's establishment in 1895, it has concentrated mainly on civil litigation and offers tax planning, estate planning and corporate services. The firm has a support staff consisting of paralegals and represents small businesses, individuals and corporations throughout North Carolina. The firm is dedicated to delivering top quality legal services at a reasonable cost.

J. WESLEY COVINGTON, born Durham, North Carolina, May 20, 1950; admitted to bar, 1981, North Carolina. *Education:* Duke University (B.A., 1972); North Carolina Central University (J.D., 1981). Adjunct Assistant Professor of Law, North Carolina Central School of Law, 1984-1986. Assistant District Attorney, 14th Judicial District, 1981-1987. *Member:* North Carolina Academy of Trial Lawyers; The Association of Trial Lawyers of America. ***PRACTICE AREAS:*** Medical Negligence Law; Civil Litigation. **Email:** wes.covington@bpcilaw.com

ROBERT A. IDOL, born Durham, North Carolina, April 26, 1956; admitted to bar, 1981, North Carolina. *Education:* University of North Carolina (B.S., 1978; J.D., 1981); Emory University (LL.M. in Taxation, 1983). Beta Gamma Sigma. Co-Author, "Administration of the Estate in North Carolina," National Business Institute, 1991. President, Durham County Young Lawyers Division, 1988-1989. *Member:* Durham/Orange Estate Planning Council (President, 1990-1991). ***PRACTICE AREAS:*** Taxation Law; Estate Planning Law; Probate Law; Business Law; Nonprofit Corporations. **Email:** bob.idol@bpcilaw.com

DAVID O. LEWIS, born Asheville, North Carolina, June 2, 1956; admitted to bar, 1981, North Carolina. *Education:* University of North Carolina-Wilmington (B.S., 1978); University of North Carolina, Chapel Hill (J.D., 1981). Lecturer, Business Law, University of North Carolina at Wilmington, 1981-1982. Assistant Professor, Business Law, University of North Carolina at Wilmington, 1982-1987. *Member:* North Carolina Association of Defense Lawyers; Defense Research Institute. (Certified as a Civil Trial Advocate, National Board of Trial Advocacy). ***PRACTICE AREAS:*** Trials and Appeals; Negligence Law; Civil Litigation; Commercial Litigation; Insurance Defense; Commercial Real Estate. **Email:** david.lewis@bpcilaw.com

(This Listing Continued)

JEREMY D. LINDSLEY, born Poughkeepsie, New York, August 26, 1971; admitted to bar, 1999, North Carolina. *Education:* Boston University (B.A., 1993); Rutgers University Law School (J.D., 1998). ***PRACTICE AREAS:*** Civil Litigation; Insurance Defense; Personal Injury; Negligence; Criminal Law; Workers' Compensation; Traffic Violations. ***Email:*** jeremy.lindsley@bpcilaw.com

P. LEE CRAVEN, III, born Raleigh, North Carolina, November 19, 1975; admitted to bar, 2002, North Carolina. *Education:* University of North Carolina at Chapel Hill (B.A., 1998; J.D., 2002). Order of the Barristers. ***PRACTICE AREAS:*** Insurance Defense; Civil Litigation. ***Email:*** lee.craven@bpcilaw.com

ANDREW L. PETERSON, born Garden City, Kansas, May 22, 1974; admitted to bar, 2003, North Carolina. *Education:* Clemson University (B.A., 1997); North Carolina Central University School of Law (J.D., 2003). Adjunct Professor: Business and Employment Law, Vance Granville Community College (2003—); Business Law, Louisburg College (2004). ***PRACTICE AREAS:*** Civil Litigation; Criminal Law; Traffic Violations. ***Email:*** andrew.peterson@bpcilaw.com

REPRESENTATIVE CLIENTS: BioSage Group, LLC; Central Carolina Bank; Cree Research, Inc.; International Divers Alert Network, Inc.; Lawyers Mutual Insurance Co.; Nationwide Mutual Insurance Co.; North Carolina Museum of Life and Science; BB&T; Utica National Insurance Co.; Virginia Mutual Insurance Company; Wachovia Bank, N.A.; YMCA of Greater Durham; Topsail Technologies, Inc.; Triangle United Way; Regional Surgical Associates, P.A.; Scottsdale Insurance Company; Residential Warranty Corporation; Southern States Police Benevolent Association.

BUGG & WOLF, P.A.

Established in 1984

SUITE 170 UNIVERSITY OFFICE PARK
411 ANDREWS ROAD
DURHAM, NORTH CAROLINA 27705
Telephone: 919-383-9431
FAX: 919-383-9771

Mailing Address: P.O. Box 2917, Durham, NC 27715

Public and Private Construction Law, including OSHA Proceedings and Litigation. General Civil and Appellate Practice in State, Federal Courts and Administrative Agencies.

FIRM PROFILE: Since the firm's establishment in 1984 by John E. Bugg, the firm has concentrated on construction law and other commercial litigation. The firm is listed in the Bar Register of Preeminent Lawyers.

JOHN E. BUGG, born Durham, North Carolina, August 27, 1944; admitted to bar, 1970, North Carolina, U.S. District Court, Eastern, Middle and Western Districts of North Carolina, U.S. Court of Appeals, Fourth Circuit and U.S. Supreme Court. *Education:* Duke University (A.B., 1966); University of North Carolina (J.D., 1970). Order of the Coif. Staff Writer, University of North Carolina Law Review, 1969-1970. Alderman-at-Large, Durham City Council, 1971-1975. Member, Panel of Arbitrators, American Arbitration Association, 1976— and the Court-Annexed Arbitration for the U.S. District Court, Middle District of North Carolina, 1986-1993. Certified Mediator by the North Carolina Dispute Resolution Committee and U.S. District Court, Middle District of North Carolina, 1994—. *Member:* North Carolina Bar Association (Member, Construction Law Section). ***PRACTICE AREAS:*** Construction Law; Commercial Law; Government Contracts.

WILLIAM J. WOLF, born Grosse Pointe, Michigan, January 1963; admitted to bar, 1987, North Carolina and U.S. District Court, Eastern, Middle and Western Districts of North Carolina. *Education:* Alma College (B.A., 1984); Wake Forest University (J.D., cum laude, 1987). Phi Delta Phi. Business Editor, Wake Forest Law Review, 1986-1987. President, Durham County Young Lawyers, 1995. *Member:* Durham County and North Carolina (Construction Law Section) Bar Associations; The Association of Trial Lawyers of America. ***PRACTICE AREAS:*** Construction Law; Government Contracts; Commercial Law; Debtor and Creditor; Civil Appeals.

WILLIAM R. SPARROW, admitted to bar, 2005, North Carolina. *Education:* University of North Carolina at Chapel Hill (B.A., Political Science, 2001); Wake Forest University (J.D., 2005). *Member:* North Carolina State Bar.

ALLEN T. WIGGINS, born Durham, North Carolina, March 16, 1969; admitted to bar, 2002, North Carolina. *Education:* Connecticut College (B.A., History, 1991); University of North Carolina at Chapel Hill (J.D., 2002). ***PRACTICE AREAS:*** Construction Law; Government Contracts; Commercial Law. ***Email:*** wiggins@buggwolf.com

REPRESENTATIVE CLIENTS: Asphalt Experts, Inc.; Bat Masonry; Bordeaux Const. Co., Inc.; Bryant-Durham Electric Co., Inc.; Bryant Electric Company; Carolina Sunrock Corporation; C.C. Woods Const. Co., Inc.; Clancy & Theys Const. Co., Inc.; Crain and Denbo, Inc.; Crosland Contractors; Dellinger, Inc.; Enpuricon Asbestos Management, Inc.; Hanson Aggregates; Hanson Brick; Harlan Laws Corporation; Jedco Construction; Jones Bros, Inc.; Maleady Builders, Inc.; Mixon Constr. Co., Inc.; Mountain State Contractors; Neilo L. Teer Co.; Park Construction Co.; Patriot Building Company; Pipeline Utilities, Inc.; Resolute Building Company; Romeo Guest Associates; Smith-Rowe, Inc.; Steward Painting & Decorating; Triangle Grading & Paving, Inc.; Van Thomas Contractors; West Durham Lumber Company; Wellons Const., Inc.

FREDERICK A. BURKE

3622 LYCKAN PARKWAY
SUITE 5008
DURHAM, NORTH CAROLINA 27707
Telephone: 919-489-7788
Fax: 919-489-2699
Email: f.burke.attorney@att.net

Corporations, Commercial Transactions and Real Estate.

(This Listing Continued)

FREDERICK A. BURKE, born New York, 1939; admitted to bar, 1964, New York and U.S. District Court, Western District of New York; 1970, U.S. Supreme Court; 1976, Ohio; 1979, Tennessee; 1980, U.S. District Court, Eastern District of Tennessee; 1984, North Carolina; 1992, U.S. District Court, Eastern, Middle and Western Districts of North Carolina. *Education:* Manhattan College; State University of New York at Buffalo (B.A., 1962; J.D., 1963). Private Law Practice, Buffalo, New York, 1964-1967. Secretary and House Counsel, Servotronics, Inc., Buffalo, New York, 1967-1975. Secretary and Corporate Counsel, North Electric Company, Galion, Ohio, 1975-1977. Vice President and General Counsel, ITT North Electric Company, Galion, Ohio, Johnson City, Tennessee and Cape Canaveral, Florida, 1977-1983. Vice President and Group General Counsel, ITT Telecom Products Corporation, Raleigh, North Carolina, 1983-1986. General Counsel, Alcatel N.A., Inc., Raleigh, North Carolina, 1987-1988. Of Counsel, Harlow, Evans & London, Research Triangle Park, North Carolina, 1989-1992. *Member:* Wake County, Durham County, North Carolina (Member Sections on: Business Law; Real Property Law) and American (Member, Business Law Section) Bar Associations; Computer Law Round Table. ***PRACTICE AREAS:*** Corporations; Commercial Transactions; Real Estate Law.

REPRESENTATIVE CLIENTS: ITT Automotive Group; Carnivore Preservation Trust; LaQunita Inns, Inc.; Bekaert Corporation; Praigg & Praigg, CPA's; Carolina Fiber Communications, Inc.; Feedback Incorporated (USA); Chatham Development Corporation; CaroTech, L.L.C.; Simulation Technologies, Inc.; Durham County Wildlife Club, Inc.; Journalistic, Inc.; RSVP Party Service, Inc.; American Craftsmen, Inc.
APPROVED ATTORNEY FOR: Investors Title Insurance Co.; Lawyers Title Insurance Corp.; Fidelity National Title Insurance Co.; Chicago Title Insurance Co.; Commonwealth Land Title Insurance Co.

HEIDI G. CHAPMAN, P.L.L.C.

DURHAM, NORTH CAROLINA

(See Chapel Hill)

Workers Compensation, Auto Accidents, Wrongful Death, Personal Injury, Social Security Disability.

CHARNS & CHARNS

123 ORANGE STREET
P.O. BOX 59
DURHAM, NORTH CAROLINA 27702
Telephone: 919-956-7564
Fax: 919-956-7409
Email: charnsandcharns@verizon.net
URL: http://www.charns-charnslaw.com

Personal Injury, Automobile Accidents, Wrongful Death, Criminal Law, Driving While Intoxicated, Drug Crimes, Felonies, Misdemeanors, Traffic Violations, Civil Rights, Police Misconduct, Freedom of Information, Public Records, Automobile Negligence, Motor Vehicle Accidents and Injuries, Plaintiff's Personal Injury, Information and Privacy, Civil Appeals, Criminal Appeals, Civil Liberties, Civil Rights Section 1983, Constitutional Law, First Amendment Law, Fourth Amendment Law, Wiretapping, Electronic Surveillance, Malicious Prosecution, Search and Seizure, Criminal Defense, Capital Offenses, Death Penalty, False Arrest, Excessive Use of Force, False Imprisonment, Police Brutality.

MEMBERS OF FIRM

M. ALEXANDER CHARNS, born Michigan, 1956; admitted to bar, 1982, North Carolina; U.S. District Court, Eastern, Middle and Western Districts of North Carolina; U.S. Court of Appeals, Fourth Circuit. *Education:* Michigan State University; University of California at Santa Barbara; University of California at Berkeley (B.A., 1978); University of North Carolina at Chapel Hill (J.D., 1982). Author: "Cloak and Gavel: FBI Wiretaps, Bugs, Informers and the Supreme Court," University. Illinois Press, 1992; articles or essays in The New York Times, The Washington Post and other publications. Former Member, Fourteenth Judicial District Grievance Committee. Member, National Writers Union. *Member:* North Carolina State Bar; National Association Criminal Defense Lawyers; North Carolina Association of Trial Lawyers. ***REPORTED CASES:*** E.g.s Brown v. Waddell, 50 F.3d 285 (4th Cir. 1995); Tucker v. Waddell, 83 F.3d 688 (4th Cir. 1996); Glenn-Robinson v. Acker, 538 S.E.2d 601 (N.C.App. 2000); N.C. v. Sanford Video & News, 553 S.E.2d 217 (N.C.App. 2001); N.C. v. Price, 611 S.E.2d 891 (N.C.App. 2005). ***Email:*** acharns@verizon.net

D. TUCKER CHARNS, born 1961; admitted to bar, 1989, North Carolina. *Education:* University of North Carolina at Chapel Hill (B.A. 1984; J.D., 1989). *Member:* North Carolina State Bar; North Carolina Academy of Trial Attorneys; Durham Criminal Defense Lawyer Association (Former President). ***Email:*** tuckercharns@verizon.net

COLEMAN, GLEDHILL, HARGRAVE & PEEK, P.C.

DURHAM, NORTH CAROLINA

(See Hillsborough)

General Civil and Criminal Trial Practice in all State and Federal Courts. Litigation, Negligence, Domestic, Real Estate, Corporate, Municipal and Probate Law, Commercial Transactions and Litigation.

WILLIAM J. COTTER, P.A.

2003 CHAPEL HILL ROAD
P.O. BOX 3507
DURHAM, NORTH CAROLINA 27702
Telephone: 919-489-0339
Fax: 919-683-3290
URL: http://www.williamjcotterlaw.com

Criminal Law, Family Law, Traffic Violations in State and Federal Courts. Personal Injury.

(This Listing Continued)

WILLIAM J. COTTER, P.A., Durham—Continued

WILLIAM J. COTTER, born Cambridge, Massachusetts, November 5, 1947; admitted to bar, 1979, North Carolina and U.S. District Court, Middle District of North Carolina; 1994, U.S. Court of Appeals, Fourth Circuit. *Education:* East Carolina University (B.S., 1976); Duke University (J.D., 1979). Arbitrator. *Member:* Durham County and North Carolina Bar Associations; North Carolina State Bar; North Carolina Academy of Trial Lawyers. [U.S. Army, Capt. Artillery, 82nd Airborne, 1st. Cavalry, 1st. Infantry, 1966-1972]. ***PRACTICE AREAS:*** Criminal Law; Domestic Relations; Traffic Violations; Family Law.

JAMES B. CRAVEN, III

Established in 1980

349 WEST MAIN STREET
P.O. BOX 1366
DURHAM, NORTH CAROLINA 27702
Telephone: 919-688-8295
Fax: 919-688-7832
Email: jbc64@mindspring.com

Federal and General Practice. International Law, Bankruptcy, Collections, Real Estate, Federal Criminal Law and Federal Appellate Practice, Federal Executive Clemency.

JAMES B. CRAVEN, III, born Portsmouth, Virginia, December 8, 1942; admitted to bar, 1967, North Carolina and U.S. District Court, Eastern District of North Carolina; 1968, U.S. Court of Appeals, 4th Circuit; 1969, U.S. District Court, Middle District of North Carolina; 1970, U.S. District Court, Western District of North Carolina; 1974, U.S. Supreme Court. *Education:* United States Naval Academy, University of North Carolina at Chapel Hill (A.B., 1964); Duke University (M.Div., 1981; J.D., 1967). Phi Alpha Delta. Visiting Professor of Law, University of North Carolina Law School, 1971-1981. Clinical Associate in Law, Duke University, 1973-1982. Law Clerk to Judge Oren R. Lewis, U.S. District Court, Eastern District of Virginia, 1967-1968. Trial Attorney, Civil Rights Division, U.S. Department of Justice, 1968-1969. Permanent Member, Judicial Conference of the Fourth Circuit. *Member:* North Carolina and American Bar Associations; North Carolina State Bar; American Law Institute (Life Member). [LCDR, JAGC, USNR (Ret.)]

REPRESENTATIVE CLIENTS: Baseball America, Inc.; The Coastal Plain League; North Carolina Mutual Life Insurance Co.; Blue Cross Blue Shield Credit Union; Joseph E. Seagram & Sons, Inc.; Atlanta Postal Credit Union; Mellon Mortgage Company; SouthTrust Mortgage Corp.
APPROVED ATTORNEY FOR: Commonwealth Land Title Insurance Co.
REFERENCE: First Union National Bank.

DANIELS DANIELS & VERDONIK, P.A.

DURHAM, NORTH CAROLINA

(See Research Triangle Park)

Business, Corporations, Venture Capital, Securities, Corporate Finance, Computers, Biotechnology, Telecommunications, Copyright, Trademark, Patent, Technology and Science, Intellectual Property, Management and Licensing, Domestic and International Taxation, Limited Liability Companies and Partnerships, Joint Ventures, International Trade and Investment, Immigration.

WILFRED F. DRAKE, P.C.

Established in 1982

1007 VICKERS AVENUE
DURHAM, NORTH CAROLINA 27707
Telephone: 919-683-8441
Email: wfd17@netzero.com
URL: http://www.lawyers.com/wdrakelaw

General Civil Practice. Estate Planning and Estate Administration.

WILFRED F. DRAKE, born Syracuse, New York, October 23, 1949; admitted to bar, 1978, Virginia; 1979, North Carolina; 1980, U.S. District Court, Middle District of North Carolina and U.S. Tax Court; 1982, U.S. Court of Appeals, Fourth Circuit and U.S. Claims Court. *Education:* Alfred University (B.A., 1971); College of William & Mary (J.D., 1978; M.L.&T., 1979). Pi Gamma Mu; Blue Key. Associate Editor, William & Mary Law Review, 1977-1978. Author: "Tax Status of Private Segregated Schools: The New Revenue Procedure," 20 William & Mary Law Review 463, 1979. Director, Legal Research & Writing Program, College of William & Mary, 1978-1979. *Member:* North Carolina Bar Association; North Carolina Academy of Trial Lawyers. [First Lt. Finance Corps, U.S. Army Reserve, 1971-1974]. ***PRACTICE AREAS:*** Trusts and Estates; Wills; Probate; Contested Wills; Personal Injury.

KENNETH J. DUKE

Established in 1984

100 EAST PARRISH STREET, SUITE 300 WEST
DURHAM, NORTH CAROLINA 27702
Telephone: 919-683-2175
Fax: 919-680-3500
Email: kennethduke.attorney@verizon.net
URL: http://www.lawyers.com/kennethduke

Workers Compensation, Traffic Violations, Driving While Intoxicated, Drivers License Suspension, Personal Injury.

FIRM PROFILE: Workers compensation, personal injury and traffic since 1984.

(This Listing Continued)

KENNETH J. DUKE, born Richmond, Virginia, November 13, 1957; admitted to bar, 1984, North Carolina and U.S. District Court, Middle and Eastern Districts of North Carolina and U.S. Court of Appeals, 4th Circuit. *Education:* Wake Forest University (B.A., 1980); Mercer University (J.D., 1983). *Member:* Durham County Bar Association; North Carolina State Bar; North Carolina Academy of Trial Lawyers (Member, Workers Compensation Section). ***LANGUAGES:*** Spanish. ***SPECIAL AGENCIES:*** N.C. Industrial Commission. ***PRACTICE AREAS:*** Workers Compensation; Traffic Violations; Personal Injury Law; Driving While Intoxicated; Drivers License Suspension.

Languages: Spanish and English.

REFERENCE: Bank of America.

EDWARDS & TRENKLE, PLLC

331 WEST MAIN STREET, SUITE 508
P.O. BOX 77
DURHAM, NORTH CAROLINA 27701-3232
Telephone: 919-688-9555
Fax: 919-683-5650
URL: http://www.edwardstrenkle.com

Pittsboro, North Carolina Office: 72 Hillsborough Street, PO Box 541, 27312. Telephone: 919-545-5626. Fax: 919-545-0991.

Criminal Law, Driving While Intoxicated (DWI), Drug Crimes, Felonies, Parole and Probation, Traffic Violations, Personal Injury, Auto Accidents, Dog Bites, Sexual Abuse, Wrongful Death.

MARK E. EDWARDS, born Mt. Airy, North Carolina, November 8, 1959; admitted to bar, 1985, Florida; 1989, North Carolina. *Education:* Surry Community College (A.A., 1980); University of North Carolina (B.A., 1982; J.D., 1985). (Board Certified Specialist in Federal Criminal Law and State Criminal Law, North Carolina State Board of Legal Specialization). ***PRACTICE AREAS:*** Criminal Law; Personal Injury. ***Email:*** medwardslaw@hotmail.com

ROBERT C. TRENKLE, born Baltimore, Maryland, May 6, 1960; admitted to bar, 1986, Florida; 1988, North Carolina; 2002, U.S. District Court, Eastern District of North Carolina. *Education:* University of Maryland (B.S., 1982); University of North Carolina at Chapel Hill (J.D., 1986). Faculty and Lecturer: Capital College, North Carolina Academy of Trial Lawyers, 1998-2001; NITA, "Representing the Accused in a Capital Trial," 1999, Chapel Hill, NC, 2001, Philadelphia, PA. Faculty: NITA "Litigation Skills," 2001-2001, Chapel Hill, NC; Florida Prosecutor and Public Defender College, 1990, Gainesville, FL. ***PRACTICE AREAS:*** Criminal Law; Personal Injury; Civil Practice; Driving While Intoxicated. ***Email:*** rctrenkle@earthlink.net

DIONNE R. GONDER, born Kalamazoo, Michigan, January 6, 1973; admitted to bar, 1997, North Carolina. *Education:* Duke University (B.A., Sociology, 1994); New York University (J.D., 1997).

EKSTRAND & EKSTRAND, LLP

811 NINTH STREET, SUITE 260
DURHAM, NORTH CAROLINA 27705
Telephone: 919-416-4590
Fax: 919-416-4591
URL: http://www.ninthstreetlaw.com
Email: sje@ninthstreetlaw.com
URL: http://www.ekstrand-law.com

Criminal Law, Driving While Intoxicated (DWI), Drug Crimes, Felonies, Misdemeanors, Traffic Violations, Personal Injury, Automobile Accidents, Wrongful Death, Medical Malpractice, Wills, Probate, Commercial Bankruptcy, Contracts, Legal Malpractice, Education.

ROBERT C. EKSTRAND, admitted to bar, 1998, Texas; 1999, North Carolina. *Education:* University of Maryland (B.A., 1992); Duke University School of Law (J.D., 1998). Phi Beta Kappa. Omicron Delta Kappa. Member, Moot Court Board. Recipient, Highest Academic Achievement Award, University of Maryland. Editor-in-Chief, Law & Contemporary Problems. Lecturing Fellow, Duke Law School, 1999. ***PRACTICE AREAS:*** Criminal Law.

SAMANTHA SPARKS EKSTRAND, born Columbia, South Carolina, July 26, 1974; admitted to bar, 2001, North Carolina and Massachusetts. *Education:* Dartmouth College (A.B., 1996); Duke University (M.A., History, 2001; J.D., 2001). ***PRACTICE AREAS:*** General Practice.

LAW OFFICE OF
JOHN C. FITZPATRICK, P.C.

116 W. MAIN STREET
DURHAM, NORTH CAROLINA 27701
Telephone: 919-683-9500
Fax: 919-683-8400
URL: http://www.johncfitzpatrick.com

DWI, Traffic, Criminal, Personal Injury.

JOHN C. FITZPATRICK, II, born Dunn, North Carolina, May 30, 1971; admitted to bar, 1996, North Carolina. *Education:* University of North Carolina at Chapel Hill (B.A, 1993; J.D., 1996). *Member:* Durham County Bar Association; 14th Judicial District; North Carolina Academy of Trial Lawyers.

LYNN FONTANA

1316 BROAD STREET
DURHAM, NORTH CAROLINA 27705
Telephone: 919-286-2500
Facsimile: 919-286-2544
Email: lyfontana@aol.com
URL: http://www.lawyers.com/lynnfontana

Plaintiff's Employment Law and Litigation including Discrimination, Wrongful Discharge, Employment Contracts and Separation Agreements.

LYNN FONTANA, born New Orleans, Louisiana, September 14, 1959; admitted to bar, 1987, North Carolina; 1988, U.S. District Court, Eastern District of North Carolina and U.S. Court of Appeals, Fourth Circuit; 1991, U.S. Supreme Court and U.S. District Court, Middle District of North Carolina; 1994, U.S. District Court, Western District of North Carolina. *Education:* University of North Carolina, Asheville (B.A., 1984); University of North Carolina at Chapel Hill (J.D., 1987). *Member:* Durham County, North Carolina (Member: Litigation Section; Labor and Employment Law Section Council, 1991-1995, 1998-2000; Chair, 2000-2001) and American Bar Associations; North Carolina Academy of Trial Lawyers; North Carolina Association of Women Attorneys (Member: Education Committee, 1989-1991; Chair, Nominating Committee, 1991-1992; Chair, Judicial Endorsement Committee, 1992-1996); American Civil Liberties Union-North Carolina (Member, Board of Directors, 1998—; Chair, Litigation Committee, 2001—). ***PRACTICE AREAS:*** Employment Law; Litigation; Professional Malpractice.

GLENN, MILLS & FISHER, P.A.

Established in 1980

SUITE 709, SOUTH BANK BUILDING
400 WEST MAIN STREET
P.O. DRAWER 3865
DURHAM, NORTH CAROLINA 27702-3865
Telephone: 919-683-2135
Fax: 919-688-9339
Email: GMF-Law.com
URL: http://www.gmf-law.com

General Civil Trial Practice in State and Federal Courts, Personal Injury, Wrongful Death, Professional Negligence, Commercial and Civil Rights Law and Employment Law.

ROBERT B. GLENN, JR., born Winston-Salem, North Carolina, January 30, 1949; admitted to bar, 1974, North Carolina and U.S. District Court, Middle, Western and Eastern Districts of North Carolina; 1984, U.S. Court of Appeals, Fourth Circuit. *Education:* Randolph-Macon College (B.A., 1971); University of North Carolina (J.D., 1974). Phi Beta Kappa. Adjunct Instructor of Law, North Carolina Central University Law School, 1985-1991. Instructor, National Institute of Trial Advocacy, 1986-1990. Senior Lecturer, Duke University School of Law, 1991—. Commissioner: Durham Housing Authority, 1985-1995, 1997—; Durham Open Space and Trails Commission, 2000—; Durham Bicycle and Pedestrian Commission, 2001—. Examiner, National Board of Trial Advocacy, 1985-1990. *Member:* North Carolina and American Bar Associations; North Carolina State Bar; North Carolina Academy of Trial Lawyers; The Association of Trial Lawyers of America; American Board of Trial Advocates. (Certified as a Civil Trial Advocacy Specialist by the National Board of Trial Advocacy). ***PRACTICE AREAS:*** Personal Injury; Medical Malpractice; Commercial Litigation. ***Email:*** rglenn@gmf-law.com

WILLIAM S. MILLS, born Roanoke, Virginia, November 12, 1952; admitted to bar, 1979, North Carolina and U.S. District Court, Middle and Eastern Districts of North Carolina. *Education:* University of North Carolina (B.A., 1975; J.D., with honors, 1979). Phi Beta Kappa. Member, University of North Carolina Law Review, 1977-1978. Continuing Legal Education Speaker, North Carolina Academy of Trial Lawyers, 1986—. Instructor, National Institute for Trial Advocacy, 1985-1988. Adjunct Professor, Trial Advocacy, University of North Carolina, Chapel Hill School of Law, 1989—. Member: City of Durham Board of Adjustments, 1985-1988; Board of Directors, Triangle Land Conservancy, 1995-1997. Commissioner, Raleigh Durham International Airport Authority, 1991-1993. Selected to be in "The Best Lawyers in America", 2003-2006; Named to North Carolina's Legal Elite by "Business North Carolina" in 2004. *Member:* 14th Judicial District (President, 1987-1988; Founding Chairman, Grievance Committee, 1989-1990), Bar Association; North Carolina State Bar; The Association of Trial Lawyers of America; American Board of Trial Advocates; North Carolina Academy of Trial Lawyers (President, 1999-2000). (Certified as a Civil Trial Advocacy Specialist by the National Board of Trial Advocacy). ***PRACTICE AREAS:*** Personal Injury; Medical Negligence; Commercial Torts. ***Email:*** wmills@gmf-law.com

STEWART W. FISHER, born Philadelphia, Pennsylvania, March 5, 1950; admitted to bar, 1982, North Carolina, U.S. District Court, Middle, Western and Eastern Districts of North Carolina, U.S. Court of Appeals, Fourth Circuit and U.S. Supreme Court. *Education:* Duke University (B.A., magna cum laude, 1972); Yale University (M.A., 1973); University of North Carolina (J.D., with honors, 1982). Phi Beta Kappa. Notes and Comment Editor, North Carolina Journal of International Law and Commercial Regulation, 1981-1982. Continuing Legal Education Speaker: North Carolina Academy of Trial Lawyers, 1991-1998; North Carolina Bar Association, 1995. Instructor, National Institute of Trial Advocacy, Depositions, 1990-2005. Named to North Carolina's Legal Elite by "Business North Carolina" in 2004. *Member:* North Carolina and American Bar Associations; North Carolina State Bar; North Carolina Academy of Trial Lawyers; The Association of Trial Lawyers of America; National Employment Lawyers Association. (Certified as a Civil Trial Advocacy Specialist by the National Board of Trial Advocacy). ***PRACTICE AREAS:*** Personal Injury; Employment Law; Civil Rights. ***Email:*** sfisher@gmf-law.com

CARLOS E. MAHONEY, born Nashville, Tennessee, June 10, 1974; admitted to bar, 1999, North Carolina and U.S. District Court, Middle District of North Carolina. *Education:* University of North Carolina at Chapel Hill (B.A., 1996; J.D., 1999). Phi Beta Kappa. Golden Key Honor Society. *Member:* Durham and North Carolina Bar Associations; North Carolina State Bar; North Carolina Academy of Trial Lawyers; The Association of Trial Lawyers of America; North Carolina Occupation Safety and Health Coalition (Member, Board of Directors); 14th Judicial District (Member, Grievance Committee). ***PRACTICE AREAS:*** Personal Injury; Civil Rights; Estate Litigation. ***Email:*** cmahoney@gmf-law.com

LAW OFFICE OF DOROTHY HAIRSTON

400 WEST MAIN STREET, SUITE 611
DURHAM, NORTH CAROLINA 27701
Telephone: 919-682-3200
Fax: 919-682-3422
Email: dhairston21@msn.com
URL: http://www.dorothyhairstonlaw.com

Family Law, Criminal Law, Traffic Violations, Personal Injury, Medical Malpractice, Workers Compensation, Real Estate, Business, Military Law, Bankruptcy.

DOROTHY HAIRSTON, born Lawton, Oklahoma, May 19, 1977; admitted to bar, 2003, North Carolina. *Education:* North Carolina Central University (B.A., 1999); North Carolina Central University School of Law (J.D., 2002). *Member:* North Carolina Bar Association; North Carolina State Bar; North Carolina Academy of Trial Lawyers; George H. White Bar Association; Durham County Family Bar.

THEODORE R. HARPER

Established in 2002

PMB 336
6409 FAYETTEVILLE ROAD, SUITE 120
DURHAM, NORTH CAROLINA 27713
Telephone: 919-544-1137
Fax: 919-544-1139
Email: ted@trianglelegalsolutions.com
URL: http://www.trianglelegalsolutions.com

Technology Contracts, Software Licensing, Mergers and Acquisitions, Business Start-Ups, Incorporation, Venture Capital, Strategic Alliances, E-commerce, Internet Licensing, Intellectual Property, Copyrights, Joint Ventures, Distribution Agreements.

FIRM PROFILE: The firm represents clients involved in the commercialization of advanced technologies on national and international levels. Clients range from start-ups to mid-sized public companies in semiconductor, software, internet, communications, and pharmaceutical industries.

THEODORE R. HARPER, born Seattle, Washington, 1951; admitted to bar, 1979, California (inactive); 1994, North Carolina; registered to practice before U.S. Patent and Trademark Office. *Education:* University of Colorado, Boulder (B.A., 1973); University of California, Berkeley (M.B.A., 1979); Boalt Hall School of Law (J.D., 1979). Sigma Pi Sigma. Attorney, 1979-1990 and Partner, 1986-1990, Graham & James in Los Angeles and Singapore. Associate General Counsel, Seer Technologies, Inc., 1992-1995. Of Counsel 1995-1997, Kilpatrick Stockton, and Partner 1998-2002. Chief Operating Officer, Radio Satellite Corp., 1990-1992. Member, Board of Directors, NC Electronics and Information Technologies Association, 1998-2001. Triangle Legal Solutions, 2002—.

HAYWOOD, DENNY & MILLER, L.L.P.

Established in 1955

3511 SHANNON ROAD
SUITE 140
DURHAM, NORTH CAROLINA 27707
Telephone: 919-403-0000
Fax: 919-403-0001
Email: hdmllp@hdmllp.com
Mailing Address: P.O. Box 51429, Durham, NC 27717

General Civil, Trial and Appellate Practice in State and Federal Courts. Insurance, Corporations, Bankruptcy, Government Relations and Probate Law.

FIRM PROFILE: The firm was established in 1955 with a primary emphasis on civil litigation and insurance defense throughout the state of North Carolina. The firm also has a large corporate practice, representing both small and large businesses, in addition to estate planning, personal injury, bankruptcy, surety matters, government relations, collections and media representation.

MEMBERS OF FIRM

EGBERT L. HAYWOOD (1911-1985)

EMERY B. DENNY, JR. (1924-1982)

GEORGE W. MILLER, JR., born Spencer, North Carolina, May 14, 1930; admitted to bar, 1957, North Carolina; U.S. Court of Appeals, Fourth Circuit and U.S. Supreme Court. *Education:* University of North Carolina (B.S., 1954; LL.B., 1957). Phi Alpha Delta. Member, North Carolina General Assembly, 1971-2000. Member, Board of Visitors, North Carolina Central University School of Law. Member: Board of Visitors, University of North Carolina; Board of Trustees, Methodist College. *Member:* North Carolina and American Bar Associations; The North Carolina State Bar; International Association of Defense Counsel; The Defense Research Institute, Inc.; American College of Trial Lawyers. ***PRACTICE AREAS:*** Litigation; Corporate Law; Government Relations; Surety; Media Law. ***Email:*** gwmjr@hdmllp.com

KEVIN W. BUTTERFIELD, born Wareham, Massachusetts, January 5, 1957; admitted to bar, 1986, North Carolina. *Education:* Kalamazoo College (B.A., cum laude, 1979);

(This Listing Continued)

HAYWOOD, DENNY & MILLER, L.L.P., Durham—Continued

University of Minnesota (M.A., Public Affairs, 1981); University of North Carolina (J.D., 1986). Member, Holderness Moot Court, 1985-1986. *Member:* Durham County, North Carolina and American Bar Associations; North Carolina State Bar; Defense Research Institute, Inc.; North Carolina Association of Defense Attorneys. ***PRACTICE AREAS:*** Litigation; General Practice; Insurance Defense; Bankruptcy; Debtor and Creditor. ***Email:*** kwbutterfield@hdmllp.com

ROBERT E. LEVIN, born Evansville, Indiana, August 28, 1961; admitted to bar, 1986, North Carolina. *Education:* North Carolina State University (B.A., cum laude with honors, 1983); University of North Carolina at Chapel Hill (J.D., 1986). *Member:* Durham County and North Carolina Bar Associations; North Carolina Association of Defense Attorneys; Defense Research Institute. ***PRACTICE AREAS:*** Litigation; Insurance Defense; General Practice. ***Email:*** rlevin@hdmllp.com

JOHN R. KINCAID, born Bristol, Tennessee, July 8, 1965; admitted to bar, 1991, North Carolina. *Education:* University of North Carolina at Chapel Hill (B.A., 1987; J.D., with honors, 1991). *Member:* Durham County, North Carolina and American Bar Associations. ***PRACTICE AREAS:*** Litigation; Insurance Defense; Coverage Issues. ***Email:*** jrk@hdmllp.com

GEORGE W. MILLER, III, born Durham, North Carolina, June 9, 1965; admitted to bar, 1996, North Carolina and U.S. District Court, Eastern Western and Middle Districts of North Carolina. *Education:* University of North Carolina (B.A., 1990); Campbell University (J.D., 1996). Phi Alpha Delta. Legislative Aide to U.S. Senator, Terry Sanford, 1990-1993. Member, Board of Trustees, North Carolina Central University. *Member:* Durham County, North Carolina and American Bar Associations; North Carolina Association of Defense Attorneys; Defense Research Institute. ***PRACTICE AREAS:*** Civil Practice; Litigation; Insurance Defense; Government Relations; Business Planning. ***Email:*** gwm3@hdmllp.com

REPRESENTATIVE CLIENTS: State Farm Mutual Insurance Cos.; Infinity Insurance Company; MetLife Auto and Home; Peerless Insurance Co.; Reliance National; Risk Management Planning Group Inc.; Jefferson Pilot Life Insurance Co.; Pepsi-Cola Bottling Co. of Roxboro; North Carolina Farm Bureau Ins.; Jefferson Ins.; Carolina Canners, Inc.; Carolina Packaging, Inc.; Pennsylvania National Insurance Co.; Blue Cross-Blue Shield of N.C.; Underwriters Adjusting, Co.; Lancer Management Co.; Lititz Mutual Ins. Co.; Deere and Company; TIAACREF; Budget Rent-A-Car, Corp.; Mainquad Broadcasting, Inc.; International Fidelity Insurance Co.; The Durham Herald Co., Inc.; Zurich American Ins. Co.; Prime Inc. Trucking Co.; Sterling Financial, Inc.; Brotherhood Mutual Insurance Company; AT & T Corporation; Liberty Mutual Group; Tyco International; American Red Cross.
APPROVED ATTORNEYS: Lawyers Title Insurance Corp.; Chicago Title Insurance Co.; Investors Title Insurance Co.; Commonwealth Land Title Insurance Co.

HEDRICK MURRAY & CHEEK PLLC

3511 SHANNON ROAD, SUITE 200
DURHAM, NORTH CAROLINA 27707
Telephone: 919-419-3300
Telecopier: 919-419-1600
Email: name@hmclegal.com
URL: http://www.hmclegal.com

Mailing Address: P.O. Box 52394, Durham, NC 27717-2394

General Practice in all State and Federal Courts. Litigation, Real Estate, Land Use and Development Law, Insurance, Labor and Employment, Commercial Transactions, Probate.

JAMES T. HEDRICK, born Durham, North Carolina, March 8, 1928; admitted to bar, 1953, North Carolina and U.S. District Court, Middle District of North Carolina; 1954, U.S. Court of Military Appeals. *Education:* Washington & Lee University (B.A., 1950); University of North Carolina (J.D., 1953). Phi Delta Phi. *Member:* Durham County and North Carolina Bar Associations; The North Carolina State Bar. Fellow, The American College of Trust and Estate Counsel. [Captain, U.S. Army, J.A.G.C., active duty, 1954-1957]. ***PRACTICE AREAS:*** Commercial Real Estate Law; Zoning, Planning and Land Use; Probate. ***Email:*** jhedrick@hmclegal.com

JOSIAH S. MURRAY, III, born Durham, North Carolina, July 11, 1935; admitted to bar, 1962, North Carolina and U.S. District Court, Middle District of North Carolina; 1964, U.S. District Court, Eastern District of North Carolina; 1967, U.S. Court of Appeals, Fourth Circuit; 1978, U.S. Supreme Court; 1997, U.S. District Court, Western District of North Carolina. *Education:* University of North Carolina (B.S., 1957); Harvard University (LL.B., 1961). Phi Beta Kappa; Beta Gamma Sigma. Senior Vice President and General Counsel, Liggett Group Inc., 1983-1996. *Member:* Durham County and North Carolina Bar Associations; The North Carolina State Bar. ***PRACTICE AREAS:*** General Civil Litigation; Complex Commercial Litigation; Trust Litigation; Estate Litigation; Personal Injury; Commercial Transactions. ***Email:*** jmurray@hmclegal.com

LEWIS A. CHEEK, born Durham, North Carolina, May 9, 1951; admitted to bar, 1976, North Carolina; 1977, U.S. District Court, Middle District of North Carolina; 1980, U.S. District Court, Eastern District of North Carolina; 1983, U.S. Court of Appeals, Fourth Circuit; 1996, U.S. Supreme Court; 2003, U.S. District Court, Western District of North Carolina. *Education:* Wake Forest University (B.A., magna cum laude, 1973; J.D., 1976). Phi Beta Kappa. North Carolina Association of Defense Attorneys; International Association of Defense Attorneys; American Board of Trial Advocates. Member: Durham City Council, 1999-2003; Durham County Board of County Commissioners, 2004—. *Member:* Durham County, North Carolina and American Bar Associations; The North Carolina State Bar. ***PRACTICE AREAS:*** Litigation. ***Email:*** lcheek@hmclegal.com

DAVID S. KENNETT, born Asheville, North Carolina, December 15, 1957; admitted to bar, 1983, North Carolina and U.S. District Court, Middle District of North Carolina. *Education:* University of North Carolina (B.S., 1980; J.D., 1983). Phi Beta Kappa. *Member:* Durham County and North Carolina Bar Associations; The North Carolina State Bar. ***PRACTICE AREAS:*** Real Estate Law; General Business Law. ***Email:*** dkennett@hmclegal.com

JOHN C. ROGERS, III, born Atlanta, Georgia, August 29, 1972; admitted to bar, 1998, North Carolina; 1999, U.S. District Court, Eastern District of North Carolina; 2000,

(This Listing Continued)

U.S. District Court, Middle District of North Carolina. *Education:* Davidson College (B.A., cum laude, 1995); Washington and Lee University School of Law (J.D., cum laude, 1998). Phi Beta Kappa; Omicron Delta Kappa. Recipient, Aldersonian of the Year Award. *Member:* Durham County and North Carolina Bar Associations; The North Carolina State Bar. ***PRACTICE AREAS:*** Litigation. ***Email:*** jrogers@hmclegal.com

---

MARTHA E. SOULE, born Pinehurst, North Carolina, December 17, 1976; admitted to bar, 2003, North Carolina and U.S. District Court, Eastern District of North Carolina. *Education:* Wake Forest University (B.S., cum laude, 1999); Boston University School of Law (J.D., with honors in Litigation and Dispute Resolution, 2003). Member, International Law Journal. *Member:* Durham County, North Carolina and American Bar Associations; North Carolina State Bar; North Carolina Association of Women Attorneys. ***PRACTICE AREAS:*** Litigation. ***Email:*** msoule@hmclegal.com

REPRESENTATIVE CLIENTS: Wachovia Bank, N.A.; Harrington Bank; Cardinal State Bank; Liggett Group Inc.; Research Triangle Foundation of North Carolina; AIG-TS; Raleigh-Durham Airport Authority; Home Depot; Duke Energy; SunTrust; Durham Technical Community College; Durham Academy; The Hill Center; The National Humanities Center.

HIGGINS, FRANKSTONE, GRAVES & MORRIS, P.A.

DURHAM, NORTH CAROLINA

(See Chapel Hill)

Estate Planning, Probate, Corporate, Real Estate, Civil Litigation, Taxation and General Business Law.

HAYES HOFLER, P.A.

1007 VICKERS AVENUE
DURHAM, NORTH CAROLINA 27707-1355
Telephone: 919-682-9663
Fax: 919-682-2016
URL: http://www.lawyers.com/hha

Business and Commercial, Construetion, Divorce, Family, Legal Malpractice, Litigation and Appeals, Medical Malpractice, Insurance, Personal Injury, Products Liability, Professional Malpractice.

R. HAYES HOFLER, born Washington, D.C., August 7, 1946; admitted to bar, 1974, North Carolina and U.S. Court of Appeals, Fourth Circuit; 1975, U.S. District Courts, Middle and Eastern Districts of North Carolina; 1979, U.S. Supreme Court; 1993, U.S. District Court, Western District of North Carolina. *Education:* Wake Forest University (B.A., cum laude, 1968); University of Virginia (J.D., 1974). *Member:* North Carolina Bar Association; North Carolina Academy of Trial Lawyers; The Association of Trial Lawyers of America. (Board Certified Civil Trial Advocate, National Board of Trial Advocacy, 1993). ***REPORTED CASES:*** Hart v. Warren, 46 N.C. App. 672, 266 S.E. 2d 53, rev. denied, 301 N.C. (1980); D.W. Ward Const. Co., Inc. v. Adams, 323 N.C. 621, 374 S.E.2d 375 (N.C. 1988); Friend - Novorska v. Novorska, 131 N.C. App. 867, 509 S.E. 2d 460 (N.C. App. 1998). ***PRACTICE AREAS:*** Business Law; Commercial Law; Construction Law; Divorce; Family Law; Legal Malpractice; Litigation; Appellate Practice; Medical Malpractice; Personal Injury; Products Liability; Professional Malpractice. ***Email:*** hayeshofler@mindspring.com

OF COUNSEL

DANIEL B. HILL, born Sioux City, Iowa, November 26, 1941; admitted to bar, 1992, North Carolina. *Education:* Ohio University (B.B.A., cum laude, 1964); Purdue University (Ph.D., Economics, 1971); University of North Carolina (J.D., with honors, 1992). Order of the Coif. Staff Member, North Carolina Law Review, 1990-1991 (Note Published). Faculty Member: Pennsylvania State University 1972-1979; University of Alabama at Birmingham, 1979-1989. Certified Mediator: Superior Court, Workers Compensation, Family Financial Issues. *Member:* Durham County and North Carolina (Member, Family Law Section; Dispute Settlement Section) Bar Associations. ***PRACTICE AREAS:*** Mediation; Family Law; Equitable Distribution; Personal Injury. ***Email:*** danbhill@mindspring.com

C. CONNOR CROOK, born Orangeburg, South Carolina; admitted to bar, 1999, South Carolina; 2003, North Carolina; 2004, U.S. District Court, Eastern District of North Carolina. *Education:* College of Charleston (B.A., 1996); University of Charlottesville (J.D., 1999). ***PRACTICE AREAS:*** Family Law; Domestic Relations; Criminal Law; Contracts; Personal Injury. ***Email:*** connor@crooklawoffice.com

HOLLOWELL LAW OFFICES, P.A.

DURHAM, NORTH CAROLINA

(See Cary)

Health Care Law, Administrative Law, Corporate Law, Business Law, Employment, Governmental Estate Planning and Collection.

HOWARD, STALLINGS, FROM & HUTSON, P.A.

DURHAM, NORTH CAROLINA

(See Raleigh)

General, Civil and Commercial Litigation, Business Law, Commercial Real Estate, Taxation, Employment Law, Computer Law, Estate Planning and Administration, Bankruptcy Law, Loan Structuring and Workouts, Intellectual Property Law, Personal Injury.

HUTSON HUGHES & POWELL, P.A.

SUITE 1500 DURHAM CENTRE
300 WEST MORGAN STREET
P.O. DRAWER 2252-A
DURHAM, NORTH CAROLINA 27702
Telephone: 919-683-1561
FAX: 919-683-1276

General Civil Practice, Bankruptcy, Reorganization, Corporate, Commercial Real Estate, Commercial Litigation, Estate Planning and Probate. Trials in all State and Federal Courts.

RICHARD M. HUTSON, II, born Bay Shore, New York, June 19, 1940; admitted to bar, 1964, North Carolina. *Education:* University of North Carolina (A.B., 1961); Wake Forest University (LL.B., 1964). Phi Delta Phi. Law Clerk to Federal Judge Edwin M. Stanley, Middle District of North Carolina, 1964-1965. U.S. Magistrate (Part-time), 1968-1976. President, National Association of Chapter 13 Trustees, 1979-1980. Project Director, North Carolina Bankruptcy Practice Manual, 1987. Member, Bankruptcy Specialization Committee, Board of Legal Specialization, 1989-1995. Fellow, American College of Bankruptcy. *Member:* Durham County (President, 1990-1991) and North Carolina (Chairman, Bankruptcy Section, 1980-1981) Bar Associations; North Carolina State Bar. (Board Certified Specialist in Bankruptcy Law, North Carolina State Board of Legal Specialization). ***PRACTICE AREAS:*** Bankruptcy (Debtor & Creditor) Law. ***Email:*** hutson@hhplaw.com

JAMES H. HUGHES, born Sutton, West Virginia, September 16, 1950; admitted to bar, 1978, North Carolina. *Education:* East Carolina University (B.A., 1972); North Carolina Central University (J.D., magna cum laude, 1978). Executive Editor, North Carolina Central University Law Journal, 1978. Certified Superior Court Mediator. *Member:* Durham County Bar Association (Secretary/Director, 1992-1993), North Carolina Bar Association (Chair, Law Practice Management Section Council, 1994-1995; Chair, Membership Services Committee, 2002—). ***PRACTICE AREAS:*** Litigation; Mediation. ***Email:*** jhhughes@mindspring.com

STEPHANIE C. POWELL, born York, Pennsylvania, July 31, 1948; admitted to bar, 1984, North Carolina. *Education:* West Virginia University (B.S., with high honors, 1970); University of North Carolina (J.D., with honors, 1984). Order of the Coif. Staff Member, North Carolina Law Review, 1982-1983. *Member:* North Carolina State Bar (Member, Sections on: Business Law; Real Property Law). ***PRACTICE AREAS:*** Commercial Real Estate Law; Corporate Law; Business Law. ***Email:*** powell@hhplaw.com

---

WILLIAM A. HATCH, born Middletown, New York, February 24, 1961; admitted to bar, 1994, North Carolina. *Education:* East Stroudsburg University (B.S., 1983); Ohio State University (M.A., 1984); North Carolina Central University (J.D., 1994). *Member:* North Carolina Bar Association (Member, Sections on: Labor and Employment Law; Education Law); North Carolina State Bar. ***PRACTICE AREAS:*** Employment Law; Special Education. ***Email:*** hatch@hhplaw.com

APPROVED ATTORNEYS FOR: Lawyers Title Insurance Corp.; Investors Title Insurance Co.; Chicago Title Insurance Co.; Commonwealth Title Insurance Co.

HYMAN, PHELPS & McNAMARA, P.C.

Established in 2001

4819 EMPEROR BOULEVARD, SUITE 400
DURHAM, NORTH CAROLINA 27703
Telephone: 919-313-4750
Fax: 919-313-4751
URL: http://www.hpm.com

Irvine, California Office: Hyman, Phelps & McNamara. 2603 Main Street, Suite 760. Telephone: 949-553-7400. Fax: 949-553-7433.
Washington, D.C. Office: Hyman, Phelps & McNamara, P.C. 700 Thirteenth Street, N.W., Suite 1200. Telephone: 202-737-5600. Fax: 202-737-9329.

Practice before all Courts, Government Agencies and International Regulatory Authorities involving Foods, Drugs, Cosmetics, Medical Devices, Biologics, Pesticides, Controlled Substances and Consumer Products.

(For Complete Biographical Data on all Personnel, see Professional Biographies at Washington, D.C.)

JENKINS, WILSON & TAYLOR, P.A.

Established in 1984

UNIVERSITY TOWER, SUITE 1400
3100 TOWER BOULEVARD
DURHAM, NORTH CAROLINA 27707
Telephone: 919-493-8000
Fax: 919-419-0383
URL: http://www.jenkinswilsontaylor.com

Raleigh, North Carolina Office: NCSU Centennial Campus, Suite 101, Venture II, 920 Main Campus Drive, 27606. Telephone: 919-424-3710. Fax: 919-424-3711.

Patent, Trademark and Copyright Law.

FIRM PROFILE: The firm is a specialized law practice with over two decades of experience providing intellectual property services to clients with respect to patent, trademark, copyright, and unfair competition law. The firm assists clients in recognizing, defining and safeguarding intellectual property and acting to preserve that property for full commercial exploitation.

(This Listing Continued)

Serving U.S. and foreign clients in intellectual property matters, the firm has a client base that is diverse and includes large corporations and research universities as well as small businesses. A primary objective of the firm is to provide high-quality legal services in a cost-efficient and personal manner. The firm is listed in the Bar Register of Preeminent Lawyers.

RICHARD E. JENKINS, born Newport News, Virginia, January 12, 1946; admitted to bar, 1975, North Carolina; 1976, Virginia; 1977, U.S. District Court, Western District of North Carolina; 1984, U.S. District Court, Middle District of North Carolina; registered to practice before U.S. Patent and Trademark Office. *Education:* North Carolina State University (B.S., with honors, 1968); University of North Carolina (J.D., 1975). Phi Kappa Phi. Adjunct Lecturer, 1985-1989 and Adjunct Associate Professor, 1989—, Duke University. Adjunct Assistant Professor, North Carolina State University, 1992-1996. Member: Board of Directors, University of North Carolina School of Law Alumni Association, 1991-1994; Board of Trustees (appointed by Governor James G. Martin), North Carolina Central University, 1992-1995; Board of Trustees, Peace College, 2002—; Board of Directors, North Carolina State Foundation, 2002—. *Member:* North Carolina (Member: Patents, Trademarks and Copyrights Committee, 1979-1985; Intellectual Property Law Section, 1986—) and American (Member, Patent, Trademark and Copyright Law Section, 1975—) Bar Associations; Virginia State Bar; North Carolina State Bar; Carolina Patent, Trademark and Copyright Law Association (Co-Founder; Treasurer, 1979-1984); American Intellectual Property Law Association; Association of University Technology Managers. ***PRACTICE AREAS:*** Patents; Trademarks; Copyrights. ***Email:*** rjenkins@jenkinswilsontaylor.com

JEFFREY L. WILSON, born Dillon, South Carolina, February 18, 1965; admitted to bar, 1990, North Carolina and South Carolina; 1992, U.S. Court of Appeals, Federal Circuit; 1994, U.S. Court of Appeals, Fourth Circuit; 1995, U.S. District Court, District of South Carolina; 2000, U.S. District Court, Middle and Eastern Districts of North Carolina; registered to practice before U.S. Patent and Trademark Office. *Education:* University of North Carolina (B.A., Biology, 1987); Campbell University (J.D., 1990). *Member:* North Carolina (Member, Intellectual Property Law Section) and American (Member, Patent, Trademark and Copyright Law Section) Bar Associations; South Carolina Bar; American Intellectual Property Law Association; Carolina Patent, Trademark and Copyright Law Association (Board of Managers, 1992-1994; President, 1998-1999); Association of University Technology Managers. ***PRACTICE AREAS:*** Patents; Trademarks; Copyrights. ***Email:*** jwilson@jenkinswilsontaylor.com

ARLES A. TAYLOR, JR., born Pinehurst, North Carolina, September 5, 1968; admitted to bar, 1994, Tennessee; 1998, North Carolina; 2000, U.S. District Court, Middle and Eastern Districts of North Carolina; registered to practice before the U.S. Patent and Trademark Office. *Education:* North Carolina State University (B.S., Biochemistry, B.A., Chemistry, summa cum laude, 1990); University of North Carolina (J.D., 1994). Phi Kappa Phi. Research Assistant, NIEHS (NIH), 1990-1991. *Member:* North Carolina, Tennessee and American Bar Associations; American Intellectual Property Law Association; Carolina Patent, Trademark & Copyright Law Association; Association of University Technology Managers. ***PRACTICE AREAS:*** Patents; Trademarks; Copyrights. ***Email:*** ataylor@jenkinswilsontaylor.com

GREGORY A. HUNT, born Charlotte, North Carolina, October 19, 1969; admitted to bar, 1996, North Carolina; 1997, District of Columbia; U.S. Court of Appeals for the Federal Circuit; registered to practice before U.S. Patent and Trademark Office. *Education:* North Carolina State University (B.S.E.E., summa cum laude, 1993; M.S., Computer Networking, 2002); University of North Carolina School of Law (J.D., with honors, 1996). Tau Beta Pi; Phi Alpha Delta. Recipient, American Jurisprudence Award. *Member:* American Bar Association; Carolina Patent Trademark and Copyright Law Association; American Intellectual Property Law Association; Association of University Technology Managers; Institute of Electrical and Electronics Engineers. ***PRACTICE AREAS:*** Patents; Trademarks; Copyrights. ***Email:*** ghunt@jenkinswilsontaylor.com

---

BENTLEY J. OLIVE, born Raleigh, North Carolina, March 16, 1975; admitted to bar, 2001, North Carolina; registered to practice before U.S. Patent and Trademark Office. *Education:* North Carolina State University (B.S., Electrical Engineering; B.S., Computer Engineering, magna cum laude, 1997); University of North Carolina School of Law (J.D., 2000). *Member:* American Bar Association; American Intellectual Property Law Association; Carolina Patent, Trademark and Copyright Law Association. ***PRACTICE AREAS:*** Patents; Trademarks; Copyrights. ***Email:*** bolive@jenkinswilsontaylor.com

E. ERIC MILLS, born Raleigh, North Carolina, June 20, 1970; admitted to bar, 2001, North Carolina; registered to practice before U.S. Patent and Trademark Office. *Education:* North Carolina State University (B.S., Civil Engineering; B.S., Environmental Engineering, cum laude, 1993; M.C.E., Civil Engineering, 1998); University of North Carolina (J.D., 2001). *Member:* American Bar Association; American Intellectual Law Association; Carolina Patent Trademark and Copyright Law Association; American Society of Civil Engineers. ***PRACTICE AREAS:*** Patents; Trademarks; Copyrights. ***Email:*** emills@jenkinswilsontaylor.com

CHRISTOPHER P. PERKINS, PH.D., born Tenafly, New Jersey, August 23, 1963; admitted to bar, 2001, California; registered to practice before U.S. Patent and Trademark Office (Not admitted in North Carolina). *Education:* Swarthmore College (B.A., Biology, 1985); Columbia University (M.S., 1991; Ph.D., Genetics and Development, 1993); University of Southern California (J.D., 2001). *Member:* State Bar of California; American Bar Association; American Intellectual Property Law Association. ***PRACTICE AREAS:*** Patents; Trademarks; Copyrights. ***Email:*** cperkins@jenkinswilsontaylor.com

JAMES DALY IV, PH.D., born Dearborn, Michigan, September 2, 1968; admitted to bar, 2001, Kentucky; registered to practice before the U.S. Patent and Trademark Office (Not admitted in North Carolina). *Education:* Bellarmine College (B.A., Biology, 1991); University of Louisville, School of Medicine (Ph.D., Microbiology and Immunology, 1998); University of Louisville (J.D., cum laude, 2001). *Member:* Louisville, Kentucky and American Bar Associations; American Association for the Advancement of Science; American Intellectual Property Law Association. ***PRACTICE AREAS:*** Patents; Trademarks; Copyrights. ***Email:*** jdaly@jenkinswilsontaylor.com

(This Listing Continued)

JENKINS, WILSON & TAYLOR, P.A., Durham—Continued

JEFFREY W. CHILDERS, Ph.D., born Owensboro, Kentucky, July 25, 1958; admitted to bar, 2003, North Carolina. *Education:* West Virginia University (B.S., Chemistry, 1980); Duke University (Ph.D., 1985); University of North Carolina at Chapel Hill (J.D., with honors, 2003). Law Review, Articles Editor. *Member:* North Carolina State Bar; North Carolina Bar Association; American Intellectual Property Law Association. ***PRACTICE AREAS:*** Patents; Trademarks; Copyrights. ***Email:*** jchilders@jenkinswilsontaylor.com

P. ASHLEY DARDEN, born Wilmington, North Carolina, August 13, 1974; admitted to bar, 2003, North Carolina. *Education:* North Carolina State University (B.A., Chemistry, 1997; B.S., Biochemistry, 1997; M.S., Biochemistry, 2004); Campbell University (J.D., 2003). *Member:* North Carolina State Bar. ***PRACTICE AREAS:*** Patents; Patent Applications; Patent Litigation; Patent Licensing. ***Email:*** adarden@jenkinswilsontaylor.com

REPRESENTATIVE CLIENTS: Böwe Bell and Howell Mail Co.; Duke University; Freudenberg Spunweb Co.; GlaxoSmithKline, Inc.; Huesker, Inc.; North Carolina State University; Sumitomo Electric Lightwave Corp.; The University of North Carolina at Chapel Hill; Vanderbilt University.

JOHNSON, HEARN, VINEGAR, GEE & GLASS, PLLC

Established in 1955

GENERATION PLAZA
SUITE 200
1822 N.C. HIGHWAY 54 EAST
DURHAM, NORTH CAROLINA 27713
Telephone: 919-544-3302
Fax: 919-544-5920
Email: jhvgg@jhvgglaw.com

Raleigh, North Carolina Office: Two Hannover Square, 434 Fayetteville Street Mall, Suite 2200, P.O. Box 1776, 27602. Telephone: 919-743-2200. Fax: 919-743-2201. Email: jhvgm@jhvgmlaw.com

Civil trial and appellate practice before all state and federal courts and administrative agencies, administrative law, including occupational licensing, alternative dispute resolution, automobile dealer law, business and corporate law, franchise law, government relations, including representation before the General Assembly and regulatory agencies, insurance insolvency, state and local taxation, trade association law, wills, trusts and estates and unfair competition.

RICHARD J. VINEGAR

REPRESENTATIVE CLIENTS: Anderson Automotive Investments, Inc. d/b/a Fred Anderson Toyota; Asbury Villanova, LLC; Capital Associated Industries, Inc.; Carolina Power & Light Company; Carolina/Virginia Dairy Products Association, Inc.; David O'Neal Chrysler Jeep/ Eagle; Eckerd Drugs; Fred Anderson Nissan Lincoln-Mercury; Fulcrum Financial Advisors, Inc.; Hendrick Automotive Group; International Paper; Laidlaw Transit Services, Inc.; Leith, Inc.; McLaurin Parking Company; Measurements Group., Inc.; Morgan Stanley Dean Witter, Inc.; Noble Oil, Inc.; North Carolina Associated Industries; North Carolina Association of Certified Public Accountants; North Carolina Association of Pharmacists; North Carolina Automobile Dealers Association; North Carolina Chapter of the American Institute of Architects; North Carolina Veterinary Medical Board; Sara Lee Corp.; Sir Walter Chevrolet Co.; Universal Chevrolet Co.; Wake Technical Community College.

(For complete biographical data on all personnel, see Professional Biographies at Raleigh, North Carolina)

DANA G. JONES

14 GROVE PARK
DURHAM, NORTH CAROLINA 27705
Telephone: 919-309-2411
Fax: 919-383-2078
Email: loodgj@aol.com
URL: http://www.keepthefaithlawfirm.com

Divorce, Child Custody and Child Support, Bankruptcy, Adoption.

DANA G. JONES, born Chicago, Illinois; admitted to bar, 1998, North Carolina; 1999, U.S. District Court, Middle and Eastern Districts of North Carolina. *Education:* University of Wisconsin-Madison (B.S., 1990); North Carolina Central University School of Law (J.D., 1997). *Member:* North Carolina and American Bar Associations.

KENNON, CRAVER, BELO, CRAIG & McKEE, PLLC

4011 UNIVERSITY DRIVE, SUITE 300
P.O. BOX 51579
DURHAM, NORTH CAROLINA 27717-1579
Telephone: 919-490-0500
Telecopier: 919-490-0873
Email: name@kennoncraver.com
URL: http://www.kennoncraver.com

General Practice in all State and Federal Courts. Corporation, Health Care, Insurance, Labor and Employment, Land Use and Development Law, Litigation, Probate, Real Estate, Taxation, Banking Law.

A. WILLIAM KENNON, born Durham, North Carolina, November 22, 1940; admitted to bar, 1967, North Carolina; 1970, U.S. Tax Court and U.S. District Courts, Middle and Eastern Districts of North Carolina; 1983, U.S. Court of Appeals, Fourth Circuit. *Education:* Duke University (A.B., 1962); University of North Carolina (J.D., with honors in Taxation, 1967). Phi Delta Phi. *Member:* North Carolina (Chairman, Retirement Plan Committee, 1980-1981; Member, Executive Council, Estate Planning and Fiduciary Law Section, 1998-2001) and American (Member, Exempt Organizations Committee, 1983-2003) Bar Associations; American Counsel Association. Fellow, American College of Trust and Estate Counsel. [Lieutenant, USNR, active duty, 1962-1964]. ***PRACTICE AREAS:*** Closely Held Business Law; Business Taxation; Nonprofit and Charitable Organizations; Estate Planning; Tax Planning; Estate Administration; Trust Administration; Charitable Giving. ***Email:*** wkennon@kennoncraver.com

KATHERINE L. McKEE, born Rock Hill, South Carolina, August 22, 1951; admitted to bar, 1976, North Carolina and U.S. District Court, Middle District of North Carolina. *Education:* Queens College and University of North Carolina (B.A., 1973); University of North Carolina (J.D., with honors, 1976). Phi Beta Kappa. Staff Editor, North Carolina Law Review, 1975-1976. Member: Professional Advisors Committee Triangle Community Foundation; Planned Giving Council, University of North Carolina Educational Foundation; Junior League of Durham and Orange Counties. *Member:* Durham County and North Carolina (Member, Sections on: Estate Planning and Fiduciary Law; Taxation) Bar Associations. ***PRACTICE AREAS:*** Business Law; Nonprofit and Charitable Organizations; Estate Planning; Tax Planning; Estate Administration; Trust Administration. ***Email:*** kmckee@kennoncraver.com

ROBERT O. BELO, born Apex, North Carolina, January 26, 1950; admitted to bar, 1979, North Carolina and U.S. District Court, Middle District of North Carolina. *Education:* University of North Carolina (B.S., 1972; J.D., 1978). Phi Beta Kappa. Listed in: The Best Lawyers in America. Member, Habitat for Humanity. *Member:* North Carolina Bar Association; North Carolina State Bar (Councilor, 14th Judicial District). ***PRACTICE AREAS:*** Commercial Law; Banking; Real Estate. ***Email:*** rbelo@kennoncraver.com

JOEL M. CRAIG, born Durham, North Carolina, November 20, 1954; admitted to bar, 1980, North Carolina and U.S. District Courts, Middle and Eastern Districts of North Carolina; 1981, U.S. Court of Appeals, Fourth Circuit; 1992, U.S. Tax Court. *Education:* University of North Carolina (A.B., 1977; J.D., with honors, 1980). Phi Beta Kappa; Order of the Coif. Member of Staff, North Carolina Law Review, 1979-1980. *Member:* Durham County and North Carolina (Member, Sections on: Litigation; Health Law) Bar Associations; Defense Research Institute; North Carolina Defense Attorney's Association. ***PRACTICE AREAS:*** Civil Litigation; Personal Injury Defense; Professional Liability; Civil Rights. ***Email:*** jcraig@kennoncraver.com

G. RHODES CRAVER, born Charlotte, North Carolina, May 30, 1956; admitted to bar, 1982, North Carolina. *Education:* University of Richmond; University of North Carolina (B.S., 1979); Wake Forest University (J.D., 1982). Community Board Member, Central Carolina Bank. Member, Durham Kiwanis Club. *Member:* North Carolina Bar Association (Member, Sections on: Estate Planning; Fiduciary Law); North Carolina Association of Certified Public Accountants. ***PRACTICE AREAS:*** Closely Held Business Law; Closely Held Business Taxation; Estate Planning; Tax Planning; Estate Administration; Trust Administration. ***Email:*** rcraver@kennoncraver.com

J. ALAN CAMPBELL, born Lake Norman, North Carolina, April 8, 1970; admitted to bar, 1995, North Carolina. *Education:* Wake Forest University (B.S., 1992); Duke University (J.D., with honors, 1995). Phi Beta Kappa. Order of the Coif. Recipient, Estate Planning Council Scholarship. Treasurer, Durham/Orange Estate Planning Council. Member: North Carolina Bar Specialist Committee. Board Member, Volunteers for Youth. *Member:* North Carolina Bar Association (Tax, Estates and Business Sections). (Board Certified Specialist in Estate Planning and Probate Law, North Carolina State Board of Legal Specialization). ***PRACTICE AREAS:*** Closely Held Business Law; Tax Planning; Nonprofit and Charitable Organizations; Estate Planning; Estate Administration; Trust Administration. ***Email:*** acampbell@kennoncraver.com

JAMES R. EASTHOM, born Weisbaden, Germany, December 6, 1963; admitted to bar, 1991, Virginia; 1993, District of Columbia; 1996, North Carolina. *Education:* Duke University (A.B., Economics, magna cum laude, 1985); University of Virginia (J.D., 1991). Board of Directors: Durham Central Park; Downtown Durham, Inc.; Urban Ministries of Durham. *Member:* North Carolina Bar Association. ***PRACTICE AREAS:*** Corporate Law; Private Equity Transactions; Business Transactions; Employment Law; Trademarks; Copyright Law. ***Email:*** jeasthom@kennoncraver.com

WILLIAM T. HUTCHINS, JR., born Durham, North Carolina, October 7, 1970; admitted to bar, 1995, North Carolina. *Education:* University of North Carolina at Chapel Hill (B.A., with distinction, 1992; J.D., with honors, 1995). Member: Phi Beta Kappa; Phi Eta Sigma. Staff Member, North Carolina Law Review, 1993-1994. Board Member, Durham YMCA. *Member:* Durham County (Board Member) and North Carolina Bar Associations. (Board Certified Specialist in Real Property, Business, Commercial and Industrial Transactions, North Carolina State Board of Legal Specialization). ***PRACTICE AREAS:*** Commercial Real Estate; Business Real Estate; Industrial Real Estate Law. ***Email:*** whutchins@kennoncraver.com

GWENDOLYN C. BROOKS, Ph.D., born Augsburg, West Germany, February 9, 1964; admitted to bar, 1999, North Carolina. *Education:* Princeton University (B.A., summa cum laude, 1986); Duke University (Ph.D., English Literature, 1996); Duke University School of Law (J.D., 1999). Board Member, The Forest at Duke. *Member:* North Carolina Bar Association (Member: Estate Planning Section; Legislative Committee); Durham/Orange Estate Planning Council. ***PRACTICE AREAS:*** Nonprofit and Charitable Organizations; Estate Planning; Tax Planning; Estate Administration; Trust Administration. ***Email:*** wbrooks@kennoncraver.com

WILLIAM ALBERT ANDERSON, III, born Cambridge, Massachusetts, October 26, 1972; admitted to bar, 2000, North Carolina. *Education:* University of North Carolina at Chapel Hill (B.A., English/Political Science, 1995; J.D., 2000). Phi Beta Kappa. Staff Member, North Carolina Law Review. Member: Durham City/County Environmental Affairs Board; Historic Preservation Society of Durham Board. *Member:* Durham County and North Carolina Bar Associations. ***PRACTICE AREAS:*** Commercial Real Estate; Land Use; Business Formation. ***Email:*** wanderson@kennoncraver.com

---

ERIN M. LOCKLEAR, born Fairmont, North Carolina, June 7, 1975; admitted to bar, 2002, North Carolina. *Education:* Princeton University (A.B., cum laude, 1999); University of North Carolina at Chapel Hill (J.D., 2002). Member, Triangle Native American Society. Board Member: Durham Jaycees; Independent Animal Rescue. *Member:* Durham

(This Listing Continued)

County and North Carolina (Member, Durham Young Lawyers Division) Bar Associations. ***PRACTICE AREAS:*** Litigation; Foreclosures; Real Estate; Business Law. ***Email:*** elocklear@kennoncraver.com

REPRESENTATIVE CLIENTS: Sun Trust Banks, Inc.; Wachovia Bank, N.A.; Harrington Bank; Cardinal State Bank; Liggett Group, Inc.; National Humanities Center; Research Triangle Foundation of North Carolina; City of Durham; Blue Cross and Blue Shield or North Carolina; American Football Coaches Foundation; American Football Coaches Association; Medical Mutual Insurance Company of N.C.; Durham Internal Medicine Associates, P.A.; Podiatry Insurance Co. of America; Elon University; Divers Alert Network, Inc.; North Carolina State University; East West Partners; Real Estate Associates, Inc.; Branch Banking & Trust (BB & T); Chicago Title Insurance Company.

KESTENBAUM LAW FIRM, P.C.

P.O. BOX 51939
DURHAM, NORTH CAROLINA 27717
Telephone: 919-459-2360
Fax: 919-459-2365

Workers' Compensation, Employment Law, Appellate Practice.

JANE KESTENBAUM, born Newark, New Jersey, June 11, 1955; admitted to bar, 1983, New York; 1989, North Carolina. *Education:* Barnard College (A.B., cum laude, with honors in Political Science, 1977); Case Western Reserve University (J.D., 1982). Member, Case Western Reserve Law Review, 1980-1982. Lecturer: Duke University Physician Assistant Certificate Program in Occupational and Environmental Medicine, 2001, 2002, 2003 and 2004; Council on Education in Management, 2003 and 2004. Assistant District Attorney, Manhattan District Attorney's Office, New York, NY, 1983-1987. *Member:* North Carolina Association of Defense Attorneys. ***PRACTICE AREAS:*** Workers' Compensation; Employment Law; Appellate Practice. ***Email:*** jak@kestenbaumlaw.com

JOHN W. STRANGE, born Batesville, Indiana, September 12, 1974; admitted to bar, 2001, North Carolina. *Education:* DePauw University (B.A., 1997); Cumberland School of Law of Samford University (J.D., cum laude, 2001). *Member:* Wake County and North Carolina Bar Associations. ***PRACTICE AREAS:*** Workers' Compensation; Employment Law; Appellate Practice. ***Email:*** jws@kestenbaumlaw.com

REPRESENTATIVE CLIENTS: Broyhill Furniture Industries; Eaton Corp.; American Red Cross; City of Durham; Gallagher Bassett Services; Gates McDonald; Comp Management; Key Risk Management; Southeastern Claims Services, Inc.; Express Personnel; Hallmark Management.

KNOTT, CLARK & BERGER, L.L.P.

DURHAM, NORTH CAROLINA

(See Raleigh)

General Practice in State and Federal Courts. Medical Malpractice, Nursing Malpractice, Hospital Liability, Plaintiffs Personal Injury, Wrongful Death, Automobile Accidents and Injuries, Commercial Vehicle Liability, Nursing Home Negligence, Workers Compensation, Insurance Bad Faith, Insurance Litigation.

LAW OFFICES OF KARL E. KNUDSEN

DURHAM, NORTH CAROLINA

(See Raleigh)

Criminal Law, Driving While Intoxicated, Drug Crimes, Felonies, Homicide, Misdemeanors, Traffic Violations, Personal Injury, Medical Malpractice, Auto Accidents, Wrongful Death, Products Liability, Workers Compensation.

THE KORNBLUTH LAW FIRM, P.A.

120 EAST PARRISH STREET, SUITE 210
DURHAM, NORTH CAROLINA 27702
Telephone: 919-680-8575
Fax: 919-688-4335
Email: mak@kornbluthlaw.com
URL: http://www.lawyers.com/kornbluthlaw

Personal Injury, Automobile Accidents, Wrongful Death, Workers Compensation, Employment Law, Discrimination, Sexual Harassment, Employee Benefits, Civil Litigation, Criminal, Satellite Litigation, Traffic.

MICHAEL A. KORNBLUTH, born Alexandria, Virginia, August 27, 1973; admitted to bar, 2001, North Carolina; US District Court, Eastern, Middle and Western Districts of North Carolina. *Education:* University of Rochester (B.A., 1995); George Washington University Law School (J.D., with honors, 2001). Legal Intern to U.S. District Judge Thomas F. Hogan, Washington, D.C., 1999. Member, The Public Contract Law Journal, 1999-2001. Vice President, Alternative Dispute Resolution Board. *Member:* North Carolina and American Bar Associations; North Carolina State Bar; North Carolina Academy of Trial Lawyers.

LEWIS, ANDERSON, PHILLIPS, GREENE & HINKLE, PLLC

DURHAM, NORTH CAROLINA

(See Chapel Hill)

Business Law, Commercial Litigation, Family Law, Divorce, Estate Planning and Administration, Probate, Wills, Civil Litigation, Intellectual Property Litigation, Copyright, Trademark, Personal Injury, Real Estate Litigation, Construction, Condemnation, Employment Contracts,

(This Listing Continued)

Corporate Taxation, Corporate Finance, Partnership Taxation, Mediation, Arbitration, Computer Law.

MAITLAND & MAITLAND, PLLC

DURHAM, NORTH CAROLINA

(See Chapel Hill)

Real Estate, Closings, Residential, Commercial, Business Law, Entrepreneurial, Partnerships, Small Business, Entrepreneur, Business Formation, Immigration, Naturalization, Citizenship, Permanent Resident, Investor, Teacher Visas, H1B, J1, Visa Petitions, Litigation, Banking, Contracts, Foreclosure, Mortgages, Personal Injury, Traffic Violations, DWI, DUI, Liquor License, Alcohol Permit, Wills, Banking, Collection, Sports, Entertainment Law.

MARTIN & JONES

UNIVERSITY TOWERS, SUITE 526
3100 TOWER BOULEVARD
DURHAM, NORTH CAROLINA 27707
Telephone: 919-544-3000
URL: http://www.MartinandJones.com

Raleigh, North Carolina Office: 410 Glenwood Avenue, 27603. Telephone: 919-821-0005.
Wilmington, North Carolina Office: 1213 Culbreth Drive, Suite 121, 28405. Telephone: 910-256-4005.
Atlanta, Georgia Office: 3353 Peachtree Road, NE, Suite 510, 30326. Telephone: 404-257-1117.

Asbestos Litigation, Bad Faith and Unfair Competition, Business Litigation, Construction Site Injuries, Inadequate Security, Medical Malpractice, Nursing/Rest Home Negligence, Personal Injury, Pharmaceutical and Medical Device Litigation, Product Liability, Social Security Disability, Toxic Torts, Trucking Accidents, Workers' Compensation and Wrongful Death, Land Condemnation, FELA (Federal Employers' Liability Act), Securities Fraud.

HOYT G. TESSENER, admitted to bar, 1988, North Carolina, U.S. District Court, Eastern, Middle and Western Districts of North Carolina and U.S. Court of Appeals, Fourth Circuit. *Education:* North Carolina State University (B.S., 1983); Campbell University (J.D., with honors, 1988). ***PRACTICE AREAS:*** Nursing Home Negligence; Securities Fraud; Automobile Accidents and Injuries. ***Email:*** HGT@M-J.COM

(For complete biographical data on other personnel, see Professional Biographies at Raleigh, North Carolina)

GABRIELA J. MATTHEWS & ASSOCIATES, P.A.

100 EAST PARRISH STREET
SUITE 400
DURHAM, NORTH CAROLINA 27701
Telephone: 919-956-7888
Fax: 919-956-7833
Email: attorney.gmatthews@verizon.net
URL: http://www.ncdivorcelawfirm.com

Family Law, Child Custody, Child Support, Divorce, Personal Injury, Adoption Law, Domestic Violence, Visitation Rights.

GABRIELA J. MATTHEWS, born Buenos Aires, Argentina, May 23, 1963; admitted to bar, 1989, Maryland; 1991, North Carolina; 1995, U.S. District Court, Middle District of North Carolina. *Education:* University of North Carolina (B.A., 1985); Georgetown University Law Center (J.D., 1989). Member, Jessup International Law Moot Court Team, 1988. *Member:* Durham County (Chair, Family Law Section, 1993-1995) and North Carolina (Member, Family Law Section) Bar Associations; North Carolina State Bar; North Carolina Academy of Trial Lawyers (Chair, Family Law Section, 1995-1996); North Carolina Academy of Trial Lawyers (Member, Family Law Section); North Carolina Association of Women Attorneys (Chair, Durham County Chapter, 1998-1999). ***LANGUAGES:*** Spanish. ***PRACTICE AREAS:*** Litigation; Child Custody; Visitation Rights; Child Support; Divorce; Personal Injury; Adoption Law; Domestic Violence; Collaborative Family Law; Mediation.

MAUPIN TAYLOR, P.A.

DURHAM, NORTH CAROLINA

(See Research Triangle Park)

Agribusiness, Administrative, Alcoholic Beverages, Alternative Dispute Resolution, Antitrust and Trade Regulation, Aviation Law, Bankruptcy, Banking Law, Business Litigation, Charitable Organizations, Collective Bargaining, Commercial Leases, Commercial Real Estate, Computers and Software, Construction Law, Copyrights, Corporate Finance, Corporate Law, Creditors' Rights, Employee Benefits, Employer Liability, Employment Discrimination, Employment Law, Employment Litigation, Environmental Law, Franchises and Franchising, Government Contracts, Governmental (State and Local) Law, Health Law, Hospital Law, Immigration and Naturalization, Industrial Accidents, Industrial Relations, Intellectual Property, Labor Arbitration, Labor Law, Labor Legislation, Labor Relations, Management Labor Law, Medical Malpractice Defense, Mergers and Acquisitions, Occupational Health and Safety, Patent Litigation, Products Liability, Real Estate Finance, Secured Lending, Securities Regulation, Sports Law, Taxation, Technology Law, Trademark, Trusts and Estates, Venture Capital, Zoning Law.

MAXWELL, FREEMAN & BOWMAN, P.A.

2741 UNIVERSITY DRIVE
P.O. BOX 52396
DURHAM, NORTH CAROLINA 27717-2396
Telephone: 919-493-6464
Telecopier: 919-493-1218

Medical and Legal Negligence, Professional Responsibility, Wrongful Death and Serious Personal Injury, Business and Corporate Law, Residential and Commercial Real Estate, Estate Planning and Estate and Trust Administration, Domestic Relations, Family and Divorce Mediation and Collaborative Family Law, Civil Litigation and Traffic Violations.

FIRM PROFILE: The present firm was founded in 1975. It has an emphasis of practice in the areas of professional negligence, catastrophic injury and wrongful death, primarily representing plaintiffs throughout the state of North Carolina. The firm also has a substantial residential real estate in addition to commercial real estate, estate planning, estate and trust administration, business and corporate, domestic relations, family and divorce mediation, and collaborative family law, civil litigation and traffic violations. Our office building was fashioned after an older home including a working fireplace in our waiting area. Client's enjoy high-quality legal representation in a relaxed and family-like atmosphere. The Firm is committed to participating in activities of the organized bar with its members having served in leadership positions at both the state and local level and in service to the community.

JAMES B. MAXWELL, born Hampton, Virginia, August 22, 1941; admitted to bar, 1966, North Carolina; U.S. District Court, Eastern, Middle and Western Districts of North Carolina; U.S. Court of Appeals, Fourth Circuit. *Education:* Randolph-Macon College (B.A., 1963); Duke University (LL.B., 1966). Phi Delta Phi; Omicron Delta Kappa. Advocate, American Board of Trial Advocates; North Carolina College of Advocacy. Listed in: "Best Lawyers in America - Civil Litigation," 1987—. *Member:* Durham County, North Carolina (Chairman: Family Law Section, 1980-1981; Lecturer, Practical Skills Course, 1973-1988, 1993—; Board of Governors, 1994-1997; President Elect, 1999-2000; President, 2000-2001) and American Bar Associations; The Association of Trial Lawyers of America; North Carolina Academy of Trial Lawyers (Member, Board of Governors, 1981-1988; Vice President, 1983-1985; President Elect, 1985-1986; President, 1986-1987); Legal Aid of North Carolina (Chairman, 2003-2004). Fellow: American College of Trial Lawyers; International Society of Barristers. ***PRACTICE AREAS:*** Professional Responsibility; Catastrophic Injury; Medical Negligence; Personal Injury; Wrongful Death. ***Email:*** jmaxwell@mfbpa.com

HOMA J. FREEMAN, JR., born Durham, North Carolina, July 30, 1949; admitted to bar, 1974, North Carolina. *Education:* University of North Carolina (A.B., 1971; J.D., 1974). Phi Beta Kappa; Omicron Delta Epsilon; Phi Delta Phi. *Member:* Durham County (Secretary, 1978-1979), North Carolina (Member, Practical Skills Curriculum Committee 1985-1996 and Chairman, 1993-1994, 1995-1996; Education Law Section Membership Chairman, 1989-1990, Treasurer 1990-1991, Section Chair, 1991-1992) and American Bar Associations. ***PRACTICE AREAS:*** Residential Real Estate; Commercial Real Estate; Estate Planning Law; Elder Law; Estate Administration Law; Trust Administration Law; Business Transactions; Contracts; Corporate Law. ***Email:*** hfreeman@mfbpa.com

JOHN A. BOWMAN, born Richmond, Virginia, June 29, 1956; admitted to bar, 1987, North Carolina; 1988, U.S. District Court, Eastern and Middle Districts of North Carolina. *Education:* Virginia Military Institute (B.A., 1978); Campbell University School of Law (J.D., 1984). Member, Executive Committee, North Carolina Conference of Bar Presidents, 1998-2001. *Member:* Durham County (Vice President, 1995-1996; President-Elect, 1996-1997; President, 1997-1998) and North Carolina (Member, Sections on: Litigation, Dispute Resolution and Family Law; Family Law Council Member, 2000-2003) Bar Associations; North Carolina Academy of Trial Lawyers; Association for Conflict Resolution (Family Section); International Association of Collaborative Professionals. ***PRACTICE AREAS:*** Family Law; Family Mediation; Collaborative Family Law; Civil Litigation. ***Email:*** jbowman@mfbpa.com

REPRESENTATIVE CLIENTS: Triangle Transit Authority; Long Beverage, Inc.; Duke University; East Coast Metal Distributors, Inc.
APPROVED ATTORNEYS FOR: Lawyers Title Insurance Corp.; Investors Title Insurance Co.; Chicago Title Insurance Co.; First American Title Insurance Co.; The Title Company of North Carolina, Inc.

McKISSICK & McKISSICK

THE BB&T BUILDING
4011 UNIVERSITY DRIVE, SUITE 203
DURHAM, NORTH CAROLINA 27707
Telephone: 919-490-5373
Fax: 919-493-0488
URL: http://www.FloydMcKissick.com
URL: http://www.lawyers.com/mckissicklaw

Family Law, Premarital Agreements, Equitable Distribution, Divorce, Child Custody, Child Support, Separation and Property Settlement Agreements, Contracts Disputes, Criminal Law, Civil Litigation, Business Law, Commercial Litigation, Zoning, Planning and Land Use, Governmental Relations, Construction Litigation.

FLOYD B. McKISSICK, JR., born Durham, North Carolina, November 21, 1952; admitted to bar, 1984, North Carolina; 1985, U.S. District Court, Middle and Eastern Districts of North Carolina; U.S. District Court, District of Columbia. *Education:* Clark University (A.B., 1974); University of North Carolina, School of City and Regional Planning (M.R.P., 1975); Harvard University, John F. Kennedy School of Government (M.P.A., 1979); Duke University (J.D., 1983). James A. Bell Scholar. Author: Termination: "When An Owner May Terminate A Contract Because of Delay," Construction Law Adviser, May, 1984. Former Member, Durham Board of Adjustment and Durham Planning Commission. Member, City Council, Durham, North Carolina, 1993-2001. Chairman of the Board, Triangle J, Council of Governments, 2001. *Member:* Durham County and North Carolina Bar Associations. ***Email:*** FmcKissick@aol.com

(This Listing Continued)

McPHERSON & ROCAMORA, PLLC

3211 SHANNON ROAD
SUITE 620
DURHAM, NORTH CAROLINA 27707
Telephone: 919-493-0584
Facsimile: 919-493-0856

Estate Planning, Probate Administration Law, Taxation.

WILLIAM V. McPHERSON, JR., born Wilmington, North Carolina, February 27, 1942; admitted to bar, 1969, North Carolina; 1970, U.S. District Court, District of South Dakota; 1973, U.S. District Court, Middle District of North Carolina; 1976, U.S. District Court, Eastern District of North Carolina and U.S. Court of Appeals, Fourth Circuit; 1979, U.S. Supreme Court; 1988, U.S. Tax Court. *Education:* Duke University (A.B., 1966); University of North Carolina (J.D., with honors, 1969). Order of the Coif. Articles Editor, North Carolina Law Review, 1968-1969. Trial Attorney, Tax Division, U.S. Department of Justice, 1969-1971. District Administrative Assistant to Nick Galifianakis, Member of Congress, 1971-1972. *Member:* Durham County, North Carolina (Member, Sections on: Taxation, Estate Planning and Fiduciary Law) and American (Member, Sections on: Taxation; Real Property, Probate and Trust Law) Bar Associations; North Carolina State Bar; Durham Orange Estate Planning Council (President, 1996-1997). Fellow, American College of Trust and Estate Counsel. (Board Certified Specialist in Estate Planning and Probate Law, North Carolina State Board of Legal Specialization). ***PRACTICE AREAS:*** Estate Planning; Trust Administration; Estate Administration; Charitable Giving. ***Email:*** wmcpherson@macroclaw.com

LARRY H. ROCAMORA, born Asheville, North Carolina, February 14, 1958; admitted to bar, 1988, North Carolina. *Education:* University of North Carolina (B.S., 1981); Hastings College of the Law, University of California (J.D., summa cum laude, 1988). Order of the Coif. Member, Hastings Law Review, 1987-1988. Certified Public Accountant, 1984. *Member:* Durham County, North Carolina (Member, Sections on: Business Law; Elder Law; Estate Planning and Fiduciary Law; Taxation Law) and American (Member, Sections on: Taxation; Real Property, Probate and Trust Law) Bar Associations. Fellow, American College of Trust and Estate Counsel. (Board Certified Specialist in Estate Planning and Probate Law, North Carolina State Board of Legal Specialization). ***PRACTICE AREAS:*** Estate Planning; Business Organizations; Taxation Law; Trust Administration; Estate Administration; Elder Law. ***Email:*** lrocamora@macroclaw.com

---

KATHRYN T. CURRAN, born Charlotte, North Carolina, June 6, 1959; admitted to bar, 1985, North Carolina. *Education:* University of North Carolina at Chapel Hill (B.S., 1981; J.D., 1984). *Member:* North Carolina Bar Association (Member, Probate Section). ***PRACTICE AREAS:*** Estate Planning; Probate. ***Email:*** kcurran@macroclaw.com

MITCHELL, EYSTER & WARNER, P.A.

2004 S. MIAMI BOULEVARD
DURHAM, NORTH CAROLINA 27703
Telephone: 919-598-9000
Facsimile: 919-598-9090
Email: attorney@nchealthlaw.com
URL: http://www.nchealthlaw.com

Comprehensive Health Care Law including Administrative Law, Corporate Law, Business Law, Tax Law, Employment, Estate Planning, Trusts and Estates, Collections.

JOAN M. MITCHELL, born Bremerton, Washington, July 31, 1943; admitted to bar, 1991, North Carolina. *Education:* University of North Carolina at Chapel Hill (B.A., 1988; J.D., with honors, 1991). ***PRACTICE AREAS:*** Litigation; Collections; Estate Planning; Estate Administration.

DONNA TURNER EYSTER, born St. Louis, Missouri, February 14, 1948; admitted to bar, 2001, North Carolina. *Education:* Meredith College (B.A., 1993); University of North Carolina at Chapel Hill (J.D., 2000). ***PRACTICE AREAS:*** Health Law; Employment Law; Administrative Law; Civil Law.

H. LAWRENCE WARNER, JR., born Walkertown, North Carolina, May 31, 1961; admitted to bar, 1992, Pennsylvania and District of Columbia; 1993, North Carolina. *Education:* University of North Carolina (B.S., 1983); Catholic University of America (J.D., 1991); George Washington University (M.B.A., 1992).

MOORE & VAN ALLEN PLLC

DURHAM, NORTH CAROLINA
(See Research Triangle Park)

MORRIS, MANNING & MARTIN, LLP

A Limited Liability Partnership
Established in 1976
1000 PARK 40 PLAZA, SUITE 300
DURHAM, NORTH CAROLINA 28262
Telephone: 704-369-7012
Fax: 704-369-7071
Email: kburns@mmmlaw.com
URL: http://www.mmmlaw.com

Charlotte, NC Office: 201 South College Street, Suite 2300, 28244. Telephone: 704-554-7070. Fax: 704-556-5050.

(This Listing Continued)

Charlotte, NC Office: 10150 Mallard Creek Drive, Suite 105, 28262. Telephone: 704-369-7012. Fax: 704-369-7071.
Washington, D.C. Office: City Center Building, 1401 H Street, N.W., Suite 760, 20005. Telephone: 202-408-5153. Fax: 202-408-5146.
Princeton, NJ Office: 601 Ewing Street, Suite C-8, 08540. Telephone: 609-430-1414. Fax: 609-430-1411.
Georgia Office Addresses:
Atlanta (Buckhead) Office: 1600 Atlanta Financial Center, 3343 Peachtree Road, N.E., Atlanta, GA 30326. Telephone: 404-233-7000.
Peachtree Dunwoody Office: 5775-C Peachtree Dunwoody Road, Suite 150, Atlanta, GA 30342. Telephone: 404-255-6900. Fax: 404-843-2317.
Duluth Office: 2180 Satellite Boulevard, Suite 180, Duluth, GA 30097. Telephone: 678-987-2800. Fax: 678-417-0056.
Cumming Office: 307 Atlanta Highway, Cumming, GA 30040. Telephone: 770-781-3000. Fax: 770-781-3007.
Alpharetta Office: 5780 Windward Parkway, Suite 225, Alpharetta, GA 30005. Telephone: 770-781-3000. Fax: 770-781-3007.

Benefits and Compensation, Commercial Lending, Construction, Corporate, Corporate Technology, Creditor's Rights and Bankruptcy, Emerging Companies, Employment, Environmental, Healthcare, Hospitality, Insurance and Reinsurance, Insurance and Reinsurance Dispute Resolution, Intellectual Property, International, Life Sciences, Litigation, Medical Device, Mergers and Acquisitions, Privacy and Security, Products Liability and Toxic Torts, Real Estate Capital Markets, Real Estate Development and Finance, Residential Real Estate, Securities, Taxation, Technology, Technology Litigation, Telecommunications, Wealth Planning.

FIRM PROFILE: Since 1976, Morris, Manning & Martin has represented some of the most active real estate developers and builders in the region. Since its formation, MMM's real estate practice has steadily grown. Our residential real estate development practice provides a full array of services that will assist developers from acquisition of raw land through the ultimate sale of a finished home to a developer's customer. The number of client representations we have handled and the value of the transactions we have closed is a testament to our experience and quality of work, as well as the confidence and trust clients place in us. Our attorneys have helped clients close commercial real estate deals valued in the billions of dollars and handled millions of dollars worth of residential closings.

LAW FIRM ALLIANCES/ASSOCIATIONS: **LAWYERS ASSOCIATED WORLDWIDE (L.A.W.)**

OF COUNSEL

KEITH D. BURNS, born Laurinburg, North Carolina, 1968; admitted to bar, 1993, North Carolina. *Education:* University of North Carolina at Chapel Hill (B.A., 1989); Wake Forest University School of Law (J.D., 1993). Order of the Barristers. Member, National Trial Team, 1992-1993. Recipient, Robert Goldberg Award in Trial Advocacy. *Member:* North Carolina (Member, Sections on: Employment Law; Business Law; Real Property Law) and American (Member, Business Law Section; Fellow) Bar Associations; Braxton Craven Inn of Court (President, 2004-2005). ***PRACTICE AREAS:*** Corporate Litigation; Commercial Litigation; Employment Law; Real Estate Development; Real Estate Finance. ***Email:*** kburns@mmmlaw.com

ASSOCIATE

KANDAS D. BURNETT, born Latrobe, Pennsylvania, 1976; admitted to bar, 2001, North Carolina. *Education:* University of North Carolina at Charlotte (B.A., Political Science, with honors, 1998); University of Tulsa (J.D., 2000). ***PRACTICE AREAS:*** Residential Real Estate. ***Email:*** kburnett@mmmlaw.com

OLIVE AND OLIVE, P.A.

Established in 1957
500 MEMORIAL STREET
P.O. BOX 2049
DURHAM, NORTH CAROLINA 27702-2049
Telephone: 919-683-5514
Fax: 919-688-3781
URL: http://www.lawyers.com/oliveandolive
Email: iplaw@oliveandolive.com
URL: http://www.oliveandolive.com

Intellectual Property, Patent, Trademark, Copyright, Computer and Biotechnology Law and Related Litigation.

FIRM PROFILE: The firm of Olive and Olive, P.A. limits its practice to intellectual property law. This includes traditional services in the patent, trademark, copyright and trade secret fields, and related areas of practice; and covers litigation in addition to counseling and protection. The firm assists its clients both with conventional and with highly advanced technologies.

Olive and Olive, P.A. works with a broad range of scientific and industrial technologies, including, but not limited to biotechnology (instruments, cultures and assays, diagnostic methods and apparatus, pharmaceuticals, etc.); computer hardware and software; electronics and robotics; chemistry; packaging and other machinery; plastics; agricultural and horticultural methods, machines and equipment, as well as plants themselves; lasers; textile products and apparatus; and airplane, automobile, and boat components.

B. B. OLIVE, born Fuquay-Springs, North Carolina, November 5, 1921; admitted to bar, 1953, New York; 1956, North Carolina; 1958, U.S. District Court, Eastern, Western and Middle Districts of North Carolina; 1974, U.S. Court of Appeals, Fourth Circuit; U.S. Supreme Court; registered to practice before U.S. Patent and Trademark Office. *Education:* The Pennsylvania State College and Duke University (B.S.E.E., with honors, 1948); St. John's University (LL.B., 1953; J.D., 1968). Tau Beta Pi; Pi Mu Epsilon; Omicron Delta Kappa; Sigma Xi. Recipient: Duke University Distinguished Engineering Alumnus Award, 1970 and Trustee Recognition, 1983; Governor's Volunteer Award, 1980. Author: "Acquiring and Establishing Proprietary Rights," North Carolina Bar Association Institute, 1960; "Transportation Policy and Energy Considerations," Energy Technologies and Policies for North Carolina, 1978; "Patents, Trademarks and Copyrights For The Entrepreneur," Duke University Conference on Entrepreneurship, 1986. Adjunct Professor in Engineering and Patent Law, Duke University, 1957-1972; Chairman, Duke University Alumni Committee on Publications, 1963-1964. President, Duke Engineering Alumni Association, 1964-1965. Member, North Carolina Academy of Science, 1977-1982. Board Member, Council For Entrepreneurial Development, 1985-1987. Secretary/Director, Member Executive Committee, Triangle Land Conservancy, 1983-1988 and 1990-1994. Board Member and Member, Development Committee, Durham Historic Preservation Society, 1993-1998. *Member:* Durham County, North Carolina (Member and Chairman, Patent, Trademark and Copyright Committee, 1966-1968) Bar Associations; Fourteenth Judicial District and The North Carolina State Bars; Carolina Patent, Trademark and Copyright Law Association (Member, Board of Managers, 1980-1982, 1987-1990. Member, Fourteenth Judicial District Grievance Committee, 1993-1995; North Carolina Bar Association Continuing Legal Education, Long Range Planning and Publication Committees, 1994-1998; Program chairman and Newsletter Editor, Senior Lawyers Division, 1990-1998; Member and Legal Subcommittee Co-Chair, North Carolina Biotechnology Center Advisory Council, 1995). ***PRACTICE AREAS:*** Patents. ***Email:*** iplaw@oliveandolive.com

SUSAN FREYA OLIVE, born Durham, North Carolina, June 26, 1952; admitted to bar, 1976, North Carolina and U.S. Court of Military Appeals; 1977, U.S. District Court, Eastern and Middle District of North Carolina; 1984, U.S. District Court, Western District of North Carolina; U.S. Court of Appeals, Fourth and Federal Circuits; U.S. Supreme Court. *Education:* Brown University (A.B., 1974); Duke University (J.D., with distinction, 1977). Editor, The Durham Docket, Bar Newsletter, 1977-1983. Author: "When and How to Seek Rule 11 and Rule 37 Sanctions," 2000; "Limitations on Trademark Protection: Fair Use and the First Amendment," 1994; "Copyrightability of Compilations," 1992; "Integrated Protection for Computer Programs," 1990; "Work for Hire Issues, Who Owns What?" 1990; "Publishing Contracts," 1989; "Copyright Basics," 1988; "Trademark Basics," 1988; "Copyright Basics for the General Practitioner," 1986; "Protection of the Computer Hardware and Software Product: A Primer," 1986; "Brief Introduction to Trademarks and Copyrights," 1988, North Carolina Bar Association. Special Counsel, Ninth Judicial District of North Carolina, 1977-1979. Regional Chairperson, Brown University National Alumni Schools Program, 1977-2004. Member, Board of Directors, 1979-1983 and Chairperson, Legislation Committee, 1980-1982, Mental Health Association in Durham County. Member, Board of Directors, Durham Young Lawyers Association, 1978-1979. Member, Board of Directors, 1980—, Treasurer, 1989-1990 and President, 1990-1992, North Carolina Prisoners' Legal Services, Inc. Member, 1985-1993 Secretary, 1985-1987 and Chairman, 1989-1990, Federal Bar Advisory Council. Member, Research Committee for Court Annexed Arbitration, U.S. Middle District Court of North Carolina, 1985-1989. Member, Attorney Qualification Review Committee, U.S. District Court, Middle District of North Carolina, 1984—. Member, 1993— and First Woman Chair, 2003-2004, North Carolina Board of Law Examiners; Commissioner, North Carolina General Statutes Commission, 1991-1998. Permanent Member, Fourth Circuit Judicial Conference. *Member:* Durham County (President, 1983-1984; First Vice President, 1982-1983; Secretary, 1981-1982), North Carolina (Member, Board of Governors, 1988-1991; Chairman, Long Range Plan Implementation Committee, 1997-1999, Chairman, Technology & The Law Committee, 1989-1991; Chairman, Intellectual Property Law Committee, 1984-1987; Chairman, Mental Health Law Committee, 1982-1984; Member, Intellectual Property Law Committee, 1983-1989; Member, 1989— and Member, Section Council, 1989-1993, Intellectual Property Law Section; Member: Litigation Section, 1987—; Member, Constitutional Rights and Responsibilities Section, 1995—; Bar Center Cabinet, 1994-1996; Bar Steering Committee, 1987-1988; Nominations Committee, 1983-1984), American (Member: Intellectual Property Law Section and Co-Chair, Subcommittee on Patent/Trade Dress Interface; Franchising Section; Forum Committee on Science and Technology) and Federal Bar Associations; Fourteenth Judicial District (President, 1983-1984; First Vice President, 1982-1983; Secretary, 1981-1982) and North Carolina State (Member, Out of State Mergers Committee, 1984-1985) Bars; North Carolina Academy of Trial Lawyers; North Carolina Association of Women Attorneys (President, 1993; President-Elect, 1992); The Association of Trial Lawyers of America; Carolina Patent, Trademark and Copyright Law Association. ***REPORTED CASES:*** 21 USPQ 2d 1388 (CAFC 1992). ***PRACTICE AREAS:*** Intellectual Property Law and Related Litigation.

VEDIA JONES-RICHARDSON, born Brooklyn, New York, February 16, 1956; admitted to bar, 1983, District of Columbia; 1985, Illinois; 1992, North Carolina; registered to practice before U.S. Patent and Trademark Office. *Education:* Howard University (B.F.A., 1978); Georgetown University (J.D., 1982). President, Durham Arts Council, 1999-2000. Board Member, Kenan Institute for the Arts. Vice-President, Durham Library Foundation. *Member:* Durham County (Member, Grievance Committee, 1997—), North Carolina (Member, Committee on Women in the Legal Profession, 1998), National (Member, Intellectual Property Section, 1998—) and American (Member, Commission on Responsibility in Client Development; Member, Sections on: Law Practice Management, 1985—; Science and Technology, 1993—; Intellectual Property, 1993—; Council Member, 1998— Section Officer, 2004—) Bar Associations; North Carolina Association of Women Attorneys; North Carolina Association of Black Lawyers; George White Bar Association; Durham and Orange Women Attorneys (President). ***PRACTICE AREAS:*** Business Law; Trademarks; Copyrights; Computer Law.

JOSHUA L. PRICE, born Portland, Oregon, July 15, 1975; admitted to bar, 2002, North Carolina; registered to practice before U.S. Patent and Trademark Office. *Education:* Oregon State University (B.S., 1998); University of Oregon School of Law (J.D., 2001). Phi Alpha Delta. Member, Oregon Review of International Law. *Member:* North Carolina Bar Association; American Intellectual Property Law Association; Association of Trial Lawyers of America. ***PRACTICE AREAS:*** Patent Prosecution; Patent Litigation; Copyrights; Trademarks. ***Email:*** jprice@oliveandolive.com

ANDREW T. PROKOPETZ, born Trenton, New Jersey, March 8, 1955; admitted to bar, 1988, North Carolina; registered to practice before U.S. Patent and Trademark Office.

(This Listing Continued)

OLIVE AND OLIVE, P.A., Durham—Continued

Education: Rider University (B.S., 1978); University of North Carolina at Chapel Hill (M.S., 1983); North Carolina Central University (JD, 1988). Lecturer: "Got My Patent, How About Licensing: Licensing 101" at the Laws of Science, NC Biotechnology Center, Research Triangle Park, NC, 2003. Former Member: American Chemical Society; ACGIH. *Member:* North Carolina Bar Association (Co-Chair, Chemical/Biotech Patent Law Committee). ***LANGUAGES:*** French. ***PRACTICE AREAS:*** Patent Prosecution; Patent Drafting; Licensing; Contract Negotiations and Drafting; Intellectual Property. ***Email:*** aprokopetz@oliveandolive.com

DEVON E. WHITE, born White Plains, New York; admitted to bar, 2002, North Carolina; registered to practice before U.S. Patent and Trademark Office. *Education:* University of North Carolina at Wilmington (B.A., 1993; M.A., 1995); North Carolina Central University (J.D., with Honors, 2002). Board Member, Wake County Commission for Women, 2004-2006. *Member:* North Carolina Bar Association; North Carolina Association of Women Attorneys; Wake Women Attorneys (Treasurer, 2004); Durham Orange Women Attorneys Association. ***PRACTICE AREAS:*** Intellectual Property.

S. MATTHEW EDWARDS, born Troy, North Carolina, August 18, 1980; admitted to bar, 2005, North Carolina. *Education:* Campbell University (B.S., 2002; J.D., 2005). ***PRACTICE AREAS:*** Patent Prosecution Litigation; Trademarks; Copyrights. ***Email:*** sme@oliveandolive.com

REFERENCES: North Carolina Bar Assn.; Durham County Bar Assn.; Centura Bank & Trust Co., Durham.

J. KIRK OSBORN

DURHAM, NORTH CAROLINA

(See Chapel Hill)

General Civil and Criminal Litigation in State and Federal Courts. Criminal, Drug Crimes, Driving While Intoxicated (DWI), White Collar Crimes, Homicide, Traffic Violations, Premises Liability, Personal Injury and Nursing Home Litigation, Wrongful Death, Civil Rights.

POE & HOOF PLLC

Established in 1989

3612 SHANNON ROAD, SUITE 101

P.O. BOX 51909

DURHAM, NORTH CAROLINA 27717

Telephone: 919-489-9100

Fax: 919-489-9090

Email: postmaster@phalaw.com

URL: http://www.phalaw.com

General Civil Trial and Appellate Practice, Commercial Litigation, Insurance Defense, Personal Injury, Plaintiff's and Workers Compensation.

MEMBERS OF FIRM

G. JONA POE, JR., born Portsmouth, Virginia, August 6, 1945; admitted to bar, 1970, New York; 1972, U.S. District Court, Southern and Eastern Districts of New York; 1974, U.S. Supreme Court; 1975, North Carolina; 1977, U.S. District Court, Middle District of North Carolina; 1978, U.S. District Court, Eastern District of North Carolina and U.S. Court of Appeals, Fourth Circuit. *Education:* Duke University (B.S., 1967); Columbia University (J.D., 1970); New York University (LL.M., 1975). Assistant District Attorney, Bronx County, New York, 1970-1975. Special Deputy Attorney General of North Carolina, 1975-1977. *Member:* Durham County, North Carolina and New York State Bar Associations; North Carolina State Bar; North Carolina Academy of Trial Lawyers. ***PRACTICE AREAS:*** Trial Practice; Personal Injury; Commercial Litigation. ***Email:*** gjp@phalaw.com

J. BRUCE HOOF, born Boston, Massachusetts, May 25, 1948; admitted to bar, 1973, North Carolina; 1975, U.S. District Court, Middle District of North Carolina; 1978, U.S. District Court, Eastern District of North Carolina; 1989, U.S. District Court, Western District of North Carolina. *Education:* Kingswood School, Bath, England; Deerfield Academy; University of North Carolina (A.B., 1970); Vanderbilt University (J.D., 1973). Phi Beta Kappa; Phi Eta Sigma; Phi Alpha Theta. Patrick Wilson Scholar. *Member:* Durham County Bar Association; North Carolina State Bar; North Carolina Association of Defense Attorneys. ***PRACTICE AREAS:*** Civil Litigation; Insurance Defense. ***Email:*** jbh@phalaw.com

REPRESENTATIVE CLIENTS: Alliance Mutual Insurance Co.; Alterman Transport Lines, Inc.; American Freightways, Inc.; Church Mutual Insurance Company; City of Durham, North Carolina; CNI Claim Service; County of Durham, N.C.; CVS Pharmacy, Inc.; Dollar Rent A Car Systems, Inc.; Durham County Sheriff's Department; Enterprise Leasing Company; Erie Insurance Group; E.R.M.C., L.P.; Farmers Insurance Group; Federated Rural Electric Insurance Company; Foremost Insurance Co.; GRE Insurance Group; The Guardian Insurance Company of Canada; Harford Mutual Insurance Company; HCM Claim Management; Hertz Corporation; Integon Insurance Co.; James C. Greene Co.; Lawyers Mutual Ins. Co.; Leaseway Personnel Corp.; Leaseway Transportation Corp.; Metropolitan Property & Casualty Company; Motors Insurance Co.; National Casualty Co.; NCI Transportation Services; Network Adjusters, Inc.; Newark Insurance Co.; New Jersey Manufacturers Insurance Co.; Ohio Casualty Group, Inc.; Penn-America Insurance Company; Pennsylvania Lumbermens Mutual Insurance Co.; Progressive Insurance Co.; Prudential Carolinas Realty; R.E. Pratt & Company; Rea Construction Company; Revco Discount Drug Centers, Inc.; Rider Insurance Company; Ryder Transportation Services; Ryder Truck Rental, Inc.; Spartan Express, Inc.; University Ford, Inc.; Vimasco Corporation; Wachovia Bank and Trust Co.; Ward North America, Inc.

PULLEY, WATSON, KING & LISCHER, P.A.

Established in 1982

21-F BRIGHTLEAF SQUARE

905 WEST MAIN STREET

P.O. BOX 3600

DURHAM, NORTH CAROLINA 27702

Telephone: 919-682-9691

Telecopier: 919-688-9107

URL: http://www.pwkl.com

General Civil and Criminal Trial and Appellate Practice, Personal Injury, Commercial Litigation, Commercial Real Estate, Corporate, Bankruptcy, Environmental Law, Government Contracts Law, Professional Negligence.

FIRM PROFILE: Pulley, Watson, King & Lischer, P.A. was formed by merger in 1982. A full service practice, the firm serves the state of North Carolina. Areas of concentration include Personal Injury, Medical Malpractice, and Commercial/Corporate. The firm encourages continuing legal education, professional development and participation in professional association activities and civic affairs.

MALVERN F. KING, JR., born Roanoke Rapids, North Carolina, January 26, 1943; admitted to bar, 1968, North Carolina, U.S. District Court, Middle, Western and Eastern Districts of North Carolina, U.S. Court of Appeals, Fourth Circuit, U.S. Court of Appeals for the Armed Forces and U.S. Supreme Court. *Education:* University of North Carolina at Chapel Hill (A.B., 1965; J.D., 1968). Delta Theta Phi (President, 1967-1968). *Member:* North Carolina (Chairman, Young Lawyers Section, 1978-1979; Chairman, General Practice Section, 1998-1999; Board of Governors, 2002-2005) and American (Member, Executive Council, Young Lawyers Division, 1977-1978) Bar Associations; Fourteenth Judicial District and North Carolina State Bars. [U.S. Navy, Active Duty, 1968-1972; Ret. Captain, JAGC, U.S. Naval Reserve (1975-1993)]. ***PRACTICE AREAS:*** Corporate Law; Business Litigation; Zoning, Planning and Land Use; Commercial Real Estate. ***Email:*** MFK@PWKL.com

RICHARD N. WATSON, born Lumberton, North Carolina, January 13, 1946; admitted to bar, 1974, North Carolina; 1975, U.S. District Court, Eastern and Middle Districts of North Carolina, U.S. Court of Appeals, Fourth Circuit, U.S. Court of Appeals for the Armed Forces and U.S. Supreme Court. *Education:* University of North Carolina at Chapel Hill (B.A., 1968; J.D., 1974). Certified Superior Court Mediator. *Member:* North Carolina and American Bar Associations; Fourteenth Judicial District Bar Association; North Carolina State Bar; North Carolina Academy of Trial Lawyers; The Association of Trial Lawyers of America; The American Board of Trial Advocates; The Triangle Circle of Advocates; The Academy of Catastrophic Injury Attorneys. [Capt., U.S. Army, 1968-1971]. ***PRACTICE AREAS:*** Personal Injury; Environmental Law; Litigation. ***Email:*** RNW@PWKL.com

TRACY KENYON LISCHER, born St. Louis, Missouri, October 3, 1944; admitted to bar, 1984, North Carolina and U.S. District Court, Eastern and Middle Districts of North Carolina, U.S. Court of Appeals, Fourth Circuit, U.S. Court of Appeals for the Armed Forces and U.S. Supreme Court. *Education:* University of Missouri (B.A., with honors, 1965); St. Louis University (M.A., 1967; Ph.D., 1977); University of North Carolina at Chapel Hill (J.D., with honors, 1984). Phi Beta Kappa. Recipient, American Jurisprudence Awards in Torts and Evidence. Staff Member, 1982-1983 and Executive Editor, 1983-1984, North Carolina Journal of International Law and Commercial Regulation. Author: "U.S. v Falvey: A Constitutionality Test for Foreign Electronic Intelligence Surveillance," North Carolina Journal of International Law, Vol. 8, No. 1, 1982; "Extending the Rule of Reason to Pendent Jurisdiction," North Carolina Journal of International Law, Vol. 9, No. 3, 1984. Law Clerk to Hon. Willis P. Whichard, North Carolina Court of Appeals, 1984-1985. *Member:* North Carolina Bar Association; North Carolina State Bar; North Carolina Academy of Trial Lawyers; The Association of Trial Lawyers of America; North Carolina Association of Women Attorneys (Past President). ***PRACTICE AREAS:*** Medical Malpractice; Personal Injury; Wrongful Death; Kernicterus cases. ***Email:*** TKL@PWKL.com

MICHAEL J. O'FOGHLUDHA, born Ann Arbor, Michigan, December 25, 1956; admitted to bar, 1982, North Carolina; 1988, U.S. District Court, Eastern District of North Carolina, U.S. Court of Appeals for the Armed Forces, U.S. Supreme Court and U.S. Court of Federal Claims. *Education:* Duke University (A.B., cum laude, 1978); University of North Carolina at Chapel Hill (J.D., with honors, 1982). Assistant Public Defender, 12th Judicial District, 1984-1987. Certified Superior Court Mediator. *Member:* Durham County and North Carolina Bar Associations; The Association of Trial Lawyers of America; North Carolina Academy of Trial Lawyers. ***LANGUAGES:*** French. ***REPORTED CASES:*** Electric Supply v. Swain Electric 328 NC 651 (1991); State v. Lockear 84 NC App. 637 (1987) In RE: Bavnhill 72 NC App. 530 (1985). ***PRACTICE AREAS:*** Personal Injury; Litigation; Workers Compensation. ***Email:*** MJO@PWKL.com

CHARLES F. CARPENTER, born Raleigh, North Carolina, April 3, 1957; admitted to bar, 1982, North Carolina, U.S. District Court, Eastern, Western and Middle Districts of North Carolina and U.S. Court of Appeals, Fourth Circuit. *Education:* University of North Carolina at Chapel Hill (B.A., with honors, 1979; J.D., 1982). Phi Eta Sigma; Phi Beta Kappa. Certified Superior Court Mediator. *Member:* Durham County, North Carolina (Member, Litigation and Bankruptcy Sections) and American Bar Associations (Member, Litigation Section); North Carolina State Bar. ***PRACTICE AREAS:*** Personal Injury Law; Bankruptcy; Creditors Rights. ***Email:*** cfc@pwkl.com

GUY W. CRABTREE, born Durham, North Carolina, September 4, 1948; admitted to bar, 1978, North Carolina, U.S. District Court, Eastern, Middle and Western Districts of North Carolina, U.S. Court of Appeals, Fourth Circuit, U.S. Tax Court and U.S. Court of Appeals for the Federal Circuit. *Education:* University of North Carolina at Chapel Hill (B.A., 1975); North Carolina Central University (J.D., cum laude, 1978). Recipient, American Jurisprudence Award in Civil Procedure. Member, North Carolina Central University Law Journal, 1976-1978. Certified Superior Court Mediator. *Member:* Durham County and North Carolina Bar Associations; North Carolina State Bar; North Carolina Academy of Trial Lawyers (Member, Board of Governors, 1993—; Vice-President of Education, 1997-1999, 2002-2005; Vice-President of Public Education, 2005—; Continuing Legal Education Committee, 1988-1999; Chair, Auto Torts Section, 1999-2000; Political Action Com-

(This Listing Continued)

mittee, 2001-2004); The Association of Trial Lawyers of America. ***PRACTICE AREAS:*** Civil Practice; Trial Practice; Personal Injury Law; Wrongful Death; Insurance Law; Environmental Litigation; Malpractice Law; Business Torts. ***Email:*** gwc@pwkl.com

DIETER MAUCH, born Leonberg, Germany, December 3, 1959; admitted to bar, 1989, North Carolina, U.S. District Court, Eastern, Middle and Western Districts of North Carolina and U.S. Court of Appeals, Fourth Circuit. *Education:* University of North Carolina at Chapel Hill (B.A., 1982; J.D., 1989). Member: Holderness Moot Court Bench; Phillip C. Jessup Moot Court Team. Recipient, American Jurisprudence Award in Contracts. Listed in, Who's Who Among American Law Students. Instructor, Research and Writing, University of North Carolina School of Law, 1994-1995. *Member:* Durham County and North Carolina Bar Associations. ***PRACTICE AREAS:*** Commercial Litigation; Business Torts; Condemnation; Insurance Law; Personal Injury. ***Email:*** DMauch@PWKL.com

OF COUNSEL

W. PAUL PULLEY, JR., born Durham, North Carolina, August 30, 1936; admitted to bar, 1961, North Carolina, U.S. District Court, Eastern, Middle and Western Districts of North Carolina, U.S. Court of Appeals, Fourth Circuit, U.S. Court of Appeals for the Armed Forces and U.S. Supreme Court. *Education:* University of North Carolina at Chapel Hill (A.B., 1958; LL.B., 1961). Delta Theta Phi. Listed in Who's Who in American Law and The Best Lawyers in America. Member, North Carolina General Assembly, 1979-1986; Chairman, Judiciary IV Committee, 1983-1986. Chairman, Durham Educational Development Council, 1971-1972. *Member:* North Carolina and American Bar Associations; 14th Judicial District (Member, Executive Committee, 1970-1971) and North Carolina State Bars; North Carolina Academy of Trial Lawyers; The Association of Trial Lawyers of America. ***PRACTICE AREAS:*** Litigation; Medical Malpractice. ***Email:*** wppulley@ec.rr.com

MARK E. FOGEL, born New York, N.Y., November 28, 1942; admitted to bar, 1974, North Carolina; 1977, U.S. District Court, Eastern District of North Carolina; 1985, U.S. Court of Appeals, Fourth Circuit. *Education:* The Cooper Union (B.C.E., 1965); University of North Carolina at Chapel Hill (M.S., Environmental Engineering, 1967; J.D., 1974). Counsel, North Carolina Department of Natural and Economic Resources, 1974-1977. *Member:* North Carolina (Member, Environmental Law Section) and American (Member: Sections on: Environment, Energy and Resources) Bar Associations. (Also practicing individually at Raleigh, North Carolina). ***PRACTICE AREAS:*** Groundwater Contamination; Hazardous Waste Management; Superfund; Toxic Torts; Underground Storage Tanks; Water Pollution. ***Email:*** mef@pwkl.com

WILLIAM L. STANFORD, JR., born Rome, Georgia, June 23, 1941; admitted to bar, 1971, Florida; 1974, U.S. District Court, Middle District of Florida; 1977, North Carolina; 1987, U.S. District Court, Middle District of North Carolina; 1988, U.S. District Court, Eastern District of North Carolina; 1989, U.S. District Court, Western District of North Carolina and U.S. Tax Court; 1995, U.S. Court of Appeals, for the Armed Forces and U.S. Supreme Court. *Education:* University of Florida (B.A., 1963); University of Oregon (J.D., 1967). Phi Delta Phi (President, 1966-1967). *Member:* Durham County and North Carolina Bar Associations (Member, Estate Planning and Fiduciary Law Section, 1987); North Carolina State Bar. ***PRACTICE AREAS:*** Probate; Trusts and Estates; Commercial Transactions; Corporate. ***Email:*** WLS@PWKL.com

JAMES A. CLARK, born Jacksonville, North Carolina, March 25, 1967; admitted to bar, 1999, North Carolina, U.S. District Court, Eastern, Middle and Western Districts of North Carolina, U.S. Court of Appeals, Fourth Circuit and U.S. Supreme Court. *Education:* Columbus College (B.S., 1989); University of Arkansas (J.D., 1999). Quarterfinalist, Craven Memorial Moot Court Competition, University of North Carolina, 1999. Recipient, Mitchell Williams Board of Advocates Scholarship. Author: "Collections In North Carolina," chapter of the 2004 North Carolina Bar Association General Practice Section Deskbook. CLE Speaker, Preparing For Deposition and Using Deposition At Trial, N.C. Bar Association General Practice Section, 2004. CLAE Speaker: Service of Process/Rule 45 Subpoenas, N.C. Paralegal Association, 2004; Parties, Pleadings and Motions, N.C. Academy of Trial Lawyers, 2004; Applying the Federal Rules of Evidence to Litigation and Federal Rules of Civil Procedure - The path of Litigation, N.C. Paralegal Association, 2002. Symposium Speaker, Survival Skills for the New Attorney, Duke University, 2002. Chairman, Board of Advocates, 1999. *Member:* Durham County and North Carolina (Member: Construction Law Section; Technology Subcommittee) Bar Associations; North Carolina Academy of Trial Lawyers. [STG2, USN, 1990-1996; SGT, USARNG, 1996-1999]. ***PRACTICE AREAS:*** Commercial Litigation; Construction Law; Corporate Law; Bankruptcy Creditor Representation; Estate Litigation; Intellectual Property. ***Email:*** jac@pwkl.com

APPROVED ATTORNEYS FOR: Lawyers Title Insurance Corp.; AMI Title Insurance Co.; Chicago Title Insurance Co.; Investors Title Insurance Co.; Commonwealth Land Title Insurance Co.
REPRESENTATIVE CLIENTS: Carolina Learning Services Corp.; SEHED Development Corp.; Montrose Capital; Durham Products, Inc.; Durham Convention & Visitors Bureau.
REFERENCE: NationsBank of North Carolina.

THE RICHARDSON LAW FIRM, PLLC

Established in 1996

125 EAST PARRISH STREET
DURHAM, NORTH CAROLINA 27701
Telephone: 919-680-2300
Fax: 919-680-2500
URL: http://www.kwrlaw.net
Email: info@kwrlaw.net
URL: http://www.lawyers.com/katwilliamslaw

Personal Injury, Family Law, Traffic Violations, Civil Practice, Criminal Law, Collection.

KATHY WILLIAMS RICHARDSON, born Okinawa, Japan, August 2, 1965; admitted to bar, 1992, North Carolina. *Education:* East Carolina University (B.S., 1987); Wake Forest University (J.D., 1992). Attorney, Gastonia Public Defenders Office, 1992-1994. Attorney, Durham Public Defenders Office, 1994-1996. *Member:* Durham County, North Carolina and American Bar Associations; George White Bar Association; North Carolina Academy of Trial Lawyers; National Association of Criminal Defense Lawyers; Association of Trial Lawyers of America. [Captain. U.S. Army, 1987-1996]. ***PRACTICE AREAS:*** Criminal Law; Drivers License Suspension; Driving While Intoxicated; Criminal Defense; Traffic Violations; Family Law; Divorce; Separation Agreements; Uncontested Divorce; Spousal Support; Premarital Agreements; Paternity; Marital Property Distribution; Alimony; Annulment. ***Email:*** kwr@kwrlaw.net

(This Listing Continued)

SANDS ANDERSON MARKS & MILLER

A PROFESSIONAL CORPORATION

3622 LYCKAN PARKWAY, SUITE 4005
P.O. BOX 51266 (27717)
DURHAM, NORTH CAROLINA 27707
Telephone: 919-401-6818
Facsimile: 919-401-8114
URL: http://www.SandsAnderson.com

Radford, Virginia Office: 101 W. Main Street, P.O. Box 1052, 24143-1052. Telephone: 540-639-1601. Facsimile: 540-639-6802.
Richmond, Virginia Office: 801 East Main Street, Suite 1800, P.O. Box 1998, 23218-1998. Telephone: 804-648-1636. Facsimile: 804-783-7291.
Fredericksburg, Virginia Office: 904 Princess Anne Street, Suite 407, P.O. Box 907, 22404-0907. Telephone: 540-373-2504. Fax: 540-371-8158.
McLean, Virginia Office: 1481 Chain Bridge Road, Suite 200, 22101. Telephone: 703-893-3600. Facsimile: 703-893-8484.

Government, Municipal Law, Securities, Environmental Law, Civil Litigation, Construction Law.

PRINCIPAL

PAUL C. JACOBSON, born Huntington, NY, 1956; admitted to bar, 1981, Arizona; 1991, Virginia; 2000, North Carolina. *Education:* Pomona College (B.A., 1978); Arizona State University (J.D., 1981). Special Projects Editor, Arizona State Law Journal, 1980-1981. *National Association of Bond Lawyers; North Carolina Association of Municipal Attorneys; Local Government Attorneys of Virginia.* ***PRACTICE AREAS:*** Government; Public Finance; Securities Law; Municipal Law. ***Email:*** PJacobson@SandsAnderson.com

COUNSEL

DAILEY J. DERR, born 1941; admitted to bar, 1972, North Carolina; 1975, District of Columbia. *Education:* University of North Carolina (B.A., 1964; J.D., 1971); George Washington University (M.A., 1966). *Member:* Durham County, North Carolina and American Bar Associations; North Carolina State Bar; The District of Columbia Bar; American Arbitration Association; Professional Construction Estimators Association of America, Inc. (Triangle Chapter); The Associated General Contractors of America; Carolinas AGC Chapter and Fourth Circuit Judicial Conference. ***PRACTICE AREAS:*** Construction Law; Commercial Real Estate; Regulatory Law; Negotiation; Litigation; Alternative Dispute Resolution. ***Email:*** DDerr@SandsAnderson.com

ASSOCIATE

CELIE B. RICHARDSON, born Clinton, NC, 1951; admitted to bar, 1998, North Carolina; U.S. District Court, Eastern, Middle and Western Districts of North Carolina; U.S. Court of Appeals, Fourth Circuit. *Education:* University of North Carolina at Chapel Hill (A.B., with highest honors, Phi Beta Kappa, 1973; J.D., with honors, 1998); University of Minnesota (M.A., 1975). Articles Editor, North Carolina Law Review, 1997-1998. *Member:* Durham County and North Carolina Bar Associations; Orange-Chatham Bar; North Carolina Association of Women Attorneys; North Carolina Association of Municipal Attorneys; American Agricultural Law Association. ***PRACTICE AREAS:*** Civil Litigation; Business and Professional Litigation; Commercial Litigation; Civil Rights Litigation; Employment; Personal Injury Law; Construction Litigation. ***Email:*** CRichardson@SandsAnderson.com

All Attorneys are Members of the North Carolina State Bar.

SESSOMS & ROGERS, P.A.

3326 CHAPEL HILL BLVD., SUITE A-200
DURHAM, NORTH CAROLINA 27707
Telephone: 919-688-1000
Fax: 919-688-9000
Email: mail@sessomslaw.com
URL: http://www.sessomslaw.com
Mailing Address: P.O. Box 52508, Durham, NC 27717

Collections, Civil Litigation, Commercial Litigation, Banking Law, Consumer Bankruptcy, Traffic Violations.

STUART M. SESSOMS, JR., born Baltimore, Maryland, November 4, 1947; admitted to bar, 1974, North Carolina. *Education:* University of North Carolina at Chapel Hill (A.B., 1969); Duke University School of Law (J.D., 1974). Psi Chi; Phi Alpha Delta. *Member:* North Carolina State Bar; American Bar Association; North Carolina Academy of Trial Lawyers; Commercial Law League of America; National Association of Retail Collection Attorneys. ***PRACTICE AREAS:*** Collections; Civil Litigation; Commercial Litigation; Banking Law.

LEE C. ROGERS, born Syracuse, New York, March 1, 1955; admitted to bar, 1982, North Carolina. *Education:* Duke University (B.A., 1977); North Carolina Central University (J.D., 1982). *Member:* Durham County Bar Association; North Carolina Academy of Trial Lawyers; National Association of Consumer Bankruptcy Attorneys. ***PRACTICE AREAS:*** Consumer Bankruptcy; Traffic Violations; Collections.

(This Listing Continued)

SESSOMS & ROGERS, P.A., Durham—Continued

REPRESENTATIVE CLIENTS: Providian National Bank; Branch Banking & Trust Co.; First Select, Inc.

LAW OFFICE OF NICOLE D. SLADE

315 EAST CHAPEL HILL STREET, SUITE 204
DURHAM, NORTH CAROLINA 27702
Telephone: 919-680-6521
Fax: 919-680-6704
Email: attyndslade@verizon.net
URL: http://www.sladelawofc.com

Family Law, Civil Litigation, Bankruptcy, Personal Injury, Traffic.

NICOLE D. SLADE, born Chapel Hill, North Carolina, November 13, 1971; admitted to bar, 2001, North Carolina. *Education:* University of North Carolina at Chapel Hill (B.A., 1993); North Carolina Central University School of Law (J.D., with honors, 2000). ***PRACTICE AREAS:*** Family Law (70%); Civil Litigation (10%); Bankruptcy (10%); Personal Injury (5%); Traffic Violations (5%).

SOLOMON & MITCHELL, PLLC

5850 FAYETTEVILLE ROAD - SUITE 210
DURHAM, NORTH CAROLINA 27713
Telephone: 919-687-4577
Fax: 919-687-4578
URL: http://www.solomonmitchell.com

General Civil Practice. Business Transactions, Family Law, Real Property, Personal Injury, Estate Planning, Creditors' Rights, Health Care, Litigation and Appeals.

LAUREL E. SOLOMON, born Queens, New York, March 17, 1962; admitted to bar, 1988, New York, District of Columbia and North Carolina; 1989, U.S. District Court, Middle District of North Carolina; 1990, U.S. District Court, Eastern District of North Carolina and U.S. Court of Appeals, Fourth Circuit; 1993, U.S. District Court, Western District of North Carolina. *Education:* State University of New York at Albany (B.A., magna cum laude, 1983); Duke University (M.A., 1987; J.D., 1987). Law Clerk, New York Supreme Court, Appellate Division, 1987-1988. *Member:* Durham County, North Carolina (Member, Family Law Section) and American Bar Associations; North Carolina Academy of Trial Lawyers (Member, Family Law Section); The Association of Trial Lawyers of America. (Board Certified Specialist in Family Law, North Carolina State Board of Legal Specialization). ***PRACTICE AREAS:*** Family Law; Creditors' Rights; Personal Injury; Civil Litigation. ***Email:*** lesolomon@mindspring.com

HENRY A. MITCHELL, III, born Greensboro, North Carolina, December 15, 1962; admitted to bar, 1991, North Carolina and U.S. District Court, Middle District of North Carolina; 1992, U.S. District Court, Eastern District of North Carolina. *Education:* Davidson College (B.A., 1985); Wake Forest University (J.D., 1991); Campbell University (Master of Trust and Investment Management, 2004). Omicron Delta Epsilon; Phi Delta Phi. *Member:* Durham County (President, Young Lawyers Division, 1997-1998; Member, Board of Directors, 1997-1998), North Carolina (Member, Sections on: Real Property; Business Law) and American (Delegate, House of Delegates, 1997-1999; Member, Sections On: Real Property and Probate) Bar Associations. ***PRACTICE AREAS:*** Commercial Transactions; Estate Planning; Estate Administration; Corporate Law; Real Property. ***Email:*** hamitchell@mindspring.com

ASSOCIATE

MARTY S. McCONCHIE, born Alexandria, Virginia, April 5, 1975; admitted to bar, 2000, North Carolina; 2004, U.S. District Court, Eastern, Middle and Western Districts of North Carolina. *Education:* Wake Forest University (B.A., 1997); George Mason University (J.D., 2000). *Member:* Durham County (President, Young Lawyers Division, 2004), North Carolina (Member, Real Property Section; Member, Public Service Advisory and Chair, Small Firm and Solo Practice Committees) and American (Member, Sections on: Real Property; Probate) Bar Associations. ***LANGUAGES:*** Spanish. ***PRACTICE AREAS:*** Real Property; Estate Planning; Corporate. ***Email:*** mmcconch@mindspring.com

REPRESENTATIVE CLIENTS: Self-Help Credit Union; GKN Automotive, Inc.; Blackhorse Run of Durham Homeowners' Association; Colvard Farms Development Company, LLC; Parkwood Association.

STARK LAW GROUP, PLLC

DURHAM, NORTH CAROLINA

(See Chapel Hill)

Construction, Commercial and Corporate Litigation. Personal Injury Litigation, Environmental Law, Computer and Intellectual Property Law, Corporate Acquisitions and Real Property Law, Real Estate Closings, Business Law.

STUBBS, COLE, BREEDLOVE, PRENTIS & BIGGS, P.L.L.C.

Established in 1932
122 EAST PARRISH STREET
P.O. BOX 376
DURHAM, NORTH CAROLINA 27702
Telephone: 919-682-9331
Fax: 919-682-5590
Real Estate Fax: 919-688-0277
Email: stubbscole@aol.com
URL: http://www.stubbscole.com

General Civil and Criminal Trial Practice. Banking, Corporate, Real Estate, Wills and Estates, Estate Planning, Construction and Personal Injury Law.

ALLSTON J. STUBBS (1909-2003)
IRVIN P. BREEDLOVE, JR. (1946-2003)

MEMBERS OF FIRM

JAMES A. COLE, JR., born Spartanburg, South Carolina, September 13, 1935; admitted to bar, 1961, North Carolina. *Education:* Catawba College and University of North Carolina (A.B., 1957); University of North Carolina (LL.B., 1961). Delta Theta Phi. *Member:* Durham County, North Carolina and American Bar Associations; The North Carolina State Bar; North Carolina Academy of Trial Lawyers; American Judicature Society. ***PRACTICE AREAS:*** Wills; Trusts and Estates; Business Law; Banking; Commercial. ***Email:*** jacole@stubbscole.com

RICHARD F. PRENTIS, JR., born St. Petersburg, Florida, May 8, 1946; admitted to bar, 1973, Florida; 1974, North Carolina. *Education:* Duke University (A.B., 1968); University of North Carolina (J.D., 1972). Law Clerk to the Honorable Gerald Bard Tjoflat, U.S. District Judge, Middle District Of Florida, 1972-1973. *Member:* North Carolina Bar Association; The North Carolina State Bar; The Florida Bar; North Carolina Academy of Trial Lawyers. ***PRACTICE AREAS:*** Commercial Law; Real Estate; Banking; Litigation. ***Email:*** rfprentis@stubbscole.com

C. THOMAS BIGGS, born Durham, North Carolina, November 8, 1937; admitted to bar, 1962, North Carolina. *Education:* Duke University (B.S.C.E., 1959; LL.B., 1962). Delta Theta Phi. *Member:* Durham County and North Carolina Bar Associations; The North Carolina State Bar. ***PRACTICE AREAS:*** Real Estate. ***Email:*** ctbiggs@stubbscole.com

JONATHAN W. BIGGS, born Durham, North Carolina, December 1, 1964; admitted to bar, 1990, North Carolina, U.S. Court of Appeals, Fourth Circuit and U.S. District Court, Middle, Eastern and Western Districts of North Carolina. *Education:* Duke University (A.B., 1987); Wake Forest University School of Law (J.D., 1990). *Member:* Durham County (Young Lawyers Division, President, 1993; Vice President, 1992; Secretary, 1991), North Carolina and American Bar Associations; North Carolina State Bar. ***PRACTICE AREAS:*** Banking; Commercial; Business. ***Email:*** jwbiggs@stubbscole.com

ASSOCIATES

C. SCOTT HOLMES, born Ft. Levenworth, Kansas, January 2, 1972; admitted to bar, 1998, North Carolina; 2001, U.S. District Court, Middle and Eastern District of North Carolina. *Education:* University of North Carolina at Chapel Hill (B.A., with highest honors, 1994; J.D. with honors, 1998). Phi Beta Kappa. Law Clerk to the Honorable Judge John C. Martin of the North Carolina Court of Appeals. State Court Appointed Lists for Criminal Felonies, Appeals and Capital Cases. *Member:* Durham county and North Carolina Bar Association; North Carolina State Bar; National Lawyer's Guild; North Carolina Academy of Trial Lawyers; American Civil Liberties Union. ***PRACTICE AREAS:*** Criminal Law; Trial Practice; Appellate Practice; Civil Litigation; Personal Injury; Civil Rights.

WILLIAM H. PATE, born Southern Pines, North Carolina, October 18, 1978; admitted to bar, 2004, North Carolina. *Education:* University of North Carolina at Chapel Hill (B.S., Business Administration, 2001); Campbell University (J.D., cum laude, 2004; M.B.A., 2004). Staff Member, Notes and Comments Editor, Campbell Law Review. Author, "To Sanction or Not To Sanction: Why Arguing Against the Court's Precedent Is Not An Automatic Rule II Violation According To Hunter v. Earthgrains Co. Bakery," 25 Campbell L. Rev. 115, 2002. ***PRACTICE AREAS:*** Business Law; Corporate Law; Estate Planning; Tax Planning. ***Email:*** whpate@stubbscole.com

ROBIN M. BAREFOOT, born Elmhurst, New York, February 6, 1958; admitted to bar, 1985, North Carolina. *Education:* University of North Carolina at Chapel Hill (B.A., 1980); North Carolina Central University School of Law (J.D., 1985). *Member:* North Carolina State Bar (Member, Real Property and Estate Planning Sections). ***PRACTICE AREAS:*** Estate Planning; Wills.

ATTORNEYS FOR: National Commerce Financial Corp.; Central Carolina Bank and Trust Company; North Carolina Mutual Wholesale Drugs Co. L.A. Downey & Son Construction Co.; Howerton-Bryan Co., Inc.; Cimarron Capital, Inc.; Durham Association of Realtors, Inc.
APPROVED ATTORNEYS FOR: St. Paul Title Insurance Company; Pioneer Title Insurance Co.; Chicago Title Insurance Co.; Lawyers Title Insurance Corp.; Commonwealth Title Insurance Co.; Investors Title Insurance Co.; United Title Insurance Co.

THARRINGTON SMITH

DURHAM, NORTH CAROLINA

(See Raleigh)

Civil and Criminal Trials and Appeals in all State and Federal Courts, Mediation and Alternative Dispute Resolution, Education Law, Constitutional Law, Employment Law, Family Law, Professional Licensure Proceedings, Personal Injury, Voting Rights, Local Government Law, Construction Contracts and Litigation, Business and Corporate Law, Commercial Litigation, Alcoholic Beverage Control Law, Administrative Law, Tax Litigation, Unfair Competition, Copyright, Legislative and Lobbying, Sports and Entertainment Law.

TWIGGS, BESKIND, STRICKLAND & RABENAU, P.A.

DURHAM, NORTH CAROLINA

(See Raleigh)

Personal Injury, Products Liability, Business Torts, Medical and other Professional Negligence, Federal and State Tort Claims, Environmental Torts, Insurance Bad Faith, Aviation Law and Wrongful Death.

THE LAW OFFICES OF H. WOOD VANN AND EDWARD J. FALCONE

SUITE 200, 120 EAST PARRISH STREET
DURHAM, NORTH CAROLINA 27701
Telephone: 919-682-9273; 919-682-4638
Facsimile: 919-683-5533
URL: http://www.lawyers.com/vannandfalcone

Criminal Law, Personal Injury, Auto Accidents, Family Law, Divorce, Traffic Violations, Driving While Intoxicated..

FIRM PROFILE: The law offices of H. Wood Vann and Edward J. Falcone have been serving Durham and the surrounding counties in excess of twenty (20) years. The firm operates primarily in Durham County, but will travel to other local counties. The firm practices in all State Courts and in Federal Court (primarily criminal). Edward J. Falcone and H. Wood Vann are life long residents of Durham. Tyler S. Pokrass has resided in Durham since law school. The firm's original founder was Arthur Vann, II, who practiced with distinction for almost fifty (50) years. The firm concentrates its practice in Criminal, Traffic, Personal Injury, Family Law and Workers Compensation and is experienced in both jury and non-jury litigation.

H. WOOD VANN, born Durham, North Carolina, July 20, 1957; admitted to bar, 1982, North Carolina and U.S. District Court, Eastern and Middle Districts of North Carolina; U.S. Court of Appeals, Fourth Circuit. *Education:* Wake Forest University (B.A., 1979); University of North Carolina (J.D., 1982). Phi Delta Phi. *Member:* Durham County Bar Association; North Carolina State Bar; North Carolina Academy of Trial Lawyers. ***PRACTICE AREAS:*** Personal Injury; Criminal Law; Family Law; Traffic Violations. **Email:** hwoodvanlawoffice@verizon.net

EDWARD J. FALCONE, born Durham, North Carolina, February 20, 1952; admitted to bar, 1979, North Carolina; 1983, U.S. District Court, Middle District of North Carolina. *Education:* Duke University (B.A., 1974); University of South Carolina (J.D., 1978). *Member:* North Carolina Academy of Trial Lawyers. ***PRACTICE AREAS:*** Automobile Accidents and Injuries; Criminal Law; Traffic Violations; Family Law; Personal Injury; Workers Compensation. **Email:** edwardjfalcone@verizon.net

ASSOCIATE

TYLER SETH POKRASS, born Lusaka, Zambia, Africa, October 23, 1970; admitted to bar, 1997, North Carolina. *Education:* University of North Carolina at Chapel Hill (B.A., 1992); North Carolina Central University (J.D., 1996). President, 1995-1999 and Member, 1994-1995, Phi Delta Phi. *Member:* Durham County Bar Association; North Carolina State Bar; North Carolina Academy Trial Lawyers. ***PRACTICE AREAS:*** Personal Injury; Criminal Law; Traffic Violations.

THE VIRA LAW FIRM, PA

133 CELESTE CIRCLE
DURHAM, NORTH CAROLINA 27517
Telephone: 919-918-8000
Fax: 919-918-7887
Email: lisa_vira@nc.rr.com
URL: http://www.lisakvira.com

Carrboro Office: 205 W. Main Street, Suite 207, 27510. Telephone: 919-918-8000. Fax: 919-918-7887.

Trusts and Estates, Probate, Wills, Real Estate, Taxation, Business Law.

(For complete biographical data on all personnel, see Professional Biographies at Carrboro, North Carolina)

WALKER & LAMBE, P.L.L.C.

Established in 1983

SOUTH SQUARE CORPORATE CENTRE II
3708 MAYFAIR STREET, SUITE 100
P.O. BOX 51549
DURHAM, NORTH CAROLINA 27717-1549
Telephone: 919-493-8411
Fax: 919-493-2047
URL: http://www.WalkerLambe.com

Business Law, Corporate Law, Corporation, Taxation, Real Estate, Estate Planning and Probate Law, Trusts Administration.

FIRM PROFILE: Walker & Lambe, has served the Durham, Chapel Hill, Raleigh and Research Triangle area for more than twenty years, providing established support for clients in matters relating to business, estate planning, estate trust administration, commercial real estate and financial services law.

(This Listing Continued)

MEMBERS OF FIRM

WILLIAM H. LAMBE, JR., born Winston-Salem, North Carolina, December 8, 1946; admitted to bar, 1973, North Carolina. *Education:* Wake Forest University (B.A., 1969; J.D., 1973). Phi Delta Phi. Member, 1971-1972 and Managing Editor, 1972-1973, Wake Forest Law Review. *Member:* 14th Judicial District Bar (Treasurer, 1986-1987; Vice President, 1990-1992; President, 1992-1993) and North Carolina Bar Associations; North Carolina State Bar (Trustee, IOLTA Program, 1998-2003). ***PRACTICE AREAS:*** Corporate Law; Business Law; Business Transactions; Contracts; Real Estate Law; Personnel Law; Employment Law. **Email:** whl@walkerlambe.com

EDWIN J. WALKER, JR., born Concord, North Carolina, May 7, 1944; admitted to bar, 1969, North Carolina; 1980, U.S. Tax Court; U.S. District Court, Middle District of North Carolina. *Education:* Davidson College (B.A., 1966); University of North Carolina (J.D., 1969). Phi Delta Phi. Duke University Estate Planning Council. *Member:* North Carolina and American (Member, Section of Taxation; Adjunct Member, Committee on Employee Benefits and Committee on Estate and Gift Taxes, 1979—) Bar Associations; Fourteenth Judicial District Bar (Treasurer, 1982-1983); North Carolina Society of Hospital Attorneys. (Board Certified Specialist in Estate Planning and Probate Law, North Carolinas State Board of Legal Specialization). ***PRACTICE AREAS:*** Tax Law; Estate Planning Law; Nonprofit and Charitable Organizations; Corporate Law. **Email:** ejw@walkerlambe.com

STEPHEN C. RHUDY, born Schenectady, New York, September 4, 1951; admitted to bar, 1977, North Carolina; 1980, U.S. Tax Court. *Education:* State University of New York at Binghamton (B.A., with honors, 1973); Duke University (J.D., with distinction, 1977). Phi Beta Kappa. Lecturer, North Carolina State University, 1988-1992. *Member:* Durham County, North Carolina and American Bar Associations. ***PRACTICE AREAS:*** Estate Planning; Estate and Trust Administration; Business Transactions; Tax Law; Tax Exempt Organizations. **Email:** scr@walkerlambe.com

MARK O. COSTLEY, born Stillwater, Oklahoma, June 12, 1960; admitted to bar, 1985, Oklahoma; U.S. District Court, Northern and Western Districts of Oklahoma; 1990, North Carolina; U.S. District Court, Middle and Western Districts of North Carolina; U.S. Court of Appeals, Tenth Circuit. *Education:* Oklahoma State University; Duke University (A.B., magna cum laude, 1982; J.D., 1985). Editor, Duke University Legal Research Program, 1984-1985. National Moot Court Team. Trustee, Duke University, 1982-1985. Certified Court Mediator, North Carolina, 1993—. *Member:* Oklahoma, North Carolina and American Bar Associations; North Carolina State Bar. ***PRACTICE AREAS:*** Estate Planning; Estate and Trust Administration; Business Law; Non-Profit Organizations; Business Transactions; Mediation; Estate Litigation; Business Litigation.

OF COUNSEL

RALPH LEE McCAUGHAN, born Gainesville, Florida, November 14, 1939; admitted to bar, 1966, Florida; 1970, U.S. District Court, Southern District of Florida; 1971, U.S. Tax Court; 1984, District of Columbia; 1988, North Carolina. *Education:* Duke University (A.B., 1961; LL.B., 1966). Senior Lecturer in Law, Duke University School of Law, 1985-1989. President, Durham/Orange Estate Planning Council, 1986-1987. Member, The Duke University Estate Planning Council, 1981—. *Member:* Durham County, North Carolina and American Bar Associations. [U.S. Navy Reserve, LCDR (SC) 1961-1972]. ***PRACTICE AREAS:*** University Law; Estate and Trust Law; Tax Law; Technology Licensing and Research Law.

KATHARINE B. BUCHANAN, born Boulder, Colorado, November 6, 1970; admitted to bar, 2001, Virginia; 2002, North Carolina. *Education:* Duke University (A.B., cum laude, 1992); University of Virginia (J.D., 2001). Hardy C. Dillard Fellow, University of Virginia. Member, Managing Board, Virginia Tax Review. *Member:* Durham County, North Carolina, Virginia and American Bar Associations; Durham-Orange Estate Planning Council. ***PRACTICE AREAS:*** Taxation; Estate Planning; Estate Administration; Nonprofit and Charitable Organizations. **Email:** kbb@walkerlambe.com

CHARLES W. WHITE (Retired)

LISA HOLLAND POWELL (Retired)

ASSOCIATES

DONNA RAY CHMURA, born Greensboro, North Carolina, July 8, 1967; admitted to bar, 1995, North Carolina. *Education:* Northwestern University (B.S.J., Sigma Delta Chi, 1989); The George Washington University (J.D., cum laude, 1995). Member, The George Washington University Law Review, 1994-1995. *Member:* Durham County and North Carolina Bar Associations; North Carolina State Bar (Member, Sections on: Business Law; Intellectual Property). ***PRACTICE AREAS:*** Commercial Real Estate Acquisitions; Commercial Conveyancing; Commercial Real Estate Contracts; Commercial Real Estate Sales; Business Development; Business Dissolutions; Business Formation; Business Organization; Business Planning; Business Start-Ups; Business Succession Planning; Buy-Sell Agreements; Buying and Selling of Businesses; Family Business Successions; Limited Liability Company Law; Professional Practices; Small Business Law; Sole Proprietorships; Strategic Alliances; Commercial Transactions; Sale of Goods; Secured Transactions; Uniform Commercial Code; Computer Contracts; Information Technology Contracts; Information Technology Licensing; Software Licensing; Intellectual Property Licensing; Confidentiality Agreements; Employment Contracts; Personnel Policies; Restrictive Covenants; Trademark Licensing; Trademark Prosecution. **Email:** drc@walkerlambe.com

JENNIFER WESTERHAUS ADAMS, born Des Moines, Iowa, December 20, 1974; admitted to bar, 2002, Georgia; 2005, North Carolina; U.S. District Court, Northern District of Georgia; U.S. District Court, Middle District of North Carolina. *Education:* University of Southern California (B.A./B.A., 1998); Duke University (A.M., 2002; J.D., 2002). Previously with Troutman Sanders LLP, Atlanta, Georgia. *Member:* State Bar of Georgia; North Carolina State Bar; American Bar Association. ***PRACTICE AREAS:*** Estate Planning; Business Law; Trademarks; Copyrights; Business Litigation. **Email:** jwa@walkerlambe.com

(This Listing Continued)

WALKER & LAMBE, P.L.L.C., Durham—Continued

REPRESENTATIVE CLIENTS: Woodland Associates, Inc.; Newton Instrument Co.; C.T. Wilson Construction Co.; Centurion Construction Co.; Carolina Door Controls, Inc.; Morgan Motors, Inc.; Insurance Accounting & Systems Association, Inc.; Durham Health Partners; Triangle Community Foundation.
APPROVED ATTORNEYS FOR: Lawyers Title of North Carolina; Investors Title Insurance Co.; Chicago Title Insurance Co.; Security Union Title Insurance Co.; The Title Company of North Carolina; United Title Insurance Co.; First American Title Insurance Co.; Commonwealth Land Title Insurance Co.; Fidelity National Title Insurance Co.

LAW OFFICE OF ANNE PAGE WATSON, PLLC

3500 WESTGATE DRIVE, SUITE 604
DURHAM, NORTH CAROLINA 27707
Telephone: 919-489-9058
Fax: 919-489-9309
URL: http://www.apwatson.com
Email: annepagewatson@apwatson.com
URL: http://www.lawyers.com/annepagewatson

Estate Planning, Estate Administration, Estate and Gift Taxation, Asset Protection, Small Business Law, Commercial Real Estate, Residential Real Estate, Condominium Law, Charitable Giving, Wills and Probate.

ANNE PAGE WATSON, born Louisville, Kentucky, 1949; admitted to bar, 1975, North Carolina. *Education:* University of North Carolina (A.B. 1972); Wake Forest University (J.D., 1975). Served on Durham Co. Equalization and Review Board, and Board of Directors for Durham Technical Community College Foundation, Inc. Member, WealthCounsel, LLC, a national organization of estate planning attorneys. *Member:* Durham and Orange County North Carolina Estate Planning Council.

THE WELLONS LAW FIRM

DURHAM, NORTH CAROLINA

(See Raleigh)

Corporate Law, Taxation, Employment Law, Family Law, Estate Planning, Estate Administration.

JAMES A. WILSON

Established in 2001
5322 HIGHGATE DRIVE, SUITE 243
DURHAM, NORTH CAROLINA 27713
Telephone: 919-361-4300
Fax: 919-361-4305
Email: jim@jamesawilson.com
URL: http://www.jamesawilson.com

Physicians Licensing, Medical Disciplinary Proceedings, Controlled Substances Law, Professional Conduct, Professional Discipline, Professional Sexual Misconduct, Hospital Peer Review, Hospital Privilege, Medical Staff Credentialing, Health Law, Medical Ethics, Medical-Legal Law, Physicians Rights, Professional Licensing, Professional Licensing Regulation, Health Care Licensing, Nurses Licensing.

FIRM PROFILE: Mr. Wilson is a former Chief Prosecutor and General Counsel for the North Carolina Medical Board.

JAMES A. WILSON, born Nashville, Tennessee, January 13, 1961; admitted to bar, 1989, North Carolina. *Education:* University of North Carolina (B.S., 1982; J.D., with honors, 1989). Order of the Coif. Business Manager, North Carolina Law Review, 1988-89. *Member:* North Carolina Bar Association (Member, Health Law Section Council, 1996-1999); North Carolina Society of Health Care Attorneys (Vice President, 2000-2001; President, 2001-2002); Susie M. Sharp Inn of Court; American Health Lawyers Association. ***PRACTICE AREAS:*** Physicians Licensing; Medical Disciplinary Proceedings; Controlled Substances Law; Professional Conduct; Professional Discipline; Professional Sexual Misconduct; Hospital Peer Review; Hospital Privilege; Medical Staff Credentialing; Health Law; Medical Ethics; Medical Law; Physicians Rights; Professional Licensing; Professional Licensing Regulation; Health Care Licensing; Nurses Licensing.

WINSTON & MAHER

DURHAM, NORTH CAROLINA

(See Chapel Hill)

General Civil, Criminal Trial Practice in all State and Federal Courts, Felonies, Misdemeanors, Drugs and Narcotics, White Collar Crime, Traffic Violations, Driving While Intoxicated.

THE DEUTERMAN LAW GROUP, P.A.

EDEN, NORTH CAROLINA

(See Greensboro)

Workers Compensation, Auto Accidents, Social Security Disability, Wrongful Death, Nursing Home Neglect, Slip and Fall, Products Liability.

C. ORVILLE LIGHT

407 S. VAN BUREN ROAD, SUITE C-D
EDEN, NORTH CAROLINA 27288
Telephone: 336-627-4566
Email: orvillelight@earthlink.net
URL: http://www.corvillelightlaw.com

General Practice. Workers Compensation, Real Estate, Corporation, Business Law, Family, Divorce, Adoptions, Child Custody and Support, Automobile Accidents, Wrongful Death, Trusts and Estates, Wills and Probate, Estate Planning and Personal Injury Law.

C. ORVILLE LIGHT, admitted to bar, 1960, North Carolina; 1977, U.S. Supreme Court. *Education:* Elon College; Wake Forest University (J.D., cum laude, 1960). Phi Alpha Delta. *Member:* North Carolina State Bar; North Carolina Academy of Trial Lawyers.

MADDREY ETRINGER & SMITH, L.L.P.

Established in 1984
610 HENRY STREET
P.O. BOX 507
EDEN, NORTH CAROLINA 27288
Telephone: 336-623-4491
Fax: 336-623-7308
Email: edenlawfirm@earthlink.net

General Trial Practice in all State and Federal Courts. Personal Injury, Automobile Accidents, Wrongful Death, Real Estate, Banking, Business and Corporate Law, Probate Law, Family Law, Divorce, Child Custody, Bankruptcy, Collections, Criminal, DWI, Traffic, Zoning, Planning and Land Use Law, Construction Law, Foreclosures.

MEMBERS OF FIRM

JOSEPH G. MADDREY, born Raleigh, North Carolina, October 6, 1941; admitted to bar, 1967, North Carolina. *Education:* Wake Forest University (B.A., 1964; J.D., 1967). (Board Certified Specialist in Real Property Law, North Carolina State Board of Legal Specialization). ***PRACTICE AREAS:*** Real Estate; Land Use; Banking Law; Business Law; Corporate Law; Probate; Foreclosures; Administrative Law.

WALTER J. ETRINGER, born Brooklyn, New York, December 23, 1947; admitted to bar, 1976, North Carolina. *Education:* North Carolina State University (B.A., with high honors, 1972); Wake Forest University (J.D., 1976). [Captain, U.S. Army, 1968-1972]. ***PRACTICE AREAS:*** Criminal Law; Family Law; Bankruptcy; Civil Litigation; Personal Injury.

MATTHEW W. SMITH, born Burlington, North Carolina, September 6, 1973; admitted to bar, 1998, North Carolina. *Education:* Campbell University (B.A., cum laude, 1995; J.D., 1998). ***PRACTICE AREAS:*** Construction Law; Business Law; Corporate Law; Real Estate; Civil Practice; Civil Litigation; Wills.

LOCAL COUNSEL FOR: Branch Banking & Trust Company; Brian Center Nursing Home; Spray Water Power and Land Company; Eden Mall; Rockingham County Association of Realtors; Citizens Economic Development, Inc. of Rockingham County; Eden Chamber of Commerce.
STATE COUNSEL FOR: First Mortgage of North Carolina, Inc.; Dominion Pipeline, LLC; Hutchins Petroleum Corp.
REPRESENTATIVE COUNSEL FOR: Branch Banking & Trust Company; Wachovia Bank and Trust Company; CMH Homes, Inc.; First Greensboro Home Equity, Inc.; Osborne Construction Company; The Wright Co. of N.C., Inc (residential and commercial construction and development); First National Bank Southeast.
APPROVED ATTORNEYS FOR: First American Title Insurance Company; Lawyers Title Insurance Company; Investors Title Insurance Company; Chicago Title Insurance Company; Fidelity National Title.
REFERENCES: Branch Banking and Trust Company; First National Bank.

WALKER & MELVIN, LLP

640 FAGG DRIVE
P.O. BOX 528
EDEN, NORTH CAROLINA 27289
Telephone: 336-623-3138
Fax: 336-623-2023
Email: walkermelvin@earthlink.net
URL: http://www.walkermelvin.com

Civil Practice, Criminal Law, Driving While Intoxicated, Traffic Violations, Wrongful Death, Probate, Real Estate, Personal Injury, Automobile Accidents, Corporate Law, Family Law, Divorce, Child Custody, Adoptions.

MEMBERS OF FIRM

JAMES R. WALKER, born Leaksville, North Carolina, May 9, 1940; admitted to bar, 1965, North Carolina. *Education:* Wake Forest University (A.B., 1962; LL.B., 1965). *Member:* Rockingham County and North Carolina Bar Associations; Seventeenth Judicial District and North Carolina State Bars. ***PRACTICE AREAS:*** Estate Planning Law; Probate Law; Criminal Law; Domestic Relations Law; Real Property; Commercial Law; Residential Law. **Email:** jwalkeredenlaw@yahoo.com

R. MARTIN MELVIN, born Reidsville, North Carolina, March 25, 1948; admitted to bar, 1973, North Carolina. *Education:* University of North Carolina (B.S. in B.A., 1970; J.D., 1973). *Member:* Rockingham County (President, 1986-1987) and North Carolina Bar Associations; Seventeenth Judicial District and North Carolina State Bar. ***PRACTICE AREAS:*** Real Property-Commercial and Residential Law; Domestic Relations Law; Corporation Law; Foreclosure Law; Collection Law. **Email:** mmelvinedenlaw@yahoo.com

LOCAL COUNSEL FOR: Wachovia Bank & Trust Co., N.A.; Washington Mutual Finance Co.; American General Finance, Inc.; First Citizen Bank & Trust Co.

(This Listing Continued)

REPRESENTATIVE CLIENTS: Morehead Memorial Hospital; Bank of America; Home Savings Bank; Branch Banking & Trust Co.; Dyer's Plumbing, Inc.; Farmers Home Administration; Rockingham Opportunity Corp; State Employees Credit Union; American General Finance Inc.; First Citizens Bank and Trust Co.; Ralph Barrow Automobiles, Inc.; FNB Southeast.
APPROVED ATTORNEYS FOR: Lawyers Title Insurance Corp.; Chicago Title Insurance Co.; Investors Title Insurance Co.; Fidelity National Insurance Co.; First American Title Insurance Company.
REFERENCE: First Citizens Bank and Trust Co.

SAMUEL BOBBITT DIXON

117 WEST EDEN STREET
EDENTON, NORTH CAROLINA 27932
Telephone: 252-482-8696
Fax: 252-482-1493
Email: dixonlaw@thedixonlawfirm.com

Real Estate, Buying and Selling a Home, Criminal Law, Traffic and DWI Offenses, Drug Crimes, Capital Offenses, Murder, Historic Preservation, Juvenile Law, Personal Injury, Automobile Accidents, and Wrongful Death.

SAMUEL BOBBITT DIXON, born Edenton, North Carolina, December 17, 1961; admitted to bar, 1988, North Carolina. *Education:* University of North Carolina at Chapel Hill (B.A., 1984); Wake Forest University (J.D., 1988). *Member:* North Carolina State Bar; North Carolina Bar Association (Board of Director, Preservation Foundation of North Carolina). ***PRACTICE AREAS:*** Real Estate; Criminal Law; Historic Preservation; Juvenile Law.

THE VINCENT LAW FIRM, PC

EDENTON, NORTH CAROLINA

(See Southern Shores)

Workers Compensation, Personal Injury, Auto Accidents, Social Security Disability, Wrongful Death and Admiralty Longshores.

ALEXY, FLETCHER, WILLS & WILLS, P.C.

ELIZABETH CITY, NORTH CAROLINA

(See Point Harbor)

HORNTHAL, RILEY, ELLIS & MALAND, L.L.P.

301 EAST MAIN STREET
P.O. BOX 220
ELIZABETH CITY, NORTH CAROLINA 27907-0220
Telephone: 252-335-0871
Fax: 252-335-4223
URL: http://www.hrem.com

Nags Head, North Carolina Office: 2502 South Croatan Highway, P.O. Box 310, 27959-0310. Telephone: 252-441-0871. Telefax: 252-441-8822.

General Trial and Appellate Practice in all Courts. Personal Injury, Products Liability, Professional Malpractice, Corporate, Tax, Bankruptcy, Employment, Education, Criminal, Insurance, Construction, Real Estate, Environmental, Elder, Local Government, Wills and Trusts, Probate and Admiralty Law.

FIRM PROFILE: Hornthal, Riley, Ellis & Maland, L.L.P. was created in 1985 from a merger of two firms, each founded before 1920. From its members have come two State Superior Court Judges, a current sitting Federal Judge, and Presidents of the North Carolina State Bar, the North Carolina Bar Association and the North Carolina Association of Defense Attorneys. The firm practices throughout northeastern North Carolina, representing a broad local, regional and national clientele. The practice is general, with emphasis on civil litigation and real estate. The firm emphasizes continuing legal education, with members frequently serving as faculty in such programs.

L. P. HORNTHAL, JR., born Tarboro, North Carolina, October 16, 1936; admitted to bar, 1963, North Carolina; 1975, U.S. Court of Appeals, Fourth Circuit; 1978, U.S. Supreme Court. *Education:* University of North Carolina (A.B., 1958; LL.B., 1963). Phi Delta Phi. Research Assistant, North Carolina Supreme Court, 1963-1964. Member of Staff, Attorney General of North Carolina, 1964-1965. Member, Legislative Study Commission, North Carolina Futures Commission, 1997-1998. Certified Mediator, North Carolina Dispute Resolution Commission and U.S. District Court, Eastern District of North Carolina. Board of Directors, NCIOLTA, 1999-2003. *Member:* North Carolina (President, 1996-1997) and American Bar Associations; North Carolina State Bar (Member, Disciplinary Hearing Commission, 1986-1992); American College of Trial Lawyers; International Association of Insurance Counsel; Association of Insurance Attorneys; North Carolina Association of Defense Attorneys (President, 1984-1985); Lawyers Mutual Liability Insurance Company of North Carolina (1988—); Georgia Lawyers Insurance Company (2002—). ***PRACTICE AREAS:*** Civil Litigation; Employment Litigation; Business Litigation; Commercial Litigation; Education; Personal Injury.

M. H. HOOD ELLIS, born Raleigh, North Carolina, November 6, 1949; admitted to bar, 1975, North Carolina; 1976, U.S. Court of Appeals, Fourth Circuit. *Education:* North Carolina State University (B.S., with high honors, 1972); Wake Forest University (J.D., cum laude, 1975). Tau Beta Pi; Phi Kappa Phi; Phi Delta Phi. Editor, Wake Forest Law Review, 1974-1975. Author: Note, "Assignments Which Purport to Assign an Entire Executory Bilateral Contract," Wake Forest Law Review, Vol. 10, p. 179, 1974. City Attorney, Elizabeth City, 1981-1989. Chairman, North Carolina State Board of Elections, 1989-1993. Certified Mediator, North Carolina Dispute Resolution Commission. *Member:* First Judicial District (President, 1982-1983) and North Carolina Bar Associations; North Carolina State Bar; North Carolina Association of Defense Attorneys. ***PRACTICE AREAS:*** Civil Litigation; Municipal; Local Government Law; Real Estate; Construction.

MARK M. MALAND, born New Hyde Park, New York, September 30, 1948; admitted to bar, 1977, North Carolina and U.S. Tax Court; 1978, U.S. Court of Appeals, Fourth Circuit. *Education:* University of North Carolina at Chapel Hill (A.B., 1970); University of Connecticut at Storrs (M.B.A., 1972); Wake Forest University (J.D., cum laude, 1977). Managing Editor, Wake Forest Law Review, 1976-1977. Author: Note, "Qualified Immunity for School Board Members - A Standard for Determining Good Faith Under 42 U.S.C. Section 1983," Wake Forest Law Review, Vol. 11, P. 720, 1975. Adjunct Faculty Member, College of the Albemarle, 1979—. Estate and Gift Tax Group, Internal Revenue Service, Greensboro, North Carolina, 1975-1977. Trustee, Chapter 7 Bankruptcy Panel, Eastern District of North Carolina, 1985-1991. *Member:* North Carolina Bar Association (Member, Estate Planning and Fiduciary Law Section). ***PRACTICE AREAS:*** Bankruptcy; Estate Planning; Administrative; Corporate; Taxation; Elder.

DONALD C. PRENTISS, born Middletown, New York, October 19, 1955; admitted to bar, 1981, North Carolina and U.S. District Court, Eastern District of North Carolina; 1987, U.S. Court of Appeals, Fourth Circuit. *Education:* Wake Forest University (B.A., 1977; J.D., 1981). Phi Delta Phi. Legislative Counsel to North Carolina Bar Association, 1982-1985. Member: Board of Directors, Legal Services of North Carolina, 1990-1995; Board of Directors, Client Security Fund, 2001—. North Carolina State Bar Councilor, 2005—. *Member:* First Judicial District (President, 1991-1992), North Carolina and American (Member, Sections on: Litigation; Torts and Insurance) Bar Associations; North Carolina State Bar; North Carolina Association of Defense Attorneys (Board of Directors, 1997-2002); Defense Research Institutes. ***PRACTICE AREAS:*** Civil Litigation; Insurance; Commercial; Contract Litigation; Personal Injury.

ROBERT B. HOBBS, JR., born Richmond, Virginia, December 31, 1960; admitted to bar, 1986, North Carolina. *Education:* University of North Carolina at Chapel Hill (B.A., 1983); Campbell University (J.D., 1986). Phi Alpha Delta. Staff Member, Campbell Law Review, 1984-1986. Case Law Editor, Campbell Law Observer, 1985. Author: Note, "Cable TV's 'Must Carry' Rules: The Most Restrictive Alternative," 8 Campbell Law Review 339, 1986. Member, Board of Governors, North Carolina Bar Association, 1993-1996. Member: Executive Council, 1988-1993 and Chair, 1991-1992, Law Practice Management Section, Executive Council, 2004-2007, Real Property Section, North Carolina Bar Association. *Member:* North Carolina State Bar; North Carolina (Member, Sections on: Real Property; Estate Planning and Fiduciary Law) and American (Member, Sections on: Real Property; Probate and Trust Law) Bar Associations. (Also at Nags Head Office) (Board Certified Specialist in Real Property Law-Residential, Business, Commercial and Industrial Transactions, North Carolina State Bar Board of Legal Specialization). ***PRACTICE AREAS:*** Real Property; Estate Planning; Business.

DONALD I. McREE, JR., born Hampton, Virginia, May 29, 1961; admitted to bar, 1987, North Carolina; 1989, U.S. District Court, Eastern District of North Carolina. *Education:* St. Andrews Presbyterian College (B.A., 1983); Campbell University School of Law (J.D., 1986). Phi Alpha Delta. Member of Staff, North Carolina Local Government Commission, 1986-1989. County Attorney: Currituck County, 1989-1992; Pasquotank County, 1992-2000, Tyrrell County, 2004—. Town Attorney, Towns of Hertford, Nags Head and Southern Shores, 2001—; Town Attorney, Town of Duck, 2002—. *Member:* First Judicial District, North Carolina and American Bar Associations; North Carolina State Bar; International Municipal Lawyers Association; North Carolina Association of Municipal Attorneys; North Carolina Association of County Attorneys. ***PRACTICE AREAS:*** Municipal Law; Land Use.

JOHN D. LEIDY, born Albion, Michigan, February 15, 1962; admitted to bar, 1987, North Carolina and U.S. District Court, Eastern District of North Carolina; 1989, U.S. Court of Appeals, Fourth Circuit; 2000, U.S. Court of Appeals, Fifth Circuit. *Education:* Denison University (B.A., 1984); University of North Carolina (J.D., 1987). Staff Member, North Carolina Journal of International Law and Commercial Regulation, 1985-1986. *Member:* North Carolina (Section Council, Labor and Employment, 1999—; Member, Sections on: Workers Compensation, Litigation and Antitrust and Trade Regulations) and American (Member, Sections on: Litigation; Labor and Employment Law; Torts and Insurance Practice) Bar Associations; North Carolina State Bar. ***PRACTICE AREAS:*** Civil Litigation; Employment; Employee Benefits; Workers Compensation; Wrongful Termination; Education Law; Commercial.

MICHAEL P. SANDERS, born Elizabeth City, North Carolina, August 13, 1964; admitted to bar, 1990, North Carolina and U.S. District Court, Eastern District of North Carolina. *Education:* University of North Carolina (B.A., 1986); Campbell University (J.D., cum laude, 1990). Phi Kappa Phi; Phi Alpha Delta. Member, 1988-1990 and Notes and Comments Editor, 1989-1990, Campbell University Law Review. *Member:* North Carolina and American Bar Associations; North Carolina State Bar; North Carolina Academy of Trial Lawyers. ***PRACTICE AREAS:*** Criminal Litigation; Civil Litigation.

L. PHILLIP HORNTHAL III, born Elizabeth City, North Carolina, 1967; admitted to bar, 1993, North Carolina; 1995, U.S. District Court, Eastern District of North Carolina; 2000, U.S. Court of Appeals, 4th Circuit. *Education:* University of North Carolina at Chapel Hill (B.A., 1989) Phi Eta Sigma; Campbell University (J.D., 1993). Notes and Comments Editor, Campbell Law Review, 1992-1993. Author: Note, "Another Step Towards Ending Discrimination In The Jury Selection Process—*"Powers v. Ohio,"* 14 Campbell Law Review, 369, 1992. Research Assistant to the Honorable Justice John Webb, North Carolina Supreme Court, 1993-1994. *Member:* North Carolina Bar Association; North Carolina State Bar; First Judicial District Bar Association; Defense Research Institute; North Carolina Association of Defense Attorneys. ***PRACTICE AREAS:*** Civil Litigation; Insurance Defense; Personal Injury; Worker's Compensation; Construction Litigation; Land Litigation.

WILLIAM BROCK MITCHELL, born Goldsboro, North Carolina, December, 19, 1973; admitted to bar, 2002, North Carolina. *Education:* College of Charleston (B.A., 1996); Mississippi College School of Law (J.D., 2000); University of Denver (LL.M., Taxa-

(This Listing Continued)

HORNTHAL, RILEY, ELLIS & MALAND, L.L.P., Elizabeth City—Continued

tion, 2001). *Member:* North Carolina Bar Association; North Carolina State Bar; First Judicial District Bar Association. ***PRACTICE AREAS:*** Real Property; Estate Planning; Business Law; Taxation.

CLAYTON W. CHEEK, born Durham, North Carolina, March 9, 1973; admitted to bar, 2003, North Carolina. *Education:* Wake Forest University (B.A., 1995; J.D., M.B.A., 2002). *Member:* North Carolina Bar Association; North Carolina State Bar; First Judicial District Bar; American Bar Association. ***PRACTICE AREAS:*** Estate Planning; Estate Administration; Corporate Law; Taxation; Elder Law; Bankruptcy.

OF COUNSEL

J. FRED RILEY, born Salisbury, North Carolina, October 18, 1938; admitted to bar, 1967, North Carolina. *Education:* Wake Forest University (A.B., 1960); University of North Carolina (J.D., 1967). Phi Delta Phi. Research Assistant, North Carolina Supreme Court, 1967-1968. *Member:* North Carolina (Member, Real Property Section) and American (Member, Section on Real Property, Probate and Trust Law) Bar Associations; North Carolina State Bar (Member, Board of Legal Specialization, 1989-1995). [Lt. U.S. Navy, 1960-1962]. ***PRACTICE AREAS:*** Real Property; Corporations; Wills; Trusts; Administrative.

THOMAS L. WHITE, JR., born Raleigh, North Carolina, June 6, 1938; admitted to bar, 1970, North Carolina; 1978, U.S. District Court, Eastern District of North Carolina and U.S. Supreme Court; 1984, U.S. Court of Appeals, Fourth Circuit. *Education:* University of North Carolina (A.B., 1960; J.D., 1970). Phi Alpha Delta. Town Attorney: Nags Head, 1971-2001; Southern Shores, 1979-2001. *Member:* Dare County (President, 1975-1976), First Judicial District (Vice President, 1979; President, 1980), and North Carolina Bar Associations; North Carolina State Bar; North Carolina Association of Municipal Attorneys. [U.S. Navy, 1960-1967; Capt., USNR, 1967-1989]. (Resident, Nags Head Office). ***PRACTICE AREAS:*** Education Law; Government Law; Municipal Law.

REPRESENTATIVE CLIENTS: Wachovia Bank of North Carolina, N.A.; North Carolina Power Co.; College of the Albemarle; Elizabeth City-Pasquotank County Board of Education; Camden County Board of Education; Elizabeth City Housing Authority; Southern Railway System; Lawyers Title Insurance Corp.; Chicago Title Insurance Co.; Old Republic Title Insurance Co.; Federal Land Bank Association of Columbia; State Farm Mutual; Travelers Insurance Co.; Government Employees Insurance Co.; Crum and Forster; Great American Insurance Co.; USF&G; Kemper Insurance Group; Pennsylvania National Insurance Group; Employers' Mutual Casualty Co.; Grain Dealers Mutual Insurance Co.; Ohio Casualty Insurance Group; Chubb and Son Group; Firemen's Fund Insurance Co.; Dare County Airport Authority; North Carolina Professional Liability Pool; Branch Banking & Trust Co.; N.C. Insurance Guaranty Association; N.C. Interlocal Risk Financing Fund; Horace Mann Insurance Companies; Carmike Cinemas, Inc.; Town of Nags Head; Town of Southern Shores; Town of Duck; Town of Hertford.
APPROVED ATTORNEYS FOR: Lawyers Title Insurance Corp.; United Title Insurance Co.; Commonwealth Land Title Insurance Co.; Old Republic Title Insurance Co.; Investors Title Insurance; Ticor Title Insurance Co.; First American Title Insurance Co.; Stewart Title Co.; Chicago Title Co.; Atlantic Casualty Insurance Group; Universal Underwriters Insurance Group.

THE VINCENT LAW FIRM, PC

ELIZABETH CITY, NORTH CAROLINA

(See Southern Shores)

Workers Compensation, Personal Injury, Auto Accidents, Social Security Disability, Wrongful Death and Admiralty Longshores.

LAW OFFICES OF WILLIAM S. BRITT

ELIZABETHTOWN, NORTH CAROLINA

(See Lumberton)

Medical Malpractice, Wrongful Death, Automobile Accidents and Injuries, Truck Accidents, Motorcycle Accidents, Construction Accidents, Dog Bites and Personal Injury Law.

BRUMBAUGH, MU & KING, P.A.

Established in 1978

102 WEST BROAD STREET

ELIZABETHTOWN, NORTH CAROLINA 28337-0995

Telephone: 910-862-2211

URL: http://www.bmklaw.net

Practice Limited to Injury Cases. Automobile, Wrongful Death, Medical Malpractice, Workers' Compensation, Products Liability and Social Security Claims.

(For complete biographical data on all personnel, see professional biographies, Jacksonville, North Carolina)

HESTER, GRADY & HESTER, P.L.L.C.

Established in 1926

115 COURTHOUSE DRIVE

P.O. DRAWER 130

ELIZABETHTOWN, NORTH CAROLINA 28337

Telephone: 910-862-3191

FAX: 910-862-4802

URL: http://www.lawyers.com/hestergradyhester

General Practice. Domestic, Real Estate, Personal Injury, Negligence, Workers Compensation, Corporate Law, Criminal Law, Municipal Law, School Law, Divorce, Driving While Intoxicated, Child Support, Contracts, Business Law, Automobile Accidents and Injuries, Wills, Probate, Insurance.

(This Listing Continued)

FIRM PROFILE: Hester, Grady & Hester, P.L.L.C. was founded by R.J. Hester in 1926. Serving clients throughout Bladen, Brunswick, Columbus and surrounding counties, the firm engages in a general practice with individual lawyers practicing in specific areas of law.

MEMBERS OF FIRM

GARY A. GRADY, born Elizabethtown, North Carolina, July 11, 1954; admitted to bar, 1979, North Carolina. *Education:* Appalachian State University (B.A., 1976); North Carolina Central University (J.D., 1979). Phi Delta Phi. Assistant District Attorney, Fourth Judicial District of North Carolina, 1978-1980. *Member:* North Carolina State Bar; American Bar Association. ***PRACTICE AREAS:*** Criminal Law; Domestic Relations Law; Personal Injury. ***Email:*** ggrady@hghgp.com

H. CLIFTON HESTER, born Bladen County, North Carolina, September 19, 1956; admitted to bar, 1981, Georgia and U.S. District Court, Northern and Middle Districts of Georgia; 1983, North Carolina and U.S. District Court, Eastern District of North Carolina. *Education:* Davidson College (A.B., 1978); University of North Carolina at Chapel Hill (J.D., 1981). Phi Delta Phi. Town Attorney: Clarkton, 1965—; White Lake, 1983—. *Member:* North Carolina and American Bar Associations; State Bar of Georgia; North Carolina State Bar; North Carolina Academy of Trial Lawyers. ***PRACTICE AREAS:*** Personal Injury Law; Workers Compensation Law; Civil Trial; Social Security Disability. ***Email:*** chester@hghgp.com

OF COUNSEL

WORTH H. HESTER, born Bladenboro, North Carolina, April 6, 1923; admitted to bar, 1950, North Carolina. *Education:* Wake Forest University (B.S., 1948; J.D., 1950). Phi Delta Phi. Solicitor, Bladen County Recorder's Court, 1953-1954. Attorney for Bladen County Board of Education, 1965—. *Member:* Bladen County and North Carolina Bar Associations; 13th Judicial District and North Carolina State (Councilor, 13th District, 1973—) Bars. ***PRACTICE AREAS:*** Real Estate Law; Estates Law.

FRANK T. GRADY, born Rocky Mount, North Carolina, June 3, 1919; admitted to bar, 1949, North Carolina. *Education:* Campbell College and University of North Carolina (A.B., 1947); University of North Carolina (J.D., 1949). Phi Alpha Delta. Judge of Bladen County, Recorder's Court, 1952-1954. Chief District Judge, 1975-1980. *Member:* 13th Judicial District and North Carolina State Bars. [With U.S. Army, 1941-1944]

MYRA GOODEN PATE, born Lumberton, North Carolina; admitted to bar, 2002, North Carolina. *Education:* Salem College (B.A., 1999); Campbell University (J.D., 2002). ***PRACTICE AREAS:*** Real Estate; Wills; Estate Administration. ***Email:*** myrapate@hotmail.com

SCOTI L. USSERY, born August 16, 1971; admitted to bar, 2003, North Carolina. *Education:* University of North Carolina at Wilmington (B.A., 1993); North Carolina Central University (J.D., 2002). *Member:* North Carolina and American Bar Associations; North Carolina State Bar. ***PRACTICE AREAS:*** Criminal Law; Family Law; Personal Injury; Collections; Civil Litigation.

REPRESENTATIVE CLIENTS: Bladen Electric; Wachovia Bank & Trust; International Paper Company; C.S. Sholar & Sons' Chipping & Logging; Bladen Housing Assn., Inc.; Farmers Cooperative Exchange; Bladen Builders Supply; First Investors Savings & Loan, Whiteville; Westwood Manufacturing; J. Earl Faircloth Construction Co.; Elizabethtown Commerce & Development Co.; Carolina Power & Light Co.; Bank of America, N.A.; State Highway Commission (North Carolina); Town of Clarkton, N.C.; General Motors Acceptance Corp.; Ward Lumber Co.; Town of White Lake; Cape Craftsman Inc.; Nature Conservancy; Murphy Farms, Inc.; Browns of Carolina, Inc.
APPROVED ATTORNEYS FOR: Cape Fear Farm Credit, ACA; Cooperative Bank for Savings; Nationwide Insurance Co.; Lawyers Title Insurance Corp.; The Federal Land Bank of Columbia, South Carolina; Southern Title Insurance Co.; Jefferson-Pilot Title Insurance Co.; American Title Insurance Co.; Commercial Standard Title Insurance Co.; First Title Insurance Co.; VA, FHA and Farmers Home Administration; Investors Title Insurance Cos.; The Title Company of North Carolina.
REFERENCES: First Citizens Bank and Trust Co.; United Carolina Bank; Wachovia Bank of North Carolina; Bank of America, N.A.; Branch Banking and Trust Co.

GREG JONES & ASSOCIATES, P.A.

ELIZABETHTOWN, NORTH CAROLINA

(See Wilmington)

Personal Injury, Automobile Accidents, Brain Injury, Motorcycle Accidents, Wrongful Death, Medical Malpractice, Spinal Cord Injuries, Drug and Medical Device Litigation, Pharmacists Liability, Head Injuries, Products Liability, Medical and Nursing Home Negligence, Workers Compensation, Toxic Torts, Nursing Home Abuse, Stock Fraud.

THE MAYNARD LAW FIRM

Established in 1986

101 COURTHOUSE DRIVE

P.O. BOX 875

ELIZABETHTOWN, NORTH CAROLINA 28337

Telephone: 910-862-8461

FAX: 910-862-6171

Email: maynard_alan@hotmail.com

General Practice. Civil and Criminal Litigation. Family, Probate, Real Estate, Corporate Law, Workman's Compensation, Social Security Law and Personal Injury Law .

MEMBER OF FIRM

ALAN I. MAYNARD, born Wilmington, North Carolina, November 21, 1957; admitted to bar, 1983, North Carolina; 1985, U.S. District Court, Eastern District of North Carolina. *Education:* University of North Carolina at Chapel Hill (B.A., 1980; J.D., 1983). Judicial District Representative, North Carolina Young Lawyers Division, 1986-1989. *Member:* Bladen County, North Carolina and American Bar Associations; Thirteenth Judicial

(This Listing Continued)

District Bar Association (Secretary, 1986-1987; Vice-President, 1989-1990; President, 1990-1991); North Carolina State Bar; North Carolina Academy of Trial Lawyers. **PRACTICE AREAS:** Civil Litigation; Family Law; Probate; Real Estate; Corporate Law; Social Security. **Email:** maynard_alan@hotmail.com

ASSOCIATES

MATTHEW J. DIXON, born Wilmington, Delaware, September 22, 1970; admitted to bar, 1996, Oklahoma; 1997, North Carolina. *Education:* University of North Carolina at Chapel Hill (B.A., 1992); Oklahoma City University School of Law (J.D., 1996). *Member:* North Carolina State Bar; North Carolina Academy of Trial Lawyers. **PRACTICE AREAS:** Personal Injury; Workers Compensation; Civil Litigation; Real Estate. **Email:** dixonlaw@intrstar.net

IRENE G. RIEL, born Fayetteville, North Carolina, October 5, 1957; admitted to bar, 1992, North Carolina. *Education:* Methodist College (B.A., 1979); Campbell University (J.D., 1992). *Member:* North Carolina Bar Association. **PRACTICE AREAS:** Criminal Defense (90%).

OF COUNSEL

REUBEN L. MOORE, JR., born Florence, South Carolina, June 11, 1941; admitted to bar, 1965, North Carolina; 1975, U.S. District Court, Eastern District of North Carolina. *Education:* University of North Carolina (B.A., 1963; LL.B., 1965). *Member:* Bladen County, North Carolina and American Bar Associations; Thirteenth Judicial District Bar Association; North Carolina State Bar.

REPRESENTATIVE CLIENTS: Byrd Field Farms; Bladenboro Housing Authority; Elizabethtown Housing Authority; Clarkton Housing Authority; Town of East Arcadia.
REFERENCES: Branch Bank and Trust Co.; First Citizen Bank and Trust Co.; Cooperative Bank for Savings; Wachovia Bank and Trust Co.; Bank of America; Cape Fear Farm Credit.

J. MICHAEL McGUINNESS

2034 HIGHWAY, 701 NORTH LAKEWOOD PLAZA
P.O. BOX 952
ELIZABETHTOWN, NORTH CAROLINA 28337-0952
Telephone: 910-862-7087
Fax: 910-862-8865
Email: jmichael@mcguinnesslaw.com
URL: http://www.mcguinnesslaw.com

Washington, D.C. Office: 1300 Pennsylvania Avenue, N.W., Suite 700. 20004.
Boston, Massachusetts Office: 28 State Street, Suite 1100, 02109.

Personal Injury Law, Products Liability, Wrongful Death, Automobile Accidents, Labor and Employment, Civil Rights, Law Enforcement Liability, Criminal Law, Constitutional Law.

FIRM PROFILE: J. Michael McGuinness has served plaintiff and defense clients in personal injury, civil rights, employment and law enforcement litigation for over 20 years. Mr. McGuinness has served as lead counsel in over one hundred and fifty litigated cases, in jury trials or appeals, in numerous jurisdictions. Board Certified Civil Trial Advocate, National Board of Trial Advocacy.

J. MICHAEL McGUINNESS, born Elizabethtown, North Carolina, July 3, 1957; admitted to bar, 1984, North Carolina, 1985, District of Columbia; 1991, Massachusetts; U.S. District Court, Eastern, Middle and Western Districts of North Carolina; U.S. Court of Appeals, for the District of Columbia, First, Second, Third, Fourth, Fifth and Seventh Circuits; 1987, U.S. Supreme Court. *Education:* University of North Carolina (B.A., cum laude, 1979); North Carolina Central University (J.D., 1983); George Washington University, 1984-1985. Special Counsel, Appellate Litigation, National Troopers Coalition. Litigation Counsel, Southern States Police Benevolent Association. Board of Editors: National Trial Lawyer Magazine, N.C. and Massachusetts Academy of Trial Lawyers. Former Adjunct Professor of Law, Instructor: Labor Relations Information Systems; National Association of Police Organizations; Georgetown University Law Center; Williams College; Practising Law Institute; N.C. Bar Association; Massachusetts Academy of Trial Attorneys; National Troopers Coalition. Former Assistant District Attorney and Counsel for the U.S. Government.

EVERETT & EVERETT, PLLC

1106 N. BRIDGE STREET
POST OFFICE DRAWER 189
ELKIN, NORTH CAROLINA 28621
Telephone: 336-835-1210
Facsimile: 336-835-7177
Email: jeverett@riverto.net
URL: http://www.everettlawoffice.com

Specializing in injury related cases.

JAMES A. EVERETT, born Williamston, North Carolina, January 6, 1948; admitted to bar, 1974, North Carolina and U.S. District Court, Eastern, Middle and Western Districts of North Carolina; U.S. Court of Appeals, Fourth Circuit. *Education:* University of North Carolina at Chapel Hill (B.A., 1971); Wake Forest University (J.D., 1974). **PRACTICE AREAS:** Personal Injury. **Email:** jeverett@riverto.net

WILLIAM HARRELL EVERETT, born Williamston, North Carolina, 1934; admitted to bar, 1962, North Carolina. *Education:* University of North Carolina at Chapel Hill (B.A., 1957; J.D., 1962). (Also Member, Everett, Womble, Finan, Lawrence & Brown, Goldsboro, North Carolina). **PRACTICE AREAS:** Civil Litigation.

LAW OFFICES OF THOMAS C. FLIPPIN, PC

1435 N. BRIDGE STREET
ELKIN, NORTH CAROLINA 28621-2334
Telephone: 336-526-2280
Fax: 336-526-5612
Email: tom@flippinlaw.com
URL: http://www.flippinlawfirm.com

Bankruptcy, Real Estate.

THOMAS CLAY FLIPPIN, born Winston-Salem, North Carolina, April 2, 1975; admitted to bar, 2000, North Carolina. *Education:* Appalachian State University (B.S., Political Science, 1999); Campbell University (J.D., 2000). Recipient, Edward Allen Scholarship. *Member:* North Carolina Bar Association (Bankruptcy and Family Law Sections); North Carolina Academy of Trial Lawyers. **PRACTICE AREAS:** Bankruptcy; Real Estate. **Email:** tom@flippinlaw.com

JAMES N. FREEMAN, JR., P.C.

117 CHURCH STREET
P.O. BOX 347
ELKIN, NORTH CAROLINA 28621
Telephone: 336-835-4407
Fax: 336-526-3908
Email: jnfheel@hotmail.com

Civil Litigation, Appellate Practice, General Practice, Trusts & Estates, Wills & Probate, Real Estate, Traffic Offenses, Business, Corporate, Personal Injury, Wrongful Death, Automobile Accidents.

JAMES N. FREEMAN, JR., born Mt. Airy, North Carolina, February 9, 1966; admitted to bar, 1991, North Carolina. *Education:* University of North Carolina (B.A., 1988; J.D., 1991). Pi Sigma Alpha, Phi Delta Phi. Order of the Barristers. Holderness Moot Court Bench. Law Clerk to the Honorable Burley B. Mitchell, Jr., Associate Justice, North Carolina Supreme Court, 1991-1992. *Member:* North Carolina Bar Association; North Carolina State Bar. **PRACTICE AREAS:** Civil Litigation; General Practice; Trusts and Estates; Wills; Probate; Real Estate; Traffic Violations; Business Law; Corporate Law; Personal Injury; Wrongful Death; Automobile Accidents; Appellate Practice.

COLLINS AND MOORE, PLLC

EMERALD ISLE, NORTH CAROLINA

(See Jacksonville)

Personal Injury including Wrongful Death, Automobile Accidents and Injuries, Medical Malpractice, Premises Liability; Corporate and Business Law including Contracts, Disputes, Commercial Litigation, Taxation; Estate Planning including Wills, Trusts, Retirement Planning, Wealth Preservation; Criminal Defense including Felonies, Misdemeanors, Drugs, Traffic Violations, Speeding, Parole and Probation, DWI; Family Law including Divorce, Child Custody, Alimony, Separation Agreements; Workers Compensation.

HUX, LIVERMON & ARMSTRONG, L.L.P.

Established in 1959
114 WHITFIELD STREET
P.O. BOX 217
ENFIELD, NORTH CAROLINA 27823
Telephone: 252-445-5188
Fax: 252-445-3285
Email: hla@hlalaw.net

General Practice. Criminal including DWI, Traffic Offenses, and Civil Trials in all Courts. Wills and Probate, Trusts and Estates, Corporation, Insurance and Real Property Law, Personal Injury, Automobile Accidents, Family Law.

MEMBERS OF FIRM

JAMES S. LIVERMON, JR., born Scotland Neck, North Carolina, September 24, 1943; admitted to bar, 1967, North Carolina. *Education:* Wake Forest University (B.A., 1965; J.D., 1967). Phi Delta Phi. *Member:* Halifax County Bar Association (President, 1984 and 1989); North Carolina State Bar; North Carolina Academy of Trial Lawyers. **PRACTICE AREAS:** Criminal Law; Personal Injury; Traffic Violations; Driving While Intoxicated; Civil Liability; General Practice.

H. LAWRENCE ARMSTRONG, JR., born Rocky Mount, North Carolina, May 23, 1950; admitted to bar, 1975, North Carolina. *Education:* University of North Carolina (A.B., 1972; J.D., 1975). Phi Beta Kappa. Member, National Order of the Barristers. *Member:* Halifax County (Secretary/Treasurer, 1982-1984), North Carolina and American Bar Associations; North Carolina State Bar; North Carolina Academy of Trial Lawyers. **PRACTICE AREAS:** Civil Practice; Personal Injury; Education; Family Law; Electric Cooperatives Law; Real Estate; Decedents Estates.

REPRESENTATIVE CLIENTS: Centura Bank; Halifax Electric Membership Corp.; Enfield Grain and Fertilizer Co.; Halifax County School Board.
APPROVED TITLE ATTORNEYS FOR: Lawyers Title Insurance Corp.; First Title Insurance Co.; Commonwealth Land Title Co.; Investors Title Insurance Co.; Tarheel Farm Credit Service; Chicago Title Ins. Co.

OWENS & NELSON, P.L.L.C.

FARMVILLE, NORTH CAROLINA

(See Greenville)

General Civil and Criminal Trial Practice before all State and Federal Courts. Alternative Dispute Resolution, Civil Practice, Commercial Real Estate, Criminal Law, Domestic Relations, DUI and DWI Law, Eminent Domain, Estates, Family Law, Fraud and Deceit, General Practice, Guardianship Law, Insurance, Litigation, Medical Malpractice, Mortgages, Negligence, Personal Injury, Premises Liability, Probate, Professional Liability, Property Law, Real Estate, Torts, Traffic, Trusts and Estates, Unfair Competition, White Collar Crime, Wills and Workers Compensation Law.

ANDERSON, JOHNSON, LAWRENCE, BUTLER & BOCK, L.L.P.

Established in 1945

SUITE 204 FIRST-CITIZENS BANK BUILDING
P.O. DRAWER 2737
FAYETTEVILLE, NORTH CAROLINA 28302-2737
Telephone: 910-483-1171
FAX: 910-483-5005
Email: ajlbb@andersonjohnson.com
URL: http://www.andersonjohnson.com

Civil Trials in all Courts, State and Federal. General Insurance Defense, Medical Malpractice and Professional Malpractice Claims, Product Liability Claims, Drug and Medical Device Claims, Construction Claims, Fire, Arson and Fraud Claims, Fidelity and Surety Claims, Life, Accident and Health Insurance Coverage Claims, Personal Injury and Worker's Compensation, Business and Insurance Litigation, Excess and Reinsurance, Health and Hospital Law.

FIRM PROFILE: Anderson, Johnson, Lawrence, Butler & Bock, L.L.P. was founded by Henry Anderson in 1945, serving clients throughout southeastern North Carolina. The firm focuses its practice in Insurance Defense Work.

MEMBERS OF FIRM

HENRY L. ANDERSON (1911-1986)

HAL W. BROADFOOT (1929-1994)

LEE BEST JOHNSON, born Dunn, N.C., November 1, 1946; admitted to bar, 1974, North Carolina. *Education:* University of North Carolina (B.S., 1969); Cumberland School of Law of Samford University (J.D., 1974). Delta Theta Phi. Assistant District Attorney, Twelfth Judicial District, North Carolina, 1975. *Member:* Cumberland County, North Carolina and American Bar Associations; The North Carolina State Bar; North Carolina Association of Defense Attorneys; American Counsel Association; Defense Research Institute. ***PRACTICE AREAS:*** Civil Litigation; Personal Injury Litigation; Insurance Defense Litigation; Professional Malpractice Defense; Premises Liability Defense; General Liability Defense; Insurance Coverage. ***Email:*** leejohnson@andersonjohnson.com

JOHN HUSKE ANDERSON, II, born Fayetteville, N.C., March 15, 1946; admitted to bar, 1975, North Carolina. *Education:* North Carolina State University (B.S., 1968); Wake Forest University (J.D., cum laude, 1975). Phi Delta Phi. Member, Wake Forest Law Review, 1974-1975. Assistant District Attorney, 12th Judicial District, Cumberland County, 1975-1976. *Member:* Cumberland County and North Carolina, Federal And American Bar Associations; The North Carolina State Bar; North Carolina Association of Defense Attorneys; Association of Defense Trial Attorneys; Defense Research Institute. ***PRACTICE AREAS:*** Civil Litigation; Personal Injury Litigation; Insurance Litigation; Legal Malpractice Defense; Premises Liability Defense; General Liability Defense; Insurance Coverage; Subrogation. ***Email:*** janderson@andersonjohnson.com

STEVEN C. LAWRENCE, born Raleigh, N.C., March 30, 1959; admitted to bar, 1984, North Carolina. *Education:* East Carolina University; University of North Carolina (B.A., 1981); Campbell University (J.D., 1984). Phi Alpha Delta. *Member:* Cumberland County, North Carolina and American Bar Associations; The North Carolina State Bar; North Carolina Association of Defense Attorneys; The Association of Trial Lawyers of America. ***PRACTICE AREAS:*** Civil Litigation; Personal Injury; Insurance Defense; Professional Negligence; Premises Liability; Construction Law; Workers Compensation; Contracts. ***Email:*** slawrence@andersonjohnson.com

J. STEWART BUTLER, III, born Fayetteville, N.C., April 18, 1957; admitted to bar, 1985, North Carolina. *Education:* University of North Carolina (B.A., 1979); North Carolina Central University (J.D., 1985). Phi Delta Phi. Assistant District Attorney, 12th Judicial District, 1986. *Member:* Cumberland County, North Carolina and American Bar Associations; The North Carolina State Bar; North Carolina Association of Defense Attorneys. ***PRACTICE AREAS:*** Insurance Litigation; Personal Injury Defense; General Liability Defense; Plaintiffs Personal Injury Defense; Governmental Liability; Premises Liability Defense. ***Email:*** jsbutler@andersonjohnson.com

A. DAVID BOCK, born Winchester, Virginia, January 18, 1958; admitted to bar, 1987, North Carolina. *Education:* University of North Carolina (B.A., 1980); Campbell University (J.D., 1987). Delta Theta Phi. Member, The Order of Barristers. *Member:* Cumberland County (Treasurer, 1988-1989), North Carolina and American Bar Associations; North Carolina State Bar; North Carolina Association of Defense Attorneys; American Counsel Association. ***PRACTICE AREAS:*** Civil Litigation; Personal Injury Litigation; Insurance Defense Litigation; Premises Liability Defense; General Liability Defense. ***Email:*** adavidbock@andersonjohnson.com

ASSOCIATE

ROBERT A. HASTY, JR., born Fayetteville, N.C., January 16, 1966; admitted to bar, 1998, North Carolina. *Education:* East Carolina University (B.S., 1988); Cumberland School of Law of Samford University (J.D., 1998). Phi Alpha Delta. *Member:* Cumberland County (Secretary, 2000-2002) and North Carolina Bar Associations; North Carolina State Bar; North Carolina Association of Defense Attorneys; Defense Research Institute. ***PRACTICE AREAS:*** Personal Injury Defense; Premises Liability Defense; Insurance Coverage; Subrogation. ***Email:*** rhasty@andersonjohnson.com

(This Listing Continued)

REPRESENTATIVE CLIENTS: ALEXSIS; All American Life & Casualty; Allied Corp.; Allstate Insurance Co.; American International Recovery, Inc.; American Modern Home Group; American Psychiatric Association (Professional Risk Mgmt.); American States Insurance Co.; Amerisure Companies; Armed Forces Insurance; Auto Owners Ins.; Avis Rent-A-Car Systems, Inc.; Balboa Insurance Co.; Bankers & Shippers Ins. Co.; Bituminous Ins. Co.; Budget Rent-A-Car; Canal Insurance Co.; Carolina Casualty Group; Carriers Insurance Co.; Cherokee Insurance Co.; Chubb/Pacific Insurance Group; Cincinnati Insurance; CNA Insurance Cos.; Cumis Insurance Society, Inc.; Employers Casualty Co.; Employers Mutual of Wausau; Erie Insurance Group; Essex Ins. Co.; Farmers Insurance Group; First of Georgia Insurance Co.; Foremost Insurance Co.; Gay & Taylor; General Accident Group; Georgia-Pacific Corp.; GEICO; Grain Dealers Mutual Insurance Co.; Home Insurance Cos.; Integon Ins. Co.; Iowa Mutual; Jefferson Pilot Fire & Casualty Co.; John Hancock Life Insurance Co.; Lawyers Mutual Liability Ins. Co.; Lumber Mutual Insurance Co.; Merchants and Business Men's Mut. Ins. Co.; Metropolitan Ins. Co.; Mutual of Omaha Insurance Co.; National Casualty Ins. Co.; National Fire & Marine Insurance Co.; National Foundation Insurance Co.; Nationwide Insurance Co.; New York Central Mutual Fire Insurance Co.; North Carolina Farm Bureau Mutual Ins. Co.; North Carolina Grange Mutual Ins.; Occidental Fire & Casualty Co. of N.C.; Peerless Insurance Co.; Preferred Mutual Ins. Co.; Professional Risk Management (American Psychiatric Assoc.); Progressive Casualty Ins. Co.; Protective Insurance Co.; Providence Washington Insurance Co.; Providian Auto & Home Insurance Co.; Provident General Insurance (Provident Life & Acc. Ins.); Prudential Insurance Co.; Ryder Truck Rental, Inc.; Safeco Insurance Co.; Seibels, Bruce & Co. (South Carolina Ins. Co.); Sentry Insurance Co.; Shelby Insurance Co.; South Carolina Farm Bureau Ins. Co.; Southern General Ins. Co.; Southern Home Ins. Co.; State Auto Group; State Capitol Insurance Co.; Transamerica Insurance Group; Transit Casualty Co.; Transport Ins. Co. (TICO); U.S. Insurance Group; Underwriters Adjusting Co.; Unigard Ins. Group; Utica Mutual Ins. Group; Vanliner Ins.; Wausau Insurance Cos.
REFERENCE: First Citizens Bank and Trust Co.

ANDERSON, JONES & GENGO, PLLC

FAYETTEVILLE, NORTH CAROLINA

(See Raleigh)

Construction Law, Construction Litigation, Collections, OSHA Defense, Contracts, Administrative Law, Administrative Litigation, Real Estate, Environmental Law, Environmental Litigation, Toxic Mold Litigation.

BAER & BAER ATTORNEYS AT LAW, P.A.

Established in 1992

SUITE 211, MCNAIRY BUILDING
EUTAW VILLAGE NORTH 823 ELM STREET
P.O. BOX 35110
FAYETTEVILLE, NORTH CAROLINA 28303
Telephone: 910-483-8066
Fax: 910-483-7261
Email: baer.baer@earthlink.net
URL: http://www.lawyers.com/baerattorneyatlaw

General Civil Practice. Trials in all Courts. Personal Injury Litigation, Probate, Estate Planning, Corporate, Business and Tax Law, Real Estate, Bankruptcy.

FIRM PROFILE: Baer & Baer Attorneys have been serving clients for more than 30 years throughout Cumberland and its contiguous counties. The firm engages in a general civil practice with emphasis on Commercial and Residential Real Estate, Creditors' Rights, Business Law, Estate Planning and Estate Administration.

ERVIN I. BAER (1928-2004)

BRUCE F. BAER, born Fayetteville, North Carolina, March 1, 1957; admitted to bar, 1984, North Carolina. *Education:* University of North Carolina at Chapel Hill (B.S.B.A., 1979; J.D., 1984). Phi Delta Phi. Fayetteville Area Habit For Humanity, Inc. (Board Attorney, 1992—). *Member:* Cumberland County, North Carolina and American Bar Associations; North Carolina State Bar. ***PRACTICE AREAS:*** Real Property Law; Bankruptcy Law; Litigation; Corporate Law; Business Law; Trusts and Estates. ***Email:*** bfbaer@earthlink.net

JENNIFER R. COONEY, born Fayetteville, North Carolina; admitted to bar, 2003, North Carolina. *Education:* University of North Carolina at Chapel Hill (B.S.B.A., 1994); Campbell University (J.D., 2003). Delta Theta Phi. *Member:* North Carolina State Bar. ***PRACTICE AREAS:*** Real Estate; Estate Administration; Corporate Law. ***Email:*** cooneyjr@earthlink.net

REPRESENTATIVE CLIENTS: Branch Banking and Trust Co.; Powers-Swain Chevrolet, Inc.; Stout Properties, Inc. (Holiday Inn-Bordeaux); Eutaw Shopping Center, Inc.; McDonald Lumber Co., Inc.; V-Point Super Markets, Inc.; Bobby Taylor Oil Co., Inc.; Paris and Potter Management Corporation (Kentucky Fried Chicken); NTR Group, LLC (Cici's Pizza); Cape Fear Cardiology Associates, P.A.; Parker House of Music, Inc.; Physicians' Total Rehab of Fayetteville; Highland Health of North Carolina, P.A.; Bordeaux Center, Inc.; LaFayette Realty; Warren's Air Conditioning and Heating Service, Inc.; Drose Investments, Inc.; Park N' Shop Food Mart, Inc.; The Hawley Company; Hawley's Bicycle World, Inc; /Hawley's Cycle & Camping Center, Inc.; McLaurin Company, Inc.; Fayetteville Psychiatric Associates, Inc.
REFERENCES: First Citizens Bank & Trust Co.; Branch Banking & Trust Co.; RBC Centura; Bank of America; Wachovia Bank, N.A.; New Century Bank of Fayetteville.

BEAVER HOLT STERNLICHT & COURIE, P.A.

Established in 1979

230 GREEN STREET

FAYETTEVILLE, NORTH CAROLINA 28301

Telephone: 910-323-4600
FAX: 910-323-3403
Email: info@beaverholt.com
URL: http://www.beaverholt.com

Raeford, North Carolina Office: 127 West Edinborough Avenue. Telephone: 910-875-3379. FAX: 910-875-4030.

Civil and Criminal Litigation in all State and Federal Courts. Personal Injury, Medical Negligence, Wrongful Death, Workers Compensation, Criminal Defense, Corporate Litigation, Commercial Litigation, Employment and Labor Law, DWI, Traffic Violations.

FIRM PROFILE: Beaver Holt has grown substantially over the last two decades. In civil practice, the firm's areas of concentration include plaintiff's personal injury, malpractice and commercial matters. The firm offers a full spectrum of criminal defense ranging from traffic offenses in State courts to white-collar criminal defense at the Federal level and a wide-ranging appellate practice in both State and Federal forums. Members of the firm maintain active membership in specialized professional organizations including the American Bar Association, the Association of Trial Lawyers of America, the National Association of Criminal Defense Lawyers, the North Carolina Academy of Trial Lawyers, and all state and local bar organizations. In addition, the firm has access to a Spanish interpreter.

H. GERALD BEAVER, born Albemarle, North Carolina, July 13, 1947; admitted to bar, 1973, North Carolina, U.S. District Court, Eastern District of North Carolina, U.S. District Court, Middle District of North Carolina and U.S. Court of Appeals, Fourth Circuit; 1980, U.S. Supreme Court. *Education:* East Carolina University (B.A., 1969); University of North Carolina (J.D., 1973). Delta Theta Phi. Listed in: Best Lawyers in America; National Directory of Criminal Lawyers, 1991—. Author: "Police Misconduct, One North Carolina City's Story," Trial Briefs, Journal of the N.C. Academy of Trial Lawyers, Vol. 19, No. 4, 4th Quarter, 1987; "Technicolor Trial, The Use of Gory Photographs in Homicide Prosecutions," The Champion, Journal of the National Association of Criminal Defense Lawyers, Vol. XII, No. 8, Sept/Oct 1988; "Expert Testimony, Four Criteria for Determining Admissibility," The Champion, Journal of the National Association of Criminal Defense Lawyers, Volume XIV, No. 1, Jan./Feb. 1990; "Police Brutality, A Call to Arms," The Champion, July, 1991; "Presumptive Testing for the Presence of Blood: Limiting the "Glow" of Misleading Expert Testimony" Trial Briefs Journal of the North Carolina Academy of Trial Lawyers, Spring, 1996; "Effectively Dealing with Trial by Ambush: Combating Late Discovery in Criminal Cases," Trial Briefs, Journal of the N.C. Academy of Trial Lawyers, September, 2000; "Expert Testimony: From Frye to Daubert to Kumbo Tire and Beyond," The Implications of Revised Rule 702 - The True Bill, N.C. Bar Association, Criminal Section, Spring, 2001. Assistant Public Defender, 12th Judicial District, 1973-1975. *Member:* Cumberland County, 12th Judicial District (Counselor to North Carolina State Bar, 1991—) and North Carolina Bar Associations; North Carolina State Bar; National Association of Criminal Defense Lawyers; North Carolina Academy of Trial Lawyers; The Association of Trial Lawyers of America. ***REPORTED CASES:*** Graham v. Connor, 490 U.S. 1 (1989); Spell v. McDaniel, 824 F.2d1 1380 (4th Cir. 1987); State v. Hennis, 323 N.C. 279, 372 S.E. 2d 523 (1988); Pinckney v. Van Damme, 116 N.C. App. 139, 447 S.E. 2d 825 (1994). ***PRACTICE AREAS:*** Federal Criminal Law; State Criminal Law; Civil Litigation. ***Email:*** hgb@beaverholt.com

F. THOMAS III HOLT, born New York, New York, December 29, 1952; admitted to bar, 1980, North Carolina, U.S. District Court, Eastern District of North Carolina and U.S. Court of Appeals, Fourth Circuit. *Education:* University of North Carolina (A.B., 1974); Campbell University (J.D., with distinction, 1980). Omicron Delta Kappa; Delta Theta Phi. Associate Editor, Campbell Law Review, 1979-1980. *Member:* Cumberland County, North Carolina and American Bar Associations. ***PRACTICE AREAS:*** Business Law; Mediation; Arbitration. ***Email:*** fth@beaverholt.com

MARK A. STERNLICHT, born Portsmouth, Virginia, September 24, 1954; admitted to bar, 1978, North Carolina; 1982, Pennsylvania, U.S. Court of Appeals, Third and Fourth Circuits, U.S. District Court, Middle and Eastern Districts of North Carolina and U.S. District Court, Eastern District of Pennsylvania. *Education:* University of North Carolina (A.B., with honors, 1975; J.D., 1978). Phi Beta Kappa. Staff Member, North Carolina Law Review, 1976-1978. Author: "Military Law-Right To Counsel At A Summary Court Martial: Middendorf v. Henry," 55 North Carolina Law Review 300, 1977. Co-Author: "Judge Braxton Craven, Jr.: Portrait Of A Pragmatist," 56 North Carolina Law Review 211, 1978. Listed in Personal Injury Litigation Section, The Best Lawyers in America. *Member:* Cumberland County, North Carolina, Pennsylvania and American Bar Associations; North Carolina State Bar; North Carolina Academy of Trial Lawyers; The Association of Trial Lawyers of America. ***PRACTICE AREAS:*** Medical and Professional Negligence; Personal Injury; Workers' Compensation; Commercial Litigation. ***Email:*** mas@beaverholt.com

DAVID T. COURIE, born Fayetteville, North Carolina, July 9, 1970; admitted to bar, 1997, North Carolina, U.S. Court of Appeals, Fourth Circuit and U.S. District Court, Eastern District of North Carolina. *Education:* Campbell University (B.B.A., 1993; J.D., 1997). Phi Alpha Delta. Voted, Fayetteville's Best Lawyer, Fayetteville Observer Reader's Choice, 2001. Chairman, Attorneys Division, Cumberland United Way, 1998. Special Assistant to U.S. Senator Jesse Helms, 1993-1994. Chair, City of Fayetteville, North Carolina Board of Adjustment, 2000-2003. Member: Board of Directors, American Lung Association; Board of Directors, Fayetteville Downtown Development Corporation, 2001—; Board of Directors, Boys and Girls Club of Cumberland County; Board of Visitors, Methodist College. *Member:* Cumberland County, North Carolina and American Bar Associations; North Carolina Academy of Trial Lawyers; Cumberland County Young Lawyers (President, 1999-2001); Cumberland County Criminal Defense Lawyers Association (Member, Executive Committee, 2000—); National Association of Criminal Defense Attorneys; Association of

(This Listing Continued)

Trial Lawyers of America. ***PRACTICE AREAS:*** Criminal Defense; Driving While Intoxicated; Drugs and Narcotics; Traffic Violations; Civil Litigation; Personal Injury. ***Email:*** dtc@beaverholt.com

HAL BROADFOOT JR., born Fayetteville, North Carolina, October 11, 1962; admitted to bar, 2002, North Carolina. *Education:* University of North Carolina at Chapel Hill (B.S.B.A., 1984); Campbell University (J.D., 2002). *Member:* Cumberland County, North Carolina and American Bar Associations. ***PRACTICE AREAS:*** Civil Litigation; Personal Injury. ***Email:*** hwb@beaverholt.com

MARK HEARP, admitted to bar, 2001, North Carolina. *Education:* University of North Carolina at Chapel Hill (B.A., Economics, 1998); Campbell University (J.D., 2001). ***PRACTICE AREAS:*** Criminal Law; Traffic Violations; Misdemeanors; Driving While Intoxicated; Federal Criminal Law. ***Email:*** mlh@beaverholt.com

OF COUNSEL

JANET HOLLAND DOWNING, born Winston Salem, North Carolina; admitted to bar, 1977, North Carolina. *Education:* Pfeiffer College (B.A., 1973); University of North Carolina at Chapel Hill (J.D., 1977). Trial Attorney, National Labor Relations Board, 1977-1986. Assistant District Attorney, Forsyth County, N.C., 1987-1991. Private Practice, 1992—. ***PRACTICE AREAS:*** Workers Compensation. ***Email:*** jhd@beaverholt.com

REFERENCES: Available Upon Request.

BLACKWELL & EDWARDS, P.A.

300 DICK STREET, HERITAGE SQUARE
P.O. BOX 469

FAYETTEVILLE, NORTH CAROLINA 28302

Telephone: 910-483-5176
Fax: 910-483-9653
Email: TDEdwards@nc.rr.com
URL: http://www.blackwellandedwards.com

Family Law, Probate.

FIRM PROFILE: John V. Blackwell and his brother Hector C. Blackwell founded a law firm in 1929 as Blackwell & Blackwell. John V. Blackwell, Jr. joined the firm in 1955. All were graduates of Wake Forest University's School of Law. That Timothy D. Edwards joined the law firm in 1995 and continues to practice in the firms area of concentration which is Family Law.

JOHN V. BLACKWELL, JR., born Fayetteville, North Carolina, December 12, 1932; admitted to bar, 1955, North Carolina. *Education:* Wake Forest University (B.A., 1953; LL.B., 1955). Phi Alpha Delta. Trustee, Cape Fear Valley Hospital, 1979-1982. Member, Estate Planning Committee, Campbell University, 1979-1981. *Member:* Cumberland County (President, 1977-1978), North Carolina and American Bar Associations; 12th Judicial District (President, 1974-1975) and North Carolina State (Council, Family Law Section, 1988-1991) Bars. (Retired). ***PRACTICE AREAS:*** Family Law; Probate Law. ***Email:*** JVBlackwell@nc.rr.com

TIMOTHY D. EDWARDS, born Springfield, Missouri, December 16, 1969; admitted to bar, 1995, North Carolina. *Education:* Liberty University (B.S., 1992); Campbell University School of Law (J.D., 1995). Delta Theta Phi. *Member:* North Carolina (Member, Family Law Section) and American Bar Associations; North Carolina Academy of Trial Lawyers; Young Lawyers Association. ***PRACTICE AREAS:*** Family Law; Criminal Law. ***Email:*** TDEdwards@nc.rr.com

REPRESENTATIVE CLIENTS: Furnished Upon Request.
REFERENCES: Wachovia Bank and Trust Co.; B.B.&T; Bank First Citizens Bank and Trust Co., Fayetteville, N.C.

MICHAEL C. BOOSE

Established in 1983

214 DICK STREET

FAYETTEVILLE, NORTH CAROLINA 28302

Telephone: 910-486-9292
Fax: 910-221-0750
URL: http://www.boose-law.com

Criminal Law, Personal Injury, Family Law.

FIRM PROFILE: Trial practice firm specializing in traffic defenses (speeding, revoked license, driving while impaired); criminal defense (felony and misdemeanor); and personal injury/automobile accidents.

MICHAEL C. BOOSE, born Fort Devens, Massachusetts, April 26, 1955; admitted to bar, 1981, North Carolina. *Education:* East Carolina University (B.S., 1977); Campbell University (J.D., 1981). Phi Alpha Delta. Instructor: Campbell University, 1982; Fayetteville Technical Institute, 1983. Assistant District Attorney, Twelfth Judicial District of North Carolina, 1981-1983. Member, 1988-2002 and Chairman, 1992, 1993, 1994, 2002, Board of Education, Cumberland County. *Member:* Cumberland County, North Carolina (Member, Section on Criminal Law) and American Bar Associations; North Carolina State Bar; North Carolina Academy of Trial Lawyers (Member, Sections on: Criminal Law; Auto Torts); The Association of Trial Lawyers of America. ***PRACTICE AREAS:*** Criminal Law (50%); Traffic Violations (25%); Personal Injury (25%).

REPRESENTATIVE CLIENTS: Show and Pro Auto; Diamond's Body Shop; North Carolina State Veteran's Home; Bramble Builders; Dave's Transmission; Moonlight Communications.
APPROVED ATTORNEYS FOR: Pre-paid Legal Services; NCAE Referral Service; North Carolina Lawyer Referral Service; NEA Referral Service.

CARL L. BRITT, JR., ATTORNEY AT LAW

224 DICK STREET
FAYETTEVILLE, NORTH CAROLINA 28302
Telephone: 910-483-1176
Fax: 910-483-5201
Email: carl@carlbritt.com
URL: http://www.carlbrittjr.com

Personal Injury, Wrongful Death, Traffic Violations, Driving While Intoxicated, Driving Under the Influence, Criminal Law.

CARL L. BRITT, JR. (WOODY), born Lumberton, North Carolina, March 29, 1955; admitted to bar, 1980, North Carolina and U.S. District Court, Eastern District of North Carolina. *Education:* University of North Carolina at Chapel Hill (B.A., 1977); Campbell University School of Law (J.D., 1980). Delta Theta Phi. *Member:* North Carolina Bar Association; North Carolina State Bar; North Carolina Academy of Trial Lawyers; The Association of Trial Lawyers of America. ***Email:*** carl@carlbritt.com

BROWN & MOSS, P.A.

Established in 1989

SUITE 302, NEW FIRST CITIZENS BANK BUILDING
109 GREEN STREET
FAYETTEVILLE, NORTH CAROLINA 28301-5044
Telephone: 910-433-2800
Fax: 910-433-4427
Email: mosspr@aol.com
URL: http://www.lawyers.com/mosspr

Traffic Offenses, Criminal, DWI, Bond Reductions, Misdemeanors, Felonies, Criminal Practice in State and Federal Courts.

FIRM PROFILE: In practice since 1989, Patricia R. Moss offers clients in Fayetteville and Cumberland County a full service traffic, DWI, bond reduction and criminal trial practice in State and Federal Courts. Ms. Moss is active in State and National Trial Lawyers Associations.

PATRICIA R. MOSS, born Harnett County, North Carolina, May 4, 1947; admitted to bar, 1982, North Carolina. *Education:* Campbell University (B.A., 1979; J.D., 1982). Delta Theta Phi. *Member:* Cumberland County, North Carolina and American Bar Associations; North Carolina State Bar; North Carolina Academy of Trial Lawyers; The Association of Trial Lawyers of America. ***PRACTICE AREAS:*** Criminal Law; Driving While Intoxicated; Traffic Violations; Bond Reductions; Misdemeanors; Felonies. ***Email:*** mosspr@aol.com

BRUMBAUGH, MU & KING, P.A.

Established in 1978

609 EXECUTIVE PLACE
FAYETTEVILLE, NORTH CAROLINA 28305
Telephone: 910-630-2099
URL: http://www.bmklaw.net

Practice Limited to Injury Cases. Automobile, Wrongful Death, Medical Malpractice, Workers' Compensation, Products Liability and Social Security Claims.

(For complete biographical data on all personnel, see professional biographies, Jacksonville, North Carolina)

GREGORY M. BYRD

214 DICK STREET, SUITE B
P.O. BOX 332
FAYETTEVILLE, NORTH CAROLINA 28302-0332
Telephone: 910-678-0966
1-800-793-1962
Fax: 910-678-0677
URL: http://www.ncdrunkdriving.com
Email: gbyrdlaw@aol.com
URL: http://www.lawyers.com/gregorymbyrd-com

Criminal Law, Criminal Defense, Drugs and Narcotics, Traffic Violations/Speeding, DWI, Personal Injury, Automobile Accidents and Injuries, Employment Law, Unemployment Compensation, Wrongful Termination.

GREGORY M. BYRD, born Raleigh, North Carolina, November 12, 1963; admitted to bar, 1995, North Carolina and U.S. District Court, Eastern District of North Carolina. *Education:* North Carolina State University (B.S., 1987); Campbell University (J.D., 1995). *Member:* Cumberland County (Member, Criminal Defense Section) and North Carolina Bar Associations; North Carolina State Bar; North Carolina Association of Trial Lawyers.

WILLIAM E. CLARK

2850 VILLAGE DRIVE, SUITE 204
FAYETTEVILLE, NORTH CAROLINA 28304
Telephone: 910-323-2020
FAX: 910-485-8320
Email: weclark@earthlink.net

General Civil Practice. Wills, Estate Planning and Probate. Corporate and Business Law. Real Estate Closings and Development.

WILLIAM E. CLARK, born Fayetteville, North Carolina, January 12, 1943; admitted to bar, 1968, North Carolina. *Education:* Davidson College (B.A., 1965); University of North Carolina at Chapel Hill (J.D., 1968). Member, North Carolina General Assembly, 1969-1986. *Member:* North Carolina and American Bar Associations; North Carolina State Bar. ***PRACTICE AREAS:*** Real Estate; Residential Real Estate Closings; Commercial Real Estate Closings; Foreclosures; Landlord and Tenant Law; Contracts; Litigation; Wills; Estates.

REPRESENTATIVE CLIENTS: Cape Fear Farm Credit; Carolina Model Home Corp.; Highland Lumber Company; Cohen & Green Salvage Company.
APPROVED ATTORNEY FOR: Investor's Title Insurance Co.; Chicago Title Insurance Co.; Lawyers Title Insurance Corp.

ROGER R. COMPTON

5311 RAEFORD ROAD
P.O. BOX 42836
FAYETTEVILLE, NORTH CAROLINA 28309-2836
Telephone: 910-424-6393
Fax: 910-424-2212
Email: adminoffice@nc.rr.com
URL: http://www.rogercompton.com

Family Law, including Divorce, Child Custody, Child Support, Spousal Support; Consumer Bankruptcy Chapter 7,11 and 13; Criminal Defense, Traffic Violations.

ROGER R. COMPTON, born Prim, Arkansas, July 5, 1946; admitted to bar, 1979, North Carolina; 1980, U.S. District Court, Eastern District of North Carolina. *Education:* Campbell University (B.S., 1973; J.D., 1979). *Member:* North Carolina Bar Association; North Carolina Academy of Trial Lawyers. [(U.S. Army, 1966-1976, Major; N.C. National Guard, 1976-1987, Major)]. ***PRACTICE AREAS:*** Family Law; Consumer Bankruptcy; Traffic Violations; Criminal.

ASSOCIATE

MELINDA C. FLINN, admitted to bar, 2002, North Carolina. *Education:* Campbell University (B.S., 1999; J.D., 2002).

THE CROSBY LAW FIRM

210 EAST RUSSELL STREET, SUITE 105
FAYETTEVILLE, NORTH CAROLINA 28302
Telephone: 910-483-0458
Fax: 910-483-8689
Email: rcrosby@crosbylawoffices.com
URL: http://www.crosbylawfirms.com

Traffic Violations, Criminal Law, Driving While Intoxicated, Military Law, Personal Injury.

RONALD C. CROSBY, JR., born New York, N.Y., February 16, 1971; admitted to bar, 1997, North Carolina; 2004, U.S. District Court, Eastern District of North Carolina. *Education:* University of North Carolina at Chapel Hill (B.A., 1993); Wake Forest University (J.D., 1997). ***PRACTICE AREAS:*** Criminal Law; Traffic Violations; Driving While Intoxicated; Military Law; Personal Injury. ***Email:*** rcrosby@crosbylawoffices.com

R. GREGG EDWARDS

1003 HAY STREET, SUITE 3
P.O. BOX 53885
FAYETTEVILLE, NORTH CAROLINA 28305
Telephone: 910-483-3399
Fax: 910-483-9585
Email: rgrdedwards@hotmail.com
URL: http://www.lawyers.com/rgedwards

Bankruptcy (including Small Business), Personal Injury, Automobile Accidents and Injuries, Workers Compensation, Back Injuries, Medical Malpractice, Civil Litigation.

R. GREGG EDWARDS, born Raleigh, North Carolina, November 27, 1957; admitted to bar, 1983, North Carolina; 1984, U.S. District Court, Eastern District of North Carolina; 2000, U.S. District Court, Middle District of North Carolina. *Education:* North Carolina State University (B.S., 1980); Wake Forest University (J.D., 1983). Member, Moot Court. *Member:* Cumberland County and North Carolina (Member, Sections on: Bankruptcy; Family Law; Litigation, Workers Compensation) Bar Associations; North Carolina Academy of Trial Lawyers. ***PRACTICE AREAS:*** Personal Injury; Automobile Accidents and Injuries; Workers Compensation; Civil Litigation; Bankruptcy Chapter 7; Bankruptcy Chapter 13; Bankruptcy Litigation.

PATRICIA A. WILSON FERGUSON

201 SOUTH MCPHERSON CHURCH ROAD
SUITE 209
FAYETTEVILLE, NORTH CAROLINA 28303
Telephone: 910-860-2889
Fax: 910-860-2880
Email: tfergie@earthlink.net
URL: http://www.fergusonhyattlaw.com
Mailing Address: P.O. Box 816, Fayetteville, NC 28302

Workers Compensation, Family Law, Domestic Law, Civil Litigation, Corporate Law, Business Law, Criminal, Real Estate, Zoning.

PATRICIA A. WILSON FERGUSON, born Fayetteville, North Carolina, February 15, 1951; admitted to bar, 2001, North Carolina. *Education:* North Carolina State University (B.A., honors program, magna cum laude, 1997); University of North Carolina (J.D.,

(This Listing Continued)

2000). *Member:* North Carolina Bar Association (Member, Family Law Section, 2001—). ***PRACTICE AREAS:*** Workers Compensation; Family Law; Domestic Law.

GEORGE J. FRANKS, P.A.

Established in 2001

115 SOUTH COOL SPRING STREET

FAYETTEVILLE, NORTH CAROLINA 28301

Telephone: 910-323-2834

Fax: 910-323-4923

Email: frankstrafficlaw@nc.rr.com

URL: http://.georgejfranks.com

Criminal Law, Traffic Law, Personal Injury, Representation of Professionals before Boards, Representation of Law Enforcement Officers.

FIRM PROFILE: Specializing in Criminal Law, Traffic Law, Personal Injury. Representation of Professionals before Boards, representation of Law Enforcement Officers.

GEORGE J. FRANKS, born Philadelphia, Pennsylvania, September 28, 1948; admitted to bar, 1983, North Carolina and U.S. District Court, Eastern District of North Carolina; 1988, U.S. Court of Appeals, Fourth Circuit. *Education:* University of Florida (B.S., 1970); West Virginia University (Ph.D., 1976); Campbell University (J.D., 1983). Licensed Practicing Psychologist and Health Service Provider, Psychology, North Carolina 1978. Member, North Carolina Psychological Association. *Member:* North Carolina Bar Association; North Carolina Academy of Trial Lawyers. ***PRACTICE AREAS:*** Criminal Law; Traffic Violations; Professional Discipline; Law Enforcement; Personal Injury. ***Email:*** frankstrafficlaw@nc.rr.com

REPRESENTATIVE CLIENTS: International Union of Police Associations.

HARDISON & LEONE, L.L.P.

Established in 1997

1014 HAY STREET

DRAWER 53037

FAYETTEVILLE, NORTH CAROLINA 28305-5316

Telephone: 910-223-3022

Toll Free: 800-782-3145

Fax: 910-223-9006

URL: http://www.hardisonandleone.com

Personal Injury, Auto and Trucking Accidents, Pedestrian Accidents, Catastrophic Injury, Medical Malpractice, Workers' Compensation, Social Security Disability, Nursing Home Negligence, Security Investment Fraud, Inadequate Security Claims, Premises Liability, Mass Torts, Drug Liability Claims, Employment Law, Appellate Practice.

(For complete information on all personnel, see Professional Biographies at Raleigh, North Carolina)

PAUL F. HERZOG

Established in 2000

210 EAST RUSSELL STREET, SUITE 101-103

P.O. BOX 3097

FAYETTEVILLE, NORTH CAROLINA 28302-3097

Telephone: 910-483-9500

Fax: 910-483-9524

URL: http://www.lawyers.com/theherzogfirm

Email: paulfherzog@hotmail.com

URL: http://www.theherzogfirm.com

Criminal Defense, Traffic Violations, Drug Crimes, Narcotics, DWI, Homicide, Assault, Sexual Assault, Personal Injury.

FIRM PROFILE: Paul Herzog concentrates in criminal and traffic law. His practice centers in Fayetteville, North Carolina (adjacent to Ft. Bragg). He is the former head of the Public Defender's Office for the 12th Judicial District in Southeastern North Carolina and has handled a number of first degree murder cases involving the death penalty, including State v. Malcolm-Wright, a case which was televised on Court TV. He is a published author and has lectured extensively on a number of criminal law subjects on the east coast.

PAUL F. HERZOG, born Augusta, Georgia, February 16, 1953; admitted to bar, 1978, North Carolina. *Education:* Duke University (B.A. in History, 1975); University of North Carolina at Chapel Hill (J.D., 1978). *Member:* North Carolina and American Bar Associations; North Carolina Academy of Trial Lawyers; Cumberland County Association of Criminal Lawyers. ***PRACTICE AREAS:*** Criminal Law; Drugs and Narcotics; Personal Injury.

THE LAW FIRM OF HUTCHENS, SENTER & BRITTON, P.A.

4317 RAMSEY STREET

FAYETTEVILLE, NORTH CAROLINA 28311

Telephone: 910-864-6888

Facsimile: 910-864-6848

Email: lawfirm@hutchensandsenter.com

URL: http://www.hutchensandsenter.com

Mailing Address: P.O. Box 2505, Fayetteville, NC 28302

Wilmington, North Carolina Office: Suite 210, 1437 Military Cutoff Road, P.O. Box 12969. Telephone: 910-509-7480. Fax: 910-509-7448.

(This Listing Continued)

Raleigh, North Carolina Office: Suite 1540, Two Hanover Square. Telephone: 919-834-2688. Fax: 919-834-3373.

General Civil Practice, Trials in all State and Federal Courts, Creditor Bankruptcy, Foreclosures and Collection, Personal Injury, Wrongful Death, Worker's Compensation, Insurance Law, Corporation, Business and Real Estate.

H. TERRY HUTCHENS, born San Antonio, Texas, September 18, 1950; admitted to bar, 1977, North Carolina; 1978, U.S. District Court, Eastern, Middle and Western Districts of North Carolina and U.S. Court of Military Appeals; 1982, U.S. Supreme Court. *Education:* North Carolina State University (B.A., 1972); Wake Forest University (M.B.A., 1974; J.D., 1977). Phi Delta Phi. Member: North Carolina Board of Transportation, 1985-1990; North Carolina Board of Economic Development, 1990-1992. *Member:* Cumberland County, North Carolina (Member, Real Property and Bankruptcy Sections) and American Bar Associations; North Carolina State Bar. ***PRACTICE AREAS:*** Civil Practice; Real Property; Creditors Rights; Business Law. ***Email:*** thutchens@hutchensandsenter.com

WILLIAM L. SENTER, born Raeford, North Carolina, March 21, 1950; admitted to bar, 1975, North Carolina. *Education:* University of North Carolina (B.S., Beta Gamma Sigma, 1972) ; Morehead Scholar; Wake Forest University (J.D., 1975). Phi Delta Phi. Member, Wake Forest Law Review, 1974-1975. Author: Note, "Implied Warranty of Habitability in North Carolina," 11 Wake Forest Law Review 155, 1975. Certified Mediator. *Member:* Cumberland County, North Carolina (Member, Dispute Resolution Committee) and American (Member, Section of Litigation) Bar Associations; North Carolina State Bar; North Carolina Academy of Trial Lawyers; The Association of Trial Lawyers of America. ***PRACTICE AREAS:*** Personal Injury Law; Medical Negligence Litigation; Mediation; Arbitration; Worker's Compensation. ***Email:*** bsenter@hutchensandsenter.com

JOHN H. BRITTON, born Bethesda, Maryland, March 14, 1962; admitted to bar, 1995, North Carolina; U.S. District Court, Eastern, Middle and Western Districts of North Carolina. *Education:* University of Maine at Presque Isle (B.S., 1984); Duke University (M.B.A., 1988); Campbell Law School (J.D., 1995). *Member:* Cumberland County, North Carolina (Member, Real Property Section) and American Bar Associations; North Carolina State Bar; North Carolina Academy of Trial Lawyers. ***PRACTICE AREAS:*** Civil Practice; Real Property; Foreclosures. ***Email:*** jbritton@hutchensandsenter.com

JOSEPH J. VONNEGUT, born Whiteman AFB, Missouri, December 22, 1963; admitted to bar, 1989, Georgia; 2004, North Carolina and U.S. District Court, Eastern, Middle and Western Districts of North Carolina; 1993, U.S. Court of Appeals, Seventh Circuit; 1994, U.S. District Court, Middle District of Illinois; 1989, U.S. Army Court of Criminal Appeals. *Education:* The Citadel (B.A., 1986); Mercer University (J.D., 1989). *Member:* State Bar of Georgia; Cumberland County and North Carolina Bar Associations; North Carolina State Bar (Member, Bankruptcy and Real Property Sections). [Major, U.S. Army J.A.G. Corps, 1989-1998; USAR, 1998—]. ***PRACTICE AREAS:*** Bankruptcy; Creditors Rights in Bankruptcy; Civil Practice. ***Email:*** jvonnegut@hutchensandsenter.com

REBECCA J. BRITTON, born Poughkeepsie, New York, August 12, 1963; admitted to bar, 1992, North Carolina, U.S. District Court, Eastern and Middle Districts of North Carolina, U.S. Court of Appeals, Fourth Circuit and U.S. Supreme Court,. *Education:* University of Maine (B.A., with distinction, 1989); Campbell University (J.D, 1992). Order of the Barristers. Adjunct Professor, Campbell University School of Law. *Member:* Cumberland County (Secretary, 1995-1998), North Carolina and American Bar Associations; North Carolina State Bar; North Carolina Academy of Trial Lawyers (Vice President, Public Education); The Association of Trial Lawyers of America. ***PRACTICE AREAS:*** Medical Negligence; Personal Injury; Civil Litigation; Civil Rights.

SHAWNA Y. STATON, born Sealevel, North Carolina, August 11, 1966; admitted to bar, 1991, North Carolina and U.S. District Court, Western, Eastern and Middle Districts of North Carolina; 1992, U.S. Court of Appeals, Fourth Circuit. *Education:* University of North Carolina at Chapel Hill (B.A., 1988; J.D., 1991). Phi Alpha Delta. Editor, Disclosure Statement, Bankruptcy Section Newsletter, North Carolina Bar Association, 2001-2003. Panel Member: Chapter 7 Bankruptcy Trustees for Eastern District of North Carolina, 1998—; Local Bankruptcy Rules Committee for the Eastern District of North Carolina. *Member:* Wake County, North Carolina (Member, Young Lawyers Section; Member, Executive Council, 1998— and Chair, Ethics Committee, 1999, Bankruptcy Section) and American Bar Associations; American Bankruptcy Institute. (Resident, Raleigh, North Carolina Office). ***PRACTICE AREAS:*** Bankruptcy; Commercial Litigation. ***Email:*** Shawna.Staton@hutchensandsenter.com

ASSOCIATES

WENDY H. HUGHES, born Lumberton, North Carolina, October 10, 1969; admitted to bar, 1999, North Carolina. *Education:* University of North Carolina (B.S., 1991); Campbell University (M.B.A., 1999); Campbell Law School (J.D., 1999). *Member:* Cumberland County and North Carolina Bar Associations; North Carolina State Bar (Member, Real Property Section); North Carolina Land Title Association. ***PRACTICE AREAS:*** Real Property; Foreclosures. ***Email:*** whughes@hutchensandsenter.com

LONNIE M. PLAYER, JR., born Fayetteville, North Carolina, August 1, 1970; admitted to bar, 1998, North Carolina, U.S. District Court, Eastern, Middle and Western Districts of North Carolina and Cherokee Supreme Court. *Education:* Duke University (A.B., cum laude, 1993); University of Texas at Austin (M.A., 1995); University of North Carolina (J.D., 1998). Phi Delta Phi. *Member:* Cumberland County (Treasurer, 2002-2003), 12th Judical District (Vice President, 2005-2006), North Carolina and American Bar Associations; North Carolina State Bar; Commercial Law League of America; Twelfth Judicial District Bar (Treasurer, 2001-2002); National Association of Retail Collection Attorneys. ***PRACTICE AREAS:*** Corporate Transactions; Commercial Litigation; Collections. ***Email:*** lplayer@hutchensandsenter.com

JAMES C. HUFF, born Wilmington, North Carolina, November 8, 1969; admitted to bar, 1999, North Carolina; U.S. District Court, Eastern, Middle and Western Districts of North Carolina. *Education:* Campbell University (B.B.A., 1994; J.D., 1999). *Member:* Cumberland County and North Carolina (Member, Real Estate Section, 1999—) Bar Associations; North Carolina State Bar. ***PRACTICE AREAS:*** Real Estate Foreclosure; Real Estate Litigation; Real Estate Loan Closings. ***Email:*** jchuff@hutchensandsenter.com

(This Listing Continued)

THE LAW FIRM OF HUTCHENS, SENTER & BRITTON, P.A., Fayetteville—Continued

JOHN A. MANDULAK, born Fairbanks, Alaska, December 4, 1976; admitted to bar, 2002, North Carolina; 2004, U.S. District Court, Eastern, Middle and Western Districts of North Carolina. *Education:* University of North Carolina at Chapel Hill (B.A., 1999); Dayton Law School (J.D., 2002). *Member:* Cumberland County, North Carolina and American Bar Associations; North Carolina State Bar. ***PRACTICE AREAS:*** Real Estate; Litigation; Business Law. ***Email:*** jmandulak@hutchensandsenter.com

SARAH MIRANDA, born Lumberton, North Carolina, November 8, 1972; admitted to bar, 1999, Virginia; 2000, North Carolina; U.S. District Court, Eastern, Middle and Western Districts of North Carolina. *Education:* University of North Carolina at Chapel Hill (B.A., 1995); Regent University (J.D., cum laude, 1999). *Member:* North Carolina (Member, Bankruptcy Section) and American Bar Associations. ***PRACTICE AREAS:*** Creditor Bankruptcy; Civil Practice. ***Email:*** sarah.miranda@hutchensandsenter.com

J. SCOTT FLOWERS, born Fayetteville, North Carolina, October 28, 1977; admitted to bar, 2003, North Carolina and U.S. District Court, Eastern, Middle and Western Districts of North Carolina. *Education:* East Carolina University (B.A., 2000); Campbell University (J.D., 2003). Order of Old Kivett. Listed, Assistant District Attorney, Twelfth Judicial District, 2004. *Member:* Cumberland County and North Carolina (Member, Real Property Section) Bar Associations; North Carolina State Bar; North Carolina Academy of Trial Lawyers. ***PRACTICE AREAS:*** Civil Litigation; Foreclosures. ***Email:*** jsflowers@hutchensandsenter.com

ERIK T. BENNINGTON, born Wheeling, West Virginia, January 2, 1978; admitted to bar, 2003, North Carolina and U.S. District Court, Eastern and Western Districts of North Carolina. *Education:* Campbell University (B.B.A., 2000); Wake Forest University (J.D., 2003). *Member:* North Carolina Bar Association (Real Property and Young Lawyers Sections); New Hanover County Bar Association. (Also at Wilmington, North Carolina Office). ***PRACTICE AREAS:*** Civil Litigation; Foreclosures; Real Estate. ***Email:*** erik.bennington@hutchensandsenter.com

STEPHEN BAILEY, born Eden, North Carolina, February 4, 1975; admitted to bar, 2003, North Carolina. *Education:* Appalachian State University (B.S., 1997); Mercer University (J.D., 2003). *Member:* Hanover County and North Carolina Bar Associations. (Also at Wilmington, North Carolina Office). ***PRACTICE AREAS:*** Real Estate.

OF COUNSEL

RUDOLPH G. SINGLETON, JR., born Lexington, Kentucky, May 24, 1930; admitted to bar, 1954, North Carolina; U.S. District Court, Eastern and Middle Districts of North Carolina; U.S. Supreme Court. *Education:* Mars Hill College and Wake Forest University (A.B., 1952); Wake Forest University (J.D., 1954). Phi Alpha Delta. North Carolina Certified Mediator, 1995—. Assistant District Attorney, Cumberland County Superior Court, 1955-1956. Member of Panel, American Arbitration Association. Fayetteville City Attorney, 1972-1974. *Member:* Cumberland County (President, 1980-1981), North Carolina and American Bar Associations; Twelfth Judicial District State Bar; The North Carolina State Bar; North Carolina Academy of Trial Lawyers (Governor, 1975-1977). [U.S. Army Intelligence, 1956-1957]. ***PRACTICE AREAS:*** Personal Injury Law; Civil Litigation; Condemnation; Mediation; Arbitration; Estate Administration. ***Email:*** rsingleton@hutchensandsenter.com

REPRESENTATIVE CLIENTS: Available Upon Request.

COLLEEN J. KELLY

350 DICK STREET
FAYETTEVILLE, NORTH CAROLINA 28302
Telephone: 910-424-6699
Fax: 910-426-8463
Email: ckellylaw@earthlink.net

Family Law, Domestic Relations, Juvenile Law, Traffic Violations.

COLLEEN J. KELLY, born Grand Rapids, Michigan, April 4, 1966; admitted to bar, 2001, North Carolina. *Education:* Fayetteville State University (B.S., 1995); Campbell University (J.D., 2001). ***PRACTICE AREAS:*** Family Law; Domestic Relations; Juvenile Law; Traffic Violations.

LEDBETTER & TITSWORTH, P.A.

FAYETTEVILLE, NORTH CAROLINA

(See Cary)

Workers Compensation, Personal Injury, Automobile Accidents, Trucking Accidents, Medical Malpractice.

MAXWELL & MELVIN

Established in 1990

116 NORTH COOL SPRING STREET
FAYETTEVILLE, NORTH CAROLINA 28301
Telephone: 910-483-1414
FAX: 910-483-7443

General Practice, Personal Injury, Wrongful Death, Medical Malpractice, Real Estate, Workers Compensation, Collections, Bankruptcy, Criminal, Traffic, Corporations, Elder Law, Wills and Estates.

MEMBERS OF FIRM

C. DOUGLAS MAXWELL, JR., born Cumberland County, North Carolina, October 17, 1940; admitted to bar, 1970, North Carolina. *Education:* Wake Forest University and St. Andrews Presbyterian College (B.S., 1963); University of North Carolina (J.D., 1970). Phi Delta Phi (Magister, 1969-1970). *Member:* Twelfth Judicial District, North Carolina and American Bar Associations; North Carolina State Bar; National Association of Elder Law Attorneys. ***PRACTICE AREAS:*** Elder Law; Wills and Estates; Personal Injury; Corporations; Collections. ***Email:*** cdmaxwell@nc.rr.com

STEPHEN R. MELVIN, born Fayetteville, North Carolina, November 4, 1952; admitted to bar, 1981, North Carolina. *Education:* Wake Forest University (B.A., 1975); Campbell University (J.D., 1981). Member, Campbell University Law Review, 1980-1981. Member, Cumberland County Area Mental Health Board of Directors, (1987-1993). Chairman, Cumberland County Board of Elections, 1997-1999. *Member:* Cumberland County, North Carolina and American Bar Associations; North Carolina State Bar; North Carolina Academy of Trial Lawyers; The Association of Trial Lawyers of America. ***PRACTICE AREAS:*** Personal Injury; Medical Malpractice; Wrongful Death; Workers Compensation; Criminal; Civil Litigation. ***Email:*** srmelvin@nc.rr.com

REPRESENTATIVE CLIENTS: B.B.& T.; Horne's Furniture and Appliance, Inc.; Rhudy's, Inc.; M.J. Noonan, P.A.; Rental Uniform Services, Inc.; Briggs & Sons Tires; City Cab of Fayetteville, Inc.; AAA Moving & Storage; Piedmont Moving & Storage; Stedman-Wade Health Services; Cumberland Pharmacies, Inc.; The Learning License Inc.; Gill Security Systems, Inc.; Snowhill Turf Farm, Inc.; BLS Holdings, Inc.; Sandy Ridge Electric, Inc.; Graham Battery Co., Inc.
APPROVED ATTORNEYS FOR: Lawyers Title Insurance Corp.; Chicago Title Insurance; Investors Title Insurance Co.; Jefferson-Pilot Title Insurance Co.; Farmers Home Administration; Centura Bank; 1st Citizens Bank & Trust Co.; Branch Banking & Trust Co.

McCOY WEAVER WIGGINS CLEVELAND ROSE RAY PLLC

Established in 1955

202 FAIRWAY DRIVE
P.O. BOX 87009
FAYETTEVILLE, NORTH CAROLINA 28304
Telephone: 910-483-8104
FAX: 910-483-0094
Email: office@mccoyrose.com

Civil Litigation, Corporate, Wills and Estates, Taxation, Municipal and Institutional Bonds, Real Estate and Immigration.

FIRM PROFILE: The firm is a combination of two of the oldest firms in southeastern North Carolina with the law practice of Charles G. Rose beginning in the 1800's and the practice of Sanford, Phillips McCoy and Weaver beginning in the late 1950's. Charles G. Rose, Jr. practiced law in Fayetteville for many years and served as a member of the N.C. General Assembly. His son, Charles G. Rose III, became a U.S. Congressman. Terry Sanford became Governor of North Carolina, a U.S. Senator and President of Duke University. Dickson Phillips became Dean of the University of North Carolina School of Law and later a Judge on the Fourth Circuit Court of Appeals. The firm has consistently been listed in the Bar Register of Preeminent Lawyers.

MEMBERS OF FIRM

DONALD W. McCOY (1919-1995)

CHARLES G. ROSE, JR. (1912-1996)

RICHARD M. WIGGINS, born Fayetteville, North Carolina, August 20, 1933; admitted to bar, 1958, North Carolina; U.S. District Court, Eastern, Middle and Western Districts of North Carolina; U.S. Court of Appeals, Fourth Circuit and U.S. Supreme Court. *Education:* University of North Carolina (A.B., 1955; J.D., 1958). Delta Theta Phi. *Member:* Cumberland County (President, 1985-1986), North Carolina and American Bar Associations; The North Carolina State Bar. ***PRACTICE AREAS:*** Commercial Litigation; Insurance Defense; Corporate Law; Construction Law. ***Email:*** rmwiggins@mccoyrose.com

ALFRED E. CLEVELAND, born Richmond, Virginia, July 14, 1935; admitted to bar, 1959, North Carolina. *Education:* Georgetown University (B.S. in F.S., 1956); University of North Carolina (J.D., 1959). Phi Alpha Delta. Member, Board of Editors, University of North Carolina Law Review, 1959. Listed in The Best Lawyers in America. *Member:* Cumberland County (President, 1990-1991), North Carolina and American Bar Associations; The North Carolina State Bar. [Lt. USAR, 1964-1967]. ***PRACTICE AREAS:*** Corporate; Banking Law; Trusts and Estates. ***Email:*** aecleveland@mccoyrose.com

ROBERT G. RAY, born Portsmouth, Virginia, April 9, 1943; admitted to bar, 1968, North Carolina; 1973, U.S. District Court, Eastern District of North Carolina and U.S. Tax Court. *Education:* University of North Carolina (B.S., 1965; J.D., 1968); New York University (LL.M. in Taxation, 1972). Phi Alpha Delta. Certified Public Accountant, North Carolina, 1970. *Member:* Cumberland County and North Carolina Bar Associations; American Institute of Certified Public Accountants. Fellow, American College of Trust and Estate Counsel. (Board Certified Specialist in Estate Planning and Probate Law, North Carolina State Board of Legal Specialization). ***PRACTICE AREAS:*** Taxation Law; Estate Planning and Probate Law; Business Law. ***Email:*** rray@mccoyrose.com

STEVEN J. O'CONNOR, born Burlington, North Carolina, May 16, 1958; admitted to bar, 1983, North Carolina; 1984, U.S. District Court, Eastern District of North Carolina and U.S. Tax Court; 1991, U.S. Court of Appeals, Fourth Circuit; 1993, U.S. District Court, Middle District of North Carolina. *Education:* University of North Carolina (B.A., 1980; J.D., 1983). *Member:* Cumberland County, North Carolina and American Bar Associations; North Carolina Academy of Trial Lawyers; American Immigration Lawyers Association. ***PRACTICE AREAS:*** Business Law; Civil Litigation; Immigration and Naturalization; Commercial Real Estate. ***Email:*** sjoco@mccoyrose.com

ANNE MAYO EVANS, born Raleigh, North Carolina, June 12, 1956; admitted to bar, 1987, North Carolina. *Education:* University of North Carolina (B.A., 1978); Campbell University (J.D., with honors, 1987). Phi Alpha Delta. Member, Editorial Board, Campbell Law Review, 1986-1987. *Member:* Cumberland County and North Carolina Bar Associations; North Carolina State Bar. ***PRACTICE AREAS:*** Construction Law; Real Estate Law; Bankruptcy; Corporate; Real Estate Litigation. ***Email:*** cwburris@mccoyrose.com

(This Listing Continued)

JEFF DUNHAM, born Biloxi, Mississippi, June 4, 1960; admitted to bar, 1985, North Carolina. *Education:* Wake Forest University (B.A., 1982); University of North Carolina (J.D., 1985). *Member:* Cumberland County Bar Association; North Carolina Bar Association (Member, Real Property Section Council); North Carolina State Bar. (Board Certified Specialist in Real Property Law; Business, Commercial and Industrial Transactions; and Residential Transactions, North Carolina State Board of Legal Specialization). ***PRACTICE AREAS:*** Commercial Real Estate; Residential Real Estate; Business Law; Commercial Law. ***Email:*** jdunham@mccoyrose.com

JIM WADE GOODMAN, born Fayetteville, North Carolina, September 28, 1963; admitted to bar, 1988, North Carolina, U.S. District Court, Eastern and Middle Districts of North Carolina; 1991, U.S. Court of Appeals, Fourth Circuit. *Education:* University of North Carolina (B.S., 1985; J.D., 1988). Phi Beta Kappa. Recipient, American Jurisprudence Award in Civil Procedure. *Member:* Cumberland County, North Carolina and American Bar Associations; North Carolina State Bar. ***PRACTICE AREAS:*** Commercial Litigation; Corporate Law; Construction Law; Condemnation. ***Email:*** jgoodman@mccoyrose.com

R. WILLIFORD McCAULEY, born Asheboro, North Carolina, June 15, 1965; admitted to bar, 1991, North Carolina. *Education:* Davidson College (B.A., 1987); Wake Forest University (J.D., M.B.A., 1991); New York University (LL.M. Taxation, 1995). *Member:* Cumberland County and North Carolina Bar Associations. ***PRACTICE AREAS:*** Estate Planning; Estate Administration; Taxation; Business Law. ***Email:*** rwm@mccoyrose.com

JAMES ALBERT McLEAN, III, born Fayetteville, North Carolina, July 7, 1976; admitted to bar, 2001, North Carolina; 2002, U.S. District Court, Eastern District of North Carolina and U.S. Court of Appeals, 4th Circuit. *Education:* Duke University (A.B., 1998); University of North Carolina School of Law (J.D., 2001). Duke University Golden Key. *Member:* Cumberland, North Carolina and American Bar Associations. ***PRACTICE AREAS:*** Corporate Law; Commercial Law; Estate Litigation; Real Estate; Commercial Litigation; Business Litigation; Real Estate Litigation. ***Email:*** jmclean@mccoyrose.com

OF COUNSEL

L. STACY WEAVER, JR., born Morganton, North Carolina, May 23, 1929; admitted to bar, 1953, North Carolina. *Education:* Duke University (A.B., 1951; J.D., 1953). Delta Theta Phi. Member, Editorial Board, Duke Bar Journal, 1952-1953. Instructional Assistant, Legal Aid Clinic of Duke University, 1953-1954. *Member:* Cumberland County (President, 1976-1977), North Carolina and American Bar Associations; The North Carolina State Bar. ***PRACTICE AREAS:*** Commercial Real Estate; Corporate; Estates; Estate Planning; Zoning; Education Law. ***Email:*** lsweaver@mccoyrose.com

REPRESENTATIVE CLIENTS: North Carolina Natural Gas Corporation; Branch Banking & Trust Company; Hercules Steel Corporation; Fay Block Co.; Methodist College; Fayetteville Technical Community College; Barnhill Contracting Company; John Koeing Realtors, Inc.; Chicago Title Insurance Company; Investors Title Insurance Company; First American Title Insurance Company.
APPROVED ATTORNEYS FOR: Lawyers Title Insurance Corp.; Chicago Title Insurance Co.; Farmers Home Administration; Federal Land Bank; Investors Title Insurance Co.

THE McLEOD LAW FIRM, P.A.

Established in 1972

FIRST CITIZENS BANK BUILDING
SUITE ONE
109 GREEN STREET
P.O. BOX 1539
FAYETTEVILLE, NORTH CAROLINA 28302
Telephone: 910-323-1425
800-446-8259
Fax: 910-323-4582
Email: theMcLeodlawfirm@aol.com

Practice limited to Civil Litigation in State and Federal Courts.

FIRM PROFILE: The McLeod Law Firm was founded by Joe McLeod in 1972. The firm has been serving clients throughout North Carolina, with a focus on civil litigation.

JOE McLEOD, born Raeford, North Carolina, November 30, 1937; admitted to bar, 1963, North Carolina and U.S. District Court, Eastern District of North Carolina; 1968, U.S. Court of Appeals, 4th Circuit; 1972, U.S. Supreme Court. *Education:* University of North Carolina (A.B., 1960; J.D., 1962). Phi Delta Phi (President, 1961-1962). Member, 1970-1978; Vice Chairman, 1975-1976; Chairman, 1976-1978, North Carolina Human Relations Commission. *Member:* Cumberland County (Vice President, 1988-1989; President, 1989-1990) and North Carolina (Member: Courts and Civil Litigation Committee, 1970-1976; Appellate Rules Study Committee, 1973-1975) Bar Associations; 12th Judicial Circuit and North Carolina State Bars; North Carolina Academy of Trial Lawyers (Member, Board of Governors, 1981-1986); The Association of Trial Lawyers of America (State Committeeman, 1981-1982; Co-Chair, Ethical Conduct Committee, 1996—). Fellow, International Society of Barristers (Member, Board of Governors, 1992-2002; President, 2001-2002). Certified Civil Trial Advocate by National Board of Trial Advocacy (Member, Board of Directors, 1992-2002). ***PRACTICE AREAS:*** Wrongful Death; Personal Injury Law; Medical Negligence Litigation; Federal Tort Claims; Corporate Litigation; Aviation; Products Liability. ***Email:*** wojocloud@aol.com

CATHERINE H. LESICA, born Baltimore, Maryland, July 8, 1956; admitted to bar, 1981, District of Columbia, U.S. Court of Appeals for the District of Columbia Circuit and U.S. District Court for the District of Columbia; 1983, Hawaii and U.S. District Court, District of Hawaii; 1994, North Carolina. *Education:* Pennsylvania State University (B.S., with highest honors, 1978); Washington College of Law of American University (J.D., magna cum laude, 1981). Phi Alpha Delta. Member, Moot Court. *Member:* Cumberland County and Hawaii State Bar Associations; North Carolina State Bar; North Carolina Academy of Trial Lawyers. ***PRACTICE AREAS:*** Civil Litigation.

WILLIAM W. AYCOCK, JR., born Greenville, North Carolina, June 29, 1937; admitted to bar, 1961, North Carolina. *Education:* Presbyterian College (B.S., 1960); Wake

(This Listing Continued)

Forest College (LL.B., 1961). Phi Alpha Delta. Member, Tarboro City Board of Education, 1981-1985. *Member:* Cumberland County and North Carolina Bar Associations; Twelfth Judicial District and North Carolina State Bars. [Capt., U.S. Army, 1961-1963]. ***PRACTICE AREAS:*** Wrongful Death; Personal Injury Law; Medical Negligence Litigation; Federal Tort Claims; Corporate Litigation; Aviation; Class Action Litigation; Products Liability.

REFERENCE: First Citizens Bank & Trust Co.

MITCHELL BREWER RICHARDSON, PLLC

2950 VILLAGE DRIVE
FAYETTEVILLE, NORTH CAROLINA 28304
Telephone: 910-678-7100
Fax: 910-678-9099

Other Fayetteville Office: 2950 Village Drive, 28304. Telephone: 910-678-7100. Fax: 910-678-9099.

Personal Injury, Medical Malpractice, Traffic, Criminal, Workers Compensation, Appellate Law, General Civil and Criminal Practice, Trials in all State and Federal Courts.

MEMBERS OF FIRM

RONNIE MONROE MITCHELL, born Clinton, North Carolina, November 10, 1952; admitted to bar, 1978, North Carolina; 1983, U.S. Court of Appeals, Fourth Circuit; 1984, U.S. Supreme Court. *Education:* Wake Forest University (B.A., cum laude, 1975; J.D., cum laude, 1978). Carswell Scholar. Articles Editor, Wake Forest Law Review, 1977-1978. Author and Contributor: North Carolina Family Law Practice Handbook, Wake Forest University CLE, 1980-1984; North Carolina Family Law Forms Manual, Wake Forest University CLE, 1981; North Carolina Criminal Defense Manual, Wake Forest University CLE, 1984; North Carolina DUI Manual, Wake Forest University CLE, 1982; North Carolina Criminal Practice Manual, 1988. Adjunct Professor of Law, Norman Adrian Wiggins School of Law, Campbell University. *Member:* Cumberland County (Treasurer, 1979-1980), North Carolina and America Bar Associations; Twelfth Judicial District (President, 1988-1989) and North Carolina State (Member, North Carolina State Bar Board of Legal Specialization Family Law Certification Committee) Bars; National Association of Criminal Defense Lawyers; North Carolina Academy of Trial Lawyers; The Association of Trial Lawyers of America. ***PRACTICE AREAS:*** Personal Injury; Criminal Law; Appellate Practice; Medical Malpractice; Business Litigation. ***Email:*** ronnie.mitchell@mbr-law.com

COY E. BREWER, JR., born Durham, North Carolina, November 15, 1947; admitted to bar, 1972, North Carolina. *Education:* Wake Forest University (B.A., American History, 1969); University of North Carolina (J.D., with honors, 1972). Order of the Coif. Recipient, Outstanding North Carolina Trial Judge, North Carolina Academy of Trial Lawyers, 1984. Editor, North Carolina Law Review, 1971-1972. Research Assistant to Justice Dan K. Moore, North Carolina Supreme Court. Author: "Racial Discrimination in Housing," North Carolina Law Review, 1970; "Retention by Police of Arrest Records," North Carolina Law Review, 1971; "Relational Privileges," North Carolina Law Review, 1972; "Judicial Review of Settlements," North Carolina Bar Association CLE, View from the Bench, 1990; "Direct Examination," North Carolina Bar Association CLE, 1994; "Jury Selection," Bar Notes, North Carolina Bar Association, 1997. Associate: Murchison, Fox & Newton, Wilmington, NC, 1973-1974; Rose, Thorpe & Rand, 1975. Assistant District Attorney, 1974-1975, District Court Judge, 1976-1977, Superior Court Judge, 1977-1992 and Senior Superior Court Judge, 1992-1998, 12th Judicial District. President, Eckerd's Wilderness Therapeutic Camps, 1981-1984. Member: Citizens Commission on Alternatives to Incarceration, 1985-1987; Joint Legislative Study Commission on North Carolina Criminal Procedure, 1992-1995; North Carolina Drugs Task Force, 1997—; Board of Governors, Summit House, Inc., 1998—. Superior Court Representative, Commission on Court Ordered Mediation, 1992-1994. Vice Chair, Commission on Mental Health Alternatives, 1993-1995. Chair: North Carolina Courts and Drugs Task Force (appointed by Chief Justice), 1995-1997; Cumberland County Community Penalties Program, 1996-1998; Commission on Model Continuance Policy (appointed by Chief Justice), 1997-1998; Commission on Death Penalty, Indigent Defense (appointed by Chief Justice), 1997-1998. *Member:* North Carolina and American Bar Associations; North Carolina Academy of Trial Lawyers. ***PRACTICE AREAS:*** Civil Practice; Criminal Law; Appellate Practice; Personal Injury. ***Email:*** coy.brewer@mbr-law.com

WILLIAM O. RICHARDSON, born New Bern, North Carolina, June 9, 1955; admitted to bar, 1980, North Carolina; 1982, U.S. District Court, Eastern District of North Carolina. *Education:* University of North Carolina at Chapel Hill (B.A., 1977); Campbell University (J.D., 1980). Delta Theta Phi. Assistant District Attorney, 12th Judicial District, 1980-1982. Member, North Carolina House of Representatives, 1993—. *Member:* Cumberland County (Secretary, 1981-1982) and North Carolina Bar Associations; North Carolina Academy of Trial Lawyers; National Association of Criminal Defense Lawyers; The Association of Trial Lawyers of America. ***PRACTICE AREAS:*** Personal Injury; Civil Litigation; Civil Rights Law; Employment Law; Administrative Law. ***Email:*** billy.richardson@mbr-law.com

ASSOCIATE

CHARLES M. BRITTAIN, born Hickory, North Carolina, January 15, 1969; admitted to bar, 1996, North Carolina. *Education:* University of North Carolina, Chapel Hill (B.A., 1991); Norman A. Wiggins School of Law (J.D., 1996). Delta Theta Phi. *Member:* Cumberland County and North Carolina Bar Associations; North Carolina State Bar. ***PRACTICE AREAS:*** Personal Injury; Civil Litigation. ***Email:*** charles.brittain@mbr-law.com

MURRAY, CRAVEN & INMAN, L.L.P.

HIGHLAND PLACE
2517 RAEFORD ROAD
P.O. DRAWER 53007
FAYETTEVILLE, NORTH CAROLINA 28305-3007
Telephone: 910-483-4990
FAX: 910-483-6822

General Civil and Criminal Trial Practice before all State and Federal Courts. Corporation, Insurance, Bankruptcy, Personal Injury, Probate, Taxation, Estate Planning, Construction Law.

MEMBERS OF FIRM

OCIE F. MURRAY, JR., born Virgilina, Virginia, December 25, 1941; admitted to bar, 1967, Virginia; 1971, North Carolina. *Education:* Elon University (A.B., 1964); College of William and Mary (J.D., 1967); Georgetown University (LL.M., in Taxation, 1969). Trial Attorney in the Office of Chief Counsel, Internal Revenue Service, 1967-1972. *Member:* Cumberland County, North Carolina (Chairman, Tax Section, 1985) and Virginia Bar Associations. ***PRACTICE AREAS:*** Taxation; Bankruptcy; Business; Corporation Law; Estate Planning; Probate.

RICHARD T. CRAVEN, born New York, N.Y., April 26, 1953; admitted to bar, 1979, North Carolina. *Education:* University of North Carolina (B.A., 1975); Cumberland School of Law of Samford University (J.D., 1979). Delta Theta Phi. Assistant District Attorney, 1979-1980. *Member:* Twelfth Judicial District (Secretary, 1980-1981), Cumberland County (Vice President, 2004-2005), North Carolina and American Bar Associations; North Carolina State Bar; North Carolina Academy of Trial Lawyers; Cumberland County Young Lawyers (President, 1987-1988). ***PRACTICE AREAS:*** Personal Injury Law; Civil and Criminal Litigation.

STEPHEN G. INMAN, born Wilmington, North Carolina, February 3, 1947; admitted to bar, 1988, North Carolina. *Education:* University of North Carolina at Chapel Hill (A.B., 1969); Medical College of Virginia (D.D.S., 1973); Campbell School of Law (J.D., 1988). *Member:* Cumberland County and North Carolina Bar Associations; North Carolina State Bar. ***PRACTICE AREAS:*** Bankruptcy; Business; Corporation Law.

THOMAS WAITT PLEASANT, born Lumberton, North Carolina, November 1, 1970; admitted to bar, 1996, North Carolina; 2002, U.S. District Court, Eastern District of North Carolina and U.S. Court of Appeals, Eighth Circuit. *Education:* Wake Forest University (B.A., 1993; J.D., 1996). Member, Moot Court Board. *Member:* Cumberland County and North Carolina (Member, Litigation and Construction Law Sections) Bar Associations. ***PRACTICE AREAS:*** Commercial Litigation; Civil Litigation; Business Law; Construction Law.

REPRESENTATIVE CLIENTS: Putt Putt Golf Courses of America, Inc.; Metropolitan Life Insurance Co.; State Farm Insurance Cos.; Westwood Shopping Center; CIGNA Property and Casualty Cos.; ERIE Insurance Group; Carolina Model Homes Corp.; D.K. Taylor Oil Co.; Animal Hospital, P.A.; N.C. Farm Bureau Ins. Co.; GEICO Ins. Co.; Strickland Ins. Group; Orion Insurance Co.; Nationwide Insurance Company.
REFERENCES: Wachovia Bank; Fayetteville Area Chamber of Commerce; Branch Banking & Trust Co.

HEATHER D. MILLER NICHOLS

Established in 2005
213 DICK STREET, SUITE 204
P.O. BOX 2302
FAYETTEVILLE, NORTH CAROLINA 28302
Telephone: 910-484-4876
Fax: 910-484-7352
Email: heather@heathernicholslaw.com
URL: http://www.heathernicholslaw.com
Mailing Address: P.O. Box 2302, Fayetteville, NC 28302

Family Law, Civil Litigation, Real Estate Litigation, Wills, Estates.

HEATHER D. MILLER NICHOLS, born Bucyrus, Ohio, October 14, 1972; admitted to bar, 2003, North Carolina. *Education:* Drury University (A.S., with honors, 1994); Methodist College (B.A., cum laude, 1998); Campbell University (J.D., 2003). *Member:* Cumberland County, North Carolina and American Bar Associations; North Carolina State Bar; North Carolina Academy of Trial Lawyers. ***PRACTICE AREAS:*** Family Law; Civil Litigation; Real Estate Litigation; Wills; Estates.

TIMOTHY A. NOE, P.A.

Established in 1982
507 OWEN DRIVE
FAYETTEVILLE, NORTH CAROLINA 28304
Telephone: 910-485-8805
Fax: 910-485-8807
Email: timothynoe@aol.com
URL: http://www.lawyers.com/noelaw

Personal Injury, Criminal Law, Traffic Violations, Driving While Intoxicated, Medical Malpractice, Wrongful Death.

TIMOTHY A. NOE, born Louisville, Kentucky, May 3, 1951; admitted to bar, 1982, North Carolina. *Education:* Duke University (A.B., History, 1973); Campbell University (J.D., 1982). *Member:* Cumberland County and North Carolina Bar Associations; North Carolina State Bar; North Carolina Academy of Trial Lawyers. [U.S. Navy, 1969-1977].

(This Listing Continued)

PRACTICE AREAS: Personal Injury; Criminal Law; Traffic Violations; Driving While Impaired.

THE RAPER LAW FIRM PLLC

2543 RAVENHILL DRIVE, SUITE C
FAYETTEVILLE, NORTH CAROLINA 28303
Telephone: 910-764-9200
Fax: 910-486-5358
Mailing Address: P.O. Box 87409, Fayetteville, NC 28304

Corporate Law, Tax Law, Trusts and Estates, Commercial Real Estate, Finance, Business and Construction Litigation.

MEMBER OF FIRM

JOHN E. RAPER, JR., born Lexington, North Carolina, December 11, 1935; admitted to bar, 1961, North Carolina; U.S. District Court, Eastern, Middle and Western Districts of North Carolina; U.S. Court of Appeals, Fourth Circuit; U.S. Supreme Court; U.S. Tax Court. *Education:* University of North Carolina (A.B., 1958); University of Goettingen, Germany; New York University (J.D., 1961). Phi Beta Kappa. President, The Lawyers of North Carolina, 1978-1980. Board of Directors, Executive Committee and Claims Committee, Lawyers Mutual Liability Insurance Company of North Carolina, 1988—. Member, Board of Trustees and Executive Committee, Blue Cross Blue Shield of North Carolina, 1979—. *Member:* Cumberland County (President, 1988-1989), North Carolina (Member, Board of Governors, Executive Committee, 1981-1984) and American Bar Associations; North Carolina State Bar. ***PRACTICE AREAS:*** Corporate Law; Tax Law; Trusts and Estates; Commercial Real Estate; Finance; Business Litigation; Construction Litigation; Condemnation. ***Email:*** jraper@raperlawfirm.com

ASSOCIATE

SARILYN HARDEE LEARY, born Dunn, North Carolina, September 15, 1978; admitted to bar, 2003, North Carolina. *Education:* Campbell University (B.A., summa cum laude, 2000; J.D., summa cum laude, 2003). Order of Barristers. Editor in Chief, Campbell Law Review, 2002-2003. Author: "Why the United States Supreme Court's Ruling in Kyllo v. United States is Not the Final Word on the Constitutionality of Thermal Imaging," Note, 34 Campbell Law Review 53 (2002). *Member:* North Carolina and Cumberland County Bar Associations. ***PRACTICE AREAS:*** Corporate Law; Commercial Law; Real Estate; Estate Planning; Business Litigation. ***Email:*** sleary@raperlawfirm.com

REPRESENTATIVE CLIENTS: Lee-Moore Oil Company; Li'l Thrift Food Marts Inc., d/b/a Short Stop; Tri-Arc Food Systems, Inc.; Governors Club Development Corp.; Governors Club L.P.; Ellis-Walker Builders, Inc.; Huffman Mill Plaza L.P.; Estate of Truby G. Proctor, Jr.; Healy Wholesale Co., Inc.; Keefe Enterprises, Inc.; Skibo Properties LLC; Taylor Express, Inc.; Carolina Trace Gated Properties, LLC; Anvil Iron Works, Inc.; VanStory-Exum Agency, Inc.; Cape Fear Neonatology Service PA; Fayetteville Children's Clinic PA; Carolina Crating, Inc.; Gainey Grain, Inc.; JK Food Enterprises, LLC.

REID, LEWIS, DEESE, NANCE & PERSON, L.L.P.

Established in 1970
330 DICK STREET, HERITAGE SQUARE
FAYETTEVILLE, NORTH CAROLINA 28301
Telephone: 910-323-3500
Fax: 910-323-0066
URL: http://www.rldnp.com
Mailing Address: P.O. Drawer 1358, Fayetteville, NC 28302

General Civil and Criminal Trial Practice in State and Federal Courts. Personal Injury, Negligence, Family Law, Construction Insurance, Corporation, Probate and Real Estate Law.

FIRM PROFILE: Reid, Lewis, Deese, Nance & Person, L.L.P. was originally founded in 1970 by Marland C. Reid and Richard M. Lewis, Jr. Serving clients throughout Cumberland, Sampson, Harnett, Hoke, Bladen and surrounding counties, it is a full service firm excluding complex tax matters and securities work.

MEMBERS OF FIRM

MARLAND C. REID (1934-1998)

RICHARD M. LEWIS, JR., born Whiteville, North Carolina, January 15, 1935; admitted to bar, 1963, North Carolina; 1964, U.S. District Court, Eastern District of North Carolina. *Education:* University of Notre Dame (A.B., 1957); University of North Carolina (LL.B., 1963). Phi Delta Phi. Assistant Solicitor, Superior Court, 1964-1965. Attorney For: Public Works Commission for City of Fayetteville, 1971—; Airborne & Special Operations Museum, 1997—; Fayetteville Redevelopment Commission, 1969—. *Member:* Cumberland County (President, 1993-1994; Chairman, Real Estate Section, 1977-1985), North Carolina (Member, Real Estate Council, 1985-1987, Treasurer, 1989-1990) and American Bar Associations; North Carolina State Bar. [LTJG, U.S. Navy, 1957-1960]. ***PRACTICE AREAS:*** Real Estate Law; Wills; Corporate Law; Trusts and Estates; Eminent Domain. ***Email:*** rmlewis@rldnp.com

RENNY W. DEESE, born Rotenburg, Germany, February 8, 1946; admitted to bar, 1971, North Carolina and U.S. Court of Military Appeals; 1976, U.S. District Court, Eastern District of North Carolina; 1981, U.S. Court of Appeals, Fourth Circuit. *Education:* The Citadel (B.A., 1968); Wake Forest University (J.D., 1971). Pi Sigma Alpha; Phi Alpha Delta. Author: Note, "The Exempt Status of Cash Surrender-Value of Life Insurance in N.C.," 7 Wake Forest Law Review 515, 1971. Adjunct Professor, Constitutional Issues in Criminal Justice and Legal Issues in Management, Webster College, 1975-1981. *Member:* Cumberland County and North Carolina (Treasurer, Family Law Council, 1995-2000) Bar Associations; North Carolina State Bar (Chairman, Family Law Specialization Committee, 1995-2000; Councilor, 2001—). Fellow, American Academy of Matrimonial Lawyers. [Capt., JAGC, U.S. Army, 1971-1975]. (Board Certified Specialist in Family Law, North

(This Listing Continued)

Carolina State Board of Legal Specialization). ***LANGUAGES:*** German. ***PRACTICE AREAS:*** Family Law; Civil Litigation; Appellate Practice. ***Email:*** rwdeese@rldnp.com

JAMES R. NANCE, JR., born Lumberton, North Carolina, May 26, 1940; admitted to bar, 1965, North Carolina. *Education:* Wake Forest University (B.A., 1962; J.D., 1965). Phi Delta Phi. *Member:* Cumberland County (President, 1997-1998), North Carolina and American Bar Associations; 12th Judicial District (President, 1984-1985, 1997-1998); North Carolina State Bar; North Carolina Academy of Trial Lawyers. ***PRACTICE AREAS:*** Civil Litigation; Personal Injury; Defense Litigation; Employment Law; Professional Liability; Civil Rights; Eminent Domain; Construction Law; Workers Compensation. ***Email:*** jrnance@rldnp.com

REBECCA F. PERSON, born Fayetteville, North Carolina, September 20, 1958; admitted to bar, 1983, North Carolina and U.S. District Court, Eastern District of North Carolina. *Education:* University of North Carolina (B.S., 1980); Wake Forest University (J.D, 1983). *Member:* Cumberland County (Secretary, 1984; Vice President/President, 2000) and North Carolina (Chair, N.C. Twelfth Judicial District Grievance Committee, 1994, 1996 and 1997; Member, Real Property Committee); Member, N.C. Twelfth Judicial District Bar Candidate Review Committee) Bar Associations. ***PRACTICE AREAS:*** Real Estate; Business Law; Banks and Banking; Corporate Law. ***Email:*** rfperson@rldnp.com

ASSOCIATE

JAMES KIRKMAN NANCE, born Fayetteville, North Carolina, July 8, 1970; admitted to bar, 2001, North Carolina and U.S. District Court, Eastern District of North Carolina. *Education:* University of North Carolina at Wilmington (B.A., 1995); Regent University (J.D., 1999). Secretary, 12th Judicial District Bar, 2002-2003. *Member:* Cumberland County and North Carolina Bar Associations; North Carolina State Bar. ***PRACTICE AREAS:*** Criminal Law; Traffic Violations; Domestic Relations; Civil Litigation; Driving While Impaired. ***Email:*** jknance@rldnp.com

REPRESENTATIVE CLIENTS: Callahan & Rice Insurance Group, Inc.; Fayetteville Redevelopment Commission; Public Works Commission, City of Fayetteville; Fayetteville Investments, Inc.; Airborne and Special Operations Museum Foundation; AAA Glass Co., Inc.; Westarea Fire Dept. Inc.; Pa. Lumbermans Mutual; Farmers Insurance Group; OMNI National Bank; Transportation Claims Inc.; Lee Hyundai; Great West Insurance Company.
APPROVED ATTORNEYS FOR: Lawyers Title Insurance Corp.; North Carolina Title Insurance Co.; Chicago T.I. Co.; Stewart Title Ins. Co.; First Title Insurance Co.; Commonwealth Land Title Insurance Co.; First American Title Insurance Co.; Investors Title Insurance Co.; American Title Insurance Co.
REFERENCES: Wachovia Bank Branch Banking & Trust Co.; First Citizens Bank; Omni National Bank; Centura Bank.

J.B. ROUSE III & ASSOCIATES

1300 A PAMALEE DRIVE
FAYETTEVILLE, NORTH CAROLINA 28303
Telephone: 910-488-2100
Fax: 910-488-5515
URL: http://www.jbrouselaw.com

Personal Injury, Automobile Accidents, Serious Accidents, Lemon Law, Traffic Violations, DWI, Wills, Probate, Trusts and Estates, Business Litigation.

J. B. (MICKEY) ROUSE, born Dunn, North Carolina, October 12, 1946; admitted to bar, 1983, North Carolina. *Education:* Campbell University (B.B.A., 1978; J.D., 1982). *Member:* Cumberland County, North Carolina and American Bar Associations; North Carolina State Bar; The Association of Trial Lawyers of America; North Carolina Academy of Trial Lawyers; National Association of Retail Collections Attorneys; Commercial Law League of America. [U.S. Army - Special Forces, 1967-1970]. ***PRACTICE AREAS:*** Personal Injury; Automobile Accidents and Injuries; Lemon Law; Traffic Violations; Driving While Intoxicated; Wills; Probate; Trusts and Estates; Business Litigation.

THORP, CLARKE & NEVILLE, P.A.

150 N. MCPHERSON CHURCH ROAD, SUITE B
FAYETTEVILLE, NORTH CAROLINA 28303
Telephone: 910-323-4111
Fax: 910-483-1247
Email: thorpclark@aol.com
URL: http://www.lawyers.com/thorpclarke

General and Trial Practice. Personal Injury, Medical Negligence, Real Estate, Probate, Criminal, Corporate and Bankruptcy Law.

FIRM PROFILE: The firm was established in 1982, the members having had many years of practice before that. The firm offers clients in the Cumberland County area a general practice with emphasis on a civil trial practice in all courts, business and corporate law and real estate. Mr. Thorp served as the president of the Cumberland County Bar Association as well as the 12th Judicial District Bar. Mr. Clarke served as US Magistrate Judge for the US District Court, Eastern District, North Carolina from 1973-1983. Members of the firm continue to actively serve in the legal community.

MEMBERS OF FIRM

HERBERT H. THORP (1932-1996)

F. STUART CLARKE, born Danville, Virginia, November 2, 1942; admitted to bar, 1971, North Carolina. *Education:* University of North Carolina (A.B., 1965; J.D., 1971). Delta Theta Phi. Law Clerk to Hon. John D. Larkins, Jr., U.S. District Judge, Eastern District of North Carolina, 1971. Assistant U.S. Attorney, Eastern District of North Carolina, 1971-1972. U.S. Magistrate, U.S. District Court, Eastern District of North Carolina, 1973-1983. *Member:* North Carolina Bar Association; North Carolina State Bar; North Carolina Academy of Trial Lawyers. [1st Lt., 1966-1969; U.S. Army]. ***PRACTICE AREAS:*** Plaintiff and Defendant Litigation; Real Property Law and Estates and Trusts Law; Corporate Law; Foreclosures; Commercial Law; Bankruptcy Law.

(This Listing Continued)

J. THOMAS NEVILLE, born Riegelwood, North Carolina, August 3, 1966; admitted to bar, 2004, North Carolina. *Education:* North Carolina State University (P.S.; B.A., 1988); Norman Adrian Wiggins - Campbell University Law School (J.D., 2004). *Member:* Cumberland County and North Carolina Bar Associations; North Carolina State Bar. [U.S. Marine Corp., 1988-1992, final rank Captain]. ***PRACTICE AREAS:*** Construction Litigation (30%); Property Litigation (20%); Business Litigation (15%); Personal Injury (15%); Estate (20%). ***Email:*** JTNeville@thorpclarke.com

COUNSEL FOR: W.S. Wellons Realty, Inc.; A/E Builders; Cape Fear Theatres, Inc. d/b/a Loyd & Bradford; L/E Construction, Inc.; All American Mortgage Co., Inc.; Ace Construction Co., Inc; Ashton Development Group, Inc.; Remax Premier Properties; Homeowners, Ltd.; Remax Allstars; Hope Mills.
APPROVED ATTORNEY FOR: Lawyers Title Insurance Co.; Investors Title Insurance Co.; Commercial Standard Title Insurance Co.; Commonwealth Title Insurance Co.; Carolina Title Co.; American Title Insurance Co.; Chicago Title Insurance Co.; Federal National Mortgage Insurance Co.; Pioneer Title Insurance Co.; Stewart Title.
REFERENCES: RBC Centura Bank; NationsBank; Branch Banking and Trust Company.

H. MAC TYSON, II

FAYETTEVILLE, NORTH CAROLINA

(See Shallotte)

General Practice including General Civil Trial, Traffic Violations, Criminal Defense, Personal Injury, Corporate, Municipal, Military Law, Equitable Distribution, Domestic Law, Workers Compensation, Real Estate (Commercial and Residential), Probate, Wills and Estates, Taxation, Business Litigation, Zoning Law, Governmental Law and Ethics.

THE LAW OFFICES OF CHRISTOPHER V. VAUGHAN

FAYETTEVILLE, NORTH CAROLINA

(See Raeford)

Criminal Law, Traffic, DWI, Family Law, Divorce, Child Support and Child Custody.

WAPLE & ASSOCIATES

NO. 6, GEORGETOWN SQUARE
120 WESTLAKE ROAD
FAYETTEVILLE, NORTH CAROLINA 28314
Telephone: 910-864-3737
Fax: 910-864-3284
Email: waplelaw@earthlink.net
URL: http://www.waplelaw.com

Medical Negligence, including Obstetric Malpractice, Birth Trauma, Surgical Malpractice, Oncological Malpractice, Failure to Diagnose Disease, Medication Errors, Military Medical Negligence; Armed Forces Law, including practice in all Military Trials and Appellate Courts, all Service Boards for Correction of Military Records, Military Personnel Law, Personal Injury.

FIRM PROFILE: Mark L. Waple has been practicing medical negligence cases in the Armed Forces health care system, overseas and in the United States for twenty years. Particular emphasis is placed on obstetrical negligence. In addition Mr. Waple handles all areas of Armed Forces Law.

MARK L. WAPLE, born Washington, D.C., May 7, 1945; admitted to bar, 1974, North Carolina; 1975, U.S. District Court, Eastern District of North Carolina; 1979, U.S. Court of Appeals, Fourth Circuit; 1982, U.S. Supreme Court and U.S. Court of Federal Claims; 1987, U.S. Army and Air Force Courts of Criminal Appeals; 1997, U.S. Court of Appeals, Federal Circuit. *Education:* United States Military Academy-West Point (B.S., 1969); University of North Carolina (J.D., 1974); Boston University (M.A., 1975). Author, "Is There Adequate Due Process for Military Personnel?," The Federal Lawyer, Vol. 42, No. 3 (1995). *Member:* North Carolina State Bar; North Carolina Academy of Trial Lawyers; Association of Trial Lawyers of America (Military Advocacy and Professional Negligence Sections); North Carolina Governor's Advisory Committee of Military Affairs. ***REPORTED CASES:*** May v. Gray, 708 F. Supp. 716 (E.D.N.C. 1988); U.S. v. Summerset, 37 M.J. 695 (ACMR 1993).

JOHN MICHAEL WINESETTE

202 FAIRWAY DRIVE, SUITE A
FAYETTEVILLE, NORTH CAROLINA 28305
Telephone: 910-433-2400
Fax: 910-433-2618
Email: MikeWnst@prodigy.net

Personal Injury, Automobile Accidents, Aviation, Products Liability, Medical Negligence including Obstetric, Emergency Room and Surgical Negligence, Wrongful Death Litigation.

JOHN MICHAEL WINESETTE, born San Marcos, Texas, September 20, 1952; admitted to bar, 1978, North Carolina; 1981, U.S. District Court, Eastern District of North Carolina. *Education:* University of North Carolina (B.A., 1974); North Carolina Central University (J.D., cum laude, 1978). *Member:* Cumberland County (Member, Ethics Committee, 1980-1981) and North Carolina (Counsel Member, Litigation Section, 1987-1990) Bar Associations; North Carolina State Bar; North Carolina Academy of Trial Lawyers (Member, Sections on: Litigation; Professional Negligence); The Association of Trial Lawyers of America (Member, Professional Negligence Section).

THE YARBOROUGH LAW FIRM

115 EAST RUSSELL STREET
FAYETTEVILLE, NORTH CAROLINA 28301
Telephone: 910-433-4433
Fax: 910-433-2233
Email: gnyesq@yarboroughlawfirm.com
URL: http://www.yarboroughlawfirm.com

General Civil Trial Practice in all State and Federal Courts. Construction, Municipal, Real Estate, Land Condemnation, Corporation, Collections, Personal Injury, Administrative and Probate Law.

GARRIS NEIL YARBOROUGH, born Dunn, North Carolina, May 7, 1951; admitted to bar, 1977, North Carolina; 1978, U.S. District Court, Eastern District of North Carolina; 1983, U.S. Court of Appeals, Fourth Circuit; 1993, U.S. District Court, Middle District of North Carolina; 1995, U.S. Supreme Court; 2001, U.S. Court of Federal Claims. *Education:* University of North Carolina (B.A., 1973; J.D., 1977); Duke University (M.P.P.S., 1977). Phi Alpha Delta. Assistant County Attorney of Cumberland County, 1977-1982. County Attorney of Cumberland County, 1982-1988 and 1994-1999. Town Attorney of Saint Pauls, 1991—. County Attorney of Hoke County 1993—. Town Attorney, Parkton, 2002—. Town Attorney, Lumber Bridge, 2003—. Attorney, Cumberland County ABC System, 2003—. Attorney, North Carolina Indian Housing Authority, 2004—. Member, North Carolina Administrative Procedures Study Commission, 1980-1981. Trustee, Cape Fear Valley Medical Center, 1991-1994. Member of Panel, American Arbitration Association. Certified Superior Court Mediator. President of North Carolina Association of County Attorneys, 1996-1997. *Member:* Cumberland County (President, 1999-2000), North Carolina (Member, Sections on: Construction, Real Estate and Administrative Law) and American Bar Associations; North Carolina Academy of Trial Lawyers; Association of Trial Lawyers of America; North Carolina Municipal Attorney's Association; Professional Construction Estimators Association of America. ***Email:*** gnyesq@yarboroughlawfirm.com

ASSOCIATES

HUGH ADDISON WINTERS, III, born Philadelphia, Pennsylvania, October 16, 1957; admitted to bar, 1985, North Carolina and U.S. Court of Appeals, Fourth Circuit. *Education:* Georgetown University (B.A., 1980); University of North Carolina at Chapel Hill (J.D., 1983). Member, Editorial Board, National Institute of Construction Law, Inc., 1985-1994. Co-Author "Construction and Design Law," Michie, 1985-1994; Managing Editor, Construction and Design Law Digest," 1988-1994. Certified Superior Court Mediator. *Member:* Cumberland County and North Carolina (Member, Sections on Construction Law, Litigation and Alternative Dispute Resolution) Bar Associations; Construction Law Section Council; Professional Construction Estimators Association of America. ***Email:*** awinters@yarboroughlawfirm.com

JOHN HAMILTON JACKSON, born Gurdon, Arkansas, September 28, 1939; admitted to bar, 1971, Arkansas and U.S. District Court, Western District of Arkansas; 1993, North Carolina; 1994, U.S. District Court, Eastern District of North Carolina. *Education:* Henderson State University (B.S.E., 1962); University of Arkansas (J.D., 1971); SMU-Southwestern School of Banking (Graduate, Trust Major). City Attorney, Gurdon, Arkansas, 1971-1989. Juvenile Judge, Clark County, Arkansas, 1982-1988; Town Attorney, Town of Stedman, 1993—; Counsel, Mid-Carolina Council of Governments, Fayetteville, North Carolina, 1993—; Town Attorney, Spring Lake, 1998—; Town Attorney, Town of Wade, 2000—. Town Attorney, Town of Linden, 2004—. *Member:* Cumberland County (Member, Real Estate Section), North Carolina Bar Association; Arkansas Bar Foundation. [Col. U.S. Army - Special Forces, 1957-1993 (Retired)]. ***Email:*** jjackson@yarboroughlawfirm.com

CHUCK SWEENY, admitted to bar, 1972, North Carolina; 1984, U.S. Supreme Court. *Education:* Colgate University (B.A., 1966); Wake Forest University (J.D., cum laude, 1972). *Member:* Cumberland County, North Carolina and American Bar Associations; North Carolina State Bar; North Carolina Academy of Trial Lawyers; The Association of Trial Lawyers of America. [1st Lt., U.S. Marine Corps, 1966-1969]. ***Email:*** chucksweeny@yarboroughlawfirm.com

---

BLANCHARD, NEWMAN & HAYES

FLETCHER, NORTH CAROLINA

(See Hendersonville)

General Civil Litigation, Family Law, Divorce, Criminal in all State and Federal Courts, Traffic, DWI.

HAMRICK, BOWEN, MEBANE, GREENWAY & LLOYD, L.L.P.

FOREST CITY, NORTH CAROLINA

(See Rutherfordton)

General Trial and Appellate Practice in all State and Federal Courts, Business, Collections and Creditor's Rights, Commercial, Construction, Corporations, DWI, Traffic Offenses, Criminal, Family, Divorce, Equitable Distribution, Child Custody, Child Support, Domestic, Employment, Insurance, Personal Injury, Real Estate, Social Security, Trusts and Estates and Workers Compensation.

PRICE, SMITH, HARGETT, PETHO & ANDERSON

Established in 1979
552 OAK STREET
FOREST CITY, NORTH CAROLINA 28043
Telephone: 828-248-1448
Fax: 828-248-4405
Email: priceatty@aol.com
URL: http://www.lawyers.com/pshp&a

Plaintiffs Catastrophic Personal Injury, Medical Malpractice, Wrongful Death, Workers Compensation, Insurance Litigation for Plaintiff, Motor Vehicle Accidents, Criminal Defense.

(For Complete Biographical Data on all Personnel, see Professional Biographies at Charlotte, North Carolina)

THE YARBOROUGH LAW FIRM

FORT BRAGG, NORTH CAROLINA

(See Fayetteville)

General Civil Trial Practice in all State and Federal Courts. Construction, Municipal, Real Estate, Land Condemnation, Corporation, Collections, Personal Injury, Administrative and Probate Law.

RUSSELL R. BOWLING

77 WEST MAIN STREET
FRANKLIN, NORTH CAROLINA 28734
Telephone: 828-524-5070
Fax: 828-524-5380
Email: rbowling@russellbowling.com
URL: http://www.russellbowling.com

General Civil and Criminal Practice. Real Estate, Wills, Estates and Estate Administration, Criminal and Traffic and Motor Vehicle Law, Social Security Disability.

RUSSELL R. BOWLING, born Ft. Sill, Oklahoma, October 28, 1954; admitted to bar, 1979, North Carolina and U.S. District Court, Western District of North Carolina. *Education:* Wake Forest University (B.A., 1976; J.D., 1979). Phi Alpha Delta. *Member:* 30th Judicial District and North Carolina Bar Associations; North Carolina State Bar; North Carolina Academy of Trial Lawyers; The Association of Trial Lawyers of America; National Organization of Social Security Claimants' Representatives (NOSSCR).

REPRESENTATIVE CLIENTS: Furnished Upon Request.

COLLINS & HENSLEY, P.A.

Established in 1995
217 IOTLA STREET
FRANKLIN, NORTH CAROLINA 28734
Telephone: 828-524-0017
Telecopier: 828-524-0024
Email: colhen@dnet.net
URL: http://www.lawyers.com/colhen

Civil Litigation, Criminal, Real Property, Personal Injury, Automobile Accidents and Injuries, Wrongful Death, Domestic Relations Family Law, Divorce, Child Custody, Equitable Distribution, Adoption Law, Social Security Disability Law, Workers Compensation.

FIRM PROFILE: Our firm is a small firm limiting its practice to western North Carolina in all counties west of Asheville, North Carolina. Areas of practice are the defense of criminal cases (including DUI and Traffic offenses), real property, family law, personal injury and workers compensation.

JOSEPH M. COLLINS, born Franklin, North Carolina, July 11, 1955; admitted to bar, 1987, North Carolina. *Education:* University of North Carolina at Chapel Hill (B.A., 1977); Campbell University School of Law (J.D., 1987). *Member:* Macon County and North Carolina Bar Associations; 30th Judicial District and North Carolina State Bars. ***PRACTICE AREAS:*** Real Property; Adoption Law; Civil Litigation; Workers Compensation; Family Law. ***Email:*** colhen@dnet.net

ROBERT E. HENSLEY, born Jacksonville, North Carolina; April 29, 1963; admitted to bar, 1988, North Carolina. *Education:* University of North Carolina at Wilmington (B.A., 1985); Campbell University (J.D., 1988). Assistant District Attorney, 1988-1995. *Member:* North Carolina State Bar; 30th Judicial District Bar Association; National Association of Criminal Defense Lawyers; North Carolina Academy of Trial Lawyers (Criminal Justice Section). (Board Certified Specialist in Criminal Law, North Carolina State Board of Legal Specialization). ***PRACTICE AREAS:*** Criminal; Driving While Intoxicated; Traffic Violations; Family Law; Divorce; Child Custody; Equitable Distribution. ***Email:*** colhen@dnet.net

---

COWARD, HICKS & SILER, P.A.

Established in 1951
43 WEST MAIN STREET
FRANKLIN, NORTH CAROLINA 28734
Telephone: 828-524-6475
Fax: 828-524-9833

Sylva, North Carolina Office: 705 West Main Street, 28779. Telephone: 828-586-2147. Fax: 828-586-2605.
Cashiers, North Carolina Office: 211 Cashiers School Road, P.O. Box 1918, 28717. Telephone: 828-743-2401. Fax: 828-743-2403.

(This Listing Continued)

General Practice in all Courts. Trials, Eminent Domain, Personal Injury and Workers Compensation, Probate, Estate Planning, Real Estate, Corporations, Family Law.

COUNSEL FOR: Cullasaja Club; Highlands Country Club; Fairfield Communities Inc.; Country Club of Sapphire Valley, Inc.; Highlands Falls Country Club, Inc.; Mill Creek Golf Club of Franklin, Inc.; Smoky Mountain Area Mental Health; Zickgrat Enterprises, Inc.; Nantahala Lumber Co.; Golf Properties, Inc.; Franklin Board of Realtors, Inc.; Highland-Cashiers Board of Realtors, Inc.; Signal Ridge Yacht & Country Club; Town of Highlands; Village of Forest Hills; Angel Medical Center.
REPRESENTATIVE CLIENTS: Wachovia Bank and Trust Co.; TransAmerica Title Insurance Co.; Stewart Title Insurance Co.; Fidelity National Title Insurance Co.
APPROVED ATTORNEYS FOR: Lawyers Title Insurance Corp.; Federal Land Bank of Columbia; Farmers Home Administration; Fidelity National Title Insurance Co.; Stewart Title Insurance Co.; National Title Insurance Co.; Safeco Title Insurance Co.; Investors Title Insurance Co.; Title Insurance Company of Minnesota; American Title Insurance Co.; Chicago Title Insurance Co.; TransAmerica Title Insurance Co.; Wachovia Bank and Trust Co.; First Citizens Bank and Trust Co.; Macon Bank, Inc.; Centura Bank; First National Bank of Gainesville d/b/a/ The Mortgage Source; Rabun County Bank.
REFERENCES: First Citizens Bank and Trust Co.; Macon Bank, Inc.; Wachovia Bank and Trust Co.

(For complete biographical data on all personnel, see Professional Biographies at Sylva, North Carolina)

LAW OFFICES OF KENNETH W. FROMKNECHT, II P.A.

Established in 1998

29 IOTLA STREET
P.O. DRAWER 1146
FRANKLIN, NORTH CAROLINA 28744-1146
Telephone: 888-349-9911
Telecopier: 828-349-9944
Email: kwflaw@dnet.net
URL: http://www.lawyers.com/fromknechtlaw

Real Estate, Land Use, Inheritance, Business Formation, Construction Litigation, Complex Commercial Litigation, Catastrophic Injury, Insurance Litigation.

KENNETH W. FROMKNECHT, II, born Clearwater, Florida, October 17, 1958; admitted to bar, 1989, Florida; 1991, U.S. District Court, Southern District of Florida; 1996, North Carolina; 1997, U.S. District Court, Western District of North Carolina and U.S. Court of Federal Claims. *Education:* University of South Florida (B.A., Economics, 1986); Stetson University College of Law (J.D., 1989). Dana Scholar. Member, Local Government Digest Committee, Stetson Law Review. Author: Essays and Digests, Stetson Law Review, Volume 18, 1989. Co-Author: "North Carolina Lien Law: Beyond the Basics", North Carolina Bar Association. Adjunct Professor: Western Carolina University; Southwestern Community College. Past President, Franklin Daybreak Rotary Club. Past President, Port St. Lucie Bar Association. *Member:* North Carolina Bar Association (Council Member, Construction Law Section); The Florida Bar; Macon County Builder's Association. (Board Certified Lawyer, Civil Trial, Florida Bar Board of Legal Specialization and Education). ***REPORTED CASES:*** Buchanan v. Weber, 567 S.E.2d 413, 34 A.L.R. 3d 962 (2002); Berkman v. Foley, 709 So.2d 628 (Fla. 4th DCA 1998). ***PRACTICE AREAS:*** Real Property; Land Use; Business Formation; Construction Litigation; Complex Commercial Litigation; Catastrophic Injury; Insurance Litigation.

REPRESENTATIVE CLIENTS: Rabun County Bank; Fidelity National Title Insurance Company; CNA Pro Insurance;Sullivan Construction & Development, Co.; Unicom Communications, Inc.; State Farm Fire & Casualty; Land America/Commonwealth Land Title Insurance Company; United Community Bank.
APPROVED ATTORNEY FOR: Commonwealth Land Title Insurance Company of North Carolina; Fidelity National Title Insurance Company; Investors Title Insurance Company; Statewide Title Co.; Land Title Insurance Company; Macon Bank; RBC Centura Bank; United Community Bank; Centura Bank; Regions Bank; State Employees Credit Union; Rabun County Bank; Wachovia; Bank of America; Wells Fargo Mortgage Corporation.

JONES, KEY, MELVIN & PATTON, P.A.

Established in 1878

61 EAST MAIN STREET
FRANKLIN, NORTH CAROLINA 28734
Telephone: 828-524-4444
Fax: 828-369-7343
Email: jkmp@smnet.net
URL: http://www.joneskey.com

Highlands, North Carolina Office: Professional Building, Suite 3, South Street, 28741. Telephone: 828-526-3762.

Civil Trial Practice in all Courts. Real Estate, Insurance, Corporate Law, Probate, Family Law, Divorce, Adoptions, Equitable Distribution, Pre-Nuptial Agreements, Child Custody, Child Support, Domestic Violence, Alimony, Personal Injury, Auto Accidents, Wrongful Death, Estate and Gift Taxation, Taxation, Government, Mediation; Business Law, Litigation, Trusts and Estates, Wills, Criminal Law, DWI, Traffic Offenses.

FIRM PROFILE: George Andrew Jones commenced the practice of law in Franklin, Macon County, North Carolina, in the year 1878. He was thereafter associated with, or followed in the practice by three of his sons, his grandson and in the year 1992, by his great-grandson. The law firm founded by Judge Jones has been continuous in its service to the western part of North Carolina for more than 125 years and has expanded in number, in order to create a full service, general practice firm. The Partners and Associates participate in professional, governmental, political and community affairs and actively provide leadership in all such areas.

RICHARD S. JONES, JR., born Asheville, North Carolina, May 20, 1934; admitted to bar, 1961, North Carolina. *Education:* Davidson College (B.S., 1956); University of North Carolina (J.D., 1961). Phi Delta Phi (President, 1960-1961). Attorney, Macon County, 1969— and Town of Highlands, 1969-1974; Counsel, Macon Bank, Inc., 1972—. Member, North Carolina Board of Law Examiners, 1982-1995; Chairman, 1994-1995. Inducted into North Carolina Bar Association General Practice Hall of Fame, 1999. *Member:* North Carolina (Vice President, 2002-2004) and American Bar Associations; North Carolina State Bar; North Carolina Academy of Trial Lawyers. ***PRACTICE AREAS:*** Litigation; Trusts and Estates; Probate. ***Email:*** rsjones@smnet.net

BOBBY JOE KEY, born Surry County, North Carolina, March 29, 1933; admitted to bar, 1964, North Carolina. *Education:* Davidson College (B.S., 1955); University of North Carolina (J.D., 1964). Attorney, Town of Franklin. *Member:* Macon County and North Carolina Bar Associations; North Carolina State Bar. [LTJG, U.S. Navy, 1955-1959]. ***PRACTICE AREAS:*** Real Estate; Civil Trial Practice; Trusts and Estates; Probate. ***Email:*** bjkey@smnet.net

RICHARD F. MELVIN, born June 3, 1941; admitted to bar, 1966, Florida and U.S. Court of Military Appeals; 1969, North Carolina. *Education:* Duke University (A.B., 1963); University of Florida (J.D., 1966). *Member:* North Carolina State Bar; The Florida Bar. [Lieut., U.S. Navy, 1966-1971]. (Resident, Highlands Office). ***PRACTICE AREAS:*** Real Estate; Probate. ***Email:*** melvin@smnet.net

LAWRENCE M. PATTON, JR., born Franklin, North Carolina, May 16, 1946; admitted to bar, 1973, North Carolina. *Education:* Davidson College (A.B., 1968); University of North Carolina (J.D., 1973). President, 30th Judicial District Bar Association, 2002-2004. *Member:* Macon County and North Carolina Bar Associations; North Carolina State Bar. [1st Lieut., AGC, US Army, 1968-1970]. ***PRACTICE AREAS:*** Real Estate. ***Email:*** lmpatton@smnet.net

FRED HOWELL JONES, born Asheville, North Carolina, March 22, 1965; admitted to bar, 1990, North Carolina. *Education:* University of North Carolina at Chapel Hill (B.A., 1987; J.D., 1990). Phi Delta Phi. Morehead Scholar. Articles Editor, North Carolina Journal of International Law and Commercial Regulation, 1989-1990. Author: Comment, "U.S. Tobacco Goes Abroad: Section 301 of the 1974 Trade Act as a Tool For Achieving Access to Foreign Tobacco Markets," 14 North Carolina Journal of International Law and Commercial Regulation 439, 1989. Law Clerk to Hon. Willis P. Whichard, North Carolina Supreme Court, 1990-1992. *Member:* North Carolina State Bar; North Carolina and American Bar Associations; North Carolina Academy of Trial Lawyers. ***PRACTICE AREAS:*** Civil Litigation; Mediation; General Practice; Personal Injury; Automobile Accidents and Injuries; Wrongful Death. ***Email:*** fhjones@smnet.net

CHESTER M. JONES, born Atlanta, Georgia, March 13, 1959; admitted to bar, 1983, North Carolina. *Education:* Oxford College of Emory University (A.A., 1979); Emory University (B.B.A., 1980); Wake Forest University (J.D., 1983). Beta Gamma Sigma. Recipient, Wall Street Journal Award in Finance. Former Graham County Attorney, 1994-2004. Clay County Attorney, 2005. *Member:* North Carolina Bar Association; North Carolina State Bar. ***PRACTICE AREAS:*** Civil Litigation; Appellate Practice; Business Law; Corporate Law; Local Government Law; Personal Injury; Construction Law. ***Email:*** chestermjones@smnet.net

CAMILA J. WRIGHT, born Franklin, North Carolina, January 8, 1978; admitted to bar, 2003, North Carolina. *Education:* University of Tennessee (B.A., Honors Political Science, 2000); University of North Carolina School of Law (J.D., 2003). *Member:* North Carolina and American Bar Associations. ***PRACTICE AREAS:*** Trusts and Estates; Wills; Real Estate; General Practice; Child Support; Civil Litigation. ***Email:*** cwright@smnet.net

GREGORY F. BOYER, born Framingham, Massachusetts, February 28, 1949; admitted to bar, 1986, Florida; 2004, North Carolina. *Education:* Florida State University (B.S., 1972); Oral Roberts University (J.D., 1985); Regent University (Juris Doctorate Certificate of Confirmation, 1991). *Member:* North Carolina and American Bar Associations; The Florida Bar; Association of Trial Lawyers of America; North Carolina Trial Lawyers Association. ***PRACTICE AREAS:*** Family Law; Litigation; Corporate Law; Personal Injury; Immigration Law; Real Estate; Criminal Defense; General Practice. ***Email:*** gfboyer@smnet.net

REPRESENTATIVE CLIENTS: Regions Bank of Clayton; John C. Campbell Folk School; County of Macon; First Citizens Bank and Trust Co.; First Clayton Bank & Trust; Macon Bank; Town of Franklin; Wachovia Bank and Trust Co., N.A.; Wildcat Cliffs Country Club.
APPROVED ATTORNEYS FOR: American Title Insurance Co.; Chicago Title Insurance Co.; First Title Insurance Co.; Lawyers Title Insurance Corp.; Fidelity National Title Insurance Co.; Investors Title Insurance Company; Southern Title Insurance Co.

PHILO & SPIVEY, P.A.

Established in 1984

587 WEST MAIN STREET
FRANKLIN, NORTH CAROLINA 28734
Telephone: 828-524-6377
Fax: 828-369-8054
Email: sphilo@mchsi.com
Email: s.philo@mchsi.com
URL: http://www.lawyers.com/philo&spiveypa

Criminal Law, DWI, Traffic Violations, Civil Trial and Appellate Practice in all Courts. Real Property, Probate, Corporate Law, Domestic Relations and Family Law, Divorce.

STEVEN E. PHILO, born Winston-Salem, North Carolina, December 24, 1942; admitted to bar, 1974, North Carolina. *Education:* U.S. Military Academy (B.S., 1965); Duke University; Wake Forest University (J.D., 1974). Phi Alpha Delta. Member, Wake Forest Law Review, 1973-1974. Chief Trial Judge, Eastern Band of Cherokee Indians, 1993—. *Member:* North Carolina Bar Association (Member, Sections on: Real Property; General Practice); North Carolina State Bar (Chairman, PALS, Lawyers Assistance Program, 1996-2001). [Capt., U.S. Army, active duty, 1965-1970]. ***PRACTICE AREAS:*** Real Property; Probate; Corporate Law. ***Email:*** s.philo@mchsi.com

DAVID C. SPIVEY, born Burlington, North Carolina, June 2, 1957; admitted to bar, 1982, North Carolina and U.S. District Court, Western District of North Carolina. *Education:* Wake Forest University (B.S., 1979; J.D., 1982). Phi Delta Phi. Member: Order of Barristers; Wake Forest National Trial Court Team. Recipient: Lewis F. Powell, Jr. National Moot Court Award; American College of Trial Lawyers Medal of Excellence in Trial Advocacy. Arbitrator, 30th Judicial District, 1990—. *Member:* Macon County, North Carolina (Member, Sections on: Criminal Justice, Litigation and Domestic Relations) and American

(This Listing Continued)

PHILO & SPIVEY, P.A., Franklin—Continued

(Member, Section on Criminal Justice) Bar Associations; 30th Judicial District (Secretary, 1986-1987) and North Carolina State Bars; North Carolina Academy of Trial Lawyers; The Association of Trial Lawyers of America; National Organization of Social Security Claimant's Representative. ***PRACTICE AREAS:*** Litigation; Family Law; Divorce; Adoption Law; Child Custody; Child Support; Equitable Distribution; Alimony; Social Security Disability; Criminal Law; Driving While Intoxicated; Traffic Violations. ***Email:*** spiveydavid@msn.com

APPROVED ATTORNEYS FOR: Investors Title Insurance Co.; Fidelity National Title Insurance Co.; Lawyers Title Insurance Co.
REFERENCES: Macon Savings Bank; First Citizens Bank & Trust Co.; Wachovia Bank; Carolina Community Bank; RBC Centura Bank.

JONATHAN D. BREEDEN

INT. 1-40, HIGHWAY 42, EXIT 312
100 PROFESSIONAL COURT, SUITE 2
GARNER, NORTH CAROLINA 27529
Telephone: 919-661-4970
Fax: 919-661-4971
URL: http://www.jbreedenlaw.com
Email: jonathan@breedenlaw.com
URL: http://www.breedenlaw.com
Mailing Address: P.O. Box 967, Clayton, NC 27528

Criminal Law, Driving While Intoxicated (DWI), Drug Crimes, Traffic Violations, Family Law, Child Custody, Child Support, Divorce, Education Law, Contracts, Wills.

JONATHAN D. BREEDEN, born 1975; admitted to bar, 2000, North Carolina. *Education:* North Carolina State University (B.A., 1996); Campbell University (J.D., 2000). *Member:* North Carolina Bar Association (Chairman, Small Firm/Solo Practice Committee, Young Lawyers Division, 2001-2002); North Carolina Academy of Trial Lawyers. ***PRACTICE AREAS:*** Criminal Law; Traffic Violations; Family Law.

THE HILBERT LAW FIRM, PLLC

GARNER, NORTH CAROLINA

(See Raleigh)

Family Law, Child Custody, Divorce Litigation, Child Support, Domestic Violence, Equitable Distribution, Alimony, Post-Separation Support, Separation Agreements Premarital Agreements, Adoptions, Visition Rights, Divorce.

PRATHER LAW FIRM, P.C.

402 ST. MARY'S STREET
GARNER, NORTH CAROLINA 27529
Telephone: 919-772-0699
Fax: 919-772-0682
Email: jdp@pratherlaw.com

Workers Compensation, Social Security Disability, Disability Claims, Personal Injury, Automobile Accidents, Slip and Fall, Wrongful Death, Toxic Tort, Mold Exposure.

J. D. PRATHER, born Meadville, Pennsylvania, August 29, 1962; admitted to bar, 1988, North Carolina. *Education:* Duke University (A.B., 1984; J.D., 1988); Boston University. Certified Mediator. *Member:* Wake County Bar Association (Member, Workers Compensation Section); The North Carolina State Bar. ***Email:*** jdp@pratherlaw.com

THE LAW OFFICE OF JONATHAN RICHARDSON

GARNER, NORTH CAROLINA

(See Cary)

Personal Injury, Real Estate, Closings, Workers Compensation, Injuries, Traffic Violations, Tickets, Wrongful Death.

CHRISTINA RIVENBARK & ASSOCIATES

5533 NC HIGHWAY 42 WEST
GARNER, NORTH CAROLINA 27529
Telephone: 1-800-561-9221

Wilmington, North Carolina Office: 4009 Oleander Drive, 28403. Telephone: 1-800-806-8896.
Clinton, North Carolina Office: 603A Northeast Boulevard, 28328. Telephone: 1-800-777-5159.

Personal Injury, Automobile Accidents, Workers Compensation, Wrongful Death, Medical Malpractice, Slip and Fall, Criminal Law, Driving While Intoxicated, Traffic Violations, Drug Offenses, Misdemeanors, Felonies, Sexual Assaults, Assaults, Burglary, Motorcycle Accidents, Head Injuries.

(For Complete Biographical Data on Personnel, see Professional Biography at Wilmington, North Carolina)

ARTHURS & FOLTZ

Established in 1989
420 EAST LONG AVENUE
P.O. BOX 2206
GASTONIA, NORTH CAROLINA 28053-2206
Telephone: 704-865-1900
Fax: 704-854-9323
Email: dpa@arthursfoltz.com

General Civil and Trial Practice before all State Courts. Real Estate, Eminent Domain, Buying or Selling, Commercial Leasing, Construction, Landlord and Tenant, Zoning and Land Use, Insurance Defense, Personal Injury, Automobile Accidents, Dog Bites, Slip and Fall, Wrongful Death, Insurance, Property Damage, Domestic/Family Law, Adoptions, Child Support, Child Custody, Divorce, Domestic Violence, Visitation Rights, Wills and Estates, Zoning, Planning and Land Use, Debt and Credit, Collections, Creditors Rights.

MEMBERS OF FIRM

DOUGLAS P. ARTHURS, born Lincolnton, North Carolina, May 13, 1954; admitted to bar, 1982, North Carolina. *Education:* Gaston College (A.A., 1977); University of North Carolina (B.A., 1978); Wake Forest University (J.D., magna cum laude, 1982). Member, Wake Forest Moot Court Board. Member, Wake Forest Law Review, 1981-1982. Author: Notes, "The Preemptive Provision as a Valid Restraint on Alienation," 17 Wake Forest Law Review 682, 1981; "Spousal Testimony in Criminal Proceedings," 17 Wake Forest Law Review 990, 181. *Member:* Gaston County (President, 1991-1992) and North Carolina Bar Associations; North Carolina State Bar. ***PRACTICE AREAS:*** Civil Litigation; Personal Injury; Insurance Defense; Zoning, Planning and Land Use; Automobile Accidents and Injuries; Dog Bites; Slip and Fall; Wrongful Death; Debt Finance; Collections; Creditors Rights. ***Email:*** dpa@arthursfoltz.com

NANCY EWINGER FOLTZ, born Burlington, Iowa, February 2, 1954; admitted to bar, 1980, North Carolina. *Education:* University of Iowa (B.S., with distinction, 1976); University of Houston and Wake Forest University (J.D., cum laude, 1980). Phi Beta Kappa. Member, Houston Law Review, 1977-1978. Member, Advisory Committee for Volunteer Lawyers Program of Gaston County. *Member:* Gaston County (President, 1995) and North Carolina Bar Associations; North Carolina State Bar. ***PRACTICE AREAS:*** Civil Litigation; Personal Injury; Insurance Defense; Family Law. ***Email:*** nef@arthursfoltz.com

ANN BRITTIAN GREEN, born Alexandria, Virginia, March 9, 1971; admitted to bar, 1996, North Carolina. *Education:* University of North Carolina at Chapel Hill (B.A., 1993); Wake Forest University (J.D., 1996). *Member:* Gaston County (Secretary, 2000-2001) and North Carolina Bar Associations; North Carolina State Bar. ***PRACTICE AREAS:*** Real Estate; Buying and Selling; Foreclosures; Wills and Estates; Collections; Creditors Rights; Probate. ***Email:*** abm@arthursfoltz.com

ASSOCIATE

TARA REAVIS SAIN, born Henderson, North Carolina, May 11, 1972; admitted to bar, 1998, North Carolina. *Education:* University of North Carolina at Chapel Hill (B.A., 1994); Norman A. Wiggins School of Law (J.D., 1998). *Member:* Gaston County (Secretary, 2002) and North Carolina Bar Associations; North Carolina State Bar. ***PRACTICE AREAS:*** Adoption Law; Child Support; Child Custody; Divorce; Visitation Rights; Equitable Distribution; Landlord and Tenant Law; Family Law. ***Email:*** trs@arthursfoltz.com

REPRESENTATIVE CLIENTS: Allstate Insurance Company; Auto Owners Insurance Company; State Auto Insurance Co.; North Carolina Insurance Guaranty Association; BB&T; First Gaston Bank.

BOGLE, ANTHONY & LEACH, P.A.

223 WEST MAIN AVENUE, SUITE A
P.O. BOX 981
GASTONIA, NORTH CAROLINA 28053-0981
Telephone: 704-867-3688
800-422-4988
Fax: 704-867-1938
Email: WilliamAAnthony@aol.com
URL: http://www.bogleanthonylaw.com

Workers Compensation, Personal Injury, Wrongful Death, Criminal Defense, Traffic Violations, Driving While Intoxicated, Corporate Law, Wills, Trust Law, Family Law/Domestic, Divorce, Child Custody, Child Support.

EDGAR F. BOGLE, born Charlotte, North Carolina, October 23, 1968; admitted to bar, 1995, North Carolina and U.S. District Court, Western District of North Carolina. *Education:* University of North Carolina (B.A., with honors, 1991); Wake Forest University (J.D., 1995). *Member:* North Carolina Trial Lawyers Association. ***PRACTICE AREAS:*** Criminal Defense; Traffic Violations; Felonies; Civil Practice; Corporate Law; Personal Injury; Wills; Trust Law.

WILLIAM A. ANTHONY, III, born Gastonia, North Carolina, March 3, 1964; admitted to bar, 1996, North Carolina. *Education:* University of North Carolina at Charlotte (B.A., 1992); Cumberland School of Law (J.D., 1996). *Member:* Gaston County Bar Association; North Carolina State Bar. ***PRACTICE AREAS:*** Criminal Defense; Traffic Violations; Civil Practice; Civil Litigation; Juvenile Law; Workers Compensation. ***Email:*** WilliamAAnthony@aol.com

TIMOTHY T. LEACH, born Brooklyn, New York, September 25, 1966; admitted to bar, 1991, North Carolina. *Education:* University of North Carolina at Charlotte (B.A., cum laude, 1988); Duke University (J.D., 1991). Certified Mediator. *Member:* Mecklenburg County, Gaston County and North Carolina Bar Associations; North Carolina State Bar; North Carolina Association of Defense Attorneys. ***PRACTICE AREAS:*** Insurance Defense; Alternative Dispute Resolution; Domestic Relations; Commercial Litigation. ***Email:*** timtleach@aol.com

BOLLINGER & PIEMONTE, PC

GASTONIA, NORTH CAROLINA

(See Charlotte)

Workers Compensation, Social Security Disability, Personal Injury, Disability Insurance, General Civil Litigation, Wrongful Death, Railroad Disability.

LAW OFFICE OF AARON E. BRADSHAW

313 S. SOUTH STREET
P.O. BOX 1072
GASTONIA, NORTH CAROLINA 28053
Telephone: 704-866-8289
Fax: 704-866-9429
Email: info@gastonlaw.com
URL: http://www.gastonlaw.com

Civil Litigation, Insurance Defense, General Liability, Automobile Liability, Product Liability, Construction Litigation, Commercial Litigation, Insurance Law.

FIRM PROFILE: The Law Office of Aaron E. Bradshaw, established in 1995, focuses exclusively on civil litigation and dispute resolution. The firm provides professional legal services to businesses and individuals in Western North Carolina.

We provide representation in all courts in Western North Carolina, including Superior and District Courts in the following counties: Gaston, Mecklenburg, Lincoln, Cleveland, Catawba, Rutherford, Polk, Union, Carbarrus, Iredell, Alexander, Caldwell, and Burke and the U.S. District Court for the Western District of North Carolina. The following cities lie within our service area: Gastonia, Charlotte, Hickory, Newton, Lenoir, Monroe, Morganton, Lincolnton, Shelby, Rutherfordton, Columbus, Taylorsville, Concord and Statesville.

AARON E. BRADSHAW, born Lincolnton, North Carolina, October 4, 1956; admitted to bar, 1985, North Carolina; 1987, Alabama. *Education:* Appalachian State University (B.A., 1981); Cumberland School of Law of Samford University (J.D., magna cum laude, 1985). Phi Kappa Phi. Member, Curia Honoris. Editor in Chief, American Journal of Trial Advocacy, 1984-1985. Law Clerk to Hon. Virgil Pittman, Senior U.S. District Judge for the Southern District of Alabama, 1985-1987. Certified Mediator and Arbitrator. *Member:* Gaston County, North Carolina and American Bar Associations; North Carolina State Bar; Alabama State Bar.

DON H. BUMGARDNER

Established in 1988
219 WEST MAIN AVENUE
GASTONIA, NORTH CAROLINA 28052
Telephone: 704-868-9293
Fax: 704-868-9296
Email: bumgardd@bellsouth.net
URL: http://www.bumgardner.lawoffice.com

General Civil and Appellate Practice in all State and Federal Courts. Personal Injury, Products Liability, Workers Compensation and Medical Malpractice.

FIRM PROFILE: Mr. Bumgardner is a member of the American Board of Trial Advocates.

DON H. BUMGARDNER, born Charlotte, North Carolina, February 7, 1945; admitted to bar, 1970, North Carolina, U.S. Court of Appeals, Fourth Circuit and U.S. District Court, Western District of North Carolina. *Education:* University of North Carolina (A.B. with Honors, 1967; J.D., 1970). Phi Alpha Theta. *Member:* Gaston County (President, 1978-1979) and 27-A Judicial District (President, 1979-1980) Bar Associations; North Carolina State Bar; The Association of Trial Lawyers of America; North Carolina Academy of Trial Lawyers; American Board of Trial Advocates (Advocate). ***PRACTICE AREAS:*** Personal Injury; Medical Negligence; Products Liability; Workmen's Compensation.

J. BOYCE GARLAND, JR.

Established in 2005
223 WEST MAIN AVENUE, SUITE M
P.O. BOX 1657
GASTONIA, NORTH CAROLINA 28053
Telephone: 704-867-1113
Fax: 704-867-4792
Email: jboycejr@bellsouth.net
URL: http://www.jboycegarland.com

General Civil and Criminal Practice in all Courts. Corporations, Business, Estate Planning and Administration, Probate, Real Estate, Personal Injury, Automobile Accidents, and Criminal.

FIRM PROFILE: General Civil and Criminal Practice in all courts with 17 years of trial experience.

JAMES B. GARLAND, born Gastonia, North Carolina, June 16, 1920. (1920-2002)

J. BOYCE GARLAND, JR., born Gastonia, North Carolina, November 29, 1959; admitted to bar, 1987, North Carolina. *Education:* University of North Carolina (B.A., 1982); Cumberland School of Law of Samford University; Campbell University School of Law (J.D., 1987). National German Honor Society. Delta Theta Phi. *Member:* Gaston County Bar Association; North Carolina State Bar; North Carolina Association of District Attorneys; North Carolina Academy of Trial Lawyers. ***LANGUAGES:*** German. ***PRACTICE AREAS:*** Real Estate; General Civil Litigation; Personal Injury; Estate Administration; Criminal. ***Email:*** jboycejr@bellsouth.net

LEGAL SUPPORT PERSONNEL

PRISCILLA ANDERSON, (Legal Assistant)

Language: German.

REPRESENTATIVE CLIENTS: SET Enterprises, Inc.; R & M Homes, Inc.; Wachovia Bank, N.A.; Branch Banking and Trust Company; Massey Plumbing, Inc.; Puestial Homes of Gastonia.
REFERENCES: Wachovia, N.A.; RBC Centura Bank; Branch Banking and Trust Company.

GRAY, LAYTON, KERSH, SOLOMON, SIGMON, FURR & SMITH, P.A.

Established in 1991
516 SOUTH NEW HOPE ROAD
P.O. BOX 2636
GASTONIA, NORTH CAROLINA 28053-2636
Telephone: 704-865-4400
FAX: 704-866-8010
URL: http://www.gastonlegal.com

General Civil Trial Practice, Arbitration, Corporation Law, Construction Law, Real Estate Law, Mediation, Municipal and Zoning Law, Mergers and Acquisitions, Bankruptcy, Family, Tax, Estate Planning and Probate Law, Personal Injury Law, Traffic, Professional Sports Representation, Community Association Law.

DAVID A. LAYTON, born Tulsa, Oklahoma, February 6, 1943; admitted to bar, 1968, North Carolina. *Education:* University of North Carolina (A.B., 1965; J.D., 1968). Delta Theta Phi. Member, 1980-1984 and President, 1983-1984, Board of Directors, Legal Services of South Piedmont, Inc. Member, Panel of Construction Arbitrators, American Arbitration Association, 1987-2004. Certified Mediator, North Carolina. *Member:* Gaston County, North Carolina (Member of Council, Business Law Section, 1986-1989; Real Property Section, 1994-1997; Construction Law Section, 1998-2001; Chair, Revise Lien Law Committee, 2001—) and American Bar Associations; North Carolina State Bar. ***PRACTICE AREAS:*** Construction Law; Real Estate Law; Debtor and Creditor; Alternative Dispute Resolution; Corporate Law. ***Email:*** dlayton@gastonlegal.com

JOHN D. KERSH, JR., born Gastonia, North Carolina, June 16, 1950; admitted to bar, 1978, North Carolina. *Education:* University of North Carolina (B.A., 1972); Wake Forest University (J.D., 1978); Emory University (LL.M., in Taxation, 1979). Instructor, North Carolina Association Certified Public Accountants, 1981-1995. (Board Certified Specialist in Estate Planning and Probate Law, North Carolina State Board of Legal Specialization). ***PRACTICE AREAS:*** Estate Planning Law; Federal Income, Estate and Gift Taxation Law; Mergers and Acquisitions. ***Email:*** dkersh@gastonlegal.com

T. J. SOLOMON, II, born Uniontown, Pennsylvania, September 2, 1949; admitted to bar, 1974, South Carolina; 1975, U.S. Court of Military Appeals; 1979, North Carolina, U.S. District Court, Western District of North Carolina and U.S. District Court, District of South Carolina. *Education:* Coe College (B.A., 1971); University of South Carolina (J.D., 1974). *Member:* 27A Judicial District (President, 1986, 1987), North Carolina and American Bar Associations; South Carolina Bar; North Carolina State Bar; North Carolina Academy of Trial Lawyers; The Association of Trial Lawyers of America. [Capt. USAF, 1975-1980; Lt. Colonel USAFR, 1980-1996]. ***LANGUAGES:*** Spanish. ***PRACTICE AREAS:*** Personal Injury Law; Litigation; Commercial Law; Traffic Violations. ***Email:*** tjsolomon@gastonlegal.com

P. WAYNE SIGMON, born Charlotte, North Carolina, November 26, 1949; admitted to bar, 1976, North Carolina and Florida. *Education:* North Carolina State University (B.S.I.E., with honors, 1972); Stetson University (J.D., with honors, 1976). (Board Certified Specialist in Bankruptcy Law, North Carolina State Board of Legal Specialization). ***PRACTICE AREAS:*** Bankruptcy Law. ***Email:*** wsigmon@siglawfirm.com

DAVID M. FURR, born Charlotte, North Carolina, November 15, 1957; admitted to bar, 1982, North Carolina, 1983, Florida, U.S. Tax Court; 1984, U.S. Court of Appeals, Fourth Circuit and U.S. Supreme Court. *Education:* Wake Forest University (B.A., 1980; J.D., 1982); University of Florida (LL.M., Taxation, 1983). Member, Wake Forest Law Review, 1981-1982. *Member:* Gaston County, North Carolina and American Bar Associations; North Carolina State Bar; The Florida Bar. ***PRACTICE AREAS:*** Taxation Law; Sports Law; Sports Licensing. ***Email:*** dfurr@gastonlegal.com

DAVID W. SMITH, III, born Gastonia, North Carolina, July 16, 1954; admitted to bar, 1980, North Carolina and U.S. District Court, Middle and Western Districts of North Carolina. *Education:* Furman University (B.A., 1976); Wake Forest University (J.D., 1979). Certified Mediator, North Carolina. City Attorney, Bessemer City, North Carolina. Author, "Collecting the Judgment," National Business Institute, 2000. *Member:* Gaston County and North Carolina Bar Associations; North Carolina Academy of Trial Lawyers (Member, Council Construction Law Section, 2000—). ***PRACTICE AREAS:*** Civil Litigation; Debtor Creditor Law; Real Estate. ***Email:*** dsmith@gastonlegal.com

WILLIAM E. MOORE, JR., born Chapel Hill, North Carolina, October 22, 1958; admitted to bar, 1981, North Carolina, U.S. District Court, Western, Middle and Eastern Districts of North Carolina and U.S. Court of Appeals, Fourth Circuit. *Education:* Utah State University; University of Florida (B.A., with high honors, 1978); Duke University (J.D., 1981). Phi Beta Kappa. *Member:* Gaston County, North Carolina and American Bar Associations; North Carolina State Bar. ***PRACTICE AREAS:*** Civil Litigation. ***Email:*** bmoore@gastonlegal.com

JOHN H. GRIFFING, born Youngstown, Ohio, January 24, 1962; admitted to bar, 1988, North Carolina; 1989, U.S. Tax Court; 1993, South Carolina. *Education:* University of North Carolina (B.S., 1984); Wake Forest University (J.D., cum laude, 1987); Babcock Graduate School of Management (M.B.A., with distinction, 1988). Certified Public Accountant, North Carolina, 1989. Certified Management Accountant, North Carolina, 1992.

(This Listing Continued)

GRAY, LAYTON, KERSH, SOLOMON, SIGMON, FURR & SMITH, P.A., Gastonia—Continued

Chartered Financial Analyst, 1992. Member, Graduate Faculty of the University of North Carolina at Charlotte. (Board Certified Specialist in Estate Planning and Probate Law, North Carolina State Board of Legal Specialization). ***PRACTICE AREAS:*** Taxation; Real Estate Development; Syndication; Securities Arbitration; Mergers and Acquisitions; Estate Planning. ***Email:*** jgriffing@gastonlegal.com

EMILY H. LEAZER, born Raleigh, North Carolina, March 22, 1969; admitted to bar, 1994, North Carolina; 1997, U.S. Tax Court. *Education:* University of North Carolina (B.S.B.A., 1991); Campbell University (J.D., 1994; M.B.A., 1994); Villanova University (LL.M., in Taxation, 1995). Delta Theta Phi. Certified Public Accountant, North Carolina. Member: North Carolina Association of Certified Public Accountants; American Institute of Certified Public Accountants. *Member:* Gaston County, North Carolina and American Bar Associations; North Carolina State Bar; Western Piedmont Estate Planning Council. ***PRACTICE AREAS:*** Taxation; Tax Controversies; Corporate; Mergers and Acquisitions; Estate Planning. ***Email:*** eleazer@gastonlegal.com

TED F. MITCHELL, born Hickory, North Carolina, October 17, 1967; admitted to bar, 1996, North Carolina, South Carolina and U.S. District Court, Western District of North Carolina; 1997, U.S. Court of Appeals, Fourth Circuit. *Education:* Clemson University (B.A., 1990; M.A., 1992); Campbell University (J.D., 1996). *Member:* Gaston County Bar Association; North Carolina State Bar; South Carolina Bar. ***PRACTICE AREAS:*** Civil Litigation; Debtor and Creditor; Construction Law; Community Association Law; Employment Law. ***Email:*** tmitchell@gastonlegal.com

OF COUNSEL

CHARLES D. GRAY, III, born Gastonia, North Carolina, August 13, 1938; admitted to bar, 1963, North Carolina. *Education:* University of North Carolina (A.B., 1960); New York University (LL.B., 1963).

REPRESENTATIVE CLIENTS: Action Performance Companies, Inc.; Bryant Electric Supply Inc.; Cablevision of Gastonia; Carlisle Chiropractic Clinic, P.A.; Choice, USA; Concrete Supply Co.; Digital Recorders, Inc.; First Gaston Bank; Fleischman's Yeast Corp.; Gaston Country Club; Good Will Publishers, Inc.; Gough Econ, Inc.; Sonny Hancock Automotive Group, Inc.; Independence Nissan; M & M Electric Service, Inc.; Neuroscience & Spine Center of the Carolinas, PA; RBC Centura; Standard Distrubuters, Inc.; Wachovia Bank & Trust Company, N.A.; Webb Metal, Ltd.; Witten Lumber Co., Inc.; McKenney Chevrolet, Inc.
REFERENCES: RBC Centura; Wachovia Bank & Trust Company, N.A.

HELMS, HENDERSON & ASSOCIATES, P.A.

GASTONIA, NORTH CAROLINA

(See Charlotte)

General, Civil and Criminal Trial Practice in State and Federal Courts and Agencies, Corporation, Real Estate, Probate, Insurance, Bankruptcy, Commercial, Personal Injury, Collections and Tax.

THOMAS B. KAKASSY, P.A.

Established in 1985

414 SOUTH STREET
P.O. BOX 2436
GASTONIA, NORTH CAROLINA 28053
Telephone: 704-867-1795
Fax: 704-867-1820
Email: ThomasKakassy@Carolina.rr.com
URL: http://www.kakassy.com

Civil Litigation, Personal Injury, Workers Compensation, Social Security Disability, Bankruptcy, Business, Domestic Relations, Family Law, Criminal, Traffic, Real Estate, Estates and Guardianships.

THOMAS B. KAKASSY, born Evanston, Illinois, August 13, 1955; admitted to bar, 1980, North Carolina; U.S. District Courts, Eastern, Western and Middle Districts of North Carolina; U.S. Court of Appeals, Fourth Circuit. *Education:* University of North Carolina at Chapel Hill (B.A., 1977); Wake Forest University (J.D., 1980). President: Gastonia Jaycees, 1982; Kiwanis Club of Gastonia, 1988; Gaston County Humane Society, 1989. Chairman, Parish Council, St. Michael's Catholic Church, 1991-1992. Board Member, Gaston Literacy Council, Inc., 1990-1998. Past President and Member, Gaston County Family Services Advisory Board, 1995—. Member, Department of Social Services Community Performance Advocacy Committee, 1998—. Member Chairman of the Board of Cornerstone Christian Center, Gastonia, North Carolina, 2002—. Board Member, Gaston County Heart Society, 2003—. *Member:* Gaston County and North Carolina Bar Associations; North Carolina State Bar. ***PRACTICE AREAS:*** Civil Litigation; Personal Injury; Workers Compensation; Social Security Disability; Bankruptcy; Business Law; Family Law; Criminal Law; Traffic Violations; Real Estate; Adoption Law; Child Abuse and Neglect; Child Custody; Child Support; Termination of Parental Rights; Guardianship. ***Email:*** ThomasKakassy@Carolina.rr.com

MORRIS W. KEETER

309 SOUTH STREET
P.O. BOX 1575
GASTONIA, NORTH CAROLINA 28053-1575
Telephone: 704-864-5425
Telecopier: 704-864-5426
Email: mwkeeter@bellsouth.net
URL: http://www.lawyers.com/morriswkeeter

FIRM PROFILE: Mr. Keeter has been in private practice in Gastonia, North Carolina since 1978.

MORRIS W. KEETER, born Hickory, North Carolina, February 24, 1950; admitted to bar, 1975, North Carolina and U.S. District Court, Middle District of North Carolina; 1977, U.S. Court of Appeals, Fourth Circuit; 1981, U.S. Supreme Court. *Education:* Lenoir-Rhyne College (A.B., 1972); Wake Forest University (J.D., 1975). Phi Delta Phi. City Attorney, City of Lowell, 1980-1992. Legal Counsel, Gaston County Home Builders Association. *Member:* Gaston County and North Carolina Bar Associations; The North Carolina State Bar; National Academy of Elder Law Attorneys. ***PRACTICE AREAS:*** Real Estate; Construction Law; Contracts; Business Law; Wills; Trusts & Estates; Elder Law; Medicare and Medicaid; Corporate Law; Civil Litigation; Collections; Zoning, Planning and Land Use; Municipal Law.

REPRESENTATIVE CLIENTS: A list of Representative Clients and References will be Furnished upon Request.

THE KING LAW FIRM PLLC

GASTONIA, NORTH CAROLINA

(See Huntersville)

Bankruptcy, Domestic, Family, Wills, Trusts, Criminal.

RICHARD D. LAWS, P.A.

418 SOUTH STREET
GASTONIA, NORTH CAROLINA 28052
Telephone: 704-861-0575
Facsimile: 704-868-9132
Email: rlaws92022@aol.com
URL: http://www.lawyers.com/rlaws

Mailing Address: P.O. Box 1985, Gastonia, NC 28053

Residential Real Estate, Commercial Real Estate, Estate Planning, Estate Administration, Wills, Probate, Trusts.

RICHARD D. LAWS, born Cleveland, Ohio, March 2, 1954; admitted to bar, 1979, North Carolina. *Education:* Wake Forest University (B.S., 1976; J.D., 1979). *Member:* Gaston County, North Carolina (Member, Real Property, Estate Planning and Fiduciary Law Sections) and American Bar Associations. ***PRACTICE AREAS:*** Residential Real Estate; Commercial Real Estate; Estate Planning; Estate Administration; Wills; Probate; Trusts.

MULLEN HOLLAND & COOPER P.A.

301 SOUTH YORK STREET, P.O. BOX 488
GASTONIA, NORTH CAROLINA 28053
Telephone: 704-864-6751
Facsimile: 704-861-8394
URL: http://www.mhc-law.com

General Civil Trial and Appellate Practice, all Federal and State Courts. Banking, Bankruptcy and Reorganization, Construction, Corporate and Commercial, Employment Discrimination, Estate Planning and Administration, Health Care, Insurance, Mergers and Acquisitions, Negligence, Personal Injury, Professional Malpractice, Real Estate, Workers' Compensation.

FIRM PROFILE: The law firm of Mullen Holland & Cooper P.A. is a full-service law firm handling a broad range of individual and business civil matters. Founded in 1950 by James Mullen and J. Mack Holland, its partners have included a North Carolina Bar Association President, three Gaston County Bar Association Presidents, three members of the Board of Governors of the North Carolina Bar Association, a member of the North Carolina Board of Law Examiners and a Federal District Court Judge. Its members frequently lecture at continuing legal education programs.

LANGDON M. COOPER, born April 27, 1941; admitted to bar, 1969, North Carolina; 1973, U.S. Tax Court; 1987, U.S. District Court, Eastern, Middle and Western Districts of North Carolina and U.S. Court of Appeals, Third and Fourth Circuits; 1992, U.S. Supreme Court. *Education:* Duke University (A.B., 1964); University of North Carolina at Chapel Hill (J.D., 1969). Co-Author and Lecturer: J. Nelson Young Tax Institute, 1994; N.C. Bar Foundation; Bankruptcy Institute, 1994. Member, United States Bankruptcy Trustee Panel, Western District of North Carolina, 1978—. *Member:* Gaston County, North Carolina (Member, Board of Governors, 1985-1988) and American Bar Associations; North Carolina State Bar; American Bankruptcy Institute. (Board Certified Specialist in Bankruptcy Law by North Carolina State Board of Legal Specialization) (Board Certified Business and Consumer Bankruptcy Law Specialist by American Bankruptcy Board of Certification). ***PRACTICE AREAS:*** Bankruptcy; Creditors Rights; Corporate Law; Commercial Law; Banking; Civil Trial. ***Email:*** lcooper@mhc-law.com

H. RANDOLPH SUMNER, born March 13, 1957; admitted to bar, 1982, North Carolina; 1987, U.S. District Court, Western District of North Carolina; 1993, U.S. Supreme Court. *Education:* University of North Carolina at Chapel Hill (B.A., 1979); Wake Forest University (J.D., 1982). Phi Delta Phi. Recipient: Lawyer 1989 Distinguished Service Award; Volunteer Service Award, North Carolina Bar Association, 1988-1998. *Member:*

(This Listing Continued)

Gaston County (President, 1993) and North Carolina Bar Associations; North Carolina State Bar (Member, Workers' Compensation Committee). ***PRACTICE AREAS:*** Workers Compensation; Insurance Defense Law; Civil Trial. ***Email:*** dsumner@mhc-law.com

NANCY BORDERS PASCHALL, born May 10, 1960; admitted to bar, 1985, North Carolina, and U.S. District Court, Eastern, Middle and Western Districts of North Carolina; 1992, U.S. Court of Appeals, Fourth Circuit; 1993, U.S. Supreme Court. *Education:* Wake Forest University (B.A., cum laude, 1982; J.D., cum laude, 1985). Order of the Barristers. Member: National Moot Court Team, 1984-1985; William and Mary Moot Court Team, 1983-1984; Moot Court Board, 1983-1985. Member, Wake Forest Law Review, 1983-1985. Published two comments in Wake Forest L. Rev. *Member:* Gaston County, North Carolina and American Bar Associations; North Carolina State Bar; North and South Carolina Association of Housing Authority Attorneys (Founding Member; President, 1992-1993). ***PRACTICE AREAS:*** Commercial Law; Bankruptcy; Landlord and Tenant Law; Personal Injury; Health Law; Mental Health Law; Civil Trial. ***Email:*** npaschall@mhc-law.com

J. MARK HEAVNER, born February 24, 1959; admitted to bar, 1984, North Carolina; 1986, U.S. District Court, Eastern and Western Districts of North Carolina; 1988, U.S. Court of Appeals, Fourth Circuit; 1998, U.S. Supreme Court. *Education:* Davidson College (A.B., 1981); Wake Forest University (J.D., 1984). Editorial Staff Member, Wake Forest Law Review, 1982-1984. Research Assistant, North Carolina Supreme Court, 1984-1986. *Member:* North Carolina Bar Association; North Carolina State Bar; National Lawyers Association. ***PRACTICE AREAS:*** Commercial Law; Corporate Law; Real Estate Law; Business Law; Collections. ***Email:*** mheavner@mhc-law.com

J. REID McGRAW, JR., born October 13, 1962; admitted to bar, 1989, North Carolina; U.S. Court of Appeals, Fourth Circuit; U.S. District Court, Middle and Western Districts of North Carolina; U.S. Supreme Court. *Education:* University of North Carolina at Charlotte (B.A., 1984); Wake Forest University (J.D., 1989). Phi Delta Phi. Certified Mediator. *Member:* Gaston County and American Bar Associations; North Carolina State Bar; North Carolina Bar Association (Member, Worker's Compensation Section). ***PRACTICE AREAS:*** Workers Compensation; Mediation; Civil Trial; Insurance Defense. ***Email:*** rmcgraw@mhc-law.com

JESSE V. BONE, JR., born March 10, 1960; admitted to bar, 1991, North Carolina and U.S. District Court, Western District of North Carolina. *Education:* University of North Carolina, Chapel Hill (B.A., 1982); Duke University (M.Div., 1986); Wake Forest University (J.D., 1991). Certified Mediator. *Member:* Gaston County and North Carolina Bar Associations; North Carolina State Bar. ***PRACTICE AREAS:*** Workers' Compensation; Mediation; Insurance Defense. ***Email:*** jbone@mhc-law.com

ELIZABETH NEISLER SUMNER, born May 27, 1958; admitted to bar, 1982, North Carolina. *Education:* Davidson College (A.B., cum laude, 1979); Universite De Montpellier, France; Wake Forest University (J.D., 1982). Phi Beta Kappa. *Member:* Gaston County and North Carolina Bar Associations; North Carolina State Bar; Western Piedmont Estate Planning Council. (Board Certified Specialist in Estate Planning and Probate Law, North Carolina State Board of Legal Specialization). ***PRACTICE AREAS:*** Estate Planning; Probate; Estate Administration; Corporate Law; Partnership Law. ***Email:*** lsumner@mhc-law.com

JAMES R. MARTIN, born November 20, 1971; admitted to bar, 1997, North Carolina; 1998, South Carolina. *Education:* Cornell University (B.A., 1994); Wake Forest University (J.D., cum laude, 1997). Order of Coif. Member, Wake Forest Law Review, 1995-1997. ***LANGUAGES:*** Spanish. ***PRACTICE AREAS:*** Workers Compensation; Civil Litigation; Mental Health Law; Insurance Defense; Personal Injury. ***Email:*** jmartin@mhc-law.com

JANE FOY PAINTER, born December 10, 1960; admitted to bar, 1986, North Carolina. *Education:* University of North Carolina at Chapel Hill (B.A., 1983; J.D., 1986). *Member:* Gaston County and North Carolina Bar Associations; North Carolina State Bar. ***PRACTICE AREAS:*** Commercial Real Estate; Corporate Law. ***Email:*** jpainter@mhc-law.com

JOHN H. RUSSELL, JR., born March 25, 1967; admitted to bar, 1993, North Carolina. *Education:* Princeton University (B.A., 1989); University of North Carolina at Chapel Hill (J.D., 1992). *Member:* North Carolina State Bar. ***PRACTICE AREAS:*** Workers Compensation; Landlord and Tenant Law; Social Security Disability. ***Email:*** jrussell@mhc-law.com

LEE A. PEINDL, born October 30, 1976; admitted to bar, 2003, North Carolina; 2004, U.S. District Court, Western District of North Carolina. *Education:* Westminster College (B.A., 1999); Case Western Reserve University (J.D., 2002). Order of the Barristers. Chairman, Moot Court Board. Senator, Student Bar Association. *Member:* Gaston County, North Carolina and American Bar Associations; North Carolina State Bar. ***PRACTICE AREAS:*** Construction Law; Workers Compensation Defense; Collections; Civil Litigation. ***Email:*** lpeindl@mhc-law.com

JASON R. SHOEMAKER, born January 4, 1978; admitted to bar, 2003, North Carolina; 2004, U.S. District Court, Western District of North Carolina. *Education:* Wake Forest University (B.A., magna cum laude, 2000; J.D., 2003). Phi Beta Kappa. Member and Research Editor, Wake Forest Law Review, published, 2002. *Member:* Gaston County, North Carolina and American Bar Associations; North Carolina State Bar. ***PRACTICE AREAS:*** Workers Compensation; Civil Litigation; Insurance Defense; Corporate Law; Collections. ***Email:*** jshoemaker@mhc-law.com

D. BRAD COLLINS, born March 2, 1978; admitted to bar, 2004, North Carolina. *Education:* University of Manchester School of Management, Manchester, England (1998-1999); University of North Carolina at Greensboro (B.A., cum laude, 2000); University of Tennessee at Knoxville (J.D., 2004). Member, Tennessee Law Review, 2002-2004. ***PRACTICE AREAS:*** Workers Compensation; Civil Litigation; Traffic Violations. ***Email:*** bcollins@mhc-law.com

REPRESENTATIVE CLIENTS: American & Efird; Bellsouth; CIGNA; Cameron M. Harris & Co.; City of Gastonia; Concrete Supply Co.; Crawford & Co.; Duke Energy; First Gaston Bank; First National Bank of Shelby; Gastonia Housing Authority; Gaston Lincoln Cleveland Mental Health Substance Abuse Development Disabilities Area Program D/B/A Pathways; The Hartford; Helmsman Management Services; Hewitt-Coleman; Integon Insurance Co.; Liberty Mutual Insurance Company; FMC Corporation; Lithium Division; Norfolk Southern Railway; North Carolina Guaranty Fund; Pharr Yarns; The PMA Group; Prepaid Legal Services; PSNC Energy; SCANA; Shelby Savings Bank; Sherman Textiles; Spectrum Dyed Yarns; Travelers Insurance Co.; W.D. Lee & Co., Inc.; Witten Lumber Co., Inc.; Zenith Insurance Company; Zurich-American Group.

NICHOLS AND AUSTELL L.L.P.

600 EAST FRANKLIN BOULEVARD
GASTONIA, NORTH CAROLINA 28054
Telephone: 704-868-4340
Fax: 704-868-4342
URL: http://www.nicholsaustell.com

Wills, Probate, Real Estate, Residential Real Estate.

MEMBERS OF FIRM

NICOLE L. NICHOLS, born 1973; admitted to bar, 1998, North Carolina. *Education:* University of North Carolina, Charlotte (B.A., 1995); Campbell University School of Law (J.D., 1998). *Member:* Gaston County and North Carolina Bar Associations; North Carolina State Bar. ***PRACTICE AREAS:*** Real Estate; Residential Real Estate; Wills; Probate.

STACEY PARKER AUSTELL, born Gastonia, North Carolina, June 15, 1977; admitted to bar, 2002, North Carolina. *Education:* Duke University (A.B., 1999); University of North Carolina at Chapel Hill (J.D., 2002). *Member:* Gaston County, North Carolina and American Bar Associations; North Carolina State Bar. ***PRACTICE AREAS:*** Wills; Probate; Real Estate; Residential Real Estate.

PARKER, POE, ADAMS & BERNSTEIN L.L.P.

GASTONIA, NORTH CAROLINA

(See Charlotte)

Administrative and Regulatory, Antitrust and Trade Regulation, Arbitration, Banking, Bankruptcy, Insolvency and Reorganization, Biotechnology, Capital Markets, Computer, Construction, Copyright, Corporate, Corporate Finance, Education, Employee Benefits and Compensation Plans, Employment, Environmental, Estate Planning and Administration, Governmental Contracts and Procurement, Governmental Relations, Health Care, Immigration, Insurance, Intellectual Property, International Trade and Investment, Joint Ventures, Lending and Finance, Limited Liability Companies and Partnerships, Litigation, Malpractice Defense, Mergers and Acquisitions, Municipal, Products Liability, Project Development, Project Finance, Public Finance, Commercial Real Estate, Securities, Tax Exempt Organizations, Taxation, Technology Management and Licensing, Telecommunications, Trademark, Transportation, Utilities Regulation, Zoning.

PATTERSON AND ADAMS PLLC

1305 EAST GARRISON BOULEVARD
GASTONIA, NORTH CAROLINA 28054
Telephone: 704-867-1955
Fax: 704-853-1875
URL: http://www.patterson-adams.com
URL: http://www.pattersonadamslawoffice.com

Concord, North Carolina Office: 433 Church Street North, 28025. Telephone: 704-795-4317. Fax: 704-795-5738.

Salisbury, North Carolina Office: 710 North Main Street, 28144. Telephone: 704-795-4317.

Personal Injury, Automobile Accidents, Wrongful Deaths, Workers Compensation, Medical Malpractice.

(For complete biographical data on all personnel, see Professional Biographies at Concord, North Carolina)

RAGAN & RAGAN PLLC

Established in 2005
616 COX ROAD
P.O. BOX 249
GASTONIA, NORTH CAROLINA 28053-0249
Telephone: 704-864-3409
Fax: 704-853-1040
Email: info@ragan-ragan.com
URL: http://www.ragan-ragan.com

Personal Injury, Workers Compensation, Medical Malpractice, Wrongful Death, Automobile Accidents, Products Liability.

MEMBERS OF FIRM

JERRY NEIL RAGAN, born Norfolk, Virginia, May 28, 1955; admitted to bar, 1980, Virginia and West Virginia; 1987, North Carolina. *Education:* University of Virginia (B.A., with distinction, 1977); Marshall-Wythe School of Law, College of William & Mary (J.D., 1980). *Member:* West Virginia State Bar; Virginia State Bar; North Carolina State Bar; North Carolina Academy of Trial Lawyers; International Society of Primerus Law Firms. ***PRACTICE AREAS:*** Personal Injury; Medical Malpractice; Products Liability; Workers Compensation; Wrongful Death. ***Email:*** jnragan@ragan-ragan.com

JAMES W. RAGAN, born Norfolk, Virginia, June 12, 1951; admitted to bar, 1977, Virginia; 1997, North Carolina; 1999, South Carolina. *Education:* University of Virginia (B.A, 1973); University of South Carolina (J.D., 1976); University of Houston (M.B.A., 1982; PhD., Organizational Behavior, 1988). *Member:* North Carolina State Bar; South Carolina Bar; Virginia State Bar. ***PRACTICE AREAS:*** Personal Injury; Workers Com-

(This Listing Continued)

RAGAN & RAGAN PLLC, Gastonia—Continued

pensation; Medical Malpractice; Wrongful Death; Automobile Accidents. ***Email:*** jwragan@ragan-ragan.com

BRENT D. RATCHFORD

Established in 1997

223 W. MAIN AVENUE, SUITE B
P.O. BOX 726
GASTONIA, NORTH CAROLINA 28053-0726
Telephone: 704-868-3434
Fax: 704-868-3225
Email: bdrattorneyatlaw@aol.com
URL: http://www.brentratchford.com

Criminal Law, Juvenile Law, Traffic Law, Federal Law.

BRENT D. RATCHFORD, born 1970; admitted to bar, 1996, North Carolina. *Education:* University of North Carolina (B.S., 1992); Norman A. Wiggins School of Law (J.D., 1996). *Member:* Gaston County Bar Association (Former President and Treasurer); North Carolina State Bar; North Carolina Academy of Trial Lawyers. ***PRACTICE AREAS:*** Criminal Law; Juvenile Law; Traffic Violations; Federal Criminal Law; Driving While Intoxicated; Trial Practice; Personal Injury; Wrongful Death.

THE ROBERTS LAW FIRM, P.A.

302 SOUTH YORK STREET
P.O. BOX 2335
GASTONIA, NORTH CAROLINA 28053-2335
Telephone: 704-865-1271
Fax: 704-865-1488

Trial Practice. Personal Injury, Workers Compensation, Social Security Disability, Medical Malpractice, Nursing home Litigation, Products Liability and Wrongful Death.

FIRM PROFILE: The Roberts Law Firm, P.A. has built a reputation of always putting the interests of its clients ahead of anything else. We are stewards of the rights and needs of our clients, and we do not forget this. The firm has been actively engaged in civil litigation since 1964, in all state and federal courts. We are licensed to appear before the Fourth Circuit Court of Appeals and the U.S. Supreme Court, and have had more than 50 cases reach the Appellate Court. Our firm is community oriented and active on civic boards.

JOSEPH B. ROBERTS, III, born Gastonia, North Carolina, May 24, 1940; admitted to bar, 1964, North Carolina; 1971, U.S. Supreme Court, U.S. Court of Appeals, Fourth Circuit and U.S. Claims Court. *Education:* University of North Carolina (A.B., 1962; LL.B., 1964). Phi Alpha Delta. William T. Phillips Scholar. Member, National Transportation Safety Board, 1976. Chairman, Gaston-Lincoln Mental Health Board. Member, Flynn Homes, Inc. Chairman, Gaston County Board of Elections, 1977. Lay Member, Appointed by Governor Jim Hunt, North Carolina Pharmacy Board, 1982-1988. Member, North Carolina House of Representatives, 1983. Editor, "Course and Scope," Chairman, Workers Compensation Section, North Carolina Bar Association (September 1998-1999). *Member:* Gaston County, 27th Judicial District (President, 1970; 1980-1982), North Carolina (Chairman, Workers Compensation Section, 1998-1999) and American Bar Associations; North Carolina State Bar; North Carolina Academy of Trial Lawyers; The Association of Trial Lawyers of America. ***REPORTED CASES:*** Sizemore v. Raxter, 344 S.E.2d 391, 314 N.C. 527; Sizemore v. Raxter, 327 S.E.2d 258, 73 N.C.App. 531; Ross v. Young Supply Co., 322 S.E.2d 648, 71 N.C.App. 532; Bush v. BASF Wyandotte Corp., 306 S.E.2d 562, 64 N.C.App. 41; Hughey v. Cloninger, 253 S.E.2d 898, 297 N.C. 86; Phillips v. Phillips, 252 S.E.2d 790, 34 N.C.App. 428; Henderson County v. Osteen, 235 S.E.2d 166, 292 N.C. 692; In re Robinson, 215 S.E.2d 631, 26 N.C.App. 341; Gastonia Personnel Corp. v. Rogers, 172 S.E.2d 19, 276 N.C. 279; Gastonia Personnel Corp. v. Rogers, 168 S.E.2d 31, 5 N.C.App. 219; State v. Gibson, 162 S.E.2d 627, 2 N.C.App. 187. ***PRACTICE AREAS:*** Litigation; Worker's Compensation; Medical Malpractice; Torts; Products Liability; Wrongful Death. ***Email:*** joe@robertsfirm.com

SCOTT W. ROBERTS, born Gastonia, North Carolina, August 28, 1968; admitted to bar, 1994, South Carolina; 1995, North Carolina. *Education:* North Carolina University, Chapel Hill (B.A., 1991); South Carolina Law School (J.D., 1994). Chairman and Vice President, Finance Committee, Legal Services of the Southern Piedmont. *Member:* Gaston County (President, 2002-2003; Vice President, 2001-2002) and North Carolina Bar Associations; South Carolina Bar; North Carolina Academy of Trial Lawyers; The Association of Trial Lawyers of America. ***PRACTICE AREAS:*** Litigation; Workers Compensation; Personal Injury; Products Liability; Medical Malpractice; Social Security. ***Email:*** scott@robertsfirm.com

LAW OFFICES OF J. NEAL RODGERS, PLLC

GASTONIA, NORTH CAROLINA

(See Charlotte)

Personal Injury, Wrongful Death, Automobile Accidents, Medical Malpractice, Jail Injury Cases, Employment Law, Civil Rights.

SCOTT R. ROSENBERG

201 WEST SECOND AVENUE, SUITE B
GASTONIA, NORTH CAROLINA 28052
Telephone: 704-865-3600
Fax: 704-865-3792
Email: rosenbergscottra@bellsouth.net
Mailing Address: P.O. Box 278, Gastonia, NC 28053-0278

Criminal Law, Traffic, Driving While Intoxicated, Juvenile Crimes, Parole and Probation.

SCOTT R. ROSENBERG, born Michigan, 1970; admitted to bar, 1997, North Carolina and U.S. District Court, Western District of North Carolina. *Education:* University of Alabama (B.A., 1992); Thomas M. Cooley Law School (J.D., 1997). Recipient, American Jurisprudence Award. Certificate of Merit, Juvenile Law, Moot Court. Assistant District Attorney, Gaston County. *Member:* Gaston County, Mecklenburg County and North Carolina Bar Associations; North Carolina State Bar. ***PRACTICE AREAS:*** Criminal Law; Traffic Violations; Driving While Intoxicated; Juvenile Criminal Law; Parole and Probation.

STOTT, HOLLOWELL, PALMER & WINDHAM, L.L.P.

401 EAST FRANKLIN BOULEVARD
P.O. BOX 995
GASTONIA, NORTH CAROLINA 28053-0995
Telephone: 704-864-3425
Fax: 704-864-0478

General Civil and Trial Practice in all Courts. Corporation, Real Estate, Estate Planning and Probate, Insurance, Commercial Law, Municipal Law, Worker Compensation, Bankruptcy, Labor and Employment Law.

MEMBERS OF FIRM

L. B. HOLLOWELL (1904-1981)

GRADY B. STOTT, born Bailey, North Carolina, September 19, 1921; admitted to bar, 1952, North Carolina. *Education:* Duke University (A.B., 1947; LL.B., 1952). Delta Theta Phi. Solicitor, Gastonia Municipal Recorders Court, 1954-1956. Solicitor, 14th Solicitorial District of North Carolina, 1957-1961. *Member:* Gaston County (President, 1955), North Carolina and American Bar Associations; North Carolina State Bar (President, 1979). Fellow: American College of Trial Lawyers; American Bar Foundation. ***PRACTICE AREAS:*** Civil Litigation; Insurance Defense; Workers Compensation; Municipal Law. ***Email:*** gbs@shpw.com

JAMES C. WINDHAM, JR., born Gastonia, North Carolina, July 30, 1947; admitted to bar, 1972, North Carolina. *Education:* Furman University (B.A., 1969); University of North Carolina (J.D., 1972). Municipal Attorney, Stanley, N.C., Lowell, N.C. and High Shoals, N.C. *Member:* Gaston County, North Carolina and American Bar Associations; North Carolina State Bar; North Carolina Association of Defense Attorneys. [Capt. U.S. Army, 1972-1973]. ***PRACTICE AREAS:*** Civil Litigation; Insurance Defense; Business Law; Municipal Law. ***Email:*** jwindham@shpw.com

H. WILLIAM PALMER, born Rocky Mount, North Carolina, October 3, 1930; admitted to bar, 1954, North Carolina. *Education:* University of North Carolina (A.B., 1952; LL.B., 1954; now J. D). Phi Alpha Delta. *Member:* Gaston County Bar Association; North Carolina State Bar. [LTJG, U.S. Navy, 1955-1958]. ***PRACTICE AREAS:*** Corporate Law; Estate Planning; Probate Law. ***Email:*** bpalmer@shpw.com

MARTHA R. THOMPSON, born Mount Holly, New Jersey, March 7, 1963; admitted to bar, 1988, North Carolina; U.S. District, Western District of North Carolina. *Education:* Furman University (B.A., cum laude, 1985); University of South Carolina (J.D., 1988). Phi Beta Kappa; Omicron Delta Kappa. *Member:* Gaston County (President, 1998) and North Carolina Bar Associations; North Carolina State Bar; North Carolina Association of Defense Attorneys; Defense Research Institute. ***PRACTICE AREAS:*** Civil Litigation; Insurance Defense; Municipal Law; Labor and Employment. ***Email:*** mthompson@shpw.com

CHARLTON K. TORRENCE, III, born Gastonia, North Carolina, October 5, 1962; admitted to bar, 1989, North Carolina. *Education:* University of North Carolina (B.A., 1985; J.D., 1989). *Member:* Gaston County and North Carolina Bar Associations; North Carolina State Bar. ***PRACTICE AREAS:*** Probate Law; Estate Planning; Corporate Law. ***Email:*** ckt3@shpw.com

JACK D. DRUM, born Gaston County, North Carolina, June 25, 1948; admitted to bar, 1974, North Carolina and U.S. District Court, Eastern District and Western District of North Carolina. *Education:* University of North Carolina at Chapel Hill (B.S.B.A., 1970; J.D., with honors, 1974). Order of the Coif. Member, North Carolina Law Review, 1972-1974. Member, 1988-1993 and Chairman, 1991-1992 Bank Counsel Committee of North Carolina Bankers Association. Research Assistant to North Carolina Supreme Court, 1974-1975. Author: "Student Suffrage: The Illusory Right to Vote," 51 NC Law Rev. 1060, 1973. *Member:* Gaston County and North Carolina Bar Associations; North Carolina State Bar. ***REPORTED CASES:*** Carolinas-Virginia's Association of Building Owners and Managers v. Ingram, 39 N.C. App. 688, 251 S.E.2d 910, cert. denied 297 N.C. 299, 257S.E.2d 910 (1979); Coley v. North Carolina National Bank, 41 N.C. App. 121, 254 S.E.2d 217 (1979). ***PRACTICE AREAS:*** Real Estate; Commercial Law; Civil Litigation; Education Law. ***Email:*** jdrum@shpw.com

D. KEVIN JOYCE, born Walkertown, North Carolina, February 13, 1973; admitted to bar, 1998, North Carolina. *Education:* University of North Carolina at Chapel Hill (B.S., 1995); North Carolina Central University (J.D., summa cum laude, 1998). Phi Delta Phi. *Member:* North Carolina State Bar. ***PRACTICE AREAS:*** Residential Real Estate; General Practice. ***Email:*** kjoyce@shpw.com

(This Listing Continued)

ASSOCIATE

DAVID W. AYCOCK, born Morganton, North Carolina, 1976; admitted to bar, 2005, North Carolina. *Education:* Davidson College (A.B., 1998); Wake Forest University (J.D., 2005). *Member:* Gaston County Bar; North Carolina State Bar. [Capt., U. S. Army, 1998-2002.]. ***PRACTICE AREAS:*** Insurance Defense; Litigation; Workers Compensation.

OF COUNSEL

LINWOOD BRANTON HOLLOWELL, JR., born Gastonia, North Carolina, November 15, 1937; admitted to bar, 1963, North Carolina. *Education:* Duke University (A.B., 1959; LL.B., 1962). Certified Mediator. ***Email:*** lhollowell@shpw.com

CHARLES L. GRAHAM, JR., born Gastonia, North Carolina, July 6, 1961; admitted to bar, 1986, North Carolina. *Education:* Belmont Abbey College (B.A., cum laude, 1983); Campbell University (J.D., cum laude, 1986). ***Email:*** cgraham@shpw.com

REPRESENTATIVE CLIENTS: Wix Corp.; Parkdale Mills Inc.; Gaston County; North Carolina League of Municipalities; Citizens South Bank; Nationwide Insurance Co.; State Farm Insurance Co.; Gastonia ABC Board; Town of Stanley; GMAC Insurance.
APPROVED ATTORNEYS FOR: Lawyers Title Insurance Corp.; Investors Title Insurance Company; Chicago Title Insurance Company. References: Branch Banking & Trust Co.; Citizens South Bank.

REGINA MITCHELL TAYLOR

1568-E UNION ROAD
GASTONIA, NORTH CAROLINA 28054
Telephone: 704-861-0700
Fax: 704-861-0488
Email: rmtatty@bellsouth.net
URL: http://www.regina-taylorlaw.com

Business Law, Corporate Law, Family Business Law, Small Business Law, Bankruptcy, Fair Debt Collections Act, Creditors Rights, Landlord and Tenant Law, Criminal, DWI, Traffic Violations, Domestic Relations, Family Law, Divorce, Child Custody, Adoptions, Child Support, Religious Institutions, Non Profit Organizations, Real Estate Title Examinations, Land Acquisitions, Wills, Decedents Estates.

REGINA MITCHELL TAYLOR, born Hickory, North Carolina, November 9, 1965; admitted to bar, 1991, North Carolina; 1994, U.S. District Court, Western District of North Carolina. *Education:* North Carolina A&T State University (B.S., 1988); North Carolina Central University School of Law (J.D., 1991). Chairperson, Moot Court Board Law Journal. Staff Attorney, Catawba County Department of Social Services, 1999-2001. *Member:* Gaston County and North Carolina Bar Associations; North Carolina State Bar; North Carolina Association of Black Lawyers.

PENNIE M. THROWER

GASTONIA, NORTH CAROLINA

(See Dallas)

Residence Real Estate, Traffic Offenses, Wills, Powers of Attorney, Living Wills, Incorporations.

YELTON, FARFOUR, McCARTNEY, LUTZ & CRAIG, P.A.

GASTONIA, NORTH CAROLINA

(See Shelby)

General Practice. Corporation, Estate Planning, and Personal Injury Law. Trial and appellate practice in all courts. Creditors" Rights and Bankruptcy law. Domestic and Family Law.

BADDOUR, PARKER & HINE, P.C.

208 SOUTH WILLIAM STREET
P.O. DRAWER 916
GOLDSBORO, NORTH CAROLINA 27530
Telephone: 919-735-7275
Fax: 919-736-3297
Email: info@goldsborolawyers.com
URL: http://www.lawyers.com/baddourparkerhine&orander

Automobile Accidents and Injuries, Personal Injury, Wrongful Death, Workers Compensation, Real Estate, Social Security Disability, Wills, Trusts and States, Taxation, Family Law, Divorce, Business Law, Civil Litigation, Products Liability.

FIRM PROFILE: Baddour, Parker & Hine, PC serves individuals, business, municipalities and county governments throughout Wayne County and Eastern North Carolina.

PHILIP A. BADDOUR, JR., born Goldsboro, North Carolina, August 5, 1942; admitted to bar, 1967, North Carolina and U.S. Supreme Court. *Education:* University of North Carolina (A.B., 1964; J.D., 1967). Delta Theta Phi. Member: North Carolina House of Representatives, 1993-1994, 1997-2002; North Carolina State Bar Disciplinary Hearing Commission, 1980-1986. Certified Mediator. *Member:* Wayne County, North Carolina and American Bar Associations; North Carolina State Bar; North Carolina Academy of Trial Lawyers (Member, Board of Governors, 1990-1995; Vice President, 2004—); The Association of Trial Lawyers of America. [Col., JAGC, NCARNG, 1967-1999]. ***PRACTICE AREAS:*** Personal Injury Law; Civil Litigation; Corporate Law; Mediation. ***Email:*** pbaddour@goldsborolawyers.com

E. B. BORDEN PARKER, born Goldsboro, North Carolina, February 5, 1944; admitted to bar, 1969, North Carolina, U.S. Supreme Court and U.S. Court of Military Appeals. *Education:* University of North Carolina (A.B., 1966; J.D., 1969). Phi Delta Phi. Wayne County Attorney, 1975—; Greene County Attorney, 2000— . *Member:* Wayne County, North Carolina and American Bar Associations; North Carolina State Bar. [Capt., U.S. Army, 1969-1973]. ***PRACTICE AREAS:*** Civil Litigation; Governmental Law; Family Law; Divorce; Equitable Distribution. ***Email:*** bparker@goldsborolawyers.com

JOHN C. HINE, born Winston-Salem, North Carolina, December 30, 1948; admitted to bar, 1974, North Carolina; 1975, U.S. Tax Court; 1980, U.S. Supreme Court; 1989, U.S. Court of Military Appeals. *Education:* University of North Carolina (B.S., 1971); University of Tennessee (J.D., 1974); New York University (LL.M. in Taxation, 1977). Phi Alpha Delta. Attorney, Internal Revenue Service, Raleigh, North Carolina, 1974-1976. *Member:* Wayne County, North Carolina (Member, Estate Administration Manual Subcommittee, 1987-1990) and American Bar Associations; North Carolina State Bar (Member, Estate Planning and Probate Specialization Committee, 1985). Fellow, American College of Trust and Estate Counsel. Certified Mediator. [Lt. Col., JAGC, USAFR, 1974-2000]. (Board Certified Specialist in Estate Planning and Probate Law, North Carolina State Board of Legal Specialization). ***REPORTED CASES:*** Goldsboro Art League v. Commissioner, 75 T.C. 337 (1980); Denise v. Cornell, 324 S.E.2d 305 (1985). ***PRACTICE AREAS:*** Estate Planning; Wills; Probate; Tax; Corporate Law. ***Email:*** jhine@goldsborolawyers.com

REPRESENTATIVE CLIENTS: Wayne County; Wayne County Department of Social Services; Housing Authority of the City of Goldsboro; Village of Walnut Creek; J. Isaac Gurley Farms, Inc.; Quality Forest Products, Inc.; Wayne Realty & Insurance Co.; Seegars Fence Co.; Shepherd Electric Supply Co., Inc.; Southeastern Medical Oncology Center, P.A.; Goldsboro Medical Clients, P.A.; Goldsboro Eye Clinic; Eastern Carolina Surgical Associates, P.A.; Goldsboro Neurological Surgery, P.A.; Coldwell Banker/Crawford-Norwood Realty, Inc.; Goldsboro Builders Supply, Inc.; Centrex Properties; Greene County; Greene County Department of Social Services; Jeffreys Seed Company; Southco Distributing Company; Pittard Perry & Crone, Inc.; Jerry G. Williams & Sons, Inc.
APPROVED ATTORNEYS FOR: Lawyers Title Insurance Corp.; Chicago Title Insurance Co.; First American Title Insurance Company; Investors Title Insurance Company; Statewide Title; Title Company of North Carolina; United Title Insurance Co.; Commonwealth Land Title Insurance Co.
REFERENCES: Branch Banking & Trust Co.; Wachovia Bank & Trust Co.; First-Citizens Bank & Trust Co.; New Century Bank.

BRANTLEY, JENKINS, RIDDLE, HARDEE & HARDEE

601 NORTH SPENCE AVENUE
GOLDSBORO, NORTH CAROLINA 27534
Telephone: 919-778-9700
Fax: 919-778-1938
URL: http://www.bjrhhlawyers.com
URL: http://www.bjrhhatty.com

Greenville, North Carolina Office: 202 East Arlington Boulevard, P.O. Box 924, 27858. Telephone: 252-355-1998. Fax: 252-321-2948.
Jacksonville, North Carolina Office: 901 Hargett Street, P.O. Box 7070, 28540. Telephone: 910-455-5599. Fax: 910-455-7191.
Kinston, North Carolina Office: 2506 Heritage Street, Suite A, 28501. Telephone: 252-522-1500.

Personal Injury, Wrongful Death, Automobile Accidents, Head and Spinal Injury, Nursing Home Abuse and Neglect, Workers Compensation, Insurance, Products Liability, Social Security Disability, Medical Malpractice.

FIRM PROFILE: Brantley, Jenkins, Riddle, Hardee & Hardee L.L.P. is a progressive firm known for its tireless efforts protecting the rights of people injured by the negligence of others. Our firm has years of knowledge and experience in the field of personal injury law. Four of our six Attorneys are members of the prestigious Million Dollar Advocates Forum.

J. CHRISTOPHER BRANTLEY, born Goldsboro, North Carolina, May 17, 1966; admitted to bar, 1993, North Carolina. *Education:* East Carolina University (B.A., 1989); Campbell University (J.D., 1993). *Member:* North Carolina and American Bar Associations; North Carolina Academy of Trial Lawyers. ***PRACTICE AREAS:*** Workers Compensation.

EUGENE G. JENKINS (1961-2003)

GENE A. RIDDLE, born Albemarle, North Carolina, July 7, 1959; admitted to bar, 1985, North Carolina. *Education:* University of North Carolina (B.A., 1981); Wake Forest University (J.D., 1985). Member, Moot Court. Recipient, American Jurisprudence Book Award. Member, Campbell University Law Review, 1983-1984. *Member:* Wayne County Bar Association; North Carolina State Bar; North Carolina Academy of Trial Lawyers. (Also at Goldsboro Office). ***PRACTICE AREAS:*** Personal Injury; Automobile Accidents and Injuries; Wrongful Death; Workers Compensation.

CHARLES R. HARDEE, born Kinston, North Carolina, January 11, 1956; admitted to bar, 1981, North Carolina; 1982, U.S. District Court, Eastern District of North Carolina and U.S. Court of Appeals, Fourth Circuit; 1983, U.S. Supreme Court. *Education:* University of North Carolina at Chapel Hill (B.S., 1978); Campbell University (J.D., 1981). Member, Campbell University Law Review. Certified Mediator. *Member:* Pitt County (President, 1997-1998) and North Carolina Bar Associations; North Carolina Academy of Trial Lawyers (Member, Board of Governors); The Association of Trial Lawyers of America. ***PRACTICE AREAS:*** Personal Injury; Wrongful Death; Nursing Home Abuse and Neglect; Premises Liability; Insurance Coverage.

G. WAYNE HARDEE, born Kinston, North Carolina, June 15, 1957; admitted to bar, 1982, North Carolina, U.S. District Court, Eastern District of North Carolina and U.S. Court of Appeals, Fourth Circuit; 1985, U.S. Supreme Court. *Education:* University of North Carolina at Chapel Hill (B.S., 1979); Campbell University (J.D., 1982). Arbitrator, North Carolina, 1991—. Certified Mediator, North Carolina Dispute Resolution Commission, 1996—. *Member:* Pitt County, North Carolina and American Bar Associations; North Carolina State Bar; North Carolina Academy of Trial Lawyers; The Association of Trial Lawyers of America. ***PRACTICE AREAS:*** Personal Injury; Wrongful Death; Insurance Coverage.

(This Listing Continued)

(This Listing Continued)

BRANTLEY, JENKINS, RIDDLE, HARDEE & HARDEE, Goldsboro—Continued

ASSOCIATES

BRIAN CHRISTOPHER (CHRIS) DANIELS, born Henderson, North Carolina, April 6, 1972; admitted to bar, 2000, North Carolina. *Education:* North Carolina Weselyan College (B.A., 1997); Thomas M. Cooley Law School (J.D., 2000). Member, Thomas M. Cooley Law Review, 1997-1999.*Member:* Onslow County and North Carolina Bar Associations; North Carolina State Bar; Association of Trial Lawyers of America. ***PRACTICE AREAS:*** Personal Injury.

THOMAS MOORE, born Charlotte, North Carolina; admitted to bar, 2003, North Carolina. *Education:* North Carolina State University (B.A., 1999); Loyola University (J.D, 2003). Managing Substance and Citing Editor, Maritime Law Journal. Member, Moot Court Board. Best Oralist, Moot Court Intramural Champion, 2001. ***PRACTICE AREAS:*** Personal Injury; Automobile Accidents and Injuries; Wrongful Death; Workers Compensation.

DEES, SMITH, POWELL, JARRETT, DEES & JONES

Established in 1914
100 NORTH WILLIAM STREET
POST OFFICE DRAWER 8
GOLDSBORO, NORTH CAROLINA 27533-0008
Telephone: 919-735-8311
Fax: 919-735-0234
Email: emilyp@deeslaw.com
URL: http://www.deeslaw.com

General Trial and Appellate Practice in all State and Federal Courts, Personal Injury, Medical Malpractice, Workers Compensation, Dispute Resolution, Corporate Law and Business Law, Contracts, Traffic Offenses, DWI, Commercial, Environmental, Banking, Real Property, Timber Transactions, Estate Administration, Trusts and Estates, Wills and Probate, Negligence and Traffic Law.

FIRM PROFILE: Dees, Smith, Powell, Jarrett, Dees & Jones was founded by William Archie Dees in 1914 and has earned a reputation for professional excellence and client service throughout North Carolina. Its members have been involved extensively in the business, governmental, political and civic life of North Carolina.

MEMBERS OF FIRM

W. ARCHIE DEES (1887-1979)

WILLIAM A. DEES, JR., born Goldsboro, North Carolina, June 10, 1920; admitted to bar, 1948, North Carolina; U.S. District Court, Eastern District of North Carolina. *Education:* University of North Carolina (A.B., 1941; J.D., with honors, 1948). Phi Delta Phi. Associate Editor, North Carolina Law Review, 1947-1948. Member, Board of Aldermen, City of Goldsboro, 1950-1957. Member and Chairman, Goldsboro City Board of Education, 1963-1972. Member, 1963-1965 and Chairman, 1964-1965, North Carolina State Board of Higher Education. Member, 1972-1990 and Chairman, 1972-1976, Board of Governors, University of North Carolina. *Member:* Wayne County, North Carolina and American Bar Associations; North Carolina State Bar. ***PRACTICE AREAS:*** Wills and Estates. ***Email:*** deesw@deeslaw.com

WILLIAM W. SMITH (Retired)

WILLIAM L. POWELL, JR. (Retired)

TOMMY W. JARRETT, born Hayesville, North Carolina, February 28, 1943; admitted to bar, 1967, North Carolina; U.S. District Court, Eastern District of North Carolina, U.S. Court of Appeals, Fourth Circuit, U.S. Court of Military Appeals and U.S. Supreme Court. *Education:* University of North Carolina (A.B., 1965; J.D., 1967). Delta Theta Phi. Member, Board of Editors, North Carolina Law Review, 1966-1967. Wayne County Commissioner, 1988-1992. Past Chair, Wayne County Board of Elections, 1993-1999. Member, Board of Trustees, Wayne Community College. *Member:* Wayne County, North Carolina and American Bar Associations; North Carolina State Bar (Councilor, 1980-1988; President, 1990-1991); The Association of Trial Lawyers of America. [Capt., USMCR, Judge Advocate, 1967-1970]. ***PRACTICE AREAS:*** Civil Litigation; Business Law. ***Email:*** jarrett@deeslaw.com

JOHN W. DEES, born Durham, North Carolina, June 15, 1947; admitted to bar, 1972, North Carolina; U.S. District Court, Eastern District of North Carolina. *Education:* University of North Carolina (A.B., 1969; J.D., with honors, 1972). Phi Beta Kappa; Order of the Coif; Phi Delta Phi. Associate Editor, North Carolina Law Review, 1971-1972. Law Clerk to Judge James B. McMillan, U.S. District Court, Western District of North Carolina. Past President, Eastern Carolina Legal Services. *Member:* Wayne County, North Carolina and American Bar Associations; North Carolina State Bar. ***PRACTICE AREAS:*** Real Estate; Timber and Logging Law. ***Email:*** deesj@deeslaw.com

MICHAEL M. JONES, born Bonne Terre, Missouri, November 22, 1953; admitted to bar, 1979, North Carolina; U.S. District Court, Eastern District of North Carolina. *Education:* University of North Carolina (A.B., 1976; J.D., 1979). Phi Beta Kappa. Projects Editor, North Carolina Law Review, 1978-1979. Member, North Carolina Dispute Resolution Commission, 1995-1997. *Member:* Wayne County, North Carolina (Past Chair, General Practice Section Council) and American Bar Associations; North Carolina State Bar. ***PRACTICE AREAS:*** Civil Litigation; Alternative Dispute Resolution. ***Email:*** jones@deeslaw.com

ASSOCIATES

JOYCE ANN KELLER, born Toccoa, Georgia, September 25, 1950; admitted to bar, 1978, Georgia; 1979, North Carolina. *Education:* University of Georgia (B.A., 1972); Emory University (M.A., 1973; J.D., 1978). Phi Beta Kappa; Omicron Delta Kappa. *Member:* Wayne County and North Carolina Bar Associations; North Carolina State Bar; State Bar of Georgia. ***PRACTICE AREAS:*** Real Estate; Collections. ***Email:*** kellerjoyce@hotmail.com

BILLY J. STRICKLAND II, born Orlando, Florida, December 12, 1973; admitted to bar, 2005, North Carolina. *Education:* Campbell University (B.S., 2000); Regent University (J.D., 2004). Law Clerk to Judge John M. Tyson, North Carolina Court of Appeals. *Member:* North Carolina State Bar; North Carolina and American Bar Associations. ***PRACTICE AREAS:*** Civil Practice; Criminal Defense; Domestic Relations; Appellate Practice.

REPRESENTATIVE CLIENTS: Branch Banking & Trust Co.; Franklin Baking Co. (Sunbeam); North Carolina Community Federal Credit Union (formerly known as Seymour Johnson Federal Credit Union); Crawford-Norwood Co. (Realtors); General Industries, Inc.; Georgia Pacific Corporation; Neuse Lumber Company, Inc.; The Timber Harvester, Inc.
APPROVED ATTORNEYS FOR: Lawyers Title Insurance Corp.; Chicago Title Insurance Co.; Investors Title Insurance Co.; First American Title Insurance Company; Fidelity National Title.

KELLUM LAW FIRM

2005 EAST ASH STREET
P.O. BOX 1085
GOLDSBORO, NORTH CAROLINA 27533
Telephone: 919-722-6955
Fax: 919-722-6922
Email: ckeenhold@kellumlawfirm.com
URL: http://www.lawyers.com/kellumlawfirm

State and Federal Civil Trial Practice, Personal Injury Law, Wrongful Death, Workers' Compensation, Social Security, Defective Products, Mass Torts and Insurance Law.

(For complete biographical data on all personnel, see Professional Biographies at New Bern)

ROSE RAND ATTORNEYS, P.A.

GOLDSBORO, NORTH CAROLINA

(See Wilson)

General Practice, all Courts. Corporation, Labor and Insurance Law. Trials, including Personal Injury, Wrongful Death and Workers Compensation, Eminent Domain, Tax, Estate Planning and Administration, Municipal, Environmental, Real Estate, Bankruptcy.

SMITH AND STRICKLAND, PLLC

104 S. WILLIAM STREET, SUITE A
P.O. BOX 1657
GOLDSBORO, NORTH CAROLINA 27533
Telephone: 919-735-5252
Fax: 919-735-5696
URL: http://www.smithandstrickland.com

Criminal Defense, Driving While Impaired, DUI, DWI, Traffic Violations, Parole and Probation, Drug Crimes, White Collar Crimes, Juvenile Crimes, Personal Injury, Military Law.

ROBERT MORGAN SMITH, born Kinston, North Carolina, November 3, 1969; admitted to bar, 2003, North Carolina. *Education:* Mount Olive College (B.S., 2000); Thomas M. Cooley Law School (J.D., 2002). Member, Juvenile Crime Prevention Council. *Member:* Wayne County Bar Association; North Carolina State Bar; North Carolina Association of Trial Lawyers; Eighth District Bar Association. ***PRACTICE AREAS:*** Criminal Defense; Driving While Intoxicated; Traffic Violations; Parole and Probation; Drug Crimes; White Collar Crime; Juvenile Criminal Law; Personal Injury. ***Email:*** smith_law@bellsouth.net

DONALD B. STRICKLAND, born Rich Square, North Carolina, February 25, 1931; admitted to bar, 1956, North Carolina; 1963, U.S. Court of Military Appeals; 1964, U.S. Supreme Court. *Education:* Duke University (B.A., 1953; J.D., 1956); University of Maryland (M.A., 1970). Delta Theta Phi. Instructor: Administrative Law, Central Michigan University, 1978; Business Law and Law & Society, St. Leo's University, 1979-1982. Chief Trial Judge, United States Air Force, 1982-1984. *Member:* North Carolina State Bar. [Judge Advocate General's Department, U.S. Air Force, 1963-1984; Colonel, Retired]. ***PRACTICE AREAS:*** Criminal Law; Military Law.

WALLACE, MORRIS, BARWICK, LANDIS & STROUD, P.A.

GOLDSBORO, NORTH CAROLINA

(See Kinston)

General Civil and Trial Practice in all State and Federal Courts. Aviation, Banking, Corporate Law, Insurance, Personal Injury, Probate, Product Liability, Real Estate and Taxation.

WARREN, KERR, WALSTON, TAYLOR & SMITH, L.L.P.

117 ORMOND AVENUE
P.O. BOX 1616
GOLDSBORO, NORTH CAROLINA 27533-1616
Telephone: 919-734-1841
Fax: 919-734-4215

General Civil Practice. Corporate and Business Law, Wills and Probate, Trusts and Estates, Banking, Tax, Labor, Insurance, Collections, Real Estate, and Traffic Violations.

(This Listing Continued)

WILLIAM R. ALLEN (1896-1972)

WALTER FRANK TAYLOR (1889-1977)

OF COUNSEL

LINDSAY C. WARREN, JR., born Washington, North Carolina, October 8, 1924; admitted to bar, 1951, North Carolina. *Education:* University of North Carolina (B.S., 1948; J.D., 1951). Phi Delta Phi; Order of the Coif. Associate Editor, North Carolina Law Review, 1950-1951. Member, Board of Trustees, Wayne County Memorial Hospital, 1958-1969. Member, Goldsboro School Board, 1959-1962. Member, North Carolina State Senate, 1963-1970. *Member:* Wayne County, North Carolina (President, 1969-1970) and American Bar Associations; North Carolina State Bar.

MEMBERS OF FIRM

JOHN H. KERR, III, born Richmond, Virginia, February 28, 1936; admitted to bar, 1961, North Carolina. *Education:* University of North Carolina (A.B., 1958; LL.B. with honors, 1961). Phi Delta Phi; Order of the Coif; Phi Beta Kappa. Member: Board of Editors, North Carolina Law Review, 1960-1961; N.C. House of Representatives, 1987-1992; N.C. Senate, 1993—. *Member:* Wayne County and North Carolina Bar Association; North Carolina State Bar. **Email:** kerr@warrenkerr.com

JOHN T. WALSTON, born Wilson County, North Carolina, January 5, 1952; admitted to bar, 1977, North Carolina. *Education:* University of North Carolina (A.B., with honors, 1974; J.D., 1977). *Member:* Wayne County (President, 1999-2000) and North Carolina Bar Associations; North Carolina State Bar. **Email:** walston@warrenkerr.com

L. E. (TREY) TAYLOR, III, born Faison, North Carolina, April 21, 1962; admitted to bar, 1987, North Carolina and U.S. District Court, Eastern District of North Carolina. *Education:* University of North Carolina (B.S., 1984; J.D., 1987). Phi Eta Sigma; Phi Delta Phi. *Member:* Wayne County and North Carolina Bar Associations; North Carolina State Bar. **Email:** taylor@warrenkerr.com

HENRY C. SMITH, born Goldsboro, North Carolina, February 4, 1956; admitted to bar, 1981, North Carolina. *Education:* University of North Carolina at Chapel Hill (B.S., 1978; J.D., 1981). Phi Delta Phi; Beta Gamma Sigma. Assistant District Attorney, Eleventh Prosecutorial District of North Carolina, 1981-1985. *Member:* Wayne County, North Carolina and American Bar Associations; North Carolina State Bar. **Email:** smith@warrenkerr.com

REPRESENTATIVE CLIENTS: *General Counsel for:* Mt. Olive College, Inc.; H. Weil & Bros.; Goldsboro Milling Co.; R.A. Jeffreys Distributing Co.; Wooten Oil Co.; Mt. Olive Pickle Co.; Pate-Dawson Co.; Wayne Printing Co.; T.A. Loving Co.; *Local Counsel for:* Progress Energy Service Co.; Bell South; Ted Lansing Corp.
APPROVED ATTORNEYS FOR: Lawyers Title Insurance Corp.; Chicago Title Co.; Investors Title Insurance Co.; First American Title Insurance Co.

GEORGE B. DANIEL, P.A.

GRAHAM, NORTH CAROLINA

(See Yanceyville)

Criminal Law, Felonies, Misdemeanors, Traffic Violations, Driving While Intoxicated, Automobile Accidents, Truck Accidents, Personal Injury, Wrongful Death, Civil Litigation, Real Estate, Residential Real Estate, Commercial Real Estate, Real Estate Litigation, Workers Compensation, Estate Planning, Estate Administration, Drug Crimes.

WILLIAM H. DANIEL, P.A.

GRAHAM, NORTH CAROLINA

(See Yanceyville)

Criminal Law, Felonies, Misdemeanors, Traffic Violations, Driving While Intoxicated, Drug Crimes, Personal Injury, Automobile Accidents, Truck Accidents, Motorcycle Accidents, Wrongful Death, Workers Compensation, Real Estate, Wills, Estate Administration.

LAW OFFICE OF DOROTHY HAIRSTON

GRAHAM, NORTH CAROLINA

(See Durham)

Family Law, Criminal Law, Traffic Violations, Personal Injury, Medical Malpractice, Workers Compensation, Real Estate, Business, Military Law, Bankruptcy.

McENTIRE & DiLELLO

103 WEST ELM STREET
P.O. DRAWER 471
GRAHAM, NORTH CAROLINA 27253
Telephone: 336-228-1341
Fax: 336-229-7465
Email: mmmfirm@aol.com

Criminal and Traffic, DWI, Municipal, Personal Injury and Estates.

MITCHELL M. McENTIRE, born Old Fort, North Carolina, February 7, 1945; admitted to bar, 1970, North Carolina and U.S. District Court, Middle District of North Carolina; 1994, U.S. Supreme Court. *Education:* University of North Carolina (B.A., 1967; J.D., 1970). Phi Alpha Delta. Town Attorney, Haw River, North Carolina, 1979—. President, Alamance County Bar Association, 1994. *Member:* Alamance County, North Carolina and American Bar Associations; North Carolina State Bar; North Carolina League of Municipalities; North Carolina Academy of Trial Lawyers. ***PRACTICE AREAS:*** Criminal Defense; Traffic Violations; Personal Injury; Automobile Accidents and Injuries; Wrongful Death; Wills; Trusts; Probate; Municipal law.

(This Listing Continued)

ANTHONY C. DiLELLO, born Yonkers, New York, May 21, 1970; admitted to bar, 1995, North Carolina. *Education:* North Carolina State University (B.A., magna cum laude, 1992); North Carolina Central University (J.D., cum laude, 1995). Corpus Juris Secundum, Civil Procedure. *Member:* Alamance County and American Bar Associations; North Carolina State Bar; North Carolina Academy of Trial Lawyers. ***PRACTICE AREAS:*** Personal Injury; Automobile Accidents and Injuries; Traffic Violations; Driving While Intoxicated.

STEDMAN LAW FIRM

GRAHAM, NORTH CAROLINA

(See Burlington)

Personal Injury, Workers Compensation Injuries, Commercial & Residential Real Estate, Trusts, Estates & Wills, Business & Corporate Law.

ADAMS KLEEMEIER HAGAN HANNAH & FOUTS PLLC

GREENSBORO, NORTH CAROLINA

(See Nexsen Pruet Adams Kleemeier, PLLC)

ADAMS & OSTEEN

BB&T BUILDING-SUITE 410
201 WEST MARKET STREET
GREENSBORO, NORTH CAROLINA 27401-2527
Telephone: 336-274-2947
Fax: 336-274-2940
Email: osteena@bellsouth.net

Civil and Criminal Trial and Appeals in all State and Federal Courts. Real Estate, Corporation and Wills and Probate, Commercial Law, Business and Construction Law.

J. PATRICK ADAMS, born Farmer, North Carolina, April 7, 1936; admitted to bar, 1961, North Carolina. *Education:* University of North Carolina (A.B., 1958; LL.B., 1961). *Member:* Greensboro and North Carolina Bar Associations; North Carolina State Bar. ***PRACTICE AREAS:*** Real Estate; Corporate Law; Wills; Probate.

WILLIAM L. OSTEEN, JR., born Greensboro, North Carolina, August 8, 1960; admitted to bar, 1987, North Carolina and U.S. District Court, Eastern, Middle and Western Districts of North Carolina; U.S. Court of Appeals, 4th Circuit. *Education:* University of North Carolina (B.S., 1983; J.D., 1987). *Member:* Greensboro, North Carolina (Chair, Criminal Justice Council, 2000-2001) and American Bar Associations; North Carolina State Bar; National Association of Criminal Defense Lawyers; American Board of Trial Advocates. ***PRACTICE AREAS:*** Criminal Law; Federal Criminal Law; Civil Trials and Appeals.

ALEXANDER RALSTON, SPECKHARD & SPECKHARD, L.L.P.

221 COMMERCE PLACE, SUITE D
GREENSBORO, NORTH CAROLINA 27401
Telephone: 336-379-9302
Fax: 336-370-1232
URL: http://www.speckhardandspeckhard.com

General Practice in all Courts. Corporate, Bankruptcy, Commercial, Personal Injury, Medical Malpractice, Product Liability, Wrongful Death, Brain Injury, Real Estate, Wills, Probate and Estate Planning, Civil Litigation, Workers Compensation and Appellate Law.

DONALD K. SPECKHARD, born Chicago, Illinois, October 4, 1941; admitted to bar, 1970, North Carolina and U.S. District Court, Middle District of North Carolina; 1974, U.S. District Court, Eastern District of North Carolina; 1980, U.S. District Court, Western District of North Carolina; 1982, U.S. Court of Appeals, Fourth Circuit; 1992, U.S. Court of Appeals, Federal Circuit. *Education:* Lenoir-Rhyne College (B.A., 1963); University of North Carolina (J.D., 1970). *Member:* Greensboro and North Carolina (Member, Sections on: Business Law, Wills and Estates; Real Property) Bar Associations; North Carolina Academy of Trial Lawyers. [With U.S. Army, 1963-1966]. ***PRACTICE AREAS:*** Real Estate Law; Commercial Law; Collections; Probate and Estate; Appellate Practice; Corporate Law; Bankruptcy. **Email:** sarahgbarker@bellsouth.net

STANLEY E. SPECKHARD, born Carrollton, Illinois, July 6, 1949; admitted to bar, 1975, North Carolina and U.S. District Court, Middle District of North Carolina; 1982, U.S. Court of Appeals, Fourth Circuit. *Education:* University of North Carolina (B.A., 1971; J.D., 1975). Phi Delta Phi; Phi Beta Kappa. Certified Superior Court and Workers Compensation Mediator.*Member:* Greensboro and North Carolina (Member, Sections on: Civil Litigation) Bar Associations; North Carolina Academy of Trial Lawyers; The Association of Trial Lawyers of America. ***PRACTICE AREAS:*** Civil Litigation; Medical Malpractice; Personal Injury Law; Products Liability Law; Worker's Compensation; Wrongful Death. **Email:** sspeckhard@bellsouth.net

---

ANDERSON KORZEN & ASSOCIATES, P.C.

GREENSBORO, NORTH CAROLINA

(See Kernersville)

Complex Litigation and Trials, Long Term Care and Nursing Home Abuse and Neglect, Serious Personal Injuries, Wrongful Death, Medical Malpractice, Aviation Torts and Air Crash Disasters, Serious Professional Negligence, Tractor Trailer Collisions, Product Liability.

BAILEY & THOMAS, P.A.

GREENSBORO, NORTH CAROLINA

(See Winston-Salem)

General Civil and Criminal Practice. Trials in all State and Federal Courts. Probate, Real Estate and Property Law. Wills, Trust and Estate Planning, Corporation, Insurance Law and Personal Injury Law.

BARRON & BERRY, L.L.P.

Established in 1991

301 SOUTH GREENE STREET, SUITE 310
GREENSBORO, NORTH CAROLINA 27401
Telephone: 336-274-4782
Fax: 336-379-8592
URL: http://www.barronberry.com
Email: barronberry@bellsouth.net
URL: http://www.lawyers.com/barronberrylaw

Mailing Address: P.O. Box 2370, Greensboro, NC 27402-2370

Personal Injury, Medical Malpractice, Automobile Accidents, Wrongful Death, Products Liability and Brain Injury.

VANCE BARRON, JR., born Gainesville, Georgia, May 22, 1943; admitted to bar, 1973, North Carolina. *Education:* University of North Carolina at Chapel Hill (B.A., with honors, 1965; J.D., with honors, 1973). Phi Beta Kappa; Order of the Coif. Named to 2003 Legal Elite in Litigation, Business North Carolina magazine. Editor-in-Chief, North Carolina Law Review, 1972-1973. Author: "A Probing View of Cross-Examination," Litigation, Fall, 1989; "How Do I Evade Thee? Let Me Count the Ways," Litigation, Spring, 1990; "The Poisoned Question," Litigation, Summer, 1990. John Motley Morehead Fellow. *Member:* Greensboro, North Carolina and American Bar Associations; North Carolina State Bar; North Carolina Academy of Trial Lawyers; The Association of Trial Lawyers of America; Guilford Inn of Court (President, 2003—). [LCDR, U.S. Navy, active duty, 1968-1970]. ***PRACTICE AREAS:*** Personal Injury; Medical Malpractice; Products Liability. ***Email:*** vance.barron@barronberry.com

FREDERICK L. BERRY, born Greensboro, North Carolina, July 24, 1956; admitted to bar, 1981, North Carolina. *Education:* Wake Forest University (B.A., cum laude, 1978; J.D., 1981). *Member:* Greensboro and North Carolina (Member, Sections on: Real Estate; Litigation) Bar Associations; North Carolina State Bar; North Carolina Academy of Trial Lawyers. ***PRACTICE AREAS:*** Personal Injury; Medical Malpractice; Products Liability; Wrongful Death; Insurance Defense; Brain Injury. ***Email:*** fred.berry@barronberry.com

ASSOCIATE

JAMIE LISA FORBES, born Laramie, Wyoming, July 14, 1955; admitted to bar, 2001, North Carolina. *Education:* University of Colorado at Boulder (B.A., with honors, 1977); University of North Carolina at Chapel Hill (J.D., 2001). Phi Beta Kappa. *Member:* Greensboro and North Carolina Bar Associations; Guilford County Association of Women Attorneys; North Carolina Association of Women Attorneys. ***PRACTICE AREAS:*** Personal Injury; Civil Litigation; Employment Law; Medical Malpractice. ***Email:*** jamie.forbes@barronberry.com

MATHEW E. BATES, P.A.

Established in 1984

5501 ADAMS FARM LANE, SUITE D
P.O. BOX 7219
GREENSBORO, NORTH CAROLINA 27417
Telephone: 336-854-9500
Fax: 336-854-9566
URL: http://www.lawyers.com/mathewbates

Taxation, Securities Arbitration, Commodities Arbitration, Bankruptcy, Business, Corporate and Wills, Chapter 7 Bankruptcy, Chapter 13 Bankruptcy.

FIRM PROFILE: Matthew E. Bates, P.A., former Senior Trial Attorney for the I.R.S., has been in private practice since 1984 and represents taxpayers in tax matters, investors with security claims and handles businesses and individuals in bankruptcy.

MATHEW E. BATES, born Woodbury, New Jersey, October 2, 1948; admitted to bar, 1974, North Carolina, U.S. District Court, Middle District of North Carolina and U.S. Tax Court; 1985, U.S. Court of Federal Claims; 1988, U.S. Court of Appeals, Fourth Circuit; 1991, U.S. District Court, Eastern District of North Carolina. *Education:* Pfeiffer College (A.B., magna cum laude, 1971); Wake Forest University (J.D., cum laude, 1974). Phi Alpha Delta. Staff Member, Wake Forest Law Review, 1972-1974. Auditor, A.M. Pullen & Company, CPAs, 1970. Trial Attorney, District Counsels Office, Internal Revenue Service, 1974-1984. *Member:* North Carolina Bar Association (Member, Tax Section); North Carolina State Bar; Public Investors Arbitration Bar Association. ***REPORTED CASES:*** Alonso v. Commissioner, 78 T.C. 577 (1982); Shelby U.S. Distributors, Inc. v. Commissioner, 71 T.C. 874 (1979); Hughes v. Commissioner, 65 T.C. 566 (1975); Estate of Sullivan v. Commissioner, T.C. Memo. 1983-185. ***PRACTICE AREAS:*** Taxation; Securities; Bankruptcy; Business Law; Corporate Law; Wills; Trusts and Estates.

WALTER L. BEAVERS

326 SOUTH EUGENE STREET
GREENSBORO, NORTH CAROLINA 27401
Telephone: 336-275-7601
Facsimile: 336-275-2009
Email: wbeavers@bellsouth.net

Practice Limited to Intellectual Property Law including Patent, Trademark, Copyright and Unfair Competition.

(This Listing Continued)

WALTER L. BEAVERS, born Winston-Salem, North Carolina, March 23, 1938; admitted to bar, 1972, North Carolina; registered to practice before U.S. Patent and Trademark Office. *Education:* Guilford College (B.S., Chemistry, 1963); Memphis State University (J.D., 1972). *Member:* North Carolina State Bar; American Intellectual Property Law Association. [With USMC, active duty, 1956-1958]

BENSON & MARSHALL, L.L.P.

221 COMMERCE PLACE
GREENSBORO, NORTH CAROLINA 27401
Telephone: 336-691-1044
Fax: 336-691-1428
URL: http://www.bensonandmarshall.com

General Civil Practice, Corporation, Commercial, Personal Injury and Insurance, Real Estate, Business Acquisitions, Probate, Wills and Estate Planning, Elder Law, Business, Contracts, Collections, Civil Litigation, Domestic Relations, Family Law, Divorce, Adoptions, Foreclosures, General Practice.

ROBERT A. BENSON, born Portsmouth, Virginia, June 1, 1950; admitted to bar, 1975, North Carolina. *Education:* Wake Forest University (B.A., 1972; J.D., 1975). Phi Delta Phi. Printing Manager, Wake Forest University Law Review, 1974-1975. *Member:* Greensboro and North Carolina Bar Associations; North Carolina State Bar; North Carolina Academy of Trial Lawyers. ***PRACTICE AREAS:*** Civil Litigation; Personal Injury Law; Corporate Law; Domestic Relations; Adoptions. ***Email:*** bbenson@btitelecom.net

MICHAEL T. MARSHALL, born Manhattan, New York, March 29, 1949; admitted to bar, 1974, North Carolina and U.S. District Court, Middle District of North Carolina. *Education:* University of North Carolina (A.B., 1971); Memphis State University (J.D., 1974). *Member:* Greensboro and North Carolina (Member, Sections on: Real Estate; Health Law) Bar Associations; North Carolina State Bar; North Carolina Academy of Trial Lawyers. ***PRACTICE AREAS:*** Real Estate Law; Collections; Medical Collections; Hospital Collections; Civil Litigation; Personal Injury Law; Automobile Accidents and Injuries; Trusts and Estates; Business Law. ***Email:*** mmarshall@btitelecom.net

JEFFREY S. BERMAN

216 COMMERCE PLACE
GREENSBORO, NORTH CAROLINA 27401
Telephone: 336-691-0054
Fax: 336-691-0530
Email: jberman@triad.rr.com
URL: http://www.jeffreybermanlawfirm.com

Family Law, Divorce, Child Custody, Alimony, Criminal Law, Traffic Violations, Driving While Intoxicated, Civil Litigation, Personal Injury, Wills and Estates.

JEFFREY S. BERMAN, born Buffalo, New York, July 7, 1951; admitted to bar, 1988, North Carolina. *Education:* Alfred University (B.A., 1973); University of Maryland (M.A., 1976); University of Toledo (J.D., 1987). *Member:* Greensboro, North Carolina and American Bar Associations; North Carolina State Bar.

BOOTH HARRINGTON & JOHNS, LLP

Established in 1979

239 N. EDGEWORTH STREET
P.O. BOX 3585
GREENSBORO, NORTH CAROLINA 27402
Telephone: 336-275-9567
Fax: 336-373-8747
Email: kdm@nc-law.com
URL: http://www.nc-law.com

State and Federal Civil Litigation, Personal Injury, Elder Law, Estate Planning, Trusts and Probate, Special Needs Trusts, Guardianships, Education and Disability Law.

MEMBERS OF FIRM

ROY M. BOOTH (1911-1995)

E. JACKSON HARRINGTON, JR., born Barnesville, Georgia, August 10, 1944; admitted to bar, 1969, North Carolina. *Education:* University of North Carolina at Chapel Hill (A.B., 1966; J.D., 1969). Phi Beta Kappa; Phi Delta Phi. President, 18th Judicial District Bar, 1986-1987. *Member:* American Board of Trial Advocates; North Carolina Academy of Trial Lawyers; The Association of Trial Lawyers of America. [Capt., USAF, JAGC, 1969-1973]. ***PRACTICE AREAS:*** Civil Litigation; Trusts and Estates; Elder Law. ***Email:*** jharrington@nc-law.com

A. FRANK JOHNS, born Jacksonville, Florida, October 26, 1945; admitted to bar, 1977, North Carolina; 1984, U.S. Court of Appeals, Fourth Circuit; 1985, U.S. Supreme Court. *Education:* Florida State University (B.S., 1968; J.D., 1971). Certified Elder Law Attorney by National Elder Law Foundation. *Member:* North Carolina Bar Association (Member, Sections on: Elder Law, Chair, 1996-1998; Estate Planning and Fiduciary); National Academy of Elder Law Attorneys (NAELA)(Fellow, National President, 1999-2000); American College of Trust and Estates Counsel (ACTEC); National Guardianship Association (Charter Member, National Board, 1988-1991). ***PRACTICE AREAS:*** Elder Law; Guardianship; Disabilities; Education Law; Special Needs Trusts; Fiduciary Litigation. ***Email:*** afj@nc-law.com

R. HARBOUR PARTESOTTI, born Ocean Springs, Mississippi, February 23, 1977; admitted to bar, 2003, North Carolina. *Education:* University of Alabama (B.S., summa

(This Listing Continued)

cum laude and honors, 1999); University of North Carolina at Chapel Hill (J.D., 2003; M.P.H., 2003). Phi Alpha Delta. Delta Omega Public Health Honorary. ***PRACTICE AREAS:*** Elder Law; Guardianship; Special Needs Trusts; Trusts and Estates.

All Attorneys are members of the North Carolina and American Bar Associations.

BRANNON STRICKLAND, PLLC

GREENSBORO, NORTH CAROLINA

(See Raleigh)

Appellate Advocacy, Civil Litigation. Constitutional Law, Criminal Defense, District Court/ Traffic Violations, Divorce, Family Law, Juvenile/DSS, Real Estate.

PETER J. BREVORKA

1515 WEST CORNWALLIS DRIVE, SUITE 101
GREENSBORO, NORTH CAROLINA 27408
Telephone: 336-271-4016
Fax: 336-271-8448
Email: brevorka@bellsouth.net

Probate, Estate Planning, Trusts and Estates.

PETER J. BREVORKA, admitted to bar, 1968, New York; 1976, Florida, U.S. Tax Court and U.S. Tax Court; 1999, North Carolina. *Education:* University of Buffalo (J.D., cum laude, 1968). *Member:* Erie County (President, 1989-1990), Greensboro, New York State and American Bar Associations; American College of Trust & Estate Counsel; National Academy of Elder Law Attorneys. (Board Certified Specialist in Estate Planning and Probate Law, North Carolina State Board of Legal Specialization)

BROOKS, PIERCE, McLENDON, HUMPHREY & LEONARD, L.L.P.

Established in 1897

2000 RENAISSANCE PLAZA
230 NORTH ELM STREET (27401)
P.O. BOX 26000
GREENSBORO, NORTH CAROLINA 27420-6000
Telephone: 336-373-8850
Facsimile: 336-378-1001
URL: http://www.brookspierce.com

Raleigh, North Carolina Office: 1600 Wachovia Capitol Center, 150 Fayetteville Street Mall, 27601, P.O. Box 1800, 27602-1800. Telephone: 919-839-0300. Facsimile: 919-839-0304.

General Practice in State and Federal Courts. Administrative, Antitrust, Banking, Bankruptcy, Bonds, Business Litigation, Communications and Media, Corporate, Corporate Finance, Energy, Environmental, Foundations, Insurance, Intellectual Property, Internet, Labor, Legislative, Mergers and Acquisitions, Probate, Public Utilities, Real Estate, Securities, Taxation, Telecommunications and Trade Associations Law.

AUBREY L. BROOKS (1872-1958)
WILLIAM H. HOLDERNESS (1904-1965)
LENNOX P. McLENDON (1890-1968)
KENNETH M. BRIM (1898-1974)
C. THEODORE LEONARD, JR. (1929-1983)
CLAUDE C. PIERCE (1913-1988)
THORNTON H. BROOKS (1912-1988)
G. NEIL DANIELS (1911-1997)
HUBERT HUMPHREY (1928-2003)

OF COUNSEL

HENRY E. FRYE, born August 1, 1932; admitted to bar, 1959, North Carolina. *Education:* North Carolina Agricultural & Technical State University (B.S., summa cum laude, 1953); University of North Carolina (J.D., with honors, 1959). Board of Editors, North Carolina Law Review, 1958-59. Associate Justice, 1983-99 and Chief Justice, 1999-00, North Carolina Supreme Court. Member, North Carolina House of Representatives, 1968-80 and North Carolina Senate, 1981-82. ***Email:*** hfrye@brookspierce.com

SPECIAL COUNSEL

J. LEE LLOYD, born December 2, 1959; admitted to bar, 1986, North Carolina. *Education:* University of North Carolina at Chapel Hill (B.S.B.A., 1982; J.D., with honors, 1986). Phi Beta Kappa. Staff Member, North Carolina Law Review, 1984-85. Vice President, Investment Banking Division, Goldman, Sachs & Co., 1986-91. ***PRACTICE AREAS:*** Mergers and Acquisitions; Corporate Finance; Corporate Law. ***Email:*** leelloyd@brookspierce.com

MEMBERS OF FIRM

LENNOX P. McLENDON, JR., born February 2, 1921; admitted to bar, 1948, North Carolina. *Education:* Baylor School, Chattanooga, Tennessee; University of North Carolina (A.B., 1942; J.D., 1948). Order of the Golden Fleece. Staff Member, North Carolina Law Review, 1946-48. North Carolina Senate, 1965-69, 1971-73. Counsel, North Carolina Savings and Loan League, 1973-85. Division Counsel for North Carolina for Norfolk Southern Railway Company, 1980—. ***PRACTICE AREAS:*** Civil Litigation; General Corporate Law; Legislative Representation Law. ***Email:*** lmclendon@brookspierce.com

(This Listing Continued)

EDGAR B. FISHER, JR., born August 5, 1935; admitted to bar, 1961, North Carolina. *Education:* Duke University (A.B., 1957; LL.B., 1961); Yale University (1958). Editorial Board Member, Duke Law Journal, 1960-61. ***PRACTICE AREAS:*** Real Estate Law; Estate Planning Law; Estate Administration Law; General Corporate Law. ***Email:*** efisher@brookspierce.com

W. ERWIN FULLER, JR., born July 23, 1938; admitted to bar, 1964, North Carolina. *Education:* University of North Carolina (B.S., 1960); Pembroke College, Oxford University, England (1960-61); Duke University (LL.B., with honors, 1964). Order of the Coif; Phi Beta Kappa. Articles Editor, Duke Law Journal, 1963-64. Law Clerk to Judge J. Spencer Bell, U.S. Court of Appeals, Fourth Circuit, 1964-65. Trustee, 1982-91, and Board of Trustees Chairman, 1990-91, Lees-McRae College. Listed in The Best Lawyers in America, Trusts and Estates. Councilor, North Carolina State Bar, 1987-94. Member, North Carolina General Statutes Commission, 2001-05. ***PRACTICE AREAS:*** Real Estate Law; Estate Administration Law; General Corporate Law. ***Email:*** efuller@brookspierce.com

JAMES T. WILLIAMS, JR., born July 21, 1940; admitted to bar, 1966, North Carolina. *Education:* Wake Forest University (B.A., 1962; LL.B., cum laude, 1966). Associate Editor, Wake Forest Law Review, 1965-66. Trustee, Wake Forest University, 2002—. Listed in The Best Lawyers in America, Antitrust Law and Commercial Litigation. Fellow, American College of Trial Lawyers (Chair, North Carolina Committee, 2002-04). ***PRACTICE AREAS:*** Civil Litigation; General Corporate Law. ***Email:*** jwilliams@brookspierce.com

WADE H. HARGROVE, born March 6, 1940; admitted to bar, 1965, North Carolina; 1967, District of Columbia; 1968, U.S. Supreme Court. *Education:* University of North Carolina (A.B., with honors, 1962; J.D., 1965). Jefferson Foundation Scholar. Board of Editors, Federal Communications Bar Journal, 1968-72. Governor's Council on State Goals and Policy, 1974-79. Special Advisor to United States at the International Telecommunications Union Communications Satellite Conference, Geneva, 1983. Commissioner, North Carolina Milk Commission, 1976-78. Chair: North Carolina Security and Privacy Board, 1976-78; North Carolina News Media-Administration of Justice Council, 1978-80. Board of Commissioners, North Carolina Agency for Public Telecommunications, 1988-00. Member: Governor's Telecommunications Policy Task Force, 1978-79; Legislative Study Commission on Open Government, 1990; Member, Board of Visitors University of North Carolina, 1991-94. Member, Board of Trustees, Peace College, 2003. President: North Carolina Center for Public Policy Research, 1994; University of North Carolina Law Alumni Association, 1991. Listed in The Best Lawyers in America in Corporate Law, First Amendment Law, and Energy Law. ***PRACTICE AREAS:*** Communications Law; Intellectual Property; Corporate Law; Public Utility Law; Legislative Representation Law; Energy. ***Email:*** whargrove@brookspierce.com

M. DANIEL McGINN, born July 30, 1942; admitted to bar, 1967, North Carolina. *Education:* Wake Forest University (A.B., magna cum laude, 1964; J.D., cum laude, 1967). Phi Beta Kappa. Associate Editor, Wake Forest Law Review, 1966-67. Attorney, National Labor Relations Board, 1967, 1970. Listed in The Best Lawyers in America, Labor and Employment Law. Chair, Labor and Employment Law Section, North Carolina Bar Association, 1987-88. Fellow, American College of Trial Lawyers. ***PRACTICE AREAS:*** Labor Law; Employment Law; Civil Litigation. ***Email:*** dmcginn@brookspierce.com

MICHAEL D. MEEKER, born June 13, 1947; admitted to bar, 1972, North Carolina. *Education:* University of North Carolina (B.S., 1969; J.D., with honors, 1972). Order of the Coif. Staff Member, North Carolina Law Review, 1971-72. ***PRACTICE AREAS:*** Partnership Law; Real Estate Syndication Law. ***Email:*** mmeeker@brookspierce.com

WILLIAM G. McNAIRY, born September 20, 1943; admitted to bar, 1973, North Carolina. *Education:* University of North Carolina (B.S., 1965); University of Virginia (M.B.A., 1967); College of William and Mary in Virginia (J.D., 1973). Certified Public Accountant, North Carolina, 1970. Listed in The Best Lawyers in America, Tax Law and Trusts and Estates. ***PRACTICE AREAS:*** Taxation Law; Banking Law; Corporate Finance Law. ***Email:*** bmcnairy@brookspierce.com

EDWARD C. WINSLOW, III, born May 11, 1946; admitted to bar, 1974, North Carolina. *Education:* Davidson College (B.A., 1968); University of Montpellier, Montpellier, France; University of North Carolina (J.D., with high honors, 1974). Order of the Coif. Staff Member, North Carolina Law Review, 1973-74. Listed in The Best Lawyers in America, Financial Institutions Law. Chair, Business Law Section, North Carolina Bar Association, 1987-89. Member, North Carolina General Statutes Commission, 1998—. ***PRACTICE AREAS:*** Banking Law; Civil Litigation; General Corporate Law. ***Email:*** ewinslow@brookspierce.com

HOWARD L. WILLIAMS, born November 14, 1945; admitted to bar, 1972, North Carolina. *Education:* North Carolina State University (B.S., with honors, 1969); Wake Forest University (J.D., cum laude, 1972); George Washington University (LL.M., with highest honors, 1975). Member, Board of Editors, Wake Forest Law Review, 1971-72. Attorney, Office of Chief Counsel, Internal Revenue Service, 1972-76. Listed in The Best Lawyers in America, Tax Law. ***PRACTICE AREAS:*** Taxation Law; Employee Benefits Law; General Corporate Law. ***Email:*** hwilliams@brookspierce.com

GEORGE W. HOUSE, born December 7, 1946; admitted to bar, 1973, Virginia; 1977, North Carolina. *Education:* Davidson College (B.A., cum laude, 1969); University of Virginia (J.D., 1972). Editor, Virginia Journal of International Law, 1971-72. Listed in The Best Lawyers in America, Energy Law, Environmental Law, and Natural Resources Law. Chair, Environment and Natural Resource Law Section, North Carolina Bar Association, 2001-02. ***PRACTICE AREAS:*** Environmental and Natural Resources Law; Construction Law; Civil Litigation. ***Email:*** ghouse@brookspierce.com

WILLIAM P. H. CARY, born September 8, 1949; admitted to bar, 1976, Virginia; 1977, North Carolina. *Education:* University of Virginia (B.A., 1971; M.B.A., 1976; J.D., 1976). Listed in The Best Lawyers in America, Labor and Employment Law. ***PRACTICE AREAS:*** Labor Law; Employment Law; Civil Litigation. ***Email:*** wcary@brookspierce.com

REID L. PHILLIPS, born July 21, 1952; admitted to bar, 1977, North Carolina. *Education:* University of North Carolina (B.A., with honors, 1974); University of Texas (J.D., with honors, 1977). Phi Beta Kappa. Listed in The Best Lawyers in America, Commercial Litigation. Fellow, American College of Trial Lawyers. Member, Board of Governors and Chair, Young Lawyers Division, North Carolina Bar Association, 1985-86. Delegate,

(This Listing Continued)

BROOKS, PIERCE, McLENDON, HUMPHREY & LEONARD, L.L.P., Greensboro—Continued

American Bar Association House of Delegates, 1986-88. Member, Board of Directors, American Judicature Society, 1986-89. ***PRACTICE AREAS:*** Business Law; Class Actions; Complex and Multi-District Litigation. ***Email:*** rphillips@brookspierce.com

ROBERT A. SINGER, born August 26, 1952; admitted to bar, 1979, North Carolina. *Education:* University of North Carolina (B.A., 1974); Wake Forest University (J.D., magna cum laude, 1979). Editorial Staff Member, Wake Forest Law Review, 1977-79. ***PRACTICE AREAS:*** Banking Law; Securities; Corporate Finance. ***Email:*** rsinger@brookspierce.com

JOHN H. SMALL, born January 28, 1954; admitted to bar, 1979, North Carolina; 1982, U.S. Supreme Court. *Education:* University of North Carolina (B.A., 1976); Yale University (J.D., 1979). Phi Beta Kappa. Editorial Staff Member, Yale Law Journal, 1977-79. Listed in The Best Lawyers in America, Bankruptcy and Creditor-Debtor Rights Law. Member, Bankruptcy Specialization Committee of the Board of Legal Specialization, North Carolina State Bar, 2004—. Member, Bankruptcy Section Council, North Carolina Bar Association, 1986-1989. (Board Certified Specialist in Business and Consumer Bankruptcy Law, North Carolina State Board of Legal Specialization). ***PRACTICE AREAS:*** Bankruptcy Law; General Corporate Law. ***Email:*** jsmall@brookspierce.com

RANDALL A. UNDERWOOD, born October 8, 1952; admitted to bar, 1979, North Carolina. *Education:* University of North Carolina (B.S., 1974); University of Virginia (J.D., 1979). Phi Beta Kappa. Listed in The Best Lawyers in America, Financial Institutions Law. Fellow, American College of Mortgage Attorneys. ***PRACTICE AREAS:*** Banking Law; Real Estate Law; General Corporate Law. ***Email:*** runderwood@brookspierce.com

S. LEIGH RODENBOUGH, IV, born September 30, 1955; admitted to bar, 1980, North Carolina. *Education:* University of North Carolina (B.A., 1977; J.D., with high honors, 1980). Order of the Coif. Editor-in-Chief, North Carolina Law Review, 1979-80. Law Clerk to Judge J. Dickson Phillips, U.S. Court of Appeals, Fourth Circuit, 1980-81. Listed in The Best Lawyers in America, Commercial Litigation. ***PRACTICE AREAS:*** Civil Litigation; General Corporate Law; Real Estate Law. ***Email:*** brodenbough@brookspierce.com

MARK J. PRAK, born May 8, 1955; admitted to bar, 1980, North Carolina; 1986, U.S. Supreme Court. *Education:* Duke University (A.B., magna cum laude, 1977; J.D., 1980). Editorial Board, Duke Law Journal, 1979-80. Visiting Lecturer in Public Policy, Duke University Terry Sanford Institute of Policy Sciences and Public Affairs, 1992—. The Best Lawyers in America, First Amendment Law. Chair, Constitutional Rights and Responsibilities Section, North Carolina Bar Association, 2003-04. ***PRACTICE AREAS:*** Communications Law; Civil Litigation; Intellectual Property Law. ***Email:*** mprak@brookspierce.com

JILL R. WILSON, born January 28, 1957; admitted to bar, 1982, North Carolina. *Education:* Hillsdale College (B.A., with honors, 1979); Wake Forest University (J.D., 1982). Staff Member, Wake Forest Law Review, 1981-82. ***PRACTICE AREAS:*** Education Law; Civil Litigation; Insurance Law. ***Email:*** jwilson@brookspierce.com

MARC D. BISHOP, born September 6, 1959; admitted to bar, 1984, North Carolina. *Education:* University of North Carolina (B.A., 1981; J.D., 1984). Phi Beta Kappa. Note and Comment Editor, North Carolina Law Review, 1983-84. Listed in The Best Lawyers in America, Corporate Law. ***PRACTICE AREAS:*** Mergers and Acquisitions; Corporate Finance; Venture Capital; General Corporate. ***Email:*** mbishop@brookspierce.com

JIM W. PHILLIPS, JR., born April 6, 1957; admitted to bar, 1984, North Carolina. *Education:* University of North Carolina (B.A., 1979); Wake Forest University (J.D., magna cum laude, 1984). Listed in The Best Lawyers in America, Commercial Litigation. Editor-in-Chief, Wake Forest Law Review, 1983-84. Legislative Counsel to North Carolina Governor James B. Hunt, Jr., 1993-94, 1996. Member, University of North Carolina Board of Governors, 1997—. ***PRACTICE AREAS:*** Civil Litigation; Legislative Representative Law; Intellectual Property Law. ***Email:*** jphillips@brookspierce.com

MACK SPERLING, born September 23, 1958; admitted to bar, 1983, North Carolina; 1996, Maryland. *Education:* Union College (B.A., 1980); University of North Carolina (J.D., with honors, 1983). Order of the Coif. Note and Comment Editor, North Carolina Law Review, 1982-83. Law Clerk to Judge Frank W. Bullock, Jr., U.S. District Court for the Middle District of North Carolina, 1983-84. Listed in The Best Lawyers in America, Commercial Litigation. ***PRACTICE AREAS:*** Civil Litigation; Intellectual Property. ***Email:*** msperling@brookspierce.com

JEFFREY E. OLEYNIK, born July 22, 1958; admitted to bar, 1983, Texas; 1987, North Carolina. *Education:* College of William and Mary in Virginia (B.A., 1980); University of Virginia (J.D., 1983). Phi Beta Kappa; Order of the Coif. Editorial Board Member, Virginia Law Review, 1982-83. Council Member, 1996-99, and Chair, 2001-02, Bankruptcy Law Section; Council Member, 1997—, and Chair, 2004-05, Antitrust and Trade Regulation Law Section, North Carolina Bar Association. ***PRACTICE AREAS:*** Civil Litigation; Commercial Bankruptcy; Antitrust. ***Email:*** joleynik@brookspierce.com

MARK DAVIDSON, born November 6, 1957; admitted to bar, 1983, Texas; 1988, North Carolina. *Education:* University of North Carolina (B.A., 1980); University of Virginia (J.D., 1983). Phi Beta Kappa; Order of the Coif. Executive Editor, Virginia Tax Review, 1982-83. Chair, Business Law Section, North Carolina Bar Association, 2005—. ***PRACTICE AREAS:*** Corporate Taxation Law; Estate Planning Law; Business Associations Law. ***Email:*** mdavidson@brookspierce.com

JOHN W. ORMAND, III, born June 24, 1962; admitted to bar, 1987, North Carolina. *Education:* Wake Forest University (B.A., magna cum laude, 1984); University of North Carolina (J.D., with honors, 1987). ***PRACTICE AREAS:*** Litigation; Construction Law; Personal Injury; Insurance Coverage; Occupational Safety and Health. ***Email:*** jormand@brookspierce.com

ROBERT J. KING, III, born July 10, 1962; admitted to bar, 1988, North Carolina. *Education:* University of North Carolina at Charlotte (B.A., 1984); Wake Forest University (J.D., magna cum laude, 1988). Articles Editor, Wake Forest Law Review, 1987-88. ***PRACTICE AREAS:*** Civil Litigation; Environmental and Natural Resources Law. ***Email:*** rking@brookspierce.com

V. RANDALL TINSLEY, born February 8, 1958; admitted to bar, 1987, North Carolina. *Education:* Ohio State University (B.S., with honors, 1980); Virginia Polytechnic Institute and State University (M.S., 1984); University of Virginia (J.D., 1987). Council Member, Environmental and Natural Resources Section, North Carolina Bar Association, 1994-97. ***PRACTICE AREAS:*** Environmental and Natural Resources Law; Water Rights; Water and Sewer Utilities. ***Email:*** rtinsley@brookspierce.com

S. KYLE WOOSLEY, born February 8, 1954; admitted to bar, 1980, North Carolina. *Education:* University of Washington; University of North Carolina (B.A., 1976); Stanford University (J.D., 1980); University of North Carolina at Greensboro. Phi Beta Kappa. ***PRACTICE AREAS:*** Environmental and Natural Resources Law; Civil Litigation. ***Email:*** kwoosley@brookspierce.com

FORREST W. CAMPBELL, JR., born April 12, 1955; admitted to bar, 1990, North Carolina. *Education:* North Carolina School of the Arts (B.M., 1976); University of Michigan (M.M., 1978); Wake Forest University (J.D., cum laude, 1990). Notes and Comments Editor, Wake Forest Law Review, 1989-90. ***PRACTICE AREAS:*** Health Care Law; Administrative Law. ***Email:*** fcampbell@brookspierce.com

MARCUS W. TRATHEN, born June 14, 1965; admitted to bar, 1990, North Carolina. *Education:* University of North Carolina at Chapel Hill (B.A., with highest honors and highest distinction, 1987; J.D., with honors, 1990). Phi Beta Kappa. North Carolina Journal of International Law and Commercial Regulation, Member, 1988-89, Senior Staff, 1989-90. ***PRACTICE AREAS:*** Communications Law; Public Utilities Law; Internet Law; Corporate Law; Intellectual Property Law. ***Email:*** mtrathen@brookspierce.com

JEAN C. BROOKS, born June 3, 1947; admitted to bar, 1991, North Carolina. *Education:* Hollins College, University of North Carolina; University of North Carolina at Greensboro (B.A., summa cum laude, 1982); Wake Forest University (J.D., magna cum laude, 1991). Member, 1989-91, and Symposium Editor, 1990-91, Wake Forest Law Review. ***PRACTICE AREAS:*** Corporate Transactions; Securities Law; General Corporate Law; Corporate Finance Law; Banking. ***Email:*** jbrooks@brookspierce.com

JAMES C. ADAMS, II, born March 8, 1966; admitted to bar, 1991, North Carolina. *Education:* University of North Carolina (B.A., with honors and with distinction, 1988); Georgetown University (J.D., magna cum laude, 1991). Phi Beta Kappa; Order of the Coif. Articles Editor, Georgetown Law Journal, 1990-91. Law Clerk to Judge Frank W. Bullock, Jr., U.S. District Court, Middle District of North Carolina, 1991-92. ***PRACTICE AREAS:*** Civil Litigation. ***Email:*** jadams@brookspierce.com

ALLISON M. GRIMM, born February 5, 1963; admitted to bar, 1990, North Carolina. *Education:* University of North Carolina (B.S., 1985); Wake Forest University (J.D., cum laude, 1990). Staff Member, Wake Forest Law Review, 1988-90. Law Clerk to Chief Judge Sam J. Ervin, III, U.S. Court of Appeals, Fourth Circuit, 1990-91. ***PRACTICE AREAS:*** Employee Benefits Law; Civil Litigation; Appellate Matters. ***Email:*** agrimm@brookspierce.com

ELIZABETH S. BREWINGTON, born March 5, 1965; admitted to bar, 1992, North Carolina. *Education:* Davidson College (B.A., 1987); University of North Carolina (J.D., with high honors, 1992). Order of the Coif. Staff Member, North Carolina Law Review, 1990-91. ***PRACTICE AREAS:*** Corporate Law; Business Law; Corporate Finance Law. ***Email:*** ebrewington@brookspierce.com

H. ARTHUR BOLICK, II, born May 1, 1969; admitted to bar, 1994, North Carolina. *Education:* University of North Carolina (B.A., 1991; J.D., with honors, 1994). Order of the Coif. Staff Member, North Carolina Law Review, 1992-94. ***PRACTICE AREAS:*** Civil Litigation; Bankruptcy Law. ***Email:*** abolick@brookspierce.com

J. EDWIN TURLINGTON, born April 25, 1957; admitted to bar, 1982, North Carolina. *Education:* Duke University (B.A., cum laude, 1979); University of North Carolina (J.D., 1982). Law Clerk to Judge Gerald Arnold, N.C. Court of Appeals, 1982-83. Special Assistant/Counsel to U.S. Senator Terry Sanford, 1986-87. Chief of Staff for N.C. Lt. Governor Bob Jordan, 1987-89. Executive Assistant (Chief of Staff) for N.C. Governor James B. Hunt, Jr., 1993-96. Coordinator, Office of former U.S. Senator Bill Bradley, 1997-98. Commissioner, North Carolina Rural Internet Access Authority, 2000-03. ***PRACTICE AREAS:*** Communications Law; Legislative Practice; Government; Technology Law; Corporate Law. ***Email:*** eturlington@brookspierce.com

JOHN M. CROSS, JR., born May 28, 1970; admitted to bar, 1995, North Carolina. *Education:* University of North Carolina (B.S., 1992; J.D., with honors, 1995). Staff Member, North Carolina Law Review, 1994-95, and North Carolina Journal of International Law and Commercial Regulation, 1993-94. ***PRACTICE AREAS:*** Corporate Law; Corporate Finance; Mergers and Acquisitions; Securities. ***Email:*** jcross@brookspierce.com

JENNIFER K. VAN ZANT, born April 28, 1969; admitted to bar, 1994, North Carolina. *Education:* Duke University (B.S., 1991); Wake Forest University (J.D., magna cum laude, 1994). Managing Editor, Wake Forest Law Review, 1993-94. Law Clerk to Judge N. Carlton Tilley, Jr., U.S. District Court, Middle District of North Carolina, 1994-95. ***PRACTICE AREAS:*** Civil Litigation; Labor and Employment. ***Email:*** jvanzant@brookspierce.com

DAVID W. SAR, born August 12, 1971; admitted to bar, 1996, North Carolina. *Education:* Duke University (B.A., magna cum laude, 1992); Yale University (J.D., 1996). Phi Beta Kappa. Articles Editor, Yale Journal on Regulation, 1995-96. ***PRACTICE AREAS:*** Civil Litigation; Intellectual Property. ***Email:*** dsar@brookspierce.com

BRIAN J. McMILLAN, born February 19, 1957; admitted to bar, 1997, North Carolina and California. *Education:* University of Denver (B.S.B.A., 1982); University of California at Los Angeles (J.D., 1996). ***PRACTICE AREAS:*** Civil Litigation; Eminent Domain; Condemnation; Corporate Law. ***Email:*** bmcmillan@brookspierce.com

NATALIE KAY SANDERS, born February 18, 1970; admitted to bar, 1995, Texas; 1999, North Carolina. *Education:* Buena Vista College (B.A., 1992); Duke University (J.D., with honors, 1995). Order of the Coif. Staff Member, Duke Law Journal, 1993-95. ***PRACTICE AREAS:*** Labor Law; Employment Law; Civil Litigation. ***Email:*** nsanders@brookspierce.com

(This Listing Continued)

DAVID KUSHNER, born March 3, 1963; admitted to bar, 1996, North Carolina; U.S. Supreme Court. *Education:* University of North Carolina (A.B., with honors, 1985); Princeton University (Ph.D., 1990); Duke University (J.D., with high honors, 1996). Phi Beta Kappa; Morehead Scholar; Order of the Coif. Senior Editor, Alaska Law Review, 1995-96. Law Clerk to Judge Sam J. Ervin, III, U.S. Court of Appeals, Fourth Circuit, 1996-97. ***PRACTICE AREAS:*** Communications; Intellectual Property; Commercial Litigation; Appellate Practice. ***Email:*** dkushner@brookspierce.com

DEREK J. ALLEN, born June 3, 1971; admitted to bar, 1997, North Carolina. *Education:* University of North Carolina at Asheville (B.A., magna cum laude, 1993); University of North Carolina (J.D., 1997). Chair, Arts, Entertainment & Sports Section, North Carolina Bar Association, 2004—. ***Email:*** dallen@brookspierce.com

CLINTON R. PINYAN, born October 5, 1968; admitted to bar, 1995, North Carolina; 1998, District of Columbia. *Education:* Wake Forest University (B.A., summa cum laude, 1991); University of Chicago (J.D., with high honors, 1995). Phi Beta Kappa; Order of the Coif. Law Clerk to Chief Judge Frank W. Bullock, U.S. District Court, Middle District of North Carolina, 1995-96. ***Email:*** cpinyan@brookspierce.com

TERESA DeLOATCH BRYANT, born September 17, 1968; admitted to bar, 1993, North Carolina. *Education:* North Carolina State University (B.A., cum laude, 1990); Duke University (J.D., 1993). Law Clerk to Justice Henry E. Frye, North Carolina Supreme Court, 1993-94. ***Email:*** tbryant@brookspierce.com

COE W. RAMSEY, born July 5, 1972; admitted to bar, 1998, North Carolina. *Education:* University of North Carolina (B.A., 1994); Wake Forest University (J.D., cum laude, 1998). Order of the Coif. Managing Editor, Wake Forest Law Review, 1997-98. ***Email:*** cramsey@brookspierce.com

ROBERT W. SAUNDERS, born March 3, 1959; admitted to bar, 1987, North Carolina. *Education:* University of North Carolina (B.A., 1982); University of Virginia (J.D., 1987). Daniel Caplin Tax Award, 1987. Editor-in-Chief, Virginia Tax Review, 1986-87. Staff Attorney, Associate Chief Counsel (Litigation), Internal Revenue Service, 1988-89. ***PRACTICE AREAS:*** Tax Exempt Organizations; Public Finance; Taxation; Corporate Law; Estate Planning. ***Email:*** rsaunders@brookspierce.com

ELIZABETH V. LaFOLLETTE, born September 11, 1972; admitted to bar, 1997, North Carolina. *Education:* University of Arizona (B.A., magna cum laude, 1994); University of North Carolina (J.D., with high honors, 1997). Phi Beta Kappa; Order of the Coif. Articles Editor, North Carolina Law Review, 1996-97. ***Email:*** llafollette@brookspierce.com

GINGER S. SHIELDS, born November 11, 1971; admitted to bar, 1997, North Carolina. *Education:* Davidson College (B.A., magna cum laude, 1994); Duke University (J.D., with honors, 1997). Phi Beta Kappa; Order of the Coif. Staff Member, Duke Law Journal, 1995-97. ***Email:*** gshields@brookspierce.com

JENNIFER T. HARROD, born March 28, 1968; admitted to bar, 1997, Georgia; 1998, Missouri; 1999, North Carolina. *Education:* University of North Carolina (B.A., 1991; M.A., 1993); Duke University (J.D., with high honors, 1996). Order of the Coif. Member, Journal of Law and Contemporary Problems. Law Clerk to: Senior Judge John A. MacKenzie, U.S. District Court, Eastern District of Virginia, 1996-97; Judge Joel F. Dubina, U.S. Court of Appeals, Eleventh Circuit, 1997-98. ***Email:*** jharrod@brookspierce.com

CHARLES E. COBLE, born October 30, 1972; admitted to bar, 1998, North Carolina. *Education:* Yale University (B.A., magna cum laude, 1995); Harvard University (J.D., magna cum laude, 1998). Law Clerk to Chief Judge Frank W. Bullock, Jr., U.S. District Court, Middle District of North Carolina, 1998-99. ***Email:*** ccoble@brookspierce.com

CHARLES F. MARSHALL, III, born May 26, 1970; admitted to bar, 1996, North Carolina. *Education:* University of North Carolina at Chapel Hill (B.A., with distinction, 1992; J.D., with honors, 1996). Phi Beta Kappa. Staff Member, North Carolina Journal of International Law and Commercial Regulation, 1995-96. Law Clerk to Judge John D. Butzner, Jr., U.S. Court of Appeals, Fourth Circuit, 1996-97. Attorney, Appellate Section, Tax Division, U.S. Department of Justice, 1997-01. Legislative Assistant to U.S. Senator Mitch McConnell, 2001-02. ***Email:*** cmarshall@brookspierce.com

PATRICK J. JOHNSON, born September 10, 1969; admitted to bar, 1994, Virginia; 1996, New York; 2005, North Carolina. *Education:* University of Virginia (B.A., 1991; J.D., 1994). Managing Board, Virginia Tax Review, 1993-94. ***PRACTICE AREAS:*** Corporate Law; Mergers, Acquisitions and Divestitures; Securities. ***Email:*** pjohnson@brookspierce.com

JOHN M. DeANGELIS, born December 4, 1968; admitted to bar, 1998, North Carolina. *Education:* Harvard University (A.B., cum laude, 1991); University of North Carolina (J.D., with high honors, 1998). Order of the Coif. Staff Member, North Carolina Law Review, 1996-97; Articles Editor, North Carolina Banking Institute, 1997-98. Law Clerk to Chief Judge Terrence W. Boyle, U.S. District Court, Eastern District of North Carolina, 1998-99. ***Email:*** jdeangelis@brookspierce.com

STEPHEN G. HARTZELL, born February 20, 1969; admitted to bar, 2000, North Carolina. *Education:* University of Houston (B.A., magna cum laude, 1991); University of North Carolina (J.D., with high honors, 2000). Order of the Coif. Articles Editor, North Carolina Law Review, 1999-00. ***Email:*** shartzell@brookspierce.com

JESSICA M. MARLIES, born May 23, 1969; admitted to bar, 2000, North Carolina. *Education:* Columbia University (B.A., cum laude, 1993); University of North Carolina (J.D., with high honors, 2000). Order of the Coif. Staff Member, North Carolina Law Review, 1998-99. ***Email:*** jmarlies@brookspierce.com

ANDREW J. HAILE, born August 1, 1972; admitted to bar, 2000, North Carolina. *Education:* Davidson College (B.S., magna cum laude, 1994); Stanford University (J.D., with distinction, 2000). Phi Beta Kappa; Order of the Coif. Staff Member, Stanford Law Review, 1998-00. Law Clerk to Judge Frank W. Bullock, Jr., U.S. District Court, Middle District of North Carolina, 2000-01. ***Email:*** ahaile@brookspierce.com

J. BENJAMIN DAVIS, born October 24, 1971; admitted to bar, 1998, North Carolina. *Education:* Wake Forest University (B.A., magna cum laude, 1994); Yale University (J.D., 1998). Phi Beta Kappa. Managing Editor, Yale Journal of Law and the Humanities, 1996-97. Assistant to the General Counsel, U.S. Army Office of General Counsel, 1998-02. ***PRACTICE AREAS:*** Banking and Financial Services; Communications and Media; Securities; Administrative and Regulatory Law. ***Email:*** bdavis@brookspierce.com

CAROLINE ELIZABETH RITCHIE, born August 20, 1974; admitted to bar, 2001, North Carolina. *Education:* Davidson College (B.A., 1996); University of South Carolina (J.D., 2001). Editor-in-Chief, South Carolina Law Review, 2000-01. Law Clerk to Judge Carlton N. Tilley, Jr., U.S. District Court, Middle District of North Carolina, 2001-02. ***Email:*** critchie@brookspierce.com

KATHERINE A. MURPHY, born August 11, 1958; admitted to bar, 1999, North Carolina. *Education:* State University of New York at Binghamton (B.A., 1979); Brown University (Sc.M., 1981; Ph.D., 1983); University of North Carolina (J.D., with high honors, 1999). Phi Beta Kappa; Order of the Coif. Articles Editor, North Carolina Law Review, 1998-99. Law Clerk to: Judge Sam J. Ervin, III, U.S. Court of Appeals, Fourth Circuit, 1999; Judge William W. Wilkins, Jr., U.S. Court of Appeals, Fourth Circuit, 1999-00; Judge Rebecca Beach Smith, U.S. District Court, Eastern District of Virginia, 2000-01; Judge Robin Hudson, North Carolina Court of Appeals, 2001-02. ***Email:*** kmurphy@brookspierce.com

SARA R. VIZITHUM, born January 16, 1975; admitted to bar, 2002, North Carolina. *Education:* Hope College (B.A., magna cum laude, 1997); University of North Carolina (J.D., with high honors, 2002). Order of the Coif. Articles Editor, North Carolina Law Review, 2001-02. ***Email:*** svizithum@brookspierce.com

C. SCOTT MEYERS, born January 10, 1972; admitted to bar, 2001, Virginia; 2002, North Carolina. *Education:* Virginia Polytechnic Institute and State University (B.A., 1994); George Mason University School of Law (J.D., magna cum laude, 2001). Articles Editor, George Mason Law Review, 2000-01. Law Clerk to Judge William S. Osteen, Sr., U.S. District Court, Middle District of North Carolina, 2001-02. ***PRACTICE AREAS:*** Litigation; Bankruptcy; Environmental Law. ***Email:*** cmeyers@brookspierce.com

JOHN S. BUFORD, born November 10, 1977; admitted to bar, 2002, North Carolina. *Education:* University of Virginia (B.A., 1999); Washington & Lee University (J.D., cum laude, 2002). Executive Editor, Washington & Lee Law Review, 2001-02. Law Clerk to Senior Judge Jackson L. Kiser, U.S. District Court, Western District of Virginia, 2002-03. ***Email:*** jbuford@brookspierce.com

NICOLE A. CRAWFORD, born August 31, 1969; admitted to bar, 2003, North Carolina. *Education:* University of California at Los Angeles (B.A., with departmental highest honors, 1994); Duke University (J.D., 2003; M.P.P., 2003). Staff Editor, Duke Environmental Law and Policy Forum, 2000-03. ***Email:*** ncrawford@brookspierce.com

ALEXANDER ELKAN, born August 27, 1969; admitted to bar, 2003, North Carolina. *Education:* Union College (B.S., 1991); Duke University (M.E.M., 1996); University of North Carolina (J.D., 2003). ***Email:*** aelkan@brookspierce.com

C. ROBIN BRITT, JR., born October 27, 1972; admitted to bar, 2001, North Carolina. *Education:* University of North Carolina (B.A., 1995; M.B.A., 2001; J.D., 2001). Order of the Coif. ***PRACTICE AREAS:*** Education Law. ***Email:*** rbritt@brookspierce.com

KATHERINE J. CLAYTON, born September 17, 1949; admitted to bar, 2004, North Carolina. *Education:* Vanderbilt University (B.E., Mechanical Engineering, cum laude, 1971); Duke University (M.B.A., 1980); University of North Carolina (J.D., with honors, 2004). Managing Editor, North Carolina Journal of Law and Technology, 2003-04. ***Email:*** kclayton@brookspierce.com

JENNIFER ANN GALASSI, born June 3, 1979; admitted to bar, 2004, North Carolina. *Education:* University of North Carolina (B.A., with highest honors and highest distinction, 2001; J.D., with honors, 2004). Phi Beta Kappa; Order of the Coif. Staff Member, 2002-03, Articles Editor, and Member, Board of Editors, 2003-04, North Carolina Law Review. ***Email:*** jgalassi@brookspierce.com

KATHLEEN A. GLEASON, born March 21, 1964; admitted to bar, 2003, North Carolina. *Education:* University of Wisconsin (B.S., 1986); North Carolina Central University (J.D., summa cum laude, 2003). Articles Editor, 2002-03, and Staff Editor, 2001-02, North Carolina Central Law Journal. Law Clerk to: Judge Allyson K. Duncan, U.S. Court of Appeals, Fourth Circuit, 2003-04; Judge W. Earl Britt, U.S. District Court, Eastern District of North Carolina, 2002. ***Email:*** kgleason@brookspierce.com

JANICE L. KOPEC, born September 14, 1977; admitted to bar, 2004, North Carolina. *Education:* College of the Holy Cross (B.A., 1999); Washington & Lee University (J.D., 2004). ***Email:*** jkopec@brookspierce.com

SUSAN M. YOUNG, born February 18, 1977; admitted to bar, 2004, North Carolina. *Education:* University of Wisconsin (B.A., 1999); Wake Forest University (J.D., 2004). Staff Member, 2002-03 and Notes and Comments Editor, 2003-04, Wake Forest Law Review. ***Email:*** syoung@brookspierce.com

DARRELL A. FRUTH, born June 24, 1972; admitted to bar, 2001, California; 2005, North Carolina; registered to practice before U.S. Patent and Trademark Office. *Education:* Massachusetts Institute of Technology (S.B., 1994); University of California at Berkeley (M.S., 1995); Yale University (J.D., 2000). Essays Editor, Yale Journal on Regulation, 1998-99. ***PRACTICE AREAS:*** Intellectual Property Litigation; Environmental Litigation. ***Email:*** dfruth@brookspierce.com

IAIN MacSWEEN, born August 16, 1972; admitted to bar, 1996, Scotland; 2004, New York; 2005, North Carolina. *Education:* University of Glasgow (LL.B., with honors, 1995); Emory University (LL.M., 2005). ***Email:*** imacsween@brookspierce.com

BENJAMIN R. NORMAN, born April 14, 1978; admitted to bar, 2005, North Carolina. *Education:* University of North Carolina at Chapel Hill (B.A., 2000); Wake Forest University (J.D., 2004). Managing Editor, Wake Forest Law Review, 2003-2004. Law Clerk to the Hon. Ben F. Tennille, Chief Special Superior Court Judge for Complex Business Cases, North Carolina Business Court, 2004-2005. ***Email:*** bnorman@brookspierce.com

ELIZABETH E. SPAINHOUR, born July 31, 1973; admitted to bar, 2005, North Carolina. *Education:* Dartmouth College (B.A., cum laude, 1995); University of North Carolina at Chapel Hill (M.A., 2002; J.D., with honors, 2005). Comments Editor, North Carolina Law Review, 2004-2005. ***Email:*** espainhour@brookspierce.com

All Attorneys are Members of the American, North Carolina and Local Bar Associations and The North Carolina State Bar.

(This Listing Continued)

BROOKS, PIERCE, McLENDON, HUMPHREY & LEONARD, L.L.P., Greensboro—Continued

REPRESENTATIVE CLIENTS: ABC, Inc.; ABC-TV Network Affiliates Association; Associated Press; Bank of New York; City of Greensboro; Deloitte & Touche LLP; Electronic News Directors Association; FNB Financial Services Corporation; Greensboro College; Guilford County Board of Education; Hearst-Argyle Television; KPMG, LLP; Leggett & Platt, Incorporated; Lorillard Tobacco Co.; MCNC, Inc.; Norfolk Southern Railway Co.; NC Association of Broadcasters; NC Association of Convenience Stores; NC Bankers Association; NC Cable Telecommunications Association; NC Technology Association; Northstar Travel Media, LLC; Performance, Inc.; Piedmont Triad Airport Authority; Red Hat, Inc.; The Hearst Corporation; The New York Times Co.; Time Warner; University of North Carolina; US Greenfiber, LLC; Weyerhaeuser Co.

BROTHERTON FORD YEOMAN & WORLEY, PLLC

Established in 2004

127 NORTH GREENE STREET, FOURTH FLOOR
P.O. BOX 21327
GREENSBORO, NORTH CAROLINA 27401
Telephone: 336-346-1116
Fax: 336-346-1117
URL: http://www.bfyandw.com

Employment Litigation, Medical Malpractice, Commercial Claims, Business Torts, General Liability Claims, Insurance Defense, Workers Compensation, Insurance Coverage, Business Litigation, Commercial Litigation, Professional Malpractice.

JOSEPH F. BROTHERTON, born Brevard, North Carolina, July 10, 1954; admitted to bar, 1979, North Carolina. *Education:* University of North Carolina (B.A., 1976; J.D., 1979). Phi Beta Kappa. Author: "Recent Case Law Developments," N.C. Adjuster's Report, 1984. *Member:* Greensboro, North Carolina and American Bar Associations; North Carolina State Bar; North Carolina Association of Defense Attorneys. ***PRACTICE AREAS:*** General Insurance Litigation; Insurance Coverage Law; Workers Compensation Litigation; Business Law; Corporate Litigation. **Email:** brotherton@brothertonford.com

ROBERT A. FORD, born Ft. Chaffee, Arkansas, August 9, 1955; admitted to bar, 1984, North Carolina. *Education:* Washington & Lee University (B.A., magna cum laude, 1977); Wake Forest University (J.D., magna cum laude, 1984). Phi Beta Kappa. Member, Wake Forest Law Review, 1982-1984. *Member:* Greensboro, North Carolina and American Bar Associations; North Carolina State Bar; North Carolina Association of Defense Attorneys; Defense Research Institute. [U.S. Army, 1977-1981]. ***PRACTICE AREAS:*** Employment Litigation; Medical Malpractice; Commercial Law; Business Torts; General Liability. **Email:** ford@brothertonford.com

RICHARD D. YEOMAN, born Fort Ord, California, April 17, 1970; admitted to bar, 1997, North Carolina; U.S. District Court, Eastern, Western and Middle Districts of North Carolina and U.S. Court of Appeals, Fourth Circuit. *Education:* Brigham Young University (B.A., 1994); Brigham Young University, J. Reuben Clark Law School (J.D., cum laude, 1997). Member, Brigham Young University Law Review, 1995-1997. *Member:* Greensboro, North Carolina and American Bar Associations; North Carolina Association of Defense Attorneys. ***LANGUAGES:*** Portuguese. ***PRACTICE AREAS:*** Medical Malpractice; Insurance Defense; Workers Compensation; Professional Malpractice; Employment Litigation; Business Litigation; Commercial Litigation. **Email:** yeoman@brothertonford.com

DEMETRIUS L. WORLEY, born Lumberton, North Carolina, August 31, 1972; admitted to bar, 1997, North Carolina; U.S. District Court, Western and Middle Districts of North Carolina and U.S. Court of Appeals, Fourth Circuit. *Education:* Campbell University (B.A., summa cum laude, 1994); University of North Carolina at Chapel Hill (J.D., 1997). Holderness Moot Court Bench, 1996-1997. Member, National Moot Court Team. *Member:* Greensboro and North Carolina Bar Associations; North Carolina Association of Defense Attorneys (Member, Board of Directors, 2004-2007). ***PRACTICE AREAS:*** Medical Malpractice; Insurance Defense; Workers Compensation; Professional Malpractice; Business Litigation; Commercial Litigation. **Email:** worley@brothertonford.com

---

STEVEN P. WEAVER, born Raleigh, North Carolina, October 13, 1976; admitted to bar, 2002, North Carolina and U.S. District Court, Middle District of North Carolina; 2003, U.S. Court of Appeals, Fourth Circuit. *Education:* University of North Carolina at Chapel Hill (B.A., 1999; J.D., 2002). Phi Beta Kappa. Member, Holderness Moot Court. *Member:* Greensboro and North Carolina Bar Associations; Guilford Inn of Court. ***PRACTICE AREAS:*** Business Litigation; Commercial Litigation; Insurance Defense; Workers Compensation; Medical Malpractice; Professional Malpractice. **Email:** weaver@brothertonford.com

MARIAN SMITH KSHETRAPAL, born Greenville, North Carolina, June 6, 1978; admitted to bar, 2004, North Carolina; 2005, U.S. District Court, Middle District of North Carolina. *Education:* University of North Carolina at Chapel Hill (B.A., History, 2000); Wake Forest University (J.D., 2003). *Member:* Guilford County, North Carolina (Member, Workers Compensation Section) and American Bar Associations. ***PRACTICE AREAS:*** Workers Compensation; Insurance Defense; Medical Malpractice. **Email:** kshetrapal@brothertonford.com

BURTON & SUE, L.L.P.

Established in 1996

419 NORTH ELM STREET
P.O. BOX 20083
GREENSBORO, NORTH CAROLINA 27420
Telephone: 336-275-0512
Facsimile: 336-378-1390
Email: burtnsue@bellsouth.net

General Practice. Trials in all State and Federal Courts. Negligence, Automobile, Workers' Compensation, Medical, Legal and Professional Malpractice, Products Liability, Fire, Casualty, Surety and General Insurance Defense Practice.

FIRM PROFILE: Established in 1996, Burton & Sue, L.L.P. devotes 90% of its practice to General Insurance Defense. The firm represents a wide diversity of state and nationwide clients, and is listed in the Bar Register of Preeminent Lawyers.

MEMBERS OF FIRM

GARY K. SUE, born Big Springs, Texas, December 20, 1958; admitted to bar, 1985, North Carolina; U.S. District Court, Middle District of North Carolina; 1993, U.S. District Court Western District of North Carolina; 1997, U.S. Court of Appeals, Fourth Circuit. *Education:* Wake Forest University (B.A., 1981); Mississippi College School of Law (J.D., 1985). Phi Alpha Delta. Member, Mississippi College Law Review, 1984-1985. *Member:* ; Defense Research Institute. ***PRACTICE AREAS:*** Civil Litigation; Commercial Litigation; Products Liability Law; Personal Injury and Wrongful Death; Environmental Law; Insurance Defense.

WALTER K. BURTON, born Bluefield, West Virginia, September 27, 1959; admitted to bar, 1984, Illinois and North Carolina; 1991, U.S. District Court, Middle District of North Carolina; 1997, U.S. Court of Appeals, Fourth Circuit and U.S. District Court, Eastern District of North Carolina. *Education:* Marshall University (B.A., cum laude, 1981); John Marshall Law School (J.D., 1984). *Member:* Defense Research Institute. ***PRACTICE AREAS:*** Civil Litigation; Personal Injury and Wrongful Death; Products Liability Law; Insurance Defense.

ASSOCIATES

STEPHANIE W. ANDERSON, born Burlington, North Carolina, November 2, 1971; admitted to bar, 2001, North Carolina. *Education:* Elon University (B.A., magna cum laude, 1993; M.B.A., with honors, 1998); Campbell University (J.D., 2001). Pi Sigma Alpha Honor Society. Certificate in General Insurance, 1996. Formerly with: Bankers & Shippers Insurance Company; Pennsylvania National Insurance Company; Seibels Bruce Group. **Email:** andersonstephie@hotmail.com

JULIE A. CONNOLLY, born Bristol, Tennessee, November 25, 1977; admitted to bar, 2004, North Carolina. *Education:* University of North Carolina (B.A., 2000); Florida State University College of Law (J.D., 2004). Member, Journal of Transnational Law and Policy. **Email:** burtnsue@bellsouth.net

DESIRÉ E. CARTER, born Sylva, North Carolina, June 7, 1977; admitted to bar, 2004, North Carolina. *Education:* Salem College (B.A., 1999); University of North Carolina School of Law (J.D., 2004). Member, North Carolina Law Review, 2002-2003. **Email:** burton.sue@bellsouth.net

C. MICHAEL DAY, born Mooresville, North Carolina, January 19, 1961; admitted to bar, 1991, North Carolina and U.S. District Court, Middle District of North Carolina; 1993, Virginia; U.S. District Court, Western District of Virginia and U.S. Court of Appeals, 4th Circuit. *Education:* University of North Carolina at Charlotte (B.A., magna cum laude, 1988); Wake Forest School of Law (J.D., 1991). *Member:* Virginia Bar Association. ***PRACTICE AREAS:*** Civil Practice.

All attorneys are members of the Greensboro, North Carolina and American Bar Associations and the North Carolina State Bar.

REPRESENTATIVE CLIENTS: Alliance Mutual Insurance Co.; Allstate Insurance Co.; American Auto Club; CIGNA; Century Mutual Ins. Co.; Crum & Forster Group; Direct Insurance Co.; Encompass Insurance Companies; Erie Insurance Group; Grain Dealers Mutual Ins. Co.; Horace Mann Co.; Lincoln General Ins. Co.; N.C. Farm Bureau Mutual Ins. Co.; Seibels Bruce/Universal Insurance Group; Southern General Financial Group; U.S. Auto Services; Virginia Farm Bureau Ins. Services; Virginia Mutual Ins. Co.

CARRUTHERS & ROTH, P.A.

Established in 1937

235 NORTH EDGEWORTH STREET (27401)
P.O. BOX 540
GREENSBORO, NORTH CAROLINA 27402
Telephone: 336-379-8651
Fax: 336-273-7885
Email: rrk@crlaw.com
URL: http://www.crlaw.com

Business and Civil Trial Practice. Trials in all State and Federal Courts. Administrative, Hearings, Arbitration, Business, Corporation, Partnership, Limited Liability Company, Secured Transactions, Banking, Pension, Profit-Sharing and Employee Benefits, Employment, International, Intellectual Property, Corporate Reorganization, Bankruptcy, Debtors' and Creditors' Rights, Estate Planning, Probate and Trust, Elder Law, Medicaid Planning, Real Estate, Administrative, Environmental, Taxation, Construction, Product Liability, Professional Liability, Negligence, Insurance, Personal Injury and Workers Compensation Law.

FIRM PROFILE: Carruthers & Roth, P.A. was founded in 1937. The firm has a full service civil practice and represents clients throughout the state and region. The firm is divided into three practice groups, commercial real estate and finance, business and estates, and litigation. Four

(This Listing Continued)

of the firm's attorneys and 2 of the paralegals are licensed as Certified Public Accountants. The firm's attorneys are active both in professional organizations and a wide variety of civic affairs. The firm is listed in the Bar Register of Preeminent Lawyers.

JOSEPH T. CARRUTHERS, JR. (1906-1992)

CHARLES E. ROTH (1917-1992)

KENNETH M. GREENE, born Martinsville, Virginia, May 5, 1945; admitted to bar, 1970, Virginia; 1974, North Carolina. *Education:* Washington & Lee University (B.S., magna cum laude, 1967); University of Virginia (J.D., 1970). Order of the Coif; Phi Beta Kappa; Phi Eta Sigma; Beta Gamma Sigma. Member, 1968-1969 and Associate Editor, 1969-1970, Virginia Law Review. Fellow: American College of Commercial Finance Attorneys; Turnaround Management Association. *Member:* Association of Commercial Finance Attorneys. [Lt. USNR, active duty, 1970-1974]. ***PRACTICE AREAS:*** Banking; Secured Lending; Commercial Finance and Factoring; Bankruptcy; Insolvency. ***Email:*** kmg@crlaw.com

RICHARD L. VANORE, born Bronxville, New York, September 25, 1947; admitted to bar, 1973, North Carolina. *Education:* University of North Carolina (A.B., 1969; J.D., with honors, 1973). Order of the Coif. Member, North Carolina Law Review, 1972-1973. *Member:* North Carolina Association of Defense Attorneys; Defense Research Institute; American Board of Trial Advocates. ***PRACTICE AREAS:*** Litigation; Professional Liability; Insurance Defense. ***Email:*** rlv@crlaw.com

KENNETH R. KELLER, born Ames, Iowa, November 17, 1946; admitted to bar, 1974, North Carolina. *Education:* North Carolina State University (B.A., with high honors, 1969); University of North Carolina (J.D., with honors, 1974). Phi Kappa Phi. Research Editor, North Carolina Law Review, 1973-1974. *Member:* North Carolina Association of Defense Attorneys. ***PRACTICE AREAS:*** Employment; Commercial and Construction Litigation; Insurance Defense. ***Email:*** krk@crlaw.com

L. WORTH HOLLEMAN, JR., born Raleigh, North Carolina, April 26, 1948; admitted to bar, 1974, North Carolina. *Education:* University of North Carolina (B.S., 1970; J.D., 1974). Phi Delta Phi. Member, Greensboro Transit Authority, 1995-1997. Member, Greensboro Zoning Commission, 1997-2001. Member, Greensboro War Memorial Coliseum Commission 2001—. ***PRACTICE AREAS:*** Real Property; Zoning, Planning and Land Use; Leasing; Foreclosure; Corporate; Banking; Land Development. ***Email:*** lwh@crlaw.com

JACK B. BAYLISS, JR., born Cocoa Beach, Florida, January 9, 1954; admitted to bar, 1979, North Carolina. *Education:* University of North Carolina (A.B., 1976; J.D., 1979). *Member:* International Association of Defense Counsel; North Carolina Association of Defense Attorneys; Defense Research Institute. ***PRACTICE AREAS:*** Civil Litigation; Professional Liability; Commercial Litigation; Environmental Litigation; Insurance Defense; Workers Compensation. ***Email:*** jbayliss@crlaw.com

HOWARD L. BORUM, born Greensboro, North Carolina, December 24, 1955; admitted to bar, 1980, North Carolina. *Education:* North Carolina State University (B.S., with honors, 1977); Wake Forest University (J.D., cum laude, 1980). Phi Eta Sigma; Tau Beta Pi. Member of Council, 1988-1995 and Chair, 1994-1995, Real Property Section, North Carolina Bar Association. Member, International Council of Shopping Centers. (Board Certified Specialist in Real Property Law-Business, Commercial and Industrial Transactions, North Carolina State Board of Legal Specialization). ***PRACTICE AREAS:*** Real Property; Secured Lending; Foreclosures; Leasing. ***Email:*** hlb@crlaw.com

J. SCOTT DILLON, born Charlotte, North Carolina, November 24, 1956; admitted to bar, 1983, North Carolina. *Education:* North Carolina State University (B.S., cum laude, 1979); University of North Carolina (J.D., 1983). Recipient, Block Award for Outstanding Achievement in Legal Studies, 1983. ***PRACTICE AREAS:*** Employee Benefits; Pension and Profit Sharing; Business; Corporate; Taxation. ***Email:*** jsd@crlaw.com

J. STANLEY ATWELL, born Ft. Bragg, North Carolina, January 16, 1956; admitted to bar, 1984, North Carolina. *Education:* University of North Carolina (B.S., 1978); Wake Forest University (J.D., 1984). Fellow, American College of Trust and Estate Counsel. Business Editor, Wake Forest Law Review, 1983-1984. Certified Public Accountant, North Carolina, 1981. Member of Council, 1988-1995 and Chair, 1994-1995, Estate Planning and Fiduciary Law Section, North Carolina Bar Association. *Member:* North Carolina Association of Certified Public Accountants; American Institute of Certified Public Accountants. (Board Certified Specialist in Estate Planning and Probate Law, North Carolina State Board of Legal Specialization). ***PRACTICE AREAS:*** Estate Planning; Probate and Trust; Corporate; Business; Taxation. ***Email:*** jsa@crlaw.com

KENNETH L. JONES, born Raleigh, North Carolina, June 7, 1960; admitted to bar, 1985, North Carolina. *Education:* University of North Carolina (B.S., 1982; J.D., with honors, 1985). Phi Eta Sigma; Phi Beta Kappa. Order of the Coif. Member, North Carolina Law Review, 1983-1984. *Member:* North Carolina Association of Defense Attorneys; Defense Research Institute. ***PRACTICE AREAS:*** Professional Liability; Medical Malpractice; Dental Malpractice; Commercial Litigation; Bankruptcy; Insurance Defense. ***Email:*** klj@crlaw.com

JUNE L. BASDEN, born Graham, North Carolina, March 15, 1953; admitted to bar, 1986, North Carolina. *Education:* University of North Carolina at Greensboro (B.S., summa cum laude, 1983); University of North Carolina (J.D., 1986). Member, Holderness Moot Court Board, 1984-1986. Order of Barristers. Certified Public Accountant, North Carolina, 1991. *Member:* North Carolina Bar Association (Council Member: Bankruptcy Law Section, 1992-1995; Business Law Section, 1995-1998; Vice Chair, 2001-2003 and Chair, 2003—); North Carolina Association of Certified Public Accountants; American Institute of Certified Public Accountants. ***PRACTICE AREAS:*** Secured Lending; Commercial Finance and Factoring; Bankruptcy; Creditors Rights; Insolvency; Business Law; Corporate Law. ***Email:*** jlb@crlaw.com

MICHAEL J. ALLEN, born Elmhurst, Illinois, February 27, 1960; admitted to bar, 1985, Illinois; 1991, North Carolina. *Education:* Westminster College (B.A., magna cum laude, 1982); University of Notre Dame (J.D., 1985). Thomas J. White Scholar. Articles Editor, Journal of Legislation, 1984-1985; Senior Editor, Notre Dame Journal of Law, Ethics and Public Policy, 1984-1985. Author: "The Role of Actual Confusion Evidence in Federal Trademark Infringement Litigation," 83 Trademark Reporter 267 (1993) and 16 Campbell Law Review 19 (1994); "Who Must Be Confused and When?: The Scope of Confusion Actionable Under Federal Trademark Law", 81 Trademark Reporter 209 (1991), and 26 Wake Forest Law Review 321 (1991). Co-Author: "Application of the Antitrust Laws to the Activities of Insurance Companies: Heavier Risks, Expanded Coverage, and Greater Liability," 63 North Carolina Law Review 321 (1985). ***PRACTICE AREAS:*** Commercial Litigation; Intellectual Property; Antitrust; Insurance Defense. ***Email:*** mja@crlaw.com

GREGORY S. WILLIAMS, born Eglin Air Force Base, Florida, April 20, 1965; admitted to bar, 1990, North Carolina. *Education:* University of Virginia (B.A., 1987); College of William & Mary (J.D., 1990). *Member:* North Carolina Bar Association (Member, Estate Planning and Fiduciary Law Section). (Board Certified Specialist in Estate Planning and Probate Law, North Carolina State Board of Legal Specialization). ***PRACTICE AREAS:*** Business; Corporate; Partnership; Limited Liability Company; Estate Planning; Probate; Trust Law. ***Email:*** gsw@crlaw.com

JOHN M. FLYNN, born Asheville, North Carolina, November 12, 1964; admitted to bar, 1990, North Carolina. *Education:* Wake Forest University (B.A., magna cum laude, 1987; J.D., 1990). Phi Beta Kappa. Member, 1988-1989 and Articles Editor, 1989-1990, Wake Forest Law Review. Law Clerk, Honorable Hiram H. Ward, U.S. District Court, Middle District of North Carolina, 1990-1992. ***PRACTICE AREAS:*** Secured Lending; Commercial Finance; Factoring Law; Environmental. ***Email:*** jmf@crlaw.com

KEITH A. WOOD, born Burlington, North Carolina, July 30. 1965; admitted to bar, 1991, North Carolina. *Education:* University of North Carolina (B.S., 1987; J.D., with honors, 1991). Business Manager, North Carolina Journal of International Law and Commercial Regulation, 1990-1991. Certified Public Accountant, North Carolina, 1994. Board Certified Specialist in Estate Planning and Probate Law. *Member:* North Carolina Association of Certified Public Accountants (Member, Board of Directors, 2001-2004); American Institute of Certified Public Accountants. ***PRACTICE AREAS:*** Taxation; Business; Corporate; Partnership; Estate Planning. ***Email:*** kaw@crlaw.com

CHRISTOPHER J. VAUGHN, born Easley, South Carolina, April 1, 1968; admitted to bar, 1994, North Carolina. *Education:* University of North Carolina (B.S., and Master of Accounting, highest distinction, 1991); Duke University (J.D., 1994). Phi Beta Kappa. Member of Council, 2001-2005, Real Property Section, North Carolina Bar Association. Member of Real Property Section Forms Manual Project. Chair of Real Property Section Legislative Committee, 2003-2004. Vice Chair, Real Property Section, 2004-2005. ***PRACTICE AREAS:*** Real Estate; Secured Lending; Commercial Finance; Foreclosures; Leasing. ***Email:*** cjv@crlaw.com

NORMAN F. KLICK, JR., born Rochester, New York, April 16, 1971; admitted to bar, 1997, North Carolina. *Education:* North Carolina State University (B.A., 1994); Wake Forest University (J.D., cum laude, 1997). Order of the Coif. Member: Wake Forest Law Review, 1996-1997; Wake Forest National Trial Team, 1996-1997. *Member:* Defense Research Institute; North Carolina Association of Defense Attorneys; Association of Trial Lawyers of America. ***PRACTICE AREAS:*** Litigation; Professional Liability; Personal Injury; Insurance Defense; Employment Litigation; Commercial Litigation. ***Email:*** nfk@crlaw.com

---

CAREY A. McALISTER, born Gastonia, North Carolina, December 30, 1974; admitted to bar, 2000, North Carolina. *Education:* Davidson College (A.B., 1997); Campbell University at Buies Creek (J.D., cum laude, 2000). Order of Old Kivett. Omicron Delta Kappa. Member, National Moot Court Team. Membership Editor, Campbell University Law Review, 1999-2000. *Member:* North Carolina Bar Association (Chair, Young Lawyers Division Task Force on Law and Aging; Liaison and Member, Elder Law Council; Member, Estate and Elder Law Section); Guilford County and North Carolina Associations of Women Attorneys; National Association of Elder Law Attorneys; Greensboro Estate Planning Council. ***PRACTICE AREAS:*** Estate Planning; Elder Law; Medicaid Planning; Business Law; Estate Administration. ***Email:*** cam@crlaw.com

J. PATRICK HAYWOOD, born Winston-Salem, North Carolina, June 1, 1972; admitted to bar, 2001, North Carolina. *Education:* North Carolina State University (B.A., History, magna cum laude, 1994); University of North Carolina at Chapel Hill (J.D., 2001). Member, Holderness Moot Court, 1999-2001. *Member:* North Carolina Association of Defense Attorneys; North Carolina Bar Association (Member, Construction Law Section). ***PRACTICE AREAS:*** Construction Litigation; Commercial Litigation. ***Email:*** jph@crlaw.com

CRAIG A. TAYLOR, born Sparta, North Carolina, April 8, 1976; admitted to bar, 2001, North Carolina. *Education:* Wake Forest University (B.A., History, magna cum laude, 1998; J.D., cum laude, 2001). Order of the Coif. Staff Member, Wake Forest Law Review, 2000-2001. *Member:* Greensboro Bar Association (Member, Board of Directors, Young Lawyers' Division). ***PRACTICE AREAS:*** Business Law; Corporate Law; Taxation; Partnership Law; Limited Liability Company Law. ***Email:*** cat@crlaw.com

C. MARK STEVENSON, born Titusville, Florida, August 21, 1973; admitted to bar, 2002, North Carolina. *Education:* University of Central Florida (B.S., 1996); University of Miami (J.D., with honors, 2000; M.B.A., Corporate Finance, 2001); University of Florida (LL.M., Taxation, 2001). Phi Kappa Phi; Beta Gamma Sigma. Member, University of Miami-Business Law Review, 1998-2000. *Member:* North Carolina Bar Association. ***PRACTICE AREAS:*** Taxation; Corporate Law; Limited Liability Company Law; Partnership Law; Estate Planning; Employee Benefits. ***Email:*** cms@crlaw.com

ELIZABETH S. JESTER, born Honolulu, Hawaii, July 20, 1973; admitted to bar, 2003, North Carolina. *Education:* University of North Carolina at Chapel Hill (B.A., 1996); Wake Forest University (J.D., 2003); New York University (LL.M., Taxation, 2004). Member, Wake Forest Law Review, 2001-2004. ***PRACTICE AREAS:*** Real Property; Foreclosures; Secured Lending; Leasing; Like Kind Exchanges. ***Email:*** esj@crlaw.com

RICHARD M. BOTWRIGHT, born Reading, Pennsylvania, December 3, 1970; admitted to bar, 2004, North Carolina. *Education:* Kutztown University of Pennsylvania (B.S., magna cum laude, 1994); University of North Carolina at Chapel Hill (J.D., with honors, 2004). ***PRACTICE AREAS:*** Banking Law; Secured Lending; Commercial Finance; Bankruptcy; Insolvency. ***Email:*** rmb@crlaw.com

(This Listing Continued)

CARRUTHERS & ROTH, P.A., Greensboro—Continued

OF COUNSEL

WILLIAM L. TANKERSLEY, III, born Greensboro, North Carolina, July 14, 1948; admitted to bar, 1974, North Carolina. *Education:* Furman University (B.A., 1970); University of North Carolina (J.D., with honors, 1974). Order of the Coif; Phi Delta Phi. Member, North Carolina Law Review, 1973-1974. Certified Public Accountant, North Carolina, 1976. Member, Board of Directors, Guilford Center, 2002. Treasurer, Family Life Council of Greater Greensboro, 1998—. *Member:* North Carolina Bar Association; North Carolina Association of Certified Public Accountants (Member, Board of Directors, 1997-2002); American Institute of Certified Public Accountants. ***PRACTICE AREAS:*** Taxation; Business; Corporate; Partnership; Commercial Real Estate. ***Email:*** wlt@crlaw.com

All Attorneys are Members of the Greensboro, North Carolina and American Bar Associations and the North Carolina State Bar.

REPRESENTATIVE CLIENTS: *Business:* AC Corporation; American Society of Composers, Authors and Publishers; American South Construction Co.; Burlington Chemical Co.; Colfax Furniture; DLH Nordisk, Inc.; Donathan Properties, Inc.; Glenwood Development Company; H.V. McCoy and Company; Industries of the Blind, Inc.; Kisco Senior Living; Schiffman's, Inc.; *Banks and Financial Institutions:* Branch Banking and Trust Company; Capital Factors, Inc.; GE Capital Commercial Services, Inc.; FNB Southeast; Fleet Capital Corporation; Foothill Capital Corporation; General Electric Capital Corporation.; Lighthouse Financial Corp.; Principal Life Insurance Company; The CIT Group; Wachovia Bank, National Association; Wells Fargo Business Corp. *Insurance:* Amerisure Insurance Cos.; Lawyer's Mutual Liability Insurance Co.; Medical Mutual Insurance Company; North Carolina Farm Bureau Insurance Co.; Northland Insurance Companies; Royal & Sunalliance Insurance Company; Safeco Select Markets; St. Paul Insurance Cos.; TIG Insurance Co.; W.R. Berkley Group.

EWING CARTER III, P.A.

GREENSBORO, NORTH CAROLINA

(See High Point)

Personal Injury, Workers Compensation, Driving While Intoxicated, Driving While License Revoked, Speeding Tickets, Auto Accidents, Wrongful Death, Traffic Violations, Slip and Fall.

AMES C. CHAMBERLIN

FIRST CITIZENS BUILDING
SUITE 430
100 SOUTH ELM STREET
GREENSBORO, NORTH CAROLINA 27401
Telephone: 336-272-6867
Fax: 336-272-7778
Email: ameschamberlin@msn.com
URL: http://www.chamberlinlaw.com

Drug Cases, Drunk Driving Cases, Homicide/Capital Cases, Traffic Cases, Federal Cases; Assault Cases, Expunctions, Probation Violation Cases, Fraud Cases; White Collar Crime, and Domestic Violence Cases.

AMES C. CHAMBERLIN, born Rochester, New York, June 19, 1967; admitted to bar, 1995, North Carolina and U.S. District Court, Middle District of North Carolina; 2004, U.S. Court of Appeals, Fourth Circuit. *Education:* Berry College (B.A., in Psychology, 1991); Campbell University (J.D., 1995). *Member:* North Carolina Bar Association (Criminal Justice Section, 2004); Greensboro Criminal Defense Bar Association (President, 2005); North Carolina Academy of Trial Lawyers (District Representative, Criminal Division). (Board Certified Specialist in State Criminal Law and Federal Criminal Law, North Carolina State Board of Legal Specialization)

PETER CHASTAIN & ASSOCIATES, P.A.

Established in 2001

3705 WEST MARKET STREET, SUITE C
GREENSBORO, NORTH CAROLINA 27403
Telephone: 336-297-0711
Fax: 336-297-4099
Email: pchastain@chastain-law.com
URL: http://www.hudclosingagentnc.com

Real Estate, Commercial Law.

FIRM PROFILE: This firm specializes in Real Estate Title Examinations for Real Property Closings. It represents mortgage lenders and assists them through workout agreements and foreclosure proceedings.

PETER F. CHASTAIN, born Lowell, Massachusetts, October 25, 1945; admitted to bar, 1974, North Carolina. *Education:* University of South Carolina (A.B., 1967); University of North Carolina at Chapel Hill (J.D., 1973). Administrative Law Judge, North Carolina Occupational Safety and Health Review Board, 1985-1986. Closing Agent, U.S. Department of Housing & Urban Development, 1990-1994, 1999-2005. *Member:* American Bar Association. [Lt., U.S. Naval Reserve, active duty, 1968-1970]. (Also, Member, Hahn & Chastain, P.A.). ***PRACTICE AREAS:*** Real Estate; Commercial Law; Creditors Rights. ***Email:*** pchastain@chastain-law.com

---

MOSHERA MOHAMED, born Cairo, Egypt, June 18, 1975; admitted to bar, 2002, North Carolina. *Education:* University of North Carolina at Greensboro (B.S., Economics, 1997); North Carolina Central University (J.D., 2001). ***PRACTICE AREAS:*** Real Estate. ***Email:*** mmohamed@chastain-law.com

(This Listing Continued)

OF COUNSEL

CHARLES B. HAHN, born Augusta, Georgia, February 13, 1947; admitted to bar, 1971, North Carolina. *Education:* Erskine College (B.A., cum laude, 1970); Tulane University (J.D., 1971). Phi Alpha Delta. Member, Board of Student Editors, Tulane Law Review, 1969-1971. (Board Certified Specialist in Estate Planning and Probate Law, North Carolina State Bar Board of Legal Specialization) (Also Member, Hahn & Chastain, P.A.). ***PRACTICE AREAS:*** Corporate Law; Business Law; Taxation; Wills; Trusts and Estates; Probate.

REPRESENTATIVE CLIENTS: U.S. Department of Housing and Urban Development; Investors Title Insurance Co.; Chicago Title Insurance Co.; Commonwealth Land Title Co.; First American Title Insurance Co.; Stewart Title Insurance Co.; Lawyers Title Insurance Co.; Fidelity Title Insurance Co.; GMAC Commercial Mortgage Corp.; Bank of North Carolina; Attorneys Title Insurance Company.

MERCEDES OGLUKIAN CHUT

201 WEST MARKET STREET, SUITE 409
GREENSBORO, NORTH CAROLINA 27401
Telephone: 336-274-0352
Fax: 336-373-0947
Email: MercedesChut@aol.com

Civil Litigation in State and Federal Courts, Appellate Law, Bankruptcy, Business, Local Government, Employment (Employer), Divorce.

MERCEDES OGLUKIAN CHUT, born Edwards A.F.B., California, April 16, 1963; admitted to bar, 1990, Florida; 1991, North Carolina; U.S. District Court, Eastern, Western and Middle Districts of North Carolina and U.S. Court of Appeals, Fourth Circuit. *Education:* Davidson College (B.A., magna cum laude, 1986); Duke University (J.D., 1989). Phi Beta Kappa. Recipient, American Jurisprudence Award, Constitutional Law. Special Counsel, North Carolina Banking Commission, 1992-1994. Partner, Chut & Chut, P.A., 1994-1999. With Office of Guilford County Attorney, 1999-2003. *Member:* Greensboro and North Carolina Bar Associations; North Carolina State Bar; The Florida Bar; North Carolina Academy of Trial Lawyers; Guilford Inn of Court. ***PRACTICE AREAS:*** Civil Litigation; Appellate Practice; Bankruptcy; Business; Local Government; Employment; Employer; Divorce.

CLARK BLOSS & WALL, PLLC

Established in 1968

600 DIXIE BUILDING
125 SOUTH ELM STREET
P.O. BOX 1349
GREENSBORO, NORTH CAROLINA 27402
Telephone: 336-275-7275
Fax: 336-275-7276
Email: cbw@cbw-law.com

General Practice. Trials in all State and Federal Courts. Commercial, Securities, Corporations, Personal Injury, Medical Malpractice, Professional Liability, Insurance, Contracts, Class Actions, and Probate Law.

DAVID M. CLARK, born Greenville, North Carolina, September 1, 1929; admitted to bar, 1958, North Carolina; 1959, U.S. District Court, Middle District of North Carolina; 1961, U.S. Court of Appeals, 4th Circuit, U.S. Supreme Court. *Education:* Wake Forest College (A.B., 1951); New York University (LL.B., 1957). Phi Delta Phi; Omicron Delta Kappa. Managing Editor, New York University Law Review, 1956-1957. Law Clerk to Justice Black, U.S. Supreme Court, 1957-1959. Chairman, Board of Trustees, The Greensboro Legal Aid Foundation, 1965-1968. Director, Legal Services of North Carolina, Inc., 1976-1982. *Member:* Greensboro, North Carolina (Member, Board of Governors, 1982-1985) and American Bar Associations; North Carolina Academy of Trial Lawyers; American Board of Trial Advocates (Member, National Board of Directors, 1997—). ***PRACTICE AREAS:*** Civil Litigation; Securities; Commercial; Personal Injury; Malpractice.

JOHN F. BLOSS, born Leesville, Louisiana, September 12, 1965; admitted to bar, 1993, Virginia; 1997, North Carolina; U.S. District Court, Middle, Eastern and Western Districts of North Carolina; U.S. District Court, Western District of Virginia and U.S. District Court, District of Colorado; U.S. Supreme Court; U.S. Court of Appeals, 3rd, 4th, 11th and District of Columbia Circuits. *Education:* College of William & Mary (B.S., 1987); George Mason University School of Law (J.D., 1993). Author: "Lowering A Mighty FDIC Shield," 18 Legal Times 51 (Sept 25, 1995). *Member:* Greensboro, North Carolina and American Bar Associations; North Carolina Academy of Trial Lawyers. ***PRACTICE AREAS:*** Civil Litigation; Securities Law; Contracts; Commercial Law. ***Email:*** jbloss@cbw-law.com

JONATHAN WALL, born St. Joseph, Missouri, January 3, 1964; admitted to bar, 1994, District of Columbia; 1996, North Carolina; U.S. District Court, Middle and Eastern Districts of North Carolina; U.S. Court of Appeals, Fourth Circuit. *Education:* Duke University (B.A., 1986); Washington & Lee University (J.D., 1989). Author: "Verdicts & Settlements," Trial Briefs, 1998—. *Member:* Greensboro (Member, Young Lawyers Board, 1999-2000) and North Carolina (Ed., Labor and Employment, 2002—) Bar Associations; North Carolina Academy of Trial Lawyers (Member, Board of Governors, 2003—; Member, 1998— and Chair, 2003—, Publications Committee); Association of Trial Lawyers of America (NLD Board of Governors, 2002—). ***PRACTICE AREAS:*** Medical Malpractice; Commercial Law; Labor and Employment; Civil Litigation; Personal Injury. ***Email:*** jwall@cbw-law.com

REPRESENTATIVE CLIENTS: Johnson Controls, Inc.; Hampshire Hosiery, Inc.; GBF, Inc.; Wall Industries, Inc.; Binswanger Glass Co. (ACI America); Guardian Life Insurance Co.; Filtration Technology, Inc.; Carolina Cast Stone Co.; Chicago Grain & Financial Futures Co.; Tubular Textile Machinery Corp.; ITT Corporation.
APPROVED ATTORNEYS FOR: Lawyers Title Insurance Corp.; Jefferson Title Insurance Co.
REFERENCE: Branch Banking and Trust Co.

CLIFFORD CLENDENIN O'HALE & JONES, LLP

Established in 1971

415 WEST FRIENDLY AVENUE
GREENSBORO, NORTH CAROLINA 27401
Telephone: 336-378-1212
Fax: 336-333-9820
Email: frontdesk@ccojcd.com
URL: http://www.ccojcd.com
Email: coachclendenin@aol.com
URL: http://www.greensborocriminallawyers.com

General Civil and Criminal Practice. Trials in all State and Federal Courts. Personal Injury, Wrongful Death, Products Liability, Workers Compensation, Criminal Trials and Appeals, Federal Forfeitures, Grand Jury Practice, Criminal Law, Drugs and Narcotics, Fraud and Deceit, Money Laundering, white Collar Crime, Occupational Safety and Health, Workers Compensation, Premises Liability, Personal Injury, Criminal Appeals, Capital Offenses.

FIRM PROFILE: Clifford Clendenin O'Hale & Jones, LLP is a firm of four trial lawyers (all partners), with eight support staff, limiting its practice to criminal defense, personal injury, wrongful death and workers compensation. The firm was founded in 1973 by R. Walton McNairy and Locke T. Clifford, classmates at the UNC School of Law, Class of 1967.

Locke Clifford, Robert O'Hale and Walter Jones are certified by the North Carolina State Bar as specialists in Federal and State Criminal Law. They represent individuals and corporate clients in matters ranging from sex offenses, financial crimes, arson, federal grand jury and regulatory agency investigations, drug conspiracies, federal tax and bankruptcy fraud, record expunctions, probation and parole violations, death penalty homicides to DWI and traffic tickets.

Harry Clendenin, who became a partner in 1975, specializes in representing claimants in workers compensation matters and in personal injury and wrongful death claims, and is chair of the Workers' Compensation Section of the North Carolina Bar Association.

Robert O'Hale also represents personal injury claimants.

The firm members have deep involvement in community affairs including Boy Scouts, church activities, Class A professional baseball ownership, coaching high school and youth baseball, and girls' soccer.

Foreign language translation is provided under a firm contract with a professional translator in Spanish, French, German and Italian. Korean language translation is also available.

MEMBERS OF FIRM

LOCKE T. CLIFFORD, born Cincinnati, Ohio, July 27, 1942; admitted to bar, 1967, North Carolina; 1970, Georgia. *Education:* University of North Carolina at Chapel Hill (A.B., 1964; J.D., 1967). Listed in, Best Lawyers in America, published by Woodward/White, Inc., 1989-2004 editions. Assistant Solicitor, 18th Judicial District, 1971-1973. Member, Board of Directors, National Association of Counsel for Children, 1978. Member, North Carolina Sentencing and Policy Advisory Commission, 1997—. Member, North Carolina Legal Elite, Business North Carolina, 2004. *Member:* Greensboro Bar Association (President, Young Lawyers Section, 1973-1974; Member: Board of Directors, 1995-1996; Quality of Life Committee, 1996-1997; President Elect, 1999-2000; President, 2000-2001), 18th Judicial District Bar Association (President, 1998-1999; Nominating Committee Chairman, 2001-2002; Member, Fee Dispute Resolution Committee, 2002-2003); North Carolina State Bar (Member, Criminal Law Certification Specialization Committee, 2001-2002); American Bar Association (Member, Criminal Justice Section, 1973—); American Board of Trial Advocates (Associate, 1999—); Federal Bar Advisory Committee; Guilford Inn of Court, American Inns of Court (Master of the Bench). Fellow, American College of Trial Lawyers (Member: Federal Criminal Procedure Committee, 1999-2003; NC State Committee, 2000-2004). [Infantry Officer, U.S. Army, 1969-1971]. (Board Certified Specialist in Criminal Law, North Carolina State Board of Legal Specialization). ***REPORTED CASES:*** State v. Watkins, 11 N.C.App.766, 433 S.E.2d 817 (1993); 337 N.C. 437, 446 S.E .2d 67 (1994); 120 N.C.App.804, 463 S.E.2d. 802 (1995). ***PRACTICE AREAS:*** Bank Fraud; Check Fraud; Credit Fraud; Juvenile Criminal Law; Fifth Amendment Law; Fourth Amendment Law; Criminal Law; Assault and Battery; Burglary; Capital Offenses; Civil Forfeiture; Criminal Conspiracy; Criminal Defense; Criminal Fraud; Criminal Investigation; Criminal Prosecution; Extortion; Federal Criminal Law; Felonies; Forensic Accounting; Forgery; Grand Jury Practice; Habeas Corpus; Homicide; Mail Fraud; Manslaughter; Misdemeanors; Murder; Post-Conviction Remedies; Search and Seizure; Sex Crimes; Sexual Assault; Theft; Weapons Charges; Drugs and Narcotics; Civil Drug Forfeiture; Controlled Substances Law; Drug Crimes; Drug Forfeiture; Drug Trafficking; Financial Fraud; Fraud and Deceit; Health Care Fraud; Insurance Fraud; Money Laundering; Securities Fraud; Tax Fraud; White Collar Crime; Embezzlement; White Collar Criminal Defense; White Collar Fraud. ***Email:*** frontdesk@ccojcd.com

HARRY H. CLENDENIN, III, born Raleigh, North Carolina, January 6, 1945; admitted to bar, 1970, North Carolina. *Education:* North Carolina State University (B.A., 1967); Wake Forest University (J.D., with honors, 1970). Phi Delta Phi. Recipient, American Jurisprudence Awards in: Civil Procedure; Mortgages; Negotiable Instruments. Recipient, West Publishing Company Awards in: Evidence; Insurance; Administrative Law. Recipient, Corpus Juris Secundum Award; Constitutional Law. Associate Editor, Wake Forest Law Review, 1969-1970. Member, Wake Forest Law Alumni Council, 1990-1993. Member, Board of Directors, Greensboro Palomino Baseball, Inc., 1992-1994. Junior Varsity Baseball Coach, 1996— and Assistant Varsity Baseball Coach, 1996—, Walter Hines Page High School. Baseball Coach, Pony System, 1986-1998. Girls' Soccer Coach, Greensboro Youth Soccer Association, 1978-1991. North Carolina Industrial Commission approved Mediator. *Member:* Greensboro (President, Young Lawyers Section, 1974-1975; Co-Chair, Membership and Professional Relations Committee, 1999-2000 and 2000-2001), North Carolina (State Coordinator, Young Lawyers Section, 1974-1975; Member, Workers' Compensation Committee, Litigation Section, 1980-1995; Workers Compensation Section (Membership Chair, 1999-2000), 1995—; Workers Compensation Section Council (Section Vice Chair, 2001-2002; Section Chair, 2002-2003), 1997—; Chairman, Products Liability Committee, Litigation Section, 1983-1985; Chairman, Membership Committee, Litigation Section, 1985; Member, Task Force on Dispute Resolution, 1985; Member, Council, Litigation Section, 1984-1987) and American Bar Associations; North Carolina Academy of Trial Lawyers (Member, Workers' Compensation Section, 1982—; Membership Committee, 2000-2001); The Association of Trial Lawyers of America; North Carolina Industrial Commission approved Mediator. ***REPORTED CASES:*** Poe v. Acme Builders, 69 NC App. 147, 316 SE 2nd 338 (1984); Barham v. Foodworld, 300 NC 329, 266 SE 2nd 676 (1980); Roberts v. Burlington Industries, 321 NC 150, 364 SE 2nd 417 (1988). ***PRACTICE AREAS:*** Occupational Safety and Health; Industrial Accidents; Occupational Disease; Occupational Injuries; Personal Injury; Accidents; Automobile Accidents and Injuries; Automobile Negligence; Bodily Injury; Brain Injury; Carpal Tunnel Syndrome; Catastrophic Injury; Commercial Vehicle Liability; Cumulative Trauma; Electrical Injury; Head Injury; Motor Vehicle Accidents and Injuries; Motorcycle Accidents; Pedestrian Injuries; Personal Injury Mediation; Plaintiffs Personal Injury; Repetitive Stress Injury; Slip and Fall; Third Party Wrongful Death; Wrongful Death; Premises Liability; Negligent Security; Workers Compensation; Industrial Insurance; Workers Compensation Mediation. ***Email:*** coachclendenin@aol.com

ROBERT O'HALE, born Cleveland, Ohio, April l, 1954; admitted to bar, 1981, North Carolina; 1992, U.S. District Court, Middle District of North Carolina. *Education:* University of North Carolina (B.A., 1976); Campbell University (J.D., 1981). Member, Campbell University Law Review. Assistant District Attorney, 1982-1987. Assistant Public Defender, 1987-1992. *Member:* Greensboro Bar Association; Greensboro Criminal Defense Lawyers. (Board Certified Specialist in Criminal Law, North Carolina State Board of Legal Specialization). ***REPORTED CASES:*** State v. Fleming, 106 N.C.App.165, 415 S.E. 2d. 782 (1992). ***PRACTICE AREAS:*** Assault and Battery; Burglary; Civil Forfeiture; Crime Victims Compensation; Criminal Antitrust; Criminal Appeals; Criminal Conspiracy; Criminal Defense; Criminal Forfeiture; Criminal Fraud; Criminal Investigation; Criminal Prosecution; Death Penalty; Drivers License Suspension; Driving While Intoxicated; Electronic Surveillance; Extortion; Extradition; Federal Criminal Law; Felonies; Forensic Accounting; Forensic DNA; Forensic Medicine; Forensic Science; Forgery; Grand Jury Practice; Habeas Corpus; Homicide; International Criminal Law; International Extradition; Mail Fraud; Malicious Prosecution; Manslaughter; Misdemeanors; Murder; Parole and Probation; Post-Conviction Remedies; Search and Seizure; Sex Crimes; Sexual Assault; Theft; Traffic Violations; Victims Rights; Weapons Charges; Wiretapping; Personal Injury; Automobile Accidents and Injuries; Wrongful Death. ***Email:*** robert@ccojcd.com

WALTER L. JONES, born Radford, Virginia, September 28, 1964; admitted to bar, 1989, North Carolina; 1992, U.S. District Court, Middle District of North Carolina. *Education:* North Carolina State University (B.A., 1986); Campbell University (J.D., 1989). Member: Campbell Law Observer; Campbell Law Review; Dean Robert Bryan Senate of Delta Theta Phi Trial Team. Law Clerk to the Honorable P. Trevor Sharp, U.S. Magistrate Judge, 1989-1991. Assistant Public Defender, 1991-1996. *Member:* Greensboro and North Carolina Bar Associations; Greensboro Criminal Defense Lawyers (Board of Directors, 1993—; President, 2000); North Carolina Academy of Trial Lawyers. ***REPORTED CASES:*** State v. Bunning 346 NC 253, 485 SE 2d 290 (1997); State v. Pearson 348 NC 272 498 SE 2d 599 (1998); United States v. Hassouneh 199 F3d 175 (4th Cir 2000); Williams v. Currie, 103 fSupp 2d 858 (MDNC 2000). ***PRACTICE AREAS:*** Computer Crime; Fifth Amendment Law; Fourth Amendment Law; Criminal Law; Assault and Battery; Burglary; Capital Offenses; Criminal Appeals; Criminal Defense; Death Penalty; Extortion; Federal Criminal Law; Felonies; Forgery; Grand Jury Practice; Habeas Corpus; Homicide; Mail Fraud; Manslaughter; Misdemeanors; Murder; Post-Conviction Remedies; Search and Seizure; Sex Crimes; Sexual Assault; Theft; Traffic Violations; Weapons Charges; Drugs and Narcotics; Drug Crimes; Drug Trafficking; Fraud and Deceit; Internet Crimes; Law Enforcement Officers Rights; Embezzlement. ***Email:*** walt@ccojcd.com

All attorneys are Members of the North Carolina State Bar.

COLTRANE AYCOCK & OVERFIELD, PLLC

106 NORTH ELM STREET, SUITE 300
GREENSBORO, NORTH CAROLINA 27401
Telephone: 336-279-8707
Fax: 336-279-8849

Family Law, Civil Litigation, Equitable Distribution, Domestic Relations, Real Property, Creditors Rights, Collections, Corporate Law, Business Law, Trusts and Estates.

CHARLES W. COLTRANE, born May 21, 1963; admitted to bar, 1990, North Carolina; 1991, Georgia. *Education:* University of North Carolina (B.S.B.A., 1985); Wake Forest University (J.D., 1990). Phi Delta Phi. Law Review Editorial Staff. Moot Court Board. Chair, Family Law Council, Family Law Section, North Carolina Bar Association, 2001-2002. (Board Certified Specialist in Family Law, North Carolina State Board of Legal Specialization). ***PRACTICE AREAS:*** Family Law; Civil Litigation. ***Email:*** coltrane@caolaw.com

GEORGE W. (TREY) AYCOCK, III, born Goldsboro, North Carolina, December 1, 1967; admitted to bar, 1994, North Carolina; U.S. District Court, Middle District of North Carolina; U.S. Court of Appeals, Fourth Circuit. *Education:* University of North Carolina (B.A., 1991); Valparaiso University (J.D., 1994). Valparaiso University Law Review, 1992-1994. *Member:* Greensboro and North Carolina (Member, Family Law Section) Bar Associations. (Board Certified Specialist in Family Law, North Carolina State Board of Legal Specialization). ***PRACTICE AREAS:*** Civil Litigation; Family Law. ***Email:*** aycock@caolaw.com

JOHN COVINGTON OVERFIELD, born Nashville, Tennessee, June 17, 1970; admitted to bar, 1995, North Carolina and U.S. District Court, Middle District of North Carolina; 1996, U.S. District Court, Eastern and Western Districts of North Carolina. *Education:* Vanderbilt University (B.A., cum laude, 1991; M.B.A., 1992); Wake Forest University (J.D., 1995). Beta Gamma Sigma. Member, Moot Court Board, 1993-1995. Recipient: Moot Court Board Award, 1995. *Member:* Greensboro, North Carolina and American Bar

(This Listing Continued)

COLTRANE AYCOCK & OVERFIELD, PLLC, Greensboro—Continued

Associations; North Carolina State Bar. ***PRACTICE AREAS:*** Creditors Rights; Collections; Corporate Law; Business Law; Real Property; Wills; Estates. ***Email:*** overfield@caolaw.com

CONNER GWYN SCHENCK PLLC

306 E. MARKET STREET, SUITE ONE
GREENSBORO, NORTH CAROLINA 27401
Telephone: 336-691-9222
Fax: 336-691-9259
URL: http://www.cgspllc.com
Mailing Address: P.O. Box 20744, Greensboro, NC 27420

Raleigh, North Carolina Office: 2626 Glenwood Avenue, Suite 180, 27608. Telephone: 919-789-9242. Fax: 919-789-9210.

Construction Law, Trials, Contract Law, Mediation, Arbitration.

FIRM PROFILE: Co-author, "Construction Damages and Remedies," ABA Book Publishing, 2004. Member, Editorial Board, "Construction and Design Law Digest," Michle Bunerworth, 1986-1998. Assistant U.S. Attorney, Middle District of North Carolina, 1976-1980. Certified Mediator and Arbitrator: NC AOC; NC US Distr. Cts.; AAA Carolinas Construction Mediation Panel of Neutrals; AAA Large Complex Case Program Panel of Arbitrators. Charter Member, Board of Trustees, NC Clean Water Management Trust Fund, 1996-2003.

Member: Greensboro, North Carolina (Founding Member, Construction Law Section) and American (Chair, Forum on the Construction Industry, 1999-2000; Governing Committee, 1995-2001; ABA Standing Committee on Publishing Oversight 2000—; Contributing Editor, ABA Construction Forum Law Journal, The Construction Lawyer, 1990-1997) Bar Associations. Fellow, American College of Construction Lawyers (Board of Governors, 2003—).

RICHARD D. CONNER, born Richmond, Virginia, February 8, 1945; admitted to bar, 1973, North Carolina; U.S. District Court, Middle, Western and Eastern Districts of North Carolina; 1982, U.S. Court of Appeals, 4th Circuit. *Education:* Guilford College (A.B., 1970); University of North Carolina (J.D., 1973). Delta Theta Phi. General Counsel, Construction Management Association of America, Inc., 1982-1999. Chairman, Board of Elections, Guilford County, North Carolina, 1985-1989. Arbitrator, Court Annexed Arbitration Plan for the U.S. District Court, Middle District of North Carolina, 1985—. Member, Greensboro, North Carolina Transit Authority, 1991-1995. Member, Construction Industry Panel of Arbitrators, Complex Cases, American Arbitration Association. Member, Board of Governors, American College of Construction Lawyers. Private Judge, Private Adjudication Center, Duke University Law School. Dispute Resolution Board Member, Public Toll Road Authority. Court Certified Mediator, North Carolina Federal and State Courts. *Member:* Greensboro, North Carolina (Director, Construction Law Section) and American (Forum on the Construction Industry, Division Chair, 1994-1995) Bar Associations. (Resident). ***PRACTICE AREAS:*** Construction Law. ***Email:*** rconner@cgspllc.com

ALLEN HOLT GWYN, born Winston Salem, North Carolina, September 11, 1949; admitted to bar, 1976, North Carolina; U.S. District Court, Eastern, Middle and Western Districts of North Carolina; U.S. Court of Appeals, 4th Circuit; U.S. Supreme Court. *Education:* University of North Carolina, Chapel Hill (A.B., 1971); Wake Forest University (J.D., 1976). Assistant U.S. Attorney, Middle District of North Carolina, 1976-1980. Fellow, American College of Construction Lawyers (Board of Governors, 2003—). Certified Mediator and Arbitrator: NC AOC; NC US Distr. Cts.; AAA Carolinas Construction Mediation Panel of Neutrals; AAA Large Complex Case Program Panel of Arbitrators; Charter Member, Board of Trustees, NC Clean Water Management Trust Fund, 1996-2003. Co-Author: CONSTRUCTION DAMAGES AND REMEDIES, ABA Book Publishing, 2004. Member Editorial Board, "Construction and Design Law Digest," Michie Butterworth, 1986-1998. *Member:* Greensboro, North Carolina (Founding Member, Construction Law Section) and American (Chair, Forum on the Construction Industry, 1999-2000; Governing Committee, 1995-2001; ABA Standing Committee on Publishing Oversight, 2000—; Contributing Editor, ABA Construction Forum Law Journal, The Construction Lawyer, 1990-1997) Bar Associations. (Resident). ***PRACTICE AREAS:*** Construction Law; Environmental Law. ***Email:*** ahgwyn@cgspllc.com

JAMES S. SCHENCK, IV, born Greensboro, North Carolina, July 22, 1955; admitted to bar, 1982, North Carolina; 1983, U.S. District Court, Middle District of North Carolina; 1984, U.S. District Court, Eastern District of North Carolina and U.S. Court of Appeals, Fourth Circuit; 1991, U.S. District Court, Western District of North Carolina. *Education:* University of North Carolina (A.B., 1976; J.D., 1982); Duke University (M.A.P.P.S., 1982). Member, Wake County Citizens Energy Advisory Commission, 1996—. Certified Mediator, North Carolina Superior Courts. Member, Construction Industry Panel of Arbitrators and Mediators, American Arbitration Association. *Member:* Wake County, North Carolina (Chair: Construction Law Section, 1991-1992; Communications Committee, 1996-1998, 2000-2002; Member, Board of Governors, 2002—) and American (Forum on the Construction Industry Division Chair, 2001-2002) Bar Associations. (Resident, Raleigh Office). ***PRACTICE AREAS:*** Construction Law; Administrative Law. ***Email:*** jschenck@cgspllc.com

C. HAMILTON JARRETT, III, born Charlotte, North Carolina, February 19, 1952; admitted to bar, 1983, North Carolina. *Education:* Clemson University (B.S., Civil Engineering, 1975); Mercer University (J.D., cum laude, 1983). Member of Staff, 1981-1982 and Lead Articles II Editor, 1982-1983, Mercer Law Review. *Member:* North Carolina (Council Member, Construction Law Section, 1995-1998) and American (Member: Fidelity and Surety Law Committee, Tort and Insurance Practice Section; Forum Committee on the Construction Industry) Bar Associations; Associated General Contractors of America (Member, Surety Bonding Committee). (Resident, Raleigh Office). ***Email:*** hjarrett@cgspllc.com

(This Listing Continued)

PAUL E. DAVIS, born Brooklyn, New York, April 23, 1957; admitted to bar, 1984, North Carolina; U.S. District Court, Eastern and Middle Districts of North Carolina. *Education:* University of North Carolina (B.A., 1979; J.D., 1984). Co-Author: Fifty State Public Construction Contracting - North Carolina Chapter (Aspen Law & Business); Fifty State Construction Lien and Bond Law, North Carolina Chapter (Aspen Law & Business); State Public Construction Law Sourcebook, North Carolina Chapter, (CCH, Inc.). *Member:* North Carolina (Chair, Construction Law Section, 2002-2003; Council Member, 1996-1999; Newsletter Editor, 1990-1991) and American (Member, Forum on the Construction Industry) Bar Associations. (Resident, Raleigh Office). ***PRACTICE AREAS:*** Construction Law; Litigation. ***Email:*** pdavis@cgspllc.com

JAY M. WILKERSON, admitted to bar, 1992, North Carolina, U.S. District Court, Eastern, Middle and Western Districts of North Carolina and U.S. Court of Appeals, Fourth Circuit. *Education:* University of North Carolina, Chapel Hill (B.S., 1989; J.D., 1992). Staff Writer, Journal of International Law & Commerce, 1990-1992. *Member:* North Carolina (Member, Construction Law Section) and American (Member, Forum on the Construction Industry) Bar Associations. (Resident). ***PRACTICE AREAS:*** Construction Law; OSHA; Litigation; Government Contracts. ***Email:*** jwilkerson@cgspllc.com

---

EDWARD N. POLLARD, admitted to bar, 1993, North Carolina and U.S. District Court, Middle District of North Carolina. *Education:* North Carolina State University (B.S.C.E., 1982); Wake Forest University (J.D., 1993). Law Clerk to Hon. Hiram H. Ward, U.S. District Court, Middle District of North Carolina, 1993-1996. Registered Professional Engineer, 1986. *Member:* North Carolina Bar Association (Member, Construction Law Section). (Resident). ***PRACTICE AREAS:*** Construction Law; Litigation. ***Email:*** epollard@cgspllc.com

OF COUNSEL

JEFFREY B. PARSONS, born Greensboro, North Carolina, November 5, 1962; admitted to bar, 1988, North Carolina; 1989, U.S. District Court, Eastern District of North Carolina; 1992, U.S. District Court, Middle District of North Carolina and U.S. Supreme Court; 1993, U.S. Court of Appeals, Fourth Circuit and U.S. Court of Military Appeals. *Education:* University of North Carolina at Chapel Hill (B.A., with highest honors, 1985; J.D., 1988). Member, Holderness Moot Court, Honor Court. Assistant Attorney General, Property and Construction, State of North Carolina, 1998-2003. Special Deputy Attorney General, Property and Construction, State of North Carolina, 2003-2004. Member, Raleigh Human Relations Commission, 1994-1997. *Member:* North Carolina State Bar; North Carolina Bar Association (Chair, Real Property Curriculum Committee, 2002—; Member: Continuing Legal Education Committee; Construction Law Section; Litigation Section). (Resident, Raleigh Office). ***Email:*** jparsons@cgspllc.com

CONSTANGY, BROOKS & SMITH, LLC

GREENSBORO, NORTH CAROLINA

(See Winston-Salem, North Carolina)

Labor Relations, Employment Litigation, Employee Benefits Law, Wage and Hour, OSHA Law, Business Immigration, Affirmative Action.

COOKE & COOKE, LLP

Established in 1948

SUITE 301 FIRST CITIZENS BANK BUILDING
100 SOUTH ELM STREET
P.O. BOX 187
GREENSBORO, NORTH CAROLINA 27402
Telephone: 336-272-4514
Facsimile: 336-272-4516

General Civil Practice, Trials in all State Courts, Business, Corporate, Limited Liability, Partnership Trust and Estates, Estate Planning and Administration, Wills and Probate, Real Estate, Eminent Domain, Landlord Tenant, Foreclosures.

MEMBERS OF FIRM

ARTHUR O. COOKE (1916-1983)

WILLIAM OWEN COOKE, born Greensboro, North Carolina, October 8, 1917; admitted to bar, 1941, North Carolina. *Education:* Davidson College (A.B., 1938); University of North Carolina (J.D., 1941). Phi Delta Phi; Order of the Coif. Assistant Editor, University of North Carolina Law Review, 1940-1941. Judge, Civil Division, Municipal County Court, 1948-1952. *Member:* Greensboro (President, 1970-1971) and North Carolina Bar Associations; The North Carolina State Bar. Fellow, The American College of Trust and Estate Counsel. [Capt., A.U.S., 1942-1946]

BARDEN W. COOKE, born Greensboro, North Carolina, December 9, 1949; admitted to bar, 1976, North Carolina. *Education:* Davidson College (B.A., 1972); Wake Forest University (J.D., 1976). Member, Wake Forest Law Review, 1975-1976. *Member:* Greensboro (Board of Directors, 2002-2005) and North Carolina Bar Associations; The North Carolina State Bar. ***Email:*** barcooke@bellsouth.net

WILLIAM O. COOKE, JR., born Greensboro, North Carolina, April 13, 1952; admitted to bar, 1978, North Carolina. *Education:* Amherst College (B.A., 1974); Duke University (J.D., 1978). Phi Beta Kappa. *Member:* Greensboro and North Carolina Bar Associations; The North Carolina State Bar. ***Email:*** wocjr@bellsouth.net

REPRESENTATIVE CLIENTS: N. C. Grange Mutual Insurance Co.; Piedmont Triad Airport Authority; Brown-Gardiner Drug Co.; Engineered Plastics, Inc.; Strandberg Engineering Laboratories; ICBT, Inc.

CRUMLEY & ASSOCIATES

2400 FREEMAN MILL ROAD, SUITE 200
GREENSBORO, NORTH CAROLINA 27406
Telephone: Toll Free: 800-288-1529
Fax: 336-333-9894
URL: http://www.crumleyandassociates.com

Workers' Compensation, Automobile Accidents, Nursing Home Abuse, Social Security Disability, Traumatic Brain Injury, Wrongful Death, Slip and Fall Injury, Drug Injury, Product Liability and Consumer Fraud.

BOBBY J. CRUMLEY, born Elizabethton, Tennessee, December 28, 1956; admitted to bar, 1980, North Carolina. *Education:* Appalachian State University (B.A., cum laude, 1977); Wake Forest University (J.D., 1980). Member: Moot Court Board; International Law Moot Court Team. Licensed Real Estate Broker, North Carolina, 1983. Licensed Insurance Broker, North Carolina, 1987. Author: "How to Avoid COBRA's Bite," Journal of International Hospitality Accountants, Fall, 1987. Manager and Attorney, Randolph County, North Carolina, 1982-1984. *Member:* Randolph County, North Carolina and American Bar Associations; North Carolina State Bar; North Carolina Trial Lawyers Association. ***PRACTICE AREAS:*** Workers Compensation (40%, 100); Automobile Accidents and Injuries; Nursing Home Abuse and Neglect; Social Security Disability; Brain Injury; Wrongful Death; Slip and Fall; Drug Injury; Products Liability; Consumer Fraud.

DAIL & LINTON

GREENSBORO, NORTH CAROLINA

(See High Point)

Personal Injury, Automobile Accidents, Slip and Fall, Wrongful Death, Family Law, Adoption Law, Child Custody, Child Support, Divorce, Domestic Violence, Criminal Law, Driving While Intoxicated, Drug Crimes, Traffic Violations, Business Litigation, Trial Practice, General Practice, Workers Compensation.

CHERYL K. DAVID

Established in 1990
5606 WEST FRIENDLY AVENUE
GREENSBORO, NORTH CAROLINA 27410
Telephone: 336-275-0804
Fax: 336-272-2441
URL: http://www.cheryldavid.com
Email: cheryl@cheryldavid.com
URL: http://www.greensboroestateplanning.com

Estate Planning, Elder Law, Asset Protection, Trusts and Estates, Wills and Probate, Guardianship.

FIRM PROFILE: Estate and Elder Law attorney, protecting your future, preserving your past.

CHERYL K. DAVID, born Little Rock, Arkansas, May 8, 1962; admitted to bar, 1987, Maryland; 1989, North Carolina. *Education:* University of North Carolina at Chapel Hill (B.S., 1984); University of Baltimore School of Law (J.D., 1986). Ellin & Baker, Baltimore, Maryland 1986-1987, U.S. Government, Appointed, Administrative Judge Equal Employment Opportunity Commission 1987-1988. Egerton, Quinn & David 1989-1992, David & Quinn 1992-1994. Law Offices of Cheryl K. David (Practice devoted exclusively to Estate Planning) 1995—. Member, Board of Governors, American Academy of Estate Planning Attorneys, 1999-2002. Member, Board of Trustees, Beth David Synagogue, 1999-2002. Member: American Academy of Estate Planning Attorneys, 1997—; National Academy of Elder Law; Greensboro Estate Planning Council. Member, American Bar Association, Probate and Property. Member, North Carolina, Probate and Property. North Carolina Licensed Long Term Care/ Medicare, Insurance. Securities Licensed Series 7 and Series 66, National Association of Securities Dealers. Employee Benefit Group Practitioner ARAG, CLC, GE. *Member:* North Carolina State Bar; North Carolina Bar Foundation.

DAVID AND ASSOCIATES, PLLC

529 COLLEGE ROAD, SUITE G
GREENSBORO, NORTH CAROLINA 27410
Telephone: 336-354-1040
Toll Free: 1-800-856-9927
Email: aeverhart@davidandassociates.com
URL: http://www.wilmingtonpiattorneys.com

Jacksonville, North Carolina Office: 405-B Western Boulevard. 28546. Telephone: 910-219-4878.
Supply, North Carolina Office: Highway 17. 28462. Telephone: 910-754-8465.
Wallace, North Carolina Office: 107 North Norwood Street. 28466. Telephone: 910-285-8777.
Clinton, North Carolina Office: 610 Beaman Street. 28328. Telephone: 910-592-8400.
Winston-Salem, North Carolina Office: 1100-A South Stratford Road. 27103. Telephone: 336-354-1040.
Wilmington, North Carolina Office: 1516 Dawson Street. 28401. Telephone: 910-251-8088.

Personal Injury, Medical Malpractice, Wrongful Death, Products Liability, Workers Compensation, Aviation, Airplane Crashes, Negligence, Class Actions, Maritime Accidents, Boating Accidents, Bicycle Accidents, Motorcycle Accidents, Truck Accidents, School Bus Accidents, Railroad Accidents, Dog Bites, Slip and Fall, Birth Trauma, Brain Injury, Spinal Injury, Head Injury, Catastrophic Injury, Vehicular Homicide, Personal Injury Mediation, Products Liability, Drug and Medical Device Litigation, Product Defects, Automobile Liability, Motorcycle Products Liability, Amusement Park Liability, Hotel Liability, Marina Liability, Sports Injury.

(For complete biographical data on all personnel, see Professional Biographies, Wilmington, North Carolina)

THE DEUTERMAN LAW GROUP, P.A.

Established in 2003
101 SOUTH ELM STREET, SUITE 170
GREENSBORO, NORTH CAROLINA 27401
Telephone: Toll Free: 866-373-1130
Fax: 336-373-1466
URL: http://www.lawyers.com/deutermanlaw
Email: info@deutermanlaw.com
URL: http://www.deutermanlaw.com

Workers Compensation, Auto Accidents, Social Security Disability, Wrongful Death, Nursing Home Neglect, Slip and Fall, Products Liability.

FIRM PROFILE: North Carolina lawyers experienced in handling workers' compensation (injured workers) auto accidents, social security disability, wrongful death, slip and fall, nursing home neglect/abuse, and products liability.

Our attorneys bring 17 years of Trial Law experience. 5 of these years were spent representing insurance companies and employers and over 12 years representing injured people. Mr. Deuterman is a Board Certified Specialist in Workers' Compensation Law. We know how the system works, know how to deal with the insurance companies and adjusters, and our experience allows us to get the most favorable decisions in your case.

Our professional experienced paralegals are multi-lingual, speaking not only English but Spanish and Russian. The Deuterman Law Group is dedicated to providing our clients with not only the best in legal expertise, but excellent customer service. This is why most of our cases come from referrals from previous clients and other attorneys.

We strive to create a pleasant experience for our clients during a difficult time. Our goal is to get the best for you, based on what YOU want and need. We will help you get the best medical treatment and the best cash settlement.

We offer a free consultation and there is no attorney fee unless we win your case.

We are easy to find in downtown Greensboro. We are located in The Law Center Building on the corner of South Elm & Market Street. We offer free parking across the street in the parking deck. Please keep in mind that although we are located in Greensboro, we routinely handle client's cases throughout North Carolina.

Call us toll free today! You have nothing to lose and everything to gain.

DANIEL L. DEUTERMAN, born Highland Park, Illinois, September 22, 1965; admitted to bar, 1991, North Carolina. *Education:* University of North Carolina at Chapel Hill (B.A., 1987; J.D., 1991). Phi Delta Phi. Member, Holderness Moot Court Bench, 1990-1991. *Member:* North Carolina Academy of Trial Lawyers; Association of Trial Lawyers of America; North Carolina Bar Association; Workplace Injury Litigation Group; Greensboro Bar Association; Guilford Inn of Court; National Organization of Social Security Claimant's Representatives. (Board Certified Specialist in Workers' Compensation, North Carolina State Board of Legal Specialization). ***PRACTICE AREAS:*** Workers Compensation; Automobile Accidents and Injuries; Social Security Disability; Wrongful Death; Nursing Home Abuse and Neglect; Slip and Fall; Products Liability. ***Email:*** dan@deutermanlaw.com

JOEL W. DAVIS, born Kissimmee, Florida, June 28, 1974; admitted to bar, 2000, North Carolina. *Education:* Georgia Southern College (B.B.A., 1996); Tulane University (J.D., 2000). *Member:* North Carolina Academy of Trial Lawyers; Association of Trial Lawyers of America; North Carolina Bar Association; Workplace Injury Litigation Group; Greensboro Bar Association; National Organization of Social Security Claimant's Representatives. ***PRACTICE AREAS:*** Automobile Accidents; Social Security Disability; Workers Compensation; Wrongful Death; Nursing Home Abuse and Neglect; Slip and Fall; Products Liability. ***Email:*** joel@deutermanlaw.com

Languages: Spanish and Russian.

DONALDSON & BLACK, P.A.

Established in 1988
208 WEST WENDOVER AVENUE
GREENSBORO, NORTH CAROLINA 27401-1307
Telephone: 336-273-3812
N.C. Toll Free: 800-531-9191
Fax: 336-379-9415
Email: postmaster@donaldsonandblack.com
URL: http://www.donaldsonandblack.com

Personal Injury, Wrongful Death, Products Liability, Worker's Compensation, Professional Malpractice, Nursing Home Neglect and Abuse, Inadequate Security, Eminent Domain, Qui Tam Fraud, Lead Poisoning and Domestic.

FIRM PROFILE: In 1967, Arthur J. Donaldson opened his general civil and criminal practice as a sole practitioner in Salisbury, North Carolina. When Donaldson moved his practice to Greensboro, North Carolina in 1985, he began concentrating in personal injury and wrongful death claims. Over the years that followed, the law firm that eventually became Donaldson & Black has grown to seven attorneys.

(This Listing Continued)

DONALDSON & BLACK, P.A., Greensboro—Continued

As the firm has grown in size, the firm has also expanded the scope of its practice. Along with the firm's longstanding experience in personal injury and wrongful death cases, the attorneys of Donaldson & Black routinely handle cases involving Worker's Compensation, Products Liability, Medical & Legal Malpractice, Nursing Home Litigation, Mass Torts (e.g. asbestos, breast implants, lead, contraceptive implants, diet drugs, medical devices, environmental exposures and pharmaceuticals), Eminent Domain, Insurance and State and Federal Criminal Charges.

From an office in the Piedmont Triad, North Carolina, the firm practices before a number of state and federal courts and administrative agencies in the Southeast.

ARTHUR J. DONALDSON, born New York, N.Y., March 29, 1938; admitted to bar, 1965, District of Columbia; 1967, North Carolina. *Education:* Catholic University of America (B.A., 1960; J.D., 1963). Special Agent FBI, 1963-1967. Prosecuting Attorney, 1967-1968. *Member:* The Association of Trial Lawyers of America (State Delegate, 1975-1986); National Lawyers Association; American Board of Trial Advocacy. ***PRACTICE AREAS:*** Personal Injury Law; Products Liability Law; Inadequate Security. ***Email:*** adonaldson@donaldsonandblack.com

JANET WARD BLACK, born Concord, North Carolina, February 15, 1959; admitted to bar, 1985, North Carolina. *Education:* Davidson College (B.A., cum laude, 1982); Duke University (J.D., 1985). Omicron Delta Epsilon. Charles A. Cannon Scholar in Chemistry and Economics, Lunsford Richardson Honors Scholar, Davidson College. North Carolina Co-Liaison Counsel for Federal Breast Implant Litigation, 1992-1995. Member, North Carolina General Assembly Civil Procedure Study Commission, 1999-2001. Member, North Carolina Business Court Rules Committee. Co-Chair, Access to Justice Campaign for Legal Services, 1998-1999. *Member:* Greensboro Bar Association (Chair: Health Committee, 1994-1996; Chair: Speakers Committee, 1997-1998, 2003-2004; Nominating Committee, 1998-1999), Rowan County Bar Association (President, 1992; President Elect, 1990-1991) and North Carolina Bar Association (Co-Chair, NCBA Task Force on Tort Reform, 2003-2004; Chair, Strategic Planning Committee, 2001-2002; Member, Task Force on Women in the Profession, 1999-2001; Member, Board of Governors, 1998-2001; Member, NCBA Executive Committee, 1998-2000; Chair, Section Advisory Group, 1997-1998; Chair, Litigation Section, 1996-1997; Member, Litigation Section Council, 1994-1997; Vice Chair, Litigation Section, 1995-1996; Co-Chair, Ethics Committee, Litigation Section, 1994-1995); The Association of Trial Lawyers of America (Co-Chair, PAC Task Force, 1998-1999); North Carolina Academy of Trial Lawyers (President, 2002-2003; President-Elect, 2001-2002; Vice President, Membership, 1998-2000; Vice President, Legislative, 2000-2001; Member, Board of Governors, 1995-1998); Joseph Branch Inn of Court (Master of the Bench, 1995—). ***PRACTICE AREAS:*** Personal Injury; Products Liability. ***Email:*** jwblack@donaldsonandblack.com

---

RACHEL SCOTT DECKER, born Mountain View, California, October 20, 1971; admitted to bar, 1995, North Carolina, South Carolina and U.S. District Court, Middle District of North Carolina; 2000, Virginia. *Education:* University of North Carolina (B.A., with distinction, 1992); University of South Carolina (J.D., cum laude, 1995). Phi Beta Kappa. Order of Coif; Order of Wig and Robe. Student Member, John Belton O'Neall Inn of Court. Recipient, American Jurisprudence Award Contracts. Student Works Editor, South Carolina Law Review. *Member:* North Carolina Bar Association; South Carolina Bar; North Carolina Academy of Trial Lawyers (President, Young Lawyer's Division, 2001-2002); Virginia Trial Lawyers Association; The Association of Trial Lawyers of America; Guilford Inn of Court; Guilford County Association of Women Attorneys; North Carolina Association of Women Attorneys. ***PRACTICE AREAS:*** Personal Injury; Wrongful Death; Nursing Home Litigation; Elder Abuse. ***Email:*** rdecker@donaldsonandblack.com

PHYLLIS J. LILE-KING, born Hopkinsville, Kentucky, September 15, 1964; admitted to bar, 1992, Virginia; 1994, District of Columbia; 1995, North Carolina. *Education:* Georgetown College (B.A., summa cum laude, 1986); University of Virginia (J.D., 1992). Dillard Fellow. Recipient, Oral Advocacy Award. Law Clerk, the Honorable Pierce Lively, United States Court of Appeals, 6th Circuit, 1992-1993. *Member:* Virginia State Bar (Access to Legal Svcs. Committee); District of Columbia Bar; North Carolina State Bar (Labor and Employment Section Council; Lawyer Effectiveness and Quality of Life Committee); American Bar Association; North Carolina Academy of Trial Lawyers; The Association of Trial Lawyers of America; National Employment Lawyers Association; Joseph Branch Inn of Court. ***PRACTICE AREAS:*** Products Liability; Toxic Torts; Environmental Contamination; Lead Poisoning. ***Email:*** plileking@donaldsonandblack.com

S. CAMILLE PAYTON, born Kinston, North Carolina, September 22, 1962; admitted to bar, 1993, North Carolina. *Education:* University of North Carolina at Chapel Hill (B.A., 1984); University of Texas at Austin (J.D., 1993). Associate Editor, The Review of Litigation, 1992-1993. *Member:* Greensboro Bar Association; North Carolina Bar Association (Membership Committee; Bar Cares Committee; Workers' Compensation Section Council); Guilford County Association of Black Lawyers (Treasurer); North Carolina Association of Black Lawyers; North Carolina Academy of Trial Lawyers; North Carolina Association of Women Attorneys; The Association of Trial Lawyers of America; Guilford County Association of Women Attorneys (Vice President, 2003-2004). ***REPORTED CASES:*** Robinson v. State of North Carolina, 351 N.C. 38; Bason v. Kraft Food Service, Inc., 535 S.E. 2d 606. ***PRACTICE AREAS:*** Workers' Compensation. ***Email:*** scpayton@donaldsonandblack.com

JOHN T. O'NEAL, born New Bern, North Carolina, March 23, 1971; admitted to bar, 1996, North Carolina. *Education:* University of North Carolina at Greensboro (B.A., 1993); University of North Carolina at Chapel Hill (J.D., 1996). *Member:* Greensboro Bar Association; North Carolina State Bar; 18th Judicial District Bar; Guilford County Association of Black Lawyers; North Carolina Association of Black Lawyers; North Carolina Academy of Trial Lawyers (Chair, Hispanic/Latino Issues Division, 2003-2004); The Association of Trial Lawyers of America. ***PRACTICE AREAS:*** Personal Injury; Products Liability; Professional Negligence; Civil Litigation. ***Email:*** joneal@donaldsonandblack.com

(This Listing Continued)

DOUGLAS, RAVENEL, HARDY, CRIHFIELD & HOYLE, L.L.P.

Established in 1936
110 COMMERCE PLACE
P.O. BOX 419
GREENSBORO, NORTH CAROLINA 27402-0419
Telephone: 336-378-0580
Fax: 336-378-0886
URL: http://www.drhch.com

General Civil Practice. Trials in all State Courts. Corporation, Real Estate, Estate Planning, Probate, Family, Child Support, Child Custody, Divorce, Arbitrations, Personal Injury, and Mediation Law.

FIRM PROFILE: The firm traces its history to the year 1936 when the late R. D. Douglas, Sr. and his son, R. D. Douglas, Jr., founded the firm. The firm presently has 4 full-time attorneys practicing in the areas of Family Law, Wills, Estate Planning and Administration, Real Estate, Corporate and Business, Commercial and Personal Injury.

MEMBERS OF FIRM

R. D. DOUGLAS, SR. (1875-1960)

THOMAS P. RAVENEL (1916-1992)

GLENN STEVENSON CRIHFIELD, born Morristown, Tennessee, May 9, 1936; admitted to bar, 1963, North Carolina; 1964, U.S. District Court, Middle District of North Carolina; 1967, U.S. Supreme Court; 1968, U.S. District Court, Eastern District of North Carolina; 1972, U.S. District Court, Western District of North Carolina. *Education:* Duke University (A.B., 1959); University of North Carolina (LL.B., 1963). Phi Delta Phi. *Member:* Greensboro (President, Young Lawyers Section, 1967-1968; President, 1988-1989), 18th Judicial District (Chairman, Grievance Committee, 1988-1993, President, 2000-2001) and North Carolina (Family Law Council, 1993-1994, Lawyer Effectiveness and Quality of Life Committee, 1989—, 2004, Chairman, 1995-1997) Bar Associations; North Carolina State Bar (Councilor 2001—); The Guilford Inn of Court (Master; President, 1995-1999). ***PRACTICE AREAS:*** Litigation; Family Law; Child Custody; Child Support; Divorce. ***Email:*** scrihfield@drhch.com

ROBERT D. DOUGLAS, III, born Washington, D.C., February 21, 1943; admitted to bar, 1968, North Carolina and U.S. District Court, Middle District of North Carolina; 1988, U.S. Court of Appeals, Fourth Circuit. *Education:* University of North Carolina (A.B., 1965; J.D., 1968). Phi Delta Phi. Assistant Public Defender, 18th Judicial District, 1970-1971. *Member:* Greensboro (Treasurer, 1971 and President, 1972, Young Lawyers Section) and North Carolina (Member, Sections of Real Property and Estate Planning and Fiduciary Law) Bar Associations; North Carolina State Bar. ***PRACTICE AREAS:*** Real Estate Law; Estate Planning; Wills; Probate and Fiduciary Law. ***Email:*** rdouglas@drhch.com

WILLIAM R. HOYLE, born Greensboro, North Carolina, August 20, 1941; admitted to bar, 1966, North Carolina and U.S. District Court, Middle District of North Carolina. *Education:* University of North Carolina (A.B., 1963). Delta Theta Phi. *Member:* Greensboro and North Carolina Bar Associations; North Carolina State Bar (Councilor, 18th Judicial District, 1991-1997). [CAPT., USNR (retired), active duty, 1966-1969]. ***PRACTICE AREAS:*** Real Estate; Estate Planning; Wills; Probate; Fiduciary Law. ***Email:*** whoyle@drhch.com

AMANDA L. FIELDS, born Asheboro, North Carolina, April 8, 1965; admitted to bar, 1998, North Carolina. *Education:* University of North Carolina at Greensboro (B.A., summa cum laude, 1995); University of North Carolina at Chapel Hills (J.D., with honors, 1998). Phi Beta Kappa. Recipient: Eugene Gressman and Daniel H. Pollitt Award for Appellate Advocacy, 1996. Senior Staff Member, North Carolina Journal of International Law and Commercial Regulation, 1997-1998. *Member:* Greensboro and North Carolina Bar Associations. ***PRACTICE AREAS:*** Family Law; Civil Litigation. ***Email:*** afields@drhch.com

OF COUNSEL

R. D. DOUGLAS, JR.
JOHN W. HARDY
ROBERT P. WORTH

ELLIS & WINTERS LLP

100 N. GREENE STREET, SUITE 102
GREENSBORO, NORTH CAROLINA 27401
Telephone: 336-217-4193
Facsimile: 336-217-4198
URL: http://www.elliswinters.com

Cary, North Carolina Office: 1100 Crescent Green, Suite 200, 27511-8105. Telephone: 919-865-7000. Facsimile: 919-865-7010.

Raleigh, North Carolina Office: P.O. Box 33550, 27636. Telephone: 919-865-7000. Facsimile: 919-865-7010.

Trial and Appellate Practice in all State and Federal Courts. Commercial Litigation, Administrative Litigation, Medical Malpractice, Products Liability, Antitrust, Corporate, Real Estate and Finance.

ANDREW S. CHAMBERLIN, born Rochester, New York, December 18, 1964; admitted to bar, 1990, North Carolina. *Education:* University of Georgia (B.A., 1987; J.D., cum laude, 1990). Member, Georgia Journal of International and Comparative Law, 1989-

(This Listing Continued)

1990. *Member:* North Carolina and American Bar Associations; Defense Research Institute; International Association of Defense Counsel; North Carolina Association of Defense Attorneys. ***PRACTICE AREAS:*** Products Liability; Civil Litigation; Commercial Litigation; Trade Secrets Litigation. ***Email:*** andrew_chamberlin@elliswinters.com

CURTIS J. SHIPLEY, born Chariton, Iowa, February 21, 1963; admitted to bar, 1990, Illinois; 1991, District of Columbia; 1992, North Carolina. *Education:* Northwestern University (B.S., 1985); University of Iowa (J.D., with high distinction, 1988). Articles Editor, Iowa Law Review, 1987-1988. *Member:* North Carolina State Bar; American Bar Association. ***PRACTICE AREAS:*** Commercial Litigation; Products Liability; Environmental Litigation; Construction Litigation. ***Email:*** curtis_shipley@elliswinters.com

ASSOCIATE

JOHN A. CHILSON, born Wellsboro, Pennsylvania, 1969; admitted to bar, 1999, Michigan; 2003, North Carolina. *Education:* U.S. Naval Academy (B.S., 1991); University of Michigan at Ann Arbor (J.D., cum laude, 1999). Author: "Keeping Clean Waters Clean: Making the Clean Water Act's Antidegradation Policy Work," Vol. 32, University of Michigan Journal of Law Reform. *Member:* North Carolina and American Bar Associations; State Bar of Michigan; Defense Research Institute. [Lt. Commander, U.S. Navy, 1991-2003]. ***PRACTICE AREAS:*** Products Liability; Commercial Litigation; Civil Rights Litigation; Criminal Defense. ***Email:*** john_chilson@elliswinters.com

(For complete biographical data on other personnel, see Professional Biographies at Cary, North Carolina and Raleigh, North Carolina)

THE ELLISON LAW FIRM

GREENSBORO, NORTH CAROLINA

(See Winston-Salem)

Real Estate, Landlord Tenant, Criminal Law, Traffic Violations, Divorce.

ELROD LAWING & SHARPLESS, P.A.

GREENSBORO, NORTH CAROLINA

(See Sharpless & Stavola, P.A.)

LAW OFFICE OF JODI A. ERNEST

3703-D W. MARKET STREET
GREENSBORO, NORTH CAROLINA 27403
Telephone: 336-315-2266
Fax: 336-315-2257
Email: earnestlaw@hotmail.com
URL: http://www.ernestlaw.com
Mailing Address: P.O. Box 1738, Greensboro, NC 27402-1738

Real Estate, Residential, Buying or Selling Home, Commercial Real Estate, Conveyancing, Living Wills, Wills.

JODI A. ERNEST, born Fairfax, Virginia, July 30, 1970; admitted to bar, 1996, North Carolina. *Education:* Colby College (B.A., 1992); California Western School of Law (J.D., 1994). *Member:* Greensboro, North Carolina (Member, Real Estate and Juvenile Sections) and American Bar Associations. ***PRACTICE AREAS:*** Residential Real Estate; Commercial Real Estate; Conveyancing; Living Wills; Wills.

EVANS & CO.

101 WEST FRIENDLY AVENUE, SUITE 500
GREENSBORO, NORTH CAROLINA 27401
Telephone: 336-275-1400
Fax: 336-275-1401
URL: http://www.evanslawfirm.com

New Orleans, Louisiana Office: 629 Cherokee Street, 70118. Telephone: 504-522-1400. Fax: 504-522-1401.
Durango, Colorado Office: 823 East 4th Avenue, 81301. Telephone: 970-375-9300. Fax: 970-375-9301. .
Houston, Texas Office: 13700 Veterans Memorial Drive, Suite 250, 77014. Telephone: 713+522-1400. Fax: 713-522-1401.

General Insurance Defense, Admiralty, Aviation, Comprehensive General Liability, Cargo, Construction, Energy, Environmental, Toxic Torts, Errors and Omissions, Excess and Umbrella, Motor Carriers, Railroad, Insurance Coverage, Oil and Gas, Products Liability, Professional Liability, Directors and Officers Liability, Property and Casualty.

MEMBER OF FIRM

ROBERT C. EVANS, born 1954; admitted to bar, 1980, Louisiana and Maryland; U.S. District Court, Eastern, Middle and Western Districts of Maryland; U.S Court of Appeals, Fifth Circuit; 1991, U.S Court of Appeals, Eleventh Circuit; 1999, Colorado (Not admitted in North Carolina). *Education:* Columbia University (B.A., 1975); University of Maryland School of Law (J.D., with honors, 1980). *Member:* New Orleans, Louisiana State, Maryland State and Colorado Bar Associations; New Orleans Association of Defense Counsel; Louisiana Association of Defense Counsel; Lawyer-Pilots Bar Association; The Maritime Law Association of the United States; Defense Research Institute. ***Email:*** REVANS@EVANSLAWFIRM.COM

(This Listing Continued)

ASSOCIATE

JEFFERY M. DAVIS, admitted to bar, 2003, North Carolina. *Education:* Clemson University (B.A., 2000); University of North Carolina at Chapel Hill (J.D., 2003). *Member:* North Carolina Bar Association.

(For complete biographical data on all personnel, see Professional Biographies at New Orleans, Louisiana, Durango, Colorado and Houston, Texas)

FORMAN ROSSABI BLACK, P.A.

Established in 1962

3623 NORTH ELM STREET, SUITE 200
P.O. BOX 41027
GREENSBORO, NORTH CAROLINA 27455-2586
Telephone: 336-378-1899; 1-800-805-0425
Fax: 336-378-1850
Email: firm@frb-law.com
URL: http://www.frb-law.com

Appellate Practice, Business Law, Commercial Law, Community Association Law, Construction Law, Contracts, Corporate Law, Debtor and Creditor, Family Law, Insurance, Labor and Employment, Litigation, Parliamentary Law, Personal Injury, Real Estate, Taxation, Trusts and Estates, Trial Practice in all State and Federal Courts.

FIRM PROFILE: Founded in 1962, the firm conducts a diverse civil practice with each lawyer maintaining a different area of primary emphasis with concentrations in the areas listed above.

AMIEL J. ROSSABI, born New York, N.Y., February 3, 1963; admitted to bar, 1988, New York; 1989, North Carolina, U.S. Supreme Court, U.S. Court of Appeals, Fourth, Fifth and Seventh Circuits, U.S. District Court, Southern, Eastern and Western Districts of New York, Cherokee Supreme Court and U.S. District Court, Middle, Eastern and Western Districts of North Carolina. *Education:* University of North Carolina at Chapel Hill (B.A., 1984); St. Johns University Law School (J.D., 1987). Chief Justice, Moot Court Board, 1986-1987. *Member:* Greensboro, North Carolina and New York State Bar Associations; North Carolina State Bar. ***LANGUAGES:*** French. ***PRACTICE AREAS:*** Business Litigation; Commercial Litigation; Appellate Litigation; Products Liability; Personal Injury; Estate Litigation. ***Email:*** arossabi@frb-law.com

T. KEITH BLACK, born Ponca City, Oklahoma, March 1, 1959; admitted to bar, 1984, North Carolina; 1994, U.S. Court of Appeals, Fourth Circuit. *Education:* University of North Carolina (B.S., 1981; J.D., 1984). *Member:* Greensboro (Secretary, 2000; President, Young Lawyer's Section, 1989) and North Carolina Bar Associations; North Carolina State Bar; The North Carolina Trial Lawyers Association. ***PRACTICE AREAS:*** Civil Litigation; Domestic Relations Law; Commercial Collections; Real Estate; Personal Injury. ***Email:*** tkblack@frb-law.com

JAMES H. SLAUGHTER, born Kannapolis, North Carolina, July 29, 1964; admitted to bar, 1989, North Carolina, U.S. District Court, Middle and Western Districts of North Carolina, U.S. Court of Appeals, Federal Circuit and U.S. Supreme Court. *Education:* University of North Carolina at Chapel Hill (B.A., with highest honors, 1986; J.D., 1989). Phi Beta Kappa; Phi Eta Sigma. Harry S. Truman Scholar. Member, Order of the Barristers. Member, Holderness Moot Court Bench, 1988-1989. Member, University of North Carolina National Moot Court Team, 1988-1989. Member, University of North Carolina National Trial Competition Team, 1988-1989. Real Estate Broker, North Carolina, 1982. Certified Professional Parliamentarian, American Institute of Parliamentarians, 1993. Professional Registered Parliamentarian, National Association of Parliamentarians, 1995. Certified Mediator and Arbitrator. *Member:* Greensboro (Treasurer, 1991-1992; Board Member, 2002-2005) and North Carolina Bar Associations; American Inns of Court (Barrister). ***PRACTICE AREAS:*** Civil Litigation; Business Litigation; Personal Injury; Real Estate Litigation; Community Association Law; Homeowners Association Law; Condominium Association Law; Unfair Competition; Parliamentary Law. ***Email:*** jslaughter@frb-law.com

STEVEN E. BLACK, born Lexington, Kentucky, October 2, 1971; admitted to bar, 1999, North Carolina. *Education:* University of North Carolina at Greensboro (B.S., in Political Science, 1995); Thomas M. Cooley Law School (J.D., cum laude, 1999). Recipient: Distinguished Student Award, Thomas M. Cooley Law School; John D. Voelker Award. Editor, Thomas M. Cooley Law School Law Review, 1998-1999. *Member:* Greensboro Bar Association (Member, Executive Board; Board Member, Young Lawyers Division Executive); North Carolina State Bar. ***PRACTICE AREAS:*** Community Association Law; Homeowners Association Law; Condominium Association Law; Real Estate; Civil Litigation. ***Email:*** sblack@frb-law.com

WILLIAM F. PATTERSON, JR., born Washington, North Carolina, November 28, 1954; admitted to bar, 1982, District of Columbia; 1984, Pennsylvania; 1987, North Carolina; U.S. Court of Appeals, Fourth Circuit; U.S. District Court, Middle, Eastern and Western Districts of North Carolina. *Education:* University of North Carolina (B.A., 1977; J.D., 1982). Phi Beta Kappa. John Motley Morehead Scholar. Member, North Carolina Law Review, 1980-1981. *Member:* North Carolina Bar Association (Member, Litigation and Labor and Employment Sections; Chair, Technology Advisory Committee, 1998-2000); American Bar Association (Member, Litigation and Tort and Insurance Practice Sections). ***PRACTICE AREAS:*** Civil Litigation; Civil Appeals; Complex Business Litigation; Commercial Litigation; Personal Injury; Employment Law; Insurance Coverage. ***Email:*** wfp@frb-law.com

Emily Jeffords Meister
Barbara Lynn Stewart (Corporate Counsel)
Theodora A. Vaporis
Jason M. Goins
Erinn McKee Hannigan

OF COUNSEL

RICHARD C. FORMAN, born Cleveland, Ohio, September 9, 1929; admitted to bar, 1953, Georgia; 1957, U.S. Tax Court; 1960, North Carolina; 1964, U.S. Supreme Court.

(This Listing Continued)

FORMAN ROSSABI BLACK, P.A., Greensboro—Continued

Education: University of Georgia (A.B., 1950); Emory University (J.D., 1954). Phi Alpha Delta. Member, Bryan Society. Tax Attorney, Office of Chief Counsel, Internal Revenue Service, Boston, Massachusetts and Greensboro, North Carolina, 1956-1961. Chairman, Greensboro Human Relations Commission, 1971-1972. President, Greensboro Estate Planning Council, 1972. Author and Lecturer, "Statutory Based Fringe Benefits," N.Y.U. Tax Institute (1979). *Member:* Greensboro (Secretary, 1970; Treasurer, 1984), North Carolina, Federal (President, 1963) and American Bar Associations. ***PRACTICE AREAS:*** Income, Estate and Gift Taxation Law; Estate Planning and Administration; Corporations Law; Wills and Trusts; Pension and Profit Sharing; Executive Compensation. ***Email:*** rcforman@frb-law.com

PAUL E. MARTH, born Philadelphia, Pennsylvania, February 27, 1950; admitted to bar, 1975, North Carolina, U.S. Court of Appeals, Fourth Circuit, Federal Circuit U.S. Court of Military Appeals and U.S. Supreme Court. *Education:* Wake Forest University (B.A., cum laude, 1972; J.D., cum laude, 1975); New York University (LL.M., 1978). Phi Alpha Delta. Associate Editor, Wake Forest Law Review, 1974-75. Author: Comment, 11 Wake Forest Law Review 459, 1975; Note, Wake Forest Law Review 589, 1973. *Member:* Greensboro (Treasurer, 1989), North Carolina Bar Association. [LTC., Retired, U.S. Army Reserves]. ***PRACTICE AREAS:*** Labor and Employment Law; Business Law; Debtor Creditor Law; Estate Planning and Administration; Administrative Law. ***Email:*** pmarth@frb-law.com

REPRESENTATIVE CLIENTS: ADA Computer Products, Inc.; Carson Dellosa Publishing Company, Inc.; Curtis Packing Co.; Greensboro Painting Company, Inc.; I.T.M. Ltd., South; Jamestown International, Inc.; John Kavanagh Company; Kindley's Office Furniture, Inc.; Laddie and Duke's Family Grill & Pub; Martin's Systems, Inc.; P.M. Segal & Co.; Port City Chop House, L.L.C.; Sherrill Inc.; Specialty Transportation Services, Inc.; Supreme Maintenance Organization, L.L.C.; Wajax Limited; West Market Street Development Co.; Wolfe Construction, Inc.; Wysong & Miles Company; Rent-A-Car, Inc.; Ross Angel Associates, LLC.
LOCAL COUNSEL FOR: American Honda Finance Corporation; First Specialty Insurance; Girl Scouts Tarheel Triad Council, Inc.; Honda North America, Inc.; Westport Insurance Corp.
REFERENCES: Merrill Lynch; First Citizens Bank.

FRASSINETI AND GLOVER

Established in 1957

SUITE 403, 201 WEST MARKET STREET
P.O. DRAWER 1799
GREENSBORO, NORTH CAROLINA 27402
Telephone: 336-273-9794
Fax: 336-273-1570
Email: dmglover@bellsouth.net

Business Litigation, Bankruptcy, Collections, Incorporation, Probate and Real Estate.

JORDAN J. FRASSINETI (1929-1996)

DURANT M. GLOVER, born Wilmington, North Carolina, March 6, 1951; admitted to bar, 1976, North Carolina; 1977, U.S. Court of Appeals, Fourth Circuit; 1980, U.S. Supreme Court. *Education:* Duke University (A.B., cum laude, 1973); University of North Carolina at Chapel Hill (J.D., with honors, 1976). Order of the Coif. Staff Editor, North Carolina Law Review, 1975-1976. Author: Note, "Damages— Retail Prices for Damaged Goods— A Double Recovery?" 53 North Carolina Law Review 1043, 1975; Comment, "Real Property— Changes in North Carolina's Foreclosure Law," 54 North Carolina Law Review 903, 1976; North Carolina Digest Section, National Mortgage Servicer's Reference Directory, 1985—. Recipient, Chief Justice Walter Clark Award, 1976. Editor in Chief, Greensboro Bar News, 1984-1987. *Member:* Greensboro (Member, Board of Directors, 1987-1989; Member, Section on Real Property) and North Carolina (Member, Sections on: Bankruptcy; General Practice; Real Property) Bar Associations; North Carolina State Bar.

FRAZIER & FRAZIER, LLP

SUITE 206 SOUTHEASTERN BUILDING
102 NORTH ELM STREET
P.O. DRAWER 1559
GREENSBORO, NORTH CAROLINA 27402
Telephone: 336-378-9411
Telecopier: 336-274-7358
URL: http://www.frazier-lawnc.com

General Practice. Trials in all State and Federal Courts, Corporate and Commercial Transactions, Estate Planning and Administration, Civil Litigation, Personal Injury and Insurance Litigation, Taxation and Real Estate Development, Commercial and Residential Transactions.

MEMBERS OF FIRM

C. CLIFFORD FRAZIER (1884-1967)

ROBERT H. FRAZIER (1899-1978)

CYRUS CLIFFORD FRAZIER, JR., born Greensboro, North Carolina, September 30, 1923; admitted to bar, 1951, North Carolina. *Education:* University of North Carolina (A.B., 1948; LL.B., 1951). Phi Delta Phi. Special Assistant to Attorney General of U.S., 1953-58. Member, Guilford County Board of Elections, 1965-1974. *Member:* Greensboro (Secretary, 1963-1964; President, 1976-1977), 18th Judicial District (President, 1970-1971), North Carolina and American Bar Associations; North Carolina State Bar. Fellow, American College of Trust and Estate Counsel. [Lt. (j.g.), U.S. Navy, 1946]. ***PRACTICE AREAS:*** Corporate and Commercial Transactions; Estate and Trust Planning; Probate and Administration; Real Estate. ***Email:*** frazier@frazierlawnc.com

ROBERT A. FRANKLIN, born Morganton, North Carolina, November 12, 1942; admitted to bar, 1972, North Carolina. *Education:* University of North Carolina-Chapel Hill (A.B., 1965); Wake Forest University (J.D., 1972). Phi Delta Phi. Attorney, District Attorney's Office, Greensboro, North Carolina, 1972-1975. Public Defender, 1975-1978. *Member:* Greensboro Bar Association; North Carolina State Bar; North Carolina Association of

(This Listing Continued)

Defense Attorneys. ***PRACTICE AREAS:*** Insurance Defense Law; Personal Injury Law; Criminal Law; Civil Litigation; Wrongful Death. ***Email:*** franklin@frazierlawnc.com

TORIN LANE FURY, born Fort Ord, California, July 28, 1964; admitted to bar, 1991, North Carolina. *Education:* North Carolina State University (B.A., 1987); Campbell University (J.D., 1991). Delta Theta Phi; Phi Kappa Phi; Omicron Delta Kappa. Articles Editor, Campbell Law Review, 1990-1991. Associate Case Law Editor and Perspectives Staff, Campbell Law Observer. *Member:* Greensboro, North Carolina and American Bar Associations; North Carolina State Bar. ***PRACTICE AREAS:*** Civil Trial; Personal Injury Law; Insurance Defense Law; Administrative Law. ***Email:*** fury@frazierlawnc.com

G. CLARK HERING, IV, born Wilmington, Delaware, November 24, 1962; admitted to bar, 1992, Delaware; 1993, U.S. District Court, District of Delaware; 1995, North Carolina; 1996, U.S. District Court, Middle District of North Carolina and 1997, U.S. District Court, Western District of North Carolina. *Education:* Wake Forest University (B.A., 1985); Dickinson School of Law (J.D., 1992). Member, Dickinson Journal of International Law. *Member:* Greensboro, North Carolina and American Bar Associations; North Carolina State Bar. ***PRACTICE AREAS:*** Civil Litigation; Personal Injury Law; Insurance Defense Law; Real Estate. ***Email:*** hering@frazierlawnc.com

REPRESENTATIVE CLIENTS: Bank of America (Trust Dept.); Wachovia Bank Of North Carolina (Trust Dept.); RBC-Centura Bank; State Farm Mutual Automobile Insurance Co.; State Farm Fire & Casualty Co.; Atlantic Casualty Insurance Co.; Orion Auto; GMAC Insurance; Foremost Insurance Co.; United Services Automobile Association (USAA); Prudential Property and Casualty Insurance Company; GEICO Direct; Virginia Farm Bureau Mutual Insurance Company; Revco Discount Drug Centers, Inc.; Neese Country Sausage, Inc.; Geoffrey Bodine New World Racing, Inc.; Unifi, Inc.; Atlantic Mobilehome & Recreational Vehicle Suppliers Corp.; Richard Petty-Petty Enterprises, Inc.
APPROVED ATTORNEYS FOR: Lawyers Title of North Carolina, Inc.; Fidelity National Title Insurance Co.; First American Title Insurance Co.; Common Wealth Land Title Company of North Carolina; Chicago Title Insurance Co.; Investors Title Insurance Co.
REFERENCES: Wachovia Bank of North Carolina, N.A.; RBC-Centura Bank; Bank of America.

GABRIEL BERRY & WESTON, L.L.P.

Established in 1978

214 COMMERCE PLACE
GREENSBORO, NORTH CAROLINA 27401
Telephone: 336-275-9381
Fax: 336-275-7864
URL: http://www.gabrielberryweston law.com
URL: http://www.lawyers.com/gbwlaw

General Civil Practice in all Courts. Insurance, Real Estate, Civil Litigation, Personal Injury, Family, Divorce, Custody, Taxation, Probate, Estate Planning Corporation Law.

FIRM PROFILE: The law firm of Gabriel Berry & Weston, a Limited Liability Partnership, was formed in 1980 with a commitment to hard work and prompt service at a competitive price.

We can assist you in a broad range of legal services: simple traffic matters, probate of estates, tax or corporate matters, domestic and family law, financing and purchase of real estate, litigation, workers' compensation, personal injury and property damage insurance claims, contracts, and business tax planning. Our clients include regional and international concerns.

MEMBERS OF FIRM

RICHARD W. GABRIEL, born Greensboro, North Carolina, November 2, 1949; admitted to bar, 1975, North Carolina; 1978, U.S. Supreme Court; 1981, U.S. Tax Court. *Education:* Duke University (A.B., 1971); University of North Carolina (M.B.A., 1977); Wake Forest University (J.D., 1975). Phi Alpha Delta. Editor-in-Chief, Wake Forest Jurist, 1975. Listed in Who's Who in American Law, 1994. Co-Author: "Proving Damages in North Carolina," National Business Institute, 1989; "Trial Advocacy in North Carolina," National Business Institute, 1990; "Trying the Automobile Injury Case in N.C.," National Business Institute, 1992, 1993, 1995; "Counseling the Small Business Client in N.C.," National Business Institute, 1996. Negotiating and Drafting Acquisitions Agreements in N.C., 1999. Visiting Lecturer, Guilford College, 1977-1981. *Member:* Greensboro and North Carolina Bar Associations; North Carolina Academy of Trial Lawyers. [North Carolina National Guard, 1971-1977]. ***PRACTICE AREAS:*** Personal Injury Law; Business Law; Taxation; Trusts and Estates; Probate. ***Email:*** rgabriel@gbwlaw.com

M. DOUGLAS BERRY, born Greensboro, North Carolina, December 16, 1948; admitted to bar, 1975, North Carolina and U.S. District Court, Middle District of North Carolina; 1977, U.S. Court of Appeals, Fourth Circuit; U.S. Supreme Court. *Education:* University of North Carolina (B.A., 1971; J.D., 1975). Phi Delta Phi; Order of the Barrister. *Member:* Greensboro, North Carolina (Member, Family Law and Litigation Sections) and American Bar Associations; North Carolina Academy of Trial Lawyers; The Association of Trial Lawyers of America. [North Carolina National Guard, 1971-1977]. (Board Certified Specialist in Family Law, North Carolina State Board of Legal Specialization). ***PRACTICE AREAS:*** Personal Injury Law; Family Law; Civil Litigation. ***Email:*** dougberry@gbwlaw.com

ROBERT A. WELLS, born Hopewell, Virginia, September 6, 1970; admitted to bar, 1996, North Carolina and U.S. District Court, Middle District of North Carolina. *Education:* Virginia Polytechnic Institute and State University (B.A., 1992); Wake Forest University (J.D., 1996). *Member:* Greensboro and North Carolina Bar Associations; North Carolina Academy of Trial Lawyers. ***PRACTICE AREAS:*** Business; Estate and Probate; Personal Injury; Litigation. ***Email:*** rwells@gbwlaw.com

REPRESENTATIVE CLIENTS: Trust Department for the Wachovia Bank & Trust Company, N.A.; The City of Greensboro; International Home Furnishings Representatives Assn.; Personal Legal Plans; Southeast Fuels, Inc.; Greensboro Regional Realtors Association; Stock Building Supply; N.C. Grange Mutual Insurance Co.
REFERENCE: Wachovia Bank & Trust Co., N.A.

JAY GERVASI, P.A.

910 NORTH ELM STREET
GREENSBORO, NORTH CAROLINA 27401
Telephone: 336-574-0174
Fax: 336-574-2541
Email: jay@gervasilaw.com
URL: http://www.jgervasilaw.com

Workers Compensation, Personal Injury.

JAY A. GERVASI, JR., born Charleston, West Virginia, May 18, 1958; admitted to bar, 1986, North Carolina; 1988, South Carolina. *Education:* Duke University (B.S., cum laude, 1980); Vanderbilt University (J.D., 1986). *Member:* Greensboro, North Carolina (Member, Workers Compensation Section) and American Bar Associations; North Carolina Academy of Trial Lawyers (Member, Executive Committee, Workers Rights Section, 1995—); The Association of Trial Lawyers of America. (Board Certified, Specialist in Worker's Compensation Law, North Carolina State Bar, Board of Legal Specialization). ***PRACTICE AREAS:*** Workers Compensation; Personal Injury.

GOULDER IMMIGRATION LAW FIRM

3200 NORTHLINE AVENUE, SUITE 130
GREENSBORO, NORTH CAROLINA 27408
Telephone: 336-808-1119
Fax: 336-294-3063
Toll Free Voice/Fax: 1-866-878-4727
Email: Goulder@gouldervisa.com
URL: http://www.gouldervisa.com

Immigration and Naturalization, Visas, U.S. Citizenship, Student Visa, HI-B, L Visas, E Visas, Employment Visa, J-Visa, Fiancée Visas, all Family-Based Immigration Visas and Adjustments of Status.

GERALD P. GOULDER, born Columbus, Ohio, April 30, 1953; admitted to bar, 1979, Ohio and U.S. District Court, Southern District of Ohio; 1984, North Carolina. *Education:* The Ohio State University (B.A., 1975); Washington University School of Law (J.D., 1978). *Member:* North Carolina State Bar; American Immigration Lawyers Association. ***PRACTICE AREAS:*** Immigration and Naturalization; Visas; Citizenship; Employment Visas. ***Email:*** goulder@gouldervisa.com

GRACE HOLTON TISDALE & CLIFTON P.A.

GREENSBORO, NORTH CAROLINA

(See Winston-Salem)

Criminal Law in all State and Federal Courts. Traffic Violations, White Collar Crime.

GRAY LEGAL GROUP

108 N. ELM STREET
GREENSBORO, NORTH CAROLINA 27401
Telephone: 336-691-9200
Fax: 336-691-0888
Email: markvlgray@gnjblaw.com
URL: http://www.graylegalgroup.com

Workers Compensation, Injuries, Wrongful Death, Life and Disability Insurance Claims, Auto Accidents.

MARK V.L. GRAY, born Washington, North Carolina, October 26, 1956; admitted to bar, 1982, North Carolina, U.S. Court of Appeals, 4th Circuit, U.S. District Court, Eastern, Middle and Western Districts of North Carolina. *Education:* East Carolina University (B.A., History, 1974); University of North Carolina at Chapel Hill (J.D., 1982). Omega Psi Phi Fraternity, Inc; Alpha Theta Phi; Psi Sigma Tau. *Member:* Greensboro Bar Association; North Carolina State Bar; North Carolina Academy of Trial Lawyers; North Carolina Association of Black Lawyers; Guilford County Black Lawyers Association; American Trial Lawyers Association. ***PRACTICE AREAS:*** Personal Injury; Wrongful Death; Medical Malpractice; Workers Compensation; Nursing Home Litigation; Insurance Litigation; Traffic Law; Criminal Law.

GRIMES & GRIMES OF NORTH CAROLINA, P.A.

307 SOUTH SWING ROAD
GREENSBORO, NORTH CAROLINA 27409
Telephone: 336-232-5921
Fax: 336-217-4357

Mailing Address: P.O. Box 8009, Greensboro, NC 27419

Entertainment Law, Entertainment Litigation, Business and Commercial Litigation, Administrative Agency Practice, Construction Law and Collections and Business Law.

FIRM PROFILE: Grimes & Grimes of North Carolina, P.A. is a firm dedicated to serving the legal needs of our clients. Our firm is unique in that we handle complex business litigation, particularly in the entertainment industry. Our firm focuses on entertainment law and entertainment litigation disputes such as copyright infringement, breach of contract, and unfair trade practices. We are legal counsel to entertainers and professionals working in entertainment fields, and represent movie production companies that produce quality films, videos and other media.

L. CHARLES GRIMES, born Fayetteville, North Carolina, November 28, 1962; admitted to bar, 1989, North Carolina. *Education:* University of North Carolina at Chapel Hill

(This Listing Continued)

(B.S., with highest honors and distinction, 1986; J.D., 1989). Member, North Carolina Law Review, 1988-1989. First Prize, University of North Carolina School of Law, Nathan Burkan Memorial Competition in Intellectual Property, 1989. *Member:* Greensboro, North Carolina and American Bar Associations; North Carolina State Bar. ***PRACTICE AREAS:*** Entertainment Law; Civil Litigation; Business Law; Construction Law; Collections; Administrative Agency Practice. ***Email:*** cgrimes@grimesandgrimes.com

ELIZABETH G. GRIMES, born Winston-Salem, North Carolina, April 25, 1964; admitted to bar, 1989, North Carolina. *Education:* University of North Carolina at Chapel Hill (B.A., 1985); Wake Forest University (J.D., 1989). Member, Moot Court Board. Member, Wake Forest University Law Review, 1987-1988. Adjunct Associate Professor, Broadcasting and Cinema Department, University of North Carolina at Greensboro, 2004—. Visiting Assistant Professor, Media Law and Ethics, Production Distribution and Finance, and Media Communication Theory, University of North Carolina at Greensboro, 2003-2004. *Member:* Greensboro (Past President, Young Lawyers Division, 1994-1995), North Carolina (Workers' Compensation Council Member, 1999-2002) and American Bar Associations; North Carolina State Bar; Guilford Inn of Court. ***PRACTICE AREAS:*** Entertainment Law; Entertainment Litigation; Commercial Litigation. ***Email:*** egrimes@grimesandgrimes.com

HAHN & CHASTAIN, P.A.

3705 WEST MARKET STREET, SUITE C
GREENSBORO, NORTH CAROLINA 27403
Telephone: 336-297-0530
URL: http://www.hahnchastainlaw.com

Corporate Law, Taxation, Estate Planning, Wills, Probate, Elder Law, Real Estate, Trusts and Estates, Business Law, Commercial Law.

CHARLES B. HAHN, born Augusta, Georgia, February 13, 1947; admitted to bar, 1971, North Carolina. *Education:* Erskine College (B.A., cum laude, 1970); Tulane University (J.D., 1971). Phi Alpha Delta. Member, Board of Student Editors, Tulane Law Review, 1969-1971. (Board Certified Specialist in Estate Planning and Probate Law, North Carolina State Bar Board of Legal Specialization) (Also Of Counsel, Peter Chastain & Associates, P.A.). ***PRACTICE AREAS:*** Corporate Law; Business Law; Taxation; Wills; Trusts and Estates; Probate.

PETER F. CHASTAIN, born Lowell, Massachusetts, October 25, 1945; admitted to bar, 1974, North Carolina. *Education:* University of South Carolina (A.B., 1967); University of North Carolina at Chapel Hill (J.D., 1973). *Member:* American Bar Association. [Lt., U.S. Naval Reserve, active duty, 1968-1970]. (Also Member, Peter F. Chastain & Associates, P.A.). ***PRACTICE AREAS:*** Real Estate; Commercial Law; Creditors Rights.

HANDLER & BROWN, P.L.L.C.

GREENSBORO, NORTH CAROLINA

(See Winston-Salem)

Business Law, Commercial Law, Insurance Premium Finance Law, Factoring, Leasing, Licensing, Franchise Law, Intellectual Property Law, Trademarks, Copyrights, Unfair Competition, Real Estate, Condominium Law, Association Law, Land Use, Environmental Law, Commercial Litigation, Unfair Trade Practice Law, Creditors Rights, Civil Trial Practice, Appellate Practice, Arbitration, Class Actions, Constitutional Law, Professional Liability, Medical Malpractice, Products Liability, Personal Injury, Civil Rights, Labor and Employment, Wrongful Discharge and Discrimination Law.

ANN E. HANKS

GREENSBORO, NORTH CAROLINA

(See High Point)

Trusts and Estates, Asset Protection, Estate Planning, Guardianship, Wills and Probate, Tax Planning, Elder Law.

A. WAYNE HARRISON

101 S. ELM STREET, SUITE 230
GREENSBORO, NORTH CAROLINA 27401
Telephone: 336-378-0616
Fax: 336-378-1172
Email: wayno@triad.rr.com
URL: http://www.lawyers.com/harrisenlaw

Criminal Law, Constitutional Law, Civil Forfeiture, Criminal Forfeiture, Criminal Appeals, White Collar Crimes.

A. WAYNE HARRISON, born Salisbury, North Carolina, January 25, 1942; admitted to bar, 1969, North Carolina and U.S. District Court, Middle, Eastern and Western Districts of North Carolina; U.S. Court of Appeals, Fourth Circuit and U.S. Supreme Court. *Education:* University of North Carolina (LL.B., 1969). Phi Delta Phi (President, 1968-1969). Visiting Lecturer, Constitutional Law, The Fourth Amendment, Guilford College, 1980. *Member:* Greensboro and American Bar Associations; North Carolina State Bar; Greensboro Criminal Defense Lawyers Association (President, 1978-1979; Member, Board of Directors, 1979—); North Carolina Academy of Trial Lawyers.

MARK E. HAYES

101 SOUTH ELM STREET, SUITE 142
GREENSBORO, NORTH CAROLINA 27401
Telephone: 336-333-2900
Fax: 336-333-2995
URL: http://www.markhayeslaw.com

Criminal Law. Trials and Appeals in all State Courts. DUI/DWI, Traffic Violations, Drug Crimes, Felonies, Misdemeanors, Sexual Assault, White Collar Crime.

FIRM PROFILE: Mark E. Hayes is a solo practitioner in all areas of criminal law. He has over 18 years experience with the North Carolina court system, with 11 years as an Assistant Public Defender.

MARK E. HAYES, born November 3, 1958; admitted to bar, 1986, Georgia; 1987, North Carolina. *Education:* Elon College (B.A., 1981); Mercer University (J.D., 1985). Previous Employment: Womble Carlyle Sandridge & Rice, 1986-1989. Assistant Public Defender, 18th Judicial District, 1989-2000. *Member:* Greensboro Criminal Lawyers Association (President, 2001); American Inns of Court.

HAYNSWORTH BALDWIN JOHNSON & GREAVES LLC

GREENSBORO, NORTH CAROLINA

(See Ogletree, Deakins, Nash, Smoak & Stewart, P.C.)

HENSON & HENSON, L.L.P.

SUITE 600, THE PIEDMONT BUILDING
114 NORTH ELM STREET
GREENSBORO, NORTH CAROLINA 27401
Telephone: 336-275-0587
Facsimile: 336-273-2585
Email: phenson@hensonlawyers.com
URL: http://www.lawyers.com/hensonandhenson
Mailing Address: P.O. Box 3525, Greensboro, NC 27402-3525

General Civil Practice, Trials and Appeals in all State and Federal Courts, Personal Injury, Automobile, Workers' Compensation, Wrongful Death, Medical Malpractice, Legal Malpractice, Insurance, Professional Malpractice, Products Liability, Fire, ERISA and Insurance Defense.

PERRY C. HENSON (1922-2003)

PERRY C. HENSON, JR., born Greensboro, North Carolina, September 27, 1952; admitted to bar, 1977, North Carolina. *Education:* University of North Carolina at Chapel Hill (A.B., 1974; J.D., 1977). Order of the Barristers; Holderness Moot Court Bench, 1977. University of North Carolina Mock Trial Team, 1977. *Member:* International Association of Insurance Defense Counsel; North Carolina Association of Defense Attorneys; Defense Research Institute. ***PRACTICE AREAS:*** Civil Litigation; Commercial Litigation; Personal Injury; Wrongful Death; Trucking Law; Insurance Coverage Law; Workers' Compensation; Legal Malpractice Defense; Insurance Defense. ***Email:*** phenson@hensonlawyers.com

THOMAS D. CARRUTHERS, born Greensboro, North Carolina, May 16, 1960; admitted to bar, 1986, North Carolina. *Education:* Duke University (B.A., 1982); Campbell University Law School (J.D., 1986). ***PRACTICE AREAS:*** Civil Litigation; Commercial Litigation; Personal Injury; Wrongful Death; Workers' Compensation; Insurance Defense; Medical Malpractice. ***Email:*** tcarruthers@hensonlawyers.com

KAREN STROM TALLEY, born Flushing, New York, June 15, 1977; admitted to bar, 2002, North Carolina. *Education:* University of North Carolina at Greensboro (B.A., cum laude, 1999); University of North Carolina at Chapel Hill (J.D., with honors, 2002). Articles Editor, North Carolina Journal of International Law and Commercial Regulation, 2001-2002. *Member:* North Carolina Association of Defense Attorneys; Guilford County Association of Women Attorneys; North Carolina Association of Women Attorneys. ***PRACTICE AREAS:*** Civil Litigation; Commercial Litigation; Personal Injury; Wrongful Death; Insurance Coverage Law; Trucking Law; Insurance Defense. ***Email:*** ktalley@hensonlawyers.com

All Attorneys are Members of the Greensboro, North Carolina and American Bar Associations and the North Carolina State Bar.

REPRESENTATIVE CLIENTS: A.I. Transport; Allgood Construction Co. Inc.; Atlantic Mutual Insurance Company; Baldwin & Lyons, Inc.; Cambridge Integrated Services Group, Inc.; *Canal Insurance Company; Carolina Bank Holdings, Inc.;* Carolina Farmers Mut. Ins. Co.; Colony Insurance Group; Discovery Insurance Company; Epes Transport System, Inc.; GEICO Direct Insurance Company; Grange Mutual Casualty Company; Kmart Corporation; Lawyers Mutual Liability Insurance Company of North Carolina; Midwestern Insurance Alliance; North Carolina Farm Bureau Mutual Insurance Company; Old Dominion Freight Line, Inc.; Protective Insurance Company; Sedgwick Claims Management Services, Inc.; Vanliner Insurance Company.

HILL, EVANS, DUNCAN, JORDAN & BEATTY

A Professional Limited Liability Company
Established in 1948
1400 RENAISSANCE PLAZA
230 NORTH ELM STREET
P.O. BOX 989
GREENSBORO, NORTH CAROLINA 27402
Telephone: 336-379-1390
Fax: 336-379-1198
Email: generalmail@hillevans.com
URL: http://www.hillevans.com

General Civil Practice. Banking, Bankruptcy, Construction, Corporation, Mediation, Employment, Environmental, Estate Planning, Family, Insurance, Labor, Personal Injury, Product Liability, Real Estate, Surety, Taxation, Trade Regulation, Wills and Trusts, Workers Compensation Law, Municipal and Police Liability, Criminal and Traffic.

MEMBERS OF FIRM

WELCH JORDAN (1912-1976)

WILLIAM D. CAFFREY (1928-1991)

KARL N. HILL, JR., born February 16, 1930; admitted to bar, 1958, North Carolina. *Education:* University of North Carolina (B.S., 1952; J.D., with honors, 1958). Member of Staff, North Carolina Law Review, 1957-1958. Member, North Carolina Board of Law Examiners, 1987-2001; International Association of Defense Counsel; Defense Research Institute; North Carolina Association of Defense Attorneys. ***PRACTICE AREAS:*** Insurance Defense Litigation; Workers Compensation Law; Professional Liability Defense Litigation; Products Liability Defense. ***Email:*** khill@hillevans.com

THOMAS C. DUNCAN, born April 10, 1945; admitted to bar, 1969, North Carolina. *Education:* University of North Carolina (A.B., 1967; J.D., 1969). Phi Delta Phi. Certified Mediator. ***PRACTICE AREAS:*** Business Litigation; Corporate; Civil Litigation; Workers Compensation; Mediation. ***Email:*** duncan@hillevans.com

WILLIAM WELCH JORDAN, born August 28, 1945; admitted to bar, 1970, North Carolina. *Education:* Emory University; University of North Carolina (A.B., 1967; J.D., 1970). Phi Delta Phi. Listed in Best Lawyers in America, Family Law. *Member:* Greensboro (Chairman, Family Law Committee, 1978-1980; Family Law Section Council, 1988-1991; Family Law Section Curriculum Committee, 1986-2000) and American Bar Associations. (Board Certified Specialist in Family Law, North Carolina State Board of Legal Specialization). ***PRACTICE AREAS:*** Family Law; Equitable Distribution Law; Civil Litigation. ***Email:*** wwjordan@hillevans.com

JOSEPH R. BEATTY, born July 12, 1944; admitted to bar, 1969, North Carolina. *Education:* University of North Carolina (A.B., 1966); Duke University (J.D., with distinction, 1969). Phi Eta Sigma; Phi Beta Kappa. *Member:* Defense Research Institute; North Carolina Association of Defense Attorneys. [Capt., JAGC, U.S. Army Reserve, Active Duty, 1970-1974]. ***PRACTICE AREAS:*** Products Liability Law; Tort Litigation; Commercial Litigation; Insurance Defense Litigation; Municipal Liability; Police Liability. ***Email:*** joe.beatty@hillevans.com

R. THOMPSON WRIGHT, born December 17, 1949; admitted to bar, 1975, North Carolina. *Education:* Haverford College (A.B., 1972); University of North Carolina (J.D., with honors, 1975). Order of the Coif. *Member:* North Carolina Association of Defense Attorneys. ***PRACTICE AREAS:*** Commercial Litigation; General Litigation; Environmental Law; Real Estate; Employment Law. ***Email:*** tom.wright@hillevans.com

EVERETT B. SASLOW, JR., born June 1, 1951; admitted to bar, 1976, North Carolina. *Education:* Davidson College; University of North Carolina, Chapel Hill (B.A., 1973; J.D., with honors, 1976). Phi Beta Kappa; Order of the Coif. Staff Member, North Carolina Law Review. Member, Panel of Standing Trustees for U.S. Bankruptcy Court, Middle District of North Carolina. (Board Certified Specialist in Business and Consumer Bankruptcy Law, North Carolina State Board of Legal Specialization). ***PRACTICE AREAS:*** Bankruptcy; Commercial Law; Real Estate; Corporate; Business. ***Email:*** saslow@hillevans.com

POLLY D. SIZEMORE, born August 29, 1952; admitted to bar, 1988, North Carolina. *Education:* Appalachian State University (B.A., 1973); University of North Carolina at Greensboro (M.Ed., 1980); Wake Forest University (J.D., 1988). Certified Mediator. *Member:* Greensboro Bar Association (President, 2004-2005); Greensboro Criminal Defense Attorneys Association. ***PRACTICE AREAS:*** Civil Litigation; Municipal Liability; Mediation; Police Liability; Criminal Defense; Traffic. ***Email:*** sizemore@hillevans.com

MICHELE G. SMITH, born October 12, 1951; admitted to bar, 1993, North Carolina. *Education:* Appalachian State University (B.S., cum laude, 1973); Wake Forest University (J.D., cum laude, 1993). Alpha Chi; Phi Alpha Theta. Research Editor, Wake Forest Law Review. ***PRACTICE AREAS:*** Family Law; Adoption; Litigation. ***Email:*** msmith@hillevans.com

JOSEPH P. GRAM, born September 1, 1970; admitted to bar, 1995, North Carolina. *Education:* University of North Carolina at Chapel Hill (B.A. with honors, 1992; J.D., with honors, 1995). Phi Alpha Delta. Holderness Moot Court. ***PRACTICE AREAS:*** Civil Litigation; Construction Law. ***Email:*** jpg@hillevans.com

ELAINE HEDRICK ASHLEY, born Charlotte, North Carolina, April 7, 1954; admitted to bar, 1998, North Carolina. *Education:* University of North Carolina (B.M., 1976); Southern Methodist University (M.M., summa cum laude, 1977); North Carolina Central University (J.D., 1998). Phi Delta Phi. Member, North Carolina Central Law Journal, 1996-1998. Member, North Carolina Central University Trial Advocacy Board. ***PRACTICE AREAS:*** Family Law; Insurance Defense Litigation. ***Email:*** eashley@hillevans.com

RICHARD T. GRANOWSKY, born December 11, 1964; admitted to bar, 1999, North Carolina. *Education:* Appalachian State University (B.A., 1986); University of North Carolina (M.Ed., 1990; J.D., with honors, 1999). Order of the Coif. North Carolina

(This Listing Continued)

Journal of International Law and Business Regulation. ***PRACTICE AREAS:*** Civil Litigation; Products Liability; Insurance Defense Litigation; Workers Compensation. **Email:** rgranowsky@hillevans.com

G. MARLIN EVANS (Retired)

ASSOCIATES

MARTHA R. SACRINTY, born Lynchburg, Virginia, May 19, 1979; admitted to bar, 2004, North Carolina. *Education:* University of North Carolina at Chapel Hill (B.A., with honors and distinction, 2001; J.D., with honors, 2004). Member, Holderness Moot Court. Circulation Editor, First Amendment Law Review. Member, Board of Governors, Student Bar Association. ***PRACTICE AREAS:*** Bankruptcy; Litigation. **Email:** sacrinty@hillevans.com

ROBERT E. GRAY, III, born San Antonio, Texas, April 21, 1961; admitted to bar, 2004, North Carolina. *Education:* High Point University (B.A., summa cum laude, 1993); University of North Carolina (J.D., 2004). Member, City Council, City of Archdale, North Carolina. ***PRACTICE AREAS:*** Family Law; Equitable Distribution Law. **Email:** regray@hillevans.com

SHAWN C. TROXLER, born Greensboro, North Carolina, September 14, 1978; admitted to bar, 2005, North Carolina. *Education:* North Carolina State University (B.S., summa cum laude, 2000; M.S., 2002); University of North Carolina (J.D., 2005). ***PRACTICE AREAS:*** Civil Litigation; General Practice. **Email:** stroxler@hillevans.com

All Attorneys are members of the Greensboro, North Carolina and American Bar Associations.

REPRESENTATIVE CLIENTS: American International Group, Inc.; American International Adjustment Company; Anthem Insurance Co.; Bruce-Terminix Company; Central Insurance Companies; Children's Home Society of N.C., Inc.; Cincinnati Insurance Company; City of Greensboro, N.C.; Clayson Knitting Company, Inc.; Crawford & Company; Friends Homes, Inc.; Ford Motor Credit Co.; GAB Business Services; Gilbarco Inc.; Hedgecock Lumber Company; Jefferson-Pilot Corp.; Jefferson Smurfit Corporation; K-Mart Corporation; Lawyers Mutual Liability Insurance Company; Liberty Embroidery, Inc.; Liberty Finance Company; Overnight Transportation Co.; Pennsylvania National Insurance Group; Rheem Manufacturing Company; Ryder Truck Lines; Sentry Insurance Group; Unigard Insurance Group; Universal Underwriters Insurance Co.
APPROVED ATTORNEYS FOR: First American Title Insurance Co.; Lawyers Title Insurance Corp.

THE HODGMAN LAW FIRM

Established in 1993

FIRST CITIZENS BANK BUILDING
100 SOUTH ELM STREET, SUITE 514
P.O. BOX 3245
GREENSBORO, NORTH CAROLINA 27402
Telephone: 336-373-0934
Fax: 336-373-0160
URL: http://www.hodgmanlaw.com
Email: rshodgman@aol.com
URL: http://www.lawyers.com/hodgmanlawfirm

Workers Compensation, Personal Injury, Automobile Accidents and Injuries, Products Liability, Social Security.

ROBERT S. HODGMAN, born Cambridge, Massachusetts, January 17, 1947; admitted to bar, 1972, North Carolina and U.S. District Court, Eastern and Middle Districts of North Carolina; 1976, U.S. Court of Appeals, Third and Fourth Circuits. *Education:* Duke University (A.B., 1969); University of North Carolina (J.D., 1972). *Member:* Greensboro and North Carolina (Past Chair, Workers Compensation Section, 1997) Bar Associations; North Carolina Academy of Trial Lawyers (Past Trustee; Member: Worker's Rights Committee; Executive Committee, 1997-2003); Workplace Injury Law and Advocacy Group (Charter Member; 1997-2005; Member, Board of Directors, 2004—); The Association of Trial Lawyers of America; North Carolina College of Advocacy. (Board Certified Specialist in Workers Compensation Law, North Carolina State Board of Legal Specialization). ***PRACTICE AREAS:*** Workers Compensation; Personal Injury; Automobile Accidents and Injuries. **Email:** RSHodgman@aol.com

HEATHER PAIGE HODGMAN, born Greensboro, NC, April 25, 1979; admitted to bar, 2004, North Carolina. *Education:* Duke University (A.B., 2001); William & Mary Law School (J.D., 2004). *Member:* Greensboro Bar Association; North Carolina Academy of Trial Lawyers; Workplace Injury Law and Advocacy Group. ***PRACTICE AREAS:*** Workers Compensation; Personal Injury.

Language: Spanish.

WILLIAM F. HORSLEY, P.A.

500-D STATE STREET
GREENSBORO, NORTH CAROLINA 27405
Telephone: 336-691-0077; 1-800-953-2542
Fax: 336-691-8083
URL: http://www.lawyers.com/horsleylawfirm
Email: wfh@horsleylawfirm.com
URL: http://www.horsleylawfirm.com

Personal Injury, Product Liability, Auto Accidents, Wrongful Death, Nursing Home Negligence, Medical Malpractice, Premises Liability, Inadequate Security, Land Condemnation.

FIRM PROFILE: William F. Horsley, P.A. is dedicated to the protection of the rights of individuals injured by the carelessness of others. The firm's philosophy is to provide professional, personal services to our clients. Bill Horsley is a past President of the North Carolina Academy of Trial Lawyers and has long been recognized by his peers as one of the outstanding trial lawyers in North Carolina. He is listed in "The Best Lawyers in America." He is a frequent speaker at programs to educate other lawyers in the representation of injured people.

(This Listing Continued)

WILLIAM F. HORSLEY, born Birmingham, Alabama, October 2, 1947; admitted to bar, 1972, North Carolina; 1973, U.S. Court of Appeals, Fourth Circuit; 2001, U.S Supreme Court. *Education:* Peabody College (B.A., 1969); Wake Forest University (J.D., 1972). Best Lawyers in America, 1992—. Advocate, American Board of Trial Advocates. *Member:* North Carolina Bar Association; North Carolina Academy of Trial Lawyers (Member, Board of Governors, 1986-1987, 1999-2000; Vice President, Membership, 1987-1989; Vice President, Education, 1989-1990; Chair, Small Office Practice Section, 1998-1999; Chair, Political Action Committee, 1995-1997; President-Elect, 1990-1991; President, 1991-1992); The Association of Trial Lawyers of America; Academy of Catastrophic Injury Attorneys. ***PRACTICE AREAS:*** Personal Injury; Wrongful Death; Nursing Home Negligence; Medical Malpractice; Automobile Accidents and Injuries; Products Liability. **Email:** wfh@horsleylawfirm.com

HUNTER, HIGGINS, MILES, ELAM & BENJAMIN, PLLC

Established in 2002

101 WEST FRIENDLY AVENUE, SUITE 500
GREENSBORO, NORTH CAROLINA 27401
Telephone: 336-273-1600
Fax: 336-274-4650
URL: http://www.greensborolaw.com
Email: hjeb@greensborolaw.com
URL: http://www.lawyers.com/hunterhiggins

Mailing Address: P.O. Box 20570, Greensboro, NC 27420

General Business, Commercial, Real Estate, Arbitration and Mediation, Securities, Election Law, Business Bankruptcy and Workouts, Business and Civil Litigation, Appeals, Personal Injury, Wrongful Death, Medical Malpractice, Criminal Defense, Family Law, Insurance, Construction, Employment, Education, Environmental Law, Tax, Estate Planning, Estate Administration, Intellectual Property Law.

JOHN T. HIGGINS, JR., born Mineola, New York, 1947; admitted to bar, 1972, North Carolina. *Education:* University of Pennsylvania (B.A., 1969); University of North Carolina (J.D., 1972). Member, City of Greensboro Zoning Commission, 2001-2004. Chairman of Triad Real Estate and Building Industry Coalition, 2005. *Member:* North Carolina Bar Association (Member, Sections on: Real Property, Zoning, Planning and Land Use). ***PRACTICE AREAS:*** Real Estate; Finance; Zoning, Planning and Land Use. **Email:** jhiggins@greensborolaw.com

ROBERT N. HUNTER, JR., born Greensboro, North Carolina, March 30, 1947; admitted to bar, 1973, North Carolina, U.S. District Court, Western, Middle and Eastern Districts of North Carolina; 1976, U.S. Court of Appeals, Fourth Circuit; 1985, U.S. Supreme Court. *Education:* University of North Carolina (B.A., 1969; J.D., 1973). Public Administrator, Guilford County, 1981-1994. Chairman, North Carolina State Board of Elections, 1985-1989. NASD Securities Arbitrator. *Member:* Greensboro, North Carolina (Member, Committee on Constitutional Rights) and American (Member, Sections on: Real Property, Probate and Trust; Public Contract) Bar Associations; North Carolina State Bar (Chairman); North Carolina Academy of Trial Lawyers; American Inns of Court; American Board of Trial Advocates. ***PRACTICE AREAS:*** Estate Law; Probate Law; Litigation; Arbitration; Securities; Real Property; Civil Rights. **Email:** rnhunterjr@greensborolaw.com

JAMES W. MILES, JR., born Roanoke, Virginia, 1948; admitted to bar, 1973, North Carolina; U.S. District Court, Western, Middle and Eastern Districts of North Carolina; U.S. Court of Appeals, Fourth Circuit. *Education:* University of North Carolina (B.A., 1970; J.D., 1973). *Member:* Greensboro Bar Association; North Carolina Bar Association (Member, Sections on: Business; Litigation; Environmental); North Carolina State Bar. ***PRACTICE AREAS:*** Business Law; Litigation; Environmental Law. **Email:** jmiles@greensborolaw.com

RAYFORD K. ADAMS III, born Annapolis, Maryland, July 9, 1950; admitted to bar, 1979, North Carolina and U.S. District Court, Western, Middle and Eastern Districts of North Carolina; 1985, U.S. Court of Appeals, Fourth Circuit; 2002, U.S. Supreme Court. *Education:* Davidson College (B.S., 1972); Wake Forest University (J.D., 1979). Member, Moot Court Board. Chapter 13 Standing Trustee, Middle District of North Carolina (Winston-Salem Division), 1979-1980. Adjunct Professor of Law, Wake Forest University School of Law, 1998. Director, Middle District Bankruptcy Institute. *Member:* Greensboro, North Carolina (Member, Bankruptcy Section Council, 1988-1991; Treasurer, 2002-2004) and American Bar Associations; North Carolina State Bar (Member, Bankruptcy Specialization Committee, 1991-1998; Chair, 1995-1998); American Bankruptcy Institute. (Board Certified Specialist in Business and Consumer Bankruptcy Law, North Carolina State Bar Board of Legal Specialization). ***PRACTICE AREAS:*** Bankruptcy Law; Bankruptcy Chapter 11; Bankruptcy Chapter 7; Commercial Bankruptcy; Debtor Bankruptcy; Creditors Rights; Bankruptcy Appeals; Bankruptcy Litigation; Workouts; Commercial Law. **Email:** rkadams@greensborolaw.com

WILLIAM P. BENJAMIN, born New Orleans, Louisiana, December 27, 1953; admitted to bar, 1979, Louisiana; 1984, North Carolina. *Education:* University of North Carolina, Chapel Hill (B.S., 1976); Tulane University (J.D., 1979). Certified Public Accountant, Louisiana, 1980—and North Carolina, 1982—. *Member:* North Carolina State Bar; Greensboro, North Carolina, Louisiana State and American Bar Associations. ***PRACTICE AREAS:*** Business Law; Corporate Law; Estates; Real Estate; Probate; Tax. **Email:** wbenjamin@greensborolaw.com

WILLIAM A. EAGLES, born Kinston, North Carolina, 1948; admitted to bar, 1979, North Carolina; 1980, District of Columbia; 1983, Arkansas; U.S. Supreme Court. *Education:* North Carolina State University (B.S., 1970); University of North Carolina (M.A., 1975); Wake Forest University (J.D., 1979). Phi Alpha Delta. Golden Chain, Business Editor, Wake Forest Law Review, 1979. Certified Mediator. *Member:* Greensboro, North Carolina and American Bar Associations. ***PRACTICE AREAS:*** Litigation; Mediation. **Email:** weagles@greensborolaw.com

(This Listing Continued)

HUNTER, HIGGINS, MILES, ELAM & BENJAMIN, PLLC, Greensboro—Continued

JOHN C. ELAM, born Chapel Hill, North Carolina, March 21, 1953; admitted to bar, 1981, North Carolina and U.S. District Court, Middle District of North Carolina. *Education:* University of North Carolina at Chapel Hill (B.A., 1975); Wake Forest University (J.D., 1981). Certified Public Mediator. *Member:* Greensboro and North Carolina Bar Associations; North Carolina State Bar. ***PRACTICE AREAS:*** Personal Injury Litigation; Civil Litigation; Criminal Litigation; Mediation; Traffic Violations; Criminal Law; Eminent Domain; Medical Malpractice. ***Email:*** jelam@greensborolaw.com

ROBERT G. McIVER, born Greensboro, North Carolina, November 2, 1952; admitted to bar, 1981, Louisiana and U.S. District Court, Eastern District of Louisiana; 1982, U.S. Court of Appeals, 5th Circuit; 1984, U.S. District Court, Western District of Louisiana; 1986, North Carolina, U.S. District Court, Middle, Western and Eastern Districts of North Carolina and U.S. Court of Appeals, 4th Circuit. *Education:* Harvard University (B.A., cum laude, 1975); Trinity College, Dublin, Ireland (Diploma, 1976); University of Virginia (J.D., 1980). *Member:* Greensboro and American Bar Associations; North Carolina State Bar. ***PRACTICE AREAS:*** Construction Law; Medical Malpractice; Insurance Issues; General Liability. ***Email:*** rmciver@greensborolaw.com

GILBERT J. ANDIA, JR., born Bay Shore, New York, June 1, 1960; admitted to bar, 1989, North Carolina; 1996, U.S. District Court, Middle District of North Carolina; 1999, U.S. District Court, Western District of North Carolina and U.S. Supreme Court; 1998, U.S. Court of Appeals, Fourth Circuit; registered to practice before U.S. Patent and Trademark Office. *Education:* Virginia Polytechnic Institute and State University (B.S., 1982); Wake Forest University (J.D., cum laude, 1989). Order of Barristers. Member, 1988-1989 and Articles Editor, 1989, Wake Forest Law Review. National Trial Team, 1989.*Member:* North Carolina and Federal Bar Association; Joseph Branch Inn of Court. [Lt. Col., U.S.A.F.R.]. ***PRACTICE AREAS:*** Patent, Trademark and Copyright; Business Litigation; Litigation; Unfair Competition. ***Email:*** bandia@greensborolaw.com

RONDA L. LOWE, born Thomasville, North Carolina, 1957; admitted to bar, 1990, North Carolina; 1992, U.S. District Court, Middle District of North Carolina; 1993, U.S. District Court, Eastern and Western Districts of North Carolina and U.S. Court of Appeals, Fourth Circuit. *Education:* University of North Carolina at Greensboro (B.A., 1980); Campbell Law School (J.D., cum laude, 1990). Phi Kappa Phi; Order of the Barristers; National Moot Court Team; Member, Campbell Law Review, 1989-1990. *Member:* North Carolina Bar Association (Labor and Employment Sections). ***PRACTICE AREAS:*** Labor and Employment Law; Education Law; Litigation. ***Email:*** rlowe@greensborolaw.com

BRIAN TOMLIN, born Lynchburg, Virginia, July 26, 1960; admitted to bar, 1996, North Carolina; U.S. District Court, Middle District of North Carolina; U.S. Court of Appeals, Fourth Circuit. *Education:* University of Virginia (B.A., 1983); University of North Carolina, Greensboro (M.Ed., 1991); North Carolina Central University (J.D., cum laude, 1996). ***PRACTICE AREAS:*** Criminal Law; Traffic Violations; Personal Injury; Family Law. ***Email:*** btomlin@greensborolaw.com

JEFFREY M. DAVIS, born Greensboro, North Carolina, March 19, 1978; admitted to bar, 2003, North Carolina, U.S. District Court, Western, Middle, Eastern Districts of North Carolina. *Education:* Clemson University (B.A., 2000); University of North Carolina at Chapel Hill (J.D., 2003). President, Clemson University Student Senate. Algernon Sydney Sullivan Award for Service to the Community. Eugene Gressman and Daniel H. Pollitt Award for Appellate Advocacy. Craven Bench, Holderness Moot Court. *Member:* Greensboro and North Carolina Bar Associations, North Carolina State Bar; Guilford Inn of Court. ***PRACTICE AREAS:*** Debtor and Creditor Collections; Commercial Litigation; Commercial Law; Civil Litigation. ***Email:*** jdavis@greensborolaw.com

ASSOCIATES

JENNIFER F. ADAMS, born Concord, North Carolina, May 1, 1976; admitted to bar, 2001, North Carolina, U.S. Court of Appeals, Fourth Circuit; 2002, U.S. District Court, Middle and Eastern Districts of North Carolina. *Education:* Davidson College (B.A., 1998); Wake Forest University (J.D., 2001). ***PRACTICE AREAS:*** Bankruptcy Law; Bankruptcy Appeals. ***Email:*** jadams@greensborolaw.com

LISA JOHNSON-TONKINS, born Greensboro, North Carolina, June 20, 1972; admitted to bar, 2003, North Carolina. *Education:* North Carolina Agricultural & Technical State University (B.A., 1994); North Carolina Central University (J.D., 2003). *Member:* North Carolina Bar Association; American Bar Association; Black Lawyers Association; Guilford Inns of Court. ***PRACTICE AREAS:*** Bankruptcy (10%); Real Estate (5%); Traffic Violations (20%); General Practice (65%). ***Email:*** ljohnson-tonkins@greensborolaw.com

AMANDA M. PATTY, born Greensboro, North Carolina, 1978; admitted to bar, 2004, North Carolina. *Education:* University of North Carolina (B.A., Psychology, 2000); University of Pittsburgh (J.D., 2004). *Member:* Greensboro, North Carolina and American Bar Associations; North Carolina State Bar; Guilford County Association of Women Attorneys; North Carolina Association of Women Attorneys. ***PRACTICE AREAS:*** Business Law; Corporate Law; Estate Planning; Trusts and Estates; Taxation. ***Email:*** apatty@greensborolaw.com

OF COUNSEL

JAMES N. ROGERS, born Olean, New York, 1941; admitted to bar, 1966, New York; 1990, Virginia; 1991, West Virginia (Not admitted in North Carolina). *Education:* Northeastern University (B.S., 1963); State University of New York at Buffalo (J.D., 1966); George Washington University (LL.M., 1972). Certified North Carolina Mediator. *Member:* West Virginia State Bar. [Capt. USN, U.S. Navy JAG, (Retired)]. ***PRACTICE AREAS:*** Real Estate; Finance; Estate Planning; Mediation.

ISAACSON ISAACSON & SHERIDAN, LLP

SUITE 400 BANK OF AMERICA BUILDING
101 WEST FRIENDLY AVENUE
P.O. BOX 1888
GREENSBORO, NORTH CAROLINA 27402
Telephone: 336-275-7626
Fax: 336-273-7293
URL: http://www.lawyers.com/iislaw

General Practice in State and Federal Courts. Business & Corporate, Real Estate (Residential and Commercial), Municipal/Zoning, Commercial, Tax, Probate and International Law.

MEMBERS OF FIRM

HENRY H. ISAACSON, born Greensboro, North Carolina, April 29, 1933; admitted to bar, 1958, North Carolina. *Education:* University of North Carolina (A.B., 1955; J.D., with honors, 1958). Phi Delta Phi. Member, Student Board of Editors, North Carolina Law Review, 1956-1957. Member: Greensboro Human Relations Commission, 1967-1969; Governmental Center Commission, 1967-1972; Greensboro Alcoholic Beverage Control Board, 1979-1988 and Chairman, 1980-1988. Piedmont Triad Airport Authority, 1999—and Chairman, 2003—. President, North Carolina Association of ABC Boards, 1987-1988. Board of Trustees, North Carolina, A&T State University, 1999—. *Member:* Greensboro, North Carolina and American Bar Associations. [Capt., JAGD, Active Duty, 1958-1961]. ***PRACTICE AREAS:*** Zoning; Land Use and Regulation; Civil Litigation; General Corporate Law. ***Email:*** hisaacson@iislaw.com

MARC L. ISAACSON, born Chapel Hill, North Carolina, October 15, 1956; admitted to bar, 1983, North Carolina. *Education:* University of North Carolina (B.A., 1978); Wake Forest University (J.D., 1982). Member, 1981-1982 and Member, Editorial Staff, 1982, Wake Forest Law Review. Author: "Article 9: U.C.C.-Secured Transactions," 18 Wake Forest Law Review 390, Symposium Issue, 1982. Member, Greensboro Parks & Recreation Commission, 1985-1991. Chairman, Board of Trustees Natural Science Center of Greensboro, Inc., 1993—. Member, Guilford County Board of Elections, 1992-2002; Secretary, 1995; Chairman, 1996-2002. Member, War Memorial Coliseum Commission, 1994-2001. *Member:* Greensboro, North Carolina (Member, Sections on Business Law, Environmental, Real Property and Tax; Member, Real Property Section Council, 1998-2002) and American Bar Associations. ***PRACTICE AREAS:*** General Corporate Law; Mergers and Acquisitions; Real Property Law (Commercial and Residential); Estate Planning and Administration. ***Email:*** misaacson@iislaw.com

DESMOND G. SHERIDAN, born Barbados, West Indies, November 2, 1957; admitted to bar, 1986, North Carolina. *Education:* University of Florida (B.S., 1978; M.B.A., 1980); University of North Carolina (J.D., with honors, 1986). Order of the Coif. Member, North Carolina Law Review, 1984-1985. Certified Public Accountant, North Carolina, 1984 and Florida, 1981. *Member:* Greensboro, North Carolina (Member, Sections on Business Law, Real Property and Tax; Member, Tax Section Council, 1997-2000) and American (Member, Tax Section) Bar Associations; North Carolina Association of Certified Public Accountants (Member Board of Directors, 1992-1995); American Institute of Certified Public Accountants. ***PRACTICE AREAS:*** Taxation; Business; Corporate; Partnership; Limited Liability Company; Commercial Real Estate. ***Email:*** dsheridan@iislaw.com

JENNIFER N. FOUNTAIN, born Lexington, North Carolina, July 3, 1972; admitted to bar, 1999, North Carolina. *Education:* University of Georgia (B.A., 1994); University of Richmond (J.D., with honors, 1999). Recipient, CALI Award for Insurance Law. Member, Journal of Law and the Public Interest. *Member:* Greensboro, North Carolina and American (Member, Litigation Section) Bar Associations. ***PRACTICE AREAS:*** Litigation; Employment Law; Corporate Law; Real Property. ***Email:*** jfountain@iislaw.com

ASSOCIATES

DEBBI L. ABERMAN, born Miami, Florida, February 19, 1956; admitted to bar, 1981, Florida and U.S. District Court, Southern District of Florida; 1994, North Carolina. *Education:* University of Florida (B.A., 1977; J.D., 1981). Phi Beta Kappa. *Member:* Dade County and American Bar Associations; The Florida Bar. ***PRACTICE AREAS:*** Commercial Real Estate; Residential Real Estate.

JOAN M. BERGMAN, born New York, N.Y., September 13, 1972; admitted to bar, 1998, Florida; 2004, North Carolina. *Education:* Loyola College (B.A., 1994); Widener University (J.D., 1997). Member, Moot Court Honor Society. ***PRACTICE AREAS:*** Commercial Real Estate; Residential Real Estate. ***Email:*** jbergman@iislaw.com

REPRESENTATIVE CLIENTS: Ace / Avant Concrete Construction Co.; Alliance Properties; Autozone; Bank of America; BellSouth Corporation; Biscuitville; Blue Ridge Companies; BP Amoco; Carmike Theaters; Dixie Sales Co.; D.R. Horton, Inc. (Arrapco Homes); Fairway Outdoor Advertising; The Faison Company; Fortis Homes; Gibbs Machine Co.; Japan Tech. Inc.; Jefferson-Pilot Corporation; Key Risk Management Services; Merrill Lynch Pierce Fenner & Smith, Inc.; Morrisette Paper Co.; Pearce Financial Group, Inc.; Portrait Homes; The Sadolin Cos. (Denmark); Sandhills Foods, Inc.; Sav-Way Stores; Shionogi Qualicaps, Inc.; Southeastern Eye Center; Southern Rubber Co.; Triad Freightliner of Greensboro, Inc.; Tournament Hosts of Greensboro, Inc.; Westminster Homes, Inc.; Z. Bavelloni U.S.A., Inc.
APPROVED ATTORNEYS FOR: First American Title Insurance Co.; Wachovia Mortgage Co.; Lawyers Title Insurance Co.; Bank of America; Ticor Title Insurance Co.; Investors Title Insurance Co.

IVEY, McCLELLAN, GATTON & TALCOTT, L.L.P.

121 SOUTH ELM STREET
P.O. BOX 3324
GREENSBORO, NORTH CAROLINA 27402
Telephone: 336-274-4658
Telefax: 336-274-4540

General Practice in all State and Federal Courts. Litigation, Insurance, Tax, Bankruptcy, Commercial, Corporation, Real Estate, Domestic, Criminal and Probate Law.

(This Listing Continued)

MEMBERS OF FIRM

CHARLES M. IVEY, JR. (1914-1993)

CHARLES M. IVEY, III, born Greensboro, North Carolina, February 11, 1953; admitted to bar, 1978, North Carolina. *Education:* University of North Carolina (A.B., 1975); Wake Forest University (J.D., 1978). Member, Panel of Trustees, Bankruptcy Court, Middle District of North Carolina, 1980—. Contributing Author: *North Carolina Bankruptcy Manual,* (1987). *Member:* Greensboro and North Carolina (Counsel Member, Bankruptcy Section, 1981-1984) Bar Associations; American Bankruptcy Institute; The North Carolina State Bar; Turnaround Management Association; Commercial Law League of America (Counsel Member, Bankruptcy and Insolvency Section, 1986-1987). (Board Certified Specialist in Business and Consumer Bankruptcy Law, North Carolina State Bar Board of Legal Specialization). ***PRACTICE AREAS:*** Bankruptcy Law; Commercial Litigation; Business Law. ***Email:*** cmi@imgt-law.com

ROBERT L. McCLELLAN, born Greensboro, North Carolina, July 27, 1952; admitted to bar, 1978, North Carolina. *Education:* University of North Carolina (B.A., 1974); Wake Forest University (J.D., 1978). Phi Alpha Delta. Assistant Public Defender, 1979-1986. *Member:* Greensboro and North Carolina (Litigation and Criminal Law Sections) Bar Associations; The North Carolina State Bar; Greensboro Criminal Defense Lawyers Association; North Carolina Academy of Trial Lawyers. ***PRACTICE AREAS:*** Criminal Law; Traffic Law; Civil Litigation; Personal Injury Law. ***Email:*** rlm@imgt-law.com

EDWIN R. GATTON, born Statesville, North Carolina, July 11, 1947; admitted to bar, 1973, North Carolina; U.S. District Court, Middle and Eastern Districts of North Carolina; U.S. Court of Appeals, Fourth Circuit. *Education:* Appalachian State University (B.S., 1969); Wake Forest University (J.D., 1973). Phi Alpha Delta. Staff Member, Wake Forest Law Review, 1971-1973. Author: "Constitutional Law-Free Speech Regulated in Shopping Centers," 8 Wake Forest Law Review 590, 1972. *Member:* Greensboro and North Carolina (Member: Corporate Counsel Committee, 1978-1988; Labor and Employment Law Section) Bar Associations; North Carolina State Bar; Association of Life Insurance Counsel. ***PRACTICE AREAS:*** Civil Litigation; Estate Planning Law; Personal Injury Law; Domestic Law; General Commercial Law. ***Email:*** erg@imgt-law.com

JAMES K. TALCOTT, born Ft. Myers, Florida, July 15, 1946; admitted to bar, 1985, North Carolina and U.S. District Court, Middle District of North Carolina. *Education:* University of Florida (B.S., 1969); Wake Forest University (J.D., 1985). Certified Public Accountant, North Carolina, 1979. *Member:* Greensboro and North Carolina (Counsel Member, Bankruptcy Section, 2001-2004) Bar Associations; North Carolina State Bar; American Bankruptcy Institute; Turnaround Management Association. (Board Certified Specialist in Business and Consumer Bankruptcy Law, North Carolina State Bar Board of Legal Specialization). ***PRACTICE AREAS:*** Bankruptcy Law; Corporate Law; Commercial Law. ***Email:*** jkt@imgt-law.com

DIRK W. SIEGMUND, born Plainfield, New Jersey, November 18, 1959; admitted to bar, 1994, North Carolina and U.S. District Court, Middle District of North Carolina. *Education:* University of Delaware (B.S.B.A., 1983); University of Wisconsin at Madison (M.B.A., 1984); Wake Forest University (J.D., 1994). *Member:* Greensboro Bar Association; North Carolina Bar Association (Counsel Member, Bankruptcy Section, 1999-2002); American Bar Association; American Bankruptcy Institute. (Board Certified Specialist in Business and Consumer Bankruptcy Law, North Carolina State Board of Legal Specialization). ***PRACTICE AREAS:*** Bankruptcy; Business Litigation; Corporate; Tax. ***Email:*** dws@imgt-law.com

ERIC A. RICHARDSON, born Norristown, Pennsylvania, December 15, 1968; admitted to bar, 1996, North Carolina and U.S. District Court, Middle District of North Carolina. *Education:* College of William & Mary (B.A., 1991); Wake Forest University (J.D., 1996). Staff Member, 1994-1995 and Senior Notes and Comments Editor, 1995-1996, Wake Forest Law Review. Author: Note, "Of Presumed Presidential Quality: Who Should Succeed to the Presidency When the President and Vice President Are Gone?" 30 Wake Forest Law Review 617. *Member:* Greensboro and North Carolina (Member, Family Law Section) Bar Associations; North Carolina Academy of Trial Lawyers (Member, Family Law and Workers Compensation Sections). ***PRACTICE AREAS:*** Civil Litigation; Family Law; Personal Injury; Workers Compensation. ***Email:*** ear@imgt-law.com

ASSOCIATES

JOHN M. BLUST, born Hamilton, Ohio, June 4, 1954; admitted to bar, 1982, North Carolina and U.S. District Court, Middle, Western and Eastern District of North Carolina. *Education:* University of North Carolina at Chapel Hill (B.S., 1979; J.D., 1982). State Senator, North Carolina, 1996-1998. State Representative, 2001—. *Member:* Greensboro and North Carolina (Member, Sections on: Bankruptcy; Tax) Bar Associations; North Carolina State Bar. [Captain, U.S. Army, 1982-1985 active duty]. ***PRACTICE AREAS:*** Bankruptcy Law; Tax Law; Estate Planning Law; Fiduciary Law; Corporate Law; Commercial Law; Business Law. ***Email:*** jmb@imgt-law.com

MARY BETH B. SWECKER, born Staunton, Virginia, September 5, 1961; admitted to bar, 1988, North Carolina; 1989, U.S. Court of Appeals, Fourth Circuit and U.S. District Court, Middle District of North Carolina; 1994, Pennsylvania. *Education:* University of Virginia (B.S., 1983); Wake Forest University (J.D., 1988). Member, 1986-1988 and Notes and Comments Editor, 1987-1988, Wake Forest University Law Review. Member: Moot Court Board; Trial Bar. *Member:* Greensboro (Member, Family Law Section, Secretary-Treasurer, 1992-1993), North Carolina (Member, Family Law Section) and American Bar Associations. ***LANGUAGES:*** French. ***PRACTICE AREAS:*** Domestic Relations; Family Law; Bankruptcy. ***Email:*** mbs@imgt-law.com

J. MARSHALL SHELTON, born Greensboro, North Carolina, July 18, 1975; admitted to bar, 2003, North Carolina, U.S. District Court, Middle District of North Carolina and U.S. Court of Appeals, Fourth Circuit. *Education:* University of North Carolina at Chapel Hill (B.S., 1998); Ohio Northern University (J.D., 2003). Member, Ohio Northern University Law Review, 2000-2003. Presiding Judge, Board of Advocates, Ohio Northern University, Moot Court Executive Board, International Law. *Member:* Greensboro, North Carolina (Member, Young Lawyers Division and Bankruptcy Section) and American Bar Associations. ***PRACTICE AREAS:*** Bankruptcy; Federal Criminal Law. ***Email:*** jms@imgt-law.com

(This Listing Continued)

REPRESENTATIVE CLIENTS: Laurel Hill Paper Company; Alexander Community Hospital, Inc.; Rite Industries, Inc.; Mercedes-Benz Credit Corporation; Sedgewick Industries, Inc.; Greensboro Academy; Oak Ridge Military Academy; Computer Net Inc.; Guilford Assembly, Inc.; Phoenix Grill Company; Whitin Roberts Company; Harley Davidson Credit Corp.
APPROVED ATTORNEYS FOR: Jefferson-Pilot Title Insurance Co.; Lawyers Title Insurance Corp.

JOHNSON, PEDDRICK, KANTLEHNER & McDONALD, P.L.L.C.

440 WEST MARKET STREET, SUITE 300
GREENSBORO, NORTH CAROLINA 27401
Telephone: 336-574-9720
Telefax: 336-574-9734
URL: http://www.lawyers.com/jpmck

Estate Planning, Estate and Trust Administration, Probate, Corporate and Business Law, Tax Services, Elder Law, Guardianship.

RONALD P. JOHNSON, born Clinton, South Carolina, July 28, 1949; admitted to bar, 1974, North Carolina. *Education:* University of South Carolina (B.A., magna cum laude, 1971; J.D., cum laude, 1974). Phi Beta Kappa; Omicron Delta Kappa; Phi Eta Sigma; Order of Wig and Robe, 1973-1974. Member of Staff, 1972-1973, Contributor, 1973 and Comments Editor, 1973-1974, South Carolina Law Review. *Member:* Greensboro, North Carolina and American Bar Associations; Greensboro Estate Planning Council (President, 2002-2003). (Board Certified Specialist in Estate Planning and Probate Law, North Carolina Board of Legal Specialization). ***PRACTICE AREAS:*** Estate Planning; Estate Administration; Business Law. ***Email:*** rjohnson@jplegal.net

MARTHA TAYLOR PEDDRICK, born Wilmington, Delaware, June 7, 1950; admitted to bar, 1984, North Carolina. *Education:* Pennsylvania State University; University of Delaware (B.A., with honors, 1971); University of North Carolina (M.S.W., 1974); Wake Forest University (J.D., 1984). Member, Moot Court Board. *Member:* Greensboro, North Carolina and American Bar Associations; Greensboro Estate Planning Council. (Board Certified Specialist in Estate Planning and Probate Law, North Carolina Board of Legal Specialization). ***PRACTICE AREAS:*** Estate Planning; Estate Administration; Guardianship; Business Law. ***Email:*** mpeddrick@jplegal.net

MARGARET ROBISON KANTLEHNER, born Atlanta, Georgia, August 27, 1959; admitted to bar, 1984, North Carolina. *Education:* Dartmouth College (A.B., 1981); Campbell University (J.D., 1984). Delta Theta Phi. Clerk of Courts, Campbell University School of Law, 1983-1984. U.S. Supreme Court Editor, Campbell Law Observer. *Member:* Greensboro (Treasurer and Secretary, Real Property Section, 1997-2000; Director, 2000-2003, Secretary, 2004-2005), North Carolina (Chair, Young Lawyers Division, 1995-1996) and American Bar Associations; Greensboro Estate Planning Council. ***PRACTICE AREAS:*** Estate Planning; Estate Administration; Guardianship; Real Estate. ***Email:*** mkantlehner@jplegal.net

DAVIS McDONALD, born Houston, Texas, October 4, 1957; admitted to bar, 1986, North Carolina. *Education:* Haverford College (A.B., 1979); University of North Carolina at Chapel Hill (J.D., 1986; M.B.A., 1986). *Member:* Greensboro, North Carolina and American Bar Associations; Greensboro Estate Planning Council. ***PRACTICE AREAS:*** Corporate Law; Estate Planning; Probate. ***Email:*** dmcdonald@jplegal.net

DAVID B. McLEAN, born Middletown, Ohio, September 28, 1966; admitted to bar, 1999, North Carolina. *Education:* Furman University (B.A., 1988); Southern Baptist Theological Seminary (M.Div., 1992); Wake Forest University (J.D., 1999). *Member:* North Carolina (Member: Elder Law Section Legislative Committee; Estate Planning Section) and American Bar Associations. ***LANGUAGES:*** French. ***PRACTICE AREAS:*** Elder Law; Estate Planning; Estate Administration; Guardianship. ***Email:*** dmclean@jplegal.net

---

HORACE M. KIMEL, JR.

BB&T BUILDING
201 W. MARKET STREET, SUITE 409
GREENSBORO, NORTH CAROLINA 27401
Telephone: 336-389-0830
Fax: 336-373-0947

Criminal, Traffic Offenses, Traffic Violations, Drug Offense, Homicide and Serious Offenses Against Persons. Personal Injury, Felonies, Misdemeanors, DWI, DMV Hearings, Driving While License Revoked.

FIRM PROFILE: Long term Guilford County District Attorney with over 24 years of criminal experience in District Attorney's Office. Put Jim Kimel's experience and knowledge to work for you.

HORACE M. KIMEL, JR., born Winston-Salem, North Carolina, September 24, 1948; admitted to bar, 1973, North Carolina, 1974, U.S. District Court, Western District North Carolina, 2002, U.S. District Court, Middle District of North Carolina. *Education:* University of North Carolina, Chapel Hill (B.A., 1970; J.D., 1973); National College of District Attorneys, Houston (Executive Prosecutors Course, Diploma). District Attorney, 1987-2001. President, NC Conference of District Attorneys, 1992-1993. ***PRACTICE AREAS:*** Criminal Law; Personal Injury; Traffic Violations; Driving While Intoxicated; Drivers License Suspension.

ALETA B. KISER

GREENSBORO, NORTH CAROLINA

(See High Point)

Bankruptcy, Traffic Violations, Criminal, Real Estate, Buying or Selling a Home, Personal Injury, Estate Planning, Social Security, Wills and Probate, Trusts and Estates, Probate, Estate Planning and General Practice.

CLAYTON B. KROHN

100 SOUTH ELM STREET, SUITE 430
GREENSBORO, NORTH CAROLINA 27401
Telephone: 336-379-7159
Fax: 336-272-7778

Email: claytonkrohn@yahoo.com
URL: http://www.claytonkrohnlaw.com

Civil Litigation, Juvenile Delinquency, Insurance, Copyrights, Trademarks, Collections, Traffic Violations, Personal Injury.

CLAYTON B. KROHN, born Cynthiana, Indiana, July 29, 1963; admitted to bar, 1998, North Carolina. *Education:* Michigan State University (B.A., 1986); University of North Carolina of Greensboro (M.M., 1991); Washington & Lee University (J.D., 1997). Member, Washington & Lee University School of Law National Mock Trial Team, 1997. Recipient, Fletcher Fellowship, 1988. *Member:* North Carolina Bar Association; North Carolina State Bar. ***PRACTICE AREAS:*** Litigation; Insurance; Copyrights; Trademarks; Collections; Juvenile Delinquency.

THE LAWING FIRM, P.A.

3859 BATTLEGROUND AVENUE, SUITE 210
GREENSBORO, NORTH CAROLINA 27410
Telephone: 336-288-0808
Fax: 336-288-0858
Email: sally@lawingfirm.com

Medical Malpractice.

SALLY A. LAWING, born Charlotte, North Carolina, October 23, 1954; admitted to bar, 1982, North Carolina. *Education:* University of North Carolina at Charlotte (B.A., with honors, 1977); University of North Carolina at Chapel Hill (J.D., with honors, 1982). Order of Barristers. Member: Holderness Moot Court Bench; National Moot Court Team. *Member:* Greensboro and North Carolina Bar Associations; North Carolina State Bar; American College of Trial Lawyers; American Board of Trial Advocates; North Carolina Academy of Trial Lawyers. ***PRACTICE AREAS:*** Medical Malpractice. ***Email:*** sally@lawingfirm.com

---

LAWING SHARPLESS & STAVOLA, P.A.

GREENSBORO, NORTH CAROLINA

(See Sharpless & Stavola, P.A.)

LAW OFFICES OF REBECCA A. LEIGH

301 SOUTH GREENE STREET, SUITE 201
GREENSBORO, NORTH CAROLINA 27401
Telephone: 336-389-1800
Fax: 336-389-0060;
URL: http://www.leighlawnc.com
Email: rebecca@leighlaw.com
URL: http://www.leighlaw.com

Business Litigation, Creditors Rights, Creditor Bankruptcy, Corporate Law, Banking Law, Civil Litigation, Equipment Financing and Leasing.

REBECCA A. LEIGH, born Kansas City, Missouri, March 17, 1951; admitted to bar, 1984, Texas; U.S. District Court, Southern District of Texas; 1986, U.S. District Court, Western District of Texas; 1988, U.S. District Court, Eastern and Northern Districts of Texas; 1993, U.S. Court of Appeals, Fifth Circuit; 1995, Florida and Supreme Court of Florida; 1997, North Carolina; U.S. District Court, Middle District of North Carolina; 1998, Eastern and Western Districts of North Carolina. *Education:* Elmira College (B.A., 1973); State University of New York at Oneonta (M.S., in Education, 1977); South Texas College of Law (J.D., 1983). Psi Chi Honor Society. *Member:* Greensboro and North Carolina Bar Associations; State Bar of Texas (Former Member, Grievance Committee District 4C); State Bar of North Carolina; The Florida Bar; American Bar Association; American Bankruptcy Institute. ***PRACTICE AREAS:*** Commercial Litigation; Bankruptcy Law; Commercial Leasing Law; Commercial Lending; Corporate Litigation.

KATHRYN S. LINDLEY

314 S. EUGENE STREET
GREENSBORO, NORTH CAROLINA 27402
Telephone: 336-333-9600
Fax: 336-274-6956
Email: lindleylaw@mindspring.com
URL: http://www.lindleylawfirm.com

Mailing Address: P.O. Box 3272, Greensboro, NC 27402

Family Law, Divorce, Visitation Rights, Domestic Violence, Child Support, Child Custody, Adoptions, Criminal Law, Driving While Intoxicated, Traffic Violations, Trusts and Estates, Estate Planning, Wills and Probate, Corporate, Business, Real Estate, Collections.

FIRM PROFILE: Ms. Lindley is an attorney, CPA, and certified Family Financial Mediator. She graduated from Wake Forest School of Law and opened her law practice in 1997 in Guilford County, North Carolina. While attending law school, Ms. Lindley worked as a Paramedic and for a local C.P.A. firm. She received her undergraduate degree in Accounting for UNC-Greensboro.

(This Listing Continued)

She is a member of the North Carolina and Greensboro Bar Association, The North Carolina Academy of Trial Lawyers, The North Carolina Association of Professional Family Mediators, The Guilford Inn of Court and several other professional organizations. She currently serves on the Board of the Greensboro Bar Association. Her primary areas of practice include Family Law Wills, Estates, & Trusts and Criminal Law.

Ms. Lindley is an active member of the Carolina Piedmont Chapter of the American Business Women's Association and has served in many offices within the chapter. She received national recognition as one of the 2000 Top Ten Business Women of ABWA, having been chosen from a field of 70,000 working women.

Her civic activities include: Second Vice President of the Family Life Council board; Treasurer of the Summit House Board; and Member and past president of The Guilford Center Board (formerly called Area Mental Health).

KATHRYN S. LINDLEY, born High Point, North Carolina, July 17; admitted to bar, 1997, North Carolina and U.S. District Court, Middle District of North Carolina. *Education:* Gulfford Technical Community College (A.D., 1980); University of North Carolina, Greensboro (B.S., 1989); Wake Forest University (J.D., 1997). 1995 Woman of the Year of Carolina Piedmont Chapter of ABWA. Treasurer, Carolina Piedmont Chapter, ABWA, 1997-1998. National Top Ten Business Woman of ABWA, 2000. Guilford Center Board Member, 2000—. Board Member: Family Life Council. Board Advisor, Sanctuary House; The Evergreens. Attorney Volunteer for Women's Resource Center. Parenting Children of Divorce Presenter. Past President and Secretary of Carolina Piedmont Chapter of ABWA. *Member:* Greensboro (Board of Directors), Eighteenth Judicial District and North Carolina Bar Associations; North Carolina State Bar; North Carolina Academy of Trial Lawyers.

CHARLES A. LLOYD

301 SOUTH GREENE STREET
SUITE 100
GREENSBORO, NORTH CAROLINA 27401
Telephone: 336-275-9358
Fax: 336-273-0502
URL: http://www.lawyers.com/charleslloyd

Criminal, Traffic, Driving While Impaired, Conspiracy, Felony, Drug Cases. Trials and Appeals in State and Federal Courts.

FIRM PROFILE: Over 90 reported cases including: State v. Humphries, 82 N.C. App. 749, 348 S.E. 2d 167 (1986) discretionary rev. dismissed 320 N.C. 165, 357 S.E. 2d 359 (1987); State v. Johnson, 317 N.C. 343, 346 S.E. 2d 596 (1986); State v. Trexler, 316 N.C. 528, 342 S.E. 2d 878 (1986).

CHARLES A. LLOYD, born Hickory, North Carolina, March 27, 1944; admitted to bar, 1969, North Carolina; 1970, U.S. District Court, Eastern, Middle and Western Districts; 1972, U.S. Court of Appeals, Fourth Circuit; 1974, U.S. Supreme Court. *Education:* Davidson College (B.A., 1966); University of North Carolina (J.D., 1969). *CLE Faculty:* North Carolina Academy of Trial Lawyers, North Carolina Bar Association; Greensboro Criminal Defense Lawyers, Wake Forest University. Law Clerk to the Honorable Algernon L. Butler, Chief Judge, U.S. District Court, Eastern District of North Carolina, 1969-1970. Assistant Attorney General, North Carolina Attorney General's Office, 1970-1974. Listed in Barry Tarlow's National Directory of Criminal Lawyers. The Best Lawyers in America, 1995-2002. *Member:* North Carolina (Chairman, Criminal Justice Section, 1986-1988; Committee Member, Criminal Specialization) and American Bar Associations; North Carolina State Bar; National Association of Criminal Defense Lawyers; Greensboro Criminal Defense Lawyers Association (President, 1983, 1988, 1994). (Board Certified Specialist in Criminal Law, North Carolina State Board of Legal Specialization). ***PRACTICE AREAS:*** Criminal Defense; Driving While Intoxicated; Federal Criminal Law; Felonies; Misdemeanors; Traffic Violations; Drug Crimes; White Collar Crime; Medicare Fraud.

LLOYD MILLER & ASSOCIATES, P.A.

PIEDMONT NATURAL GAS BUILDING
806 GREEN VALLEY ROAD, SUITE 203
GREENSBORO, NORTH CAROLINA 27408-7076
Telephone: 336-373-5991
Fax: 336-272-2180
URL: http://www.lloydmiller.com
URL: http://www.lloydmillerlaw.com

Mailing Address: P.O. Box 29247, Greensboro, NC 27429-9247

Trust Administration, Estate Administration, Estate Planning, Probate Administration, Taxation, Corporate Law, Limited Liability Company Law, Employee Benefits, Business Start Up, Partnership Law, Mergers and Acquisitions, Wills and Probate.

ROBERT B. LLOYD, JR., born York, Pennsylvania, July 20, 1926; admitted to bar, 1950, North Carolina. *Education:* Harvard University (A.B., cum laude, 1947); Duke University (J.D., LL.B., 1950). Phi Delta Phi. Listed in: The Best Lawyers in America; Who's Who in America (current ed.). Member, North Carolina State Bar Board of Legal Specialization, 1992-1998. Chairman: Probate Division Committee on Technology and Economics in Planning and Probate Administration, Section of Real Property, Probate and Trust Law, American Bar Association, 1975-1985; Chairman, Section of Estate Planning and Fiduciary Law, North Carolina Bar Association, 1980-1981. Vice Chairman, 1984-1986 and Chairman, 1987-1990, Specialty Committee on Probate and Fiduciary Law of North Carolina Board of Legal Specialization. *Member:* Judicial Conference of 4th Federal Circuit Court of Appeals. Fellow, American College of Trust and Estate Counsel, 1976—(North Carolina State Chairman, 1985; Member, Practice Committee and Editorial Board, 1996—). (Board Certified Specialist in Estate Planning and Probate Law, North Carolina

(This Listing Continued)

State Board of Legal Specialization). ***PRACTICE AREAS:*** Estate Planning; Probate Administration; Taxation; Corporate Law; Mergers and Acquisitions. ***Email:*** rbl@lloydmillerlaw.com

PETER J. MILLER, born Brooklyn, New York, November 20, 1956; admitted to bar, 1983, North Carolina; 1987, U.S. Tax Court. *Education:* Wake Forest University (B.A., 1978); University of North Carolina at Greensboro (M.B.A., 1983); Campbell University (J.D., cum laude, 1983). Omicron Delta Kappa; Phi Alpha Delta. Recipient, Prentice-Hall, Inc. Student Award in Taxation. Member, Campbell Law Review, 1981-1983. (Board Certified Specialist in Estate Planning and Probate Law, North Carolina State Board of Legal Specialization). ***PRACTICE AREAS:*** Estate Planning; Trust Administration; Estate Administration; Taxation; Employee Benefits; Corporate Law; Partnership Law; Limited Liability Company Law. ***Email:*** pjm@lloydmillerlaw.com

LEGAL SUPPORT PERSONNEL

LINDA S. CARY. *Education:* University of North Carolina at Greensboro (B.S., 1981; M.S., 2001). Certified Public Accountant. (CPA and Paralegal). ***Email:*** lsc@lloydmillerlaw.com

MACCORD MASON PLLC

Established in 1987

300 NORTH GREENE STREET, SUITE 1600
P.O. BOX 2974
GREENSBORO, NORTH CAROLINA 27402
Telephone: 336-273-4422
Fax: 336-271-2830
URL: http://www.maccordmason.com

Wilmington, North Carolina Office: 1209 Culbreth Drive, Suite 103, 28405. Telephone: 910-256-3557. Fax: 910-256-0523.

Raleigh, North Carolina Office: 510 Glenwood Avenue, Suite 321, 27611. Telephone: 919-664-8624. Fax: 919-664-8625.

Patent, Trademark, Copyright and Unfair Competition. Trade Secret Practice before all Courts. Intellectual Property Law, Litigation.

FIRM PROFILE: MacCord Mason PLLC is a law firm with offices in Greensboro, Raleigh and Wilmington, North Carolina. The firm concentrates in intellectual property and technology-related law, including United States and international patents, trademarks, copyrights, trade secrets, unfair competition, licensing and related litigation and contract matters. The attorneys making up the firm have diverse backgrounds in corporate and private practice in the intellectual property field, bringing to the firm a wide scope of experience in handling the range of issues faced in connection with intellectual property law, such as procurement, exploitation and enforcement of rights, In addition, defense against infringement claims is an important part of the firm's practice. The geographic scope of the practice is unlimited, with clients throughout North Carolina, the United States and the world. Intellectual property rights in foreign countries are obtained in cooperation with the firm's foreign associate law firms.

MEMBERS OF FIRM

EDWARD W. RILEE, born Newport News, Virginia, July 1, 1949; admitted to bar, 1982, Ohio; 1988, North Carolina; registered to practice before U.S. Patent and Trademark Office. *Education:* Virginia Polytechnic Institute (B.S., 1971; M.S., 1977; Phi Eta Sigma); Akron University Law School (J.D., 1982). Member, University of Akron Law Review, 1981-1982. Author: "The Protection of Property Rights in Computer Software," 14 Akron Law Review 85, 1980. *Member:* Greensboro, North Carolina and American Bar Associations; North Carolina State Bar; American Institute of Chemical Engineers; American Intellectual Property Law Association. ***PRACTICE AREAS:*** Patent Law; Trademark Law; Copyright Law; Unfair Competition Law; Trade Secrets Law; Intellectual Property Law. ***Email:*** erilee@maccordmason.com

HOWARD A. MACCORD, JR., born Dayton, Kentucky, August 10, 1950; admitted to bar, 1978, District of Columbia; 1982, U.S. Court of Appeals for the Federal Circuit; 1988, North Carolina; registered to practice before U.S. Patent and Trademark Office. *Education:* University of Virginia (B.A., with distinction, 1972); George Washington University (J.D., 1978). Sigma Pi Sigma. Delegate, National Council of Intellectual Property Law Associations, 1985-1990; Chair, 1996-1997. Board of Directors, National Inventors Hall of Fame Foundation, Inc. *Member:* Greensboro (Secretary, 1994-1995), North Carolina (Council Member, Intellectual Property Law Section, 1989-1993; Chairman, 1995-1996) and American Bar Associations; North Carolina State Bar; American Intellectual Property Law Association; Carolina Patent, Trademark & Copyright Law Association (President, 1992-1993). ***PRACTICE AREAS:*** Patent Law; Trademark Law; Copyright Law; Trade Secrets Law; Intellectual Property Law. ***Email:*** amaccord@maccordmason.com

WILLIAM J. MASON, born Morrison, Tennessee, June 13, 1940; admitted to bar, 1968, District of Columbia; 1973, North Carolina; registered to practice before U.S. Patent and Trademark Office. *Education:* Tennessee Technological University (B.S., 1962); George Washington University (J.D., 1967). *Member:* New Hanover and North Carolina Bar Associations. (Resident, Wilmington Office). ***PRACTICE AREAS:*** Patent Law; Trademark Law; Copyright Law; Licensing Law. ***Email:*** wmason@mmpatent.com

JAMES L. LESTER, born Rapid City, South Dakota, June 17, 1957; admitted to bar, 1982, Virginia; 1988, North Carolina; 1999, U.S. Supreme Court; registered to practice before U.S. Patent and Trademark Office. *Education:* Massachusetts Institute of Technology (S.B., Civil Engineering, 1979); Duke University (J.D., 1982). Chi Epsilon. North Carolina Certified Mediator. *Member:* Greensboro and North Carolina Bar Associations; American Intellectual Property Law Association. ***PRACTICE AREAS:*** Litigation; Patent Law; Trademark Law; Trade Secret Law. ***Email:*** jlester@maccordmason.com

(This Listing Continued)

ASSOCIATES

DEAN TURMAN, born Richmond, Virginia, January 23, 1969; admitted to bar, 2001, Florida; 2004, North Carolina; registered to practice before the U.S. Patent and Trademark Office. *Education:* North Carolina State University (B.S., with honors, 1992); University of Hawaii (J.D., 2001). *Member:* Greensboro and North Carolina Bar Associations; North Carolina State Bar; The Florida Bar. ***PRACTICE AREAS:*** Patents; Trademarks; Copyrights; Unfair Competition; Trade Secrets; Intellectual Property Law. ***Email:*** dturman@maccordmason.com

NANCY K. BURNS, born Winston-Salem, North Carolina, November 10, 1978; admitted to bar, 2005, North Carolina. *Education:* Wake Forest University (B.A., with honors, 2001); Wake Forest University School of Law (J.D., 2004). Minor in Biology, inorganic and organic chemistry and physics. Studied marine biology in London, England and Biological Field Research at the Dale Fort Field Centre, Haverfordwest, Pembrokeshire, Wales, 2000. Technology Editor, Wake Forest Intellectual Property Law Journal. *Member:* Wake Forest Chapter of Women in Law; Greensboro Bar Association; State Bar of North Carolina. ***PRACTICE AREAS:*** Patents; Trademarks; Copyrights; Unfair Competition; Trade Secrets; Intellectual Property. ***Email:*** nburns@maccordmason.com

R. KODY JONES, born Greensboro, North Carolina, September 23, 1977; admitted to bar, 2005, North Carolina; registered to practice before the U.S. Patent and Trademark Office. *Education:* University of North Carolina at Chapel Hill (B.S., Biology, 1999); University of Hawaii at Manoa (M.S., Microbiology, 2002); Franklin Pierce Law Center (J.D., cum laude, 2005). *Member:* North Carolina Bar Association; American Intellectual Property Law Association. ***PRACTICE AREAS:*** Patents; Copyrights; Trademarks; Unfair Competition; Trade Secrets; Intellectual Property.

OF COUNSEL

JINAN GLASGOW, born Meadville, Pennsylvania, May 4, 1968; admitted to bar, 1999, North Carolina; registered to practice before U.S. Patent and Trademark Office. *Education:* North Carolina State University (B.S., Textile Engineering, with distinction, 1990); University of North Carolina (J.D., 1999); Duke University (M.T.S., with distinction, 2000). Former United States Patent Examiner. *Member:* North Carolina and American Bar Associations; Triangle Intellectual Property Law Association; American Intellectual Property Law Association; Carolina Intellectual Property Law Association (Founder and President, 1996-1997). ***PRACTICE AREAS:*** Patents; Trademarks; Copyrights; Patent Licensing. ***Email:*** jinang@trianglepatents.com

LEGAL SUPPORT PERSONNEL

BEN FRINK, born Wilmington, North Carolina, August 19, 1961. *Education:* North Carolina State University (B.S., in Electrical Engineering, 1985); North Carolina State Continuing Education Program (Fiber Optics and Applications); North Hampton Community College (IPC cerified Surface Mount Solder Training); Georgia Tech (RF and Wireless Engineering, 1999). Registered to practice before U.S. Patent and Trademark Office. Founder, Remote Data Systems, Inc., 1993. (Resident, Wilmington Office). ***Email:*** bfrink@mmpatent.com

ANTHONY C. McLAUGHLIN

125 SOUTH ELM STREET, SUITE 604
P.O. BOX 217
GREENSBORO, NORTH CAROLINA 27402
Telephone: 336-274-8441
Fax: 336-274-8422
URL: http://www.lawyers.com/ncdirtlawyer
Email: dirt_law@bellsouth.net
URL: http://www.ncdirtlawyer.com

General Practice, Residential Real Estate, Commercial Real Estate, Wills and Probate.

ANTHONY C. McLAUGHLIN, born 1955; admitted to bar, 1980, North Carolina. *Education:* Rutgers University (B.A., business administration, 1977); St. John's University (J.D., 1980). Omicron Delta Epsilon. Editor, Tax Forum, St. John's University Publication, 1979-1980. Partner, Forrester & McLaughlin, 1982-1986. Partner, Rightsell, Forrester, McLaughlin & Knight, 1986-1987. Partner, Rightsell, McLaughlin & Shumate, 1987-1993. Solo Practitioner, 1993—. ***PRACTICE AREAS:*** Residential Real Estate; Commercial Real Estate; Corporate Law.

APPROVED ATTORNEY FOR: First American Title Ins. Co.; Stewart Title Guananty Co.; Investor's Title Insurance Agencies; Lawyer's Title Insurance Company; Commonwealth Land Title Insurance Company; American Title Insurance Company; Fidelity National Title Insurance Company; Chicago Title Insurance Company.

MORGAN, HERRING, MORGAN, GREEN, ROSENBLUTT & GILL, LLP

GREENSBORO, NORTH CAROLINA

(See High Point)

General Civil and Criminal Trial Practice in all State and Federal Courts. Interstate Commerce, Probate, Real Estate, Corporation and Tax Law. Torts. Traffic Violations and Driving Under the Influence, Personal Injury, Auto Accidents, Wills and Estates, Family Law, Divorce, Custody, Support, Adoption, Workers Compensation, Bankruptcy, Social Security, Employment Discrimination.

MORGENSTERN & BONUOMO, PLLC

Established in 1998

419 NORTH EDGEWORTH STREET

GREENSBORO, NORTH CAROLINA 27401

Telephone: 336-379-5006

Telefax: 336-275-3901

Practice Limited to Family and Domestic Relations Law.

BARBARA R. MORGENSTERN, born New York, N.Y., December 30, 1954; admitted to bar, 1986, North Carolina. *Education:* Indiana University (A.B., 1977); University of North Carolina (J.D., 1986). Listed in The Best Lawyers in America, Family Law Section, 1997—. Staff Member, 1984-1985 and Editor in Chief, 1985-1986, North Carolina Journal of International Law and Commercial Regulation. *Member:* Greensboro (Vice Chair, 1989-1991, Chair, 1991-1992 and Secretary-Treasurer, 1993-1994, Family Law Section), North Carolina (Vice Chair, 1992-1993 and Chair, 1993-1994, Family Law Section; Member: Continuing Legal Education Committee) and American (Member, Family Law Section) Bar Associations; North Carolina State Bar. Fellow, American Academy of Matrimonial Lawyers. (Board Certified Specialist in Family Law, North Carolina State Board of Legal Specialization). ***LANGUAGES:*** Spanish. ***PRACTICE AREAS:*** Family Law. ***Email:*** barbara@barkimlaw.com

KIM R. BONUOMO, born Memphis, Tennessee, October 28, 1961; admitted to bar, 1988, North Carolina; 1993, U.S. Court of Military Appeals; 1994, U.S. District Court, Middle District of North Carolina. *Education:* University of Richmond (B.A., magna cum laude, 1983); University of Virginia (J.D., 1988). Phi Beta Kappa. Justice Joseph Branch Inn of Court, 1997-2000. *Member:* Greensboro (Vice Chair, 1994-1995 and Chair, 1995-1996, Family Law Section) and North Carolina (Vice-Chair 2001-2002; Chair 2002-2003; Council Member, 1998-2004, Family Law Section,) Bar Associations; North Carolina State Bar. [Capt., U.S. Army JAGC, 1988-1993]. (Board Certified Specialist in Family Law, North Carolina State Board of Legal Specialization). ***PRACTICE AREAS:*** Family Law. ***Email:*** kim@barkimlaw.com

MORRIS YORK WILLIAMS SURLES & BARRINGER, L.L.P.

GREENSBORO, NORTH CAROLINA

(See Charlotte)

Civil, Business and Commercial Litigation. Insurance Defense Litigation, Insurance Coverage and Workers Compensation. Medical and Professional Malpractice Defense. Land Condemnation and Alternative Dispute Resolution Services.

MOSS, MASON & HILL

Established in 1997

BANK OF AMERICA BUILDING

101 WEST FRIENDLY AVENUE

SUITE 602

GREENSBORO, NORTH CAROLINA 27429

Telephone: 336-370-1282

Fax: 336-271-6838

Civil Litigation, Construction Litigation, Criminal Defense, Insurance Litigation, Workers Compensation, Personal Injury, Products Liability, Civil Rights, Law Enforcement Liability.

FIRM PROFILE: The firm has a civil trial practice with strong emphasis on litigation in the areas of civil rights and law enforcement liability, business, insurance defense, construction and products liability.

MATTHEW L. MASON, born Greensboro, North Carolina, 1965; admitted to bar, 1990, North Carolina. *Education:* North Carolina State University; Guilford College (B.S., with high honors, 1987); University of Virginia (J.D., 1990). Guilford Scholarship Society. Member, Moot Court Board. *Member:* North Carolina Bar Association; Defense Research Institute. ***PRACTICE AREAS:*** Civil Litigation; Insurance Litigation; Commercial Litigation; Appellate Practice; Civil Rights Litigation. **Email:** mmason@mossmasonandhill.com

WILLIAM L. HILL, born Hampton Bays, New York, April 8, 1965; admitted to bar, 1994, North Carolina and U.S. District Court, Eastern, Western and Middle Districts of North Carolina; 1998, U.S. Court of Appeals, Fourth Circuit. *Education:* University of North Carolina at Charlotte (B.S., cum laude, 1989); University of Louisville (J.D., cum laude, 1994). Member, 1992-1993 and Periodical Editor, 1993-1994, The Journal of Law and Education. President, Brandeis Academic Honors Society, 1993-1994. *Member:* North Carolina Bar Association; North Carolina Association of Defense Attorneys; Defense Research Institute. ***PRACTICE AREAS:*** Civil Litigation; Criminal Defense; Workers Compensation; Personal Injury; Civil Rights Litigation; Administrative Trial Practice. ***Email:*** whill@mossmasonandhill.com

OF COUNSEL

JOSEPH W. MOSS, born Gainesville, Georgia, April 6, 1941; admitted to bar, 1966, North Carolina. *Education:* Duke University (B.A., 1963); Mercer University and Wake Forest University (LL.B., 1966). Phi Delta Phi. Research Assistant, North Carolina Supreme Court, 1966-1967. *Member:* Greensboro, North Carolina (Chairman, Young Lawyers Section, 1974-1975) and American Bar Associations; North Carolina Association of Defense Attorneys; Defense Research Institute. Fellow, American College of Trial Lawyers. ***PRACTICE AREAS:*** Civil Litigation; Insurance Litigation; Construction Litigation; Securities Litigation; Real Property Litigation; Intellectual Property Litigation. ***Email:*** jmoss@mossmasonandhill.com

(This Listing Continued)

ASSOCIATE

MEGAN E. CALLAHAN, born Greensboro, North Carolina, January 23, 1978; admitted to bar, 2004, North Carolina. *Education:* North Carolina State University (B.A., 2000); Campbell University (J.D., cum laude, 2004). Member, Order of Old Kivett. Recipient, Calhoun Advocacy Award. Team Member, ATLA Trial Team and Moot Court. *Member:* North Carolina Bar Association; Defense Research Institute. ***PRACTICE AREAS:*** Civil Defense Litigation. ***Email:*** mcallahan@mossmasonandhill.com

NEXSEN PRUET ADAMS KLEEMEIER, PLLC

Established in 1945

701 GREEN VALLEY ROAD, SUITE 100

P.O. BOX 3463 (27402)

GREENSBORO, NORTH CAROLINA 27408

Telephone: 336-373-1600

Facsimile: 336-273-5357

URL: http://www.npaklaw.com

Acquisitions, Administrative Law, Alternative Dispute Resolution, Antitrust Law, Appellate Practice, Arbitration, Bankruptcy Law, Business Law, Collections Law, Construction Law, Commercial Law, Commercial Real Estate, Computers, Contracts, Copyrights, Corporate Law, Creditor-Debtor Rights, Disabilities, Domestic Relations Law, Economic Development Law, Education Law, Election, Eminent Domain Employee Benefits Law, Employment Law, Environmental Law, Estate Planning, Family Law, Fidelity Law, Finance Law, Governmental Representation, Health Care Law, Hospital Law, Immigration Law, Insurance Law, Insurance Defense, Intellectual Property Law, International Law, Internet Law, Investments, Labor Law, Land Use, Leasing Law, Litigation, Maritime Law, Mediation, Mergers, Naturalization Law, Partnership Law, Patents, Personal Injury, Probate, Products Liability Law, Professional Liability, Public Contracts, Public Finance, Real Estate Law, Real Estate Planning, Regulatory Law, Securities, Surety Law, Taxation Law, Technology Law, Torts, Trade Regulation, Trade Secrets, Trademarks, Transportation, Trusts, Utility Law, Wills, Workers' Compensation and Zoning Law.

FIRM PROFILE: Nexsen Pruet Adams Kleemeier is the Carolinas Law Firm. With 7 offices in North and South Carolina, Nexsen Pruet Adams Kleemeier attorneys can, and do, handle a broad range of legal needs for those doing business in the Carolinas. Our attorneys are licensed to practice in state and federal courts and before the U.S. Patent and Trademark Office. The firm's website is www.npaklaw.com.

LAW FIRM ALLIANCES/ASSOCIATIONS: ***LAWORLD:*** *http://www.LaWorld.com.*

WILBURN BREWER, JR. (1939-2003)
C. ALVIN BROWN (1940-1978)
PAUL A. COOPER (1889-1956)
FRANK B. GARY (1900-1971)
JOHN A. KLEEMEIER, JR. (1911-1973)
WILLIAM J. ADAMS, JR. (1908-1993)
ELIZABETH DUNN WHITE (1954-1995)
DANIEL W. FOUTS (1932-2003)

MEMBERS OF FIRM

J. ALEXANDER S. BARRETT, admitted to bar, 1985, North Carolina; 1986, South Carolina. *Education:* Emory University (B.A., with honors, 1980); Vanderbilt University (J.D., 1985). *Member:* South Carolina Bar. ***PRACTICE AREAS:*** Business Litigation; Employment Litigation. ***Email:*** ABarrett@npaklaw.com

ROBERT G. BAYNES, admitted to bar, 1964, North Carolina. *Education:* University of North Carolina (B.A., 1961; J.D., with honors, 1964). Member, North Carolina Law Review. President, North Carolina State Bar, 1988-1989. Chairman, Board of Trustees, North Carolina Client Security Fund, 1992-1994. Member, House of Delegates, American Bar Association, 1993-1996. Former Member, Governor's Commission on Business Laws and the Economy. Fellow, American Bar Foundation. Certified Superior Court Mediator. ***PRACTICE AREAS:*** Mergers and Acquisitions; Corporate Finance; Fiduciary Liability Defense; Securities. ***Email:*** RBaynes@npaklaw.com

GARY L. BEAVER, born Havelock, North Carolina, December 1, 1955; admitted to bar, 1982, North Carolina. *Education:* U.S. Naval Academy (B.S., with distinction, 1977); Duke University (J.D., 1982). *Member:* North Carolina (Member, Appellate Rules Study Committee) and American Bar Associations; North Carolina State Bar. [Colonel, USMCR]. ***PRACTICE AREAS:*** Commercial Litigation; E-Commerce; Products Liability; Intellectual Property Litigation; Torts; Appellate Practice; Pharmacists Liability; False Advertising. ***Email:*** GBeaver@npaklaw.com

JAMES W. BRYAN, born February 19, 1958; admitted to bar, 1989, North Carolina. *Education:* University of North Carolina at Chapel Hill (B.A., 1981); Wake Forest University (J.D., 1989). Member, Moot Court Board. Member, Wake Forest Law Review. Member: Insurance Coverage Committee, Tort Trial and Insurance Practice Section; Environmental, Energy and Resources Section, American Bar Association. Council Member, Environmental and Natural Resources Law Section; Litigation Section, North Carolina Bar Association. *Member:* Defense Research Institute; North Carolina Association of Defense Attorneys. ***REPORTED CASES:*** Ayers v. Patz, 2002 WL 1901906, N.C.App., Aug. 20, 2002; Polo Ralph Lauren Corp. v. Gulf Ins. Co., 2001 WL 34000140, 2001 NCBC 3, N.C. Super., Jan. 31, 2001; Markham v. Nationwide Ins. Co., 125 N.C.App. 443, 481 S.E.2d 349 (1997); Hunter v. Newsom, 121 N.C.App. 564, 468 S.E.2d 802 (1996); Fidelity National Title Ins. Co. of Tenn. v. Kidd, 99 N.C.App. 737, 394 S.E.2d 225 (1990). ***PRACTICE AREAS:*** Insurance; Insurance Defense; Commercial Law; Environmental Law; Litigation; Torts; Toxic Torts; Transportation; Fidelity and Surety. ***Email:*** JBryan@npaklaw.com

MARGARET SHEA BURNHAM, admitted to bar, 1983, North Carolina. *Education:* Virginia Polytechnic Institute and State University (B.A., 1980); Wake Forest University

(This Listing Continued)

(J.D., 1983). Member, National Moot Court Competition. Order of Barristers. Research Editor, Wake Forest Law Review. Certified Mediator, Dispute Resolution Commission. *Member:* North Carolina Bar Association (Chair, Real Property Section Council; Member, Litigation Section Council; Member, Board of Governors); North Carolina State Bar (Councilor, Eighteenth Judicial District); American College of Real Estate Lawyers. (Board Certified Specialist in Real Property Law, Business, Commercial and Industrial Transactions, North Carolina State Board of Legal Specialization). ***PRACTICE AREAS:*** Civil Litigation; Professional Liability; Commercial Real Estate. ***Email:*** MBurnham@npaklaw.com

W. B. RODMAN DAVIS, admitted to bar, 1978, North Carolina. *Education:* University of North Carolina (B.A., 1975); Emory University (J.D., 1978; M.B.A., 1978). Certified Public Accountant, North Carolina, 1979. Member, Board of Advisors, U.N.C. Tax Institute, 1987—. *Member:* North Carolina Bar Association (Chair, Tax Section, 1996-1997; Member, Drafting Committee, Limited Liability Company Act); North Carolina State Bar; North Carolina Association of Certified Public Accountants; American Institute of Certified Public Accountants. ***PRACTICE AREAS:*** Taxation; Limited Liability Companies; Corporate Law; Venture Capital; Mergers and Acquisitions; Estate Planning; Technology. ***Email:*** RDavis@npaklaw.com

M. JAY DeVANEY, admitted to bar, 1971, North Carolina. *Education:* Wake Forest University (B.A., 1969; J.D., 1971). Member, Wake Forest Law Review. Member, Board of Governors, 1992-1995 and Chairman, Real Property Section, 1982-1983, North Carolina Bar Association. Selected among Best Lawyers in America in Real Estate Law. *Member:* American College of Real Estate Lawyers (Chair, Land Use / Environmental Committee; Member, Board of Governors). American College of Mortgage Attorneys. (Board Certified Specialist in Real Property Law, Business, Commercial and Industrial Transactions, North Carolina State Board of Legal Specialization). ***PRACTICE AREAS:*** Commercial Real Estate Transactions; Land Use Litigation; Real Estate Secured Lending. ***Email:*** JDevaney@npaklaw.com

TRUDY A. ENNIS, admitted to bar, 1987, North Carolina. *Education:* Western Carolina University (B.A., summa cum laude, 1973; M.A.Ed., 1976); University of North Carolina at Chapel Hill (J.D., with honors, 1987). Order of the Coif. Member, North Carolina Law Review. Selected for inclusion in Best Lawyers in America in Family Law. (Board Certified Specialist in Family Law, North Carolina State Board of Legal Specialization). ***PRACTICE AREAS:*** Family Law; Civil Litigation; Alternative Dispute Resolution; Collaborative Law. ***Email:*** TEnnis@npaklaw.com

CHARLES T. HAGAN III, admitted to bar, 1977, North Carolina; 1980, Florida. *Education:* University of North Carolina (B.A., 1970); Wake Forest University (J.D., 1977). Editor-in-Chief, Wake Forest Law Review. Past Chairman, Greensboro Area Chamber of Commerce, 1998-1999. Chairman, Leadership North Carolina, 1999—. *Member:* The Florida Bar. [Lt., USN, 1970-1974]. ***PRACTICE AREAS:*** Banks and Banking; Business Law; Mergers, Acquisitions and Divestitures; Corporate Law; International Trade. ***Email:*** CHagan@npaklaw.com

J. SCOTT HALE, admitted to bar, 1996, North Carolina. *Education:* University of North Carolina at Chapel Hill (B.A., 1990); Mercer University (J.D., cum laude, 1996). Articles Editor, Mercer Law Review. ***PRACTICE AREAS:*** Business Litigation; Utility Law; Banking Litigation. ***Email:*** SHale@npaklaw.com

R. HARPER HECKMAN, admitted to bar, 1991, North Carolina. *Education:* University of North Carolina (B.A., 1988; J.D., with honors, 1991). Former Chair, Construction Law Section of the North Carolina Bar Association. Contract Documents Steering Committee, ABA Forum on the Construction Industry. Holderness Moot Court Invitational Team. Co-author: "Time is Money: Recovery of Liquidated Damages by the Owner," The Construction Lawyer, ABA Forum on Construction. ***PRACTICE AREAS:*** Construction Law; Civil Litigation; Commercial Litigation; Utility Law. ***Email:*** HHeckman@npaklaw.com

STEVEN D. HEDGES, admitted to bar, 1982, Virginia; 1988, North Carolina; 1994, Colorado. *Education:* Virginia Polytechnic Institute and State University (B. Arch., magna cum laude, 1979); Wake Forest University (J.D., 1982). Member, Editorial Staff, Wake Forest Law Review. Member, ABA Forum on the Construction Industry. Certified Mediator. *Member:* Greensboro, North Carolina and Virginia (Member, Sections on: Construction Law; Litigation) Bar Associations. ***PRACTICE AREAS:*** Construction Law; Commercial Litigation; Environmental Law. ***Email:*** SHedges@npaklaw.com

A. SCOTT JACKSON, admitted to bar, 1988, North Carolina. *Education:* Marshall University (B.B.A., magna cum laude, 1985); University of North Carolina at Chapel Hill (J.D., 1988). Staff Member, North Carolina Journal of International Law and Commercial Regulation. ***PRACTICE AREAS:*** Corporate Law; Mergers, Acquisitions and Divestitures; Finance; Business Law; Computers and Software; Electronic Commerce; Technology. ***Email:*** SJackson@npaklaw.com

BENJAMIN A. KAHN, admitted to bar, 1993, North Carolina. *Education:* University of North Carolina at Chapel Hill (B.A., 1990; J.D., with honors, 1993). Law Clerk to Hon. Jerry G. Tart, Chief Judge, U.S. Bankruptcy Court, Middle District of North Carolina, 1993-1995; Hon. Catharine R. Carruthers, U.S. Bankruptcy Court, Middle District of North Carolina. Secretary, Bankruptcy Section Council, North Carolina Bar Association, 2002-2003. (Board Certified Specialist in Business and Consumer Bankruptcy, North Carolina State Board of Legal Specialization). ***PRACTICE AREAS:*** Commercial Litigation; Bankruptcy and Creditors Rights; Corporate Litigation. ***Email:*** BKahn@npaklaw.com

D. BETH LANGLEY, admitted to bar, 1992, North Carolina. *Education:* Wake Forest University (B.A., cum laude, 1986; J.D., cum laude, 1992). Member, Moot Court Board. Editor-in-Chief, Wake Forest Law Review. Adjunct Professor of Law, Wake Forest University School of Law. Chair, Labor and Employment Law Section, North Carolina Bar Association, 2001-2002. ***PRACTICE AREAS:*** Labor and Employment Law; Civil Rights; Commercial Litigation; Immigration. ***Email:*** BLangley@nexsenpruet.com

HENRY B. MANGUM, JR., born Monroe, North Carolina, December 17, 1955; admitted to bar, 1981, North Carolina. *Education:* Wake Forest University (B.S., 1978; J.D., cum laude, 1981). Certified Public Accountant, North Carolina, 1984. *Member:* North Carolina Association of Certified Public Accountants; American Institute of Certified Public Accountants. ***PRACTICE AREAS:*** Business Organizations; Mergers, Acquisitions and Divestitures; Financial Transactions; Taxation. ***Email:*** HMangum@npaklaw.com

CHRISTINE L. MYATT, admitted to bar, 1982, North Carolina. *Education:* Wake Forest University (B.A., 1979; J.D., 1982). Law Clerk to the Honorable James B. Wolfe, Jr., U.S. Bankruptcy Court, Middle District of North Carolina. Former Chair, North Carolina State Bar Board of Legal Specialization. *Member:* Greensboro, North Carolina (Chair, Bankruptcy Section) and American (Member, Standing Committee on Legal Specialization) Bar Associations; North Carolina State Bar. (Certified in Business Bankruptcy Law by the American Board of Certification) (Board Certified Specialist in Business Bankruptcy Law, North Carolina State Board of Legal Specialization). ***TRANSACTIONS:*** Receiver for SEC in Ponzi scheme involving over $42 million and 2000 investors. Local counsel for secured creditor owed in excess of $172 million in convenience store bankruptcy case involving over 450 stores throughout southeast. ***PRACTICE AREAS:*** Bankruptcy; Creditors Rights; Asset Protection; Workouts; Receiverships. ***Email:*** CMyatt@npaklaw.com

PETER G. PAPPAS, admitted to bar, 1982, North Carolina. *Education:* North Carolina State University; University of North Carolina (B.A., with highest honors, 1978; J.D., 1982). Law Clerk to the Hon. W. Earl Britt, U.S. District Judge for the Eastern District of North Carolina, 1982-1984. American Bar Association, Delegate, House of Delegates, 1988-1989. North Carolina Bar Association, Chairman, Young Lawyers Division, 1991-1992 and Member, Board of Governors, 1991-1992. North Carolina Bar Association, Chair, Litigation Section, 1997-1998. North Carolina Bar Association, Member, Litigation Section Council, 1994-1999. Member, 2001— and Chair, 2004—, Bench/Bar Liaison Committee. American Bar Association, Member, Litigation Section, Labor and Employment Law Section, and Tort and Insurance Practice Section. Defense Research Institute, Member, Fidelity and Surety Committee, Labor and Employment Law Committee and Business Litigation Section. ***PRACTICE AREAS:*** Business Litigation; Civil Litigation; Commercial Litigation; Labor and Employment; Insurance Litigation; ERISA Litigation; Fidelity and Surety; Federal Civil Practice. ***Email:*** PPappas@npaklaw.com

DAVID S. POKELA, admitted to bar, 1992, North Carolina. *Education:* University of North Carolina (B.S., 1987); Wake Forest University (J.D., 1992). Member, Wake Forest Law Review. Member, Moot Court Board. Newsletter Co-Chair, The Real Estate and Probate Litigation Committee, American Bar Association. Past Chair, Real Property Litigation Committee, Real Property Section Council, North Carolina Bar Association. ***PRACTICE AREAS:*** Real Estate Litigation; Land Use Litigation; Commercial Litigation; Civil Appeals. ***Email:*** DPokela@npaklaw.com

TONYA BUNN POWELL, admitted to bar, 1996, North Carolina. *Education:* Wake Forest University (B.A., summa cum laude, 1993); University of North Carolina at Chapel Hill (J.D., with honors, 1996). Phi Beta Kappa; Order of the Barristers. Holderness Moot Court National Team. (Board Certified Specialist in Real Property Law: Business, Commercial and Industrial Transactions, North Carolina State Board of Legal Specialization). ***PRACTICE AREAS:*** Real Estate; Secured Financing. ***Email:*** TPowell@npaklaw.com

RANDALL W. REAVIS, admitted to bar, 1989, North Carolina. *Education:* Catawba College (B.A., cum laude, 1986); University of North Carolina (J.D., 1989). Member, Holderness Moot Court National Team. ***PRACTICE AREAS:*** Litigation; Professional Liability; Construction Law. ***Email:*** RReavis@npaklaw.com

DAVID A. SENTER, admitted to bar, 1984, North Carolina. *Education:* Wake Forest University (B.S., cum laude, 1981; J.D., cum laude, 1984). Member, National Moot Court Competition. Order of Barristers. Wake Forest Law Review. Member, Construction Law Section Council, North Carolina Bar Association, 1992-1995. Member, Panel of Arbitrators, American Arbitration Association. Member, ABA Forum on the Construction Industry (Governing Committee, 2004—; Chair, Division 9 Steering Committee, 2000-2004) and ABA Litigation Section and Construction Litigation Committee (4th Circuit and North Carolina Casenote Editor). Selected for inclusion in Best Lawyers in America for Construction Law. ***PRACTICE AREAS:*** Construction Law; Fidelity and Surety; Commercial Litigation; Collections; Debtor and Creditor. ***Email:*** DSenter@npaklaw.com

THOMAS S. THORNTON, JR., admitted to bar, 1969, North Carolina. *Education:* Duke University (B.A., 1966); Wake Forest University (J.D., 1969). Law Clerk to Chief Judge Edwin M. Stanley, U.S. District Court, Middle District of North Carolina, 1969-1971. Member, Construction Law Section Council, North Carolina Bar Association, 1991-1994. Member, Panel of Arbitrators, American Arbitration Association. Member, ABA Forum on the Construction Industry. ***PRACTICE AREAS:*** Construction Law; Commercial Law; Business Law; Debtor and Creditor Rights. ***Email:*** TThornton@npaklaw.com

WILLIAM M. WILCOX IV, admitted to bar, 1983, North Carolina; 1986, U.S. Tax Court. *Education:* Washington & Lee University; Miami University, Ohio (B.S., 1975); Wake Forest University (J.D., 1982). Certified Public Accountant, North Carolina, 1985. Member, 1992— and Chair, 2001-2002, Tax Section Council, North Carolina Bar Association. *Member:* American Institute of Certified Public Accountants; North Carolina Association of Certified Public Accountants. ***PRACTICE AREAS:*** Taxation; Business Law; Employee Benefits. ***Email:*** BWilcox@npaklaw.com

OF COUNSEL

F. COOPER BRANTLEY, admitted to bar, 1973, North Carolina. *Education:* Davidson College (B.A., 1970); University of North Carolina (J.D., 1973). ***PRACTICE AREAS:*** Real Estate Development. ***Email:*** CBrantley@npaklaw.com

CHARLES T. HAGAN, JR., admitted to bar, 1936, North Carolina. *Education:* University of North Carolina; University of Virginia (J.D., 1936). District Attorney, 12th Judicial District. Member, North Carolina Judicial Council. Councillor, North Carolina State Bar. President, Greensboro Bar Association. Fellow, American College of Trial Lawyers. [Major General, U.S.M.C.R., Retired]. ***PRACTICE AREAS:*** Civil Litigation.

WALTER L. HANNAH, admitted to bar, 1953, North Carolina. *Education:* Virginia Polytechnic Institute and State University; Washington & Lee University (J.D., 1950). North Carolina Bar Association's General Practice Hall of Fame, 2002. Evelyn Corman Distinguished Service Award of the Construction Law Section of the North Carolina Bar Association. Certified Mediator by Courts. Member, ABA Forum on the Construction Industry. Member, ABA, Alternate Dispute Resolution Section. Member, National Panel of

(This Listing Continued)

NEXSEN PRUET ADAMS KLEEMEIER, PLLC, Greensboro—Continued

Arbitrators for Large Complex Case Program at the American Arbitration Association. Fellow: American Bar Foundation; American College of Construction Lawyers. ***PRACTICE AREAS:*** Mediation; Arbitration. ***Email:*** WHannah@npaklaw.com

DANIEL K. HICKS, admitted to bar, 1997, South Carolina and North Carolina. *Education:* Bob Jones University (B.A., magna cum laude, 1992; M.A., 1994); University of North Carolina at Chapel Hill (J.D., 1997). *Member:* South Carolina Bar (Member, CLE Committee and Legislative Committee, 2004-2005); North Carolina State Bar (Vice-Chair, CLE Committee, 2004-2005 and Member, Legislative Committee, 2003-2005, Estate Planning and Fiduciary Law Section). ***PRACTICE AREAS:*** Estate Planning; Tax Law; Estate Administration; Nonprofit Organizations. ***Email:*** DHicks@npaklaw.com

W. WINBURNE KING III, admitted to bar, 1975, North Carolina. *Education:* University of North Carolina (B.A., 1968; J.D., 1975). Member, Panel of Construction Arbitrators, American Arbitration Association. [Captain, USNR]. ***PRACTICE AREAS:*** Civil Litigation; Construction Law. ***Email:*** WKing@npaklaw.com

JOHN N. OGBURN, JR., admitted to bar, 1957, North Carolina. *Education:* University of North Carolina (B.S., 1955; J.D., 1957). Certified Mediator, State Court and North Carolina Industrial Commission. ***PRACTICE AREAS:*** Mediation. ***Email:*** JOgburn@npaklaw.com

SPECIAL COUNSEL

J. PHILLIPS L. JOHNSTON, admitted to bar, 1963, North Carolina. *Education:* Duke University (A.B., Economics, 1961); University of North Carolina School of Law (J.D., 1963); New York University, Stern School of Business, 1963-1965; Harvard University, John F. Kennedy School of Government, Senior Managers in Government; Stanford University, Directors' College. Founder and co-director of the University of North Carolina School of Law Initiative for Corporate Governance. Former Chief Executive Officer of NASDAQ-listed Digital Recorders. Served on the board of directors of five publicly traded companies including a NYSE-listed public company and 15 private boards. SEC Audit Committee Financial Expert. Named Entrepreneur of the Year by the Council for Entrepreneurial Development, 1997. Enterpreneurial Fellow, Wake Forest University. Founding Chairman, NCEITA, (the electronic trade association representing over 374 companies including several 500 Fortune companies). Author: best-selling book, *Success in Small Business is a Laughing Matter* and has published numerous articles on Corporate Governance. *Member:* North Carolina State Bar. ***PRACTICE AREAS:*** Corporate Law. ***Email:*** pjohnston@npaklaw.com

R. SCOTT TOBIN, admitted to bar, 1981, Georgia; 2005, North Carolina. *Education:* Tulane University, 1972-1974; University of London, 1974; University of North Carolina at Chapel Hill (B.A., 1975; J.D., 1981). Former Georgia Assistant Attorney General. Served as: General Counsel and Chief Strategic Officer for ICC, a leading provider of manufacturing execution system software for the aerospace and electronic assembly industries; Executive Vice President for global strategies and managing director; General Counsel for private equity investments for Premiere Global Services, a publicly traded provider of conferencing, e-mail, fax, and voice messaging services to global Fortune 1000 companies; Chairman and CEO of the wood furniture manufacturer Wellington Hall Designs, Lexington, NC. Recognized as one of the Top 10 Business People in the Triad Region of North Carolina, 2003. Director, University of North Carolina School of Law Foundation. Founding Director, University of North Carolina School of Law Initiative for Corporate Governance. Member, University of North Carolina School of Law Council for Entrepreneurial Law. Director, Piedmont Triad Entrepreneurial Network. *Member:* State Bar of Georgia. ***PRACTICE AREAS:*** Corporate Governance. ***Email:*** stobin@npaklaw.com

ASSOCIATES

ERIC H. BIESECKER, admitted to bar, 1996, North Carolina. *Education:* Wake Forest University (B.A., magna cum laude, 1993); University of North Carolina (J.D., with honors, 1996). Order of the Coif. Staff Member, North Carolina Law Review. *Member:* Guilford County, Greensboro and North Carolina Bar Associations; North Carolina State Bar. ***PRACTICE AREAS:*** Business Law; Construction Law; Commercial Law; Real Estate Litigation. ***Email:*** EBiesecker@npaklaw.com

BROOKS F. BOSSONG, admitted to bar, 1993, North Carolina. *Education:* University of North Carolina (B.A., 1984); Louisiana State University (J.D., 1993). ***PRACTICE AREAS:*** Commercial Litigation; Creditors' Rights. ***Email:*** BBossong@npaklaw.com

BRIAN S. CLARKE, admitted to bar, 1999, North Carolina and U.S. District Court, Middle District of North Carolina; 2000, U.S. Court of Appeals, Fourth Circuit and U.S. District Court, Eastern and Western Districts of North Carolina. *Education:* University of North Carolina at Chapel Hill (B.A., 1995); Washington & Lee University (J.D., magna cum laude, 1999). Order of the Coif. Omicron Delta Kappa. Executive Editor, Capital Defense Journal, 1998-1999. Case Notes Editor, Environmental Law Digest, 1997-1998. Board of Directors and Vice President, Preservation Greensboro, Inc. *Member:* North Carolina Bar Association (Member: Labor and Employment Law Section Council; Pro Bono Committee, Labor and Employment Law Section). ***REPORTED CASES:*** Enoch v. Alamance County Dep't of Social Services, 595 S.E.2d 744 (N.C. Ct. App. 2004); McRae v. Rogosin Converters, Inc., 301 F. Supp.2d 471 (M.D.N.C. 2004); Freeman v. Duke Power Co., 174 L.R.R.M. (BNA) 2468 (M.D.N.C. 2003). ***PRACTICE AREAS:*** Labor and Employment; ERISA Litigation; Employee Benefits Litigation; Civil Litigation. ***Email:*** BClarke@npaklaw.com

LEIGH COUGHENOUR, admitted to bar, 2004, North Carolina. *Education:* University of North Carolina (B.S., Psychology, with honors, 1999); Wake Forest University (J.D., 2004). *Member:* American Bar Association; North Carolina Bar Association (Member, Real Estate Section); Greensboro Bar Association; North Carolina Association of Women Attorneys. ***PRACTICE AREAS:*** Commercial Real Estate. ***Email:*** LCoughenour@npaklaw.com

STEPHANIE RENEE ENNIS, admitted to bar, 2004, North Carolina. *Education:* University of North Carolina (B.A., 1996; J.D., 2004). Author of "Section 307 of the Sarbanes-Oxley Act: Eroding the Legal Profession's System of Self-Governance?," 7 North Carolina Banking Institute 155. ***PRACTICE AREAS:*** Commercial Litigation. ***Email:*** SEnnis@npaklaw.com

STUART C. GAUFFREAU, admitted to bar, 1996, North Carolina. *Education:* Duke University (B.A., summa cum laude, 1988); University of North Carolina at Chapel Hill (J.D., with honors, 1996). Managing Editor, North Carolina Journal of International Law and Commercial Regulation. Law Clerk, Honorable Graham C. Mullen, Chief U.S. District Judge for the Western District of North Carolina. *Member:* Greensboro, North Carolina (Member, Litigation Section) and American (Member, Litigation Section) Bar Associations; North Carolina State Bar. [Capt., U.S. Army, 1988-1993 (Military Intelligence); Army Reserve, 1993 —, Major, JAGC]. ***PRACTICE AREAS:*** Litigation; Appellate Practice. ***Email:*** SGauffreau@npaklaw.com

ELIZABETH DAVIS HALL, admitted to bar, 2002, North Carolina. *Education:* Davidson College (B.A., with honors, magna cum laude, 1999); University of Virginia (J.D., 2002). Phi Beta Kappa. Executive Editor, Virginia Law Review. ***PRACTICE AREAS:*** Business and Tax; Estate Planning. ***Email:*** LHall@npaklaw.com

GREGORY T. HIGGINS, born Gainesville, Florida; admitted to bar, 2000, North Carolina. *Education:* University of Florida (B.A., 1995); Wake Forest University (J.D., 2000). Articles Editor, Wake Forest Law Review, 1998-2000. Member, Wake Forest Moot Court Board, 1998-2000. Winner, George K. Walker Moot Court Competition, 1998. Finalist, Kaufman Securities Law Moot Court Competition, 1999. Author: "Persian Gulf War Genetic Birth Defects and Inherited Injustice in Minns v. United States," 34 Wake Forest L. Rev. 935, 1999; "Construction Manager Contract Form Issues for Public and Private Projects," 17 Change Order 1, (NCBA, 2002). Chairman, Board of Directors, Gate City Community Development Corporation, 2002-2003. Editor, "The Change Order," North Carolina Bar Association's Construction Law Section Newsletter. Member, Board of Directors, Preservation Greensboro, Inc. *Member:* North Carolina (Member, Sections on: Construction Law; Litigation) and American (Member, Litigation Section) Bar Associations; North Carolina State Bar. ***REPORTED CASES:*** City of New Bern v. Carteret-Craven Elec. Membership Corp., 356 N.C. 123, 567 S.E.2d 131 (2002). ***PRACTICE AREAS:*** Construction Law; Commercial Litigation; Fidelity and Surety; Utility Law. ***Email:*** GHiggins@npaklaw.com

JOSEPH M. KAHN, admitted to bar, 2000, South Carolina; 2001, North Carolina. *Education:* Washington University (B.A., 1997); University of South Carolina (J.D., 2000). Member, South Carolina Law Review. *Member:* North Carolina, South Carolina and American Bar Associations; North Carolina State Bar; American Health Lawyers Association. ***PRACTICE AREAS:*** Health Care Facility Regulation; Health Care Reimbursement; Commercial Litigation. ***Email:*** JKahn@npaklaw.com

DANIEL W. KOENIG, admitted to bar, 1997, North Carolina. *Education:* Duke University (A.B., 1994); Southern Methodist University (J.D., 1997). Articles Editor, The International Law Review Association. *Member:* American Bar Association (Member, Sections on: Tort Trial and Insurance Practice; Litigation); North Carolina Bar Association (Member, Litigation Section); Greensboro Bar Association; Guilford Inn of Court. ***PRACTICE AREAS:*** Business Litigation; Insurance Litigation; Personal Injury; Wrongful Death. ***Email:*** DKoenig@npaklaw.com

BRIAN T. PEARCE, admitted to bar, 2003, North Carolina; U.S. District Court, Middle District of North Carolina. *Education:* Clemson University (B.S., cum laude, 2000); Wake Forest University School of Law (J.D., 2003). Member, Greensboro Jaycees. *Member:* Greensboro and North Carolina Bar Associations; Greensboro Young Lawyers Association. ***PRACTICE AREAS:*** Real Estate. ***Email:*** BPearce@npaklaw.com

JAMES DAVID YARBROUGH, JR., admitted to bar, 2002, North Carolina. *Education:* University of North Carolina at Chapel Hill (B.A., 1999); Tulane University School of Law (J.D., 2002). Senior Associate Editor, Tulane Law Review. Law Clerk, Honorable Graham C. Mullen and Honorable Richard L. Voorhees, United States District Court for the Western District of North Carolina. ***PRACTICE AREAS:*** Bankruptcy; Litigation. ***Email:*** DYarbrough@npaklaw.com

NIXON & ASSOCIATES

GREENSBORO, NORTH CAROLINA

(See High Point)

Traffic Violations, Criminal Defense, DWI, Drug Charges, License Restoration, Personal Injury, Auto Accidents, Domestic Law.

OGLETREE, DEAKINS, NASH, SMOAK & STEWART, P.C.

Established in 1972

2725 HORSE PEN CREEK ROAD
SUITE 101
GREENSBORO, NORTH CAROLINA 27410-8392
Telephone: 336-375-9737
Facsimile: 336-375-4430
Email: clientservices@ogletreedeakins.com
URL: http://www.ogletreedeakins.com

Mailing Address: P.O. Box 13310, Greensboro, NC

Atlanta, Georgia Office: 600 Peachtree Street, N.E., Suite 2100. Telephone: 404-881-1300.
Austin, Texas Office: 301 Congress Avenue, Suite 1250. Telephone: 512-344-4700.
Birmingham, Alabama Office: One Federal Place, Suite 1000, 1819 Fifth Avenue North. Telephone: 205-328-1900.
Charleston, South Carolina Office: 134 Meeting Street, Suite 160, P.O. Box 1808. Telephone: 843-853-1300.
Charlotte, North Carolina Office: 400 West Trade Street. Telephone: 704-342-2588.

(This Listing Continued)

Chicago, Illinois Office: Twenty-Fifth Floor, Two First National Plaza, 20 South Clark Street. Telephone: 312-558-1220.
Columbia, South Carolina Office: 1320 Main Street, Suite 600. Telephone: 803-252-1300.
Dallas, Texas Office: 700 Preston Commons, 8117 Preston Road. Telephone: 214-987-3800.
Greenville, South Carolina Office: The Ogletree Building, 300 North Main Street, P.O. Box 2757. Telephone: 864-271-1300.
Houston, Texas Office: One Allen Center, 500 Dallas Street, Suite 3000. Telephone: 713-655-0855.
Kansas City, Missouri Office: 4717 Grand Avenue, Suite 300. Telephone: 816-471-1301.
Los Angeles, California Office: 633 West Fifth Street, Suite 5300. Telephone: 213-239-9800.
Indianapolis, Indiana Office: Suite 4600, 111 Monument Circle. Telephone: 317-916-1300.
Miami, Florida Office: 80 S.W. 8th Street, Suite 1830. Telephone: 305-374-0506.
Morristown, New Jersey Office: 10 Madison Avenue, Suite 402. Telephone: 973-656-1600.
Nashville, Tennessee Office: SunTrust Center, Suite 800, 424 Church Street. Telephone: 615-254-1900.
Phoenix, Arizona Office: 2415 East Camelback Road, Suite 800. Telephone: 602-778-3700.
Raleigh, North Carolina Office: 2301 Sugar Bush Road, Suite 600, P.O. Box 31608. Telephone: 919-787-9700.
San Antonio, Texas Office: 2600 Weston Centre, 112 East Pecan Street. Telephone: 210-354-1300.
St. Thomas, U.S. Virgin Islands Office: The Tunick Building, 1336 Beltjen Road, Suite 202. Telephone: 340-714-1235.
Tampa, Florida Office: 100 North Tampa Street, Suite 3600. Telephone: 813-289-1247.
Washington, D.C. Office: Fifth Floor, 2400 N Street, N.W. Telephone: 202-887-0855.

Labor Relations, Employment Litigation, Workers' Compensation. Civil Litigation in all State and Federal Courts and Administrative Agencies.

BRIAN M. FREEDMAN, born Washington, D.C., August 6, 1964; admitted to bar, 1989, North Carolina. *Education:* Duke University (B.A., 1984; M.B.A., 1986); Wake Forest University (J.D., 1989). Phi Delta Phi. *Member:* North Carolina State Bar. ***PRACTICE AREAS:*** Employment Discrimination; Employment Law; Labor Arbitration; Workers' Compensation Defense. ***Email:*** brian.freedman@ogletreedeakins.com

REPRESENTATIVE CLIENTS: Alcoa, Inc.; Carolina Forge; Frontier Spinning Mills; GKN Automotive, Inc.; Harris Teeter, Inc.; Honda Power Equipment Mfg., Inc.; K. Hovnanian Companies, Inc.; Kentucky Derby Hosiery; Lexington Home Brands; New Breed Corporations; Owens Corning Corporation; Perdue Farms, Inc.; Purolater/Facet Enterprises, Inc.; Rowan Regional Medical Center; Stanley Furniture Co.; The May Department Stores Company; Unifi, Inc.; Vaughan Bassett Furniture; VF Corp.; Volvo Trucks North America, Inc.; WestPoint Stevens Inc.

OTT CONE & REDPATH, P.A.

1501 HIGHWOODS BOULEVARD, SUITE 101
GREENSBORO, NORTH CAROLINA 27410
Telephone: 336-373-1300
Fax: 336-273-9353
URL: http://www.ottconeredpath.com

Trial and Appellate Practice in all State and Federal Courts. Administrative, Regulatory, Health Care, Hospital, Labor and Employment Law.

THOMAS E. CONE, born Greensboro, North Carolina, June 24, 1954; admitted to bar, 1981, North Carolina. *Education:* Amherst College (B.A., 1977); Duke University (J.D., with distinction, 1981). Member, Health Law Section, American Bar Association. *Member:* North Carolina Society of Health Care Attorneys (President, 1994). ***PRACTICE AREAS:*** Hospital Law; Health Care; Administrative Law. ***Email:*** tec@ocrlaw.com

MELANIE MARTIN HAMILTON, born Bay City, Michigan, October 10, 1968; admitted to bar, 1993, North Carolina. *Education:* Alma College (B.A., magna cum laude, 1990); Wake Forest University (J.D., cum laude, 1993). Phi Beta Kappa; Omicron Delta Kappa; Order of Barristers. Member, Wake Forest Law Review, 1991-1993. Council Member, Health Law Section, North Carolina Bar Association, 2002—. *Member:* North Carolina Bar Association; American Health Lawyers Association. ***PRACTICE AREAS:*** Civil Litigation; Administrative Law; Hospital Law; Health Care. ***Email:*** mmh@ocrlaw.com

WENDELL H. OTT, born Osyka, Mississippi, August 12, 1940; admitted to bar, 1976, North Carolina. *Education:* University of Southern Mississippi (B.S., 1962); Tulane University of Louisiana (M.S.W., 1967); University of North Carolina (J.D., with honors, 1976). Pi Gamma Mu; Order of the Coif. Managing Editor, North Carolina Law Review, 1976. Council Member, Health Law Section, 1985-1987, North Carolina Bar Association. *Member:* American Health Lawyers Association; North Carolina Society of Health Care Attorneys (President, 1988). ***PRACTICE AREAS:*** Hospital Law; Health Care; Administrative Law. ***Email:*** who@ocrlaw.com

RANDOLPH A. REDPATH, born Midland, Texas, May 16, 1952; admitted to bar, 1983, North Carolina. *Education:* University of Kansas (B.A., 1974); Duke University (M.H.A., 1976); Wake Forest University (J.D., 1982). Member, Wake Forest Law Review, 1981-1982. Chair, Health Law Section, 1992-1993, North Carolina Bar Association. Chair, Health Law Committee, Board of Legal Specialization, North Carolina State Bar, 1996-2001. *Member:* American Health Lawyers Association; North Carolina Society of Health Care Attorneys. [Captain, Medical Service Corps, USNR, 1976-1997]. ***PRACTICE AREAS:*** Hospital Law; Health Care; Administrative Law. ***Email:*** rar@ocrlaw.com

LAURIE S. TRUESDELL, born Raleigh, North Carolina, August 29, 1958; admitted to bar, 1987, North Carolina. *Education:* University of North Carolina (B.S., 1980; J.D., 1987). Editor-in-Chief, The North Carolina Journal of International Law and Commercial Regulation, 1986-1987. Council Member, Health Law Section, North Carolina Bar Association, 1994-1997. *Member:* North Carolina Society of Health Care Attorneys. ***PRACTICE AREAS:*** Civil Litigation; Hospital Law; Administrative Law; Health Care; Insurance. ***Email:*** lst@ocrlaw.com

(This Listing Continued)

RICHARD L. WELLS, born Punxsutawney, Pennsylvania, May 10, 1947; admitted to bar, 1974, Michigan; 1977, North Carolina. *Education:* Michigan State University (B.S., 1969); University of Michigan (J.D., 1974). Vice President, Secretary and General Counsel, 1981-1986 and Vice President, Human Resources, 1995-1997, Volvo GM Heavy Truck Corporation. *Member:* State Bar of Michigan. ***PRACTICE AREAS:*** Business Law; Corporate Law; Commercial Law; Health Care; Employment Law. ***Email:*** rlw@ocrlaw.com

OF COUNSEL

HERMAN G. ENOCHS, JR., born Hickory, North Carolina, May 20, 1929; admitted to bar, 1956, North Carolina. *Education:* Guilford College (A.B., 1952); University of North Carolina (LL.B., 1956). Delta Theta Phi. Senior Judge, Municipal County Court of Greensboro, 1962-1968. North Carolina District Judge, 18th Judicial District, 1968-1972. ***PRACTICE AREAS:*** Civil Litigation; Vehicle Law; Wills; Estates. ***Email:*** hge@ocrlaw.com

A. L. MEYLAND, born Wilmington, North Carolina, August 3, 1919; admitted to bar, 1948, North Carolina. *Education:* University of North Carolina (LL.B., 1948). Phi Delta Phi. Member, Student Board of Editors, North Carolina Law Review, 1947-48. President, Greensboro Bar Association, 1975. ***PRACTICE AREAS:*** Corporate Law; Commercial Litigation; Construction Law; Bankruptcy. ***Email:*** alm@ocrlaw.com

REPRESENTATIVE CLIENTS: Carolinas Healthcare System; Cleveland Regional Medical Center; Duke University Medical Center; Lexington Memorial Hospital; Mission Health, Inc.; Moses Cone Health System; New Hanover Regional Medical Center; North Carolina Baptist Hospital; Wake Medical Center; WilMed Healthcare, Inc.; Blumenthal Jewish Home for the Aged, Inc.; Cape Fear Valley Health System; Pitt County Memorial Hospital, Inc.; Wake Forest University Health Sciences; Piedmont Paper Stock.

PATTERSON HARKAVY LLP

101 SOUTH ELM STREET
P.O. BOX 29269
GREENSBORO, NORTH CAROLINA 27429-9269
Telephone: 336-370-4200
Facsimile: 336-274-8490
URL: http://www.pathlaw.com

Raleigh, North Carolina Office: 414 West Jones Street, P.O. Box 27927, 27611. Telephone: 919-755-1812. Facsimile: 919-755-0124.
Chapel Hill, North Carolina Office: 100 Europa Drive, Suite 250, 27517. Telephone: 919-942-5200. Toll Free: 800-458-2541. Fax: 919-942-5256.

Dispute Resolution Practice in all State and Federal Courts.

JONATHAN R. HARKAVY, born Los Angeles, California, January 19, 1943; admitted to bar, 1969, New York; 1972, U.S. Supreme Court; 1973, North Carolina. *Education:* University of Kansas (A.B., cum laude, 1965); Columbia University (LL.B., 1968). Author: "Privatizing Workplace Justice: The Advent of Mediation in Resolving Sexual Harassment Disputes," 34 Wake Forest L.Rev. 135 (1999); "Larson Employment Discrimination Practice Appendix," Matthew Bender, 1992. Lecturer in Law, Duke University School of Law, 1980-1981. Visiting Lecturer, University of North Carolina School of Law, Chapel Hill, 1979-1980. Adjunct Professor, Wake Forest University School of Law, 1986-1998. Law Clerk to Hon. Richard T. Rives, U.S. Court of Appeals for the Fifth Circuit, 1968-1969. Arbitrator and Mediator, State and Federal Courts, 1985—. Certified Mediator, North Carolina. *Member:* The Association of the Bar of the City of New York; North Carolina State Bar (President, 18th Judicial District, 1993-1994); North Carolina (Chairman, Section of Labor and Employment Law, 1983-1985) and American (Subcommittee Co-Chair, Section of Labor and Employment Law, 1982-1985) Bar Associations. (Resident). ***Email:*** jharkavy@aol.com

OF COUNSEL

NAHOMI HARKAVY, born New York, N.Y., August 30, 1945; admitted to bar, 1972, New York; 1974, North Carolina; 1980, U.S. Supreme Court. *Education:* Barnard College (B.A., cum laude, 1967); Columbia University (J.D., 1971). Certified Mediator, North Carolina. *Member:* North Carolina State Bar; North Carolina and American (Member, Labor and Employment Law Section) Bar Associations. (Resident). ***Email:*** nharkavy@aol.com

(For Complete Biographical Data on all Personnel see Professional Biographies at Raleigh, North Carolina)

THE LAW OFFICES OF JEFFREY K. PERALDO, P.A.

500-D STATE STREET
GREENSBORO, NORTH CAROLINA 27405
Telephone: 336-458-0058
Fax: 336-691-8083
URL: http://www.greensborolawyer.com
Email: jkp@greensborolawyer.com
URL: http://www.jkperaldolaw.com

Serious Personal Injury, Wrongful Death, Automobile Accidents, Trucking Accidents, Medical Malpractice, Hospital Malpractice, Nursing Home Neglect and Abuse, Product Liability, Construction Accidents, Consumer Fraud, Land Condemnation, Negligent Security.

JEFFREY K. PERALDO, born Welch, West Virginia, March 27, 1958; admitted to bar, 1990, North Carolina and U.S. District Court, Middle, Eastern and Western Districts of North Carolina; 1999, U.S. Court of Appeals, Fourth Circuit. *Education:* Wake Forest University (B.A., 1980; J.D., 1990). Staff Member, Wake Forest Law Review, 1989-1990. Member, Wake Forest Moot Court Board, 1988-1990. *Member:* North Carolina and American Bar Associations; North Carolina Academy of Trial Lawyers (Member: Education Committee; Executive Committee; Chair, Products Liability Section, 2004-2005; Member:

(This Listing Continued)

THE LAW OFFICES OF JEFFREY K. PERALDO, P.A., Greensboro—Continued

Auto Torts, Nursing Home, Products Liability, Professional Malpractice and Eminent Domain Sections); The Association of Trial Lawyers of America (Member: Inadequate Security, Auto Torts and Professional Malpractice Litigation Groups). ***PRACTICE AREAS:*** Arbitration; Mediation; Consumer Fraud; Eminent Domain; Hospital Negligence; Insurance Litigation; Medical Malpractice; Nursing Malpractice; Personal Injury; Automobile Accidents and Injuries; Catastrophic Injury; Wrongful Death; Premises Liability; Negligent Security; Professional Liability; Products Liability; Automotive Crashworthiness; Drug and Medical Device Litigation. ***Email:*** jkp@greensborolawyer.com

PINTO COATES KYRE & BROWN, PLLC

Established in 1994

3203 BRASSFIELD ROAD

GREENSBORO, NORTH CAROLINA 27410

Telephone: 336-282-8848

Facsimile: 336-282-8409

URL: http://www.pckb-law.com

Mailing Address: P.O. Box 4848, Greensboro, NC 27404

Civil Litigation, Insurance Defense, Insurance Coverage, Commercial Litigation, Personal Injury, Products Liability, Wrongful Death, Medical Malpractice, Workers Compensation, Labor and Employment, Appellate Practice.

MEMBERS OF FIRM

RICHARD L. PINTO, born New Brunswick, New Jersey, 1955; admitted to bar, 1980, North Carolina and U.S. District Court, Middle District of North Carolina; 1981, U.S. District Court, Eastern District of North Carolina. *Education:* Wake Forest University (B.A., cum laude, 1977; J.D., 1980). Phi Alpha Theta. *Member:* Greensboro and North Carolina Bar Associations; North Carolina State Bar; North Carolina Association of Defense Attorneys; Defense Research Institute and Trial Lawyers Association (DRI); Federation of Defense and Corporate Counsel. ***PRACTICE AREAS:*** Insurance Coverage; Insurance Defense; Personal Injury; Construction Litigation; Commercial Litigation; Wrongful Death; Products Liability; Medical Malpractice; Motor Carrier Defense.

PAUL D. COATES, born Deep River, Ontario, Canada 1956; admitted to bar, 1981, North Carolina and U.S. District Court, Middle District of North Carolina. *Education:* University of North Carolina at Greensboro (B.S., magna cum laude, 1978); University of North Carolina (J.D., 1981). Omicron Delta Epsilon. Graduate of Insurance Counsel Trial Academy, 1985. Recipient, G. Duffield Smith Award for Outstanding Publication, DRI, 1993. *Member:* Greensboro, North Carolina and American Bar Associations; North Carolina State Bar; Association of Trial Lawyers of America (ATLA); North Carolina Academy of Trial Lawyers (NCATL). ***PRACTICE AREAS:*** Insurance Coverage; Insurance Defense; Personal Injury; Uninsured and Underinsured Motorists; Wrongful Death; Medical Malpractice.

KENNETH KYRE, JR., born Dayton, Ohio, 1951; admitted to bar, 1977, North Carolina; 1979, U.S. District Court, Middle and Eastern Districts of North Carolina; 1980, U.S. Court of Appeals, Fourth Circuit; 1981, Supreme Court; 1983, U.S. District Court, Western District of North Carolina. *Education:* Shenandoah University (A.A., summa cum laude, 1972); St. Andrews Presbyterian College (B.A., with high honors, 1974); Wake Forest University (J.D., cum laude, 1977). Member, 1975-1976 and Research Editor, 1976-1977, Wake Forest Law Review. Law Clerk to U.S. District Judge Hiram H. Ward, U.S. District Court, Middle District of North Carolina, 1977-1979. Certified Mediator, North Carolina.*Member:* Greensboro, North Carolina and American Bar Associations; North Carolina State Bar; North Carolina Association of Defense Attorneys (Board Member, 2002-2005); Defense Research Institute and Trial Lawyers Association (DRI); American Judicature Society. ***PRACTICE AREAS:*** Products Liability; Commercial Litigation; Insurance Defense; Personal Injury; Wrongful Death.

DAVID L. BROWN, born Yadkinville, North Carolina, 1966; admitted to bar, 1992, North Carolina and U.S. District Court, Middle District of North Carolina. *Education:* University of North Carolina at Greensboro (B.A., summa cum laude, Economics, 1988); University of North Carolina (J.D., 1992). Phi Beta Kappa; Beta Gamma Sigma; Omicron Delta Epsilon; Phi Delta Phi. *Member:* Greensboro and North Carolina Bar Associations; North Carolina State Bar; North Carolina Association of Defense Attorneys (Chair, Young Lawyers Committee, 1998-2000); Defense Research Institute and Trial Lawyers Association (DRI). ***PRACTICE AREAS:*** Insurance Coverage; Personal Injury; Construction Litigation; Commercial Litigation.

MARTHA P. BROWN, born Bridgeport, Connecticut, 1968; admitted to bar, 1993, North Carolina and U.S. District Court, Middle District of North Carolina; 1994, U.S. Court of Appeals, Fourth Circuit; 1995, U.S. District Court, Eastern District of North Carolina. *Education:* Fairfield University (B.A., summa cum laude, 1990); University of North Carolina (J.D., with honors, 1993). Alpha Sigma Nu. Staff Member, North Carolina Law Review, 1992-1993. *Member:* Greensboro and North Carolina Bar Associations; North Carolina State Bar; North Carolina Association of Defense Attorneys; Defense Research Institute and Trial Lawyers Association (DRI). ***PRACTICE AREAS:*** Labor and Employment; Workers Compensation; Civil Litigation; Insurance Defense.

NANCY R. MEYERS, born Greensboro, North Carolina, 1969; admitted to bar, 1995, Kentucky; 1996, North Carolina and U.S. District Court, Middle District of North Carolina. *Education:* University of North Carolina (B.S., Biology, 1991); University of Louisville (J.D., cum laude, 1995). Alpha Epsilon Delta Pre-Medical Honor Society; Phi Kappa Phi, Member, University Of Louisville Journal of Law and Education, 1994-1995. Member, *1993-1995* and Secretary, *1993-1994,* Brandeis Honor Society. Member, Environmental Law Society, 1993-1995. *Member:* Greensboro, Kentucky and North Carolina Bar Associations; North Carolina State Bar; North Carolina Association of Defense Attorneys. ***PRACTICE AREAS:*** Insurance Defense; Personal Injury; Medical Malpractice; Civil Litigation.

(This Listing Continued)

JOHN I. MALONE, JR., born Philadelphia, Pennsylvania, August 26, 1968; admitted to bar, 1995, North Carolina and U.S. District Court, Middle District of North Carolina; 1999, U.S. District Court, Eastern and Western Districts of North Carolina. *Education:* Wake Forest University (B.A., 1990; J.D., 1995). Phi Delta Phi. *Member:* Greensboro and North Carolina Bar Associations; North Carolina State Bar; North Carolina Association of Defense Attorneys; Defense Research Institute and Trial Lawyers Association (DRI). ***PRACTICE AREAS:*** Insurance Defense; Commercial Litigation; Construction Litigation; Personal Injury.

DEBORAH J. BOWERS, born Freeport, Texas, 1952; admitted to bar, 1980, Texas; 1981, New Jersey; 1998, North Carolina; 2000, U.S. District Court, Middle District of North Carolina; 2001, U.S. District Court, Eastern District of North Carolina. *Education:* University of Texas (B.A., 1974); University of Houston (J.D., cum laude, 1980). Phi Delta Phi. Member, Order of the Barons. Member: International Law Journal, 1978-1980; The Advocates, 1978-1980. Civil Mediation Training, Seton Hall Law School, Institute for Dispute Resolution, 1995. *Member:* Greensboro and North Carolina Bar Associations; State Bar of Texas; North Carolina State Bar; North Carolina Association of Defense Attorneys; Defense Research Institute and Trial Lawyers Association (DRI). ***PRACTICE AREAS:*** Insurance Defense; Insurance Coverage; Commercial Litigation; Construction Litigation; Workers Compensation.

BRADY A. YNTEMA, born Flint, Michigan, 1973; admitted to bar, 1998, North Carolina and U.S. District Court, Middle District of North Carolina. *Education:* Elon College (B.S., cum laude, 1995); University of Dayton (J.D., 1998). Omicron Delta Kappa. Law Clerk to Judge Catharine R. Carruthers, United States Bankruptcy Court, Middle District of North Carolina, 1998-1999. *Member:* Greensboro and North Carolina Bar Associations; North Carolina State Bar; North Carolina Association of Defense Attorneys. ***PRACTICE AREAS:*** Civil Litigation; Personal Injury; Insurance Defense.

ASSOCIATES

BRYAN G. SCOTT, born Winston-Salem, North Carolina, January 7, 1979; admitted to bar, 2004, North Carolina and U.S. District Court, Middle District of North Carolina; 2005, U.S. District Court, Eastern and Western Districts of North Carolina and U.S. Court of Appeals, 4th Circuit. *Education:* Appalachian State University (B.A., magna cum laude, 2001); Wake Forest University (J.D., 2004). *Member:* Greensboro, North Carolina and American Bar Associations; North Carolina Association of Defense Attorneys. ***PRACTICE AREAS:*** Civil Litigation; Insurance Defense; Commercial Litigation; Personal Injury.

KIMBERLY A. SCHELL, born San Jose, California, July 12, 1979; admitted to bar, 2005, North Carolina. *Education:* University of Richmond (B.A., 2001); Wake Forest University (J.D., 2004). Pi Sigma Alpha. *Member:* North Carolina Bar Association. ***PRACTICE AREAS:*** Civil Litigation; Personal Injury; Insurance Defense.

REPRESENTATIVE CLIENTS: Penn National Insurance Co.; St. Paul Travelers; Grain Dealers Mutual Insurance Co.; Harleysville Mutual Insurance Co.; Lowes Companies, Inc.; N.C. Farm Bureau Mutual Insurance Co.; Piedmont Natural Gas Co.; Selective Insurance; Auto-Owners Insurance Co.; General Casualty Insurance Co.; Virginia Mutual Insurance Co.; Builders Mutual Insurance Co.; Specialty Risk Services; Southeastern Claims Services.

KENNETH L. POORTVLIET

318 S. EUGENE STREET, SUITE 103

GREENSBORO, NORTH CAROLINA 27405

Telephone: 336-370-1614

Fax: 336-370-1732

Email: ken@poortvlietlaw.com

URL: http://www.kpoortvlietlaw.com

Family Law, Divorce, Child Custody, Child Support, Adoptions, Domestic Violence, Visitation Rights, Criminal Law, Traffic Violations and Driving While Intoxicated.

KENNETH L. POORTVLIET, born Seattle, Washington, May 9, 1961; admitted to bar, 1999, North Carolina. *Education:* Seattle Pacific University (B.A., Political Science and Journalism, 1996); Regent University (J.D., 1999). *Member:* Guilford County Bar Association; North Carolina State Bar (Member, Family Law Section). ***PRACTICE AREAS:*** Family Law; Divorce; Child Custody; Child Support; Adoptions; Domestic Violence; Visitation Rights; Criminal Law; Traffic Violations; Driving Intoxicated.

PURRINGTON MOODY LLP

301 NORTH ELM STREET, SUITE 115

GREENSBORO, NORTH CAROLINA 27401

Telephone: 336-510-5880

Fax: 336-510-5888

URL: http://www.purringtonmoody.com

New York, New York Office: 105 Hudson Street, Suite 304, 10013. Telephone: 212-431-7129. Fax: 212-431-7124.

Investments, Investment Funds, Private Equity, Corporate Law, Partnership Law, Limited Liability Companies, Securities, Business Law, Finance, Mergers and Acquisitions.

MEMBERS OF FIRM

ALFRED NICHOLAS PURRINGTON, born Raleigh, North Carolina, March 14, 1966; admitted to bar, 1994, New York; 1999, North Carolina. *Education:* Princeton University (A.B., 1988); Georgetown University (J.D., magna cum laude, 1993). Order of the Coif. Recipient, RIA Tax Award. *Member:* Greensboro, North Carolina, New York State and American Bar (Member, Business Law Section) Associations. **Email:** npurrington@purringtonmoody.com

DAVID K. MOODY, born Burlington, Vermont, April 1, 1961; admitted to bar, 1992, New York; 2003, North Carolina. *Education:* Swarthmore College (B.A., 1983); Cornell

(This Listing Continued)

University (J.D., magna cum laude, 1991). Order of the Coif. Note Editor, Cornell Law Review. Law Clerk, Hon. Frank M. Johnson, U.S. Court of Appeals, Eleventh Circuit. (Resident, New York, New York Office)

JAMES S. FELT, born Charleston, South Carolina, May 8, 1967; admitted to bar, 1993, New York and New Jersey; 1994, District of Columbia; 1996, U.S. Court of Appeals, Fourth Circuit; 1999, U.S. Supreme Court; 2001, North Carolina. *Education:* Emory University (B.A., 1989); Georgetown University (J.D., cum laude, 1992). *Member:* The District of Columbia Bar; Greensboro, North Carolina and American Bar Associations. ***REPORTED CASES:*** Wilson v. Lane, 526 U.S. 603 (1999). ***Email:*** jfelt@purringtonmoody.com

NEIL M. FREEMAN, born Memphis, Tenn. October 15, 1967; admitted to bar, 1993, New York; 1995, District of Columbia (Not admitted in North Carolina). *Education:* Duke University (B.A., 1989); Georgetown University (J.D., cum laude, 1992). (Resident, New York, New York Office). ***Email:*** nfreeman@purringtonmoody.com

JEFFREY A. JONES, born Salem, Illinois, April 3, 1964; admitted to bar, 1992, Connecticut; 2001, Arizona; 2002, North Carolina. *Education:* Trinity University (B.S., cum laude, 1986); Georgetown University Law Center (J.D., 1992). *Member:* Greensboro, Pima County, North Carolina, Arizona and American Bar Associations. ***Email:*** jjones@purringtonmoody.com

STEPHEN L. PAMPUSH, born Lakewood, Ohio, March 15, 1965; admitted to bar, 1992, Ohio; 1994, New Jersey; 2001, New York. *Education:* University of Notre Dame (B.S., 1987); Georgetown University (J.D., 1992). (Resident, New York, New York Office). ***Email:*** spampush@purringtonmoody.com

CHRISTOPHER E. LINDSEY, born Beaumont, Texas, August 19, 1966; admitted to bar, 1993, Texas; 2003, North Carolina. *Education:* University of Virginia (B.A., 1988); University of Texas (J.D., 1993; M.B.A., 2003). Jefferson Scholar and Echols Scholar, University of Virginia. ***LANGUAGES:*** German. ***Email:*** clindsey@purringtonmoody.com

ASSOCIATE

HARRISON M. HALL, born Cincinnati, Ohio; admitted to bar, 2002, North Carolina. *Education:* Davidson College (A.B., 1999); Wake Forest University Law School (J.D., 2002). *Member:* Greensboro, North Carolina and American (Member, Business Law Section) Bar Associations. ***Email:*** hhall@purringtonmoody.com

SENIOR COUNSEL

ALFRED L. PURRINGTON, III, born Raleigh, North Carolina, August 31, 1933; admitted to bar, 1961, North Carolina. *Education:* University of North Carolina (A.B., 1955); Harvard University (LL.B., 1961). Phi Beta Kappa. Chancellor, Episcopal Diocese of North Carolina, 2000—. *Member:* Wake County, North Carolina (Chairman, Commercial Banking and Business Law Section, 1981-1983) and American (Member, Small Business Committee, Legal Opinions Committee, Business Law Section, 1973—) Bar Associations. ***Email:*** apurrington@purringtonmoody.com

THE QUINN LAW FIRM

315 SPRING GARDEN STREET, SUITE 1D
GREENSBORO, NORTH CAROLINA 27401
Telephone: 336-272-9072
Fax: 336-272-2289
Email: quinnlaw@triadbiz.rr.com
URL: http://www.quinnlawnc.com

Workers Compensation, Personal Injury, Automobile Accidents and Injuries, Employment Discrimination, Immigration.

NANCY P. QUINN, born Muscatine, Iowa, November 29, 1956; admitted to bar, 1989, North Carolina. *Education:* University of North Florida (B.A., 1981); Wake Forest University (J.D., 1989). *Member:* Guilford County, North Carolina, and American Bar Associations; North Carolina State Bar (Member, Sections on: Workers Compensation; Labor and Employment). ***PRACTICE AREAS:*** Workers Compensation; Personal Injury; Automobile Accidents and Injuries; Employment Discrimination.

ROBERSON, HAWORTH & REESE, P.L.L.C.

GREENSBORO, NORTH CAROLINA

(See High Point)

General and Trial Practice in State and Federal Courts. Banking, Corporation, Probate, Real Estate, Bankruptcy, Commercial, Municipal Corporations, Personal Injury, Products Liability, Zoning and Land Use, Condemnation.

ROBINSON & LAWING, L.L.P.

GREENSBORO, NORTH CAROLINA

(See Winston-Salem)

General Civil and Complex Litigation in All Courts. Business, Corporate, Antitrust and Trade, Intellectual Property, Products Liability, Personal Injury, Professional Malpractice, Workers Compensation, Bankruptcy, Family Law, Wrongful Death, Insurance, Employee Benefits Law, Employment and Labor Law, Business Law, Estate and Tax Law.

GERALD S. SCHAFER

Established in 1971
220 COMMERCE PLACE
GREENSBORO, NORTH CAROLINA 27401
Telephone: 336-273-9309
Fax: 336-273-2700

General Civil Practice. Bankruptcy, Debtor/Creditors Rights Law, Collection and Criminal Law.

(This Listing Continued)

GERALD S. SCHAFER, born Mount Airy, North Carolina, November 4, 1944; admitted to bar, 1970, North Carolina; 1971, U.S. District Court, Middle District of North Carolina; 1976, U.S. Court of Appeals, Fourth Circuit. *Education:* University of North Carolina (A.B., 1967; J.D., 1970). Phi Alpha Delta. *Member:* Greensboro and North Carolina (Member, Bankruptcy Section) Bar Associations; North Carolina State Bar; North Carolina Trial Lawyers Associations (Member, Panel of Chapter 7 Bankruptcy Trustees for Middle District of North Carolina); Commercial Law League of America.

REPRESENTATIVE CLIENTS: Williamson Heating & Cooling, Inc.; Branch Banking & Trust Co.; Environmental Air Systems Inc.; Lewis Systems & Services, Inc.; Envirotrol Inc.; Corporate America; Family Credit Union.
APPROVED ATTORNEY FOR: Fidelity National Title; Investors Title Insurance Co.
REFERENCE: Wachovia Bank.

SCHELL BRAY AYCOCK ABEL & LIVINGSTON P.L.L.C.

Established in 1987
1500 RENAISSANCE PLAZA
230 NORTH ELM STREET
P.O. BOX 21847
GREENSBORO, NORTH CAROLINA 27420
Telephone: 336-370-8800
Fax: 336-370-8830
Email: Info@sbaal.com
URL: http://www.sbaal.com

Corporate, Taxation, Securities Regulation, Venture Capital, Real Estate and Real Estate Finance, Mergers and Acquisitions, Health Care, Antitrust and Trade Regulation, Banking, Commercial, Employee Benefits, Estate Planning and Administration.

FIRM PROFILE: Schell Bray Aycock Abel & Livingston P.L.L.C. serves as regular outside counsel to public and privately held businesses with diverse interests in local, national and international markets. Clients of the firm operate in a variety of organizational structures, including corporations, partnerships, limited liability companies and joint ventures. Attorneys have significant experience in the areas of mergers and acquisitions, securities offerings, business restructurings, estate and tax-planning, employee benefits, health care, commercial real estate development and tax exempt organizations. The firm is listed in the Bar Register of Preeminent Lawyers.

MEMBERS OF FIRM

BRAXTON SCHELL, born Raleigh, North Carolina, February 24, 1924; admitted to bar, 1951, North Carolina. *Education:* North Carolina State University; University of North Carolina (B.S., 1948; J.D., with honors, 1951). Beta Gamma Sigma; Phi Delta Phi; Phi Beta Kappa; Order of the Coif. Associate Editor, North Carolina Law Review, 1950-1951. Fellow: American Bar Foundation. [A.A.F., Active Duty, 1943-1945]. ***PRACTICE AREAS:*** Corporate Practice; Mergers and Acquisitions Law; Exempt Organizations. ***Email:*** bschell@sbaal.com

DORIS R. BRAY, born Reidsville, North Carolina, January 7, 1938; admitted to bar, 1966, North Carolina. *Education:* Lake Erie College (A.B., summa cum laude, 1959); Yale University (M.A., 1960); University of North Carolina (LL.B., with high honors, 1966). Order of the Coif. Editor-in-Chief, North Carolina Law Review, 1965-1966. Woodrow Wilson Fellow. Law Clerk to Judge J. Spencer Bell, U.S. Court of Appeals, Fourth Circuit, 1966-1967. Member, North Carolina General Statute Commission, 1982-2002; Chairman, 1997-2002. Member, Board of Governors, 1977-1980 and Chairman, Section on Commercial Banking and Business Law, 1980-1981, North Carolina Bar Association. ***PRACTICE AREAS:*** Corporate Practice; Securities Regulation Law; Mergers and Acquisitions Law; Corporate Governance; Venture Capital. ***Email:*** dbray@sbaal.com

WILLIAM P. AYCOCK, II, born Anniston, Alabama, March 5, 1943; admitted to bar, 1970, North Carolina. *Education:* University of North Carolina (A.B., 1965; J.D., with honors, 1970). Order of the Coif. Research Editor, North Carolina Law Review, 1969-1970. Certified Mediator, North Carolina Dispute Resolution Commission. *Member:* North Carolina Bar Association (Council Member, Real Estate Section, 1989-1992). [U.S. Navy, Active Duty, 1965-1967]. (Board Certified Specialist in Real Property Law - Business, Commercial and Industrial Transactions, North Carolina State Board of Legal Specialization). ***PRACTICE AREAS:*** Real Estate Development and Finance; Commercial Real Estate; Real Property Acquisitions; Leasing. ***Email:*** wpaycock@sbaal.com

MICHAEL R. ABEL, born York, Pennsylvania, July 6, 1945; admitted to bar, 1970, North Carolina. *Education:* Davidson College (A.B., 1967); University of North Carolina (J.D., with high honors, 1970). Order of the Coif. Articles Editor, North Carolina Law Review, 1969-1970. Adjunct Professor of Law, University of North Carolina School of Law, 1979—. Member, North Carolina General Statutes Commission, 2002—; North Carolina General Statues Commission Drafting Committees for Business Corporation Act, Nonprofit Corporation Act and Uniform Partnership Act. North Carolina Bar Association Drafting Committee for Limited Liability Company Act. ***PRACTICE AREAS:*** Taxation; Mergers and Acquisitions; Antitrust; Exempt Organizations; Employee Benefits. ***Email:*** mrabel@sbaal.com

PAUL H. LIVINGSTON, JR., born Laurinburg, North Carolina, May 27, 1946; admitted to bar, 1971, North Carolina. *Education:* University of North Carolina (B.S., 1968); Wake Forest University (J.D., cum laude, 1971). Phi Alpha Delta. Notes Editor, Wake Forest Law Review, 1970-1971. Certified Public Accountant, North Carolina, 1972. Chairman, Tax Section, North Carolina Bar Association, 1983-1984. *Member:* North Carolina Association of Certified Public Accountants; American Institute of Certified Public Accountants. Fellow, American College of Trust and Estate Counsel. (Board Certified Specialist in Estate Planning and Probate Law, North Carolina State Board of Legal Specialization). ***PRACTICE AREAS:*** Estate Planning; Estate Administration; Taxation Law; Exempt Organizations. ***Email:*** plivingston@sbaal.com

(This Listing Continued)

SCHELL BRAY AYCOCK ABEL & LIVINGSTON P.L.L.C., Greensboro—Continued

THOMAS C. WATKINS, born Wilmington, North Carolina, May 30, 1951; admitted to bar, 1978, North Carolina. *Education:* University of North Carolina at Chapel Hill (B.S., 1973; J.D., with honors, 1978). Beta Gamma Sigma. Staff Member, North Carolina Law Review, 1976-1978. *Member:* North Carolina Bar Association (Business Law Section, Chair, 2001-2003; Chair, Business Organizations Committee, 1997-1998). ***PRACTICE AREAS:*** Mergers and Acquisitions Law; Corporate Law; Banking Law. ***Email:*** tcwatkins@sbaal.com

MICHAEL H. GODWIN, born Dunn, North Carolina, January 9, 1949; admitted to bar, 1974, North Carolina. *Education:* University of North Carolina (B.A., 1971; J.D., with honors, 1974). Phi Beta Kappa. Member, North Carolina Law Review, 1973-1974. Chair, Estate Planning and Fiduciary Law Section, 1988-1989, North Carolina Bar Association. Fellow, American College of Trust and Estate Counsel (State Chair). Board Certified Specialist in Estate Planning and Probate Law, North Carolina State Board of Legal Specialization. ***PRACTICE AREAS:*** Estate Planning; Business Planning; Tax Planning; Estate and Trust Administration; Tax Exempt Organizations. ***Email:*** mgodwin@sbaal.com

BARBARA R. CHRISTY, born Tampa, Florida, May 30, 1958; admitted to bar, 1983, North Carolina. *Education:* Appalachian State University (B.S., magna cum laude, 1980); University of North Carolina (J.D., 1983). ***PRACTICE AREAS:*** Real Estate Development and Finance; Commercial Real Estate; Apartment Projects; Shopping Center Acquisitions; Section 1031 Exchanges; Real Estate Title Examination. ***Email:*** bchristy@sbaal.com

JOHN A. McLENDON, JR., born Boston, Massachusetts, June 2, 1958; admitted to bar, 1987, North Carolina. *Education:* Middlebury College (B.A., cum laude, 1980); University of North Carolina (J.D., with honors, 1987). Order of the Coif. Staff Member, North Carolina Law Review, 1985-1986. ***PRACTICE AREAS:*** Real Estate Development and Finance; Condominium Law; Planned Unit Development Law; Commercial Real Estate. ***Email:*** jmclendon@sbaal.com

MELANIE SAMSON TUTTLE, born Amityville, New York, December 2, 1954; admitted to bar, 1983, Pennsylvania and U.S. District Court, Western District of Pennsylvania; 1985, Ohio and U.S. Court of Appeals, Third Circuit; 1986, U.S. District Court, Northern District of Ohio; 1996, U.S. District Court, Northern District of Indiana; 2000, North Carolina and U.S. District Court, Middle District of North Carolina. *Education:* University of Michigan (B.S.E., cum laude, 1977); University of Cincinnati (J.D., 1983). Tau Beta Pi; Pi Tau Sigma. Member, Order of the Coif. Recipient, University Prize. Editor-in-Chief, University of Cincinnati Law Review, 1982-1983. Law Clerk to the Hon. Ruggero J. Aldisert, U.S. Court of Appeals, Third Circuit, 1983-1985. ***REPORTED CASES:*** In Re Auto-Train Corp., Inc., 810 F.2d 270 (D.C.Cir. 1987); Goltz v. University of Notre Dame, 177 F.R.D. 638 (N.D. Ind. 1997). ***PRACTICE AREAS:*** Business Transactions; Securities Regulation; Corporate Governance; Employment Law. ***Email:*** mtuttle@sbaal.com

JENNIFER L.J. KOENIG, born Wittenberg, Wisconsin, April 8, 1972; admitted to bar, 1997, North Carolina. *Education:* University of North Carolina at Chapel Hill (A.B., Mathematics, highest distinction, 1994; J.D., 1997). Phi Beta Kappa; Pi Mu Epsilon. *Member:* North Carolina Bar Association (Estate Planning and Fiduciary Law Section; Council Member, 2001-2004; Chair, Pro Bono Committee, 1998-2001; Chair, Public Relations and Education Committee, 2003—). (Board Certified Specialist in Estate Planning and Probate Law, North Carolina State Board of Legal Specialization). ***PRACTICE AREAS:*** Estate Planning; Estate Administration; Business Law; Exempt Organizations; Taxation. ***Email:*** jkoenig@sbaal.com

HOLLY H. ALDERMAN, born Shreveport, Louisiana, October 13, 1964; admitted to bar, 1989, Georgia; 1994, North Carolina. *Education:* University of North Carolina at Chapel Hill (B.S., 1986; J.D., 1989). *Member:* North Carolina (Corporate Counsel; Member and Real Property Counsel, Real Property Section) and American Bar Associations; State Bar of Georgia (Member, Real Property Section). (Resident, Chapel Hill, North Carolina Office) (Board Certified Specialist in Real Property Law: Business, Commercial and Industrial Transactions, North Carolina State Board of Legal Specialization). ***PRACTICE AREAS:*** Commercial Real Estate; Real Estate Development. ***Email:*** halderman@sbaal.com

MARK T. CAIN, born Dearborn, Michigan, May 15, 1961; admitted to bar, 1987, Tennessee; 1988, North Carolina. *Education:* University of Michigan (B.A., with high distinction, 1983); University of North Carolina at Chapel Hill (J.D., 1987). Associate and Partner, Schell Bray Aycock Abel & Livingston, LLP, 1988-1997. *Member:* North Carolina and American Bar Associations. ***PRACTICE AREAS:*** Business Transactions; Finance; Corporate Law; Mortgage Banking Law. ***Email:*** mcain@sbaal.com

ASSOCIATES

GARLAND G. GRAHAM, born Manila, Philippines, September 14, 1975; admitted to bar, 1999, North Carolina. *Education:* University of Florida (B.A., with honors, 1996; J.D., with honors, 1999). *Member:* North Carolina Bar Association (Business Law Section, Treasurer 2004-2005, Council Member 2005—); Greensboro Bar Association (President 2004, Young Lawyers Division). ***PRACTICE AREAS:*** Corporate; Finance; Mergers and Acquisitions. ***Email:*** ggraham@sbaal.com

STACEY A. BRADY, born New York, 1972; admitted to bar, 1998, North Carolina. *Education:* Clemson University (B.A., summa cum laude, senior departmental honors, 1995); University of North Carolina at Chapel Hill (J.D., with honors, 1998). Phi Alpha Delta. Staff Member, 1996-1997 and Note and Comment Editor, 1997-1998, North Carolina Journal of International Law and Commercial Regulation. ***PRACTICE AREAS:*** Pass-Through Entities; Mergers and Acquisitions; Corporate Law; Taxation. ***Email:*** sbrady@sbaal.com

JILL L. RASPET, born Upland, California, August 8, 1978; admitted to bar, 2002, North Carolina. *Education:* University of North Carolina at Wilmington (B.S., summa cum laude, 1999); Wake Forest University School of Law (J.D., magna cum laude, 2002). Order of the Coif. Notes and Comments Editor, Wake Forest Law Review, 2000-2002. *Member:* North Carolina Bar Association (Estate Planning & Fiduciary Law Section; Chair, Technology Committee); Greensboro Bar Association (Young Lawyers Division). ***PRACTICE AREAS:*** Estate Planning; Estate Administration; Tax Exempt Organizations. ***Email:*** jraspet@sbaal.com

(This Listing Continued)

JOHN CRAIG KISER, born Statesville, North Carolina, January 13, 1976; admitted to bar, 2002, North Carolina. *Education:* University of North Carolina at Chapel Hill (B.A., 1998); Wake Forest University School of Law (J.D., 2002). ***PRACTICE AREAS:*** Commercial Real Estate; Real Estate Development; Real Estate Finance. ***Email:*** ckiser@sbaal.com

CHRISTINA N. FREEMAN, born Lexington, North Carolina; admitted to bar, 1998, North Carolina; 2002, Massachusetts and U.S. Tax Court. *Education:* University of North Carolina, Greensboro (B.S.W., 1990); North Carolina Central University School of Law (J.D., magna cum laude, 1998); Boston University School of Law (LL.M. in Taxation, 2002). Assistant Associate Editor, NCCU Law Journal. *Member:* North Carolina Bar Association (Taxation and Real Property Law Sections). ***PRACTICE AREAS:*** Commercial Real Estate; Real Estate Acquisitions; Real Estate Development; Real Estate Finance; Taxation. ***Email:*** cfreeman@sbaal.com

SAMANTHA G. STEFFEN, born London, England, August 13, 1973; admitted to bar, 1998, Florida and U.S. District Court, Middle District of Florida; 1999, Georgia and U.S. District Court, Northern District of Georgia; 2000, North Carolina and U.S. District Court, Middle, Eastern and Western District of North Carolina. *Education:* University of Central Florida (B.S.B.A., magna cum laude, 1994); University of Florida (J.D., with honors, 1997). Chair: ABA/IPL Federal Legislation Committee, 2005—; ABA/ILP Online Trademark Issues Committee, 2004—; ABA/IPL Special 401 Actions Subcommittee, 2002-2003. Member, INTA Subcommittee Information Resources Committee, 2004—. Formerly With: Kilpatrick Stockton LLP, Winston-Salem, NC, 2000-2005; Kilpatrick Stockton LLP, Augusta, GA, 1999-2000; Fisher, Rushmer, Werrenrath, Dickson, Tallt & Dunlap, P.A., Orlando, FL., 1998-1999. *Member:* The Florida Bar; State Bar of Georgia; American Bar Association; National Order of Barristers. ***PRACTICE AREAS:*** Intellectual Property; Trademarks; Corporate Transactions; Commercial Transactions. ***Email:*** ssteffen@sbaal.com

All Attorneys are Members of Greensboro, North Carolina and American Bar Associations and North Carolina State Bar.

REPRESENTATIVE CLIENTS: Acme-McCrary Corporation; Anderson Bauman Tourtellot Vos and Co.; The Breakers Palm Beach, Inc.; Buzz-Off Insect Shield, LLC; Carolina Container Company; Cherokee Investment Partners; Confluence Holdings Corp.; Dick Broadcasting Company; D.P. Solutions, Inc.; The Ellison Company, Inc.; First Greensboro Home Equity, Inc.; First National Bank and Trust Company; Flagler Systems, Inc.; Franklin Street Trust Company; Gate City Motor Company; Hunt Electrical Supply Company; Kenan Family Foundation; Kenan Management Inc.; Kenan Transport Company; Klaussner Furniture Industries, Inc.; Landfall Associates; Michael Thomas Furniture; Natuzzi Americas, Inc.; Osborne Company Inc.; Piedmont Financial Trust Company; Restoration Systems, LLC; St. James Plantation; Sapona Manufacturing Company; Southeast Capital, LLC; Steven D. Bell & Company; Tencarva Machinery Company; TriPath Imaging, Inc.; United Brass Works, Inc.; Universal Furniture International, Inc.; University of North Carolina at Chapel Hill Foundation, Inc.; The William R. Kenan, Jr. Fund.

SCHLOSSER & PRITCHETT

5709 W. FRIENDLY AVENUE
GREENSBORO, NORTH CAROLINA 27410
Telephone: 336-292-4076
Fax: 336-292-8003
URL: http://www.schlosserpritchett.com

Criminal Law, Wrongful Death, Automobile Accidents, Felonies, Misdemeanors, Traffic, Personal Injury, Litigation in State and Federal Courts.

MICHAEL A. SCHLOSSER, born Greensboro, North Carolina, May 1, 1945; admitted to bar, 1973, North Carolina and U.S. District Court, Middle District of North Carolina. *Education:* Virginia Military Institute (B.A., 1967); Wake Forest University (J.D., 1973). Phi Alpha Delta. Guilford County Assistant District Attorney, 1973-1978 and District Attorney, 1978-1982. *Member:* Greensboro, Guilford County and American Bar Associations; North Carolina State Bar; North Carolina Academy of Trial Lawyers. [1st Lt., U.S. Army, 1967-1970]. ***PRACTICE AREAS:*** Criminal Law; Wrongful Death; Automobile Accidents and Injuries; Felonies; Misdemeanors. ***Email:*** mike@greensborolawyer.net

JAN ELLIOTT PRITCHETT, born Durham, North Carolina, August 20, 1968; admitted to bar, 1995, North Carolina, U.S. District Court, Eastern and Middle Districts of North Carolina and U.S. Court of Appeals, 4th Circuit. *Education:* Winston-Salem State University (B.A., 1991); Southern University Law Center (J.D., 1994). Delta Sigma Pi. Moot Court. Assistant District Attorney, Guilford County, 1996-2000. *Member:* Greensboro, North Carolina and American Bar Associations; National Bar Association; Guilford County Black Lawyers Association (Treasurer, 2000; Executive Board, 2000). ***PRACTICE AREAS:*** Criminal Law; Traffic Violations; Personal Injury; Litigation. ***Email:*** jpritchett@greensborolawyer.net

ASSOCIATES

L. STEVEN WAYNE, born Durham, North Carolina, August 29, 1972; admitted to bar, 1998, North Carolina. *Education:* University of North Carolina at Chapel Hill (B.A., 1995); Campbell University (J.D., 1998). ***PRACTICE AREAS:*** Criminal Law. ***Email:*** swayne@greensborolawyer.net

SCOTT G. GALIGER, born Elgin, Illinois, January 8, 1969; admitted to bar, 1994, Georgia; 1995, North Carolina and U.S. District Court, Middle District of North Carolina; 1997, U.S. District Court, Eastern District of North Carolina. *Education:* Ursinus College (B.A., 1991); Emory University (J.D., with distinction, 1994). *Member:* North Carolina State Bar; North Carolina Academy of Trial Lawyers. ***PRACTICE AREAS:*** Workers Compensation; Automobile Accidents and Injuries; Social Security Disability. ***Email:*** sgaliger@greensborolawyer.net

SHARPLESS & STAVOLA, P.A.

Established in 1990

826 NORTH ELM STREET
P.O. BOX 22106
GREENSBORO, NORTH CAROLINA 27420
Telephone: 336-333-6400
Facsimile: 336-333-6399
URL: http://www.sharpless-stavola.com

General Civil Litigation, Trials and Appeals in all State and Federal Courts, Professional and Medical Malpractice, Construction and Commercial Litigation, Business Torts, Hospitals and Health Care, Employment and Administrative Law, Insurance Coverage, Wrongful Death, Product Liability Defense, Toxic Torts, Environmental Litigation.

FREDERICK K. SHARPLESS, born Pennsylvania; admitted to bar, 1984, North Carolina. *Education:* Dartmouth College (A.B., 1980); University of North Carolina (J.D., with high honors, 1984). Order of the Coif. Articles Editor, North Carolina Law Review, 1983-1984. *Member:* Greensboro, North Carolina and American Bar Associations; North Carolina State Bar. ***PRACTICE AREAS:*** Business Torts; Construction Litigation; Insurance; Commercial Litigation; Professional Malpractice; Products Liability. ***Email:*** fks@sharpless-stavola.com

PAMELA A. ROBERTSON, born Salisbury, North Carolina, October 26, 1955; admitted to bar, 1982, Georgia and North Carolina. *Education:* Meredith College (B.A., 1978); Mercer University (J.D., 1982). Member, Moot Court Board. Member, Mercer Law Review, 1980-1982. Law Clerk to The Honorable James C. Fox, U.S. District Judge, Eastern District of North Carolina, 1982-1984. *Member:* Greensboro and North Carolina Bar Associations; North Carolina State Bar; State Bar of Georgia. ***PRACTICE AREAS:*** Medical Malpractice; Wrongful Death; Personal Injury; Long Term Care; Insurance Coverage. ***Email:*** par@sharpless-stavola.com

JOSEPH M. STAVOLA, born New York, N.Y.; admitted to bar, 1979, New York; 1991, North Carolina. *Education:* State University of New York at Albany (B.A., cum laude, 1975); New York Law School (J.D., 1978). Recipient: American Jurisprudence Award and Jackson Award in Labor Law. *Member:* Greensboro, North Carolina and New York State Bar Associations; North Carolina State Bar. ***PRACTICE AREAS:*** Personal Injury; Wrongful Death; Medical Malpractice; Products Liability; Construction Accidents; Fire Loss. ***Email:*** jms@sharpless-stavola.com

BRENDA S. McCLEARN, born Denver, Colorado; admitted to bar, 1994, North Carolina. *Education:* University of Colorado at Boulder (B.S., magna cum laude, 1990); George Washington University National Law Center (J.D., with honors, 1994). Beta Gamma Sigma; Sigma Iota Epsilon; Golden Key. Moot Court. Editor-in-Chief, Commercial Protection Reporting Service, 1994. *Member:* Greensboro, North Carolina and American Bar Associations; North Carolina State Bar. ***PRACTICE AREAS:*** Commercial Litigation; Products Liability; Dental Malpractice Defense; Medical Malpractice Defense; Construction Litigation; Professional Malpractice; Insurance Defense; Workers Compensation Defense. ***Email:*** bsm@sharpless-stavola.com

JOSEPH P. BOOTH, III, born Gastonia, North Carolina, August 26, 1969; admitted to bar, 1997, North Carolina. *Education:* University of North Carolina at Wilmington (B.S., 1992); Syracuse University (J.D., cum laude, 1997). Articles Editor, The Labor Lawyer, 1996-1997. *Member:* Greensboro, North Carolina and American Bar Associations; North Carolina State Bar. ***PRACTICE AREAS:*** Medical Malpractice Defense; Construction Litigation; Commercial Litigation; Products Liability. ***Email:*** jpb@sharpless-stavola.com

BRIAN H. ALLIGOOD, born Fayetteville, North Carolina, July 30, 1967; admitted to bar, 1992, Georgia; 2000, North Carolina. *Education:* University of North Carolina (B.A., with honors, 1989); Duke University (J.D., 1992). Phi Beta Kappa. *Member:* Greensboro, North Carolina and American Bar Associations; State Bar of Georgia; North Carolina State Bar. ***PRACTICE AREAS:*** Medical Malpractice Defense; Employment Discrimination; Long Term Care; Workers Compensation. ***Email:*** bha@sharpless-stavola.com

EUGENE E. LESTER, III, born Southampton, New York, March 31, 1971; admitted to bar, 1996, North Carolina. *Education:* Binghamton University (B.S., summa cum laude, 1993); Wake Forest University (J.D., 1996). 1996-1998, Law Clerk to the Honorable P. Trevor Sharp, U.S. Magistrate Judge, Middle District of North Carolina. *Member:* Greensboro, North Carolina and American Bar Associations; North Carolina State Bar. ***PRACTICE AREAS:*** Business Torts; Construction Litigation; Insurance; Commercial Litigation; Professional Malpractice; Products Liability; Employment Law; Workers Compensation; Federal Criminal Law. ***Email:*** eel@sharpless-stavola.com

---

CHRISTINA L. LEWIS, born Kansas City, Missouri; admitted to bar, 2002, North Carolina. *Education:* University of Texas (B.A., with honors, 1999); Duke University (J.D., 2002). Phi Beta Kappa. Member, Alaska Law School Law Review. *Member:* Greensboro, North Carolina and American Bar Associations; North Carolina State Bar. ***PRACTICE AREAS:*** Medical Malpractice Defense; Products Liability; Commercial Litigation; Workers Compensation. ***Email:*** cll@sharpless-stavola.com

REPRESENTATIVE CLIENTS: Jefferson Pilot Corporation; Cornerstone Healthcare, P.A.; Church Mutual Insurance Co.; CNA Insurance Group; Davenport, Marvin, Joyce & Co., L.L.P.; Dixon Hughes, P.L.L.C.; High Point Regional Hospital; Senergy, Inc.; The Medical Protective Company; AIG Companies; Northeast Medical Center; Chem Rex, Inc.; Beverly Enterprises.
REFERENCE: Branch Banking & Trust Co.

DAVID B. SMITH

Established in 1997

FIRST CITIZENS BANK BUILDING
100 SOUTH ELM STREET, SUITE 520
GREENSBORO, NORTH CAROLINA 27402
Telephone: 336-574-2533
Fax: 336-574-3378
Email: dbsmithattorney@msn.com
URL: http://www.dbsmithattorney.net

Mailing Address: P.O. Box 2097, Greensboro, NC 27402-2097

Criminal Practice in all State and Federal Courts, Criminal Law, Driving While Intoxicated (DWI), Drug Crimes, Juvenile Crimes, Parole and Probation, Traffic Violations, White Collar Crimes, Federal Appellate, Federal Forfeitures, Fraud.

FIRM PROFILE: David B. Smith is a member of the Bar Register of Preeminent Lawyers in Criminal Trial Practice.

DAVID B. SMITH, born 1948; admitted to bar, 1973, North Carolina. *Education:* North Carolina Agricultural & Technical State University (B.S); University of North Carolina (J.D.). Assistant District Attorney, 1975-1978. Assistant United States Attorney, 1978-1996. *Member:* Guilford County, North Carolina and American Bar Associations; North Carolina Association of Black Lawyers; North Carolina Academy of Trial Lawyers.

SMITH, JAMES, ROWLETT & COHEN, L.L.P.

101 SOUTH ELM STREET, SUITE 310
P.O. BOX 990
GREENSBORO, NORTH CAROLINA 27402
Telephone: 336-274-2992
FAX: 336-274-8490
Email: sjrclaw@earthlink.net
URL: http://www.sjrclaw.com

General Practice in all State and Federal Courts. Antitrust, Employment, Labor, Constitutional, Divorce, Environmental, Probate, Workers Compensation, Negligence, Personal Injury, Product Liability; Shareholder and Investor Rights; Civil and Criminal Trial and Appellate Practice, Wills.

MEMBERS OF FIRM

J. DAVID JAMES, born Louisville, Kentucky, 1944; admitted to bar, 1971, North Carolina; 1974, U.S. Supreme Court. *Education:* Davidson College (B.A., 1966); University of North Carolina (J.D., with honors, 1971). Order of the Coif. Member, Board of Editors and Business Manager, North Carolina Law Review, 1970-1971. Listed in the Best Lawyers of America, Labor and Employment Law Section. *Member:* North Carolina and American Bar Associations; North Carolina Academy of Trial Lawyers. [U.S. Army, active duty, 1966-1968]. ***PRACTICE AREAS:*** Civil Litigation; Labor Law; Employment Law; Constitutional Rights.

MARGARET F. ROWLETT, born Abingdon, Virginia, 1964; admitted to bar, 1990, North Carolina. *Education:* Emory & Henry College (B.A., summa cum laude, 1986); Duke University (M.A., Public-Policy Sciences, 1990; J.D., 1990). *Member:* North Carolina State Bar; The Association of Trial Lawyers of America; North Carolina Academy of Trial Lawyers; North Carolina Association of Women Attorneys. ***PRACTICE AREAS:*** Civil Litigation; Workers Compensation; Negligence; Employment Law.

SETH R. COHEN, born Atlanta, Georgia, 1957; admitted to bar, 1991, North Carolina; 1997, U.S. Supreme Court. *Education:* University of Georgia (B.A., magna cum laude, 1978; A.B.J., Journalism, 1979); University of North Carolina at Chapel Hill (J.D., with highest honors, 1991). Phi Beta Kappa; Phi Kappa Phi; Order of the Coif; Order of the Barristers; Carolyn B. Davis Society. Adjunct Professor, Wake Forest University School of Law, 1999—. General Counsel, American Civil Liberties Union of North Carolina. *Member:* Greensboro and American Bar Associations; North Carolina State Bar; North Carolina Academy of Trial Lawyers. ***PRACTICE AREAS:*** Civil Litigation; State and Federal Criminal Defense; Civil and Constitutional Rights; Labor and Employment Law; Capital Litigation.

OF COUNSEL

NORMAN B. SMITH, born Iron Mountain, Michigan, 1938; admitted to bar, 1965, North Carolina; 1969, U.S. Supreme Court. *Education:* University of North Carolina (A.B., 1960); Harvard University (LL.B., cum laude, 1965). Phi Beta Kappa. Listed in the Best Lawyers of America, first amendment law and labor and employment law sections. Recipient: Norman B. Smith Award, The North Carolina Civil Liberties Union, January, 1993; Frank Porter Graham Award, The North Carolina Civil Liberties Union, 1978. *Member:* Greensboro, North Carolina (Chair, Antitrust and Trade Regulation Section, 1997-1998) and American Bar Associations; North Carolina Academy of Trial Lawyers. [U.S. Navy, active duty, 1960-1962]. ***PRACTICE AREAS:*** Civil Trials; Antitrust; Employment; Constitutional; Environmental; Shareholder and Investor Rights; Negligence; Product Liability.

SMITH MOORE LLP

Established in 1919

WACHOVIA TOWER
300 NORTH GREENE STREET, SUITE 1400
P.O. BOX 21927
GREENSBORO, NORTH CAROLINA 27420
Telephone: 336-378-5200
Fax: 336-378-5400
Email: smith.moore@smithmoorelaw.com
URL: http://www.smithmoorelaw.com

Raleigh, North Carolina Office: 2800 Two Hannover Square, P.O. Box 27525. Telephone: 919-755-8700. Fax: 919-755-8800.

(This Listing Continued)

SMITH MOORE LLP, Greensboro—Continued

Atlanta, Georgia Office: One Atlantic Center, Suite 3700, 1201 West Peachtree Street. Telephone: 404-962-1000. Fax: 404-962-1200.
Wilmington, North Carolina Office: 300 North Third Street, Suite 301. Telephone: 910-251-7001. Fax: 910-251-7007.

General, Trial and Appellate Practice in All State and Federal Courts, Dispute Resolution, Corporate, Taxation, Securities Regulation, Real Property and Finance, Labor and Employment (Management) Law, Employee Benefits, International and Immigration, Antitrust and Trade Regulation, Negligence, Products Liability, Insurance Coverage, Media, Banking, Commercial, Bankruptcy, Administrative, Environmental, Hospital and Health Care, Public Authority and Public Finance, Estate Planning and Administration, Probate, Legislative, Intellectual Property, Education, and Sports Law.

LAW FIRM ALLIANCES/ASSOCIATIONS: **TERRALEX, THE WORLDWIDE NETWORK OF INDEPENDENT LAW FIRMS**

PARTNERS

D. ERIK ALBRIGHT, born February 12, 1965; admitted to bar, 1990, North Carolina. *Education:* Duke University (A.B., 1987); Vanderbilt University (J.D., 1990). Patrick Wilson Scholar. ***PRACTICE AREAS:*** Civil Litigation; White Collar Crime; Sports Law. ***Email:*** erik.albright@smithmoorelaw.com

BRUCE P. ASHLEY, born January 20, 1961; admitted to bar, 1986, North Carolina. *Education:* University of North Carolina (A.B., 1983); University of Michigan (J.D., cum laude, 1986). ***PRACTICE AREAS:*** Civil Litigation; Construction Law; Condemnation Litigation; Real Property Litigation. ***Email:*** bruce.ashley@smithmoorelaw.com

EVAN KENT AUBERRY, born July 17, 1956; admitted to bar, 1982, North Carolina. *Education:* University of North Carolina (A.B., 1978; J.D., with highest honors, 1982). Phi Beta Kappa. Order of the Coif. Editor-in-Chief, North Carolina Law Review, 1981-1982. Visiting Lecturer of Law, Business Planning, University of North Carolina School of Law, 1987-1990. Member, Editorial Board, U.S. Trademark Reporter, International Trademark Association, 1996-1999. ***PRACTICE AREAS:*** Corporate Law; Securities Regulation; Intellectual Property. ***Email:*** kent.auberry@smithmoorelaw.com

W. ALEXANDER AUDILET, born June 17, 1961; admitted to bar, 1988, North Carolina. *Education:* University of Virginia (B.A., 1983); Wake Forest University (J.D., 1988). Notes and Comments Editor, Wake Forest Law Review, 1987-1988. ***PRACTICE AREAS:*** Mergers and Acquisitions; Corporate Law; Construction Law; Securities. ***Email:*** alex.audilet@smithmoorelaw.com

JONATHAN A. BERKELHAMMER, born February 11, 1955; admitted to bar, 1982, North Carolina. *Education:* University of North Carolina at Greensboro (B.S., summa cum laude, 1979); University of North Carolina at Chapel Hill (J.D., with honors, 1982). Order of the Coif. Member, University of North Carolina Law Review, 1981-1982. Clerk to Chief Judge Franklin T. Dupree, Jr., U.S. District Court, Eastern District of North Carolina, 1982-1984. *Member:* North Carolina Association of Defense Counsel; Defense Research Institute. ***PRACTICE AREAS:*** Civil Litigation; Products Liability; Insurance Litigation; Commercial Litigation; Lanham Act Litigation; Trade Secret Litigation; Personal Injury Litigation. ***Email:*** jon.berkelhammer@smithmoorelaw.com

CAROLE WATKINS BRUCE, born August 24, 1945; admitted to bar, 1980, North Carolina. *Education:* Auburn University (B.S., with honors, 1967; M.B.A., 1968); Wake Forest University (J.D., cum laude, 1980). Phi Kappa Phi. Director, Greensboro Chamber of Commerce, 1997—. Trustee: Moses Cone Health System, 1989—; North Carolina A&T State University, 1998—. ***PRACTICE AREAS:*** Taxation; Estate Planning; Estate Administration; Nonprofit and Charitable Organizations. ***Email:*** carole.bruce@smithmoorelaw.com

WILLIAM E. BURTON III, born November 11, 1968; admitted to bar, 1993, North Carolina; 1994, District of Columbia. *Education:* North Carolina State University (B.S., 1990; B.A., 1990); Wake Forest University (J.D., 1993). *Member:* Greensboro, North Carolina and American Bar Associations. ***PRACTICE AREAS:*** Environmental Law; Corporate Law; Alcoholic Beverage Licensing; Alcoholic Beverage Regulation. ***Email:*** will.burton@smithmoorelaw.com

HAROLD N. BYNUM, born May 22, 1939; admitted to bar, 1969, North Carolina. *Education:* Davidson College (B.S., 1961); North Carolina State University (M.S., 1963); University of North Carolina (J.D., with honors, 1969). Phi Delta Phi; Order of the Coif. Business Manager, North Carolina Law Review, 1968-1969. [U.S. Army Reserve, Active Duty, 1964-1966]. ***PRACTICE AREAS:*** Environmental Law; Occupational Safety and Health; Administrative Law. ***Email:*** harold.bynum@smithmoorelaw.com

MANNING A. CONNORS, III, born Bloomington, Indiana, September 23, 1970; admitted to bar, 1995, North Carolina. *Education:* Furman University (B.A., 1992); Wake Forest University (J.D., 1995). ***PRACTICE AREAS:*** Litigation. ***Email:*** manning.connors@smithmoorelaw.com

RICHARD A. COUGHLIN, born April 10, 1968; admitted to bar, 1993, North Carolina. *Education:* Furman University (B.A., 1990); University of Georgia (J.D., cum laude, 1993). ***PRACTICE AREAS:*** Civil Litigation; Insurance Litigation; Commercial Litigation; Personal Injury. ***Email:*** rick.coughlin@smithmoorelaw.com

J. DONALD COWAN, JR., born November 14, 1943; admitted to bar, 1968, North Carolina and U.S. Court of Military Appeals; 1972, U.S. Supreme Court; 1975, U.S. Court of Federal Claims. *Education:* Wake Forest University (B.A., 1965; J.D., with honors, 1968). Phi Delta Phi. Editor-in-Chief, Wake Forest Law Review. Fellow, American College of Trial Lawyers (State Chair, 1998-2000). Trustee, Wake Forest University, 1994-1998, 1999—. Legal Services of North Carolina (Board of Directors, 1993-1999; President, 1998-1999); Product Liability Advisory Council. Permanent Member, Fourth Circuit Judicial Conference. Adjunct Instructor of Trial Practice, Duke University School of Law. *Member:* North Carolina Bar Association (Board of Governors, 1982-1985; Chairman, Young Lawyers Division, 1979-1980; Chairman, Litigation Section, 1985-1986; President, 1992-1993); American Judicature Society; American Board of Trial Advocates (Chapter President, 1999-2000); The American Law Institute; American Academy of Appellate Lawyers. [Capt., U.S. Army, Active Duty, 1968-1973]. (Also at Raleigh, North Carolina). ***PRACTICE AREAS:*** Litigation; Products Liability; Intellectual Property Litigation. ***Email:*** don.cowan@smithmoorelaw.com

GERARD H. DAVIDSON, JR., born October 7, 1943; admitted to bar, 1968, North Carolina. *Education:* Wake Forest University (B.A., cum laude, 1965; J.D., 1968). Phi Delta Phi. Hankins Scholar. Business Manager, Wake Forest Law Review, 1967-1968. *Member:* Defense Research Institute. [Capt., JAGC, U.S. Army, 1968-1973]. ***PRACTICE AREAS:*** Civil Litigation; Products Liability Litigation; Toxic Torts; Environmental Litigation. ***Email:*** gerard.davidson@smithmoorelaw.com

HERBERT O. DAVIS, born June 11, 1935; admitted to bar, 1960, North Carolina. *Education:* University of North Carolina (A.B., 1957); Duke University (J.D., 1960). Phi Beta Kappa. Editor-in-Chief, Duke Law Journal, 1959-1960. ***PRACTICE AREAS:*** Corporate Law; Commercial Finance; Mergers and Acquisitions. ***Email:*** bert.davis@smithmoorelaw.com

ALAN W. DUNCAN, born April 3, 1954; admitted to bar, 1979, North Carolina. *Education:* Davidson College (A.B., cum laude, 1976); Vanderbilt University (J.D., 1979). Phi Beta Kappa. Executive Editor, Vanderbilt Law Review, 1978-1979. *Member:* North Carolina Bar Association (Chair, Litigation Section, 1993-1994; Chair, Trial Practice Curriculum Committee, 1989-1991); North Carolina Association of Defense Attorneys (President, 1994-1995); International Trademark Association; Defense Research Institute. ***PRACTICE AREAS:*** Civil Litigation; Media Law; Intellectual Property; Health Care Law. ***Email:*** alan.duncan@smithmoorelaw.com

STEPHEN W. EARP, born September 12, 1952; admitted to bar, 1977, Virginia and North Carolina. *Education:* Davidson College (B.A., cum laude, 1974); University of Virginia (J.D., 1977). Phi Beta Kappa. Notes Editor, Virginia Journal of International Law, 1976-1977. *Member:* North Carolina Bar Association (Chair, Environmental Section, 1997-1998); Environmental Law Institute. ***PRACTICE AREAS:*** Environmental Law; Civil Litigation. ***Email:*** steve.earp@smithmoorelaw.com

MARTIN N. ERWIN, born May 4, 1938; admitted to bar, 1967, North Carolina. *Education:* Wake Forest College (B.A., 1959); University of North Carolina (M.A., 1965; J.D., with high honors, 1967). Phi Delta Phi; Order of the Coif. Associate Editor, North Carolina Law Review, 1966-1967. Clerk to Honorable J. Braxton Craven, Jr., U.S. Court of Appeals, Fourth Circuit, 1967-1968. [U.S. Navy, Active Duty, 1960-1963]. ***PRACTICE AREAS:*** Labor and Employment (Management) Law. ***Email:*** martin.erwin@smithmoorelaw.com

MARILYN FEUCHS-MARKER, born October 21, 1953; admitted to bar, 1988, North Carolina. *Education:* University of Maryland at College Park (B.A., 1975); University of Maryland at Baltimore (M.S.W., 1981); Loyola Law School (J.D., cum laude, 1988). Member, St. Thomas More Law Honor Society. Member, Loyola of Los Angeles Law Review, 1986-1987. ***PRACTICE AREAS:*** Family Law; International Family Law. ***Email:*** marilyn.feuchs-marker@smithmoorelaw.com

SUSAN McNEAR FRADENBURG, born May 9, 1968; admitted to bar, 1993, North Carolina. *Education:* University of Kansas (B.A., with highest distinction, 1990); Wake Forest University (J.D., 1993). Phi Beta Kappa. Order of Barristers. Law Clerk to Justice Louis Meyer, N.C. Supreme Court, 1993-1994; Justice Sarah Parker, N.C. Supreme Court, 1994-1995. Council Member, Health Law Section, North Carolina Bar Association. *Member:* National Health Lawyers Association. ***PRACTICE AREAS:*** Health Care; Civil Litigation. ***Email:*** susan.fradenburg@smithmoorelaw.com

LISA FRYE GARRISON, born March 24, 1969; admitted to bar, 1994, North Carolina. *Education:* University of North Carolina, (B.A., with highest honors, 1991; J.D., with honors, 1994). Phi Beta Kappa. Order of the Golden Fleece; Order of the Grail-Valkyries. Executive Articles Editor, North Carolina Law Review, 1993-1994. ***PRACTICE AREAS:*** Litigation; Health Care. ***Email:*** lisa.garrison@smithmoorelaw.com

TERRILL JOHNSON HARRIS, born August 15, 1965; admitted to bar, 1990, North Carolina; 1991, District of Columbia. *Education:* Wake Forest University (B.A., magna cum laude, 1987); Duke University (J.D., with honors, 1990). Phi Beta Kappa; Pi Sigma Alpha. Member, Editorial Board, Duke Law Journal, 1989-1990. *Member:* North Carolina (Member, Health Law Section) and American Bar Associations; American Health Lawyers Association. ***PRACTICE AREAS:*** Health Care; Civil Litigation. ***Email:*** terri.harris@smithmoorelaw.com

GREGORY G. HOLLAND, born December 6, 1967; admitted to bar, 1992, North Carolina and Georgia. *Education:* Emory University (B.A., 1989); University of Georgia (J.D., cum laude, 1992). Notes Editor, Georgia Law Review, 1991-1992. *Member:* State Bar of Georgia; North Carolina and American Bar Associations; Defense Research Institute. ***PRACTICE AREAS:*** Complex Civil Litigation; Products Liability; Commercial Litigation; Construction Litigation. ***Email:*** greg.holland@smithmoorelaw.com

MICHAEL E. KELLY, born June 17, 1949; admitted to bar, 1974, North Carolina. *Education:* University of North Carolina (A.B., 1971; J.D., with high honors, 1974). Phi Beta Kappa; Phi Eta Sigma; Order of the Coif. Morehead Scholar. Associate Editor, North Carolina Law Review, 1973-1974. *Member:* American Judicature Society. ***PRACTICE AREAS:*** Environmental Law; Products Liability; Toxic Torts; Labor and Employment (Management). ***Email:*** mike.kelly@smithmoorelaw.com

STEPHEN E. KLEE, born December 25, 1968; admitted to bar, 1993, North Carolina. *Education:* Emory University (B.A., 1990); Wake Forest University (J.D., 1993). Wake Forest Moot Court Board, 1992-1993. Member, Wake Forest Law Review, 1991-1993. ***PRACTICE AREAS:*** Business Law; Commercial Finance; Venture Capital; Mergers and Acquisitions; Commercial Real Estate. ***Email:*** steve.klee@smithmoorelaw.com

DAVID L. KYGER, born March 30, 1955; admitted to bar, 1979, West Virginia; 1995, Virginia; 1997, North Carolina. *Education:* Vanderbilt University (A.B., summa cum laude, 1976); University of Virginia (J.D., 1979; M.Ed., 1994). Phi Beta Kappa. ***PRACTICE AREAS:*** Tax Exempt Organizations; Corporate Law; Mergers and Acquisitions; Taxation. ***Email:*** david.kyger@smithmoorelaw.com

MICHAEL V. LEE, admitted to bar, 1997, South Carolina; 1998, North Carolina. *Education:* University of North Carolina at Chapel Hill (B.A., 1991); Wake Forest University (J.D., cum laude, 1997). (Resident, Wilmington Office). ***PRACTICE AREAS:*** Business; Real Estate Development. ***Email:*** michael.lee@smithmoorelaw.com

(This Listing Continued)

CAROLINE HUDSON LOCK, born September 10, 1956; admitted to bar, 1981, North Carolina. *Education:* Duke University (A.B., summa cum laude, 1978); Vanderbilt University (J.D., 1981). Phi Beta Kappa; Order of the Coif. Angier B. Duke Scholar; Patrick Wilson Scholar. Executive Student Writing Editor, Vanderbilt Law Review, 1980-1981. *Member:* North Carolina Bar Association; North Carolina Association of Defense Attorneys. ***PRACTICE AREAS:*** Civil Litigation; Workers Compensation. ***Email:*** caroline.lock@smithmoorelaw.com

ROBERT R. MARCUS, born August 6, 1968; admitted to bar, 1993, North Carolina. *Education:* Hamilton College (B.A., cum laude, 1990); Duke University (J.D., with honors, 1993). *Member:* North Carolina Bar Association; Defense Research Institute; North Carolina Association of Defense Attorneys. ***PRACTICE AREAS:*** Commercial Litigation; Land Use Litigation; Appellate; Tort Defense. ***Email:*** rob.marcus@smithmoorelaw.com

ALEXANDER L. MAULTSBY, born February 23, 1965; admitted to bar, 1991, North Carolina. *Education:* Davidson College (B.A., cum laude, 1987); University of North Carolina (J.D., with honors, 1991). Phi Beta Kappa; Omicron Delta Kappa. Member, Order of the Barristers. ***PRACTICE AREAS:*** Labor and Employment Law; Education Law. ***Email:*** alex.maultsby@smithmoorelaw.com

PHILIP P. McCANN, born May 7, 1949; admitted to bar, 1984, Ohio; 1987, Pennsylvania; 2002, North Carolina; registered to practice before U.S. Patent and Trademark Office. *Education:* Brock University, St. Catharine's, Ontario, Canada (B.S., 1974); Gannon University (M.S., 1977); Drake University (M.B.A., 1980); University of Akron (J.D., 1984). *Member:* Akron Bar Association; Association of Corporate Patent Counsel. ***PRACTICE AREAS:*** Intellectual Property. ***Email:*** phil.mccann@smithmoorelaw.com

JAMES A. MEDFORD, born May 25, 1945; admitted to bar, 1971, North Carolina. *Education:* University of North Carolina (A.B., 1967); Johannes Gutenberg Universität, Mainz, West Germany; Harvard University (J.D., cum laude, 1971). Phi Beta Kappa; Phi Eta Sigma. Morehead Scholar; Fulbright Scholar. Clerk to Honorable J. Braxton Craven, Jr., U.S. Court of Appeals, Fourth Circuit, 1971-1972. Member, Wong Sun Society of San Francisco. *Member:* American Law Institute. ***LANGUAGES:*** German. ***PRACTICE AREAS:*** International Law; Intellectual Property Litigation; White Collar Criminal Defense; Commercial Law. ***Email:*** jim.medford@smithmoorelaw.com

MAUREEN DEMAREST MURRAY, born June 2, 1955; admitted to bar, 1980, North Carolina and Florida. *Education:* Duke University (A.B., magna cum laude, 1977); Vanderbilt University (J.D., 1980). Patrick Wilson Scholar. Best Lawyers in America. *Member:* North Carolina State Bar (Member, Disciplinary Hearing Commission, 1986-1995; Chairperson, 1990-1995); North Carolina Bar Association (Member of Council, Health Law Section, 1989-1991); American Health Lawyers Association; North Carolina Society of Health Care Attorneys. ***PRACTICE AREAS:*** Health Law; Administrative Law; Civil Litigation. ***Email:*** maureen.murray@smithmoorelaw.com

RAMONA CUNNINGHAM O'BRYANT, born April 16, 1958; admitted to bar, 1985, North Carolina. *Education:* Alderson-Broaddus College (B.A., summa cum laude, 1979); University of North Carolina at Chapel Hill (J.D., with honors, 1985). Order of the Coif. Member, University of North Carolina Law Review, 1983-1984. *Member:* North Carolina Bar Association (Council Member, Environmental Law Section). ***PRACTICE AREAS:*** Environmental Law. ***Email:*** mona.o'bryant@smithmoorelaw.com

TIMOTHY PECK, born April 26, 1955; admitted to bar, 1981, North Carolina. *Education:* Davidson College (B.A., 1978); Wake Forest University (J.D., cum laude, 1981). Research Editor, Wake Forest Law Review, 1980-1981. *Member:* North Carolina Bar Association; North Carolina Association of Defense Attorneys; Defense Research Institute. ***PRACTICE AREAS:*** Civil Litigation; Products Liability Litigation. ***Email:*** tim.peck@smithmoorelaw.com

BARBARA C. RUBY, born February 4, 1949; admitted to bar, 1976, North Carolina; 1980, U.S. Tax Court. *Education:* Duke University (B.A., 1971); University of North Carolina at Chapel Hill (J.D., with honors, 1976). Staff Member, North Carolina Law Review, 1975-1976. (Board Certified Specialist in Estate Planning and Probate Law, North Carolina State Board of Legal Specialization). ***PRACTICE AREAS:*** Estate Planning and Administration; ERISA; Business Transactions. ***Email:*** barbara.ruby@smithmoorelaw.com

LARRY B. SITTON, born January 20, 1940; admitted to bar, 1964, North Carolina. *Education:* Wake Forest University (B.A., cum laude, 1961; LL.B., cum laude, 1964). Phi Beta Kappa; Phi Delta Phi. Hankins Scholar; Babcock Scholar. Clerk to Honorable Eugene A. Gordon, U.S. District Court, Middle District of North Carolina, 1966-1967. Permanent Member, Fourth Circuit Judicial Conference. Master of the Bench, Justice Joseph Branch Inn of Court. *Member:* North Carolina Bar Association (President, 1998-1999); American Bar Foundation. Fellow, American College of Trial Lawyers. [U.S. Army, Active Duty, 1964-1966]. ***PRACTICE AREAS:*** Commercial Litigation. ***Email:*** larry.sitton@smithmoorelaw.com

THOMAS E. TERRELL, JR., born March 6, 1957; admitted to bar, 1985, North Carolina and U.S. District Court, Middle District of North Carolina. *Education:* University of North Carolina (B.A., 1979; J.D., 1985); University of Chicago (M.A., 1980). ***PRACTICE AREAS:*** Municipal Law; Land Use Litigation; Administrative Law; Zoning Law. ***Email:*** tom.terrell@smithmoorelaw.com

JULIANNA C. THEALL, born July 27, 1961; admitted to bar, 1986, Georgia and North Carolina. *Education:* University of Georgia (B.B.A., summa cum laude, 1983; J.D., magna cum laude, 1986). Phi Kappa Phi; Order of the Coif. Member, Georgia Law Review, 1984-1985. Member, Labor and Employment Section, Litigation Section, North Carolina Bar Association. Chair, Advisory Council, Federal Bar, 1998. ***PRACTICE AREAS:*** Labor and Employment Law (Management); Civil Litigation. ***Email:*** julie.theall@smithmoorelaw.com

ALLISON OVERBAY VAN LANINGHAM, born July 15, 1971; admitted to bar, 1996, North Carolina; 1998, U.S. Court of Appeals, Eleventh Circuit. *Education:* Wake Forest University (B.A., cum laude, 1993; J.D., cum laude, 1996). ***PRACTICE AREAS:*** Litigation; First Amendment and Media; Appellate. ***Email:*** allison.vanlaningham@smithmoorelaw.com

E. GARRETT WALKER, born October 19, 1950; admitted to bar, 1975, North Carolina. *Education:* University of North Carolina (A.B., 1972; J.D., with high honors, 1975). Phi Beta Kappa; Phi Eta Sigma; Order of the Coif. Associate Editor, North Carolina Law Review, 1974-1975. Clerk to Chief Justice Susie Sharp, North Carolina Supreme Court, 1975-1976. *Member:* North Carolina Bar Association (Chairman, Real Property Section, 1985); American College of Real Estate Lawyers. ***PRACTICE AREAS:*** Real Property; Mortgage Lending; Real Estate and Title Insurance Litigation. ***Email:*** garrett.walker@smithmoorelaw.com

JERI L. WHITFIELD, born September 21, 1950; admitted to bar, 1977, North Carolina. *Education:* Cornell University (B.S., with honors, 1972); Duke University; George Washington University (J.D., with honors, 1977). Master, Guilford Inn of Court. *Member:* North Carolina Bar Association (Member, Litigation Section and Council Member, Worker's Compensation Section); North Carolina Association of Defense Attorneys (Member, Board of Directors); Defense Research Institute. (Board Certified Specialist in Worker's Compensation Law, North Carolina State Board of Legal Specialization). ***PRACTICE AREAS:*** Civil Litigation; Workers Compensation; Insurance Law. ***Email:*** jeri.whitfield@smithmoorelaw.com

ASSOCIATES

Drew Brown	***Amy H. Kincaid***
Laura Deddish Burton	***Bailey King***
Brian W. Byrd	***Angela L. Little***
Crystal Bowman Crews	***Travis W. Martin***
James M. Dewey	***Jordan Nance***
James R. Faucher	***Patricia Carole Perkins***
Kimberly Bullock Gatling	***Caroline Collins Pickup***
Eileen King Gillis	***Patti West Ramseur*** (Resident)
L. Cooper Harrell	***Edward R. Sharp***
Jonathan Heyl	***Lisa Kaminski Shortt***
Neale T. Johnson	***Harriett T. Smalls***
Robert D. Kidwell	***Heather Howell Wright***

COUNSEL

STANISLAV ANTOLIN, admitted to bar, 1994, Pennsylvania; 2000, North Carolina; registered to practice before U.S. Patent and Trademark Office. *Education:* Drexel University (B.S., 1983); Carnegie-Mellon University (M.S., 1985); Widener University (J.D., 1994). *Member:* National Association of Patent Practitioners; Association of University Technology Managers. ***LANGUAGES:*** German and Slovenian. ***PRACTICE AREAS:*** Intellectual Property; Patents. ***Email:*** stan.antolin@smithmoorelaw.com

WALTER Y. BOYD JR., born February 14, 1956; admitted to bar, 1984, North Carolina and U.S. Court of Appeals, Ferderal Circuit; 1985, District of Columbia and U.S. Court of Federal Claims; 1988, U.S. Supreme Court; registered to practice before the U.S. Patent and Trademark Office. *Education:* Elon College (B.A., cum laude, 1976); University of North Carolina (M.A., 1980); North Carolina Central University School of Law (J.D., cum laude, 1983); The George Washington University National Law Center (LL.M., 1985). Member, North Carolina Central University Law Review, 1982-1983. Law Clerk to the Honorable Edward S. Smith and the Honorable Marion T. Bennett, Circuit Judges, U.S. Court of Appeals for the Federal Circuit, 1985-1986. *Member:* The District of Columbia Bar; American and Federal Circuit Bar Associations. ***PRACTICE AREAS:*** Intellectual Property; Intellectual Property Litigation; Patents. ***Email:*** walter.boyd@smithmoorelaw.com

JAMES G. EXUM, JR., born 1935; admitted to bar, 1960, North Carolina. *Education:* University of North Carolina (A.B.); New York University (LL.B.). Former Chief Justice of the North Carolina Supreme Court, Raleigh, North Carolina. ***PRACTICE AREAS:*** Appellate Practice. ***Email:*** jim.exum@smithmoorelaw.com

BYNUM M. HUNTER, born June 13, 1925; admitted to bar, 1949, North Carolina. *Education:* University of North Carolina (A.B., 1945; J.D., 1949). Phi Delta Phi. President, Greensboro Bar Association, 1965-1966. Member, Fourth Circuit Judicial Conference. *Member:* North Carolina Association of Defense Counsel; International Association of Defense Counsel; American Judicature Society; Sports Lawyers Association. Fellow: American College of Trial Lawyers; American Bar Foundation (Life Member). [U.S. Navy, Active Duty, 1943-1946; 1951-1953]. ***PRACTICE AREAS:*** Civil Litigation; Commercial Litigation; Insurance Defense; Sports Law. ***Email:*** bynum.hunter@smithmoorelaw.com

AMY SMITH KLASS, born October 2, 1962; admitted to bar, 1987, North Carolina. *Education:* Duke University; University of North Carolina (B.S., 1984; J.D., with honors, 1987). Phi Beta Kappa; Order of the Coif. Member, North Carolina Law Review, 1985-1986. ***PRACTICE AREAS:*** Estate Planning and Administration. ***Email:*** amy.klass@smithmoorelaw.com

CHARLES E. MELVIN, JR., born July 13, 1929; admitted to bar, 1956, North Carolina. *Education:* University of North Carolina (B.S., 1951; J.D., with honors, 1956). Delta Theta Phi. Member, Board of Editors, North Carolina Law Review, 1955-1956. *Member:* North Carolina Bar Association (Chairman, Real Property Section, 1980-1981); American College of Real Estate Lawyers. [U.S. Army, Active Duty, 1952-1954]. ***PRACTICE AREAS:*** Real Property; Land Use Law and Regulations; Finance; International Law. ***Email:*** charlie.melvin@smithmoorelaw.com

STEPHEN PERRY MILLIKIN, born February 20, 1926; admitted to bar, 1952, North Carolina. *Education:* University of North Carolina (B.S., 1949; J.D., with honors, 1952). Phi Delta Phi; Order of the Coif. Associate Editor, North Carolina Law Review, 1951-1952. *Member:* Fourth Circuit Judicial Conference; International Association of Defense Counsel; North Carolina Association of Defense Attorneys; American Board of Trial Advocates. Fellow: American College of Trial Lawyers. [U.S. Navy, Active Duty, 1944-1946]. ***PRACTICE AREAS:*** Civil Litigation; Commercial Litigation; Insurance Defense. ***Email:*** steve.millikin@smithmoorelaw.com

DAVID M. MOORE II, born July 31, 1944; admitted to bar, 1969, North Carolina. *Education:* University of North Carolina (A.B., 1966; J.D., with honors, 1969). Phi Beta Kappa; Phi Alpha Delta; Order of the Coif. Morehead Scholar; Morehead Fellow. Member, North Carolina Law Review, 1968-1969. Clerk to Honorable J. Braxton Craven, Jr., U.S. Court of Appeals, Fourth Circuit, 1969-1970. ***PRACTICE AREAS:*** Civil Litigation; Environmental Law; Products Liability. ***Email:*** david.moore@smithmoorelaw.com

(This Listing Continued)

SMITH MOORE LLP, Greensboro—Continued

SAMUEL M. MOORE, admitted to bar, 1970, North Carolina. *Education:* Mercer University; University of North Carolina at Chapel Hill. ***Email:*** samuel.moore@smithmoorelaw.com

D. MARSH PRAUSE, born January 23, 1968; admitted to bar, 1993, North Carolina. *Education:* Princeton University (B.S.E., 1990); Wake Forest University (J.D., 1993). National Merit Scholar. Member, Wake Forest Moot Court Board, 1991-1993. Articles Editor, Wake Forest Law Review, 1992-1993. *Member:* North Carolina (Member, Sections on: Environmental Law; Litigation) and American (Member, Sections on: Natural Resources, Energy and Environmental Law; Litigation) Bar Associations; Defense Research Institute. ***PRACTICE AREAS:*** Environmental Law; Environmental and Toxic Tort Litigation; Products Liability. ***Email:*** marsh.prause@smithmoorelaw.com

REPRESENTATIVE CLIENTS: AIG Insurance Group; Atlantic Coast Conference; Branch Banking and Trust Co.; Board of Commissioners of Douglas County; Board of Commissioners of Georgia County; Digital Optics; Dixon Hughes LLP; Eli Lilly and Co.; General Electric Co.; General Motors Corp.; Greensboro News & Record Co.; Miller Brewing Co.; North Carolina Hospital Association; Penn Western Benefits; Prime Care Health Networks; Royal & SunAlliance; Stafford Development Company; Stockhausen, Inc.; The Coca-Cola Co.; The Moses H. Cone Memorial Hospital; The Procter & Gamble Co.; United Dominion Industries, Inc.; Warner-Lambert Co.; Watauga Medical Center; Wayne Memorial Hospital.

SPARROW WOLF & SPARROW, P.A.

812 NORTH ELM STREET
P.O. BOX 308
GREENSBORO, NORTH CAROLINA 27401
Telephone: 336-544-5080
Fax: 336-544-5085
URL: http://www.sparrowwolflaw.com

General Trial Practice in all State and Federal Courts. Business Law, Corporate Law, Commercial Finance, Real Estate, Construction Law, Personal Injury, Motor Vehicle Law.

DONALD G. SPARROW, born Greensboro, North Carolina, January 16, 1945; admitted to bar, 1970, North Carolina. *Education:* University of North Carolina (A.B., 1967; J.D., 1970). Member, University of North Carolina Law Review, 1969-1970. Member: Board of Directors, Greensboro Mental Health Association, 1975-1980; City of Greensboro Board of Adjustments, 1979-1988; 2001-2004. ***PRACTICE AREAS:*** Construction Law; Business Law; Commercial Real Estate; Litigation. ***Email:*** dsparrow@sparrowwolf.com

GARY R. WOLF, born Washington, D.C., April 8, 1954; admitted to bar, 1984, North Carolina. *Education:* North Carolina State University (B.E.D., Architecture, with honors, 1976); Wake Forest University (J.D., 1984). Order of Barristers. Member, 1990-1997 and Chairman, 1995-1997, City of Greensboro Board of Adjustments. Member, 2000— and Chair, 2003, City of Greensboro Zoning Commission. ***PRACTICE AREAS:*** Corporate Law; Commercial Litigation; Construction Law; Real Property; Zoning, Planning and Land Use; Land Use Regulation. ***Email:*** gwolf@sparrowwolf.com

JASON B. SPARROW, born Greensboro, North Carolina, September 23, 1971; admitted to bar, 1998, North Carolina and U.S. District Court, Middle District of North Carolina. *Education:* University of North Carolina at Chapel Hill (B.A., 1994; J.D., 1998). Recipient, Best Brief Award, International Moot Court Competition. *Member:* Greensboro, North Carolina (Council Member, Small Firm Section) and American Bar Associations; Guilford Inn of Court. ***PRACTICE AREAS:*** Civil Litigation; Trial Practice; Collections; Corporate Law; Wills; Real Estate Litigation; Traffic Violations. ***Email:*** jsparrow@sparrowwolf.com

DANIEL SROKA, P.C.

Established in 2002
3625 NORTH ELM STREET, SUITE 107A
P.O. BOX 1658
GREENSBORO, NORTH CAROLINA 27402
Telephone: 336-282-5584
Facsimile: 336-282-5796
Email: Dan@Srokaweb.com
URL: http://www.Srokaweb.com

Corporate Law, Mergers and Acquisitions, Commercial Transactions, Franchise Law, Intellectual Property Licensing, Business Law, Commercial Real Estate.

FIRM PROFILE: Representation of businesses with respect to matters of corporate law, mergers and acquisitions and commercial real estate with emphasis on emerging companies, startup businesses and closely held entities.

DANIEL M. SROKA, born Milwaukee, Wisconsin, October 12, 1962; admitted to bar, 1989, North Carolina. *Education:* University of Wisconsin (B.B.A., 1985); Wake Forest University (J.D., 1989). Articles Editor, Wake Forest Law Review, 1988-1989. *Member:* North Carolina Bar Association. ***PRACTICE AREAS:*** Corporate Law; Mergers and Acquisitions; Commercial Real Estate. ***Email:*** Dan@Srokaweb.com

LAW OFFICE OF LAURIE R. STEGALL, P.A.

529 COLLEGE ROAD, SUITE C
GREENSBORO, NORTH CAROLINA 27410
Telephone: 336-299-0170
Facsimile: 336-299-0740
Email: stegalllaw@aol.com
URL: http://www.lauriestegalllaw.com

Residential Real Estate, Real Estate Closings, Estate Planning, Wills.

(This Listing Continued)

LAURIE R. STEGALL, born Greensboro, North Carolina, June 28, 1968; admitted to bar, 1993, North Carolina. *Education:* Guilford College (B.A., 1990); University of North Carolina at Chapel Hill (J.D., 1993). *Member:* Greensboro and North Carolina State (Member, Real Property Section) Bar Associations. ***PRACTICE AREAS:*** Residential Real Estate; Real Estate Contracts; Estate Planning; Wills.

STERN, KLEPFER & WRIGHT, PLLC

101 WEST FRIENDLY AVENUE, SUITE 600
GREENSBORO, NORTH CAROLINA 27401
Telephone: 336-373-1500
Fax: 336-272-8258

General Practice in State and Federal Courts, before Administrative Tribunals. Adoptions, Business, Closely Held Business, Limited Liability Companies, Contracts, Real Property, Real Estate, Commercial Leasing, Trusts and Estates, Estate Planning, Wills, Probate, Elder Law.

SIDNEY J. STERN, JR. (1914-1991)

JOHN L. RENDLEMAN (1932-1983)

MEMBERS OF FIRM

ROBERT O. KLEPFER, JR., born Lenoir, North Carolina, 1942; admitted to bar, 1966, North Carolina. *Education:* University of North Carolina (A.B., 1964; J.D., with honors, 1966). Order of the Coif. Member, Student Board of Editors, North Carolina Law Review, 1965-1966. Chair, National Mental Health Association, 1996-1998. *Member:* North Carolina Bar Association. ***PRACTICE AREAS:*** Business Law; Real Estate; Nonprofit and Charitable Organizations. ***Email:*** bklepfer@sternlawnc.com

BRINTON D. WRIGHT, born Springhill, Louisiana, 1949; admitted to bar, 1976, North Carolina; 1977, U.S. Tax Court. *Education:* Johns Hopkins University (B.A., 1971); University of New Hampshire (M.B.A., 1973); Wake Forest University (J.D., cum laude, 1976). *Member:* North Carolina Bar Association; American Academy of Adoption Attorneys. ***PRACTICE AREAS:*** Taxation; Probate; Children. ***Email:*** bwright@sternlawnc.com

ASSOCIATES

SALLY B. CONE, born Greenville, North Carolina, 1954; admitted to bar, 1978, North Carolina. *Education:* University of North Carolina at Chapel Hill (B.A., 1976; J.D., 1978). *Member:* Greensboro and North Carolina Bar Associations. ***PRACTICE AREAS:*** Estate Planning; Estate Administration; Fiduciary Law. ***Email:*** sallycone@sternlawnc.com

MAUREEN BREEN GERHARDT, born New York, N.Y., 1956; admitted to bar, 1984, Tennessee; 1990, North Carolina. *Education:* University of Virginia (B.S.N., with honors, 1978); Vanderbilt University (J.D., 1984). Registered Nurse: Virginia, 1978; Tennessee, 1981; North Carolina, 1989. *Member:* North Carolina Bar Association. ***PRACTICE AREAS:*** Taxation; Probate. ***Email:*** mgerhardt@sternlawnc.com

KATHLEEN MURPHY BRINKEY, born Albany, New York, 1963; admitted to bar, 1989, New York and U.S. District Court, Northern District of New York; 1990, Michigan and U.S. District Court, Eastern District of Michigan; 2003, North Carolina and U.S. District Court, Middle District of North Carolina. *Education:* College of St. Rose (B.S., Business Administration, 1985); University of Tennessee College of Law (J.D., 1988). *Member:* North Carolina Bar Association (Member, Elder Law, Estate Planning/Fiduciary and General Practice Sections, 2003—). ***PRACTICE AREAS:*** Estate Planning; Estate Administration; Elder Law; Contracts; Real Property. ***Email:*** kbrinkey@sternlawnc.com

REPRESENTATIVE CLIENTS: *Financial:* RBC Centura Bank. *Institutional:* Bennett College; Tannenbaum-Sternberger Foundation; Carolina Adoption Services; William A. Stern Foundation. *Insurance:* Robins & Weill, Inc. *Retail/Chain Stores:* Carlyle & Co. Jewelers. *Contractors:* Bostian Builders, Inc.; Residence Development Company.
APPROVED ATTORNEYS FOR: Lawyer's Title Insurance Corp.; Chicago Title Insurance Co.; Investors Title Insurance Co.; First American Title Insurance Co.; Fidelity National Title Insurance Co.; *References:* Branch Banking and Trust Company; Bank of America; Wachovia Bank & Trust Co.

LAW OFFICE OF MATT A. STOCKDALE, PLLC

Established in 2005
313 SOUTH GREENE STREET, SUITE 303
GREENSBORO, NORTH CAROLINA 27401
Telephone: 336-510-0941
Fax: 336-510-0967
URL: http://www.mattstockdalelaw.com
Email: matt@mattstockdalelaw.com
URL: http://www.mstockdalelaw.com

Criminal Law, Traffic Violations, Driving While Intoxicated, Drug Crimes, Parole and Probate, White Collar Crime, Trust and Estates, Estate Planning, Business Law, Child Support.

MEMBER OF FIRM

MATTHEW ALAN STOCKDALE, born Canton, Ohio, February 22, 1975; admitted to bar, 2000, North Carolina. *Education:* Albion College (B.A., 1997); Wake Forest University (J.D., 2000). Assistant Public Defender, 2000-2005. Private Practice, 2005—. *Member:* North Carolina Academy of Trial Lawyers; Guilford County Criminal Defense Bar; National Association of Criminal Defense Lawyers; American Trial Lawyers Association. ***PRACTICE AREAS:*** Criminal Law (80%); Business Law (10%); Wills (10%). ***Email:*** matt@mattstockdalelaw.com

LAW OFFICES OF KATHLEEN G. SUMNER

Established in 1996

9 TERRACE WAY, SUITE B
GREENSBORO, NORTH CAROLINA 27403
Telephone: 336-294-9388
Toll Free: 800-376-9718
Fax: 336-294-9144
Email: KSumner@sumnerlaw.net
URL: http://www.sumnerlaw.net

Mailing Address: P.O. Box 7915, Greensboro, NC 27417-0915

Worker Compensation, Appellate Practice.

FIRM PROFILE: The Law Offices of Kathleen G. Sumner is a law firm which places the highest priority on providing personalized services to each client. The firm has its main office in Greensboro, North Carolina, but practices throughout the State of North Carolina at the convenience of each client.

To better serve our clients, we have exclusively dedicated our practice to the area of workers" compensation and the related cases involving the employment rights of our clients who many times face loss not only due to injury but also the loss of employment rights.

We handle our clients cases from beginning to end. This may include mediation, a hearing before the Deputy Commissioner, a hearing before the Full Commission, an appeal before the North Carolina Court of Appeals, and/or an appeal or petition before the North Carolina Supreme Court.

All our fee agreements are solely on a contingency fee basis. This means that if we do not prevail, we are not paid a fee. Costs are always the responsibility of the client. However, costs are generally very low for workers' compensation cases.

We put our clients first. We recognize that each client has unique needs. Our success depends upon understanding each client's specific needs and achieving a successful resolution of the unique legal problems faced by each client. Feedback from our clients indicates that their relationship with our firm reflects a positive experience. Our clients enjoy working with our experienced and competent attorneys and our friendly and efficient office staff.

We believe that the attorney you choose to represent you does make a difference. If you choose us to represent you we believe that we can make a difference for you.

ATTORNEYS

KATHLEEN G. SUMNER, born Rochester, New York, October 9, 1950; admitted to bar, 1990, North Carolina and U.S. District Court, Eastern and Middle Districts of North Carolina; 1991, Hawaii and U.S. District Court, District of Hawaii; 1992, U.S. Court of Appeals, Fourth Circuit; 1994, District of Columbia; 2000, U.S. Supreme Court. *Education:* San Diego State University (B.A., 1971); Campbell University (J.D., 1990). *Member:* North Carolina Bar Association; The District of Columbia Bar; Hawaii Bar Association; North Carolina Academy of Trial Lawyers; The Association of Trial Lawyers of America. ***REPORTED CASES:*** Salaam v. North Carolina DOT, 122 N.C. App. 83, 468 S.E.2d 536 (1996), pet. improvidently allowed, 345 N.C. 494, 480 S.E.2d 51 (1997) Atkins v. Kelly Springfield Tire Co., 154 N.C. App. 512, 571 S.E.2d 865 (2002), aff'd, 358 N.C. 540, 597 S.E.2d 128 (2004) Reinninger v. Prestige Fabricators, Inc., 136 N.C. App. 255, 523 S.E.2d 720 (1999) Porter v. Fieldcrest Cannon, Inc., 133 N.C. App. 23, 514 S.E.2d 517 (1999) Terry v. PPG Indus., 156 N.C. App. 512, 577 S.E.2d 326 (2003) Arnold v. Wal-Mart Stores, Inc., 154 N.C. App. 482, 571 S.E.2d 888 (2002); Arnold v. Wal-Mart Stores, Inc., 596 S.E.2d 472, 2004 N.C. App. LEXIS 1053 (N.C. Ct. App., June 1, 2004) McAllister v. Wellman, Inc., 162 N.C. App. 146, 590 S.E.2d 311 (2004) Valles de Portillo v. D.H. Griffin Wrecking Co., 134 N.C. App. 714, 518 S.E.2d 555 (1999) Calhoun v. Wayne Dennis Heating & Air Conditioning, 129 N.C. App. 794, 501 S.E.2d 346 (1998) Parsons v. Pantry, Inc., 126 N.C. App. 540; 485 S.E.2d 867 (1997) Rose v. Rose, 108 N.C. App. 90, 422 S.E.2d 446 (1992) Surles v. Surles, 113 N.C. App. 32, 437 S.E.2d 661 (1993). ***PRACTICE AREAS:*** Workers Compensation (90%, 150); Appellate Practice (10%, 10). ***Email:*** ksumner@sumnerlaw.net

JEANETTE F. GRAY, born Greensboro, North Carolina, October 1, 1974; admitted to bar, 1999, North Carolina and U.S. District Court, Eastern and Middle Districts of North Carolina. *Education:* University of North Carolina at Chapel Hill (B.A., 1996); Campbell University Norman Adrian Wiggins School of Law (J.D., 1999). *Member:* North Carolina Bar Association; North Carolina Academy of Trial Lawyers; The Association of Trial Lawyers of America. ***PRACTICE AREAS:*** Workers Compensation (98%, 150); Labor and Employment (2%, 2). ***Email:*** jgray@sumnerlaw.net

---

TATE, GAYLORD, LUCAS, PURDOM & WORKMAN, L.L.P.

Established in 1969

SUITE 101, FRIENDLY HOLDEN BUILDING
3608 WEST FRIENDLY AVENUE
GREENSBORO, NORTH CAROLINA 27410
Telephone: 336-218-0602
Fax: 336-218-0025

Mailing Address: P.O. Box 4544, Greensboro, NC 27404

General Practice. Trials in all State and Federal Courts. Business, Corporate, Commercial, Real Estate, Foreclosure, Construction, Probate, Bankruptcy, Personal Injury, Wrongful Death, Estate Planning and Administration, Mediation, Collections.

(This Listing Continued)

MEMBERS OF FIRM

CHARLES M. TATE, born Greensboro, North Carolina, February 1, 1943; admitted to bar, 1968, North Carolina. *Education:* University of North Carolina (A.B., 1965; J.D., 1968). *Member:* Greensboro and North Carolina Bar Associations; North Carolina State Bar. [Captain, JAGD, U.S. Air Force, 1968-1972]. ***PRACTICE AREAS:*** Business and Commercial Matters; Trusts and Estates Law; Litigation. ***Email:*** cmtatesr@bellsouth.net

T.M. (MARK) GAYLORD, JR., born Reidsville, North Carolina, August 30, 1954; admitted to bar, 1979, North Carolina. *Education:* University of North Carolina (B.S., 1976; J.D., 1979). Phi Beta Kappa; Beta Gamma Sigma; Phi Eta Sigma. *Member:* Greensboro (President, 2003-2004) and North Carolina (Section Member, Litigation; Business Law; Construction) Bar Associations; North Carolina State Bar; North Carolina Academy of Trial Lawyers. ***PRACTICE AREAS:*** Litigation; Personal Injury; Wrongful Death; Construction Law; Business Law; Collections; Commercial Law. ***Email:*** tmgaylord@bellsouth.net

KENNETH S. LUCAS, JR., born Roanoke, Virginia, April 18, 1960; admitted to bar, 1985, North Carolina. *Education:* Washington and Lee University (B.A., cum laude, 1982); Wake Forest University (J.D., 1985). *Member:* Greensboro and North Carolina Bar Associations; North Carolina State Bar. ***PRACTICE AREAS:*** Commercial Real Estate; Residential Real Estate; Corporate Law; Bankruptcy Law; Traffic Defense; Personal Injury Law; Foreclosure. ***Email:*** kslucas@bellsouth.net

EUGENE W. PURDOM, born Greensboro, North Carolina, November 1, 1941; admitted to bar, 1968, North Carolina. *Education:* University of North Carolina (A.B., 1963; J.D., with honors, 1968). Member of Staff, North Carolina Law Review, 1966-1967. Law Clerk to Judge Eugene A. Gordon, U.S. District Court, Middle District of North Carolina, 1968-1969. *Member:* Greensboro and North Carolina Bar Associations. ***PRACTICE AREAS:*** Commercial Real Estate; Residential Real Estate; Mediation. ***Email:*** ewpurdom@bellsouth.net

JEFFREY T. WORKMAN, born Greensboro, North Carolina, October 14, 1969; admitted to bar, 1995, North Carolina. *Education:* University of North Carolina, Chapel Hill (B.A., 1992); Wake Forest University (J.D., 1995). Phi Delta Phi. *Member:* Greensboro, North Carolina and American Bar Associations. ***PRACTICE AREAS:*** Civil Litigation; Business Law; Commercial Law; Construction Law; Personal Injury; Wrongful Death; Traffic Violations; Estate Administration. ***Email:*** jtworkman@bellsouth.net

RETIRED

JULIUS DEES, JR. (1925-2001)

H. M. GILES, JR. (Retired)

CHARLES R. TEDDER (Retired)

COUNSEL FOR: Pegram-West, Inc.; Coyne Beahm Shouse, Inc.; Offutt Systems, Inc.; Jarrett Construction Co., Inc.; R.L. Casey, Inc., General Contractors; Greensboro Roofing Co., Inc.; North Carolina Farm Credit, ACA.
REPRESENTATIVE CLIENTS: Central Carolina Bank; Wachovia Bank, N.A.; Wachovia Mortgage Corp.; Triad Freightliner of Greensboro, Inc.; Richmond Federal Savings Bank; Triad Finance Company; Fidelity Bank; Carolina Bank; Paragon Bank; Capital Bank.
REPRESENTS IN TITLE LOAN AND FORECLOSURES: Bank of America; Metropolitan Life Insurance Co.; Wachovia Bank, N.A.; USDA Rural Development.
APPROVED ATTORNEYS FOR: Lawyers Title Insurance Corp.; Chicago Title Insurance Co.; First American Title Insurance Company; ; First Title Insurance Co.; Pioneer Title Co.; Attorneys Title Co.; Investors Title Insurance Co.; American Title Insurance Co.; Fidelity National Title Insurance Co.; Title Company of North Carolina, Inc.; Statewide Title Co.

TEMPLE LAW FIRM, PLLC

GREENSBORO, NORTH CAROLINA

(See Raleigh)

Pharmaceutical and Defective Medical Devices (Fen-hen, Vioxx, Celebrex & Bextra), Environmental and Toxic Torts, Personal Injury, Products Liability, Wrongful Death, Civil Litigation.

J. MICHAEL THOMAS

318 S. EUGENE STREET, SUITE 107
GREENSBORO, NORTH CAROLINA 27401
Telephone: 336-691-8150
Fax: 336-691-8151
Email: thomasjmtlawyer@aol.com

Construction Law, Municipal Law, Civil Litigation, Alimony, Divorce, Equitable Distribution, Separation Agreements, Zoning and Land Use.

J. MICHAEL THOMAS, born Leaksville, North Carolina, January 31, 1957; admitted to bar, 1984, North Carolina. *Education:* Wake Forest University (B.A., magna cum laude, 1979); University of North Carolina (J.D., 1984). City Attorney, Reidsville, North Carolina, 1987-1999. Town Attorney, Oak Ridge, 2005—. *Member:* Greensboro and North Carolina (Member, Sections On: Family Law, 1995-2005; Construction Law, 1999—) Bar Associations; North Carolina Association of Municipal Attorneys. ***PRACTICE AREAS:*** Construction Law; Municipal Law; Civil Litigation.

REPRESENTATIVE CLIENTS: Bank of America; City of Reidsville; Town of Oak Ridge.
APPROVED ATTORNEY FOR: First American Title Insurance Co.; Chicago Title Insurance Co.; Investors Title Insurance Co.; Lawyers Title Insurance Co.

TUGGLE DUGGINS & MESCHAN, P.A.

228 WEST MARKET STREET
P.O. BOX 2888
GREENSBORO, NORTH CAROLINA 27402-2888
Telephone: 336-378-1431
Telecopier: 336-274-6590
URL: http://www.tuggleduggins.com

General Civil Practice. Corporation, Tax, Insurance, Banking, Pension and Profit Sharing, Bankruptcy and Creditors' Rights, Trust and Estate, Construction and Real Estate Law. Trials and Appeals in all State and Federal Courts.

RICHARD J. TUGGLE, born Kannapolis, North Carolina, July 24, 1930; admitted to bar, 1959, North Carolina. *Education:* University of North Carolina (B.S., 1952; J.D., with honors, 1959). Order of the Coif; Phi Beta Kappa; Beta Gamma Sigma; Phi Alpha Delta. Member, Board of Editors, North Carolina Law Review, 1958-1959. Certified Public Accountant, North Carolina, 1955. Member, Board of Trustees, 1966—; President, 1971-1972; 1991-1992, Southern Federal Tax Institute. *Member:* Greensboro, North Carolina and American Bar Associations; The North Carolina State Bar; American College of Tax Counsel; North Carolina Association of Certified Public Accountants; American Institute of Certified Public Accountants. [U.S. Army, active duty, 1952-1954]. ***PRACTICE AREAS:*** Acquisitions, Divestitures and Mergers Law; Taxation Law; Corporate Law. ***Email:*** rtuggle@tuggleduggins.com

JAMES N. DUGGINS, JR., born St. Augustine, Florida, April 26, 1943; admitted to bar, 1968, North Carolina. *Education:* University of North Carolina (B.S., 1965; J.D., with honors, 1968). Phi Eta Sigma; Beta Gamma Sigma; Phi Beta Kappa; Order of the Coif. Business Manager, North Carolina Law Review, 1967-1968. Certified Public Accountant, North Carolina, 1979. *Member:* Greensboro, North Carolina and American Bar Associations; The North Carolina State Bar; American College of Tax Counsel; North Carolina Association of Certified Public Accountants; American Institute of Certified Public Accountants. ***PRACTICE AREAS:*** Business Acquisitions, Mergers and Divestitures Law; Taxation Law; Corporate Law. ***Email:*** jduggins@tuggleduggins.com

DAVID F. MESCHAN, born Melbourne, Australia, June 28, 1944; admitted to bar, 1969, North Carolina. *Education:* Davidson College (A.B., 1966); University of North Carolina (J.D., 1969). Phi Delta Phi. Member, Holderness Moot Court Bench, National Moot Court Team, 1968-1969. *Member:* Greensboro, North Carolina and American Bar Associations; The North Carolina State Bar. [Capt., U.S. Army, active duty MACV, 1970-1971]. ***PRACTICE AREAS:*** Bankruptcy; Business Reorganization; Bankruptcy Litigation; Business Litigation; Business Arbitration. ***Email:*** dmeschan@tuggleduggins.com

J. REED JOHNSTON, JR., born Pittsburgh, Pennsylvania, April 22, 1944; admitted to bar, 1968, North Carolina; 1978, Missouri. *Education:* University of North Carolina at Chapel Hill (A.B., 1965; J.D., with high honors, 1968). Order of the Coif. Associate Editor, North Carolina Law Review, 1967-1968. *Member:* Greensboro, North Carolina and American Bar Associations; The Missouri Bar; North Carolina State Bar; North Carolina Association of Defense Attorneys. ***PRACTICE AREAS:*** Appellate Litigation; Insurance Coverage Litigation; General Business Litigation; ERISA Litigation. ***Email:*** rjohnston@tuggleduggins.com

PAUL M. DENNIS, JR., born Charlotte, North Carolina, September 2, 1950; admitted to bar, 1975, North Carolina. *Education:* Duke University (B.A., magna cum laude, 1972); University of North Carolina (J.D., with honors, 1975). Staff Member, North Carolina Law Review, 1974-1975. Certified Mediator, North Carolina. *Member:* Greensboro, North Carolina and American Bar Associations; North Carolina State Bar. ***PRACTICE AREAS:*** Banking Law; Financial Law; Commercial Real Estate; Corporate Law; Alternative Dispute Resolution. ***Email:*** pdennis@tuggleduggins.com

ROBERT C. CONE, born Greensboro, North Carolina, February 13, 1952; admitted to bar, 1978, North Carolina; 1979, U.S. District Court, Middle District of North Carolina, and U.S. Court of Appeals, Fourth Circuit; 1982, U.S. Supreme Court; 1998, U.S. District Court, Western District of North Carolina; 1999, U.S. District Court, Eastern District of North Carolina. *Education:* University of North Carolina (B.A., 1974; J.D., 1978). Morehead Scholar. Chairman, University of North Carolina Law Foundation, Inc., 1997-2001. Certified Mediator in State and Federal Courts. *Member:* Greensboro (President-elect, 2004-2005; Executive Committee Member, 1983-1984, 1992-1999 and 2004—; President, Young Lawyers Division, 1983-1984), North Carolina (Member, Dispute Resolution Section Council) and American Bar Associations; North Carolina State Bar; Guilford Inn of Court; American Inn of Court (Master of the Bench). ***PRACTICE AREAS:*** Litigation; Civil Appeals; Alternative Dispute Resolution; Construction Law; Products Liability Law; Landlord and Tenant Law. ***Email:*** rcone@tuggleduggins.com

JOHN R. BARLOW, II, born Kannapolis, North Carolina, November 1, 1941; admitted to bar, 1970, North Carolina; 1974, South Carolina. *Education:* University of North Carolina (A.B., 1963); Wake Forest University (J.D., 1970). Phi Alpha Delta. Co-Editor, *Skelton on the Legal Elements of Boundaries and Adjacent Properties,* Lexis Law Publishing, 1997. *Member:* Greensboro and North Carolina Bar Associations; South Carolina Bar. (Board Certified Specialist in Real Property Law-Residential, Business, Commercial and Industrial Transactions, North Carolina State Board of Legal Specialization). ***PRACTICE AREAS:*** Real Estate Law. ***Email:*** jbarlow@tuggleduggins.com

H. VAUGHN RAMSEY, born London, England, May 17, 1956; admitted to bar, 1983, New York; 1985, North Carolina. *Education:* University of North Carolina (B.A., 1978; J.D., with honors, 1982); New York University (LL.M. in Taxation, 1985). Order of the Coif. Member, Holderness Moot Court Bench. National Moot Court Team Member. Member, University of North Carolina Law Review, 1981-1982. *Member:* Greensboro, North Carolina and American Bar Associations; North Carolina State Bar. ***PRACTICE AREAS:*** Business Acquisitions, Mergers and Divestitures Law; Federal Taxation; State Taxation; Corporate Law. ***Email:*** vramsey@tuggleduggins.com

WILLIAM C. CONNOR, born Washington, D.C., June 6, 1954; admitted to bar, 1979, Virginia; 1989, North Carolina. *Education:* Lynchburg College (B.A., magna cum laude, 1976); Washington & Lee University (J.D., cum laude, 1979). *Member:* North Carolina, Virginia and American Bar Associations; North Carolina State Bar. ***PRACTICE AREAS:*** Commercial Law; Construction Law; Commercial Litigation; Debtor-Creditor Law. ***Email:*** wconnor@tuggleduggins.com

BRADLEY L. JACOBS, born Henderson, Kentucky, January 1, 1961; admitted to bar, 1986, North Carolina. *Education:* Indiana State University (B.S., magna cum laude, 1983); University of Kentucky (J.D., 1986). Phi Delta Phi. *Member:* Greensboro and North Carolina Bar Associations; North Carolina State Bar; North Carolina Association of Certified Public Accountants; American Institute of Certified Public Accountants. (Board Certified Specialist in Estate Planning and Probate Law, North Carolina State Board of Legal Specialization). ***PRACTICE AREAS:*** Taxation Law; Estate Planning Law; Probate Law; Corporate Law. ***Email:*** bjacobs@tuggleduggins.com

MICHAEL J. WENIG, born Wauseon, Ohio, February 21, 1958; admitted to bar, 1986, North Carolina. *Education:* Northeastern University (B.S.B.A., cum laude, 1980); Indiana University (J.D., cum laude, 1986). Certified Public Accountant, North Carolina, 1987. *Member:* Greensboro and North Carolina Bar Associations; North Carolina State Bar; American Institute of Certified Public Accountants. ***PRACTICE AREAS:*** Taxation; Corporate Law; Mergers, Acquisitions and Divestitures; Business Planning. ***Email:*** mwenig@tuggleduggins.com

DENIS E. JACOBSON, born Rochester, New York, April 16, 1957; admitted to bar, 1986, North Carolina. *Education:* Michigan State University (B.A., Government, 1980); Wake Forest University (J.D., 1986). Phi Delta Phi. Member, Moot Court Board. *Member:* Greensboro, North Carolina and American Bar Associations; North Carolina State Bar. ***PRACTICE AREAS:*** Employment Law; Litigation; General Insurance Litigation; Insurance Coverage Law; Business Law; Corporate Litigation. ***Email:*** djacobson@tuggleduggins.com

WILLIAM G. BURGIN, III, born Columbus, Mississippi, March 13, 1952; admitted to bar, 1988, North Carolina. *Education:* University of Mississippi (B.A., with special distinction, 1974); Duke University (M.A., 1977; Ph.D., 1981); University of Virginia (J.D., 1988). Recipient: Rotary International Fellowship, 1974-1975; Fulbright Fellowship, 1978-1979. *Member:* Guilford County, North Carolina and American Bar Associations. (Board Certified Specialist in Real Property Law, Residential, Business, Commercial and Industrial Transactions, North Carolina State Board of Legal Specialization). ***LANGUAGES:*** German. ***PRACTICE AREAS:*** Real Estate Law; Commercial Finance Law; Commercial Transactions. ***Email:*** bburgin@tuggleduggins.com

SCOTT C. GAYLE, born High Point, North Carolina, October 26, 1951; admitted to bar, 1977, North Carolina and U.S. District Court, Western District of North Carolina; 1980, U.S. District Court, Middle District of North Carolina; 1989, U.S. Supreme Court; 1995, U.S. District Court, Eastern District of North Carolina. *Education:* University of North Carolina (A.B., with highest honors, 1974); Duke University (J.D., 1977). Phi Beta Kappa. Morehead Scholar. *Member:* Greensboro, 18th Judicial District, North Carolina and American Bar Associations; North Carolina State Bar; North Carolina Academy of Trial Lawyers. ***PRACTICE AREAS:*** Corporate Law; Civil Litigation; Commercial Law; Real Estate; Contracts; Leases and Leasing; Business Litigation; Mergers, Acquisitions and Divestitures. ***Email:*** sgayle@tuggleduggins.com

KENNETH J. GUMBINER, born Chicago, Illinois, September 2, 1946; admitted to bar, 1971, Illinois; 1981, Massachusetts; 1985, North Carolina. *Education:* Purdue University (B.S.I.E., 1968); University of Illinois (J.D., 1971). Illinois Assistant Attorney General, Environmental Control Division, 1972-1974. Member, Litigation, Construction and Intellectual Property Sections, American Bar Association and North Carolina Bar Association. Chairman, North Carolina Bar Association Dispute Resolution Section, 2000-2001. Certified Mediator in North Carolina. *Member:* North Carolina, Illinois, Massachusetts and American Bar Associations. ***LANGUAGES:*** German. ***PRACTICE AREAS:*** Complex Litigation; Alternative Dispute Resolution; Construction Law. ***Email:*** kgumbiner@tuggleduggins.com

SARAH F. SPARROW, born Port of Spain, Trinidad, June 4, 1945; admitted to bar, 1985, North Carolina and U.S. District Court, Middle District of North Carolina; 1988, U.S. District Court, Eastern District of North Carolina; 1990, U.S. Court of Appeals, Fourth Circuit; 1993, U.S. District Court, Western District of North Carolina; 1994, U.S. Court of Appeals, Fifth Circuit and U.S. District Court, Northern District of Texas. *Education:* Duke University (B.S.N., 1967); University of North Carolina (M.S., 1973; J.D., 1985). Johnston Scholar. Law Clerk to: Judge Rufus W. Reynolds, U.S. Bankruptcy Judge, 1985-1987; Judge Jerry G. Tart, U.S. Bankruptcy Judge, 1986-1987; U.S. Bankruptcy Court, Middle District of North Carolina. Member, Editorial Board, National Institute of Construction Law, Inc., 1992-1998. *Member:* Greensboro, North Carolina and American Bar Associations; North Carolina State Bar; American Bankruptcy Institute. (Board Certified Specialist in Business and Consumer Bankruptcy Law, North Carolina State Board of Legal Specialization). ***Email:*** ssparrow@tuggleduggins.com

KENNETH M. JOHNSON, born Pittsburgh, Pennsylvania, June 30, 1959; admitted to bar, 1984, Pennsylvania; 1986, District of Columbia and Maryland, U.S. District Court, District of Maryland, U.S. District Court, District of Columbia, U.S. District Court, Eastern District of Pennsylvania; 1988, U.S. Court of Appeals, Third and Fourth Circuits; 1991, U.S. Court of Appeals, District of Columbia; 1994, U.S. District Court, Central District of Illinois; 2000, North Carolina. *Education:* University of North Carolina at Greensboro (B.A., magna cum laude, 1981); George Washington University (J.D., with honors, 1984). *Member:* Greensboro, North Carolina, Pennsylvania and American Bar Associations; The District of Columbia Bar. ***PRACTICE AREAS:*** Employee Benefits; ERISA. ***Email:*** kjohnson@tuggleduggins.com

PETER O. EVENSON, SR., born New York, N.Y., March 2, 1950; admitted to bar, 1977, North Carolina and U.S. Court of Appeals, 4th Circuit; 1978, U.S. Tax Court; 2002, U.S. Supreme Court. *Education:* College of William & Mary (A.B., 1972); Wake Forest University (J.D., 1977). Certified Public Accountant: Virginia, 1978; North Carolina, 1978. Faculty, International Law Institute (chartered by Georgetown University), Washington, D.C., 1982—. *Member:* North Carolina and American (Member: Construction Industry Forum Committee; International Law and Practice Section) Bar Associations. ***Email:*** pevenson@tuggleduggins.com

MICHAEL S. FOX, born Columbus, Georgia, October 17, 1963; admitted to bar, 1989, Georgia and U.S. District Court, Northern District of Georgia; 1992, North Carolina and

(This Listing Continued)

U.S. District Court, Eastern District of North Carolina. *Education:* Appalachian State University (B.A., summa cum laude, 1986) Phi Kappa Phi; University of North Carolina at Chapel Hill (J.D., 1989). Associate, Fisher & Phillips, Atlanta, Georgia, 1989-1991. Prosecutor, DeKalb County, Georgia, 1991-1993. Assistant Attorney General, North Carolina. 1993-1996. Deputy General Counsel and Director of Governmental Affairs, Cone Mills Corporation, 1996-2001. *Member:* Greensboro and North Carolina Bar Associations; State Bar of Georgia; North Carolina State Bar. ***PRACTICE AREAS:*** Civil Litigation; Employment Law; Corporate Law; Government Affairs; Zoning Law; Land Use. ***Email:*** mfox@tuggleduggins.com

ERIC W. HARDIN, born Hendersonville, North Carolina, November 25, 1969; admitted to bar, 1996, North Carolina. *Education:* Williams College (B.A., 1992); University of North Carolina (J.D., 1996). Recipient, J. Nelson Young Scholarship in Tax Law, 1995. ***PRACTICE AREAS:*** Corporate; Taxation. ***Email:*** ehardin@tuggleduggins.com

J. NATHAN DUGGINS III, born Greensboro, North Carolina, April 27, 1969; admitted to bar, 1995, North Carolina. *Education:* University of North Carolina (B.A., 1991); Wake Forest University (J.D., 1995). Moot Court Board.*Member:* North Carolina State Bar. ***PRACTICE AREAS:*** Employment Law; Civil Litigation; Employment Litigation. ***Email:*** nduggins@tuggleduggins.com

JANIE L. LONG, born Asheboro, North Carolina, August 16, 1960; admitted to bar, 1999, North Carolina. *Education:* High Point University (B.S., Accounting and Business Administration, summa cum laude, 1996); Campbell University (J.D., 1999). Certified Public Accountant. *Member:* Greensboro and North Carolina Bar Associations. ***PRACTICE AREAS:*** Estate Planning; Probate; Taxation; Business Law. ***Email:*** jlong@tuggleduggins.com

SCOTT A. SCHAAF, born Sterling Heights, Michigan, July 29, 1977; admitted to bar, 2002, North Carolina. *Education:* University of North Carolina at Chapel Hill (B.A., 1999; J.D., 2002). Phi Beta Kappa. Staff Member, 2000-2001 and Managing Editor, 2001-2002, North Carolina Banking Institute Journal. *Member:* Greensboro and North Carolina Bar Associations. ***PRACTICE AREAS:*** Corporate Law; Commercial Transactions; Commercial Contracts; Debtor and Creditor Rights. ***Email:*** sschaaf@tuggleduggins.com

CYNTHIA MUNK SWINDLEHURST, born Salt Lake City, Utah, May 11; admitted to bar, 2003, North Carolina. *Education:* Brigham Young University (B.A., with honors, 2000); Duke University School of Law (J.D., 2003). ***LANGUAGES:*** Portuguese. ***PRACTICE AREAS:*** Litigation. ***Email:*** cswindlehurst@tuggleduggins.com

THOMAS E. NOBLE, born San Jose, California, March 23, 1971; admitted to bar, 2001, Illinois; 2004, North Carolina. *Education:* University of California at Santa Barbara (B.A., 1994); Northwestern University (J.D., 2001). *Member:* North Carolina State Bar. ***PRACTICE AREAS:*** Civil Litigation; Employment Litigation. ***Email:*** tnoble@tuggleduggins.com

REBECCA A. NIBURG, born Evanston, Illinois, January 26, 1978; admitted to bar, 2003, Maryland; 2004, North Carolina. *Education:* University of North Carolina at Chapel Hill (B.A., 2000); Washington University (M.A., J.D., 2003). Member, Phillip C. Jessup Moot Court Team, 2nd Place Regional Oralist, 2003. Clerkship to the Honorable Ellen L. Hollander, Maryland Court of Special Appeals, 2003-2004. *Member:* North Carolina State Bar. ***LANGUAGES:*** Russian, French. ***PRACTICE AREAS:*** Litigation; Immigration Law. ***Email:*** rniburg@tuggleduggins.com

REPRESENTATIVE CLIENTS: Abacon Telecommunications Corporation; Adams Electric Company; Allen Industries, Inc.; Apollo Chemical Corporation; Beacon Technologies, Inc.; Benner & Fields, Inc.; Brown Investment Properties Inc.; CGR Products, Inc.; Camcor, Inc.; Carolina Hoisery Mills, Inc.; Chelda, Inc.; Davidson's, Inc.; The Fresh Market, Inc; Fulenwider Enterprises, Inc.; High Point Furniture Industries, Inc; Highland Industries, Inc.; Industrial Air, Inc.; Jacobs Engineering Group, Inc.; Kingsdown, Inc.; Lantal Textiles, Inc.; LaRose Properties, Inc.; Newman Machine Co., Inc.; Pace Airlines, Inc.; Pay Tel Communications, Inc.; Piedmont Aviation, Inc.; Shamrock Environmental Corporation; Southern Foods Group, Inc.; Takata Restraint Systems, Inc.; Yates Construction Company, Inc.; Zickgraf Enterprises, Inc.
APPROVED ATTORNEYS FOR: Lawyer's Title Insurance Corp.; First American Title Insurance Co.; Investors Title Insurance Co.; Fidelity National Title Insurance Co.; Chicago Title Insurance Co.; Statewide Title, Inc.
REFERENCE: Wachovia Bank, N.A.

TWIGGS, BESKIND, STRICKLAND & RABENAU, P.A.

GREENSBORO, NORTH CAROLINA

(See Raleigh)

Personal Injury, Products Liability, Business Torts, Medical and other Professional Negligence, Federal and State Tort Claims, Environmental Torts, Insurance Bad Faith, Aviation Law and Wrongful Death.

DONALD R. VAUGHAN AND ASSOCIATES

Attorneys and Counselors at Law

612 W. FRIENDLY AVENUE
GREENSBORO, NORTH CAROLINA 27401
Telephone: 336-273-1415
Fax: 336-273-1445
Email: vaughanlaw@aol.com

Traffic Violations and Criminal Law.

FIRM PROFILE: Our firm handles legal matters in the following practice areas: traffic violations, criminal law, civil litigation, personal injury, real estate.

DONALD (DON) R. VAUGHAN, born Greensboro, North Carolina, September 13, 1952; admitted to bar, 1982, North Carolina; 1986, U.S. District Court for the District of Columbia; U.S. Supreme Court. *Education:* University of North Carolina at Chapel Hill (B.A., with high honors, 1974); Wake Forest University (J.D., 1979); American University (M.P.A.). Member, Wake Forest Law Review. City Councilman, Greensboro, 1991-2004. Mayor Pro Tem. Governor's Appointee, State Banking Commission. Legislative Clerk, U.S.

(This Listing Continued)

Senator Robert Morgan. ***PRACTICE AREAS:*** Traffic Violations; Criminal Law; Civil Litigation; Personal Injury; Real Estate. ***Email:*** vaughanlaw@aol.com

R. SHANE WALKER

Established in 2005

520 SOUTH ELM STREET, SUITE 204
GREENSBORO, NORTH CAROLINA 27420
Telephone: 336-373-9902
Fax: 336-373-9903
Email: rshanewalkerlaw@yahoo.com
URL: http://www.rshanewalkerlaw.com
Mailing Address: P.O. Box 20448, Greensboro, NC 27420

Automobile Accidents and Injuries, Traffic Violations, Wills, Civil Litigation, General Practice.

FIRM PROFILE: Our firm handles legal matters in the following practice areas: Automobile Accidents and Injuries,Traffic Violations, Wills, Civil Litigation, General Practice.

R. SHANE WALKER, born Eden, North Carolina, 1974; admitted to bar, 2001, North Carolina. *Education:* University of North Carolina at Chapel Hill (B.A., 1997); Campbell University (J.D., 2000). *Member:* North Carolina Bar Association. ***PRACTICE AREAS:*** Wills; Traffic Violations; Automobile Accidents and Injuries; Civil Litigation; General Practice.

WALL LAW FIRM, P.C.

GREENSBORO, NORTH CAROLINA

(See Winston-Salem)

Health Care, Corporate Law, Commercial Transactions, Bankruptcy, Mediation.

THE WALLACE LAW FIRM

GREENSBORO, NORTH CAROLINA

(See High Point)

Real Property, Business Law, Corporate Law, Intellectual Property, Traffic.

JAMES B. WEEKS

Established in 1976

119 NORTH GREENE STREET, SUITE 100
GREENSBORO, NORTH CAROLINA 27401
Telephone: 336-272-7272
Fax: 336-275-0999
Email: weekslaw@xspedius.net
URL: http://www.lawyers.com/jamesbweeks

General Civil Practice in all State and Federal Courts. Buying and Selling Homes, Commercial Real Estate, Residential Real Estate, Civil Litigation, Personal Injury, Probate, Estate Planning, Corporate Law, Social Security Disability, Criminal Law, Traffic Violations, Driving While Intoxicated.

JAMES B. WEEKS, born Sampson County, North Carolina, June 23, 1941; admitted to bar, 1976, North Carolina and U.S. District Court, Middle District of North Carolina; U.S. Court of Appeals, Fourth Circuit. *Education:* University of North Carolina (B.A., 1963; J.D., 1976). *Member:* Greensboro, North Carolina and American Bar Associations; North Carolina Academy of Trial Lawyers; The Association of Trial Lawyers of America.

ASSOCIATE

DALMIR S. GREWAL, born Punjab, India, July 15, 1966; admitted to bar, 1998, North Carolina. *Education:* University of North Carolina at Chapel Hill (B.A., Economics, 1988); East Carolina University, Greenville (M.B.A., 1992); Mississippi College (J.D., 1995). Phi Delta Phi. *Member:* Greensboro, Guilford County and North Carolina Bar Associations; North Carolina State Bar; North Carolina Academy of Trial Lawyers. ***PRACTICE AREAS:*** Residential Real Estate; Commercial Real Estate; Criminal Law; Traffic Violations; Wills; Business Law; Civil Litigation. ***Email:*** dsg@xspeedius.net

REPRESENTATIVE CLIENTS: BB&T; Parker Orleans Homebuilders; First Carolina Mortgage; Beazer Homes, Inc.; Triumph Properties.
APPROVED ATTORNEYS FOR: Investors Title Insurance Co.; First American Title Ins. Co.; Lawyers Title Ins. Co.; BB&T; Bank of America Mortgage; Bank of America; Wells Fargo Mortgage; First Horizon Mortgage.

CHARLES L. WHITE, II

330 SOUTH GREENE STREET
GREENSBORO, NORTH CAROLINA 27401
Telephone: 336-378-2746
Fax: 336-378-2749
Email: cleroy@mindspring.com
URL: http://www.chuckwhitelaw.com
Mailing Address: P.O. Box 9518, Greensboro, NC 27429

Criminal Law, Felonies, Misdemeanors, Drug Crimes, State and Federal Court, Drug Forfeiture, Driving While Intoxicated, Traffic Violations, Mediation, Arbitration, Alternative Dispute Resolution, Juvenile Delinquency Law, Child Abuse Neglect and Dependency.

FIRM PROFILE: Mr. White is a former District Court Judge.

CHARLES L. WHITE, II, born Cleveland, Ohio, March 13, 1954; admitted to bar, 1980, North Carolina; 1982, U.S. District Court, Eastern District of North Carolina and

(This Listing Continued)

CHARLES L. WHITE, II, Greensboro—Continued

U.S. Court of Appeals Fourth Circuit; 1987, U.S. District Court, Middle District of North Carolina; 1992, U.S. Supreme Court; 2004, U.S. District Court, Western District of North Carolina and U.S. District Court, Eastern District of Tennessee. *Education:* Duke University (B.S., 1976); Wake Forest University (J.D., 1980). District Court Judge, 1992-1999. *Member:* North Carolina Academy of Trial Lawyers. ***PRACTICE AREAS:*** Criminal Law; Felonies; Misdemeanors; Drug Crimes; Drug Forfeiture; Driving While Intoxicated; Traffic Violations; Mediation; Arbitration; Alternative Dispute Resolution; Civil Practice; Workers Compensation; Juvenile Law; Juvenile Criminal Law; Child Abuse Neglect and Dependency.

Languages: Spanish.

AMANDA M. WILLIS

PLAZA STATION, BANKING STREET
P.O. BOX 9593
GREENSBORO, NORTH CAROLINA 27429
Telephone: 336-688-4638
URL: http://www.amandawillislaw.com

Business and Commercial Litigation, Bankruptcy, Debt and Credit, Real Estate, Construction, Eminent Domain, Land Lord/Tenant, Animal Law and Animal Cruelty Law.

AMANDA M. WILLIS, born Shamokin, Pennsylvania, April 6, 1968; admitted to bar, 1993, Massachusetts; 2000, North Carolina. *Education:* Cornell University (B.A., 1990); Northeastern University School of Law (J.D., 1993). *Member:* Greensboro and North Carolina Bar Associations; Guilford County Association of Women Attorneys (Founding President); North Carolina Association of Women Attorneys; Greensboro Inn of Court. ***PRACTICE AREAS:*** Business Law; Commercial Litigation; Bankruptcy; Real Estate.

WILSON & ISEMAN, L.L.P.

GREENSBORO, NORTH CAROLINA

(See Winston-Salem)

General Civil Practice, including Civil Trial and Appellate Work in all State and Federal Courts, Administrative, Aviation, Commercial, Construction, Corporate, Employee Benefits and Executive Compensation, Employment, Criminal, Federal, State and Local Taxation, Insurance Defense, Personal Injury, Probate, Wills, Trusts and Estate Planning, Products Liability and Negligence Law, Professional Malpractice and Real Estate.

WINFREE & WINFREE

201 WEST MARKET STREET
SUITE 408
GREENSBORO, NORTH CAROLINA 27401
Telephone: 336-273-8998
Fax: 336-272-3065
URL: http://www.winfreelawoffice.com

Consumer Law, Lemon Law, Consumer Rights, Collections, Family Law, Divorce, Alimony, Civil Litigation, Business Litigation, Business Property, Traffic Violations.

CHARLES H. WINFREE, born Greensboro, North Carolina, 1959; admitted to bar, 1989, North Carolina. *Education:* North Carolina State University (B.S., 1981); University of North Carolina (J.D., with honors, 1989). Note and Comment Editor, North Carolina Law Review, 1988-1989. Author, The Separation of Powers and the Power to Appoint, 66, North Carolina Law Review, 1988. Member, N.C. Board of Elections, 2001—. *Member:* Greensboro, North Carolina, and American Bar Associations. ***PRACTICE AREAS:*** Consumer Rights; Lemon Law; Collections; Family Law; Civil Litigation; Business Litigation; Traffic Violations. ***Email:*** chwinfree@aol.com

WOMBLE CARLYLE SANDRIDGE & RICE

A Professional Limited Liability Company
300 NORTH GREENE STREET
GREENSBORO, NORTH CAROLINA 27402
Telephone: 336-574-8030
Fax: 336-574-4520
Email: lawyers@wcsr.com
URL: http://www.wcsr.com

REVISER OF THE NORTH CAROLINA LAW DIGEST FOR THIS DIRECTORY.

Charlotte, North Carolina Office: 3500 One Wachovia Center, 301 South College Street. Telephone: 704-331-4900. Fax: 704-331-4955.

Winston-Salem, North Carolina Office: One West Fourth Street, 27101. Telephone: 336-721-3600. Fax: 336-721-3660.

Raleigh, North Carolina Office: 2100 First Union Capitol Center, 150 Fayetteville Street Mall, P.O. Box 831. Telephone: 919-755-2100. Fax: 919-755-2150.

Research Triangle Park, North Carolina Office: 2530 Meridian Parkway, Suite 400 (Durham), 27713, P.O. Box 13069, Research Triangle Park, 27709. Telephone: 919-484-2300. Fax: 919-484-2340.

Atlanta, Georgia Office: One Atlantic Center, 1201 West Peachtree Street, Suite 3500. Telephone: 404-872-7000. Fax: 404-888-7490.

Other Atlanta, Georgia Office: Suite 404, 2296 Henderson Mill Road, N.E. Telephone: 770-492-9030. Fax: 770-492-9609.

Washington, D.C. Office: Suite 700, 1401 Eye Street. Telephone: 202-857-4400. Fax: 202-467-6910.

(This Listing Continued)

Greenville, South Carolina Office: 700 Poinsett Plaza, 104 South Main Street, P.O. Box 10208. Telephone: 864-255-5400. Fax: 864-255-5440.

Tysons Corner, Virginia Office: 8065 Leesburg Pike, Fourth Floor. Telephone: 703-790-3310. Fax: 703-790-2623.

General Civil Practice, Trial and Appellate Litigation. Administrative, Antitrust, Aviation, Banking, Bankruptcy and Creditor's Rights, Bond Financing, Civil Rights, Commercial, Construction, Consumer Lending, Corporate, E-Commerce, Employee Benefits, Environmental, Estate Planning, Family, Government Relations, Health Care, Insurance, Intellectual Property, International, Labor and Employment, Municipal, Negligence, Probate, Product Liability, Real Estate, Retirement Plans, Securities, Taxation, Toxic Tort, Wills and Trusts Law.

FIRM PROFILE: Womble Carlyle Sandridge & Rice, PLLC, which traces its history to 1876, is a full-service law firm that delivers sophisticated and innovative legal services to a wide spectrum of business clients in industries that include information technology, health care, manufacturing, telecommunications and financial services. The Firm also represents a variety of governmental units and agencies.

Womble Carlyle's mission is to provide value to clients by combining professional skill, technology and a thorough understanding of clients' needs to deliver high quality, cost-effective and responsive service. The firm is comprised of approximately 470 lawyers and 838 staff members operating from offices in Atlanta, GA; Greenville, SC; Charlotte, Winston-Salem, Research Triangle Park, Raleigh and Greensboro, NC; Tysons Corner, VA and Washington, DC.

The Firm considers technology and the benefits it offers an integral part of the legal services it provides. All of the Firm's offices are linked for full communications by telephone, fax, electronic mail and video conference over a wide area network. The Firm takes full advantage of its sophisticated computer technology for support in large-case litigation, as well as management of complex transactions. The Director of Technology is responsible for implementing existing systems, and in some instances, developing new software applications to meet specific client needs. The firm-wide communications and computer network permit the Firm to allocate resources from all offices, as needed, as well as to establish direct, secure links with clients and their legal departments, thus enhancing the responsiveness and efficiency of the Firm's lawyers.

The lawyers of Womble Carlyle have traditionally been active in community affairs, in Bar and other professional activities, and in state government. Many lawyers assume leading roles in civic and professional organizations, and several have served the government in elected or appointed positions.

LAW FIRM ALLIANCES/ASSOCIATIONS: **TOLEDO CONFERENCE GROUP**
LEX MUNDI

MEMBERS OF FIRM

GREGORY M. CHABON, born Andrews Air Force Base, Maryland, July 18, 1959; admitted to bar, 1996, North Carolina. *Education:* Clemson University (B.S., 1981); University of San Diego (M.B.A., 1994); Florida State University (J.D., magna cum laude, 1996). Order of the Coif; Order of Barristers; Moot Court. Member, Florida State Law Review. Member: North Carolina Volunteer Lawyers for the Arts; Triad Internet Council. *Member:* North Carolina State Bar (Member, Sections on: Business Law; Intellectual Property); American Bar Association. ***PRACTICE AREAS:*** Corporate Law; Intellectual Property. ***Email:*** gchabon@wcsr.com

RONALD R. DAVIS, born Abington, Pennsylvania, December 6, 1958; admitted to bar, 1987, Texas; 1993, North Carolina; U.S. District Court, Middle and Western Districts of North Carolina, U.S. Court of Appeals, Fourth and Fifth Circuits and U.S. Supreme Court. *Education:* Davidson College (B.A., 1981); University of North Carolina at Chapel Hill (M.B.A., 1986; J.D., 1986). Phi Delta Phi. Kenan Scholar. Member, Holderness Moot Court Bench. Author, "Forged Endorsements on Checks: A Primer," 59 Tex. B.J. 30 (1996). *Member:* Forsyth County, North Carolina and American Bar Associations; North Carolina State Bar (Member, Ethics Committee); North Carolina Association of Defense Attorneys (Member, Commercial Litigation Committee); Defense Research Institute. (Also at Winston-Salem Office). ***PRACTICE AREAS:*** Business Litigation; Trial Practice; Appellate Practice. ***Email:*** rdavis@wcsr.com

HARDIN G. HALSEY, born Mouth of Wilson, Virginia, April 21, 1955; admitted to bar, 1983, North Carolina. *Education:* Virginia Polytechnic Institute and State University (B.S., with distinction, 1977); University of Kentucky School of Law (J.D., with high distinction, 1983). Pi Tau Sigma Mechanical Engineering Honor Fraternity, Vice President; Tau Beta Pi Engineering Fraternity; Phi Eta Sigma Honor Fraternity; Order of the Coif; Phi Delta Phi. Member, Kentucky Law Journal, 1981-1983. Co-author: "North Carolina Real Estate Forms - Practice and North Carolina Commercial Finance Forms - Practice," (1992, Lawyers Cooperative Publishing, Rochester, New York). Listed in "The Best Lawyers in America". *Member:* Forsyth County, North Carolina (Member, Business Law Section) and American Bar Associations. (Also at Winston-Salem Office). ***PRACTICE AREAS:*** Real Estate Finance; Commercial Finance; Secured Transactions; Commercial Law; Troubled Loans and Workouts. ***Email:*** hhalsey@wcsr.com

RANDALL A. HANSON, born Charleston, West Virginia, December 18, 1960; admitted to bar, 1985, District of Columbia; 1993, North Carolina. *Education:* University of North Carolina (A.B., 1983; J.D., with honors, 1985). Phi Beta Kappa. Clerk of the Court, Holderness Moot Court Bench, 1984-1985. Member, The Order of Barristers. Associate: Womble Carlyle Sandridge & Rice, Winston-Salem, North Carolina, 1993-1995; Piper & Marbury, Washington, D.C., 1988-1993; Winston & Strawn, Washington, D.C., 1985-1988. *Member:* North Carolina (Member, Corporate Counsel Section) and American (Member, Business Law Section; Committee on Negotiated Acquisitions) Bar Associations. (Associate General Counsel). ***LANGUAGES:*** Spanish. ***PRACTICE AREAS:*** Mergers and Acquisitions; Securities; Corporate Law; International Business Transactions. ***Email:*** rhanson@wcsr.com

JACK B. HICKS, born New Orleans, Louisiana, August 28, 1957; admitted to bar, 1987, North Carolina and U.S. District Court, Middle and Eastern Districts of North Carolina; U.S. Court of Appeals for the Federal Circuit; registered to practice before U.S. Patent

(This Listing Continued)

and Trademark Office. *Education:* University of Virginia (B.S.M.E., with high distinction, 1979; M.S.M.E., 1980); University of Texas at Austin (J.D., with honors, 1987). Tau Beta Pi; Pi Tau Sigma; Sigma Xi; Raven Society; Order of the Coif. Associate Editor, Texas Law Review, 1986-1987. Author: "Copyright and Computer Databases: Is Traditional Compilation Law Adequate?" 37 Copyright Law Symposium 85, 1990. *Member:* North Carolina Bar Association (Council Member, Intellectual Property Law Section, Litigation Section); Carolina Patent, Trademark and Copyright Law Association (Member, Board of Managers); American Society of Mechanical Engineers. ***PRACTICE AREAS:*** Intellectual Property Law; Litigation. ***Email:*** jhicks@wcsr.com

DONALD C. LAMPE, admitted to bar, 1982, Texas; 1986, North Carolina. *Education:* Massachusetts Institute of Technology (B.S., 1978); Duke University (J.D., 1982). Author: "ECOA and Spousal Guaranties," N.C. Lawyers Weekly, June 1992; "Loan Commitments: Five Steps Will Avoid Litigation," N.C. Lawyers Weekly, December 1992; "Consumer Credit Law Update," NCBA Real Property Section Newsletter, September 1994; "Sub-Prime Primer," NCBA Real Property Section Newsletter, December 1996; "Regulation of Mortgage Brokers and Mortgage Bankers in North Carolina," NCBA Real Property Section Newsletter, January 1998; "Dealer Finance," Notes Bearing Interest (NCBA Business Law Section Newsletter), May 1999; "N.C. Residential Lending Overhaul Becomes Law," NCBA Real Property Section Newsletter, November 1999; "New State Predatory Lending Law: Legislative Developments in Consumer Credit," Notes Bearing Interest (NCBA Business Law Section Newsletter), January 2000; "Predatory Lending: Analysis and Perspective," BNA Banking Law Report, April 30, 2001; "An Overview of the Uniform Electronic Transactions Act and Federal ESIGN Law," The Conference on Consumer Finance Law Quarterly Report, Spring/Summer/Fall 2001; "The North Carolina Predatory Lending Usury Statute," The Conference on Consumer Finance Law Quarterly Report, Winter 2001; "Georgia Fair Lending Act Compliance Toolkit," Georgia Bankers Association, August 2002; "Predatory Lending: Federal Legislation, State Law and Preemption," The Conference on Consumer Finance Law Quarterly Report, Winter 2002 (upcoming); Rohner and Miller, Truth in Lending, Update to Section 6.09 (High-Cost Mortgage Loans), 2002 supplement (scheduled). *Member:* American Bar Association (Chair: Access to Services Subcommittee; Consumer Financial Services Committee; Predatory Lending Task Force); North Carolina Bar Association (Member: CLE Committee, 1999—; Real Property Section Council, 1997-2000; Real Property Section Executive Committee, Treasurer, 2000-2001; Real Property Curriculum Committee, 1998-1999; Business Law Section, 1999—. (Also at Charlotte, North Carolina Office). ***PRACTICE AREAS:*** Capital Markets; Banking; Consumer Practice; Regulatory Practice. ***Email:*** dlampe@wcsr.com

JAMES M. POWELL, born Grove Hill, Alabama; admitted to bar, 1977, Alabama and U.S. Supreme Court; 1979, South Carolina and U.S. Supreme Court; 1980, U.S. District Court, District of South Carolina; 1981, U.S. Court of Appeals, Fifth, Eleventh Circuits; 1984, North Carolina and U.S. Court of Appeal for the Fourth Circuit and U.S. District Court, Middle, Western and Eastern Districts of North Carolina; 2001, U.S. Supreme Court. *Education:* Auburn University (B.A., with honors, 1974); University of Alabama (J.D., 1977). Omicron Delta Kappa; Phi Delta Phi. Law Clerk, Justice Reneau P. Almon, Alabama Supreme Court, 1977-1978. *Member:* Greensboro, North Carolina (Member, Labor and Employment Law Sections) and American (Member, Labor and Employment Law Sections) Bar Associations; Alabama State Bar; South Carolina Bar;. ***PRACTICE AREAS:*** Labor and Employment. ***Email:*** jpowell@wcsr.com

C. ROBERT RHODES, born Burlington, North Carolina, August 7, 1936; admitted to bar, 1967, Virginia; 1968, North Carolina; U.S. Court of Appeals for the Federal Circuit; registered to practice before U.S. Patent and Trademark Office. *Education:* North Carolina State University (B.S., Industrial Engineering, 1960); George Washington University Law School (LL.B., 1966). Author: "Protecting Names of Products and Services," General Practice Journal 2:1, May, 1987; Legislation to Protect Citizens from Invention Marketing Companies (North Carolina Gen. Statute - Chapter 66, Article 27). Certified Mediator. *Member:* North Carolina (Member, Advisory Council on Intellectual Property Law Section, 1987-1996, Chair, 1993-1994) and American Bar Associations; American Intellectual Property Law Association; Patent Office Society. ***PRACTICE AREAS:*** Intellectual Property Law; International Patent Law; Licensing Law; Litigation; Mediation. ***Email:*** brhodes@wcsr.com

ASSOCIATES

CRAIG H. POPALIS, born Savannah, Georgia, November 14, 1955; admitted to bar, 2000, North Carolina. *Education:* University of Florida (B.S.M.E., 1980; J.D., 2000). ***PRACTICE AREAS:*** Intellectual Property. ***Email:*** cpopalis@wcsr.com

LEWIS S. ROWELL, born Lumberton, North Carolina, February 18, 1955; admitted to bar, 1998, North Carolina and U.S. District Court, Eastern District of North Carolina; 1999, U.S. District Court, Middle District of North Carolina; registered to practice before U.S. Patent and Trademark Office. *Education:* United States Military Academy (B.S., 1977); North Carolina State University (M.S., 1993); North Carolina Central University (J.D., 1998). Recipient, Daniel G. Sampson Award for Scholarship, North Carolina Central University. *Member:* North Carolina State Bar. [Capt., U.S. Army, 1977-1982]. ***PRACTICE AREAS:*** Intellectual Property; Patents; Trademarks; Copyrights. ***Email:*** lrowell@wcsr.com

J. MARK SAMPSON, born Minneapolis, Minnesota, August 1, 1972; admitted to bar, 1999, North Carolina; 2001, U.S. District Court, Middle and Eastern Districts of North Carolina; 2002, U.S. District Court, Western District of North Carolina. *Education:* Duke University (A.B., cum laude, 1994); Wake Forest University (J.D., cum laude, 1999). Order of the Coif. Executive Editor, Wake Forest Law Review, 1998-1999. Law Clerk to The Honorable John B. Lewis, Jr., North Carolina Court of Appeals, 1999-2000. *Member:* Greensboro and North Carolina Bar Associations. ***PRACTICE AREAS:*** Labor and Employment. ***Email:*** msampson@wcsr.com

OF COUNSEL

JACQUELINE E. CAMP, born Fort Lauderdale, Florida, March 25, 1963; admitted to bar, 1988, Massachusetts; 1997, North Carolina. *Education:* University of Virginia (B.A., with highest distinction, 1985); Harvard Law School (J.D., cum laude, 1988). Phi Beta Kappa. Echols Scholar. Recipient, Educom/Ncryptal Award for Best Educational Software in Law. *Member:* North Carolina State Bar; American Bar Association. ***PRACTICE AREAS:*** Corporate Law; Securities (100%). ***Email:*** jcamp@wcsr.com

D. ROSS HAMILTON, JR., born New York, N.Y., 1969; admitted to bar, 1994, North Carolina. *Education:* Duke University (A.B., 1991); Wake Forest University (J.D., 1994). Member, Moot Court Board. *Member:* Greenboro and North Carolina Bar Associations. ***PRACTICE AREAS:*** Labor and Employment. ***Email:*** rhamilton@wcsr.com

LILLIAN H. PINTO, born Greenville, South Carolina, 1958; admitted to bar, 1983, North Carolina. *Education:* Wake Forest University (B.A., cum laude, 1980); Wake Forest University School of Law (J.D., 1983). Staff Member and Articles Editor, Wake Forest Law Review. *Member:* North Carolina (Member, Sections on: Bankruptcy; Mediation and Alternative Dispute Resolutions) and American (Member, Business Bankruptcy Section) Bar Associations; American Bankruptcy Institute; Panel of Certified Mediators. ***PRACTICE AREAS:*** Bankruptcy; Creditors' Rights; Debtors Rights; Committee Representation. ***Email:*** lpinto@wcsr.com

LEGAL SUPPORT PERSONNEL

Terry Michael Wiley (Executive Director)
Susan DeVore (Office Administrator - Atlanta)
Keith Tedrow (Office Administrator - Winston-Salem)
John E. Turlington (Office Administrator - Research Triangle Park and Raleigh)
Cheri Edwards (Office Administrator - Tysons Corner, VA)
Patricia A. Kight (Director of Human Resources)
Charles R. Allison, III (Office Administrator - Charlotte)
John T. Boyer (Office Administrator - Washington, DC)
Hails Foster (Director of Finance and Systems)
Mark Whitley (Director, Strategic Planning and Marketing)
Julie D. Beavers (Professional Development/Recruiting Administrator - Research Triangle Park and Raleigh)
Cynthia K. Pruitt (Professional Development/Recruiting Administrator - Winston-Salem and Greensboro)
Kristin F. Carretta (Director of Professional Development and Recruiting)
Elizabeth P. Keasler (Professional Development/Recruiting Administrator - Charlotte and Greenville, SC)
Stacy H. Stephens (Professional Development/Recruiting Administrator - Atlanta)
Barbara Fountain (Office Manager - Greenville)
Melissa B. Weaver (Office Manager/Billing Coordinator - Greensboro)

GENERAL COUNSEL FOR: Brenner Companies; Charles & Colvard, Ltd.; Inmar Enterprises, Inc.; NC Biosciences Industry Organization; Piedmont Federal Savings & Loan Assn.; RF Micro Devices, Inc.; Venture First Associates.
REPRESENTATIVE CLIENTS: ALLTEL Corp.; Armstrong World Industries; Armtex, Inc.; Associated Aviation Underwriters; Bank of America; BB&T Corporation; Brad Ragan, Inc.; Budd Services, Inc.; Carolina Beverage Corporation; Carolina Biological Supply Company; Carolinas Medical; Carolina Mills, Inc.; Champion Industries, Inc.; Childress Klein Properties, Inc.; Cisco Systems, Inc.; City of Charlotte, North Carolina; The Crosland Group, Inc.; Duke University; First Factors, Inc.; Food Lion; GlaxoSmithKline; The Harris Group; Jefferson-Pilot Life Insurance Company; John Hancock Mutual Life Insurance Co.; Klaussner Furniture Industries, Inc.; Lowes Companies, Inc.; Magneti Marelli USA, Inc.; MCI Constructors, Inc.; Metropolitan Life Insurance Co.; North Carolina Association of County Commissioners; Novant Health, Inc.; Novartis Pharmaceutical Corporation; Old Dominion Freight Lines, Inc.; Phillips Industries, Inc.; RegO Claimants Trust; RJ Reynolds Tobacco Company; Rusty Wallace, Inc.; Sedgwick James; Sentry Insurance, a Mutual Company; Spectrum Properties; SQL Financials International, Inc.; Technimark, Inc.; Thomas Built Buses, Inc.; The Travelers Insurance Companies; Vulcan Materials Company; Wachovia Bank, N.A.; Wake Forest University; Wake Forest University Baptists Regional Medical Center; Zemex Industrial Minerals.

REVISER OF THE NORTH CAROLINA LAW DIGEST FOR THIS DIRECTORY.

(For Biographical Data of other Personnel, see Professional Biographies at Charlotte, Raleigh, Research Triangle Park, North Carolina, Atlanta, Georgia, Washington, D.C., Greenville, South Carolina and Tysons Corner, Virginia)

WOODRUFF LAW FIRM, P.A.

Established in 1994

420 W. MARKET STREET
GREENSBORO, NORTH CAROLINA 27401
Telephone: 336-272-9122
Telecopier: 336-272-7991
URL: http://www.lawyers.com/woodruff
Email: cwoodruff@woodrufflawfirm.com
URL: http://www.woodrufflawfirm.com

Family Law, Taxation, Divorce, Mediation and Arbitration Child Custody and Child Support.

CAROLYN J. WOODRUFF, born Tuscaloosa, Alabama; admitted to bar, 1983, North Carolina. *Education:* Duke University (J.D., with high honors, 1983). Phi Alpha Delta. Research and Managing Editor, Duke Law Journal, 1982-1983. Certified Public Accountant, North Carolina, 1985. Certified Valuation Analyst by the National Association of Certified Valuation Analysts. *Member:* Greensboro, North Carolina and American (Past Chair, Domestic Relations Committee, Tax Section) Bar Associations; North Carolina State Bar; North Carolina Association of Certified Public Accountants; American Institute of Certified Public Accountants. Fellow, American College of Tax Counsel. (Board Certified Specialist in Family Law by the North Carolina State Board of Legal Specialization). ***PRACTICE AREAS:*** Family Law; Equitable Distribution Law; Tax Law; Divorce. ***Email:*** cwoodruff@woodrufflawfirm.com

---

BONNIE E. ROSSI, born Homestead, Florida, May 10, 1948; admitted to bar, 1999, North Carolina. *Education:* Guilford College (B.S., 1996); Roger Williams University School of Law (J.D., 1999). *Member:* Greensboro (Member, Family Law and Litigation Section, 1999-2001); North Carolina State Bar. ***PRACTICE AREAS:*** Family Law. ***Email:*** brossi@woodrufflawfirm.com

(This Listing Continued)

WOODRUFF LAW FIRM, P.A., Greensboro—Continued

LUCY HARRINGTON, born Cedar Rapids, Iowa, January 10, 1964; admitted to bar, 1994, Iowa (Not admitted in North Carolina). *Education:* Coe College (B.A., 1986); University of Iowa (J.D., 1993). Phi Beta Kappa. ***PRACTICE AREAS:*** Family Law (100%).

WYATT EARLY HARRIS WHEELER L.L.P.

GREENSBORO, NORTH CAROLINA

(See High Point)

Litigation, Legal and Regulatory matters in Furniture/Home Furnishings Industries, General Civil, Insurance, Business, Securities, Taxation and Criminal Practice. Trials and Appeals in all State and Federal Courts. Probate and Estate Planning, Real Estate, Bankruptcy, Corporation, Banking, Negligence, Workers Compensation and Family Law.

YOUNCE, MOORE & MOSELEY, L.L.P.

333 NORTH GREENE STREET, SUITE 404
P.O. BOX 3486
GREENSBORO, NORTH CAROLINA 27402
Telephone: 336-379-0123
Fax: 336-379-9894
URL: http://www.ymmlaw.com

General Practice in All State and Federal Courts, Civil Litigation, Products Liability, Aviation Litigation, Personal Injury, Bankruptcy. Commercial Law, Collections, Homeowners Association Law, Mediation, Arbitration, Wills, Estates, General Practice in all State and Federal Courts, Litigation, Bankruptcy, Employment, Real Estate, Domestic Relations, Criminal.

MEMBERS OF FIRM

CHARLES P. YOUNCE, born Greensboro, North Carolina, August 5, 1937; admitted to bar, 1966, North Carolina and U.S. District Court, Middle, Eastern and Western Districts of North Carolina; 1967, U.S. Court of Appeals, Fourth Circuit; 1971, U.S. Court of International Trade; 1981, U.S. Supreme Court. *Education:* University of North Carolina at Chapel Hill (A.B., 1960). Sigma Alpha Epsilon; Phi Delta Phi. Commercial Panel Member, American Arbitration Association. North Carolina Certified Mediator. *Member:* Greensboro (President, 1996-1997), North Carolina (Board of Governors, 2003-2006) and American Bar Associations; North Carolina State Bar (Chairman, North Carolina Conference of Bar Presidents, 2001-2002; President, 18th Judicial District Bar, 2002-2003). [U.S. Marine Corps, 1959-1965]. ***PRACTICE AREAS:*** Civil Litigation; Commercial Law; Business Law; Condominium Law; Homeowners Association Law; Mold Litigation; Water Law; Personal Injury; Wrongful Death; Commercial Arbitration; Commercial Mediation. ***Email:*** cyounce@ymmlaw.com

LARRY I. MOORE III, born Wilson, North Carolina, July 1, 1948; admitted to bar, 1979, North Carolina and U.S. District Court, Middle District of North Carolina; 1993, U.S. District Court, Eastern and Western Districts of North Carolina; 1998, U.S. Court of Appeals, Fourth Circuit; 1999, U.S. Supreme Court. *Education:* United States Naval Academy (B.S., 1970); University of Houston Law Center (J.D., cum laude, 1979). Associate Editor, Houston Law Review, 1978-1979. Legal Counsel, Greensboro Urban Ministry, 1990-1996. *Member:* Greensboro (President, 1999-2000), North Carolina and American (Member, Litigation Section - Products Liability and Aviation Committees; Tort Trial and Insurance Section - Aviation and Space Law Committee) Bar Associations; Guilford American Inn of Court (President, 1999-2001). [Lt., USN, 1970-1976]. ***REPORTED CASES:*** Moore v. Coachman Industries, Inc. 129 N.C.App. 389, 499 S.E.2d 772, 35 UCC Rep Serv 2d 758, Prod. Liab. Rep. (CCH) p.15, 234 (1998); Hopkins v. Ciba-Geigy Corp., 111 N.C.App. 179, 432 S.E.2d 142, 62 USLW 2132, Prod. Liab. Rep. (CCH) p. 13, 711 (1993). ***PRACTICE AREAS:*** Civil Litigation; Products Liability; Aviation Litigation; Personal Injury; Wrongful Death; Construction Law; Traumatic Brain Injury. ***Email:*** lmoore@ymmlaw.com

WILLIAM O. MOSELEY, JR., born Clarksville, Virginia, February 1, 1935; admitted to bar, 1981, North Carolina and U.S. District Court, Middle District of North Carolina; U.S. District Court, Eastern and Western Districts of North Carolina. *Education:* University of North Carolina at Greensboro (B.S.B.A., magna cum laude, 1977); Wake Forest University (J.D., 1980). Member, Trustees Panel, U.S. Bankruptcy Court, Middle District of North Carolina, 1982-2000. *Member:* Greensboro, North Carolina and American Bar Associations; North Carolina State Bar. ***PRACTICE AREAS:*** Bankruptcy; Commercial; Collections; Wills; Estate Planning. ***Email:*** wmoseley@ymmlaw.com

OF COUNSEL

H. BRUCE BRANDON, born Lawrenceville, Virginia, September, 1950; admitted to bar, 1985, North Carolina. *Education:* United States Air Force Academy (B.S., 1972); Wake Forest University School of Law (J.D., cum laude, 1985). Airline Transport Rating; Certified Flight Instructor; Certified Instrument Instructor; Multi-engine Instructor, United States Air Force Pilot; Army Parachute Jump Wings. Adjunct Professor, Aviation Law, Wake Forest University School of Law. Former Adjunct Faculty Member, Basic Accident Investigation Class, National Transportation Safety Board. Former Air Line Pilots Accident Investigation Team. Federal Aviation Administration Safety Counselor. *Member:* North Carolina State Bar; Airline Pilots Association; National Transportations Safety Board Association (Founding Member); Lawyer Pilots Bar Association; Aircraft Owners and Pilot's Association (Legal Services Plan Attorney). [U.S. Air Force, 1972-1977; U.S. Air Force Reserve, 1977-1979]. ***PRACTICE AREAS:*** Aviation Litigation; Administrative Law; Airport Law; Civil Litigation; Personal Injury. ***Email:*** bbrandon@ymmlaw.com

BAKER, JONES, DALY, MURRAY, CARTER & DAUGHTRY, P.A.

GREENVILLE, NORTH CAROLINA

(See Ahoskie)

General Insurance Defense Civil Practice. Trials. Real Estate, Estate Planning, Probate, Business, Personal Injury Defense, Professional Liability, Insurance, Workers Compensation and Collections.

VICTORIA L. BLOCK

GREENVILLE, NORTH CAROLINA

(See New Bern)

Immigration Law, Social Security Law, Wills.

THE BLOUNT LAW FIRM, P.A.

Established in 1966
400 WEST FIRST STREET
P.O. DRAWER 58
GREENVILLE, NORTH CAROLINA 27835-0058
Telephone: 252-752-6000; 800-851-1818
Fax: 252-752-2174
URL: http://www.theblountlawfirmnc.com
Email: louise@theblountlawfirm.com
URL: http://www.theblountlawfirm.com

General Civil Practice in all State and Federal Courts. Personal Injury, Wrongful Death, Medical Malpractice, Legal Malpractice, Mass Torts, Complex and Multi-District Litigation, Class Actions, Antitrust, Products Liability, Nursing Home Negligence, Logging Truck Accidents, Spectator Injuries, Safety.

MARVIN K. BLOUNT, JR., born Greenville, North Carolina, August 21, 1939; admitted to bar, 1966, North Carolina and U.S. District Court, Eastern, Middle and Western Districts of North Carolina; U.S. Court of Appeals, Fourth Circuit and U.S. Supreme Court. *Education:* Woodberry Forest School; University of North Carolina and University of Georgia (A.B., 1963); Wake Forest University (J.D., 1966). Phi Delta Phi. Member, Wake Forest University Law Review. Listed in The Best Lawyers in America, 1987—. Former Judge, North Carolina Superior Court. National College of State Trial Judges, 1971. *Member:* Pitt County (Former President), North Carolina and American Bar Associations; Third Judicial District (Former President) and North Carolina State Bars; The Association of Trial Lawyers of America; North Carolina Academy of Trial Lawyers (Former Member, Board of Governors); American Board of Trial Advocates. Fellow: American Bar Foundation; Roscoe Pound Foundation. ***PRACTICE AREAS:*** Personal Injury; Wrongful Death; Medical Malpractice; Legal Malpractice; Mass Torts; Complex and Multi-District Litigation; Class Actions; Antitrust; Products Liability; Nursing Home Negligence; Logging Truck Accidents; Spectator Injuries; Safety. ***Email:*** mblount@theblountlawfirm.com

---

DARREN M. DAWSON, born Banbury, England, August 26, 1967; admitted to bar, 1992, North Carolina and U.S. District Court, Eastern, Middle and Western Districts of North Carolina. *Education:* Campbell University (B.A., 1989; J.D., 1992). Representative: National Evidence Moot Court Team; National Trial Team; Jerome Prince Invitational Evidence Moot Court Team. Recipient, Order of the Barristers' Advocacy Award, 1992. Listed in Who's Who Among Students in American Colleges and Universities, 1989, 1992. Case Writer, "Campbell Law Observer," Fourth Judicial Circuit. *Member:* Pitt County, North Carolina and American (Appointed, Student Liaison, Consumer Products Regulation Committee, 1990-1991) Bar Associations; North Carolina State Bar; The Association of Trial Lawyers of America; North Carolina Academy of Trial Lawyers. ***PRACTICE AREAS:*** Personal Injury; Wrongful Death; Medical Malpractice; Legal Malpractice; Complex and Multi-District Litigation; Class Actions; Antitrust. ***Email:*** dmd@theblountlawfirm.com

MARVIN K. BLOUNT, III, born Winston-Salem, North Carolina, October 28, 1964; admitted to bar, 1996, North Carolina and U.S. District Court, Eastern, Middle and Western Districts of North Carolina. *Education:* East Carolina University (B.S.B.A., magna cum laude, 1993); Wake Forest University (J.D., 1996). Counsel to Chief of Staff, U.S. Department of Justice, Antitrust Division, 1998-1999. Assistant Advocate, U.S. Small Business Administration, Office of Advocacy, 1997-1998. Member, North Carolina Board of Transportation, 2003-2007. Member, Board of Visitors, East Carolina University, 2003-2008. *Member:* Pitt County and North Carolina Bar Associations; North Carolina State Bar; North Carolina Academy of Trial Lawyers; The Association of Trial Lawyers of America. ***PRACTICE AREAS:*** Personal Injury; Wrongful Death; Medical Malpractice; Legal Malpractice; Mass Torts; Complex and Multi-District Litigation; Class Actions; Antitrust. ***Email:*** mblount3@theblountlawfirm.com

REBECCA C. BLOUNT, born Tuscaloosa, Alabama, August 11, 1971; admitted to bar, 2001, North Carolina and U.S. District Court, Eastern, Middle and Western Districts of North Carolina. *Education:* University of Virginia (1993); Wake Forest University School of Law (J.D., 2001). Board Member, Wake Forest University Moot Court, 1999-2001. Recipient: CALI Awards: Conflict of Laws; Clinic for the Elderly; Family Law. Winner, Edwin M. Stanley Moot Court Competition, 1999. Member, Wake Forest Law Review, 1999-2001. *Member:* Pitt County and North Carolina State Bar Associations; The Association of Trial Lawyers of America; North Carolina Academy of Trial Lawyers; North Carolina Association of Women Attorneys. ***PRACTICE AREAS:*** Complex and Multi-District Litigation; Class Actions; Antitrust; Personal Injury; Wrongful Death. ***Email:*** rebecca@theblountlawfirm.com

HARRY HUMPHREY ALBRITTON, JR., born Riverdale, Georgia, August 5, 1976; admitted to bar, 2002, North Carolina and U.S. District Court, Eastern, Middle and Western Districts of North Carolina. *Education:* East Carolina University (B.A., Psychol-

(This Listing Continued)

ogy, 1998); Ohio Northern University (J.D., 2002). *Member:* Pitt County and North Carolina Bar Associations; North Carolina State Bar; Eastern North Carolina Inn of Court. ***PRACTICE AREAS:*** Civil Litigation; Complex and Multi-District Litigation; Class Actions. ***Email:*** harry@theblountlawfirm.com

REFERENCE: First Citizens Bank, Greenville, N.C.

BRANTLEY, JENKINS, RIDDLE, HARDEE & HARDEE

202 EAST ARLINGTON BOULEVARD
P.O. BOX 924
GREENVILLE, NORTH CAROLINA 27858
Telephone: 252-355-1998
Fax: 252-321-2948
URL: http://www.bjrhhlawyers.com
URL: http://www.bjrhhatty.com

Goldsboro, North Carolina Office: 601 North Spence Avenue, 27534. Telephone: 919-778-9700. Fax: 919-778-1938.

Jacksonville, North Carolina Office: 901 Hargett Street, P.O. Box 7070, 28540. Telephone: 910-455-5599. Fax: 910-455-7191.

Kinston, North Carolina Office: 2506 Heritage Street, Suite A, 28501. Telephone: 252-522-1500.

Personal Injury, Wrongful Death, Automobile Accidents, Head and Spinal Injury, Nursing Home Abuse and Neglect, Workers Compensation, Insurance, Products Liability, Social Security Disability, Medical Malpractice.

(For complete biographical data on all personnel, see Professional Biographies at Goldsboro, North Carolina)

RODDEY M. BROWN III & ANGELA H. BROWN, P.A.

123 WEST THIRD STREET
GREENVILLE, NORTH CAROLINA 27858
Telephone: 252-317-4000
Fax: 252-317-4444
URL: http://www.roddeyandangelabrownattorneys.com

Criminal Law, DWI, Drug Crimes, Juvenile Crimes, Parole and Probation, Traffic Violations, White Collar Crime, Education, Elder Law, Nursing Home Abuse, Workers Compensation, Medical Malpractice, Personal Injury, Automobile Accidents, Sexual Abuse, Slip and Fall, Wrongfull Death and Appellate Practice.

RODDEY MIDDLETON BROWN, III, born Winston Salem, North Carolina, April 14, 1962; admitted to bar, 1994, North Carolina. *Education:* Chaminade University of Honolulu (B.A., 1990); Thomas M. Cooley Law School (J.D., 1994). ***PRACTICE AREAS:*** Criminal; Personal Injury; Workers Compensation.

ANGELA H. BROWN, born Chicago, Illinois; admitted to bar, 1995, North Carolina; 2000, U.S. District Court, Eastern, Western and Middle Districts of North Carolina; U.S. Court of Appeals, Fourth Circuit. *Education:* University of Illinois (B.S., 1988); Thomas M. Cooley Law School (J.D., magna cum laude, 1994). Recipient, American Jurisprudence Awards in Contracts, Secured Transactions and Criminal Procedure. *Member:* Pitt County, Judicial District Three-A, and North Carolina Bar Associations; North Carolina State Bar. ***PRACTICE AREAS:*** Criminal Law; Appellate Practice; Traffic Violations.

BURCH LAW OFFICE

311 SOUTH EVANS STREET
GREENVILLE, NORTH CAROLINA 27858
Telephone: 252-830-5291
Fax: 252-830-9234
Email: tim@burchlawoffice.com
URL: http://www.burchlaw-office.com

Personal Injury, Automobile Accidents, Wrongful Death, Medical Malpractice, Criminal Law, Driving While Intoxicated, Drug Crimes, Traffic Violations, White Collar Crime, Worker Compensation, Adoptions, Child Custody, Child Support, Divorce, Visitation Rights, Wills and Probate, Trust and Estates, Estate Planning, Social Security Disability, Eminent Domain, Zoning and Planning, Traumatic Brain Injury, Corporate-Business Formation.

TIMOTHY E. BURCH, born 1968; admitted to bar, 1996, North Carolina; 2003, Texas. *Education:* Washington State University (B.A., Finance and B.A., Political Science, 1992); Arizona State University (J.D., 1995). *Member:* North Carolina State Bar; American Bar Association; Association of Trial Lawyers of America; North Carolina Academy of Trial Lawyers; State Bar of Texas. ***PRACTICE AREAS:*** Personal Injury; Automobile Accidents and Injuries; Wrongful Death; Medical Malpractice; Criminal Law; Driving While Intoxicated; Drug Crimes; Traffic Violations; White Collar Crime; Workers Compensation; Adoption Law; Child Custody; Child Support; Divorce; Visitation Rights; Wills; Probate; Trusts and Estates; Estate Planning; Social Security Disability; Eminent Domain; Zoning, Planning and Land Use. ***Email:*** tim@burchlawoffice.com

PHILLIP R. DIXON, P.A.

Established in 1978
110 EAST ARLINGTON BOULEVARD
P.O. DRAWER 8668
GREENVILLE, NORTH CAROLINA 27835-8668
Telephone: 252-355-8100
Telecopier: 252-355-0271
Email: phildixon@coastalnet.com
URL: http://www.downeast-law.com

Administrative Law, Business Law, Construction Law, Corporate Law, Education Law, Elder Law, Eminent Domain, Franchise Law, General Practice, Land Use Law, Municipal and Zoning Law, Partnership Law, Public Utilities Law, Real Estate Law, Trusts and Estates, Wills and Probate.

FIRM PROFILE: Established in 1978, Phillip R. Dixon, P.A., is a general practice law firm with specialized expertise in Education and Administrative law, and Municipal and Utilities Law, including zoning. The firm also devotes substantial effort to Business and Real Estate Law, and Estate Planning and Administration. The firm has achieved and maintained Martindale-Hubbell's highest rating for legal ability and ethical standard, and provides legal services throughout eastern North Carolina. The firm is actively involved in charitable, civic, and community activities at both the local and state level.

PHILLIP R. DIXON, SR., born Wake Forest, North Carolina, March 26, 1949; admitted to bar, 1974, North Carolina; 1976, U.S. District Court, Eastern District of North Carolina; 1981, U.S. Court of Appeals, Fourth Circuit; 1982, U.S. Supreme Court; 1996, U.S. District Court, Middle and Western Districts of North Carolina. *Education:* East Carolina University (B.S.B.A., 1971); University of North Carolina at Chapel Hill (J.D., 1974). Omicron Delta Epsilon; Phi Delta Phi; Phi Kappa Phi; Beta Gamma Sigma. Author: "A Study of Looseleaf and Pocketpart Supplementation of Law Books," American Bar Association Student Lawyer Journal, 1971. Special Education Local Due Process and State Review Hearing Officer, North Carolina Department of Public Instruction, 1982-1988. Arbitrator, Judicial District 3A, 1987—. Mediator, Justice Center of Atlanta, Georgia, 1988—. Elected, University of North Carolina Board of Governors, 2005. *Member:* Pitt County, North Carolina (Board of Governors) and American Bar Associations; North Carolina State Bar; North Carolina Academy of Trial Lawyers. ***REPORTED CASES:*** Redevelopment Commission of City of Greenville v. Hannaford, 222 S.E.2d 752 (N.C.App. 1976); Waters v. North Carolina Phosphate Corp., 232 S.E.2d 275 (N.C.App. 1977); Williams v. Wachovia Bank & Trust Co., 233 S.E.2d 589 (N.C. 1977); State v. Chambers, 255 S.E.2d 294 (N.C.App. 1979); DeJaager v. DeJaager, 267 S.E.2d 399 (N.C.App. 1980); Bell Arthur Water Corporation, et. al., 173 F.3d 517 (4th Cir. 1999); Town of Muldrow, et. al. v. Sequayah County Rural Water District No. 7, 191 F.3d. 1192 (10th Cir. 2000). ***PRACTICE AREAS:*** Administrative Law; Business Law; Construction Law; Corporate Law; Education Law; Elder Law; Eminent Domain; Franchise Law; General Practice; Land Use; Municipal Law; Zoning Law; Partnership Law; Public Utility Law; Real Estate; Trusts and Estates; Wills; Probate. ***Email:*** phildixon@coastalnet.com

REPRESENTATIVE CLIENTS: Greenville Utilities Commission; Pitt County and Washington County Boards of Education; Pitt County, Martin County and Halifax County Community Collages; Carolina Donor Services; Town of Ayden; Tar-Pamlico Basin Association; North Carolina Association of Community College Trustees; East Carolina University Educational Foundation, Inc.; East Carolina University Foundation, Inc.; Hyatt Legal Services, Inc.; ARAG Legal Services, Inc.; RBC Centura Bank.

W. GREGORY DUKE

119 WEST FOURTH STREET
GREENVILLE, NORTH CAROLINA 27835
Telephone: 252-758-4444
Fax: 252-758-4080
Email: wgd1070@aol.com
URL: http://www.wgdukelaw.com

General Trial and Appellate in all State and Federal Courts. Criminal Law, Drug Crimes, Felonies, Homicide, Misdemeanors, Driving While Intoxicated, Traffic Violations, Domestic Relations, Divorce, Child Custody, Child Support, Alimony, Equitable Distribution.

W. GREGORY DUKE, born Jacksonville, North Carolina, March 26, 1965; admitted to bar, 1990, North Carolina; 1992 U.S. District Court, Eastern District of North Carolina; 1996, U.S. Court of Appeals, Fourth Circuit. *Education:* University of North Carolina at Chapel Hill (B.A. in Political Science, 1987; J.D., 1990). Pi Sigma Alpha. Recipient, American Jurisprudence Award in Remedies, 1990. *Member:* Pitt County and North Carolina Bar Associations; North Carolina State Bar; Pitt County Academy of Criminal Defense Attorneys; North Carolina Academy of Trial Lawyers. ***REPORTED CASES:*** Garrison v. Connor 122 N.C. App. 702 (1996); State v. Ward 338 N.C. 64 (1994); Dalton Moran Shook, Inc. v. Pitt Develop Co. 113 N.C. App. 707 (1994); Barclays Amer. Mortgage Corp. v. BECA Enterprise 116 N.C. App. 100 (1994). ***PRACTICE AREAS:*** Criminal; Civil Forfeiture; Murder; Family Law; Divorce; Child Custody; Alimony; Equitable Distribution.

EDWARDS & EDWARDS, L.L.P.

2192 SOUTH EVANS STREET
P.O. DRAWER 1425
GREENVILLE, NORTH CAROLINA 27835-1425
Telephone: 252-353-1200
Telecopier: 252-353-1301
Email: Edwards.attys@earthlink.net
URL: http://www.edwardsattorneys.com

General Civil Practice in all State and Federal Courts. Personal Injury and Wrongful Death, Automobile Accidents, Professional Malpractice and Products Liability.

(This Listing Continued)

EDWARDS & EDWARDS, L.L.P., Greenville—Continued

MEMBERS OF FIRM

JOSEPH T. EDWARDS, born Raleigh, North Carolina, June 27, 1960; admitted to bar, 1985, North Carolina and U.S. District Court, Eastern District of North Carolina. *Education:* University of North Carolina-Chapel Hill (B.S. in B.A., 1982; J.D., 1985). *Member:* Pitt County, North Carolina and American Bar Associations; North Carolina State Bar; The Association of Trial Lawyers of America; North Carolina Academy of Trial Lawyers. ***PRACTICE AREAS:*** Personal Injury; Wrongful Death; Products Liability; Medical Malpractice; Automobile Accidents and Injuries. ***Email:*** Edwards.attys@earthlink.net

SHARRON R. EDWARDS, born Greensboro, North Carolina, January 6, 1962; admitted to bar, 1987, North Carolina, U.S. District Court, Eastern and Middle Districts of North Carolina and U.S. Court of Appeals, Fourth Circuit. *Education:* University of North Carolina-Chapel Hill (B.A., 1984; J.D., with honors, 1987). Phi Beta Kappa; Order of the Coif. Member, Holderness Moot Court. *Member:* Pitt County (Past-President), North Carolina and American Bar Associations; North Carolina State Bar; The Association of Trial Lawyers of America; North Carolina Academy of Trial Lawyers. ***PRACTICE AREAS:*** Personal Injury; Wrongful Death; Products Liability; Medical Malpractice; Automobile Accidents and Injuries. ***Email:*** Edwards.attys@earthlink.net

GAYLORD, McNALLY, STRICKLAND, SNYDER & HOLSCHER, L.L.P.

Established in 1947
498 RED BANKS ROAD
P.O. DRAWER 545
GREENVILLE, NORTH CAROLINA 27835-0545
Telephone: 252-321-7111
Fax: 252-321-7112
URL: http://www.lawyers.com/gmsslaw

General Practice, Civil Practice, Real Estate, Real Property, Residential Real Estate, Commercial Real Estate, Commercial Law, Business Law, Business Transactions, Construction Law, Corporate Law, Contracts, Debtor and Creditor, Collections, Insurance, Litigation, Trial Practice, Personal Injury, Automobile Accidents and Injuries, Wrongful Death, Probate, Trusts and Estates, Estate Administration, Estate Planning, Wills, Contested Wills.

MEMBERS OF FIRM

LOUIS W. GAYLORD, JR. (Retired)

DANNY D. McNALLY, born Brenham, Texas, May 9, 1946; admitted to bar, 1973, North Carolina. *Education:* University of North Carolina (B.S., 1968; J.D., 1973). *Member:* Pitt County (President, 1978-1979) and North Carolina Bar Associations; North Carolina State Bar; North Carolina Academy of Trial Lawyers. [With U.S. Army, 1969-1971]. ***REPORTED CASES:*** Griffin v. Woodard, 126 N.C. App 649, 486 S.E. 2d 240; Tyson v. Henry, 133 N.C. App 415, 514 S.E. 2d 564; Moore v. Wachovia Bank & Trust Co., 30 N.C. App. 390, 226 S.E. 2d 833; Dozier v. Crandall, 105 N.C. App. 74, 411 S.E. 2d 635. ***PRACTICE AREAS:*** Insurance Defense; Litigation; Personal Injury; Real Estate; Business Law; Trusts and Estates; Contested Wills. ***Email:*** dannymcnally@earthlink.net

D. MICHAEL STRICKLAND, born Smithfield, North Carolina, August 10, 1953; admitted to bar, 1978, North Carolina. *Education:* North Carolina State University (B.S., cum laude, 1975); Wake Forest University (J.D., 1978). Phi Delta Phi. Member, Moot Court Board, 1977-1978. *Member:* Pitt County (President, 1987-1988) and North Carolina Bar Associations; North Carolina State Bar. ***PRACTICE AREAS:*** Real Estate; Business Law; Wills; Trusts and Estates; Litigation. ***Email:*** mikestrickland@earthlink.net

VERNON G. SNYDER, III, born Greensboro, North Carolina, March 23, 1952; admitted to bar, 1980, North Carolina. *Education:* University of North Carolina (A.B., 1977); Campbell University (J.D., cum laude, 1980). Phi Kappa Phi; Phi Alpha Delta. Recipient, American Jurisprudence Award in Criminal Law, Agency and Partnership. Member, Board of Editors, Campbell Law Review, 1978-1980. *Member:* Pitt County and North Carolina Bar Associations; North Carolina State Bar. ***PRACTICE AREAS:*** Personal Injury; Litigation; Real Estate; Trusts and Estates; Business Law. ***Email:*** vernsnyder@earthlink.net

EMMA STALLINGS HOLSCHER, born Washington, North Carolina, October 7, 1969; admitted to bar, 1997, North Carolina. *Education:* University of North Carolina at Chapel Hill (B.A., 1991); Campbell University School of Law (J.D., magna cum laude, 1997). Phi Kappa Phi. Vice Justice, Phi Alpha Delta, 1996-1997. Order of Barristers. Member, Campbell Law Review, 1995-1997. *Member:* Pitt County and North Carolina Bar Associations; North Carolina State Bar. ***PRACTICE AREAS:*** Trusts and Estates; Contested Wills; Real Estate; Personal Injury; Wills. ***Email:*** emmaholscher@earthlink.net

REPRESENTATIVE CLIENTS: Wachovia Bank, N.A.; Bank of America; The St. Paul Insurance Co.; The Daily Reflector, Inc.; Nationwide Mutual Insurance Co.; Greenbrier Realty Co., Inc.; Harleysville Mutual Insurance Co.; Garris-Evans Lumber Company, Inc.; Ironwood Development, Inc.; Optometric Eye Care Center; Pitt County Memorial Hospital; Lawyers Title Insurance Corp.; Chicago Title Insurance Co.
APPROVED ATTORNEYS FOR: Lawyers Title Insurance Corp.; Investors Title Insurance Co.; Statewide Insurance Company; Chicago Title Insurance Co.
REFERENCES: Wachovia Bank, N.A.; Bank of America; Branch Banking and Trust Company; First Citizens Bank & Trust Co.

L. ALLEN HAHN, P.A.

Established in 1973
504-A RED BANKS ROAD
DRAWER 665
GREENVILLE, NORTH CAROLINA 27835-0665
Telephone: 252-756-6970
Fax: 252-756-2837
Email: packages@earthlink.net
URL: http://www.lallenhahn.com

Real Property, Real Estate, Corporations, Collections, Wills and Estates Law, Loan Closings.

L. ALLEN HAHN, born Wilmington, North Carolina, September 2, 1948; admitted to bar, 1973, North Carolina and U.S. District Court, Eastern District of North Carolina. *Education:* University of North Carolina (A.B., 1970); University of Tennessee (J.D., 1973). Phi Alpha Delta. *Member:* Pitt County (Treasurer, 1973-1975), North Carolina and American Bar Associations; North Carolina State Bar. ***Email:*** packages@earthlink.net

WILLIAM F. HILL, P.A.

Established in 1998
2470 EMERALD PLACE DRIVE
SUITE D
GREENVILLE, NORTH CAROLINA 27834
Telephone: 252-355-4277
Fax: 252-355-2797
Email: billhill@williamfhillpa.com
URL: http://www.williamfhillpalaw.com

Creditor's Rights, Collections, Small Business, Buying or Selling a Business, Employment Contracts, General Business, Contracts, Starting a Business, Corporate Law, Family Law, Divorce.

FIRM PROFILE: William F. Hill has over twenty (20) years of legal experience representing banks, finance companies, businesses and individuals in complex commercial and consumer bankruptcies. He also has extensive experience with commercial foreclosures and all aspects of state court collections. The firm has helped clients form and grow many small businesses. Mr. Hill also handles various types of business and domestic litigation.

WILLIAM F. HILL, born Harrisburg, Pennsylvania, February 28, 1958; admitted to bar, 1984, North Carolina. *Education:* Washington and Lee University (B.A., magna cum laude, 1980); University of Virginia (J.D., 1983). Phi Beta Kappa. *Member:* North Carolina State Bar (Bankruptcy Section). ***LANGUAGES:*** English. ***PRACTICE AREAS:*** Bankruptcy; Banks and Banking; Business Law; Collections; Commercial Real Estate; Construction Law; Debtor and Creditor; Family Law; Labor and Employment; Litigation; Real Estate; Wills. ***Email:*** billhill@williamfhillpa.com

HOPF & HIGLEY, P.A.

1694 EAST ARLINGTON BOULEVARD, SUITE E
GREENVILLE, NORTH CAROLINA 27858
Telephone: 252-756-1883
Fax: 252-756-1797
URL: http://www.hopfhigley.com

Environmental, Toxic Tort, Plaintiffs' Personal Injury and other Complex Litigation in all State and Federal Courts.

JAMES F. HOPF, born U.S. Naval Hospital, Taipei, Taiwan, December 21, 1961; admitted to bar, 1986, North Carolina, U.S. District Court, Eastern and Middle Districts of North Carolina and U.S. Court of Appeals, Fourth Circuit. *Education:* Campbell University (B.A., summa cum laude, 1983); University of North Carolina (J.D., 1986). Phi Kappa Phi; Omicron Delta Kappa. Member, Order of the Barristers. Member, International Law Moot Court Team, 1984-1985. Holderness Moot Court Bench, Chief Justice, 1985-1986. *Member:* Pitt County, North Carolina (Member, Environmental and Natural Resources Law Section, 1996—; Executive Council, 1996-1999.) and American Bar Associations; North Carolina State Bar; North Carolina Academy of Trial Lawyers (Sustaining Patron); The Association of Trial Lawyers of America (Sustaining Member; Toxic, Environmental and Pharmaceutical Torts Section, 1996—); Court Certified Mediator. ***PRACTICE AREAS:*** Groundwater Contamination; Hazardous Waste; Underground Storage Tanks; Toxic Torts; Mediation. ***Email:*** jim@hopfhigley.com

DONALD S. HIGLEY, II, born Hillsdale, Michigan, December 10, 1963; admitted to bar, 1994, North Carolina and U.S. District Court, Middle and Eastern Districts of North Carolina; 1998, U.S. Court of Appeals, Fourth Circuit; 2001, U.S. Tax Court. *Education:* University of North Carolina at Chapel Hill (B.A., 1990); Campbell University (J.D., cum laude, 1994). Phi Kappa Phi; Omicron Delta Kappa. John J. Broderick Scholar. Editor in Chief, Campbell Law Review, 1993-1994. Court Certified Mediator. *Member:* Pitt County (President, 2003-2004), North Carolina and American Bar Associations; The Association of Trial Lawyers of America; North Carolina Academy of Trial Lawyers. ***PRACTICE AREAS:*** Plaintiffs' Personal Injury; Complex Litigation; Environmental Litigation; Trial Practice; Construction Litigation. ***Email:*** don@hopfhigley.com

---

CHARLES C. EDWARDS, JR., born Washington, North Carolina, January 8, 1978; admitted to bar, 2004, North Carolina, U.S. District Court, Eastern District of North Carolina. *Education:* North Carolina State University (B.S., magna cum laude, 2001); Campbell University (J.D., 2004). Member, International Law Moot Court Team, 2002-2003. National Negotiation Team, 2003-2004. *Member:* Pitt County, North Carolina and American Bar Associations; North Carolina State Bar; North Carolina Academy of Trial Lawyers; The

(This Listing Continued)

Association of Trial Lawyers of America. **PRACTICE AREAS:** Plaintiffs' Personal Injury; Complex Litigation; Environmental; Toxic Torts; Collections; General Practice. **Email:** chip@hopfhigley.com

KELLUM LAW FIRM

205 S.W. GREENVILLE BOULEVARD
P.O. BOX 20727
GREENVILLE, NORTH CAROLINA 27858
Telephone: 252-353-4100
Fax: 252-353-8754
Email: ckeenhold@kellumlawfirm.com
URL: http://www.lawyers.com/kellumlawfirm

State and Federal Civil Trial Practice, Personal Injury Law, Wrongful Death, Workers' Compensation, Social Security, Defective Products, Mass Torts and Insurance Law.

(For complete biographical data on all personnel, see Professional Biographies at New Bern)

The LeonLaw Firm

Established in 2005
P.O. BOX 20338
GREENVILLE, NORTH CAROLINA 27858
Telephone: 252-830-5366
Email: maleon@leonlaw.org
URL: http://www.leonlaw.org

Employment Law, Personal Injury, Workers Compensation, Contracts.

FIRM PROFILE: The Leon Law Firm serves employees and small businesses seeking equity in their work places, as well as individuals injured in work place and motor vehicle accidents.

MEMBER OF FIRM

MARY-ANN LEON, admitted to bar, 1999, North Carolina; 2000, U.S. District Court, Eastern and Middle Districts of North Carolina. *Education:* University of North Carolina at Chapel Hill (J.D., 1999); University of Kansas (Ph.D., 1986); University of New Mexico (M.A., 1980); California State University, Fullerton (B.A., 1979);. *Member:* North Carolina Bar Association; Association of Trial Lawyers of America; North Carolina Academy of Trial Lawyers; North Carolina Association of Women Attorneys; National Employment Lawyers Association. **PRACTICE AREAS:** Employment Law (35%); Employment Litigation; Employment Discrimination; Fair Employment Practices; Personnel Policies; Covenants Not To Compete; Retaliatory Discharge; Sexual Harassment; Whistleblower Litigation; Wrongful Termination; Wage and Hour Law; Personal Injury (35%); Automobile Accidents and Injuries; Workers Compensation (30%). **Email:** maleon@leonlaw.org

OWENS & NELSON, P.L.L.C.

Established in 1963
201 WEST THIRD STREET
P.O. BOX 36
GREENVILLE, NORTH CAROLINA 27834
Telephone: 252-757-3300
Fax: 252-758-9777
URL: http://www.owensrouseandnelson.com

General Civil and Criminal Trial Practice before all State and Federal Courts. Alternative Dispute Resolution, Civil Practice, Commercial Real Estate, Criminal Law, Domestic Relations, DUI and DWI Law, Eminent Domain, Estates, Family Law, Fraud and Deceit, General Practice, Guardianship Law, Insurance, Litigation, Medical Malpractice, Mortgages, Negligence, Personal Injury, Premises Liability, Probate, Professional Liability, Property Law, Real Estate, Torts, Traffic, Trusts and Estates, Unfair Competition, White Collar Crime, Wills and Workers Compensation Law.

FIRM PROFILE: Owens & Nelson, P.L.L.C. and its attorneys have practiced law in Greenville and the state and federal courts of eastern North Carolina since 1963. It is a full service law firm which has been privileged to represent individuals as well as domestic and foreign companies and public entities in all types of legal matters. The firm emphasizes prompt, efficient and personal service for its clients. The firm is unique in combining a strong criminal defense practice while meeting the needs of its clients relative to business and personal affairs, all levels of civil litigation, as well as commercial and residential real estate matters.

MEMBERS OF FIRM

MARK W. OWENS, JR., born Greene County, North Carolina, March 6, 1937; admitted to bar, 1963, North Carolina. *Education:* University of North Carolina (A.B., 1960); Wake Forest College (LL.B., 1963). Phi Alpha Delta. Chairman, Pitt County Board of County Commissioners; Pitt County Board of Education, Chairman (1970-1987), All-State School Board (1986); North Carolina Bar Association General Practice Hall of Fame (2002). *Member:* Pitt County, Third Judicial District, North Carolina and American Bar Associations; The North Carolina State Bar (Councilor, Third Judicial District); North Carolina Academy of Trial Lawyers. **PRACTICE AREAS:** Civil Trials; Personal Injury Law; Estates; Traffic DUI/DWI; Criminal Law.

JAMES A. NELSON, JR., born Bethel, North Carolina, December 10, 1954; admitted to bar, 1980, North Carolina and U.S. District Court, Eastern District of North Carolina; 1983, U.S. Supreme Court. *Education:* University of North Carolina at Chapel Hill, Morehead Scholar (B.A., 1977); Campbell University School of Law (J.D., 1980). Campbell Law Observer Staff, Delta Theta Phi. Public Guardian, Pitt County, 1985—. Trustee, Pitt Community College. *Member:* Pitt County, Third Judicial District, North Carolina (Real Property Section) and American Bar Associations; The North Carolina State Bar; North Carolina Academy of Trial Lawyers. **PRACTICE AREAS:** Real Estate Law; Personal Injury Law; Estates.

MARK W. OWENS, III, born Wilson, North Carolina, July 20, 1961; admitted to bar, 1986, North Carolina. *Education:* University of North Carolina (B.A., 1983); Wake Forest University (J.D., 1986). Phi Delta Phi. Legal Assistant to Justice John Webb, N. C. Supreme Court. *Member:* Pitt County, Third Judicial District and North Carolina Bar Associations; North Carolina State Bar; North Carolina Academy of Trial Lawyers. **PRACTICE AREAS:** Personal Injury Law; Civil Trials; Criminal Law; Real Estate Law; Estates.

JOSEPH B. DUPREE, II, born Johnson County, North Carolina, October 2, 1968; admitted to bar, 1993, North Carolina. *Education:* University of North Carolina at Chapel Hill (A.B., 1990); Campbell University (J.D., 1993). Phi Alpha Delta. Member, Moot Court. *Member:* Pitt County, North Carolina and American Bar Associations; North Carolina State Bar; Criminal Defense Bar; North Carolina Academy of Trial Lawyers; Third Judicial District. **PRACTICE AREAS:** Personal Injury Law; Civil Trial; Criminal Law; Real Estate Law; Traffic DUI/DWI; Wills; Estate Planning; Real Property; Family Law; Domestic Relations; Contracts; Negotiations.

REPRESENTATIVE CLIENTS: First Citizens Bank, Greenville, North Carolina; N.C. Department of Transportation; Blount Petroleum Corporation; Farmville Housing Authority; Tucker Farms, Inc.; State Employees Credit Union; Bank of America.
APPROVED ATTORNEYS FOR: Lawyers Title Insurance Corp.; Federal Land Bank of Columbia; Investors Title Insurance; Chicago Title Insurance Company; First Title Insurance Company; Farmers Home Administration; Commonwealth Land Title.
REFERENCE: First Citizens Bank, Greenville, North Carolina.

THE ROBINSON LAW FIRM, P.A.

1510 EAST ARLINGTON BOULEVARD
GREENVILLE, NORTH CAROLINA 27858
Telephone: 252-758-4100
Fax: 252-758-0876
Email: contactus@therobinsonlawfirm.com
URL: http://www.therobinsonlawfirm.com

Criminal Law, Driving While Intoxicated, Alcohol Violations, Controlled Substance Violations.

FIRM PROFILE: The Robinson Law Firm, P.A. concentrates its practice in representing those persons/entities charged with various Alcohol, Drug and Narcotic Offenses.

LESLIE S. ROBINSON, born Greenville, North Carolina, April 10, 1961; admitted to bar, 1986, North Carolina. *Education:* East Carolina University (B.S., 1983); Campbell University (J.D., 1986). Omicron Delta Kappa; Phi Alpha Delta; Order of the Barristers; 1985 Appellate Advocacy Competitor. American Jurisprudence Award, Campbell Law Review. Author, Continuing Legal Education Publications: Advanced Issues for a State District Court Practice: A Checklist Seminar DWI General Update (North Carolina Bar Association, November 1997); A Checklist Seminar II: DWI General Update: Cross-Examination Points (North Carolina Bar Association, November 1999); DWI: Attacking the State's Case through Motions (Academy of Trial Lawyers, January 2000); Hot Issues in DWI Defense (Academy of Trial Lawyers, January 2000); How to Successfully Defend a DWI Case: DWI Checklist Update (North Carolina Bar Association, November 2000); Staying on Top of Your Game: Challenging Blood Tests in DWI Cases (North Carolina Bar Association, June 2001); DWI General Update/Cross Examination: The Sequel Checklist Seminar III (North Carolina Bar Association, October 2001); Criminal Justice Checklist IV: Hot Topics and Old Standbys (North Carolina Bar Association, November 2004); Professionalism From Your Bar Councilor's Perspective (Chief Justice: Commission on Professionalism, December 2004). Member: Pitt County Substance Abuse Coalition; Coastal Conservation Association (East Carolina Chapter); East Carolina University Pirate Club (Pitt County Chapter, Pirate Club Representative); Fellowship of Christian Athletes (Board Member). National Wild Turkey Federation; North Carolina Waterfowl Association; North Carolina Wildlife Commission (Lifetime Licensee). Oakmont Baptist Church Member, Usher. Charter Member, The Mattamuskeet Foundation, Inc. *Member:* Pitt County (Former President, Vice President), North Carolina (Member, Criminal Justice Section Committee Member, 1999-2002 and 2005-2008) and American (Member, Criminal Justice Section) Bar Associations; North Carolina State Bar (Councilor, Three-A Judicial District, 2002—; Grievance Committee, 2002—; Authorized Practice Committee, 2002-2004; Client Assistance Committee, 2005); Three-A Judicial District Bar (Vice President, 1995-1996, President, 1996-1997), North Carolina Academy of Trial Lawyers (Member, Criminal Law Section; DWI Task Force Committee Member); The Association of Trial Lawyers of America; Pitt County Academy of Criminal Defense Trial Lawyers (Founding Member; Secretary/Treasurer, 1990-1991; Vice President, 1991-1992; President, 1992-1993); National Association of Criminal Defense Lawyers); Eastern North Carolina Inn of Court. **REPORTED CASES:** State v. Bowes, 159 N.C. App 18, 583 S.E. 2d 294 (2003), 596 S.E. 2d 813 (2004); State v. Madry, 140 N.C. App 600, 537 S.E. 2d 827 (2000); State v. Morris, 103 N.C. App 246, 405 S.E. 2d 351 (1991). **PRACTICE AREAS:** Criminal Law; Traffic Violations; Misdemeanors; Felonies; Wildlife Law; White Collar Crime; Drugs and Narcotics; Alcohol Violations; Controlled Substances Violations; Driving While Intoxicated.

LAW OFFICES OF ROBERT D. ROUSE, III PLLC

610 LYNNDALE COURT, SUITE D.
GREENVILLE, NORTH CAROLINA 27858
Telephone: 252-752-4200
Fax: 252-752-9200
URL: http://www.rrouselaw.com

Personal Injury, Property Damage, Premises Liability, Auto Accidents, Bus Accidents, Motorcycle Accidents, Truck and Tractor-Trailer Collisions, Wrongful Death Claims, Dog Bites, Head and Spinal Injuries, Civil Litigation, Medical Malpractice, Nursing Home Abuse/Negligence, Bad Faith, Unfair Competition.

FIRM PROFILE: A Tradition of Providing Legal Advice and Representation Since 1973.

(This Listing Continued)

LAW OFFICES OF ROBERT D. ROUSE, III PLLC, Greenville—Continued

ROBERT D. ROUSE, III, admitted to bar, 1973, North Carolina; 1994, U.S. District Court, Eastern District of North Carolina. *Education:* University of North Carolina (A.B., 1969; J.D., 1973). Delta Theta Phi. Certified Superior Court Mediator. *Member:* Pitt County, Third Judicial District, North Carolina Bar Associations; North Carolina State Bar; North Carolina Academy of Trial Lawyers. ***PRACTICE AREAS:*** Personal Injury; Premises Liability; Automobile Accidents and Injuries; Wrongful Death; Dog Bites; Head Injury; Spinal Injury; Civil Litigation; Medical Malpractice; Nursing Home Abuse and Neglect.

SUMRELL, SUGG, CARMICHAEL, HICKS & HART, P.A.

GREENVILLE, NORTH CAROLINA

(See New Bern)

General Civil. Trials and Appeals in all Civil Courts. Wills and Estates, Real Estate, Corporate Law, Financial Transactions, Insurance and Negligence, Employment Law, Municipal Law, Law Enforcement Liability Defense, Health Care Law and Intellectual Property.

WALLACE, MORRIS, BARWICK, LANDIS & STROUD, P.A.

GREENVILLE, NORTH CAROLINA

(See Kinston)

General Civil and Trial Practice in all State and Federal Courts. Aviation, Banking, Corporate Law, Insurance, Personal Injury, Probate, Product Liability, Real Estate and Taxation.

WARD AND SMITH, P.A.

Established in 1895

120 WEST FIRE TOWER ROAD
P.O. BOX 8088
GREENVILLE, NORTH CAROLINA 27835-8088
Telephone: 252-215-4000
Facsimile: 252-215-4077
Email: wardsmith@wardandsmith.com
URL: http://www.wardandsmith.com

New Bern, North Carolina Office: 1001 College Court, P.O. Box 867. Telephone: 252-672-5400. Facsimile: 252-672-5477.

Raleigh, North Carolina Office: Suite 2400, Two Hannover Square, Fayetteville Street Mall, P.O. Box 2091. Telephone: 919-836-4260. Facsimile: 919-836-4277.

Wilmington, North Carolina Office: University Corporate Center, 127 Racine Drive, P.O. Box 7068. Telephone: 910-794-4800. Facsimile: 910-794-4877.

General and Trial Practice. Admiralty Law; Bankruptcy; Banks and Banking; Business Law; Civil Rights; Commercial Law; Construction Law; Contracts; Copyrights; Corporate Law; Debtor and Creditor; Elder Law; Eminent Domain; Employee Benefits; Environmental Law; Family Law including Divorce; Finance; Franchise Law; Government; Government Contracts; Health Care Law; Immigration and Naturalization; Insurance; International Law; International Trade; Investments; Labor and Employment including Discrimination, Sexual Harassment, and Workers' Compensation; Landlord and Tenant; Litigation; Personal Injury including Automobile Accidents, Legal Malpractice and Medical Malpractice; Products Liability; Real Estate; Securities; Taxation; Technology and Science including Internet Law, Trademarks, and Patents; Trusts and Estates including Estate Planning and Wills and Probate; Zoning and Land Use.

FIRM PROFILE: Located in Greenville, New Bern, Raleigh, and Wilmington, we are successor to a practice founded in New Bern, North Carolina in 1895. Our firm has grown to over 60 attorneys and more than 160 support staff members who are committed to quality and responsiveness. We strive to deliver a product that is tailored to our clients' unique needs wherever and whenever the need should arise. Our attorneys may be contacted by either a phone call or a confidential email, in or out of the office and at home. Attorney availability reinforces our commitment to a strong attorney-client relationship and a proactive and preventive approach to our clients' legal issues. Our philosophy is to utilize other attorneys in the firm whose knowledge and expertise allows a more efficient and timely delivery of our clients' legal services. In summary, the collective mission of our attorneys, legal assistants, and administrative staff is to provide our clients with the highest quality legal service at an affordable cost.

W. L. ALLEN, III, admitted to bar, 1992, North Carolina. *Education:* East Carolina University (B.S., 1989); Wake Forest University (J.D., 1992). *Member:* North Carolina and American Bar Associations; North Carolina State Bar; North Carolina Academy of Trial Lawyers. [Captain, JAGC, USAR]. ***PRACTICE AREAS:*** Family Law; Litigation; Personal Injury; Wrongful Death; Immigration. ***Email:*** wla@wardandsmith.com

DEBORAH B. ANDREWS, admitted to bar, 1997, North Carolina; 1999, Georgia. *Education:* North Carolina State University (B.A., with honors, 1989); University of North Carolina (J.D., 1997); Georgetown University (LL.M., Taxation, 2003). Certified Public Accountant, North Carolina, 1993. *Member:* North Carolina and American Bar Associations; North Carolina State Bar; State Bar of Georgia; North Carolina Association of Certified Public Accountants. ***PRACTICE AREAS:*** Business Law; Tax Law. ***Email:*** dba@wardandsmith.com

MARY V. CAVANAGH, admitted to bar, 1989, Colorado; 1993, North Carolina. *Education:* Wake Forest University (B.A., summa cum laude, 1986); University of Virginia

(This Listing Continued)

(J.D., 1989). Phi Beta Kappa. *Member:* North Carolina State Bar; Colorado State Bar. ***PRACTICE AREAS:*** Appellate Practice; Litigation; Construction Law; Civil Litigation. ***Email:*** mvc@wardandsmith.com

DONALT J. EGLINTON, admitted to bar, 1982, North Carolina. *Education:* Texas A. & M. University (B.E.D., magna cum laude, 1974); Central Michigan University (M.A., 1980); Wake Forest University (J.D., 1982). Staff Member, 1980-1981 and Research Editor, 1981-1982, Wake Forest Law Review. *Member:* North Carolina and American Bar Associations; North Carolina State Bar; North Carolina Academy of Trial Lawyers; Association of Trial Lawyers of America; American Institute of Architects. ***PRACTICE AREAS:*** Litigation; Business Law; Copyrights; Commercial Law; Contracts; Intellectual Property; Construction Law; Products Liability; Trade Secrets; Trademarks; Unfair Competition; Commercial Litigation; Trusts and Estates Litigation; Dealer/Distributor and Franchising; Environmental; Technology. ***Email:*** dje@wardandsmith.com

A. CHARLES ELLIS, admitted to bar, 1983, North Carolina. *Education:* University of North Carolina (B.A., 1980); Campbell University (J.D., cum laude, 1983). Member, Campbell University Law Review, 1980-1983. Listed in *The Best Lawyers in America. Member:* Pitt County (President, 1990-1991), North Carolina and American Bar Associations; North Carolina State Bar; North Carolina Academy of Trial Lawyers; Association of Trial Lawyers of America. ***PRACTICE AREAS:*** Personal Injury; Wrongful Death; Litigation; Insurance; Medical Malpractice; Products Liability. ***Email:*** ace@wardandsmith.com

E. BRADLEY EVANS, admitted to bar, 2002, North Carolina. *Education:* Woodberry Forest School, 1994; University of Westminster; Wake Forest University (B.A., cum laude, 1998; J.D., 2002). Order of the Coif. Member, Wake Forest Law Review. Law Clerk to the Honorable Malcolm J. Howard, U.S. District Judge, Eastern District of North Carolina, 2002-2003. *Member:* North Carolina and American Bar Associations; North Carolina State Bar. ***PRACTICE AREAS:*** Litigation. ***Email:*** ebe@wardandsmith.com

LYNWOOD P. EVANS, admitted to bar, 1999, North Carolina. *Education:* University of North Carolina (B.S., Business Administration, 1996); Campbell University (J.D., cum laude, 1999). Member, 1996-1999, Business Editor, 1998-1999, Campbell Law Review. *Member:* North Carolina and American Bar Associations; North Carolina State Bar; Association of Trial Lawyers of America; North Carolina Academy of Trial Lawyers. ***PRACTICE AREAS:*** Litigation; Insurance; Medical Malpractice; Personal Injury; Wrongful Death; Professional Liability; Business Litigation. ***Email:*** lpe@wardandsmith.com

PAUL A. FANNING, admitted to bar, 1998, North Carolina. *Education:* University of North Carolina-Asheville (B.A., 1993); Wake Forest University (J.D., 1998). *Member:* North Carolina Bar Association; North Carolina State Bar. ***PRACTICE AREAS:*** Bankruptcy; Commercial Law; Debtor and Creditor. ***Email:*** paf@wardandsmith.com

J. MICHAEL FIELDS, admitted to bar, 1991, North Carolina. *Education:* University of North Carolina (B.S., 1988; J.D., with honors, 1991). Staff Member, N.C. Journal of International Law and Commercial Regulation, 1989-1991. *Member:* North Carolina Bar Association (Member, Bankruptcy Section Council, 1997-1999); North Carolina State Bar; American Bankruptcy Institute. ***PRACTICE AREAS:*** Business; Health Care; Real Estate - Community Associations; Creditors' Rights; Debtor and Creditor; Contracts; Bankruptcy. ***Email:*** jmf@wardandsmith.com

MICHAEL P. FLANAGAN, admitted to bar, 1971, Florida; 1972, North Carolina. *Education:* University of North Carolina (A.B., 1968; J.D., 1971). Member, National Moot Court Team; Holderness Moot Court Bench, 1970-1971. Listed in *The Best Lawyers in America.. Member:* North Carolina (Member, Bankruptcy Section Council, 1979-1984; Vice Chairman, 1987-1988; Chairman, 1988-1989, Bankruptcy Section) and American Bar Associations; North Carolina State Bar; The Florida Bar; American Bankruptcy Institute. ***PRACTICE AREAS:*** Creditors' Rights; Debtor and Creditor; Bankruptcy; Commercial Law. ***Email:*** mpf@wardandsmith.com

MERRILL G. JONES II, admitted to bar, 1997, North Carolina. *Education:* Wake Forest University (B.S., 1990); East Carolina University (M.B.A., 1993); Wake Forest University (J.D., 1997). Member, Moot Court Board, 1995-1997. Articles Editor, 1996-1997, Staff Member, 1995-1996, Wake Forest Law Review. Certified Public Accountant, North Carolina, 1994. *Member:* North Carolina and American Bar Associations; North Carolina State Bar; North Carolina Association of Certified Public Accountants; East Carolina Estate Planning Council. ***PRACTICE AREAS:*** Business Law; Construction Law; Health Care; Contracts; Corporate Law; Mergers and Acquisitions; Tax Law. ***Email:*** mgj@wardandsmith.com

KATHERINE EVANS LEWIS, admitted to bar, 1993, Tennessee; 1994, Arkansas; 1999, North Carolina. *Education:* Arkansas State University (B.S., magna cum laude, 1989); University of Mississippi (J.D., magna cum laude, 1993). Associate Articles Editor, 1992-1993 and Staff Member, 1991-1992, Mississippi Law Journal. *Member:* North Carolina, Arkansas and American Bar Associations; North Carolina State Bar. ***PRACTICE AREAS:*** Creditors' Rights; Debtor and Creditor; Real Estate; Bankruptcy. ***Email:*** kel@wardandsmith.com

JOHN M. MARTIN, admitted to bar, 1975, North Carolina. *Education:* North Carolina State University (B.A., with high honors, 1972); Wake Forest University (J.D., 1975). Associate Editor, Wake Forest Law Review, 1974-1975. Listed in *The Best Lawyers in America. Member:* North Carolina and American Bar Associations; North Carolina State Bar; The Association of Trial Lawyers of America; North Carolina Academy of Trial Lawyers. ***PRACTICE AREAS:*** Business Litigation; Litigation; Family Law; Personal Injury; Wrongful Death; Professional Liability. ***Email:*** jmm@wardandsmith.com

LANCE P. MARTIN, admitted to bar, 1995, Louisiana; 2000, North Carolina. *Education:* Spring Hill College (B.S., summa cum laude, 1992); Tulane University (J.D., magna cum laude, 1995). Order of the Coif. *Member:* North Carolina and American Bar Associations; North Carolina State Bar. ***PRACTICE AREAS:*** Creditors' Rights; Debtor and Creditor; Bankruptcy; Commercial Law; Litigation. ***Email:*** lpm@wardandsmith.com

GREGORY T. PEACOCK, admitted to bar, 1996, North Carolina. *Education:* University of North Carolina (B.S, Business Administration, 1990); Wake Forest University (J.D., 1996). Member, Moot Court Board, 1994-1996. Member, Wake Forest Law Review, 1994-1996. *Member:* North Carolina Bar Association; North Carolina State Bar; National Academy of Elder Law Attorneys; East Carolina Estate Planning Council. (Board Certified

(This Listing Continued)

Specialist in Estate Planning and Probate Law, North Carolina State Board of Legal Specialization). ***PRACTICE AREAS:*** Trusts and Estates; Wills and Probate; Taxation; Elder Law. ***Email:*** gtp@wardandsmith.com

GARY J. RICKNER, admitted to bar, 1974, Indiana; 1998, North Carolina. *Education:* Taylor University (B.A., 1971); Cumberland School of Law of Samford University (J.D., cum laude, 1974). Associate Editor, Cumberland-Samford Law Review, 1972-1974. Listed in *The Best Lawyers in America.* Instructor, National Institute for Trial Advocacy. *Member:* North Carolina, Indiana State and American Bar Associations; North Carolina State Bar; Defense Research Institute; American College of Trial Lawyers. ***PRACTICE AREAS:*** Business Litigation; Commercial Litigation; Financial Institutions; Civil Litigation; Litigation; Products Liability; Banking Law. ***Email:*** gjr@wardandsmith.com

STANLEY M. SAMS, admitted to bar, 1979, North Carolina. *Education:* East Carolina University (B.S., Business Administration, 1976); University of North Carolina (J.D., 1979). Member, Holderness Moot Court Bench. Lecturer, in Business Law, East Carolina University, 1979-1991. *Member:* North Carolina and American Bar Associations; North Carolina State Bar; East Carolina Estate Planning Council. ***PRACTICE AREAS:*** Real Estate; Trusts and Estates; Wills and Probate; Business Law. ***Email:*** sms@wardandsmith.com

J. TROY SMITH, JR., admitted to bar, 1967, North Carolina; 1979, U.S. Supreme Court; 1983, U.S. Tax Court. *Education:* University of North Carolina (A.B., 1965; J.D., with highest honors, 1967). Order of the Coif. Editor-in-Chief, North Carolina Law Review, 1966-1967. Recipient, Chief Justice Walter Clark Award. Member, General Statutes Commission Code Committee, 1978-1981. Listed in *Best Lawyers in America* . *Member:* North Carolina Bar Association (Member, Board of Governors, 1973-1976; Chairman, Real Property Committee, 1973-1979; Chairman, Special Committee on Recodification of General Statutes, 1976-1981; General Practice Hall of Fame); North Carolina State Bar; American College of Real Estate Lawyers. ***PRACTICE AREAS:*** Business Law; Corporate Law; Health Care Law. ***Email:*** jts@wardandsmith.com

H. L. STEPHENSON, III, admitted to bar, 1982, North Carolina. *Education:* University of North Carolina (B.A., 1979; J.D., 1982); College of William & Mary (LL.M., Taxation, 1983). *Member:* North Carolina (Member, Tax Section Council, 1986-1988, 1993-1995) and American Bar Associations; North Carolina State Bar; East Carolina Estate Planning Council; North Carolina Economic Developers Association. ***PRACTICE AREAS:*** Business Law; Tax Law; Mergers and Acquisitions; Trusts and Estates. ***Email:*** hls@wardandsmith.com

BENJAMIN E. F. B. WALLER, admitted to bar, 1998, Alabama; 2001, North Carolina. *Education:* Goucher College (B.A., with honors, 1992); Washington University (M.A., 1995); Duke University (J.D., 1998). *Member:* North Carolina State Bar; Alabama State Bar; North Carolina and American Bar Associations; North Carolina Academy of Trial Lawyers. ***PRACTICE AREAS:*** Creditors' Rights; Debtor and Creditor; Bankruptcy; Commercial Law; Business Litigation; Commercial Litigation. ***Email:*** bew@wardandsmith.com

KENNETH R. WOOTEN, admitted to bar, 1979, North Carolina. *Education:* North Carolina State University (B.A., with high honors, 1976); University of North Carolina (J.D., with honors, 1979). Order of the Coif. Staff Member, North Carolina Law Review, 1977-1978. Member, Invitational Moot Court Team, Holderness Moot Court Bench, 1978-1979. Research Assistant to Justice J. William Copeland, North Carolina Supreme Court, 1979-1980. *Member:* North Carolina (Construction Law Section, Chair, 1992-1993, Vice Chair, 1991-1992, Secretary, 1988-1991) and American (Member, Litigation Section) Bar Associations; North Carolina State Bar; North Carolina Association of Defense Attorneys; Defense Research Institute; Christian Legal Society. ***PRACTICE AREAS:*** Construction Law; Litigation; Housing Authority Law; Commercial Law; Insurance. ***Email:*** krw@wardandsmith.com

REPRESENTATIVE CLIENTS: Amital Spinning Corp.; Atlantic Coast Contracting; Atlantic States Bank; Barnhill Contracting Company; Cape Fear Community College; Central Carolina Bank and Trust Co.; Chubb Insurance; City of Havelock; Craven Community College; Daedong- USA, Inc.; East Carolina Bank; Eastern Carolina Regional Housing Authority; Eastern Radiologists, Inc.; First-Citizens Bank & Trust Company; First Flight Federal Credit Union; Fountain Powerboats, Inc.; Hatteras Yachts; Ironstone Bank; Janus Development Group; Mountainbank Financial Corp.; NC State Firemen's Association; Neuse Regional Water & Sewer; Physicians East, P.A.; Potash Corp.; Southern Banc & Trust Co.; State of North Carolina; Weyerhaeuser Co.; Wilmington Cardiology, PLLC.

(For complete biographical data on all personnel, see professional biographies at, New Bern, North Carolina).

RALPH G. WILLEY, P.A.

GREENVILLE, NORTH CAROLINA

(See Rocky Mount)

Workers Compensation, Board Certified, Personal Injury, Civil and Criminal Trial Practice in all Courts, Traffic, Mediation, Arbitration.

LAW OFFICES OF
KEITH A. WILLIAMS, P.A.

Established in 1998

321 SOUTH EVANS STREET, SUITE 103
P.O. BOX 1965
GREENVILLE, NORTH CAROLINA 27835-1965
Telephone: 252-931-9362
Fax: 252-830-5155
Email: kwlaw@earthlink.net
URL: http://www.lawyers.com/keithwilliams

Criminal and Civil Litigation in Federal and State Courts.

KEITH ALAN WILLIAMS, born Camden, New Jersey, April 30, 1967; admitted to bar, 1992, North Carolina; 1994, U.S. District Court, Eastern District of North Carolina;

(This Listing Continued)

1996, U.S. Court of Appeals, Fourth Circuit; 2001, U.S. Supreme Court. *Education:* Messiah College (B.A., Political Science, 1989); University of North Carolina, Chapel Hill (J.D., 1992). Law Clerk for U.S. District Judge Malcom J. Howard, Eastern District of North Carolina, 1992-1994. Assistant District Attorney, 1994-1996. *Member:* North Carolina State Bar; North Carolina Bar Association; National Association of Criminal Defense Lawyers; Christian Legal Society; North Carolina Academy of Trial Lawyers. (Board Certified Specialist in Federal and State Criminal Law, North Carolina State Board of Legal Specialization). ***REPORTED CASES:*** State v. Bowes, 159 N.C. App. 18 (2003); State v. Hilbert, 145 N.C. App. 440 (2001). ***PRACTICE AREAS:*** Federal Criminal Law; Criminal Law. ***Email:*** kwlaw@earthlink.net

HUX, LIVERMON & ARMSTRONG, L.L.P.

HALIFAX, NORTH CAROLINA

(See Enfield)

General Practice. Criminal including DWI, Traffic Offenses, and Civil Trials in all Courts. Wills and Probate, Trusts and Estates, Corporation, Insurance and Real Property Law, Personal Injury, Automobile Accidents, Family Law.

LAW OFFICE OF
FRANKLIN L. JONES, JR.

462 HIGHWAY 301 SOUTH
P.O. BOX 556
HALIFAX, NORTH CAROLINA 27839
Telephone: 252-583-1515
Fax: 252-583-1818
Email: fjoneslaw@coastalnet.com
URL: http://www.franklinljones.com

Criminal Defense, Personal Injury, Workers Compensation.

FRANKLIN L. JONES, JR., born Roanoke Rapids/Halifax, North Carolina, March 1, 1966; admitted to bar, 1995, North Carolina. *Education:* University of North Carolina at Chapel Hill (B.S., 1990); Campbell University, School of Law (J.D., 1995). *Member:* North Carolina State Bar. ***PRACTICE AREAS:*** Criminal Defense; Personal Injury; Workers Compensation.

MOSELEY, ELLIOTT & DICKENS, L.L.P.

HALIFAX, NORTH CAROLINA

(See Roanoke Rapids)

Real Estate, Probate, Criminal Law, Misdemeanors, Traffic Violations, Domestic Relations, Family Law, Municipal Corporations, Corporate Law, Civil Litigation.

BRUMBAUGH, MU & KING, P.A.

Established in 1978

404 EAST MAIN STREET
HAVELOCK, NORTH CAROLINA 28532
Telephone: 252-447-4445
URL: http://www.bmklaw.net

Practice Limited to Injury Cases. Automobile, Wrongful Death, Medical Malpractice, Workers' Compensation, Products Liability and Social Security Claims.

(For complete biographical data on all personnel, see professional biographies, Jacksonville, North Carolina)

MILLS & WILLEY

HAVELOCK, NORTH CAROLINA

(See New Bern)

Accident, Personal Injury Law, Workers Compensation, Criminal Law, General Civil and Criminal Litigation in State and Federal Courts.

STUBBS & PERDUE, P.A.

HAVELOCK, NORTH CAROLINA

(See New Bern)

General Practice in all Courts. Probate, Real Estate, Personal Injury, Bankruptcy Reorganization, Domestic Relations, Corporation and Criminal Law, Environmental Law, Toxic Torts.

SUMRELL, SUGG, CARMICHAEL, HICKS & HART, P.A.

HAVELOCK, NORTH CAROLINA

(See New Bern)

General Civil. Trials and Appeals in all Civil Courts. Wills and Estates, Real Estate, Corporate Law, Financial Transactions, Insurance and Negligence, Employment Law, Municipal Law, Law Enforcement Liability Defense, Health Care Law and Intellectual Property.

BEVIN W. WALL

HAVELOCK, NORTH CAROLINA

(See Newport)

Bankruptcy, Real Estate, Traffic, DWI, Juvenile.

LARRY J. FORD
ATTORNEY AT LAW

46 CHURCH STREET, SUITE 22
P.O. BOX 750
HAYESVILLE, NORTH CAROLINA 28904-0750
Telephone: 828-389-3726
Fax: 828-389-3816
Email: fordlaw@usa.net
URL: http://www.lfordlaw.com

Real Estate, Trusts and Estates, Elder Law, Business Law, Corporate Law, Wills & Probate.

LARRY J. FORD, admitted to bar, 1976, North Carolina. *Education:* Western Carolina University (B.A., magna cum laude, 1973); University of North Carolina (J.D., 1976). Albert Ellis Fellowship, 1973-1976. Legal Counsel, Commonwealth Land Title, 1983-1985. General Counsel, Blue Ridge Pharmaceuticals, Inc., 1995-1998. *Member:* North Carolina State Bar. ***PRACTICE AREAS:*** Real Estate; Trusts and Estates; Elder Law; Business Law; Corporate Law; Wills; Probate.

LAW OFFICES OF
MERINDA SWANSON WOODY, P.A.

137 TUSQUITTEE STREET
P.O. BOX 1519
HAYESVILLE, NORTH CAROLINA 28904
Telephone: 828-389-0202
URL: http://www.lawyers.com/woody

Residential and Commercial Real Estate, Buying or Selling a Home or Business, Business Law, Construction Law, Contract Law, Estate Planning, Wills and Probate, Trusts and Estates, Asset Protection.

MERINDA SWANSON WOODY, born Murphy, North Carolina, September 19, 1952; admitted to bar, 1983, North Carolina; 1984, U.S. District Court, Western District of North Carolina; 1986, U.S. Supreme Court; 1988, U.S. Court of Appeals, Fourth Circuit. *Education:* University of North Carolina (B.A., 1973); Campbell University (J.D., 1983).

DAVIS, STURGES & TOMLINSON

HENDERSON, NORTH CAROLINA

(See Louisburg)

General Civil and Criminal Trial Practice in State and Federal Courts. Estate and Probate, Real Estate and Corporation Law. Personal Injury, Automobile Accidents, Truck Accidents, Wrongful Death, Traffic Violations, DWI, Litigation, Land Condemnation.

HARVEY D. JACKSON
ATTORNEY AT LAW

125 N. GARNETT STREET
HENDERSON, NORTH CAROLINA 27536
Telephone: 252-492-7929
Fax: 252-492-4799
Email: hjackson@inet4u.com
URL: http://www.harveyjacksonlaw.com

Worker's Compensation, Personal Injury, Auto Accident and Insurance Claims, Wrongful Death, Traffic Violations.

HARVEY D. JACKSON, born Gastonia, North Carolina, June 5, 1947; admitted to bar, 1978, North Carolina. *Education:* Davidson College (B.A., 1969); University of Chapel Hill (J.D., 1978). ***PRACTICE AREAS:*** Workers Compensation; Personal Injury; Automobile Accidents and Injuries; Wrongful Death; Traffic Violations.

JOHN H. PIKE

HENDERSON, NORTH CAROLINA

(See Oxford)

Traffic Violations, DWI, Criminal Law (all except capital), Family Law, Child Custody, Divorce, Adoptions, Personal Injury, Automobile Accidents, Truck and Motorcycle Accidents, Civil Litigation, Wrongful Death.

STAINBACK & SATTERWHITE

Established in 1979
115 N. GARNETT STREET
P.O. BOX 1820
HENDERSON, NORTH CAROLINA 27536-4637
Telephone: 252-438-4136
FAX: 252-438-6044

General Civil and Criminal Practice. Trials in all Courts. Probate, Real Estate, Corporation, Commercial and School District Law.

(This Listing Continued)

MEMBERS OF FIRM

PAUL J. STAINBACK, born Henderson, North Carolina, May 26, 1949; admitted to bar, 1976, North Carolina and U.S. District Court, Eastern District of North Carolina. *Education:* Wake Forest University (B.A., 1971; J.D., 1974). Phi Delta Phi. Moot Court Board (Justice, 1973-1974). *Member:* Vance County, North Carolina and American Bar Associations; North Carolina State Bar; North Carolina Academy of Trial Lawyers. ***PRACTICE AREAS:*** Criminal Law; Personal Injury; Workman's Compensation. ***Email:*** jstain@stainbacksatterwhite.com

MICHAEL E. SATTERWHITE, born Henderson, North Carolina, August 28, 1952; admitted to bar, 1977, Georgia and North Carolina; 1979, U.S. District Court, Eastern District of North Carolina. *Education:* University of North Carolina (B.A., 1974); Walter F. George School of Law (J.D., 1977). Phi Delta Phi. Member, 1975-1976, Managing Editor, 1976-1977, Mercer Law Review. *Member:* Vance County, North Carolina and American Bar Associations; North Carolina State Bar; North Carolina Academy of Trial Lawyers. ***PRACTICE AREAS:*** Real Estate Law; Probate Law; Traffic Law; Business Law. ***Email:*** msatter@stainbacksatterwhite.com

ASSOCIATE

CAROLINE SLATER BURNETTE, born South Williamson, Kentucky; admitted to bar, 2004, North Carolina. *Education:* Transylvania University (B.A., Philosophy, magna cum laude, 1999)); Norman A. Wiggins School of Law, Campbell University (J.D., 2004). Order of the Barristers. Membership Editor, Campbell Law Review. Moot Court Team. Author, "Making Specimen Cups as Normal as Prom Night," 25 Campbell L. Rev. 71 (2002). *Member:* North Carolina Bar Association. ***PRACTICE AREAS:*** General Practice. ***Email:*** cburnette@stainbacksatterwhite.com

APPROVED ATTORNEYS FOR: Investors Title Insurance Co.; First Title Insurance Co.; Lawyers Title Insurance Co.; United Title Insurance Co.; The Federal Land Bank of Columbia; Rural Housing.
REPRESENTATIVE CLIENTS: First-Citizens Bank & Trust Co.; Vance County ABC Board; Vance County Board of Education; Carolina Cooling and Heating, Inc.; Town of Middleburg.
REFERENCES: First-Citizens Bank & Trust Co.; Branch Banking & Trust Company; RBC Centura Bank; Bank of America, N.A.

ZOLLICOFFER LAW OFFICE

Established in 1881
215 NORTH GARNETT STREET
P.O. DRAWER 19
HENDERSON, NORTH CAROLINA 27536
Telephone: 252-438-4134
Fax: 252-438-2700

General Practice, Litigation Torts, Trials, Personal Injury, Corporation, Insurance Law, Trusts and Estates, Wills, Traffic Citations; Real Estate, Mediation.

MEMBERS OF FIRM

ALLISON C. ZOLLICOFFER (1854-1922)
JERE P. ZOLLICOFFER (1890-1944)
JOHN H. ZOLLICOFFER (1902-1975)
A. AUGUSTUS ZOLLICOFFER, JR. (1924-1991)

JOHN H. ZOLLICOFFER, JR., born Henderson, North Carolina, April 15, 1936; admitted to bar, 1961, North Carolina. *Education:* University of North Carolina (A.B. in History, 1958); Duke University (J.D., 1961). Phi Beta Kappa; Delta Theta Phi. John Motley Morehead Scholar. Member, Board of Editors, Duke Law Journal, 1960-1961. City Attorney, City of Henderson, 1972—. Certified Superior Court Mediator, 1996—. *Member:* Vance County (President, 1974-1975) and North Carolina Bar Associations; The North Carolina State Bar; North Carolina Academy of Trial Lawyers; The Association of Trial Lawyers of America. ***PRACTICE AREAS:*** General Practice; Trusts and Estates; Wills; Civil Litigation; Torts; Corporate Law; Insurance; Personal Injury; Real Estate; Municipal Law; Mediation.

REPRESENTATIVE CLIENTS: City of Henderson; Greystone Concrete Products, Inc.; Owen E. Gupton, Inc.; Rose Oil Co., Inc.; Sanford Milling Co.; Senior Citizens Home, Inc.; Vance Construction Co.
APPROVED ATTORNEYS FOR: Commonwealth Land Title Insurance Co.; First American Title Insurance Co.; First Title Insurance Co.; Investors Title Insurance Co.; Lawyers Title Insurance Corp.; Ticor Title Insurance Co.; Farmers Home Administration; United Title Insurance.

BLANCHARD, NEWMAN & HAYES

112 SOUTH WASHINGTON STREET
P.O. BOX 868
HENDERSONVILLE, NORTH CAROLINA 28793
Telephone: 828-693-0222
Fax: 828-693-0454
Email: bcbattys@brinet.com
URL: http://www.lawyers.com/bbn&j

General Civil Litigation, Family Law, Divorce, Criminal in all State and Federal Courts, Traffic, DWI.

MEMBERS OF FIRM

RONALD G. BLANCHARD, born July 14, 1948; admitted to bar, 1977, North Carolina. *Education:* Wake Forest University (B.A.); North Carolina Central University (J.D., 1976). *Member:* Henderson County and North Carolina Bar Associations; North Carolina State Bar; The Association of Trial Lawyers of America; Criminal Defense Attorneys; North Carolina Academy of Trial Lawyers. [U.S. Army, 1970]. ***LANGUAGES:*** Spanish. ***PRACTICE AREAS:*** General Civil Litigation; Domestic Relations; Family Law; Di-

(This Listing Continued)

vorce; Adoption Law; Child Custody; Child Support; Equitable Distribution; Premarital Agreements; Separation Agreements; Domestic Violence; Criminal Law; Traffic Violations; Driving While Intoxicated. **Email:** battys@brinet.com

GREGORY A. NEWMAN, born Hendersonville, North Carolina, November 25, 1961; admitted to bar, 1989, Ohio; 1995, Tennessee; 2000, North Carolina. *Education:* University of North Carolina at Asheville (B.A., 1986); University of Dayton (J.D., 1989). Assistant Prosecuting Attorney, Ashland County, Ohio, 1991-1995. Assistant Attorney General, Tennessee, 1995-2000. *Member:* Henderson County, North Carolina, Tennessee and Ohio State Bar Associations. ***LANGUAGES:*** Spanish. ***PRACTICE AREAS:*** Criminal Law; Federal Criminal Law; Appellate Practice; Traffic Violations; Driving While Intoxicated; Family Law. ***Email:*** battys@brinet.com

JASON RANDOLPH HAYES, born Winston-Salem, North Carolina, December 25, 1972; admitted to bar, 2001, North Carolina. *Education:* East Carolina University (B.A., Psychology, 1996); Wake Forest University (J.D., 2001). *Member:* Henderson County, North Carolina and American Bar Associations; North Carolina State Bar. ***LANGUAGES:*** Spanish. ***PRACTICE AREAS:*** Criminal Law; Federal Criminal Law; Driving While Intoxicated; Traffic Violations; Juvenile Law; Family Law; Divorce; Child Custody; Child Support; Equitable Distribution; Domestic Violence; Separation Agreements; Personal Injury. ***Email:*** battys@brinet.com

WALTER C. CARPENTER

132 SOUTH MAIN STREET
HENDERSONVILLE, NORTH CAROLINA 28792
Telephone: 628-692-1919
Fax: 628-692-2647

Civil and Criminal Litigation, Traffic Violations, Driving While Intoxicated, Real Estate, Buying and Selling a Home, Commercial Real Estate, Wills, Probate, Estate Planning, Trusts and Estates.

WALTER C. CARPENTER, admitted to bar, 1985, North Carolina. *Education:* Furman University; University of North Carolina, Chapel Hill (B.A., 1980); Mercer University (J.D., cum laude, 1985). Phi Delta Phi.

TIMITHY R. COSGROVE

Established in 1976
100-A CHADWICK SQUARE COURT
HENDERSONVILLE, NORTH CAROLINA 28739
Telephone: 828-696-7993
Facsimile: 828-696-7928
Email: doryyoung@aol.com

Civil and Criminal Litigation in all State and Federal Courts. Real Estate, Probate, Estate Planning, Traffic Matters, DWI, Family Law, Divorce, Equitable Distribution, Adoption, Personal Injury Litigation.

TIMITHY R. COSGROVE, born Helena, Montana, June 9, 1948; admitted to bar, 1975, North Carolina. *Education:* Brown University (A.B., 1971); Wake Forest University (J.D., 1975). Phi Alpha Delta. Member, State of North Carolina Administrative Procedure Act Study Commission, 1980-1981. *Member:* Henderson County Bar Association; North Carolina State Bar; North Carolina Academy of Trial Lawyers. ***PRACTICE AREAS:*** Criminal Law; Driving While Intoxicated; Traffic Violations; Family Law; Divorce; Equitable Distribution; Adoption Law; Civil Litigation; Real Estate; Personal Injury; Litigation.

ROBERT J. DEUTSCH, P.A.

HENDERSONVILLE, NORTH CAROLINA
(See Asheville)

General Civil Trial Practice. Wills and Probate, Business, Family Law, Equitable Distribution, Real Estate, Corporate Law, Zoning, Personal Injury, Products Liability, Wrongful Death, Computer Law.

JACOB C. EHRMANN

HENDERSONVILLE, NORTH CAROLINA
(See Asheville)

Domestic Violence, Family Law, Divorce, Child Custody, Child Support, Entertainment Law, Copyrights, Contracts.

ELKINS & ELKINS

Established in 2000
228 6TH AVENUE EAST, SUITE 1B
HENDERSONVILLE, NORTH CAROLINA 28792
Telephone: 828-692-2205
Fax: 828-692-8469
Email: htelkins@prodigy.net

Bankruptcy, Real Estate, Residential Real Estate, Buying and Selling a Home, Probate, Corporation, Civil Trial Practice, Out of Court Debt Restructuring.

MEMBERS OF FIRM

DON H. ELKINS, born Burlington, North Carolina, January 8, 1939; admitted to bar, 1969, North Carolina. *Education:* Catawba College (A.B., 1962); Wake Forest University

(This Listing Continued)

(J.D., 1969). Phi Alpha Delta. *Member:* North Carolina State Bar; American Bar Association. [1st Lt., USAF, 1962-1965]. ***PRACTICE AREAS:*** Real Estate; Probate; Corporate Law. ***Email:*** htelkins@prodigy.net

H. TRADE ELKINS, born 1974; admitted to bar, 2000, North Carolina and U.S. District Court, Western District of North Carolina. *Education:* Western Carolina University (B.S., 1996; B.A., 1996); Widener University (J.D., cum laude, 2000). Chief Editor, Widener Journal of Public Law. *Member:* North Carolina State Bar; American Bankruptcy Institute. ***PRACTICE AREAS:*** Bankruptcy; Real Estate; Foreclosures; Bankruptcy Chapter 7; Bankruptcy Chapter 11; Bankruptcy Chapter 12; Bankruptcy Chapter 13; General Civil Litigation. ***Email:*** htelkins@prodigy.net

REFERENCES: Chicago Title Insurance Co.; Fidelity National Title Insurance Co.; Hometrust Bank.

MICHAEL C. EUBANKS

HENDERSONVILLE, NORTH CAROLINA
(See Brevard)

Family Law, Divorce, Child Custody, Equitable Distribution, Personal Injury, Wrongful Death, Automobile Accidents, Business, Estate and Real Property Litigation.

FERIKES & BLEYNAT, PLLC

HENDERSONVILLE, NORTH CAROLINA
(See Asheville)

Business Litigation, Business Torts, Construction Litigation, Appellate Practice, Property Law and Litigation; Personal Injury and Medical Malpractice, Automobile Accidents, Wrongful Death, Brain Injury, Torts, Commercial Liability, Commercial Real Estate Litigation, Construction Defects and Liens, Contract Litigation, Corporate Litigation, Workers Compensation.

THE FRUE LAW FIRM, PLLC

HENDERSONVILLE, NORTH CAROLINA
(See Asheville)

General Civil Practice, Real Estate, Probate, Corporate Law, Business Law.

DAVID GANTT LAW OFFICE

HENDERSONVILLE, NORTH CAROLINA
(See Asheville)

Insurance Claims, Personal Injury, Automobile, Social Security Claims, Workers' Compensation.

WILLIAM L. GARDO, II

921 OAKLAND STREET
HENDERSONVILLE, NORTH CAROLINA 28791
Telephone: 828-697-9964
Fax: 828-697-9495
URL: http://www.lawyers.com/gardolaw

General Civil Trial Practice, Personal Injury, Automobile Accidents, Wrongful Death, Family Law, Divorce, Child Custody, Child Support, Adoptions, Workers Compensation, Criminal Law, Driving While Intoxicated, Traffic Violations, Drug Offenses.

WILLIAM L. GARDO, II, born Tryon, North Carolina, February 16, 1962; admitted to bar, 1987, North Carolina; 1989, U.S. District Court, Western District of North Carolina. *Education:* Appalachian State University (B.A., 1984); University of North Carolina at Chapel Hill (J.D.,1987). Phi Delta Phi. *Member:* Henderson County (President, 1994) and North Carolina Bar Associations; North Carolina Academy of Trial Lawyers; National Association of Criminal Defense Lawyers; Association of Trial Lawyers of America. ***LANGUAGES:*** Spanish.

GRIMES & TEICH

HENDERSONVILLE, NORTH CAROLINA
(See Asheville)

Personal Injury, Automobile Accidents, Trucking Accidents, Motorcycle Accidents, Boating Accidents, Brain and Head Injuries, Dog Bites, Products Liability, Catastrophic Injury, Pedestrian Injuries, Slip and Fall Injuries, Workers Compensation, Social Security Law, Social Security Disability, Medical Malpractice, Nursing Home Negligence, Nursing Home Abuse, Wrongful Death, Fire Injuries.

THOMAS N. HIX

422 N. CHURCH STREET
HENDERSONVILLE, NORTH CAROLINA 28792
Telephone: 828-697-5410
Fax: 828-692-5373
URL: http://www.thomashix.com

Family Law, Divorce, Equitable Distribution, Child Custody, Child Support, Adoption, Prenuptial Agreements, Domestic Violence, Criminal Law, DWI, Traffic Violations, Drug Offenses, Civil Litigation, Wills.

(This Listing Continued)

THOMAS N. HIX, Hendersonville—Continued

THOMAS N. HIX, born Lynchburg, Virginia, June 8, 1950; admitted to bar, 1976, North Carolina. *Education:* University of Richmond (B.A., History, 1972); Cumberland School of Law (J.D., 1975). *Member:* North Carolina Bar Association; The Association of Trial Lawyers of America.

HOWE, WATERS & MOXLEY, P.A.

Established in 1954

P.O. BOX 586

HENDERSONVILLE, NORTH CAROLINA 28793

Telephone: 828-692-9636

Email: HWCM@bellsouth.net

General Civil Practice. Civil and Criminal Litigation, Real Estate, Residential and Commercial Real Estate, Guardianships, Wills and Probate, Trusts and Estates, Business Law, Contracts.

WILLIAM B. W. HOWE (1928-2003)

R. CHARLES WATERS, born 1938; admitted to bar, 1968, North Carolina. *Education:* Duke University (A.B., 1961); University of North Carolina (J.D., 1968). Omicron Delta Kappa. *Member:* Henderson County and North Carolina Bar Associations; North Carolina State Bar.

LINDA A. MOXLEY, born 1952; admitted to bar, 1994, North Carolina. *Education:* Clemson University (B.A., 1975); Mercer University (J.D., 1994). Phi Alpha Delta. *Member:* Henderson County, North Carolina and American Bar Associations.

LAW OFFICES OF FRANK B. JACKSON

Established in 1980

422 NORTH CHURCH STREET

P.O. BOX 1666

HENDERSONVILLE, NORTH CAROLINA 28792

Telephone: 828-697-5410

Fax: 828-692-5373

URL: http://www.frankbjacksonlaw.com

Mailing Address: P.O. Box 1666, Hendersonville, NC

Civil Litigation in all State and Federal Courts. Domestic Litigation, Divorce, Child Custody, Child Support, Equitable Distribution, Spousal Support, General Civil Practice, Appeals, Probate and Estate Planning.

FRANK B. JACKSON, born Hendersonville, North Carolina, May 26, 1947; admitted to bar, 1972, North Carolina and U.S. District Court, Eastern District of North Carolina; 1976, U.S. District Court, Middle District of North Carolina; 1980, U.S. District Court, Western District of North Carolina and U.S. Court of Appeals, Fourth Circuit. *Education:* University of North Carolina (A.B., 1969; J.D., 1971). Recipient: American Jurisprudence Award in Bills and Notes. Author: "The Public Trust Doctrine," 49 North Carolina Law Review 973, 1971. Contributor, North Carolina Complaints Manual, 1985. Contributor, North Carolina Advanced Litigation Skills for Paralegals, 2000. Contributor, Basics of Legal Assisting in North Carolina, 2002. Member, North Carolina College of Advocacy, 1981. Certified Mediator. *Member:* Henderson County (Past President), North Carolina (Member, Sections on: Family Law; Estate Planning; Civil Litigation) and American Bar Associations; North Carolina State Bar (Member, Unauthorized Practice of Law Committee, 1987); North Carolina Academy of Trial Lawyers; The Association of Trial Lawyers of America. ***PRACTICE AREAS:*** Civil Litigation; Family Law; Divorce; Child Custody; Child Support; Equitable Distribution; Spousal Support; Personal Injury; Automobile Accidents and Injuries; Wrongful Death; Probate; Business Law.

ASSOCIATE

JAMES LAMAR PALMER, born Wilmington, North Carolina, 1976; admitted to bar, 2002, North Carolina. *Education:* University of North Carolina at Chapel Hill (B.A., History and Economics, with honors, 1999); North Carolina Central University (J.D., cum laude, 2002). Formerly with: University of North Carolina Office of Economic Development, Research Division, North Carolina General Assembly; Land Loss Prevention Project, Durham North Carolina. **Email:** jameslamarpalmer@hotmail.com

LEGAL SUPPORT PERSONNEL

DOROTHY GARLAND. PRACTICE AREAS: Civil Litigation; Appellate Practice.

JUDITH TURNER, (Office Manager). ***PRACTICE AREAS:*** Estate Administration; Probate.

JENNI HONECKER. PRACTICE AREAS: Civil Litigation.

THERESA McCALL, (Legal Assistant). ***PRACTICE AREAS:*** Civil Litigation.

REPRESENTATIVE CLIENTS: Duke Power Co.; Hendersonville Surgical Associates, PLLC; Globe Treks, Inc.; Boyd Pontiac Cadillac, Inc.; W.R. Case & Sons Cutlery Co.; Pisgah Associates of Pathology and Laboratory Medicine; Hendersonville Hematology & Oncology Associates, LLC; West Publishing Corp. Media com.

LAW OFFICES OF E.K. MORLEY, PLLC

104 FIRST AVENUE EAST

HENDERSONVILLE, NORTH CAROLINA 28792

Telephone: 828-697-6285

Fax: 828-697-6287

Email: ekmorley@ioa.com

URL: http://www.lawyers.com/ekmorley

Contested Wills, Will Contests, Estate Litigation, Decedents Estates, Inheritance, Successions, Trusts and Estates, Surrogates Court Practice, Contested Trusts and Estates, Estate Administration, Estate Settlements, Fiduciary Law, Fiduciary Liability, Fiduciary Litigation, Trust Law, Trust Litigation, Ancillary Probate, Probate Litigation.

E.K. MORLEY, born Warren, Pennsylvania, March 15, 1931; admitted to bar, 1982, North Carolina, U.S. Tax Court and U.S. Court of Appeals, 4th Circuit; 1985, U.S. District Court, Western District of North Carolina. *Education:* Pennsylvania State University (B.A., 1953); University of Geneva; Wake Forest University (J.D., 1982). *Member:* North Carolina Bar Association; The Association of Trial Lawyers of America. (Board Certified Specialist in Estate Planning and Probate Law, North Carolina State Board of Legal Specialization). ***LANGUAGES:*** French, Italian. ***REPORTED CASES:*** Estate of Mamie Beatrice Wells, Deceased v. James H. Toms, 500 S.E.2d 105, 129 N.C. App. 413 (N.C. App. 1998). **Email:** ekmorley@ioa.com

REPRESENTATIVE CLIENTS: American Legion Post 77; Die-Tronic Metal Castings, Inc.; Jones Tree Farm, Inc.; Looking Glass Associates.
REFERENCES: Bank of America; Centura Bank.

D. SAMUEL NEILL

Established in 1976

222 THIRD AVENUE WEST

HENDERSONVILLE, NORTH CAROLINA 28739

Telephone: 828-693-1739

Faxline: 828-696-9163

Email: samneill@bellsouth.net

URL: http://www.samneilllaw.com

Estate Planning, Wills and Probate, Trusts and Estates, Real Estate, Residential Real Estate, Commercial Real Estate, Personal Injury, Business Law and Elder Law.

D. SAMUEL NEILL, born Sylva, North Carolina, December 10, 1949; admitted to bar, 1975, North Carolina; 1977, U.S. District Court, Western District of North Carolina and U.S. Court of Appeals, 4th Circuit; 1981, U.S. Supreme Court and U.S. Tax Court; 2002, Cherokee Supreme Court (Eastern Band). *Education:* Wake Forest University (B.A., 1972; J.D., 1975). Attorney, Town of Laurel Park, 1977—. Member, Board of Governors, The University of North Carolina (16 campus), 1985-1997; Chairman, 1995-1996. HomeTrust Bank, Board of Directors, 1990—; Chairman, Investment Committee, 2004—. Member, Western North Carolina Regional Economic Development Commission (Advantage West), 1997—. Member, Board of Trustees, North Carolina School of the Arts (1999—; Chairman, 2005—). Arbitrator, 1987-1997. Chairman, Western North Carolina Film Commission, 2002—. *Member:* North Carolina (Chairman, Disaster Legal Services, 1981-1985) and American Bar Associations. ***PRACTICE AREAS:*** Real Estate; Real Property; Estate Planning; Estate Administration; Business Law; Personal Injury; Elder Law.

REPRESENTATIVE CLIENTS: Hendersonville Internists; Town of Laurel Park; Hendersonville Pediatrics; Kanuga Episcopal Conferences; State of North Carolina; Southeastern Sureties; Fifth Avenue Travel; Pack Square Investors.
APPROVED ATTORNEY FOR: Lawyers Title Insurance Co.; Chicago Title Insurance Co.; Investors Title Insurance.
REFERENCE: Carolina First Bank.

SCOTT D. NEUMANN

HENDERSONVILLE, NORTH CAROLINA

(See Brevard)

Family Law, Divorce, Child Custody and Support, Adoptions, Domestic Violence, Visitation Rights, Civil Practice, Criminal Law, Driving While Intoxicated, Traffic Violations, Drug Crimes, Juvenile Crimes, Parole and Probation, White Collar Crime, Real Estate, Buying or Selling a Home, Construction, Commercial Real Estate, Bankruptcy, Business Law, Buying or Selling a Business, Immigration and Naturalization, Visas, Trusts and Estates, Estate Planning, Wills and Probate.

PRINCE, YOUNGBLOOD & MASSAGEE

240 THIRD AVENUE, WEST

HENDERSONVILLE, NORTH CAROLINA 28739

Telephone: 828-692-2595

FAX: 828-693-0177

General Practice. Probate, Civil Litigation, Commercial, Residential Real Estate, Corporate, Arbitration, Mediation, Healthcare, Employment Law, Family Law, Equitable Distribution, Child Custody, Adoptions.

FIRM PROFILE: Price, Youngblood & Massagee is one of the counties oldest and well respected law firms. Located in Hendersonville, they also service all of the surrounding counties including Buncombe, Transylvania, Polk, Rutherford and McDowell. The firm maintains a general litigation practice and admitted to practice before all state and federal courts.

MEMBERS OF FIRM

L. B. PRINCE (1898-1982)

KENNETH R. YOUNGBLOOD, born Fletcher, North Carolina, January 16, 1931; admitted to bar, 1955, North Carolina and U.S. District Court, Western District of North

(This Listing Continued)

Carolina. *Education:* University of North Carolina (A.B., 1953; LL.B., 1955); Western Carolina University (M.Ed., 1987). Phi Delta Phi. Chairman, North Carolina General Statutes Commission, 1984-1994. Counselor to the North Carolina State Bar for the 29th Judicial District of North Carolina, 1972-1983. *Member:* Henderson County, North Carolina and American Bar Association; North Carolina State Bar (Member, Sections on: Taxation; Estate Planning and Fiduciary Law; Member, Council on Estate Planning and Probate Law Section; Member, Board of Continuing Legal Education). Life Fellow, American Bar Foundation. ***PRACTICE AREAS:*** Estate Planning & Administration; Corporate and Real Estate.

BOYD B. MASSAGEE, JR., born Greenville, North Carolina, September 25, 1932; admitted to bar, 1959, North Carolina. *Education:* Davidson College (B.S., 1954); University of North Carolina (LL.B., 1959). Delta Theta Phi. Member, Board of Editors, University of North Carolina Law Review, 1958-1959. *Member:* Henderson County and North Carolina (Member, Sections on: Family Law; Litigation) Bar Associations; North Carolina State Bar (Member, Sections on: Domestic Law); North Carolina Academy of Trial Lawyers. ***PRACTICE AREAS:*** Civil Trial; Domestic Law.

B. B. MASSAGEE, III, born Charlotte, North Carolina, March 18, 1954; admitted to bar, 1979, North Carolina; U.S. District Court, Western District of North Carolina; U.S. Court of Appeals, Fourth Circuit. *Education:* Wake Forest University (B.A., in Philosophy, 1976; J.D., 1979). *Member:* North Carolina Bar Association (Member, Sections on: Estate Planning; Real Property; Domestic Law); North Carolina State Bar; North Carolina Academy of Trial Lawyers; 29th Judicial Bar (President, 1994-1995). ***PRACTICE AREAS:*** Civil Litigation; Family Law; Estates and Real Estate; Equitable Distribution; Child Custody; Adoption Law.

SHARON B. ALEXANDER, born Pensacola, Florida, December 19, 1956; admitted to bar, 1981, North Carolina; U.S. District Court, Middle and Western Districts of North Carolina; U.S. Court of Appeals, Fourth Circuit. *Education:* Carson-Newman College (B.A., summa cum laude, 1978); University of Tennessee (J.D., 1981). Alpha Chi; Order of the Coif; Phi Kappa Phi; Phi Delta Phi. Recipient, American Jurisprudence Awards in Criminal Procedure, Evidence, Future Interests and Property. *Member:* North Carolina Bar Association (Member, Sections on: Bankruptcy and Health Law); North Carolina State Bar. ***PRACTICE AREAS:*** Appellate Practice; Municipal Law; Civil Litigation; Health Care Law; Estates; Real Estate.

REPRESENTATIVE CLIENTS: Margaret R. Pardee Memorial Hospital; First Citizens Bank and Trust Co.; Blue Ridge Community College; Blue Ridge Community College Foundation; Fletcher Motor Company, Inc.; Fletcher BMW; Hunter Chevrolet-Volvo-Subaru Company, Inc.; Hunter Chevrolet Co.; Carolina Village, Inc.; Etowah Realty, Inc.; Ducote Realty; Mark White Auctions & Realty; Arrington Properties; Habitat Realty; Western North Carolina Apple Growers, Inc.; Carolina Apple Processors Cooperative, Inc.; Industrial Maintenance Overflow Corporation, Inc.; Village of Flat Rock; Town of Mills River.

CURTIS ALAN SLUDER

HENDERSONVILLE, NORTH CAROLINA

(See Asheville)

Criminal Law, Traffic Violations, Driving While Intoxicated, Expunction.

VAN WINKLE, BUCK, WALL, STARNES AND DAVIS, P.A.

422 SOUTH MAIN STREET
HENDERSONVILLE, NORTH CAROLINA 28792
Telephone: 828-697-6196
FAX: 828-693-3999
Email: vw@vwlawfirm.com
URL: http://www.vwlawfirm.com

Asheville, North Carolina Office: 11 North Market Street, P.O. Box 7376. Telephone: 828-258-2991. FAX: 828-255-0255; 257-2767.

Administrative, Banking, Bankruptcy, Business Law, Creditor's Rights, Estates and Trusts, Litigation, Real Estate, Taxation.

ROBERT H. HAGGARD, born Alexandria, Virginia, August 12, 1949; admitted to bar, 1974, North Carolina; 1975, Florida; 1988, U.S. Tax Court. *Education:* Davidson College (B.A., 1971); Florida State University (J.D., 1974). Frequent Lecturer, Probate and Fiduciary Law Seminar, Manuscript, "The Caveat in North Carolina." Chair, North Carolina State Bar Estate Planning and Probate Law Specialization Committee, 2000. Listed, Trusts and Estates, "Best Lawyers in America." *Member:* North Carolina Bar Association (Member, Estate Planning and Fiduciary Law Section, Secretary 2001-2002; Member, Council, 1986-1988; 1997-2001); 29th Judicial District and North Carolina State Bar; Land of the Sky Estate Planning Council (President, 1983). Fellow, American College of Trust and Estate Council. (Board Certified Specialist in Estate Planning and Probate Law, North Carolina State Board of Legal Specialization). ***PRACTICE AREAS:*** Estate Planning; Fiduciary Law; Estate Administration; Trust Administration. ***Email:*** rhaggard@vwlawfirm.com

MICHAEL M. THOMPSON, born Hendersonville, North Carolina, October 12, 1957; admitted to bar, 1985, North Carolina. *Education:* University of North Carolina (B.S., 1980); Campbell University (J.D., 1984). *Member:* Henderson County (President, 2000-2001 and 2002-2003) and North Carolina (Council Member, Real Property Section) Bar Associations; North Carolina State Bar. ***PRACTICE AREAS:*** Real Property Law. ***Email:*** mthompson@vwlawfirm.com

ADAM L. SHEALY, born Stuttgart, Germany, October 27, 1968; admitted to bar, 1996, North Carolina. *Education:* College of Charleston (B.S., Business Administration, 1991); University of Georgia (J.D. with honors, 1996). Editorial Board, 1994-1995 and Notes Editor, 1995-1996, Georgia Law Review. Certified Public Accountant. *Member:* North Carolina Bar Association (Council Member, Estate Planning and Fiduciary Law Section); American Bar Association. (Board Certified Specialist in Estate Planning and Probate

(This Listing Continued)

[redacted]olina State Board of Legal Specialization). ***PRACTICE AREAS:*** Estate [redacted]e Administration; Trust Administration; Business Planning; Business Trans- [redacted]***l:*** ashealy@vwlawfirm.com

[redacted]***E T. KNOX,*** born Norfolk, Virginia, June 29, 1970; admitted to bar, 2000, [redacted]a. *Education:* College of William & Mary (B.A., 1992); Wake Forest Uni- [redacted] 2000). Notes and Comments Editor, Wake Forest University Law Review, [redacted]*ember:* North Carolina Bar Association (Member Sections on: Estate Plan- [redacted]ry Law, Elder Law); National Academy of Elder Law Attorneys. ***PRACTICE*** [redacted]ate Planning (40%); Estate Administration (40%); Elder Law (20%). ***Email:*** [redacted]wfirm.com

[redacted]NTATIVE CLIENTS: Asheville Cardiology Associates; Carolina Power & Light Co., [redacted]nergy Company; Central Carolina Restaurants, Inc.; Champion Hills Associates; [redacted]wen Mfg. Co.; Chicago Title Insurance Co.; Chrysler Corp.; Columbia Carolina [redacted]Revco Drug Centers; EchoStar Communications Companies; E.I. Du Pont de [redacted] Company; First Citizens Bank and Trust Co.; First Union National Bank of North Carolina; Haywood Regional Medical Center; Hedrick Industries Group; High Street Banking Co.; The Hometown Bank; Kenmure Properties, Ltd.; Lawyers Title Insurance Co.; Lowe's Corporation; MCI; McDonald's Corporation; Mission-St. Joseph's Health System, Inc.; Mountain Area Health Education Center; Mountain Energy Corporation; P.H. Glatfelter Company; Public Service Company of N.C. (a SCANA Company); Regional Water Authority of Asheville, Buncombe and Henderson; Steelcase, Inc.; Verizon; Wachovia Bank, N.A.; Westcare Health System.

(For Biographical Data on all Personnel, see Professional Biographies at Asheville, North Carolina)

WHITMIRE BEEKER & TOWNSEND

120 WEST ALLEN STREET
HENDERSONVILLE, NORTH CAROLINA 28792
Telephone: 828-692-8201
Fax: 828-692-7032
URL: http://www.wbtlawfirm.com

Real Estate - Residential and Commercial, Local Government Law, Land Development, Business and Corporations, Wills and Estates, Bankruptcy, Family Law, Environmental Law, Litigation.

ANGELA SKERRETT BEEKER, born Hendersonville, North Carolina; admitted to bar, 1991, North Carolina; 1993, U.S. District Court, Western District of North Carolina. *Education:* Duke University (B.S.E., 1988); Campbell University, Norman Adrian Wiggins School of Law (J.D., 1991). *Member:* North Carolina Bar Association (Member, Sections on: Preal Property; Wills and Estates; Local Government Law). ***PRACTICE AREAS:*** Real Estate; Residential Real Estate; Commercial Law; Local Government Law; Land Development; Business Law; Corporate Law; Wills; Trusts and Estates; Bankruptcy. ***Email:*** beekera@bellsouth.net

TERESA L. TOWNSEND, born Lima, Ohio, August 17, 1950; admitted to bar, 1986, North Carolina. *Education:* Eastern Kentucky University (B.S., 1972); Ohio State University (M.A., 1976); Wake Forest University (J.D., 1986); Vermont Law School (LL.M., 2005). *Member:* North Carolina Bar Association (Member, Sections on: Family Law; Environmental Law). ***PRACTICE AREAS:*** Family Law (50%); Environmental Law (25%); Litigation (25%). ***Email:*** tltownsend@bellsouth.net

THE VINCENT LAW FIRM, PC

HERTFORD, NORTH CAROLINA

(See Southern Shores)

Workers Compensation, Personal Injury, Auto Accidents, Social Security Disability, Wrongful Death and Admiralty Longshores.

DON H. BUMGARDNER

HICKORY, NORTH CAROLINA

(See Gastonia)

General Civil and Appellate Practice in all State and Federal Courts. Personal Injury, Products Liability, Workers Compensation and Medical Malpractice.

SCOTT D. CONRAD

HICKORY, NORTH CAROLINA

(See Newton)

Criminal, Domestic/Family, Child Custody, Juvenile, Traffic, Divorce, Real Estate, Wills.

CORNE, CORNE & GRANT, P.A.

HICKORY, NORTH CAROLINA

(See Newton)

Personal Injury, Automobile Accidents, Slip and Fall, Wrongful Death, Medical Malpractice, Family Law, Child Custody, Child Support, Divorce, Visitation Rights, Real Estate, Residential Real Estate, Criminal Law, Business Law, Joint Ventures, Limited Liability Company Law, Partnership, Corporate Law, Trusts and Estates.

L. TALTON DARK, III

HICKORY, NORTH CAROLINA

(See Morganton)

Criminal Law, Driving While Intoxicated, Traffic Violations.

EAKER & FULKERSON, PC

Established in 2004

110 N. CENTER STREET, SUITE 203
HICKORY, NORTH CAROLINA 28603-9249
Telephone: 828-267-2923
Fax: 828-267-2924

Criminal Law, Driving Under the Influence, Real Estate, Domestic

JENNIFER EAKER, born Cherryville, North Carolina, December 11, 19 to bar, 2003, North Carolina. *Education:* University of North Carolina at Chap English and Political Science, 1997); Cumberland School of Law of Samfo (J.D., 2001). ***PRACTICE AREAS:*** General Practice; Real Estate; Domestic Law. ***Email:*** jeakerunc@aol.com

DANIEL R. FULKERSON, born Du Bois, Pennsylvania; admitted to ba consin and Georgia; 2002, North Carolina. *Education:* University of North C 1997); University of Wisconsin-Madison (J.D., with honors, 2001). *Member* lina Bar Association. ***PRACTICE AREAS:*** Criminal Defense; Driving Whil Traffic Violations. ***Email:*** danrfulkerson@yahoo.com

J. BRYAN ELLIOTT

21 FIRST STREET NW, SUITE 400
P.O. BOX 2047
HICKORY, NORTH CAROLINA 28603-2047
Telephone: 828-324-5200
Fax: 828-324-0498
Email: elliottbk@earthlink.net
URL: http://www.jbryanelliottlawfirm.com

Bankruptcy, Social Security Disability.

J. BRYAN ELLIOTT, born Roanoke Rapids, North Carolina, March ted to bar, 1975, North Carolina; 1977, U.S. District Court, Western Distr lina. *Education:* University of North Carolina at Chapel Hill (A.B., 1971; J.D., 1975). *Member:* North Carolina Bar Association (Bankruptcy Section); American Bankruptcy Institute. ***PRACTICE AREAS:*** Bankruptcy (85%); Social Security Disability (15%).

GORHAM, CRONE, MACE, GREEN & CODY, LLP

Established in 1975

FIDELITY PROFESSIONAL BUILDING
27 FIRST AVENUE, N.E., SUITE 203
P.O. BOX 2507
HICKORY, NORTH CAROLINA 28603-2507
Telephone: 828-322-5505
Telefax: 828-328-1882

General Practice, Bankruptcy, Criminal, Driving While Intoxicated, Drug Crimes, Parole and Probation, Traffic Violations, White Collar Crime, Family Law, Adoption Law, Child Custody, Child Support, Divorce, Domestic Violence, Visitation Rights, Municipal Law, Personal Injury, Automobile Accidents, Wrongful Death, Real Estate, Buying or Selling a Home, Construction, Eminent Domain, Zoning and Land Use, Trust and Estates, Asset Protection, Estate Planning, Wills and Probate. Litigation in all State and Federal Courts.

MEMBERS OF FIRM

J. SAMUEL GORHAM, III, born Rocky Mount, NC December 27, 1942; admitted to bar, 1971, North Carolina; 1976, U.S. Court of Appeals, Fourth Circuit. *Education:* University of North Carolina (B.S.B.A., 1966); Wake Forest University (J.D., 1971). Winner, NCNB Will and Trust Drafting Contest, 1971. Law Clerk to Hon. Woodrow W. Jones, Chief Judge, U.S. District Court, Western District of NC, 1971-1973. *Member:* Catawba County, North Carolina (Council Member, Bankruptcy Section, 1978-1981, 1987-1989) and American Bar Associations; NC State Bar. [Captain, JAGC, U.S. Naval Reserves, Ret.]. (Board Certified Specialist in Business and Consumer Bankruptcy Law, North Carolina State Board of Legal Specialization). ***PRACTICE AREAS:*** Bankruptcy; Estate Planning; Corporate Law; Real Estate. ***Email:*** jsgorham@charter.net

JOHN W. CRONE, III, born Hickory, NC, March 13, 1954; admitted to bar, 1980, NC and U.S. District Court, Western District of NC; 1985, U.S. Court of Appeals, Fourth Circuit; U.S. Supreme Court. *Education:* University of North Carolina at Chapel Hill (B.A., 1976); Wake Forest University (J.D., 1980). Member, Moot Court Board. Recipient, NC Academy of Trial Lawyers Award. City Attorney, Hickory. *Member:* Catawba County (President, 1987-1988) North Carolina and American Bar Associations; NC State Bar; NC Academy of Trial Lawyers; The Association of Trial Lawyers of America; NC Association of Municipal Attorneys. ***PRACTICE AREAS:*** Municipal Law; Civil Litigation; Corporate Law; Personal Injury; Real Estate. ***Email:*** jcrone@charter.net

DEREK L. MACE, born Valdese, NC, September 8, 1972; admitted to bar, 1997, NC and U.S. District Court, Western District of NC. *Education:* Lenoir-Rhyne College (B.A., 1994); University of North Carolina (J.D., 1997). Phi Alpha Delta. Member, NC Journal of International Law and Commercial Regulation. *Member:* North Carolina and American Bar Associations; NC State Bar. ***LANGUAGES:*** Spanish. ***PRACTICE AREAS:*** Criminal Law; Family Law; Corporate Law; Civil Litigation; Traffic Violations. ***Email:*** dlmace@charter.net

DANIEL R. GREEN, JR., born Winston-Salem, NC, August 11, 1954; admitted to bar, 1979, North Carolina; 1982, U.S. District Court, Western District of NC; 2002, U.S. Court of Appeals, Fourth Circuit. *Education:* Lenoir-Rhyne College (B.A., 1976); University of North Carolina at Chapel Hill (J.D., 1979). District Court Judge, 25th Judicial District, 1984-1986; Superior Court Judge, Judicial District 25B, NC, 2002. *Member:* Catawba County and North Carolina Bar Associations; NC State Bar; NC Academy of Trial Lawyers.

(This Listing Continued)

PRACTICE AREAS: Family Law; Civil Litigation; Personal Injury; Residential Real Estate; Commercial Real Estate; Wills; Estate Administration; Corporate Law; Criminal Law; Traffic Violations. ***Email:*** danrgreen@charter.net

BLAIR E. CODY, III, born Hickory, NC, November 11, 1974; admitted to bar, 2000, North Carolina. *Education:* Lenoir-Rhyne College (B.A., 1997); North Carolina Central University (J.D., 2000). *Member:* NC State Bar; NC Academy of Trial Lawyers; Association of Trial Lawyers of America; National Association of Criminal Defense Lawyers. ***PRACTICE AREAS:*** Criminal Law; Family Law; Juvenile Law; Real Estate; Civil Litigation. ***Email:*** becody@charter.net

ASSOCIATE

B. GREGORY GORHAM, born Hickory, NC, April 10, 1974; admitted to bar, 1999, North Carolina. *Education:* University of Virginia (B.S. in Commerce, 1996); University of North Carolina School of Law (J.D., 1999). Beta Gamma Sigma; Phi Alpha Delta. *Member:* Catawba County Bar Association; NC State Bar. ***Email:*** bggorham@charter.net

REPRESENTATIVE CLIENTS: Alex Lee, Inc.; Merchants Distributors, Inc.; Institution Food House, Inc.; Lowe's Food Stores, Inc.; Region E Development Corp.; Johnson Hosiery Mills, Inc.; Western Piedmont Council of Governments; Poteat Motor Lines, Inc.; McKinley Leather of Hickory, Inc.; Stewart Leather, Inc.; Sign Systems, Inc.; City of Hickory; Gastroenterology Associates, LLC; Mid-Atlantic Wood Products, Inc.
APPROVED ATTORNEYS FOR: Chicago Title Insurance Co.; Lawyers Title Insurance Corp.; Investors Title Insurance Co.;
REFERENCES: Catawba Valley Bank; Bank of Granite; Bank of America.

GRAY, LAYTON, KERSH, SOLOMON, SIGMON, FURR & SMITH, P.A.

HICKORY, NORTH CAROLINA

(See Gastonia)

General Civil Trial Practice, Arbitration, Corporation Law, Construction Law, Real Estate Law, Mediation, Municipal and Zoning Law, Mergers and Acquisitions, Bankruptcy, Family, Tax, Estate Planning and Probate Law, Personal Injury Law, Traffic, Professional Sports Representation, Community Association Law.

LYNDON R. HELTON PLLC

827 HIGHLAND AVENUE NE
P.O. BOX 909
HICKORY, NORTH CAROLINA 28601
Telephone: 828-328-9966
Fax: 828-328-9996
URL: http://www.lyndonheltonlaw.com

Workers Compensation, Personal Injury.

LYNDON R. HELTON, born Hickory, North Carolina, July 15, 1965; admitted to bar, 1993, Virginia; 1994, Maryland; 1996, North Carolina. *Education:* Lenior-Rhyne College (B.A., 1988); Wake Forest University (J.D., 1993). Judicial Law Clerk, Hon. James C. Cacheris, Chief Judge, U.S. District Court, Eastern District of Virginia, 1993-1995. *Member:* North Carolina State Bar. [U.S. Navy, 1988; Lieutenant, 1990]. ***PRACTICE AREAS:*** Workers Compensation (50%); Personal Injury (50%).

LOVEKIN, YOUNG & ORNDOFF, PC

Established in 2004

27 FIRST AVENUE, N.E.
HICKORY, NORTH CAROLINA 28601
Telephone: 828-322-5435
Toll Free: 1-800-241-2001
Fax: 828-322-3973
Email: lovekin@charter.net
URL: http://www.stephenlovekinlaw.com
Mailing Address: P.O. Box 2087, Hickory, NC 28603

Personal Injury, Automobile Accidents, Bodily Injury, Wrongful Death, Workers Compensation, Products Liability, Family Law, Divorce, Child Custody, Child Support, Step-Parent Adoptions, Employment Insurance, Traffic Violations, Wills.

MEMBERS OF FIRM

STEPHEN L. LOVEKIN, born Bala Cynwyd, Pennsylvania, August 1, 1940; admitted to bar, 1968, North Carolina. *Education:* Catawba College (B.A., 1964); Wake Forest University (J.D., 1967). Phi Alpha Delta. Member, Catawba County Board of Elections, 1971-1972. Member, Catawba County Board of Zoning Adjustment, 1982-2000. *Member:* Catawba County, North Carolina and American Bar Associations; North Carolina State Bar; North Carolina Academy of Trial Lawyers; The Association of Trial Lawyers of America. ***PRACTICE AREAS:*** Personal Injury Law; Bodily Injury; Workman's Compensation; Traffic Matters; Wills; Wrongful Death; Products Liability. ***Email:*** lovekin@charter.net

GARY F. YOUNG, born Brooklyn, New York, November 24, 1954; admitted to bar, 1979, North Carolina. *Education:* Northwestern University (B.A., Economics, with honors, 1976); University of North Carolina (J.D., 1979). Associate Justice, Holderness Moot Court Board. *Member:* Catawba County Bar Association, North Carolina Bar Association, North Carolina Academy of Trial Lawyers. ***PRACTICE AREAS:*** Civil Litigation; Personal Injury; Workers Compensation; Domestic Relations. ***Email:*** gfy-law@charter.net

JASON ALEXANDER ORNDOFF, born Spruce Pine, North Carolina, 1975; admitted to bar, 2001, North Carolina. *Education:* University of North Carolina at Chapel Hill (B.A., 1997; J.D., 2001). *Member:* Catawba County Bar Association; North Carolina State Bar; North Carolina Academy Trial Lawyers. ***PRACTICE AREAS:*** Personal Injury; Workers Compensation; Wills; Traffic Violations. ***Email:*** orndoff@charter.net

(This Listing Continued)

LEGAL SUPPORT PERSONNEL

SANDY BARKER-BRYANT, (Paralegal)

ANN BANKS, (Legal Administrator)

MULLEN HOLLAND & COOPER P.A.

HICKORY, NORTH CAROLINA

(See Gastonia)

General Civil Trial and Appellate Practice, all Federal and State Courts. Banking, Bankruptcy and Reorganization, Construction, Corporate and Commercial, Employment Discrimination, Estate Planning and Administration, Health Care, Insurance, Mergers and Acquisitions, Negligence, Personal Injury, Professional Malpractice, Real Estate, Workers' Compensation.

PATRICK, HARPER & DIXON L.L.P.

Established in 1946

CENTURA BANK BUILDING
34 SECOND STREET, N.W.
P.O. BOX 218
HICKORY, NORTH CAROLINA 28603
Telephone: 828-322-7741
Fax: 828-322-9340

General Practice, State and Federal Courts. Insurance, Tax, Probate, Estate Planning and Corporation Law. Real Property and Litigation.

MEMBERS OF FIRM

BAILEY PATRICK (1898-1989)

JAMES T. PATRICK (1936-1990)

F. GWYN HARPER, JR. (1911-1994)

STEPHEN MASON THOMAS, born Asheville, North Carolina, September 22, 1945; admitted to bar, 1970, North Carolina. *Education:* University of North Carolina (B.A., 1967; J.D., 1970). Phi Alpha Delta. John M. Morehead Scholar. Member of Staff, North Carolina Law Review, 1969-1970. Certified Mediator. *Member:* Catawba County, North Carolina and American Bar Associations; North Carolina Association of Defense Attorneys; Defense Research Institute; American Board of Trial Advocates (Advocate). ***PRACTICE AREAS:*** Civil Litigation; Corporate Law; Construction Law; Insurance. ***Email:*** sthomas@phd-law.com

DONALD R. FULLER, JR., born Lumberton, North Carolina, August 20, 1948; admitted to bar, 1973, North Carolina. *Education:* University of North Carolina (B.S., 1970); University of Virginia (J.D., 1973). Phi Beta Kappa; Beta Gamma Sigma. John M. Morehead Scholar. *Member:* Catawba County, North Carolina and American Bar Associations. ***PRACTICE AREAS:*** Business Law; Corporate Law; Creditors Rights; Real Estate; Civil Litigation; Estate Planning. ***Email:*** dfuller@phd-law.com

ELOISE DeLANEY BRADSHAW, born Charlotte, North Carolina, May 26, 1955; admitted to bar, 1980, North Carolina; 1982, Kentucky. *Education:* University of North Carolina at Chapel Hill (A.B., 1977; J.D., with honors, 1980). Phi Beta Kappa; Order of the Coif. Staff Member, University of North Carolina at Chapel Hill Law Review, 1978-1980. Law Clerkship, Judge J. Phil Carlton, N.C. Supreme Court, 1980-1982. *Member:* Catawba County, North Carolina and American Bar Associations. ***PRACTICE AREAS:*** Corporate Law; Real Estate; Trusts and Estates; Business Law. ***Email:*** ebradshaw@phd-law.com

DAVID WALLACE HOOD, born Charlotte, North Carolina, February 9, 1966; admitted to bar, 1991, North Carolina. *Education:* University of North Carolina at Chapel Hill (B.A., 1988; J.D., with honors, 1991). Recipient, American Jurisprudence Awards in Torts, Business Associations, Constitutional Law, Probate, Criminal Procedure, Income Taxation and Trial Advocacy. Staff Member, North Carolina Journal of International Law and Commercial Regulation. Associate Justice, Holderness Moot Court Bench. *Member:* Catawba County and North Carolina Bar Associations. ***PRACTICE AREAS:*** Civil Litigation; Insurance Defense; Construction Law; Collections. ***Email:*** dhood@phd-law.com

KIMBERLY H. WHITLEY, born Chapel Hill, North Carolina, October 26, 1967; admitted to bar, 1993, North Carolina. *Education:* University of North Carolina at Chapel Hill (B.A., with honors and distinction, 1990; J.D., with high honors, 1993). Phi Beta Kappa; Phi Alpha Delta. John M. Morehead Scholar. Order of the Coif. Member, 1991-1992, and Note Editor, 1992-1993, North Carolina Law Review. Law Clerk, Judge Clyde H. Hamilton, United States Court of Appeals, Fourth Circuit, 1993-1994. *Member:* Catawba County, North Carolina and American Bar Associations. ***PRACTICE AREAS:*** Corporate Law; Civil Litigation; Elder Law; Trusts and Estates. ***Email:*** kwhitley@phd-law.com

EVANS W. FISHER, born Winston-Salem, North Carolina, November 15, 1952; admitted to bar, 1978, North Carolina. *Education:* Davidson College (B.A., 1975); Duke University (J.D., 1978). *Member:* Catawba County and North Carolina Bar Associations; American Health Lawyers Association; North Carolina Society of Healthcare Attorneys. ***PRACTICE AREAS:*** Health Care; Corporate Law; Business Law. ***Email:*** efisher@phd-law.com

L. OLIVER NOBLE, JR., born Kinston, North Carolina, January 24, 1946; admitted to bar, 1970, North Carolina. *Education:* North Carolina State University (B.S., 1967); University of North Carolina at Chapel Hill (J.D., 1970). Research Assistant to Judge Earl Vaughn, North Carolina Court of Appeals, 1970-1971. Recipient, Foundation for the Improvement of Justice Award, 1998. District Court Judge, 1977-1986. Chief District Court Judge, 1987-1998. Senior Resident Superior Court Judge, 1999-2002. Past President, North Carolina Association of District Court Judges. *Member:* North Carolina State Bar; North Carolina Bar Association. ***PRACTICE AREAS:*** Mediation; Civil Litigation; Corporate Law; Domestic Relations; Traffic Violations. ***Email:*** onoble@phd-law.com

(This Listing Continued)

ASSOCIATES

PTOLEMY TAYLOR ALLPORT, born Monroe, Louisiana, 1963; admitted to bar, 1993, Arizona; 1996, Georgia; 1999, North Carolina. *Education:* Texas A&M University (B.S., 1984); London School of Economics (M.S., 1989); Tulane University of Louisiana (J.D., 1993). Moot Court Oralist, Moot Court Board, 1991-1993. Notes and Comments Editor, Tulane Law Review, 1992-1993. *Member:* Catawba County and North Carolina Bar Associations; North Carolina State Bar. ***PRACTICE AREAS:*** Civil Litigation; Insurance Defense. ***Email:*** pallport@phd-law.com

MICHAEL J. BARNETT, born Weirton, West Virginia, April 8, 1977; admitted to bar, 2002, Pennsylvania; 2004, North Carolina. *Education:* State University of New York at Albany (B.A., 1998); University of North Carolina at Chapel Hill (J.D., with honors, 2002). Staff Member, 2001-2002 and Symposium Editor, 2001-2002, University of North Carolina Law Review. *Member:* Catawba County and North Carolina Bar Associations. ***PRACTICE AREAS:*** Civil Litigation; Insurance Defense; Construction Law; Collections. ***Email:*** mbarnett@phd-law.com

MICHAEL P. THOMAS, born Hickory, North Carolina, March 2, 1976; admitted to bar, 2001, North Carolina; 2002, Georgia. *Education:* Princeton University (A.B., 1998); Washington and Lee University School of Law (J.D., 2001). Law Clerk, Hon. Lacy H. Thornburg, United States District Court, Western District of North Carolina, Asheville, North Carolina, 2001-2002. *Member:* Catawba County and American Bar Associations; North Carolina State Bar; State Bar of Georgia. ***PRACTICE AREAS:*** Civil Litigation; Insurance; Employment; Construction. ***Email:*** mthomas@phd-law.com

SARAH M. WHITE, born Decatur, Georgia, June 9, 1978; admitted to bar, 2003, North Carolina. *Education:* University of North Carolina at Chapel Hill (B.A., with highest distinction, 2000; J.D., 2003). Phi Beta Kappa. John M. Morehead Scholar. Law Clerk, Judge Linda M. McGee, North Carolina Court of Appeals, 2003-2004. *Member:* Catawba County, North Carolina and American Bar Associations. ***PRACTICE AREAS:*** Real Estate; Corporate Law; Trusts and Estates. ***Email:*** swhite@phd-law.com

OF COUNSEL

CHARLES D. DIXON, born York County, South Carolina, December 12, 1926; admitted to bar, 1952, North Carolina. *Education:* University of North Carolina (A.B., 1949); Harvard University (LL.B., 1952). Tau Beta Pi; Phi Beta Kappa. Certified Mediator. *Member:* Catawba County, North Carolina and American Bar Associations. Fellow: American College of Trust and Estate Counsel. (Board Certified Specialist in Estate Planning and Probate Law, North Carolina State Board of Legal Specialization). ***PRACTICE AREAS:*** Estate Planning; Taxation; Corporate Law; Hospital Law. ***Email:*** cdixon@phd-law.com

GENERAL COUNSEL FOR: Shuford Mills, Inc.; Hickory Springs Manufacturing Co.; Century Furniture Co.; Southern Furniture Company of Conover, Inc.; Hickory Construction Co.; Catawba Valley Medical Center; Snyder Paper Co.; Joan Fabrics Corp.; Hickory Printing Group, Inc.; Regal Manufacturing Co.; Classic Leather, Inc.; Drillers Service, Inc.; Plastic Packaging, Inc.; Hickory Chair Co.; Neuville Industries, Inc.; Valdese Weavers, Inc.; Ingold Company, Inc.; McCreary Modern, Inc.; Vanguard Furniture Co., Inc.; Catawba County; Shurtape Technologies, Inc.; C.R. Laine Furniture, Inc.; Neill Grading and Construction Co.; Matthews Construction Co.; Moss-Marlow Building Co.; Huffman Grading Co.
SPECIAL COUNSEL FOR: Norfolk-Southern Railway Co.
LOCAL COUNSEL FOR: Duke Power Co.; Martin Marietta Corp.; Wal-Mart Stores, Inc.; Bassett Furniture Industries Inc.; The Lane Co.; Sarstedt, Inc.; Crum & Forster Insurance Cos.; Nationwide Insurance Co.; The Employers Group; State Farm Insurance Cos.; Security Insurance Group; Lumbermens Mutual Casualty Co.; Fireman's Fund American Insurance Co.; Aetna Insurance Co.; Great American Insurance Co.; GMHC Insurance Cos.; Amerisure Insurance Co.; Kmart Corp.; USAA Insurance; State Auto Insurance Cos.; Crawford and Co.; Lowes Companies, Inc.; GAB Robbins; Interlocal Risk Financing Fund of N.C.; NC Farm Bureau Insurance Co.; Alfa Virginia Mutual Insurance Co.; Sentry Insurance Group.

LAW OFFICE OF KEITH W. RIGSBEE, PLLC

HICKORY, NORTH CAROLINA

(See Morganton)

Family Law, Criminal Law, Personal Injury, Small Business Corporations, Real Estate.

SIGMON, CLARK, MACKIE, HUTTON, HANVEY & FERRELL, P.A.

Established in 1963

420 THIRD AVENUE, N.W.
P.O. DRAWER 1470
HICKORY, NORTH CAROLINA 28603
Telephone: 828-328-2596
FAX: 828-328-6876
URL: http://www.sigmonclark.com

General Practice. Probate, Corporate, Trials concerning all phases of the law and Real Estate Law.

FIRM PROFILE: Sigmon, Clark, Mackie, Hutton, Hanvey & Ferrell, P.A. enjoys an excellent reputation for Trial Advocacy, Business Development and Corporate Law, Estate Planning and Administration and all phases of Real Estate Law. We practice throughout the 25th Judicial District and across the state. All attorneys are active in County, State and Local Bar Associations.

WILLIAM R. SIGMON, born Morganton, North Carolina, September 7, 1935; admitted to bar, 1963, North Carolina and U.S. District Court, Western District of North Carolina; 1977, U.S. Supreme Court. *Education:* Lenoir-Rhyne College; Wake Forest College (LL.B., 1963). Phi Alpha Delta. *Member:* Catawba County, North Carolina and American Bar Associations; Twenty-Fifth Judicial District (Secretary-Treasurer, 1963-1964); North

(This Listing Continued)

SIGMON, CLARK, MACKIE, HUTTON, HANVEY & FERRELL, P.A., Hickory—Continued

Carolina State Bar; American Judicature Society. ***PRACTICE AREAS:*** Business and Corporate; Estate Planning and Administration; Real Estate. ***Email:*** bill.sigmon@sigmonclark.com

JEFFREY T. MACKIE, born Winston-Salem, North Carolina, June 28, 1947; admitted to bar, 1973, North Carolina and U.S. District Court, Western and Middle Districts of North Carolina. *Education:* Wake Forest University (B.A., 1969); University of North Carolina (J.D., 1972). Phi Delta Phi. Attorney, Hickory City Schools Board of Education, Hickory, North Carolina, 1994—. *Member:* Catawba County, 25th Judicial District (President, 1981-1982) and North Carolina Bar Associations; North Carolina State Bar; North Carolina Academy of Trial Lawyers. ***PRACTICE AREAS:*** Personal Injury; Workers Compensation; Medical Negligence; Insurance Law; Civil Litigation; Education Law; Mediation. ***Email:*** jeff.mackie@sigmonclark.com

WARREN A. HUTTON, born Hickory, North Carolina, July 15, 1957; admitted to bar, 1983, North Carolina, U.S. District Court, Western and Middle Districts of North Carolina and U.S. Supreme Court. *Education:* Tulane University (B.A., 1979); Wake Forest University (J.D., 1982). Phi Delta Phi. *Member:* Catawba County, 25th Judicial District (President, 1991-1992) and North Carolina Bar Associations; North Carolina State Bar. ***REPORTED CASES:*** Dale K. Cline CPA, LLC v. Dahle, No. COA01-94, Slip Op. (N.C. App. May 7, 2002); Ann A. Reece v. The Estate of Edward Filmore Swann, Jr., No. COA99-1152, Slip Op. (N.C. App. December 2000). ***PRACTICE AREAS:*** Civil Litigation; Business and Corporate Law; Business Transactions; Mergers and Acquisitions; Real Estate; Eminent Domain. ***Email:*** warren.hutton@sigmonclark.com

J. SCOTT HANVEY, born Charlotte, North Carolina, February 12, 1967; admitted to bar, 1992, North Carolina and U.S. District Court, Western District of North Carolina. *Education:* University of North Carolina at Chapel Hill (B.A., 1989); Campbell University (J.D., 1992). Phi Alpha Delta. *Member:* Catawba County, North Carolina and American Bar Associations; North Carolina State Bar Association; North Carolina Academy of Trial Lawyers. ***PRACTICE AREAS:*** Family Law; Civil Litigation; Criminal Litigation; Personal Injury. ***Email:*** scott.hanvey@sigmonclark.com

FORREST A. FERRELL, born Greensboro, North Carolina, August 26, 1938; admitted to bar, 1963, North Carolina. *Education:* High Point University (A.B., 1960); University of North Carolina at Chapel Hill (LL.B). North Carolina Superior Court Judge, 1975-1998. President Conference of Superior Court Judges, 1989. North Carolina Court Commission, 1980. Executive Committee, North Carolina Judicial Conference. *Member:* North Carolina Bar Association (Vice President). ***PRACTICE AREAS:*** Civil Litigation; Criminal Litigation; Business Law; Corporate Law; Personal Injury; Administrative Law; Employment Law. ***Email:*** forrest.ferrell@sigmonclark.com

STEPHEN L. PALMER, born Albany, Georgia, June 14, 1970; admitted to bar, 1997, North Carolina; U.S. District Court, Western and Eastern Districts of North Carolina; U.S. Court of Appeals, 4th Circuit and U.S. Supreme Court. *Education:* Clemson University (B.S., 1992); Campbell University (J.D., magna cum laude, 1997). Articles Editor, Campbell Law Review; Member, ABA and National Moot Court Teams. *Member:* Catawba County and North Carolina Bar Associations; North Carolina State Bar. ***PRACTICE AREAS:*** Business Law; Corporate Law; Real Estate; Estate Planning; Probate; Civil Litigation; Appellate Practice. ***Email:*** stephen.palmer@sigmonclark.com

---

R. JASON WHITE, born Taylorsville, North Carolina, April 25, 1977; admitted to bar, 2003, North Carolina. *Education:* University of North Carolina, Asheville (B.A., Political Science, 1999); Campbell University, Norman A. Wiggins School of Law (J.D., 2003). Order of the Kivett. Member, National Moot Court Competition Team. Articles Editor, Campbell Law Review. *Member:* Catawba County, 25th Judicial District and North Carolina (Member, Young Lawyers Division) Bar Associations. ***PRACTICE AREAS:*** Criminal Law; Civil Litigation; Business Law; Traffic Violations. ***Email:*** jason.white@sigmonclark.com

NANCY L. HUEGERICH, born Orlando, Florida, November 26, 1976; admitted to bar, 2003, North Carolina. *Education:* North Carolina State University (B.A., 2000); University of North Carolina at Chapel Hill (J.D., 2003). ***PRACTICE AREAS:*** Civil Litigation; Real Estate; Criminal Law; Business Law. ***Email:*** nancy.huegerich@sigmonclark.com

OF COUNSEL

MARSHALL V. YOUNT, born Hickory, North Carolina, January 21, 1917; admitted to bar, 1940, North Carolina. *Education:* University of North Carolina (B.S., 1938; LL.B., 1940). *Member:* Catawba County, 25th Judicial District (Past President) and North Carolina (Member, General Practice Hall of Fame) Bar Associations. [U.S. Army, 1942-1946, Captain]. ***PRACTICE AREAS:*** Real Estate; Estate Planning; Probate. ***Email:*** marshall.yount@sigmonclark.com

REPRESENTATIVE CLIENTS: Hickory Throwing Co.; Sherrill Furniture Company; Gaines Motor Lines Inc.; Hickory Sheet Metal Company, Inc.; Cox Manufacturing Co.; Associated Hardwoods, Inc.; Jordan-Holman Lumber Co., Inc.; Hickory City Board of Education; Taylor King Furniture; Velco Industries, Inc.; Alba Waldensian, Inc.; Hancock & Moore, Inc.; CBSA Architects, Inc.; Branch Banking and Trust Co.
LOCAL COUNSEL FOR: Erie Insurance Co.
APPROVED ATTORNEYS FOR: Lawyers Title Insurance Corp.; Chicago Title Insurance; AMI Title Insurance; Pioneer National Title Insurance Co.; Stewart Title Guaranty Co.; Commonwealth Title; Investors Title.
REFERENCES: Wachovia Bank; Bank of Granite.

STOTT, HOLLOWELL, PALMER & WINDHAM, L.L.P.

HICKORY, NORTH CAROLINA

(See Gastonia)

General Civil and Trial Practice in all Courts. Corporation, Real Estate, Estate Planning and Probate, Insurance, Commercial Law, Municipal Law, Worker Compensation, Bankruptcy, Labor and Employment Law.

LAW OFFICES OF JASON E. TAYLOR

120 THIRD STREET, NE
HICKORY, NORTH CAROLINA 28601
Telephone: 828-327-9004; Toll Free: 800-351-3008
Fax: 828-327-9008
URL: http://www.jasonetaylor.com
Email: Jason@JasonETaylor.com

Mailing Address: P.O. Box 2688 28603-2688

Charlotte, North Carolina Office: 200 North McDowell, 28204. Telephone: 704-350-1646. Fax: 704-350-1648. Toll Free: 1-877-350-1646.

Personal Injury, Automobile Accidents, Motorcycle Accidents, Wrongful Death, Slip and Fall, Medical Malpractice, Workers Compensation, Criminal.

JASON E. TAYLOR, born Fairfax, Virginia, December 20, 1967; admitted to bar, 1993, North Carolina. *Education:* Hobart College (B.A., 1989); Washington College of Law (J.D., cum laude, 1993). Listed in, Strathmore's Who's Who. *Member:* Mecklenburg County and North Carolina Bar Associations; Mecklenburg Trial Lawyers Association (Past President); North Carolina Trial Lawyers Association; Association of Trial Lawyers of America. ***PRACTICE AREAS:*** Personal Injury; Medical Malpractice; Workers Compensation; Criminal Law.

RUFUS F. WALKER, JR.

110 THIRD STREET, NORTH EAST
HICKORY, NORTH CAROLINA 28601
Telephone: 828-328-8101
Fax: 828-328-8103
Email: rfw@charter.net
URL: http://www.lawyers.com/rufuswalkerlaw

General Civil Practice. Trials. Real Estate, Corporation, Estate Planning, Probate, Elder Law and Personal Injury.

RUFUS F. WALKER, JR., born Boston, Massachusetts, November 26, 1946; admitted to bar, 1975, North Carolina and Massachusetts. *Education:* Boston University (A.B., 1969); Suffolk University (J.D., 1975). Public Defender, Mecklenburg County, 1975-1977. *Member:* Catawba County, North Carolina and American Bar Associations; North Carolina Trial Lawyers Association. ***PRACTICE AREAS:*** Corporate Law; Contracts; Probate; Elder Law; Estate Planning; Personal Injury; Civil Litigation; Real Estate.

LOCAL COUNSEL FOR: Bank of Granite.
REPRESENTATIVE CLIENTS: Catawba Valley Association of Realtors, Inc.; Multiple Listing Service of Catawba Valley, Inc.; The Flowers Co.; Edelweiss Manufacturing Co., Inc.; Paramount Motor Sales, Inc.

YOUNG, MORPHIS, BACH AND TAYLOR, L.L.P.

Established in 1949

FIRST LAWYERS BUILDING
400 SECOND AVENUE, N.W.
P.O. DRAWER 2428
HICKORY, NORTH CAROLINA 28603
Telephone: 828-322-4663
FAX: 828-322-2023
Email: lawyers@hickorylaw.com
URL: http://www.hickorylaw.com

General, Civil and Criminal Practice. Trials in all State and Federal Courts and the U.S. Supreme Court. Corporations, Taxation, Probate, Trusts, Real Estate, Commercial, Complex Business and Commercial, Municipal, Family Law, Complex Matrimonial Law, Negligence, Products Liability, Personal Injury, Workers Compensation, Insurance Law, Bankruptcy, Patent Law.

MEMBERS OF FIRM

CHARLES R. YOUNG, born Greenville, South Carolina, October 8, 1942; admitted to bar, 1968, North Carolina. *Education:* Wofford College (B.A., 1965); Wake Forest University (J.D., 1968). Director, 1972— and President, 1979, Greater Hickory United Fund. Member: Real Property Section Council, North Carolina Bar Association, 1973-1980, 1982-1986; Board of Directors, Ten Broeck Hospital, 1979—; Board of Trustees, North Carolina Baptist Hospital, Inc., 1994-1997; Board of Directors (Chairman in 2001), Frye Regional Medical Center; Board of Directors, Deacon Club, Wake Forest University. Presented, Order of Long Leaf Pine, 1987. Vice President/Director, Shareholder, Hickory Baseball, Inc. "Hickory Crawdads" minor league team, 1993—. *Member:* North Carolina and American Bar Associations; North Carolina State Bar. ***PRACTICE AREAS:*** Corporate Law; Real Estate Law; Commercial Transactions. ***Email:*** charlesy@hickorylaw.com

(This Listing Continued)

THOMAS C. MORPHIS, SR., born Greensboro, North Carolina, September 20, 1947; admitted to bar, 1972, North Carolina. *Education:* Guilford College (B.A., 1969); University of North Carolina (J.D., 1972). Delta Theta Phi. *Member:* Catawba County, North Carolina (Member, Professionalism Committee, 2005-2006) and American (Member, Sections on: Litigation and Family Law) Bar Associations; North Carolina State Bar; North Carolina Trial Lawyers Association. **PRACTICE AREAS:** Personal Injury Law; Matrimonial Law; Construction Law; Business Litigation; Commercial Litigation. **Email:** tomm@hickorylaw.com

WAYNE M. BACH, born Washington, D.C., June 6, 1946; admitted to bar, 1973, Virginia; 1974, U.S. Tax Court; 1978, North Carolina and U.S. District Court, Middle District of North Carolina. *Education:* East Carolina University (A.B., 1968); University of Louisville (J.D., cum laude, 1973); College of William & Mary (LL.M. in Taxation, 1974). Phi Kappa Phi. Editor, Law Journal, University of Louisville, 1973. Senior Trial Attorney, Office of Regional Counsel, I.R.S., 1974-1978. *Member:* North Carolina, Virginia and American Bar Associations; North Carolina State Bar (Member, Section on Taxation). **PRACTICE AREAS:** Taxation Law; Estate Planning Law; Probate Law.

TERRY M. TAYLOR, born Hinsdale, Illinois, January 25, 1955; admitted to bar, 1984, North Carolina. *Education:* Western Illinois University (B.S., with high honors, 1977; M.A., with highest honors, 1978) Phi Kappa Phi; Wake Forest University (J.D., 1984). Town Attorney, Sawmills, 1988—. Paralegal Instructor, Caldwell Community College and Technical Institute. Rural Initiative Project Director, Neuse River COG, New Bern, NC, 1978-1980. Special Assistant for Rural Affairs, U.S. Department of HUD, Washington, D.C., 1980-1981. *Member:* Catawba County (Treasurer, 1990 and 1991; Vice President, 1992; President, 1993), 25th District, North Carolina (Member, Real Property and Business Sections) and American Bar Associations; North Carolina State Bar; North Carolina Municipal Attorneys Association. (Certified Specialist, Real Property Law, North Carolina State Board of Legal Specialization). **PRACTICE AREAS:** Municipal Law; Real Estate Law; Wills and Estates Law; Commercial Transactions. **Email:** terryt@hickorylaw.com

T. DEAN AMOS, born Chapel Hill, North Carolina, November 29, 1960; admitted to bar, 1987, North Carolina. *Education:* University of North Carolina at Chapel Hill (B.S., 1983); Wake Forest University (J.D., 1987). *Member:* Catawba County (Secretary, 1998; Vice President, 1999; President, 2001), North Carolina and American Bar Associations; North Carolina State Bar (Member, Family Law and Litigation Sections); Young Lawyers Judicial District Representation (1992-1993), 25th District Treasurer (1994—). **PRACTICE AREAS:** Civil Litigation; Criminal Law; Personal Injury Litigation; Business Litigation; Corporate Law; Family Law.

PAUL E. CULPEPPER, born Greenville, Mississippi, June 28, 1967; admitted to bar, 1993, North Carolina and U.S. District Court, Eastern, Western and Middle Districts of North Carolina; U.S. Court of Appeals, Fourth District; U.S. Supreme Court. *Education:* Wake Forest University (B.A., 1990); Norman A. Wiggins/Campbell University School of Law (J.D., 1993). *Member:* Catawba County, North Carolina and American Bar Associations; North Carolina State Bar; North Carolina Academy of Trial Lawyers. **PRACTICE AREAS:** Civil Litigation; Business Litigation; Employment Law; Workers Compensation. **Email:** paulc@hickorylaw.com

KEVIN C. McINTOSH, born Marion, North Carolina, December 15, 1967; admitted to bar, 1993, North Carolina. *Education:* University of North Carolina at Chapel Hill (B.S., Business Administration, 1990); Campbell University (J.D., 1993). Recipient, Dean's Scholarship. *Member:* Catawba County, North Carolina (Former Judicial Districts Representative, Young Lawyers Division; Member, Sections on: Business Law; Real Property Law; Tax Law; Health Law; Elder Law) and American Bar Associations. **PRACTICE AREAS:** Real Estate; Business Law; Elder Law; Commercial Transactions; Health Care; Health Law. **Email:** kevinm@hickorylaw.com

ASSOCIATES

VALEREE R. ADAMS, born Methuen, Massachusetts, September 27, 1975; admitted to bar, 2000, North Carolina. *Education:* Catawba College (B.A., cum laude, 1997); Campbell University at Buies Creek (J.D., cum laude, 2000). Recipient, Law Review Scholarship, Campbell University. *Member:* Catawba County, North Carolina and American Bar Associations; Christian Legal Society; North Carolina Academy of Trial Lawyers (Member, Sections on: Family Law; Young Lawyers Division). **PRACTICE AREAS:** Civil Litigation; Family Law. **Email:** vadams@hickorylaw.com

JIMMY R. SUMMERLIN, JR., born Tarboro, North Carolina, December 8, 1973; admitted to bar, 2003, North Carolina. *Education:* North Carolina State University (B.S., cum laude, 1995; M.S., 1998); University of Tennessee (Ph.D., 2000; J.D., magna cum laude, Business Transactions Concentration, 2003). Phi Kappa Phi. The Order of the Coif. Recipient: Hilton A. Smith Graduate Fellowship, University of Tennessee; Hunton & Williams Legal Writing Award, University of Tennessee. Staff Editor, Transactions, The Tennessee Journal of Business Law. *Member:* Catawba County, North Carolina and American Bar Associations. **PRACTICE AREAS:** Consumer Bankruptcy; Business Bankruptcy; Debtor and Creditor; Corporate Law; Business Law; Commercial Real Estate; Residential Real Estate; Commercial Transactions; Wills; Estate Administration. **Email:** jimmys@hickorylaw.com

FRANK W. LEAK, born Charlotte, North Carolina, January 30, 1968; admitted to bar, 2001, North Carolina; registered to practice before U.S. Patent and Trademark Office. *Education:* University of North Carolina at Chapel Hill (B.A., 1990; J.D., 2001); North Carolina State University (M.S., Microbiology/Molecular Biology, 1997). Former Associate, Alston & Bird LLP. **PRACTICE AREAS:** Intellectual Property; Patents; Civil Litigation. **Email:** frankl@hickorylaw.com

REPRESENTATIVE CLIENTS: First Citizens Bank & Trust Co.; Donald C. Beaver; Graystone Ophthalmology Associates, P.A.; Hyalyn, Inc.; Shuford Mills, Inc.; A. Klein & Co.; Cramer Lumber Co.; Mutual Insurance Co. of Sawmills; Pepsi-Cola Bottling Company of Hickory, Inc.; Piedmont Natural Gas Co.; Carolina Specialty Tools; DeFeet International, Inc.; Branch Banking and Trust; Cox Mfg.; Enterprise Healthcare; Auto Owners Ins. Co.; Bank of Granite; Lawrence Lumber Co., Inc.; Prism Development, LLC; Hickory-Conover Tourism development Authority; Hospitality Group of Hickory, Inc.; Rock Barn Club of Golf, Inc.; Pierre Foods, Inc.; Hewitt Coleman and Assoc.; North Carolina Forestry Mutual; City of Hickory Public Housing Authority; David E. Looper & Co.; Hickory Yarns; Cajah Mountain Hosler Mill; Record Properties, Inc.; Commercial First, LLC; Hickory Baseball, Inc.; Exodus Outreach Foundation; Rubberflex Sdn. Bhd.; Lutheran Services for the Aging, Inc.; Valley Nursing Center.

(This Listing Continued)

APPROVED ATTORNEYS FOR: Lawyers Title Insurance Corp.; First Title Insurance Co.; Pilot Title Insurance Co.; Investors Title Insurance Co.; Chicago Title Insurance Co.; Commonwealth Land & Title Co.; Fidelity National Title Insurance. References: First Citizens Bank & Trust; Bank of Granite.

LAW OFFICES OF LEONARD F. BAER, PLLC

511 SMALLWOOD AVENUE
P.O. BOX 2619
HIGHLANDS, NORTH CAROLINA 28741
Telephone: 828-526-8411
Fax: 826-526-9834
Email: LegalBaer@aol.com
URL: http://www.LegalBaer.com

Construction Law, Employment Law, Elder Law, Immigration Law.

LEONARD F. BAER, born Troy, New York; admitted to bar, 1977, New York; 1978, Florida and District of Columbia; 2005, North Carolina and Georgia. *Education:* Ithaca College (B.S., Cum Laude, 1964) New England School of Law (J.D., 1973); University of Miami (M.S., with Honors, 1994). Phi Delta Phi. Order of the Coif. Recipient: Trial Advocacy Award; Recipient Moot Court Award. Adjunct Professor, Sports Law, University of Miami, 1994-1998. Select Panel Committee Member to the Federal Courts, Southern District of Florida, Numerous articles for the National Association of Criminal Defense Lawyers. Deputy Chief Major Crimes United States Attorney's Office, Southern District of Florida. *Member:* New York State and North Carolina Bar Association; The Florida Bar (Member, Eminent Domain Committee, 2000-2003); The District of Columbia Bar; State Bar of Georgia; National Association of Criminal Defense Lawyers; American Immigration Lawyers Association; National Academy of Elder Law Attorneys; American Trial Lawyers Association; North Carolina Trial Lawyers Association. **LANGUAGES:** English and Spanish. **PRACTICE AREAS:** Construction Law (60%); Elder Law (20%); Immigration Law (20%). **Email:** LegalBaer@aol.com

JOHN R. MAYER ATTORNEY AT LAW, PLLC

511 SMALLWOOD AVENUE
P.O. BOX 750
HIGHLANDS, NORTH CAROLINA 28741
Telephone: 828-526-3731
Fax: 828-526-3734
Email: jack@jackmayerlaw.com

General Practice including Civil Rights, Class Actions, Employment Law, Personal Injury, Products Liability, Professional Liability, Toxic Torts, Wrongful Death.

JOHN R. MAYER, born Louisville, Kentucky, December 13, 1939; admitted to bar, 1970, Kentucky; 1971, U.S. District Court of the Virgin Islands; 1972, U.S. Court of Appeals, Third Circuit; 1981, North Carolina; 1982, U.S. Court of Appeals, Sixth Circuit. *Education:* University of Louisville (B.A., 1967; J.D., 1970). Reviser, Martindale-Hubbell's Virgin Islands Law Digest, 1972-1980. Town Attorney, Highlands, North Carolina, 1986-1994. *Member:* Kentucky, Virgin Islands (Member, 1976-1979, and Chairman, 1978-1979, Committee on Professional Ethics and Grievances) and American Bar Associations; North Carolina State Bar; Association of Trial Lawyers of America; North Carolina Academy of Trial Lawyers; American Civil Liberties Union; Amnesty International USA; Southern Poverty Law Center.

CREIGHTON W. SOSSOMON

125 PINE STREET
P.O. BOX 9
HIGHLANDS, NORTH CAROLINA 28741
Telephone: 828-526-2101
Fax: 828-526-3654

General Civil Trial Practice. Civil Litigation, Real Estate, Estate Planning and Probate Law.

CREIGHTON W. SOSSOMON, born Charlotte, North Carolina, September 28, 1944; admitted to bar, 1969, North Carolina; 1970, Georgia; 1978, U.S. Court of Appeals, Fourth Circuit. *Education:* University of North Carolina (A.B., 1966; J.D., 1969). *Member:* North Carolina and American Bar Associations; State Bar of Georgia; North Carolina State Bar.

A List of Representative Clients will be furnished upon request.

BAKER LAW OFFICES, PLLC

820 NORTH ELM STREET
HIGH POINT, NORTH CAROLINA 27262
Telephone: 336-885-0111
Fax: 336-885-1460
URL: http://www.baker-lawoffices.com
URL: http://www.lawyers.com/bakerlawofficepllc

General Civil and Criminal Trial Practice. Personal Injury, Criminal, Traffic, Worker's Compensation, Social Security, Estate and Probate.

WALTER W. BAKER, JR., born Raleigh, North Carolina, July 27, 1942; admitted to bar, 1966, North Carolina; 1974, U.S. Supreme Court. *Education:* University of North Carolina (A.B., 1964; J.D., 1966). Phi Alpha Delta. Listed in: The Best Lawyers in America (Personal Injury), 1997—. Research Assistant to Chief Justice R. Hunt Parker, North Caro-

(This Listing Continued)

BAKER LAW OFFICES, PLLC, High Point—Continued

lina Supreme Court, 1966-1967. Adjunct Professor, Trial Advocacy, Wake Forest University, 1998—. Contributing Editor: Wake Forest University, School of Law: North Carolina Civil Trial Book, 1983; North Carolina New Rules of Evidence Handbook, 1985. Continuing Legal Education Lecturer: Medical Workshops, 1976-1977; Lawyer Disciplinary Proceedings, 1977; Law Office Economics and Administration, 1979; Psychological Jury Techniques, 1981; Negotiation Techniques, 1986; Malpractice Prevention, 1986; Persuasion, 1987; Cross-Examination, 1988; Direct Examination, 1989; Personal Injury Damages Law of North Carolina, 1992, 1996, 2000, 2001 and 2004; Preparation of Neck and Back Injury Cases, 1993; Recovering Damages for Enhanced Injuries Due To Plaintiffs Peculiar Susceptibility, 1994; Proving Soft Tissue Damages, 1994; The Opening Statement: A Legitimate Forensic Weapon, 1995; Presenting Plaintiff's Case-in-Chief, 1997; Evidence for Trial Lawyers, 1997; Civil Law Update, 1998; Winning Ways With Cross-Examination, 1998; Trial of Soft Tissue Cases, 1999; Advocacy: The Structure, Setting, and Bounds, 2000; Powerful Courtroom Evidence, 2004; Practical Trial Skills Workshop for Lawyers and Students, annually; NITA Southeastern Trial Advocacy Faculty, 2000—; Evidentiary Foundations 2003; Q&A Testimonial Evidence 2003; Artful Witness Examination: Question Structure and Testimony Control, 2004. Ethics Lecturer and Facilitator: Negotiations, 1992; Litigation, 1993; General Practice: A Primer, 1994; Ethics for Trial Lawyers, 1995. Ethics of Advocacy, 2004. *Member:* High Point (President, 1986), North Carolina and American Bar Associations; North Carolina State Bar (Councilor, 18th Judicial District, 1991-1999); North Carolina Academy of Trial Lawyers (President, 1985); The Association of Trial Lawyers of America; Justice Joseph Branch Inn of Court (Master); American Board of Trial Advocates (Advocate and President, North Carolina Western Chapter, 2001); Million Dollar Advocates Forum. ***PRACTICE AREAS:*** Personal Injury; Civil Litigation. ***Email:*** walt@baker-lawoffices.com

JEFFREY L. MABE, born Greensboro, North Carolina, December 16, 1956; admitted to bar, 1982, North Carolina and U.S. District Court, Middle District of North Carolina. *Education:* University of North Carolina at Greensboro (B.A., magna cum laude, 1979); Wake Forest University (J.D., 1982). Phi Beta Kappa. Member, Editorial Staff, Wake Forest Law Review, 1982. *Member:* High Point and North Carolina Bar Associations; North Carolina State Bar; North Carolina Academy of Trial Lawyers. ***PRACTICE AREAS:*** Workers Compensation; Social Security Claims. ***Email:*** jeff@baker-lawoffices.com

ASSOCIATE

WALTER W. (TRIP) BAKER III, born High Point, North Carolina, August 9, 1977; admitted to bar, 2004, North Carolina. *Education:* University of North Carolina at Asheville (B.A., 1999); Wake Forest University (J.D., 2003). *Member:* High Point, North Carolina and American Bar Associations; North Carolina Academy of Trial Lawyers; The Association of Trial Lawyers of America. ***Email:*** trip@baker-lawoffices.com

---

BARRON & BERRY, L.L.P.

HIGH POINT, NORTH CAROLINA

(See Greensboro)

Personal Injury, Medical Malpractice, Automobile Accidents, Wrongful Death, Products Liability and Brain Injury.

JEFFREY S. BERMAN

HIGH POINT, NORTH CAROLINA

(See Greensboro)

Family Law, Divorce, Child Custody, Alimony, Criminal Law, Traffic Violations, Driving While Intoxicated, Civil Litigation, Personal Injury, Wills and Estates.

BOOTH HARRINGTON & JOHNS, LLP

HIGH POINT, NORTH CAROLINA

(See Greensboro)

LAW OFFICES OF JOSEPH E. BRUNER

Established in 1982

510 FERNDALE BOULEVARD, SUITE 101
HIGH POINT, NORTH CAROLINA 27262
Telephone: 336-889-7277
Fax: 336-889-5155
URL: http://wwwbrunerlawfirm.com
Email: joebruner@brunerlaw.com
URL: http://www.brunerlaw.com

Criminal Defense, Felonies, Drug Crimes, White Collar Crimes, Driving While Impaired, Traffic Violations, Automobile Accidents, Personal Injury, Medical Malpractice, Workers Compensation, Business Law, Tax Law.

JOSEPH E. BRUNER, born Salisbury, North Carolina, September 29, 1948; admitted to bar, 1974, North Carolina; U.S. District Court, Middle District of North Carolina. *Education:* University of Georgia (B.B.A., 1970); University of North Carolina (J.D., 1974). Special Agent: Internal Revenue Service Intelligence Division, 1974-1975; Federal Bureau of Investigation, 1975-1978. Assistant District Attorney, Guilford County, 1978-1980. Assistant Public Defender, Guilford County, 1980-1982. *Member:* Greensboro/High Point and North Carolina Bar Associations; North Carolina State Bar; North Carolina Academy of Trial Lawyers; Greensboro Criminal Defense Lawyers Association. [With U.S. Marine Corps, 1970-1971]. ***PRACTICE AREAS:*** Criminal Law; Personal Injury; Medical Malpractice; Traffic Violations; Driving While Impaired.

(This Listing Continued)

ASSOCIATE

JUAN F. ZULUAGA, born Medellin, Colombia, June 3, 1972; admitted to bar, 2003, Florida; 2005, North Carolina. *Education:* University of North Carolina, Greensboro (B.S., magna cum laude, 1999); University of North Carolina at Chapel Hill (J.D., 2003). Recipient: M. & W. Johnson Law Scholarship; Dixie Atwater Law Scholarship. President, Hispanic Latino Law Student Association. Member, Law School Minority Advisory Committee. Participant: Trial Law Academy Competition; Carolina Mediation Society Competition. Financial Specialist, First Union National Bank, 1999-2000. International Sales Representative, USAirways, 1996-1998. *Member:* North Carolina and American Bar Associations; The Florida Bar; North Carolina Academy of Trial Lawyers Association; Broward County Hispanic Bar Association. [Operation Iraqi Freedom II, 2004-2005 and Airborne Infantry, 1990-1994, U.S. Army; Engineer, Army National Guard, 1994—]. ***LANGUAGES:*** Spanish. ***PRACTICE AREAS:*** Criminal Defense; Traffic Violations; Driving While Intoxicated; Personal Injury; Workers Compensation. ***Email:*** jfzuluaga@brunerlaw.com

Languages: Spanish.

RON BUTLER

Established in 1986

322 SOUTH WRENN STREET
P.O. BOX 2594
HIGH POINT, NORTH CAROLINA 27261
Telephone: 336-841-7915
Fax: 336-885-5152
Email: hplaw@prodigy.net
URL: http://www.ronbutlerlawfirm.com

Traffic Violations, Criminal Law, Driving While Intoxicated, Family Law, Divorce and Juvenile Law. Wills.

RONALD P. BUTLER, born Roanoke, Virginia, December 30, 1952; admitted to bar, 1982, North Carolina. *Education:* Elon University (B.A., 1975); North Carolina Central University (J.D., 1982). Phi Alpha Delta. Assistant Public Defender, Guilford County, 1982-1985. District Court Arbitrator, Guilford County. *Member:* North Carolina and American Bar Associations; North Carolina Academy of Trial Lawyers. ***PRACTICE AREAS:*** Traffic Violations; Criminal Law; Driving While Intoxicated; Family Law; Divorce; Personal Injury; Juvenile Law; Wills.

CARRUTHERS & ROTH, P.A.

HIGH POINT, NORTH CAROLINA

(See Greensboro)

Business and Civil Trial Practice. Trials in all State and Federal Courts. Administrative, Hearings, Arbitration, Business, Corporation, Partnership, Limited Liability Company, Secured Transactions, Banking, Pension, Profit-Sharing and Employee Benefits, Employment, International, Intellectual Property, Corporate Reorganization, Bankruptcy, Debtors' and Creditors' Rights, Estate Planning, Probate and Trust, Elder Law, Medicaid Planning, Real Estate, Administrative, Environmental, Taxation, Construction, Product Liability, Professional Liability, Negligence, Insurance, Personal Injury and Workers Compensation Law.

EWING CARTER III, P.A.

1004 N. MAIN STREET, SUITE 102
HIGH POINT, NORTH CAROLINA 27262
Telephone: 336-883-2247
Fax: 336-883-2696
Email: lawoffice@ecarterlaw.com

Personal Injury, Workers Compensation, Driving While Intoxicated, Driving While License Revoked, Speeding Tickets, Auto Accidents, Wrongful Death, Traffic Violations, Slip and Fall.

EWING CARTER III, born Springfield, Ohio, February 24, 1959; admitted to bar, 1991, North Carolina. *Education:* Wilmington College (B.A., 1981); Miami University (M.S., 1987); University of Cincinnati College of Law (J.D., 1991). *Member:* High Point, North Carolina and American Bar Associations; Association of Trial Lawyers of America; North Carolina Academy of Trial Lawyers. ***PRACTICE AREAS:*** Personal Injury (35%); Workers Compensation (35%); Driving While Intoxicated (10%); Driving While License Revoked (10%); Speeding Tickets (10%); Automobile Accidents; Wrongful Death; Traffic Violations; Slip and Fall. ***Email:*** lawoffice@ecarterlaw.com

---

AMES C. CHAMBERLIN

HIGH POINT, NORTH CAROLINA

(See Greensboro)

Drug Cases, Drunk Driving Cases, Homicide/Capital Cases, Traffic Cases, Federal Cases; Assault Cases, Expunctions, Probation Violation Cases, Fraud Cases; White Collar Crime, and Domestic Violence Cases.

MERCEDES OGLUKIAN CHUT

HIGH POINT, NORTH CAROLINA

(See Greensboro)

Civil Litigation in State and Federal Courts, Appellate Law, Bankruptcy, Business, Local Government, Employment (Employer), Divorce.

CLIFFORD CLENDENIN O'HALE & JONES, LLP

HIGH POINT, NORTH CAROLINA

(See Greensboro)

General Civil and Criminal Practice. Trials in all State and Federal Courts. Personal Injury, Wrongful Death, Products Liability, Workers Compensation, Criminal Trials and Appeals, Federal Forfeitures, Grand Jury Practice, Criminal Law, Drugs and Narcotics, Fraud and Deceit, Money Laundering, white Collar Crime, Occupational Safety and Health, Workers Compensation, Premises Liability, Personal Injury, Criminal Appeals, Capital Offenses.

DAIL & LINTON

407 FERNDALE BOULEVARD
HIGH POINT, NORTH CAROLINA 27262
Telephone: 336-889-0138
Fax: 336-889-0341
Email: dail-linton@northstate.net
URL: http://www.dailandlinton.com

Personal Injury, Automobile Accidents, Slip and Fall, Wrongful Death, Family Law, Adoption Law, Child Custody, Child Support, Divorce, Domestic Violence, Criminal Law, Driving While Intoxicated, Drug Crimes, Traffic Violations, Business Litigation, Trial Practice, General Practice, Workers Compensation.

MEMBERS OF FIRM

RICHARD T. DAIL, born Clinton, North Carolina, April 3, 1963; admitted to bar, 1998, North Carolina and U.S. District Court, Middle District of North Carolina. *Education:* Embry-Riddle Aeronautical University (B.S., 1988); Campbell University (J.D., 1998). *Member:* North Carolina State Bar; North Carolina Academy of Trial Lawyers. [Former Captain, U.S. Air Force]. ***PRACTICE AREAS:*** Personal Injury; Criminal Law; Domestic Relations; Business Litigation; Family Law; Divorce; Child Custody.

WILBUR L. LINTON, JR., born Syracuse, New York, May 1, 1967; admitted to bar, 1998, North Carolina and U.S. Court of Appeals, Fourth Circuit. *Education:* Greensboro College (B.A., 1995); Campbell University (J.D., 1998). Delta Theta Phi. *Member:* North Carolina Bar Association; North Carolina State Bar; North Carolina Academy of Trial Lawyers. [U.S. Army, 1986-1990]. ***PRACTICE AREAS:*** Business Litigation; Personal Injury; Criminal Law; Automobile Accidents; Domestic Relations; Family Law; Child Custody; Divorce.

REPRESENTATIVE CLIENTS: Galaxy Motor Sports; Global Airways; Hydraulics, Inc.; MLP Construction; First Aide Restorations; Homes 'R' Us; Slipknot, Inc.

CHERYL K. DAVID

HIGH POINT, NORTH CAROLINA

(See Greensboro)

Estate Planning, Elder Law, Asset Protection, Trusts and Estates, Wills and Probate, Guardianship.

THE DEUTERMAN LAW GROUP, P.A.

HIGH POINT, NORTH CAROLINA

(See Greensboro)

Workers Compensation, Auto Accidents, Social Security Disability, Wrongful Death, Nursing Home Neglect, Slip and Fall, Products Liability.

DOUGLAS, RAVENEL, HARDY, CRIHFIELD & HOYLE, L.L.P.

HIGH POINT, NORTH CAROLINA

(See Greensboro)

General Civil Practice. Trials in all State Courts. Corporation, Real Estate, Estate Planning, Probate, Family, Child Support, Child Custody, Divorce, Arbitrations, Personal Injury, and Mediation Law.

LAW OFFICE OF JODI A. ERNEST

HIGH POINT, NORTH CAROLINA

(See Greensboro)

Real Estate, Residential, Buying or Selling Home, Commercial Real Estate, Conveyancing, Living Wills, Wills.

FISHER, CLINARD & CORNWELL, PLLC

Established in 1924
SUITE 800 GE CAPITAL BUILDING
101 S. MAIN STREET
P.O. BOX 1150
HIGH POINT, NORTH CAROLINA 27261
Telephone: 336-883-9156
Fax: 336-886-8593
URL: http://www.highpointlaw.com

Corporation and Business, General Trial and Appellate Practice, Estate Planning and Administration, Taxation, Bankruptcy, Inter-creditor workouts, Commercial Real Estate, Banking, Commercial and Construction Litigation, Municipal Law, Zoning, Mediation and Dispute Resolution, Criminal, Traffic, Personal Injury and Wrongful Death.

FIRM PROFILE: Founded in 1924, making it one of High Point's oldest law offices, the firm provides a broad range of legal services to corporations and businesses throughout the Piedmont Triad area; and, advises and represents national and international clients, many of which are involved in the home furnishings industry. Additionally, the Fisher firm has a long-standing working relationship with two law firms, one of which specializes in Trademark, Patent and Copyright law and the other in Immigration and Naturalization law. Listed in the Bar Register of Preeminent Lawyers.

LOUIS J. FISHER, SR. (1901-1981)

LOUIS J. FISHER, JR. (1935-2004)

AARON NEAL CLINARD, born Thomasville, North Carolina, March 19, 1947; admitted to bar, 1977, North Carolina and U.S. District Court, Middle District of North Carolina; 1989, U.S. Supreme Court. *Education:* University of North Carolina (A.B., 1972); Wake Forest University (J.D., 1976). General Counsel for High Point Chamber of Commerce. Board of Directors, High Point Economic Development Corporation. Chairman, High Point Downtown Improvement Committee (2000—). Director, High Point Showroom Association (Design Center). Town Attorney for Wallburg, N.C. Board of Visitors, High Point University. Certified Mediator, North Carolina. *Member:* High Point, 18th Judicial District and North Carolina Bar Associations; North Carolina State Bar. [Sergeant E-5, U.S. Army Vietnam, 1969 . Army Commendation Medal]. ***PRACTICE AREAS:*** Corporate Law; Municipal Law; Zoning Law; Estate Administration; Wills; Civil and Commercial Litigation; Wrongful Death; Personal Injury. ***Email:*** aclinard@highpointlaw.com

RICK CORNWELL, born Shawnee, Oklahoma, April 7, 1949; admitted to bar, 1974, Oklahoma; 1980, U.S. District Court, Western District of Oklahoma; 1981, U.S. Tax Court; 1988, North Carolina and U.S. District Court, Middle District of North Carolina. *Education:* Oklahoma State University (B.A., 1971); University of Oklahoma (J.D., 1974). Phi Kappa Phi; Phi Delta Phi; Order of the Coif; Member, High Point Estate Planning Council. *Member:* Oklahoma Bar Association; North Carolina State Bar; American Institute of Certified Public Accountants; North Carolina Association of Certified Public Accountants. ***PRACTICE AREAS:*** Trusts and Estates; Taxation; Business Law; Wills. ***Email:*** rcornwell@highpointlaw.com

SHANE T. STUTTS, born Falls Church, Virginia, May 14, 1972; admitted to bar, 1997, North Carolina. *Education:* University of North Carolina (B.A., with honors, 1994); University of Richmond, T.C. Williams School of Law (J.D., 1997). Former Assistant District Attorney for Guilford County. *Member:* High Point, 18th Judicial District and North Carolina Bar Associations; North Carolina State Bar; Guilford Inn of Court (Associate); Association of Trial Lawyers of America. ***PRACTICE AREAS:*** Civil Litigation; Commercial Litigation; Collections Law; Personal Injury; Criminal Law. ***Email:*** sstutts@highpointlaw.com

---

ROBERT A. LEFKOWITZ, born Richmond, Virginia, December 24, 1958; admitted to bar, 1984, Virginia; 1994, North Carolina. *Education:* University of Richmond (B.A., with honors, summa cum laude, 1981); College of William & Mary (J.D., 1984). Phi Beta Kappa. Law Clerk to the Honorable Hal J. Bonney, Jr., U.S. Bankruptcy Judge, Eastern District of Virginia, and the Honorable Douglas O. Tice, Jr., Chief U.S. Bankruptcy Judge for the Eastern District of Virginia. Past Contributing Author: Collier Bankruptcy Exemption Guide and Collier on Bankruptcy. *Member:* North Carolina (Past Member, Business Law Curriculum Committee; Past Councilor and Past Seminar Chairperson, Bankruptcy Section) and American Bar Associations. (Board Certified Specialist in Business Bankruptcy Law, North Carolina State Board of Legal Specialization). ***REPORTED CASES:*** Patterson v. Shumate, 504 U.S. 753, 112 S.Ct. 2242, 199 L.Ed 2nd 519 (1992); Old Salem Foreign Car Serv. v. Webb et al., 582 S.E.2d 673 (N.C. App. 2003). ***PRACTICE AREAS:*** Bankruptcy Law; General Corporate; Commercial Litigation; Commercial Workouts; Creditor Bankruptcy; Debtor Bankruptcy; Pre-Bankruptcy Workouts. ***Email:*** rlefkowitz@highpointlaw.com

JAY W. WAGNER, born High Point, North Carolina, June 17, 1968; admitted to bar, 1998, North Carolina and U.S. District Court, Middle District of North Carolina. *Education:* University of North Carolina (A.B., 1990); North Carolina Central University (J.D., 1998). Member, Moot Court Board. Member, North Carolina Central University Law Journal. Vice Chairman, Planning & Zoning Commission, City of High Point, 2005-2006. Member, Rotary Club of High Point. *Member:* High Point Bar and North Carolina Bar Associations; North Carolina State Bar; 18th Judicial District Bar,. ***PRACTICE AREAS:*** Real Estate (70%); Civil Litigation (15%); Wills (5%); Trusts and Estates (5%); Corporate Law (5%). ***Email:*** jwagner@highpointlaw.com

REPRESENTATIVE CLIENTS:
COUNSEL FOR: High Point Chamber of Commerce, Inc., High Point Community Foundation; Town of Wallburg, N.C.; and High Point Country Club, Inc.; Showplace! LLC; Hamilton Properties; Arpel Leather, Inc.; Niroflex Imp. Exp. Ltda; Giovanni Leather, Inc.; Branch Banking and Trust Co.(BB&T); Bekaert Textiles U.S.A., Inc.; Calia Maxim U.S.A., Incorporated; LC Mobili S.r.l.; Carolina Cardiology Associates, P.A.; Pinewest OB-GYN, Inc.; Phillips Interests, Inc.; Carolina Process Piping; Sharrard McGee and Co., P.A.; Odom & Company, LLP; Ledford Productions, Inc.; Furnitureland South, Inc.

(This Listing Continued)

FISHER, CLINARD & CORNWELL, PLLC, High Point—Continued

APPROVED ATTORNEYS FOR: Lawyers Title; First American Title; Commonwealth Title; Chicago Title; Investors Title.

FRAZIER & FRAZIER, LLP

HIGH POINT, NORTH CAROLINA

(See Greensboro)

General Practice. Trials in all State and Federal Courts, Corporate and Commercial Transactions, Estate Planning and Administration, Civil Litigation, Personal Injury and Insurance Litigation, Taxation and Real Estate Development, Commercial and Residential Transactions.

GABRIEL BERRY & WESTON, L.L.P.

HIGH POINT, NORTH CAROLINA

(See Greensboro)

General Civil Practice in all Courts. Insurance, Real Estate, Civil Litigation, Personal Injury, Family, Divorce, Custody, Taxation, Probate, Estate Planning Corporation Law.

GOULDER IMMIGRATION LAW FIRM

HIGH POINT, NORTH CAROLINA

(See Greensboro)

Immigration and Naturalization, Visas, U.S. Citizenship, Student Visa, HI-B, L Visas, E Visas, Employment Visa, J-Visa, Fiancée Visas, all Family-Based Immigration Visas and Adjustments of Status.

HANDLER & BROWN, P.L.L.C.

HIGH POINT, NORTH CAROLINA

(See Winston-Salem)

Business Law, Commercial Law, Insurance Premium Finance Law, Factoring, Leasing, Licensing, Franchise Law, Intellectual Property Law, Trademarks, Copyrights, Unfair Competition, Real Estate, Condominium Law, Association Law, Land Use, Environmental Law, Commercial Litigation, Unfair Trade Practice Law, Creditors Rights, Civil Trial Practice, Appellate Practice, Arbitration, Class Actions, Constitutional Law, Professional Liability, Medical Malpractice, Products Liability, Personal Injury, Civil Rights, Labor and Employment, Wrongful Discharge and Discrimination Law.

ANN E. HANKS

202 W. LEXINGTON AVENUE
HIGH POINT, NORTH CAROLINA 27262
Telephone: 336-812-3073
Fax: 1-866-521-5296
Email: ahanks@triad.rr.com
URL: http://www.annhankslaw.com

Mailing Address: P.O. Box 5064, High Point, NC 27262

Trusts and Estates, Asset Protection, Estate Planning, Guardianship, Wills and Probate, Tax Planning, Elder Law.

ANN E. HANKS, born Winston-Salem, North Carolina, January 23, 1954; admitted to bar, 1979, North Carolina. *Education:* University of North Carolina at Chapel Hill (A.B., 1976; J.D., 1979). Phi Beta Kappa. Certified Financial Planner, 1986. Certified Public Accountant, North Carolina, 1988. Chartered Life Underwriters, 1988. Chartered Financial Consultant, 1988. Member, High Point Estate Planning Council. *Member:* North Carolina Bar Association; North Carolina Association of Certified Public Accountants. Fellow, American College of Trust and Estate Counsel. (Board Certified Specialist in Estate Planning and Probate Law, North Carolina State Board of Legal Specialization). ***PRACTICE AREAS:*** Probate; Wills; Trusts and Estates.

HENSON & HENSON, L.L.P.

HIGH POINT, NORTH CAROLINA

(See Greensboro)

General Civil Practice, Trials and Appeals in all State and Federal Courts, Personal Injury, Automobile, Workers' Compensation, Wrongful Death, Medical Malpractice, Legal Malpractice, Insurance, Professional Malpractice, Products Liability, Fire, ERISA and Insurance Defense.

HILL, EVANS, DUNCAN, JORDAN & BEATTY

HIGH POINT, NORTH CAROLINA

(See Greensboro)

General Civil Practice. Banking, Bankruptcy, Construction, Corporation, Mediation, Employment, Environmental, Estate Planning, Family, Insurance, Labor, Personal Injury, Product Liability, Real Estate, Surety, Taxation, Trade Regulation, Wills and Trusts, Workers Compensation Law, Municipal and Police Liability, Criminal and Traffic.

THE HOWARD LAW FIRM, P.C.

SPRING TREE OFFICE PARK
2115 EASTCHESTER DRIVE
HIGH POINT, NORTH CAROLINA 27265
Telephone: 336-885-3124
Fax: 336-885-3116

Family Law, Adoptions, Child Custody, Divorce, Child Support, Domestic Violence, Alimony, Contempt, Interstate Child Custody Matters, Termination of Parental Rights.

MOLLY NALL HOWARD, born South Boston, Virginia, July 9, 1969; admitted to bar, 1994, North Carolina. *Education:* Duke University (B.A., 1991); Wake Forest University (J.D., 1994). Lecturer, "Children of Divorce," Program, High Point Family Services. *Member:* High Point, North Carolina (Member, Family Law Section) and American Bar Associations. ***LANGUAGES:*** French and Italian. ***PRACTICE AREAS:*** Family Law; Children; Child Custody; Alimony; Equitable Distribution. ***Email:*** molly@triadbiz.rr.com

D. DARREN HOWARD, born 1968; admitted to bar, 1997, North Carolina. *Education:* Duke University (B.A., 1990); Wake Forest University (J.D., 1997); Johns Hopkins University (M.S., Finance). *Member:* North Carolina Academy of Trial Lawyers. ***PRACTICE AREAS:*** Personal Injury; Workers Compensation; Collections; Family Law.

LEGAL SUPPORT PERSONNEL

CHERILYN McCRAY, Certified Legal Assistant.
SHERRY DIXON, (Legal Assistant)

DAVID H. IDOL

704 NORTH MAIN STREET
P.O. BOX 1776
HIGH POINT, NORTH CAROLINA 27261-1776
Telephone: 336-889-8111
Fax: 336-889-7764

Personal Injury, General Civil and Criminal Practice, Bankruptcy, Real Estate, Commercial, Wills and Estates, Corporations and Partnerships, Traffic Violations, Driving While Intoxicated, Social Security Disability.

DAVID H. IDOL, born High Point, North Carolina, May 20, 1946; admitted to bar, 1973, North Carolina and U.S. District Court, Middle District of North Carolina; 1977, U.S. Supreme Court. *Education:* Woodberry Forest School; King's College, Taunton, Somerset, England; Yale University; University of North Carolina (B.A., honors in English, 1969; J.D., 1972). Phi Alpha Delta. Law Clerk, U.S. Court of Appeals, Fourth Circuit, 1972-1973. Assistant District Attorney, Eighteenth Judicial District, 1973-1982. *Member:* High Point and North Carolina Bar Associations; Eighteenth Judicial District and North Carolina State Bars; North Carolina Academy of Trial Lawyers.

KEZIAH, GATES & SAMET, L.L.P.

Established in 1977
SUITE 400 HIGH POINT BANK & TRUST BUILDING
300 NORTH MAIN STREET
P.O. BOX 2608
HIGH POINT, NORTH CAROLINA 27261-2608
Telephone: 336-889-6900
336-889-7055
Email: info@keziahgates.com
URL: http://www.keziahgates.com

General Civil Practice in State and Federal Courts. Trials and Appeals, Real Estate, Banking, Corporate Law, Estate Planning and Probate, Construction Law, Taxation, Commercial Law and Collections.

FIRM PROFILE: Keziah, Gates & Samet was founded in 1977. Its principal areas of practice are (I) business and tax planning and transactions for privately held businesses and their owners, (II) commercial loans and transactions, (III) estate planning and probate, (IV) commercial and residential real property development and transactions, (V) commercial, corporate and business litigation, including construction litigation and arbitration (VI) commercial and retail collections, including representation of creditors in bankruptcy proceedings. The firm's normal practice is to refer personal injury, criminal, family law and workers' compensation matters to others.

PARTNERS

S. PERRY KEZIAH, born High Point, North Carolina, November 18, 1930; admitted to bar, 1954, North Carolina and U.S. District Court, Middle District of North Carolina; 1958, U.S. Tax Court; 1971, Florida. *Education:* Duke University (A.B., 1952; J.D., 1954). Delta Theta Phi. Business Editor and Editorial Board Member, Duke Bar Journal, 1953-1954. Listed in The Best Lawyers in America, Taxation Section. Staff Attorney and Instructor of Legal Aid, Duke Law School, 1954-1955. Special Agent, U.S. Army Counterintelligence Corps, Active Duty, 1955-1957. Special Trial Attorney, Office of Chief Counsel, U.S. Internal Revenue Service, 1957-1961. Member, 1962-1964 and Chairman, 1963, High Point, North Carolina, Municipal Election Board. Member and Secretary, Guilford County Board of Elections, 1964-1970. Board Member, Duke University Estate Planning Council. *Member:* High Point, North Carolina (Member: CLE Committee, 1979-1982; Southeastern Region IRS Tax Liaison, 1977-1979; Continuing Legal Education Seminar Lecturer, 1977-1978, 1980) and American Bar Associations; 18th Judicial District (President, 1985-1986) and North Carolina State Bars; The Florida Bar. Fellow, The American College of Trust and Estate Counsel. ***PRACTICE AREAS:*** Corporations Law; Taxation Law; Estate Planning Law. ***Email:*** keziah@keziahgates.com

(This Listing Continued)

GILBERT L. GATES, born Essex County, New Jersey, December 15, 1942; admitted to bar, 1968, North Carolina; 1969, U.S. District Court, Middle District of North Carolina; 1971, U.S. Tax Court; 1975, U.S. Court of Appeals, Fourth Circuit; 1976, U.S. Supreme Court. *Education:* Duke University (B.A., 1965; J.D., 1968). Phi Delta Phi. *Member:* High Point (Secretary, 1977-1978; Vice President, 1986-1987; President, 1987-1988), 18th Judicial District (Secretary, 1974-1975; President, 1991-1992), North Carolina (Member, Real Property Section Council, 1995-1997) and American Bar Associations; North Carolina State Bar. ***PRACTICE AREAS:*** Commercial Leasing; Commercial Real Property; Zoning, Planning and Land Use Law; Estate Planning Law. ***Email:*** gates@keziahgates.com

JAN H. SAMET, born Lumberton, North Carolina, June 3, 1945; admitted to bar, 1973, North Carolina, U.S. District Court, Eastern District of North Carolina; 1975, U.S. District Court, Middle District of North Carolina and U.S. Court of Appeals, Fourth Circuit; 1985, U.S. Supreme Court. *Education:* High Point University and University of North Carolina at Greensboro (B.A., 1967); University of North Carolina at Chapel Hill (J.D., 1973). Recipient, North Carolina Bar Association Centennial Award, 2003. Author: *The Latin American Approach to the Law of the Sea.* Law Clerk to Algernon L. Butler, Chief Judge, U.S. District Court, Eastern District of North Carolina, 1973-1975. *Member:* High Point (Member, Young Lawyers Section; President, 1976-1977; Secretary, 1981-1982; Vice President, 1992-1993; President, 1993-1994; Chairman, Grievance Committee, 1996-1999), North Carolina (Member, Young Lawyers Section: Vice-Chairman Youth and Law Committee, 1976-1977; Law Practice Management Council; Local Bar Services Council) ; North Carolina State Bar; 18th Judicial District Bar (Vice President, 1996-1997; President, 1997-1998; Council of Bar President, 1999-2006; State Bar Counselor, 1999-2006); Guilford Inns of Court (President, 2001-2003). ***PRACTICE AREAS:*** Commercial Law; Trial Practice. ***Email:*** jsamet@keziahgates.com

CHARLES E. LYNCH, JR., born Bennettsville, South Carolina, January 22, 1947; admitted to bar, 1971, South Carolina; 1972, North Carolina. *Education:* University of North Carolina (A.B., 1968); University of South Carolina (J.D., 1971); New York University (LL.M. in Taxation, 1973). *Member:* High Point and North Carolina (Member, Taxation Section) Bar Associations; North Carolina State Bar; South Carolina Bar. ***PRACTICE AREAS:*** Corporate Law; Taxation Law; Mergers, Acquisitions and Divestitures; Business; Commercial Transactions; Estate Planning. ***Email:*** cel@keziahgates.com

ANDREW S. LASINE, born High Point, North Carolina, February 24, 1957; admitted to bar, 1983, North Carolina and U.S. District Court, Middle and Eastern Districts of North Carolina; 1985, U.S. Court of Appeals, Fourth Circuit. *Education:* Duke University (A.B., cum laude, 1979); Washington & Lee University (J.D., 1983). *Member:* High Point and North Carolina (Secretary, General Practice Council, 1987-1993) Bar Associations; 18th Judicial District and North Carolina State Bars. ***PRACTICE AREAS:*** Construction Law; Commercial Law; Trial Practice. ***Email:*** sam@keziahgates.com

STEVEN H. BOULDIN, born High Point, North Carolina, December 16, 1962; admitted to bar, 1988, North Carolina and U.S. District Court, Middle District of North Carolina. *Education:* Duke University (A.B., magna cum laude, 1985); Wake Forest University (J.D., 1988). *Member:* High Point (Secretary-Treasurer, 1995-1996) and North Carolina Bar Associations; North Carolina State Bar. ***PRACTICE AREAS:*** Business; Commercial Transactions; Real Estate; Estate Planning. ***Email:*** sbouldin@keziahgates.com

ALAN N. POST, born High Point, North Carolina, October 10, 1958; admitted to bar, 1986, North Carolina and U.S. District Court, Middle District of North Carolina. *Education:* The Lawrenceville School; Brown University (A.B., 1981); Cumberland School of Law at Samford University (J.D., 1984). Member, Local Advisory Board, First Bank. *Member:* High Point, Guilford County, North Carolina and American Bar Associations; North Carolina State Bar. ***PRACTICE AREAS:*** Real Estate Law; Real Estate Finance; Condemnation; Trials; Probate; Trust Law; Corporate; Zoning, Planning and Land Use. ***Email:*** apost@keziahgates.com

OF COUNSEL

MAURICE S. S. HULL, born Greensboro, North Carolina, February 14, 1953; admitted to bar, 1979, North Carolina, U.S. District Court, Middle District of North Carolina and U.S. Court of Appeals, Fourth Circuit; 1985, U.S. Supreme Court. *Education:* Wofford College (B.A., 1975); Wake Forest University (J.D., 1979). Phi Delta Phi. *Member:* High Point and North Carolina Bar Associations; 18th Judicial District and North Carolina State Bars. ***PRACTICE AREAS:*** Real Property Law; Leases and Leasing; Zoning, Planning and Land Use; Environmental Law; Corporate Law.

ASSOCIATE

GRANT W. ALMOND, born Raleigh, North Carolina, November 12, 1976; admitted to bar, 2002, North Carolina and U.S. District Court, Middle District of North Carolina. *Education:* University of North Carolina at Chapel Hill (B.A., 1999); Campbell University, Norman Adrian Wiggins School of Law (J.D., 2002). *Member:* High Point and North Carolina Bar Associations; North Carolina State Bar. ***PRACTICE AREAS:*** Business Law; Commercial Transactions; Estate Planning. ***Email:*** galmond@keziahgates.com

COUNSEL FOR: Atlantic Insurance & Realty Co.; Bank of America, N.A.; Beeson Hardware & Lumber Co.; BURCO Welding & Cutting Products, Inc.; Carolyn Fabrics, Inc.; CBL & Associates; Colonial, LLC; Commonwealth Hosiery Mills, Inc.; First Bank; Four Star Hosiery, Ltd.; Freud America, Inc.; Fulterer USA, Incorporated; Furniture Manufacturers Credit Assn., Inc.; Harris Teeter, Inc.; Guy M. Turner, Inc.; Harriss & Covington Hosiery Mills, Inc.; High Point Bank & Trust Co.; High Point Fiber, Inc.; High Point Regional Health Systems; High Point Sprinkler Inc.; High Point University; Honbarrier, Inc.; IHFC Properties, LLC; Latham Entertainment, Inc.; La-Z-Boy Incorporated; Lighting & Accessories, Inc.; Lighting Creations, Inc.; Mann Media, Inc.; Mickey Truck Bodies, Inc.; Miller Desk, Inc.; North State Communications Inc; ; North Pointe Partners, L.L.C.; Old Dominion Freight Line, Inc.; Ornamental Products, LLC; Ornamenetal Mouldings, LLC; Quality Hardware, Inc. and Affiliates; Samples, Inc.; Sealy, Inc.; Smith General Contractors, Inc.; Spence & Lester of High Point, Inc.; Sunland Fire Protection Inc.; Triad Steel Co.; Vann York Pontiac, Inc.; Vann York Toyota, Inc.; WGHP-TV, Inc.; J.B. White Construction Co.; Williard-Stewart, Inc.; Woodworkers Supply, Inc.

APPROVED ATTORNEYS FOR: Chicago Title Insurance Co.; Lawyers Title Insurance Corp.; First American Title Insurance Co.; First Title Insurance Co.; Commonwealth Land Title Co.; Investors Title Insurance Co.; Old Republic Title Insurance Co.; Stewart Title Insurance Corp. References: High Point Bank & Trust Co.; First-Citizens Bank & Trust Co.; Bank of America, N.A.; Branch Banking & Trust; SouthTrust Bank.

HORACE M. KIMEL, JR.

HIGH POINT, NORTH CAROLINA

(See Greensboro)

Criminal, Traffic Offenses, Traffic Violations, Drug Offense, Homicide and Serious Offenses Against Persons. Personal Injury, Felonies, Misdemeanors, DWI, DMV Hearings, Driving While License Revoked.

ALETA B. KISER

2201 EASTCHESTER DRIVE, SUITE 105
HIGH POINT, NORTH CAROLINA 27265
Telephone: 336-885-5580
Fax: 336-885-8592
Email: aletakiser@northstate.net

Bankruptcy, Traffic Violations, Criminal, Real Estate, Buying or Selling a Home, Personal Injury, Estate Planning, Social Security, Wills and Probate, Trusts and Estates, Probate, Estate Planning and General Practice.

ALETA B. KISER, born Abingdon, Virginia, November 25, 1961; admitted to bar, 1995, Ohio; 1997, North Carolina. *Education:* Virginia Polytechnic Institute and State University (B.A., cum laude, 1984); Wake Forest School of Law (J.D., 1987). Recipient, American Jurisprudence Awards: Torts, 1984; Estate Planning, 1987. Listed in Who's Who in American Law Students, 1986. *Member:* High Point and North Carolina Bar Associations. ***PRACTICE AREAS:*** Estate Planning; Wills; Trusts and Estates; Probate; Bankruptcy; Traffic Violations; Criminal Law; Real Estate; Personal Injury; Social Security; General Practice.

CLAYTON B. KROHN

HIGH POINT, NORTH CAROLINA

(See Greensboro)

Civil Litigation, Juvenile Delinquency, Insurance, Copyrights, Trademarks, Collections, Traffic Violations, Personal Injury.

CHARLES A. LLOYD

HIGH POINT, NORTH CAROLINA

(See Greensboro)

Criminal, Traffic, Driving While Impaired, Conspiracy, Felony, Drug Cases. Trials and Appeals in State and Federal Courts.

MANGER LAW FIRM

THE ARBORETUM, SUITE 230
1208 EASTCHESTER DRIVE
HIGH POINT, NORTH CAROLINA 27265
Telephone: 336-889-4334
Fax: 336-889-3977
Email: ram@mangerlaw.com
URL: http://www.mangerlawfirm.com

Personal Injury, Workers Compensation, Wrongful Death, Automobile Accidents, Trucking Accidents.

RICHARD A. MANGER, born Lansdowne, Pennsylvania, May 25, 1952; admitted to bar, 1977, North Carolina; 1978, Pennsylvania; 1979, U.S. District Court, Middle District of North Carolina; 1995, U.S. District Court, Western District of North Carolina. *Education:* Wake Forest University (B.A., 1974; J.D., 1977). *Member:* High Point (President, 1996-1997) and North Carolina Bar Associations; North Carolina State Bar (Chair, 18th Judicial District High Point Grievance Committee, 2001-2004); North Carolina Academy of Trial Lawyers (Vice President, 1996-1998; Chair, Small Office Practice Section, 2000—; Member: Board of Governors, 1994-2004; Public Education Committee, 1991—; Membership Committee, 1994-1998; Education Committee, 1998—; Editorial Board, 2001—); The Association of Trial Lawyers of America; Guilford Inn of Court (Master; Membership Chair, 2005-2006). ***Email:*** ram@mangerlaw.com

---

THE MCALLISTER FIRM, PLLC

Established in 2004

201 NEAL PLACE
P.O. BOX 5006
HIGH POINT, NORTH CAROLINA 27262
Telephone: 336-882-4300
Fax: 336-882-4306
Email: kmcallister@mcallisterlawfirm.com
URL: http://www.mcallisterlawfirm.com

General Civil and Criminal Trial Practice in State and Federal Court. Traffic Violations, White Collar Crime, Corporation and Business, Trusts and Estates, Wills and Probate, Estate Planning and Administration, Banking, Family Law, Personal Injury.

KENNETH W. MCALLISTER, born High Point, North Carolina, January 3, 1949; admitted to bar, 1974, North Carolina and U.S. District Court, Middle District of North Carolina; 1980, U.S. Court of Appeals, Fourth Circuit and U.S. Supreme Court. *Education:* University of North Carolina (A.B., 1971); Duke University (J.D., 1974). Phi Beta Kappa. Morehead Scholar. U.S. Attorney, Middle District of North Carolina, 1981-1986. Member, 1983-1986 and Vice Chairman, 1986, Attorney General's Advisory Committee of U.S. At-

(This Listing Continued)

THE McALLISTER FIRM, PLLC, High Point—Continued

torneys. General Counsel, 1988-2001 and Senior Executive Vice President, 1997-2001, Wachovia Corporation. Member, Board of Visitors: Wake Forest University School of Law, 1989-1996; University of North Carolina, Chapel Hill, 1989-1993; Duke University School of Law, 1996—. Director, Piedmont Triad Airport Authority, 1998-2001. Member, North Carolina Commission on Business Laws and the Economy, 1994-2000. Member, Board of Advisors, UNC School of Law Banking Institute, 1998-2002. NCDRC Certified Superior Court Mediator. *Member:* North Carolina (Member, Board of Governors, 2000-2003) and American Bar Associations; North Carolina State Bar; National Association of Former U.S. Attorneys; Fourth Circuit Judicial Conference (Permanent Member). Fellow, American Bar Foundation. ***PRACTICE AREAS:*** Litigation; White Collar Crime; Business Law; Corporate Law; Personal Injury. ***Email:*** kmcallister@mcallisterlawfirm.com

ATTORNEY

MARC R. TYREY, born Durham, North Carolina, April 16, 1971; admitted to bar, 1997, North Carolina. *Education:* Guilford College (B.A., 1994); Campbell University (J.D., cum laude, 1997). Articles Editor, Campbell Law Review, 1996-1997. Research Assistant, North Carolina Conference of Superior Court Judges; Pattern Jury Instruction Committee, 1995-1997. Assistant District Attorney, State of North Carolina, 1998-2001. *Member:* High Point and North Carolina Bar Associations; North Carolina State Bar. ***PRACTICE AREAS:*** Civil Litigation; Criminal Law; Traffic Offenses; Personal Injury; Construction Law. ***Email:*** mtyrey@mcallisterlawfirm.com

MORGAN, HERRING, MORGAN, GREEN, ROSENBLUTT & GILL, LLP

Established in 1942

1801 WESTCHESTER DRIVE, SUITE 200
P.O. BOX 2756
HIGH POINT, NORTH CAROLINA 27262
Telephone: 336-883-6177
FAX: 336-883-6647

General Civil and Criminal Trial Practice in all State and Federal Courts. Interstate Commerce, Probate, Real Estate, Corporation and Tax Law. Torts. Traffic Violations and Driving Under the Influence, Personal Injury, Auto Accidents, Wills and Estates, Family Law, Divorce, Custody, Support, Adoption, Workers Compensation, Bankruptcy, Social Security, Employment Discrimination.

MEMBERS OF FIRM

J.V. MORGAN (1918-1982)

W. DAN HERRING, born Rocky Mount, North Carolina, March 3, 1933; admitted to bar, 1963, North Carolina; 1965, U.S. District Court, Middle District of North Carolina; 1969, U.S. Supreme Court. *Education:* Wake Forest College (B.S., 1959; J.D., 1962). Phi Delta Phi. *Member:* High Point and North Carolina Bar Associations; North Carolina State Bar; The Association of Trial Lawyers of America; North Carolina Academy of Trial Lawyers. ***PRACTICE AREAS:*** Personal Injury; Family Law; Civil Litigation.

JAMES F. MORGAN, born High Point, North Carolina, June 21, 1943; admitted to bar, 1969, North Carolina; 1970, U.S. District Court, Middle District of North Carolina. *Education:* Guilford College (B.A., 1966); Cumberland School of Law of Samford University (J.D., 1969). Phi Alpha Delta. Young Man of the Year, City of High Point, 1973, 1974. Chosen One of Five Outstanding Young Men of North Carolina, State of North Carolina, 1973, 1974. Citizen of the Year, High Point, 1991. Distinguished Citizen, High Point Chamber of Commerce, 1998. 2002 Humanitarian of the Year, High Point Human Relations Commission. Member, North Carolina House of Representatives, 1977-1982. *Member:* High Point (Secretary-Treasurer, 1970-1971; President, 1989-1990), 18th Judicial District (Treasurer, 1970-1971; 18th Judicial President, 1995-1996), North Carolina and American (Member, Awards Committee, 1971) Bar Associations; North Carolina State Bar (Chairman; President, 1995-2000); North Carolina Trial Lawyers Association. ***PRACTICE AREAS:*** Personal Injury; Probate; Wills; Trials; Zoning; Governmental Law. ***Email:*** jimmorgan@morganherring.com

JAMES M. GREEN, JR., born High Point, North Carolina, April 4, 1946; admitted to bar, 1972, North Carolina; 1975, U.S. District Court, Middle District of North Carolina; 1976, U.S. Supreme Court. *Education:* Guilford College (B.A., 1968); Cumberland School of Law of Samford University (J.D., 1972). Delta Theta Phi. Attorney, Assistant District Attorney's Office, 18th Judicial District, North Carolina, 1975-1979. *Member:* High Point (President, 1992-1993), Guilford County and North Carolina Bar Associations; North Carolina State Bar; North Carolina Academy of Trial Lawyers. ***PRACTICE AREAS:*** Bankruptcy; Civil Litigation; Criminal; Domestic; Personal Injury. ***Email:*** jackgreen@morganherring.com

DAVID K. ROSENBLUTT, born Caldwell, New Jersey, September 16, 1952; admitted to bar, 1977, Massachusetts; 1979, North Carolina. *Education:* Williams College (B.A., cum laude, 1974); Boston University (J.D., 1977). *Member:* High Point, North Carolina and Massachusetts Bar Associations; North Carolina State Bar; The Association of Trial Lawyers of America; North Carolina Academy of Trial Lawyers. ***LANGUAGES:*** French. ***PRACTICE AREAS:*** Personal Injury; Civil Litigation; Bankruptcy; Probate; Corporate. ***Email:*** dblutt@morganherring.com

JAMES E. GILL, JR., born Detroit, Michigan, March 7, 1944; admitted to bar, 1971, North Carolina; 1974, U.S. District Court, Middle District of North Carolina; 1976, U.S. Supreme Court; 1977, U.S. Tax Court. *Education:* Guilford College (B.A., 1967); Cumberland Law School of Samford University (J.D., 1970). Phi Alpha Delta. *Member:* High Point (Secretary, 1972-1973; President, 1994-1995), North Carolina (Member, Real Property Section) and American (Member, Real Property, Probate and Trust Law Section) Bar Associations; 18th Judicial District and North Carolina State Bars. ***PRACTICE AREAS:*** Real Property; Probate; Trust Law; Corporate Law. ***Email:*** jegill@morganherring.com

(This Listing Continued)

ASSOCIATES

TODD J. COMBS, born Sumter, South Carolina, July 26, 1968; admitted to bar, 1996, North Carolina; 2003, U.S. District Court, Middle District of North Carolina. *Education:* College of Charleston (B.S., 1991); Oklahoma City University School of Law (J.D., 1996). Phi Delta Phi. North Carolina Real Estate License. *Member:* High Point, North Carolina and Eighteenth Judicial District Bar Associations; North Carolina State Bar. ***PRACTICE AREAS:*** Personal Injury Law; Employment Discrimination; Family Law; Civil Litigation; Wills; Probate. ***Email:*** tcombs@morganherring.com

JOHN S. COALTER, born Dallas, Texas, My 17, 1965; admitted to bar, 1996, North Carolina and U.S. District Court, Middle District of North Carolina. *Education:* University of Texas at Austin (B.A., cum laude, 1989); Campbell University (J.D., cum laude, 1996). Research Editor, Campbell Law Review. Author: "Vicarious Liability of a Physician for the Negligence of Other Medical Professionals- North Carolina Charts a Middle Course- The Effect of Harris v. Miller," Campbell Law Review, Vol. 17, Number 2. Assistant Public Defender, 1997-2001. Assistant District Attorney, 18th Judicial District, 2001-2003. *Member:* 18th Judicial District Bar Association; North Carolina State Bar; Guilford Inn of Court. [Spec. Fourth Class, U.S. Army, 1983-1989]. ***PRACTICE AREAS:*** Criminal Law; Civil Litigation; Personal Injury; Traffic Violations; Driving While Intoxicated. ***Email:*** scoalter@morganherring.com

OF COUNSEL

JOHN HAWORTH, born High Point, North Carolina, February 12, 1927; admitted to bar, 1950, North Carolina and U.S. District Court, Eastern, Middle and Western Districts of North Carolina; 1962, U.S. Tax Court and U.S. Court of Appeals, Fourth Circuit; 1963, U.S. Court of Appeals, District of Columbia and U.S. Supreme Court; 1977, U.S. Claims Court. *Education:* Guilford College (A.B., 1947); University of North Carolina (LL.B., 1950). Phi Delta Phi. Author: "Premises Liability— Trip and Fall" 10 Am Jur Trials, 1965; "How To Handle A Will Case: Trial," Wake Forest Seminar, 1993, 1996, 2000, 2003. Member, High Point City Council, 1953-1959. Certified Mediator. *Member:* High Point, North Carolina (Chairman, Committees on: Continuing Legal Education, 1961-1964; Courts and Civil Litigation, 1975-1979; Member, Board of Governors, 1962-1965; President, 1979-1980) and American (Member, House of Delegates, 1982-1986) Bar Associations; North Carolina State Bar; North Carolina Academy of Trial Lawyers; Fourth Circuit Judicial Conference. Fellow, American College of Trial Lawyers. ***PRACTICE AREAS:*** Civil Trial Practice; Products Liability Law; Motor Vehicle Law; Probate Law; Business Law; Personal Injury Law. ***Email:*** hawjo@morganherring.com

JOHN C. RIGGS, born Mt. Airy, North Carolina, December 5, 1927; admitted to bar, 1956, North Carolina; 1957, U.S. District Court, Middle District of North Carolina; 1962, U.S. Court of Appeals, Fourth Circuit; 1964, U.S. Supreme Court; 1974, U.S. District Court, Western District of North Carolina. *Education:* High Point College and Wake Forest College (B.S., 1952); Wake Forest College (LL.B., 1956). Phi Delta Phi (Magister, Ruffin Inn, 1955-1956). *Member:* High Point (President, 1968-1969), North Carolina and American Bar Associations; 18th Judicial District (Secretary, 1960; Vice President, 1982-1983; President, 1983-1984) and North Carolina State Bars. ***PRACTICE AREAS:*** Trusts and Estates; Real Estate; Business Law. ***Email:*** hrkhattys@aol.com

REPRESENTATIVE CLIENTS: High Point Merchants Assn.; North State Telephone Co.; Arthur A. Oliver and Son, Inc.; Cain Veneer Co; Global Veneer Co., Mattress Guild Inc.; Precision Laser, Inc.; Royals, Inc.; Duke Power Co.; Crown Printing Co.; McNeil Veneer, Inc.; Simanco, Inc.
LOCAL COUNSEL FOR: *Mortgage Loans:* Pilot Life Insurance Co.; Federal National Mortgage Assn.; Federal Housing Administration; First Bank; High Point Bank & Trust Co.; Norwest Mortgage; Northwestern Life Insurance Co.; NCNB National Bank of North Carolina; Bank of America; Equitable Life Assurance Society of the United States; Metropolitan Life Insurance Co.; Wachovia Bank & Trust Co.
APPROVED ATTORNEYS FOR: Chicago Title Insurance Co.; Investors Title Insurance Co.; Lawyers Title Insurance Corp.; First American Title Insurance Co.; American Title Insurance Co.
REFERENCES: National Bank; High Point Bank & Trust Co.; Wachovia Bank & Trust Co.; First Citizens Bank & Trust Co.; BB&T.

NIXON & ASSOCIATES

210 EAST LEXINGTON AVENUE
HIGH POINT, NORTH CAROLINA 27262
Telephone: 336-885-5959
Fax: 336-885-7400
Email: gnixon@northstate.net
URL: http://www.nixonlawoffices.com

Traffic Violations, Criminal Defense, DWI, Drug Charges, License Restoration, Personal Injury, Auto Accidents, Domestic Law.

GEORGIA S. NIXON, born High Point, North Carolina, August 4, 1965; admitted to bar, 1991, North Carolina. *Education:* North Carolina State University (B.A., 1987); Norman A. Wiggins School of Law (J.D., 1990). Former Assistant District Attorney, 1992-1995. *Member:* North Carolina and American Bar Association; North Carolina State Bar; Academy of Trial Lawyers; National Academy of Criminal Defense Attorneys; Inns of Court. (Board Certified Specialist in Criminal Law, North Carolina State Board of Legal Specialization). ***LANGUAGES:*** Greek. ***PRACTICE AREAS:*** Criminal Defense.

THE LAW OFFICES OF JEFFREY K. PERALDO, P.A.

HIGH POINT, NORTH CAROLINA

(See Greensboro)

Serious Personal Injury, Wrongful Death, Automobile Accidents, Trucking Accidents, Medical Malpractice, Hospital Malpractice, Nursing Home Neglect and Abuse, Product Liability, Construction Accidents, Consumer Fraud, Land Condemnation, Negligent Security.

KENNETH L. POORTVLIET

HIGH POINT, NORTH CAROLINA

(See Greensboro)

Family Law, Divorce, Child Custody, Child Support, Adoptions, Domestic Violence, Visitation Rights, Criminal Law, Traffic Violations and Driving While Intoxicated.

J. BROOKS REITZEL, JR.

Established in 1998

SUNTRUST BANK BUILDING
1301 EASTCHESTER DRIVE, SUITE 201
P.O. BOX 5544
HIGH POINT, NORTH CAROLINA 27265
Telephone: 336-885-7900
Fax: 336-885-7925
URL: http://www.reitzellaw.com

Bankruptcy, Debtor/Creditor Relations, Banking Law, Commercial Law, Corporate Law, Wills, Probate, Trust and Estate, Estate Planning, Real Estate, Trial Practice in State and Federal Courts. Representing Furniture Designers, Importers, Manufacturers, Retailers throughout the United States.

FIRM PROFILE: Mr. Reitzel began his practice in 1971 with the law firm Roberson Haworth & Reese. While practicing with that firm as a partner, Mr. Reitzel focused his practice upon real estate, wills and estates, banking and general business matters. During this time, Mr. Reitzel was counsel for several local banks including High Point Bank and Trust Company, Wachovia Bank and Trust Company, First Citizen's Bank and BB&T. Mr. Reitzel was appointed to the Chapter 7 Bankruptcy Panel of Trustees for the Middle District of North Carolina, and during this time liquidated many corporate entities, both as a Chapter 7 Trustee and for the banks which he represented. In 1994, Mr. Reitzel left Roberson Haworth & Reese and joined the regional law firm Wyatt Early Harris Wheeler as a partner. During the next four years, Mr. Reitzel continued with his established practice and added commercial litigation. In 1998, Mr. Reitzel started his solo practice to allow him to limit the number of clients that he represents to enable him to provide more personalized service for those clients.

J. BROOKS REITZEL, JR., born High Point, North Carolina, October 20, 1945; admitted to bar, 1971, North Carolina. *Education:* Stetson University; University of North Carolina (B.A., 1968; J.D., 1971). Arbitrator/Mediator, NC. Formerly with: Robeson Haworth & Reese, High Point, North Carolina, 1971-1994; Wyatt Early Harris & Wheeler, High Point, North Carolina, 1995-1997. *Member:* High Point and North Carolina Bar Associations; The North Carolina State Bar. ***PRACTICE AREAS:*** Bankruptcy; Debtor/Creditor Relations; Banking Law; Commercial Law; Corporate Law; Wills and Estates; Real Estate.

REPRESENTATIVE CLIENTS: BB&T; SunTrust Bank; First Citizens Bank and Trust Company; Wachovia Bank & Trust, NA; Phillips Factors Corp.; Rose Furniture Co.; Main Street Pennsylvania House, Inc.; Holton Furniture Gallery; Optics, Inc.

ROBERSON, HAWORTH & REESE, P.L.L.C.

Established in 1925

HIGH POINT BANK & TRUST COMPANY BUILDING, SUITE 300
300 NORTH MAIN STREET
P.O. BOX 1550
HIGH POINT, NORTH CAROLINA 27261
Telephone: 336-889-8733
FAX: 336-885-1280
Email: mail@rhrlaw.com
URL: http://www.rhrlaw.com

General and Trial Practice in State and Federal Courts. Banking, Corporation, Probate, Real Estate, Bankruptcy, Commercial, Municipal Corporations, Personal Injury, Products Liability, Zoning and Land Use, Condemnation.

MEMBERS OF FIRM

WESCOTT ROBERSON (1875-1938)
HORACE S. HAWORTH (1892-1978)
OWEN REESE (1896-1970)
ARTHUR M. UTLEY, JR. (1923-1987)

ROBERT A. BRINSON, born High Point, North Carolina, June 17, 1950; admitted to bar, 1976, North Carolina and U.S. District Court, Middle District of North Carolina. *Education:* The McCallie School; Wofford College (A.B., 1972); Wake Forest University (J.D., 1976). Certified Superior Court Mediator. *Member:* High Point (President, 1997-1998), North Carolina and American Bar Associations; North Carolina State Bar; Commercial Law League; North Carolina Academy of Trial Lawyers; American Academy of Trial Lawyers. ***PRACTICE AREAS:*** Civil Litigation; Mediation; Wills; Estate Litigation; Condemnation; Employment Law; Personal Injury; Products Liability; Shareholder Disputes; Real Estate Brokerage Law. ***Email:*** bbrinson@rhrlaw.com

ELIZABETH MacLEAN KOONCE, born High Point, North Carolina, November 19, 1954; admitted to bar, 1980, North Carolina. *Education:* Salem College; University of North Carolina (B.A., 1977; J.D., 1980). Chairman, High Point Planning and Zoning Commission, 1989-1991. *Member:* High Point Bar Association; The North Carolina State Bar (Member: Section on, Real Property; Estate Planning). ***PRACTICE AREAS:*** Real Estate Law; Municipal Corporations Law; Zoning Law; Estate Planning; Probate. ***Email:*** bkoonce@rhrlaw.com

DAVID L. MAYNARD, born Gastonia, North Carolina, April 10, 1937; admitted to bar, 1963, North Carolina. *Education:* Duke University (A.B., 1959; LL.B., 1962). City

(This Listing Continued)

Attorney, City of Jamestown. President, 18th Judicial Bar, 1993-1994. Member, North Carolina Sports Development Commission. *Member:* High Point (Past President) and North Carolina (Member, Real Property Section Council) Bar Associations; The North Carolina State Bar. ***PRACTICE AREAS:*** Real Estate Law; Estates Law; Municipal Corporations Law.

WILLIAM P. MILLER, born Mount Airy, North Carolina, April 27, 1955; admitted to bar, 1980, North Carolina. *Education:* Woodberry Forest School; Duke University (A.B., cum laude, 1977); University of North Carolina (J.D., 1980). Phi Delta Phi. Member, Holderness Moot Court Board. Chief Justice of Honor Court, University of North Carolina School of Law, 1979-1980. City Attorney, City of Archdale, 1987—. Chapter 7 Panel Trustee for the U.S. Bankruptcy Court, Middle District of North Carolina. *Member:* High Point and North Carolina (Bankruptcy Section) Bar Associations; 18th Judicial District Bar; North Carolina State Bar; National Association of Bankruptcy Trustees; American Bankruptcy Institute. ***PRACTICE AREAS:*** Commercial Law; Banking Law; Bankruptcy Law; Municipal Corporations Law; Commercial Real Estate; Zoning; Planning and Land Use. ***Email:*** bmiller@rhrlaw.com

ALAN B. POWELL, born Southport, North Carolina, April 7, 1965; admitted to bar, 1990, North Carolina; 1991, U.S. District Court, Eastern, Western and Middle Districts of North Carolina. *Education:* Vanderbilt University (B.A., 1987); Wake Forest University (J.D., 1990). Member, National Moot Court Team, 1990. Publications: "Conducting Valuation Hearings After Rash" (1998); "Recovery of Attorney's Fees in Chapter 13," Consumer Bankruptcy Law Symposium, 1999; "North Carolina Foreclosure Law," 2003 Publication and Legal Seminar. Certified Superior Court Mediator. *Member:* High Point and North Carolina (Member, Bankruptcy, Business Law and Real Property Sections) Bar Associations; American Bankruptcy Institute. ***PRACTICE AREAS:*** Commercial Law; Bankruptcy; Civil Litigation; Banking; Creditors Rights; Foreclosures; Title Insurance Litigation. ***Email:*** apowell@rhrlaw.com

COLIN D. MERRITT, born Roanoke, Virginia, October 9, 1972; admitted to bar, 1998, North Carolina. *Education:* Wake Forest University (B.S., cum laude, 1994; J.D., 1998; M.B.A., 1998). *Member:* High Point and North Carolina Bar Associations; North Carolina State Bar. ***PRACTICE AREAS:*** Corporate Law; Business Law; Commercial Law; Contracts; Foreclosures; Mergers and Acquisitions. ***Email:*** cmerritt@rhrlaw.com

CHRISTOPHER C. FINAN, born Hayward, California, October 12, 1975; admitted to bar, 2001, North Carolina and U.S. District Court, Eastern, Middle and Western Districts of North Carolina; U.S. Tax Court. *Education:* Pennsylvania State University (B.S., 1997); Wake Forest University (J.D., 2001). Member, Moot Court Board, 1999-2001. *Member:* High Point (Treasurer, 2002-2003) and North Carolina Bar Associations; North Carolina State Bar. ***PRACTICE AREAS:*** Civil Litigation; Bankruptcy Law; Commercial Law; Creditors Rights; Real Estate Law; Title Insurance Litigation. ***Email:*** cfinan@rhrlaw.com

ASSOCIATES

LISA W. POWELL, born Denver, Colorado, February 23, 1965; admitted to bar, 1991, North Carolina. *Education:* University of Colorado at Boulder (B.A., 1987); Wake Forest University (J.D., 1990). Member, Wake Forest Law Review. Note Author, "Mallard v. U.S. District Court," 25 Wake Forest L. Rev. 642, 1990. *Member:* High Point and North Carolina (Member, Real Estate Section) Bar Associations. ***PRACTICE AREAS:*** Real Estate; Foreclosures. ***Email:*** lpowell@rhrlaw.com

THOMAS F. FOSTER, born Winston-Salem, North Carolina, September 14, 1948; admitted to bar, 1977, North Carolina. *Education:* University of North Carolina at Chapel Hill (B.A., 1970; J.D., 1977). Certified Public Accountant, North Carolina, 1979. [E-5, U.S. Air Force, 1970-1974]. ***PRACTICE AREAS:*** Taxation; Estate Planning and Administration; Business Law. ***Email:*** tfoster@rhrlaw.com

JAMES C. LANIK, born Cedar Rapids, Iowa, February 8, 1969; admitted to bar, 1995, Colorado; U.S. District Court, District of Colorado; 2002, North Carolina; 2003, U.S. District Court, Eastern, Western and Middle Districts of North Carolina. *Education:* United States Air Force Academy; Lawrence University (B.A., 1992); University of Denver (J.D., 1995). Author, "Stopping the Tailspin: Use of Oligopolistic and Oligopsonistic Power to Produce Profits in the Airline Industry" 22 Trans. L.J. 509 (1995). President, American Society of Corporate Secretaries, Rocky Mountain Chapter, 2001-2002. *Member:* Denver, High Point, Colorado and North Carolina Bar Associations. ***PRACTICE AREAS:*** Corporate Law; Employment Law; Creditors Rights; Bankruptcy. ***Email:*** jlanik@rhrlaw.com

SPECIAL COUNSEL: Southern Railway Co.
COUNSEL FOR: Wachovia Bank of North Carolina, N.A.; Marsh Furniture Co.; Triad MLS, Inc.; High Point Regional Association of Realtors, Inc.; Town of Jamestown; City of Archdale; Sedgefield Sanitary District; Town of Jamestown Alcohol Beverage Control Board; Vecoplan, LLC.
APPROVED ATTORNEYS FOR: The Lawyers Title Insurance Corp. of Richmond; First American Title Insurance Company; Chicago Title Insurance Co.; Investors Title Co.; Commonwealth Land Title Insurance Co.; First Title Insurance Co.; The Title Company of North Carolina.
APPROVED REAL ESTATE MORTGAGE ATTORNEYS FOR: Wachovia Mortgage Corp.; NationsBank; Branch Banking & Trust Company; Norwest Mortgage Corp.
REPRESENTATIVE CLIENTS: High Point Bank and Trust Co.; Branch Banking & Trust Company; Centura Park; United Carolina Bank; Bank of North Carolina, N.A.; Piedmont Triad Regional Water Authority; Veterans Administration; U.S. Small Business Administration; Bottlers Services, Inc.; CIGNA Insurance Company; Rea Construction Co.; Household International and Subsidiaries; Stewart Title; Swaim Originals, Inc.; Furnitureland South, Inc.

ROBINSON & LAWING, L.L.P.

HIGH POINT, NORTH CAROLINA

(See Winston-Salem)

General Civil and Complex Litigation in All Courts. Business, Corporate, Antitrust and Trade, Intellectual Property, Products Liability, Personal Injury, Professional Malpractice, Workers Compensation, Bankruptcy, Family Law, Wrongful Death, Insurance, Employee Benefits Law, Employment and Labor Law, Business Law, Estate and Tax Law.

SCHELL BRAY AYCOCK ABEL & LIVINGSTON P.L.L.C.

HIGH POINT, NORTH CAROLINA

(See Greensboro)

Corporate, Taxation, Securities Regulation, Venture Capital, Real Estate and Real Estate Finance, Mergers and Acquisitions, Health Care, Antitrust and Trade Regulation, Banking, Commercial, Employee Benefits, Estate Planning and Administration.

SCHLOSSER & PRITCHETT

HIGH POINT, NORTH CAROLINA

(See Greensboro)

Criminal Law, Wrongful Death, Automobile Accidents, Felonies, Misdemeanors, Traffic, Personal Injury, Litigation in State and Federal Courts.

SCHOCH & SCHOCH

Established in 1936

500 EAST GREEN DRIVE
P.O. BOX 1893
HIGH POINT, NORTH CAROLINA 27261
Telephone: 336-884-4151
Telecopier: 336-883-7151

General Civil Trial Practice. Personal Injury, Automobile Accidents, Wrongful Death, Civil Litigation, Criminal Defense, Traffic Violations, Condemnation.

MEMBERS OF FIRM

ARCH K. SCHOCH (1909-1980)

LOUISE RODES SCHOCH (1909-1995)

ARCH K. SCHOCH IV, born High Point, North Carolina, April 4, 1940; admitted to bar, 1964, North Carolina, U.S. District Court, Middle District of North Carolina, U.S. Court of Appeals, Fourth Circuit and U.S. Supreme Court. *Education:* University of Virginia; University of North Carolina (B.A., 1962; LL.B., with honors, 1964). Phi Beta Kappa; Order of the Coif; Phi Delta Phi. Member of Staff and Member, Board of Editors, North Carolina Law Review, 1963-1964. Listed, Best Lawyers of America, 1983—. Member, 1980-1992, Chairman, 1990-1992 and Emeritus Member, 1993—, North Carolina Board of Law Examiners. Founding Member, North Carolina Personal Injury Referral Service, 1984. *Member:* High Point (President, 1980-1981) and North Carolina Bar Associations; Eighteenth Judicial District Bar (President, 1976-1977); North Carolina State Bar (Member, Council, 1969-1972); Master, Joseph Branch Inn of Court; North Carolina Academy of Trial Lawyers (Member, Board of Governors, 1978-1979); The Association of Trial Lawyers of America. Fellow: International Academy of Trial Lawyers; American College of Trial Lawyers. ***PRACTICE AREAS:*** Personal Injury; Wrongful Death; Condemnation.

ARCH K. SCHOCH V, born High Point, North Carolina, July 9, 1967; admitted to bar, 1997, North Carolina. *Education:* University of Virginia (B.A., 1990); Cumberland School of Law (J.D., 1996). *Member:* High Point (Secretary-Treasurer, 1998-1999) and North Carolina Bar Associations; Eighteenth Judicial District Bar Association (Secretary-Treasurer, 2001-2002); North Carolina State Bar; North Carolina Academy of Trial Lawyers; The Association of Trial Lawyers of America; The Guilford Inn of Court. ***PRACTICE AREAS:*** Criminal Law; Traffic Violations; Personal Injury; Civil Litigation.

REPRESENTATIVE CLIENTS: Archdale Oil Co.; Classic Gallery, Inc.; Cramer Wood Products, Inc.; Jones & Peacock Insurance, Inc.; Phillips Industries, Inc.; Piedmont Chemical Industries, Inc.

LAW OFFICE OF LAURIE R. STEGALL, P.A.

HIGH POINT, NORTH CAROLINA

(See Greensboro)

Residential Real Estate, Real Estate Closings, Estate Planning, Wills.

LAW OFFICE OF MATT A. STOCKDALE, PLLC

HIGH POINT, NORTH CAROLINA

(See Greensboro)

Criminal Law, Traffic Violations, Driving While Intoxicated, Drug Crimes, Parole and Probate, White Collar Crime, Trust and Estates, Estate Planning, Business Law, Child Support.

TUGGLE DUGGINS & MESCHAN, P.A.

HIGH POINT, NORTH CAROLINA

(See Greensboro)

General Civil Practice. Corporation, Tax, Insurance, Banking, Pension and Profit Sharing, Bankruptcy and Creditors' Rights, Trust and Estate, Construction and Real Estate Law. Trials and Appeals in all State and Federal Courts.

THE WALLACE LAW FIRM

Established in 2003

300 N. LINDSAY STREET, SUITE 101
HIGH POINT, NORTH CAROLINA 27262
Telephone: 336-882-4940
Fax: 336-882-4945
Email: Mercy@wlfnc.com
URL: http://www.WLFCarolinas.com

Real Property, Business Law, Corporate Law, Intellectual Property, Traffic.

FIRM PROFILE: The Wallace Law Firm is a small firm with the strength of one much larger. By maintaining the highest of standards, our legal representation holds genuine concern for each client at its heart. Representation may take many forms, but always reflects the Wallace Law Firm's attention to responsiveness and courtesy. We forge strong relationships based on reasonable expectations and sturdy boundaries creating a new definition of the attorney-client relationship.

STEPHEN F. WALLACE, born High Point, North Carolina, August 15, 1969; admitted to bar, 2003, North Carolina and U.S. District, Middle District of North Carolina; 2004, South Carolina. *Education:* North Carolina State University (B.A., International Business, 1992); High Point University (M.S., International Business, 1998); Regent University (J.D., 2002); National Trial Advocacy College of the University of Virginia School of Law (2004). Sole Practitioner, 2003. Superior Court Mediator, 2003. *Member:* American Bar Association; North Carolina State Bar; The Association of Trial Lawyers of America; High Point Bar Association. ***PRACTICE AREAS:*** Real Property; Business Law; Corporate Law; Intellectual Property; Traffic Violations. ***Email:*** steve@wlfnc.com

Languages: English and Spanish.

REPRESENTATIVE CLIENTS: Homelegance USA LLC; Piedmont Recovery Inc.; CJC Enterprises Inc.; Phatty's LLC; Best Deal Homes LLC; GDW Investments LLC; Craven & Wilson LLC; Y.F. Drywall.

CHARLES L. WHITE, II

HIGH POINT, NORTH CAROLINA

(See Greensboro)

Criminal Law, Felonies, Misdemeanors, Drug Crimes, State and Federal Court, Drug Forfeiture, Driving While Intoxicated, Traffic Violations, Mediation, Arbitration, Alternative Dispute Resolution, Juvenile Delinquency Law, Child Abuse Neglect and Dependency.

WINFREE & WINFREE

HIGH POINT, NORTH CAROLINA

(See Greensboro)

Consumer Law, Lemon Law, Consumer Rights, Collections, Family Law, Divorce, Alimony, Civil Litigation, Business Litigation, Business Property, Traffic Violations.

WOODRUFF LAW FIRM, P.A.

HIGH POINT, NORTH CAROLINA

(See Greensboro)

Family Law, Taxation, Divorce, Mediation and Arbitration Child Custody and Child Support.

WYATT EARLY HARRIS WHEELER L.L.P.

Established in 1930

1912 EASTCHESTER DRIVE, SUITE 400
P.O. DRAWER 2086
HIGH POINT, NORTH CAROLINA 27261
Telephone: 336-884-4444
Fax: 336-889-5232
URL: http://www.wehwlaw.com

Litigation, Legal and Regulatory matters in Furniture/Home Furnishings Industries, General Civil, Insurance, Business, Securities, Taxation and Criminal Practice. Trials and Appeals in all State and Federal Courts. Probate and Estate Planning, Real Estate, Bankruptcy, Corporation, Banking, Negligence, Workers Compensation and Family Law.

FIRM PROFILE: Founded in 1930, Wyatt Early Harris Wheeler, L.L.P. is a full-service firm, which has experienced progressive growth over the years. Its lawyers provide a full complement of legal services to a broad range of clients. Because the firm is located in the heart of the International Furniture/Home Furnishings Market, it is uniquely positioned to provide special counseling on Litigation and other legal and regulatory matters affecting the furniture/home furnishings and related industries. The firm has a Furniture Practice Group comprised of attorneys and support personnel who dedicate a significant portion of their practice to advising the furniture industry concerning the design, manufacture, marketing, and sale of furniture and home furnishings.

MEMBERS OF FIRM

FRANK BURKHEAD WYATT, born Greenville, North Carolina, January 16, 1934; admitted to bar, 1959, North Carolina and U.S. District Court, Middle District of North Carolina; 1964, U.S. Court of Military Appeals, U.S. Court of Federal Claims and U.S. Supreme Court. *Education:* Wake Forest University (B.S., 1956; J.D., 1958). Omicron Delta Kappa. Trustee, Wake Forest University. *Member:* High Point (President, 1972-1973), 18th Judicial District (President, 1987), North Carolina (Member, Board of Governors, 1975-1978) and American Bar Associations; Fourth Circuit Judicial Conference (Permanent

(This Listing Continued)

Member); North Carolina Academy of Trial Lawyers; North Carolina Defense Attorneys Association. Fellow: American College of Trial Lawyers; Federation of Insurance Counsel; Association of Defense Trial Attorneys; International Society of Barristers. [Captain, U.S. Army, J.A.G.C., active duty, 1956-1957]. ***PRACTICE AREAS:*** Condemnation; Personal Injury; Products Liability. ***Email:*** fwyatt@wehwlaw.com

WILLIAM P. HARRIS, born Pinehurst, North Carolina, September 23, 1942; admitted to bar, 1968, North Carolina; 1970, U.S. District Court, Middle District of North Carolina; 1977, U.S. Tax Court. *Education:* High Point College (A.B., 1965); Wake Forest University (J.D., 1968). *Member:* High Point (President, 1988-1989) and American Bar Associations. ***PRACTICE AREAS:*** Business Law; Mergers and Acquisitions; Commercial Transactions. ***Email:*** wharris@wehwlaw.com

A. DOYLE EARLY, JR., born Guilford County, North Carolina, January 27, 1943; admitted to bar, 1967, North Carolina; 1970, U.S. District Court, Middle District of North Carolina and U.S. Supreme Court. *Education:* Wake Forest University (B.A., 1965; J.D., 1967). *Member:* High Point (President, 1986-1987), North Carolina (Member, Fiduciary Law Committee) and American Bar Associations; 18th Judicial District (President, 1999); North Carolina Academy of Trial Lawyers; American Academy of Matrimonial Lawyers. (Board Certified Specialist in Family Law, North Carolina State Board of Legal Specialization). ***PRACTICE AREAS:*** Divorce; Alimony; Equitable Distribution. ***Email:*** dearly@wehwlaw.com

WILLIAM E. WHEELER, born Wilson, North Carolina, October 24, 1945; admitted to bar, 1975, North Carolina and U.S. District Court, Middle District of North Carolina; 1980, U.S. Tax Court and U.S. Supreme Court. *Education:* University of North Carolina at Chapel Hill (A.B., 1972); Wake Forest University (J.D., 1975). Phi Beta Kappa. Associate Editor, Wake Forest Law Review, 1974-1975. Federal Arbitrator. *Member:* American Bar Association. [1st Lt., U.S. Army, 1966-1969]. ***PRACTICE AREAS:*** Probate Litigation; Contract Litigation. ***Email:*** bwheeler@wehwlaw.com

DAVID B. ASHCRAFT, born Clarksburg, West Virginia, July 9, 1947; admitted to bar, 1974, North Carolina and U.S. District Court, Middle District of North Carolina; 1977, U.S. Supreme Court. *Education:* Wake Forest University (B.S., cum laude, 1969; J.D., 1974). Omicron Delta Kappa. Staff Member, Wake Forest Law Review, 1974. *Member:* American Bar Association. ***PRACTICE AREAS:*** Business Law; Banking. ***Email:*** dashcraft@wehwlaw.com

KIM W. GALLIMORE, born High Point, North Carolina, September 28, 1955; admitted to bar, 1980, North Carolina and U.S. District Court, Middle District of North Carolina; 1981, U.S. Tax Court. *Education:* Duke University (A.B., magna cum laude, 1977); Wake Forest University (J.D., 1980). *Member:* American Bar Association; North Carolina League of Savings Institutions; North Carolina Land Title Association. (Board Certified Specialist in Real Property Law: Business, Commercial, Industrial and Residential Transactions, North Carolina State Board of Legal Specialization). ***PRACTICE AREAS:*** Commercial Real Estate; Residential Real Estate. ***Email:*** kgallimore@wehwlaw.com

KIM R. BAUMAN, born Tupelo, Mississippi, May 15, 1955; admitted to bar, 1980, North Carolina, U.S. District Court, Eastern, Middle and Western Districts of North Carolina and U.S. Court of Appeals, Fourth Circuit. *Education:* Duke University (A.B., 1977); Wake Forest University (J.D., 1980). Phi Beta Kappa. *Member:* North Carolina Association of Defense Attorneys. ***PRACTICE AREAS:*** Labor and Employment; Workers Compensation; Insurance. ***Email:*** kbauman@wehwlaw.com

R. BRUCE LANEY, born Lenoir, North Carolina, January 9, 1949; admitted to bar, 1973, North Carolina. *Education:* University of North Carolina at Chapel Hill (A.B., 1970; J.D., 1973). Recipient, Morehead Scholar, 1970. Member, High Point Board of Education, 1986-1993. ***PRACTICE AREAS:*** Commercial Real Estate; Residential Real Estate.

CHARLES A. ALT, born Winchester, Virginia, April 9, 1955; admitted to bar, 1980, Virginia and U.S. Tax Court; 1984, U.S. District Court, Western District of Virginia; 1985, North Carolina and U.S. District Court, Middle District of North Carolina. *Education:* Washington & Lee University (B.S., 1977); College of William & Mary (J.D., 1980; M.L.T., 1981). *Member:* Virginia State Bar; American Bar Association. ***PRACTICE AREAS:*** Corporate Law; Investments; Taxation; Employee Benefits.

FREDERICK G. SAWYER, born High Point, North Carolina, July 26, 1959; admitted to bar, 1984, North Carolina and U.S. District Court, Middle District of North Carolina. *Education:* University of North Carolina at Chapel Hill (B.S., 1981; J.D., 1984). Phi Beta Kappa. *Member:* American Bar Association. ***PRACTICE AREAS:*** Construction Law; Environmental Law. ***Email:*** rsawyer@wehwlaw.com

JAMES R. HUNDLEY, born Daytona Beach, Florida, August 22, 1956; admitted to bar, 1985, North Carolina, U.S. District Court, Middle District of North Carolina, U.S. Court of Appeals, Fourth Circuit and U.S. Supreme Court. *Education:* University of North Carolina-Greensboro (B.A., magna cum laude, 1982); Wake Forest University (J.D., 1985). Certified Mediator. *Member:* American Bar Association; American Bankruptcy Institute. ***PRACTICE AREAS:*** Bankruptcy; Foreclosures; Collections; Debtor and Creditor; Landlord and Tenant Law. ***Email:*** jhundley@wehwlaw.com

EDGAR S. LEVY, III, born Baton Rouge, Louisiana, October 13, 1955; admitted to bar, 1980, Virginia; 1982, District of Columbia; 1987, U.S. Tax Court; 2000, North Carolina. *Education:* University of Virginia (B.S., 1977); College of William & Mary (J.D., 1980). Order of the Coif. Member, William and Mary Law Review. Certified Public Accountant, Virginia, 1982. *Member:* District of Columbia Bar; Virginia State Bar. (Board Certified Specialist in Estate Planning and Probate Law, North Carolina State Board of Legal Specialization). ***PRACTICE AREAS:*** Trusts and Estates; Wills and Probate; Tax Law. ***Email:*** plevy@wehwlaw.com

JOHN D. BRYSON, born Ephrata, Pennsylvania, May 26, 1958; admitted to bar, 1985, North Carolina, U.S. District Court, Eastern, Middle and Western Districts of North Carolina, U.S. Court of Appeals, Fourth Circuit and U.S. Supreme Court. *Education:* Wake Forest University (B.A., 1980; J.D., 1985). Adjunct Professor, Wake Forest University, School of Law, 1994—. *Member:* National Association of Criminal Defense Lawyers; North Carolina Academy of Trial Lawyers. (Board Certified Specialist in Criminal Law including Appellate Practice, North Carolina State Board of Legal Specialization). ***PRACTICE AREAS:*** Criminal Defense; Criminal Appeals; Driving While Intoxicated; Traffic Violations. ***Email:*** jbryson@wehwlaw.com

(This Listing Continued)

STANLEY F. HAMMER, born Columbia, South Carolina, February 25, 1953; admitted to bar, 1984, North Carolina; 1985, South Carolina, U.S. District Court, Middle District of North Carolina, U.S. Court of Appeals, Fourth Circuit and U.S. Supreme Court. *Education:* University of South Carolina (B.A., 1974; M.Lib., 1977); Campbell University (J.D., 1984). Law Clerk to the Hon. Louis B. Meyer, Associate Justice, North Carolina Supreme Court, 1986-1987. Director of Research and Assistant Professor of Law, Campbell University, School of Law, 1985. *Member:* South Carolina Bar; North Carolina Academy of Trial Lawyers. (Board Certified Specialist in Criminal Law including Appellate Practice, North Carolina State Board of Legal Specialization). ***PRACTICE AREAS:*** Personal Injury; Criminal Defense; Civil Rights; Medical Malpractice. ***Email:*** shammer@wehwlaw.com

SCOTT FITZGERALD WYATT, born High Point, North Carolina, August 1, 1966; admitted to bar, 1992, North Carolina and U.S. Court of Appeals, Fourth Circuit; 1993, U.S. District Court, Eastern District of North Carolina. *Education:* Wake Forest University (B.A., Economics, cum laude, 1988; J.D., 1991). Law Clerk to the Hon. W. Earl Britt, U.S. District Court, Eastern District of North Carolina, 1991-1993. *Member:* North Carolina Academy of Trial Lawyers. ***PRACTICE AREAS:*** Condemnation; Personal Injury; Business Litigation; Class Actions. ***Email:*** swyatt@wehwlaw.com

DAVID NEAL WOODS, born Valdese, North Carolina, January 22, 1975; admitted to bar, 2000, North Carolina. *Education:* Lenoir-Rhyne College (B.A., 1997); University of North Carolina at Chapel Hill (J.D., 2000). ***PRACTICE AREAS:*** Real Property. ***Email:*** dwoods@wehwlaw.com

CHRISTOPHER M. KROGER, born Charleston, West Virginia, August 26, 1963; admitted to bar, 1994, West Virginia and U.S. District Court, Southern District of West Virginia; 1997, North Carolina and U.S. Court of Appeals, Fourth Circuit; 1998, U.S. District Court, Eastern, Middle and Western Districts of North Carolina. *Education:* Marshall University (B.B.A., Accounting, cum laude, 1985); West Virginia University (J.D., 1994). Order of the Coif. *Member:* West Virginia State Bar. ***PRACTICE AREAS:*** Business Law; Commercial Law; Bankruptcy; Entertainment Law. ***Email:*** ckroger@wehwlaw.com

MATTHEW C. JOBE, born Rocky Mount, North Carolina, June 11, 1971; admitted to bar, 2001, North Carolina. *Education:* University of North Carolina at Chapel Hill (B.S.B.A., 1994; M.A.C., 1994); Wake Forest University (J.D., 2001). Member, Moot Court. Certified Public Accountant, North Carolina, 1996. ***PRACTICE AREAS:*** Business Law; Taxation. ***Email:*** mjobe@wehwlaw.com

ARLENE W. REARDON, born Delaware County, Pennsylvania, November 23, 1975; admitted to bar, 2001, North Carolina and U.S. District Court, Middle District of North Carolina. *Education:* C.W. Post Campus of Long Island University (B.A.M.A., summa cum laude, 1998); Wake Forest University (J.D., 2001). ***PRACTICE AREAS:*** Family Law. ***Email:*** awiegner@wehwlaw.com

JASON E. MOSS, born Atlanta, Georgia, May 28, 1974; admitted to bar, 1999, North Carolina and U.S. District Court, Middle District of North Carolina; 2000, U.S. Court of Appeals, Fourth Circuit. *Education:* Wake Forest University (B.A., cum laude, 1996; J.D. 1999). Member, Moot Court Board. Member, Wake Forest Law Review. Law Clerk to the Hon. Judge William L. Osteen, U.S. District Court, Middle District of North Carolina, 1999-2000. ***PRACTICE AREAS:*** Commercial Litigation; Elder Law. ***Email:*** jmoss@wehwlaw.com

CORY A. RAYBORN, born Greensboro, North Carolina, November 12, 1975; admitted to bar, 2003, North Carolina. *Education:* Duke University (B.S., 1998); University of North Carolina at Chapel Hill (J.D., 2003). *Member:* American Bar Association. ***PRACTICE AREAS:*** Wills; Trust Planning; Estate Planning. ***Email:*** crayborn@wehwlaw.com

MARTHA C. MASSIE, born Lexington, Virginia, January 27, 1960; admitted to bar, 2003, North Carolina. *Education:* Guilford College (B.S., Psychology, 1983; B.A., English, 1984); University of North Carolina at Chapel Hill (M.A., Mass Communications, 1988; J.D., 2003). Dana Scholar. *Member:* American Bar Association. ***PRACTICE AREAS:*** Family Law. ***Email:*** mmassie@wehwlaw.com

OF COUNSEL

CALVIN B. BRYANT, born Roanoke Rapids, North Carolina, September 13, 1928; admitted to bar, 1955, North Carolina and U.S. District Court, Middle District of North Carolina. *Education:* University of North Carolina at Chapel Hill (A.B., 1953; J.D., 1955). Member, University of North Carolina Law Review, 1954-1955. *Member:* American Bar Association. (Board Certified Specialist in Estate Planning and Probate Law, North Carolina State Board of Legal Specialization). ***PRACTICE AREAS:*** Probate; Wills; Estate Administration.

All attorneys are members of the High Point and North Carolina Bar Associations and the North Carolina State Bar.

REPRESENTATIVE CLIENTS: Allstate Insurance Co.; Banner Pharmacaps, Inc.; BB&T Factors Corp.; Davis Furniture Industries; Dar-Ran Furniture Industries; Mid-State Petroleum; J & S Cafeterias; The Presbyterian Homes, Inc.; British Vita; Palliser Furniture Corp.
APPROVED ATTORNEYS FOR: Lawyers Title Insurance Corp.; Chicago Title Insurance Co.; Jefferson-Pilot Title Insurance Co.; American Title Insurance Co.; AMI Title Insurance Co.; Investors Title Insurance Co.; First Title Insurance Co.; Farmers Home Administration.

COLEMAN, GLEDHILL, HARGRAVE & PEEK, P.C.

Established in 1969

129 EAST TRYON STREET
P.O. DRAWER 1529
HILLSBOROUGH, NORTH CAROLINA 27278
Telephone: 919-732-2196
FAX: 919-732-7997
URL: http://www.cgandh.com

General Civil and Criminal Trial Practice in all State and Federal Courts. Litigation, Negligence, Domestic, Real Estate, Corporate, Municipal and Probate Law, Commercial Transactions and Litigation.

(This Listing Continued)

COLEMAN, GLEDHILL, HARGRAVE & PEEK, P.C., Hillsborough—Continued

GEOFFREY E. GLEDHILL, born Philadelphia, Pennsylvania, August 16, 1944; admitted to bar, 1975, North Carolina; 1980, U.S. Court of Appeals, 4th Circuit; 1983, U.S. District Court, Middle District of North Carolina. *Education:* Widener University (B.S., 1966); North Carolina Central University (J.D., cum laude, 1975). Member of Staff, North Carolina Central University Law Journal, 1973-1975. Orange County Attorney, 1976—. General Counsel, Lumbee River Electric Membership Corporation, 1983-1989. *Member:* Orange County Bar Association; 15B Judicial District and North Carolina State Bars; North Carolina Association of County Attorneys (Past President). ***PRACTICE AREAS:*** Municipal; Zoning and Planning; Corporate; Small Business. ***Email:*** GeoffreyGledhill@CGandH.com

DOUGLAS HARGRAVE, born Philadelphia, Pennsylvania, March 28, 1950; admitted to bar, 1976, North Carolina; 1977, U.S. District Court, Middle District of North Carolina; 1998, U.S. Supreme Court. *Education:* Wake Forest University (B.A., cum laude, 1972); University of North Carolina (J.D., 1976). Orange County Attorney, 1976. Member: Board of Directors, American Red Cross, 1993-1994; Branch Banking & Trust Advisory Board, 1994—. *Member:* Orange County (President, 1982) and North Carolina Bar Association; 15B Judicial District and North Carolina State Bars; North Carolina Academy of Trial Lawyers; Academy of Trial Lawyers of America. ***PRACTICE AREAS:*** Personal Injury; Civil Litigation; Real Estate; Trusts and Estates; Commercial Litigation. ***Email:*** DouglasHargrave@CGandH.com

SAMUEL E. COLEMAN, born Durham, North Carolina, September 29, 1963; admitted to bar, 1994, North Carolina. *Education:* University of North Carolina (B.A., 1991; J.D., 1994). *Member:* 15B Judicial District (President, 2002), Orange County and North Carolina (Member, Criminal Law Section Council) Bar Associations; North Carolina Academy of Trial Lawyers. ***PRACTICE AREAS:*** Criminal Law; Contracts; Construction Law; Trusts and Estates. ***Email:*** SamuelColeman@CGandH.com

LEIGH ANN PEEK, born Quantico, Virginia, September 1, 1960; admitted to bar, 1995, North Carolina. *Education:* East Carolina University (B.A., cum laude, 1981); The University of North Carolina at Chapel Hill (M.A., 1992; J.D., 1995). *Member:* Orange County and 15B Judicial District Bar Associations; North Carolina State Bar. ***PRACTICE AREAS:*** Domestic Relations Law; Criminal Law; Civil Litigation; Juvenile Law; Immigration. ***Email:*** LeighAnnPeek@CGandH.com

S. SEAN BORHANIAN, born November 12, 1958; admitted to bar, 1991, South Carolina; 1998, North Carolina. *Education:* Rutgers University (B.A., Zoology, 1983); University of South Carolina (J.D., 1991). *Member:* Orange County, 15B Judicial District and North Carolina (Member, Administrative Law Section) Bar Associations; North Carolina State Bar. ***PRACTICE AREAS:*** Municipal; Zoning, Planning and Land Use; Corporate; Health Law. ***Email:*** SeanB@CGandH.com

MARKEE L. SQUIRE, born Emporia, Virginia, September 18, 1977; admitted to bar, 2002, North Carolina; 2003, U.S. District Court, Middle District of North Carolina. *Education:* North Carolina Agricultural & Technical State University (B.S., summa cum laude, 1998; M.S., 1999); University of North Carolina at Chapel Hill (J.D., 2002). *Member:* 15B Judicial District, Orange County and North Carolina Bar Associations; North Carolina Academy of Trial Lawyers. ***PRACTICE AREAS:*** Civil Litigation; Small Business Law; Corporate Law; Real Estate; Foreclosures. ***Email:*** MarkeeSquire@CGandH.com

DONALD R. DICKERSON, P.A.

106 NORTH CHURTON STREET
HILLSBOROUGH, NORTH CAROLINA 27278
Telephone: 919-644-0021
Toll Free: 888-920-0021
Facsimile: 919-732-1002
Email: lodickerson@mindspring.com
Email: drdpa@earthlink.net
URL: http://www.dickerson-law-firm.com

General Civil and Criminal Trial Practice. Criminal, Civil, Domestic Relations, Family, Personal Injury, Traffic Violations.

DONALD R. DICKERSON, born Henderson, North Carolina, May 2, 1948; admitted to bar, 1973, North Carolina. *Education:* University of North Carolina (B.A., 1970; J.D., 1973). *Member:* Orange County and North Carolina Bar Associations; 15B Judicial District Bar Association (Member, Executive Committee, 1981); North Carolina State Bar. ***PRACTICE AREAS:*** Criminal Law; Federal Criminal Law; Domestic Relations; Civil Litigation; Family Law; Traffic Violations. ***Email:*** drdpa@earthlink.net

LAUREN O. DICKERSON, born Durham, North Carolina, January 28, 1975; admitted to bar, 2001, North Carolina. *Education:* University of North Carolina at Chapel Hill (B.A., 1997); Campbell University Law School (J.D., 2001). The Order of Barristers. *Member:* Orange County and North Carolina Bar Associations; 15B Judicial District Bar Association; North Carolina State Bar; North Carolina Academy of Trial Lawyers. ***PRACTICE AREAS:*** Criminal Defense; Family Law; Domestic Relations; Traffic Violations; Drivers License Suspension; Juvenile Law. ***Email:*** lodickerson@mindspring.com

EPTING & HACKNEY

HILLSBOROUGH, NORTH CAROLINA

(See Chapel Hill)

General Civil and Criminal Practice, Trials, Family Law, Real Estate, Business and Corporations, Wills, Probate, Estate Planning.

LAW OFFICE OF JOHN C. FITZPATRICK, P.C.

HILLSBOROUGH, NORTH CAROLINA

(See Durham)

DWI, Traffic, Criminal, Personal Injury.

FRANKLIN LAW CENTER, PLLC

HILLSBOROUGH, NORTH CAROLINA

(See Chapel Hill)

Divorce, Alimony, Spousal Support, Separation Agreements, Marital Property Settlements, Equitable Distribution of Assets, Cohabitation Agreements, Community Property Law, Non-Traditional Family Law, Divorce Mediation, Divorce Arbitration, Collaborative Family Law, Adoption, International Family Law, Child Custody, Military Divorce, Military Family Law, Trial Practice in all Courts.

LAW OFFICE OF DOROTHY HAIRSTON

HILLSBOROUGH, NORTH CAROLINA

(See Durham)

Family Law, Criminal Law, Traffic Violations, Personal Injury, Medical Malpractice, Workers Compensation, Real Estate, Business, Military Law, Bankruptcy.

JUDITH M. HAUSER

127 WEST KING STREET
HILLSBOROUGH, NORTH CAROLINA 27278-2543
Telephone: 919-732-6131
Fax: 919-732-6229
Email: closings@mindspring.com

General Practice. Real Estate, Wills and Estates.

JUDITH M. HAUSER, born Avon Park, Florida; admitted to bar, 1985, North Carolina. *Education:* University of Richmond; Atlantic Christian College; University of North Carolina at Chapel Hill (B.A., 1981; J.D., 1984). *Member:* North Carolina (Member, Real Estate, Bankruptcy and General Section), Orange County and American Bar Associations; North Carolina State Bar.

LOFTIN AND LOFTIN, P.A.

117 NORTH CHURTON STREET
P.O. BOX 733
HILLSBOROUGH, NORTH CAROLINA 27278
Telephone: 919-732-9748
Fax: 919-732-4241
Email: jdloftin@mindspring.com
URL: http://www.jdloftinlaw.com

General Practice, General Civil and Criminal Trial and Appellate Practice. Personal Injury, Real Estate, Contracts, Constitutional, American Indian Law, Condemnation, Subdivision, Zoning, Family, Probate and Corporation Law.

JOHN D. LOFTIN, born Warwick, Virginia, September 26, 1955; admitted to bar, 1989, North Carolina. *Education:* East Carolina University; University of North Carolina (A.B., 1977; J.D., 1989) Harvard Divinity School; Duke University (Ph.D., 1983). Phi Beta Kappa. Recipient, American Jurisprudence Award for Constitutional Law. Author: "Anglo-American Jurisprudence and the Native American Tribal Quest for Religious Freedom," American Culture and Research Journal, Vol. 13, No. 1., 1989: 1-52. Visiting Assistant Professor, University of North Carolina at Greensboro, 2000—. Visiting Lecturer, Duke University, 1996-1998. *Member:* Orange County (President, 2000-2001), 15B District (Director, 2000—), North Carolina and American Bar Associations; North Carolina State Bar; North Carolina Academy of Trial Lawyers; The Association of Trial Lawyers of America; National Association of Criminal Defense Lawyers; Native American Rights Fund; Daniel Pollitt Criminal Defense Bar (President, 1998-1999). ***PRACTICE AREAS:*** Personal Injury; Condemnation; Family Law; Litigation; Criminal Defense. ***Email:*** JDLoftin@mindspring.com

OF COUNSEL

DALTON HARTWELL LOFTIN, born 1931; admitted to bar, 1959, North Carolina. *Education:* University of North Carolina (B.S., 1954; J.D., 1959). ***PRACTICE AREAS:*** Contracts; Wills and Estates; Real Estate; Commercial Law; Corporate Law; Probate.

REPRESENTATIVE CLIENTS: Hillsborough Savings Bank; Orange County Medical Foundation, Inc.
REFERENCES: Hillsborough Savings Bank; Central Carolina Bank; NationsBank; Federal Land Bank; Farmers Home Administration.

THE LAW OFFICE OF JONATHAN RICHARDSON

HOLLY SPRINGS, NORTH CAROLINA

(See Cary)

Personal Injury, Real Estate, Closings, Workers Compensation, Injuries, Traffic Violations, Tickets, Wrongful Death.

WILLIAM E. CLARK

HOPE MILLS, NORTH CAROLINA

(See Fayetteville)

General Civil Practice. Wills, Estate Planning and Probate. Corporate and Business Law. Real Estate Closings and Development.

THE BOLDUC LAW FIRM, PLLC

HUNTERSVILLE, NORTH CAROLINA

(See Charlotte)

NASD Arbitration, Business Litigation, Securities Fraud, Corporate Malfeasance, Mutual Fund Disputes, Wrongful Termination, Banking and Finance Law, and Accounting.

ELLIOTT LAW FIRM, P.C.

Established in 2004

P.O. BOX 1821

HUNTERSVILLE, NORTH CAROLINA 28078

Telephone: 704-491-0365

URL: http://www.mkelliott-law.com

Email: mikeelliott@legalemail.com

URL: http://www.elliottlawfirm.net

Business Law, Limited Liability Company Law, Incorporations, Corporate Law, Mergers and Acquisitions, Tax Law, Real Estate, Construction Law, Trusts and Estates, Asset Protection, Estate Planning, Guardianship, Bankruptcy, Traffic Violations.

FIRM PROFILE: Elliott Law Firm strives to provide individualized service to clients. Practice areas include: Business Law, Corporation Law, Limited Liability Company, Mergers and Acquisitions, Tax, Real Estate, Bankruptcy, Traffic Defense and Estate Planning.

MICHAEL K. ELLIOTT, born Columbia, South Carolina, May 13, 1967; admitted to bar, 2003, North Carolina and U.S. District Court, Western District of North Carolina; U.S. District Court, Middle District of North Carolina; U.S. Tax Court. *Education:* North Carolina A&T State University (B.S., summa cum laude, 2000); Regent University (J.D., 2003). *Member:* Mecklenburg County and North Carolina Bar Associations; North Carolina Bar. **PRACTICE AREAS:** Business Formation; Tax; Wills; Trusts; Estate Planning. ***Email:*** mikeelliott@legalemail.com

REPRESENTATIVE CLIENTS: Kare Pertmers, LLC; Polycom User Group, Inc.; The Riverdell Center, Inc.

RAY A. HAYES II P.A.

HUNTERSVILLE, NORTH CAROLINA

(See Cornelius)

Business Transactions, Business Litigation, Corporate Law, Business Planning, Buying or Selling a Business, Securities, Contracts, Trusts and Estates, Wills and Probate, Bankruptcy, Consumer Bankruptcy, Traffic Violations.

BRUCE L. JAMES

Established in 2002

ROSEDALE COMMONS EXECUTIVE SUITES

10105 HICKORYWOOD HILL AVENUE

SUITE B-3

HUNTERSVILLE, NORTH CAROLINA 28078

Telephone: 704-992-6556

Facsimile: 704-992-6559

Charlotte: 704-372-1202

Email: bruceljames1@aol.com

URL: http://www.brucejameslaw.com

Mailing Address: P.O. Box 657, Huntersville, NC 28070

Estate Planning, Asset Protection, Estate Litigation, Tax, Wills and Probate, Non Profit and Charitable Organizations, Business Law, Corporate Law, Collections, Eminent Domain, Employee Benefits, Civil Litigation, Taxation.

FIRM PROFILE: Representing business and individuals in estate planning, estate administration, tax matter and business matters, serious counseling, advice and implementation of client's legal strategies. Experienced in planning for and disposing of business, as well as ongoing matters of litigation.

BRUCE L. JAMES, born Salisbury, North Carolina, June 18, 1961; admitted to bar, 1986, North Carolina; 1990, U.S. District Court, Western District of North Carolina; 1991, U.S. Tax Court. *Education:* University of North Carolina at Charlotte (B.S., 1983); Campbell University (J.D., 1986). Beta Alpha Psi. Certified Public Accountant, North Carolina, 1988. Lt. Governor, North Carolina West Optimist. BSA Leader. Member, Board of Director, Charlotte Optimist Club. KPMG Tax Alumnus. *Member:* North Carolina and American (Member, Sections on: Tax; Business Law) Bar Associations; North Carolina State Bar.

THE KING LAW FIRM PLLC

7930 W. KENTON CIRCLE, SUITE 100

HUNTERSVILLE, NORTH CAROLINA 28078

Telephone: 704-892-5533

Fax: 704-892-9191

Email: bking@brentkinglaw.com

URL: http://www.brent-kinglawfirm.com

Bankruptcy, Domestic, Family, Wills, Trusts, Criminal.

(This Listing Continued)

BRENT F. KING, born Mooresville, North Carolina, November 16, 1970; admitted to bar, 1996, North Carolina. *Education:* University of North Carolina at Chapel Hill (B.A., 1993); Wake Forest University (J.D., 1996). Phi Alpha Delta. *Member:* Mecklenburg County, North Carolina (Member, Sections on: Bankruptcy; Real Estate) and American Bar Associations; North Carolina State Bar; North Carolina Academy of Trial Lawyers. **PRACTICE AREAS:** Bankruptcy; Domestic Partnerships; Family Law; Wills; Trust Law; Criminal Law. ***Email:*** bking@brentkinglaw.com

G. PATTESON WILLIAMS

HUNTERSVILLE, NORTH CAROLINA

(See Cornelius)

Real Estate, Residential Real Estate, Commercial Real Estate, Wills, Estates, Estate Administration, Business, Corporate, Automobile Accidents, Personal Injury.

MOSELEY, ELLIOTT & DICKENS, L.L.P.

JACKSON, NORTH CAROLINA

(See Roanoke Rapids)

Real Estate, Probate, Criminal Law, Misdemeanors, Traffic Violations, Domestic Relations, Family Law, Municipal Corporations, Corporate Law, Civil Litigation.

VICTORIA L. BLOCK

JACKSONVILLE, NORTH CAROLINA

(See New Bern)

Immigration Law, Social Security Law, Wills.

BRANTLEY, JENKINS, RIDDLE, HARDEE & HARDEE

901 HARGETT STREET

P.O. BOX 7070

JACKSONVILLE, NORTH CAROLINA 28540

Telephone: 910-455-5599

Fax: 910-455-7191

URL: http://www.bjrhhlawyers.com

URL: http://www.bjrhhatty.com

Goldsboro, North Carolina Office: 601 North Spence Avenue, 27534. Telephone: 919-778-9700. Fax: 919-778-1938.

Greenville, North Carolina Office: 202 East Arlington Boulevard, P.O. Box 924, 27858. Telephone: 252-355-1998. Fax: 252-321-2948.

Kinston, North Carolina Office: 2506 Heritage Street, Suite A, 28501. Telephone: 252-522-1500.

Personal Injury, Wrongful Death, Automobile Accidents, Head and Spinal Injury, Nursing Home Abuse and Neglect, Workers Compensation, Insurance, Products Liability, Social Security Disability, Medical Malpractice.

(For complete biographical data on all personnel, see Professional Biographies at Goldsboro, North Carolina)

BRUMBAUGH, MU & KING, P.A.

Established in 1978

112 OLD BRIDGE STREET

P.O. BOX 1088

JACKSONVILLE, NORTH CAROLINA 28541-1088

Telephone: 910-455-4065; 800-635-1683

Fax: 910-455-5539

URL: http://www.lawyers.com/brumbaughmuandking

URL: http://www.bmklaw.net

Wilmington, North Carolina Office: 2018 South 16th Street. Telephone: 910-763-2111.

Elizabethtown, North Carolina Office: 102 West Broad Street. Telephone: 910-862-2211.

Fayetteville, North Carolina Office: 609 Executive Place. Telephone: 910-630-2099.

New Bern, North Carolina, Office: McCarthy Square Office Suites, 790 Cardinal Road, Suite 6. Telephone: 252-636-2099.

Shallotte, North Carolina Office: 143 Holden Beach Rd., Suite #6-A. Telephone: 910-754-3660.

Washington, North Carolina Office: 110 West Third Street, P.O. Box 338. Telephone: 252-946-0793.

Havelock, North Carolina Office: 404 East Main Street, 28532. Telephone: 252-447-4445.

Kinston, North Carolina Office: 414 South Queen Street, 28501. Telephone: 252-939-1800.

Rocky Mt., North Carolina Office: 876 Country Club Rd., 27804. Telephone: 252-451-4090.

Practice Limited to Injury Cases. Automobile, Wrongful Death, Medical Malpractice, Workers' Compensation, Products Liability and Social Security Claims.

FIRM PROFILE: In 1989, our firm limited its practice to injury law. We maintain offices in Jacksonville, Wilmington, Elizabethtown, Fayetteville, Shallotte, New Bern, Washington, Havelock, Kinston and Rocky Mount and provide services to the surrounding counties.

We employ an accident investigator, paralegals and secretaries who are experienced in injury law.

(This Listing Continued)

BRUMBAUGH, MU & KING, P.A., Jacksonville—Continued

Our firm has an active trial practice in both federal and state courts. We have extensive experience in Federal Tort claims involving negligence of government employees. Arbitration of personal injury cases is a routine part of our practice. Our attorneys and staff participate in continuing legal education, professional activities and civic affairs.

RICHARD A. MU, born Buffalo, New York, March 23, 1950; admitted to bar, 1980, North Carolina; 1983, U.S. District Court, Eastern District of North Carolina. *Education:* United States Naval Academy (B.S., 1972); St. Mary's University; Wake Forest University (J.D., 1980). *Member:* Onslow County, North Carolina and American Bar Associations; North Carolina Academy of Trial Lawyers (Patron); Association of Trial Lawyers of America. [Major, U.S. Marine Corps Reserve, 1972-1977]. ***PRACTICE AREAS:*** Personal Injury Litigation; Wrongful Death; Federal Tort Claims; Trials in State and Federal Courts; Arbitration Hearings. ***Email:*** RAMu@BMKLaw.Net

CLAY A. BRUMBAUGH, born Oroville, Washington, February 2, 1940; admitted to bar, 1972, California; 1978, North Carolina; 1979, U.S. District Court, Eastern District of North Carolina and U.S. Supreme Court. *Education:* University of Colorado at Boulder (B.A., 1963); Hastings College of the Law, University of California (J.D., 1972). Phi Alpha Delta. *Member:* New Hanover County Bar Association; North Carolina State Bar; State Bar of California (inactive); North Carolina Academy of Trial Lawyers; North Carolina College of Advocacy; The Association of Trial Lawyers of America. [U.S. Marine Corps, 1958-1978, JAG Corps, 1973-1978, Retired Major, Special Courts Martial Judge]. ***PRACTICE AREAS:*** Personal Injury; Wrongful Death Claims; Arbitration Hearings. ***Email:*** CABrumbaugh@BMKLaw.Net

KENNETH W. KING, JR., born Honolulu, Hawaii, May 3, 1961; admitted to bar, 1986, Georgia and North Carolina; 1990, U.S. District Court, Eastern District of North Carolina and U.S. Court of Appeals, Fourth Circuit. *Education:* University of North Carolina at Chapel Hill (B.S., 1983); Mercer University (J.D., cum laude, 1986); Naval Justice School, Newport, Rhode Island, graduated with honors, 1987. Phi Alpha Delta; Order of the Barristers. Member: Moot Court Board; National Moot Court Competition Team. Recipient, James C. Estes Moot Court Award. Member, Mercer University Law Review. Author: "Becker v. IRM Corp: The Beginning of Caveat Lessor," 37 Mercer Law Review 1145, 1986. *Member:* Onslow County, New Hanover County and North Carolina Bar Associations; North Carolina State Bar; State Bar of Georgia; North Carolina Academy of Trial Lawyers; The Association of Trial Lawyers of America. [Capt., USMC JAG Corps, 1986-1990]. (Board Certified Specialist in Workers' Compensation, North Carolina State Board of Legal Specialization). ***PRACTICE AREAS:*** Personal Injury Litigation; Wrongful Death; Workers Compensation; Trials in State and Federal Courts; Arbitrations. ***Email:*** KWKing@BMKLaw.Net

LEAH L. KING, born Rocky Mount, North Carolina, September 3, 1967; admitted to bar, 1992, North Carolina. *Education:* East Carolina University (B.S., 1989); Campbell University (J.D., 1992). Gamma Beta Phi; Alpha Phi Sigma; Phi Alpha Delta. Intramural Moot Court Competition. Campbell Law Observer. *Member:* Onslow County, New Hanover County and North Carolina Bar Associations; North Carolina Academy of Trial Lawyers. (Board Certified Specialist in Workers' Compensation, North Carolina State Board of Legal Specialization). ***PRACTICE AREAS:*** Personal Injury; Workers Compensation; Trials in State and Federal Courts; Arbitrations. ***Email:*** LLKing@BMKLaw.Net

ASSOCIATES

NICOLE D. WRAY, born Fayetteville, North Carolina, April 26, 1970; admitted to bar, 1995, North Carolina. *Education:* East Carolina University (B.A., cum laude, 1992); Campbell University (J.D., 1995). Phi Alpha Delta. Member, National Moot Court Team. Member, Moot Court Board. Campbell Law Observer. Recipient, Rick Edmondson Memorial Award for Moot Court. *Member:* Onslow County Bar Association; North Carolina State Bar; North Carolina Academy of Trial Lawyers. ***PRACTICE AREAS:*** Personal Injury; Workers Compensation; Arbitration; Social Security; Social Security Disability. ***Email:*** NDWray@BMKLaw.Net

ANGELA D. VANDIVIER-STANLEY, born Connersville, Indiana, August 19, 1970; admitted to bar, 2000, North Carolina. *Education:* Ball State University (B.S., 1993); Thomas M. Cooley Law School (J.D., 1999). *Member:* Onslow County and North Carolina Bar Associations; North Carolina Academy of Trial Lawyers. ***PRACTICE AREAS:*** Personal Injury; Workers Compensation. ***Email:*** ADVStanley@BMKLaw.Net

C. MARK BALDWIN, born Burlington, North Carolina, June 21, 1951; admitted to bar, 1980, North Carolina; 1983, U.S. District Court, Eastern District of North Carolina. *Education:* University of North Carolina at Chapel Hill (A.B., Political Science, 1973); Duke University (J.D., 1980). Phi Delta Phi. Special Assistant U.S. Attorney: Southern District of California, 1989-1990; Eastern District of North Carolina, 1991-1993. *Member:* Onslow County, North Carolina and American Bar Associations; North Carolina State Bar; North Carolina Academy of Trial Lawyers. [U.S.M.C., 1973-1993; Retired Major]. ***PRACTICE AREAS:*** Personal Injury; Workers Compensation. ***Email:*** MBaldwin@BMKLaw.Net

REFERENCE: First Citizens Bank, Jacksonville, NC.

COLLINS AND MOORE, PLLC

Established in 1983

634 COURT ST.

JACKSONVILLE, NORTH CAROLINA 28540

Telephone: 910-347-7100
Fax: 910-455-1496
URL: http://www.collinsandmoore.com
Email: glcatty@earthlink.net
URL: http://www.lawyers.com/collinsandmoore

Personal Injury including Wrongful Death, Automobile Accidents and Injuries, Medical Malpractice, Premises Liability; Corporate and Business Law including Contracts, Disputes, Commercial Litigation, Taxation; Estate Planning including Wills, Trusts, Retirement Planning, Wealth Preservation; Criminal Defense including Felonies, Misdemeanors, Drugs, Traffic Violations, Speeding, Parole and Probation, DWI; Family Law including Divorce, Child Custody, Alimony, Separation Agreements; Workers Compensation.

FIRM PROFILE: Prior to establishing his law practice in 1983, Mr. Collins was a Certified Public Accountant in Jacksonville. As the only CPA/JD in the county, Mr. Collins brings an extensive knowledge of tax law pertaining to business and estate related matters. In addition, the firm serves its clients in a traditional general practice.

MEMBERS OF FIRM

GEORGE L. COLLINS, born Rocky Mount, North Carolina, April 7, 1944; admitted to bar, 1983, North Carolina; 1984, U.S. Tax Court; 1986, U.S. District Court, Eastern and Middle Districts of North Carolina, U.S. Supreme Court and U.S. Court of Appeals, Federal Circuit. *Education:* University of North Carolina (B.S., 1970); Campbell University (J.D., 1983). Certified Public Accountant, North Carolina, 1972. Superior Court Certified Mediator. *Member:* Onslow County Bar Association; North Carolina State Bar; Fourth Judicial District Bar Association; North Carolina Academy of Trial Lawyers; North Carolina Association of Certified Public Accountants. ***PRACTICE AREAS:*** Personal Injury; Wills and Estates; Civil Litigation; Corporation. ***Email:*** glcatty@earthlink.net

JAMES L. MOORE, JR., born Rocky Mount, North Carolina, September 14, 1959; admitted to bar, 1985, North Carolina. *Education:* University of North Carolina (B.A., 1981); Campbell University (J.D., 1985). Member, Campbell University Law Review, Honor Court. *Member:* Onslow County, North Carolina and American Bar Associations; North Carolina State Bar; North Carolina Academy of Trial Lawyers. ***PRACTICE AREAS:*** Criminal; Workers Compensation; Personal Injury.

ANN D. MAREADY, born Raleigh, North Carolina, June 28, 1968; admitted to bar, 1993, North Carolina. *Education:* Wake Forest University (B.A., 1990); Campbell University Law School (J.D., 1993). Phi Alpha Delta. *Member:* Onslow County Bar Association (Treasurer/Secretary, 1995-1998). ***PRACTICE AREAS:*** Domestic Relations; Criminal Law; Juvenile Law. ***Email:*** annatty@earthlink.net

REFERENCES: NationsBank; Wachovia Bank and Trust Co.

DAVID AND ASSOCIATES, PLLC

405-B WESTERN BOULEVARD

JACKSONVILLE, NORTH CAROLINA 28546

Telephone: 910-219-4878
Toll Free: 1-800-856-9927
Email: aeverhart@davidandassociates.com
URL: http://www.wilmingtonpiattorneys.com

Wilmington, North Carolina Office: 1516 Dawson Street. 28401. Telephone: 910-251-8088.

Supply, North Carolina Office: Highway 17. 28462. Telephone: 910-754-8465.

Wallace, North Carolina Office: 107 North Norwood Street. 28466. Telephone: 910-285-8777.

Clinton, North Carolina Office: 610 Beaman Street. 28328. Telephone: 910-592-8400.

Winston-Salem, North Carolina Office: 1100-A South Stratford Road. 27103. Telephone: 336-354-1040.

Greensboro, North Carolina Office: 529 College Road. Suite G. 27410. Telephone: 336-354-1040.

Personal Injury, Medical Malpractice, Wrongful Death, Products Liability, Workers Compensation, Aviation, Airplane Crashes, Negligence, Class Actions, Maritime Accidents, Boating Accidents, Bicycle Accidents, Motorcycle Accidents, Truck Accidents, School Bus Accidents, Railroad Accidents, Dog Bites, Slip and Fall, Birth Trauma, Brain Injury, Spinal Injury, Head Injury, Catastrophic Injury, Vehicular Homicide, Personal Injury Mediation, Products Liability, Drug and Medical Device Litigation, Product Defects, Automobile Liability, Motorcycle Products Liability, Amusement Park Liability, Hotel Liability, Marina Liability, Sports Injury.

(For complete biographical data on all personnel, see Professional Biographies, Wilmington, North Carolina)

ERWIN, SIMPSON & STROUD, P.L.L.C.

Established in 1983

825 GUM BRANCH ROAD, SUITE 115

JACKSONVILLE, NORTH CAROLINA 28540

Telephone: 910-455-1800
Facsimile: 910-346-5883
URL: http://www.essnc.com

Cedar Point, North Carolina Office: 708 Cedar Point Boulevard, 28584. Telephone: 910-326-4008.

Appellate Practice, Bankruptcy, Civil Practice, Commercial Real Estate, Condominium Law, Construction Law, Contracts, Corporate Law, Criminal Law, Debtor and Creditor, Family Law, Real Estate Foreclosure, Homeowners Association Law, Civil Litigation, Municipal Law, Personal Injury, Real Estate, Trusts and Estates, Wills.

FRANK W. ERWIN, born Laurinburg, North Carolina, August 4, 1952; admitted to bar, 1977, North Carolina; 1980, U.S. Court of Appeals, Fourth Circuit and U.S. Court of Military Appeals; 1981, U.S. Supreme Court; 1985, U.S. Claims Court. *Education:* Davidson College (A.B., Political Science, 1974); Duke University (J.D., 1977). Omicron Delta Kappa. Member, Onslow County Hospital Authority, 1981-1989. Member, Neuse River Economic Development Council, 1983-1986. Member, Panel of Arbitrators, American Arbitration Association. *Member:* Onslow County, North Carolina and American Bar Associations; North Carolina State Bar; North Carolina College of Advocacy (Member Council, Real Property Residential Forms Committee, 1998-2002; Real Property Law Section).

(This Listing Continued)

(Board Certified Specialist in Real Property Law, Residential Transactions, North Carolina State Board of Legal Specialization). ***PRACTICE AREAS:*** Real Estate; Homeowner Association Law; Business Law. ***Email:*** ferwin@essnc.com

JOHN P. SIMPSON, born Durham, North Carolina, November 14, 1945; admitted to bar, 1972, North Carolina, U.S. District Court, Eastern, Middle and Western Districts of North Carolina, U.S. Court of Appeals, Fourth Circuit and U.S. Supreme Court. *Education:* Wake Forest University (B.A., 1968; J.D., 1972). Phi Alpha Delta. Editor-in-Chief, Wake Forest Jurist, 1971-1972. Certified Mediator, Civil and N.C. Industrial Commission Worker Compensation Cases. *Member:* Onslow County and North Carolina (Member, Sections on: Alternative Dispute Resolution; Family Law; Bankruptcy Law; Worker Compensation) Bar Associations; North Carolina State Bar; National Association of Consumer Bankruptcy Attorneys. ***PRACTICE AREAS:*** Bankruptcy; Debtor and Creditor; Wills; Civil Practice; Family Law; Business Law; Contract Law; Mediation. ***Email:*** jsimpson@essnc.com

JOSEPH E. STROUD, JR., born Raleigh, North Carolina, January 4, 1951; admitted to bar, 1977, North Carolina; 1983, U.S. District Court, Eastern District of North Carolina. *Education:* East Carolina University (B.A., 1973; Graduate Studies, 1973-1974); Wake Forest University (J.D., 1977). Phi Alpha Delta. *Member:* Onslow County and North Carolina Bar Associations; North Carolina State Bar; North Carolina Academy of Trial Lawyers; National Association of Criminal Defense Lawyers. (Board Certified Specialist in State Criminal Law, North Carolina State Board of Legal Specialization). ***PRACTICE AREAS:*** Criminal Law; Family Law; Civil Litigation; Homeowners Association Law; Municipal Law. ***Email:*** jstroud@essnc.com

REPRESENTATIVE CLIENTS: Carolina Forest Developers, LLC; Emerald Plantation Master Association, Inc.; Gum Branch Square II Owners Association; Heron Cay Owners' Association Inc.; Hunters Creek CSA, Inc.; Hunter Development Corporation; Bank of America; New River Plantation CSA, Inc.; Ocean Bay Village Townhome Owners Association; Spinnakers Reach Realty, Inc.; Viking Utility Corp.; Town of Swansboro; Town of Cape Carteret; Town of Holly Ridge; Williams Farm CSA, Inc.; Williamsburg Plantation HOA; Topsail Reef HOA; Debby Crayton, Inc.; Emerald Sands, Inc.
APPROVED ATTORNEYS FOR: Investors Title Insurance Co.; Chicago Title Insurance Co.; Fidelity National Title Insurance Co.; First Citizens Bank; Investors Title; Lawyers Title; Bank of America; Stewart Title Insurance Co.; Wachovia Bank; Wells Fargo Home Mortgage; RBC Centura; BB&T; The Little Bank.

GLENN O'KEITH FISHER
ATTORNEY AT LAW

2505 HENDERSON DRIVE
JACKSONVILLE, NORTH CAROLINA 28546-5253
Telephone: 910-347-8800
Fax: 910-455-4440
Email: fmlaw@coastalnet.com

Real Estate, Criminal Law, Civil Litigation, Probate, Corporation, Personal Injury, Municipal Law.

GLENN O'KEITH FISHER, born Jacksonville, North Carolina, July 8, 1957; admitted to bar, 1982, North Carolina. *Education:* University of North Carolina (B.S., Business Administration, 1979); Wake Forest University (J.D., 1982). Member, Wake Forest University Law Review, 1981-1982. *Member:* Onslow County and Fourth Judicial District Bar Associations; North Carolina State Bar; North Carolina Academy of Trial Lawyers. ***PRACTICE AREAS:*** Civil Litigation; Probate; Corporate Law; Personal Injury; Municipal Law; Real Estate.

GAYLOR, EDWARDS AND VATCHER

Established in 1978
219 NEW BRIDGE STREET
P.O. BOX 1057
JACKSONVILLE, NORTH CAROLINA 28541-1057
Telephone: 910-455-9494
FAX: 910-455-0117

General Civil and Criminal Practice. Real Estate, Personal Injury, Traffic Violation, DWI, Felonies, Misdemeanor, Driver License Restoration, Medical Malpractice, Auto Accidents, Wrongful Death, Trust & Estate.

FIRM PROFILE: Since the predecessor firm was established in 1978, Gaylor, Edwards and Vatcher has offered clients in Jacksonville and Onslow County a general civil and criminal trial practice. The firm concentrates on personal injury law, including automobile accidents, medical malpractice and wrongful death, as well as criminal defense and drivers license restoration. The firm also handles matters of real estate, wills and trusts and contract law.

JIMMY F. GAYLOR, born Johnston County, North Carolina, August 15, 1949; admitted to bar, 1974, North Carolina; 1979, U.S. District Court, Eastern District of North Carolina; 1981, U.S. Court of Appeals, Fourth Circuit. *Education:* East Carolina University (B.A., 1971); Wake Forest University (J.D., 1974). Phi Delta Phi. Certified Mediator, State Court of North Carolina, 1998. *Member:* Onslow County (Vice President, 1981-1982; President, 1982-1983) and North Carolina (Member, Litigation Section) Bar Associations; Fourth Judicial District and North Carolina State Bar; North Carolina Academy of Trial Lawyers. ***PRACTICE AREAS:*** Personal Injury Law; Civil Litigation; Criminal Law.

J. DEWEY EDWARDS, JR., born Jacksonville, North Carolina, September 20, 1951; admitted to bar, 1976, North Carolina. *Education:* Wake Forest University (B.A., 1973; J.D., 1976). Phi Delta Phi. *Member:* Onslow County (President, 1990-1991), North Carolina (Member, Real Property Section) and 4th Judicial District Bar Associations; North Carolina State Bar. ***PRACTICE AREAS:*** Real Estate Law; Wills Law; Contract Law. ***Email:*** jde@bizec.rr.com

WALTER W. VATCHER, born Anaheim, California, March 12, 1952; admitted to bar, 1979, North Carolina; 1980, U.S. District Court, Eastern District of North Carolina. *Education:* University of North Carolina (B.S., 1974); Campbell University (J.D., 1979). Delta Theta Phi. Assistant District Attorney, 4th Judicial District, 1979-1984. Member, Military Affairs Committee, Chamber of Commerce. Member, Board of Directors, Pretrial Resource Center, Inc. *Member:* Onslow County (Vice President, 1998-1999; President, 1999-2000) and North Carolina (Member, Section on Criminal Law) Bar Associations; Fourth Judicial District Bar; North Carolina State Bar; North Carolina Academy of Trial Lawyers. ***PRACTICE AREAS:*** Criminal Law; Personal Injury Law; Civil Litigation. ***Email:*** wvatcher@bizec.rr.com

GENERAL COUNSEL FOR: National Dodge, Inc.; CTS Software, Inc.; Investco, Inc.
REPRESENTATIVE CLIENTS: HDX Corp.; Western Boulevard Properties, Inc.; Mercer Building Co.; Mercer Design; Hancock Builders; Richard Ray Real Estate; Old Towne Realty; Federal Land & Timber Corp; Delta Investors, Inc.; Onslow Investors, LLC; Western Boulevard, LLC.; JLP Investments, LLC; ABA Rental Properties, Inc.
APPROVED ATTORNEYS FOR: Fidelity Title Insurance Co.; Investors Title Insurance Co.; Lawyers Title Insurance Co.; Chicago Title Insurance Co.
REFERENCES: First Citizens Bank & Trust Co.; Wachovia Bank & Trust Co., N.A.; HDX Corp.

KELLUM LAW FIRM

445-A WESTERN BOULEVARD
P.O. BOX 12155
JACKSONVILLE, NORTH CAROLINA 28546
Telephone: 910-455-4546
Fax: 910-455-2422
Email: ckeenhold@kellumlawfirm.com
URL: http://www.lawyers.com/kellumlawfirm

State and Federal Civil Trial Practice, Personal Injury Law, Wrongful Death, Workers' Compensation, Social Security, Defective Products, Mass Torts and Insurance Law.

(For complete biographical data on all personnel, see Professional Biographies at New Bern)

MAKO & ASSOCIATES, P.A.

JACKSONVILLE, NORTH CAROLINA

(See Wilmington)

Personal Injury, Automobile Accidents, Wrongful Death, Trucking Accidents, Head Trauma, Spinal Cord Injuries, Motorcycle Accidents, Workers Compensation, Mediation and Arbitration, Birth Trauma, Medical Malpractice, Construction Accidents, Nursing Home Negligence, Nursing Home Abuse and Neglect and Dog Bites.

McNAMARA & SMITH, P.C.

Established in 1997
309 NEW BRIDGE STREET
JACKSONVILLE, NORTH CAROLINA 28540-4757
Telephone: 910-938-7191
Fax: 910-938-7833
Email: thomasmcnamara1@earthlink.net
URL: http://www.lawyers.com/mcnamaraandsmith

Family Law, including Divorce, Separation Agreements, Child Custody, Child Support, Alimony, Property Distribution.

THOMAS D. McNAMARA, born Houston, Texas, November 26, 1954; admitted to bar, 1993, North Carolina. *Education:* U.S. Naval Academy (B.S., 1977); Campbell University (J.D., 1993). *Member:* Onslow County and North Carolina (Member, Family Law Section) Bar Associations. [Lieutenant Colonel, U.S. Marine Corps (Retired)]. (Board Certified Specialist in Family Law, North Carolina State Board of Legal Specialization). ***PRACTICE AREAS:*** Family Law. ***Email:*** thomasmcnamara1@earthlink.net

M. LYNN SMITH, born Jacksonville, North Carolina, July 17, 1969; admitted to bar, 1995, North Carolina. *Education:* University of North Carolina at Chapel Hill (B.S., 1991; M.P.A., 1995; J.D., 1995). *Member:* Onslow County and North Carolina (Member, Family Law Section) Bar Associations; North Carolina State Bar; North Carolina Academy of Trial Lawyers. (Board Certified Specialist in Family Law, North Carolina State Board of Legal Specialization). ***PRACTICE AREAS:*** Family Law. ***Email:*** msmith15519@earthlink.net

ROGER A. MOORE

Established in 1977
100 OLD BRIDGE STREET
P.O. DRAWER 886
JACKSONVILLE, NORTH CAROLINA 28540
Telephone: 910-455-0448; 455-0449
Fax: 910-347-6343
Email: rogermooreatty4u@earthlink.net
URL: http://www.ncbankruptcylaw.com

Bankruptcy, Municipal Law.

FIRM PROFILE: We are a debt relief agency filing bankruptcies for consumers.

ROGER A. MOORE, born Charlotte, North Carolina, November 8, 1946; admitted to bar, 1973, North Carolina. *Education:* Woodberry Forest School; University of North Carolina (A.B., 1968; J.D., 1973). Phi Delta Phi. Law Clerk to Hon. John D. Larkins, Jr., U.S. District Court, Eastern District of North Carolina, 1974-1975. County Attorney, Onslow County, 1977-2004. President, North Carolina Association of County Attorneys, 1986. Member, Judicial Conference for the Fourth Circuit, 1978—. *Member:* Onslow County (President, 1994-1995), North Carolina and American Bar Associations; North Carolina State Bar. (Board Certified Specialist in Bankruptcy Law, North Carolina State Board of Legal Specialization). ***PRACTICE AREAS:*** Bankruptcy; Municipal Law.

VICTOR H.E. MORGAN, JR.
ATTORNEY AT LAW

732 COURT STREET
P.O. BOX 746
JACKSONVILLE, NORTH CAROLINA 28541
Telephone: 910-455-6555
Facsimile: 910-455-5149

Personal Injury, Auto Accidents, Workers' Compensation, Social Security Disability, Domestic Relations, Divorce, Criminal, Traffic Violations, DWI.

VICTOR H.E. MORGAN, JR., born Washington, D.C., August 15, 1957; admitted to bar, 1983, North Carolina; 1984, U.S. District Court, Eastern District of North Carolina; 1987, U.S. District Court, Western District of North Carolina. *Education:* University of North Carolina at Wilmington (B.A., with honors, 1980); Wake Forest University School of Law (J.D., 1983). Pi Sigma Alpha. Associate Attorney General, State of North Carolina, 1983-1985; Assistant Attorney General, State of North Carolina, 1985-1991. Member, Workplace Injury Litigation Groups. *Member:* Onslow County and North Carolina (Council Member, Workers Compensation and Member, Sections on: Litigation; Workers Compensation) Bar Associations; North Carolina Academy of Trial Lawyers (Member, Sections on: Workers Compensation, Auto Torts and Disability Advocacy); Fourth Judicial District Bar (President, 2002-2003); The Association of Trial Lawyers of America.

WILLIAM J. MORGAN, P.A.

127 CHANEY AVENUE
P.O. DRAWER 700
JACKSONVILLE, NORTH CAROLINA 28541-0700
Telephone: 910-989-1234
Fax: 910-455-8988
URL: http://www.morganlaw-nc.com
Email: wjm@morganlaw-nc.com
URL: http://morganlawfirm-nc.com

Personal Injury Law, General Civil Litigation, Medical Negligence Law, Major Criminal Defense.

FIRM PROFILE: Sole practitioner with 37 years experience representing injured persons and estates of persons killed by negligence. Also represents defendants in major criminal cases.

WILLIAM J. MORGAN, born Jacksonville, North Carolina, August 24, 1941; admitted to bar, 1967, North Carolina. *Education:* Davidson College (A.B., 1964); University of North Carolina (J.D., 1967). Phi Delta Phi. Listed, Best Lawyers in America, Personal Injury Section, 2002—. *Member:* Onslow County, North Carolina and American Bar Associations; The North Carolina State Bar; North Carolina Academy of Trial Lawyers (Former Member, Board of Governors; Former Vice-President). ***PRACTICE AREAS:*** General Civil Litigation; Medical Negligence Law; Criminal Defense; Plaintiffs Personal Injury; Personal Injury Mediation; Wrongful Death. ***Email:*** wjm@morganlaw-nc.com

SAMUEL STUART POPKIN

1007 HARGETT STREET, SUITE 1
JACKSONVILLE, NORTH CAROLINA 28540
Telephone: 910-347-0100
Fax: 910-989-1202
Email: spopkinattrny@ec.rr.com
URL: http://www.popkinlaw.com

Criminal Law, Traffic Violations, Juvenile Delinquency, Divorce, Negligence, Abuse.

SAMUEL STUART POPKIN, born Wilmington, North Carolina, April 13, 1952; admitted to bar, 1978, North Carolina; 1979, U.S. District Court, Eastern District of North Carolina. *Education:* Duke University (B.A., Political Science, 1974); North Carolina Central University (J.D., 1977); New York University School of Law (LL.M., Taxation, 1979). *Member:* North Carolina Bar Association; North Carolina State Bar. ***PRACTICE AREAS:*** Criminal Law; Traffic Violations; Juvenile Delinquency; Divorce; Negligence; Elder Abuse.

BRUCE H. ROBINSON, JR.

JACKSONVILLE, NORTH CAROLINA

(See Wilmington)

TAYLOR AND BASHAM

Established in 1981

SUITE 117, 825 GUM BRANCH ROAD
JACKSONVILLE, NORTH CAROLINA 28540
Telephone: 910-455-6300
Fax: 910-455-3012
Email: vaughantaylor@att.net
URL: http://www.lawyers.com/militarylaw

Military Law, Military Courts Martial, Military Criminal Law, Military Justice and Military Administrative Law.

FIRM PROFILE: Vaughan E. Taylor started this practice in 1981 after he served for eleven years as an Army Judge Advocate. The practice is dedicated to the representation of United States military personnel worldwide before military trial and appellate courts, administrative boards, and all military tribunals. Range of practice includes trials by court-martial; appeals to the Judge Advocates General, Service Secretaries, Courts of Criminal Appeals and the Court of Appeals for the Armed Forces; administrative separation and reduction boards; evaluation and fitness report appeals; medical boards; professional credentials review boards (physicians, aviators, etc.); applications for correction of military and naval records. Mr. Taylor has over thirty years experience practicing nothing but military law. The firm is also fully staffed with paralegals, with a wide range of military law-related backgrounds.

VAUGHAN E. TAYLOR, born Portland, Maine, October 3, 1947; admitted to bar, 1972, Virginia and Maine; 1980, U.S. Court of Federal Claims; 1983, North Carolina, U.S. Supreme Court, U.S. Court of the Armed Forces. *Education:* Dartmouth College (B.A., cum laude, 1969); University of Virginia (J.D., 1972); The Judge Advocate General's School, Army (Graduate Course, Masters of Law Program, 1977). Author: "The Competency of Counsel," The Army Lawyer, October, 1977; "Building The Cuckoo's Nest," The Army Lawyer, June, 1978; "Using The Cuckoo's Nest," The Army Lawyer, July, 1979; "Witnesses: The Ultimate Weapon," The Army Lawyer, May, 1987. Contributing Author, "Principles and Practice of Military Forensic Psychiatry," 1997. *Member:* Onslow County and North Carolina Bar Associations. [U.S. Army, JAGC, 1969-1980; Officer in Charge, Aschaffenburg Branch SJA Office, 1974-1976; Instructor, Criminal Law Division, The Judge Advocate General's School, Army, 1977-1980. Certified as Military Judge, 1979. The Army's JAG School is responsible for the initial training of all the military's judges, as well as continuing legal education for the JAGS of all the armed services . U.S. Army Reserves, JAGC, 1980-1989; Senior Reserve Instructor, Criminal Law Division, The Judge Advocate General's School, Army, 1980-1989; Retired Reserve, 1989—. Army Commendation Medal, 1976; Meritorious Service Medal 1980; Army Achievement Medal, 1987]. ***LANGUAGES:*** Spanish. ***REPORTED CASES:*** United States v: Woolheater; Babbitt; Lips; Benedict; Cox; Garwood; Washington; Saul; Brakebush; Bair. ***PRACTICE AREAS:*** Military Law; Military Courts Martial; Military Criminal Law; Military Justice; Military Administrative Law. ***Email:*** vaughantaylor@att.net

OWEN D. BASHAM, born Daviess County, Kentucky, May 23, 1942; admitted to bar, 1967, Kentucky; 1973, U.S. Supreme Court; 1989, Virginia; U.S. Court of the Armed Forces (Not admitted in North Carolina). *Education:* Murray State University (B.A., 1965); University of Kentucky (J.D., 1967); The Judge Advocate General's School (Army, Graduate Course Masters of Law Program, 1974); U.S. Army Command and General Staff College (1985). Recipient, ROTC Military Honors; Military Appellate Judge, 1988-1989; Military Judge, 1974-1977; Legion of Merit, 1989; and other military awards and decorations. *Member:* Virginia State Bar. [Lt. Col., U.S. Army, 1965-1982; Senior Instructor, United States Army JAGC School, 1977-1982]. ***REPORTED CASES:*** U.S. v. SCHWAB, 27 M.J. 559 (ACMR 1988); U.S. v. JOHNSON, 27 M.J. 553 (ACMR 1988); U.S. v. BARBER, 27 M.J. 885 (ACMR 1989). ***PRACTICE AREAS:*** Military Law; Military Courts Martial; Military Criminal Law; Military Justice; Military Administrative Law. ***Email:*** bashamlaw@aol.com

WALLACE, MORRIS, BARWICK, LANDIS & STROUD, P.A.

JACKSONVILLE, NORTH CAROLINA

(See Kinston)

General Civil and Trial Practice in all State and Federal Courts. Aviation, Banking, Corporate Law, Insurance, Personal Injury, Probate, Product Liability, Real Estate and Taxation.

WARD AND SMITH, P.A.

JACKSONVILLE, NORTH CAROLINA

(See New Bern)

General and Trial Practice. Admiralty Law; Bankruptcy; Banks and Banking; Business Law; Civil Rights; Commercial Law; Construction Law; Contracts; Copyrights; Corporate Law; Debtor and Creditor; Elder Law; Eminent Domain; Employee Benefits; Environmental Law; Family Law including Divorce; Finance; Franchise Law; Government; Government Contracts; Health Care Law; Immigration and Naturalization; Insurance; International Law; International Trade; Investments; Labor and Employment including Discrimination, Sexual Harassment, and Workers' Compensation; Landlord and Tenant; Litigation; Personal Injury including Automobile Accidents, Legal Malpractice and Medical Malpractice; Products Liability; Real Estate; Securities; Taxation; Technology and Science including Internet Law, Trademarks, and Patents; Trusts and Estates including Estate Planning and Wills and Probate; Zoning and Land Use.

LANA S. WARLICK

410 NEW BRIDGE STREET
SUITE 1A
P.O. BOX 1393
JACKSONVILLE, NORTH CAROLINA 28540
Telephone: 910-347-4400
Fax: 910-347-3736

Family Law, Divorce Law, Separation Agreements, Custody, Child Support, Alimony, Property Distribution, Adoption and Appellate Practice.

LANA S. WARLICK, born Charlotte, North Carolina, September 18, 1951; admitted to bar, 1976, North Carolina. *Education:* University of North Carolina at Chapel Hill (A.B., 1973; J.D., 1976). *Member:* Onslow County, North Carolina and American Bar Associations; North Carolina State Bar; North Carolina Academy of Trial Lawyers; The Association of Trial Lawyers of America. Fellow: American Academy of Matrimonial Lawyers. (Board Certified Specialist in Family Law, North Carolina State Board of Legal Specialization). ***PRACTICE AREAS:*** Family Law; Children.

REFERENCES: First Citizens Bank and Trust Co.; BB & T; RBC Centura.

THE LAW OFFICES OF JOHN DREW WARLICK, P.A.

313 NEW BRIDGE STREET
JACKSONVILLE, NORTH CAROLINA 28540
Telephone: 910-455-7700
Fax: 910-455-4068
Email: jdw@warlicklaw.com
URL: http://www.warlicklawoffice.com

Personal Injury Law, Medical Negligence Law, General Civil Litigation, Automobile Accidents and Injuries, Wrongful Death, DWI, Traffic and Family Law.

JOHN D. WARLICK, JR., born Wilmington, North Carolina, September 10, 1934; admitted to bar, 1962, North Carolina. *Education:* University of North Carolina (A.B., 1958; J.D., with honors, 1962). Delta Theta Phi; Order of the Coif. Associate Editor, The North Carolina Law Review, 1961-1962. Member, North Carolina Judicial Nominating Committee, North Carolina Superior Court, 1978-1984. Member, North Carolina Board of Law Examiners, 1979-1987. Listed in Personal Injury Section, Best Lawyers in America, 1987—. *Member:* Onslow County, North Carolina and American Bar Associations; The North Carolina State Bar; The Association of Trial Lawyers of America (State Delegate, 1986-1988); North Carolina Academy of Trial Lawyers (Member, Board of Governors, 1976-1988; President, 1982-1983). Fellow, American College of Trial Lawyers; International Society of Barristers. ***PRACTICE AREAS:*** Personal Injury; Medical Malpractice; Civil Litigation. ***Email:*** jdw@warlicklaw.com

ROBERT A. WARLICK, born Jacksonville, North Carolina, May 3, 1971; admitted to bar, 1997, North Carolina. *Education:* University of North Carolina at Wilmington (B.A., 1994); Campbell University (J.D., 1997). General Counsel, Jones-Onslow Electric Membership Corporation. *Member:* Onslow County Bar Association; North Carolina State Bar; North Carolina Academy of Trial Lawyers. ***PRACTICE AREAS:*** Personal Injury; Civil Litigation; DWI and Traffic Offenses. ***Email:*** raw@warlicklaw.com

---

DEKE SLAYTON OWENS, born Birmingham, Alabama, June 30, 1971; admitted to bar, 1996, North Carolina. *Education:* East Carolina University (B.S., magna cum laude, 1993); Samford University (J.D., 1996). *Member:* Onslow County Bar Association; North Carolina State Bar; North Carolina Academy of Trial Lawyers (Chairman, Young Lawyers Division; Auto Torts Section). ***PRACTICE AREAS:*** Personal Injury; Criminal Defense; Family Law; Civil Litigation. ***Email:*** dso@warlicklaw.com

THE WELCH LAW FIRM, P.C.

220 OLD BRIDGE STREET
JACKSONVILLE, NORTH CAROLINA 28540
Telephone: 910-347-0161
Fax: 910-347-0164

Criminal Law, General Practice.

CHRISTOPHER J. WELCH, born Washington, D.C., June 1, 1975; admitted to bar, 2000, North Carolina. *Education:* Trinity College (B.A., 1997); Wake Forest University (J.D., 2000). *Member:* Onslow County (Member, Teen Court Board of Directors) and North Carolina Bar Associations; North Carolina Academy of Trial Lawyers. ***PRACTICE AREAS:*** Criminal Law (100%).

HARTSELL & WILLIAMS, P.A.

Established in 1896
708 MCLAIN ROAD
P.O. BOX 2
KANNAPOLIS, NORTH CAROLINA 28082
Telephone: 704-932-3157
Facsimile: 704-932-9597

Concord, North Carolina Office: 71 McCachern Boulevard, S.E., P.O. Box 368, 28025. Telephone: 704-786-5161. Facsimile: 704-788-8058.

General Civil and Criminal Practice in all Courts. Workers Compensation, Corporation, Insurance, Real Estate, Taxation, Probate Law, Estate Planning, Family Law and Motor Sports (Racing).

FIRM PROFILE: Established in 1896, Hartsell & Williams, P.A. is a regional firm with a small-town personality, providing excellence in legal services to individuals and businesses. The firm has achieved and maintained Martindale-Hubbell's highest rating for legal ability and ethical conduct and is committed to providing quality, cost-effective representation, reflecting the highest diligence and integrity. The attorneys of Hartsell & Williams, P.A. focus on civil and criminal litigation, estate planning, probate, administrative, government, banking, motor sports (racing), corporate law and real estate transactions of all types.

LUTHER T. HARTSELL (1870-1961)

LUTHER T. HARTSELL, JR. (1902-1961)

JOHN HUGH WILLIAMS (1913-1995)

THOMAS MYERS GRADY, born Concord, North Carolina, July 25, 1941; admitted to bar, 1966, North Carolina. *Education:* Pfeiffer College (B.S., 1963); Wake Forest College (J.D., 1966). Phi Delta Phi. *Member:* Cabarrus County (President, 1981-1982), North Carolina and American Bar Associations; 19-A Judicial District (President, 1981-1982) and North Carolina State Bars. ***PRACTICE AREAS:*** Motor Sports Law (Racing); Personal Injury; Traffic Violations; Criminal. ***Email:*** tgrady@hwplaw.com

(This Listing Continued)

J. MERRITT WHITE, III, born Savannah, Georgia, October 6, 1959; admitted to bar, 1987, North Carolina and U.S. District Court, Western District of North Carolina. *Education:* Campbell University (B.B.A., 1982; J.D., 1987); University of North Florida (M.B.A., 1984). Omicron Delta Kappa. Member: The Order of the Barristers; National Trial Team; National Moot Court Team; International Moot Court Team; Campbell University Law Review, 1986-1987. *Member:* North Carolina State Bar; American Bar Association. ***PRACTICE AREAS:*** Insurance Litigation; Civil Litigation; Domestic Law; Criminal Law. ***Email:*** mwhite@hwpalaw.com

MICHAEL R. BURGNER, born Boulder, Colorado, September 15, 1972; admitted to bar, 1999, North Carolina. *Education:* Duke University (A.B., 1995); Georgetown University (J.D., 1998). Member: Georgetown University Student Intellectual Property Law Association, 1995-1998; Health Care and Biotechnology Law Association, 1995-1998. *Member:* North Carolina State Bar. ***PRACTICE AREAS:*** Probate; Estate Planning; Corporate Law; Intellectual Property. ***Email:*** mburgner@hwpalaw.com

ASSOCIATE

CHRISTY E. WILHELM, born Salisbury, North Carolina; admitted to bar, 2002, North Carolina. *Education:* Duke University (B.A., 1995); Campbell University (J.D., 2002). ***PRACTICE AREAS:*** Criminal Law; Personal Injury; Appellate Practice. ***Email:*** cwilhelm@hwpalaw.com

GENERAL COUNSEL: Board of County Commissioners, Cabarrus County; Cabarrus Regional Chamber of Commerce; NorthEast Medical Center; Cabarrus Health Alliance (Public Health Authority of Cabarrus County); Water and Sewer Authority of Cabarrus County, North Carolina.

REPRESENTATIVE CLIENTS: South Trust Bank; First Charter National Bank; Central Carolina Bank; CTC Communications; Duke Energy Co.; Cabarrus County Board of Education; The Mills Corporation (Concord Mills Mall); The Shoe Show, Inc.; Schrader Racing, Inc.; Wallace Racing, Inc.; Camp & Associates, Inc.; Rickey Craven Racing, Inc.; Bodine Racing, Inc.; Fitz-Bradshaw Racing, Inc.; Habitat for Humanity Cabarrus County, Inc.; Sparks Chrysler-Plymouth-Jeep, Inc.; Hilbish (Ford) Motor Co.; Ben Mynatt Chevrolet-Cadillac-GMC, Inc.; Beasley-Cross Chevrolet; E.L. Morrison Lumber Co., Inc.; R.S. Braswell Co.; Probst Construction Co.; Public Service Company of North Carolina; Norfolk & Southern Railway; Lawyers Mutual Liability Company of North Carolina; Allstate Insurance Co.; Nationwide Insurance Co.; Integon Insurance Co.; South Carolina Insurance Companies; Moss & Moore, Inc.; Gullege Building Supply; Sundrop Bottling Co. of Concord.

APPROVED ATTORNEYS FOR: AMI Title Insurance Co.; Pioneer Title Insurance Co.; First Title Insurance Co.; St. Paul Title Insurance Co.; Chicago Title Insurance Co.; Lawyers Title Insurance Corp.; Investors Title Insurance Co.; First American Title Co.; State Land Title Co.; The Title Company of North Carolina; Statewide Title Insurance Co.

(For complete biographical data on all other personnel, see Professional Biographies at Concord, North Carolina)

THE LAW OFFICE OF RANDELL F. HASTINGS

KANNAPOLIS, NORTH CAROLINA

(See Concord)

Family Law, Divorce, Child Custody, Child Support, Visitation Rights, Domestic Violence, Personal injury, Automobile Accidents, Wrongful Death, Civil Litigation.

KOONTZ, HAWKINS, NIXON & MILLER

KANNAPOLIS, NORTH CAROLINA

(See Concord)

Civil Trial Practice, Criminal Trial Practice, Driving While Intoxicated, Drug Crimes, Juvenile Crimes, Parole and Probation, Traffic Violations, White Collar Crimes, Personal Injury, Automobile Accidents, Wrongful Death, Social Security Disability, Workers Compensation, Family Law, Divorce, Domestic Violence, Child Support, Child Custody.

MILLS LAW, P.A.

KANNAPOLIS, NORTH CAROLINA

(See Concord)

Trusts and Estates, Asset Protection, Estate Planning, Probate, Taxation, Corporate Law, Real Estate.

MARK E. SHELLEY

KANNAPOLIS, NORTH CAROLINA

(See Concord)

Tax, IRS Audits, Property Tax, Tax Planning, Trust and Estates, Asset Protection, Estate Planning, Wills and Probate.

HALE & HARRELL

KENANSVILLE, NORTH CAROLINA

(See Burgaw)

Family Law, Criminal Law, Civil Litigation, Driving While Intoxicated, Traffic Offenses.

LUDLUM LAW FIRM

KENANSVILLE, NORTH CAROLINA

(See Warsaw)

Driving While Intoxicated and Traffic Violations. Criminal Defense, Real Estate, Divorce and Family Law, Accidents and Personal Injury, Litigation, Wills, Commercial Transactions.

PHILLIPS & PHILLIPS

112 FRONT STREET
P.O. BOX 720
KENANSVILLE, NORTH CAROLINA 28349
Telephone: 910-296-0215
Fax: 910-296-0923
Email: phillipsattn@earthlink.net

Traffic Violations, Driving While Intoxicated, Personal Injury, Probate, Estate Planning, Real Estate, General Practice.

MEMBER OF FIRM

DAVID T. PHILLIPS, born Goldsboro, North Carolina, August 20, 1952; admitted to bar, 1981, North Carolina. *Education:* Campbell University (B.S., 1974); Wake Forest University (J.D., 1978). Counsel, Duplin County Board of Education. *Member:* North Carolina State Bar (Counselor, Division 1); North Carolina Academy of Trial Lawyers. ***PRACTICE AREAS:*** Traffic Violations; Driving While Intoxicated; Personal Injury; Probate; Estate Planning; Real Estate; General Practice. ***Email:*** phillipsattn@earthlink.net

ATTORNEY FOR: Duplin County Board of Education; State Bar Councilor for the 4th Judicial District.
APPROVED TITLE ATTORNEY FOR: Farm Credit Bank; FHA.

ROBIN NEIL RHODES PLLC

310 N. MAIN STREET
P.O. BOX 717
KENANSVILLE, NORTH CAROLINA 28349
Telephone: 910-296-6090
Fax: 910-296-6091
Email: rhodeslawfirm@earthlink.net

Criminal Law, Traffic Violations, Driving While Intoxicated, Felonies, Misdemeanors. Real Estate, Personal Injury, Divorce.

MEMBER OF FIRM

ROBIN NEIL RHODES, born Charlotte, North Carolina, April 10, 1963; admitted to bar, 1998, North Carolina. *Education:* University of North Carolina at Chapel Hill (B.A., 1985); University of Arkansas at Little Rock (J.D., 1998). *Member:* Duplin County, Fourth Judicial District and North Carolina Bar Associations; North Carolina Academy of Trial Lawyers. ***PRACTICE AREAS:*** Criminal Law; Traffic Violations; Driving While Intoxicated; Felonies; Misdemeanors; Real Estate; Personal Injury; Divorce.

THOMPSON & THOMPSON, P.C.

KENANSVILLE, NORTH CAROLINA

(See Warsaw)

Criminal Law, Driving While Intoxicated, Traffic Violations, Civil Litigation, Medical Malpractice, Real Estate.

WALLACE, MORRIS, BARWICK, LANDIS & STROUD, P.A.

KENANSVILLE, NORTH CAROLINA

(See Kinston)

General Civil and Trial Practice in all State and Federal Courts. Aviation, Banking, Corporate Law, Insurance, Personal Injury, Probate, Product Liability, Real Estate and Taxation.

THE WELCH LAW FIRM, P.C.

KENANSVILLE, NORTH CAROLINA

(See Jacksonville)

Criminal Law, General Practice.

ANDERSON KORZEN & ASSOCIATES, P.C.

Established in 1997

233 WEST MOUNTAIN STREET
KERNERSVILLE, NORTH CAROLINA 27284
Telephone: 336-993-7958
Fax: 336-993-7964
URL: http://www.lawyers.com/anderson
Email: janderson@andersonkorzen.com
URL: http://www.andersonkorzen.com

Complex Litigation and Trials, Long Term Care and Nursing Home Abuse and Neglect, Serious Personal Injuries, Wrongful Death, Medical Malpractice, Aviation Torts and Air Crash Disasters, Serious Professional Negligence, Tractor Trailer Collisions, Product Liability.

JOSEPH L. ANDERSON, born San Luis Obispo, California, September 30, 1962; admitted to bar, 1989, California; U.S District Court, Northern, Eastern, Central and Southern Districts of California; 1993, North Carolina; U.S. District Court, Eastern, Western and Middle Districts of North Carolina; U.S. Court of Appeals, Fourth and Ninth Circuits; 2001, Kentucky, District of Columbia and West Virginia. *Education:* University of California at Berkeley (B.A., summa cum laude, 1986); Harvard Law School (J.D., cum laude, 1989). Judicial Clerk for Chief Justice Jay A. Rabinowitz, Supreme Court of Alaska, 1989-1990. Licensed pilot, North Carolina, 2001. Trial Specialist, National Board of Trial Advocacy.

(This Listing Continued)

Member: Forsyth County, North Carolina, Kentucky and West Virginia Bar Associations; State Bar of California; District of Columbia Bar; Lawyer - Pilots Bar Association; North Carolina Academy of Trial Lawyers; Association of Trial Lawyers of America. ***PRACTICE AREAS:*** Complex Litigation; Catastrophic Injury; Wrongful Death; Long Term Care; Nursing Home Abuse and Neglect; Medical Malpractice; Aviation Torts; Professional Negligence. ***Email:*** janderson@andersonkorzen.com

---

JEFFREY G. WEBER, born Detroit, Michigan, January 27, 1958; admitted to bar, 1991, North Carolina. *Education:* Columbia International University (B.A., 1986); University of South Carolina (J.D., 1990); Reformed Theological Seminary (M.Div., 2004). Managing Editor, Journal of Law & Education, 1988-1990. Certified Diver, 2000. Certified Arbitrator. *Member:* Greensboro and North Carolina (Member, Elder Law Division) Bar Associations; Lawyers-Pilot Bar Association; North Carolina Academy of Trial Lawyers (Member, Sections on: Professional Negligence; Nursing Home Abuse); The Association of Trial Lawyers of America; Christian Legal Society; Aircraft Owners and Pilots Association. ***PRACTICE AREAS:*** Nursing Home Abuse and Neglect (20%); Medical Malpractice (20%); Wrongful Death (20%); Aviation Accidents (20%); Catastrophic Injury (20%). ***Email:*** jweber@andersonkorzen.com

KATHERINE FLYNN HENRY, born Wadsworth, Ohio, January 16, 1973; admitted to bar, 1998, North Carolina and U.S. District Court, Middle District of North Carolina; 2004, Ohio; U.S. Court of Appeals, Fourth Circuit. *Education:* Miami University (B.A., 1995); Wake Forest University (J.D., 1998). Member, Moot Court Board, 1997-1998. Judicial Intern, Butler County Court of Common Pleas, Honorable Michael J. Sage, 1994. *Member:* North Carolina and Ohio State Bar Associations; Association of Trial Lawyers of America; North Carolina Academy of Trial Lawyers; Ohio Academy of Trial Lawyers. ***PRACTICE AREAS:*** Complex Litigation; Nursing Home Abuse and Neglect; Aviation Torts; Medical Malpractice; Wrongful Death; Catastrophic Injury; Professional Negligence. ***Email:*** khenry@andersonkorzen.com

OF COUNSEL

JOHN J. KORZEN, born East Orange, New Jersey, April 24, 1960; admitted to bar, 1991, North Carolina; U.S. District Court, Middle District of North Carolina and U.S. Court of Appeals, Fourth Circuit. *Education:* Wake Forest University (B.A., cum laude, 1981; J.D., cum laude, 1991). Executive Editor, Wake Forest Law Review, 1990-1991. Member, Jessup International Moot Court Team. Clerk, Honorable Sam J. Ervin, III, U.S. Court of Appeals, Fourth Circuit, 1991-1992, Summer Clerk, Honorable James B. McMillan, U. S. District Court, Western District of North Carolina, 1989. *Member:* North Carolina and American (Member: Litigation Section, Appellate Practice Committee; Tort and Insurance Practice Section, Appellate Advocacy Committee) Bar Associations; North Carolina Academy of Trial Lawyers; Guilford Inn of Court. ***PRACTICE AREAS:*** Appellate Practice; Civil Litigation; Workers Compensation; Federal Criminal Defense; Sports Agency Law.

LAW OFFICES OF MICHAEL J. PANGIA, born Brooklyn, New York, January 5, 1942; admitted to bar, 1967, New York; 1977, District of Columbia, U.S. Supreme Court and U.S. Claims Court (Not admitted in North Carolina). *Education:* United States Merchant Marine Academy (B.S. in Engineering, 1963); St. John's University (J.D., 1967). Recipient: The John Marshall Award by U.S. Attorney General for Outstanding Achievement in the Development of Aviation Law; Meritorious Award from FAA for Chicago DC-10 Hearings; Highest Professional Achievement Award for USMMA Class '63. Author: "Post-traumatic Stress Disorder, Litigation Strategies," Journal of Air Law & Commerce, 1999; "Litigating Air Crash Cased, "The Digest, Syracuse University School of Law, 1999; "Pilot Judgement: Training, Current Development and Future Issues in Aviation Cases," Journal of Air Law and Commerce, Spring 1983; "A Clear Approach to Aviation Cases," Trial Magazine, Vol. 17, No. 2, 1981; "Handling FAA Enforcement Proceedings, A View From the Inside," Journal of Air Law and Commerce, Spring 1981; "Aviation Accident Investigation in a Litigation Environmental." Adjunct Professor, Business Law, Long Island University, 1969-1971. Airline Transport Pilot Certificate, Single, Multiengine, Instrument Rated, Flight and Ground School Instructor, FAA Certificated Aircraft and Powerplant Mechanic. Trial Attorney, Admiralty, Senior Trial Attorney, Aviation and Chief of Aviation Unit, U.S. Department of Justice, 1970-1979. Chief of Litigation Counsel and Accident Investigation Spokesman of Federal Aviation Administration, 1979-1982. FAA Designated Accident Prevention Counselor, 1982—. Director of Air Safety of Congressional Squadron of Civil Air Patrol, 1983. General Counsel and Member of the Board of National Aviation Club, 1984—. Member, Experimental Aircraft Association Advisory Council, 1989-1992. Advisor to Airline Passenger Association, 1989-1990. Member and Counsel, International Society of Air Safety Investigators. *Member:* District of Columbia Bar; Bar Association of the District of Columbia Bar; Association of the Bar of the City of New York; Federal (Chairman, Aviation Committee, 1986—) and American Bar Associations; The Association of Trial Lawyers of America; National Head Injury Foundation; Lawyer-Pilots Bar Association; National Transportation Safety Board Bar Association (Founding Member; President, 1988-1990). Certified as a Civil Trial Advocate by the National Board of Trial Advocacy. ***PRACTICE AREAS:*** Aviation Accidents; Aviation Injuries; Aviation Torts; Helicopter Litigation; Marine Law; Products Liability; Medical Malpractice and Administrative Proceedings.

JERRY D. JORDAN

KERNERSVILLE, NORTH CAROLINA

(See Winston-Salem)

Criminal, Drug Crimes, DWI, Traffic Violations, Family Law, Child Custody, Child Support.

DEAN B. RUTLEDGE

KERNERSVILLE, NORTH CAROLINA

(See Winston-Salem)

Family Law, Adoptions, Child Custody, Child Support, Divorce, Equitable Distribution, Premarital Agreements, Spousal Support, Mediation, Felonies, Misdemeanors, Drug Crimes, Traffic Violations.

SURRATT & THOMPSON, PLLC

KERNERSVILLE, NORTH CAROLINA

(See Winston-Salem)

General Civil Practice in all State and Federal Courts. Corporate Law, Business Law, Collections, Wills, Probate, Trusts and Estates, Taxation, Real Estate, Commercial Law, Bankruptcy, Family Law and Litigation.

WINFREE & WINFREE

KERNERSVILLE, NORTH CAROLINA

(See Greensboro)

Consumer Law, Lemon Law, Consumer Rights, Collections, Family Law, Divorce, Alimony, Civil Litigation, Business Litigation, Business Property, Traffic Violations.

ROY A. ARCHBELL, JR.

KILL DEVIL HILLS, NORTH CAROLINA

(See Kitty Hawk)

General Civil Trial Practice in State and Federal Courts. Family, Personal Injury, Collection, Corporate, Construction, Insurance, Real Estate, Domestic Relations, Divorce.

RONALD E. DEVEAU, P.C.

KILL DEVIL HILLS, NORTH CAROLINA

(See Nags Head)

General Civil and Trial Practice in State and Federal Courts, Personal Injury and Negligence, Workers Compensation, Family Law, Business Torts, Estates.

HORNTHAL, RILEY, ELLIS & MALAND, L.L.P.

KILL DEVIL HILLS, NORTH CAROLINA

(See Elizabeth City)

General Trial and Appellate Practice in all Courts. Personal Injury, Products Liability, Professional Malpractice, Corporate, Tax, Bankruptcy, Employment, Education, Criminal, Insurance, Construction, Real Estate, Environmental, Elder, Local Government, Wills and Trusts, Probate and Admiralty Law.

KELLOGG AND EVANS, P.A.

KILL DEVIL HILLS, NORTH CAROLINA

(See Manteo)

General Civil Practice in State Courts, Family Law, Probate, Real Estate, Business Law, Vessel Documentation and Financing, and Estate Planning and Administration.

THE VINCENT LAW FIRM, PC

KILL DEVIL HILLS, NORTH CAROLINA

(See Southern Shores)

Workers Compensation, Personal Injury, Auto Accidents, Social Security Disability, Wrongful Death and Admiralty Longshores.

DAVID MARK HULLENDER

Established in 2001

235 S. BATTLEGROUND AVENUE
KINGS MOUNTAIN, NORTH CAROLINA 28086
Telephone: 704-739-2965
Fax: 704-739-2966
Email: Hullylaw@bellsouth.net
URL: http://www.hullenderlaw.com

General Practice, Traffic Violations, Driving While Intoxicated, Real Estate, Family Law, Divorce, Wills, Probate.

DAVID MARK HULLENDER, born March 27, 1962; admitted to bar, 1989, North Carolina; U.S. District Court, Western District of North Carolina. *Education:* University of North Carolina at Chapel Hill (B.A., 1984); North Carolina Central University Law School (J.D., 1989); University of Florida (LL.M., 1990). Phi Delta Phi. Member, Moot Court Board. Member, Law Journal of North Carolina Central Law School. *Member:* North Carolina State Bar; North Carolina and American Bar Associations. ***PRACTICE AREAS:*** General Practice; Traffic Violations; Driving While Intoxicated; Real Estate; Family Law; Divorce; Wills; Probate.

BRANTLEY, JENKINS, RIDDLE, HARDEE & HARDEE

2506 HERRITAGE STREET, SUITE A
KINSTON, NORTH CAROLINA 28501
Telephone: 252-522-1500
Fax: 252-522-0556
URL: http://www.bjrhhlawyers.com
URL: http://www.bjrhhatty.com

Goldsboro, North Carolina Office: 601 North Spence Avenue, 27534. Telephone: 919-778-9700. Fax: 919-778-1938.

(This Listing Continued)

Greenville, North Carolina Office: 202 East Arlington Boulevard, P.O. Box 924, 27858. Telephone: 252-355-1998. Fax: 252-321-2948.

Jacksonville, North Carolina Office: 901 Hargett Street, P.O. Box 7070, 28540. Telephone: 910-455-5599. Fax: 910-455-7191.

Personal Injury, Wrongful Death, Automobile Accidents, Head and Spinal Injury, Nursing Home Abuse and Neglect, Workers Compensation, Insurance, Products Liability, Social Security Disability, Medical Malpractice.

(For complete biographical data on all personnel, see Professional Biographies at Goldsboro, North Carolina)

BRUMBAUGH, MU & KING, P.A.

Established in 1978

414 SOUTH QUEEN STREET
KINSTON, NORTH CAROLINA 28501
Telephone: 252-939-1800
URL: http://www.bmklaw.net

Practice Limited to Injury Cases. Automobile, Wrongful Death, Medical Malpractice, Workers' Compensation, Products Liability and Social Security Claims.

(For complete biographical data on all personnel, see professional biographies, Jacksonville, North Carolina)

BURCH LAW OFFICE

KINSTON, NORTH CAROLINA

(See Greenville)

Personal Injury, Automobile Accidents, Wrongful Death, Medical Malpractice, Criminal Law, Driving While Intoxicated, Drug Crimes, Traffic Violations, White Collar Crime, Worker Compensation, Adoptions, Child Custody, Child Support, Divorce, Visitation Rights, Wills and Probate, Trust and Estates, Estate Planning, Social Security Disability, Eminent Domain, Zoning and Planning, Traumatic Brain Injury, Corporate-Business Formation.

GEORGE L. JENKINS, JR.

Established in 1982

111 EAST GORDON STREET
P.O. BOX 303
KINSTON, NORTH CAROLINA 28502-0303
Telephone: 252-523-4000
Fax: 252-523-0980
Email: kinstonlawyer@mac.com
URL: http://www.lawyers.com/georgejenkins

Real Estate, Traffic Tickets, Divorce, Adoption, Real Estate Acquisition and Real Estate Foreclosure.

GEORGE L. JENKINS, JR., born Kinston, North Carolina, February 22, 1952; admitted to bar, 1982, North Carolina. *Education:* University of North Carolina (B.A., 1974); North Carolina State University; Campbell University (J.D., 1981). Town Attorney: Town of LaGrange; Town of Pink Hill. *Member:* Lenoir County, North Carolina and American Bar Associations; North Carolina State Bar;. ***PRACTICE AREAS:*** Real Estate; Traffic Violations; Divorce; Adoption Law; Real Estate Acquisitions; Real Estate Foreclosure.

REPRESENTATIVE CLIENTS: City of Kinston Tax Collector; Lenoir County Tax Office; Town of Pink Hill; Town of La Grange; State Employees' Credit Union; Wachovia Bank & Trust Co.; Wachovia Mortgage Co.; N.C. Administrative Office of the Courts-GAL Services; Branch Banking & Trust Co.
REFERENCES: Wachovia Bank of North Carolina, N.A.; Branch Banking & Trust Co.

ROSE RAND ATTORNEYS, P.A.

KINSTON, NORTH CAROLINA

(See Wilson)

General Practice, all Courts. Corporation, Labor and Insurance Law. Trials, including Personal Injury, Wrongful Death and Workers Compensation, Eminent Domain, Tax, Estate Planning and Administration, Municipal, Environmental, Real Estate, Bankruptcy.

SMITH AND STRICKLAND, PLLC

KINSTON, NORTH CAROLINA

(See Goldsboro)

Criminal Defense, Driving While Impaired, DUI, DWI, Traffic Violations, Parole and Probation, Drug Crimes, White Collar Crimes, Juvenile Crimes, Personal Injury, Military Law.

SUMRELL, SUGG, CARMICHAEL, HICKS & HART, P.A.

KINSTON, NORTH CAROLINA

(See New Bern)

General Civil. Trials and Appeals in all Civil Courts. Wills and Estates, Real Estate, Corporate Law, Financial Transactions, Insurance and Negligence, Employment Law, Municipal Law, Law Enforcement Liability Defense, Health Care Law and Intellectual Property.

WALLACE, MORRIS, BARWICK, LANDIS & STROUD, P.A.

131 SOUTH QUEEN STREET
P.O. BOX 3557
KINSTON, NORTH CAROLINA 28502-3557
Telephone: 252-523-2000
Fax: 252-523-0408
URL: http://www.wmbattorneys.com

General Civil and Trial Practice in all State and Federal Courts. Aviation, Banking, Corporate Law, Insurance, Personal Injury, Probate, Product Liability, Real Estate and Taxation.

FITZHUGH E. WALLACE, JR. (Retired)

THOMAS H. MORRIS, born Halifax, North Carolina, April 25, 1936; admitted to bar, 1963, North Carolina. *Education:* Wake Forest University (B.A., 1958; J.D., 1963). Phi Delta Phi. *Member:* Lenoir County, North Carolina (Member, Board of Governors, 1980-1981) and American Bar Associations; North Carolina State Bar; North Carolina Association of Defense Attorneys; American Board of Trial Advocates. ***PRACTICE AREAS:*** Products Liability Law; Corporate Law; Insurance Defense Law. ***Email:*** thm@wmbattorneys.com

P. C. BARWICK, JR., born Kinston, North Carolina, June 28, 1937; admitted to bar, 1961, North Carolina. *Education:* Wake Forest University (B.A., 1959; LL.B., 1960). Phi Delta Phi. *Member:* Lenoir County, North Carolina and American Bar Associations; North Carolina State Bar (Councillor, 1989-1994); North Carolina Association of Defense Attorneys. ***PRACTICE AREAS:*** Insurance Law; Commercial Law; Real Estate Law; Civil Litigation. ***Email:*** pcb@wmbattorneys.com

RICHARD F. LANDIS, II, born York, Pennsylvania, April 27, 1948; admitted to bar, 1973, North Carolina. *Education:* Catawba College (A.B., 1970); Wake Forest University (J.D., 1973). Phi Delta Phi. Certified Public Accountant, North Carolina, 1982. *Member:* Lenoir County, North Carolina and American Bar Associations; North Carolina State Bar; North Carolina Association of Certified Public Accountants. ***PRACTICE AREAS:*** Probate Law; Corporate Law; Tax Planning Law; Real Estate. ***Email:*** rfl@wmbattorneys.com

STUART L. STROUD, born Kinston, North Carolina, July 18, 1967; admitted to bar, 1992, North Carolina. *Education:* University of North Carolina at Chapel Hill (B.A., 1989); Campbell University (J.D., 1992). Delta Theta Phi. Certified Superior Court Mediator. *Member:* Lenoir County and North Carolina Bar Associations; North Carolina Association of Defense Attorneys. ***PRACTICE AREAS:*** Civil Litigation; Insurance Defense Law; Criminal Law; Real Estate; Mediation. ***Email:*** sls@wmbattorneys.com

---

KIMBERLY A. CONNOR, born San Antonio, Texas, August 6, 1977; admitted to bar, 2002, North Carolina. *Education:* DePauw University (B.A., cum laude, 1999); Valparaiso University School of Law (J.D., magna cum laude, 2002). Phi Delta Phi. Member, Valparaiso Law Review. Author: Note, "A Critique of the Marital Privileges. An Explanation of the Marital Privileges in the United States Military Through the State and Federal Approaches to the Marital Privileges," 36 Valparaiso University Law Review 119. *Member:* Lenoir County and North Carolina Bar Association; North Carolina State Bar. ***PRACTICE AREAS:*** Family Law; Appellate Practice; Civil Litigation; Criminal Law; Collections. ***Email:*** kac@wmbattorneys.com

PAYTON D. HOOVER, born Charlotte, North Carolina, October 1, 1971; admitted to bar, 2003, North Carolina. *Education:* University of North Carolina at Chapel Hill (B.A., 1994); Campbell University (J.D., 2003). *Member:* North Carolina Bar Association. ***PRACTICE AREAS:*** Civil Litigation; Criminal Defense. ***Email:*** paytonhl@yahoo.com

REPRESENTATIVE CLIENTS: Bank of America; Branch Banking & Trust Co.; City of Kinston; E.I. DuPont de Nemours & Co., Inc.; First Citizens Bank & Trust Co.; General Motors Corp; Kmart Corporation; Kinston Daily Free Press Co.; Progress Energy; Town of Dover.
INSURANCE CLIENTS: Allstate Insurance Co.; American Modern Home Insurance Co.; Berkeley Insurance; Cambridge Integrated Services Group, Inc.; Carolina Casualty Co.; CGU Insurance Co.; Continental Insurance Group; Discover RE; Empire Fire & Marine Insurance Co.; Farmland Insurance; GMAC Insurance; Great American Insurance Cos.; Horace Mann Insurance Co.; Lawyers Mutual of N.C.; Liberty Mutual Insurance Co.; MetLife Property & Casualty Insurance Co.; Nationwide Mutual Insurance Co.; North Carolina Farm Bureau Insurance Co.; Ohio Casualty Insurance Co.; Orion Auto; Pennsylvania National Mutual Casualty Insurance Co.; Progressive Insurance Co.; Rockingham Casualty Co.; Safeco Insurance Co.; Scottsdale Insurance Co.; Seibels Bruce Group, Inc.; Southern Guaranty Insurance Co.; State Farm Insurance Cos.; Transport Insurance Co.; USAA Insurance Co.; Universal Underwriters; Utica Mutual Insurance Co.
APPROVED ATTORNEYS FOR: ATI Title Company; Chicago Title Insurance Co.; Commonwealth Land Title Insurance Company; Consumers Title Company; First American Title Company; Investors Title Insurance Co.; Lawyers Title Insurance Corp.; Statewide Title, Inc.; Stewart Title Insurance Co.; The Title Company of North Carolina; United Title Insurance Company.

WARD AND SMITH, P.A.

KINSTON, NORTH CAROLINA

(See New Bern)

General and Trial Practice. Admiralty Law; Bankruptcy; Banks and Banking; Business Law; Civil Rights; Commercial Law; Construction Law; Contracts; Copyrights; Corporate Law; Debtor and Creditor; Elder Law; Eminent Domain; Employee Benefits; Environmental Law; Family Law including Divorce; Finance; Franchise Law; Government; Government Contracts; Health Care Law; Immigration and Naturalization; Insurance; International Law; International Trade; Investments; Labor and Employment including Discrimination, Sexual Harassment, and Workers' Compensation; Landlord and Tenant; Litigation; Personal Injury including Automobile Accidents, Legal Malpractice and Medical Malpractice; Products Liability; Real Estate; Securities; Taxation; Technology and Science including Internet Law, Trademarks, and Patents; Trusts and Estates including Estate Planning and Wills and Probate; Zoning and Land Use.

WHITE & ALLEN, P.A.

Established in 1927
106 SOUTH MCLEWEAN STREET
P.O. BOX 3169
KINSTON, NORTH CAROLINA 28501
Telephone: 252-527-8000
Telecopier: 252-527-8128
Email: law@whiteandallen.com
URL: http://www.whiteandallen.com

Snow Hill, North Carolina Office: 109 S.E. Second Street. 28580. Telephone: 252-747-5152. Telecopier: 252-747-4657. Email: law@whiteandallen.com.

General Civil Practice in all State and Federal Courts. Personal Injury, Automobile Accidents, Wrongful Death, Insurance, Real Estate, Corporation, Taxation, Commercial, Trusts and Estates, Wills and Probate.

FIRM PROFILE: Established in 1927, the law firm of White & Allen, P.A. has been serving the people of eastern North Carolina for over 70 years. The firm is committed to providing the highest quality legal services.

THOMAS J. WHITE (1903-1991)

WILLIAM A. ALLEN, JR. (1920-2001)

JOHN R. HOOTEN, born June 10, 1935; admitted to bar, 1963, North Carolina; U.S. District Court, Eastern, Middle and Western Districts of North Carolina and U.S. Court of Appeals, Fourth Circuit; U.S. Supreme Court. *Education:* University of North Carolina (B.S., 1957); Wake Forest University of School of Law (J.D., 1963). Law Clerk to Hon. John D. Larkins, Jr., U.S. District Judge, 1963. Assistant U.S. Attorney, Eastern District of North Carolina. North Carolina Dispute Resolution Committee Certified Superior Court and Family Financial Mediator. *Member:* Lenoir County, Eighth Judicial District, North Carolina and American Bar Associations; North Carolina State Bar; North Carolina Academy of Trial Lawyers. ***PRACTICE AREAS:*** Personal Injury Litigation; Wrongful Death; Health Law. ***Email:*** hooten@whiteandallen.com

JOHN C. ARCHIE, born December 9, 1951; admitted to bar, 1978, North Carolina. *Education:* University of North Carolina (B.A., 1973); Cumberland School of Law of Samford University (J.D., 1978). *Member:* North Carolina State Bar; North Carolina (Member, Health Section) and American (Member, Sections on: Business Law; Health Law) Bar Associations. ***PRACTICE AREAS:*** Employment Law; Health Law; Business Transactions. ***Email:*** jarchie@whiteandallen.com

C. GRAY JOHNSEY, born March 1, 1949; admitted to bar, 1978, North Carolina. *Education:* University of North Carolina (B.A., 1971); East Carolina University (M.B.A., 1975); Cumberland School of Law of Samford University (J.D., cum laude, curia honoris, 1978); University of Florida (LL.M. in Taxation, 1979). Instructor, Southeastern Trust School. *Member:* North Carolina and American Bar Associations; North Carolina State Bar. Fellow, American College of Trust and Estate Counsel. (Board Certified Specialist in Estate Planning and Probate Law, North Carolina State Board of Legal Specialization). ***PRACTICE AREAS:*** Tax Law; Estate Planning; Business Planning; Administration of Estates; Corporations. ***Email:*** gjohnsey@whiteandallen.com

JOSEPH SIDNEY BOWER, born January 1, 1951; admitted to bar, 1979, North Carolina. *Education:* University of North Carolina (B.A., 1973); East Carolina University (M.B.A., 1976); Cumberland School of Law of Samford University (J.D., cum laude, 1979). *Member:* Lenoir County (Chairman, Bar Candidate Committee, 1988-1996), North Carolina (Member, Sections on: Real Property; Bankruptcy) and American Bar Association; Eighth Judicial District Bar (President, 1987); North Carolina State Bar. ***PRACTICE AREAS:*** Commercial Real Estate; Residential Real Estate; Zoning Law; Corporate Law; Commercial Transactions; Collections; Creditors Rights in Bankruptcy; Foreclosures. ***Email:*** jsbower@whiteandallen.com

DAVID J. FILLIPPELI, JR., born August 15, 1960; admitted to bar, 1985, North Carolina; 1987, U.S. District Court, Eastern District of North Carolina; 1992, U.S. Court of Appeals, Fourth Circuit and U.S. Supreme Court. *Education:* North Carolina State University (B.A., magna cum laude, 1982); University of North Carolina (J.D., 1985). *Member:* Lenoir County (President, 1990), North Carolina and American Bar Associations; Eighth Judicial District Bar (President, 1993); North Carolina State Bar; North Carolina Academy of Trial Lawyers (Member, Sections on: Civil Litigation; Domestic Law; Criminal Law). ***PRACTICE AREAS:*** Domestic Litigation; Personal Injury Litigation; Criminal Litigation; Commercial Litigation; General Civil Litigation. ***Email:*** djf@whiteandallen.com

MATTHEW S. SULLIVAN, born January 1, 1968; admitted to bar, 1995, North Carolina. *Education:* Virginia Commonwealth University (B.S., magna cum laude, 1990); Campbell University (J.D., magna cum laude, 1995). Wiggins Scholar. Staff Member, 1993-1994, Editor-in-Chief, 1994-1995, Campbell Law Review. Author: Published Note, Campbell Law Review, 1993. Member, Order of Barristers. *Member:* Lenoir County (President, 1997-1998), North Carolina (Member, Business Law and Litigation Sections) and American Bar Associations; Eighth Judicial District Bar; North Carolina State Bar; North Carolina Academy of Trial Lawyers; Eastern North Carolina Inn of Court; International Trial Lawyers. ***PRACTICE AREAS:*** Catastrophic Injury; Industrial Accidents; Wrongful Death; Workers Compensation; Civil Litigation. ***Email:*** msullivan@whiteandallen.com

SHERWOOD C. HENDERSON, born September 15, 1970; admitted to bar, 1996, Georgia and North Carolina. *Education:* Davidson College (B.A., 1992); Campbell University (J.D, 1996); Villanova University (LL.M. in Taxation, 1997). *Member:* North Carolina and American Bar Associations; State Bar of North Carolina; State Bar of Georgia. ***LANGUAGES:*** Spanish. ***PRACTICE AREAS:*** Tax Law; Retirement Planning; Estate Planning; Administration; Business Planning; Corporations. ***Email:*** chenderson@whiteandallen.com

RICHARD J. ARCHIE, born January 12, 1967; admitted to bar, 1991, North Carolina; U.S. District Court, Eastern District of North Carolina. *Education:* University of North Carolina (B.A., 1988; J.D., 1991). Phi Delta Phi. *Member:* Lenoir County, Eighth Judicial

(This Listing Continued)

District and North Carolina Bar Associations. ***PRACTICE AREAS:*** Real Property Law; Corporate; Business Law; Commercial Transactions. ***Email:*** dickarchie@whiteandallen.com

WILLIAM E. MANNING, JR., born Morehead City, North Carolina, July 18, 1966; admitted to bar, 1991, North Carolina. *Education:* University of North Carolina (B.S.B.A., 1988; J.D., 1991). Phi Alpha Delta. *Member:* Lenoir County (President, 1995), Eighth Judicial District, North Carolina and American Bar Associations; North Carolina State Bar. (Board Certified Specialist in Real Property Law-Residential Transactions, North Carolina State Board of Legal Specialization). ***PRACTICE AREAS:*** Residential Real Estate; Commercial Real Estate; Business Law; Creditors Rights; Foreclosures; Construction Law. ***Email:*** wem@whiteandallen.com

DELAINA DAVIS BOYD, born August 29, 1974; admitted to bar, 1999, North Carolina; U.S. District Court, Eastern District of North Carolina. *Education:* North Carolina State University (B.S., cum laude, 1995); Campbell University (J.D., 1999). Phi Alpha Delta. *Member:* Lenoir County, Eighth Judicial District and North Carolina Bar Associations; North Carolina Academy of Trial Lawyers. ***PRACTICE AREAS:*** Domestic Litigation; Criminal Litigation; Juvenile Law; Social Security Disability; General Civil Litigation. ***Email:*** deedavis@whiteandallen.com

THOMAS J. WHITE, III, born Kinston, North Carolina, April 16, 1941; admitted to bar, 1966, North Carolina; 1978, Alabama. *Education:* Woodberry Forest School; University of North Carolina at Chapel Hill (B.A., 1963; LL.B., 1966). Morehead Scholar. Law Clerk to Hon. John D. Larkins, Jr., U.S. District Judge, Eastern District of North Carolina, 1966-1967. Permanent Member, Fourth Circuit Judicial Conference. DRC Certified Mediator. *Member:* North Carolina State Bar; Alabama State Bar; Lawyer-Pilots Bar Association; North Carolina Academy of Trial Lawyers; Eastern North Carolina Inn of Court. ***PRACTICE AREAS:*** Tort Liability; Aviation Litigation; Railroad Litigation; Complex Business Litigation; Mediation; Arbitration. ***Email:*** twhite@whiteandallen.com

J. MARK HERRING, born Clinton, North Carolina, August 27, 1974; admitted to bar, 2000, North Carolina; U.S. District Court, Eastern District of North Carolina, U.S. Court of Appeals, Fourth Circuit. *Education:* North Carolina State University (B.A., 1996); Cumberland School of Law of Samford University (J.D., 2000). Assistant District Attorney, Fourth Prosecutorial District of North Carolina, 2000-2002. *Member:* Lenoir County, Eighth Judicial District, North Carolina and American Bar Associations; The Association of Trial Lawyers of America; National Association of Criminal Defense Lawyers. ***PRACTICE AREAS:*** State and Federal Criminal Defense; White Collar Criminal Defense; Civil Litigation. ***Email:*** mherring@whiteandallen.com

E. WYLES JOHNSON, JR., born January 22, 1956; admitted to bar, 2002, North Carolina, U.S. District Court, Eastern District of North Carolina and U.S. Court of Appeals, Fourth Circuit. *Education:* Old Dominion University (B.S., cum laude, 1981; M.B.A., 1982); Campbell University (J.D., 2001). *Member:* North Carolina State Bar; Lenoir County, Eighth Judicial District, North Carolina and American Bar Associations; North Carolina Academy of Trial Lawyers; Association of Trial Lawyers of America. ***PRACTICE AREAS:*** Commercial Litigation; Civil Litigation; Elder Law; Construction Law; Employment Law; Workers Compensation. ***Email:*** wjohnson@whiteandallen.com

GREGORY E. FLOYD, born November 28, 1976; admitted to bar, 2002, North Carolina; U.S. District Court, Eastern District of North Carolina and U.S. Court of Appeals, Fourth Circuit. *Education:* Reed College (B.A., 1999); Campbell University (J.D., 2002). *Member:* North Carolina State Bar; Lenoir County, Eighth Judicial District, North Carolina and American Bar Associations; North Carolina Academy of Trial Lawyers; Association of Trial Lawyers of America. ***PRACTICE AREAS:*** Civil Litigation; Commercial Litigation; Employment Law; Workers Compensation; Personal Injury. ***Email:*** gfloyd@whiteandallen.com

REPRESENTATIVE CLIENTS: Kinston Medical Specialists, P.A.; Coastal Neurological Associates, P.A.; Carolina Power & Light Co.; Kinston Housing Authority; Tands, Inc.; Kinston Indians/Sluggers; First Citizens Bank & Trust Co.; Wachovia Bank & Trust Co. N.A.; NationsBank, N.A.; Kemper National Group; Hampton Industries, Inc.; Sale Chevrolet Buick-BMW, Inc.; Massey Motor Co.; Kinston Clinic Properties, Inc.; The Sherwin Williams Company; Associated Bank; Beneficial North Carolina; Branch Banking & Trust Co.; Harleysville Mutual Insurance Co.; Morehead Block & Tile Co., Inc.; North Lenior Water Corp.; Pennsylvania National Mutual Casualty Insurance Co.; USAA Property and Casualty Insurance; Avco Financial Services; Deep Run Water Corporation; Brambles Equipment Services, Inc.; Homebuilders Association of Kinston; Kinston Board of Realtors; Jones County Cotton Gin; Evans Ford, Inc.; Hillco Ltd.; Britthaven, Inc.
APPROVED ATTORNEYS FOR: Lawyers Title Insurance Corp.; First Title Insurance Co.; Jefferson-Pilot Title Insurance Co.; AMI Title Insurance Co.; American Title Insurance Co.; Commonwealth Land Title Insurance Co.; Title Co. of NC; Investors Title Insurance Co.; United Title Co.

WHITLEY, RODGMAN & WHITLEY

Established in 2003

2902-B NORTH HERRITAGE STREET
P.O. BOX 5309
KINSTON, NORTH CAROLINA 28503-5309
Telephone: 252-523-3000
Fax: 252-523-3433
URL: http://www.wrwlaw.com
Email: rew@wrwlaw.com
URL: http://www.whitleyrodgmanwhitley.com

New Bern, North Carolina Office: 701 McCarthy Boulevard, P.O. Box 12550. Telephone: 252-633-6601. Fax: 252-635-6621.

Raleigh, North Carolina Office: 3605 Glenwood Avenue, Suite 350. Telephone: 919-785-5000. Fax: 919-785-3729.

Jacksonville, North Carolina Office: 200 Valencia Drive, Suite 101. Telephone: 910-219-1000. Fax: 910-219-1111.

Greenville, North Carolina Office: 1702-A E. Arlington Boulevard, Suite 100. Telephone: 252-353-5500. Fax: 252-352-0405.

Personal Injury, Wrongful Death, Workers' Compensation, Social Security Disability, Nursing Home Negligence.

(This Listing Continued)

FIRM PROFILE: We've been providing information and protecting families in NC since 1974. Our lawyers will work hard for you, always telling you the truth and giving you the close, personal service you need.

PARTNERS

ROBERT E. WHITLEY, born Greenville, North Carolina, May 28, 1949; admitted to bar, 1974, North Carolina. *Education:* East Carolina University (B.S.B.A., 1972); Wake Forest University (J.D., 1974). Phi Sigma Pi. *Member:* North Carolina State Bar; North Carolina Bar Association; The Association of Trial Lawyers of America; North Carolina Academy of Trial Lawyers. ***LANGUAGES:*** English. ***PRACTICE AREAS:*** Plaintiffs Personal Injury; Wrongful Death; Workers Compensation; Nursing Home Negligence; Premises Liability; Medical Malpractice; Social Security Disability. ***Email:*** rew@wrwlaw.com

PAUL A. RODGMAN, born Toronto, Ontario, September 13, 1950; admitted to bar, 1976, North Carolina. *Education:* Duke University (B.A., 1972); University of North Carolina (J.D., 1976). Assistant District Attorney, 1977-1979. Certified Arbitrator. S*Member:* Lenoir County, North Carolina and American Bar Associations; North Carolina State Bar; North Carolina Academy of Trial Lawyers. ***LANGUAGES:*** English. ***PRACTICE AREAS:*** Personal Injury; Insurance Law; Workers Compensation. ***Email:*** par@wrwlaw.com

ROBERT E. WHITLEY, JR., born Kinston, North Carolina, March 29, 1969; admitted to bar, 1995, North Carolina. *Education:* Appalachian State University (B.A., 1991); Campbell University (J.D., 1995). *Member:* North Carolina State Bar; North Carolina Bar Association; North Carolina Academy of Trial Lawyers; North Carolina Brain Injury Association. (Also at New Bern Office). ***LANGUAGES:*** English. ***PRACTICE AREAS:*** Social Security Disability; Personal Injury; Workers Compensation. ***Email:*** whit@wrwlaw.com

---

BENJAMIN H. WHITLEY, born Kinston, North Carolina, September 13, 1977; admitted to bar, 2003, North Carolina. *Education:* University of North Carolina at Chapel Hill (B.A., 2000); Mississippi College School of Law (J.D., 2003). *Member:* North Carolina State Bar; North Carolina Academy of Trial Lawyers. (Resident, Raleigh Office). ***LANGUAGES:*** English. ***PRACTICE AREAS:*** Motor Vehicle Accidents and Injuries; Plaintiffs Personal Injury; Wrongful Death; Workers Compensation; Premises Liability; Social Security Disability; Civil Litigation. ***Email:*** bhw@wrwlaw.com

BRIAN E. CLEMMONS, born Wilmington, North Carolina, October 30, 1961; admitted to bar, 1987, North Carolina. *Education:* University of North Carolina (B.A., 1984; J.D., 1987). Member, North Carolina Law Review, 1986-1987. Law Clerk to Hon. James C. Fox, United States District Court, Eastern District of North Carolina, 1987-1989. *Member:* Wake County, North Carolina and American Bar Associations; North Carolina State Bar; North Carolina Academy of Trial Lawyers. (Resident, Raleigh Office). ***LANGUAGES:*** English. ***PRACTICE AREAS:*** Personal Injury; Automobile Accidents; Wrongful Death; Workers Compensation; Products Liability; Civil Litigation. ***Email:*** bec@wrwlaw.com

JUAN A. FLORES, born Chattanooga, Tennessee; admitted to bar, 1988, North Carolina. *Education:* University of Tennessee at Chattanooga (B.S., Psychology, 1976); University of North Carolina at Chapel Hill (J.D., 1987). (Resident, Raleigh Office). ***LANGUAGES:*** English. ***PRACTICE AREAS:*** Social Security Disability. ***Email:*** jaf@wrwlaw.com

ALEXY, FLETCHER, WILLS & WILLS, P.C.

KITTY HAWK, NORTH CAROLINA

(See Point Harbor)

ROY A. ARCHBELL, JR.

12 JUNIPER TRAIL CENTER
P.O. BOX 57
KITTY HAWK, NORTH CAROLINA 27949
Telephone: 252-261-7555
Fax: 252-261-6444
Email: archbell.roy@earthlink.net
URL: http://www.lawyers.com/archbell

General Civil Trial Practice in State and Federal Courts. Family, Personal Injury, Collection, Corporate, Construction, Insurance, Real Estate, Domestic Relations, Divorce.

FIRM PROFILE: Roy A. Archbell, Jr. has practiced law in northeastern North Carolina since 1974. The firm's practice is primarily focused on the handling of civil litigation matters including personal injury, wrongful death, malpractice, domestic relations, real property, contract, construction and insurance. The firm is dedicated to providing quality legal representation and rendering personalized attention.

ROY A. ARCHBELL, JR., born Aurora, North Carolina, July 14, 1949; admitted to bar, 1974, North Carolina; 1975, U.S. District Court, Eastern District of North Carolina; 1982, U.S. Court of Appeals, Fourth Circuit; 1985, U.S. Supreme Court. *Education:* Wake Forest University (B.A., 1971; J.D., 1974). Phi Delta Phi. Member, Wake Forest Law Review, 1972-1974. Author: "No Fault Divorce—Iowa's Elimination of Fault Concept in Alimony Awards," Volume 9 No. 1, Wake Forest Law Review, December 1972. *Member:* North Carolina and American Bar Associations; North Carolina Academy of Trial Lawyers. ***REPORTED CASES:*** (selected): Va. Electric and Power Co. v. Tillett, 316 N.C. 73, 340 S.E.2d 62 (1986) and 80 N.C. App. 383, S.E.2d 188 (1986); Nugent v. Beckham, 37 N.C. App. 557, 246 S.E.2d 541 (1978); Loy v. Lorm Corp., 52 N.C. App. 428, 278 S.E.2d 897 (1981); Garrett v. Garrett & Garrett Farms, 39 N.C. App. 210, 249 S.E.2d 808 (1978); Pan-

(This Listing Continued)

ROY A. ARCHBELL, JR., Kitty Hawk—Continued

nill Knitting Co. v. Golden Corral Corp., 89 N.C. App. 675 (1988) 366 S.E.2d 891; Sharp v. Sharp, 84 N.C. App. 128 (1987) 351 S.E.2d 799; Rawls v. Lampert, 58 N.C. App. 399 (1982) 293 S.E.2d 620.

REPRESENTATIVE CLIENTS: Lawyers Title Insurance Co.; Commonwealth Land Title Co.; Bear Drugs, Inc.; Freedom Insulation, Inc.; Colington Harbor Property Owners Association; Dare Building Supply Company; Stonehaven, Inc.; Coastal Engineering & Surveying, Inc.; R. O. Givens Signs, Inc.

RONALD E. DEVEAU, P.C.

KITTY HAWK, NORTH CAROLINA

(See Nags Head)

General Civil and Trial Practice in State and Federal Courts, Personal Injury and Negligence, Workers Compensation, Family Law, Business Torts, Estates.

HORNTHAL, RILEY, ELLIS & MALAND, L.L.P.

KITTY HAWK, NORTH CAROLINA

(See Elizabeth City)

General Trial and Appellate Practice in all Courts. Personal Injury, Products Liability, Professional Malpractice, Corporate, Tax, Bankruptcy, Employment, Education, Criminal, Insurance, Construction, Real Estate, Environmental, Elder, Local Government, Wills and Trusts, Probate and Admiralty Law.

THE MOORE LAW FIRM, P.C.

KITTY HAWK, NORTH CAROLINA

(See Manns Harbor)

Real Estate, Corporate Law.

SHARP, MICHAEL, OUTTEN AND GRAHAM

Established in 1985

4417 NORTH CROATAN HIGHWAY

P.O. DRAWER 1027

KITTY HAWK, NORTH CAROLINA 27949

Telephone: 252-261-2126

Fax: 252-261-1188

URL: http://www.lawyers.com/smo&glaw

General Civil and Criminal Practice, Commercial and Residential Real Estate, Municipal and Administrative, Family and Domestic Relations, Personal Injury, Probate, Banking, Corporations, Traffic, Driving While Intoxicated, Mediation, Arbitration, Ship Documentation, Estate Planning, Elder Law.

MEMBERS OF FIRM

STARKEY SHARP, born Fort Belvoir, Virginia, May 20, 1952; admitted to bar, 1977, North Carolina. *Education:* Southern Methodist University (B.B.A., 1974); Duke University (J.D., 1977). Certified Mediator, North Carolina Dispute Resolution Commission. Certified Arbitrator, Administrative Office of the Courts. *Member:* Dare County, North Carolina and American Bar Associations; First Judicial District and North Carolina State Bars. ***PRACTICE AREAS:*** Real Estate Law; Corporations; Commercial Law; Estates Law; Regulatory Law; Mediation; Arbitration; Ship Documentation. ***Email:*** starkey@smogobx.com

STEVEN D. MICHAEL, born Lexington, North Carolina, January 23, 1949; admitted to bar, 1975, North Carolina and U.S. District Court, Eastern District of North Carolina; 1976, U.S. Court of Appeals, Fourth Circuit. *Education:* East Carolina University (B.S., 1971); University of North Carolina (J.D., 1975). Assistant District Attorney, 10th Judicial District, 1978-1980. Resident Superior Court Judge, First Judicial District, 1991-1992. Certified Mediator, North Carolina Dispute Resolution Commission. Certified Arbitrator, Administrative Office of the Courts. Member, Chief Justice's Committee on Political Conduct by Judges and Judicial Candidates, 2004. *Member:* Dare County (President, 1983-1984), North Carolina (Council Member, Criminal Justice Section, 1982-1985; Bench, Bar Law School Liaison Committee, 1992-1995; Administration of Justice Task Force, 1999-2001) and American Bar Associations; First Judicial District Bar; North Carolina State Bar (Councilor, 1996-2004, Vice President, 2004-2005). ***PRACTICE AREAS:*** Civil Litigation; Personal Injury Law; Family Law; Collections Law; Mediation; Arbitration. ***Email:*** michael@smogobx.com

ROBERT L. OUTTEN, born Plymouth, North Carolina, November 14, 1956; admitted to bar, 1982, North Carolina. *Education:* University of North Carolina (B.S.B.A., 1979); Wake Forest University (J.D., 1982). Phi Delta Phi. Recipient, American Jurisprudence Award. Town Attorney for Town of Kill Devil Hills, 1998—; County Attorney for Dare County, 2001-2003, 2005—. Member, Dare County Board of Adjustments, 2003-2005. Attorney, Currituck County Board of Adjustments, 2004—. *Member:* Dare County (Vice President, 1985—), North Carolina and American Bar Associations; First Judicial District and North Carolina State Bars; North Carolina Academy of Trial Lawyers. ***PRACTICE AREAS:*** Real Estate Law; Civil Litigation; Administrative; Regulatory Law; Municipal Law; Arbitration. ***Email:*** outten@smogobx.com

JOHN C. GRAHAM, III, born Charlotte, North Carolina, January 14, 1960; admitted to bar, 1985, North Carolina, U.S. District Court, Eastern District of North Carolina and U.S. Court of Appeals, Fourth Circuit. *Education:* North Carolina State University (B.A., 1982); Mercer University (J.D., 1985). Phi Delta Phi. *Member:* Dare County (Secretary and Treasurer, 1985—), North Carolina and American Bar Associations; North Carolina State Bar; The Association of Trial Lawyers of America; North Carolina Academy of Trial Lawyers. ***PRACTICE AREAS:*** Criminal and Civil Litigation; Personal Injury Law. ***Email:*** graham@smogobx.com

JEANINE C. EVANS, born Huntsville, Alabama, June 1, 1970; admitted to bar, 1995, North Carolina. *Education:* University of North Carolina at Chapel Hill (B.A., English, 1992); Campbell University (J.D., 1995). Phi Alpha Delta; American Bar Association, President, Campbell Chapter; John Marshall National Moot Court Team. *Member:* Dare County, North Carolina and American Bar Associations; First Judicial District Bar; North Carolina Academy of Trial Lawyers. ***PRACTICE AREAS:*** Family Law; Juvenile Law. ***Email:*** evans@smogobx.com

MICHAEL C. REEVES, born West Point, Georgia, February 11, 1947; admitted to bar, 1973, North Carolina and U.S. District Court, Western District of North Carolina; 1978, U.S. Supreme Court. *Education:* Presbyterian College (B.A., 1969); Wake Forest University (J.D., 1973). Phi Alpha Delta. Vice President, AMIC Title Insurance Company, 1978-1983. Chairman and President, The Title Company of North Carolina, Inc., 1983-1991. *Member:* Dare County and North Carolina Bar Associations; North Carolina State Bar; First Judicial District Bar. ***PRACTICE AREAS:*** Estate Planning Law; Elder Law; Commercial Real Estate Law; Residential Real Estate Law. ***Email:*** reeves@smogbx.com

REPRESENTATIVE CLIENTS: Town of Kill Devil Hills, Dare County; Dare County Dept. Social Services; Griggs Lumber & Produce Co., Inc.; Beach Realty & Construction, Inc.; Atlantic Realty; Centura Bank; Southern Bank; Ocracoke Sanitary District; Town of Nags Head Board of Adjustment; Beach Medical Center.
APPROVED ATTORNEYS FOR: Lawyers Title Insurance Corp.; Chicago Title Insurance Co.; First Title Insurance Co.; Commonwealth Land Title Insurance Co.; Investors Title Insurance Co.
REFERENCES: Centura Bank; Southern Bank; East Carolina Bank; Wachovia Bank; Bank of America.

NORMAN W. SHEARIN, JR.

KITTY HAWK, NORTH CAROLINA

(See Vandeventer Black LLP, Norfolk, Virginia)

VANDEVENTER BLACK LLP

SOUTHERN SHORES LAW BUILDING

6 JUNIPER TRAIL

P.O. BOX 1042

KITTY HAWK, NORTH CAROLINA 27949

Telephone: 252-261-5055

Facsimile: 252-261-8444

Email: nshearin@vanblk.com

URL: http://www.vanblk.com

Norfolk, Virginia Office: 500 World Trade Center, 23510-1699. Telephone: 757-446-8600. Telecopier: 757-446-8670.

Richmond, Virginia Office: Eighth & Main Building, 707 East Main Street, P.O. Box 1558, 23218-1558. Telephone: 804-237-8800. Fax: 804-237-8801.

Roanoke Island, North Carolina Office: 305 Essex Square, Sir Walter Raleigh Street. Telephone: 252-473-1888. Fax: 252-261-5374.

London, England Office: Blackwell House, 23 Guildhall Yard, EC2V 5AE. Telephone: 011 44 020 7917 6053. Facsimile: 011 44 020 7917 6054.

Raleigh, North Carolina Office: Two Hannover Square, Suite 1530, 434 Fayetteville Street Mall, P.O. Box 2599. Telephone: 919-754-1171. Fax: 919-754-1317.

Admiralty, Arbitration and Mediation, Aviation, Banking, Bankruptcy and Creditors' Rights, Commercial Transactions, Community Associations, Construction Law, Environmental Law, Estate Planning, General Litigation in State and Federal Courts, Government/Public Contracts, Health Care Law, Immigration Law, International, Intellectual Property, Insurance Defense, Labor and Employment Law, Land Use, Local Government/Municipal Law, Malpractice, Maritime, Mergers and Acquisitions, Products Liability, Public Utilities, Real Estate, Taxation, Technology, Workers' Compensation.

PARTNERS

G. WILLIAM BIRKHEAD, born Baltimore, Maryland, October 9, 1941; admitted to bar, 1966, Virginia; 1994, North Carolina. *Education:* Webb Institute (B.S., 1963); University of Virginia (LL.B., 1966). Pi Delta Epsilon. Co-Author: "Maritime Contract Claims Against the United States Government," Southeastern Admiralty Law Institute, 1996. *Member:* Norfolk and Portsmouth, Virginia, North Carolina and American Bar Associations; Virginia State Bar; North Carolina State Bar; The Maritime Law Association of the United States (Member, Board of Directors, 1994-1997; Chairman, Fisheries Committee, 1998-2001); Hampton Roads Maritime Association; Society of Naval Architects and Maritime Engineers. [LCDR USCGR, 1966-1975]. ***PRACTICE AREAS:*** Admiralty Law; Vessel Financing Law; Fisheries Regulation; Financial Transactions. ***Email:*** bbirkhead@vanblk.com

DEAN T. BUCKIUS, born Agana, Guam, December 17, 1959; admitted to bar, 1984, Virginia; 1993, North Carolina. *Education:* College of William & Mary (B.A., 1981); Wake Forest University (J.D., cum laude, 1984). Member, Wake Forest Law Review, 1982-1984. Member: Hampton Roads Chamber of Commerce; Society for Human Resource Management; Downtown Norfolk Council. Alumnus, Leadership Hampton Roads. Co-Chairperson-City of Norfolk Employee Grievance Panel. *Member:* Norfolk, Portsmouth, Virginia Beach, Virginia (Member: Labor and Employment Law Section Council; Litigation Section), North Carolina (Member: Labor and Employment Law Section; Litigation Section) and American (Member: Labor and Employment Law Section; Litigation Section) Bar Associations; North Carolina State Bar; Virginia State Bar. ***PRACTICE AREAS:*** Labor and Employment Law; Litigation. ***Email:*** dbuckius@vanblk.com

PATRICK A. GENZLER, born Chicago Heights, Illinois, October 31, 1949; admitted to bar, 1978, Virginia; 1979, U.S. District Court, Eastern District of Virginia; U.S. Court of Appeals, Fourth Circuit; 1995, U.S. Court of Federal Claims; 1997, North Carolina. *Education:* Virginia Polytechnic Institute (B.S., Mechanical Engineering, 1971); College of

(This Listing Continued)

William & Mary (J.D., 1978); George Washington University (LL.M., Environmental Law, 1989). Managing Editor, William & Mary Law Review, 1977-1978. Certified Mediator by Virginia Supreme Court for Circuit Court cases; Certified as Mediator by North Carolina Resolution Commission for Superior Court Cases. General Counsel, Hampton Roads Technology Council. *Member:* Norfolk and Portsmouth, Virginia (Member, Environmental and Construction Sections), North Carolina (Member, Environmental and Construction Law Sections) and American (Member, Section on: Natural Resources, Energy and Environmental Law) Bar Associations; Virginia State Bar. [U.S. Navy, 1972-1992, Commander, JAGC, (Ret.)]. ***PRACTICE AREAS:*** Environmental Law; Construction Law; Public Contracts Law; Litigation; Alternative Dispute Resolution. ***Email:*** pgenzler@vanblk.com

RICHARD S. GUY, born Summit, New Jersey, February 2, 1951; admitted to bar, 1982, North Carolina; 1995, Virginia. *Education:* Dartmouth College (A.B., magna cum laude, 1973); University of Virginia (M.B.A., 1982; J.D., 1982). Phi Beta Kappa. *Member:* Norfolk and Portsmouth, Virginia Beach, Virginia, North Carolina and American Bar Associations; North Carolina State Bar; Virginia State Bar. ***LANGUAGES:*** English, Spanish and French. ***PRACTICE AREAS:*** Business Law; Commercial Transactions; Mergers, Acquisitions and Divestitures; Banks and Banking; Commercial Finance; Commercial Real Estate; Health Care. ***Email:*** rguy@vanblk.com

PATRICK W. HERMAN, born Charlotte, North Carolina, September 12, 1952; admitted to bar, 1982, Virginia; 1998, North Carolina. *Education:* Virginia Polytechnic Institute and State University (B.A.,1974); George Washington University (M.S., 1979); College of William & Mary (J.D., 1982; M.L.T., 1984). Phi Delta Phi. Publications: "Private Inurement: The Basics," Tax Exempt Organizations; "Private Benefit, Private Inurement and Inurement per se: Avoiding the Loss of Your Organization's Tax-Exempt Status," Tax Exempt Organizations. General Counsel, Angel Kiss Foundation, 1990-1998. Tax Counsel, Outer Banks Community Foundation. Director, Elizabeth River Restoration Trust, 2004—. *Member:* Norfolk and Portsmouth, Virginia and American Bar Associations; Virginia State Bar (Member, Tax Sections); Hampton Roads Tax Forum; Tidewater Estate Planning Council. [Capt., JAGC, USAR, 1974-1986]. ***PRACTICE AREAS:*** Tax; Wills; Trust and Estates; Exempt Organizations; ERISA. ***Email:*** pherman@vanblk.com

DANIEL D. KHOURY, born Columbus, Ohio, September 15, 1950; admitted to bar, 1977, North Carolina, Ohio, U.S. District Court, Eastern District of North Carolina, U.S. Court of Appeals, Fourth Circuit and U.S. Supreme Court. *Education:* Ohio State University (B.S.Ed., 1973); Wake Forest University (J.D., 1976). Municipal Attorney: Town of Columbia, 1979-1981; Town of Manteo, 1985-1995. Town Attorney for the Town of Manteo 2002—. Member, *Faculty & Lecturer*, North Carolina Bar Association Real Estate and Residential Real Property Seminars. Lecturer, Business Law, College of Albemarle. *Member:* Dare County Bar Association; North Carolina State Bar (Member, Board of Legal Specialization, 2000-2003; Councilor for the First Judicial District, 1990-1996; Ethics Committee Chairman, 1995; Chairman of the Of Counsel Committee, 1994; Member, Board of Continuing Legal Education; Vice Chairman, 1993-1994; Chairman, Accreditations Committee, 1988-1994); North Carolina (Member: Board of Governors, 1999-2002; Section Chairman, Real Property Council, 1990-1991; President, 1988; President, First District Judicial Bar, 1985) and American Bar Associations. (Board Certified Specialists in Real Property Law-Business, Commercial and Industrial Transactions). ***PRACTICE AREAS:*** Real Property; Business Law; International Law; Securities Law. ***Email:*** dkhoury@vanblk.com

NEIL S. LOWENSTEIN, born Richmond, Virginia, April 26, 1963; admitted to bar, 1989, Virginia, U.S. District Court, Eastern District of Virginia and U.S. Court of Appeals, Fourth Circuit; 1994, U.S. Court of Federal Claims; 1999, North Carolina and U.S. District Court, Eastern, Middle and Western Districts of North Carolina; 2001, U.S. Court of Appeals for the Federal Circuit; 2004, District of Columbia and U.S. District Court, District of Columbia; 2005, U.S. Court of Appeals for the District of Columbia Circuit. *Education:* Virginia Military Institute (B.A., with distinction, 1985); University of Richmond (J.D., 1989). State Board, ABC Virginia; Trustee, ABC Virginia PAC; Past Chairman, Hampton Roads Leadership Committee, ABC Virginia; Past Chairman, Legislative Committee, Hampton Roads Utility & Heavy Contractors Association. Virginia Bar Association Representative, Virginia Continuing Legal Education Committee; Past Board Member, Tidewater Heart Association; and Board Member, Hampton Roads Youth Center. *Member:* Norfolk & Portsmouth, Virginia Beach, Virginia (Member, Sections on: Construction Law; Litigation), North Carolina (Member, Sections on: Construction and Public Contracts Law; Litigation) and American (Member, Sections on: Construction Law Forum; Litigation) Bar Associations; Virginia State Bar; North Carolina State Bar; District of Columbia Bar; Associated General Contractors; Associated Builders & Contractors; Hampton Roads Utility & Heavy Contractors Association. [Infantry and Civil Affairs, U.S. Army Reserve, 1985—]. ***PRACTICE AREAS:*** Construction Law; Public Contracts; General Litigation; Alternative Dispute Resolution. ***Email:*** nlowenstein@vanblk.com

ROBERT L. O'DONNELL, born Akron, Ohio, January 30, 1946; admitted to bar, 1975, Virginia; 1993, North Carolina. *Education:* Spring Hill College (B.S., summa cum laude, 1968); University of Virginia (J.D., 1975). *Member:* Norfolk and Portsmouth, Virginia and American Bar Associations; Virginia State Bar; North Carolina State Bar. [Capt., U.S. Marine Corps., 1969-1972]. ***PRACTICE AREAS:*** Toxic Torts Litigation; Products Liability; Commercial Litigation; Land Use Litigation; Personal Injury. ***Email:*** rodonnell@vanblk.com

EDWARD J. POWERS, born Boston, Massachusetts, February 11, 1965; admitted to bar, 1990, Virginia, U.S. District Court, Eastern District of Virginia and U.S. Court of Appeals, Fourth Circuit; 1998, North Carolina; U.S. District Court, Eastern and Middle Districts of North Carolina; U.S. Supreme Court; 2000, U.S. Court of Appeals, First Circuit. *Education:* Virginia Polytechnic Institute and State University (B.A., 1987); University of Richmond (J.D., 1990). Associate Editor: University of Richmond Law Review, 1989-1990; American Maritime Cases, 2000—. Law Clerk for the Hon. Richard B. Kellam, U.S. District Judge for the Eastern District of Virginia, Norfolk Division, 1990-1991. *Member:* Norfolk and Portsmouth, Virginia, Federal and American Bar Associations; Southeastern Admiralty Law Institute; The Maritime Law Association of the United States; Hampton Roads Maritime Association; Judicial Conference of the U.S. Court of Appeals, Fourth Circuit. ***PRACTICE AREAS:*** Admiralty Law; Civil Litigation. ***Email:*** epowers@vanblk.com

NORMAN W. SHEARIN, JR., born Rocky Mount, North Carolina, February 17, 1945; admitted to bar, 1971, North Carolina and U.S. District Court, Eastern District of

(This Listing Continued)

North Carolina; 1974, U.S. Court of Appeals, Fourth Circuit. *Education:* University of North Carolina at Chapel Hill (B.S., Business Administration, 1967); Wake Forest University (J.D., 1971). Phi Alpha Delta. Research Editor, Wake Forest Law Review, 1970-1971. *Member:* Dare County and American Bar Associations; First Judicial District Bar; North Carolina State Bar; North Carolina Electric Membership Corporations Counsel Association. (Board Certified Specialist in Real Property Law- Business, Commercial and Industrial Transactions, North Carolina State Board of Legal Specialization). ***PRACTICE AREAS:*** Commercial Real Estate; Condemnation and Land Use Litigation; Public Utilities; Real Estate Development; Zoning Law; Land Use. ***Email:*** nshearin@vanblk.com

ASSOCIATES

WYATT M. BOOTH, admitted to bar, 2001, Virginia; 2002, North Carolina. *Education:* North Carolina State University (B.S.Chem.Eng., 1998); Washington & Lee University (J.D., 2001). Staff Writer, Washington & Lee Law Review. *Member:* North Carolina Bar Association; North Carolina State Bar; Virginia State Bar. ***PRACTICE AREAS:*** Civil Litigation; Eminent Domain; Municipal Law. ***Email:*** wbooth@vanblk.com

DAVID P. FERRELL, born Albemarle, North Carolina, July 1, 1971; admitted to bar, 1996, North Carolina and U.S. District Court, Eastern District of North Carolina; 2003, U.S. District Court, Middle and Western Districts of North Carolina. *Education:* University of North Carolina (B.A., 1993); Campbell University (J.D., 1996). Phi Alpha Delta. CLE Course Planner, Update on Legislative Law and Lobbying, 2001—. Fellow, Education Policy Fellowship Program, Institute for Professional Leadership, 1999-2000. Member, YMCA Youth Legislature Bill Selection Committee, 1996—. *Member:* Wake County (Member: Bench/Bar Committee; Professionalism Committee), North Carolina (Chair, Young Lawyers Division Legislative Committee; Member: Communications Committee; Member: Administrative Law Section; Business Law Section) and American (Member: Administrative Law and Regulatory Practice Section; Civil Litigation Section) Bar Associations. ***PRACTICE AREAS:*** Administrative and Regulatory Law; Civil Litigation; Business Law; Cooperative Law; Public Utility Law; Trade and Professional Associations; Legislative Representation. ***Email:*** dferrell@vanblkral.com

TERRY C. FRANK, born June 22, 1973; admitted to bar, 2003, North Carolina. *Education:* Mary Washington College (B.A., 1996); University of Richmond (J.D., 2003). *Member:* Dare County and American Bar Associations; North Carolina Bar Association; First Judicial District Bar Association. (Resident, Kitty Hawk, North Carolina Office). ***PRACTICE AREAS:*** Civil Litigation; Municipal Government Law; Eminent Domain. ***Email:*** tfrank@vanblk.com

ROBERT P. TRIVETTE, born Hickory, North Carolina, June 6, 1956; admitted to bar, 1989, North Carolina; 2005, U.S. District Court, Eastern District of North Carolina. *Education:* Virginia Intermont College (B.A. Eng., 1981); University of North Carolina, Chapel Hill (M.A., Journalism,1987; J.D., 1989). Recipient, American Jurisprudence Award in Constitutional Law. Articles Editor, North Carolina Journal of International Law & Commercial Regulation; Law Clerk, Judge Gerald Arnold, North Carolina Court of Appeals. Assistant District Attorney, First Judicial District in North Carolina, 1991-2004. *Member:* First Judicial District Bar Association (Secretary, 2004—); North Carolina State Bar. ***PRACTICE AREAS:*** Civil Litigation; Criminal Law. ***Email:*** rtrivette@vanblk.com

GENERAL COMMERCIAL REPRESENTATION: Cape Hatteras Electric Membership Cooperative; Hipage Co., Inc.; Flagship Group, Ltd.; General Foam Plastics Corp.; Hampton Roads Shipping Association - ILA Pension Fund; Iceland Seafood, Corp.; Liberty Property Trust; Norfolk Airport Authority; Owens-Illinois; TECNICO Corp.; The CSL Group; The Town of Kitty Hawk; Virginia International Terminals, Inc.
BANKING: Branch Banking and Trust (BB&T); RCB-Centura; Wachovia.
CONSTRUCTION & GOVERNMENT/PUBLIC CONTRACTS: Atlantic Drydock; Chicago Bridge & Iron; Colonial Mechanical Corp.; Davis Boat Works, Inc.; E.L. Hamm & Associates, Inc.; English Construction Co., Inc.; Gilbert Southern Corp.; Globe Iron Construction Corp.; Glover Construction Co., Inc.; Management Consulting, Inc.; McKenzie Construction Corp.; McLean Contracting Co., Inc.; Mid-Eastern Builders, Inc.; Milcom, Inc.; Peter Kiewit Sons', Inc.; SB Ballard Construction Co., Inc.; Shirley Construction Corp.; The Bionetics Corporation; Tidewater - SKANSKA Inc.; Bayshore Concrete Products Corp.; Palmetto Bridge Construction; VIRTEXCO Corp.; W.M., Jordan Company.
LABOR & EMPLOYMENT/WORKERS' COMPENSATION: Hampton Roads Shipping Association; The Hartford; Metro Machine Corp.; Signal Administration, Inc.; New Dominion Pictures, Inc.; American International Group; The Travelers Companies.
MARITIME: Allied Marine Industries, Inc.; Atlantic Yacht Basin; Britannia Steam Ship Insurance Assoc., Ltd.; Chesapeake Yachts Inc.; Crofton Diving Corp.; Hampton Roads Maritime Association; Osprey Associates; London United Marine Agency; Maersk Line Ltd.; Marine Claims Handling Agencies GmbH; Moran Towing of Virginia; Noord Nederlandsche Protectie Club; North of England P & I Assn. Ltd.; The Standard Steamship Owners Protection and Indemnity Assn. Ltd.; The Steamship Mutual Underwriting Assn. (Bermuda) Ltd.; The American Club; The Swedish Club; United Kingdom Mutual Steam Ship Owners Mutual Assurance Assn. (Bermuda) Ltd.; Transport Mutual Services, Inc.; West of England Ship Owners Mutual Insurance Assn. (Luxembourg); Sunderland Steamship; British Marine Mutual Hull Assoc., Ltd.; UK Defense Club; Virginia Pilot Association.
APPROVED ATTORNEYS FOR: Chicago Title Insurance Co.; Lawyers Title Insurance Corp.; Ticor Title Insurance Co.; Zurich American Insurance.

(For complete biographical data on all personnel, see professional biographies at Norfolk, Virginia)

THE VINCENT LAW FIRM, PC

KITTY HAWK, NORTH CAROLINA

(See Southern Shores)

Workers Compensation, Personal Injury, Auto Accidents, Social Security Disability, Wrongful Death and Admiralty Longshores.

DAVIS & McCABE, P.A.

KNIGHTDALE, NORTH CAROLINA

(See Raleigh)

Personal Injury, Automobile Accidents and Injuries, Trucking Accidents, Medical Malpractice, Products Liability, Workers Compensation.

DEBBIE GORONET BAKER

LAURINBURG, NORTH CAROLINA

(See Raeford)

General Practice, Personal Injury, Automobile Accidents and Injuries, Wrongful Death, Criminal Defense, Misdemeanors, Felonies, DWI, Traffic Violations, Revoked Licenses/DMV Hearings, Uncontested Divorces, Workers Compensation, Child Support, Child Custody.

LAW OFFICES OF WILLIAM S. BRITT

LAURINBURG, NORTH CAROLINA

(See Lumberton)

Medical Malpractice, Wrongful Death, Automobile Accidents and Injuries, Truck Accidents, Motorcycle Accidents, Construction Accidents, Dog Bites and Personal Injury Law.

LAW OFFICE OF JOHN R. DANIEL

LAURINBURG, NORTH CAROLINA

(See Rockingham)

General Civil Trial Practice in all State and Federal Courts and Administrative Agencies. Personal Injury, Workers Compensation, Social Security Disability, Real Estate and Traffic.

GORDON, HORNE, HICKS AND FLOYD, P.A.

Established in 1968

609 SOUTH ATKINSON STREET
P.O. BOX 587
LAURINBURG, NORTH CAROLINA 28352
Telephone: 910-276-7825
Fax: 910-277-8430
URL: http://www.lawyers.com/ghandhlaw

General, Civil and Criminal Trial Practice, Probate, Corporation, Real Estate, Personal Injury, Estate Planning, Social Security Disability, Workers' Compensation and Family Law.

FIRM PROFILE: Gordon, Horne, Hicks and Floyd, P.A. serves clients with over 35 years of experience throughout Scotland, Hoke, Robeson, Richmond and surrounding counties.

The firm engages in a General Practice and has achieved and maintained Martindale-Hubbell's highest rating for legal ability and ethical conduct.

J. ROBERT GORDON, born Hamlet, North Carolina, August 26, 1939; admitted to bar, 1964, North Carolina. *Education:* Davidson College (B.A., 1961); University of North Carolina (J.D., 1964). Phi Delta Phi. Chairman, North Carolina Wildlife Resources Commission, 1977-1985. Certified Superior Court Mediator. Member, North Carolina Wildlife Resources Commission, 1995-2001. Member, North Carolina Natural Heritage Trust Fund Board, 2001—. *Member:* North Carolina and American Bar Associations; 16A Judicial District and North Carolina State Bars. [Captain, U.S. Army, 1964-1966]. ***PRACTICE AREAS:*** Corporate Law; Estate Planning; Real Estate; Probate; Social Security Disability. ***Email:*** bobgordon@ghhf.com

JOHN H. HORNE, JR., born Wadesboro, North Carolina, December 30, 1946; admitted to bar, 1972, North Carolina. *Education:* University of North Carolina (A.B., 1968; J.D., 1972). Phi Delta Phi (President, 1971-1972). *Member:* Scotland County and North Carolina Bar Associations; 16A Judicial District and North Carolina State Bars; North Carolina Academy of Trial Lawyers; The National Association of Criminal Defense Lawyers. ***PRACTICE AREAS:*** Criminal Law; Personal Injury; Real Estate. ***Email:*** johnhorne@ghhf.com

CHARLES L. HICKS, JR., born Asheboro, North Carolina, June 9, 1956; admitted to bar, 1981, North Carolina. *Education:* North Carolina State University; University of North Carolina (A.B., 1978; J.D., 1981). Phi Beta Kappa. *Member:* North Carolina Bar Association; 16A Judicial District and North Carolina State Bars; North Carolina Academy of Trial Lawyers. ***PRACTICE AREAS:*** Criminal Law; Personal Injury; Real Estate; Family Law. ***Email:*** chuckhicks@ghhf.com

WILLIAM P. FLOYD, JR., born Lumberton, North Carolina, October 26, 1964; admitted to bar, 1994, North Carolina. *Education:* University of North Carolina (B.A., 1987); Wake Forest University (J.D., 1994). ***PRACTICE AREAS:*** Business Law; Personal Injury; Workers Compensation; Elder Law; Real Estate. ***Email:*** billfloyd@ghhf.com

REPRESENTATIVE CLIENTS: Branch Banking and Trust Co.; City of Laurinburg; Wachovia Bank, N.A.; RBC Centura Bank; First Capital Bank; Remax Connection Realty; Wallace Trucking Co.; Farmland AG-Services, Inc.; Graham and Grubbs Realty; Hasty Realty, Inc.; Riggins Enterprises, Inc.; Barrons, Inc.; Gibson Construction Co., Inc.; Electrical Equipment Co.; Eaton Corp.; Scotland Motors, Inc.; Scotland Orthopedics, P.A.; Campbell Soup.
APPROVED ATTORNEYS FOR: Lawyers Title Insurance Corp.; Fidelity National Title Insurance Co.; Investors Title Insurance Co.; United Title Co.; Chicago Title Co.; Wachovia Bank, N.A.; Branch Banking and Trust Co.; RBC Centura Bank; Cape Fear Farm Credit, A.C.A.
REFERENCES: Branch Banking and Trust Co.; RBC Centura Bank; First Capital Bank.

GRIFFIN LAW OFFICE

LAURINBURG, NORTH CAROLINA

(See Red Springs)

Abuse and Neglect, Juvenile Law, Real Estate Transactions, Traffic, Traffic Violations, DWI, Criminal Law, Domestic and Family Law.

GREG JONES & ASSOCIATES, P.A.

LAURINBURG, NORTH CAROLINA

(See Wilmington)

Personal Injury, Automobile Accidents, Brain Injury, Motorcycle Accidents, Wrongful Death, Medical Malpractice, Spinal Cord Injuries, Drug and Medical Device Litigation, Pharmacists Liability, Head Injuries, Products Liability, Medical and Nursing Home Negligence, Workers Compensation, Toxic Torts, Nursing Home Abuse, Stock Fraud.

MOSER, GARNER, BRUNER & WANSKER, P.A.

600 E. SOUTH MAIN STREET, SUITE E
P.O. BOX 1827
LAURINBURG, NORTH CAROLINA 28353-1827
Telephone: 910-276-2631
Fax: 910-276-0326
Email: emgbw@carolina.net
URL: http://www.lawyers.com/emgblaw

General Civil and Criminal Trial Practice, Insurance, Social Security, Disability Law, Workers Compensation, Administrative, Corporate Law, Commercial and Residential Real Estate, Probate Law, Personal Injury and Negligence Litigation, Family Law, Motor Vehicle Law.

FIRM PROFILE: The firm has been in existence over 60 years providing service to clients in Scotland, Hoke, Richmond, Robeson and surrounding counties.

WILLIAM F. MOSER, born Winston-Salem, North Carolina, February 3, 1942; admitted to bar, 1967, North Carolina. *Education:* Wake Forest College (B.A., 1964; J.D., 1967). Law Clerk to Justice I. Beverly Lake, North Carolina Supreme Court, 1967-1968. ***PRACTICE AREAS:*** Real Estate; Probate; Estate Planning; Corporate Law; Personal Injury; General Civil Practice.

TERRY R. GARNER, born Newport, North Carolina, March 21, 1947; admitted to bar, 1972, North Carolina. *Education:* University of North Carolina (A.B., 1969; J.D., 1972). Morehead Scholar. Law Clerk to Judge Algernon L. Butler, Chief Judge, U.S. District Court, Eastern District of North Carolina, 1972-1974. *Member:* National Organization of Social Security Claimants Representatives. ***PRACTICE AREAS:*** Insurance; Personal Injury; Workers Compensation; Family Law; Social Security Disability; General Civil Practice.

JERRY L. BRUNER, born Lumberton, North Carolina, August 16, 1961; admitted to bar, 1986, North Carolina. *Education:* East Carolina University (B.S., cum laude, 1983); Campbell University (J.D., 1986). *Member:* North Carolina Academy of Trial Lawyers. ***PRACTICE AREAS:*** Criminal Trial Practice; Workers Compensation; Personal injury; Family Law; Motor Vehicle Law; Social Security Disability; General Civil Practice.

OF COUNSEL

HENRY B. WANSKER, born Durham, North Carolina, September 15, 1952; admitted to bar, 1978, North Carolina. *Education:* University of North Carolina at Chapel Hill (B.A., 1974); Wake Forest University School of Law (J.D., 1978). *Member:* The Association of Trial Lawyers of America (Chairperson, Social Security Disability Law Section, 1998-1999). (Also practicing individually, Salt Lake City, Utah)

(All Attorneys are Members of the North Carolina State Bar, North Carolina and American Bar Associations)

REPRESENTATIVE CLIENTS: Bob's Jewel Shop, Inc.; Branch Banking & Trust Company; Cape Fear Farm Credit ACA; RCB Centura Bank; Cooper Petroleum, Inc.; First Bank; First National Bank and Trust Company; Laurinburg-Maxton Airport Commission; McDougald Funeral Home. Inc.; Nic's Pic Kwik, Inc.; Quality Oil Company; Scotland Container, Inc.; Scottish Food Systems, Inc.; Town of Wagram; Wachovia Bank, N.A.; Z.V. Pate, Inc.
APPROVED ATTORNEYS FOR: Chicago Title Insurance Company; First American Title Insurance Company; Investors Title Insurance Company; Lawyers Title Insurance Corporation; Statewide Title, Inc.; Stewart Title Company; United Title Insurance Company.

PURCELL & GRISWOLD, LLP

210 WEST CRONLY STREET
P.O. BOX 1567
LAURINBURG, NORTH CAROLINA 28353
Telephone: 910-277-1980
Fax: 910-277-1480
URL: http://www.purcellandgriswold.com

General Civil and Criminal Litigation, Health Care, Criminal Law, Traffic Violations, Personal Injury, Real Estate, Business Law, Wills and Estates.

WILLIAM R. PURCELL, II, born Charleston, South Carolina, May 15, 1960; admitted to bar, 1985, North Carolina; U.S. District Court, Eastern, Middle and Western Districts of North Carolina; U.S. Court of Appeals, Fourth Circuit and U.S. Supreme Court. *Education:* Davidson College (A.B., cum laude, 1982); University of North Carolina (J.D., with honors, 1985). Omicron Delta Kappa; Order of the Coif. Member, North Carolina Law Review, 1983-1984. Member, Board of Visitors, University of North Carolina at Chapel Hill. *Member:* North Carolina and American Bar Associations. ***PRACTICE AREAS:*** Civil Litigation; Health Care; Real Estate; Personal Injury; Wills; Estates; Business Law; Insurance Defense. ***Email:*** wrp@purcellandgriswold.com

LISA D. GRISWOLD, born Des Moines, Iowa, October 14, 1966; admitted to bar, 1992, North Carolina. *Education:* University of North Carolina (B.A., 1988; J.D., 1992). Phi Beta Kappa. Recipient, Athletic Directors Scholar Athlete Award. *Member:* North Carolina and American Bar Associations; North Carolina Academy of Trial Lawyers. ***PRACTICE AREAS:*** Criminal Law; Traffic Violations; Personal Injury; Real Estate. ***Email:*** ldg@purcellandgriswold.com

(This Listing Continued)

COUNSEL FOR: Scotland Memorial Hospital; St. Andrews Presbyterian College; Scotland County Department of Social Services; Hasty Plywood; Healthkeeperz, Inc.; The Morgan Co.
REPRESENTATIVE CLIENTS: BB & T; Wachovia Bank, N.A.; Longleaf Community Bank; First National Bank & Trust Co.; First Bank; RBCCentura Bank.
APPROVED ATTORNEYS FOR: United Title; Stewart Title; First American; Chicago Title; Lawyers Title; Investors Title.
REFERENCES: BB & T; First National Bank & Trust Co.

THE LAW OFFICES OF CHRISTOPHER V. VAUGHAN

LAURINBURG, NORTH CAROLINA

(See Raeford)

Criminal Law, Traffic, DWI, Family Law, Divorce, Child Support and Child Custody.

WILLIAMSON, DEAN, WILLIAMSON & SOJKA, L.L.P.

213C EAST CRONLY STREET
P.O. BOX 1627
LAURINBURG, NORTH CAROLINA 28353
Telephone: 910-276-8082
Fax: 910-276-1011
URL: http://www.williamsondean.com

General Civil and Criminal Practice. Real Estate, Business Law, Probate, Workers Compensation, Personal Injury, Traffic, Education, Labor and Employment, Construction and Family Law. Trials in all Courts.

ANDREW G. WILLIAMSON (Retired)

MEMBERS OF FIRM

DANIEL B. DEAN, born Laurinburg, North Carolina, March 12, 1947; admitted to bar, 1975, North Carolina. *Education:* Davidson College (B.S., 1969); University of North Carolina (J.D., with honors, 1975). Staff Member, North Carolina Law Review, 1974-1975. Member, North Carolina State Bar Council, 1995-2000. *Member:* North Carolina and American Bar Associations. [Capt., U.S. Army, 1969-1972]. **PRACTICE AREAS:** Real Estate; Estate Planning; Business Law; Education Law. **Email:** ddean@williamsondean.com

ANDREW G. WILLIAMSON, JR., born Laurinburg, North Carolina, May 2, 1958; admitted to bar, 1984, North Carolina. *Education:* University of North Carolina (B.A., 1980); Wake Forest University (J.D., 1983). Law Clerk to Honorable S. Gerald Arnold, North Carolina Court of Appeals, 1983-1984. *Member:* North Carolina Bar Association; North Carolina Academy of Trial Lawyers. **PRACTICE AREAS:** Personal Injury; Social Security; Workers Compensation; Insurance Defense. **Email:** dwilliamson@williamsondean.com

NICKOLAS J. SOJKA, JR., born Durham, North Carolina August 30, 1962; admitted to bar, 1987, North Carolina; 1993, South Carolina; U.S. District Court, Eastern, Middle and Western Districts of North Carolina; U.S. Court of Appeals, Fourth Circuit. *Education:* College of William and Mary (B.A., 1984); University of Virginia (J.D., 1987). Phi Beta Kappa; Omicron Delta Kappa. *Member:* North Carolina and American Bar Associations; South Carolina Bar. **PRACTICE AREAS:** Civil Litigation; Labor and Employment; Personal Injury; Construction; Education Law. **Email:** nsojka@williamsondean.com

COUNSEL FOR: Scotland County Board of Education; Hoke County Board of Education; Hoke County Department of Social Services; Kordsa USA, Inc.; InterKordsa, Inc.; Laurinburg Housing Authority; Southern Pines Housing Authority; Laurinburg Board of Realtors.
REPRESENTATIVE CLIENTS: St. Andrews Presbyterian College; The Morgan Co.; McCarter Electrical Company; Charles Craft Inc.; Cooper Petroleum, Inc.; Carolmet, Inc.; GMAC/Integon Insurance Co.; McArthur Construction Company; RBC Centura Bank; BB & T; Wachovia Bank, N.A.; First Bank.
APPROVED ATTORNEYS FOR: Lawyers Title Insurance Co.; First American Title Insurance Co.; Investors Title Insurance Co.; Chicago Title Insurance Co.; Stewart Title Insurance Co.; Old Republic Title Insurance Co.
REFERENCES: Wachovia Bank, N.A.; First Bank.

MAKO & ASSOCIATES, P.A.

LELAND, NORTH CAROLINA

(See Wilmington)

Personal Injury, Automobile Accidents, Wrongful Death, Trucking Accidents, Head Trauma, Spinal Cord Injuries, Motorcycle Accidents, Workers Compensation, Mediation and Arbitration, Birth Trauma, Medical Malpractice, Construction Accidents, Nursing Home Negligence, Nursing Home Abuse and Neglect and Dog Bites.

L. TALTON DARK, III

LENOIR, NORTH CAROLINA

(See Morganton)

Criminal Law, Driving While Intoxicated, Traffic Violations.

EAKER & FULKERSON, PC

LENOIR, NORTH CAROLINA

(See Hickory)

Criminal Law, Driving Under the Influence, Real Estate, Domestic.

J. BRYAN ELLIOTT

LENOIR, NORTH CAROLINA

(See Hickory)

Bankruptcy, Social Security Disability.

GROOME, TUTTLE, PIKE & BLAIR

Established in 1978
210 RIDGE STREET, N.W.
P.O. BOX 776
LENOIR, NORTH CAROLINA 28645
Telephone: 828-758-0141
Fax: 828-758-5326

MEMBERS OF FIRM

H. HOUSTON GROOME, JR., admitted to bar, 1965, North Carolina; 1968, U.S. Tax Court; 1969, U.S. District Court, Western District of North Carolina; 1980, U.S. Court of Appeals, Fourth Circuit. *Education:* Duke University (A.B., 1960); University of North Carolina (J.D., 1964). Councilor, North Carolina State Bar, 1998—. **PRACTICE AREAS:** Public Utilities Law; Corporate Law; Commercial Law; Estate Planning; Estate Administration.

CARROLL D. TUTTLE, admitted to bar, 1974, North Carolina; 1979, U.S. District Court, Western District of North Carolina. *Education:* Appalachian State University (B.S., 1969); University of North Carolina at Chapel Hill (J.D., 1974). (Board Certified Specialist in Real Property Law-Residential Transactions, North Carolina Board of Legal Specialization). **PRACTICE AREAS:** Real Estate; Real Estate Litigation; Corporate; Business; Bankruptcy Law; Chapter 13; Chapter 7; General Civil Litigation; Estate Administration.

FRED D. PIKE, admitted to bar, 1979, North Carolina; 1980, South Carolina; 1982, U.S. District Court, Western District of North Carolina. *Education:* The Citadel (B.A., 1976); University of South Carolina (J.D., 1979). **PRACTICE AREAS:** Real Estate Law; Collections; Social Security Law.

EDWARD H. BLAIR, JR., admitted to bar, 1978, North Carolina; U.S. District Court, Western and Middle Districts of North Carolina; U.S. Supreme Court. *Education:* University of North Carolina, Chapel Hill (A.B., 1968); University of South Carolina (M.B.A., 1969; J.D., 1977). North Carolina District Court Judge, 1983-1986. **PRACTICE AREAS:** Municipal and Education Law; Family Law; Divorce; Child Custody; Civil Litigation; Traffic Court; Personal Injury.

GENERAL COUNSEL FOR: Caldwell Memorial Hospital; Blue Ridge Electric Membership Corp; Town of Hudson; City of Lenoir; Caldwell County Bd. of Education.

LYNDON R. HELTON PLLC

LENOIR, NORTH CAROLINA

(See Hickory)

Workers Compensation, Personal Injury.

TODD, VANDERBLOEMEN AND BRADY, P.A.

214 RIDGE STREET, NORTHWEST
P.O. DRAWER 1320
LENOIR, NORTH CAROLINA 28645-5227
Telephone: 828-758-0044
Fax: 828-758-8467

General Civil and Criminal Practice. Trials in all Courts. Real Estate, Probate, Corporation, Administrative, Family and Personal Injury Law.

FIRM PROFILE: Todd, Vanderbloemen and Brady, P.A. is a well established law firm and has been since 1952. They focus on Civil and Criminal law in all courts. They also specialize in Family Law, Personal Injury and Real Estate. This firm is well respected and reputable in the entire Caldwell County area.

FOLGER L. TOWNSEND (1899-1973)

JAMES R. TODD, JR., born Lenoir, North Carolina, September 23, 1920; admitted to bar, 1951, North Carolina. *Education:* University of North Carolina (A.B., 1946). Caldwell County Tax Attorney, 1955-1965. *Member:* Caldwell County, North Carolina and American Bar Associations; 25th Judicial District and North Carolina State Bars. [U.S. Air Force, active duty, 1942-1944]. **PRACTICE AREAS:** General Civil Litigation; Insurance Law; Real Estate Law; Educational and Charitable Institutions Law.

BRUCE W. VANDERBLOEMEN, born Indianapolis, Indiana, May 9, 1947; admitted to bar, 1971, North Carolina. *Education:* Davidson College (A.B., 1968); University of North Carolina (J.D., 1971). Research Assistant to North Carolina Supreme Court Justice Dan K. Moore, 1971-1972. *Member:* Caldwell County (President, 1975-1976), North Carolina and American Bar Associations; 25th Judicial District (President, 1981-1982) and North Carolina State Bars; North Carolina Academy of Trial Lawyers. **PRACTICE AREAS:** General Civil Litigation; Corporations Law; Real Estate Law; Probate Law.

CHARLES A. BRADY, III, born Hickory, North Carolina, August 25, 1955; admitted to bar, 1981, North Carolina. *Education:* University of North Carolina (B.A., 1977); Wake Forest University (J.D., 1981). *Member:* North Carolina and American Bar Associations; North Carolina State Bar; North Carolina Academy of Trial Lawyers. **PRACTICE AREAS:** General Civil Litigation; Workmen's Compensation; Personal Injury Law; Family Law; Divorce; Child Custody; Child Support; Equitable Distribution; Automobile Accidents and Injuries.

DISTRICT COUNSEL FOR: Southern Bell Telephone & Telegraph Co.

(This Listing Continued)

TODD, VANDERBLOEMEN AND BRADY, P.A., Lenoir—Continued

REPRESENTATIVE CLIENTS: NationsBank; First Union National Bank; Caldwell Savings Bank, Inc.; Duke Power Co.; Norfolk-Southern Railway; Furniture City Broadcasters, Inc.; General Motors Corp.; Western Carolina Tire, Inc.; Bush Oldsmobile, Inc.; Koinonia, Inc.; Commercial Union Assurance Cos.; Fireman's Fund Insurance Co.; Integon Insurance Co.; Nationwide Mutual Insurance Co.; Travelers Insurance Co.; Caldwell Community College & Technical Institute; Anderson Truck Lines, Inc.; Lenoir Women's Clinic, P.A.; Broyhill Furniture Rentals, Inc.; Blowing Rock Furniture; Stevens Furniture Co.; Lenoir Living Center, Inc.; Lawyers Mutual Insurance Co., Inc.; Universal Underwriters Insurance Co.; Bush-Parsons Chrysler-Plymouth, Inc.; Bankers and Shippers Insurance; Selective Insurance Co.; The Morgan School at Patterson Preserve; General Mills, Inc.
APPROVED ATTORNEYS FOR: Lawyers Title Insurance Corp.; Transamerica Title Insurance Services; Chicago Title Insurance Co.
REFERENCES: NCNB NationsBank; First Union National Bank; Bank of Granite.

DAVIS ELDER & DISABILITY LAW

6620 SHALLOWFORD ROAD
P.O. BOX 754
LEWISVILLE, NORTH CAROLINA 27023
Telephone: 336-946-0266
Fax: 336-946-0499
URL: http://www.tatedavis.com
Email: tate@daviselderlaw.com
URL: http://www.daviselderlawoffice.com

Elder Law.

V. TATE DAVIS, born Havre de Grace, Maryland, March 11, 1968; admitted to bar, 2000, North Carolina and U.S. District Court, Middle District of North Carolina. *Education:* Frostburg State University (B.S., summa cum laude, 1997); Wake Forest University (J.D., 2000). *Member:* North Carolina Bar Association (Member, Elder Law Section); North Carolina State Bar; National Academy of Elder Law Attorneys; North Carolina Academy of Trial Lawyers (Member, Disability Advocacy Section); National Organization of Social Security Claimants Representatives. ***PRACTICE AREAS:*** Long Term Care; Medicaid Planning; Special Needs Trusts; Wills; Probate; Trusts and Estates; Estate Planning; Asset Protection; Guardianship. ***Email:*** tate@daviselderlaw.com

THE LAW PRACTICE OF DANIEL B. ANTHONY PC

LEXINGTON, NORTH CAROLINA

(See Winston-Salem)

Workers Compensation, Personal Injury, Criminal Defense, Disability Claims, Civil Litigation.

BARNES, GRIMES, BUNCE & FRALEY, PLLC

20 SOUTH MAIN STREET
P.O. BOX 476
LEXINGTON, NORTH CAROLINA 27292-0476
Telephone: 336-249-9128
Fax: 336-249-9129
Email: linwoodbunce@bgblawoffice.com
URL: http://www.lawyers.com/bgblawoffice

Personal Injury, Auto Accidents, Wrongful Death, Workers Compensation, Criminal Law, DWI, Drug Crimes, Traffic Violations, Real Estate, Mortgages, Landlord and Tenant Law, Wills and Probate, Family Law, Child Custody, Child Support, Divorce, Elder Law.

BEAMER H. BARNES, admitted to bar, 1940, North Carolina. (1915-2002)

JERRY B. GRIMES, born 1938; admitted to bar, 1963, North Carolina. *Education:* Wake Forest University (LL.B., 1963; J.D., 1970). ***PRACTICE AREAS:*** Criminal Law; General Practice. ***Email:*** jerrygrimes@bgblawoffice.com

D. LINWOOD BUNCE, II, born 1953; admitted to bar, 1979, North Carolina. *Education:* Campbell University (B.S., 1975; J.D., 1979). ***PRACTICE AREAS:*** Family Law; Wills; Estate Planning; Real Estate; Personal Injury; Workers Compensation. ***Email:*** linwoodbruce@bgblawoffice.com

SHAWN L. FRALEY, born 1975; admitted to bar, 2001, North Carolina. *Education:* University of North Carolina at Chapel Hill (B.A., 1998; J.D., 2001). ***PRACTICE AREAS:*** Criminal Law; General Practice. ***Email:*** shawnfraley@bgblawoffice.com

JEFFREY J. BERG

401 WEST CENTER STREET
LEXINGTON, NORTH CAROLINA 27292
Telephone: 336-249-3870
Fax: 336-243-3059
Email: lawyer@jberglaw.com
URL: http://www.jberglaw.com

Criminal Defense, Driving While Intoxicated (DWI), Misdemeanors, Traffic Violations, Speeding Tickets, Residential Real Estate, Commercial Real Estate, Mortgages, Deeds, Land Sales, Trusts and Estates, Corporations, Wills and Probate.

JEFFREY J. BERG, born Missoula, Montana, October 30, 1961; admitted to bar, 1989, Oklahoma; 1990, North Carolina. *Education:* Southwestern Oklahoma State University (B.S., Computer Science, 1984); University of Oklahoma (J.D., 1989). Assistant District Attorney, Davidson County, 1991-1993. *Member:* Davidson County and American Bar Associations; North Carolina State Bar; North Carolina Academy of Trial Lawyers; National Association of Criminal Defense Attorneys.

COUNSEL FOR: Lexington Housing Authority.
REFERENCES: Lexington State Bank; Industrial Federal Savings Bank; Davidson Mortgage.
APPROVED ATTORNEYS: Investors Title; Statewide Title; Lawyers Title Insurance Company; Commonwealth and Title.

BRINKLEY WALSER, PLLC

Established in 1886

10 LSB PLAZA
P.O. BOX 1657
LEXINGTON, NORTH CAROLINA 27292
Telephone: 336-249-2101
Fax: 336-249-4572

General Practice in State and Federal Courts. Insurance, Corporation, Probate, Real Estate Law, Medical Malpractice Defense, Personal Injury Litigation, Workers' Compensation, Elder Law, Social Security, Criminal Law, Domestic Relations, Banking Law.

ZEB VANCE WALSER (1863-1940)

DON A. WALSER (1899-1977)

GAITHER S. WALSER (1934-2001)

WALTER F. BRINKLEY, born Lexington, North Carolina, June 22, 1926; admitted to bar, 1949, North Carolina; 1951, U.S. Court of Appeals, Fourth Circuit. *Education:* University of North Carolina (LL.B., 1949). Phi Delta Phi. Recipient, John J. Parker Award, 2000. Staff of Attorney General of North Carolina, 1950-51. President, Legal Services of North Carolina, Inc., 1976-1979. Member, North Carolina Board of Law Examiners, 1981-1994 and Chairman, 1992-1994. North Carolina General Practice Hall of Fame, 1996. *Member:* North Carolina (President, 1974) and American Bar Associations; International Association of Defense Counsel; International Academy of Trial Lawyers. Fellow, American College of Trial Lawyers. Fellow, American Bar Foundation. ***PRACTICE AREAS:*** Civil Litigation; Business; Probate.

CHARLES H. McGIRT, born Bennettsville, South Carolina, May 5, 1936; admitted to bar, 1961, North Carolina and U.S. District Court, Middle District of North Carolina; 1969, U.S. Court of Appeals, Fourth Circuit; 1971, U.S. Supreme Court. *Education:* Lenoir Rhyne College (A.B., 1958); University of North Carolina (J.D., 1961). Delta Theta Phi. Member, Fourth Circuit Judicial Conference, Permanent. *Member:* North Carolina and American Bar Associations; North Carolina State Bar; Federation of Insurance and Corporate Counsel; North Carolina Association of Defense Attorneys. ***PRACTICE AREAS:*** Civil Litigation; Banking; Probate; Corporate Law; Estate Planning; Real Property Law. ***Email:*** cmcgirt@brinkleywalser.com

G. THOMPSON MILLER, born Lexington, North Carolina, May 12, 1946; admitted to bar, 1972, North Carolina and U.S. District Court, Middle District of North Carolina; 1981, U.S. Court of Appeals, Fourth Circuit. *Education:* Wake Forest University (B.A., cum laude, 1968; J.D., 1972). Phi Delta Phi. Writer, Wake Forest Intramural Law Review, 1969-1970. *Member:* Davidson County, North Carolina and American Bar Associations; 22nd Judicial District and North Carolina State Bars. [Capt., USAR, 1971-1979]. ***PRACTICE AREAS:*** Civil Litigation; Workers' Compensation; Social Security Disability. ***Email:*** tmiller@brinkleywalser.com

D. CLARK SMITH, JR., born Lexington, North Carolina, June 15, 1950; admitted to bar, 1975, North Carolina and U.S. District Court, Middle and Eastern Districts of North Carolina. *Education:* Wake Forest University (B.S., cum laude, 1972; J.D., cum laude, 1975). Phi Delta Phi. Listed in The Best Lawyers in America, 1993—. Member of Staff, Wake Forest Law Review, 1974-1975. *Member:* Davidson County, North Carolina (Executive Committee, 1996-1997; Board of Governors, 1994-1997) and American Bar Associations; 22nd Judicial District and North Carolina State Bars; North Carolina Association of Defense Attorneys (Board of Directors, 1995-2004; Treasurer, 1998-2000; Executive V.P., 2000-2001; President-Elect, 2001-2002; President, 2002-2003; Immediate Past President, 2003-2004). Fellow, American College of Trial Lawyers; Defense Research Institute. ***PRACTICE AREAS:*** Medical Malpractice Defense; Civil Litigation; Commercial Litigation; Corporate Law. ***Email:*** csmith@brinkleywalser.com

STEPHEN W. COLES, born Toronto, Ontario, September 22, 1956; admitted to bar, 1980, North Carolina and U.S. District Court, Middle, Western and Eastern Districts of North Carolina; U.S. Court of Appeals, Fourth Circuit. *Education:* Wake Forest University (B.A., cum laude, 1977; J.D., 1980). Phi Alpha Theta; Phi Delta Phi. Listed in The Best Lawyers in America, 2001—. Board of Directors, Central Carolina Legal Services, Inc. (Director, 1981-1997, President, 1992-1993). *Member:* Davidson County, 22nd Judicial District, North Carolina (Member, Medico-Legal Liaison Committee, 1997—) and American Bar Associations; North Carolina State Bar; North Carolina Association of Defense Attorneys (Board of Directors, 2004—); International Association of Defense Counsel; Defense Research Institute; National School Boards Association Council of School Attorneys. ***PRACTICE AREAS:*** Medical Malpractice Defense; Civil Litigation; Commercial Litigation; Education Law. ***Email:*** scoles@brinkleywalser.com

DAVID E. INABINETT, born Salisbury, North Carolina, March 16, 1970; admitted to bar, 1996, North Carolina. *Education:* Wake Forest University (B.A., cum laude, 1992; J.D., 1996). Phi Delta Phi. Member, Moot Court Board. *Member:* Davidson County and North Carolina (Member, Elder Law Section; Estate Planning Section) Bar Associations; National Academy of Elder Law Attorneys. ***PRACTICE AREAS:*** Elder Law; Medicaid Planning; Long Term Care Planning; Wills and Estates; Real Property Law; Civil Litigation; Education Law. ***Email:*** dinabinett@brinkleywalser.com

STEPHEN D. BARNHILL, born Winston-Salem, North Carolina, September 8, 1958; admitted to bar, 1990, North Carolina. *Education:* High Point University (B.S., Business Administration, cum laude, 1984); Wake Forest University (J.D., 1990). Assistant District Attorney, 22nd Prosecutorial District, 1990-1998. *Member:* Davidson County and North Carolina Bar Associations; North Carolina State Bar; North Carolina Association of Defense Attorneys; American Board of Trial Advocates. [U.S. Army, 1984-1987, 1st Lieuten-

(This Listing Continued)

ant; North Carolina Army National Guard, Captain, 1988-1995]. ***PRACTICE AREAS:*** Civil Litigation; Criminal Law; Felonies; Drug Crimes; Misdemeanors; Driving While Impaired; Traffic Violations. ***Email:*** sbarnhill@brinkleywalser.com

ASSOCIATES

APRIL D. CRAFT, born Ronceverte, West Virginia, May 3, 1971; admitted to bar, 2001, North Carolina. *Education:* Elon College (B.A., History, magna cum laude, 1993); Wake Forest University (J.D., 2001). Omicron Delta Kappa. Member, Wake Forest Moot Court Board. *Member:* Davidson County and North Carolina (Member, Sections on: Family Law; Education Law) Bar Associations. ***PRACTICE AREAS:*** Family Law; Civil Litigation; Education Law; Medicaid Planning. ***Email:*** acraft@brinkleywalser.com

BRADLEY S. HUNT, born High Point, North Carolina, December 30, 1975; admitted to bar, 2002, West Virginia; 2003, North Carolina. *Education:* University of North Carolina at Chapel Hill (B.A., Political Science, 1998); West Virginia University (J.D., 2002). *Member:* Davidson County, West Virginia and North Carolina Bar Associations; North Carolina State Bar; North Carolina Association of Defense Attorneys. ***PRACTICE AREAS:*** Civil Litigation; Banking; Medical Malpractice Defense. ***Email:*** bhunt@brinkleywalser.com

GENERAL COUNSEL: Lexington State Bank; Davidson County Board of Education; Davidson County Community College, Inc.; G.W. Mountaincastle Agency, Inc.; Lexington City Board of Education; Lexington Memorial Hospital; The Dispatch Publishing Co.; Davis Chevrolet, Inc.; Fletcher Machine Co.; Housing Management, Inc.; Dalcor Management, Inc.; Southern Services of Lexington, Inc.; Don Mays Buick-Pontiac, Inc.; Turlington & Company, LLP.; Billings Freight Systems, Inc.; Brian Vickers, LLC.
LOCAL COUNSEL: Duke Energy Corporation; The New York Times Co.; The Gillette Co.; Duracell Inc.; Kimberly-Clark Corp.; Wake Forest University Baptist Medical Center; Medical Mutual Insurance Co.; MAG Mutual Insurance Co.; Lawyers Mutual Liability Insurance Co.; Mutual of Omaha; GMAC Insurance Co.; St. Paul Fire and Marine Insurance Co.; Magna Fabrics, Inc.; CV Products, Inc.; KEJ Marketing, Inc.
REFERENCE: Lexington State Bank.

LAW OFFICE OF DARYL G. DAVIDSON, SR., PC

LEXINGTON, NORTH CAROLINA

(See Statesville)

Family Law, Child Support, Child Custody, Divorce, Domestic Violence, Visitation Rights, Criminal Law, Driving While Intoxicated (DWI); Drug Crimes, Traffic Violations, Immigration, Automobile Accidents.

HANDLER & BROWN, P.L.L.C.

LEXINGTON, NORTH CAROLINA

(See Winston-Salem)

Business Law, Commercial Law, Insurance Premium Finance Law, Factoring, Leasing, Licensing, Franchise Law, Intellectual Property Law, Trademarks, Copyrights, Unfair Competition, Real Estate, Condominium Law, Association Law, Land Use, Environmental Law, Commercial Litigation, Unfair Trade Practice Law, Creditors Rights, Civil Trial Practice, Appellate Practice, Arbitration, Class Actions, Constitutional Law, Professional Liability, Medical Malpractice, Products Liability, Personal Injury, Civil Rights, Labor and Employment, Wrongful Discharge and Discrimination Law.

KETNER & DEES, P.A.

LEXINGTON, NORTH CAROLINA

(See Salisbury)

General Civil Practice State and Federal Courts, Real Estate, Zoning, Planning and Land Use, Corporate and Business Law, Elder Law, Trusts and Estates, Estate Planning, Probate, Wills, Health Care Law.

MORGAN, HERRING, MORGAN, GREEN, ROSENBLUTT & GILL, LLP

LEXINGTON, NORTH CAROLINA

(See High Point)

General Civil and Criminal Trial Practice in all State and Federal Courts. Interstate Commerce, Probate, Real Estate, Corporation and Tax Law. Torts. Traffic Violations and Driving Under the Influence, Personal Injury, Auto Accidents, Wills and Estates, Family Law, Divorce, Custody, Support, Adoption, Workers Compensation, Bankruptcy, Social Security, Employment Discrimination.

JAMES EUGENE SNYDER, JR.

Established in 1970

16 WEST 1ST AVENUE
P.O. BOX 482
LEXINGTON, NORTH CAROLINA 27293
Telephone: 336-249-3399
Fax: 336-243-7800
Email: JamesSnyder@jamesesnyderjr.com
URL: http://www.jamesesnyderjr.com

General Civil and Criminal Trial Practice in State and Federal Courts. Corporations, Real Property, Family and Probate Law with Personal Injury and Medical Malpractice concentration.

(This Listing Continued)

JAMES EUGENE SNYDER, JR., born Lexington, North Carolina, June 30, 1945; admitted to bar, 1970, North Carolina and U.S. Tax Court; 1971, U.S. District Court, Middle District of North Carolina; 1978, U.S. Court of Appeals, Fourth Circuit and U.S. Supreme Court. *Education:* Wake Forest University (B.A., 1967; J.D., 1970). Omicron Delta Kappa. Author: *North Carolina Automobile Insurance Law,* The Harrison Company, 3rd Edition, 1999; *N.C. Corporation Law, and Practice Forms,* West, A. Thomson Business, 4th Ed., 2003; *N.C. Corporation Law and Practice,* West, A. Thomson Business, 4th Edition, 2003; Take Counsel, Universal Publishing Co., 2000; *A Lawyer Prays God's Will for His Clients,* Universal Publishing Co., 2000; *The Saga of Joe Monk,* Universal Publishing Co., 2000; *The Conservation Mind,* Universal Publishing Co., 2004. Author and Lecturer: Insurance and Criminal Law, Wake Forest Continuing Legal Education, 1991; Corporations, Wake Forest Continuing Legal Education, 1991, 1992, 1993, 1994, 1995, 1996, 1997, 1998, 1999, 2000 and 2001. Member, North Carolina House of Representatives, 1971. Trustee, Davidson County Community College, 1973-1981. Candidate: (pri.), U.S. Senate, N. C., 2002; (gen. elect.), Lt. Gov., N.C. 2004. Member, Select Committee, N. C. Bd. of Law Examiners. *Member:* North Carolina State Bar; North Carolina Trial Lawyers Association.

REPRESENTATIVE CLIENTS: Central Carolina Bank (Lexington); Valendrawers, Inc.

MICHAEL A. SWANN, P.A.

Established in 1981

21 VANCE CIRCLE
P.O. BOX 1503
LEXINGTON, NORTH CAROLINA 27293
Telephone: 336-249-7777
Facsimile: 336-249-9988
Email: michaelswann@lexcominc.net

Practice Limited to: Workers' Compensation, Personal Injury, Civil Litigation, Mediation.

FIRM PROFILE: Michael began his practice in Raleigh, North Carolina in 1977 with the firm of Ragsdale, Ligbett & Cheshire. The Lexington office was established in 1984 and the practice was limited to personal injury and worker's compensation. He was certified in mediation in 1998 and arbitration in 2003. He has handled cases in many southeastern states, now dividing his practice equally between advocacy and mediation/arbitration.

MICHAEL A. SWANN, born Honolulu, Hawaii, November 14, 1947; admitted to bar, 1977, North Carolina; 1982, U.S. District Court, Middle District of North Carolina. *Education:* University of North Carolina (A.B., 1969; J.D., 1977). Member, 1975-1976 and Staff Editor, 1976, North Carolina Law Review. Member, North Carolina OSHA Review Board, 1979-1982. *Member:* Davidson County and North Carolina (Workers' Compensation Council, 2002—) Bar Associations; North Carolina State Bar; North Carolina Academy of Trial Lawyers; The Association of Trial Lawyers of America. [Capt., USAF, 1970-1974]. ***REPORTED CASES:*** Craver v. Dixie Furniture Co./Liberty Mutual, 447 S.E.2d 789 (N.C. App. 1994). ***PRACTICE AREAS:*** Workers' Compensation; Personal Injury; Civil Litigation; Mediation. ***Email:*** michaelswann@lexcominc.net

LEGAL SUPPORT PERSONNEL

TERESA COBLE, (Legal Assistant)

DONETTE THORE, (Administrative Assistant)

REFERENCE: Bank of North Carolina, Lexington.

WYATT EARLY HARRIS WHEELER L.L.P.

LEXINGTON, NORTH CAROLINA

(See High Point)

Litigation, Legal and Regulatory matters in Furniture/Home Furnishings Industries, General Civil, Insurance, Business, Securities, Taxation and Criminal Practice. Trials and Appeals in all State and Federal Courts. Probate and Estate Planning, Real Estate, Bankruptcy, Corporation, Banking, Negligence, Workers Compensation and Family Law.

LAW OFFICES OF WILLIAM H. FLOWE, JR.

124 S. FAYETTEVILLE STREET
LIBERTY, NORTH CAROLINA 27298-1315
Telephone: 336-622-2278
Fax: 336-622-5944
Email: flowe51@rtelco.net
URL: http://www.williamflowelaw.com

Real Estate, Closings, Buying and Selling, Wills, Trust and Estates, Estates Planning, Small Business, Limited Liability Companies, Business Enterprises, Family Law, Divorce.

WILLIAM H. FLOWE, JR., born Concord, North Carolina, October 13, 1951; admitted to bar, 1976, North Carolina. *Education:* Wake Forest University (B.A., 1973; J.D., 1976). ***PRACTICE AREAS:*** Real Estate; Closely Held Business Estate Planning; Buying and Selling of Businesses; Wills; Trusts and Estates; Estate Planning; Small Business Law; Limited Liability Company Law; Business Enterprises; Family Law; Divorce.

BAIN, BUZZARD & McRAE, LLP

Established in 1961

65 BAIN STREET

LILLINGTON, NORTH CAROLINA 27546

Telephone: 910-893-5111

Fax: 910-893-6956

URL: http://www.bainlawyers.com

URL: http://www.bainandmcrae.com

General Civil and Criminal Practice. Trials in all State and Federal Courts. Real Estate, Trusts and Estates, Wills and Probate, Medicaid Planning, Elder Law, Business and Corporate Law, Taxation, Tax Planning, Personal Injury, Automobile Accidents, Wrongful Death, Medical Malpractice, Criminal Law, DWI, Traffic Offenses.

FIRM PROFILE: Bain, Buzzard & McRae, LLP was founded by Edgar R. Bain in 1961. Serving clients throughout Harnett, Lee and Johnston Counties. The firm engages in a general civil and criminal practice and is listed in the Bar Register of Preeminent Lawyers.

MEMBERS OF FIRM

EDGAR R. BAIN, born Harnett County, North Carolina, January 1, 1933; admitted to bar, 1957, North Carolina. *Education:* Campbell College (A.A., 1953); Wake Forest College (B.S., 1955; LL.B., 1957). Phi Delta Phi; Epsilon Pi Eta. Town Attorney, Town of Lillington, North Carolina, 1961-1981. Awarded Town of Lillington Community Service Award, Man of the Year, 1966. *Member:* Harnett County Bar Association (President, 1964-1965) Eleventh Judicial District and North Carolina State Bars. ***PRACTICE AREAS:*** Civil Litigation; Torts; Estate and Probate; Real Estate. ***Email:*** ebain@bainlawyers.com

ALTON D. BAIN, born Raleigh, North Carolina, June 3, 1960; admitted to bar, 1985, North Carolina. *Education:* Duke University (A.B., summa cum laude, 1982); University of North Carolina (J.D., 1985); University of Florida (LL.M. in Taxation, 2001). Phi Beta Kappa. Member, Order of Golden Fleece. Law Clerk to Hon. Gerald Arnold, North Carolina Court of Appeals, 1985-1986. Attorney, Harnett County Public Utilities and Town of Coats. *Member:* Harnett County (President, 1992-1993), North Carolina (Member, Estate Planning, Fiduciary Law, Elder Law, Tax Sections) and American (Member, Taxation, Probate and Trust Sections) Bar Associations; Eleventh Judicial District (President, 2005). ***PRACTICE AREAS:*** Taxation; Trusts and Estates; Wills; Probate; Estate Planning; Estate Administration; Medicaid Planning; Elder Law. ***Email:*** abain@bainlawyers.com

ROBERT A. BUZZARD, born Chapel Hill, North Carolina, September 29, 1965; admitted to bar, 1991, North Carolina. *Education:* Illinois State University (B.S., 1988); Campbell University (J.D., 1991). Illinois State Scholar. *Member:* North Carolina State Bar; Harnett County Bar Association (President, 1996-1998); Eleventh Judicial District Bar Association; North Carolina Academy of Trial Lawyers. ***PRACTICE AREAS:*** Criminal Law; Personal Injury; Civil Litigation; Medical Malpractice; Workers Compensation. ***Email:*** tbuzzard@bainlawyers.com

DAVID F. McRAE, born Harnett County, North Carolina, December 29, 1957; admitted to bar, 1989, North Carolina. *Education:* Lees-McRae College (A.A., 1978); East Carolina University (B.A., 1981); Campbell University (J.D., 1989). *Member:* Harnett County and North Carolina Bar Associations; North Carolina Academy of Trial Lawyers. ***PRACTICE AREAS:*** Criminal Law; Real Estate; Personal Injury; Estate and Probate. ***Email:*** dmcrae@bainlawyers.com

---

L. STACY WEAVER, III, born Fayetteville, North Carolina, December 16, 1956; admitted to bar, 2004, North Carolina. *Education:* Duke University (B.A., cum laude, 1980); Campbell University (J.D., 2004). *Member:* North Carolina State Bar; North Carolina Academy of Trial Lawyers. ***PRACTICE AREAS:*** Criminal Law; Civil Litigation; Family Law. ***Email:*** sweaver@bainlawyers.com

JONATHAN D. BREEDEN

LILLINGTON, NORTH CAROLINA

(See Garner)

Criminal Law, Driving While Intoxicated (DWI), Drug Crimes, Traffic Violations, Family Law, Child Custody, Child Support, Divorce, Education Law, Contracts, Wills.

CHARLENE EDWARDS LAW OFFICE

Established in 1999

CAPE FEAR PLAZA

133C WEST CORNELIUS HARNETT BOULEVARD

LILLINGTON, NORTH CAROLINA 27546

Telephone: 910-893-1128

Fax: 910-893-1138

Email: edwardslaw1@earthlink.net

URL: http://www.lillingtonlawyers.com

Mailing Address: P.O. Box 2446, Lillington, NC 27546

Family Law, Divorce, Domestic Relations, Personal Injury, Automobile Accidents, Wrongful Death, Construction Accidents, Criminal Law, Workers Compensation, Social Security Disability, Traffic Law.

FIRM PROFILE: Charlene Edwards Law Office is a full service law firm that represents clients in a variety of legal needs including family/domestic law; criminal/traffic law; personal injury; workers compensation; and social security disability.

CHARLENE EDWARDS, born Henderson, North Carolina, July 29, 1968; admitted to bar, 1993, North Carolina; 1995, U.S. District Court, Eastern District of North Carolina; 1998, U.S. District Court, Middle District of North Carolina; 1999, U.S. District Court, Western District of North Carolina. *Education:* Campbell University (B.A., 1990; J.D., 1993). Pi Gamma Mu; Epsilon Pi Eta; Delta Theta Phi. Listed in, Who's Who in American Universities. Formerly with, Hartley and Edwards. Member, Federalist Society. Lecturer, Campbell University Government/History Department, Intro to Trials/Mock Trials, 1995-2001. Certified Family Financial Mediator, 2003. *Member:* North Carolina and American Bar Associations; North Carolina State Bar; North Carolina Association of Women Attorneys; North Carolina Association of Trial Lawyers. ***LANGUAGES:*** Greek. ***REPORTED CASES:*** Liller vs. Quick Stop Food Mart, Inc. -NCAPP-, 1998. ***PRACTICE AREAS:*** Domestic Relations; Family Law; Divorce; Personal Injury; Criminal Law; Workers Compensation; Social Security Disability.

(This Listing Continued)

ASSOCIATE

BEN L. ROBERTS, born Shelby, North Carolina, May 25, 1979; admitted to bar, 2004, North Carolina and U.S. District Court, Eastern District of North Carolina. *Education:* Campbell University (B.A., 2001; J.D., 2004). Delta Theta Phi; Bailiff. ***PRACTICE AREAS:*** Juvenile Law; Social Security Disability; Divorce; Criminal Law; Traffic Violations. ***Email:*** logan.roberts@earthlink.net

L. HOLT FELMET, P.A.

Established in 1993

32 EAST FRONT STREET

P.O. BOX 1689

LILLINGTON, NORTH CAROLINA 27546

Telephone: 910-893-2999

Fax: 910-893-3255

Email: hfelmet@aol.com

URL: http://www.felmetlaw.com

General Civil and Criminal Trial Practice in all Courts. Personal Injury Litigation, Domestic Relations and Family Law, Real Estate, Criminal Defense (including traffic) and Estate Administration.

FIRM PROFILE: L. Holt Felmet established his own firm in 1993 after 19 years in practice. He offers clients in Lillington and Harnett County a civil and criminal trial practice, including criminal defense. In addition, Mr. Felmet is experienced in real estate matters and family law including domestic relations.

L. HOLT FELMET, born Raleigh, North Carolina, March 8, 1946; admitted to bar, 1974, North Carolina. *Education:* Wake Forest University (B.A., 1968; J.D., 1974). Phi Delta Phi. Associate Editor, Wake Forest Law Review, 1973-1974. Author: "Consignment Transactions Under the Uniform Commercial Code-Conflicting Rights of the Consignee's Creditors and the Consignor in Consigned Goods," Vol. 9, No. 2, Wake Forest Law Review, p. 256, 1973. Assistant District Attorney, 11th Judicial District, 1979-1980. Trust Officer, First Citizens Bank, 1976-1979. Attorney for Harnett County Child Support Enforcement Agency, 1981—. *Member:* Harnett County, Eleventh Judicial District (President, 1999-2000) and North Carolina Bar Associations; North Carolina State Bar; North Carolina Academy of Trial Lawyers. [Lt. J.G., U.S. Navy, active duty, 1968-1971]. ***REPORTED CASES:*** Doxol Gas of Angier, Inc. v. Howard, 28 N.C.App. 132, 220 S.E.2d 203 (1975); Howard v. Federal Crop Ins. Corp., 540 F.2d 695 (4th Cir., 1976); In re Lee, 69 N.C.App. 277, 317 S.E.2d 75 (1984); Patterson v. Markam & Associates, 123 N.C.App. 448, 474 S.E.2d 400 (1996) cert. denied 344 N.C. 734, 478 S.E.2d 5 (1996); State v. Walston, 140 N.C.App. 327, 536 S.E.2d 630 (2000). ***PRACTICE AREAS:*** Criminal Law; Traffic Violations; Driving While Intoxicated; Personal Injury; Domestic Relations; Family Law; Divorce; Civil Litigation; Real Estate; Probate Law. ***Email:*** hfelmet@aol.com

APPROVED ATTORNEY FOR: Commonwealth Land Title Insurance Co.; Lawyers Title Insurance Co.; Jefferson-Pilot Insurance Co.; Chicago Title Insurance Co.; Investors Title Insurance Co.; Old Republic Title Insurance Co.

THE LAW OFFICES OF HALES & CONAWAY, PLLC

LILLINGTON, NORTH CAROLINA

(See Clinton)

Family Law, Divorce, Adoption, Custody, Child Support, Premarital Agreements, Separation Agreements, Criminal Defense, Social Security Disability, Collections, Debtor, Creditor, Juvenile Law, Estate Administration and Estate Planning, Civil Litigation, Workers Compensation, Personal Injury, Traffic, DWI.

HAYES, WILLIAMS, TURNER & DAUGHTRY, P.A.

Established in 1969

950 MAIN STREET

LILLINGTON, NORTH CAROLINA 27546

Telephone: 910-814-1111

Fax: 910-891-1198

Mailing Address: 804 West Broad Street, Dunn, NC 28334

General Criminal and Civil Practice. Traffic Court, Personal Injury, Real Estate, Probate, Family and Corporation Law. Trials in all Courts.

REPRESENTATIVE CLIENTS: Amerigas Propane/Petrolane; Warren Oil Co.; Godwin Manufacturing, Inc.; Time Warner Cablevision; Police Benevolent Assn.; Quail Run Homes, Inc.; Cape Fear Quail Unlimited, Inc.; Alternate Harnett County IVD Child Support Enforcement Agency; New Century Bank Corp.
APPROVED ATTORNEYS FOR: Lawyers Title Insurance Corp.; Investors Title Insurance Co.; Farmers Home Administration; Federal Land Bank of Columbia.
REFERENCES: New Century Bank; Central Carolina Bank.

(For complete biographical data on all personnel, see Professional Biographies at Dunn, North Carolina)

JESSE W. JONES

700 SOUTH 8TH STREET
LILLINGTON, NORTH CAROLINA 27546
Telephone: 910-814-2661
Fax: 910-814-3709
Email: jessejoneslaw@yahoo.com
URL: http://www.jessejoneslaw.com

Criminal Law, Felonies, Misdemeanors, Murder, Manslaughter, Parole and Probation, Sex Crimes, Capital Offenses, Personal Injury, Automobile Accidents and Injuries, Wrongful Death, Family Law, Child Custody, Divorce, Alimony, Spousal Support, Traffic Violations, Driving While Intoxicated.

JESSE W. JONES, born Fuquay-Varina, North Carolina, May 14, 1964; admitted to bar, 1994, North Carolina. *Education:* North Carolina State University (B.S., Zoology, 1990); Campbell University (J.D., 1994). *Member:* North Carolina Bar Association. ***PRACTICE AREAS:*** Criminal Law; Felonies; Misdemeanors; Murder; Manslaughter; Parole and Probation; Sex Crimes; Capital Offenses; Personal Injury; Automobile Accidents and Injuries; Wrongful Death; Family Law; Child Custody; Divorce; Alimony; Spousal Support; Traffic Violations; Driving While Intoxicated.

KELLY & WEST, P.A.

Established in 1982
900 S. MAIN STREET
P.O. BOX 1118
LILLINGTON, NORTH CAROLINA 27546
Telephone: 910-893-8183
Toll Free: 1-800-936-3133
Fax: 910-893-5814
Email: info@kelly-west.com
URL: http://www.kelly-westlaw.com

Personal Injury and Wrongful Death Litigation, Automobile Negligence, Medical Negligence, Workers Compensation, Trials and Appeals, Real Estate, Wills, Traffic and DWI Law.

FIRM PROFILE: Kelly & West was founded in 1982 by Reggie Kelly and Thomas West, former classmates and graduates of Campbell University School of Law. David Lewis became associated in 1995. Our primary areas of concentration are Personal Injury and Wrongful Death Litigation, Criminal Defense and Real Estate Loans and Transactions.

REGINALD B. KELLY, born Erwin, North Carolina, November 27, 1950; admitted to bar, 1981, North Carolina, U.S. Tax Court and U.S. Supreme Court. *Education:* North Carolina State University (B.S., magna cum laude, 1976); Campbell University (J.D., cum laude, 1981). *Member:* Harnett County, North Carolina and American Bar Associations; North Carolina State Bar; North Carolina Academy of Trial Lawyers; The Association of Trial Lawyers of America. [North Carolina National Guard, 1970-1976, Sp-5]. ***PRACTICE AREAS:*** Real Estate; Criminal Law; Wills. ***Email:*** reggie@kelly-west.com

J. THOMAS WEST, born Dunn, North Carolina, April 8, 1951; admitted to bar, 1981, North Carolina, U.S. District Court, Eastern District of North Carolina and U.S. Court of Appeals, Fourth Circuit; 1984, U.S. Supreme Court; 1999, U.S. Court of Federal Claims. *Education:* Campbell University (B.B.A., magna cum laude, 1973; J.D., cum laude, 1981). Phi Kappa Phi; Phi Alpha Delta. Recipient: Corpus Juris Secundum Award; American Jurisprudence Book Awards. *Member:* Harnett County and North Carolina Bar Associations; North Carolina State Bar; North Carolina Academy of Trial Lawyers; The Association of Trial Lawyers of America. (Managing Partner). ***PRACTICE AREAS:*** Personal Injury; Automobile Accidents and Injuries; Slip and Fall; Premises Liability; Dog Bites; Wrongful Death; Medical Malpractice; Workers Compensation. ***Email:*** thomas@kelly-west.com

ASSOCIATE

J. DAVID LEWIS, born Jefferson, North Carolina, December 10, 1961; admitted to bar, 1988, North Carolina and U.S. District Court, Middle District of North Carolina; 1991, U.S. District Court, Western District of North Carolina. *Education:* University of North Carolina at Chapel Hill (B.A., 1984); Wake Forest University (J.D., 1988). *Member:* Harnett County and North Carolina Bar Associations; North Carolina State Bar; Lincoln Forum; North Carolina Academy of Trial Lawyers; The Association of Trial Lawyers of America. ***PRACTICE AREAS:*** Civil Litigation; Insurance; Appellate Practice; Personal Injury; Workers Compensation. ***Email:*** david@kelly-west.com

APPROVED ATTORNEYS FOR: Investors Title Ins. Co.; First Title Ins. Co.; Network Title Ins. Co.; Cape Fear Farm Credit; Chicago Title Ins. Co.; Statewide Title Ins. Co.
REFERENCES: First Bank; J. E. Worable & Sons, Inc.; B B & T; RBC Century.

STEWART LAW FIRM

LILLINGTON, NORTH CAROLINA

(See Dunn)

Personal Injury, Automobile Accidents, Criminal Law, Traffic Violations, Real Estate, Corporate Law, Family Law, Divorce, Child Custody and Child Support.

DAVID M. BLACK, P.A.

333 EAST MAIN STREET, SUITE 105
P.O. BOX 2000
LINCOLNTON, NORTH CAROLINA 28093
Telephone: 704-732-1778
Fax: 704-732-9927
Email: dblack@davidmblack.com
URL: http://www.dblacklaw.com

DAVID M. BLACK, born Chatsworth, Georgia, February 18, 1957; admitted to bar, 1983, North Carolina; 1984, U.S. District Court, Western District of North Carolina. *Education:* Appalachian State University (B.S., Criminal Justice, 1979); University of North Carolina at Chapel Hill (J.D., 1983). Former Commander, Lincolnton Unit, North Carolina National Guard. *Member:* Lincoln County, North Carolina and American Bar Associations; North Carolina State Bar. ***PRACTICE AREAS:*** Traffic Violations; Driving While Intoxicated; Wills; Probate; Estate Administration. ***Email:*** dblack@davidmblack.com

J. BRYAN ELLIOTT

LINCOLNTON, NORTH CAROLINA

(See Hickory)

Bankruptcy, Social Security Disability.

J. BOYCE GARLAND, JR.

LINCOLNTON, NORTH CAROLINA

(See Gastonia)

General Civil and Criminal Practice in all Courts. Corporations, Business, Estate Planning and Administration, Probate, Real Estate, Personal Injury, Automobile Accidents, and Criminal.

GRAY, LAYTON, KERSH, SOLOMON, SIGMON, FURR & SMITH, P.A.

LINCOLNTON, NORTH CAROLINA

(See Gastonia)

General Civil Trial Practice, Arbitration, Corporation Law, Construction Law, Real Estate Law, Mediation, Municipal and Zoning Law, Mergers and Acquisitions, Bankruptcy, Family, Tax, Estate Planning and Probate Law, Personal Injury Law, Traffic, Professional Sports Representation, Community Association Law.

HUFFSTETLER LAW OFFICES

LINCOLNTON, NORTH CAROLINA

(See Cherryville)

General Practice, Real Estate, Loan Closings, Estates, Wills, Criminal Law, Traffic, Uncontested Divorce, Separation Agreements, Business Law.

THE JONAS LAW FIRM, P.L.L.C.

Established in 1913
210 EAST MAIN STREET
P.O. BOX 38
LINCOLNTON, NORTH CAROLINA 28092
Telephone: 704-735-1423
Fax: 704-735-1490
URL: http://www.jonaslawfirm.com

General Civil and Criminal Litigation Practice. Corporation, Banking, Real Estate, Probate Estate Planning, Elder and Family Law.

MEMBERS OF FIRM

CHARLES A. JONAS (1876-1955)

CHARLES R. JONAS (1904-1988)

RICHARD E. JONAS, born Raleigh, North Carolina, March 18, 1943; admitted to bar, 1968, North Carolina. *Education:* University of North Carolina (B.A., 1965); Duke University (J.D., 1968). ***PRACTICE AREAS:*** Residential and Commercial Real Estate; Corporations; Estates and Probate. ***Email:*** rjonas@jonaslaw.com

JOHNATHAN L. RHYNE, JR., born Charlotte, North Carolina, June 6, 1955; admitted to bar, 1981, North Carolina. *Education:* Davidson College (B.A., 1977); Campbell University (J.D., 1981). Phi Alpha Delta. Member, North Carolina House of Representatives, 1985-1992. House Minority Leader, 1988-1992. Chairman, 1986-1993, North Carolina Courts Commission. Member, Advisory Budget Commission, 1989-1990. Member, Commission for the Future of Justice and the Courts in North Carolina, 1995-1996. (Board Certified Specialist in Family Law, North Carolina State Board of Legal Specialization). ***PRACTICE AREAS:*** Family Law; Civil Litigation. ***Email:*** jrhyne@jonaslaw.com

W. TODD POMEROY, born Waynesboro, Virginia, November 9, 1970; admitted to bar, 1996, North Carolina. *Education:* Vanderbilt University (B.S., 1993); Cumberland School of Law of Samford University (J.D., 1996). ***PRACTICE AREAS:*** Criminal Law; Felonies; Misdemeanors; Civil Litigation; Domestic Law; Traffic Offense; Child Support; Personal Injury. ***Email:*** tpomeroy@jonaslaw.com

REBECCA J. POMEROY, born Gastonia, North Carolina, March 29, 1971; admitted to bar, 1996, North Carolina. *Education:* University of North Carolina at Chapel Hill (B.A., 1992); Cumberland School of Law of Samford University (J.D., 1996). Attorney for the Lincoln County Department of Social Services in Child Protective Services and Adult Protective Services Divisions. ***PRACTICE AREAS:*** Residential Real Estate; Estate Planning; Probate; Elder Law; Juvenile Law. ***Email:*** rpomeroy@jonaslaw.com

OF COUNSEL

HARVEY A. JONAS, JR., born Lincolnton, North Carolina, May 12, 1919; admitted to bar, 1942, North Carolina. *Education:* University of North Carolina (A.B., 1940; J.D., 1942). Charter Member, General Practice Hall of Fame, 1989. ***PRACTICE AREAS:*** Estates; Probate; Elder Law. ***Email:*** hjonas@jonaslaw.com

(This Listing Continued)

THE JONAS LAW FIRM, P.L.L.C., Lincolnton—Continued

ASSOCIATE

JEREMY S. WILSON, born Brevaro, North Carolina, May 5, 1978; admitted to bar, 2003, North Carolina. *Education:* Methodist College (B.S., 2000); Campbell University (J.D., 2003). Phi Alpha Delta. *Member:* North Carolina State Bar. ***PRACTICE AREAS:*** Family Law; Domestic Partnerships; Civil Litigation; Criminal Law. ***Email:*** jwilson@jonaslaw.com

REPRESENTATIVE CLIENTS: First Federal Savings Bank; Aburnethy Chevrolet, Inc.; Lincoln Health Systems; Kings Office Supply, Inc.
APPROVED ATTORNEYS FOR: Lawyers Title Insurance Corp.; Investors Title Co.
REFERENCES: First Citizens Bank & Trust Co.; Bank of America.

KENNEDY & WULFHORST, P.A.

LINCOLNTON, NORTH CAROLINA

(See Denver)

Residential and Commercial Real Estate, Corporate and Business Law, Wills, Probate, Estate Planning, Domestic and Family Law, Criminal Law, Traffic, Juvenile, Divorce, Collections.

PATTERSON AND ADAMS PLLC

LINCOLNTON, NORTH CAROLINA

(See Concord)

Personal Injury, Automobile Accidents, Wrongful Deaths, Workers Compensation, Medical Malpractice.

SINGLETARY LAW FIRM, PLLC

LINCOLNTON, NORTH CAROLINA

(See Cornelius)

Immigration, Sports and Entertainment, Business Law, Business Formation, Buying and Selling a Business.

LAW OFFICE OF LYNN BROADWAY WILKIE

214 EAST MAIN STREET
LINCOLNTON, NORTH CAROLINA 28054
Telephone: 704-732-7417
Fax: 704-732-7418
URL: http://www.wilkielawfirm.com
Email: lynn@wilkie.net
URL: http://www.wilkielaw.com

LYNN BROADWAY WILKIE, born Shelby, North Carolina, September 21, 1965; admitted to bar, 1993, North Carolina; 1996, U.S. District Court, Eastern District of North Carolina. *Education:* Appalachian State University (B.S., Criminal Justice, 1987; B.A., English, 1987); Wake Forest University (J.D., 1993). District Attorney, Lincoln and Cleveland County, 1998-2004. *Member:* Lincoln County and Cleveland County Bar Associations; North Carolina State Bar. ***PRACTICE AREAS:*** Criminal Law; Traffic Violations; Driving While Intoxicated; Drug Crimes. ***Email:*** lynn@wilkie.net

YELTON, FARFOUR, McCARTNEY, LUTZ & CRAIG, P.A.

LINCOLNTON, NORTH CAROLINA

(See Shelby)

General Practice. Corporation, Estate Planning, and Personal Injury Law. Trial and appellate practice in all courts. Creditors" Rights and Bankruptcy law. Domestic and Family Law.

DAVIS, STURGES & TOMLINSON

Established in 1968
DSS BUILDING
101 NORTH CHURCH STREET
P.O. DRAWER 708
LOUISBURG, NORTH CAROLINA 27549
Telephone: 919-496-2137
Telecopier: 919-496-6291
Email: name@dstattys.com
URL: http://www.louisburglawyers.com

General Civil and Criminal Trial Practice in State and Federal Courts. Estate and Probate, Real Estate and Corporation Law. Personal Injury, Automobile Accidents, Truck Accidents, Wrongful Death, Traffic Violations, DWI, Litigation, Land Condemnation.

MEMBERS OF FIRM

CHARLES M. DAVIS, born Louisburg, North Carolina, January 3, 1936; admitted to bar, 1961, North Carolina. *Education:* University of North Carolina (A.B., 1958); Wake Forest College (LL.B., 1961). Phi Alpha Delta; Phi Alpha Theta. Franklin County Attorney, 1963-1968. Solicitor, Franklin County Court, 1966-1968. Certified Mediator. *Member:* Franklin County, 9th Judicial District, North Carolina and American (Member, House of Delegates, 1996-2000) Bar Associations; North Carolina State Bar (Counselor, 1986-1992; Vice President, 1993; President-Elect, 1994; President, 1995); North Carolina Trial Lawyers Association; North Carolina Judicial Standards Commission, 1996-2002.

AUBREY S. TOMLINSON, JR., born Laurinburg, North Carolina, July 28, 1943; admitted to bar, 1968, North Carolina. *Education:* Wake Forest College (B.A., 1965); University of North Carolina (J.D., 1968). Assistant Solicitor, Ninth Solicitorial District, 1971-1972. County Attorney, Franklin County, 1988-1992. Attorney for Town of Youngsville. President, 9th Judicial Bar, 2003. *Member:* Franklin County and North Carolina Bar Associations; North Carolina State Bar; North Carolina Trial Lawyers Association. ***PRACTICE AREAS:*** Real Estate; Civil Litigation; Criminal Law; Business Law; Personal Injury; Municipal Law. ***Email:*** ptomlinson@davissturgestomlinson.com

C. BOYD STURGES, III, born Henderson, North Carolina, January 30, 1969; admitted to bar, 1995, North Carolina. *Education:* Wake Forest University (B.A., cum laude, 1991; J.D., 1995). Phi Alpha Theta. Recipient, Am-Jur Award-Constitutional Law. Treasurer/Secretary, Ninth Judicial Bar, 1998. Town Councilman, Louisburg, North Carolina, 2001—. Attorney, Franklin School Board. *Member:* Franklin County and North Carolina Bar Associations; North Carolina State Bar; North Carolina Trial Lawyers Association. ***PRACTICE AREAS:*** Real Estate; Criminal Law; Civil Litigation; Business Law; Domestic Law; Personal Injury; Land Condemnation; Buying and Selling of Businesses; Probate; Wills; Estate Administration; Traffic Violations; Driving While Intoxicated; DUI/DWI. ***Email:*** bsturges@dstattys.com

REPRESENTATIVE CLIENTS: Toney Lumber Co., Inc.; Franklin County Board of Education; Pruitt Lumber Co.; IMD-European, LIP; Lawyer's Mutual Insurance Co.; Arbor Recycling and Equipment Co., Inc.; Town of Youngsville; Joyner Manufacturing Inc.; Richards Oil Company; United County Realty.
APPROVED ATTORNEYS FOR: Lawyers Title Insurance Corp.; Fidelity National Title Insurance Co.; First Citizens Bank & Trust Co.; Branch Bank & Trust Co.; In Venture Title Ins. Co.; Statewide Title Ins. Co.; Investors Title Insurance Co.; Chicago Title Insurance Co.
REFERENCES: First Citizens Bank & Trust Co.; Branch Bank & Trust Co.

JOLLY, WILLIAMSON & WILLIAMSON

Established in 1879
106 EAST NASH STREET
LOUISBURG, NORTH CAROLINA 27549
Telephone: 919-496-4152
Fax: 919-496-5270
Email: jollywilliamson@aol.com

General Practice in State and Federal Courts. Trials. Wills, Trusts, Probate, Civil, Criminal, DWI, Real Estate, Personal Injury Law, Automobile Accidents and Wrongful Death.

JOHN P. WILLIAMSON, JR., born Louisburg, North Carolina, 1943; admitted to bar, 1969, North Carolina. *Education:* University of North Carolina (A.B., 1966); University of Tennessee (J.D., 1969). Town Attorney, Franklinton, 1986—. *Member:* North Carolina Bar Association; North Carolina State Bar.

BENJAMIN N. WILLIAMSON, III, born Franklinton, North Carolina, 1943; admitted to bar, 1969, North Carolina. *Education:* University of North Carolina (B.S., 1967); University of Tennessee (J.D., 1969). Attorney, Franklinton City Board of Education, 1979-1992. Town Attorney, Bunn, 1987—. *Member:* North Carolina Bar Association; North Carolina State Bar; North Carolina Academy of Trial Lawyers.

APPROVED ATTORNEYS FOR: Lawyers Title Insurance Corporation; AMI Title Insurance Company; First Citizens Bank and Trust Company; BB & T; Stockton, White and Co.; Federal Land Bank of Columbia; American Title Insurance Co.; First Title Insurance Co.; Home Savings & Loan Assn.; Transamerica Title Insurance Co.; Investors Title Insurance Co.; Chicago Title Ins. Co.
REPRESENTATIVE CLIENTS: First Citizens Bank and Trust Company; Farm Bureau Insurance Co.; Edwards and Foster Fertilizer, Inc.; Champion International Corp.; Federal Land Bank of Columbia; Canal Wood Corp.; Town of Bunn; Town of Franklinton; Louisburg Hardwood, Inc; Tar River Hardwood, Inc.; Mack Cooper Enterprises; Brown & Gupton Co., Inc.

LAW OFFICES OF WILLIAM S. BRITT

106 W. FIFTH STREET
LUMBERTON, NORTH CAROLINA 28358
Telephone: 910-739-7141
Fax: 910-739-7906
URL: http://www.wsbritt.com

Medical Malpractice, Wrongful Death, Automobile Accidents and Injuries, Truck Accidents, Motorcycle Accidents, Construction Accidents, Dog Bites and Personal Injury Law.

WILLIAM S. BRITT, born Lumberton, North Carolina, December 4, 1954; admitted to bar, 1981, North Carolina. *Education:* Wake Forest University (B.A., 1977; J.D., 1980). *Member:* North Carolina and American Bar Associations; North Carolina State Bar; North Carolina Academy of Trial Lawyers; The Association of Trial Lawyers of America.

R. GREGG EDWARDS

LUMBERTON, NORTH CAROLINA

(See Fayetteville)

Bankruptcy (including Small Business), Personal Injury, Automobile Accidents and Injuries, Workers Compensation, Back Injuries, Medical Malpractice, Civil Litigation.

GORDON, HORNE, HICKS AND FLOYD, P.A.

LUMBERTON, NORTH CAROLINA

(See Laurinburg)

General, Civil and Criminal Trial Practice, Probate, Corporation, Real Estate, Personal Injury, Estate Planning, Social Security Disability, Workers' Compensation and Family Law.

GRIFFIN LAW OFFICE

LUMBERTON, NORTH CAROLINA

(See Red Springs)

Abuse and Neglect, Juvenile Law, Real Estate Transactions, Traffic, Traffic Violations, DWI, Criminal Law, Domestic and Family Law.

GREG JONES & ASSOCIATES, P.A.

LUMBERTON, NORTH CAROLINA

(See Wilmington)

Personal Injury, Automobile Accidents, Brain Injury, Motorcycle Accidents, Wrongful Death, Medical Malpractice, Spinal Cord Injuries, Drug and Medical Device Litigation, Pharmacists Liability, Head Injuries, Products Liability, Medical and Nursing Home Negligence, Workers Compensation, Toxic Torts, Nursing Home Abuse, Stock Fraud.

J.B. ROUSE III & ASSOCIATES

LUMBERTON, NORTH CAROLINA

(See Fayetteville)

Personal Injury, Automobile Accidents, Serious Accidents, Lemon Law, Traffic Violations, DWI, Wills, Probate, Trusts and Estates, Business Litigation.

C. CHRISTOPHER SMITH, P.A.

Established in 1973

4850 FAYETTEVILLE ROAD, SUITE C
LUMBERTON, NORTH CAROLINA 28358
Telephone: 910-738-8131
Fax: 910-738-6078
Email: smithlaw@carolina.net
URL: http://www.cchristophersmith.com

Real Estate, Bankruptcy, Wills, Estate Administration, Business Law, Corporation Law, Limited Liability Company Law, Partnership Law, General Practice.

FIRM PROFILE: C. Christopher Smith has been serving clients for over 30 years throughout Robeson and its contiguous counties. The firm engages in a General Civil Trial Practice.

C. CHRISTOPHER SMITH, born Havre de Grace, Maryland, September 30, 1946; admitted to bar, 1972, North Carolina; 1988, U.S. District Court, Eastern, Middle and Western Districts of North Carolina and U.S. Court of Appeals, Fourth Circuit. *Education:* University of North Carolina—Chapel Hill (A.B., 1969); University of Mississippi and University of South Carolina Law School (J.D., 1972). Phi Alpha Delta. *Member:* Robeson County (President, 1985), North Carolina and American Bar Associations; North Carolina State Bar. ***PRACTICE AREAS:*** Real Estate; Bankruptcy; Wills; Estate Administration; Business Law; Corporate Law; Limited Liability Company Law; Partnership Law; General Practice. ***Email:*** smithlaw@carolina.net

APPROVED ATTORNEY FOR: Chicago Title Insurance Co.; Lawyerstitle; Investors Title; Statewide Title; Network Title.

J. RICHARD TOWNSEND

Established in 1999

SALEM SQUARE PROFESSIONAL PARK
4904 FAYETTEVILLE ROAD
LUMBERTON, NORTH CAROLINA 28358
Telephone: 910-739-7518
1-800-542-2664
Fax: 910-671-8433
URL: http://www.lawyers.com/richardtownsend

Personal Injury, Automobile Accidents, Truck Accidents, Motorcycle Accidents, Bicycle Accidents, Dog Bites, Hospital Negligence, Nursing Home Negligence, Criminal Law, Misdemeanors, Assaults, Traffic Violations, Driving While Intoxicated, Estate Planning, Wills, Trusts and Estates.

FIRM PROFILE: Our firm concentrates in the areas of personal injury, traffic offenses and estates.

J. RICHARD TOWNSEND, born Lumberton, North Carolina, September 29, 1952; admitted to bar, 1978, North Carolina; 1979, U.S. District Court, Eastern District of North Carolina. *Education:* East Carolina University (B.A., 1975); Wake Forest University (J.D., 1978). District Attorney, 16-B District, 1989-1994. *Member:* North Carolina Bar Association; North Carolina State Bar; North Carolina Trial Lawyers Association. ***PRACTICE AREAS:*** Personal Injury; Automobile Accidents and Injuries; Truck Accidents; Motorcycle Accidents; Bicycle Accidents; Dog Bites; Hospital Negligence; Nursing Home Abuse and Neglect; Criminal Law; Misdemeanors; Assault and Battery; Traffic Violations; Driving While Intoxicated; Probate; Estate Planning; Wills; Trusts and Estates.

FOLGER & TUCKER, P.A.

Established in 1951

117 EAST MURPHY STREET
MADISON, NORTH CAROLINA 27025
Telephone: 336-548-2309
Fax: 336-548-1751
Email: fthlaw@earthlink.net

General Civil and Criminal Practice in State Courts. Personal Injury, Automobile Accidents, Wrongful Death, Workers Compensation, Real Estate, Family Law, Divorce, Child Custody, Traffic Violations, Corporations and Probate Law.

(This Listing Continued)

MEMBERS OF FIRM

ALONZO D. FOLGER, JR. (1922-2000)

BENJAMIN F. TUCKER, born Lynchburg, Virginia, May 11, 1951; admitted to bar, 1976, North Carolina. *Education:* University of North Carolina (A.B., 1973); University of Richmond (J.D., 1976). Phi Delta Phi. *Member:* Rockingham County (President, 1983-1984) and North Carolina Bar Associations; 17-A Judicial District (Vice President, 1983-1994; President, 1997) Bar Association; North Carolina State Bar; North Carolina Academy of Trial Lawyers; Association of Trial Lawyers of America. ***PRACTICE AREAS:*** Personal Injury; Workers Compensation; Corporate; Traffic Violations; Real Estate. ***Email:*** fthlaw@erthlink.net

REPRESENTATIVE CLIENTS: Branch Banking and Trust Co.; Guaranteed Systems, Inc.; McMichael Mills, Inc; FNB Southeast; Western Rockingham Properties; Riverview Commons, LLC.
APPROVED ATTORNEYS FOR: First American Title Insurance Co.; Investors Title Insurance Co.; Federal Land Bank of Columbia; Branch Banking and Trust Co.; First Citizens Bank; Central Carolina Bank; FNB Southeast.
REFERENCES: Branch Banking and Trust Company, Madison, North Carolina; FNB Southeast, Madison, North Carolina.

THE MOORE LAW FIRM, P.C.

Established in 2004

6983 OLD MANNS HARBOR ROAD
P.O. BOX 150
MANNS HARBOR, NORTH CAROLINA 27953
Telephone: 252-473-9777
Fax: 252-473-9801
Email: rondamoore@charter.net
URL: http://www.mooreouterbankslaw.com

Real Estate, Corporate Law.

FIRM PROFILE: Established in 2004, The Moore Law Firm, P.C., is dedicated to providing innovative legal services with a traditional flair to real estate and corporate clients. The foundation of this firm is service, value, quality and communication.

RONDA G. MOORE, born Huntington, West Virginia, October 24, 1968; admitted to bar, 1994, West Virginia; 1999, North Carolina. *Education:* Washington & Lee University (B.S., 1990); Ohio Northern University (J.D., 1994). Order of Barristers. Moot Court, Administrative Justice, 1993-1994. Faculty, College of the Albemarle, Business Law, 2001-2002. *Member:* North Carolina and American Bar Associations; West Virginia State Bar; First Judicial District and North Carolina State Bars. ***PRACTICE AREAS:*** Real Estate; Corporate Law. ***Email:*** rondamoore@charter.net

ALDRIDGE, SEAWELL, SPENCE & FELTHOUSEN, L.L.P.

Established in 1977

805 NORTH MAIN HIGHWAY
P.O. BOX 339
MANTEO, NORTH CAROLINA 27954
Telephone: 252-473-3484
Facsimile: 252-473-2046
URL: http://www.lawyers.com/aldridgeseawellfelthousen

General Civil and Criminal Trial Practice. Real Estate, Wills and Probate, Corporate, Domestic Relations Law, Family, Divorce, Child Custody, Personal Injury, Automobile Accidents and Wrongful Death.

MEMBERS OF FIRM

GEORGE IRVIN ALDRIDGE (Retired)

CHRISTOPHER L. SEAWELL, born Greensboro, North Carolina, October 12, 1946; admitted to bar, 1971, North Carolina, U.S. District Court, Eastern District of North Carolina, U.S. Court of Appeals, Fourth Circuit and U.S. Supreme Court. *Education:* University of North Carolina (B.S., 1968; J.D., 1971). Chairman, Board of Trustees for the College of the Albemarle. *Member:* North Carolina and American Bar Associations; North Carolina State Bar; North Carolina Academy of Trial Lawyers. ***PRACTICE AREAS:*** General Civil Litigation Practice; Real Estate Law; Corporate Law; Estate Planning; Probate Law. ***Email:*** cseawell@usaairnet.net

W. MARK SPENCE, born Elizabeth City, North Carolina, November 2, 1951; admitted to bar, 1979, North Carolina, U.S. District Court, Eastern and Middle Districts of North Carolina, U.S. Court of Appeals, Fourth Circuit and U.S. Supreme Court. *Education:* Atlantic Christian College (B.S., 1973); Campbell University (J.D., 1979). *Member:* North Carolina State Bar; North Carolina Bar Association; North Carolina Academy of Trial Lawyers. ***PRACTICE AREAS:*** Family; Domestic Law; Personal Injury; Wrongful Death; Criminal Law. ***Email:*** mspence@usaairnet.net

KRIS J. FELTHOUSEN, born Fort Belvoir, Virginia, April 7, 1966; admitted to bar, 1992, North Carolina. *Education:* University of Virginia (B.A., 1989); George Mason University School of Law (J.D, 1992). Member, Thomas More Society. Past President, First Flight Rotary Club. *Member:* North Carolina (Litigation Section), First Judicial District (Officer) and American Bar Associations; North Carolina Academy of Trial Lawyers. ***PRACTICE AREAS:*** Criminal Defense; Civil Litigation. ***Email:*** kfelthousen@usaairnet.net

ASSOCIATES

PADDISON P. HUDSPETH, born Winston-Salem, North Carolina, September 18, 1979; admitted to bar, 2004, North Carolina. *Education:* University of North Carolina

(This Listing Continued)

ALDRIDGE, SEAWELL, SPENCE & FELTHOUSEN, L.L.P., Manteo—Continued

(B.A., 2001; J.D., 2004). *Member:* North Carolina (Member, Young Lawyers Division) and American Bar Associations; North Carolina State Bar. ***PRACTICE AREAS:*** Civil Litigation; Real Estate; Criminal Defense. ***Email:*** phudspeth@beachlink.com

THOMAS P. ROUTTEN, born Newport News, Virginia, June 5, 1978; admitted to bar, 2004, North Carolina. *Education:* University of Virginia (B.A., 2000); University of Richmond (J.D., 2003). *Member:* North Carolina (Member, Young Lawyers Division) and American Bar Associations; North Carolina State Bar. ***PRACTICE AREAS:*** Criminal Defense; Domestic Relations; General Practice. ***Email:*** troutten@beachlink.com

REPRESENTATIVE CLIENTS: Manteo Motel Corp.; Davis Boat Works, Inc.; Roanoke Island Historical Association; Midgett Realty, Inc.; Outer Beaches Realty, Inc.; Wanchese Fish Co., Inc; Outer Banks Chrysler; Bruruh Bank & Trust Co.; Spencer Yachts; Bayliss Boatworks, Kellogg Supply Co.; Ace Hardware.
REFERENCES: East Carolina Bank; RBC Centura; Cooperative Savings Bank; Wachovia Bank.

ROY A. ARCHBELL, JR.

MANTEO, NORTH CAROLINA

(See Kitty Hawk)

General Civil Trial Practice in State and Federal Courts. Family, Personal Injury, Collection, Corporate, Construction, Insurance, Real Estate, Domestic Relations, Divorce.

RONALD E. DEVEAU, P.C.

MANTEO, NORTH CAROLINA

(See Nags Head)

General Civil and Trial Practice in State and Federal Courts, Personal Injury and Negligence, Workers Compensation, Family Law, Business Torts, Estates.

HORNTHAL, RILEY, ELLIS & MALAND, L.L.P.

MANTEO, NORTH CAROLINA

(See Elizabeth City)

General Trial and Appellate Practice in all Courts. Personal Injury, Products Liability, Professional Malpractice, Corporate, Tax, Bankruptcy, Employment, Education, Criminal, Insurance, Construction, Real Estate, Environmental, Elder, Local Government, Wills and Trusts, Probate and Admiralty Law.

KELLOGG AND EVANS, P.A.

Established in 1931

201 ANANIAS DARE STREET
P.O. BOX 189
MANTEO, NORTH CAROLINA 27954
Telephone: 252-473-2171
Fax: 252-473-1214, 2157
Email: kandelaw@kelloggandevans.com
URL: http://www.lawyers.com/kelloggandevans

General Civil Practice in State Courts, Family Law, Probate, Real Estate, Business Law, Vessel Documentation and Financing, and Estate Planning and Administration.

MEMBERS OF FIRM

MARTIN KELLOGG, JR. (1908-2001)

CHARLES D. EVANS, born Manteo, N.C., October 8, 1944; admitted to bar, 1973, North Carolina. *Education:* University of North Carolina (B.A., 1967; J.D., 1971). Member, North Carolina General Assembly, 1979-1986. Board of Governors, University of North Carolina, 1987-1995. Trustee of the University of North Carolina at Wilmington, Director of the North Carolina Community Foundation and the UNC Coastal Studies Institute. *Member:* North Carolina and American Bar Associations; First Judicial District and North Carolina State Bars. ***PRACTICE AREAS:*** Real Estate; Estates and Probate; Estate Planning; Corporations. ***Email:*** charlese@kelloggandevans.com

ASSOCIATE

SUSAN HARMAN-SCOTT, born Montgomery, Alabama, July 3, 1954; admitted to bar, 1986, North Carolina; 1993, U.S. District Court, Eastern District of North Carolina. *Education:* University of North Carolina-Greensboro (B.A. 1975; M.F.A., 1979); Wake Forest University (J.D., 1986). Member, Moot Court Board. Certified Family Financial Mediator. *Member:* North Carolina and American (Member, Family Law Section, 1987—) Bar Associations; North Carolina State Bar; First Judicial District Bar Association; North Carolina Academy of Trial Lawyers. ***PRACTICE AREAS:*** Family Law; Alternative Dispute Resolution; Civil Litigation; General Practice. ***Email:*** susanhs@kelloggandevans.com

REPRESENTATIVE CLIENTS: RBC Centura Bank; Dare County Department of Social Services; The Island Art Gallery and Christmas Shop, Ltd.; Outer Banks Ventures, Inc.; Nags Head Hammocks, Inc.;Food-A-Rama, Inc.; Wachovia Bank; East Carolina Bank.
APPROVED ATTORNEYS FOR: Lawyers Title Insurance Corp.; Chicago Title Insurance Co.; First Title Insurance Co.; American Title Insurance Co.; Commonwealth Land Title Insurance Co.; Investors Title Insurance Co.; United Title; Title Company of North Carolina, Inc.; Statewide Title Insurance Company.
REFERENCES: RBC Centura Bank; First South Bank; Southern Bank; Bank of America; East Carolina Bank; Cooperative Savings Bank, F.S.B.; Wachovia Bank; Chase Manhattan Mortgage Corporation; Firstmark Mortgage Corp.; Branch Banking and Trust Co.; First Citizens Bank; Wells Fargo Mortgage.

SHARP, MICHAEL, OUTTEN AND GRAHAM

MANTEO, NORTH CAROLINA

(See Kitty Hawk)

General Civil and Criminal Practice, Commercial and Residential Real Estate, Municipal and Administrative, Family and Domestic Relations, Personal Injury, Probate, Banking, Corporations, Traffic, Driving While Intoxicated, Mediation, Arbitration, Ship Documentation, Estate Planning, Elder Law.

VANDEVENTER BLACK LLP

MANTEO, NORTH CAROLINA

(See Kitty Hawk)

Admiralty, Arbitration and Mediation, Aviation, Banking, Bankruptcy and Creditors' Rights, Commercial Transactions, Community Associations, Construction Law, Environmental Law, Estate Planning, General Litigation in State and Federal Courts, Government/Public Contracts, Health Care Law, Immigration Law, International, Intellectual Property, Insurance Defense, Labor and Employment Law, Land Use, Local Government/Municipal Law, Malpractice, Maritime, Mergers and Acquisitions, Products Liability, Public Utilities, Real Estate, Taxation, Technology, Workers' Compensation.

THE VINCENT LAW FIRM, PC

MANTEO, NORTH CAROLINA

(See Southern Shores)

Workers Compensation, Personal Injury, Auto Accidents, Social Security Disability, Wrongful Death and Admiralty Longshores.

WHELESS & WHELESS, PLLC

101 SOUTH VIRGINIA DARE ROAD
P.O. BOX 500
MANTEO, NORTH CAROLINA 27954
Telephone: 252-473-5500
Fax: 252-473-1154
Real Estate Processing Email: whelesslawfirm@earthlink.net
Email: whelesslawfirm@earthlink.net
URL: http://www.whelesslawfirm.com

Columbia, North Carolina Office: 402 Main Street, 27925. Telephone: 252-796-5500. Fax: 252-796-1154.

Traffic Violations, General Practice. Real Estate, Driving While Intoxicated, Civil Litigation, County Government Law, Insurance Defense, Real Estate Development, Residential Real Estate Development, Waterfront Development, Zoning Law, Ship Documentation and Ship Finance and Family Law.

FIRM PROFILE: Wheless & Wheless, PLLC is a general practice law firm with attorneys licensed to practice in state and federal courts. The father/son team strives to provide prompt, personalized service and each is active in professional associations and civic affairs. Located in Manteo, the county seat of Dare County, Wheless & Wheless, PLLC handles a variety of matters throughout Dare, Currituck, Hyde and Tyrrell Counties.

MEMBERS OF FIRM

DWIGHT H. WHELESS, born High Point, North Carolina, November 16, 1940; admitted to bar, 1967, North Carolina. *Education:* University of North Carolina (A.B., 1963; J.D., 1967). Phi Alpha Delta. Member, Order of the Golden Fleece. President, Student Bar Association, University of North Carolina, 1966-1967. County Attorney, Dare County, 1972-1993. Named Outstanding County Attorney by North Carolina County Commissioners, 1977-1978 and 1990-1991. Town Attorney, Columbia, N.C. Attorney, The Albemarle Commission and Albemarle Regional Solid Waste Management Authority. *Member:* North Carolina Bar Association; First Judicial District (President, 1976-1977) and North Carolina State Bars; North Carolina Association of County Attorneys President, 1990-1991). [National Commander, U.S. Civil Air Patrol]. (Also at Columbia Office). ***PRACTICE AREAS:*** Real Estate; Corporate Law; Municipal Law; Wills; Estate Administration; County Government Law. ***Email:*** dhwheless@earthlink.net

W. JAY WHELESS, born Durham, North Carolina, February 19, 1964; admitted to bar, 1989, North Carolina. *Education:* University of North Carolina (A.B., 1986); Campbell University (J.D., 1989). Phi Alpha Delta. Member, The Order of Barristers. Member, 1989 National Trial Advocacy Team, Finalist in Southeastern Region. Vice-President, Student Bar Association, Campbell University, 1988-1989. Attorney, Dare County Tourism Board, 1993—. *Member:* Dare County (Secretary, 1990-1991), North Carolina Bar Association; North Carolina State Bar; Lawyer-Pilots Bar Association. ***PRACTICE AREAS:*** Real Estate; Traffic Violations; Civil Litigation; Insurance Defense. ***Email:*** wjwheless@earthlink.net

---

MATTHEW J. HARDEN, born Louisville, Kentucky, September 15, 1976; admitted to bar, 2002, Kentucky; 2005, North Carolina. *Education:* Old Dominion University (B.S., 1998); Regent University School of Law (J.D., 2002). Secretary, American Bar Association Law Student Division, 2001-2002. *Member:* Kentucky and North Carolina Bar Associations. ***PRACTICE AREAS:*** Civil Litigation; Family Law; Criminal Law. ***Email:*** mattjharden@earthlink.net

REPRESENTATIVE CLIENTS: R.D. Sawyer Motor Co., Inc.; Midgett Realty, Inc.; Dare County Tourism Board; Roanoke Properties Limited Partnership; Pirate's Cove Subdivision; Oregon Inlet Charter Captains Association, Town of Columbia; The Albemarle Commission.

(This Listing Continued)

APPROVED ATTORNEYS FOR: Lawyers Title Insurance Co.; Title Company of North Carolina; Commonwealth Land Title Insurance Co.; Investors' Title Insurance Co.; United Title Insurance Co.; Old Republic Title Insurance Company; Chicago title Insurance Company.

DAMERON, BURGIN & PARKER, P.A.

26 WEST COURT STREET
P.O. DRAWER 1049
MARION, NORTH CAROLINA 28752
Telephone: 828-652-2441
Telecopier: 828-652-9579
Email: dameronburgin@dameronburginlaw.com
URL: http://www.dameronburginlaw.com

General Practice and Litigation in all State and Federal Courts, Medical Malpractice, Municipal Law; Education Law, Health Care, Corporate Law, Insurance, Real Estate, Probate Law, and Professional Liability.

FIRM PROFILE: Dameron, Burgin & Parker, P.A. has its origins in western North Carolina and has evolved through a number of partnerships over the course of more than 70 years. The firm has maintained a general practice throughout its history, and since the 1970's has specialized in the defense of medical malpractice and other professional liability claims. Dameron, Burgin & Parker, P.A. represents a larger number of professional liability insurers than any other firm of its size in North Carolina.

EMERSON P. DAMERON (1909-2000)

CHARLES E. BURGIN, born Marion, North Carolina, December 16, 1938; admitted to bar, 1965, North Carolina; 1975, U.S. Supreme Court. *Education:* University of North Carolina (A.B., 1961); Duke University (LL.B., 1964). Phi Alpha Delta. Law Clerk to: Hon. J. Braxton Craven, Jr. for U.S. District Court, Western District of North Carolina, 1964-1966; U.S. Court of Appeals, 4th Circuit, 1966. Listed: The Best Lawyers in America, 1995—; Legal Elite in North Carolina Litigation, 2004. Solicitor, McDowell County Criminal Court, 1966-1968. City Attorney, Marion, North Carolina, 1969—. *Member:* McDowell County (Past President), North Carolina (Member, Board of Governors, 1982-1985; President, 1993) and American Bar Associations; North Carolina State Bar; North Carolina Association of Defense Attorneys; American Society of Hospital Attorneys; International Society of Barristers. Fellow, American College of Trial Lawyers (State Chair, 1996-1998). ***PRACTICE AREAS:*** Medical Malpractice Defense; Defense Litigation; Hospital Law; Product Liability; Corporate Law; Municipal Law. ***Email:*** cburgin@dameronburginlaw.com

SHARON L. PARKER, born Madison, Wisconsin, March 1, 1959; admitted to bar, 1987, Georgia and North Carolina. *Education:* University of North Carolina (B.A., 1981; J.D., with honors, 1987). Board of Directors: Lawyers Mutual Liability Insurance Company of North Carolina, 1999—; The McDowell Foundation, 2000—; Catawba Valley Legal Services, 1995-2001 (President, 2000-2001). Certified Civil Superior Court Mediator. *Member:* McDowell County, North Carolina (Member, Board of Governors, 1992-1995; Health Law Section Council, 1992-1995 and 2001; Litigation Section Council, 1997-2000; Co-Chair, Commission on the Status of Women in the Legal Profession, 1990-1993) and American Bar Associations; North Carolina State Bar (Advisory Member, Ethics Committee, 1992-1996); State Bar of Georgia; North Carolina Association of Defense Attorneys (Board of Directors, 1997-2000); North Carolina Association of Women Attorneys. ***PRACTICE AREAS:*** Hospital Law; Medical Malpractice Defense; Defense Litigation; Education Law; Municipal Law; Nonprofit and Charitable Organizations; Mediation. ***Email:*** sparker@dameronburginlaw.com

MARGARET A. LORENZ, born Nashua, New Hampshire, November 25, 1967; admitted to bar, 1993, North Carolina. *Education:* College of William & Mary (B.A., 1989); Wake Forest University School of Law (J.D., 1993). Phi Alpha Delta. *Member:* McDowell County, North Carolina and American Bar Associations; North Carolina State Bar; National Academy of Elder Law Attorneys. ***PRACTICE AREAS:*** Contracts; Corporate Law; Guardianship and Conservatorship; Municipal Law; Nonprofit and Charitable Organizations; Probate; Real Estate; Trusts and Estates; Wills. ***Email:*** mlorenz@dameronburginlaw.com

PHILLIP T. JACKSON, born Hendersonville, North Carolina, March 7, 1968; admitted to bar, 1994, North Carolina; 1995, U.S. District Court, Western District of North Carolina; 1999, U.S. Court of Appeals, Fourth Circuit. *Education:* North Carolina State University (B.A., 1991); University of North Carolina at Chapel Hill (J.D., 1994). Member, Holderness Moot Court; National Moot Court Team. The Order of Barristers. With North Carolina Attorneys General's Office, 2000-2001. *Member:* McDowell County and North Carolina Bar Associations; North Carolina State Bar; North Carolina Association of Defense Attorneys; Defense Research Institute. ***REPORTED CASES:*** Suarez v. Wotring, 155 NC App. 20, 573 S.E. 2d. 746 (2002); Pulliam v. Smith, 348 N.C. 616, 501 S.E.2d 898 (1998); Stafford v. Stafford, 133 N.C. App. 163, 515 S.E. 2d 43 (1999), aff'd 351 N.C. 94, 520 S.E. 2d 785 (1999); Glaspy v. Glaspy, 143 N.C. App.782, 545 S.E. 2d 782 (2001); Cantrell v. Wishon, 141 N.C. App. 340, 540 S.E. 2d 804 (2000); Onuska v. Barnwell, 140 N.C. App. 590, 537 S.E. 2d 840 (2000); State v. Smith 139 N.C. App. 209, 533 S.E. 2d 518 (2000); Royce v. Rushco Food Stores, Inc., 139 N.C. App. 322,533 S.E. 2d 284 (2000); Ice v. Ice, 136 N.C. App. 787, 525 S.E. 2d 843 (2000); Alexander v. Quattlebaum, 135 N.C. App. 622, 522 S.E.2d 88 (1999); Lang v. Lang, 132 N.C. App. 580, 512 S.E. 2d 788 (1999); Lang v. Lang, 125 N.C. App. 573, 481 S.E. 2d 280 (1997). ***PRACTICE AREAS:*** Medical Malpractice Defense; Civil Litigation; Corporate Litigation; Appellate Practice; Workers Compensation. ***Email:*** pjackson@dameronburginlaw.com

---

JENNIFER O. JACKSON, born Anderson, South Carolina, September 15, 1968; admitted to bar, 1993, North Carolina. *Education:* Clemson University (B.S., 1990); University of North Carolina (J.D., 1993). Phi Delta Phi. *Member:* McDowell County and North Carolina Bar Associations; North Carolina State Bar. ***PRACTICE AREAS:*** Real Estate; Business Law; Contracts; Employment Law; Local Government Law; Nonprofit and Charitable Organizations; Probate; Trusts and Estates; Wills; School Law. ***Email:*** jjackson@dameronburginlaw.com

AARON G. WALKER, born Asheville, North Carolina, May 8, 1979; admitted to bar, 2004, North Carolina. *Education:* Appalachian State University (B.S., 2001); University of North Carolina at Chapel Hill (J.D., 2004). *Member:* McDowell County and North Carolina Bar Associations; North Carolina State Bar; North Carolina Association of Defense Attorneys; Defense Research Institute. ***PRACTICE AREAS:*** Medical Malpractice Defense; Criminal Defense; Civil Litigation. ***Email:*** awalker@dameronburginlaw.com

COUNSEL FOR: McDowell County Schools; Town of Old Fort, North Carolina; City of Marion, North Carolina; Ford Motor Company; Ford Leasing and Development Company; Hospice of MCDowell County; Coats American; Norfolk Southern Railway Co.; Jefferson-Pilot Insurance Cos.; Security Life & Trust Co.; The McDowell Hospital, Inc.; Marion Machine Co.; North American Van Lines; CSX Transportation; Polk-Rutherford-McDowell District Board of Health; St. Paul Fire and Marine Insurance Company; Medical Mutual Insurance Company of North Carolina; Chubb Specialty; The Aetna Casualty and Surety Co.; The Medical Protective Insurance Company; MAG Mutual Insurance Co.; Lawyers Mutual Liability Insurance Company of North Carolina; Michigan Mutual Insurance Co.; Kentucky Medical Insurance Co.; CNA Insurance Co.; Employers Reinsurance Co.; Western Indemnity Insurance Co.; Integon Insurance Co.; Church Insurance Co.; H.F.I.C. Management Co.; Phico Insurance Co.; Zurich American Insurance Group; AIGTS Insurance; Adventist Hospital System; Allied Claims Administration, Inc.; Professional Underwriters Liability Insurance Co.
APPROVED ATTORNEYS FOR: Lawyers Title Insurance Corp.; Asheville Savings Bank; Farmers Home Administration; Federal Land Bank of Columbia; First Citizens Bank & Trust Company; Chicago Title Insurance Co.; Commonwealth Title Insurance Co.; Wachovia; Bank of America; Stewart Title Insurance Co.; Branch Banking and Trust Co.; Prudential Mortgage Corporation; Fidelity National Title Insurance Company.

GOLDSMITH, GOLDSMITH & DEWS, P.A.

Established in 1979
57 SOUTH MAIN STREET
P.O. BOX 1107
MARION, NORTH CAROLINA 28752
Telephone: 828-652-3000
Fax: 828-652-9196
Email: lawfirm@GoldsmithDews.com
URL: http://www.GoldsmithDews.com

General Trial and Appellate Practice, Civil and Criminal, before all State and Federal Courts. Personal Injury, Workers Compensation, Family, Employment, Real Estate, Probate, Commercial and Constitutional Law.

C. FRANK GOLDSMITH, JR., born Asheville, North Carolina, August 26, 1945; admitted to bar, 1970, North Carolina; 1973, U.S. Court of Appeals, 4th Circuit and U.S. Supreme Court. *Education:* Davidson College (A.B., 1967); Université de Montpellier, Montpellier, France; University of North Carolina (J.D., cum laude, 1970); National Institute for Trial Advocacy (Harvard Teacher Training Program, 1988; National Program Faculty, 1994). Order of the Coif. Associate Editor, North Carolina Law Review, 1969-1970. Senior Lecturing Fellow, Duke University School of Law, 1993-1994. Listed in Best Lawyers in America. *Member:* North Carolina Bar Association (Member, Board of Governors, 1990-1993; Chair, Labor and Employment Law Section, 1986-1987); North Carolina Academy of Trial Lawyers (Member, Board of Governors, 1988-1995). Fellow, American College of Trial Lawyers. [Capt., U.S. Army, JAGC, 1970-1972]. ***LANGUAGES:*** French and Spanish. ***PRACTICE AREAS:*** Commercial Litigation; Personal Injury; Employment Law; Criminal Law; Mediation. ***Email:*** frank@GoldsmithDews.com

JAMES W. GOLDSMITH, born Marion, North Carolina, March 12, 1948; admitted to bar, 1975, North Carolina. *Education:* North Carolina State University (B.S., cum laude, 1970); University of North Carolina (J.D., 1975); National Institute for Trial Advocacy, 1979. *Member:* North Carolina and 29th Judicial District (President, 1990-1991) Bar Associations; North Carolina Academy of Trial Lawyers. [1st Lt., U.S. Army, 1970-1972]. ***PRACTICE AREAS:*** Litigation; Personal Injury; Automobile Accidents and Injuries; Real Estate; Probate. ***Email:*** jim@GoldsmithDews.com

JULIE DEWS, born Albany, Georgia, October 16, 1951; admitted to bar, 1990, North Carolina; 1990, U.S. District Court, Western District of North Carolina. *Education:* University of North Carolina at Asheville (B.A., with distinction, 1974); Northeastern University (J.D., 1990). *Member:* North Carolina Bar Association; North Carolina State Bar; North Carolina Academy of Trial Lawyers. ***PRACTICE AREAS:*** Litigation; Automobile Accidents and Injuries; Personal Injury; Workers Compensation; Social Security. ***Email:*** julie@GoldsmithDews.com

LEAKE & SCOTT

MASHBURN BUILDING
P.O. BOX 451
MARSHALL, NORTH CAROLINA 28753
Telephone: 828-649-3883
Email: harrell_leake@law.com
Asheville, North Carolina Office: 501 BB&T Building, 28801. Telephone: 828-253-3661.

General Practice and Trial in all Courts. Interstate Commerce, Insurance, Corporation, Real Estate, Governmental, Medical Malpractice, Personal Injury, Taxation Law.

LARRY B. LEAKE, born Asheville, North Carolina, May 19, 1950; admitted to bar, 1974, North Carolina and U.S. District Court, Western District of North Carolina; 1979, U.S. Court of Appeals, Fourth Circuit and U.S. Supreme Court. *Education:* University of North Carolina (B.A., 1972; J.D., 1974). Phi Beta Kappa. Recipient, Order of the Long Leaf Pine, presented by Governor James B. Hunt, 1980, 2000. Attorney, Madison County Board of Commissioners, 1976-1994, 1998—. Attorney, Madison County Board of Education, 1976-1987. Attorney: Town of Hot Springs, 1976-1989, 1991—; Town of Mars Hill, 1994—; Town of Marshall, 1997—. Member: North Carolina State Goals and Policy Board, 1978-1985; North Carolina State Senate, 1979-1981; North Carolina Commission on the Future, 1981-1983. North Carolina State Board of Elections, Member, 1993—;

(This Listing Continued)

LEAKE & SCOTT, Marshall—Continued

Chairman, 1997—. Board, Blue Ridge Mental Health, Member, 1999-2001. Mars Hill College Board of Advisors, Member, 1992—, Chairman, 2001-2004. *Member:* Buncombe County (Secretary, 1975-1976), North Carolina and American Bar Associations; North Carolina State Bar; North Carolina Association of Defense Attorneys. ***PRACTICE AREAS:*** Civil Defense; Governmental Law; Medical Malpractice; Personal Injury; Wrongful Death. ***Email:*** leakeandscott@bellsouth.net

(For complete biographical data on all personnel, see Professional Biographies at Asheville, North Carolina)

CURTIS ALAN SLUDER

MARSHALL, NORTH CAROLINA

(See Asheville)

Criminal Law, Traffic Violations, Driving While Intoxicated, Expunction.

JAMES H. CARTER

131 MATTHEWS STATION STREET, SUITE 2C
MATTHEWS, NORTH CAROLINA 28105
Telephone: 704-844-8926
Fax: 704-844-8936
Email: jamescarterlaw@alltel.net
Mailing Address: P.O. Box 2638, Matthews, NC 28206

Construction Law, Personal Injury.

JAMES H. CARTER, born Charlotte, North Carolina, March 11, 1946; admitted to bar, 1979, North Carolina and U.S. District Court, Western District of North Carolina; 1982, U.S. Supreme Court. *Education:* University of North Carolina at Charlotte (B.A., 1974); Campbell University (J.D., 1979). *Member:* North Carolina State Bar. ***PRACTICE AREAS:*** Construction Law; Personal Injury.

GARIS LAW FIRM

MATTHEWS, NORTH CAROLINA

(See Charlotte)

Corporate Law, Business Law, Contracts, Collections, Employment, Real Estate, Foreclosure, Trusts and Estates, Wills, Bankruptcy, Debtor and Creditor, Personal Injury, Automobile Accidents, Workers Compensation, Uncontested Divorces, Family Law, Construction, Litigation.

C. WAYNE HEASLEY

MATTHEWS, NORTH CAROLINA

(See Charlotte)

Family Law, Divorce, Alimony, Equitable Distribution, Expungements, Child Support, Child Custody, Visitation Rights, Criminal, Driving While Intoxicated (DWI), Traffic Violations.

SPERRY & TYSON, PLLC

100-E WEST JOHN STREET
MATTHEWS, NORTH CAROLINA 28105
Telephone: 704-845-2600
Fax: 704-845-1339
Mailing Address: P.O. Box 2475, Matthews, NC 28106

Real Estate, Residential Real Estate, Commercial Real Estate, Mortgages, Trusts and Estates, Estate Planning, Business Law, Partnerships, Contracts, Collections, Corporate, Taxation, Bankruptcy.

GEORGE H. SPERRY, JR., born Wilmington, North Carolina, June 20, 1966; admitted to bar, 1999, North Carolina. *Education:* University of North Carolina at Wilmington (B.S., cum laude, in Accounting, 1994); University of North Carolina at Chapel Hill (J.D., 1999). Beta Gamma Sigma. Certified Public Accountant, 1996. *Member:* Mecklenburg County and North Carolina Bar Associations; North Carolina State Bar. ***PRACTICE AREAS:*** Business Formation; Tax Planning; Corporate Law; Estate and Gift Taxation; Real Estate. ***Email:*** gsperry@sperrylaw.net

ADAM M. TYSON, born Stamford, Connecticut, January 22, 1966; admitted to bar, 2002, North Carolina. *Education:* Southern Connecticut State University (B.S., 1991); North Carolina Central University (J.D., 2002). *Member:* North Carolina (Member, Real Property Section) and American Bar Associations; North Carolina Bar. [Army National Guard, 1986-1994]. ***PRACTICE AREAS:*** Real Estate; Estate Planning; Contracts; Litigation. ***Email:*** atyson@sperrylaw.net

VANN LAW FIRM, P.A.

9930 MONROE ROAD, SUITE 103
MATTHEWS, NORTH CAROLINA 28105
Telephone: 704-846-6050
Fax: 704-845-1662
URL: http://www.vannlawfirm.com

Business Law, Corporate, Limited Liability Companies, Small Business, Contracts, Collections, Creditor Rights, Employment, Discrimination, Driving While Intoxicated, Traffic Violations and Wrongful Termination Law.

(This Listing Continued)

MEMBER OF FIRM

CHRISTOPHER M. VANN, born Greensboro, North Carolina, March 3, 1968; admitted to bar, 1993, North Carolina. *Education:* Duke University (B.A., 1990); University of North Carolina at Chapel Hill (J.D., 1993). Law Clerk: Hon. James A. Wynn, Jr., North Carolina Court of Appeals, 1993-1995; Hon. James A. Beaty, Jr., U.S. District Court, 1995-1996. *Member:* North Carolina Bar Association. ***REPORTED CASES:*** Estate of Iteel v. Darby, 500 S.E.2d 759, 1998; Haight v. Travelers/Aetna Casualty, 514 S.E.2d 102, 1999. ***PRACTICE AREAS:*** Business Litigation. ***Email:*** chrisvannatty@alltel.net

THE VIRA LAW FIRM, PA

MEBANE, NORTH CAROLINA

(See Carrboro)

Trusts and Estates, Probate, Wills, Real Estate, Taxation, Business Law.

MARTIN & VAN HOY LLP

10 COURT SQUARE
MOCKSVILLE, NORTH CAROLINA 27028-2415
Telephone: 336-751-2171
Fax: 336-751-1773

General Civil Practice. Trials. Probate, Real Estate, Corporation, Insurance and Personal Injury Law, Criminal Defense, Family Law, Estate Planning, Business Law, Mediation.

MEMBERS OF FIRM

GEORGE W. MARTIN, born Mocksville, North Carolina, April 24, 1927; admitted to bar, 1952, North Carolina. *Education:* Duke University (A.B., 1948; J.D., 1951); Cambridge University, England. Phi Delta Phi. Rotary Foundation Fellow, Cambridge University, England, 1953. *Member:* North Carolina Bar Council. ***PRACTICE AREAS:*** Real Estate.

HENRY P. VAN HOY, II, born Winston-Salem, North Carolina, July 21, 1949; admitted to bar, 1974, North Carolina. *Education:* University of North Carolina (A.B., 1971; J.D., 1974). Town Attorney, Town of Mocksville, 1974—. *Member:* North Carolina Bar Association (President, 2001). ***PRACTICE AREAS:*** Estate Planning; Business Litigation; Civil Litigation. ***Email:*** hvh@mvhlaw.com

SALLY WOMACK SMITH, born Coral Gables, Florida, February 15, 1957; admitted to bar, 1982, North Carolina. *Education:* University of Florida (B.A., 1979); Wake Forest University (J.D., 1982). Court Certified Mediator. ***PRACTICE AREAS:*** Family Law; Civil Litigation; Real Property; Mediation. ***Email:*** sws@mvhlaw.com

ROBERT H. RAISBECK, JR., born Charleston, West Virginia, March 30, 1963; admitted to bar, 1989, North Carolina. *Education:* Wake Forest University (B.A., 1985; J.D., 1989). ***PRACTICE AREAS:*** Criminal; Bankruptcy; Family Law. ***Email:*** rhr@mvhlaw.com

TAMARA ALLEN FLEMING, born Mocksville, North Carolina, January 27, 1961; admitted to bar, 1986, North Carolina. *Education:* Peace College (A.A., 1981); University of North Carolina-Chapel Hill (B.A., 1983); Campbell University (J.D., 1986). Phi Alpha Delta. ***PRACTICE AREAS:*** Real Estate; Workers Compensation; Social Security Disability. ***Email:*** taf@mvhlaw.com

BRIAN F. WILLIAMS, born 1971; admitted to bar, 1999, North Carolina. *Education:* University of North Carolina at Chapel Hill (B.A., 1994); Wake Forest University (J.D., 1999). *Member:* North Carolina State Bar. ***PRACTICE AREAS:*** Elder Law; Civil Litigation. ***Email:*** bfw@mvhlaw.com

All Members belong to Davie County, North Carolina and American Bar Associations; 22nd Judicial District and North Carolina State Bar.

REPRESENTATIVE CLIENTS: Central Carolina Bank and Trust Co.; Funder America, Inc.; Town of Mocksville.
APPROVED ATTORNEYS FOR: Lawyers Title Insurance; Commonwealth Title Insurance; Jefferson Pilot Title Insurance; Investors Title Insurance; Chicago Title Insurance.
REFERENCE: Central Carolina Bank.

TEETER LAW FIRM

MOCKSVILLE, NORTH CAROLINA

(See Winston-Salem)

Appellate Practice, Criminal Law, Civil Litigation, Domestic Relations, Personal Injury, Trusts and Estates and Wills.

ROBERT C. ADAMS

MONROE, NORTH CAROLINA

(See Charlotte)

Wills, Living Wills, Trust Law, Trusts and Estates, Estate Planning, Estate Administration, Trust Administration, Probate, Taxation, Tax Law, Income Tax, Business Law, Corporate Law, Business Formation, Incorporation, Contracts Breach of Contract, Contract Litigation.

HAL BERGER, P.A.

A PROFESSIONAL LAW CORPORATION

MONROE, NORTH CAROLINA

(See Charlotte)

Real Estate Closings, Residential Real Estate, Commercial Real Estate, Estate Planning, Trusts and Estates, Business Law, Corporate Law.

CHARLES B. BROOKS, II

313 NORTH MAIN STREET
MONROE, NORTH CAROLINA 28112
Telephone: 704-283-9363
Fax: 704-289-8327

Criminal Defense, Driving While Intoxicated (DWI Defense), Drug Crimes, Assault, Traffic Violations, Child Custody, Child Support, Divorce, Products Liability, Medical Malpractice, Automobile Accidents, Wrongful Death, Products Liability and Medical Malpractice. Litigation.

CHARLES B. BROOKS, II, born Monroe, North Carolina, 1960; admitted to bar, 1985, North Carolina. *Education:* Guilford College (A.B., 1982); University of North Carolina (J.D., 1985). *Member:* Union County and North Carolina Bar Associations; North Carolina State Bar; The Association of Trial Lawyers of America. ***PRACTICE AREAS:*** Criminal Defense; DWI Defense; Personal Injury; Products Liability; Medical Malpractice.

BROOKS LAW OFFICE

MONROE, NORTH CAROLINA

(See Charlotte)

Medical Malpractice, Wrongful Death, Personal Injury, Automobile Accidents, Slip and Fall, Employment Law, Employment Discrimination, Wrongful Termination, Sexual Harassment, Contracts, Employment Contracts, Sports, Entertainment.

RICHARD L. BROWN, JR.

310 N. CHURCH STREET
P.O. BOX 3326
MONROE, NORTH CAROLINA 28112
Telephone: 704-283-6800
Fax: 704-291-7725
Email: arichardbrownl@carolina.rr.com
URL: http://www.richardbrownlaw.com

Real Estate-Buying and Selling, Landlord and Tenant, Personal Injury, Automobile Accidents, Dog Bites, Criminal Law, White Collar Crime, Traffic Violations, Driving While Intoxicated, Employment Law, Wrongful Terminations, Bankruptcy, Civil Rights, Health Care, Nursing Home Issues.

RICHARD L. BROWN, JR., born Lancaster, South Carolina, May 28, 1969; admitted to bar, 1996, North Carolina; 2002, U.S. Court of Appeals, 4th Circuit. *Education:* Morehouse College (B.A., English, cum laude, 1991); University of North Carolina at Chapel Hill (J.D., 1995). *Member:* Union County and North Carolina Bar Associations; The Association of Trial Lawyers of America.

CLODFELTER LAW OFFICE

MONROE, NORTH CAROLINA

(See Wadesboro)

Criminal Law, Domestic, Family Law, Child Custody, Divorce, Personal Injury, Wrongful Death, Traffic Violations, Driving While Intoxicated.

ZACHARY A. COHEN

201 N. MAIN STREET, SUITE 101
MONROE, NORTH CAROLINA 28112
Telephone: 704-283-9090
Email: zcohen@lawyer.com
URL: http://www.zachcohenlaw.com

Criminal Law, Traffic Violations, Drug Crimes, Driving While Intoxicated, Sex Crimes.

ZACHARY A. COHEN, admitted to bar, 2005, North Carolina. *Education:* Wingate University (B.A., History, 2000); Texas Wesleyan University (J.D., 2004). Moot Court. Trial Advocacy. *Member:* Union County and North Carolina Bar Associations. ***PRACTICE AREAS:*** Criminal Law; Traffic Violations; Drug Crimes; Driving While Intoxicated; Sex Crimes.

SHAWNA DAVIS COLLINS

315-A N. MAIN STREET
SUITE 201
MONROE, NORTH CAROLINA 28112
Telephone: 704-289-3250
Facsimile: 704-283-9539
Email: info@shawnacollins.com
URL: http://www.lawyers.com/sdcollins

Family Law, Adoption Law, Child Custody, Child Support, Divorce, Criminal Law, Driving While Intoxicated, Drug Crimes, Felonies, Traffic Violations, Trusts and Estates, Wills, Probate.

SHAWNA DAVIS COLLINS, born Columbus, Ohio, March 22, 1970; admitted to bar, 1995, North Carolina; 1999, South Carolina. *Education:* College of Charleston (B.A., cum laude, 1992); University of Florida (J.D., 1995). *Member:* Beaufort County and Union County Bar Associations; North Carolina State Bar; South Carolina Bar; North Carolina

(This Listing Continued)

Academy of Trial Lawyers. ***REPORTED CASES:*** State v. Bobby Neal Helms, 348 N.C. 578, 504 S.E.2d 293 (1998).

KOY E. DAWKINS, P.A.

Established in 1966
212 EAST JEFFERSON STREET
P.O. DRAWER 399
MONROE, NORTH CAROLINA 28111-0399
Telephone: 704-283-8501
Fax: 704-283-1371
Email: kdawkins@koydawkins.com
URL: http://www.koydawkins.com

General Practice in all State and Federal Courts. Real Estate, Commercial and Business Law. Construction Law, Education Law, Personal Injury, Trusts and Estates, Civil Litigation, Wills and Probate.

KOY E. DAWKINS, born Richmond County, North Carolina, October 13, 1934; admitted to bar, 1959, North Carolina; 1962, U.S. District Court, Western District of North Carolina; 1977, U.S. Court of Appeals, 4th Circuit; 1979, U.S. District Court, Eastern District of North Carolina; 1980, U.S. District Court, Middle District of North Carolina. *Education:* High Point College (B.S., 1956); Wake Forest University (LL.B., 1959). Phi Alpha Delta. Member, Construction Professionals Network. *Member:* Union County (President, 1982-1983), North Carolina and American Bar Associations; North Carolina State Bar; North Carolina Academy of Trial Lawyers; North Carolina Counsel of School Attorneys (Chairman); American Board of Trial Advocates. ***PRACTICE AREAS:*** Real Estate; Commercial Law; Business Law; Education Law; Civil Litigation; Construction Law; Trusts and Estates; Wills; Probate; Corporate Law. ***Email:*** kdawkins@koydawkins.com

REPRESENTATIVE CLIENTS: Goulston Technologies, Inc.; John M. Campbell Company; Monroe Mall; Union County Public Schools; Monroe Oil Co.; Catawla Oil Co.; Potter & Co., CPA; Montieth Construction Corp.; Ryder Truck Rental, Inc.; The Sansbury Company; Site Prep, Inc. of NC.
APPROVED ATTORNEY FOR: Lawyers Title Insurance Co.; Chicago Title Insurance Co.; Investors Title Insurance Co.; First Title Insurance Co.; Fidelity Title Insurance Co.
REFERENCE: First Citizens Bank.

KERRY B. EVERETT

MONROE, NORTH CAROLINA

(See Charlotte)

Adoptions, Real Estate, Buying or Selling a Home, Buying or Selling a Business, State and Federal Appellate and Civil Practice, Wills and Probate.

GARIS LAW FIRM

MONROE, NORTH CAROLINA

(See Charlotte)

Corporate Law, Business Law, Contracts, Collections, Employment, Real Estate, Foreclosure, Trusts and Estates, Wills, Bankruptcy, Debtor and Creditor, Personal Injury, Automobile Accidents, Workers Compensation, Uncontested Divorces, Family Law, Construction, Litigation.

LAW OFFICES OF WILLIAM K. GOLDFARB

Established in 1996
301 SOUTH CHARLOTTE AVENUE
P.O. BOX 3200
MONROE, NORTH CAROLINA 28111
Telephone: 704-296-0055
Fax: 704-296-0053
Email: goldfarb_law@hotmail.com

Personal Injury, Professional Negligence, Medical Malpractice, Workers' Compensation, Traffic Violations.

WILLIAM K. GOLDFARB, born Charlotte, North Carolina, April 25, 1964; admitted to bar, 1991, North Carolina. *Education:* North Carolina State University (B.A., Gymnastic's Scholarship, 1987); Campbell University (J.D., 1991). Delta Theta Phi. Recipient: American Jurisprudence Book Award, Torts II; North Carolina Trial Advocacy Achievement Award. Chief Justice of Honor Court, Campbell Law School 1990-1991. Honor Court Review Board for Campbell Law School, 1989-1990. *Member:* Union County Bar Association; North Carolina State Bar; American Trial Lawyers Association; North Carolina Academy of Trial Lawyers; Mecklenburg Trial LAwyers Association. ***PRACTICE AREAS:*** Personal Injury; Professional Negligence; Medical Malpractice; Workers' Compensation; Traffic Violations.

GRIFFIN, SMITH, CALDWELL, HELDER & HELMS, P.A.

314 NORTH HAYNE STREET
P.O. DRAWER 99
MONROE, NORTH CAROLINA 28111-0099
Telephone: 704-289-4577
Toll Free from Charlotte: 704-372-4808
Fax: 704-289-4218 (Real Estate); 704-283-1122 (General)
URL: http://www.griffinsmithcaldwell.com

Personal Injury, Worker's Compensation, General Civil Litigation, Residential and Commercial Real Estate Finance and Development, Land Use Planning and Zoning, Wills, Trusts, Estate Planning and Administration, Business and Corporate Law, General Practice, Family Law, Traffic.

(This Listing Continued)

GRIFFIN, SMITH, CALDWELL, HELDER & HELMS, P.A., Monroe—Continued

THOMAS J. CALDWELL, born Charlotte, North Carolina, February 27, 1946; admitted to bar, 1971, North Carolina. *Education:* Davidson College (A.B., 1968); University of North Carolina (J.D., 1971). President, Union County Bar Association, 1984. *Member:* North Carolina State Bar; North Carolina Bar Association. (Certified Mediator). ***PRACTICE AREAS:*** Corporate Law; Real Estate Law; Civil Litigation; Estate Planning; Estate Administration. ***Email:*** tcaldwell@griffinsmithcaldwell.com

JAKE C. HELDER, born Charlotte, North Carolina, February 26, 1945; admitted to bar, 1970, North Carolina. *Education:* University of North Carolina (B.S., 1967); Wake Forest University (J.D., 1970). Phi Alpha Delta. Member, Wake Forest University Law Review, 1969-1970. *Member:* North Carolina State Bar. [Capt., USA, JAGC, 1970-1974]. ***PRACTICE AREAS:*** Real Estate Law; Corporate Law; Civil Litigation. ***Email:*** jhelder@griffinsmithcaldwell.com

R. KENNETH HELMS, JR., born Monroe, North Carolina, October 26, 1962; admitted to bar, 1988, North Carolina. *Education:* University of North Carolina at Chapel Hill (B.A., 1985); Wake Forest University (J.D., 1988). *Member:* Union County and North Carolina Bar Associations; North Carolina State Bar. ***PRACTICE AREAS:*** Civil Litigation; Personal Injury; Estate Administration; Worker's Compensation. ***Email:*** khelms@griffinsmithcaldwell.com

---

TREY ROBISON, born Midwest City, Oklahoma, April 6, 1967; admitted to bar, 1996, North Carolina. *Education:* University of Oklahoma (B.A., 1989); Wake Forest University (J.D., 1996). Assistant District Attorney, 20th Pros. Dist., 1996-2002. ***PRACTICE AREAS:*** Civil Litigation; Personal Injury; Criminal Defense. ***Email:*** trobison@griffinsmithcaldwell.com

REBECCA L. ROBISON, born Midland, Michigan, 1970; admitted to bar, 1998, North Carolina. *Education:* St Mary's College; The Ohio State University (B.A., 1994); Capital University Law School (J.D., 1997). Assistant District Attorney, Union County, North Carolina, 1998-2001. *Member:* Union County, 20th District and North Carolina Bar Associations; North Carolina Academy of Trial Lawyers. ***PRACTICE AREAS:*** Domestic Relations (80%); Criminal Law (5%); Traffic Violations (5%); Civil Litigation (10%). ***Email:*** rrobison@griffinsmithcaldwell.com

KIMBERLY B. LOIA, born Charlotte, North Carolina, March 6, 1975; admitted to bar, 2001, North Carolina. *Education:* College of Charleston (B.S., 1997); Thomas Jefferson School of Law (J.D., 2000). *Member:* North Carolina State Bar; Union County and 20th District Bar Associations. ***PRACTICE AREAS:*** Real Estate. ***Email:*** kloia@griffinsmithcaldwell.com

JAMES A. LEE, III, born Monroe, North Carolina, October 11, 1975; admitted to bar, 2005, North Carolina. *Education:* North Carolina State University (B.S., 1998); Campbell University, Norman Adrian Wiggins School of Law (J.D., 2005). *Member:* Union County and North Carolina Bar Associations; North Carolina State Bar. ***PRACTICE AREAS:*** Corporate Law; Real Estate; Civil Litigation; Estate Planning; Estate Administration; Elder Law. ***Email:*** jalee@griffinsmithcaldwell.com

OF COUNSEL

C. FRANK GRIFFIN
HENRY B. SMITH, JR.

HARRINGTON LAW FIRM

Established in 1947
315 A NORTH MAIN STREET
P.O. BOX 1003
MONROE, NORTH CAROLINA 28112
Telephone: 704-289-2548
Fax: 704-283-9539
URL: http://www.lawyers.com/larryeharrington

Civil and Criminal Trials in all Courts. Corporation, Wills, Probate and Estates, Insurance Law, Personal Injury, Traffic Violations.

LARRY E. HARRINGTON, born Lilesville, North Carolina, March 26, 1940; admitted to bar, 1964, North Carolina. *Education:* Lenoir-Rhyne College; Wake Forest College (LL.B., cum laude, 1964). With Federal Bureau of Investigation, 1964-1966. *Member:* Union County and American Bar Associations; North Carolina State Bar; National Association of Criminal Defense Lawyers. ***PRACTICE AREAS:*** Personal Injury; Wills; Trusts; Estates; Criminal Trials; Civil Litigation; Traffic Violations.

JAMES J. HARRINGTON, born Monroe, North Carolina, 1973; admitted to bar, 2002, North Carolina. *Education:* Wofford College (J.D., 1995); Cumberland School of Law (J.D., 2002). *Member:* Union County Bar Association; North Carolina State Bar; North Carolina Academy of Trial Lawyers. ***PRACTICE AREAS:*** Wills; Trusts; Estates; Personal Injury; Criminal Trials; Civil Litigation; Traffic Violations; Driving While Intoxicated.

HELMS, HENDERSON & ASSOCIATES, P.A.

MONROE, NORTH CAROLINA
(See Charlotte)

General, Civil and Criminal Trial Practice in State and Federal Courts and Agencies, Corporation, Real Estate, Probate, Insurance, Bankruptcy, Commercial, Personal Injury, Collections and Tax.

THE HONNOLD LAW FIRM, P.A.

MONROE, NORTH CAROLINA
(See Charlotte)

Family Law, Domestic Relations, Civil Litigation, Separation Agreements, Divorce, Child Custody, Child Support, Alimony, Post Separation Support, Property Division, Domestic Violence, Premarital Agreements.

JACK G. LEZMAN, P.A.

MONROE, NORTH CAROLINA
(See Charlotte)

PERRY, BUNDY, PLYLER & LONG, L.L.P.

Established in 1980
316 NORTH HAYNE STREET
P.O. BOX 7
MONROE, NORTH CAROLINA 28111-0007
Telephone: 704-289-2519
Fax: 704-282-0105

General Practice. Trials in all State and Federal Courts. Real Estate and Probate, Corporation, Worker's Compensation, Personal Injury, Family Law, Local Government Law, Traffic Violations, Social Security Disability.

MEMBERS OF FIRM

DONALD C. PERRY, born Union County, North Carolina, May 17, 1940; admitted to bar, 1964, North Carolina; 1967, U.S. Supreme Court. *Education:* Wingate College (A.A., 1960); Wake Forest University (B.A., 1962; J.D., 1964). Phi Alpha Delta. Instructor, Business Law II, Wingate College, 1980. County Attorney, 1994—. *Member:* Union County (President, 1981), North Carolina (Member, Sections on: Real Estate; Construction; Probate; Government Law) and American Bar Associations; North Carolina State Bar. [Capt., Office of the Judge Advocate General, USAF, 1965-1968]. ***PRACTICE AREAS:*** Real Estate; Wills and Estates; Corporate Law; Local Government Law. ***Email:*** dperry@pbpl-llp.com

H. LIGON BUNDY, born Harriman, Tennessee, November 2, 1949; admitted to bar, 1976, North Carolina. *Education:* University of North Carolina (B.A., with honors, 1972; J.D., 1976). *Member:* Union County (President, 1986) and North Carolina (Member, Sections on: Litigation, Worker's Compensation and Family Law) Bar Associations; North Carolina State Bar; North Carolina Academy of Trial Lawyers. ***PRACTICE AREAS:*** Personal Injury; Worker's Compensation; Local Government Law; Civil Litigation. ***Email:*** ligonbundy@pbpl-llp.com

DALE ANN WILKINSON PLYLER, born Reidsville, North Carolina, June 7, 1964; admitted to bar, 1990, North Carolina. *Education:* Western Carolina University (B.S., 1986); Campbell University (J.D., 1990). Delta Theta Phi. Legislative Representative, Student Bar Association, 1988-1990. Law Day Chairperson, 1990. *Member:* Union County (Treasurer, 1991-1993, President, 1995; Young Lawyers Division), North Carolina and American (Member, Family Law Section) Bar Associations; North Carolina Academy of Trial Lawyers. ***PRACTICE AREAS:*** Domestic Relations Law; Civil Litigation; Traffic Violations; Social Security. ***Email:*** dplyler@pbpl-llp.com

RICHARD G. LONG, JR., born Roxboro, North Carolina, June 27, 1957; admitted to bar, 1982, North Carolina. *Education:* Elon College; University of North Carolina (B.A., 1979); Wake Forest University (J.D., 1982). Phi Delta Phi. Certified Family Law Mediator. *Member:* Union County (Treasurer, 1986; President, 1996) and North Carolina Bar Associations; North Carolina State Bar; North Carolina Academy of Trial Lawyers. ***PRACTICE AREAS:*** Real Estate; Domestic Relations; Civil Litigation. ***Email:*** rlong@pbpl-llp.com

REPRESENTATIVE CLIENTS: Union County; Town of Wingate; Town of Stallings; Union County Department of Social Services; Union County Board of Realtors; Windsor Window Co, Monroe.
APPROVED ATTORNEYS FOR: Lawyers Title Insurance Corp.; Chicago Title Insurance Co.; Investors Title Insurance Co. and other title companies; list of lenders furnished upon request.
REFERENCES: Bank of America; First Citizens Bank.

THE SCHATTENFIELD LAW FIRM, PLLC

MONROE, NORTH CAROLINA
(See Charlotte)

Trust and Estates, Estate Planning, Asset Protection, Estate and Trust Administration, Fiduciary Law, Business, Family Business, Limited Liability, Wills and Probate, Taxation.

SPERRY & TYSON, PLLC

MONROE, NORTH CAROLINA
(See Matthews)

Real Estate, Residential Real Estate, Commercial Real Estate, Mortgages, Trusts and Estates, Estate Planning, Business Law, Partnerships, Contracts, Collections, Corporate, Taxation, Bankruptcy.

LAW OFFICE OF DONNA B. STEPP, P.C.

Established in 1998

105 C EAST JEFFERSON STREET
P.O. BOX 2526
MONROE, NORTH CAROLINA 28111
Telephone: 704-283-5353
Fax: 704-289-2528
Email: dbstepp@gte.net

Family Law, Divorce, Separation, Child Custody, Traffic Violations, DWI, Criminal Defense.

DONNA B. STEPP, born China Lake, California, May 31, 1969; admitted to bar, 1993, North Carolina. *Education:* George Mason University (B.A., 1990); Campbell University (J.D., 1993). Delta Theta Phi; Omicron Delta Kappa. *Member:* North Carolina Bar Association; North Carolina State Bar; North Carolina Association of Trial Lawyers. **LANGUAGES:** Spanish.

LAW OFFICE OF ANNA N. WESTMORELAND

MONROE, NORTH CAROLINA

(See Charlotte)

Family Law, Divorce, Child Support, Employment Law, Employment Contracts, Wrongful Termination, Severance, Employment Benefits, Bankruptcy, Wills, Probate, Trusts and Estates.

WILSON & JONES

111 WINCHESTER AVENUE
MONROE, NORTH CAROLINA 28110
Telephone: 704-283-1500
URL: http://www.wilsonjoneslaw.com

Criminal Law, Bankruptcy, Workers Compensation, Personal Injury, Family Law, Traffic Violations, Social Security, Automobile Accidents, Elder Law.

MEMBERS OF FIRM

TIFFANY N. WILSON, born Monroe, North Carolina, January 22, 1977; admitted to bar, 2003, North Carolina. *Education:* Howard University (B.A., Political Science, 1999); North Carolina Central University Law School (J.D., 2003). Pi Sigma Alpha; Delta Sigma Theta. *Member:* 20th District and North Carolina Bar Associations; North Carolina State Bar; North Carolina Trial Advocacy Team; North Carolina Association of Women's Attorney. **PRACTICE AREAS:** Criminal Law; Bankruptcy; Workers Compensation; Personal Injury; Family Law; Traffic Violations; Social Security; Automobile Accidents and Injuries. **Email:** TiffanyWilson04@hotmail.com

DANIELL JONES, born Monroe, North Carolina, September 20, 1979; admitted to bar, 2004, North Carolina. *Education:* North Carolina Agricultural & Technical State University (B.A., Economics, 2001); Wake Forest University Law School (J.D., 2004). *Member:* 20th District and North Carolina Bar Associations; North Carolina State Bar. **PRACTICE AREAS:** Criminal Law; Traffic Violations; Bankruptcy; Elder Law; Family Law; Personal Injury; Workers Compensation; Social Security.

THE BARONE LAW FIRM, P.A.

MOORESVILLE, NORTH CAROLINA

(See Cornelius)

Real Estate, Buying and Selling a Home, Construction, Landlord and Tenant, Zoning Planning and Land Use, Business Law, Corporate, Limited Liability Companies, Partnerships, Trusts and Estates, Asset Protection, Estate Planning, Bankruptcy, Foreclosures, Personal Injury, Automobile Accidents, Dog Bites, Wrongful Death, Criminal Law, Traffic Violations, Driving While Intoxicated, Parole and Probation, Federal Criminal Law, Collections, Contracts, Intellectual Property.

THE BOLDUC LAW FIRM, PLLC

MOORESVILLE, NORTH CAROLINA

(See Charlotte)

NASD Arbitration, Business Litigation, Securities Fraud, Corporate Malfeasance, Mutual Fund Disputes, Wrongful Termination, Banking and Finance Law, and Accounting.

LAW OFFICE OF WILLIAM T. CORBETT, JR.

755 NORTH MAIN STREET, SUITE A
P.O. BOX 1227
MOORESVILLE, NORTH CAROLINA 28115
Telephone: 704-799-7076
Fax: 704-663-5455
Email: billcorbettlaw@msn.com
URL: http://www.billcorbettlaw.com

Insurance Defense, Wills and Probate, Estates, Criminal Law, Traffic Violations, General Civil Litigation.

(This Listing Continued)

WILLIAM T. CORBETT, JR., born Windsor, North Carolina, March 17, 1964; admitted to bar, 1989, North Carolina, U.S. District Court, Eastern District of North Carolina and U.S. Court of Appeals, Fourth Circuit. *Education:* Campbell University (B.A., magna cum laude, 1986); Campbell University School of Law (J.D., 1989). Omicron Delta Kappa; Pi Gamma Mu; Phi Kappa Phi; Delta Theta Phi. *Member:* Iredell County and North Carolina Bar Associations; North Carolina State Bar; North Carolina Association of Defense Attorneys. **PRACTICE AREAS:** Insurance Defense; Workers Compensation; Criminal Law; Personal Injury; Family Law; Products Liability; Professional Malpractice.

JUDY DALTON

MOORESVILLE, NORTH CAROLINA

(See Troutman)

Family Law, Child Custody, Child Support, Visitation Rights, Divorce, Property Distribution, Restraining Orders, Adoptions, Criminal Defense, Felonies and Misdemeanors, DWI, Traffic Violations, Drug Crimes, Probation Violations, Civil Litigation, Wills, Debt Collections.

LAW OFFICE OF DARYL G. DAVIDSON, SR., PC

MOORESVILLE, NORTH CAROLINA

(See Statesville)

Family Law, Child Support, Child Custody, Divorce, Domestic Violence, Visitation Rights, Criminal Law, Driving While Intoxicated (DWI); Drug Crimes, Traffic Violations, Immigration, Automobile Accidents.

HARTSELL & WILLIAMS, P.A.

MOORESVILLE, NORTH CAROLINA

(See Concord)

General Civil and Criminal Practice in all Courts. Workers Compensation, Corporation, Insurance, Real Estate, Taxation, Probate Law, Estate Planning, Family Law and Motor Sports (Racing).

RAY A. HAYES II P.A.

MOORESVILLE, NORTH CAROLINA

(See Cornelius)

Business Transactions, Business Litigation, Corporate Law, Business Planning, Buying or Selling a Business, Securities, Contracts, Trusts and Estates, Wills and Probate, Bankruptcy, Consumer Bankruptcy, Traffic Violations.

HOMESLEY GOODMAN & WINGO, PLLC

Established in 2002

330 SOUTH MAIN STREET
MOORESVILLE, NORTH CAROLINA 28115
Telephone: 704-664-2162
Fax: 704-664-0267
Email: HGWinfo@lakenormanlaw.com
URL: http://www.lakenormanlaw.com

Contract Law, Commercial and Business Law, Trademark Law, Civil Litigation, Corporate Law, Residential and Commercial Real Estate, Domestic and Family Law, Elder Law, Estate Planning and Administration, Wills and Trusts, Personal Injury, Worker's Compensation, Traffic and Criminal Law.

FIRM PROFILE: The firm serves Mooresville, Lake Norman, Iredell County and the surrounding counties including Mecklenburg, Rowan, Cabarrus, Lincoln, Catawba and Davie. The firm is a full service general practice law firm capable of handling all of your legal matters.

The firm's office is located at 330 South Main Street in the historic Isaac Harris House, built around 1875 by Mooresville's first elected mayor.

For Reported Cases and Representative Clients see www.lakenormanlaw.com.

MEMBERS OF THE FIRM

CLIFTON W. HOMESLEY, born Bremerhaven, West Germany, March 25, 1960; admitted to bar, 1986, North Carolina. *Education:* University of North Carolina at Chapel Hill (B.S., 1982); Campbell University (J.D., 1986). Member, Magistrate's Selection Committee, Western District of North Carolina. Past President, 22nd District Bar. *Member:* Iredell County and North Carolina (Member, Law Practice Management Section; President, 2002) Bar Associations; North Carolina State Bar; North Carolina Academy of Trial Lawyers. **PRACTICE AREAS:** Criminal Law; Contracts; Civil Litigation; Motor Sports Law; Commercial Real Estate; Family Law; Personal Injury; Trademarks. **Email:** cliff@lakenormanlaw.com

ANDREW J. WINGO, born Greenwood, South Carolina, December 15, 1972; admitted to bar, 1998, North Carolina and South Carolina. *Education:* Catawba College (B.A., cum laude, 1995); Campbell University (J.D., 1998; M.B.A., 1998). Member, All South Atlantic Academic Football Team; Order of the Blue and White. Recipient, Honors, Lawyers and The Law Firm Book Award. *Member:* Iredell County, North Carolina, South Carolina and American Bar Associations; North Carolina State Bar; Lake Norman Homebuilders Association (Board of Directors Legal Counsel). **PRACTICE AREAS:** Civil Litigation; Criminal Law; Business Law; Commercial Real Estate; Contracts; Family Law; Personal Injury; Workers Compensation. **Email:** andrew@lakenormanlaw.com

(This Listing Continued)

HOMESLEY GOODMAN & WINGO, PLLC, Mooresville—Continued

NANCY BARLOW GOODMAN, born September 19, 1966; admitted to bar, 1994, South Carolina; 1998, North Carolina. *Education:* Emory University (B.A., 1988); University of South Carolina (J.D., 1994). Member, Student Editorial Board, American Bar Association Real Property Probate and Trust Journal, 1992-1994. Recipient, Legal Writing and Research, American Jurisprudence Award (Most Outstanding Student). Attorney, Senate Judiciary Committee, Joint Legislative Committee for Judicial Screening and South Carolina Hunley Commission, 1992-1996. Commended on motion of the Senate's President Pro Tempore for outstanding service. *Member:* North Carolina Bar Association; South Carolina Bar (Member, Estate Planning Section); North Carolina State Bar (Member, Sections on: Estate Planning; Elder Law); National Academy of Elder Law Attorneys. ***PRACTICE AREAS:*** Estate Planning; Estate Administration; Probate; Elder Law. ***Email:*** nancy@lakenormanlaw.com

ASSOCIATES

CHRISTOPHER C. "KIT" ANDERSON, born Columbia, South Carolina, August 6, 1977; admitted to bar, 2004, North Carolina. *Education:* Wake Forest University (B.A., cum laude, 1999); University of Georgia (J.D., cum laude, 2004). Omicron Delta Epsilon. Author, "The Dangerous Lives of Teachers," The Education Law Consortium, University of Georgia, Spring 2004, also found at http://www.educationlawconsortium.org/studentpubs.html. Member, Habitat for Humanity, Winston-Salem, NC and Charlotte, NC Chapters, 1998-2001. *Member:* Iredell County, North Carolina and American Bar Associations; North Carolina State Bar. ***PRACTICE AREAS:*** General Practice; Civil Litigation; Personal Injury; Breach of Contract; Real Estate. ***Email:*** kit@lakenormanlaw.com

RONNIE D. CRISCO, JR., born Kannapolis, North Carolina, June 3, 1980; admitted to bar, 2005, North Carolina. *Education:* Duke University (B.A., Public Policy, magna cum laude, 2002); University of North Carolina at Chapel Hill (J.D., 2005). President, Duke Democrats, 2000-2001. Member: UNC Civil Assistance Clinic; Hart Leadership Program in New York, Public Policy and the Arts. Member, Broun National Mock Trial Team. Staff Writer, UNC Journal of Law and Technology, 2003-2004. Author, "Follow the Leaders: A Constructive Examination of Existing Regulatory Tools That Could Be Applied to Internet Gambling," 5 N.C.J.L. & Tech. 155 (Fall 2003). *Member:* Iredell County and North Carolina Bar Associations; North Carolina State Bar. ***PRACTICE AREAS:*** General Practice; Criminal Law; Corporate Law; Civil Litigation; Family Law. ***Email:*** ronnie@lakenormanlaw.com

Languages: Spanish.

HOMESLEY, JONES, GAINES, DUDLEY, McLURKIN & DONALDSON, PLLC

236 RACEWAY DRIVE
SUITE 7, LAKESIDE BUSINESS PARK
MOORESVILLE, NORTH CAROLINA 28117
Telephone: 704-664-1127
Real Estate Telephone: 704-664-2145
Fax: 704-663-0939
Real Estate Fax: 704-664-6596
Real Estate Email: lakenormanrealestate@alltel.net
URL: http://www.mooresvillelakelaw.com
Mailing Address: P.O. Box 3010, Mooresville, NC 28117

Statesville, North Carolina Office: 316 East Broad Street, P.O. Box 149. Telephone: 704-873-2172. Fax: 704-924-2103; 704-873-5908. Email: hjgd@statesville.net. Real Estate Email: realestate@statesville.net.

General Civil and Criminal Trial Practice in all State and Federal Courts. Probate, Real Estate, Personal Injury, Family, Corporation, Insurance, Negligence.

TROY C. HOMESLEY, JR., born Cherryville, North Carolina, December 22, 1934; admitted to bar, 1958, North Carolina; 1959, U.S. Court of Military Appeals. *Education:* University of North Carolina (B.S., 1956; J.D., 1958). Phi Delta Phi. Solicitor, Mooresville Recorder's Court, 1963. *Member:* Iredell County, North Carolina and American Bar Associations; 22nd Judicial District and North Carolina State Bars; North Carolina Academy of Trial Lawyers; The Association of Trial Lawyers of America; American Judicature Society. [Capt. JAGC, U.S. Army, 1958-1962]. ***PRACTICE AREAS:*** Criminal Law; Domestic Law; Personal Injury Law; Civil Litigation.

WALTER H. JONES, JR., admitted to bar, 1966, North Carolina and U.S. Court of Military Appeals. *Education:* University of North Carolina at Chapel Hill (B.A., 1963); Wake Forest University (J.D., 1966). Phi Delta Phi. Chairman, Mooresville Board of Elections, 1973-2000. Attorney, Mooresville Graded School District, 1985-2000. City Attorney, Mooresville, North Carolina, 2000-2002. *Member:* Iredell County, North Carolina and American Bar Associations; North Carolina State Bar. ***PRACTICE AREAS:*** Residential Real Estate; Commercial Real Estate; Municipal Law; Corporate Law; Civil Litigation; Probate; Estate Planning; Elder Law; Contract Law. ***Email:*** walterjones@alltel.net

ELISE B. McLURKIN, born Columbia, South Carolina, June 20, 1970; admitted to bar, 1997, North Carolina and South Carolina. *Education:* Erskine College (B.S., 1992); Campbell University School of Law (J.D., 1997). Attorney, Mooresville Graded School District. United Way of Central Carolinas, Inc.; Mooresville-South Iredell Board of Directors; Mooresville YMCA Board of Managers; Mooresville Foundation for Excellence in Education Board of Directors. *Member:* Iredell County and North Carolina State Bar Associations; South Carolina Bar; North Carolina State Bar. ***PRACTICE AREAS:*** Civil Litigation; Probate; Wills; Residential Real Estate; Commercial Real Estate; Corporate Law; Workers Compensation; Social Security Disability; Personal Injury; Contracts; Construction Law. ***Email:*** emclurkin@alltel.net

KEVIN C. DONALDSON, born Troutman, North Carolina, October 3, 1973; admitted to bar, 1999, North Carolina. *Education:* Erskine College (B.A., 1996); Campbell University School of Law (J.D., 1999). President, Mooresville-South Iredell Chamber of Commerce, 2004. Member, Top of the Lake Rotary. Member, Board of Directors, MSI Chamber of Commerce, 2002-2005. *Member:* Iredell County and North Carolina Bar Association; North Carolina State Bar; North Carolina Academy of Trial Lawyers; Association of Trial Lawyers of America. ***PRACTICE AREAS:*** Civil Litigation; Residential Real Estate; Commercial Real Estate; Wills; Estates; Criminal Law; Estate Planning; Corporate Law; Personal Injury; Contracts; Landlord and Tenant Law; Construction Law. ***Email:*** kcdonaldson@alltel.net

JOHN P. STUTTS, born Statesville, North Carolina, July 10, 1977; admitted to bar, 2003, North Carolina. *Education:* Virginia Military Institute (B.A., 1999); Campbell University (J.D., cum laude, 2003). Articles Editor, Campbell Law Review, 2002-2003. ***PRACTICE AREAS:*** Real Estate; Civil Litigation; Personal Injury; Corporate Law; Estate Planning. ***Email:*** patrickstutts@alltel.net

REPRESENTATIVE CLIENTS: Branch Bank and Trust Co.; Wooten's Jewelers; City of Statesville; JMS Southeast, Inc.; Statesville Process Instruments; NGK Ceramics; Mooresville Savings Bank; Best Sweets, Inc; Crescent Resources; Custom Products, Inc.; Mooresville Graded School District; Northlake Lumber Company, Inc.; J.T. Alexander & Son, Inc.; Piedmont Investors, Inc.; RSR Team, Inc.; R.L. Smith Development, Inc.; Spectrum Financial Systems, Inc; Southern Container, Inc.; Bob Rudisill Homes, Inc.; Bay State Milling Company, Inc.; Cavin Funeral Home; Neill Funeral Home; Motorsports Image Paint & Body, Inc.; First Charter National Bank; Southern Door of Mooresville, Inc.; Hicks Companies, L.L.C.; Dane Construction, Inc; Lake Norman Regional Medical Center; Mooresville Foundation for Excellence in Education; Piedmont Pacific Industries, Inc.; The Point on Norman, LLC; Don Allen Surveyors; Crosslake Park Property Owners Association, Inc.; ET Homes, Inc.; G.D. Smith Development Group, Inc.; Realticorp, Inc.; Plaza Lake, LLC; Callaway Service Company, Inc; D.M. Bowman Trucking Company, Inc.; Aldelphia Business Solutions; Fox Den Country Club; Genesis Eldercare; Piedmont Fiberglass, Inc.; Bonanza Development Company, Inc.; Profit Technologies Corporation; Sponsorlogic, Inc.; Piedmount Bank; Carter County Bank; Consolidated Financial Resources; Amity Development and Realty Services; Fox Den Development, LLC; Regency Lake, LLC.
REFERENCES: Branch Bank and Trust Co., Statesville, North Carolina; Piedmont Bank, Mooresville, North Carolina; First Charter Bank, Charlotte, North Carolina.
APPROVED ATTORNEYS FOR: Chicago Title Insurance Company; Investors Title Insurance Company; Lawyers Title Insurance Company; Fidelity National Title Insurance Company; Colonial Insurance Company; Commonwealth Land Title Insurance Company; Stewart Title Insurance Company; First American Title Insurance Company; Old Republic Title Insurance Company; Statewide Title Insurance Company; Land America/Lawyers Title, Charlotte, North Carolina.

(For Other Biographical Information, see Professional Biographies at Statesville, North Carolina)

KLUTTZ, REAMER, HAYES, RANDOLPH & ADKINS, L.L.P.

MOORESVILLE, NORTH CAROLINA

(See Salisbury)

General Civil Practice. Trials. Employment Law, Corporation, Taxation, Real Estate, Estate Planning, Probate and Trusts, Traffic, Criminal Law, Mediation, Personal Injury, Driving While Impaired, Workers Compensation.

THE McINTOSH LAW FIRM, P.C.

MOORESVILLE, NORTH CAROLINA

(See Davidson)

Adoptions, Appeals, Bankruptcy, Business Law, Civil Litigation, Commercial and Consumer Collections, Commercial and Residential Real Estate, Corporate Law, Foreclosures, Insurance Subrogation, Estate Administration, Family Law, Personal Injury, Wrongful Death, Wills, Workers Compensation, Planning and Land Use.

BRADLEY C. MORRIS, PLLC

Established in 2005
174 NORTH MAIN STREET
MOORESVILLE, NORTH CAROLINA 28115
Telephone: 704-799-6662
Fax: 704-799-6554
Email: brad@bradmorrislaw.com
URL: http://www.bradmorrislaw.com

Civil Litigation, Complex Business Litigation, Construction Law, Employment Contract Disputes, Business Law.

BRADLEY C. MORRIS, born Gary, Indiana, February 12, 1954; admitted to bar, 1989, Indiana; 2002, North Carolina. *Education:* Purdue University (B.A., with distinction, 1986); Indiana University (J.D., cum laude, 1989). Alpha Chi. Senior Managing Editor, Indiana Law Journal, 1988-1989. *Member:* North Carolina Bar Association (Member, Litigation and Construction Law Sections). ***PRACTICE AREAS:*** Civil Litigation; Complex Business Litigation; Construction Law; Employment Contracts; Trade Secrets; Real Estate. ***Email:*** brad@bradmorrislaw.com

SINGLETARY LAW FIRM, PLLC

MOORESVILLE, NORTH CAROLINA

(See Cornelius)

Immigration, Sports and Entertainment, Business Law, Business Formation, Buying and Selling a Business.

(This Listing Continued)

DOUGLAS A. SMITH

MOORESVILLE, NORTH CAROLINA

(See Salisbury)

Criminal Law, Felonies, Misdemeanors, Family Law, Divorce, Child Custody, Child Support, Separation, Traffic Violations, Driving While Intoxicated, Construction Law, Children, Child Abuse and Neglect, Child Care, Grandparents Custody, Grandparents Visitation Rights, Juvenile Criminal Law, Step Parent Adoptions, Criminal Defense, Drivers License Suspension, Theft, Weapons Charges, Drug Crimes, Alimony, Domestic Violence, Equitable Distribution, Military Divorce, Name Changes, Paternity, Qualified Domestic Relations Orders, Separation Agreements, Spousal Support, Uncontested Divorce, Guardianship and Conservatorship, Guardian Ad Litem, Incompetency Proceedings, Personal Injury, Accidents, Automobile Accidents and Injuries, Motor Vehicle Accidents and Injuries, Pedestrian Injuries.

WHITFIELD & MOCK, P.A.

609 EAST CENTER AVENUE
P.O. BOX 1616
MOORESVILLE, NORTH CAROLINA 28115
Telephone: 704-663-5350
Fax: 704-663-4001
URL: http://www.whitfieldandmocklaw.com

Personal Injury, Workers Compensation, Traffic Violations, Driving While Intoxicated, Criminal Law, Civil Litigation, Family Law, Social Security Disability, Wills and Probate.

M. GREGORY WHITFIELD, born Fayetteville, North Carolina, July 30, 1965; admitted to bar, 1991, North Carolina. *Education:* University of North Carolina, Chapel Hill (B.S.B.A., 1987; J.D., 1990). Phi Delta Phi. *Member:* Iredell County and North Carolina Bar Associations; North Carolina State Bar; North Carolina Academy of Trial Lawyers (Board of Governors, Young Lawyers Division; Vice President, 2000-2001; Secretary, 1999-2000).

FRANKLIN MOCK, born Lexington, North Carolina, July 13, 1974; admitted to bar, 1999, North Carolina. *Education:* University of North Carolina, Chapel Hill (B.A., History and Political Science, 1996); Wake Forest University (J.D., 1999). Board Member: Legal Aid of Northwest North Carolina; Health Clinic of Mooresville. *Member:* Iredell County and North Carolina Bar Associations; North Carolina State Bar; North Carolina Academy of Trial Lawyers. ***PRACTICE AREAS:*** Family Law; Social Security Disability; Criminal Law; Driving While Intoxicated; Traffic Violations; Civil Litigation; Contracts; Liens; Wills. ***Email:*** jfmlaw@alltel.net

G. PATTESON WILLIAMS

MOORESVILLE, NORTH CAROLINA

(See Cornelius)

Real Estate, Residential Real Estate, Commercial Real Estate, Wills, Estates, Estate Administration, Business, Corporate, Automobile Accidents, Personal Injury.

WILLIAM M. WILLIS IV
ATTORNEY AT LAW

201 N. CHURCH STREET, SUITE 501
P.O. BOX 707
MOORESVILLE, NORTH CAROLINA 28115
Telephone: 704-660-8019
Fax: 704-663-5914
URL: http://www.willislaw-office.com
URL: http://www.willislawyer.com
Email: william@willislawyer.com
URL: http://www.willislawoffice.com

Criminal Law, Traffic Violations, Drug Crimes, Personal Injury, Automobile Accidents, Family Law, Workers Compensation.

WILLIAM M. WILLIS, IV, born Greenville, South Carolina, 1970; admitted to bar, 1995, North Carolina and U.S. District Court, District of North Carolina. *Education:* Clemson University (B.S., 1991); University of Georgia School of Law (J.D., cum laude, 1994). Vice-Justice, Phi Alpha Delta Law Fraternity, 1992-1993. Alexander D. Stevens Chapter delegate to the fraternity's 49th Biennial Convention, 1992. Notes Editor, 1993-1994 and Member, 1992-1994, Managing Board, Georgia Journal of International and Comparative Law. Chairman of the Board, 1995-2002 and Member, 2000-2001, Hospice of Iredell County. Board Member, Statesville Jaycees, 1995-1997. ***PRACTICE AREAS:*** Criminal Law; Domestic Relations; Personal Injury.

BESWICK, GOINES & STEPHENSON, P.A.

Established in 1980
911 ARENDELL STREET
MOREHEAD CITY, NORTH CAROLINA 28557
Telephone: 252-726-2134
Facsimile: 252-726-7438
Email: bmg@coastalaw.com
URL: http://www.coastalaw.com

General Civil and Trial Practice, Personal Injury, Wrongful Death, Medical Malpractice, Workers Compensation, Civil Litigation, Business and Commercial Litigation, Construction, Real Estate (Commercial and Residential), Wills, Trust, Estates, Traffic Matters, Criminal Law, Juvenile Matters, Domestic (Divorce, Alimony, Child Custody, Child Support), Social Security Disability.

(This Listing Continued)

FIRM PROFILE: Beswick, Goines & Stephenson, P.A. was founded by George W. Beswick, a 1974 graduate of the University of North Carolina Law School, after leaving the District Attorney's office. The firm is a general civil and trial practice. Firm members are experienced in their respective areas of expertise, participate regularly in continuing legal education seminars, and are active in professional association and civic affairs.

GEORGE W. BESWICK, born Newport, Rhode Island, July 29, 1941; admitted to bar, 1975, North Carolina; 1980, U.S. District Court, Eastern and Middle Districts of North Carolina; 1982, U.S. Supreme Court; 1983, U.S. Court of Military Appeals; 1986, U.S. Tax Court. *Education:* University of North Carolina (A.B., with honors, 1972; J.D., 1974). Phi Beta Kappa. Member, Carrboro Board of Aldermen, 1975-1977. Assistant District Attorney, 3rd and 18th Judicial Districts, North Carolina, 1978-1980. *Member:* Carteret County and North Carolina Bar Associations; North Carolina State Bar; North Carolina Academy of Trial Lawyers. [Sergeant, U.S. Army, 1959-1964]. ***PRACTICE AREAS:*** Criminal Law; Civil Litigation; Personal Injury; Family Law; Medical Malpractice; Construction Litigation. ***Email:*** pbeswick@coastalaw.com

M. DOUGLAS GOINES, born Charlotte, North Carolina, August 13, 1947; admitted to bar, 1975, North Carolina and U.S. District Court, Western District of North Carolina; 1987, U.S. District Court, Eastern District of North Carolina. *Education:* University of North Carolina (B.S.B.A., 1969); University of Georgia (M.B.A., 1972); Wake Forest University (J.D., cum laude, 1975). Phi Kappa Phi; Beta Gamma Sigma; Phi Alpha Delta. Member, Wake Forest University Law Review, 1974-1975. Author: "The Application of the Fairness Doctrine to Editorial Advertising," Wake Forest Law Review, 1974. *Member:* Carteret County (President, 1987), Third Judicial District (President, 1988) and North Carolina (Member, Business Law Section) Bar Associations; North Carolina State Bar. [1st Lt., U.S. Army, 1969-1971]. ***PRACTICE AREAS:*** Commercial Law; Real Estate; Probate; Civil Practice; Collections; Business Law; Commercial. ***Email:*** dgoines@coastalaw.com

SUNDEE G. STEPHENSON, born Denver, Colorado, August 7, 1970; admitted to bar, 2001, North Carolina. *Education:* North Carolina State University (B.A., 1992; B.S.W., 1993); Campbell University, Norman Adrian Wiggins School of Law (J.D., 2001). *Contract Attorney, Carteret County Department of Social Services. Member:* Carteret County, North Carolina, American and Third Judicial District Bar Associations (Secretary and Treasurer); North Carolina State Bar. ***PRACTICE AREAS:*** Criminal Law; Traffic Violations; Family Law; Divorce; Social Security Disability; Civil Litigation; Business Litigation; Personal Injury; Juvenile Law; Parental Rights; Elder Law; Guardianship. ***Email:*** sstephenson@coastalaw.com

REPRESENTATIVE CLIENTS: Tetterton Resort Management; First Flight Federal Credit Union; Alpha and Omega Construction Company; Alan Shelor Realty, Kurtis Chevrolet; Leader Home Sales N.C. Coast Communications, Inc.; Carteret County Department of Social Services.
APPROVED ATTORNEYS FOR: Lawyer's Title Insurance; Statewide Title Insurance Company; Chicago Title Insurance Company; Investors Title Insurance Company; Fidelity National Title Insurance Company.
REFERENCE: Branch Banking and Trust Company.

MARGARET ANN GARNER

3332 BRIDGES STREET, SUITE # 2B
MOREHEAD CITY, NORTH CAROLINA 28557
Telephone: 252-726-1810
Fax: 252-726-0980
Email: mgarner@coastalnet.com
URL: http://www.lawyers.com/margaretanngarner

Estate Planning, Probate and Estate Administration, Commercial and Residential Real Estate, Corporations, Partnerships and LLCs, Bankruptcy.

FIRM PROFILE: Margaret Ann Garner practiced law with the international firm Gibson, Dunn & Crutcher for eleven years in both its Los Angeles and Washington, DC offices before returning home to Carteret County.

MARGARET ANN GARNER, born Newport, North Carolina, December 4, 1954; admitted to bar, 1982, Arizona; 1988, California; 1990, District of Columbia; 1991, Virginia, 1997, North Carolina. *Education:* University of Arizona (B.A., with distinction, 1977; J.D., 1982). *Member:* Carteret County and North Carolina Bar Associations; State Bar of Arizona; State Bar of California; Virginia State Bar; District of Columbia Bar. ***PRACTICE AREAS:*** Estate Planning; Probate; Estate Administration; Commercial Real Estate; Residential Real Estate; Corporate Law; Partnership Law; Limited Liability Company Law; Bankruptcy.

KELLUM LAW FIRM

5178 HIGHWAY 70 WEST
MOREHEAD CITY, NORTH CAROLINA 28557
Telephone: 252-726-7000
Fax: 252-726-8888
Email: ckeenhold@kellumlawfirm.com
URL: http://www.lawyers.com/kellumlawfirm

State and Federal Civil Trial Practice, Personal Injury Law, Wrongful Death, Workers' Compensation, Social Security, Defective Products, Mass Torts and Insurance Law.

(For complete biographical data on all personnel, see Professional Biographies at New Bern)

KIRKMAN, WHITFORD, BRADY & BERRYMAN, P.A.

Established in 1978
710 ARENDELL STREET - SUITE 105
P.O. DRAWER 1347
MOREHEAD CITY, NORTH CAROLINA 28557-4240
Telephone: 252-726-8411
Fax: 252-726-6974
Email: kirkwhit@mail.clis.com
URL: http://www.kirkmanwhitford.com

General Civil Practice. Real Estate, Development and Land Use, Condominium, Corporate, Probate, Municipal, Business, Education, Civil Litigation, Environmental Law.

NEIL B. WHITFORD, born Raleigh, North Carolina, June 13, 1951; admitted to bar, 1976, North Carolina; 1977, U.S. District Court, Eastern District of North Carolina; 1983, U.S. Court of Appeals, Fourth Circuit and U.S. Supreme Court. *Education:* North Carolina State University (B.A., with honors, 1973); University of North Carolina (J.D., 1976). ***PRACTICE AREAS:*** Municipal Law; Education Law; Construction Law; Homeowner Association Law; Civil Litigation. ***Email:*** nwhitford@ec.rr.com

CAROLYN BARNETT BRADY, born Macon, Georgia, October 7, 1959; admitted to bar, 1985, Georgia; 1988, North Carolina. *Education:* Davidson College (B.A., 1981); Wake Forest University (J.D., 1985). ***PRACTICE AREAS:*** Civil Trial Practice; Criminal Trial Practice; Municipal Law; Education Law. ***Email:*** kirkwhit@clis.com

MELISSA BERRYMAN, born Suffolk, Virginia, August 11, 1973; admitted to bar, 1998, North Carolina. *Education:* Hollins College (B.A., 1995); Campbell University (J.D., 1998). ***PRACTICE AREAS:*** Real Estate; Corporate Law; Municipal Law. ***Email:*** mberryman@ec.rr.com

REPRESENTATIVE CLIENTS: Carteret County Board of Education; Harkers Island Electric Membership Corp.; Bogue Banks Water & Sewer Corp.; Town of Pine Knoll Shores; Town of Indian Beach; Town of Beaufort.
REFERENCES: Wachovia Bank and Trust Company; Branch Banking and Trust Company; Chicago Title Insurance Company.

DENNIS M. MARQUARDT, PA

1210 ARENDELL STREET
MOREHEAD CITY, NORTH CAROLINA 28557
Telephone: 252-726-4114
Fax: 252-726-4720
Email: dmmlaw@ec.rr.com

Real Estate, Real Estate Foreclosure, Condominiums, Probate, Wills & Estates, Corporate Law.

DENNIS M. MARQUARDT, born Elyria, Ohio, November 5, 1941; admitted to bar, 1970, North Carolina and U.S. District Court, Eastern District of North Carolina. *Education:* Capital University (B.A., 1963); University of North Carolina at Chapel Hill (J.D., 1970). Phi Alpha Delta. [LTJG, U.S. Navy 1963-1967]. ***PRACTICE AREAS:*** Real Estate; Real Estate Foreclosure; Condominium Law; Probate; Wills; Estate Administration; Corporate Law.

MASON & MASON, P.A.

225 PROFESSIONAL CIRCLE
P.O. DRAWER 99
MOREHEAD CITY, NORTH CAROLINA 28557
Telephone: 252-247-5303
Fax: 252-240-4848
Email: pat@masonattorneys.com

General Civil Trial Practice. Real Estate Law, Admiralty, Probate, Corporate.

L. PATTEN MASON, born New Bern, North Carolina, March 22, 1941; admitted to bar, 1967, North Carolina; 1979, U.S. Supreme Court. *Education:* University of North Carolina (B.S., 1964; J.D., 1967). Law Clerk to U.S. District Court Judge A.L. Butler, 1967-1968. Carteret County Attorney, 1970-1976. North Carolina State Bar Councilor for the 3rd Judicial District, 1984-1994. *Member:* Carteret County (President, 1970), Third Judicial District (President, 1976), North Carolina and American Bar Associations; The North Carolina State Bar. ***PRACTICE AREAS:*** Admiralty and Maritime Law; Banks and Banking; Business Law; Commercial Law; Corporate Law; Insurance; Leases and Leasing; Litigation; Personal Injury; Probate; Trusts and Estates; Wills. ***Email:*** pat@masonattorneys.com

EDITH W. MASON, born Smithfield, North Carolina, February 6, 1950; admitted to bar, 1980, North Carolina and U.S. District Court, Eastern District of North Carolina. *Education:* Meredith College (B.A., 1972); Wake Forest University Law School (J.D., 1980). Staff Member, 1978-1979, and Business Editor, 1979-1980, Wake Forest Law Review. *Member:* Carteret County (Secretary, 1981; President, 1982) and North Carolina (Member, Real Property Section) Bar Associations; North Carolina State Bar. ***PRACTICE AREAS:*** Real Estate; Probate; Wills; Corporate Law. ***Email:*** edith@masonattorneys.com

REPRESENTATIVE CLIENTS: Branch Banking & Trust Co.; McQueens Interiors, Inc.; Atlantic Veneer Corp.; Sanitary Fish Market & Restaurant, Inc.; Barbour's Marine & Supply Co.; Morehead Sports Marina; Morehead Block & Tile Co.; Wickes Lumber Company; Bistro by the Sea, L.L.C.; Southwinds Homeowners Association; The Cedars Inc.; Veneer Technologies, Inc.; Joyce & Associates Construction; Baker Construction, Inc.; Brooks Funeral Home; Carteret OBGYN Association.
APPROVED ATTORNEYS FOR: North Carolina Title Co.; Lawyers Title Co.; First Title Insurance Co.; Investors Title Insurance Co.; Security Union Title Insurance Co.; Chicago Title Insurance Co.
REFERENCES: Branch Banking and Trust Co.; Wachovia Bank & Trust Co.; First Citizens Bank & Trust Co.

SUMRELL, SUGG, CARMICHAEL, HICKS & HART, P.A.

MOREHEAD CITY, NORTH CAROLINA
(See New Bern)

General Civil. Trials and Appeals in all Civil Courts. Wills and Estates, Real Estate, Corporate Law, Financial Transactions, Insurance and Negligence, Employment Law, Municipal Law, Law Enforcement Liability Defense, Health Care Law and Intellectual Property.

BEVIN W. WALL

MOREHEAD CITY, NORTH CAROLINA
(See Newport)

Bankruptcy, Real Estate, Traffic, DWI, Juvenile.

WALLACE, MORRIS, BARWICK, LANDIS & STROUD, P.A.

MOREHEAD CITY, NORTH CAROLINA
(See Kinston)

General Civil and Trial Practice in all State and Federal Courts. Aviation, Banking, Corporate Law, Insurance, Personal Injury, Probate, Product Liability, Real Estate and Taxation.

WARD AND SMITH, P.A.

MOREHEAD CITY, NORTH CAROLINA
(See New Bern)

General and Trial Practice. Admiralty Law; Bankruptcy; Banks and Banking; Business Law; Civil Rights; Commercial Law; Construction Law; Contracts; Copyrights; Corporate Law; Debtor and Creditor; Elder Law; Eminent Domain; Employee Benefits; Environmental Law; Family Law including Divorce; Finance; Franchise Law; Government; Government Contracts; Health Care Law; Immigration and Naturalization; Insurance; International Law; International Trade; Investments; Labor and Employment including Discrimination, Sexual Harassment, and Workers' Compensation; Landlord and Tenant; Litigation; Personal Injury including Automobile Accidents, Legal Malpractice and Medical Malpractice; Products Liability; Real Estate; Securities; Taxation; Technology and Science including Internet Law, Trademarks, and Patents; Trusts and Estates including Estate Planning and Wills and Probate; Zoning and Land Use.

BYRD, BYRD, ERVIN, WHISNANT & McMAHON, P.A.

Established in 1950
ONE NORTHSQUARE
301 EAST MEETING STREET
MORGANTON, NORTH CAROLINA 28655
Telephone: 828-437-4220
Fax: 828-438-4517
Email: skp@byrdlaw.com
URL: http://www.lawyers.com/byrdbyrdervin

Business Law, Business Dissolutions, Business Estate Planning, Business Formation, Buy-Sell Agreements, Closely Held Business Estate Planning, Civil Litigation, Commercial Litigation, Common Carrier Liability Law, Contested Wills, Corporate Law, Closely Held Corporations, Corporate Dissolutions, Corporate Formation, Criminal, Drivers' License Suspension, Driving While Intoxicated, Motor Carrier Liability, Partnership Law, Limited Liability Partnerships, Partnership Dissolution, Partnership Formation, Personal Injury, Accidents, Auto Accidents, Auto Negligence, Bodily Injury, Brain Injury, Carpal Tunnel Syndrome, Catastrophic Injury, Commercial Vehicle Liability, Head Injury, Motor Vehicle Accidents & Injuries, Motorcycle Accidents, Pedestrian Injuries, School Bus Accident, Severe Burns, Slip and Fall, Spinal Injury, Third Party Wrongful Death, TMS Dysfunction, Wrongful Death, Social Security, Social Security Disability, Truck Accidents, Trusts & Estates, Decedent's Estate, Estate Administration, Estate Planning, Workers' Compensation, Industrial Insurance, Workers' Compensation Appeals.

FIRM PROFILE: Founded in 1950 by Joe K. Byrd, the firm has grown from an individual practitioner to a diversified firm providing specialized legal services to clients throughout western N.C.. Employing a highly experienced support staff, the member attorneys concentrate their practice in the specific areas outlined above. To insure collective professional development and to best serve its clients, the firm emphasizes participation in professional, cultural, charitable and civic organizations at all levels. Professional memberships include the Burke County Bar, the 25th Judicial District Bar, the North Carolina Bar Association, General Practice Hall of Fame, 1993, the North Carolina State Bar, the North Carolina Academy of Trial Lawyers and the Association of Trial Lawyers of America. Firm members have held various positions of responsibility in local and state associations.

JOE K. BYRD (Retired)

ROBERT B. BYRD (1930-2002)

JOHN W. ERVIN, JR., born Morganton, North Carolina, March 28, 1937; admitted to bar, 1962, North Carolina; 1964, U.S. Court of Appeals, Fourth Circuit. *Education:* University of North Carolina (A.B., 1959; J.D., 1962). ***PRACTICE AREAS:*** Business Law; Business Dissolutions; Business Estate Planning; Business Formation; Buy-Sell Agreements; Closely Held Business Estate Planning; Commercial Litigation; Corporate Law; Closely Held Corporations; Corporate Dissolutions; Corporate Formation; Partnership

(This Listing Continued)

Law; Limited Liability Partnerships; Partnership Dissolution; Partnership Formation; Trusts and Estates; Decedents Estates; Estate Administration; Estate Planning. **Email:** jwe@byrdlaw.com

C. SCOTT WHISNANT, born Morganton, North Carolina, August 11, 1950; admitted to bar, 1975, North Carolina; 1981, U.S. Court of Appeals, Fourth Circuit. *Education:* University of North Carolina (B.A., 1972); Cumberland School of Law of Samford University (J.D., 1975). ***PRACTICE AREAS:*** Workers Compensation; Workers Compensation Appeals; Industrial Insurance; Social Security Disability; Civil Litigation. **Email:** csw@byrdlaw.com

LAWRENCE D. McMAHON, JR., born Morganton, North Carolina, February 26, 1953; admitted to bar, 1978, North Carolina; 1981, U.S. Court of Appeals, Fourth Circuit. *Education:* University of North Carolina (B.A., 1975; J.D., with honors, 1978). Morehead Scholar, 1975. Coordinating Editor, "Trial Briefs," NCATL, October 2002. Author: "The Expert Witness and Discovery," NCATL Expert Witness Seminar, 1991; "Service of Process: Pre-Trial Procedure," NCATL Pre-Trial Procedure Seminar, 1989; "Motor Vehicle Law: Using Jury Instructions," NCATL Motor Vehicle Law Seminar, 1989; "Insurance Law: Dram Shop Liability," NCATL Insurance Law Seminar, 1988. Co-Chair, Seminar "Nuts & Bolts of Dollars & Cents," NCATL, 2001. Program Chair, Seminar "Disbursement of Tort Recoveries," NCATL, 2002. ***PRACTICE AREAS:*** Civil Litigation; Common Carrier Liability Law; Contested Wills; Insurance; Automobile Insurance; Automobile Liability; Uninsured and Underinsured Motorists; Motor Carrier Liability; Personal Injury; Accidents; Automobile Accidents and Injuries; Automobile Negligence; Bodily Injury; Carpal Tunnel Syndrome; Catastrophic Injury; Commercial Vehicle Liability; Head Injury; Motor Vehicle Accidents and Injuries; Motorcycle Accidents; Pedestrian Injuries; Plaintiffs Personal Injury; School Bus Accidents; Severe Burns; Slip and Fall; Spinal Injury; Third Party Wrongful Death; TMJ Dysfunction; Wrongful Death; Truck Accidents. **Email:** ldm@byrdlaw.com

---

MICHELLE C. PRITCHARD, born Morganton, North Carolina, May 6, 1970; admitted to bar, 1996, California and U.S. District Court, Central District of California; 1997, U.S. Court of Appeals, Ninth Circuit; 1999, North Carolina. *Education:* Davidson College (B.A., 1992); Pepperdine University (J.D., 1995). Law Clerk to the Honorable Lance A. Ito during the case People v. Orenthal James Simpson: Associate Attorney on Federal Computer Fraud Case of United States v. Keith David Mitnick. *Member:* Burke County Bar Association; North Carolina Academy of Trial Lawyers. ***PRACTICE AREAS:*** Criminal Law; Drivers License Suspension; Driving While Intoxicated; Traffic Violations; Social Security; Social Security Disability; Workers Compensation; Industrial Insurance; Workers Compensation Appeals. **Email:** mcp@byrdlaw.com

ROBERT K. DENTON, born Morganton, North Carolina, October 9, 1974; admitted to bar, 2003, North Carolina. *Education:* University of North Carolina (B.A., 1996); Duke University (M.A., 2000); Campbell University (J.D., 2003). Recipient, M.J. Calhoun Trial Advocacy Award, North Carolina Academy of Trial Lawyers, 2003. Assistant Editor: North Carolina Appellate Advocacy, 2002-2003; North Carolina Law of Damages, 2002-2003. *Member:* North Carolina and American Bar Associations; North Carolina Academy of Trial Lawyers. ***PRACTICE AREAS:*** Personal Injury; Wrongful Death; Criminal Law. **Email:** rkd@byrdlaw.com

---

L. TALTON DARK, III

211 EAST UNION STREET
MORGANTON, NORTH CAROLINA 28655-3449
Telephone: 828-433-0103
Fax: 828-437-9397
Toll Free #: 1-888-433-0103
Email: darklaw@bellsouth.net
URL: http://www.taltondark.com

Criminal Law, Driving While Intoxicated, Traffic Violations.

L. TALTON DARK, III, born 1953; admitted to bar, 1979, North Carolina. *Education:* Appalachian State University (B.S.B.A., 1975); Wake Forest University (J.D., 1979). Assistant District Attorney, 25th District, 1983-1994. Private Practice, 1995—. *Member:* Burke County Bar Association; North Carolina State Bar; North Carolina Academy of Trial Lawyers. ***PRACTICE AREAS:*** Criminal Law; Driving While Intoxicated; Traffic Violations; Drug Crimes.

EAKER & FULKERSON, PC

MORGANTON, NORTH CAROLINA

(See Hickory)

Criminal Law, Driving Under the Influence, Real Estate, Domestic.

J. BRYAN ELLIOTT

MORGANTON, NORTH CAROLINA

(See Hickory)

Bankruptcy, Social Security Disability.

HALL & HALL ATTORNEYS AT LAW, P.C.

SUITE 200
305 S. GREEN STREET
MORGANTON, NORTH CAROLINA 28655
Telephone: 828-433-9100
Fax: 828-433-9339
Email: hallandhall@bellsouth.net

Newland, North Carolina Office: 118 Elk Street, 28657. Telephone: 828-733-9222.

Estates, Real Estate, Workers Compensation, Family Law, Divorce, Equitable Distribution, Personal Injury, Traffic Violations, Driving While Intoxicated, Criminal Law, Collections, Child Custody, Corporate Law, Employment Discrimination.

DOUGLAS L. HALL, admitted to bar, 1995, North Carolina; U.S. District Court, Western District of North Carolina and U.S.Court of Appeals, 4th Circuit. *Education:* Guilford College (B.A., 1992); Campbell University (J.D., 1995). Phi Alpha Theta; Phi Alpha Delta. *Member:* North Carolina State Bar. **Email:** hallandhall@bellsouth.net

SUSAN P. HALL, admitted to bar, 1995, North Carolina, South Carolina and U.S. District Court, Eastern and Western Districts of North Carolina. *Education:* Furman University (B.A., 1992); Campbell University (J.D., 1995).

LYNDON R. HELTON PLLC

MORGANTON, NORTH CAROLINA

(See Hickory)

Workers Compensation, Personal Injury.

LAW OFFICE OF KEITH W. RIGSBEE, PLLC

204 SOUTH GREEN STREET
MORGANTON, NORTH CAROLINA 28655
Telephone: 828-430-7540
Fax: 828-430-7540
Email: rigsbeek@bellsouth.net
URL: http://www.rigsbeelawoffice.com

Family Law, Criminal Law, Personal Injury, Small Business Corporations, Real Estate.

KEITH W. RIGSBEE, born Durham, North Carolina, August 16, 1965; admitted to bar, 1990, North Carolina. *Education:* Wake Forest University (B.A., 1987); Wake Forest University School of Law (J.D., 1990). *Member:* Burke County (Past President), North Carolina and American Bar Associations; North Carolina State Bar; North Carolina Academy of Trial Lawyers. ***PRACTICE AREAS:*** Family Law (50%); Criminal Law (25%); Personal Injury (10%); Small Business Corporations (5%); Real Estate (5%). **Email:** rigsbeek@bellsouth.net

---

PEGGY M. SAUNDERS

Established in 2001
500 SOUTH GREEN STREET
P.O. BOX 790
MORGANTON, NORTH CAROLINA 28680-0790
Telephone: 828-437-8333
Facsimile: 828-430-9333
Email: psaunders@hci.net

Real Property, Real Estate, Probate, Trusts, Wills and Estates.

PEGGY M. SAUNDERS, born Rutherfordton, North Carolina, June 11, 1952; admitted to bar, 1989, North Carolina. *Education:* Berea College (B.A., 1973); University of North Carolina, Greensboro (M.A., 1976); University of North Carolina (J.D., 1989). Staff Member, University of North Carolina Law Review, 1987-1988. ***PRACTICE AREAS:*** Real Property; Real Estate; Probate; Trusts; Wills and Estates.

STARNES, AYCOCK, HAIRE & EINSTEIN, P.A.

Established in 1926
118 NORTH STERLING STREET
MORGANTON, NORTH CAROLINA 28655
Telephone: 828-437-3335
Fax: 828-438-4929; 828-437-9832

General Civil Trial Practice in all Courts, Business Law, Real Estate, Probate, Trusts and Estates Wills.

THOMAS M. STARNES, born Concord, North Carolina, March 9, 1936; admitted to bar, 1963, North Carolina and U.S. District Court, Western District of North Carolina; 1965, U.S. Court of Appeals, Fourth Circuit. *Education:* University of North Carolina (B.S., 1958; LL.B., with honors, 1962). Board of Editors, North Carolina Law Review, 1961-1962. Certified Mediator, North Carolina Dispute Resolution Commission. *Member:* North Carolina, Burke County and American Bar Associations; North Carolina State Bar; U.S. Fourth Circuit Judicial Conference. Fellow, American College of Trial Lawyers. ***PRACTICE AREAS:*** Arbitration; Mediation; Real Estate; Business Law; Estate Planning; Probate; Trusts and Estates; Civil Litigation. **Email:** tom_lawfirm@bellsouth.net

SAMUEL E. AYCOCK, born Smithfield, North Carolina, December 28, 1946; admitted to bar, 1972, North Carolina. *Education:* Davidson College (A.B., 1969); University of

(This Listing Continued)

STARNES, AYCOCK, HAIRE & EINSTEIN, P.A., Morganton—Continued

North Carolina (J.D., 1972). Omicron Delta Kappa. Who's Who Among Students in American Colleges and Universities. Past President, 25th District Bar. Certified Mediator, North Carolina Dispute Resolution Commission. Member, Commercial Arbitration Panel, American Arbitration Association. *Member:* Burke County (Past President) and North Carolina Bar Associations; North Carolina State Bar. ***PRACTICE AREAS:*** Personal Injury Law; Civil Litigation; Education Law; Mediation; Arbitration; Insurance Defense; Litigation; Real Estate. ***Email:*** kathy_lawfirm@bellsouth.net

SUSAN L. HAIRE, born Burke County, North Carolina, August 19, 1970; admitted to bar, 1996, North Carolina. *Education:* University of North Carolina at Chapel Hill (B.S., 1992); North Carolina Central University (J.D., with honors, 1995). Phi Sigma Pi. Staff Member, North Carolina Central University Law Journal. *Member:* Burke County and American Bar Associations; North Carolina State Bar. ***PRACTICE AREAS:*** Real Estate; Wills; Civil Litigation; Criminal Defense; Corporate Law; Commercial Law; Insurance Defense; Litigation; Traffic Violations; Probate. ***Email:*** susan_lawfirm@bellsouth.net

NANCY L. EINSTEIN, born Northville, Michigan, August 26, 1955; admitted to bar, 1984, North Carolina. *Education:* Michigan State University (B.A., 1977); University of Baltimore School of Law (J.D., 1983). North Carolina District Court Judge, 25th Judicial District, 1988-2000. *Member:* North Carolina State Bar. ***PRACTICE AREAS:*** Juvenile; Criminal Defense; Civil Litigation; Wills and Estates; Family Law; Traffic Violations; Child Custody; Divorce; Equitable Distribution; Divorce Mediation. ***Email:*** neinstein@bellsouth.net

REPRESENTATIVE CLIENTS: Burke County Board of Education; Duke Energy Corp.; Crescent Resources, LLC; USAA Insurance; Wilkie Construction Co.; Wachovia Bank; Far Research, Inc.; Kemper Insurance Group; North Carolina Farm Bureau Insurance Co.; Leviton Manufacturing Co., Inc.; Morganton Federal S & L Assn.; Western Piedmont Community College; Triangle Contractors, Inc.
APPROVED ATTORNEYS FOR: Lawyers Title Insurance Corp.; Investors Title Insurance; Ticor Title Insurance; Chicago Title Insurance; Stewart Title Insurance Co.; Commonwealth Title Insurance;
REFERENCES: Wachovia Bank, Morganton, North Carolina; Central Carolina Bank, Morganton, North Carolina.

YOUNG, MORPHIS, BACH AND TAYLOR, L.L.P.

MORGANTON, NORTH CAROLINA

(See Hickory)

General, Civil and Criminal Practice. Trials in all State and Federal Courts and the U.S. Supreme Court. Corporations, Taxation, Probate, Trusts, Real Estate, Commercial, Complex Business and Commercial, Municipal, Family Law, Complex Matrimonial Law, Negligence, Products Liability, Personal Injury, Workers Compensation, Insurance Law, Bankruptcy, Patent Law.

THE LAW OFFICE OF JONATHAN RICHARDSON

MORRISVILLE, NORTH CAROLINA

(See Cary)

Personal Injury, Real Estate, Closings, Workers Compensation, Injuries, Traffic Violations, Tickets, Wrongful Death.

KAREN J. ADAMS

MOUNT AIRY, NORTH CAROLINA

(See Dobson)

Criminal Law, Divorce, Speeding Tickets, DUI, DWI.

DAVIS ELDER & DISABILITY LAW

MOUNT AIRY, NORTH CAROLINA

(See Lewisville)

Elder Law.

FAW, FOLGER & JOHNSON, P.C.

Established in 1970

BRANCH BANKING AND TRUST BUILDING
541 NORTH MAIN STREET
P.O. DRAWER 512
MOUNT AIRY, NORTH CAROLINA 27030
Telephone: 336-786-2401
Fax: 336-786-2620
Email: fawfolger1@earthlink.net
URL: http://www.fgjohnson.com

General and Trial Practice. Business and Corporate, Commercial, Education, Municipal, Trusts and Estates, Wills, Probate, Real Estate Law.

CHARLES L. FOLGER (1911-1998)

FREDRICK G. JOHNSON, born Mount Airy, North Carolina, January 4, 1948; admitted to bar, 1973, North Carolina. *Education:* Wake Forest University (B.A., 1969); University of North Carolina (J.D., 1973). Author: "Program Inequality Within School Districts: A Constitutional Violation," Popular Government, March 1973; "Contracts," Education Law in North Carolina, 1988. *Member:* Surry County, North Carolina and American Bar Associations; North Carolina State Bar; North Carolina Council of School Attorneys (Chairman, 1984, 1994). ***PRACTICE AREAS:*** Education Law; Business Law; Commercial Law; Estate Litigation.

OF COUNSEL

THOMAS M. FAW, born North Wilkesboro, North Carolina, September 13, 1924; admitted to bar, 1954, North Carolina. *Education:* Davidson College (A.B., 1948); Wake Forest University (LL.B., 1954). *Member:* Surry County, North Carolina and American Bar Associations; North Carolina State Bar. Fellow, American College of Trial Lawyers. ***PRACTICE AREAS:*** Business Law; Commercial Law; Estate Litigation.

COUNSEL FOR: North Carolina Foam Industries, Inc., a Division of Barnhardt Manufacturing Company; Kentucky Derby Hosiery Company, Inc.; Surry Chemicals, Inc.; Petroleum Transport Company, Inc.; Surry Community College; Alleghany County Board of Education; Elkin City Board of Education; Mount Airy City Board of Education; Stokes County Board of Education; Surry County Board of Education; Wilkes County Board of Education; Northwest Regional Educational Service Alliance.
REPRESENTATIVE CLIENTS: Yoco, Inc.; Johnny C. Johnson, Inc.; Blue Ridge Enterprises, Inc.; Harrell Oil Co., Inc.; First Union National Bank; Branch Banking & Trust ("BB&T"); Ashe County Board of Education; Davie County Board of Education; Yadkin County Board of Education; J. G. Coram Company, Inc.
APPROVED ATTORNEYS FOR: American Title Insurance Co.; Investors Title Insurance Company; Commonwealth Title Insurance Co.; Chicago Title Insurance Co.; Lawyers Title Insurance Co.; United Title Insurance Co.; Jefferson-Pilot Title Insurance Co.
REFERENCES: First Union National Bank; Branch Banking & Trust ("BB&T").

GARDNER, GARDNER AND CAMPBELL PLLC

Established in 1956

304 FRANKLIN STREET
P.O. BOX 866
MOUNT AIRY, NORTH CAROLINA 27030
Telephone: 336-789-5502
Fax: 336-789-5506
URL: http://www.lawyers.com/ggs&m

General Civil and Criminal Practice in all State and Federal Courts, including Corporate and Real Property Practice.

MEMBERS OF FIRM

CARROLL F. GARDNER (1934-2004)

JOHN C. W. GARDNER, JR., born Mount Airy, North Carolina, January 4, 1958; admitted to bar, 1985, North Carolina. *Education:* Wake Forest University (B.A., cum laude, 1981; J.D., 1984). *Member:* North Carolina State Bar; North Carolina Academy of Trial Lawyers. ***PRACTICE AREAS:*** Civil Trial Practice Law; Negligence; Personal Injury; Workers Compensation. ***Email:*** malawyer@surry.net

HUGH B. CAMPBELL, III, born Charlotte, North Carolina, May 26, 1967; admitted to bar, 1992, North Carolina. *Education:* Davidson College (B.A., 1989); Wake Forest University (J.D., 1992). Recipient, American Jurisprudence Book Award for Trial Advocacy. City Attorney, City of Mount Airy. *Member:* North Carolina State Bar; North Carolina Bar Association (Member, Education Section). ***PRACTICE AREAS:*** Civil Trial Practice; Personal Injury; Commercial Law; Business Law; Municipal Law; Real Estate. ***Email:*** hbcampbell@surry.net

OF COUNSEL

JOHN C. W. GARDNER, born Dobson, North Carolina, November 13, 1929; admitted to bar, 1956, North Carolina; 1957, U.S. District Court, Middle District of North Carolina. *Education:* Lenoir-Rhyne College (A.B., 1951); Wake Forest University (J.D., 1956). Phi Delta Phi. City Attorney, 1962-1986. Elected to North Carolina General Practice Hall of Fame, 2005. *Member:* North Carolina State Bar; North Carolina and American Bar Associations; North Carolina Academy of Trial Lawyers. ***PRACTICE AREAS:*** Commercial Law; Probate Law; Corporate Law; Business Law.

MATTHEW J. MIDDLETON, born Ruston, Louisiana, January 25, 1974; admitted to bar, 2004, North Carolina. *Education:* Appalachian State University (B.A., 1997); University of Tulsa College of Law (J.D., 2003). Editor, Tulsa Law Review. *Member:* North Carolina Bar Association. ***PRACTICE AREAS:*** Civil Litigation; Criminal Law; Family Law. ***Email:*** mmiddleton3_2000@yahoo.com

LEGAL SUPPORT PERSONNEL

Nancy Gordon ***Sharon Dorminy***
Angela Grubb ***Shirley Mustin***

LOCAL COUNSEL FOR: Housing Authority of the Town of Mt. Airy; City of Mt. Airy; Cooke Trucking Co.; North Carolina Granite Corp.; Federal Land Bank of Columbia; Wachovia Bank; Scenic Motors, Inc.; Northern Hospital of Surry County.
APPROVED ATTORNEYS FOR: Lawyers Title Insurance Corp.; Jefferson-Pilot Title Insurance Co.; Commercial Standard Title Insurance Co.; American Title Insurance Co.; Chicago Title Insurance Co.; West Jersey Title & Guaranty Co.; Inter-County Title Guaranty & Mortgage Company of New York; Town of Dobson, (Local Council).
REFERENCES: Wachovia Bank, Mt. Airy, N.C.; Bank of America, Mt. Airy, N.C.

THE LAW OFFICES OF RON L. JESSUP

132 MOORE AVENUE
MOUNT AIRY, NORTH CAROLINA 27030
Telephone: 336-786-5200
Fax: 336-786-1504
Email: jessuplaw@hotmail.com

Consumer Protection Law, Unfair and Deceptive Trade Practices, Employment and Labor Law, Sexual Harassment and Discrimination, U.S. Title VII Discrimination, Criminal Law, Civil and Criminal Trial Litigation, State and Federal Courts.

(This Listing Continued)

FIRM PROFILE: Successfully represented clients in over 1,000 consumer protection, employment and labor law, and criminal law cases.

RON L. JESSUP, born Forsyth County, North Carolina, February 17, 1953; admitted to bar, 1991, North Carolina; 1992, U.S. District Court, Middle District of North Carolina. *Education:* North Carolina State University (B.A., 1975; M.A., Public Affairs, 1976); North Carolina Central University (J.D., 1990). Recipient, Eagle Scout Rank, Boy Scouts of America, 1968. Law Clerk for North Carolina Attorney General's Office, 1989. Appointed, Magistrate Judge, North Carolina, 1984-1987, 1991-1993. Student Body President, Ex-Officio Member, Board of Trustees, North Carolina State University, 1974-1975. English Teacher and English Department Chair, East Surry High School, Pilot Mountain, 1977-1983. Candidate, North Carolina State Senate, 12th State Legislative District, 1998. *Member:* Surry County, 17-B Judicial District, North Carolina and American Bar Associations; North Carolina State Bar.

ROYSTER AND ROYSTER

Established in 1979
851 MARSHALL STREET
P.O. BOX 1005
MOUNT AIRY, NORTH CAROLINA 27030
Telephone: 336-789-5127
Fax: 336-789-6650
Email: sgr@roysterandroyster.com
URL: http://www.lawyers.com/roysterandroyster

Pilot Mountain, North Carolina Office: 110 South Davis Street, P.O. Box 1396. Telephone: 919-368-4455. Fax: 919-368-1279. Email: mroyster@surry.net.

General Civil and Criminal Trial Practice. DWI, Traffic Offenses, Felonies. Personal Injury, Automobile Accidents, Wrongful Death, Real Estate Law, Trusts and Estates, Wills and Probate, Probate Law and Workers Compensation.

MEMBERS OF FIRM

STEPHEN G. ROYSTER, born Shelby, North Carolina, September 11, 1946; admitted to bar, 1974, North Carolina. *Education:* Wake Forest University (B.A., 1968); Cumberland School of Law of Samford University (J.D., 1974). Phi Delta Phi. Associate Editor, The Cumberland Lawyer, 1973-1974. Chairman, Cumberland School of Law Speakers Program, 1972-1973. Vice-President, Cumberland Student Bar Association, 1973-1974. Member, 1974-1976 and Chairman, 1976-1980, Surry County Board of Elections. Member, Surry County School Board, 1984-1988. *Member:* Surry County Bar Association (Secretary-Treasurer, 1974—); North Carolina State Bar; North Carolina Academy of Trial Lawyers. **PRACTICE AREAS:** Personal Injury Law; Criminal Law. **Email:** sgr@roysterandroyster.com

MICHAEL F. ROYSTER, born Shelby, North Carolina, September 11, 1946; admitted to bar, 1975, North Carolina. *Education:* Wake Forest University (B.A., 1968); Cumberland School of Law of Samford University (J.D., cum laude, 1975). Phi Delta Phi. Member, Curia Honoris. Associate Editor, 1973-1974 and Alumni Editor, 1974-1975, The Cumberland Lawyer. Assistant District Attorney for Mecklenburg County, North Carolina, 1975-1979. *Member:* North Carolina State Bar. **PRACTICE AREAS:** Real Estate Law; Estates. **Email:** mikey_27041@yahoo.com

ASSOCIATE

MICHAEL D. BEAL, born Lenoir, North Carolina, December 12, 1966; admitted to bar, 1991, North Carolina. *Education:* North Carolina State University (B.A., 1988); Wake Forest University (J.D., 1991). Phi Delta Phi. Member, Mount Airy City School Board, 1999—. *Member:* Surry County and North Carolina Bar Association (Member, Young Lawyers Division); North Carolina State Bar; North Carolina Academy of Trial Lawyers. **PRACTICE AREAS:** Personal Injury Law; Criminal Law; Real Estate; Workers Compensation. **Email:** mdb@roysterandroyster.com

REPRESENTATIVE CLIENTS: Sanders McHone Farm Service; Hull Brothers Lumber Co., Inc.; S and C Pools, Inc.; Cox-Needham Funeral Home; Corder Transportations, Inc.; Pilot Engines, Inc.; Pilot Mountain Animal Hospital; Farm Credit Services.

CLONINGER LAW OFFICE

1453 N. MAIN STREET
MOUNT PLEASANT, NORTH CAROLINA 28124
Telephone: 704-436-2233
Fax: 704-436-2244
Email: bcloninger@ctc.net
URL: http://www.cloningerlawfirm.com

Mailing Address: P.O. Box 1518, Mount Pleasant, NC 28124

Criminal, Traffic, Driving While Intoxicated, Family Law, Custody, Divorce, Child Support, Visitation Rights, Wills and Probate.

BRENT CLONINGER, born Concord, North Carolina, 1963; admitted to bar, 1993, North Carolina. *Education:* University of North Carolina at Chapel Hill (B.A., 1986); Campbell University School of Law (J.D., 1993). Phi Alpha Delta. Member, Moot Court. Volunteer, Cabarrus County Teen Court. Intern, Mecklenburg County District Attorney's Office. *Member:* Cabarrus County Bar Association; North Carolina State Bar. **PRACTICE AREAS:** Criminal; Traffic; Driving While Intoxicated; Family Law; Custody; Divorce; Child Support; Visitation Rights; Wills; Probate. **Email:** bcloninger@ctc.net

The LeonLaw Firm

MURFREESBORO, NORTH CAROLINA

(See Greenville)

Employment Law, Personal Injury, Workers Compensation, Contracts.

REVELLE & LEE, LLP

Established in 1936
201 EAST MAIN STREET
P.O. BOX 448
MURFREESBORO, NORTH CAROLINA 27855
Telephone: 252-398-4171
Fax: 252-398-4051
Email: revellelawfirm@coastalnet.com

Probate, Real Estate, Corporation, Taxation and Municipal Corporations Law.

MEMBERS OF FIRM

ROBERT EDWARD LEE, JR., born Murfreesboro, North Carolina, December 5, 1945; admitted to bar, 1972, North Carolina. *Education:* Wake Forest University (B.A., 1968; J.D., 1972). Phi Delta Phi. Town Attorney, Town of Murfreesboro, 1978—. Adjunct Professor, Chowan College, Murfreesboro, North Carolina, 1992—. *Member:* Hertford County, North Carolina and Sixth Judicial District (Vice-President, 1988; President, 1989) Bar Associations; North Carolina State Bar. **PRACTICE AREAS:** General Practice; Real Property; Probate; Local Government.

CHARLES L. REVELLE, III, born Suffolk, Virginia, June 15, 1952; admitted to bar, 1977, North Carolina. *Education:* University of North Carolina (A.B., 1974); Duke University (J.D., 1977). County Attorney, Hertford County, 1998—. General Counsel: Chowan College, 1998—; Hertford County Department of Social Services, 1980—. *Member:* North Carolina and American Bar Associations; Sixth Judicial District and The North Carolina State Bars. **PRACTICE AREAS:** Real Property Law; Estate Planning; Commercial Law; Municipal Law.

ASSOCIATE

J. JERRY VICK, JR.

OF COUNSEL

J. GUY REVELLE, JR.

GENERAL COUNSEL FOR: Hertford County; Chowan College; Town of Murfreesboro; Town of Como; Murfreesboro Historical Assn., Inc.; Hertford County Department of Social Services; Hertford County Planning Board; Severn Peanut Co.; Meherrin Agricultural & Chemical Co.
REPRESENTATIVE CLIENTS: Centura Bank; Southern Bank and Trust Co.; Revelle Agri-Products, Inc.; Revelle Grain Co., Inc.; Jenkins Insurance Agency; Murfreesboro Peanut Cooperative; Brown's Mobile Homes, Inc.; Resinall (Chemicals); United Turf, Inc.; Revelle Builders of NC, Inc.

RUDOLPH A. BATA, JR., P.A.

Established in 1978
225 VALLEY RIVER AVENUE
SUITE A
MURPHY, NORTH CAROLINA 28906
Telephone: 828-837-8684
Fax: 828-837-2174
Email: batalaw@yahoo.com
URL: http://www.lawyers.com/batalaw

General Civil Practice, Civil Litigation in State and Federal Courts, Personal Injury, Negligence, Real Estate Litigation, Residential and Commercial Transactions, Probate Law.

RUDOLPH A. BATA, JR., born Akron, Ohio, January 9, 1947; admitted to bar, 1973, District of Columbia; 1978, North Carolina; 1991, U.S. District Court, Western District of North Carolina and U.S. Court of Appeals, Fourth Circuit, U.S. Supreme Court. *Education:* Southern College (B.S., 1969); Emory University (J.D., 1972). Member, Editorial Board, Emory Law Journal, 1971-1972. Certified Mediator. *Member:* North Carolina (Member, Pro Bono Committee) and American Bar Associations; The District of Columbia Bar; North Carolina State Bar. **PRACTICE AREAS:** Mediation; Real Estate; Family; Corporate; Business; Banking; Probate; Estates; Civil Litigation. **Email:** batalaw@dnet.net

LEGAL SUPPORT PERSONNEL

AMANDA CARROLL (Paralegal)

REPRESENTATIVE CLIENTS: Boyd's Cabinets; W & H Development, Inc.; David R. Silverstein, D.D.S.; James W. Vollmer, D.D.S.; River Ridge of Murphy, N.C. Homeowner's Association; Ralph L. Crisp Realty Company, Inc.; Prince Land and Development Corp.; Sunset Mountain Development Co.; Murphy Mountain Land Co.; Granny Squirrel Mountain Club Homeowners Association; Higdon Construction Co.; W & H Development, Inc.; Wisley Investments, Ltd.; The 409 Building, LLC; Ziyd H. Mugharbil, M.D., P.A.; Otter Creek Land Company; Otter Creek Excavating Company; Kush Investments, LLC; Jacky Jones Pontiac, Buick, GMC Trucks, Inc.; Hayesville Mountain Mercantile, Inc.; Jacky Jones Ford of Andrews, Inc.; Riverbend Property Owners Assn., Inc.; Quail Cove Property Owners Assn., Inc.; Whispering Springs Property Owners Assn., Inc.; Mt. Shaddai Homeowners Assn., Inc.; Nantahala Shores Property Owners Assn., Inc.
REFERENCES: First Citizens Bank; First Union National Bank; First Title Insurance Co.; Title Insurance Company of Minnesota; Lawyer's Title Insurance Co.; Stewart Title Insurance Co.; Ticor Title Insurance Co.; Investors Title Insurance Co.; Commonwealth Land Title Insurance Co.; Transamerica Title Insurance Co.

COWAN & COWAN, P.A.

26 TENNESSEE STREET
P.O. BOX 579
MURPHY, NORTH CAROLINA 28906-0579
Telephone: 828-873-2332
Fax: 828-837-2336
Email: cowanlawyers@brmemc.net

Civil Litigation, Criminal Defense, Traffic Violations, Real Estate, Residential Transactions, Commercial Transactions.

(This Listing Continued)

COWAN & COWAN, P.A., Murphy—Continued

RONALD M. COWAN, born Sylva, North Carolina, March 26, 1950; admitted to bar, 1975, North Carolina. *Education:* Wingate College (A.A., 1970); University of North Carolina (B.S., 1972); Wake Forest University (J.D., cum laude, 1975). Phi Beta Kappa. *Member:* North Carolina State Bar; North Carolina Bar Association; North Carolina Academy of Trial Lawyers. ***PRACTICE AREAS:*** Civil Litigation; Criminal Defense; Traffic Violations.

DAVID E. COWAN, born Pinehurst, North Carolina, October 13, 1976; admitted to bar, 2002, North Carolina. *Education:* Western Carolina University (B.S., cum laude, 1999); Campbell University (J.D., 2002). *Member:* North Carolina State Bar; North Carolina Bar Association. ***PRACTICE AREAS:*** Real Estate; Residential Transactions; Commercial Transactions.

LARRY J. FORD
ATTORNEY AT LAW

MURPHY, NORTH CAROLINA

(See Hayesville)

Real Estate, Trusts and Estates, Elder Law, Business Law, Corporate Law, Wills & Probate.

ALEXY, FLETCHER, WILLS & WILLS, P.C.

NAGS HEAD, NORTH CAROLINA

(See Point Harbor)

ROY A. ARCHBELL, JR.

NAGS HEAD, NORTH CAROLINA

(See Kitty Hawk)

General Civil Trial Practice in State and Federal Courts. Family, Personal Injury, Collection, Corporate, Construction, Insurance, Real Estate, Domestic Relations, Divorce.

RONALD E. DeVEAU, P.C.

2224 S. CROATAN HIGHWAY, #14
NAGS HEAD, NORTH CAROLINA 27959
Telephone: 252-480-2828
Fax: 252-480-2929
Email: ron@deveaulaw.com
URL: http://www.lawyers.com/deveaulaw

General Civil and Trial Practice in State and Federal Courts, Personal Injury and Negligence, Workers Compensation, Family Law, Business Torts, Estates.

RONALD E. DeVEAU, born New Kensington, Pennsylvania, November 22, 1944; admitted to bar, 1970, Ohio; 1986, North Carolina; U.S. District Court, Eastern District of North Carolina. *Education:* Lehigh University (B.S., with honors, 1966); Duke University (J.D., 1969). Phi Alpha Delta. Assistant Professor of Law, Ohio University, 1969-1971. Acting Judge, Athens County Municipal Court, 1980-1986. Arbitrator, First Judicial District. *Member:* North Carolina Academy of Trial Lawyers (Member, Auto Torts and Workers Compensation Sections); American Trial Lawyers Association. ***PRACTICE AREAS:*** Personal Injury; Workers Compensation; Business Litigation; Collections; Marital Property Settlements. ***Email:*** ron@deveaulaw.com

HORNTHAL, RILEY, ELLIS & MALAND, L.L.P.

2502 SOUTH CROATAN HIGHWAY
P.O. BOX 310
NAGS HEAD, NORTH CAROLINA 27959-0310
Telephone: 252-441-0871
Telefax: 252-441-8822
Email: hrem@hrem.com
URL: http://www.hrem.com

Elizabeth City, North Carolina Office: 301 East Main Street, P.O. Box 220. Telephone: 252-335-0871. Fax: 252-335-4223.

General Trial and Appellate Practice in all Courts. Personal Injury, Products Liability, Professional Malpractice, Corporate, Tax, Bankruptcy, Employment, Education, Family, Construction, Real Estate, Environment, Elder, Local Government, Wills and Trusts, Probate and Admiralty Law.

ROBERT B. HOBBS, JR., born Richmond, Virginia, December 31, 1960; admitted to bar, 1986, North Carolina. *Education:* University of North Carolina at Chapel Hill (B.A., 1983); Campbell University (J.D., 1986). Phi Alpha Delta. Staff Member, Campbell Law Review, 1984-1986. Case Law Editor, Campbell Law Observer, 1985. Author: Note, "Cable TV's 'Must Carry' Rules: The Most Restrictive Alternative," 8 Campbell Law Review 339, 1986. Member, Board of Governors, North Carolina Bar Association, 1993-1996. Member: Executive Council, 1988-1993 and Chair, 1991-1992, Law Practice Management Section, Executive Council, 2004-2007, Real Property Section, North Carolina Bar Association. *Member:* North Carolina State Bar; North Carolina (Member, Sections on: Real Property; Estate Planning and Fiduciary Law) and American (Member, Sections on: Real Property; Probate and Trust Law) Bar Associations. (Also at Elizabeth City Office) (Board Certified Specialist in Real Property Law-Residential, Business, Commercial and Industrial Transactions, North Carolina State Bar Board of Legal Specialization). ***PRACTICE AREAS:*** Real Property; Estate Planning; Business.

(This Listing Continued)

DONALD I. McREE, JR., born Hampton, Virginia, May 29, 1961; admitted to bar, 1987, North Carolina; 1989, U.S. District Court, Eastern District of North Carolina. *Education:* St. Andrews Presbyterian College (B.A., 1983); Campbell University School of Law (J.D., 1986). Phi Alpha Delta. Member of Staff, North Carolina Local Government Commission, 1986-1989. County Attorney: Currituck County, 1989-1992; Pasquotank County, 1992-2000, Tyrrell County, 2004—. Town Attorney: Towns of Hertford, Nags Head and Southern Shores, 2001—; Town of Duck, 2002—. *Member:* First Judicial District, North Carolina and American Bar Associations; North Carolina State Bar; International Municipal Lawyers Association; North Carolina Association of Municipal Attorneys; North Carolina Association of County Attorneys. ***PRACTICE AREAS:*** Municipal Law; Land Use.

OF COUNSEL

THOMAS L. WHITE, JR., born Raleigh, North Carolina, June 6, 1938; admitted to bar, 1970, North Carolina; 1978, U.S. District Court, Eastern District of North Carolina and U.S. Supreme Court; 1984, U.S. Court of Appeals, Fourth Circuit. *Education:* University of North Carolina (A.B., 1960; J.D., 1970). Phi Alpha Delta. Town Attorney: Nags Head, 1971-2001; Southern Shores, 1979-2001. *Member:* Dare County (President, 1975-1976), First Judicial District (Vice-President, 1979; President, 1980), and North Carolina Bar Associations; North Carolina State Bar; North Carolina Association of Municipal Attorneys. [U.S. Navy, 1960-1967; Capt., USNR, 1967-1989]. (Resident). ***PRACTICE AREAS:*** Education Law; Government Law; Municipal Law.

REPRESENTATIVE CLIENTS: Wachovia Bank of North Carolina, N.A.; North Carolina Power Co.; College of the Albemarle; Elizabeth City-Pasquotank County Board of Education; Camden County Board of Education; Elizabeth City Housing Authority; Southern Railway System; Lawyers Title Insurance Corp.; Chicago Title Insurance Co.; Old Republic Title Insurance Co.; Federal Land Bank Association of Columbia; State Farm Mutual; Travelers Insurance Co.; Government Employees Insurance Co.; Crum and Forster; Great American Insurance Co.; USF&G; Kemper Insurance Group; Pennsylvania National Insurance Group; Employers' Mutual Casualty Co.; Grain Dealers Mutual Insurance Co.; Ohio Casualty Insurance Group; Chubb and Son Group; Firemen's Fund Insurance Co.; Dare County Airport Authority; North Carolina Professional Liability Pool; Branch Banking & Trust Co.; N.C. Insurance Guaranty Association; N.C. Interlocal Risk Financing Fund; Horace Mann Insurance Companies; Carmike Cinemas, Inc.; Town of Nags Head; Town of Southern Shores; Town of Duck; Town of Hertford.
APPROVED ATTORNEYS FOR: Lawyers Title Insurance Corp.; United Title Insurance Co.; Commonwealth Land Title Insurance Co.; Old Republic Title Insurance Co.; Investors Title Insurance; Ticor Title Insurance Co.; First American Title Insurance Co.; Stewart Title Co.; Chicago Title Co.; Atlantic Casualty Insurance Group; Universal Underwriters Insurance Group.

(For complete biographical data on personnel, see Professional Biographies at Elizabeth City, North Carolina)

KELLOGG AND EVANS, P.A.

NAGS HEAD, NORTH CAROLINA

(See Manteo)

General Civil Practice in State Courts, Family Law, Probate, Real Estate, Business Law, Vessel Documentation and Financing, and Estate Planning and Administration.

THE MOORE LAW FIRM, P.C.

NAGS HEAD, NORTH CAROLINA

(See Manns Harbor)

Real Estate, Corporate Law.

SHARP, MICHAEL, OUTTEN AND GRAHAM

NAGS HEAD, NORTH CAROLINA

(See Kitty Hawk)

General Civil and Criminal Practice, Commercial and Residential Real Estate, Municipal and Administrative, Family and Domestic Relations, Personal Injury, Probate, Banking, Corporations, Traffic, Driving While Intoxicated, Mediation, Arbitration, Ship Documentation, Estate Planning, Elder Law.

VANDEVENTER BLACK LLP

NAGS HEAD, NORTH CAROLINA

(See Kitty Hawk)

Admiralty, Arbitration and Mediation, Aviation, Banking, Bankruptcy and Creditors' Rights, Commercial Transactions, Community Associations, Construction Law, Environmental Law, Estate Planning, General Litigation in State and Federal Courts, Government/Public Contracts, Health Care Law, Immigration Law, International, Intellectual Property, Insurance Defense, Labor and Employment Law, Land Use, Local Government/Municipal Law, Malpractice, Maritime, Mergers and Acquisitions, Products Liability, Public Utilities, Real Estate, Taxation, Technology, Workers' Compensation.

THE VINCENT LAW FIRM, PC

NAGS HEAD, NORTH CAROLINA

(See Southern Shores)

Workers Compensation, Personal Injury, Auto Accidents, Social Security Disability, Wrongful Death and Admiralty Longshores.

JOHN E. DAVENPORT, P.A.

207 WEST WASHINGTON STREET
P.O. BOX 938
NASHVILLE, NORTH CAROLINA 27856
Telephone: 252-459-2124
Fax: 252-459-7691

General Civil and Criminal Practice. Probate, Real Estate, and Taxation.

FIRM PROFILE: Firm established by Louis L. Davenport in 1912. Later Davenport and Davenport, John E. Davenport, P.A., 1982.

JOHN E. DAVENPORT, born Nashville, North Carolina, April 28, 1928; admitted to bar, 1952, North Carolina. *Education:* University of North Carolina (A.B., 1948; J.D., 1951). Delta Theta Phi (District Chancellor, 1957-1973). Prosecuting Attorney, Nash County, 1956-1957. Real Property Attorney, State of North Carolina, 1957-1959. Member: House of Representatives. North Carolina General Assembly, 1973-1978. Member, Board of Governors, University of North Carolina, 1979-1985. Member, North Carolina Statute Commission, 1994-1996. Inducted into North Carolina Bar Association General Practitioner's Hall of Fame, June, 2004. *Member:* Nash-Edgecombe County (President, 1969-1970), North Carolina and American (Member, Real Estate and Probate Section) Bar Associations; Seventh Judicial District State Bar (President, 1991-1994). [Capt., J.A.G., U.S.A.F., 1951-1953]

APPROVED ATTORNEY FOR: First Title Co.; Lawyers Title Insurance Corp.; Chicago Title Insurance Co.; A.M.I. Title Co.; Commonwealth Land Title Insurance Co.; First American Title Insurance Co.
REFERENCE: Centura Bank.

FIELDS & COOPER, PLLC

113 COURT STREET
P.O. BOX 757
NASHVILLE, NORTH CAROLINA 27856
Telephone: 252-459-2121
Fax: 252-459-2123

Rocky Mount, North Carolina Office: 422 Sunset Avenue, P.O. Box 4538. Telephone: 252-442-3115. Fax: 252-442-4170. Email: nashville.fclaw@earthlink.net.

General Civil and Trial Practice in State and Federal Courts. Personal Injury, Creditor Bankruptcy and Collections, Construction, Corporation, Probate, Real Estate, Traffic, and Elder Law.

(For complete biographical data on all personnel, see Professional Biographies at Rocky Mount, North Carolina)

MICHAEL P. MURPHY, P.A.

NASHVILLE, NORTH CAROLINA

(See Rocky Mount)

Commercial Collections, Wills, Trust Law, Estate Planning, Personal Injury, Automobile Accidents and Injuries, Truck Accidents, Bankruptcy Chapter 7, Bankruptcy Chapter 13, Corporate Law, Limited Liability Company Law, Business Law, Criminal Law, Traffic Violations.

VALENTINE, ADAMS & LAMAR, L.L.P.

203 SOUTH BARNES STREET
P.O. BOX 847
NASHVILLE, NORTH CAROLINA 27856
Telephone: 252-459-1111
Email: 2lewis@nashvillenc.com

Personal Injury, Automobile Accidents, Wrongful Death, Criminal, DWI, Traffic, Real Estate, Business, Wills, Trusts, Estate, Elder Law, Education Law.

MEMBERS OF FIRM

I.T. "TIM" VALENTINE (Retired) (U.S. Congressman)

FRANKLIN L. ADAMS, JR., born Lumberton, North Carolina, 1939; admitted to bar, 1963, North Carolina. *Education:* University of North Carolina (B.A., 1961; LL.B., 1963). *Member:* Nash-Edgecombe (President, 1975) and North Carolina Bar Associations; North Carolina State Bar. [JAGD, U.S.A.F; Capt.]

L. WARDLAW LAMAR, born Montgomery, Alabama, 1936; admitted to bar, 1968, North Carolina; 1992, Alabama. *Education:* Auburn University (B.A., 1959; M.A., 1969); Emory University and University of North Carolina (J.D., 1968). Clerk to Hon. Algernon L. Butler, U.S. District Court. Distinguished Service Award-NC Bar Association, 1997. Work with various North Carolina School Boards and Community Colleges. *Member:* North Carolina Bar Association; North Carolina State Bar; North Carolina Council of School Attorneys (President, 1991-1992). [Capt., USMC, 1959-1962]. ***PRACTICE AREAS:*** Education Law; Personal Injury; Wills; Estates; Real Estate.

LEWIS W. LAMAR, JR., born Chapel Hill, North Carolina, 1968; admitted to bar, 1995, North Carolina. *Education:* University of North Carolina, Chapel Hill (B.A., English, 1990); Campbell University (J.D., 1995). *Member:* North Carolina State Bar; North Carolina Bar Association; North Carolina Council of School Attorneys. ***PRACTICE AREAS:*** Education Law; Real Property; Civil Litigation; Traffic Violations. ***Email:*** lewis.valfirm@gmail.com

VICTORIA L. BLOCK

Established in 2003
315 METCALF STREET
NEW BERN, NORTH CAROLINA 28562
Telephone: 252-636-0600
Fax: 252-636-0527
Email: vblock@mindspring.com
URL: http://www.victoriablocklaw.com

Immigration Law, Social Security Law, Wills.

VICTORIA L. BLOCK, born Chicago, Illinois, September 6, 1948; admitted to bar, 1977, California; 1983, U.S. Court of Appeals, Sixth Circuit; 1988, U.S. District Court, Northern District of California; 2000, District of Columbia and Maryland; 2003, North Carolina. *Education:* Stanford University (A.B., 1970); University of California at Los Angeles (J.D., 1975). Judicial Nominating Commission for the Commonwealth of Kentucky, 1984-1988. *Member:* Craven County and American (Member, Law Practice Management Committee) Bar Associations; State Bar of California (Member, Litigation Section); American Immigration Lawyers Association. ***LANGUAGES:*** French and Italian. ***PRACTICE AREAS:*** Immigration Law; Real Estate; Wills; Litigation; Family Law.

BRUMBAUGH, MU & KING, P.A.

Established in 1978
MCCARTHY SQUARE OFFICE SUITES
790 CARDINAL ROAD, SUITE 6
NEW BERN, NORTH CAROLINA 28562
Telephone: 252-636-2099
URL: http://www.bmklaw.net

Practice Limited to Injury Cases. Automobile, Wrongful Death, Medical Malpractice, Workers' Compensation, Products Liability and Social Security Claims.

(For complete biographical data on all personnel, see professional biographies, Jacksonville, North Carolina)

CHESNUTT, CLEMMONS, THOMAS & PEACOCK, P.A.

Established in 1994
225-C BROAD STREET
P.O. BOX 12530
NEW BERN, NORTH CAROLINA 28561
Telephone: 252-633-6868
Fax: 252-637-2450
Email: gary@nclegalnet.com

General Practice in all State and Federal Courts. Personal Injury, Wrongful Death, Civil Litigation, DWI, Traffic Offenses, Family and Domestic Law. Social Security, Workers' Compensation, Homeowners Associations, Criminal Defense, DMV Hearings.

MARCUS W. CHESNUTT, born Lumberton, North Carolina, August 31, 1953; admitted to bar, 1978, North Carolina. *Education:* University of North Carolina (B.A., 1975); Cumberland School of Law of Sanford University (J.D., 1978). Delta Theta Phi. Senior Law Clerk to Chief U.S. District Judge John D. Larkins, Jr., 1978-1979 and Member, Local Rules Committee, Civil Rules Section, 1979, U.S. District Court, Eastern District of North Carolina. Member, Trial Advocacy Board, Cumberland School of Law, 1977-1978. Permanent Delegate, 4th Circuit Judicial Conference, 1980—. President, Third Judicial District, 1983-1984. *Member:* Craven County and North Carolina Bar Associations; North Carolina State Bar; North Carolina Academy of Trial Lawyers. ***PRACTICE AREAS:*** Criminal; Traffic; Domestic; Personal Injury.

GARY H. CLEMMONS, born Wilmington, North Carolina, July 5, 1955; admitted to bar, 1981, North Carolina. *Education:* University of North Carolina at Chapel Hill (B.A., 1977); Campbell University (J.D., 1981). Listed, Swarthmore's Who's Who, 2000-2001. Member, Editorial Board, Campbell Law Review, 1979-1981. Law Clerk to Senior U.S. District Court Judge John D. Larkins, Jr., 1981-1982. Assistant U.S. Attorney, Eastern District of North Carolina, 1982-1985. Permanent Delegate, 4th Circuit Judicial Conference, 1985—. *Member:* Craven County Bar Association (Secretary, 1991-1993; President, 1993-1994; Attorney, Home Health and Hospice); North Carolina Bar Association (Litigation Section Council); North Carolina State Bar; North Carolina Academy of Trial Lawyers (Member, Board of Governors, 2002—); Eastern Inn of Court. ***PRACTICE AREAS:*** Personal Injury; Wrongful Death; Automobile Accidents and Injuries; Federal Criminal Defense; Civil Litigation; Worker's Compensation; Social Security Disability; Homeowners Associations. ***Email:*** gary@nclegalnet.com

SCOTT E. THOMAS, born New Bern, North Carolina, July 19, 1966; admitted to bar, 1992, North Carolina. *Education:* East Carolina University (B.S., 1988); North Carolina Central University (J.D., 1992). Law Clerk to North Carolina Supreme Court Justice, John Webb, 1992-1993. Legal Intern to State Bureau of Investigation Director, Robert B. Morgan, 1990. Assistant District Attorney, Craven County, 1993-1994. Member, North Carolina House of Representatives, 1999-2000. Member, North Carolina Senate, 2001— *Member:* Third Judicial District and North Carolina Bar Associations; North Carolina Academy of Trial Lawyers. ***PRACTICE AREAS:*** Criminal; Traffic; Domestic; Personal Injury; DMV Hearings.

CAROLYN TAYLOR PEACOCK, born Orlando, Florida, November 14, 1972; admitted to bar, 1996, North Carolina. *Education:* Florida State University (B.S., 1993); Wake Forest University (J.D., 1996). Member, Moot Court Board. Assistant District Attorney, Craven County District Attorney's Office, 1996-1998. *Member:* Craven County (Secretary, 1999; President, 2000) and North Carolina Bar Associations; North Carolina State Bar (Counsel, Criminal Law Section; Member, Family Law; President, Judicial District 3-B)

(This Listing Continued)

CHESNUTT, CLEMMONS, THOMAS & PEACOCK, P.A., New Bern—Continued

North Carolina Academy of Trial Lawyers. ***PRACTICE AREAS:*** Family Law; Domestic Relations; Child Support; Criminal Law. ***Email:*** carolyn@nclegalnet.com

EMANUEL & DUNN, PLLC

3230 COUNTRY CLUB ROAD
P.O. BOX 1389
NEW BERN, NORTH CAROLINA 28563
Telephone: 252-633-3800
Fax: 252-633-6669

Raleigh, North Carolina Office) 130 South Salisbury Street, P.O. Box 426, 27602. Telephone: 919-832-0329; 919-832-0320.

Civil Trials in all State and Federal Courts. Business Litigation, Employment Litigation, Personal Injury Litigation, ERISA Litigation, Business Law, Contracts, Real Estate, Estate Planning and Probate, Employment Law.

FIRM PROFILE: Established over 75 years ago, the firm of Emanuel & Dunn, PLLC has grown into a strong practice serving North Carolina with special emphasis on litigating and resolving employment, complex business and computer related disputes; wealth transfer planning and wills and estates; and business transactions.

MEMBERS OF FIRM

J. L. EMANUEL (1894-1968)

RAYMOND E. DUNN (1922-2001)

ROBERT L. EMANUEL (Resident, Raleigh Office)

STEPHEN A. DUNN (Resident, Raleigh Office)

JAMES M. MASON

RAYMOND E. DUNN, JR., born Durham, North Carolina, February 27, 1951; admitted to bar, 1979, North Carolina and U.S. District Court, Eastern District of North Carolina. *Education:* University of North Carolina (B.A., 1973; M.R.P., 1976); Wake Forest University (J.D., 1979). Member, Wake Forest Law Review, 1977-1979. Author: "The Standard of Commercial Reasonableness in The Sale of Repossessed Collateral," 15 Wake Forest Law Review 71, 1979. Member, Panel of Arbitrators, American Arbitration Association. *Member:* Craven County, North Carolina and American (Member, Litigation Section) Bar Associations; North Carolina State Bar. ***PRACTICE AREAS:*** Business Litigation; Employment Litigation; Personal Injury Litigation. ***Email:*** rdunn@emanuelanddunn.com

PAT LEIGH PITTMAN, born Fairmont, North Carolina, April 6, 1963; admitted to bar, 1988, North Carolina. *Education:* Wake Forest University (B.A., cum laude, 1985); University of North Carolina, Chapel Hill School of Law (J.D., 1988). George Foster Hankins Scholar. *Member:* North Carolina and American (Member, Real Property Section; Probate and Trust Law Sections) Bar Associations; North Carolina State Bar. ***PRACTICE AREAS:*** Business Law; Estate Planning Law; Probate Law; Real Estate. ***Email:*** plpittman@emanuelanddunn.com

ANNE DUNCAN EDWARDS, born Norfolk, Virginia, December 5, 1955; admitted to bar, 1991, North Carolina and U.S. District Court, Eastern and Middle Districts of North Carolina; 1996, U.S. Court of Appeals, Fourth Circuit. *Education:* Virginia Polytechnic Institute and State University (B.S., 1979; M.S., 1983); College of William and Mary (J.D., 1991). Issue Editor, Administrative Law Review, 1989-1991. Certified Superior Court Mediator. *Member:* Craven County, Third Judicial District, North Carolina, and American Bar Associations; North Carolina State Bar. ***PRACTICE AREAS:*** Employment Litigation; Business Litigation; Complex Litigation; Labor and Employment; Computer and Software; Civil Litigation; Appellate Practice; Insurance Defense; Mediation. ***Email:*** adedwards@emanuelanddunn.com

JOANNE K. PARTIN, born Mansfield, Ohio, September 8, 1946; admitted to bar, 1981, North Carolina. *Education:* Wake Forest University (B.A., cum laude, 1969); University of North Carolina (J.D., 1981). *Member:* Craven County and North Carolina (Member, Sections on: Estate Planning and Fiduciary Law; Elder Law) Bar Associations; North Carolina State Bar. (Board Certified Specialist in Estate Planning and Probate Law, North Carolina State Board of Legal Specialization). ***PRACTICE AREAS:*** Estate Planning; Estate Planning for the Elderly; Family Trusts; Family Wealth Transfer; Estate Administration; Probate. ***Email:*** jpartin@emanuelanddunn.com

LEE W. BETTIS, JR., born Los Angeles, California, September 22, 1964; admitted to bar, 2001, New York; 2004, North Carolina. *Education:* Slippery Rock University (B.A., 1987); Brooklyn Law School (J.D., 2000). *Member:* Craven County, North Carolina and New York State Bar Associations; North Carolina State Bar. ***PRACTICE AREAS:*** Business Litigation; Insurance Defense Litigation; Personal Injury Litigation; Workers Compensation.

MARY THOMPSON SKINNER, born Durham, North Carolina, January 2, 1954; admitted to bar, 1981, North Carolina. *Education:* University of North Carolina (B.S., 1976; J.D., 1981). *Member:* Craven, Pamlico and North Carolina (Member, Estate Planning; Tax Sections) Bar Associations. ***PRACTICE AREAS:*** Estate Planning; Estate Administration; Probate; Income Tax; Tax Planning; Business Law. ***Email:*** mskinner@emanuelanddunn.com

REPRESENTATIVE CLIENTS: Admiral Insurance Co.; Aegon, USA Group of Insurance Co.; American Bankers Insurance Group; American Centennial Insurance Company; The Atlantic Cos.; Carolina Rehabilitation and Evaluation Center, Inc.; Carteret Community College; Chicago Insurance Co.; The Chubb Group of Insurance Cos.; Economy Fire and Casualty Co.; Erie Insurance Co.; Federal Insurance Co.; Fireman's Fund Insurance Cos.; Gay and Taylor, Inc.; Georgia International Life Insurance Co.; Integon General Insurance Corp.; Iowa Mutual Insurance Co.; J.E. Jones Lumber Co., Inc.; Kemper Group of Insurance Co.; The Maryland Insurance Group; Metropolitan Fire and Casualty Co.; MS Insurance Co.; New York Mutual Fire Insurance Co.; North Carolina Land and Timber Co.; Old Dominion Freight Line Inc.; Ramsay Health Care, Inc.; Seibels Bruce & Co.; Selective Insurance Company; Sentry Claims Service; Craven Regional Airport Authority; State Farm Fire and Casualty Co.; State Farm Mutual Automobile Insurance Co.; Universal Insurance Co.; USAA Insurance Group; Zaytoun and Raines Construction Co; Continental Life Insurance Co.; Universal Under Writers Group; North Carolina Insurance Guaranty Association; Bituminous Insurance Companies; Centennial Life Insurance Company; California Insurance Guaranty; Florida Insurance Guaranty; Virginia Insurance Guaranty; The Hanover Insurance Companies.
APPROVED ATTORNEYS FOR: AMIC Title Insurance Co.; Chicago Title Insurance Co.; First Title Insurance Co.; Investors Title Insurance Co.; Jefferson-Pilot Title Insurance Co.; Lawyers Title Insurance Co.
REFERENCES: State Farm Insurance Cos.; Branch Banking & Trust Co.; Wachovia Bank & Trust Co., N.A.; Bank of America.

HARRIS, CREECH, WARD & BLACKERBY, P.A.

325 POLLOCK STREET
P.O. DRAWER 1168
NEW BERN, NORTH CAROLINA 28563-1168
Telephone: 252-638-6666
Facsimile: 252-638-3542
Email: info@hcwb.net

Greenville, North Carolina Office: 219 Commerce Street, Suite C. 27858.

General Practice.

FIRM PROFILE: The firm represents health care providers; defends professional negligence claims and generally limits its litigation practice to the defense of non-domestic litigation. Several members of the firm engage in a general practice, including wills, estates, corporations and real estate.

THOMAS E. HARRIS, born Lexington, Kentucky, January 12, 1940; admitted to bar, 1965, Kentucky; 1971, U.S. Supreme Court; 1978, North Carolina. *Education:* University of Kentucky (B.S., 1962; J.D., 1965). Fellow, American College of Trial Lawyers. Certified Mediator. ***PRACTICE AREAS:*** Civil Practice; Professional Liability.

C. DAVID CREECH, born Smithfield, North Carolina, March 21, 1959; admitted to bar, 1988, North Carolina and U.S. Court of Appeals, Fourth Circuit. *Education:* East Carolina University (B.S., 1985); University of North Carolina (J.D., with honors, 1988). Editor, North Carolina Law Review, 1987-1988. ***PRACTICE AREAS:*** Civil Practice; Professional Liability; Automobile Accidents and Injuries; Insurance Coverage; Property Claims.

THOMAS M. WARD, born Raleigh, North Carolina, March 6, 1952; admitted to bar, 1978, North Carolina; U.S. District Court, Eastern, Middle and Western Districts of North Carolina. *Education:* University of North Carolina at Chapel Hill (B.S., 1974; J.D., 1978). ***PRACTICE AREAS:*** General Practice; Bankruptcy Litigation; Estate Planning; Tax.

R. BRITTAIN BLACKERBY, born New Bern, North Carolina, April 29, 1965; admitted to bar, 1992, North Carolina; U.S. District Court, Eastern District of North Carolina. *Education:* University of North Carolina at Wilmington (B.A., 1989); Campbell University School of Law (J.D., 1992). ***PRACTICE AREAS:*** Civil Practice; Professional Liability.

CHARLES EVERETT SIMPSON, JR., born Winston-Salem, North Carolina, May 19, 1968; admitted to bar, 1993, North Carolina and U.S. Court of Appeals, 4th Circuit. *Education:* University of North Carolina at Chapel Hill (B.A., Economics, 1990); Campbell University (J.D., 1993). Order of Barristers. Certified Mediator. ***PRACTICE AREAS:*** Civil Practice; Professional Liability.

BONNIE J. REFINSKI-KNIGHT, born Milwaukee, Wisconsin, December 14, 1960; admitted to bar, 1990, North Carolina; U.S. District Court, Eastern District of North Carolina; U.S. Court of Appeals, Fourth Circuit. *Education:* University of Wisconsin-Madison (B.A., 1983; J.D., 1990). ***PRACTICE AREAS:*** Civil Practice; Professional Liability.

WALTER GREGORY MERRITT, born Anderson, South Carolina, September 4, 1968; admitted to bar, 1996, North Carolina, U.S. District Court, Eastern, Middle and Western Districts of North Carolina and U.S. Supreme Court. *Education:* University of North Carolina (B.S.B.A., 1990); Campbell University (J.D., magna cum laude, 1996). Law Clerk, the Honorable Malcolm J. Howard, United States District Court, Eastern District of North Carolina, 1996-1998. ***PRACTICE AREAS:*** Professional Liability.

MARIE C. MOSELEY, born San Francisco, California, August 5, 1954; admitted to bar, 2000, North Carolina. *Education:* University of North Carolina at Chapel Hill (B.S.N., 1996; M.Ph., J.D., 2000). ***PRACTICE AREAS:*** Health Law; Professional Liability; Hospital Law.

NICHOLE G. BOOKER, born Rutherfordton, North Carolina, November 10, 1974; admitted to bar, 2004, North Carolina. *Education:* University of North Carolina at Greensboro (B.A., 1998; M.Ed., 1999); Campbell University (J.D., 2004). ***PRACTICE AREAS:*** Civil Practice; Professional Liability.

JENNIFER M. ARNO-WOOD, born Syracuse, New York; admitted to bar, 2004, North Carolina. *Education:* LeMoyne College (B.A., 2001); State University of New York at Buffalo (J.D., 2004). ***PRACTICE AREAS:*** Civil Litigation.

REPRESENTATIVE CLIENTS: Pitt County Memorial Hospital; St. Paul Fire and Marine Insurance Co.; The Medical Protective Insurance Company; Lawyers Mutual Liability Insurance Company of North Carolina; North Carolina Farm Bureau Mutual Insurance; Medical Mutual Insurance Company of North Carolina; Wachovia Bank and Trust Co.; Wachovia Mortgage Corp.

HENDERSON, BAXTER, TAYLOR & GATCHEL, P.A.

1319 COMMERCE DRIVE
NEW BERN, NORTH CAROLINA 28562
Telephone: 252-638-5792
Fax: 252-637-7548
URL: http://www.ncfirm.com

Mailing Address: Post Office Drawer U, New Bern, NC 28653

(This Listing Continued)

General Civil and Criminal Practice in all State and Federal Courts. Estate Planning, Estate Administration, Real Estate Law, Corporations, Collections, Social Security Law, Foreclosure, Business Law, Family Law and Administrative Law.

DAVID S. HENDERSON, born New Bern, North Carolina, August 21, 1933; admitted to bar, 1959, North Carolina. *Education:* Washington & Lee University (B.A., 1956); Wake Forest University (LL.B., 1959). Phi Delta Phi. U.S. Magistrate, 1972-1973. *Member:* North Carolina Council of School Attorneys. ***PRACTICE AREAS:*** Real Estate Litigation; Administrative Law; Estates Law.

BRIAN ZACHARY TAYLOR, born Sioux City, Iowa, March 24, 1964; admitted to bar, 1991, North Carolina and U.S. District Court, Eastern District of North Carolina; 2001 U.S. Supreme Court. *Education:* University of North Carolina at Chapel Hill (B.S., 1986); Campbell University (J.D., 1991). Delta Theta Phi. Recipient, Campbell University Book Award in Real Property Planning. Instructor, Craven Community College (Business and Real Estate Law, 1994—). President, 3B Judicial District Bar Association, 2000-2001. ***PRACTICE AREAS:*** Real Property; Business Law; Collections; Foreclosures. ***Email:*** btaylor@ncfirm.com

BRIAN J. GATCHEL, born Charleston, West Virginia, August 22, 1968; admitted to bar, 1995, North Carolina. *Education:* Davidson College (B.A., 1990); University of Kentucky (J.D., 1995). Recipient, American Jurisprudence Book Award, Land Use Planning. Publication, "Informational and Procedural Standing After" Lijan v. Defenders of Wildlife, 11 J. Land Use & Envtl. L. 75 (1995) cited in Sierra Club v. Hawaii Tourism Authority 59 P3d 877 (2002). *Member:* Craven County and American Bar Associations; North Carolina State Bar. ***PRACTICE AREAS:*** Estate Administration; Estate Planning; Elder Law; Wills; Real Estate; Business Law; Education Law. ***Email:*** bgatchel@ncfirm.com

REPRESENTATIVE CLIENT: Craven County Board of Education.

HOWARD, STALLINGS, FROM & HUTSON, P.A.

Established in 1983

2407 GRACE AVENUE
P.O. BOX 975
NEW BERN, NORTH CAROLINA 28563
Telephone: 252-633-3006
Fax: 252-633-3097
URL: http://www.howardstallings.com

Raleigh, North Carolina Office: Suite 400, 4000 Westchase Boulevard, 27607, P.O. Box 12347. Telephone: 919-821-7700. Fax: 919-821-7703.

General, Civil and Commercial Litigation, Business Law, Construction Law, Family and Domestic Relations Law, Commercial Real Estate, Taxation, Employment Law, Computer Law, Estate Planning and Administration, Employment Law, Computer Law, Representation of Creditors, Debtors and Trustees in Bankruptcy Cases, Out-of-Court Debt Restructuring, Foreclosure Proceedings, Project Finance, Landlord-Tenant Law, Intellectual Property; Contract Litigation; Contracts.

FIRM PROFILE: Since 1983, we have served our clients in New Bern, throughout North Carolina, and elsewhere with efficient, professional representation. Our firm has successfully litigated complex business matters all across the nation. We also provide a large array of legal services to our business and banking clients, and their owners. As a compliment to our commercial practice, our firm includes attorneys experienced in such diverse areas as estate planning, estate litigation, insurance law, and personal injury law, as well as a Board Certified Specialist in business and bankruptcy law.

JOSEPH H. STALLINGS, born New Bern, North Carolina, January 9, 1950; admitted to bar, 1976, New York; 1979, North Carolina; U.S. District Court, Southern and Eastern Districts of New York; U.S. District Court, Eastern, Middle and Western Districts of North Carolina; U.S. Court of Appeals, Fourth and Fifth Circuits; U.S. Tax Court; U.S. Court of Federal Claims. *Education:* University of North Carolina (A.B., 1972; J.D., with honors, 1975). Morehead Scholar; Student Body President, 1971-1972. Phi Beta Kappa; Order of the Coif. Editor-in-Chief, North Carolina Law Review, 1974-1975. Associate: Mudge Rose Guthrie & Alexander, 1976-1977; Ford Marrin Esposito & Witmeyer, 1977-1979. Member, University of North Carolina Board of Governors, 1991-1995. ***PRACTICE AREAS:*** Business Law; Business Litigation; Business Lending; Mergers and Acquisitions. ***Email:*** jstallings@hsfh.com

BETH FEREBEE ATKINS, born New Bern, North Carolina, July 8, 1960; admitted to bar, 1985, North Carolina. *Education:* University of North Carolina (B.S., 1982); University of Virginia (J.D., 1985). Director, New Bern Area Chamber of Commerce. Craven County Distinguished Women of the Year 1994. ***PRACTICE AREAS:*** Corporate; Business Law; Real Estate; Business Lending; Mergers and Acquisitions. ***Email:*** batkins@hsfh.com

MARY Z. HANDY, born Okinawa, Japan, January 10, 1974; admitted to bar, 1999, North Carolina; U.S. District Court, Eastern, Middle and Western Districts of North Carolina. *Education:* University of North Carolina (B.A., 1996); Emory University (J.D., 1999). Dean's Fellow. Articles Editor, Emory International Law Review. ***PRACTICE AREAS:*** Business Law; Corporate Law; Mergers and Acquisitions; Civil Practice. ***Email:*** mhandy@hsfh.com

REPRESENTATIVE CLIENTS: Marmon Industrial Corp; Eckerd Corp; VR Business Brokers; Microspace Communications Corp.; Extend Stay America, Inc.; Tricor Development Corp.; L&M Brokerage, Inc.; CRTS, Inc.; Executive Staffing Services; Branch Banking & Trust Co.

(For complete biographical data on all personnel, see Professional Biographies at Raleigh, North Carolina)

HUNTER BIRCHER, LLP

Established in 2000

220 EAST FRONT STREET
P.O. BOX 567
NEW BERN, NORTH CAROLINA 28563
Telephone: 252-638-3222
Facsimile: 252-638-1113
Email: jcb@hunterbircher.com

Debtor Creditor Law, Family Law, Bankruptcy, Federal Law, Administrative, Civil Litigation, Corporate Law, Small Business, Divorce, Child Custody, Commercial Law, Collections.

J. RANDAL HUNTER, born Columbia, South Carolina, September 24, 1954; admitted to bar, 1979, North Carolina and U.S. District Court, Eastern District of North Carolina. *Education:* Davidson College (B.A., with honors, 1976); Wake Forest University (J.D., 1979). Phi Delta Phi. District Court Judge, District 3B, 1984-1988. *Member:* Craven County and North Carolina Bar Associations; North Carolina State Bar; North Carolina Academy of Trial Lawyers. (Board Certified Specialist in Family Law, North Carolina State Board of Legal Specialization). ***PRACTICE AREAS:*** Family Law; Civil Practice; Child Custody; Marital Property Law; Separation Agreements. ***Email:*** randy@hunterbircher.com

JOHN C. BIRCHER III, born Columbia, South Carolina, September 23, 1970; admitted to bar, 1997, North Carolina; U.S. District Court, Eastern District of North Carolina; 1999, U.S. Tax Court; 2002, U.S. District Court, Middle and Western Districts of North Carolina; 2004, Tennessee, Georgia and U.S. District Court, Northern District of Georgia, 2004. *Education:* University of North Carolina (B.S.C.J., 1992); Campbell University (J.D., 1997). National Finalist, Client Counseling, 1997. Case Law Editor, Campbell Law Observer, 1996-1997. Honor Court Defense Counsel, 1996. Member, Panel of Chapter 7 Bankruptcy Trustees, Eastern District of North Carolina. Member, Local Rules Committee, United States Bankruptcy Court, Eastern District of North Carolina 2005. Speaker, Interaction of Bankruptcy and Domestic Practice, EBI 2004, North Carolina State Bankruptcy Annual Meeting, 2005. *Member:* Craven County (President, 2001-2002), Tennessee and North Carolina (Member, Bankruptcy Section) Bar Associations; State Bar of Georgia; National Association of Bankruptcy Trustees; Eastern Bankruptcy Institute. ***PRACTICE AREAS:*** Bankruptcy; Government; Civil Litigation; Creditors Rights; Collections; Federal Administrative Law; Administrative Hearings and Appeals; Business Planning; Business Law. ***Email:*** jcb@hunterbircher.com

AISHA PRIDGEN, born Portsmouth, Virginia, November 6, 1976; admitted to bar, 2002, North Carolina. *Education:* University of North Carolina at Greensboro (B.A., 1998); University of North Carolina at Chapel Hill (J.D., 2001). *Member:* Craven County and North Carolina Bar Associations; North Carolina State Bar. ***PRACTICE AREAS:*** Family Law. ***Email:*** aisha@hunterbircher.com

REPRESENTATIVE CLIENTS: Core Creek Drainage District; Big Brothers Big Sisters of the Lower Neuse; Reeds Jewelers; Cyprus Financial Company, Inc.; The Money Store; The Harold Bate Foundation, Inc.; Branch Banking & Trust; First USA; East Carolina Bank; Household Automotive Finance Corporation; Transamerica Commercial Financial Corporation; MBNA America Bank, NA; Household Bank, NA.

KELLUM LAW FIRM

219 BROAD STREET
P.O. BOX 866
NEW BERN, NORTH CAROLINA 28563
Telephone: 252-633-2550
Fax: 252-672-0536
Email: ckeenhold@kellumlawfirm.com
URL: http://www.lawyers.com/kellumlawfirm

Jacksonville, North Carolina Office: 445-A Western Boulevard, P.O. Box 12155, 28546. Telephone: 910-455-4546. Fax: 910-455-2422.
Greenville, North Carolina Office: 205 S.W. Greenville Boulevard, P.O. Box 20727, 27858. Telephone: 252-353-4100. Fax: 252-353-8754.
Goldsboro, North Carolina Office: 2005 East Ash Street, P.O. Box 1085, 27533. Telephone: 919-722-6955. Fax: 919-722-6922.
Rocky Mount, North Carolina Office: 3250 Zebulon Road, 27804. Telephone: 252-442-3975. Fax: 252-442-7309.
Morehead City, North Carolina Office: 5178 Highway 70 West, 28557. Telephone: 252-726-7000. Fax: 252-726-8888.

State and Federal Civil Trial Practice, Personal Injury Law, Wrongful Death, Workers' Compensation, Social Security, Defective Products, Mass Torts and Insurance Law.

FIRM PROFILE: John W. Beaman began the general practice of law in New Bern, North Carolina in 1937 and continued, without interruption, but for World War II army service, until his death in 1984. In February, 1968, the partnership of Beaman & Kellum was formed with the addition of Norman B. Kellum, Jr. The firm has undergone several name changes through the years but has been the Kellum Law Firm since January, 2000. The firm limits its practice to Personal Injury, Wrongful Death, Social Security, Defective Products, Mass Torts, Workers' Compensation Cases and Insurance Law. John T. Briggs joined the firm in December, 1994 after serving as a U.S. Navy JAGC Officer in Japan. Russell L. Needell joined the firm in March, 1997 after practicing in New Jersey and Charlotte, North Carolina. J. Kevin Jones joined the firm in July, 1998 after practicing in Carteret County for over 5 years in the areas of personal injury and workers' compensation. Douglas Bruce Johnson joined the firm in March, 2000 after several years of practice in Albemarle, North Carolina. The practice is conducted mainly in eastern North Carolina with offices in New Bern, Jacksonville, Greenville, Goldsboro and Rocky Mount.

JOHN W. BEAMAN (1911-1984)

(This Listing Continued)

KELLUM LAW FIRM, New Bern—Continued

NORMAN B. KELLUM, JR., born Maysville, North Carolina, August 12, 1937; admitted to bar, 1965, North Carolina; 1966, U.S. District Court, Eastern District of North Carolina; 1967, U.S. Court of Appeals, Fourth Circuit; 1994, U.S. Supreme Court. *Education:* Wake Forest University (B.S., 1959; J.D., 1965). Phi Delta Phi. Recipient, Wake Forest Law School Outstanding Alumni Award, 1993. Research Assistant for Chief Justice Emery B. Denny, North Carolina Supreme Court and Associate Justice J. Will Pless, 1965-1966. Member: Wake Forest University Law Alumni Executive Committee, 1983-1986; Meredith College Board of Trustees, 1988-1992, 1994-1997, 1999-2002; Chairman, Board of Trustees Meredith College, 1996, 1997; Wake Forest University Law School Board of Visitors, 1992-1999. Listed in *The Best Lawyers in America.* Member, 1996-2000 and President, 1998-1999, Craven Regional Medical Center Foundation. Member, Craven Regional Medical Authority, 2001—; Vice-Chairman, 2002-2004; Chairman, 2004—. Formerly with: Beaman & Kellum; Beaman Kellum Mills & Kafer; Beaman Kellum Stallings & Hollows; Kd Jones. *Member:* Craven County (3B District) and North Carolina Bar Associations; North Carolina State Bar; North Carolina Academy of Trial Lawyers (Member, Board of Governors, 1978-1981, 1983-1987); The Association of Trial Lawyers of America; The American Board of Trial Advocates (President, 2002, 2003); Eastern North Carolina Inn of Court (President, 1995). [First Lt., 101st Airborne Military Intelligence Detachment, U.S. Army, 1960-1962]. (Also at Jacksonville, Greenville, Rocky Mount, Goldsboro and Morehead City Offices). ***PRACTICE AREAS:*** Personal Injury Law; Wrongful Death; Workers Compensation; General Practice. ***Email:*** nkellum@kellumlawfirm.com

---

JOHN T. BRIGGS, born Durham, North Carolina, January 26, 1965; admitted to bar, 1991, North Carolina; 1993, U.S. Court of Military Appeals; 2001, South Carolina. *Education:* East Carolina University (B.S., 1988); Campbell University (J.D., 1991) Delta Theta Phi; Naval Justice School (1991). *Member:* North Carolina (Member, Disability Law Section) and American Bar Associations; North Carolina State Bar; South Carolina Bar; North Carolina Academy of Trial Lawyers; The Association of Trial Lawyers of America (Member, Toxic, Environmental and Pharmaceutical Torts Section). [Lieut. U.S. Navy, JAGC, 1991-1994]. ***PRACTICE AREAS:*** Personal Injury Law; Workers' Compensation; Social Security Disability; Insurance Law.

RUSSELL L. NEEDELL, born New York, N.Y., February 14, 1956; admitted to bar, 1981, New Jersey, Pennsylvania and U.S. District Court, District of New Jersey; 1982, Ohio; 1993, North Carolina. *Education:* Franklin Pierce College (B.A., 1978); Capital University (J.D., 1981). Phi Alpha Delta. Research Assistant to Law Faculty, 1980-1981. Judicial Clerk, Hon. Richard J. S. Barlow, Jr., New Jersey Superior Court, 1981-1982. Assistant City Attorney, Columbus, Ohio, 1982-1984. Trustee, 1986-1988, Treasurer, 1987-1988, Vice President, 1988-1989, President, 1989-1990, Mercer County Legal Aid Society. *Member:* North Carolina State Bar; American Bar Association; North Carolina Academy of Trial Lawyers; American Board of Trial Advocates (President, Eastern North Carolina Chapter, 2001-2001); American Trial Lawyers Association. (Also at Greenville and Rocky Mount Offices). ***PRACTICE AREAS:*** Personal Injury Law; Insurance Law.

J. KEVIN JONES, born Morehead City, North Carolina, June 7, 1967; admitted to bar, 1992, North Carolina and U.S. District Court, Eastern District of North Carolina. *Education:* University of North Carolina at Chapel Hill (B.S., 1989); Campbell University School of Law (J.D., 1992). Inaugural Member, Eastern North Carolina Inn of Court. *Member:* Craven County and North Carolina (Member, Workers' Compensation Section) Bar Associations; North Carolina State Bar; North Carolina Academy of Trial Lawyers (Member, Sections on: Workers' Compensation; Auto Torts); The Association of Trial Lawyers of America. (Board Certified Specialist in Workers' Compensation Law, North Carolina State Board of Legal Specialization). ***PRACTICE AREAS:*** Workers' Compensation; Personal Injury.

DOUGLAS B. JOHNSON, JR., born New Bern, North Carolina, March 27, 1966; admitted to bar, 1997, North Carolina. *Education:* East Carolina University (B.A., 1990); Campbell University School of Law (J.D., 1997). *Member:* Craven County and North Carolina Bar Association; North Carolina State Bar; North Carolina Academy of Trial Lawyers. ***PRACTICE AREAS:*** Workers Compensation; Personal Injury.

JEFFREY W. PHILLIPS, born Rocky Mount, North Carolina, October 2, 1977; admitted to bar, 2003, North Carolina and U.S. District Court, Eastern District of North Carolina. *Education:* University of North Carolina at Chapel Hill (B.A., 2000); Wake Forest University School of Law (J.D., 2003). *Member:* Craven County, North Carolina and American Bar Associations; North Carolina Bar; North Carolina Academy of Trial Lawyers (Member, Section on: Auto Torts and Disability Advocacy). ***PRACTICE AREAS:*** Personal Injury; Social Security Disability.

EDWIN M. BRASWELL, JR., born Fayetteville, North Carolina, March 6, 1952; admitted to bar, 1978, North Carolina. *Education:* University of North Carolina (B.S., 1973); North Carolina Central University (J.D., cum laude, 1978). Delta Theta Phi. Law Clerk to Judge Mitchell, North Carolina Court of Appeals, 1978-1979. Assistant District Attorney, 1979-1982. Certified Mediator. *Member:* Lenoir County and North Carolina Bar Associations; North Carolina State Bar. ***PRACTICE AREAS:*** Mediation; Civil Litigation; Personal Injury. ***Email:*** edbraswell@justice.com

---

The LeonLaw Firm

NEW BERN, NORTH CAROLINA

(See Greenville)

Employment Law, Personal Injury, Workers Compensation, Contracts.

McCOTTER, ASHTON & SMITH, P.A.

3515 TRENT ROAD, SUITE 10
P.O. BOX 12800
NEW BERN, NORTH CAROLINA 28561
Telephone: 252-635-1005
Fax: 252-635-5050
Email: maslaw@justice.com
URL: http://www.lawyers.com/mmalaw

General Civil and Criminal Practice and Appeals in all State and Federal Courts. Probate, Real Property, Corporation, Business, Construction, Administrative, Negligence, Workers' Compensation, Admiralty and Maritime, Federal and State Criminal Defense, Mediation and Arbitration.

FIRM PROFILE: The firm of McCotter, Ashton & Smith, P.A. serves clients throughout the state of North Carolina offering a comprehensive practice in all state and federal courts. In addition to an active civil and criminal trial practice, the firm represents clients in matters of admiralty and maritime law and offers services in arbitration and mediation. The firm is committed to provide personalized, yet cost-effective representation, reflecting high standards of diligence and integrity.

MEMBERS

CHARLES K. McCOTTER, JR., born New Bern, North Carolina, October 29, 1946; admitted to bar, 1971, North Carolina and U.S. District Court, Eastern District of North Carolina. *Education:* University of North Carolina (B.S., 1968; J.D.,1971). U.S. Magistrate Judge, 1979-1995. Member, Fourth Circuit Judicial Conference. Proctor in Admiralty. Certified Mediator, North Carolina State and Federal Courts. Member, Eastern North Carolina Inns of Court. *Member:* Craven County, District 3B, North Carolina and American Bar Associations; North Carolina State Bar; Maritime Law Association; UNC Law Alumni Board; UNC Marine Sciences Board of Visitors. ***PRACTICE AREAS:*** Admiralty and Maritime Law; Civil Practice; Trial Practice; Mediation; Corporate Law; Land Disputes. ***Email:*** ckm@justice.com

RUDOLPH ALEXANDER ASHTON, III, born Washington, D.C., October 12, 1946; admitted to bar, 1971, North Carolina; 1979, U.S. Supreme Court; 1980, U.S. Court of Appeals, Fourth Circuit. *Education:* Wake Forest University (B.S., 1968); University of Virginia (J.D., 1971). Phi Delta Phi. *Member:* Craven County and North Carolina Bar Associations; North Carolina State Bar; North Carolina Academy of Trial Lawyers. [1st Lt., U.S. Army, 1970-1972]. ***PRACTICE AREAS:*** Insurance Defense; Appellate Practice; Criminal Defense; Mediation; Arbitration; Personal Injury. ***Email:*** raa111@justice.com

KIRBY H. SMITH, III, born Salisbury, North Carolina, September 7, 1965; admitted to bar, 1992, North Carolina; 1995, U.S. District Court, Eastern District of North Carolina; 2000, U.S. District Court, Middle District of North Carolina. *Education:* University of North Carolina (B.S., 1987); Wake Forest University (J.D., 1992). Phi Delta Phi. Series 7 Brokerage License, 1989. Assistant District Attorney, 1992-1995. *Member:* Craven County and North Carolina Bar Associations; North Carolina Academy of Trial Lawyers. ***PRACTICE AREAS:*** Criminal Law; Civil Litigation; Appellate Practice. ***Email:*** kirbyhsmith@yahoo.com

ASSOCIATE

TERRI WOODARD SHARP, born Portsmouth, Virginia, August 31, 1962; admitted to bar, 2000, North Carolina. *Education:* North Carolina Wesleyan College (B.S., magna cum laude, 1996); North Carolina Central University (J.D., cum laude, 2000). Real Estate Sales, North Carolina, 1989—. *Member:* Craven County, North Carolina and American Bar Associations; North Carolina Association of Trial Lawyers. ***PRACTICE AREAS:*** Real Estate Transactions; Real Estate Litigation; Estate Planning and Administration; Corporate Law. ***Email:*** rtsharp@justice.com

---

MILLS & WILLEY

Established in 1995

201 BROAD STREET
DRAWER 1638
NEW BERN, NORTH CAROLINA 28563
Telephone: 252-638-1111
Telecopier: 252-638-8499
Email: mills@cconnect.net

Accident, Personal Injury Law, Workers Compensation, Criminal Law, General Civil and Criminal Litigation in State and Federal Courts.

FIRM PROFILE: The firm was established in 1995 when Michael Mills and Joshua Willey, Jr. left large law firms to be able to concentrate on a civil trial practice including personal injury and workers' compensation matters. Practicing in both state and federal courts, the firm also handles criminal litigation. It is committed to provide cost-effective representation reflecting high standards of diligence and integrity.

J. MICHAEL MILLS, born Wilson, North Carolina, November 28, 1964; admitted to bar, 1990, North Carolina. *Education:* University of North Carolina at Chapel Hill (B.A., 1987); Wake Forest University (J.D., 1990). Phi Delta Phi. Member: Eastern North Carolina Inn of Court. *Member:* Craven County, Third Judicial District (President, 1999-2000) and North Carolina Bar Associations; North Carolina State Bar; North Carolina Academy of Trial Lawyers. ***PRACTICE AREAS:*** Personal Injury; Workers Compensation; Criminal. ***Email:*** jmmillshsd@earthlink.net

JOSHUA W. WILLEY, JR., born Norfolk, Virginia, February 29, 1952; admitted to bar, 1977, North Carolina; 1978, U.S. District Court, Eastern District of North Carolina; 1982, U.S. Court of Appeals, Fourth Circuit; 2001, U.S. Supreme Court. *Education:* Wake Forest University (B.A., cum laude, 1974; J.D., 1977). Phi Alpha Theta; Phi Delta Phi. Certified Superior Court Mediator, 2001-2005. *Member:* Craven County, Third Judicial Dis-

(This Listing Continued)

trict (Secretary, 1987-1988) and North Carolina Bar Associations; North Carolina State Bar (Councilor for District 3B, 2001-2005); North Carolina Academy of Trial Lawyers; The Association of Trial Lawyers of America; Eastern North Carolina Inn of Court. ***PRACTICE AREAS:*** Civil Litigation; Personal Injury; Workers Compensation; Criminal Law; Mediation. ***Email:*** jwwilleyjr@earthlink.net

STUBBS & PERDUE, P.A.

310 CRAVEN STREET
P.O. BOX 1654
NEW BERN, NORTH CAROLINA 28563-1654
Telephone: 252-633-2700
Fax: 252-633-9600
URL: http://www.stubbsperdue.com
Email: law@stubbsperdue.com
URL: http://www.lawyers.com/stubbsperdue

Raleigh, North Carolina Office: Two Hannover Square, 434 Fayetteville Street Mall, Suite 1630, P.O. Box 1630, 27602-1630. Telephone: 919-856-9400. Fax: 919-856-9300. Email: law@stubbsperdue.com

General Practice in all Courts. Probate, Real Estate, Personal Injury, Bankruptcy Reorganization, Domestic Relations, Corporation and Criminal Law, Environmental Law, Toxic Torts.

FIRM PROFILE: The predecessor to Stubbs & Perdue, P.A., was founded by T.H. Stubbs, Jr. on July 1, 1971. The firm originated as a general practice with an emphasis on criminal law, bankruptcy, and a general specialty in the federal courts. The present firm serves the eastern district of North Carolina for bankruptcy and criminal cases and offers a full range of legal services locally as specified herein. The firm emphasizes continuing legal education for all partners and associates. Partners of the firm have served as speakers and have otherwise participated in educational seminars. All lawyers in the firm are active in professional and political activities and local civic affairs.

GARY R. PERDUE, SR. (1947-1997)

TRAWICK H. STUBBS, JR., born Atlanta, Georgia, September 1, 1942; admitted to bar, 1967, North Carolina. *Education:* University of North Carolina (A.B., 1964); Duke University (J.D., 1967). Phi Delta Phi. Member, Order of the Coif. Member, Editorial Board, Duke Law Journal, 1966-1967. Law Clerk to U.S. District Judge John D. Larkins, Jr., 1969-1970. Speaker, Organizer and Founder, Eastern Bankruptcy Institute. Member, Bankruptcy Specialist, N.C. State Bar. Permanent Delegate, Fourth Circuit Judicial Conference, 1971—. County Attorney for Craven County, 1995-1998. N.C. State Bar Board of Specialization (Member, Bankruptcy Committee, 1984-1990). *Member:* Craven County and North Carolina (Member, Bankruptcy Section, 1986-1989) Bar Associations; North Carolina State Bar; North Carolina Academy of Trial Lawyers; The Association of Trial Lawyers of America; National Association of Chapter 13 Trustees; NCATT Statistical Data Committee (Member, Chairman); Eastern Inn of Court. ***PRACTICE AREAS:*** Bankruptcy Reorganization; Debtor and Creditor; Workouts; Litigation; Personal Injury; Tax Law; Federal Civil Practice; Federal Criminal Law; Commercial Law; Contracts; Toxic Torts; Business Formation. ***Email:*** law@stubbsperdue.com

JOHN W. KING, JR., born Louisburg, North Carolina, November 19, 1954; admitted to bar, 1980, North Carolina; 1981, U.S. District Court, Eastern District of North Carolina; 1983, U.S. Supreme Court. *Education:* Louisburg College (A.A., magna cum laude, 1975); Wake Forest University (B.A., cum laude, 1977); Campbell University (J.D., with honors, 1980). Delta Theta Phi. North Carolina Real Estate Broker, 1979—. Attorney, Habitat for Humanity of Greater New Bern, Inc., 1995—. Attorney, Town of Dover, 1994—. Attorney, New Bern Board of Realtors, 2001—. *Member:* Craven County, North Carolina (Member, Probate and Real Property Section) and American (Member, Probate and Real Property Section) Bar Associations; North Carolina State Bar; North Carolina Academy of Trial Lawyers. ***PRACTICE AREAS:*** Elder Law; Foreclosures; Business Formation; Guardianship; Charitable Trusts and Foundations; Real Estate Exchanges; Real Property; Estate and Gift Taxation; Civil Litigation; Trusts and Estates; Estate Administration; Estate Planning; Successions. ***Email:*** jking@stubbsperdue.com

KELLY L. GREENE, born Raleigh, North Carolina, March 20, 1973; admitted to bar, 1999, North Carolina. *Education:* Wake Forest University (B.A., 1996); Campbell University (J.D., 1999). Member: Moot Court Competition and Trial Advocacy Program; Guardian Ad Litem Program. Editor, Campbell Law Observer. Certified Mediator, District Court. *Member:* Craven County and North Carolina Bar Associations; North Carolina State Bar; North Carolina Academy of Trial Lawyers. ***PRACTICE AREAS:*** Guardianship; Personal Injury; Federal Criminal Law; Criminal Law; Family Law; Workers Compensation. ***Email:*** kgreene@stubbsperdue.com

GEORGE MASON OLIVER, born Jacksonville, Florida, September 3, 1974; admitted to bar, 1999, North Carolina, U.S. District Court, Western District of North Carolina; 2001; U.S. District Court, Eastern District of North Carolina and U.S. Court of Appeals, 4th Circuit. *Education:* University of North Carolina (B.A., 1996; J.D., 1999). *Member:* North Carolina State Bar; The Association of Trial Lawyers of America; North Carolina Academy of Trial Lawyers. ***PRACTICE AREAS:*** Bankruptcy Reorganization; Federal Civil Law; State Civil Law; Federal Criminal Law. ***Email:*** goliver@stubbsperdue.com

RODNEY A. CURRIN, admitted to bar, 1976, North Carolina; 1977, U.S. District Court, Eastern District of North Carolina; 1978, U.S. District Court, Middle District of North Carolina; 1980, U.S. Court of Appeals, Fourth Circuit; 1984, U.S. Tax Court. *Education:* University of North Carolina at Chapel Hill (B.S., 1972; J.D., 1976). Formerly with Ward and Smith, P.A. *Member:* North Carolina and American Bar Associations. ***PRACTICE AREAS:*** Business Law; Banking; Trademark.

THOMAS R. WILSON, born St. Louis, Missouri, November 5, 1976; admitted to bar, 2003, North Carolina; 2004, U.S. District Court, Eastern District of North Carolina; 2005, U.S. Court of Appeals, 4th Circuit. *Education:* Miami University of Ohio (B.A., English, cum laude, 1999); St. Louis University (J.D., magna cum laude, 2003). Law Clerk, North Carolina Court of Appeals, 2003-2004. Faculty Fellow, Saint Louis University, 2002-2003. *Member:* North Carolina State Bar; North Carolina Bar Association (Member, Environmental Division). ***LANGUAGES:*** Japanese. ***PRACTICE AREAS:*** Civil Litigation; Bankruptcy; Environmental Law; Administrative Law. ***Email:*** twilson@stubbsperdue.com

APPROVED ATTORNEYS FOR: Lawyers Title Insurance Corp.
REFERENCES: Investors Title Insurance Company; Lawyers Title Ins. Co.; Chicago Title Insurance Co.

SUMRELL, SUGG, CARMICHAEL, HICKS & HART, P.A.

416 POLLOCK STREET
P.O. DRAWER 889
NEW BERN, NORTH CAROLINA 28563
Telephone: 252-633-3131
Fax: 252-633-3507
Email: email@nclawyers.com
URL: http://www.nclawyers.com

General Civil. Trials and Appeals in all Civil Courts. Wills and Estates, Real Estate, Corporate Law, Financial Transactions, Insurance and Negligence, Employment Law, Municipal Law, Law Enforcement Liability Defense, Health Care Law and Intellectual Property.

RAYMOND E. SUMRELL (1924-2004)

JAMES R. SUGG, born Snow Hill, North Carolina, July 4, 1931; admitted to bar, 1959, North Carolina; U.S. Court of Appeals, Fourth Circuit. *Education:* High Point College (A.B., 1952); Wake Forest University (J.D., 1959). Phi Delta Phi. Member, North Carolina General Assembly, 1967. Craven County Attorney. *Member:* Craven County (President, 1972-1973) and North Carolina Bar Associations; Third Judicial District and North Carolina State Bars; North Carolina Academy of Trial Lawyers; American Board of Trial Advocates. [Capt., U.S. Marine Corps, 1953-1956]. ***PRACTICE AREAS:*** Litigation; Municipal Law; Insurance Defense Law; Workers' Compensation Defense. ***Email:*** jsugg@nclawyers.com

FRED M. CARMICHAEL, born New Bern, North Carolina, March 2, 1937; admitted to bar, 1965, North Carolina; 1972, U.S. Court of Appeals, Fourth Circuit; 1994, U.S. Supreme Court. *Education:* Wake Forest University (B.A., 1959); University of North Carolina (J.D., 1965). Phi Delta Phi. Member, Board of Directors: North Carolina Society of Hospital Attorneys, 1976-1984; Solid Waste Association of North America. *Member:* Craven County (President, 1967-1968), Third Judicial District (President, 1970-1971) and American Bar Associations; North Carolina State Bar; American Health Lawyers Association. [1st Lt., U.S. Army, 1959-1961]. ***PRACTICE AREAS:*** Health Care and Hospital Law; Real Estate; Business Law; Corporate Law; Municipal Law; Municipal Solid Waste. ***Email:*** fmc@nclawyers.com

JIMMIE B. HICKS, JR., born New Bern, North Carolina, May 20, 1965; admitted to bar, 1991, North Carolina; 1994, U.S. Court of Appeals, Fourth Circuit; 1995, U.S. Supreme Court. *Education:* North Carolina State University (C.S.C., cum laude, 1988); University of North Carolina Law School (J.D., 1991). Alpha Sigma Pi; Phi Delta Phi. Winner, Nathan Burkan Memorial Competition. Member, North Carolina Information Highway Advisory Committee. *Member:* Craven County (President, 1995-1996; Secretary, 1994-1995), North Carolina (Chair, 1996-1997, Multimedia and Computer Law Committee) and American (Science and Technology, Intellectual Property, Business Law and Local Government Law Sections) Bar Associations. ***PRACTICE AREAS:*** Corporate and Commercial Law; Municipal Law; Wills; Estate Law; Intellectual Property; Real Estate; Environmental Law. ***Email:*** jhicks@nclawyers.com

SCOTT C. HART, born Landstuhl, West Germany, October 7, 1968; admitted to bar, 1992, North Carolina; 1994, U.S. Court of Appeals, Fourth Circuit; 1995, U.S. Supreme Court. *Education:* University of North Carolina, Chapel Hill (B.A., 1989; J.D. 1992). *Member:* Craven County (Secretary, 1997-1998; President, 1998-1999), North Carolina and American Bar Associations; North Carolina Association of Defense Attorneys; Defense Research Institute; Eastern North Carolina Inn of Court. ***PRACTICE AREAS:*** Civil Litigation; Personal Injury Litigation; Law Enforcement Liability Defense; Municipal Defense; Appellate Law; Insurance Defense. ***Email:*** shart@nclawyers.com

JILL QUATTLEBAUM BYRUM, born Columbia, South Carolina, August 25, 1968; admitted to bar, 1992, South Carolina; 1997, North Carolina; 1999, U.S. Court of Appeals, Fourth Circuit. *Education:* University of South Carolina (B.S., Finance and Real Estate, magna cum laude, 1989; J.D., 1992). Delta Sigma Pi; Carolina Scholar; National Merit Scholar; Roy A. Webster Scholar. *Member:* Craven County, North Carolina and American Bar Associations; South Carolina Bar; North Carolina State Bar; North Carolina Association of Defense Attorneys; American Health Lawyers Association. ***LANGUAGES:*** Spanish. ***PRACTICE AREAS:*** Employment Law; Workers Compensation Defense; Insurance Defense Litigation; Health Care; Hospital Law. ***Email:*** jqbyrum@nclawyers.com

AREY W. GRADY, III, born Kinston, North Carolina, December 25, 1972; admitted to bar, 1998, North Carolina. *Education:* University of North Carolina, Chapel Hill (B.A., with distinction, 1995; J.D., with honors, 1998). Articles Editor and Staff Member, Journal of International Law and Commercial Regulation, 1996-1998. *Member:* Craven County and North Carolina Bar Associations. ***PRACTICE AREAS:*** Estate Planning; Estate Administration; Residential Real Estate; Commercial Real Estate; Municipal Law; Local Government Law; Law Enforcement; Municipal Liability; Local Government Liability; Commercial Law; Business Law; Civil Litigation. ***Email:*** agrady@nclawyers.com

B. KYLE DICKERSON, born Durham, North Carolina, March 28, 1974; admitted to bar, 2000, North Carolina. *Education:* University of North Carolina at Chapel Hill (B.A., 1996); University of Memphis (J.D., cum laude, 2000). Member, University of Memphis

(This Listing Continued)

SUMRELL, SUGG, CARMICHAEL, HICKS & HART, P.A., New Bern—Continued

Law Review, 1999-2000. *Member:* Craven County, North Carolina and American Bar Associations; North Carolina State Bar; American Health Lawyers Association. ***PRACTICE AREAS:*** Health Care; Hospital Law; Estate Planning; Estate Administration; Probate; Workers Compensation Defense; Municipal Law. ***Email:*** bkdickerson@nclawyers.com

REPRESENTATIVE CLIENTS: *Real Estate:* Tryon Realty Company, Inc.; Crayton & Company; Zaytoun-Raines Construction; Neuse Builders. *Municipal:* Craven, Pamlico and Jones Counties; Towns of River Bend, Bridgeton, Minnesott Beach and Cove City; Coastal Regional Solid Waste Management Authority; Craven and Jones County Economic Development Commission; New Bern Police Department; City of Kinston; Craven County Committee of 100; North Carolina League of Municipalities; North Carolina Association of County Commissioners. *Health Care:* Onslow Memorial Hospital; Craven Regional Medical Authority; Beaufort County Hospital; Pungo District Hospital; Shriners Hospitals for Children; Washington County Hospital. *Insurance:* St. Paul Fire & Marine Insurance Company; Network Adjusters; Gulf Insurance Company; Essex Insurance Company; Kemper Insurance Company; The Reciprocal Group; Zurich Insurance Company; JWF Specialty Company; MetLife Auto & Home Insurance Company; Companion Property and Casualty Group; Discovery Insurance Company; Hewitt Coleman and Associates; North Carolina Guaranty Association; North Carolina League of Municipalities; North Carolina Association of County Commissioners. *General:* Nicholas Sparks Enterprises; Maola Milk and Ice Cream Company; Norfolk Southern Corporation; Mallard Oil and Propane Co.; TESI; Crown American Properties; Dominion N.C. Power. *Authorized to Close Loans for:* Wachovia; Bank of America; First Citizens Bank; Branch Bank & Trust Company; Countrywide Mortgage; Centura; Eastern N.C. Natural Gas Co.; Stewart Title Guaranty Company.
REFERENCES: First Citizens Bank; Branch Bank & Trust Company; Wachovia.

WALLACE, MORRIS, BARWICK, LANDIS & STROUD, P.A.

NEW BERN, NORTH CAROLINA

(See Kinston)

General Civil and Trial Practice in all State and Federal Courts. Aviation, Banking, Corporate Law, Insurance, Personal Injury, Probate, Product Liability, Real Estate and Taxation.

WARD AND SMITH, P.A.

Established in 1895
1001 COLLEGE COURT
P.O. BOX 867
NEW BERN, NORTH CAROLINA 28563-0867
Telephone: 252-672-5400
Facsimile: 252-672-5477
Email: wardsmith@wardandsmith.com
URL: http://www.wardandsmith.com

Greenville, North Carolina Office: 120 West Fire Tower Road, P.O. Box 8088. Telephone: 252-215-4000. Facsimile: 252-215-4077.
Raleigh, North Carolina Office: Suite 2400, Two Hannover Square, Fayetteville Street Mall, P.O. Box 2091. Telephone: 919-836-4260. Facsimile: 919-836-4277.
Wilmington, North Carolina Office: University Corporate Center, 127 Racine Drive, P.O. Box 7068. Telephone: 910-794-4800. Facsimile: 910-794-4877.

General and Trial Practice. Admiralty Law; Bankruptcy; Banks and Banking; Business Law; Civil Rights; Commercial Law; Construction Law; Contracts; Copyrights; Corporate Law; Debtor and Creditor; Elder Law; Eminent Domain; Employee Benefits; Environmental Law; Family Law including Divorce; Finance; Franchise Law; Government; Government Contracts; Health Care Law; Immigration and Naturalization; Insurance; International Law; International Trade; Investments; Labor and Employment including Discrimination, Sexual Harassment, and Workers' Compensation; Landlord and Tenant; Litigation; Personal Injury including Automobile Accidents, Legal Malpractice and Medical Malpractice; Products Liability; Real Estate; Securities; Taxation; Technology and Science including Internet Law, Trademarks, and Patents; Trusts and Estates including Estate Planning and Wills and Probate; Zoning and Land Use.

FIRM PROFILE: Located in Greenville, New Bern, Raleigh, and Wilmington, we are successor to a practice founded in New Bern, North Carolina in 1895. Our firm has grown to over 60 attorneys and more than 160 support staff members who are committed to quality and responsiveness. We strive to deliver a product that is tailored to our clients' unique needs wherever and whenever the need should arise. Our attorneys may be contacted by either a phone call or a confidential email, in or out of the office and at home. Attorney availability reinforces our commitment to a strong attorney-client relationship and a proactive and preventive approach to our clients' legal issues. Our philosophy is to utilize other attorneys in the firm whose knowledge and expertise allows a more efficient and timely delivery of our clients' legal services. In summary, the collective mission of our attorneys, legal assistants, and administrative staff is to provide our clients with the highest quality legal service at an affordable cost.

D. L. WARD (1903-1971)

W. L. ALLEN, III, admitted to bar, 1992, North Carolina. *Education:* East Carolina University (B.S., 1989); Wake Forest University (J.D., 1992). *Member:* North Carolina and American Bar Associations; North Carolina State Bar; North Carolina Academy of Trial Lawyers. [Captain, JAGC, USAR]. ***PRACTICE AREAS:*** Family Law; Litigation; Personal Injury; Wrongful Death; Immigration. ***Email:*** wla@wardandsmith.com

DEBORAH B. ANDREWS, admitted to bar, 1997, North Carolina; 1999, Georgia. *Education:* North Carolina State University (B.A., with honors, 1989); University of North Carolina (J.D., 1997); Georgetown University (LL.M., Taxation, 2003). Certified Public Accountant, North Carolina, 1993. *Member:* North Carolina and American Bar Associations; North Carolina State Bar; State Bar of Georgia; North Carolina Association of Certified Public Accountants. ***PRACTICE AREAS:*** Business Law; Tax Law. ***Email:*** dba@wardandsmith.com

(This Listing Continued)

WILLIAM JOSEPH AUSTIN, JR., admitted to bar, 1978, North Carolina; 1981, U.S. Tax Court. *Education:* University of North Carolina (A.B., 1973; J.D., 1978); Duke University (M.A., 1978). Phi Beta Kappa. Member, National Moot Court Team; Holderness Moot Court Bench, 1977-1978. Staff Member, North Carolina Law Review, 1977-1978. *Member:* North Carolina (Litigation Section Council, 2001—) and American Bar Associations; North Carolina State Bar. ***PRACTICE AREAS:*** Education Law; Labor and Employment; Litigation; Workers' Compensation. ***Email:*** wja@wardandsmith.com

ADAM M. BEAUDOIN, admitted to bar, 2001, North Carolina. *Education:* James Madison University (B.A., magna cum laude, 1998); University of Richmond (J.D., cum laude, 2001). *Member:* Craven County (President, 2004-2005), North Carolina and American Bar Associations; North Carolina State Bar. ***PRACTICE AREAS:*** Business Law; Corporate Law; Nonprofit Organizations Law; Limited Liability Company Law; Real Estate - Community Associations; Dealer/Distributor and Franchising. ***Email:*** amb@wardandsmith.com

ALBERT R. BELL, JR., admitted to bar, 1975, North Carolina. *Education:* Campbell University (B.S., 1966); Wake Forest University (J.D., 1975). Managing Editor, Wake Forest Law Review, 1974-1975. Listed in *The Best Lawyers in America* . Wage and Hour Investigator, U.S. Department of Labor, 1966-1969. *Member:* North Carolina (Member, Labor and Employment Law Section; Labor and Employment Law Section Council, Chair, 1991-1992, Member, 1985-2000) and American (Member, Sections on: Labor and Employment Law; Public Contract Law; Health Law) Bar Associations; North Carolina State Bar. [USAR, 1966-1972]. ***PRACTICE AREAS:*** Labor and Employment; Employment Benefits; Government Affairs; Government Contracts; Wage and Hour Law. ***Email:*** arb@wardandsmith.com

JENNIFER LYNN BOWMAN, admitted to bar, 1993, North Carolina. *Education:* University of North Carolina (A.B., with honors, 1990; J.D., with high honors, 1993). Order of the Coif. Phi Beta Kappa. Staff Member, North Carolina Law Review, 1991-1993. *Member:* North Carolina and American Bar Associations; North Carolina State Bar; American Intellectual Property Law Association; North Carolina World Trade Association (President Elect, 2004-2005). ***PRACTICE AREAS:*** Government Affairs; Intellectual Property; International Law; Technology; Business; Housing Authority Law; Dealer/Distributor and Franchising; Financial Institutions; Banking Law. ***Email:*** jlb@wardandsmith.com

JENNA FRUECHTENICHT BUTLER, admitted to bar, 1996, North Carolina and Georgia. *Education:* Wake Forest University (B.A., magna cum laude, 1992; J.D., cum laude, 1995). Member, Moot Court Board. Notes and Comments Editor, Wake Forest Law Review. Law Clerk to the Honorable Malcolm J. Howard, U.S. District Judge, Eastern District of North Carolina, 1995-1996. *Member:* North Carolina Bar Association; North Carolina State Bar; State Bar of Georgia; North Carolina Association of Defense Attorneys; National Association of Women in Construction. ***PRACTICE AREAS:*** Business Litigation; Construction Law; Contract Litigation; Community Associations; Civil Litigation; Family Law. ***Email:*** jfb@wardandsmith.com

MARY V. CAVANAGH, admitted to bar, 1989, Colorado; 1993, North Carolina. *Education:* Wake Forest University (B.A., summa cum laude, 1986); University of Virginia (J.D., 1989). Phi Beta Kappa. *Member:* North Carolina State Bar; Colorado State Bar. ***PRACTICE AREAS:*** Appellate Practice; Litigation; Construction Law; Civil Litigation. ***Email:*** mvc@wardandsmith.com

ALEXANDER C. DALE, admitted to bar, 2001, North Carolina. *Education:* University of North Carolina (B.A., 1998; M.A., 2001); Duke University (J.D., 2001). Phi Beta Kappa. Research Editor, Duke Journal of Comparative and International Law. *Member:* North Carolina and American Bar Associations; North Carolina State Bar; North Carolina Academy of Trial Lawyers. ***PRACTICE AREAS:*** Litigation; Business; Technology; Intellectual Property; Civil Litigation; Administrative Law; Alternative Dispute Resolution; Appellate Practice; Communications and Media; Computers and Software; Copyrights; Investments; Libel, Slander and Defamation; Media Law; Privacy Law; Trademarks; Unfair Competition; Trusts and Estates Litigation; Securities Litigation; Business Disolution Litigation; Community Associations. ***Email:*** acd@wardandsmith.com

JAMES LEE DAVIS, admitted to bar, 1971, North Carolina; 2001, U.S. Supreme Court. *Education:* Woodberry Forest School; University of North Carolina; Guilford College (A.B., with high honors, 1968); University of North Carolina (J.D., with honors, 1971). Order of the Coif. Member, North Carolina Law Review, 1969-1970. Listed in *The Best Lawyers in America* . *Member:* North Carolina Bar Association (Chairman, Real Property Section, 1981-1982); North Carolina State Bar; North Carolina Land Title Association. ***PRACTICE AREAS:*** Business Law; Government Affairs. ***Email:*** jld@wardandsmith.com

STUART B. DORSETT, admitted to bar, 1985, North Carolina. *Education:* Davidson College (A.B., cum laude, 1982); University of North Carolina (J.D., with honors, 1985). Phi Beta Kappa; Order of the Coif. Member, International Law Moot Court Team, Jessup Competition, 1984-1985. Listed in *The Best Lawyers in America*. *Member:* North Carolina (Chair, Young Lawyers Division, 1994-1995; Vice Chair, 2003-2004; Chair, 2004-2005, Estate Planning and Fiduciary Law Section Council) and American (Member, Executive Council, Young Lawyers Division, 1988-1990) Bar Associations; North Carolina State Bar; American Counsel Association. The American College of Trusts and Estates Counsel. (Board Certified Specialist in Estate Planning and Probate Law, North Carolina State Board of Legal Specialization). ***PRACTICE AREAS:*** Trusts and Estates; Taxation; Wills and Probate; Business. ***Email:*** sbd@wardandsmith.com

RICHARD J. CROW, admitted to bar, 2004, North Carolina. *Education:* University of North Carolina (B.A., 2000); North Carolina Central University (J.D., summa cum laude, 2004); University of Florida (LL.M., 2005). *Member:* North Carolina and American Bar Associations. ***PRACTICE AREAS:*** Business Law; Taxation. ***Email:*** rjc@wardandsmith.com

WILLIAM S. DURR, admitted to bar, 1991, New York; 2001, North Carolina. *Education:* University of Rochester (B.A., 1987); Washington University (J.D., 1990). Order of Barristers. *Member:* North Carolina (Member: Litigation; Family Law Sections), New York State and American Bar Associations; North Carolina State Bar. ***PRACTICE AREAS:*** Family Law; Divorce; Civil Litigation. ***Email:*** wsd@wardandsmith.com

(This Listing Continued)

DONALT J. EGLINTON, admitted to bar, 1982, North Carolina. *Education:* Texas A. & M. University (B.E.D., magna cum laude, 1974); Central Michigan University (M.A., 1980); Wake Forest University (J.D., 1982). Staff Member, 1980-1981 and Research Editor, 1981-1982, Wake Forest Law Review. *Member:* North Carolina and American Bar Associations; North Carolina State Bar; North Carolina Academy of Trial Lawyers; Association of Trial Lawyers of America; American Institute of Architects. ***PRACTICE AREAS:*** Litigation; Business Law; Copyrights; Commercial Law; Contracts; Intellectual Property; Construction Law; Products Liability; Trade Secrets; Trademarks; Unfair Competition; Commercial Litigation; Trusts and Estates Litigation; Dealer/Distributor and Franchising; Environmental; Technology. ***Email:*** dje@wardandsmith.com

A. CHARLES ELLIS, admitted to bar, 1983, North Carolina. *Education:* University of North Carolina (A.B., 1980); Campbell University (J.D., cum laude, 1983). Member, Campbell University Law Review, 1980-1983. Listed in *The Best Lawyers in America. Member:* Pitt County (President, 1990-1991), North Carolina and American Bar Associations; North Carolina State Bar; North Carolina Academy of Trial Lawyers; Association of Trial Lawyers of America. ***PRACTICE AREAS:*** Personal Injury; Wrongful Death; Litigation; Insurance; Medical Malpractice; Products Liability. ***Email:*** ace@wardandsmith.com

E. BRADLEY EVANS, admitted to bar, 2002, North Carolina. *Education:* Woodberry Forest School, 1994; University of Westminster; Wake Forest University (B.A., cum laude, 1998; J.D., 2002). Order of the Coif. Member, Wake Forest Law Review. Law Clerk to the Honorable Malcolm J. Howard, U.S. District Judge, Eastern District of North Carolina, 2002-2003. *Member:* North Carolina and American Bar Associations; North Carolina State Bar. ***PRACTICE AREAS:*** Litigation; Appellate Practice; Civil Practice; Construction Law; Contracts; Intellectual Property; Trade Secrets; Trusts and Estates Litigation; Business Law. ***Email:*** ebe@wardandsmith.com

LYNWOOD P. EVANS, admitted to bar, 1999, North Carolina. *Education:* University of North Carolina (B.S., Business Administration, 1996); Campbell University (J.D., cum laude, 1999). Member, 1996-1999, Business Editor, 1998-1999, Campbell Law Review. *Member:* North Carolina and American Bar Associations; North Carolina State Bar; Association of Trial Lawyers of America; North Carolina Academy of Trial Lawyers. ***PRACTICE AREAS:*** Litigation; Insurance; Medical Malpractice; Personal Injury; Wrongful Death; Professional Liability; Business Litigation. ***Email:*** lpe@wardandsmith.com

PAUL A. FANNING, admitted to bar, 1998, North Carolina. *Education:* University of North Carolina-Asheville (B.A., 1993); Wake Forest University (J.D., 1998). *Member:* North Carolina Bar Association; North Carolina State Bar. ***PRACTICE AREAS:*** Bankruptcy; Commercial Law; Debtor and Creditor; Creditors' Rights. ***Email:*** paf@wardandsmith.com

J. MICHAEL FIELDS, admitted to bar, 1991, North Carolina. *Education:* University of North Carolina (B.S., 1988; J.D., with honors, 1991). Staff Member, N.C. Journal of International Law and Commercial Regulation, 1989-1991. *Member:* North Carolina Bar Association (Member, Bankruptcy Section Council, 1997-1999); North Carolina State Bar; American Bankruptcy Institute. ***PRACTICE AREAS:*** Business; Health Care; Real Estate - Community Associations; Creditors' Rights; Debtor and Creditor; Contracts; Bankruptcy. ***Email:*** jmf@wardandsmith.com

MICHAEL P. FLANAGAN, admitted to bar, 1971, Florida; 1972, North Carolina. *Education:* University of North Carolina (A.B., 1968; J.D., 1971). Member, National Moot Court Team; Holderness Moot Court Bench, 1970-1971. Listed in *The Best Lawyers in America.. Member:* North Carolina (Member, Bankruptcy Section Council, 1979-1984; Vice Chairman, 1987-1988; Chairman, 1988-1989, Bankruptcy Section) and American Bar Associations; North Carolina State Bar; The Florida Bar; American Bankruptcy Institute. ***PRACTICE AREAS:*** Creditors' Rights; Debtor and Creditor; Bankruptcy; Commercial Law. ***Email:*** mpf@wardandsmith.com

GEORGE K. FREEMAN, JR., admitted to bar, 1955, North Carolina. *Education:* University of North Carolina (B.S.B.A., 1952); Harvard University (J.D., cum laude, 1955). *Member:* North Carolina and American Bar Associations; North Carolina State Bar; American Arbitration Association; National Panel of Arbitrators. ***PRACTICE AREAS:*** Construction Law; Litigation; Family Law; Civil Litigation. ***Email:*** gkf@wardandsmith.com

S. McKINLEY GRAY, III, admitted to bar, 1993, North Carolina. *Education:* University of North Carolina (B.S., 1990); Campbell University (J.D., magna cum laude, 1993). Business Editor, Campbell Law Review. *Member:* North Carolina and American Bar Associations; North Carolina State Bar. ***PRACTICE AREAS:*** Labor and Employment; Litigation; Employee Benefits; Occupational Health and Safety; Workers' Compensation; Wage and Hour Law; Immigration. ***Email:*** smg@wardandsmith.com

BARRY P. HARRIS, IV, admitted to bar, 1979, Georgia; 2005, North Carolina. *Education:* University of Georgia (B.A., magna cum laude with general honors, 1976; J.D., magna cum laude, 1979). *Member:* North Carolina and American Bar Associations; State Bar of Georgia. ***PRACTICE AREAS:*** Financial Institutions; Banking Law. ***Email:*** bph@wardandsmith.com

CONSTANTINE C. HINGSON, admitted to bar, 2004, North Carolina. *Education:* University of North Carolina (B.A., 1998); Campbell University (J.D., 2004). *Member:* North Carolina State Bar. ***PRACTICE AREAS:*** Litigation. ***Email:*** cch@wardandsmith.com

THOMAS H. JOHNSON, JR., admitted to bar, 1985, North Carolina; 1988, U.S. District Court, Eastern District of North Carolina; 1993, U.S. Court of Appeals, Fourth Circuit; 1995, U.S. Court of Appeals for Veteran's Claims. *Education:* University of North Carolina at Chapel Hill (B.S., 1982; J.D., 1985). Phi Beta Kappa. *Member:* Pitt County (President, 1994-1995), North Carolina (Member: Business Law Section; Real Property Law Section; Estate Planning and Fiduciary Law Section; Law Practice Management Section; Zoning, Planning and Land Use Section) and American (Member: Business Law Section; Real Property and Probate Law Section; General Practice, Solo, and Small Firm Section) Bar Associations; North Carolina State Bar. ***PRACTICE AREAS:*** Real Estate. ***Email:*** thj@wardandsmith.com

MERRILL G. JONES II, admitted to bar, 1997, North Carolina. *Education:* Wake Forest University (B.S., 1990); East Carolina University (M.B.A., 1993); Wake Forest University (J.D., 1997). Member, Moot Court Board, 1995-1997. Articles Editor, 1996-1997,

(This Listing Continued)

Staff Member, 1995-1996, Wake Forest Law Review. Certified Public Accountant, North Carolina, 1994. *Member:* North Carolina and American Bar Associations; North Carolina State Bar; North Carolina Association of Certified Public Accountants; East Carolina Estate Planning Council. ***PRACTICE AREAS:*** Business Law; Construction Law; Health Care; Contracts; Corporate Law; Mergers and Acquisitions; Tax Law. ***Email:*** mgj@wardandsmith.com

WILLIAM R. LATHAN, JR., admitted to bar, 1975, North Carolina. *Education:* University of North Carolina (A.B., 1972; J.D., 1975). Assistant General Counsel, 1975-1980 and General Counsel and Secretary, 1980-1987, United Carolina Bancshares Corporation. Member, Board of Advisors, University of North Carolina School of Law, Center for Banking and Finance. *Member:* North Carolina and American Bar Associations; North Carolina State Bar; North Carolina Bankers Association. ***PRACTICE AREAS:*** Business Law; Financial Institutions; Finance; Securities; Corporate Law; Banks and Banking. ***Email:*** wrl@wardandsmith.com

KATHERINE EVANS LEWIS, admitted to bar, 1993, Tennessee; 1994, Arkansas; 1999, North Carolina. *Education:* Arkansas State University (B.S., magna cum laude, 1989); University of Mississippi (J.D., magna cum laude, 1993). Associate Articles Editor, 1992-1993 and Staff Member, 1991-1992, Mississippi Law Journal. *Member:* North Carolina, Arkansas and American Bar Associations; North Carolina State Bar. ***PRACTICE AREAS:*** Creditors' Rights; Debtor and Creditor; Real Estate; Bankruptcy. ***Email:*** kel@wardandsmith.com

CHERYL A. MARTENEY, admitted to bar, 1989, North Carolina. *Education:* West Virginia Wesleyan College (B.A., magna cum laude, 1981); College of William & Mary (J.D., 1989). *Member:* North Carolina and American Bar Associations; North Carolina State Bar; Defense Research Institute; North Carolina Association of Defense Attorneys. ***PRACTICE AREAS:*** Banking Law; Business Litigation; Construction; Litigation; Appellate Practice. ***Email:*** cam@wardandsmith.com

JOHN M. MARTIN, admitted to bar, 1975, North Carolina. *Education:* North Carolina State University (B.A., with high honors, 1972); Wake Forest University (J.D., 1975). Associate Editor, Wake Forest Law Review, 1974-1975. Listed in *The Best Lawyers in America. Member:* North Carolina and American Bar Associations; North Carolina State Bar; The Association of Trial Lawyers of America; North Carolina Academy of Trial Lawyers. ***PRACTICE AREAS:*** Business Litigation; Litigation; Family Law; Personal Injury; Wrongful Death; Professional Liability. ***Email:*** jmm@wardandsmith.com

LANCE P. MARTIN, admitted to bar, 1995, Louisiana; 2000, North Carolina. *Education:* Spring Hill College (B.S., summa cum laude, 1992); Tulane University (J.D., magna cum laude, 1995). Order of the Coif. *Member:* North Carolina and American Bar Associations; North Carolina State Bar. ***PRACTICE AREAS:*** Creditors' Rights; Debtor and Creditor; Bankruptcy; Commercial Law; Litigation. ***Email:*** lpm@wardandsmith.com

W. DANIEL MARTIN, III, admitted to bar, 1973, North Carolina. *Education:* North Carolina State University (B.A., 1969); University of North Carolina (J.D., 1973). *Member:* North Carolina Bar Association (Member, Real Property Section Council, 1984-1987); North Carolina State Bar; Community Associations Institute; North Carolina Land Title Association. ***PRACTICE AREAS:*** Business Law; Community Associations; Real Estate; Commercial Real Estate; Planning and Land Use. ***Email:*** wdm@wardandsmith.com

WILLIAM E. MARTIN, admitted to bar, 1975, North Carolina. *Education:* Wake Forest University (B.A., magna cum laude, 1971; J.D., cum laude, 1975). Phi Beta Kappa. Associate Professor of Law, Campbell University School of Law, 1976-1983. Assistant U.S. Attorney, Eastern District of North Carolina, 1983-1985. Deputy Federal Public Defender, 1985-1986 and Federal Public Defender, 1986-1993, Eastern District of North Carolina. Federal Public Defender, 1993-1997, Middle District of North Carolina. *Member:* North Carolina Bar Association; North Carolina State Bar. ***PRACTICE AREAS:*** Real Estate; Commercial Real Estate. ***Email:*** wem@wardandsmith.com

JAMES W. NORMENT, admitted to bar, 2001, North Carolina. *Education:* University of North Carolina (B.A., 1992; J.D., 2001). Articles Editor, North Carolina Law Review. *Member:* North Carolina and American Bar Associations; North Carolina State Bar; American Health Lawyers Association. ***PRACTICE AREAS:*** Business Law; Construction; Financial Institutions; Government Affairs; Housing Authority Law; Banking Law. ***Email:*** jwn@wardandsmith.com

WILLIAM A. ODEN, III, admitted to bar, 2004, North Carolina. *Education:* University of North Carolina (B.A., 2001); Campbell University (J.D., 2004). Member, Moot Court Board. Business Editor, Campbell Law Review, 2003-2004. ***PRACTICE AREAS:*** Construction; Litigation; Environmental Law; Intellectual Property; Trusts and Estates Litigation; Labor and Employment. ***Email:*** wao@wardandsmith.com

HUGH R. OVERHOLT, admitted to bar, 1957, Arkansas; 1988, District of Columbia; 1989, North Carolina. *Education:* University of Arkansas (A.B., 1955; J.D., 1957); U.S. Army Judge Advocate General's School (1965); Command and General Staff College (1969); National Defense University (1976). Comments Editor, University of Arkansas Law Review. Chief, Criminal Law Division, The Judge Advocate General School. The Judge Advocate General Corps, 1957-1989. Major General of the U.S. Army, 1981-1989. The Judge Advocate General U.S. Army, 1985-1989. *Member:* North Carolina, Arkansas and American Bar Associations; North Carolina State Bar; District of Columbia Bar. [Major General, U.S. Army, Retired]. ***PRACTICE AREAS:*** Business; Government Affairs; Litigation; Administrative Law; Government Contracts; Military Law; International Law. ***Email:*** hro@wardandsmith.com

JEANNETTE A. PARROTT, admitted to bar, 1990, North Carolina. *Education:* Duke University (B.A., magna cum laude, 1983); University of Virginia (J.D., 1990). Law Clerk to Honorable Robert F. Orr, North Carolina Court of Appeals, 1990-1992. *Member:* North Carolina Bar Association; North Carolina State Bar. ***PRACTICE AREAS:*** Trusts and Estates; Wills and Probate. ***Email:*** jap@wardandsmith.com

CLIFFORD P. PARSON, admitted to bar, 1992, North Carolina. *Education:* Hampden-Sydney College (B.A., magna cum laude, 1989); Wake Forest University (J.D., 1992). Phi Beta Kappa. *Member:* North Carolina and American Bar Associations; North Carolina State Bar. ***PRACTICE AREAS:*** Real Estate; Commercial Real Estate. ***Email:*** cpp@wardandsmith.com

(This Listing Continued)

WARD AND SMITH, P.A., New Bern—Continued

GREGORY T. PEACOCK, admitted to bar, 1996, North Carolina. *Education:* University of North Carolina (B.S., Business Administration, 1990); Wake Forest University (J.D., 1996). Member, Moot Court Board, 1994-1996. Member, Wake Forest Law Review, 1994-1996. *Member:* North Carolina Bar Association; North Carolina State Bar; National Academy of Elder Law Attorneys; East Carolina Estate Planning Council. (Board Certified Specialist in Estate Planning and Probate Law, North Carolina State Board of Legal Specialization). ***PRACTICE AREAS:*** Trusts and Estates; Wills and Probate; Taxation; Elder Law. ***Email:*** gtp@wardandsmith.com

SAMUEL H. POOLE, admitted to bar, 1962, North Carolina. *Education:* University of North Carolina at Chapel Hill (A.B., 1959; LL.B., 1962). Board of Governors, 1983-1999, Chairman, 1990-1994, University of North Carolina. *Member:* North Carolina and American Bar Associations; North Carolina State Bar. ***PRACTICE AREAS:*** Business Law; Government Affairs; International Law; Administrative Law; Dealer/Distributor and Franchising. ***Email:*** shp@wardandsmith.com

C. H. POPE, JR., admitted to bar, 1972, North Carolina. *Education:* University of North Carolina (B.S., 1968; J.D., with high honors, 1972). Order of the Coif. Associate Editor, North Carolina Law Review, 1971-1972. Research Assistant to Associate (later Chief) Justice Susie Sharp, North Carolina Supreme Court, 1972-1973. *Member:* North Carolina and American Bar Associations; North Carolina State Bar. ***PRACTICE AREAS:*** Construction Law; Real Estate; Commercial Real Estate; Zoning, Planning and Land Use; Wetlands. ***Email:*** chp@wardandsmith.com

E. KNOX PROCTOR V, admitted to bar, 1987, North Carolina. *Education:* Davidson College; University of North Carolina (A.B., 1984; J.D., with high honors, 1987). Order of the Coif. Member, Board of Editors, North Carolina Law Review, 1986-1987. *Member:* North Carolina and American Bar Associations; North Carolina State Bar. ***PRACTICE AREAS:*** Financial Institutions; Business Law; Banks and Banking; Insurance; Securities. ***Email:*** ekp@wardandsmith.com

CINDI M. QUAY, admitted to bar, 2000, North Carolina. *Education:* North Carolina Wesleyan College (B.A., summa cum laude, 1994); North Carolina Central University (J.D., magna cum laude, 2000). Member, North Carolina Central University Law Journal, 1999-2000. Member, Susie Sharp Inns of Court. *Member:* North Carolina and American Bar Associations; North Carolina State Bar; The Association of Trial Lawyers of America; Eastern Carolina Inns of Court. ***PRACTICE AREAS:*** Business Litigation; Family Law; Litigation; Civil Litigation. ***Email:*** cmq@wardandsmith.com

ERIC J. REMINGTON, admitted to bar, 1993, Virginia; 1999, North Carolina. *Education:* Iowa State University (B.S., 1986); Creighton University (J.D., 1993). Trial Advocacy Team; International Moot Court Board. *Member:* North Carolina and American Bar Associations; North Carolina State Bar; Virginia State Bar; Defense Research Institute; North Carolina Association of Defense Attorneys. [Capt., U.S. Marine Corps, 1986-1996]. ***PRACTICE AREAS:*** Litigation; Business Litigation; Commercial Litigation; Civil Litigation; Insurance; Products Liability. ***Email:*** ejr@wardandsmith.com

JULIANA CLELAND RICHARDS, admitted to bar, 2005, North Carolina. *Education:* United States Naval Academy (B.S., 1992); Duke University (J.D., magna cum laude, 2004). Order of the Coif. *Member:* North Carolina and American Bar Associations. [Lieutenant Commander, U.S. Navy, 1992-2000]. ***PRACTICE AREAS:*** Business Law; Financial Institutions; Technology; Intellectual Property; Information; Securities; Banking Law. ***Email:*** jcr@wardandsmith.com

GARY J. RICKNER, admitted to bar, 1974, Indiana; 1998, North Carolina. *Education:* Taylor University (B.A., 1971); Cumberland School of Law of Samford University (J.D., cum laude, 1974). Associate Editor, Cumberland-Samford Law Review, 1972-1974. Listed in *The Best Lawyers in America.* Instructor, National Institute for Trial Advocacy. *Member:* North Carolina, Indiana State and American Bar Associations; North Carolina State Bar; Defense Research Institute; American College of Trial Lawyers. ***PRACTICE AREAS:*** Business Litigation; Commercial Litigation; Financial Institutions; Civil Litigation; Litigation; Products Liability; Banking Law. ***Email:*** gjr@wardandsmith.com

CLINT D. ROUTSON, admitted to bar, 1983, North Carolina. *Education:* Centre College of Kentucky (B.S., 1980); College of William & Mary (J.D., 1983). Order of the Coif. *Member:* North Carolina (Chair, Real Property Section, 1997-1998) and American Bar Associations; North Carolina State Bar. ***PRACTICE AREAS:*** Construction; Real Estate; Commercial Real Estate; Zoning, Planning and Land Use. ***Email:*** cdr@wardandsmith.com

STANLEY M. SAMS, admitted to bar, 1979, North Carolina. *Education:* East Carolina University (B.S., Business Administration, 1976); University of North Carolina (J.D., 1979). Member, Holderness Moot Court Bench. Lecturer, in Business Law, East Carolina University, 1979-1991. *Member:* North Carolina and American Bar Associations; North Carolina State Bar; East Carolina Estate Planning Council. ***PRACTICE AREAS:*** Real Estate; Construction; Commercial Real Estate; Business Law; Wills and Probate. ***Email:*** sms@wardandsmith.com

JEREMY R. SAYRE, admitted to bar, 1998, Ohio; 2004, North Carolina. *Education:* John Carroll University (B.S., 1994); Ohio State University (J.D., 1998). National Moot Court Team. Herman Moot Court. *Member:* Ohio State and American Bar Associations; North Carolina State Bar. ***PRACTICE AREAS:*** Labor and Employment. ***Email:*** js@wardandsmith.com

FRANK H. SHEFFIELD, JR., admitted to bar, 1974, Texas; 1989, North Carolina. *Education:* University of Texas at Austin (B.A., 1968; J.D., 1974). Listed in *The Best Lawyers in America*. Chair, North Carolina Ports Advisory Council. Mayor, Hillsborough, North Carolina, 1983-1987. *Member:* North Carolina (Past Chair, Environmental and Natural Resources Law Section, 1999-2000) and American Bar Associations; North Carolina State Bar; State Bar of Texas; American Agricultural Law Association; North Carolina Ports Advisory Council. ***PRACTICE AREAS:*** Environmental Law; Government Affairs; Agricultural Law; Natural Resources; Toxic Torts; Land Use and Zoning; Labor and Employment. ***Email:*** fhs@wardandsmith.com

JOHN REEVES SLOAN, admitted to bar, 1990, Virginia; 1994, North Carolina. *Education:* University of North Carolina (A.B., 1987; J.D., with honors, 1990). National Moot Court Team; Holderness Moot Court Bench. *Member:* North Carolina, Virginia and American Bar Associations; Virginia State Bar; North Carolina State Bar. (Board Certified Specialist in Estate Planning and Probate Law, North Carolina State Board of Legal Specialization). ***PRACTICE AREAS:*** Trusts and Estates; Wills and Probate; Taxation. ***Email:*** jrs@wardandsmith.com

J. TROY SMITH, JR., admitted to bar, 1967, North Carolina; 1979, U.S. Supreme Court; 1983, U.S. Tax Court. *Education:* University of North Carolina (A.B., 1965; J.D., with highest honors, 1967). Order of the Coif. Editor-in-Chief, North Carolina Law Review, 1966-1967. Recipient, Chief Justice Walter Clark Award. Listed in *The Best Lawyers in America.* Member, General Statutes Commission Code Committee, 1978-1981. *Member:* North Carolina Bar Association (Member, Board of Governors, 1973-1976; Chairman, Real Property Committee, 1973-1979; Chairman, Special Committee on Recodification of General Statutes, 1976-1981; General Practice Hall of Fame); North Carolina State Bar; American College of Real Estate Lawyers. ***PRACTICE AREAS:*** Business Law; Government Affairs; Health Care; Corporate Law; Mergers and Acquisitions; Taxation. ***Email:*** jts@wardandsmith.com

H. L. STEPHENSON, III, admitted to bar, 1982, North Carolina. *Education:* University of North Carolina (A.B., 1979; J.D., 1982); College of William & Mary (LL.M., Taxation, 1983). *Member:* North Carolina (Member, Tax Section Council, 1986-1988, 1993-1995) and American Bar Associations; North Carolina State Bar; East Carolina Estate Planning Council; North Carolina Economic Developers Association. ***PRACTICE AREAS:*** Business Law; Tax Law; Mergers and Acquisitions; Trusts and Estates. ***Email:*** hls@wardandsmith.com

JOHN P. SWART, admitted to bar, 1981, North Carolina. *Education:* East Tennessee State University (B.S., magna cum laude, 1974); University of Tennessee (J.D., 1980). Order of the Coif. *Member:* North Carolina State Bar. ***PRACTICE AREAS:*** Litigation; Personal Injury; Wrongful Death; Civil Litigation. ***Email:*** jps@wardandsmith.com

RYAL W. TAYLOE, admitted to bar, 1982, North Carolina. *Education:* University of North Carolina (A.B., 1979); Wake Forest University (J.D., 1982). *Member:* North Carolina and American Bar Associations; North Carolina State Bar; North Carolina Academy of Trial Lawyers; The Association of Trial Lawyers of America. ***PRACTICE AREAS:*** Community Associations; Construction Law; Business Litigation; Commercial Litigation; Real Estate; Eminent Domain. ***Email:*** rwt@wardandsmith.com

MATTHEW W. THOMPSON, admitted to bar, 2004, North Carolina. *Education:* University of Delaware (B.A., 2000); William and Mary School of Law (J.D., 2004). Phi Beta Kappa. *Member:* North Carolina State Bar. ***PRACTICE AREAS:*** Trusts and Estates. ***Email:*** mwt@wardandsmith.com

BENJAMIN E. F. B. WALLER, admitted to bar, 1998, Alabama; 2001, North Carolina. *Education:* Goucher College (B.A., with honors, 1992); Washington University (M.A., 1995); Duke University (J.D., 1998). *Member:* North Carolina State Bar; Alabama State Bar; North Carolina and American Bar Associations; North Carolina Academy of Trial Lawyers. ***PRACTICE AREAS:*** Creditors' Rights; Debtor and Creditor; Bankruptcy; Commercial Law; Business Litigation; Commercial Litigation. ***Email:*** bew@wardandsmith.com

AMY P. WANG, admitted to bar, 1996, North Carolina. *Education:* University of Virginia (B.A., 1992); Wake Forest University (J.D., 1996). *Member:* North Carolina and American Bar Associations; North Carolina State Bar; North Carolina Association of Women Attorneys. ***PRACTICE AREAS:*** Litigation; Trust Litigation; Estate Litigation; Environmental Law. ***Email:*** apw@wardandsmith.com

DAVID L. WARD, JR., admitted to bar, 1962, North Carolina. *Education:* University of North Carolina (B.S., 1957); Duke University (J.D., 1962). Phi Beta Kappa. Member, Editorial Board, Duke Law Journal, 1961-1962. Listed in *The Best Lawyers in America.* Inducted into Hall of Fame of the General Practice Section, North Carolina Bar Association. Chair of Directors, Research Triangle Foundation, 2000—. Member, 1989-1993 and Vice Chairman, 1991-1993, Board of Trustees, University of North Carolina at Chapel Hill. *Member:* North Carolina and American Bar Associations; North Carolina State Bar; North Carolina Association of Defense Attorneys; The American College of Trust and Estate Counsel. ***PRACTICE AREAS:*** Business Law; Financial Institutions; Government Affairs; Housing Authority Law; Labor and Employment; Banking Law; Finance. ***Email:*** dlw@wardandsmith.com

LEIGH ALLRED WILKINSON, admitted to bar, 1985, North Carolina. *Education:* North Carolina State University (B.S., magna cum laude, 1982); University of North Carolina (J.D., 1985). *Member:* North Carolina and American Bar Associations; North Carolina State Bar; American Health Lawyers Association; Health Care Compliance Association; Medical Group Management Association; North Carolina Hospital Association; North Carolina Society of Healthcare Attorneys. ***PRACTICE AREAS:*** Business Law; Health Care Law; Corporate Law. ***Email:*** law@wardandsmith.com

A. REXFORD WILLIS, III, admitted to bar, 1980, North Carolina; 1986, U.S. Tax Court. *Education:* University of North Carolina (B.S., 1977; J.D., 1980). Certified Public Accountant, North Carolina, 1982. *Member:* North Carolina and American Bar Associations; North Carolina State Bar; North Carolina Association of Certified Public Accountants. ***PRACTICE AREAS:*** Business Law; Trusts and Estates; Corporate Law; Tax Law. ***Email:*** arw@wardandsmith.com

KENNETH R. WOOTEN, admitted to bar, 1979, North Carolina. *Education:* North Carolina State University (B.A., with high honors, 1976); University of North Carolina (J.D., with honors, 1979). Order of the Coif. Staff Member, North Carolina Law Review, 1977-1978. Member, Invitational Moot Court Team, Holderness Moot Court Bench, 1978-1979. Research Assistant to Justice J. William Copeland, North Carolina Supreme Court, 1979-1980. *Member:* North Carolina (Construction Law Section, Chair, 1992-1993, Vice Chair, 1991-1992, Secretary, 1988-1991) and American (Member, Litigation Section) Bar Associations; North Carolina State Bar; North Carolina Association of Defense Attorneys; Defense Research Institute; Christian Legal Society. ***PRACTICE AREAS:*** Construction Law; Litigation; Housing Authority Law; Commercial Law; Insurance. ***Email:*** krw@wardandsmith.com

REPRESENTATIVE CLIENTS: Amital Spinning Corp.; Atlantic Coast Contracting; Atlantic States Bank; Barnhill Contracting Company; Cape Fear Community College; Central Carolina Bank and Trust Co.; Chubb Insurance; City of Havelock; Craven Community College;

(This Listing Continued)

Daedong- USA, Inc.; East Carolina Bank; Eastern Carolina Regional Housing Authority; Eastern Radiologists, Inc.; First-Citizens Bank & Trust Company; First Flight Federal Credit Union; Fountain Powerboats, Inc.; Hatteras Yachts; Ironstone Bank; Janus Development Group; Mountainbank Financial Corp.; NC State Firemen's Association; Neuse Regional Water & Sewer; Physicians East, P.A.; Potash Corp.; Southern Banc & Trust Co.; State of North Carolina; Weyerhaeuser Co.; Wilmington Cardiology, PLLC.

DI SANTI WATSON CAPUA & WILSON

Established in 1971
102 ELK STREET
NEWLAND, NORTH CAROLINA 28657
Telephone: 828-733-9273
URL: http://www.lawyers.com/disantiwatson&capua

Boone, North Carolina Office: 642 West King Street, P.O. Box 193, 28607-4040. Telephone: 828-264-6126.

General Civil Practice and in all State and Federal Courts. Corporation, Real Property, Insurance, Family, Municipal, Personal Injury, Automobile Accidents and Injuries, Estate Planning, Probate, Real Estate Development and Interstate Land Sales.

FIRM PROFILE: Di Santi Watson Capua & Wilson is a very well established firm since 1971. They have a complete general civil practice in State and Federal Courts. This firm is a very reputable and credible in the Boone Area.

COUNSEL FOR: Boone Industries, Inc.; Boone Mall, Ltd.; Northwestern Regional Housing Authority; Linville Ridge Country Club; Elk River Development Corp.; Log Homes of America, Inc., WJ Office City; High Country Bank.
REPRESENTATIVE CLIENTS: Insurance Company of North America; Fireman's Fund; Shelby Mutual Insurance Co.; Tweetsie Railroad, Inc.; Midwest Mutual Insurance Co.; Piedmont Savings & Loan Assn.; U.S.F. & G. Insurance Co.; Allstate Insurance Co.; First Union National Bank; The Pantry, Inc.; Seibels Bruce Insurance Group; Lloyd's, London; Indiana Lumberman's Insurance Co.; Tenn. Farmers Mutual Insurance Co.; Nationwide Homes, Inc.; Pennsylvania National Insurance Co.; Integon Insurance Co.; Cincinnati Insurance Co.; KM Administrative Services.
APPROVED ATTORNEYS FOR: Lawyers Title Insurance Corp.; Chicago Title Insurance Co.; American Title Insurance Co.; Commonwealth Title Insurance.
REFERENCE: Bank of America, Boone, N.C.

(For Complete Biographical Data on all Personnel, see Professional Biographies at Boone, North Carolina)

HALL & HALL ATTORNEYS AT LAW, P.C.

118 ELK STREET
P.O. BOX 898
NEWLAND, NORTH CAROLINA 28657
Telephone: 828-733-9222
Fax: 828-737-9009
Email: hallandhall@bellsouth.net

Morganton, North Carolina Office: 305 S. Green Street, 28655. Telephone: 828-433-9100. Fax: 828-433-9339

Estates, Real Estate, Workers Compensation, Family Law, Divorce, Equitable Distribution, Personal Injury, Traffic Violations, Driving While Intoxicated, Criminal Law, Collections, Child Custody, Corporate Law, Employment Discrimination.

DOUGLAS L. HALL, admitted to bar, 1995, North Carolina; U.S. District Court, Western District of North Carolina and U.S.Court of Appeals, 4th Circuit. *Education:* Guilford College (B.A., 1992); Campbell University (J.D., 1995). Phi Alpha Theta; Phi Alpha Delta. *Member:* North Carolina State Bar. ***Email:*** hallandhall@bellsouth.net

KATHRYN G. HEMPHILL

299 SOKOSSA ROAD
P.O. DRAWER 849
NEWLAND, NORTH CAROLINA 28657
Telephone: 828-733-6004
Fax: 828-733-2091
Email: khemphill@goboone.net

General Trial Practice. Civil Practice in State Courts. Domestic Relations and Real Estate Law. Estates and Wills.

KATHRYN G. HEMPHILL, born Hickory, North Carolina, September 1, 1946; admitted to bar, 1981, North Carolina. *Education:* Sweet Briar College (B.A., 1969); Appalachian State University (M.A., 1974); Wake Forest University (J.D., 1980).

REPRESENTATIVE CLIENTS: Linville Resorts, Inc.; Grandfather Golf & Country Club; Apple Orchard, Ltd.; Rocky Knob. *Approved Title Attorney For:* LandAmerica Title Insurance; Investors Title; First American Title.

GERALD R. McKINNEY, P.A.

Established in 1988
390 SOKASSA ROAD
P.O. BOX 9
NEWLAND, NORTH CAROLINA 28657
Telephone: 828-733-5199; 733-5299
Fax: 828-733-1582
Email: geraldlaw1@bellsouth.net

General Civil and Criminal Trial Practice. Workers Compensation, and Personal Injury Law. Mediation; Real Estate.

(This Listing Continued)

GERALD R. McKINNEY, born Marion, North Carolina, March 11, 1955; admitted to bar, 1980, North Carolina. *Education:* University of North Carolina at Chapel Hill (B.S., 1977; J.D., 1980). Town Attorney: Village of Sugar Mountain, 1985-1990; Town of Banner Elk, 2003—. Attorney: Toe River Health District; Linville Land Harbor Property Owners Association. Certified Mediator: North Carolina Dispute Resolution Commission and North Carolina Industrial Commission. *Member:* Avery County and North Carolina Bar (Governing Council Member, General Practice Section Chair, 1994-1995; General Practice Hall of Fame Selection Committee Chair, 1997; Member, Board of Governors, 1998-2001) Associations; North Carolina State Bar; 24th Judicial District (President, 1997) Bar Association. ***PRACTICE AREAS:*** Driving While Intoxicated; Traffic Violations; Criminal Litigation; Civil Litigation; Real Estate; Personal Injury; Automobile Accidents and Injuries; Wrongful Death; Mediation.

JOSEPH W. SEEGERS

125 PINEOLA
P.O. BOX 490
NEWLAND, NORTH CAROLINA 28657
Telephone: 828-733-9206
Fax: 828-733-3291

General Civil and Criminal Trial Practice before all Courts. Criminal Law, Capital Offenses, D.U.I., Traffic Violations, Probate, Estates, Estate Planning, Business and Commercial Law, Negligence Law, Workers Compensation, Municipal Law, Juvenile Law, Family Law, Divorce, Child Custody.

JOSEPH W. SEEGERS, born Raleigh, North Carolina, April 26, 1947; admitted to bar, 1972, North Carolina. *Education:* Hampden-Sydney College (B.S., 1969); University of South Carolina (J.D., 1972). Town Attorney, Elk Park, 1986—. Avery County Attorney, 1990-1996. *Member:* State Bar of North Carolina; 24th Judicial District Bar Association (President, 1985-1987); Avery County and North Carolina Bar Associations; North Carolina Academy of Trial Lawyers.

REPRESENTATIVE CLIENTS: Avery County Ambulance & Resque Squad Association, Inc.; Southern Balsam, Inc.; ERA Resort Real Estate and Rentals; Property Management, Inc.; Sugar Mountain Village.
APPROVED ATTORNEYS FOR: Lawyers Title Insurance Corp.; First American Title Insurance Co.; American Title Insurance Co.; Safeco Title Insurance Co.; Commonwealth Land Title Insurance Co.; Jefferson-Pilot Title Insurance Co.; First Title Insurance Co.; Investors Title Insurance Co.; Transamerica Title Insurance Co.

BEVIN W. WALL

OCEAN WAY PLAZA, SUITE F
7025 HIGHWAY 70
NEWPORT, NORTH CAROLINA 28570
Telephone: 252-223-4411
Fax: 252-223-5104

Bankruptcy, Real Estate, Traffic, DWI, Juvenile.

BEVIN W. WALL, born Newport, North Carolina, July 18, 1963; admitted to bar, 1988, North Carolina. *Education:* St. Andrews Presbyterian College (B.A., with Honors, 1985); University of North Carolina (J.D., 1988). *Member:* Carteret County (Secretary and Treasurer, 1998-2001; President, 2003), North Carolina and American Bar Associations; North Carolina State Bar; 3rd Judicial District Bar; North Carolina Academy of Trial Lawyers; Association of Trial Lawyers of America; Eastern Bankruptcy Institute. ***PRACTICE AREAS:*** Bankruptcy; Real Estate; Traffic Violations; Driving While Intoxicated; Juvenile Law.

SCOTT D. CONRAD

11 EAST "A" STREET
P.O. BOX 42
NEWTON, NORTH CAROLINA 28658
Telephone: 828-466-3858
Fax: 828-466-3808
Email: Killian&Reilley@w3link.com
URL: http://www.lawyers.com/scottdconrad

Criminal, Domestic/Family, Child Custody, Juvenile, Traffic, Divorce, Real Estate, Wills.

SCOTT D. CONRAD, born Franklin Lakes, New Jersey, November 18, 1968; admitted to bar, 1996, North Carolina. *Education:* Appalachian State University (B.S. and B.A., 1992); Campbell University Norman A. Wiggins School of Law (J.D., 1996). Phi Alpha Delta. *Member:* Catawba County Bar Association; North Carolina State Bar; North Carolina Academy of Trial Lawyers. ***PRACTICE AREAS:*** Criminal Defense; Family Law; Divorce; Real Estate; Traffic Violations.

CORNE, CORNE & GRANT, P.A.

217 NORTH MAIN AVENUE
P.O. DRAWER 166
NEWTON, NORTH CAROLINA 28658
Telephone: 828-464-2371
Fax: 828-465-5422
Email: ccg@newtonslaw.com
URL: http://www.newtonslaw.com

Personal Injury, Automobile Accidents, Slip and Fall, Wrongful Death, Medical Malpractice, Family Law, Child Custody, Child Support, Divorce, Visitation Rights, Real Estate, Residential Real Estate, Criminal Law, Business Law, Joint Ventures, Limited Liability Company Law, Partnership, Corporate Law, Trusts and Estates.

(This Listing Continued)

CORNE, CORNE & GRANT, P.A., Newton—Continued

FIRM PROFILE: Corne, Corne & Grant, P.A. is a full service, general practice law firm situated in Catawba County.

STANLEY J. CORNE (1924-2003)

RAY GARRISON CORNE, born Newton, North Carolina, September 26, 1952; admitted to bar, 1977, North Carolina. *Education:* Davidson College (B.A., 1974); University of Capetown, South Africa; Wake Forest University (J.D., 1977). Instructor, Business Law, Catawba Valley Community College. Certified District and Superior Court Mediator. *Member:* Catawba County and American Bar Associations; North Carolina State Bar; North Carolina Trial Lawyers Association. ***LANGUAGES:*** Spanish. ***PRACTICE AREAS:*** Family Law; Elder Law; Personal Injury. ***Email:*** rgc@twave.net

ROBERT M. GRANT, JR., born Statesville, North Carolina, March 7, 1949; admitted to bar, 1974, North Carolina. *Education:* Wake Forest University (B.A., 1971; J.D., 1974). Phi Alpha Delta. Member, Moot Court. Assistant District Attorney, 25th Prosecutorial District, 1974-1978. Part-time Instructor, Tort, Criminal and Domestic Law, Trial Preparation and Evidence, Central Piedmont Community College and Catawba Valley Community College, 1983-1985. *Member:* Catawba County and North Carolina Bar Associations; North Carolina State Bar; North Carolina Academy of Trial Lawyers; The Association of Trial Lawyers of America. ***LANGUAGES:*** French. ***PRACTICE AREAS:*** Governmental Law; Personal Injury; Civil Litigation; Medical Malpractice; Commercial Real Estate; Residential Real Estate; Trusts and Estates; Business Law; Corporate Law; Limited Liability Partnerships. ***Email:*** rmgrant@newtonslaw.com

CHRYSTAL N. DEHART, born Rutherford, North Carolina, May 7, 1976; admitted to bar, 2001, North Carolina. *Education:* University of North Carolina at Chapel Hill (B.A., 1998); Emory University School of Law (J.D., 2001). Phi Alpha Delta. *Member:* Catawba County (Secretary), North Carolina and American Bar Associations; North Carolina State Bar Association. ***PRACTICE AREAS:*** Estate Planning; Estate Administration; Real Estate; Taxation; Business Law; Elder Law; Guardianship; Adoption Law. ***Email:*** chrystaldehart@charter.net

REPRESENTATIVE CLIENTS: Carolina Glove Co.; City of Claremont; Conover Lumber Co.; Hendrick Motors.
REFERENCES: Bank of Granite; Peoples Bank; Branch Banking & Trust.

EAKER & FULKERSON, PC

NEWTON, NORTH CAROLINA

(See Hickory)

Criminal Law, Driving Under the Influence, Real Estate, Domestic.

GORHAM, CRONE, MACE, GREEN & CODY, LLP

NEWTON, NORTH CAROLINA

(See Hickory)

General Practice, Bankruptcy, Criminal, Driving While Intoxicated, Drug Crimes, Parole and Probation, Traffic Violations, White Collar Crime, Family Law, Adoption Law, Child Custody, Child Support, Divorce, Domestic Violence, Visitation Rights, Municipal Law, Personal Injury, Automobile Accidents, Wrongful Death, Real Estate, Buying or Selling a Home, Construction, Eminent Domain, Zoning and Land Use, Trust and Estates, Asset Protection, Estate Planning, Wills and Probate. Litigation in all State and Federal Courts.

ISENHOWER, WOOD & CILLEY, P.A.

Established in 1991
7 EAST SECOND STREET
P.O. BOX 145
NEWTON, NORTH CAROLINA 28658
Telephone: 828-465-2100
Fax: 828-465-3707
Email: iwc@iwc-law.com

Aged and Aging, Bankruptcy, Commercial, Corporate, Foreclosures, Probate, Real Estate, Trusts and Estates and Wills.

DAVID L. ISENHOWER, born Hickory, North Carolina, January 4, 1948; admitted to bar, 1974, North Carolina; 1977, U.S. District Court, Western District of North Carolina. *Education:* Lenoir-Rhyne College (A.B., 1971); University of North Carolina-Chapel Hill (J.D., 1974). Member, Catawba County Industrial Development Commission, 1981-1987. Member, Board of Directors, Love-N-Care Child Development Center, 1981-1988; 1996-1998. Member, Abernethy Laurels Advisory Council, 1991-1998 and 2003—. Member, Catawba County Mental Health Board, 2000—. Member, Board of Directors, United Church Homes and Services, 2004—. *Member:* Catawba County (Treasurer, 1975) and North Carolina Bar Associations; North Carolina State Bar. (Managing Partner). ***PRACTICE AREAS:*** Aged and Aging; Corporate Law; Probate; Real Estate; Trusts and Estates; Wills. ***Email:*** disenhower@iwc-law.com

ALLEN W. WOOD, III, born Fayetteville, North Carolina, December 3, 1951; admitted to bar, 1977, North Carolina and U.S. District Court, Western District of North Carolina; 1978, U.S. District Court, Middle District of North Carolina; 1979, U.S. Court of Appeals, Fourth Circuit. *Education:* Wake Forest University (B.A., 1974); University of North Carolina-Chapel Hill (J.D., 1977). Phi Delta Phi (Member, Vance Inn). Member, North Carolina Law Review, 1976-1977. Member: Catawba County Board of Elections, 1993-1996, 1999-2001 and 2003—; Board of Directors, Green Room Community Theatre, 1992-2003 and 2004—; Catawba County Council for the Arts, 2001—. *Member:* Catawba County and North Carolina Bar Associations; North Carolina State Bar. ***PRACTICE AREAS:*** Bankruptcy Law; General Business Law. ***Email:*** awood@iwc-law.com

(This Listing Continued)

JOHN H. CILLEY, IV, born Charlotte, North Carolina, November 8, 1959; admitted to bar, 1985, North Carolina. *Education:* Georgetown University (B.S.F.S., 1982); Wake Forest University (J.D., 1985). Member, Hickory Jaycees, 1990-1996. Chairman, Catawba County Democratic Party, 1990-1993. Member, Board of Directors, Adult Life Programs, 2003-2005. Instructor, Real Estate Law, Institute of Financial Education. Commissioner, Employment Security Commission of N.C., 1995—. Trustee, Teachers and State Employees' Retirement System of NC, 1995-2005. *Member:* Catawba County, North Carolina and American Bar Associations; North Carolina State Bar. ***PRACTICE AREAS:*** Real Estate Law; Corporate Law; Probate Law; Foreclosures. ***Email:*** jcilley@iwc-law.com

REPRESENTATIVE CLIENTS: Branch Banking and Trust Company; Catawba Valley Bank; Corning Cable Systems Credit Union; Lee Industries, Inc.
APPROVED ATTORNEYS FOR: Chicago Title; First American Title; Investors Title; Lawyers Title; Statewide Title.

PATRICK, HARPER & DIXON L.L.P.

NEWTON, NORTH CAROLINA

(See Hickory)

General Practice, State and Federal Courts. Insurance, Tax, Probate, Estate Planning and Corporation Law. Real Property and Litigation.

SIGMON, CLARK, MACKIE, HUTTON, HANVEY & FERRELL, P.A.

NEWTON, NORTH CAROLINA

(See Hickory)

General Practice. Probate, Corporate, Trials concerning all phases of the law and Real Estate Law.

SIGMON, SIGMON & ISENHOWER

P.O. BOX 88
NEWTON, NORTH CAROLINA 28658
Telephone: 828-464-0101
Fax: 828-464-9062

General Civil and Criminal Practice, Driving While Intoxicated, Felonies, Traffic Violations, Probate, Real Estate, Corporation, Business Law, Family Law, Adoptions, Child Custody, Child Support, Divorce, Personal Injury, Tort Law.

MEMBERS OF FIRM

JESSE C. SIGMON (1885-1967)

JESSE C. SIGMON, JR. (1922-1997)

GENE SIGMON, born Iredell County, North Carolina, August 3, 1941; admitted to bar, 1967, North Carolina; 1976, U.S. Court of Appeals, Fourth Circuit and U.S. Supreme Court. *Education:* University of North Carolina (B.A., 1964; J.D., 1967). Law Clerk, U.S. District Court, 1967-1968. Judge, District Court, 25th Judicial District, 1970-1973. Attorney, Catawba County School Board, 1974-1978. Catawba County Attorney, 1978—. ***PRACTICE AREAS:*** Trial Practice; Torts; Municipal Law; Corporate Law.

C. RANDALL ISENHOWER, born Newton, North Carolina, December 22, 1953; admitted to bar, 1979, North Carolina. *Education:* North Carolina State University (B.S.C.E., 1976); University of North Carolina (J.D., 1979). Phi Kappa Phi. Attorney, Town of Maiden, 1989—. Member, North Carolina Board of Certified Public Accountant Examiners, 1988-1994. Member, 1997— and Chairman, 2003—, Newton-Conover City Schools Board of Education. ***PRACTICE AREAS:*** Trial Practice; Real Estate; Probate; Family Law; Corporate Law. ***Email:*** cheryl@ssi-law.com

ASSOCIATE

WESLEY W. BARKLEY, born Pensacola, Florida, January 19, 1978; admitted to bar, 2003, North Carolina. *Education:* Gardner-Webb University (B.A., 1999); Campbell University (J.D., 2003). ***PRACTICE AREAS:*** Criminal Law; Traffic Law; Real Estate; Trial Practice; Torts. ***Email:*** wes@ssi-law.com

All Members belong to the Catawba County and North Carolina Bar Associations and the North Carolina State Bar.

REPRESENTATIVE CLIENTS: Furnished Upon Request.

YOUNG, MORPHIS, BACH AND TAYLOR, L.L.P.

NEWTON, NORTH CAROLINA

(See Hickory)

General, Civil and Criminal Practice. Trials in all State and Federal Courts and the U.S. Supreme Court. Corporations, Taxation, Probate, Trusts, Real Estate, Commercial, Complex Business and Commercial, Municipal, Family Law, Complex Matrimonial Law, Negligence, Products Liability, Personal Injury, Workers Compensation, Insurance Law, Bankruptcy, Patent Law.

VANNOY, COLVARD, TRIPLETT & VANNOY, P.L.L.C.

922 "C" STREET
P.O. BOX 1388
NORTH WILKESBORO, NORTH CAROLINA 28659
Telephone: 336-667-7201
Fax: 336-838-7250
URL: http://www.vannoylaw.com

Civil and Criminal Litigation, Corporations, Personal Injury, Automobile Accidents, Traffic, Driving While Intoxicated, DWI, Real Estate, Wills, Trusts and Estates, Workers' Compensation, Social Security Disability.

MEMBERS OF FIRM

J. GARY VANNOY, born Wilkes County, North Carolina, August 23, 1940; admitted to bar, 1964, North Carolina; 1967, U.S. Supreme Court. *Education:* Mars Hill College and Wake Forest University (B.A., 1962); Wake Forest University (LL.B., 1964). Phi Alpha Delta. Judge, Wilkes County Court, 1965-1968. Certified Superior Court Mediator. *Member:* Wilkes County and North Carolina Bar Associations; North Carolina State Bar; North Carolina Academy of Trial Lawyers. ***PRACTICE AREAS:*** Civil Litigation; Criminal Litigation. ***Email:*** gvannoy@vannoylaw.com

HOWARD C. COLVARD, JR., born Iredell County, North Carolina, September 15, 1946; admitted to bar, 1971, North Carolina. *Education:* Wake Forest University (B.A., 1968; J.D., 1971). Phi Delta Phi. *Member:* Wilkes County and North Carolina Bar Associations; North Carolina State Bar; North Carolina Academy of Trial Lawyers. ***PRACTICE AREAS:*** Corporate; Estate Planning; Commercial Real Estate; Corporate Litigation; Civil Litigation. ***Email:*** bcolvard@vannoylaw.com

ANTHONY R. TRIPLETT, born Wilkes County, North Carolina, October 22, 1955; admitted to bar, 1981, North Carolina. *Education:* University of North Carolina (B.S. in Business Administration, 1978; J.D., 1981). Phi Beta Kappa; Phi Eta Sigma; Beta Gamma Sigma. Member, North Carolina State Board of Examiners for Nursing Home Administrators, 1985-1991. County Attorney, Wilkes County, 1990—. *Member:* Wilkes County and North Carolina Bar Associations; North Carolina State Bar; North Carolina Academy of Trial Lawyers. ***PRACTICE AREAS:*** Contracts; Corporate Law; Real Estate; Wills and Estates; Municipal Law; General Civil Practice. ***Email:*** ttriplett@vannoylaw.com

JOHN G. (JAY) VANNOY, JR., born North Wilkesboro, North Carolina, January 31, 1967; admitted to bar, 1992, North Carolina; U.S. District Court, Western and Middle Districts of North Carolina; U.S. Court of Appeals, 4th Circuit. *Education:* Guilford College (B.S., 1989); Campbell University (J.D., 1992). Phi Alpha Delta. Order of Old Kivett. American Bar Association Criminal Justice Trial Team. Board Certified Specialist in State Criminal Law. *Member:* Wilkes County and North Carolina Bar Associations; North Carolina State Bar; National Association of Criminal Defense Attorneys; Association of Trial Lawyers of America; North Carolina Academy of Trial Lawyers. ***PRACTICE AREAS:*** Criminal Defense; Traffic Violations; Civil Litigation. ***Email:*** jay@vannoylaw.com

---

DANIEL STUART JOHNSON, born Williamston, North Carolina, July 2, 1975; admitted to bar, 2000, North Carolina; 2002, U.S. District Court, Western District of North Carolina. *Education:* University of North Carolina at Chapel Hill (B.S.B.A., 1997); Wake Forest University (J.D., 2000). *Member:* Wilkes County and North Carolina Bar Associations; North Carolina State Bar; North Carolina Academy of Trial Lawyers. ***PRACTICE AREAS:*** Civil Practice. ***Email:*** djohnson@vannoylaw.com

CARMEN ELIZABETH JAMES, born Wilkes County, North Carolina, June 23, 1958; admitted to bar, 2001, North Carolina. *Education:* Wake Forest University (B.A., 1997); North Carolina Central University (J.D., 2000). Phi Theta Kappa; Phi Alpha Theta. Licensed 3rd class restricted R-TV operator. *Member:* Wilkes County and North Carolina Bar Associations; North Carolina State Bar. ***PRACTICE AREAS:*** Real Estate. ***Email:*** carmen@vannoylaw.com

APPROVED ATTORNEYS FOR: Investors Title Insurance Company; Lawyers Title Insurance Corporation; Chicago Title Insurance Company; American Title Insurance Company; First Title Insurance Company; The Title Company; First American Title Company; Statewide Title Company.
REPRESENTED CLIENTS: Wilkes County; Key City Furniture Company; Jenkins Properties, Inc.; East Coast Millwork Distributors, Inc.
REFERENCES: 1st Citizens Bank & Trust Co.; Branch Banking & Trust Co.

ROGER LEE EDWARDS, P.A.

Established in 1983

7201 EAST OAK ISLAND DRIVE
OAK ISLAND, NORTH CAROLINA 28465
Telephone: 910-278-3100
Fax: 910-278-3320
Email: rledwardsesq@bellsouth.net

General Civil State and Federal Courts. Municipal and Local Government Law, Real Estate, Corporate, Commercial, Probate, Family, Personal Injury.

ROGER LEE EDWARDS, born Sparta, North Carolina, October 29, 1953; admitted to bar, 1979, North Carolina, U.S. District Court, Western and Middle Districts of North Carolina, U.S. Court of Appeals, Fourth Circuit and U.S. Supreme Court. *Education:* Surry Community College (A.A., 1973); Appalachian State University (B.A., 1975); Campbell University (J.D., 1979). Pi Gamma Mu; Phi Kappa Phi; Alpha Chi. Town Attorney, Town of Oak Island. *Member:* North Carolina and American Bar Associations; North Carolina State Bar; North Carolina Academy of Trial Lawyers; The Association of Trial Lawyers of America. ***Email:*** rledwardsesq@bellsouth.net

(This Listing Continued)

APPROVED ATTORNEYS FOR: Commonwealth Land Title; Commonwealth Land Title Insurance Co.; Stewart Title Guaranty Company; Investors Title Insurance Company; Chicago Title Insurance Company; Lawyers Title of North Carolina.

KATHERINE S. PARKER-LOWE

35 MISS ELECIA LANE, SUITE 101
P.O. BOX 730
OCRACOKE, NORTH CAROLINA 27960-0730
Telephone: 252-928-1000
Fax: 252-928-3037
Email: katherine@parker-lowe.net

Real Estate, Civil Practice, Consumer Law, Traffic, Bankruptcy, Business.

KATHERINE PARKER-LOWE, admitted to bar, 1986, North Carolina, U.S. District Court, Eastern District of North Carolina, U.S. Court of Appeals, Fourth Circuit and U.S. Bankruptcy Court, Eastern District of North Carolina. *Education:* University of North Carolina at Greensboro (B.A., 1981); Campbell University (J.D., 1985). *Member:* North Carolina State Bar; Second Judicial District Bar Association. ***PRACTICE AREAS:*** Real Estate; Civil Practice; Banking Law; Consumer Law. ***Email:*** katherine@parker-lowe.net

---

CURRIN & DUTRA, LLP

118 MAIN STREET
P.O. BOX 1226
OXFORD, NORTH CAROLINA 27565
Telephone: 919-693-8011
Fax: 919-690-1415
Email: oxfordlaw@earthlink.net

General Practice, Civil Litigation in all Courts, Criminal Litigation in all Courts, Traffic Offenses, Personal Injury, Small Business Law, Corporate Law, Residential Real Estate, Commercial Real Estate, Land Use Planning, Estate Planning, Probate, Workers Compensation and Social Security Disability.

MEMBERS OF FIRM

THOMAS L. CURRIN, born Oxford, North Carolina, July 30, 1951; admitted to bar, 1976, North Carolina; 1978, U.S. District Court, Eastern District of North Carolina; 1997, U.S. District Court, Middle District of North Carolina. *Education:* University of North Carolina at Chapel Hill (B.A., 1973; J.D., 1976). John Motley Morehead Scholar, 1969-1973. *Member:* Granville County, Ninth Judicial District and North Carolina (Member, General Practice Section) Bar Associations; North Carolina State Bar; North Carolina Academy of Trial Lawyers (Member, Criminal Law Section). ***PRACTICE AREAS:*** Trial Practice; Personal Injury; Traffic Violations; Commercial Real Estate; Residential Real Estate; Estate Planning; Probate; Municipal Law.

LORI A. DUTRA, born St. Louis, Missouri, September 24, 1960; admitted to bar, 1987, Florida; 1990, North Carolina. *Education:* University of North Carolina, Charlotte (B.A., cum laude, 1982); University of North Carolina, Chapel Hill (M.R.P., 1987; J.D., with honors, 1987). Member, National Moot Court Competition Team. *Member:* The Florida Bar; North Carolina State Bar; North Carolina Bar Association; North Carolina Academy of Trial Lawyers. ***PRACTICE AREAS:*** Trial Practice; Land Use; Zoning Law; Personal Injury; Domestic Relations; Workers Compensation; Social Security Disability; Commercial Real Estate; Residential Real Estate; Municipal Law.

ASSOCIATE

AMY R. EDGE, born Charlotte, North Carolina, January 17, 1969; admitted to bar, 1995, North Carolina; 1997, U.S. District Court, Eastern and Middle Districts of North Carolina. *Education:* Duke University (A.B., 1991); University of North Carolina (J.D., 1995). Articles Editor, The North Carolina Journal of International Law and Commercial Regulation, 1994-1995. Author: Comment, "Preventing Software Piracy Through Regional Trade Agreements: The Mexican Example," The North Carolina Journal of International Law and Commercial Regulation, Fall, 1994 Vol. 20 Number 1. *Member:* North Carolina Bar Association (Council Member, Real Property Section); North Carolina State Bar. ***PRACTICE AREAS:*** Commercial Real Estate; Residential Real Estate; Appellate Practice; Trial Practice; Probate; Personal Injury; Small Business Law; Corporate Law.

LEGAL SUPPORT PERSONNEL

LISA J. NEWTON, born Oxford, North Carolina, September 11, 1972. *Education:* Meredith College (B.S.B.A., 1994). Certified Legal Assistant, 1999.

REPRESENTATIVE CLIENTS: City of Creedmoor; Town of Stovall; Granville County Board of Elections; Georgia Pacific Corporation; Ellington-Brim Chevrolet; Al Sandling Chevrolet.
APPROVED ATTORNEYS FOR: Investor's Title Insurance Company; Chicago Title Insurance Company; Fidelity National Title Insurance Company; Consumers Title; Statewide Title.
REFERENCES: Central Carolina Bank; Branch Banking and Trust; Fidelity Bank; RBC-Centura Bank.

HOPPER & HICKS, L.L.P.

111 GILLIAM STREET
P.O. BOX 247
OXFORD, NORTH CAROLINA 27565
Telephone: 919-693-8161
Fax: 919-693-9938
URL: http://www.hopperhicks.com

General Civil and Criminal Practice. Trials in all Courts. Probate, Wills and Probate, Real Estate, Automobile Accidents, Wrongful Death, Personal Injury, Family Law, Divorce, Child Custody, Adoptions, Business and Corporate Law, Administrative Law, Immigration Law, Taxation.

(This Listing Continued)

HOPPER & HICKS, L.L.P., Oxford—Continued

MEMBERS OF FIRM

WILLIAM L. HOPPER, born La Porte, Indiana, September 13, 1941; admitted to bar, 1966, Arkansas; 1970, U.S. District Court, Western District of Arkansas; 1977, North Carolina; 1978, U.S. District Court, Eastern District of North Carolina; 1981, U.S. Tax Court; 1985, U.S. Court of Appeals, Fourth Circuit. *Education:* College of the Ozarks (B.S., 1963); University of Arkansas (J.D., 1966). Phi Alpha Delta. Member, Arkansas Law Review, 1963-1966. Special Agent Federal Bureau of Investigation, 1966-1969. *Member:* Granville County, Arkansas and North Carolina Bar Associations; Ninth Judicial District and North Carolina State Bars; The Association of Trial Lawyers of America; North Carolina Academy of Trial Lawyers. ***PRACTICE AREAS:*** Administrative Law; Civil Litigation; Municipal Law; Business Associations; Health Care Law; Personal Injury; Estate Planning; Probate. ***Email:*** wlh@hopperhicks.com

N. KYLE HICKS, born Durham, North Carolina, November 26, 1958; admitted to bar, 1984, North Carolina; 1985, U.S. District Court, Eastern District of North Carolina. *Education:* University of North Carolina (B.S., 1981); Walter F. George School of Law, Mercer University; Wake Forest University School of Law (J.D., 1984). *Member:* Granville County and North Carolina Bar Associations; Ninth Judicial District and North Carolina State Bars. (Board Certified Specialist in Residential Transactions and Real Property Law, North Carolina State Board of Legal Specialization). ***PRACTICE AREAS:*** Real Estate Law; Traffic Violations; Criminal Law; Family Law; Divorce; Adoption Law; Probate. ***Email:*** nkh@hopperhicks.com

---

JAMES C. WRENN, JR., born Henderson, North Carolina; admitted to bar, 2000, North Carolina; 2001, U.S. Court of Appeals, Fourth Circuit; 2002, U.S. District Court, Eastern and Middle Districts of North Carolina. *Education:* Virginia Military Institute (B.A., 1997); Harvard Law School (J.D., cum laude, 2000). Executive Editor, Harvard Journal of Law and Public Policy. Law Clerk to the Honorable Karen J. Williams, U.S. Court of Appeals, Fourth Circuit, 2000-2001. Author: "Passing the Buck: The Supreme Court's Failure to Clarify Qualified Immunity Doctrine to Protect Public Officials," 22 Harv. J.L. & Public Policy, 1031. *Member:* American Immigration Lawyers Association. ***PRACTICE AREAS:*** Civil Litigation; Municipal Law; Business Associations Law; Health Care Law; Immigration Law; Taxation; Appellate Practice; Personal Injury; Estate Planning; Probate. ***Email:*** jcw@hopperhicks.com

COUNSEL FOR: Capital Bank; Granville County; Granville Medical Center; Granville County Department of Social Services; Kerr-Tar Regional Council of Governments; North Carolina Association Long Term Care Facilities; RBC Centura Bank.
REPRESENTATIVE CLIENTS: Capital Bank; Centura Bank; BB&T; The Fidelity Bank; Premier Quilting Corp.; Nelms Electric Corp.; Carolina Sunrock Corp.; Ideal Fastener Corp.; Lace Lastic & Co.; Pierce Management Group; Triad Packaging, Inc.; Diversicare Assisted Living Services of North Carolina, LLC.
APPROVED ATTORNEYS FOR: Lawyer's Title Insurance Corp.; North Carolina Title Insurance Corp.; Commercial Title Insurance Corp.; St. Paul Title Insurance Corp.; First Title Insurance Corp.; Investor's Title Insurance Corp.; Chicago Title Insurance Co.
REFERENCES: RBC Centura Bank; BB&T; Capital Bank.

HARVEY D. JACKSON
ATTORNEY AT LAW

OXFORD, NORTH CAROLINA

(See Henderson)

Worker's Compensation, Personal Injury, Auto Accident and Insurance Claims, Wrongful Death, Traffic Violations.

JOHN H. PIKE

Established in 1976

129 WILLIAMSBORO STREET
SUITE 1
P.O. BOX 1165
OXFORD, NORTH CAROLINA 27565
Telephone: 919-693-2412
Fax: 919-693-1652
Email: JPIKE@GLORYROAD.net
URL: http://www.lawyers.com/johnhpike

Traffic Violations, DWI, Criminal Law (all except capital), Family Law, Child Custody, Divorce, Adoptions, Personal Injury, Automobile Accidents, Truck and Motorcycle Accidents, Civil Litigation, Wrongful Death.

FIRM PROFILE: John H. Pike has appeared on behalf of hundreds of individual clients, in their absence, to resolve traffic violations and DWI's in Granville and Vance Counties.

JOHN H. PIKE, born Raleigh, North Carolina, February 20, 1947; admitted to bar, 1976, North Carolina; 1978, U.S. District Court, Eastern District of North Carolina. *Education:* University of North Carolina (B.S., 1970; J.D., 1976). *Member:* Granville County and North Carolina Bar Associations; Ninth Judicial District and North Carolina State Bars; North Carolina Academy of Trial Lawyers. ***PRACTICE AREAS:*** Traffic Violations; Driving While Intoxicated; Criminal Law; Family Law; Divorce; Personal Injury; Civil Litigation.

ROYSTER, CROSS & CURRIN, LLP

Established in 1888

135 COLLEGE STREET
P.O. DRAWER 1168
OXFORD, NORTH CAROLINA 27565
Telephone: 919-693-3131
Fax: 919-693-2919

Business Law, Corporate Law, Wills and Probate, Trusts and Estates, Commercial and Residential Real Estate, Personal Injury, Traffic, Family Law, Divorce, Child Custody, Adoptions.

MEMBERS OF FIRM

THOMAS S. ROYSTER, JR., born Oxford, North Carolina, May 21, 1937; admitted to bar, 1961, North Carolina. *Education:* Wake Forest University (B.S., 1959; LL.B., 1961). Member, Governor's Crime Commission, 1986-1995. *Member:* North Carolina (Member, Estate Planning and Fiduciary Law Section) and Ninth Judicial District Bar Associations; North Carolina State Bar. (Board Certified Specialist in Estate Planning and Probate Law, North Carolina State Board of Legal Specialization). ***PRACTICE AREAS:*** Estate Planning and Administration; Wills and Trusts; Business Law. ***Email:*** samroyster@aol.com

JAMES E. CROSS, JR., born Greensboro, North Carolina, November 16, 1947; admitted to bar, 1973, North Carolina; 2001, U.S. Supreme Court. *Education:* Wake Forest University (B.A., 1970; J.D., 1973). Chairman, The North Carolina State Bar Board of Legal Specialization, 1994-1997. Granville County School Board Attorney. *Member:* Ninth Judicial District and North Carolina (Member, Education Law, Real Estate Law Sections) and American Bar Associations; North Carolina State Bar. (Board Certified Specialist in Real Property Law-Residential Transactions, North Carolina State Board of Legal Specialization). ***PRACTICE AREAS:*** Commercial Real Estate; Residential Real Estate; Business Law; Wills and Estates. ***Email:*** jcross@rccattorneys.com

HUGH M. CURRIN, JR., born August 25, 1951; admitted to bar, 1980, North Carolina. *Education:* North Carolina State University (B.A., 1973); Campbell University (J.D., 1980). Counselor, North Carolina State Bar, Ninth Judicial District, 1993-1994. DRC Certified Mediator, Superior Court and Family Financial. *Member:* Ninth Judicial District Bar Association (President, 1989-1990); North Carolina State Bar (Member, Family Law Section); North Carolina Academy of Trial Lawyers. ***PRACTICE AREAS:*** Family Law; Personal Injury; Criminal Law; Litigation; Mediation. ***Email:*** hcurrin@rccattorneys.com

DALE W. HENSLEY, born Asheville, North Carolina, June 30, 1969; admitted to bar, 1998, North Carolina. *Education:* University of North Carolina, Asheville (B.A., cum laude, 1995); University of North Carolina, Chapel Hill (J.D., 1998). *Member:* Ninth Judicial District (Secretary-Treasurer, 1998-2000) and North Carolina (Member, General Practice Section) Bar Associations. ***PRACTICE AREAS:*** Trusts and Estates; Real Estate; Wills; Litigation; Traffic Violations. ***Email:*** dhensley@rccattorneys.com

---

H. NORMAN THORP, III

133 WILLIAMSBORO STREET
P.O. BOX 1027
OXFORD, NORTH CAROLINA 27565
Telephone: 919-693-3232
Telecopier: 919-693-2322
Email: hnthorp@gloryroad.net
URL: http://www.lawyers.com/hnthorp

Criminal Law, Traffic Violations, DWI, Drug Violations, Theft, Personal Injury, Automobile Accidents, Residential Real Estate, Creditor Bankruptcy, Small Business Law, Business Startup, Wills and Probate.

H. NORMAN THORP, III, born Oxford, North Carolina, April 17, 1963; admitted to bar, 1988, North Carolina. *Education:* Appalachian State University (B.S., Criminal Justice, 1985); Campbell University School of Law (J.D., 1988). Phi Alpha Delta. *Member:* Granville County and North Carolina Bar Association; North Carolina State Bar; North Carolina Academy of Trial Lawyers; Association of Trial Lawyers of America. ***PRACTICE AREAS:*** Criminal Law; Traffic Violations; Driving While Intoxicated; Drug Crimes; Theft; Personal Injury; Automobile Accidents and Injuries; Residential Real Estate; Creditor Bankruptcy; Small Business Law; Business Start-Ups; Wills; Probate.

JOHN W. WATSON, JR.

Established in 1985

204 WILLIAMSBORO STREET
P.O. BOX 100
OXFORD, NORTH CAROLINA 27565-0100
Telephone: 919-693-5697
Facsimile: 919-693-1192
Email: jwwatsonjr@earthlink.net
URL: http://www.jwatsonlaw.com

Workers Compensation Law, Criminal Law, Estates, Personal Injury, Automobile Accidents, Wrongful Death, Traffic Violations, DWI, Family Law, Divorce, Child Custody.

JOHN W. WATSON, JR., born Richmond, Virginia, January 16, 1954; admitted to bar, 1982, North Carolina; 1985, U.S. District Court, Eastern District of North Carolina; 1986, U.S. Supreme Court. *Education:* University of North Carolina (B.A., 1976); Mercer University; Campbell University (J.D., 1982). Delta Theta Phi. Member, Campbell University Law Review, 1981-1982. Author: Note, "Tort Law-Merchant's Duty to Protect Invitees From Third Party Criminal Acts," Campbell Law Review, Volume 4, Number 2, Spring, 1982. President, Ninth Judicial District Bar Association, 1994-1995. Former Director and Vice-President, North Central Legal Services of North Carolina. *Member:* Granville County and North Carolina Bar Associations; North Carolina State Bar; North Carolina Academy of Trial Lawyers; The Association of Trial Lawyers of America. ***LANGUAGES:***

(This Listing Continued)

Spanish. ***REPORTED CASES:*** Jones v. Murdoch Center, NCAPP, 327, SE2d 294, 74 NCAPP 128-Work Comp 803, 847, 876; Hilliard v. Manitowoc, 61 F3d 900, 1995 WL 434828 4th Circuit South Carolina; Hooper v. Pizzagalli Const. Co., NCApp, 436 SE2d 145, 112 NCAPP 400, review den 442 SE2d 516, 335 NC 770.-App & E 875; Judgm 181 (2), 185 (6), 345; Mast & S 315, 318 (1), 319; Neglig 22, 55; Pretrial Proc 695; Work Comp 2084. ***PRACTICE AREAS:*** Civil Practice; Estates; Personal Injury; Automobile Accidents and Injuries; Wrongful Death; Workers Compensation Law; Traffic Violations.

ASSOCIATE

JOHN M. DUNLOW, born Gaston, North Carolina, March 21, 1968; admitted to bar, 1994, North Carolina. *Education:* Appalachian State University (B.S. cum laude, 1990); Campbell University (J.D. magna cum laude, 1994). Gamma Beta Phi; Pi Gamma Mu. Who's Who Among American Law School Students. Clerk, Judge Sidney S. Eagles, Jr., 1993. President, Oxford Jaycees, 1998-1999. *Member:* Granville County (President, 2004-2005) and American Bar Associations; North Carolina State Bar; North Carolina Association of Trial Lawyers. ***PRACTICE AREAS:*** Family Law; Divorce; Child Custody; Child Support; Adoption Law; Criminal Law; Traffic Violations; Guardian Ad Litem; Driving While Impaired; Felonies. ***Email:*** jmdunlow@earthlink.net

THOMAS W. ANDERSON

214 E. MARION STREET
P.O. BOX 1273
PILOT MOUNTAIN, NORTH CAROLINA 27041
Telephone: 336-368-9621
Fax: 336-368-9168
Email: thanderson54@hotmail.com
URL: http://www.lawyers.com/thomaswandersonlaw

Bankruptcy, Mediation, Employment Law and Criminal.

THOMAS W. ANDERSON, born Burgaw, North Carolina, August 5, 1954; admitted to bar, 1979, North Carolina; 1980, U.S. District Court, Middle District of North Carolina; 1991, U.S. District Court, Eastern District of North Carolina; 1994, U.S. District Court, Western District of North Carolina. *Education:* Wake Forest University; University of North Carolina, Wilmington; University of North Carolina, Chapel Hill (B.A., Economics, 1976; J.D., 1979). Phi Delta Phi. Assistant District Attorney, Judicial District 17B, 1983-1990. Member, 1991-1997, Chair, 1995-1997, Surry County Board of Elections. Past Member, Board of Directors, Hospice of Surry County, Inc. *Member:* Surry County and North Carolina Bar Associations; North Carolina State Bar; National Association of Chapter 13 Trustees (Associate Member); National Association of Consumer Bankruptcy Attorneys; National Association of Consumer Attorneys. ***PRACTICE AREAS:*** Bankruptcy; Criminal; Personal Injury; Mediation.

M. ANN ANDERSON, born Elkin, North Carolina, March 1, 1955; admitted to bar, 1981, North Carolina and U.S. District Court, Middle District of North Carolina; 1983, U.S. District Court, Eastern District of North Carolina; 1985, U.S. Court of Appeals, Fourth Circuit; 1995, U.S. District Court, Western District of North Carolina. *Education:* University of North Carolina, Chapel Hill (B.A., Psychology, 1976; J.D., with honors, 1981). Research Editor, 1980-1981, Staff Member, 1979-1980, North Carolina Law Review. Co-Editor, Dispute Resolution Newsletter, 2001-2003. Adjunct Instructor, Clinical Program, Wake Forest University School of Law, 1989. Adjunct Instructor, Spring, 2002. Past Member, Board of Trustees, University of North Carolina School of Law, 1989-1991. President, 1998-2001. Board Member, 1992—, Board of Directors, Triad United Methodist Home. Secretary/Treasurer, Charles H. Stone Memorial Library, 1995-1999. Member, 1998—, Treasurer, 2003-2004 and Secretary, 2004-2005, Dispute Resolution Council Board of Directors, Pilot Mountain Foundation. *Member:* Surry County and North Carolina Bar Associations. ***SPECIAL AGENCIES:*** Guardian at Litem, Attorney Advocate, 1996-1999. ***PRACTICE AREAS:*** Employment Discrimination Law; Labor Law; Mediation. ***Email:*** annanderson681@hotmail.com

MORRIS LAW OFFICE

PINEHURST, NORTH CAROLINA

(See Whispering Pines)

Criminal Law, Felonies and Misdemeanors, Traffic Violations and Tickets, Trucks, Motorcycles, Driving While Intoxicated, DUI, Animal Law, Equine, Horse Rights and Trusts, Veterans Benefits and Appeals.

PATE & SCARBOROUGH, L.L.P.

15 CHINQUAPIN ROAD
P.O. BOX 1669
PINEHURST, NORTH CAROLINA 28370
Telephone: 910-295-2161
Fax: 910-295-3247

Real Property, Trust and Estate Planning and Administration, Business Formation.

W. DANIEL PATE, born Rowland, North Carolina, December 15, 1948; admitted to bar, 1974, North Carolina. *Education:* McCallie School; University of North Carolina (B.S., 1971); Wake Forest University (J.D., 1974). Phi Delta Phi. Staff Member, Wake Forest Law Review, 1973-1974. Author: "Evidence-Admissibility of Computer Print-Outs as Business Records," 9 Wake Forest Law Review 428, 1974. *Member:* Moore County (President, 1982-1983) and North Carolina Bar Associations; North Carolina State Bar; National Association of Elder Law Attorneys. ***PRACTICE AREAS:*** Trusts and Estates; Estate Planning; Estate Administration; Commercial and Residential Real Estate.

(This Listing Continued)

DEWITT TALMADGE SCARBOROUGH, III, born Pinehurst, North Carolina, January 10, 1950; admitted to bar, 1975, North Carolina; 1976, U.S. District Court, Middle District of North Carolina. *Education:* University of North Carolina (A.B., 1972; J.D., 1975). Phi Beta Kappa. *Member:* 20th Judicial District (President, 1983-1984), North Carolina (Council Member, Real Property Section, 1990-1993; Treasurer, 1994) and American Bar Associations; North Carolina State Bar (District Representative, Legal Aid Committee, 1978-1979; Board of Directors, North State Legal Services Corporation, 1982-1984). (Board Certified Specialist in Real Property Law-Residential, North Carolina State Board of Legal Specialization). ***PRACTICE AREAS:*** Commercial and Residential Real Estate; Community Associations.

APPROVED ATTORNEYS FOR: Chicago Title Insurance Co.; Fidelity National Title Company of NY; First American Title Insurance Co.; Investors Title Insurance Co.; Lawyers Title Insurance Corp.; The Title Company of N.C., Inc.
REFERENCES: Branch Banking and Trust Company; Centura Bank.

ROBBINS MAY & RICH LLP

120 APPLECROSS ROAD
PINEHURST, NORTH CAROLINA 28374
Telephone: 910-692-4900
Fax: 910-692-4286 (Real Estate and Corporate)
Fax: 910-692-1768 (Trusts and Estates and Litigation)
URL: http://www.rmrattorneys.com

General Civil and Criminal Litigation in all Courts. Traffic Violations, Real Property, Trust and Estate Planning and Administration, Commercial and Residential Real Estate Transactions, Banking, Taxation, Personal Injury, Family Law, Divorce, Worker's Compensation, Business Formations and Transactions and Social Security Disability.

PARTNERS

PHILLIP WAYNE ROBBINS, born Winston-Salem, North Carolina; admitted to bar, 1966, North Carolina. *Education:* Columbia University (A.B., 1963); University of North Carolina (J.D., 1966). Delta Theta Phi. Certified Mediator; 20th Judicial District (President, 1978-1979). *Member:* Moore County, North Carolina and American Bar Associations; North Carolina State Bars; North Carolina Academy of Trial Lawyers. ***PRACTICE AREAS:*** Civil Litigation; Criminal Litigation; Traffic Violations; Commercial Litigation; Domestic Relations; Bankruptcy; Collections. ***Email:*** pwrobbins@rmrattorneys.com

JOHN M. MAY, born Raleigh, North Carolina; admitted to bar, 1972, North Carolina. *Education:* Wake Forest University (B.A., 1970; J.D., 1972); New York University (LL.M. in Taxation, 1985). Councilor, 20th Judicial District, 1989-1995. *Member:* Moore County and North Carolina Bar Associations; North Carolina State Bar (Chairman, CLE Board, 2000-2001; Member, Disciplinary Hearing Committee, 2003—). ***PRACTICE AREAS:*** Taxation; Business Transactions; Real Estate. ***Email:*** jmay@rmrattorneys.com

CAROL M. WHITE, born Carthage, North Carolina; admitted to bar, 1988, North Carolina. *Education:* Meredith College; University of North Carolina-Chapel Hill (B.S., 1982); Campbell University School of Law (J.D., cum laude, 1988). *Member:* North Carolina State Bar; North Carolina Bar Association. ***PRACTICE AREAS:*** Civil Litigation; Domestic Relations; Personal Injury; Workers Compensation. ***Email:*** cwhite@rmrattorneys.com

MARK D. VAUGHN, born Oak Park, Illinois; admitted to bar, 1988, North Carolina. *Education:* Wheaton College (B.A., 1985); Wake Forest University (J.D., 1988). *Member:* Moore County and North Carolina Bar Associations; North Carolina State Bar. ***PRACTICE AREAS:*** Trust Planning; Estate Planning; Trust Administration; Estate Administration. ***Email:*** mdvaughn@rmrattorneys.com

VICTORIA P. BRENNER, born West Palm Beach, Florida; admitted to bar, 1981, Florida; 1992, California; 1993, North Carolina. *Education:* Emory University (B.A., 1978); University of Miami (J.D., cum laude, 1981). *Member:* Moore County, North Carolina (Member, Estate Planning and Fiduciary Law Section Council) and American Bar Associations. ***PRACTICE AREAS:*** Trust Planning; Estate Planning; Trust Administration; Estate Administration. ***Email:*** vpbrenner@rmrattorneys.com

ROBERT M. FRIESEN, born Kansas City, Missouri; admitted to bar, 1990, North Carolina. *Education:* Westminster College; University of Kansas (B.A., 1984; J.D., 1989). Phi Delta Phi. *Member:* Moore County, North Carolina (Former Member, Real Property Council) and American Bar Associations. ***PRACTICE AREAS:*** Commercial Real Estate; Residential Real Estate; Business Law. ***Email:*** bfriesen@rmrattorneys.com

STEPHEN F. LATER, born Hartford, Connecticut; admitted to bar, 1994, North Carolina; 1996, District of Columbia; 1997, U.S. Supreme Court. *Education:* Columbia University (B.A., cum laude, 1990); University of Virginia (M.A., 1991); University of North Carolina (J.D., cum laude, 1994). Notes Editor, North Carolina Law Review, 1993-1994. Counsel to U.S. Senator Lauch Faircloth, 1995-1998. *Member:* North Carolina State Bar; District of Columbia Bar. ***PRACTICE AREAS:*** Business Law; Business Transactions; Labor and Employment; Health Care; Real Estate. ***Email:*** sflater@rmrattorneys.com

RETIRED PARTNER

DEAN A. RICH, born Galesburg, Illinois; admitted to bar, 1957, North Carolina. *Education:* Knox College (B.A., 1951); University of North Carolina (J.D., 1957). Chairman, Estate Planning and Fiduciary Law Section, 1981-1982, and Chair, Senior Lawyers Division, 1995-1996, North Carolina Bar Association. Fellow, American College of Trust and Estate Counsel.

ASSOCIATE

JANET C. SMITH, born Washington, D.C., December 4, 1959; admitted to bar, 1995, North Carolina; 2001, U.S. Supreme Court. *Education:* Duke University (A.B., 1982); Ohio State University (M.A., 1983); Columbus School of Law, Catholic University of America (J.D., 1995). Certified Superior Court Mediator. Village Attorney, Village of Pinehurst, 2002-2004. ***PRACTICE AREAS:*** Municipal Law; Zoning Law; Land Use; Estate Administration; Mediation. ***Email:*** jsmith@rmrattorneys.com

(This Listing Continued)

ROBBINS MAY & RICH LLP, Pinehurst—Continued

APPROVED ATTORNEYS FOR: The Title Company of N.C., Inc.; Commonwealth Title Insurance Co.; First Title Insurance Co.; Lawyers Title Insurance Corp.; Chicago Title Insurance Co.; Investors Title; Fidelity National Title Insurance Company.
REFERENCES: Branch Banking & Trust Company; N.G. Purvis Farms, Inc.; Bank of America; Sandhills Community College; The Country Club of North Carolina, Inc.; Wachovia Bank, National Association; Bill Smith Ford Lincoln Mercury, Inc.; Eastover Capital Management, Inc.; First Bank; First Bank Insurance Services, Inc.; First Health of the Carolinas, Inc.; Longworth Industries, Inc.; McBrayer Chrysler Dodge Jeep, Inc.; McDonald Brothers, Inc.; The Pilot, LLC; Pinehurst, Inc.; Pinewild Property Owners Association; Scotland Container Corp.; Sterling Transport, Inc.

HURLEY E. THOMPSON, JR.

PINEHURST, NORTH CAROLINA

(See Carthage)

Residential Real Property, Foreclosure, Traffic Offenses, Wills, Estates, Personal Injury.

ROBERT S. THOMPSON, P.A.

PINEHURST, NORTH CAROLINA

(See Southern Pines)

Estate Planning Law, Business Law, Corporate Law, Probate Law, Wills, Trusts and Estates, Commercial and Residential Real Estate Law.

VAN CAMP, MEACHAM & NEWMAN, PLLC

Established in 1976

TWO REGIONAL CIRCLE
PINEHURST, NORTH CAROLINA 28374
Telephone: 910-295-2525
Fax: 910-295-2001; 910-295-1520 (Litigation)
URL: http://www.lawyers.com/vancampmeacham&newman

General Civil and Criminal Litigation and Appellate Practice in State and Federal Courts. Personal Injury, Commercial, Medical Malpractice, Wrongful Death, Worker's Compensation, Insurance, Land Condemnation, Constitutional and Civil Rights, Family, Corporate, Real Estate, Administrative, Social Security Disability, Construction Law, Labor and Employment, Wills, Estate Planning and Probate Law.

FIRM PROFILE: Founded by James R. Van Camp in 1976, Van Camp, Meacham & Newman, PLLC engages in the general practice of law and offers a full range of services to individual and corporate clients. The firm employs a highly experienced support staff, including paralegals. The firm emphasizes participation in continuing legal education activities as well as professional, cultural, charitable, and civic associations.

JAMES R. VAN CAMP, born Orange, New Jersey, June 11, 1940; admitted to bar, 1965, North Carolina; 1966, U.S. District Court, Middle, Eastern and Western Districts of North Carolina; U.S. Court of Appeals, Fourth Circuit; U.S. District Court, District of Maine; U.S. Court of Appeals, First Circuit; U.S. Supreme Court. *Education:* Atlantic Christian College (A.B., 1962); Wake Forest University (LL.B., 1965). Phi Delta Phi. The Order of Barristers, 1991—. Member, Board of Editors, Wake Forest Intramural Law Review, 1964-1965. Co-Author: "North Carolina Criminal Procedure Forms," Van Camp, Eagles and Corbett, 1975; 3d Edition, 1989. Member: Governor's Committee on Law and Order, 1970-1973; North Carolina Criminal Code Commission, 1973-1982. Member, 1977-1986, Vice Chairman, 1979 and Chairman, 1980-1986, Governor's North Carolina Crime Commission. Member, North Carolina Courts Commission, 1981-1982. Member, International Society of Barristers, 1989—; Member, Commission for the Future of Justice and the Courts, 1994—. Member, School Board of Visitors, Wake Forest University Law School, 1995—. Member, North Carolina Board of Law Examiners, 2005. *Member:* Moore County (President, 1974) and North Carolina Bar Associations; The Association of Trial Lawyers of America; North Carolina Academy of Trial Lawyers (Member, Board of Governors, 1974-1985; Vice President, 1977-1983; President, 1983-1984); American Academy of Criminal Defense Attorneys; American Board of Trial Advocates. ***PRACTICE AREAS:*** Civil Litigation; Commercial; Personal Injury; Administrative; Wrongful Death; Land Condemnation; Appellate Practice; Corporate; Criminal Defense; Domestic Law; Litigation. ***Email:*** jamesv@vancamplaw.com

EDDIE H. MEACHAM, born Danville, Virginia, May 8, 1958; admitted to bar, 1983, North Carolina. *Education:* Elon College (B.A., cum laude, 1980); Wake Forest University (J.D., 1983). Alpha Chi; Pi Gamma Mu. Assistant District Attorney, 20th Prosecutorial District, 1984-1987. *Member:* 20th Judicial District Bar (Vice President, 1988-1989; President, 1990) and Moore County Bar Associations; The Association of Trial Lawyers of America; North Carolina Academy of Trial Lawyers. ***PRACTICE AREAS:*** Criminal Defense.

MICHAEL J. NEWMAN, born Abilene, Texas, May 24, 1962; admitted to bar, 1988, North Carolina, U.S. District Court, Middle, Western and Eastern Districts of North Carolina. *Education:* Western Carolina University (B.S., magna cum laude, 1985); Wake Forest University (J.D., 1988). Member: A.B.A. National Moot Court Team, 1987; Wake Forest Law Review, 1987-1988. *Member:* Moore County and North Carolina Bar Associations. ***PRACTICE AREAS:*** Civil Litigation; Personal Injury; Insurance Litigation; Land Condemnation; Wrongful Death. ***Email:*** michaeln@vancamplaw.com

THOMAS M. VAN CAMP, born Dobbs Ferry, New York, January 30, 1963; admitted to bar, 1989, North Carolina and U.S. District Court, Middle, Eastern and Western Districts of North Carolina, U.S. Court of Appeals, Fourth Circuit. *Education:* Franklin and Marshall College (B.A., with honors, 1986); Wake Forest University (J.D., 1989). Member, Wake Forest Law Review, 1988-1989. Secretary-Treasurer, Twentieth Judicial District Bar, 1994-1995. *Member:* Moore County, North Carolina and American Bar Associations; North Carolina State Bar; North Carolina Academy of Trial Lawyers. ***PRACTICE AREAS:*** General Civil Litigation; Personal Injury; Constitutional and Civil Rights Law; Construction Law; Insurance Litigation; Employment Law; Workers Compensation. ***Email:*** thomasv@vancamplaw.com

(This Listing Continued)

LAURA S. CREED, born Lake City, Florida, August 5, 1973; admitted to bar, 1998, Alabama and U.S. District Court, Middle District of Alabama; 1999, North Carolina. *Education:* Auburn University (B.S., 1995); Mississippi College (J.D., 1998). Delta Theta Phi. Law Clerk to Chief Justice Hooper, Supreme Court of Alabama. *Member:* Moore County Bar Association; North Carolina State Bar; Alabama State Bar. ***PRACTICE AREAS:*** Civil Litigation; Juvenile Law; Family Law; Social Security Disability. ***Email:*** laurac@vancamplaw.com

RYAN D. OXENDINE, born Pinehurst, North Carolina, June 23, 1975; admitted to bar, 2001, North Carolina. *Education:* University of North Carolina at Chapel Hill (B.A., 1997); New England School of Law, North Carolina Central University (J.D., 2000). Phi Alpha Delta. *Member:* North Carolina State Bar; Moore County Bar Association; North Carolina Bar Association; American Bar Association. ***PRACTICE AREAS:*** Commercial Real Estate; Corporate Law; Estate Administration; Business Law; Estate Planning; Residential Real Estate. ***Email:*** ryano@vancamplaw.com

TIFFANY J. SKILLMAN, born Laurinburg, North Carolina, June 14, 1977; admitted to bar, 2002, North Carolina. *Education:* University of North Carolina at Chapel Hill (B.A., 1999); Campbell University School of Law (J.D., cum laude, 2002). Member, Campbell Law Review, 2000-2002. *Member:* Moore County Bar Association; North Carolina State Bar. ***PRACTICE AREAS:*** Civil Litigation. ***Email:*** tiffanys@vancamplaw.com

CRAIG A. SLAGLE, born Hollywood, Florida, 1976; admitted to bar, 2005, North Carolina. *Education:* Appalachian State University (B.S., 1997); Campbell University (J.D., cum laude, 2005). *Member:* Moore County, North Carolina and American Bar Associations; North Carolina State Bar.

REPRESENTATIVE CLIENTS: Carolina Eye Associates; Country Club of Whispering Pines; High Falls Oil Co., Inc.; Lee Electrical Construction, Inc.; Mid Pines Resort; Pine Needles Resort; Pinehurst Medical Clinic; Pinehurst Neurology; Pinehurst Pathology Center; Pinehurst Radiology Group; Resorts of Pinehurst; Sandhills Center for Mental Health; Southeastern Regional Mental Health; Village of Pinehurst.

WEST & SMITH, L.L.P.

PINEHURST, NORTH CAROLINA

(See Southern Pines)

Personal Injury, Wrongful Death, Civil Litigation, Insurance Litigation, Contested Wills, Worker's Compensation, Social Security Disability, Land Condemnation, Commercial Litigation, Construction Litigation, Mediation and Arbitration.

BRADSHAW & ROBINSON, L.L.P.

HALL-LONDON HOUSE
128 HILLSBORO STREET
P.O. BOX 607
PITTSBORO, NORTH CAROLINA 27312
Telephone: 919-542-2400
Fax: 919-542-1319
Email: law@bradshawrobinson.com

Civil and Criminal Practice. Development and Zoning, Business, Corporation, Bankruptcy, Wills, Probate, Estate Administration, Real Estate and Traffic Law.

PATRICK E. BRADSHAW, born Goldsboro, North Carolina, October 4, 1964; admitted to bar, 1989, Georgia; 1992, North Carolina. *Education:* University of North Carolina (B.A., with distinction, 1986; J.D., 1989). Phi Beta Kappa. *Member:* North Carolina State Bar; State Bar of Georgia; North Carolina and American Bar Associations. ***PRACTICE AREAS:*** Zoning, Planning and Land Use; Business Law; Corporate Law; Real Estate. ***Email:*** bradshaw@bradshawrobinson.com

NICOLAS P. ROBINSON, born Madrid, Spain, May 20, 1964; admitted to bar, 1989, Georgia; 1991, North Carolina. *Education:* University of North Carolina, Chapel Hill (B.A., with honors, 1985; J.D., with honors, 1989). Phi Beta Kappa. Donald Seawell Scholar. Holderness Moot Court Board (National Team). Member, Board of Directors: Carolina Meadows, 2002—; Joint Orange Chatham Community Action, 1998—. *Member:* State Bar of Georgia; North Carolina State Bar; North Carolina Bar Association; Pro Bono Planning Committee, 1994-1995; Pro Bono Recruitment and Activation Subcommittee, (Chairman, 1994-1995, Third Grade Education Project Committee, 1994-1996). ***LANGUAGES:*** Spanish. ***PRACTICE AREAS:*** Zoning, Planning and Land Use; Business Law; Creditors Rights; Litigation. ***Email:*** robinson@bradshawrobinson.com

ASSOCIATE

COURTNEY A. BOWEN, born Belmont, North Carolina, December 19, 1977; admitted to bar, 2003, North Carolina. *Education:* University of North Carolina at Chapel Hill (B.A., with distinction, 2000; J.D., 2003). Member, NC Journal of International Law and Commercial Regulation, 2001-2003. *Member:* North Carolina Bar Association. ***PRACTICE AREAS:*** Real Estate; Wills; Estate Administration; Traffic Law. ***Email:*** bowen@bradshawrobinson.com

REPRESENTATIVE CLIENTS: Governors Club Limited Partnership; Jordan Lake Preserve Corporation; Bluegreen Carolina Lands, LLC; Toll Brothers, Inc.; Powell Place Development Company; Chatham County partnership for Children; Keisler Land Co., LLC.

FRANKLIN LAW CENTER, PLLC

60 WEST STREET
P.O. BOX 685
PITTSBORO, NORTH CAROLINA 27312
Telephone: 919-942-0800
Fax: 919-942-0607
Email: sfranklin@franklinlawcenter.com
URL: http://www.franklinlawcenter.com

Chapel Hill Office: Exchange West at Meadowmont, 1414 Raleigh Road, Suite 290. 27517-8834. Telephone: 919-942-0800. Fax: 919-942-0607.

Divorce, Alimony, Spousal Support, Separation Agreements, Marital Property Settlements, Equitable Distribution of Assets, Cohabitation Agreements, Community Property Law, Non-Traditional Family Law, Divorce Mediation, Divorce Arbitration, Collaborative Family Law, Adoption, International Family Law, Child Custody, Military Divorce, Military Family Law, Trial Practice in all Courts.

FIRM PROFILE: Serving Orange and Chatham Counties in all family law related matters.

(For complete biographical data on all personnel, see Professional Biographies at Chapel Hill, North Carolina)

GUNN & MESSICK, LLP

90 WEST SALISBURY STREET
P.O. BOX 880
PITTSBORO, NORTH CAROLINA 27312-0880
Telephone: 919-542-3253
Fax: 919-542-0257

General Civil and Criminal Practice. Trials in all State Courts. Estate Planning, Corporation, Personal Injury, Real Estate and Administrative Law.

MEMBERS OF FIRM

ROBERT L. GUNN, born Millry, Alabama, September 29, 1931; admitted to bar, 1963, North Carolina. *Education:* University of North Carolina (B.S., 1961; J.D./LL.B., 1962). Delta Theta Phi. Author: "Chemical Tests and Implied Consent," University of North Carolina Law Review, 1964; "North Carolina Motor Vehicle Law and the Uniform Vehicle Code," A Comparative Analysis for the State of North Carolina, 1970. Assistant Professor of Public Law, University of North Carolina at Chapel Hill, 1962-1965. Assistant Attorney General of North Carolina, 1967-1968. Chatham County Attorney, 1973—. *Member:* Chatham County and North Carolina Bar Associations; North Carolina State Bar; North Carolina Academy of Trial Lawyers. ***PRACTICE AREAS:*** Personal Injury; Traffic Violations; Estate Planning; Administrative Law; Litigation. ***Email:*** bg@gunnmessick.com

PAUL S. MESSICK, JR., born Chattanooga, Tennessee, August 22, 1946; admitted to bar, 1971, North Carolina. *Education:* Duke University (A.B., 1968); University of North Carolina (J.D., 1971). Town Attorney, Town of Pittsboro, 1973—. *Member:* Chatham County (President, 1977-1978); North Carolina and American Bar Associations; The North Carolina State Bar; North Carolina Academy of Trial Lawyers. ***PRACTICE AREAS:*** Real Estate; Local Government; Personal Injury. ***Email:*** pmessick@emji.net

REPRESENTATIVE CLIENTS: First Citizens Bank & Trust Company, Pittsboro; Chatham County Housing Authority.
REFERENCE: First Citizens Bank & Trust Company, Pittsboro.

DANA G. JONES

PITTSBORO, NORTH CAROLINA
(See Durham)

Divorce, Child Custody and Child Support, Bankruptcy, Adoption.

MAITLAND & MAITLAND, PLLC

PITTSBORO, NORTH CAROLINA
(See Chapel Hill)

Real Estate, Closings, Residential, Commercial, Business Law, Entrepreneurial, Partnerships, Small Business, Entrepreneur, Business Formation, Immigration, Naturalization, Citizenship, Permanent Resident, Investor, Teacher Visas, H1B, J1, Visa Petitions, Litigation, Banking, Contracts, Foreclosure, Mortgages, Personal Injury, Traffic Violations, DWI, DUI, Liquor License, Alcohol Permit, Wills, Banking, Collection, Sports, Entertainment Law.

CHARLES W. MILLER

Established in 2004

288 EAST STREET, SUITE 2004
P.O. BOX 1549
PITTSBORO, NORTH CAROLINA 27312
Telephone: 919-542-9820
Fax: 919-542-5624
URL: http://www.pittsborolaw.com
Email: charlesmiller@pittsborolaw.com
URL: http://www.lawyers.com/pittsborolaw

Collections, Bankruptcy, Commercial Litigation, Business Contracts, Credit Law, Administrative Law, Real Estate, Mediation, Securities Arbitration, Investment Fund.

FIRM PROFILE: Law firm emphasizing bankruptcy, collections, litigation, real estate, administrative law, mediation, and securities arbitration in the trial and triad regions of North Carolina.

(This Listing Continued)

CHARLES W. MILLER, born Detroit, Michigan, August 20, 1958; admitted to bar, 1998, North Carolina and U.S. District Court, Middle, Eastern and Western Districts of North Carolina. *Education:* Western Michigan University (B.B.A., 1978); Wayne State University (J.D., 1981). Certified as Superior Court Mediator, North Carolina Dispute Resolution Commission. NASD Arbitrator. *Member:* North Carolina State Bar; North Carolina Bar Association. ***PRACTICE AREAS:*** Bankruptcy; Collections; Commercial Litigation; Contracts; Leases and Leasing; Real Estate; NASD Arbitration; Securities Arbitration; Securities Consumer Arbitration; Securities Fraud; Securities Fraud Arbitration.

THE VIRA LAW FIRM, PA

PITTSBORO, NORTH CAROLINA
(See Carrboro)

Trusts and Estates, Probate, Wills, Real Estate, Taxation, Business Law.

LAW OFFICES OF ROBERT J. WILLIS

PITTSBORO, NORTH CAROLINA
(See Raleigh)

Workers Compensation, Criminal Defense, Driving While Intoxicated, Traffic Violations, Automobile Accidents, Wage and Hour Disputes.

WINSTON & MAHER

PITTSBORO, NORTH CAROLINA
(See Chapel Hill)

General Civil, Criminal Trial Practice in all State and Federal Courts, Felonies, Misdemeanors, Drugs and Narcotics, White Collar Crime, Traffic Violations, Driving While Intoxicated.

RALPH G. WILLEY, P.A.

PLYMOUTH, NORTH CAROLINA
(See Rocky Mount)

Workers Compensation, Board Certified, Personal Injury, Civil and Criminal Trial Practice in all Courts, Traffic, Mediation, Arbitration.

ALEXY, FLETCHER, WILLS & WILLS, P.C.

8845 CARATOKE HIGHWAY
POINT HARBOR, NORTH CAROLINA 27964
Telephone: 252-491-8497
Fax: 252-491-8723
URL: http://www.obxlawfirm.com

Business Law, Child Custody, Civil Litigation, Criminal Law, Domestic Relations, Divorce Law, Family Law, Medical Malpractice, Personal Injury, Real Estate Law and Workers Compensation Law, Traffic Violations, Driving While Intoxicated, Buying or Selling a Home, Buying or Selling a Business, Corporate, Small Business.

GRANT E. FLETCHER, born Detroit, Michigan, April 27, 1965; admitted to bar, 1995, Michigan; 1999, North Carolina. *Education:* University of Detroit Mercy (B.A., 1988); Michigan State University (J.D., 1995). *Member:* Oakland County and North Carolina Bar Associations; North Carolina State Bar. ***PRACTICE AREAS:*** Real Estate Litigation; Business Law. ***Email:*** gfletcher@obxlaw.com

GREGORY E. WILLS, born Bangkok, Thailand, March 25, 1964; admitted to bar, 1993, Texas; 1994, North Carolina. *Education:* George Mason University (B.A., 1986); Campbell University (J.D., 1994). *Member:* North Carolina Bar Association; North Carolina State Bar; North Carolina Academy of Trial Lawyers. ***PRACTICE AREAS:*** General Practice; Civil Litigation; Personal Injury; Medical Malpractice; Workers Compensation. ***Email:*** gwills@obxlaw.com

JAMES R. WILLS, III, born Washington, D.C., February 28, 1961; admitted to bar, 1993, Oklahoma; 1994, North Carolina and U.S. District Court, Eastern District of North Carolina. *Education:* George Mason University (B.S., 1989); Oklahoma City University (J.D., 1993). *Member:* North Carolina and Oklahoma Bar Associations; North Carolina State Bar; 1st Judicial District Bar Association. ***PRACTICE AREAS:*** Criminal Law; Family Law; Business Law. ***Email:*** jwills@obxlaw.com

BERNARD "B.J." B. McAVOY, JR., born Johnson City, New York, June 30, 1976; admitted to bar, 2004, North Carolina. *Education:* North Carolina State University (B.S., Accounting, 1998); Campbell University (J.D., 2004). *Member:* North Carolina Bar Association; North Carolina State Bar; 1st Judicial District Bar Association; North Carolina Academy of Trial Lawyers. ***PRACTICE AREAS:*** Criminal Law; Domestic Relations; Family Law; Divorce; Child Custody. ***Email:*** bmcavoy@obxlaw.com

DEBBIE GORONET BAKER

Established in 1994

112 E. ELWOOD AVENUE
RAEFORD, NORTH CAROLINA 28376
Telephone: 910-904-5585; Toll Free: 866-423-6084
Fax: 910-904-5589
URL: http://www.debbiebaker.com
Email: DBakerattorney@aol.com
URL: http://www.hoke-raeford.com/debbiebaker
Mailing Address: P.O. Box 726, Raeford, NC 28376

(This Listing Continued)

DEBBIE GORONET BAKER, Raeford—Continued

General Practice, Personal Injury, Automobile Accidents and Injuries, Wrongful Death, Criminal Defense, Misdemeanors, Felonies, DWI, Traffic Violations, Revoked Licenses/DMV Hearings, Uncontested Divorces, Workers Compensation, Child Support, Child Custody.

DEBBIE GORONET BAKER, born Raeford, North Carolina, December 6, 1968; admitted to bar, 1994, North Carolina. *Education:* University of North Carolina at Chapel Hill (B.A., 1991); North Carolina Central University (J.D., 1994). *Member:* North Carolina Bar Association; North Carolina State Bar; North Carolina Academy of Trial Lawyers. ***PRACTICE AREAS:*** Criminal Defense; Traffic Violations; Personal Injury; Civil.

LAW OFFICES OF WILLIAM S. BRITT

RAEFORD, NORTH CAROLINA

(See Lumberton)

Medical Malpractice, Wrongful Death, Automobile Accidents and Injuries, Truck Accidents, Motorcycle Accidents, Construction Accidents, Dog Bites and Personal Injury Law.

GREGORY M. BYRD

RAEFORD, NORTH CAROLINA

(See Fayetteville)

Criminal Law, Criminal Defense, Drugs and Narcotics, Traffic Violations/Speeding, DWI, Personal Injury, Automobile Accidents and Injuries, Employment Law, Unemployment Compensation, Wrongful Termination.

GORDON, HORNE, HICKS AND FLOYD, P.A.

RAEFORD, NORTH CAROLINA

(See Laurinburg)

General, Civil and Criminal Trial Practice, Probate, Corporation, Real Estate, Personal Injury, Estate Planning, Social Security Disability, Workers' Compensation and Family Law.

GRIFFIN LAW OFFICE

RAEFORD, NORTH CAROLINA

(See Red Springs)

Abuse and Neglect, Juvenile Law, Real Estate Transactions, Traffic, Traffic Violations, DWI, Criminal Law, Domestic and Family Law.

THE LAW OFFICES OF CHRISTOPHER V. VAUGHAN

131 WEST EDINBOROUGH AVENUE
RAEFORD, NORTH CAROLINA 28376
Telephone: 910-875-0955
Fax: 910-875-0233
Email: izzydaddy@hotmail.com
URL: http://www.vaughanlawoffice.com

Mailing Address: P.O. Box 35590, Fayetteville, NC 28303

Criminal Law, Traffic, DWI, Family Law, Divorce, Child Support and Child Custody.

CHRISTOPHER V. VAUGHAN, born Tacoma, Washington, October 3, 1969; admitted to bar, 2001, North Carolina. *Education:* Pembroke State University (B.S., 1992); Norman A. Wiggins School of Law (J.D., 2000). *Member:* North Carolina State Bar; North Carolina Bar Association; 16th Judicial Bar. ***PRACTICE AREAS:*** Criminal Law; Traffic Violations; Driving While Intoxicated; Family Law; Divorce; Child Custody; Child Support.

WILLCOX, McFADYEN, FIELDS & SUTHERLAND

Established in 1969

112 E. EDINBOROUGH AVENUE
RAEFORD, NORTH CAROLINA 28376
Telephone: 910-875-4065
Fax: 910-875-6710
Email: wmfs@nc.rr.com
URL: http://www.racefordlawyers.com

General Civil and Criminal Trial Practice. Personal Injury, Probate and Real Estate Law.

FIRM PROFILE: Willcox, McFadyen, Fields & Sutherland was founded by R. Palmer Willcox in 1969, and serves clients in Raeford and throughout Hoke, Scotland and surrounding counties with a full civil and criminal trial practice in all state courts.

MEMBERS OF FIRM

R. PALMER WILLCOX (Retired)

DUNCAN B. McFADYEN, III, born Lumberton, North Carolina, April 20, 1948; admitted to bar, 1973, North Carolina. *Education:* Presbyterian College (B.A., 1970); University of North Carolina (J.D., 1973). Phi Delta Phi. Assistant District Attorney, District Attorney's Office, Fayetteville, North Carolina, 1973-1976. Attorney, Hoke County, 1979-1993. *Member:* Hoke County Bar Association; 16-A Judicial District (Bar Councilor,

(This Listing Continued)

2001—) and North Carolina State Bars; North Carolina Academy of Trial Lawyers. ***REPORTED CASES:*** County of Hoke v. Byrd. ***PRACTICE AREAS:*** Civil Litigation; Traffic Violations; Driving While Intoxicated; Criminal Law; Business Law; Corporate Law; Partnership Law; Estate Planning; Wills; Personal Injury.

WILLIAM CORBETT FIELDS, JR., born Lumberton, North Carolina, December 9, 1966; admitted to bar, 1992, North Carolina. *Education:* Appalachian State University (B.A., 1989); Campbell University (J.D., 1992). City Attorney, City of Raeford, 2000—. *Member:* Hoke County and North Carolina Bar Associations; 16-A Judicial District and North Carolina State Bars. ***PRACTICE AREAS:*** Civil Practice; Personal Injury; Accidents; Wrongful Death; Collections. ***Email:*** wmfs@nc.rr.com

REGINA ROBERTS SUTHERLAND, born Honolulu, Hawaii, December 4, 1971; admitted to bar, 2000, North Carolina. *Education:* East Carolina University (B.S.C.J., 1995); Campbell University (J.D., 2000). *Member:* Hoke County (President) and 16-A Judicial District Bar Associations; North Carolina State Bar. ***PRACTICE AREAS:*** Real Estate; Domestic; Family Law; Divorce; Adoption Law; Child Custody; Child Support; Equitable Distribution; Alimony; Domestic Violence; Civil Practice.

APPROVED ATTORNEYS FOR: Investors Title Insurance Co.; Stewart Title Insurance Co.; Consumers Title; Fidelity Title; Chicago Title; Lawyers Title.
REPRESENTATIVE CLIENTS: Farm Credit Service; Progressive State Bank; The Fidelity Bank; Branch Banking & Trust; Centura Bank; State Employees Credit Union; The City of Raeford.

ABRAMS & ABRAMS, P.A.

414 WEST JONES STREET
RALEIGH, NORTH CAROLINA 27603
Telephone: 919-755-9166
Fax: 919-755-9396
URL: http://www.abramslawfirm.com
Email: dabrams@abramslawfirm.com
URL: http://www.lawyers.com/abramslawfirm

Mailing Address: P.O. Box 26025, Raleigh, NC 27611

Catastrophic Personal Injury, Tractor Trailer Wrecks, Traumatic Brain Injury, Products Liability, Wrongful Death, Electrocutions, Toxic Torts, Insurance Litigation, Industrial/Construction Explosions, Railroad Litigation, Professional Negligence, Maritime Litigation.

FIRM PROFILE: Abrams & Abrams, P.A. is a law firm handling catastrophic personal injury, tractor trailer wrecks, traumatic brain injury, products liability, wrongful death, electrocutions, toxic torts, insurance litigation, industrial/construction explosions, railroad litigation, professional negligence, maritime litigation or environmental torts.

DOUGLAS B. ABRAMS, born Greenville, South Carolina, March 18, 1954; admitted to bar, 1979, North Carolina, South Carolina, U.S. District Court, Eastern, Middle and Western Districts of North Carolina and U.S. Court of Appeals, Fourth Circuit; 1995, U.S. Supreme Court. *Education:* Wake Forest University (B.A., magna cum laude, 1976; J.D., 1979). Phi Beta Kappa. Member, 1977-1978 and Research Editor, 1978-1979, Wake Forest Law Review. Listed: "The Best Lawyers in America." Contributing Author: "Anatomy of a Personal Injury Lawsuit," 3rd Edition, ATLA Press, 1991. Co-Author: Blanchard & Abrams, "North Carolina's New Products Liability Act: A Critical Analysis," Wake Forest University Law Review, Vol. 16, 1980. Member, Board of Directors, North Carolina Consumers Council, 1981-1986. Associate, American Board of Trial Advocates. *Member:* Wake County and North Carolina Bar Associations; North Carolina State Bar; South Carolina Bar; North Carolina Academy of Trial Lawyers (President's Club, President, 1995-1996; Benefactor; Vice President, Education, 1993-1994; Vice President, Public Service and Information, 1990-1993; Co-Chairman, Amicus Curiae Committee, 1983-1986; Board of Governors, 1987—; Faculty, Civil Trial Advocacy, 1988-1993); The Association of Trial Lawyers of America (Leadership Forum, Sustaining Member; Presidents' Club; Co-Chair: Exchange Committee, 1990-1991; 1996-1997; Sections to Litigation Group Coordination Council, 1991-1994; Communications, Computers and Law Office Technology Committee, 1992-1994; Subcommittee Chairperson, Computers in Products Liability, Products Liability Advisory Committee, 1989-1991); American Trial Lawyers Association (State Delegate, 2003). ***PRACTICE AREAS:*** Catastrophic Injury; Brain Injury; Products Liability; Wrongful Death; Toxic Torts; Insurance Litigation; Industrial/Construction Explosions; Railroad Litigation; Professional Negligence; Maritime Litigation; Environmental Law. ***Email:*** dabrams@abramslawfirm.com

MARGARET SMITH ABRAMS, born Monmouth County, New Jersey, September 8, 1954; admitted to bar, 1980, North Carolina and U.S. District Court, Eastern, Middle and Western Districts of North Carolina. *Education:* Wake Forest University (B.A., 1976; J.D., 1980); Duke University. Law Clerk to Judge Willis P. Whichard, North Carolina Court of Appeals, 1980-1982. Certified Superior Court Mediator. *Member:* Wake County and North Carolina Bar Associations; North Carolina Academy of Trial Lawyers (President's Club, Education Committee; Benefactor); The Association of Trial Lawyers of America (Leadership Forum). ***PRACTICE AREAS:*** Catastrophic Injury; Brain Injury; Products Liability; Wrongful Death; Toxic Torts; Insurance Litigation; Industrial Explosions; Construction Accidents; Railroad Litigation; Professional Negligence; Maritime Litigation; Environmental Law. ***Email:*** mabrams@abramslawfirm.com

ADAMS, McCULLOUGH & BEARD

RALEIGH, NORTH CAROLINA

(See Parker, Poe, Adams & Bernstein L.L.P.)

R. L. ADAMS, PLLC

3737 GLENWOOD AVENUE, SUITE 100
RALEIGH, NORTH CAROLINA 27612
Telephone: 919-573-1868
Telefax: 919-239-2687
Email: rl@rladams.com
URL: http://www.rladams.com

Mailing Address: P.O. Box 31703, Raleigh, NC, 27622-1703

Equine Law, Civil Litigation, Real Estate Litigation, Business Torts, Products Liability.

R. L. ADAMS, born Sharon, Pennsylvania, August 22, 1957; admitted to bar, 1983, North Carolina. *Education:* University of North Carolina (B.A., with honors, 1979; J.D., with honors, 1983). Morehead Scholar. [U.S. Army, JAGC, 1983-1988]. ***PRACTICE AREAS:*** Equine Law; Civil Litigation; Real Estate Litigation; Business Torts; Products Liability.

ALEXANDER & DOYLE, P.A.

RALEIGH, NORTH CAROLINA

(See Cary)

Family Law, Child Custody, Child Support, Spousal Support, Domestic Violence, Adoptions, Termination of Parental Rights, Wills, Trusts and Estates, Probate Law, Criminal Law (Misdemeanors), Traffic Law.

ALLEN & MOORE, L.L.P.

Established in 1996

3700 COMPUTER DRIVE, SUITE 320
RALEIGH, NORTH CAROLINA 27609-8627
Telephone: 919-783-8023
Fax: 919-783-8282
Email: ALLNMOORE@AOL.COM

General Civil Practice. Administrative, Business and Corporate Law, Insurance Law, Construction Law and Litigation in all State and Federal Courts.

ARCH T. ALLEN, III, born Raleigh, North Carolina, March 27, 1940; admitted to bar, 1965, North Carolina. *Education:* University of North Carolina (B.S., 1962; J.D., with honors, 1965). Order of the Coif. Editor-in-Chief, North Carolina Law Review, 1964-1965. Member: Board of Visitors, 1980-1988, and Board of Trustees, 1989-1991, University of North Carolina at Chapel Hill. Vice Chancellor for Development and University Relations, University of North Carolina at Chapel Hill, 1991-1995. Certified Mediator, Mediated Settlement Conferences, 1996—. [Capt. JAGC, USAR, Active Duty, 1965-1968]

JOSEPH C. MOORE, III, born Raleigh, North Carolina, May 2, 1948; admitted to bar, 1974, North Carolina. *Education:* University of North Carolina (A.B., 1971); Wake Forest University (J.D., cum laude, 1974). Editor-in-Chief, Wake Forest Law Review, 1973-1974. Lecturer: American Arbitration Association; North Carolina Bar Association. *Member:* North Carolina Bar Association (Member: C.L.E. Committee; Litigation Section Council; Administration of Justice Committee; Civil Practice & Procedure Committee).

ANN STRADER HANLEY, born Winston-Salem, North Carolina, January 14, 1959; admitted to bar, 1985, North Carolina. *Education:* Wake Forest University (B.A., 1981; J.D., 1985). Law Clerk to Associate Justice (Later Chief Justice) Burley B. Mitchell, Jr., North Carolina Supreme Court, 1985-1986. Certified Mediator. ***Email:*** annstrader@aol.com

All firm members are members of North Carolina Bar Association.

ALLEN AND PINNIX, P.A.

Established in 1977

333 FAYETTEVILLE STREET MALL
SUITE 1200
RALEIGH, NORTH CAROLINA 27601
Telephone: 919-755-0505
Facsimile: 919-829-8098
Email: tmr@allen-pinnix.com
URL: http://www.allen-pinnix.com

Antitrust, Immigration, Administrative, International Trade, Corporate, Construction, Insurance, Employment, Arbitration, Mediation, Franchise, Unfair Trade Practices, Unfair Competition, Mergers and Acquisitions, Business Litigation and Appellate Practice in all State and Federal Courts.

NOEL L. ALLEN, born Greensboro, North Carolina, October 23, 1947; admitted to bar, 1974, North Carolina; 1978, U.S. Supreme Court; 1981, District of Columbia; 1983, U.S. Court of International Trade. *Education:* Elon University (B.A., 1969); University of North Carolina at Chapel Hill (J.D., 1973); University of Amsterdam (Dip., Int'l. L., 1974). Recipient, International Service Award, N.C. World Trade Association. Listed in, *Best Lawyers in America,* Antitrust. Fellow, Center for International Legal Studies. Author: *North Carolina Unfair Business Practice,* 1995, 3rd Edition 2004. U.S. Editor, *Competition Law in Western Europe and the U.S.,* Kluwer, 1989—. Member, North Carolina Tax Review Board. Trustee, 1985—, Elon University, and Chair, 2001-2003. Adjunct Professor, Antitrust and Trade Regulation Law, Campbell University School of Law, 1979—. *Member:* Wake County, North Carolina (Chair, Antitrust Section, 1998-1999; Chair, International Section, 1992-1994; Vice-Chair, Administrative Section, 2005-2006) and American Bar Associations. ***PRACTICE AREAS:*** Antitrust; Trade Regulation; Unfair Trade; International Law; Administrative Law; Regulatory Law; Professional Licensing; Business Litigation. ***Email:*** nla@allen-pinnix.com

(This Listing Continued)

JOHN L. PINNIX, born Reidsville, North Carolina, October 8, 1947; admitted to bar, 1973, North Carolina and District of Columbia. *Education:* University of North Carolina at Greensboro (B.A., 1969; M.A., 1975); Wake Forest University (J.D., 1973). Listed in *Best Lawyers in America,* Immigration Law. Former Vice-Chair, American Immigration Law Foundation. Adjunct Professor, Immigration Law, North Carolina Central University School of Law, 1997, 2002 and 2005. Senior Lecturer, Duke School of Law, 1999. *Member:* North Carolina and American Bar Associations; American Immigration Lawyers Association (President, 2002-2003; Member, National Executive Committee, 1997-2004; Board of Governors, 1993—). (Board Certified Specialist in Immigration Law, North Carolina State Board of Legal Specialization). ***PRACTICE AREAS:*** Immigration and Naturalization Law. ***Email:*** jlp@allen-pinnix.com

C. LYNN CALDER, born Pirmasens, Germany, December 5, 1959; admitted to bar, 1984, North Carolina. *Education:* East Carolina University (B.A., 1981); Campbell University (J.D., 1984). Listed in *Best Lawyers in America*, Immigration Law. Speaker and Writer on Immigration Issues: American Immigration Lawyers Association (AILA); North Carolina Bar Association; North Carolina Academy of Trial Lawyers; Wake Forest University School of Law Continuing Legal Education and other Legal Education Programs. Adjunct Professor, Immigration Law, North Carolina Central University School of Law, 1997, 2003, 2005. Trustee Emeritus, American Immigration Law Foundation. *Member:* North Carolina Bar Association (Former Chair, Immigration and Nationality Law Committee); American Immigration Lawyers Association (Member and Former Chair, Carolinas Chapter). (Board Certified Specialist in Immigration Law, North Carolina State Board of Legal Specialization). ***PRACTICE AREAS:*** Immigration and Naturalization Law. ***Email:*** lcalder@allen-pinnix.com

M. JACKSON NICHOLS, born Quantico, Virginia, September 13, 1951; admitted to bar, 1977, North Carolina; U.S. District Court, Eastern, Middle and Western Districts of North Carolina; U.S. Court of Appeals, Fourth Circuit and U.S. Supreme Court. *Education:* Davidson College (B.A., 1973); Duke University (M.A., 1977); Wake Forest University (J.D., 1977). Author: "The New North Carolina APA: A Practical Guide to Understanding and Using It," Campbell Law Review, Spring 1987. Visiting Professor, Administrative and Constitutional Law, University of North Carolina Political Science Department, Fall 1987, Spring 1989, Spring 1992. Board of County Commissioners, Wake County, 1990-1994. Deputy Legislative Liaison to Governor James B. Hunt, Jr., 1982-1985. Member and Vice Chair, Administrative Rules Review Commission, 1985-1988. Eagle Scout. *Member:* Wake County and North Carolina Bar Associations (Member, Administrative Law Section Council, 1990—; Chair, 1994-1995). ***LANGUAGES:*** Spanish. ***REPORTED CASES:*** North Carolina Board of Mortuary Science v. Crown Memorial Park, L.L.C., 162 N.C. App.316, 590 S.E.2d 467 (2004); Davenport v. N.C. DOT, 102 N.C. App. 476, 402 S.E. 477 (1991); Davenport v. N.C. DOT, 3 F.2d 89 (4th Cir. 1990). ***PRACTICE AREAS:*** Administrative Law; Civil Litigation; Employment Law; Non-Profit Organizations. ***Email:*** mjn@allen-pinnix.com

J. HEYDT PHILBECK, born Statesville, North Carolina, February 4, 1967; admitted to bar, 1992, North Carolina; 1993, U.S. District Court, Eastern District of North Carolina; 2000, U.S. District Court, Middle and Western Districts of North Carolina; U.S. Court of Appeals, Fourth Circuit; U.S. Court of International Trade; U.S. Tax Court; U.S. Supreme Court. *Education:* Elon College (B.A., magna cum laude, 1989); Valparaiso University (J.D., 1992); Georgetown University, Institute of Comparative Political and Economic Systems (1987). Alpha Chi. Pi Gamma Mu; Phi Delta Theta. Griswald-Watts Scholar. Intern, Hon. Sidney S. Eagles, Jr., N.C. Court of Appeals, 1990. *Member:* Wake County and North Carolina (Member, Litigation Section) Bar Associations; North Carolina Academy of Trial Lawyers (Member, Employment Law Section); The Association of Trial Lawyers of America; National Institute of Trial Advocacy; Braxton Craven American Inn of Court (Barrister). Fellow, North Carolina Institute of Political Leadership (1996); Leadership Triangle (1998); Leadership North Carolina (2001). ***PRACTICE AREAS:*** Trial Practice; Civil Litigation; Civil Rights; Discrimination; Employment Law; Unfair Business Practices; Business Law; Contracts. ***Email:*** hphilbeck@allen-pinnix.com

D. JAMES JONES, JR., born Raleigh, North Carolina, May 18, 1943; admitted to bar, 1968, North Carolina; 1972, U.S. Supreme Court; 1975, U.S. District Court, Eastern and Middle Districts of North Carolina; 1995, U.S. Court of Appeals, Fourth Circuit. *Education:* Davidson College (A.B., 1965); University of North Carolina (J.D., 1968). Phi Delta Phi. Member, Board of Editors, North Carolina Law Review, 1967-1968. Legislative Assistant to U.S. Representative Richardson Preyer, 1971-1973. Member, Tenth Judicial District Grievance Committee, 1995-1997. Former Adjunct Professor of Political Science, Peace College. Certified Mediator. Certified Arbitrator. *Member:* Wake County, North Carolina (Member, Sections on: Business Law; Dispute Resolution; Litigation) and American Bar Associations; North Carolina Association of Defense Attorneys. [Capt., USAR, active duty, 1968-1970]. ***PRACTICE AREAS:*** Mediation; Arbitration; Civil Litigation; Insurance Defense; Unfair Business Practices; Administrative Law. ***Email:*** djj@allen-pinnix.com

ALICE S. GLOVER, born Durham, North Carolina, February 5, 1960; admitted to bar, 1994, North Carolina. *Education:* University of North Carolina at Chapel Hill (B.A., 1982); North Carolina Central University School of Law, Evening Program (J.D., cum laude, 1994). Senior Staff Member, North Carolina Central Law Journal. Law Clerk, North Carolina Court of Appeals, 1994-1997; Immigration Staff Assistant to U.S. Senator Terry Sanford, 1986-1992. *Member:* American Immigration Lawyers Association (Past Chair, Carolinas Chapter); North Carolina Association of Women Attorneys. ***PRACTICE AREAS:*** Immigration and Naturalization Law. ***Email:*** asg@allen-pinnix.com

KENNETH C. DAY, born Greensboro, North Carolina, September 8, 1947; admitted to bar, 1973, New York; 1977, North Carolina. *Education:* University of North Carolina (A.B., 1969; J.D., with high honors, 1972). Phi Beta Kappa; Order of the Coif. Morehead Fellow. Member, North Carolina Law Review, 1971. *Member:* Wake County, North Carolina and American Bar Associations. ***PRACTICE AREAS:*** Administrative Law. ***Email:*** kcd@allen-pinnix.com

ANGELA LONG CARTER, born Bluefield, West Virginia, May 24, 1975; admitted to bar, 2000, North Carolina. *Education:* Elon College (B.A., summa cum laude, 1997); University of North Carolina (J.D., 2000). *Member:* Wake County, North Carolina and American (Administrative Law Council, Co-Editor, Section Newsletter; Nominating Committee) Bar Associations. ***REPORTED CASES:*** N.C. Bd. of Mortuary Science v. Crown Memo-

(This Listing Continued)

ALLEN AND PINNIX, P.A., Raleigh—Continued

rial Park, LLC, 162 NC App 316, 590 SE 2d 467 (2004); Caves v. N.C. Department of Corrections, 2002 N.C. App. Lexis 1945 (2002). ***PRACTICE AREAS:*** Trial Practice; Civil Litigation; Employment Law; Administrative Law. ***Email:*** acarter@allen-pinnix.com

ALSTON & BIRD LLP

Established in 1893

3201 BEECHLEAF COURT, SUITE 600
RALEIGH, NORTH CAROLINA 27604-1062
Telephone: 919-862-2200
Telecopier: 919-862-2260
Cable Address: AMGRAM GA
Telex: 54-2 996
Easylink: 62985848
Email: info@alston.com
URL: http://www.alston.com

Atlanta, Georgia Office: One Atlantic Center, 1201 West Peachtree Street, 30309-3424. Telephone: 404-881-7000. Telecopier: 404-881-7777.
Washington, D.C. Office: 601 Pennsylvania Avenue, N.W., North Building, 10th Floor, 20004-2601. Telephone: 202-756-3300. Telecopier: 202-756-3333.
Charlotte, North Carolina Office: Bank of America Plaza, 101 South Tryon Street, Suite 4000, 28280-4000. Telephone: 704-444-1000. Fax: 704-444-1111.
New York, New York Office: 90 Park Avenue, 10016-1387. Telephone: 212-210-9400. Fax: 212-210-9444.
(Liaison) Munich, Germany Office: Brienner Strasse 11/V, 80333 Munich. Telephone: (49) (89) 238-0-70. Telecopier: (49) (89) 238-0-7110.

Administrative Law, Alternative Dispute Resolution, Antitrust and Trade Regulation, Appellate Practice, Bankruptcy, Banks and Banking, Biotechnology, Business Law, Class Actions, Commercial Real Estate, FCC Licensing, FCC Regulation, Wireless Communications, Complex and Multi-District Litigation, Computers and Software, Constitutional Law, Construction Law, Copyrights, Corporate Ethics, Corporate Governance, Corporate Law, Criminal Law, Debtor and Creditor, Electronic Commerce, Emerging Growth Companies, Employee Benefits, Employment Law, Entertainment Law, ERISA, ERISA Litigation, Energy, Environmental Law, Environmental Litigation, Executive Compensation; Finance, Franchises and Franchising, Government Investigations; Health Care Corporate Law, Health Care Regulation, Immigration Law, Insurance Defense, Intellectual Property, International Finance, International Law, International Taxation, International Trade, Internet Law, Labor Law, Labor and Employment, Land Use, Legislative Practice, Life Sciences, Litigation, Local Taxation, Medical Malpractice, Mergers, Acquisitions and Divestitures, Multimedia Law, Municipal Law, Nonprofit and Charitable Organizations, Occupational Safety and Health, Partnership Law, Patents, Privacy Law, Products Liability, Professional Liability, Public Finance, Public Policy, Real Estate Finance, Regulatory Law, RICO, Securities, Securities Litigation, State Taxation, Taxation, Tax Litigation, Technology and Science, Telecommunications Law, Trademarks, Trusts and Estates, Utility Law, Venture Capital, White Collar Crime, Zoning.

LAW FIRM ALLIANCES/ASSOCIATIONS: **LEX MUNDI**

MEMBERS OF FIRM

W. MURRAY SPRUILL, born Columbia, North Carolina, March 24, 1954; admitted to bar, 1992, Virginia; 1993, District of Columbia; 1996, North Carolina; registered to practice before U.S. Patent and Trademark Office. *Education:* East Carolina University (B.S., 1976); North Carolina State University (Ph.D., 1981); George Washington University (J.D., 1992). ***PRACTICE AREAS:*** Pharmaceutical Intellectual Property; Biotechnology Patents; Intellectual Property Portfolio Management; Intellectual Property Infringement; Intellectual Property Licensing; International Intellectual Property; Chemical Intellectual Property; Intellectual Property Litigation; International Licensing. ***Email:*** mspruill@alston.com

CHRISTOPHER M. HUMPHREY, born Raleigh, North Carolina, September 3, 1971; admitted to bar, 1998, Georgia and North Carolina; 2000, District of Columbia; registered to practice before U.S. Patent and Trademark Office. *Education:* North Carolina State University (B.S., magna cum laude, 1993); University of North Carolina (J.D., 1997). ***PRACTICE AREAS:*** Intellectual Property; Patents; Chemical Patents; Biotechnology Patents; Mechanical Patents; Patent Prosecution; International Patent Prosecution.

OF COUNSEL

JASPER L. CUMMINGS, JR., born Rocky Mount, North Carolina, May 11, 1946; admitted to bar, 1972, North Carolina; 2000, District of Columbia. *Education:* Duke University (A.B., summa cum laude, 1968); Yale University (J.D., 1971); New York University (LL.M., Taxation, 1987). ***PRACTICE AREAS:*** Federal Taxation; State Taxation.

ASSOCIATES

RYAN W. CAGLE, born Pryor, OK, March 17, 1972; admitted to bar, 2002, North Carolina; registered to practice before U.S. Patent and Trademark Office. *Education:* Northeastern University (B.S., 1995); University of Tulsa (J.D., 2002).

MICHELLE L. CUNNINGHAM, admitted to bar, 2003, North Carolina; registered to practice before U.S. Patent and Trademark Office. *Education:* University of Dayton (B.S., 1995); University of North Carolina (Ph.D., 2000; J.D., 2003). ***Email:*** mcunningham@alston.com

EDWARD R. ERGENZINGER, JR., born April 21, 1972; admitted to bar, 2002, North Carolina; registered to practice before U.S. Patent and Trademark Office. *Education:* Wake Forest University (B.A., 1994; Ph.D., 1999; J.D., 2002).

KEVIN R. LYN, born Port Maria, Jamaica, West Indies, October 25, 1966; admitted to bar, 1998, North Carolina; registered to practice before U.S. Patent and Trademark Office. *Education:* Duke University (B.S.E., cum laude, 1987; M.S., 1989); University of North Carolina (J.D., 1998).

JASON O. PICHE, born Charlotte, North Carolina, January 21, 1975; admitted to bar, 2003, North Carolina. *Education:* Duke University (B.S.E., 1997); University of Virginia (J.D., 2003).

DAVID M. SARAVITZ, born Scranton, Pennsylvania; admitted to bar, 2003, North Carolina; registered to practice before U.S. Patent and Trademark Office. *Education:* Pennsylvania State University (B.S., with distinction, 1984); North Carolina State University (M.S., 1986); Duke University (Ph.D., 1993); North Carolina Central University (J.D., magna cum laude, 2003). ***PRACTICE AREAS:*** Intellectual Property; Biotechnology; Biotechnology Patents.

LEIGH W. THORNE, born December 10, 1964; admitted to bar, 2001, North Carolina; 2003, District of Columbia; registered to practice before U.S. Patent and Trademark Office. *Education:* Cornell University (B.S., 1986); University of Washington (Ph.D., 1992); Duke University (J.D., 2001).

Languages: Bangla, Bulgarian, Croatian, French, German, Gujarati, Hindi, Italian, Japanese, Korean, Portuguese, Russian, Spanish, Tamil, Thai, Turkish, Urdu.

REPRESENTATIVE CLIENTS: AFLAC, Inc.; AIG; ALCOA; Allegiance Healthcare Corporation; Allied Systems; Altana Inc.; ARCADIS; Arthritis Foundation; Assurant, Inc.; BB&T; Belk Store Services, Inc.; BellSouth Corporation; Bertelsmann AG; GBF Industries, Inc.; BNP Residential Properties, Inc.; The Boeing Company; Boral Industries, Inc.; Borden, Inc.; Bose Corporation; Cable News Network; CGW Southeast Partners & Affiliates; Cingular Wireless LLC; The Community Foundation for Greater Atlanta, Inc.; Delta Air Lines, Inc.; Dimension Data Holdings, Inc.; The Dow Chemical Company; Duke University; Emory University and Emory Healthcare; The Fulton-DeKalb Hospital Authority; Genuine Parts Co. Inc.; Georgia Hospital Association; Georgia-Pacific Corporation; Global Payments, Inc.; Gold Kist Inc.; Goldman, Sachs & Co.; Group Bruxelles Lambert; HealthSouth Corporation; H. Stern Jewelers, Inc.; i:FAO Aktiengesellschaft; IMERYS; Industrial Developments International, Inc. (IDI); INEOS; ING Americas; InterContinental Hotels Group; JDN Realty Corporation; Johns Hopkins University; Knology; Komatsu America Corp.; Lend Lease Real Estate Investments, Inc.; Lowrance Electronics. Inc.; MAG Mutual Insurance Company; Malcolm Pirnie; MANN + HUMMEL Group; Matsushita Electric Corporation of America / Panasonice U.S.A.; MBIA Insurance Corporation; MCNC; Metso Paper, Inc.; Mirant Corporation; Mohawk Industries, Inc.; Municipal Electric Authority of Georgia (MEAG Power); Municipal Gas Authority of Georgia (MGAG); National Association for Stock Car Auto Racing, Inc. (NASCAR); The National Business Coalition on E-Commerce and Privacy; National Industries for the Blind; NDCHealth Corporation; Nokia; Paragon Trade Brands, Inc.; Porcher Industries, S.A.; The Prudential Insurance Company of America; Regions Financial Corporation; Renal Care Group, Inc.; Rexam Corporation; Robert W. Baird & Co.; Rodenstock GmbH; The Rouse Company; Sabre; Saks Incorporated; Shearwater Corporation (nka Nektar Therapeutics); Silhouette Modell; Silicon Valley Bank; Skanska USA Building Inc.; Sonoco Products Company; Southwire Company; Springs Industries, Inc.; SunTrust Banks, Inc.; SunTrust Robinson Humphrey; TAPPI; Turner Broadcasting System, Inc.; Uniden America Corporation; Union Planters Corporation; University of California at Berkeley; University of North Carolina at Charlotte; UnumProvident Corporation; UPS; Verizon Wireless; Visa; Vulcan Materials Company; Wachovia Corporation; Waffle House, Inc.; WebMD Corporation; XL Capital Assurance Inc.

(For complete biographical data on other personnel, see professional biographies at Atlanta, Georgia, Washington, D.C., Charlotte, North Carolina, New York, New York, and Munich, Germany).

ANDERSON, JONES & GENGO, PLLC

Established in 2003

1305 NAVAHO DRIVE, SUITE 103
RALEIGH, NORTH CAROLINA 27609
Telephone: 919-277-2541
Fax: 919-277-2544
Email: lgengo@ajgpllc.com
URL: http://www.ajgpllc.com

Construction Law, Construction Litigation, Collections, OSHA Defense, Contracts, Administrative Law, Administrative Litigation, Real Estate, Environmental Law, Environmental Litigation, Toxic Mold Litigation.

MEMBERS OF THE FIRM

VICTOR A. ANDERSON, JR., born Dunn, North Carolina, May 19, 1952; admitted to bar, 1988, North Carolina and U.S. District Court, Eastern and Middle Districts of North Carolina. *Education:* University of North Carolina at Chapel Hill; Campbell University (B.A., 1985; J.D., 1988). *Member:* North Carolina State Bar (Member: Construction Law and Bankruptcy Sections, 1988; Construction Law, Section Council, 2005—). ***PRACTICE AREAS:*** Construction Law; Construction Litigation; Collections; OSHA Defense; Contracts; Administrative Law; Administrative Litigation. ***Email:*** aanderson@ajgpllc.com

TODD ALLEN JONES, born Durham, North Carolina, October 5, 1971; admitted to bar, 1998, North Carolina; 1999, District of Columbia; 2000, U.S. Court of Appeals, Fourth Circuit. *Education:* University of North Carolina at Chapel Hill (B.S.P.H., 1993); Campbell University School of Law (J.D., 1998). *Member:* North Carolina Bar Association (Member: Young Lawyers Division, 1998—; Construction Law Section, 1998— Chair, Law Day Committee, 2001—); District of Columbia Bar. ***PRACTICE AREAS:*** Construction Law; Construction Litigation; Contract Law; Real Estate; Collections; Employment Law; Homeowners Association Law. ***Email:*** tjones@ajgpllc.com

LAURIE B. GENGO, born Jamestown, New York, August 18, 1958; admitted to bar, 1986, Indiana and U.S. District Court, Northern and Southern Districts of Indiana; 1988, North Carolina and U.S. District Court, Eastern District of North Carolina. *Education:* State University of New York at Geneseo (B.A., summa cum laude, 1980); State University of New York at Buffalo (J.D., 1985). Instructor, State University of New York at Buffalo, 1985. Certification in Local Government Law at Buffalo. *Member:* North Carolina Bar Association (Member, Sections on: Construction Law; Environmental Law (Council Member, 1998-1999); Litigation, Real Estate); North Carolina Association of Women Attorneys; North Carolina Academy of Trial Lawyers; Waterproofing Contractors Association; Associated Builders and Contractors of the Carolinas; North Carolina Home Builder's Associa-

(This Listing Continued)

tion; Wake County Home Builder's Association. ***REPORTED CASES:*** American Canoe Association v. Murphy Farms, Inc., 210 F.3d 360 (4th Cir. N.C.2000); North Carolina ex.tel. Haves v. W.R. Peele, Sr. Trust, 876 F.Supp.733 (1995). ***PRACTICE AREAS:*** Construction Law; Construction Litigation; Environmental Law; Environmental Litigation; Toxic Torts; Mold Litigation; Real Estate; Administrative Law; Collections. ***Email:*** lgengo@ajgpllc.com

ARANEDA LAW FIRM, P.C.

Established in 1994

4600 MARRIOTT DRIVE, SUITE 350
RALEIGH, NORTH CAROLINA 27612
Telephone: 919-788-9225
Fax: 919-788-9151
Email: alf-law@att.net
URL: http://www.aranedalaw.com
Mailing Address: P.O. Box 31383, Raleigh, NC 27622-1383

New York, New York Office: 48 Wall Street, Suite 1100. 10005. Telephone: 212-918-4625. Fax: 212-918-4801.

Immigration Law, Business Immigration, Citizenship, Consular Law, Employment Authorizations, Employment Immigration, Employment Visas, Family Immigration Law, Labor Certifications, Permanent Visas, Religious Visas, Visas, Federal Criminal Law, Immigration Defense.

FIRM PROFILE: The Araneda Law Firm offers Immigration services, both for clients currently in the U.S. and abroad.

JORGELINA ELCIRA ARANEDA, born Rosario, Argentina; admitted to bar, 1990, North Carolina; 1991, District of Columbia; 1993, U.S. District Court, Eastern District of North Carolina and U.S. Court of Appeals, Fourth Circuit; 2003, U.S. Court of Appeals, Eleventh Circuit and U.S. Supreme Court. *Education:* University of North Carolina at Chapel Hill (B.A., 1985; J.D., 1989); The National Law Center, George Washington University (LL.M., International and Comparative Law, 1992). Immigration Law Training, George Washington University Immigration Law Clinic, Washington D.C. Recipient: 2004 North Carolina Businesswoman of the Year Award by the National Republican Congressional Committee Business Advisory Council. *Member:* Wake County, North Carolina, American and International Bar Associations; District of Columbia Bar; North Carolina State Bar (Appointed, Immigration Law Specialty Committee); American Immigration Lawyers Association; Hispanic National Bar Association. (Board Certified Specialist in Immigration Law, North Carolina State Board of Legal Specialization),. ***LANGUAGES:*** Spanish. ***PRACTICE AREAS:*** Immigration Law; Business Immigration; Citizenship; Consular Law; Employment Authorizations; Employment Immigration; Employment Visas; Family Immigration Law; Labor Certifications; Permanent Visas; Religious Visas; Visas; Federal Immigration Litigation; Federal Criminal Law. ***Email:*** alf-law@att.net

Languages: English and Spanish.

BAGWELL, HOLT & SMITH, P.A.

RALEIGH, NORTH CAROLINA
(See Chapel Hill)

Commercial and Residential Real Estate, Business, Civil Litigation, Estate Planning, Creditor's Rights, Collections, Workers Compensation, Automobile Accidents, Personal Injury, Wrongful Death, Wills, Probate.

BAILEY & DIXON, L.L.P.

Established in 1948

2500 TWO HANNOVER SQUARE
434 FAYETTEVILLE STREET MALL
P.O. BOX 1351
RALEIGH, NORTH CAROLINA 27602
Telephone: 919-828-0731
Facsimile: 919-828-6592
Email: info@bdixon.com
URL: http://www.bdixon.com

General Civil Trial, Appellate and Administrative Practice. Litigation: Insurance Regulation, Defense of Personal Injury and Professional Malpractice Claims, Commercial Litigation, Including Environmental Law, Employment Law, Insurance Coverage Disputes, Construction, Land Use, Municipal and Police Liability, Products Liability, Drug and Medical Device Liability, Business Torts, and Workers' Compensation. Administrative Law: Public Utilities, Including Electric, Telecommunications, Gas, Transportation, Water and Sewer. Professional and Occupational Licensing, Healthcare, Labor and Employment Law, Business and Corporate Law, Commercial Real Estate, Estate Administration and Taxation.

FIRM PROFILE: Bailey & Dixon, L.L.P. has served local, national and international clients in North Carolina's capital, across the state and in neighboring states for fifty years. The Firm practices primarily in civil litigation, administrative law, business law and governmental relations. Its experience in these chosen practice fields exceeds firms of far greater size and encompasses representation in a variety of complex business, tort and regulatory matters. By blending prudent growth with selectivity in its practice areas, it has earned a reputation as one of the most effective, efficient firms in the region. Founded by a former Chair of the North Carolina Utilities Commission, the Firm has a proud history of public and professional service. Bailey & Dixon's lawyers have served in the State's General Assembly, on its appellate courts, on government commissions and committees, as councillor and president of its State Bar and in diverse capacities in national, state and local bar organizations.

(This Listing Continued)

MEMBERS OF FIRM

RALPH McDONALD, born Raleigh, North Carolina, February 1, 1940; admitted to bar, 1964, North Carolina; U.S. District Court, Eastern and Middle Districts of North Carolina; U.S. Court of Appeals, Fourth Circuit; U.S. Supreme Court. *Education:* University of North Carolina (A.B., 1961; LL.B., 1964). Phi Delta Phi. Member, Legislative Research Commission's Committee on the Administrative Procedure Act's Rule-Making Process, The Office of Administrative Hearings and The Administrative Rules Review Commission, 1989-1990. *Member:* Wake County, North Carolina (Chair, Administrative Law Section, 1989-1990) and American Bar Associations. ***PRACTICE AREAS:*** Public Utilities Law; Business Law; Administrative Law; Real Estate. ***Email:*** rmcdonald@bdixon.com

GARY S. PARSONS, born Erwin, North Carolina, July 16, 1952; admitted to bar, 1977, North Carolina; U.S. District Court, Eastern, Western and Middle Districts of North Carolina; U.S. Court of Appeals, Fourth Circuit; U.S. Supreme Court. *Education:* North Carolina State University (B.S., 1974); University of North Carolina (J.D., 1977). Member, National Moot Court Team, 1976-1977. Law Clerk to Associate Justice J. William Copeland, North Carolina Supreme Court, 1977-1978. Voted, Top Business Litigation Attorney in North Carolina, Business North Carolina Magazine, 2005. Listed in The Best Lawyers in America, Business Litigation, Legal Malpractice Law, Personal Injury Litigation. *Member:* Wake County (Member, Board of Directors, 1989-1990), North Carolina (Member, Committees on: Appellate Rules, 1982-1995; Civil Practice and Procedure Study, 1999-2000) and American Bar Associations; North Carolina Association of Defense Attorneys (Member, Board of Directors, 1998-2001; Executive Vice President, 2001-2002; President-Elect, 2002-2003; President, 2003-2004); Defense Research Institute. ***PRACTICE AREAS:*** Trial Practice; Civil Litigation; Products Liability; Drug and Medical Device Defense; Appellate Practice; Commercial Litigation; Insurance Bad Faith; Insurance Coverage; Legal Malpractice Defense; Corporate Insurance; Attorney Discipline; Police Liability Defense; Insurance Litigation; Aquatic Injuries; Land Use Litigation; Local Government Defense; Catastrophic Injury. ***Email:*** gparsons@bdixon.com

CARSON CARMICHAEL, III, born Abingdon, Virginia, September 29, 1954; admitted to bar, 1981, North Carolina; U.S. District Court, Eastern and Middle Districts of North Carolina; U.S. Court of Appeals, Fourth Circuit. *Education:* North Carolina State University (B.S. with honors, Pulp and Paper, Science and Technology, Chemical Engineering, 1976); Wake Forest University (J.D., 1980). Phi Eta Sigma; Xi Sigma Pi; Phi Alpha Delta. Member, Wake Forest Law Review. Author: "Directing a Verdict in Favor of the Party with the Burden of Proof," 16 Wake Forest L. Rev. 607, 1980; "Preservation of Trade Secret Protection During a Patent Application Appeal," 15 Wake Forest L. Rev. 559, 1979. Member, Governor's Waste Management Board Legal Committee, 1986-1989. *Member:* Wake County, North Carolina (Member, Environmental Law Committee, 1984-1987; Construction Law Section, Chair, 1999-2000, Vice Chair, 1998-1999, Treasurer, 1993-1995, Council Member, 1990-1993; Administrative Law Section, Council Member, 1995-1998) and American Bar Associations; North Carolina Society of Health Care Attorneys; American Society of Pharmacy Law. ***PRACTICE AREAS:*** Public Utilities Law; Environmental Law; Administrative Law. ***Email:*** ccarmichael@bdixon.com

ROBERT H. MERRITT, JR., born San Antonio, Texas, July 29, 1948; admitted to bar, 1974, Texas; 1977, North Carolina; U.S. District Court, Eastern, Middle and Western Districts of North Carolina, U.S. Court of Appeals, Fourth Circuit and U.S. Tax Court. *Education:* Choate School, Wallingford, Connecticut; University of North Carolina (B.A., 1971); Southern Methodist University (J.D., 1974; LL.M. in Taxation, 1976). Member, Legislative Study Committee on Revenue Laws, 1979-1984. *Member:* North Carolina (Chairman, Legislative Committee, 1985-1987) and American (Taxation Section) Bar Associations. ***PRACTICE AREAS:*** Taxation; Corporate; Banking; Real Estate; Health Law; Commercial Litigation. ***Email:*** rmerritt@bdixon.com

PATRICIA P. KERNER, born Elizabeth City, North Carolina, January 4, 1960; admitted to bar, 1985, North Carolina; U.S. District Court, Eastern, Western and Middle Districts of North Carolina; U.S. Supreme Court. *Education:* Wake Forest University (B.A., cum laude, 1982); University of North Carolina (J.D., 1985). Articles Editor, North Carolina Journal of International Law and Commercial Regulation, 1984-1985. Law Clerk to Chief Judge R.A. Hedrick, North Carolina Court of Appeals, 1985-1987. Author: "Case Disposition in Entry of Judgement," North Carolina Trial and Appeal, American Inns of Court Civil Procedure Series. Listed, "Best Lawyers in America," 2003-2004. *Member:* Wake County, North Carolina and American Bar Associations; North Carolina Association of Defense Attorneys; Defense Research Institute. ***PRACTICE AREAS:*** Trial Practice; Commercial Litigation; Insurance Coverage; General Liability; Insurance Litigation; Products Liability; Business Torts; Personal Injury Defense; Insurance Bad Faith; Professional Malpractice Defense; Drug and Medical Device Defense; Governmental Defense; Insurance Regulation; Appellate Practice; Administrative Law. ***Email:*** pkerner@bdixon.com

CATHLEEN M. PLAUT, born Cincinnati, Ohio, November 22, 1960; admitted to bar, 1986, North Carolina; U.S. District Court, Eastern, Western and Middle Districts of North Carolina. *Education:* Miami University (B.S., cum laude, 1982); University of North Carolina at Chapel Hill (J.D., 1986). Phi Kappa Phi. Member: Order of Barristers; Holderness Moot Court Bench, 1985-1986. Law Clerk to Judge S. Gerald Arnold, North Carolina Court of Appeals, 1986-1988. Instructor, "Legal Research and Writing," University of North Carolina, School of Law, 1987-1988. *Member:* Wake County and North Carolina Bar Associations. ***PRACTICE AREAS:*** Labor and Employment Law; Telecommunications Law; Health Care; Utility Law; Telephone Utilities; Electric Utilities; Gas Utilities; Water Utilities; Business Law; Corporate Law. ***Email:*** cplaut@bdixon.com

DAVID S. COATS, born New Orleans, Louisiana, February 20, 1962; admitted to bar, 1988, North Carolina; U.S. District Court, Eastern, Middle and Western Districts of North Carolina; U.S. Court of Appeals, Fourth Circuit; U.S. Supreme Court. *Education:* Guilford College (B.S., 1984); Wake Forest University (J.D., 1988). Phi Alpha Theta. Law Clerk to Hon. Eugene H. Phillips, North Carolina Court of Appeals, 1988-1989. *Member:* Wake County (Member, Board of Directors, 2002-2004), North Carolina (Member, Appellate Rules Study Committee, 1994-2000; Chair, Environmental Issues Committee, 1994-1995), and American Bar Associations; North Carolina Association of Defense Attorneys; Defense Research Institute. ***PRACTICE AREAS:*** Trial Practice; Commercial Litigation; Construction Law; Appellate Practice; Insurance; Insurance Coverage; Insurance Defense; Insurance Bad Faith; Personal Injury Litigation. ***Email:*** dcoats@bdixon.com

(This Listing Continued)

BAILEY & DIXON, L.L.P., Raleigh—Continued

M. DENISE STANFORD, born San Jose, Costa Rica, July 10, 1961; admitted to bar, 1990, North Carolina; U.S. District Court, Eastern and Middle Districts of North Carolina; U.S. Supreme Court. *Education:* University of North Carolina (B.A., 1983; J.D., 1990). *Member:* Wake County, North Carolina (Council Member, Administrative Law Section, 1998-2004) and American Bar Associations; North Carolina State Bar; American Association of Dental Examiners. ***PRACTICE AREAS:*** Administrative Law; Health Law; Professional Discipline; Appellate Practice; Business Law. ***Email:*** dstanford@bdixon.com

DAVID S. WISZ, born Tonawanda, New York, September 6, 1969; admitted to bar, 1994, Kentucky; U.S. District Court, Eastern District of Kentucky; 1996, North Carolina; U.S. District Court, Eastern District of North Carolina; U.S. Court of Appeals, Fourth and Sixth Circuit; U.S. Supreme Court. *Education:* St. Bonaventure University (B.B.A., summa cum laude, 1991); University of Kentucky (J.D. with high distinction, 1994). Order of Coif. Notes Editor, Kentucky Law Journal, 1993-1994. Author: "States Rights to Confine 'Not Guilty by Reason of Insanity' Acquittees After Foucha v. Louisiana," 82 Kentucky L. Jou. 315, 1993. *Member:* Wake County, North Carolina and American Bar Associations; Kentucky Bar Association; North Carolina Association of Defense Attorneys; Defense Research Institute. ***PRACTICE AREAS:*** Civil Litigation; Insurance; Negligence; Premises Liability; Torts; Litigation; Construction Law; Appellate Practice; Contracts; Insurance Defense; Personal Injury; Commercial Litigation; Products Liability; Professional Liability; Mold Litigation. ***Email:*** dwisz@bdixon.com

WARREN TOBIN SAVAGE, IV, born Auburn, Alabama, April 13, 1964; admitted to bar, 1996, North Carolina; U.S. District Court, Eastern, Western and Middle Districts of North Carolina; U.S. Court of Appeals, Fourth Circuit. *Education:* University of Virginia (B.A., 1986); University of North Carolina at Chapel Hill (M.A.T., 1989); Campbell University (J.D., magna cum laude, 1996). Managing Editor, Campbell Law Review, 1995-1996. *Member:* Wake County, North Carolina and American Bar Associations; North Carolina Association of Defense Attorneys; Defense Research Institute. ***PRACTICE AREAS:*** Trial Practice; Civil Litigation; Insurance Coverage; Administrative Law; Health Law; Securities Litigation; Securities Arbitration; Professional Liability; Professional Discipline; Appellate Practice. ***Email:*** wsavage@bdixon.com

DAYATRA T. KING, born Brooklyn, New York, June 28, 1972; admitted to bar, 1997, North Carolina; 1998, U.S. District Court, Eastern District of North Carolina; 1999, U.S. Court of Appeals, Fourth Circuit. *Education:* University of North Carolina at Chapel Hill (B.A., magna cum laude, 1994); Duke University (J.D., 1997). Phi Beta Kappa. Law Clerk to Judge James A. Wynn, North Carolina Court of Appeals, 1997-1998. *Member:* Wake County, North Carolina and American Bar Associations; North Carolina Association of Black Attorneys; North Carolina Association of Defense Attorneys; Defense Research Institute. ***PRACTICE AREAS:*** Trial Practice; Civil Litigation; Insurance Coverage; Personal Injury Defense; Appellate Practice; General Liability Defense; Labor Law; Employment Litigation. ***Email:*** dking@bdixon.com

ASSOCIATES

ANNA BAIRD CHOI, born Raleigh, North Carolina, March 14, 1968; admitted to bar, 1994, North Carolina; U.S. District Court, Eastern District of North Carolina. *Education:* University of North Carolina at Chapel Hill (B.A., 1990); Campbell University, School of Law (J.D., 1994). *Member:* Wake County and North Carolina Bar Associations; American Immigration Lawyers Association. ***PRACTICE AREAS:*** Business Immigration; Administrative Law. ***Email:*** achoi@bdixon.com

DONALD T. O'TOOLE, born Brooklyn, New York, September 13, 1960; admitted to bar, 2000, North Carolina; U.S. District Court, Eastern, Western and Middle Districts of North Carolina; U.S. Court of Appeals, Fourth Circuit; U.S. Supreme Court. *Education:* Brown University (Sc.B., 1982); North Carolina State University (B.S.C.E., summa cum laude, 1988); University of North Carolina at Chapel Hill (J.D., 2000). Registered Professional Engineer, North Carolina, 1992. *Member:* North Carolina and American Bar Associations; North Carolina Association of Defense Attorneys; Defense Research Institute. ***PRACTICE AREAS:*** Commercial Litigation; Construction Litigation; Fair Housing; Local Government Liability; Mold Litigation. ***Email:*** dotoole@bdixon.com

GAVIN B. PARSONS, born Raleigh, North Carolina, November 23, 1975; admitted to bar, 2001, North Carolina; U.S. District Court, Eastern, Western and Middle Districts of North Carolina; U.S. Court of Appeals, Fourth Circuit. *Education:* North Carolina State University (B.A., 1998); Wake Forest University (J.D., 2001). Member, Moot Court Board. *Member:* Wake County and North Carolina Bar Associations; North Carolina Association of Defense Attorneys; Defense Research Institute. ***PRACTICE AREAS:*** Trial Practice; Civil Litigation; Products Liability; Commercial Litigation; Insurance Law; Insurance Coverage; Insurance Bad Faith; Local Government Liability; Police Liability Defense; General Liability; Legal Ethics and Professional Responsibility; Employment Law; Fair Housing; Professional Liability; Legal Malpractice Defense. ***Email:*** gbparsons@bdixon.com

HANNAH G. STYRON, born Morehead City, North Carolina, July 14, 1973; admitted to bar, 2002, North Carolina. *Education:* University of North Carolina at Chapel Hill (B.A., 1994); Campbell University (J.D., 2002). Phi Alpha Delta (Chief Justice, Iredell Chapter, 2001-2002). Order of Barristers. *Member:* Wake County and North Carolina Bar Associations; North Carolina Association of Defense Attorneys; Defense Research Institute. ***PRACTICE AREAS:*** Trial Practice; Civil Litigation; General Liability Defense; Legal Ethics; Legal Malpractice Defense; Employment Law; Personal Injury Defense; Insurance Coverage; Criminal Law; Traffic Violations; Appellate Practice; Criminal Taxation; Criminal Tax Audits. ***Email:*** hstyron@bdixon.com

REPRESENTATIVE CLIENTS: Abbott Laboratories Inc.; Aetna Life and Casualty Insurance Co.; American International Group; Carolina Industrial Groups For Fair Utility Rates; Colonial Insurance Co.; Erie Insurance Co.; GAB Business Services, Inc.; Southern Pilot Insurance Co.; Hartford Insurance Group; American Insurance Association; Employers Casualty Co.; Nationwide Insurance Co.; MCI; Lawyers Mutual Liability Insurance Co. of North Carolina; North Carolina League of Municipalities Risk Management Services; Scottsdale Insurance Co.; State Auto Insurance Co.; State Employees' Credit Union; State Farm Insurance Cos.; N.C. Board of Pharmacy; North Carolina Medical Board; North Carolina Licensing Board for General Contractors; North Carolina Board of Registration for Professional Engineers and Land Surveyors; North Carolina State Board of Dental Examiners; North Carolina Medical Board; City of Raleigh; West Bend Co.; Sta-Rite Industries; The Great West Life Insurance Co.; Graward General Cos.; Bank of America, N.A.; SCANA Corp.; Peace College; City of Raleigh Board of Adjustment; Qwest Communications Corp.; Integrated Laboratory Systems, Incorportated; Great American E&S Insurance Co.; RLI Insurance Co.; Jefferson Pilot Financial Insurance Co.; Riverstone Claims Management, L.L.C.; Public Service Co. North Carolina, Incorporated; Builders Mutual Insurance Co.; North Carolina Farm Bureau Mutual Insurance Co.

(This Listing Continued)

APPROVED ATTORNEYS FOR: Lawyers Title Insurance Corp.; Fidelity National Title Insurance Co.; Security Union Title Insurance Co.; Stewart Title Insurance Co.; United Title Insurance Co.; Commonwealth Land Title Insurance Co.; Investors Title Insurance Co.; Surety Land Title Co.; Consumers Title Co.

THE LAW OFFICES OF OMAR BALOCH

Established in 2004

5104 WESTERN BOULEVARD, SUITE C
RALEIGH, NORTH CAROLINA 27606
Telephone: 919-233-4999
Fax: 919-859-5321
Email: mobaloch@balochlaw.com
URL: http://www.balochlaw.com

Immigration, Traffic Violations, Personal Injury, Small Business and Business Enterprises.

FIRM PROFILE: A practice dedicated to Family and Employment based Immigration. Serving families and companies in the triangle for all their Immigration needs.

OMAR BALOCH, admitted to bar, 2004, North Carolina. *Education:* University of North Carolina at Chapel Hill (B.A., 1999); Ohio State University College of Law (J.D., 2003). *Member:* Wake County and North Carolina Bar Associations; American Immigration Lawyers Association. ***LANGUAGES:*** Hindi and Urdu. ***PRACTICE AREAS:*** Immigration; Traffic Violations; Personal Injury; Small Business; Business Enterprises.

Languages: Hindi and Urdo.

NIGLE B. BARROW, JR.

1635 TWO HANOVER SQUARE
P.O. BOX 2714
RALEIGH, NORTH CAROLINA 27602-2714
Telephone: 919-834-2116
Fax: 919-831-4789
Email: texbarrow@att.net
URL: http://www.lawyers.com/niglebbarrowjr
Mailing Address: P.O. Box 2714, Raleigh, NC 27602-2714

Complex Commercial Litigation, Civil Litigation, Trial Practice, Construction Litigation, Class Actions Litigation, Personal Injury Litigation.

NIGLE B. BARROW, JR., born Bryan, Texas, November 8, 1949; admitted to bar, 1977, North Carolina. *Education:* Campbell College (B.A., summa cum laude, 1972); University of North Carolina (J.D., with honors, 1977). Staff Member, University of North Carolina Law Review, 1977. *Member:* Wake County, North Carolina and American Bar Associations; North Carolina State Bar.

REPRESENTATIVE CLIENTS: Bayer Corporation; Bovis Lend Lease, Inc.; The Goodyear Tire and Rubber Company; C.T. Wilson Construction Company, Inc.; PBM Graphics, Inc.; Corrugated Container Corporation.

BASHYAM & SPIRO, LLP

4101 LAKE BOONE TRAIL, SUITE 200
RALEIGH, NORTH CAROLINA 27607
Telephone: 919-833-0840
Fax: 919-833-4722
URL: http://www.lawyers.com/immigrationcounsel

U.S. and Foreign Immigration and Nationality Law.

MEMBERS OF FIRM

MURALI BASHYAM, born Brampton, Ontario, Canada, August 13, 1970; admitted to bar, 1995, North Carolina, District of Columbia and U.S. District Court, Middle District of North Carolina. *Education:* University of Texas; Wake Forest University (B.A., cum laude, 1992; J.D., 1995). *Member:* The District of Columbia Bar; North Carolina State Bar; American Bar Association; American Immigration Lawyers Association. ***PRACTICE AREAS:*** Immigration Law. ***Email:*** mbashyam@bashyamspiro.com

ROBERT B. SPIRO, born Jacksonville, Florida, October 11, 1968; admitted to bar, 1995, North Carolina. *Education:* Florida Southern College; University of North Florida (B.A., 1991); Wake Forest University (J.D., 1995). Phi Alpha Delta; Phi Kappa Phi. *Member:* North Carolina State Bar; American Immigration Lawyers Association. ***PRACTICE AREAS:*** Immigration and Nationality Law. ***Email:*** rspiro@bashyamspiro.com

ASSOCIATE

CARRIE AMELIA (AME) COATS, born Lancaster, Pennsylvania, October 5, 1970; admitted to bar, 2002, North Carolina. *Education:* University of North Carolina at Chapel Hill (B.A., 1993); Campbell University (J.D., 2002). *Member:* North Carolina State Bar; American Immigration Lawyers Association. ***PRACTICE AREAS:*** Immigration Law. ***Email:*** acoats@bashyamspiro.com

BASS, BRYANT & FANNEY, P.L.L.C.

Established in 1988

16 WEST MARTIN STREET, SUITE 900

DRAWER 909

RALEIGH, NORTH CAROLINA 27602

Telephone: 919-832-9661

Fax: 919-831-9211

URL: http://www.lawyers.com/bassbryant&fanney

General Trial Practice in all Courts, Criminal Law, Driving While Impaired, (DWI), Federal Criminal Offenses, Felonies, Misdemeanors, Traffic Violations, Personal Injury, Wrongful Death, Professional Malpractice, Construction Law, Corporate, Business Litigation, Collections, Landlord/Tenant, Appellate, Administrative, Contract, Fiduciary, Estates and Wills.

JOHN WALTER BRYANT, born Scotland Neck, North Carolina, May 6, 1953; admitted to bar, 1986, North Carolina; 1988, U.S. District Court, Eastern District of North Carolina; 1993, U.S. District Court, Middle District of North Carolina; 1994, U.S. Court of Appeals, Fourth Circuit. *Education:* Wake Forest University (B.A., 1976; J.D., 1986). Phi Delta Phi. Law Clerk: U.S. District Court, Eastern District of North Carolina, 1986-1987; North Carolina Court of Appeals, 1987; Eagle Scout. *Member:* Wake County and North Carolina Bar Associations; North Carolina State Bar; The Association of Trial Lawyers of America. ***PRACTICE AREAS:*** Civil Litigation; Products Liability; Contracts; Complex Commercial Litigation; Professional Malpractice; Trust and Fiduciary Law; Construction Law; Business Law; Administrative Law; Appellate Practice. **Email:** jbryant@bbf-law.com

JOHN K. FANNEY, born Emporia, Virginia, April 27, 1965; admitted to bar, 1991, North Carolina; 1994, U.S. District Court, Eastern District of North Carolina; 2000, U.S. Court of Appeals, Fourth Circuit. *Education:* University of North Carolina, Chapel Hill (B.A., 1987); Campbell University (J.D., 1991). Phi Alpha Delta. *Member:* Wake County, North Carolina (Member, Pro Bono Committee, 1992-1993) and American (Member, Homeless Issue Committee, 1994-1995) Bar Associations; North Carolina Academy of Trial Lawyers (Member, Criminal Section; Co-Chair, DUI Task Force); National Association of Criminal Defense Lawyers (NACDL); National College for DWI Defense (NCDD). (Board Certified Specialist in Federal Criminal Law and State Criminal Law, North Carolina State Board of Legal Specialization). ***PRACTICE AREAS:*** Criminal Law; Driving While Intoxicated; Traffic Violations; Federal Criminal Law. **Email:** jfanney@bbf-law.com

ASSOCIATES

JAMES K. JACKSON, born Raleigh, North Carolina, June 2, 1976; admitted to bar, 2002, North Carolina. *Education:* North Carolina State University (B.A., 1998); Mercer University (J.D., 2001). ***PRACTICE AREAS:*** General Practice; Criminal Defense; Civil Litigation. **Email:** jjackson@bbf-law.com

EVA C. CURRIN, born Willow Spring, North Carolina, September 3, 1978; admitted to bar, 2003, North Carolina and U.S. District Court, Eastern District of North Carolina; U.S. Court of Appeals, Fourth Circuit. *Education:* North Carolina State University (B.A., summa cum laude, 2000); University of North Carolina at Chapel Hill (J.D., 2003). Phi Beta Kappa; Phi Kappa Phi. *Member:* North Carolina Bar Association. ***PRACTICE AREAS:*** Civil Litigation; Business Law; Corporate Law; Construction Law; Contracts; Landlord and Tenant Law; Collections; Appellate Practice; Administrative Law. **Email:** ecurrin@bbf-law.com

OF COUNSEL

GERALD L. BASS, born Wilson, North Carolina, December 27, 1933; admitted to bar, 1962, North Carolina; 1963, U.S. District Court, Eastern District of North Carolina and U.S. Court of Appeals, Fourth Circuit; 1964, U.S. District Court, Middle District of North Carolina. *Education:* University of North Carolina (B.S., 1959; LL.B., 1962). Delta Theta Phi. Law Clerk, U.S. District Court, Eastern District of North Carolina, 1962-1963. Assistant U.S. Attorney, Eastern District of North Carolina, 1963-1968. *Member:* Wake County (Member, Executive Committee, 1972-1974; Vice-Chairman, 1986-1987; Chairman, 1987-1988) and North Carolina Bar Associations; North Carolina State Bar; North Carolina Academy of Trial Lawyers. ***PRACTICE AREAS:*** Criminal Law; Civil Litigation. **Email:** gbass@bbf-law.com

BATTLE, WINSLOW, SCOTT & WILEY, P.A.

Established in 1911

3737 GLENWOOD AVENUE, SUITE 100

RALEIGH, NORTH CAROLINA 27612

Telephone: 919-573-1877

Facsimile: 919-573-1878

Rocky Mount, North Carolina Office: 2343 Professional Drive, PO Box 7100, 27804. Telephone: 252-937-2200. Facsimile: 252-937-8100.

Administrative, Alternative Dispute Resolution, Banking, Bankruptcy, Construction, Commercial, Corporate, Environmental, Estate Planning, General Trial and Appellate Practice in all State and Federal Courts. Health Care, Insurance, Insurance Defense, Labor and Employment, Local Government Law, Personal Injury, Probate and Estate Planning, Real Estate, Tax, Workers' Compensation.

FIRM PROFILE: Battle, Winslow, Scott & Wiley, P.A. is one of the oldest law firms in North Carolina, with the original partnership having been formed by Kemp D. Battle and Francis E. Winslow in 1911. The practice encompasses Eastern North Carolina, serving clients in a large geographic area. The firm provides a broad spectrum of the highest quality of legal services.

GENERAL COUNSEL FOR: Nash County; Nash County Business Development Authority; Nash Health Care Systems; Rocky Mount Redevelopment Commission.

(This Listing Continued)

REPRESENTATIVE CLIENTS: Barcalounger; Bay Foods, Inc.; Boddie-Noell Enterprises, Inc.; Boseman Farms, Inc.; Branch Banking & Trust Company; Carolina Regional Orthopaedics, PA; Crown Carriers, Inc.; Eastern Carolina Broadcasting Company, Inc.; E-B Grain, Inc.; First Carolina State Bank; Lambert Properties, LLC; Lee Motor Company, Inc.; North Carolina Wesleyan College; RBC Centura Bank; Rocky Mount Recyclers, Inc.; Simmons & Harris, Inc.; Simmons & Harris Insurance Agency; Stretchlon Industries; Texas Steak, Ltd.
REPRESENTATIVE INSURANCE CLIENTS: Alliance Mutual; Atlantic Claims Service; Atlantic Risk Management; Bituminous; Canal Insurance; Commonwealth Dealers Life Insurance; Crawford & Company; Erie Insurance; Essex Insurance; Fireman's Fund; GAB; Galligher-Bassett Services; GMAC Insurance; Great American Insurance Group; Hanover Insurance; Infinity Insurance; John Deere; Kemper; Lawyers Mutual Liability Insurance Company of North Carolina; MSI; N.C. Farm Bureau; OrionAuto; State Auto Insurance Company; State Farm; United American Insurance; United Services Automobile Association.

(For complete biographical data on all personnel, see Professional Biographies at Rocky Mount)

BECTON, SLIFKIN & BELL, P.A.

4000 WESTCHASE BOULEVARD

SUITE 500

RALEIGH, NORTH CAROLINA 27607

Telephone: 919-755-1068

Fax: 919-828-7543

Email: bsb@bsblawfirm.com

URL: http://www.lawyers.com/bsblawfirm

Personal Injury and Wrongful Death, Vehicle Collisions, Medical Malpractice and Product Liability.

FIRM PROFILE: The firm's practice is primarily directed towards settlement and trial of major personal injury cases. Most of these involve vehicle collisions, defective products, and professional negligence. It is our goal to work diligently and zealously to protect our clients' rights and to hold accountable and responsible those individuals, corporations, and governmental bodies who engage in conduct that is unsafe, negligent, and criminal. Because of a commitment to making justice for all a reality, the firm has worked as cooperating counsel with NC Legal Services, the NAACP Legal Defense Fund, the Southern Poverty Law Center, and the American Civil Liberties Union.

MEMBERS OF FIRM

CHARLES L. BECTON, born Morehead City, North Carolina, May 4, 1944; admitted to bar, 1969, North Carolina; U.S. District Court, Eastern, Middle and Western Districts of North Carolina; U.S. Court of Appeals, Fourth Circuit; U.S. Supreme Court. *Education:* Howard University (B.A., 1966); Duke University (J.D., 1969); University of Virginia (LL.M., 1986). Served as Judge on the North Carolina Court of Appeals, 1981-1990. John Scott Cansler Lecturer in Trial Advocacy, University of North Carolina School of Law, 1976—. Senior Lecturer in Law, Duke University School of Law, Durham, North Carolina, 1980—. Instructor at Trial Advocacy Skills Institutes Nationwide and in the Republic of South Africa. Recipient: Outstanding Trial Advocate, North Carolina Academy of Trial Lawyers, November 1984; North Carolina Appellate Judge of the Year, 1985; Distinguished Alumni Award, Duke University Black Law Students Association, April 1987; Justice William J. Brennan, Jr. Trial Advocacy Award, January 1988; North Carolina Association of Educators "Excellence in Equity" Award, January 1990; Charles L. Becton Trial Advocacy Award, given annually by the North Carolina Academy of Trial Lawyers, 1st recipient; Roscoe Pound Foundation's Richard S. Jacobson Award from the Association of Trial Lawyers of America recognizing the nation's best trial advocacy teachers, July 1990. NITA's Robert Keeton Trial Advocacy Teaching Award, 1995. Listed in The Best Lawyers in America, 1993. *Member:* North Carolina and American Bar Associations; National Bar Association; North Carolina Association of Black Lawyers (President, 1980); North Carolina Academy of Trial Lawyers (President, 1994); The Association of Trial Lawyers of America; International Society of Barristers; American Board of Trial Advocates; American College of Trial Lawyers. **Email:** c.becton@bsblawfirm.com

ANNE R. SLIFKIN, born Urbana, Illinois, June 12, 1951; admitted to bar, 1976, North Carolina; 1979, U.S. District Court, Eastern District of North Carolina and U.S. Court of Appeals, Fourth Circuit. *Education:* Brandeis University (B.A., 1973); University of North Carolina at Chapel Hill (J.D., 1976). Phi Beta Kappa; Order of Coif. Member: Chapel Hill Board of Adjustment, 1974; Chapel Hill Planning Board, 1974-1976. Instructor, National Institute for Trial Advocacy, 1988—. Certified Superior Court Mediator. Private Arbiter. *Member:* North Carolina State Bar; North Carolina Academy of Trial Lawyers; The Association of Trial Lawyers of America; North Carolina Association of Women Attorneys (Vice President, 1978-1979). ***LANGUAGES:*** French. ***PRACTICE AREAS:*** Personal Injury; Wrongful Death; Medical Malpractice Litigation; Arbitration; Mediation. **Email:** a.slifkin@bsblawfirm.com

ASA L. BELL, JR., born Tarboro, North Carolina, September 26, 1965; admitted to bar, 1991, North Carolina; 1992, U.S. District Court, Eastern and Middle Districts of North Carolina. *Education:* University of North Carolina at Chapel Hill (B.A., 1987; M.B.A., 1991; J.D., 1991). Phi Alpha Delta. CLE Presenter: North Carolina Bar Association; North Carolina Association of Trial Lawyers; North Carolina Association of Black Lawyers. Instructor, National Institute of Trial Advocacy. *Member:* Wake County, North Carolina (Member, Litigation Council, 1995-1998) and American Bar Associations; North Carolina State Bar (Chairman, Judicial District 10-B Bar Candidate Committee, 1994); North Carolina Association of Black Lawyers (President, 1998-2000; First Vice President, 1996-1998; Parliamentarian, 1994-1996); National Bar Association; North Carolina Academy of Trial Lawyers (Member, YLD Board of Governors; Co-Organizer, Young Lawyers Steering Committee; Membership Committee); The Association of Trial Lawyers of America (State Governor, New Lawyers Division, 1993-1997). ***PRACTICE AREAS:*** Plaintiffs Personal Injury; Trucking Collisions; Wrongful Death; Medical Malpractice. **Email:** a.bell@bsblawfirm.com

ASSOCIATE

JUDITH M. POPE, born Bridgetown, Barbados, September 21, 1964; admitted to bar, 2000, Belgium; 2003, North Carolina. *Education:* University College, University of Lon-

(This Listing Continued)

BECTON, SLIFKIN & BELL, P.A., Raleigh—Continued

don (B.A., 1987); University of Bordeaux (LL.B., 1993); University of Paris, Sorbonne (LL.M., 1996); College of William and Mary (LL.M., 2002). *Member:* Belgian Bar Association; Wake County and North Carolina Bar Associations; American Bar Association; North Carolina Academy of Trial Lawyers; The Association of Trial Lawyers of America. **Email:** j.pope@bsblawfirm.com

SHERRI D. BELK

THE CAPITAL CLUB BUILDING
16 WEST MARTIN STREET, SUITE 604
RALEIGH, NORTH CAROLINA 27601
Telephone: 919-834-3533
Fax: 919-829-1600
Email: sherribelklaw@aol.com

Family Law, Divorce, Child Custody, Child Support, Visitation Rights, Criminal Law, Traffic Violations, Driving While Intoxicated, Misdemeanors, Wills, Probate, Personal Injury, Automobile Accidents.

SHERRI D. BELK, born Camden, New Jersey, March 28, 1973; admitted to bar, 2003, North Carolina. *Education:* University of North Carolina (B.A., 1996); South Texas College of Law (J.D., 2002). *Member:* North Carolina State Bar; North Carolina and American Bar Associations.

BENDER LAW OFFICES

Established in 1986
6608-204 SIX FORKS ROAD
RALEIGH, NORTH CAROLINA 27615
Telephone: 919-870-9600
Fax: 919-847-2473
Email: info@benderlaw.com
URL: http://www.benderlaw.com

Family Law, Divorce, Child Custody, Child Support, Spousal Support, Alimony, Equitable Distribution, Domestic Violence.

FIRM PROFILE: Ms. Bender has practiced family law for over 20 years.

VICTORIA BENDER, born Wisconsin; admitted to bar, 1978, California; 1983, North Carolina. *Education:* State University of New York at Stony Brook (B.A., cum laude, 1971); Hastings College of Law, University of California, San Francisco. Board Certified Family Law Practitioner, 2003. *Member:* Wake County, 10th Judicial District and North Carolina Bar Associations; The State Bar of California; North Carolina State Bar. ***PRACTICE AREAS:*** Family Law (100%). **Email:** vbender@benderlaw.com

LAW OFFICES OF JOHN T. BENJAMIN, JR.

Established in 1994
227 WEST MARTIN STREET
RALEIGH, NORTH CAROLINA 27601
Telephone: 919-755-0060
Fax: 919-755-0069
Email: benjamin@lawjtb.com

Civil Litigation, Commercial Litigation, Construction Litigation, Banking Litigation, Commercial Leasing Litigation, Commercial Debt, Creditors Rights, Negligence Defense, Business Law, Contracts, Appellate Practice.

FIRM PROFILE: The Firm was created by John T. Benjamin, Jr. in 1994. The firm specializes in civil litigation and is heavily involved in litigation in both state and federal courts.

JOHN T. BENJAMIN, JR., born New York, N.Y., January 19, 1966; admitted to bar, 1992, North Carolina and U.S. District Court, Eastern and Middle Districts of North Carolina; U.S. District Court, Western District of North Carolina and U.S. Court of Appeals, Fourth Circuit. *Education:* Bucknell University (B.A., 1988); Boston University (J.D., 1991). Selected to Legal Elite for Construction Law, Business North Carolina, January 2004. *Member:* Wake County Bar Association; North Carolina State Bar; American Bar Association (Member, Litigation Section). ***REPORTED CASES:*** Lewis v. Estate of Lewis, 137 N.C. App. 112 (2000); North Carolina Farm Partnership et al. v. Pig Improvement Company 163 N.C. App. 318, 593 S.E.2d 126 (2004); Coastal Caissan v. Kline Iron & Steel, 02-1319 (August 5, 2003) (unpublished); Brown v. Centex Homes, 615 S.E.2d 86, (N.C. App. July 19, 2005); Appel v. Food Lion, L.L.C., 608 S.E.2d 415 (Table) 2005 WL 351148 (N.C.App.; Feb. 15, 2005, No. COA04-423) (unpublished). ***PRACTICE AREAS:*** Civil Litigation; Construction Law; Contracts; Business Law; Banking Litigation; Commercial Litigation; Creditors Rights.

ASSOCIATES

WILLIAM E. HUBBARD, admitted to bar, 1996, North Carolina and U.S. District Court, Eastern, Middle and Western Districts of North Carolina. *Education:* University of Edinburgh, Scotland, U.K.; Appalachian State University (B.S., 1992); Campbell University (J.D., 1996). *Member:* Wake County and American Bar Associations; North Carolina State Bar. ***REPORTED CASES:*** Lewis v. Estate of Lewis, 137 N.C. App. 112 (2000); Brown v. Centex Homes, 615 S.E.2d 86, (N.C. App. July 19, 2005); Appel v. Food Lion, L.L.C. 608 S.E.2d 415 (Table) 2005WL 351148 (N.C. App.; Feb. 15, 2005, No. COA4-423) (unpublished). ***PRACTICE AREAS:*** Civil Litigation; Construction Law; Contracts; Mechanics Liens; Creditors Rights; Commercial Law. **Email:** hubbard@lawjtb.com

MITCHELL A. MEYERS, born Farmington, Michigan, July 11, 1971; admitted to bar, 1998, Florida; 1999, U.S. District Court, Southern District of Florida; 2001, North Carolina, U.S. District Court, Eastern, Middle and Western Districts of North Carolina. *Education:* University of Florida (B.A., Political Science, 1993); Nova Southeastern University (J.D., 1997). Author: "A Defense of Unilateral or Multi-Lateral Intervention When Human Rights Violations Constitute an Implied Waiver of Sovereignty," (ILSA) Journal of Comparative and International Law, Spring, 1997. *Member:* North Carolina State Bar Association; Commercial Law League of America; American Collector's Association. ***PRACTICE AREAS:*** Commercial Litigation; Creditors Rights; Construction Litigation; Banking Litigation; Commercial Lease Litigation. **Email:** meyers@lawjtb.com

REPRESENTATIVE CLIENTS: Food Lion, LLC; Kash n' Karry; Kimco, Inc.; EMC Mortgage Corp.; LaSalle Bank, N.A.; Wells Fargo; Ohio Savings Bank; M.B. Kahn Construction Co., Inc.; Centex Homes; St. Lawrence Homes, Inc.; Washington Homes; Fortis Homes; Westminster Homes; Keystone Homes; M/I Schottenstein Homes, Inc.; David Weekley Homes; Warren Distributing Co.; American Drywall Co.; Capital Drywall Co.; Topside Construction Co.; Tilesetters of Raleigh, Inc.; Harold G. Bagwell; Bagwell Properties; Shooting Sports, LLC; Select Portfolio Servicing Inc.; DLC Management; Irwin Mortgage; Radio Shack Corporation; River Crest Realty; State Employees Credit Union; Soil and Environmental Consultants; Wilshire Corporation; World Omni Financial Corporation; Smithfield Barbeque.

CALVIN B. BENNETT, III

Established in 1997
P.O. BOX 90574
RALEIGH, NORTH CAROLINA 27675
Telephone: 919-844-3989
Fax: 919-848-6261
Email: cal@bennett-law.com
URL: http://www.bennett-law.com

Mediation, Real Estate Investment and Executive Compensation.

CALVIN B. BENNETT, III, born Opelika, Alabama, May 5, 1962; admitted to bar, 1991, North Carolina; 1997, U.S. District Court, Eastern, Middle and Western Districts of North Carolina; 1998, U.S. Court of Veterans Appeals. *Education:* Auburn University (B.A., 1984); Duke University (J.D., with highest honors, 1991). Recipient, American Jurisprudence Awards: Evidence, 1989; Bankruptcy, 1990. Senior Editor, Law and Contemporary Problems, 1990-1991. Certified Mediator, North Carolina Dispute Resolution Commission. *Member:* Wake County and North Carolina Bar Associations. [USMC, 1984-1997; Lt. Col., USMCR, Retired, 1997-2004]. ***PRACTICE AREAS:*** Mediation; Real Estate Investment; Real Estate Mediation; Real Estate Sales; Executive Compensation; Alternative Dispute Resolution.

BLANCHARD, JENKINS, MILLER, LEWIS & STYERS, P.A.

1117 HILLSBOROUGH STREET
RALEIGH, NORTH CAROLINA 27603-1505
Telephone: 919-755-3993
Fax: 919-755-3994
URL: http://www.bjmls-law.com

Civil and Business Litigation, Administrative Law, Serious Personal Injury and Wrongful Death in following areas: Nursing Home Negligence, Medical and Professional Negligence, Automobile and Trucking Accidents, and Premises Liability, Commercial Torts, Utilities Law, Land Use and Zoning; Alcoholic Beverage Control Law, Federal and State Criminal Defense, Federal Grand jury Practice, Appellate Practice.

FIRM PROFILE: The firm has an extensive litigation and administrative law practice representing clients in areas as diverse as commercial and business disputes, serious personal injury, utilities regulation, wrongful death, zoning and land use hearings, medical and professional negligence, nursing home abuse and neglect, and criminal defense. The firm's lawyers have represented clients in the state and federal courts at all levels and before state and local regulatory agencies, boards and commissions. They are experienced not only in litigation and administrative matters, but are well-regarded appellate lawyers, handling appeals in both the state and federal courts. The firm takes an active interest in both trial and non-trial matters affecting public policy, frequently serving as counsel for citizen groups or as counsel for amici curiae.

ROBERT O. JENKINS, born Boiling Springs, North Carolina, March 18, 1962; admitted to bar, 1992, North Carolina; U.S. District Court, Eastern, Middle and Western Districts of North Carolina. *Education:* University of North Carolina, Chapel Hill (B.A., 1984; J.D., with honors, 1992); North Carolina State University (M.P.A., with honors, 1988). Order of the Coif. Recipient: William T. Joyner Award for Excellence in Student Writing, 1992. Member, Staff, North Carolina Law Review, 1990-1991. Author: The Litigator "Protecting Willful and Wanton Conduct," Vol. 16, No. 2, June 1996; Campbell Law Observer "A Summary of 1995 Legislative Changes, Medical Malpractice, Punitive Damages and Products Liability", Volume 17, Number 2, March, 1996; Note, Constitutionally Mandated Southern Hospitality, 69 N.C.L. Rev. 1001 (1991). Adjunct Faculty, UNC School of Law, 2004. *Member:* Wake County and North Carolina (Litigation Section Council, 2000-2003; Trial Practice Committee, 2004—) Bar Associations; North Carolina Academy of Trial Lawyers (Board of Governors, 1998—); The Association of Trial Lawyers of America; Southern Trial Lawyers Association; Susic Sharp Inn of Court. ***PRACTICE AREAS:*** Personal Injury; Medical Negligence; Commercial Litigation; Products Liability; Wrongful Death. **Email:** rjenkins@bjmls-law.com

PHILIP R. MILLER, III, born Winston-Salem, North Carolina, May 15, 1966; admitted to bar, 1992, North Carolina; U.S. District Court, Eastern District of North Carolina; U.S. Court of Appeals, Fourth Circuit. *Education:* University of North Carolina (B.A., 1988); Campbell University School of Law (J.D., 1992). Phi Alpha Delta. Recipient, Order of Old Kivett Award for Excellence in Advocacy in Trial Competition. Case Summary Writer, Articles Editor, Campbell Law Observer. ATLA Trial Team. Author: Campbell Law

(This Listing Continued)

Observer "A Summary of 1995 Legislative Changes, Medical Malpractice, Punitive Damages and Product Liability", Volume 17, Number 2, March 1996; "North Carolina AIC Evidence §11," Exhibits (1998); "North Carolina AIC Civil Procedure Pretrial 2 §22, Physical and Mental Examination of Persons" (1998). Lecturer: Automobile Tort Litigation and Nursing Home Litigation. *Member:* Wake County and North Carolina (Litigation Section Council) Bar Associations; North Carolina Academy of Trial Lawyers; The Association of Trial Lawyers of America; National Citizens Coalition for Nursing Home Reform; Friends of Residents of Long Term Care; Braxton Craven Inn of Court; American Judicature Society. ***PRACTICE AREAS:*** Personal Injury; Medical Negligence; Nursing Home Litigation; Wrongful Death; Products Liability. ***Email:*** pmiller@bjmls-law.com

E. HARDY LEWIS, born Fayetteville, North Carolina, May 1, 1965; admitted to bar, 1991, North Carolina; U.S. District Court, Eastern, Middle and Western Districts of North Carolina; U.S. Court of Appeals, Fourth Circuit, District of Columbia Circuit; U.S. Supreme Court. *Education:* University of Notre Dame (B.A., 1987); University of North Carolina (J.D., 1991). Articles Editor, 1990-1991, North Carolina Law Review. Author: "Municipal Ownership of Cable Television Systems", 68 N.C.L. Rev. 1295, 1990. *Member:* Wake County (10th Judicial District Fee Arbitration Committee, 1994-2003), North Carolina (Member, Appellate Rules Study Committee, 1996-1999; Co-Chair, Legislative Committee of Litigation Section, 1997-1998) and American Bar Associations; North Carolina Academy of Trial Lawyers (Member, Legal Affairs Committee). ***PRACTICE AREAS:*** Business Litigation; Commercial Litigation; Automobile Negligence; Professional Negligence; Products Liability; Criminal Defense; Administrative Law; Alcoholic Beverage Control Law; Appellate Practice. ***Email:*** hlewis@bjmls-law.com

M. GRAY STYERS, JR., born Hickory, North Carolina, November 11, 1962; admitted to bar, 1989, North Carolina; U.S. District Court, Eastern and Middle Districts of North Carolina; U.S. Court of Appeals, Fourth Circuit; U.S. Supreme Court. *Education:* Wake Forest University (B.A., magna cum laude, 1985); University of North Carolina at Chapel Hill (M.B.A., J.D., with honors, 1989). Phi Beta Kappa. Articles Editor, North Carolina Law Review, 1988-1989. Author: "Pre-Trial Detention Seen Through the Looking Glass," 66 N.C.L. Rev. 610 (1988). *Member:* Wake County Bar Association; North Carolina Bar Association (Former Chair, Administrative Law Section); American Bar Association; Susie Sharpe Inn of Court. ***PRACTICE AREAS:*** Government Relations; Utility Law; Zoning, Planning and Land Use; Administrative Law; Commercial Litigation. ***Email:*** gstyers@bjmls-law.com

OF COUNSEL

CHARLES F. BLANCHARD, born Richmond County, North Carolina, October 3, 1923; admitted to bar, 1950, District of Columbia and North Carolina; U.S. District Court, Eastern, Middle and Western Districts of North Carolina; U.S. Court of Appeals, Fourth Circuit; U.S. Supreme Court. *Education:* Duke University (A.B., 1947; J.D., 1949). Phi Delta Phi; Omicron Delta Kappa. Recipient, Southern Trial Lawyers Warhorse Award, 1993. Listed in Best Lawyers of America, all editions. Lecturer, Trial Advocacy Skills, North Carolina Bar Association and North Carolina Academy of Trial Lawyers. Chairman, North Carolina Supreme Court Historical Society, 1994-1996. President, Braxton Craven Inn of Court. 1994-1995. *Member:* Wake County (President, 1977; Recipient, Chief Justice Joseph Branch Professional Award, 1994), North Carolina (Member, Board of Governors, 1983-1986; Chairman, Litigation Section, 1982-1983) and American Bar Associations; North Carolina State Bar (Councillor, 1980-1985); North Carolina Academy of Trial Lawyers (President, 1969-1971; Recipient of Academy's Highest Honor, the Chief Justice Walter Clark Award for Pursuit of Justice, 1993); The Association of Trial Lawyers of America (Governor, 1965-1967; 1970-1973; Chairman, National Speakers Committee, 1971). Fellow: International Society of Barristers (President, 1994-1995); International Academy of Trial Lawyers. [Lt. (j.g.), U.S.N.R., active duty, 1944-1946]. ***PRACTICE AREAS:*** Commercial Litigation; Personal Injury; Product Liability; Medical Malpractice.

ERIC MILLER REEVES, born Oklahoma, October 18, 1963; admitted to bar, 1989, North Carolina. *Education:* Duke University (B.A., 1986); Wake Forest University (J.D., 1989). Member, Editorial Board, Wake Forest Law Review, 1988-1989. Author: "Note," Volume 23, Wake Forest Law Review. Law Clerk to Justice Burley B. Mitchell, North Carolina Supreme Court, 1989-1990. Member, City Council, Raleigh, 1993-1996. Member, 1996—and Chair, Senate Information Technology Committee, State Senate. *Member:* Wake County and North Carolina Bar Associations. ***PRACTICE AREAS:*** Civil Trials; Real Estate; Corporate Law. ***Email:*** ereeves@bjmls-law.com

ASSOCIATE

KAREN KEMERAIT PRATHER, born Rockledge, Florida, May 2, 1966; admitted to bar, 1991, North Carolina. *Education:* Davidson College (B.A., 1988); Wake Forest University School of Law (J.D., 1991). Phi Delta Phi. Law Clerk to Judge Elizabeth G. McCrodden, North Carolina Court of Appeals, 1991-1993. *Member:* Wake County and North Carolina Bar Associations; North Carolina Academy of Trial Lawyers. ***PRACTICE AREAS:*** Utility Law; Zoning, Planning and Land Use; Administrative Law; Commercial Litigation; Personal Injury; Nursing Home Litigation. ***Email:*** Kprather@bjmls-law.com

BODE, CALL & STROUPE, L.L.P.

Established in 1977

3105 GLENWOOD AVENUE, SUITE 300
P.O. BOX 6338
RALEIGH, NORTH CAROLINA 27628-6338
Telephone: 919-881-0338
Telecopier: 919-881-9548

General Civil and Trial Practice. Utility Regulation, Energy, Corporation, Contract, Commercial Law, Real Estate, Hospital, Health Care and Administrative Law, Legislative Representation, Securities and Municipal Finance, Trials and Appeals in all State and Federal Courts, Land Use and Insurance Regulation.

(This Listing Continued)

MEMBERS OF FIRM

DAVID P. GREEN (1945-1985)

JOHN V. HUNTER III (Retired)

JOHN T. BODE, born Cleveland, Ohio, January 27, 1941; admitted to bar, 1970, New York; 1973, North Carolina. *Education:* United States Military Academy (B.S., 1962); University of North Carolina (J.D., 1969). Order of the Coif. Member, North Carolina Medical Care Commission, 1978-1983. *Member:* Wake County and American Bar Associations; North Carolina State Bar. [Capt., U.S. Army, 1962-1966]. ***PRACTICE AREAS:*** Legislative Practice; Securities Regulation; Corporate Finance; Municipal Finance.

W. DAVIDSON CALL, born Lynchburg, Virginia, August 5, 1942; admitted to bar, 1968, Virginia; 1972, North Carolina. *Education:* University of Virginia (B.A., 1965); University of Richmond (LL.B., 1968). Phi Delta Phi. *Member:* Wake County and North Carolina Bar Associations; Virginia State Bar; North Carolina State Bar. [Capt., USAR, 1968-1970]. ***PRACTICE AREAS:*** Real Estate; Commercial Law; Corporate Law. ***Email:*** call@bcs-law.com

ROBERT V. BODE, born Raleigh, North Carolina, October 11, 1948; admitted to bar, 1974, North Carolina. *Education:* University of North Carolina (B.A., 1970; J.D., 1974). Morehead Scholar. Co-Author, "Coastal Zone Management in North Carolina," published under grant from the North Carolina Law Center, 1973. Member, North Carolina Health Care Society. Member, Panel of Arbitrators, American Arbitration Association, 1989—. *Member:* Wake County Bar Association; North Carolina State Bar; Federation of Regulatory Counsel. [LTJG, U.S. Navy, 1970-1971]. ***PRACTICE AREAS:*** Litigation; Health Care; Administrative Law. ***Email:*** rbode@bcs-law.com

ODES L. STROUPE, JR., born Charlotte, North Carolina, March 10, 1946; admitted to bar, 1971, North Carolina; 1986, New York. *Education:* North Carolina State University (B.A., 1968); University of North Carolina (J.D., with honors, 1971). Phi Delta Phi. Member, Board of Editors, North Carolina Law Review, 1969-1970. Permanent Member, Federal Judicial Conference for the Fourth Circuit. *Member:* Wake County (Chairman, Young Lawyers Section, 1975), North Carolina (Council Member, Litigation Section, 1985-1993), New York State and American Bar Associations; North Carolina State Bar; National Association of Railroad Trial Counsel; Defense Research and Trial Lawyers Association. ***PRACTICE AREAS:*** Civil Litigation; Commercial Law. ***Email:*** stroupe@bcs-law.com

V. LANE WHARTON, JR., born Jackson, Mississippi, August 22, 1947; admitted to bar, 1974, North Carolina. *Education:* University of Louisiana at Lafayette (B.A., with high distinction, 1969); University of Chicago (J.D., 1974). Phi Eta Sigma; Phi Kappa Phi; Blue Key. Member, North Carolina Insurance Advisory Board, 1978-1985. Appeals and Hearing Officer, CHAMPUS, U.S. Department of Defense, 1978-1981. *Member:* Wake County (Vice Chairman, Young Lawyers Section, 1978-1981), North Carolina (Member, Law Office and Economics Committee, 1980-1987; Chairman, Executive Council, Young Lawyers in Practice Committee, Younger Lawyers Division, 1981-1984) and American Bar Associations; North Carolina State Bar. [1st Lt., USMCR, 1970-1976]. ***LANGUAGES:*** French. ***PRACTICE AREAS:*** Insurance Regulation; Insurance Insolvency. ***Email:*** wharton@bcs-law.com

S. TODD HEMPHILL, born Hickory, North Carolina, March 27, 1956; admitted to bar, 1982, North Carolina. *Education:* Dartmouth College (A.B., cum laude, 1978); University of North Carolina (M.B.A., 1982; J.D., 1982). Law Clerk to the Honorable Franklin T. Dupree, Jr., U.S. District Court, Eastern District of North Carolina, 1984-1986. *Member:* Wake County and North Carolina (Council Member: Administrative Law Section, 2005-2006; Health Care) Bar Associations; North Carolina State Bar; North Carolina Health Care Society. ***PRACTICE AREAS:*** Litigation; Administrative Law; Health Care. ***Email:*** hemphill@bcs-law.com

DIANA EVANS RICKETTS, born Raleigh, North Carolina, July 22, 1949; admitted to bar, 1974, North Carolina. *Education:* University of North Carolina (B.A., English, 1971; J.D., 1974). Phi Beta Kappa. *Member:* Wake County Bar Association; North Carolina State Bar; North Carolina Health Care Society. ***PRACTICE AREAS:*** Litigation; Administrative Law; Health Care. ***Email:*** ricketts@bcs-law.com

ASSOCIATES

JOHN S. BYRD, II, born Wilson, North Carolina, December 13, 1965; admitted to bar, 2001, North Carolina. *Education:* North Carolina State University (B.A., 1990); University of North Carolina at Wilmington (M.B.A., with honors, 1998); University of Miami School of Law (J.D., cum laude, 2001). *Member:* Wake County and North Carolina Bar Associations; North Carolina State Bar; North Carolina Association of Defense Attorneys; Defense Research Institute. ***PRACTICE AREAS:*** Civil Litigation; Commercial Litigation. ***Email:*** jbyrd@bcs-law.com

MATTHEW A. FISHER, born Asheville, North Carolina, April 13, 1976; admitted to bar, 2001, North Carolina. *Education:* University of Tennessee at Knoxville (B.A., 1998); University of North Carolina at Chapel Hill (J.D., 2001). Phi Beta Kappa. *Member:* Wake County and American Bar Associations; North Carolina Association of Defense Attorneys; Defense Research Institute; North Carolina State Bar. ***PRACTICE AREAS:*** Litigation; Administrative Law; Health Care. ***Email:*** fisher@bcs-law.com

REPRESENTATIVE CLIENTS: Accenture LLP; Alltel Communications, Inc.; Banc One Corporation; BellSouth Telecommunications, Inc.; Bobbitt Design Build, Inc.; Caldwell Memorial Hospital; California Wine Institute; Capitol Travel, Inc.; Centex Rooney Construction Co.; Central Carolina Hospital; Circle K Corp.; Commissioner of Insurance of State of North Carolina; Cormetech, Inc.; Corning, Inc.; County Electric Supply Company, Ltd.; Craven Regional Medical Center; Harris Wholesale, Inc.; Health Systems Management, Inc.; Liberty Life Insurance Corporation; McGraw-Hill, Inc.; Medical Facilities of North Carolina, Inc.; MedQuest Associates, Inc.; Metro Air Conditioning, Inc.; Munich American Reinsurance Co.; Norfolk Southern Corporation; Norfolk Southern Railway Co.; North Carolina Academy of Physicians Assistants, North Carolina Baptist Hospital; North Carolina Hospital Association; Onslow Memorial Hospital; Piedmont Medical Center; Progress Energy; Raleigh Neurology Associates, P.A.; Scott-Madden & Associates, Inc.; Service Experts, Inc.; Service Express; Sports & Recreation, Inc.; The Biltmore Co.; The Stanley Works; TSC Leasing; Union Bankers Insurance Co.; U.S. Oncology; Wake Forest University School of Medicine.
COUNSEL FOR: Attorney's Title Insurance Company; Independent Insurance Agents of North Carolina, Inc.; North Carolina Chapter of the American College of Radiology; Pines of Carolina Girl Scout Council, Inc.; Tenet HealthSystem.

(This Listing Continued)

BODE, CALL & STROUPE, L.L.P., Raleigh—Continued

APPROVED ATTORNEYS FOR: Chicago Title Insurance Co.; Commonwealth Land Title Insurance Co.; First Title Insurance Co.; Investors Title Insurance Co., Lawyers Title Insurance Corp.
REFERENCE: Bank of America.

BOXLEY, BOLTON, GARBER & HAYWOOD, L.L.P.

Established in 1981

THE NASH SQUARE BUILDING
227 WEST MARTIN STREET
P.O. DRAWER 1429
RALEIGH, NORTH CAROLINA 27602
Telephone: 919-832-3915
Fax: 919-832-3918

General Civil Trial Practice in State and Federal Courts. Probate, Family, Personal Injury, Administrative, Corporation, Taxation, Real Estate, Eminent Domain, Business, Legislative and Construction.

JOHN MACLACHLAN BOXLEY, born Raleigh, North Carolina, February 2, 1942; admitted to bar, 1967, North Carolina. *Education:* University of North Carolina (B.A., 1964; J.D., 1967). Certified Mediator. Professor, Business Law, Peace College, 1984-1988. Chairman, North Carolina State Board of Paroles, 1973-1974. Member, North Carolina Board of Ethics, 1977-1979. *Member:* North Carolina State Bar (Vice-Chair, Disciplinary Hearing Commission, 1975-1981); North Carolina Academy of Trial Lawyers. Fellow, American Academy of Matrimonial Lawyers. ***PRACTICE AREAS:*** Family Law; Personal Injury; Legislative Practice; Health Law.

LAWRENCE E. BOLTON, born Queens, New York, August 23, 1943; admitted to bar, 1968, Virginia; 1971, North Carolina. *Education:* College of William & Mary (B.A., 1965; J.D., 1968). Phi Delta Phi. Attorney, Estate Tax Division, Internal Revenue Service, 1968-1974. (Board Certified Specialist in Estate Planning and Probate Law, North Carolina State Board of Legal Specialization). ***PRACTICE AREAS:*** Estate Planning; Taxation; Corporate Law; Real Property. ***Email:*** lebolton@earthlink.net

RONALD HILL GARBER, born Albemarle, North Carolina, November 9, 1951; admitted to bar, 1977, North Carolina. *Education:* University of North Carolina (B.A., 1974; J.D., 1977). Phi Eta Sigma. Phi Beta Kappa. Member, Holderness Moot Court Bench, 1976-1977. *Member:* Wake County Bar Association (Member, Board of Directors, 1995-1996); North Carolina Bar Association (Member: Board of Governors, 1988-1991; Endowment Committee, 1991—; Executive Council, Law Office Management Section, 1986-1988; Executive Council, Young Lawyers Division, 1982-1988; Recipient, Outstanding Young Lawyer, 1988); North Carolina State Bar; North Carolina Academy of Trial Lawyers. ***REPORTED CASES:*** Hobby & Son v. Family Homes, 302 N.C. 64 (1981); N.C. Farm Partnership v. Pig Improvement Company, 162 N.C. App. 318 (2004); W.A. Dail Plumbing, Inc. v. Roger Baker & Associates, 78 N.C. App. 664 (1986). ***PRACTICE AREAS:*** Personal Injury; Commercial Litigation; Real Property Litigation.

KENNETH C. HAYWOOD, born Raleigh, North Carolina, January 31, 1966; admitted to bar, 1992, North Carolina; 1999, U.S. District Court, Eastern District of North Carolina. *Education:* University of North Carolina at Chapel Hill (B.A., 1989); Wake Forest University (J.D., 1992). Order of the Golden Fleece. Law Clerk to Justice I. Beverly Lake, Jr. (now Chief Justice), North Carolina Supreme Court, 1992-1993. *Member:* Wake County (Member: Bench-Bar Committee, 2001—; Professionalism Committee, 2000—) and North Carolina (Member, Section on Zoning and Land Use) Bar Associations. ***PRACTICE AREAS:*** Business Litigation; Real Estate Litigation; Construction Litigation; Eminent Domain; Zoning Law; Land Use. ***Email:*** khaywood@bbghlaw.com

ASSOCIATES

BRIAN C. SETLIFF, born Reidsville, North Carolina, March 16, 1972; admitted to bar, 1999, Georgia; 2004, North Carolina. *Education:* Appalachian State University (B.A., 1994); John Marshall Law School (J.D., 1999); University of Denver School of Law (LL.M., Environmental Law, 2003). *Member:* Wake County Bar Association; State Bar of Georgia; North Carolina State Bar. ***PRACTICE AREAS:*** Real Estate Litigation; Commercial Real Estate; Environmental Law; Personal Injury. ***Email:*** bsetliff@bbghlaw.com

EVERETT M. BOLTON, born Raleigh, North Carolina, December 8, 1973; admitted to bar, 2005, North Carolina. *Education:* Wake Forest University (B.A., Politics, 1996); Campbell Law School (J.D., 2005). ***PRACTICE AREAS:*** Family Law; Domestic Relations; Estate Planning. ***Email:*** ebolton@bbghlaw.com

REPRESENTATIVE CLIENTS: Carolinas Ready Mixed Concrete Association; Sirchie Finger Print Laboratories, Inc.; N.C. Podiatric Medical Society; N.C. Aggregates Assn.; Triangle Radiation Oncology Services, Inc.; Home Builders Association of Raleigh and Wake County; First Title Insurance Co.; Fidelity National Title Insurance Co. ; Lawyers Mutual Liability Insurance Company of North Carolina; Rockett Burkhead & Winslow; R.W. Moore Equipment Company; Wake County Board of Education.
APPROVED ATTORNEYS FOR: First Title Insurance Co.; Fidelity National Title Insurance Co.; Commonwealth Land Title Insurance Company. Lawyers Title Insurance Co.
REFERENCES: Wachovia Bank; Branch Banking & Trust Co.

BOYCE & ISLEY, PLLC

LAWYERS WEEKLY BUILDING, SUITE 100
107 FAYETTEVILLE STREET MALL
P.O. BOX 1990
RALEIGH, NORTH CAROLINA 27602-1990
Telephone: 919-833-7373
Fax: 919-833-7536
Email: pisley@boyceisley.com
URL: http://www.boyce-isleylaw.com

Civil Litigation, Class Actions, Taxation, Complex Litigation, Commercial Litigation, Criminal Law, Insurance Defense, Appellate Practice, Employment Law.

(This Listing Continued)

G. EUGENE BOYCE, born Clinton, North Carolina, July 12, 1932; admitted to bar, 1956, North Carolina; 1957, U.S. District Court, Eastern and Middle Districts of North Carolina and U.S. Supreme Court; 1976, District of Columbia. *Education:* Wake Forest University (B.S., summa cum laude, 1954; LL.B., magna cum laude, 1956). Phi Beta Kappa; Phi Alpha Delta. Lecturer, Annual Review Institute, 1979-1990. Assistant Chief Counsel, Watergate Committee (Sen. Sam J. Ervin Staff), 1973. *Member:* Wake County (President, 1979-1980) and North Carolina Bar Associations; The North Carolina State Bar (Councillor, 1980-1988); American College of Trial Lawyers; American Board of Trial Attorneys. [Capt., U.S. Army, JAGC, 1957-1960]. ***PRACTICE AREAS:*** Class Action; Litigation; Commercial Litigation; Constitutional Law. ***Email:*** gboyce@boyceisley.com

R. DANIEL BOYCE, born Fayetteville, North Carolina, December 8, 1958; admitted to bar, 1984, North Carolina; 1985, U.S. District Court, Eastern District of North Carolina; 1988, U.S. Court of Appeals, Fourth Circuit; 1995, U.S. District Court, Middle District of North Carolina. *Education:* Wake Forest University (B.A., cum laude, 1981); University of North Carolina (J.D., 1984). Licensed Private Investigator, State of North Carolina, 1994. Assistant U.S. Attorney, 1987-1994. *Member:* Wake County Bar Association (Past President, Young Lawyers Division; Member, Board of Directors); North Carolina State Bar (Member, Board of Directors, Criminal Section); North Carolina Academy of Trial Lawyers (Member, Board of Directors, Criminal Section); Wake County Academy of Trial Lawyers. (Board Certified Specialist in State and Federal, Criminal Law, North Carolina State Board of Legal Specialization). ***PRACTICE AREAS:*** Civil Litigation; Class Action Litigation; Criminal Law. ***Email:*** dboyce@boyceisley.com

PHILIP R. ISLEY, born Martinsville, Virginia, August 20, 1967; admitted to bar, 1992, North Carolina and U.S. District Court, Eastern District of North Carolina. *Education:* Washington and Lee University (B.A., cum laude, 1989); University of Mississippi (J.D., 1992). Phi Delta Phi. Associate Editor, Mississippi Law Journal. Member, Moot Court Board, 1991-1992; Honor Council, 1990-1992; Prosecutor, Honor Council, 1991-1992. Member, Raleigh City Council, 2001—. *Member:* Wake County (President Young Lawyers Division, 1995-1997) and North Carolina (Leadership Network Committee, 1993-1997) Bar Associations. ***PRACTICE AREAS:*** Commercial Litigation; Class Action Litigation; Insurance Defense; Employment Law; Real Estate Litigation. ***Email:*** pisley@boyceisley.com

LAURA BOYCE ISLEY, born Raleigh, North Carolina, November 20, 1966; admitted to bar, 1992, North Carolina. *Education:* Wake Forest University (B.A., cum laude, 1989; J.D., 1992). Research Assistant, North Carolina Supreme Court. Staff Attorney, North Carolina Court of Appeals. ***PRACTICE AREAS:*** Civil Appeals. ***Email:*** lisley@boyceisley.com

BRADY, NORDGREN, KLYM & MORTON, PLLC

Established in 2003

2301 SUGAR BUSH ROAD, SUITE 450
RALEIGH, NORTH CAROLINA 27612
Telephone: 919-782-3500
Fax: 919-573-1430
Email: lawyers@bradynordgren.com
URL: http://www.bradynordgren.com

Trusts and Estates, Estate Planning, Estate Litigation, Personal Injury, Civil Litigation, Commercial Litigation, Wills, Probate, Corporate Law, Business Law, Taxation, Elder Law.

MEMBERS OF FIRM

R. DANIEL BRADY, born Raleigh, North Carolina, November 19, 1953; admitted to bar, 1982, North Carolina, U.S. Tax Court, U.S. Claims Court and U.S. District Court, Eastern District of North Carolina. *Education:* University of North Carolina (B.S., 1976); Wake Forest University (J.D., 1982). *Member:* Wake County and North Carolina (Estate Planning and Fiduciary Law) Bar Associations; North Carolina Association of Certified Public Accountants. (Board Certified Specialist in Estate Planning and Probate Law, North Carolina State Board of Legal Specialization). ***PRACTICE AREAS:*** Trusts and Estates; Taxation; Wills; Probate; Elder Law; Estate Planning; Estate Planning for Unmarried Couples; Living Trusts; Probate Litigation; Special Needs Trusts; Estate Litigation; Family Corporations; Corporate Law; Powers of Attorney; Family Partnerships. ***Email:*** dan@danbrady.com

MARK R. KLYM, born Parma, Ohio, February 18, 1970; admitted to bar, 1995, North Carolina. *Education:* University of Vermont (B.A., 1992); Ohio Northern University; Pettit College of Law (J.D., with distinction, 1995). *Member:* Wake County and North Carolina (Member, Sections on Estate Planning and Fiduciary Law) Bar Associations. [U.S. Navy JAG Corps Lieutenant, 1995-1998]. (Board Certified Specialist in Estate Planning and Probate Law, North Carolina State Board of Legal Specialization). ***PRACTICE AREAS:*** Trusts and Estates; Wills; Probate; Guardianship; Estate Planning for Parents of Handicapped Children; Estate Settlements; Family Trusts; Living Trusts; Trust Planning; Business Successions; Business Formation; Family Limited Partnerships. ***Email:*** mark@markklym.com

TRAVIS K. MORTON, born West Palm Beach, Florida, February 8, 1969; admitted to bar, 1994, North Carolina. *Education:* North Carolina State University (B.A. with honors, 1991); University of North Carolina at Chapel Hill (J.D., 1994). AOC Certified Mediator, Alternative Dispute Resolution. *Member:* Wake County, North Carolina and American Bar Associations. ***PRACTICE AREAS:*** Civil Litigation; Personal Injury; Commercial Litigation; Estate Litigation; Contested Wills; Fiduciary Liability; Contested Trusts and Estates. ***Email:*** travis@travismorton.com

TIMOTHY A. NORDGREN, born Providence, Rhode Island, August 6, 1969; admitted to bar, 1995, Tennessee; 1998, North Carolina. *Education:* University of Iowa (B.B.A., with distinction, 1991); University of North Carolina (J.D., 1994). Phi Eta Sigma; Beta Gamma Sigma; Pi Kappa Alpha. *Member:* Wake County, North Carolina (Member, Sections on Estate Planning and Fiduciary Law) and Tennessee Bar Associations; North Carolina State Bar. (Board Certified Specialist in Estate Planning and Probate Law, North Carolina State Board of Legal Specialization). ***PRACTICE AREAS:*** Trusts and Estates; Estate Planning; Living Trusts; Wills; Probate; Like Kind Exchanges; Business Formation; Busi-

(This Listing Continued)

ness Successions; Charitable Giving; Adult Guardianship; Special Needs Trusts; Trust Litigation; Fiduciary Liability; Trusts and Estates Taxation; Family Limited Partnerships. **Email:** tim@timnordgren.com

J. MICHAEL MALONE, born York, Pennsylvania, January 15, 1968; admitted to bar, 1999, North Carolina. *Education:* North Carolina State University (B.S.C.E., 1991; M.S.C.E., 1993; Ph.D., 1996); University of North Carolina, Chapel Hill (J.D., 1999). *Member:* North Carolina Bar Association; North Carolina Academy of Trial Lawyers. ***PRACTICE AREAS:*** Personal Injury; Toxic Torts; Lead Poisoning; Chemical Exposure; Hazardous Materials and Substances; Litigation. **Email:** mmalonelaw@aol.com

BRANNON STRICKLAND, PLLC

107 FAYETTEVILLE STREET MALL, SUITE 201
RALEIGH, NORTH CAROLINA 27601
Telephone: 919-838-5295
Fax: 919-838-5299
URL: http://www.brannonstrickland.com

Appellate Advocacy, Civil Litigation. Constitutional Law, Criminal Defense, District Court/ Traffic Violations, Divorce, Family Law, Juvenile/DSS, Real Estate.

ANTHONY M. BRANNON, born Los Angeles, California, October 28, 1964; admitted to bar, 2001, North Carolina; U.S. Court of Appeals, Fourth Circuit; U.S. District Court, Eastern District of North Carolina. *Education:* North Carolina State University (B.S., 1998); Campbell University (J.D., 2001). Phi Beta Kappa. Law Clerk, North Carolina Court of Appeals. (Also Member, Wake County Traffic & DWI Center, PLLC). ***PRACTICE AREAS:*** Appellate Practice; Constitutional Law; Civil Litigation; Criminal; Child Custody; Adoptions; Personal Injury. **Email:** abrannon@brannonstrickland.com

ROBIN EASON STRICKLAND, born Raleigh, North Carolina, July 31, 1977; admitted to bar, 2002, North Carolina. *Education:* North Carolina State University (B.A., French, 1998); Campbell University (J.D., 2002). *Member:* Wake County, North Carolina and American Bar Associations; Wake County Academy of Trial Lawyers. ***PRACTICE AREAS:*** Juvenile Law; Real Estate; Personal Injury; Collections. **Email:** rstrickland@brannonstrickland.com

ASSOCIATE

MARLET MASSEY EDWARDS, born Raleigh, North Carolina, November 21, 1975; admitted to bar, 2002, North Carolina. *Education:* North Carolina State University (B.A., 1998); Campbell University (J.D., 2002). ***PRACTICE AREAS:*** Criminal Defense; Juvenile Criminal Law. **Email:** medwards@brannonstrickland.com

THE BREWER LAW FIRM

619 NORTH PERSON STREET
RALEIGH, NORTH CAROLINA 27604
Telephone: 919-832-2288; 1-800-899-3328
Fax: 919-834-2011
URL: http://www.brewerlawyers.com
Email: info@brewerwright.com
URL: http://www.debtrelief.com

Bankruptcy (Debtors and Noninstitutional Creditors), Consumer and Business Bankruptcy.

FIRM PROFILE: Mr. Brewer and Ms. Wright are both Board Certified in Consumer Bankruptcy. Mr. Brewer has practiced law in Raleigh since 1977, first as a general practitioner and as a Board Certified Specialist in Consumer Bankruptcy since 1993. Ms. Wright served as the law clerk to Judge A. Thomas Small for 3 years prior to joining the firm in August 1997.

Our first goal is to educate individuals and small businesses that are in financial difficulty about all of their legal options. We provide personal consultations to prospective clients to thoroughly analyze their particular circumstances and to better advise them. When clients retain us, our aim is to represent them in a professional manner, for reasonable fees, throughout the bankruptcy process.

WILLIAM E. BREWER, born Kinston, North Carolina, September 13, 1951; admitted to bar, 1976, North Carolina. *Education:* University of North Carolina (A.B., Econ., 1973; J.D., with honors, 1976). Phi Beta Kappa. *Member:* North Carolina Bar Association; North Carolina State Bar; National Association of Consumer Bankruptcy Attorneys (Director); North Carolina Academy of Trial Lawyers. (Board Certified Specialist in Consumer Bankruptcy Law, North Carolina Board of Legal Specialization). ***PRACTICE AREAS:*** Bankruptcy Law. **Email:** wbrewer@brewerwright.com

VICTORIA S. WRIGHT, born Milwaukee, Wisconsin, November 19, 1956; admitted to bar, 1994, North Carolina; 1995, U.S. District Court, Eastern District of North Carolina and U.S. Court of Appeals, Fourth Circuit. *Education:* Northwestern University (B.S.S., 1978); Wake Forest University (J.D., 1994). Wake Forest University Law Review. Law Clerk, Honorable A. Thomas Small, Chief Bankruptcy Judge, Eastern District of North Carolina, 1994-1997. *Member:* Wake County and North Carolina Bar Associations; North Carolina State Bar; National Association of Consumer Bankruptcy Attorneys. (Board Certified Specialist in Consumer Bankruptcy, North Carolina State Board of Legal Specialization). ***PRACTICE AREAS:*** Bankruptcy Law. **Email:** vwright@brewerwright.com

F. BRYAN BRICE, JR.

Established in 1999

19 WEST HARGETT STREET, SUITE 600
RALEIGH, NORTH CAROLINA 27601
Telephone: 919-754-1600
Fax: 919-832-0301
URL: http://www.attybryanbrice.com
Email: bryan_brice@yahoo.com
URL: http://www.lawyers.com/bryanbrice

Environmental Law, Brownfields Redevelopment, Underground Storage Tanks, Wetlands, Toxic Torts, Administrative Law, Criminal Law, Driving While Intoxicated (DWI), Traffic Violations, Personal Injury, Condemnation, Eminent Domain.

F. BRYAN BRICE, JR., born Wilson, North Carolina, July 6, 1962; admitted to bar, 1991, North Carolina; 1993, District of Columbia. *Education:* University of North Carolina at Chapel Hill (B.A., 1985; J.D., 1990). Law Clerk to Justice John Webb, North Carolina Supreme Court, 1990-1991. Staff Attorney, United States Environmental Protection Agency, Washington, D.C., 1991-1996. Environmental Attorney, Transportation Section, North Carolina Attorney General's Office, 1996-1999. *Member:* Wake County, North Carolina (Member, Environmental and Natural Resources Section; Council Member, 2004—) and American (Member: Environmental, Energy and Natural Resources Section; Administrative Law Section) Bar Associations; North Carolina State Bar.

ASSOCIATE

HEATHER L. SPURLOCK, born Rolla, Missouri; admitted to bar, 2002, North Carolina. *Education:* University of North Carolina at Chapel Hill (B.S., Public Health, 1998); Vermont Law School (J.D., Masters in Env. Law, 2002). Albert Schweitzer Fellow, 2000-2001. Member: Debevoise Moot Court Board, 2001-2002); Negotiations Moot Court Board, 1999-2002; Environmental Law Society, 1999-2002. *Member:* Wake County, North Carolina (Member, Environmental and Natural Resources Section) and American (Member, Environmental, Energy and National Resources Section) Bar Associations; North Carolina State Bar. ***PRACTICE AREAS:*** Environmental Law; Underground Storage Tanks; Toxic Torts; Brownfields Redevelopment; Wetlands Protection; Administrative Law; Criminal Law; Products Liability; Traffic Violations; Personal Injury. **Email:** hspurlock@attybryanbrice.com

REPRESENTATIVE CLIENTS: Kodak (Qualex); GreenVest; Soil, Water & Environmental Group; Blount Feed and Fertilizer; Restoration Systems; Triangle Wetlands; Lawn Master; TAO Auto; The Garden Path; The Dilweg Company; Empire Properties; Eagle Cleaner I.

DEWEY P. BRINKLEY

5 WEST HARGETT STREET, SUITE 904
RALEIGH, NORTH CAROLINA 27601
Telephone: 919-616-1269
Fax: 919-833-6106
Email: brinkleylawfirm@bellsouth.net
URL: http://www.brinkleylawfirm.com

Criminal Law, Driving While Intoxicated, DWI, Traffic Violations, Drug Crimes, Parole and Probation, Juvenile Crimes, White Collar Crimes.

DEWEY P. BRINKLEY, born Raleigh, North Carolina, May 9, 1972; admitted to bar, 2002, North Carolina. *Education:* University of North Carolina at Chapel Hill (B.A., 1994); Tulane University (J.D., 2002). Assistant District Attorney, Wake County, North Carolina, 2002-2005. *Member:* Wake County, North Carolina and American Bar Associations. ***PRACTICE AREAS:*** Criminal Law; Driving While Intoxicated; DWI; Traffic Violations; Drug Crimes; Parole and Probation; Juvenile Criminal Law; White Collar Crime.

BROOKS, PIERCE, McLENDON, HUMPHREY & LEONARD, L.L.P.

Established in 1897

1600 WACHOVIA CAPITOL CENTER
150 FAYETTEVILLE STREET MALL (27601)
P.O. BOX 1800
RALEIGH, NORTH CAROLINA 27602-1800
Telephone: 919-839-0300
Facsimile: 919-839-0304
URL: http://www.brookspierce.com

Greensboro, North Carolina Office: 2000 Renaissance Plaza, 230 North Elm Street, 27401, P.O. Box 26000, 27420-6000. Telephone: 336-373-8850. Facsimile: 336-378-1001.

General Practice in State and Federal Courts. Administrative, Antitrust, Banking, Bankruptcy, Bonds, Business Litigation, Communications and Media, Corporate, Corporate Finance, Energy, Environmental, Foundations, Insurance, Intellectual Property, Internet, Labor, Legislative, Mergers and Acquisitions, Probate, Public Utilities, Real Estate, Securities, Taxation, Telecommunications and Trade Associations Law.

OF COUNSEL

HENRY E. FRYE, born August 1, 1932; admitted to bar, 1959, North Carolina. *Education:* North Carolina Agricultural & Technical State University (B.S., summa cum laude, 1953); University of North Carolina at Chapel Hill (J.D., with honors, 1959). Board of Editors, North Carolina Law Review, 1958-59. Associate Justice, 1983-99 and Chief Justice, 1999-00, North Carolina Supreme Court. Member, North Carolina House of Representatives, 1968-80 and North Carolina Senate, 1981-82. **Email:** hfrye@brookspierce.com

(This Listing Continued)

BROOKS, PIERCE, McLENDON, HUMPHREY & LEONARD, L.L.P., Raleigh—Continued

MEMBERS OF FIRM

WADE H. HARGROVE, born March 6, 1940; admitted to bar, 1965, North Carolina; 1967, District of Columbia; 1968, U.S. Supreme Court. *Education:* University of North Carolina (A.B., with honors, 1962; J.D., 1965). Jefferson Foundation Scholar. Board of Editors, Federal Communications Bar Journal, 1968-72. Governor's Council on State Goals and Policy, 1974-79. Special Advisor to United States at the International Telecommunications Union Communications Satellite Conference, Geneva, 1983. Commissioner, North Carolina Milk Commission, 1976-78. Chair: North Carolina Security and Privacy Board, 1976-78; North Carolina News Media-Administration of Justice Council, 1978-80. Board of Commissioners, North Carolina Agency for Public Telecommunications, 1988-00. Member: Governor's Telecommunications Policy Task Force, 1978-79; Legislative Study Commission on Open Government, 1990; Member, Board of Visitors University of North Carolina, 1991-94. Member, Board of Trustees, Peace College, 2003. President: North Carolina Center for Public Policy Research, 1994; University of North Carolina Law Alumni Association, 1991. Listed in The Best Lawyers in America in Corporate Law, First Amendment Law, and Energy Law. ***PRACTICE AREAS:*** Communications Law; Intellectual Property; Corporate Law; Public Utility Law; Legislative Representation Law; Energy. ***Email:*** whargrove@brookspierce.com

MARK J. PRAK, born May 8, 1955; admitted to bar, 1980, North Carolina; 1986, U.S. Supreme Court. *Education:* Duke University (A.B., magna cum laude, 1977; J.D., 1980). Editorial Board, Duke Law Journal, 1979-80. Visiting Lecturer in Public Policy, Duke University Terry Sanford Institute of Policy Sciences and Public Affairs, 1992—. The Best Lawyers in America, First Amendment Law. Chair, Constitutional Rights and Responsibilities Section, North Carolina Bar Association, 2003-04. ***PRACTICE AREAS:*** Communications Law; Civil Litigation; Intellectual Property Law. ***Email:*** mprak@brookspierce.com

JOHN W. ORMAND, III, born June 24, 1962; admitted to bar, 1987, North Carolina. *Education:* Wake Forest University (B.A., magna cum laude, 1984); University of North Carolina (J.D., with honors, 1987). ***PRACTICE AREAS:*** Litigation; Construction Law; Personal Injury; Insurance Coverage; Occupational Safety and Health. ***Email:*** jormand@brookspierce.com

MARCUS W. TRATHEN, born June 14, 1965; admitted to bar, 1990, North Carolina. *Education:* University of North Carolina at Chapel Hill (B.A., with highest honors and highest distinction, 1987; J.D., with honors, 1990). Phi Beta Kappa. North Carolina Journal of International Law and Commercial Regulation, Member, 1988-89, Senior Staff, 1989-90. ***PRACTICE AREAS:*** Communications Law; Public Utilities Law; Internet Law; Corporate Law; Intellectual Property Law. ***Email:*** mtrathen@brookspierce.com

J. EDWIN TURLINGTON, born April 25, 1957; admitted to bar, 1982, North Carolina. *Education:* Duke University (B.A., cum laude, 1979); University of North Carolina (J.D., 1982). Law Clerk to Judge Gerald Arnold, N.C. Court of Appeals, 1982-83. Special Assistant/Counsel to U.S. Senator Terry Sanford, 1986-87. Chief of Staff for N.C. Lt. Governor Bob Jordan, 1987-89. Executive Assistant (Chief of Staff) for N.C. Governor James B. Hunt, Jr., 1993-96. Coordinator, Office of former U.S. Senator Bill Bradley, 1997-98. Commissioner, North Carolina Rural Internet Access Authority, 2000-03. ***PRACTICE AREAS:*** Communications Law; Legislative Practice; Government; Technology Law; Corporate Law. ***Email:*** eturlington@brookspierce.com

DAVID KUSHNER, born March 3, 1963; admitted to bar, 1996, North Carolina; U.S. Supreme Court. *Education:* University of North Carolina (A.B., with honors, 1985); Princeton University (Ph.D., 1990); Duke University (J.D., with high honors, 1996). Phi Beta Kappa; Morehead Scholar; Order of the Coif. Senior Editor, Alaska Law Review, 1995-96. Law Clerk to Judge Sam J. Ervin, III, U.S. Court of Appeals, Fourth Circuit, 1996-97. ***PRACTICE AREAS:*** Communications; Intellectual Property; Commercial Litigation; Appellate Practice. ***Email:*** dkushner@brookspierce.com

COE W. RAMSEY, born July 5, 1972; admitted to bar, 1998, North Carolina. *Education:* University of North Carolina (B.A., 1994); Wake Forest University (J.D., cum laude, 1998). Order of the Coif. Managing Editor, Wake Forest Law Review, 1997-98. ***Email:*** cramsey@brookspierce.com

ROBERT W. SAUNDERS, born March 3, 1959; admitted to bar, 1987, North Carolina. *Education:* University of North Carolina (B.A., 1982); University of Virginia (J.D., 1987). Daniel Caplin Tax Award, 1987. Editor-in-Chief, Virginia Tax Review, 1986-87. Staff Attorney, Associate Chief Counsel (Litigation), Internal Revenue Service, 1988-89. ***PRACTICE AREAS:*** Tax Exempt Organizations; Public Finance; Taxation; Corporate Law; Estate Planning. ***Email:*** rsaunders@brookspierce.com

CHARLES E. COBLE, born October 30, 1972; admitted to bar, 1998, North Carolina. *Education:* Yale University (B.A., magna cum laude, 1995); Harvard University (J.D., magna cum laude, 1998). Law Clerk to Chief Judge Frank W. Bullock, Jr., U.S. District Court, Middle District of North Carolina, 1998-99. ***Email:*** ccoble@brookspierce.com

CHARLES F. MARSHALL, III, born May 26, 1970; admitted to bar, 1996, North Carolina. *Education:* University of North Carolina at Chapel Hill (B.A., with distinction, 1992; J.D., with honors, 1996). Phi Beta Kappa. Staff Member, North Carolina Journal of International Law and Commercial Regulation, 1995-96. Law Clerk to Judge John D. Butzner, Jr., U.S. Court of Appeals, Fourth Circuit, 1996-97. Attorney, Appellate Section, Tax Division, U.S. Department of Justice, 1997-01. Legislative Assistant to U.S. Senator Mitch McConnell, 2001-02. ***Email:*** cmarshall@brookspierce.com

PATRICK J. JOHNSON, born September 10, 1969; admitted to bar, 1994, Virginia; 1996, New York; 2005, North Carolina. *Education:* University of Virginia (B.A., 1991; J.D., 1994). Managing Board, Virginia Tax Review, 1993-94. ***PRACTICE AREAS:*** Corporate Law; Mergers, Acquisitions and Divestitures; Securities. ***Email:*** pjohnson@brookspierce.com

STEPHEN G. HARTZELL, born February 20, 1969; admitted to bar, 2000, North Carolina. *Education:* University of Houston (B.A., magna cum laude, 1991); University of North Carolina (J.D., with high honors, 2000). Order of the Coif. Articles Editor, North Carolina Law Review, 1999-00. ***Email:*** shartzell@brookspierce.com

(This Listing Continued)

J. BENJAMIN DAVIS, born October 24, 1971; admitted to bar, 1998, North Carolina. *Education:* Wake Forest University (B.A., magna cum laude, 1994); Yale University (J.D., 1998). Phi Beta Kappa. Managing Editor, Yale Journal of Law and the Humanities, 1996-97. Assistant to the General Counsel, U.S. Army Office of General Counsel, 1998-02. ***PRACTICE AREAS:*** Banking and Financial Services; Communications and Media; Securities; Administrative and Regulatory Law. ***Email:*** bdavis@brookspierce.com

KATHERINE J. CLAYTON, born September 17, 1949; admitted to bar, 2004, North Carolina. *Education:* Vanderbilt University (B.E., Mechanical Engineering, cum laude, 1971); Duke University (M.B.A., 1980); University of North Carolina (J.D., with honors, 2004). Managing Editor, North Carolina Journal of Law and Technology, 2003-04. ***Email:*** kclayton@brookspierce.com

ELIZABETH E. SPAINHOUR, born July 31, 1973; admitted to bar, 2005, North Carolina. *Education:* Dartmouth College (B.A., cum laude, 1995); University of North Carolina at Chapel Hill (M.A., 2002; J.D., with honors, 2005). Comments Editor, North Carolina Law Review, 2004-2005. ***Email:*** espainhour@brookspierce.com

JAMES T. WILLIAMS, JR., born July 21, 1940; admitted to bar, 1966, North Carolina. *Education:* Wake Forest University (B.A., 1962; LL.B., cum laude, 1966). Associate Editor, Wake Forest Law Review, 1965-66. Trustee, Wake Forest University, 2002—. Listed in The Best Lawyers in America, Antitrust Law and Commercial Litigation. Fellow, American College of Trial Lawyers (Chair, North Carolina Committee, 2002-04). (Also at Greensboro Office). ***PRACTICE AREAS:*** Civil Litigation; General Corporate Law; Public Utilities Law; Education Law. ***Email:*** jwilliams@brookspierce.com

M. DANIEL McGINN, born July 30, 1942; admitted to bar, 1967, North Carolina. *Education:* Wake Forest University (A.B., magna cum laude, 1964; J.D., cum laude, 1967). Phi Beta Kappa. Associate Editor, Wake Forest Law Review, 1966-67. Attorney, National Labor Relations Board, 1967, 1970. Listed in The Best Lawyers in America, Labor and Employment Law. Chair, Labor and Employment Law Section, North Carolina Bar Association, 1987-88. Fellow, American College of Trial Lawyers. (Also at Greensboro Office). ***PRACTICE AREAS:*** Labor Law; Employment Law; Civil Litigation. ***Email:*** dmcginn@brookspierce.com

WILLIAM G. McNAIRY, born September 20, 1943; admitted to bar, 1973, North Carolina. *Education:* University of North Carolina (B.S., 1965); University of Virginia (M.B.A., 1967); College of William and Mary in Virginia (J.D., 1973). Certified Public Accountant, North Carolina, 1970. Listed in The Best Lawyers in America, Tax Law and Trusts and Estates. (Also at Greensboro Office). ***PRACTICE AREAS:*** Taxation Law; Banking Law; Corporate Finance Law. ***Email:*** bmcnairy@brookspierce.com

EDWARD C. WINSLOW, III, born May 11, 1946; admitted to bar, 1974, North Carolina. *Education:* Davidson College (B.A., 1968); University of Montpellier, Montpellier, France; University of North Carolina (J.D., with high honors, 1974). Order of the Coif. Staff Member, North Carolina Law Review, 1973-74. Listed in The Best Lawyers in America, Financial Institutions Law. Chair, Business Law Section, North Carolina Bar Association, 1987-89. Member, North Carolina General Statutes Commission, 1998—. (Also at Greensboro Office). ***PRACTICE AREAS:*** Banking Law; Civil Litigation; General Corporate Law. ***Email:*** ewinslow@brookspierce.com

GEORGE W. HOUSE, born December 7, 1946; admitted to bar, 1973, Virginia; 1977, North Carolina. *Education:* Davidson College (B.A., cum laude, 1969); University of Virginia (J.D., 1972). Editor, Virginia Journal of International Law, 1971-72. Listed in The Best Lawyers in America, Energy Law, Environmental Law, and Natural Resources Law. Chair, Environment and Natural Resource Law Section, North Carolina Bar Association, 2001-02. (Also at Greensboro Office). ***PRACTICE AREAS:*** Environmental and Natural Resources Law; Construction Law; Civil Litigation. ***Email:*** ghouse@brookspierce.com

MARC D. BISHOP, born September 6, 1959; admitted to bar, 1984, North Carolina. *Education:* University of North Carolina (B.A., 1981; J.D., 1984). Phi Beta Kappa. Note and Comment Editor, North Carolina Law Review, 1983-84. Listed in The Best Lawyers in America, Corporate Law. (Also at Greensboro Office). ***PRACTICE AREAS:*** Mergers and Acquisitions; Corporate Finance; Venture Capital; General Corporate. ***Email:*** mbishop@brookspierce.com

JIM W. PHILLIPS, JR., born April 6, 1957; admitted to bar, 1984, North Carolina. *Education:* University of North Carolina (B.A., 1979); Wake Forest University (J.D., magna cum laude, 1984). Listed in The Best Lawyers in America, Commercial Litigation. Editor-in-Chief, Wake Forest Law Review, 1983-84. Legislative Counsel to North Carolina Governor James B. Hunt, Jr., 1993-94, 1996. Member, University of North Carolina Board of Governors, 1997—. (Also at Greensboro Office). ***PRACTICE AREAS:*** Civil Litigation; Legislative Representative Law; Intellectual Property Law. ***Email:*** jphillips@brookspierce.com

JEFFREY E. OLEYNIK, born July 22, 1958; admitted to bar, 1983, Texas; 1987, North Carolina. *Education:* College of William and Mary in Virginia (B.A., 1980); University of Virginia (J.D., 1983). Phi Beta Kappa; Order of the Coif. Editorial Board Member, Virginia Law Review, 1982-83. Listed in The Best Lawyers in America, Antitrust Law. Council Member, 1996-99, and Chair, 2001-02, Bankruptcy Law Section; Council Member, 1997—, and Chair, 2004-05, Antitrust and Trade Regulation Law Section, North Carolina Bar Association. (Also at Greensboro Office). ***PRACTICE AREAS:*** Civil Litigation; Commercial Bankruptcy; Antitrust. ***Email:*** joleynik@brookspierce.com

DAVID W. SAR, born August 12, 1971; admitted to bar, 1996, North Carolina. *Education:* Duke University (B.A., magna cum laude, 1992); Yale University (J.D., 1996). Phi Beta Kappa. Articles Editor, Yale Journal on Regulation, 1995-96. (Also at Greensboro Office). ***PRACTICE AREAS:*** Civil Litigation; Intellectual Property. ***Email:*** dsar@brookspierce.com

REPRESENTATIVE CLIENTS: ABC, Inc.; ABC-TV Network Affiliates Association; Associated Press; Bank of New York; City of Greensboro; Deloitte & Touche LLP; Electronic News Directors Association; FNB Financial Services Corporation; Greensboro College; Guilford County Board of Education; Hearst-Argyle Television; KPMG, LLP; Leggett & Platt, Incorporated; Lorillard Tobacco Co.; MCNC, Inc.; NC Association of Broadcasters; NC Association of Convenience Stores; NC Bankers Association; NC Cable Telecommunications Association; NC Technology Association; Norfolk Southern Railway Co.; Northstar Travel Media, LLC; Performance, Inc.; Piedmont Triad Airport Authority; Red Hat, Inc.; The Hearst Corpo-

(This Listing Continued)

ration; The New York Times Co.; Time Warner; University of North Carolina; US Greenfiber, LLC; Weyerhaeuser Co.

(For complete biographical data on all personnel, see Professional Biographies at Greensboro)

BROOKS, STEVENS & POPE, P.A.

RALEIGH, NORTH CAROLINA

(See Cary)

General Civil and Appellate Practice, Employment Law, OSHA, Workers' Compensation, Insurance, Self-Insurance, Municipal and Family Law.

BROUGHTON & FERNANDEZ

Established in 1993

4030 WAKE FOREST ROAD, SUITE 300
RALEIGH, NORTH CAROLINA 27609
Telephone: 919-719-2722
Fax: 919-719-2799
Email: johnfernandez@raleightriallawyers.com
URL: http://www.raleightriallawyers.com

Civil Litigation, Personal Injury, Automobile Accidents, Truck Accidents, Wrongful Death.

ALLEN L. BROUGHTON, born Texas City, Texas, October 8, 1968; admitted to bar, 1993, Georgia; 1994, District of Columbia (Not admitted in North Carolina). *Education:* University of North Carolina, Chapel Hill (B.S./B.A., 1990; J.D., 1993). President, University of North Carolina Law Class of 1993. Associate, Hawkins & Parnell, Atlanta, Georgia, 1993-1999. *Member:* State Bar of Georgia; North Carolina State Bar; District of Columbia Bar; American Bar Association; The Association of Trial Lawyers of America; Georgia Trial Lawyers Association. (Resident, Roswell, Georgia Office). ***PRACTICE AREAS:*** Personal Injury; Civil Litigation; Business Law; Government; Civil Rights; Premises Liability; Insurance; Medical Malpractice; Products Liability. ***Email:*** alb@atlantatriallawyers.com

JOHN P. FERNANDEZ, born Boston, Massachusetts, July 18, 1963; admitted to bar, 1993, North Carolina and U.S. District Court, Middle District of North Carolina. *Education:* North Carolina Central University (B.A., magna cum laude, 1990); University of North Carolina at Chapel Hill (J.D., 1993). Court Appointed Arbitrator, Wake County Judicial System. *Member:* North Carolina State Bar; North Carolina Academy of Trial Lawyers; The Association of Trial Lawyers of America; Raleigh Trial Lawyers Partnership. [U.S. Marine Corp., 1981-1985]. ***LANGUAGES:*** Spanish. ***PRACTICE AREAS:*** Personal Injury; Wrongful Death. ***Email:*** johnfernandez@raleightriallawyers.com

STEPHANIE J. BROWN

Established in 1992

916 ROCK QUARRY ROAD, SUITE 116
RALEIGH, NORTH CAROLINA 27610
Telephone: 919-836-9444
Fax: 919-836-9409
Email: sjbrown_law@hotmail.com
URL: http://www.sjbrown-law.com

Criminal Law, Driving While Intoxicated, Drug Crimes, Felonies, Misdemeanors, Parole and Probation, Traffic Violations, Family Law, Child Custody, Child Support, Divorce, Visitation Rights, Automobile Accidents, Social Security Disability.

STEPHANIE J. BROWN, born Iredel County, October 20, 1966; admitted to bar, 1992, North Carolina. *Education:* North Carolina State University (B.A., 1989); Wake Forest University (J.D., 1992). *Member:* North Carolina Bar Association; North Carolina State Bar; North Carolina Academy of Trial Lawyers; Capital City Lawyers. ***PRACTICE AREAS:*** Family Law; Criminal Law; Social Security Disability.

BROWN & BUNCH, PLLC

4900 FALLS OF NEUSE ROAD, SUITE 210
POST OFFICE BOX 19409
RALEIGH, NORTH CAROLINA 27619-9409
Telephone: 919-878-8060
FAX: 919-878-8062
Email: brownandbunch@mindspring.com

Chapel Hill, North Carolina Office: 101 North Columbia Street, 27514. Telephone: 919-968-1111. Fax: 919-968-1444.
Durham, North Carolina Office: 21 West Colony Place, Suite 250, 27705. Telephone: 919-490-9700. Fax: 919-419-9736.

General Practice in all State and Federal Courts, Administrative Law, Antitrust Litigation, Appeals, Collections, Commercial Litigation, Commercial Transactions, Construction, Corporate Practice, Creditors' Rights, Employment Law, Estates and Trusts, Health Law, Lender Liability Defense, Mediation, Municipal and Land Use Law, Real Estate, State and Federal Taxation, Trade Regulation and Trials.

MEMBERS OF FIRM

CHARLES GORDON BROWN, born Winston-Salem, North Carolina, July 31, 1950; admitted to bar, 1975, Georgia; 1978, North Carolina, U.S. District Court, Eastern, Middle and Western Districts of North Carolina and Northern District of Georgia and U.S. Court of Appeals, Fourth Circuit. *Education:* University of North Carolina (A.B., summa cum laude, 1972); University of Virginia (J.D., 1975). Phi Beta Kappa; Order of the Coif; Phi Delta Phi. Member, Editorial Board, Virginia Law Review, 1974-1975. Assistant Professor of Law, 1978-1981 and Visiting Assistant Professor of Law, 1977-1978, University of North Carolina. Visiting Assistant Professor of Law, University of Texas, 1979. Bar Examination Lecturer, North Carolina Bar Association, 1981-1985. Recipient, Frederick B. McCall Award for Excellence in Teaching, 1980 and 1981. Reporter for N.C. Pattern Jury Instructions Committee, 1979-1981 and 1985-2003. Member, North Carolina State Bar Ethics Committee, 1997-2002. *Member:* Orange County and North Carolina (Member, Antitrust, Real Estate and Business Sections) Bar Associations; North Carolina State Bar; State Bar of Georgia. (Resident, Chapel Hill Office). ***PRACTICE AREAS:*** Trade Regulation; Commercial Litigation; Commercial Transactions. ***Email:*** gbrown@brownandbunch.com

(This Listing Continued)

WILLIAM W. BUNCH, III, born Edenton, North Carolina, October 18, 1954; admitted to bar, 1980, North Carolina, U.S. District Court, Eastern District of North Carolina and U.S. Court of Appeals, Fourth Circuit. *Education:* University of North Carolina (B.S., 1977; J.D., 1980). Beta Gamma Sigma; Phi Delta Phi. *Member:* Wake County, North Carolina (Member, Real Property Section) and American Bar Associations; North Carolina State Bar. (Resident). ***PRACTICE AREAS:*** Commercial Real Estate; Real Estate Development. ***Email:*** bbunch@brownandbunch.net

WILLIAM D. BERNARD, born Minneapolis, Minnesota, May 14, 1956; admitted to bar, 1982, Tennessee and U.S. District Court, Middle District of Tennessee; 1984, North Carolina and U.S. District Court, Middle and Eastern Districts of North Carolina; 1986, U.S. District Court, Western District of North Carolina. *Education:* University of North Carolina (B.A., 1978; M.B.A., 1982; J.D., 1982). *Member:* Orange County, North Carolina (Member, Real Property and Business Law Sections) and American Bar Associations; North Carolina State Bar. (Resident, Chapel Hill Office). ***PRACTICE AREAS:*** Commercial Law; Residential and Commercial Real Estate. ***Email:*** wbernard@brownandbunch.com

A. VANN IRVIN, born Shelby, North Carolina, January 14, 1951; admitted to bar, 1982, Tennessee; 1984, Georgia; 1986, North Carolina; 1993, U.S. Tax Court and U.S. Court of Appeals, Fourth and Sixth Circuits. *Education:* College of Albemarle (A.A., 1971); University of North Carolina (B.A., 1973; J.D., 1982). *Member:* Durham County, North Carolina and American Bar Associations; State Bar of Georgia; North Carolina State Bar. (Board Certified Specialist in Estate Planning and Probate Law, North Carolina State Board of Legal Specialization) (Resident, Durham Office). ***PRACTICE AREAS:*** Trusts and Estates; Wills; Business Law; Probate; Taxation; Corporate Law. ***Email:*** vannirvin@aol.com

LEANN NEASE BROWN, born Greensboro, North Carolina, May 7, 1955; admitted to bar, 1984, North Carolina, U.S. District Court, Eastern and Middle Districts of North Carolina, U.S. Court of Appeals, Fourth Circuit and U.S. Tax Court. *Education:* University of North Carolina (B.A., 1977); University of North Carolina School of Medical Allied Health Sciences (M.S., 1981); University of North Carolina School of Law (J.D., 1984). *Member:* Orange County, North Carolina (Member, Sections on: Litigation; Dispute Resolution; Health Law; Chair, 1996-1997, Antitrust and Trade Regulation; Chair, Trial Practice Curriculum Committee, 2002-2005; Member, CLE Committee, 2002—; Zoning, Planning and Land Use, Secretary 2005—) and American Bar Associations; North Carolina State Bar. D.R.C. Certified Mediator, Superior Court Matters and Family Financial Matters, North Carolina. (Resident, Chapel Hill Office). ***PRACTICE AREAS:*** Litigation; Zoning, Planning and Land Use; Health Law; Employment Law; Mediation. ***Email:*** lnease@brownandbunch.com

SCOTT D. ZIMMERMAN, born Berea, Ohio, June 1, 1963; admitted to bar, 1989, North Carolina, U.S. District Court, Eastern and Middle Districts of North Carolina and U.S. Court of Appeals, Fourth Circuit. *Education:* University of North Carolina (B.A., 1985; J.D., with honors, 1989). *Member:* Orange County, North Carolina and American Bar Associations; North Carolina State Bar; The Association of Trial Lawyers of America. (Resident, Chapel Hill Office). ***PRACTICE AREAS:*** Civil Litigation. ***Email:*** szimmerman@brownandbunch.com

COUNSEL FOR: Bank of America, N.A.; Mellon Bank, N.A.; SunTrust Bank; Chicago Title Insurance Company; Investors Title Insurance Company; Kenan Enterprises, Inc.; Town of Cary; Dycom Industries, LLC; ANSCO & Associates, LLC; Globe Communications, LLC; Hydro Tube Corp.; Fidelity National Title Insurance Company; Horton Enterprises, LLC; Meadowlands Associates; Buckhorn Ridge Associates, LLC; Strategic Properties, LLC; Ford Motor Credit Company; Carolina Hosiery Mills, Inc.
GENERAL COUNSEL FOR: Affordable Care, Inc.; Chapel Hill Internal Medicine, L.L.P.; Crossroads Ford, Inc.; The Educational Foundation, Inc.; Home Health Foundation of Chapel Hill, Inc.; Maximum Advantage Corp.; Orange-Person-Chatham Mental Health, Developmental Disabilities and Substance Abuse Authority; Vicious Cycle Software, Inc.; Winston Hotels, Inc. (NYSE); Worden Bros., Inc.; Centrex Properties, Inc.; First Oakland Properties, Inc.
APPROVED ATTORNEYS FOR: Commonwealth Land Title Insurance Co.; Lawyers Title Insurance Co.; First Title Insurance Co.; Investors Title Insurance Co.; Chicago Title Insurance Co.; Title Company of North Carolina, Inc.; Fidelity National Title Insurance Company.
REFERENCES: Centura Bank; Bank of America; SunTrust Bank.

BROWNLEE LAW FIRM

2501 BLUE RIDGE ROAD, SUITE 150
RALEIGH, NORTH CAROLINA 27607
Telephone: 919-863-4305
Fax: 919-863-4315
Email: will@wkblawfirm.com
URL: http://www.wkblaw-firm.com

Residential and Commercial Real Estate, Landlord-Tenant Law, Business Law, Contracts, Debtor and Creditor, Commercial Leasing, Mechanics Liens.

WILLIAM K. BROWNLEE, born Charleston, South Carolina, February 19, 1971; admitted to bar, 1999, North Carolina. *Education:* The Citadel (B.A., 1993); North Carolina Central University (J.D., 1999). *Member:* Wake County and North Carolina Bar Associations; North Carolina State Bar. ***PRACTICE AREAS:*** Landlord/Tenant Law. ***Email:*** will@wkblawfirm.com

BUMGARDNER & ROSE, P.A.

Established in 1988

3948 BROWNING PLACE, SUITE 100

RALEIGH, NORTH CAROLINA 27609

Telephone: 919-571-1866

Fax: 919-571-0096

Email: bumrose@bumgardner-rose.com

URL: http://www.bumgardner-rose.com

Family Law, Domestic Relations, Divorce, Premarital Agreement, Separation Agreement, Child Custody, Child Support, Visitation Rights, Mediation, Collaborative Law.

FIRM PROFILE: Bumgardner & Rose, P.A. is conveniently located in Raleigh, N.C. We have been in practice since 1988 and have limited our area of concentration primarily to domestic/family law. Our practice includes litigation, mediation and collaborative law.

KATHRYN V. BUMGARDNER, born Winston-Salem, North Carolina, July 4, 1951; admitted to bar, 1988, North Carolina and U.S. District Court, Eastern District of North Carolina. *Education:* North Carolina State University (B.A., 1984); North Carolina Central University School of Law (J.D., 1988). Omicron Delta Epsilon. Phi Alpha Delta. Author: Manuscript, National Business Institute, November 2000. Instructor, Institute for Paralegal Studies, 1982-1991. *Member:* North Carolina Bar Association; North Carolina State Bar; Wake County Family Lawyers Association. ***PRACTICE AREAS:*** Family Law (100%). ***Email:*** kathryn@bumgardner-rose.com

MARGIE E. ROSE, born Asheville, North Carolina, March 11, 1939; admitted to bar, 1988, North Carolina and U.S. District Court, Eastern District of north Carolina. *Education:* Duke University (B.A., 1961); University of North Carolina School of Public Health (MSPH, 1968); North Carolina Central University School of Law (J.D., 1987). Delta Omega. Member, American Public Health Association. Instructor, Regional Family Planning Training Center, Emory University, 1989-1997 and University of North Carolina School of Public Health, 1989-1997. ***PRACTICE AREAS:*** Family Law. ***Email:*** margie@bumgardner-rose.com

BURNS, DAY & PRESNELL, P.A.

Established in 1987

SUITE 560, 2626 GLENWOOD AVENUE

P.O. BOX 10867

RALEIGH, NORTH CAROLINA 27605

Telephone: 919-782-1441

Fax: 919-782-2311

URL: http://www.burnsdaylaw.com

General Practice in State and Federal Courts and Administrative Agencies. Commercial, Construction and Insurance Litigation, Arbitration and Mediation, Public Utilities, Telecommunication, Real Property, Corporate and Probate Law, Bankruptcy and Business Reorganizations.

DAVID W. BOONE, born Raleigh, North Carolina, July 19, 1953; admitted to bar, 1979, North Carolina; U.S. District Court, Eastern, Middle and Western Districts of North Carolina; U.S. Court of Appeals, Fourth Circuit. *Education:* East Carolina University (B.A., 1974; European Studies Minor earned in Bonn, Germany; M.A., 1976); Wake Forest University (J.D., 1979). Pi Sigma Alpha; Order of Barristers. Moot Court Board (Chief Justice, 1978-1979). Certified Mediator, Court-Ordered Mediation. ***PRACTICE AREAS:*** Business Reorganizations; Commercial Litigation; Mediation. ***Email:*** dboone@bdppa.com

JAMES M. DAY, born Lafayette, Indiana, September 14, 1950; admitted to bar, 1975, North Carolina and U.S. District Court, Eastern District of North Carolina; 1980, U.S. District Court, Middle District of North Carolina and U.S. Supreme Court. *Education:* Purdue University (B.S.A.E., 1972); Wake Forest University (J.D., 1975). Phi Delta Phi. Recipient: American Jurisprudence Award in Corporations and Real Property; Bureau of National Affairs, Inc., Third Year Class Award. Member, American Institute of Aeronautics and Astronautics, 1971-1974. *Member:* Wake County and North Carolina (Member, Sections on: Business Law; Real Property) Bar Associations; North Carolina State Bar; Wake County Real Property Lawyers Association (President, 1990). ***PRACTICE AREAS:*** Real Estate-Commercial Law; Corporate Law; Business Law. ***Email:*** jday@bdppa.com

DANIEL C. HIGGINS, born Orange, Virginia, August 22, 1954; admitted to bar, 1981, North Carolina and Virginia; 1982, U.S. District Court, Western and Eastern Districts of North Carolina; 1984, U.S. Court of Appeals, Fourth Circuit; 1985, U.S. District Court, Middle District of North Carolina. *Education:* Madison College (B.A., 1976) Omicron Delta Kappa; College of William & Mary (J.D., 1981). Assistant Attorney General, State of North Carolina, 1981-1986. *Member:* Wake County and North Carolina (Member, Construction and Litigation Sections) Bar Associations; North Carolina State Bar; Virginia State Bar. ***PRACTICE AREAS:*** Public Utility Law; Telecommunications Law; Business Law; Commercial Litigation. ***Email:*** dhiggins@bdppa.com

GREG L. HINSHAW, born Burlington, North Carolina, April 19, 1950; admitted to bar, 1975, North Carolina; 1977, U.S. District Court, Eastern District of North Carolina. *Education:* University of North Carolina (B.S., 1972); Wake Forest University (J.D., 1975). Phi Delta Phi. *Member:* Wake County and North Carolina (Member, Real Property, Construction and Probate Sections) Bar Associations; North Carolina State Bar; Wake County Real Property Lawyers Association. ***PRACTICE AREAS:*** Estate Planning Law; Probate Law; Real Estate-Residential Law; Real Estate-Commercial Law. ***Email:*** ghinshaw@bdppa.com

LACY M. PRESNELL III, born Asheboro, North Carolina, June 28, 1951; admitted to bar, 1976, North Carolina; 1980, U.S. District Court, Eastern and Middle Districts of North Carolina and U.S. Supreme Court; 1981, U.S. Court of Appeals, Fourth Circuit. *Education:* University of North Carolina at Chapel Hill (A.B., 1973); Wake Forest University (J.D., 1976). Phi Delta Phi. Associate Editor, Wake Forest Law Review, 1975-1976. Assistant Investigator, U.S. Senate Select Committee on Presidential Campaign Activities, 1973. Woodward/White: The Best Lawyers in America (Personal Injury Law). Certified Mediator, Court-Ordered Mediation. *Member:* Wake County (President, 2003), 10th Judicial District, North Carolina and American Bar Associations; North Carolina State Bar; North Carolina Academy of Trial Lawyers. (Certified as a Civil Trial Specialist by the National Board of Trial Advocacy). ***PRACTICE AREAS:*** Litigation in State and Federal Courts; Arbitration and Mediation. ***Email:*** lpresnell@bdppa.com

JULIA M. YOUNG, born Whiteville, North Carolina, November 12, 1973; admitted to bar, 2000, North Carolina; 2001, U.S. District Court, Eastern, Middle and Western Districts of North Carolina and U.S. Court of Appeals, Fourth Circuit. *Education:* North Carolina State University (B.A., 1996); Campbell University (J.D., 2000). *Member:* Wake County, North Carolina (Member, Litigation and Employment Law Sections; Co-Chair, 2002-2005, Peer Mediation Task Force; Member, Young Lawyers Division Executive Council) and American Bar Associations; North Carolina State Bar. ***PRACTICE AREAS:*** Employment Law; Construction Law; Commercial Litigation. ***Email:*** jyoung@bdppa.com

RETIRED

F. KENT BURNS, born Winston-Salem, North Carolina, September 2, 1929; admitted to bar, 1955, North Carolina; 1959, U.S. District Court, Eastern and Middle Districts of North Carolina; 1966, U.S. Court of Appeals, Fourth Circuit; 1973, District of Columbia; 1975, U.S. Supreme Court; 1977, U.S. Court of Appeals, Fifth Circuit. *Education:* Duke University (A.B., 1950); University of North Carolina (J.D., 1955). (Retired). ***PRACTICE AREAS:*** Public Utility Law; Transportation Law.

REPRESENTATIVE CLIENTS: Alltel Corp.; Alltel Communications, Inc.; Wachovia Bank; Regions Bank; Tier One Bank; Mid Carolina Bank; First Indiana Bank; Beazer Homes Corp.; Randolph Telephone Co.; Ellerbe Telephone Co.; Citizens Telephone Company; Town of Pineville; United States Cellular Telephone Co.; Austin-Mullins Associates; Benchmark Homes Co.; Dan C. Austin & Associates, Inc.; Precision Walls, Inc.; Keystone Corp.; TDS Telecom, Inc.; DTE Biomass Energy, Inc.
APPROVED ATTORNEYS FOR: Lawyers Title Insurance Corp.; Stewart Title Insurance Corp.; Commonwealth Land Title Insurance Corp.; Fidelity National Title Insurance Corp.; Safeco Title; Investors Title; Chicago Title; Republic National Title; Surety Title.
REFERENCE: Branch Banking and Trust Company.

THE BUSSIAN LAW FIRM PLLC

WACHOVIA CAPITOL CENTER

16TH FLOOR

150 FAYETTEVILLE STREET MALL

RALEIGH, NORTH CAROLINA 27601

Telephone: 919-829-4900

Fax: 919-829-2165

Constitutional, Intellectual Property, Corporate and Securities Law in all Courts.

JOHN A. BUSSIAN III, admitted to bar, 1980, Florida; 1983, U.S. Supreme Court; 1985, District of Columbia; 1988, North Carolina; 1993, Texas. *Education:* Duke University (B.A., 1976); Georgetown University Law Center (J.D., 1979). Co-Author: Florida Press Association's *Reporter's Handbook,* North Carolina Media Law Handbook. Chairman, Southern Newspaper Publishers' Association First Amendment Committee; Member, American Society of Newspapers Editors Freedom of Information Committee. ***PRACTICE AREAS:*** Constitutional Law; Media Law; Intellectual Property Law. ***Email:*** jbussian@bellsouth.net

LAW OFFICE OF DEREK R. CALDWELL, P.A.

Established in 2002

211 EAST SIX FORKS ROAD, SUITE 210-A

P.O. BOX 19242

RALEIGH, NORTH CAROLINA 27619

Telephone: 919-838-9400

Fax: 919-834-1031

Email: derekcaldwell_attorney@yahoo.com

Email: derek@derekcaldwelllaw.com

URL: http://www.derekcaldwelllaw.com

Bankruptcy, Personal Bankruptcy, Chapter 7, Chapter 13, Consumer and Business Bankruptcy, Personal Injury, Automobile Accidents, Wrongful Death, Mediation, Business Law, Consumer Law, Lemon Law, Fair Debt Collection Practices.

DEREK R. CALDWELL, born Fort Walton Beach, Florida, July 25, 1959; admitted to bar, 1995, North Carolina. *Education:* University of Colorado (B.A., 1990); Chicago-Kent College of Law (J.D., 1995). Phi Beta Kappa. Certified Superior Court Mediator. *Member:* Wake County, North Carolina and American Bar Associations; North Carolina State Bar; National Association of Consumer Bankruptcy Attorneys. ***LANGUAGES:*** French. ***Email:*** derek@derekcaldwelllaw.com

JOHN E. CAMPION

5 WEST HARGETT STREET

SUITE 810

P.O. BOX 2656

RALEIGH, NORTH CAROLINA 27602

Telephone: 919-239-0260

Fax: 919-239-0261

Email: john@johncampionlaw.com

URL: http://www.johncampionlaw.com

Employment Law, Discrimination, Sexual Harassment, Non-Compete Agreements, Wage and Hour Law, Employment Severance Agreements.

(This Listing Continued)

JOHN E. CAMPION, born Atlanta, Georgia, January 8, 1947; admitted to bar, 1976, Ohio; 1984, North Carolina; 1990, U.S. Supreme Court. *Education:* Ohio State University (B.A., 1969); Case Western Reserve University (J.D., 1976). Order of the Coif. Editor, Case Western Reserve University Law Review, 1975-1976. Author: "Ohio Landlord and Tenant Reform Act," 25 Case Western Reserve University Law Review 876, 1976. Formerly, Assistant General Counsel, Burroughs Wellcome Co., 1982-1995; Glaxo Wellcome Inc., 1995-2001. *Member:* North Carolina State Bar; American Bar Association; North Carolina Academy of Trial Lawyers; National Employment Lawyers Association.

CAPITOL DISTRICT LAW OFFICES

Established in 1992

11 SOUTH BLOUNT STREET
P.O. BOX 25096
RALEIGH, NORTH CAROLINA 27611-5096
Telephone: 919-828-0363
Fax: 919-832-5205
Email: rweaver@capitolaw.com
URL: http://www.capitolaw.com

Civil Practice in State and Federal Courts. Trials and Appeals. Employment Law, including Discrimination, Retaliatory Discharge, Whistleblower Litigation, Sexual Harassment, Contracts, Covenants Not To Compete, Executive Severance Contracts, Professional Licensing. False Claims Act, Qui Tam Litigation, Wrongful Death, Personal Injury, Arbitration and Mediation, Wrongful Termination, Title VII Discrimination, Equal Employment Opportunity Law.

FIRM PROFILE: Capitol District Law Offices was founded in 1992 by Reagan H. Weaver. It is primarily an employment law firm that focuses on employee rights. The firm's predominant practice is in the representation of employees, both government and corporate. The firm maintains a personal injury practice as well. Mr. Weaver is a practicing certified Mediator and Arbitrator.

MEMBER OF FIRM

REAGAN HALE WEAVER, born Greensboro, North Carolina, August 29, 1951; admitted to bar, 1984, North Carolina. *Education:* University of North Carolina at Chapel Hill (B.A., 1973; M.B.A., 1984; J.D., 1984). Recipient, Center for Public Resources Legal Program Award for Excellence and Innovation in Alternative Dispute Management, 1983 for article "Orders of Reference: Ready and Waiting for Imaginative Lawyers?" Author: "Interracial and Cross-Cultural Relations," Journal of Intergroup Relations, 1980. Member, Commercial Panel of Arbitrators, American Arbitration Association. Administrative Law Judge, North Carolina Safety and Health Review Board, 2004—. *Member:* Wake County, North Carolina (Chair and Vice-Chair, Dispute Resolution Section, 1993-1995) and American Bar Associations; North Carolina State Bar; North Carolina Academy of Trial Lawyers; American Academy of Trial Lawyers. ***PRACTICE AREAS:*** Employment Law; Personal Injury; Workers Compensation; Civil Rights; False Claims Act; Arbitration; Mediation. ***Email:*** rweaver@capitolaw.com

LEGAL SUPPORT PERSONNEL

BARBARA L. WESTPHAL. *Education:* Nassau Community College (A.A., Paralegal Studies, 1990). (Paralegal). ***Email:*** bwestphal@capitolaw.com

PAUL CARRUTH

Established in 1974

5834 FARINGDON PLACE, SUITE 1
RALEIGH, NORTH CAROLINA 27609
Telephone: 919-872-8225
Fax: 919-872-8335
Email: carruthlaw@aol.com
URL: http://www.lawyers.com/carruthlaw

Real Estate, Wills, Trusts and Estates, Probate, Family Law, Mediation and Arbitration, General Practice.

FIRM PROFILE: A General Civil Family Practice Firm convenient to clients in Wake County and surrounding counties in central North Carolina.

PAUL CARRUTH, born Raleigh, North Carolina, July 30, 1948; admitted to bar, 1974, North Carolina; 1975, U.S. District Court, Eastern District of North Carolina. *Education:* North Carolina State University-Raleigh; Duke University (B.A., 1970); University of North Carolina-Chapel Hill (J.D., 1973). Certified Trial Court Mediator, North Carolina, 1995. Court appointed Arbitrator, Wake County, North Carolina District Court, 1998-1999. *Member:* Wake County (Member, Board of Directors, 1999-2000, Member, Fee Arbitration Committee), North Carolina (Lawyer Effectiveness and Quality of Life Committee) and American Bar Associations. ***PRACTICE AREAS:*** Real Estate; Wills; Trusts and Estates; Arbitration and Mediation.

REPRESENTATIVE CLIENTS: Central Carolina Bank; GMAC Mortgage; Branch Banking and Trust; Sister's Catering; United Methodist Church; Zest, Inc.; Carolina Cardiology Consulatnts, P.A.; Mumford Restoration, Inc.; Freedom Properties, LLC; Preservation Homes, LLC; Primary Relocation, L.L.C.

DAVID R. CHAMBERS

3110 EDWARDS MILL ROAD, SUITE 340
RALEIGH, NORTH CAROLINA 27612
Telephone: 919-277-2200
Fax: 919-277-2525
Email: drcestate@aol.com
URL: http://www.davidrchambers.com

Estate Planning, Wealth Transfer, Asset Protection, Tax Planning, Charitable Giving.

(This Listing Continued)

FIRM PROFILE: The mission of David R. Chambers, J.D., LL.M., Attorney and Counselor at Law, is to satisfy my clients by providing the highest quality estate planning services possible, I do this by constantly keeping abreast of changes in estate planning and tax law by working closely with my clients and their financial advisors.

DAVID R. CHAMBERS, born Durham, North Carolina, August 6, 1953; admitted to bar, 1981, South Carolina; 1982, North Carolina. *Education:* University of North Carolina (B.A., 1976); North Carolina Central University (J.D., 1979); University of Miami (LL.M., Estate Planning, 1998). *Member:* North Carolina State Bar; South Carolina State Bar; North Carolina Bar Association; Christian Legal Society. ***PRACTICE AREAS:*** Estate Planning; Wills; Trust; Tax Planning.

PETER CHASTAIN & ASSOCIATES, P.A.

RALEIGH, NORTH CAROLINA

(See Greensboro)

Real Estate, Commercial Law.

CHESHIRE, PARKER, SCHNEIDER, BRYAN & VITALE

Established in 1978

133 FAYETTEVILLE STREET MALL, SUITE 500
P.O. BOX 1029
RALEIGH, NORTH CAROLINA 27602-1029
Telephone: 919-833-3114
Fax: 919-832-0739

Federal and State Criminal Trials and Appeals. Professional Discipline and Regulatory Law, Ethics. Family Law, Divorce, Alimony, Child Custody, Equitable Distribution, Civil Trial Defense.

MEMBERS OF FIRM

JOSEPH B. CHESHIRE, V, born Raleigh, North Carolina, May 19, 1947; admitted to bar, 1973, North Carolina and U.S. District Court, Eastern, Middle and Western Districts of North Carolina; U.S. Court of Appeals, Fourth Circuit; U.S. Supreme Court. *Education:* Groton School, Groton, Massachusetts; University of North Carolina (B.A., 1970); Wake Forest University (J.D., 1973). Chief Justice and Founding Member, Wake Forest Moot Court. Member, The International Society of Barristers. Lecturer: The Association of Trial Lawyers of America; Law Education Institute; Florida Criminal Defense Association; North Carolina Academy of Trial Lawyers; South Carolina Academy of Trial Lawyers; North Carolina Bar Association; North Carolina State Bar; Wake Forest University, School of Law; University of North Carolina at Chapel Hill; Campbell University School of Law; North Carolina State University; Superstars Seminar, Atlanta, Georgia Association of Trial Lawyers of America; Professor of Litigation, Meredith College Legal Assistants School, 1980-1982. Special Prosecutor for Wake County, 1977. Member, Committee on Indigent Appointments, 1977-1981. Member, Magistrate Selection Commission, U.S. District Court. Member, Discretionary Fund Commission, U.S. District Court. Member: Legislative Indigent Fund Study Commission, 1999-2000. Chair, 2003— and Commissioner, 2001—, Indigent Defense Services Commission for the State of North Carolina. *Member:* Wake County (Member, Board of Directors, 1977-1978 and 2005—), North Carolina (Member, Criminal Justice Section Board Member, 1982-1983 and 1997-2004; Chair, 1998-2000; Board of Governors, 2001-2004; Executive Committee, 2002-2003) and American Bar Associations; North Carolina State Bar (Founding Chairman, Criminal Law Specialization Committee, 1988-1995); Wake County Academy of Criminal Trial Lawyers; North Carolina Academy of Trial Lawyers (Member, Board of Governors, 1985-1994; Executive Committee, 2004—; Founder and Chairman, Criminal Law Section, 1985-1989); National Association of Criminal Defense Lawyers; Fellow, American Board of Criminal Lawyers; Association of Professional Responsibility Lawyers. (Board Certified Specialist in Criminal Law, North Carolina State Board of Legal Specialization). ***PRACTICE AREAS:*** Criminal Trials and Appeals; Professional Discipline Law; Legal Ethics; Civil Trial Defense. ***Email:*** joe.cheshire@cheshirepark.com

JOHN H. PARKER, born High Point, North Carolina, February 1, 1944; admitted to bar, 1969, North Carolina; U.S. District Court, Eastern District of North Carolina; U.S. Court of Appeals, Fourth Circuit and U.S. Supreme Court. *Education:* University of North Carolina at Chapel Hill (B.A., 1966); University of Tennessee at Knoxville (J.D., 1969). Private practice, 1969-1976. District Court Judge, 10th Judicial District, North Carolina, 1976-1982. *Member:* Wake County and North Carolina (Vice Chairman, 1983-1984 and Chairman, 1984-1985, Family Law Section; Editor, Family Law Forum, 1983-1988; Member, Family Law Continuing Legal Education Curriculum Committee, 1979—, Chairman, 1986, 1987, 1996, 1997, 1998; Member, Trial Practice Curriculum Committee, 2003—) Bar Associations; North Carolina State Bar; North Carolina Academy of Trial Lawyers; American Academy of Matrimonial Lawyers (Member, Ethics Committee, 1995-1996; President, N.C. Chapter, 1999-2000); American College of Family Trial Lawyers (Diplomat). ***PRACTICE AREAS:*** Family Law; Divorce; Alimony, Child Custody and Equitable Distribution. ***Email:*** john.parker@cheshirepark.com

ALAN MARC SCHNEIDER, born New York, N.Y., May 10, 1964; admitted to bar, 1990, North Carolina and U.S. District Court, Eastern and Middle Districts of North Carolina. *Education:* State University of New York at Binghamton, (B.A., 1986); California Western School of Law (J.D., 1990). *Member:* Wake County and North Carolina Bar Associations (Ethics Chair, Criminal Justice Section, 2001—); North Carolina State Bar; North Carolina Academy of Trial Lawyers; Wake County Criminal Trial Lawyers Association; Association of Professional Responsibility Lawyers. ***PRACTICE AREAS:*** Professional Discipline Defense. ***Email:*** alan.schneider@cheshirepark.com

KIMBERLY W. BRYAN, born High Point, North Carolina; admitted to bar, 1992, North Carolina and U.S. District Court, Eastern District of North Carolina. *Education:* North Carolina State University (B.A., 1980); Campbell University (J.D., 1992). Lecturer

(This Listing Continued)

CHESHIRE, PARKER, SCHNEIDER, BRYAN & VITALE, Raleigh—Continued

and Author: "When Is It Deceptive Not To Disclose?" Trial Briefs, July 1999; "How to Try a Custody Case Without Vilifying the Other Spouse," N.C. Academy of Trial Lawyers, October 2000. Certified Mediator, N.C. Dispute Resolution Commission. *Member:* Wake County, North Carolina (Member, Section on: Family Law; Member, CLE Committee) and American (Member, Family Law Section) Bar Associations; North Carolina State Bar; North Carolina Association of Women Attorneys; North Carolina Academy of Trial Lawyers; The Association of Trial Lawyers of America; Wake Collaborative Family Law Group; International Academy of Collaborative Professionals. (Board Certified Specialist in Family Law, North Carolina State Board of Legal Specialization). ***REPORTED CASES:*** Doan v. Doan, 156 N.C. App. 570, 577 S.E.2d 146 (2003). ***PRACTICE AREAS:*** Family Law; Child Custody; Child Support; Equitable Distribution; Spousal Support; Civil Litigation. ***Email:*** kimberly.bryan@cheshirepark.com

JONATHAN GORDON McGIRT, born Chapel Hill, North Carolina, September 27, 1963; admitted to bar, 1993, North Carolina; 1996, U.S. District Court, Eastern District of North Carolina. *Education:* University of North Carolina, Chapel Hill, (B.A., with highest honors, 1988); University of North Carolina Law School (J.D., 1993). Recipient, American Jurisprudence Award for Advanced Family Law. Author: "Recent Opinions, N.C. Court of Appeals," Family Forum, v. 14, no. 3-, Nov. 1993- (regular feature), with Jaye Meyer. Member, Governor's Task Force on Domestic Violence, 1998-1999. *Member:* Wake County, North Carolina (Member, Sections on: Family Law and Family Law Section Council, 1996—) and American (Member, Section on: Family Law, 1996—) Bar Associations; Tenth Judicial District and North Carolina State Bars; North Carolina Association of Trial Lawyers; Association of Trial Lawyers of America. (Board Certified Specialist in Family Law, North Carolina Board of Legal Specialization). ***LANGUAGES:*** German, French, Russian, Latin. ***REPORTED CASES:*** Eluhu v. Rosenhaus, 159 N.C. App. 355, 583 S.E.2d 707 (2003), aff'd per curiam 595 S.E.2d 146 (N.C. 2004); Long v. Long 160 N.C. App. 664, 588 S.E.2d 1 (2003); Rice v. Rice, 159 N.C. App. 484, 584 S.E.2d 317 (2003); Vadala v. Vadala, 145 N.C. App. 478, 550 S.E.2d 536 (2001); Embler v. Embler, 143 N.C. App. 162, 545 S.E.2d 259 (2001); Hubbard v. OPM, 247 F.3d 1236, reh'g and reh'g en banc denied (Fed. Cir. 2001). ***PRACTICE AREAS:*** Family Law; Qualified Domestic Relations Orders; Appellate Practice; Civil Appeals. ***Email:*** jonathan.mcgirt@cheshirepark.com

LORION MACRAE VITALE, born Ft. Walton Beach, Florida, April 21, 1970; admitted to bar, 1995, North Carolina; U.S. District Court, Middle and Eastern Districts of North Carolina. *Education:* Randolph-Macon Woman's College (B.A., 1992); Wake Forest University (J.D., 1995). Lecturer and Author: "Child Support, Domestic Violence and Ex Parte Contact," N.C. Academy of Trial Lawyers, January 1999; "Post Trial Practice," Wake Forest University, October 2000; "Legal Traps in Bankruptcy, Real Property and Domestic Violence," N.C. Bar Assoc., November 2000; "Parole Evidence," N.C. Bar Assoc., May 2001; "Enforcing Your Order and Judgment Through Contempt and Proper Filing of Judgments," N.C. Academy of Trial Lawyers, September 2001; "Interstate Child Support," Wake Forest University, October 2001. Program Planner for, "Hot Topics in Family Law: Evidentiary Issues in Child Custody Cases," N.C. Bar Association, September 2004. Member, North Carolina Child Support Study Committee, 2000. *Member:* Wake County, North Carolina (Chair, Equitable Distribution Committee, Family Law Section, 2000—; Member, Family Law Council; Member, Continuing Legal Education Committee) and American Bar Associations; North Carolina State Bar. Fellow, North Carolina Academy of Trial Lawyers. (Board Certified Specialist in Family Law, North Carolina State Board of Legal Specialization). ***PRACTICE AREAS:*** Family Law; Divorce; Child Custody; Alimony; Child Support; Separation Agreements. ***Email:*** lori.vitale@cheshirepark.com

JOHN KEATING WILES, born Louisville, Kentucky, September 1, 1950; admitted to bar, 1995, North Carolina; 1996, U.S. District Court, Eastern District of North Carolina; 1997, U.S. District Court, Western and Middle Districts of North Carolina and U.S. Court of Appeals, Fourth Circuit. *Education:* Oklahoma Baptist University (B.M., 1972); University of North Carolina at Chapel Hill (J.D., 1995); Midwestern Baptist Theological Seminary (M.Div, 1977); The Southern Baptist Theological Seminary (Ph.D., 1982). Recipient, American Jurisprudence Award for Criminal Law. Lecturer and Author: "When Political Speech Meets State Regulation: The Case of Farmers for Fairness," N.C. Bar Association, October 2001; "A Case of Probable Cause Protecting Free Speech," TRIALBriefs, N.C. Academy of Trial Lawyers, Fall 1997. *Member:* North Carolina and American Bar Associations; North Carolina Academy of Trial Lawyers; National Association of Criminal Defense Lawyers. ***LANGUAGES:*** Indonesian, Malaysian. ***REPORTED CASES:*** State v. Coble, 351 N.C. 448, 527 S.E.2d 45 (2000); United States v. Rhynes, 206 F.3d 349 (4th Cir. 2000). ***PRACTICE AREAS:*** Criminal Defense; State and Federal Appeals; Election Law; Administrative Law. ***Email:*** keat.wiles@cheshirepark.com

BRADLEY J. BANNON, born New York, N.Y., August 20, 1970; admitted to bar, 1997, North Carolina; 2000, U.S. District Court, Eastern District of North Carolina. *Education:* University of South Carolina (B.A., 1993); Campbell University (J.D., 1997); National Criminal Defense College, Mercer Law School (1999). Published Articles, "Pretrial Publicity: Know the Rules," December 2003 Trial Briefs; "Advocating for Those Left Behind: The Need for Discovery Reform in Non-Capital Post-Conviction Cases," April 2005 Trial Brief (with Maitri "Mike" Klinkosum). Guest Lecturer, North Carolina Criminal Procedure, Campbell University Law School, 2000—. *Member:* Wake County, North Carolina (Executive Committee, Criminal Justice Section), 10th Judicial District (Liaison), and American Bar Associations; North Carolina Academy of Trial Lawyers (Vice-Chairman, Criminal Defense Section, 2005—). ***REPORTED CASES:*** State v. White, 135 N.C. App. 349, 520 S.E.2d. 70 (1999). ***PRACTICE AREAS:*** Criminal Defense; Appellate Practice. ***Email:*** brad.bannon@cheshirepark.com

ASSOCIATE

DORIS K. JORDAN, born Raleigh, North Carolina; admitted to bar, 2004, North Carolina. *Education:* Appalachian State University (B.A., magna cum laude, 2000); University of North Carolina School of Law (J.D., 2004). *Member:* Wake County, North Carolina (Member, Family Law Section) and American Bar Associations; Tenth Judicial District Bar; North Carolina State Bar. ***LANGUAGES:*** German. ***PRACTICE AREAS:*** Family Law; Divorce; Child Custody; Equitable Distribution; Child Support; Separation Agreements. ***Email:*** dori.jordan@cheshirepark.com

(This Listing Continued)

LAW OFFICES OF GREGORY P. CHOCKLETT

Established in 1988

711 HARVEY STREET
RALEIGH, NORTH CAROLINA 27608-2403
Telephone: 919-856-0100
Fax: 919-856-0799
Email: chocklett@bellsouth.net
URL: http://www.chocklettlaw.com

Commercial Litigation, Bankruptcy/Creditor, Collections, Contracts, Civil Trials and Appeals, Personal Injury. Medical Malpractice, ERISA, Repossessions, Foreclosures.

GREGORY P. CHOCKLETT, born Charlotte, North Carolina, December 15, 1956; admitted to bar, 1984, North Carolina and South Carolina; 1986, U.S. District Court, Middle, Eastern and Western Districts of North Carolina; U.S. Court of Appeals, Fourth Circuit; U.S. Bankruptcy Court. *Education:* University of North Carolina (A.B., with honors in English, 1979; J.D., 1984). Best Oralist, Voluntary Moot Court Competition. *Member:* Wake County and North Carolina (Member, Sections on: Bankruptcy; Litigation; Workers Compensation) Bar Associations; North Carolina State Bar; South Carolina Bar. ***REPORTED CASES:*** CIT Communications Finance Corp. v. Midway Airlines Corp., Case #04-1502, (4th Cir. May, 2005). ***PRACTICE AREAS:*** Creditors Rights; Creditor Bankruptcy; Repossessions; Commercial Litigation; Lender Law; Business Litigation; Commercial Collections; Secured Transactions; Mortgage Foreclosure; Contract Litigation; Civil Forfeiture; ERISA; Plaintiffs Personal Injury; Automobile Liability; Government Tort Liability; Insurance Litigation; Medical Negligence; Professional Malpractice; Mobile Home Law; Truck Accidents; Estate Litigation; Real Estate Litigation.

REPRESENTATIVE CLIENTS: General Electric Capital Corp.; G.E. Capital Asset Management Corp.; Citicorp National Services, Inc.; The C.I.T. Group; Transamerica Commercial Finance Corp.; Ford Consumer Finance; W.F.S. Financial; Cooper Leasing, Inc.; Nations Credit Financial Services Corp.; Eastman Kodak Co.; Southern States Co-Op., Inc.; Key Bank; Onyx Acceptance Corp.; Nuvell Financial Services Corp.; Loan Servicing Enterprise, Inc.; Summit Acceptance Corp.; Consumer Portfolio Services, Inc.; Wells Fargo Bank; Tyco Capital Corporation; Champion Window Company; Origen Financial L.L.C.; Lockheed Martin Lender Services, Inc.

CLIFTON & SINGER, L.L.P.

Established in 1978

4900 FALLS OF NEUSE ROAD, SUITE 160
RALEIGH, NORTH CAROLINA 27609
Telephone: 919-790-7000
URL: http://www.cliftonsingerlaw.com

Personal Injury, Medical Malpractice, Wrongful Death, Catastrophic Injury, Residential Real Estate, Commercial Real Estate, Family Law, Divorce, Child Custody, Criminal Law, DWI, Traffic Violations.

FIRM PROFILE: Clifton & Singer, L.L.P. is a small law firm with a special emphasis in serious civil, administrative and family law litigation. In addition, it has a separate real estate section to serve home buyers and sellers in fast growing Wake County.

MEMBERS OF FIRM

BENJAMIN F. CLIFTON, JR., born Harnett County, North Carolina, April 28, 1943; admitted to bar, 1970, North Carolina; 1973, U.S. District Court, Eastern District of North Carolina. *Education:* University of North Carolina (B.A., 1966; J.D., 1970). Phi Alpha Delta. Law Clerk, Judge Naomi Morris, North Carolina Court of Appeals, 1970-1971. *Member:* Wake County and North Carolina Bar Associations; North Carolina State Bar; North Carolina Academy of Trial Lawyers. ***PRACTICE AREAS:*** Residential Real Estate; Civil Litigation; Criminal Defense. ***Email:*** bclifton@cliftonsingerlaw.com

RICHARD G. SINGER, born Chambersburg, Pennsylvania, January 1, 1943; admitted to bar, 1969, North Carolina and U.S. District Court, Eastern and Middle Districts of North Carolina. *Education:* University of North Carolina (B.A., 1965; J.D., 1969). Delta Theta Phi. Law Clerk to Judge Earl W. Vaughn, Court of Appeals of North Carolina, 1969-1970. *Member:* Wake County, North Carolina and American Bar Associations; The North Carolina State Bar; North Carolina Academy of Trial Lawyers. ***PRACTICE AREAS:*** Real Estate; Personal Injury Litigation; Business Law; Commercial Law; Medical Malpractice.

ASSOCIATES

LANCE R. FIFE, born Rexburg, Idaho, May 3, 1970; admitted to bar, 1999, North Carolina. *Education:* Utah State University (B.S., 1994); Oklahoma City University (J.D., 1997). ***PRACTICE AREAS:*** Real Estate; Litigation; Estate Planning. ***Email:*** lfife@cliftonsingerlaw.com

LUCY T. BREWER, born Rocky Mount, North Carolina, February 17, 1975; admitted to bar, 2003, North Carolina. *Education:* University of North Carolina at Chapel Hill (B.A., 1997); Campbell University (J.D., 2003). Phi Alpha Delta. *Member:* North Carolina and American Bar Associations. ***PRACTICE AREAS:*** Real Estate.

REPRESENTATIVE CLIENTS: Beazer Homes; Beazer Mortgage Co.; Atkinson & Associates, Inc.; Biscuitville, Inc.; Darryl Burke Chevrolet, Inc.; Dunn Automotive Group; Comstock Homes; John Deere Co.; Gulledge Building Co.; Mid-South Title Company; Nationwide Homes; Royal Pontiac, G.M.C., Isuzu, Inc.; Colonial Carton Co.; Charter Industries; Bill Clark Construction Co.; U.S. Case Corp.; Weichert Relocation Co., Inc.; Pulte Homes; Pulte Mortgages; Remax Property Associates; Bassett Furniture Industries of N.C., Inc.; Chicago Title Insurance Co.; Crane Co.; Duke University; Empire Relocation; Executrans; Fantis Foods, Inc.; First Indiana Bank; Nationwide Homes, Inc.; Nations Bank; Remax; Republic Bank, Dallas, N.A.; Security Union Insurance Co.; Travelers Relocation; United Carolina Bank; U.S. Fidelity and Guaranty Co.; Vulcan Life Insurance Co.; Wachovia Bank and Trust Co.; Surety

(This Listing Continued)

Title Insurance Company; Title Company of North Carolina; Regents Bank; Cendant Mobility Services, Inc.; Certified Closing Network; Fannie Mae; Fidelity Financial Title Insurance.

COATS & BENNETT, PLLC

RALEIGH, NORTH CAROLINA

(See Cary)

Patent, Trademark, Copyright and Unfair Competition Practice before all Courts.

COLEMAN, GLEDHILL, HARGRAVE & PEEK, P.C.

RALEIGH, NORTH CAROLINA

(See Hillsborough)

General Civil and Criminal Trial Practice in all State and Federal Courts. Litigation, Negligence, Domestic, Real Estate, Corporate, Municipal and Probate Law, Commercial Transactions and Litigation.

CONNER GWYN SCHENCK PLLC

2626 GLENWOOD AVENUE, SUITE 180
RALEIGH, NORTH CAROLINA 27608
Telephone: 919-789-9242
Facsimile: 919-789-9210
URL: http://www.cgspllc.com
Mailing Address: P.O. Box 30933, Raleigh, NC 27622

Greensboro, North Carolina Office: 306 E. Market Street, Suite One, 27401. Telephone: 336-691-9222. Fax: 336-691-9259.

Construction Law, Trials, Contract Law, Mediation, Arbitration.

RICHARD D. CONNER, born Richmond, Virginia, February 8, 1945; admitted to bar, 1973, North Carolina and U.S. District Court, Middle, Western and Eastern Districts of North Carolina; 1982, U.S. Court of Appeals, 4th Circuit. *Education:* Guilford College (A.B., 1970); University of North Carolina (J.D., 1973). Delta Theta Phi. General Counsel, Construction Management Association of America, Inc., 1982-1999. Chairman, Board of Elections, Guilford County, North Carolina, 1985-1989. Arbitrator, Court Annexed Arbitration Plan for the U.S. District Court, Middle District of North Carolina, 1985—. Member, Greensboro, North Carolina Transit Authority, 1991-1995. Member, Construction Industry Panel of Arbitrators, Complex Cases, American Arbitration Association. Member, Board of Governors, American College of Construction Lawyers. Private Judge, Private Adjudication Center, Duke University Law School. Dispute Resolution Board Member, Public Toll Road Authority. Certified Mediator, North Carolina Federal and State Courts. *Member:* Greensboro, North Carolina (Director, Construction Law Section) and American (Forum on the Construction Industry, Division Chair, 1994-1995) Bar Associations. (Resident, Greensboro Office). ***PRACTICE AREAS:*** Construction Law. ***Email:*** rconner@cgspllc.com

ALLEN HOLT GWYN, born Winston Salem, North Carolina, September 11, 1949; admitted to bar, 1976, North Carolina; U.S. District Court, Eastern, Middle and Western Districts of North Carolina, U.S. Court of Appeals, 4th Circuit, U.S. Supreme Court. *Education:* University of North Carolina, Chapel Hill (A.B., 1971); Wake Forest University (J.D., 1976). Co-author, "Construction Damages and Remedies," ABA Book Publishing, 2004. Member, Editorial Board, "Construction and Design Law Digest," Michle Bunerworth, 1986-1998. Assistant U.S. Attorney, Middle District of North Carolina, 1976-1980. Certified Mediator and Arbitrator: NC AOC; NC US Distr. Cts.; AAA Carolinas Construction Mediation Panel of Neutrals; AAA Large Complex Case Program Panel of Arbitrators. Charter Member, Board of Trustees, NC Clean Water Management Trust Fund, 1996-2003. *Member:* Greensboro, North Carolina (Founding Member, Construction Law Section) and American (Chair, Forum on the Construction Industry, 1999-2000; Governing Committee, 1995-2001; ABA Standing Committee on Publishing Oversight 2000—; Contributing Editor, ABA Construction Forum Law Journal, The Construction Lawyer, 1990-1997) Bar Associations. Fellow, American College of Construction Lawyers (Board of Governors, 2003—). (Resident, Greensboro Office). ***PRACTICE AREAS:*** Construction Law. ***Email:*** ahgwyn@cgspllc.com

JAMES S. SCHENCK, IV, admitted to bar, 1982, North Carolina; 1983, U.S. District Court, Middle District of North Carolina; 1984, U.S. District Court, Eastern District of North Carolina and U.S. Court of Appeals, Fourth Circuit; 1991, U.S. District Court, Western District of North Carolina. *Education:* University of North Carolina (A.B., 1976; J.D., 1982); Duke University (M.A.P.P.S., 1982). Member, Wake County Citizens Energy Advisory Commission, 1996—. Certified Mediator, North Carolina Superior Courts. Member, Construction Industry Panel of Arbitrators and Mediators, American Arbitration Association. *Member:* Wake County, North Carolina (Chair: Construction Law Section, 1991-1992; Communications Committee, 1996-1998, 2000-2002; Member, Board of Governors, 2002—) and American (Forum on the Construction Industry Division Chair, 2001-2002) Bar Associations. (Resident). ***PRACTICE AREAS:*** Construction Law; Administrative Law. ***Email:*** jschenck@cgspllc.com

C. HAMILTON JARRETT, III, born Charlotte, North Carolina, February 19, 1952; admitted to bar, 1983, North Carolina. *Education:* Clemson University (B.S., Civil Engineering, 1975); Mercer University (J.D., cum laude, 1983). Member of Staff, 1981-1982 and Lead Articles II Editor, 1982-1983, Mercer Law Review. *Member:* North Carolina (Council Member, Construction Law Section, 1995-1998) and American (Member: Fidelity and Surety Law Committee, Tort and Insurance Practice Section; Forum Committee on the Construction Industry) Bar Associations; Associated General Contractors of America (Member, Surety Bonding Committee). (Resident). ***Email:*** hjarrett@cgspllc.com

PAUL E. DAVIS, admitted to bar, 1984, North Carolina; U.S. District Court, Eastern, Middle and Western Districts of North Carolina. *Education:* University of North Carolina (B.A., 1979; J.D., 1984). Co-Author: Fifty State Public Construction Contracting - North Carolina Chapter (Aspen Law & Business); Fifty State Construction Lien and Bond Law,

(This Listing Continued)

North Carolina Chapter (Aspen Law & Business); State Public Construction Law Sourcebook, North Carolina Chapter, (CCH, Inc.). *Member:* North Carolina (Chair, Construction Law Section, 2002-2003; Council Member, 1996-1999; Newsletter Editor, 1990-1991) and American (Member, Forum on the Construction Industry) Bar Associations. (Resident). ***PRACTICE AREAS:*** Construction Law; Litigation. ***Email:*** pdavis@cgspllc.com

JAY M. WILKERSON, admitted to bar, 1992, North Carolina, U.S. District Court, Eastern, Middle and Western Districts of North Carolina and U.S. Court of Appeals, Fourth Circuit. *Education:* University of North Carolina, Chapel Hill (B.S., 1989; J.D., 1992). Staff Writer, Journal of International Law & Commerce, 1990-1992. *Member:* North Carolina (Member, Construction Law Section) and American (Member, Forum on the Construction Industry) Bar Associations. (Resident, Greensboro Office). ***PRACTICE AREAS:*** Construction Law; OSHA; Litigation; Government Contracts. ***Email:*** jwilkerson@cgspllc.com

EDWARD N. POLLARD, admitted to bar, 1993, North Carolina and U.S. District Court, Middle District of North Carolina. *Education:* North Carolina State University (B.S.C.E., 1982); Wake Forest University (J.D., 1993). Law Clerk to Hon. Hiram H. Ward, U.S. District Court, Middle District of North Carolina, 1993-1996. Registered Professional Engineer, 1986. *Member:* North Carolina Bar Association (Member, Construction Law Section). (Resident, Greensboro Office). ***PRACTICE AREAS:*** Construction Law; Litigation. ***Email:*** epollard@cgspllc.com

OF COUNSEL

JEFFREY B. PARSONS, born Greensboro, North Carolina, November 5, 1962; admitted to bar, 1988, North Carolina; 1989, U.S. District Court, Eastern District of North Carolina; 1992, U.S. District Court, Middle District of North Carolina and U.S. Supreme Court; 1993, U.S. Court of Appeals, Fourth Circuit and U.S. Court of Military Appeals. *Education:* University of North Carolina at Chapel Hill (B.A., with highest honors, 1985; J.D., 1988). Member, Holderness Moot Court, Honor Court. Assistant Attorney General, Property and Construction, State of North Carolina, 1998-2003. Special Deputy Attorney General, Property and Construction, State of North Carolina, 2003-2004. Member, Raleigh Human Relations Commission, 1994-1997. *Member:* North Carolina State Bar; North Carolina Bar Association (Chair, Real Property Curriculum Committee, 2002—; Member: Continuing Legal Education Committee; Construction Law Section; Litigation Section). ***Email:*** jparsons@cgspllc.com

WILLIAM J. COTTER, P.A.

RALEIGH, NORTH CAROLINA

(See Durham)

Criminal Law, Family Law, Traffic Violations in State and Federal Courts. Personal Injury.

CRANFILL, SUMNER & HARTZOG, L.L.P.

HILLSBOROUGH PLACE
225 HILLSBOROUGH STREET, SUITE 300
P.O. BOX 27808
RALEIGH, NORTH CAROLINA 27611-7808
Telephone: 919-828-5100
Fax: 919-828-2277
URL: http://www.cshlaw.com

Charlotte, North Carolina Office: 227 West Trade Street, Suite 600. Telephone: 704-332-8300. Fax: 704-332-9994.

Wilmington, North Carolina Office: 1209 Culbreth Drive, Suite 200, 28405. Telephone: 910-509-9778. Fax: 910-509-9676.

General Trial and Appellate Practice before all State and Federal Courts. Litigation of Insurance Law, Personal Injury, Medical Malpractice, Nursing Home Negligence, Professional Malpractice, Products Liability, Premises Liability, Municipal and Police Liability, Intentional Torts, Commercial Litigation, Workers' Compensation, Employment, Education, Construction and Land Condemnation Law.

MEMBERS OF THE FIRM

PAUL L. CRANFILL, admitted to bar, 1969, North Carolina. *Education:* University of North Carolina at Chapel Hill (B.S., 1965; J.D., 1969).

ROBERT W. SUMNER, admitted to bar, 1970, North Carolina. *Education:* Wake Forest University (B.A., 1967; J.D., 1970).

DAN M. HARTZOG, admitted to bar, 1973, North Carolina. *Education:* University of North Carolina at Chapel Hill (A.B., 1969; J.D., 1972). (Managing Partner)

ALENE M. MERCER, admitted to bar, 1977, North Carolina. *Education:* University of North Carolina at Chapel Hill (B.S., 1970); New York University (J.D., 1977).

RICHARD T. BOYETTE, admitted to bar, 1977, North Carolina. *Education:* University of North Carolina at Chapel Hill (B.A., 1974; J.D., 1977).

DAVID D. WARD, admitted to bar, 1975, North Carolina. *Education:* Wake Forest University (B.A., 1972; J.D., 1975).

PATRICIA L. HOLLAND, admitted to bar, 1979, North Carolina. *Education:* Wittenberg University (B.A., 1976); Wake Forest University (J.D., 1979).

DAVID H. BATTEN, admitted to bar, 1983, North Carolina. *Education:* University of North Carolina at Chapel Hill (B.A., 1979); Wake Forest University (J.D., 1983).

H. LEE EVANS, JR., admitted to bar, 1984, North Carolina. *Education:* University of North Carolina at Chapel Hill (B.S., 1981; J.D., 1984).

C. D. TAYLOR PACE, admitted to bar, 1985, North Carolina. *Education:* University of North Carolina at Chapel Hill (B.A., 1982; J.D., 1985).

(This Listing Continued)

CRANFILL, SUMNER & HARTZOG, L.L.P., Raleigh—Continued

SUSAN K. BURKHART, admitted to bar, 1982, North Carolina. *Education:* University of Michigan (B.A., 1977); Wayne State University (J.D., 1981).

BUXTON S. COPELAND, admitted to bar, 1985, North Carolina. *Education:* University of North Carolina at Chapel Hill (B.A., 1981); Campbell University (J.D., 1985).

P. COLLINS BARWICK, III, admitted to bar, 1988, North Carolina. *Education:* Wake Forest University (B.A., 1983; J.D., 1987).

ROBERT H. GRIFFIN, admitted to bar, 1986, North Carolina. *Education:* Wake Forest University (B.A., 1983; J.D., 1986).

KARI RUSSWURM JOHNSON, admitted to bar, 1988, North Carolina. *Education:* East Carolina University (B.S., 1984); Wake Forest University (J.D., 1988).

DAVID A. RHOADES, admitted to bar, 1989, North Carolina. *Education:* University of North Carolina at Chapel Hill (B.A., 1985); Wake Forest University (M.B.A./J.D., 1989).

BRADY W. WELLS, admitted to bar, 1991, North Carolina. *Education:* University of North Carolina at Chapel Hill (B.A., 1987; J.D., 1990).

JOSEPH B. CHAMBLISS, JR., admitted to bar, 1985, North Carolina. *Education:* University of North Carolina at Chapel Hill (B.A., 1977); Campbell University (J.D., 1985).

W. SCOTT FULLER, admitted to bar, 1992, North Carolina. *Education:* University of North Carolina at Chapel Hill (B.A., 1988; J.D., 1992).

ROBIN H. TERRY, admitted to bar, 1990, North Carolina. *Education:* University of North Carolina at Wilmington (B.A., 1987); Campbell University (J.D., 1990).

WILLIAM W. POLLOCK, admitted to bar, 1992, North Carolina. *Education:* Wake Forest University (B.A., 1984); University of South Carolina (J.D., 1987).

STEPHANIE HUTCHINS AUTRY, admitted to bar, 1987, North Carolina. *Education:* University of North Carolina at Greensboro (B.A., 1984); University of North Carolina at Chapel Hill (J.D., 1987).

LEIGH ANN G. SMITH, admitted to bar, 1995, North Carolina. *Education:* University of North Carolina at Chapel Hill (B.A., 1991); Campbell University (J.D., 1995).

JONATHAN C. ANDERS, admitted to bar, 1996, North Carolina. *Education:* University of North Carolina at Chapel Hill (B.A., 1992); Campbell University (J.D., 1996).

MARANDA J. FREEMAN, admitted to bar, 1996, North Carolina. *Education:* University of North Carolina at Charlotte (B.S., 1993); Wake Forest University (J.D., 1996).

H. VANCE BARNETTE, III, admitted to bar, 1997, North Carolina. *Education:* Wake Forest University (B.A., 1992); Widener University (J.D., 1997).

KIRK D. KUHNS, admitted to bar, 1994, North Carolina. *Education:* University of North Carolina at Chapel Hill (B.S., 1990); New England School of Law (J.D., 1994).

JAYE ELIZABETH BINGHAM, admitted to bar, 1997, North Carolina. *Education:* Duke University (A.B., 1994); University of North Carolina at Chapel Hill (J.D., 1997).

BETH R. FLEISHMAN, admitted to bar, 1977, North Carolina. *Education:* University of North Carolina at Chapel Hill (A.B., 1972; M.A., 1974; J.D., 1977).

ANN SMITH ESTRIDGE, admitted to bar, 1996, North Carolina. *Education:* North Carolina State University (B.A., 1991); University of North Carolina at Chapel Hill (J.D., 1996).

J. GREGORY NEWTON, admitted to bar, 1996, North Carolina. *Education:* University of North Carolina at Chapel Hill (B.A., 1992); Campbell University (J.D., 1996).

DONNA R. RASCOE, admitted to bar, 1993, North Carolina. *Education:* University of North Carolina, Greensboro (B.A., 1980); University of Iowa (M.A., 1982); University of North Carolina at Chapel Hill (J.D., 1993).

C. HOUSTON FOPPIANO, admitted to bar, 1999, North Carolina. *Education:* University of Texas at Austin (B.S., 1991); University of Tennessee at Knoxville (J.D., 1995).

JAMES BELL BLACK, IV, admitted to bar, 1999, North Carolina. *Education:* University of North Carolina at Chapel Hill (B.S.B.A., 1995); Wake Forest University (J.D., 1999).

ERIN FLEMING TAYLOR, born Ft. Monmouth, New Jersey, October 5, 1974; admitted to bar, 1999, North Carolina. *Education:* University of North Carolina at Greensboro (B.A., 1995); Campbell University School of Law (J.D., 1999).

F. MARSHALL WALL, admitted to bar, 1999, North Carolina. *Education:* University of North Carolina at Chapel Hill (A.B., 1996); Campbell University (J.D., 1999).

JESSE M. TILLMAN, III, admitted to bar, 1999, North Carolina. *Education:* University of North Carolina at Chapel Hill (B.A., 1986); Campbell University (J.D., 1999). [Lt., U.S. Navy, 1986-1993; LCDR, U.S. Naval Reserve, 1993—]

MICHAEL C. ALLEN, admitted to bar, 1999, North Carolina. *Education:* University of North Carolina at Chapel Hill (B.S., 1980); Campbell University School of Law (J.D., 1999).

MELISSA ROBIN DAVIS, admitted to bar, 1990, North Carolina. *Education:* University of Louisville (B.A., 1987); Georgetown University (J.D., 1990).

DANIEL G. KATZENBACH, admitted to bar, 1997, North Carolina. *Education:* Washington & Lee University (B.A., 1994); Wake Forest University (J.D., 1997).

GLORIA TAFT BECKER, admitted to bar, 2000, North Carolina. *Education:* University of North Carolina at Chapel Hill (B.A., 1996); Campbell University (J.D., 2000).

GEORGE L. SIMPSON, IV, admitted to bar, 2000, North Carolina. *Education:* University of North Carolina at Chapel Hill (B.A., 1996; J.D., 2000).

RANDOLPH L. LEE, admitted to bar, 1999, North Carolina. *Education:* Northwestern University (B.A., 1982); North Carolina Central University (J.D., 1999).

GEORGE B. AUTRY, JR., admitted to bar, 1991, North Carolina. *Education:* University of Texas at Austin (B.A., 1991); University of North Carolina at Chapel Hill (J.D., 1991).

(This Listing Continued)

KATHERINE HILKEY-BOYATT, admitted to bar, 2001, North Carolina. *Education:* University of North Carolina at Chapel Hill (B.A., 1997; J.D., 2001).

JENNIFER C. POLLEY-ABRAMSON, admitted to bar, 2002, North Carolina. *Education:* University of Kentucky (B.A., 1991); University of Utah (J.D., 1998).

J. GREER VANDERBERRY, JR., admitted to bar, 2001, North Carolina. *Education:* University of North Carolina at Chapel Hill (B.A., 1995); Wake Forest University (J.D., 2001).

TRACY C. MYATT, admitted to bar, 1994, North Carolina. *Education:* North Carolina State University (B.A., 1986); University of North Carolina at Chapel Hill (J.D., 1994).

KATHLEEN MANNING MILES, admitted to bar, 1998, North Carolina. *Education:* North Carolina State University (B.A., 1994); Campbell University (J.D., 1998).

ROY G. PETTIGREW, admitted to bar, 2001, North Carolina. *Education:* University of North Carolina at Chapel Hill (B.A., 1995); Wake Forest University School of Law (J.D., 2000).

RACHEL K. ESPOSITO, admitted to bar, 2000, North Carolina. *Education:* Elon College (B.A., 1993); University of North Carolina at Chapel Hill (J.D., 2000).

DAWN CONGER-LANE, admitted to bar, 1996, North Carolina. *Education:* Campbell University (B.B.A., 1991); North Carolina Central University (J.D., 1996).

LEANNE L. MULLIS, admitted to bar, 2002, North Carolina. *Education:* Vassar College (B.A., 1994); Campbell University (J.D., 2002).

AMY HARRISON NUTTALL, admitted to bar, 2002, North Carolina. *Education:* University of Miami (B.S., 1992); Campbell University (J.D., 2002).

JOHN MICHAEL RICCI, admitted to bar, 2002, North Carolina. *Education:* University of North Carolina at Chapel Hill (B.A., 1999); Campbell University (J.D., 2002).

ALYCIA S. LEVY, admitted to bar, 2002, Viginia; 2003, North Carolina. *Education:* Emory University (B.A., 1998); University of Richmond (J.D., 2002).

MEREDITH T. BLACK, admitted to bar, 1998, North Carolina. *Education:* Meredith College (B.A., 1995); Wake Forest University (J.D., 1998).

DEXTER M. CAMPBELL, III, admitted to bar, 2003, North Carolina. *Education:* University of North Carolina at Chapel Hill (B.A., 2000); Campbell University (J.D., 2003).

GINGER BAGLEY HUNSUCKER, admitted to bar, 2003, North Carolina. *Education:* University of North Carolina at Chapel Hill (B.S., B.A., 1993; J.D., 2003).

JENNIFER A. ADDLETON, admitted to bar, 2003, North Carolina. *Education:* University of North Carolina at Wilmington (B.A., 1999); Campbell University (J.D., 2003).

STEPHANIE A. GASTON, admitted to bar, 2003, North Carolina. *Education:* Furman University (B.A., 2000); Campbell University (J.D., 2003).

MICHAEL C. CONNELL, admitted to bar, 1986, North Carolina. *Education:* University of North Carolina at Chapel Hill (B.A., 1981; J.D., 1985).

AMY L. PFEIFFER, admitted to bar, 1991, North Carolina. *Education:* North Carolina State University (B.A., magna cum laude, 1988); Columbus School of Law of the Catholic University of America (J.D., 1991).

ERICA JONA THOMAS, admitted to bar, 2004, North Carolina. *Education:* Davdison College (B.A., 1998); University of Richmond (J.D., 2004).

KATIE J. WEAVER, admitted to bar, 2004, North Carolina. *Education:* University of North Carolina at Chapel Hill (B.A., 2001); Campbell University (J.D., 2004).

ASHLEY KAMPHAUS BRATHWAITE, admitted to bar, 2005, North Carolina and U.S. District Court, Eastern District of North Carolina. *Education:* Furman University (B.A., 2000); Campbell University (J.D., 2005). *Member:* North Carolina State Bar.

CHRISTOPHER A. BROOK, admitted to bar, 2005, North Carolina and U.S. District Court, Eastern District of North Carolina. *Education:* University of North Carolina at Chapel Hill (B.A., 2002; J.D., 2005). *Member:* North Carolina State Bar.

PAUL HOLSCHER, admitted to bar, 2005, North Carolina. *Education:* University of North Carolina at Chapel Hill (B.A., 2000); Campbell University (J.D., 2005). *Member:* North Carolina State Bar.

REPRESENTATIVE CLIENTS: ABB; ACE, USA; Aegis Administrative Services; AIG; Allstate; Amerisure; Amica; Ashland Construction Co.; Boddie-Noell Enterprises, Inc.; Bridgestone/Firestone; Builders Mutual; Carquest; CIGNA; Cincinnati Insurance; CNA; Companion Insurance; CompCarolina; Crawford & Company; Crum & Forster; Dennis & Associates; Discovery Insurance Co.; Dow Chemical; Duke University Medical Center; Erie Insurance; Estes Express Lines; Food Lion, Inc.; Forestry Mutual; GAB Robins North America, Inc.; Gallagher-Bassett; Golden Corral; Great American; Guaranty National; Hardee's Food Systems, Inc.; Harleysville Insurance; ITT Hartford; Highland Insurance Group; Homebuilders Mutual; Horace Mann; IHDS Corporation; James C. Greene Co., Inc.; Kemper; Key Risk Management Services, Inc.; Lawyers Mutual; Liberty Mutual; Lowe's; Lumbermens Underwriting Alliance; Medical Protective; National Chiropractic Mutual; Nationwide; NC Association of County Commissioners; NC Housing Authority Risk Retention Pool; NC Joint Underwriting Association; NC League of Municipalities; NC School Boards Trust; North Carolina Association of Self-Insurers; North Carolina Farm Bureau; OCG; Health Care Indemnity, Inc.; Penn National Insurance; Royal Insurance; Safeco; Scott Wetzel Services, Inc.; Sentry Insurance; Shoney's; Southern Risk Services; St. Paul; Sumitomo Marine Management USA; Travelers; Tultex; Tyson Foods, Inc.; UNC Hospitals; Unigard; Universal Underwriters; USAA; Vanliner Insurance; V.F. Corporation; VFS Insurance Co.; Wausau, Wrangler; Zenith; Zurich.

CRAWFORD LAW OFFICE

Established in 2002

LANDMARK CENTER

4601 SIX FORKS ROAD, SUITE 500

RALEIGH, NORTH CAROLINA 27609

Telephone: 919-510-8140

Facsimile: 919-785-4152

URL: http://www.lawyers.com/crawfordlawoffice

Medical Malpractice Defense, Professional and Occupational Licensing and Discipline Defense, Administrative Law, Employment Law, Insurance Defense, Business Litigation, Civil Appeals.

(This Listing Continued)

FIRM PROFILE: Crawford Law Office focuses its practice on the defense of physicians in medical malpractice actions. It defends professionals in disciplinary actions before their respective licensing boards. The firm also defends employers in discrimination actions. The firm also handles other civil and administrative litigation and appeals, as well as general business litigation.

RENEE BILLINGS CRAWFORD, born Durham, North Carolina, September 10, 1960; admitted to bar, 1996, North Carolina; U.S. District Court, Eastern District of North Carolina; U.S. Court of Appeals, 4th Circuit. *Education:* Temple University (B.A., 1983); University of Oregon (M.F.A., 1986); Duke University (J.D., 1996). *Member:* Wake County, Tenth Judicial District and North Carolina Bar Associations; The North Carolina State Bar; Defense Research Institute; North Carolina Association of Defense Attorneys. ***REPORTED CASES:*** Stewart v. Southeastern Regional Medical Center, 142 N.C. App. 456, S.E. 543 S.E. 2d 517 (2001). ***PRACTICE AREAS:*** Medical Malpractice Defense; Professional Liability Defense; Business Litigation.

ROBERT O. CRAWFORD, III, born Claremont, North Carolina, December 29, 1958; admitted to bar, 1984, North Carolina, U.S. District Court, Eastern, Western and Middle Districts of North Carolina, U.S. Court of Appeals, 4th Circuit and U.S. Supreme Court. *Education:* Wake Forest University (B.A., cum laude, 1981; J.D., 1984). Assistant Attorney General, 1994-1998 and Special Deputy Attorney General, 1998-2004, North Carolina Department of Transportation and North Carolina Board of Law Examiners. *Member:* Wake County, Tenth Judicial District and North Carolina (Administrative Law Section) Bar Associations; North Carolina State Bar; Defense Research Institute; North Carolina Association of Defense Attorneys. ***REPORTED CASES:*** Hodge v. N.C. Dept. of Transp., 161 N.C. App. 726, 589 S.E.2d 737 (2003); In re Gordon, 352 N.C. 349, 531 S.E.2d 795 (2000); In re Braun, 352 N.C. 327, 531 S.E.2d 213 (2000); Powell v. N.C. Dept. of Transp., 347 N.C. 614, 499 S.E.2d 180 (1998); Sidney v. Allen, 114 N.C. App. 138, 441 S.E. 2d 561 (1994). ***PRACTICE AREAS:*** Professional Licensing; Professional Discipline; Medical Disciplinary Proceedings; Attorney Discipline; Administrative Law; Employment Law; Employment Litigation; Employment Defense; Public Sector Employment Law; Insurance Defense; Business Litigation; Civil Appeals; Medical Malpractice Defense; Libel, Slander and Defamation; Law Enforcement Disciplinary; Covenants Not To Compete.

REPRESENTATIVE CLIENT: Medical Mutual Insurance Company of North Carolina.

PAUL P. CREECH
ATTORNEY AT LAW PLLC

3605 GLENWOOD AVENUE
SUITE 220
RALEIGH, NORTH CAROLINA 27612
Telephone: 919-787-7766
Fax: 919-787-7793
Email: paul@creechlaw.com
URL: http://www.creechlawfirm.com

Business, Corporate, Tax, Estate Planning, Real Estate, Wills Buying and Selling of Businesses.

PAUL P. CREECH, born Tarboro, North Carolina, September 3, 1951; admitted to bar, 1977, North Carolina; 1980, U.S. Tax Court; 1989, U.S. District Court, Eastern District of North Carolina. *Education:* University of North Carolina (A.B., 1974); University of South Carolina (J.D., 1977); University of Miami (LL.M., 1978). Co-Author: "Basic Probate in North Carolina"; "Sophisticated Section 1031 Transactions in North Carolina." Lecturer for CLE on Estate Planning and Probate matters. *Member:* Wake County, North Carolina (Member, Sections on: Tax Law; Business Law; Real Property; Estate Planning); Wake County Real Property Lawyers Association. ***PRACTICE AREAS:*** Business; Corporate; Tax; Estate Planning; Real Estate; Wills; Buying and Selling of Businesses. **Email:** paul@creechlaw.com

---

CRISP PAGE & CURRIN, LLP

1305 NAVAHO DRIVE, SUITE 302
RALEIGH, NORTH CAROLINA 27609-7444
Telephone: 919-876-8282
Fax: 919-876-8285
URL: http://www.cpclaw.com
URL: http://crisppageandcurrin.com

General Civil Practice in State and Federal Courts, Trial Practice, Appellate Practice, Civil Litigation, Business Litigation, Utilities, Cellular Telephone, Communications, Corporate Law, Cooperative, Non-Profit Organizations, Employment, Mediation, Administrative Law, Social Security Disability.

FIRM PROFILE: Crisp Page & Currin, L.L.P. was founded in 1960 by William T. Crisp. Through his efforts, and with the support of his other partners, the firm now serves as general counsel to several electric cooperatives and a telephone cooperative in North Carolina, and represents rural electric and telephone cooperatives in several other states. The firm now services clients in several areas of practice: general business and corporate, employment, cellular and long distance telephone communications, civil litigation, social security disability, mediation. Crisp Page & Currin teaches educational seminars for attorneys, cooperatives, managers, directors, and executives across North Carolina and the nation.

WILLIAM T. CRISP (1924-1992)

MEMBERS OF THE FIRM

ROBERT F. PAGE, born Pinehurst, North Carolina, March 27, 1944; admitted to bar, 1969, North Carolina; 1971, U.S. District Court, Eastern District of North Carolina; 1973, U.S. Court of Appeals, Fourth Circuit; 1974, U.S. Court of Appeals, District of Columbia Circuit; 1985, U.S. Supreme Court. *Education:* Duke University (B.A., 1966; J.D., 1969). Pi Sigma Alpha; Phi Delta Phi. Assistant District Attorney, Fayetteville, North Carolina, 1970-1971. Private Practice, 1971-1973. Staff Attorney and Hearing Officer, 1973-1977, North Carolina Utilities Commission. Staff Counsel, 1977-1980; Chief Counsel, 1980-1981; Public Staff, North Carolina Utilities Commission, Raleigh, North Carolina. Qualified Arbitrator, District 10. *Member:* Wake County, North Carolina and American Bar Associations; North Carolina Academy of Trial Lawyers; North Carolina EMC Counsel Association. ***REPORTED CASES:*** Nantahala Power & Light Co. et al v. Thornburg, Attorney General of North Carolina et al., 477 U.S. 902, 106 S. Ct. 3268, 91 L.Ed.2d 559 (1986); State ex rel. Utilities Comm'n v. Heater Util., Inc., 288 N.C. 457, 219 S.E. 2d 56 (1975). ***PRACTICE AREAS:*** Communications Law; Utility Law; Administrative Law; Cooperative Law; Corporate Law.

CYNTHIA M. CURRIN, born Oxford, North Carolina, November 18, 1954; admitted to bar, 1980, North Carolina, U.S. District Court, Eastern District of North Carolina, U.S. Court of Appeals, Fourth Circuit and U.S. Supreme Court. *Education:* University of North Carolina (A.B., 1977; J.D., 1980). Phi Beta Kappa. Clerk of Court, Holderness Moot Court Bench. Editor: Currin Energy Page, 1998—; NRECA Legal Reporting Service, 1993-1998. Member, Board of Editors, Trial Briefs, The Journal of North Carolina Academy of Trial Lawyers. Certified to Conduct Court-Ordered Mediation in Superior Court pursuant to Rules of the North Carolina Supreme Court. Qualified Arbitrator, District 10. Member, University of North Carolina Law School Mentoring Program, 1996-1997. *Member:* Wake County, North Carolina (Member, Lawyer Referral Committee) and American Bar Associations; North Carolina Academy of Trial Lawyers; The Association of Trial Lawyers of America; North Carolina Association of Women Attorneys; North Carolina EMC Counsel Association; Electric Cooperative Bar Association. ***REPORTED CASES:*** Springer-Eubank Company v. Four County Electric Membership Corporation and Four County ServicePlus, Inc., 543 S.E. 2d 197 (N.C. App. 2001); City of Charlotte v. Cook, 479 S.E. 2d 503 (N.C. App. 1997); Peace River Elec. Co-op. v. Ward Trans. 116 N.C. App. 493, 449 S.E.2d 202 (1994), disc. rev. denied, 339 N.C. 739, 454 S.E.2d 655 (1995); Weston v. Daniels, 442 S.E.2d 69 (N.C. App., 1994), disc. rev. denied 447 S.E.2d 433 (1994); Barbara S. Batts v. Louis W. Sullivan, M.D., 818 F.Supp. 138 (E.D.N.C., 1993); American Aluminum Products, Inc. v. John Richard Pollard and Calvin W. Morrison, 97 N.C. App. 541, 389 S.E. 2d 589 (1990); Janet M. Proctor v. The State Government of North Carolina, et al. 689 F. 2d 491 (4th Cir. 1982); Janet M. Proctor v. The State of North Carolina, et al. 830 F.2d 514 (4th Cir. 1987); Maureen Schneider and Thomas Schneider v. William B. Brunk, D.D.S.; Bruce V. Wainwright, D.D.S. and Bruce V. Wainwright, D.D.S., P.A. 72 N.C. App. 560, 324 S.E. 2d 922 (1985). ***PRACTICE AREAS:*** Civil Litigation; Utility Law; Cooperative Law; Corporate Law; Mediation; Social Security Disability Law.

REPRESENTATIVE CLIENTS: Central, Four County, Jones-Onslow, Tideland and Wake Electric Membership Cooperatives; Triangle Services Group, Inc.; Piedmont Telephone Membership Corporation; Piedmont Cable Services, Inc.; Carolina West Wireless.

CROUSE LAW OFFICES

Established in 2000

TWO HANOVER SQUARE, SUITE 2350
434 FAYETTEVILLE STREET MALL
RALEIGH, NORTH CAROLINA 27601
Telephone: 919-861-0500
Fax: 919-861-0504
Email: JTC@CrouseLaw.com
URL: http://www.crouselaw.com

National and International Aviation Litigation, Mass Disaster, Products Liability, Personal Injury Litigation, Appeals in all Courts.

JAMES T. CROUSE, born Asheville, North Carolina, August 12, 1949; admitted to bar, 1981, Louisiana; 1983, New York; 1986, District of Columbia; 1990, Texas; 1996, North Carolina; 1997, Virginia. *Education:* Davidson College (B.A., 1971); Duke University (J.D., 1980). Adjunct Professor of Aviation Law, Duke University School of Law, 2002—. Commercial Helicopter Pilot with Instrument Ratings, United States, 1973. Graduate, United States Army Helicopter Maintenance Test Pilot School, 1974. *Member:* North Carolina Bar Association, International Society of Air Safety Investigators (ISASI); American Helicopter Society; Helicopter Association International; American Institute of Aeronautics and Astronautics. [Capt., U.S. Army Aviator, Active Flight Duty, 1973-1977; Lieutenant Colonel, U.S. Army National Guard U.S. Army Reserve Aviator, Active Flight Duty, 1977-1987; Retired, 1997]. ***PRACTICE AREAS:*** Aviation Accidents Litigation; Personal Injury; Wrongful Death; Products Liability. **Email:** jtc@crouselaw.com

---

CURRIN LAW FIRM, PLLC

CURRIN LAW BUILDING
20 MARKET PLAZA
P.O. BOX 269
RALEIGH, NORTH CAROLINA 27602-0269
Telephone: 919-833-0888
Facsimile: 919-833-8171
URL: http://www.currinlaw.com
URL: http://www.lawyers.com/currinlaw
Mailing Address: P.O. Box 269, Raleigh, NC

Wilmington, North Carolina Office: Goolsby Law Building, 620 Market Street, 28401. Telephone: 910-763-3339. Fax: 910-763-1720.

Federal and State Criminal Defense, Civil and Criminal Forfeitures, Serious Personal Injury/Wrongful Death, Medical Malpractice, Government Relations.

SAMUEL T. CURRIN, born Oxford, North Carolina, December 13, 1948; admitted to bar, 1974, North Carolina; 1975, U.S. District Court, Eastern, Middle and Western Districts of North Carolina and U.S. Court of Appeals, Fourth Circuit; 1980, U.S. Supreme Court. *Education:* Wake Forest University (B.A., cum laude, 1971); University of North Carolina

(This Listing Continued)

CURRIN LAW FIRM, PLLC, Raleigh—Continued

(J.D., 1974). National Judicial College, 1988. Adjunct Professor of Law, Campbell University School of Law. Co-Author: "Regulation of Pornography-The North Carolina Approach," 21 Wake Forest Law Review 263, 1986. Superior Court Judge, 1987-1990. U.S. Attorney, Eastern District of North Carolina, 1981-1987. Assistant U.S. Attorney, Eastern District of North Carolina, 1976-1978. Legislative Counsel, U.S. Senate, 1978-1981. Presidential Elector, 1972, 2000. Chairman, North Carolina Republican Party, 1996-1999. *Member:* International Bar Association; North Carolina Academy of Trial Lawyers; National Association of Criminal Defense Lawyers; Association Internationale De Droit Penal; National Association of Former United States Attorneys. ***PRACTICE AREAS:*** Federal Criminal Law; Criminal Defense; Criminal Forfeiture; Wrongful Death; Personal Injury; Medical Malpractice; Government Relations. ***Email:*** sam@currinlaw.com

THOMAS C. GOOLSBY, born Dothan, Alabama, September 11, 1961; admitted to bar, 1992, North Carolina. *Education:* The Citadel (B.S., cum laude, with honors, 1984); Golden Gate University (M.B.A., 1987); University of North Carolina at Chapel Hill (J.D., 1991). Davis Honor Society. Air Traffic Control FAA Certified Tower Operator, 1985. Author: "Le Rôle Du Minist ère Public Am éricain, Revue Internationale De Droit Penal, 3 et 4 Trimestres 1992. Adjunct Professor of Law, Campbell University School of Law. Legal Counsel, North Carolina Governor's Crime Commission, 1992-1993. *Member:* North Carolina and International Bar Associations; Association Internationale De Droit Penal; Million Dollar Advocates Forum (Life Member). [USMC, 1984-1988, Recalled For Gulf War, Capt.]. ***PRACTICE AREAS:*** Federal Criminal Law; Criminal Defense; Personal Injury; Wrongful Death; Medical Malpractice. ***Email:*** thom@currinlaw.com

THE DALTON LAW FIRM, P.A.

2501 BLUE RIDGE ROAD
SUITE 390
RALEIGH, NORTH CAROLINA 26707
Telephone: 919-755-0255
Fax: 919-785-3422
Email: maryann@daltonlawyer.com
URL: http://www.daltonelderlawfirm.com

Elder Law, Medicaid Planning, Estate Planning, Asset Protection, Wills, Probate, Trusts, Collaborative Law, Elder Law Mediation.

MARY ANN DALTON, born Bryn Mawr, Pennsylvania, August 23, 1971; admitted to bar, 1999, North Carolina; 2000, Hawaii; 2002, Washington. *Education:* University of North Carolina at Chapel Hill (B.A., 1993); Campbell University (J.D., 1999). *Member:* North Carolina, Washington State, Hawaii State and American Bar Associations; National Academy of Elder Law Attorneys. ***PRACTICE AREAS:*** Elder Law; Estate Planning; Estate Administration; Asset Protection; Guardianship; Wills; Probate; Nursing Home Abuse; Elder Mediation; Collaborative Law.

DANIELS DANIELS & VERDONIK, P.A.

RALEIGH, NORTH CAROLINA

(See Research Triangle Park)

Business, Corporations, Venture Capital, Securities, Corporate Finance, Computers, Biotechnology, Telecommunications, Copyright, Trademark, Patent, Technology and Science, Intellectual Property, Management and Licensing, Domestic and International Taxation, Limited Liability Companies and Partnerships, Joint Ventures, International Trade and Investment, Immigration.

JOYCE L. DAVIS & ASSOCIATES

TWO HANNOVER SQUARE
SUITE 1730
P.O. BOX 709
RALEIGH, NORTH CAROLINA 27602
Telephone: 919-834-6534
Facsimile: 919-834-6536
Email: jldAssoc@jldavis.com
URL: http://www.jldavis.com

Employment Law, Civil Litigation, Cooperative Law, Non-Profit Law, and Business Law, including Board of Directors Legal Liability.

JOYCE L. DAVIS, born Charlotte, North Carolina, August 30, 1948; admitted to bar, 1974, North Carolina and U.S. District Court, Eastern, Middle and Western Districts of North Carolina; U.S. Court of Appeals, Fourth Circuit and U.S. Supreme Court. *Education:* University of North Carolina at Chapel Hill (B.S., 1970; J.D., 1974). Order of the Golden Fleece. Editor, NRECA Personnel Practice Pointers, 1981—. Instructor, NRECA Continuing Series, Employee & Labor Relations Update. Author: NRECA Employee & Labor Relations Manual, 1984-1992 and 1996—. President, Student Bar Association, 1973-1974. Member and President, Board of Directors, 1981-1983, East Central Community Legal Services Board. Appointed by Chief Judge to U.S. District Court, Eastern District Advisory Group for Civil Justice Reform Act of 1990, 1991-1995. *Member:* Wake County (President, Board of Directors, 1981), North Carolina and American Bar Associations; North Carolina Academy of Trial Lawyers (Member, Board of Governors, 1981-1987); North Carolina Association of Women Attorneys; The Association of Trial Lawyers of America. ***REPORTED CASES:*** Cozart v. Chapin, 39 N.C. App. 503, 251 S.E. 2d 681, pet. disc. rev. denied, 297 N.C. 29, 254 S.E. 2d 920 (1979); Janet M. Proctor v. The State Government of North Carolina, et al. 689 F.2d 491 (4th Cir. 1982); Janet M. Proctor v. The State of North Carolina, et al. 830 F 2d 514 (4th Cir. 1987); Duke v. Uniroyal, 743 F Supp. 1218 (E.D.N.C. 1990), modified, 928 F 2d 1413, cert. denied, 112 S Ct. 429 (4th Cir. 1991). ***PRACTICE AREAS:*** Labor Law; Employment Law; Personnel Law; Civil Litigation; Cooperative Law.

(This Listing Continued)

ASSOCIATES

EVERETTE P. WINSLOW, admitted to bar, 1997, North Carolina. *Education:* Howard University (B.A., summa cum laude, 1989); University of Iowa (J.D., 1997). President, Iowa Student Bar Association. *Member:* North Carolina and American Bar Associations; North Carolina Association of Black Lawyers. ***PRACTICE AREAS:*** Employment Law; Nonprofit and Charitable Organizations; Entertainment Law. ***Email:*** ewinslow@jldavis.com

C. ANDREW McGUFFIN, born Tucson, Arizona, August 25, 1969; admitted to bar, 2003, North Carolina. *Education:* Humboldt State University (B.A. History, 1998); Hastings College of the Law, University of California (J.D., 2002). *Member:* Wake County and American (Member, Young Lawyers Division) Bar Associations; North Carolina State Bar; North Carolina Academy of Trial Lawyers. [USMC, 1990-1994]. ***LANGUAGES:*** Spanish. ***PRACTICE AREAS:*** Employment; Personal Injury; Workers Compensation; Immigration and Naturalization. ***Email:*** amcguffin@jldavis.com

OF COUNSEL

LAURA J. WETSCH, born Fargo, North Dakota, November 18, 1959; admitted to bar, 1985, North Dakota; 1987, U.S. District Court, District of North Dakota; 1993, North Carolina and U.S. District Court, Eastern District of North Carolina. *Education:* Bismarck State College (A.A., 1980); University of North Dakota (B.A.; 1982, J.D., 1985). Member, North Dakota Law Review, 1984-1985. Law Clerk to the Hon. Patrick A. Conmy, Chief Judge, U.S. District Court, District of North Dakota, 1985-1988. Instructor, University of North Dakota, 1989. *Member:* North Carolina State Bar. ***PRACTICE AREAS:*** Litigation; Commercial Transactions; Employment Law. ***Email:*** lwetsch@jldavis.com

ADRIAN J. DAVIS
ATTORNEY AT LAW

234 FAYETTEVILLE STREET MALL
SUITE 200
RALEIGH, NORTH CAROLINA 27601
Telephone: 919-755-2274
Fax: 919-755-2274
Email: adavis.cclg@notrials.com
URL: http://www.wakefamilylawfirm.com

Family Law, Divorce, Child Custody, Child Support, Collaborative Law.

ADRIAN JAYE DAVIS, born Winston Salem, North Carolina, December 30, 1973; admitted to bar, 2000, North Carolina. *Education:* University of North Carolina at Chapel Hill (B.A., 1996; J.D., 1999). Member, Carolina Collaborative Law Group. *Member:* Wake County and North Carolina Bar Associations.

DAVIS & McCABE, P.A.

1115 HILLSBOROUGH STREET
RALEIGH, NORTH CAROLINA 27603
Telephone: 919-833-3370
Fax: 919-833-3371
URL: http://www.davismccabe.com

Personal Injury, Automobile Accidents and Injuries, Trucking Accidents, Medical Malpractice, Products Liability, Workers Compensation.

FIRM PROFILE: Davis & McCabe represents those seriously injured or killed as a result of others negligence.

BRIAN F. DAVIS, born Asheville, North Carolina; admitted to bar, 1991, North Carolina and U.S. District Court, Eastern District of North Carolina; 1993, U.S. District Court, Middle and Western Districts of North Carolina; 1996, U.S. Supreme Court. *Education:* University of North Carolina at Chapel Hill (B.A., 1987); Wake Forest University School of Law (J.D., 1991). Recipient: American Jurisprudence Award in Trial Practice, 1991; Association of Trial Lawyers of America, Weidemann Wysocki Citation of Excellence Award, 1994 & 1996. *Member:* Wake County, North Carolina and American Bar Associations; North Carolina Academy of Trial Lawyers (Member, Board of Governors, 1998 —); Association of Trial Lawyers of America. ***PRACTICE AREAS:*** Catastrophic Injury; Wrongful Death; Commercial Vehicle Liability; Automobile Accidents; Fraud and Deceit; Medical Malpractice; Professional Liability; Airplane Crash Litigation. ***Email:*** bdavis@davismccabe.com

JOHN MATTHEW McCABE, born Alameda, California; admitted to bar, 1994, North Carolina; U.S. District Court, Eastern District of North Carolina. *Education:* University of North Carolina (A.B., 1991); Campbell University (J.D., cum laude, 1994). *Member:* Wake County and North Carolina Bar Associations; North Carolina Academy of Trial Lawyers; Association of Trial Lawyers of America. ***PRACTICE AREAS:*** Personal Injury; Automobile Accidents; Products Liability; Nursing Home Litigation.

DEMENT, ASKEW, GAMMON & DEMENT

SUITE 1513 BRANCH BANK BUILDING
333 FAYETTEVILLE STREET MALL
P.O. BOX 711
RALEIGH, NORTH CAROLINA 27602
Telephone: 919-833-5555
Fax: 919-832-8287
Email: lawdagdo@aol.com

Criminal and General Civil Practice in State and Federal Courts and before State Departments and Commissions. Corporation, Real Estate Law, Trusts and Estates.

MEMBERS OF FIRM

RUSSELL W. DEMENT, JR., born Wake County, North Carolina, February 22, 1940; admitted to bar, 1965, North Carolina and U.S. District Court, Middle and Eastern Districts of North Carolina. *Education:* Wake Forest University (B.A., 1962; LL.B., 1965). Phi Delta Phi. Listed, "The Best Lawyers in America", 1990—. Lecturer: North Carolina Academy of Trial Lawyers; North Carolina Bar Association, 1976—; Assistant District Attorney, Wake County Superior Court, 1966-1967. Member, North Carolina Criminal Code Commission, 1976—. Susie Sharp Inns of Court. *Member:* Wake County, North Carolina and American Bar Associations; The North Carolina State Bar; Wake County Academy of Criminal Trial Lawyers; North Carolina Academy of Trial Lawyers; The Association of Trial Lawyers of America. ***PRACTICE AREAS:*** Criminal and Civil Litigation. ***Email:*** rdement@dagdo.com

GARLAND L. ASKEW, born Colerain, North Carolina, December 23, 1943; admitted to bar, 1969, North Carolina. *Education:* East Carolina University (A.B., 1966); University of North Carolina (J.D., 1969). Delta Theta Phi. Member, Grievance Committee, Tenth Judicial District. *Member:* Wake County and North Carolina Bar Associations; The North Carolina State Bar; Wake County Real Property Lawyers Association. ***PRACTICE AREAS:*** Real Estate; Probate; Business Law. ***Email:*** gaskew@dagdo.com

RICHARD T. GAMMON, born Raleigh, North Carolina, April 19, 1954; admitted to bar, 1981, North Carolina, U.S. District Court, Eastern, Middle and Western Districts of North Carolina and U.S. Court of Appeals, Fourth Circuit. *Education:* Campbell University (B.S., 1978; J.D., 1981). Law Clerk to United States Attorney, Eastern District of North Carolina, 1980-1981. Listed in "The Best Lawyers in America," 1999-2000. *Member:* Wake County (Member, Board of Directors, 1986 and 1994), North Carolina and American Bar Associations; The North Carolina State Bar (Member, North Carolina Disciplinary Hearing Commission); North Carolina Academy of Trial Lawyers. ***PRACTICE AREAS:*** Criminal Law (State and Federal Courts). ***Email:*** rgammon@dagdo.com

ANGELA L. DEMENT, born Winston-Salem, North Carolina, January 2, 1963; admitted to bar, 1988, North Carolina, U.S. District Court, Western, Middle and Eastern Districts of North Carolina and U.S. Court of Appeals, Fourth Circuit. *Education:* Wake Forest University (B.A., cum laude, 1985; J.D., 1988). Member: Moot Court Board; The Order of Barristers. ABA National Moot Court Team, 1987. Winner and Best Oralist, Polsky National Moot Court Competition, 1987. *Member:* Wake County, North Carolina (Member, Litigation Section) and American Bar Associations; North Carolina State Bar Association; North Carolina Academy of Trial Lawyers. ***PRACTICE AREAS:*** Personal Injury; Wrongful Death; General Civil Litigation.

RUSSELL W. DEMENT, III, born 1971; admitted to bar, 1997, North Carolina. *Education:* Wake Forest University (B.A., 1994; J.D., 1997). ***PRACTICE AREAS:*** Criminal Law; Civil Litigation. ***Email:*** rdementiii@dagdo.com

BERRYMAN J. FITZHUGH, III, born Richmond, Virginia, April 18, 1972; admitted to bar, 1998, North Carolina. *Education:* University of North Carolina (B.A., 1994); Norman A. Wiggins School of Law (J.D., 1998). *Member:* Wake County, North Carolina and American Bar Associations. ***PRACTICE AREAS:*** Criminal Law; Traffic Violations; Driving While Intoxicated.

REPRESENTATIVE CLIENTS: Branch Banking & Trust Co.; Myrick Construction Co.; Custom Homes of Raleigh, Inc.; The Title Company of North Carolina.
APPROVED ATTORNEYS FOR: Lawyers Title Insurance Corp.; Federal Land Bank; Chicago Title Insurance Co.; North Carolina State Highway Commission; Jefferson Pilot Title Insurance Co.; Fidelity National Title Insurance Company; Commonwealth Land Title Insurance Co.
REFERENCES: First Union National Bank; Branch Bank and Trust Co.; Bank of North Carolina (Raleigh Branch).

DLA PIPER RUDNICK GRAY CARY US LLP

SIX FORKS CENTER I
4700 SIX FORKS ROAD, SUITE 200
RALEIGH, NORTH CAROLINA 27609
Telephone: 919-786-2000
FAX: 919-786-2200
Email: info@dlapiper.com
URL: http://www.dlapiper.com

Annapolis, Maryland Office: 60 West Street, Suite 401, 21401-2434. Telephone: 443-482-3830. FAX: 443-482-3848.
Baltimore, Maryland Office (Downtown): 111 South Calvert Street, Suite 1950, 21202-6174. Telephone: 410-580-3000. FAX: 410-580-3665.
Baltimore, Maryland Office (Mt. Washington): 6225 Smith Avenue, 21209-3600. Telephone: 410-580-3000. FAX: 410-580-3001.
Boston, Massachusetts Office: One International Place, 21st Floor, 02110-2613. Telephone: 617-406-6000. FAX: 617-406-6100.
Chicago, Illinois Office: 203 North La Salle Street, Suite 1900, 60601-1293. Telephone: 312-368-4000. FAX: 312-236-7516.
Dallas, Texas Office: 1717 Main Street, Suite 4600, 75201-4605. Telephone: 214-743-4500. FAX: 214-743-4545.
Easton, Maryland Office: 117 Bay Street, 21601-2703. Telephone: 410-820-4460. FAX: 410-820- 4463.

(This Listing Continued)

Edison, New Jersey Office: Piper Rudnick LLP, A New Jersey Limited Liability Partnership, Robert A. Assuncao, Managing Partner, 379 Thornall Street, Eighth Floor, 08837-2226. Telephone: 732-590-1850. FAX: 732-590-1860.
La Jolla, California Office: 1200 Prospect Street, Suite 575, 92037. Telephone: 858-638-6806. Fax: 858-456-3075.
Las Vegas, Nevada Office: Hughes Center, 3960 Howard Hughes Parkway, Suite 400, 89109. Telephone: 702-737-3433. FAX: 702-737-1612.
Los Angeles, California Office (Century City): 1999 Avenue of the Stars, Fourth Floor, 90067-6022. Telephone: 310-595-3000. FAX: 310-595-3300.
Los Angeles, California Office (Downtown): 550 South Hope Street, Suite 2300, 90071-2631. Telephone: 213-330-7700. FAX: 213-330-7701.
New York, New York Office: 1251 Avenue of the Americas, 10020-1104. Telephone: 212-835-6000. FAX: 212-835-6001.
Paris, France Office: Cariddi, Mee, Rue, Association d'Avocats au Barreau de Paris, Correspondants de Piper Rudnick LLP, 12 rue de la Paix, 75002 Paris, France. Telephone: +33-1 42.61.57.71. FAX: +33-1 42.61.79.21.
Philadelphia, Pennsylvania Office: One Liberty Place, 1650 Market Street, Suite 4900, 19103. Telephone: 215-656-3300. FAX: 215-656-3301.
Reston, Virginia Office: 1775 Wiehle Avenue, Suite 400, 20190-5159. Telephone: 703-773-4000. FAX: 703-773-5000.
San Francisco, California Office: 333 Market Street, Suite 3200, 94105-2150. Telephone: 415-659-7000. FAX: 415-659-7300.
Tampa, Florida Office: 101 East Kennedy Boulevard, Suite 2000, 33602-5149. Telephone: 813-229-2111. FAX: 813-229-1447.
Washington, District of Columbia Office: 1200 Nineteenth Street, NW, Main Reception on 7th Floor, 20036-2412. Telephone: 202-861-3900. FAX: 202-223-2085.

Advertising, Promotion and Trade Practices; Aerospace and Defense; Antitrust and Trade Regulation; Aviation; Bankruptcy and Business Reorganization; Biosciences; Business and Technology; Class Action Litigation; Communications; Construction; Copyrights; Corporate Governance and Protective Practices; Corporate and Securities; Domain Name Practice; Drug and Medical Device; Electronic Commerce and Privacy; Employee Benefits and Executive Compensation; Energy; Environmental; Federal Affairs and Legislative; Finance; Finance, Financial Services and Bankruptcy; Franchise and Distribution; Franchise and Distribution-International; Franchise and Distribution-Litigation; Franchise and Distribution-Technology; Government Contracts; Government Controversies; Governmental Affairs, Land Use and Development; HIPAA Privacy and Security; Health Care; Homeland Security; Information Technology; Insurance and Reinsurance; Insurance and Surety Litigation; Intellectual Property; International Commerce and Litigation; Iraq Reconstruction; Labor and Employment Law; Leasing; Legislative Financial Services; Litigation; Lodging and Timeshare; Medical Malpractice Defense; Mergers and Acquisitions; Multifamily Housing and Community Development Law; Nonprofit Organizations; Outsourcing; Patent Litigation; Patent Prosecution; Pesticide; Private Client Services; Product Liability and Toxic Torts; Professional Liability; Project Finance; Public Finance; REITs and Real Estate Securitization; Real Estate; Real Estate Finance; Securities Litigation; Sports Facilities Development; State Legislation and Public Policy; Tax; Tax Policy and Legislation; Technology Transfer; Trademark Litigation; Trademarks; Transportation; Venture Capital and Emerging Companies; White Collar; Workout Experience.

FIRM PROFILE: As an organization, we place the highest value on building close working relationships with our clients. To accomplish that, we offer you lawyers who are culturally attuned to the business demands and legal requirements of their countries, who have excellent legal skills, and who are totally committed to our client service ethic. Our clients say that this commitment is what really sets us apart.

We provide an extensive range of legal services through seven global practice groups:

Corporate and Finance - On the corporate and finance side, we operate significant transactional-based practices and serve not only some of the world's largest companies but numerous middle and upper-mid market clients. The firm is on the panels of a number of major banks and financial institutions and has a substantial bankruptcy and restructuring practice.

We are relationship-driven lawyers meeting the ongoing legal needs of our clients wherever they choose to do business. Operating across the US, Europe and Asia, we offer you 2,700 lawyers in 49 cities in 18 countries. We act for enterprises across the full spectrum of business, including local, national and multinational companies in a wide range of business sectors. Our clients range from single-owner startups to household name companies known worldwide.

Commercial - The group will be a market leader in European Public Private Partnerships (PPPs) and the provision of infrastructure and project finance services to sponsors and funders internationally. The group has lawyers who are particularly experienced in energy, sports, water, defense, healthcare and transportation, and is also recognized worldwide for its top-ranked franchise and distribution practice.

Human Resources - With more than 200 lawyers located in key jurisdictions around the world, our human resources and labor lawyers are equipped to handle both local employment issues and complex cross-border transactions.

Legislative and Regulatory - At the federal and state level in the US, and in the individual countries of Europe as well as the EU, our people understand the legislative and regulatory process. To the strengths of our team, which includes our chairman, Senator George J. Mitchell, we add the firm's alliance with The Cohen Group, the international business consulting firm.

Litigation - The group brings together more than 800 top litigators in the US, Europe and Asia and offers lawyers experienced in patent, class action, securities, antitrust, banking and finance, technology, telecommunications and insurance disputes.

Real Estate - With over 200 real estate lawyers in both the US and the UK, our real estate practice is one of the most highly ranked in the world, serving the needs of developers, corporations, retailers and investors.

(This Listing Continued)

DLA PIPER RUDNICK GRAY CARY US LLP, Raleigh—Continued

Technology, Media and Communications (TMC) - This global practice represents a combination of market-leading teams in information technology/outsourcing, telecommunications, patent, trademark, copyright, media, e-business, sport, data protection and privacy. With over 420 lawyers globally, it will be one of the leading global TMC/TMT practices.

PARTNERS

ROBERT H. BERGDOLT, admitted to bar, 1991, New York; 1993, North Carolina. *Education:* Duke University (A.B., magna cum laude, 1987); Yale Law School (J.D., 1990). ***PRACTICE AREAS:*** Real Estate Investment Trusts; Corporate Law; Securities; Mergers, Acquisitions and Divestitures. ***Email:*** robert.bergdolt@dlapiper.com

WILLIAM R. KLAPP, JR., admitted to bar, 1986, New York, U.S. District Court, Southern and Eastern Districts of New York; 1988, Georgia; 2000, North Carolina. *Education:* Virginia Polytechnic Institute and State University (B.A., 1972); Florida State University (M.F.A., 1977); Fordham University (J.D., cum laude, 1985). ***LANGUAGES:*** Italian and French. ***PRACTICE AREAS:*** Structured Finance; Real Estate Joint Ventures; Real Estate Investment Trusts; Mergers and Acquisitions. ***Email:*** william.klapp@dlapiper.com

BRAD S. MARKOFF, admitted to bar, 1982, Missouri; 1984, U.S. Tax Court; 1985, North Carolina. *Education:* Duke University (A.B., with distinction, 1979); Washington University (J.D., 1982). Member, Washington University Law Quarterly, 1980-1982 (Editor, 1981-1982). Co-Chair, National REIT Practice, DLA Piper Rudnick Gray Cary US LLP. Managing Partner, DLA Piper Rudnick Gray Cary US LLP, Raleigh, North Carolina Office. *Member:* North Carolina Bar Association; American Bar Association; National Association of Real Estate Investment Trusts (Member, Board of Advisors); National Association of Bond Lawyers; Council for Entrepreneurial Development (Member, Board of Directors). (Partner-in-Charge, Alston & Bird LLP, Research Triangle Park Office). ***PRACTICE AREAS:*** Securities; Mergers, Acquisitions and Divestitures; Real Estate Investment Trusts; Emerging Growth Companies; Corporate Law; Business Law; Partnership Law; Tax Exempt Finance. ***Email:*** brad.markoff@dlapiper.com

JEFFREY D. MILLER, admitted to bar, 1996, North Carolina. *Education:* Pennsylvania State University (B.A., 1992); Wake Forest University (J.D., 1996; M.B.A., 1996). ***PRACTICE AREAS:*** Securities; Mergers and Acquisitions; Real Estate Investment Trusts. ***Email:*** jeffrey.miller@dlapiper.com

JEFFREY M. SULLIVAN, admitted to bar, 1995, Tennessee; 1998, North Carolina. *Education:* University of North Carolina at Chapel Hill (B.A., 1992); Vanderbilt University (J.D., 1995). Order of the Coif. ***Email:*** jeffrey.sullivan@dlapiper.com

OF COUNSEL

CHRISTINE C. LEHR, admitted to bar, 1996, Georgia; 1999, North Carolina. *Education:* University of North Carolina at Chapel Hill (B.S., Business Administration with highest distinction, 1993); Duke University (J.D., 1996). *Member:* Wake County, North Carolina and American Bar Associations; North Carolina State Bar; State Bar of Georgia. ***PRACTICE AREAS:*** Corporate; Securities; Mergers; Acquisitions; Divestitures. ***Email:*** christine.lehr@dlapiper.com

BRADFORD R. LENOX, admitted to bar, 1996, North Carolina. *Education:* College of William & Mary (B.B.A., 1988); Duke University (J.D., cum laude, 1996). Member, Alaska Law Review. Samuel Fox Mordecai Scholar. Certified Public Accountant, North Carolina, 1992. Co-Author: "Twas the Night Before Christmas When We Adopted Plain English," REIT Report, Spring 1998. *Member:* North Carolina and American Bar Associations; American Institute and North Carolina Association of Certified Public Accountants. ***PRACTICE AREAS:*** Real Estate Investment Trusts; Corporate and Securities; Emerging Growth and Venture Capital; Mergers and Acquisitions; Life Science; Life Science, Computers, and Software; Partnerships and Limited Liabilities Companies. ***Email:*** bradford.lenox@dlapiper.com

ASSOCIATES

KERRY E. CAMDEN, admitted to bar, 2005, North Carolina. *Education:* University of Pennsylvania (B.A., 2002); Wake Forest University School of Law (J.D., 2005). ***PRACTICE AREAS:*** Real Estate Capital Markets. ***Email:*** kerry.camden@dlapiper.com

CARRIE JOAN HARTLEY, admitted to bar, 2001, North Carolina. *Education:* University of North Carolina at Chapel Hill (B.A., with honors and highest distinction, 1998); Harvard University (J.D., magna cum laude, 2001). ***PRACTICE AREAS:*** Corporate Law; Securities. ***Email:*** carrie.hartley@dlapiper.com

DAMON M. McLEAN, admitted to bar, 2002, North Carolina. *Education:* Princeton University (A.B., 1999); Duke University (M.A., 2002; J.D., 2002). ***Email:*** damon.mclean@dlapiper.com

MICHAEL S. O'SULLIVAN, admitted to bar, 2002, North Carolina. *Education:* Pennsylvania State University (B.A., 1997); University of North Carolina at Chapel Hill (J.D., 2002). ***Email:*** michael.osullivan@dlapiper.com

DOUGLASS & DOUGLASS

Established in 1911

TWO HANNOVER SQUARE, SUITE 2050
P.O. BOX 362
RALEIGH, NORTH CAROLINA 27602-0362
Telephone: 919-832-1620
FAX: 919-833-8182
Email: douglassatty@earthlink.com
URL: http://www.lawyers.com/douglass&douglass

General Civil Litigation, Personal Injury, Automobile Accidents and Injuries, Traffic Violations, Wills, Trusts and Estates, Estate Administration, Real Estate.

(This Listing Continued)

CLYDE A. DOUGLASS (1889-1973)

CLYDE A. DOUGLASS, II (1923-1994)

THOMAS G. DOUGLASS, born Raleigh, North Carolina, December 22, 1956; admitted to bar, 1983, North Carolina. *Education:* Hampden-Sydney College (B.A., 1979); Campbell University (J.D., 1983). Arbitrator, National Association of Securities Dealers, American Stock Exchange. *Member:* Wake County and North Carolina Bar Associations; North Carolina State Bar; North Carolina Academy of Trial Lawyers. ***PRACTICE AREAS:*** General Practice; Personal Injury Law.

APPROVED ATTORNEYS: First Title Insurance Co.; Land America Lawyers Title; Commonwealth Title Insurance Co.
REFERENCES: First Citizens Bank and Trust Co.; Bank of America; RBC-Centrua Bank; Branch Banking & Trust Co.; Wachovia Bank & Trust Co.

WAYNE BUCHANAN EADS

715 WEST JOHNSON STREET
RALEIGH, NORTH CAROLINA 27603
Telephone: 919-833-3703
Fax: 919-833-0337
Email: waynebuchananeads@yahoo.com
Mailing Address: P.O. Box 25789, Raleigh, NC 27611-25789

Criminal Defense in State and Federal Courts. All Major Crimes, White Collar Crimes, Drug Offenses, Firearms Offenses, Trials and Appeals.

MEMBER OF FIRM

WAYNE B. EADS, born 1950; admitted to bar, 1975, Florida (inactive); 1979, North Carolina; 1984, U.S. Supreme Court; U.S. District Court, Eastern, Middle and Western Districts of North Carolina; U.S. Court of Appeals, Fourth Circuit; U.S. District Court, Eastern District of Tennessee. *Education:* East Carolina University (B.A., 1971); University of North Carolina at Chapel Hill (J.D., 1974). *Member:* National Association of Criminal Defense Lawyers. ***LANGUAGES:*** Spanish, Russian. ***PRACTICE AREAS:*** Criminal Defense Law; Major Crimes; White Collar Crimes; Drug Offenses; Firearms Litigation; Trials and Appeals. ***Email:*** waynebuchananeads@yahoo.com

THE EDMISTEN & WEBB LAW FIRM

133 FAYETTEVILLE STREET MALL, SUITE 300
P.O. BOX 1509
RALEIGH, NORTH CAROLINA 27602
Telephone: 919-831-8700
Fax: 919-831-8749
Email: rufus@rufusedmisten.com
Email: woodywebb@ew-law.com
URL: http://www.edmisten-webblaw.com

Other Raleigh Office: 132 South Salisbury Street, Suite 300. 27601. Telephone: 919-829-1988. Fax: 919-829-1983.

Civil and Criminal Litigation, Business and Corporate Law, Government Relations and Legislative Law, Administrative Law, Sports Law, Real Estate.

RUFUS L. EDMISTEN, born Boone, North Carolina, July 12, 1941; admitted to bar, 1967, North Carolina, U.S. District Court for the District of Columbia and U.S. Court of Appeals for the District of Columbia Circuit; 1968, U.S. Court of Military Appeals; 1970, U.S. Supreme Court; 1975, U.S. District Court, Eastern District of North Carolina. *Education:* University of North Carolina at Chapel Hill (B.A., with honors, 1963); George Washington University Law School (J.D., with honors, 1966). Phi Delta Phi. Member, George Washington University Law Review, 1965-1966. Member: Scottish Rite Bodies and York Rite Masonic Bodies of Raleigh; Amran Temple Shriners; NC Film Council; Preservation North Carolina; Wake County Society for the Prevention of Cruelty to Animals. Founder: General Counsel, Foundation for Good Business; Extra Special Super Kids Scholarship Program. President: Southern Appalachian Historical Association; North Carolina Capitol Foundation. Director, Capital Bank, Raleigh. Visiting Professor, Political Science, Greensboro College, 1985-1986. Aide and Chief Counsel to U.S. Senator Sam J. Ervin, Jr., 1964-1974. North Carolina Attorney General, 1974-1984. North Carolina Secretary of State, 1989-1996. Chairman, Information Resources Management Commission, North Carolina, 1992-1995. *Member:* North Carolina, District of Columbia, Federal and American Bar Associations; North Carolina State Bar. ***PRACTICE AREAS:*** Administrative Law; State and Federal Lobbying; Executive Lobbying; Legislative Lobbying; Personal Injury; Representation of High-Tech Companies before NGA, NASS and NAAG. ***Email:*** rufus@rufusedmisten.com

WILLIAM WOODWARD WEBB, born Birmingham, Alabama, November 21, 1945; admitted to bar, 1971, North Carolina; 1972, District of Columbia, U.S. District Court, Eastern, Middle and Western Districts of North Carolina, Cherokee Indian Tribal Supreme Court, U.S. Court of Appeals, Fourth, Sixth and D.C. Circuits, U.S. Supreme Court. *Education:* The Lawrenceville School; Stanford University (B.A., 1968); University of North Carolina (J.D., 1971). Phi Delta Phi. Co-Author: "Some Practical Implications of Civil Rico Cases," 7 Campbell Law Review 299, 1985; "Practice and Procedure Under Amended Rule 11 of the Federal Rules of Civil Procedure," 9 Campbell Law Review 11, 1986. Visiting Assistant Professor, North Carolina State University, 1975-1977. Panel Member, Georgetown University Law School Civil RICO Seminar, 1986. Presenter, "Introduction to Federal Practice in North Carolina," 2001. Associate Attorney General, Assistant Attorney General and Special Deputy Attorney General, North Carolina Department of Justice, 1973-1979. Assistant United States Attorney, Chief, Civil Section, Eastern District of North Carolina, 1979-1981. Member, Board of Directors, North State Legal Services, 1976-1981. Member, North Carolina Society of Health Care Attorneys, 1982. Member, North Carolina Boxing Commission, Appointed by Governor Eisley, 2001. *Member:* Wake County and North Carolina Bar Associations; The District of Columbia Bar; North

(This Listing Continued)

Carolina State Bar; Business Advisory Council (N.C. Secretary of State); Court TV Commentator. ***PRACTICE AREAS:*** Litigation (Civil and Criminal); Corporate Law; Legislative Law; Sports Law. ***Email:*** woodywebb@ew-law.com

WILLIAM WOODWARD WEBB, JR., born Durham, North Carolina, December 20, 1970; admitted to bar, 1999, North Carolina, U.S. District Court, Eastern, Middle and Western Districts of North Carolina, Cherokee Indian Tribel Supreme Court. *Education:* University of North Carolina-Chapel Hill (B.A., 1994); University of Richmond, T.C. Williams School of Law (J.D., 1998). Intern, U.S. Attorney's Office, Eastern District of North Carolina, 1997. Professional Tennis Player, 1994-1996. Member, Criminal Justice Act Panel Attorneys (Federal Criminal Cases). *Member:* Wake County and North Carolina Bar Association. ***PRACTICE AREAS:*** Civil Litigation; Criminal Litigation; Federal Criminal Law; Business Law; Corporate Law; Administrative Law; Sports Law. ***Email:*** woodywebbjr@ew-law.com

ASSOCIATES

GARDNER MARSHALL PAYNE, born Albemarle, North Carolina, July 15, 1972; admitted to bar, 2001, North Carolina. *Education:* North Carolina State University (B.A., 1994); Campbell University School of Law (J.D., 2001). Phi Delta Phi. Member: Campbell University School of Law Student Bar Association (President, 2000-2001); Institute of Political Leadership, 2005; North Carolina Big Sweep Board of Directors; Extra Special Super Kids Foundation. Board of Director, Finance Director for Lieutenant Governor Beverly Perdue. *Member:* North Carolina and Tenth Judicial District Bar Associations; North Carolina Young Lobbyist Association. ***PRACTICE AREAS:*** Lobbying; Government Relations; Corporate; Administrative Law; State Legislative Practice. ***Email:*** gardner@rufusedminsten.com

VIRGINIA DOCKERY WEBB, born Ft. Lauderdale, Florida, March 30, 1972; admitted to bar, 1997, North Carolina. *Education:* University of North Carolina, Chapel Hill (B.A., 1994); Wake Forest University School of Law (J.D., 1997). *Member:* Wake County (Member, Real Estate Section) and North Carolina Bar Associations. ***PRACTICE AREAS:*** Real Estate. ***Email:*** jennawebb@mindspring.com

EDWARDS & EDWARDS, L.L.P.

RALEIGH, NORTH CAROLINA

(See Greenville)

General Civil Practice in all State and Federal Courts. Personal Injury and Wrongful Death, Automobile Accidents, Professional Malpractice and Products Liability.

ELLIS & WINTERS LLP

P.O. BOX 33550
RALEIGH, NORTH CAROLINA 27636
Telephone: 919-865-7000
Fax: 919-865-7010
URL: http://www.elliswinters.com

Cary, North Carolina Office: 1100 Crescent Green, Suite 200, 27511-8105. Telephone: 919-865-7000. Facsimile: 919-865-7010.
Greensboro, North Carolina Office: 100 N. Greene Street, Suite 102, 27401. Telephone: 336-217-4193. Facsimile: 336-217-4198.

Trial and Appellate Practice in all State and Federal Courts. Commercial Litigation, Administrative Litigation, Medical Malpractice, Products Liability, Antitrust, Corporate, Real Estate and Finance.

RICHARD W. ELLIS, born Raleigh, North Carolina, April 20, 1942; admitted to bar, 1969, North Carolina. *Education:* University of North Carolina (A.B., 1964; J.D., with high honors, 1969). Order of the Coif. Associate Editor, North Carolina Law Review, 1968-1969. *Member:* International Association of Defense Counsel; Defense Research Institute; North Carolina Association of Defense Attorneys. Fellow: American College of Trial Lawyers. [U.S. Naval Reserve, Active Duty, 1964-1966]. ***PRACTICE AREAS:*** Products Liability; Civil Litigation; Commercial Litigation; Media Law; Antitrust. ***Email:*** dick_ellis@elliswinters.com

MICHAEL G. WINTERS, born Raleigh, North Carolina, January 6, 1953; admitted to bar, 1978, North Carolina. *Education:* University of North Carolina (B.S., 1975; J.D., 1978). Beta Gamma Sigma. Morehead Scholar. ***PRACTICE AREAS:*** Commercial Real Estate; Real Estate Development. ***Email:*** mike_winters@elliswinters.com

JONATHAN D. SASSER, born Monroe, North Carolina, March 1, 1956; admitted to bar, 1981, North Carolina; 1983, New York. *Education:* University of North Carolina at Chapel Hill (B.A., with honors, Political Science, 1978; J.D., with honors, 1981). Phi Beta Kappa. Morehead Fellow in Law. Morehead Scholar. North Carolina Law Review, 1980-1981. Law Clerk to Hon. Burley B. Mitchell, Jr., Associate Justice, 1982; Hon. J. Frank Huskins, Associate Justice, North Carolina Supreme Court, 1981. *Member:* North Carolina Bar Association (Chair, Constitutional Law Section, 2002-2003). ***PRACTICE AREAS:*** Intellectual Property Litigation; Toxic Torts; Environmental Litigation; Constitutional Law; Commercial Litigation; Securities Litigation. ***Email:*** jon_sasser@elliswinters.com

LESLIE C. O'TOOLE, born Chicago, Illinois, November 14, 1961; admitted to bar, 1986, North Carolina. *Education:* Brown University (A.B., with honors, magna cum laude, 1982); University of North Carolina (J.D., with high honors, 1986). Phi Beta Kappa; Order of the Coif. Morehead Fellow. Research Editor, North Carolina Law Review, 1985-1986. Secretary, Special Olympics World Summer Games, 1999. President, Raleigh Professional Women's Forum, 1988-1989. Board Chair, Special Olympics North Carolina. *Member:* North Carolina Association of Defense Attorneys (Executive Vice President); Defense Research Institute. ***PRACTICE AREAS:*** Civil Litigation; Products Liability; Medical Malpractice. ***Email:*** leslie_otoole@elliswinters.com

CHARLES N. ANDERSON, JR., born Raleigh, North Carolina, April 25, 1956; admitted to bar, 1986, North Carolina. *Education:* North Carolina State University (B.A., with honors, 1978); University of North Carolina (J.D., with high honors, 1986). Order of the Coif. Member, North Carolina Law Review, 1984-1985. ***PRACTICE AREAS:*** Corporate; Finance; Real Property. ***Email:*** chuck_anderson@elliswinters.com

PAUL K. SUN, JR., born Toledo, Ohio, May 28, 1957; admitted to bar, 1989, North Carolina. *Education:* Wittenberg University (B.A., magna cum laude, 1979); Vanderbilt University (M.B.A., 1981); Duke University (J.D., with highest honors, 1989). Order of the Coif. Founder's Medalist, Vanderbilt University. Articles Editor, Duke Law Journal, 1988-1989. Clerk to Judge J. Dickson Phillips, Jr., U.S. Court of Appeals, Fourth Circuit, 1989-1990. ***PRACTICE AREAS:*** Civil Litigation; Administrative Litigation; Criminal Litigation; Appellate Practice. ***Email:*** paul_sun@elliswinters.com

MATTHEW W. SAWCHAK, born Washington, D.C., June 3, 1962; admitted to bar, 1989, North Carolina. *Education:* Harvard University (A.B., cum laude, 1984); Duke University (J.D., with honors, 1989; LL.M., 1989). Order of the Coif. Editor-in-Chief, Duke Law Journal, 1988-1989. Clerk to Judge Clarence Thomas, U.S. Court of Appeals, District of Columbia Circuit, 1990. *Member:* North Carolina Bar Association (Past Chair, Appellate Rules Study Committee; Past Chair, Antitrust and Trade Regulation Section). ***LANGUAGES:*** Russian. ***PRACTICE AREAS:*** Business Litigation; Appellate Practice; Antitrust. ***Email:*** matt_sawchak@elliswinters.com

ALEX J. HAGAN, born Winston-Salem, North Carolina, February 7, 1965; admitted to bar, 1992, North Carolina. *Education:* University of North Carolina (B.A., 1987; J.D., with honors, 1992). Holderness Moot Court. Order of the Barristers. Clerk to Chief Justice James G. Exum, Jr., North Carolina Supreme Court. *Member:* North Carolina and American Bar Associations; North Carolina Association of Defense Attorneys; Defense Research Institute. ***PRACTICE AREAS:*** Civil Litigation; Medical Malpractice; Products Liability. ***Email:*** alex_hagan@elliswinters.com

JULIA F. YOUNGMAN, born Roanoke, Virginia, March 23, 1965; admitted to bar, 1994, North Carolina; 1996, District of Columbia. *Education:* Duke University (B.S., 1987; M.A., Environmental Science, 1994; J.D., with high honors, 1994). Order of the Coif. Managing Editor, Duke Law Journal. Law Clerk, Judge J. Dickson Phillips, Jr., U.S. Court of Appeals, Fourth Circuit, 1994-1995. Certified Mediator. [U.S. Army, 1987-1991, Captain]. ***PRACTICE AREAS:*** Commercial Litigation; Construction Law; First Amendment Law; Appellate Practice; Mediation. ***Email:*** julie_youngman@elliswinters.com

THOMAS D. BLUE, JR., born Charlottesville, Virginia, October 17, 1960; admitted to bar, 1997, North Carolina. *Education:* University of North Carolina at Asheville (B.A., summa cum laude, 1989); University of North Carolina at Chapel Hill (J.D., with honors, 1997). Staff Member, North Carolina Law Review, 1995-1997. ***PRACTICE AREAS:*** Civil Litigation. ***Email:*** tom_blue@elliswinters.com

CURTIS J. SHIPLEY, born Chariton, Iowa, February 21, 1963; admitted to bar, 1990, Illinois; 1991, District of Columbia; 1992, North Carolina. *Education:* Northwestern University (B.S., 1985); University of Iowa (J.D., with high distinction, 1988). Articles Editor, Iowa Law Review, 1987-1988. *Member:* North Carolina State Bar; American Bar Association. ***PRACTICE AREAS:*** Commercial Litigation; Products Liability; Environmental Litigation; Construction Litigation. ***Email:*** curtis_shipley@elliswinters.com

ASSOCIATES

SUZANNE COLLINS LAGERHOLM, born Laurinburg, North Carolina, November 15, 1967; admitted to bar, 1999, Pennsylvania; 2004, North Carolina. *Education:* University of North Carolina (B.A., 1994; J.D., 1999). Articles Editor, The North Carolina Journal of International Law and Commercial Regulation, 1998-1999. Former Associate, Buchanan Ingersoll, P.C. Author: In re Jenoptiak AG, 23 NCJILCR 691, Summer 1998. ***PRACTICE AREAS:*** Real Estate; Corporate Law. ***Email:*** suzanne_lagerholm@elliswinters.com

WENDY I. SEXTON, born Toronto, Ontario, Canada, January 17, 1973; admitted to bar, 1999, North Carolina; 2003, U.S. District Court, Eastern District of North Carolina; U.S. Court of Appeals, Fourth Circuit; 2004, U.S. District Court, Western and Middle Districts of North Carolina. *Education:* University of North Carolina at Chapel Hill (B.A., 1995); Wake Forest University School of Law (J.D., 1999). Member, Wake Forest University Law Review, 1997-1999. Member, Wake Forest University Moot Court Board, 1997-1999. *Member:* North Carolina and American Bar Associations; North Carolina Association of Defense Attorneys; Defense Research Institute. ***PRACTICE AREAS:*** Civil Litigation; Products Liability; Professional Malpractice; Antitrust; Commercial Litigation; Appellate Practice. ***Email:*** wendy_sexton@elliswinters.com

GEORGE F. SANDERSON, III, born Carson City, Nevada, June 9, 1973; admitted to bar, 2000, New York; 2001, U.S. District Court, Southern and Eastern Districts of New York; 2004, North Carolina and U.S. District Court, Eastern, Middle and Western Districts of North Carolina. *Education:* Georgetown University (A.B., 1995); New York University (J.D., 1999). Phi Beta Kappa. Law Clerk, Hon. Stephen L. St. John, Eastern District of Virginia Bankruptcy Court, 1999-2000. Author: "Congressional Involvement in Class Action Reform," 2, NYU J. Legis. & Pub. Pol., 315 (1999). ***PRACTICE AREAS:*** Commercial Litigation; Arbitration; Securities Litigation; Antitrust. ***Email:*** george_sanderson@elliswinters.com

DANIELLE ENG ROSE, born Albany, New York, April 13, 1972; admitted to bar, 2000, North Carolina. *Education:* College of William & Mary (B.A., summa cum laude, 1993); Duke University (J.D., with high honors, 2000). Phi Beta Kappa. *Member:* American, North Carolina, and Wake County Bar Associations. ***LANGUAGES:*** Spanish. ***PRACTICE AREAS:*** Business Litigation; Education Law. ***Email:*** danielle_rose@elliswinters.com

THOMAS H. SEGARS, born Wilmington, Delaware, 1975; admitted to bar, 2000, North Carolina; 2001, U.S Court of Appeals, Third Circuit. *Education:* Wake Forest University (B.A., magna cum laude, 1997); University of North Carolina (J.D., with high honors, 2000). Chancellors Scholar. Order of the Coif. Clerk to Judge Jane R. Roth, U.S. Court of Appeals, Third Circuit. ***PRACTICE AREAS:*** Litigation. ***Email:*** tom_segars@elliswinters.com

(This Listing Continued)

ELLIS & WINTERS LLP, Raleigh—Continued

BRIAN C. VICK, born Raleigh, North Carolina, April 22, 1972; admitted to bar, 2002, North Carolina. *Education:* Vassar College (B.A., 1994); University of Georgia School of Law (J.D., summa cum laude, 2002). Clerk to Judge Joel F. Dubina, U.S. Court of Appeals, Eleventh Circuit. **Email:** brian_vick@elliswinters.com

STEPHEN C. KEADEY, born Mt. Vernon, Ohio, September 26, 1969; admitted to bar, 2003, North Carolina. *Education:* University of North Carolina at Chapel Hill (A.B., summa cum laude, 1991); North Carolina State University (M.A., 1994); University of North Carolina at Chapel Hill School of Law (J.D., with honors, 2002). Clerk to Judge William Osteen, U.S. District Court, Middle District of North Carolina. **Email:** steve_keadey@elliswinters.com

JOHN A. CHILSON, born Wellsboro, Pennsylvania, 1969; admitted to bar, 1999, Michigan; 2003, North Carolina. *Education:* U.S. Naval Academy (B.S., 1991); University of Michigan at Ann Arbor (J.D., cum laude, 1999). Author: "Keeping Clean Waters Clean: Making the Clean Water Act's Antidegradation Policy Work," Vol. 32, University of Michigan Journal of Law Reform. *Member:* North Carolina and American Bar Associations; State Bar of Michigan; Defense Research Institute. [Lt. Commander, U.S. Navy, 1991-2003]. **PRACTICE AREAS:** Products Liability; Commercial Litigation; Civil Rights Litigation; Criminal Defense. **Email:** john_chilson@elliswinters.com

OF COUNSEL

DONNA K. BLUMBERG, born Lafayette, Louisiana, May 31, 1959; admitted to bar, 1985, North Carolina. *Education:* University of North Carolina (B.A., 1981; J.D., 1985). Order of the Coif. **PRACTICE AREAS:** Commercial Real Estate. **Email:** donna_blumberg@elliswinters.com

(For Complete Biographical Data on all Personnel, see Professional Biographies at Cary, North Carolina and Greensboro, North Carolina)

ELMORE & WALL, P.A.

3737 GLENWOOD AVENUE, SUITE 100
RALEIGH, NORTH CAROLINA 27612
Telephone: 919-865-9500
Fax: 919-865-9501
Email: keith.coltrain@elmorewall.com
URL: http://www.elmorewall.com

Mailing Address: P.O. Box 10937, Raleigh, NC 27605

Charleston, South Carolina Office: 145 King Street, Suite 302. 29401. Telephone: 843-329-9500. Fax: 843-329-9501.

Greenville, South Carolina Office: 301 North Main Street, Suite 2000, 29601. Telephone: 864-255-9500. Fax: 864-255-9505.

Construction, Surety, Complex Litigation, Medical Malpractice, Products Liability, Toxic Torts, Class Actions, Insurance Defense, Arbitration, Mediation.

FIRM PROFILE: Elmore & Wall, P.A. handles legal matters in the following practice areas: Construction, Surety, Complex Litigation, Arbitration, Mediation, Insurance Defense and the Defense of Medical Malpractice, Products Liability, Toxic Torts and Class Actions.

KEITH E. COLTRAIN, born Bethel, North Carolina, December 17, 1964; admitted to bar, 1995, North Carolina. *Education:* North Carolina State University (B.S., summa cum laude, Chemical Engineering, 1988); University of North Carolina at Chapel Hill (J.D., 1995). Member: The Order of the Barristers; Holderness Moot Court Bench; Environmental Negotiation Team, 1993-1995. Staff Member, North Carolina Journal of International Law and Commercial Regulation, 1994-1995. Member, Carolinas AGC. Member, Construction Specifications Institute. *Member:* North Carolina Bar Association (Member, Sections on: Construction; Litigation); American Bar Association (Member, Construction Law Section); Defense Research Institute. **PRACTICE AREAS:** Construction Law; Civil Litigation. **Email:** keith.coltrain@elmorewall.com

EMANUEL & DUNN, PLLC

130 SOUTH SALISBURY STREET
RALEIGH, NORTH CAROLINA 27602
Telephone: 919-832-0329; 919-832-0320
Fax: 919-832-6731

New Bern, North Carolina Office: 3230 Country Club Road, P.O. Drawer 1389, 28563. Telephone: 252-633-3800. Fax: 252-633-6669.

Civil Trials in all State and Federal Courts. Business Litigation, Employment Litigation, Personal Injury Litigation, ERISA Litigation, Business Law, Contracts, Real Estate, Estate Planning and Probate, Employment Law.

FIRM PROFILE: Established over 75 years ago, the firm of Emanuel & Dunn, PLLC has grown into a strong practice serving North Carolina with special emphasis on litigating and resolving employment, complex business and computer related disputes; wealth transfer planning and wills and estates; and business transactions.

MEMBERS OF FIRM

ROBERT L. EMANUEL, born Raleigh, North Carolina, August 28, 1926; admitted to bar, 1951, North Carolina; U.S. District Court, Eastern, Middle and Western Districts of North Carolina; U.S. Court of Appeals, Fourth Circuit. *Education:* University of North Carolina (A.B., 1948; LL.B., 1951). Phi Delta Phi. Member, Staff of State Attorney General, 1952-1954. Solicitor, Cary, North Carolina, Recorders Court, 1956-1962. *Member:* Wake County and North Carolina Bar Associations; North Carolina Bar; North Carolina Association of Defense Attorneys. **PRACTICE AREAS:** Business Law; Business Transactions. **Email:** remanuel@emanuelanddunn.com

(This Listing Continued)

STEPHEN A. DUNN, born New Bern, North Carolina, January 16, 1956; admitted to bar, 1984, North Carolina; 1986, Georgia; U.S. District Court, Eastern, Middle and Western Districts of North Carolina; U.S. Court of Appeals, Fourth Circuit. *Education:* North Carolina State University (B.A., 1981); Cumberland School of Law of Samford University (J.D., 1984). *Member:* Wake County and North Carolina Bar Associations; North Carolina State Bar; State Bar of Georgia. (Resident, Raleigh Office). **PRACTICE AREAS:** Business Litigation; ERISA; Insurance Defense; Contracts; Real Estate. **Email:** sdunn@emanuelanddunn.com

RAYMOND E. DUNN, JR., born Durham, North Carolina, February 27, 1951; admitted to bar, 1979, North Carolina and U.S. District Court, Eastern District of North Carolina. *Education:* University of North Carolina (B.A., 1973; M.R.P., 1976); Wake Forest University (J.D., 1979). Member, Wake Forest Law Review, 1977-1979. Author: "The Standard of Commercial Reasonableness In The Sale of Repossessed Collateral," 15 Wake Forest Law Review 71, 1979. Member, Panel of Arbitrators, American Arbitration Association. *Member:* Craven County, North Carolina and American (Member, Litigation Section) Bar Associations; North Carolina State Bar. **PRACTICE AREAS:** Business Litigation; Employment Litigation; Personal Injury Litigation. **Email:** rdunn@emanuelanddunn.com

JAMES M. MASON, born La Jolla, California, March 2, 1972; admitted to bar, 2004, North Carolina and U.S. District Court, Eastern District of North Carolina; 2005, U.S. District Court, Western and Middle Districts of North Carolina and U.S. Court of Appeals, Fourth Circuit. *Education:* Duke University (B.A., History, 1994); Wake Forest University (J.D., 2004). **PRACTICE AREAS:** Business Litigation; ERISA; Employment; Federal Practice; Environmental Law. **Email:** jmason@emanuelanddunn.com

COUNSEL FOR: Ads Infinitum; Auto Interiors & Tops; Bell South Communications, Inc.; Capitol City Lumber Company; Cargill, Incorporated; Chicago Southern Management, Inc.; Davis Landscape, Ltd.; Fidelity Mutual Life Insurance Company; Hertzburg Furs; Interior Distributors, Inc.; J.W. Buress, Inc.; John Hancock Mutual Life Insurance Company; Lone Wolf Publishing, Inc.; Massachusetts Mutual Life Insurance Company; Mckinney & Silver; Metropolitan Life Insurance Company; Modern Woodmen of America; Mutual Benefit Life Insurance Company; New England Mutual Life Insurance Company; Nextec Communications; Penn-America Insurance Company; Principal Mutual Life Insurance Company; Quality Air Service, Inc.; Shenandoah Life Insurance Company; Stan Taylor Insurance Agency, Inc.; Stratton Tire; Sunlink, Inc.; The Equitable Tire America; The Great West Life Assurance Company; The Prudential Insurance Company of America; Turf Transport; United Turf, Inc.; Western Electric Co.; William Penn Life Insurance Company.

(For complete biographical data on all personnel, see Professional Biographies at New Bern, North Carolina)

EVERETT, GASKINS, HANCOCK & STEVENS, LLP

Established in 1905
THE PROFESSIONAL BUILDING, SUITE 600
127 WEST HARGETT STREET
P.O. BOX 911
RALEIGH, NORTH CAROLINA 27602-0911
Telephone: 919-755-0025
Fax: 919-755-0009
URL: http://www.eghs.com

Administrative Law, Appellate Practice, Bankruptcy, Business Law, Biotechnology, Commercial Law, Commercial Litigation, Communications and Media Law, Construction Law, Corporate Law, Debtor and Creditor Law, Education Law, First Amendment Law, Franchise Law, Intellectual Property, Insurance Law, International Trade Law, Internet Law, Litigation, Lobbying, Non-Profit Corporations and Charitable Organizations, Parliamentary Law, Tax and Estate Planning, Tax Controversies, Taxation, Toxic Torts, Trade Association Law.

FIRM PROFILE: Everett, Gaskins, Hancock & Stevens, LLP, is a multi-faceted law firm that emphasizes technology, quality of service and value for its clients, and quality of life for its attorneys and staff. The firm's practice is guided by written principles which articulate its values. For example, the firm purposely controls growth by focusing its practice in selected areas in which its lawyers have proven expertise; nevertheless, it provides a broad array of services, including litigation in state and federal courts; media law; legislative representation; bankruptcy; tax and estate planning; business law; and administrative law. A significant portion of the firm's litigation and transactional work involves matters in which the firm's lawyers team with out-of-state and foreign law firms to provide North Carolina representation to clients based in New York, Chicago, London and other world commercial centers.

The firm's diverse trial practice includes complex commercial and construction litigation; the representation of news organizations in libel, privacy and other First Amendment cases; disputes related to insurance and reinsurance brokerage and coverage; and suits on behalf of individuals or businesses injured or affected by toxic mold. Through Trial View, an affiliated entity, the firm helps other lawyers prepare for trial by arranging and evaluating mock trials, practice arguments and focus groups.

The firm's legislative practice focuses on the North Carolina General Assembly, where Everett, Gaskins represents the North Carolina travel and tourism industry and the school districts in 77 of the state's 100 counties. The firm represents various organizations in the bioscience industry, including the North Carolina Life Sciences Development Corporation. The firm also handles administrative matters before a variety of local, state and federal regulatory agencies, including occupational licensing boards.

The firm's comprehensive bankruptcy practice includes service as a bankruptcy trustee, the representation of debtors and creditors, business reorganization and work-outs, and the prosecution and defense of bankruptcy-related adversary proceedings.

The firm's business and estate planning practice provides clients with sophisticated counsel on a wide variety of issues related to business planning and business succession, individual, corporate and partnership taxation and estate planning and administration.

(This Listing Continued)

The firm's attorneys regularly practice before state and federal courts and administrative agencies throughout North Carolina. Members of the firm are admitted to practice in Georgia, the District of Columbia, and Louisiana, and before the Supreme Court of the United States, the Fourth U.S. Circuit Court of Appeals, the U.S. Tax Court, and the U.S. Court of Claims.

The firm's principles and other information about the firm are available at www.eghs.com. References and a list of representative clients will be provided on request.

PARTNERS

R.O. EVERETT (1878-1971)

KATHRINE R. EVERETT (1893-1992)

HUGH CANNON (1931-2005)

ED GASKINS, JR., born New Bern, North Carolina, May 15, 1941; admitted to bar, 1966, North Carolina; 1979, District of Columbia; 1983, U.S. Supreme Court. *Education:* Wake Forest University (B.A., 1963); Duke University (J.D., 1966). ***PRACTICE AREAS:*** Administrative Law; Bankruptcy Litigation; Debtor and Creditor; Commercial Litigation; Complex Litigation; Construction Law; Mold Litigation. ***Email:*** ed@eghs.com

WILLIAM GERRY HANCOCK, JR., born Charlotte, North Carolina, July 29, 1943; admitted to bar, 1971, North Carolina. *Education:* University of North Carolina (A.B., 1965); Duke University (J.D., 1968). ***PRACTICE AREAS:*** Lobbying; Government; Travel and Tourism; Nonprofit and Charitable Organizations; Public School Law; Trade Association Law. ***Email:*** gerry@eghs.com

HUGH STEVENS, born Burlington, North Carolina, August 29, 1944; admitted to bar, 1968, North Carolina; 1970, U.S. Court of Military Appeals; 1979, U.S. Supreme Court. *Education:* University of North Carolina (A.B., 1965; J.D., with honors, 1968). ***PRACTICE AREAS:*** Civil Litigation; First Amendment Law; Insurance; Libel, Slander and Defamation; Media Law; Reinsurance. ***Email:*** hugh@eghs.com

PAUL C. RIDGEWAY, born 1960; admitted to bar, 1986, North Carolina. *Education:* North Carolina State University (B.S., 1982; M.P.A., 1989); Campbell University (J.D., cum laude, 1986); University of Amsterdam (D. Int'l. L., 1987). Editor-in-Chief, Campbell Law Review, 1986. *Member:* Wake County Bar Association (President, 2002). ***PRACTICE AREAS:*** Trade Regulation; Business Law; Franchises and Franchising; International Trade; Litigation; Internet Law. ***Email:*** paul@eghs.com

C. AMANDA MARTIN, born Raleigh, North Carolina, July 22, 1967; admitted to bar, 1992, Georgia; 1994, North Carolina. *Education:* University of Florida (B.S., 1989); University of North Carolina (J.D., with honors, 1992). ***PRACTICE AREAS:*** Media Law; Libel, Slander and Defamation; Internet Litigation; Labor and Employment; Trademarks; Nonprofit and Charitable Organizations; First Amendment Law; Communications and Media; Internet Law. ***Email:*** amartin@eghs.com

LOUIS E. WOOTEN, III, born Raleigh, North Carolina, April 6, 1963; admitted to bar, 1988, Georgia; 1990, District of Columbia; 1992, North Carolina. *Education:* University of North Carolina at Chapel Hill (B.A./B.S., 1985); Wake Forest University (J.D., 1988); Emory University (LL.M., Taxation, 1990). ***PRACTICE AREAS:*** Business Planning; Estate and Gift Taxation; Tax Litigation; Estate Administration; Estate Planning; Tax Planning; Wills; Real Estate Foreclosure. ***Email:*** Louis@eghs.com

WILLIAM P. JANVIER, born New Orleans, Louisiana, March 8, 1967; admitted to bar, 1993, Louisiana; 1994, North Carolina. *Education:* Rice University (B.A., 1989); University of North Carolina (J.D., with honors, 1992). Member, North Carolina Bankruptcy Council, Panel of Chapter 7 Trustees. (Board Certified Specialist in Business and Consumer Bankruptcy Law, North Carolina State Board of Legal Specialization). ***PRACTICE AREAS:*** Creditor Bankruptcy; Debtor Bankruptcy; Bankruptcy Litigation; Commercial Litigation. ***Email:*** Bill@eghs.com

K. MATTHEW VAUGHN, born Eden, North Carolina, August 22, 1968; admitted to bar, 1993, North Carolina. *Education:* University of North Carolina (B.S., Business Administration, 1990); University of Texas at Austin (J.D., 1993). ***PRACTICE AREAS:*** Business Litigation; Insurance Agents and Brokers Errors and Omissions; Insurance Coverage; Insurance Litigation; Unfair Insurance Practices; Civil Appeals; Complex Business Litigation; Uniform Commercial Code; Bankruptcy; Commercial Litigation. ***Email:*** matt@eghs.com

MICHAEL J. TADYCH, born Berea, Ohio, June 22, 1968; admitted to bar, 1997, North Carolina and U.S. District Court, District of South Carolina; U.S. Court of Appeals, Fourth Circuit. *Education:* Indiana University (B.A., Telecommunications, 1990); Case Western Reserve University (J.D., cum laude, 1997). ***PRACTICE AREAS:*** Agricultural Law; Trade Regulation; Commercial Law; Communications and Media; Entertainment and the Arts; Copyrights; Trademarks; Insurance Bad Faith; Sports Law. ***Email:*** mike@eghs.com

ASSOCIATE

ASHLEY MATLOCK, admitted to bar, 2001, North Carolina. *Education:* University of North Carolina at Chapel Hill (B.A., 1998; J.D., 2001). Phi Beta Kappa; Kappa Tau Alpha. Recipient: Brandeis Law School Scholarship; Alala Law School Scholarship. ***PRACTICE AREAS:*** Civil Litigation. ***Email:*** ashley@eghs.com

OF COUNSEL

ROBINSON O. EVERETT, born Durham, North Carolina, March 18, 1928; admitted to bar, 1950, North Carolina; 1954, District of Columbia. *Education:* Harvard University (A.B., magna cum laude, 1947); Harvard Law School (J.D., magna cum laude, 1950); Duke Law School (LL.M., 1959). ***PRACTICE AREAS:*** Administrative Law; Civil and Criminal Appeals; Commercial Real Property; Commercial Litigation; Construction Litigation; Zoning and Land Use Regulation.

All members of the firm are admitted to all state and federal courts in North Carolina and the United States Court of Appeals for the Fourth Circuit.

FERGUSON, STEIN, CHAMBERS, GRESHAM & SUMTER, P.A.

RALEIGH, NORTH CAROLINA

(See Charlotte)

Civil Rights, Employment and Labor, General Civil, Criminal, Plaintiff's Medical Malpractice, Trial and Appellate Practice. Probate and Real Estate Law.

LAW OFFICE OF JOHN C. FITZPATRICK, P.C.

RALEIGH, NORTH CAROLINA

(See Durham)

DWI, Traffic, Criminal, Personal Injury.

THE FLEXNER LAW FIRM, P.A.

300 W. MILLBROOK ROAD, SUITE 101
RALEIGH, NORTH CAROLINA 27609
Telephone: 919-787-1661; 1-800-FLEXNER
Fax: 919-787-1771
Email: flexlaw@flexlaw.com
URL: http://www.flexlaw.com

Personal Injury, Products Liability, Medical Malpractice, Automobile Accidents and Injuries, Truck Accidents, Motorcycle Accidents, Workers Compensation, Social Security Disability, Wrongful Death, Civil Litigation, Insurance Litigation, Hospital Negligence, Nursing Home Negligence, Catastrophic Injury.

FIRM PROFILE: The Flexner Law Firm, P.A. practices in a wide range of matters involving serious personal injuries and wrongful death. Richard M. Flexner, the firm's founder, has more than twenty five years of experience successfully representing injured persons and their families.

The firm places the highest emphasis on its relationship with its clients. This client-focused approach to personal injury law results in representation that identifies and responds to client needs.

RICHARD M. FLEXNER, born Newark, New Jersey, January 24, 1953; admitted to bar, 1977, New Jersey, Pennsylvania and U.S. District Court, District of New Jersey; 1983, District of Columbia; 1997, North Carolina. *Education:* Pennsylvania State University (B.A., with high distinction, 1974); Villanova University (J.D., 1977). Adjunct Professor, Montclair State University, 1985-1987. Arbitrator, New Jersey Superior Court, 1990-1996. Arbitrator, North Carolina General Court of Justice, 1999—. *Member:* Wake County, North Carolina, Pennsylvania and New Jersey State Bar Associations; North Carolina State Bar; District of Columbia Bar; North Carolina Academy of Trial Lawyers. ***PRACTICE AREAS:*** Personal Injury; Products Liability; Medical Malpractice; Automobile Accidents and Injuries; Wrongful Death; Truck Accidents; Motorcycle Accidents; Premises Liability; Social Security Disability; Workers Compensation; Civil Litigation; Insurance Litigation; Hospital Negligence; Nursing Home Negligence; Catastrophic Injury. ***Email:*** rflexner@flexlaw.com

TONYA LYNETTE FORD

16 WEST MARTIN STREET, SUITE 604
RALEIGH, NORTH CAROLINA 27601
Telephone: 919-829-1500
Fax: 919-829-1600
Email: tlford@tlfordlaw.com
URL: http://www.tlfordlaw.com

Employment Law, Discrimination, Employee Benefits, Sexual Harassment, Wrongful Termination, Criminal Law, Driving While Intoxicated, Juvenile Crimes, Traffic Violations, Business Law, Personal Injury.

TONYA LYNETTE FORD, born Winston-Salem, North Carolina, February 1, 1974; admitted to bar, 1999, North Carolina; U.S. District Court, Middle District of North Carolina; 2004, U.S. District Court, Eastern and Western Districts of North Carolina; U.S. Court of Appeals, Fourth Circuit. *Education:* Hampton University (B.A., with honors, 1996); North Carolina Central University School of Law (J.D., 1999). Author: "Sexual Harassment of School Employees by Other School Employees," National Council of School Attorneys, March 2001; "Effective Training on Sexual Harassment by Employees." Member, North Carolina Central University School of Law Alumni Board. *Member:* Wake County, North Carolina State and American Bar Associations; North Carolina Academy of Trial Lawyers.

FRANCIS & AUSTIN, PLLC

TWO HANNOVER SQUARE
434 FAYETTEVILLE STREET MALL
SUITE 2300
P.O. BOX 164
RALEIGH, NORTH CAROLINA 27602-0164
Telephone: 919-828-0801
Fax: 919-828-0804
URL: http://www.lawyers.com/francis&austin

Appellate Advocacy, Automobile Accidents and Personal Injuries, Business Organization, Complex Business Litigation, Federal Civil Practice, Unfair and Deceptive Trade Practices, Debtor and Creditor Collections, Commercial Litigation, Construction Litigation, Insurance

(This Listing Continued)

FRANCIS & AUSTIN, PLLC, Raleigh—Continued

Law, Public Housing, Trial Practice, Medical Negligence, Birth Injury, Civil Litigation, Personal Injury, Wrongful Death, Public Finance, Private Finance, Toxic and Environmental Torts, Defamation and Media Torts.

CHARLES T. FRANCIS, born 1963; admitted to bar, 1989, North Carolina; U.S. District Court, Estern, Middle and Western Districts of North Carolina; U.S. Court of Appeals, Fourth Circuit. *Education:* Princeton University (A.B., 1985); Duke University (J.D., 1988). Law Clerk to the Hon. Richard C. Erwin, Chief Judge, Middle District of North Carolina, 1988-1989. Assistant U.S. Attorney, Middle District of North Carolina, 1989-1990. Member, Board of Directors, Capital Economic Development Corporation, 1990-1992. Member of Board, Mechanics & Farmers Bank, Raleigh, 1991-1993. Vice Chair, Wake County Democratic Party, 1991-1992. City of Raleigh Planning Commissioner, 1991-1992. Member, Raleigh City Council, 1993. Member, Rex Healthcare, Board of Trustees, 1998-2002. Trustee, Rex Endowment. Director and Vice Chairman, North State Bank, 2000—. *Member:* Wake County (Board of Directors, 1995—) and North Carolina Bar Associations; North Carolina Academy of Trial Lawyers; North Carolina Association of Black Lawyers. ***PRACTICE AREAS:*** Civil Litigation; Personal Injury; Medical Negligence; Birth Trauma; Insurance Law; Legislative Representation; Business Crimes Law; Business Representation; Utility Regulation; Employment Law. ***Email:*** cfrancis@francisandaustin.com

JOHN SCOTT AUSTIN, born Atlanta, Georgia, May 9, 1964; admitted to bar, 1994, North Carolina; 1995, U.S. District Court, Eastern District of North Carolina. *Education:* North Carolina State University (B.A., 1990); Campbell University School of Law (J.D., 1994). Delta Theta Phi. Managing Editor, Campbell Law Review, 1993-1994. Law Clerk to Burley B. Mitchell, Chief Justice of the North Carolina Supreme Court, 1994-1995. Author: "Prosecutorial Discretion and Substantial Assistance: The Power and Authority of Judicial Review - United States v. Wade," 15 Campbell Law Review 263 (Summer, 1993). Associate Editor, Litigation News, 2002—. *Member:* Wake County, North Carolina (Member, Environmental Law Section, 1995-1997; Executive Council, Young Lawyers Division, 1997-2000) and American (Member, Section on Litigation, 2000—; Tort Trial & Insurance Practice Section; Executive Council, Young Lawyers Division, 1998-2000) Bar Associations; North Carolina Association of Black Lawyers. ***PRACTICE AREAS:*** Automobile Accidents; Business Litigation; Defamation; Media Law; Torts; Collections; Insurance; Commercial Litigation; Personal Injury; Medical Negligence; Civil Litigation; Appellate Advocacy; Toxic Tort Litigation; Environmental Litigation; Creditors Rights; Real Estate Litigation. ***Email:*** jaustin@francisandaustin.com

OF COUNSEL

ALAN D. WOODLIEF, JR., born Oxford, North Carolina, January 5, 1969; admitted to bar, 1994, North Carolina. *Education:* University of North Carolina (B.A., 1991); Campbell University (J.D., magna cum laude, 1994). Order of Barristers. Listed in *Who's Who Among American Colleges and Universities.* Articles Editor, Campbell Law Review. Revising Author, *Hightowers North Carolina Law of Damages* (Harrison Publishing Co). Assistant Professor of Law, Legal Research and Writing, Campbell University, 1995—. *Member:* North Carolina (Member, Appellate Rules Study Commission) and American Bar Associations. ***PRACTICE AREAS:*** Business Litigation; Business Representation; Unfair Trade Practice; Civil Litigation.

STACIE S. WATSON, admitted to bar, 1997, North Carolina. *Education:* Tuskegee University (B.S., 1987); University of Arizona (J.D., 1995).

GAILOR, WALLIS & HUNT, PLLC

THE 1903 BUILDING
1101 HAYNES STREET, SUITE 201
RALEIGH, NORTH CAROLINA 27604
Telephone: 919-832-8488
Fax: 919-832-8283
URL: http://www.gailorwallis.com

Equitable Distribution, Divorce Litigation, Child Custody, Child Support, Hague Convention Proceedings, Domestic Relations Appeals, Divorce Mediation, Arbitration and Adoption, Family Law.

CAROLE S. GAILOR, born Boston, Massachusetts, April 14, 1945; admitted to bar, 1977, Virginia, U.S. Court of Appeals, Fourth and Fifth Circuits and U.S. District Court, Eastern District of Virginia; 1978, District of Columbia and U.S. District Court, Western District of Virginia; 1983, North Carolina. *Education:* American University (B.A., 1967; J.D., cum laude, 1977). *Member:* The District of Columbia Bar; North Carolina Bar Association; Virginia State Bar. Fellow, American Academy of Matrimonial Lawyers. (Board Certified Specialist in Family Law, North Carolina State Board of Legal Specialization). ***PRACTICE AREAS:*** Family Law; Divorce; Equitable Distribution; Domestic Relations Appeals; Divorce Mediation; Divorce Arbitration; Hague Convention Proceedings. ***Email:*** cgailor@gailorwallis.com

KIMBERLY ANN WALLIS, born Alexandria, Virginia, August 14, 1969; admitted to bar, 1995, North Carolina. *Education:* North Carolina State University (B.A., magna cum laude, 1991); Wake Forest University School of Law (J.D 1995). Law Clerk to the Honorable Ralph A. Walker, North Carolina Court of Appeals, 1995-1996. *Member:* Wake County, Sixteenth Judicial District and North Carolina State Bar. ***PRACTICE AREAS:*** Family Law; Appellate Practice; Domestic Relations Litigation; Equitable Distribution; Adoption. ***Email.*** kwallis@gailorwallis.com

CATHY CUBBON HUNT, born Ft. Belvoir, Virginia, June 20, 1961; admitted to bar, 1996, North Carolina; 1997, Virginia; 1998, District of Columbia. *Education:* University of North Carolina (B.S., magna cum laude, 1993); University of Memphis (J.D., 1996). Listed in: Who's Who of College Students; Who's Who of Law Students. Recipient, Chancellor's Award for Academic Excellence. Member, University of Memphis Law Review. *Member:* North Carolina Bar Association; Virginia State Bar; The District of Columbia Bar. ***PRACTICE AREAS:*** Family Law; Domestic Relations; Equitable Distribution. ***Email:*** chunt@gailorwallis.com

JAIME HUMPHRIES DAVIS, born Raleigh, North Carolina, August 4, 1976; admitted to bar, 2001, North Carolina. *Education:* University of North Carolina at Chapel Hill (B.A., with distinction, 1998; J.D., 2001). *Member:* North Carolina State Bar; North Carolina, Wake County and American Bar Associations. ***PRACTICE AREAS:*** Family Law; Domestic Relations Litigation; Equitable Distribution; Support. ***Email:*** jdavis@gailorwallis.com

STEPHANIE THOMAS JENKINS, born Greeneville, Tennessee, March 16, 1966; admitted to bar, 1992, North Carolina. *Education:* Davidson College (B.A., 1988); University of North Carolina at Chapel Hill (J.D., 1992). Assistant District Attorney, Tenth Judicial District, 1996-2002. *Member:* Wake County and American Bar Associations; North Carolina State Bar; Tenth Judicial District Bar. ***PRACTICE AREAS:*** Family Law; Domestic Relations; Equitable Distribution; Criminal Law; Criminal Defense. ***Email:*** sjenkins@gailorwallis.com

STEPHANIE J. GIBBS, born Albany, New York, January 11, 1958; admitted to bar, 2003, North Carolina. *Education:* State University of New York at Brockport (B.A., magna cum laude, 1980); University of North Carolina School of Law at Chapel Hill (J.D., 2003). Recognition for pro bono service. Law Clerk to the Honorable Martha A. Geer, North Carolina Court of Appeals, 2003-2004. *Member:* North Carolina State Bar; North Carolina Bar Association (Chair, Policy and Legislation Subcommittee; Disability Law Committee). ***PRACTICE AREAS:*** Family Law; Domestic Relations; Criminal Defense; Disabilities; Guardianship. ***Email:*** sjgibbs@gailorwallis.com

ROSEMARY GODWIN

434 FAYETTEVILLE STREET MALL
RALEIGH, NORTH CAROLINA 27601
Telephone: 919-834-6161
Fax: 919-834-6269
Email: rosemarygodwin@bellsouth.net
URL: http://www.rosemarygodwinlaw.com

Criminal Law in all State and Federal Courts. Federal Criminal Law, White Collar Crime, Driving While Intoxicated, Drug Crimes, Felonies, Homicide, Misdemeanors, Sexual Assault, Traffic.

ROSEMARY GODWIN, born Erwin, North Carolina, August 16, 1958; admitted to bar, 1991, North Carolina. *Education:* University of North Carolina (B.S.B.A., 1980); Campbell University (J.D., cum laude, 1991). Member, National Trial Team, Campbell University. *Member:* Wake County Bar Association; North Carolina State Bar; Wake County Criminal Trial Lawyers (Treasurer, 1999; Vice-President, 2000); North Carolina Academy of Trial Lawyers; National Association Criminal Defense Lawyers.

KEITH O. GREGORY

TWO HANNOVER SQUARE
434 FAYETTEVILLE STREET MALL, SUITE 2310
RALEIGH, NORTH CAROLINA 27601
Telephone: 919-832-3148
Email: attykeithgregory@aol.com
URL: http://www.kogregorylaw.com

Criminal Law, Driving While Intoxicated, Drug Crimes, Felonies, Homicide, Sexual Assault, Traffic Violations, Personal Injury, Automobile Accidents, Wrongful Death, Uncontested Divorces, Entertainment Law, Music Contracts, Athletic Contracts.

KEITH O. GREGORY, born Emporia, Virginia, April 21, 1966; admitted to bar, 1995, North Carolina. *Education:* University of Virginia (B.A., 1988); North Carolina Central University (J.D., 1994). Assistant Public Defender, Cumberland County, 1995-1996. Assistant District Attorney, Wake County, 1996-2000. *Member:* Wake County Bar Association; North Carolina State Bar; Susie Sharpe Inns of Court. ***LANGUAGES:*** Spanish. ***PRACTICE AREAS:*** Criminal Law; Driving While Intoxicated; Drug Crimes; Felonies; Homicide; Sexual Assault; Traffic Violations; Personal Injury; Automobile Accidents and Injuries; Wrongful Death; Divorce; Entertainment Law; Music Law; Sports Contracts; Separation Agreements; Wills.

HAAS McNEIL & ASSOCIATES, P.A.

Established in 1992
801 OBERLIN ROAD
SUITE 250
RALEIGH, NORTH CAROLINA 27605
Telephone: 919-783-9669
Fax: 919-783-7235
URL: http://www.carolinafamilylaw.com
Email: inquiry@carolinfamilylaw.com
URL: http://www.haasmcneil.com

Family Law, Divorce, Separation Agreements, Child Support, Child Custody, Alimony, Domestic Violence, Visitation Rights, Spousal Support, Property Distribution, Prenuptial Agreements, Alimony, Domestic Law, Adoption, Litigation, Mediation, Collaborative Law, Alternative Dispute Resolution, LGBT Law, and Non-Traditional Family Law.

FIRM PROFILE: The law firm of Haas McNeil & Associates, P.A. represents clients in the many facets of Family Law. From separation through Divorce, the law firm prides itself in effective communications with all parties, tough effective representation, and resolution to family issues whether through settlement, mediation, collaboration, or litigation. We utilize the many resources available to effectively serve our clients.

(This Listing Continued)

ANGELA L. HAAS, born Raleigh, North Carolina; admitted to bar, 2002, North Carolina; U.S. District Court, Eastern District of North Carolina. *Education:* Appalachian State University (B.S., Psychology, 1988; B.S., Criminal Justice, 1988); Campbell University (J.D., 2002). Phi Alpha Delta; Order of Barristers. Speaker, GALA Continuing Legal Education, Spring 2005. Co-Founder, Carolina Collaborative Law Group, 2002. *Member:* North Carolina State Bar; North Carolina Bar Association (Member, Sections on: ADR; Family Law); 10th Judicial District; Carolina Collaborative Law Group (Member and Co-founder); North Carolina Association of Women Attorneys; North Carolina GALA (Treasurer, Board of Directors); International Academy of Collaborative Law Professionals; Wake County Bar Association. ***PRACTICE AREAS:*** Family Law; Divorce; Separation Agreements; Child Custody; Child Support; Alimony; Collaborative Law; Domestic Partnerships; Non-Traditional Family Law; Premarital Agreements; Uncontested Divorce. ***Email:*** inquiry@carolinafamilylaw.com

JOHN P. McNEIL, born Miami, Florida, February 2, 1968; admitted to bar, 2001, North Carolina and U.S. District Court, Middle District of North Carolina. *Education:* University of North Carolina at Wilmington (B.A., 1998); Wake Forest University School of Law (J.D., 2001). Phi Alpha Delta. Executive Board Member, Post 1, American Legion. Member, Veterans of Foreign Wars. *Member:* North Carolina Bar Association (Member, Family Law Section); North Carolina Academy of Trial Lawyers; 10th Judicial District Bar Association. [Sgt., U.S. Marine Corps Infantry, 1986-1992]. ***REPORTED CASES:*** Long v. Long (October 2003); Evans v. Evans (June 2003); Scott v. Scott (May 2003). ***PRACTICE AREAS:*** Family Law; Divorce; Domestic Relations; Domestic Violence; Equitable Distribution; Civil Litigation; Criminal Law; Traffic Law; Military Divorce; Litigation; Alimony; Marital Property Distribution; Post Divorce Modification; Restraining Orders; Separation Agreements; Spousal Support. ***Email:*** jmcneil@carolinafamilylaw.com

L. ALLEN HAHN, P.A.

RALEIGH, NORTH CAROLINA

(See Greenville)

Real Property, Real Estate, Corporations, Collections, Wills and Estates Law, Loan Closings.

KYLE S. HALL

5 WEST HARGETT STREET
SUITE 810
P.O. BOX 2211
RALEIGH, NORTH CAROLINA 27602
Telephone: 919-831-8901
Fax: 919-831-8719
Email: khall@mindspring.com
URL: http://www.lawyers.com/ks-hall

Criminal Law, Homicide, Sexual Assault, Drug Crimes, Felonies, Misdemeanors, Driving While Intoxicated, Traffic Violations, Parole and Probation, Personal Injury, Products Liability, Automobile Accidents and Injuries, Wrongful Death, Railroad Accidents.

KYLE S. HALL, born Sampson County, North Carolina, December 9, 1944; admitted to bar, 1970, North Carolina, U.S. District Court, Eastern and Middle Districts of North Carolina and U.S. Court of Appeals, Fourth Circuit. *Education:* University of North Carolina (A.B., 1967; J.D., 1970). Law Clerk, North Carolina Court of Appeals, 1970-1971. Assistant District Attorney, Wake County, 1971-1978. *Member:* Wake County, North Carolina and American Bar Associations; North Carolina Academy of Trial Lawyers; The Association of Trial Lawyers of America; Wake County Academy of Criminal Defense Lawyers (President, 1984); National Association of Criminal Defense Lawyers.

HARDISON & LEONE, L.L.P.

225 HILLSBOROUGH PLACE, SUITE 400
P.O. BOX 27843
RALEIGH, NORTH CAROLINA 27603-7843
Telephone: 919-829-0449
Toll Free: 1-800-738-0449
Fax: 919-835-1379
Email: ken@hardisonandleone.com
URL: http://www.hardisonandleone.com

Dunn, North Carolina Office: 212 S. Wilson Avenue, P.O. Box 759, 28335. Telephone: 910-892-1181. Toll Free: 1-888-892-1181. Fax: 910-892-7874.
Fayetteville, North Carolina Office: 1014 Hay Street, Post Office Drawer 53037, 28305-5316. Telephone: 910-223-3022. Toll Free: 800-782-3145. Fax: 910-223-9006.
Southern Pines, North Carolina Office: 235 E. Pennsylvania Avenue, Sandhills Executive Center, 28387. Telephone: 910-695-1183. Toll Free: 800-600-7969. Fax: 919-835-1379.
Greensboro, North Carolina Office: 7B Corporate Center Court, 27408. Telephone: 336-370-1299. Toll Free: 800-600-7969. Fax: 919-835-1379.
Charlotte, North Carolina Office: 6047 Tyvola Glen Circle, 28217. Telephone: 704-377-3190. Toll Free: 800-600-7969. Fax: 919-835-1379.
Myrtle Beach, South Carolina Office: 115 48th Avenue, Suite 122, 29577. Telephone: 843-467-2100. Toll Free: 800-600-7969. Fax: 919-835-1379.
Durham, North Carolina Office: 2530 Meridian Parkway, Suit 3.

Personal Injury, Auto and Trucking Accidents, Pedestrian Accidents, Catastrophic Injury, Medical Malpractice, Workers' Compensation, Social Security Disability, Nursing Home Negligence, Security Investment Fraud, Inadequate Security Claims, Premises Liability, Mass Torts, Drug Liability Claims, Employment Law, Appellate Practice, Immigration.

FIRM PROFILE: Hardison & Leone, L.L.P. represents clients in every level of state and federal courts with a reputation for legal excellence in the representation of plaintiffs in its practice areas.

(This Listing Continued)

KENNETH L. HARDISON, born Dunn, North Carolina, December 23, 1956; admitted to bar, 1982, North Carolina. *Education:* Campbell University (B.S., cum laude, 1975; J.D., 1982). Delta Theta Phi; Epsilon Pi Eta. Member, Campbell Law Review, 1981-1982. Author: Workers Compensation, "You Take (45%) of My Breath Away," Campbell Law Review Vol. 4, Pg. 107, 1982; Numerous Manuscripts for NCATL Seminars, 2002-2004. Co-Author: "The ABC's of Law Office Management, 2003; "4 The Client," 2004; "Claimants for Life," North Carolina Paralegal Association State Convention, 2004. Speaker: Client Service: "From Expert to Advocate," NCATL Law Office Management Seminar, September 2002; Numerous NCATL Seminars. *Member:* Harnett County (Secretary/Treasurer, 1983-1984), Wake County, North Carolina and American Bar Associations (Member, Sections on: Auto Torts; Workers Compensation); North Carolina Academy of Trial Lawyers; The Association of Trial Lawyers of America; Million Dollar Advocates Forum. ***PRACTICE AREAS:*** Catastrophic Injury; Wrongful Death; Automobile Accidents and Injuries; Workers Compensation; Mass Torts; Investment Fraud. ***Email:*** ken@hardisonandleone.com

ELIZABETH A. LEONE, born Jacksonville, North Carolina, February 20, 1969; admitted to bar, 1998, North Carolina. *Education:* Campbell University (B.S., cum laude, 1995; J.D., 1998). Speaker: Numerous NCATL Seminars; Gerry Spence Trial Lawyers College, Dubois, Wyoming, 2000. Presenter, "How to Try Soft Tissue Cases," NCATL, 2004. *Member:* Wake County, North Carolina and American Bar Associations; Eleventh Judicial Bar Association; North Carolina Academy of Trial Lawyers (Past Chair, Auto Torts Section; Chair, Fall Mountain Magic Convention, 2004); Association of Trial Lawyers of America (Member, Sections on: Motor Vehicle Liability); Million Dollar Advocates Forum. ***PRACTICE AREAS:*** Trial Practice; Automobile Accidents and Injuries; Wrongful Death; Medical Malpractice; Catastrophic Injury; Nursing Home Abuse and Neglect. ***Email:*** beth@hardisonandleone.com

BENJAMIN T. COCHRAN, born Rocky Mount, North Carolina, December 28, 1976; admitted to bar, 2002, North Carolina. *Education:* University of North Carolina at Chapel Hill (B.A., 1999); Norman A. Wiggins School of Law, Campbell University (J.D., 2002). Phi Alpha Delta. Speaker, "Medical Records Management for North Carolina Paralegals," IPE Institute for Paralegal Education, June 2004. *Member:* Wake County Bar Association; North Carolina State Bar; Tenth Judicial Bar Association; North Carolina Academy of Trial Lawyers. (Managing Attorney, Workers' Compensation). ***PRACTICE AREAS:*** Workers Compensation; Personal Injury. ***Email:*** btcochran@hardisonandleone.com

JENNIFER H. SEATE, born Amherst, Ohio; admitted to bar, 1996, North Carolina. *Education:* Campbell University (B.A., summa cum laude, 1993); Norman A. Wiggins School of Law, Campbell University (J.D., 1996). North Carolina Claims Adjustor, 1996-2002. Former Allstate Insurance Company Legal Claims Adjustor. *Member:* Harnett County Bar Association; North Carolina State Bar; North Carolina Academy of Trial Lawyers. ***PRACTICE AREAS:*** Automobile Accidents and Injuries; Personal Injury. ***Email:*** jhseate@hardisonandleone.com

JOSEPH W. OSMAN, born Knoxville, Tennessee, August 17, 1970; admitted to bar, 1996, North Carolina; U.S. Court of Appeals, Fourth Circuit; U.S. District Court, Eastern and Middle Districts of North Carolina. *Education:* University of North Carolina at Pembroke (B.A., 1993); Campbell University (J.D., 1996). *Member:* Cumberland County, Robeson County, North Carolina and American Bar Associations; North Carolina Academy of Trial Lawyers; The Association of Trial Lawyers of America. ***PRACTICE AREAS:*** Medical Negligence; Personal Injury; Professional Negligence; Civil Litigation. ***Email:*** jwosman@hardisonandleone.com

C. MICHAEL MILLARD, born Goldsboro, North Carolina, April 30, 1957; admitted to bar, 1993, North Carolina. *Education:* Bob Jones University (B.S., Business Administration, cum laude, 1989); University of South Carolina (J.D., 1992). *Member:* North Carolina Bar Association; North Carolina Academy of Trial Lawyers. ***Email:*** cmmillard@hardisonandleone.com

K. GREGORY GUNTER, born Bryson City, North Carolina, March 17, 1973; admitted to bar, 2001, North Carolina; U.S. District Court, Eastern District of North Carolina. *Education:* Western Carolina University (B.S., magna cum laude, 1996); University of North Carolina at Chapel Hill (J.D., 2001). Author, "Computerized Credit Scoring's Effect on The Lending Industry," 4 North Carolina Banking Institute 443, 2000; "Three Guideposts to Representing Hispanic Clients," North Carolina Lawyers Weekly, June 14, 2004 at 17. *Member:* North Carolina State Bar. ***PRACTICE AREAS:*** Personal Injury (5%); Workers Compensation (95%). ***Email:*** kggunter@hardisonandleone.com

CHRISTOPHER R. NICHOLS, born Southampton, New York, July 11, 1969; admitted to bar, 1994, North Carolina and U.S. District Court, Western District of North Carolina. *Education:* Wake Forest University (B.A., cum laude, 1991; J.D., 1994). Outstanding Member, Moot Court Board; Order of the Barristers; American Inns of Court. *Member:* Henderson County (President, 1997-1998) and Wake County Bar Associations; The Association of Trial Lawyers of America; North Carolina Academy of Trial Lawyers (Board of Governors, 1999-2000; Chair, Young Lawyers Division, 1999-2000; Chair, Auto Torts Division, 2004-2005); National College of Advocacy. ***PRACTICE AREAS:*** Medical Malpractice; Trucking Liability; Automobile Liability; Arbitration; Insurance Litigation; Brain Injury; Sexual Abuse. ***Email:*** cnichols@hardisonandleone.com

SHARON K. DOW, born Gastonia, North Carolina, February 12, 1973; admitted to bar, 1997, North Carolina. *Education:* Wingate University (B.A., 1994); Norman A. Wiggins School of Law (J.D., 1997). *Member:* American Immigration Lawyers Association. ***PRACTICE AREAS:*** Immigration Law. ***Email:*** skd@hardisonandleone.com

MORGAN CARRIDY GUTSHALL, born Greensboro, North Carolina, June 24, 1980; admitted to bar, 2005, North Carolina. *Education:* University of Tennessee at Knoxville (B.A., 2002); Campbell University (J.D., 2005). Order of Barristers. Member, 2002-2005 and Secretary, 2005, Phi Alpha Delta. ***PRACTICE AREAS:*** Automobile Accidents and Injuries. ***Email:*** mcg@hardisonandleone.com

OF COUNSEL

RICHARD B. GLAZIER, born Allentown, Pennsylvania, June 16, 1955; admitted to bar, 1981, North Carolina; 1984, U.S. District Court, Eastern District of North Carolina;

(This Listing Continued)

HARDISON & LEONE, L.L.P., Raleigh—Continued

1989, U.S. Supreme Court and U.S. Court of Appeals, Fourth Circuit. *Education:* Pennsylvania State University (B.A., 1977); University of Virginia; Wake Forest University (J.D., 1981). Elected to the North Carolina House of Representatives, 2003—. *Member:* Cumberland County, North Carolina and American (Member, Criminal Justice Section) Bar Associations; North Carolina State Bar; The Association of Trial Lawyers of America; North Carolina Academy of Trial Lawyers. ***PRACTICE AREAS:*** Appellate Practice; Civil Rights; Employment. ***Email:*** rbg@hardisonandleone.com

JAMES T. IRVIN, JR., born Shelby, North Carolina, March 29, 1940; admitted to bar, 1967, South Carolina and U.S. District Court, District of South Carolina; 1969, U.S. Court of Appeals, Fourth Circuit. *Education:* University of Georgia (B.S., Business Administration, 1963); University of South Carolina (J.D., 1966). *Member:* South Carolina Bar; National Association of Criminal Defense Lawyers; National Association of Federal Defense Lawyers. (Also practicing individually, North Myrtle Beach). ***PRACTICE AREAS:*** Criminal Law; Personal Injury; Automobile Accidents and Injuries; Construction Accidents; Medical Malpractice; Wrongful Death.

Languages: English and Spanish.

MALCOLM E. HARRIS, P.A.

RALEIGH, NORTH CAROLINA

(See Wake Forest)

HARRIS & WINFIELD, llp

Established in 1999

1044 WASHINGTON STREET
RALEIGH, NORTH CAROLINA 27605
Telephone: 919-546-8788
Fax: 919-546-8789
URL: http://www.harriswinfield.com
Email: email@harriswinfield.com
URL: http://www.harris-winfield.com

Business Litigation, Breach of Contract, Trademark and Copyright Litigation, Technology Litigation, Medical Malpractice, Wrongful Death, Unfair Trade Practices Litigation, Catastrophic Injury.

DONALD J. HARRIS, born 1962; admitted to bar, 1988, North Carolina; 1989, U.S. District Court, Eastern and Middle Districts of North Carolina; 1995, U.S. Court of Appeals, Fourth Circuit. *Education:* State University of New York at Geneseo (B.S., 1983); State University of New York at Buffalo (J.D., 1988). *Member:* North Carolina Bar Association; American Trial Lawyers Academy. ***PRACTICE AREAS:*** Business Litigation; Technology Litigation; Trademark Litigation; Copyright Litigation; Medical Malpractice; Wrongful Death; Catastrophic Injury. ***Email:*** dharris@harriswinfield.com

MARGARET WINFIELD HARRIS, born 1969; admitted to bar, 1994, North Carolina; 1995, U.S. District Court, Eastern and Middle Districts of North Carolina; U.S. Court of Appeals, Fourth Circuit. *Education:* University of Virginia (B.A., 1991; J.D., 1994). Phi Beta Kappa. Recipient, Waggenheim Memorial Scholarship. *Member:* North Carolina Bar Association. ***PRACTICE AREAS:*** Business Litigation; Technology Litigation. ***Email:*** mwh@harriswinfield.com

CLAY HODGES, born Elizabeth City, North Carolina, August 4, 1968; admitted to bar, 2000, North Carolina. *Education:* University of North Carolina at Chapel Hill (B.A., with honors, 1990; J.D., 2000). Judicial Law Clerk, Judge John C. Martin, North Carolina Court of Appeals, 2000-2002. English Instructor, Coastal Carolina Community College, 1994-1997. ***PRACTICE AREAS:*** Education Law; Business Litigation; Wage and Hour Law; Medical Malpractice; Wrongful Death; Catastrophic Injury. ***Email:*** chodges@hariswinfield.com

LEGAL SUPPORT PERSONNEL

KATRINA ARRUDA, (Legal Assistant)
CAROL YORK, (Legal Assistant)

Language: Spanish, Portuguese.

HARTZELL & WHITEMAN, L.L.P.

2626 GLENWOOD AVENUE, SUITE 500
RALEIGH, NORTH CAROLINA 27608
Telephone: 919-571-8300
Fax: 919-571-1004
URL: http://www.hwlawyers.com

Business Litigation, Securities Claims and Arbitration, Business Ownership Disputes, Consumer Class Actions, Disability/Insurance Claims, Employee Benefits and Workplace Injuries, Wage and Hour/Overtime Disputes, Intellectual Property Claims, Consumer and Employment Disputes, Professional Malpractice.

FIRM PROFILE: Hartzell & Whiteman, L.L.P. was formed in 1994 by three experienced litigation attorneys. The bulk of its work is in the federal and state courts sitting in North Carolina. The firm is experienced in complex litigation, class actions, trial and appellate practice, and is committed to providing high quality, cost-effective advocacy, particularly in disputes arising out of business matters, including shareholder disputes, securities claims, intellectual property disputes, and cases alleging misrepresentation or breach of fiduciary duty.

(This Listing Continued)

MEMBERS OF FIRM

J. JEROME HARTZELL, born Gettysburg, Pennsylvania, 1950; admitted to bar, 1977, North Carolina. *Education:* Phillips Academy; University of North Carolina (B.A., 1972; J.D., with honors, 1977; M.B.A., 1977). Phi Beta Kappa; Beta Gamma Sigma; Order of the Coif. Morehead Scholar. Member, and Staff Editor, North Carolina Law Review, 1975-1977. Law Clerk to Justice J. Frank Huskins, Supreme Court of North Carolina, 1977-1978. *Member:* Wake County, North Carolina (Past Legislative Chair and Council Member, Section of Business Law; Member, Litigation Section) and American (Member, Business and Litigation Sections) Bar Associations; National Association of Consumer Advocates. ***PRACTICE AREAS:*** Business Litigation; Consumer Class Actions. ***Email:*** jjh@hwlawyers.com

ANDREW O. WHITEMAN, born Cleveland, Ohio, 1955; admitted to bar, 1980, North Carolina; U.S. District Court, Middle, Eastern and Western Districts of North Carolina; U.S. Court of Appeals, Fourth Circuit and U.S. Tax Court; U.S. Supreme Court. *Education:* Miami University (B.S., cum laude, 1977); The Ohio State University (J.D., 1980). Member, The Order of Barristers. Staff Member, Ohio State Law Journal, 1979-1980. *Member:* Tenth Judicial District Bar (Fee Arbitration Committee, 1997—; Grievance Committee, 2000—); Wake County and North Carolina (Member, Sections on: Litigation and Business Law) Bar Associations; North Carolina State Bar; Public Investors Arbitration Bar Association; Member, NASD Panel of Arbitrators. ***PRACTICE AREAS:*** Securities Litigation; Broker-Dealer Arbitration; Commercial Litigation; ERISA; Disabilities; Employee Benefits; Workplace Injuries; Class Actions; Malpractice; Wrongful Death; Professional Liability; Employment Law; Insurance Claims. ***Email:*** aow@hwlawyers.com

JOHN R. RITTELMEYER, born Jackson, Mississippi, 1955; admitted to bar, 1988, Mississippi; 1990, North Carolina. *Education:* Georgetown University (B.S., 1977); University of Mississippi (J.D., 1988). ICCP Certificate of Data Processing (CDP), 1985. Law Clerk to Hon. James L. Robertson, Mississippi Supreme Court, 1988-1989. *Member:* Wake County, North Carolina and American Bar Associations; The Mississippi Bar. ***PRACTICE AREAS:*** Business Litigation; Intellectual Property Law. ***Email:*** jrr@hwlawyers.com

HATCH, LITTLE & BUNN, L.L.P.

327 HILLSBOROUGH STREET
P.O. BOX 527
RALEIGH, NORTH CAROLINA 27602
Telephone: 919-856-3940
Fax: 919-856-3950
URL: http://www.hatchlittlebunn.com

General Practice in all Courts. Bankruptcy, Civil, Commercial, Corporate, Criminal, Driving While Intoxicated, Traffic Violations, Family, Divorce, Child Custody, Child Support, Insurance, Interstate Commerce, Municipal, Zoning, Personal Injury, Probate, Real Property, Utility Law, Home Owners Associations, Foreclosure.

MEMBERS OF FIRM

J. WILBUR BUNN (1883-1969)
WILLIAM T. HATCH (1905-1979)
JAMES C. LITTLE (1917-1977)

HAROLD W. BERRY, JR., born Union, South Carolina, December 21, 1945; admitted to bar, 1971, North Carolina. *Education:* University of North Carolina (A.B., 1967; J.D., 1971). Special Lecturer, Business Law, North Carolina State University, 1976. ***PRACTICE AREAS:*** Business Law; Environmental Law; Regulatory Law; Estate Planning. ***Email:*** hwberry@hatchlittlebunn.com

THOMAS D. BUNN, born Raleigh, North Carolina, January 17, 1925; admitted to bar, 1950, North Carolina. *Education:* North Carolina State College; Wake Forest College (J.D., 1950). Member, North Carolina General Assembly, 1963-1968. ***PRACTICE AREAS:*** Real Property Litigation; Probate Law; Estate Litigation; Domestic Relations Law. ***Email:*** tdbunn@hatchlittlebunn.com

JOHN N. McCLAIN, JR., born Chattanooga, Tennessee, July 28, 1949; admitted to bar, 1974, North Carolina. *Education:* University of North Carolina (A.B., 1971); University of Tennessee (J.D., 1974). ***PRACTICE AREAS:*** Banking Litigation; Personal Injury Law; Domestic Relations Law; General Litigation; Alternative Dispute Resolution; Arbitration Law. ***Email:*** jnmcclain@hatchlittlebunn.com

TINA FRAZIER PACE, born Wake Forest, North Carolina, March 15, 1968; admitted to bar, 1994, North Carolina. *Education:* Duke University (A.B., 1990); University of North Carolina at Chapel Hill (J.D., 1994). ***PRACTICE AREAS:*** Environmental; Administrative; General Litigation. ***Email:*** tfpace@hatchlittlebunn.com

DAVID H. PERMAR, born Columbus, Ohio, June 5, 1943; admitted to bar, 1972, North Carolina. *Education:* Duke University and University of Maryland (B.S., 1969); George Washington University (J.D., 1972). [Capt., U.S. Army, active duty, 1964-1968]. ***PRACTICE AREAS:*** Civil Litigation; Transportation Law; Insurance Regulation; Real Estate; Administrative Law. ***Email:*** dhpermar@hatchlittlebunn.com

A. BARTLETT WHITE, born Norfolk, Virginia, August 3, 1954; admitted to bar, 1981, Virginia and North Carolina. *Education:* Virginia Military Institute (B.A., 1977); University of Richmond (J.D., 1981). ***PRACTICE AREAS:*** Civil Litigation; Criminal Litigation; Landlord and Tenant Law; Construction Litigation; Environmental Litigation. ***Email:*** abwhite@hatchlittlebunn.com

DOUGLAS Q. WICKHAM, born Chicago, Illinois, August 11, 1941; admitted to bar, 1966, Illinois; 1984, Tennessee; 1987, North Carolina. *Education:* Yale University (B.A., 1963; LL.B., 1966); Harvard University (LL.M., 1971). (Board Certified in Business Bankruptcy Law and Consumer Bankruptcy Law, North Carolina State Board of Legal Specialization). ***PRACTICE AREAS:*** Bankruptcy; Workouts; Commercial Litigation. ***Email:*** dqwickham@hatchlittlebunn.com

(This Listing Continued)

WILLIAM D. YOUNG, IV, admitted to bar, 1991, North Carolina. *Education:* North Carolina State University (B.A., B.S.W., 1985); North Carolina Central University (J.D., 1991). ***PRACTICE AREAS:*** Criminal Law; Landlord/Tenant Law; General Litigation. ***Email:*** wdyoung@hatchlittlebunn.com

ASSOCIATES

ELIZABETH T. MARTIN, born Redwood City, California, March 3, 1976; admitted to bar, 2002, North Carolina. *Education:* Drew University (B.A., Political Science, 1998); University of North Carolina (J.D., 2002). Phi Beta Kappa; Pi Sigma Alpha. *Member:* North Carolina Bar Association; North Carolina Association of Women Attorneys; Wake County Women Attorneys (Vice President, 2004). ***PRACTICE AREAS:*** Landlord and Tenant Law; Civil Litigation. ***Email:*** etmartin@hatchlittlebunn.com

JOHN E. McKNIGHT, born Greensboro, North Carolina, February 13, 1973; admitted to bar, 2004, North Carolina. *Education:* University of Central Florida (B.A., 1999); Wake Forest University (J.D., 2004). Order of Barristers. Chief Justice, 2003-2004 and Board Member, 2002-2003, Moot Court Board. ***PRACTICE AREAS:*** Family Law. ***Email:*** jemcknight@hatchlittlebunn.com

GENERAL COUNSEL FOR: United Energy, Inc.; North Carolina Petroleum Marketers Assoc.; Carolina Asphalt Pavement Assoc.; Triangle J Council of Governments; R.L. Dresser, Inc.; McCracken Enterprises.
REPRESENTATIVE CLIENTS: First-Citizens Bank; Peace College; J.M. Thompson Company, General Contractors.
REFERENCE: First Citizens Bank.

EMMETT BONEY HAYWOOD

3700 NATIONAL DRIVE, SUITE 112
RALEIGH, NORTH CAROLINA 27612
Telephone: 919-781-1371
Fax: 919-781-1373
Email: ehaywood@landlaw-nc.com
URL: http://www.landlaw-nc.com

Eminent Domain, Land Condemnation, Land Use, Contracts, Civil Litigation and Dispute Resolution.

EMMETT BONEY HAYWOOD, born Wilmington, North Carolina, June 14, 1955; admitted to bar, 1982, North Carolina; 2004, U.S. Supreme Court. *Education:* University of North Carolina (A.B., with honors in International Studies, 1977; J.D., 1982). Assistant Attorney General, Transportation Section, North Carolina Department of Justice, 1991-2000. Certified Mediator, State of North Carolina. *Member:* Wake County and North Carolina Bar Associations; North Carolina Academy of Trial Lawyers.

HEDRICK EATMAN GARDNER & KINCHELOE, L.L.P.

4011 WESTCHASE BOULEVARD, SUITE 300
RALEIGH, NORTH CAROLINA 27607
Telephone: 919-832-9424
Fax: 919-832-9425
URL: http://www.hedrickeatman.com

Charlotte, North Carolina Office: 6000 Fairview Road, Suite 1000, 28210. Mailing Address: P.O. Box 30397, 28230. Telephone: 704-366-1101. Fax: 704-366-6181.
Wilmington, North Carolina Office: 1508 Military Cutoff Road, Suite 202, 28403. Telephone: 910-509-9664. Fax: 910-509-9630.
Columbia, South Carolina Office: 1201 Main Street, Suite 1200, 29201. Mailing Address: P.O. Box 11267, 29211. Telephone: 803-727-1200. Fax: 803-727-1259.

General Civil Litigation and Insurance Defense, Legal and Professional Malpractice, Motor Vehicle Negligence, Premises Liability, Product Liability, Construction, Insurance Coverage Disputes, Arson and Fraud, Employment Law, Trucking and Transportation and Worker's Compensation.

FIRM PROFILE: Hedrick Eatman Gardner & Kincheloe, L.L.P. is a full-service litigation defense firm which serves insurance and business clients. Founded in North Carolina in 1956, the firm's four offices allow us to provide cost-effective representation throughout North and South Carolina. Our attorneys have superior litigation and dispute resolution skills. We zealously represent our loyal client base, while maintaining a high degree of ethics and professionalism. Client satisfaction is a priority, which is how we preserve long-term relationships. We strive for continued growth while maintaining our solid reputation before the bench and the Bar, our focus on client service, and qualifty of life for our attorneys and staff.

PARTNERS

JEFFREY A. DOYLE, admitted to bar, 1993, North Carolina and U.S. District Court, Western and Eastern Districts of North Carolina. *Education:* University of North Carolina at Chapel Hill (B.A., 1990; J.D., with honors, 1993). (Resident). ***PRACTICE AREAS:*** Personal Injury Defense; Products Liability Defense; Insurance Coverage; Workers Compensation. ***Email:*** jdoyle@hedrickeatman.com

THOMAS M. MORROW, admitted to bar, 1997, North Carolina and U.S. District Court, Eastern District of North Carolina. *Education:* University of Virginia (B.S., 1991); Wake Forest University (J.D., 1997). (Resident). ***PRACTICE AREAS:*** Workers Compensation; Civil Litigation. ***Email:*** tmorrow@hedrickeatman.com

ASSOCIATES

JESSICA C. SMYTHE, admitted to bar, 1996, North Carolina and U.S. District Court, Eastern District of North Carolina. *Education:* Meredith College (B.A., magna cum laude, 1993); Campbell University (J.D., 1996). ***PRACTICE AREAS:*** Insurance Defense; Workers Compensation; Products Liability.

(This Listing Continued)

ERIN DANCY EVESON, admitted to bar, 2000, North Carolina and U.S. District Court, Eastern District of North Carolina. *Education:* Catawba College (B.A., summa cum laude, 1997); University of North Carolina at Chapel Hill (J.D., 2000).

JENNIFER S. JERZAK, admitted to bar, 1997, North Carolina. *Education:* University of Virginia (B.A., 1994); Wake Forest University (J.D., 1997). ***PRACTICE AREAS:*** Workers Compensation; Insurance Defense. ***Email:*** jjerzak@hedrickeatman.com

TONYA D. DAVIS, admitted to bar, 2001, North Carolina and U.S. District Court, Eastern and Middle Districts of North Carolina. *Education:* University of North Carolina at Chapel Hill (B.A., 1996; J.D., 2001).

JENNIFER VEGA RUIZ, admitted to bar, 2002, North Carolina. *Education:* Peace College (B.A., 1999); University of North Carolina at Chapel Hill (J.D., 2002). ***PRACTICE AREAS:*** Litigation; Workers Compensation.

BARRY C. JENNINGS, admitted to bar, 2003, North Carolina and U.S. District Court, Eastern District of North Carolina. *Education:* North Carolina State University (B.S., 2000); University of North Carolina at Chapel Hill (J.D., with honors, 2003). ***PRACTICE AREAS:*** Civil Litigation; Motor Vehicle Accidents and Injuries; Workers Compensation. ***Email:*** bjennings@hedrickeatman.com

BETTINA MUMME, admitted to bar, 2001, North Carolina. *Education:* Pennsylvania State University (B.S. 1998); University of North Carolina at Chapel Hill (J.D., 2001).

ERIKA D. TAYLOR, admitted to bar, 2003, North Carolina. *Education:* North Carolina Agricultural & Technical State University (B.A., magna cum laude, 1998); North Carolina Central University (J.D., 2002).

STACY M. RACE, admitted to bar, 2003, North Carolina. *Education:* University of South Carolina (B.A., magna cum laude, 1998); Dalhousie University (M.A., 1999); Boston College (J.D., cum laude, 2003).

DANA C. MOODY, admitted to bar, 2001, North Carolina. *Education:* University of North Carolina at Chapel Hill (B.A., 1998; J.D., 2001). ***PRACTICE AREAS:*** Workers Compensation.

SUSAN J. VanDERWEERT, admitted to bar, 2002, North Carolina. *Education:* University of Minnesota (B.A., 1979); Duke University (M.A., 1999); University of North Carolina at Chapel Hill (J.D., 2002).

KYLA K. BLOCK, admitted to bar, 2005, North Carolina and U.S. District Court, District of South Carolina. *Education:* Colgate University (B.A., 2000); Wake Forest University (J.D., 2005).

REPRESENTATIVE CLIENTS: Ace-USA; Food Lion; Great American Insurance Co.; PMA Group; St. Paul Travelers Insurance Co.; Waffle House.
REFERENCE: Bank of America.

(For Complete biographical data on all personnel, see Professional Biographies at Charlotte)

HEDRICK MURRAY & CHEEK PLLC

RALEIGH, NORTH CAROLINA

(See Durham)

General Practice in all State and Federal Courts. Litigation, Real Estate, Land Use and Development Law, Insurance, Labor and Employment, Commercial Transactions, Probate.

HEDSPETH LAW FIRM, PLLC

410 N. BOYLAN AVENUE, SUITE 145
RALEIGH, NORTH CAROLINA 27603
Telephone: 919-256-3645
Fax: 919-256-3745
URL: http://www.trianglefamilylaw.com
Email: mhedspeth@hedspethlaw.com
URL: http://www.hedspethlaw.com

Family Law, Traffic Violations, Criminal Law, Misdemeanors.

MISTY COBLE HEDSPETH, born Lynchburg, Virginia, February 16, 1978; admitted to bar, 2003, North Carolina. *Education:* North Carolina State University (B.S., Accounting, 2000); Campbell University, Norman Adrian Wiggins School of Law (M.B.A., 2003; J.D., 2003). *Member:* North Carolina State Bar; Wake County, North Carolina and American Bar Associations; Christian Legal Society; North Carolina Association of Trial Lawyers. ***PRACTICE AREAS:*** Family Law (95%); Traffic Violations (4%); Misdemeanors (1%). ***Email:*** mhedspeth@hedspethlaw.com

C. D. HEIDGERD

3737 GLENWOOD AVENUE, SUITE 100
RALEIGH, NORTH CAROLINA 27612
Telephone: 919-861-2484
Fax: 919-861-2486
URL: http://cdheidgerdlaw.com/
Email: cdh@heidgerdlaw.com
URL: http://www.heidgerdlaw.com

Civil Trials and Appeals, Personal Injury, Wrongful Death, Eminent Domain, Administrative Law, Professional and Occupational Licensing, Family Law.

FIRM PROFILE: Dick Heidgerd has served people, their families and their businesses for over 30 years. He has appeared in every state and federal trial and appeals court as well as in many state and federal agencies.

C. D. HEIDGERD, born Sewickley, Pennsylvania, January 19, 1947; admitted to bar, 1972, North Carolina and U.S. District Court, Middle District of North Carolina; 1973, U.S. District Court, Western District of North Carolina; 1975, U.S. District Court, Eastern Dis-

(This Listing Continued)

C. D. HEIDGERD, Raleigh—Continued

trict of North Carolina; 1977, U.S. Supreme Court; 1981, U.S. Court of Appeals, Fourth Circuit. *Education:* Wake Forest University (B.A., 1969; J.D., 1972). Phi Delta Phi. Associate Attorney General, North Carolina Department of Justice, 1972-1975. Hearing Officer, OCHAMPUS, 1984-1997. *Member:* Wake County (Member, Board of Directors, 1977-1979) and North Carolina (Member, Litigation Section) Bar Associations; North Carolina State Bar; North Carolina Academy of Trial Lawyers. ***PRACTICE AREAS:*** Civil Practice; Litigation; Administrative Law; Family Law.

REPRESENTATIVE CLIENT: Capital Ford, Inc.; Capital Lincoln-Mercury, Inc.

HELMS MULLISS & WICKER, PLLC

Established in 1922

2600 TWO HANNOVER SQUARE

RALEIGH, NORTH CAROLINA 27601

Telephone: 919-755-6600

Fax: 919-755-6699.

Telex: 572460

URL: http://www.hmw.com

Mailing Address: P.O. Box 27507, Raleigh, NC 27611

Charlotte, North Carolina Office: 201 North Tryon Street, P.O. Box 31247 (28231). Telephone: 704-343-2000. Fax: 704-343-2300. Telex: 572460.

Wilmington, North Carolina Office: 127 Grace Street, P.O. Box 599 (28402). Telephone: 910-254-3800. Fax: 910-254-3900.

Banking, Finance, Corporate, Government Relations, Business Litigation, Tax, Securities, Real Property and Finance, Labor and Employment (Management) Law, Employee Benefits, International, Technology, Insurance Coverage, Media, Commercial Bankruptcy, Environmental, Public Finance, ERISA, Estate Planning and Administration, Education, Venture Capital, Intellectual Property.

MEMBERS OF FIRM

DAVID V. OTTERSON, born Merced, California, October 4, 1953; admitted to bar, 1980, California; 1998, North Carolina. *Education:* California State University at Chico (B.A., 1977); Hastings College of the Law, University of California (J.D., 1980). Articles Editor, Hastings Law Journal, 1979-1980. Board Member, Council for Entrepreneurial Development, 1998—. Member, Technology Committee, University of North Carolina, Charlotte, 1999—. *Member:* North Carolina (Chair, Information Technology Law Committee, Intellectual Property Law Section) and American (Business and Intellectual Property Sections) Bar Associations; State Bar of California (Member: Business, Intellectual Property and International Sections). ***PRACTICE AREAS:*** Corporate; Securities; Venture Capital; Mergers and Acquisitions; Technology Transfer; Technology Licensing. ***Email:*** David.Otterson@hmw.com

MACK A. PAUL, IV, born Raleigh, North Carolina, November 21, 1962; admitted to bar, 1991, North Carolina. *Education:* Dartmouth College (B.A., with high honors, 1985); Columbia University (J.D., 1991). Harlan Fiske Stone Scholar. ***LANGUAGES:*** French. ***PRACTICE AREAS:*** Government Relations; Administrative Law. ***Email:*** Mack.Paul@hmw.com

DAVID F. PAULSON, JR., born Durham, North Carolina, September 16, 1964; admitted to bar, 1991, North Carolina. *Education:* Duke University (B.A., 1987); Babcock Graduate School of Management, Wake Forest University (M.B.A., 1991); Wake Forest University (J.D., 1991). *Member:* North Carolina (Member: Business and Health Care Law Sections) and American (Member: Business Law and Health Care Law Sections) Bar Associations. ***PRACTICE AREAS:*** Corporate Law; Mergers and Acquisitions; Health Care Law; Venture Capital; Technology Law; Corporate Finance. ***Email:*** David.Paulson@hmw.com

ROBERT H. TILLER, born Appalachia, Virginia, 1955; admitted to bar, 1989, District of Columbia; 1991, North Carolina. *Education:* Oberlin College (B.A., 1977); University of Virginia (J.D., 1986). Phi Beta Kappa. Order of the Coif. Law Clerk to: the Hon. Antonin Scalia, U.S. Supreme Court, 1987-1988; the Hon. Stephen F. Williams, U.S. Court of Appeals, District of Columbia Circuit, 1986-1987. *Member:* North Carolina and American Bar Associations. ***PRACTICE AREAS:*** Commercial Litigation; Constitutional Law; Appellate Practice; Intellectual Property. ***Email:*** rob.tiller@hmw.com

DENNIS A. WICKER, born Lee County, North Carolina, June 14, 1952; admitted to bar, 1978, North Carolina. *Education:* University of North Carolina (B.A., with honors, 1974); Wake Forest University (J.D., 1978). Phi Beta Kappa; Phi Alpha Delta. Member, North Carolina House of Representatives, 1981-1992. House Majority Leader, 1989-1992. North Carolina Lieutenant Governor, 1993-2000. *Member:* North Carolina and American Bar Associations; North Carolina State Bar; North Carolina Academy of Trial Lawyers. ***PRACTICE AREAS:*** Government Relations; Bond Finance; Corporate Law. ***Email:*** Dennis.Wicker@hmw.com

ROBERT A. WICKER, born Sanford, North Carolina, October 18, 1944; admitted to bar, 1969, North Carolina; 1988, District of Columbia, U.S. Court of Appeals, Fourth Circuit, U.S. Court of Military Appeals and U.S. District Court, Eastern, Middle and Western Districts of North Carolina. *Education:* University of North Carolina (A.B., 1966; J.D., with honors, 1969). *Member:* North Carolina and American Bar Associations. [Capt., JAGC, U.S. Army, 1969-1974]

ASSOCIATES

Keith P. Anthony	***Jason R. Schneider***
Mathias H. "Matt" Hunoval	***Aaron G. Spencer***
Andrew E. Kristianson	***Guilford Mattern York***

Attorneys in the Raleigh Office Are Members of: Mecklenburg County, North Carolina Bar Associations and North Carolina State Bar.

(This Listing Continued)

REPRESENTATIVE CLIENTS: Bank of America; Branch Banking and Trust Co.; Digital Optics; Kitty Hawk Capital; Royal & SunAlliance; Compass Group USA, Inc.; Harris Teeter; Johnson & Wales University; The Charlotte Observer; First Charter Corporation; Continental Tire; Central Carolina Bank.

(For biographical data on other personnel, see Professional Biographies at Charlotte and Wilmington, North Carolina)

HENSON & FUERST, P.A.

Established in 1972

2501 BLUE RIDGE ROAD, SUITE 390

RALEIGH, NORTH CAROLINA 27607

Telephone: 919-781-1107

Fax: 919-781-8048

Email: henson-fuerst@lawmed.com

URL: http://www.lawmed.com

Rocky Mount Office: 2317 Sunset Avenue, P.O. Box 7008, 27804-2529. Telephone: 252-443-2111. Fax: 252-443-9429.

Civil Trial Practice, Medical Malpractice, Nursing Home Liability, Nursing Home Abuse and Neglect, Personal Injury, Automobile Accidents, Wrongful Death.

FIRM PROFILE: Henson & Fuerst, P.A., since 1972, is a North Carolina law firm with principal offices in Raleigh and Rocky Mount. We limit our practice to nursing home abuse and neglect, health care negligence and personal injury. All of our lawyers are licensed to practice in North Carolina and are dedicated to helping injured people.

(For complete biographical data on all personnel, see Professional Biographies at Rocky Mount, North Carolina)

HERRING McBENNETT MILLS & FINKELSTEIN, PLLC

TWO HANNOVER SQUARE

RALEIGH, NORTH CAROLINA 27601

Telephone: 919-821-1860

Fax: 919-821-1816

Email: hermcb@hermcb.com

URL: http://www.hermcb.com

Mailing Address: P.O. Box 1677, Raleigh, NC 27602

Comprehensive Business, Litigation, Real Estate, Domestic and Adoption Practice including, Trial and Appellate Litigation, Administrative, Antitrust, Business Law, Business Crimes, Civil Rights, Commercial, Construction, Corporate, Business Formation, E-Commerce, Employment, Environmental, Estate Planning, Family, Adoption, Equitable Distribution, Divorce, Health Care, Intellectual Property, Negligence, Probate, Products Liability, Real Estate, Toxic Tort, Wills and Trusts Law, Business Ownership Disputes, Disability, Insurance Claims, Wage and Hour, Overtime Disputes, Franchise Disputes, Contracts Disputes, Unfair Trade Practices, Breach of Fiduciary Duty, Partnership Disputes, Non-Compete Covenants, Tortious Interference with Contract, Mergers and Acquisitions, White Collar Criminal Defense, Regulatory Law, Professional Licensing, Eminent Domain and Land Condemnation.

FIRM PROFILE: Herring McBennett Mills & Finkelstein, PLLC is a full service law firm located in Raleigh, North Carolina. Today, our firm serves as counsel to both individuals and business entities, handling both litigation and transactional legal matters for these clients. Our firm focuses on handling our clients' specific needs in both state and federal courts. We also have experience serving as local counsel for out-of-state law firms in both state and federal courts. Herring McBennett has received Martindale-Hubbell's highest rating from our peers in the practice of law. We are proud of our rating from the oldest and most respected law firm rating service.

E. PARKER HERRING, born Goldsboro, North Carolina, March 20, 1953; admitted to bar, 1986, North Carolina; 1987, U.S. District Court, Eastern District of North Carolina. *Education:* University of North Carolina at Chapel Hill (B.A., 1975); Wake Forest University (J.D., 1985). Order of the Barristers. Executive Counsel, Moot Court Board. Member, National Moot Court Team. Winner of Best Brief, Edwin A. Stanley Memorial Moot Court Competition. Law Clerk to the Hon. Eugene H. Phillips, North Carolina Court of Appeals, 1986-1987. *Member:* Wake County, North Carolina and American Bar Associations; Wake County Family Lawyers (Past President); North Carolina Academy of Trial Lawyers. (Board Certified Specialist, Family Law, North Carolina State Board of Legal Specialization). ***PRACTICE AREAS:*** Family Law; Adoption Law. ***Email:*** pherring@hermcb.com

LARRY D. McBENNETT, born Fayetteville, North Carolina, September 6, 1949; admitted to bar, 1977, North Carolina and District of Columbia. *Education:* University of North Carolina at Chapel Hill (B.A., 1972; J.D., 1977; M.R.P., 1977). Phi Beta Kappa. *Member:* Wake County, North Carolina and District of Columbia Bar Associations; The District of Columbia Bar. ***PRACTICE AREAS:*** Real Estate; Trusts and Estates; Business Transactions. ***Email:*** lmcbennett@hermcb.com

BOBBY D. MILLS, born Morganton, North Carolina, July 2, 1960; admitted to bar, 1985, North Carolina and U.S. District Court, Eastern District of North Carolina. *Education:* University of North Carolina at Asheville (B.A., 1982); Wake Forest University (J.D., 1985). *Member:* Wake County and North Carolina Bar Associations; North Carolina State Bar; North Carolina Academy of Trial Lawyers; American Academy of Adoption Attorneys. [Capt., JAGC, U.S. Army, 1987-1991]. (Board Certified Specialist in Family Law, North Carolina State Board of Legal Specialization). ***PRACTICE AREAS:*** Family Law; Adoption. ***Email:*** bmills@hermcb.com

MARK A. FINKELSTEIN, born West Point, New York, 1959; admitted to bar, 1985, North Carolina; 1988, U.S. Supreme Court. *Education:* Grinnell College (B.A., with honors, 1982); University of North Carolina at Chapel Hill (J.D., with honors, 1985). Author of numerous articles regarding Litigation, Business, Environmental and Administrative Matters. Listed in Who's Who in American Law. Law Clerk to Chief Judge R.A. Hedrick, North

(This Listing Continued)

Carolina Court of Appeals, 1985-1986. Instructor, Civil Litigation, Meredith College Legal Assistants Program, 1988. Supervising Attorney, Duke University Law School Environmental Law Clinic, 1992. Member, North Carolina Low Level Radioactive Waste Management Authority. Instructor, National Institute for Trial Advocacy, 1993—. Board of Directors Member, Carolina Legal Assistance, Mediation Services of Wake County and National Association of Environmental Professionals. *Member:* Wake County and North Carolina Bar Associations; American Academy of Political and Social Sciences; National Institute of Trial Advocacy (Diplomate). ***PRACTICE AREAS:*** Litigation; Business Law; Administrative Law. ***Email:*** mfinkelstein@hermcb.com

STEPHEN W. PETERSEN, born Conway, Arkansas, July 12, 1952; admitted to bar, 1996, North Carolina. *Education:* Guilford College (A.B., 1974); North Carolina State University (B.S., high honors, 1978); University of North Carolina (D.D.S., 1982; J.D., 1996). Phi Kappa Phi. Member, Civil Trial Competition Team, University of North Carolina School of Law, 1995-1996. Licensed Dentist, North Carolina, 1982. Licensed General Contractor, North Carolina, 1989-1999. *Member:* Wake County (Member, Board of Directors 2002—), North Carolina (Member: 10th Judicial District Grievance Committee, 1999-2001; 10th Judicial District Board of Directors, 2002—; Investment Committee, 2002—; Sections on Business Law; Antitrust; Health Law;) and American (Member, Sections on: Health Law; Antitrust) Bar Associations. ***REPORTED CASES:*** Erie Ins. Exch. v. Bledsoe, 141 N.C. App. 331, 540 S.E.2d 57 (2000), cert. denied, 353 N.C. 371, 547 S.E. 2d 442 (2001). Gibson v. Mena, 144 N.C. App. 125, 548 S.E. 2d 745 (2001). ***PRACTICE AREAS:*** Business Litigation; White Collar Crime; Professional Ethics; Professional Licensing and Discipline; Health Care; Grand Jury Proceedings. ***Email:*** spetersen@hermcb.com

ASSOCIATE

ANNA E. WORLEY, born San Antonio, Texas, February 9, 1971; admitted to bar, 1996, North Carolina. *Education:* Wake Forest University (B.A., 1993; J.D., 1996). Phi Alpha Delta. *Member:* 18th Judicial District and North Carolina Bar Associations; North Carolina Academy of Trial Lawyers. ***LANGUAGES:*** Spanish. ***PRACTICE AREAS:*** Family Law.

THE HILBERT LAW FIRM, PLLC

410 N. BOYLAN AVENUE, SUITE 152
RALEIGH, NORTH CAROLINA 27603
Telephone: 919-256-3970
Fax: 919-256-3971
Email: maryhilbertlaw@yahoo.com
URL: http://www.raleighdivorcelawfirm.com

Family Law, Child Custody, Divorce Litigation, Child Support, Domestic Violence, Equitable Distribution, Alimony, Post-Separation Support, Separation Agreements Premarital Agreements, Adoptions, Visition Rights, Divorce.

MARY LIFSON HILBERT, born Annapolis, Maryland, October 24, 1973; admitted to bar, 1999, North Carolina and U.S. District Court, Eastern District of North Carolina. *Education:* Vanderbilt University (B.A., 1995); Washington University School of Law (J.D., 1999). *Member:* Wake County and North Carolina Bar Associations; North Carolina Academy of Trial Lawyers; North Carolina Association of Women Attorneys. ***PRACTICE AREAS:*** Family Law; Child Custody; Divorce Litigation; Child Support; Domestic Violence; Equitable Distribution; Alimony; Post Separation Support; Separation Agreements; Premarital Agreements; Adoptions; Visitation Rights; Divorce. ***Email:*** maryhilbertlaw@yahoo.com

RANDOLPH J. HILL

434 FAYETTEVILLE STREET
SUITE 2350
RALEIGH, NORTH CAROLINA 27601
Telephone: 919-861-0507
Fax: 919-861-0504
Email: rjhlaw@earthlink.net
URL: http://www.lawyers.com/rjhilllaw

Criminal, Personal Injury, Automobile Accidents, Civil, Appeals, Business Litigation, Traffic, Driving While Intoxicated, Drug Crimes, Felonies, Homicide, Misdemeanors.

RANDOLPH J. HILL, born Bath, New York, March 9, 1962; admitted to bar, 1987, North Carolina and U.S. Court of Military Appeals; 1997, U.S. District Court, Eastern District of North Carolina; 2003, U.S. Court of Appeals, 4th Circuit. *Education:* University of Notre Dame (B.A., 1984); Wake Forest University (J.D., 1987). Chairman, Committee on Indigent Appointments, 2003-2004. *Member:* North Carolina Bar Association; Wake County Academy of Criminal Trial Lawyers (Vice President. 1997; President, 1998). [Captain U.S. Army, JAG Corp, 1987-1992]

HOLLOWELL LAW OFFICES, P.A.

5511 CAPITAL CENTER DRIVE, SUITE 104
RALEIGH, NORTH CAROLINA 27606
Telephone: 919-852-2211
Fax: 919-852-2233
Email: edhollowell@bellsouth.net
URL: http://www.hollowell-lawoffices.com

Health Care Law, Administrative Law, Corporate Law, Business Law, Employment, Governmental Estate Planning and Collection.

(This Listing Continued)

MEMBER

EDWARD E. HOLLOWELL, born Aurora, North Carolina, December 26, 1933; admitted to bar, 1961, North Carolina. *Education:* University of North Carolina (B.S., 1959; J.D., 1961). ***PRACTICE AREAS:*** Health Law; Administrative Law; Corporate; Business Law; Employment; Governmental Law; Collections. ***Email:*** edhollowell@bellsouth.net

HOLM LAW FIRM, PLLC

TWO HANNOVER SQUARE, SUITE 2406
RALEIGH, NORTH CAROLINA 27601
Telephone: 919-833-4000
Fax: 919-833-0731
Email: dave@holmlawoffice.com
URL: http://www.holmlawoffice.com

Family Law, Child Support, Child Custody, Divorce, Alimony, Visitation Rights, Collaborative Law, Trusts and Estates, Asset Protection, Guardianship and Wills.

DAVID E. HOLM, born 1970; admitted to bar, 2000, North Carolina, U.S. District Court, Eastern and Middle Districts of North Carolina, U.S. Tax Court. *Education:* North Carolina State University (B.A., 1992; Master of Economics, 1995); University of Miami (J.D., cum laude, 2000). *Member:* Wake County, North Carolina and American Bar Associations; North Carolina State Bar. ***PRACTICE AREAS:*** Family Law; Wills; Probate; Trusts and Estates. ***Email:*** dave@holmlawoffice.com

HOLT YORK McDARRIS & HIGH, LLP

TWO HANNOVER SQUARE, SUITE 2010
434 FAYETTEVILLE STREET MALL
RALEIGH, NORTH CAROLINA 27601
Telephone: 919-420-7826; Toll Free: 888-285-7634
Fax: 919-420-7838
URL: http://www.hymh.com
Mailing Address: P.O. Box 2060, Raleigh, NC 27602

Edenton, North Carolina Office: 102 East Queen Street, P.O. Box 92, 27932. Telephone: 252-482-4422, Toll-free: 888-256-0219. Fax: 252-482-4423.

Municipal/Administrative Law, Zoning and Land Use, Real Property, Government Regulations, Condemnation Defense, Corporate Law, Trusts and Estates, Wills and Probate, Alcoholic Beverages, General Trial and Appellate Practice before all State and Federal Courts and Agencies. Legislative Representation before the North Carolina General Assembly.

FIRM PROFILE: The emphasis of the Holt York McDarris & High, LLP practice is the representation of companies and individuals in regard to business matters and in dealings with government agencies. The firm's attorneys have extensive involvement in the Research Triangle area's governmental, judicial, political and civic life. Firm clientele are located in and around the state capital, including regional and national firms who do business there, as well as municipalities and other government agencies across eastern North Carolina.

The firm's dedicated support staff are vital to its operation. The expertise of all attorneys within the firm is utilized to best serve its clients in a cost-effective manner.

PARTNERS

JEFFREY P. GRAY, born Sylva, North Carolina, August 1, 1959; admitted to bar, 1986, North Carolina; U.S. District Court, Eastern, Middle and Western Districts of North Carolina; U.S. Court of Appeals, Fourth Circuit and U.S. Supreme Court. *Education:* Western Carolina University (B.S., 1981); Campbell University (J.D., 1985). Benton National Moot Court Competition. Recipient, I. Beverly Lake Award, Excellence in Constitutional Law. Author of published articles in the *Campbell Law Observer,* The Campbell Law Review, the North Carolina *State Bar Journal,* the Supreme Court Historical Society's *Juridicus,* the North Carolina Bar Association JLD Newsletter, *Popular Government,* and various law enforcement and trade journals. Author of numerous publications for distribution by the N.C. Department of Justice to local and state government agencies. Instructor, Wake Technical Community College, Raleigh, North Carolina, 1996-1998. Legal Counsel, Auctioneer Licensing Board, 1994—. Special Assistant to Attorney General (now U.S. District Judge) Lacy H. Thornburg, 1985-1991. Assistant Attorney General, 1992-1998. Attorney, North Carolina Alcoholic Beverage Control Commission, 1996-1998. *Member:* Wake County, Tenth Judicial and North Carolina (Member, Administrative Law Section) Bar Associations; North Carolina State Bar. ***PRACTICE AREAS:*** Administrative Law; Litigation; Government; Legislative Practice. ***Email:*** jgray@hymh.com

W. HACKNEY HIGH, JR., born Robersonville, North Carolina, February 4, 1965; admitted to bar, 1990, North Carolina. *Education:* University of North Carolina (B.S., 1987); Campbell University (J.D., 1990). Phi Alpha Delta (Vice President, 1989-1990). *Member:* Chowan County, North Carolina and American Bar Associations; North Carolina State Bar; North Carolina Trial Lawyers Association; North Carolina Municipal Lawyers Association; North Carolina Council of School Attorneys. ***PRACTICE AREAS:*** General Practice; Litigation; Real Estate; Municipal Law. ***Email:*** hhigh@hymh.com

CLYDE HOLT, III, born Beaver, Pennsylvania, September 16, 1947; admitted to bar, 1972, North Carolina. *Education:* Northwestern University (B.A., 1969); University of North Carolina (J.D., 1972). Associate City Attorney, City of Raleigh, 1972-1976. Chairman, Wake County Library Commission. Chairman, City of Raleigh Civil Service Commission. Vice-Chairman, Triangle Sports Authority. Director, Wake County SPCA. Director, Elizabeth City State University Foundation. General Counsel, The Centennial Authority. Town Attorney, Knightdale, North Carolina. Member, North Carolina General Assembly Building Code Issues Committee. Registered Lobbyist, North Carolina General Assembly. Co-Author: "Zoning and Other Local Government Regulations Affecting Residential Building Contractors in Wake County", Home Builders Association of Raleigh, Wake County, 1989; "Major Land Use Laws in North Carolina", National Business Institute, Inc., 1992. *Member:* Wake County and North Carolina Bar Associations; The North Carolina

(This Listing Continued)

HOLT YORK McDARRIS & HIGH, LLP, Raleigh—Continued

State Bar; North Carolina Municipal Attorneys Association (Director); Academy of Trial Lawyers. ***PRACTICE AREAS:*** Municipal Law; Land Use Law; Environmental Law; Zoning and Planning; Real Property Law. ***Email:*** cholt@hymh.com

CHARLES F. McDARRIS, born Waynesville, North Carolina, May 4, 1963; admitted to bar, 1991, North Carolina; 1996, U.S. District Court, Eastern District of North Carolina; 1998, U.S. Supreme Court and U.S. Court of Appeals, Fourth Circuit. *Education:* Presbyterian College (B.S., 1985); Wake Forest University (J.D., 1990). Recipient, American Jurisprudence Award in Trial Practice, 1990. Associate Attorney General, North Carolina Department of Justice, 1991-1992. Legal Counsel: North Carolina Private Protective Services, 1991—; North Carolina Alarm Systems Licensing Board, 1991—; Hearing Board for North Carolina Board of Funeral Services. General Counsel, North Carolina Board of Landscape Architects. *Member:* Wake County and North Carolina (Member, Administrative Law Section) Bar Associations; North Carolina State Bar; Tenth Judicial Bar. ***PRACTICE AREAS:*** Administrative Law; Litigation. ***Email:*** cmcdarris@hymh.com

ELIZABETH CARR TRAHOS, born Fairfax, Virginia, March 6, 1972; admitted to bar, 1997, North Carolina; 1998, Virginia. *Education:* University of Richmond (B.A., 1994; J.D., 1997); Virginia Commonwealth University (M.U.R.P., 1997). Vice Chair, Wake County Planning Board, 2005—. *Member:* Wake County (Member, Bench-Bar Committee), North Carolina and American Bar Associations; North Carolina State Bar; Virginia State Bar (Member, Local Government Section); American Planning Association (Secretary-Treasurer, Planning and Law Division, 1998-2000). ***PRACTICE AREAS:*** Zoning, Planning and Land Use; Municipal Law; Real Property; Administrative Law. ***Email:*** etrahos@hymh.com

DAVID L. YORK, born New Orleans, Louisiana, April 10, 1963; admitted to bar, 1989, North Carolina and U.S. District Court, Eastern District of North Carolina. *Education:* North Carolina State University (B.S., 1985); Campbell University (J.D., 1989). Phi Alpha Delta. Raleigh Civil Service Commission, 1995—. *Member:* Wake County, North Carolina and American (Member, Real Property Section, 2005—; Vice Chair, Zoning, Planning and Land Use Section) Bar Associations; American Planning Association (Member, Planning and Law Division). ***PRACTICE AREAS:*** Municipal Law; Land Use Law; Zoning and Planning; Real Property Law; Estates. ***Email:*** dyork@hymh.com

WILLIAM M. CROWE, born 1966; admitted to bar, 2002, North Carolina. *Education:* University of North Carolina at Chapel Hill (B.A., 1988); North Carolina State University (M.P.A., 1995); North Carolina Central University (J.D., 2002). Pi Alpha Alpha. *Member:* Chowan County, Fifth Judicial District, North Carolina and American Bar Associations; North Carolina Academy of Trial Lawyers. ***PRACTICE AREAS:*** Civil Practice; Criminal Law; Real Estate; Local Government Law; Municipal Law; Family Law; Probate. ***Email:*** wcrowe@hymh.com

COLLEEN KOCHANEK, born Fontana, California, June 17, 1967; admitted to bar, 1992, North Carolina; 1993, U.S. District Court, Eastern District of North Carolina. *Education:* Indiana University (B.A., 1989); Wake Forest University (J.D., 1992). *Member:* Wake County and North Carolina Bar Associations; North Carolina State Bar; North Carolina Association of Women Attorneys; Association of Professional Lobbyists. ***PRACTICE AREAS:*** Association Law; Legislative Representation; Lobbying; Professional and Occupational Licensing; Administrative Law; Business Law. ***Email:*** ckochanek@hymh.com

BENJAMIN R. KUHN, born 1970; admitted to bar, 1997, North Carolina. *Education:* University of North Carolina at Charlotte (B.A., 1992); Temple University School of Law (J.D., 1996). Business Editor, Temple International and Comparative Law Journal. Author: "Negotiating Broadcast Deals with Major League Professional Sports Franchises," Broadcast Law Report, Feb. 2001, at 1; "Dilemma in Cyberspace and Beyond: Copyright Law for the Information Superhighways of Today and Tomorrow," 10 Temp. Int'l Comp. L.J. 171, 1996. *Member:* Wake County, North Carolina and American Bar Associations. ***PRACTICE AREAS:*** Administrative Law; Litigation; Land Use; Real Property; Business Law. ***Email:*** bkuhn@hymh.com

CLAUDIA N. McCLINTON, born Charlotte, North Carolina, August 20, 1976; admitted to bar, 2004, North Carolina. *Education:* University of North Carolina at Chapel Hill (B.A., 2000; J.D., 2003). Dean's List; Order of the Barristers. Recipient: Bicentennial Challenge (Ivey) Scholarship; Gressman-Pollitt Award for Oral Advocacy. Teaching Assistant, Legal Education Advancement Program, 2002-2003.*Member:* Wake County Bar Association; North Carolina Bar Association (Bar Exam Committee, 2004); North Carolina State Bar; National Bar Association; North Carolina Association of Women Attorneys. ***PRACTICE AREAS:*** Local Government Relations; Land Use; Commercial Litigation. ***Email:*** cmcclinton@hymh.com

DAVID J. NEILL, born Baltimore, Maryland, January 20, 1973; admitted to bar, 2004, North Carolina. *Education:* University of North Carolina at Chapel Hill (A.B., 1995; J.D., 2004). *Member:* North Carolina State Bar. ***PRACTICE AREAS:*** Zoning, Planning and Land Use; Commercial Real Estate; Municipal Law. ***Email:*** dneill@hymh.com

BRADFORD A. WILLIAMS, born Little Rock, Arkansas, November 23, 1974; admitted to bar, 1999, North Carolina. *Education:* University of North Carolina at Chapel Hill (B.A., 1996; J.D., 1999). *Member:* Wake County and North Carolina Bar Associations; North Carolina State Bar. ***PRACTICE AREAS:*** Municipal Law; Administrative Law; Zoning, Planning and Land Use; Real Property. ***Email:*** bwilliams@hymh.com

OF COUNSEL

F. EUGENE HAFER, born Charlotte, North Carolina, January 21, 1934; admitted to bar, 1966, North Carolina; 1973, U.S. Supreme Court. *Education:* University of North Carolina (B.S., 1955; J.D., 1966). Law Clerk to Justice William H. Bobbitt, North Carolina Supreme Court, 1966-1967. Assistant Attorney General, State of North Carolina, 1970-1973. *Member:* Wake County and North Carolina Bar Associations; North Carolina State Bar. ***PRACTICE AREAS:*** Association Law; Business Law. ***Email:*** ehafer@hymh.com

EDMOND W. CALDWELL, JR., born Hickory, North Carolina, August 30, 1955; admitted to bar, 1982, North Carolina. *Education:* University of North Carolina (B.S., 1977); Campbell University (J.D., 1981). Phi Alpha Delta. Recipient, Bureau of National Affairs (BNA) Student Advocacy Award for Outstanding Achievement. Law Clerk to United States Attorney, Eastern District of North Carolina, 1981. Assistant District Attorney, 1982. Special Deputy Attorney General, 1983-1989. Legal Counsel to the North Carolina Speaker of the House of Representatives, 1989-1991. Commissioner, North Carolina Criminal Justice Education and Training Standards Commission, 1991—. Member of the Human Rights Committee for the Governor Morehead School for Blind Children, 1991-1999. Executive Vice President and General Counsel, North Carolina Sheriff's Association, 2004—. *Member:* Wake County, North Carolina and American Bar Associations; North Carolina State Bar. ***PRACTICE AREAS:*** Legislative Representation; Lobbying; Association Law; Professional and Occupational Licensing; Administrative Law. ***Email:*** ecaldwell@hymh.com

HOPPER LAW FIRM

4601 SIX FORKS ROAD, SUITE 127
RALEIGH, NORTH CAROLINA 27609
Telephone: 919-829-5600
Fax: 919-510-5152
URL: http://www.HopperLawfirm.com
URL: http://www.hopperlawoffice.com

Family Law, Business Litigation, Construction Law, Child Custody, Divorce, Criminal Law, Traffic Violations, DWI, Commercial Litigation, Alimony and Misdemeanors.

MEMBER OF FIRM

KEVIN P. HOPPER, born Beaumont, Texas, March 17, 1967; admitted to bar, 1994, North Carolina and U.S. District Court, Eastern District of North Carolina. *Education:* Stephen F. Austin State University (B.S., 1989); Texas Tech University (J.D., 1993). Sigma Chi (Member, Raleigh Alumni Chapter). Member, Moot Court Program. Winner, Undergraduate Moot Court Competition, State of Texas, 1989. Recognized by the National Institute for Trial Advocacy, for Completion of a Trial Advocacy Skills Program, 1998. Member, The Sacred Heart Church. Member of the Contemporaries, North Carolina Museum of Art. *Member:* Wake County and American Bar Associations; North Carolina State Bar; North Carolina Academy of Trial Lawyers. (Managing Partner). ***PRACTICE AREAS:*** Family Law; Business Litigation; Construction Law; Child Custody; Divorce; Alimony; Commercial Law; DWI; Traffic Violations; Criminal Law. ***Email:*** kevin@HopperLawfirm.com

HOWARD, GREEN & MOYE, L.L.P.

4000 WESTCHASE BOULEVARD
SUITE 200
P.O. BOX 10305
RALEIGH, NORTH CAROLINA 27605
Telephone: 919-833-2422
Fax: 919-833-2430
Email: howardandgreen@mindspring.com
URL: http://www.lawyers.com/howardandgreen

General Civil Practice. Real Estate, Family and Domestic Relations Law. Custody and Support and Equitable Distribution Law.

ROBERT E. HOWARD SR., born Raleigh, North Carolina, April 25, 1945; admitted to bar, 1970, North Carolina; 1971, U.S. District Court, Eastern District of North Carolina; 1973, U.S. District Court, Middle District of North Carolina. *Education:* University of North Carolina (LL.B., 1970). Wake County Chief Legal Aid Attorney, 1970-1972. Solicitor, Wake County District Courts, 1970-1972. Author: "The Alimony Complaint," North Carolina Bar Foundation, 1987; "Challenging Social Services," Family Law In Bush's America, "Challenging the System," North Carolina Family Law Specialist Group, 2005. Speaker, "CPA on the Hot Seat," CPA/Law Forum, 2004. *Member:* Wake County (Chairman, Legal Aid Committee, 1970-1972) and North Carolina (Chairman, Legislative Committee of Family Law Section, 1986-1987; Member, Family Law Counsel, 1987-1988) Bar Associations. ***PRACTICE AREAS:*** Family Law; Equitable Distribution Law.

KATHERINE S. MOYE, born New Orleans, Louisiana, December 26, 1968; admitted to bar, 1994, North Carolina. *Education:* Louisiana State University (B.A., magna cum laude, 1991); University of North Carolina at Chapel Hill (J.D., 1994). Phi Beta Kappa; Phi Kappa Phi. *Member:* Wake County and North Carolina (Member, Family Law Section) Bar Associations; North Carolina State Bar. ***PRACTICE AREAS:*** Family Law; Equitable Distribution.

ASSOCIATE

ROBERT E. HOWARD, JR., born Raleigh, North Carolina, October 13, 1976; admitted to bar, 2003, North Carolina. *Education:* Wake Forest University (B.A., cum laude, 1999); University of South Carolina (J.D., 2003). Assistant in Preparation, "Challenging the System," North Carolina Family Law Specialist Group, 2005. *Member:* Wake County Bar Association; North Carolina Bar Association (Member, Family Law Section). ***PRACTICE AREAS:*** Family Law; Equitable Distribution; Civil Practice; Business Law.

OF COUNSEL

CHARLES P. GREEN, JR., born Gatesville, North Carolina, July 2, 1941; admitted to bar, 1965, North Carolina. *Education:* Woodberry Forest School; University of North Carolina (A.B., 1962; LL.B., 1965). Phi Delta Phi. *Member:* Wake County and North Carolina Bar Associations; North Carolina State Bar (Advisory Member, Consumer Protection Committee, 1995-1998). ***PRACTICE AREAS:*** Real Estate; Corporate Law; Wills; Estates.

REPRESENTATIVE CLIENTS: North Carolina Assn.; Long Term Care Facilities; Clearscapes Architects; Tingen Technical Sales; Hofler Enterprises; Gowenn Chemical.

(This Listing Continued)

APPROVED ATTORNEYS FOR: Lawyers Title of North Carolina, Inc.; The Title Company of North Carolina; Commonwealth Title; United Title.
REFERENCES: Bank of America; First Citizens Bank & Trust, Wachovia Bank.

HOWARD, STALLINGS, FROM & HUTSON, P.A.

Established in 1983

4000 WESTCHASE BOULEVARD, SUITE 400
P.O. BOX 12347
RALEIGH, NORTH CAROLINA 27607
Telephone: 919-821-7700; 800-822-4182
Fax: 919-821-7703; 834-8481
URL: http://www.hsfh.com

New Bern, North Carolina Office: 2407 Grace Avenue, 28563, P.O. Box 975. Telephone: 252-633-3006. Fax: 252-633-3097.

General, Civil and Commercial Litigation, Business Law, Commercial Real Estate, Taxation, Employment Law, Computer Law, Estate Planning and Administration, Bankruptcy Law, Loan Structuring and Workouts, Intellectual Property Law, Personal Injury.

FIRM PROFILE: Since 1983, we have served our nationwide clients with efficient, professional representation in the Triangle, throughout North Carolina and elsewhere. Our firm has successfully litigated complex business matters all across the nation. We also provide a large array of legal services to our business and banking clients, and their owners. As a complement to our commercial practice, our firm includes attorneys experienced in such diverse areas as estate planning, estate litigation, employment law, and personal injury law, as well as a Board Certified Specialist in business and bankruptcy law. Members of the firm include noted legal author John Hutson, Co-Author of the Authoritative Treatise North Carolina Contract Law (www.nocontractlaw.com).

EDWARD CADER HOWARD, born Wilmington, North Carolina, April 13, 1948; admitted to bar, 1972, North Carolina. *Education:* Davidson College (A.B., 1969); University of North Carolina (J.D., 1972). Member of Staff, North Carolina Law Review, 1971-1972. [Capt., U.S. Army, Retired]. ***PRACTICE AREAS:*** Real Estate Law; Civil Practice; Debtor and Creditor Law; Business Law. ***Email:*** choward@hsfh.com

I. ALLAN FROM, born Union, South Carolina, January 9, 1950; admitted to bar, 1975, South Carolina; 1978, North Carolina; U.S. Tax Court; U.S. District Court, Eastern District of North Carolina; U.S. Court of Federal Claims. *Education:* George Washington University (B.B.A., in Accounting, 1972); University of South Carolina (J.D., 1975); Georgetown University (LL.M. in Taxation, 1976). Member, Legal Staff, Internal Revenue Service, Estate and Gift Tax Division, 1974-1975. President, Wake County Jewish Federation, 1993-1995. Member, Board of Trustees, George Washington University, 2004—. ***PRACTICE AREAS:*** Taxation Law; Business Law; Estate Planning Law. ***Email:*** afrom@hsfh.com

JOSEPH H. STALLINGS, born New Bern, North Carolina, January 9, 1950; admitted to bar, 1976, New York; 1979, North Carolina; U.S. District Court, Southern and Eastern Districts of New York; U.S. District Court, Eastern, Middle and Western Districts of North Carolina;U.S. Court of Appeals, Fourth and Fifth Circuits; U.S. Tax Court; U.S. Court of Federal Claims. *Education:* University of North Carolina (A.B., 1972; J.D., with honors, 1975). Morehead Scholar; Student Body President, 1971-1972. Phi Beta Kappa; Order of the Coif. Editor-in-Chief, North Carolina Law Review, 1974-1975. Associate: Mudge Rose Guthrie & Alexander, 1976-1977; Ford Marrin Esposito & Witmeyer, 1977-1979. Member, University of North Carolina Board of Governors, 1991-1995. ***PRACTICE AREAS:*** Business Law; Business Litigation; Business Lending; Mergers and Acquisitions. ***Email:*** jstallings@hsfh.com

JOHN N. HUTSON, JR., born Birmingham, Alabama, September 24, 1955; admitted to bar, 1981, North Carolina, U.S. District Court, Eastern, Middle and Western Districts of North Carolina and U.S. Court of Appeals, Fourth Circuit. *Education:* University of North Carolina (B.A., 1977; J.D., 1981). Co-Author: "North Carolina Contract Law," Lexis Publishing, 2001. ***PRACTICE AREAS:*** Contracts; Contract Litigation; Business Litigation; Estate Litigation; Trust Litigation; Landlord and Tenant Law; Real Estate Litigation. ***Email:*** jhutson@hsfh.com

BETH FEREBEE ATKINS, born New Bern, North Carolina, July 8, 1960; admitted to bar, 1985, North Carolina. *Education:* University of North Carolina (B.S., 1982); University of Virginia (J.D., 1985). Director, New Bern Area Chamber of Commerce. Craven County Distinguished Women of the Year 1994. ***PRACTICE AREAS:*** Business Law; Real Estate; Business Lending; Mergers and Acquisitions. ***Email:*** batkins@hsfh.com

JAMES B. ANGELL, born Delaware, Ohio, November 18, 1956; admitted to bar, 1985, North Carolina; U.S. District Court, Eastern, Middle and Western Districts of North Carolina; U.S. Court of Appeals, Fourth Circuit. *Education:* University of North Carolina (B.A., 1979; J.D., 1985). North Carolina Certified Public Accountant. Chapter 7 Panel Trustee, Eastern District of North Carolina. Chair, Bankruptcy Law Specialty Committee, North Carolina State Bar Board of Legal Specialization. (Board Certified Specialist in Business Bankruptcy Law, North Carolina State Board of Legal Specialization). ***PRACTICE AREAS:*** Bankruptcy; Debtor and Creditor; Commercial Litigation; Commercial Transactions; Tax; Construction Law. ***Email:*** jangell@hsfh.com

PEGGY S. VINCENT, born Jefferson City, Missouri, August 4, 1951; admitted to bar, 1988, North Carolina; U.S. District Court, Eastern, Western and Middle Districts of North Carolina; U.S. Supreme Court. *Education:* University of Missouri (B.S., 1973); University of North Carolina (J.D., 1988). Certified Mediator. ***PRACTICE AREAS:*** Business Law; Collections; Employment Law; Computer Law; Intellectual Property. ***Email:*** pvincent@hsfh.com

B. JOAN DAVIS, born Kinston, North Carolina, September 3, 1965; admitted to bar, 1990, North Carolina; U.S. District Court, Eastern, Middle and Western Districts of North Carolina; U.S. Court of Appeals, Fourth Circuit. *Education:* Peace College (A.A., with honors, 1985); University of North Carolina (B.A., with honors, 1987; J.D., with honors, 1990). ***PRACTICE AREAS:*** Civil Litigation; Commercial Litigation; Corporate Law; Business Law; Business Lending; Creditors Rights; Bankruptcy. ***Email:*** jdavis@hsfh.com

BRIAN E. MOORE, born Farmville, North Carolina, February 22, 1974; admitted to bar, 1999, North Carolina; U.S. District Court, Eastern, Middle and Western Districts of North Carolina. *Education:* University of North Carolina (B.A., 1996); Campbell University (J.D., 1999). Member, Campbell Law Review, 1997-1998, Editor-in-Chief, 1998-1999. ***PRACTICE AREAS:*** Commercial Litigation; Estate Litigation; Business Law. ***Email:*** bmoore@hsfh.com

PHILIP W. PAINE, born Roanoke, Virginia, August 21, 1977; admitted to bar, 2003, North Carolina; U.S. District Court, Eastern, Middle and Western Districts of North Carolina; U.S. Court of Appeals, Fourth Circuit. *Education:* University of South Carolina (B.S., 1999); University of North Carolina (J.D., 2003). ***PRACTICE AREAS:*** Bankruptcy; Commercial Litigation; Employment Law; Construction Law; Business Law. ***Email:*** ppaine@hsfh

MARY Z. HANDY, born Okinowa, Japan, January 10, 1974; admitted to bar, 1999, North Carolina; U.S. District Court, Eastern, Middle and Western Districts of North Carolina. *Education:* University of North Carolina (B.A., 1996); Emory University (J.D., 1999). Dean's Fellow. Articles Editor, Emory International Law Review. ***PRACTICE AREAS:*** Business Law; Mergers and Acquisitions; Civil Practice. ***Email:*** mhandy@hsfh.com

RUSSELL W. JOHNSON, born Charleston, West Virginia, March 18, 1977; admitted to bar, 2004, North Carolina. *Education:* West Virginia University (B.A., 1999); University of North Carolina (J.D., 2004). Phi Beta Kappa; Phi Kappa Phi; Golden Key. Author: "One Nation Under God?" Issue 1 First Amendment Law Review, 2003. ***PRACTICE AREAS:*** Civil Litigation; Immigration Law; Personal Injury. ***Email:*** rjohnson@hsfh.com

OF COUNSEL

EDWIN P. FRIEDBERG, born Nassau County, New York, May 25, 1920; admitted to bar, 1948, North Carolina and U.S. Tax Court; U.S. Court of Federal Claims and U.S. Court of Appeals, Fourth Circuit. *Education:* Duke University (B.A., 1943; J.D., 1948). Certified Public Accountant, North Carolina. Lecturer, Tax Practice and Procedure, Duke Law School, 1970. Trial Attorney, Chief Counsel Office, Bureau of Internal Revenue Service, 1948-1952. [Lt., U.S.M.C.R., Retired]

REPRESENTATIVE CLIENTS: Eckerd Corp.; Marmon Industrial Corp.; Branch Banking & Trust Co.; First Union National Bank; VR Business Brokers; Executive Staffing Services; Extended Stay America, Inc; CBL & Associates Properties; The Castleton Group; Bank of America; Big Rock Sports, LLC; Howard Perry & Walston; Cary Orthopedic; Kemper Insurance Company; Neuse River Development Authority, Inc.; Neuse Center for Mental Health.
APPROVED ATTORNEYS FOR: Jefferson Pilot Title; Attorneys Title; Chicago Title; Stewart Title; First American Title; Lawyers Title of N.C.; Fidelity National Title; Investors Title; The Title Company of N.C.

BRETT A. HUBBARD

RALEIGH, NORTH CAROLINA

(See Cary)

Family Law, Separation Agreements, Child Custody, Child Support, Divorce, Bankruptcy, Bankruptcy Chapter 7, Bankruptcy Chapter 13, Wills, Estate Planning, Probate, Estate Administration, Traffic Violations, Criminal Law, Driving While Intoxicated, Real Estate, Employment Law, Small Business Law, Personal Injury.

RICHARD S. HUNTER, JR.

133 FAYETTEVILLE STREET MALL, SUITE 300
P.O. DRAWER 470
RALEIGH, NORTH CAROLINA 27602-0470
Telephone: 919-831-8722
Fax: 919-831-8734
Email: hunteratty@aol.com
URL: http://www.rshunteratty.com

Litigation, Personal Injury, Wrongful Death, Professional Negligence, Product Liability.

RICHARD S. HUNTER, JR., born Montgomery, Alabama, May 8, 1954; admitted to bar, 1980, North Carolina; 1981, U.S. District Court, Eastern and Middle Districts of North Carolina. *Education:* Berklee College of Music; University of North Carolina at Chapel Hill (B.A., 1977); Cumberland School of Law of Samford University (J.D., 1980). Phi Alpha Delta. President, North Carolina Academy of Trial Lawyers, 1993-1994, Board, 1984-1994 and Chair, Auto Torts Section, 1998-1999. Certified, American Board of Trial Advocates (Vice President, 2004). Certified Mediator. Speaker: "Handling Wrongful Death Claims in N.C.," Lorman Education Systems, Inc., 2005; "Case Evaluation, Picking The Right Number," 2001; "Masters In Advocacy: Settlement Techniques," N.C. Academy of Trial Lawyers, 1994; "Semi-Litigated Settlement Conferences," Southern Trial Lawyers Association, New Orleans, 1994; "Wrongful Death," 2004; "Trying the Soft Injury Case," NBI Seminars, 2001. Author: "Insurance Law for the General Practitioner," North Carolina Bar Association Desk Book, 1992: "Pre-suit Preparation," Trial Briefs Magazine, 1992. Chairman, NCATL Seminars: "Inadequate Offer? Try That P.I. Case!", 1995; "Traumatic Medicine," 1988; "How to Try a Civil Law Case," 1986; "Masters In Advocacy Settlement Techniques," 1994; "Case Evaluation," 2001. Speaker, NCATL Seminars on: "Settlement Techniques: Mediation, Arbitration, Mini-Trials", 1995; "Underinsured Motorist Coverage," 1986; "Closed Head Injuries," 1988; "Chronic Pain Syndrome," 1989; "Practical Solutions to Insurance Problems"; "A P.I. System: Brochure and Trial Exhibits," 1991; "Handling Liens and Subrogation Claims," 1993. Speaker: North Carolina Black Lawyers Association on "Insurance Law," 1993; "The Uncivil Practice of Civil Law," NC Association of Insurance Defense Attorneys, Hilton Head, 1994. Faculty, NCATL Trial Advocacy Clinic, November 1987. Listed Who's Who in American Law (1987—). *Member:* Wake County (Member, Board of Directors, 1987 and 1988; Chairman of Board, 1988); North

(This Listing Continued)

(This Listing Continued)

RICHARD S. HUNTER, JR., Raleigh—Continued

Carolina (Member: Litigation Section) North Carolina State Bar; The Association of Trial Lawyers of America; American Board of Trial Advocates (Eastern District of North Carolina Chapter; Diplomate, President, 2005; Vice President, 2004).

OF COUNSEL

KAREN BRITT PEELER

HUNTON & WILLIAMS LLP

ONE BANK OF AMERICA PLAZA
421 FAYETTEVILLE STREET MALL, SUITE 1400
RALEIGH, NORTH CAROLINA 27601
Telephone: 919-899-3000
FAX: 919-833-6352; 919-899-3096
URL: http://www.hunton.com

Washington, D.C. Office: 1900 K Street, N.W., 20006-1109. Telephone: 202-955-1500. Fax: 202-778-2201.
Miami, Florida Office: 1111 Brickell Avenue, Suite 2500, 33131. Telephone: 305-810-2500. Fax: 305-810-2460.
Atlanta, Georgia Office: Bank of America Plaza, 600 Peachtree Street, N.E., Suite 4100, 30308-2216. Telephone: 404-888-4000. Fax: 404-888-4190 and Georgia-Hill Office: Southside Legal Center, 250 Georgia Avenue, S.E., Suite 211, 30312. Telephone: 404-688-5512; 404-688-5513.
New York, New York Office: 200 Park Avenue, 43rd Floor, 10166-0136. Telephone: 212-309-1000. Fax: 212-309-1100.
Charlotte, North Carolina Office: Bank of America Plaza, 101 South Tryon Street, Suite 3500, 28280. Telephone: 704-378-4700. Fax: 704-378-4890.
Knoxville, Tennessee Office: 2000 Riverview Tower, 900 South Gay Street, 37902. Telephone: 865-549-7700. Fax: 865-549-7704.
Dallas, Texas Office: Energy Plaza, 30th Floor, 1601 Bryan Street, 75201-3402. Telephone: 214-979-3000. Fax: 214-880-0011.
Richmond, Virginia Office: Riverfront Plaza, East Tower, 951 East Byrd Street, 23219-4074. Telephone: 804-788-8200. Fax: 804-788-8218; 804-788-8219 and Church Hill Office: 2300 East Marshall Street, 23223. Telephone: 804-775-2248.
McLean, Virginia Office: 1751 Pinnacle Drive, Suite 1700, Tysons Corner, 22102. Telephone: 703-714-7400. Fax: 703-714-7410.
Norfolk, Virginia Office: 500 East Main Street, Suite 1000, 23510-3889. Telephone: 757-640-5300. Fax: 757-625-7720.
Brussels, Belgium Office: Ave Louise 326, B6, 1050 Brussels, Belgium. Telephone: +32 0-2-643-5800. Fax: +32 0-2-643-5822.
Bangkok, Thailand Office: 34/F Abdulrahim Place, 990 Rama IV Road, Bangkok, Thailand, 1050. Telephone: +011 662 636-2366. Fax: +011 662 636-2377.
London, England Office: Fleetway House, 25 Farringdon Street, London EC4A 4AB, England. Telephone: +44 (0)20 7246 5700. Fax: +44 (0)20 7246 5772.
Singapore, Singapore Office: 6 Battery Road, #24-01, Singapore, 049909. Telephone: +65 6534-5608. Fax: +65 6534-5532.
Beijing, China Office: 517-520 South Office Tower, Beijing Kerry Centre, No. 1 Guanghua Road, Chaoyang District, Beijing, PRC 100020, China. Telephone: +86 10 5863 7500. Fax: +86 10 5863 7591.

General Practice. Administrative/Regulatory Law, Admiralty, Antitrust, Unfair Trade Practices, Bankruptcy, Business, Corporation, Environmental, Insurance, International, Labor, Municipal Bond and Finance Law, Non-Criminal Trials and Appeals, Real Property, Condemnation, Securities Regulation, Taxation, Trademarks, Copyright, Utilities, Probate and Estate Planning.

FIRM PROFILE: Hunton & Williams provides legal counsel to corporations, financial institutions, governments and individuals as well as a broad array of other entities. Founded in 1901, Hunton & Williams is a US law firm with a significant international presence. More than 850 attorneys in 16 offices have served clients in over 100 countries around the world.

SENIOR COUNSEL

ROBERT C. HOWISON, JR., born Baltimore, Maryland, July 26, 1915; admitted to bar, 1939, North Carolina. *Education:* University of North Carolina (A.B., 1937; J.D., with honors, 1939). Phi Beta Kappa; Phi Delta Phi; Order of the Coif. Associate Editor, 1937-1938 and Editor-in-Chief, 1938-1939, North Carolina Law Review. Chairman, North Carolina State Board of Public Welfare, 1965-1969. Member, 1968-1980 and Chairman, 1977-1980, North Carolina Board of Law Examiners. President, Wake County Bar Association, 1968. President, 10th Judicial District, North Carolina State Bar, 1960. Fellow, American College of Trial Lawyers. ***PRACTICE AREAS:*** Energy. ***Email:*** rhowison@hunton.com

WALTON K. JOYNER, born Raleigh, North Carolina, April 1, 1933; admitted to bar, 1960, North Carolina. *Education:* University of North Carolina (A.B., 1955; J.D., with honors, 1960). Phi Beta Kappa; Phi Delta Phi; Order of the Coif. Associate Editor, North Carolina Law Review, 1959-1960. Chairman, Board of Directors, Wake County Bar Association, 1977. Certified Mediator. ***PRACTICE AREAS:*** Trusts and Estates; Insurance Regulation. ***Email:*** wjoyner@hunton.com

PARTNERS

CRAIG A. BROMBY, born Elizabeth, New Jersey, 1949; admitted to bar, 1975, North Carolina; 1984, Florida; 1991, U. S. District Court, Eastern District of North Carolina. *Education:* North Carolina State University (B.S., with honors, 1971); University of North Carolina (J.D., with honors, 1975). Phi Kappa Phi. Member, North Carolina Law Review, 1974-1975. President, N.C. Association of Environmental Professionals, 1993-1994. Member: Administrative Law and Environmental Law Sections, North Carolina Bar Association; Environmental and Land Use Law Section, Florida Bar; Section on Environment, Energy, and Resources, American Bar Association. ***PRACTICE AREAS:*** Environmental Law; Administrative Law; Natural Resources. ***Email:*** cbromby@hunton.com

JEAN GORDON CARTER, born Fort Belvoir, Virginia, 1955; admitted to bar, 1983, North Carolina. *Education:* Wake Forest University (B.S., magna cum laude, with honors in Accountancy, 1977); Duke University (J.D., with high honors, 1983). Order of the Coif; Phi Beta Kappa. Carswell Scholar. Member, Board of Editors, Duke Law Journal, 1981-1983. Certified Public Accountant, North Carolina, 1979. Fellow, American College of Trust and Estates Counsel. (Board Certified Specialist in Estate Planning and Probate Law). ***PRACTICE AREAS:*** Taxation; Trusts and Estates. ***Email:*** jcarter@hunton.com

CHARLES D. CASE, born Manning, South Carolina, 1952; admitted to bar, 1977, North Carolina. *Education:* North Carolina State University (B.S., Physics, with high honors, 1973); Harvard University (J.D., 1977). Phi Beta Kappa. Member, Board of Editors, Harvard CR-CL Law Review, 1976-1977. Adjunct Professor of Environmental Law, Campbell University, 1980-1984. Co-Editor and Contributing Author, "Toxic Tort and Hazardous Substance Litigation," Michie 1995. Member: Environmental Law Section, American Bar Association. Member and Chair, Environmental and Natural Resources Section and Member and Past Chair, Administrative Law Section, North Carolina Bar Association; Groundwater Professionals of North Carolina; Carolinas Air Pollution Control Association. Member and Past Chair, Board of Visitors, N.C. State University. Member, Advisory Board, Industrial Extension Service. Member and Past Chair, Foundation for the College of Physical and Mathematical Sciences. Past Member, North Carolina Legislative Study Commission, Hazardous Waste Liability. ***REPORTED CASES:*** Deep River Citizens v. DENR, (N.C. Ct. App. NO. COA02-16570) (6 July 2004), and 149 N.C. App. 211; 560 S.E.2d 814 (2002); N.C. Forestry Assoc. v. DENR, 357 N.C. 640; 588 SE2d 880 (2003); In re Request for Declaratory Ruling, 155 N.C. App. 408; 573 S.E.2d 732 (2002); In re Denial of Request for a Full Administrative Hearing, 146 N.C. App. 258; 552 S.E.2d 230 (2001); sc. rev. den., 354 NC 573; 558 S.E.2d 867 (2001); Arrowood v. Health and Human Services, 353 N.C. 351; 543 S.E.2d 481 (2001); Smith Chapel v. City of Durham, 350 N.C. 805; 517 S.E.2d 874 (1999); Richmond County v. North Carolina Low-level Radioactive Waste Management Auth., disc. rev. den. (1992); 108 N.C. App. 700; 425 S.E.2d 468 (1993); Chatham County v. North Carolina Low-level Radioactive Waste Management Auth., 413 S.E.2d 548 (1992); In re Appeal from the Environmental Management Commission, 80 N.C. App. 1; 341 S.E.2d 588, disc. rev. den. 317 N.C. 334; 346 S.E.2d 139 (1986); Park v. Sleepy Creek Turkeys, Inc., 60 N.C. App. 545; 299 S.E.2d 670 (1983); Underwriters National v. N.C. Life & Accident & Health Insurance Guaranty, 455 U.S. 691; 102 S. Ct. 1357 (1982); The Banking Center v. American Mortgage Insurance Co., Inc., 1982 U.S. App. LEXIS 19155 (4th Cir. 1982); New Hope Community Assoc. v. U.S. Dept. of Housing and Urban Development, 509 F. Supp. 525 (1981). ***PRACTICE AREAS:*** Environmental; Natural Resources; Utility Law; Agricultural Law; Occupational Safety and Health; Administrative Law; Regulatory Law; Zoning, Planning and Land Use; Lobbying; Electric Power; Energy Acquisitions; Energy Facility Siting; Energy Project Development; Hydroelectricity Licensing; Nuclear Energy; Biotechnology. ***Email:*** ccase@hunton.com

WILLIAM D. DANNELLY, born Andalusia, Alabama, 1951; admitted to bar, 1977, North Carolina. *Education:* Massachusetts Institute of Technology (S.B., 1973); University of North Carolina (J.D., 1977). Order of the Coif. Member, North Carolina Law Review, 1975-1977. Law Clerk to Hon. James B. McMillan, U.S. District Court for the Western District of North Carolina, 1977-1978. Contributing Author, "Toxic Tort and Hazardous Substance Litigation," Michie 1995. ***PRACTICE AREAS:*** Environmental; Toxic Torts; Litigation. ***Email:*** wdannelly@hunton.com

L. NEAL ELLIS, JR., born Washington, D.C., August 1, 1948; admitted to bar, 1975, Virginia; 1976, U. S. Claims Court; 1978, District of Columbia; 1985, North Carolina; 2000, U.S. Supreme Court. *Education:* United States Military Academy (B.S., 1970); University of Virginia (J.D., 1975). Phi Delta Phi. Managing Editor, Virginia Journal of International Law, 1974-1975. Member of Section Council, ABA Tort Trial and Insurance Practice Section, 2003—. Chair, ABA Trial Techniques Committee, Tort and Insurance Section, 2000-2001. Chair, ABA Commercial Torts Committee, Tort and Insurance Section, 1992-1993; Chair, ABA Tort and Trial Practice Steering Committee, 2001-2003. Editor-in-Chief, ABA Tort and Insurance Law Journal, 1997-1999. Editor-in-Chief, ABA Tort Source, 2001-2003. Member, The American Jury Project, 2004. Member, North Carolina Bar Association Task Force on Administration of Justice. Member and Chairman, 1986-1993, Wake County Board of Elections. [Colonel, U.S. Army Reserve]. ***PRACTICE AREAS:*** Commercial Litigation; Environmental Litigation and Toxic Torts; Products Liability; Medical Devices; Pharmaceuticals. ***Email:*** nellis@hunton.com

EDWARD S. FINLEY, JR., born North Wilkesboro, North Carolina, March 24, 1949; admitted to bar, 1974, North Carolina. *Education:* University of North Carolina (A.B., 1971; J.D., with honors, 1974). Phi Beta Kappa; Order of the Coif. Member, North Carolina Law Review, 1973-1974. ***PRACTICE AREAS:*** Energy. ***Email:*** efinley@hunton.com

WILLIAM M. FLYNN, born St. Louis, Missouri, June 21, 1949; admitted to bar, 1977, Pennsylvania; 1980, North Carolina. *Education:* Georgetown University, School of Foreign Service (B.S.F.S., 1971); College of William & Mary (J.D., 1977). Member, William & Mary Law Review, 1975-1977. Member, North Carolina Bar Association: Board of Governors, 1997-2000; Chairman, Membership Recruitment and Retention Committee, 2000-2002; Member, Strategic Planning Committee, 2001-2002; Chairman, Large Law Firm Committee, 2005-2006; Chairman, Business Law Section, 1995-1997; Chairman, Business Section Continuing Legal Education Committee, 1994-1995; Chairman, Business Section Ethics Committee, 1993-1994; Chairman, Business Section Financial Institutions Committee, 1991-1993. Member, Business Law/Organizations Specialty Committee, North Carolina State Bar Board of Legal Specialization, 1995. Member, Business Law Section, American Bar Association. ***PRACTICE AREAS:*** Corporate Law; Commercial Law; Mergers, Acquisitions and Divestitures; Finance; Securities. ***Email:*** wflynn@hunton.com

DAVID R. FRICKE, born Bloomfield Hills, Michigan, 1961; admitted to bar, 1986, North Carolina. *Education:* University of Vermont (B.A., 1983); Wake Forest University (J.D., 1986). Adjunct Professor, Meredith College, 1992-1995. *Member:* National Association of Bond Lawyers. ***PRACTICE AREAS:*** Commercial Real Estate; Public Finance. ***Email:*** dfricke@hunton.com

(This Listing Continued)

TIMOTHY S. GOETTEL, born Cooperstown, New York, December 2, 1961; admitted to bar, 1987, North Carolina. *Education:* Duke University (B.A., magna cum laude, 1983); University of Virginia (J.D., 1987). Member, Business Law Sections of North Carolina Bar Association and American Bar Associations. ***PRACTICE AREAS:*** Mergers and Acquisitions; Securities. ***Email:*** tgoettel@hunton.com

DOUGLAS WAYNE KENYON, born Fort Lauderdale, Florida, April 15, 1954; admitted to bar, 1979, Virginia; 1986, North Carolina. *Education:* University of Notre Dame (B.A., 1976; J.D., with honors, 1979). Pi Sigma Alpha. Member, Sections on: Antitrust Law; Litigation, 1979—; Patent Trademark and Copyright Law, 1983—, American Bar Association. Chair, Antitrust and Trade Regulation Section, 1992—, 1987-1989; Member, Trial Practice and Curriculum Committee, 1992—, North Carolina Bar Association. *Member:* Virginia State Bar; Virginia Bar Association; American Judicature Society; American Law Institute. ***PRACTICE AREAS:*** Intellectual Property; Antitrust. ***Email:*** dkenyon@hunton.com

THOMAS J. MANLEY, born Montgomery, Alabama, January 23, 1946; admitted to bar, 1972, Virginia; 1979, U.S. Supreme Court; 1983, North Carolina. *Education:* University of North Carolina (A.B., 1969); Harvard Law School (J.D., 1972). Phi Beta Kappa. Mediator, Certified North Carolina, 1991. ***PRACTICE AREAS:*** Labor and Employment; Alternative Dispute Resolution. ***Email:*** tmanley@hunton.com

WILLIAM H. McBRIDE, born San Antonio, Texas, August 8, 1948; admitted to bar, 1976, Texas; 1977, Virginia; 1981, North Carolina. *Education:* Princeton University (A.B., 1970); University of Texas (J.D., 1976). Associate Editor, University of Texas Law Review, 1975-1976. Chairman, Bond Attorneys' Workshop, 1988. *Member:* National Association of Bond Lawyers (Director, 1987-1988, 1991-1997; President, 1995-1996); American College of Bond Counsel. [Sergeant, U. S. Army, 1970-1973]. ***PRACTICE AREAS:*** Public Finance; Municipal Bonds; Tax Audits. ***Email:*** wmcbride@hunton.com

WILLIAM S. PATTERSON, born Kings Mountain, North Carolina, July 16, 1947; admitted to bar, 1973, North Carolina. *Education:* Wake Forest University (B.A., 1969); University of North Carolina (J.D., with honors, 1973). Order of the Coif. Member, North Carolina Law Review, 1972-1973. Staff Attorney, Interpretative Division, 1973-1975; Tax Court Litigation Division, 1975-1977, Office of the Chief Counsel, United States Department of the Treasury. ***PRACTICE AREAS:*** Corporate; Securities. ***Email:*** bpatterson@hunton.com

MARY NASH KELLY RUSHER, born Norfolk, Virginia, May 25, 1958; admitted to bar, 1985, North Carolina. *Education:* Wake Forest University (B.A., magna cum laude, 1980); University of Virginia (J.D., 1984). Order of the Coif; Omicron Delta Kappa; Phi Beta Kappa; Mortar Board. Law Clerk to the Hon. John D. Butzner, Jr., U.S. Court of Appeals, 4th Circuit, 1984-1985. Member, Committee on Women in the Profession, North Carolina Bar Association. *Member:* National Association of Bond Lawyers. ***LANGUAGES:*** German. ***PRACTICE AREAS:*** Banking and Finance; Public Finance. ***Email:*** mnrusher@hunton.com

COUNSEL

WILLIAM P. ANDREWS, JR., born Fort Worth, Texas, 1949; admitted to bar, 1975, North Carolina; 1983, Massachusetts; 1985, U.S. District Court, Eastern District of North Carolina; 2000, U.S. Court of International Trade. *Education:* University of North Carolina (B.A., 1971; J.D., 1975). Assistant Editor, University of North Carolina Sea Grant Publications. Member, North Carolina Law Review, 1974-1975. Co-Chair, ABA International Section Inter-American Law Committee, 1993-1995. *Member:* Wake County, North Carolina and American Bar Associations. ***LANGUAGES:*** Spanish. ***PRACTICE AREAS:*** Intellectual Property; Corporate Law; International Law; Computers and Software. ***Email:*** jandrews@hunton.com

STEVEN B. EPSTEIN, born New York, N.Y., April 2, 1965; admitted to bar, 1990, North Carolina; 1992, U.S. District Court, Eastern District of North Carolina and U.S. Court of Appeals, Fourth Circuit; 1997, U.S. District Court, Western District of North Carolina; 1998, U.S. District Court, Middle District of North Carolina. *Education:* University of North Carolina at Chapel Hill (B.A., with highest honors, 1987; J.D., with highest honors, 1990). Chair, Litigation Section, North Carolina Bar Association, 2003-2004. Special NCBA Special Tort Reform Study Committee, 2003-2006. DRC Certified Mediator. ***PRACTICE AREAS:*** Litigation; Products Liability; Construction. ***Email:*** sepstein@hunton.com

WILLIAM E. GRAHAM, JR., born Jackson Springs, North Carolina, December 31, 1929; admitted to bar, 1956, North Carolina. *Education:* University of North Carolina (A.B., 1952; J.D., with honors, 1956). Phi Delta Phi; Order of the Coif. Associate Editor, North Carolina Law Review. Judge of North Carolina Court of Appeals, 1969-1973. Law Clerk to Hon. John J. Parker, Chief Judge, U. S. Court of Appeals, 4th Cir., 1956-1957; Vice Chairman, General Counsel (and various executive positions) Carolina Power & Light Co. 1973-1993. Chairman, ABA Section on Public Utility, Communications and Transportation Law, 1990-1991. ***PRACTICE AREAS:*** Regulated Industries; Governmental Relations. ***Email:*** dgraham@hunton.com

ASSOCIATES

CHRISTOPHER J. AYERS, born Rutherfordton, North Carolina, July 20, 1977; admitted to bar, 2002, North Carolina; 2003, U.S. District Court, Eastern District of North Carolina. *Education:* Duke University (B.A., magna cum laude, 1999); University of North Carolina at Chapel Hill (J.D., with honors, 2002). Managing Editor, North Carolina Law Review, 2001-2002. Law clerk, Judge Linda M. McGee, North Carolina Court of Appeals, 2002-2003. *Member:* Wake County and North Carolina Bar Associations; North Carolina State Bar. ***PRACTICE AREAS:*** Utilities; Regulatory Law; Appellate Practice; Administrative Law. ***Email:*** cayers@hunton.com

JULIE BEDDINGFIELD, born Winter Haven, Florida, July 30, 1968; admitted to bar, 2000, North Carolina. *Education:* Loyola University (B.A., cum laude, 1992); University of Florida (J.D., with honors, 2000). ***PRACTICE AREAS:*** Environmental Law. ***Email:*** jbeddingfield@hunton.com

ALISON J. BENGE, born 1976; admitted to bar, 2005, North Carolina. *Education:* Hanover College (B.A., summa cum laude, 1998) Duke University (J.D., cum laude, 2002). ***PRACTICE AREAS:*** Public Finance; Bond Finance; Industrial Development Bonds; Public Authority Finance; Public Finance Taxation; Tax Exempt Bonds; Tax Exempt Finance. ***Email:*** abenge@hunton.com

DANIELLE BENNETT, born Boston, Massachusetts, June 5, 1973; admitted to bar, 1999, North Carolina. *Education:* Duke University (A.B., cum laude, 1994); North Carolina Central University (J.D., summa cum laude, 1999). ***PRACTICE AREAS:*** Corporate Law; Securities.

ZACHARY R. BISHOP, born Durham, North Carolina, December 5, 1975; admitted to bar, 2001, Georgia; 2004, North Carolina. *Education:* Duke University (A.B., 1998); Tulane University (J.D., magna cum laude, 2001). *Member:* State Bar of Georgia; North Carolina State Bar. ***PRACTICE AREAS:*** Technology Law; Intellectual Property; Corporate Law. ***Email:*** zbishop@hunton.com

JOHN D. BURNS, born Heidelberg, Germany, October 14, 1970; admitted to bar, 1997, North Carolina. *Education:* Davidson College (A.B., Political Science, 1992); Wake Forest University (J.D., 1997). Rotary International Ambassadorial Scholar, 1993-1994. Governor, Fourth Circuit, ABA Law Student Division, 1996-1997. Staff Member, Wake Forest Law Review, 1995-1997. Law Clerk to Honorable W. Earl Britt, U.S. District Judge, EDNC, 1997-1999. Author, "The Eight Million Little Pigs - A Cautionary Tale: Statutory and Regulatory Responses to Concentrated Hog Farming," 31 WLFR 851 (1996). *Member:* Wake County, North Carolina and American Bar Associations; American Bankruptcy Institute; North Carolina Academy of Trial Lawyers. ***LANGUAGES:*** French. ***PRACTICE AREAS:*** Civil Trial Practice (65%); Bankruptcy (35%). ***Email:*** jburns@hunton.com

J. KEITH COATES, JR., born Roanoke, Virginia, November 4, 1972; admitted to bar, 1998, Georgia (Not admitted in North Carolina). *Education:* University of the South (B.A., with honors, 1995); University of Tennessee (J.D., summa cum laude, 1998). Phi Kappa Phi; Order of the Barristers. Member, Moot Court Board. ***PRACTICE AREAS:*** Labor and Employment. ***Email:*** kcoates@hunton.com

JOHN T. EARWOOD, born Richmond, Virginia, August 16, 1969; admitted to bar, 1997, North Carolina. *Education:* Wake Forest University (B.A., 1992; M.B.A., 1997; J.D., 1997). ***PRACTICE AREAS:*** Corporate; Public Finance. ***Email:*** jearwood@hunton.com

KELLI DUTROW JACKSON, born Apple Valley, California, September 10, 1965; admitted to bar, 2002, Georgia (Not admitted in North Carolina). *Education:* Duke University (B.A., Political Science, 1987); University of North Carolina at Chapel Hill (M.A., Exercise Physiology, 1992); Georgia State University (J.D., cum laude, 2002). Editor-in-Chief, Georgia State University Law Review, 2001-2002. Author: "Working at Home at Your Own Risk: Employer Liability for Teleworkers Under the Occupational Safety and Health Act of 1970," 18 Ga. St. U. L. Rev. 955, 2002; "Relationship Between Blood Testosterone Concentrations and Body Composition in Physically Active Men," Medicina Sportiva (Bohemica & Slovaca), 4(3): 65-67, 1996 (with A.C. Hackney, Ph.D.). ***PRACTICE AREAS:*** Labor and Employment. ***Email:*** kjackson@hunton.com

ELIZABETH H. JOHNSON, born 1977; admitted to bar, 2003, North Carolina. *Education:* Coe College (B.A., 1999); Duke University (M.E.M., 2003; J.D., 2003). ***PRACTICE AREAS:*** Administrative Law; Environmental Law; Privacy Law; Regulatory Law. ***Email:*** e.johnson@hunton.com

TIMOTHY D. JOHNSON, born April 21, 1975; admitted to bar, 2001, Washington 2004, North Carolina. *Education:* Taylor University (B.A., 1997); Duke University (J.D., 2001). ***PRACTICE AREAS:*** Corporate Law; Securities; Technology and Science; Real Estate. ***Email:*** tdjohnson@hunton.com

CHRISTOPHER R. STAMBAUGH, born Los Angeles, California; admitted to bar, 2004, New York (Not admitted in North Carolina). *Education:* Duke University (B.S.E., 1997; M.E.M., 2000); Fordham University (J.D., 2003). *Member:* New York State Bar Association. ***PRACTICE AREAS:*** Corporate Law; Securities. ***Email:*** cstambaugh@hunton.com

RAY A. STARLING, born Fayetteville, North Carolina, August 8, 1976; admitted to bar, 2002, North Carolina; 2003, U.S. District Court, Eastern, Middle and Western Districts of North Carolina. *Education:* North Carolina State University (B.S., magna cum laude, 1999); University of North Carolina at Chapel Hill (J.D., with honors, 2002). Chief Justice, Holderness Moot Court Bench, 2001-2002; National Trial Team, 2000-2002; James and Carolyn B. Davis Society, 2002. Best Overall: Holderness Moot Court Invitational Team Competition, 2001; National Trial Team Competition, 2001. Law Clerk to Hon. Mark D. Martin, North Carolina Supreme Court, 2002-2003. Member, Young Adults Ministry Council, Edenton Street UMC. *Member:* Wake County (Member, Professionalism Committee) and North Carolina Bar Associations; North Carolina State Bar; American Agricultural Law Association. ***PRACTICE AREAS:*** Commercial Litigation. ***Email:*** rstarling@hunton.com

JASON S. THOMAS, born Lansing, Michigan, 1954; admitted to bar, 1991, North Carolina; 1992, U.S. District Court, Eastern District of North Carolina; 1994, U.S. Court of Appeals, Fourth Circuit; 1995, U.S. District Court, Middle and Western Districts of North Carolina. *Education:* Oberlin College Conservatory of Music (B.Mus., 1976); State University of New York at Stony Brook (M.M., 1978); University of North Carolina (J.D., 1991); University of Wisconsin, Madison (D.M.A., 1992). ***PRACTICE AREAS:*** Environmental Law; Administrative Law; Litigation. ***Email:*** jsthomas@hunton.com

JENNIFER J. TUNG, admitted to bar, 2005, North Carolina. *Education:* Stanford University (B.A., 2001); Harvard Law School (J.D., 2005). ***Email:*** jtung@hunton.com

ROBERT C. VAN ARNAM, born Albany, New York, October 15, 1966; admitted to bar, 2002, North Carolina and U.S. District Court, Eastern and Middle Districts of North Carolina. *Education:* Dickinson College (B.A., 1989); American University (M.A., 1994); University of North Carolina (J.D., 2002). Special Assistant, U.S. Department of Justice: Office of Intelligence Policy; Office of International Affairs, Criminal Division; Department Budget Staff, 1994-1999. Staff Associate, Association of American Medical Colleges,

(This Listing Continued)

HUNTON & WILLIAMS LLP, Raleigh—Continued

1989-1994. *Member:* North Carolina and American Bar Associations. ***LANGUAGES:*** French. ***PRACTICE AREAS:*** Antitrust and Trade Regulation (40%); Intellectual Property (35%); Litigation (25%). ***Email:*** rvanarnam@hunton.com

Most lawyers are admitted in North Carolina and are members of the Mecklenburg or Wake County, North Carolina State Bar, North Carolina and American Bar Associations.

(For complete biographical data on other personnel, see Professional Biographies at other locations)

THE LAW FIRM OF HUTCHENS, SENTER & BRITTON, P.A.

SUITE 1540
TWO HANOVER SQUARE
RALEIGH, NORTH CAROLINA 27601
Telephone: 919-834-2688
Facsimile: 919-834-3373
Email: lawfirm@hutchensandsenter.com
URL: http://www.hutchensandsenter.com

Mailing Address: P.O. Box 2505, Fayetteville, NC 28302

Fayetteville, North Carolina Office: 4317 Ramsey Street, P.O. Box 2505. Telephone: 910-864-6888. Fax: 910-864-6848.

Wilmington, North Carolina Office: Suite 210, 1437 Military Cutoff Road, P.O. Box 12969. Telephone: 910-509-7480. Fax: 910-509-7448.

General Civil Practice, Trials in all State and Federal Courts, Creditor Bankruptcy, Foreclosures and Collection, Personal Injury, Wrongful Death, Worker's Compensation, Insurance Law, Corporation, Business and Real Estate.

SHAWNA Y. STATON, born Sealevel, North Carolina, August 11, 1966; admitted to bar, 1991, North Carolina and U.S. District Court, Western, Eastern and Middle Districts of North Carolina; 1992, U.S. Court of Appeals, Fourth Circuit. *Education:* University of North Carolina at Chapel Hill (B.A., 1988; J.D., 1991). Phi Alpha Delta. Editor, Disclosure Statement, Bankruptcy Section Newsletter, North Carolina Bar Association, 2001-2003. Panel Member: Chapter 7 Bankruptcy Trustees for Eastern District of North Carolina, 1998—; Local Bankruptcy Rules Committee for the Eastern District of North Carolina. *Member:* Wake County, North Carolina (Member, Young Lawyers Section; Member, Executive Council, 1998— and Chair, Ethics Committee, 1999, Bankruptcy Section) and American Bar Associations; American Bankruptcy Institute. ***PRACTICE AREAS:*** Bankruptcy; Commercial Litigation. ***Email:*** Shawna.Staton@hutchensandsenter.com

REPRESENTATIVE CLIENTS: Available Upon Request.

(For complete biographical data on all personnel, see Professional Biographies at Fayetteville, North Carolina)

HUTCHISON & MASON PLLC

Established in 1996

3110 EDWARDS MILL ROAD, SUITE 100
RALEIGH, NORTH CAROLINA 27612
Telephone: 919-829-9600
Fax: 919-829-9696
Email: info@hutchlaw.com
URL: http://www.hutchlaw.com

Business, Corporate, Securities and Commercial Law, including Start-Up and Emerging Growth Companies, Software and Computer Law, Corporate Finance, including Venture Capital Financings and Private Placements, Public Offerings, Corporate Governance, Corporate Mergers, Acquisitions and Dispositions, Joint Ventures, Intellectual Property (Patents, Trademarks, Copyright, Licensing and Trade Secrets), Executive Employment, Compensation and Termination.

FIRM PROFILE: A law firm focused on life sciences and information technology companies, Hutchison & Mason PLLC provides strategic legal advice, connections and support to its clients.

Hutchison & Mason PLLC has a strategic relationship with Wilmer Cutler Pickering Hale and Dorr LLP.

FRED D. HUTCHISON, born Maryville, Tennessee, 1949; admitted to bar, 1975, North Carolina; 1976, District of Columbia. *Education:* University of North Carolina (B.S., 1971); University of Virginia (J.D., 1975). Phi Beta Kappa; Order of the Coif. Member, Board of Editors, Virginia Law Review, 1973-1975. Member: Governor's Task Force on Development of Private Seed Capital Sources, 1987-1988; Business Review Panel, North Carolina Technological Development Authority, 1984-1985. Business Reviewer, N.C. Biotechnology Center, 1987. Member, Board of Directors and Chairman, Business Innovation and Technology Advancement Center, 1988-1991. President, 1984-1985, Member, Executive Committee, 1984—, and Member, Board of Directors, 1984—, Council for Entrepreneurial Development. Member, Board of Directors, 1988-1997, Member, Executive Committee, 1990-1997, and Chairman, 1993-1994, Greater Raleigh Chamber of Commerce. Chairman, North Carolina Venture Capital Conference, 1992. Member, Board of Directors, Raleigh-Durham Regional Partnership, 1993-1994. General Counsel, North Carolina Electronics and Information Technologies Association, 1993-1996. Member, External Advisory Team, North Carolina Biotechnology Center, 1995-2002. Director, Raleigh Little Theatre, 1995-1997. Chairman, 1995, and Member, Executive Committee, 1998, Duke Conference on Entrepreneurship. Chairman, 1997-1999 and Member, Executive Committee, 1997-2004, The Sports Council. Member, Board of Directors, Pan Am Games Bid Committee for the Triangle, 1998-1999. Member, 1995-2001, Executive Committee, and President, 1998-2000, The Fifty Group. Member, Board of Directors, 1998 and Chairman-Elect, 2000-2002; Chairman, 2002-2004, Triangle Community Foundation. Chairman, Entrepreneurial Advisory Committee, The Catalyst Project, 1999-2003. Raleigh Little Theatre's Advisory Board, 2003—. Co-Chairman, Venture, 2005. Chairman, First Flight Venture Charter, 2004—. *Member:* Wake County, North Carolina and American Bar Associations. ***PRACTICE AREAS:*** Corporate Law; Business Law; Venture Capital; Mergers and Acquisitions; Commercial Law; Securities. ***Email:*** fhutchison@hutchlaw.com

MERRILL McCALL MASON, born Melbourne, Florida, 1960; admitted to bar, 1989, North Carolina. *Education:* University of North Carolina (B.A., 1982; J.D., 1986). Adjunct Instructor, Kenan-Flagler Business School, 2000—; UNC Law School, 2001—. Council for Entrepreneurial Development; Board of Advisors, 1997; Program Committee Chairman, 1994-1997; Venture '97 Selection Committee; Board of Directors, 2001—, Executive Committee, 2002—, Co-Chair, CED Biotech Conference, 1999. Volunteer Coordinator Committee, Special Olympics World Game, 2001. Member: Wake County, North Carolina and American Bar Associations. ***PRACTICE AREAS:*** Business Law; Corporate Law; Mergers and Acquisitions; Commercial Law; Securities. ***Email:*** mmason@hutchlaw.com

HELGA LURA LEFTWICH, born Lynchburg, Virginia, April 4, 1952; admitted to bar, 1993, North Carolina. *Education:* Duke University (B.A., magna cum laude, 1974); University of North Carolina at Chapel Hill (M.S.L.S., 1977; J.D., with high honors, 1993). Order of the Coif. Editor-in-Chief, North Carolina Law Review, 1992-1993. Recipient: E.S.W. Dameron Merit Scholarship; Chief Justice Walker Clark Award. Author: "The Intentional—Tort Exception To The Workers' Compensation Exclusive Remedy Immunity Provision," 70 N.C. Law Review 849 (1992). Member, Council for Entrepreneurial Development; Presentation Enhancement Committee, Venture Conference, 1997-2001. Co-Chair, Enhancement Committee, Venture Conferences, 2002, 2003. Chair, Company Recruitment Committee, Member, Venture Conferences, 2005; Chair, Venture Conference, 2004; Streak Venture Forum Program Committee, 1998; Streak Selection Committee, 1999-2000. Co-Chair, Biotech Conference, 2003. Member, United Arts Council of Raleigh and Wake County, Inc., 2001-2004, Board of Directors, 2001—; Executive Committee of Board of Directors, 2004—. Member, Business Friends, The North Carolina Museum of Art. Member: Business Law Section Council, 2000-2003; Executive Committee, 2002-2003, North Carolina Bar Association. Member, Forum Committee and Coaching Co-Chair, Springboard Venture Forum: Southeast, September 2002. *Member:* Wake County, 14th Judicial District Bar Association (Member, Business Law Section), North Carolina and American Bar Associations. ***LANGUAGES:*** German. ***PRACTICE AREAS:*** Business Law; Corporate Law; Securities Law; Venture Capital; Mergers and Acquisitions. ***Email:*** hleftwich@hutchlaw.com

J. ROBERT TYLER, III, born Charlottesville, Virginia, April 14, 1961; admitted to bar, 1989, Virginia; 1996, North Carolina. *Education:* University of Richmond (B.S., 1984; J.D., cum laude, 1989). McNeill Honor Society. Editor-in-Chief, University of Richmond Law Review, 1988-1989. Recipient, Corpus Juris Secundum Award for Most Significant Contribution to Legal Scholarship; Best Brief Award, Carrico Moot Court Competition. Member, Business Law Section Council, North Carolina Bar Association. President, Business Friends Council, North Carolina Museum of Art. Chairman, Summit on the Park, North Carolina Museum of Art, 2003; Chairman, Public Affairs Subcommittee; Council For Entrepreneurial Development. Executive-In-Residence, North Carolina State University College of Management's Technology Education and Commercialization Program. *Member:* Wake County, North Carolina and American Bar Associations. ***PRACTICE AREAS:*** Corporate Law; Venture Capital; Intellectual Property Licensing; Mergers and Acquisitions; Securities Law. ***Email:*** rtyler@hutchlaw.com

RANDALL M. WHITMEYER, born Baton Rouge, Louisiana, December 6, 1963; admitted to bar, 1991, Illinois, U.S. District Court, Northern District of Illinois, U.S. Court of Appeals, Seventh Circuit and U.S. Court of Appeals for the Federal Circuit; 1997, North Carolina. *Education:* Duke University (B.S., summa cum laude, 1984); Northwestern University (J.D., magna cum laude, 1991). Phi Beta Kappa; Order of the Coif; Recipient, John Paul Stevens Award for Academic Excellence. Author: "A Plea For Due Processes: Defining The Proper Scope of Patent Protection for Computer Software," 85 Northwestern University Law Review 1103, 1991; "Digital Images and Copyright Law," ImageBase Magazine, 5, July, 1993; "The Reno Decision and its Aftermath: Limiting Censorship on the Net," Computer Law Association Bulletin, Vol. 12, No.4, 1997. Law Clerk to the Honorable Walter J. Cummings, U.S. Court of Appeals, Seventh Circuit, 1991-1992. United States Recent Developments Editor, Computer Law Association Bulletin, 1999-2002. Member, Board of Directors, Communities in Schools of Wake County, 2001—. *Member:* North Carolina and American Bar Associations; Computer Law Association; International Trademark Association. ***PRACTICE AREAS:*** Computer Law; Intellectual Property Law; Intellectual Property Licensing; Commercial Law; Information Technology Law; Trademarks. ***Email:*** rwhitmeyer@hutchlaw.com

ALLEN R. BAUM, born Chicago, Illinois, August 29, 1967; admitted to bar, 1992, Virginia and U.S. Court of Appeals, Fourth Circuit; 1994, U.S. Court of Appeals for the Federal Circuit; 1998, North Carolina and U.S. District Court, Middle District of North Carolina; 1999, U.S. District Court, Eastern District of North Carolina; registered to practice before U.S. Patent and Trademark Office. *Education:* Muhlenberg College (B.S., Chemistry, 1989); Widener University (J.D., 1992). *Member:* Virginia State Bar; North Carolina State Bar; American Bar Association (Member, Patent, Trademark and Copyright Section); American Intellectual Property Law Association (Trustee, 2001-2003; Vice President, 2003—); Licensing Executives Society; Triangle Intellectual Property Law Association. ***LANGUAGES:*** German. ***Email:*** abaum@hutchlaw.com

JOHN M. FOGG, born Oakland, California, September 11, 1968; admitted to bar, 1994, California (Not admitted in North Carolina). *Education:* Yale University (B.A., cum laude, 1991); Columbia University (J.D., 1994). Member, Editorial Board & Business Manager, Columbia Journal of Law and The Arts, 1992-1994. Charter Member, The Indus Entrepreneurs Silicon Valley. *Member:* State Bar of California; American Bar Association. ***PRACTICE AREAS:*** Corporate Law; Securities; Mergers and Acquisitions; Venture Capital. ***Email:*** jfogg@hutchlaw.com

WILLIAM N. WOFFORD, born Coral Gables, Florida, May 10, 1967; admitted to bar, 1995, New York; 1997, North Carolina. *Education:* University of Virginia (B.A., 1989; J.D., 1994). Recipient, Ford Foundation International Law Scholarship, 1993. Member, Editorial Board and Executive Editor, Virginia Journal of International Law, 1992-1994.

(This Listing Continued)

Member, Council for Entrepreneurial Development; Presentation Enhancement Committee, Venture Conference, 2002—. Member, North Carolina Bioscience Industry Organization. Member, Advisory Board, Carrboro Parks Project, 2001—. Member, Board of Directors, Krquden Institute, 2003—. *Member:* North Carolina (Member, Business Section) and American (Member, Business Law and Science and Technology Sections; Biotechnology Committee) Bar Associations. ***PRACTICE AREAS:*** Business Law; Corporate Law; Securities Law; Mergers and Acquisitions; Venture Capital; Intellectual Property Licensing; Technology Law. ***Email:*** bwofford@hutchlaw.com

KATHLEEN NOWACK WORM, born Newark, New Jersey, August 20, 1960; admitted to bar, 1991, Texas; 1994, North Carolina. *Education:* Randolph Macon-Woman's College (B.A., 1982); Emory University (J.D., 1990). *Member:* North Carolina Bar Association. ***PRACTICE AREAS:*** Business Law; Labor and Employment Law; Real Estate Law. ***Email:*** kworm@hutchlaw.com

---

NEIL S. BAGCHI, born Toronto, Canada, January 9, 1977; admitted to bar, 2004, North Carolina. *Education:* University of North Carolina-Chapel Hill (B.A., 1999; J.D., 2004). Morehead Scholar. ***PRACTICE AREAS:*** Corporate Law; Venture Capital; Mergers and Acquisitions; Business Law. ***Email:*** nbagchi@hutchlaw.com

HOLLY ANN COLDIRON, born New London, Pennsylvania, October 30, 1963; admitted to bar, 1997, North Carolina. *Education:* University of North Carolina (B.A., 1984; J.D., 1996). *Member:* North Carolina (Member, Intellectual Property Committee) and American Bar Associations; International Trademark Association. ***PRACTICE AREAS:*** Computer Law; Intellectual Property Law; Trademark; Intellectual Property Licensing; Copyright; Unfair Competition; Corporate Law; Business Law; Mergers and Acquisitions; Securities Law. ***Email:*** hcoldiron@hutchlaw.com

L. AYLETT COLSTON, born Durham, North Carolina, March 15, 1972; admitted to bar, 1999, North Carolina and U.S. District Court, Eastern District of North Carolina. *Education:* Davidson College (B.A., 1994); Washington & Lee University (J.D., 1999). ***PRACTICE AREAS:*** Corporate Law; Business Law; Securities Law; Venture Capital; Mergers and Acquisitions. ***Email:*** acolston@hutchlaw.com

JOSHUA T. ELLIOTT, born Washington, North Carolina, January 9, 1973; admitted to bar, 1999, Ohio; 2001, North Carolina; registered to practice before U.S. Patent and Trademark Office. *Education:* University of North Carolina at Chapel Hill (B.S., Chemistry, with distinction, 1995); University of Dayton (J.D., cum laude, 1999). *Member:* North Carolina Bar Association; American Intellectual Property Law Association. ***Email:*** jelliott@hutchlaw.com

AARON P. GOLUB, born Philadelphia, Pennsylvania, 1974; admitted to bar, 2002, California; 2003, North Carolina. *Education:* George Washington University (B.A., 1996; J.D., 2002). *Member:* North Carolina State Bar; State Bar of California; North Carolina and American Bar Associations;. ***PRACTICE AREAS:*** Intellectual Property; Trademarks; Copyrights; Unfair Competition; Computer Law; Corporate Law; Venture Capital; Mergers and Acquisitions; Securities; Finance.

JUSTYN J. KASIERSKI, born Worcester, Massachusetts, December 1, 1972; admitted to bar, 2000, Massachusetts (Not admitted in North Carolina). *Education:* University of Rhode Island (B.A., 1997); Duke University (J.D., 2000). *Member:* Massachusetts and American Bar Associations. ***PRACTICE AREAS:*** Business Law; Corporate Law; Venture Capital; Mergers and Acquisitions; Securities; Finance. ***Email:*** jkasierski@hutchlaw.com

D. KAREN MAREADY, born Wilmington, North Carolina, February 19, 1974; admitted to bar, 2003, North Carolina. *Education:* Brigham Young University, Hawaii (B.A., 1996); University of Mississippi (J.D., 2003). *Member:* North Carolina and American (Member, Labor and Employment Section) Bar Associations. ***PRACTICE AREAS:*** Labor and Employment; Business Law. ***Email:*** dmaready@hutchlaw.com

DONALD L. NOVAJOSKY, born New Brunswick, New Jersey, February 28, 1971; admitted to bar, 2000, New Jersey; 2003, New York (Not admitted in North Carolina). *Education:* Pennsylvania State University (B.S., Finance, 1993); New York Law School (J.D., magna cum laude, 2000). Member and Editor, New York Law School Law Review, 1998-2000. ***PRACTICE AREAS:*** Corporate Law; Securities; Intellectual Property Licensing; Mergers and Acquisitions.

OF COUNSEL

MARY B. GRANT, born Kokomo, Indiana, February 13, 1961; admitted to bar, 1989, District of Columbia; 1993, North Carolina; registered to practice before U.S. Patent and Trademark Office. *Education:* Purdue University (B.S., 1983); George Washington University (J.D., with high honors, 1987). *Member:* North Carolina State Bar; North Carolina Bar Association; American Intellectual Property Law Association. ***PRACTICE AREAS:*** Patents; Intellectual Property. ***Email:*** mgrant@hutchlaw.com

REPRESENTATIVE CLIENTS: AlphaVax, Inc.; Amphora Discovery Corp.; Bloodhound Software, Inc.; Blue 292, Inc.; Coventor, Inc.; Elumens Corporation; Gentris Corporation; Hatteras Networks, Inc.; ICAgen, Inc.; Industrial Microwave Systems, Inc.; Intelli-Mark Technologies, Inc.; Kyma Technologies, Inc.; LipoScience, Inc.; LVL7 Systems, Inc.; LiveWire Logic, Inc.; MERIX Bioscience, Inc.; Micell Technologies, Inc.; Paradigm Genetics, Inc.; PeopleClick.com, Inc.; POZEN Inc.; Quill Medical, Inc.; Sicel Technologies, Inc; Serenex, Inc.; Southern Assisted Living, Inc.; Scynexis, Inc.; Transzyme, Inc.; United Emergency Services, Inc.; XS, Inc.; Ziptronix, Inc.

THE LAW OFFICE OF MARK W. ISHMAN, P.C.

9660 FALLS OF NEUSE ROAD
SUITE 138-350
RALEIGH, NORTH CAROLINA 27615
Telephone: 919-468-3266
Email: mishman@ishmanlaw.com
URL: http://www.ishmanlawfirm.com

Internet Law, E-Commerce, Intellectual Property, Copyrights, Licensing Agreements, Patents, Trade Secrets, Trademarks, Unfair Trade Practice, Corporate, Cyber Law.

(This Listing Continued)

MARK W. ISHMAN, born LaGrange, Illinois, 1970; admitted to bar, 2001, North Carolina. *Education:* Northern Illinois University (B.S., 1992); The John Marshall Law School (LL.M., Information Technology and Privacy Law, 2001; J.D., 2001). *Member:* North Carolina and American (Member, Electronic Commerce Law Society and Science and Technology Law Society) Bar Associations; Executive Licensing Society; Computer Law Association; Copyright Law Association; ICANN Membership. ***PRACTICE AREAS:*** Internet Law; E-Commerce; Intellectual Property; Copyrights; Licensing Agreements; Patents; Trade Secrets; Trademarks; Unfair Trade Practice; Corporate Law; Cyber Law.

JANAK LAW FIRM, P.A.

7404-D CHAPEL HILL ROAD
RALEIGH, NORTH CAROLINA 27607
Telephone: 919-233-0358
Fax: 919-233-0323
Email: cjanak@janaklaw.com

Bankruptcy, Consumer Bankruptcy, Foreclosures, Real Estate, Buying and Selling, Landlord and Tenant, Business Law, Collections, Creditors Rights.

CRAIG M. JANAK, born Cheektowaga, New York, July 27, 1971; admitted to bar, 1998, New York; 1999, North Carolina, New Jersey and U.S. District Court, Western District of New York; 2000, U.S. District Court, Eastern and Middle Districts of North Carolina. *Education:* State University of New York at Buffalo (B.A., Economics, 1994); Rutgers University Law School-Camden (J.D., 1997). *Member:* North Carolina Bar Association; National Association of Consumer Bankruptcy Attorneys. ***PRACTICE AREAS:*** Land Trusts; Real Estate Foreclosure; Real Estate Investment; Business Formation; Small Business Law; Fair Credit Reporting Act; Consumer Credit; Wills; Estate Planning; Consumer Bankruptcy. ***Email:*** cjanak@janaklaw.com

---

JENKINS, WILSON & TAYLOR, P.A.

Established in 1984
NCSU CENTENNIAL CAMPUS, SUITE 101 VENTURE 11
920 MAIN CAMPUS DRIVE
RALEIGH, NORTH CAROLINA 27606
Telephone: 919-424-3710
Fax: 919-424-3711
URL: http://www.jenkinswilsontaylor.com

Durham, North Carolina Office: University Tower, Suite 1400, 3100 Tower Boulevard, 27707-6226. Telephone: 919-493-8000. Fax: 919-419-0383.

Patent, Trademark and Copyright Law.

FIRM PROFILE: The firm is a specialized law practice with over two decades of experience providing intellectual property services to clients with respect to patent, trademark, copyright, and unfair competition law. The firm assists clients in recognizing, defining and safeguarding intellectual property and acting to preserve that property for full commercial exploitation.

Serving U.S. and foreign clients in intellectual property matters, the firm has a client base that is diverse and includes large corporations and research universities as well as small businesses and individuals. A primary objective of the firm is to provide high-quality legal services in a cost-efficient and personal manner. The firm is listed in the Bar Register of Preeminent Lawyers.

REPRESENTATIVE CLIENTS: Appalachian State University; Böwe Bell and Howell Co.; Central Carolina Bank; Costa & Grissom Machinery Co., Inc.; Coventor, Inc.; Cree Inc.; Duke University; Freudenberg Spunweb Company; GlaxoSmithKline, Inc.; Harvard University; Honda Power Equipment; Huesker, Inc.; Kinetikos Medical, Inc.; North Carolina State University; Sumitomo Electric Lightwave Corp.; Syngenta; Tekelec Inc.; Troxler Electronics; The University of North Carolina at Chapel Hill; University of Tennessee Research Corp.; VSL International; VStructural; Vanderbilt University; Varian, Inc.; Weck (Teleflex).
REFERENCES: Centura Bank; North Carolina State Bar.

(For Complete Personnel and Biographical data, see Professional Biographies at Durham, North Carolina)

THE JERNIGAN LAW FIRM

A PROFESSIONAL LAW CORPORATION
Established in 1988
WACHOVIA CAPITOL CENTER
SUITE 1910
150 FAYETTEVILLE STREET MALL
P.O. BOX 847
RALEIGH, NORTH CAROLINA 27602
Telephone: 919-833-1283
Fax: 919-833-1059
Email: ltj@jernlaw.com
URL: http://www.jernlaw.com

Trial and Appellate Practice before State and Federal Courts and Agencies, Personal Injury, Workers' Compensation, Toxic Torts (Asbestos), Products Liability.

LEONARD T. JERNIGAN, JR., born Durham, North Carolina, February 13, 1950; admitted to bar, 1976, North Carolina and U.S. District Court, Eastern, Middle and Western Districts of North Carolina. *Education:* Deerfield Academy (1968); University of North Carolina (B.A., 1972); North Carolina Central University (J.D., 1976). Articles Editor, North Carolina Central Law Journal, 1976. Author: *North Carolina Workers' Compensation Law and Practice,* West Publishing, 1988. Adjunct Professor of Law, North Carolina Central University Law School, 2003. Listed in Best Lawyers in America. *Member:* Wake County (Board of Directors, 1988-1990) and North Carolina Bar Associations; North Caro-

(This Listing Continued)

THE JERNIGAN LAW FIRM, A PROFESSIONAL LAW CORPORATION, Raleigh—Continued

lina Academy of Trial Lawyers (Board of Governors, 1990-1997); The Association of Trial Lawyers of America (Chair, Workers' Compensation Section, 1997-1998); National Football League Players' Association Workers' Compensation Panel (1996—); Workers Injury Law and Advocacy Group (President, 2001). (Board Certified Specialist in Workers Compensation, North Carolina State Board of Legal Specialization). ***PRACTICE AREAS:*** Personal Injury Law; Workers' Compensation Law; Toxic Torts (Asbestos); Products Liability. ***Email:*** ltj@jernlaw.com

N. VICTOR FARAH, born Flint, Michigan, May 13, 1954; admitted to bar, 1981, Michigan (Inactive); 1987, North Carolina. *Education:* University of Michigan (B.A., 1976); Wayne State University (J.D., 1981). *Member:* Wake County and North Carolina Bar Associations (Member, Medico-Legal Liaison Committee, 1996-2004, Chair, 2002-2004); North Carolina State Bar (Peer Counselor, PALS Committee); North Carolina Academy of Trial Lawyers (Member, Workers' Compensation Section; Secretary, 1995-1997; Vice-Chair, 1997-2000; Chair, 2000-2001; Member, Board of Governors, 2001—); Workplace Injury Litigation Group. (Board Certified Specialist in Workers Compensation, North Carolina State Board of Legal Specialization). ***PRACTICE AREAS:*** Workers' Compensation Law; Personal Injury Law. ***Email:*** nvf@jernlaw.com

GINA E. CAMMARANO, born Flushing, New York, September 23, 1968; admitted to bar, 1995, North Carolina. *Education:* University of Notre Dame (B.B.A., 1990); University of North Carolina at Chapel Hill (J.D., 1995). Member: National Football League Players' Association; Workers' Compensation Panel, Professional Hockey Players' Association; Workers' Compensation Panel. *Member:* North Carolina Bar Association (Member, Workers' Compensation Section Council, 2002—); North Carolina Academy of Trial Lawyers (Member, Workers Compensation Section); North Carolina Association of Women Attorneys; Workplace Injury Litigation Group. ***PRACTICE AREAS:*** Workers' Compensation; Personal Injury. ***Email:*** gec@jernlaw.com

LAUREN R. TRUSTMAN, born Raleigh, North Carolina, November 12, 1974; admitted to bar, 2001, North Carolina. *Education:* Brown University (B.A., 1997); Johnson and Wales University (A.S., 1998); University of North Carolina (J.D., 2001). Member, North Carolina Law Review, 1999-2000. Member, Workplace Injury Litigation Group. *Member:* Wake County and North Carolina (Member, Workers Compensation Section; Medico-Legal Liaison Committee) Bar Associations; North Carolina Academy of Trial Lawyers (Member, Sections on: Workers Compensation; Auto-Torts); American Trial Lawyers Association. ***PRACTICE AREAS:*** Workers Compensation; Personal Injury. ***Email:*** lrt@jernlaw.com

JOHNSON, HEARN, VINEGAR, GEE & GLASS, PLLC

Established in 1955

TWO HANNOVER SQUARE
434 FAYETTEVILLE STREET MALL, SUITE 2200
P.O. BOX 1776
RALEIGH, NORTH CAROLINA 27602
Telephone: 919-743-2200
Fax: 919-743-2201
Email: jhvgg@jhvgglaw.com

Durham Office: Generation Plaza, Suite 200, 1822 N.C. Highway 54 East, 27713. Telephone: 919-544-3302. Fax: 919-544-5920. Email: richard@vinegarlaw.com.

Civil trial and appellate practice before all state and federal courts and administrative agencies, administrative law, including occupational licensing, alternative dispute resolution, automobile dealer law, business and corporate law, franchise law, government relations, including representation before the General Assembly and regulatory agencies, insurance insolvency, state and local taxation, trade association law, wills, trusts and estates and unfair competition, landlord tenant, property tax appeals, e-commerce, business enterprises, closely held businesses, limited liability companies, partnerships, small businesses, buying or selling a business, employment contracts, human resources, business planning, lawsuits, licensing agreements, internet, starting a business, strategic alliances, joint venture.

SAMUEL H. JOHNSON, born 1927; admitted to bar, 1953, North Carolina and U.S. District Court, Eastern District of North Carolina and U.S. Supreme Court. *Education:* Pfeiffer College, Mexico City College and University of North Carolina (A.B., 1950); University of North Carolina (J.D., 1953). Phi Delta Phi. Member, North Carolina General Assembly, 1965-1974. Trustee, University of North Carolina, 1967-1972. Chairman, North Carolina Local Government Study Commission, 1967-1973. Member: North Carolina Joint Select Commission on Fiscal Trends and Reform, 1992-1993; Advisory Budget Commission of North Carolina, 1969-1971. Special Counsel to Speaker of House of Representatives and Lt. Governor, 1975-1977. *Member:* Wake County, North Carolina and American Bar Associations; North Carolina State Bar; North Carolina Academy of Trial Lawyers (Director, 1976-1981). [U.S.N., Naval Research Laboratory, 1946-1948]. ***PRACTICE AREAS:*** Legislative Practice; Estate Planning; Business Law; Trade Association Law. ***Email:*** sjohnson@jhvgglaw.com

GEORGE G. HEARN, born Burlington, North Carolina, September 8, 1949; admitted to bar, 1974, North Carolina. *Education:* University of North Carolina (A.B., 1971; J.D., 1974). Phi Delta Phi. Holderness Moot Court Bench, 1973-1974. Research Assistant to Hon. Frank M. Parker, North Carolina Court of Appeals, 1974-1975. *Member:* Wake County (Director, 1990-1991; 2002, 2003; President, 2005) and North Carolina Bar Associations; North Carolina State Bar; North Carolina Academy of Trial Lawyers. ***PRACTICE AREAS:*** Administrative Law. ***Email:*** ghearn@jhvgglaw.com

RICHARD J. VINEGAR, born New York, N.Y., February 28, 1954; admitted to bar, 1979, North Carolina; 1986, New York. *Education:* Duke University (A.B., magna cum laude, 1976); Cornell University (J.D., 1979). Author: "Presidents on Television: The Effect of Instant Analysis," Public Opinion Quarterly, Winter, 1977-1978. Research Assistant to Hon. Burley B. Mitchell, Jr. and Hon. Hugh A. Wells, North Carolina Court of Appeals, 1979-1980. Chairman, Board of Trustees, Lenox Baker Children's Hospital, 1983—. *Member:* Wake County, North Carolina and American Bar Associations; North Carolina State Bar. (Resident, Research Triangle Park Office). ***PRACTICE AREAS:*** Automobile Dealership Law; Contracts; Employment Law; Administrative Law; Appellate Practice; Franchising. ***Email:*** richard@vinegarlaw.com

M. BLEN GEE, JR., born Chicago, Illinois, February 4, 1950; admitted to bar, 1981, North Carolina; 1984, U.S. District Court, Eastern District of North Carolina; 1988, U.S. District Court, Middle District of North Carolina. *Education:* University of North Carolina (A.B., 1972; J.D., with honors, 1981). Articles Editor, North Carolina Journal of International Law and Commercial Regulation, 1980-1981. Author: Note, "North Carolina Foreign-Trade Zones: Problems and Prospects," 5 North Carolina Journal of International Law and Commercial Regulation 521, 1980. Member, U.S. Peace Corps, 1975-1977. DRC Certified Mediator. *Member:* Wake County and North Carolina Bar Associations; North Carolina State Bar. ***LANGUAGES:*** French. ***PRACTICE AREAS:*** Business Law; Commercial Law; Contracts; Corporate Law; Mergers and Acquisitions; International Law; Civil Litigation; Arbitration; Mediation; Appellate Practice; Insurance Insolvency; Automotive Franchises and Dealerships; Franchise Law. ***Email:*** bgee@jhvgglaw.com

F. STEPHEN GLASS, born Asheboro, North Carolina, October 17, 1940; admitted to bar, 1966, North Carolina, U.S. District Court, Eastern, Middle and Western Districts of North Carolina, U.S. Court of Appeals, Fourth Circuit, U.S. Court of Appeals for the Armed Forces and U.S. Supreme Court. *Education:* Wake Forest University (B.A., 1963; J.D., 1966). First Place, North Carolina Wills & Trust Drafting, Omicron Delta Kappa Leadership. Law Clerk to the Hon. Justice I Beverly Lake, Sr., and the Hon. Justice Susie Sharp, North Carolina Supreme Court, 1966-1967. Faculty, National Institute of Trial Advocacy Southeastern Deposition Training, Duke University Law School. Contributing Author: North Carolina Will Drafting and Probate Practice Handbook, Wake Forest University School of Law, CLE, 1985; "Computerized Litigation Support-Death of The Paper Chase," North Carolina Defense Lawyers CLE, 1990. Author: "Automation: The Great Equalizer," North Carolina Bar CLE, 1995; "Winning the Gang-Busters Litigation Through Information Management," NC Bar CLE, 1998; Tax Reform Act of 2001-Seminar for CPA's, 2001; North Carolina Probate and Estate Planning Skills for Paralegals, 2003; The Legal Handbook for North Carolina Businesses; Your Estate Planning Handbook; Limited Liability Companies Updated: Formation and Operation, State Law LLC Issues, LLC Tax Issues, LLC Securities Law Issues, Special Uses of LLCs, 2004. President, Randolph County Bar Association, 1973-1974. President, 19th Judicial District Bar Association, 1974-1975. Executive Director, North Carolina Democratic Party, 1977-1978; Deputy Commissioner, North Carolina Industrial Commission, 1978. Special Assistant, 4th Congressional District, North Carolina, 1979. Certified Superior Court Mediator, 2000+. Member: Board of Directors and Incoming Chairman, Cary Chamber of Commerce. Board of Directors: Capital Bank, Cary; Executive Board, Boy Scouts of America; National Alliance of Trust & Estate Professionals. Member, Governor's Commission on Military Affairs. *Member:* North Carolina and American Bar Associations; North Carolina State Bar; Wake County Estate Planning Council. [Rear Admiral, JAGC, USNR]. ***PRACTICE AREAS:*** Business Law; Corporate Law; Employment Law; Health Care; Elder Law; Commercial Law; Contracts; Mergers and Acquisitions; Trusts and Estates; Wills; Probate. ***Email:*** sglass@jhvgglaw.com

OF COUNSEL

JEAN WINBORNE BOYLES, born Raleigh, North Carolina, January 13, 1945; admitted to bar, 1973, North Carolina and U.S. District Court, Eastern and Middle Districts of North Carolina; U.S. Court of Appeals, Fourth Circuit. *Education:* Bradford Junior College; University of North Carolina (B.A., 1966; J.D., 1973). Certified Superior Court Mediator. Assistant Town Attorney, Town of Chapel Hill, North Carolina, 1973-1977. Assistant Attorney General, State of North Carolina and Hospital Attorney, N.C. Memorial Hospital, 1977-1981. *Member:* Wake County Bar Association (History and Scholarship Committee); Tenth Judicial District Bar Association; North Carolina Bar Association (Member: Health Law Section; Council, 1979-1983; Bankruptcy Section); North Carolina State Bar; North Carolina Society of Health Care Attorneys (Vice President, 1978-1979). ***PRACTICE AREAS:*** Bankruptcy; Creditors Rights; Health Law; Corporate Law; Commercial Leasing; Franchise Law; Administrative Law; Mediation. ***Email:*** jboyles@jhvgglaw.com

REPRESENTATIVE CLIENTS: Anderson Automotive Investments, Inc. d/b/a Fred Anderson Toyota; Asbury Villanova, LLC; Board Retailers Association; Carolina/Virginia Dairy Products Association, Inc.; David O'Neal Chrysler Jeep/Eagle; Eckerd Drugs; Fred Anderson Nissan Lincoln-Mercury; Fulcrum Financial Advisors, Inc.; Hendrick Automotive Group; Leith, Inc.; McLaurin Parking Company; Vishay-Measurements Group, Inc.; Measurements Group., Inc.; Morgan Stanley & Co.; Noble Oil, Inc.; North Carolina Association of Certified Public Accountants; North Carolina Association of Pharmacists; North Carolina Automobile Dealers Association; North Carolina Chapter of the American Institute of Architects; North Carolina Veterinary Medical Board; The Pharmacy Franchise Owners Association; Ri Ra Holdings, LLC; Roof Consultants Institute, Inc.; Sara Lee Corp.; Sir Walter Chevrolet Co.; Sonic Automotive, Inc.; The TBM Consulting Group, Inc.; Universal Chevrolet Co.; Wake Technical Community College.

JAMES T. JOHNSON, P.A.

THE PILOT MILL BUILDING
1101 HAYNES STREET, SUITE 103
RALEIGH, NORTH CAROLINA 27604
Telephone: 919-833-8133
Fax: 919-833-8305
Email: jjohnson@jtjlaw.com
URL: http://www.jtjlaw.com

Mailing Address: P.O. Box 886, Raleigh, NC 27602

Personal Injury, Automobile Accidents, Wrongful Death, Nursing Home Litigation, Medical Malpractice, Insurance Litigation, Commercial Litigation, Construction Litigation.

(This Listing Continued)

JAMES T. JOHNSON, born Savannah, Georgia, May 25, 1966; admitted to bar, 1992, North Carolina, U.S. District Court, Eastern, Middle and Western Districts of North Carolina, U.S. Court of Appeals, Fourth Circuit. *Education:* Duke University (B.A., 1988); University of North Carolina Law School (J.D., 1992). Assistant District Attorney, Wake County, 1993-1995. North Carolina Associate Attorney General, North Carolina, 1995-1997. *Member:* Wake County, North Carolina and American Bar Associations; North Carolina Academy of Trial Lawyers.

JONES MARTIN PARRIS & TESSNER LAW OFFICES, PLLC

RALEIGH, NORTH CAROLINA

(See Martin & Jones)

JORDAN PRICE WALL GRAY JONES & CARLTON

A Professional Limited Liability Company
1951 CLARK AVENUE
P.O. BOX 10669
RALEIGH, NORTH CAROLINA 27605-0669
Telephone: 919-828-2501
Telecopier: 919-834-8447
Email: law@jordanprice.com
URL: http://www.jordanprice.com

General Practice in all State and Federal Courts. Trials. Banking, Insurance, Health and Hospital Law. Corporate Practice and Administrative Law, Creditors' Rights and Bankruptcy, Insurance Defense. Condominium and Homeowners' Association Law. Estate Planning. Legislative Representation, Commercial Real Estate and Local Government Law.

MEMBERS OF FIRM

JOSEPH E. WALL, born Mebane, North Carolina, January 16, 1945; admitted to bar, 1972, North Carolina. *Education:* Duke University (A.B., 1967); University of North Carolina (J.D., 1972). Phi Alpha Delta. Member of Staff, North Carolina Law Review, 1972. Member, Moot Court Bench, 1969-1972. DRC Certified Superior Court Mediator. AOC Certified District Court Arbitrator.*Member:* Wake County and North Carolina (Member, Sections on: Litigation; Business Law; Dispute Resolution) Bar Associations; North Carolina State Bar; North Carolina Association of Defense Attorneys; Defense Research Institute (Member, Trucking Law Committee). [With U.S. Army, 1969-1971]. ***PRACTICE AREAS:*** Insurance Defense; Civil Litigation; Commercial Law; General Business Practice. ***Email:*** jwall@jordanprice.com

R. FRANK GRAY, born Jacksonville, Florida, September 23, 1948; admitted to bar, 1973, North Carolina; 1982, U.S. Supreme Court; 1988, U.S. Court of Appeals, 4th Circuit. *Education:* Davidson College (B.A., 1970); University of Florida (J.D., with honors, 1973). Phi Kappa Phi. Member, Wake County Board of Adjustment, 1984-1991. *Member:* Wake County, North Carolina (Member: Local Government Law Committee, 1982-1984; Administrative Law Section Council, 1985-1987) and American Bar Associations; North Carolina State Bar; North Carolina Academy of Trial Lawyers; North Carolina Association of Municipal Attorneys (President, 1998-1999). ***PRACTICE AREAS:*** General Business Practice; Administrative Law; Legislative Representation Law; Employment Law. ***Email:*** fgray@jordanprice.com

HENRY W. JONES, JR., born Raleigh, North Carolina, October 13, 1952; admitted to bar, 1978, North Carolina. *Education:* North Carolina State University (B.A., with honors, 1974); University of Richmond (J.D., 1978). Phi Alpha Delta. Member: National Moot Court Team; Moot Court Board. Author: "The Future of Multi-Prime Projects in Public Works," American Bar Association Forum on the Construction Industry, 1998. Member, City of Raleigh Planning Commission, 1986-1988; Treasurer, 1985-1987 and Chairman, 1987-1991, Wake County Democratic Party. *Member:* Wake County, North Carolina and American Bar Associations; North Carolina State Bar; North Carolina Academy of Trial Lawyers; Community Association Institute. ***PRACTICE AREAS:*** Civil Litigation; Legislative Law; Construction Law; Condominium Law. ***Email:*** hjones@jordanprice.com

PAUL T. FLICK, born Hagerstown, Maryland, April 15, 1961; admitted to bar, 1986, North Carolina and U.S. District Court, Western, Middle and Eastern Districts of North Carolina. *Education:* Wake Forest University (B.A., cum laude, 1983; J.D., 1986). *Member:* Wake County, North Carolina and American Bar Associations; North Carolina State Bar. ***PRACTICE AREAS:*** Civil Litigation; Commercial Law. ***Email:*** pflick@jordanprice.com

TERRY J. CARLTON, born Tecumseh, Michigan, March 16, 1961; admitted to bar, 1986, California; 1990, North Carolina and Michigan. *Education:* Michigan State University (B.A., 1983); Wake Forest University (J.D., 1986). *Member:* Orange County, Wake County (Member, Estate Planning Council), North Carolina and American Bar Associations; North Carolina State Bar; State Bar of California; State Bar of Michigan. ***PRACTICE AREAS:*** Business; Estate Planning; Real Estate. ***Email:*** tcarlton@jordanprice.com

HOPE DERBY CARMICHAEL, born Chapel Hill, North Carolina, January 28, 1966; admitted to bar, 1991, North Carolina. *Education:* Salem College (B.A., cum laude, 1988); University of North Carolina (J.D., 1991). Phi Delta Phi. Member: Holderness Moot Court; Order of the Barristers. *Member:* Wake County and North Carolina Bar Associations; North Carolina State Bar; North Carolina Academy of Trial Lawyers. ***PRACTICE AREAS:*** Community Associations Law; Civil Litigation. ***Email:*** hcarmichael@jordanprice.com

JONATHAN P. CARR, born Washington, D.C., May 14, 1966; admitted to bar, 1992, North Carolina. *Education:* University of North Carolina at Chapel Hill (B.S., Business Administration, 1988); Campbell University (J.D., 1992). Member, Association of Executives of North Carolina, 1993—. *Member:* North Carolina and American Bar Associations; North Carolina State Bar. ***PRACTICE AREAS:*** Legislative Representation; Business Law; Construction Law; Civil Litigation. ***Email:*** jcarr@jordanprice.com

(This Listing Continued)

WILLIAM K. HALE, born Spokane, Washington, April 14, 1947; admitted to bar, 1974, North Carolina; 1980, U.S. District Court, Eastern District of North Carolina; 1981, U.S. Court of Appeals, Fourth Circuit. *Education:* North Carolina State University (B.A., 1969); University of North Carolina (J.D., 1974). Deputy Insurance Commissioner and Legislative Counsel, North Carolina, 1985-2002. *Member:* Wake County, North Carolina and American Bar Associations; North Carolina State Bar. ***PRACTICE AREAS:*** Legislative Lobbying; Insurance Regulation; Health Care Legislation; Administrative Lobbying; Administrative Agency Practice. ***Email:*** bhale@jordanprice.com

JEFFREY R. ELLINGER, born Pittsburgh, Pennsylvania, August 5, 1954; admitted to bar, 1986, North Carolina, U.S. District Court, Eastern, Western and Middle District of North Carolina and U.S. Court of Appeals, 4th Circuit; U.S. Court of Federal Claims. *Education:* Pennsylvania State University (B.A., 1981); North Carolina Central University (J.D., cum laude, 1986). Phi Delta Phi. Law Journal. *Member:* North Carolina Academy of Trial Lawyers. [U.S. Army, 1974-1977]. ***PRACTICE AREAS:*** Litigation; Medical Malpractice; Legal Malpractice; Family Law; Construction Law.

ASSOCIATES

STEPHEN R. DOLAN, born Bryn Mawr, Pennsylvania, March 8, 1949; admitted to bar, 1974, North Carolina; 1976, Illinois. *Education:* Kenyon College (A.B., magna cum laude, 1971); Northwestern University (J.D., 1974). Phi Beta Kappa. *Member:* Wake County and North Carolina Bar Associations; North Carolina State Bar. ***PRACTICE AREAS:*** Health and Hospital Law; Regulatory Law; Administrative Law; General Corporate Law. ***Email:*** sdolan@jordanprice.com

SARA C. MOESTA, born Jacksonville, North Carolina, January 15, 1976; admitted to bar, 2000, North Carolina. *Education:* James Madison University (B.A., 1996); Wake Forest University School of Law (J.D., 2000). *Member:* North Carolina Bar Association. ***PRACTICE AREAS:*** Corporate Law; Commercial Real Estate.

BRIAN S. EDLIN, born Lynchburg, Virginia, September 12, 1974; admitted to bar, 2000, North Carolina. *Education:* Western Carolina University (B.S., with honors, magna cum laude, 1997); Villanova University School of Law (J.D., 2000). Phi Alpha Delta. Member, Board of Directors, Western Carolina University Alumni Association, 2000-2002. *Member:* North Carolina and American Bar Associations. ***PRACTICE AREAS:*** Civil Litigation; Commercial Law.

JEFFREY JOHN GOEBEL, born Memphis, Tennessee, June 3, 1969; admitted to bar, 2000, North Carolina and U.S. District Court, Western District of North Carolina. *Education:* Marquette University (B.A., International Affairs, 1991); University of Arkansas School of Law (J.D., 2000). *Member:* Wake County and North Carolina (Member, Sections on: Real Property; International Law) Bar Associations. ***PRACTICE AREAS:*** Real Estate; Debtor and Creditor; Commercial Law. ***Email:*** jgoebel@jordanprice.com

JOSEPH E. PROPST, born Hickory, North Carolina, July 23, 1969; admitted to bar, 1999, North Carolina; 2001, U.S. District Court, Eastern, Middle and Western Districts of North Carolina. *Education:* University of North Carolina at Chapel Hill (B.A., 1991); Cumberland School of Law of Samford University (J.D., 1998). Recipient, Leadership Scholarship, Cumberland School of Law, 1997-1998. Author: "NSF Checks and the Automatic Stay: Is Debt Collection a Crime?" Credit Today, January 2004. *Member:* Wake County (Secretary, 2003-2004; President, Young Lawyers Division, 2004) and North Carolina (Member, Board of Governors, 2004-2006; Secretary, Young Lawyers Division, 2004-2005) Bar Associations; North Carolina State Bar. ***PRACTICE AREAS:*** Construction Law; Creditors Rights; Bankruptcy; Workers Compensation. ***Email:*** jpropst@jordanprice.com

ROBERT L. ANGE, born Wilson, North Carolina, June 7, 1978; admitted to bar, 2003, North Carolina. *Education:* University of North Carolina at Chapel Hill (B.A., Management and Society, 2000); Norman Adrian Wiggins Campbell University (J.D., 2003). Phi Alpha Delta. Order of Old Kivett. *Member:* North Carolina State Bar. ***PRACTICE AREAS:*** Corporate Law; Business Law; Mergers and Acquisitions. ***Email:*** range@jordanprice.com

JESSICA E. COOLEY, born Pinehurst, North Carolina, 1979; admitted to bar, 2005, North Carolina. *Education:* Pensacola Christian College (B.A., Pre-Law, 2000); Campbell University (J.D., cum laude, 2005). President, Innocence Project, Campbell Law Division, 2004-2005. Articles Editor, Campbell Law Review, 2004-2005. *Member:* North Carolina State Bar. ***PRACTICE AREAS:*** Civil Litigation; Commercial Law. ***Email:*** jcooley@jordanprice.com

OF COUNSEL

JOHN R. JORDAN, JR., born Winton, North Carolina, January 16, 1921; admitted to bar, 1948, North Carolina; 1960, U.S. Supreme Court. *Education:* University of North Carolina (B.A., 1942); University of North Carolina School of Law (J.D., 1948). *Member:* Wake County, North Carolina and American Bar Associations; American Judicature Society; The Association of Trial Lawyers of America; Fourth Circuit Judicial Conference (Permanent Member). ***PRACTICE AREAS:*** Banking Law; Insurance Law. ***Email:*** law@jordanprice.com

ROBERT R. PRICE, born Eden, North Carolina, August 25, 1949; admitted to bar, 1974, North Carolina; 1984, U.S. Court of Appeals, 4th Circuit. *Education:* Guilford College (B.A., 1971); Northwestern University (J.D., 1974). *Member:* Wake County, North Carolina and American Bar Associations; North Carolina State Bar. ***PRACTICE AREAS:*** General Corporate Law; Insurance Law; Employment Law; Legislative Representation Law. ***Email:*** rprice@jordanprice.com

KAREN KELLY CARLTON, born Washington, North Carolina, August 21, 1961; admitted to bar, 1986, California; 1990, North Carolina and U.S. District Court, Eastern District of North Carolina. *Education:* Old Dominion University (B.A., 1982); Wake Forest University (J.D., 1986). *Member:* Wake County Bar Association; North Carolina State Bar. ***PRACTICE AREAS:*** Civil Litigation; Real Estate. ***Email:*** kcarlton@jordanprice.com

(This Listing Continued)

JORDAN PRICE WALL GRAY JONES & CARLTON, Raleigh—Continued

GENERAL COUNSEL FOR: The North Carolina Association of Alcoholic Beverage Control Boards; North Carolina Manufactured Housing Institute, Inc.; Family Health International; Paragon Commercial Bank; NC Association of Plumbing - Heating - Cooling Contractors; House of Raeford Farms, Inc.; North Carolina Restaurant Association.
COUNSEL FOR: Town of Morrisville; First Citizens Bank and Trust Company; Wachovia Bank & Trust Company, N.A.; American Council of Life Insurance; Jefferson-Pilot Life Insurance Company; Canal Insurance Company; United Insurance Company of America; Carolinas Electrical Contractors Association; WATCO Corporation; Associated Builders and Contractors of the Carolinas, Inc.; Greentree Servicing LLC; Lancer Insurance Company; Metro Telecom, Inc.; NC Association of Personnel Services; United Church Retirement Homes, Inc.; Carol Woods Retirement Community; Alliance Life Care Corporation; Integrated Health Services, Inc.; Daimler Chrysler Corp. and Alliance of Automobile Manufacturers.
APPROVED ATTORNEYS FOR: Lawyers Title Insurance Corp.; Commonwealth Land Title Company; Fidelity National Title Co.; Chicago Title Insurance Co.; Investors Title Insurance Co.

LAW OFFICES OF GREGORY M. KASH

Established in 2001

TWO HANNOVER SQUARE
434 FAYETTEVILLE STREET, SUITE 2350
RALEIGH, NORTH CAROLINA 27601
Telephone: 919-861-2006
Facsimile: 919-861-0504
Email: gregkash@mindspring.com
URL: http://www.gkashlaw.com

Civil Litigation, Personal Injury, Medical Malpractice, Products Liability, Automobile Accidents, Wrongful Death, Premises Liability, Workers Compensation, Animal Law, Consumer Law, Business Law, Labor and Employment, Military Law.

FIRM PROFILE: General Civil Trial Practice, State and Federal Courts of North Carolina, in all areas of personal injury, medical malpractice, product liability, commercial litigation, school law, premises liability, employment law and workers compensation administrative practice.

GREGORY M. KASH, born Lexington, Kentucky, September 27, 1962; admitted to bar, 1987, North Carolina; 1988, South Carolina; 1990, U.S. Court of Military Appeals; 1991, U.S. District Court, Eastern, Middle and Western Districts of North Carolina; 1998, U.S. Court of Appeals, Fourth Circuit. *Education:* Davidson College (B.A., 1984); Campbell University (J.D., 1987). Delta Theta Phi. *Member:* Wake County and North Carolina Bar Associations; South Carolina Bar; North Carolina Association of Defense Attorneys; Defense Research Institute. [U.S. Naval Reserve, 1987-1991, LCDR (Judge Advocate General Corps)]

REPRESENTATIVE CLIENTS: Universal Underwriters Ins. Co.; Horace Mann Ins. Group; Pharmacist Mutual Ins. Co.; Florist Mutual Ins. Co.; Employers Mutual Ins. Co.

ROBERT W. KAYLOR, P.A.

Established in 1996

225 HILLSBOROUGH STREET, SUITE 480
RALEIGH, NORTH CAROLINA 27603
Telephone: 919-828-5250
Fax: 919-828-5240
Email: bkaylor@rwkaylorlaw.com

Public Utility Regulation, State Legislative Practice, Administrative Agency Practice, Workers Compensation.

ROBERT W. KAYLOR, born Wilmington, North Carolina, January 7, 1944; admitted to bar, 1974, North Carolina and U.S. District Court, Eastern and Middle Districts of North Carolina. *Education:* East Carolina University (B.A., 1966); University of North Carolina School of Law (J.D., 1974). Registered Lobbyist with North Carolina Secretary of State for: Alltel Communications; Duke Energy Corporation; Dominion North Carolina Power; Verizon South, Inc.; Verizon Wireless; North Carolina Association of Defense Attorneys, North Carolina Association of Self-Insurers; McLane Company, Inc. *Member:* Wake County and North Carolina Bar Associations; North Carolina State Bar; North Carolina Association of Defense Attorneys. [Capt., USAF, 1967-1971]. ***PRACTICE AREAS:*** Public Utility Regulation; Electric Utilities; Gas Utilities; Telephone Utilities; Wireless Communications; State Legislative Practice; Administrative Agency Practice.

REPRESENTATIVE CLIENTS: Alltell Communications; Dominion Resources, Inc.; Verizon Wireless; Verizon South, Inc.; Dominion North Carolina Power; Duke Energy Corporation; BellSouth Telecommunications, Inc.; North Carolina Association of Self-Insurers; North Carolina Association of Defense Attorneys; IBM; McLane Company, Inc.

KELLY & WEST, P.A.

RALEIGH, NORTH CAROLINA

(See Lillington)

KENNEDY COVINGTON LOBDELL & HICKMAN, L.L.P.

Established in 1957

434 FAYETTEVILLE STREET MALL, 19TH FLOOR
P.O. BOX 1070
RALEIGH, NORTH CAROLINA 27602-1070
Telephone: 919-743-7300
Fax: 919-743-7358
URL: http://www.kennedycovington.com

Charlotte, North Carolina Office: Hearst Tower, 214 North Tryon Street, 47th Floor, 28202. Telephone: 704-331-7400. Fax: 704-331-7598.

(This Listing Continued)

Research Triangle Park, North Carolina Office: P.O. Box 14210, Research Triangle Park, 27709-4210, 2801 Slater Road, Suite 120, Morrisville, 27560. Telephone: 919-466-1190. Fax: 919-831-7040.

Columbia, South Carolina Office: NBSC Building, Suite 850, 1122 Lady Street, 29201. Telephone: 803-251-2300. Fax: 803-251-2315.

Rock Hill, South Carolina Office: 140 East Main Street, Suite 220, P.O. Box 11429, 29731-1429. Telephone: 803-329-7600. Fax: 803-329-7677.

Administrative Law, Alternative Dispute Resolution, Antitrust and Trade Regulation, Bankruptcy, Banks and Banking, Business Law, Commercial Law, Commercial Real Estate Development, Construction Law, Corporate Law, Debt and Equity Finance, Emerging Growth Companies, Employee Benefits, Employment Law, Entrepreneurial Business Law, Environmental Law, Family Law, Finance, Governmental, Health Care, Immigration and Naturalization, Intellectual Property, International Law, Labor and Employment, Land Sales, Land Use Regulation, Limited Liability Companies and Partnerships, Litigation, Medical Malpractice, Mergers, Acquisitions and Divestitures, Non-Profit and Charitable Organizations, Patents, Private Equity, Products Liability, Professional Liability, Public Utility Law, Real Estate Development, Real Estate Leasing, Real Estate Finance, Securities, Taxation, Technology Law, Trademarks, Trial Practice, Trusts and Estates, Utility Law, Venture Capital, Zoning, Planning and Land Use.

FIRM PROFILE: Kennedy Covington Lobdell & Hickman, L.L.P. is one of the largest full service law firms in the Carolinas, with offices in Charlotte, Columbia, Raleigh, Research Triangle Park and Rock Hill. Our lawyers bring a depth of experience and a knowledge of the law to bear in solving problems and leveraging opportunities for clients in varied industries such as banking, real estate, technology and manufacturing. At Kennedy Covington, we give more than a legal opinion; we provide a business perspective.

PARTNERS

STANFORD D. BAIRD, admitted to bar, 1995, North Carolina. *Education:* Duke University (A.B., cum laude, 1992); Wake Forest University (J.D., cum laude, 1995). ***PRACTICE AREAS:*** Environmental Law; Commercial Real Estate Development; Environmental Compliance. ***Email:*** sbaird@kennedycovington.com

F. DANIEL BELL, III, admitted to bar, 1980, North Carolina; 2001, New York. *Education:* University of North Carolina at Chapel Hill (B.S., 1976); Loyola University (J.D., 1979); East Carolina University (M.B.A., 1981). ***PRACTICE AREAS:*** Securities Regulatory Defense; Broker-Dealer Regulation and Defense; Investment Advisor Regulation and Defense; Securities Arbitration; Securities Offerings. ***Email:*** dbell@kennedycovington.com

CURTIS C. BREWER, IV, admitted to bar, 1995, North Carolina. *Education:* University of North Carolina (B.A., 1991); Wake Forest University (J.D., cum laude, 1995). ***PRACTICE AREAS:*** Business Law; Corporate Law; Corporate Finance; Emerging Business Law; Private Equity; Venture Capital; Mergers and Acquisitions. ***Email:*** cbrewer@kennedycovington.com

WILLIAM J. BRIAN, admitted to bar, 1989, North Carolina. *Education:* Washington University (A.B., History, cum laude, 1984); George Washington University (M.A., International Affairs, 1987); Duke University (J.D., with high honors, 1989). (Also at Research Triangle Park, North Carolina Office). ***PRACTICE AREAS:*** Zoning, Planning and Land Use; Real Estate Litigation. ***Email:*** bbrian@kennedycovington.com

AMIE FLOWERS CARMACK, admitted to bar, 1995, North Carolina. *Education:* Wake Forest University (B.A., cum laude, with honors in History, 1991; J.D., 1995). ***PRACTICE AREAS:*** Labor and Employment; Litigation; Commercial Law; Appellate Practice. ***Email:*** acarmack@kennedycovington.com

KENT F. CHRISTISON, admitted to bar, 1971, Ohio; 1976, North Carolina. *Education:* Wittenberg University (A.B., magna cum laude, 1968); University of Virginia (J.D., 1971). Order of the Coif. ***PRACTICE AREAS:*** Business Law; Entrepreneurial Business Law; Corporate Law; Partnership Law; Limited Liability Company Law; Strategic Alliances; Mergers and Acquisitions; Venture Capital; Debt and Equity Finance. ***Email:*** kchristison@kennedycovington.com

DAVID SCOTT COWARD, admitted to bar, 1989, North Carolina; 1990, District of Columbia. *Education:* University of North Carolina (B.S., Business Administration, 1986); Columbia University (J.D., 1989). Phi Beta Kappa. Harlan Fisk Stone Scholar. Member, Columbia Law Review, 1987-1989. Partner, 1991-1995 and 1995-2002, Smith Anderson, Raleigh, North Carolina; Attorney, IBM, Research Triangle Park, North Carolina, 1994-1995; Associate, Covington & Burling, Washington, D.C., 1989-1991. ***PRACTICE AREAS:*** Corporate Law; Mergers and Acquisitions; Life Sciences. ***Email:*** scoward@kennedycovington.com

A. LEE HOGEWOOD III, admitted to bar, 1990, North Carolina. *Education:* Harvard University (A.B., cum laude, 1987); Wake Forest University (J.D., cum laude, 1990). ***PRACTICE AREAS:*** Litigation; Bankruptcy; Debtor and Creditor Rights; Creditors Rights. ***Email:*** lhogewood@kennedycovington.com

ALAN H. PETERSON, admitted to bar, 1977, North Carolina. *Education:* Macalester College (B.A., 1971); Johns Hopkins School of Advanced International Studies; University of North Carolina (J.D., 1977). ***PRACTICE AREAS:*** Commercial Real Estate; Real Estate Finance; Real Estate Development; Zoning, Planning and Land Use; Land Use Regulation. ***Email:*** apeterson@kennedycovington.com

LACY H. REAVES, admitted to bar, 1972, North Carolina. *Education:* University of North Carolina (A.B., 1969; J.D., with honors, 1972). ***PRACTICE AREAS:*** Business Law; Corporate Law; Creditor Bankruptcy Law; Zoning, Planning and Land Use; Commercial Real Estate. ***Email:*** lreaves@kennedycovington.com

JOHN L. SARRATT, admitted to bar, 1972, North Carolina. *Education:* University of North Carolina (B.A., with highest honors, 1969); Harvard University (J.D., cum laude, 1972). ***PRACTICE AREAS:*** Commercial Litigation; Business Litigation. ***Email:*** jsarratt@kennedycovington.com

WILLIAM G. SCOGGIN, admitted to bar, 1989, Georgia; 1991, District of Columbia; 1993, North Carolina. *Education:* Wake Forest University (B.A., cum laude, 1986); Uni-

(This Listing Continued)

versity of North Carolina (J.D., 1989). ***PRACTICE AREAS:*** Election, Campaign and Political Law; Lobbying; Government Contracts; Administrative Law; Regulatory Agency Practice; Business Law; Information Technology. ***Email:*** bscoggin@kennedycovington.com

MICHAEL R. THORNTON, admitted to bar, 1995, New York; 1997, North Carolina. *Education:* University of North Carolina - Chapel Hill (A.B., with honors, 1991); Georgetown University (J.D., cum laude, 1994). ***PRACTICE AREAS:*** Commercial Real Estate; Real Estate Finance; Real Estate Development; Zoning, Planning and Land Use; Land Use Regulation. ***Email:*** mthornton@kennedycovington.com

ROBERT B. WOMBLE, admitted to bar, 1979, North Carolina. *Education:* Wake Forest University (B.A., cum laude, 1976); Washington & Lee University (J.D., cum laude, 1979); Georgetown University (LL.M. in Taxation, 1982). ***PRACTICE AREAS:*** Business Law; Corporate Law; Partnership Law; Debt and Equity Finance; Venture Capital; Mergers and Acquisitions; Technology Law; Emerging Business Law. ***Email:*** rwomble@kennedycovington.com

SPECIAL COUNSEL

ERIC M. BRAUN, admitted to bar, 1993, North Carolina; 1996, U.S. District Court, Eastern District of North Carolina; 2001, U.S. District Court, Middle District of North Carolina; 1998, U.S. Supreme Court and U.S. Court of Appeals, Fourth Circuit. *Education:* James Madison University (B.S., Public Administration, cum laude, 1990); Wake Forest University (J.D., 1993); University of Georgia (M.A., Public Administration, 1995). (Also at Research Triangle Park, North Carolina Office). ***PRACTICE AREAS:*** Zoning, Planning and Land Use; Real Estate Litigation. ***Email:*** ebraun@kennedycovington.com

PATRICK L. BYKER, admitted to bar, 1992, North Carolina. *Education:* Calvin College (B.A., Classical Studies, 1987); University of North Carolina at Chapel Hill (J.D., 1992; M.A., Regional Planning, concentration in Economic Development, 1994). (Also at Research Triangle Park, North Carolina Office). ***PRACTICE AREAS:*** Zoning, Planning and Land Use. ***Email:*** pbyker@kennedycovington.com

BRETT T. HANNA, admitted to bar, 1997, North Carolina. *Education:* United States Air Force Academy (B.S., 1989); Wake Forest University (J.D., 1997). [U.S. Air Force Active Duty, 1989-1994]. ***PRACTICE AREAS:*** Real Estate Development; Real Estate Leasing; Real Estate Finance. ***Email:*** bhanna@kennedycovington.com

THOMAS I. LYON, admitted to bar, 1998, North Carolina. *Education:* University of North Carolina (B.S.B.A., with distinction, 1995); University of Kentucky (J.D., cum laude, 1998). Beta Gamma Sigma; Order of the Coif. Associate Editor, Kentucky Law Journal. ***PRACTICE AREAS:*** Corporate Law; Enterpreneurial Business; Mergers and Acquisitions; Private Equity; Venture Capital.

JOHN E. (JACK) MARKHAM, JR., admitted to bar, 1973, North Carolina; 1979, U.S. District Court, Middle District of North Carolina. *Education:* University of North Carolina at Chapel Hill (A.B., History, 1967; J.D., 1973). (Also at Research Triangle Park, North Carolina Office). ***PRACTICE AREAS:*** Zoning, Planning and Land Use; Real Estate Development. ***Email:*** jmarkham@kennedycovington.com

NEAL B. WOLGIN, admitted to bar, 1999, North Carolina; registered to practice before U.S. Patent and Trademark Office. *Education:* Lehigh University (B.S., 1984); Duke University (M.B.A., 1992); University of North Carolina (J.D., 1999). ***PRACTICE AREAS:*** Intellectual Property; Technology and Science. ***Email:*** nwolgin@kennedycovington.com

ASSOCIATES

ANN M. ANDERSON, admitted to bar, 2001, North Carolina. *Education:* University of North Carolina (B.A., 1997; J.D., 2001). ***PRACTICE AREAS:*** Litigation. ***Email:*** aanderson@kennedycovington.com

JASON L. BARRON, admitted to bar, 2002, North Carolina. *Education:* North Carolina State University (B.A., 1999); Wake Forest University School of Law (J.D., 2002). ***PRACTICE AREAS:*** Commercial Litigation. ***Email:*** jbarron@kennedycovington.com

JAMES EWING, (admission pending); admitted to bar, 2005, North Carolina. *Education:* Colby College (cum laude, 2002); Wake Forest University School of Law (J.D., 2005). ***PRACTICE AREAS:*** Finance. ***Email:*** jewing@kennedycovington.com

BRIAN FORK, admitted to bar, 2005, North Carolina. *Education:* Davidson College (B.A., 2001); University of North Carolina (J.D., 2005). ***PRACTICE AREAS:*** Litigation; Civil Litigation. ***Email:*** bfork@kennedycovington.com

GRAYSON S. HALE, admitted to bar, 1998, Texas; 2002, North Carolina. *Education:* Arkansas Tech University (B.S., 1991; B.S., 1995); University of Central Arkansas (M.B.A., 1992); University of Arkansas (J.D., cum laude, 1998); Southern Methodist University (LL.M., Taxation, 2000). ***PRACTICE AREAS:*** Corporate; Entrepreneurial Business; Life Sciences; Mergers and Acquisitions; Securities; Venture Capital. ***Email:*** ghale@kennedycovington.com

DAVID N. JONSON, admitted to bar, 1997, South Carolina; 2001, North Carolina. *Education:* Washington & Lee University (B.A., cum laude, 1985); University of South Carolina (J.D., 1997). ***PRACTICE AREAS:*** Securities Arbitration; Securities Regulation; Broker-Dealer Regulation; Investment Regulation; Securities Offerings; Blue Sky Law; Government Relations. ***Email:*** djonson@kennedycovington.com

MICHAEL F. KING, admitted to bar, 1998, North Carolina. *Education:* Princeton University (A.B., 1991); University of Texas (J.D., with honors, 1998). ***PRACTICE AREAS:*** Commercial Real Estate Development; Commercial Real Estate Finance. ***Email:*** mking@kennedycovington.com

KATHERINE STUKES McKENZIE, admitted to bar, 2003, North Carolina. *Education:* University of North Carolina at Chapel Hill (B.A., with distinction, 1999; J.D.,with honors, 2003). ***PRACTICE AREAS:*** Real Estate; Real Estate Development; Real Estate Leasing. ***Email:*** kmckenzie@kennedycovington.com

(This Listing Continued)

CHARLOTTE MITCHELL, (admission pending). *Education:* University of North Carolina (B.A., 2000; J.D., 2005); Duke University, Nicholas School of the Environment (Masters of Environmental Management, 2005). ***PRACTICE AREAS:*** Real Estate Development. ***Email:*** cmitchell@kennedycovington.com

DANIEL J. PALMIERI, admitted to bar, 2004, North Carolina. *Education:* University of North Carolina (B.A., Economics, with highest distinction, 2000; J.D., with high honors, 2003). Order of the Coif. Articles Editor, North Carolina Law Review, 2002-2003. ***PRACTICE AREAS:*** Litigation; Employment Law. ***Email:*** dpalmieri@kennedycovington.com

CRAIGIE D. SANDERS, admitted to bar, 2003, North Carolina. *Education:* University of Kentucky (B.A., Political Science, 1987); Murray State University (M.P.A., 1992); North Carolina Central University (J.D., 2000). (Also at Research Triangle Park, North Carolina Office). ***PRACTICE AREAS:*** Zoning, Planning and Land Use. ***Email:*** csanders@kennedycovington.com

DAVID E. WAGNER, admitted to bar, 2000, North Carolina. *Education:* University of North Carolina at Chapel Hill (B.A., 1991); University of South Carolina (J.D., magna cum laude, 2000). ***PRACTICE AREAS:*** Real Estate Development; Real Estate Finance; Leasing; Land Use. ***Email:*** dwagner@kennedycovington.com

MARGARET ROSE WESTBROOK, admitted to bar, 1996, North Carolina. *Education:* University of North Carolina (B.A., 1993; J.D., with honors, 1996). ***PRACTICE AREAS:*** Bankruptcy; Creditors Rights; Commercial Litigation; Government Relations. ***Email:*** mwestbrook@kennedycovington.com

C. ALLEN YORK, admitted to bar, 2004, North Carolina. *Education:* University of North Carolina (B.A., English, 1998; J.D., with honors, 2004). Staff Member, North Carolina Law Review, 2002-2003. ***PRACTICE AREAS:*** Real Estate Development; Real Estate Leasing. ***Email:*** cayork@kennedycovington.com

(For complete biographical data on all firm personnel and representative clients, see biographical card at Charlotte, North Carolina)

KENNON, CRAVER, BELO, CRAIG & McKEE, PLLC

RALEIGH, NORTH CAROLINA

(See Durham)

General Practice in all State and Federal Courts. Corporation, Health Care, Insurance, Labor and Employment, Land Use and Development Law, Litigation, Probate, Real Estate, Taxation, Banking Law.

KESTENBAUM LAW FIRM, P.C.

RALEIGH, NORTH CAROLINA

(See Durham)

Workers' Compensation, Employment Law, Appellate Practice.

KILPATRICK STOCKTON LLP

SUITE 400, 3737 GLENWOOD AVENUE
RALEIGH, NORTH CAROLINA 27612
Telephone: 919-420-1700
Facsimile: 919-420-1800
Email: info@KilpatrickStockton.com
URL: http://www.KilpatrickStockton.com

Atlanta, Georgia Office: Suite 2800, 1100 Peachtree Street. Telephone: 404-815-6500. Facsimile: 404-815-6555. Telex: 54-2307.

Augusta, Georgia Office: 699 Broad Street, Suite 1400, 30903-2043. Telephone: 706-724-2622. Facsimile: 706-722-0219.

Charlotte, North Carolina Office: Suite 2500, 214 North Tryon Street, 28202. Telephone: 704-338-5000. Facsimile: 704-338-5125.

London, England Office: 39th Floor, One Canada Square, London E145 NZ. Telephone: 44 (0)20 7154 6000. Facsimile: 44 (0)20 7154 6100.

New York, New York Office: 805 Third Avenue, 20th Floor, 10022. Telephone: 212-912-3527.

Stockholm, Sweden Office: Box 5421, SE-114 84. Telephone: 46-8-505-646-00. Facsimile: 46-8-505-646-99.

Washington, D.C. Office: Suite 900, 607 14th Street, N.W., 20005-2018. Telephone: 202-508-5800. Facsimile: 202-508-5858.

Winston-Salem, North Carolina Office: 1001 West Fourth Street, 27101-2400. Telephone: 336-607-7300. Facsimile: 336-607-7500.

Civil Trial and Appellate Practice in all State and Federal Courts, Federal State and Local Taxation, Probate, Trust and Estate Planning, Real Estate, Environmental, Corporate, Corporate Reorganization, Securities, Banking Commercial, Antitrust, Labor, Employment, Administrative, Bankruptcy, Construction, Healthcare, Intellectual Property, Professional Malpractice, Products Liability and Negligence Law, Domestic Law and Equitable Distribution, Employee Benefits and Executive Compensation, Entrepreneurial Development, Franchising, Insurance Defense, Sports and Entertainment, State Agency and Lobbying Practice.

FIRM PROFILE: Kilpatrick Stockton LLP is a full-service international law firm with more than 470 attorneys in nine offices across the globe: Atlanta and Augusta, GA; Charlotte, Raleigh and Winston-Salem, NC; New York, NY; Washington, DC; London, England; and Stockholm, Sweden. Kilpatrick Stockton's delivery of innovative business solutions provides results-oriented counsel for corporations, from the challenging demands of financial transactions and securities to the disciplines of intellectual property management. Collaboration among Kilpatrick Stockton's corporate, tax, employment and employee benefit attorneys provides knowledgeable and proactive guidance for companies at every stage of the business life cycle.

(This Listing Continued)

KILPATRICK STOCKTON LLP, Raleigh—Continued

MEMBERS OF FIRM

RANDALL DAVID AVRAM, admitted to bar, 1986, North Carolina. *Education:* University of North Carolina (B.A., 1981); Wake Forest University School of Law (J.D., magna cum laude, 1986). Phi Delta Phi. Robert E. Lee Scholar. Member, Wake Forest Law Review, 1984-1986. Member, Labor and Employment Law Section of North Carolina and American Bar Associations. ***PRACTICE AREAS:*** Labor and Employment; Litigation. ***Email:*** RAvram@KilpatrickStockton.com

JEFFREY A. BENSON, admitted to bar, 1993, North Carolina. *Education:* Middlebury College (B.A., cum laude, 1988); Terry Sanford Institute of Public Policy, Duke University (M.A., 1993); Duke University School of Law (J.D., with honors, 1993). ***PRACTICE AREAS:*** Real Estate; Zoning, Planning and Land Use. ***Email:*** JBenson@KilpatrickStockton.com

ALFRED P. CARLTON, JR., admitted to bar, 1975, North Carolina; 1993, U.S. Supreme Court. *Education:* University of North Carolina at Chapel Hill (B.S., Business Administration, 1969); University of Dayton (M.P.A., 1973); University of North Carolina (J.D., 1975); Stetson University (LL.D, 2002); California Western School of Law (2002); University of Denver (LL.D, 2003). First Lieutenant, USA Medical Service Corps, 1970-1973. Counsel, NC Bankers Association, 1976-1979. Secretary and General Counsel, Bancshares of NC, 1979-1983. Adjunct Professor of Law, Campbell University Law School, 1979-1982. Trustee, University of North Carolina, Wilmington, 1997—. *Member:* North Carolina Bar Association (Chair, Young Lawyers Division, 1981-1982; Member, Board of Governors, 1992-1995); American Bar Association (President 2002-2003; Chair, Standing Committees on Continuing Education of the Bar, 1990-1993 and Judicial Independence, 1998-2001; Member, House of Delegates, 1982-1984, 1987—, Chair of House of Delegates, 1996-1998); American Law Institute. Fellow, American Bar Foundation. ***PRACTICE AREAS:*** General Corporate; Corporate Finance and Securities; Public Finance; Regulated Industries; Financial Institutions; Nonprofit Organizations. ***Email:*** APCarlton@KilpatrickStockton.com

LOIS W. COLBERT, admitted to bar, 1988, Illinois; 1990, District of Columbia; 1994, North Carolina. *Education:* University of Illinois (B.S., with high honors, 1985); University of Michigan (J.D., 1988). Member, Southern Employee Benefits Conference. *Member:* North Carolina (Member, Tax Section Council; Editor, Tax Section Newsletter), Illinois State and American Bar Associations; The District of Columbia Bar. ***PRACTICE AREAS:*** Employee Benefits. ***Email:*** LColbert@KilpatrickStockton.com

LISA J. DIXON, admitted to bar, 1987, North Carolina. *Education:* North Carolina State University (B.A., magna cum laude, 1984); University of North Carolina (J.D., 1987). ***PRACTICE AREAS:*** Corporate; Real Estate. ***Email:*** LDixon@KilpatrickStockton.com

THEODORE C. EDWARDS, II, admitted to bar, 1994, North Carolina. *Education:* Duke University (A.B., 1991; J.D., 1994). ***PRACTICE AREAS:*** OSHA; Mold Litigation; Construction Litigation. ***Email:*** TEdwards@KilpatrickStockton.com

SARAH WESLEY FOX, admitted to bar, 1983, North Carolina. *Education:* Tulane University; Sophie Newcomb College (B.A., 1977); Wake Forest University (J.D., cum laude, 1983). Phi Alpha Theta. Wilson Scholar. Member, Wake Forest University Law Review, 1982-1983. Permanent Member, Fourth Circuit Judicial Conference. President, Badger-Iredell Foundation. Member, Board of Directors, 1992-1995, Community Vice President, 1993-1994, Member, Executive Committee, 1993-1994, Provisional Chair, 1994-1995, President, 1997, Inaugural Ball Co-Chair, 2000-2001 and Member, Junior League of Raleigh. Member, Board of Directors, Executive Committee, 1995-1996, 1999-2000 and 2002-2003 and Member, SAFEchild. Member, Board of Directors, Prevent Blindness North Carolina, 2003-2004. Co-Chair, "Eyes of March" Gala, 2003. *Member:* Wake County, North Carolina and American (Member, Employee Rights and Responsibilities Committee) Bar Associations. (Resident). ***PRACTICE AREAS:*** Labor and Employment. ***Email:*** SFox@KilpatrickStockton.com

PATRICIA W. GOODSON, admitted to bar, 1996, North Carolina. *Education:* Wake Forest University (B.A., magna cum laude, 1992; J.D., 1996). ***PRACTICE AREAS:*** Litigation; Labor and Employment. ***Email:*** TGoodson@KilpatrickStockton.com

RICHARD DAVID HAYGOOD, admitted to bar, 1997, North Carolina; U.S. District Court, Eastern and Western Districts of North Carolina and U.S. Court of Appeals, Fourth Circuit. *Education:* University of North Carolina, Greensboro (B.A., cum laude, 1993); University of North Carolina, Chapel Hill (J.D., with honors, 1997). Order of the Coif. Craven Bench, Holderness Moot Court. Note and Comment Editor, North Carolina Journal of International Law and Commercial Regulation. ***PRACTICE AREAS:*** Labor and Employment. ***Email:*** RHaygood@KilpatrickStockton.com

CARL W. HIBBERT, admitted to bar, 1972, North Carolina. *Education:* Wake Forest University (B.A., 1970; J.D., 1972). (Resident). ***PRACTICE AREAS:*** Probate; Taxation; Business. ***Email:*** CHibbert@KilpatrickStockton.com

GERALD A. "JEB" JEUTTER, JR., admitted to bar, 1985, Mississippi; 1987, Texas; 1990, North Carolina. *Education:* College of William & Mary (B.A., 1982); Mississippi College School of Law (J.D., 1985); Georgetown University (LL.M., Securities Regulation, 1987). (Resident). ***PRACTICE AREAS:*** Business Law; Creditors' Rights; Financial Restructuring. ***Email:*** JJeutter@KilpatrickStockton.com

GARY K. JOYNER, admitted to bar, 1982, North Carolina. *Education:* University of North Carolina (B.A., 1979); Wake Forest University (J.D., 1982). (Resident). ***PRACTICE AREAS:*** Real Estate; Corporate. ***Email:*** GJoyner@KilpatrickStockton.com

DAVID M. KRASNOW, admitted to bar, 1988, Virginia; 1989, Pennsylvania; 1990, U.S. Court of Appeals for the Federal Circuit and U.S. Court of Appeals, Fourth Circuit; 1998, North Carolina; registered to practice before U.S. Patent and Trademark Office. *Education:* Southampton College of Long Island University (B.S. Chemistry, 1982); George Mason University School of Law (J.D., 1988). Past-Patent Counsel, Bausch & Lomb, Inc. Member, Intellectual Property Group, Kilpatrick Stockton. *Member:* Virginia and Pennsylvania Bar Associations; Virginia State Bar; North Carolina State Bar. ***PRACTICE AREAS:*** Intellectual Property; Patents; Trademark; Copyright. ***Email:*** DKrasnow@KilpatrickStockton.com

(This Listing Continued)

WILLIAM F. LANE, admitted to bar, 1997, North Carolina; registered to practice before U.S. Patent and Trademark Office. *Education:* University of Notre Dame (B.S., 1987); University of Texas (M.S., 1991); University of North Carolina (J.D., with honors, 1997). ***PRACTICE AREAS:*** Environmental; Administrative; Intellectual Property. ***Email:*** BLane@KilpatrickStockton.com

STEVEN J. LEVITAS, admitted to bar, 1983, North Carolina. *Education:* University of North Carolina (B.A., 1976); Harvard University (J.D., cum laude, 1982). Listed in: Best Lawyers in America, 2004; Chambers USA: America's Leading Business Lawyers, 2004-2005 edition. Selected as a Member of the North Carolina Legal Elite, 2003 and 2004. Law Clerk to the Hon. James B. McMillan, U.S. District Court, Western District of North Carolina, 1982-1983. Deputy Secretary, North Carolina Department of Environment and Natural Resources, 1993-1996. Publications: "Point/Nonpoint Source Trading: A New Approach to Reducing Nutrient Pollution," Journal of Environmental Permitting, Winter, 1992-1993. *Member:* North Carolina State Bar; North Carolina (Member, Environmental Law Section) and American (Member: Standing Committee on Environmental Law; Environment, Energy and Resources Section) Bar Associations. ***PRACTICE AREAS:*** Environmental and Natural Resources Law; Administrative Law; Legislative Practice. ***Email:*** SLevitas@KilpatrickStockton.com

W. CHRISTOPHER MATTON, admitted to bar, 1994, North Carolina. *Education:* Univ. of Pennsylvania, Wharton (B.S.E., 1991); Wake Forest Univ. (J.D., 1994). ***PRACTICE AREAS:*** Corporate; Securities; Technology. ***Email:*** CMatton@KilpatrickStockton.com

ALAN H. McCONNELL, admitted to bar, 1988, North Carolina, Virginia and District of Columbia. *Education:* University of Georgia (B.S., 1982); George Washington University (J.D., 1988). (Resident). ***PRACTICE AREAS:*** Environmental; Administrative. ***Email:*** AMcconnell@KilpatrickStockton.com

GREGG E. McDOUGAL, admitted to bar, 1987, Georgia; 2000, North Carolina. *Education:* Miami University (B.S., 1984); Wake Forest University (J.D., 1987). Recipient, North Carolina Academy of Trial Lawyers Award, 1987. Leadership Georgia, 1996 (Program Chair, 1999). Named to *Business North Carolina's* 2003 "Legal Elite" for litigation. *Member:* Wake County Bar Association; North Carolina State Bar; State Bar of Georgia. (Resident). ***PRACTICE AREAS:*** Complex Commercial Litigation; Catastrophic Injury; Wrongful Death; Products Liability. ***Email:*** GMcdougal@KilpatrickStockton.com

ALAN D. McINNES, admitted to bar, 1994, North Carolina. *Education:* Duke University (B.A., cum laude, 1986); University of North Carolina at Chapel Hill School of Law (J.D., with honors, 1994). ***PRACTICE AREAS:*** Litigation; Construction; Bankruptcy. ***Email:*** AMcinnes@KilpatrickStockton.com

MARTHA L. SEWELL, admitted to bar, 1993, North Carolina. *Education:* University of North Carolina (B.A., 1987); Wake Forest University (J.D., 1993). ***PRACTICE AREAS:*** Employee Benefits. ***Email:*** MSewell@KilpatrickStockton.com

HAYDEN J. SILVER, III, admitted to bar, 1981, North Carolina; 1984, U.S. Supreme Court. *Education:* Davidson College (B.A., magna cum laude, 1978); University of Virginia (J.D., 1981). Law Clerk to the Hon. James C. Turk, Chief Judge, United States District Court, Western District of Virginia, 1981-1982. *Member:* North Carolina and American Bar Associations;. ***PRACTICE AREAS:*** Commercial Litigation; Intellectual Property; Business Torts. ***Email:*** JaySilver@KilpatrickStockton.com

JEFFREY T. SKINNER, admitted to bar, 1996, Georgia; 2000, North Carolina. *Education:* Duke University (A.B., 1993); University of North Carolina, Chapel Hill (J.D., 1996). ***PRACTICE AREAS:*** Securities; Investment Management; Investment Advisers; Investment Companies. ***Email:*** JSkinner@KilpatrickStockton.com

CRAIG B. WHEATON, admitted to bar, 1981, North Carolina. *Education:* University of Virginia (B.A., with honors, 1978); Wake Forest University (J.D., 1981). (Resident). ***PRACTICE AREAS:*** Employee Benefits; Corporate. ***Email:*** CWheaton@KilpatrickStockton.com

COUNSEL

MICHAEL L. SCHENK, admitted to bar, 1996, North Carolina. *Education:* Eastern Michigan University (B.B.A., 1987); Wake Forest University (J.D., cum laude, 1996). Order of the Coif; Phi Delta Phi. Member, North Carolina Association of CPA's. *Member:* Wake County, North Carolina (Member, Tax Section) and American Bar Associations. ***PRACTICE AREAS:*** Executive Compensation; ERISA; Employee Benefits. ***Email:*** MSchenk@KilpatrickStockton.com

RESIDENT ASSOCIATES

CAROLYN A. BACHL, admitted to bar, 2004, North Carolina. *Education:* University of North Carolina (B.S., Geology, 1993); Vanderbilt University (M.S., Geology, 1997); University of North Carolina School of Law (J.D., with honors, 2004). ***PRACTICE AREAS:*** Environment; Energy; Land Use. ***Email:*** CBachl@KilpatrickStockton.com

BETSY COOKE, admitted to bar, 1998, North Carolina. *Education:* University of North Carolina-Chapel Hill (B.A., with distinction, 1993; J.D., with honors, 1998). ***PRACTICE AREAS:*** Employment Law; Commercial Litigation; Business Torts. ***Email:*** BCooke@KilpatrickStockton.com

LORIEN GOLASKI, admitted to bar, 2005, North Carolina. *Education:* Northwestern University (B.S., Journalism, 1995); Tulane University School of Law (J.D., magna cum laude, 2005). ***PRACTICE AREAS:*** Business Law; Corporate Law.

LAWRENCE J. GOULD, admitted to bar, 1994, Georgia; 2005, North Carolina. *Education:* Wesleyan University (B.A., with honors, 1987); Duke University (J.D., 1993). ***PRACTICE AREAS:*** Real Estate.

MARCELLA A. HARSHBARGER, admitted to bar, 2003, New York; 2005, North Carolina. *Education:* Wright State University (B.A., Financial Services and Marketing, summa cum laude); Duke University (J.D.; LL.M., International and Comparative Law, 2002). ***LANGUAGES:*** Spanish and Icelandic. ***PRACTICE AREAS:*** Corporate Law. ***Email:*** MHarshbarger@KilpatrickStockton.com

(This Listing Continued)

ROBERT G. HENSLEY, JR., admitted to bar, 2003, North Carolina. *Education:* University of Southern Mississippi (B.A., with general honors, 1992; M.A., 2000); University of North Carolina School of Law (J.D., with honors, 2002). *Member:* North Carolina State Bar. ***PRACTICE AREAS:*** Labor and Employment. ***Email:*** RHensley@KilpatrickStockton.com

J. CHRISTOPHER JACKSON, admitted to bar, 1999, North Carolina. *Education:* University of North Carolina at Chapel Hill (B.A., Political Science, with distinction, 1995; J.D., with honors, 1999). ***PRACTICE AREAS:*** Commercial Litigation; Personal Injury. ***Email:*** CJackson@KilpatrickStockton.com

KIRSTEN E. KENNEY, admitted to bar, 2003, North Carolina. *Education:* Wellesley College (B.A., magna cum laude, 1998); Duke University School of Law (J.D., 2003). ***LANGUAGES:*** German. ***PRACTICE AREAS:*** Real Estate. ***Email:*** KKenney@KilpatrickStockton.com

DAVID C. LINDSAY, admitted to bar, 1997, North Carolina. *Education:* University of North Carolina (B.A., 1994); Duke University (J.D., 1997). ***PRACTICE AREAS:*** Labor and Employment. ***Email:*** DLindsay@KilpatrickStockton.com

STEPHEN S. LOGUE, admitted to bar, 2005, North Carolina. *Education:* North Carolina State University (B.S. Management, Concentration in Finance, summa cum laude, 2000); University of North Carolina School of Law (J.D., with honors, 2004); New York University (LL.M. Taxation, 2005). ***PRACTICE AREAS:*** Real Estate. ***Email:*** SLogue@KilpatrickStockton.com

EMILY A. MOSELEY, admitted to bar, 1998, North Carolina. *Education:* Pomona College (B.A., 1995); Vanderbilt University (J.D., 1998). ***PRACTICE AREAS:*** Litigation; Labor and Employment.

JENNIFER S. O'CONNOR, admitted to bar, 1998, Florida; 2001, Georgia (Not admitted in North Carolina). *Education:* Duke University (B.A., 1995); Suffolk University (J.D., cum laude, 1998); Stetson College of Law (Transient Student, 1998). *Member:* Lakeland Bar Association, The Florida Bar; State Bar of Georgia. ***PRACTICE AREAS:*** Finance; Securitization; Real Estate. ***Email:*** JOConnor@KilpatrickStockton.com

MS. DORINDA L. PEACOCK, admitted to bar, 1998, North Carolina. *Education:* Davidson College (A.B., 1990); University of North Carolina (M.R.P., 1998; J.D., with honors, 1998). ***PRACTICE AREAS:*** Business; Corporate. ***Email:*** DPeacock@KilpatrickStockton.com

DEBORAH L. PRITCHARD, admitted to bar, 2004, North Carolina and U.S. District Court, Eastern District of North Carolina. *Education:* University of Delaware (B.S., Chemistry, 1987); University of North Carolina at Chapel Hill (Ph.D., Inorganic Chemistry, 1994); North Carolina Central University (J.D., magna cum laude, 2004). ***LANGUAGES:*** German. ***PRACTICE AREAS:*** Litigation. ***Email:*** DPritchard@KilpatrickStockton.com

B. FORD ROBERTSON, admitted to bar, 1996, Georgia; 2000, North Carolina. *Education:* University of Virginia (B.A., 1993); Wake Forest University (J.D., magna cum laude, 1996). ***PRACTICE AREAS:*** Real Estate. ***Email:*** FRobertson@KilpatrickStockton.com

SABRINA PRESNELL ROCKOFF, admitted to bar, 2002, North Carolina. *Education:* University of North Carolina at Chapel Hill (B.S., with honors, 1999; J.D., with honors, 2002). Chancellor's Scholar. Publication Editor, North Carolina Law Review, 2001-2002. *Member:* North Carolina State Bar. ***PRACTICE AREAS:*** Labor and Employment. ***Email:*** SRockoff@KilpatrickStockton.com

CATHERINE L. THOMAS, admitted to bar, 2003, North Carolina and U.S. District Court, Eastern District of North Carolina. *Education:* Sweet Briar College (B.A., Government, Business Management Certificate, 1998); American University, Washington College of Law (J.D., 2003); American University, Kogod School of Business (M.B.A., Real Estate and Finance, with honors, 2004). Recipient, Dean's Scholarship, Sweet Briar College. ***PRACTICE AREAS:*** Finance. ***Email:*** CThomas@KilpatrickStockton.com

LINDA B. TIGGES, born January 28, 1965; admitted to bar, 1999, North Carolina. *Education:* University of North Carolina at Chapel Hill (B.S., 1987; J.D., 1999). *Member:* North Carolina State Bar. ***PRACTICE AREAS:*** Finance; Corporate. ***Email:*** LTigges@KilpatrickStockton.com

ELIZABETH C. WILLIAMSON, admitted to bar, 1997, Georgia; 1998, Florida; 2002, North Carolina. *Education:* Florida State University (B.S., magna cum laude, 1994; J.D., with honors, 1997). Author: "City of Boerne v. Flores and the Religious Freedom Restoration Act: The Delicate Balance Between Religious Freedom and Historic Preservation," Journal of Land Use & Enviromental Law, Vol. 13 Issue 1 (1997); "The 1996 Florida Administrative Procedure Acts Attorney's Fees Reform: Creating Innovative Solutions or New Problems?" 24 FSU L. Rev. Issue 2 (1996); "EAC's and U.S. Ozone Regulation," The National Law Journal (2004). ***PRACTICE AREAS:*** Environmental; Commercial Litigation. ***Email:*** EWilliamson@KilpatrickStockton.com

W. SWAIN WOOD, admitted to bar, 1997, Georgia; 2003, North Carolina. *Education:* Georgetown University (A.B., magna cum laude, 1992); Harvard Law School (J.D., cum laude, 1997). ***PRACTICE AREAS:*** Litigation; Intellectual Property; Copyright Law. ***Email:*** SWood@KilpatrickStockton.com

(For complete biographical data on all personnel, see Professional Biographies at Atlanta and Augusta, Georgia; Washington, D.C.; Charlotte and Winston Salem, North Carolina; Stockholm, Sweden and London, England).

KIRBY & HOLT, L.L.P.

(Formerly Edwards & Kirby)

SUITE 100
3201 GLENWOOD AVENUE
P.O. BOX 31665
RALEIGH, NORTH CAROLINA 27622
Telephone: 919-881-2111
Fax: 919-781-8630
URL: http://www.kirby-holt.com

Personal injury, including medical malpractice, products liability and catastrophic injury, and business torts.

(This Listing Continued)

DAVID F. KIRBY, born Goldsboro, North Carolina, March 4, 1951; admitted to bar, 1977, North Carolina; 1978, U.S. District Court, Eastern District of North Carolina; 1988, U.S. District Court, Middle District of North Carolina. *Education:* University of North Carolina (A.B., 1973; J.D., 1977). Recipient, Steven J. Sharp Public Service Award, The Association of Trial Lawyers of America, 1997. Research Assistant to John Webb, Judge, North Carolina Court of Appeals, 1978. Co-Author: "North Carolina, Preparing and Trying the Automobile Accident Case," 1991. Named: 1996 Lawyers Weekly USA Lawyer of the Year; Best Lawyers in America; North Carolina's Legal Elite by Business North Carolina Magazine, 2001-2003. Member: Editorial Board, Trial; Inner Circle of Advocates. *Member:* Wake County (Member, Board of Directors, 1986-1987; 1995-1996); North Carolina (Member, Section on Litigation) and American (Member, Section on Litigation) Bar Associations; North Carolina State Bar; North Carolina Academy of Trial Lawyers (Member, Auto Torts Section); American Board of Trial Advocacy; The Association of Trial Lawyers of America (Member: Liquor Liability Group, 1990; Aquatic Injury Safety Group, 1989; Inadequate Security Group). Fellow, American College of Trial Lawyers. ***Email:*** dkirby@kirby-holt.com

C. MARK HOLT, born Oxford, North Carolina, October 29, 1960; admitted to bar, 1987, North Carolina. *Education:* Wake Forest University (B.A., 1983); University of Essex, England (M.A., 1984); University of North Carolina (J.D., with honors, 1987). Hankins Scholar. Omicron Delta Kappa. Rotary Foundation Scholar. Order of the Coif. Jessup Cup International Law Moot Court Team, 1986-1987. North Carolina Law Review, 1985-1986. Wake Forest University Board of Trustees, 1980-1982. Governor's Advocacy Council on Children and Youth, 1977-1981. Outstanding Young Lawyer Award, Young Lawyers Division of North Carolina Bar Association, 1990-1991. Chair, (Professional Negligence Section) North Carolina Academy of Trial Lawyers, 1999-2000. *Member:* Wake County, North Carolina and American Bar Associations; North Carolina Academy of Trial Lawyers; The Association of Trial Lawyers of America. Barrister, Chief Justice Susie M. Sharp Inn of Court. ***Email:*** mholt@kirby-holt.com

WILLIAM B. BYSTRYNSKI, born Springfield, Massachusetts, August 26, 1957; admitted to bar, 1994, North Carolina. *Education:* Hofstra University (B.A., magna cum laude, 1979); University of North Carolina (J.D., with honors, 1994). Phi Beta Kappa. Member, North Carolina Law Review. Wake County Bar Association Scholar. Author: "Riggins v. Nevada: Toward a Standard for Medicating the Incompetent Defendant to Competence," 71 North Carolina Law Review 1206, 1993. *Member:* Wake County (Chair, Scholarship Fund), North Carolina and American Bar Associations. North Carolina State Bar; The North Carolina Academy of Trial Lawyers; The Association of Trial Lawyers of America. ***PRACTICE AREAS:*** Catastrophic Injury; Personal Injury; Medical Malpractice; Products Liability. ***Email:*** bbystrynski@kirby-holt.com

ISAAC L. THORP, born Rocky Mount, North Carolina, January 20, 1957; admitted to bar, 1987, New York; 1991, North Carolina. *Education:* Hampshire College (B.A., 1981); New York University (J.D., 1986). Co-Author, Thorp's North Carolina Trial Practice Forms, 4th Edition, 1998. Assistant District Attorney, Sex Crimes Bureau, Brooklyn, New York, 1986-1990. *Member:* Wake County, North Carolina and American Bar Associations; Association of Trial Lawyers of America (Member, Sections on: Professional Negligence; Product Liability; Auto Torts; Member, Electrical Accident Litigation Group). ***PRACTICE AREAS:*** Negligence; Products Liability; Premises Liability. ***Email:*** ithorp@kirby-holt.com

---

LAURIE G. ARMSTRONG, admitted to bar, 2004, North Carolina. *Education:* University of North Carolina at Chapel Hill (B.S., 1988; J.D., 2003).

KNOTT, CLARK & BERGER, L.L.P.

Established in 1985

4800 SIX FORKS ROAD, SUITE 100
RALEIGH, NORTH CAROLINA 27609
Telephone: 919-783-5900
Telecopier: 919-783-9650
URL: http://www.knottclarkberger.com
URL: http://www.lawyers.com/pncb

General Practice in State and Federal Courts. Medical Malpractice, Nursing Malpractice, Hospital Liability, Plaintiffs Personal Injury, Wrongful Death, Automobile Accidents and Injuries, Commercial Vehicle Liability, Nursing Home Negligence, Workers Compensation, Insurance Bad Faith, Insurance Litigation.

FIRM PROFILE: Knott, Clark & Berger, L.L.P., are trial attorneys. The firm concentrates its practice on serious personal injury and wrongful death litigation arising from medical negligence, tractor-trailer and other motor vehicle crashes, nursing home negligence, defective products and in bad faith litigation against insurance companies. The firm practices trial and appellate litigation in state and federal courts throughout North Carolina.

MEMBERS OF FIRM

JOE THOMAS KNOTT, III, born Raleigh, North Carolina, July 25, 1951; admitted to bar, 1980, North Carolina, U.S. District Court, Eastern District of North Carolina and U.S. Court of Appeals, Fourth Circuit; 1989, U.S. District Court, Middle District of North Carolina. *Education:* University of North Carolina (B.S., Business Administration, 1974; J.D., 1980); Trinity Evangelical Divinity School (M. Div., 1978). Assistant U.S. Attorney, 1981-1985, Chief of Civil Section, 1981-1983 and Criminal Prosecutor, 1983-1985, Eastern District of North Carolina. Member, Board of Directors: Southern Baptist Sunday School Board, 1984-1992; Board of Directors, Hale High School, 1989—. Chairman, 1998-2002 and Member, Board of Directors, 1994-2002, St. Timothy's Elementary School. *Member:* Wake County and North Carolina Bar Associations; North Carolina State Bar; North Carolina Academy of Trial Lawyers. ***PRACTICE AREAS:*** Personal Injury; Medical Malpractice; Federal Tort Claims; Torts. ***Email:*** jtk.pkcb@intrex.net

MICHAEL WOOD CLARK, born Wilmington, North Carolina, November 5, 1959; admitted to bar, 1990, North Carolina and U.S. Court of Appeals, Fourth Circuit; 1993, U.S.

(This Listing Continued)

KNOTT, CLARK & BERGER, L.L.P., Raleigh—Continued

District Court, Eastern District of North Carolina. *Education:* University of North Carolina at Greensboro (B.S.N., 1982); Campbell University (J.D., 1990). Recipient, Fred O. Dennis Award. Registered Nurse, 1982. *Member:* Wake County and North Carolina Bar Associations; North Carolina State Bar. ***PRACTICE AREAS:*** Medical Malpractice; Nursing Malpractice; Personal Injury. ***Email:*** mwc.pkcb@intrex.net

BRUCE W. BERGER, born Beech Grove, Indiana, September 29, 1955; admitted to bar, 1980, West Virginia; 1981, U.S. District Court, Southern and Northern Districts of West Virginia and U.S. Court of Appeals, Fourth Circuit; 1988, North Carolina and U.S. District Court, Eastern and Middle Districts of North Carolina. *Education:* Vanderbilt University (B.A., cum laude, with honors, 1977); Southern Methodist University (J.D., 1980). Member: Defense Trial Counsel of West Virginia, 1983-1987; Defense Research Institute, 1990-1997. *Member:* Wake County and North Carolina Bar Associations; West Virginia State Bar; North Carolina State Bar; North Carolina Academy of Trial Lawyers. ***PRACTICE AREAS:*** Medical Malpractice; Personal Injury; Insurance Bad Faith; Insurance Litigation. ***Email:*** bwb.pkcb@intrex.net

KENNETH R. MURPHY, III, born Charlotte, North Carolina, July 7, 1969; admitted to bar, 1999, North Carolina; 2000, U.S. District Court, Eastern District of North Carolina. *Education:* University of North Carolina at Chapel Hill (B.A., 1991; J.D., 1999). *Member:* Durham County and North Carolina Bar Associations. ***PRACTICE AREAS:*** Personal Injury; Medical Malpractice. ***Email:*** krm.pkcb@intrex.net

LAW OFFICES OF KARL E. KNUDSEN

Established in 1987

FIVE WEST HARGETT STREET, SUITE 1100
P.O. BOX 2386
RALEIGH, NORTH CAROLINA 27601
Telephone: 919-828-5566
Fax: 919-834-3343
Email: kknudsen@karlkudsenlaw.com
URL: http://www.knudsen-law.com

Criminal Law, Driving While Intoxicated, Drug Crimes, Felonies, Homicide, Misdemeanors, Traffic Violations, Personal Injury, Medical Malpractice, Auto Accidents, Wrongful Death, Products Liability, Workers Compensation.

FIRM PROFILE: We are dedicated to providing competent, caring representation of people who have been injured by others or who have been charged with criminal offenses.

KARL E. KNUDSEN, born Atlanta, Georgia, December 14, 1952; admitted to bar, 1978, North Carolina; 2001, U.S. District Court, Eastern District of North Carolina. *Education:* North Carolina State University (B.A., Politics, 1975); University of North Carolina (J.D., 1978). Author: "DNA Fingerprinting: Prosecutors Dream Come True- Nightmare for the Defense," The True Bill, Vol. 11, No. 1, Nov. 1990; "DNA Fingerprinting: Part Two, The Making and the Meaning of a Match," The True Bill, Vol. 11, No. 2, March 1991. Faculty Advisor, Career Prosecutor Course, National College of District Attorneys, 1985. Assistant District Attorney, North Carolina 10th Judicial District, 1978-1982, 1983-1987. Member, Public Defender Qualifications Committee, 10th Judicial District, 2004-2005. *Member:* North Carolina Bar Association (Member, Sections on: Criminal Justice; Litigation); North Carolina State Bar; North Carolina Academy of Trial Lawyers (Member, Sections on: Criminal Justice; Auto Torts); Association of Trial Lawyers of America (Member, Sections on: Criminal Law; Motor Vehicle Collision; Highway and Premises Liability); National Association of Criminal Defense Lawyers; Wake County Academy of Criminal Trial Lawyers. (Board Certified Specialist in State Criminal Law, North Carolina State Board of Legal Specialization). ***PRACTICE AREAS:*** Criminal Defense (60%); Personal Injury (30%); Medical Malpractice (10%).

ASSOCIATE

EILEEN A. MULLEN, born Bronx, New York, January 26, 1970; admitted to bar, 1997, North Carolina. *Education:* Syracuse University (B.A., 1992); Duquesne University School of Law, (J.D., 1996). *Member:* Wake County, Tenth Judicial District and North Carolina Bar Associations; North Carolina Academy of Trial Lawyers (Member, Sections on: Workers Compensation; Auto Torts; Professional Negligence; Nursing Home Negligence). ***PRACTICE AREAS:*** Workers Compensation (60%); Plaintiffs Personal Injury (30%); Medical Malpractice (10%). ***Email:*** emullen@karlknudsenlaw.com

HOWARD A. KRAMER

Established in 1980

300 WEST MILLBROOK ROAD, SUITE 101
RALEIGH, NORTH CAROLINA 27609
Telephone: 919-821-4600
Fax: 919-787-1771
Email: hk11772003@yahoo.com
URL: http://www.lawyers.com/kramerlaw

Administrative Law, Health Care Law, Government Relations, Lobbying, Representation before State Agencies and Boards, Professional Licensing.

HOWARD A. KRAMER, born Great Neck, New York, May 11, 1944; admitted to bar, 1971, New York; 1972, North Carolina; 1977, U.S. Supreme Court. *Education:* University of Wisconsin-Madison (B.S., 1966); University of North Carolina at Chapel Hill (J.D., 1969). Chief Deputy Attorney General, State of North Carolina, 1975-1980. Executive Director, North Carolina Sheriff's Association, 1980-1987. General Counsel, North Carolina Board of Nursing, 1981—. Charter Member, North Carolina Professional Lobbyists Association. *Member:* Wake County and North Carolina (Member, Sections on: Health Law; Administrative Law; Government and Public Sector) Bar Associations; Society of Health Care Attorneys.

(This Listing Continued)

KUNIHOLM LAW FIRM

Established in 1991

1500 SUNDAY DRIVE, SUITE 208
P.O. BOX 30303
RALEIGH, NORTH CAROLINA 27622
Telephone: 919-854-4454
Telecopier: 919-854-4450
Email: kuniholmlaw@kuniholmlaw.com
URL: http://www.kuniholmlaw.com

Asheville, North Carolina Office: 46 Haywood Street, Suite 250. Telephone: 800-350-7574.

Civil Trial and Appellate Practice in all State and Federal Courts, Personal Injury and Wrongful Death, Medical and Professional Negligence, Obstetric and Pediatric Malpractice, Brain Injury. Trucking Accidents, Automobile Accidents. Insurance Litigation. Sexual Abuse.

FIRM PROFILE: The Kuniholm Law Firm's practice is devoted to the settlement or trial of major personal injury cases. Most cases involve medical negligence, hospital liability, pediatric malpractice or obstetric malpractice. We also dedicate a portion of the practice to claims for victims of automobile and trucking wrecks. The firm also pursues claims against sexual abusers, both individuals and institutions. The firm has offices in Raleigh and Asheville and will pursue claims in any of North Carolina's 100 counties.

ELIZABETH F. KUNIHOLM, born New Haven, Connecticut, May 7, 1947; admitted to bar, 1981, North Carolina. *Education:* Duke University (A.B., 1970; M.A., 1980; J.D., 1980); Oberlin College. Order of the Coif. Editorial Board, Duke Law Journal, 1979-1980. Senior Lecturer, Duke University School of Law, 1987—. Law Clerk to the Honorable J. Dickson Phillips, Jr., U.S. Court of Appeals for the Fourth Circuit, 1980-1981. Co-Author: "Sexual Abuse" in *Litigating Tort Cases,* West/Association of Trial Lawyers of America, 2003. *Member:* Wake County, North Carolina (Member: Medical-Legal Liaison Committee, 1990-1991, 1996-1997; Chair, Litigation Section, 1992-1993; Board of Governors, 1993-1996) and American Bar Associations; The Association of Trial Lawyers of America; North Carolina Academy of Trial Lawyers (Board of Governors, 1991-1993; Vice President, Legal Affairs, 1993-1996; Vice President, Public Education, 1996-1997; President, 1998-1999); National Crime Victims Bar Association (Member, Board of Advisors, 2003—); National Alliance of Victim's Rights Attorneys; North Carolina Association of Women Attorneys; American Board of Trial Advocates. ***SPECIAL AGENCIES:*** Member: Birth-Related Neurological Impairment Study Commission, North Carolina General Assembly, 1991-1992; Medical Malpractice Study Committee, Legislative Research Commission, North Carolina General Assembly, 1998-1999. ***PRACTICE AREAS:*** Medical Malpractice; Hospital Liability; Obstetric Malpractice; Pediatric Malpractice; Personal Injury; Wrongful Death; Brain Injury; Sexual Abuse. ***Email:*** kuniholmlaw@kuniholmlaw.com

LUCY N. INMAN, born Indianapolis, Indiana, May 7, 1961; admitted to bar, 1990, North Carolina and U.S. District Court, Eastern District of North Carolina; 1992, California; 1993, U.S. District Court, Central District of California. *Education:* North Carolina State University (B.A., with highest honors, 1984); University of North Carolina at Chapel Hill (J.D., with honors, 1990). Articles Editor, North Carolina Law Review, 1989-1990. Law Clerk to the Honorable James G. Exum, Jr., Chief Justice, North Carolina Supreme Court, 1990-1992. *Member:* North Carolina Bar Association; North Carolina State Bar; North Carolina Academy of Trial Lawyers. ***PRACTICE AREAS:*** Professional Negligence; Personal Injury. ***Email:*** linman@kuniholmlaw.com

ASHLEY BROWNING YOUNG, born Henderson, North Carolina, November 16, 1970; admitted to bar, 1998, North Carolina. *Education:* University of North Carolina at Chapel Hill (B.A., 1993); North Carolina Central University (J.D., cum laude, 1998). Member: N.C.C.U. Law Journal, 1997-1998; N.C.C.U. Trial Advocacy Board, 1996-1998; Co-Chair, N.C.C.U. Women's Caucus, 1995-1996. Executive Board, North Carolina Association of Women Attorneys, 1997-1998. *Member:* Wake County and North Carolina Bar Associations; North Carolina Academy of Trial Lawyers; The Association of Trial Lawyers of America. ***PRACTICE AREAS:*** Medical Malpractice; Personal Injury; Sexual Abuse; Truck Accidents; Automobile Accidents and Injuries; Professional Negligence. ***Email:*** ayoung@kuniholmlaw.com

PATRICK F. BALESTRIERI, born Washington, D.C., June 12, 1968; admitted to bar, 1994, New York and District of Columbia; 1998, North Carolina. *Education:* University of North Carolina at Chapel Hill (B.A., 1990) Pi Sigma Alpha; Mercer University (J.D., 1993); New York Law School (Visiting Third Year Student). *Member:* Wake County, North Carolina and New York State Bar Associations; The District of Columbia Bar; North Carolina Academy of Trial Lawyers; The Association of Trial Lawyers of America. ***PRACTICE AREAS:*** Civil Litigation; Medical Malpractice; Personal Injury; Wrongful Death; Hospital Liability. ***Email:*** pbalestrieri@kuniholmlaw.com

OF COUNSEL

KIM CHURCH, born Lexington, North Carolina, August 7, 1956; admitted to bar, 1982, North Carolina. *Education:* University of North Carolina at Greensboro (B.A., summa cum laude, 1979); University of North Carolina at Chapel Hill (J.D., 1982). Phi Beta Kappa. Winfield Scholar in English. Recipient, Student Excellence Award. Co-Author, "Sexual Abuse", in *Litigating Tort Cases,* West /Association of Trial Lawyers of America, 2003. Author, "The Discretionary Factor in the Equitable Distribution Act," 60 N.C.L.Rev. 1399 (1982). Mediator, North Carolina Dispute Resolution Commission. *Member:* North Carolina Bar Association; North Carolina Academy of Trial Lawyers; The Association of Trial Lawyers of America; National Alliance of Victim's Rights Attorneys. ***PRACTICE***

(This Listing Continued)

AREAS: Civil Litigation; Sexual Abuse; Foster Care Negligence. ***Email:*** kchurch@kuniholmlaw.com

KURTZ & BLUM, PLLC

16 WEST MARTIN STREET, 10TH FLOOR
RALEIGH, NORTH CAROLINA 27601
Telephone: 919-832-7700; Toll Free: 888-505-7780
Facsimile: 919-832-2740
URL: http://www.lawyers.com/kurtzandblum
Email: info@kurtzandblum.com
URL: http://www.KurtzandBlum.com

Criminal Law, DWI, Drug Crimes, Felonies, Homicides, Misdemeanors, Parole and Probation, Sexual Assaults, Traffic Violations, White Collar Crimes, Family Law, Child Custody, Child Support, Divorce, Domestic Violence, Spousal Support, Personal Injury, Auto Accidents, Sexual Abuse, Wrongful Death, Legal Malpractice, Medical Malpractice, Immigration.

HOWARD A. KURTZ, born Philadelphia, Pennsylvania, April 30, 1967; admitted to bar, 1992, North Carolina, U.S. District Court, Eastern District of North Carolina and U.S. Court of Appeals, Fourth Circuit. *Education:* University of North Carolina at Chapel Hill (B.A., 1989; J.D., 1992). Assistant Public Defender, Fayetteville, N.C., 1992-1998. Partner, Kurtz & Blum, Raleigh, N.C., 1998—. Publications: Editor, The True Bill, publication of the Criminal Justice Section of the North Carolina Bar Association, 1998-1999; 2000-2001. *Member:* North Carolina State Bar; North Carolina and American Bar Associations; North Carolina Academy of Trial Lawyers; National Association of Criminal Defense Lawyers; Association of Trial Lawyers of America. ***PRACTICE AREAS:*** Criminal Defense; Traffic; DWI; Trial Practice; Appellate Practice; Death Penalty Post-conviction work; Personal Injury; Professional Negligence; Medical Malpractice; Legal Malpractice. ***Email:*** H.Kurtz@KurtzandBlum.com

SETH A. BLUM, born Williamsport, Pennsylvania, September 30, 1968; admitted to bar, 1993, North Carolina, U.S. District Court, Eastern District of North Carolina and U.S. Court of Appeals, Fourth Circuit. *Education:* Tufts University (B.S., 1990); Duke University (J.D., M.A., 1993). Publications: Editor, The True Bill, publication of the Criminal Justice Section of the North Carolina Bar Association, 1999-2000. Assistant Public Defender: Fayetteville, N.C., 1993-1995; Carrboro, N.C., 1997-1998. Litigation Associate, Law Offices of G. Michael Malone, Raleigh, N.C., 1995-1996. Partner, Kurtz & Blum, Raleigh, N.C., 1998—. Member: Mensa. *Member:* North Carolina State Bar; North Carolina and American Bar Associations; North Carolina Academy of Trial Lawyers; National Association of Criminal Defense Lawyers; Association of Trial Lawyers of America. ***PRACTICE AREAS:*** Criminal Defense; Traffic; Driving While Impaired; Trial Practice; Appellate Practice; Death Penalty; Personal Injury; Immigration Law. ***Email:*** S.Blum@KurtzandBlum.com

ASSOCIATES

MEREDITH S. NICHOLSON, born Greensboro, North Carolina, July 23, 1973; admitted to bar, 2000, North Carolina. *Education:* University of North Carolina-Chapel Hill (B.A., 1995; J.D., 1999). Recipient, Carolina Law Pro Bono Award for service performed. *Member:* North Carolina State Bar; National Lawyers Guild (Chair, UNC-Chapel Hill chapter); North Carolina Academy of Trial Lawyers; National Association of Criminal Defense Lawyers; Wake County Academy of Criminal Trial Lawyers; Hispanic/Latino Lawyers Committee; Durham and Orange Women Attorneys; The North Carolina Association of Women Attorneys. ***LANGUAGES:*** French and Spanish. ***PRACTICE AREAS:*** Criminal Defense; Driving While Impaired; Traffic Violations; Personal Injury. ***Email:*** M.Nicholson@KurtzandBlum.com

PAULA K. McGRANN, admitted to bar, 2001, North Carolina. *Education:* Methodist College (B.A., 1983); North Carolina Central University Law School (J.D., 2001). Associate, Kurtz & Blum, Raleigh, North Carolina, 2001. *Member:* North Carolina State Bar; North Carolina and American Bar Associations; North Carolina Academy of Trial Lawyers; The Association of Trial Lawyers of America. ***PRACTICE AREAS:*** Family Law; Civil Appeals; Criminal Appeals; Post Conviction. ***Email:*** P.McGrann@KurtzandBlum.com

ADAM P. SOLTYS, born Boston, Massachusetts, April 27, 1978; admitted to bar, 2003, North Carolina; 2004, West Virginia. *Education:* Davidson College (B.A., 2000); University of North Carolina at Chapel Hill Law School (J.D., 2003). Formerly with John N. Frigulietti, LLC. ***PRACTICE AREAS:*** Criminal Defense; Driving While Intoxicated; Traffic Violations. ***Email:*** A.Soltys@kurtzandblum.com

LAW OFFICE OF ROBERT J. LANE III

107 FAYETTEVILLE STREET MALL, SUITE 201
RALEIGH, NORTH CAROLINA 27601
Telephone: 919-835-9095
Fax: 919-838-5299
Email: rlane@lawyer.com
URL: http://www.robertjlanelaw.com

Criminal Law, Driving While Intoxicated (DWI), Drug Crimes, Felonies, Assault, Traffic, Personal Injury, Auto Accidents, Wrongful Death, Employment, Discrimination, Harassment.

ROBERT J. LANE, III, born Erwin, North Carolina, May 12, 1964; admitted to bar, 1989, North Carolina and U.S. District Court, Eastern District of North Carolina. *Education:* Campbell University (B.B.A., 1986); University of North Carolina School of Law (J.D., 1989). *Member:* Wake County and North Carolina Bar Associations; North Carolina State Bar. (Also Member, Wake County Traffic & DWI Center, PLLC). ***PRACTICE AREAS:*** Criminal Law; Driving While Intoxicated; Traffic Violations; Personal Injury; Automobile Accidents and Injuries.

LARCADE, HEISKELL AND ASKEW PLLC

3716 NATIONAL DRIVE, SUITE 118
RALEIGH, NORTH CAROLINA 27612
Telephone: 919-785-3494
Facsimile: 919-785-3221

JODEE SPARKMAN LARCADE, born Edison, New Jersey, May 8, 1954; admitted to bar, 1979, North Carolina and U.S. District Court, Eastern, Middle and Western Districts of North Carolina. *Education:* Duke University (B.A., magna cum laude, 1976); Oxford University, Oxford, England (1975); Southern Methodist University (J.D., 1979). Editor, Duke Law Journal, 1978-1979. Case Note and Comment Editor, Journal of Air Law & Commerce, 1978-1979. *Member:* Wake County and North Carolina Bar Associations; Defense Research Institute; North Carolina Association of Defense Attorneys. ***PRACTICE AREAS:*** Trial Practice; Civil Litigation; Medical Malpractice; Professional Liability; Insurance Defense; Mediation. ***Email:*** jslarcade@aol.com

CHRISTOPHER NEIL HEISKELL, born Enid, Oklahoma, July 7, 1968; admitted to bar, 1993, North Carolina. *Education:* Guilford College (B.S. 1990); Campbell University (M.B.A., 1993; J.D., 1993). *Member:* North Carolina State Bar; North Carolina Association of Defense Attorneys; Defense Research Institute. ***PRACTICE AREAS:*** Insurance Defense; Negligence Litigation; General Civil Practice. ***Email:*** cnheiskell@netscape.net

ROGER ALLAN ASKEW, born Ahoskie, North Carolina, June 8, 1964; admitted to bar, 1991, North Carolina; U.S. District Court, Eastern and Middle Districts of North Carolina; U.S. Supreme Court. *Education:* Chowan College (A.A., 1984); Campbell University (B.A., 1986); Norman A. Wiggins School of Law (J.D., 1991). *Member:* North Carolina State Bar; North Carolina Association of Defense Attorneys. (Resident, Rocky Mount Office). ***PRACTICE AREAS:*** Insurance Defense. ***Email:*** askewra@bjjlawoffices.com

MARGARET P. EAGLES, born March 2, 1973; admitted to bar, 2000, North Carolina and U.S. District Court, Eastern, Middle and Western Districts of North Carolina. *Education:* Wake Forest University (B.A., 1995); Campbell University (J.D., cum laude, 2000). Phi Kappa Phi; Omicron Delta Kappa; Phi Alpha Delta. Editor-in-Chief, Campbell Law Review, 1999-2000. Law Clerk to the Honorable George L. Wainwright, Jr., Associate Justice, North Carolina Supreme Court, 1999-2001. *Member:* Wake County and North Carolina Bar Associations. ***PRACTICE AREAS:*** Insurance Defense; Civil Practice; Environmental Law.

REPRESENTATIVE CLIENTS: North Carolina Farm Bureau Insurance Co.; Allstate Insurance Co.; State Farm Insurance Co.; St. Paul Insurance Co. Orion Auto Insurance; Nationwide Mutual Insurance Company; Windsor Group.

THE LAW OFFICE OF JAMES P. LAURIE III, PLLC

Established in 1999
8311 SIX FORKS ROAD,
SUITE 111
RALEIGH, NORTH CAROLINA 27615
Telephone: 919-256-4455
Fax: 919-256-4466
Email: jameslaurie@laurielaw.com
URL: http://www.laurielaw.com

Construction Law, Mechanics Liens and Bond Claims, Construction Litigation, Construction Defects, Arbitration, Commercial Law.

FIRM PROFILE: Construction Industry representation including Owners, Developers, Sureties, General Contractors, Subcontractors, Suppliers, Factors, Architects, Engineers, and Construction Industry Associations. Licensed Attorney in North Carolina, Tennessee, and the District of Columbia.

JAMES P. LAURIE, III, born Roanoke, Virginia, October 11, 1962; admitted to bar, 1992, North Carolina and Tennessee; 1993, District of Columbia. *Education:* Washington & Lee University (B.A., 1984); Campbell University School of Law (J.D., 1992). Certified, OSHA Instructor, Private Sector Safety & Health Compliance, OSHA School, Des Plaines, Illinois. Author: Note, ABA Public Contractor Newsletter, Fall 1991; Note, ABA Forum on Construction, Spring 1992; "North Carolina Lien & Bond Law in the Fifty States," 1994-2004; "North Carolina Prompt Pay Laws in the Fifty States," 1994-2004; "'North Carolina' Reference Guide to Licensing and Registration Requirements in the Fifty States and the District," 1998, American Subcontractors Association; "Advanced Construction Law, National Business Institute, 1999-2002; "Construction Defects and Mold Litigation," National Business Institute, 2003; "North Carolina Lien and Bond Claim Strategies," National Business Institute, 2004. Member, Attorney's Council, American Subcontractors Association. Certified Arbitrator, Wake County District Court Arbitration Program. Chair, Public Safety Liaison Committee and Board Member, Eastside Neighborhood Task Force, City of Raleigh, North Carolina; Board Member: Glenwood South Redevelopment Area Advisory Board, City of Raleigh; Exploris-Southeast Raleigh Advisory Board, 1998-1999; Board Member, Southeast Raleigh Assembly, 2001-2003. President, 1996-1998; Board Member, 1995-1999; Treasurer, 1998-1999; Reserve Study Chairman, 1995, Founders Row Condominium Association. Member, Downtown Raleigh Alliance Advisory Committee, 1999-2000. Precinct Judge, Wake County, Board of Elections, 2003. *Member:* American (Member, Construction Forum, Division 9 Specialty Trade Contractors Steering Committee and Liaison, Young Lawyers Committee) Bar Association. ***PRACTICE AREAS:*** Construction Law. ***Email:*** jameslaurie@laurielaw.com

ASSOCIATES

JINA B. PROPST, born Smithfield, North Carolina, March 8, 1970; admitted to bar, 1998, North Carolina. *Education:* Wake Forest University (B.A., cum laude, 1992); Campbell University (J.D., 1998). Author: Campbell Law Observer, September 2000. Lecturer,

(This Listing Continued)

THE LAW OFFICE OF JAMES P. LAURIE III, PLLC, Raleigh—Continued

"Mechanics Lien & Bond Claim Strategies," National Business Institute, 2001. Volunteer, Guardian Ad Litem, 1996-1997. Advocate, Arbitration and Mediation. *Member:* Wake County (Social Chair, Young Lawyers Division, 1999-2003; 10th Judicial District Representative, Young Lawyers Division, 2003—; Eastern Regional Moot Court Competition; Co-Chair, Law Week, Young Lawyers Division, 1999—), North Carolina (Member, Construction Law Section, 1998—) and American (Member, Construction Forum, 2001—) Bar Associations; Attorney's Council, American Subcontractors Association. ***PRACTICE AREAS:*** Construction Law. ***Email:*** jinapropst@laurielaw.com

ANDREW T. CORNELIUS, born Salisbury, North Carolina, May 7, 1979; admitted to bar, 2004, North Carolina. *Education:* University of North Carolina at Chapel Hill (B.A., 2001); Campbell University School of Law (J.D., 2004). Author: "Construction Payment Remedies in North Carolina," National Business Institute, 2004. *Member:* North Carolina State Bar. ***PRACTICE AREAS:*** Construction Law. ***Email:*** andrewcornelius@laurielaw.com

LEWIS & ROBERTS, P.L.L.C.

1305 NAVAHO DRIVE, SUITE 400
RALEIGH, NORTH CAROLINA 27609-7482
Telephone: 919-981-0191
888-981-0939
Facsimile: 919-981-0199
URL: http://www.lewis-roberts.com

Mailing Address: P.O. Box 17529, Raleigh, NC 27619-7529

Charlotte, North Carolina Office: 128 South Tryon Street, Suite 1100, 28202-5012. Telephone: 704-347-8990. Facsimile: 704-347-8929.

Workers' Compensation Law, Commercial Litigation, Construction Law, Surety Law, Civil Trial Practice.

RICHARD M. LEWIS, born Wilmington, Delaware, May 14, 1950; admitted to bar, 1975, North Carolina. *Education:* Wake Forest University (B.A., 1972; J.D., 1975). Member, Board of Editors, Wake Forest Law Review, 1974-1975. Selected, Best Lawyers in America. *Member:* North Carolina Bar Association (Member, Litigation Section; Chairman, Workers' Compensation Section, 1999-2000); North Carolina Association of Defense Attorneys (Board of Directors, 1999-2002). ***PRACTICE AREAS:*** Workers Compensation Law. ***Email:*** ricklewis@lewis-roberts.com

JAMES A. ROBERTS, III, born Decatur, Alabama, September 5, 1956; admitted to bar, 1982, North Carolina. *Education:* Wake Forest University (B.A., cum laude, 1979; J.D., 1982). Selected, Best Lawyers in America. *Member:* North Carolina (Member: Litigation Section; Construction Law Section) and American (Member: Litigation Section; Construction Law Section, Fidelity and Surety Law Committee) Bar Associations. ***PRACTICE AREAS:*** Commercial Litigation; Construction Law; Surety Law; Business Torts; Insurance Law. ***Email:*** jimroberts@lewis-roberts.com

WINSTON L. PAGE, JR., born Raleigh, North Carolina, April 16, 1948; admitted to bar, 1975, North Carolina. *Education:* University of North Carolina (B.A., 1970; J.D., 1974). Selected, Best Lawyers in America. Deputy Commissioner, North Carolina Industrial Commission, 1981-1989. *Member:* North Carolina Bar Association (Member, Litigation Section and Council Member, Workers' Compensation Section); North Carolina Association of Defense Attorneys. ***PRACTICE AREAS:*** Workers Compensation Law. ***Email:*** winstonpage@lewis-roberts.com

TIMOTHY S. RIORDAN, born Lincoln Park, Michigan, December 9, 1960; admitted to bar, 1987, North Carolina. *Education:* Hillsdale College (B.A., magna cum laude, 1983); University of Notre Dame (J.D., 1986). *Member:* North Carolina Bar Association; North Carolina Association of Defense Attorneys. ***PRACTICE AREAS:*** Workers' Compensation Law. ***Email:*** timriordan@lewis-roberts.com

JACK SPAIN HOLMES, born Washington, D.C., January 5, 1962; admitted to bar, 1987, North Carolina. *Education:* University of North Carolina (B.S., 1984); College of William and Mary (J.D., 1987). *Member:* North Carolina Bar Association; North Carolina Association of Defense Attorneys. ***PRACTICE AREAS:*** Workers Compensation Law. ***Email:*** jackholmes@lewis-roberts.com

DANIEL K. BRYSON, born Asheville, North Carolina, December 3, 1960; admitted to bar, 1988, North Carolina. *Education:* University of North Carolina (B.A., 1983); University of North Carolina at Greensboro (M.B.A., 1986); Wake Forest University (J.D., cum laude, 1988). Member, Wake Forest Law Review, 1987-1988. *Member:* North Carolina (Chair, Construction Law Section, Council, 2001-2002) and American (Member, Construction Law Section, Fidelity and Surety Law Committee) Bar Associations; North Carolina Academy of Trial Lawyers; The Association of Trial Lawyers of America (Member, Construction Defects and Mold Litigation Sections). ***PRACTICE AREAS:*** Construction Defects; Construction Law; Surety Law; Consumer Class Actions; Commercial Litigation. ***Email:*** danbryson@lewis-roberts.com

JOHN D. ELVERS, born Grand Forks, North Dakota, December 27, 1963; admitted to bar, 1989, North Carolina. *Education:* University of North Carolina (B.A., 1986; J.D., 1989). *Member:* North Carolina Bar Association (Member, Litigation and Worker's Compensation Section). ***PRACTICE AREAS:*** Workers Compensation Law. ***Email:*** johnelvers@lewis-roberts.com

BRIAN D. LAKE, born Dover, New Jersey, May 15, 1958; admitted to bar, 1987, North Carolina. *Education:* Virginia Military Institute (B.A., 1980); Wake Forest University (J.D., 1987). Finalist, Stanley Cup Moot Court Competition, 1985. *Member:* North Carolina Bar Association. [Capt., USMC, 1980-1984]. ***PRACTICE AREAS:*** Workers Compensation Law; Litigation. ***Email:*** brianlake@lewis-roberts.com

(This Listing Continued)

JOHN H. RUOCCHIO, born Beacon, New York, July 25, 1965; admitted to bar, 1995, North Carolina. *Education:* University of North Carolina (B.A., 1987); Campbell University School of Law (J.D., 1995). *Member:* North Carolina Bar Association. ***PRACTICE AREAS:*** Workers Compensation Law. ***Email:*** johnruocchio@lewis-roberts.com

GARY VANCE MAUNEY, born Tampa, Florida, May 14, 1965; admitted to bar, 1995, North Carolina. *Education:* North Carolina State University (B.A., Business Management; B.A., Economics, 1988); American University, Washington College of Law (J.D., 1995). Paul J. Sedgewick Scholar, American University, Washington College of Law. Law Clerk to the Honorable: Jack Cozort and Donald L. Smith, North Carolina Court of Appeals, 1995-1997. *Member:* North Carolina (Newsletter Committee Chairperson for the Litigation Section, 2003-2004; Chair, Disaster Legal Services Committee, 1997-1998) and American Bar (Member, Sections on: Business Law, Litigation, Tort and Insurance Law) Associations; Mecklenburg and American Trial Lawyers Association (Member, Professional Negligence Section; Chair, Abusive Tax Shelter Litigation Group); North Carolina Academy of Trial Lawyers. Joseph Brown Inn of Court. (Resident, Charlotte Office). ***PRACTICE AREAS:*** Complex Civil Litigation; Catastrophic Injury; Personal Injury; Professional Malpractice; Nursing Home Negligence; Products Liability; Aviation Litigation; Business Torts; Class Actions; Tax Shelters. ***Email:*** garymauney@lewis-roberts.com

SCOTT J. LASSO, born North Kingstown, Rhode Island, March 13, 1967; admitted to bar, 1992, North Carolina, U.S. District Court, Eastern District of North Carolina. *Education:* University of Mississippi (B.B.A., 1989); Wake Forest University (J.D., 1992). *Member:* North Carolina Bar Association (Member, Workers Compensation Section); North Carolina Association of Defense Attorneys. ***PRACTICE AREAS:*** Workers Compensation (100%). ***Email:*** scottlasso@lewis-roberts.com

KIMBERLY R. WILSON, born Beckley, West Virginia, June 9, 1969; admitted to bar, 1995, West Virginia; 1996, U.S. District Court, Northern District of West Virginia; 2001, North Carolina; U.S. District Court, Eastern District of North Carolina. *Education:* West Virginia University (B.A., 1991; J.D., 1995). Author: "Mycotokins: Ingestion Inhalation and Injury," Mealeys, Mold Litigation Report, July 2003. *Member:* West Virginia State Bar; North Carolina State Bar; American Trial Lawyers Association. ***PRACTICE AREAS:*** Toxic Torts; Pharmaceutical Law; Products Liability; Personal Injury.

JEFFREY ALLEN MISENHEIMER, born Raleigh, North Carolina, November 19, 1973; admitted to bar, 1999, North Carolina. *Education:* Hampden-Sydney College (B.A., 1996); Cumberland School of Law of Samford University (J.D., 1999). Member: Justice Richard "Red" Jones National Moot Court Team, 1998-1999; Henry Upson Sims Moot Court Board, 1998-1999. *Member:* North Carolina Bar Association (Member, Workers Compensation Section); North Carolina Association of Defense Attorneys. ***PRACTICE AREAS:*** Workers Compensation Law. ***Email:*** jeffreymisenheimer@lewis-roberts.com

PAUL R. DICKINSON, JR., born Suffolk, Virginia, April 3, 1960; admitted to bar, 1990, Texas; 1994, North Carolina. *Education:* University of South Florida (B.A., 1986); South Texas College of Law (J.D., 1990). *Member:* North Carolina Bar Association (Member, Litigation and Professional Negligence Sections); North Carolina Academy of Trial Lawyers; The Association of Trial Lawyers of America (Member, Professional Negligence Section). (Resident, Charlotte Office). ***PRACTICE AREAS:*** Construction Defects; Stucco Litigation; Truck Accidents; Nursing Home Abuse and Neglect; Nursing Negligence; Medical Malpractice; Construction Litigation; Construction Products Liability; Products Liability; Catastrophic Injury; Birth Trauma; Obstetric Malpractice. ***Email:*** pauldickinson@lewis-roberts.com

GEORGE V. BURNS, born Boston, Massachusetts, November 15, 1967; admitted to bar, 1994, Massachusetts; 1999 North Carolina. *Education:* Stonehill College (B.A., 1989); New England School of Law (J.D., 1994). *Member:* North Carolina Bar Association. ***PRACTICE AREAS:*** Construction Litigation; Commercial Litigation. ***Email:*** georgeburns@lewis-roberts.com

J. ANDREW FINE, born West Palm Beach, Florida, November 13, 1971; admitted to bar, 1997, Florida (Not admitted in North Carolina). *Education:* University of Florida (B.A., 1994; J.D., 1997). ***PRACTICE AREAS:*** Construction Law; Construction Litigation; Technology Law; Litigation. ***Email:*** jaf@lewis-roberts.com

BRYANT D. PARIS, III, born Raleigh, North Carolina, April 26, 1975; admitted to bar, 2002, North Carolina. *Education:* University of North Carolina at Chapel Hill (A.B., 1997); University of Mississippi, Oxford (J.D., 2002). *Member:* North Carolina Bar Association (Member: Workers' Compensation Section; Appellate Rules Committee). ***PRACTICE AREAS:*** Workers Compensation. ***Email:*** bryantparis@lewis-roberts.com

GEOFFREY S. PROUD, born Bryn Mawr, Pennsylvania, May 27, 1977; admitted to bar, 2003, Massachusetts; 2004, North Carolina. *Education:* Wake Forest University (B.A., 1999); Boston College Law School (J.D., 2003). *Member:* North Carolina, Massachusetts and American Bar Associations. ***PRACTICE AREAS:*** Civil Litigation; Commercial Litigation; Construction Law; Pharmacy Law. ***Email:*** gsp@lewis-roberts.com

SARAH E. CONE, born Jacksonville, North Carolina, March 14, 1978; admitted to bar, 2005, North Carolina. *Education:* North Carolina State University (B.A., 2000); Campbell University (J.D., 2004). *Member:* North Carolina and American Bar Associations. ***PRACTICE AREAS:*** Workers Compensation. ***Email:*** sarahcone@lewis-roberts.com

REPRESENTATIVE CLIENTS: Collins & Aikman Corp.; Springs Industries; Great American Insurance Co.; Builders Mutual Ins. Co.; J.M. Thompson Const. Co., Inc.; St. Paul Fire & Marine Ins. Co.; RSKCo.; Kemper Insurance Companies; Zenith Insurance Co.; Key Risk Management Services; Hewitt, Coleman & Associates, Inc.; Southern States Insurance Exchange; Overnite Transportation; RPC Contracting, Inc.; Eaton Corp.; Central Insurance Companies; J.W. Grand Const. Co.; Travelers Insurance Co.; Smithfield Foods; The Lundy Packing Co.; Glaxo-Wellcome, Inc.; NACCO Materials Handling Group, Inc.; Zurich US Inc.; ITT-Hartford; Erie Insurance Group; Food Lion; Discovery Insurance; Crawford and Co.; City of Durham; Carolina Holding, Inc.; Abbott Laboratories; Dupont; Carolina Builders Corp.; Forestry Mutual Insurance Co.; Pella Corp.; Blue Rhino Corp.; NC Association of Home Inspectors; Royal & Sunalliance Insurance Co.

THE LAW OFFICES OF LOWRY & ASSOCIATES

8358 SIX FORKS ROAD, SUITE 104
RALEIGH, NORTH CAROLINA 27615
Telephone: 919-518-0783
Fax: 919-518-8375

Residential Real Estate, Commercial Real Estate, Trusts and Estates, Estate Planning, Asset Protection, Wills, Probate, Business Law, Limited Liability Company Law, Tax Law, Non-Profit and Charitable Organizations.

STEPHEN D. LOWRY, born Oklahoma City, Oklahoma, December 17, 1955; admitted to bar, 1980, Ohio; 1986, North Carolina. *Education:* David Lipscomb College (B.A., magna cum laude, 1976); Duke University (J.D., 1980). *Member:* North Carolina State Bar (Member, Sections on: Real Estate; Estate Planning); American Bar Association (Member, Sections on: Taxation; Business Law). **Email:** stevelowry@nc.rr.com

LYNCH & EATMAN, L.L.P.

CAROLINA CORPORATE CENTER, SUITE 201
5400 GLENWOOD AVENUE
P.O. BOX 30515
RALEIGH, NORTH CAROLINA 27622-0515
Telephone: 919-571-3332
Fax: 919-571-9983
URL: http://www.lyncheatman.com

Business and Corporate Law, Mergers and Acquisitions, Zoning and Real Estate, Probate, Wills and Estate Administration and Taxation Law.

MEMBERS OF FIRM

MARIA M. LYNCH, born Nashville, Tennessee, November 7, 1953; admitted to bar, 1979, North Carolina. *Education:* University of Tennessee (B.A., with high honors, 1974); University of North Carolina (J.D., with honors, 1979). Order of the Coif. Research Editor, University of North Carolina Law Review, 1978-1979. Law Clerk to Hon. J. Dickson Phillips, Jr., U.S. Circuit Judge, U.S. Court of Appeals for the Fourth Circuit, 1979-1980. Adjunct Professor of Law, University of North Carolina School of Law, 2005. *Member:* Wake County and North Carolina (Member, Council, Estate Planning and Fiduciary Law Section, 1987-1990; 2004—) Bar Associations; North Carolina State Bar (Councilor, 1993-2001). Fellow, American College of Trust and Estate Counsel. (Board Certified Specialist, Estate Planning and Probate Law, North Carolina State Board of Legal Specialization). **PRACTICE AREAS:** Estate Planning; Taxation. **Email:** mml@lyncheatman.com

JEROME R. EATMAN, JR., born Cheyenne, Wyoming, December 4, 1956; admitted to bar, 1982, North Carolina; 1985, U.S. Tax Court. *Education:* University of North Carolina (A.B., 1979; J.D., 1982). *Member:* North Carolina Bar Association. **PRACTICE AREAS:** Land Use and Zoning; Commercial Real Property; Business Acquisitions and Financing. **Email:** jre@lyncheatman.com

KATHERINE B. WILKERSON, born Winston-Salem, North Carolina, May 10, 1967; admitted to bar, 1992, North Carolina, U.S. District Court, Eastern District of North Carolina and U.S. Court of Appeals, Fourth Circuit. *Education:* Smith College (A.B., 1989); University of North Carolina at Chapel Hill (J.D., 1992). *Member:* Wake County and North Carolina (Chair, Young Lawyers Division, 2002-2003; Member: Board of Governors, 2002-2003; Real Property Section;) Bar Associations; North Carolina State Bar. **PRACTICE AREAS:** Commercial Real Estate; Business; Land Use and Zoning. **Email:** kbw@lyncheatman.com

REPRESENTATIVE CLIENTS: BrodyCo., Inc.; Hughes/Weingarten Development Company; The Medical Foundation of North Carolina; Sprint PCS; York Properties, Inc.

MACCORD MASON PLLC

Established in 1987
510 GLENWOOD AVENUE, SUITE 321
RALEIGH, NORTH CAROLINA 27611
Telephone: 919-664-8624
Fax: 919-664-8625
URL: http://www.maccordmason.com

Wilmington, North Carolina Office: 1209 Culbreth Drive, Suite 103, 28405. Telephone: 910-256-3557. Fax: 910-256-0523.
Greensboro, North Carolina Office: 300 North Greene Street, Suite 1600, 27402. Telephone: 336-273-4422. Fax: 336-271-2830.

Patent, Trademark, Copyright and Unfair Competition. Trade Secret Practice before all Courts. Intellectual Property Law, Litigation.

FIRM PROFILE: MacCord Mason PLLC is a law firm with offices in Greensboro, Raleigh and Wilmington, North Carolina. The firm concentrates in intellectual property and technology-related law, including United States and international patents, trademarks, copyrights, trade secrets, unfair competition, licensing and related litigation and contract matters. The attorneys making up the firm have diverse backgrounds in corporate and private practice in the intellectual property field, bringing to the firm a wide scope of experience in handling the range of issues faced in connection with intellectual property law, such as procurement, exploitation and enforcement of rights, In addition, defense against infringement claims is an important part of the firm's practice. The geographic scope of the practice is unlimited, with clients throughout North Carolina, the United States and the world. Intellectual property rights in foreign countries are obtained in cooperation with the firm's foreign associate law firms.

(This Listing Continued)

OF COUNSEL

JINAN GLASGOW, born Meadville, Pennsylvania, May 4, 1968; admitted to bar, 1999, North Carolina; registered to practice before U.S. Patent and Trademark Office. *Education:* North Carolina State University (B.S., Textile Engineering, with distinction, 1990); University of North Carolina (J.D., 1999); Duke University (M.T.S., with distinction, 2000). Former United States Patent Examiner. *Member:* North Carolina and American Bar Associations; Triangle Intellectual Property Law Association; American Intellectual Property Law Association; Carolina Intellectual Property Law Association (Founder and President, 1996-1997). **PRACTICE AREAS:** Patents; Trademarks; Copyrights; Patent Licensing. **Email:** jinang@trianglepatents.com

(For complete biographical data on all personnel, see Professional Biographies at Greensboro, North Carolina)

MAITIN LAW FIRM

8396 SIX FORKS ROAD, SUITE 201
RALEIGH, NORTH CAROLINA 27615
Telephone: 919-846-1057
Fax: 919-846-1058
Email: Larry@Maitinlaw.com

Creditors Rights, Real Estate, Foreclosures, Collections, Bankruptcy.

LAWRENCE S. MAITIN, born Brooklyn, New York, October 25, 1968; admitted to bar, 1994, North Carolina, U.S. District Courts, Eastern, Western and Middle Districts of North Carolina. *Education:* State University of New York at Stony Brook (B.A., Economics, 1991); Ohio Northern University College of Law (J.D., 1994). Recipient, American Jurisprudence Award, Law and Accounting. Author: "NC Real Property Foreclosure Procedures," National Business Institute, 2004. *Member:* North Carolina Bar Association (Member, Bankruptcy and Real Estate Sections). **Email:** Larry@Maitinlaw.com

MAITLAND & MAITLAND, PLLC

RALEIGH, NORTH CAROLINA

(See Chapel Hill)

Real Estate, Closings, Residential, Commercial, Business Law, Entrepreneurial, Partnerships, Small Business, Entrepreneur, Business Formation, Immigration, Naturalization, Citizenship, Permanent Resident, Investor, Teacher Visas, H1B, J1, Visa Petitions, Litigation, Banking, Contracts, Foreclosure, Mortgages, Personal Injury, Traffic Violations, DWI, DUI, Liquor License, Alcohol Permit, Wills, Banking, Collection, Sports, Entertainment Law.

MANNING & CROUCH

CAPITAL CLUB BUILDING, SUITE 1104
16 WEST MARTIN STREET
P.O. BOX 350
RALEIGH, NORTH CAROLINA 27602
Telephone: 919-828-5778
Fax: 919-828-5045
Email: manninglaw@att.net
URL: http://www.lawyers.com/manning&crouch

Criminal Trials in State and Federal Courts, Criminal Fraud, Criminal Tax Matters, Grand Jury Investigation, Homicide, Federal Grand Jury, Criminal and Regulatory Investigations, Driving While Intoxicated (DWI), Driving While Impaired, Traffic Violations, Homicide, Sex Crimes, Drug Crimes.

FIRM PROFILE: Manning & Crouch, with practice limited to criminal defense matters, was founded in 1995 by Thomas C. Manning following an eighteen-year career as federal judicial law clerk, federal prosecutor, and criminal defense specialist with a prominent general practice law firm. James A. Crouch joined the firm in 1997 after serving for several years as trial counsel with North Carolina Prisoner Legal Services. The firm's practice is exclusively criminal defense, handling criminal cases and other criminal matters ranging from complex federal grand jury and trial matters in white-collar and controlled substances cases, to homicide and other violent felonies, domestic and sexual assaults, fraud and controlled substances cases, and traffic offenses such as Driving While Impaired, Revoked License and other serious misdemeanors. Both members are active in Bar matters. Thomas C. Manning is a frequent CLE lecturer and has served as an officer in a variety of local and statewide legal organizations. The firm carries the highest rating from Martindale-Hubbell and is listed in the Bar Register of Preeminent Lawyers.

THOMAS C. MANNING, born Durham, North Carolina, January 4, 1952; admitted to bar, 1977, North Carolina, South Carolina and U.S. District Court, Eastern District of North Carolina; 1979, U.S. Court of Appeals, Fourth Circuit; 1980, U.S. District Court, Middle and Western Districts of North Carolina; 1984, U.S. Supreme Court; 1986, U.S. District Court, District of South Carolina. *Education:* Virginia Episcopal School; University of North Carolina (A.B., 1974); University of South Carolina Law School (J.D., 1977). Phi Delta Phi. Senior Law Clerk to Chief Judge John D. Larkins, Jr., U.S. District Court, Eastern District of North Carolina, 1977-1978. Lecturer: Federal Public Defender Panel Lawyer Seminars. Assistant U.S. Attorney, Eastern District of North Carolina, 1978-1980. U.S. Commissioner, 1980. Permanent Delegate, Fourth Circuit Judicial Conference. Member, North Carolina Sentencing and Policy Advisory Commission, 1993-2000. Member and Secretary, Committee on Local Rules of Practice, 1978-1980 and Member, Pretrial Services Study Committee, 1983-1984, U.S. District Court, Eastern District of North Carolina. Chair, Committee on Indigent Appointments, Tenth Judicial District of North Carolina, 1984-1987 and 2002-2003. *Member:* Wake County (Board of Directors, 1988-1989; Public Defender Selections Committee, 2005), North Carolina (Board Member, Criminal Justice Section, 1984—and Chair, 1994; Annual Lecturer, Criminal Law) and American Bar As-

(This Listing Continued)

MANNING & CROUCH, Raleigh—Continued

sociations; South Carolina Bar; The North Carolina State Bar (Member, Criminal Law Specialization Examiners, 1992-1995; 2000-2003; Chair, 2003-2005); The Association of Trial Lawyers of America; National Association of Criminal Defense Lawyers; North Carolina Academy of Trial Lawyers; North Carolina College of Advocacy; Wake County Academy of Criminal Trial Lawyers (President, 2004). (Board Certified Specialist in Criminal Law, North Carolina State Board of Legal Specialization). ***PRACTICE AREAS:*** Homicide; Federal Criminal Law; Criminal Fraud; Drug Crimes.

JAMES A. CROUCH, born Winston-Salem, North Carolina, August 22, 1966; admitted to bar, 1992, North Carolina; 1993, U.S. District Court, Eastern District of North Carolina; 1994, U.S. District Court, Middle District of North Carolina and U.S. Court of Appeals, Fourth Circuit; 1995, U.S. District Court, Western District of North Carolina. *Education:* East Carolina University (B.A., Economics and Political Science); Campbell University School of Law (J.D., 1992). *Member:* North Carolina Bar Association; Wake County Academy of Criminal Defense Lawyers; North Carolina Academy of Trial Lawyers; National Academy of Criminal Defense Lawyers. ***PRACTICE AREAS:*** Driving While Intoxicated; Traffic Violations.

LEGAL SUPPORT PERSONNEL

CHRISTY BOLING (Paralegal)

NICHOLE STEPHENSON, (Paralegal)

MANNING, FULTON & SKINNER, P.A.

Established in 1954

GLENWOOD PLAZA
SUITE 500, 3605 GLENWOOD AVENUE
P.O. BOX 20389
RALEIGH, NORTH CAROLINA 27619-0389
Telephone: 919-787-8880
Telecopier: 919-787-8902 (Litigation); 781-0811 (Real Estate); 571-2504 (Business-Tax)
Email: manager@manningfulton.com
URL: http://www.manningfulton.com

Alternative Dispute Resolution, Appellate; Bankruptcy, Condemnation, Corporate/Business Entities, Corporate Finance, Employee Benefits/ERISA, Employment, Estate/Trust Administration, Estate Planning/Wealth Transfer, Family Law, Franchise, Government Relations, Litigation, Mergers/Acquisitions, Real Property, Sports/Entertainment, Tax Controversies, Tax Planning.

FIRM PROFILE: The firm of Manning, Fulton & Skinner, P.A. was formed in 1954 by Howard E. Manning and Charles L. Fulton, joined shortly by William P. Skinner, Jr. It is a general practice firm, offering a wide range of legal services with extensive experience in the following industries: Agribusiness, Automotive, Construction, Financial Services, Franchise, Government, Hospitality, Insurance, Manufacturing/Sales, Medical Practices, Publishing, Real Estate, Sports/Entertainment, Technology, and Warehouse/Distribution. It's members serve in numerous leadership roles in bar organizations, participate in continuing legal education seminars, and are involved in community, church and civic activities.

The firm is listed in the Bar Register of Preeminent Lawyers.

HOWARD E. MANNING (1914-2002)

CHARLES L. FULTON, born Highlands, North Carolina, December 11, 1927; admitted to bar, 1950, North Carolina. *Education:* University of North Carolina (A.B., 1947; J.D., 1950). Order of the Coif; Phi Delta Phi. Associate Editor, North Carolina Law Review, 1949-1950. *Member:* Wake County and North Carolina (Member, Board of Governors, 1980-1985; President, 1983-1984) Bar Associations; North Carolina State Bar (Member, 1984-1989 and Chairman, 1984-1985, Client Security Fund Board of Trustees; Member, Board of Legal Specialization, 1989-1992); American College of Real Estate Lawyers. Fellow, American College of Mortgage Attorneys. (Board Certified Specialist in Real Property Law-Business, Commercial and Industrial Transactions, North Carolina State Board of Legal Specialization). ***PRACTICE AREAS:*** Commercial Real Estate; Financing and Leasing Law. ***Email:*** fulton@manningfulton.com

WILLIAM P. SKINNER, JR., born Elizabeth City, North Carolina, July 31, 1929; admitted to bar, 1956, North Carolina. *Education:* University of North Carolina (A.B., 1951; J.D., 1956). Phi Delta Phi. Member, Staff of the North Carolina Law Review, 1954-1956. *Member:* Wake County and North Carolina (Chairman, Probate and Fiduciary Law Section, 1982) Bar Associations. ***PRACTICE AREAS:*** Estate Planning Law; Probate Law; Fiduciary Law. ***Email:*** skinner@manningfulton.com

JOHN B. McMILLAN, born Rochester, Minnesota, August 31, 1942; admitted to bar, 1967, North Carolina. *Education:* University of North Carolina (A.B., 1964; J.D., 1967). Phi Delta Phi. *Member:* Wake County (President, 1985) and North Carolina Bar Associations; North Carolina State Bar (Councilor, 1998—; Member, Disciplinary Hearing Commission, 1981-1990; Chairman, 1986-1990); North Carolina Academy of Trial Lawyers. ***PRACTICE AREAS:*** Litigation; Administrative Law; Legislative Law; Matrimonial Law. ***Email:*** mcmillan@manningfulton.com

W. GERALD THORNTON, born Clinton, North Carolina, May 13, 1942; admitted to bar, 1967, North Carolina and U.S. Tax Court. *Education:* University of North Carolina (B.S., 1964; J.D., 1967). Attorney, Office of Chief Counsel, Internal Revenue Service, 1967-1970. *Member:* Wake County, North Carolina (Chairman, Taxation Section, 1981-1983; Member, Board of Governors, 1988-1991; Tax Section Council Member, 1979-1988; Chairman, Estate Planning and Taxation CLE Curriculum Advisory Committee, 1985-1987) and American Bar Associations. Fellow: American College of Trust and Estate Counsel; American College of Tax Counsel. ***PRACTICE AREAS:*** Tax Law; Estate Planning Law; Business Planning Law. ***Email:*** thornton@manningfulton.com

CHARLES B. MORRIS, JR. (1936-1995)

(This Listing Continued)

M. MARSHALL HAPPER III, born Kinston, North Carolina, July 11, 1938; admitted to bar, 1963, North Carolina; 1968, U.S. District Court, Eastern District of North Carolina; 1979, U.S. District Court, Middle District of North Carolina; 1981, New York; 1996, Connecticut. *Education:* University of North Carolina (A.B., 1961; LL.B./J.D., 1963). Phi Delta Phi. *Member:* Wake County (Director, 1972), North Carolina (Member, Real Property Committee, 1973-1980; Chairman, Modernization of Land Record Committee, 1977-1978; Chairman, Standard Real Estate Forms Subcommittee, 1975-1981; Vice Chairman, Real Property Section, 1980-1981; Chairman, Sports and Entertainment Law Section, 2000-2001) and American Bar Associations; North Carolina State Bar. ***REPORTED CASES:*** Pipkin v. Thomas & Hill, 33 NC App. 710 (1977), 298 NC 278 (1979) (breach of contract to lend money); Furst v. Loftin 29 NC App. 268 (1976) (wrongful foreclosure). ***TRANSACTIONS:*** Contracts for U.S. Open Tennis Championships for the sales of television rights, sponsorship rights, and various other sports and business contracts for the U.S. Open and the United States Tennis Association. ***PRACTICE AREAS:*** Sports Law; Entertainment Law; Contracts; Corporate Law; Real Estate; Litigation. ***Email:*** happer@manningfulton.com

MICHAEL T. MEDFORD, born Waynesville, North Carolina, April 29, 1951; admitted to bar, 1976, North Carolina. *Education:* University of North Carolina (A.B., 1973); Columbia University (J.D., 1976). Phi Beta Kappa. Recipient: Morehead Scholar; Harlan Fiske Stone Scholar. Member, Board of Editors, Columbia Law Review, 1975-1976. Law Clerk to Judge Donald Russell, U.S. Court of Appeals, Fourth Circuit, 1976-1977. Member, Federal Bar Advisory Council, 1993-1996. *Member:* Wake County, North Carolina and American Bar Associations. ***PRACTICE AREAS:*** Commercial Litigation; Insurance Litigation; Employment Litigation; ERISA. ***Email:*** medford@manningfulton.com

SAMUEL T. OLIVER, JR., born Greensboro, North Carolina, February 28, 1952; admitted to bar, 1979, North Carolina. *Education:* Wake Forest University (B.A., magna cum laude, 1974); University of North Carolina (J.D., 1979). Phi Beta Kappa. Adjunct Associate Professor of Law, University of North Carolina School of Law, 1998—. *Member:* Wake County and North Carolina Bar Associations; American College of Real Estate Lawyers. (Board Certified Specialist in Real Property Law-Business, Commercial and Industrial Transactions, North Carolina State Board of Legal Specialization). ***TRANSACTIONS:*** Multistate Real Estate Acquisitions and Financings. ***PRACTICE AREAS:*** Real Estate Law; Business Law; Real Estate Finance; Leases. ***Email:*** oliver@manningfulton.com

DAVID D. DAHL, born Burlington, North Carolina, June 14, 1952; admitted to bar, 1980, Ohio and U.S. Tax Court; 1983, North Carolina. *Education:* Washington & Lee University (B.A., 1973); Bristol University, England; University of North Carolina (J.D., 1979). Phi Beta Kappa; Omicron Delta Epsilon. Attorney, Office of Chief Counsel, Internal Revenue Service, 1979-1982. *Member:* Wake County, North Carolina and American (Council Member, Tax Section, 1987—; Chairman, 1991-1992) Bar Associations. ***PRACTICE AREAS:*** Tax Controversies Law; Trusts and Estates; General Corporate. ***Email:*** dahl@manningfulton.com

CHARLES E. NICHOLS, JR., born Greensboro, North Carolina, August 11, 1956; admitted to bar, 1982, North Carolina. *Education:* Duke University (B.A., magna cum laude, 1978); University of North Carolina (M.B.A. and J.D., with honors, 1982). Beta Gamma Sigma. *Member:* Wake County, North Carolina and American Bar Associations. (Board Certified Specialist in Real Property Law: Business, Commercial and Industrial Transactions, North Carolina State Board of Legal Specialization). ***PRACTICE AREAS:*** Real Estate Law; Land Use; Construction Law. ***Email:*** nichols@manningfulton.com

BARRY D. MANN, born Morehead City, North Carolina, December 30, 1956; admitted to bar, 1982, North Carolina. *Education:* University of North Carolina (B.S., 1979; J.D., 1982). Beta Gamma Sigma; Phi Delta Phi. *Member:* Wake County, North Carolina (Council Member, Real Property Section, 1999—; Chair, 2003-2004) and American Bar Associations. ***PRACTICE AREAS:*** Real Estate Law; Title Matters. ***Email:*** mann@manningfulton.com

JOHN C. DORSEY, born Cleveland, Ohio, June 4, 1946; admitted to bar, 1972, Ohio (Inactive); 1980, U.S. Tax Court; 1986, North Carolina. *Education:* Wittenberg University (B.A., 1968); George Washington University (J.D., with honors, 1972). *Member:* Wake County, North Carolina (Council Member, Tax Section, 1993—; Vice Chair, 2004-2005) and American Bar Associations; North Carolina State Bar. ***PRACTICE AREAS:*** ERISA Law; Estate Planning Law; Corporate Law; Health Law. ***Email:*** dorsey@manningfulton.com

WILLIAM C. SMITH, JR., born Wilson, North Carolina, February 24, 1961; admitted to bar, 1987, North Carolina. *Education:* University of North Carolina at Chapel Hill (B.A., 1983; J.D., 1987). Phi Delta Phi. *Member:* Wake County and North Carolina Bar Associations. ***PRACTICE AREAS:*** Civil Litigation; Bankruptcy. ***Email:*** smith@manningfulton.com

DEBORAH L. HILDEBRAN-BACHOFEN, born Albemarle, North Carolina, July 12, 1953; admitted to bar, 1984, North Carolina and U.S. Tax Court. *Education:* Wingate College (A.A., 1973); University of North Carolina (B.S.B.A., 1976; J.D., 1984). Phi Theta Kappa. Certified Public Accountant, North Carolina, 1978. Attorney, Office of Chief Counsel, Internal Revenue Service, 1984-1987. Special Assistant U.S. Attorney, Middle District, 1986-1987. *Member:* Wake County, North Carolina (Council Member, 2002-2004; Treasurer, 2004-2005; Chair, Estate Administration Manual Committee, 2001-2004; Council Member, Estate Planning and Fiduciary Law Section; Council Member, Tax Section, 1997-2000) and American Bar Associations. Fellow, American College of Trust and Estate Counsel. (Board Certified Specialist in Estate Planning and Probate Law, North Carolina State Board of Legal Specialization). ***PRACTICE AREAS:*** Tax Law; Estate Planning and Probate Law; Business Planning Law; Mergers and Acquisitions; Corporate Finance. ***Email:*** hildebran@manningfulton.com

STEPHEN T. BYRD, born Roanoke Rapids, North Carolina, July 4, 1957; admitted to bar, 1984, North Carolina. *Education:* University of North Carolina at Chapel Hill (B.S., 1979; J.D., 1984). Phi Beta Kappa; Beta Alpha Psi; Beta Gamma Sigma; Phi Eta Sigma. Member of Staff, North Carolina Journal of International Law and Commercial Regulation, 1983-1984. Certified Public Accountant, North Carolina, 1982. Author: "Tax Consequences of Distributions of Appreciated Property by Pass-Through Entities," Journal of Partnership Taxation, Spring, 1989. *Member:* Wake County and North Carolina (Editor, Tax Section Newsletter, 1989-1991; Council Member, 1990-1993, 1994-1996, Chair,

(This Listing Continued)

1999-2000, Tax Section; Director, Young Lawyers Division, 1990-1992; Member, Young Lawyers Division Executive Council, 1987-1992) Bar Associations; North Carolina Association of Certified Public Accountants; Wake County Estate Planning Council. (Board Certified Specialist in Estate Planning and Probate Law, North Carolina State Board of Legal Specialization). ***PRACTICE AREAS:*** Tax; Estate Planning; Corporate; Partnership; Limited Liability Company Law; Corporate Finance. ***Email:*** byrd@manningfulton.com

MICHAEL S. HARRELL, born Norfolk, Virginia, December 20, 1962; admitted to bar, 1990, North Carolina. *Education:* Old Dominion University (B.A., 1985); Wake Forest University (M.A., 1987); University of Virginia (J.D., 1990). Member, National Communications Association, 1987-2004. *Member:* Wake County (10th Judicial District Committee on Professionalism, 1998—), North Carolina and American Bar Associations; North Carolina State Bar. ***PRACTICE AREAS:*** Commercial Litigation; Appellate Practice; Collections; Domestic Relations; Alternative Dispute Resolution. ***Email:*** harrell@manningfulton.com

ALISON R. CAYTON, born Charlotte, North Carolina, July 5, 1964; admitted to bar, 1991, North Carolina. *Education:* University of the South (B.A., cum laude, 1986); University of North Carolina at Chapel Hill (J.D., 1991; M.R.P., 1991). Omicron Delta Kappa. *Member:* Wake County, North Carolina and American Bar Associations; American Planning Association. (Board Certified Specialist in Real Property Law: Business, Commercial and Industrial Transactions, North Carolina State Board of Legal Specialization). ***PRACTICE AREAS:*** Real Estate Law; Real Estate Finance; Title Matters. ***Email:*** cayton@manningfulton.com

CARY ELIZABETH CLOSE, born Norfolk, Virginia, August 4, 1959; admitted to bar, 1991, North Carolina. *Education:* University of North Carolina at Chapel Hill (B.A., 1981); Campbell University (J.D., cum laude, 1991). Notes and Comments Editor, Campbell Law Review, 1991. *Member:* Wake County and North Carolina Bar Associations. ***PRACTICE AREAS:*** Family Law; Appellate Practice. ***Email:*** close@manningfulton.com

KRISTEN GARDNER LINGO, born North Wilkesboro, North Carolina, August 5, 1967; admitted to bar, 1993, North Carolina. *Education:* University of North Carolina at Chapel Hill (B.A., 1989; J.D., with honors, 1993). Morehead Scholar. Phi Beta Kappa. Member: Invitational Moot Court Team, 1992-1993; Holderness Moot Court Bench, 1992-1993. Staff Member, North Carolina Law Review, 1992-1993. *Member:* Wake County, North Carolina (Division Director, Young Lawyers Division, 2000-2003) and American Bar Associations. ***PRACTICE AREAS:*** Civil Litigation; Employment Litigation and Counseling. ***Email:*** lingo@manningfulton.com

THOMAS C. KILPATRICK, born Johnson City, Tennessee, May 25, 1971; admitted to bar, 1996, North Carolina. *Education:* University of North Carolina at Chapel Hill (B.S., with honors, 1993; J.D., with honors, 1996). Phi Beta Kappa; Beta Gamma Sigma; Phi Alpha Delta; Order of the Barristers. Member: Environmental Law Negotiation Moot Court Team; Holderness Moot Court Bench, 1994-1996.*Member:* Wake County, North Carolina and American Bar Associations. ***PRACTICE AREAS:*** Litigation. ***Email:*** kilpatrick@manningfulton.com

S. NICOLE TAYLOR, born Elizabeth City, North Carolina, June 9, 1970; admitted to bar, 1996, North Carolina. *Education:* East Carolina University (B.A., magna cum laude, 1992); University of North Carolina (J.D., 1996). *Member:* Wake County, North Carolina and American Bar Associations. ***PRACTICE AREAS:*** Civil Litigation; Family Law; Alternative Dispute Resolution. ***Email:*** ntaylor@manningfulton.com

JUDSON A. WELBORN, born Durham, North Carolina, April 8, 1973; admitted to bar, 1998, North Carolina. *Education:* University of North Carolina at Chapel Hill (B.A., 1995); Campbell University (J.D., 1998). Phi Alpha Delta. Recipient, North Carolina Academy of Trial Lawyers Calhoun Advocacy Award, 1998. *Member:* Wake County (Member, Public Service Committee, 2002—; Member, Professionalism Committee, 2002—), North Carolina and American Bar Associations; North Carolina Young Lawyers Division (Member: Lawyer Effectiveness Committee, 1998—; Co-Chair, 2002-2004; Executive Council, 2002—). ***PRACTICE AREAS:*** Commercial Litigation; Real Property Litigation. ***Email:*** welborn@manningfulton.com

SANDRA M. CLARK, born Orlando, Florida, September 21, 1963; admitted to bar, 1994, North Carolina. *Education:* Campbell University (B.B.A., cum laude, 1985; J.D., cum laude, 1994). Business Editor, Campbell University Law Review, 1993-1994. Certified Public Accountant, 1990. Dean, Delta Theta Phi, 1993-1994. *Member:* Wake County and North Carolina Bar Associations; North Carolina Association of Certified Public Accountants; Wake County Estate Planning Council. (Board Certified Specialist in Estate Planning and Probate Law, North Carolina State Board of Legal Specialization). ***PRACTICE AREAS:*** Estate Planning; Probate; Corporate Law; Taxation. ***Email:*** clark@manningfulton.com

LEANOR BAILEY HODGE, born Philadelphia, Pennsylvania, May 23, 1971; admitted to bar, 1997, Pennsylvania; 1998, Illinois, 2000, North Carolina. *Education:* Howard University (B.B.A., 1993); Temple University School of Law (J.D., 1996). *Member:* Wake County, North Carolina and American Bar Associations; North Carolina Association of Black Lawyers. ***PRACTICE AREAS:*** Civil Litigation; Condemnation. ***Email:*** hodge@manningfulton.com

RITCHIE W. TAYLOR, born Greensboro, North Carolina; admitted to bar, 1999, North Carolina; 2000, U.S. Tax Court. *Education:* Brigham Young University (B.S., 1996; J.D., cum laude, 1999). Phi Delta Phi. Managing Editor, Brigham Young University Journal of Public Law, 1998-1999. Author: "Domestic Asset Protection Trusts: The Estate Planning Tool of the Decade or a Charlatan?" 13 Brigham Young University Journal of Public Law 163 (1998). Co-Author: Modifying and Terminating Irrevocable Trusts - Navigating the Statutory Maze," The Will and the Way, Vol. 21 No. 4 June 2002, p 12 (2002). *Member:* North Carolina State Bar. ***LANGUAGES:*** Portuguese. ***PRACTICE AREAS:*** Taxation; Corporate Finance; Partnership Law; Corporate Law; Franchise Law. ***Email:*** rtaylor@manningfulton.com

ANSLEY CHAPMAN CELLA, born August 18, 1973; admitted to bar, 1998, South Carolina; 2001, North Carolina. *Education:* Clemson University (B.A., 1994); University of South Carolina (J.D., 1998); University of Miami (LL.M., in Estate Planning, 2000). Phi Delta Phi. Law Clerk, Hon. Paula H. Thomas, Fifteenth Judicial Circuit of South Carolina, 1998-1999. *Member:* Wake County and North Carolina Bar Associations; South Carolina Bar. ***PRACTICE AREAS:*** Estate Planning; Taxation; Corporate. ***Email:*** acella@manningfulton.com

DAVID G. MARTIN, born Chapel Hill, North Carolina, July 8, 1965; admitted to bar, 1996, North Carolina. *Education:* University of North Carolina at Chapel Hill (B.A., 1991); Campbell University School of Law (J.D., 1996); Boston University (LL.M., Taxation, 1997). *Member:* New Hanover County and North Carolina Bar Associations. ***PRACTICE AREAS:*** Real Estate; Finance. ***Email:*** martin@manningfulton.com

FRANKLIN E. MARTIN, born Fayetteville, North Carolina, April 19, 1938; admitted to bar, 1968, North Carolina; 1972, U.S. Supreme Court and U.S. District Court, Eastern District of North Carolina; 1979, U.S. Court of Appeals, 4th Circuit. *Education:* University of North Carolina at Chapel Hill (B.A., 1960; J.D., 1967). Phi Delta Phi. Lecturer, Wake Forest University Law School Continuing Legal Education Series on Will Drafting, Probate and Estate Planning, 1983, 1984, 1987, 1990 and 1991. Speaker: North Carolina Bar Foundation, Continuing Legal Education Seminar on Real Property, 1993, 2004. *Member:* New Hanover County (President, 1988-1989) and North Carolina (Member, Board of Governors, 1996-1999; Member, Secretary, Vice Chair and Chair of Council, Real Property Section) Bar Associations; Fifth Judicial District Bar (Member, 1982-1997 and Chair, 1986-1997, Bar Candidate Committee); North Carolina State Bar (Member, Lawyers Trust Accounts Committee, 1989-1993; Disciplinary Hearing Commission, 1995-2000; Vice Chair, Chair 2004 and Member, 2000—,Board of Legal Specialization). [Lieutenant, U.S. Naval Reserve, active duty, 1960-1964]. (Board Certified Specialist in Real Property Law - Residential Transactions, North Carolina State Board of Legal Specialization). ***Email:*** fmartin@manningfulton.com

---

NICOLE SABOURIN LOEFFLER, born Bitburg, Germany, June 27, 1973; admitted to bar, 2000, North Carolina. *Education:* University of Oregon (B.I.arc, 1996); Robert D. Clark Honors College (with distinction, 1996); University of North Carolina (J.D., 2000). Note Editor, North Carolina Law Review, 1999-2000. *Member:* Wake County; North Carolina and American Bar Associations. ***PRACTICE AREAS:*** Civil Litigation. ***Email:*** loeffler@manningfulton.com

EVAN B. HORWITZ, born Raleigh, North Carolina, June 27, 1975; admitted to bar, 2001, North Carolina. *Education:* Indiana University (B.A., 1997); Campbell University (J.D., 2001). Managing Editor, Campbell Law Review, 2000-2001. Law Clerk to Justice Robert F. Orr, North Carolina Supreme Court. *Member:* Wake County (Member, North Carolina Young Lawyers Division, 2001—) and North Carolina Bar Associations; North Carolina State Bar;. ***PRACTICE AREAS:*** Commercial Litigation; Family Law; Appellate Practice; Alternative Dispute Resolution. ***Email:*** horwitz@manningfulton.com

JOHN R. CELLA, JR., born Raleigh, North Carolina; admitted to bar, 2000, South Carolina; 2001, North Carolina. *Education:* University of North Carolina (B.A., 1994); University of South Carolina (B.A., 1996; J.D., 1999); John Marshall Law School (LL.M., with honors, Employee Benefits, 2003). Phi Delta Phi. Ellis, Lawhorne & Sims Journal Competition Writing Award. Member, Student Editorial Board, American Bar Association Real Property, Probate and Trust Journal, 1998-1999. Author: "The Pursuit of Proceeds by Plans, Participants, and Plaintiffs' Lawyers: Dissonant Solutions to an Alliterative Problem," 22 Campbell Law Review 317 (2000). Member, Triangle Benefits Forum. *Member:* North Carolina; South Carolina and Wake County Bar Associations. ***PRACTICE AREAS:*** ERISA; Employee Benefits; Executive Compensation; ERISA Litigation. ***Email:*** jcella@manningfulton.com

JENNIFER L. WEAVER, born Kodiak, Alaska, August 4, 1971; admitted to bar, 2001, North Carolina. *Education:* Smith College (B.A., 1993); Duke University School of Law (J.D., 2001). *Member:* Wake County, Durham County and North Carolina Bar Associations. ***PRACTICE AREAS:*** Estate Planning; Taxation; Corporate Law. ***Email:*** weaver@manningfulton.com

DAVID B. EFIRD, born Augusta, Georgia, September 19, 1978; admitted to bar, 2004, North Carolina. *Education:* University of North Carolina at Chapel Hill (B.S.B.A., 2001; J.D., 2004). ***PRACTICE AREAS:*** Commercial Litigation; Insurance Litigation. ***Email:*** efird@manningfulton.com

REPRESENTATIVE CLIENTS: International Business Machines Corp.; Anheuser-Busch Cos.; Employees Reinsurance Corp.; General Parts, Inc. ("CARQUEST"); Pharmaceutical Research and Manufacturers of America, Inc.; Fonville Morisey Realty, Inc.; Jordan Lumber Company; Highwoods, Properties, Inc.; Prestage Farms, Inc.; United States Tennis Association.

ROGER MANUS

Established in 1998

1312 ANNAPOLIS DRIVE, SUITE 103
RALEIGH, NORTH CAROLINA 27608-2146
Telephone: 919-833-4600
Fax: 919-833-4726
Email: manuslaw@bellsouth.net
URL: http://www.manuslaw.com

Nursing Home Negligence, Class Actions, Mental Disability Law, Medicaid Appeals, Wrongful Death, Medical Malpractice, Disability Rights, Americans with Disabilities Act (ADA), Employment Discrimination, False Claims Act, Mental Health Law.

FIRM PROFILE: Our mission is to provide personalized legal representation in order to advance justice, self determination and respect for individuals with disabilities and others who have been seriously injured in care-giving settings, wrongfully deprived of supports, services or employment, or discriminated against.

ROGER MANUS, admitted to bar, 1979, North Carolina, U.S. Supreme Court, U.S. Court of Appeals, Fourth Circuit, U.S. District Court, Eastern, Western and Middle Districts of North Carolina. *Education:* Macalester College (B.A., 1974) Phi Beta Kappa; New York University (J.D., 1977). Wingspread Fellow, Macalester College. Root Tilden Public Interest Scholar, New York University. Author of Articles and CLE Lecturer regarding Mental

(This Listing Continued)

ROGER MANUS, Raleigh—Continued

Disability Law and Nursing Home Abuse Litigation. Adjunct Faculty, Law School, University of North Carolina at Chapel Hill, 1987 and 1988. Faculty, Developmental Disabilities Training Institute, University of North Carolina at Chapel Hill, 1977-1979. Class action lead attorney, 1982-1998, Thomas S.v. Bruton, F2d (4th Cir. 1986). President, Friends of Residents in Long Term Care (2004). Member, National Citizens Coalition for Nursing Home Reform. Recipient, Distinguished Service Awards, Mental Health Association of North Carolina and Community Living Association. *Member:* North Carolina State Bar; North Carolina Bar Association; North Carolina Academy of Trial Lawyers (Member, Nursing Home Litigation Group).

PARALEGALS

ROZANNE K. REYNOLDS, Assistant, Special Master, Federal Court, 1992-1996. ***Email:*** rozanne2@bellsouth.net

GERI LYN CROSS. *Education:* Central Pennsylvania Business College (A.S., 1982). ***Email:*** gerilyncross@bellsouth.net

ANDREW S. MARTIN

1026 WASHINGTON STREET
P.O. BOX 10406
RALEIGH, NORTH CAROLINA 27605-0406
Telephone: 919-828-5620
Telecopier: 919-828-5211
Email: asm@martinlaw.net

Residential and Commercial Real Estate Transactions, Estate Planning, Probate and Trusts, Corporations, Limited Liability Companies.

ANDREW S. MARTIN, born Washington, D.C., November 3, 1943; admitted to bar, 1969, North Carolina; 1976, U.S. Tax Court. *Education:* University of North Carolina at Chapel Hill (B.S., 1966); Wake Forest University (J.D., 1969). Phi Alpha Delta. *Member:* Wake County and North Carolina Bar Associations. ***PRACTICE AREAS:*** Residential Real Estate; Commercial Real Estate; Probate Law; Estate Planning; Business Enterprises.

APPROVED ATTORNEY FOR: Lawyers Title Insurance Co.; Commonwealth Land Title Insurance Co.; Investors Title Insurance Co.; Stewart Title Guaranty Co.; Fidelity National Title Insurance Co.; Chicago Title Insurance Co.
REFERENCES: Wachovia Bank, NA; The Fidelity Bank.

MARTIN & JONES

Established in 1982
SUITE 200
410 GLENWOOD AVENUE
RALEIGH, NORTH CAROLINA 27603
Telephone: 919-821-0005
URL: http://www.MartinandJones.com

Durham, North Carolina Office: University Towers, Suite 526. 3100 Tower Boulevard, 27707. Telephone: 919-544-3000.

Wilmington, North Carolina Office: 1213 Culbreth Drive, Suite 121, 28405. Telephone: 910-256-4005.

Atlanta, Georgia Office: 3353 Peachtree Road, NE, Suite 510, 30326. Telephone: 404-257-1117.

Asbestos Litigation, Bad Faith and Unfair Competition, Business Litigation, Construction Site Injuries, Inadequate Security, Medical Malpractice, Nursing/Rest Home Negligence, Personal Injury, Pharmaceutical and Medical Device Litigation, Product Liability, Social Security Disability, Toxic Torts, Trucking Accidents, Workers' Compensation and Wrongful Death, Land Condemnation, FELA (Federal Employers' Liability Act), Securities Fraud.

FIRM PROFILE: Martin & Jones is one of the largest law firms in North Carolina, limiting its practice to representation of plaintiffs in tort and insurance claims. The firm is comprised of 16 attorneys litigating claims in state and federal courts. The firm has offices in Raleigh, Durham and Wilmington, North Carolina, as well as Atlanta, Georgia, but its practice is by no means limited to these areas. Firm lawyers have represented plaintiffs from more than thirty states in courts throughout North Carolina, Georgia, California, New York, South Carolina, Tennessee, Rhode Island, Texas, Virginia, Wisconsin and other venues.

Martin & Jones has successfully represented individuals in claims against more than 30 of the 100 largest corporations in America. We are proud to represent people from all walks of life, and the firm has the experience and resources to aggressively do so, regardless of the size of the defendant.

JOHN ALAN JONES, born Pine Level, North Carolina, November 17, 1956; admitted to bar, 1982, North Carolina, U.S. District Court, Eastern, Middle and Western Districts of North Carolina and U.S Court of Appeals, 4th Circuit. *Education:* University of North Carolina at Chapel Hill (B.A., 1979; J.D., 1982). Phi Eta Sigma; Phi Beta Kappa; Holderness Moot Court Member. *Member:* Wake County, North Carolina and American Bar Associations; North Carolina State Bar; Association of Trial Lawyers of America; North Carolina Academy of Trial Lawyers. ***PRACTICE AREAS:*** Medical Malpractice; Obstetric Malpractice; Drug and Medical Device Litigation; Pediatric Malpractice; Products Liability; Surgeons Liability; Hospital Liability. ***Email:*** JAJ@M-J.COM

GREGORY M. MARTIN, born Concord, North Carolina, March 11, 1957; admitted to bar, 1982, North Carolina. *Education:* University of North Carolina at Chapel Hill (B.A., 1979; J.D., with honors, 1982). James M. Johnson Scholar. Phi Beta Kappa; Order of the Coif. Staff, North Carolina Law Review, 1980-1981. *Member:* Wake County and North Carolina Bar Associations; North Carolina State Bar; Association of Trial Lawyers of America; North Carolina Academy of Trial Lawyers. ***PRACTICE AREAS:*** Motor Vehicle Accidents and Injuries; Diet Drug Litigation; Brain Injury; Wrongful Death; Products Liability. ***Email:*** GMM@M-J.COM

E. SPENCER PARRIS, born Columbia, South Carolina, May 26, 1950; admitted to bar, 1983, South Carolina and North Carolina; 1996, Texas; U.S. Court of Appeals, Fourth and Eleventh Circuits; U.S. District Court, District of South Carolina and U.S. District Court, Eastern, Middle and Western Districts of North Carolina. *Education:* Clemson University (B.S., 1976); University of South Carolina (J.D., 1983). Associate Editor-in-Chief, South Carolina Law Review, 1982-1983. Recipient, Victor A. Michaelwitz for Excellence in Legal Writing. Instructor Legal Writing, University of South Carolina Law School, 1982-1983. Adjunct Professor, Meredith College. Law Clerk to U.S. District Judge Franklin T. Dupree, Jr., Eastern District of North Carolina, 1983-1985. *Member:* Wake County, North Carolina and South Carolina Bar Associations; North Carolina State Bar; Association of Trial Lawyers of America (State Delegate, 1997 & 2001—); North Carolina Academy of Trial Lawyers (Vice President Legal Affairs, 1999-2001; Vice President Legislative Affairs, 2001—). ***PRACTICE AREAS:*** Asbestos Litigation; Occupational Cancer; Mass Torts; Products Liability; Complex Litigation. ***Email:*** ESP@M-J.COM

HOYT G. TESSENER, admitted to bar, 1988, North Carolina, U.S. District Court, Eastern, Middle and Western Districts of North Carolina and U.S. Court of Appeals, Fourth Circuit. *Education:* North Carolina State University (B.S., 1983); Campbell University (J.D., with honors, 1988). ***PRACTICE AREAS:*** Nursing Home Negligence; Securities Fraud; Automobile Accidents and Injuries. ***Email:*** HGT@M-J.COM

H. FOREST HORNE, JR., born Munich, Germany, October 19, 1960; admitted to bar, 1989, North Carolina, U.S. District Court, Eastern, Middle and Western Districts of North Carolina and U.S. Court of Appeals, 4th Circuit. *Education:* University of Kentucky (B.A., 1982); Campbell University School of Law (J.D., 1989). Member: The Order of Barristers; National Moot Court Team. Articles Editor, Campbell Law Review, 1988-1989. *Member:* North Carolina State Bar; North Carolina Academy of Trial Lawyers (Co-Chair, Auto Torts, 1998-1999); Association of Trial Lawyers of America. ***PRACTICE AREAS:*** Professional Negligence; Defective Products; Business Fraud; Federal Employers Liability Act (FELA). ***Email:*** HFH@M-J.COM

JOHN MICHAEL RILEY, born Chapel Hill, North Carolina, April 11, 1966; admitted to bar, 1991, North Carolina; U.S. District Court, Eastern and Western Districts of North Carolina and U.S. Court of Appeals, Fourth Circuit. *Education:* Wake Forest University (B.S., 1988); University of North Carolina at Chapel Hill (J.D., 1991). *Member:* North Carolina Bar Association; North Carolina State Bar; The Association of Trial Lawyers of America; North Carolina Academy of Trial Lawyers. ***PRACTICE AREAS:*** Occupational Disease; Asbestos Litigation; Products Liability. ***Email:*** JMR@M-J.COM

THOMAS E. BARWICK, born Kinston, North Carolina, December 24, 1954; admitted to bar, 1980, North Carolina, and U.S. District Court, Eastern District of North Carolina. *Education:* East Carolina University (B.A., 1977); University of Richmond (J.D., 1980). Phi Sigma Pi; Delta Theta Phi. Member, University of Richmond Law Review, 1979-1980. *Member:* Wayne County (President, 1984-1985; Secretary, 1980-1981) and North Carolina Bar Associations; North Carolina Academy of Trial Lawyers; Association of Trial Lawyers of America. ***PRACTICE AREAS:*** Medical Malpractice; Obstetric Malpractice; Hospital Liability; Pediatric Malpractice; Surgeons Liability; Wrongful Death. ***Email:*** TEB@M-J.Com

G. CHRISTOPHER OLSON, born Durham, North Carolina, December 3, 1967; admitted to bar, 1994, North Carolina; 1996, U.S. District Court, Eastern, Middle and Western Districts of North Carolina and U.S. Court of Appeals, Fourth Circuit. *Education:* University of North Carolina at Chapel Hill (B.A., 1990); Campbell University (J.D., magna cum laude, 1994). Member, Campbell Law Review. Recipient, American Jurisprudence Book Awards: Civil Procedure, Federal Jurisdiction, Constitutional Law and Pretrial Litigation. Author: "State v. Garner: North Carolina Adopts the Inevitable Discovery Exception to the Exclusionary Rule," Campbell Law Review, Vol. 15, No. 3, Fall 1993. Law Clerk to the Honorable Franklin T. Dupree, U.S. District Judge for the Eastern District of North Carolina, 1994-1996. *Member:* North Carolina State Bar; North Carolina Bar Association; The Association of Trial Lawyers of America; North Carolina Academy of Trial Lawyers; Wake County Bar Association. ***PRACTICE AREAS:*** Personal Injury; Motor Vehicle Accidents and Injuries; Products Liability; Civil Rights. ***Email:*** gco@m-j.com

SCOTT BARTLEY GOODSON, born Chapel Hill, North Carolina, April 2, 1967; admitted to bar, 1996, North Carolina; U.S. District Court, Eastern and Middle Districts of North Carolina. *Education:* University of North Carolina at Chapel Hill (B.S.B.A., 1989); Wake Forest University (J.D., 1996). Phi Delta Phi. Wake Forest Law Review. National Moot Court Team. Order of Barristers. *Member:* North Carolina Academy of Trial Lawyers; The Association of Trial Lawyers of America. ***PRACTICE AREAS:*** Medical Malpractice; Hospital Liability; Drug and Medical Device Litigation; Civil Litigation. ***Email:*** SBG@M-J.COM

ELIZABETH TODD BEALL, born Atlanta, Georgia, March 15, 1968; admitted to bar, 1996, North Carolina. *Education:* University of North Carolina at Greensboro (B.A., 1990); Wake Forest University (J.D., 1996). *Member:* North Carolina State Bar; North Carolina and American Bar Associations; The Association of Trial Lawyers of America; North Carolina Association of Trial Lawyers. ***PRACTICE AREAS:*** Nursing Home Negligence; Automobile Accidents and Injuries; Truck Accidents; Commercial Vehicle Liability; Wrongful Death. ***Email:*** ECT@M-J.COM

SEAN A.B. COLE, born Oakwood, Virginia, April 29, 1971; admitted to bar, 1997, North Carolina. *Education:* King College (B.A., history, cum laude, 1994); Wake Forest University (J.D., 1997). Order of Barristers. Member: Moot Court; National Moot Court Team; Student Trial Bar. *Member:* Wake County and North Carolina Bar Associations; North Carolina Academy of Trial Lawyers; The Association of Trial Lawyers of America. ***PRACTICE AREAS:*** Automobile Accidents and Injuries; Truck Accidents; Commercial Vehicle Liability; Wrongful Death; Construction Injuries; Insurance Bad Faith; Products Liability; Sulzer Hip Litigation. ***Email:*** SAC@M-J.COM

KATHERINE N. BRICIO, born Raleigh, North Carolina, September 25, 1971; admitted to bar, 1999, North Carolina; U.S. District Court, Eastern, Western and Middle Districts of North Carolina. *Education:* University of North Carolina at Chapel Hill (B.A., 1992; J.D., with honors, 1999). Member, Holderness Moot Court. *Member:* North Carolina

(This Listing Continued)

Bar Association; North Carolina Academy of Trial Lawyers; North Carolina Association of Women Attorneys; Association of Trial Lawyers of America. ***PRACTICE AREAS:*** Medical Malpractice; Products Liability; Civil Litigation. ***Email:*** KNB@M-J.COM

JULIA ELLEN DIXON, born Raleigh, North Carolina, April 7, 1969; admitted to bar, 2001, North Carolina. *Education:* Meredith College (B.A., 1991); North Carolina State University (M.P.A., 1995); University of North Carolina at Chapel Hill (J.D., 2001). *Member:* North Carolina State Bar; North Carolina Association of Trial Lawyers. ***PRACTICE AREAS:*** Workers Compensation; Products Liability; Asbestos Litigation. ***Email:*** jed@m-j.com

MARTIN A. RAMEY, born Rome, Georgia, October 31, 1966; admitted to bar, 2002, California and U.S. District Court, Southern District of California; 2003, U.S. District Court, Central District of California and U.S. District Court, Southern District of Indiana; 2005, North Carolina. *Education:* Arizona State University (B.A., 1999); University of San Diego (J.D., 2002). Executive Comments Editor, 2001-2002, Member, 2000-2001, San Diego Law Review. Author: "Putting the Cart Before the Horse: The Need to Examine Damage Caps in California's Elder Abuse Act," 39 San Diego L. Rev. 599, 2002. ***LANGUAGES:*** Spanish. ***PRACTICE AREAS:*** Products Liability. ***Email:*** mar@m-j.com

CLINT W. SITTON, born Atlanta, Georgia, December 7, 1957; admitted to bar, 1983, Georgia; 1984, Georgia Court of Appeals and Supreme Court of Georgia; 1985, U.S. District Court, Southern District of Georgia and U.S. Court of Appeals, 11th Circuit; 1987, U.S. District Court, Northern and Middle Districts of Georgia (Not admitted in North Carolina). *Education:* Emory University (B.A., 1979; J.D., 1983). Law Clerk to Honorable John J. Bruner, Judge, State Court of Fulton County, Atlanta, Georgia, 1983-1984. *Member:* Savannah (Co-Chairman, Law Day Committee, Young Lawyers Section, 1985) and American Bar Associations; State Bar of Georgia; The Association of Trial Lawyers of America; Georgia Trial Lawyers Association (Law-Pac Chairman, 1991-1992; State Bar Liaison, 1992-1993; Long-Range Planning, 1993-1994; Publications Committee, 2001-2002); Trial Lawyers for Public Justice; Savannah Trial Lawyers Association. (Also practicing individually). ***PRACTICE AREAS:*** Asbestos Litigation; Products Liability; Personal Injury; Professional Negligence; Medical Malpractice; Aviation. ***Email:*** sittonlaw@atlanta-ics.com

SAMUEL L. STARKS, born Columbia, South Carolina, August 27, 1966; admitted to bar, 1994, District of Columbia; 1999, Georgia; U.S. District Court, Northern and Middle Districts of Georgia; U.S. Court of Appeals, 11th Circuit (Not admitted in North Carolina). *Education:* University of South Carolina (B.A., cum laude, 1989); Duke University (J.D., 1992). Phi Beta Kappa. Note Editor, Duke Law Journal, 1991-1992. Law Clerk to the Honorable Damon Keith, U.S. Court of Appeals, 6th Circuit, 1992-1993. Author: "Understanding Government Affirmative Action and Metro Broadcasting, Inc. v. FCC," 41 Duke L.J. 933 (1992). *Member:* State Bar of Georgia; District of Columbia Bar; The Association of Trial Lawyers of America; Georgia Trial Lawyers Association; Gate City Bar Association of Atlanta. [U.S. Army, 1984-1986]. ***PRACTICE AREAS:*** Civil Practice; Personal Injury; Products Liability; Medical Malpractice; Toxic Torts; Consumer Litigation. ***Email:*** sls@gsllaw.com

MAUPIN TAYLOR, P.A.

Established in 1870

HIGHWOODS TOWER ONE, SUITE 500
3200 BEECHLEAF COURT
P.O. DRAWER 19764
RALEIGH, NORTH CAROLINA 27604-1064
Telephone: 919-981-4000
Telecopier: 919-981-4300
URL: http://www.maupintaylor.com

Research Triangle Park, North Carolina Office: 480 Beta Building, Headquarters Park, Post Office Box 13646, 27709-3646. Telephone: 919-361-4900. Telecopier: 919-361-2262.

Wilmington, North Carolina Office: Landfall Park North, 1985 Eastwood Road, Suite 200, 28403. Telephone: 910-256-5135. Telecopier: 910-256-6451.

Agribusiness, Administrative, Alcoholic Beverages, Alternative Dispute Resolution, Antitrust and Trade Regulation, Aviation Law, Bankruptcy, Banking Law, Business Litigation, Charitable Organizations, Collective Bargaining, Commercial Leases, Commercial Real Estate, Computers and Software, Construction Law, Copyrights, Corporate Finance, Corporate Law, Creditors' Rights, Employee Benefits, Employer Liability, Employment Discrimination, Employment Law, Employment Litigation, Environmental Law, Franchises and Franchising, Government Contracts, Governmental (State and Local) Law, Health Law, Hospital Law, Immigration and Naturalization, Industrial Accidents, Industrial Relations, Intellectual Property, Labor Arbitration, Labor Law, Labor Legislation, Labor Relations, Management Labor Law, Medical Malpractice Defense, Mergers and Acquisitions, Occupational Health and Safety, Patent Litigation, Products Liability, Real Estate Finance, Secured Lending, Securities Regulation, Sports Law, Taxation, Technology Law, Trademark, Trusts and Estates, Venture Capital, Zoning Law.

FIRM PROFILE: The law firm of Maupin Taylor, P.A., embodies a legacy of leadership and legal excellence that dates back to 1870. The firm has a long history of serving its clients, large and small, with integrity and success. To better serve its clients it maintains offices in Raleigh, Research Triangle Park and Wilmington. It is one of the largest firms in the area. From start-up companies cultivating new ideas and technologies to venerable companies whose roots are embedded in North Carolina history, Maupin Taylor provides the experience, depth and diversity to help them all thrive.

Maupin Taylor is a full service corporate law firm that concentrates in business law, litigation, labor and employment matters, health law, environmental, commercial real estate, trusts and estates, and banking law. The firm takes great pride in its rich history and its ability to apply the practice of law to the technological demands of 21st century business.

ARMISTEAD J. MAUPIN (1914-2005)
WILLIAM W. TAYLOR, JR. (Retired)

(This Listing Continued)

CHARLES B. NEELY, JR., born Raleigh, NC, December 11, 1943; admitted to bar, 1970, NC. *Education:* Univ. of North Carolina (A.B., with honors, 1965); Duke Univ. (J.D., 1970). Co-Author: "Sales and Use Taxation of Computer Software," Journal of Multi-State Taxation, No. 5, 1992. "Can Contingent-Fee Property Tax Audits Be Challenged on Due Process Grounds?" Journal of Multistate Taxation, No. 2, 1994; "Care in Classifying Computer Software Can Avoid or Reduce Property Taxes," Journal Multistate Taxation No. 2, 1995; "Toward A Better Understanding of Value In Use In Property Tax Appraisals," Journal of Property Tax Management, Winter 1997;" "North Carolina Property Tax Assessment and Appeals Procedures," North Carolina State Bar Journal, Winter 2001. Member, Fourth Circuit Judicial Conference. Fellow, American Bar Foundation. Member, NC General Assembly, 1995-1999. *Member:* NC (Member, Board of Governors, 1995-1998) and American (Member, Taxation Section) Bar Associations; Institute of Professionals in Taxation. [Capt., USNR, 1965-1989]. ***PRACTICE AREAS:*** State and Local Taxation; Civil Litigation; Corporate Law. ***Email:*** cneely@maupintaylor.com

THOMAS WILLIS HAYWOOD ALEXANDER, born Raleigh, NC, February 27, 1940; admitted to bar, 1968, NC. *Education:* Univ. of North Carolina (A.B., 1962); Wake Forest Univ. (J.D., 1968). Morehead Scholar, 1958-1962. Clerk to Chief Justice of NC, 1968-1969. Assistant Solicitor, 10th Judicial District, 1969-1971. *Member:* NC Bar Association; Defense Research Institute; NC Association of Defense Attorneys (Past President); Lawyer Pilots Bar Association. [Sgt., USMCR, 1961-1967]. ***PRACTICE AREAS:*** Aviation Law; Products Liability Defense; Construction Law; Personal Injury Litigation. ***Email:*** talexander@maupintaylor.com

ROBERT A. VALOIS, born New York, NY, May 13, 1938; admitted to bar, 1972, NC and FL. *Education:* Univ. of Miami (B.B.A., 1962); Wake Forest Univ. (J.D., 1972). Associate Editor, Wake Forest Law Review, 1971-1972. Labor-Management Relations Examiner, National Labor Relations Board, 1962-1970. Vice Chairman, Legislative Study Commission, Fair Employment Practices, 1980-1981. Vice-Chairman, Legal Services Corporation, 1984-1989, Director, 1984-1990. *Member:* NC Bar Association (Member, Labor and Employment Law Section, Labor Law Committee, 1973—); The Florida Bar. [U.S.N., 1956-1959]. ***PRACTICE AREAS:*** Labor and Employment Law; Employment Discrimination Law. ***Email:*** rvalois@maupintaylor.com

JOHN T. WILLIAMSON, born Booneville, KY, December 16, 1945; admitted to bar, 1973, NC. *Education:* United States Naval Academy (B.S., 1967); Duke Univ. (J.D., with honors, 1973). *Member:* NC Bar Association; Association of Defense Attorneys. [1st Lt., USMC., 1967-1969, retired]. ***PRACTICE AREAS:*** Medical Malpractice Defense; Civil Litigation; Products Liability Defense; Aviation Law.

FRANK P. WARD, JR., born Detroit, MI, January 10, 1944; admitted to bar, 1971, NC; 1973, FL. *Education:* Yale Univ. (A.B., 1966); Duke Univ. (J.D., 1971); New York Univ. (LL.M., Labor Law, 1972). Member, U.S. Department of Education Civil Rights Reviewing Authority, 1985-1989. *Member:* NC (Member: Labor Law Committee, 1980-1982, Labor and Employment Law Section, 1982—; Employment Law Section Council, 1982-1986; Constitutional Rights and Responsibilities Section, Member, 1996—; Council Member, 1996-1998; Vice-Chairman, 1996-1997; Chairman, 1997-1998) and American (Member, Labor and Employment Law Section, Committee on Equal Employment Opportunity Law, 1979—) Bar Associations; The Florida Bar (Member, Labor Relations Law Committee, 1975—). ***PRACTICE AREAS:*** Labor and Employment Law; Employment Discrimination Law; Equal Opportunity Employment Law; Age Discrimination Law; Disability Discrimination Law. ***Email:*** fward@maupintaylor.com

NANCY S. RENDLEMAN, born Greensboro, NC, April 17, 1952; admitted to bar, 1977, IL; 1981, NC. *Education:* Univ. of North Carolina (B.S., 1974; J.D., 1977). Phi Beta Kappa; Order of the Coif. Co-Author: "Sales and Use Taxation of Computer Software," Journal of Multistate Taxation, No. 5, 1992; "Can Contingent-Fee Property Tax Audits Be Challenged On Due Process Grounds?" Journal of Multistate Taxation, No. 2, 1994; "Care in Classifying Computer Software Can Avoid or Reduce Property Taxes," Journal of Multistate Taxation, No. 1, 1995; "Toward a Better Understanding of Value-In-Use," Journal of Property Tax Management, Winter 1997; "North Carolina Property Tax Assessment and Appeals Procedures," North Carolina State Bar Journal, Winter 2001. *Member:* NC (Member, Sections on: Taxation; Estate Planning and Fiduciary Law; Member, Estate Planning and Fiduciary Law Section Council, 1990-1993; Chair, Estate Planning and Fiduciary Law Legislative Committee, 1993-1995; Treasurer, Estate Planning and Fiduciary Law Section, 1995-1997) and American (Member, Sections on: Taxation; Real Estate, Probate and Trust Law) Bar Associations; Institute of Property Taxation; American College of Trust and Estate Counsel. (Board Certified Specialist in Estate Planning and Probate Law, North Carolina State Board of Legal Specialization). ***PRACTICE AREAS:*** State and Local Taxation; Estate Planning and Administration. ***Email:*** nrendleman@maupintaylor.com

MARGIE TOY CASE, born New Kensington, PA, October 25, 1952; admitted to bar, 1978, PA; 1981, NC. *Education:* Dickinson College (B.A., magna cum laude, 1974); McMaster Univ. (M.A., 1975); Univ. of Pittsburgh (J.D., 1978). Phi Beta Kappa. Staff Member, Univ. of Pittsburgh Law Review, 1978. *Member:* NC (Member, Labor and Employment Law Section and PA Bar Associations. ***PRACTICE AREAS:*** Labor and Employment Law. ***Email:*** mcase@maupintaylor.com

M. KEITH KAPP, born Winston-Salem, NC, November 28, 1953; admitted to bar, 1979, NC. *Education:* Univ. of North Carolina (A.B., with honors, 1976; J.D., with honors, 1979). Phi Beta Kappa. Member, Order of Barristers. Morehead Scholar. Staff Member, 1977-1978 and Research Editor, 1978-1979, NC Journal of International Law and Commercial Regulation. Law Clerk to: Judge Earl W. Vaughn, NC Court of Appeals, 1979-1980; Justice J. Frank Huskins, NC Supreme Court, 1980-1981. NC State Bar Councilor. *Member:* Wake County (President, 1996), NC (Member, Board of Governors, 1983-1986) and American (Member, Antitrust Section and Forum on Franchising) Bar Associations; NC Association of Defense Attorneys. ***PRACTICE AREAS:*** Commercial Litigation; Administrative Litigation; Antitrust; Franchise Law. ***Email:*** kkapp@maupintaylor.com

MARK S. THOMAS, born Leaksville, NC, October 28, 1952; admitted to bar, 1978, NC. *Education:* Wake Forest Univ. (B.A., magna cum laude, 1975; J.D., cum laude, 1978). Phi Beta Kappa. Member, Order of Barristers. Guy T. Carswell Scholar. Irving E. Carlyle Scholar. Staff Member, Wake Forest Law Review, 1976-1978. *Member:* NC Bar Association (Labor and Employment Law Section: Chair, 2003-2004; Intellectual Property Law Section) and American Bar Association (Member, Tort and Insurance Section); Defense

(This Listing Continued)

MAUPIN TAYLOR, P.A., Raleigh—Continued

Research Institute; NC Association of Defense Attorneys. [Capt., USA, 1978-1981]. ***PRACTICE AREAS:*** Employee Benefits Law; Insurance Litigation; Intellectual Property Litigation. ***Email:*** mthomas@maupintaylor.com

DAVID R. DORTON, born Concord, NC, June 10, 1953; admitted to bar, 1979, NC. *Education:* Wake Forest Univ. (B.A., magna cum laude, 1975); Univ. of North Carolina (J.D., 1979). Phi Beta Kappa. Guy T. Carswell Scholar. *Member:* NC Bar Association (Member: Real Property Section; Real Property Section Council; Vice-Chairman, 1991-1992; Chairman, 1992-1993). (Board Certified Specialist in Real Property Law, Business, Commercial and Industrial Transactions, North Carolina State Board of Legal Specialization). ***PRACTICE AREAS:*** Commercial Real Estate; Real Property Development; Real Estate Finance Law. ***Email:*** ddorton@maupintaylor.com

HOLMES P. HARDEN, born Greensboro, NC, January 14, 1956; admitted to bar, 1981, NC. *Education:* Davidson College (B.A., cum laude, 1978); Univ. of North Carolina (J.D., 1981). Dana Scholar. Law Clerk to Hon. Naomi E. Morris, Chief Judge, NC Court of Appeals, 1981-1982. Member, Panel of Bankruptcy Trustees, Eastern District of NC, 1983—. *Member:* NC Bar Association (Member, Sections on: Bankruptcy; Business, Banking and Commercial Law). (Certified Specialist, Business and Consumer Bankruptcy Law, North Carolina State Board of Legal Specialization; Certified Specialist, Business Bankruptcy Law, American Bankruptcy Board of Certification). ***PRACTICE AREAS:*** Bankruptcy and Creditors' Rights. ***Email:*** hharden@maupintaylor.com

D. ROYCE POWELL, born Raleigh, NC, November 21, 1951; admitted to bar, 1979, NC; 1981, U.S. Tax Court; 1985, U.S. Court of Federal Claims; 1988, DC; 1989, NY. *Education:* Univ. of North Carolina (B.S., 1974; J.D., 1979); Emory Univ. (LL.M., Taxation, 1985). Phi Beta Kappa. Adjunct Professor, UNC Graduate School of Business, 1989-1992. Board of Advisors, UNC-Chapel Hill Law School Tax Institute, 1991—. Management Analyst, U.S. General Accounting Office, 1974-1976. Co-Author: "Is Income of Exempt Scientific Research Organizations From Unrelated Business?" 64 J. Tax 210, 1986. Author: "Will S Shareholders Guarantees Ever Increase Basis?" 69 Journal of Taxation 12, 1988; "Unexpected Tax Consequences of Utility Contributions by Developers," 47 Urban Land No. 7, 1988; "Buy-Sell Agreements," Duke Univ. School of Law Tax and Estate Planning Conference, 1991. *Member:* NC (Chairman, 1997-1998 and Council Member, Taxation Section) and American (Member, Sections on: Taxation; Corporation; Banking and business Law; Committees: Tax Court Procedure; Corporate Tax) Bar Associations. ***PRACTICE AREAS:*** Federal Taxation Law; Mergers and Acquisitions Law; Securities Law. ***Email:*** rpowell@maupintaylor.com

WILLIAM B. GWYN, JR., born North Wilkesboro, NC, February 14, 1950; admitted to bar, 1981, NC; 1982, U.S. Tax Court; 1986, U.S. Court of Federal Claims and U.S. Court of Appeals for the Federal Circuit. *Education:* Wake Forest Univ. (B.S., 1972; M.B.A., 1975; J.D., 1981). Co-Author: "Foreign Corporations in North Carolina: The 'Doing Business' Standards of Qualification, Taxation and Jurisdiction," 17 Wake Forest Law Review 711, 1980; "The Duty to Update the Forecasts, Predictions and Projections of Public Companies," 24 Securities Regulation Law Journal 366, 1994. *Member:* NC and American (Member, Sections on: Business Law; Taxation) Bar Associations. ***PRACTICE AREAS:*** Corporate Law; Tax Law; Mergers and Acquisitions; Corporate Finance; International Transactions. ***Email:*** bgwyn@maupintaylor.com

JAMES E. GATES, born Los Angeles, CA, November 18, 1954; admitted to bar, 1981, DC; 1982, VA; 1985, NC. *Education:* Ursinus College (B.A., summa cum laude, 1977); Georgetown Univ. (J.D., 1981; M.Sc., 1985). Law Clerk to the Hon. Frank W. Bullock, Jr., U.S. District Judge, Middle District of NC, 1983-1985. Co-Author: *North Carolina Civil Trial Guide,* Matthew Bender, 1993. Spanish Instructor, Wake Technical Community College, 1996. Certified Mediator, NC. *Member:* NC (Secretary Dispute Resolution Section, 1995-1997; Vice Chair, 1997-1998; Chair, 1998-1999) and American Bar Associations; Alternative Dispute Resolution (Committee of State Judicial Council, 2000—); Foreign Language Advisory Committee of Administrative Office of the Courts (1999—); Carolina Association of Translators and Interpreters. ***LANGUAGES:*** Spanish. ***PRACTICE AREAS:*** Health Care Litigation; Commercial Litigation; Alternative Dispute Resolution. ***Email:*** jgates@maupintaylor.com

AMOS C. DAWSON, III, born Southern Pines, NC, February 15, 1948; admitted to bar, 1975, NC; 1980, SC. *Education:* Univ. of North Carolina (B.A., 1969; J.D., 1975). Phi Beta Kappa. Author: "Environmental Regulation in North Carolina—How to Cope with the New Regulatory Jungle," Institute of Business Law, 1993; "Third Party Litigation—Toxic Torts and Cost Recovery," Environmental Law Handbook, Wake Forest School of Law, 1992; "The Attorney-Consultant Relationship in CERCLA and RCRA Litigation," NC Bar Foundation, 1991. Visiting Professor of Law, UNC School of Law, 1978-1979. Staff Attorney, NC Coastal Resources Commission, 1975-1976. Assistant Attorney General, Environmental Protection Section, NC Department of Justice, 1976-1980. *Member:* NC (Member, Environmental and Natural Resources Law Section) and American (Member, Natural Resources, Energy and Environmental Law Section) Bar Associations. [Lt. U.S.N.R. (Ret.), 1969-1971]. ***PRACTICE AREAS:*** Environmental Law; Litigation; Administrative Law; Alternative Dispute Resolution. ***Email:*** adawson@maupintaylor.com

GILBERT C. LAITE, III, born Camden, ME, October 28, 1957; admitted to bar, 1984, NC; 1986, ME. *Education:* Univ. of Southern Maine (B.S., Business Adm., 1980); Wake Forest Univ. (J.D., cum laude, 1984). Real Estate Broker, 1977-1981. Co-Author: "Real Estate Litigation in North Carolina, 1990; "Construction Lien Law in North Carolina," 1994, 1996; "Trial Book-Civil," Wake Forest Univ., 1994. Law Clerk to the Honorable Russell A. Eliason, U.S. Magistrate Judge, Middle District of NC, 1984-1986. *Member:* NC and American Bar Associations. ***PRACTICE AREAS:*** Commercial Litigation; Contracts; Sales; Lender Liability; Uniform Commercial Code; Products Liability; Construction; Railroad Real Property; Eminent Domain; Landlord and Tenant; Title and Boundary Disputes. ***Email:*** glaite@maupintaylor.com

RONALD R. ROGERS, born Princeton, NJ, September 3, 1960; admitted to bar, 1986, NC. *Education:* Wake Forest Univ. (B.A., magna cum laude, 1982); Univ. of North Carolina (J.D., 1986). Phi Beta Kappa. Staff Member, NC Journal of International Law and Commercial Regulation, 1984-1985. *Member:* NC and American Bar Associations. ***PRACTICE AREAS:*** Commercial Real Estate; Land Use; Foreclosure Law. ***Email:*** rrogers@maupintaylor.com

ELIZABETH DAVENPORT SCOTT, born Raleigh, NC, December 28, 1960; admitted to bar, 1986, NC. *Education:* Univ. of North Carolina (B.A., 1983; J.D., with honors, 1986). Law Clerk: Honorable Willis P. Whichard, Justice, NC Supreme Court; Honorable Robert F. Orr, Judge of the NC Court of Appeals. Certified Mediator, NC. *Member:* NC Bar Association; NC Association of Defense Counsel. ***PRACTICE AREAS:*** Commercial Litigation; Personal Injury Litigation; Alternative Dispute Resolution; Insurance Coverage. ***Email:*** escott@maupintaylor.com

REUBEN G. CLARK, III, born Washington, DC, June 27, 1952; admitted to bar, 1980, DE and PA; 1988, NC. *Education:* Stanford Univ. (B.A., 1974); Univ. of Pennsylvania (J.D., 1979). Recipient: Jefferson Fordham Human Rights Award; Reginald Heber Smith Fellowship. *Member:* NC and American (Member, Sections on: Business Law; Real Property; Probate and Trust Law) Bar Associations. ***PRACTICE AREAS:*** Commercial Real Estate; Real Estate Development; Commercial Leasing; Business Law. ***Email:*** rclark@maupintaylor.com

ARLENE J. DIOSEGY, born Pittsburgh, PA, September 13, 1949; admitted to bar, 1974, PA; 1981, CO; 1983, NC. *Education:* Allegheny College (B.A., 1971); Temple Univ. (J.D., 1974). Editor and Author, Body Medical/Body Legal, 1989—. Adjunct Instructor, Department of Health Policy and Administration, UNC at Chapel Hill, 1989—. *Member:* NC (Member, board of Governors, 1989-1992; Health Benefit Trust Trustee, 1990-1994) and American Bar Associations; National Health Lawyers Association; NC Society of Health Care Attorneys. ***PRACTICE AREAS:*** Health Care Law; Corporate and Business Law; Administrative Law. ***Email:*** adiosegy@maupintaylor.com

MICHAEL C. LORD, born London, England, August 21, 1963; admitted to bar, 1988, NC. *Education:* Washington & Lee Univ. (B.A., magna cum laude, 1985); Wake Forest Univ. (J.D., cum laude, 1988). Phi Beta Kappa. Member, Wake Forest Law Review, 1987-1988. Law Clerk, Hon. Eugene A. Gordon, Senior U.S. District Court Judge, Middle District of NC, 1988-1989. *Member:* NC (Member, Sections on: Labor; Litigation) and American (Member, Litigation Section) Bar Associations. ***PRACTICE AREAS:*** Occupational Safety and Health Law; Labor and Employment Law. ***Email:*** mlord@maupintaylor.com

KARON B. THORNTON, born Pasadena, CA, May 26, 1965; admitted to bar, 1990, NC. *Education:* Centre College of Kentucky (B.A., 1987); Univ. of Kentucky (J.D., 1990). *Member:* NC (Member, Sections on: Litigation; Health Care) and American Bar Associations. ***PRACTICE AREAS:*** Civil Litigation; Medical Malpractice Defense. ***Email:*** kthornton@maupintaylor.com

THERON McK. vanDUSEN, born Detroit, MI, March 26, 1957; admitted to bar, 1991, NC. *Education:* Univ. of Pennsylvania (B.A., magna cum laude, 1979); Duke Univ. (J.D., with honors, 1991). Editor, Law and Contemporary Problems, 1989-1991. *Member:* NC (Member, Sections on: Business; Tax Law) and American (Member, Sections on: Business: Tax Law) Bar Associations. ***LANGUAGES:*** French. ***PRACTICE AREAS:*** Corporate and Securities Law; Mergers and Acquisitions; Technology Law; Federal Taxation. ***Email:*** tvandusen@maupintaylor.com

WILLIAM P. BARRETT, born Evanston, IL, April 30, 1963; admitted to bar, 1988, MO; 1993, NC. *Education:* Univ. of Missouri (B.J., cum laude, 1985; J.D., 1988). Field Attorney, National Labor Relations Board, 1988-1992. *Member:* NC Bar Association (Member, Labor and Employment Law Section Council); The Missouri Bar. ***PRACTICE AREAS:*** Labor and Employment Law. ***Email:*** bbarrett@maupintaylor.com

KURT J. OLSON, born Amityville, NY, April 21, 1952; admitted to bar, 1984, VA; 1985, DC; 1996, NC. *Education:* Univ. of Mass. (B.S., cum laude, 1976); Catholic Univ. of America (J.D., 1984). Faculty Award, Highest GPA. Co-Author: "The Shrinking World of Hazardous Waste Exports: A Guide Through the Conundrum," Journal of Environmental Regulation, Autumn, 1994; "The Fight to Save Sweeden's Swamp in Light of New Wetlands Management Initiatives," Journal of Environmental Regulations, Autumn 1995. Symposium, Shell Oil v. EPA, Chemical Waste Litigation Reporter, January 1992. NPDES Permit Challenge. Counsel's Advisory, Washington Legal Foundation, May 19, 1995. *Member:* NC and American Bar Associations; DC Bar; VA State Bar. ***PRACTICE AREAS:*** Environmental Law; Insurance Law. ***Email:*** kolson@maupintaylor.com

JOHN W. (JACK) MARIN, born Sharon, PA, October 12, 1944; admitted to bar, 1980, NC. *Education:* Duke Univ. (A.B., 1966; J.D., 1980). Co-Author: "Lending to Professional Athletes," 63 J. Comm. Bk. Lndg. 9, 16, 1981. Certified Player Representative, NBPA. *Member:* NC Bar Association. ***LANGUAGES:*** Italian. ***PRACTICE AREAS:*** Sports Law. ***Email:*** jmarin@maupintaylor.com

JOHN I. MABE, JR., born Norfolk, VA, November 27, 1954; admitted to bar, 1980, NC. *Education:* Univ. of North Carolina (B.A., 1977; J.D., 1980). Morehead Scholar. *Member:* NC (Member: Construction Law Section, Chairman, 1997-1998; Board of Governors, 2002—) and American (Member, Forum on Construction Industry) Bar Associations. ***PRACTICE AREAS:*** Commercial Litigation; Construction Law; Litigation. ***Email:*** jmabe@maupintaylor.com

DAVID A. BOOKHOUT, born Cooperstown, NY, January 20, 1948; admitted to bar, 1974, MA; 1978, NY; 1998, NC. *Education:* Amherst College (B.A., magna cum laude, 1970); Harvard Univ. (J.D., 1974). *Member:* NC and American Bar Associations. ***PRACTICE AREAS:*** Corporate Law; Venture Capital; Corporate Finance; Biotechnology Law; Mergers and Acquisitions; International Business. ***Email:*** dbookhout@maupintaylor.com

CHARLES L. STEEL, IV, born Greensboro, NC, 1945; admitted to bar, 1970, NC. *Education:* Davidson College (A.B., 1967); Vanderbilt Univ. (J.D., 1970); New York Univ. (LL.M., Taxation, 1972). Council, Tax Section, Chair, 2002-2003, NC Bar Association. Director and Past President, Fourteenth Judicial District Bar. Member, Planning Committee, J. Nelson Young Tax Institute at the UNC School of Law; Petitioner's Counsel in Jao Montoro and Neuza Paula v. Commissioner, 73TCM 3110, Filed June 23, 1997. ***PRACTICE AREAS:*** Taxation Law; Estate Planning Law; Corporate Law. ***Email:*** csteel@maupintaylor.com

STEVEN B. LONG, born New Bern, NC, August 29, 1960; admitted to bar, 1991, NC and DC. *Education:* Univ. of North Carolina (B.S., 1982); Georgetown Univ. (J.D., cum laude, 1991; LL.M., Tax, 1998). Associate Editor, Georgetown Law Journal, 1990-1991.

(This Listing Continued)

Author: "State Withholding Taxes on the Personal Service Income of Nonresident Independent Contractors," 4 The State and Local Tax Lawyer 87 (1999). *Member:* NC Bar Association (Member, Tax Section). ***PRACTICE AREAS:*** Taxation; Employee Benefits; Corporate Law. ***Email:*** slong@maupintaylor.com

LAURA A. EDGERTON, born Washington, DC, September 30, 1968; admitted to bar, 1993, GA; 1995, NC. *Education:* NC State Univ. (B.A., magna cum laude, 1990); Univ. of Georgia (J.D., cum laude, 1993). Editor, Georgia Journal of International and Comparative Law, 1991-1993. Law Clerk to the Honorable Glen E. Conrad, Magistrate Judge, U.S. District Court, Western District of Virginia, 1993-1994. *Member:* NC (Member, Immigration Law Subcommittee, 1996—) and American Bar Associations; American Immigration Lawyers Association. ***PRACTICE AREAS:*** Immigration; Employment. ***Email:*** ledgerton@maupintaylor.com

RONALD D. RAXTER, born Greenville, SC, February 14, 1953; admitted to bar, 1977, NC. *Education:* Univ. of North Carolina (B.A., 1973; J.D., 1977). Attorney, NC Department of Insurance, 1977-1985. General Counsel, NC Savings Institutions Division, 1985-1992. Author: "Why Convert to A State Savings Bank?" Fall Issue, NC Alliance of Community Financial Institutions, 1992. Vice Chairman, Wake County Board of Adjustment. *Member:* Wake County; Tenth Judicial District and NC Bar Associations. ***PRACTICE AREAS:*** Banking; Securities; Insurance; Administrative Law; Corporate Law; Corporate Finance; Nonprofit Organizations; Mergers and Acquisitions. ***Email:*** rraxter@maupintaylor.com

GERALD A. TINGEN, born Roxboro, NC, August 5, 1958; admitted to bar, 1984, NC. *Education:* Univ. of North Carolina (B.A., 1981; J.D., 1984). James M. Johnston Scholar. ***PRACTICE AREAS:*** Commercial Real Estate; Commercial Real Estate Finance; Commercial Leasing. ***Email:*** ttingen@maupintaylor.com

ROY H. WYMAN, JR., born San Diego, CA, December 5, 1963; admitted to bar, 1993, MI; 1995, NC. *Education:* Wheaton College (B.S., cum laude, 1986); Univ. of Michigan (J.D., cum laude, 1993). ***PRACTICE AREAS:*** Health Care; Business; Corporate Transactions; Medicare; Medicaid; Health Care Fraud. ***Email:*** rwyman@maupintaylor.com

KEVIN W. BENEDICT, born Vestal, NY, August 2, 1969; admitted to bar, 1995, NC. *Education:* NC State Univ. (B.S., Civil Engineering with construction option, 1992); Univ. of Tennessee (J.D., 1995). Staff Member, 1993-1994 and Research Editor, 1994-1995, Univ. of Tennessee Law Review. Member, Univ. of Tennessee Moot Court Board, 1994-1995. Law Clerk to the Hon. Sidney S. Eagles, Jr., NC Court of Appeals, 1995-1997. ***PRACTICE AREAS:*** Construction; Aviation; Environmental; Litigation. ***Email:*** kbenedict@maupintaylor.com

JOSHUA M. KRASNER, born New York, NY, February 5, 1967; admitted to bar, 1992, NC. *Education:* Univ. of North Carolina (B.S., 1989); Wake Forest Univ. (J.D., 1992). Member: Wake Forest Law Review, 1990-1992; Wake Forest Moot Court Board. Law Clerk to the Hon. I. Beverly Lake, Jr., Associate Justice, Supreme Court of North Carolina, 1995-1997. ***PRACTICE AREAS:*** Labor and Employment Law. ***Email:*** jkrasner@maupintaylor.com

CAMDEN R. WEBB, born Raleigh, NC, July 19, 1970; admitted to bar, 1995, NC. *Education:* Univ. of Richmond (B.A., magna cum laude, 1992); Univ. of North Carolina (J.D., with honors, 1995). Phi Beta Kappa. Staff Member, 1993-1994 and Note and Comment Editor, 1994-1995, North Carolina Journal of International Law and Commercial Regulation. [Capt., U.S. Army JAGC, 1995-1999]. ***PRACTICE AREAS:*** Commercial Litigation; Food and Drug Law. ***Email:*** cwebb@maupintaylor.com

TERENCE D. FRIEDMAN, born Philadelphia, PA, September 2, 1969; admitted to bar, 1998, NC and TX. *Education:* Univ. of Missouri (B.A., 1992; B.J., 1992); Baylor Univ. (J.D., 1997). Senior Notes and Comments Editor, Baylor Univ. Law Review. Co-Author: "The Anti-Retaliation Provisions of Title VII, The ADA & The ADEA," Missouri Law Review, Spring 1998. Author: "Celotex Corp. V. Edwards: Go Directly to Bankruptcy Court. Do Not Pass District Court. Do Not Collect Your Judgement," Baylor Law Review, Spring 1996. Law Clerk to the Hon. James T. Trimble, U.S. District Court, Western District of LA, 1997-1998. ***LANGUAGES:*** Spanish. ***PRACTICE AREAS:*** Labor; Employment. ***Email:*** tfriedman@maupintaylor.com

WILLIAM SAM BYASSEE, born Paducah, KY, June 3, 1950; admitted to bar, 1982, NC; 1984, U.S. Court of Appeals, Fourth Circuit; 1998, U.S. Court of Appeals for the Federal Circuit. *Education:* Univ. of Tennessee (B.A., cum laude, 1973); Univ. of Kentucky; Vanderbilt Univ. (J.D., 1982). Recipient: Law Review Award, 1982; The Morgan Prize, 1983. Executive Articles Editor, The Vanderbilt Law Review, 1981-1982. Clerk to Senior Judge Eugene A. Gordon, U.S. District Court, Middle District of North Carolina, 1982-1983. *Member:* NC (Chair: Technology Advisory Committee, 1991-1996; Intellectual Property Section, 1999-2000) and American (Member and Chair Elect, 2001-2002, Science and Technology Section) Bar Associations. ***PRACTICE AREAS:*** Information Technology; Internet; Intellectual Property Law; First Amendment and Media Law. ***Email:*** sbyassee@maupintaylor.com

---

MARK A. WHITSON, born Winston-Salem, NC, June 29, 1965; admitted to bar, 1996, NC. *Education:* Univ. of North Carolina (B.A., 1983; J.D., with honors, 1996). [USMC, 1987-1999; Major, USMCR, 1999—]. ***PRACTICE AREAS:*** Litigation; Aviation Law. ***Email:*** mwhitson@maupintaylor.com

MARCUS C. HEWITT, born Charlotte, NC, May 7, 1971; admitted to bar, 1996, NC. *Education:* Univ. of North Carolina (B.A., with distinction, 1993; J.D., 1996). Holderness Moot Court. [Capt., USMC, 1996-2000]. ***PRACTICE AREAS:*** Civil Litigation; Computer Law; Medical Malpractice Defense. ***Email:*** mhewitt@maupintaylor.com

HANS H. HUANG, born Madison, WI, October 4, 1973; admitted to bar, 1998, NC. *Education:* Univ. of North Carolina (B.A., 1994; J.D., 1998). Phi Delta Phi; Holderness Moot Court; Trial Law Academy. ***PRACTICE AREAS:*** Civil Litigation; Health Law; Commercial Litigation. ***Email:*** hhuang@maupintaylor.com

HEATHER E. BRIDGERS, born Lakeland, FL, July 11, 1970; admitted to bar, 2000, NC. *Education:* Univ. of Florida (B.A., 1993); Southern Methodist Univ. (J.D., cum laude,

(This Listing Continued)

2000). Moot Court Chief Justice, 1999. Staff Member, The International Lawyer, 1998-1999. ***PRACTICE AREAS:*** Commercial Litigation. ***Email:*** hbridgers@maupintaylor.com

SHANA G. R. FISHER, born Ann Arbor, MI, May 17, 1973; admitted to bar, 1998, MI; 2000, NH; 2005, NC. *Education:* University of Michigan (B.A., summa cum laude, 1995; J.D., cum laude, 1998). Law Clerk, U.S. District Court, Western District of Michigan. ***PRACTICE AREAS:*** Commercial Real Estate. ***Email:*** sfisher@maupintaylor.com

MATTHEW F. FUSSA, born Elizabeth, NJ, July 28, 1968; admitted to bar, 1993, PA; 2001, DC and NC. *Education:* Muhlenberg College (B.A., 1990); Widener University (J.D., 1993). [USMC, 1994-2004; Major, USMC Judge Advocate]. ***PRACTICE AREAS:*** Litigation. ***Email:*** mfussa@maupintaylor.com

W. WINBORNE BOYLES, born Chapel Hill, NC, April 5, 1977; admitted to bar, 2003, NC. *Education:* University of North Carolina at Chapel Hill (B.A., 1999; J.D., 2003). Articles and Notes Editor, North Carolina Banking Institute. Law Clerk to the Hon. J. Rich Leonard, Chief Judge, U.S. Bankruptcy Court, Eastern District of NC. ***PRACTICE AREAS:*** Litigation. ***Email:*** wboyles@maupintaylor.com

JONATHAN R. BUMGARNER, born Winston-Salem, NC, September 1, 1978; admitted to bar, 2003, NC. *Education:* Campbell University (B.A., magna cum laude, 2000; J.D., cum laude, 2003). Member, Campbell Law Review. Law Clerk to the Hon. Frank W. Bullock, Jr., District Judge, U.S. District Court, Middle District of NC. ***PRACTICE AREAS:*** Litigation. ***Email:*** jbumgarner@maupintaylor.com

BRENDA J. THISSEN, born St. Paul, MN, March 8, 1961; admitted to bar, 2004, DC (Not admitted in North Carolina). *Education:* University of Minnesota (B.A., 1986); University of North Carolina at Chapel Hill (M.A., 1988; J.D., 2003). Articles and Notes Editor, First Amendment Law Review. Law Clerk to the Hon. Wallace W. Dixon, U.S. Magistrate Judge, U.S. District Court, Middle District of NC. ***PRACTICE AREAS:*** Litigation. ***Email:*** bthissen@maupintaylor.com

ROBERT W. SHAW, born Columbus, OH, February 16, 1977; admitted to bar, 2004, NC. *Education:* Wake Forest University (B.S., 1999); University of North Carolina at Chapel Hill (J.D., 2004). Law Clerk to the Hon. Malcolm Howard, U.S. District Court, Eastern District of NC. ***PRACTICE AREAS:*** State and Local Taxation; Litigation. ***Email:*** rshaw@maupintaylor.com

JENNIFER A. MORGAN, born Lynchburg, VA, November 27, 1979; admitted to bar, 2005, NC. *Education:* North Carolina State University (B.S., 2002); Campbell University (J.D., 2005). Member, Campbell Law Review. Susie Sharp Inn of Court. ***PRACTICE AREAS:*** Litigation. ***Email:*** jmorgan@maupintaylor.com

NICHOLAS A. NANCE, born Charlotte, NC, June 16, 1979; admitted to bar, 2005, NC. *Education:* Appalachian State University (B.S.B.A., 2002); Campbell University (J.D., 2005; M.B.A., 2005). ***PRACTICE AREAS:*** Litigation; Corporate Law. ***Email:*** nnance@maupintaylor.com

OF COUNSEL

DANIEL LEE BRAWLEY, born Greensboro, NC, March 31, 1942; admitted to bar, 1967, NC. *Education:* University of North Carolina (A.B., 1964; J.D., 1967). Listed in *The Best Lawyers in America (Business Litigation, Maritime Law, Personal Injury and Civil Litigation).* Member, National Panel of Arbitrators, American Arbitration Association. *Member:* North Carolina and American Bar Associations; Southeastern Admiralty Law Institute (Member, Board of Governors, 1972-1974, 1988-1990, 1994, 1996, 1998-1999; Treasurer, 1975; Secretary, 1976; Vice Chairman, 1977; Chairman, 1978); Maritime Law Association of the United States (Proctor); North Carolina Association of Defense Attorneys (Member, Board of Directors, 1992-1995). ***PRACTICE AREAS:*** Construction Law; Commercial Litigation; Business Litigation; Admiralty Law; Personal Injury. ***Email:*** dbrawley@maupintaylor.com

ROBERT B. BROUGHTON, born Raleigh, NC, November 28, 1924; admitted to bar, 1951, NC and U.S. Court of Appeals, Fourth Circuit; 1986, U.S. Supreme Court. *Education:* Univ. of North Carolina (A.B., 1948); Wake Forest Univ. (J.D., 1951). Legal Staff, NC Attorney General, 1951-1952. Assistant District Attorney, NC Superior Court, Seventh District, 1953-1954. Commissioner, 1958-1963 and Chairman, 1963-1973, Housing Authority of the City of Raleigh. General Counsel, NC Farm Bureau Federation and NC Farm Bureau Mutual Insurance Co., 1981-1993. [U.S. Navy, active duty, 1943-1946, Lt. j.g.; USNR]. ***PRACTICE AREAS:*** Agricultural Law; Insurance Law; Corporate Law.

SANTO J. COSTA, born New York, NY, May 22, 1945; admitted to bar, 1972, NY; 1980, OH; 1988, NC. *Education:* St. John's Univ. (B.S., 1968; J.D., 1971). Senior Vice President, Administration and General Counsel, Glaxo, Inc., 1986-1993; President and COO, 1994-1999 and Vice Chairman, 1999-2001, Quintiles Transactional Corporation; Member, Board of Directors, Quintiles Transactional Corporation; NPS Pharmaceuticals; Pilot Therapeutics; AgroMed. Member, Board of Advisors, A.M. Pappas and Associates. Member, Board of Directors: The Duke Medical Center Children's Classic; NC Outward Bound School; Duke Brain Tumor Advisory Committee; Duke University Medical Center Board of Visitors; Food and Drug Law Institute Advisory Board. ***PRACTICE AREAS:*** Business Law; Corporate Law; Pharmaceutical and Biotechnology Law. ***Email:*** scosta@maupintaylor.com

ROBERT K. IMPERIAL, born Norfolk, VA, December 6, 1962; admitted to bar, 1988, GA (Not admitted in North Carolina). *Education:* Old Dominion University (B.A., cum laude, 1985); Mercer University (J.D., 1988). ***PRACTICE AREAS:*** Bankruptcy; Creditors Rights. ***Email:*** rimperial@maupintaylor.com

W. TRAVIS PORTER, born Lumberton, NC, 1931; admitted to bar, 1960, NC. *Education:* Univ. of North Carolina (A.B., 1953; J.D., with high honors, 1960). Order of the Coif. Member, Board of Editors, North Carolina Law Review, 1959-1960. Adjunct Professor, Graduate School of Business, Duke Univ., 1974-1981. President, Durham, NC Chamber of Commerce, 1984-1985. Member, UNC System: Board of Governors, 1987-1995; Vice-Chairman, 1990-1994; Chairman, 1994-1995. Member, Board of Trustees, 1979-1987; Chairman, 1983-1984, UNC Chapel Hill. Member: 1983-1987 and Chairman, 1983-1984, UNC Endowment Board; UNC Public Television Foundation Board of Directors,

(This Listing Continued)

MAUPIN TAYLOR, P.A., Raleigh—Continued

1997—; UNC Board of Visitors, 1987—. [Captain, USMC, Active Duty, 1953-1956]. ***PRACTICE AREAS:*** Corporate Law; Administrative Law; Governmental Law; Land Use Law; Contracts Law. ***Email:*** tporter@maupintaylor.com

KEVIN A. PRAKKE, born Ashville, NC, August 27, 1968; admitted to bar, 1993, NC. *Education:* University of North Carolina (B.S., with distinction, 1990; J.D., 1993). *Member:* North Carolina State Bar (Member, Business Section). ***PRACTICE AREAS:*** Public Offerings; Private Placements; Securities Law; Mergers, Acquisitions and Divestitures; Business Law; Corporate Law; Venture Capital. ***Email:*** kprakke@maupintaylor.com

REPRESENTATIVE CLIENTS: A I G Aviation, Inc.; Ajinomoto USA, Inc.; Alcoa, Inc.; Bandag Incorporated; Blue Cross/Blue Shield of North Carolina; City of Durham; City of Raleigh; Cornerstone Health Care, P.A.; CSX Transportation; DaimlerChrysler Corporation; Duke University; E & J Gallo Winery; Eastman Kodak Company; Ford Motor Company; GlaxoSmithKline; HealthSouth Corporation; Hog Slat, Inc.; McDonald's Corporation; Nash Finch Company, Inc.; North Carolina Hospital Association; North Carolina Housing Finance Agency; North Carolina Museum of Life and Science; Nortel; Reichhold Chemical Co., Inc.; Sampson Regional Medical Center; Seaboard Group II; SouthTrust Bank; SpectraSite Communications, Inc.; The New Kerr Drugs; J. M. Thompson Company.

THE LAW OFFICE OF ANDREW McCOPPIN, P.A.

RALEIGH, NORTH CAROLINA

(See Cary)

Driving While Intoxicated, Traffic Violations, Violent Crimes, Drug Crimes, White Collar Crimes, Domestic Violence and Federal Criminal Law.

McDANIEL & ANDERSON, L.L.P.

LAFAYETTE SQUARE
4942 WINDY HILL DRIVE
P.O. BOX 58186
RALEIGH, NORTH CAROLINA 27658
Telephone: 919-872-3000
Fax: 919-790-9273

Civil Trials and Appeals, Corporations, Securities, Administrative, Personal Injury, Construction Law, Insurance, Negligence, Zoning and Municipal Law.

MEMBERS OF FIRM

L. BRUCE McDANIEL, born Dillon, South Carolina, May 26, 1933; admitted to bar, 1958, North Carolina; 1963, Georgia; 1971, U.S. Supreme Court. *Education:* Wake Forest College (B.S., 1955; J.D., 1958). Omicron Delta Kappa (President, 1955-1956); Phi Delta Phi (Vice President, 1957-1958). Author: "Basic Requirements and Prohibitions of Securities Law," North Carolina Bar Association Bar Notes, February and May, 1970; "Private Placements of Securities," The North Carolina Bar, Vol. 22, No. 3, 1975 and The Barrister, Winter, 1976. Guest Lecturer on Securities Law, University of Georgia, 1965 and Emory University, 1966. Staff Attorney, U.S. Securities and Exchange Commission, Atlanta Regional Office, Atlanta, Georgia, 1962-1966. *Member:* Wake County, North Carolina (Member, Business Law Section), Federal and American Bar Associations; North Carolina State Bar; State Bar of Georgia; North Carolina Academy of Trial Lawyers. [Captain, JAG, USAF, 1959-1961]. ***PRACTICE AREAS:*** Securities Law; Corporations Law. ***Email:*** mcdas@mcdas.com

WILLIAM EUGENE ANDERSON, born Marion, North Carolina, August 23, 1944; admitted to bar, 1969, North Carolina; 1973, U.S. District Court, Eastern and Middle Districts of North Carolina; 1977, U.S. Supreme Court; 1979, U.S. Court of Appeals, Fourth Circuit. *Education:* Duke University (B.A., 1966); University of North Carolina (J.D., 1969). Law Clerk, North Carolina Court of Appeals, 1969-1970. Assistant Commission Attorney, 1970-1973 and Hearing Examiner, 1971-1973, North Carolina Utilities Commission. Hearing Officer, Civilian Health and Medical Program of the Uniformed Services, Department of Defense, 1978-1995. Town Attorney, Town of Garner, 1987—. Member, Panel of Arbitrators, American Arbitration Association. *Member:* Wake County, North Carolina and American Bar Associations; North Carolina State Bar; North Carolina Association of Defense Attorneys; Defense Research Institute; North Carolina Association of Municipal Attorneys. ***PRACTICE AREAS:*** Civil Litigation; Insurance Defense; Insurance Law; Municipal Law; Zoning Law. ***Email:*** weanderson@mcdas.com

---

JOHN M. KIRBY, born Charlotte, North Carolina, November 3, 1966; admitted to bar, 1994, North Carolina; 1995, U.S. District Court, Eastern District of North Carolina; U.S. Court of Appeals, 4th Circuit. *Education:* North Carolina State University (B.A., summa cum laude, 1988); University of North Carolina at Chapel Hill (J.D., with honors, 1993). Author: 72 N.C.L.Rev. 666, 1993. Judicial Clerk to Chief Justice James G. Exum, North Carolina Supreme Court, 1993-1994. *Member:* Wake County Bar Association; North Carolina State Bar. ***LANGUAGES:*** Spanish. ***PRACTICE AREAS:*** Insurance Defense; Litigation. ***Email:*** jmkirby@mcdas.com

JOHN C. LLOYD, admitted to bar, 1997, North Carolina. *Education:* University of Scranton (B.A., 1992); Widener University School of Law (J.D., 1996). Society of Forensics. *Member:* Wake County Bar Association; North Carolina State Bar. ***PRACTICE AREAS:*** Insurance Defense. ***Email:*** jclloyd@mcdas.com

REPRESENTATIVE CLIENTS: Dean-Witter Reynolds, Inc.; Peat, Marwick, Mitchell & Co.; Prudential-Bache Securities, Inc.; Century Surety Company; Deed South Surplus of Tennessee, Inc.; Federal Insurance (Chubb Group); Harleysville Mutual Insurance Company; Huron Insurance Company; National American Insurance Company; Ohio Casualty Insurance Companies; St. Paul Insurance Companies.

McMILLAN, SMITH & PLYLER

Established in 1949
205 WEST MARTIN STREET
RALEIGH, NORTH CAROLINA 27602
Telephone: 919-821-5124
Fax: 919-821-5129
Email: plyler@mspraleigh.com

Civil and Criminal Trials and Appeals in all State and Federal Courts. Commercial Litigation, False Claims Act Litigation, Business Torts, Antitrust, Personal Injury, Negligence, Criminal Defense and White Collar Criminal Defense, N.C. Election Law.

MEMBERS OF FIRM

ROBERT L. McMILLAN, born Raleigh, North Carolina, September 4, 1923; admitted to bar, 1949, North Carolina. *Education:* Wake Forest University (B.S., 1943); University of North Carolina (LL.B., 1949). Phi Delta Phi. Prosecutor, Municipal Court, Raleigh, 1954-1957; First Recipient, Joseph Branch Professionalism Award presented by Wake County Bar Association, 1991. *Member:* Wake County (President, 1976) and North Carolina (Member, General Practice Hall of Fame, 1992) Bar Associations; North Carolina State Bar (Councillor, Tenth Judicial District, 1984-1992); Wake County Academy of Criminal Trial Lawyers (President, 1974). [Capt., U.S. Marine Corps, 1943-1946; 1951-1952]. ***PRACTICE AREAS:*** Criminal Law.

STEPHEN T. SMITH, born Raleigh, North Carolina, August 26, 1947; admitted to bar, 1973, North Carolina; 1976, U.S. Supreme Court. *Education:* East Carolina University (A.B., with honors, 1969); University of North Carolina (J.D., with honors, 1973). North Carolina Law Review, 1972-1973. Listed in The Best Lawyers in America. *Member:* North Carolina State Bar (Disciplinary Hearing Commission, 1990-1996; Tenth Judicial District Grievance Committee, 1988-1990, Chairman, 1990); Wake County (President, 1992), North Carolina (Chairman, Criminal Justice Section, 1984-1985) and American (Member: Litigation Section; White Collar Crime Committee, Criminal Justice Section) Bar Associations; Wake County Academy of Criminal Trial Lawyers (President, 1979-1980); National Association of Criminal Defense Lawyers. [Sgt., U.S. Army, Active Duty, 1969-1971]. ***PRACTICE AREAS:*** Civil and Criminal Trials; White Collar Criminal Defense; Antitrust; False Claim Act Litigation; State Election Law; Professional Discipline. ***Email:*** smith@mspraleigh.com

DUNCAN A. McMILLAN, born Durham, North Carolina, August 25, 1952; admitted to bar, 1977, North Carolina. *Education:* Wake Forest University (B.A., cum laude, 1974); University of North Carolina (J.D., 1977). Listed in Best Lawyers in America, Criminal Law. *Member:* Wake County (Member, Executive Committee, 1981-1983; 1991-1992) and North Carolina Bar Associations; North Carolina State Bar (Member, Tenth Judicial District Grievance Committee, 1996-1999); North Carolina Academy of Trial Lawyers; Wake County Academy of Criminal Trial Lawyers (President, 1983). ***LANGUAGES:*** Spanish. ***PRACTICE AREAS:*** Criminal Trials. ***Email:*** dmcmillan@mspraleigh.com

WILLIAM WEBB PLYLER, born Wilson, North Carolina, November 3, 1955; admitted to bar, 1982, North Carolina. *Education:* University of North Carolina (A.B., 1978; J.D., 1982). Assistant District Attorney, Tenth Judicial District, 1982-1985. *Member:* Wake County (President, 2000), 10th Judicial District (President, 2000; Member, Tenth Judicial District Grievance Committee, 2003—) and North Carolina Bar Associations; North Carolina State Bar; North Carolina Academy of Trial Lawyers; The Association of Trial Lawyers of America; Fourth Circuit Judicial Conference. ***PRACTICE AREAS:*** Personal Injury; Civil Litigation; Fraud and Deceit; Negligence; Products Liability; Torts. ***Email:*** plyler@mspraleigh.com

Languages: Spanish and English.

McNAIR LAW FIRM, P.A.

LANDMARK CENTER, SUITE 500
4601 SIX FORKS ROAD
RALEIGH, NORTH CAROLINA 27609
Telephone: 919-786-4061
Facsimile: 919-786-4076
Email: cfort@mcnair.net
URL: http://www.mcnair.net

Columbia, South Carolina Office: 1301 Gervais Street, P.O. Box 11390, 29211. Telephone: 803-799-9800. Facsimile: 803-799-9804.
Anderson, South Carolina Office: 500 South McDuffie Street, P.O. Box 4086, 29621. Telephone: 864-226-1688. Facsimile: 864-225-6456.
Bluffton, South Carolina Office: 5 Belfair Village Drive, 29910-2605. Telephone: 843-815-2171. Facsimile: 843-815-5991.
Charleston, South Carolina Office: 100 Calhoun Street, Suite 400, 29401. Telephone: 843-723-7831. Facsimile: 843-722-3227.
Georgetown, South Carolina Office: 121 Screven Street, P.O. Drawer 418, 29442. Telephone: 843-546-6102. Facsimile: 843-546-0096.
Greenville, South Carolina Office: Bank of America Plaza, 7 North Laurens Street-Suite 600, P.O. Box 447. 29602. Telephone: 864-271-4940. Facsimile: 864-233-0423; 864-271-4015.
Hilton Head Island, South Carolina Office: Shelter Cove Executive Park, 23-B Shelter Cove Lane, Suite 400, P.O. Drawer 3, 29938-0003. Telephone: 843-785-2171. Facsimile: 843-686-5991.
Myrtle Beach, South Carolina Office: Founders Centre, 2411 Oak Street, Suite 206, 29577. Telephone: 843-444-1107. Facsimile: 843-444-4729.
Charlotte, North Carolina Office: Two Wachovia Center, 301 South Tryon Street, Suite 1615, 28282. Telephone: 704-347-1170. Facsimile: 704-347-4467.

Administrative, Admiralty, Antitrust, Banking, Bankruptcy, Civil and Criminal Practice in all State and Federal Courts of Record, Corporate, Environmental, ERISA, Estate Planning, Health Care, Intellectual Property, Immigration, International, Interstate Land Sales, Labor

(This Listing Continued)

and Employment Relations, Legislative/Governmental (National and State), Mergers and Acquisitions, Municipal Finance, Probate, Real Estate, Regulatory, Securities, Tax, Telecommunications, and Utility Law.

CHARLES S. CARTER, admitted to bar, 1974, North Carolina, District of Columbia and U.S. Supreme Court. *Education:* Duke University (B.S., in Engineering, 1970); University of North Carolina School of Law (J.D., 1974). Associate Director of Congressional Liaison Office, USEPA, 1981-1982; Assistant General Counsel, USEPA, 1982-1990. *Member:* North Carolina (Member, Environmental and Administrative Law Sections) and American (Chair and Vice Chair, Air Quality Committee, SONREEL, 1990— Judicial Review Committee, Administrative Law Section) Bar Associations; Air and Waste Management Association RTP Chapter Board Member); Environmental Law Institute (Associate); Carolinas Pollution Control Association. ***PRACTICE AREAS:*** Environmental; Regulatory; Business. ***Email:*** ccarter@mcnair.net

REPRESENTATIVE CLIENTS: Bank of America; Brunswick County, North Carolina; Colonial Life & Accident Insurance Company; Food Lion, Inc.; Fuji Photo Film, Inc.; Georgetown Steel Corp.; Georgia-Pacific Corporation; International Paper; McDevitt & Street Co.; Milliken & Co.; Norfolk Southern Corporation; Palmetto Health Alliance; Palmetto Seed Capital Corporation; Piedmont Municipal Power Agency; Pirelli Cable Corporation; Safety-Kleen Corp.; SCANA Corporation; Showa Denko Carbon, Inc.; South Carolina Electric & Gas Company; South Carolina State Ports Authority; Union Camp Corporation; UNISYS Corporation; Westinghouse Electric Corporation.

(For complete biographical data on Columbia, Anderson, Bluffton, Charleston, Georgetown, Greenville, Hilton Head Island and Myrtle Beach, South Carolina and Charlotte, North Carolina personnel, see Professional Biographies of those cities)

MEDIRATTA LAW FIRM

5 WEST HARGETT STREET, SUITE 700
RALEIGH, NORTH CAROLINA 27601
Telephone: 919-833-6105
Fax: 919-833-6106
URL: http://www.medirattalawoffice.com
Email: medirattalawfirm@bellsouth.net
URL: http://www.medirattalawfirm.com

Criminal Law, Driving While Intoxicated, Traffic Violations, Personal Injury, Civil Litigation, Immigration, Automobile Accidents, Juvenile Law.

PAUL MEDIRATTA, admitted to bar, 2003, North Carolina and U.S. District Court, Eastern District of North Carolina. *Education:* University of Maryland, College Park (B.S., Psychology, 1995); Thomas M. Cooley Law School (J.D., 2000). *Member:* North Carolina and American Bar Associations; The Association of Trial Lawyers of America. ***PRACTICE AREAS:*** Criminal Law; Driving While Intoxicated; Traffic Violations; Personal Injury; Civil Litigation; Immigration and Naturalization; Automobile Accidents and Injuries; Juvenile Law. ***Email:*** medirattalawfirm@bellsouth.net

MILLBERG, GORDON & STEWART, PLLC

1101 HAYNES STREET, SUITE 104
RALEIGH, NORTH CAROLINA 27604-1455
Telephone: 919-836-0090
Fax: 919-836-8027
Email: mgsfirm@mgsattorneys.com
URL: http://www.mgsattorneys.com

Civil Trial, Product Liability, Railroad Litigation, Trucking Liability, Construction Litigation, Toxic Torts, Professional Liability and Professional Ethics, Occupational Licensing and Discipline.

FIRM PROFILE: Millberg, Gordon & Stewart's attorneys have engaged in an active civil trial practice in the Carolinas for many years. The firm's clients include railroads, heavy equipment manufacturers, trucking companies, construction companies, insurance companies, and other businesses, large and small. The firm has successfully represented its clients in a wide variety of cases, including class actions, multiple fatality claims, toxic torts and severe brain damage cases, to name a few.

The firm also represents professional clients in licensing, disciplinary, and ethical matters, in other administrative proceedings, and in professional malpractice litigation.

JOHN C. MILLBERG, born New London, Connecticut, January 4, 1956; admitted to bar, 1980, Texas; 1986, North Carolina; 2000, South Carolina. *Education:* Bowling Green State University (B.A., cum laude, 1977); Wake Forest University School of Law (J.D., 1980). *Member:* North Carolina Bar Association; State Bar of Texas; South Carolina Bar; North Carolina Association of Defense Attorneys; National Association of Railroad Trial Counsel; Transportation Research Board. ***REPORTED CASES:*** McNair v. Lend Lease Trucks, Inc., 95 F.3d 325 (4th Cir. 1996) (en banc); McNair v. Lend Lease Trucks, Inc., 62 F.3d 651 (4th Cir. 1995); Collins v. CXX Transp., Inc., 114 N.C.App. 14, 441 S.E.2d 150, disc rev. denied 336 N.C. 603, 447 S.E.2d 388 (1994); Robinson v. Seaboard System R.R., Inc., 87 N.C.App. 512, 361 S.E.2d 909 (1987), disc. rev. denied, 321 N.C. 474, 364 S.E.2d 924 (1988); Wilkerson v. Norfolk Southern Ry. Co., 606 S.E.2d 187 (N.C.App. 2004); Sharp v. CSX Transp., Inc., 160 N.C.App. 241, 584 S.E.2d 888 (2003); Jackson v. Associated Scaffolders and Equip. Co., Inc., 152 N.C.App. 687, 568 S.E.2d 666 (2002); Turner v. Norfolk Southern Corp., 137 N.C.App. 138, 526 S.E.2d 666 (2000); Pinckney v.Van Damme, 116 N.C.App. 139, 447 S.E.2d 825 (1994); McKeithan v. CSX Transp., Inc., 113 N.C.App. 818, 440 S.E.2d 312 (1994); McClain v. Otis Elevator Co., Inc., 106 N.C.App. 45, 415 S.E.2d 312 (1992); Strickland v. Jacobs, 88 N.C.App. 397, 363 S.E.2d 229 (1988); Flores v. Coffield Warehouse Co., 683 S.W.2d 31, (Tx.Ct.App.-Texarkana, 1984); Smith v. Aberdeen, Carolina and Western Ry. Co., 859 F.Supp. 188 (W.D.N.C. 1994); McCallum v. CSX Tramsp., Inc., 149 F.R.D. 104 (M.D.N.C. 1993); Ward v. CSX Transp., Inc., 161 F.R.D. 38, 32 Fed.R.Serv.3d 408 (E.D.N.C. 1995); Ford v. CSX Transportation, Inc., 162 F.R.D. 108 (E.D.N.C. 1995). ***PRACTICE AREAS:*** Railroad Litigation; Products Liability; Professional Liability. ***Email:*** jmillberg@mgsattorneys.com

(This Listing Continued)

FRANK J. GORDON, born Hickory, North Carolina, April 7, 1962; admitted to bar, 1988, North Carolina, U.S. District Court, Eastern, Western and Middle Districts of North Carolina; 2003, South Carolina, U.S. District Court, District of South Carolina, U.S. Court of Appeals, Fourth Circuit, U.S. Supreme Court. *Education:* North Carolina State University (B.S.Ch.E., 1985); Wake Forest University School of Law (J.D., 1988). Harry S. Truman Scholar. James F. Hoge Scholar of Law. Member, Wake Forest University Law Review, 1986-1988. Law Clerk to Hon. Frank W. Bullock, Jr., U.S. District Judge, Middle District of North Caroline. *Member:* North Carolina Bar Association; South Carolina Bar; North Carolina Association of Defense Attorneys; National Association of Railroad Trial Counsel; Defense Research Institute. ***REPORTED CASES:*** Loredo v. CSX Transp., Inc., 2005 WL 756 352 (N.C.App., April 5, 2005); Warnock v. CSX Transp., Inc.,159 N.C.app. 215, 582 S.E.2d 386, disc. rev. denied, 357 N.C. 582, 589 S.E.2d 725 (2003); Turner v. Norfolk Southern Corp., 137 N.C.App. 138, 526 S.E.2d 666 (2000); Goodrum v. Green, 334 N.C. 620, 435 S.E.2d 335 (1993); Clinton v. Wake County Bd. of Educ., 108 N.C.App. 616, 424 S.E.2d 691, 80 Ed. Law Rep. 319 disc. rev. denied 333 N.C. 574, 429 S.E.2d 570 (1993); Collins v. CSX Transp., Inc., 114 N.C.App. 14, 441 S.E.2d 150 disc. rev. denied 336 N.C. 603, 447 S.E.2d 388 (1994); Smith v. Aberdeen, Carolina and Western Ry. Co., 859 F.Supp. 188 (W.D.N.C. 1994); McCallum v. CSX Transp., Inc., 149 F.R.D.104 (M.D.N.C. 1993). ***PRACTICE AREAS:*** Railroad Litigation; Products Liability; Trucking Law. ***Email:*** fgordon@mgsattorneys.com

WILLIAM W. STEWART, JR., born Charlotte, North Carolina, December 30, 1964; admitted to bar, 1994, North Carolina; 2004, South Carolina. *Education:* Mississippi College (B.S., 1987); Mississippi College School of Law (J.D. with distinction, 1993). Managing Editor, Mississippi College Law Review, 1992-1993. Law Clerk to Hon. Franklin T. Dupree, Jr., Senior U.S. District Judge, Eastern District of NC. Note, "'Sweeping the Buses': Florida's Search for the Appropriate Test in Determining What Constitutes a Seizure in Regard to Their Own Drug Interdiction Program," 13 Miss. C.L.Rev. 385 (1993). *Member:* North Carolina and American Bar Associations; South Carolina Bar; National Association of Railroad Trial Counsel; North Carolina Association of Defense Attorneys; Defense Research Institute. ***REPORTED CASES:*** Virgil v. Montgomery, 353 F.Supp.2d 620 (E.D.N.C. 2005); Jackson v. Associated Scaffolders and Equip. Co., Inc., 152 N.C.App. 687, 568 S.E.2d 666 (2002); Pontoon v. National R.R. Passenger Corp., 194 F.R.D. 521, 44 Fed.R.Law.3d 676, 48 Fed.R.Serv.3d 1198 (M.D.N.C. 1999); Denty v. CSX Transp., Inc., 168 F.R.D. 549 (E.D.N.C. 1996). ***PRACTICE AREAS:*** Railroad Litigation; Personal Injury; Trucking Liability; Products Liability. ***Email:*** bstewart@mgsattorneys.com

DOUGLAS J. BROCKER, born York, Pennsylvania, January 7, 1967; admitted to bar, 1992, Illinois, 1994, U.S. District Court, Northern District of Illinois; 1996, North Carolina, U.S. District Court, Eastern and Middle Districts of North Carolina and U.S. Court of Appeals, Fourth Circuit. *Education:* University of Rochester (B.A., magna cum laude, 1989); University of North Carolina at Chapel Hill (J.D., with honors, 1992). Phi Beta Kappa. Member, North Carolina Law Review. Law Clerk, Honorable Franklin T. Dupree, Jr., U.S. District Court, Eastern District of North Carolina. *Member:* Wake County, North Carolina (Member, Administrative Law Section), Illinois State Bar Associations. North Carolina State Bar. ***PRACTICE AREAS:*** Professional Licensing; Professional Discipline; Corporate Ethics; Professional Liability; Professional Malpractice; Administrative Law. ***Email:*** dbrocker@mgsattorneys.com

SETH C. TURNER, born Raleigh, North Carolina, June 6, 1980; admitted to bar, 2005, North Carolina. *Education:* University of North Carolina at Chapel Hill (B.A., with distinction and highest honors, 2002; J.D., with honors, 2005). Phi Beta Kappa; Order of the Barristers. Chief Justice, Holderness Moot Court, 2004-2005. Member: Invitational Moot Court Team, 2003-2005; Broun National Trial Team, 2003-2005. Recipient: Frany Ryan Prize; James H. Morrow Award. *Member:* Wake County and North Carolina Bar Associations; North Carolina State Bar. ***PRACTICE AREAS:*** Railroad Litigation.

ELIZABETH H. POREMBA, born Fayetteville, North Carolina, November 18, 1977; admitted to bar, 2003, North Carolina; 2004, South Carolina. *Education:* Appalachian State University (B.S.C.J., cum laude, 1999); Campbell University (J.D., 2003). Phi Alpha Delta. *Member:* Wake County and North Carolina Bar Associations; National Association of Railroad Trial Counsel; North Carolina Association of Defense Attorneys; Defense Research Institute. ***PRACTICE AREAS:*** Railroad Litigation; Premises Liability; Products Liability. ***Email:*** eporemba@mgsattorneys.com

REPRESENTATIVE CLIENTS: Carolina Crane and Equipment, LLC; Caterpillar Inc.; Centex Homes; CNA Insurance Companies; CSX Transportation, Inc.; Dixie Pipeline Co.; La Personelle Assurance; Midlands Claims Administrators, Inc.; National Railroad Passenger Corporation (Amtrak); North Carolina Board of Dental Examiners; North Carolina Mutual Wholesale Drug Company; Royal Sun Alliance; Shelby-Vesta Insurance Group; United Dominion Industries, Inc.; Volkswagon of America, Inc.

CHARLES W. MILLER

RALEIGH, NORTH CAROLINA

(See Pittsboro)

Collections, Bankruptcy, Commercial Litigation, Business Contracts, Credit Law, Administrative Law, Real Estate, Mediation, Securities Arbitration, Investment Fund.

MILLER & SHEDOR, PLLC

RALEIGH, NORTH CAROLINA

(See Cary)

Criminal Law, Driving While Intoxicated, Juvenile Crimes, Traffic Violations, Bankruptcy, Foreclosures, Family Law, Adoptions, Child Support, Child Custody, Divorce, Visitation Rights, Real Estate, Landlord and Tenant Law, Wills, Probate, Collections, Personal Injury, Automobile Accidents, Slip and Fall, Wrongful Death, Workers Compensation, Discrimination, Sexual Harassment, Wrongful Termination.

MINEO & MINEO

TWO HANOVER SQUARE, SUITE 2350
434 FAYETTEVILLE STREET MALL
RALEIGH, NORTH CAROLINA 27601
Telephone: 919-861-0501
Fax: 919-861-0504
URL: http://www.airlawus.com

National and International Aviation Litigation, Aircraft Crash and Regulatory Law, Mass Disaster, Product Liability, and Personal Injury Litigation. Appeals in all Courts.

FIRM PROFILE: For complete information, visit our website at www.airlawus.com.

MEMBERS OF FIRM

ROBERT A. MINEO, born Oriental, North Carolina, November 30, 1948; admitted to bar, 1981, North Carolina and U.S. District Court, Eastern District of North Carolina; 1982, U.S. District Court, Middle and Western Districts of North Carolina, U.S. District Court, District of Maryland and U.S. Court of Appeals, Fourth Circuit; 1983, U.S. Court of Appeals for the District of Columbia Circuit and U.S. Claims Court; 1984, U.S. District Court, Eastern District of Texas; 1986, U.S. Supreme Court; 1988, District of Columbia. *Education:* North Carolina State University (B.S., in Aerospace Engineering, 1970); University of Notre Dame; Campbell University (J.D., 1981). Member, Campbell Law Review, 1980-1981. Adjunct Professor of Aviation Law, Norman A. Wiggins School of Law, Campbell University. *Member:* North Carolina State Bar; District of Columbia Bar, American Institute of Aeronautics and Astronautics; International Society of Air Safety Investigators. [Aerospace Engineer, U.S. Navy, 1970-1978]. ***PRACTICE AREAS:*** Aviation Accidents Litigation; Personal Injury; Wrongful Death; Products Liability. ***Email:*** ncairlaw@aol.com

ATHENA R. MINEO, born Greensboro, North Carolina, January 26, 1957; admitted to bar, 1982, North Carolina. *Education:* University of North Carolina at Chapel Hill (B.A., Psychology and Drama, with honors, 1978); University of Notre Dame; Campbell University (J.D., 1982). President, Women in Law, Campbell Law Journal. Senate Legal Counsel, Senator Jesse Helms, Washington, D.C., 1982-1983. Professor of Business Law, Wake Community College, 1994. Licensed Realtor, North Carolina, 1994—. Corporate Counsel, Society Brand Industries, U.S. and Puerto Rico, 1984-1986. *Member:* North Carolina State Bar. ***PRACTICE AREAS:*** Corporate Law; Business Law; Personal Injury; Regulatory Law.

DAVID R. MINGES

Established in 2003
4401 REVERE DRIVE
RALEIGH, NORTH CAROLINA 27609
Telephone: 919-782-4476
Fax: 919-782-4277
Email: dminges@nc.rr.com
URL: http://www.lawyers.com/davidminges
Eminent Domain, Condemnation, Real Estate.

FIRM PROFILE: Specializes in land condemnation, eminent domain, real estate and civil litigation. Former condemnation trial attorney for N.C. Department of Transportation; extensive trial and appellate experience; numerous million dollar acquisitions.

DAVID R. MINGES, born Rocky Mount, North Carolina, April 2, 1956; admitted to bar, 1982, North Carolina. *Education:* East Carolina University (B.S., Business Administration, with honors, 1978); Campbell University (J.D., 1982). Assistant Attorney General, North Carolina Department of Justice, Attorney General's Office, 1982-2002. *Member:* North Carolina Bar Association. ***REPORTED CASES:*** Southern Furniture Co. v. NC-DOT, 133 NCApp 400, 516 SE 2d 383 (1999); DOT v. Haggerty, 127 NCApp 499, 492 SE2d 770 (1997). ***PRACTICE AREAS:*** Eminent Domain; Condemnation; Real Estate.

MITCHELL, EYSTER & WARNER, P.A.

RALEIGH, NORTH CAROLINA

(See Durham)

Comprehensive Health Care Law including Administrative Law, Corporate Law, Business Law, Tax Law, Employment, Estate Planning, Trusts and Estates, Collections.

MITCHINER LAW FIRM, PLLC

3110 EDWARDS MILL ROAD, SUITE 340
RALEIGH, NORTH CAROLINA 27612-5419
Telephone: 919-277-2600
Fax: 919-277-2626
Email: joe.mitchiner@mitchinerlaw.com

Wills, Trusts and Estates, including Estate Planning, Family Wealth Transfer, Living Trusts, Trust Planning and Wealth Preservation.

FIRM PROFILE: Began with DeMent Redwine & Yeargan (1976-78), formed Yeargan & Mitchiner (1978-82), expanded to Yeargan, Thompson & Mitchiner (1982-96), solo (1996-1999), Of Counsel to Wallis & Morton, P.A. (1999-2004), formed Mitchiner Law Firm, PLLC, in 2004 to limit scope of practice.

JOSEPH H. MITCHINER, born Smithfield, North Carolina, June 10, 1951; admitted to bar, 1977, North Carolina; 1978, Florida; U.S. Supreme Court, U.S. Court of Appeals, Fourth and Eleventh Circuits, U.S. District Court, Eastern and Middle Districts of North Carolina and Southern District of Florida and U.S. Tax Court. *Education:* University of North Carolina, Chapel Hill (B.S., in Business Administration, 1973); North Carolina Central University, Durham (J.D., magna cum laude, 1976). *Member:* Wake County and North Carolina (Member, Sections on: Estate Planning and Fiduciary Law) Bar Associations; North Carolina State Bar; The Florida Bar. ***Email:*** joe.mitchiner@mitchinerlaw.com

LAW OFFICES OF CHARLES H. MONTGOMERY

RALEIGH, NORTH CAROLINA

(See Cary)

Family Law, Civil Litigation, Civil Appeals, Mediation, Arbitration, Divorce, Separation Agreements, Child Custody, Spousal Support, Marital Property Distribution, Premarital Agreements.

MOORE & ALPHIN, PLLC

3716 NATIONAL DRIVE, SUITE 100
RALEIGH, NORTH CAROLINA 27612
Telephone: 919-787-8812
Facsimile: 919-787-3312
URL: http://www.lawyers.com/moorealphin

Durham, North Carolina Office: 1000 Park Forty Plaza, Suite 100, 27713. Telephone: 919-544-0092. Facsimile: 919-544-1059.

Residential and Commercial Real Estate, Zoning, Planning and Land Use, Corporate, Business Law, Small Business, Estate Planning, Wills.

RICHARD W. MOORE, born Atlanta, Georgia, February 15, 1947; admitted to bar, 1977, Georgia; 1984, North Carolina. *Education:* Auburn University (B.S., with high honor, 1969); University of Virginia (J.D., 1977). Member, Virginia Law Review, 1976-1977. Court Certified Mediator. *Member:* Wake County and North Carolina (Member, Real Property Section) Bar Associations; North Carolina State Bar. ***PRACTICE AREAS:*** Real Estate Law; Corporate Law. ***Email:*** rwm@moorealphin.com

G. MARK TEAGUE, born Salisbury, North Carolina, November 26, 1967; admitted to bar, 1993, North Carolina; 1996, U.S. District Court, Eastern and Middle Districts of North Carolina. *Education:* University of North Carolina (B.A., 1990); Wake Forest University School of Law (J.D., 1993). *Member:* North Carolina State Bar; North Carolina Bar Association (Member, Real Property Section). ***PRACTICE AREAS:*** Real Estate. ***Email:*** gmt@moorealphin.com

S. AMANDA PALMER, born Plainfield, New Jersey, March 10, 1970; admitted to bar, 1998, North Carolina. *Education:* American University (B.A., 1992); George Mason University School of Law (J.D., 1998). *Member:* Wake County and North Carolina Bar Associations. ***PRACTICE AREAS:*** Real Estate. ***Email:*** amanda@moorealphin.com

OF COUNSEL

OLIVER W. ALPHIN, born Duplin County, North Carolina, July 16, 1933; admitted to bar, 1961, North Carolina. *Education:* University of North Carolina (B.S., 1959; J.D., with honors, 1961). Order of the Coif. Board of Editors, North Carolina Law Review, 1959-1961. Law Clerk to Hon. A.L. Butler, U.S. District Court, Eastern District of North Carolina, 1961-1962. Adjunct Professor, Real Estate Law, University of North Carolina School of Law, 1982-1984 . Hearing Examiner, North Carolina Occupational Safety and Health Review Board, 1976-1989. Member, North Carolina Property Tax Commission, 1989-1993. *Member:* Durham County and North Carolina (Member, Real Estate Section) Bar Associations. ***PRACTICE AREAS:*** Real Estate.

MOORE & VAN ALLEN PLLC

RALEIGH, NORTH CAROLINA

(See Research Triangle Park)

MORRIS YORK WILLIAMS SURLES & BARRINGER, L.L.P.

RALEIGH, NORTH CAROLINA

(See Charlotte)

Civil, Business and Commercial Litigation. Insurance Defense Litigation, Insurance Coverage and Workers Compensation. Medical and Professional Malpractice Defense. Land Condemnation and Alternative Dispute Resolution Services.

MYERS BIGEL SIBLEY & SAJOVEC, P.A.

4140 PARKLAKE AVENUE, SUITE 600
RALEIGH, NORTH CAROLINA 27612
Telephone: 919-854-1400
Fax: 919-854-1401
Email: mbss@myersbigel.com
URL: http://www.myersbigel.com

Intellectual Property Law: Patents, Trademarks, Copyrights and related Litigation.

FIRM PROFILE: Myers Bigel Sibley & Sajovec, P.A. is devoted to the practice of intellectual property law and is the largest independent intellectual property law firm in North Carolina. Each of its attorneys has a technical background, including electronics, computers, chemistry, biotechnology and mechanical engineering. Myers Bigel Sibley & Sajovec is located in the heart of North Carolina's Research Triangle Park, and is experienced in patent preparation and prosecution, trademark registration practice and intellectual property litigation.

(This Listing Continued)

The firm's clients include regional, national and international corporations, research consortia, universities and technology start-up companies.

D. RANDAL AYERS, born Washington, D.C., 1963; admitted to bar, 1994, North Carolina; registered to practice before U.S. Patent and Trademark Office. *Education:* University of Virginia (B.S.E.E., 1986); George Mason University (M.S.E.E., 1990); University of Virginia (J.D., 1994). Order of the Coif. Member, Virginia Law Review. ***PRACTICE AREAS:*** Patent, Trademark and Copyright; Litigation. ***Email:*** rayers@myersbigel.com

DAVID D. BEATTY, born Asheboro, North Carolina, 1968; admitted to bar, 1993, North Carolina; registered to practice before U.S. Patent and Trademark Office. *Education:* The North Carolina School of Science and Mathematics; North Carolina State University (B.S., Nuclear Engineering, 1990); University of North Carolina (J.D., 1993). *Member:* Carolina Patent, Trademark and Copyright Law Association (Member, Board of Directors). ***PRACTICE AREAS:*** Patent, Trademark and Copyright. ***Email:*** dbeatty@myersbigel.com

MITCHELL S. BIGEL, born Brooklyn, New York, 1953; admitted to bar, 1982, District of Columbia; 1983, New York; 1989, North Carolina; registered to practice before U.S. Patent and Trademark Office. *Education:* City College of the City University of New York (B.E.E., cum laude, 1977); George Washington University (J.D., with high honors, 1982). Recipient: Ranked as the #1 Patent and Intellectual Property Lawyer in North Carolina by Business North Carolina Magazine, 2002, 2003; Inducted into the "Legal Elite" Hall of Fame, Business North Carolina Magazine. Former Chair, AIPLA Law Practice Management Committee. Former President, Carolina Patent, Trademark and Copyright Law Association. *Member:* American Bar Association (Former Chair, Economics Committee, Intellectual Property Law Section). ***PRACTICE AREAS:*** Patent; Trademark; Copyright; Electrical Intellectual Property; Electronics; Computer Technology. ***Email:*** mbigel@myersbigel.com

NEEDHAM J. BODDIE, II, born Durham, North Carolina, 1956; admitted to bar, 1994, North Carolina; registered to practice before U.S. Patent and Trademark Office. *Education:* Duke University (B.S.M.E., 1979); Wake Forest University (M.B.A., 1989; J.D., cum laude, 1994). Professional Engineer, North Carolina, 1986. ***PRACTICE AREAS:*** Patent, Trademark and Copyright. ***Email:*** nboddie@myersbigel.com

LYNNE A. BORCHERS, born Rhinebeck, New York, 1964; admitted to bar, 1991, New York; 2001, New Jersey; 2004, North Carolina; registered to practice before U.S. Patent and Trademark Office. *Education:* State University of New York Maritime College (B.E.E.E., 1985); Seton Hall University School of Law (J.D., 1991). ***PRACTICE AREAS:*** Intellectual Property Litigation. ***Email:*** lborchers@myersbigel.com

JAMES R. CANNON, born Tulsa, Oklahoma, December 2, 1960; admitted to bar, 1991, North Carolina; registered to practice before U.S. Patent and Trademark Office. *Education:* Texas Christian University (B.S. summa cum laude, 1982); Washington University (B.S.M.E., cum laude, 1984); Duke University (J.D., with honors, 1991). Recipient, Named to the "Legal Elite," Business North Carolina Magazine, 2004. Technical Editor, Law & Contemporary Problems. Author: "Novelty and the Public Domain," *The Law and Strategy of Biotechnology Patents*, 1994. *Member:* North Carolina Bar Association (Former CLE Chairman, Secretary, Vice Chair and Chair, Intellectual Property Law Section). ***PRACTICE AREAS:*** Patent, Trademark and Copyright. ***Email:*** jcannon@myersbigel.com

ROBERT N. CROUSE, born Boston, Massachusetts, 1960; admitted to bar, 1997, North Carolina; registered to practice before the U.S. Patent and Trademark Office. *Education:* Northeastern University (B.S.E.E., with honors, 1983); Wake Forest University (J.D., 1997). *Member:* IEEE. ***PRACTICE AREAS:*** Patent, Trademark and Copyright. ***Email:*** bcrouse@myersbigel.com

ROBERT W. GLATZ, born Rochester, New York, 1958; admitted to bar, 1991, North Carolina; registered to practice before U.S. Patent and Trademark Office. *Education:* Massachusetts Institute of Technology (S.B.M.E., 1980); Rochester Institute of Technology (M.S.E.E., 1983); University of North Carolina at Charlotte (M.B.A., 1987); University of North Carolina (J.D., with high honors, 1991). Order of the Coif. Member, North Carolina Law Review. Recipient, Named to the "Legal Elite," Business North Carolina Magazine, 2004. Co-Author: "Substantive Aspects of Patent Litigation" and "Procedural Aspects of Patent Litigation," *The Law and Strategy of Biotechnology Patents*, 1994. ***PRACTICE AREAS:*** Patent, Trademark and Copyright. ***Email:*** rglatz@myersbigel.com

SCOTT C. HATFIELD, born Memphis, Tennessee, 1965; admitted to bar, 1993, North Carolina; registered to practice before U.S. Patent and Trademark Office. *Education:* Vanderbilt University (B.E.E.E., summa cum laude, 1987; J.D., 1993). ***PRACTICE AREAS:*** Patent, Trademark and Copyright. ***Email:*** shatfield@myersbigel.com

DR. KAREN A. MAGRI, born Smithtown, New York, 1963; admitted to bar, 1996, North Carolina; registered to practice before U.S. Patent and Trademark Office. *Education:* Cornell University (B.S., with distinction, 1985); Pennsylvania State University (M.S., 1988); Syracuse University (Ph.D., 1993); Duke University (J.D., with highest honors, 1996). Order of the Coif. Duke Law Journal. ***PRACTICE AREAS:*** Patent, Trademark and Copyright; Biotechnology. ***Email:*** kmagri@myersbigel.com

ROBERT M. MEEKS, born Denver, Colorado, 1959; admitted to bar, 1995, North Carolina; registered to practice before U.S. Patent and Trademark Office. *Education:* Georgia Institute of Technology (B.S.E.E., 1984; M.S.E.E., 1986); University of Georgia (J.D., cum laude, 1995). Articles Editor, Journal of Intellectual Property Law. ***PRACTICE AREAS:*** Patent, Trademark and Copyright. ***Email:*** bmeeks@myersbigel.com

DR. MARY L. MILLER, born Gary, Indiana, 1956; admitted to bar, 1997, Georgia; 2004, North Carolina; registered to practice before the U.S. Patent and Trademark Office. *Education:* University of South Florida (B.A., in Microbiology, 1982); University of Texas at Austin (Ph.D., in Microbiology, 1991); Georgia State University (J.D., 1997). ***PRACTICE AREAS:*** Biotechnology Patents. ***Email:*** mmiller@myersbigel.com

D. SCOTT MOORE, born Knoxville, Tennessee, 1963; admitted to bar, 1996, Illinois; 1998, Georgia; 2000, North Carolina; registered to practice before U.S. Patent and Trademark Office. *Education:* University of Illinois (B.S.E.E., with high honors, 1985; M.S.E.E., 1987); Chicago-Kent College of Law (J.D., with honors, 1996). ***PRACTICE AREAS:*** Patent, Trademark and Copyright. ***Email:*** smoore@myersbigel.com

(This Listing Continued)

JAMES D. MYERS, born Columbia, South Carolina, 1940; admitted to bar, 1972, South Carolina; 1974, North Carolina; registered to practice before U.S. Patent and Trademark Office. *Education:* University of South Carolina (B.S.Ch.E., 1963; J.D., cum laude, 1972). Recipient, Named to the "Legal Elite," Business North Carolina Magazine, 2004. Co-Author: "Substantive Aspects of Patent Litigation" and "Procedural Aspects of Patent Litigation," *The Law and Strategy of Biotechnology Patents*, 1994. Author: "Conflicting Rights in the Same Trademark in Different Geographical Areas," 37 Federal Bar Journal 82, 1978; "EEC Antitrust Law," 5 North Carolina Journal of International Law & Commercial Regulation 37, 1980; "Biotechnology in the Courts," 40 Society for Industrial Microbiology News 189, 1990. Law Clerk to Hon. Clement F. Haynsworth Jr., Chief Judge, U.S. Court of Appeals, Fourth Circuit, 1972-1973. Member, Panel of Patent Dispute Arbitrators, American Arbitration Association. ***PRACTICE AREAS:*** Intellectual Property Litigation. ***Email:*** jmyers@myersbigel.com

TIMOTHY J. O'SULLIVAN, born Kirkwood, Missouri, 1961; admitted to bar, 1990, North Carolina; registered to practice before U.S. Patent and Trademark Office. *Education:* University of Missouri-Rolla (B.S.E.E., magna cum laude, honor scholar, 1984); Duke University (J.D., 1990). ***PRACTICE AREAS:*** Patent, Trademark and Copyright. ***Email:*** tosullivan@myersbigel.com

DAVID K. PURKS, born Ft. Rucker, Alabama, 1963; admitted to bar, 1994, Colorado; 1997, North Carolina; registered to practice before U.S. Patent and Trademark Office. *Education:* Virginia Polytechnic Institute and State University (B.S., Electrical Engineering, 1987; B.S., Aerospace Engineering, 1987); St. Louis University (J.D., 1994). Recipient, First Prize in Nathan Burkan Memorial Competition for paper entitled "Copyright Infringement: A Computer Software Developer's Guide to Protection.". ***PRACTICE AREAS:*** Patents. ***Email:*** dpurks@myersbigel.com

JULIE H. RICHARDSON, born Evansville, Indiana, 1959; admitted to bar, 1995, North Carolina; registered to practice before U.S. Patent and Trademark Office. *Education:* Purdue University (B.S.M.E., 1981); Duke University (J.D., with honors, 1995). Recipient, Named to the "Legal Elite," Business North Carolina Magazine, 2004. ***PRACTICE AREAS:*** Patent, Trademark and Copyright. ***Email:*** jrichardson@myersbigel.com

F. MICHAEL SAJOVEC, born Newport News, Virginia, 1959; admitted to bar, 1986, North Carolina; registered to practice before U.S. Patent and Trademark Office. *Education:* Carnegie Mellon University (B.S., 1981); Cleveland Marshall College of Law (J.D., 1986). Recipient, Named to the "Legal Elite," Business North Carolina Magazine, 2004. *Member:* The Licensing Executives Society. ***PRACTICE AREAS:*** Patent, Trademark and Copyright. ***Email:*** msajovec@myersbigel.com

GRANT J. SCOTT, born White Plains, New York, 1962; admitted to bar, 1991, North Carolina; registered to practice before U.S. Patent and Trademark Office. *Education:* University of Virginia (B.S.E.E., summa cum laude, 1984); University of Illinois (M.S.E.E., 1986); University of North Carolina (J.D., 1991). ***PRACTICE AREAS:*** Patent, Trademark and Copyright. ***Email:*** gscott@myersbigel.com

KENNETH D. SIBLEY, born White Plains, New York, 1956; admitted to bar, 1985, North Carolina; registered to practice before U.S. Patent and Trademark Office. *Education:* Lycoming College (B.A., magna cum laude, Biology, 1979); University of Rochester (M.A., 1982); Duke University (J.D., 1985). Senior Lecturing Fellow, Duke University School of Law, 1995—. Editor: *The Law and Strategy of Biotechnology Patents*, 1994 (Butterworth Heinemann). Recipient: Ranked as the #1 Patent and Intellectual Property Lawyer in North Carolina by Business North Carolina Magazine, 2004. Author: "Practical Utility: Evolution Suspended?" 32 IDEA 203, 1992; "Patent Strategy For Corporations Pursuing World Markets," 40 SIM Indust. Microbiol. News 139, 1990; "Factual Inquiries in Deciding the Question of Enablement," 70 J. Pat. Off. Soc'y. 115, 1988. Co-Author: "Legal Aspects of Product Protection," In Drug Development, 2d ED., C. Hamner ED., 1990. *Member:* Association of University Technology Managers. ***PRACTICE AREAS:*** Patent, Trademark and Copyright; Biotechnology; Intellectual Property. ***Email:*** ksibley@myersbigel.com

RICHARD P. VITEK, born Detroit, Michigan, 1960; admitted to bar, 1985, Michigan; 1989, California; 2001, North Carolina; registered to practice before U.S. Patent and Trademark Office. *Education:* Stanford University (B.S., Industrial Engineering, 1982); University of Michigan School of Law (J.D., 1985). ***PRACTICE AREAS:*** Intellectual Property Litigation. ***Email:*** rvitek@myersbigel.com

---

JARETT K. ABRAMSON, born Livingston, New Jersey, 1971; admitted to bar, 1997, Utah; 2003, North Carolina; registered to practice before U.S. Patent and Trademark Office. *Education:* University of Pennsylvania (B.A., 1994); University of Utah (J.D., 1997; M.S. Chemistry, Biological, 2000). Staff Member, Journal of Energy, Natural Resources and Environmental Law. ***PRACTICE AREAS:*** Patent, Trademark and Copyright; Biotechnology. ***Email:*** jabramson@myersbigel.com

DR. ALICE M. BONNEN, born Lansing, Michigan, 1956; admitted to bar, 2004, North Carolina. *Education:* Michigan State University (B.S., with high honors, 1978); University of Minnesota (M.S., 1981); Michigan State University (Ph.D., 1988); Wake Forest University (J.D., 2004). ***PRACTICE AREAS:*** Patents; Trademarks; Copyrights.

ANNA CARR, born Morristown, New Jersey, 1975; admitted to bar, 2003, North Carolina. *Education:* College of William & Mary (B.S., 1997); University of Texas Graduate School of Biomedical Sciences at Houston (M.S., 2000); Wake Forest University (J.D., 2003). Moot Court Board. ***PRACTICE AREAS:*** Intellectual Property Litigation; Patents; Trademarks; Copyrights. ***Email:*** acarr@myersbigel.com

LAURA M. KELLEY, born Tacoma, Washington, 1974; admitted to bar, 2000, North Carolina; registered to practice before U.S. Patent and Trademark Office. *Education:* College of William & Mary (B.S. in Physics, 1996); Duke University (J.D., high honors, 2000). Phi Beta Kappa. ***PRACTICE AREAS:*** Patents; Intellectual Property; Trademarks. ***Email:*** lkelley@myersbigel.com

DR. SHAWNA CANNON LEMON, born Columbia, South Carolina, 1968; admitted to bar, 2001, North Carolina; registered to practice before U.S. Patent and Trademark Office. *Education:* Wofford College (B.S. in Biology, 1990); University of South Carolina

(This Listing Continued)

MYERS BIGEL SIBLEY & SAJOVEC, P.A., Raleigh—Continued

School of Medicine (Ph.D. in Biomedical Science/Pharmacology, 1995); University of North Carolina at Chapel Hill (J.D., 2001). ***PRACTICE AREAS:*** Patents; Trademarks; Copyrights. ***Email:*** slemon@myersbigel.com

ROHAN G. SABAPATHYPILLAI, born Brooklyn, New York, 1974; admitted to bar, 2003, North Carolina; registered to practice before U.S. Patent and Trademark Office. *Education:* Virginia Polytechnic Institute (B.S.E.E., cum laude, 1997); University of North Carolina (J.D., 2003). ***PRACTICE AREAS:*** Patents; Trademarks; Copyrights. ***Email:*** rsaba@myersbigel.com

ELIZABETH A. STANEK, born Glen Cove, New York, 1975; admitted to bar, 2000, North Carolina; 2002, New York; registered to practice before U.S. Patent and Trademark Office. *Education:* North Carolina State University (B.S., cum laude, Electrical Engineering, 1997); University of North Carolina at Chapel Hill (J.D., 2000). ***PRACTICE AREAS:*** Patent, Trademark and Copyright. ***Email:*** lstanek@myersbigel.com

THE LAW OFFICES OF ADAM NEIJNA, PLLC

8601 SIX FORKS ROAD, SUITE 400
RALEIGH, NORTH CAROLINA 27615
Telephone: 919-844-0900
Fax: 919-882-2110
Email: amn@amnlawfirm.com
URL: http://www.amnlawfirm.com

Civil Litigation, Construction Law, Commercial Law, Products Liability, Personal Injury.

MEMBER

ADAM M. NEIJNA, born 1966; admitted to bar, 1991, Florida; 1997, Colorado; 1998, U.S. District Court, Southern District of Florida; 2002, North Carolina; U.S. District Courts, Eastern, Middle and Western Districts of North Carolina. *Education:* Emory University (B.A., 1988); University of Miami (J.D., 1991). Phi Delta Phi. Prosecutor State Attorneys Office, Miami, Florida, 1991-1997. *Member:* North Carolina State Bar; North Carolina Bar Association; The Florida Bar; Defense Research Instiitute (Member, Construction Law Section); American Bar Association. ***LANGUAGES:*** Spanish. ***PRACTICE AREAS:*** Construction Law (30%); Construction Claims; Construction Arbitration; Construction Litigation (45%); Complex Litigation; Wills (5%); Personal Injury (5%); Wrongful Death; Business Law (15%). ***Email:*** amn@amnlawfirm.com

NELSON MULLINS RILEY & SCARBOROUGH LLP

GLENLAKE ONE, SUITE 200
4140 PARKLAKE AVENUE
RALEIGH, NORTH CAROLINA 27612
Telephone: 919-877-3800
Telecopy: 919-877-3799
URL: http://www.nelsonmullins.com

Atlanta, Georgia Office: 999 Peachtree Street, N.E., Suite 1400, 30309-3964. P.O. Box 77707, 30357-0707. Telephone: 404-817-6000. Telecopy: 404-817-6050.

Charleston, South Carolina Office: Liberty Center, Suite 600, 151 Meeting Street, 29401-2239. P.O. Box 1806, 29402-1806. Telephone: 843-853-5200. Telecopy: 843-722-8700.

Charlotte, North Carolina Office: Bank of America Corporate Center, Suite 2400, 100 North Tryon Street, 28202-4007. Telephone: 704-417-3000. Telecopy: 704-377-4814.

Columbia, South Carolina Office: Meridian, 17th Floor, 1320 Main Street, 29201, P.O. Box 11070, 29211-1070. Telephone: 803-799-2000. Telecopy: 803-256-7500.

Greenville, South Carolina Office: Poinsett Plaza, 104 South Main Street, Suite 900, 29601. P.O. Box 10084, 29603-0084. Telephone: 864-250-2300. Telecopy: 864-232-2925.

Myrtle Beach, South Carolina Office: Founders Centre, Suite 301, 2411 North Oak Street, 29577-3165. P.O. Box 3939, 29578-3939. Telephone: 843-448-3500. Telecopy: 843-448-3437.

Washington, D.C. Office: 101 Constitution Avenue, NW, Suite 900, 20001. Telephone: 202-712-2800. Fax: 202-712-2860.

Winston-Salem, North Carolina Office: The Knollwood, 380 Knollwood Street, Suite 530, 27103. Telephone: 336-774-3300. Fax: 336-774-3299.

Health Care; Intellectual Property; labor and Employment; Low Income Housing Tax Credits.

OF COUNSEL

CATHARINE W. CUMMER, born Dallas, Texas, January 4, 1972; admitted to bar, 1996, California (inactive status); 1998, District of Columbia; 2000, North Carolina. *Education:* Stanford University (A.B., with distinction, 1993); Boalt Hall School of Law, University of California (J.D., 1996). ***PRACTICE AREAS:*** Health Care; Labor and Employment; Litigation. ***Email:*** catharine.cummer@nelsonmullins.com

REED J. HOLLANDER, born Evanston, Illinois, August 21, 1972; admitted to bar, 1996, North Carolina. *Education:* University of Illinois (B.A. with honors and distinction in English, 1993); Duke University (J.D., cum laude, 1996). Vice-Chair, North Carolina Bar Association Constitutional Rights and Responsibilities Section; Legal Counsel, North Carolina Jaycees, 2000-2005; Legal Counsel, Raleigh Jaycees, 2003-2004. *Member:* Wake County (Member, Professionalism Committee), Tenth Judicial District, North Carolina (Member, Sections on: Constitutional Rights; Litigation) and American (Member, Sections on: Tort and Insurance Practice; Litigation) Bar Associations. ***PRACTICE AREAS:*** Administrative and State Tax Litigation; Commercial and Business Litigation; Intellectual Property Litigation; Constitutional Law; Construction Law. ***Email:*** reed.hollander@nelsonmullins.com

(This Listing Continued)

PARTNERS

BARRY D. ALEXANDER, admitted to bar, 1994, Virginia; 1999, District of Columbia; 2001, North Carolina. *Education:* George Mason University (B.S., 1989; J.D., 1994). ***PRACTICE AREAS:*** Health Law; Medicare and Medicaid Reimbursement; Health Care Fraud. ***Email:*** barry.alexander@nelsonmullins.com

CHRISTOPHER J. BLAKE, born Yonkers, New York, October 9, 1961; admitted to bar, 1986, District of Columbia; 1989, North Carolina. *Education:* Pace University (B.A., 1983); Catholic University of America (J.D., 1986). *Member:* State Bar of North Carolina, Bar Association of North Carolina, American Bar Association (Member, Litigation Section, Construction Industry Forum). ***PRACTICE AREAS:*** Commercial Litigation; Insurance; Insolvency; Communications and Media; Construction Law. ***Email:*** chris.blake@nelsonmullins.com

STEVEN CARR, born Winfield, Kansas, June 15, 1954; admitted to bar, 1979, Kansas; 1985, U.S. Court of Appeals, Eighth Circuit; 1986, Florida; 1992, U.S. Court of Appeals, Tenth Circuit; 1993, Iowa; 1994, North Carolina and U.S. Court of Appeals, Fourth Circuit. *Education:* Washburn University of Topeka (B.A., magna cum laude, 1976; J.D., with honors, 1979). Phi Kappa Phi. Assistant Attorney General, Kansas, 1979-1981. Attorney and Director of Litigation, Kansas Power and Light Company (now Western Resources, Inc.), Topeka, Kansas, 1981-1986. Senior Attorney, Florida Power & Light Co., Miami, Florida, 1986-1991. General Counsel and Secretary, IES Industries Inc., Cedar Rapids, Iowa, 1992-1993. Member: American Society of Corporate Secretaries, 1992-1993; Edison Electric Institute Legal Committee, 1992-1993. Director, The Contemporary Science Center, Inc. *Member:* Wake County, North Carolina (Member: Continuing Legal Education Committee; Sections on: Antitrust, Corporate Counsel), Kansas and American (Member: Electricity Committee; Communications Committee; Corporate Finance Committee; Sections on: Public Utility, Communications and Transportation) Bar Associations; The Florida Bar; North Carolina State Bar; American Corporate Counsel Association. ***REPORTED CASES:*** State, ex rel. v. Palmgren, 231 Kan. 524, 646 P.2d 1091 (1982); Bell v. Gas Service Co., 778 F.2d 512 (8th Cir. 1985); Broadhead v. Kansas Power & Light Co., 671 F.2d 1264 (10th Cir. 1982). ***PRACTICE AREAS:*** Corporate Law; Securities; Commercial Transactions; Corporate Governance; Energy Regulation; Telecommunications; Technology Law. ***Email:*** steven.carr@nelsonmullins.com

MELISSA J. COPELAND, born Orangeburg, South Carolina, September 9, 1969; admitted to bar, 1994, South Carolina and U.S. Court of Appeals, Fourth Circuit; 1995, U.S. District Court, District of South Carolina; 2000,U.S. District Court, Eastern District of Michigan (Not admitted in North Carolina). *Education:* College of Charleston (B.A., 1991); University of South Carolina (J.D., 1994). Omicron Delta Kappa, Pi Sigma Alpha. *Member, American Bar Association (Member, Section on, Public Contract Law).* ***SPECIAL AGENCIES:*** Special Assistant Solicitor, Eleventh Judicial Circuit Solicitor's Office. ***PRACTICE AREAS:*** Administrative Law; Government Procurement; Food Products Liability. ***Email:*** missy.copeland@nelsonmullins.com

THEODORE E. CORVETTE, born 1945; admitted to bar, 1973, North Carolina; 1991, Oregon; 1992, Washington. *Education:* University of Delaware (B.A., 1967); Duke University (J.D., 1973). ***PRACTICE AREAS:*** Computers and Software; Construction Law; Intellectual Property; Technology Law. ***Email:*** ted.corvette@nelsonmullins.com

JOSEPH W. EASON, born Durham, North Carolina, May 20, 1953; admitted to bar, 1977, North Carolina; 1978, District of Columbia (inactive). *Education:* University of North Carolina (B.A., 1974; J.D., with honors, 1977). Phi Beta Kappa. Order of the Coif. North Carolina Law Review, 1975-1977. Law Clerk to Hon. Susie Sharp, Chief Justice, North Carolina Supreme Court, 1977-1978. *Member:* Wake County (Chairman, Fee Arbitration Committee, Tenth Judicial District Bar), North Carolina and American Bar Associations; Energy Bar Association; Electric Cooperative Bar Association. ***PRACTICE AREAS:*** Commercial Litigation; Insurance; Insolvency; Utilities. ***Email:*** joe.eason@nelsonmullins.com

SUSAN Y. ELLINGER, born 1953; admitted to bar, 1992, North Carolina; 1994, South Carolina. *Education:* University of South Carolina (B.A., 1974); North Carolina Central University (J.D., magna cum laude, 1992). Notes and Comments Editor, North Carolina Central University Law Journal. Law Clerk to the Hon. Robert F. Orr, North Carolina Court of Appeals, 1993-1994. Adjunct Professor of Law, North Carolina Central University, Labor and Employment Law. State Chair, Affordable Housing and Community Development Forum. ***PRACTICE AREAS:*** Affordable Housing; Labor and Employment; Municipal Law; Community Development; Business; Commercial Real Estate; Low Income Housing Tax Credits. ***Email:*** susan.ellinger@nelsonmullins.com

WILLIAM H. GAMMON, born 1948; admitted to bar, 1973, North Carolina; 1980, Virginia; 1982, District of Columbia. *Education:* Davidson College (A.B., 1970); University of North Carolina (J.D., 1973); George Washington University (LL.M., 1977). Law Clerk to Hon.Carlisle W. Higgins, Senior Associate Justice, North Carolina Supreme Court, 1973-1974. Trial Attorney, Contract Appeals Division, Office of the Judge Advocate General, 1975-1978. Co-Author: North Carolina Construction Law Deskbook, Federal Contracting and State Contracting Chapters, 2003; Postaward Relief for Mistakes in Bids, Briefing Papers, Federal Publications, Inc., 1988. Co-Chair, CAGC/NCBA Joint Committee. *Member:* North Carolina (Member, Vice Chair 2004-2005 and Chair 2005-2006, Construction Law Section) and American (Member, Forum Committee on Construction Industry and Public Contract Law Section) Bar Associations. [Capt., U.S. Army, JAGC, 1974-1978]. ***PRACTICE AREAS:*** Government Contracts; Construction. ***Email:*** bill.gammon@nelsonmullins.com

DAVID A. HARLOW, born 1943; admitted to bar, 1968, New Jersey; 1971, North Carolina; registered to practice before U.S. Patent and Trademark Office. *Education:* Lehigh University (B.A., 1965); Duke University (J.D., 1968); National Institute for Trial Advocacy at Boulder (National Program, 1978). Special Trial Counsel, U.S. Army Corps of Engineers, 1976-1977. Chair, Intellectual Property Section, North Carolina Bar Association, 1994-1995. [Special Trial Counsel, U.S. Army Corps of Engineers, 1976-1977]. ***PRACTICE AREAS:*** Intellectual Property; Litigation; Corporate; Computer Law. ***Email:*** david.harlow@nelsonmullins.com

FRANK A. HIRSCH, JR., born Chattanooga, Tennessee, December 12, 1960; admitted to bar, 1987, North Carolina. *Education:* University of North Carolina at Chapel Hill

(This Listing Continued)

(B.A., Political Science/History, 1983); Vanderbilt University (J.D., 1986). Director, Mergers and Acquisitions, RBC Centura Bank, Raleigh, North Carolina, 2001; General Counsel and Corporate Secretary, Centura Banks, Inc., Rocky Mount, North Carolina, 2000-2001; Partner and Litigation Department Team Head, Hunton & Williams, Charlotte, North Carolina, 1996-2000; Parker Poe Adams & Bernstein, L.L.P., Charlotte, North Carolina, 1986-1996; Research Editor, Vanderbilt Journal of Transnational Law; "Fast 40 Under 40" Award recipient, Charlotte Business Journal, 1997. *Member:* North Carolina (Member, Sections on: Litigation and Business Law,) and American (Member: Sections on: Litigation; Business Law; Litigation Section Committees on Class Actions and Business Torts; Subcommittees on Consumer Financial Services, Banking and Finance, and Commercial Lending; Tort and Insurance Practice Section Committee on Unfair Competition). ***PRACTICE AREAS:*** Alternative Dispute Resolution; Business Litigation; Consumer Finance; Financial Institutions Law. ***Email:*** frank.hirsch@nelsonmullins.com

WALLACE C. HOLLOWELL, III, born Elizabeth City, North Carolina, June 24, 1971; admitted to bar, 1997, North Carolina. *Education:* University of North Carolina, Chapel Hill (B.A., 1993); University of Virginia (J.D., 1997). Phi Beta Kappa. Member, University of Virginia Law Review. Member, Board of Directors: North Carolina Society of Healthcare Attorneys; Triangle Chapter, American Red Cross. *Member:* North Carolina (Member, Health Law Section) and American (Member, Health Law Forum) Bar Associations. ***REPORTED CASES:*** Williamson v. Liptzin, 539 S.E.2d 313 (N.C. 2000). ***PRACTICE AREAS:*** Health; Litigation; Hospital. ***Email:*** chuck.hollowell@nelsonmullins.com

NOAH H. HUFFSTETLER, III, born Charlotte, North Carolina, March 26, 1951; admitted to bar, 1976, North Carolina; 1980, U.S. Court of Appeals, Fourth Circuit; 1983, U.S. Supreme Court. *Education:* University of North Carolina (A.B., 1973; J.D., 1976). Phi Beta Kappa. Morehead Scholar. Listed in Best Lawyers in America, 1991—. Member, North Carolina Law Review, 1975-1976. Member, Board of Advisors, University of North Carolina School of Public Health, 1985-1993. Member, Board of Visitors, University of North Carolina at Chapel Hill. Member, Commercial and Construction Panel of Arbitrators, American Arbitration Association. *Member:* Wake County and North Carolina (Chairman, Health Law Section, 1984-1985; Member, Committee on Health Law Specialization) Bar Associations; American Health Lawyers Association; North Carolina Society of Healthcare Attorneys. (Managing Partner, Raleigh Office). ***PRACTICE AREAS:*** Health; Hospital; Litigation. ***Email:*** noah.huffstetler@nelsonmullins.com

LEON M. KILLIAN, III, born Newport News, Virginia, 1944; admitted to bar, 1969, North Carolina. *Education:* University of North Carolina (B.S., 1966; J.D., 1969). Phi Delta Phi. Attorney: Haywood County, 1972—; Town of Hazelwood, 1972-1984; Haywood County Department of Social Services, 1973-1990. *Member:* 30th Judicial District (President, 1985-1987) and North Carolina State Bars; North Carolina (Member of Council, Real Property Section, 1982-1985, Vice-Chairman, 1986-1987 and Chairman, 1987-1988; Member, Board of Governors, 1989-1992) and American Bar Associations; North Carolina Land Title Association; North Carolina Association of County Attorneys; North Carolina Professional Lobbyists Association. (Board Certified Specialist in Real Property Law, Residential, Business, Commercial and Industrial Transactions, North Carolina State Board of Legal Specialization). ***PRACTICE AREAS:*** Commercial Real Property; Legislative Practice; Regulatory Law; Local Government Law; Business Law. ***Email:*** chip.killian@nelsonmullins.com

MATTHEW P. McGUIRE, born East Point, Georgia, June 7, 1966; admitted to bar, 1993, North Carolina. *Education:* University of Notre Dame (B.A., magna cum laude, 1988); University of North Carolina at Chapel Hill (M.A., 1990; J.D., with honors, 1993). Order of the Coif. Articles Editor, North Carolina Law Review, 1992-1993. Staff Member, North Carolina Journal of International Law & Commercial Regulation. Author: "Baker v. Martin and the Constitutionality of Partisan Qualifications for Appointment to District Court," 70 N.C. Law Review 1916, 1992; "Direct Effect Jurisdiction in the 90's: Weltover, Inc., v. Republic of Argentina and a Broad Interpretation of the Foreign Sovereign Immunities Act of 1976," 17 N.C. Journal of Int'l. Law & Commercial Regulation 383, 1992. Vice Chair, Trial Techniques Committee, Former Young Lawyers Division Liaison to the Membership Committee, Tort, Trial & Insurance Practice Section and North Carolina District Representative, Young Lawyers Division, American Bar Association. *Member:* North Carolina Bar Association (Former Chair, Young Lawyers Division); North Carolina State Bar; American Bar Association. ***LANGUAGES:*** French. ***PRACTICE AREAS:*** Alternative Dispute Resolution; Business Litigation; Consumer Finance; Financial Institutions Law. ***Email:*** matt.mcguire@nelsonmullins.com

CHARLES H. MERCER, JR., born Wilmington, North Carolina, August 11, 1947; admitted to bar, 1975, North Carolina; 1985, Pennsylvania (inactive). *Education:* University of North Carolina at Chapel Hill (A.B., 1969); University of Miami (J.D., 1974); New York University (LL.M., 1977); Harvard University (M.P.A., 1984). Law Clerk to Judge Earl W. Vaughn, North Carolina Court of Appeals, 1974-1975. Instructor, New York University School of Law, 1975-1977. Adjunct Professor of Law, Campbell University School of Law, 1978-1980. Lecturer, Duke University School of Law, 1979-1982. Special Counsel, United States Congressman Ike F. Andrews, 1980-1983. Chair, Legal Committee, Institute for Professionals in Taxation, 1997-1998. Chairman, North Carolina Property Tax Commission, 1980-1981. Member, North Carolina State Banking Commission, 1991-1995. Member, University of North Carolina Board of Governors, 2001—. Member, Duke University Divinity School Board of Visitors, 1998—. Member, Board of Trustees, Louisburg College, 1988-1999. Member, Governor's Commission to Modernize State Finances, 2002. Member, North Carolina Local Government Commission, 1984-1985. Member, Board of Directors, Greater Raleigh Chamber of Commerce, 2000-2001. Member, Salvation Army Community Center Advisory Council (Raleigh), 1993-1998. Member, Board of Trustees, North Carolina Conference of the United Methodist Church, 1990-1998. Member, Rotary Club of Raleigh. *Member:* American Bar Association; North Carolina Bar Association; North Carolina State Bar; Institute for Professionals in Taxation. ***PRACTICE AREAS:*** Litigation; State and Local Taxation; Administrative Law; Government Relations; Economic Relations; Product Liability; Class Action Defense; Taxation. ***Email:*** charles.mercer@nelsonmullins.com

ROBERT A. MEYNARDIE, born 1959; admitted to bar, 1991, Georgia; 1994, North Carolina. *Education:* University of Pennsylvania (B.S., 1981); University of San Francisco (M.B.A., 1985); Emory University (J.D., 1991). Order of the Coif. Emory Law Journal. Clerk for Hon. Susan H. Black, United States District Court for the Middle District of Florida and the United States Court of Appeals for the Eleventh Circuit. ***PRACTICE AREAS:*** Litigation; Contracts; Construction Law; Commercial Law; Regulatory Law; Utility Law; Trade Secrets. ***Email:*** bob.meynardie@nelsonmullins.com

CATHY M. RUDISILL, admitted to bar, 1984, North Carolina; 1985, U.S. Tax Court; 1986, District of Columbia. *Education:* University of North Carolina at Chapel Hill (B.A., 1980; J.D., 1984); Georgetown University (M.L.T., 1987). Phi Beta Kappa. Member, Holderness Moot Court Bench, 1983-1984. Note and Comment Editor, North Carolina Journal of International Law and Commercial Regulation, 1983-1984. Law Clerk, U.S. Tax Court, 1984-1986. *Member:* Wake County, North Carolina (Member, Real Property Section) and American Bar Associations; Wake County Real Property Lawyers Association. ***PRACTICE AREAS:*** Real Estate; Corporate Law; Banking Law; Finance; Education Law. ***Email:*** cathy.rudisill@nelsonmullins.com

GEORGE M. TEAGUE, born 1945; admitted to bar, 1971, North Carolina. *Education:* University of North Carolina (A.B., 1968); Vanderbilt University (J.D., 1971). Phi Beta Kappa. Morehead Scholar. Associate Editor, Vanderbilt Law Review, 1970-1971. ***PRACTICE AREAS:*** Administrative and Regulatory; Legislative Lobbying; Commercial Litigation. ***Email:*** george.teague@nelsonmullins.com

ASSOCIATES

SEAGRUMN L. GILBERT, born Charlotte, North Carolina, March 2, 1979; admitted to bar, 2004, North Carolina and U.S. District Court, Eastern District of North Carolina. *Education:* University of North Carolina (B.A., cum laude, 2001); Duke University School of Law (J.D., 2004; LL.M., 2004). *Member:* Wake County and American Bar Associations; North Carolina State Bar. ***PRACTICE AREAS:*** Real Estate; Litigation; Corporate. ***Email:*** seagrumn.gilbert@nelsonmullins.com

LISA R. GORDON, admitted to bar, 1999, California; 2002, North Carolina; U.S. Court of Appeals, Ninth Circuit; U.S. District Court, Middle District of California and Eastern, Western and Middle Districts of North Carolina. *Education:* University of California at Davis (A.B., summa cum laude, 1994); University of Minnesota (J.D., magna cum laude, 1998). Phi Beta Kappa. Order of the Coif. University of Minnesota Law Review, Note and Comment Editor, 1997-1998. Prognosis Health Law Journal, Co-Editor, 2002-2004. Law Clerk, Michael Daly Hawkins, U.S. Court of Appeals for the Ninth Circuit, 1998-1999 Term. Recipient: Award of Merit, National Center for Missing & Exploited Children, 2004; Claude M. Scarborough, Jr. Pro Bono Award, 2004; North Carolina Bar Association Young Lawyers Division Pro Bono Service Award, 2005. *Member:* Wake County, North Carolina (Member, Sections on: Health Law; Labor Law; Litigation; Member, Bench and Bar Committee 2004—) and American (Member, Advisory Council, Committee on Judicial Independence, 2002—) Bar Associations; State Bar of California. ***PRACTICE AREAS:*** Litigation; Health Care; Employment; International Family Law; Hague Convention Proceedings. ***Email:*** lisa.gordon@nelsonmullins.com

AMY L. KEEGAN, born Martinsburg, West Virginia, February 8, 1977; admitted to bar, 2002, South Carolina; 2003, North Carolina. *Education:* Virginia Tech (B.A., History and Political Science, summa cum laude, 1999); Duke University School of Law (J.D., 2002). *Member:* North Carolina State Bar; South Carolina Bar; Greenville and American Bar Associations. ***PRACTICE AREAS:*** Labor and Employment. ***Email:*** amy.keegan@nelsonmullins.com

CHRISTOPHER M. KINDEL, born 1975; admitted to bar, 2001, North Carolina. *Education:* University of Texas at Austin (B.A., with high honors, 1998); University of North Carolina (J.D., with honors, 2001). Chancellors Scholar, University of North Carolina School of Law. Comments Editor, North Carolina Law Review. Author, Note, "When Digital Contacts Equal Minimum Contacts: How Fourth Circuit Courts Should Assess Personal Jurisdiction in Trademark Disputes Over Internet Domain Names," 78 N.C. Law Review 2105 (2000). *Member:* North Carolina Bar Association; American Bar Association; Young Lawyers Division of North Carolina Bar Association; International Trademark Association (INTA). ***PRACTICE AREAS:*** Litigation; Intellectual Property; Intellectual Property Litigation. ***Email:*** chris.kindel@nelsonmullins.com

LESLIE C. LANE, born Athens, Georgia, September 19, 1978; admitted to bar, 2004, North Carolina. *Education:* University of North Carolina at Chapel Hill (B.A., Journalism and Mass Communications, 2001; B.A., Political Science, 2001); University of Georgia School of Law (J.D., magna cum laude, 2004). Member, Editorial Board, Georgia Law Review. Recipient, Verner F. Chaffin Award for Excellence in Fiduciary Law. *Member:* Wake County, North Carolina and American Bar Associations; North Carolina State Bar. ***PRACTICE AREAS:*** Business Litigation. ***Email:*** leslie.lane@nelsonmullins.com

STEPHEN D. MARTIN, born Akron, Ohio, January 23, 1975; admitted to bar, 2002, North Carolina; 2003, District of Columbia. *Education:* Ohio Wesleyan University (B.A., summa cum laude, 1997); Northwestern University School of Law (J.D., 2002). *Member:* North Carolina and American Bar Associations; District of Columbia Bar; American Health Lawyers Association. ***PRACTICE AREAS:*** Litigation. ***Email:*** steve.martin@nelsonmullins.com

ROSS E. SALLADE, born Newport News, Viriginia, November 20, 1969; admitted to bar, 2000, North Carolina and U.S. District Court, Western District of North Carolina. *Education:* Hampden-Sydney College (B.S., cum laude, Honors, 1992); Virginia Commonwealth University (M.H.A., 1997); University of Virginia (J.D., 2000). *Member:* North Carolina State Bar (Member, Health Law Section); American Health Lawyers Association; American College of Health Care Executives. ***PRACTICE AREAS:*** Health Care; Medicare and Medicaid; Hospital Law. ***Email:*** ross.sallade@nelsonmullins.com

CHRISTOPHER M. THOMAS, born Cleveland, Ohio, June 21, 1968; admitted to bar, 2003, North Carolina; U.S. District Court, Eastern, Middle and Western Districts of North Carolina. *Education:* Allegheny College (B.A., 1991); Georgia State University (M.B.A., 1999); University of Georgia (J.D., cum laude, 2003). Recipient, ABA-BNA Award for Excellence in the Study of Intellectual Property, 2002 and 2003. Senior Articles

(This Listing Continued)

NELSON MULLINS RILEY & SCARBOROUGH LLP, Raleigh—Continued

Editor, Journal of Intellectual Property Law, 2002-2003. ***PRACTICE AREAS:*** Copyright; Intellectual Property; Litigation; Entertainment Law. ***Email:*** chris.thomas@nelsonmullins.com

All Raleigh Attorneys are Members of the North Carolina State Bar unless indicated otherwise.

(For biographical data on Atlanta, Georgia, Charleston, South Carolina, Columbia, South Carolina, Greenville, South Carolina, Myrtle Beach, South Carolina, Charlotte, North Carolina, Washington, D.C. and Winston-Salem, North Carolina, see Professional Biographies of those cities)

NICHOLLS & CRAMPTON, P.A.

4300 SIX FORKS ROAD
SUITE 700
P.O. BOX 18237
RALEIGH, NORTH CAROLINA 27609
Telephone: 919-781-1311
Telecopier: 919-782-0465
URL: http://www.nichollscrampton.com

Trust, Estate Planning, Probate, Bankruptcy and Business Law, Civil Trial Practice, Construction Litigation, Commercial Trial Practice, Corporation, Criminal Trial Practice, Employment Law, Family Law, Personal Injury, Products Liability, Real Estate and Wrongful Death.

W. SIDNEY ALDRIDGE, born Raleigh, North Carolina, April 26, 1952; admitted to bar, 1977, North Carolina; U.S. Supreme Court. *Education:* University of North Carolina (A.B., 1974; J.D., with honors, 1977). Phi Eta Sigma; Phi Beta Kappa. Staff Member, 1975-1976 and Business Manager and Member, Board of Editors, 1976-1977, North Carolina Law Review. Author: "Adversary Proceedings," in N.C. Bankruptcy Guide, 1987. *Member:* Wake County (Treasurer, 1978-1979; Member, Board of Directors, 1981-1982; President, 1995), North Carolina (Council Member, Law Office Management Section, 1985-1990; Chairman, 1989; Council Member, Bankruptcy Section, 1990-1993; Chairman, Bankruptcy Section, 1994-1995; Chairman, Membership Services, 1996-1998) and American Bar Associations; North Carolina State Bar. ***PRACTICE AREAS:*** Civil Law; Commercial Litigation; Bankruptcy Law; Business Law. ***Email:*** wsaldridge@ipass.net

ROBIN ADAMS ANDERSON, born Cambridge, Massachusetts, June 18, 1958; admitted to bar, 1990, North Carolina, U.S. District Court, Eastern, Middle and Western Districts of North Carolina, U.S. Court of Appeals, Fourth Circuit and U.S. Supreme Court. *Education:* University of Massachusetts (B.A., cum laude, 1984); University of North Carolina (J.D., 1990). The Order of Barristers. Member: Holderness Moot Court Bench; National Moot Court Team. Law Clerk to Senior Justice Louis B. Meyer, Supreme Court of North Carolina, 1990-1991. Adjunct Professor, Business Law, The John E. Weems Graduate School of Business, Meredith College. Chair, State Personnel Commission. *Member:* Wake County, North Carolina (Member, Labor and Employment Law Section) and American (Member, EEO Committee) Bar Associations; North Carolina Association of Women Attorneys. ***PRACTICE AREAS:*** Employment Law; Discrimination; Personnel Law; Civil Litigation. ***Email:*** RAnderson@nichollscrampton.com

GREGORY B. CRAMPTON, born Washington, D.C., August 7, 1947; admitted to bar, 1972, North Carolina; U.S. Supreme Court. *Education:* Washington and Lee University (B.A., 1969); University of North Carolina (J.D., 1972). Law Clerk to Chief Judge Walter E. Brock, Court of Appeals of North Carolina, 1972-1973. Member, Panel of Trustees, U.S. Bankruptcy Court, Eastern District of North Carolina 1979—. Fellow, American College of Bankruptcy. *Member:* Wake County, North Carolina (Council Member, Bankruptcy Section, 1979-1981, 1983-1986) and American Bar Associations; The North Carolina State Bar; North Carolina Academy of Trial Lawyers; Mid-Atlantic Business Bankruptcy Institute (Member, Planning Committee, 1986-1995); American Bankruptcy Institute (Certified in Business Bankruptcy Law by the American Board of Bankruptcy Certification). (Board Certified Specialist in Bankruptcy Law, North Carolina State Board of Legal Specialization). ***PRACTICE AREAS:*** Business Bankruptcy; Reorganizations; Civil Practice; Land Use; Commercial Litigation. ***Email:*** gcrampton@nichollscrampton.com

NICHOLAS J. DOMBALIS, II, born Raleigh, North Carolina, June 17, 1950; admitted to bar, 1975, North Carolina, U.S. Supreme Court, U.S. Tax Court and U.S. District Court, Eastern and Middle Districts of North Carolina. *Education:* Hampden-Sydney College (B.A., 1972); Wake Forest University (J.D., 1975). Phi Delta Phi. Assistant District Attorney, Wake County, 1975-1979. *Member:* Wake County Bar Association (Member, Board of Directors, 1983-1984, 1996-1998); North Carolina State Bar; North Carolina Academy of Trial Lawyers. ***PRACTICE AREAS:*** Criminal; Personal Injury; Domestic Law; Family Law. ***Email:*** ndombalis@ipass.net

STEPHANI WILSON HUMRICKHOUSE, born Monticello, New York, 1956; admitted to bar, 1980, North Carolina; U.S. District Court, Eastern, Western and Middle Districts of North Carolina; U.S. Court of Appeals, Fourth Circuit. *Education:* Cornell University (B.S.I.L.R., 1977); University of North Carolina (J.D., 1980). Phi Delta Phi. Chair: Attorney Advisory Group, U.S. Bankruptcy Court, Eastern District of North Carolina, 1996; Chair, Local Rules Committee, U.S. Bankruptcy Court, Eastern District of North Carolina, 1996-2000. *Member:* Wake County, Tenth Judicial District (Member, Board of Directors, 1999; Grievance Committee, 1996-1998) and North Carolina (Board of Directors, 1999; Member, Bench/Bar Committee, 1997-2001; Member, Swearing-In Committee, 2000-2005) Bar Associations; North Carolina State Bar (Council Member, Bankruptcy Section, 1988-1990); The American Bankruptcy Institute. (Board Certified Specialist in Bankruptcy Law, North Carolina State Board of Legal Specialization; Certified Specialist, Business Bankruptcy Law, American Bankruptcy Board of Certification). ***PRACTICE AREAS:*** Bankruptcy; Civil Litigation; Commercial Litigation. ***Email:*** shumrickhouse@nichollscrampton.com

(This Listing Continued)

F. TIMOTHY NICHOLLS, born Canton, North Carolina, April 1, 1943; admitted to bar, 1967, North Carolina, U.S. Tax Court and U.S. District Court, Eastern District of North Carolina. *Education:* University of North Carolina (B.A., 1965; J.D., 1967). Attorney, Office of Chief Counsel, I.R.S., 1967-1971. Phi Delta Phi. *Member:* Wake County, North Carolina (Member, Board of Directors, Tax Council, 1979-1983) and American (Member, Section of Taxation) Bar Associations. ***PRACTICE AREAS:*** Taxation; Estate Planning; Corporation; Commercial Real Estate. ***Email:*** TNicholls@nichollscrampton.com

KEVIN L. SINK, born Lexington, North Carolina, November 22, 1969; admitted to bar, 1994, North Carolina and U.S. District Court, Eastern, Western and Middle Districts of North Carolina; 1998, U.S. Court of Appeals, Fourth Circuit. *Education:* North Carolina State University (B.A., summa cum laude, Accounting, 1991); University of North Carolina at Chapel Hill (J.D., with honors, 1994). Phi Kappa Phi. Member, Senior Member, North Carolina Law Review, 1992-1994. *Member:* North Carolina Bar Association (Member, Bankruptcy Section); American Bar Association; American Bankruptcy Institute. (Board Certified Specialist in Business Bankruptcy Law, North Carolina State Board of Legal Specialization). ***PRACTICE AREAS:*** Bankruptcy Law; Commercial Litigation; Bankruptcy Litigation; Commercial Transactions.

NODELL, GLASS & HASKELL, L.L.P.

5540 CENTERVIEW DRIVE, SUITE 416
RALEIGH, NORTH CAROLINA 27606
Telephone: 919-821-2600
Fax: 919-821-7744
URL: http://www.nodglahaslaw.com

Creditor Bankruptcy, Creditor Rights, Secured Transactions, Foreclosure, Collections, Commercial Litigation and Workouts.

MEMBERS OF FIRM

THEODORE A. NODELL, born Charlotte, North Carolina, January 1, 1947; admitted to bar, 1972, North Carolina. *Education:* Wake Forest University (B.A., 1969; J.D., 1972). Associate Member of National Association of Chapter 13 Trustees, 1981-1993. Chairman, 1984, 1991 and 1995. Eastern Bankruptcy Institute Creditors' Workshop. Member, Board of Directors, Eastern Bankruptcy Institute, 1989-1995. *Member:* North Carolina Bar Association. ***PRACTICE AREAS:*** Creditor Bankruptcy Law; Creditor Rights; Secured Transactions; Commercial Litigation; Workouts.

PHILIP A. GLASS, born Detroit, Michigan, April 27, 1959; admitted to bar, 1984, Florida; 1986, North Carolina. *Education:* Miami University (B.A., magna cum laude, 1981); University of North Carolina (J.D., 1984). Phi Beta Kappa; Phi Kappa Phi. Assistant County Attorney, Office of County Attorney, Pinellas County, Florida, 1984-1987. Attorney Advisor General, Office of General Counsel, U.S. Department of Agriculture, 1987-1988. Member, Clearwater, Florida Bar Association, 1984-1987 (Local Government Section, 1986-1987). *Member:* Wake County and North Carolina Bar Associations; The Florida Bar. ***PRACTICE AREAS:*** Creditor Bankruptcy Law; Creditor Rights; Foreclosure; Collections; Commercial Litigation. ***Email:*** pglass@nghlaw.org

CRAIG S. HASKELL, born New York, N.Y., March 11, 1966; admitted to bar, 1990, North Carolina. *Education:* University of Pennsylvania (B.A., 1987); University of North Carolina (J.D., 1990). *Member:* Wake County and North Carolina (Member, Bankruptcy and Real Property Sections) Bar Associations. ***PRACTICE AREAS:*** Creditor Bankruptcy Law; Creditor Rights; Foreclosure; Collections; Commercial Litigation. ***Email:*** chaskell@nghlaw.org

ASSOCIATE

JAMES R. WHITE, born Seaboard, North Carolina, March 18, 1975; admitted to bar, 2000, North Carolina. *Education:* University of North Carolina (B.A., 1997); Wake Forest University (J.D., 2000). *Wake County and North Carolina Bar Associations.* ***PRACTICE AREAS:*** Creditors Rights; Foreclosures; Collections. ***Email:*** jwhite@nghlaw.org

REPRESENTATIVE CLIENTS: Select Portfolio Servicing, Inc.; JP Morgan Chase Bank; Citigroup; GreenPoint Credit, L.L.C.; Vanderbilt Mortgage & Finance, Inc.; Green Tree Servicing, L.L.C.; 21st Mortgage; Wachovia Bank; Origen Financial Inc.; Bombardier Capital, Corp.; Wells Fargo Home Mortgage, EMC Mortgage Corp.; Fidelity National Foreclosure Solutions; Provident Consumer Financial Services, Inc.; GMAC Mortgage Corp.; Foreclosure Management Company; The CIT Group/Consumer Finance, Inc.; American General Finance, Inc.; First National Acceptance Company; Ohio Savings Bank.
REFERENCE: Branch Banking and Trust Company.

OETTINGER & PEEBLES, LLP

3737 GLENWOOD AVENUE, SUITE 100
RALEIGH, NORTH CAROLINA 27612
Telephone: 919-573-1860
Fax: 919-573-1861

MEMBERS OF THE FIRM

KENNETH B. OETTINGER, born Washington, D.C., January 7, 1944; admitted to bar, 1971, North Carolina; U.S. District Court, Eastern, Middle and Western Districts of North Carolina; 1976, U.S. Court of Appeals, Fourth Circuit; 1980, U.S. Supreme Court. *Education:* University of North Carolina at Chapel Hill (A.B., 1966; J.D., 1971). *Member:* Wake County and North Carolina Bar Associations; North Carolina State Bar; North Carolina Academy of Trial Lawyers. ***PRACTICE AREAS:*** Medical Malpractice; Wrongful Death; Nursing Home Abuse and Neglect; Catastrophic Injury; Business Litigation; Civil Litigation. ***Email:*** kbo@o-plaw.com

MONIQUE M. PEEBLES, born New York, N.Y., January 27, 1968; admitted to bar, 1994, North Carolina; U.S. District Court, Eastern District of North Carolina; U.S. Court of Appeals, Fourth Circuit. *Education:* North Carolina State University (B.A., 1990); North Carolina Central University (J.D., 1994). Staff Member, North Carolina Central Law Journal, 1992-1994. Recipient, Albert Turner Award. *Member:* Wake County and North Caro-

(This Listing Continued)

lina Bar Associations; North Carolina State Bar; Black Lawyers Association; Capital City Lawyers. **PRACTICE AREAS:** Medical Negligence; Personal Injury; Automobile Accidents and Injuries; Truck Accidents; Head Injury. ***Email:*** mmp@o-plaw.com

OGLETREE, DEAKINS, NASH, SMOAK & STEWART, P.C.

2301 SUGAR BUSH ROAD
SUITE 600
RALEIGH, NORTH CAROLINA 27612
Telephone: 919-787-9700
Facsimile: 919-783-9412
Immigration Telephone: 919-760-3000
Immigration Facsimile: 919-787-2934
URL: http://www.visatrax.com
Email: clientservices@ogletreedeakins.com
URL: http://www.ogletreedeakins.com

Mailing Address: P.O. Box 31608, Raleigh, NC 27622

Atlanta, Georgia Office: 600 Peachtree Street, N.E., Suite 2100. Telephone: 404-881-1300.
Austin, Texas Office: 301 Congress Avenue, Suite 1250. Telephone: 512-344-4700.
Birmingham, Alabama Office: One Federal Place, Suite 1000, 1819 Fifth Avenue North. Telephone: 205-328-1900.
Charleston, South Carolina Office: 134 Meeting Street, Suite 160, P.O. Box 1808. Telephone: 843-853-1300.
Charlotte, North Carolina Office: 400 West Trade Street. Telephone: 704-342-2588.
Chicago, Illinois Office: Twenty-Fifth Floor, Two First National Plaza, 20 South Clark Street. Telephone: 312-558-1220.
Columbia, South Carolina Office: 1320 Main Street, Suite 600. Telephone: 803-252-1300.
Dallas, Texas Office: 700 Preston Commons, 8117 Preston Road. Telephone: 214-987-3800.
Greensboro, North Carolina Office: 2725 Horse Pen Creek Road, Suite 101. Telephone: 336-375-9737.
Greenville, South Carolina Office: The Ogletree Building, 300 North Main Street, P.O. Box 2757. Telephone: 864-271-1300.
Houston, Texas Office: One Allen Center, 500 Dallas Street, Suite 3000. Telephone: 713-655-0855.
Kansas City, Missouri Office: 4717 Grand Avenue, Suite 300. Telephone: 816-471-1301.
Los Angeles, California Office: 633 West Fifth Street, Suite 5300. Telephone: 213-239-9800.
Indianapolis, Indiana Office: Suite 4600, 111 Monument Circle. Telephone: 317-916-1300.
Miami, Florida Office: 80 S.W. 8th Street, Suite 1830. Telephone: 305-374-0506.
Morristown, New Jersey Office: 10 Madison Avenue, Suite 402. Telephone: 973-656-1600.
Nashville, Tennessee Office: SunTrust Center, Suite 800, 424 Church Street. Telephone: 615-254-1900.
Phoenix, Arizona Office: 2415 East Camelback Road, Suite 800. Telephone: 602-778-3700.
San Antonio, Texas Office: 2600 Weston Centre, 112 East Pecan Street. Telephone: 210-354-1300.
St. Thomas, U.S. Virgin Islands Office: The Tunick Building, 1336 Beltjen Road, Suite 202. Telephone: 340-714-1235.
Tampa, Florida Office: 100 North Tampa Street, Suite 3600. Telephone: 813-289-1247.
Washington, D.C. Office: Fifth Floor, 2400 N Street, N.W. Telephone: 202-887-0855.

Labor Relations, Employment Litigation, Workers' Compensation. Civil Litigation in all State and Federal Courts and Administrative Agencies.

GUY F. DRIVER (1940-2001)

JOHN S. BURGIN, born Lexington, Kentucky, August 14, 1951; admitted to bar, 1977, Kentucky; 1977, South Carolina; 1982, U.S. Supreme Court; 1986, North Carolina. *Education:* Transylvania University (B.A., 1974); University of Kentucky (J.D., 1976). Phi Delta Phi. Member, Moot Court Board, 1975-1976. *Member:* Greenville County, Wake County and North Carolina Bar Associations; South Carolina Bar; Kentucky Bar; North Carolina State Bar. **PRACTICE AREAS:** Labor and Employment; Affirmative Action; Employment Litigation; NLRB Elections. ***Email:*** john.burgin@ogletreedeakins.com

C. MATTHEW KEEN, born Goldsboro, North Carolina, January 8, 1961; admitted to bar, 1987, North Carolina and U.S. District Court, Eastern, Middle and Western Districts of North Carolina; 1990, U.S. Court of Appeals, Fourth Circuit; 1996, U.S. Court of Appeals, Eleventh Circuit; 2001, U.S. Supreme Court; 2004, U.S. Court of Appeals, Fifth Circuit. *Education:* North Carolina State University (B.S., 1983); University of North Carolina (J.D., 1987). Phi Delta Phi; Order of the Coif. Recipient: Chief Justice Walter J. Clark Award. Member, North Carolina Law Review, 1986-1987. *Member:* American Bar Association (Member, Committee on WARN Act); Wake County and North Carolina (Member: Labor and Employment Law Section; Litigation Section) Bar Associations; North Carolina State Bar; American Employment Law Council. **PRACTICE AREAS:** Labor and Employment; Employment Litigation; National Labor Relations Act. ***Email:*** matt.keen@ogletreedeakins.com

ANDREW W. MERRILLS, born Montreal, Quebec, Canada, September 13, 1965; admitted to bar, 1991, North Carolina. *Education:* Duke University (A.B., 1988); Walter F. George School of Law, Mercer University (J.D., 1991). *Member:* North Carolina Bar Association; American Immigration Lawyers Association. **PRACTICE AREAS:** Immigration and Naturalization; Business Immigration; Citizenship; Employment Visas; Permanent Visas. ***Email:*** andrew.merrills@ogletreedeakins.com

ROBERT A. SAR, born Roanoke, Virginia, May 30, 1968; admitted to bar, 1995, North Carolina. *Education:* Wake Forest University (B.S., 1990); Campbell University (J.D. cum laude, 1995). Phi Kappa Phi; Order of the Barristers. ATLA Trial Team, Moot Court Team. Managing Editor, Campbell Law Review. Staff Assistant to the Chief of Staff, The White House, 1990-1991. *Member:* Member: North Carolina Bar Association (Membership Chairman, Labor and Employment Section; Technology Chairman, Litigation Section). **PRACTICE AREAS:** Labor and Employment; Employment Litigation. ***Email:*** robert.sar@ogletreedeakins.com

BRUCE A. PETESCH, born Chicago, Illinois, March 7, 1943; admitted to bar, 1969, Illinois and U.S. Court of Military Appeals; 1976, South Carolina; 1977, U.S. Court of Appeals, Fourth and Fifth Circuits; 1985, North Carolina; 1990, U.S. Supreme Court. *Education:* Ripon College (A.B., 1966); DePaul University (J.D., 1969). Editor-in-Chief, De Paul Law Review, Fall, 1968. *Member:* Wake County, Illinois State and North Carolina Bar Associations; South Carolina Bar; North Carolina State Bar. [Capt., U.S. Army, JAGC, 1969-1973]. **PRACTICE AREAS:** Management Labor and Employment Law; National Labor Relations Act; Unfair Labor Practices; Collective Bargaining and Strikes; Union Elections; Employment Discrimination. ***Email:*** bruce.petesch@ogletreedeakins.com

THOMAS A. FARR, born Cincinnati, Ohio, October 24, 1954; admitted to bar, 1979, Georgia; 1980, Virginia; 1983, North Carolina. *Education:* Hillsdale College (B.L.S., summa cum laude, 1976); Emory University (J.D., 1979); Georgetown University (LL.M., Labor Law, 1983). Permanent Member, U.S. Court of Appeals, Fourth Circuit Judicial Council. Adjunct Professor of Labor and Employment Law, Norman Adrian Wiggins School of Law, Campbell University, 1990-1997. Staff Attorney, National Right to Work Legal Defense Foundation, 1979-1981. Counsel to Senator John P. East, U.S. Senate Committee on Labor and Human Resources, 1981-1982. Law Clerk to the Hon. Frank W. Bullock, Jr., U.S. District Judge, Middle District of North Carolina, 1983. Member, North Carolina State Board of Elections, 1986-1987. Member, U.S. Federal Service Impasses Panel, 1983-1989. *Member:* North Carolina Bar Association; North Carolina State Bar; State Bar of Georgia; Virginia State Bar. **PRACTICE AREAS:** Class / Collective Action Defense; Complex Litigation / Non-Compete Cases; Constitutional and Election Law; Employment Law. ***Email:*** thomas.farr@ogletreedeakins.com

GREGORY P. McGUIRE, born Hazleton, Pennsylvania, August 11, 1962; admitted to bar, 1987, North Carolina; U.S. Court of Appeals, Fourth and Eleventh Circuits; U.S. District Court, Middle, Eastern and Western Districts of North Carolina; U.S. Supreme Court. *Education:* Cornell University (B.S., 1984); University of North Carolina (J.D., 1987). *Member:* Wake County and North Carolina Bar Associations; North Carolina State Bar. **PRACTICE AREAS:** Employment Discrimination; Sexual Harassment; Defense Litigation; Affirmative Action. ***Email:*** greg.mcguire@ogletreedeakins.com

RODOLFO R. AGRAZ, born Chattanooga, Tennessee, June 30, 1962; admitted to bar, 1988, Georgia and North Carolina. *Education:* Duke University (B.S., 1984); University of Georgia (J.D., 1988). Blue Key. *Member:* Wake County, North Carolina (Member, Labor and Employment Law Section Council, 1997—) and American Bar Associations; State Bar of Georgia; North Carolina State Bar. **LANGUAGES:** Spanish. **PRACTICE AREAS:** Affirmative Action; Employment Discrimination; National Labor Relations Act; Occupational Safety and Health. ***Email:*** fito.agraz@ogletreedeakins.com

GRETCHEN W. EWALT, born Arlington, Virginia, September 14, 1962; admitted to bar, 1988, North Carolina. *Education:* Virginia Commonwealth University (B.A., cum laude, 1985); University of Virginia (J.D., 1988). *Member:* North Carolina State Bar. **PRACTICE AREAS:** Affirmative Action; Employer Rights; Employee Discipline; Employee Drug Testing; Employment Litigation Defense; Family and Medical Leave Act. ***Email:*** gretchen.ewalt@ogletreedeakins.com

STEPHEN H. SMALLEY, born Xenia, Ohio, September 16, 1970; admitted to bar, 1995, Alabama; 1998, District of Columbia; 2001, North Carolina; U.S. District Court, Eastern and Central Districts of North Carolina. *Education:* Rhodes College (B.A., 1991); Cumberland School of Law of Samford University (J.D., 1995). Winner: Parham Williams Trial Competition and American Bar Association Negotiation (ADR) Competition; Regional Finalist, The Association of Trial Lawyers of America National Trial Competition. Director, Cumberland Trial Advocacy Board. *Member:* Alabama State Bar; Bar Association of the District of Columbia; North Carolina (Member, Pro Bono Steering Committee, YLD) and American Bar Associations; American Immigration Lawyers Association. **PRACTICE AREAS:** Immigration Law; Immigration and Naturalization; Business Immigration; Employer Regulatory Compliance; Labor and Employment Law. ***Email:*** stephen.smalley@ogletreedeakins.com

MARIFRANCES MORRISON, born Pittsfield, Massachusetts, November 25, 1968; admitted to bar, 1994, Massachusetts; 1999, North Carolina. *Education:* University of Massachusetts (B.A., 1990); New England School of Law (J.D., cum laude, 1994). **PRACTICE AREAS:** Business Immigration; Employment Immigration; Employment Visas; Permanent Visas. ***Email:*** fran.morrison@ogletreedeakins.com

---

RACHEL B. MARCH, born Columbus, Ohio; admitted to bar, 1997, North Carolina and Georgia. *Education:* Wake Forest University (B.A., summa cum laude, 1992; J.D., 1996). Phi Beta Kappa. Member, Moot Court Board. Research Editor, Wake Forest Law Review. Law Clerk to Honorable Russell A. Eliason, Magistrate Judge, Middle District of North Carolina, 1996-1997. *Member:* State Bar of Georgia; North Carolina Bar Association. **PRACTICE AREAS:** Labor and Employment; Employment Litigation. ***Email:*** rachel.march@ogletreedeakins.com

PHILLIP J. STRACH, born Weisbaden, West Germany, March 1, 1973; admitted to bar, 2000, North Carolina. *Education:* Campbell University (B.A., summa cum laude, 1996); University of North Carolina (M.P.A., 2000); University of North Carolina School of Law (J.D., with honors, 2000). Member, North Carolina Law Review, 1998-2000. Author: "Ohio Adult Parole Authority v. Woodard: Breathing New "Life" Into An Old Fourteenth Amendment Controversy," 77 North Carolina Law Review 891, January 1999; "Too Far Too Fast?" The North Carolina Supreme Court Eliminates The Common Law Distinction Between Invitees and Licensees in Nelson v. Freeland," 77 North Carolina Law Review 2377, September 1999. *Member:* North Carolina State Bar; American Bar Association. **PRACTICE AREAS:** Labor and Employment. ***Email:*** phil.strach@ogletreedeakins.com

KEVIN S. JOYNER, born Greenville, North Carolina, March 30, 1971; admitted to bar, 1998, North Carolina and U.S. District Court, Eastern and Middle Districts of North Carolina. *Education:* East Carolina University (B.S.B.A, magna cum laude, 1993; M.B.A., 1994); Campbell University (J.D., 1998). Beta Gamma Sigma; Phi Kappa Phi; Omicron

(This Listing Continued)

OGLETREE, DEAKINS, NASH, SMOAK & STEWART, P.C., Raleigh—Continued

Delta Kappa. Listed: Who's Who Among American University and Colleges. Articles Editor, 1997-1998 and Staff Member, 1996-1997, Campbell Law Review. Author: "The Use of Race in the Admissions of Higher Educational Institutions - A Violation of the Equal Protection Clause?" 19 Campbell Law Review 489, 1997. *Member:* Wake County and North Carolina Bar Associations; North Carolina State Bar. ***PRACTICE AREAS:*** Employment Litigation; Commercial Litigation. ***Email:*** kevin.joyner@ogletreedeakins.com

BERNHARD MUELLER, born Bad Kissingen, Germany, February 9, 1968; admitted to bar, 2001, South Carolina; 2002, North Carolina. *Education:* University of South Carolina (B.A., 1995; J.D., 2001; MIBS, 2001). Phi Beta Kappa. Order of the Coif. Wig and Robe. *Member:* Wake County, North Carolina and American Bar Associations; South Carolina Bar; North Carolina State Bar; American Immigration Lawyers Association. ***LANGUAGES:*** German. ***PRACTICE AREAS:*** Employment Law; Immigration Law; National Labor Relations Act. ***Email:*** bernhard.mueller@ogletreedeakins.com

DAVID B. HAWLEY, born Bedford, Pennsylvania, August 8, 1958; admitted to bar, 1999, North Carolina and U.S. District Court, Eastern District of North Carolina; 2005, U.S. District Court, Middle and Western Districts of North Carolina and U.S Court of Appeals, Fourth Circuit. *Education:* West Virginia University (B.A., 1981); Florida State University (M.S.P., 1984); University of North Carolina at Chapel Hill (J.D., 1999). Staff Member, 1997-1998 and Managing Editor, 1998-1999, North Carolina Law Review. *Member:* North Carolina (Member, Labor and Employment Section) and American (Member, Labor and Employment Section) Bar Associations; North Carolina State Bar. ***PRACTICE AREAS:*** Labor and Employment. ***Email:*** david.hawley@ogletreedeakins.com

KEVIN J. O'SULLIVAN, born Teaneck, New Jersey; admitted to bar, 2003, New York (Not admitted in North Carolina). *Education:* Lafayette College (B.A., 1996); Fordham University School of Law (J.D., 2002). ***PRACTICE AREAS:*** Immigration. ***Email:*** kevin.osullivan@ogletreedeakins.com

JOHN E. BRANCH, born Atlanta, Georgia; admitted to bar, 2004, North Carolina; 2005, U.S. District Court, Eastern, Middle and Western Districts of North Carolina and U.S. Court of Appeals, Fourth Circuit. *Education:* University of North Carolina at Chapel Hill (B.A., 2001; J.D., 2004). Member, 2002-2003 and Symposium Editor, 2002-2003, North Carolina Law Review. Author: "Statutory Misinterpretation: The Foreign Intelligence Surveillance Court of Review's Interpretation of the 'Significant Purpose' Requirement of the Foreign Intelligence Surveillance," Act, 81 N.C. L. Rev. 2075 (2003). Law Clerk, Honorable Glen M. Williams, Senior U.S. District Judge, Abingdon, Virginia. *Member:* Wake County, North Carolina and American Bar Associations. ***PRACTICE AREAS:*** Employment Litigation; Labor Law. ***Email:*** john.branch@ogletreedeakins.com

CHARLES RYAN COOK, born Seoul, South Korea; admitted to bar, 1997, Washington (Not admitted in North Carolina). *Education:* University of California (B.A., 1991); University of Arizona (J.D., 1996). Phi Delta Phi. Chair, Department of Labor Liaison Committee, Washington State Chapter of American Immigration Lawyers Association, 2002-2004. *Member:* American Bar Association; American Immigration Lawyers Association. ***PRACTICE AREAS:*** Corporate Immigration; Business Law. ***Email:*** ryan.cook@ogletreedeakins.com

OF COUNSEL

DEBRA L. DEWAR, admitted to bar, 1995, Georgia; 2002, North Carolina and U.S. District Court, Eastern, Western and Middle Districts of North Carolina. *Education:* University of North Carolina at Chapel Hill (B.S., with highest distinction, Phi Beta Kappa, 1991; J.D., with honors, 1994). National Mock Trial Team. Former Member, Board of Directors, Atlanta Volunteer Lawyers Foundation. Former Treasurer, Atlanta Bar Association - Atlanta Council of Young Lawyers. *Member:* North Carolina Bar Association; Atlanta Bar Association (Former Member, Board of Directors and Treasurer, Atlanta Council of Younger Lawyers). ***PRACTICE AREAS:*** Labor and Employment; Employment Discrimination; Age Discrimination in Employment; Title VII Discrimination. ***Email:*** debra.dewar@ogletreedeakins.com

THOMAS F. ELLIS, born Alameda, California, August 10, 1920; admitted to bar, 1947, Virginia; 1948, North Carolina. *Education:* University of North Carolina (B.S., 1943); University of Virginia (LL.B., 1948). Assistant United States Attorney, Eastern District of North Carolina, 1952-1954. Special Counsel, Governor's Advisory Committee on Education, 1955-1956. President, 10th Judicial District, 1960. Chairman, U.S. Condemnation Commissions, Eastern District of North Carolina, 1963-1966. Member, Administrative Conference of the United States, 1982-1985. Permanent Member, Fourth Circuit Judicial Conference. *Member:* North Carolina and Virginia Bar Associations; National Association of Railroad Trial Counsel; North Carolina Association of Defense Attorneys. [Lt., USNR, 1943-1946]. ***PRACTICE AREAS:*** Civil Litigation; Constitutional Law; Election Law; Land Condemnation Law. ***Email:*** tom.ellis@ogletreedeakins.com

REPRESENTATIVE CLIENTS: ABB, Inc.; Baptist State Convention; Boddie-Noell Enterprises, Inc.; Campbell Soup Co.; Coty, Inc.; Deere-Hitachi Construction Machinery Corp.; Duke Energy Corp.; Duke University; Eastman Kodak Co.; Farm Bureau of North Carolina; FedEx Ground; General Electric Co.; General Parts, Inc. (CarQuest); GlaxoSmithKline; Glen Raven Mills, Inc.; W. R. Grace & Co.; Hendrick Automotive Group; Hoechst Celanese Corporation; Honeywell International; International Business Machines; ITT Hartford Insurance Group; Deere & Company; Lockheed Martin Services Group; Mercedes-Benz U.S. International, Inc.; Moen, Incorporated; Nissan Motor Manufacturing Corporation U.S.A.; Nortel Networks, Inc.; Novant Health, Inc.; Pfizer; PSNC Energy; Reichhold Chemicals, Inc.; Rockwell International; St. Gobain Glass; SAS Institute Inc.; Square D Co.; Sumitomo Electric Fiber Optics Corp.; TYCO; Wachovia Corp.; WestPoint Stevens, Inc.

OLIVE AND OLIVE, P.A.

RALEIGH, NORTH CAROLINA

(See Durham)

Intellectual Property, Patent, Trademark, Copyright, Computer and Biotechnology Law and Related Litigation.

J. KIRK OSBORN

RALEIGH, NORTH CAROLINA

(See Chapel Hill)

General Civil and Criminal Litigation in State and Federal Courts. Criminal, Drug Crimes, Driving While Intoxicated (DWI), White Collar Crimes, Homicide, Traffic Violations, Premises Liability, Personal Injury and Nursing Home Litigation, Wrongful Death, Civil Rights.

PARKER, POE, ADAMS & BERNSTEIN L.L.P.

WACHOVIA CAPITOL CENTER
150 FAYETTEVILLE STREET MALL, SUITE 1400
P.O. BOX 389
RALEIGH, NORTH CAROLINA 27602-0389
Telephone: 919-828-0564
Facsimile: 919-834-4564
Email: info@parkerpoe.com
URL: http://www.parkerpoe.com

Charlotte, North Carolina Offices: Three Wachovia Center, 401 South Tryon Street, Suite 3000, 28202. Telephone: 704-372-9000. Facsimile: 704-334-4706.
Columbia, South Carolina Office: 1201 Main Street, Suite 1450, 29201. Telephone: 803-255-8000. Facsimile: 803-255-8017.
Spartanburg, South Carolina Office: 101 W. St. John Street, Suite 203, 29306. Telephone: 803-591-2030. Facsimile: 803-591-2050.
Charleston, South Carolina Office: 200 Meeting Street, Suite 301, 29401. Telephone: 843-727-2650. Facsimile: 843-727-2680.

Administrative and Regulatory, Antitrust and Trade Regulation, Arbitration, Banking, Bankruptcy, Insolvency and Reorganization, Biotechnology, Capital Markets, Computer, Construction, Copyright, Corporate, Corporate Finance, Education, Employee Benefits and Compensation Plans, Employment, Environmental, Estate Planning and Administration, Governmental Contracts and Procurement, Governmental Relations, Health Care, Immigration, Insurance, Intellectual Property, International Trade and Investment, Joint Ventures, Lending and Finance, Limited Liability Companies and Partnerships, Litigation, Malpractice Defense, Mergers and Acquisitions, Municipal, Products Liability, Project Development, Project Finance, Public Finance, Commercial Real Estate, Securities, Tax Exempt Organizations, Taxation, Technology Management and Licensing, Telecommunications, Trademark, Transportation, Utilities Regulation, Zoning.

FIRM PROFILE: Parker, Poe, Adams & Bernstein L.L.P. is one of the oldest and largest firms in the Carolinas. From our Raleigh, Charlotte, Charleston, Spartanburg and Columbia offices we serve a region recognized as an emerging center for business and industry. For information contact Allison L. Karp, Development Director, 704-372-9000.

PARTNERS

CATHARINE BIGGS ARROWOOD, born Lumberton, North Carolina, 1951; admitted to bar, 1976, North Carolina. *Education:* Wake Forest University (B.A., cum laude, 1973; J.D., cum laude, 1976). Phi Beta Kappa. Former Associate Attorney General, North Carolina Department of Justice, Antitrust Section. Former Chair, North Carolina Federal Bar Advisory Council. Former Chair, Civil Justice Reform Act Committee (EDNC). Listed in the Best Lawyers in America, Business Litigation and Alternative Dispute Resolution. Member, Fourth Circuit Judicial Conference. Member, Panel of Neutrals, American Arbitration Association. *Member:* American Bar Association. Fellow, American College of Trial Lawyers. ***PRACTICE AREAS:*** Commercial Litigation; Antitrust and Trade Regulation; Intellectual Property; Corporate Law; Alternative Dispute Resolution; International Dispute Resolution. ***Email:*** cbarrowood@parkerpoe.com

PATRICIA T. BARTIS, born York, Pennsylvania, 1965; admitted to bar, 1994, North Carolina. *Education:* Bucknell University (B.A., summa cum laude, 1987); University of North Carolina at Chapel Hill (J.D., with honors, 1994). Phi Beta Kappa. *Member:* Employment Law Alliance (North Carolina Representative). ***PRACTICE AREAS:*** Labor and Employment; Litigation; Business Torts. ***Email:*** pattibartis@parkerpoe.com

BRANDON G. BORDEAUX, born Aberdeen, Washington, 1970; admitted to bar, 1995, North Carolina. *Education:* Syracuse University (B.S., cum laude, 1991); Wake Forest University (J.D., 1995). Law Clerk to the Hon. K. Edward Greene, North Carolina Court of Appeals, 1995-1997. ***PRACTICE AREAS:*** Real Estate; Commercial Real Estate Development. ***Email:*** brandonbordeaux@parkerpoe.com

BRIAN R. BROWN, born 1952; admitted to bar, 1979, Georgia; 1986, District of Columbia; 1988, North Carolina. *Education:* Virginia Polytechnic Institute and State University (B.A., with distinction, 1974); Emory University (J.D., 1979); Georgetown University Law Center (LL.M., 1988). *Member:* Bar Association of North Carolina (Member, Tax, Business and Estate Planning Sections); State Bar of North Carolina; State Bar of Georgia; Bar Association of the District of Columbia; American Bar Association (Member, Tax and Business Sections). [Capt., U.S. Air Force, 1982-1987]. ***PRACTICE AREAS:*** Business Law; Trusts and Estates; Probate; Taxation. ***Email:*** brianbrown@parkerpoe.com

JOHN J. BUTLER, born Arlington, Virginia, 1957; admitted to bar, 1983, North Carolina. *Education:* University of North Carolina at Greensboro (B.A., summa cum laude, 1979); Harvard University (J.D., 1983). Phi Beta Kappa. Law Clerk to Honorable Sam J. Ervin, III, U.S. Fourth Circuit Court of Appeals. ***LANGUAGES:*** French. ***PRACTICE AREAS:*** Environmental Law; Litigation; Commercial Contracts. ***Email:*** jaybutler@parkerpoe.com

HENRY C. CAMPEN, JR., born Fayetteville, North Carolina, 1949; admitted to bar, 1986, North Carolina; 1987, District of Columbia. *Education:* Wake Forest University (B.A., 1971); American University (M.P.A., 1978); North Carolina Central University (J.D., summa cum laude, 1986). ***PRACTICE AREAS:*** Telecommunications; Land Use Regulation; State and Local Taxation. ***Email:*** henrycampen@parkerpoe.com

KEVIN L. CHIGNELL, born Washington, D.C., 1970; admitted to bar, 1995, North Carolina. *Education:* University of North Carolina at Chapel Hill (B.S., with highest dis-

(This Listing Continued)

tinction, 1992; J.D., with honors, 1995). Phi Beta Kappa. Law Clerk to the Hon. William L. Osteen, Sr., U.S. District Court, Middle District of North Carolina, 1995-1996. *Member:* North Carolina and American Bar Associations; North Carolina Association of Defense Attorneys. ***LANGUAGES:*** German. ***REPORTED CASES:*** Central Carolina Bank and Trust Company v. Security Life of Denver Insurance Company, 247 F. Supp. 2d 791 (M.D.N.C. 2003). ***PRACTICE AREAS:*** Tort Defense; Trucking and Transportation; Products Liability; Insurance Coverage; Premises Liability; Construction Law. ***Email:*** kevinchignell@parkerpoe.com

JACK L. COZORT, born Valdese, North Carolina, 1950; admitted to bar, 1975, North Carolina. *Education:* North Carolina State University (B.A., 1972); Wake Forest University (J.D., 1975). Former Judge, North Carolina Court of Appeals. Former Director, North Carolina Administrative Office of the Courts. Former Legal Counsel, Governor James B. Hunt. Former Associate Attorney General, North Carolina Department of Justice. Former Vice President, North Carolina Judicial Conference. Former Board of Directors, Wake County Bar Association. Member: Board of Directors, North Carolina Forum for Research and Economic Education, 1999—; Board of Visitors, Wake Forest University School of Law; Board of Visitors, North Carolina State University. ***PRACTICE AREAS:*** Government Relations; Government Contracts; Constitutional Law. ***Email:*** jackcozort@parkerpoe.com

MELANIE BLACK DUBIS, born Kernersville, North Carolina, 1970; admitted to bar, 1995, North Carolina; U.S. District Court, Eastern and Middle District of North Carolina; 1996, U.S. Court of Appeals, Fourth Circuit; 2002, U.S. Court of Appeals, Federal Circuit. *Education:* University of North Carolina at Chapel Hill (B.A., with honors, 1992); Vanderbilt University (J.D., 1995). Phi Beta Kappa. John W. Wade Scholar. Senior Student Writing Editor, Vanderbilt Law Review, 1994-1995. *Member:* North Carolina (Member, Appellate Rules Advisory Committee, Chair, Civil Practice and Procedure Committee, Litigation Section) and American Bar Associations. ***PRACTICE AREAS:*** Antitrust; Trade Regulation; Business Torts; Commercial Litigation; Securities Litigation. ***Email:*** melaniedubis@parkerpoe.com

JOHN R. ERWIN, born Morganton, North Carolina, 1957; admitted to bar, 1983, North Carolina. *Education:* Phillips Universität (1978); Davidson College (B.A., 1979); University of North Carolina at Chapel Hill (J.D., 1983). ***LANGUAGES:*** German. ***PRACTICE AREAS:*** Mergers and Acquisitions; Biotechnology; Health Care. ***Email:*** johnerwin@parkerpoe.com

RUSSELL B. KILLEN, born Hampton, Virginia, 1969; admitted to bar, 1994, North Carolina. *Education:* University of North Carolina at Chapel Hill (B.A., 1991); Phi Beta Kappa; Duke University (J.D., 1994). Town Councilman, Town of Knightdale. Member: Board of Directors, Wake Education Partnership; Wake Med Champions Board; Board of Trustees, National Multiple Sclerosis Society, Eastern North Carolina Chapter, 2001-2004; Board of Directors, Knightdale Chamber of Commerce, 2001-2004. Member, Construction Professionals Network. *Member:* North Carolina Bar Association(Member, Construction Section and Land Use & Zoning Section) and American (Member: Construction Forum; Litigation Section) Bar Associations. ***PRACTICE AREAS:*** Construction Law; Commercial Litigation; Zoning, Planning and Land Use. ***Email:*** russellkillen@parkerpoe.com

CHARLES C. MEEKER, born Washington, D.C., 1950; admitted to bar, 1975, North Carolina; 1984, District of Columbia. *Education:* Yale University (B.A., 1972); Columbia University (J.D., 1975). Former Member, Raleigh City Council. Mayor, City of Raleigh, 2001—. ***PRACTICE AREAS:*** Municipal Law; Municipal Taxation; Commercial Litigation; Government Relations. ***Email:*** charlesmeeker@parkerpoe.com

RENEE J. MONTGOMERY, born Cleveland, Ohio, 1950; admitted to bar, 1978, North Carolina. *Education:* Duke University (B.A., 1971; J.D., with distinction, 1978). Member: American Health Lawyers Association. Former President and Board Member, N.C. Society of Health Care Attorneys. *Member:* North Carolina Bar Association (Council Member, Health Law and Administrative Law Sections). ***PRACTICE AREAS:*** Health Care; Employment Law; Government Relations. ***Email:*** reneemontgomery@parkerpoe.com

WILLIAM G. PAPPAS, born Fayetteville, North Carolina, 1952; admitted to bar, 1977, North Carolina. *Education:* University of North Carolina at Chapel Hill (B.A., 1974; J.D., 1977). Phi Beta Kappa. Law Clerk to U.S. District Court, Eastern District of North Carolina: Judge Franklin T. Dupree, Jr., 1978-1979; Magistrate Logan D. Howell, 1977-1978. Former Chairman, Business Law Section, North Carolina Bar Association. General Counsel, Research Triangle Chapter, National Association of Corporate Directors. ***PRACTICE AREAS:*** Mergers and Acquisitions; International; Biotechnology. ***Email:*** billpappas@parkerpoe.com

FRANK E. SILBER, born Raleigh, North Carolina, December 3, 1972; admitted to bar, 1997, North Carolina. *Education:* University of North Carolina at Chapel Hill (B.S., 1994); Wake Forest University (J.D., magna cum laude, 1997). Order of the Coif. Executive Editor, Wake Forest Law Review, 1996-1997. ***PRACTICE AREAS:*** Corporate Law; Intellectual Property Licensing; Computers and Software. ***Email:*** franksilber@parkerpoe.com

ROBERT W. SPEARMAN, born Durham, North Carolina, 1943; admitted to bar, 1971, North Carolina; 1979, District of Columbia. *Education:* University of North Carolina at Chapel Hill (A.B., with highest honors, 1965); Oxford University (M.A., First Class Honors, 1967); Yale University (LL.B., 1970). Phi Beta Kappa. Morehead Scholar. Rhodes Scholar. Law Clerk to the Hon. Hugo L. Black, U.S. Supreme Court, 1970-1971. Former Board of Director, American Judicature Society. Former Chairman, North Carolina State Board of Elections. Listed in Best Lawyers in America, Antitrust Law, Business Litigation and Intellectual Property Law. Named to Business North Carolina's Legal Elite, Antitrust Law. *Member:* American College of Trial Lawyers. ***PRACTICE AREAS:*** Antitrust and Trade Regulation; Commercial Litigation; Professional Malpractice. ***Email:*** bobspearman@parkerpoe.com

JAMES A. THOMAS, admitted to bar, 1987, North Carolina; 1989, Georgia; 2004, District Of Columbia. *Education:* Asbury College (A.B., magna cum laude, 1984); Duke University (J.D., magna cum laude, 1987). Order of the Coif. Member, Editorial Board, Duke Law Journal, 1986-1987. *Member:* The District of Columbia Bar; International Trademark Association; British American Business Council; Pharmaceutical Trade Marks Group. ***PRACTICE AREAS:*** Intellectual Property Licensing; International Licensing; Intellectual Property Portfolio Management; International Pharmaceutical Intellectual Property; Trademarks; International Trademarks; Copyrights; International Copyright Law; Business Transactions; Corporate Contracts. ***Email:*** jamesthomas@parkerpoe.com

R. BRUCE THOMPSON, II, born Greenville, North Carolina, 1967; admitted to bar, 1994, North Carolina. *Education:* Wake Forest University (B.A., 1988; J.D., 1994). Law Clerk to the Hon. Jack L. Cozort, North Carolina Court of Appeals, 1994-1995. Former Assistant Attorney General, North Carolina Department of Justice, Education Section. Former Campaign Manager, The Mike Easley Committee. Town Attorney, Town of Clayton, North Carolina. *Member:* Wake County, North Carolina and American Bar Associations; North Carolina Professional Lobbyists Association; North Carolina Municipal Attorneys Association. (Government Practice Group Leader). ***PRACTICE AREAS:*** Government Relations; Municipal Law; Litigation; Eminent Domain; Land Use; Zoning Law; Election, Campaign and Political Law. ***Email:*** brucethompson@parkerpoe.com

JAMES C. THORNTON, born Huntington, West Virginia, 1964; admitted to bar, 1989, North Carolina. *Education:* University of Kentucky (B.S., with high distinction, 1986; J.D., 1989). *Member:* North Carolina Association of Defense Attorneys. ***PRACTICE AREAS:*** Tort Defense; Insurance Coverage; Personal Injury; Wrongful Death. ***Email:*** jamesthornton@parkerpoe.com

CYNTHIA LEIGH WITTMER, born Raleigh, North Carolina, 1953; admitted to bar, 1981, North Carolina. *Education:* University of North Carolina at Chapel Hill (B.A., 1975); Duke University (J.D., 1981). Phi Beta Kappa; Order of the Coif; Order of the Valkyries. Member, Duke Law Journal. Chair, Tenth Judicial District Grievance Committee. Former Chair, Tenth Judicial District Fee Arbitration Committee. Former Member, Board of Directors, Tenth Judicial District Bar. *Member:* North Carolina and American Bar Associations. ***PRACTICE AREAS:*** Commercial Litigation; Intellectual Property; Government Contracts. ***Email:*** cindywittmer@parkerpoe.com

SPECIAL COUNSEL

REBECCA BLACKMON JOYNER, born Valdosta, Georgia, Feburary 22, 1974; admitted to bar, 2004, North Carolina. *Education:* University of North Carolina at Chapel Hill (B.A., with honors, 1996); Columbia University (M.P.A., 1998); Fordham University (J.D., magna cum laude, 2004). *Member:* North Carolina State Bar; North Carolina and American Bar Associations; National Association of Bond Lawyers. ***PRACTICE AREAS:*** Public Finance; Government. ***Email:*** rebeccajoyner@parkerpoe.com

TODD M. RUBIN, born Buffalo, New York, 1954; admitted to bar, 1985, New York and District of Columbia; 1997, North Carolina. *Education:* Pitzer College (B.A., 1976); State University of New York at Buffalo (J.D., 1984). ***PRACTICE AREAS:*** Immigration Law. ***Email:*** toddrubin@parkerpoe.com

OF COUNSEL

J. ALLEN ADAMS, born Greensboro, North Carolina, 1932; admitted to bar, 1954, North Carolina; U.S. District Court, Eastern, Western and Middle Districts of North Carolina, U.S. Court of Appeals, 4th Circuit, U.S. Court of the Armed Forces and U.S. Supreme Court. *Education:* Boston University; University of North Carolina at Chapel Hill (A.B., 1952; J.D., 1954). Former Member, North Carolina House of Representatives and Former Chairman, Appropriations Committee (Base Budget). *Member:* Wake County, North Carolina and American Bar Associations. [Capt., JAGC, USNR, Retired]. ***PRACTICE AREAS:*** Government Relations; Government Contracts. ***Email:*** aladams@parkerpoe.com

JOHN F. GRAYBEAL, born Richmond, Virginia, 1937; admitted to bar, 1962, District of Columbia; 1987, North Carolina. *Education:* Oberlin College (B.A., 1959); Harvard Law School (LL.B., 1962). ***PRACTICE AREAS:*** Antitrust Law; Commercial Litigation. ***Email:*** johngraybeal@parkerpoe.com

WILLIAM H. McCULLOUGH, born Chattanooga, Tennessee, 1934; admitted to bar, 1959, North Carolina. *Education:* Lenoir-Rhyne College (A.B., 1956); University of North Carolina at Chapel Hill (J.D., with honors, 1959). (Board Certified Specialist in Real Property Law and Business, Commercial and Industrial Transactions, North Carolina Board of Legal Specialization). ***PRACTICE AREAS:*** Real Estate; Creditors Rights; Contracts; Bankruptcy Reorganization. ***Email:*** billmccullough@parkerpoe.com

ASSOCIATES

NICHOLLE ALLEN-STEELE, born Washington, D.C., April 14, 1970; admitted to bar, 1999, District of Columbia; 2000, North Carolina. *Education:* Drexel University (B.S., 1992); Columbus School of Law of The Catholic University of America (J.D., 1996). Member, Triangle Commercial Real Estate Women (TCREW). *Member:* Wake County, North Carolina (Member, Real Property Section) and American Bar Associations. ***PRACTICE AREAS:*** Real Estate; Commercial Real Estate Development; Telecommunications Law; Commercial Loans. ***Email:*** nicholleasteele@parkerpoe.com

JEFFREY A. BANDINI, born Camden, New Jersey, May 31, 1971; admitted to bar, 1998, North Carolina. *Education:* University of North Carolina at Chapel Hill (B.A., with highest honors, 1993; J.D., 1997; M.R.P., 1997). *Member:* North Carolina State Bar; North Carolina and American Bar Associations. ***PRACTICE AREAS:*** Land Use; Zoning Law; Public Transportation Law; Municipal Law; Government; Commercial Real Estate. ***Email:*** jeffbandini@parkerpoe.com

SCOTT E. BAYZLE, born Wilmington, North Carolina, September 17, 1977; admitted to bar, 2005, North Carolina. *Education:* Wake Forest University (B.S., 2000); Wake Forest School of Law (J.D., 2005). Order of the Barristers; Order of the Coif. ***PRACTICE AREAS:*** Antitrust; Business Torts; Intellectual Property. ***Email:*** scottbayzle@parkerpoe.com

GEORGE T. BRADY III, born Queens, New York, February 9, 1972; admitted to bar, 1998, North Carolina. *Education:* University of North Carolina at Chapel Hill (B.S.B.A., with honors, 1994; J.D., with honors, 1998). Phi Beta Kappa. Member, International Law Journal. ***PRACTICE AREAS:*** Mergers, Acquisitions and Divestitures; Corporate Law; Securities. ***Email:*** georgebrady@parkerpoe.com

(This Listing Continued)

PARKER, POE, ADAMS & BERNSTEIN L.L.P., Raleigh—Continued

MELISSA S. DAIGNEAULT, born New Orleans, Louisisana, July 11, 1978; admitted to bar, 2003, Texas; 2004, North Carolina. *Education:* Texas A & M University (B.S., summa cum laude, 1999); Wake Forest University (J.D., 2003). *Member:* State Bar of Texas; Wake County, North Carolina (Member, Construction Law Section) and American (Member, Sections on: Construction Law; Dispute Resolution) Bar Associations; Texas Young Lawyers Association; Aggie Bar Association. ***PRACTICE AREAS:*** Construction Law; Debtor and Creditor. ***Email:*** melissadaigneault@parkerpoe.com

BRIAN D. DARER, born New York, January 12, 1973; admitted to bar, 1998, North Carolina and U.S. District Court, Eastern District of North Carolina; 1999, U.S. District Court, Middle and Western Districts of North Carolina; 2000, U.S. Court of Appeals, Fourth Circuit. *Education:* University of Virginia (B.A., with honors, 1995; J.D. 1998). *Member:* North Carolina (Member, Bankruptcy Section) and American (Member, Litigation Section) Bar Associations; North Carolina State Bar. ***PRACTICE AREAS:*** Bankruptcy; Construction Law. ***Email:*** briandarer@parkerpoe.com

SUSAN L. DUNATHAN, born Philadelphia, Pennsylvania, August 28, 1959; admitted to bar, 2001, North Carolina. *Education:* Emory University (B.A., 1982); North Carolina Central University (J.D., magna cum laude, 2001). *Member:* Wake County, North Carolina and American Bar Associations; American Health Lawyers Association. ***PRACTICE AREAS:*** Health Care Regulation; Civil Litigation. ***Email:*** susandunathan@parkerpoe.com

SARAH L. FORD, born Oxford, Ohio, July 23, 1973; admitted to bar, 2003, North Carolina. *Education:* Miami University (B.A., magna cum laude, 1996); New York University (J.D., cum laude, 2003). *Member:* North Carolina and American Bar Associations. ***PRACTICE AREAS:*** Antitrust and Business Torts. ***Email:*** sarahford@parkerpoe.com

AMANDA A. HAYES, born East Stroudsburg, Pennsylvania; admitted to bar, 2002, North Carolina. *Education:* University of Delaware (B.A., magna cum laude, 1999); University of North Carolina at Chapel Hill (J.D., with honors, 2002). Phi Beta Kappa. Comments Editor, 2001-2002 and Staff Member, 2000-2001, North Carolina Law Review. *Member:* Wake County, North Carolina and American Bar Associations; North Carolina State Bar. ***PRACTICE AREAS:*** Business Law; Mergers and Acquisitions; Joint Ventures; Commercial Law. ***Email:*** amandahayes@parkerpoe.com

TRACY WOOD KIMBRELL, born Evanston, Illinois, March 23, 1980; admitted to bar, 2005, North Carolina. *Education:* North Carolina State University (B.A., 2002); University of North Carolina at Chapel Hill (J.D., 2005). ***PRACTICE AREAS:*** Government Relations; Municipalities; Commercial Litigation. ***Email:*** tracykimbrell@parkerpoe.com

KATHRYN S. LEHMAN, admitted to bar, 2004, North Carolina. *Education:* North Carolina State University (B.A., B.S., summa cum laude, 2001); University of North Carolina at Chapel Hill (J.D., 2004). *Member:* North Carolina State Bar. ***PRACTICE AREAS:*** Tort Defense; Insurance Coverage; Personal Injury; Wrongful Death. ***Email:*** katylehman@parkerpoe.com

BRENTON W. McCONKEY, born Memphis, Tennessee, November 17, 1978; admitted to bar, 2004, North Carolina. *Education:* Wake Forest University (B.A., summa cum laude, 2001); University of North Carolina at Chapel Hill (J.D., with honors, 2004). *Member:* North Carolina State Bar. ***PRACTICE AREAS:*** Government. ***Email:*** brentmcconkey@parkerpoe.com

CHARLES E. RAYNAL, IV, born Durham, North Carolina, December 17, 1973; admitted to bar, 2000, Georgia; 2001, U.S. District Court, Northern District of Georgia; 2004, North Carolina and U.S. District Court, Eastern District of North Carolina; 2005, U.S. District Court, Middle District of North Carolina. *Education:* Davidson College (B.A., 1995); Wake Forest University (J.D., 2000). Order of the Barristers. Member, National Trial Team, 1999-2000. Finalist, Kauffman Securities Litigation Moot Court Competition, 1999. Recipient, American Jurisprudence Awards in Torts, Trial Advocacy, Bankruptcy. Member, Wake Forest University Law Review, 1998-2000. *Member:* Wake County and American Bar Associations; State Bar of Georgia; North Carolina State Bar. ***PRACTICE AREAS:*** Litigation; Government; Municipal Law. ***Email:*** charlesraynal@parkerpoe.com

REPRESENTATIVE CLIENTS: Accor Hotels; Association for Home and Hospice Care of North Carolina; Atlantic Partners, LLC; Attorneys Liability Protection Society; Asahi Glass America; Ashtead Group plc; Aston Properties; AVX; Bank of America, N.A.; Barnhardt Manufacturing Co.; Bauer International Inc.; Blackbaud, Inc.; Board of Governors of the University of North Carolina; Bombardier Capital Inc.; BP, Inc.; Burroughs & Chapin Company, Inc.; Brunswick County; Cardinal Health, Inc.; Carolina Federal Savings Bank; Charlotte Mecklenburg Hospital Authority; Childress Klein Properties; City of Charlotte; City of Durham; City of Winston-Salem; Coen Capital, Inc.; Collins & Aikman; Conseco, Inc.; Consulting Engineers Council; Crescent Resources; DAK Americas; Domnick Hunter; Duke Energy; DukeNet Communication; DyStar LP; Family Dollar Stores; First State Management; Fluor Corporation; Freightliner Corporation; Freudenberg Group; Gaston Memorial Hospital; Genpharm; Gibbs International; Golf Trust of America, L.P.; Great Harvest Franchising; Hilton Hotels Corporation; Horace Mann Insurance; Hospitality Management Group, Inc.; Invista S.a.r.l., John Wieland Homes; Johnson C. Smith University; Kiawah Resort Associates, L.P.; Klerk"s Plastic Products Manufacturing, Inc.; Laboratory Corporation of America Holdings; Legg Mason; Lowe"s Motor Speedway; MAG Mutual Insurance; Media General, Inc.; Merit Group; National Spinning Co.; National Welders Supply Co.; Nextel Communications; NGK Ceramics USA; NICCA, USA; North Carolina Biotechnology Center; North Carolina State University; N. Schlumberger USA; Nucor Corporation; Osram Sylvania; Otto Industries; Pergo; Progress Energy; Rack Room Shoes; Reeves Brothers; Robinson-Humphrey; Roper St. Francis HealthCare; Self Regional HealthCare; SGL Carbon Group; Sonic Automotive; South Carolina Federal Credit Union; Speedway Motorsports; St. Paul Travelers; Suburban Propane; Sunbelt Rentals, Inc. ; Sun Microsystems; Tanner Companies; The Crosland Group; Trammell Crow Companies; Triangle Transit Authority; U-Haul International, Inc.; University Medical Associates; University of North Carolina; Union County North Carolina; Wachovia; Wood Partners.

(For biographical data on other personnel, see Professional Biographies at Charlotte, North Carolina, Columbia, South Carolina, Spartanburg, South Carolina and Charleston, South Carolina)

PASSÉ INTELLECTUAL PROPERTY, LLC

1717 BRASSFIELD ROAD
RALEIGH, NORTH CAROLINA 27614-9448
Telephone: 919-256-8196
Fax: 919-878-0101
Email: jpasse@passeip.com

Patent Drafting, Patent Prosecution, Patents, Intellectual Property, Trademarks.

JAMES G. PASSÉ, born Chicago, Illinois, November 26, 1951; admitted to bar, 1979, Michigan & Illinois; registered to practice before U.S. Patent and Trademark Office (Not admitted in North Carolina). *Education:* University of Illinois (B.S., Pharmacology, 1974); Chicago-Kent College of Law, Illinois Institute of Technology (J.D. 1979). *Member:* North Carolina (Past Chairman, Biotechnology Committee) Illinois State, Michigan and American Bar Associations; American Intellectual Property Lawyers Association; Triangle Intellectual Property Lawyers Association. ***LANGUAGES:*** French. ***PRACTICE AREAS:*** Patents; Patent Prosecution; Intellectual Property; Trademarks. ***Email:*** jpasse@passeip.com

---

MICHAEL W. PATRICK

RALEIGH, NORTH CAROLINA

(See Chapel Hill)

Products Liability, Malpractice, Environmental, Toxic Torts, Asbestos, Federal Criminal Law.

PATTERSON, DILTHEY, CLAY, BRYSON & ANDERSON, L.L.P.

Established in 1992

4020 WESTCHASE BOULEVARD, SUITE 550
RALEIGH, NORTH CAROLINA 27607
Telephone: 919-821-4020
Fax: 919-829-0055
URL: http://www.pattersondilthey.com

Wilmington, North Carolina Office: 2516 Independence Boulevard, Suite 200. Telephone: 910-452-2797. Toll-Free: 877-731-5007. Fax: 910-452-4151.

General Trial and Appellate Practice before all State and Federal Courts. Litigation of Insurance Law, Personal Injury, Medical Malpractice, Legal Malpractice, Workers Compensation and Intentional Torts, Construction Law and Litigation, Products Liability and General Civil and Commercial Litigation.

FIRM PROFILE: This firm is comprised of trial lawyers who actively engage in the defense of civil litigation throughout the state of North Carolina.

MEMBERS OF FIRM

GRADY S. PATTERSON, JR. (Retired)

RONALD C. DILTHEY, born New York, June 5, 1935; admitted to bar, 1960, North Carolina. *Education:* Wake Forest College (B.S., 1957; LL.B., 1960). Phi Delta Phi. Adjunct Professor of Law, Campbell University School of Law, 1979—. *Member:* Wake County, North Carolina (Lecturer, Annual Practical Skills Course, 1969-1995; Chairman, Committee on Medico-Legal Liaison, 1976-1979; Member, Board of Governors, 1982-1985; Chairman, Litigation Section, 1983-1984; Chairman, Administration of Justice Study Committee, 1992-1993; Chairman, Administration of Justice Study Task Force, 1993-1996; Vice President, 1996-1998) and American Bar Associations; Fellow, American College of Trial Lawyers. [Capt., U.S. Army Reserves]. ***PRACTICE AREAS:*** Personal Injury Litigation; Products Liability; Mediator; Legal Malpractice; Business Litigation.

ROBERT M. CLAY, born Tillsonburg, Ontario, Canada, September 13, 1935; admitted to bar, 1961, North Carolina. *Education:* University of North Carolina (A.B., 1959; J.D., 1961). Phi Alpha Delta. Member, North Carolina General Statutes Commission, 1977-1980. Member, North Carolina Courts Commission, 1980-1985. *Member:* Wake County (Member, Executive Committee, 1971-1972), North Carolina (Chairman, Administration of Justice Study Committee, 1979-1981; Chairman, Subcommittee on Merit Selection of Judges, 1977-1978; Member, Torts and Civil Litigation Committee, 1974-1977; Member, Litigation Section; Lecturer, CLE Programs on: Rules of Civil Procedure, 1973; Products Liability, 1979; Code of Evidence, 1984; Civil Practice and Procedure, 1984) and American (Member: Torts and Insurance Practice Section; Committee on Medicine and Law, 1984—) Bar Associations; North Carolina Association of Defense Attorneys; North Carolina Society of Health Care Attorneys; American Society for Healthcare Risk Management; Defense Research and Trial Lawyers Association; International Association of Defense Counsel. Fellow, American College of Trial Lawyers. ***PRACTICE AREAS:*** Medical Malpractice Defense. ***Email:*** RClay@pattersondilthey.com

E. C. BRYSON, JR., born Durham, North Carolina, July 16, 1936; admitted to bar, 1964, North Carolina and U.S. District Court, Middle and Eastern Districts of North Carolina. *Education:* Duke University (B.A., 1958); University of North Carolina (LL.B., 1964). *Member:* Durham County and North Carolina Bar Associations; Fourteenth Judicial District and North Carolina State Bars; North Carolina Association of Defense Attorneys; Fellow, American College of Trial Lawyers. [Captain, USMCR, active duty, 1958-1961]. ***PRACTICE AREAS:*** Medical Malpractice Defense; Dental Malpractice Defense; Products Liability; Insurance Defense. ***Email:*** EBryson@pattersondilthey.com

REID RUSSELL, born Lewes, Delaware, July 25, 1952; admitted to bar, 1980, North Carolina. *Education:* Union College and University (B.A., cum laude, 1975); University of North Carolina (J.D., 1980). *Member:* Wake County and North Carolina Bar Associations; North Carolina Association of Defense Attorneys. [Capt., U.S. Army JAGC, 1981-1984]. ***PRACTICE AREAS:*** Insurance Defense; Personal Injury; Products Liability. ***Email:*** RRussell@pattersondilthey.com

(This Listing Continued)

MARK E. ANDERSON, born Durham, North Carolina, April 22, 1963; admitted to bar, 1988, North Carolina and U.S. District Court, Eastern District of North Carolina; 1991, U.S. District Court, Middle District of North Carolina; U.S. District Court, Western District of North Carolina; U.S. Court of Appeals, Fourth Circuit; 2005, U.S. Supreme Court. *Education:* Duke University (A.B., 1985); University of North Carolina (J.D., 1988). Phi Delta Phi. Holderness Moot Court Bench. *Member:* Durham County, North Carolina and American Bar Associations; North Carolina State Bar; Defense Research Institute; American Society for Healthcare Risk Management; North Carolina Association of Defense Attorneys. ***PRACTICE AREAS:*** Personal Injury; Insurance Law; Medical Malpractice Defense; Complex and Multi-District Litigation. ***Email:*** MAnderson@pattersondilthey.com

DONNA RENFROW RUTALA, born Smithfield, North Carolina, December 16, 1957; admitted to bar, 1989, North Carolina and U.S. District Court, Eastern and Middle Districts of North Carolina. *Education:* University of North Carolina (B.S.N., 1980); North Carolina Central University (J.D., 1989). Sigma Theta Tau. Registered Nurse, North Carolina, 1980. Recipient, American Jurisprudence Award in Appellate Advocacy. Member, North Carolina Chapter, American Society for Healthcare Risk Management. *Member:* Wake County, North Carolina and American (Sections on: Litigation; Health Law) Bar Associations; Defense Research Institute; North Carolina Association of Defense Attorneys. ***PRACTICE AREAS:*** Insurance Defense; Medical Malpractice Defense; Health Law. ***Email:*** DRutala@pattersondilthey.com

PHILLIP J. ANTHONY, born Akron, Ohio, May 30, 1958; admitted to bar, 1992, North Carolina and U.S. District Court, Eastern District of North Carolina; U.S. Court of Appeals, Fourth Circuit. *Education:* University of Akron (B.A., 1981); Webster University (M.A., 1988); Campbell University (J.D., 1992). Phi Kappa Phi; Omicron Delta Kappa; Delta Theta Phi. Member, Law Review. *Member:* Wake County and North Carolina Bar Associations; Defense Research Institute. ***PRACTICE AREAS:*** Insurance Defense Litigation; Products Liability; Workers Compensation; General Tort; Employment. ***Email:*** PAnthony@pattersondilthey.com

G. LAWRENCE REEVES, JR., born Charlotte, North Carolina, November 9, 1952; admitted to bar, 1978, North Carolina and U.S. District Court, Western, Eastern and Middle Districts of North Carolina; U.S. Supreme Court. *Education:* University of North Carolina at Chapel Hill (B.S., 1975; J.D., 1978). Assistant District Attorney, Charlotte, North Carolina, 1980-1983. Special Agent, Federal Bureau of Investigation, 1983-1986. Associate/Assistant Attorney General, 1986-1993. *Member:* Wake County and North Carolina Bar Associations. ***PRACTICE AREAS:*** Insurance Defense; Personal Injury; Workers Compensation; Professional and Medical Malpractice Defense; Coverage Disputes. ***Email:*** LReeves@pattersondilthey.com

CHARLES GEORGE, born New York, N.Y., June 22, 1966; admitted to bar, 1994, North Carolina and U.S. District Court, Eastern District of North Carolina; U.S. District Court, Middle District of North Carolina and U.S. Court of Appeals, Fourth Circuit. *Education:* University of Michigan (B.A., 1988); Pennsylvania State University (M.B.A., 1990); University of Miami (J.D., cum laude, 1994). *Member:* Wake County, North Carolina and American Bar Associations; North Carolina Association of Defense Attorneys; Defense Research Institute. ***PRACTICE AREAS:*** Insurance Coverage; Insurance Defense Litigation; Professional and Medical Malpractice Defense. ***Email:*** CGeorge@pattersondilthey.com

MARY McHUGH WEBB, born Raleigh, North Carolina, December 30, 1966; admitted to bar, 1992, North Carolina and U.S. District Court, Eastern, Middle and Western Districts of North Carolina. *Education:* University of North Carolina at Chapel Hill (B.A., Psychology, 1989); Campbell University (J.D., 1992). *Member:* Wake County, North Carolina and American (Member, Litigation Section) Bar Associations; North Carolina Association of Defense Attorneys; Defense Research Institute. ***PRACTICE AREAS:*** Civil Litigation; Insurance Defense; Professional Malpractice; Premises Liability; Construction Law. ***Email:*** MWebb@pattersondilthey.com

CHRISTIAN MICHAEL KENNEDY, born Danbury, Connecticut, September 14, 1963; admitted to bar, 1997, North Carolina. *Education:* Trinity University (B.A., 1985); Campbell University (J.D., 1997). ***PRACTICE AREAS:*** General Liability; Medical Malpractice Litigation; Commercial Litigation; Products Liability Litigation. ***Email:*** CKennedy@pattersondilthey.com

CHRISTOPHER J. DERRENBACHER, born Atlanta, Georgia, May 23, 1972; admitted to bar, 1998, North Carolina; U.S. District Court Eastern, Middle and Western Districts of North Carolina. *Education:* East Carolina University (B.A., 1994); Norman A. Wiggins School of Law (J.D., cum laude, 1998). *Member:* Wake County and North Carolina (Member, Litigation Section) Bar Associations; North Carolina Association of Defense Attorneys; Defense Research Institute. ***PRACTICE AREAS:*** Civil Defense Litigation; Medical Malpractice; Workers Compensation; Insurance Coverage; Construction Litigation. ***Email:*** CDerrenbacher@pattersondilthey.com

CHRISTOPHER M. HINNANT, born Wilson, North Carolina, June 29, 1972; admitted to bar, 1997, North Carolina and U.S. District Court, Eastern District of North Carolina. *Education:* University of North Carolina (B.A., 1994); Campbell University (J.D., 1997). Phi Alpha Delta. Order of the Barristers. Member, Moot Court Competition. *Member:* North Carolina and American Bar Associations; North Carolina Academy of Trial Lawyers; International Academy of Trial Lawyers. ***LANGUAGES:*** Spanish. ***PRACTICE AREAS:*** Insurance Defense; Civil Litigation; Coverage Disputes; Medical Malpractice; Workers Compensation. ***Email:*** CHinnant@pattersondilthey.com

PATRICK M. MEACHAM, born Roanoke, Virginia, April 1, 1966; admitted to bar, 1999, North Carolina. *Education:* University of Kansas (B.A., 1988); Campbell University (J.D., 1999). Order of Barristers. Member: John Marshall Moot Court Team; ATLA Trial Team. ***PRACTICE AREAS:*** Civil Defense Litigation; Medical Malpractice Litigation. ***Email:*** PMeacham@pattersondilthey.com

JULIE L. BELL, born Greensboro, North Carolina, April 22, 1967; admitted to bar, 1992, North Carolina; 1997, U.S. District Court, Eastern District of North Carolina; 2000, U.S. District Court, Middle and Western Districts of North Carolina. *Education:* University of North Carolina, Greensboro (B.A., 1989); University of North Carolina, Chapel Hill (J.D., 1992). Davis Society. Former Assistant District Attorney, Wake County. *Member:* Wake County and North Carolina Bar Associations; North Carolina Association of Black

(This Listing Continued)

Attorneys; North Carolina Association of Defense Attorneys; Defense Research Institute. ***PRACTICE AREAS:*** Insurance Defense; Medical Malpractice Defense; Civil Litigation; Criminal Defense; Premises Liability. ***Email:*** JBell@pattersondilthey.com

CARRIE E. MEIGS, born Wright Patterson, A.F.B., May 19, 1974; admitted to bar, 1998, North Carolina. *Education:* University of North Carolina at Chapel Hill (B.A., 1995; J.D., 1998). Member, Invitational Moot Court Team, Order of the Barristers. *Member:* North Carolina State Bar; North Carolina Association of Defense Attorneys; Defense Research Institute. ***PRACTICE AREAS:*** Insurance Defense Litigation; Insurance Coverage; Medical Malpractice Defense. ***Email:*** CMeigs@pattersondilthey.com

THOMAS M. BUCKLEY, born Washington, D.C., December 22, 1964; admitted to bar, 1990, California; 1999, North Carolina. *Education:* Boston College (B.A., magna cum laude, 1987); Hastings College of the Law, University of California (J.D., 1990). Recipient, American Jurisprudence Award in Conflict of Laws. Assistant Articles Editor, Hastings Journal of Communications and Entertainment Law, 1989-1990. CLE Speaker on Construction, Insurance and Maritime issues. Judge, National Maritime Moot Court Competition, 1994. Moot Court Instructor, Oakland College of Law, 1992-1996. *Member:* Wake County (Member, Litigation Section) and North Carolina (Member, Sections on: Litigation and Construction Law) Bar Associations; State Bar of California; North Carolina State Bar; Defense Research Institute (Construction Law Committee). ***PRACTICE AREAS:*** Insurance Defense; Medical Malpractice Defense; Commercial Law Disputes; Construction Litigation; Maritime Law. ***Email:*** TBuckley@pattersondilthey.com

ASSOCIATES

HEATHER R. WILSON, born Thomasville, North Carolina, March 8, 1975; admitted to bar, 2001, North Carolina. *Education:* University of North Carolina at Charlotte (B.A., 1997); Campbell University (J.D., 2001). Order of Barristers. *Member:* Wake County Bar Association (Young Lawyers Division). ***PRACTICE AREAS:*** Civil Defense Litigation. ***Email:*** HWilson@pattersondilthey.com

KATHRINE E. DOWNING, born Columbus, Ohio, August 4, 1968; admitted to bar, 2001, North Carolina; U.S. District Court, Eastern District of North Carolina; U.S. Court of Appeals, Fourth Circuit; U.S. Supreme Court. *Education:* Ohio State University (B.S.L.A., 1991); Campbell University (J.D., 2001). Phi Alpha Delta; Order of Barristers. John Marshall Moot Court Team. Law Clerk to the Hon. John M. Tyson, North Carolina Court of Appeals, 2001. *Member:* North Carolina State Bar; North Carolina Association of Defense Attorneys. ***PRACTICE AREAS:*** Workers Compensation; Medical Malpractice Defense; Insurance Defense. ***Email:*** KDowning@pattersondilthey.com

HELEN D. MEELHEIM, born Charleston, West Virginia, March 25, 1952; admitted to bar, 1995, North Carolina. *Education:* University of North Carolina at Chapel hill (B.S.N., 1974; J.D., 1992); East Carolina University (M.S.N., 1982). Sigma Theta Tau. Registered Nurse, 1974—. *Member:* North Carolina Bar Association. [LTC ANC, USAR, 1984—]. ***PRACTICE AREAS:*** Medical Malpractice Defense; Administrative Law. ***Email:*** HMeelheim@pattersondilthey.com

KIMBERLY K. PARKMAN, born Albuquerque, New Mexico, October 30, 1975; admitted to bar, 2003, North Carolina. *Education:* Texas Christian University (B.S.N., 1998); University of North Carolina at Chapel Hill School of Law (J.D., 2003). Phi Delta Phi; Sigma Theta Tau (International Nursing Honor Society). Member, The Order of Barristers. Registered Nurse, 1999. *Member:* North Carolina and American Bar Associations. ***PRACTICE AREAS:*** Medical Malpractice Defense; Civil Litigation. ***Email:*** KParkman@pattersondilthey.com

KRISTIE L. HEDRICK, born Conover, North Carolina, April 15, 1974; admitted to bar, 2003, North Carolina. *Education:* University of North Carolina at Chapel Hill (B.A., 1999); University of North Carolina at Chapel Hill School of Law (J.D., 2003). Member and Officer, Broun National Trial Team. ***PRACTICE AREAS:*** Civil Litigation; Insurance Defense; Medical Malpractice; Commercial Litigation. ***Email:*** KHedrick@pattersondilthey.com

JUSTIN D. HOWARD, born Abilene, Texas, January 23, 1973; admitted to bar, 2003, North Carolina and U.S. District Court, Eastern District of North Carolina. *Education:* University of North Carolina at Wilmington (B.S., 2000); University of North Carolina at Chapel Hill School of Law (J.D., 2003). Member, The Order of Barristers. Recipient, James William Morrow, III Award. Chief Justice, Holderness Moot Court Bench. Broun National Trial Team. Law Clerk to the North Carolina Civil Pattern Jury Instruction Committee, 2001-2003. *Member:* Wake County, North Carolina and American Bar Associations; Defense Research Institute; North Carolina Association of Defense Attorneys; The Federalist Society for Law and Public Policy Studies. [United States Marine Corps, 1993-1997]. ***PRACTICE AREAS:*** Civil Litigation; Insurance Defense; Medical Malpractice Defense; Legal Malpractice Defense; Products Liability; Premises Liability; Construction Litigation. ***Email:*** JHoward@pattersondilthey.com

TOBIAS S. HAMPSON, born Basingstone, England, December 20, 1975; admitted to bar, 2002, North Carolina; 2003, U.S. District Court, Eastern District of North Carolina. *Education:* American University (B.A., 1998); Norman A. Wiggins School of Law, Campbell University (J.D., 2002). Law Clerk to the: Hon. K. Edward Greene, North Carolina Court of Appeals, 2002; Hon. Wanda Bryant, North Carolina Court of Appeals, 2003; Hon. Robert Hunter, North Carolina Court of Appeals, 2003-2004. *Member:* North Carolina State Bar; North Carolina Bar Association. ***PRACTICE AREAS:*** Civil Litigation; Workers Compensation. ***Email:*** THampson@pattersondilthey.com

EDWARD K. BROOKS, born Pembroke, North Carolina, April 5, 1974; admitted to bar, 2004, North Carolina. *Education:* University of North Carolina at Chapel Hill (B.A., 1996); North Carolina Central University (J.D., 2003). Chair, Trial Advocacy Board, 2003. ***PRACTICE AREAS:*** General Liability Defense; Medical Malpractice. ***Email:*** EBrooks@pattersondilthey.com

JENNIFER M. ST. CLAIR, born Statesville, North Carolina, May 29, 1979; admitted to bar, 2004, North Carolina. *Education:* University of North Carolina at Chapel Hill (B.A., 2001); Norman A. Wiggins School of Law, Campbell University (J.D., 2004). Omicron Delta Kappa National Honor Society. Member, Order of the Barristers. Recipient, Interna-

(This Listing Continued)

PATTERSON, DILTHEY, CLAY, BRYSON & ANDERSON, L.L.P., Raleigh—Continued

tional Academy of Trial Lawyers Trial Advocacy Award. Team Member: National Civil Trial Competition; The Association of Trial Lawyers of America. ***PRACTICE AREAS:*** Civil Defense Litigation. ***Email:*** JStClair@pattersondilthey.com

MINDI L. SCHULZE, born Scottsdale, Arizona, June 10, 1980; admitted to bar, 2004, North Carolina. *Education:* Appalachian State University (B.S., 2001); Norman A. Wiggins School of Law, Campbell University (J.D., 2004). Williston Scholar. Team Member: The Association of Trial Lawyers of America, 2004; National Civil Trial Competition, 2003. Notes and Comments Editor, 2003-2004 and Member, 2002-2003, Campbell Law Review. ***PRACTICE AREAS:*** Civil Defense Litigation. ***Email:*** MSchulze@pattersondilthey.com

LORI P. JONES, born Raleigh, North Carolina, December 7, 1973; admitted to bar, 2004, North Carolina. *Education:* North Carolina State University (B.S., 1997; B.A., 1997; Master of Zoology, 1999); University of North Carolina at Chapel Hill (J.D., with honors, 2004). Thomas Jefferson Scholar, North Carolina State University, 1992-1997. Member, National Moot Court Team, University of North Carolina at Chapel Hill, 2003-2004. Member, North Carolina Law Review, 2002-2003. Author: "A Call for Uniform Regulation of Intentional Introductions of Non-Indigenous Species: The Suminoe Oyster," North Carolina Law Review, Vol. 81(6), 2003. ***PRACTICE AREAS:*** Civil Defense Litigation; Medical Malpractice Defense. ***Email:*** LJones@pattersondilthey.com

HOLLY A. MANTLE, born Pinehurst, North Carolina, July 23, 1976; admitted to bar, 2005, North Carolina. *Education:* University of North Carolina at Chapel Hill (B.S., 2002); Whittier Law School (J.D., 2005). Sigma Theta Tau International Nursing Honor Society. Critical Care Nurse in the Open Heart Intensive Care and Surgical ICU. Registered Nurse License, 1997. Charge nurse in the Post Anesthesia Care Unit. President and Member, Trial Team, Health Law Society. *Member:* North Carolina State Bar; American Bar Association. ***PRACTICE AREAS:*** Medical Malpractice Defense; Civil Litigation.

JESSICA M. LEWIS, born Augsburg, Germany, September 3, 1976; admitted to bar, 2005, North Carolina. *Education:* University of North Carolina at Chapel Hill (B.S., Nursing, 1998; J.D., 2005). Member, Holderness Moot Court Invitational Team. Selected as best overall Competitor and Oralist. Recipient, Gressman-Pollit Award for excellence in oral advocacy. Publication Editor, North Carolina Banking Institute Journal, published HIPPA: Demystifying the Implications for Financial Institutions. Law School Honors Writing Scholar. Research Assistant, Research Division of the North Carolina General Assembly. *Member:* North Carolina and American Bar Associations. [U.S. Army Nurse Corps, 1998-2002]. ***PRACTICE AREAS:*** Medical Malpractice Defense; Civil Litigation.

OF COUNSEL

CLAIRE A. MODLIN, born Wilson, North Carolina, August 14, 1970; admitted to bar, 1995, North Carolina and U.S. District Court, Eastern and Middle Districts of North Carolina; U.S. Court of Appeals, Fourth Circuit. *Education:* University of North Carolina at Chapel Hill (B.S., 1992); Campbell University (J.D., 1995). Member, John Marshall Moot Court Team. Notes and Comments Editor, Campbell Law Review. *Member:* Wake County, North Carolina and American Bar Associations; North Carolina Association of Defense Attorneys; Defense Research Institute. ***PRACTICE AREAS:*** Insurance Defense; Medical Malpractice Defense; Products Liability Defense.

REPRESENTATIVE CLIENTS: Amica Mutual Insurance Company; Cambridge Integrated Services Group; Carolina Casualty Insurance Co.; Carolina Power and Light; Cincinnati Insurance Cos.; CNA Insurance Co.; Connecticut Specialty Insurance Group; The Doctor's Company; Dollar General; Employers Mutual Casualty Co.; Food Lion; Gallagher Bassett; Kemper Insurance Group; Liberty Mutual Insurance Co.; Medical Protective Insurance Co.; North Carolina Farm Bureau; Ohio Casualty Group; Risk Management Services; State Farm Mutual Insurance Company; St. Paul Insurance Co.; Utica Mutual; The Virginia Insurance Reciprocal; Zurich.

PATTERSON HARKAVY LLP

414 WEST JONES STREET
RALEIGH, NORTH CAROLINA 27603
Telephone: 919-755-1812
Facsimile: 919-755-0124
URL: http://www.pathlaw.com

Mailing Address: P.O. Box 27927, Raleigh, NC 27611

Greensboro, North Carolina Office: 101 South Elm Street, P.O. Box 29269, 27429-9269. Telephone: 336-370-4200. Facsimile: 336-274-8490.

Chapel Hill, North Carolina Office: 100 Europa Drive, Suite 250, 27517. Telephone: 919-942-5200. Toll Free: 800-458-2541. Fax: 919-942-5256.

Trial, Appellate and Dispute Resolution Practice in all State and Federal Courts. Personal Injury, Wrongful Death, Medical Malpractice, Workers' Compensation, Labor, Employment, Civil Rights, and Criminal.

FIRM PROFILE: The firm is dedicated to providing high quality, energetic advocacy in a few specialized areas of practice: personal injury, wrongful death, medical malpractice, workers' compensation, labor and employment, civil rights, and criminal defense. The firm has extensive experience in complex litigation, class actions, trial and appellate practice, and advocacy before a variety of administrative bodies and the North Carolina General Assembly. Members of the firm regularly provide mediation and arbitration services, teach at law schools, universities and professional education seminars and are active in bar and public interest organizations. The firm has litigated in affiliation with the American Civil Liberties Union, the North Carolina Academy of Trial Lawyers, the NAACP Legal Defense and Education Fund Inc., and local and international unions.

MEMBERS OF FIRM

HENRY N. PATTERSON, JR. (Resident, Chapel Hill, North Carolina Office)

LETO COPELEY (Resident, Chapel Hill, North Carolina Office)

(This Listing Continued)

VALERIE ALSTON JOHNSON (Resident, Chapel Hill, North Carolina Office)

BURTON CRAIGE, born Boston, Massachusetts, April 6, 1949; admitted to bar, 1980, North Carolina. *Education:* Harvard University (B.A, cum laude, 1971); University of North Carolina (M.P.H., 1974; J.D., with high honors, 1980). Trial Attorney, Civil Rights Division, United States Department of Justice, 1980-1984. *Member:* North Carolina Academy of Trial Lawyers (Vice President for Legal Affairs, 1996-1998; Vice President for Legislative Affairs, 1998-2000; President, 2001-2002); Association of Trial Lawyers of America; American Civil Liberties Union of North Carolina (Chair, Legal Committee, 1990-1993; President, 1993-1994); North Carolina Civil Procedure Study Commission (Co-Chair, 1997-1998); Legal Aid of North Carolina (Board of Governors, 2002—). ***PRACTICE AREAS:*** Medical Malpractice; Personal Injury; Employment; Civil Rights. ***Email:*** bcraige@pathlaw.com

ANN ELIZABETH GRONINGER, born Cleveland, Ohio, May 1, 1969; admitted to bar, 1995, North Carolina. *Education:* Michigan State University (B.S., Engineering Arts, with honors, 1991); Tulane University of Louisiana (J.D., cum laude, 1994). Order of the Coif. Public Interest Law Fellow, 1992. Member, Fayetteville Human Relations Commission, 1997-2000. *Member:* Wake County and North Carolina Bar Associations; North Carolina Academy of Trial Lawyers; North Carolina Association of Women Attorneys; The Association of Trial Lawyers of America; National Association of Criminal Defense Lawyers. ***PRACTICE AREAS:*** Criminal Defense; Civil Litigation; Personal Injury; Employment Litigation. ***Email:*** agroninger@pathlaw.com

JONATHAN R. HARKAVY (Resident, Greensboro, North Carolina Office)

MICHAEL G. OKUN, born Boston, Massachusetts, December 14, 1947; admitted to bar, 1980, North Carolina; 1984, U.S. Supreme Court. *Education:* Antioch College (B.A., 1977); University of North Carolina (J.D., with honors, 1980). James O. Bowman Scholar, 1979-1980. Member, North Carolina Law Review, 1978-1980. Attorney, Appellate Court Branch, Office of General Counsel, National Labor Relations Board, 1980-1981. Law Clerk, Honorable J. Dickson Phillips, U.S. Court of Appeals for the Fourth Circuit, 1981-1982. Adjunct Professor, Wake Forest University School of Law, 1997—. *Member:* North Carolina Bar Association (Chair, Labor and Employment Section, 1994-1995); National Employment Lawyers Association (Member, Executive Board, 1985; Chair, Advisory Board, Lawyers Coordinating Committee, 1987-1988). ***Email:*** mokun@pathlaw.com

OF COUNSEL

NAHOMI HARKAVY (Resident, Greensboro, North Carolina Office)

THE PECK LAW FIRM, P.A.

Established in 1997
7511 MOURNING DOVE ROAD, SUITE 104
RALEIGH, NORTH CAROLINA 27615-5097
Telephone: 919-376-5411
Telecopier: 919-782-9493
Email: Chris@PeckLawFirm.Net
URL: http://www.pecklawfirm.net

Business Acquisitions and Divestitures, Corporation, Finance and Commercial Law, Real Property, Construction Law, Franchise Law, Entertainment Law and Intellectual Property.

FIRM PROFILE: Located in the heart of the rapidly growing Research Triangle area, our firm is uniquely adept at working with both new entrepreneurs and existing companies to assist them through our experience, knowledge and creativity to reach their goals. We are committed to providing high quality legal services and personal attention to the individual and corporate needs of our clients. We strive to learn as much as possible about the business objectives and operations of our clients in order to anticipate potential problems and develop a full range of options and innovative solutions.

MEMBER OF THE FIRM

CHRISTOPHER L. PECK, born Fairfield, Iowa, April 10, 1964; admitted to bar, 1994, North Carolina and U.S. District Court, Eastern District of North Carolina. *Education:* College of Charleston (B.A., distinguished, 1990); Vermont Law School (J.D., Master in Environmental Law, cum laude, 1994). Author: "Vermont Bench Guide: The Contempt Power," Vermont Judicial Conference, 1994. Member: Board of Directors of ThetaXM, Co.; Sabretooth Productions, Co.; North Raleigh Mountain Bike Association. Chairman, Triangle Fly Fishing Council. *Member:* North Carolina Bar Association (Member: Business, Intellectual Property and Real Property Sections; Lawyer Referral Committee); North Carolina State Bar. [EW5, U.S. Navy, U.S.S. Hoel, DDG-13, 1983-1987]. ***PRACTICE AREAS:*** Business Acquisitions; Business Divestitures; Corporate; Finance; Commercial Law; Real Property; Construction Law; Franchise Law; Entertainment Law; Intellectual Property.

REPRESENTATIVE CLIENTS: Capital Bank; Milestone Wealth Management; United Investment Group; Temecula Valley Bank; Fortress International; Advanced Audio Visual Systems; Century Small Business Solutions; Access Capital Advisors; Sunbelt Business Brokers; Lawrence Homes; Thickpenny Enterprises; Graham Allen Associates; SouthTrust Bank; North State Bank; ReMax United; Carolina Realty Group; Triangle Community Assistance; Community Solutions; DKR Restaurant Group; CIT Small Business Lending Corp.

PENDERGRASS LAW FIRM, PLLC

4101 LAKE BOONE TRAIL, SUITE 202
RALEIGH, NORTH CAROLINA 27607
Telephone: 919-510-9559
Fax: 919-510-0190
Email: mailbox@pendergrasslawfirm.com
URL: http://www.lawyers.com/pendergrasslaw

Commercial Real Estate, Residential Real Estate, Real Estate Litigation, Legal Malpractice Defense, Corporate and Banking Law.

(This Listing Continued)

JAMES K. PENDERGRASS, JR., born Sanford, North Carolina, December 10, 1960; admitted to bar, 1987, North Carolina and South Carolina; 1988, District of Columbia. *Education:* Elon College (B.S., cum laude, 1983); Wake Forest University School of Law (J.D., 1986). Member, Small Business and Technology Center Advisory Board. Vice-Chairman, City of Raleigh Planning Commission, 1993-1997. (Board Certified Specialist in Residential, Business, Commercial and Industrial Transactions, North Carolina State Board of Legal Specialization). ***PRACTICE AREAS:*** Real Estate Litigation; Real Estate Title Insurance; Legal Malpractice Defense; Corporate Real Estate; Land Use Regulation; Banking Law; Creditors Rights. ***Email:*** jpendergrass@pendergrasslawfirm.com

BERNARD RICHARDS, JR., born San Angelo, Texas, April 18, 1967; admitted to bar, 1993, North Carolina. *Education:* University of Georgia (B.A., 1989); Campbell University (J.D., 1993). Phi Alpha Delta. *Member:* North Carolina State Bar; North Carolina Bar Association (Real Property Section); North Carolina Land Title Association. ***PRACTICE AREAS:*** Real Estate. ***Email:*** rrichards@pendergrasslawfirm.com

MICHAEL SCOTT PETTY

Established in 1995

133 FAYETTEVILLE STREET MALL, SUITE 300
RALEIGH, NORTH CAROLINA 27602
Telephone: 919-821-5959
Facsimile: 919-821-9303
URL: http://www.michaelpettylaw.com
Email: mpetty@michaelpettylaw.com
URL: http://www.michaelscottpetty.com

Mailing Address: P.O. Box 2298, Raleigh, NC 27602

Criminal Defense in State and Federal Courts, White Collar Crimes, Sexual Offenses, Traffic Offenses, Personal Injury, Auto Accidents, Products Liability, Unfair and Deceptive Trade Practice, Antitrust Litigation, Premises Liability, Intentional Torts, Dental and Medical Malpractice, Unfair and Deceptive Trade Practice Litigation.

MICHAEL SCOTT PETTY, born Mountain Home, Idaho, April 29, 1967; admitted to bar, 1995, North Carolina; 1996, U.S. District Court, Eastern District of North Carolina; 1998, U.S. Court of Appeals, 4th Circuit. *Education:* University of North Carolina (B.A., 1989); Campbell University School of Law (J.D., 1995). *Member:* Wake County and North Carolina Bar Associations; North Carolina Academy of Trial Lawyers; North Carolina State Bar; Wake County Academy of Criminal Trial Lawyers.

PINNA JOHNSTON & BURWELL, P.A.

Established in 1975

2601 OBERLIN ROAD, SUITE 100
P.O. BOX 31788
RALEIGH, NORTH CAROLINA 27622
Telephone: 919-755-1317; 782-0450
Fax: 919-782-0452
URL: http://www.pjb-law.com
URL: http://www.pinnajohnstonburwell.com

Corporation, Mergers and Acquisitions, Probate, Trusts, Real Estate Law, Taxation and Estate Planning, Wills and Trusts. General Civil Practice in all State and Federal Courts.

FIRM PROFILE: Pinna Johnston & Burwell, P.A. is a broad-based law firm delivering sophisticated and innovative counseling to a wide spectrum of clients. The firm was founded in 1975 by William P. Pinna, who built the firm upon a singular premise: providing all clients with the highest level of legal representation and service, efficiently and cost effectively, by carefully assessing each clients needs and tailoring our services to meet those needs.

WILLIAM P. PINNA, born Chicago, Illinois, August 11, 1943; admitted to bar, 1968, Illinois; 1970, North Carolina and U.S. Tax Court; 1978, U.S. District Court, Eastern District of North Carolina. *Education:* DePaul University (B.S.C., magna cum laude, 1966); Duke University (J.D., 1968). Phi Eta Sigma; Beta Alpha Psi; Phi Alpha Delta. Author: "Partnerships, Their Formation and Taxation," September, 1978; "Incorporation of Farm Business," October, 1971 and "Estate Planning for North Carolina Families," June, 1977, both published through Economics Information Report for North Carolina State University; "Fee Collections," Legal Economics, March/April, 1979; "The Use of Credit Cards in the Law Firm," Legal Economics, July/August, 1980. Recipient, Outstanding Teacher Award, North Carolina State University, 1969-1970; 1975-1976. Assistant Professor, North Carolina State University, 1968-1981. Adjunct Associate Professor, Corporate and Partnership Planning and Drafting and Business Planning, Duke University School of Law, 1978-1985. Chairman, North Carolina Property Tax Commission, 1988-1990. *Member:* Chicago, Wake County, North Carolina, Illinois State and American (Member, Committee on Accounting Problems, Agricultural Tax Laws, Section of Taxation, 1968-1985; Chairman, Committees on: Accounts Receivable and Billing; Personal Computers; Money Management and Investments, Economics of Law Practice Section, 1978; Section 2032A, 1983-1985) Bar Associations; North Carolina State Bar; National Association of Accountants; American Association of Accountants. ***PRACTICE AREAS:*** Taxation Law; Estate Planning Law; Corporation Law. ***Email:*** bpinna@pjb-law.com

MARGARET G. JOHNSTON, born Syracuse, New York, December 9, 1947; admitted to bar, 1974, North Carolina; 1980, U.S. Tax Court. *Education:* State University of New York at Binghamton (B.A., 1969); University of North Carolina (J.D., with honors, 1974). Order of the Coif. Staff Member, University of North Carolina Law Review, 1973-1974. *Member:* North Carolina Bar Association (Member, Sections on: Taxation; Law Practice Management; Estate Planning). ***PRACTICE AREAS:*** Estate Planning; Taxation; Business Law. ***Email:*** mjohnston@pjb-law.com

WALTER BRODIE BURWELL, JR., born Henderson, North Carolina, March 11, 1953; admitted to bar, 1983, North Carolina, U.S. Tax Court and U.S. District Court, Eastern and Middle Districts of North Carolina. *Education:* University of North Carolina (B.A., 1975); North Carolina State University; Campbell University (J.D., 1982). Lecturer on Law, North Carolina State University College of Veterinary Medicine. *Member:* North Carolina State Bar; North Carolina (Member, Section of Taxation) and American (Member, Section of Taxation) Bar Associations; North Carolina Association of Certified Public Accountants. ***PRACTICE AREAS:*** Taxation Law; Partnership Law; Corporate Law; Charitable Trusts and Foundations. ***Email:*** bburwell@pjb-law.com

ROBIN E. PIPKIN, born Raleigh, North Carolina, February 7, 1956; admitted to bar, 1981, North Carolina; 1989, U.S. Tax Court. *Education:* University of North Carolina (B.S., 1978; J.D., 1981). Delta Phi Alpha; Beta Gamma Sigma; Beta Alpha Psi. Adjunct Lecturer in Law, University of North Carolina School of Law, 1992—. *Member:* Wake County and North Carolina Bar Associations; North Carolina State Bar. ***PRACTICE AREAS:*** Estate Planning Law; Taxation Law; Corporate Law; Real Estate Law. ***Email:*** rpipkin@pjb-law.com

MATTHEW S. BLACK, born Norfolk, Virginia, March 24, 1973; admitted to bar, 1998, North Carolina. *Education:* University of North Carolina at Chapel Hill (B.S., with distinction, 1995); Wake Forest University (J.D., 1998). *Member:* Wake County Bar Association; North Carolina State Bar. ***PRACTICE AREAS:*** Corporate Law; Contracts; Mergers and Acquisitions. ***Email:*** mblack@pjb-law.com

---

DANIEL B. FINCH, born Oxford, North Carolina, February 28, 1975; admitted to bar, 2001, North Carolina. *Education:* North Carolina State University (B.A., 1997); Campbell University (J.D., 2001; M.B.A., 2001). Phi Alpha Delta (Vice Justice). *Member:* Wake County, North Carolina and American Bar Associations. ***PRACTICE AREAS:*** Estate Planning; Estate and Gift Taxation; Income Tax; Business Law. ***Email:*** dfinch@pjb-law.com

ROBERT CHARLES LAWSON, born Greensboro, North Carolina, October 4, 1976; admitted to bar, 2003, North Carolina and U.S. District Court, Eastern District of North Carolina. *Education:* University of Virginia (B.A., 1999); Babcock Graduate School of Management at Wake Forest University (M.B.A., 2003); Wake Forest University School of Law (J.D., 2003). Phi Alpha Delta. *Member:* North Carolina and American Bar Associations. ***PRACTICE AREAS:*** Corporate Law; Estate Planning; Business Litigation. ***Email:*** rlawson@pjb-law.com

REPRESENTATIVE CLIENTS: McDonalds Corp.; Braswell Milling Co., Inc.; H. Stadiem, Inc.; Graedon Enterprises, Inc.; Capital Planning Associates; Swan Acre Farms, Inc.; Sunnybrook Farms, Inc.; Tunnell Farms, Inc.; Tiny Oak Farms, Inc.; Circle Grove Seed Farms, Inc.; Boerema Dairy, Inc.; Basic Machinery, Inc.; Financial Analysts, Inc.; Taylors Nursery, Inc.; The Medical & Professional Center; Whitener Capital, Inc.; Triangle Lithotripsy Corp.; D.R. Allen & Sons, Inc.; Premier Quilting Company.

POYNER & SPRUILL LLP

3600 GLENWOOD AVENUE
P.O. BOX 10096
RALEIGH, NORTH CAROLINA 27605-0096
Telephone: 919-783-6400
Telecopier: 919-783-1075
URL: http://www.poynerspruill.com

Rocky Mount, North Carolina Office: 130 S. Franklin Street, P.O. Box 353, 27802-0353. Telephone: 252-446-2341. Telecopier: 252-972-7045.
Charlotte, North Carolina Office: One Wachovia Center, 301 South College Street, Suite 2300, 28202. Telephone: 704-342-5250. Telecopier: 704-342-5264.
Southern Pines, North Carolina Office: 135 West New Hampshire Avenue, 28388-0371. Telephone: 910-692-6866. Telecopier: 910-695-3036.

Comprehensive business and litigation practice including: Appellate, Arbitration, Banking, Bankruptcy/Creditors' Rights, Complex Business Litigation, Construction, Credit and Financial Services, Eminent Domain/Condemnation, Employment Benefits, Employment Practices, Entertainment Law, Environmental, Estate, Exempt Organizations, General Corporate, Governmental Relations, Health Care, Intellectual Property Law, International, Land Use and Zoning, Limited Liability Companies, Local Government, Mediation, Partnerships, Personal and Financial Planning, Probate, Product Liability, Professional Liability, Railroad, Real Estate, Regulatory and Municipal, Securities, Sports Law, Tax, Technology and Emerging Business, Tort Litigation and Insurance Defense, Transactional including Mergers and Acquisitions, Transportation, Utilities, White Collar Criminal Defense.

FIRM PROFILE: Poyner & Spruill LLP is a multi-disciplined firm which effectively and efficiently provides a comprehensive range of business and litigation legal services. The firm is one of the largest firms in North Carolina and maintains its offices in Raleigh, Charlotte, Rocky Mount, and Southern Pines. (However, it's reputation, size, multi-disciplines, and client base has enabled it to effectively represent interests of its clients on a national and regional basis as well as in North Carolina). The firm is committed to client services based on accessibility, knowledge of the client's business and industry and timely and effective response to clients' needs. This commitment is designed to be pro-active and responsive to emerging issues and trends impacting clients in the business and industries in which they participate.

LAW FIRM ALLIANCES/ASSOCIATIONS: ***STATE CAPITAL GLOBAL LAW FIRM GROUP***

USLaw NETWORK

WORLDSERVICES GROUP (WSG)

MEMBERS OF FIRM

MARVIN D. MUSSELWHITE, JR., born Greenville, North Carolina, January 12, 1938; admitted to bar, 1963, North Carolina; 1978, U.S. Supreme Court. *Education:* Duke University (A.B., 1960; J.D., 1963). ***PRACTICE AREAS:*** Legislative Representation; Governmental Relations. ***Email:*** mmuss@poynerspruill.com

(This Listing Continued)

(This Listing Continued)

POYNER & SPRUILL LLP, Raleigh—Continued

DAVID W. LONG, born Punxsutawney, Pennsylvania, February 18, 1942; admitted to bar, 1967, North Carolina; 1979, U.S. Supreme Court. *Education:* Duke University (A.B., 1964); University of North Carolina (J.D., 1967). ***PRACTICE AREAS:*** Business Litigation; Criminal Defense. ***Email:*** dwlong@poynerspruill.com

JOHN L. SHAW, born Elkin, North Carolina, August 10, 1944; admitted to bar, 1969, North Carolina; 1973, U.S. Supreme Court. *Education:* University of North Carolina at Chapel Hill (B.S., 1966; J.D., 1969). Certified Mediator, North Carolina. Certified Master Arbitrator, American Arbitration Association. ***PRACTICE AREAS:*** ADR (40%); Construction Law (30%); Litigation (10%); Commercial Law (10%); Computer Law (10%). ***Email:*** jshaw@poynerspruill.com

CECIL W. HARRISON, JR., born New Bern, North Carolina, July 29, 1947; admitted to bar, 1973, North Carolina; 1979, U.S. Supreme Court. *Education:* University of North Carolina (A.B., 1969; J.D., 1973). ***PRACTICE AREAS:*** Litigation; Employment Discrimination Law; Appellate Practice. ***Email:*** cwharrison@poynerspruill.com

WILLIAM S. CHERRY, JR., born Windsor, North Carolina, August 9, 1950; admitted to bar, 1975, North Carolina. *Education:* North Carolina State University (B.A., 1972); Wake Forest University (J.D., 1975). ***PRACTICE AREAS:*** Financial Services; Creditor Law; Real Estate Law. ***Email:*** bcherry@poynerspruill.com

LEMUEL H. GIBBONS, III, born Wilson, North Carolina, July 22, 1952; admitted to bar, 1977, North Carolina. *Education:* University of North Carolina (B.A., 1974; J.D., 1977); New York University (LL.M. in Taxation, 1979). ***PRACTICE AREAS:*** Taxation Law; Partnership Law; Corporate Law; Business Law. ***Email:*** cgibbons@poynerspruill.com

H. GLENN DUNN, born New Bern, North Carolina, November 9, 1944; admitted to bar, 1977, North Carolina. *Education:* University of Florida (B.D., with honors, 1967); University of North Carolina (J.D., 1976; M.C.R.P., 1976). Certified Mediator, North Carolina. ***PRACTICE AREAS:*** Environmental Law; Administrative Law; Land Use Law. ***Email:*** hgdunn@poynerspruill.com

SUSANNA K. GIBBONS, born Providence, Rhode Island, January 31, 1957; admitted to bar, 1981, North Carolina; 1984, U.S. Supreme Court. *Education:* Wake Forest University (B.A., summa cum laude, 1978; J.D., cum laude, 1981). ***PRACTICE AREAS:*** Employment Law; ERISA Litigation; Commercial Litigation. ***Email:*** sgibbons@poynerspruill.com

LOUIS B. MEYER III, born Winston-Salem, North Carolina, December 14, 1957; admitted to bar, 1983, North Carolina; 1996, U.S. Supreme Court. *Education:* Wake Forest University (B.A., 1980; J.D., 1983). Certified Mediator. ***PRACTICE AREAS:*** Litigation; Healthcare; Employment Law. ***Email:*** Lbmeyer@poynerspruill.com

DAVID DREIFUS, born Memphis, Tennessee, November 14, 1952; admitted to bar, 1982, North Carolina; 1992, U.S. Supreme Court. *Education:* Tufts University (B.A., magna cum laude, 1974); Duke University (J.D., 1980). ***PRACTICE AREAS:*** Business Litigation; Complex Litigation. ***Email:*** ddreifus@poynerspruill.com

DAVID M. BARNES, born Winston-Salem, North Carolina, June 19, 1959; admitted to bar, 1985, North Carolina. *Education:* Wake Forest University (B.A., cum laude, 1982; J.D., 1985). ***PRACTICE AREAS:*** Legislative Representation; Governmental Affairs; Construction Litigation; Commercial Landlord-Tenant. ***Email:*** dmbarnes@poynerspruill.com

THOMAS H. DAVIS, JR., born Raleigh, North Carolina, June 11, 1951; admitted to bar, 1976, North Carolina; 1979, U.S. Supreme Court. *Education:* North Carolina State University (B.A., 1973); Wake Forest University (J.D., 1976). ***PRACTICE AREAS:*** Commercial Litigation; Construction Litigation; Condemnation Law; Labor and OSHA. ***Email:*** thdavis@poynerspruill.com

WILSON HAYMAN, born Durham, North Carolina, April 18, 1954; admitted to bar, 1979, North Carolina; 1984, U.S. Supreme Court. *Education:* Princeton University (A.B., magna cum laude, 1976); University of North Carolina-Chapel Hill (J.D., 1979). ***LANGUAGES:*** German and French. ***PRACTICE AREAS:*** Hospital and Health Care Law; Insurance; Managed Care Regulation; Administrative Litigation; Church Law. ***Email:*** whayman@poynerspruill.com

CRAIG G. DALTON, JR., born Winston-Salem, North Carolina, April 6, 1950; admitted to bar, 1977, North Carolina and U.S. Supreme Court. *Education:* University of North Carolina (A.B., with honors, 1972; M.B.A., 1977; J.D., 1977); Emory University (LL.M., in Taxation, 1979). Certified Public Accountant, North Carolina, 1983. ***PRACTICE AREAS:*** Taxation Law; Estate Planning Law; Corporate Law. ***Email:*** craigdalton@poynerspruill.com

EDWIN MARION SPEAS, JR., born Boonville, North Carolina, April 18, 1945; admitted to bar, 1971, North Carolina; 1979, U.S. State Supreme Court. *Education:* Wake Forest University (B.A., 1967; J.D., 1971). Chief Deputy Attorney General, 1998-2003, Senior Deputy Attorney General and Head of Special Litigation/Education Division, 1990-1998 and Special Deputy Attorney General and Head of the Education Section, 1975-1990, Office of the Attorney General of North Carolina. ***PRACTICE AREAS:*** Appellate Practice; Litigation; Government. ***Email:*** espeas@poynerspruill.com

TIMOTHY P. SULLIVAN, born Binghamton, New York, February 4, 1957; admitted to bar, 1983, North Carolina. *Education:* University of North Carolina at Chapel Hill (B.S., 1979; J.D., 1983). Certified Mediator, North Carolina. ***PRACTICE AREAS:*** Environmental Law; Land Use Planning; Administrative Law. ***Email:*** tsullivan@poynerspruill.com

HUGH W. DAVIS II, born Norfolk, Virginia, March 15, 1962; admitted to bar, 1988, North Carolina. *Education:* Duke University (B.A., 1984); University of Virginia (J.D., 1988). ***PRACTICE AREAS:*** ERISA and Employee Benefits; Qualified Retirement Plan Law. ***Email:*** hwdavis@poynerspruill.com

KEITH H. JOHNSON, born Raleigh, North Carolina, May 15, 1962; admitted to bar, 1991, North Carolina. *Education:* University of North Carolina, Chapel Hill (B.A.); University of Virginia School of Law (J.D., 1989). ***PRACTICE AREAS:*** Environmental Law; Commercial Litigation. ***Email:*** kjohnson@poynerspruill.com

(This Listing Continued)

JOSEPH B. DEMPSTER, JR., born Winston-Salem, North Carolina, June 3, 1965; admitted to bar, 1990, North Carolina. *Education:* University of North Carolina, Chapel Hill (B.A.); Wake Forest University (J.D., 1990). ***PRACTICE AREAS:*** Corporate; Real Estate; Financial Services. ***Email:*** jbdempster@poynerspruill.com

THOMAS R. WEST, born Jacksonville, North Carolina, July 6, 1954; admitted to bar, 1980, North Carolina. *Education:* University of North Carolina (B.A., 1975); Duke University (J.D., 1979). Administrative Law Judge, North Carolina Office of Administrative Hearings, 1986-1997. ***PRACTICE AREAS:*** Health Care; Mediation; Professional Licensing; Administrative Hearings and Appeals; County Government Law. ***Email:*** twest@poynerspruill.com

ERIC P. STEVENS, born Wichita, Kansas, September 6, 1965; admitted to bar, 1990, North Carolina. *Education:* Wake Forest University (B.A., 1987); Mercer University (J.D., magna cum laude, 1990). ***PRACTICE AREAS:*** Commercial Litigation; Intellectual Property. ***Email:*** estevens@poynerspruill.com

ROBIN L. TATUM, born Charlotte, North Carolina, January 20, 1961; admitted to bar, 1990, North Carolina. *Education:* North Carolina State University (B.S., 1983; M.E., 1986): North Carolina Central University (J.D., summa cum laude, 1990). ***PRACTICE AREAS:*** Land Use and Zoning Litigation. ***Email:*** rtatum@poynerspruill.com

STEVEN MANSFIELD SHABER, born Fort Wayne, Indiana, March 8, 1951; admitted to bar, 1976, North Carolina; 1980, U.S. Supreme Court. *Education:* Wabash College (B.A., magna cum laude, 1973); Duke University (J.D., 1976). ***PRACTICE AREAS:*** Health and Hospital Law; Administrative Law; Civil Litigation; Legislative Practice. ***Email:*** sshaber@poynerspruill.com

WILLIAM R. SHENTON, born Lancaster, Pennsylvania, January 17, 1949; admitted to bar, 1979, North Carolina. *Education:* University of North Carolina (B.A., 1975; J.D., 1979). ***PRACTICE AREAS:*** Health and Hospital Law; Civil Litigation; Administrative Law. ***Email:*** wshenton@poynerspruill.com

DAVID R. KROSNER, born Philadelphia, Pennsylvania, September 19, 1963; admitted to bar, 1989, Wisconsin; 2000, North Carolina. *Education:* Illinois State University (B.S., 1986); Marquette University (J.D., magna cum laude, 1989). Certified Public Accountant, Illinois, 1986. ***PRACTICE AREAS:*** Business Law; Mergers and Acquisitions; Securities. ***Email:*** dkrosner@poynerspruill.com

JAMES M. O'BRIEN, III, born Bethlehem, Pennsylvania, January 12, 1966; admitted to bar, 1992, California; 1995, North Carolina. *Education:* University of North Carolina, Chapel Hill (B.A., 1988); University of California, Berkeley (J.D., 1992). ***PRACTICE AREAS:*** Business and Corporate Law; Mergers and Acquisitions; Emerging Business; Entertainment. ***Email:*** jobrien@poynerspruill.com

JOSEPH E. ZESZOTARSKI, JR., born Jersey City, New Jersey, December 6, 1968; admitted to bar, 1994, North Carolina. *Education:* Muhlenberg College (A.B., summa cum laude, 1991); Wake Forest University (J.D., cum laude, 1994). ***PRACTICE AREAS:*** White Collar Criminal Defense; Commercial Litigation. ***Email:*** jzeszotarski@poynerspruill.com

TERRI L. GARDNER, born Mount Airy, North Carolina, May 11, 1956; admitted to bar, 1981, North Carolina. *Education:* Wake Forest University (B.A., 1978; J.D., with honors, 1981). ***PRACTICE AREAS:*** Corporate Reorganizations; Workouts; Creditors Rights. ***Email:*** tgardner@poynerspruill.com

CHARLES F. POWERS, III, born Raleigh, North Carolina, November 10, 1943; admitted to bar, 1966, North Carolina. *Education:* Belmont Abbey (A.B., 1963); University of North Carolina (LL.B., 1966). ***PRACTICE AREAS:*** Commercial Real Estate Law; Corporate Law; Employment Law; Health Law. ***Email:*** cpowers@poynerspruill.com

SUZANNE R. GRIFFIN, born Waterloo, Iowa, March 20, 1964; admitted to bar, 1989, Illinois; 2000, Colorado; 2003, North Carolina. *Education:* University of Illinois (B.S., 1986); Northwestern University (J.D., 1989). ***PRACTICE AREAS:*** Financial Services; Real Estate; Agricultural Law; Agribusiness. ***Email:*** sgriffin@poynerspruill.com

DAVID L. WOODARD, born Clinton, North Carolina, January 12, 1965; admitted to bar, 1992, North Carolina. *Education:* North Carolina State University (B.A., 1988); Campbell University (J.D., cum laude, 1992). ***PRACTICE AREAS:*** Employment Law; Commercial Litigation. ***Email:*** dlwoodard@poynerspruill.com

DANIEL G. CAHILL, born Montgomery, Alabama, August 23, 1967; admitted to bar, 1994, North Carolina. *Education:* University of North Carolina at Chapel Hill (B.A., 1989); Wake Forest University (J.D., 1994). ***PRACTICE AREAS:*** Commercial Litigation; Construction Law; Condemnation; Land Use Litigation; Appellate Practice. ***Email:*** dcahill@poynerspruill.com

LISA P. SUMNER, born Louisburg, North Carolina, September 5, 1969; admitted to bar, 1994, South Carolina; 1996, North Carolina; 1999, Virginia. *Education:* University of North Carolina (B.A., 1991); Duke University (J.D., 1994). ***PRACTICE AREAS:*** Bankruptcy; Commercial Litigation. ***Email:*** lsumner@poynerspruill.com

ASSOCIATES

PEARL B. DOHERTY, born New York, N.Y., March 26, 1955; admitted to bar, 1981, New York; 1989, District of Columbia; 1994, North Carolina. *Education:* Johns Hopkins University (B.A., 1976); State University of New York at Buffalo (J.D., magna cum laude, 1980); New York University (LL.M., 1981). ***PRACTICE AREAS:*** Taxation; Partnerships and LLCs; Nonprofit Organizations. ***Email:*** pbdoherty@poynerspruill.com

PAMELA A. SCOTT, born Louisburg, North Carolina, October 27, 1965; admitted to bar, 1998, North Carolina. *Education:* University of North Carolina at Chapel Hill (B.A., 1988; J.D., 1998). ***PRACTICE AREAS:*** Health Law; Administrative Law. ***Email:*** pscott@poynerspruill.com

ANUJA GULERIA PUROHIT, born Chandigarh, India, August 20, 1967; admitted to bar, 1993, North Carolina; 1995, California. *Education:* Denison University (B.A. summa

(This Listing Continued)

cum laude, 1989); Duke University (J.D., 1992; LL.M., 1992). ***PRACTICE AREAS:*** Employment Law; Zoning, Planning and Land Use Law. ***Email:*** apurohit@poynerspruill.com

KACEY S. RAGSDALE, born 1973; admitted to bar, 2000, North Carolina. *Education:* University of North Carolina at Chapel Hill (B.A., with honors, 1995; J.D., with honors, 2000). ***PRACTICE AREAS:*** Employment Law; Land Use; Zoning Law. ***Email:*** ksewell@poynerspruill.com

EDWARD BARDIN SIMMONS, JR., born Tarboro, North Carolina, January 13, 1978; admitted to bar, 2003, North Carolina. *Education:* Duke University (B.A., 2000); Wake Forst University (J.D., 2003). ***PRACTICE AREAS:*** Financial Services; Commercial Real Estate. ***Email:*** bsimmons@poynerspruill.com

ANNE C. SHERMAN, born Columbus, Ohio, August 18, 1972; admitted to bar, 1999, Illinois; 2004, North Carolina. *Education:* Duke University (A.B., cum laude, 1994); University of Chicago (J.D., with honors, 1999). ***PRACTICE AREAS:*** Employee Benefits. ***Email:*** asherman@poynerspruill.com

JULIE W. HAMPTON, born Kinston, North Carolina, February 16, 1977; admitted to bar, 2002, North Carolina. *Education:* University of North Carolina (B.A., 1999); Campbell University (J.D., 2002). ***PRACTICE AREAS:*** Litigation. ***Email:*** jhampton@poynershpruill.com

HEATHER F. RILEY, born Rocky Mount, North Carolina; admitted to bar, 2003, North Carolina. *Education:* University of North Carolina at Chapel Hill (B.A., 1999); Wake Forest University (J.D., 2003); Georgetown University (LL.M., Taxation, 2005). ***PRACTICE AREAS:*** Corporate Law. ***Email:*** hriley@poynerspruill.com

BRYN D. WILSON, born Lapeer, Michigan, March 31, 1979; admitted to bar, 2005, North Carolina. *Education:* University of Michigan (B.A., 2001); New York University (J.D., 2004). ***PRACTICE AREAS:*** Labor and Employment. ***Email:*** bwilson@poynerspruill.com

ADAM B. SNYDER, born Asheville, North Carolina, July 28, 1974; admitted to bar, 2002, Alabama; 2004, U.S. Tax Court (Not admitted in North Carolina). *Education:* University of North Carolina at Asheville (B.A., summa cum laude, 1997); University of Alabama (J.D., magna cum laude, 2002); University of Florida (LL.M., Taxation, 2003). Member, Alabama Law Review, 2000-2002. *Member:* Birmingham and American (Member, Tax Section) Bar Associations; Alabama State Bar. ***PRACTICE AREAS:*** Corporate Law; Taxation.

PAUL A. ARENA, born Durham, North Carolina, August 2, 1970; admitted to bar, 1996, North Carolina. *Education:* University of North Carolina at Chapel Hill (B.A., Political Science, 1993; J.D., 1996). Author, "The Electronic Transactions Act in North Carolina: A Real Estate Practitioner's Perspective," 13 N.C. Law Weekly, October 30, 2000 Real Property Supplement 1-B. Member, Real Property Law Section, Member, Business Law Section and Member, Land Use Section, North Carolina Bar Association. *Member:* Wake County and Tenth Judicial District Bar Associations. ***PRACTICE AREAS:*** Financial Law; Real Estate. ***Email:*** parena@poynerspruill.com

OF COUNSEL

ARCH E. LYNCH, JR., born Buies Creek, North Carolina, November 9, 1930; admitted to bar, 1957, North Carolina. *Education:* Wake Forest University (B.S., 1952; J.D., 1957). ***PRACTICE AREAS:*** Securities Regulation Law; Banking Law; Savings and Loan Law.

DEWITT C. MCCOTTER, III, born New Bern, North Carolina, April 6, 1939; admitted to bar, 1964, North Carolina. *Education:* University of North Carolina (B.S., 1961; J.D., with honors, 1964). ***PRACTICE AREAS:*** Business Law; Corporate Law; Mergers and Acquisitions Law; Municipal Law; Utility Law. ***Email:*** dcmccotter@poynerspruill.com

THOMAS L. NORRIS, JR., born South Mills, North Carolina, November 23, 1933; admitted to bar, 1960, North Carolina; 1975, U.S. Supreme Court. *Education:* University of North Carolina (B.S., 1955; J.D., with honors, 1960). ***PRACTICE AREAS:*** Taxation Law; Pension and Profit Sharing Law; Estate Planning Law. ***Email:*** tlnorris@poynerspruill.com

ROBERT W. WILSON, JR., born Danville, Virginia, May 23, 1939; admitted to bar, 1963, North Carolina. *Education:* University of North Carolina (A.B., 1961; LL.B., 1963). ***PRACTICE AREAS:*** Real Estate Law; Lease Law. ***Email:*** rwilson@poynerspruill.com

CHARLES H. HENDERSON, born 1940; admitted to bar, 1976, North Carolina. *Education:* East Carolina University (A.B., 1963); North Carolina Central University (J.D., summa cum laude, 1976). ***PRACTICE AREAS:*** Government; Municipal Law. ***Email:*** chenderson@poynerspruill.com

JOHN A. MACKETHAN, born Fayetteville, North Carolina, December 12, 1942; admitted to bar, 1968, North Carolina. *Education:* University of North Carolina at Chapel Hill (B.S., 1965; J.D., 1968). Certified Public Accountant, North Carolina, 1970. ***PRACTICE AREAS:*** Taxation Law; Employee Benefits Law. ***Email:*** jmackethan@poynerspruill.com

ASSOCIATE COUNSEL

BRIAN F. CORBETT, born Canandaigua, New York, September 12, 1975; admitted to bar, 2000, Maryland; 2001, North Carolina. *Education:* Loyola College (B.A., 1997); Wake Forest University (J.D., 2000). ***PRACTICE AREAS:*** Financial Services Law; Real Estate Law. ***Email:*** bcorbett@poynerspruill.com

All Attorneys are Members of The North Carolina State Bar and North Carolina Bar Association.

REPRESENTATIVE CLIENTS: American Airlines; Alliance One International; BB&T; Boddie-Noell Enterprises, Inc.; The Body Shop, Inc.; Browning-Ferris Industries; CSX Transportations, Inc.; Data General Corp.; Electricities of North Carolina, Inc.; Farm Bureau Mutual Insurance Co.; Food Lion, Inc.; General Electric Capital Corp.; General Electric Company; General Electric Mortgage Insurance Company; General Motors, Inc.; Granutec, Inc.; Guardian Corporation, Inc.; H&R Block, Inc.; Investors Holding Company (Golden Corral and affiliates); LSB Bancshares, Inc.; Martin Marietta Materials; Mitsubishi Semiconductor America, Inc.; Nomaco, Inc.; N.C. Eastern Municipal Power Agency; North Carolina Enterprise Corporation; N.C. Housing Finance Agency; North Carolina Municipal Power Agency; Pepsico, Inc.; PF Properties; Pitt County Memorial Hospital; Premium Standard Farms, Inc.; Purdue Pharmaceuticals, L.P.; RBC Centura Banks, Inc.; Research Triangle Foundation; Richardson Sports (Carolina Panthers); Roses Stores, Inc.; R.J. Reynolds Tobacco Co.; Schwarz Biosciences, Inc.; Semi-Conductor Research Corp.; T.A. Loving Company; WakeMed.

(This Listing Continued)

(For additional Personnel and Biographical data see listings at Rocky Mount, Charlotte and Southern Pines)

PRATHER LAW FIRM, P.C.

RALEIGH, NORTH CAROLINA

(See Garner)

Workers Compensation, Social Security Disability, Disability Claims, Personal Injury, Automobile Accidents, Slip and Fall, Wrongful Death, Toxic Tort, Mold Exposure.

RAGSDALE LIGGETT PLLC

A Professional Limited Liability Company

Established in 1972

CROSSPOINTE PLAZA, SUITE 400
2840 PLAZA PLACE
P.O. BOX 31507
RALEIGH, NORTH CAROLINA 27612
Telephone: 919-787-5200
Fax: 919-783-8991
URL: http://www.rl-law.com
Mailing Address: P.O. Box 31507, Raleigh, NC 27622-1507

General Civil Litigation and Administrative Law in State and Federal Courts and Agencies. Taxation, Estate Planning, Partnership, Landlord and Tenant, Real Estate, Insurance and Reinsurance Law. Corporate, Business, International, Environmental Law. Construction Law, Employment Discrimination and Administrative Hearings and Appeals.

FIRM PROFILE: Ragsdale Liggett PLLC which was established in 1972, serves clients across a broad spectrum of needs. The firm's three primary areas of concentration are: Litigation, including complex commercial litigation, professional negligence defense and insurance/reinsurance coverage matters; Business Law, including formations, acquisitions, mergers and ongoing representation of business entities related to tax, capital, financial, regulatory and international issues and Real Estate Law, including representation of commercial and development needs from acquisition through disposition.

MEMBERS OF FIRM

DAN K. MOORE (1906-1986)

GEORGE R. RAGSDALE, born 1936; admitted to bar, 1962, North Carolina. *Education:* University of North Carolina (A.B., 1958; LL.B., 1961). Phi Delta Phi. Member, Order of the Golden Fleece. Richardson Fellow, Office of United States Senator Sam J. Ervin, Jr., and Assistant to Chief Counsel, Senate Subcommittee on Constitutional Rights, 1961-1962. Legal Counsel to the Governor of North Carolina, 1965-1968. Judge of the Superior Court of North Carolina, 1968-1970. Member, 1979-1987 and Chairman, 1984-1985, Board of Trustees, University of North Carolina at Chapel Hill. Member and Chairman, 1984-1985, Board of Trustees of the Endowment of the University of North Carolina. Member, Board of Directors of the University of North Carolina Foundation, 1979-1985. ***PRACTICE AREAS:*** International Law; Civil Litigation; Complex Litigation. ***Email:*** gragsdale@rl-law.com

FRANK R. LIGGETT III, born 1940; admitted to bar, 1966, North Carolina. *Education:* Woodberry Forest School, Orange, Virginia; International Fellowship, Denstone College, Uttoxeter, Staffordshire, England, 1958-1959 and University of North Carolina (A.B., 1963); University of North Carolina (J.D., 1969, replaced LL.B. conferred, 1966). Phi Delta Phi. Member, Federation of Regulatory Counsel, Inc., 1996—. ***PRACTICE AREAS:*** Insurance Law; Corporate Law; Business Law. ***Email:*** fliggett@rl-law.com

WILLIAM A. MANN, born Los Angeles, California, 1944; admitted to bar, 1968, North Carolina and U.S. District Court, Eastern District of North Carolina. *Education:* Phillips Andover Academy and University of North Carolina (A.B., 1965; J.D., 1968). Phi Delta Phi. *Member:* Wake County (Member: Real Property and Business Sections) North Carolina (Member, Alternative Billing Commission) and American Bar Associations. ***PRACTICE AREAS:*** Real Estate; Commercial Law; Corporate Law; International Law. ***Email:*** bmann@rl-law.com

WILLIAM B. BOST III, born Columbus, Georgia, December 23, 1963; admitted to bar, 1989, Virginia; 1993, North Carolina. *Education:* University of North Carolina (B.A., 1986; J.D., with honors, 1989). Order of the Coif. Member, North Carolina Law Review, 1988-1989. John Motley Morehead Scholar. "Author: "Interstate Banking: A Guide To The Fifty States." *Member:* Wake County and North Carolina Bar Associations. ***PRACTICE AREAS:*** Corporate Law; Business Law; Banking Law. ***Email:*** bbost@rl-law.com

DOROTHY BASS BURCH, born Raleigh, North Carolina, December 27, 1965; admitted to bar, 1991, North Carolina; U.S. District Court, Eastern District of North Carolina. *Education:* Meredith College (B.A., summa cum laude, 1987); University of North Carolina at Chapel Hill (J.D., 1991). Recipient: Judge Heriot Clarkson Award; AmJur Book Award in Professional Responsibility. *Member:* Wake County, North Carolina and American Bar Associations; Wake County Real Property Lawyers Association; North Carolina Association of Women Attorneys. ***PRACTICE AREAS:*** Corporate Law; Insurance Law; Real Estate Law. ***Email:*** dburch@rl-law.com

MARY HULETT, born Mexico, Missouri, April 9, 1942; admitted to bar, 1977, District of Columbia and Virginia; 1980, California; 2001, North Carolina. *Education:* Stanford University (B.A., 1963); George Washington University (J.D., with high honors, 1977). Member, Order of the Coif. Author: "Privacy and the Freedom of Information Act," 27 Administrative Law Review, 275, 1975. Counsel to the Consumer Products Safety Commission, 1977-1980. *Member:* Los Angeles County Bar Association; State Bar of California; District of Columbia Bar; Virginia State Bar; Association of Southern California De-

(This Listing Continued)

RAGSDALE LIGGETT PLLC, Raleigh—Continued

fense Counsel (Member, Board of Directors, 1991-1993). ***PRACTICE AREAS:*** Trial and Appellate Law; Products Liability; Business; Wrongful Termination; Employment Discrimination; Environmental and Toxic Torts. ***Email:*** mhulett@rl-law.com

WALTER L. TIPPETT, JR., born Raleigh, North Carolina, March 26, 1969; admitted to bar, 1995, North Carolina. *Education:* University of North Carolina at Chapel Hill (B.S.B.A., 1991; J.D., 1995). Phi Eta Sigma; Order of Barristers. Chief Justice, Holderness Moot Court Bench, 1994-1995. Recipient, Judge Heriot Clarkson Award. *Member:* Wake County and American Bar Associations; North Carolina State Bar; North Carolina Association of Defense Attorneys; Defense Research Institute. ***PRACTICE AREAS:*** Business Law; Real Estate; Commercial Litigation. ***Email:*** wtippett@rl-law.com

DAVID K. LIGGETT, born Chapel Hill, North Carolina, June 23, 1965; admitted to bar, 1995, North Carolina and U.S. District Court, Eastern District of North Carolina; 1996, U.S. District Court, Middle and Western Districts of North Carolina. *Education:* Virginia Episcopal School; University of North Carolina (B.A., 1988; J.D., 1995). Phi Delta Phi. Member: National Mock Trial Team, 1993-1995. Merit Award, Civil Lawyering Process. *Member:* Wake County, North Carolina and American Bar Associations; North Carolina Association of Defense Attorneys; Defense Research Institute. ***PRACTICE AREAS:*** Business Law; Insurance Law; Employment Law. ***Email:*** dliggett@rl-law.com

JOHN M. NUNNALLY, born Ft. Belvoir, Virginia, April 22, 1965; admitted to bar, 1992, North Carolina; 1993, U.S. District Court, Western District of North Carolina; 1999, U.S. District Court, Eastern and Middle Districts of North Carolina. *Education:* North Carolina State University (B.A., 1988); Campbell University (J.D., 1992). Phi Alpha Delta. Notes and Comments Editor, Campbell Law Review, 1991-1992. *Member:* Wake County, North Carolina and American Bar Associations; North Carolina State Bar; North Carolina Association of Defense Attorneys. ***PRACTICE AREAS:*** Construction Law; Insurance Defense; Civil Litigation. ***Email:*** jnunnally@rl-law.com

ROBERT J. RAMSEUR, JR., born Tyndall AFB, Florida, 1970; admitted to bar, 1996, North Carolina; 2002, U.S. Supreme Court. *Education:* Wake Forest University (A.B., cum laude, 1992; J.D., 1995). Licensed Realtor, North Carolina. *Member:* Wake County and North Carolina (Member, Real Property Division) Bar Associations; North Carolina State Bar; Wake County Real Property Lawyers Association.

GREGORY W. BROWN, admitted to bar, 1999, North Carolina. *Education:* University of Virginia (B.A., 1989); Duke University (J.D., 1993). *Member:* North Carolina State Bar; Virginia State Bar. ***PRACTICE AREAS:*** Civil Litigation. ***Email:*** gbrown@rl-law.com

OF COUNSEL

JOSEPH E. JOHNSON, born 1941; admitted to bar, 1966, North Carolina. *Education:* North Carolina State University; Wake Forest University (B.B.A., 1964; J.D., 1966). Vice President and Corporate Counsel, First Union Corporation 1971-1981. Member, North Carolina General Assembly, House of Representatives, 1975-1980. Member, North Carolina Senate, 1980-1994. [1st Lt., U.S. Army, 1967-1969]. ***PRACTICE AREAS:*** Administrative Law. ***Email:*** jjohnson@rl-law.com

ASSOCIATES

SARAH E. WINSLOW, born Belvidere, North Carolina, October 16, 1973; admitted to bar, 1998, North Carolina; 1999, U.S. District Court, Eastern, Middle, Western Districts of North Carolina and U.S. Court of Appeals, Fifth Circuit. *Education:* Duke University (B.S., 1995; J.D., cum laude, 1998). *Member:* Wake County and North Carolina Bar Associations; North Carolina State Bar. ***PRACTICE AREAS:*** Commercial Litigation; Construction Law; Real Estate Litigation. ***Email:*** swinslow@rl-law.com

MELISSA DEWEY BRUMBACK, born Elmira, New York, August 30, 1972; admitted to bar, 1998, North Carolina; 2001, U.S. District Court, Eastern, Middle and Western Districts of North Carolina. *Education:* Corning Community College (A.A., with honors, 1992); University of Manchester, England; University of North Carolina-Chapel Hill (B.A., with honors and highest distinction, 1994; J.D., 1998). Phi Beta Kappa. Member, Golden Key National Honor Society. New York State Regents Scholar. Recipient: Communication Award for Excellence; Humanities Scholarship Award; History/Government/Geography Award; Gressman-Pollitt Appellate Advocacy Award. Visiting Student in Faculty of Law, University of Manchester, England, 1997. *Member:* Wake County, North Carolina and American Bar Associations; North Carolina State Bar; North Carolina Association of Women Attorneys. ***PRACTICE AREAS:*** Construction Law; Civil Litigation. ***Email:*** mbrumback@rl-law.com

JESSICA C. TYNDALL, born Roanoke, Virginia, January 13, 1977; admitted to bar, 2002, North Carolina and U.S. District Court, Eastern District of North Carolina. *Education:* Duke University (A.B., 1999); University of Richmond (J.D., cum laude, 2002). Member: Moot Court Board; Trial Advocacy Board; Journal of Law and Technology. Author: "Bloom v. Commonwealth: Identifying the Face Behind the Instant Message," 8 Rich.J.L. and Tech. 17 (Spring 2002) at http://www.lawrichmond.edu/jolt/v8i3/article17.html. ***LANGUAGES:*** Spanish. ***PRACTICE AREAS:*** Civil Litigation; Insurance Law.

SANDRA W. MITTERLING, born Morehead City, North Carolina, January 26, 1966; admitted to bar, 1995, North Carolina; 2001, U.S. District Court, Eastern District of North Carolina; 2002, U.S. Court of Appeals, Fourth Circuit. *Education:* University of North Carolina at Chapel Hill (B.A., 1988; J.D., 1991). *Member:* Wake County, North Carolina and American Bar Associations. ***PRACTICE AREAS:*** Civil Litigation; Construction Law. ***Email:*** smitterling@rl-law.com

HANNAH C. BISSETTE, admitted to bar, 2004, North Carolina. *Education:* University of North Carolina at Chapel Hill (B.A., 1999); Wake Forest University (J.D., 2004). ***PRACTICE AREAS:*** Civil Litigation (100%). ***Email:*** hbissette@rl-law.com

RICHARD O. BOLTON, born Raleigh, North Carolina, June 17, 1972; admitted to bar, 1998, North Carolina. *Education:* Wake Forest University (B.A., 1994; J.D., 1998). *Member:* North Carolina and American Bar Associations. ***PRACTICE AREAS:*** Commercial Real Estate. ***Email:*** rbolton@rl-law.com

CHARLES VAUGHAN, III, born 1977; admitted to bar, 2005, North Carolina. *Education:* University of North Carolina at Chapel Hill (B.A., 2001); University of North Carolina School of Law (J.D., 2005). ***PRACTICE AREAS:*** Business Law.

ASHLEY HUFFSTETLER, born 1976; admitted to bar, 2003, North Carolina. *Education:* University of North Carolina at Chapel Hill (B.A., 1999); University of North Carolina School of Law (J.D., 2003). ***PRACTICE AREAS:*** Civil Litigation.

CHRISTINA RIVENBARK & ASSOCIATES

RALEIGH, NORTH CAROLINA

(See Wilmington)

Personal Injury, Automobile Accidents, Workers Compensation, Wrongful Death, Medical Malpractice, Slip and Fall, Criminal Law, Driving While Intoxicated, Traffic Violations, Drug Offenses, Misdemeanors, Felonies, Sexual Assaults, Assaults, Burglary, Motorcycle Accidents, Head Injuries.

ROBERTSON IMMIGRATION LAW FIRM

Established in 1992

THE CAPITAL CLUB BUILDING
16 WEST MARTIN STREET, SUITE 1101
RALEIGH, NORTH CAROLINA 27601-2977
Telephone: 919-834-7004
Fax: 919-834-0428
Email: immigrationlaw@nc.rr.com
URL: http://www.robertsonimmigrationlaw.com

Immigration and Naturalization, Business Immigration, Citizenship, Consular Law, Employment Visas, Political Asylum, Non-Immigrant Visas.

FIRM PROFILE: Since 1992, Robertson Immigration Law Firm has represented clients for employment-based and family-based immigration, naturalization, asylum, and all types of non-immigrant visas. The law firm has staff members who are fluent in Spanish and in French. Robertson Immigration Law Firm has been on retainer by the Mexican Consulate representing North Carolina and South Carolina since that Consulate's founding in 2000. Ann Robertson is one of only seventeen Board Certified Specialists in Immigration Law in North Carolina. There are only six such specialists east of Greensboro, North Carolina.

ANN ROBERTSON, born Rocky Mount, North Carolina, May 21, 1948; admitted to bar, 1991, North Carolina. *Education:* University of North Carolina at Chapel Hill (B.A., 1970; J.D., 1989); University of North Carolina at Greensboro (M.A.); Duke University (Ph.D., 1981). Law Clerk to The Honorable John B. Lewis, Jr., N.C. Court of Appeals, 1989-1990. Deputy Campaign Manager, Congressman David Price, U.S. House of Representatives, 1991. *Member:* Wake County and North Carolina Bar Associations; American Immigration Lawyers Association; National Association of Foreign Student Advisors. (Board Certified Specialist in Immigration Law, North Carolina State Board of Legal Specialization). ***LANGUAGES:*** French. ***PRACTICE AREAS:*** Immigration and Naturalization; Business Immigration; Citizenship; Consular Law; Employment Visas; Political Asylum; All Non-Immigrant Visas.

ROSE RAND ATTORNEYS, P.A.

Established in 1944

CORPORATE PLAZA BUILDING, SUITE 1508
333 FAYETTEVILLE STREET
RALEIGH, NORTH CAROLINA 27601
Telephone: 919-832-4040
Fax: 919-832-4050

Wilson, North Carolina Office: 2500 West Nash Street, Unit C, P.O. Drawer 2367, 27894-2367. Telephone: 252-291-3848. Telecopier: 252-291-9555.

General Practice, all Courts. Corporation, Labor and Insurance Law. Trials, including Personal Injury, Wrongful Death and Workers Compensation, Eminent Domain, Tax, Estate Planning and Administration, Municipal, Environmental, Real Estate, Bankruptcy.

J. YANCEY WASHINGTON, born Oxford, North Carolina, June 11, 1976; admitted to bar, 2001, North Carolina. *Education:* Hampden-Sydney College (B.A., History, cum laude, 1998); Virginia Programmee at Oxford, Oxford, England (1998); Campbell University (J.D., 2001). Phi Alpha Delta (Clerk, Iredell Chapter). *Member:* Wilson County, North Carolina, Seventh and Tenth Judicial District Bar Associations; North Carolina State Bar; Eastern North Carolina Inn of Court. ***PRACTICE AREAS:*** Bankruptcy; Municipal Law; General Practice. ***Email:*** ywashington@rose-randlaw.com

(For complete biographical data on all personnel, see Professional Biographies at Wilson, North Carolina)

SANDLIN & DAVIDIAN

5617 DEPARTURE DRIVE
RALEIGH, NORTH CAROLINA 27616
Telephone: 919-850-9199
Fax: 919-850-9699
URL: http://www.sandlin-law.com

Family Law, Divorce, Equitable Distribution, Child Custody, Child Support, Alimony, Premarital Agreements, Domestic Partnership Agreements, Domestic Violence, Driving While Intoxicated (DWI), Drug Crimes, Parole and Probation, Traffic Violations, Appellate Practice.

(This Listing Continued)

DEBORAH SANDLIN, admitted to bar, 1998, North Carolina and U.S. District Court, Eastern District of North Carolina. *Education:* Eastern Kentucky University (B.A., Political Science, 1985); North Carolina Central University (J.D., summa cum laude, 1998). Adjunct Professor at North Carolina Central University School of Law. Guest Speaker, Meredith College. *Member:* North Carolina Bar Association (Member, Family Law Section); North Carolina Academy of Trial Lawyers (Family Law Section Chair, 2002-2003; Vice Chair, Family Law Section, 2002-2003; CLE Chair, 2002-2003; CLE presenter for North Carolina Academy of Trial Lawyers at numerous seminars and for Wake Forest University). (Board Certified Specialist in Family Law, North Carolina State Board of Legal Specialization). ***LANGUAGES:*** German. ***REPORTED CASES:*** Long v. Long, 588 S.E. 2d 1 (2003); Evans v. Evans, 581 S.E. 2d 464 (2003); Scott v. Scott, 579 S.E. 2d 431 (2003); Schmeltzle v. Schmeltzle, 535 S.E. 2d 326 (2000); Torres v. McLain, 535 S.E. 2d 623 (2000). ***PRACTICE AREAS:*** Family Law Appeals; Adoption; Alimony; Child Custody; Child Support; Equitable Distribution; Post Separation Support; Domestic Partnerships; Premarital Agreements; Separation Agreements. ***Email:*** dsandlin@sandlindavidian.com

V.A. "WOOFER" DAVIDIAN III, born Chapel Hill, North Carolina; admitted to bar, 1999, North Carolina. *Education:* University of North Carolina at Chapel Hill (B.A., Political Science, 1991); Regent University (J.D., 1999). [Lt., Judge Advocate General's Corps (JAG), U.S. Navy, 1999-2002]. ***PRACTICE AREAS:*** Family Law; Traffic Violations. ***Email:*** vadavidian@sandlin-law.com

ANDREW K. SANDMAN

7101 CREEDMOOR ROAD
SUITE 122
RALEIGH, NORTH CAROLINA 27613
Telephone: 919-845-6688
Facsimile: 919-845-6639
Email: asandlaw@bellsouth.net
URL: http://www.andrewsandmanlaw.com

Criminal Law, Drug Crimes, Driving While Intoxicated, Assaults, Traffic Violations, Personal Injury.

ANDREW K. SANDMAN, born Raleigh, North Carolina, August 11, 1968; admitted to bar, 1993, North Carolina. *Education:* North Carolina State University (B.S., 1990); Campbell College of Law (J.D., 1993). Assistant District Attorney, Wake County, 1993-1995. *Member:* Wake County, North Carolina and American Bar Associations; North Carolina State Bar; North Carolina Academy of Trial Lawyers; National Association of Criminal Defense Lawyers. ***PRACTICE AREAS:*** Criminal; Drug Trafficking; Driving While Intoxicated; Traffic Violations; Juvenile Law; Drug Crimes; Assault and Battery; Felonies.

ASSOCIATE

WILLIAM FINN, admitted to bar, 1999, North Carolina. *Education:* North Carolina State University (B.A., 1990) Campbell University (J.D., 1999). *Member:* North Carolina and Wake County Bar Associations. ***Email:*** bsandlaw@bellsouth.net

TRAVIS SASSER

RALEIGH, NORTH CAROLINA

(See Cary)

Bankruptcy, Consumer Bankruptcy, Commercial Bankruptcy, Foreclosures.

SATISKY & SILVERSTEIN, LLP

Established in 1976
900 RIDGEFIELD DRIVE
SUITE 250
RALEIGH, NORTH CAROLINA 27609
Telephone: 919-790-9102
Telecopier: 919-790-1560

Commercial Real Estate, Eminent Domain, Corporate, Civil, Commercial and Business Litigation, Leasing, Construction Law, Municipal Law, Computer Law, Administrative.

HOWARD P. SATISKY, born Raleigh, North Carolina, April 8, 1945; admitted to bar, 1969, North Carolina. *Education:* University of North Carolina (B.S., 1967; J.D., 1969). Assistant Attorney General, North Carolina Department of Justice, 1969-1973. Director, North Carolina Organized Crime Protection Council, 1972-1973. Member, 1974-1982 and Chairman, 1979, Raleigh Board of Adjustment. *Member:* Wake County (Executive Committee, 1977-1979), North Carolina and American Bar Associations; North Carolina State Bar (Councillor, 1992-2000; Chair, Consumer Protection, Advertising Committee; Member, Executive Committee); North Carolina Academy of Trial Lawyers. ***PRACTICE AREAS:*** Business Law; Commercial Real Estate; Commercial Litigation; Eminent Domain. ***Email:*** hsatisky@satiskysilverstein.com

JOHN M. SILVERSTEIN, born Baltimore, Maryland, February 1, 1946; admitted to bar, 1971, North Carolina; 1976, U.S. Supreme Court. *Education:* Colgate University (A.B., 1968); University of North Carolina (J.D., 1971). Delta Theta Phi. Assistant Attorney General, North Carolina Department of Justice, 1974-1975. Special Deputy Attorney General, North Carolina Department of Justice, 1975-1976. Member, 1982-1988, Chairman, 1984-1988 and Attorney, 1988—, Raleigh Board of Adjustment. *Member:* Wake County (Member, Executive Committee, 1982-1984; President, 1994), North Carolina (Chair, Local Bar Services Committee, 1995-1996) and American Bar Associations. ***PRACTICE AREAS:*** Property Law; Administrative Law; Municipal Law; General Practice. ***Email:*** jms@satiskysilverstein.com

KEITH A. SATISKY, born Raleigh, North Carolina, October 7, 1967; admitted to bar, 1994, North Carolina and U.S. District Court, Eastern District of North Carolina. *Education:* Duke University (A.B., 1989); Wake Forest University (J.D., 1994). *Member:* Wake County (Member, Board of Directors 2000-2002), North Carolina and American Bar Associations; North Carolina Academy of Trial Lawyers. ***PRACTICE AREAS:*** Corporate Law; Commercial Litigation; Business Litigation; Computer Law; Leases and Leasing; Construction Law. ***Email:*** ksatisky@satiskysilverstein.com

COUNSEL FOR: Drucker & Falk, LLC; Clancy & Theys Construction Co.; Mediclick, Inc.; N.C. Board of Physical Therapy Examiners; United Restaurant Equipment Co.; White Oak Properties; Raleigh Board of Adjustment; E Plus Group, Inc.; Langford Construction Company; Knightdale Board of Adjustment.

LAW OFFICE OF SALLY SCHERER

133 FAYETTEVILLE STREET, SUITE 200
P.O. BOX 106
RALEIGH, NORTH CAROLINA 27602
Telephone: 919-821-5393
Fax: 919-459-2727
Email: SSchererJD@aol.com

Trial and Appellate Practice, Domestic and Family Law, Divorce, Custody, Mediation, Arbitration.

SALLY H. SCHERER, born Richmond, Virginia, January 11, 1940; admitted to bar, 1981, North Carolina; 1986, U.S. Supreme Court. *Education:* Sweet Briar College (B.A., 1962); University of Virginia School of Medicine (Med. Tech., 1964); Franklin Pierce Law Center (J.D., 1981). Certified Mediator. *Member:* Wake County (Board of Directors, 1989-1992, 1995-1997), North Carolina and American Bar Associations; Tenth Judicial District (President, 1996) and North Carolina State Bar; North Carolina Association of Women Attorneys; North Carolina Academy of Trial Lawyers (Board of Governors, 1987-1993); North Carolina Conference of Bar Presidents (President, 1997-1998); Wake County Academy of Criminal Trial Lawyers (President, 1985); American Civil Liberties Union. ***PRACTICE AREAS:*** Trial and Appellate Practice; Family Law; Divorce; Custody; Mediation; Arbitration; Adoption Law; Child Support; Collaborative Family Law; Domestic Violence; Name Changes; Non-Traditional Family Law; Paternity.

ASSOCIATE

ANGENETTE STEPHENSON, born Salem, Oregon, July 28, 1968; admitted to bar, 2004, North Carolina and Hawaii. *Education:* Eastern Mennonite University (B.S., 1990); University of North Carolina at Chapel Hill (J.D., 2003); University of North Carolina School of Social Work, Chapel Hill (M.S.W., 2003). *Member:* North Carolina Bar Association (Member: Juvenile Justice Section; Family Law Section); America Bar Association; Association of Family and Conciliation Courts; North Carolina Association of Women Attorneys. ***PRACTICE AREAS:*** Family Law; Juvenile Law. ***Email:*** angie@sschererlaw.com

SCHILLER & SCHILLER PLLC

5540 MUNFORD ROAD, SUITE 101
RALEIGH, NORTH CAROLINA 27612
Telephone: 919-789-4677
Fax: 919-789-4469
URL: http://www.schillerandschiller.com

Appellate Practice, Automobile Accidents and Injuries, Business Disputes, Class Actions, Contracts, Deceptive Trade Practices, Defective Products, Defamation, Employment, Environment, Insurance Claims, Personal Injury, Property Damage, Retirement Benefits, Securities Fraud, Workers Compensation, Wrongful Death, Family Law, Divorce.

MEMBERS OF FIRM

MARVIN SCHILLER, born Miami, Florida, April 13, 1940; admitted to bar, 1975, North Carolina; 1979, U.S. Supreme Court. *Education:* University of Miami (B.A., 1961); University of North Carolina (Ph.D., 1970); Duke University (J.D., 1975). Assistant Professor: Department of Philosophy, Southern Methodist University, 1965-1969; Department of Philosophy, University of Toronto, 1969-1973. Assistant Attorney General, North Carolina, 1978-1981. *Member:* Wake County, North Carolina and American Bar Associations; North Carolina State Bar; North Carolina Academy of Trial Lawyers. ***REPORTED CASES:*** Simpson v. N.C. Local Gov't Employees' Retirement System, 88 N.C. App. 218, 363 S.E.2d 90 (1987) Aff'd per curiam, 323 N.C. 362, 372 S.E.2d 559 (1988); Faulkenbury v. Teachers' and State Employees' Retirement System, 345 N.C. 683, 483 S.E.2d 422 (1997). ***Email:*** marvinschiller@msn.com

CAROL M. SCHILLER

DAVID G. SCHILLER, born Toronto, Ontario Canada, April 25, 1970; admitted to bar, 1999, North Carolina and U.S. District Court, Eastern District of North Carolina. *Education:* Guilford College (B.S., 1992); University of Miami (J.D., 1998). Editor-in-Chief, Inter-American Law Review, University of Miami, 1997-1998. Author: "The North American Commission on Environmental Cooperation Review of the Cozumel Pier Submission," 28 U. Miami Inter-Am. L.Rev. 437, 1997. *Member:* Wake County and North Carolina Bar Associations; North Carolina Academy of Trial Lawyers. ***REPORTED CASES:*** Jordan v. North Carolina Department of Transportation, Division of Motor Vehicles, 353 N.C. 376, 547 S.E.2d 412 (2001); Godon v. North Carolina Crime Control & Public Safety, 238 F.3d 412, 2000 WL 1763464 (4th Cir. (N.C.) (unpublished)). ***Email:*** davidschiller@mindspring.com

SCHWARTZ & SHAW, P.L.L.C.

Established in 1991

COMMERCE BUILDING, SUITE 1000
19 WEST HARGETT STREET
P.O. BOX 2350
RALEIGH, NORTH CAROLINA 27602
Telephone: 919-821-9011
Fax: 919-821-9015
URL: http://www.lawyers.com/schwartz-shaw

Education Law, Employment Law, Civil Litigation.

MEMBERS OF FIRM

RICHARD SCHWARTZ, born Rockville Centre, New York, July 31, 1953; admitted to bar, 1978, North Carolina. *Education:* Duke University (B.A., 1975); North Carolina State University; University of North Carolina (J.D., 1978). National Order of Barristers. Lecturer, Legal Research and Writing, University of North Carolina, 1978-1979. Legislative Staff, North Carolina General Assembly (Utilities & Energy), 1975-1977. Vice Chairman, North Carolina Council on the Holocaust. *Member:* Wake County, North Carolina and American Bar Associations; National Council of School Attorneys (Member, Board of Directors, 1995-1999); North Carolina Center for the Advancement of Teaching (Chairman: Foundation Board; Holocaust Endowment Fund); North Carolina Partnership for Excellence (Member, Board of Directors); North Carolina Council of School Attorneys (Secretary-Treasurer, 1983-1984; Vice-Chairman, 1984-1985; Chairman, 1985-1986). ***PRACTICE AREAS:*** Education Law; Employment Law; Civil Litigation. ***Email:*** rschwartz@schwartz-shaw.com

BRIAN C. SHAW, born Oxnard, California, July 12, 1954; admitted to bar, 1980, California; 1984, Maine; 1993, North Carolina. *Education:* Harvard University (B.A., cum laude, 1976; J.D., cum laude, 1980). Phi Beta Kappa. Law Clerk to Hon. Edward J. Schwartz, Chief Judge, U.S. District Court, Southern District of California, 1980-1981. Author: "The Legal Implications of Values Education," Maine Policy Review, December, 1992; "Regulating Hate Speech in Public Schools," Inquiry and Analysis, National School Boards Association, July 1993; "Reasonable Accommodation of Disabled Employees: A Comprehensive Case Law Reference," National School Boards Association, February, 1996; "Sexual Harassment Law after the 1997 U.S. Supreme Court Term," Inquiry and Analysis, National School Boards Association, November 1998. *Member:* Wake County, Maine State and American Bar Associations; North Carolina State Bar; North Carolina Council of School Attorneys; National Council of School Attorneys. ***REPORTED CASES:*** Solmitz v. Maine School Administrative District No. 59, 495 A.2d 812 (Me. 1985); City of Lewiston v. Lewiston Educational Directors, 503 A.2d 210 (Me. 1985); Scribner v. Berry, 489 A.2d 8 (Me. 1985); Banks v. County of Buncombe, 500 S.E. 2d 666 (1998). ***PRACTICE AREAS:*** Education Law; Employment Law; Civil Litigation. ***Email:*** bshaw@schwartz-shaw.com

ASSOCIATES

MICHAEL R. DELAFIELD, born Portland, Maine, December 25, 1970; admitted to bar, 1999, North Carolina. *Education:* Princeton University (B.A., 1993); University of Maine School of Law (J.D., 1999). Member, Maine Law Review. *Member:* Wake County, North Carolina and American Bar Associations; National Council of School Attorneys; North Carolina Council of School Attorneys. ***PRACTICE AREAS:*** Education Law; Civil Litigation; Employment Law. ***Email:*** mdelafield@schwartz-shaw.com

CRAIG W. NOYES, born Nashville, Tennessee, June 4, 1977; admitted to bar, 2002, North Carolina. *Education:* Florida State University (B.S., summa cum laude, 1999); University of North Carolina (J.D., with honors, 2002). *Member:* Wake County, North Carolina and American Bar Associations; National Council of School Attorneys; North Carolina Council of School Attorneys. ***PRACTICE AREAS:*** Education Law; Civil Litigation; Employment Law. ***Email:*** cnoyes@schwartz-shaw.com

RACHEL B. HITCH, born West Chester, Pennsylvania, March 23, 1974; admitted to bar, 2002, North Carolina. *Education:* Bloomsburg University of Pennsylvania (B.A., 1997); Campbell University School of Law (J.D., 2002). Member Editor, Campbell Law Review, 2001-2002. Recipient: North Carolina State Bar Pro Bono Public Service Award, 2002; American Bankruptcy Institute Medal of Excellence, 2002. *Member:* Wake County, North Carolina and American Bar Associations; National Council of School Attorneys; North Carolina Council of School Attorneys. ***PRACTICE AREAS:*** Education Law; Civil Litigation; Employment Law. ***Email:*** rhitch@schwartz-shaw.com

REPRESENTATIVE CLIENTS: Moore County Board of Education; Guilford County Board of Education; Kannapolis City Board of Education; Dare County Board of Education; Pamlico County Board of Education; Avery County Board of Education; Asheville City Board of Education.

SCUDDER & HEDRICK

Established in 2001

1312 ANNAPOLIS DRIVE, SUITE 203
RALEIGH, NORTH CAROLINA 27608
Telephone: 919-828-7333
Fax: 919-828-1209
Email: shwcl@bellsouth.net

Workers Compensation, Serious Personal Injury, Mediation, Employment, Pharmacy Malpractice, Medical Malpractice.

FIRM PROFILE: Scudder & Hedrick was founded by attorneys with over twenty-five combined years experience in the practice of law. Sam Scudder and John Hedrick were practicing with The Law Offices of Robin E. Hudson when Ms. Hudson was elected to the North Carolina Court of Appeals and closed her practice. Sam, Judge Hudson's senior associate, and John, a former North Carolina Industrial Commission Deputy Commissioner, formed Scudder & Hedrick, and have since expanded the firm to include a third attorney whose nine years of experience and fluency in Spanish and in English allow us to represent a broader population of clients.

Both partners are Board Certified Specialists in Workers' Compensation Law, which means that we are very knowledgeable in the specific field of representing injured workers. The size of our firm assures that your claim will get personal, hands-on attention. We are dedicated to providing our clients with information regarding their claims every step of the way, and to open and accessible communication with the individuals we represent.

Our attorneys are members of the North Carolina Academy of Trial Lawyers, an association dedicated to protecting people's rights through advocacy and education. Our attorneys attend, write materials for, and lecture at continuing education courses regularly, assuring that they maintain knowledge of the very latest information available to assist clients.

In addition to the years of experience and education our attorneys have, we have many resources available, from electronic research assistance to the experience and dedication of our staff.

PARTNERS

SAMUEL ALAN SCUDDER, born Jacksonville, North Carolina, May 5, 1959; admitted to bar, 1990, North Carolina and U.S. District Court, Eastern and Middle Districts of North Carolina. *Education:* University of North Carolina at Greensboro; University of Florida (B.S., Pharmacy, 1982); Campbell University School of Law (J.D., 1990). Certified Mediator: North Carolina Industrial Commission; North Carolina Dispute Resolution Commission. *Member:* Wake County, 10th Judicial District and North Carolina Bar Associations; North Carolina State Bar; North Carolina Academy of Trial Lawyers. (Board Certified Specialist in Workers' Compensation, North Carolina State Board of Legal Specialization). ***REPORTED CASES:*** GOFORTH v. K-MART CORPORATION, COA03-1475 (N.C.App. 12-21-2004) 605 S.E.2d 709; JONES v. WEYERHAEUSER, 99-742 (N.C.App. 12-29-2000) 560 S.E.2d 227; CARROLL v. LIVING CENTERS SOUTHEAST, 157 N.C. App. 116 (2003) 577 S.E.2d 925; HATCHER v. DANIEL INTL. CORP., 153 N.C. App. 776 (2002) 571 S.E.2d 20; HOLLEY v. ACTS, INC., 357 N.C. 228 (2003) 581 S.E.2d 750; CLARK v. ITT GRINNELL IND. PIPING, 141 N.C. App. 417 (2000) 539 S.E.2d 369; JONES v. WEYERHAEUSER CO., 141 N.C. App. 482 (2000) 539 S.E.2d 380. ***PRACTICE AREAS:*** Workers Compensation (75%); Workers Compensation Mediation (8%); Medical Malpractice (5%); Pharmacists Liability (5%); Personal Injury Mediation (2%); Plaintiffs Personal Injury (5%).

JOHN A. HEDRICK, born Statesville, North Carolina, September 26, 1965; admitted to bar, 1991, North Carolina. *Education:* University of North Carolina at Chapel Hill (B.A., 1987); Campbell University, Norman Adrian Wiggins School of Law (J.D., 1991). Professional Experience: Government Service Law Clerk, the Honorable John Webb, Associate Justice of the North Carolina Supreme Court, August 1991-August 1993. Law Clerk, the Honorable John C. Martin, Associate Judge, North Carolina Court of Appeals, October 1993-March 1994. Associate Attorney General, North Carolina Department of Justice, April 1994-September 1995. Deputy Commissioner, North Carolina Industrial Commission, October 1994-August 2000. Private Practice Associate Attorney, Law Offices of Robin E. Hudson, September 2000-December 2000. Partner, Scudder & Hedrick, Workers' Compensation Attorneys, January 2001 -. *Member:* Wake County, 10th Judicial District and North Carolina Bar Associations; North Carolina State Bar; North Carolina Academy of Trial Lawyers (Workers' Compensation Section). (Board Certified Specialist in Workers' Compensation, North Carolina State Board of Legal Specialization). ***REPORTED CASES:*** BUTLER v. E.I. DUPONT DE NEMOURS & CO., 165 N.C. App. 705 (2004) 601 S.E.2d 330 JONES-BAILEY v. CARLISLE PLASTICS, INC., 164 N.C. App. 228 (2004) 595 S.E.2d 451 HALE v. NOVO NORDISK PHAR. INDUS., 153 N.C. App. 272 (2002) 569 S.E.2d 724. ***PRACTICE AREAS:*** Workers Compensation (100%). ***Email:*** jhedri@bellsouth.net

ASSOCIATE

ALICE J. TEJADA, born Los Angeles, California, July 23; admitted to bar, 1997, North Carolina. *Education:* Occidental College (A.B. 1993); American University, Washington College of Law (J.D. 1996). Public Interest Service: Staff Attorney, Farmworkers Legal Services of North Carolina, June 1996-December 1998; Staff Attorney, Legal Services of North Carolina-Farmworker Unit, January 1, 1999-June 30, 2002. Associate Attorney, Scudder & Hedrick, November 2002 to present. *Member:* Wake County, 10th Judicial District and North Carolina (Race Relations Implementation Committee) Bar Associations; North Carolina State Bar; North Carolina Academy of Trial Lawyers (Workers' Compensation Section, Employment Law Section and Hispanic/Latino Issues Section); North Carolina Association of Women Attorneys. ***LANGUAGES:*** Spanish. ***PRACTICE AREAS:*** Workers Compensation (80%); Labor and Employment (20%). ***Email:*** atejada@bellsouth.net

Languages: English, Spanish.

GREGORY L. SEIBERT

117 GLENWOOD AVENUE
RALEIGH, NORTH CAROLINA 27603
Telephone: 919-546-0606
Fax: 919-546-0040
Email: seibert@seibert.com
URL: http://www.seibert.com

Criminal Law, Driving While Intoxicated (DWI), Traffic Violations, Drug Crimes, Personal Injury, Automobile Accidents, Wrongful Death, Aviation Law.

GREGORY L. SEIBERT, born Pasadena, California, April 5, 1950; admitted to bar, 1986, North Carolina. *Education:* North Carolina State University (B.S.E., 1977); North Carolina Central University (J.D., 1986). Phi Delta Phi. Aerospace Engineer. Licensed Airline Transport Pilot. Attorney for Airplane Owner and Pilot Association. *Member:* Wake

(This Listing Continued)

County, North Carolina and American Bar Associations; North Carolina Academy of Trial Lawyers. ***PRACTICE AREAS:*** DWI; Traffic Tickets; Personal Injury; Aviation Law.

SHANAHAN LAW GROUP

207 FAYETTEVILLE STREET MALL
RALEIGH, NORTH CAROLINA 27601
Telephone: 919-856-9494
Fax: 919-856-9499
Email: kieran@shanahanlawgroup.com
URL: http://www.lawyers.com/shanahanlawgroup

Business Formation and Financing, Complex Business Litigation, Federal Litigation, Regulatory Investigation, Professional Liability, Health Care Law, Business Litigation, Business Fraud, White Collar Crimes, Employment Law, Non Competes, Personal Injury, Insurance Matters, Trusts and Estates.

MEMBER

KIERAN JOSEPH SHANAHAN, born Frederick, Maryland, July 13, 1956; admitted to bar, 1982, Georgia; 1983, U.S. District Court, Northern and Middle Districts of Georgia; 1986, North Carolina and U.S. Court of Appeals, Fourth Circuit; 1989, U.S. District Court, Eastern, Middle and Western Districts of North Carolina; 1990, U.S. Court of Appeals, Seventh Circuit; 1997, U.S. District Court, Southern District of Alabama; U.S. Tax Court. *Education:* East Carolina University (B.S.B.A., cum laude, 1979); University of North Carolina (J.D., 1982). Member, Holderness Moot Court Bench, 1981-1982. Member, 1980-1981 and Recent Development Editor, 1981-1982, North Carolina Journal of International Law and Commercial Regulation. Assistant U.S. Attorney: Criminal Division, U.S. Department of Justice, 1984-1989. Member, Editorial Board, "Construction and Design Law," 1991. Member, Raleigh City Council, 1995-2003. Certified Mediator, 1992. *Member:* The North Carolina State Bar; State Bar of Georgia. ***Email:*** kieran@shanahanlawgroup.com

ASSOCIATES

ROBERT BRUCE MARKWORTH, born Hanover, New Hampshire, July 2, 1967; admitted to bar, 1998, North Carolina. *Education:* University of North Carolina at Charlotte (B.A., Economics, cum laude, 1990); Indiana University (M.A., Economics, 1992); University of North Carolina at Chapel Hill (J.D., 1998). Phi Delta Phi. Phi Eta Sigma. Phi Kappa Phi. Beta Gamma Sigma. Golden Key National Honor Society. Staff Member, North Carolina Banking Institute, 1996-1997. Author: "Survival of the Federal Common Law D'Oench Doctrine," North Carolina Banking Institute, Volume 1, March 1997. *Member:* Wake County and North Carolina (Member, Business Law Section) Bar Associations; North Carolina State Bar (Member Sections on: Business Law; Real Property). ***PRACTICE AREAS:*** Corporate Law; Finance; Real Estate; Trusts and Estates. ***Email:*** rmarkworth@shanahanlawgroup.com

STEVEN K. McCALLISTER, born Durban, South Africa; admitted to bar, 1998, North Carolina and U.S. District Court, Middle and Eastern Districts of North Carolina; 1999, U.S. Court of Appeals, Fourth Circuit; 2003, New York and U.S. District Court, Southern and Eastern Districts of New York. *Education:* Appalachian State University (B.A., magna cum laude, 1995); Wake Forest University School of Law (J.D., 1998). Phi Kappa Phi; Alpha Chi. Member, Wake Forest Law Review. Member, Wake Forest Moot Court Board. *Member:* North Carolina State Bar; New York State Bar Association. ***PRACTICE AREAS:*** Civil Litigation; Personal Injury; Products Liability.

OF COUNSEL

REEF C. IVEY, II, born Wadesboro, North Carolina, January 26, 1943; admitted to bar, 1968, North Carolina; 1969, New York; 1974, Illinois; 1982, Oklahoma and U.S. Supreme Court. *Education:* North Carolina State University (B.S., 1965); University of North Carolina (J.D., 1968). Phi Delta Phi. *Member:* North Carolina, New York State, Oklahoma and Illinois State Bar Associations; North Carolina State Bar (Member, North Carolina Commission on Business Law; Chief Justice's Commission on the Future of the North Carolina Business Court). ***PRACTICE AREAS:*** Business Law; International Law; Corporate Law; Government; Trusts and Estates. ***Email:*** rivey@shanahanlawgroup.com

LAW OFFICES OF WALTER L. SHEFFIELD III, PLLC

Established in 2002

4505 FAIR MEADOW LANE, SUITE 222
RALEIGH, NORTH CAROLINA 27607
Telephone: 919-571-4398
Fax: 919-571-4368
Email: wsheffield@waltsheffield.com
URL: http://www.waltsheffield.com

Asset Protection, Long Term Care Planning, Estate Planning, Probate Avoidance, Elder Law, Guardianship, Wills, Trusts and Estates, Taxes, Maximize Income.

WALTER L. SHEFFIELD, III, born Wilmington, North Carolina, October 18, 1949; admitted to bar, 1974, Tennessee; 1978, North Carolina. *Education:* Duke University (B.A., 1971); Vanderbilt University (J.D., 1974). *Member:* Wake County and North Carolina (Member, Elder Law, Fiduciary Law and Tax Law Sections) Bar Associations; National Academy of Elder Law Attorneys; Wake County Estate Planning Council. ***PRACTICE AREAS:*** Elder Law; Trusts and Estates; Estate Planning; Long Term Care; Asset Protection. ***Email:*** wsheffield@waltsheffield.com

ERICA A. WEHNER, born Lincoln, Nebraska, January 7, 1979; admitted to bar, 2004, North Carolina. *Education:* University of Iowa (B.A., 2001; J.D., 2004). *Member:* Wake County, 10th Judicial District, North Carolina (Member Sections on: Elder Law, Trust and Estates) and American Bar Associations. ***PRACTICE AREAS:*** Elder Law; Trusts and Estates; Estate Planning; Long Term Care; Asset Protection.

SHIRLEY & ADAMS, PLLC

150 FAYETTEVILLE STREET
SUITE 520
RALEIGH, NORTH CAROLINA 27601
Telephone: 919-899-6278
Fax: 919-899-6279
URL: http://www.shirley-adamslaw.com

Civil Trial Practice, Construction Law, Commercial Litigation, Business Litigation and Surety Law.

RYAN J. ADAMS, born Raleigh, North Carolina, November 21, 1975; admitted to bar, 2001, North Carolina. *Education:* Duke University (B.A., 1998); University of North Carolina, at Chapel Hill (J.D., 2001). *Member:* North Carolina State Bar. ***PRACTICE AREAS:*** Civil Litigation; Commercial Litigation; Construction Litigation. ***Email:*** ryanadams@shirley-adams.com

A. GRAHAM SHIRLEY, born Sioux City, Iowa, March 30, 1963; admitted to bar, 1988, North Carolina. *Education:* Virginia Military Institute (B.A., History, with distinction and honors, 1985); Marshall-Wythe School of Law, College of William & Mary (J.D., 1988). Order of the Coif. *Member:* North Carolina (Member: Sections on: Construction Law; Litigation) and American (Member, Fidelity and Surety Law Committee, Construction Law Section) Bar Associations; North Carolina State Bar. [Capt., U.S. Army, JAGC, 1988-1993]. ***PRACTICE AREAS:*** Commercial Litigation; Construction Defects; Construction Law; Surety Law. ***Email:*** grahamshirley@shirley-adams.com

STEPHEN RUSSELL SIMMONS ATTORNEY AND COUNSELLOR AT LAW

19 WEST HARGETT STREET, SUITE 202
RALEIGH, NORTH CAROLINA 27601
Telephone: 919-839-5533
Fax: 919-839-0115
URL: http://www.srsimmonslaw.com
URL: http://www.srsimmons.com

Criminal Law, Traffic Violations, Driving While Intoxicated, Speeding Tickets, Driving While License Revoked.

STEPHEN RUSSELL SIMMONS, born Winston-Salem, North Carolina, November 24, 1956; admitted to bar, 1989, North Carolina. *Education:* North Carolina State University (B.S., 1980); University of Texas at Austin (J.D., 1987). *Member:* North Carolina and American Bar Associations. ***PRACTICE AREAS:*** Criminal Law; Traffic Violations; Driving While Intoxicated; Drivers License Suspension.

LAW OFFICES OF STEVEN D. SIMPSON, P.A.

Established in 1998

LANDMARK CENTER II
4601 SIX FORKS ROAD, SUITE 530
RALEIGH, NORTH CAROLINA 27609
Telephone: 919-788-9677
Telefax: 919-788-0775
Email: s.simpsonlaw@verizon.net
URL: http://www.ssimpsonlaw.com

Taxation, Nonprofit and Charitable Organizations, Tax Exempt Organizations, Municipal Finance, Health Care Law.

FIRM PROFILE: Law Offices of Steven D. Simpson, P.A., maintains a general federal and state tax practice, with an emphasis upon tax-exempt organizations, charitable giving and health care law.

STEVEN D. SIMPSON, born Sturgis, MI, September 20, 1953; admitted to bar, 1978, Florida; 1980, District of Columbia; 1984, North Carolina; U.S. Supreme Court. *Education:* Hillsdale College (B.A., cum laude, 1975); Wake Forest University (J.D., 19 78); Georgetown University (LL.M. in Taxation, 1981). Author: "Tax -Exempt Organizations: Organization and Operational Requirements," Tax Management Portfolio No. 869 (2000); "Tax-Exempt Organizations: Reporting, Disclosure and Other Procedural Aspects," Tax Management Portfolio No. 870-2d (2000); "Private Foundations: Taxable Expenditures," Tax Management Portfolio No. 877 (2000); Tax Compliance for Tax-Exempt Organizations (Aspen 2005). "When Will Corporate Sponsorship Create UBIT Liability?" 4 J. Tax. of Exempt Organizations 3 (Nov./Dec. 1992); "The Effect of the Revenue Act of 1987 on Political Campaign Activities of Public Charities," 13 Tax Management Estates, Gifts and Trusts Journal 94, 1988; "Income-Producing Activities of Tax-Exempt Organizations: The Myth of Unfair Competition," 12 Tax Management Estates, Gifts and Trusts Journal 137, 1987; "Taxation of Income from Advertising in Exempt Organizations' Publications," 10 Tax Management Estates, Gifts and Trusts Journal 184,1985. Co-Author: "Lobbying by Public Charities Under the IRS Proposed Regulations: We Know Lobbying When We See It," 12 Tax Management Estates, Gifts and Trusts Journal 39, 1987; "Is Income of Exempt Scientific Research Organization From Unrelated Business?" 64 Journal of Taxation 210, 1986. Member: American Society of Association Executives; Association Executives of North Carolina. *Member:* North Carolina (Member, Health Law Section Council, 1992-1995) and American (Member, Sections on: Taxation, Committee on Exempt Organizations; Co-Chair, Subcommittee on Important Developments, 1998—) Bar Associations.

(This Listing Continued)

LAW OFFICES OF STEVEN D. SIMPSON, P.A., Raleigh—Continued

PRACTICE AREAS: Taxation; Nonprofit and Charitable Organizations; Tax-Exempt Organizations; Municipal Finance; Health Care Law. ***Email:*** s.simpsonlaw@verizon.net

SINK & POTTER, L.L.P.

115 SOUTH ST. MARY'S STREET
P.O. BOX 1471
RALEIGH, NORTH CAROLINA 27602
Telephone: 919-828-0684
Fax: 919-828-5386
URL: http://www.lawyers.com/sink&potter
Mailing Address: P.O. Box 1471, Raleigh, NC 27602

Alcoholic Beverage Control Law, Legislative Representation, and Administrative Law, Estate Planning, Probate, and Trusts, Corporation Matters, Real Estate Law, Health Law.

MEMBERS OF FIRM

HENRY H. SINK (1918-1989)

HENRY H. SINK, JR., born Raleigh, North Carolina, August 30, 1947; admitted to bar, 1972, North Carolina. *Education:* University of North Carolina (A.B., 1969; J.D., 1972). Scholarship, University of Gottingen, Germany, 1969-1970. Phi Alpha Delta. *Member:* Wake County and North Carolina Bar Associations; The North Carolina State Bar. ***PRACTICE AREAS:*** Real Estate Law; Trusts and Estates; Wills; Probate. ***Email:*** henry@sinkpotter.com

WILLIAM H. POTTER, JR., born Morehead City, North Carolina, October 5, 1943; admitted to bar, 1969, North Carolina. *Education:* University of North Carolina (A.B., 1966; J.D., 1969). Phi Delta Phi (Reporter, 1967-1968). Author: "Services to the North Carolina General Assembly," published by the Institute of Government at the University of North Carolina in Popular Government, 1975. Director of Research, North Carolina General Assembly, 1974-1978. *Member:* Wake County, North Carolina and American Bar Associations; North Carolina State Bar. ***PRACTICE AREAS:*** Legislative Representation Law; Health Law; Corporations Law; Administrative Law; Alcoholic Beverage Control Matters.

REPRESENTATIVE CLIENTS: NC Dental Society; Carolinas/Assn. of Water Companies; N.C. Physical Therapy Association; Valentine Investments; Hillsborough Ventures, L.L.C.
APPROVED ATTORNEYS FOR: Lawyers Title Insurance Corp.; American Title Insurance Co.; Commonwealth Land Title Insurance Co.; Chicago Title Insurance Co.; Security Union Title Insurance Co.
REFERENCE: Centura Bank.

SMITH, ANDERSON, BLOUNT, DORSETT, MITCHELL & JERNIGAN, L.L.P.

Established in 1912
2500 FIRST UNION CAPITOL CENTER
P.O. BOX 2611
RALEIGH, NORTH CAROLINA 27602-2611
Telephone: 919-821-1220
Telecopier: 919-821-6800
Email: info@smithlaw.com
URL: http://www.smithlaw.com

Administrative Hearings and Appeals, Administrative Law, Admiralty and Maritime, Agricultural Law, Alternative Dispute Resolution, Antitrust and Trade Regulation, Appellate Practice, Asset Based Finance, Aviation and Aerospace, Bankruptcy, Banks and Banking, Biotechnology, Blue Sky Law, Business Law, Capital Markets, Civil Practice, Civil Rights, Closely Held Business Law, Collections, Commercial Law, Commercial Real Estate, Communications and Media, Complex and Multi-District Litigation, Computers and Software, Construction Law, Contracts, Copyrights, Corporate Law, Creditors Rights, Disabilities, Eminent Domain, Employee Benefits, Employment Discrimination, Employment Law, Energy, Environmental Law, Equipment Finance and Leasing, ERISA, Fidelity and Surety, Finance, Franchises and Franchising, General Practice, Government, Health Care, Hospital Law, Insurance, Insurance Defense, Intellectual Property, International Law, International Trade, Internet Law, Investments, Joint Ventures, Labor and Employment, Leases and Leasing, Legal Ethics and Professional Responsibility, Libel, Slander and Defamation, Litigation, Lobbying, Media Law, Medical Malpractice, Medicare and Medicaid, Mergers, Acquisitions and Divestitures, Mortgages, Nonprofit and Charitable Organizations, Mortgage Securitization, Partnership Law, Personal Injury, Premises Liability, Privatizations, Probate, Products Liability, Professional Liability, Property Law, Real Estate, Real Property, Regulatory Law, Secured Transactions, Securities, Taxation, Technology and Science, Torts, Technology Joint Ventures, Trade and Professional Associations, Trade Secrets, Trademark Infringement, Trademark Licensing, Trademark Litigation, Trademark Registration, Trademarks, Trusts and Estates, Utility Law, Wills, Workers Compensation.

FIRM PROFILE: For almost 90 years, Smith Anderson has provided high-quality legal services to a wide spectrum of clients. Continuing that tradition, our lawyers have developed significant expertise and broad experience in complex legal matters in order to help clients achieve their business goals.

Our clients include some of the largest financial institutions, insurance companies, public utilities, media enterprises, retailers, and manufacturing companies in our region and the nation. We also represent trade and professional associations and their members, small and medium-size businesses, and individuals. We understand the needs of the emerging growth and technology companies which bring so much economic vitality to our area.

(This Listing Continued)

We have assembled an excellent group of lawyers to serve the legal needs of our clients. Each lawyer concentrates in a few specific practice areas. When complex transactions or litigation require it, we bring together the knowledge and talents of lawyers with diverse expertise to meet the client's objectives efficiently. Knowing that costs are important to our clients, we are fully committed to understanding our clients' legal matters and resolving them in a cost-effective manner.

OF COUNSEL

W. LINVILLE ROACH, born Norlina, North Carolina, October 8, 1931; admitted to bar, 1955, North Carolina. *Education:* Wake Forest University (B.S., 1953; J.D., 1955). Senior Vice President and General Counsel, Jefferson-Pilot Life Insurance Company, 1987-1988. Attorney, 1959-1971, General Counsel, 1971-1986, Senior Vice President, 1986 and Member, Board of Directors, 1986, Pilot Life Insurance Company. Member, Board of Trustees; Wake Forest University, 1978-1982; Southern Baptist Theological Seminary, 1973-1984. Member, Executive Committee, North Carolina Insurance Education Foundation, 1976-1990. Member, 1970— and Member, Board of Governors, 1984-1988, American Life Insurance Counsel. Representative on Board of Directors, 1974-1988 and Chairman, 1979-1988, North Carolina Life and Health and Accident Insurance Guaranty Association. Member, South Carolina Life and Health Insurance Guaranty Association, 1987-1988. Member, Board of Directors, National Organization of Life and Health Insurance Guaranty Association, 1983-1987. *Member:* Wake County, North Carolina and American Bar Associations; North Carolina State Bar. [Lt. Comdr., USNR, active duty, 1955-1958]. ***PRACTICE AREAS:*** Administrative Law; Insurance Regulation; Government Relations.

PHILIP R. TRACY, born Lincoln, Nebraska, February 13, 1942; admitted to bar, 1967, District of Columbia; 1976, North Carolina. *Education:* University of Nebraska (B.A., 1963); George Washington University (J.D., 1966). President, Chief Executive Officer and Board Member, 1989-1995, Assistant General Counsel, 1974-1981, Secretary and General Counsel, 1981-1989, Vice President and Member, Board of Directors, 1983-1989, Burroughs Wellcome Co. Member: Board of Directors, Wellcome Plc and the Wellcome Foundation Limited, 1989-1995; The Burroughs Wellcome Fund, 1989—; Pharmaceutical Research and Manufacturers Association, 1989-1995; Non-prescription Drug Manufacturers Association, 1989-1993; North Carolina Citizens for Business and Industry, 1989-1995; Board of Trustees, North Carolina Museum of Art, 1990-1995; Board of Visitors, Duke University Medical Center, 1993-2001; Board of Visitors, University of North Carolina at Chapel Hill, 1992-1996; Board of Advisors, George Washington University Law School, 1996—. *Member:* Wake County, North Carolina and American Bar Associations; District of Columbia Bar; North Carolina State Bar. ***PRACTICE AREAS:*** Technology and Science; Corporate Law; Venture Capital. ***Email:*** ptracy@smithlaw.com

DWIGHT W. ALLEN, born Goldsboro, North Carolina, April 9, 1946; admitted to bar, 1973, North Carolina. *Education:* University of North Carolina at Chapel Hill (B.A., 1968); Wake Forest University (J.D., 1973). *Member:* Wake County, North Carolina and American Bar Associations; North Carolina State Bar. [U.S. Army, 1969-1971]. ***PRACTICE AREAS:*** Telecommunications Law; Public Utility Law. ***Email:*** dallen@smithlaw.com

MEMBERS OF FIRM

WILLIS SMITH (1887-1953)

OSCAR LEACH (1887-1967)

WILLIS SMITH, JR. (1921-1971)

JOHN H. ANDERSON (1907-1990)

JAMES K. DORSETT, JR. (1916-2001)

LEE C. SMITH, born Biltmore, North Carolina, July 15, 1926; admitted to bar, 1953, North Carolina. *Education:* Duke University (A.B., 1950; LL.B., 1953). Delta Theta Phi. Attorney, Office of Chief Counsel, U.S. Treasury Department, 1953-1957. Chairman, 1966-1969 and Member, 1973-1977, North Carolina State Board of Elections. *Member:* Wake County, North Carolina and American Bar Associations; The North Carolina State Bar. ***PRACTICE AREAS:*** Trusts and Estates; Administrative Law; Corporate Law.

JAMES D. BLOUNT, JR., born Wilson, North Carolina, January 2, 1927; admitted to bar, 1952, North Carolina. *Education:* University of North Carolina (A.B., 1950; J.D., 1952). Phi Alpha Delta. Listed in The Best Lawyers in America. Member of Staff, North Carolina Law Review, 1952. Member, Judicial Conference, Fourth Circuit Court of Appeals, 1970—. *Member:* Wake County, North Carolina and American Bar Associations; The North Carolina State Bar; International Association of Defense Counsel; American Judicature Society; North Carolina Association of Defense Attorneys (Charter Member); American Board of Trial Advocates. Fellow: American College of Trial Lawyers; American Bar Foundation. ***PRACTICE AREAS:*** Commercial Litigation; Products Liability Defense; Professional Liability Defense. ***Email:*** jblount@smithlaw.com

HENRY A. MITCHELL, JR., born High Point, North Carolina, October 18, 1935; admitted to bar, 1961, North Carolina. *Education:* Guilford College (A.B., 1957); Wake Forest University (J.D., 1961). Phi Delta Phi (President, Ruffin Inn Chapter, 1960-1961). Law Clerk to Chief Judge, U.S. District Court for the Middle District of North Carolina, 1961-1962. Deputy General Counsel, Export Import Bank of the U.S., 1970-1971. Chairman: Lawyers Mutual Liability Insurance Company of North Carolina, 1985—. Member of Board of Directors of Georgia Lawyer Insurance Company. Former Member, Board of Law Examiners of the State of North Carolina. Director, North Carolina Citizens for Business and Industry, 1999—. Trustee, North Carolina Symphony, 1992—. *Member:* Wake County, North Carolina (Vice President and Member of Board of Governors 2003—) and American Bar Associations; The North Carolina State Bar; American Counsel Association (President, 1990-1991). Fellow (Chair of North Carolina Fellows 2003—), American Bar Foundation. ***PRACTICE AREAS:*** Corporate Law; Insurance Law; Insurance Regulation; Administrative Law. ***Email:*** hmitchell@smithlaw.com

JOHN L. JERNIGAN, born Atlanta, Georgia, May 29, 1942; admitted to bar, 1967, North Carolina. *Education:* Davidson College (A.B., 1964); University of North Carolina (J.D., 1967). Phi Delta Phi. Listed in The Best Lawyers in America. Chairman, District Bar Candidate Committee of The Board of Law Examiners of the State of North Carolina, 1978-

(This Listing Continued)

1983. Member, Davidson College Board of Visitors, 1986—. Member, Board of Trustees: North Carolina Symphony Foundation, 1982-1991; Choate Rosemary Hall School, 1989-1992; Board of Advisors, Banking Law Institute, University of North Carolina School of Law. *Member:* Wake County (Member, Executive Committee, 1975-1978), North Carolina (Chairman, Business Law Section, 1985-1987; Member, Board of Governors, 1989-1992; Member, Executive Committee, 1989-1991; Chairman, Bar Center Cabinet, 1994-1998; President, 1999-2000) and American Bar Associations; North Carolina State Bar; American Judicature Society; American Counsel Association. Fellow, American College of Mortgage Attorneys. [Capt., ADA, USAR, active duty, 1967-1969]. ***PRACTICE AREAS:*** Corporate Law; Banks and Banking; Mergers, Acquisitions and Divestitures. ***Email:*** jjernigan@smithlaw.com

SAMUEL G. THOMPSON, born Wilson, North Carolina, September 18, 1943; admitted to bar, 1968, North Carolina. *Education:* University of North Carolina (B.S., 1965; J.D., 1968). Phi Delta Phi (President, 1967-1968). *Member:* Wake County, North Carolina and American Bar Associations; The North Carolina State Bar; Defense Research and Trial Lawyers Association; International Association of Defense Counsel; North Carolina Association of Defense Attorneys (President, 1986-1987). ***PRACTICE AREAS:*** Medical Malpractice Defense; Insurance Defense. ***Email:*** sthompson@smithlaw.com

CLAUDE ERNEST SIMONS, JR., born Wilson, North Carolina, October 6, 1945; admitted to bar, 1971, North Carolina. *Education:* Wake Forest University (B.A., 1968; J.D., 1971). Phi Delta Phi (Magister, Ruffin Inn Chapter, 1970-1971). Author: "Pleading Requirements Under Rule 8(a)(1) of the North Carolina Rules of Civil Procedure," 7 Wake Forest Law Review 483, June, 1971. Law Clerk to Justice I. Beverly Lake, North Carolina Supreme Court, 1971-1972. *Member:* Wake County, North Carolina and American Bar Associations; North Carolina State Bar; North Carolina Association of Defense Attorneys (Charter Member). ***PRACTICE AREAS:*** Medical Malpractice Defense; Products Liability Defense; Workers Compensation; Construction Law; Professional Liability Defense. ***Email:*** csimons@smithlaw.com

MICHAEL E. WEDDINGTON, born Detroit, Michigan, March 1, 1941; admitted to bar, 1973, North Carolina. *Education:* University of Florida (B.S., 1963); Duke University (J.D., 1973). State Certified, Mediator, 1994. State Certified, Arbitrator, 1996. Certified NASD Regulation Arbitrator, 1998. *Member:* Wake County (Member, Board of Directors: 2002—; Member, Grievance Committee: 2002—), North Carolina and American Bar Associations; The North Carolina State Bar. [Comdr., USNR (Ret.); active duty, 1966-1970]. ***PRACTICE AREAS:*** Commercial Litigation; Construction and Surety Litigation; Intellectual Property Law; Administrative Law; Appellate Practice. ***Email:*** mweddington@smithlaw.com

CARL N. PATTERSON, JR., born Durham, North Carolina, March 18, 1951; admitted to bar, 1976, North Carolina. *Education:* Davidson College (B.A., 1973); University of North Carolina (J.D., with honors, 1976). Phi Delta Phi (Magister, Vance Inn Chapter, 1975-1976). Member of Staff, North Carolina Law Review, 1975-1976. Chairman, Raleigh area Davidson College Alumni Admissions Program, 1981-1988. *Member:* Wake County, North Carolina (Member, Executive Council, 1980-1989 and Chairman, 1987-1988, Young Lawyers Division) and American Bar Associations; North Carolina State Bar; American Judicature Society. ***PRACTICE AREAS:*** Corporate Law; Complex Corporate and Commercial Litigation. ***Email:*** cpatterson@smithlaw.com

JAMES K. DORSETT, III, born Raleigh, North Carolina, November 10, 1951; admitted to bar, 1977, North Carolina. *Education:* Davidson College (B.A., 1974); Wake Forest University (J.D., 1977). Phi Delta Phi (Vice Magister, Ruffin Inn Chapter, 1976-1977). Member, Board of Directors, Legal Services of North Carolina, 1997-1998. *Member:* Wake County (Member, Board of Directors: 1982-1984, 1988-1990; Volunteer Lawyers Program, 1990-1993), North Carolina and American (Member, House of Delegates)Bar Associations; North Carolina State Bar (President, 2002—; Councilor, 1992—; Chairman, Grievance Committee); American Counsel Association (Member, Board of Governors; President-Elect); North Carolina Association of Defense Attorneys; American Board of Trial Advocates. ***PRACTICE AREAS:*** Commercial Litigation; Products Liability Defense; Personal Injury. ***Email:*** jdorsett@smithlaw.com

ROBERT MARKS ARNOLD, born Rocky Mount, North Carolina, April 4, 1951; admitted to bar, 1978, North Carolina. *Education:* Woodberry Forest School; Princeton University (B.A., 1973); Wake Forest University (J.D., 1978). Member, Wake Forest Law Review, 1976-1978. Law Clerk to Justice Joseph Branch, North Carolina Supreme Court, 1978-1979. *Member:* Wake County, North Carolina and American Bar Associations; North Carolina State Bar. ***PRACTICE AREAS:*** Corporate Law; Commercial Law; Mergers, Acquisitions and Divestitures. ***Email:*** marnold@smithlaw.com

WALTER R. ROGERS, JR., born Henderson, North Carolina, June 5, 1952; admitted to bar, 1977, Georgia; 1979, Virginia; 1984, North Carolina. *Education:* Duke University (B.A., summa cum laude, 1974); Stanford University (J.D., 1977). Phi Beta Kappa. *Member:* Wake County, North Carolina Bar Association (Chairman, Tax Section, 2000-2001); American Bar Association; North Carolina State Bar; Virginia State Bar; State Bar of Georgia. ***PRACTICE AREAS:*** Business Law; Taxation; Trusts and Estates; Nonprofit and Charitable Organizations. ***Email:*** wrogers@smithlaw.com

JULIAN D. BOBBITT, JR., born Rocky Mount, North Carolina, October 2, 1951; admitted to bar, 1977, West Virginia; 1981, North Carolina. *Education:* University of North Carolina (B.A., 1973); University of Virginia (J.D., 1977). *Member:* Wake County, North Carolina and American Bar Associations; North Carolina State Bar; West Virginia State Bar; American Society of Medical Association Counsel; American Health Lawyers Association; North Carolina Board of Legal Specialization (Member, Health Law Committee); North Carolina Society of Health Care Attorneys. ***PRACTICE AREAS:*** Health Care; Administrative Law. ***Email:*** bbobbitt@smithlaw.com

ROBIN KENTON VINSON, born Goldsboro, North Carolina, July 10, 1954; admitted to bar, 1979, North Carolina. *Education:* Wake Forest University (B.A., cum laude, 1976; J.D., 1979). Phi Delta Phi; Omicron Delta Kappa. Member, Wake Forest Law Review, 1977-1979. Author: "Intestate Succession: *Newlin v. Gill*—Limitation of Collateral Inheritance in North Carolina," 14 Wake Forest Law Review 1085 (1978); "Evidence: The State of Mind Exception to the Hearsay Rule—*United States v. Jenkins*," 15 Wake Forest Law Review 431 (1979). Law Clerk to Chief Judge Naomi E. Morris, North Carolina Court of Appeals, Raleigh, North Carolina, 1979-1980. *Member:* Wake County, North Carolina (Council Member and Officer, Section on Antitrust and Trade Regulation) and American (Member, Sections on: Health Law; Litigation; Antitrust Law; Health Law, Antitrust and Business Torts Committees) Bar Associations; North Carolina State Bar. ***PRACTICE AREAS:*** Corporate Law; Commercial Litigation; Antitrust and Trade Regulation; Health Care. ***Email:*** rvinson@smithlaw.com

STEVEN M. SARTORIO, born New York, N.Y., August 2, 1955; admitted to bar, 1981, North Carolina. *Education:* University of North Carolina (B.A., 1977); Wake Forest University (J.D., 1981). Member, Moot Court Board. *Member:* Wake County, North Carolina and American Bar Associations; North Carolina State Bar. ***PRACTICE AREAS:*** Products Liability Defense; Insurance Defense; Workers Compensation; Condemnation. ***Email:*** ssartorio@smithlaw.com

SUSAN MILNER PARKER, born Durham, North Carolina, November 13, 1951; admitted to bar, 1981, North Carolina. *Education:* Duke University (B.A., cum laude, 1974); University of North Carolina (M.P.H., 1978); University of North Carolina School of Law and Vermont Law School (J.D., with honors, 1981). Staff Member, Vermont Law Review, 1979-1980. *Member:* Wake County, North Carolina and American Bar Associations; North Carolina State Bar. ***PRACTICE AREAS:*** Labor and Employment; Appellate Practice; Administrative Law. ***Email:*** sparker@smithlaw.com

TIMOTHY P. LEHAN, born Schenectady, New York, March 2, 1951; admitted to bar, 1982, North Carolina. *Education:* Belmont Abbey College (B.A., cum laude, 1973); University of North Carolina (J.D., 1981). Member: Order of the Barristers; Holderness Moot Court Bench. *Member:* Wake County, North Carolina and American Bar Associations; North Carolina State Bar; North Carolina Association of Defense Attorneys; International Association of Defense Counsel; Defense Research Institute. ***PRACTICE AREAS:*** Medical Malpractice Defense; Products Liability Defense. ***Email:*** tlehan@smithlaw.com

AMOS U. PRIESTER, IV, born La Grange, Georgia, December 17, 1956; admitted to bar, 1982, North Carolina. *Education:* University of North Carolina (B.S., 1979; J.D., 1982). *Member:* Wake County, North Carolina (Member, Sections on: Bankruptcy, Council Member, 1992-1995, Nominations Committee, 1995-1996; Chairman, Legislative Committee, 1998-1999, and Business Law) and American (Member, Sections on: Corporation Banking and Business Law) Bar Associations; North Carolina State Bar; American Bankruptcy Institute; Turnaround Management Association. ***PRACTICE AREAS:*** Bankruptcy; Business Law; Mergers, Acquisitions and Divestitures. ***Email:*** apriester@smithlaw.com

GERALD F. ROACH, born Las Vegas, Nevada, April 24, 1958; admitted to bar, 1982, North Carolina. *Education:* Wake Forest University (B.A., cum laude, 1980; J.D., cum laude, 1982). Honorary Member, Scribes, 1983-1984. Notes and Comments Editor, Wake Forest Law Review, 1981-1982. Author: Comment, "Regulating the Sale of Franchises: The Business Opportunity Approach," 17 Wake Forest Law Review, 623, 1981. Member: Wake Forest University Law Alumni Council, 1986-1990; Wake Forest University Alumni Council, 1996-2000. Member, Board of Directors, Council for Entrepreneurial Development, 1988-1992, 1994-1996. Member, North Carolina Commission on Business and the Economy, 1994-2000. Member, Securities Advisory Council of the North Carolina Secretary of State, 1991-1992, 1994-1995. Founding Director, Triangle Chapter of Association for Corporate Growth. *Member:* Wake County, North Carolina (Member, Business Law Section; Chairman, 1993-1995; Vice Chairman, 1991-1993; Council Member, 1988-1991; Chairman, Securities Regulation Committee, 1987-1989; Chairman, Continuing Legal Education Committee, 1989-1990; Member, Appellate Survey Committee, 1983-1984) and American (Member: Business Section; Venture Capital and Private Equity Committee; Forum Committee on Franchising) Bar Associations; North Carolina State Bar. ***PRACTICE AREAS:*** Securities; Corporate Law; Mergers, Acquisitions and Divestitures; Technology and Science; Investments. ***Email:*** groach@smithlaw.com

FRANCIS C. BAGBEY, born Roanoke, Virginia, October 31, 1949; admitted to bar, 1980, New Jersey; 1983, North Carolina. *Education:* Princeton University (A.B., 1975); Marshall-Wythe School of Law, College of William & Mary (J.D., 1980). Professional Articles Editor, William & Mary Law Review, 1979-1980. *Member:* Wake County, North Carolina and American Bar Associations; North Carolina State Bar. ***PRACTICE AREAS:*** Commercial Real Estate. ***Email:*** fbagbey@smithlaw.com

R. DONAVON MUNFORD, JR., born Raleigh, North Carolina, August 15, 1954; admitted to bar, 1979, North Carolina; 1981, U.S. Tax Court. *Education:* Davidson College (A.B., 1976); University of North Carolina (J.D., 1979). Phi Delta Phi. Member, North Carolina House of Representatives, 2003-2004. *Member:* Wake County (Chairman, Young Lawyers Division, 1985; Member, Board of Directors, 1997-1998), North Carolina (Chairman, Young Lawyers Division, 1990-1991; Chairman, Development Committee, 1999-2001; Council, Estate Planning and Fiduciary Law Section, 1996-1999) and American (Member, Young Lawyers Division House of Delegates, 1990-1991) Bar Associations; North Carolina State Bar (Member, Board of Continuing Legal Education, 1991-1997); North Carolina Association of Certified Public Accountants; American Institute of Certified Public Accountants; American Counsel Association. ***PRACTICE AREAS:*** Business Law; Nonprofit Organizations; Philanthropic Planning; Trusts and Estates; Asset Protection Planning. ***Email:*** dmunford@smithlaw.com

JOHN D. MADDEN, born Lansing, Michigan, May 17, 1957; admitted to bar, 1983, North Carolina. *Education:* Davidson College (B.A., 1979); Wake Forest University (J.D., 1983). Member, Wake Forest Moot Court Board, 1981-1983; Chief Justice, 1982-1983. Member, Wake Forest Law Review, 1981-1983. Member, Order of Barristers. Recipient, North Carolina Academy of Trial Lawyers Award. *Member:* Wake County (President, Young Lawyers Division, 1987), North Carolina and American Bar Associations; North Carolina State Bar; North Carolina Association of Defense Attorneys; Defense Research Institute. ***PRACTICE AREAS:*** Medical Malpractice Defense; Commercial Litigation; Products Liability Litigation. ***Email:*** jmadden@smithlaw.com

MARK A. ASH, born Phoenix, Arizona, February 22, 1953; admitted to bar, 1979, Massachusetts; 1987, North Carolina. *Education:* Harvard College (A.B., 1975); University of Virginia (J.D., 1978). Bigelow Fellow, University of Chicago School of Law (1979). *Member:* Wake County, North Carolina, Massachusetts and American Bar Associations; North Carolina State Bar. ***PRACTICE AREAS:*** Commercial Litigation; Employment Litigation; Trade Secrets Litigation; Unfair Competition; Products Liability; Aviation Accidents. ***Email:*** mash@smithlaw.com

(This Listing Continued)

SMITH, ANDERSON, BLOUNT, DORSETT, MITCHELL & JERNIGAN, L.L.P., Raleigh—Continued

C. STEVEN MASON, born Columbia, South Carolina, March 1, 1956; admitted to bar, 1981, North Carolina. *Education:* University of North Carolina (B.A., with highest honors, 1978); University of Virginia (J.D., 1981). Phi Beta Kappa. Order of the Coif. Morehead Scholar. Notes Editor, Virginia Law Review, 1980-1981. *Member:* Wake County, North Carolina and American Bar Associations; North Carolina State Bar. ***PRACTICE AREAS:*** Commercial Real Estate; Banking; Commercial Law. ***Email:*** smason@smithlaw.com

ROSEMARY GILL KENYON, born Syracuse, New York, May 3, 1954; admitted to bar, 1979, Michigan; 1980, Virginia; 1986, North Carolina. *Education:* Saint Mary's College, Notre Dame, Indiana (B.A., magna cum laude, 1976); University of Notre Dame (J.D., 1979). Member, Moot Court Team. Law Clerk, The Honorable W. Earl Britt, U.S. District Judge for the Eastern District of North Carolina, 1985-1986. *Member:* Wake County, North Carolina (Chair, Committee on Women in the Profession, 2001—; Chair, Dispute Resolution Section, 1995-1996; Council, Corporate Counsel Section, 1989-1996, Labor and Employment Law Section) and American (Labor and Employment Law Section, Individual Rights and Responsibility Committee) Bar Associations; Virginia State Bar; State Bar of Michigan; North Carolina State Bar. ***PRACTICE AREAS:*** Labor and Employment; Commercial Litigation. ***Email:*** rkenyon@smithlaw.com

DONALD H. TUCKER, JR., born New York, N.Y., August 3, 1959; admitted to bar, 1984, North Carolina. *Education:* Duke University (B.A., magna cum laude, 1981); University of North Carolina (J.D., 1984). Phi Delta Phi. Member, Holderness Moot Court Bench, 1983-1984. National Advisory Board, Duke Children's Hospital, 2003—. *Member:* Wake County, North Carolina and American Bar Associations; North Carolina State Bar. ***PRACTICE AREAS:*** Commercial Litigation; Trade Secrets Litigation. ***Email:*** dtucker@smithlaw.com

WILLIAM H. MOSS, born Raleigh, North Carolina, June 13, 1956; admitted to bar, 1984, North Carolina. *Education:* University of North Carolina (B.A., 1978; J.D., 1984). Member, Order of the Golden Fleece. Member: Holderness Moot Court Bench, 1983-1984; International Law Moot Court Team (Jessup Competition), 1983-1984. *Member:* Wake County, North Carolina and American Bar Associations; North Carolina State Bar. ***PRACTICE AREAS:*** Medical Malpractice Defense; Products Liability Defense; Commercial Litigation; Media Law. ***Email:*** wmoss@smithlaw.com

MICHAEL W. HUBBARD, born Newport News, Virginia, April 28, 1959; admitted to bar, 1984, Virginia; 1986, North Carolina. *Education:* Randolph-Macon College (B.S. in Chemistry, 1981); University of Virginia (J.D., 1984). Research Editor, Virginia Tax Review, 1983-1984. Co-Author: American Medical Association's Field Guide to HIPAA Implementation (AMA Press 2002); American Medical Association's HIPAA Policies and Procedures Desk Reference, (AMA Press 2003). *Member:* Wake County, North Carolina and American Bar Associations; North Carolina State Bar; Virginia State Bar; American Health Lawyers Association; North Carolina Society of Health Care Attorneys, Inc. (Board of Directors); North Carolina Healthcare Information and Communications Alliance, Inc. (Assistant Secretary). ***PRACTICE AREAS:*** Health Law; HIPAA; Health Insurance Portability and Accountability Act (HIPAA); Health Informatics; e-Health; Insurance Transactions; Insurance Regulation. ***Email:*** mhubbard@smithlaw.com

KIMBERLY J. KORANDO, born Carbondale, Illinois, July 17, 1959; admitted to bar, 1986, North Carolina; 1989, U.S. Court of Appeals, Fourth Circuit; 1991, U.S. Supreme Court. *Education:* University of Oklahoma (B.S., in Psychology, 1980; J.D., with honors, 1986). Notes Editor, Oklahoma Law Review, 1984-1986. Author: Note, "Dismissal for Sexual Conduct: Are Police Officers Held to A Higher Standard Than Other Employees?" Oklahoma Law Review, Vol. 38-2, 1985. Employment Discrimination Law, BNA Chapter Editor, Chp.33 Litigation Procedure (3rd Cum. Suppl.). Lecturer, Human Resources, Peace College, Raleigh, North Carolina (2001). Advisory Board, Peace College Human Resources Degree Program (2001—). Chair, 2001-2003, and Member, 1997—, Board of Directors: Easter Seals North Carolina. *Member:* Wake County, North Carolina (Member, Labor and Employment Law Section; Co-Editor, Section Newsletter, 1993-1995) and American (Member: Equal Employment Opportunity Committee, Labor and Employment Law Section, 1990—; Disability Subcommittee, 1992—) Bar Associations; North Carolina State Bar; Defense Research Institute (Member, Employment Law Committee, 1994—). ***PRACTICE AREAS:*** Labor and Employment. ***Email:*** kkorando@smithlaw.com

WILLIAM T. BARNETT, JR., born Macon, Georgia, August 31, 1957; admitted to bar, 1985, North Carolina. *Education:* Davidson College (B.A., 1979); University of North Carolina (J.D., with honors, 1985). Member: The Order of Barristers; North Carolina Moot Court Bench and National Moot Court Competition Team, 1984-1985. Staff Assistant to U.S. Senator Sam Nunn, 1980-1982. *Member:* Wake County, North Carolina (Member, Health Law Section Council, 1996-1999) and American Bar Associations; North Carolina State Bar; American Health Lawyers Association. ***PRACTICE AREAS:*** Insurance Regulation; Health Care; Business Law. ***Email:*** wbarnett@smithlaw.com

DAVID TODD BUCKINGHAM, born Tampa, Florida, December 6, 1957; admitted to bar, 1984, Texas; 1987, Maryland; 1988, District of Columbia; 1989, North Carolina. *Education:* Duke University (B.A., 1980; J.D., 1983). External Examiner, Duke University School of Law, 1986-1990. *Member:* Wake County, Maryland State, North Carolina and American Bar Associations; State Bar of Texas; The District of Columbia Bar; North Carolina State Bar. ***PRACTICE AREAS:*** Commercial Real Estate; Secured Lending. ***Email:*** dbuckingham@smithlaw.com

BYRON B. KIRKLAND, born Wilson, North Carolina, March 29, 1961; admitted to bar, 1987, North Carolina. *Education:* University of North Carolina (B.A., 1983; J.D., with honors, 1987; M.B.A., 1987). Phi Delta Phi. North Carolina Journal of International Law and Commercial Regulation, 1985-1987. Member, Board of Directors, Council for Entrepreneurial Development, 2000—. *Member:* Wake County, North Carolina (Chair, Young Lawyers Division, 1996-1997; Member, and Chair, 2001—, Business Law Section, Securities Regulation Committee) and American (Member, Business Law Section Council, 1997-1999; Representative, Young Lawyers Division, District 9, North Carolina, 1992-1994) Bar Associations; North Carolina State Bar. ***PRACTICE AREAS:*** Securities; Corporate Law; Venture Capital; Mergers, Acquisitions and Divestitures; Technology and Science. ***Email:*** bkirkland@smithlaw.com

(This Listing Continued)

CHRISTOPHER B. CAPEL, born Thomasville, North Carolina, July 3, 1957; admitted to bar, 1985, North Carolina; 1987, New York. *Education:* University of North Carolina (A.B., 1979; J.D., with honors, 1985). Note and Comment Editor, North Carolina Law Review, 1984-1985. Law Clerk to Sam J. Ervin III, U.S. Court of Appeals, Fourth Circuit, 1985-1986. *Member:* Wake County, North Carolina (Member, Business Law Section Council; Past Chairman, Business Organizations Committee; Past Chairman, Continuing Legal Education Committee), New York State and American Bar Associations; North Carolina State Bar. ***PRACTICE AREAS:*** Securities; Corporate Law; Mergers, Acquisitions and Divestitures; Venture Capital; Technology and Science; Investments. ***Email:*** ccapel@smithlaw.com

WILLIAM W. NELSON, born Tuscaloosa, Alabama, May 30, 1960; admitted to bar, 1986, California; 1991, North Carolina. *Education:* University of North Carolina (A.B., 1982; J.D., with high honors, 1985). Phi Beta Kappa. Order of the Coif. Staff Member, North Carolina Law Review, 1983-1984. Co-Author, *2002 Guidebook to North Carolina Taxes,* (CCH Incorporated 2001). *Member:* Wake County, North Carolina (Member: Tax Section Council) and American Bar Associations; State Bar of California; North Carolina State Bar. ***PRACTICE AREAS:*** Taxation; Business Law. ***Email:*** wnelson@smithlaw.com

B. DAVIS HORNE, JR., born Fayetteville, North Carolina, August 30, 1956; admitted to bar, 1984, North Carolina; 1989, U.S. District Court, Eastern District of North Carolina; U.S. Supreme Court. *Education:* Methodist College (B.A., 1978); Campbell University (J.D., with honors, 1984). Associate General Counsel/State Legislative Director North Carolina Farm Bureau, 1985-1988. Director of Governmental Affairs, North Carolina Bar Association, 1988-1992. Campaign and Transition Director, The Honorable Michael F. Easley, North Carolina Attorney General, 1992. Campaign Chair and Treasurer, Mike Easley For Governor Campaign 2000. *Member:* Wake County, North Carolina and American Bar Associations; North Carolina State Bar. ***PRACTICE AREAS:*** Administrative Law; Government Relations. ***Email:*** dhorne@smithlaw.com

LEE M. KIRBY, JR., born Arlington, Virginia, August 4, 1956; admitted to bar, 1987, New York; 1995, North Carolina. *Education:* Carleton College (B.A., magna cum laude, with distinction, 1978); Harvard University (J.D., cum laude, 1986). *Member:* Wake County, North Carolina and American Bar Associations; North Carolina State Bar. ***PRACTICE AREAS:*** Commercial Law; Banking Law; Finance Law; Mergers, Acquisitions and Divestitures. ***Email:*** lkirby@smithlaw.com

MICHAEL W. MITCHELL, born Raleigh, North Carolina, February 15, 1964; admitted to bar, 1989, North Carolina. *Education:* Wake Forest University (B.A., 1986; J.D., 1989). Editorial Staff Member, Wake Forest Law Review, 1988-1989. Law Clerk to the Hon. Frank W. Bullock, Jr., U.S. District Court, Middle District of North Carolina, 1989-1990. Author: "North Carolina Statutory Limitation on Directors' Liability," 24 W.F.L. Rev. 117 (1989). *Member:* Wake County, North Carolina and American Bar Associations; North Carolina State Bar. ***PRACTICE AREAS:*** Medical Malpractice Defense; Commercial Litigation; Products Liability Defense. ***Email:*** mmitchell@smithlaw.com

ROBERT JOSEPH MORRIS, born Marion, North Carolina, September 18, 1963; admitted to bar, 1988, North Carolina; 1990, District of Columbia. *Education:* Duke University (A.B., magna cum laude, 1985; J.D., with high honors, 1988). Order of the Coif. Staff Editor, Law and Contemporary Problems, 1987-1988. *Member:* Wake County, North Carolina (Member, Administration of Justice Task Force) and American Bar Associations; North Carolina State Bar (Advisory Member, Ethics Committee). ***PRACTICE AREAS:*** Commercial Litigation; Aviation Litigation; Intellectual Property Litigation. ***Email:*** jmorris@smithlaw.com

ROBERT E. DUGGINS, born Nashville, Tennessee, November 9, 1965; admitted to bar, 1990, North Carolina. *Education:* North Carolina State University (B.S., cum laude, 1987); University of North Carolina (J.D., with honors, 1990). Member, Order of the Coif. Recipient, William T. Joyner Award. Note and Comment Editor, North Carolina Law Review, 1989-1990. *Member:* Wake County, North Carolina and American Bar Associations; North Carolina State Bar. ***PRACTICE AREAS:*** Corporate Law; Mergers and Acquisitions; Venture Capital; Intellectual Property. ***Email:*** rduggins@smithlaw.com

PETER J. MARINO, born Syosset, New York, January 15, 1965; admitted to bar, 1990, North Carolina. *Education:* LeMoyne College (B.A., cum laude, 1987); University of North Carolina (J.D., with honors, 1990). Member, Holderness Moot Court Bench. Managing Editor and Contributing Author: "North Carolina Construction Law Deskbook." State Certified Arbitrator 10th Judicial District. Elected Member: North Carolina Bar Association Construction Council. *Member:* Wake County (Member, Legal Education Partnership Committee), North Carolina (Member, Professionalism Committee) and American Bar Associations; North Carolina State Bar. ***PRACTICE AREAS:*** Commercial Litigation; Construction; Bankruptcy Litigation. ***Email:*** pmarino@smithlaw.com

CARYN COPPEDGE McNEILL, born Olney, Maryland, December 9, 1966; admitted to bar, 1991, North Carolina. *Education:* Davidson College (B.A., with honors in English, 1988); Duke University (J.D., 1991). Omicron Delta Kappa. Samuel H. Bell Scholar; Charles A. Dana Scholar. Member: Southern Employee Benefits Conference; Triangle Benefits Forum. *Member:* Wake County, North Carolina (Member, Board of Governors, 1999-2000 and 2001-2002; Member, Tax Section Council, 1998-2002; Chair, Young Lawyers Division, 1999-2000) and American (District Representative, Young Lawyers Division, 1996-1997) Bar Associations; North Carolina State Bar. ***PRACTICE AREAS:*** Employee Benefits; Executive Compensation. ***Email:*** cmcneill@smithlaw.com

KERRY A. SHAD, born Jacksonville, Florida, January 15, 1965; admitted to bar, 1991, North Carolina. *Education:* Florida State University (B.S., 1985); University of North Carolina (J.D., with honors, 1991). Order of the Coif. Executive Articles Editor, 1990-1991, and Staff Member, 1989-1990, North Carolina Law Review. *Member:* Wake County, North Carolina and American Bar Associations; North Carolina State Bar. ***PRACTICE AREAS:*** Employment Litigation; Commercial Litigation. ***Email:*** kshad@smithlaw.com

AMY MEYERS BATTEN, born Hackensack, New Jersey, December 5, 1967; admitted to bar, 1992, North Carolina. *Education:* The Wharton School of the University of Pennsylvania (B.S., cum laude, 1989); Duke University (J.D., with honors, 1992). *Member:* Wake County, North Carolina and American Bar Associations; North Carolina State Bar. ***PRACTICE AREAS:*** Securities; Mergers, Acquisitions and Divestitures; Investments; Corporate Law. ***Email:*** ameyers@smithlaw.com

(This Listing Continued)

STEPHEN T. PARASCANDOLA, born Brooklyn, New York, August 15, 1962; admitted to bar, 1989, New York; 1991, Florida and North Carolina. *Education:* Eckerd College (B.A., 1984); Stetson University College of Law (J.D., 1988). Omicron Delta Kappa. Staff Member, Stetson Law Review, 1987-1988. *Member:* Wake County, New York State (Member: Journal Committee on Environmental Law, 1990-1994); North Carolina (Member: Environmental Law Section, 1991—; Section Council, 1996—; Real Estate Section) and American (Member, Science and Technology Law Committee) Bar Associations; The Florida Bar; North Carolina State Bar; North Carolina Association of Environmental Professionals; North Carolina Citizens for Business and Industry (Member, Environmental Concerns Committee). ***LANGUAGES:*** Italian and Spanish. ***PRACTICE AREAS:*** Environmental, Health and Safety Law; Health and Safety Law; Life Sciences Law; Commercial Real Estate; Business Law. ***Email:*** sparascandola@smithlaw.com

MICHAEL P. SABER, born Atlantic City, New Jersey, December 3, 1961; admitted to bar, 1989, Pennsylvania and New Jersey; 1997, North Carolina. *Education:* Columbia University (B.A., 1984); Emory University (J.D., 1989). *Member:* Wake County, North Carolina and American Bar Associations; North Carolina State Bar. ***PRACTICE AREAS:*** Securities; Corporate Law; Mergers, Acquisitions and Divestitures. ***Email:*** msaber@smithlaw.com

KIRK G. WARNER, born Greenville, Ohio, March 31, 1958; admitted to bar, 1983, Ohio; 1988, North Carolina. *Education:* Ohio State University (B.S., 1980); Duke University; University of Toledo (J.D., 1983); North Carolina State University (M.A., 1999). Delta Theta Phi. Member: Moot Court Board; The Order of Barristers; Jessup Moot Court Team. Assistant Ohio Special Prosecutor, 1985-1987. *Member:* Wake County, Ohio State and North Carolina Bar Associations; The North Carolina State Bar; Product Liability Advisory Council; International Association of Defense Counsel; Defense Research Institute; North Carolina Association of Defense Attorneys; International Association of Arson Investigators, Inc. [LTC., Judge Advocate General Corps., U.S. Army Reserve, 1980—]. ***PRACTICE AREAS:*** Products Liability Defense; Insurance Defense Litigation; Construction; Environmental; General Litigation. ***Email:*** kwarner@smithlaw.com

CHRISTOPHER G. SMITH, born Greenwich, Connecticut, June 1, 1965; admitted to bar, 1992, Connecticut; 1993, District of Columbia and New York; 1996, North Carolina. *Education:* University of Pennsylvania (B.A., summa cum laude, Phi Beta Kappa, 1987; J.D., cum laude, 1992). *Member:* Wake County, North Carolina, Connecticut, New York State and American Bar Associations; The District of Columbia Bar. ***PRACTICE AREAS:*** Appellate Practice; Civil Litigation; Business Law. ***Email:*** csmith@smithlaw.com

ZEBULON D. ANDERSON, born Alexandria, Virginia, September 13, 1969; admitted to bar, 1994, North Carolina. *Education:* Duke University (B.A., magna cum laude, 1990); University of Virginia (J.D., 1994). Order of the Coif. Member, Editorial Board, Virginia Law Review, 1992-1994. *Member:* Wake County, North Carolina (Member: Labor and Employment Law and Litigation Sections; Editor, Litigation Section Newsletter, 1997-1998; Member, Litigation Section Council, 1999-2001) and American (Member: Labor and Employment Law and Litigation Sections) Bar Associations; North Carolina State Bar. ***PRACTICE AREAS:*** Employment Litigation; Commercial Litigation. ***Email:*** zanderson@smithlaw.com

JASON L. MARTINEZ, born Brooklyn, New York, May 9, 1969; admitted to bar, 1994, Connecticut; 1995, New York; 1996, District of Columbia; 1997, North Carolina. *Education:* Georgetown University (B.S., 1991); Fordham University (J.D., 1994). Member, Intellectual Property and Entertainment Law Journal, 1993-1994. *Member:* Association of the Bar of the City of New York; Wake County, Connecticut, North Carolina (Member, Sections on: Business Law; Sports and Entertainment Law) and American (Member, Business Law Section) Bar Associations; North Carolina State Bar; Sports Council of Greater Raleigh Chamber of Commerce. ***PRACTICE AREAS:*** Corporate Law; Securities; Mergers, Acquisitions and Divestitures; Corporate Finance. ***Email:*** jmartinez@smithlaw.com

SCOTT A. MISKIMON, born West Palm Beach, Florida, August 27, 1960; admitted to bar, 1992, North Carolina; U.S. District Court, Eastern and Middle Districts of North Carolina. *Education:* University of Missouri-Columbia (B.J., 1982); University of North Carolina at Chapel Hill (J.D., 1992). Board of Editors, UNC Law Review. Co-Author: "North Carolina Contract Law," (Lexis 2001). *Member:* Wake County, North Carolina (Member, Bench/Bar Liaison Committee; Communications Committee) and American Bar Associations; North Carolina State Bar. ***PRACTICE AREAS:*** Commercial Law; Litigation; Business Law; Construction Law; Estate Litigation.

MARTIN H. BRINKLEY, born Raleigh, North Carolina, September 20, 1966; admitted to bar, 1992, North Carolina. *Education:* Phillips Exeter Academy; Harvard University (A.B., Classics, summa cum laude, 1987); University of North Carolina School of Law (J.D., 1992). Staff Member and Executive Articles Editor, North Carolina Law Review (1990-92). Phi Beta Kappa. Staff Member and Executive Articles Editor, North Carolina Law Review, 1990-1992. Law Clerk to Hon. Sam J. Ervin, III, Chief Judge, United States Court of Appeals for the Fourth Circuit, 1992-1993. *Member:* Wake County (Board of Directors, 2000-2002), North Carolina (Member, Board of Governors, 2000-2003; Chair, Young Lawyers Division, 1998-1999) and American Bar Associations; North Carolina State Bar. ***PRACTICE AREAS:*** Corporate Law; Mergers and Acquisitions; Banking Law; Business Law; Appellate Litigation.

SUSAN HANEY HARGROVE, born Colorado Springs, Colorado, August 5, 1956; admitted to bar, 1992, North Carolina. *Education:* Duke University (B.A., magna cum laude, 1978); University of North Carolina (J.D., with high honors, 1982). Order of the Coif. Staff Member, UNC Law Review. Certified Superior Court Mediator. *Member:* Wake County, North Carolina and American (Litigation and Alternative Dispute Resolution Sections) Bar Associations; North Carolina State Bar. ***PRACTICE AREAS:*** Business Law; Commercial Litigation; Health Care Litigation; Mediation. ***Email:*** shargrove@smithlaw.com

DAVID W. BERRY, born Fayetteville, North Carolina, January 3, 1963; admitted to bar, 1992, North Carolina; 1994, U.S. District Court, Eastern District of North Carolina. *Education:* University of North Carolina (B.A., 1985); Tulane University (J.D., cum laude, with Certificate in Environmental Law, 1992). Production Editor, Tulane Maritime Law Journal, 1991-1992. Assistant Attorney General, Environmental Division, North Carolina Attorney General's Office, 1992-1998. *Member:* Wake County, North Carolina (Member, Environmental Law Section, 1998—; Section Council Member, Environmental Law Section, 1999-2002) and American (Member, Environment, Energy and Resources Section) Bar Associations; North Carolina State Bar. ***PRACTICE AREAS:*** Environmental Health and Safety Law and Litigation; Commercial Real Estate. ***Email:*** dberry@smithlaw.com

DEANNA DAVIS ANDERSON, born Petersburg, Virginia, January 18, 1969; admitted to bar, 1995, North Carolina; U.S. District Court, Eastern, Middle and Western Districts of North Carolina; U.S. Court of Appeals, Fourth Circuit. *Education:* California State University, Northridge (B.A., with honors, 1991); Wake For est University (J.D., 1995). Recipient, American Jurisprudence Award, Legal Writing. *Member:* Wake County, North Carolina and American Bar Associations; North Carolina State Bar. ***PRACTICE AREAS:*** Appellate Advocacy; Civil Litigation; Construction Litigation; Medical Malpractice Defense; Insurance Defense. ***Email:*** danderson@smithlaw.com

---

STEPHEN G. DRIGGERS, born Gainesville, Florida, October 19, 1950; admitted to bar, 1993, California; 1999, North Carolina. *Education:* University of Texas at Austin (B.A., 1972); Indiana University (Ph.D., 1981); Stanford University (J.D., 1992). *Member:* Wake County, North Carolina and American Bar Associations; North Carolina State Bar; State Bar of California. ***PRACTICE AREAS:*** Employee Benefits; Executive Compensation. ***Email:*** sdriggers@smithlaw.com

SEAN A. TIMMONS, born Washington, D.C., August 4, 1967; admitted to bar, 1998, North Carolina and U.S. District Court, Eastern District of North Carolina; 2001, U.S. Court of Appeals, Fourth Circuit. *Education:* Phillips Exeter Academy; Williams College (B.A., cum laude, with highest honors in Music, 1989); Duke University (J.D., 1994). *Member:* Wake County, North Carolina and American Bar Associations; North Carolina State Bar; American Health Lawyers Association. ***PRACTICE AREAS:*** Health Care Law; Health Care Fraud and Abuse; Medicare; Medicare Compliance; Medicaid; Certificates of Need. ***Email:*** stimmons@smithlaw.com

MICHAEL R. GORDON, born Long Beach, New York, August 10, 1970; admitted to bar, 1995, New York; 1999, North Carolina. *Education:* Tulane University (B.A., cum laude, 1992); Brooklyn Law School (J.D., 1995). Member, Moot Court. Assistant District Attorney, Manhattan District Attorney's Office, 1995-1998. *Member:* Wake County, North Carolina, New York State and American Bar Associations; North Carolina State Bar. ***PRACTICE AREAS:*** Medical Malpractice Defense; Commercial Litigation; White Collar Criminal Defense. ***Email:*** mgordon@smithlaw.com

DAVID B. CLEMENT, born Opelousas, Louisiana, May 26, 1959; admitted to bar, 1986, Pennsylvania; 1988, New Jersey; 2001, North Carolina. *Education:* United States Naval Academy (B.S., with honors, 1980); Villanova University School of Law (J.D., cum laude, Order of the Coif, 1986); Georgetown University Law Center (LL.M., with distinction, 1994). *Member:* Wake County, North Carolina and American Bar Associations; North Carolina State Bar. [Cmdr., U.S. Navy JAG Corps., 1980-2000]. ***PRACTICE AREAS:*** Mergers and Acquisitions; Venture Capital and Strategic Investing; Corporate; Government Contracts; Securities Compliance for Growth Companies; Taxation.

GEOFFREY WILLIAM ADAMS, born Durham, North Carolina, February 17, 1972; admitted to bar, 1998, North Carolina. *Education:* University of Utah (B.S., 1994); Duke University (J.D., 1998). *Member:* Wake County, North Carolina and American Bar Associations; North Carolina State Bar. ***PRACTICE AREAS:*** Banking; Capital Markets Transactions; Mergers and Acquisitions; Corporate Law. ***Email:*** gadams@smithlaw.com

WAYNE K. MAIORANO, born Englewood, New Jersey, April 28, 1966; admitted to bar, 1998, North Carolina. *Education:* Villanova University (B.A., 1988); University of North Carolina (J.D., with honors, 1998). *Member:* Wake County (Member, Volunteer Lawyers Program), North Carolina and American Bar Association; North Carolina State Bar; North Carolina Association of Defense Attorneys. [Capt., U.S. Marine Corps, 1988-1994]. ***PRACTICE AREAS:*** Construction Litigation; Commercial Litigation; Bankruptcy Litigation. ***Email:*** wmaiorano@smithlaw.com

KIMBERLY QUARLES SWINTOSKY, born Atlanta, Georgia, July 4, 1970; admitted to bar, 1998, North Carolina. *Education:* University of North Carolina (B.S.B.A., M.AC, 1993; J.D., with honors, 1998). Member, North Carolina Law Review, 1996-1997. Certified Public Accountant, North Carolina, 1995. *Member:* Wake County, North Carolina and American Bar Associations; North Carolina State Bar; American Institute of Certified Public Accountants; North Carolina Association of Certified Public Accountants. ***PRACTICE AREAS:*** Business Law; Taxation; Estate Planning. ***Email:*** kswintosky@smithlaw.com

BENJI TAYLOR JONES, born Raleigh, North Carolina, February 10, 1969; admitted to bar, 1999, North Carolina. *Education:* Southern Methodist University (B.F.A., magna cum laude, with honors, 1991); New York University (M.A., 1996); Columbia Law School (J.D., 1998). Staff Member, 1996-1997 and Notes Editor, 1997-1998, Columbia Law Review. *Member:* Wake County, North Carolina and American Bar Associations; North Carolina State Bar. ***PRACTICE AREAS:*** Securities; Corporate Law; Mergers, Acquisitions and Divestitures. ***Email:*** bjones@smithlaw.com

S. NIKOLE MARIENCHECK, born Athens, Georgia, May 19, 1971; admitted to bar, 1997, North Carolina and South Carolina. *Education:* University of Georgia (B.A., 1994); University of South Carolina (J.D., cum laude, 1997). Order of the Wig & Robe; Order of the Coif. Associate Editor, ABA Real Property, Probate & Trust Journal, 1996-1997. Law clerk to the Honorable A. Thomas Small, Chief Judge, United States Bankruptcy Court for the Eastern District of North Carolina, 1997-1999. Publications: "Chapter 11 Update," Eastern Bankruptcy Institute, June, 2000. S. Nikole Byrd, "Fourth Circuit Review," Norton Bankr. L. Adviser, Published in the March Issues for 1998-2003. *Member:* Wake County, North Carolina and American Bar Associations; North Carolina State Bar; South Carolina Bar. ***PRACTICE AREAS:*** Bankruptcy; Commercial Transactions. ***Email:*** nmariencheck@smithlaw.com

JAMISON H. HINKLE, born Elizabeth City, North Carolina, October 20, 1969; admitted to bar, 1996, Alabama; 1998, North Carolina. *Education:* Duke University (A.B., Public Policy Studies, cum laude, 1991); University of North Carolina (J.D., with honors, 1996). Member, North Carolina Law Review. *Member:* Wake County, North Carolina and

(This Listing Continued)

SMITH, ANDERSON, BLOUNT, DORSETT, MITCHELL & JERNIGAN, L.L.P., Raleigh—Continued

American Bar Associations; North Carolina State Bar; Alabama State Bar; Triangle Benefits Forum. ***PRACTICE AREAS:*** Employee Benefits; Executive Compensation; Estate Planning; Tax-Exempt Organizations. ***Email:*** jhinkle@smithlaw.com

JACKSON W. MOORE, born Coral Gables, Florida, 1970; admitted to bar, 1995, Texas; 2001, North Carolina. *Education:* University of Virginia (B.A., with distinction, 1992); Duke University School of Law (J.D., with honors, 1995). Member, Moot Court Board. Research Editor, Duke Environmental Law and Policy Forum. Law Clerk to the Hon. John D. Rainey, U.S. District Court, Southern District of Texas, 1995-1997. *Member:* Wake County, North Carolina and American Bar Associations; North Carolina State Bar; State Bar of Texas. ***PRACTICE AREAS:*** Intellectual Property; Employment Law; Products Liability; Litigation; Commercial Litigation. ***Email:*** jmoore@smithlaw.com

MARGARET N. ROSENFELD, born Somerset, New Jersey, March 30, 1970; admitted to bar, 2001, North Carolina; 1998, New York. *Education:* Rutgers University (B.A., 1992); George Washington University Law School (J.D., highest honors, 1997). Member: Raleigh chapter of Business and Professional Women; Council for Entrepreneurial Developments' Government Affairs Task Force. *Member:* Wake County, New York State, North Carolina and American Bar Associations; North Carolina State Bar. ***PRACTICE AREAS:*** Public Offerings; Private Placements; Securities; Corporate Finance; Mergers and Acquisitions; Technology Protection and Licensing.

BRADLEY J. DAVES, born Cheyenne, Wyoming, June 18, 1973; admitted to bar, 1998, North Carolina; 1999, District of Columbia. *Education:* North Carolina State University (B.S., Environmental Engineering, magna cum laude, 1995); University of North Carolina (J.D., with honors, 1998). *Member:* Wake County, North Carolina, North Carolina and American Bar Associations; North Carolina State Bar; District of Columbia Bar. ***PRACTICE AREAS:*** Environmental Law; Commercial Real Estate. ***Email:*** bdaves@smithlaw.com

J. MITCHELL ARMBRUSTER, born Pittsburg, Kansas, January 8, 1971; admitted to bar, 1999, North Carolina. *Education:* Cornell University (B.S., 1993); University of North Carolina (J.D., with high honors, 1999). Order of the Coif. Editor-in-Chief, North Carolina Law Review, 1998-1999. Law Clerk to the Honorable David B. Sentelle, United States Court of Appeals for the District of Columbia Circuit, 1999-2000. *Member:* Wake County, North Carolina and American Bar Associations; North Carolina State Bar. ***PRACTICE AREAS:*** Commercial Litigation; Appellate Litigation. ***Email:*** marmbruster@smithlaw.com

DANA E. SIMPSON, born Newport News, Virginia, May 8, 1974; admitted to bar, 2000, North Carolina. *Education:* University of North Carolina at Chapel Hill (B.A., highest distinction, 1996; J.D., high honors, 2000). Phi Beta Kappa; Order of the Coif. Member, North Carolina Law Review. *Member:* Wake County, North Carolina and American Bar Associations; North Carolina State Bar; American Health Lawyers Association. ***PRACTICE AREAS:*** Health Care; Administrative Law. ***Email:*** dsimpson@smithlaw.com

RACHEL S. BETTS, born Sarasota, Florida, July 26, 1975; admitted to bar, 2000, North Carolina. *Education:* University of North Carolina at Chapel Hill (B.A., 1996; J.D., 2000). Phi Beta Kappa. Staff Member, 1998-1999, and Managing Editor, 1999-2000, North Carolina Banking Institute. Author: "Brazil and the Global Financial Crisis: An Examination of the Effect from Charlotte to Sao Paolo," 3 N.C. Banking Inst. 411, 1999. *Member:* Wake County, North Carolina and American Bar Associations; North Carolina State Bar. ***PRACTICE AREAS:*** Securities; Corporate Law; Mergers, Acquisitions and Divestitures. ***Email:*** rbetts@smithlaw.com

MIRANDA R. MILLER, born Ossining, New York, March 8, 1964; admitted to bar, 1995, New York; 1997, North Carolina. *Education:* University of California at Berkeley (B.A., 1986); Columbia University (J.D., 1994). *Member:* Wake County, North Carolina, New York and American Bar Associations; North Carolina State Bar. ***PRACTICE AREAS:*** Venture Capital Investment; Securities Compliance for Growth Companies; Business Corporate; Corporate Finance. ***Email:*** mmiller@smithlaw.com

BRYAN A. McGANN, born Washington, D.C., April 12, 1961; admitted to bar, 2001, North Carolina. *Education:* East Carolina University (B.S., 1983); Campbell University (M.B.A., 1990); University of North Carolina (J.D., with honors, 2001). *Member:* Wake County, North Carolina and American Bar Associations; North Carolina State Bar. ***PRACTICE AREAS:*** Medical Malpractice Defense Litigation; Corporate Litigation.

JAMES S. HANSON, born New York, N.Y., October 28, 1971; admitted to bar, 2001, North Carolina. *Education:* Wake Forest University (B.A., with honors, 1994); University of North Carolina School of Law (J.D., with honors, 2001). *Member:* Wake County, North Carolina and American Bar Associations; North Carolina State Bar. ***PRACTICE AREAS:*** Corporate; Securities Law.

JAN L. NEWMAN, born Highpoint, North Carolina, September 8, 1973; admitted to bar, 2001, North Carolina. *Education:* Meredith College (B.A., magna cum laude, 1995); University of North Carolina School of Law (J.D., with honors, 2000). *Member:* Wake County, North Carolina and American Bar Associations; North Carolina State Bar. ***PRACTICE AREAS:*** Commercial; Corporate Law.

MATTHEW D. RHOAD, born Fayetteville, North Carolina, February 21, 1975; admitted to bar, 2000, North Carolina. *Education:* Wake Forest University (B.A., magna cum laude, 1996); University of North Carolina (J.D., 2000). Order of the Coif. *Member:* Wake County, North Carolina and American Bar Associations; North Carolina State Bar. ***PRACTICE AREAS:*** Commercial Litigation; Employment Law. ***Email:*** mrhoad@smithlaw.com

ELLEN M. JERNIGAN, admitted to bar, 2002, North Carolina. *Education:* North Carolina State University (B.S., 1998); Wake Forest University School of Law (J.D., 2002). *Member:* Wake County, North Carolina and American Bar Associations; North Carolina State Bar. ***PRACTICE AREAS:*** Corporate Law.

CHRISTOPHER R. KIGER, born Danville, Illinois, August 21, 1975; admitted to bar, 2002, North Carolina. *Education:* Elon College (B.A., summa cum laude, 1998); University of North Carolina (J.D., with honors, 2002). Order of the Coif. *Member:* Wake County, North Carolina and American Bar Associations; North Carolina State Bar. ***PRACTICE AREAS:*** Products Liability; Contracts; Commercial Litigation. ***Email:*** ckiger@smithlaw.com

KELLY L. PODGER, born Chapel Hill, North Carolina, March 7, 1974; admitted to bar, 2002, North Carolina. *Education:* University of North Carolina (B.A., 1996; J.D., 2002). *Member:* Wake County, North Carolina and American Bar Associations; North Carolina State Bar. ***PRACTICE AREAS:*** Medical Malpractice Defense Litigation; Commercial Litigation. ***Email:*** kpodger@smithlaw.com

BARTLEY A. NORMAN, born Charlotte, North Carolina, April 12, 1972; admitted to bar, 2002, North Carolina. *Education:* North Carolina State University (B.A., cum laude, 1994); Princeton Theological Seminary (M.Div., 1999); University of North Carolina (J.D., with honors, 2002). *Member:* Wake County, North Carolina and American Bar Association; North Carolina State Bar. ***PRACTICE AREAS:*** Commercial Transactions; Business Law. ***Email:*** bnorman@smithlaw.com

K. ALAN PARRY, JR., born Springfield, Missouri, April 3, 1973; admitted to bar, 1998, Texas; 2003, North Carolina. *Education:* Texas Christian University (B.S., summa cum laude, 1995); Duke University School of Law (J.D., magna cum laude, 1998). Order of the Coif. *Member:* Wake County, North Carolina and American Bar Associations; North Carolina State Bar; State Bar of Texas. ***PRACTICE AREAS:*** Civil Litigation; Administrative Litigation.

JENNIFER B. MARKHAM, born Walnut Creek, California, June 26, 1977; admitted to bar, 2003, North Carolina. *Education:* University of North Carolina at Chapel Hill (B.A., 1999); University of Richmond Law School (J.D., 2003). *Member:* Wake County, North Carolina and American Bar Associations; North Carolina State Bar. ***PRACTICE AREAS:*** Health Care.

JAMAL A. RHINEHARDT, born Sacramento, California, December 3, 1970; admitted to bar, 2003, North Carolina. *Education:* Mount Olive College (B.S., 1998); North Carolina Central School of Law (J.D., 2003). *Member:* Wake County, North Carolina and American Bar Associations; North Carolina State Bar. ***PRACTICE AREAS:*** Litigation.

ADDIE K.S. RIES, born Asheville, North Carolina, June 22, 1978; admitted to bar, 2003, North Carolina. *Education:* University of Georgia (B.A., cum laude, 1994); University of North Carolina School of Law (J.D., 2003). Order of the Coif. ***PRACTICE AREAS:*** Commercial Litigation; Securities Litigation; Products Liability; Patent Litigation; Contract Disputes.

AMY S. WALLACE, born Butler, Pennsylvania, May 29, 1975; admitted to bar, 2003, North Carolina. *Education:* Baldwin-Wallace College (B.A., 1997); University of North Carolina School of Law (J.D., with honors, 2003). *Member:* Wake County, North Carolina and American Bar Associations; North Carolina State Bar. ***PRACTICE AREAS:*** Commercial Law.

J. TRAVIS HOCKADAY, born Dunn, North Carolina, August 29, 1978; admitted to bar, 2003, North Carolina. *Education:* Campbell University (B.A., summa cum laude, 2000); University of North Carolina School of Law (J.D., 2003). *Member:* Wake County, North Carolina and American Bar Associations; North Carolina State Bar. ***PRACTICE AREAS:*** Commercial Litigation; Government Relations; Regulatory Law.

BRIAN D. MEACHAM, admitted to bar, 2003, North Carolina. *Education:* University of North Carolina at Chapel Hill (B.S., 2000); University of North Carolina School of Law (J.D., 2003). *Member:* Wake County, North Carolina and American Bar Associations; North Carolina State Bar. ***PRACTICE AREAS:*** Corporate Law.

REPRESENTATIVE CLIENTS: A.J. Fletcher Foundation; American Continental Insurance Co.; American Security Insurance Company; Ammons, Inc.; Apple Computer, Inc.; Association of N.C. Property & Casualty Insurance Companies; The Aurora Funds; Black & Decker, Inc.; Bankers Trust Commercial Corporation; Kathleen Price Bryan Family Fund; Capital Bank Corporation; Capitol Broadcasting Company, Inc.; Carolina Power & Light Company; Catalytica Pharmaceuticals, Inc.; CIGNA Corporation; Commercial Credit Corporation; Cree Research, Inc.; Daimler Chrysler; Embrex, Inc.; Equity Research Services, Inc.; Ericsson Inc.; Fidelity and Deposit Company of Maryland; First Union Corporation; First Union National Bank of North Carolina; Fleming Companies, Inc.; Flue Cured Tobacco Stabilization Corp.; FNB Financial Services Corporation; Ford Motor Company; Four Oaks Bank & Trust Company; General Motors Corp; Glaxo Wellcome, Inc.; Goodmark Foods, Inc.; Goodyear Tire and Rubber Co.; Halco Industries, Inc.; Helena Chemical Company; Honda North America; Insect Biotechnology, Inc.; JMC (USA), Inc.; Kaiser Aluminum and Chemical Corporation; Kawasaki Motor Corporation, U.S.A.; Kia Motors America; MAG Mutual Insurance Company; The Medical Protective Insurance Company; Merrill Lynch & Co., Inc.; Merrill Lynch Trust Company of North Carolina; Minnesota Mutual Life Insurance Co.; MMI Companies, Inc.; Motion Picture Association of America; The Mutual Life Insurance Company of New York; North Carolina Medical Society; Northwestern Mutual Life Insurance Company; nTouch Research Corporation; The Pantry, Inc.; A.M. Pappas & Associates, L.L.C.; Paradigm Genetics Inc.; PBV Inc.; PCS Phosphate Company, Inc.; PepCom Industries, Inc.; Protein Delivery Inc.; Quintiles Transnational Corp.; St. Paul Insurance Cos.; Snap Products, Inc.; Sumitomo Electric Industries, Ltd.; Sumitomo Electric Lightwave Corp.; Transamerica Life Companies; Unimin Corporation; U.S. Aviation Underwriters; Wachovia Bank of North Carolina, N.A.; Wachovia Corporation; Waste Management of the Carolinas, Inc.; Winston Hotels, Inc.

(This Listing Continued)

SMITH DEBNAM NARRON WYCHE SAINTSING & MYERS, L.L.P.

Established in 1972

4601 SIX FORKS ROAD, SUITE 400
RALEIGH, NORTH CAROLINA 27609
Telephone: 919-250-2000
Facsimile: 919-250-2211
Email: mail@smithdebnamlaw.com
URL: http://www.smithdebnamlaw.com

Charlotte, North Carolina Office: 4201 Congress Street, Suite 460, 28209. Telephone: 704-643-3220. Fax: 704-643-3898.

General and Appellate Practice in all State and Federal Courts. Corporation, Bankruptcy, Non-Judicial Workouts and Reorganizations, Corporate Reorganization, Construction, Equipment Leasing and Finance, Estate Planning and Administration, Commercial and Retail Collections and Litigation. Administrative and Regulatory, Government Contracts and Procure-

(This Listing Continued)

ment, Health Care, Land Use and Zoning, Limited Liability Companies and Partnerships, Public Finance, Residential and Commercial Real Estate, Family Law and Equitable Distribution, Telecommunications, Plaintiff's Personal Injury.

FIRM PROFILE: The firm began in 1972 when Fred J. Smith, Jr. joined with Thurston Debnam and two other attorneys to form a partnership in Raleigh. During the quarter century since its founding, the firm has expanded to become one of the largest law firms in the Triangle area.

MEMBERS OF FIRM

W. THURSTON DEBNAM, JR., born Raleigh, North Carolina, March 1, 1947; admitted to bar, 1972, North Carolina and U.S. Supreme Court. *Education:* Wake Forest University (B.A., 1969; J.D., cum laude, 1972). Phi Delta Phi. Associate Editor, Wake Forest Law Review, 1971-1972. Mayor, Town of Zebulon, 1989-1993. Town Attorney, Zebulon, 1976-1988. Certified Mediator. ***PRACTICE AREAS:*** Commercial Real Estate; Residential Real Estate; Corporate Law; Administrative. ***Email:*** tdebnam@smithdebnamlaw.com

JOHN W. NARRON, born Wake County, North Carolina, November 7, 1951; admitted to bar, 1977, North Carolina and Mississippi. *Education:* East Carolina University (B.A., 1974); University of Mississippi (J.D., 1977). (Board Certified Specialist in Family Law, North Carolina State Board of Legal Specialization). ***PRACTICE AREAS:*** Personal Injury Law; Family Law; Commercial Litigation; Domestic Mediation. ***Email:*** jnarron@smithdebnamlaw.com

N. HUNTER WYCHE, JR., born Greensboro, North Carolina, May 12, 1951; admitted to bar, 1980, North Carolina and U.S. District Court, Eastern District of North Carolina; 1982, U.S. District Court, Middle District of North Carolina; 1984, U.S. Supreme Court and U.S. District Court, Western District of North Carolina; 1988, U.S. Court of Appeals, Fourth Circuit. *Education:* University of North Carolina and Campbell College (B.B.A., 1976); Campbell University (J.D., 1980). Delta Theta Phi. *Member:* American Bar Association; Commercial Law League of America (Vice-Chairman, Bankruptcy Law Committee, 1986); American Bankruptcy Institute; Tenth Judicial District Bar Association (Member, Grievance Committee, 1987-1995, Chairman, 1993-1995); North Carolina State Bar (Member, Committee on Specialization in Bankruptcy Law, 1991-1994, Chairman, 1993-1995; Vice Chair, Grievance Committee, 2003). (Board Certified Specialist in Business and Consumer Bankruptcy Law, North Carolina State Board of Legal Specialization) (Certified in Business Bankruptcy Law by the American Board of Certification). ***PRACTICE AREAS:*** Creditors Rights; Business Law; Bankruptcy Law; Bankruptcy Litigation. ***Email:*** hwyche@smithdebnamlaw.com

BETTIE KELLEY SOUSA, born Henderson, North Carolina, November 16, 1956; admitted to bar, 1981, North Carolina. *Education:* University of North Carolina (B.A., 1978); Wake Forest University (J.D., 1981). Board Member, American Board of Certification. (Certified in Creditors' Rights Law by the American Board of Certification). ***PRACTICE AREAS:*** Commercial Litigation. ***Email:*** bsousa@smithdebnamlaw.com

JERRY T. MYERS, born Monroe, North Carolina, October 1, 1958; admitted to bar, 1984, North Carolina. *Education:* Wake Forest University (B.S., 1980; J.D., 1984). Phi Delta Phi. Author: Collections and Enforcement of Judgments in N.C. (Lawyers Co-op Pub., 1997). Member, Board of Governors, CLLA, 1998-1999. (Certified in Creditors' Rights Law by the American Board of Certification). ***PRACTICE AREAS:*** Creditors Rights Law; Commercial Litigation; Collection Law. ***Email:*** jmyers@smithdebnamlaw.com

ROSE H. STOUT, born Robeson County, North Carolina, January 12, 1960; admitted to bar, 1985, North Carolina. *Education:* Campbell University (B.A., summa cum laude, 1982; J.D., 1985). Member, Campbell University Law Review, 1984-1985. *Member:* North Carolina Bar Association (Family Law Council; Editor, Family Law Forum). (Board Certified Specialist in Family Law, North Carolina State Board of Legal Specialization). ***PRACTICE AREAS:*** Family Law; Equitable Distribution. ***Email:*** rstout@smithdebnamlaw.com

BYRON L. SAINTSING, born Thomasville, North Carolina, August 18, 1963; admitted to bar, 1988, North Carolina. *Education:* Wake Forest University (B.A., cum laude, honors in Economics, 1985); University of North Carolina (J.D., with honors, 1988). *Member:* North Carolina Bar Association (Council Member, Construction Law, 1995-1998; Treasurer, 2002-2003); American Bar Association (Law Practice Management and Business Law Sections); Equipment Leasing Association (Legal Forum Committee, 2003-2006). ***PRACTICE AREAS:*** Commercial Litigation; Commercial Bankruptcy; Creditor Bankruptcy; Creditors Rights Law; Construction Law; Equipment Leasing; Finance. ***Email:*** bsaintsing@smithdebnamlaw.com

FRANKLIN DRAKE, born Pinehurst, North Carolina, December 19, 1953; admitted to bar, 1978, North Carolina; 1979, Kentucky; 1986, West Virginia. *Education:* University of North Carolina (B.A., cum laude, 1975; J.D., 1978). Phi Beta Kappa. Member, North Carolina Journal of International Law, 1976-1978. ***PRACTICE AREAS:*** Creditors Rights; Bankruptcy; Litigation. ***Email:*** fdrake@smithdebnamlaw.com

GERALD H. GROON, JR., born Takoma Park, Maryland, October 26, 1960; admitted to bar, 1990, North Carolina. *Education:* University of North Carolina at Chapel Hill (B.S., 1985); Campbell University (J.D., 1990). Member, Campbell Law Review, 1989-1990. [U.S. Air Force, 1978-1982]. (Certified in Creditors' Rights Law by the American Board of Certification). ***PRACTICE AREAS:*** Commercial Litigation; Collections; Creditors Rights Law. ***Email:*** hgroon@smithdebnamlaw.com

CAREN DAVIS ENLOE, born Tallahassee, Florida, April 26, 1964; admitted to bar, 1990, North Carolina. *Education:* Appalachian State University (B.A., B.M., 1986); Campbell University (J.D., cum laude, 1990). Omicron Delta Kappa. Editorial Board, Campbell Law Review, 1990. *Member:* North Carolina Bar Association (Member, Litigation and Construction Sections); American Bar Association (Member, Litigation Section and Construction Forum). ***PRACTICE AREAS:*** Creditors' Rights; Commercial Litigation; Construction Law; Lender Liability; Bankruptcy. ***Email:*** cenloe@smithdebnamlaw.com

JEFF D. ROGERS, born South Hill, Virginia, January 22, 1962; admitted to bar, 1987, North Carolina; U.S. District Court, Middle, Eastern and Western District of North Carolina. *Education:* University of North Carolina at Wilmington (B.A., 1984); Campbell University School of Law (J.D., 1987). Member, 1989-1995 and Chairman, 1992-1995, North Carolina Private Protective Services Board. ***PRACTICE AREAS:*** Creditor Litigation; Bankruptcy Law; Foreclosures. ***Email:*** jrogers@smithdebnamlaw.com

CONNIE E. CARRIGAN, born Monterey, California, August 15, 1961; admitted to bar, 1989, North Carolina, U.S. District Court, Middle, Eastern and Western Districts of North Carolina; U.S. Court of Appeals, Fourth Circuit. *Education:* North Carolina State University (B.A. cum laude, 1983); Campbell University School of Law (J.D., 1989). Law Clerk to the Honorable Louis B. Meyer, Associate Justice, North Carolina Supreme Court, 1989-1990. *Member:* North Carolina Bar Association (Member, Bankruptcy Section); American Bankruptcy Institute; National Association of Credit Management. ***PRACTICE AREAS:*** Collections; Bankruptcy; Creditors' Rights; Commercial Litigation; Construction; Leasing. ***Email:*** ccarrigan@smithdebnamlaw.com

CYNTHIA V. McALISTER, born Greensboro, North Carolina, July 1, 1951; admitted to bar, 1996, North Carolina. *Education:* North Carolina State University (B.A., 1993); North Carolina Central University (J.D., 1996). Author: The Repressed Memory Phenomenon, 22 NC Cent LJ 56. *Member:* North Carolina Association of Women Attorneys; North Carolina Academy of Trial Lawyers (Secretary, Family Law Section, 2002-2003). (Board Certified Specialist in Family Law, North Carolina State Board of Legal Specialization). ***PRACTICE AREAS:*** Family Law. ***Email:*** cmcalister@smithdebnamlaw.com

KRISTA F. NORSTOG LEONARD, born Fargo, North Dakota, March 10, 1966; admitted to bar, 1991, North Carolina. *Education:* Pacific Lutheran University (B.A., magna cum laude, 1988); Duke University School of Law (J.D., 1991). ***PRACTICE AREAS:*** Bankruptcy; Creditors Rights; Construction Litigation; Construction Liens; Commercial Leasing; Commercial Litigation. ***Email:*** kleonard@smithdebnamlaw.com

ASSOCIATES

THOMAS A. GRAY, born Elmira, New York, May 31, 1968; admitted to bar, 1997, Massachusetts; 1999, District of Columbia (Not admitted in North Carolina). *Education:* University of Pittsburgh (B.A., 1991); University of Arkansas (J.D., 1995). Member with Cohn & Dussi, Burlington Massachusetts. *Member:* The District of Columbia Bar. ***PRACTICE AREAS:*** Creditors Rights. ***Email:*** tgray@smithdebnamlaw.com

AARON N. BAILEY, born Jacksonville, North Carolina, November 15, 1973; admitted to bar, 1999, North Carolina. *Education:* North Carolina State University (B.A., 1996); Campbell University (J.D., 1999). *Member:* Wake County Bar Association (Co-Chair, Young Lawyers Division, Education Committee); National Association of Subrogation Professionals. ***PRACTICE AREAS:*** Creditors' Rights; Commercial Litigation. ***Email:*** abailey@smithdebnamlaw.com

PEDRO J. ZABALA, II, born St. Petersburg, Florida, March 13, 1972; admitted to bar, 2000, North Carolina. *Education:* University of Florida (B.A., with honors, 1995; J.D., 1999). Public Service Law Fellow. Recipient, Political and Civil Rights Book Award. Judicial Clerk, Eighth Judicial Circuit Court. *Member:* American Bar Association. ***LANGUAGES:*** Spanish and Portuguese. ***PRACTICE AREAS:*** Creditors Rights; Commercial Litigation. ***Email:*** pzabala@smithdebnamlaw.com

STEPHANIE FOUNTAIN BYNUM, born Rocky Mount, North Carolina, January 3, 1952; admitted to bar, 1980, Connecticut; 1989, North Carolina. *Education:* University of North Carolina at Chapel Hill (B.A., Education, 1974); Campbell University (J.D., 1980). Member: Wake County Real Property Lawyers, 1992-2000; Wake County Public Service Committee. Member, Board of Directors, Kids Center, 1996-2000. ***PRACTICE AREAS:*** Residential Real Estate; Business Law. ***Email:*** sbynum@smithdebnamlaw.com

CHAD A. SHARKEY, born Basking, Ridge, New Jersey, April 12, 1971; admitted to bar, 2000, North Carolina. *Education:* North Carolina State University (B.A., 1993); University of Dayton School of Law (J.D., magna cum laude, 2000). Staff Writer, 1998-1999 and Associate Editor, 1999-2000, University of Dayton Law Review. ***PRACTICE AREAS:*** Commercial Litigation; Commercial Bankruptcy; Construction Law; Equipment Finance and Leasing. ***Email:*** csharkey@smithdebnamlaw.com

JAMES DAVID DILL, born Waukesha, Wisconsin, September 1, 1976; admitted to bar, 2002, North Carolina. *Education:* University of Richmond; University of South Carolina (B.S., Business Administration, 1998); University of Maryland School of Law (J.D., 2002). Moot Court Board. *Member:* Wake County Bar Association (Subcommittee Chairman, Young Lawyers Division; Disaster Legal Services); North Carolina State Bar. ***PRACTICE AREAS:*** Creditors Rights. ***Email:*** jdill@smithdebnamlaw.com

CHAD L. HALLIDAY, born Islip, New York, July 20, 1976; admitted to bar, 2002, North Carolina. *Education:* State University of New York at Albany (B.A., Political Science, with honors, magna cum laude, 1998); Wake Forest University (J.D., 2001). Phi Alpha Delta; Golden Key. Wake Forest Law Faculty Scholar. *Member:* North Carolina Bar Association; North Carolina State Bar. ***PRACTICE AREAS:*** Creditors Rights.

LYNN WILSON LUPTON, born Concord, North Carolina, June 14, 1976; admitted to bar, 2003, North Carolina. *Education:* University of North Carolina at Chapel Hill (B.A., 1998); Campbell University (J.D., 2003). Phi Alpha Delta. *Member:* Wake County, North Carolina Bar Association. ***PRACTICE AREAS:*** Family Law; Civil Litigation. ***Email:*** llupton@smithdebnamlaw.com

ADAM M. GOTTSEGEN, born Greensboro, North Carolina, October 14, 1975; admitted to bar, 2002, North Carolina. *Education:* Vanderbilt University (B.A., 1998); Wake Forest University (J.D., 2002). Board Member, Moot Court. Clerk to the Honorable J. Rich Leonard Chief Bankruptcy Judge Eastern District of North Carolina. ***Email:*** agottsegen@smithdebnamlaw.com

AMANDA B. BANAT, born Washington, D.C., March 12, 1978; admitted to bar, 2003, North Carolina. *Education:* Southern Methodist University (B.A., 1998); University of Arizona (J.D., 2003). Author: 19 Ariz. J. Int'l & Compl. 939 (2002). ***PRACTICE AREAS:*** Creditors Rights. ***Email:*** abanat@smithdebnamlaw.com

OF COUNSEL

FRED J. SMITH, JR., born Raleigh, North Carolina, March 27, 1942; admitted to bar, 1966, North Carolina. *Education:* Wake Forest University (B.A., 1964; J.D., cum laude,

(This Listing Continued)

SMITH DEBNAM NARRON WYCHE SAINTSING & MYERS, L.L.P., Raleigh—Continued

1966). Phi Delta Phi. Business Manager, Wake Forest Law Review, 1966. Editor in Chief, Military Law Review, 1967-1968. Member, Board of Governors, 1985-1988 and President, 1989-1990, Commercial Law League of America.

ELIZABETH B. GODFREY, born Cincinnati, Ohio, August 21, 1956; admitted to bar, 1986, North Carolina. *Education:* Hillsdale College (B.A., cum laude, 1978); Campbell University (J.D., 1985). Law Clerk to the Honorable Franklin T. Dupree, Jr., U.S. District Court Judge, Eastern District of North Carolina, 1985-1987. *Member:* North Carolina Academy of Trial Lawyers. ***PRACTICE AREAS:*** Personal Injury; Medical Malpractice; Workmen's Compensation. ***Email:*** bgodfrey@smithdebnamlaw.com

TRACY T. DEBNAM, born Dallas, Texas, January 11, 1969; admitted to bar, 1997, North Carolina. *Education:* Southern Methodist University (B.A., 1994); Oklahoma City University (J.D., magna cum laude, 1997). Phi Delta Phi. Member: Board of Governors, 1994-1995; Law Review: Staff, 1995-1996, Executive Articles Editor, 1996-1997. ***PRACTICE AREAS:*** Corporate Law; Real Property. ***Email:*** ttdebnam@smithdebnamlaw.com

JOHN P. McNEILL, born Anchorage, Alaska, October 14, 1955; admitted to bar, 1992, Virginia, U.S. Court of Appeals, Fourth Circuit; 1996, U.S. Tax Court; 2000, U.S. District Court, Eastern District of Virginia; 2001, North Carolina and U.S. District Court, Eastern District of North Carolina. *Education:* Park University (B.S. summa cum laude, 1988); George Washington University (J.D., with honors, 1992). Adjunct Professor, Business and Tax Law, Strayer University, 1994-2000, 2003—. *Member:* Virginia State Bar; North Carolina Bar Association (Sections on Intellectual Property, Litigation and Sports and Entertainment Law); Computer Law Association (CLA); Licensing Executives Society (LES). [U.S. Coast Guard, 1973-1993]. ***PRACTICE AREAS:*** Information Technology; Intellectual Property; Business Law; Estate Planning; Estate Administration; Sweepstakes; Promotion Law; Corporate Law; Tax Law. ***Email:*** jmcneill@smithdebnamlaw.com

REPRESENTATIVE CLIENTS: CitiCapital Relocation; Ford Motor Credit Co.; Carolina Builders Corp.; General Electric Capital Corp.; Advanta Leasing Corp.; N.B. Handy Co.; Oakwood Acceptance Corp.; Bank One; Chrysler Credit; Toyota Motor Credit/Lexus Financial Services; Duke University Federal Credit Union; NC Credit Union Network; United Rentals, Inc.; Citibank, N.A.; Wells Fargo Financial Leasing, Inc.; Oberlin Capital, L.P.
APPROVED ATTORNEYS FOR: Fidelity National Title; Lawyers Title Insurance Corp.; Commonwealth Land Title Insurance Co.; Chicago Title Insurance Co.; Investors Title Insurance Co.; First American Title Insurance Co.; Stewart Title Guaranty Co.
REFERENCE: Centura Bank.

SMITH MOORE LLP

Established in 1919

2800 TWO HANOVER SQUARE
P.O. BOX 27525
RALEIGH, NORTH CAROLINA 27601
Telephone: 919-755-8700
Fax: 919-755-8800
Email: smith.moore@smithmoorelaw.com
URL: http://www.smithmoorelaw.com

Mailing Address: P.O. Box 27525, Raleigh, NC 27611

Greensboro, North Carolina Office: Wachovia Tower, 300 North Greene Street, Suite 1400, P.O. Box 21927. Telephone: 336-378-5200. Fax: 336-378-5400.
Atlanta, Georgia Office: One Atlantic Center, Suite 3700, 1201 West Peachtree Street. Telephone: 404-962-1000. Fax: 404-962-1200.
Wilmington, North Carolina Office: 300 North Third Street, Suite 301. Telephone: 910-251-7001. Fax: 910-251-7007.

General, Trial and Appellate Practice in All State and Federal Courts, Dispute Resolution, Corporate, Taxation, Securities Regulation, Real Property and Finance, Labor and Employment (Management) Law, Employee Benefits, International and Immigration, Antitrust and Trade Regulation, Negligence, Products Liability, Insurance Coverage, Media, Banking, Commercial, Bankruptcy, Administrative, Environmental, Hospital and Health Care, Public Authority and Public Finance, Estate Planning and Administration, Probate, Legislative, Intellectual Property, Education, and Sports Law.

PARTNERS

DENISE S. CLINE, admitted to bar, 1983, North Carolina. *Education:* Davidson College (A.B., 1979); University of North Carolina (J.D., 1983). Certified Mediator. *Member:* Wake County, North Carolina and American Bar Associations. ***PRACTICE AREAS:*** Litigation; Health Care; Employee Benefits. ***Email:*** denise.cline@smithmoorelaw.com

J. DONALD COWAN, JR., born November 14, 1943; admitted to bar, 1968, North Carolina and U.S. Court of Military Appeals; 1972, U.S. Supreme Court; 1975, U.S. Court of Federal Claims. *Education:* Wake Forest University (B.A., 1965; J.D., with honors, 1968). Phi Delta Phi. Editor-in-Chief, Wake Forest Law Review. Fellow, American College of Trial Lawyers (State Chair, 1998-2000). Trustee, Wake Forest University, 1994-1998, 1999—. Legal Services of North Carolina (Board of Directors, 1993-1999; President, 1998-1999); Product Liability Advisory Council. Permanent Member, Fourth Circuit Judicial Conference. Adjunct Instructor of Trial Practice, Duke University School of Law. *Member:* North Carolina Bar Association (Board of Governors, 1982-1985; Chairman, Young Lawyers Division, 1979-1980; Chairman, Litigation Section, 1985-1986; President, 1992-1993); American Judicature Society; American Board of Trial Advocates (Chapter President, 1999-2000); The American Law Institute; American Academy of Appellate Lawyers. [Capt., U.S. Army, Active Duty, 1968-1973]. (Also at Greensboro, North Carolina). ***PRACTICE AREAS:*** Litigation; Products Liability; Intellectual Property Litigation. ***Email:*** don.cowan@smithmoorelaw.com

JAMES L. GALE, born August 20, 1947; admitted to bar, 1974, Georgia and North Carolina; 1989, Florida. *Education:* Florida Presbyterian College (B.A., 1969); University of Georgia (J.D., magna cum laude, 1974). Phi Kappa Phi. Developments Editor, Georgia Law Review, 1973-1974. Clerk to Honorable Franklin T. Dupree, Jr., U.S. District Court, Eastern District of North Carolina, 1974-1976. *Member:* Defense Research Institute; The

(This Listing Continued)

Association of Trial Lawyers of America; North Carolina Association of Defense Attorneys. ***PRACTICE AREAS:*** Business Litigation; Intellectual Property; Litigation; Health Care Litigation. ***Email:*** jim.gale@smithmoorelaw.com

PATRICIA A. MARKUS, born June 6, 1967; admitted to bar, 1992, Illinois; 1996, North Carolina. *Education:* Haverford College (B.A., with honors, 1989); Boston College (J.D., 1992). Law Clerk, Justice Robert W. Cook, Illinois Appellate Court, 4th District, 1993-1995. Law Clerk, Justice Willis P. Whichard, North Carolina Supreme Court, 1995-1996. *Member:* North Carolina Bar Association (Member, Health Law Section); North Carolina Society of Health Care Attorneys (Member, Board of Directors); American Health Lawyers Association. ***PRACTICE AREAS:*** Health Care Law. ***Email:*** trish.markus@smithmoorelaw.com

GEORGE J. OLIVER, born April 9, 1943; admitted to bar, 1973, North Carolina; 1985, District of Columbia; 1986, U.S. Court of Appeals, Fourth and Ninth Circuits and U.S. Supreme Court. *Education:* Campbell University (B.S., 1966); University of Tennessee (J.D., 1973). Phi Alpha Delta (Justice, 1972-1973). Assistant Attorney General, State of North Carolina, 1975-1979. Trustee, Energy and Mineral Law Foundation, 1996—. Chair, Board of Directors, United Way of North Carolina. *Member:* North Carolina Bar Association; District of Columbia Bar. [U.S. Air Force, 1966-1970]. ***PRACTICE AREAS:*** Labor and Employment (Management) Law; Railway Labor Law; OSHA. ***Email:*** jerry.oliver@smithmoorelaw.com

BRADLEY M. RISINGER, born September 27, 1964; admitted to bar, 1990, Pennsylvania; 1991, District of Columbia; 1996, North Carolina. *Education:* Indiana University (B.A., with high distinction, 1986); Georgetown University (J.D., cum laude, 1990). *Member:* Pennsylvania, North Carolina and American Bar Associations; The District of Columbia Bar; Defense Research Institute. ***PRACTICE AREAS:*** Products Liability; Medical Services Litigation; Civil Litigation; Antitrust and Trade Regulation. ***Email:*** brad.risinger@smithmoorelaw.com

SAMUEL O. SOUTHERN, born March 11, 1944; admitted to bar, 1969, North Carolina; 1971, U.S. Court of Appeals for the Armed Forces; 1973, Florida; 1980, U.S. Court of Appeals, Fourth Circuit and U.S. Supreme Court. *Education:* Duke University (A.B., 1966); University of North Carolina (J.D., 1969). Omicron Delta Kappa. Angier B. Duke Scholar; Law Alumni Scholar. Commissioner, USS North Carolina Battleship Commission, 1992—. Member, Board of Directors, Wake County Bar Association, 1985-1987. Chairman, Health Law Section, North Carolina Bar Association, 1998-1999. *Member:* Defense Research Institute; North Carolina Association of Defense Attorneys; North Carolina Society of Health Care Attorneys; American Board of Trial Advocates; Judge Advocates Association. [Capt., JAGC, U.S. Naval Reserve (Active Duty, 1969-1974); Certified Military Judge, 1973-1998]. ***LANGUAGES:*** German. ***PRACTICE AREAS:*** Civil Litigation; Health Care Law; Medical Malpractice. ***Email:*** sam.southern@smithmoorelaw.com

ROBERT L. WILSON, JR., born October 2, 1954; admitted to bar, 1981, North Carolina. *Education:* University of North Carolina (A.B., 1976); Wake Forest University (J.D., 1981). Member, Wake Forest Law Review, 1980-1981. Author: Note, "Workers' Compensation — Redefinition of Occupational Disease and the Applicable Compensation Statute — Booker v. Duke Medical Center and Wood v. J. P. Stevens & Co.," 16 Wake Forest Law Review 288, 1980; Comment, "Impeachment of the Criminal Defendant by His Acquittals — Beyond the Bounds of Reason," 17 Wake Forest Law Review 561, 1981. Research Assistant to Judge Cecil J. Hill, North Carolina Court of Appeals, 1981-1982. *Member:* North Carolina and American Bar Associations; North Carolina Society of Health Care Attorneys; American Health Lawyers Association. ***PRACTICE AREAS:*** Health Care Law. ***Email:*** bob.wilson@smithmoorelaw.com

ASSOCIATES

D. Todd Brosius
R. James Cox, Jr.
Matthew S. Cunningham
James R. Holland
Molly G. Huggins
Shannon R. Joseph
Laura Murray Loyek
John W. Mann
Elizabeth Brooks Scherer
William W. Stewart, Jr.
Marc C. Tucker

COUNSEL

SIDNEY S. EAGLES, JR., born August 5, 1939; admitted to bar, 1964, North Carolina. *Education:* Wake Forest University (B.A., 1961; J.D., 1964). *Member:* North Carolina and American Bar Associations; American Law Institute. [Ret. Col., U.S. Air Force Reserve]. ***PRACTICE AREAS:*** Litigation; Appellate. ***Email:*** sid.eagles@smithmoorelaw.com

REPRESENTATIVE CLIENTS: AIG Insurance Group; Atlantic Coast Conference; Branch Banking and Trust Co.; Board of Commissioners of Douglas County; Board of Commissioners of Georgia County; Digital Optics; Dixon Hughes LLP; Eli Lilly and Co.; General Electric Co.; General Motors Corp.; Greensboro News & Record Co.; Miller Brewing Co.; North Carolina Hospital Association; Penn Western Benefits; Prime Care Health Networks; Royal & SunAlliance; Stafford Development Company; Stockhausen, Inc.; The Coca-Cola Co.; The Moses H. Cone Memorial Hospital; The Procter & Gamble Co.; United Dominion Industries, Inc.; Warner-Lambert Co.; Watauga Medical Center; Wayne Memorial Hospital.

(For complete biographical data on all personnel, see Professional Biographies at Greensboro, North Carolina)

SOKOL McLAMB SCHILAWSKI OLIVER LADD PLLC

d/b/a Wake Family Law Group

4350 LASSITER AT NORTH HILLS AVENUE
SUITE 360
RALEIGH, NORTH CAROLINA 27609
Telephone: 919-787-4040
Facsimile: 919-787-4811
URL: http://www.wakefamilylawfirmgroup.com
URL: http://www.wakefamilylawgroup.com

Domestic Relations, Civil Litigation, Appellate Practice, Mediation, Arbitration, Family Mediation, Family Arbitration, Collaborative Law, Family Law, Divorce, Child Custody, Equitable Distribution.

MARC W. SOKOL, born 1948; admitted to bar, 1980, New York; 1982, North Carolina. *Education:* Queens College of the City University of New York (B.A., 1969); Brooklyn Law School (J.D., 1980).

CATHERINE C. McLAMB, born Raleigh, North Carolina, August 28, 1949; admitted to bar, 1975, North Carolina; U.S. District Court, Eastern and Western Districts of North Carolina; U.S. Court of Appeals, Fourth Circuit; U.S. Supreme Court. *Education:* St. Mary's Junior College; University of North Carolina (B.A., 1971; J.D., 1975). Phi Beta Kappa. Trained Collaborative Law. Family Law Mediator. (Board Certified Specialist in Family Law, North Carolina State Board of Legal Specialization). ***PRACTICE AREAS:*** Domestic Relations; Civil Litigation; Appellate Practice; Mediation; Arbitration; Family Mediation; Collaborative Law.

MICHAEL F. SCHILAWSKI, born Marinette, Wisconsin, December 19, 1948; admitted to bar, 1982, North Carolina. *Education:* University of North Carolina (B.A., 1971); North Carolina State University (M.Ed., 1976); Campbell University (J.D., cum laude, 1982). Editor-in-Chief, Campbell Law Review, 1981-1982. *Member:* Wake County and North Carolina Bar Associations; North Carolina State Bar; North Carolina Academy of Trial Lawyers. (Board Certified Specialist in Family Law, North Carolina State Board of Legal Specialization). ***PRACTICE AREAS:*** Civil Litigation; Family Law; Family Arbitration; Family Mediation.

HELEN M. OLIVER, born Springfield, Massachusetts, February 15, 1973; admitted to bar, 1997, North Carolina. *Education:* Dickinson College (B.A., 1994); Widener University School of Law (J.D., 1997). ***PRACTICE AREAS:*** Family Law; Divorce; Child Custody; Equitable Distribution.

SUZANNE R. LADD, born 1971; admitted to bar, 1997, North Carolina. *Education:* University of North Carolina at Chapel Hill (B.A., 1993; J.D., 1997).

JENNIFER M. BRADLEY, born Maryville, Tennessee, January 22, 1973; admitted to bar, 1998, North Carolina. *Education:* Emory & Henry College (B.S., magna cum laude, 1995); University of North Carolina at Chapel Hill (J.D., 1998). ***PRACTICE AREAS:*** Civil Litigation; Family Law.

JULIA B. SOUTHWICK

4024 BARRETT DRIVE
RALEIGH, NORTH CAROLINA 27609
Telephone: 919-782-8673
Fax: 919-781-7281
Email: jsouthwick@southwicklaw.com
URL: http://www.lawyers.com/southwicklaw

Bankruptcy, Consumer Bankruptcy, Personal Bankruptcy, Residential Real Estate, Wills.

FIRM PROFILE: Mrs. Southwick has provided advice and service in the area of Consumer Bankruptcy for over twenty years.

JULIA B. SOUTHWICK, born Concord, North Carolina, May 4, 1954; admitted to bar, 1982, North Carolina and U.S. District Court, Eastern District of North Carolina. *Education:* Appalachian State University (B.M., 1976); University of North Carolina at Chapel Hill (J.D., 1982). *Member:* Wake County and North Carolina (Chair, Lawyer Referral Service Committee, 1993) Bar Associations. ***PRACTICE AREAS:*** Residential Real Estate; Consumer Bankruptcy; General Practice.

SPARROW LAW FIRM

Established in 2003

19 WEST HARGETT STREET, SUITE 501
RALEIGH, NORTH CAROLINA 27601
Telephone: 919-835-3600
Fax: 919-835-3667
URL: http://www.michellesparrowlaw.com
Email: nclawyer@bellsouth.net
URL: http://www.michellesparrowattorney.com

General Civil and Criminal Law, Driving While Intoxicated, (DWI), Drug Crimes, Felonies, Homicide, Juvenile Law, Misdemeanors, Parole and Probation, Assault, Traffic Violations, Law Enforcement, Police, Personal Injury, Automobile Accidents, Medical Malpractice, Mediation and Arbitration.

R. MICHELLE SPARROW, born Chapel Hill, North Carolina, July 28, 1961; admitted to bar, 1992, North Carolina. *Education:* University of North Carolina at Wilmington (B.A., 1983); Mississippi College School of Law (J.D., 1991). Member, Better Business Bureau. Certified Mediator and Arbitrator. Assistant District Attorney, Wake County, 1994-2002. Personal Injury Attorney, 2002-2003. *Member:* Wake County and North Carolina Bar Associations; Tenth Judicial District Association; Association of Trial Lawyers, North Carolina Association of Trial Lawyers; Dispute Resolution Commission. ***PRACTICE AREAS:*** Personal Injury; Criminal Law; Civil Practice. ***Email:*** nclawyer@bellsouth.net

STARK LAW GROUP, PLLC

RALEIGH, NORTH CAROLINA

(See Chapel Hill)

Construction, Commercial and Corporate Litigation. Personal Injury Litigation, Environmental Law, Computer and Intellectual Property Law, Corporate Acquisitions and Real Property Law, Real Estate Closings, Business Law.

STEPHENSON & STEPHENSON, LLP

RALEIGH, NORTH CAROLINA

(See Cary)

Insurance Defense, Construction Litigation, Condemnation, Personal Injury, Health Care Law, Corporate Law, Estate Planning, Estate Administration, Commercial and Residential Real Estate, Foreclosures, Civil Litigation, Collections, Contract Litigation.

STUART LAW FIRM, PLLC

1033 WADE AVENUE, SUITE 202
RALEIGH, NORTH CAROLINA 27605-1155
Telephone: 919-787-6050
Fax: 919-787-9988
Email: main@stuartlawfirm.com
URL: http://www.stuartlawfirm.com

Administrative Law, Bankruptcy, Business Law, Dispute Resolution/Mediation, Government Relations, Housing Finance, Insurance Regulatory, Intellectual Property, Municipal Bond Finance, Sports Law, Tax Exempt Organizations, Workers Compensation, Workers Compensation Self Insurance.

FIRM PROFILE: The firm was established in 1995 and its two principal attorneys have collectively practiced in the Research Triangle area for more than 40 years. Mr. Stuart's housing finance practice builds on his 13 years of prior service as general counsel to the North Carolina Housing Finance Agency, His insurance practice has developed during his 18 year tenure as general counsel to Builders Mutual Insurance Company, and its predecessors. His sports practice has been primarily focused on 22 years experience representing professional football players. Ms. Stuart's practice derives from her previous litigation experience in both state and federal courts, her representation of government agencies, her tenure as general counsel and director of tax exempt organizations including the U.S. Olympic Festival, 1987 and long-standing involvement with risk management. Together, their respective practices have combined to create a unique firm that is focused in the areas of worker's compensation insurance, risk management, housing finance transactions, sports law, representation of tax exempt organizations, and alternative dispute resolution.

MEMBERS OF FIRM

JAMES L. STUART, born Asheboro, North Carolina, 1950; admitted to bar, 1975, North Carolina; 1980, U.S. Supreme Court; 1988, District of Columbia; 2001, Tennessee. *Education:* Duke University (B.S.E., with distinction, 1971); George Washington University (J.D., with honors, 1975). Adjunct Instructor, University of North Carolina School of Law, 1983-1984. Research Assistant and Professional Staff Member, United States Senate Judiciary Subcommittees on Constitutional Rights and Separation of Powers, Senator Sam J. Ervin, Jr., Staff, 1972-1974. Assistant Attorney General, State of North Carolina, 1975-1980. *Member:* Wake County, North Carolina and American Bar Associations. ***PRACTICE AREAS:*** Housing; Housing Finance; Municipal Finance; Administrative Law; Government Relations; Sports Law; Workers Compensation. ***Email:*** jstuart@stuartlawfirm.com

CATHERINE R. STUART, born New York, N.Y., August 28, 1955; admitted to bar, 1982, North Carolina; 1986, U.S. Supreme Court. *Education:* University of North Carolina at Chapel Hill (B.A., 1977); Tulane University Law School (J.D., 1981). Senior Fellow. Law Clerk, Hon. Franklin T. Dupree, U.S. District Court, Eastern District of North Carolina, 1981-1983. Assistant Attorney General, North Carolina Department of Justice, 1984-1986. Adjunct Instructor, School of Law, University of North Carolina at Chapel Hill, 1983-1984. General Counsel, Local Organizing Committee, U.S. Olympic Festival, 1986-1987. Executive Director, People For the American Way in North Carolina, 1987-1995. Certified Mediator. *Member:* Wake County, North Carolina and American Bar Associations. ***REPORTED CASES:*** Thomas S. v. Morrow 781 F.2d 367 (4th Cir., 1986). ***PRACTICE AREAS:*** Insurance Regulation; Insurance Litigation; Workers Compensation; Civil Litigation; Corporate Law; Tax Exempt Organizations; Housing Law; Sports Law; Administrative Law; Intellectual Property; Franchises and Franchising; Alternative Dispute Resolution. ***Email:*** cstuart@stuartlawfirm.com

ASSOCIATES

THERESA S. DEW, born Jacksonville, North Carolina February 15, 1975; admitted to bar, 2000, North Carolina; 2001, South Carolina. *Education:* Campbell University (B.A., summa cum laude, 1997); University of North Carolina at Chapel Hill (J.D., with honors, 2000). Phi Delta Phi. *Member:* North Carolina (Member, Business Section) and American Bar Associations; South Carolina Bar. ***PRACTICE AREAS:*** Housing Finance; Tax Exempt Organizations; Copyrights; Trademarks; Debtor and Creditor; Workers Compensation. ***Email:*** tdew@stuartlawfirm.com

CHARLES C. KYLES, born Concord, North Carolina, August 30, 1969; admitted to bar, 2001, North Carolina; 2002, Virginia. *Education:* North Carolina State University (B.A., 1991); University of North Carolina at Chapel Hill (J.D., with honors, 2001). Phi Alpha Delta; The Order of the Barristers. Member, Holderness Moot Court. *Member:*

(This Listing Continued)

STUART LAW FIRM, PLLC, Raleigh—Continued

North Carolina and American Bar Associations. ***PRACTICE AREAS:*** Workers Compensation; Civil Litigation; Corporate Law; Insurance Regulation. ***Email:*** ckyles@stuartlawfirm.com

SANDHYA G. PATEL, born Detroit, Michigan July 5, 1978; admitted to bar, 2004, North Carolina. *Education:* University of North Carolina at Chapel Hill (B.A., with distinction, 2000); University of North Carolina at Chapel Hill (J.D., 2004). *Member:* North Carolina and American Bar Associations. ***PRACTICE AREAS:*** Workers Compensation; Insurance Regulation; Civil Litigation. ***Email:*** spatel@stuartlawfirm.com

STUBBS, COLE, BREEDLOVE, PRENTIS & BIGGS, P.L.L.C.

RALEIGH, NORTH CAROLINA

(See Durham)

General Civil and Criminal Trial Practice. Banking, Corporate, Real Estate, Wills and Estates, Estate Planning, Construction and Personal Injury Law.

STUBBS & PERDUE, P.A.

TWO HANNOVER SQUARE
434 FAYETTEVILLE STREET MALL, SUITE 1630
P.O. BOX 1630
RALEIGH, NORTH CAROLINA 27602-1630
Telephone: 919-856-9400
Fax: 919-856-9300
URL: http://www.stubbsperdue.com
Email: law@stubbsperdue.com
URL: http://www.lawyers.com/stubbsperdue

New Bern, North Carolina Office: 310 Craven Street, P.O. Box 1654. Telephone: 252-633-2700. Fax: 252-633-9600. Email: law@stubbsperdue.com

General Practice in all Courts. Probate, Real Estate, Personal Injury, Bankruptcy Reorganization, Domestic Relations, Corporation and Criminal Law, Environmental Law; Toxic Tort.

GARY R. PERDUE, SR. (1947-1997)

TRAWICK H. STUBBS, JR., born Atlanta, Georgia, September 1, 1942; admitted to bar, 1967, North Carolina. *Education:* University of North Carolina (A.B., 1964); Duke University (J.D., 1967). Phi Delta Phi. Member, Order of the Coif. Member, Editorial Board, Duke Law Journal, 1966-1967. Law Clerk to U.S. District Judge John D. Larkins, Jr., 1969-1970. Speaker, Organizer and Founder, Eastern Bankruptcy Institute. Member, Bankruptcy Specialist, N.C. State Bar. Permanent Delegate, Fourth Circuit Judicial Conference, 1971—. County Attorney for Craven County, 1995-1998. N.C. State Bar Board of Specialization (Member, Bankruptcy Committee, 1984-1990). *Member:* Craven County and North Carolina (Member, Bankruptcy Section, 1986-1989) Bar Associations; North Carolina State Bar; North Carolina Academy of Trial Lawyers; The Association of Trial Lawyers of America; National Association of Chapter 13 Trustees; NCATT Statistical Data Committee (Member, Chairman); Eastern Inn of Court. ***PRACTICE AREAS:*** Bankruptcy Reorganization; Debtor and Creditor; Workouts; Litigation; Personal Injury; Tax Law; Federal Civil Practice; Federal Criminal Law; Commercial Law; Contracts; Business Formation; Toxic Torts. ***Email:*** law@stubbsperdue.com

LAURIE B. BIGGS, born Grand Rapids, Michigan, November 23, 1977; admitted to bar, 2003, North Carolina and U.S. District Court, Eastern District of North Carolina. *Education:* University of Michigan (B.A., 2000); University of Kentucky (J.D., 2003). Order of the Coif. Staff Member, 2001-2002, Technical Editor, 2002-2003, Journal of Natural Resources and Environmental Law, University of Kentucky. *Member:* Durham County and American Bar Associations; North Carolina Academy of Trial Lawyers; Association of Trial Lawyers of America. ***PRACTICE AREAS:*** Litigation; Bankruptcy; Toxic Torts. ***Email:*** lvandenbos@stubbsperdue.com

APPROVED ATTORNEYS FOR: Lawyers Title Insurance Corp.; Fidelity National Title; Chicago Title; Investors Title Insurance; State Land Title Insurance; Commonwealth Title Insurance; Lawyers Title of North Carolina; Carolina Title Insurance Agency, Inc.
REFERENCES: First Citizens Bank; Investors Title Insurance Company; Lawyers Title Ins. Co.; Chicago Title Insurance Co.

(For Complete Biographical Data on Personnel at New Bern see Professional Biographies at New Bern)

PAUL A. SUHR

Established in 1989
1110 NAVAHO DRIVE, SUITE 502
RALEIGH, NORTH CAROLINA 27609
Telephone: 919-876-4707
Fax: 919-876-4237
Email: paulsuhr@bellsouth.net
URL: http://www.lawyers.com/paulsuhr

Immigration and Naturalization, Visas, Deportation, Citizenship, Adoptions, Criminal Law, DWI, Misdemeanors, Traffic Violations, Personal Injury, Automobile Accidents, Business Law.

FIRM PROFILE: Represented Chong France in her pardon petition to governor in 1990 and won her release. Represented Erka Cray, reported to NBC, CNN, U.S. World Report, local ABC, etc.

PAUL A. SUHR, born Seoul, Korea, January 20, 1940; admitted to bar, 1989, North Carolina; 1990, District of Columbia. *Education:* Campbell University (B.A., 1968); University of North Carolina, Greensboro (M.A., 1970); University of North Carolina, Chapel Hill (M.S., 1975); North Carolina Central University (J.D., 1988). *Member:* Wake County, North Carolina and American Bar Associations; American Immigration Lawyers Association; Association of Trial Lawyers of America. ***LANGUAGES:*** Korean.

Language: Korean.

SULLIVAN & GRACE, P.A.

Established in 1978
600 WADE AVENUE
RALEIGH, NORTH CAROLINA 27605
Telephone: 919-832-8507
Fax: 919-833-2852
Email: LAW8507@aol.com
URL: http://www.ncfamilylaw.com

Family Law, Property Division, Separation Agreements, Child Custody, Child Support, Alimony, Divorce, Adoption, Domestic Violence, Premarital Agreements, Collaborative Family Law, Wills and Probate, Military Pension Division, Arbitration, Mediation and Family Law Appeals.

FIRM PROFILE: The firm (and its predecessors) date back to 1978, shortly after Mr. Sullivan completed active duty with the Army. The firm offers a wide range of services in the areas of family law. Clients are offered over sixty brochures to help explain and resolve their problems. All attorneys are computer-proficient, which enhances the thoroughness and efficiency of the client's work. The firm requires continuing legal education in family law—both teaching and attending programs—of attorneys, and an extensive bibliography of articles and manuscripts is available.

MARK E. SULLIVAN, born Cleveland, Ohio, December 20, 1945; admitted to bar, 1971, Ohio; 1972, U.S. District Court, District of Columbia and U.S. Court of the Armed Forces; 1976, North Carolina; 1978, U.S. District Court, Eastern District of North Carolina and U.S. Court of Appeals, Fourth Circuit; 2001, U.S. Court of Federal Claims. *Education:* Kenyon College (B.A., magna cum laude, 1968); University of Virginia (J.D., 1971). Phi Beta Kappa; Phi Alpha Delta. Lecturer on War Crimes, Military Justice, Wills and Consumer Protection, 1972-1976. Counsel, Energy Conservation and Air Pollution cases, Sierra Club, 1977-1982. Chief of Legal Assistance Office, Fort Bragg, North Carolina. Defense Counsel, Military Trials and Administrative Discharge Proceedings. Counsel to Vietnam-era Army deserters during President Ford's Clemency Program. Certified Arbitrator, American Academy of Matrimonial Lawyers, 2000. *Member:* Wake County, North Carolina and American (Member: Standing Committee on Legal Assistance for Military Personnel, 'LAMP,'1982-1989, Chair, 1987-1988, CLE Committee, 1994—, Family Law Section, General Practice Section, Deputy Chair, 1995—, Vice-Chair, Military Law Committee, General Practice Section, 1993-1994) Bar Associations; American Academy of Matrimonial Lawyers; North Carolina Academy of Trial Lawyers; Judges Advocates Association; Reserve Officers Association. [Colonel, U.S. Army Reserve, 1995—]. (Board Certified Specialist in Family Law, North Carolina State Board of Legal Specialization). ***LANGUAGES:*** French. ***REPORTED CASES:*** Perkins v. Perkins, 364 S.E.2d 166, 88 N.C. App. 568; Lennon v. Wahler, 351 S.E.2d. 843, 84 N.C. App. 141; Dunlap v. Dunlap, 344 S.E.2d 806, 81 N.C. App. 675; Skamarah v. Skamarak, 343 S.E.2d 559, 81 N.C. App. 125; Mims v. Mims, 310 S.E.2d 130, 65 N.C. App. 725; Settle v. Beasley, 308 S.E.2d 288, 309 N.C. 616; Settle v. Beasley, 62, 59 N.C. App. 735. ***PRACTICE AREAS:*** Family Law; Mediation; Arbitration; Wills and Probate. ***Email:*** Law8507@aol.com

NANCY L. GRACE, admitted to bar, 1996, North Carolina. *Education:* University of North Carolina School of Law (J.D. with Honors, May 1996); University of North Carolina (M.A.T. in Spanish, 1986; B.A. in Spanish, 1982). Trained in Collaborative Family Law as part of Collaborative Divorce Program. Certified Family Financial Mediator. *Member:* Wake County and North Carolina Bar Associations; North Carolina Academy of Trial Lawyers. (Board Certified Specialist in Family Law, North Carolina State Board of Legal Specialization). ***LANGUAGES:*** Spanish. ***PRACTICE AREAS:*** Family Law; Collaborative Family Law; Mediation. ***Email:*** NLG8507@aol.com

---

KATIE HARDERSEN KING, admitted to bar, 2002, North Carolina. *Education:* Meredith College (B.A., cum laude, 1999); Campbell University (J.D., 2002). Phi Alpha Delta. *Member:* Wake County and American Bar Associations; North Carolina State Bar; North Carolina Association of Women Attorneys; North Carolina Academy of Trial Lawyers. ***PRACTICE AREAS:*** Family Law; Wills; Probate; Adoption Law. ***Email:*** kghk8507@aol.com

THE LAW OFFICES OF RAYMOND MASON TAYLOR

503 OBERLIN ROAD, SUITE 203
RALEIGH, NORTH CAROLINA 27605-1327
Telephone: 919-832-8440
Fax: 919-832-8447
URL: http://www.lawyers.com/raymondmasontaylor

Elder Law, Medicare and Medicaid, Wills, Trusts and Estates, Guardianships, Small Business.

RAYMOND MASON TAYLOR, born Washington, North Carolina, January 1, 1933; admitted to bar, 1960, North Carolina and U.S. District Court, Eastern District of North Carolina; 1970, U.S. Supreme Court; 1977, U.S. Court of Appeals, Fourth, Fifth, Sixth, Seventh, Eighth, and Ninth Circuits; 1981, U.S. Court of Appeals, Eleventh Circuit; 1983, U.S. Court of Appeals for the District of Columbia Circuit; 1981, U.S. Court of International Trade; 1983, U.S. Court of Military Appeals. *Education:* University of North Carolina (A.B., 1955; J.D., 1960). Pi Sigma Alpha; Phi Delta Phi; Omicron Delta Kappa honoris cause. Order of the Golden Fleece (Jason, 1958-1959). Assistant Editor, Tar Heel Barrister, 1958-1959. Member, Student Board of Editors, North Carolina Law Review, 1960. Certi-

(This Listing Continued)

fied Law Librarian, American Association of Law Libraries, 1968. Author: Federal Court Libraries, 2 volumes, Hein, 1981. Adjunct Instructor, 1962-1963 and Adjunct Professor, 1963-1964, Business Law, Atlantic Christian College (now Barton College). Visiting Lecturer, Economics and Business Law, North Carolina State University, 1967-1985. Listed in: National Academy of Elder Law Attorneys Experience Registry; Who's Who in America; and Who's Who in American Law. Research Assistant to Justice Clifton L. Moore, Supreme Court of North Carolina, 1960-1961. Marshal and Librarian, Supreme Court of North Carolina, 1964-1977. Project Director, Federal Judicial Center, 1976-1977. Assistant U.S. Attorney and Chief, Appellate Section, Eastern District of North Carolina, 1981-1982. Superintendent of Documents, Washington, D.C., 1982-1983. Associate, Gardner, Connor & Lee, Wilson, North Carolina, 1961-1964. *Member:* North Carolina Bar Association; National Academy of Elder Law Attorneys (State Coordinator, 1991-1995). [With U.S. Army, 1955-1957; Special Agent, Counter Intelligence Corps, 1956-1957]. ***PRACTICE AREAS:*** Elder Law; Medicare and Medicaid; Wills; Trusts and Estates; Guardianships.

TAYLOR, PENRY, RASH & RIEMANN, PLLC

Established in 2001

510 GLENWOOD AVENUE, SUITE 319

RALEIGH, NORTH CAROLINA 27603

Telephone: 919-833-9449

Fax: 919-833-9448

URL: http://www.tprr.com

Charlotte, North Carolina Office: 2359 Perimeter Pointe Parkway, Suite 360, 28208. Telephone: 704-424-2900. Fax: 704-424-2999.

Construction Law, Construction Litigation, Commercial Litigation, Securities Litigation, Mediation, Arbitration, Intellectual Property Litigation, Insurance Coverage Litigation, Government Relations and Administrative Litigation.

J. ANTHONY PENRY, born Chapel Hill, North Carolina, September 7, 1954; admitted to bar, 1979, North Carolina. *Education:* University of North Carolina at Chapel Hill (B.A., 1976); Wake Forest University (J.D., 1979). Law Clerk, Hon. James C. Fox, United States District Court for the Eastern District of North Carolina, 1982-1983. *Member:* Wake County, North Carolina and American Bar Associations. ***PRACTICE AREAS:*** Construction Litigation; Securities Litigation; Commercial Litigation. ***Email:*** andy.penry@tprr.com

NEIL A. RIEMANN, born Salisbury, North Carolina, December 8, 1966; admitted to bar, 1992, North Carolina; 1993, District of Columbia (inactive). *Education:* University of North Carolina at Chapel Hill (A.B., with honors, 1989); University of Michigan (J.D., magna cum laude, 1992). Phi Beta Kappa. Order of the Coif. Member, 1990-1991, Article Editor, 1991-1992, Michigan Law Review. Law Clerk, Hon. J. Dickson Phillips, Jr., United States Court of Appeals for the Fourth Circuit, 1992-1993. *Member:* Wake County, North Carolina and American Bar Associations. ***PRACTICE AREAS:*** Commercial Litigation; Securities Litigation; Intellectual Property Litigation; Insurance Coverage. ***Email:*** neil.riemann@tprr.com

---

CYNTHIA A. O'NEAL, born Zebulon, North Carolina, April 24, 1974; admitted to bar, 1999, North Carolina. *Education:* Duke University (B.A., cum laude, 1996; J.D., 1999). Golden Key. Member, Duke University National Honor Society. Article Editor, Duke Journal of Gender Law and Policy, 1998-1999. Law Clerk, Hon. Sarah J. Parker, North Carolina Supreme Court, 1999-2000. *Member:* Wake County, North Carolina (Member: Litigation Section; Construction Section) and American (Member: Litigation Section; Tort Trial Section; Insurance Practice Section; Fidelity and Surety Law Committee) Bar Associations; National Association of Women in Construction (Legislative Industry Committee); National Association of Women Attorneys; North Carolina Association of Black Lawyers. ***LANGUAGES:*** English. ***REPORTED CASES:*** Martin & Loftis Clearing & Grading, Inc. v. Saieed Const. Systems Corp., 608 S.e.2d 124 (N.C.App, Feb 15, 2005); Hanson Aggregates Southeast, Inc. v. City of Raleigh, 259 N.C. 188, 607 S.E.2d 269 (N.C., Dec 02, 2004); Hanson Aggregates Southeast, Inc. v. City of Raleigh, 601 S.E.2d 331 (Table, Text in WESTLAW), Unpublished Diposition, 2004 WL 1725745 (N.C.App., Aug 03, 2004); Faircloth v. Scott Howell & Co., Inc., 161 N.C.App. 741, 590 S.E.2d 24 (Table, Text in WESTLAW), Unpublished Disposition, 2003 WL 22952169 (N.C.App., Dec 16, 2003). ***PRACTICE AREAS:*** Commercial Litigation; Construction Law; Securities. ***Email:*** cynthia.oneal@tprr.com

OF COUNSEL

MICHAEL L. WEISEL, born Rumford, Maine, 1957; admitted to bar, 1980, North Carolina. *Education:* Guilford College (B.S., 1977); Campbell University (J.D., 1980); North Carolina State University (M.A., 2003). Vice President, Wells Fargo Bank, N.A., 1988-1990. Vice President and Portfolio Manager, Scudder Kemper Investments, Inc., 1990-1995. Trustee: North Carolina Teachers' and State Employees' Retirement Systems, 1993-1995; North Carolina Local Governmental Employees' Retirement System, 1993-1995. Member: North Carolina Banking Commission, 1993-1997. At-Large Member, North Carolina Board of Community Colleges, 1997-2000. Chairman, Foreign Trade Zone 93, 1997—. Board Member and Secretary, North Carolina Railroad Company, 1999-2004. *Member:* Wake County and North Carolina Bar Associations. ***PRACTICE AREAS:*** Government Relations; Administrative Law; Regulatory Law; Corporate Finance; Securities Arbitration; Mergers, Acquisitions and Divestitures; Franchise; Venture Capital; Corporate Law; Partnership Law. ***Email:*** michael.weisel@tprr.com

TEAGUE, CAMPBELL, DENNIS & GORHAM, L.L.P.

Established in 1946

1621 MIDTOWN PLACE

RALEIGH, NORTH CAROLINA 27609

Telephone: 919-873-0166

Facsimile: 919-873-1814

URL: http://www.tcdg.com

Lumberton, North Carolina Office: 408 North Chestnut Street, P.O. Box 1424. Telephone: 910-738-8534.

General Civil Defense Trial and Appellate Practice, including Automobile, and Trucking Liability, Premises and Product Liability, Medical, Nursing Home, Legal, Real Estate and other Professional Liability, Construction Law, Environmental Law, including Mold and other Toxic Torts, Corporate, Non-Profit and other Business Litigation, Governmental and Municipal Law, Life, Health and Employment Law, Insurance Coverage Disputes, Dram Shop Actions, Arson and Fraud, and Workers Compensation.

MEMBERS OF FIRM

C. WOODROW TEAGUE, born Thomasville, North Carolina, May 27, 1913; admitted to bar, 1934, North Carolina and U.S. District Court, Eastern, Middle and Western Districts of North Carolina; U.S. Court of Appeals, Fourth Circuit; U.S. Supreme Court. *Education:* Wake Forest College; Wake Forest College Law School (LL.B., 1934). Permanent Member: Fourth Circuit Judicial Conference and Board of Visitors, Wake Forest University Law School, 1991—. *Member:* North Carolina State Bar (President, 1977-1978); Association of Defense Trial Attorneys; Federation of Insurance and Corporate Counsel; Defense Research and Trial Lawyers Association; North Carolina Association of Defense Attorneys; American Judicature Society; American Board of Trial Advocates. [USNR, Lt. Commander, Active Duty, 1942-1946]

GEORGE W. DENNIS III, born Brooklyn, New York, March 24, 1950; admitted to bar, 1975, North Carolina; U.S. District Court, Eastern and Middle Districts of North Carolina; U.S. Court of Appeals, Fourth Circuit; U.S. Supreme Court. *Education:* Lehigh University (B.A., summa cum laude, 1972); Duke University (J.D., with distinction, 1975). Phi Beta Kappa; Omicron Delta Epsilon; Phi Eta Sigma. Listed, The Best Lawyers in America, 1997-2006 eds. Lecturer: North Carolina Association of Defense Attorneys, 1998; North Carolina Association of Self-Insurers Educational Conferences, 1991, 1992 and 2000; North Carolina Industrial Commission Workers' Compensation Educational Conferences, 1997 and 1998; North Carolina Bar Association Seminars on Workers' Compensation, 1982, 1987 and 1993; Wake Forest University Workers' Compensation Institutes, 1989, 1993 and 1996; The Occupational Safety and Health Educational Research Institutes, 1985, 1989 and 1993; American Academy of Industrial Hygiene, 1986. *Member:* International Association of Defense Attorneys; Defense Research Institute; North Carolina Association of Defense Attorneys. ***Email:*** gdennis@tcdg.com

HENRY W. GORHAM, born Rocky Mount, North Carolina, October 3, 1948; admitted to bar, 1974, North Carolina; U.S. District Court, Eastern, Middle and Western Districts of North Carolina; U.S. Court of Appeals, Fourth Circuit. *Education:* East Carolina University (B.S.B.A., with honors, 1971); Wake Forest University (J.D., 1974). Phi Delta Phi; Beta Gamma Sigma; Omicron Delta Epsilon. Member, Panel of Arbitrators, American Arbitration Association. North Carolina Certified Mediator for North Carolina Superior Courts and the North Carolina Industrial Commission. *Member:* North Carolina Association of Defense Attorneys. [Capt., USAF, Judge Advocate Generals Corps, 1974-1978]. ***Email:*** hgorham@tcdg.com

DAYLE A. FLAMMIA, born Raleigh, North Carolina, March 25, 1953; admitted to bar, 1981, North Carolina; U.S. District Court, Eastern and Middle Districts of North Carolina; U.S. Supreme Court; U.S. Court of Appeals, Fourth Circuit. *Education:* North Carolina State University (B.A., 1975); North Carolina Central University (J.D., 1980). Listed, The Best Lawyers in America, 2003-2006 eds. *Member:* North Carolina Association of Defense Attorneys; Defense Research Institute. ***Email:*** dflammia@tcdg.com

LINDA STEPHENS, born Woodruff, South Carolina, November 13, 1950; admitted to bar, 1979, North Carolina; U.S. District Court, Eastern and Middle Districts of North Carolina; U.S. Court of Appeals, Fourth Circuit. *Education:* University of South Carolina (B.A., summa cum laude, 1973); University of North Carolina (J.D., 1979). Phi Beta Kappa. Recipient, DRI's Fred H. Sievert Award, 2002. Listed, The Best Lawyers in America, 1995-2004 eds. Lecturer: North Carolina Bar Association's Continuing Legal Education Institutes on Workers' Compensation, 1982, 1984, 1987, 1990, 1992 and 1994; Wake Forest University's Workers' Compensation Institutes, 1986, 1989, 1994 and 1996; National Business Institute on Workers' Compensation in North Carolina, 1990; North Carolina Association of Defense Attorneys, 1991, 1995 and 1998; Institute of Government, 1991, 1993, 1994 and 1995; North Carolina Association of Self-Insurers Educational Conference, 2003. Research Assistant, North Carolina Court of Appeals, 1979-1980. Deputy Commissioner, North Carolina Industrial Commission, 1980-1984. *Member:* North Carolina Association of Defense Attorneys (Board of Directors, 1993-1996; Secretary, 1997-1999; Executive Vice President, 1999-2000; President-Elect, 2000-2001; President, 2001-2002); Defense Research Institute; The National Registry of Who's Who. ***Email:*** lstephens@tcdg.com

THOMAS M. CLARE, born New York, New York, July 6, 1953; admitted to bar, 1983, North Carolina; U.S. District Court, Middle and Eastern Districts of North Carolina; U.S. Court of Appeals, Fourth Circuit. *Education:* East Carolina University (B.A., 1975); University of North Carolina (J.D., 1982). Claims Examiner, Occidental Fire and Casualty Company, 1986-1987. *Member:* North Carolina Association of Defense Attorneys. ***Email:*** tclare@tcdg.com

ROBERT C. KERNER, JR., born Ft. Leavenworth, Kansas, October 13, 1959; admitted to bar, 1986, North Carolina; U.S. District Court, Eastern District of North Carolina. *Education:* Wake Forest University (B.A., 1982); Campbell University (J.D., 1986). Member, Campbell Law Review, 1985-1986. Research Assistant, North Carolina Court of Appeals, 1986-1988. *Member:* North Carolina Association of Defense Attorneys. ***Email:*** bkerner@tcdg.com

(This Listing Continued)

TEAGUE, CAMPBELL, DENNIS & GORHAM, L.L.P., Raleigh—Continued

JOHN A. TOMEI, born Syracuse, New York, September 29, 1962; admitted to bar, 1989, North Carolina; U.S. District Court, Eastern and Middle Districts of North Carolina. *Education:* University of North Carolina (B.A., 1984; J.D., 1989). *Member:* North Carolina Association of Defense Attorneys. ***Email:*** jtomei@tcdg.com

BRUCE A. HAMILTON, born Chicago, Illinois, March 13, 1961; admitted to bar, 1986, California; 1987, Massachusetts; 1991, North Carolina; U.S. District Court, Eastern and Middle Districts of North Carolina. *Education:* Tulane University (B.S., 1983); University of Virginia (J.D., 1986). Listed, The Best Lawyers in America, 2001-2006 eds. Lecturer: North Carolina Bar Association Seminars on Workers' Compensation, 1996-2005; North Carolina Bar Association Seminar for Mediators, 2004; North Carolina Industrial Commission Workers' Compensation Educational Conference, 2002; Wake Forest University Workers' Compensation Institute, 2000; Institute of Government, 2000; Lorman Business Institute, Worker's Compensation in North Carolina, 2000; North Carolina Association of Self-Insurers Educational Conference, 2002. *Member:* North Carolina Association of Defense Attorneys. ***Email:*** bhamilton@tcdg.com

GEORGE H. PENDER, born Fayetteville, North Carolina, July 28, 1956; admitted to bar, 1991, North Carolina; U.S. District Court, Eastern and Western Districts of North Carolina. *Education:* Appalachian State University (B.S.B.A., summa cum laude, 1978); Campbell University (J.D., 1991). Business Editor, Campbell Law Review, 1990-1991. Author, Note: "The Duty to Defend-Brown v. Lumbermens Mutual Casualty Company," 13 Campbell L. Rev. 141. *Member:* North Carolina Association of Defense Attorneys. ***Email:*** gpender@tcdg.com

DONALD F. LIVELY, born Albany, Georgia, January 13, 1955; admitted to bar, 1980, Texas; 1981, U.S. Court of Appeals, Fourth and Eleventh Circuits; U.S. District Court, Northern District of Texas; 1987, North Carolina and U.S. District Court, Eastern, Middle and Western Districts of North Carolina. *Education:* University of Georgia (B.A., cum laude, 1977); Baylor University (J.D., cum laude, 1980). National Order of Barristers; Baylor Order of Barristers. *Member:* North Carolina Association of Defense Attorneys. ***Email:*** dlively@tcdg.com

BRYAN T. SIMPSON, born Raleigh, North Carolina, August 3, 1968; admitted to bar, 1993, North Carolina; U.S. District Court, Eastern, Middle and Western Districts of North Carolina. *Education:* North Carolina State University (B.A., 1990); Campbell University (J.D., 1993). Phi Alpha Delta; Order of the Barristers. *Member:* North Carolina Association of Defense Attorneys (Co-Chair, Construction Law Committee). ***Email:*** bsimpson@tcdg.com

J. MATTHEW LITTLE, born Saginaw, Michigan, October 14, 1966; admitted to bar, 1993, North Carolina; U.S. District Court, Eastern, Middle and Western Districts of North Carolina; U.S. Court of Appeals, Fourth Circuit. *Education:* University of North Carolina (B.A., 1989); Wake Forest University (J.D., 1993). *Member:* North Carolina Association of Defense Attorneys. ***Email:*** mlittle@tcdg.com

MALLORY T. UNDERWOOD, born Birmingham, Alabama, January 14, 1971; admitted to bar, 1995, North Carolina; U.S. District Court, Eastern and Western Districts of North Carolina; U.S. Court of Appeals, Fourth Circuit. *Education:* University of South Carolina (B.S., cum laude, 1992); Wake Forest University (J.D., 1995). Member, Order of Omega; Order of the Barristers. *Member:* North Carolina Association of Defense Attorneys. ***Email:*** mtaylor@tcdg.com

JAN N. PITTMAN, born Raleigh, North Carolina, July 17, 1948; admitted to bar, 1976, South Carolina; 1977, North Carolina. *Education:* East Carolina University (B.S., 1969); University of South Carolina (J.D., 1976). Deputy Commissioner, North Carolina Industrial Commission, 1990-1996. Lecturer, 1997 and Course Planner, 1998, North Carolina Bar Association Advanced Workers' Compensation Seminars. *Member:* North Carolina Bar Association (Council Member, Workers' Compensation Section, 1997-1999; CLE Chairperson, 1998; Member, Trial Curriculum Committee, 1998-2003); North Carolina Association of Defense Attorneys. ***Email:*** jpittman@tcdg.com

MELISSA R. CLEARY, born Detroit, Michigan, July 28, 1970; admitted to bar, 1995, North Carolina; U.S. District Court, Eastern, Middle and Western Districts of North Carolina. *Education:* Saint Mary's College (B.A., magna cum laude, 1992); University of North Carolina (J.D., 1995). *Member:* North Carolina Association of Defense Attorneys. ***Email:*** mcleary@tcdg.com

ASSOCIATES

TRACEY L. JONES, born Raleigh, North Carolina, January 9, 1972; admitted to bar, 1997, North Carolina. *Education:* University of North Carolina (B.A., 1994); Wake Forest University (J.D., 1997). Member, Wake Forest Law Review, 1995-1997. Research Assistant, North Carolina Court of Appeals, 1997-1999. *Member:* North Carolina Association of Defense Attorneys. ***Email:*** tjones@tcdg.com

JENNIFER B. MILAK, born Raleigh, North Carolina, November 10, 1971; admitted to bar, 1997, North Carolina. *Education:* North Carolina State University (B.A., magna cum laude, 1994); Campbell University (J.D., magna cum laude, 1997). Phi Kappa Phi. Membership Editor, Law Review, 1995-1997. *Member:* North Carolina Association of Defense Attorneys; Association of Women in Insurance. ***Email:*** jmilak@tcdg.com

TARA D. MULLER, born Washington, D.C., January 16, 1975; admitted to bar, 2000, North Carolina; 2001, U.S. District Court, Eastern District of North Carolina; 2002, U.S. District Court, Middle District of North Carolina, U.S. Court of Appeals, Fourth Circuit; registered to practice before U.S. Patent and Trademark Office. *Education:* North Carolina State University (B.A., cum laude, 1997); Campbell University (J.D., 2000). Case Summary Editor, Campbell Law Observer, 1998-1999. *Member:* North Carolina Association of Defense Attorneys. ***Email:*** tmuller@tcdg.com

SEASON D. ATKINSON, born Johnstown, Pennsylvania, November 21, 1973; admitted to bar, 2001, North Carolina, West Virginia and U.S. District Court, Southern District of West Virginia. *Education:* Marshall University (B.A., 1997); Dickinson School of Law, Pennsylvania State University (J.D., 2000). *Member:* Wake County and North Carolina Bar Associations; North Carolina Association of Defense Attorneys. ***Email:*** satkinson@tcdg.com

CARLA M. COBB, born Smithfield, North Carolina, October 31, 1974; admitted to bar, 2001, North Carolina. *Education:* University of North Carolina (B.A., 1997); Campbell University (J.D., 2001). Order of the Barristers. Member, ABA Moot Court Team; ABA Trial Team, Regional Finalist; National Trial Team.*Member:* National Academy of Trial Lawyers; North Carolina Association of Defense Attorneys. ***Email:*** ccobb@tcdg.com

JACOB H. WELLMAN, born Rocky Mount, North Carolina, August 11, 1977; admitted to bar, 2002, North Carolina; 2005, U.S. District Court, Western District of North Carolina. *Education:* University of North Carolina (B.A., 1999); Wake Forest University (J.D., 2002). Order of the Coif. Member, Moot Court Board and Joseph Branch Inn of Court. *Member:* North Carolina Association of Defense Attorneys. ***Email:*** jwellman@tcdg.com

ROBERT M. TATUM, born Ft. Bragg, North Carolina, May 24, 1968; admitted to bar, 2002, North Carolina. *Education:* University of Virginia (B.S., 1999); University of North Carolina (J.D., 2002). Member, Journal of International Law and Commercial Regulation. Member, National Moot Court. *Member:* North Carolina Association of Defense Attorneys. [U.S. Army, 1988-1992]. ***LANGUAGES:*** Spanish, French. ***Email:*** rtatum@tcdg.com

CHRISTOPHER G. LEWIS, born Washington, D.C., May 2, 1969; admitted to bar, 1998, North Carolina. *Education:* University of North Carolina (B.A., 1991); Campbell University (J.D., 1998). *Member:* North Carolina Association of Defense Attorneys. ***Email:*** clewis@tcdg.com

JOHN L. TIDBALL, V, born Lincoln, Nebraska, June 23, 1967; admitted to bar, 1999, North Carolina. *Education:* University of Montana (B.A., 1992); Campbell University (J.D., 1999). *Member:* Wake County Bar Association; North Carolina State Bar; North Carolina Association of Defense Attorneys. ***Email:*** jtidball@tcdg.com

MICHAEL D. MOORE, born Dickinson, North Dakota, January 6, 1964; admitted to bar, 1996, North Carolina. *Education:* University of North Dakota (B.A., 1986); Campbell University (J.D., 1996). *Member:* North Carolina State Bar. [Major, USMC, 1986-1993]. ***Email:*** mmoore@tcdg.com

WILLIAM A. BULFER, born Munster, Indiana, February 11, 1978; admitted to bar, 2003, North Carolina. *Education:* Purdue University (B.A., 2000); Wake Forest University (J.D., 2003). *Member:* North Carolina State Bar. ***Email:*** wbulfer@tcdg.com

JULIA S. HOOTEN, born Raleigh, North Carolina, March 9, 1972; admitted to bar, 2003, North Carolina. *Education:* Appalachian State University (B.A., 1994); Western Carolina University (M.A., 2000); Campbell University (J.D., 2003). *Member:* North Carolina State Bar. ***Email:*** jhooten@tcdg.com

KATHRYN DEITER-MARADEI, born Pittsburgh, Pennsylvania, February 5, 1978; admitted to bar, 2004, North Carolina. *Education:* Pennsylvania State University (B.S., 2000); University of North Carolina (J.D., 2003). *Member:* North Carolina State Bar. ***LANGUAGES:*** Spanish. ***Email:*** kdeiter-maradei@tcdg.com

COURTNEY C. BRITT, born Mars Hill, North Carolina, June 3, 1977; admitted to bar, 2004, North Carolina. *Education:* Wake Forest University (B.S., 1999; J.D., 2004). ***Email:*** cbritt@tcdg.com

EDWARD S. SCHENK, III, born Mount Airy, North Carolina, January 4, 1978; admitted to bar, 2004, North Carolina. *Education:* University of North Carolina at Wilmington (B.A., 2000); Campbell University (J.D., 2004). ***Email:*** eschenk@tcdg.com

MATTHEW W. SKIDMORE, born Gastonia, North Carolina, September 17, 1978; admitted to bar, 2004, North Carolina. *Education:* North Carolina State University (B.S., 2001); University of North Carolina (J.D., 2004). ***Email:*** mskidmore@tcdg.com

BRADLEY INMAN, born Fayetteville, North Carolina, November 29, 1973; admitted to bar, 2005, North Carolina. *Education:* University of North Carolina at Chapel Hill (B.S.B.A., 1996; J.D., 2005). Certified Public Accountant, 2002. *Member:* North Carolina State Bar.

OF COUNSEL

JOHN WISHART CAMPBELL, born Lumberton, North Carolina, September 6, 1923; admitted to bar, 1949, North Carolina and U.S. District Court, Eastern District of North Carolina; 1956, U.S. Supreme Court. *Education:* Davidson College; Mississippi State College; University of North Carolina (LL.B., 1949). *Member:* North Carolina (Member, Board of Governors, 1970-1973) and American Bar Associations; North Carolina State Bar (Member, State Bar Council, 1973-1979; President, 1981-1982). Fellow, American College of Trial Lawyers. (Resident at Lumberton Office)

MARILYN ELLISON TOMEI, born Poughkeepsie, New York, April 6, 1963; admitted to bar, 1987, North Carolina; 1988, U.S. District Court, Eastern District of North Carolina; 1989, U.S. District Court, Middle District of North Carolina. *Education:* University of North Carolina (B.S., 1984; J.D., 1987). Chief Justice, Law School Honor Court, 1986-1987.

REPRESENTATIVE CLIENTS: Ace USA; Acceptance Insurance Company; Acordia of North Carolina, Inc.; AIG; Allied Claims Administration, Inc.; BE&K Construction Company; Bituminous Insurance; Blockbuster Video; Brentwood Services Administrators, Inc.; Broadspire Services, Inc.; Budget Rent-A-Car Systems, Inc.; Chicago Insurance Company; CNA; Coca Cola Bottling Company Consolidated; Companion Property & Casualty Company; CompManagement; Constitution State Service Company; Crawford & Company; Eion Homes for Children, Inc.; EMC Insurance Companies; Farmers Insurance Group; Farmland Insurance Company; Federal Express; Federated Rural Electric Insurance Company; Fireman's Fund Insurance Company; Fiuor Global Services; Fresenius Medical; GAB Robins North America Inc.; Gallagher Bassett Services, Inc.; General Casualty Insurance Company; General Electric Company; General Star Management Corporation; Great American Insurance Company; Guard Insurance Group; Interstate Insurance Group; Jefferson Insurance Company; Key Risk Management Services, Inc.; Kroger Stores, Inc.; Lancer Claim Services; Lexington Insurance Company; Liberty Mutual Insurance Company; Martin Marietta; Maryland Automobile Insurance Fund; Mead Westvaco; Mitsui Sumitomo Marine Management; Mohawk Industries; MSI Risk Management Services; National Benefits Group; National Indemnity Company; National Interstate Carriers; National Union Fire Insurance Company; Nationwide Insurance Company; North American Risk Services, Inc.; North Carolina Association of County Commissioners; North Carolina Automobile Dealers Association; North

(This Listing Continued)

Carolina Insurance Guaranty Association; North Carolina League of Municipalities; Ohio Casualty Group; Pennsylvania Lumbermen's Mutual Insurance Company; Phoenix Aviation Managers, Inc.; Pitt County Memorial Hospital; Progress Energy Carolinas, Inc.; Prudential Carolinas Realty; Psychiatric Solutions, Inc.; ReMax One Realty; Royal & SunAlliance Insurance Company; Ryan's Family Steakhouses; Scottsdale Insurance Company; Sedgwick Claims Management Services, Inc.; Seibels Bruce and Company; SISCO; Southeastern Claims Services, Inc.; Southern Guaranty Insurance Company; Specialty Risk Services; St. Paul Travelers; State Automobile Mutual Insurance Company; TIG Insurance Company; Tyson Foods, Inc.; Underwriters Safety & Claims; W.R. Berkley Corporation; Wake County Public School System; Waste Management, Inc.; WestPoint Stevens, Inc.; Weyerhaeuser Company; Yellow Freight Corporation; York Claims Service, Inc.; Zenith Insurance Company; Zurich U.S.

TEMPLE LAW FIRM, PLLC

615 WILLARD PLACE
RALEIGH, NORTH CAROLINA 27603
Telephone: 919-832-5732
1-800-982-2126
Fax: 919-832-7732
URL: http://www.templelawfirm.com

Pharmaceutical and Defective Medical Devices (Fen-hen, Vioxx, Celebrex & Bextra), Environmental and Toxic Torts, Personal Injury, Products Liability, Wrongful Death, Civil Litigation.

G. HENRY TEMPLE, JR., born Raleigh, North Carolina; admitted to bar, 1974, North Carolina. *Education:* University of North Carolina at Chapel Hill (B.A., 1970); University of South Carolina (J.D., 1974). *Member:* Wake County Bar Association; North Carolina State Bar; North Carolina Academy of Trial Lawyers; The Association of Trial Lawyers of America. ***PRACTICE AREAS:*** Personal Injury; Wrongful Death; Products Liability; Environmental Land Use; Toxic Torts. ***Email:*** ghtemple@templelawfirm.com

---

RUSSELL DAVID BABB, born Wilson, North Carolina, January 12, 1973; admitted to bar, 1999, North Carolina. *Education:* University of North Carolina (B.A., 1996; J.D., 1999). John Motley Morehead Scholar. Recipient, Atlantic Coast Conference/Weaver James Postgraduate Scholarship. *Member:* Wake County Bar Association; North Carolina State Bar (Chair, Sports and Entertainment Law Council Bylaws Committee). ***PRACTICE AREAS:*** Criminal Law; Civil Litigation; Personal Injury; Products Liability; Antitrust; White Collar Crime; Sports Law; Entertainment Law. ***Email:*** rbabb@templelawfirm.com

EDITH R. SALMONY, born Charlotte, North Carolina, November 17, 1948; admitted to bar, 1986, North Carolina. *Education:* University of North Carolina at Chapel Hill (B.A., 1970); University of North Carolina Greensboro (M.A., Economics, 1976); North Carolina Central University (J.D., magna cum laude, 1986). Adjunct Professor, UNC Law School, 1987. Former Member, Edith Richards Salmony, Attorney at Law, PA. *Member:* Orange County and North Carolina (Member, Sections on: Trusts and Estates; Real Property; Health Law; Elder Law) Bar Associations; Academy of Trial Lawyers; North Carolina Association of Women Attorneys. ***PRACTICE AREAS:*** Employment Law; Venture Capital; Business Law; Business Torts. ***Email:*** esalmony@templelawfirm.com

TENNEY & TENNEY, LLP

160 WIND CHIME COURT
RALEIGH, NORTH CAROLINA 27615
Telephone: 919-841-4696
Fax: 919-841-4699
Email: tenneylaw@msn.com

Wills, Estates, Probate, Trusts, Living Trusts, Business Law, Corporate Law, Small Business, Intellectual Property, Contracts, Personal Injury, Automobile Accidents, Slip and Fall, Civil Litigation, Real Estate, Residential Real Estate, Real Estate Closings, Family Law.

MEMBERS OF THE FIRM

BRIAN H. TENNEY, born Denver, Colorado, August 17, 1948; admitted to bar, 1973, North Carolina and U.S. Court of Military Appeals; 1977, U.S. District Court, Eastern District of North Carolina; 2002, U.S. District Court, Western District of North Carolina. *Education:* North Carolina State University (B.A., History, 1970); Wake Forest University (J.D., 1973). *Member:* Wake County and North Carolina Bar Associations. [JAGC, U.S. Army, 1973-1976]. ***PRACTICE AREAS:*** Civil Practice; Wills; Estates; Corporate Law; Business Law; Civil Litigation; Real Estate; Personal Injury Law.

WALTER D. TENNEY, born Raleigh, North Carolina, December 18, 1973; admitted to bar, 2002, North Carolina and U.S. District Court, Eastern District of North Carolina. *Education:* North Carolina State University (B.A., Political Science, 1996); New England School of Law (J.D., 2000). *Member:* Wake County and North Carolina Bar Associations; Academy of Trial Lawyers. ***PRACTICE AREAS:*** Real Estate; Civil Litigation; Wills; Estates; Corporate Law; Personal Injury Law.

ALLEN R. TEW, P.A.

RALEIGH, NORTH CAROLINA

(See Clayton)

General and Trial Practice in all State and Federal Courts, Civil Litigation, Personal Injury Law, Automobile Accidents, Wrongful Death, Domestic Relations and Real Estate, Construction Litigation, Mediation.

THARRINGTON SMITH

A Registered Limited Liability Partnership
Established in 1964
209 FAYETTEVILLE STREET MALL
P.O. BOX 1151
RALEIGH, NORTH CAROLINA 27602
Telephone: 919-821-4711
Telecopier: 919-829-1583
Email: kgardner@tharringtonsmith.com
URL: http://tharringtonsmith.com

Civil and Criminal Trials and Appeals in all State and Federal Courts, Mediation and Alternative Dispute Resolution, Education Law, Constitutional Law, Employment Law, Family Law, Professional Licensure Proceedings, Personal Injury, Voting Rights, Local Government Law, Construction Contracts and Litigation, Business and Corporate Law, Commercial Litigation, Alcoholic Beverage Control Law, Administrative Law, Tax Litigation, Unfair Competition, Copyright, Legislative and Lobbying, Sports and Entertainment Law.

MEMBERS OF FIRM

CARLISLE W. HIGGINS (1887-1980)

GEORGE T. ROGISTER, JR. (1946-1995)

WADE M. SMITH, born Albemarle, North Carolina, October 9, 1937; admitted to bar, 1963, North Carolina; 1968, U.S. Supreme Court; 1979, U.S. Court of Appeals, Fourth Circuit; U.S. District Court, Eastern, Middle and Western Districts of North Carolina; U.S. District Court, Eastern District of Tennessee. *Education:* University of North Carolina (A.B., 1960; J.D., 1963). President, General Alumni Association, 1990-1991. U.N.C. Distinguished Service Award, 1993. Morehead Scholar. Member, Fourth Circuit Judicial Conference. Named Alumnus of the Year, University of North Carolina School of Law, 2000. Listed in Best Lawyers in America (Criminal Section). Law Clerk, North Carolina Supreme Court, 1963-1964. North Carolina Criminal Code Commission, 1970-1976. Lecturer, Atlanta Superstars Seminar, Atlanta, Georgia, 1988. Member, North Carolina House of Representatives, 1973-1976. North Carolina Art Museum Commission, 1982. Chairman, North Carolina Democratic Party, 1985. Past Member, Board of Trustees, North Carolina School of the Arts. Trustee, Wake County Education Partnership. Chosen by Business North Carolina Magazine, North Carolina's Number One Criminal Lawyer, based on survey of North Carolina lawyers. *Member:* Wake County (President, 1988), North Carolina and American Bar Associations; North Carolina Academy of Trial Lawyers; The Association of Trial Lawyers of America; National Association of Criminal Defense Lawyers; Wake County Academy of Criminal Trial Lawyers (President, 1972). Fellow: American College of Trial Lawyers; American Board of Criminal Lawyers; International Society of Barristers. ***PRACTICE AREAS:*** Administrative Law; Employment Law; White Collar Crime; Federal Criminal Law; Federal Civil Litigation; Civil Litigation. ***Email:*** wsmith@tharringtonsmith.com

ROGER W. SMITH, born Albemarle, North Carolina, June 15, 1941; admitted to bar, 1967, North Carolina; 1973, U.S. District Court, Eastern, Middle and Western Districts of North Carolina, U.S. Court of Appeals; 1974, U.S. Supreme Court. *Education:* University of North Carolina at Chapel Hill (A.B., 1964; J.D., 1967). Chief Justice, Holderness Moot Court Bench. Morehead Scholar. Recipient, Wettach-Van Hecke Citizenship Award. Law Clerk, Supreme Court of North Carolina, 1967-1968. Listed: Best Lawyers In America (Criminal Section). Member: Louisburg College, Board of Directors, 1998—; American Judicature Society, Director, 1997—; North Carolina Board of Legal Specialization, 1990-1996, Vice-chairman, 1996; North Carolina Sentencing and Policy Advisory Commission, 1992-1994; North Carolina Justice Needs Assessment Task Force, 1993; North Carolina Supreme Court Historical Society, President, 1998—; Summit House of North Carolina, Board of Governors, 1995—. *Member:* Wake County (Secretary, 1971-1972; President, 1993), North Carolina and American (House of Delegates, 1996—) Bar Associations; North Carolina State Bar (Council, 1980-1989; Ethics Committee, 1980-1989; Chair, Publications Study Commission, 1994-1996; Publications Committee, 1998—); Wake County Academy of Criminal Trial Lawyers (Secretary, 1971-1972; Vice-President, 1972-1973; President, 1973-1974); Association of Trial Lawyers of American. Fellow: American College of Trial Lawyers; American Academy of Appellate Lawyers. ***PRACTICE AREAS:*** Criminal Law; Civil Litigation; Professional Discipline. ***Email:*** rsmith@tharringtonsmith.com

CARLYN G. POOLE, born Taylor, Texas, August 22, 1940; admitted to bar, 1979, North Carolina. *Education:* Texas Tech University (B.A., with honors, 1962; M.A., 1963); Vanderbilt University; University of North Carolina (J.D., with honors, 1979). Order of the Coif. Managing Editor, North Carolina Law Review, 1978-1979. Editor, North Carolina Family Forum, 1984-1985. Listed: Best Lawyers in America (Family Law Section). Adjunct Instructor, University of North Carolina School of Law, 1992-1993. North Carolina Child Support Council, 1987-1989. Chair, North Carolina Conference of Bar Presidents, 1992. Certified Mediator for Family Financial Cases, Dispute Resolution Commission. *Member:* Wake County (President, 1991; Long Range Planning Committee Chair, 1996; Professionalism Committee Chair, 1996-1997) and North Carolina (Family Law Section, Chair, 1985-1986; Appellate Rules Study Committee, 1982-1986; Board of Governors, 1986-1989; Vice-President, 1992-1994; Family Law CLE Committee, 1988-2004) Bar Associations; North Carolina State Bar (Member, Family Law Specialization Committee, 1996-2001; CLE Committee, 1995-1999; Disciplinary Hearing Commission, 2000-2006). Fellow, American Academy of Matrimonial Lawyers. (Board Certified Specialist in Family Law, North Carolina State Board of Legal Specialization). ***PRACTICE AREAS:*** Family Law; Mediation. ***Email:*** cpoole@tharringtonsmith.com

DOUGLAS E. KINGSBERY, born Phoenix, Arizona, December 30, 1954; admitted to bar, 1980, North Carolina; 1981, U.S. District Court, Eastern, Western, and Middle Districts of North Carolina; 1984, U.S. Court of Appeals, Fourth Circuit; 1991, U.S. Supreme Court; 1994, U.S. Tax Court; 1996, U.S. Court of Federal Claims. *Education:* Duke University (A.B., 1977; J.D., 1980). *Member:* Wake County, North Carolina and American (Litigation and Criminal Law Sections) Bar Associations; North Carolina Academy of Trial Lawyers; The Association of Trial Lawyers of America; National Association of Criminal

(This Listing Continued)

THARRINGTON SMITH, Raleigh—Continued

Defense Lawyers; North Carolina State Bar (Member, North Carolina Medical Board; Chair, Criminal Law Specialty Committee, 1999-2000). ***PRACTICE AREAS:*** Commercial Litigation; White Collar Crime; Civil Tax Litigation; Criminal Tax Litigation. ***Email:*** dek@tharringtonsmith.com

RANDALL M. RODEN, born Iowa City, Iowa, January 30, 1946; admitted to bar, 1976, North Carolina; 1977, District of Columbia; 1980, U.S. Supreme Court; 1984, U.S. Claims Court; U.S. Tax Court; U.S. Court of Appeals, Fourth Circuit; U.S. Court of Appeals, District of Columbia Circuit; U.S. Court of Appeals for the Federal Circuit; U.S. District Court, Eastern, Middle and Western Districts of North Carolina. *Education:* Phillips Academy, Andover, Mass. (1964); University of North Carolina (B.A., 1973; J.D., 1976). Trial Attorney, Tax Division, U.S. Department of Justice, 1977-1984. *Member:* Wake County, North Carolina (Litigation and Construction Sections) and American (Litigation Section) Bar Associations; North Carolina Academy of Trial Lawyers. ***PRACTICE AREAS:*** Civil Litigation; Civil Appellate Litigation; Business and Employment Law. ***Email:*** rroden@tharringtonsmith.com

MICHAEL CROWELL, born Waco, Texas, 1945; admitted to bar, 1971, North Carolina. *Education:* University of Mississippi (Carrier Scholar); University of North Carolina (B.A., 1967); Harvard University (J.D., cum laude, 1970). Professor of Public Law and Government, 1970-1985, Institute of Government, University of North Carolina at Chapel Hill. Director of Legislative Drafting, North Carolina General Assembly, 1981. Consultant, North Carolina Criminal Code Commission, 1978-1983. Executive Director, Commission for the Future of Justice and the Courts in North Carolina, 1994-1996. Member, Election Laws Revision Commission, 1999-2001. Certified Mediator. *Member:* North Carolina Bar Association (Chair, Administrative Law Section, 1991-1992; Council; Government and Public Sector Section, 2003—); International Municipal Lawyers Association. ***PRACTICE AREAS:*** Administrative Law; Local Government Law; Elections; Mediation. ***Email:*** mcrowell@tharringtonsmith.com

ANN L. MAJESTIC, born Honolulu, Hawaii, October 20, 1952; admitted to bar, 1982, North Carolina. *Education:* Duke University (B.A., 1974; J.D., 1982); Harvard University (Ed. M., 1978). *Member:* Wake County and North Carolina (Board of Directors, Education Law Section, 1990-1992) Bar Associations; National Council of School Attorneys (Board of Directors, 1990—; Secretary, 1995-1996, Second Vice-Chairman, 1996-1997; First Vice Chairman, 1997-1998; Chairman, 1998-1999); North Carolina Council of School Attorneys (Chairman, 1988-1989). ***PRACTICE AREAS:*** Education Law; Employment Law. ***Email:*** amajestice@tharringtonsmith.com

MELISSA HILL, born Asheville, North Carolina, March 20, 1962; admitted to bar, 1987, North Carolina. *Education:* University of North Carolina (B.A., with honors, 1984; J.D., with honors, 1987). Phi Beta Kappa; Order of the Coif. Staff Member, North Carolina Law Review, 1985-1986. *Member:* Wake County, North Carolina and American Bar Associations; The Association of Trial Lawyers of America; North Carolina Academy of Trial Lawyers; Wake County Academy of Criminal Trial Lawyers. ***PRACTICE AREAS:*** Criminal Law; Civil Litigation. ***Email:*** mhill@tharringtonsmith.com

DANIEL W. CLARK, born Binghamton, New York, September 26, 1963; admitted to bar, 1988, North Carolina; U.S. Court of Appeals, Fourth Circuit; U.S. District Court, Eastern, Middle and Western Districts of North Carolina. *Education:* University of North Carolina at Chapel Hill (B.A., with honors, 1985; J.D., 1988). Member, University of North Carolina Law Review, 1987-1988. Staff Member, 1986-1987 and Editorial Board Member, 1987-1988. *Member:* Wake County, North Carolina and American Bar Associations; North Carolina Academy of Trial Lawyers. ***PRACTICE AREAS:*** Employment Law; Civil Litigation; Business Law; Intellectual Property Law. ***Email:*** dclark@tharringtonsmith.com

JONATHAN A. BLUMBERG, born Baltimore, Maryland, April 11, 1960; admitted to bar, 1986, North Carolina. *Education:* University of North Carolina at Chapel Hill (B.A., 1982; J.D., with honors, 1986). Member, University of North Carolina Law Review, 1984-1985. Law Clerk to the Honorable Eugene A. Gordon, U.S. District Court Judge, Middle District of North Carolina. *Member:* Wake County and North Carolina Bar Associations; North Carolina Council of School Attorneys; National Council of School Attorneys. ***PRACTICE AREAS:*** Education Law; Employment Law; Civil Litigation. ***Email:*** jblumberg@tharringtonsmith.com

ROD MALONE, born Raleigh, North Carolina, March 5, 1964; admitted to bar, 1989, North Carolina. *Education:* North Carolina State University (B.S.E.E., 1986); University of North Carolina at Chapel Hill (J.D., 1989). *Member:* Wake County, North Carolina (Member, Committees on: Education Law; Construction Law; Council Member, Construction Law Section) and American (Public Contract Law and Construction Industry Form Committee) Bar Associations; North Carolina Council of School Attorneys (Chairman, Executive Committee); National Council of School Attorneys. ***PRACTICE AREAS:*** Education Law; Construction Law; Employment Law. ***Email:*** rmalone@tharringtonsmith.com

JAYE POWELL MEYER, born Quantico, Virginia, January 17, 1961; admitted to bar, 1990, North Carolina. *Education:* Wake Forest University (B.A., 1983); University of North Carolina at Chapel Hill (M.S., 1985; J.D., with high honors, 1990). Editor-in-Chief, North Carolina Law Review, 1989-1990. Listed in Best Lawyers in America, 2001—. *Member:* Wake County, North Carolina (Past Chair, Family Law Section) and American (Family Law Section) Bar Associations. Fellow, American Academy of Matrimonial Lawyers. (Board Certified Specialist in Family Law, North Carolina State Board of Legal Specialization). ***PRACTICE AREAS:*** Family Law. ***Email:*** jmeyer@tharringtonsmith.com

KENNETH A. SOO, born Winston-Salem, North Carolina, June 10, 1958; admitted to bar, 1991, North Carolina and U.S. District Court, Western District of North Carolina; 1994, U.S. District Court, Eastern and Middle Districts of North Carolina; 1996, U.S. Court of Appeals, Fourth Circuit. *Education:* Duke University (A.B., 1981); University of North Carolina-Chapel Hill (J.D., with honors, 1991). Note Editor, North Carolina Law Review. *Member:* Durham County and North Carolina Bar Associations; North Carolina Council of School Attorneys; National Council of School Attorneys. ***PRACTICE AREAS:*** Education Law; Employment Law. ***Email:*** ksoo@tharringtonsmith.com

(This Listing Continued)

LYNN P. BURLESON, born 1948; admitted to bar, 1980, North Carolina. *Education:* University of North Carolina (A.B., 1970; M.P.A., 1974); Wake Forest University (J.D., 1980). Listed in: Best Lawyers in America, 2001-2002; Business North Carolina Legal Elite, 2004. North Carolina District Court Judge, 1984-1987. *Member:* Wake County, Forsyth County (Past President) and North Carolina (Past Chair, Family Law Section; Member, Board of Governors, 1994-1997) Bar Associations. Fellow, American Academy of Matrimonial Lawyers (Past President, State Chapter). ***PRACTICE AREAS:*** Family Law. ***Email:*** lburleson@tharringtonsmith.com

F. HILL ALLEN, born Louisburg, North Carolina, September 27, 1967; admitted to bar, 1992, North Carolina; U.S. Court of Appeals, Fourth Circuit; U.S. District Court, Eastern, Middle and Western Districts of North Carolina. *Education:* University of North Carolina at Chapel Hill (B.A., English, honors in Creative Writing, 1989); University of Virginia (J.D., 1992). Phi Beta Kappa. ***PRACTICE AREAS:*** Criminal Law; Civil Litigation. ***Email:*** hallen@tharringtonsmith.com

FRED M. MORELOCK, born Nuremberg, Germany, March 9, 1952; admitted to bar, 1976, North Carolina. *Education:* University of North Carolina (B.A., 1974; J.D., 1976). District Court Judge, 10th Judicial District, Wake County, 1986-2000. Certified Superior Court Mediator. *Member:* North Carolina Bar Association (Family Law Section). ***PRACTICE AREAS:*** Family Law Litigation; Mediation; Arbitration. ***Email:*** fmorelock@tsmithlaw.com

ASSOCIATES

ROGER W. SMITH, JR., born Raleigh, North Carolina, January 21, 1969; admitted to bar, 1999, North Carolina. *Education:* University of North Carolina at Chapel Hill (B.A., English, 1991); Campbell University (J.D., 1999). Order of Kivett. Member, National Trial Team. *Member:* Wake County, North Carolina and American Bar Associations; Wake County Academy of Criminal Trial Lawyers; North Carolina Academy of Trial Lawyers; National Association of Criminal Defense Lawyers; American Judicature Society. ***PRACTICE AREAS:*** Criminal Law; Personal Injury. ***Email:*** rsmithjr@tharringtonsmith.com

CAROLYN A. WALLER, born 1968; admitted to bar, 1998, North Carolina; U.S. Court of Appeals, Fourth Circuit and U.S. District Court, Eastern, Middle and Western Districts of North Carolina. *Education:* University of California at Berkeley (B.A., 1990); University of North Carolina (J.D., with honors, 1998). Daniel H. Pollitt Fellow, James E. & Carolyn B. Davis Society. Articles Editor, North Carolina Journal of International Law and Commercial Regulation, 1997-1998. *Member:* North Carolina Bar Association (Member, Education Section); National Council of School Attorneys; North Carolina Council of School Attorneys. ***PRACTICE AREAS:*** Education Law; Employment Law. ***Email:*** cwaller@tharringtonsmith.com

KARA GRICE ACREE, born Charlotte, North Carolina, October 6, 1970; admitted to bar, 2000, North Carolina. *Education:* Duke University (B.A., 1992; M.A.T., 1993); University of North Carolina at Chapel Hill (J.D., with honors, 2000). Fellow, James Madison Memorial Foundation. Staff Member, North Carolina Law Review. Author, "Striking an Unequal Balance", 77 N.C. L. Rev. 1960 (1999). *Member:* North Carolina Bar Association (Member, Education Section; Member, Education Section Council); National Council of School Attorneys; North Carolina Council of School Attorneys. ***PRACTICE AREAS:*** Education Law. ***Email:*** kacree@tharringtonsmith.com

JILL SCHNABEL JACKSON, born Clark County, Wisconsin, February 25, 1974; admitted to bar, 1999, North Carolina. *Education:* University of Minnesota (B.A., 1996); University of North Carolina at Chapel Hill (J.D., with honors, 1999). Member, National Moot Court Team; Staff Member, North Carolina Journal of International Law and Commercial Regulation. Law Clerk, Associate Justice Sarah Parker, North Carolina Supreme Court. *Member:* Wake County and North Carolina (Member, Family Law Section) Bar Associations. ***PRACTICE AREAS:*** Family Law. ***Email:*** jilljackson@tharringtonsmith.com

KRISTOPHER B. GARDNER, born Charlotte, North Carolina, August 21, 1976; admitted to bar, 2002, North Carolina and U.S. District Court, Middle and Eastern Districts of North Carolina. *Education:* University of North Carolina at Chapel Hill (B.A., 1998); North Carolina Central University (J.D., 2002). *Member:* Wake County, North Carolina and American Bar Associations. ***PRACTICE AREAS:*** Local Government Law; Litigation. ***Email:*** kgardner@tharringtonsmith.com

DEBORAH R. STAGNER, born Parma, Ohio, 1963; admitted to bar, 1997, North Carolina. *Education:* University of Kansas (B.G.S., 1992); University of North Carolina, Chapel Hill (J.D., with honors, 1997). Staff Member, North Carolina Law Review. Law Clerk, Chief Justice Henry E. Frye, North Carolina Supreme Court, 1997-2000. ***PRACTICE AREAS:*** Education Law; Election Law. ***Email:*** dstagner@tharringtonsmith.com

KATHLEEN P. TANNER, born Raleigh, North Carolina, November 18, 1975; admitted to bar, 2001, North Carolina; 2003, District of Columbia. *Education:* University of North Carolina at Chapel Hill (B.A., 1997; J.D., with honors, 2001). Phi Beta Kappa. Member, North Carolina Law Review, 1999-2000. Law Clerk, Honorable Ed. Carnes, U.S. Court of Appeals for the Eleventh Circuit. *Member:* North Carolina Bar Association (Member, Education Section); North Carolina Council of School Attorneys; National Council of School Attorneys. ***PRACTICE AREAS:*** Education; Litigation. ***Email:*** ktanner@tharringtonsmith.com

RETIRED

J. HAROLD THARRINGTON, born Raleigh, North Carolina, May 5, 1937; admitted to bar, 1963, North Carolina; 1968, U.S. Supreme Court. *Education:* University of North Carolina (A.B., 1959; J.D., with honors, 1963). North Carolina Law Review, 1962-1963. Law Clerk, North Carolina Supreme Court, 1963-1964. *Member:* North Carolina (Family Law Section) Bar Association. ***PRACTICE AREAS:*** Family Law; Mediation.

REPRESENTATIVE CLIENTS: Wake County Board of Education; Durham Public Schools Board of Education; North Carolina School Boards Assn.; North Carolina Psychological Assn.; USF&G Corporation; Exxon Corporation; The Liberty Corporation; American National Can Company; Adams Products Co.; Person County Board of Education; Crown Central Petroleum Corp.; North Carolina Beer and Wine Wholesalers Association; Northampton County Board of Education; Hertford County Board of Education; Weldon County Board of Education; Edgecombe County Board of Education; Beaufort County Board of Education; Johnston County Board of Education; North Carolina Nurses Association.

FREDERIC E. TOMS & ASSOCIATES, PLLC

RALEIGH, NORTH CAROLINA

(See Cary)

Personal Injury, Medical Malpractice, Creditor, Traffic Violations, Nursing Home Litigation, Automobile Accidents, Wrongful Death.

DANIEL T. TOWER, P.A.

Established in 2004

4700 SIX FORKS ROAD, SUITE 150
RALEIGH, NORTH CAROLINA 27609
Telephone: 919-781-2217
Fax: 919-781-7727
Email: dtower@towerlawfirm.com
URL: http://www.towerlawfirm.com

Mailing Address: P.O. Box 13011, Raleigh, NC 27609

Real Estate, Real Estate Development, Real Estate Litigation, Construction Law, Commercial Litigation.

FIRM PROFILE: A law firm dedicated to helping firms and individuals in the areas of construction and real estate law.

DANIEL T. TOWER, born Auckland, New Zealand, September 2, 1971; admitted to bar, 1998, North Carolina and U.S. District Court, Eastern, Middle and Western Districts of North Carolina; 2000, Georgia and U.S. District Court, Northern District of Georgia. *Education:* Duke University (B.A., 1993); Wake Forest University (J.D., 1998). Member, Wake Forest Moot Court Board, 1996-1998. Member, Wake Forest Law Review, 1996-1998. *Member:* Wake County, North Carolina (Member, Construction Law Section) and American Bar Associations. ***PRACTICE AREAS:*** Construction Law; Real Estate Development; Real Estate Litigation; Commercial Litigation. ***Email:*** dtower@towerlawfirm.com

APPROVED ATTORNEY FOR: Investor's Title Co.; Surety Land Title Co.; Commonwealth Land Title Co.; Title Co. of NC.

TRACHTMAN LAW FIRM, P.L.L.C.

Established in 2005

CAROLINA CORPORATE CENTRE
5400 GLENWOOD AVENUE
SUITE G-01
RALEIGH, NORTH CAROLINA 27612
Telephone: 919-781-3404
Facsimile: 919-781-3405
Email: Info@TrachtmanLawFirm.com
URL: http://www.TrachtmanLawFirm.com

Real Estate Litigation, Contract Disputes, Broker/Dealer Litigation, Derivative Actions, Securities Litigation, Business Torts, Director and Officer Liability Claims, Fiduciary Liability Claims, Intellectual Property Claims, Unfair Trade Practices, Non-competition Agreements, Employee Benefits Litigation, Catastrophic Personal Injury, Wrongful Death, Appeals.

JAMES B. TRACHTMAN, admitted to bar, 1995, North Carolina. *Education:* University of Pennsylvania, Wharton (B.S.E., magna cum laude, 1990); Duke University School of Law (J.D., 1995). Managing Editor, Alaska Law Review. Member, Moot Court Board. ***PRACTICE AREAS:*** Real Estate Litigation; Contract Disputes; Broker-Dealer Litigation; Derivatives Action; Securities Litigation; Business Torts; Directors and Officers Liability; Fiduciary Liability; Intellectual Property; Unfair Trade; Noncompetition and Non-Solicitation Agreements; Employee Benefits Litigation; Catastrophic Injury; Wrongful Death; Appellate Practice. ***Email:*** JTrachtman@TrachtmanLawFirm.com

LEGAL SUPPORT PERSONNEL

KAREN L. TRACHTMAN. *Education:* Pitt Community College (A.A.S., Paralegal Technology, 1989). ***Email:*** KTrachtman@TrachtmanLawFirm.com

TROUTMAN SANDERS LLP

434 FAYETTEVILLE STREET MALL
TWO HANNOVER SQUARE
SUITE 1100
RALEIGH, NORTH CAROLINA 27601
Telephone: 919-212-4100
Fax: 919-212-4101
Email: info@troutmansanders.com
URL: http://www.troutmansanders.com

Atlanta, Georgia Office: 600 Peachtree Street, NE, Suite 5200, Atlanta, GA 30308-2216. Telephone: 404-885-3000. Facsimile: 404-885-3900.
Washington, D.C. Office: 401 Ninth Street, N.W., Suite 1000, Washington, D.C. 20004-2134. Telephone: 202-274-2950. Facsimile: 202-274-2994.
Richmond, Virginia Office: Troutman Sanders Building, 1001 Haxall Point, Richmond, VA 23219. Telephone: 804-697-1200. Facsimile: 804-697-1339.
Other Richmond, Virginia Office: 500 Libbie Avenue, Richmond, VA 23226. Telephone: 804-697-1200. Facsimile: 804-288-8366.
McLean Virginia Office: 1660 International Drive, Suite 600, McLean, VA 22102. Telephone: 703-734-4334. Facsimile: 703-734-4340.
Norfolk, Virginia Office: 150 West Main Street, Suite 1600, Norfolk, VA 23510. Telephone: 757-687-7700. Facsimile: 757-687-7701.
Virginia Beach, Virginia Office: 222 Central Park Avenue, Suite 2000, Virginia Beach, VA 23462. Telephone: 757-687-7500. Facsimile: 757-687-7510.

(This Listing Continued)

New York, New York Office: The Chrysler Building, 405 Lexington Avenue, New York, NY 10174. Telephone: 212-704-6000. Facsimile: 212-704-6288.
Hong Kong Office: Suite 3403 Two Exchange Square, 8 Connaught Place, Central, Hong Kong. Telephone: 011-852-2533-7888. Facsimile: 011-852-2533-7898.
London, England Office: Regina House, 6th Floor, 5 Queen Street, EC4N 1SW, London. Telephone: +44 (0) 20 7038 6650. Fax: +44 (0) 20 7038 6651.

Alternative Dispute Resolution, Bankruptcy, Commercial Development and Real Estate Investments, Commercial Leasing, Community Association Law, Compensation and Employee Benefits, Complex Litigation, Construction, Corporate and Securities, Energy, Environmental and Natural Resources, Financial Institutions, Governmental, Government Business Transactions, Healthcare, International, Labor and Employment, Lending and Structured Finance, Media and Entertainment, Multifamily Housing, Nuclear Regulation, Products Liability, Project Development and Finance, Public Finance, Real Estate Finance, Special Investigations, Tax, Technology and Intellectual Property, Technology and Intellectual Property Litigation, Telecommunications and E-Commerce, Tort Liability, Transportation, Trusts and Estates.

FIRM PROFILE: Troutman Sanders LLP, founded in 1897, is an Atlanta-based international law firm with approximately 600 attorneys serving clients from offices in Atlanta, Hong Kong, London, New York, Norfolk, Raleigh, Richmond, Tysons Corner, Virginia Beach and Washington, D.C. The full-service firm offers a broad array of practice areas including corporate, finance, real estate, litigation and public law.

LAW FIRM ALLIANCES/ASSOCIATIONS: ***STATE CAPITAL GLOBAL LAW FIRM GROUP***

TERRALEX, THE WORLDWIDE NETWORK OF INDEPENDENT LAW FIRMS

PARTNERS

F. BRIAN SCHNEIDERMAN, born Huntington, West Virginia, 1965; admitted to bar, 1991, Virginia (Not admitted in North Carolina). *Education:* Duke University (A.B., 1987; M.B.A., 1991; J.D., 1991). (Also at Virginia Beach, Virginia Office). ***PRACTICE AREAS:*** Commercial Real Estate; Real Estate Development; Finance; Commercial Leasing; Sports Law; Entertainment Law. ***Email:*** brian.schneiderman@troutmansanders.com

ASHLEY H. STORY, born Washington, D.C., May 22, 1956; admitted to bar, 1982, North Carolina; 1983, U.S. District Court, Eastern District of North Carolina; 1986, U.S. Tax Court and U.S. Court of Appeals, Fourth Circuit; 1987, U.S. Supreme Court; 1988, U.S. District Court, Western District of North Carolina and U.S. Claims Court; 1993, U.S. District Court, Middle District of North Carolina. *Education:* Wake Forest University (B.A.); Campbell University (J.D., cum laude, 1982); Emory University (LL.M., with distinction, Taxation, 1985); The London School of Economics and Political Science (LL.M., 2000). Phi Kappa Phi; Phi Alpha Delta. Member, Campbell Law Review, 1980-1982. Recipient: American Jurisprudence Book Award; National Education Systems Trial Advocacy Award. Member, American Friends of the London School of Economics. *Member:* Wake County, North Carolina, American and International Bar Associations; International Council of Shopping Centers; Amercian Bankruptcy Institute. (Board Certified Specialist in Business and Bankruptcy Law, North Carolina State Board of Legal Specialization). ***PRACTICE AREAS:*** Commercial Real Estate; Bankruptcy and Insolvency Law; Land Use and Zoning. ***Email:*** ashley.story@troutmansanders.com

ASSOCIATES

JOHN D. BRISTOW, admitted to bar, 2000, North Carolina; 2001, Virginia. *Education:* University of North Carolina at Chapel Hill (B.S., 1992; M.S., 1992; J.D., with high honors, 2000). Order of the Coif. Member, University of North Carolina Law Review. Certified Public Accountant. Tax Manager, Price Waterhouse LLP, 1992-1997. Author: "Eastern Enterprises v. Apfel: Is the Court One Step Closer to Unraveling the Takings and Due Process Clauses?" 77 N.C. Law Rev. 1525, 1999. Speaker, "How to Protect Assets During Life and Avoid Estate Tax at Death in Virginia," CLE course, 2002. ***PRACTICE AREAS:*** Trust and Estate Administration; Trust and Estate Taxation; Estate Planning; Taxation. ***Email:*** john.bristow@troutmansanders.com

BENJAMIN P. FISHER, born Gainesville, Florida, February 11, 1976; admitted to bar, 2001, North Carolina. *Education:* University of North Carolina at Chapel Hill (B.A., 1998); Wake Forest University (J.D., 2001). Semi-Finalist, Trial Bar Competition, 1999. Recipient: CALI Award for Torts, 1999; CALI Award for Trademarks, 2001; James Mason Scholarship, 1999-2001. Member: Trial Bar Association, 1999-2001; Sports and Entertainment Law Association, 2001. Co-Author: "Dealing with Debt Consolidation Companies: A Creditor's Perspective," Legal Insights, Semptember 2002. *Member:* North Carolina Bar Association; North Carolina State Bar; Commercial Law League of America. ***PRACTICE AREAS:*** Commercial Real Estate and Development; Collections. ***Email:*** benjamin.fisher@troutmansanders.com

ALBERT CHEN-HUEI HWANG, born New York, N.Y., March 21, 1976; admitted to bar, 2001, North Carolina. *Education:* University of North Carolina at Chapel Hill (B.A., International Studies/Philosophy, 1997; J.D., 2000). ***LANGUAGES:*** Chinese and Taiwanese. ***PRACTICE AREAS:*** Commercial Real Estate; Corporate. ***Email:*** albert.hwang@troutmansanders.com

KEVIN G. MEEKS, born Atlanta, Georgia, 1970; admitted to bar, 1999, Georgia; 2001, District of Columbia; 2005, North Carolina. *Education:* Duke University (A.B., 1993); University of Georgia (J.D., cum laude, 1999). Member, Editorial Board, 1997-1998, and Managing Editor, 1998-1999, Georgia Law Review. Barrister, Bleckley Inn of Court. Special Assistant and Political Director, Georgia Governor Zell Miller, 1993-1996. Law Clerk to the Hon. Thomas W. Thrash, Jr., District Judge, U.S. District Court, Northern District of Georgia, 1999-2001. Author, Note, "From *Sindell* to Street Pushers: Imposing Market Share Tort Liability on Illegal Drug Dealers," 33 Ga. L. Rev. 315 (1998). *Member:* State Bar of Georgia (Member, Sections on: Administrative Law; Local Government); The District of Columbia Bar (Member, Administrative Law and Agency Practice Section); North Carolina Bar Association (Member, Administrative Law Section). (Also at Atlanta, Georgia Office). ***PRACTICE AREAS:*** Administrative Law; State and Local Government Law; Federal Practice; Appellate Practice; Government Contracts; Election, Campaign and Political Law. ***Email:*** kevin.meeks@troutmansanders.com

(This Listing Continued)

TROUTMAN SANDERS LLP, Raleigh—Continued

OF COUNSEL

ANN H. STUART, born Wilmington, North Carolina; admitted to bar, 1978, North Carolina. *Education:* University of North Carolina at Chapel Hill (B.A., 1974; J.D., with honors, 1978). *Member:* North Carolina State Bar; North Carolina Bar Association. ***PRACTICE AREAS:*** Commercial Development; Real Estate Investment. ***Email:*** ann.stuart@troutmansanders.com

(For Biographical data on all Personnel, see Professional Biographies at other offices)

TWIGGS, BESKIND, STRICKLAND & RABENAU, P.A.

Established in 1950

WACHOVIA CAPITOL CENTER
150 FAYETTEVILLE STREET MALL, SUITE 1100
P.O. DRAWER 30
RALEIGH, NORTH CAROLINA 27602-0030
Telephone: 919-828-4357
Fax: 919-833-7924
Email: nctrial@nctrial.com
URL: http://www.nctrial.com

Personal Injury, Products Liability, Business Torts, Medical and other Professional Negligence, Federal and State Tort Claims, Environmental Torts, Insurance Bad Faith, Aviation Law and Wrongful Death.

FIRM PROFILE: The firm was founded in 1950 and developed an early emphasis in plaintiffs' personal injury cases. For many years, at the referral of other members of the profession, the firm has represented plaintiffs exclusively in complex personal injury, medical malpractice, products liability, business torts, aviation and in insurance fraud and bad faith actions. The firm feels a special commitment to the activities of the organized trial bar, several of its members having served in high leadership positions at the national, state and local levels.

HOWARD F. TWIGGS, born Cincinnati, Ohio, October 27, 1932; admitted to bar, 1957, North Carolina; U.S. District Court, Eastern, Middle and Western Districts of North Carolina; U.S. Court of Appeals, Fourth Circuit. *Education:* Wake Forest University (B.S., 1954; J.D., 1957). Phi Delta Phi (President, 1956-1957); Omicron Delta Kappa. Fellow: International Society of Barristers; International Academy of Trial Lawyers; American Board of Trial Advocates. Recipient: Leonard Ring Champion of Justice, 1998 and Harry Philo Award, 1999, Association of Trial Lawyers of America; Warhorse Award, Southern Trial Lawyers Association, 1996; Walter Clark Award, North Carolina Academy of Trial Lawyers. Distinguished Alumnus Award, Wake Forest University, 2002. Member, 1965-1974, Chairman of Judiciary Committee, 1972-1974 and Vice Chairman of Courts and Judicial Districts, 1971-1972, North Carolina House of Representatives. Member: North Carolina Courts Commission; Chief Justice Commission on Professionalism. President, Wake Forest Law School Alumni Association, 1995-1996; Chairperson, Law School Board of Visitors, 2004. *Member:* Wake County (President, 1986-1987), North Carolina and American Bar Associations; The Association of Trial Lawyers of America (President, 1995-1996; Board of Governors, 1986-2000); North Carolina Academy of Trial Lawyers (President, 1980-1982; Board of Governors, 1977-2005). Listed in Best Lawyers in America, 1988-2005. [Lt., USAR, 1959-1965]. ***PRACTICE AREAS:*** Plaintiffs Personal Injury; Business Torts; Professional Negligence. ***Email:*** htwiggs@nctrial.com

DONALD H. BESKIND, born New York, N.Y., January 6, 1948; admitted to bar, 1973, Connecticut and U.S. District Court, District of Connecticut; 1974, Colorado; 1975, U.S. Court of Appeals, Tenth Circuit; 1976, U.S. Court of Appeals, Fourth Circuit; 1978, North Carolina; 1979, U.S. District Court, Eastern District of North Carolina; 1980, U.S. District Court, Middle District of North Carolina; 1983, U.S. District Court, Western District of North Carolina and U.S. Supreme Court. *Education:* George Washington University (A.B., 1969); University of Connecticut (J.D., cum laude, 1973); Duke University (LL.M., 1977). John S. Bradway Fellowship. Listed in The Best Lawyers in America, 1993—. Co-Author: "North Carolina Evidentiary Foundations," (Lexis-Nexis 1998, rev. 2005); "Effective Use of Courtroom Technology: A Lawyers Guide," (NITA 2002); "Problems in Trial Advocacy," (NITA 1996). Teaching Fellow, 1975-1977, Assistant Professor, 1977-1980, Associate Professor, 1980-1982 and Senior Lecturer in Law and Director of Trial Practice Programs, 1982—, Duke University Law School. Lecturer, University of North Carolina School of Law, 1978-1990. Program Director-at-Large, National Institute for Trial Advocacy, 1987-2003. *Member:* North Carolina State Bar; North Carolina (Member, Board of Governors, 1986-1989) and American Bar Associations; The Association of Trial Lawyers of America (President's Club Member); National College of Advocacy (Co-Chair, Board of Trustees); North Carolina Academy of Trial Lawyers (Member, Board of Governors, 1989-1993; Vice President, Education, 1998-2001). Fellow: American College of Trial Lawyers; International Society of Barristers; ABOTA. ***PRACTICE AREAS:*** Complex Personal Injury; Medical Malpractice; Business Torts; Products Liability. ***Email:*** dbeskind@nctrial.com

DONALD R. STRICKLAND, born Wake County, North Carolina, February 10, 1956; admitted to bar, 1984, North Carolina; U.S. District Court, Eastern and Middle Districts of North Carolina; U.S. Court of Appeals, Fourth Circuit. *Education:* University of North Carolina at Chapel Hill (B.S., 1978); Duke University (J.D., 1984). Listed in Best Lawyers In America. Selected by Business North Carolina in 2003 as a Member of its North Carolina Legal Elite in the field of litigation. *Member:* Wake County, North Carolina and American Bar Associations; North Carolina State Bar; North Carolina Academy of Trial Lawyers (Board of Governors, 1997—; Benefactor; Board of Editors, *Trials Briefs,* 1986-1999); The Association of Trial Lawyers of America (President's Club). ***PRACTICE AREAS:*** Complex Personal Injury; Business Torts; Professional Negligence; Products Liability. ***Email:*** dstrickland@nctrial.com

(This Listing Continued)

KAREN M. RABENAU, born Westminster, Maryland, September 14, 1967; admitted to bar, 1992, North Carolina; U.S. District Court, Eastern, Middle and Western Districts of North Carolina; U.S. Court of Appeals, Fourth Circuit. *Education:* Hollins College (B.A., cum laude, 1989); University of North Carolina at Chapel Hill (J.D., 1992). Phi Beta Kappa. Member, Holderness Moot Court National Team, 1990-1992. Barrister, Braxton Craven Inn of Court. Listed in the Best Lawyers in America, 2003—. *Member:* Wake County, North Carolina (Member, Law Week Committee, 1997—; Medico-Legal Liaison Committee, 2003—; Litigation Council, 2003—) and American Bar Associations; North Carolina Academy of Trial Lawyers (President's Club; Member, Board of Governors, 1999—; Member, Education Committee, 1999-2002; Professional Negligence Section: Chair, 2001-2002; Education Chair, 1999-2001; Secretary, 2000-2001; Young Lawyers Division: Chair, 1997-1998, Secretary, 1996-1997); The Association of Trial Lawyers of America (President's Club; New Lawyers Division Board of Governors, 2002-2003; Student Trial Advocacy Committee: Co-Chair, 1998-2000, Member, 1996-2001, Publications Committee Co-Chair, 1998-1999, Member, 1998-2000). ***PRACTICE AREAS:*** Complex Personal Injury; Business Torts; Professional Negligence; Products Liability. ***Email:*** krabenau@nctrial.com

OF COUNSEL

JEROME P. TREHY, JR., born Camp Lejeune, North Carolina, September 9, 1957; admitted to bar, 1983, North Carolina; U.S. District Court, Eastern, Middle and Western Districts of North Carolina; U.S. Supreme Court and U.S. Court of Appeals, Fourth Circuit. *Education:* Duke University (B.A., 1979); University of North Carolina (J.D., 1983). Assistant Public Defender, 12th Judicial District, 1983-1986. Contributing Author: "North Carolina General Practice Deskbook." *Member:* Wake County, North Carolina and American Bar Associations; North Carolina Academy of Trial Lawyers (Benefactor, Education Committee, 1989—; Member, Legislative Committee, 1999—; Products Liability Section Chairman, 2002-2003; Member: Board of Governors, 2001-2002, 2004—; The Association of Trial Lawyers of America (President's Club). ***PRACTICE AREAS:*** Complex Personal Injury; Products Liability; Insurance Litigation; Aviation Litigation; Industrial/Construction Accidents. ***Email:*** jtrehy@nctrial.com

CHARLES R. ULLMAN & ASSOCIATES

109 SOUTH BLOODWORTH STREET
RALEIGH, NORTH CAROLINA 27601
Telephone: 919-829-1006
Facsimile: 919-829-1078
Email: cullman@nc.rr.com

Family Law, Adoptions, Child Custody, Child Support, Divorce, Domestic Violence, Premarital Agreements, Spousal Support, Alimony, Equitable Distribution, Property Division.

CHARLES R. ULLMAN, born Burlington, North Carolina, January 21, 1968; admitted to bar, 1993, North Carolina. *Education:* Campbell University (B.A., cum laude, 1990); University of North Carolina at Chapel Hill (J.D., 1993). Epsilon Phi Eta. Member: Federalist Society, 1991—; Christian Legal Society. Trained Mediator. *Member:* North Carolina State Bar. ***Email:*** cullman@nc.rr.com

UNDERWOOD & ROBERTS, PLLC

A Professional Limited Liability Company Including A Professional Association

Established in 1983

4000 WESTCHASE BOULEVARD, SUITE 410
RALEIGH, NORTH CAROLINA 27607
Telephone: 919-664-8803
Fax: 919-664-8975
Email: runderwood@rlulaw.com
URL: http://www.rlulaw.com

Las Vegas, Nevada Office: 3230 S. Buffalo, Suite 108, 89117. Telephone: 702-699-7333. Fax: 702-699-7377.

Orlando, Florida Office: 5728 Major Boulevard, Suite 550, 32819. Telephone: 407-354-3420. Fax: 407-354-3840.

Lexington, Kentucky Office: 175 East Main Street, Suite 200, 40507. Telephone: 800-686-1615.

Federal Taxation, Automobile Dealership Law, Business Negotiation and Planning, Estate Planning, Business Transactions.

FIRM PROFILE: The Firm was organized in 1983 by Robert L. Underwood, whose previous experience and practice in the taxation field commenced in 1972. Client services in tax, business transactions, and related legal matters are provided through one firm. The firm's extensive automotive practice represents automobile dealers with all aspects of their business.

ROBERT L. UNDERWOOD, III, born Waycross, Georgia, January 10, 1946; admitted to bar, 1973, District of Columbia, U.S. Tax Court, U.S. District Court, District of Columbia, U.S. Court of Appeals, District of Columbia Circuit and U.S. Court of Federal Claims; 1996, Florida (Not admitted in North Carolina). *Education:* North Carolina State University (B.A., 1969); University of North Carolina (J.D., 1972); George Washington University (LL.M., Taxation, 1974). Stanford University, Executive Programs, 1980, 1983, 1986; Harvard University Executive Program, 1981. Certified Public Accountant, North Carolina, 1973. *Member:* District of Columbia Bar; The Florida Bar; American Bar Association (Member, Tax Committee, 1973); American Institute of Certified Public Accountants; North Carolina Association of Certified Public Accountants; International Fiscal Association. ***PRACTICE AREAS:*** Federal Tax Law; Estate Planning; Buying and Selling of Businesses; IRS Representation; International Taxation; Business Taxation. ***Email:*** runderwood@rlulaw.com

(This Listing Continued)

JEFFERY G. ROBERTS, born Lexington, Kentucky, January 8, 1969; admitted to bar, 1994, Georgia; 1996, Kentucky; 2000, North Carolina. *Education:* Wake Forest University (B.S., 1991); University of Louisville (J.D., 1994). Conference on Consumer Finance Law. *Member:* Wake County, Augusta, Louisville, Kentucky and North Carolina Bar Associations; North Carolina State Bar; Kentucky Automobile Dealers Association. ***PRACTICE AREAS:*** Automobile Dealerships and Dealers; Business Transactions; Corporate; Federal Tax Law; Business Taxation; Closely Held Business Planning. ***Email:*** jroberts@rlulaw.com

OF COUNSEL

CARL A. BERTOCH (Not admitted in North Carolina; Resident, Orlando, Florida Office)

DAVID S. COHEN (Resident, Orlando, Florida Office)

SHANNON L. EVANS (Resident, Las Vegas, Nevada Office) (Also practicing individually, Las Vegas, Nevada)

ASSOCIATES

LINCOLN H. JONES (Not admitted in North Carolina; Resident, Orlando, Florida Office)

ERIC E. PRIDGEN, born Wilmington, North Carolina, January 26, 1976; admitted to bar, 2003, North Carolina; 2005, South Carolina. *Education:* University of North Carolina (B.A., 1998); North Carolina Central University (J.D., cum laude, 2003); University of Florida (LL.M., Taxation, 2004). *Member:* Wake County, North Carolina and American Bar Associations; North Carolina State Bar; South Carolina State Bar. ***PRACTICE AREAS:*** Taxation. ***Email:*** epridgen@rlulaw.com

REPRESENTATIVE CLIENTS: Crown Capital/Anderson Automotive Companies; Poma Companies of Orlando; Farmer Automotive Group, Inc.; Puryear/World Wide Group; Beckstead Companies; Britt Worldwide Ltd.; Renfrow Companies; Kunz Companies; Webb Automotive Companies; Pearson Automotive Companies; Reed Automotive Companies; Powell Industries; Gregory Automotive Companies; Jesse Hansen Companies; MD Beauty Inc.; Bare Escentuals; Academy of Art University/Stephens; Huggins Automotive Companies; Crowley Automotive Companies; John Calhoun Wells Companies; Difiore Automotive Companies; Flethcher Jones Automotive Group; Hudson Automotive Group; The Well Project, LLC; Ascent Automotive Group.

VANDEVENTER BLACK LLP

Established in 1883
TWO HANNOVER SQUARE, SUITE 1530
434 FAYETTEVILLE STREET MALL
P.O. BOX 2599
RALEIGH, NORTH CAROLINA 27602-2599
Telephone: 919-754-1171
Fax: 919-754-1317
Email: dferrell@vanblkral.com
URL: http://www.vanblk.com

Norfolk, Virginia Office: 500 World Trade Center, 23510-1699. Telephone: 757-446-8600. Telecopier: 757-446-8670.

Richmond, Virginia Office: Eighth & Main Building, 707 East Main Street, P.O. Box 1558, 23218-1558. Telephone: 804-237-8800. Fax: 804-237-8801.

Kitty Hawk, North Carolina Office: Southern Shores Law Building, 6 Juniper Trail, P.O. Box 1042, 27949 (Dare Co.). Telephone: 252-261-5055. Fax: 252-261-8444.

Roanoke Island, North Carolina Office: 305 Essex Square, Sir Walter Raleigh Street. Telephone: 252-473-1888. Fax: 252-261-5374.

London, England Office: Blackwell House, 23 Guildhall Yard, EC2V 5AE. Telephone: 011 44 020 7917 6053. Facsimile: 011 44 020 7917 6054.

General Civil Practice and General Litigation in State and Federal Courts, Trials and Appeals, Civil and Business Litigation, Public Utilities, Landline and Mobile Communications, Corporation, Cooperative, Non-profit Organizations, Mediation, Administrative, Social Security Disability (Raleigh office only), Admiralty, Arbitration and Mediation, Aviation, Banking, Bankruptcy and Creditors' Rights, Commercial Transactions, Community Associations, Construction Law, Environmental Law, Estate Planning, General Litigation in State and Federal Courts, Government/Public Contracts, Health Care Law, Immigration Law, International, Intellectual Property, Insurance Defense, Labor and Employment Law, Land Use, Local Government/Municipal Law, Malpractice, Maritime, Mergers and Acquisitions, Products Liability, Public Utilities, Real Estate, Taxation, Technology, Workers' Compensation.

FIRM PROFILE: Vandeventer Black LLP was founded over a century ago in Norfolk, Virginia and now serves the Mid-Atlantic Region with offices in Norfolk, Richmond, North Carolina and London, England. The firm handles all aspects of general civil litigation, commercial and labor and employment law. Vandeventer Black is uniquely qualified to handle complex legal matters that involve multidisciplinary and technical issues in the areas such as construction, maritime and transportation. The firm has attorneys and staff with engineering and business degrees and who are multi-lingual.

PARTNERS

G. WILLIAM BIRKHEAD, born Baltimore, Maryland, October 9, 1941; admitted to bar, 1966, Virginia; 1994, North Carolina. *Education:* Webb Institute (B.S., 1963); University of Virginia (LL.B., 1966). Pi Delta Epsilon. Co-Author: "Maritime Contract Claims Against the United States Government," Southeastern Admiralty Law Institute, 1996. *Member:* Norfolk and Portsmouth, Virginia, North Carolina and American Bar Associations; Virginia State Bar; North Carolina State Bar; The Maritime Law Association of the United States (Member, Board of Directors, 1994-1997; Chairman, Fisheries Committee, 1998-2001); Hampton Roads Maritime Association; Society of Naval Architects and Marine Engineers. [LCDR USCGR, 1966-1975]. ***PRACTICE AREAS:*** Admiralty Law; Vessel Financing Law; Fisheries Regulation; Financial Transactions. ***Email:*** bbirkhead@vanblk.com

(This Listing Continued)

DEAN T. BUCKIUS, born Agana, Guam, December 17, 1959; admitted to bar, 1984, Virginia; 1993, North Carolina. *Education:* College of William & Mary (B.A., 1981); Wake Forest University (J.D., cum laude, 1984). Member, Wake Forest Law Review, 1982-1984. Member: Hampton Roads Chamber of Commerce; Society for Human Resource Management; Downtown Norfolk Council. Alumnus, Leadership Hampton Roads. Co-Chairperson-City of Norfolk Employee Grievance Panel. *Member:* Norfolk, Portsmouth, Virginia Beach, Virginia (Member: Labor and Employment Law Section Council; Litigation Section), North Carolina (Member: Labor and Employment Law Section; Litigation Section) and American (Member: Labor and Employment Law Section; Litigation Section) Bar Associations; North Carolina State Bar; Virginia State Bar. ***PRACTICE AREAS:*** Labor and Employment Law; Litigation. ***Email:*** dbuckius@vanblk.com

PATRICK A. GENZLER, born Chicago Heights, Illinois, October 31, 1949; admitted to bar, 1978, Virginia; 1979, U.S. District Court, Eastern District of Virginia; U.S. Court of Appeals, Fourth Circuit; 1995, U.S. Court of Federal Claims; 1997, North Carolina. *Education:* Virginia Polytechnic Institute (B.S., Mechanical Engineering, 1971); College of William & Mary (J.D., 1978); George Washington University (LL.M., Environmental Law, 1989). Managing Editor, William & Mary Law Review, 1977-1978. Certified Mediator by Virginia Supreme Court for Circuit Court cases; Certified as Mediator by North Carolina Resolution Commission for Superior Court Cases. General Counsel, Hampton Roads Technology Council. *Member:* Norfolk and Portsmouth, Virginia (Member, Environmental and Construction Sections), North Carolina (Member, Environmental and Construction Law Sections) and American (Member, Section on: Natural Resources, Energy and Environmental Law) Bar Associations; Virginia State Bar. [U.S. Navy, 1972-1992, Commander, JAGC, (Ret.)]. ***PRACTICE AREAS:*** Environmental Law; Construction Law; Public Contracts Law; Litigation; Alternative Dispute Resolution. ***Email:*** pgenzler@vanblk.com

RICHARD S. GUY, born Summit, New Jersey, February 2, 1951; admitted to bar, 1982, North Carolina; 1995, Virginia. *Education:* Dartmouth College (A.B., magna cum laude, 1973); University of Virginia (M.B.A., 1982; J.D., 1982). Phi Beta Kappa. *Member:* Norfolk and Portsmouth, Virginia Beach, Virginia, North Carolina and American Bar Associations; North Carolina State Bar; Virginia State Bar. ***LANGUAGES:*** English, Spanish and French. ***PRACTICE AREAS:*** Business Law; Commercial Transactions; Mergers, Acquisitions and Divestitures; Banks and Banking; Commercial Finance; Commercial Real Estate; Health Care. ***Email:*** rguy@vanblk.com

PATRICK W. HERMAN, born Charlotte, North Carolina, September 12, 1952; admitted to bar, 1982, Virginia; 1998, North Carolina. *Education:* Virginia Polytechnic Institute and State University (B.A.,1974); George Washington University (M.S., 1979); College of William & Mary (J.D., 1982; M.L.T., 1984). Phi Delta Phi. Publications: "Private Inurement: The Basics," Tax Exempt Organizations; "Private Benefit, Private Inurement and Inurement per se: Avoiding the Loss of Your Organization's Tax-Exempt Status," Tax Exempt Organizations. General Counsel, Angel Kiss Foundation, 1990-1998. Tax Counsel, Outer Banks Community Foundation. Director, Elizabeth River Restoration Trust, 2004—. *Member:* Norfolk and Portsmouth, Virginia and American Bar Associations; Virginia State Bar (Member, Tax Sections); Hampton Roads Tax Forum; Tidewater Estate Planning Council. [Capt., JAGC, USAR, 1974-1986]. ***PRACTICE AREAS:*** Tax; Wills; Trust and Estates; Exempt Organizations; ERISA. ***Email:*** pherman@vanblk.com

DANIEL D. KHOURY, born Columbus, Ohio, September 15, 1950; admitted to bar, 1977, North Carolina, Ohio, U.S. District Court, Eastern District of North Carolina, U.S. Court of Appeals, Fourth Circuit and U.S. Supreme Court. *Education:* Ohio State University (B.S.Ed., 1973); Wake Forest University (J.D., 1976). Municipal Attorney: Town of Columbia, 1979-1981; Town of Manteo, 1985-1995. Town Attorney for the Town of Manteo 2002—. Member, *Faculty & Lecturer*, North Carolina Bar Association Real Estate and Residential Real Property Seminars. Lecturer, Business Law, College of Albemarle. *Member:* Dare County Bar Association; North Carolina State Bar (Member, Board of Legal Specialization, 2000-2003; Councilor for the First Judicial District, 1990-1996; Ethics Committee Chairman, 1995; Chairman of the Of Counsel Committee, 1994; Member, Board of Continuing Legal Education; Vice Chairman, 1993-1994; Chairman, Accreditations Committee, 1988-1994); North Carolina (Member: Board of Governors, 1999-2002; Section Chairman, Real Property Council, 1990-1991; President, 1988; President, First District Judicial Bar, 1985) and American Bar Associations. (Partner, Kitty Hawk/Roanoke Island Offices) (Board Certified Specialists in Real Property Law-Business, Commercial and Industrial Transactions). ***PRACTICE AREAS:*** Real Property; Business Law; International Law; Securities Law. ***Email:*** dkhoury@vanblk.com

NEIL S. LOWENSTEIN, born Richmond, Virginia, April 26, 1963; admitted to bar, 1989, Virginia, U.S. District Court, Eastern District of Virginia and U.S. Court of Appeals, Fourth Circuit; 1994, U.S. Court of Federal Claims; 1999, North Carolina and U.S. District Court, Eastern, Middle and Western Districts of North Carolina; 2001, U.S. Court of Appeals for the Federal Circuit; 2004, District of Columbia and U.S. District Court, District of Columbia; 2005, U.S. Court of Appeals for the District of Columbia Circuit. *Education:* Virginia Military Institute (B.A., with distinction, 1985); University of Richmond (J.D., 1989). State Board, ABC Virginia; Trustee, ABC Virginia PAC; Past Chairman, Hampton Roads Leadership Committee, ABC Virginia; Past Chairman, Legislative Committee, Hampton Roads Utility & Heavy Contractors Association. Virginia Bar Association Representative, Virginia Continuing Legal Education Committee; Past Board Member, Tidewater Heart Association; and Board Member, Hampton Roads Youth Center. *Member:* Norfolk & Portsmouth, Virginia Beach, Virginia (Member, Sections on: Construction Law; Litigation), North Carolina (Member, Sections on: Construction and Public Contracts Law; Litigation) and American (Member, Sections on: Construction Law Forum; Litigation) Bar Associations; Virginia State Bar; North Carolina State Bar; District of Columbia Bar; Associated General Contractors; Associated Builders & Contractors; Hampton Roads Utility & Heavy Contractors Association. [Infantry and Civil Affairs, U.S. Army Reserve, 1985—]. ***PRACTICE AREAS:*** Construction Law; Public Contracts; General Litigation; Alternative Dispute Resolution. ***Email:*** nlowenstein@vanblk.com

ROBERT L. O'DONNELL, born Akron, Ohio, January 30, 1946; admitted to bar, 1975, Virginia; 1993, North Carolina. *Education:* Spring Hill College (B.S., summa cum laude, 1968); University of Virginia (J.D., 1975). *Member:* Norfolk and Portsmouth, Virginia and American Bar Associations; Virginia State Bar; North Carolina State Bar. [Capt.,

(This Listing Continued)

VANDEVENTER BLACK LLP, Raleigh—Continued

U.S. Marine Corps., 1969-1972]. ***PRACTICE AREAS:*** Toxic Torts Litigation; Products Liability; Commercial Litigation; Land Use Litigation; Personal Injury. ***Email:*** rodonnell@vanblk.com

EDWARD J. POWERS, born Boston, Massachusetts, February 11, 1965; admitted to bar, 1990, Virginia, U.S. District Court, Eastern District of Virginia and U.S. Court of Appeals, Fourth Circuit; 1998, North Carolina; U.S. District Court, Eastern and Middle Districts of North Carolina; U.S. Supreme Court; 2000, U.S. Court of Appeals, First Circuit. *Education:* Virginia Polytechnic Institute and State University (B.A., 1987); University of Richmond (J.D., 1990). Associate Editor: University of Richmond Law Review, 1989-1990; American Maritime Cases, 2000—. Law Clerk for the Hon. Richard B. Kellam, U.S. District Judge for the Eastern District of Virginia, Norfolk Division, 1990-1991. *Member:* Norfolk and Portsmouth, Virginia, Federal and American Bar Associations; Southeastern Admiralty Law Institute; The Maritime Law Association of the United States; Hampton Roads Maritime Association; Judicial Conference of the U.S. Court of Appeals, Fourth Circuit. ***PRACTICE AREAS:*** Admiralty Law; Civil Litigation. ***Email:*** epowers@vanblk.com

NORMAN W. SHEARIN, JR., born Rocky Mount, North Carolina, February 17, 1945; admitted to bar, 1971, North Carolina and U.S. District Court, Eastern District of North Carolina; 1974, U.S. Court of Appeals, Fourth Circuit. *Education:* University of North Carolina at Chapel Hill (B.S., Business Administration, 1967); Wake Forest University (J.D., 1971). Phi Alpha Delta. Research Editor, Wake Forest Law Review, 1970-1971. *Member:* Dare County and American Bar Associations; First Judicial District Bar; North Carolina State Bar; North Carolina Electric Membership Corporations Counsel Association. (Resident Partner, Kitty Hawk, North Carolina Office) (Board Certified Specialist in Real Property Law- Business, Commercial and Industrial Transactions, North Carolina State Board of Legal Specialization). ***PRACTICE AREAS:*** Commercial Real Estate; Condemnation and Land Use Litigation; Public Utilities; Real Estate Development; Zoning Law; Land Use. ***Email:*** nshearin@vanblk.com

ASSOCIATES

WYATT M. BOOTH, admitted to bar, 2001, Virginia; 2002, North Carolina. *Education:* North Carolina State University (B.S.Chem.Eng., 1998); Washington & Lee University (J.D., 2001). Staff Writer, Washington & Lee Law Review. *Member:* North Carolina Bar Association; North Carolina State Bar; Virginia State Bar. ***PRACTICE AREAS:*** Civil Litigation; Eminent Domain; Municipal Law. ***Email:*** wbooth@vanblk.com

DAVID P. FERRELL, born Albemarle, North Carolina, July 1, 1971; admitted to bar, 1996, North Carolina and U.S. District Court, Eastern District of North Carolina; 2003, U.S. District Court, Middle and Western Districts of North Carolina. *Education:* University of North Carolina (B.A., 1993); Campbell University (J.D., 1996). Phi Alpha Delta. CLE Course Planner, Update on Legislative Law and Lobbying, 2001—. Fellow, Education Policy Fellowship Program, Institute for Professional Leadership, 1999-2000. Member, YMCA Youth Legislature Bill Selection Committee, 1996—. *Member:* Wake County (Member: Bench/Bar Committee; Professionalism Committee), North Carolina (Chair, Young Lawyers Division Legislative Committee; Member: Communications Committee; Member: Administrative Law Section; Business Law Section) and American (Member: Administrative Law and Regulatory Practice Section; Civil Litigation Section) Bar Associations. ***PRACTICE AREAS:*** Administrative and Regulatory Law; Civil Litigation; Business Law; Cooperative Law; Public Utility Law; Trade and Professional Associations; Legislative Representation. ***Email:*** dferrell@vanblkral.com

TERRY C. FRANK, born June 22, 1973; admitted to bar, 2003, North Carolina. *Education:* Mary Washington College (B.A., 1996); University of Richmond (J.D., 2003). *Member:* Dare County and American Bar Associations; North Carolina Bar Association; First Judicial District Bar Association. (Resident, Kitty Hawk, North Carolina Office). ***PRACTICE AREAS:*** Civil Litigation; Municipal Government Law; Eminent Domain. ***Email:*** tfrank@vanblk.com

ROBERT P. TRIVETTE, born Hickory, North Carolina, June 6, 1956; admitted to bar, 1989, North Carolina; 2005, U.S. District Court, Eastern District of North Carolina. *Education:* Virginia Intermont College (B.A. Eng., 1981); University of North Carolina, Chapel Hill (M.A., Journalism,1987; J.D., 1989). Recipient, American Jurisprudence Award in Constitutional Law. Articles Editor, North Carolina Journal of International Law & Commercial Regulation; Law Clerk, Judge Gerald Arnold, North Carolina Court of Appeals. Assistant District Attorney, First Judicial District in North Carolina, 1991-2004. *Member:* First Judicial District Bar Association (Secretary, 2004—); North Carolina State Bar. ***PRACTICE AREAS:*** Civil Litigation; Criminal Law. ***Email:*** rtrivette@vanblk.com

GENERAL COMMERCIAL REPRESENTATION: Cape Hatteras Electric Membership Cooperative; Hipage Co., Inc.; Flagship Group, Ltd.; General Foam Plastics Corp.; Hampton Roads Shipping Association - ILA Pension Fund; Iceland Seafood, Corp.; Liberty Property Trust; Norfolk Airport Authority; Owens-Illinois; TECNICO Corp.; The CSL Group; The Town of Kitty Hawk; Virginia International Terminals, Inc.
BANKING: Branch Banking and Trust (BB&T); RCB-Centura; Wachovia.
CONSTRUCTION & GOVERNMENT/PUBLIC CONTRACTS: Atlantic Drydock; Chicago Bridge & Iron; Colonial Mechanical Corp.; Davis Boat Works, Inc.; E.L. Hamm & Associates, Inc.; English Construction Co., Inc.; Gilbert Southern Corp.; Globe Iron Construction Corp.; Glover Construction Co., Inc.; Management Consulting, Inc.; McKenzie Construction Corp.; McLean Contractiong Co., Inc.; Mid-Eastern Builders, Inc.; Milcom, Inc.; Peter Kiewit Sons', Inc.; SB Ballard Construction Co., Inc.; Shirley Construction Corp.; The Bionetics Corporation; Tidewater - SKANSKA Inc.; Bayshore Concrete Products Corp.; Palmetto Bridge Construction; VIRTEXCO Corp.; W.M., Jordan Company.
LABOR & EMPLOYMENT/WORKERS' COMPENSATION: Hampton Roads Shipping Association; The Hartford; Metro Machine Corp.; Signal Administration, Inc.; New Dominion Pictures, Inc.; American International Group; The Travelers Companies.
MARITIME: Allied Marine Industries, Inc.; Atlantic Yacht Basin; Britannia Steam Ship Insurance Assoc., Ltd.; Chesapeake Yachts Inc.; Crofton Diving Corp.; Hampton Roads Maritime Association; Osprey Associates; London United Marine Agency; Maersk Line Ltd.; Marine Claims Handling Agencies GmbH; Moran Towing of Virginia; Noord Nederlandsche Protectie Club; North of England P & I Assn. Ltd.; The Standard Steamship Owners Protection and Indemnity Assn. Ltd.; The Steamship Mutual Underwriting Assn. (Bermuda) Ltd.; The American Club; The Swedish Club; United Kingdom Mutual Steam Ship Owners Mutual Assurance Assn. (Bermuda) Ltd.; Transport Mutual Services, Inc.; West of England Ship Owners Mutual Insurance Assn. (Luxembourg); Sunderland Steamship; British Marine Mutual Hull Assoc., Ltd.; UK Defense Club; Virginia Pilot Association.

(This Listing Continued)

APPROVED ATTORNEYS FOR: Chicago Title Insurance Co.; Lawyers Title Insurance Corp.; Ticor Title Insurance Co.; Zurich American Insurance.

(For complete biographical data on all personnel, see professional biographies at Norfolk, Virginia)

VANN & SHERIDAN, LLP

Established in 1993

1720 HILLSBOROUGH STREET, SUITE 200
RALEIGH, NORTH CAROLINA 27605
Telephone: 919-510-8585
Fax: 919-510-8570
URL: http://www.vannattorneys.com

Mailing Address: P.O. Box 2445, Raleigh, NC 27602-2445

Business and Civil Litigation practice, Commercial Collections, Estate Planning and Wills, Construction Law, Creditor Rights.

FIRM PROFILE: James Vann formed the firm in 1993. The firm has grown from a solo practice to a firm of eight attorneys. The firm stands ready to meet the diverse needs of clients ranging from individuals to privately held family businesses, to corporations with national distribution. The firm represents clients throughout North Carolina and the United States.

JAMES R. VANN, born Roxboro, North Carolina, October 6, 1963; admitted to bar, 1992, North Carolina and U.S. District Court, Eastern, Middle and Western Districts of North Carolina. *Education:* Campbell University (B.A., 1986); Cumberland School of Law of Samford University (J.D., 1990). *Member:* North Carolina and American Bar Associations; North Carolina State Bar. ***PRACTICE AREAS:*** Commercial Collections; Credit Law; Business Law; Construction Law; Materialmens Liens; Creditor Bankruptcy; Corporate Law. ***Email:*** jrvann@vannattorneys.com

PAUL A. SHERIDAN, born New York, New York, April 2, 1965; admitted to bar, 1992, North Carolina and U.S. District Court, Eastern, Middle and Western Districts of North Carolina. *Education:* Bethany College (B.S., 1987); Campbell University (J.D., 1992). Phi Alpha Delta. *Member:* North Carolina Bar (Member, Construction and Lien Law Division) and American (Member, Construction Industry Division) Bar Associations; North Carolina State Bar. ***PRACTICE AREAS:*** Construction Law; Business Litigation; Civil Litigation; Commercial Collections; Contract Litigation; Materialmens Liens; Creditor Bankruptcy. ***Email:*** pasheridan@vannattorneys.com

NANCY EDMUNDS HANNAH, born Greensboro, North Carolina, October 6, 1959; admitted to bar, 1993, North Carolina, U.S. District Court, Eastern, Middle and Western Districts of North Carolina, U.S. Court of Appeals, Fourth Circuit and U.S. Supreme Court. *Education:* Furman University (B.A., cum laude, 1981); Baylor University (M.S., 1982); Washington & Lee University (J.D., 1993). Phi Alpha Delta. Research Assistant to the Honorable John Webb, North Carolina Supreme Court, 1993-1995. *Member:* North Carolina (Member: Construction Law Section; Sports and Entertainment Law Section) and American (Member, Public Contract Section, 1997—; Labor and Employment Section, 1998—) Bar Associations; North Carolina State Bar. ***PRACTICE AREAS:*** Commercial Collections; Materialmens Liens; Creditor Bankruptcy; Construction Law; Employment Law. ***Email:*** nehannah@vannattorneys.com

PAIGE CHANDLER, born Fort Smith, Arkansas, October 1, 1971; admitted to bar, 1999, North Carolina; 2000, U.S. District Court, Eastern, Middle and Western Districts of North Carolina; U.S. Court of Appeals, Fourth Circuit. *Education:* University of North Carolina at Chapel Hill (B.A., 1993); Campbell University (J.D., 1999). *Member:* Wake County and North Carolina (Member, Litigation Section) Bar Associations; North Carolina State Bar; North Carolina Academy of Trial Lawyers. ***PRACTICE AREAS:*** Commercial Collections; Construction Law; Civil Litigation; Creditor Bankruptcy; Materialmens Liens. ***Email:*** pchandler@vannattorneys.com

JAMES W. SPROUSE, JR., born Marietta, Georgia, February 11, 1969; admitted to bar, 1999, North Carolina and U.S. District Court, Eastern, Middle and Western Districts of North Carolina. *Education:* North Georgia College (B.S., Criminal Justice, 1991); University of North Carolina at Chapel Hill (J.D., 1999). Order of the Barristers.*Member:* Wake County, North Carolina and American Bar Associations. [U.S. Army Field Artillery, 1st Lieutenant]. ***PRACTICE AREAS:*** Commercial Collections; Construction Law; Creditor Bankruptcy; Business Law; Materialmens Liens. ***Email:*** jsprouse@vannattorneys.com

GILBERT W. FILE, IV, born Kinston, North Carolina, April 19, 1971; admitted to bar, 1999, North Carolina. *Education:* The Citadel (English, 1993); Campbell University (J.D., 1999). Chapter Editor, Guardianship Practice and Procedure, North Carolina Estate Administration Manual. Lecturer and Manuscript Author: "Practice Before the Clerk," McKimmon Center; "Nuts and Bolts of Civil Practice-Covering All Your Bases"; "Incompetency and Guardianship Proceedings". Guest Lecturer: Debt/Creditor and Estate Administration, Campbell University Law School; Elder Law and District Court Practice, Law 101 Committee, Wake County Bar Association. Former Clerk, Superior Court, Wake County, North Carolina, 2001-2002. ***PRACTICE AREAS:*** Business Litigation; Construction Litigation; Creditors Rights; Collections; Estate Administration; Estate Planning. ***Email:*** gwfile@vannattorneys.com

OF COUNSEL

DAVID R. COCKMAN, born Greensboro, North Carolina, October 27, 1928; admitted to bar, 1957, North Carolina. *Education:* University of North Carolina of Chapel Hill (A.B., 1951; J.D., 1957). *Member:* Wake County Bar; American Bar Association; North Carolina State Bar; Fourth Circuit Judicial Conference.

WAKE TRAFFIC CENTER

107 FAYETTEVILLE STREET MALL
SUITE 210
RALEIGH, NORTH CAROLINA 27601
Telephone: 919.833.6388
Toll Free: 866-456-traffic
Fax: 919-838-5299
URL: http://www.traffic-dwi.com

Driving While Intoxicated, Traffic Violations, Automobile Accidents and Injuries.

ANTHONY M. BRANNON, born Los Angeles, California, October 28, 1964; admitted to bar, 2001, North Carolina; U.S. Court of Appeals, Fourth Circuit; U.S. District Court, Eastern District of North Carolina. *Education:* North Carolina State University (B.S., 1998); Campbell University (J.D., 2001). Phi Beta Kappa. Law Clerk, North Carolina Court of Appeals. (Also Member, Brannon Strickland, PLLC)

ROBERT J. LANE, III, born Erwin, North Carolina, May 12, 1964; admitted to bar, 1989, North Carolina and U.S. District Court, Eastern District of North Carolina. *Education:* Campbell University (B.B.A., 1986); University of North Carolina School of Law (J.D., 1989). *Member:* Wake County and North Carolina Bar Associations; North Carolina State Bar. (Also practicing individually). ***PRACTICE AREAS:*** Criminal Law; Driving While Intoxicated; Traffic Violations; Personal Injury; Automobile Accidents and Injuries.

WARD AND SMITH, P.A.

Established in 1895
SUITE 2400, TWO HANNOVER SQUARE
FAYETTEVILLE STREET MALL
P.O. BOX 2091
RALEIGH, NORTH CAROLINA 27602-2091
Telephone: 919-836-4260
Facsimile: 919-836-4277
Email: wardsmith@wardandsmith.com
URL: http://www.wardandsmith.com

New Bern, North Carolina Office: 1001 College Court, P.O. Box 867. Telephone: 252-672-5400. Facsimile: 252-672-5400.

Greenville, North Carolina Office: 120 West Fire Tower Road, P.O. Box 8088. Telephone: 252-215-4000. Facsimile: 252-215-4077.

Wilmington, North Carolina Office: University Corporate Center, 127 Racine Drive, P.O. Box 7068. Telephone: 910-794-4800. Facsimile: 910-794-4877.

General and Trial Practice. Admiralty Law; Bankruptcy; Banks and Banking; Business Law; Civil Rights; Commercial Law; Construction Law; Contracts; Copyrights; Corporate Law; Debtor and Creditor; Elder Law; Eminent Domain; Employee Benefits; Environmental Law; Family Law including Divorce; Finance; Franchise Law; Government; Government Contracts; Health Care Law; Immigration and Naturalization; Insurance; International Law; International Trade; Investments; Labor and Employment including Discrimination, Sexual Harassment, and Workers' Compensation; Landlord and Tenant; Litigation; Personal Injury including Automobile Accidents, Legal Malpractice and Medical Malpractice; Products Liability; Real Estate; Securities; Taxation; Technology and Science including Internet Law, Trademarks, and Patents; Trusts and Estates including Estate Planning and Wills and Probate; Zoning and Land Use.

FIRM PROFILE: Located in Greenville, New Bern, Raleigh, and Wilmington, we are successor to a practice founded in New Bern, North Carolina in 1895. Our firm has grown to over 60 attorneys and more than 160 support staff members who are committed to quality and responsiveness. We strive to deliver a product that is tailored to our clients' unique needs wherever and whenever the need should arise. Our attorneys may be contacted by either a phone call or a confidential email, in or out of the office and at home. Attorney availability reinforces our commitment to a strong attorney-client relationship and a proactive and preventive approach to our clients' legal issues. Our philosophy is to utilize other attorneys in the firm whose knowledge and expertise allows a more efficient and timely delivery of our clients' legal services. In summary, the collective mission of our attorneys, legal assistants, and administrative staff is to provide our clients with the highest quality legal service at an affordable cost.

WILLIAM JOSEPH AUSTIN, JR., admitted to bar, 1978, North Carolina; 1981, U.S. Tax Court. *Education:* University of North Carolina (A.B., 1973; J.D., 1978); Duke University (M.A., 1978). Phi Beta Kappa. Member, National Moot Court Team; Holderness Moot Court Bench, 1977-1978. Staff Member, North Carolina Law Review, 1977-1978. *Member:* North Carolina (Litigation Section Council, 2001—) and American Bar Associations; North Carolina State Bar. ***PRACTICE AREAS:*** Education Law; Labor and Employment; Litigation; Workers' Compensation. ***Email:*** wja@wardandsmith.com

ALBERT R. BELL, JR., admitted to bar, 1975, North Carolina. *Education:* Campbell University (B.S., 1966); Wake Forest University (J.D., 1975). Managing Editor, Wake Forest Law Review, 1974-1975. Listed in *The Best Lawyers in America* . Wage and Hour Investigator, U.S. Department of Labor, 1966-1969. *Member:* North Carolina (Member, Labor and Employment Law Section; Labor and Employment Law Section Council, Chair, 1991-1992, Member, 1985-2000) and American (Member: Labor and Employment Law Section; Public Contract Law Section; Health Law Section) Bar Associations; North Carolina State Bar. [USAR, 1966-1972]. ***PRACTICE AREAS:*** Labor and Employment; Employment Benefits; Government Affairs; Government Contracts; Wage and Hour Law. ***Email:*** arb@wardandsmith.com

STUART B. DORSETT, admitted to bar, 1985, North Carolina. *Education:* Davidson College (A.B., cum laude, 1982); University of North Carolina (J.D., with honors, 1985). Phi Beta Kappa; Order of the Coif. Member, International Law Moot Court Team, Jessup Competition, 1984-1985. Listed in *The Best Lawyers in America. Member:* North Carolina (Chair, Young Lawyers Division, 1994-1995; Vice Chair, 2003-2004; Chair, 2004-2005, Estate Planning and Fiduciary Law Section Council) and American (Member, Executive Council, Young Lawyers Division, 1988-1990) Bar Associations; North Carolina State Bar; American Counsel Association. The American College of Trusts and Estates Counsel. (Board Certified Specialist in Estate Planning and Probate Law, North Carolina State Board of Legal Specialization). ***PRACTICE AREAS:*** Trusts and Estates; Taxation; Wills and Probate; Business. ***Email:*** sbd@wardandsmith.com

DONALT J. EGLINTON, admitted to bar, 1982, North Carolina. *Education:* Texas A. & M. University (B.E.D., magna cum laude, 1974); Central Michigan University (M.A., 1980); Wake Forest University (J.D., 1982). Staff Member, 1980-1981 and Research Editor, 1981-1982, Wake Forest Law Review. *Member:* North Carolina and American Bar Associations; North Carolina State Bar; North Carolina Academy of Trial Lawyers; Association of Trial Lawyers of America; American Institute of Architects. ***PRACTICE AREAS:*** Litigation; Business Law; Copyrights; Commercial Law; Contracts; Intellectual Property; Construction Law; Products Liability; Trade Secrets; Trademarks; Unfair Competition; Commercial Litigation; Trusts and Estates Litigation; Dealer/Distributor and Franchising; Environmental; Technology. ***Email:*** dje@wardandsmith.com

A. CHARLES ELLIS, admitted to bar, 1983, North Carolina. *Education:* University of North Carolina (A.B., 1980); Campbell University (J.D., cum laude, 1983). Member, Campbell University Law Review, 1980-1983. Listed in *The Best Lawyers in America. Member:* Pitt County (President, 1990-1991), North Carolina and American Bar Associations; North Carolina State Bar; North Carolina Academy of Trial Lawyers; Association of Trial Lawyers of America. ***PRACTICE AREAS:*** Personal Injury; Wrongful Death; Litigation; Insurance; Medical Malpractice; Products Liability. ***Email:*** ace@wardandsmith.com

WILLIAM R. LATHAN, JR., admitted to bar, 1975, North Carolina. *Education:* University of North Carolina (A.B., 1972; J.D., 1975). Assistant General Counsel, 1975-1980 and General Counsel and Secretary, 1980-1987, United Carolina Bancshares Corporation. Member, Board of Advisors, University of North Carolina School of Law, Center for Banking and Finance. *Member:* North Carolina and American Bar Associations; North Carolina State Bar; North Carolina Bankers Association. ***PRACTICE AREAS:*** Business Law; Financial Institutions; Finance; Securities; Corporate Law; Banks and Banking. ***Email:*** wrl@wardandsmith.com

SAMUEL H. POOLE, admitted to bar, 1962, North Carolina. *Education:* University of North Carolina at Chapel Hill (A.B., 1959; LL.B., 1962). Board of Governors, 1983-1999, Chairman, 1990-1994, University of North Carolina. *Member:* Wake County, North Carolina and American Bar Associations; North Carolina State Bar. ***PRACTICE AREAS:*** Administrative Law; Business Law; Government; International Law. ***Email:*** shp@wardandsmith.com

E. KNOX PROCTOR V, admitted to bar, 1987, North Carolina. *Education:* Davidson College; University of North Carolina (A.B., 1984; J.D., with high honors, 1987). Order of the Coif. Member, Board of Editors, North Carolina Law Review, 1986-1987. *Member:* North Carolina and American Bar Associations; North Carolina State Bar. ***PRACTICE AREAS:*** Financial Institutions; Business Law; Banks and Banking; Insurance; Securities. ***Email:*** ekp@wardandsmith.com

GARY J. RICKNER, admitted to bar, 1974, Indiana; 1998, North Carolina. *Education:* Taylor University (B.A., 1971); Cumberland School of Law of Samford University (J.D., cum laude, 1974). Associate Editor, Cumberland-Samford Law Review, 1972-1974. Listed in *The Best Lawyers in America.* Instructor, National Institute for Trial Advocacy. *Member:* North Carolina, Indiana State and American Bar Associations; North Carolina State Bar; Defense Research Institute; American College of Trial Lawyers. ***PRACTICE AREAS:*** Business Litigation; Commercial Litigation; Financial Institutions; Civil Litigation; Litigation; Products Liability; Banking Law. ***Email:*** gjr@wardandsmith.com

JEREMY R. SAYRE, admitted to bar, 1998, Ohio; 2004, North Carolina. *Education:* John Carroll University (B.S., 1994); Ohio State University (J.D., 1998). National Moot Court Team. Herman Moot Court. *Member:* Ohio State and American Bar Associations; North Carolina State Bar. ***PRACTICE AREAS:*** Labor and Employment. ***Email:*** js@wardandsmith.com

DAVID L. WARD, JR., admitted to bar, 1962, North Carolina. *Education:* University of North Carolina (B.S., 1957); Duke University (J.D., 1962). Phi Beta Kappa. Member, Editorial Board, Duke Law Journal, 1961-1962. Listed in *The Best Lawyers in America.* Inducted into Hall of Fame of the General Practice Section, North Carolina Bar Association. Chair of Directors, Research Triangle Foundation, 2000—. Member, 1989-1993 and Vice Chairman, 1991-1993, Board of Trustees, University of North Carolina at Chapel Hill. *Member:* North Carolina and American Bar Associations; North Carolina State Bar; North Carolina Association of Defense Attorneys; The American College of Trust and Estate Counsel. ***PRACTICE AREAS:*** Business Law; Financial Institutions; Government Affairs; Housing Authority Law; Labor and Employment; Banking Law; Finance. ***Email:*** dlw@wardandsmith.com

KENNETH R. WOOTEN, admitted to bar, 1979, North Carolina. *Education:* North Carolina State University (B.A., with high honors, 1976); University of North Carolina (J.D., with honors, 1979). Order of the Coif. Staff Member, North Carolina Law Review, 1977-1978. Member, Invitational Moot Court Team, Holderness Moot Court Bench, 1978-1979. Research Assistant to Justice J. William Copeland, North Carolina Supreme Court, 1979-1980. *Member:* North Carolina (Construction Law Section, Chair, 1992-1993, Vice Chair, 1991-1992, Secretary, 1988-1991) and American (Member, Litigation Section) Bar Associations; North Carolina State Bar; North Carolina Association of Defense Attorneys; Defense Research Institute; Christian Legal Society. ***PRACTICE AREAS:*** Construction Law; Litigation; Housing Authority Law; Commercial Law; Insurance. ***Email:*** krw@wardandsmith.com

REPRESENTATIVE CLIENTS: Amital Spinning Corp.; Atlantic Coast Contracting; Atlantic States Bank; Barnhill Contracting Company; Cape Fear Community College; Central Carolina Bank and Trust Co.; Chubb Insurance; City of Havelock; Craven Community College; Daedong- USA, Inc.; East Carolina Bank; Eastern Carolina Regional Housing Authority; Eastern Radiologists, Inc.; First-Citizens Bank & Trust Company; First Flight Federal Credit Union; Fountain Powerboats, Inc.; Hatteras Yachts; Ironstone Bank; Janus Development Group; Mountainbank Financial Corp.; NC State Firemen's Association; Neuse Regional

(This Listing Continued)

WARD AND SMITH, P.A., Raleigh—Continued

Water & Sewer; Physicians East, P.A.; Potash Corp.; Southern Banc & Trust Co.; State of North Carolina; Weyerhaeuser Co.; Wilmington Cardiology, PLLC.

(For Complete Biographical Data on all Personnel, see Professional Biographies at New Bern, North Carolina).

JEANNE H. WASHBURN

Established in 1999

3737 GLENWOOD AVENUE, SUITE 100
RALEIGH, NORTH CAROLINA 27612
Telephone: 919-821-7555
Fax: 919-573-1893
Email: jwshbrn@aol.com
URL: http://www.washburn-law.com

Civil Litigation, Personal Injury, Automobile Accidents and Injuries, Wrongful Death, Medical Malpractice, Workers Compensation.

FIRM PROFILE: Small firm specializing in advocating and litigating for the injured.

JEANNE H. WASHBURN, born Raleigh, North Carolina; admitted to bar, 1994, North Carolina. *Education:* University of North Carolina at Chapel Hill (B.A., 1991); Campbell University (J.D., 1994). *Member:* Wake County Bar Association, North Carolina Bar Association (Member, Litigation Section) and American Bar Association; North Carolina Association of Trial Attorneys (Member, Workers Compensation and Auto Torts Section). **LANGUAGES:** Spanish.

Language: Spanish.

THE WELLONS LAW FIRM

ONE EXCHANGE PLAZA, SUITE 730
RALEIGH, NORTH CAROLINA 27601
Telephone: 919-834-2712
Fax: 919-834-2713
Email: swellons@wellonslaw.com
URL: http://www.wellonslawfirm.com

Corporate Law, Taxation, Employment Law, Family Law, Estate Planning, Estate Administration.

MEMBER OF FIRM

ROBERT SHAWN WELLONS, born Roanoke, Virginia, May 1, 1968; admitted to bar, 1995, North Carolina. *Education:* Duke University (A.B., cum laude, 1990); Wake Forest University School of Law (J.D., magna cum laude, 1995); University of Florida College of Law (LL.M, Taxation, 1996). Wake Forest University School of Law Faculty Scholar. Articles Editor, Wake Forest Law Review. Student Editor, Florida Tax Review, University of Florida College of Law. *Member:* North Carolina and American Bar Associations; North Carolina State Bar. (Also, Associate, Brannon Strickland, PLLC). **PRACTICE AREAS:** Corporate Law; Taxation; Employment Law; Family Law; Estate Planning; Estate Administration. **Email:** swellons@wellonslaw.com

WEST LAW OFFICES, P.C.

SUITE 1735, TWO HANNOVER SQUARE
434 FAYETTEVILLE STREET MALL
RALEIGH, NORTH CAROLINA 27601
Telephone: 919-856-8800
Fax: 919-856-8801
Email: jpwest@westlawpc.com
URL: http://www.westlawpc.com

Utility Law, Estate Planning, Business and Employment Law.

JAMES P. WEST, born New Rochelle, New York, June 8, 1965; admitted to bar, 1991, North Carolina; 1992, District of Columbia; 1994, U.S. District Court, District of Columbia; 1996, U.S. District Court, Eastern, Middle and Western Districts of North Carolina and U.S. Court of Appeals, Fourth Circuit; 2001, U.S. Court of Appeals, District of Columbia and U.S. Supreme Court. *Education:* University of Pennsylvania (B.A., cum laude, 1986); University of North Carolina (J.D., with honors, 1991). Executive Editor, North Carolina Journal of International Law and Commercial Regulation, 1990-1991. Certified Financial Planner. Assistant District Attorney, 14th Judicial District, 1995-1996. *Member:* North Carolina and American Bar Associations; Federal Energy Bar Association; National Academy of Elder Law Attorneys.

WHITE & STRADLEY, LLP

3105 CHARLES B. ROOT WYND
RALEIGH, NORTH CAROLINA 27612
Telephone: 919-844-0400
Fax: 919-845-9745
Toll-Free: 888-666-2446
URL: http://www.injurednc.com
URL: http://www.whiteandstradleylaw.com

Personal Injury Litigation, Workers Compensation, Sports Agency Law, Sports Law, Products Liability, Medical Malpractice, Wrongful Death, Dog Bites, Automobile Accidents and Injuries.

(This Listing Continued)

NANCY P. WHITE, born Glens Falls, New York, July 23, 1960; admitted to bar, 1987, Vermont; 1989, North Carolina. *Education:* University of North Carolina at Chapel Hill (B.A., 1983); North Carolina Central University (J.D., 1986). *Member:* Wake County, Rutland County, North Carolina and Vermont Bar Associations; North Carolina State Bar; The Association of Trial Lawyers of America; North Carolina Academy of Trial Lawyers; Vermont Trial Lawyers. **PRACTICE AREAS:** Personal Injury; Workers Compensation; Sports Agency Law; Sports Law; Products Liability.

J. DAVID STRADLEY, born Statesville, North Carolina, July 8, 1969; admitted to bar, 1995, North Carolina; U.S. District Court, Eastern and Middle Districts of North Carolina. *Education:* Wake Forest University (B.A., 1991); Duke University (J.D., 1995). *Member:* North Carolina Bar Association; North Carolina Academy of Trial Lawyers; The Association of Trial Lawyers of America. **PRACTICE AREAS:** Medical Malpractice; Personal Injury; Wrongful Death; Dog Bites; Automobile Accidents and Injuries.

ASSOCIATE

CARYN MADISON, born Atlanta, Georgia, June 27, 1973; admitted to bar, 2002, North Carolina. *Education:* University of North Carolina (B.A., 1997; J.D., 2001). *Member:* North Carolina Bar Association; North Carolina Academy of Trial Lawyers; Order of the Barristers. **PRACTICE AREAS:** Civil Litigation; Workers Compensation; Consumer Law; Personal Injury. **Email:** cmadi2@yahoo.com

EDWARD V. WILLIAMS
ATTORNEY AT LAW

158 MINE LAKE COURT, SUITE 100
RALEIGH, NORTH CAROLINA 27615
Telephone: 919-844-2847
Fax: 919-844-2874
Email: nclaw@bellsouth.net
URL: http://www.evwlaw.com

Traffic Violations, Criminal Law, Driving While Intoxicated, Domestic Violence.

EDWARD V. WILLIAMS, born Port Jefferson, New York, March 28, 1962; admitted to bar, 1999, North Carolina. *Education:* The Ohio State University (B.A., 1984); North Carolina Central University (J.D., 1998). *Member:* Wake County, North Carolina and American Bar Associations. **PRACTICE AREAS:** Traffic Violations; Criminal Law; Driving While Intoxicated; Domestic Violence.

LAW OFFICES OF ROBERT J. WILLIS

5 WEST HARGETT STREET
RALEIGH, NORTH CAROLINA 27601
Telephone: 919-821-9031
Fax: 919-821-1763
Email: bnorman@jwillis-law.com
URL: http://www.rjwillislaw.com

Workers Compensation, Criminal Defense, Driving While Intoxicated, Traffic Violations, Automobile Accidents, Wage and Hour Disputes.

ROBERT J. WILLIS, born Fort Campbell, Kentucky, April 1, 1953; admitted to bar, 1979, Florida; 1983, North Carolina. *Education:* Haverford College (B.A., 1975); University of North Carolina at Chapel Hill (J.D., 1979). **PRACTICE AREAS:** Workers Compensation; Criminal Law; Driving While Intoxicated; Traffic Violations; Automobile Accidents and Injuries; Wage and Hour Law.

WILSON & ISEMAN, L.L.P.

RALEIGH, NORTH CAROLINA

(See Winston-Salem)

General Civil Practice, including Civil Trial and Appellate Work in all State and Federal Courts, Administrative, Aviation, Commercial, Construction, Corporate, Employee Benefits and Executive Compensation, Employment, Criminal, Federal, State and Local Taxation, Insurance Defense, Personal Injury, Probate, Wills, Trusts and Estate Planning, Products Liability and Negligence Law, Professional Malpractice and Real Estate.

JAMES A. WILSON

RALEIGH, NORTH CAROLINA

(See Durham)

Physicians Licensing, Medical Disciplinary Proceedings, Controlled Substances Law, Professional Conduct, Professional Discipline, Professional Sexual Misconduct, Hospital Peer Review, Hospital Privilege, Medical Staff Credentialing, Health Law, Medical Ethics, Medical-Legal Law, Physicians Rights, Professional Licensing, Professional Licensing Regulation, Health Care Licensing, Nurses Licensing.

WILSON & RATLEDGE

Professional Limited Liability Company

4600 MARRIOTT DRIVE
SUITE 400
P.O. BOX 31447
RALEIGH, NORTH CAROLINA 27622
Telephone: 919-787-7711
Fax: 919-787-7710
URL: http://www.wilsonandratledgelaw.com

Trusts and Estates, Workers Compensation.

(This Listing Continued)

THOMAS J. WILSON, born Albemarle, North Carolina, September 17, 1952; admitted to bar, 1984, North Carolina and U.S. Tax Court; 1994, U.S. Supreme Court; 2001, Florida; 2003, Colorado. *Education:* University of North Carolina at Chapel Hill (B.S., B.A., 1974); Campbell University (J.D., cum laude, 1982); Emory University (LL.M. in Taxation, 1983). Phi Kappa Phi; Phi Alpha Delta. Member, Editorial Board, Campbell University Law Review, 1981-1982. Chartered Life Underwriter. Chartered Financial Consultant. *Member:* Wake County, North Carolina (Member, Estate Planning, Fiduciary and Tax Sections) and American Bar Associations; American Society of Business Appraisers; Society of Financial Service Professionals. ***PRACTICE AREAS:*** Tax Planning; Tax Controversies; Estate Planning; Trusts and Estates; Business Law; Mergers and Acquisitions; Wealth Preservation; Business Transactions; Family Business Planning. ***Email:*** twilson@wilsonandratledge.com

JAMES E. R. RATLEDGE, born Marion, North Carolina, December 18, 1961; admitted to bar, 1988, North Carolina and U.S. District Court, Eastern District of North Carolina; 1992, U.S. Supreme Court; 1993, U.S. District Court, Middle District of North Carolina; 1996, U.S. District Court, Western District of North Carolina. *Education:* University of North Carolina at Chapel Hill (B.A., 1984; J.D., 1987). Phi Alpha Delta. Lyndon Baines Johnson Scholar, University of North Carolina. Recipient, President's Scholarship. DRC Certified Mediator. *Member:* Wake County, North Carolina and American Bar Associations; North Carolina State Bar; North Carolina Association of Defense Attorneys; Defense Research Institute. ***PRACTICE AREAS:*** Workers Compensation; Civil Litigation; Commercial Litigation; Insurance Litigation. ***Email:*** jratledge@wilsonandratledge.com

LESLEY W. BENNETT, born Goldsboro, North Carolina, June 14, 1970; admitted to bar, 1997, North Carolina. *Education:* University of North Carolina at Greensboro (B.S., cum laude, 1991); University of North Carolina at Chapel Hill (J.D., 1997). Phi Alpha Delta (Treasurer, 1995-1997). *Member:* Wake County and North Carolina Bar Associations. ***PRACTICE AREAS:*** Corporate Law; Mergers and Acquisitions; Estate Planning; Taxation; Estate Administration; Commercial Real Estate; Residential Real Estate; Trust Law. ***Email:*** lbennett@wilsonandratledge.com

HEATHER L. HAWN, born Bradford, Pennsylvania, September 16, 1970; admitted to bar, 1997, North Carolina. *Education:* University of North Carolina at Chapel Hill (A.B., 1992); Campbell University (J.D., 1997). Delta Theta Phi. Member, John Marshall Moot Court Team. Editor, Campbell Law Observer. Clerk, North Carolina Industrial Commission. *Member:* North Carolina and American Bar Associations; North Carolina Association of Defense Attorneys; Defense Research Institute. ***PRACTICE AREAS:*** Workers Compensation; Employment Law. ***Email:*** hhawn@wilsonandratledge.com

RICHARD CHARLES INLOW, born Munich, Germany, March 21, 1962; admitted to bar, 1998, New York; 2004, North Carolina; 1998, U.S. Tax Court. *Education:* University of North Carolina at Wilmington (B.S., 1987); Brooklyn Law School (J.D., 1997); New York University (LL.M., 1999). Author: Gift Tax and Real Estate Transactions Chapters, *Taxation for the General Practitioner,* 1999. *Member:* Wake County and North Carolina Bar Associations. ***PRACTICE AREAS:*** State Taxation; Federal Taxation; International Taxation; Estate Planning; Estate Administration; Corporate Organizations; Corporate Reorganizations; Asset Protection Planning; Tax Controversies; Mergers and Acquisitions. ***Email:*** rinlow@wilsonandratledge.com

PERRY J. PELAEZ, born Washington, D.C., May 30, 1961; admitted to bar, 1991, Ohio; 1992, U.S. District Court, Southern District of Ohio; 1999, North Carolina; 2002, U.S. District Court, Eastern District of North Carolina; 2003, U.S. District Court, Middle District of North Carolina and U.S. Court of Appeals, Fourth Circuit. *Education:* University of Maryland (B.A., 1987); University of Dayton (J.D., 1991). Member, Moot Court Regional Team, 1990. Assistant Prosecuting Attorney, Dayton, Ohio, 1995-1997. *Member:* Wake County, North Carolina, Ohio State and American Bar Associations. ***REPORTED CASES:*** Inman v. Inman (1995), 101 Ohio App. 3d 115, State ex rel J. Richard Gaier v. Kessler (1994), 97 Ohio App. 3d 782. ***PRACTICE AREAS:*** Civil Litigation; Complex Commercial Litigation; Insurance Litigation; Workers Compensation. ***Email:*** pjpelaez@wilsonandratledge.com

KRISTINE L. PRATI, born Rochester, New York, April 15, 1978; admitted to bar, 2003, North Carolina. *Education:* State University of New York at Buffalo (B.A., magna cum laude, 2000); University of Illinois at Urbana-Champaign (J.D., 2003). Member, JESSUP Moot Court Regional Team. *Member:* North Carolina Bar Association (Member, Workers' Compensation Section). ***PRACTICE AREAS:*** Workers Compensation. ***Email:*** kprati@wilsonandratledge.com

PAUL F. TOLAND, born Malden, Massachusetts, September 24, 1963; admitted to bar, 1993, Massachusetts; 1994, North Carolina and U.S. District Court, District of Massachusetts. *Education:* Williams College (B.A., 1985); Suffolk University (J.D., cum laude, 1993). President, Suffolk University Law School Catholic Lawyers Guild, 1992-1993. *Member:* North Carolina State Bar; Wake County Bar Association. ***PRACTICE AREAS:*** Workers' Compensation; Civil Litigation. ***Email:*** ptoland@wilsonandratledge.com

REPRESENTATIVE CLIENTS: Adecco; Fireman's Fund Insurance Co.

WINSTON & MAHER

RALEIGH, NORTH CAROLINA

(See Chapel Hill)

General Civil, Criminal Trial Practice in all State and Federal Courts, Felonies, Misdemeanors, Drugs and Narcotics, White Collar Crime, Traffic Violations, Driving While Intoxicated.

WOMBLE CARLYLE SANDRIDGE & RICE

A Professional Limited Liability Company
2100 FIRST UNION CAPITOL CENTER
150 FAYETTEVILLE STREET MALL
P.O. BOX 831
RALEIGH, NORTH CAROLINA 27602
Telephone: 919-755-2100
Fax: 919-755-2150
Email: lawyers@wcsr.com
URL: http://www.wcsr.com

REVISER OF THE NORTH CAROLINA LAW DIGEST FOR THIS DIRECTORY.

Charlotte, North Carolina Office: 3500 One Wachovia Center, 301 South College Street. Telephone: 704-331-4900. Fax: 704-331-4955.
Winston-Salem, North Carolina Office: One West Fourth Street, 27101. Telephone: 336-721-3600. Fax: 336-721-3660.
Research Triangle Park, North Carolina Office: 2530 Meridian Parkway, Suite 400 (Durham), 27713, P.O. Box 13069, Research Triangle Park, 27709. Telephone: 919-484-2300. Fax: 919-484-2340.
Greensboro, North Carolina Office: 300 North Greene Street. Telephone: 336-574-8030. Fax: 336-574-4520.
Atlanta, Georgia Office: One Atlantic Center, 1201 West Peachtree Street, Suite 3500. Telephone: 404-872-7000. Fax: 404-888-7490.
Other Atlanta, Georgia Office: Suite 404, 2296 Henderson Mill Road, N.E. Telephone: 770-492-9030. Fax: 770-492-9609.
Washington, D.C. Office: Suite 700, 1401 Eye Street. Telephone: 202-857-4400. Fax: 202-467-6910.
Greenville, South Carolina Office: 700 Poinsett Plaza, 104 South Main Street, P.O. Box 10208. Telephone: 864-255-5400. Fax: 864-255-5440.
Tysons Corner, Virginia Office: 8065 Leesburg Pike, Fourth Floor. Telephone: 703-790-3310. Fax: 703-790-2623.

General Civil Practice, Trial and Appellate Litigation. Administrative, Antitrust, Aviation, Banking, Bankruptcy and Creditor's Rights, Bond Financing, Civil Rights, Commercial, Construction, Consumer Lending, Corporate, E-Commerce, Employee Benefits, Environmental, Estate Planning, Family, Government Relations, Health Care, Insurance, Intellectual Property, International, Labor and Employment, Municipal, Negligence, Probate, Product Liability, Real Estate, Retirement Plans, Securities, Taxation, Toxic Tort, Wills and Trusts Law.

FIRM PROFILE: Womble Carlyle Sandridge & Rice, PLLC, which traces its history to 1876, is a full-service law firm that delivers sophisticated and innovative legal services to a wide spectrum of business clients in industries that include information technology, health care, manufacturing, telecommunications and financial services. The Firm also represents a variety of governmental units and agencies.

Womble Carlyle's mission is to provide value to clients by combining professional skill, technology and a thorough understanding of clients' needs to deliver high quality, cost-effective and responsive service. The firm is comprised of approximately 470 lawyers and 838 staff members operating from offices in Atlanta, GA; Greenville, SC; Charlotte, Winston-Salem, Research Triangle Park, Raleigh and Greensboro, NC; Tysons Corner, VA and Washington, DC.

The Firm considers technology and the benefits it offers an integral part of the legal services it provides. All of the Firm's offices are linked for full communications by telephone, fax, electronic mail and video conference over a wide area network. The Firm takes full advantage of its sophisticated computer technology for support in large-case litigation, as well as management of complex transactions. The Director of Technology is responsible for implementing existing systems, and in some instances, developing new software applications to meet specific client needs. The firm-wide communications and computer network permit the Firm to allocate resources from all offices, as needed, as well as to establish direct, secure links with clients and their legal departments, thus enhancing the responsiveness and efficiency of the Firm's lawyers.

The lawyers of Womble Carlyle have traditionally been active in community affairs, in Bar and other professional activities, and in state government. Many lawyers assume leading roles in civic and professional organizations, and several have served the government in elected or appointed positions.

LAW FIRM ALLIANCES/ASSOCIATIONS: ***TOLEDO CONFERENCE GROUP***
LEX MUNDI

MEMBERS OF FIRM

THOMAS B. ANDERSON, JR., born Centreville, Mississippi, November 19, 1942; admitted to bar, 1970, North Carolina; 1971, U.S. District Court, Eastern, Western and Middle Districts of North Carolina and U.S. Court of Appeals, Fourth Circuit; 1973, U.S. Supreme Court; 1984, U.S. District Court, Northern and Southern Districts of Texas and U.S. Court of Appeals, Fifth Circuit; 1985, Texas, U.S. District Court, Eastern and Western Districts of Texas; 1991, U.S. Court of Appeals, Eleventh Circuit. *Education:* Davidson College (B.A., 1965); University of North Carolina (J.D., with honors, 1970). Order of the Coif. Law Clerk to U.S. Fourth Circuit Court of Appeals Judge J. Braxton Craven, Jr., 1970-1971. Visiting Professor, North Carolina Central University School of Law, Durham, N.C., 1971-1972. Visiting Lecturer, Debtor-Creditor Relations, University of North Carolina School of Law, 1980. *Member:* North Carolina and American Bar Associations; North Carolina State Bar; State Bar of Texas. Fellow, American College of Bankruptcy. ***PRACTICE AREAS:*** Litigation; Bankruptcy and Reorganization Law. ***Email:*** tanderson@wcsr.com

SEAN E. ANDRUSSIER, born Philadelphia, Pennsylvania, June 28, 1967; admitted to bar, 1992, Pennsylvania; 1993, District of Columbia; 1998, North Carolina. *Education:* Emory University (B.A., 1989); Duke University (J.D., with high honors, 1992). Phi Beta

(This Listing Continued)

WOMBLE CARLYLE SANDRIDGE & RICE, Raleigh—Continued

Kappa; Order of the Coif. Member, Duke Law Journal. Clerkships: M. Blane Michael, U.S. Court of Appeals, 4th Circuit; Karen LeCraft Henderson, U.S. Court of Appeals, District of Columbia Circuit. ***PRACTICE AREAS:*** Litigation. ***Email:*** sandrussier@wcsr.com

PAUL H. BILLOW, born Pittsfield, Massachusetts, 1964; admitted to bar, 1989, North Carolina. *Education:* University of North Carolina at Chapel Hill (B.S., in Sociology, with honors, 1986); Wake Forest University (J.D., 1989). ***PRACTICE AREAS:*** Public Finance. ***Email:*** pbillow@wcsr.com

JOHN C. COOKE, born Raleigh, North Carolina, September 24, 1952; admitted to bar, 1978, North Carolina. *Education:* Wake Forest University (B.A., cum laude, with honors in history, 1975; J.D., 1978). Assistant Wake County Attorney, 1978-1983. *Member:* Wake County and North Carolina (Member, Sections on: Litigation; Urban, State and Local Government Law; Real Property and Trust) Bar Associations; North Carolina Academy of Trial Lawyers; The Association of Trial Lawyers of America. ***PRACTICE AREAS:*** Real Estate Litigation; Municipal Law; Zoning Law. ***Email:*** jcooke@wcsr.com

SUSAN DAVIS CROOKS, born Raleigh, North Carolina, September 15, 1950; admitted to bar, 1987, North Carolina. *Education:* University of Salamanca, American Institute for Foreign Study, Spain; North Carolina State University; Rex Hospital School of Nursing (R.N., 1974); Campbell University (J.D., cum laude, 1987). Phi Kappa Phi; Omicron Delta Kappa; Delta Theta Phi. Business Editor, Campbell Law Review, 1986-1987. Registered Nurse, North Carolina, 1974. *Member:* North Carolina Bar Association (Member, Health Law and Litigation Section). ***PRACTICE AREAS:*** Litigation; Products Liability; Environmental; Toxic Tort; Insurance Defense; Estate and Trust Litigation. ***Email:*** scrooks@wcsr.com

MARK A. DAVIS, born Jacksonville, North Carolina, October 25, 1966; admitted to bar, 1991, North Carolina; 1993, U.S. District Court, Eastern District of North Carolina; U.S. Court of Appeals, Fourth Circuit; 2002, U.S. District Court, Western District of North Carolina. *Education:* University of North Carolina (B.A., 1988; J.D., 1991). Phi Beta Kappa. Member, North Carolina Law Review. Law Clerk, Hon. Franklin T. Dupree, Jr., Eastern District of North Carolina, 1991-1993. Adjunct Professor, Campbell University, Continuing Education Program, Raleigh, N.C., 1992-1993. Member, Local Rules Committee for the Eastern District of North Carolina. *Member:* Wake County (Member, Bench Bar Committee) North Carolina (Member, Litigation Section and Constitutional and Civil Rights Section; Chairman of the Liberty Bell Award Subcommittee of the Law Week Committee of the Young Lawyers Division) and American Bar Associations. ***PRACTICE AREAS:*** Appellate Litigation; Constitutional Litigation; Employment Discrimination; Employment Law; First Amendment Civil Rights; Insurance Defense Litigation. ***Email:*** mdavis@wcsr.com

WILLIAM A. DAVIS, II, born High Point, North Carolina, May 2, 1942; admitted to bar, 1967, North Carolina. *Education:* University of North Carolina (A.B., 1964); Duke University (LL.B., 1967); New York University (LL.M. in Taxation, 1968). Listed in The Best Lawyers in America, Corporate Law Section. *Member:* Forsyth County, North Carolina and American Bar Associations. ***PRACTICE AREAS:*** Corporate Law; Mergers and Acquisitions; Executive Compensation. ***Email:*** wdavis@wcsr.com

HAMPTON Y. DELLINGER, born Oxford, Mississippi, April 30, 1967; admitted to bar, 1993, North Carolina; 1994, District of Columbia. *Education:* University of Michigan (B.A., with high honors, 1989); Yale Law School (J.D., 1993). Editor and Senior Editor, Yale Law Journal, 1991-1993. Judicial Clerk to Honorable J. Dickson Phillips, Jr., U.S. Court of Appeals, Fourth Circuit, 1993-1994. Author, "Words Are Enough: The Troublesome Use of Photographs, Maps and Other Images in Supreme Court Opinions," Harvard Law Review (Vol. 100, No. 8 (1997); "Toeing the Legal Lines," The National Law Journal (12/2/02); "Reconstruction, Muhammad Ali: The Boxer as Dissident," (Vol.2, No.3, 1994). Lecturer, Campaign and Election Law, Duke University School of Law and Terry Sanford Institute of Public Policy, 1997. Special Counsel to the Attorney General, North Carolina Department of Justice, 1996-1998. Chief Legal Counsel, NC Governor's Office, 2001-2003. Deputy Attorney General, NC Department of Justice, 1999-2001. Of Counsel, Smith Helms Mulliss & Moore, Raleigh, NC 1998-1999. Associate, Wilmer Cutler & Pickering, Washington, DC, 1994-96. ***PRACTICE AREAS:*** Litigation; Regulatory Affairs. ***Email:*** hdellinger@wcsr.com

DONALD A. DONADIO, born Hampton, Virginia, January 3, 1943; admitted to bar, 1967, Virginia; 1972, North Carolina. *Education:* Wake Forest University (B.A., cum laude, 1965; J.D., cum laude, 1967). Phi Delta Phi. Associate Editor, Wake Forest Law Review, 1966-1967. Listed in: The Directory of Municipal Bond Attorneys of the United States; The Best Lawyers in America. *Member:* Wake County, North Carolina and American Bar Associations; National Association of Bond Lawyers; American College of Real Estate Lawyers. [Capt., (JAGC), U.S. Army, 1967-1972]. (Managing Member, Raleigh Office). ***PRACTICE AREAS:*** Public Finance; Commercial Real Estate; Economic Development. ***Email:*** ddonadio@wcsr.com

CHARLES A. EDWARDS, born Lumberton, North Carolina, 1945; admitted to bar, 1970, Georgia; 1974, U.S. Supreme Court; 1981, District of Columbia; 1987, North Carolina. *Education:* Davidson College (A.B., 1967); University of North Carolina (J.D., 1970). Phi Alpha Delta. Member: Scribes; Authors' Court of Georgia (Charter Member). Listed in Who's Who in American Law, Who's Who in the South and Southwest and Who's Who in America. Author: "Georgia Employment Law," (1st ed.) The Harrison Company, 1983; "Direct Evidence of Employment Discrimination," 43 Washington & Lee Law Review 1, 1986; "International Law and Employment Discrimination," 8 Oklahoma City University Law Review 1, 1983. Member, Warrentown, North Carolina, Town Council, 2001—. *Member:* Atlanta (Chairman, Labor Law Section, 1984-1985), Ninth District, Federal, North Carolina and American Bar Associations; State Bar of Georgia; The District of Columbia Bar; Defense Research Institute (Member, EEO Committee); American Management Association; Industrial Relations Research Association. (Practice Group Leader, Labor and Employment). ***PRACTICE AREAS:*** Employment Law; Labor Law; Litigation; Fair Housing. ***Email:*** cedwards@wcsr.com

ROBERT E. FIELDS III, born Bluefield, West Virginia, November 30, 1958; admitted to bar, 1984, Georgia; 1985, North Carolina. *Education:* Davidson College (B.A., 1981); Wake Forest University (J.D., cum laude, 1984). Member, Wake Forest Law Review, 1982-1984. *Member:* Wake County, North Carolina and American Bar Associations; State Bar of Georgia; North Carolina State Bar; North Carolina Association of Defense Attorneys; Defense Research Institute. ***PRACTICE AREAS:*** Civil Litigation; Products Liability Law. ***Email:*** rfields@wcsr.com

MARILYN R. FORBES, born Latrobe, Pennsylvania, September 17, 1955; admitted to bar, 1981, North Carolina. *Education:* Pennsylvania State University (B.A., magna cum laude, 1976); Wake Forest University (J.D., 1981). Member: The Order of Barristers; Moot Court Board. Law Clerk, United States District Court, Eastern District of North Carolina, 1981-1985. *Member:* Wake County and North Carolina Bar Associations. ***PRACTICE AREAS:*** Civil Litigation. ***Email:*** mforbes@wcsr.com

CHRISTOPHER T. GRAEBE, born Indianapolis, Indiana, September 7, 1961; admitted to bar, 1990, North Carolina and U.S. District Court, Eastern and Middle Districts of North Carolina; U.S. Court of Appeals, Fourth Circuit. *Education:* Wabash College (B.A., summa cum laude, 1983); Duke University (M.Div., summa cum laude, 1986); University of North Carolina at Chapel Hill (J.D., with high honors, 1990). Phi Beta Kappa; Order of the Coif. Member, North Carolina Law Review, 1988-1990. Author: "The Federalism of James Iredell in Historical Context," North Carolina Law Review, Vol. 69, Issue 1. *Member:* Wake County, North Carolina and American Bar Associations; North Carolina State Bar. ***PRACTICE AREAS:*** Litigation. ***Email:*** cgraebe@wcsr.com

JAMES B. HUNT, JR., born Greensboro, North Carolina, May 16, 1937; admitted to bar, 1966, North Carolina and U.S. District Court, Eastern District of North Carolina. *Education:* North Carolina State University (B.S., 1959; M.S. 1962); University of North Carolina (J.D., 1964). Lieutenant Governor of North Carolina, 1973-1977. Governor of North Carolina, 1977-1985; 1993-2001. Recipient: The Education Commission of the States, James B. Conant Award; The Horace Mann League's, Friend of Education Award; The Harold W. McGraw, Jr. Prize in Education; The National Mentoring Partnership, Award for Public Leadership; The Children's Defense Fund Award; The Columbia University Teachers College Medal for Distinguished Service; The Women Executives in State Government's, "Breaking the Glass Ceiling Award"; The American Academy of Pediatrics, Child Health Advocate Award; The National Secondary Schools, Distinguished Service Award; The National State Boards of Education, Policy Leader of the Year Award; The Council of Chief State School Officers, Distinguished Service Award; The National Education Association, Friend of Education Award; The National 4-H, Outstanding Alumnus Award; The National Wildlife Federation's, Conservation Achievement Award; The Honor Award from the Soil Conservation Society of America; The National Religious Heritage Award. Chairman, National Commission on Teaching and America's Future. Member, Board of Trustees, Carnegie Corporation of New York. Past Chairman, National Education Goals Panel. Past Vice Chairman of the Board, Achieve, Inc. Chairman, National Center for Public Policy and Higher Education (at San Jose, California). Past Member, Commission on US-Japan Relations for the 21st Century. Co-Chair, National Commission on Asia in the Schools. ***Email:*** jhunt@wcsr.com

SARAH ANNE KEEFE, born New Haven, Connecticut, October 16, 1967; admitted to bar, 1992, Florida; 1993, U.S. District Court, Southern and Middle Districts of Florida; 1995, Colorado; 1996, North Carolina. *Education:* University of Miami (B.S., 1989; J.D., 1992); Georgetown University (1988). *Member:* North Carolina (Member, Intellectual Property Section) and American (Member, Intellectual Property Section) Bar Associations; The Florida Bar; International Trademark Association. ***PRACTICE AREAS:*** Intellectual Property Litigation; Trademark Prosecution. ***Email:*** skeefe@wcsr.com

G. THOMAS LEE, born Mt. Vernon, Illinois, 1957; admitted to bar, 1985, New York; 1989, North Carolina. *Education:* North Carolina State University (A.B., 1980); Wake Forest University (J.D., 1983). ***PRACTICE AREAS:*** Public Finance. ***Email:*** tlee@wcsr.com

JOHNNY M. LOPER, born Forest, Mississippi, September 25, 1952; admitted to bar, 1983, Mississippi and U.S. District Court, Northern and Southern Districts of Mississippi; 1988, North Carolina; U.S. District Court, Eastern, Middle, and Western Districts of North Carolina. *Education:* Mississippi State University (B.S., with highest distinction, 1974; M.B.A., 1975); University of Mississippi (J.D., magna cum laude, 1983). Omicron Delta Kappa; Beta Gamma Sigma; Phi Delta Phi; Phi Eta Sigma; Blue Key. Managing Editor, Mississippi Law Journal, 1982. *Member:* The Mississippi Bar; North Carolina Bar Association (Member, Litigation Section). ***PRACTICE AREAS:*** Business Litigation; Administrative Law; Professional Licensing. ***Email:*** jloper@wcsr.com

HEATHER K. MALLARD, born New Kensington, Pennsylvania, September 23, 1963; admitted to bar, 1988, North Carolina and U.S. District Court, Middle District of North Carolina. *Education:* Grove City College (B.A., summa cum laude, 1985); Washington & Lee University (J.D., summa cum laude, 1988). Omicron Delta Kappa; Order of the Coif. Member, Mortar Board. Recipient, John W. Davis Prize for Law; Washington & Lee National Trial Competition Team. *Member:* Wake County, North Carolina and American Bar Associations. ***PRACTICE AREAS:*** Partnership Law; General Business Law; Private Placement Offerings; Mergers and Acquisitions; Corporate Law. ***Email:*** hmallard@wcsr.com

WILLIAM C. MATTHEWS, JR., born Charlotte, North Carolina, May 2, 1949; admitted to bar, 1977, Connecticut; 1981, North Carolina. *Education:* Southwestern at Memphis (B.A., 1971); Yale University (M.A.R., 1973); University of Richmond (J.D., 1977). Member, University of Richmond Law Review, 1976-1977. Lecturer and Director, Legal Writing Program, The University of Connecticut School of Law, 1977-1979. Law Clerk to Hon. Lawrence W. I'Anson, Supreme Court of Virginia, 1979-1981. *Member:* Wake County, North Carolina (Member, Real Property Section) and American (Member, Real Property Section) Bar Associations. ***PRACTICE AREAS:*** Finance Law; Real Estate (Property) Law. ***Email:*** bmatthews@wcsr.com

PRESSLY M. MILLEN, born Charlotte, North Carolina, July 1, 1960; admitted to bar, 1986, New York; 1987, U.S. District Court, Southern District of New York, U.S. District Court, Western, Middle and Eastern Districts of North Carolina and U.S. Court of Appeals, Seventh Circuit; 1988, North Carolina; 1997, U.S. Supreme Court. *Education:* Yale University (A.B., magna cum laude, 1982); Duke University (J.D., high honors, 1985). Order of the Coif. Note Editor, Duke Law Journal, 1984-1985. *Member:* North Carolina and American Bar Associations. ***PRACTICE AREAS:*** Antitrust Law; Commercial and Securities Litigation. ***Email:*** pmillen@wcsr.com

(This Listing Continued)

BURLEY B. MITCHELL, JR., born Oxford, North Carolina, December 15, 1940; admitted to bar, 1969, North Carolina, U.S. District Court, Eastern, Middle and Western Districts of North Carolina; U.S. Court of Appeals, Third and Fourth Circuits; 1972, U.S. Supreme Court. *Education:* North Carolina State University (B.A., 1966; L.H.D., 1995); Campbell University (D.L., 1996); University of North Carolina (J.D., 1969);. Phi Beta Kappa; Delta Theta Phi. Chief Justice, North Carolina Supreme Court, 1995-1999; Associate Justice, 1982-1994; North Carolina Secretary of Crime Control and Public Safety (Governor's Cabinet), 1979-1982; Judge, Court of Appeals, North Carolina, 1977-1979; District Attorney, Tenth Judicial District, North Carolina (Raleigh), 1972-1977; Assistant Attorney General, North Carolina, 1969-1972. ABA Presidential Task Force on Corporate Responsibility, 2002; Board of Trustees. North Carolina State University, 2005—; Board of Directors, North State Bank, 2000—; Who's Who in America, 1982—; Best Lawyers in America 2004—; Chair, North Carolina Progress Board, 1999—; Chair, Governor's Advisory Board of Prisons and Punishment (appointed by Governor James Martin-R), 1989-1992; Governor's Crime Commission (appointed by Governor James Hunt-D), 1977-1994, (Chairman, 1977-1979); North Carolina Court's Commission, 1983-1990; North Carolina News Media Administration of Justice Council, 1976-1986. *Member:* Wake County, North Carolina (Vice President, 1986-1987) and American Bar Associations. [U.S. Navy, 1958-1962]. ***REPORTED CASES:*** San Antonio Independent School District v. Rodriguez, 411 U.S.1; 93 S. Ct., 1278; 1973 U.S. Lexis 91; 36 L.Ed. 2d 16 (1973)(establishing that U.S. Constitution does not include a right to public education) (counsel for the State of North Carolina, amicus curiae); Rhyne v. K-Mart Corp., 358 N.C. 160, 594 S.E. 2d l (2004) (constitutionality of statutory cap on punitive damages); Leandro v. State, 346 N.C. 336, 488 S.E.2d 249 (1997)(state constitutional right to public education); Gwathmey v. State, 342 N.C. 287, 464 S.E.2d 674 (1995)(public access to navigable waters under public trust doctrine); Moss v. JC Bradford & Co., 337 N.C. 315, 446 S.E.2d 799 (1994)(issue of liability of commodities merchant for liquidating plaintiff's under-margined account without prior demand or notice); In re Guess, 327 N.C. 46, 393 S.E.2d 833 (1990)(homeopathic medicine, regulation under the police power); Hall v. Post, 323 N.C. 259, 372 S.E.2d 711 (1988)(tort of invasion of privacy by public disclosure of truthful but embarrassing facts); Crow v. Citicorp Acceptance Co., 319 N.C. 274, 354 S.E.2d 459 (1987)(establishing prerequisites for class actions in North Carolina); Speck v. North Carolina Diary Foundation, 311 N.C. 679; 319 S.E.2d 139 (1984)(whether plaintiff acquired interest in secret process he discovered while employed as professor and researcher by defendants); Renwick v. News & Observer, 310 N.C. 312, 312 S.E.2d 405 (1983)(false light invasion of privacy tort). ***PRACTICE AREAS:*** Appellate Practice; Business Law; Government; Litigation. ***Email:*** bmitchell@wcsr.com

JEFFREY A. POLEY, born Cleveland, Ohio, December 26, 1970; admitted to bar, 1996, North Carolina. *Education:* Duke University (B.A., Economics, Public Policy, 1993); University of North Carolina at Chapel Hill (J.D., 1996). *Member:* National Association of Bond Lawyers. ***PRACTICE AREAS:*** Public Finance.

ALEXANDER P. SANDS, III, born Reidsville, North Carolina, October 26, 1945; admitted to bar, 1971, North Carolina. *Education:* Duke University (A.B., 1967); University of North Carolina (J.D., with honors, 1971). Phi Delta Phi. Member, Board of Editors, North Carolina Law Review, 1970-1971. Member, North Carolina Senate, 1987-1994; Chairman, Local Government and Regional Affairs Committee; Chairman, Judiciary Committee; Chairman, Committee on Rules and Operations of the Senate; Member, Legislative Advisory Committee, 1995-2001. *Member:* North Carolina Bar Association; North Carolina State Bar; The Association of Trial Lawyers of America; North Carolina Academy of Trial Lawyers. ***PRACTICE AREAS:*** Insurance Regulation; Utilities Regulation; Government Relations. ***Email:*** ssands@wcsr.com

ROBERT H. SASSER, III, born Patuxent River, Maryland, November 14, 1957; admitted to bar, 1983, North Carolina. *Education:* Wake Forest University (B.S., 1980; J.D., 1983). Member, Wake Forest Law Review, 1981-1982. *Member:* Wake County and North Carolina (Member, Litigation Section) Bar Associations; Forsyth County Young Lawyers Association (Treasurer, 1986-1987; President-elect, 1987-1988; President, 1988-1989); North Carolina Association of Defense Attorneys. ***PRACTICE AREAS:*** Products Liability. ***Email:*** rsasser@wcsr.com

NELLIE K. SHIPLEY, born Grand Forks, North Dakota, August 12, 1965; admitted to bar, 1994, North Carolina. *Education:* Yale College (B.S., Computer Science, cum laude, 1987); University of Texas, Austin (J.D., with honors, 1994). Articles Editor, Texas Law Review. *Member:* Wake County, North Carolina (Real Property Section, Law Practice Management Section) and American (Real Property, Probate and Trust Law Section; Member, State and Local Government Law Section) Bar Associations. ***LANGUAGES:*** Spanish. ***PRACTICE AREAS:*** Real Estate Acquisitions; Real Estate Finance; Real Estate Development; Redevelopment; Real Estate Leasing; Real Estate Dispositions. ***Email:*** nshipley@wcsr.com

MAURY M. TEPPER, III, born Cincinnati, Ohio, November 21, 1965; admitted to bar, 1991, North Carolina; U.S. District Court, Middle District of North Carolina. *Education:* Wake Forest University (B.A., 1988); University of Cincinnati (J.D., 1991). Order of the Coif. Student Articles Editor, University of Cincinnati Law Review, 1990-1991. Author: "Works Made for Hire and the Copyright Act of 1976: We're Finally Back Where We Started," 59 U. Cinn. L. Rev. 299, 1990; "False Advertising Claims and the Revision of the Lanham Act-A Step in Which Direction?" 59 U. Cinn. L. Rev., 1991; "Copyright Law: Integrating Successive Filtering Into the Bifurcated Substantial Similarity Inquiry in Software Copyright Infringement Cases: A Standard for Determining the Scope of Copyright Protection for Non-Literal Elements of Computer Programs," 14 Campbell L. Rev. 1, 1991; "What IP Is All About," Legal Times, August 19 and 26, 1996; "Protect Copyrights Early to Avoid Trouble Down the Line," Corporate Legal Times, November, 1996. Co-Author: *Advanced Trademark and Trade Dress Issues in Computer Software Distribution,* 1994 Computer Law Companion (Computer Law Association). *Member:* North Carolina (Immediate Past Chair, Intellectual Property Section) and American (Member, Intellectual Property Section) Bar Associations; International Trademark Association (Board of Directors; Audit Committee Chair); USPTO (Subcommittee Chair); Institute of Trademark Attorneys (Overseas Member); North Carolina Volunteer Lawyers for the Arts. (Trademark Attorney). ***PRACTICE AREAS:*** Copyright and Trademark Clearance Registration and Licensing; Computer Law; Arts and Entertainment Law.

(This Listing Continued)

KURT D. WEAVER, born Hinsdale, Illinois, December 20, 1961; admitted to bar, 1987, Ohio; 2000, North Carolina; U.S. Supreme Court; U.S. Court of Appeals, Sixth Circuit; U.S. District Court, Eastern District of North Carolina; U.S. District Court, Northern and Southern Districts of Ohio. *Education:* Hillsdale College (A.B., magna cum laude, 1984); University of Notre Dame (J.D., 1987). Member, National Trial Team. Research Editor, Notre Dame Journal of Law, Ethics and Public Policy. Law Director, Village of Peninsula, Ohio, 1998-1999; Assistant Law Director, City of Independence, Ohio, 1991-1999. Deputy Solicitor, Village of Bratenahl, Ohio, 1991-1999. *Member:* American Bar Association; Wake Coutny and North Carolina (Member, Litigation Section) Bar Associations; Defense Research Institute. ***PRACTICE AREAS:*** Products Liability; Toxic Tort Litigation; Commercial Litigation. ***Email:*** kweaver@wcsr.com

ASSOCIATES

KIMBERLY BRACKETT-JONES, born Jacksonville, Florida, 1974; admitted to bar, 1999, Georgia and North Carolina. *Education:* University of Oklahoma (B.A., 1996); University of Georgia (J.D., 1998). Phi Alpha Delta. *Member:* State Bar of Georgia; North Carolina State Bar. ***LANGUAGES:*** Spanish. ***PRACTICE AREAS:*** Products Liability Litigation. ***Email:*** kbrackett-jones@wcsr.com

JENNIFER LONG COLLINS, born Pittsburgh, Pennsylvania, July 5, 1968; admitted to bar, 1995, North Carolina. *Education:* Clemson University (B.A., English and History, 1990); University of Louisville (J.D., summa cum laude, 1995). Senior Editor, University of Louisville Journal of Family Law. Member, 1993-1995 and Vice President, 1994-1995, Brandeis Society. Author: "Hecht v. Superior Court: Recognizing a Property Right in Reproductive Material," University of Louisville Journal of Family Law, Summer 1994-1995 Issue. Law Clerk to Hon. Alexander B. Denson, U.S. District Court for the Eastern District of North Carolina, 1995-1996. *Member:* North Carolina and American Bar Associations. ***PRACTICE AREAS:*** Computer Law; Intellectual Property Licensing; Promotion Law; Sweepstakes Law. ***Email:*** jlcollins@wcsr.com

KATHRYN M. EYSTER, born Lynchburg, Virginia, September 28, 1974; admitted to bar, 2003, North Carolina; 2004; U.S. District Court, Middle District of North Carolina. *Education:* Duke University (B.S., summa cum laude, 1996); Wake Forest University (J.D., magna cum laude, 2003). Phi Beta Kappa; Phi Eta Sigma; Alpha Phi Omega Service Fraternity; Sigma Gamma Delta; Psi Chi. Member, Golden Key Honor Society. Member: Wake Forest Law Review; International Moot Court Team. A.J. Fletcher Scholarship. Recipient: CALI Awards for Academic Achievement; West Group Outstanding Achievement Award, 2001, 2002 and 2003. Member, Duke Chapel Choir, 1993-1996. Judicial Clerkship: The Honorable N. Carlton Tilley, Jr., Chief Judge, U.S. District Court, Middle District of North Carolina, 2003-2004. Member, Joseph Branch Inn of Court, 2001-2004. *Member:* North Carolina and American Bar Associations; North Carolina State Bar. ***Email:*** keyster@wcsr.com

DOUGLAS W. HANNA, born Lima, Ohio, May 25, 1966; admitted to bar, 1991, North Carolina; 1994, U.S. Court of Appeals for the Armed Forces. *Education:* University of Michigan (B.G.S., 1988); Wake Forest University (J.D., 1991). *Member:* Wake County, North Carolina and American Bar Associations; Judge Advocates Association. [LT, (JAGC), U.S. Navy, 1991-1997]. ***PRACTICE AREAS:*** Civil Litigation; Condemnation Litigation. ***Email:*** dhanna@wcsr.com

MATTHEW S. HEALEY, born Elizabeth, New Jersey, 1973; admitted to bar, 2002, North Carolina. *Education:* University of Notre Dame (B.A., 1995); University of Georgia (J.D., 2002). ***PRACTICE AREAS:*** Insurance; Government Tort Litigation. ***Email:*** mhealey@wcsr.com

BETH TYNER JONES, born Manhattan, Kansas; admitted to bar, 1988, North Carolina. *Education:* Campbell University (B.A., summa cum laude, 1985; J.D., cum laude, 1988). Omicron Delta Kappa; Phi Kappa Phi; Delta Theta Phi; The Order of Barristers. Editor-in-Chief, Campbell Law Review, 1987-1988. Former Associate, Womble Carlyle Sandridge & Rice PLLC, Raleigh, North Carolina. *Member:* North Carolina and American Bar Associations; North Carolina State Bar; American Immigration Lawyers Association (Vice-Chair, Carolina Chapter, 1994—). (Corporate Attorney). ***Email:*** bjones@wcsr.com

KELLY B. JONES, born Kingston, New York, November 7, 1971; admitted to bar, 1997, North Carolina. *Education:* University of North Carolina at Wilmington (B.S., 1994); Campbell University (J.D., 1997). *Member:* North Carolina State Bar. ***PRACTICE AREAS:*** Products Liability. ***Email:*** kjones@wcsr.com

MATTHEW K. LUNG, born Hammond, Indiana, October 8, 1971; admitted to bar, 2000, South Carolina; 2001, North Carolina. *Education:* University of South Carolina, Coastal Carolina College, Conway, S.C. (B.S., 1994); Wake Forest University (J.D., 1999). Recipient: CALI Excellence For The Future Award, Computer Law; CALI Excellence For The Future Award, Antitrust. Research Editor, Wake Forest Law Review. *Member:* Charlotte and American Bar Associations; South Carolina Bar. ***PRACTICE AREAS:*** Insurance Law; Products Liability Litigation; Toxic Torts; Medical Malpractice; Commercial Litigation. ***Email:*** mlung@wcsr.com

CATHERINE E. OTTO, born Raleigh, North Carolina, October 8, 1975; admitted to bar, 2003, North Carolina and U.S. District Court, Eastern District of North Carolina. *Education:* University of North Carolina at Chapel Hill (A.B., with honors and distinction, 1997; Masters in the Art of Teaching, 1998; J.D., 2003). Note and Comment Editor, Journal of International Law and Commerical Regulation. Summer Clerk, Federal District Judge W. Earl Britt, Raleigh, NC, 2002. Social Studies Teacher, Wake County Public School System, Southeast Raleigh High School, 1998-1999. Curriculum Specialist and Training Coordinator, LEARN NC, University of North Carolina at Chapel Hill School of Education, 1999-2000. Author: "Tracking Immigrants in the United States: Proposed and Perceived Needs to Protect the Borders of the United States," North Carolina Journal of International Law and Commercial Regulation, Vol.28, No 2, (2002). ***PRACTICE AREAS:*** Product Liability Litigation. ***Email:*** cotto@wcsr.com

VIDALIA PATTERSON, born New York, N.Y., 1975; admitted to bar, 2001, North Carolina; U.S. District Court, Eastern District of North Carolina. *Education:* Davidson College (B.A., 1997); Columbus School of Law of The Catholic University of America (J.D., 2001). *Member:* North Carolina and American Bar Associations. ***LANGUAGES:*** Spanish. ***PRACTICE AREAS:*** Products Liability; Litigation. ***Email:*** vpatterson@wcsr.com

(This Listing Continued)

WOMBLE CARLYLE SANDRIDGE & RICE, Raleigh—Continued

GARRETT R. PERDUE, born New Bern, North Carolina, September 19, 1976; admitted to bar, 2004, North Carolina. *Education:* University of North Carolina at Chapel Hill (B.A., 1999; J.D., 2004). Director, Policy and Research, Perdue for Lieutenant Governor, 1999-2001. Member: North Carolina Banking Institute; Carolina Business Institute. *Member:* North Carolina State Bar; American Constitutional Society. ***Email:*** gperdue@wcsr.com

MORGAN E. PERSINGER, born Wheeling, West Virginia, 1975; admitted to bar, 2000, West Virginia; 2001, North Carolina. *Education:* West Virginia University (B.A., 1996; J.D., 2000). *Member:* West Virginia State Bar; North Carolina State Bar; American Bar Association. ***PRACTICE AREAS:*** Product Liability Litigation; Medical Malpractice Litigation. ***Email:*** mpersinger@wcsr.com

KRISTEN S. PROVENZA BENKO, born New Orleans, Louisiana, March 25, 1974; admitted to bar, 1999, North Carolina. *Education:* Loyola University (B.A., summa cum laude, 1996); University of North Carolina at Chapel Hill (J.D., with honors, 1999). *Member:* Wake County and North Carolina Bar Associations; National Association of Bond Lawyers. ***PRACTICE AREAS:*** Public Finance. ***Email:*** kbenko@wcsr.com

MELODY C. RAY-WELBORN, born Canton, North Carolina, September 6, 1976; admitted to bar, 2001, North Carolina. *Education:* Duke University (A.B., 1998); Emory University School of Law (J.D., with honors, 2001). ***PRACTICE AREAS:*** Business Litigation. ***Email:*** mwelborn@wcsr.com

SHERI ROBERSON, born Martinsville, Virginia, November 25, 1971; admitted to bar, 1996, North Carolina. *Education:* University of Virginia (B.A., 1992); Duke University; Southern Methodist University (J.D., 1996). *Member:* Wake County and North Carolina Bar Associations; North Carolina State Bar. ***PRACTICE AREAS:*** Employment Law. ***Email:*** sroberson@wcsr.com

MARY ELIZABETH SMITH, born Knoxville, Tennessee, July 7, 1970; admitted to bar, 1998, Georgia and U.S. District Court, Northern District of Georgia; 2004, North Carolina. *Education:* Emory University (B.A., 1992); University of Georgia (J.D., cum laude, 1998). Author: "Reducing Uncertainty of the Land-Use Permitting Process," The Triangle Business Journal, April 30, 2004; Seminar Manual for Mechanics' Lien Law and Strategies in Georgia, National Business Institute, March 2000, March 2002, March 2003; Manual for Annual Update Seminar, Smith, Currie & Hancock, LLP, April, 2002, April 2003; Seminar Manual for Construction Defects & Mold Litigation, National Business Institute, May 2003. Featured Speaker: "Construction Law: Can This Job Be Saved?," Lorman Business Center, Inc., March 28, 2003; "Mechanics' Lien Law and Strategies in Georgia," National Business Institute, March 11, 2003; Annual Update Seminar, Smith, Currie & Hancock, LLP, April 2002; "Construction Claims in Georgia," Lorman Education Services, November 16, 2001; "Georgia Construction Law: From Bidding to Final Payment," Lorman Business Center, March 16, 2001; "Georgia Construction Issues" Lorman Education Services, December 14, 2000; "Georgia Construction Lien and Public Contract Bond Law," Lorman Education Services, October 13, 2000. *Member:* Atlanta and American Bar Associations; Lawyer's Club of Atlanta. ***PRACTICE AREAS:*** Real Estate Litigation; Construction Law.

THERESA M. SPRAIN, born Juneau, Alaska, May 20, 1972; admitted to bar, 1997, North Carolina. *Education:* Willamette University (B.A., 1994); Wake Forest University (J.D., 1997). National Merit Scholar. Member: National Moot Court Team; American Inns of Court; Wagner Labor Law Moot Court Team. ***PRACTICE AREAS:*** Environmental; Toxic Torts. ***Email:*** tsprain@wcsr.com

M. TODD SULLIVAN, born Detroit, Michigan, December 13, 1967; admitted to bar, 1995, New York and U.S. District Court, Western District of New York; U.S. Tax Court; U.S. Court of International Trade; 1997, North Carolina and U.S. District Court, Eastern and Middle Districts of North Carolina; 1998, U.S. Court of Appeals, Fourth Circuit; 2000, U.S. Court of Appeals, Sixth Circuit. *Education:* Lake Forest College (B.A., magna cum laude, 1990); Cornell University (J.D., 1994). Phi Beta Kappa. *Member:* North Carolina, New York State, U.S. Supreme Court and American Bar Associations. ***PRACTICE AREAS:*** Labor and Employment Litigation. ***Email:*** tsullivan@wcsr.com

ALAN K. WINDHAM, admitted to bar, 1998, North Carolina. *Education:* University of North Carolina - Chapel Hill (B.A., 1992); Indiana University School of Law - Indianapolis (J.D., 1997). Phi Alpha Delta. International Law Society, 1996-1997. *Member:* North Carolina and American Bar Associations. ***PRACTICE AREAS:*** Product Liability; Civil Litigation. ***Email:*** awindham@wcsr.com

OF COUNSEL

E. LAWRENCE DAVIS, III, born Winston-Salem, North Carolina, December 30, 1937; admitted to bar, 1963, North Carolina. *Education:* Princeton University (A.B., 1960); George Washington University (M.B.A., 1966); Duke University (LL.B., 1963). Phi Delta Phi. Member, Editorial Board, Duke Law Journal, 1962-1963. Listed in: The Best Lawyers in America, Corporate Law Section; Who's Who in America. Member: North Carolina House of Representatives, 1971-1974; North Carolina Senate, 1975-1978. Member, North Carolina Courts Commission, 1979-1985. Chairman, 1993 and Board Member, 1994—, North Carolina Family Business Forum. *Member:* Wake County, North Carolina and American Bar Associations (Member, Board of Governors, 1979-1982); American Judicature Society. [Capt., U.S. Army, active duty, 1963-1965]. ***PRACTICE AREAS:*** Business Law; Government Relations. ***Email:*** ldavis@wcsr.com

PETER J. DUFFLEY, born Omaha, Nebraska, August 13, 1967; admitted to bar, 1994, North Carolina; 1995, Illinois. *Education:* Purdue University (B.S., 1989); Wake Forest University School of Law (J.D., 1994). Partner, Poyner & Spruill LLP, Raleigh, NC, 1998-2003; Associate, Pinna Johnston & Burwell PA, Raleigh, NC, 1996-1997. *Member:* North Carolina Bar Association (Member, Sections on: Business Law, Tax Law, and Poverty Law); Illinois State Bar Association. ***PRACTICE AREAS:*** Affordable Housing and Community Development (70%); Banking Law (30%). ***Email:*** pduffley@wcsr.com

DONALD R. ESPOSITO, JR., born Greenville, South Carolina, August 2, 1969; admitted to bar, 1995, North Carolina, U.S. District Court, Western District of North Carolina and U.S. Court of Appeals, Fourth Circuit; 1997, U.S. District Court, Eastern and Middle Districts of North Carolina. *Education:* University of North Carolina at Chapel Hill (B.A., 1991); Harvard Law School (J.D., 1995). Phi Beta Kappa. John Motley Morehead Scholar. Henry Luce Scholar. Law Clerk, The Hon. Lacy H. Thornburg, U.S. District Court, W.D.N.C., 1995-1996. Assistant Attorney General, North Carolina Department of Justice, 2000-2001. ***PRACTICE AREAS:*** Antitrust; Business Litigation. ***Email:*** desposito@wcsr.com

MARY LYNNE GRIGG, born 1966; admitted to bar, 1992, North Carolina; 1993, South Carolina. *Education:* University of North Carolina, Charlotte (B.A., magna cum laude, 1989); Duke University (J.D., 1992). Omicron Delta*Member:* Wake County, North Carolina (Member, Section on Public Utility Communications and Transportation) and American Bar Associations; North Carolina State Bar; South Carolina Bar. ***PRACTICE AREAS:*** Energy; Regulated Utilities; Government Relations. ***Email:*** mgrigg@wcsr.com

JEFFREY M. HAHN, born Washington, D.C., April 20, 1962; admitted to bar, 1986, Virginia; 1987, District of Columbia; 1991, Massachusetts; 1995, North Carolina. *Education:* University of Virginia (B.A., with highest distinction, 1983); Harvard University (J.D., cum laude, 1986). Phi Beta Kappa. Author: Fasman, Dollarhide and Hahn, *What Business Must Know About the Americans with Disabilities Act* (United States Chamber of Commerce 1991); Hahn, "Pre-employment Information Services: Employers Beware?" 17 *Employee Relations Law Journal* No. 1, at 45 (Summer 1991); Hahn and Smith, "Wrongful Discharge: The Search for a Legislative Compromise," 15 *Employee Relations Law Journal* No. 4, at 515 (Spring 1990). Law Clerk, Hon. Judge James C. Cacheris, U.S. District Court, Eastern District of Virginia, 1986-1987. *Member:* American Bar Association. ***PRACTICE AREAS:*** Labor and Employment Law; Products Liability Litigation. ***Email:*** jhahn@wcsr.com

GWENDA L. LAWS, born Sanford, North Carolina, July 13, 1966; admitted to bar, 1991, North Carolina. *Education:* Duke University (B.A., 1987); University of North Carolina (J.D., 1991). Member, Moot Court Invitational Team. *Member:* Wake County, North Carolina and American Bar Associations; The North Carolina State Bar; North Carolina Association of Defense Attorneys; Defense Research Institute. ***PRACTICE AREAS:*** Products Liability Defense. ***Email:*** glaws@wcsr.com

ELIZABETH LeVAN RILEY, born St. Louis, Missouri, July 24, 1958; admitted to bar, 1983, Mississippi and U.S. District Court, Southern District of Mississippi; 1987, North Carolina, U.S. District Court, Eastern, Western and Middle Districts of North Carolina and U.S. Court of Appeals, Fourth Circuit; 1990, U.S. Supreme Court. *Education:* Vanderbilt University (B.A., magna cum laude, 1979); Oxford University, Oxford, England; University of Kentucky (J.D., 1983). Staff Member, Kentucky Law Journal, 1982-1983. Member: North Carolina Council of School Attorneys; National Association of College and University Attorneys. *Member:* North Carolina Bar Association (Member: Education Law Section; Construction Law Section) and American Bar Association (Member, Construction Industry Forum); Mississippi State Bar. ***PRACTICE AREAS:*** Commercial Litigation and Education Law. ***Email:*** lriley@wcsr.com

ELAINE M. WHITFORD, born Heidelberg, West Germany, 1964; admitted to bar, 1989, Pennsylvania; 1995, North Carolina. *Education:* University of North Carolina, Chapel Hill (B.A., 1986; J.D., 1989). *Member:* Wake County and North Carolina Bar Associations. ***PRACTICE AREAS:*** Labor and Employment; Education Law. ***Email:*** ewhitford@wcsr.com

STAFF ATTORNEYS

MELISSA DIX DONAHUE, born Campbellsville, Kentucky, June 28, 1974; admitted to bar, 2001, North Carolina. *Education:* University of Kentucky (B.A., Political Science and Psychology, cum laude, 1996; J.D., 2001). Phi Delta Phi. *Member:* North Carolina State Bar; American Bar Association. ***PRACTICE AREAS:*** Products Liability. ***Email:*** mdonahue@wcsr.com

KIMBERLY S. JUSTUS, born Atlanta, Georgia, August 25, 1972; admitted to bar, 1997, Georgia; 1999, North Carolina. *Education:* Georgia Institute of Technology (B.S., 1994); Wake Forest University (J.D., 1997). *Member:* Wake County (Member, Real Property Section) and North Carolina (Member, Real Property Section) Bar Associations; North Carolina State Bar; State Bar of Georgia. ***Email:*** kjustus@wcsr.com

LEGAL SUPPORT PERSONNEL

Terry Michael Wiley (Executive Director)
Susan DeVore (Office Administrator - Atlanta)
Keith Tedrow (Office Administrator - Winston-Salem)
John E. Turlington (Office Administrator - Research Triangle Park and Raleigh)
Cheri Edwards (Office Administrator - Tysons Corner, VA)
Patricia A. Kight (Director of Human Resources)
Charles R. Allison, III (Office Administrator - Charlotte)
John T. Boyer (Office Administrator - Washington, DC)
Hails Foster (Director of Finance and Systems)
Mark Whitley (Director, Strategic Planning and Marketing)
Julie D. Beavers (Professional Development/Recruiting Administrator - Research Triangle Park and Raleigh)
Cynthia K. Pruitt (Professional Development/Recruiting Administrator - Winston-Salem and Greensboro)
Kristin F. Carretta (Director of Professional Development and Recruiting)
Elizabeth P. Keasler (Professional Development/Recruiting Administrator - Charlotte and Greenville, SC)
Stacy H. Stephens (Professional Development/Recruiting Administrator - Atlanta)
Barbara Fountain (Office Manager - Greenville)
Melissa B. Weaver (Office Manager/Billing Coordinator - Greensboro)

GENERAL COUNSEL FOR: Brenner Companies; Charles & Colvard, Ltd.; Inmar Enterprises, Inc.; NC Biosciences Industry Organization; Piedmont Federal Savings & Loan Assn.; RF Micro Devices, Inc.; Venture First Associates.
REPRESENTATIVE CLIENTS: ABB, Inc.; Ali Group; Bank of America Corporation; BB&T Corporation; Carolinas HealthCare System; Charles & Colvard, Ltd.; Centennial Broadcasting, LLC; Cisco Systems, Inc.; City of Raleigh, North Carolina; DaimlerChrysler Corporation; Duke University; Duke University Health System, Inc.; Elster Electricity, LLC; General Electric Company; GlaxoSmithKline; Jefferson-Pilot Life Insurance Company; KIA Motors America, Inc; Lowes Companies, Inc.; Magneti Marelli Powertrain USA, Inc.; Medtronic, Inc; Motricity, Inc.; North Carolina Association of County Commissioners; North Carolina Housing Finance

(This Listing Continued)

Agency; North Carolina Railroad Company; North Carolina State University; Novartis AG; PepsiCo, Inc.; Piedmont Triad Airport Authority; Pulte Homes, Inc.; Red Hat, Inc.; Research Triangle Institute; RJ Reynolds Tobacco Company; SAS Institute Inc.; Syngenta Agribusiness; Talecris Biotherapeutics, Inc.; The Hartford Insurance Company; The Travelers Insurance Companies; University of North Carolina Health Care System; Wachovia Bank, National Association; Wake Forest University; Wake Forest University Baptist Medical Center; WakeMed; West Pharmaceutical Services, Inc.

REVISER OF THE NORTH CAROLINA LAW DIGEST FOR THIS DIRECTORY.

(For Biographical Data on other Personnel, see Professional Biographies at Winston-Salem, Charlotte, Research Triangle Park, North Carolina, Atlanta, Georgia, Washington, D.C., Greenville, South Carolina and Tysons Corner, Virginia)

RANDOLPH L. WORTH

3737 GLENWOOD AVENUE, SUITE 100
RALEIGH, NORTH CAROLINA 27612
Telephone: 919-573-6163
Fax: 919-573-6064
Email: worthlaw@bellsouth.net
Mailing Address: P.O. Box 20825, Raleigh, NC 27619-0825

Trusts and Estates, Estate Planning and Administration, Estate Litigation, Guardianship, Wills, Probate, Taxation.

RANDOLPH L. WORTH, born Washington, D.C., December 23, 1946; admitted to bar, 1972, North Carolina. *Education:* University of North Carolina (A.B., 1968); Vanderbilt University (J.D., 1972); Boston University (LL.M. in Taxation, 1981). *Member:* Wake County (Member, Board of Directors, 1975-1977), Tenth Judicial District, North Carolina and American Bar Associations; North Carolina State Bar.

WYRICK ROBBINS YATES & PONTON LLP

Established in 1979

4101 LAKE BOONE TRAIL
SUITE 300
P.O. DRAWER 17803
RALEIGH, NORTH CAROLINA 27607
Telephone: 919-781-4000
Telecopier: 919-781-4865
Email: info@wyrick.com
URL: http://www.wyrick.com

Appellate Advocacy, Arbitration, Banking, Bankruptcy and Workouts, Biotechnology, Broker-Dealer/Investment Advisor Compliance and Defense, Business, Commercial Contracts and Litigation, Commercial Real Estate, Communications, Community Associations, Computer, Construction, Copyright Licensing, Litigation and Registration, Corporate, Corporate Finance, Credit Union, Creditors Rights, Elder, Election Law, Employee Benefits, Employment, Entrepreneurial Business Law, Environmental, Estate Planning and Probate, Family Law, Franchise, Government Contracting, Health, Intellectual Property Protection and Licensing, Internet and E-Commerce, Labor, Litigation in all State and Federal Courts, Mediation, Mergers, Acquisitions and Divestitures, Municipal, Partnerships and LLC's, Private Placements, Public Offerings, Securities Arbitrations and Mediations, Securities Law, Strategic Partnerships and Collaborations, Taxation, Tax-Exempt and Non-Profit Organizations, Technology and Venture Capital Law.

FIRM PROFILE: Wyrick Robbins Yates & Ponton LLP has provided full-service legal representation on a local, regional and national basis since 1979. Our demonstrated ability to help business clients achieve their goals has earned us a reputation as one of the region's premier business law firms. The firm has specialized practice groups that provide both the depth and the flexibility to analyze and maximize the growth opportunities for all levels of business - from start-up to publicly held companies. Our commitment is to provide excellent legal skills and practical business judgment to add value to every client relationship.

D. CALDWELL BAREFOOT JR., born February 24, 1967; admitted to bar, 1994, North Carolina. *Education:* Wake Forest University (B.A., 1989); Campbell University (J.D., cum laude, 1994). Membership Editor, Campbell University Law Review. ***PRACTICE AREAS:*** Family Law; Litigation. ***Email:*** cbarefoot@wyrick.com

DONALD L. BECI, born September 21, 1954; admitted to bar, 1984, Wisconsin; 1985, Illinois; 1992, U.S. Supreme Court; 1999, U.S. Court of Appeals, Fourth Circuit; 2001, North Carolina. *Education:* University of Illinois, Urbana-Champaign (B.S.W., magna cum laude, 1977; M.S.W., 1978; J.D., cum laude, 1984). Harno Scholar. Associate Professor, 1990-1999 and Professor of the Year, 1996-1997 and 1998-1999, Campbell University School of Law. ***PRACTICE AREAS:*** Family Law; Litigation. ***Email:*** dbeci@wyrick.com

HEIDI C. BLOOM, born April 17, 1969; admitted to bar, 1996, North Carolina. *Education:* University of North Carolina-Chapel Hill (B.A., 1991); Wake Forest University (J.D., 1995). ***PRACTICE AREAS:*** Family Law; Litigation. ***Email:*** hbloom@wyrick.com

STEPHEN C. BRISSETTE, born August 1, 1957; admitted to bar, 1982, Massachusetts; 1983, U.S. District Court, District of Massachusetts; 1987, U.S. Tax Court; 1989, North Carolina. *Education:* University of North Carolina (B.A., 1979; J.D., 1982); Boston University (LL.M., Taxation, 1988). ***PRACTICE AREAS:*** Mergers, Acquisitions and Divestitures; Communications Law; Taxation. ***Email:*** sbrissette@wyrick.com

MADISON E. BULLARD, JR., born April 24, 1956; admitted to bar, 1981, North Carolina. *Education:* Wake Forest University (B.A., with honors, 1978); University of North Carolina at Chapel Hill (J.D., 1981). (Board Certified Specialist in Estate Planning and Probate Law, North Carolina State Board of Legal Specialization). ***PRACTICE AREAS:*** Estate Planning; Probate; Tax-Exempt Organizations; Taxation. ***Email:*** mbullard@wyrick.com

(This Listing Continued)

LISA K. CANFIELD, born May 12, 1972; admitted to bar, 1997, North Carolina. *Education:* Virginia Polytechnic Institute and State University (B.A., 1994); University of Virginia (J.D., 1997). ***PRACTICE AREAS:*** Estate Planning; Probate; Taxation. ***Email:*** lbark@wyrick.com

ALYSSA M. CHEN, born April 5, 1975; admitted to bar, 2003, North Carolina. *Education:* University of Colorado at Boulder (B.A., 1997); University of North Carolina (J.D., with honors, 2003). Order of the Coif. ***PRACTICE AREAS:*** Appellate Advocacy. ***Email:*** achen@wyrick.com

CHARLES W. CLANTON, born December 7, 1956; admitted to bar, 1991, North Carolina; 1992, U.S. District Court, Eastern, Western and Middle Districts of North Carolina. *Education:* Yale University; University of North Carolina at Chapel Hill (B.A., 1987; J.D., with honors, 1991). ***PRACTICE AREAS:*** Family Law; Litigation. ***Email:*** wclanton@wyrick.com

JAMES L.S. COBB, born November 14, 1952; admitted to bar, 1989, California; 1993, North Carolina. *Education:* Duke University (B.A., cum laude, 1975); Hastings College of the Law, University of California (J.D., 1989). ***PRACTICE AREAS:*** Mergers, Acquisitions and Divestitures; Venture Capital; Private Placements; Strategic Partnerships and Collaborations; Franchise Law; Business Law; Corporate Law. ***Email:*** jcobb@wyrick.com

THOMAS H. COOK, JR., born December 15, 1958; admitted to bar, 1987, Virginia; 1989, U.S. Tax Court and District of Columbia; 1990, North Carolina. *Education:* University of Virginia (B.S., 1981); University of Exeter; University of Grenoble; College of William and Mary (J.D., 1987); Georgetown University (LL.M., 1989). Certified Public Accountant, Virginia, 1983. ***PRACTICE AREAS:*** Taxation; Low Income Housing Tax Credits; Historic Rehabilitation Tax Credits; Partnership and LLC Law. ***Email:*** tcook@wyrick.com

MICHAEL D. DeFRANK, born January 17, 1974; admitted to bar, 2000, Georgia and U.S. District Court, Northern District of Georgia; 2001, U.S. District Court, Middle District of Georgia; 2004, North Carolina. *Education:* Wake Forest University (B.A., magna cum laude, 1996); Emory University (J.D., 2000). ***LANGUAGES:*** Spanish. ***PRACTICE AREAS:*** Litigation. ***Email:*** mdefrank@wyrick.com

ALEXANDER M. DONALDSON, born June 23, 1953; admitted to bar, 1984, North Carolina. *Education:* University of North Carolina, Chapel Hill (B.A., 1976); College of William and Mary (J.D., 1984). ***PRACTICE AREAS:*** Public Offerings; Private Placements; Securities Law; Banking Law; Corporate Law. ***Email:*** adonaldson@wyrick.com

CAROLYN M. DUDZIK, born November 21, 1958; admitted to bar, 1986, North Carolina; U.S. District Court, Eastern District of North Carolina; 1988, U.S. Tax Court. *Education:* Indiana University (B.A., with high distinction, 1981); University of North Carolina (J.D., with honors, 1986). ***PRACTICE AREAS:*** Mergers, Acquisitions and Divestitures; Employee Benefits; Business Law; Corporate Law. ***Email:*** cdudzik@wyrick.com

CHRISTINE S. EATMON, born October 15, 1968; admitted to bar, 2005, North Carolina. *Education:* Campbell University (B.A., 2001; J.D., 2005). ***PRACTICE AREAS:*** Family Law. ***Email:*** ceatmon@wyrick.com

KENNETH E. EHEMAN, JR., born December 28, 1965; admitted to bar, 1995, New York; 1999, North Carolina. *Education:* University of North Carolina at Chapel Hill (B.S.B.A., with honors and distinction, 1988); University of Pennsylvania (J.D., cum laude, 1994). ***PRACTICE AREAS:*** Securities Law; Biotechnology Law; Venture Capital; Public Offerings; Private Placements. ***Email:*** keheman@wyrick.com

CAROLYN L. FITZMORRIS, born September 12, 1960; admitted to bar, 1991, North Carolina. *Education:* University of California at Los Angeles (B.A., 1986); University of North Carolina (J.D. 1991). ***PRACTICE AREAS:*** Commercial Real Estate. ***Email:*** cfitzmorris@wyrick.com

JAMES E. FURR, IV, born February 19, 1974; admitted to bar, 2001, Tennessee; 2004, North Carolina. *Education:* Davidson College (B.A., 1996); University of North Carolina (J.D., with honors, 2001). Staff Member, North Carolina Law Review, 1999-2000. ***PRACTICE AREAS:*** Corporate; Securities. ***Email:*** jfurr@wyrick.com

KELLY D. FURR, born August 9, 1973; admitted to bar, 2001, Tennessee; 2005, North Carolina. *Education:* Davidson College (B.A., magna cum laude, 1995); University of North Carolina (J.D., with honors, 2001). Staff Member, North Carolina Law Review, 1999-2000. ***PRACTICE AREAS:*** Health Law. ***Email:*** kfurr@wyrick.com

JOHN M. FUSCOE, born March 22, 1958; admitted to bar, 1996, North Carolina; registered to practice before U.S. Patent and Trademark Office. *Education:* University of Virginia (B.S., Nuclear Engineering, with distinction, 1980); Carnegie Mellon University (M.B.A., 1982); Duke University School of Law (J.D., 1996). ***PRACTICE AREAS:*** Internet and E-Commerce; Intellectual Property Protection and Licensing; Computer Technology Law; Strategic Partnerships and Collaborations; Venture Capital; Private Placements; Business Law; Corporate Law. ***Email:*** jfuscoe@wyrick.com

ROBERT E. FUTRELL, JR., born May 22, 1969; admitted to bar, 1994, North Carolina. *Education:* University of North Carolina (B.S., 1991); Syracuse University (J.D., magna cum laude, 1994). Order of the Coif. Staff Member, Syracuse Law Review. ***PRACTICE AREAS:*** Mergers, Acquisitions and Divestitures; Business Law; Corporate Law; Environmental Law. ***Email:*** rfutrell@wyrick.com

JOHN R. GREEN, JR., born October 21, 1964; admitted to bar, 1992, North Carolina and U.S. District Court, Eastern and Middle Districts of North Carolina; U.S. Court of Appeals, Fourth Circuit. *Education:* North Carolina State University (B.A., 1986); Wake Forest University (J.D., 1992). ***PRACTICE AREAS:*** Litigation. ***Email:*** jgreen@wyrick.com

LISA D. INMAN, born January 5, 1966; admitted to bar, 1997, North Carolina. *Education:* Rice University (B.Mus., magna cum laude, 1988); University of North Carolina, Chapel Hill (J.D., with honors, 1997). Order of the Coif. Member, North Carolina Law Review, 1995-1996. ***PRACTICE AREAS:*** Mergers, Acquisitions and Divestitures; Business Law; Corporate Law. ***Email:*** linman@wyrick.com

JEFFREY J. JOHNSON, born October 6, 1953; admitted to bar, 1991, North Carolina. *Education:* Ohio University (B.G.S., summa cum laude, 1976); West Virginia Univer-

(This Listing Continued)

WYRICK ROBBINS YATES & PONTON LLP, Raleigh—Continued

sity (M.A., 1979); University of North Carolina (J.D., with honors, 1991). Member, University of North Carolina Law Review. ***PRACTICE AREAS:*** Commercial Real Estate. ***Email:*** jjohnson@wyrick.com

SARAH M. JOHNSON, born July 27, 1978; admitted to bar, 2004, North Carolina. *Education:* Point Loma Nazarene University (B.A., magna cum laude, 2000); Wake Forest University (J.D., cum laude, 2004). Order of the Coif. ***PRACTICE AREAS:*** Litigation. ***Email:*** sjohnson@wyrick.com

ROGER WELDON KNIGHT, born March 1, 1960; admitted to bar, 1985, North Carolina; 1986, U.S. District Court, Eastern District of North Carolina. *Education:* University of North Carolina at Wilmington (B.A., with honors, 1982); University of North Carolina at Chapel Hill (J.D., 1985). ***PRACTICE AREAS:*** Community Association Law; Municipal Law; Election Law; Bankruptcy; Litigation. ***Email:*** rknight@wyrick.com

EMIL WILLIAM KRATT, born June 12, 1962; admitted to bar, 1987, North Carolina. *Education:* Wake Forest University (B.A., 1984; J.D., 1987). (Board Certified Specialist in Estate Planning and Probate Law, North Carolina State Board of Legal Specialization). ***PRACTICE AREAS:*** Estate Planning; Probate; Elder Law. ***Email:*** bkratt@wyrick.com

WINSTON P. LLOYD, born December 9, 1966; admitted to bar, 1995, North Carolina. *Education:* University of North Carolina (B.A., 1989); Wake Forest University (J.D., magna cum laude, 1995). Member, Wake Forest Law Review, 1993-95. ***PRACTICE AREAS:*** Communications Law; Mergers, Acquisitions and Divestitures; Venture Capital; Business Law; Corporate Law. ***Email:*** wlloyd@wyrick.com

J. CHRISTOPHER LYNCH, born July 11, 1962; admitted to bar, 1988, California; 1993, North Carolina. *Education:* University of Virginia (B.A., with honors, 1984); Harvard Law School (J.D., cum laude, 1988). ***PRACTICE AREAS:*** Venture Capital; Intellectual Property Protection and Licensing; Technology Law; Strategic Partnerships and Collaborations; Mergers, Acquisitions and Divestitures; Public Offerings; Securities Law; Business Law; Corporate Law. ***Email:*** clynch@wyrick.com

W. DAVID MANNHEIM, admitted to bar, 1997, Georgia; 1998, North Carolina. *Education:* University of Georgia (B.B.A, 1994; J.D., 1997). ***PRACTICE AREAS:*** Internet and E-Commerce; Technology Law; Intellectual Property Protection and Licensing; Mergers, Acquisitions and Divestitures; Entrepreneurial Business Law; Corporate Finance. ***Email:*** dmannheim@wyrick.com

CHRISTINE F. MAYHEW, born November 26, 1975; admitted to bar, 2000, South Carolina; 2005, North Carolina. *Education:* Clemson University (B.A., summa cum laude, 1997); University of South Carolina (J.D., with honors, 2000). Member, South Carolina Law Review. ***PRACTICE AREAS:*** Litigation. ***Email:*** cmayhew@wyrick.com

DEAN M. McCORD, born September 26, 1963; admitted to bar, 1995, Wisconsin and North Carolina. *Education:* University of North Carolina (B.A., 1985; Ph.D., 1992); Marquette University (J.D., summa cum laude, 1995). Member, Marquette Law Review. ***PRACTICE AREAS:*** Health; Business Law; Corporate Law. ***Email:*** dmccord@wyrick.com

D. DONOVAN MERRITT, born March 18, 1953; admitted to bar, 1978, North Carolina; 1979, U.S. District Court, Middle District of North Carolina; 1995, U.S. District Court, Eastern District of North Carolina. *Education:* University of North Carolina (A.B., 1975; J.D., 1978). (Board Certified Specialist in Real Property Law: Residential Transactions, North Carolina State Board of Legal Specialization). ***PRACTICE AREAS:*** Commercial Real Estate. ***Email:*** dmerritt@wyrick.com

JENNIFER M. MILLER, born June 1, 1972; admitted to bar, 1998, North Carolina. *Education:* Indiana University (B.A., with highest distinction, 1994); Wake Forest University (J.D., cum laude, 1998). Member, Wake Forest Law Review, 1996-1998. ***PRACTICE AREAS:*** Government Contracting Law; Labor Law; Litigation. ***Email:*** jmiller@wyrick.com

JOSEPH H. NANNEY, JR., born March 18, 1961; admitted to bar, 1991, North Carolina. *Education:* Mars Hill College (B.M., summa cum laude, 1983); University of North Carolina (J.D., with honors, 1991). Board of Editors, North Carolina Law Review, 1990-1991. ***PRACTICE AREAS:*** Intellectual Property Litigation; Litigation; Construction Law. ***Email:*** jnanney@wyrick.com

ROBERT A. PONTON, JR., born June 9, 1954; admitted to bar, 1979, North Carolina; 1980, U.S. District Court, Eastern District of North Carolina; 1982, U.S. District Court, Middle District of North Carolina. *Education:* Maryville College and University of North Carolina (B.A., 1976); University of North Carolina (J.D., 1979). Fellow, American Academy of Matrimonial Lawyers. (Board Certified Specialist in Family Law, North Carolina State Board of Legal Specialization). ***PRACTICE AREAS:*** Family Law; Bankruptcy; Workouts. ***Email:*** rponton@wyrick.com

DANIEL S. PORPER, born November 17, 1972; admitted to bar, 1998, North Carolina. *Education:* University of South Florida (B.A., 1995); Syracuse University College of Law (J.D., 1997). ***PRACTICE AREAS:*** Intellectual Property Protection; Intellectual Property Licensing; Strategic Alliances; Health. ***Email:*** dporper@wyrick.com

DONALD R. REYNOLDS, born October 13, 1962; admitted to bar, 1989, California; 1994, North Carolina. *Education:* Whitman College (B.A., 1984); New York University (J.D., 1988). ***PRACTICE AREAS:*** Public Offerings; Private Placements; Securities Law; Venture Capital; Strategic Partnerships and Collaborations; Mergers, Acquisitions and Divestitures. ***Email:*** dreynolds@wyrick.com

LARRY E. ROBBINS, born November 4, 1951; admitted to bar, 1980, North Carolina and U.S. District Court, Eastern District of North Carolina; 1983, U.S. Tax Court. *Education:* University of North Carolina (B.A., 1974; M.B.A., 1979; J.D., 1979). ***PRACTICE AREAS:*** Venture Capital Law; Mergers, Acquisitions and Divestitures; Public Offerings; Private Placements; Intellectual Property Protection and Licensing; Strategic Partnerships and Collaborations; Securities Law; Taxation; Technology Law. ***Email:*** lrobbins@wyrick.com

(This Listing Continued)

J. KEMP SHERRON, III, born October 24, 1958; admitted to bar, 1984, North Carolina; 1985, U.S. District Court, Middle District of North Carolina; 1986, U.S. District Court, Eastern District of North Carolina. *Education:* University of North Carolina (B.S., 1981); Wake Forest University (J.D., 1984). ***PRACTICE AREAS:*** Commercial Real Estate. ***Email:*** ksherron@wyrick.com

GRADY L. SHIELDS, born October 6, 1960; admitted to bar, 1985, North Carolina and U.S. District Court, Eastern District of North Carolina; 1987, U.S. District Court, Middle District of North Carolina. *Education:* Duke University (B.A., cum laude with honors, 1982); University of North Carolina (J.D., with honors, 1985). Member of Staff, 1983-1984 and Member, Board of Editors, 1984-1985, North Carolina Law Review. ***PRACTICE AREAS:*** Construction Law; Environmental Law; Litigation. ***Email:*** gshields@wyrick.com

JEFFREY M. SMITH, born September 27, 1973; admitted to bar, 1998, Illinois; 2000 North Carolina. *Education:* DePauw University (B.A., magna cum laude, 1995); Duke University (J.D., 1998). Managing Editor, Law and Contemporary Problems. ***PRACTICE AREAS:*** Public Offerings; Private Placements; Securities; Corporate Law. ***Email:*** jsmith@wyrick.com

MICHAEL D. TANNER, born February 20, 1970; admitted to bar, 1996, Arkansas; 2001, North Carolina. *Education:* Duke University (B.A., 1992; J.D., 1996). Recipient, Duke Law Scholarship. ***PRACTICE AREAS:*** Commercial Real Estate. ***Email:*** mtanner@wyrick.com

CHARLOTTE L. TART, born December 26, 1970; admitted to bar, 1996, North Carolina. *Education:* University of North Carolina at Chapel Hill (B.A., 1993); Wake Forest University (J.D., 1996). Wake Forest University Law Review, 1994-1996. ***PRACTICE AREAS:*** Venture Capital; Private Placements; Business Law; Corporate Law. ***Email:*** ctart@wyrick.com

BENJAMIN N. THOMPSON, born March 7, 1954; admitted to bar, 1979, North Carolina and U.S. District Court, Eastern District of North Carolina; 1982, U.S. Court of Federal Claims and U.S. Supreme Court; 1983, U.S. Court of Appeals, Fourth Circuit and U.S. Court of Appeals for the Federal Circuit; 1984, U.S. District Court, Western District of North Carolina; 1990, U.S. District Court, Middle District of North Carolina. *Education:* Campbell University (B.A., 1976; J.D., 1979). ***PRACTICE AREAS:*** Litigation; Government Contracting Law; Labor Law. ***Email:*** bthompson@wyrick.com

L. DIANE TINDALL, born July 15, 1955; admitted to bar, 1986, North Carolina; 1989, U.S. District Court, Eastern District of North Carolina; 1990, U.S. District Court, Middle District of North Carolina; 1993, U.S. Court of Appeals, Fourth Circuit; 1995, U.S. District Court, Western District of North Carolina; 1996, U.S. Supreme Court. *Education:* College of William & Mary (B.A., 1977); West Virginia University (M.A., 1979); University of North Carolina at Chapel Hill (J.D., with honors, 1986). ***PRACTICE AREAS:*** Labor and Employment; Litigation. ***Email:*** dtindall@wyrick.com

S. HALLE VAKANI, born August 9, 1972; admitted to bar, 2000, Ontario, Canada; 2004, North Carolina. *Education:* University of Waterloo (B.A., 1994); Queen's University (M.A., 1996); Osgoode Hall at York University (LL.B., 1999); Widener University School of Law (LL.M., Corporate Law and Finance, cum laude, 2003). ***LANGUAGES:*** French, Spanish and Gujarati. ***PRACTICE AREAS:*** Securities; Private Placement; Public Offerings; Corporate Law. ***Email:*** hvakani@wyrick.com

ERIC A. VERNON, born November 6, 1952; admitted to bar, 1980, North Carolina and U.S. District Court, Eastern District of North Carolina. *Education:* Paul Valery University, Montpellier, France; Davidson College (B.A., with honors, 1975); University of North Carolina (M.B.A., 1979; J.D., 1979). ***LANGUAGES:*** French. ***PRACTICE AREAS:*** Commercial Real Estate; Municipal Law; Business Law; Franchise Law. ***Email:*** evernon@wyrick.com

HENRY C. WARD, born December 29, 1978; admitted to bar, 2005, North Carolina. *Education:* North Carolina State University (B.S., summa cum laude, 2001; M.S., 2002); University of North Carolina (J.D., with honors, 2005). Park Scholar. Recipient, Chancellors' Scholarship. ***PRACTICE AREAS:*** Business Law; Corporate Law. ***Email:*** hward@wyrick.com

LEE M. WHITMAN, born March 17, 1968; admitted to bar, 1993, North Carolina; 1995, U.S. District Court, Eastern, Middle and Western Districts of North Carolina and U.S. Court of Appeals, Fourth Circuit. *Education:* University of Notre Dame (B.A., with honors, 1990); University of North Carolina at Chapel Hill (J.D., with honors, 1993). ***PRACTICE AREAS:*** Litigation. ***Email:*** lwhitman@wyrick.com

JULIA R. WICKER, born February 7, 1977; admitted to bar, 2003, North Carolina. *Education:* Wake Forest University (B.A., magna cum laude, 1999; J.D., 2003). Order of the Barristers. Member: Moot Court Board; National Moot Court Team; Gabrielli Family Law Moot Court Team Champion. ***PRACTICE AREAS:*** Family Law; Litigation. ***Email:*** jwicker@wyrick.com

DAVID L. WILKE, born June 13, 1967; admitted to bar, 1997, California; 2001, North Carolina. *Education:* University of Illinois (B.A., 1989); Stanford Law School (J.D., 1997). ***PRACTICE AREAS:*** Corporate Law; Securities Law; Venture Capital Law; Public Offerings. ***Email:*** dwilke@wyrick.com

ANTHONY L. WILLIAMS, born March 22, 1971; admitted to bar, 1998, North Carolina. *Education:* University of North Carolina at Chapel Hill (B.A., 1993); Wake Forest University (J.D., 1998); Wake Forest University, Babcock Graduate School of Management (M.B.A., 1998). ***PRACTICE AREAS:*** Mergers, Acquisitions and Divestitures; Venture Capital; Business Law; Corporate Law. ***Email:*** awilliams@wyrick.com

MARY M. WILLIAMS, born March 9, 1973; admitted to bar, 1999, North Carolina. *Education:* Davidson College (B.A., with honors, 1995); University of North Carolina (J.D., 1999). Member and Publication Editor, North Carolina Law Review, 1997-1999. ***PRACTICE AREAS:*** Labor and Employment; Litigation. ***Email:*** mwilliams@wyrick.com

JASON S. WOOD, born April 2, 1971; admitted to bar, 2000, North Carolina. *Education:* Duke University (B.S., 1993); University of Virginia (J.D., 2000). Order of the Coif. Member, Editorial Board, Virginia Law Review. ***PRACTICE AREAS:*** Biotechnology Law; Venture Capital Law. ***Email:*** jwood@wyrick.com

(This Listing Continued)

ALAN E. WROBEL, born March 4, 1974; admitted to bar, 1999, North Carolina. *Education:* Michigan State University (B.A., with high honors, 1995); University of North Carolina (J.D., with honors, 1999). ***PRACTICE AREAS:*** Computer Law; Technology Law; Mergers, Acquisitions and Divestitures; Entrepreneurial Business Law; Intellectual Property Protection and Licensing. ***Email:*** awrobel@wyrick.com

JAMES M. YATES, JR., born March 11, 1954; admitted to bar, 1979, North Carolina; 1980, U.S. District Court, Eastern District of North Carolina. *Education:* University of North Carolina (B.S., 1976; J.D., 1979). ***PRACTICE AREAS:*** Mergers, Acquisitions and Divestitures; Business Law; Corporate Law; Private Equity. ***Email:*** jyates@wyrick.com

OF COUNSEL

WILEY F. BOWEN, born August 31, 1931; admitted to bar, 1961, North Carolina. *Education:* Wake Forest University (B.S., 1958; LL.B., 1961); Campbell University (M.B.A., 1986). Senior Resident Judge, North Carolina Superior Court, 1981-2003. *Member:* North Carolina Bar Association (Vice President, 1998-1999). ***PRACTICE AREAS:*** Commercial Litigation. ***Email:*** wbowen@wyrick.com

JOHN L. CRILL, born January 4, 1943; admitted to bar, 1967, Pennsylvania; 1971, North Carolina. *Education:* Allegheny College (A.B., 1964); Duke University School of Law (LL.B., 1967). ***PRACTICE AREAS:*** Health; Municipal Finance. ***Email:*** jcrill@wyrick.com

BARBARA B. GARLOCK, born June 14, 1960; admitted to bar, 1988, North Carolina. *Education:* University of Virginia (B.A., summa cum laude, 1982; J.D., 1988). ***PRACTICE AREAS:*** Health Law. ***Email:*** bgarlock@wyrick.com

K. EDWARD GREENE, born June 27, 1944; admitted to bar, 1969, North Carolina; 2002, U.S. Supreme Court. *Education:* East Carolina University (B.A., 1966); University of North Carolina School of Law (J.D., 1969); University of Virginia School of Law (LL.M., 1990). Judge, North Carolina Court of Appeals, 1986-2002. Certified Superior Court Mediator. Certified Arbitrator and Member of the American Arbitration Association's Commercial Panel of Neutrals. ***PRACTICE AREAS:*** Appellate Advocacy; Mediation; Arbitration; Equitable Distribution; Election Law. ***Email:*** egreene@wyrick.com

RICHARD A. ROGERS, JR., born April 30, 1953; admitted to bar, 1978, Virginia; 1985, North Carolina. *Education:* University of Virginia (B.A., with distinction, 1975); Washington & Lee University (J.D., 1978); Georgetown University (LL.M., 1983). *Member:* American Society of Pension Actuaries. ***Email:*** rrogers@wyrick.com

SAMUEL T. WYRICK, III, born April 25, 1944; admitted to bar, 1969, North Carolina and U.S. Court of Military Appeals; 1974, U.S. District Court, Eastern District of North Carolina; 1978, U.S. Claims Court; 1982, U.S. Court of International Trade. *Education:* Harvard University (B.A., cum laude, 1966); Duke University (J.D., 1969). Certified Mediator, North Carolina Administrative Office of Courts, 1997. ***LANGUAGES:*** French and Spanish. ***PRACTICE AREAS:*** Credit Union Law; Arbitration; Mediation; Litigation. ***Email:*** swyrick@wyrick.com

Languages: Spanish, French and Gujarati.

YARBOROUGH LAW OFFICE

RALEIGH, NORTH CAROLINA

(See Chapel Hill)

Health Care Law, Hospital Law, Managed Care Contracting and Regulatory Compliance.

YATES, McLAMB & WEYHER, L.L.P.

ONE HANNOVER SQUARE
421 FAYETTEVILLE STREET MALL
SUITE 1200
RALEIGH, NORTH CAROLINA 27601
Telephone: 919-835-0900
Fax: 919-835-0910
URL: http://www.ymwlaw.com

Mailing Address: P.O. Box 2889, Raleigh, NC 27602-2889

Trial and Appellate Practice before all State and Federal Courts. Civil Defense Litigation including Medical Malpractice, Legal Malpractice, Pharmaceutical Liability, Construction Litigation, Construction Liability Litigation, Environmental, Personal Injury and Insurance Coverage.

MEMBERS OF FIRM

JOSEPH W. YATES, III (1944-2002)

BARRY S. COBB, born Greenville, North Carolina, April 28, 1968; admitted to bar, 1992, North Carolina. *Education:* University of North Carolina at Chapel Hill (B.S., 1989; J.D., with honors, 1992). Phi Beta Kappa; Phi Delta Phi. Member, Holderness Moot Court National Team. Law Clerk to the Honorable United States District Judge Terrence W. Boyle, 1992-1993. *Member:* Wake County, North Carolina and American Bar Associations; The North Carolina State Bar; North Carolina Association of Defense Attorneys. ***PRACTICE AREAS:*** Medical Malpractice Defense; Pharmaceutical Liability Defense. ***Email:*** bcobb@ymwlaw.com

JOHN T. HONEYCUTT, born Winston-Salem, North Carolina, February 24, 1967; admitted to bar, 1992, North Carolina. *Education:* University of North Carolina at Chapel Hill (B.A., 1989; J.D., 1992). Member, University of North Carolina Holderness Moot Court, 1991-1992. *Member:* Wake County and North Carolina (Member, Technological Advisory Committee) Bar Associations; North Carolina State Bar; Defense Research Institute; North Carolina Association of Defense Attorneys. ***PRACTICE AREAS:*** Construction Litigation; Insurance Defense. ***Email:*** jhoneycutt@ymwlaw.com

MICHAEL C. HURLEY, born Baltimore, Maryland, January 19, 1958; admitted to bar, 1984, Texas; 1985, North Carolina. *Education:* University of Maryland (B.A., 1981); St. Louis University School of Law (J.D., 1984). Recipient: Kniep Award for Appellate Advocacy from Saint Louis University School of Law, 1983; Napier Award for Trial Advocacy from the Lawyers Association of St. Louis, 1984. *Member:* Wake County and North Carolina Bar Associations; State Bar of Texas; The North Carolina State Bar. ***PRACTICE AREAS:*** Medical Malpractice Defense; Nursing Home Liability Defense. ***Email:*** mhurley@ymwlaw.com

DAN J. McLAMB, born Benson, North Carolina, February 20, 1949; admitted to bar, 1974, North Carolina. *Education:* University of North Carolina at Chapel Hill (A.B., 1971; J.D., with honors, 1974). Member, National Moot Court Team National Final Rounds, 1973-1974. Listed in: The Best Lawyers in America, 1995-1996, 1997-1998, 1999-2000, 2001-2002, 2003-2004 eds. *Member:* Wake County, North Carolina (Member, Litigation Section Council, 1993-1995) and American Bar Associations; The North Carolina State Bar; Defense Research Institute; North Carolina Association of Defense Attorneys; American Board of Trial Advocates. Fellow: American College of Trial Lawyers; International Association of Trial Attorneys; International Society of Barristers. ***PRACTICE AREAS:*** Civil Litigation; Medical Malpractice Defense; Legal Malpractice Defense. ***Email:*** dmclamb@ymwlaw.com

JOHN W. MINIER, born Jersey City, New Jersey, June 19, 1962; admitted to bar, 1989, New Jersey; 1990, North Carolina. *Education:* Dartmouth College (B.A., 1984); Duke University (J.D., 1988). Member, Duke Law Journal, 1987-1988. *Member:* Wake County and North Carolina Bar Associations; The North Carolina State Bar; North Carolina Association of Defense Attorneys. ***PRACTICE AREAS:*** Medical Malpractice Defense. ***Email:*** jminier@ymwlaw.com

RODNEY E. PETTEY, born Poughkeepsie, New York, April 12, 1964; admitted to bar, 1990, North Carolina. *Education:* Bob Jones University (B.S., 1987); Wake Forest University (J.D., cum laude, 1990). Phi Alpha Delta; Order of Barristers. Member, National Trial Team and Moot Court Board. Law Clerk to Hon. Eugene A. Gordon, Senior U.S. District Judge, Middle District of North Carolina. *Member:* Wake County, North Carolina and American Bar Associations; The North Carolina State Bar; North Carolina Association of Defense Attorneys. ***PRACTICE AREAS:*** Construction Litigation; Insurance Defense Litigation; Insurance Coverage; Automobile Liability; Property Liability. ***Email:*** rpettey@ymwlaw.com

SCOTT A. SCURFIELD, born Somerset, Pennsylvania, March 29, 1963; admitted to bar, 1988, Pennsylvania; 2000, North Carolina. *Education:* University of Pittsburgh (B.A., 1985; J.D., 1988). Presidential Scholar. Attorney, Somerset County Public Defender's Office, 1991-2000. *Member:* Wake County, Pennsylvania, North Carolina and American Bar Associations; The North Carolina State Bar; North Carolina Association of Defense Attorneys. ***PRACTICE AREAS:*** Construction Litigation; Insurance Defense; Insurance Litigation; Personal Injury Defense; Automobile Liability. ***Email:*** sscurfield@ymwlaw.com

BARBARA B. WEYHER, born Glen Cove, New York, August 8, 1952; admitted to bar, 1978, New York; 1979, North Carolina. *Education:* University of North Carolina at Chapel Hill (B.A., 1973; J.D., with honors, 1977). Staff Member, University of North Carolina Law Review, 1975-1976. *Member:* Wake County (President, 1997; Member, Board of Directors, 1994-1995), North Carolina and American Bar Associations; The North Carolina State Bar (Councilor, 1998—); Tenth Judicial District Grievance Committee (Member, 1991-1993 and Chair, 1992-1993); Defense Research Institute; North Carolina Association of Defense Attorneys. ***PRACTICE AREAS:*** Insurance Coverage; Medical Malpractice Defense; Legal Malpractice Defense; Appellate Practice. ***Email:*** bweyher@ymwlaw.com

ASSOCIATES

WILLIAM T. KESLER, JR., born Goldsboro, North Carolina; admitted to bar, 2001, North Carolina. *Education:* University of North Carolina at Chapel Hill (B.A., History, 1998); Campbell University (J.D., cum laude, 2001). Kappa Alpha Order. Member, Campbell University Law Review, 2000-2001. Law Clerk to: Conference of Superior Court Judges Pattern Jury Committee, Criminal Division, 2000-2001; Honorable J. Douglas McCullough, North Carolina Court of Appeals. 2001-2002. *Member:* Wake County Bar Association; North Carolina State Bar; North Carolina Association of Defense Attorneys. ***PRACTICE AREAS:*** Insurance Defense Litigation; Automobile Liability Defense. ***Email:*** bkesler@ymwlaw.com

MONICA LANGDON LEE, born Raleigh, North Carolina, July 21, 1973; admitted to bar, 1998, North Carolina. *Education:* North Carolina State University (B.A., cum laude, History, 1995); Campbell University (J.D., 1998). Phi Alpha Delta; Phi Sigma Pi; Phi Alpha Theta; Golden Key. Scholar, College of Humanities and Social Sciences, University Scholars Program, North Carolina State University. Member, History Honors Program. Member, Moot Court Competition. Fourth Circuit Editor and Case Summary Writer, Campbell Law Observer, 1996-1998. Member, Campbell Law Republicans, 1996-1998. *Member:* Wake County (Young Lawyers Division, 1999—) and North Carolina (Member, Young Lawyers Division, 1999—) Bar Associations; North Carolina State Bar; North Carolina Association of Defense Attorneys. ***PRACTICE AREAS:*** Medical Malpractice Defense; Nursing Home Liability Defense. ***Email:*** mlee@ymwlaw.com

JENNIFER D. MALDONADO, born Asheville, North Carolina, January 2, 1972; admitted to bar, 1998, North Carolina, U.S. District Court, Western, Eastern and Middle Districts of North Carolina and U.S. Court of Appeals, Fourth Circuit. *Education:* University of North Carolina at Chapel Hill (B.A., 1994); Campbell University, School of Law (J.D., 1998). *Member:* Wake County and North Carolina Bar Associations; North Carolina State Bar. ***LANGUAGES:*** Spanish. ***PRACTICE AREAS:*** Civil Litigation; Insurance Litigation; Insurance Coverage; Construction Law. ***Email:*** jmaldonado@ymwlaw.com

ERIN D. McNEIL, born Charlotte, North Carolina, August 15, 1974; admitted to bar, 1999, North Carolina. *Education:* University of North Carolina, Greensboro (B.A., cum laude, 1996); University of North Carolina at Chapel Hill (J.D., 1999). Member, Holderness Moot Court Negotiation Team. *Member:* Wake County, North Carolina and American Bar Associations; The North Carolina State Bar; National Bar Association; North Carolina Association of Defense Attorneys. ***PRACTICE AREAS:*** Medical Malpractice Defense; Personal Injury Defense. ***Email:*** emcneil@ymwlaw.com

JOHN T. MOLLEUR, born Waterbury, Connecticut, June 9, 1964; admitted to bar, 1996, West Virginia and U.S. District Court, Southern District of West Virginia; 2000, U.S. Court of Appeals, Fourth Circuit; 2003, North Carolina; 2004, U.S. District Court, Eastern

(This Listing Continued)

(This Listing Continued)

YATES, McLAMB & WEYHER, L.L.P., Raleigh—Continued

and Middle Districts of North Carolina. *Education:* Duke University (A.B., Political Science, 1986); College of William & Mary, Marshall-Wythe (J.D., 1996). Recipient: NROTC Scholarship, Duke University. Moot Court Board. *Member:* North Carolina State Bar; West Virginia State Bar; Defense Research Institute. [U.S. Navy, 1986-1992, Lieutenant]. ***PRACTICE AREAS:*** Medical Malpractice; Employment Law. ***Email:*** jmolleur@ymwlaw.com

JAMES T. NEWMAN, JR., born Fayetteville, North Carolina; admitted to bar, 2002, North Carolina. *Education:* North Carolina State University (B.S., Business Management, 1997; B.A., Economics, 1998); Campbell University Norman Adrian Wiggins School of Law (J.D., with honors, 2002). Omicron Delta Kappa. Recipient: Campbell University Law Scholarship. Articles Editor, Campbell Law Review. Law Clerk to the Honorable I. Beverly Lake, Jr., Chief Justice, Supreme Court of North Carolina, 2002-2003. Former Claims Adjuster, Nationwide Mutual Insurance Company. *Member:* Wake County, North Carolina and American Bar Associations. ***PRACTICE AREAS:*** Medical Malpractice Defense.

JASON D. NEWTON, born Durham, North Carolina, August 2, 1972; admitted to bar, 1999, North Carolina. *Education:* University of North Carolina, Chapel Hill (B.A., 1994); Mercer University School of Law (1997); Wake Forest University School of Law (J.D., 1999). Order of the Barrister, 1999. Chief Justice Joseph Brance Inn of Court, 1998-1999. *Member:* Wake County and North Carolina (Member, Litigation Section) Bar Associations; The North Carolina State Bar; Defense Research Institute; North Carolina Association of Defense Attorneys. ***PRACTICE AREAS:*** Medical Malpractice Defense; Civil Litigation. ***Email:*** jnewton@ymwlaw.com

EDGAR MOORE PAGE, born Raleigh, North Carolina, June 17, 1975; admitted to bar, 2000, North Carolina. *Education:* University of North Carolina at Chapel Hill (B.S.B.A., 1997; J.D., 2000). Assistant District Attorney, 11th District, 2000-2004. *Member:* Lee County Bar Association (President, 2003-2004). ***PRACTICE AREAS:*** Medical Malpractice Defense; Nursing Home Liability. ***Email:*** epage@ymwlaw.com

SEAN T. PARTRICK, born Washington, D.C., February 1, 1963; admitted to bar, 1997, North Carolina; U.S. District Court, Eastern District of North Carolina. *Education:* University of North Carolina at Chapel Hill (B.A., Economics, with distinction, 1990); Campbell University, Norman Adrian Wiggins School of Law (J.D., 1996). Phi Alpha Delta. Legislative Summary Co-Editor and Editor-at-Large, Campbell Law Review, 1994-1997. *Member:* Wake County Bar Association; North Carolina State Bar; North Carolina Association of Defense Attorneys. ***PRACTICE AREAS:*** Construction Litigation; Personal Injury Litigation.

RICHARD V. STEVENS, III, born Youngstown, Ohio, December 26, 1969; admitted to bar, 1995, North Carolina; 2000, U.S. Supreme Court; 2002, U.S. District Court, Western District of North Carolina. *Education:* University of North Carolina at Chapel Hill (B.A., with Distinction, 1992; J.D., 1995). Phi Beta Kappa. *Member:* Wake County Bar Association; North Carolina State Bar; Defense Research Institute; North Carolina Association of Defense Attorneys. [Capt., U.S.A.F., 1995-2001]. ***PRACTICE AREAS:*** Medical Malpractice Defense; General Liability Defense. ***Email:*** rstevens@ymwlaw.com

SAMUEL G. THOMPSON, JR., born Raleigh, North Carolina, August 9, 1975; admitted to bar, 2004, North Carolina. *Education:* University of North Carolina at Chapel Hill (B.A., 1999); Campbell University (J.D., 2004). Member, National Order of Barristers. *Member:* Wake County and North Carolina Bar Associations; North Carolina State Bar; North Carolina Association of Defense Attorneys; Defense Research Institute. ***PRACTICE AREAS:*** Medical Malpractice Defense; Civil Litigation. ***Email:*** bthompson@ymwlaw.com

ALISSA A. WATTS, born Washington, D.C., April 25, 1967; admitted to bar, 2001, North Carolina. *Education:* University of Maryland at College Park; Old Dominion University; Catholic University of America (B.S.N., 1994); University of North Carolina at Chapel Hill (J.D., 2001). Sigma Theta Tau; Kappa Chapter. Member, International Honor Society of Nursing. Registered Nurse, North Carolina, 1994—. *Member:* Wake County Bar Association; The North Carolina State Bar; North Carolina Association of Defense Attorneys. [U.S. Navy, 1987-1998 (Hospital Corpsman, NROTC, Navy Nurse Corps); Lt., U.S. Navy Reserves]. ***PRACTICE AREAS:*** Medical Malpractice Defense. ***Email:*** awatts@ymwlaw.com

CHRISTOPHER MITCHELL WEST, born Kansas City, Missouri, August 2, 1970; admitted to bar, 2000, North Carolina. *Education:* East Carolina University (B.S., 1994); Virginia Commonwealth University (MPA, 1996); Pennsylvania State University, Dickinson Law School (J.D., 2000). Member, National Appellate Moot Court Team; National Trial Moot Court Team; Order of Barristers National Honor Society.*Member:* North Carolina Bar Association; Wake County Bar Association; North Carolina Academy of Defense Attorneys. (Also Member, Lewis & Roberts). ***PRACTICE AREAS:*** Medical Malpractice Defense; Nursing Home Liability Defense. ***Email:*** cwest@ymwlaw.com

BRIAN M. WILLIAMS, born Silver Spring, Maryland, February 9, 1977; admitted to bar, 2002, North Carolina. *Education:* University of Carolina at Chapel Hill (B.A., History, 1999); Campbell University (J.D., 2002). Phi Alpha Delta. Member, William C. Vis International Arbitration Moot Team. Case Law Editor, Campbell Law Observer, University College of London, Summer 2000. SBA Representation, 2001-2002. *Member:* Wake County, North Carolina and American Bar Associations; The North Carolina State Bar; North Carolina Association of Defense Attorneys. ***PRACTICE AREAS:*** Construction Litigation; Insurance Defense; Insurance Litigation; Personal Injury Defense; Automobile Liability. ***Email:*** bwilliams@ymwlaw.com

OF COUNSEL

SUSAN T. FOUNTAIN, born Fayetteville, North Carolina, February 28, 1972; admitted to bar, 1997, North Carolina. *Education:* University of North Carolina at Chapel Hill (B.A., with distinction, 1994; J.D., 1997). Phi Sigma Alpha; Phi Alpha Delta; Golden Key. Judicial Clerk to Chief Judge Gerald Arnold, North Carolina Court of Appeals, 1997-1998. *Member:* Wake County and North Carolina (Member, Litigation Section; Member, Young Lawyers Division; Co-Chair, Citizenship Education Committee, 1998) Bar Associations; The North Carolina State Bar. ***PRACTICE AREAS:*** Insurance Defense; General Liability; Insurance Coverage.

JULIE R. HURLEY, born Chicago, Illinois, May 1, 1959; admitted to bar, 1984, Texas; 1994, North Carolina. *Education:* University of Maryland (B.S., 1981); St. Louis University (J.D., 1984). Member, St. Louis University Public Law Forum, 1980-1981. *Member:* Wake County and North Carolina Bar Associations; The North Carolina State Bar; State Bar of Texas. ***PRACTICE AREAS:*** Medical Malpractice Defense; Nursing Home Liability Defense. ***Email:*** jhurley@ymwlaw.com

SHIRLEY MARING PRUITT, born Kalamazoo, Michigan, June 18, 1961; admitted to bar, 1992, North Carolina. *Education:* Kellogg Community College (A.D., Nursing, magna cum laude, 1984); Medical University of South Carolina (B.S., Nursing, 1989); Wake Forest University (J.D., 1992). *Member:* The North Carolina State Bar; North Carolina Bar Association; The American Association of Nurse Attorneys; North Carolina Society of Healthcare Attorneys. ***PRACTICE AREAS:*** Medical Malpractice Defense.

REPRESENTATIVE CLIENTS: Britthaven, Inc.; CVS Pharmacy, Inc.; Erie Insurance Co. Farmers Insurance Group; International Paper Co.; Lawyers Mutual Insurance Company of North Carolina; Medical Mutual Insurance Co.; Medical Protective Co.; Metropolitan Property and Casualty Co.; North Carolina School Boards Association; Northland Insurance Co.; Pitt County Memorial Hospital; Preferred Physicians Medical; Rex Hospital, Inc.; St. Paul Insurance Cos.; State Farm; The Travelers; University of North Carolina Hospitals; WakeMed; Zurich Insurance Group.

YOUNG MOORE AND HENDERSON, P.A.

Established in 1952

3101 GLENWOOD AVENUE, SUITE 200
RALEIGH, NORTH CAROLINA 27612
Telephone: 919-782-6860
Telecopier: 919-782-6753
Email: attorney@ymh.com
URL: http://www.ymh.com

Mailing Address: P.O. Box 31627, Raleigh, NC 27622

General Trial and Appellate Practice before all State and Federal Courts and Agencies. Corporate and Business Law including Litigation of Employment, Franchise, Trade Practices, Antitrust, Tax, Employment Discrimination and Labor. Insurance Law including Litigation of Regulation, Treaties, Suretyship and Bonds, Casualty and Life. Litigation of Environmental, Personal Injury, Professional Liability, Workers Compensation, Products Liability and Commercial Matters. Commercial Real Estate, Estate Planning, Probate and Taxation. Criminal Trials in State and Federal Courts.

FIRM PROFILE: Young Moore and Henderson, P.A. has been a vital part of the legal profession in North Carolina for more than eighty years. We have made and continue to make significant contributions of leadership to our profession, the administration of justice and civic improvement. Our dedication to professional excellence, integrity and service has earned us the confidence, respect and cooperation of both the bench and bar. This dedication and our reputation allow us to represent our clients effectively in diverse areas of practice and in all courts and administrative agencies throughout the state.

CHARLES H. YOUNG, JR. (1947-1992)
JOSEPH C. MOORE, JR. (1919-1988)
B. T. HENDERSON, II (1928-2000)

J. CLARK BREWER, born Greenville, North Carolina, January 15, 1942; admitted to bar, 1967, North Carolina. *Education:* University of North Carolina (B.S., 1964; J.D., 1967). Order of the Coif. *Member:* Wake County (President, Real Property Section, 1985), North Carolina (Chairman, Real Property Section, 1986-1987 and Chairman, CLE Committee, 1996-1998) and American Bar Associations; The North Carolina State Bar. [United States Air Force, 1968-1971]. (Board Certified Specialist in Real Property Law-Residential, Business, Commercial, and Industrial Transactions, North Carolina State Board of Legal Specialization). ***PRACTICE AREAS:*** Commercial Real Estate; Alternative Dispute Resolution. ***Email:*** jcb@ymh.com

JOHN N. FOUNTAIN, born High Point, North Carolina, January 26, 1944; admitted to bar, 1968, North Carolina. *Education:* Duke University (B.A., 1965); Wake Forest University (J.D., 1968). Phi Alpha Delta. Research Assistant to Judge David M. Britt, North Carolina Court of Appeals, 1968-1969. Member, North Carolina Administrative Procedures Study Commission, 1980-1981. *Member:* Wake County (President, 1989), North Carolina (Chairman, Administrative Law Committee, 1979-1982; Member, Board of Governors, 1985-1988; Chairman, Task Force on Administrative Procedure, 1987-1989; Chairman, Legislative Advisory Committee, 1989-1992 and Chairman, Alternate Billing Commission, 1996—) and American Bar Associations. ***PRACTICE AREAS:*** Administrative Law; Commercial Litigation; Real Estate. ***Email:*** jnf@ymh.com

WILLIAM M. TROTT, born Raleigh, North Carolina, July 30, 1946; admitted to bar, 1971, North Carolina. *Education:* University of North Carolina (A.B., 1968; J.D., 1971); George Washington University (LL.M., with highest honors, 1975). Phi Eta Sigma; Phi Delta Phi. Morehead Scholar. Member, North Carolina Law Review, 1969-1971. Speaker, North Carolina Bar Association Seminars, 1984, 1985, 1987; North Carolina Association of Defense Attorneys, 1986, 1989. Member and Chairman, Wake County Parks and Recreation Commission. *Member:* Wake County, North Carolina and American (Member, Sections on: Labor and Employment Law and Tort and Insurance Practices) Bar Associations; The North Carolina State Bar. [Lieut., JAGC, USNR, 1971-1975]. ***PRACTICE AREAS:*** Employment Law; Insurance Regulation. ***Email:*** wmt@ymh.com

R. MICHAEL STRICKLAND, born Raleigh, North Carolina, May 25, 1947; admitted to bar, 1972, North Carolina. *Education:* Duke University (A.B., 1969); Wake Forest College (J.D., with honors, 1972). Phi Alpha Delta. *Member:* Wake County, North Carolina and American Bar Associations; The North Carolina State Bar. ***PRACTICE AREAS:*** Insurance Regulation; Insurance Coverage; Insurance Coverage Litigation; Commercial Litigation; Appellate Practice. ***Email:*** rms@ymh.com

(This Listing Continued)

WILLIAM P. DANIELL, born Decatur, Alabama, July 27, 1951; admitted to bar, 1977, North Carolina and U.S. District Court, Middle District of North Carolina; 1981, U.S. Court of Appeals, Fourth Circuit; 1982, U.S. District Court, Eastern District of North Carolina; 1991, U.S. District Court, Western District of North Carolina. *Education:* University of North Carolina (A.B., 1973; J.D., 1977). *Member:* Durham County, North Carolina and American Bar Associations. ***PRACTICE AREAS:*** Personal Injury Law; Medical Malpractice Defense Law; Commercial Litigation; Eminent Domain.

ROBERT C. PASCHAL, born Raleigh, North Carolina, December 26, 1951; admitted to bar, 1978, North Carolina. *Education:* University of North Carolina (B.A., 1975); Duke University (J.D., 1978). Morehead Scholar. *Member:* Wake County, North Carolina and American Bar Associations; The North Carolina State Bar; Defense Research Institute. ***PRACTICE AREAS:*** Lobbying; Employee Benefits; Insurance Regulation; Administrative Law; Insurance Coverage Litigation. ***Email:*** rcp@ymh.com

WALTER E. BROCK, JR., born Wadesboro, North Carolina, November 2, 1952; admitted to bar, 1978, North Carolina. *Education:* University of North Carolina (B.A., with honors in Economics, 1975; J.D., 1978). Law Clerk to Chief Judge Naomi E. Morris, North Carolina Court of Appeals, 1978-1979. *Member:* Wake County (Board of Directors, 1991-1992; President Elect, 1997; President, 1998), North Carolina and American Bar Associations; The North Carolina State Bar; American Board of Trial Advocates (President, North Carolina Chapter, 1996; National Board of Directors, 1996-1997); North Carolina Association of Defense Attorneys; Defense Research Institute. ***PRACTICE AREAS:*** Casualty Insurance Defense; Products Liability; Insurance Coverage; Insurance Coverage Litigation; Commercial Litigation; Professional Liability; Environmental Law. ***Email:*** web@ymh.com

JOSEPH W. WILLIFORD, born Lillington, North Carolina, March 4, 1956; admitted to bar, 1981, North Carolina. *Education:* Wake Forest University (B.A., 1978; J.D., 1981). Member, 1979-1980 and Editorial Staff, 1980-1981, Wake Forest Law Review. *Member:* Wake County and North Carolina Bar Associations; The North Carolina State Bar; North Carolina Association of Defense Attorneys; Defense Research Institute. ***PRACTICE AREAS:*** Medical Liability; Nursing Home Litigation. ***Email:*** jww@ymh.com

RUDY L. OGBURN, born Raleigh, North Carolina, December 4, 1956; admitted to bar, 1982, North Carolina. *Education:* Wake Forest University (B.A., 1979; J.D., 1982). Vice President and Regional Trust Manager, 1984-1989, Trust Officer, 1982-1984, First Citizen Bank & Trust Company. *Member:* Wake County and North Carolina (Chair, Estate Planning and Fiduciary Law Section, 1997-1998) Bar Associations; North Carolina State Bar. Fellow, American College of Trust and Estate Counsel. ***PRACTICE AREAS:*** Estate Planning; Probate; Trusts and Estates; Business Law. ***Email:*** rlo@ymh.com

MARVIN M. SPIVEY, JR., born Columbus, Georgia, April 10, 1958; admitted to bar, 1983, North Carolina. *Education:* University of North Carolina (B.A., with honors, 1980; J.D., 1983). Phi Eta Sigma; Phi Beta Kappa. *Member:* Wake County and North Carolina Bar Associations; The North Carolina State Bar. ***PRACTICE AREAS:*** Insurance Regulation; Business Law. ***Email:*** mms@ymh.com

DAVID M. DUKE, born Richmond, Virginia, October 31, 1958; admitted to bar, 1984, North Carolina. *Education:* College of William & Mary (B.A., 1981); Wake Forest University (J.D., 1984). Omicron Delta Epsilon. Member, Moot Court Board, Wake Forest University. *Member:* Wake County and North Carolina Bar Associations; The North Carolina State Bar. ***PRACTICE AREAS:*** Trucking Liability; Automobile Liability; Products Liability; Casualty Insurance Defense; Aviation; Admiralty. ***Email:*** dmd@ymh.com

JOE E. AUSTIN, JR., born Monroe, North Carolina, March 13, 1965; admitted to bar, 1989, North Carolina. *Education:* North Carolina School of Science & Mathematics; Davidson College (A.B., 1986); Wake Forest University (J.D., 1989). Phi Delta Phi. Member, Moot Court Board. *Member:* Wake County, North Carolina and American Bar Associations; North Carolina State Bar. ***PRACTICE AREAS:*** Workers Compensation; Alternative Dispute Resolution. ***Email:*** jea@ymh.com

DANA H. DAVIS, born Livingston, New Jersey, April 1, 1965; admitted to bar, 1990, North Carolina. *Education:* University of North Carolina at Chapel Hill (B.A., 1987); Wake Forest University (J.D., 1990). Contributing Author: American Inns of Court Civil Procedure Series: North Carolina, 1998. *Member:* Wake County and North Carolina Bar Associations; North Carolina State Bar; North Carolina Association of Defense Attorneys. ***PRACTICE AREAS:*** Medical Liability; Professional Liability; Casualty Insurance Defense; Trucking Liability; Automobile Liability; Products Liability. ***Email:*** dhd@ymh.com

GLENN C. RAYNOR, born Clinton, North Carolina, September 8, 1965; admitted to bar, 1991, North Carolina. *Education:* University of North Carolina at Chapel Hill (B.S. in Biology, 1987; J.D., 1991). *Member:* Wake County and North Carolina Bar Associations; North Carolina State Bar. ***PRACTICE AREAS:*** Medical Liability; Casualty Insurance Defense; Insurance Coverage; Insurance Coverage Litigation; Commercial Litigation. ***Email:*** gcr@ymh.com

JAY P. TOBIN, born Excelsior Springs, Missouri, April 17, 1964; admitted to bar, 1991, North Carolina. *Education:* University of North Carolina at Chapel Hill (B.A., International Studies, 1986; J.D., 1991). Phi Delta Phi; Order of the Barristers. Member, Holderness Moot Court National Team. *Member:* Wake County and North Carolina Bar Associations; North Carolina State Bar. ***PRACTICE AREAS:*** Insurance Coverage; Insurance Coverage Litigation; Commercial Litigation; Environmental Law. ***Email:*** jpt@ymh.com

CHRISTOPHER A. PAGE, born Raleigh, North Carolina, November 6, 1966; admitted to bar, 1993, North Carolina; 1995, District of Columbia. *Education:* Duke University (B.A., summa cum laude, Political Science, 1989); Yale University Law School (J.D., 1992). Senior Editor, Yale Law Journal, 1990-1992. Law Clerk to Judge Thomas A. Wiseman, Jr., Middle District of Tennessee, 1992-1993. *Member:* Wake County, North Carolina and American Bar Associations; North Carolina State Bar; The District of Columbia Bar; Defense Research Institute. ***PRACTICE AREAS:*** Insurance Coverage; Insurance Coverage Litigation; Casualty Insurance Defense; Environmental Law; Appellate Practice; Technology Law. ***Email:*** cap@ymh.com

BRIAN O. BEVERLY, born Prince Frederick, Maryland, June 5, 1968; admitted to bar, 1995, North Carolina. *Education:* University of North Carolina (B.A. in Economics, 1992); North Carolina Central University (J.D., 1995). *Member:* Wake County and North Carolina Bar Associations; North Carolina State Bar. ***PRACTICE AREAS:*** Trucking Liability; Automobile Liability; Personal Injury Defense; Construction Liability; Insurance Coverage. ***Email:*** bob@ymh.com

JEFFREY T. LINDER, born Santa Clara, California, January 21, 1969; admitted to bar, 1995, North Carolina. *Education:* University of California, Santa Barbara (B.A., Economics and Political Science, with honors, 1992); University of North Carolina (J.D., with honors, 1995). Editorial Staff Member, North Carolina Journal of International Law and Commercial Regulation, 1993-1995. *Member:* Wake County and North Carolina Bar Associations; North Carolina State Bar. ***PRACTICE AREAS:*** Workers Compensation; Employment Law. ***Email:*** jtl@ymh.com

REED N. FOUNTAIN, born Raleigh, North Carolina, September 25, 1970; admitted to bar, 1996, North Carolina. *Education:* Duke University (B.A., Sociology and History, 1993); University of North Carolina at Chapel Hill (J.D., 1996). Member, Moot Court Board. *Member:* Wake County and North Carolina Bar Associations; North Carolina State Bar. ***PRACTICE AREAS:*** Products Liability Litigation; Commercial Litigation; Trucking Liability; Automobile Liability. ***Email:*** rnf@ymh.com

DAWN DILLON RAYNOR, admitted to bar, 1995, North Carolina. *Education:* Mary Washington College (B.A., magna cum laude, 1992); Wake Forest University (J.D., 1995). Associate Chief Justice, Moot Court Board. Law Clerk for North Carolina Court of Appeals Judges Jack Cozort and Donald Smith, 1995-1996. *Member:* Wake County and North Carolina Bar Associations; North Carolina State Bar. ***PRACTICE AREAS:*** Litigation; Administrative Law; Workers Compensation. ***Email:*** dd2@ymh.com

---

JOSEPHINE R. DARDEN, born Charlottesville, Virginia, October 3, 1952; admitted to bar, 1985, North Carolina. *Education:* Sweet Briar College; University of North Carolina (B.A., 1974); University of Virginia (M.Ed., 1976); Boston College (J.D., 1985). *Member:* Wake County and North Carolina Bar Associations; The North Carolina State Bar. ***PRACTICE AREAS:*** Estate Planning. ***Email:*** jrd@ymh.com

ZACHARY C. BOLEN, born Chapel Hill, North Carolina, January 31, 1973; admitted to bar, 2000, North Carolina. *Education:* University of North Carolina at Chapel Hill (B.A., 1995); Campbell University (J.D., 2000). Campbell University Trial Advocacy Team. *Member:* Wake County and North Carolina Bar Associations. ***PRACTICE AREAS:*** Workers Compensation. ***Email:*** zcb@ymh.com

ALEXANDER R. ATCHISON, born Salt Lake City, Utah, October 6, 1972; admitted to bar, 1998, North Carolina. *Education:* University of North Carolina at Charlotte (B.A., 1995); Cumberland School of Law of Samford University (J.D., 1998). Scholastic Chair, Phi Alpha Delta, 1995-1998. *Member:* Wake County, North Carolina and American Bar Associations; North Carolina State Bar. ***PRACTICE AREAS:*** Estate Planning; Probate; Trusts and Estates; Business Law. ***Email:*** ara@ymh.com

ROBERT C. DE ROSSET, born Belhaven, North Carolina, October 14, 1969; admitted to bar, 1996, South Carolina; 2001, North Carolina. *Education:* University of North Carolina (B.A., 1991); University of South Carolina School of Law (J.D., 1996). Order of the Wig and Robe, University of South Carolina. Recipient: American Jurisprudence Award and CALI Excellence for the Future Award, University of South Carolina. Student Editorial Board, Article and Notes Editor, Fall 1995 & Spring 1996 and Staff Member, Fall 1995 & Spring 1995, "South Carolina Environmental Law Journal." Author: Book Note, 4 S.C. Envtl. L.J. 107 (Spring 1995) (reviewing *Analyzing Superfund:* Economics, Science and Law(Richard L. Revesz and Richard B. Stuart eds., 1995); Note, "Eighth Circuit Court of Appeals Upholds Dispute Resolution Provision in Consent Decree," 4 S.C. Envtl. L.J. 75 (Spring 1995); Note, "Attorney's Fees Unavailable to Private Parties Who Bring Cost Recovery Actions under Comprehensive Environmental Response, Compensation and Liability Act" (CERCLA), 3 S.C. Envtl. L.J. 207 (Fall 1994). Graduate Teaching Assistant, Legal Research, University of South Carolina School of Law, 1995-1996. *Member:* North Carolina Bar Association; South Carolina Bar. ***PRACTICE AREAS:*** Civil Litigation. ***Email:*** rcd@ymh.com

NATHAN J. TAYLOR, born Raleigh, North Carolina, September 21, 1971; admitted to bar, 1999, North Carolina. *Education:* Wake Forest University (B.A., 1995); Campbell University (J.D., 1999). Editor, Campbell University Law Review, 1998-1999. Judicial Clerk, Western District of North Carolina, 1999-2002. *Member:* Wake County and North Carolina Bar Associations; The North Carolina State Bar. ***PRACTICE AREAS:*** Medical Malpractice; Automobile Negligence; Products Liability. ***Email:*** njt@ymh.com

JENNIFER TERRY GOTTSEGEN, born Winston-Salem, North Carolina, February 6, 1977; admitted to bar, 2002, North Carolina. *Education:* University of North Carolina (B.A., 1999); Wake Forest University (J.D., 2002). Recipient: CALI Award for Trial Advocacy; Most Outstanding Advocate, North Carolina Academy of Trial Lawyers. *Member:* North Carolina and Wake County (Member, Board of Directors, Young Lawyers Division, 2003) Bar Associations; North Carolina State Bar. ***PRACTICE AREAS:*** Workers Compensation.

MICHAEL W. BALLANCE, born Raleigh, North Carolina, October 28, 1969; admitted to bar, 1996, North Carolina. *Education:* North Carolina State University (B.A., 1992); University of North Carolina (J.D., 1996). Law Clerk to Justice I. Beverly Lake, Jr., North Carolina Supreme Court, 1996-1998. *Member:* Wake County and North Carolina Bar Associations; North Carolina Academy of Trial Lawyers (Member, Workers Compensation Section). ***PRACTICE AREAS:*** Workers Compensation; Social Security Disability; Personal Injury.

MATTHEW J. GRAY, born Charlotte, North Carolina, October 1, 1976; admitted to bar, 2003, North Carolina. *Education:* North Carolina State University (B.S., 1998); Wake Forest University (J.D., 2003). ***PRACTICE AREAS:*** Medical Liability. ***Email:*** mjg@ymh.com

ANNE ELIZABETH CROTEAU, born Harrisburg, Pennsylvania, January 19, 1971; admitted to bar, 1998, Illinois; 2002, New York; 2005, North Carolina. *Education:* Duke University (B.A., magna cum laude, 1993); Harvard University (J.D., cum laude, 1998). Phi Beta Kappa; Phi Eta Sigma. ***LANGUAGES:*** Russian and French. ***PRACTICE AREAS:*** Business Law; Insurance Regulation. ***Email:*** aec@ymh.com

(This Listing Continued)

YOUNG MOORE AND HENDERSON, P.A., Raleigh—Continued

ANGELA N. FARAG, born Wichita Falls, Texas, October 8, 1978; admitted to bar, 2004, North Carolina. *Education:* University of North Carolina at Chapel Hill (B.A., with honors and distinction, 2001; J.D., with honors, 2004). Honors Thesis, UNC Law. Member, Executive Committee, Holderness Moot Court. Semi-finalist, 2004 Robert R. Merhige, Jr., National Environmental Negotiation Competition. ***PRACTICE AREAS:*** Workers Compensation. ***Email:*** anf@ymh.com

MATTHEW B. DAVIS, born Wilmington, North Carolina, February 4, 1978; admitted to bar, 2004, North Carolina and U.S. District Court, District of North Carolina. *Education:* University of North Carolina at Chapel Hill (B.A., History, 2000; J.D., 2004). ***PRACTICE AREAS:*** Insurance Defense; Insurance Coverage; Insurance Coverage Litigation; Products Liability; Premises Liability; Construction Law. ***Email:*** mbd@ymh.com

ELIZABETH P. McCULLOUGH, born Chapel Hill, North Carolina, May 29, 1974; admitted to bar, 1999, Virginia; 2000, U.S. District Court, Eastern and Western Districts of Virginia; 2004, North Carolina; 2005, U.S. District Court, Eastern, Western and Middle Districts of North Carolina. *Education:* Davidson College (B.A., with honors, Political Science, 1996); Wake Forest University School of Law (J.D., 1999). Honors Thesis, Political Science, 1999. National Semi-Finalist, 1999 and Regional Champion, 1999, Wake Forest University Trial Team. Recipient: Lewis F. Powell Jr. Medal for Excellence in Advocacy, 1999; CALI Excellence for the Future Award in Advanced Trial Practice, 1999 and Trial Practice, 1997; North Carolina Academy of Trial Lawyers Most Outstanding Advocate Award, 1998. *Member:* Richmond, Wayne County, Tenth Judicial District, North Carolina and Virginia Bar Associations; North Carolina State Bar; Virginia State Bar; Defense Research Institute. ***REPORTED CASES:*** Perdieu v. Blackstone Family Practice Center, 264 Va. 408, 568 S.E.2d 703 (2002); Christian v. Surgical Specialists of Richmond, 268 Va. 60, 596 S.E.2d 522 (2004). ***PRACTICE AREAS:*** Medical Malpractice Defense Litigation; Premises Liability Defense Litigation; Insurance Coverage Defense; Insurance Defense. ***Email:*** epm@ymh.com

MATTHEW C. LITZ, born July 2, 1973; admitted to bar, 2003, North Carolina. *Education:* Florida International University (B.B.A., 1999); Florida State University College of Law (J.D., 2003); New York University School of Law (LL.M., Taxation, 2004). ***PRACTICE AREAS:*** Estate Planning; Trusts and Estates; Business Law; Taxation; Charitable Giving. ***Email:*** mcl@ymh.com

ELINOR JOHNSEY, born Kinston, North Carolina, June 13, 1980; admitted to bar, 2005, North Carolina. *Education:* University of North Carolina-Chapel Hill (B.A., 2002); Wake Forest University (J.D., 2005). ***PRACTICE AREAS:*** Insurance Defense. ***Email:*** emj@ymh.com

SHANNON S. FRANKEL, born Raleigh, North Carolina, April 1, 1978; admitted to bar, 2005, North Carolina. *Education:* Duke University (B.A, 2000); College of William & Mary (J.D., 2005). Member: William & Mary Moot Court Team; William & Mary Moot Court Board, Business Justice. ***PRACTICE AREAS:*** Transportation Defense; Products Liability Defense; Medical Malpractice Defense; Premises Liability Defense. ***Email:*** ssf@ymh.com

GENERAL COUNSEL FOR: North Carolina Rate Bureau; North Carolina Reinsurance Facility; State Board of Electrical Contractors; State Board of Examiners of Plumbing & Heating Contractors.
REPRESENTATIVE CLIENTS: Bridgestone/Firestone North American Holdings; Crum and Forster; Heritage Operating L.P.; Lawyers Mutual Liability Insurance Co.; Liberty Mutual Group; Lincoln General Insurance Co.; Medical Mutual Insurance Company of North Carolina; Montgomery Insurance Company; N.C. Farm Bureau Mutual Insurance Co.; Noble Oil Services; OneBeacon Insurance; Overnight Transportation Company; Pharmacists Mutual Insurance Company; ProClaim America, Inc.; Progressive Insurance Company; Ranger Fairmont Specialty; RiverStone Claims Management; Schindler Elevator Corporation; Schneider National Inc.; State Farm Insurance Companies.; Universal Insurance Company; U.S. Liability Insurance Company; Wausau; Western World Insurance Company.
APPROVED ATTORNEYS FOR: Commonwealth Title Insurance Company; First Title Insurance Company; Investors Title Insurance Company; Lawyers Title Insurance Company; Safeco Title Insurance Company; Ticor Title Insurance Company.

LAW OFFICES OF ZAYTOUN & MILLER, PLLC

414 WEST JONES STREET
RALEIGH, NORTH CAROLINA 27603
Telephone: 919-832-6690
Fax: 919-831-4793
Email: rzaytoun@zaytoun-miller.com
Email: stacymiller@zaytoun-miller.com
URL: http://www.lawyers.com/zaytoun&miller

Mailing Address: P.O. Box 307, Raleigh, NC 27602-0307

Medical Negligence, Catastrophic Personal Injury, Wrongful Deaths, Product Liability, Civil Litigation, Health Care Fraud, Business Crimes, Major Criminal Litigation, Business Torts, Managed Care Litigation and Practice in all State and Federal Courts.

ROBERT E. ZAYTOUN, born New Bern, North Carolina, September 5, 1949; admitted to bar, 1975, North Carolina; 1977, Florida; 1982, U.S. District Court, Eastern and Middle Districts of North Carolina and U.S. Court of Appeals, Fourth Circuit; U.S. Supreme Court. *Education:* University of North Carolina (A.B., 1971; J.D., 1975). Member, Wake County Christian Legal Society. Appointed by Governor Michael Easley, Health and Wellness Trust Fund Commission (Chairman, Operations and Personnel Committee). Assistant District Attorney, Wake County, 1977-1981. Mentor, University of North Carolina School of Law Mentorship Program, 1995-1996. Certified Mediator, all courts (Duke Private Adjudication Center Certification). *Member:* Wake County (Member, Board of Directors, 1988-1990), North Carolina (Member, Sections on: Health Law; Litigation; Litigation Council) and American (Member, Sections on: Health Law and Litigation) Bar Associations; North Carolina State Bar; The Florida Bar; North Carolina Academy of Trial Lawyers (Member: Board of Governors, 1989-1997; Executive Committee, 1990-1993; Professional Negligence Section; Vice Chairman 2000-2002; Chairman, 2002-2003); North Carolina College of Advocacy; National Institute for Trial Advocacy (Basic and Advanced Institutes); The Association of Trial Lawyers of America; American Board of Trial Advocates; Susie Sharp Inn of Court. ***PRACTICE AREAS:*** Medical Negligence; Catastrophic Personal Injury; Wrongful Death; Health Care Fraud and Abuse; Product Liability; Business Torts; Commercial Torts. ***Email:*** rzaytoun@zaytoun-miller.com

(This Listing Continued)

W. STACY MILLER, II, born United States Air Force Base, Bent Waters, England, March 5, 1965; admitted to bar, 1994, North Carolina, U.S. District Court, Eastern and Middle Districts of North Carolina and U.S. Court of Appeals, Fourth Circuit. *Education:* Wake Forest University (B.A., 1989); Campbell University (J.D., 1994). Phi Delta Phi, Academic Legal Fraternity. Newsletter Editor, Professional Negligence Section, Academy of Trial Lawyers of America. Member, National Trial Team; Order of Old Kevitt. District Representative, Raleigh City Counsel, 1996-1997; Christian Legal Society. Intern, Wake County District Attorneys Office, 1994. *Member:* Wake County, North Carolina (Member, Sections on: Health Law, Criminal Law and Torts) and American (Member, Sections on: White Collar Crime and Health Law) Bar Associations; North Carolina State Bar; Wake County Academy of Criminal Trial Lawyers; North Carolina Academy of Trial Lawyers (Member, Sections on: Criminal Law and Auto Torts); National Association of Criminal Defense Lawyers; National Institute for Trial Advocacy; Susie Sharp Inn of Court; The Association of Trial Lawyers of America (Member, Professional Negligence Section). ***LANGUAGES:*** Spanish. ***PRACTICE AREAS:*** Medical Negligence; Catastrophic Personal Injury; Wrongful Death; Health Care Fraud and Abuse; Products Liability; Business Torts; Commercial Torts. ***Email:*** smiller@zaytoun-miller.com

SHILOH A. DAUM, born Rochester, New York, March 24, 1975; admitted to bar, 2004, District of Columbia; 2005, North Carolina. *Education:* University of North Carolina at Chapel Hill (B.A., 1999; J.D., 2004). Member, National Moot Court Team. Note and Comment Editor, North Carolina Journal of International Law and Commercial Regulation. *Member:* Wake County and North Carolina Bar Associations; North Carolina Academy of Trial Lawyers. ***PRACTICE AREAS:*** Personal Injury; Medical Malpractice; Civil Litigation. ***Email:*** sdaum@zaytoun-miller.com

---

GRIFFIN LAW OFFICE

106 SOUTH MAIN STREET
RED SPRINGS, NORTH CAROLINA 28377
Telephone: 910-843-9600
Fax: 910-843-9701
Email: attorneyanthonydgriffin@yahoo.com
URL: http://www.griffinlaw-office.com

Abuse and Neglect, Juvenile Law, Real Estate Transactions, Traffic, Traffic Violations, DWI, Criminal Law, Domestic and Family Law.

ANTHONY D. GRIFFIN, born Lumberton, North Carolina, October 4, 1967; admitted to bar, 2000, North Carolina. *Education:* Pembroke State University (B.A., 1997); Norman A. Wiggins School of Law (J.D., 2000). *Member:* North Carolina American Trial Lawyers Association. ***Email:*** attorneyanthonydgriffin@yahoo.com

---

THE DEUTERMAN LAW GROUP, P.A.

REIDSVILLE, NORTH CAROLINA

(See Greensboro)

Workers Compensation, Auto Accidents, Social Security Disability, Wrongful Death, Nursing Home Neglect, Slip and Fall, Products Liability.

LAW OFFICES OF R. LEE FARMER, P.L.L.C.

REIDSVILLE, NORTH CAROLINA

(See Yanceyville)

General Civil and Criminal Practice in all State and Federal Courts. Probate, Real Estate, Personal Injury, Commercial, Construction, Administrative and Corporation Law.

HOLT & WATT

Established in 1976
211 GILMER STREET
P.O. BOX 728
REIDSVILLE, NORTH CAROLINA 27320
Telephone: 336-342-2997
Fax: 336-342-9158
Email: hwxandra@bellsouth.net

General Practice. Probate and Real Estate.

CLARK M. HOLT, born Reidsville, North Carolina, December 16, 1937; admitted to bar, 1964, North Carolina; 1965, U.S. District Court, Middle District of North Carolina. *Education:* Wake Forest University (A.B., 1960; LL.B., 1963). Phi Delta Phi. Chairman, Rockingham County Board of Elections, 1964-1965. Solicitor, Reidsville Recorder's Court, 1965-1970. Chief District Court Solicitor, 17th Judicial District, 1970. *Member:* Rockingham County, North Carolina (Member, Committee on Practical Training, 1967) and American Bar Associations; Seventeen-A Judicial District (Member, Executive Committee, 1971-1972; Vice President, 1973-1974; President, 1975-1976; Chairman, Bar Applicants Committee, 1978—) and North Carolina State Bars. ***PRACTICE AREAS:*** Probate Law; Real Estate Law.

ROBERT L. WATT, III, born Greensboro, North Carolina, February 24, 1946; admitted to bar, 1974, North Carolina. *Education:* Hampden-Sydney College (B.S., 1968);

(This Listing Continued)

University of North Carolina (J.D., with honors, 1974). Staff Member, North Carolina Law Review, 1973-1974. *Member:* North Carolina and American Bar Associations; Seventeen-A Judicial District (President, 1985-1986) and North Carolina State Bars. [Lt., U.S. Army, 1968-1971]. ***PRACTICE AREAS:*** Probate Law; Real Estate Law.

REPRESENTATIVE CLIENTS: Branch Banking & Trust Co. (BB&T); Bank of America; FNB Southeast.
APPROVED ATTORNEYS FOR: Lawyers Title Insurance Corp.; Chicago Title Insurance Co.; Investors Title Insurance Co.; First American Title.
REFERENCE: FNB Southeast.

C. ORVILLE LIGHT

REIDSVILLE, NORTH CAROLINA

(See Eden)

General Practice. Workers Compensation, Real Estate, Corporation, Business Law, Family, Divorce, Adoptions, Child Custody and Support, Automobile Accidents, Wrongful Death, Trusts and Estates, Wills and Probate, Estate Planning and Personal Injury Law.

MADDREY ETRINGER & SMITH, L.L.P.

REIDSVILLE, NORTH CAROLINA

(See Eden)

General Trial Practice in all State and Federal Courts. Personal Injury, Automobile Accidents, Wrongful Death, Real Estate, Banking, Business and Corporate Law, Probate Law, Family Law, Divorce, Child Custody, Bankruptcy, Collections, Criminal, DWI, Traffic, Zoning, Planning and Land Use Law, Construction Law, Foreclosures.

SCHELL BRAY AYCOCK ABEL & LIVINGSTON P.L.L.C.

REIDSVILLE, NORTH CAROLINA

(See Greensboro)

Corporate, Taxation, Securities Regulation, Venture Capital, Real Estate and Real Estate Finance, Mergers and Acquisitions, Health Care, Antitrust and Trade Regulation, Banking, Commercial, Employee Benefits, Estate Planning and Administration.

TUGGLE DUGGINS & MESCHAN, P.A.

REIDSVILLE, NORTH CAROLINA

(See Greensboro)

General Civil Practice. Corporation, Tax, Insurance, Banking, Pension and Profit Sharing, Bankruptcy and Creditors' Rights, Trust and Estate, Construction and Real Estate Law. Trials and Appeals in all State and Federal Courts.

STUART N. WATLINGTON

REIDSVILLE, NORTH CAROLINA

(See Yanceyville)

General Civil and Criminal Practice in all State and Federal Courts. DWI, Traffic Violations, Personal Injury, Wrongful Death, Probate, Real Estate.

ALLEN AND PINNIX, P.A.

RESEARCH TRIANGLE PARK, NORTH CAROLINA

(See Raleigh)

Antitrust, Immigration, Administrative, International Trade, Corporate, Construction, Insurance, Employment, Arbitration, Mediation, Franchise, Unfair Trade Practices, Unfair Competition, Mergers and Acquisitions, Business Litigation and Appellate Practice in all State and Federal Courts.

ALSTON & BIRD LLP

RESEARCH TRIANGLE PARK, NORTH CAROLINA

(See Raleigh)

Administrative Law, Alternative Dispute Resolution, Antitrust and Trade Regulation, Appellate Practice, Bankruptcy, Banks and Banking, Biotechnology, Business Law, Class Actions, Commercial Real Estate, FCC Licensing, FCC Regulation, Wireless Communications, Complex and Multi-District Litigation, Computers and Software, Constitutional Law, Construction Law, Copyrights, Corporate Ethics, Corporate Governance, Corporate Law, Criminal Law, Debtor and Creditor, Electronic Commerce, Emerging Growth Companies, Employee Benefits, Employment Law, Entertainment Law, ERISA, ERISA Litigation, Energy, Environmental Law, Environmental Litigation, Executive Compensation; Finance, Franchises and Franchising, Government Investigations; Health Care Corporate Law, Health Care Regulation, Immigration Law, Insurance Defense, Intellectual Property, International Finance, International Law, International Taxation, International Trade, Internet Law, Labor Law, Labor and Employment, Land Use, Legislative Practice, Life Sciences, Litigation, Local Taxation, Medical Malpractice, Mergers, Acquisitions and Divestitures, Multimedia Law, Municipal Law, Nonprofit and Charitable Organizations, Occupational Safety and Health, Partnership Law, Patents, Privacy Law, Products Liability, Professional Liability, Public Finance, Public Policy, Real Estate Finance, Regulatory Law, RICO, Securities, Securities Litigation, State Taxation, Taxation, Tax Litigation, Technology and Science, Telecommunications Law, Trademarks, Trusts and Estates, Utility Law, Venture Capital, White Collar Crime, Zoning.

BAILEY & DIXON, L.L.P.

RESEARCH TRIANGLE PARK, NORTH CAROLINA

(See Raleigh)

General Civil Trial, Appellate and Administrative Practice. Litigation: Insurance Regulation, Defense of Personal Injury and Professional Malpractice Claims, Commercial Litigation, Including Environmental Law, Employment Law, Insurance Coverage Disputes, Construction, Land Use, Municipal and Police Liability, Products Liability, Drug and Medical Device Liability, Business Torts, and Workers' Compensation. Administrative Law: Public Utilities, Including Electric, Telecommunications, Gas, Transportation, Water and Sewer. Professional and Occupational Licensing, Healthcare, Labor and Employment Law, Business and Corporate Law, Commercial Real Estate, Estate Administration and Taxation.

BROOKS, PIERCE, McLENDON, HUMPHREY & LEONARD, L.L.P.

RESEARCH TRIANGLE PARK, NORTH CAROLINA

(See Raleigh)

General Practice in State and Federal Courts. Administrative, Antitrust, Banking, Bankruptcy, Bonds, Business Litigation, Communications and Media, Corporate, Corporate Finance, Energy, Environmental, Foundations, Insurance, Intellectual Property, Internet, Labor, Legislative, Mergers and Acquisitions, Probate, Public Utilities, Real Estate, Securities, Taxation, Telecommunications and Trade Associations Law.

LAW OFFICES OF GREGORY P. CHOCKLETT

RESEARCH TRIANGLE PARK, NORTH CAROLINA

(See Raleigh)

Commercial Litigation, Bankruptcy/Creditor, Collections, Contracts, Civil Trials and Appeals, Personal Injury. Medical Malpractice, ERISA, Repossessions, Foreclosures.

DANIELS DANIELS & VERDONIK, P.A.

Established in 1982

SUITE 200, GENERATION PLAZA
1822 N.C. HIGHWAY 54 EAST
P.O. DRAWER 12218
RESEARCH TRIANGLE PARK, NORTH CAROLINA 27709-2218
Telephone: 919-544-5444
Fax: 919-544-5920
Email: lawinfo@d2vlaw.com
URL: http://www.d2vlaw.com

Business, Corporations, Venture Capital, Securities, Corporate Finance, Computers, Biotechnology, Telecommunications, Copyright, Trademark, Patent, Technology and Science, Intellectual Property, Management and Licensing, Domestic and International Taxation, Limited Liability Companies and Partnerships, Joint Ventures, International Trade and Investment, Immigration.

FIRM PROFILE: DANIELS DANIELS & VERDONIK, P.A. was established as the first resident law fim in the Research Triangle Park over 20 years ago. Since then the attorneys of the firm have represented growth companies, founders, management, shareholders, directors and investors in a wide range of technology industries (including software, hardware, semiconductors, medical devices, biotechnology, pharmaceuticals, chemical, chemical engineering, mechanical and telecommunications) in several billion dollars of transactions.

WALTER E. DANIELS, born Raleigh, North Carolina, 1952; admitted to bar, 1979, North Carolina. *Education:* University of North Carolina at Chapel Hill (B.A., with honors, 1975; J.D., cum laude, 1979); Duke University (M.A. in Public Policy Sciences, 1979). ***PRACTICE AREAS:*** Venture Capital; Corporate Finance; Securities; Mergers and Acquisitions; Computers and Software; Biotechnology; Telecommunications; Intellectual Property. ***Email:*** wdaniels@d2vlaw.com

LINDA MARKUS DANIELS, born Boston, Massachusetts, 1953; admitted to bar, 1983, North Carolina. *Education:* Duke University (B.A., magna cum laude, with honors in Public Policy Sciences, 1975; J.D., with honors, 1983); Johns Hopkins School of Advanced International Studies (M.A., with distinction in international economics, 1977). ***PRACTICE AREAS:*** Mergers and Acquisitions; Venture Capital; Securities; Computers; Biotechnology; Intellectual Property Transactions; International Transactions; Taxation. ***Email:*** ldaniels@d2vlaw.com

JAMES F. VERDONIK, admitted to bar, 1978, New York; 1985, North Carolina. *Education:* Fordham University (B.A., 1971; J.D., cum laude, 1977). ***PRACTICE AREAS:*** Securities; Corporate Finance; Corporate; Venture Capital; Mergers and Acquisitions. ***Email:*** jverdonik@d2vlaw.com

A. JOSE CORTINA, admitted to bar, 1979, District of Columbia; 1981, Virginia; 1992, Florida; 1999, North Carolina; registered to practice before the U.S. Patent and Trademark Office. *Education:* The American University (B.S., Physics/Distributed Sciences, 1976); The American University Washington College of Law (J.D., 1979). ***LANGUAGES:*** Spanish and French. ***PRACTICE AREAS:*** Patents; Copyrights; Trademarks; Intellectual Property Licensing. ***Email:*** jcortina@d2vlaw.com

CAROLINE HORTON ROCKAFELLOW, born Flint, Michigan, 1968; admitted to bar, 1993, Pennsylvania; 1996, Connecticut; 1998, North Carolina; registered to practice before the U.S. Patent and Trademark Office. *Education:* Drury College (B.S., 1990); Fran-

(This Listing Continued)

DANIELS DANIELS & VERDONIK, P.A., Research Triangle Park—Continued

klin Pierce Law Center (J.D., 1993; M.I.P., 1994). ***PRACTICE AREAS:*** Biotechnology; Computers; Intellectual Property Licensing; Copyrights; Trademarks; Patents. ***Email:*** crockafellow@d2vlaw.com

AMALIE L. TUFFIN, admitted to bar, 1992, Massachusetts; 1996, North Carolina. *Education:* Harvard University (A.B., cum laude, 1989); Hastings College of Law, University of California (J.D., 1992); Boston University Graduate Tax Program (LL.M., 1996). ***PRACTICE AREAS:*** Corporate and Partnership Taxation; Securities; Mergers and Acquisitions; Venture Capital; Corporations. ***Email:*** atuffin@d2vlaw.com

OF COUNSEL

JOHN C. LINDSEY, admitted to bar, 1985, District of Columbia; 1994, North Carolina. *Education:* University of North Carolina at Chapel Hill (B.A., with honors, 1972; Ph.D., Economics, 1980); Georgetown University Law Center (J.D., cum laude, 1985). ***PRACTICE AREAS:*** Immigration. ***Email:*** jlindsey@d2vlaw.coms

HOLT YORK McDARRIS & HIGH, LLP

RESEARCH TRIANGLE PARK, NORTH CAROLINA

(See Raleigh)

Municipal/Administrative Law, Zoning and Land Use, Real Property, Government Regulations, Condemnation Defense, Corporate Law, Trusts and Estates, Wills and Probate, Alcoholic Beverages, General Trial and Appellate Practice before all State and Federal Courts and Agencies. Legislative Representation before the North Carolina General Assembly.

HOWARD, STALLINGS, FROM & HUTSON, P.A.

RESEARCH TRIANGLE PARK, NORTH CAROLINA

(See Raleigh)

General, Civil and Commercial Litigation, Business Law, Commercial Real Estate, Taxation, Employment Law, Computer Law, Estate Planning and Administration, Bankruptcy Law, Loan Structuring and Workouts, Intellectual Property Law, Personal Injury.

INTELLECTUAL PROPERTY/ TECHNOLOGY LAW

RESEARCH TRIANGLE PARK, NORTH CAROLINA

(See Chapel Hill)

Intellectual Property, Technology and Biotechnology, Patents, Trademarks, Licensing and Copyright Law.

JENKINS, WILSON & TAYLOR, P.A.

RESEARCH TRIANGLE PARK, NORTH CAROLINA

(See Durham)

Patent, Trademark and Copyright Law.

KENNEDY COVINGTON LOBDELL & HICKMAN, L.L.P.

Established in 1957

P.O. BOX 14210

RESEARCH TRIANGLE PARK, NORTH CAROLINA 27709-4210

Telephone: 919-466-1190

Fax: 919-831-7040

URL: http://www.kennedycovington.com

Mailing Address: 2801 Slater Road, Suite 120, Morrisville, NC 27560

Charlotte, North Carolina Office: Hearst Tower, 214 North Tryon Street, 47th Floor, 28202. Telephone: 704-331-7400. Fax: 704-331-7598.

Raleigh, North Carolina Office: 434 Fayetteville Street Mall, 19th Floor, P.O. Box 1070, 27602-1070. Telephone: 919-743-7300. Fax: 919-743-7358.

Columbia, South Carolina Office: NBSC Building, Suite 850, 1122 Lady Street, 29201. Telephone: 803-251-2300. Fax: 803-251-2315.

Rock Hill, South Carolina Office: 140 East Main Street, Suite 220, P.O. Box 11429, 29731-1429. Telephone: 803-329-7600. Fax: 803-329-7677.

Administrative Law, Alternative Dispute Resolution, Antitrust and Trade Regulation, Bankruptcy, Banks and Banking, Business Law, Commercial Law, Commercial Real Estate Development, Construction Law, Corporate Law, Debt and Equity Finance, Emerging Growth Companies, Employee Benefits, Employment Law, Entrepreneurial Business Law, Environmental Law, Family Law, Finance, Governmental, Health Care, Immigration and Naturalization, Intellectual Property, International Law, Labor and Employment, Land Sales, Land Use Regulation, Limited Liability Companies and Partnerships, Litigation, Medical Malpractice, Mergers, Acquisitions and Divestitures, Non-Profit and Charitable Organizations, Patents, Private Equity, Products Liability, Professional Liability, Public Utility Law, Real Estate Development, Real Estate Leasing, Real Estate Finance, Securities, Taxation, Technology Law, Trademarks, Trial Practice, Trusts and Estates, Utility Law, Venture Capital, Zoning, Planning and Land Use.

(This Listing Continued)

FIRM PROFILE: Kennedy Covington Lobdell & Hickman, L.L.P. is one of the largest full service law firms in the Carolinas, with offices in Charlotte, Columbia, Raleigh, Research Triangle Park and Rock Hill. Our lawyers bring a depth of experience and a knowledge of the law to bear in solving problems and leveraging opportunities for clients in varied industries such as banking, real estate, technology and manufacturing. At Kennedy Covington, we give more than a legal opinion; we provide a business perspective.

PARTNERS

WILLIAM J. BRIAN, admitted to bar, 1989, North Carolina. *Education:* Washington University (A.B., History, cum laude, 1984); George Washington University (M.A., International Affairs, 1987); Duke University (J.D., with high honors, 1989). (Also at Raleigh, North Carolina Office). ***PRACTICE AREAS:*** Zoning, Planning and Land Use; Real Estate Litigation. ***Email:*** bbrian@kennedycovington.com

MARY BETH JOHNSTON, admitted to bar, 1986, North Carolina. *Education:* University of North Carolina (A.B., 1980); Campbell University (J.D., cum laude, 1983). ***PRACTICE AREAS:*** Health Law. ***Email:*** mjohnston@kennedycovington.com

PATRICIA T. MEADOR, admitted to bar, 1982, North Carolina; 1988, Tennessee. *Education:* Vanderbilt University (B.S.N., 1978); University of Louisville School of Law (J.D., magna cum laude, 1982); University of North Carolina (M.P.H., 1989). ***PRACTICE AREAS:*** Health Law. ***Email:*** pmeador@kennedycovington.com

GARY S. QUALLS, admitted to bar, 1989, North Carolina. *Education:* University of North Carolina-Asheville (B.S., magna cum laude, 1986); Duke University (J.D., 1989). ***PRACTICE AREAS:*** Health Law. ***Email:*** gqualls@kennedycovington.com

SPECIAL COUNSEL

ERIC M. BRAUN, admitted to bar, 1993, North Carolina; 1996, U.S. District Court, Eastern District of North Carolina; 2001, U.S. District Court, Middle District of North Carolina; 1998, U.S. Supreme Court and U.S. Court of Appeals, Fourth Circuit. *Education:* James Madison University (B.S., Public Administration, cum laude, 1990); Wake Forest University (J.D., 1993); University of Georgia (M.A., Public Administration, 1995). (Also at Raleigh, North Carolina Office). ***PRACTICE AREAS:*** Zoning, Planning and Land Use; Real Estate Litigation. ***Email:*** ebraun@kennedycovington.com

PATRICK L. BYKER, admitted to bar, 1992, North Carolina. *Education:* Calvin College (B.A., Classical Studies, 1987); University of North Carolina at Chapel Hill (J.D., 1992; M.A., Regional Planning, concentration in Economic Development, 1994). (Also at Raleigh, North Carolina Office). ***PRACTICE AREAS:*** Zoning, Planning and Land Use. ***Email:*** pbyker@kennedycovington.com

JOHN E. (JACK) MARKHAM, JR., admitted to bar, 1973, North Carolina; 1979, U.S. District Court, Middle District of North Carolina. *Education:* University of North Carolina at Chapel Hill (A.B., History, 1967; J.D., 1973). (Also at Raleigh, North Carolina Office). ***PRACTICE AREAS:*** Zoning, Planning and Land Use; Real Estate Development. ***Email:*** jmarkham@kennedycovington.com

ASSOCIATES

GINA LOUISE BERTOLINI, admitted to bar, 2000, California; 2005, North Carolina. *Education:* DePaul University (B.F.A., with honors, 1992); University of California (J.D., cum laude, 2000). ***PRACTICE AREAS:*** Health Law.

COLLEEN M. CROWLEY, admitted to bar, 1998, North Carolina. *Education:* James Madison University (B.S., summa cum laude, 1995); Wake Forest University (J.D., 1998). ***PRACTICE AREAS:*** Health Law. ***Email:*** ccrowley@kennedycovington.com

SHAWN A. McMILLAN, admitted to bar, 2002, North Carolina. *Education:* Clemson University (B.A., English, magna cum laude, 1994); Medical University of South Carolina (M.H.A., Health Administration, with honors, 1997); University of North Carolina (J.D., 2002). ***PRACTICE AREAS:*** Health Law. ***Email:*** smcmillan@kennedycovington.com

CAROLYN FIXEL MERRITT, admitted to bar, 2002, North Carolina and Tennessee. *Education:* Davidson College (B.A., cum laude, 1999); Vanderbilt University (J.D., 2002). ***PRACTICE AREAS:*** Health Care. ***Email:*** cmerritt@kennedycovington.com

CANDICE M. MURPHY-FARMER, admitted to bar, 1999, North Carolina. *Education:* University of Mississippi (B.A., Psychology, cum laude, 1991); Indiana University School of Law - Indianapolis (J.D., cum laude, 1997). ***PRACTICE AREAS:*** Health Law. ***Email:*** cmurphy-farmer@kennedycovington.com

CRAIGIE D. SANDERS, admitted to bar, 2003, North Carolina. *Education:* University of Kentucky (B.A., Political Science, 1987); Murray State University (M.P.A., 1992); North Carolina Central University (J.D., 2000). (Also at Raleigh, North Carolina Office). ***PRACTICE AREAS:*** Zoning, Planning and Land Use. ***Email:*** csanders@kennedycovington.com

All Attorneys are Members of the North Carolina and American Bar Associations with the exception of Stephen R. McCrae, Jr., who is a Member of the South Carolina Bar Association.

KIRBY & HOLT, L.L.P.

RESEARCH TRIANGLE PARK, NORTH CAROLINA

(See Raleigh)

Personal injury, including medical malpractice, products liability and catastrophic injury, and business torts.

KNOTT, CLARK & BERGER, L.L.P.

RESEARCH TRIANGLE PARK, NORTH CAROLINA

(See Raleigh)

General Practice in State and Federal Courts. Medical Malpractice, Nursing Malpractice, Hospital Liability, Plaintiffs Personal Injury, Wrongful Death, Automobile Accidents and Injuries, Commercial Vehicle Liability, Nursing Home Negligence, Workers Compensation, Insurance Bad Faith, Insurance Litigation.

MANNING & CROUCH

RESEARCH TRIANGLE PARK, NORTH CAROLINA

(See Raleigh)

Criminal Trials in State and Federal Courts, Criminal Fraud, Criminal Tax Matters, Grand Jury Investigation, Homicide, Federal Grand Jury, Criminal and Regulatory Investigations, Driving While Intoxicated (DWI), Driving While Impaired, Traffic Violations, Homicide, Sex Crimes, Drug Crimes.

MANNING, FULTON & SKINNER, P.A.

RESEARCH TRIANGLE PARK, NORTH CAROLINA

(See Raleigh)

Alternative Dispute Resolution, Appellate; Bankruptcy, Condemnation, Corporate/Business Entities, Corporate Finance, Employee Benefits/ERISA, Employment, Estate/Trust Administration, Estate Planning/Wealth Transfer, Family Law, Franchise, Government Relations, Litigation, Mergers/Acquisitions, Real Property, Sports/Entertainment, Tax Controversies, Tax Planning.

MAUPIN TAYLOR, P.A.

Established in 1870

480 BETA BUILDING, HEADQUARTERS PARK
POST OFFICE BOX 13646
RESEARCH TRIANGLE PARK, NORTH CAROLINA 27709-3646
Telephone: 919-361-4900
Telecopier: 919-361-2262
URL: http://www.maupintaylor.com

Raleigh, North Carolina: Highwoods Tower One, Suite 500, 3200 Beechleaf Court, P.O. Drawer 19764. Telephone: 919-981-4000. Telecopier: 919-981-4300.

Wilmington, North Carolina Office: Landfall Park North, 1985 Eastwood Road, Suite 200, 28403. Telephone: 910-256-5135. Telecopier: 910-256-6451.

Agribusiness, Administrative, Alcoholic Beverages, Alternative Dispute Resolution, Antitrust and Trade Regulation, Aviation Law, Bankruptcy, Banking Law, Business Litigation, Charitable Organizations, Collective Bargaining, Commercial Leases, Commercial Real Estate, Computers and Software, Construction Law, Copyrights, Corporate Finance, Corporate Law, Creditors' Rights, Employee Benefits, Employer Liability, Employment Discrimination, Employment Law, Employment Litigation, Environmental Law, Franchises and Franchising, Government Contracts, Governmental (State and Local) Law, Health Law, Hospital Law, Immigration and Naturalization, Industrial Accidents, Industrial Relations, Intellectual Property, Labor Arbitration, Labor Law, Labor Legislation, Labor Relations, Management Labor Law, Medical Malpractice Defense, Mergers and Acquisitions, Occupational Health and Safety, Patent Litigation, Products Liability, Real Estate Finance, Secured Lending, Securities Regulation, Sports Law, Taxation, Technology Law, Trademark, Trusts and Estates, Venture Capital, Zoning Law.

FIRM PROFILE: The law firm of Maupin Taylor, P.A., embodies a legacy of leadership and legal excellence that dates back to 1870. The firm has a long history of serving its clients, large and small, with integrity and success. To better serve its clients it maintains offices in Raleigh, Research Triangle Park and Wilmington. It is one of the largest firms in the area. From start-up companies cultivating new ideas and technologies to venerable companies whose roots are embedded in North Carolina history, Maupin Taylor provides the experience, depth and diversity to help them all thrive.

Maupin Taylor is a full service corporate law firm that concentrates in business law, litigation, labor and employment matters, health law, environmental, commercial real estate, trusts and estates, and banking law. The firm takes great pride in its rich history and its ability to apply the practice of law to the technological demands of 21st century business.

ARLENE J. DIOSEGY, born Pittsburgh, PA, September 13, 1949; admitted to bar, 1974, PA; 1981, CO; 1983, NC. *Education:* Allegheny College (B.A., 1971); Temple Univ. (J.D., 1974). Editor and Author, Body Medical/Body Legal, 1989—. Adjunct Instructor, Department of Health Policy and Administration, UNC at Chapel Hill, 1989—. *Member:* NC (Member, board of Governors, 1989-1992; Health Benefit Trust Trustee, 1990-1994) and American Bar Associations; National Health Lawyers Association; NC Society of Health Care Attorneys. ***PRACTICE AREAS:*** Health Care Law; Corporate and Business Law; Administrative Law. ***Email:*** adiosegy@maupintaylor.com

THERON McK. vanDUSEN, born Detroit, MI, March 26, 1957; admitted to bar, 1991, NC. *Education:* Univ. of Pennsylvania (B.A., magna cum laude, 1979); Duke Univ. (J.D., with honors, 1991). Editor, Law and Contemporary Problems, 1989-1991. *Member:* NC (Member, Sections on: Business; Tax Law) and American (Member, Sections on: Business: Tax Law) Bar Associations. ***LANGUAGES:*** French. ***PRACTICE AREAS:*** Corporate and Securities Law; Federal Taxation. ***Email:*** tvandusen@maupintaylor.com

CHARLES L. STEEL, IV, born Greensboro, NC, 1945; admitted to bar, 1970, NC. *Education:* Davidson College (A.B., 1967); Vanderbilt Univ. (J.D., 1970); New York Univ. (LL.M., Taxation, 1972). Council, Tax Section, Chair, 2002-2003, NC Bar Association. Director and Past President, Fourteenth Judicial District Bar. Member, Planning Committee, J. Nelson Young Tax Institute at the UNC School of Law; Petitioner's Counsel in Jao Montoro and Neuza Paula v. Commissioner, 73TCM 3110, Filed June 23, 1997. ***PRACTICE AREAS:*** Taxation Law; Estate Planning Law; Corporate Law. ***Email:*** csteel@maupintaylor.com

ROY H. WYMAN, JR., born San Diego, CA, December 5, 1963; admitted to bar, 1993, MI; 1995, NC. *Education:* Wheaton College (B.S., cum laude, 1986); Univ. of Michigan (J.D., cum laude, 1993). ***PRACTICE AREAS:*** Health Care; Business; Corporate Transactions; Medicare; Medicaid; Health Care Fraud. ***Email:*** rwyman@maupintaylor.com

WILLIAM SAM BYASSEE, born Paducah, KY, June 3, 1950; admitted to bar, 1982, NC; 1984, U.S. Court of Appeals, Fourth Circuit; 1998, U.S. Court of Appeals for the Federal Circuit. *Education:* Univ. of Tennessee (B.A., cum laude, 1973); Univ. of Kentucky; Vanderbilt Univ. (J.D., 1982). Recipient: Law Review Award, 1982; The Morgan Prize, 1983. Executive Articles Editor, The Vanderbilt Law Review, 1981-1982. Clerk to Senior Judge Eugene A. Gordon, U.S. District Court, Middle District of North Carolina, 1982-1983. *Member:* NC (Chair: Technology Advisory Committee, 1991-1996; Intellectual Property Section, 1999-2000) and American (Member and Chair Elect, 2001-2002, Science and Technology Section) Bar Associations. ***PRACTICE AREAS:*** Information Technology; Internet; Intellectual Property Law; First Amendment and Media Law. ***Email:*** sbyassee@maupintaylor.com

OF COUNSEL

W. TRAVIS PORTER, born Lumberton, NC, 1931; admitted to bar, 1960, NC. *Education:* Univ. of North Carolina (A.B., 1953; J.D., with high honors, 1960). Order of the Coif. Member, Board of Editors, North Carolina Law Review, 1959-1960. Adjunct Professor, Graduate School of Business, Duke Univ., 1974-1981. President, Durham, NC Chamber of Commerce, 1984-1985. Member, UNC System: Board of Governors, 1987-1995; Vice-Chairman, 1990-1994; Chairman, 1994-1995. Member, Board of Trustees, 1979-1987; Chairman, 1983-1984, UNC at Chapel Hill. Member: 1983-1987 and Chairman, 1983-1984, UNC Endowment Board; UNC Public Television Foundation Board of Directors, 1997—; UNC Board of Visitors, 1987—. [Captain, USMC, Active Duty, 1953-1956]. ***PRACTICE AREAS:*** Corporate Law; Administrative Law; Governmental Law; Land Use Law; Contracts Law. ***Email:*** tporter@maupintaylor.com

(For complete biographical data on all personnel, see Raleigh, North Carolina Professional Biographies)

MOORE & VAN ALLEN PLLC

430 DAVIS DRIVE, SUITE 500
P.O. BOX 13706
RESEARCH TRIANGLE PARK, NORTH CAROLINA 27709
Telephone: 919-286-8000
Fax: 919-286-8199
URL: http://www.mvalaw.com

Charleston, South Carolina Office: 40 Calhoun Street, Suite 300. Telephone: 843-579-7000. Fax: 843-579-7099.

Charlotte, North Carolina Office: 100 North Tryon Street, Suite 4700. Telephone: 704-331-1000. Fax: 704-331-1159.

Admiralty, Banking, Bankruptcy, Commercial Finance, Conduit Lending, Construction, Corporate, Distressed Debt Trading, Employee Benefits, Employment, Energy, Environmental, ERISA, Estate Planning and Administration, Government Contracts, Health Care, Immigration, Information Technology and E-Commerce, Insurance, Intellectual Property, International, Leasing, Litigation, Lobbying and Legislative Representation, Patent and Copyright, Real Estate, Securities, Surety, Taxation, Tax Incentives, Trusts, Utilities and Venture Capital.

FIRM PROFILE: Moore & Van Allen, PLLC is one of the largest and fastest-growing law firms in the Southeast, with approximately 250 attorneys engaged in a general business, banking, and litigation practice.

RESIDENT MEMBERS

DOMINIC J. CHIANTERA, born 1939; admitted to bar, 1974, Massachusetts; 1976, Connecticut; 1999, North Carolina; registered to practice before U.S. Patent and Trademark Office. *Education:* Fairleigh Dickinson University (B.S., 1966); Western New England College (J.D., cum laude, 1974); Rensselaer Polytechnic Institute (M.S., 1983; M.B.A., 1985). ***PRACTICE AREAS:*** Intellectual Property. ***Email:*** domchiantera@mvalaw.com

JAMES H. CLARKE, born 1954; admitted to bar, 1979, North Carolina. *Education:* University of North Carolina (B.A., with honors, 1976; J.D., with high honors, 1979). Phi Beta Kappa; Order of the Coif. North Carolina Law Review, 1978-1979. ***PRACTICE AREAS:*** Real Estate; Corporate. ***Email:*** jamieclarke@mvalaw.com

ARTHUR J. DeBAUGH, born 1963; admitted to bar, 1988, North Carolina. *Education:* University of North Carolina (B.A., with highest honors, 1985; J.D., with honors, 1988). Phi Beta Kappa. ***PRACTICE AREAS:*** Intellectual Property; Trademarks; Licensing; Trademark Trial and Appeal Board. ***Email:*** arthurdebaugh@mvalaw.com

EDWARD L. EMBREE, III, born 1947; admitted to bar, 1972, North Carolina. *Education:* Davidson College (B.A., 1969); University of North Carolina (J.D., 1972). ***PRACTICE AREAS:*** Bankruptcy; Workouts; Banking; Family Law. ***Email:*** edembree@mvalaw.com

RANDOLPH M. FLETCHER, born 1956; admitted to bar, 1984, North Carolina. *Education:* University of North Carolina (B.S., 1979; J.D., 1984). Order of the Coif. Certified Public Accountant, North Carolina, 1981. ***PRACTICE AREAS:*** Corporate; Business; Taxation; Securities. ***Email:*** randyfletcher@mvalaw.com

DAVID E. FOX, born 1956; admitted to bar, 1982, North Carolina. *Education:* University of North Carolina (B.A., 1979; J.D., 1982). Phi Beta Kappa. (Also at Raleigh Office). ***PRACTICE AREAS:*** Commercial Litigation; Construction; Suretyship; Environmental. ***Email:*** davidfox@mvalaw.com

(This Listing Continued)

MOORE & VAN ALLEN PLLC, Research Triangle Park—Continued

WILLIAM E. FREEMAN, born 1955; admitted to bar, 1980, North Carolina. *Education:* University of North Carolina (B.S., 1977; J.D., 1980). Order of the Coif. ***PRACTICE AREAS:*** Construction Litigation; Commercial Litigation; Medical Malpractice; Tort Litigation. ***Email:*** rickfreeman@mvalaw.com

ARLENE D. HANKS, born 1953; admitted to bar, 1996, North Carolina. *Education:* Louisiana State University (B.S., magna cum laude, 1974); North Carolina Central University (J.D., summa cum laude, 1996). ***PRACTICE AREAS:*** Intellectual Property. ***Email:*** arlenehanks@mvalaw.com

MICHAEL G. JOHNSTON, born 1961; admitted to bar, 1992, North Carolina; registered to practice before U.S. Patent and Trademark Office. *Education:* University of Notre Dame (B.S., 1983; M.S.E.E., 1986); North Carolina Central University (J.D., 1991). ***PRACTICE AREAS:*** Intellectual Property. ***Email:*** mikejohnston@mvalaw.com

JOSEPH D. JOYNER, JR., born 1954; admitted to bar, 1981, North Carolina. *Education:* University of North Carolina (A.B., with highest honors, 1977; M.B.A., 1981; J.D., 1981). Phi Beta Kappa. Chairman, Tax Section, North Carolina Bar Association, 1993-1994. Certified Public Accountant, North Carolina, 1982. (Also at Raleigh Office). ***PRACTICE AREAS:*** Taxation; Corporate; Trusts and Estates; Health Care. ***Email:*** jodyjoyner@mvalaw.com

WILLIAM O. KING, born 1937; admitted to bar, 1964, North Carolina and U.S. District Court, Middle and Eastern Districts of North Carolina; U.S. Court of Military Appeals. *Education:* University of North Carolina (A.B., 1959); Wake Forest University (LL.B., 1964). Phi Delta Phi. President, Student Bar Association, 1963-1964. Listed in The Best Lawyers in America. Adjunct Professor, Campbell University School of Law. Certified Mediator. Executive Council, National Conference of Bar Presidents, 1999—. *Member:* Durham County, Fourteenth Judicial District (President, 1982-1983) and American (House of Delegates, 2000—) Bar Associations; North Carolina State Bar (President, 1997-1998); North Carolina Academy of Trial Lawyers (President, 1987-1988); American Board of Trial Advocates (President, Eastern North Carolina District Chapter, 1994-1996; National Board of Governors, 1999—); The Association of Trial Lawyers of America; North Carolina Judicial Standards Commission; North Carolina Client Security Fund. [North Carolina Army National Guard (Ret. 1993); Colonel, Judge Advocate Corp; State Judge Advocate, 1989-1993]. ***PRACTICE AREAS:*** Mediation; Professional Negligence; Personal Injury; Family Law; Eminent Domain. ***Email:*** billking@mvalaw.com

MARK H. MIRKIN, born 1958; admitted to bar, 1985, Florida; 2003, North Carolina. *Education:* Duke University (B.A., cum laude, 1981; J.D., 1984). Member: Council for Entrepreneurial Development; Association for Corporate Growth; NC Entrepreneurial Association; NC Innovation Foundation. *Member:* The Florida Bar; North Carolina State Bar. ***PRACTICE AREAS:*** Business; Corporate Finance; Securities; Venture Capital; Mergers and Acquisitions. ***Email:*** markmirkin@mvalaw.com

CHARLES L. MOORE, JR., born 1952; admitted to bar, 1987, North Carolina; 1991, Ohio; registered to practice before U.S. Patent and Trademark Office. *Education:* University of Memphis (B.S.E.E., 1973; J.D., 1986); Ohio State University (M.S.E.E., 1975; M.B.A., 1977). ***PRACTICE AREAS:*** Intellectual Property. ***Email:*** chuckmoore@mvalaw.com

STEVEN B. PHILLIPS, born 1962; admitted to bar, 1993, North Carolina; registered to practice before U.S. Patent and Trademark Office. *Education:* University of Pennsylvania (B.S.E., 1984); North Carolina Central University (J.D., magna cum laude, 1993). ***PRACTICE AREAS:*** Intellectual Property. ***Email:*** stevenphilips@mvalaw.com

JAMES M. TATUM, JR., born 1947; admitted to bar, 1974, North Carolina. *Education:* University of North Carolina (B.A., 1970; J.D., 1974). Morehead Scholar. ***PRACTICE AREAS:*** Corporate; Commercial; Banking; Construction; Airport Law. ***Email:*** jimtatum@mvalaw.com

REICH L. WELBORN, born 1945; admitted to bar, 1971, North Carolina. *Education:* University of North Carolina (A.B., 1968; J.D., with honors, 1971). Order of the Coif. Board of Editors, North Carolina Law Review, 1969-1971. President, Fourteenth Judicial District Bar, 1989-1990. President, Durham County Bar Association, 1989-1990. ***PRACTICE AREAS:*** Health Care; Corporate; Finance. ***Email:*** reichwelborn@mvalaw.com

JEFFREY M. YOUNG, born 1969; admitted to bar, 1994, North Carolina. *Education:* Appalachian State University (B.A., 1991); Vanderbilt University (J.D., 1994). (Also at Raleigh Office). ***PRACTICE AREAS:*** Construction. ***Email:*** jeffyoung@mvalaw.com

RESIDENT OF COUNSEL

E. K. POWE, born 1921; admitted to bar, 1950, North Carolina. *Education:* University of North Carolina (A.B., 1948; J.D., 1950). Representative, North Carolina General Assembly, 1955-1957. North Carolina General Statutes Commission, 1956-1960. Adjunct Professor of Estate Planning, Duke University Law School, 1972-1980. Visiting Lecturer, Estate Planning, School of Law, University of North Carolina, 1979-1981. North Carolina Judicial Standards Commission, 1981-1987. Chairman, North Carolina Appellate Rules Study Committee, North Carolina Bar Association, 1984-1987. President, North Carolina State Bar, 1979-1980. Panel of Arbitrators, American Arbitration Association. ***PRACTICE AREAS:*** Corporate; Securities; Fidelity and Surety; Finance. ***Email:*** ekpowe@mvalaw.com

RESIDENT COUNSEL

WILLIAM A. BARRETT, born 1966; admitted to bar, 1997, North Carolina; registered to practice before U.S. Patent and Trademark Office. *Education:* University of North Carolina, Asheville (B.A., 1994); Wake Forest University (J.D., 1997). Member, Glaxo Wellcome, Inc., Intellectual Property Department, 1996-1997. Member, Association of University Technology Managers. *Member:* North Carolina State Bar (Member: Biotechnology and Animal Patents Committee; Intellectual Property Section). [With U.S. Air Force, 1986-1991]. ***PRACTICE AREAS:*** Intellectual Property. ***Email:*** billbarrett@mvalaw.com

(This Listing Continued)

MICHAEL J. BYRNE, born 1969; admitted to bar, 1996, North Carolina. *Education:* University of Notre Dame (B.A., 1991); University of North Carolina at Chapel Hill (J.D., with honors, 1996). Articles Editor, North Carolina Law Review, 1995-1996. Law Clerk to the Hon. John B. Lewis, Jr., North Carolina Court of Appeals, 1997-1998. ***PRACTICE AREAS:*** Commercial Litigation; Professional Malpractice Defense. ***Email:*** michaelbyrne@mvalaw.com

KEVIN M. CAPALBO, born 1963; admitted to bar, 1988, Connecticut; 1989, New York; 1990, North Carolina. *Education:* University of Pennsylvania (B.A., 1985); Tulane University (J.D., cum laude, 1988). ***PRACTICE AREAS:*** General Business Litigation; Surety; Construction Litigation. ***Email:*** kevincapalbo@mvalaw.com

GUY R. DeCARLUCCI, admitted to bar, 2003, North Carolina. *Education:* Pennsylvania State University (B.S., 1991); Duke University (J.D., 2003). ***PRACTICE AREAS:*** Business Law; Health Care. ***Email:*** guydecarlucci@mvalaw.com

CHARLES L. EVANS, born 1964; admitted to bar, 1994, North Carolina; registered to practice before the U.S. Patent and Trademark Office. *Education:* North Carolina State University (B.S., cum laude, 1991); University of North Carolina at Chapel Hill (J.D., 1994). Board of Editors, North Carolina Journal of International Law and Commercial Regulation, 1993-1994. ***PRACTICE AREAS:*** Intellectual Property Law; Computer Law. ***Email:*** chuckevans@mvalaw.com

JOYCE W. JENZANO, born 1943; admitted to bar, 1996, North Carolina. *Education:* University of North Carolina (B.S., 1965; M.S., 1973); North Carolina Central University (J.D., magna cum laude, 1996). ***PRACTICE AREAS:*** Intellectual Property. ***Email:*** joycejenzano@mvalaw.com

ELLEN A. RUBEL, born 1961; admitted to bar, 1986, Illinois; 1988, Maryland; 1991, Pennsylvania; 2001, North Carolina. *Education:* University of Pennsylvania (B.A., 1983); American University (J.D., 1986). Recipient, American Intellectual Property Association's Trademark Examining Attorney of the Year, 1991. Staff Attorney, Office of the Assistant Commissioner for Trademarks, 1992-1996. *Member:* International Trademark Association. ***SPECIAL AGENCIES:*** United States Patent and Trademark Office, 1989-1996. ***PRACTICE AREAS:*** Intellectual Property. ***Email:*** ellenrubel@mvalaw.com

JENNIFER L. SKORD, born 1948; admitted to bar, 1980, Illinois; 1985, Indiana; 1994, North Carolina; registered to practice before U.S. Patent and Trademark Office. *Education:* Bradley University (B.A., 1970); DePaul University (J.D., 1980). ***PRACTICE AREAS:*** Intellectual Property. ***Email:*** jenniferskord@mvalaw.com

GREGORY STEPHENS, born 1966; admitted to bar, 1995, North Carolina; registered to practice before U.S. Patent and Trademark Office. *Education:* Virginia Polytechnic Institute and State University (B.S.E.E., 1988); Rutgers University (J.D., 1994). ***PRACTICE AREAS:*** Intellectual Property; Patent Prosecution. ***Email:*** gregstephens@mvalaw.com

DENNIS J. WILLIAMSON, born 1959; admitted to bar, 1990, Illinois; 2002, North Carolina; registered to practice before the U.S. Patent and Trademark Office. *Education:* University of Illinois (B.S.G.E., 1982); DePaul University (J.D., with honors, 1990). (Senior Patent Licensing). ***PRACTICE AREAS:*** Intellectual Property; Patent. ***Email:*** denniswilliamson@mvalaw.com

JOHN A. ZALOOM, admitted to bar, 1996, New York and U.S. District Court, Southern and Eastern Districts of New York; 2001, U.D. District Court, Northern District of New York and U.S. Court of Appeals, Third Circuit; 2003, North Carolina. *Education:* Texas A & M University (B.A., magna cum laude, 1991); University of Texas (J.D., with honors, 1994); University of London (LL.M., with merit, 1995). Phi Kappa Phi; Sigma Phi Epsilon. Recipient, Academic Excellence and Distinguished Student Award. Texas Environmental Law Journal. ***PRACTICE AREAS:*** Litigation. ***Email:*** johnzaloom@mvalaw.com

RESIDENT ASSOCIATES

SARAH E. BUFFETT, born 1974; admitted to bar, 2000, North Carolina. *Education:* Pennsylvania State University (B.A., cum laude, 1996); Université de la Sorbonne - Paris; Cornell Institute for Comparative Law, Cornell University (J.D., 1999). Executive Bench Brief Editor, Moot Court Board. Editor, LII-NY, Cornell Online Journal. ***PRACTICE AREAS:*** International; Corporate; Immigration. ***Email:*** sarahbuffett@mvalaw.com

DALE J. DAVIS, born 1970; admitted to bar, 2005, North Carolina. *Education:* Rochester Institute of Technology (B.S.M.E., 1996); North Carolina Central University (J.D., 2004). Order of the Engineer. RIT Scholar Fellow. *Member:* American Society of Mechanical Engineers. ***PRACTICE AREAS:*** Patents; Intellectual Property. ***Email:*** daledavis@mvalaw.com

JAMES W. DYMOND, born 1975; admitted to bar, 2000, North Carolina. *Education:* State University of New York at Albany (B.S., with high honors, 1997); University of North Carolina (J.D., with high honors, 2000). ***PRACTICE AREAS:*** Business Law. ***Email:*** jimdymond@mvalaw.com

JOHN E. SLAUGHTER, III, born 1971; admitted to bar, 1997, Virginia; 2001, North Carolina; registered to practice before U.S. Patent and Trademark Office. *Education:* Virginia Polytechnic Institute and State University (B.S., B.A., 1994); University of Virginia (J.D., 1997; M.S., Coursework, 1998). Founder, Virginia Journal of Law and Technology. ***PRACTICE AREAS:*** Intellectual Property. ***Email:*** johnslaughter@mvalaw.com

JAMES C. WHITE, born 1958; admitted to bar, 2003, North Carolina. *Education:* St. John's College (B.A., 1980); Duke University (M.A., 2003; J.D., 2003). Editor-in-Chief, Law and Contemporary Problems, 2002-2003. ***PRACTICE AREAS:*** Litigation. ***Email:*** jameswhite@mvalaw.com

MATTHEW W. WITSIL, born 1965; admitted to bar, 1999, North Carolina; registered to practice before U.S. Patent and Trademark Office. *Education:* University of Virginia (B.S., 1987); Old Dominion University (M.E., 1994); Duke University (J.D., 1999). ***PRACTICE AREAS:*** Intellectual Property; Patent Law. ***Email:*** mattwitsil@mvalaw.com

LEGAL SUPPORT PERSONNEL

A. KAY LANCASTER, (Office Administrator, Durham). ***Email:*** kaylancaster@mvalaw.com

REPRESENTATIVE CLIENTS: Client references furnished upon request.

MYERS BIGEL SIBLEY & SAJOVEC, P.A.

RESEARCH TRIANGLE PARK, NORTH CAROLINA

(See Raleigh)

Intellectual Property Law: Patents, Trademarks, Copyrights and related Litigation.

OLIVE AND OLIVE, P.A.

RESEARCH TRIANGLE PARK, NORTH CAROLINA

(See Durham)

Intellectual Property, Patent, Trademark, Copyright, Computer and Biotechnology Law and Related Litigation.

PINNA JOHNSTON & BURWELL, P.A.

RESEARCH TRIANGLE PARK, NORTH CAROLINA

(See Raleigh)

Corporation, Mergers and Acquisitions, Probate, Trusts, Real Estate Law, Taxation and Estate Planning, Wills and Trusts. General Civil Practice in all State and Federal Courts.

RAGSDALE LIGGETT PLLC

RESEARCH TRIANGLE PARK, NORTH CAROLINA

(See Raleigh)

General Civil Litigation and Administrative Law in State and Federal Courts and Agencies. Taxation, Estate Planning, Partnership, Landlord and Tenant, Real Estate, Insurance and Reinsurance Law. Corporate, Business, International, Environmental Law. Construction Law, Employment Discrimination and Administrative Hearings and Appeals.

SMITH, ANDERSON, BLOUNT, DORSETT, MITCHELL & JERNIGAN, L.L.P.

RESEARCH TRIANGLE PARK, NORTH CAROLINA

(See Raleigh)

Administrative Hearings and Appeals, Administrative Law, Admiralty and Maritime, Agricultural Law, Alternative Dispute Resolution, Antitrust and Trade Regulation, Appellate Practice, Asset Based Finance, Aviation and Aerospace, Bankruptcy, Banks and Banking, Biotechnology, Blue Sky Law, Business Law, Capital Markets, Civil Practice, Civil Rights, Closely Held Business Law, Collections, Commercial Law, Commercial Real Estate, Communications and Media, Complex and Multi-District Litigation, Computers and Software, Construction Law, Contracts, Copyrights, Corporate Law, Creditors Rights, Disabilities, Eminent Domain, Employee Benefits, Employment Discrimination, Employment Law, Energy, Environmental Law, Equipment Finance and Leasing, ERISA, Fidelity and Surety, Finance, Franchises and Franchising, General Practice, Government, Health Care, Hospital Law, Insurance, Insurance Defense, Intellectual Property, International Law, International Trade, Internet Law, Investments, Joint Ventures, Labor and Employment, Leases and Leasing, Legal Ethics and Professional Responsibility, Libel, Slander and Defamation, Litigation, Lobbying, Media Law, Medical Malpractice, Medicare and Medicaid, Mergers, Acquisitions and Divestitures, Mortgages, Nonprofit and Charitable Organizations, Mortgage Securitization, Partnership Law, Personal Injury, Premises Liability, Privatizations, Probate, Products Liability, Professional Liability, Property Law, Real Estate, Real Property, Regulatory Law, Secured Transactions, Securities, Taxation, Technology and Science, Torts, Technology Joint Ventures, Trade and Professional Associations, Trade Secrets, Trademark Infringement, Trademark Licensing, Trademark Litigation, Trademark Registration, Trademarks, Trusts and Estates, Utility Law, Wills, Workers Compensation.

STARK LAW GROUP, PLLC

RESEARCH TRIANGLE PARK, NORTH CAROLINA

(See Chapel Hill)

Construction, Commercial and Corporate Litigation. Personal Injury Litigation, Environmental Law, Computer and Intellectual Property Law, Corporate Acquisitions and Real Property Law, Real Estate Closings, Business Law.

THARRINGTON SMITH

RESEARCH TRIANGLE PARK, NORTH CAROLINA

(See Raleigh)

Civil and Criminal Trials and Appeals in all State and Federal Courts, Mediation and Alternative Dispute Resolution, Education Law, Constitutional Law, Employment Law, Family Law, Professional Licensure Proceedings, Personal Injury, Voting Rights, Local Government Law, Construction Contracts and Litigation, Business and Corporate Law, Commercial Litigation, Alcoholic Beverage Control Law, Administrative Law, Tax Litigation, Unfair Competition, Copyright, Legislative and Lobbying, Sports and Entertainment Law.

TWIGGS, BESKIND, STRICKLAND & RABENAU, P.A.

RESEARCH TRIANGLE PARK, NORTH CAROLINA

(See Raleigh)

Personal Injury, Products Liability, Business Torts, Medical and other Professional Negligence, Federal and State Tort Claims, Environmental Torts, Insurance Bad Faith, Aviation Law and Wrongful Death.

VANDEVENTER BLACK LLP

RESEARCH TRIANGLE PARK, NORTH CAROLINA

(See Raleigh)

General Civil Practice and General Litigation in State and Federal Courts, Trials and Appeals, Civil and Business Litigation, Public Utilities, Landline and Mobile Communications, Corporation, Cooperative, Non-profit Organizations, Mediation, Administrative, Social Security Disability (Raleigh office only), Admiralty, Arbitration and Mediation, Aviation, Banking, Bankruptcy and Creditors' Rights, Commercial Transactions, Community Associations, Construction Law, Environmental Law, Estate Planning, General Litigation in State and Federal Courts, Government/Public Contracts, Health Care Law, Immigration Law, International, Intellectual Property, Insurance Defense, Labor and Employment Law, Land Use, Local Government/Municipal Law, Malpractice, Maritime, Mergers and Acquisitions, Products Liability, Public Utilities, Real Estate, Taxation, Technology, Workers' Compensation.

VENTURE COUNSEL

RESEARCH TRIANGLE PARK, NORTH CAROLINA

(See Raleigh)

Venture Capital, Entrepreneurial Law; Corporate Law; Securities Law; Technology and Science.

WOMBLE CARLYLE SANDRIDGE & RICE

A Professional Limited Liability Company

2530 MERIDIAN PARKWAY, SUITE 400 (DURHAM), 27713

P.O. BOX 13069

RESEARCH TRIANGLE PARK, NORTH CAROLINA 27709

Telephone: 919-484-2300

Fax: 919-484-2340

Email: lawyers@wcsr.com

URL: http://www.wcsr.com

REVISER OF THE NORTH CAROLINA LAW DIGEST FOR THIS DIRECTORY.

Winston-Salem, North Carolina Office: One West Fourth Street, 27101. Telephone: 336-721-3600. Fax: 336-721-3660.

Raleigh, North Carolina Office: 2100 First Union Capitol Center, 150 Fayetteville Street Mall, P.O. Box 831. Telephone: 919-755-2100. Fax: 919-755-2150.

Charlotte, North Carolina Office: 3500 One Wachovia Center, 301 South College Street. Telephone: 704-331-4900. Fax: 704-331-4955.

Greensboro, North Carolina Office: 300 North Greene Street. Telephone: 336-574-8030. Fax: 336-574-4520.

Atlanta, Georgia Office: One Atlantic Center, 1201 West Peachtree Street, Suite 3500. Telephone: 404-872-7000. Fax: 404-888-7490.

Other Atlanta, Georgia Office: Suite 404, 2296 Henderson Mill Road, N.E. Telephone: 770-492-9030. Fax: 770-492-9609.

Washington, D.C. Office: Suite 700, 1401 Eye Street. Telephone: 202-857-4400. Fax: 202-467-6910.

Greenville, South Carolina Office: 700 Poinsett Plaza, 104 South Main Street, P.O. Box 10208. Telephone: 864-255-5400. Fax: 864-255-5440.

Tysons Corner, Virginia Office: 8065 Leesburg Pike, Fourth Floor. Telephone: 703-790-3310. Fax: 703-790-2623.

General Civil Practice, Trial and Appellate Litigation. Administrative, Antitrust, Aviation, Banking, Bankruptcy and Creditor's Rights, Bond Financing, Civil Rights, Commercial, Construction, Consumer Lending, Corporate, E-Commerce, Employee Benefits, Environmental, Estate Planning, Family, Government Relations, Health Care, Insurance, Intellectual Property, International, Labor and Employment, Municipal, Negligence, Probate, Product Liability, Real Estate, Retirement Plans, Securities, Taxation, Toxic Tort, Wills and Trusts Law.

FIRM PROFILE: Womble Carlyle Sandridge & Rice, PLLC, which traces its history to 1876, is a full-service law firm that delivers sophisticated and innovative legal services to a wide spectrum of business clients in industries that include information technology, health care, manufacturing, telecommunications and financial services. The Firm also represents a variety of governmental units and agencies.

Womble Carlyle's mission is to provide value to clients by combining professional skill, technology and a thorough understanding of clients' needs to deliver high quality, cost-effective and responsive service. The firm is comprised of approximately 470 lawyers and 838 staff members operating from offices in Atlanta, GA; Greenville, SC; Charlotte, Winston-Salem, Research Triangle Park, Raleigh and Greensboro, NC; Tysons Corner, VA and Washington, DC.

The Firm considers technology and the benefits it offers an integral part of the legal services it provides. All of the Firm's offices are linked for full communications by telephone, fax, electronic mail and video conference over a wide area network. The Firm takes full advantage of its sophisticated computer technology for support in large-case litigation, as well as management of complex transactions. The Director of Technology is responsible for implementing existing systems, and in some instances, developing new software applications to meet specific client needs. The firm-wide communications and computer network permit the Firm to allocate resources from all offices, as needed, as well as to establish direct, secure links with clients and their legal departments, thus enhancing the responsiveness and efficiency of the Firm's lawyers.

The lawyers of Womble Carlyle have traditionally been active in community affairs, in Bar and other professional activities, and in state government. Many lawyers assume leading roles in civic and professional organizations, and several have served the government in elected or appointed positions.

LAW FIRM ALLIANCES/ASSOCIATIONS: **TOLEDO CONFERENCE GROUP**

(This Listing Continued)

WOMBLE CARLYLE SANDRIDGE & RICE, Research Triangle Park—Continued

LEX MUNDI

RESIDENT MEMBERS

M. CHRISTOPHER BOLEN, born Fort Worth, Texas, December 26, 1958; admitted to bar, 1985, Texas; 1988, North Carolina and U.S. District Court, Middle District of North Carolina. *Education:* Southern Methodist University (B.S. Engineering Management, summa cum laude, 1981; M.B.A., 1985; J.D., 1985). Order of the Coif; Phi Delta Phi; Tau Beta Pi. Assistant Editor-in-Chief, Southwestern Law Journal, 1984-1985. Member, North Carolina's "Legal Elite," named by Business North Carolina Magazine, January, 2002. Co-chair, International Trademark Association 2003 Trademark Administrator's Forum, "Negotiating the Intellecutal Property Provisions of Acquistion Agreements," Faculty for International Trademark Associations's Trademarks in Business Trasactions Forum, February 2002. Faculty for North Carolina Bar Association Seminar "Legal Guide to Cyberland: Computer Law for the Business Lawyer," Topic: "Understanding and Negotiating the Software License Agreement," February, 1999; "When Scandal Becomes Vogue," Faculty for International Trademark Association 1998 Mid-Year Meeting; Faculty for North Carolina Bar Association Seminar at Business Law Annual Meeting, "Intellectual Property Due Diligence in Mergers and Acquisitions," February, 1998; Faculty for North Carolina Bar Association Seminar at Business Law Section Annual Meeting, "Legal Potholes on the Information Superhighway: Trademark and Copyright Issues in Marketing on the Internet," February, 1996, June, 1997; Faculty for North Carolina Bar Association Seminar on Intellectual Property Law; Topic: "Copyright Law Basics," May, 1994; Faculty for Computer Law Association Seminar "Representing the Technology Client," Topic: "Advanced Trademark and Trade Dress Issues in Software Distribution," February, 1994; Faculty for North Carolina Foundation Seminar Intellectual Property for the Business Lawyer; Topic: "Technology Licensing," November, 1988. Board of Trustees, Lutheran Family Services in the Carolinas, 1994-2000, 2001—; Board of Directors, Council for Entrepeneurial Development, 1993-1994, 1995-1996; Vice Chair, Intellectual Property Section, North Carolina Bar Association. *Member:* North Carolina Bar Association (Member, Section on Intellectual Property Law); North Carolina State Bar; State Bar of Texas; Computer Law Association; International Trademark Association. ***PRACTICE AREAS:*** Technology and Computer Software Licensing; Trademarks; Copyrights. ***Email:*** cbolen@wcsr.com

JOHN J. BOWERS, born Poughkeepsie, New York, June 8, 1963; admitted to bar, 1993, New York and U.S. District Court, Southern and Eastern Districts of New York; 1997, North Carolina and U.S. District Court, Middle and Eastern Districts of North Carolina. *Education:* Rensselaer Polytechnic Institute (B.S., 1985); Duke University (J.D., 1992; M.B.A., 1992). *Member:* Forsyth County, North Carolina, New York State and American Bar Associations. ***PRACTICE AREAS:*** Litigation. ***Email:*** jbowers@wcsr.com

DAVID S. BRADIN, born Philadelphia, Pennsylvania, July 19, 1964; admitted to bar, 1995, Georgia; 1999, North Carolina; registered to practice before U.S. Patent and Trademark Office. *Education:* Wittenberg University (B.A., 1986); The Ohio State University (M.S., 1989); Rutgers University Law School, Camden (J.D., 1994). Recipient, Jurisprudence Award in Criminal Law. *Member:* State Bar of Georgia (Member, Intellectual Property Section); American and North Carolina (Member, Intellectual Property Section) Bar Associations; American Chemical Society; American Association for the Advancement of Science; American Intellectual Property Law Association. ***LANGUAGES:*** Spanish. ***PRACTICE AREAS:*** Intellectual Property. ***Email:*** dbradin@wcsr.com

LESLIE E. BROWDER, born Vicksburg, Mississippi, August 31, 1930; admitted to bar, 1954, North Carolina. *Education:* Duke University (A.B., 1952); Wake Forest University (LL.B., 1954). Phi Delta Phi. Best Lawyers in America, 1987-1998. Member, North Carolina Bankers Association, Attorneys Section, 1982—. Lecturer in Law, Wake Forest University, 1990-1992, 1997. *Member:* Forsyth County, North Carolina (Real Property, Construction Law, Environmental Law and Senior Lawyers Section) and American (Real Property, Probate and Trust Law Section) Bar Associations; American Judicature Society; National Association of College and University Attorneys. ***PRACTICE AREAS:*** Real Estate Development Law; Mortgage and Finance Law; Financial Institutions Law. ***Email:*** lbrowder@wcsr.com

KENNETH G. CARROLL, born Winston-Salem, North Carolina, February 1, 1952; admitted to bar, 1985, North Carolina. *Education:* Wake Forest University (B.A., 1982; J.D., 1985). Notes and Comments Editor, Wake Forest Law Review, 1984-1985. Recipient, James F. Hoge Award, 1984. *Member:* Durham County, North Carolina (Member, Business Section) and American (Member, Business Section) Bar Associations. (Managing Member, Research Triangle Park Office). ***PRACTICE AREAS:*** Acquisitions, Divestitures and Mergers; General Corporate Law. ***Email:*** kcarroll@wcsr.com

M. LEE CHENEY, born New Orleans, Louisiana, December 11, 1951; admitted to bar, 1983, Georgia; 1987, North Carolina; 1988, District of Columbia. *Education:* Harvard (A.B., cum laude, 1980); University of Virginia (J.D., 1983). Associate, American Board of Trial Advocates, 1997. Publications: L. Cheney, Legal Controversies in Nursing, 6(1) MEDICOLEGAL NEWS 18-19 (Spring 1978); M.L. Cheney and D.B. Mark, Medico-Legal Principles of Emergency and Intensive Medical Care, in ACUTE CORONARY CARE 1987, R.M. Califf and G.S. Wagner (eds.), Martinus Nijhoff Publishing, Boston; W.E. Brock Jr. and M.L. Cheney, seminar papers entitled Recent Developments in Liability Insurance Law Affecting Coverage for Environmental Pollution, June 1988, and Liability Insurance Coverage for Environmental Pollution, October 1988; M.L. Cheney, seminar paper entitled North Carolina Rules of Professional Responsibility Regarding Legal Assistants, April 1990; M.L. Cheney, Medicolegal Issues in Intervention Cardiology, in PRINCIPLES AND PRACTICE OF INTERVENTIONAL CARDIOLOGY, O'Neill, Roubin, Califf, Stack, Phillips, Churchill Livingstone, Inc., New York, N.Y.; M.L. Cheney and D.B. Mark, Medicolegal Aspects, in TEXTBOOK OF INTERVENTIONAL CARDIOLOGY, 2d Edition, E.J. Topol (ed.), W.B. Saunders Co., Philadelphia, P.A.; M.L. Cheney, Medicolegal Issues, in ACUTE CORONARY CARE 1992, Califf, Mark, and Wagner (eds.), Mosby-Yearbook, Inc., St. Louis, Mo.; M.L. Cheney, Medicolegal Considerations in Cardiovascular Medicine, in TEXTBOOK OF CARDIOVASCULAR MEDICINE 1997, 3d edition, E.J. Topol (ed.), Lippincott-Raven Publishers, Philadelphia, PA.; M. Lee Cheney, Medicolegal Issues in Interventional Cardiology in PRINCIPLES AND PRACTICE OF INTERVENTIONAL CARDIOLOGY, 2d edition, O'Neill, Roubin, Califf, Stack, Phillips, Churchill, Livingstone, Inc., New York, N.Y.; M.L. Cheney, Medicolegal Aspects, in TEXTBOOK OF INTERVENTIONAL CARDIOLOGY, 3d Edition, E.J. Topol (ed.). W.B. Saunders Co., Philadelphia, PA. (in press). *Member:* Wake County, North Carolina (Member: Medical Liaison Committee, Health Law Section; Litigation Section) and American Bar Associations; State Bar of Georgia; The District of Columbia Bar; The North Carolina State Bar; Defense Research Institute; North Carolina Association of Defense Attorneys (Member, Board of Directors, 1995-1998). ***PRACTICE AREAS:*** Civil Litigation; Products Liability; Medical Malpractice Defense. ***Email:*** lcheney@wcsr.com

NEILL EDWARDS, born Chapel Hill, North Carolina, January 20, 1968; admitted to bar, 1993, Georgia; 1999, North Carolina. *Education:* University of Virginia (B.A., with distinction, 1990; J.D., 1993). Phi Beta Kappa; Wagenheim Scholar; Echols Scholar; Golden Key. Listed in Who's Who in American Colleges and Universities. Author: "Building to Suit: Economic Development Makes for a Better Future," Southeast Real Estate Business, September, 2002; "Starting and Operating A Business in Georgia," PSI Research/Oasis Press, 1995; "Yucca Mountain, Or: How We Learn to Stop Worrying and Love the Department of Energy's High-Level Waste Disposal Guidelines," 12 Va. Envtl. L.J., 271, Winter 1993; "The Georgia Guide to Financing & Incentives," Georgia Center for Site Selection, 1996. *Member:* State Bar of Georgia; North Carolina State Bar. ***PRACTICE AREAS:*** Corporate; Economic Development; Multistate and Local Taxation. ***Email:*** nedwards@wcsr.com

CHARLES R. HOLTON, born Washington, DC, January 11, 1950; admitted to bar, 1973, North Carolina; U.S. District Court, Middle, Eastern and Western Districts of North Carolina, U.S. Court of Appeals, Fourth Circuit and the U.S. Supreme Court. *Education:* Abilene Christian University (B.A., summa cum laude, 1970); Duke University (J.D., with distinction, 1973). Panel of Arbitrators, American Arbitration Association. *Member:* North Carolina (Member, Construction Law Section) and American Bar Associations; Defense Research Institute; North Carolina Association of Defense Attorneys; Legal Aid of North Carolina; Braxton Craven Inn of Court; American Arbitration Association. ***PRACTICE AREAS:*** Products Liability Litigation; Professional Malpractice Defense; General Commercial Litigation. ***Email:*** cholton@wcsr.com

DEBORAH J. HYLTON, born Springfield, Missouri, May 20, 1958; admitted to bar, 1983, North Carolina. *Education:* Baylor University (B.A., magna cum laude, 1979); Duke University (J.D., with high honors, 1983). Phi Beta Kappa; Order of the Coif. Vice-President, Moot Court Board. Senior Editor, Law & Contemporary Problems, Duke University, 1982-1983. Listed in Best Lawyers in America, Corporate Law. Director, North Carolina Biosciences Organization. *Member:* North Carolina and American Bar Associations; NCBA Business Law Section Council; Past Chair, NCBA Securities Regulation Committee. ***PRACTICE AREAS:*** Mergers and Acquisitions; Securities Regulation; Corporate Law. ***Email:*** dhylton@wcsr.com

W. H. JOHNSON, III, born Durham, North Carolina, January 3, 1966; admitted to bar, 1994, North Carolina and U.S. District Court, Eastern District of North Carolina. *Education:* Duke University (A.B., summa cum laude, 1988); Duke University School of Law (J.D., with high honors, 1994); Fuqua School of Business, Duke University (M.B.A., 1994). Phi Beta Kappa; Order of the Coif. Fuqua Scholar. Author: "Proving a Criminal Predisposition: Separating the Unwary Innocent From the Unwary Criminal," 43 Duke Law Journal 384 (1993). *Member:* Durham County, North Carolina (Member, Business Section) and American (Member, Business Section) Bar Associations. ***PRACTICE AREAS:*** Corporate; Securities; Venture Capital Finance. ***Email:*** wjohnson@wcsr.com

FREDERICK W. ROM, born New York, N.Y., October 2, 1954; admitted to bar, 1979, New Jersey; 1983, Pennsylvania; 1999, North Carolina. *Education:* College of the Holy Cross (B.A. in Economics, cum laude, 1976); Boston College (J.D., 1979). Phi Beta Kappa; Omicron Delta Epsilon. Staff Member, 1977-1978 and Editor, 1978-1979, Uniform Commercial Code Reporter Digest, Boston College. *Member:* American Bar Association (Vice Chairman, Federal Practice Committee, Young Lawyers Division 1984-1985); North Carolina Bar Association; Wake County Bar Association; Defense Research Institute; North Carolina Academy of Defense Attorneys. ***PRACTICE AREAS:*** Civil Litigation; Product Liability. ***Email:*** from@wcsr.com

KENNETH N. SHELTON, born Burlington, North Carolina, September 4, 1956; admitted to bar, 1982, North Carolina. *Education:* University of North Carolina (B.S., with honors, 1978; M.B.A. and J.D., 1982). Phi Beta Kappa. Member, Board of Arbitrators, National Association of Securities Dealers, Inc., 1989-1999. *Member:* North Carolina (Chairman, Securities Regulation Committee, 1995-1997 and Business Law Section) and American (Member, Business Law Section) Bar Associations. ***PRACTICE AREAS:*** Securities Regulation Law; Corporate Finance; Venture Capital; Mergers and Acquisitions; Corporate Practice. ***Email:*** kshelton@wcsr.com

JACQUELINE TERRY, born Bronx, New York, June 30, 1965; admitted to bar, 1991, New York; 1992, New Jersey and U.S. District Court, Southern and Eastern Districts of New York; 1998, North Carolina. *Education:* State University of New York at Oneonta (B.A., 1986); Brooklyn Law School (J.D., 1990). Order of the Barristers. Executive Board Member, Moot Court. *Member:* Wake County, Tenth Judicial District, North Carolina and American Bar Associations. ***PRACTICE AREAS:*** Products Liability; Litigation. ***Email:*** jaterry@wcsr.com

F. BRUCE WILLIAMS, born Stamford, Connecticut, September 3, 1957; admitted to bar, 1988, Florida; 1991, U.S. District Court, Southern District of Florida; 1993, North Carolina, U.S. District Court, Eastern and Middle Districts of North Carolina. *Education:* University of South Florida (B.A., summa cum laude, 1984); Duke University (J.D., 1988). Phi Kappa Phi. Co-Author: "Burden Placed on Drug Manufacturers to Establish Exemption from Strict Liability for Prescription Products," Florida Bar Journal, October, 1991. Commissioner, North Carolina General Statutes Commission, August 1997- May 2001. *Member:* North Carolina and American Bar Associations; The Florida Bar; Defense Research Institute. [U.S. Army, 1975-1979]. ***PRACTICE AREAS:*** Litigation; Products Liability. ***Email:*** bwilliams@wcsr.com

(This Listing Continued)

RESIDENT ASSOCIATES

DAVID B. BADDOUR, born Chapel Hill, North Carolina, 1973; admitted to bar, 2002, North Carolina. *Education:* University of North Carolina (A.B., 1995; J.D., high honors, 2002). *Member:* North Carolina State Bar (Member, Young Lawyers Division). ***PRACTICE AREAS:*** Corporate Law; Securities. ***Email:*** dbaddour@wcsr.com

G. CAROL BRANI, admitted to bar, 2000, North Carolina and U.S. District Court, Middle District of North Carolina; U.S. Court of Appeals, Fourth Circuit. *Education:* University of Virginia (B.A., Psychology and English, 1983); Washington & Lee University (J.D., 2000). Judicial Clerk, Honorable Judge Willett & Judge Strickland, 23rd Judicial Circuit, Roanoke, Virginia, 1998-1999; Clerk, Hunton & Williams, Richmond, Virginia, 1998. Paralegal, Jones, Day, Reavis & Pogue, Washington, DC, 1995-1997; Litigation Support, Temps & Co., Washington, DC, 1995. District Manager, Lillie Rubin Affiliates, Washington, DC, 1991-1994. Author: Civil Rights and Mortgage Lending Discrimination, Race and Ethnic Ancestry Law Journal (Spring 1999). *Member:* North Carolina (Member, Antitrust Section) and American (Member, Sections on: Antitrust; Franchises) Bar Associations; Forsyth County Young Lawyers Association. ***PRACTICE AREAS:*** Intellectual Property Licensing; Promotion Law; Sweepstakes; Antitrust; Franchise Law; Dealership Law. ***Email:*** cbrani@wcsr.com

RICHARD J. CAIRA, JR., born Poughkeepsie, New York, June 19, 1969; admitted to bar, 1998, North Carolina; U.S. District Court, Eastern and Middle Districts of North Carolina. *Education:* Flagler College (B.A., 1991); Franklin Pierce Law Center (J.D., 1998). Law Clerk, SAS Institute Inc., Cary, NC, 1997. Legal Intern, National Public Radio, Inc., Washington, DC, 1997. Member, Franklin Pierce Law Journal, 1997-1998. Business Editor, IDEA: The Journal of Law and Technology. Attorney: SAS Institute Inc., 2000-2004; Womble Carlyle Sandridge & Rice, PLLC, 1998-2000. *Member:* Wake County (Member, Sections on: Intellectual Property; Business Law), North Carolina (Member: Intellectual Property Section; Young Lawyers' Division; Chair, Pro Bono Committee, 2003—) and American (Member: Intellectual Property Section; Young Lawyers' Division) Bar Associations; North Carolina State Bar; Triangle Intellectual Property Law Association. ***PRACTICE AREAS:*** Intellectual Property; Intellectual Property Licensing; Computer Law. ***Email:*** rcaira@wcsr.com

SUSAN J. GIAMPORTONE, born Brooklyn, New York, December 21, 1963; admitted to bar, 1997, North Carolina. *Education:* New England College (B.A., 1985); Wake Forest University (J.D., 1997). *Member:* North Carolina State Bar; Federal and American Bar Associations; Defense Research Institute. ***PRACTICE AREAS:*** Pharmaceutical; Insurance; Government; Tort Litigation. ***Email:*** sgiamportone@wcsr.com

LEIGH R. JOHNSON, born Hopkinsville, Kentucky 1977; admitted to bar, 2002, North Carolina and U.S. District Court, Eastern District of North Carolina. *Education:* Centre College of Kentucky (B.A., Religion, 1999); University of Kentucky (J.D., 2002). Phi Delta Phi. ***PRACTICE AREAS:*** Corporate Law; Securities. ***Email:*** lejohnson@wcsr.com

GENE A. JONES, JR., born Charlotte, North Carolina, October 15, 1969; admitted to bar, 1997, North Carolina. *Education:* Davidson College (B.A., with honors, 1992); University of Edinburgh; Cambridge University; University of North Carolina (J.D., 1997). Managing Editor, North Carolina Journal of International Law and Commercial Regulation. Member, UNC National Moot Court Team. *Member:* Wake County Bar Association; North Carolina Bar Association; North Carolina State Bar. ***PRACTICE AREAS:*** Venture Capital; Mergers and Acquisitions; Securities; Corporate Law; Technology Law. ***Email:*** gjones@wcsr.com

KIMBERLY LICATA, born Washington, D.C., July 23, 1972; admitted to bar, 1996, North Carolina; 1997, District of Columbia. *Education:* University of Virginia (B.A., with distinction, 1993); University of North Carolina (J.D., with honors, 1996). Phi Delta Phi. Order of the Coif. Chancellor's Scholar; Echols Scholar. Staff Member, North Carolina Law Review, 1994-1995. Co-Author: "Perpetuities Reform in North Carolina: The Uniform Statutory Rule Against Perpetuities, Nondonative Transfers, and Honorary Trusts," 74 N.C. L. Rev. 1783, 1996; "Holding Decision Makers Liable: Assessing Liability under a Managed Health Care System," 51 Admin. L.Rev. 199, 1999. *Member:* North Carolina Bar Association (Member, Sections on: Health Law and Administrative Law); The District of Columbia Bar (Member, Sections on: Courts, Lawyers and Administration of Justice; Health Law); American Bar Association (Member, Sections on: Health Law, Government and Public Sector Lawyers Division; State and Local Government Law); American Health Lawyers Association; North Carolina Society of Health Care Attorneys. ***PRACTICE AREAS:*** Health Care; Products Liability; Complex and Multi-District Litigation. ***Email:*** kmartinez@wcsr.com

LEIGHTON P. ROPER, III, born Norfolk, Virginia, September 8, 1968; admitted to bar, 2000, North Carolina. *Education:* University of Virginia (B.A., 1990); Duke University (J.D., 1999). *Member:* North Carolina State Bar; North Carolina Bar Association; American Health Lawyers Association. ***LANGUAGES:*** Spanish. ***PRACTICE AREAS:*** Health Care; Corporate; Securities; Civil Litigation. ***Email:*** lroper@wcsr.com

PANKAJ KASHIRAM SHERE, born Queens, New York, January 30, 1975; admitted to bar, 2001, Georgia; 2002, North Carolina. *Education:* North Carolina State University (B.S., Zoology, 1997); University of Richmond, T.C. Williams School of Law (J.D., 2001). Order of the Barristers. Client Counseling and Negotiations Champion, 2001. *Member:* State Bar of Georgia (Member, Litigation Section); North Carolina State Bar. ***LANGUAGES:*** Hindi. ***PRACTICE AREAS:*** Medical Malpractice Defense; Products Liability; Business Litigation. ***Email:*** pshere@wcsr.com

MITCH TUCHMAN, born Passaic, New Jersey, July 17, 1945; admitted to bar, 2002, North Carolina. *Education:* Occidental College (B.A., 1967); Yale University (M.Phil., 1969; Ph.D., 1973); Stanford University Law School (M.L.S., 1997); Washington College of Law of American University (J.D., 2001). Phi Beta Kappa. Author: "Inauthentic Works of Art: Why *Bridgeman* May Ultimately Be Irrelevant to Art Museums," 24 Columbia-VLA Journal of Law & the Arts, 2001; Kelly v. Arrbia Soft: "The More Things Change...," August 13, 2002. ***PRACTICE AREAS:*** Copyrights; Trademarks; Publishing Law; Copyright Licensing; Trademark Licensing. ***Email:*** mtuchman@wcsr.com

(This Listing Continued)

RESIDENT OF COUNSEL

BRYAN C. BARTNIK, admitted to bar, 1994, North Carolina. *Education:* University of North Carolina (B.A., 1991); Ohio Northern University (J.D., 1994). ***PRACTICE AREAS:*** Products Liability Litigation. ***Email:*** bbartnik@wcsr.com

SUSAN M. EASTER, born Raleigh, North Carolina, December 15, 1964; admitted to bar, 1993, Virginia; 1996, North Carolina. *Education:* University of North Carolina at Chapel Hill (B.S.N., 1987); University of Richmond (J.D., 1993). Sigma Theta Tau; Phi Alpha Delta. Member, Moot Court Board. Manuscripts Editor, University of Richmond Law Review. *Member:* American Bar Association; Defense Research Institute. ***PRACTICE AREAS:*** Products Liability; Medical Malpractice Defense. ***Email:*** seaster@wcsr.com

GARTH A. GERSTEN, born Boston, Massachusetts, October 14, 1959; admitted to bar, 1986, California; 1998, North Carolina. *Education:* University of California, Berkeley (B.A., with distinction, 1981); Hastings College of the Law, University of California (J.D., 1986). Adjunct Faculty Member, Golden Gate University. *Member:* North Carolina Bar Association; State Bar of California. ***PRACTICE AREAS:*** Insurance Coverage; Litigation; Risk Management. ***Email:*** ggersten@wcsr.com

LAURA B. LUGER, born Scranton, Pennsylvania, June 14, 1954; admitted to bar, 1981, North Carolina; U.S. District Court, Eastern, Western and Middle Districts of North Carolina; U.S. Court of Appeals, Fourth Circuit; U.S. Supreme Court. *Education:* Bryn Mawr College (A.B., cum laude, 1976); Boalt Hall School of Law, University of California at Berkeley (J.D., 1981). Certified Mediator. *Member:* North Carolina Bar Association (Construction Law Section); Durham County Bar Association; 14th Judicial District Bar; American Arbitration Association National Panel of Arbitrators; North Carolina Association of Women Attorneys. ***PRACTICE AREAS:*** Construction; Labor and Employment; General Business Litigation; Technology and Commerce. ***Email:*** lluger@wcsr.com

STAFF ATTORNEY

KELLY I. GREEN, admitted to bar, 1996, North Carolina. *Education:* University of North Carolina at Chapel Hill (B.A., 1993); Wake Forest University (J.D., 1996). ***PRACTICE AREAS:*** Products Liability Litigation. ***Email:*** kgreen@wcsr.com

LEGAL SUPPORT PERSONNEL

Terry Michael Wiley (Executive Director)
Susan DeVore (Office Administrator - Atlanta)
Keith Tedrow (Office Administrator - Winston-Salem)
John E. Turlington (Office Administrator - Research Triangle Park and Raleigh)
Cheri Edwards (Office Administrator - Tysons Corner, VA)
Patricia A. Kight (Director of Human Resources)
Charles R. Allison, III (Office Administrator - Charlotte)
John T. Boyer (Office Administrator - Washington, DC)
Hails Foster (Director of Finance and Systems)
Mark Whitley (Director, Strategic Planning and Marketing)
Julie D. Beavers (Professional Development/Recruiting Administrator - Research Triangle Park and Raleigh)
Cynthia K. Pruitt (Professional Development/Recruiting Administrator - Winston-Salem and Greensboro)
Kristin F. Carretta (Director of Professional Development and Recruiting)
Elizabeth P. Keasler (Professional Development/Recruiting Administrator - Charlotte and Greenville, SC)
Stacy H. Stephens (Professional Development/Recruiting Administrator - Atlanta)
Barbara Fountain (Office Manager - Greenville)
Melissa B. Weaver (Office Manager/Billing Coordinator - Greensboro)

GENERAL COUNSEL FOR: Brenner Companies; Charles & Colvard, Ltd.; Inmar Enterprises, Inc.; NC Biosciences Industry Organization; Piedmont Federal Savings & Loan Assn.; RF Micro Devices, Inc.; Venture First Associates.
REPRESENTATIVE CLIENTS: Alsco Metals Corporation; Amarr Company; American Honda Motor Co., Inc.; Bank of America Corporation; BB&T Corporation; Carolinas HealthCare System; Charles & Colvard, Ltd.; Cisco Systems, Inc.; Dow Reichhold Specialty Latex LLC; Duke University; Duke University Health System; Genentech, Inc.; GlaxoSmithKline; Jefferson-Pilot Life Insurance Company; KIA Motors America, Inc.; Lowes Companies, Inc.; Magneti Marelli USA, Inc.; Medtronic, Inc.; Microfibres, Inc.; Motricity, Inc.; North Carolina Association of County Commissioners; Novartis AG; Porsche Cars North America, Inc.; Red Hat, Inc.; Research Triangle Institute; RJ Reynolds Tobacco Company; SAS Institute Inc.; Sto Corp.; Targacept, Inc.; The Forestland Group; The Travelers Insurance Companies; University of North Carolina Health Care System; Wachovia Bank, National Association; Wake Forest University; Wake Forest University Baptist Medical Center; WakeMed; West Pharmaceutical Services, Inc.

REVISER OF THE NORTH CAROLINA LAW DIGEST FOR THIS DIRECTORY.

(For Biographical Data on other Personnel, see Professional Biographies at Winston-Salem, Charlotte, Raleigh, North Carolina, Atlanta, Georgia, Washington, D.C., Greenville, South Carolina and Tysons Corner, Virginia)

WYRICK ROBBINS YATES & PONTON LLP

RESEARCH TRIANGLE PARK, NORTH CAROLINA

(See Raleigh)

Appellate Advocacy, Arbitration, Banking, Bankruptcy and Workouts, Biotechnology, Broker-Dealer/Investment Advisor Compliance and Defense, Business, Commercial Contracts and Litigation, Commercial Real Estate, Communications, Community Associations, Computer, Construction, Copyright Licensing, Litigation and Registration, Corporate, Corporate Finance, Credit Union, Creditors Rights, Elder, Election Law, Employee Benefits, Employment, Entrepreneurial Business Law, Environmental, Estate Planning and Probate, Family Law, Franchise, Government Contracting, Health, Intellectual Property Protection and Licensing, Internet and E-Commerce, Labor, Litigation in all State and Federal Courts, Mediation, Mergers, Acquisitions and Divestitures, Municipal, Partnerships and LLC's, Private Placements, Public Offerings, Securities Arbitrations and Mediations, Securities Law, Strategic Partnerships and Collaborations, Taxation, Tax-Exempt and Non-Profit Organizations, Technology and Venture Capital Law.

VICTOR H.E. MORGAN, JR.
ATTORNEY AT LAW

RICHLANDS, NORTH CAROLINA

(See Jacksonville)

Personal Injury, Auto Accidents, Workers' Compensation, Social Security Disability, Domestic Relations, Divorce, Criminal, Traffic Violations, DWI.

WILLIAM J. MORGAN, P.A.

RICHLANDS, NORTH CAROLINA

(See Jacksonville)

Personal Injury Law, General Civil Litigation, Medical Negligence Law, Major Criminal Defense.

SAMUEL STUART POPKIN

RICHLANDS, NORTH CAROLINA

(See Jacksonville)

Criminal Law, Traffic Violations, Juvenile Delinquency, Divorce, Negligence, Abuse.

BATTLE, WINSLOW, SCOTT & WILEY, P.A.

ROANOKE RAPIDS, NORTH CAROLINA

(See Rocky Mount)

Administrative, Alternative Dispute Resolution, Banking, Bankruptcy, Construction, Commercial, Corporate, Environmental, Estate Planning, General Trial and Appellate Practice in all State and Federal Courts. Health Care, Insurance, Insurance Defense, Labor and Employment, Local Government Law, Personal Injury, Probate and Estate Planning, Real Estate, Tax, Workers' Compensation.

CHICHESTER & WALKER

500 JACKSON STREET
ROANOKE RAPIDS, NORTH CAROLINA 27870
Telephone: 252-535-4477
Fax: 252-537-8060
Email: marsiglilaw@earthlink.net
URL: http://www.lawyers.com/marsiglilaw
Mailing Address: P.O. Box 8574, Rocky Mount, NC 27804

Rocky Mount Office: 105 Candlewood Road, Suite A, P.O. Box 8574, 27804. Telephone: 252-451-4055. Fax: 252-451-4088.

Criminal Defense, Drug Crimes, Felonies, Misdemeanors, Traffic Violations, Driving While Intoxicated, Personal Injury, Automobile Accidents, Slip and Falls, Worker's Compensation, Wrongful Death, General Practice.

FIRM PROFILE: Serving clients for nearly 30 years, Chichester & Walker offers a variety of legal services with the professionalism and courtesy that one should expect from his or her attorney. Our attorneys strive to protect your interests and help you through almost any legal issue. Contact one of our offices today to have a free consultation with one of our attorneys.

GILBERT W. CHICHESTER, born Halifax County, North Carolina, January 5, 1947; admitted to bar, 1975, Virginia; 1977, North Carolina. *Education:* North Carolina Wesleyan (B.A., 1972); University of Richmond (J.D., 1974). *Member:* North Carolina State Bar; Virginia State Bar; North Carolina Bar Association; North Carolina Academy of Trial Lawyers; Virginia Trial Lawyers Association. ***PRACTICE AREAS:*** Personal Injury; Criminal Law; General Practice. ***Email:*** chiwalklaw@coastalnet.com

JAMES E. PASCHAL WALKER, born Richmond, Virginia, March 31, 1967; admitted to bar, 1992, North Carolina. *Education:* East Carolina University (B.A., cum laude, 1989); Wiggins, Norman A., School of Law (J.D., 1992). *Member:* Halifax County and North Carolina Bar Associations; North Carolina State Bar; North Carolina Academy of Trial Lawyers. ***PRACTICE AREAS:*** Criminal Law; Domestic Relations; Personal Injury; Worker's Compensation; Traffic Violations.

THE DALTON LAW FIRM, P.A.

ROANOKE RAPIDS, NORTH CAROLINA

(See Raleigh)

Elder Law, Medicaid Planning, Estate Planning, Asset Protection, Wills, Probate, Trusts, Collaborative Law, Elder Law Mediation.

JANET B. DUDLEY
ATTORNEY AT LAW

ROANOKE RAPIDS, NORTH CAROLINA

(See Scotland Neck)

Family Law, Divorce, Adoption Law, Child Custody, Child Support, Domestic Violence, Visitation Rights, Traffic Violations, Consumer Fraud, Warranties.

HUX, LIVERMON & ARMSTRONG, L.L.P.

ROANOKE RAPIDS, NORTH CAROLINA

(See Enfield)

General Practice. Criminal including DWI, Traffic Offenses, and Civil Trials in all Courts. Wills and Probate, Trusts and Estates, Corporation, Insurance and Real Property Law, Personal Injury, Automobile Accidents, Family Law.

JAMES, WELLMAN & WHITE

644 ROANOKE AVENUE
P.O. BOX 2018
ROANOKE RAPIDS, NORTH CAROLINA 27870
Telephone: 252-535-4545
Fax: 252-535-5959
Email: jwwrrlaw@charter.net

General Civil Trial Practice in State and Federal Courts. Personal Injury, Corporation, Real Estate, Probate, Trust, Estates, Bankruptcy Law.

MEMBERS OF FIRM

JOHN A. JAMES (1923-1988)

THOMAS H. WELLMAN, born Durham, North Carolina, November 17, 1950; admitted to bar, 1976, North Carolina. *Education:* University of North Carolina at Chapel Hill (A.B., Phi Beta Kappa, 1973; J.D., 1976). *Member:* Halifax County and North Carolina Bar Associations; North Carolina State Bar. ***PRACTICE AREAS:*** Real Estate Law; Probate Law; Trusts Law; Estates Law; Wills; Corporate Law; Municipal Law. ***Email:*** thwellman@charter.net

WILLIAM O. WHITE, JR., born Lumberton, North Carolina, September 25, 1948; admitted to bar, 1974, North Carolina; U.S. District Court, Eastern, Middle and Western Districts of North Carolina; 1988, U.S. Court of Appeals, Fourth Circuit. *Education:* Guilford College (A.B., 1970); University of North Carolina at Chapel Hill (J.D., 1974). Phi Delta Phi. *Member:* Halifax County, North Carolina and American Bar Associations; North Carolina State Bar. ***PRACTICE AREAS:*** Corporation Law; Real Estate Law; Personal Injury Law; Probate Law; Bankruptcy Law. ***Email:*** wowhite@charter.net

ASSOCIATE

HOLLY N. WILSON, born Roanoke Rapids, North Carolina, March 6, 1974; admitted to bar, 1999, North Carolina. *Education:* North Carolina State University (B.A., 1996); Campbell University (J.D., 1999). *Member:* Halifax County and North Carolina Bar Associations; North Carolina State Bar. ***PRACTICE AREAS:*** Real Estate; Estate Planning; Civil Practice. ***Email:*** hnwilson@charter.net

REPRESENTATIVE CLIENTS: Branch Banking and Trust Company; Coastal Lumber Company; Becker Mall Properties; Westmoreland-LGÆ Partners; Roanoke Rapids Housing Authority; Harris Development Co. of Wilson, Inc.; New Republic Savings Bank; Roanoke Valley Board of Realtors.
REFERENCES: Branch Banking and Trust Company; LandAmerica/Lawyers Title of North Carolina, Inc.

LAW OFFICE OF FRANKLIN L. JONES, JR.

ROANOKE RAPIDS, NORTH CAROLINA

(See Halifax)

Criminal Defense, Personal Injury, Workers Compensation.

The LeonLaw Firm

ROANOKE RAPIDS, NORTH CAROLINA

(See Greenville)

Employment Law, Personal Injury, Workers Compensation, Contracts.

MOSELEY, ELLIOTT & DICKENS, L.L.P.

928 ROANOKE AVENUE
ROANOKE RAPIDS, NORTH CAROLINA 27870
Telephone: 252-537-3534
Fax: 252-535-3063
URL: http://www.med-lawfirm.com

Real Estate, Probate, Criminal Law, Misdemeanors, Traffic Violations, Domestic Relations, Family Law, Municipal Corporations, Corporate Law, Civil Litigation.

MEMBERS OF THE FIRM

WENDELL C. MOSELEY, born Roanoke Rapids, North Carolina, February 27, 1938; admitted to bar, 1963, North Carolina. *Education:* University of North Carolina at Chapel Hill (B.S., 1960; B.L., 1963). Phi Alpha Delta. *Member:* Halifax County and North Carolina Bar Associations; North Carolina State Bar; North Carolina Academy of Trial Lawyers. ***PRACTICE AREAS:*** Real Estate (30%); Probate (20%); Criminal Law (15%); Traffic Violations; Domestic Relations (15%); Family Law (20%).

BRADLEY A. ELLIOTT, born Norfolk, Virginia, July 30, 1953; admitted to bar, 1981, North Carolina; 1986, U.S. Supreme Court. *Education:* Virginia Wesleyan College (B.A., 1975); Campbell University (J.D., 1981). Delta Theta Phi. *Member:* Halifax County (Vice President, 1983) and North Carolina Bar Associations; North Carolina State Bar. ***PRACTICE AREAS:*** Real Estate (60%, 200); Probate (25%, 30); Municipal Corporation Law (10%, 20); Corporate Law (5%, 20).

(This Listing Continued)

WILLIAM F. DICKENS, JR., born Rocky Mount, North Carolina, October 7, 1941; admitted to bar, 1967, North Carolina. *Education:* Wake Forest College (B.A., 1964); Wake Forest University (LL.B., 1967). Phi Delta Phi. *Member:* Halifax County (President, 1969; Secretary, 1977-1983) and North Carolina Bar Associations; North Carolina State Bar. ***PRACTICE AREAS:*** Real Estate (30%, 45); Probate (10%, 12); Criminal Law; Misdemeanors (40%, 150); Civil Litigation (20%, 24).

RALPH G. WILLEY, P.A.

ROANOKE RAPIDS, NORTH CAROLINA

(See Rocky Mount)

Workers Compensation, Board Certified, Personal Injury, Civil and Criminal Trial Practice in all Courts, Traffic, Mediation, Arbitration.

CLODFELTER LAW OFFICE

ROCKINGHAM, NORTH CAROLINA

(See Wadesboro)

Criminal Law, Domestic, Family Law, Child Custody, Divorce, Personal Injury, Wrongful Death, Traffic Violations, Driving While Intoxicated.

LAW OFFICE OF JOHN R. DANIEL

501 EAST BROAD AVENUE
ROCKINGHAM, NORTH CAROLINA 28380
Telephone: 910-895-1929
Fax: 910-895-1996
Email: johndaniellaw@carolina.rr.com
URL: http://www.johnrdaniel.com

General Civil Trial Practice in all State and Federal Courts and Administrative Agencies. Personal Injury, Workers Compensation, Social Security Disability, Real Estate and Traffic.

JOHN R. DANIEL, born Erwin, North Carolina, August 27, 1952; admitted to bar, 1982, North Carolina and U.S. District Court, Eastern, Middle and Western Districts of North Carolina. *Education:* Western Carolina University (B.S., 1974); Campbell University (J.D., 1982). *Member:* North Carolina Academy of Trial Lawyers (Member, Workers Right Section). ***PRACTICE AREAS:*** Personal Injury; Workers Compensation; Social Security Disability; Real Estate; Traffic.

ASSOCIATE

JOHN W. ROEBUCK, JR., born Raleigh, North Carolina, January 28, 1971; admitted to bar, 2003, North Carolina. *Education:* University of North Carolina at Wilmington (B.A., 1993); Campbell Law School (J.D., 2003). ***PRACTICE AREAS:*** Criminal Defense; Traffic Violations; Employment Law; Family Law. ***Email:*** johnroebuck@carolina.rr.com

GORDON, HORNE, HICKS AND FLOYD, P.A.

ROCKINGHAM, NORTH CAROLINA

(See Laurinburg)

General, Civil and Criminal Trial Practice, Probate, Corporation, Real Estate, Personal Injury, Estate Planning, Social Security Disability, Workers' Compensation and Family Law.

POISSON POISSON & BOWER, PLLC

ROCKINGHAM, NORTH CAROLINA

(See Wadensboro)

PURCELL & GRISWOLD, LLP

ROCKINGHAM, NORTH CAROLINA

(See Laurinburg)

General Civil and Criminal Litigation, Health Care, Criminal Law, Traffic Violations, Personal Injury, Real Estate, Business Law, Wills and Estates.

BAKER, JONES, DALY, MURRAY, CARTER & DAUGHTRY, P.A.

Established in 1980

140 NORTH FRANKLIN STREET
P.O. BOX 68
ROCKY MOUNT, NORTH CAROLINA 27802-0068
Telephone: 252-442-1977
Facsimile: 252-442-5175
Email: rockymount@bjjlawoffices.com

Ahoskie, North Carolina Office: 304 W. Sunset Street, P.O. Box 986. Telephone: 252-332-2181. Facsimile: 252-332-8354.

General Insurance Defense Civil Practice. Trials. Real Estate, Estate Planning, Probate, Business, Personal Injury Defense, Professional Liability, Insurance, Workers Compensation and Collections.

REPRESENTATIVE CLIENTS: North Carolina Farm Bureau Mutual Insurance Co.; Nationwide Mutual Insurance Co.; Great American Insurance Cos.; Travelers Property Casualty Insurance Company; North Carolina League of Municipalities Co.; Orion Auto Insurance Co.; Grain Dealers Mutual Insurance Co.; Employers Mutual Insurance Group; Integon Insurance

(This Listing Continued)

Co.; Allstate Insurance Co.; Crawford and Co.; Universal Insurance Company; Erie Insurance Co.; Millers Mutual Insurance Co.; Claims Control, Inc.; Roanoke-Chowan Medical Practices; Town of Kelford; A. T. Byrum & Son, Inc.; Commercial Ready Mix Products, Inc.; Harrellsville Metal Works, Inc.; Georgia-Pacific Corp.; Transport Insurance Co.; Lawyers Mutual Liability Insurance Company of North Carolina; Rose Brothers Paving Co., Inc.
APPROVED ATTORNEYS FOR: Stewart Title; Chicago Title Insurance; Investors Title Insurance Company; First American Title Insurance Co.
REFERENCES: First Citizens Bank and Trust Co; Centura Bank.

(For Complete Biographical Data on All Personnel, See Professional Biographies at Ahoskie, North Carolina)

BATTLE, WINSLOW, SCOTT & WILEY, P.A.

Established in 1911

2343 PROFESSIONAL DRIVE
P.O. BOX 7100
ROCKY MOUNT, NORTH CAROLINA 27804-0100
Telephone: 252-937-2200
Telecopier: 252-937-8100
Email: battlewinslow@bwsw.com

Raleigh, North Carolina Office: 3737 Glenwood Avenue, Suite 100, 27612. Telephone: 919-573-1877. Facsimile: 919-573-1878.

Administrative, Alternative Dispute Resolution, Banking, Bankruptcy, Construction, Commercial, Corporate, Environmental, Estate Planning, General Trial and Appellate Practice in all State and Federal Courts. Health Care, Insurance, Insurance Defense, Labor and Employment, Local Government Law, Personal Injury, Probate and Estate Planning, Real Estate, Tax, Workers' Compensation.

FIRM PROFILE: Battle, Winslow, Scott & Wiley, P.A. is one of the oldest law firms in North Carolina, with the original partnership having been formed by Kemp D. Battle and Francis E. Winslow in 1911. The practice encompasses Eastern North Carolina, serving clients in a large geographic area. The firm provides a broad spectrum of the highest quality of legal services.

KEMP D. BATTLE (1888-1973)
FRANCIS E. WINSLOW (1888-1976)
HERMAN S. MERRELL (1908-1966)
ROBERT MASON WILEY (1925-1998)

J. BRIAN SCOTT, born Rocky Mount, North Carolina, August 11, 1927; admitted to bar, 1951, North Carolina. *Education:* Wake Forest College (LL.B., with honors, 1951). Phi Alpha Delta. President, Wake Forest Law Alumni, 1963-1965. Chairman, North Carolina State Board of Elections, 1969-1973. *Member:* Nash-Edgecombe County (President, 1967-1968), North Carolina (Vice President, 1987-1988) and American Bar Associations; American College of Trial Lawyers. ***PRACTICE AREAS:*** Civil Litigation; Federal Practice; Insurance; Insurance Defense; Personal Injury.

SAMUEL S. WOODLEY, JR., born Columbia, North Carolina, February 3, 1939; admitted to bar, 1963, North Carolina. *Education:* University of North Carolina (A.B., 1961; J.D., with honors, 1963). Phi Alpha Delta; Order of the Coif. Member, Board of Editors, University of North Carolina Law Review, 1962-1963. North Carolina Board of Law Examiners, 2004—. Court Approved Mediator. *Member:* North Carolina Bar Association; Defense Research Institute; North Carolina Association of Defense Attorneys (President, 1997-1998). [Judge Advocate with U.S.A.F., active duty, 1963-1966]. ***PRACTICE AREAS:*** Civil Litigation; Insurance; Insurance Defense; Personal Injury Defense; Product Liability Defense. ***Email:*** swoodley@bwsw.com

LEON HENDERSON, JR., born Washington, D.C., March 11, 1938; admitted to bar, 1964, North Carolina. *Education:* North Carolina State University (B.S., 1960); Wake Forest University (J.D., cum laude, 1964). Phi Alpha Delta. Chairman, Nash Law Library Committee, 1972-1985. Member, 1974-1981 and Secretary, 1974-1977, Nash County Board of Elections. Senior Resident Superior Court Judge, District 7A, 1989-1990. *Member:* Nash-Edgecombe (President, 1991), North Carolina and American Bar Associations. ***PRACTICE AREAS:*** Alternative Dispute Resolution; Business Law; Business Litigation; Commercial Real Estate. ***Email:*** lhendson@bwsw.com

MARSHALL AUBREY GALLOP, JR., born Elizabeth City, North Carolina, May 8, 1945; admitted to bar, 1975, North Carolina. *Education:* Duke University (B.S., 1967; Ph.D., 1971); Suffolk University (J.D., magna cum laude, 1976); Boston University (LL.M., 1977). Member, Suffolk University Law Review, 1975-1976. *Member:* North Carolina (Chairman, Litigation Section, 1989-1990. Member, Board of Governors, 1990-1993) and American Bar Associations; North Carolina Association of Defense Attorneys (Board of Directors, 2000-2003). ***PRACTICE AREAS:*** Arbitration; Mediation; Civil Litigation; Business Litigation; Labor and Employment; Insurance Coverage. ***Email:*** mgallop@bwsw.com

G. VINCENT DURHAM, JR., born Lexington, North Carolina, August 12, 1951; admitted to bar, 1976, North Carolina. *Education:* University of North Carolina (A.B., 1973); Wake Forest University (J.D., 1976). Phi Delta Phi. Member, Wake Forest Law Review, 1975-1976. Law Clerk to Judge David M. Britt, North Carolina Court of Appeals, 1976-1977. *Member:* North Carolina and American Bar Associations; North Carolina Association of Defense Attorneys; Counsel for Nash County. ***PRACTICE AREAS:*** Business Litigation; Local Government Law; Real Estate; Zoning and Land Use. ***Email:*** vdurham@bwsw.com

JOSEPH NEWTON CALLAWAY, born Clinton, North Carolina, July 23, 1958; admitted to bar, 1983, North Carolina. *Education:* University of North Carolina (B.A., 1980; J.D., 1983). Order of Barristers. Member, Panel of Chapter 7 Trustees for the United States Bankruptcy Court, Eastern District of North Carolina. Member: Holderness Moot Court; Invitational Moot Court Team. *Member:* North Carolina and American Bar Associations; National Association of Bankruptcy Trustees; American Bankruptcy Institute. (Board Certified Specialist in Consumer Bankruptcy Law and Business Bankruptcy Law, North Caro-

(This Listing Continued)

BATTLE, WINSLOW, SCOTT & WILEY, P.A., Rocky Mount—Continued

lina State Board of Legal Specialization). ***PRACTICE AREAS:*** Banking Litigation; Bankruptcy; Business Litigation; Debtor and Creditor Law. ***Email:*** jcallaway@bwsw.com

RANDALL B. PRIDGEN, born Rocky Mount, North Carolina, April 7, 1957; admitted to bar, 1983, North Carolina. *Education:* University of North Carolina at Chapel Hill (B.A., 1979; J.D., 1983). Phi Beta Kappa. Chairman, Nash County Planning Board, 2002. *Member:* Nash-Edgecombe District and North Carolina Bar Associations; 7th Judicial District and The North Carolina State Bar. ***PRACTICE AREAS:*** Business Law; Business Litigation; Communications Law; Wills; Probate Law; Commercial Real Estate. ***Email:*** rpridgen@bwsw.com

M. GREG CRUMPLER, born Fayetteville, North Carolina, December 6, 1958; admitted to bar, 1984, North Carolina. *Education:* University of North Carolina (B.A., with honors, 1981); Campbell University School of Law (J.D., cum laude, 1984). Member, Board of Editors, Campbell Law Review, 1982-1984. Law Clerk to: Justice Burley Mitchell, North Carolina Supreme Court, 1984-1985; Justice Louis Meyer, North Carolina Supreme Court, 1985-1986. *Member:* North Carolina and American Bar Associations; North Carolina Association of Defense Attorneys. ***PRACTICE AREAS:*** Appellate Practice; Civil Litigation; Insurance Defense; Workers Compensation.

W. DUDLEY WHITLEY, III, born Rocky Mount, North Carolina, November 18, 1960; admitted to bar, 1986, North Carolina. *Education:* North Carolina State University (B.A., 1983); Campbell University (J.D., 1986). Phi Alpha Delta (Justice, 1985-1986), Iredell Chapter. Campbell Law Observer, Campbell University Law Review, 1985-1986. *Member:* Nash County, North Carolina and American Bar Associations; North Carolina Association of Defense Attorneys. ***PRACTICE AREAS:*** Civil Litigation; Collections; Debtor and Creditor; Insurance Defense; Personal Injury. ***Email:*** deewhit@bwsw.com

J. McLAIN WALLACE, JR., born Elizabethtown, North Carolina, December 2, 1962; admitted to bar, 1988, North Carolina. *Education:* Wake Forest University (B.A., 1985; J.D., 1988). Phi Delta Phi (Magister, 1987-1988). Law Clerk to Judge Gerald Arnold, North Carolina Court of Appeals. *Member:* North Carolina and American Bar Associations; American Health Lawyers Association; North Carolina Society of Health Care Attorneys; Nash-Rocky Mount School Board. ***PRACTICE AREAS:*** Health Care; Hospital. ***Email:*** mwallace@bwsw.com

CURTIS L. BENTZ, born Jeffersonville, Indiana, December 3, 1950; admitted to bar, 1976, Ohio; 1992, North Carolina. *Education:* United States Air Force Academy (B.S., 1972); Case Western Reserve University (J.D., 1976); George Washington University (LL.M., in Labor Law, with highest honors, 1982). *Member:* North Carolina and American Bar Associations; North Carolina Association of Defense Attorneys. [U.S. Air Force, 1972-1992, Lt. Colonel (Ret.)]. ***PRACTICE AREAS:*** Civil Litigation; Federal Practice; Labor and Employment; Insurance Defense. ***Email:*** cbentz@bwsw.com

JACOB REID PARROTT, III, born Kinston, North Carolina, January 17, 1967; admitted to bar, 1992, North Carolina. *Education:* University of North Carolina at Chapel Hill (B.A., 1989; J.D., with honors, 1992). Phi Delta Phi. Member, University of North Carolina Holderness Moot Court Bench. *Member:* North Carolina and American Bar Associations. ***PRACTICE AREAS:*** Commercial Real Estate; Residential Real Estate; Foreclosures; Real Estate Secured Lending; Real Estate Development; Business Law; Collections. ***Email:*** jparrot@bwsw.com

KATHERINE WIGGINS FISHER, born Rocky Mount, North Carolina, June 27, 1967; admitted to bar, 1992, North Carolina and U.S. District Court, Eastern and Middle Districts of North Carolina. *Education:* University of North Carolina at Chapel Hill (B.A., 1989); Campbell University (J.D., 1992). Phi Alpha Delta (Secretary, 1991-1992). *Member:* North Carolina Bar Association; North Carolina Academy of Trial Lawyers; North Carolina Association of Defense Attorneys. ***PRACTICE AREAS:*** Civil Litigation; Family Law; Insurance Defense; Personal Injury; Criminal Law; Traffic Violations. ***Email:*** kwiggins@bwsw.com

---

A. SCOTT McKELLAR, born Winston-Salem, North Carolina, March 7, 1975; admitted to bar, 2001, North Carolina. *Education:* University of North Carolina at Chapel Hill (B.A., 1997; J.D., 2001). *Member:* North Carolina and American Bar Associations. ***PRACTICE AREAS:*** Bankruptcy; Commercial Litigation; Insurance Defense; Debtor and Creditor; Collections. ***Email:*** smckellar@bwsw.com

OF COUNSEL

THOMAS L. YOUNG, born Davidson County, North Carolina, August 8, 1930; admitted to bar, 1954, North Carolina. *Education:* University of North Carolina (B.S., 1952; J.D., with honors, 1954). Order of the Coif. Associate Editor, University of North Carolina Law Review, 1953-1954. *Member:* North Carolina and American Bar Associations. ***PRACTICE AREAS:*** Administrative; Commercial Real Estate; Corporate; Health Care; Hospitals.

THOMAS G. DILL, born New Bern, North Carolina, January 19, 1922; admitted to bar, 1947, North Carolina. *Education:* University of North Carolina (B.A., 1943; J.D., 1947). Phi Beta Kappa; Phi Delta Phi. Member, Board of Editors, North Carolina Law Review, 1946-1947. Prosecuting Attorney, Rocky Mount, 1950-1955. Representative, General Assembly, Edgecombe County, 1955, 1957 and 1959. *Member:* Nash-Edgecombe (President, 1959) and North Carolina Bar Associations; 7th Judicial District (President, 1965) and The North Carolina State Bar. [Lieut., (j.g.) U.S.N.R., 1943-1946]. ***PRACTICE AREAS:*** Wills; Probate Law; Business Law; Corporate Law; Commercial Real Estate Law.

GENERAL COUNSEL FOR: Nash County; Nash County Business Development Authority; Nash Health Care Systems; Rocky Mount Redevelopment Commission.
REPRESENTATIVE CLIENTS: Barcalounger; Bay Foods, Inc.; Boddie-Noell Enterprises, Inc.; Boseman Farms, Inc.; Branch Banking & Trust Company; Carolina Regional Orthopaedics, PA; Crown Carriers, Inc.; Eastern Carolina Broadcasting Company, Inc.; E-B Grain, Inc.; First Carolina State Bank; Lambert Properties, LLC; Lee Motor Company, Inc.; North Carolina Wesleyan College; RBC Centura Bank; Rocky Mount Recyclers, Inc.; Simmons & Harris, Inc.; Simmons & Harris Insurance Agency; Stretchlon Industries; Texas Steak, Ltd.
REPRESENTATIVE INSURANCE CLIENTS: Alliance Mutual; Atlantic Claims Service; Atlantic Risk Management; Bituminous; Canal Insurance; Commonwealth Dealers Life Insurance; Crawford & Company; Erie Insurance; Essex Insurance; Fireman's Fund; GAB; Galligher-Bassett Services; GMAC Insurance; Great American Insurance Group; Hanover Insurance; Infinity Insurance; John Deere; Kemper; Lawyers Mutual Liability Insurance Company of North Carolina; MSI; N.C. Farm Bureau; OrionAuto; State Auto Insurance Company; State Farm; United American Insurance; United Services Automobile Association.

(This Listing Continued)

LAW OFFICES OF W. THOMAS BOYD, JR., P.A.

ROCKY MOUNT, NORTH CAROLINA

(See Wilson)

Commercial Real Estate, Real Estate, Corporate Law, Business Law.

SHARON ROSE BRITT, P.L.L.C.

3210 ZEBULON ROAD
ROCKY MOUNT, NORTH CAROLINA 27804
Telephone: 252-451-4422
Fax: 252-451-4322
Email: srbattorneyatlaw@earthlink.net

Family Law, Divorce, Child Custody, Adoptions, Family Law Mediation.

SHARON R. BRITT, born Wayne County, North Carolina, March 16, 1964; admitted to bar, 1989, North Carolina. *Education:* University of North Carolina (B.A., 1985); North Carolina Central University School of Law (J.D., 1989). Seventh Judicial District Family Law Council. Board Certified, Family Law Mediator. *Member:* Nash-Edgecombe (Treasurer, 1992 and 1993) and North Carolina Bar Associations; North Carolina State Bar. ***PRACTICE AREAS:*** Divorce; Child Custody; Child Support; Adoption; Alimony; Equitable Distribution; Real Estate; Wills. ***Email:*** srbattorneyatlaw@earthlink.net

---

BRUMBAUGH, MU & KING, P.A.

Established in 1978

876 COUNTRY CLUB ROAD
ROCKY MOUNT, NORTH CAROLINA 27804
Telephone: 252-451-4090
URL: http://www.bmklaw.net

Practice Limited to Injury Cases. Automobile, Wrongful Death, Medical Malpractice, Workers' Compensation, Products Liability and Social Security Claims.

(For complete biographical data on all personnel, see professional biographies, Jacksonville, North Carolina)

CHICHESTER & WALKER

105 CANDLEWOOD ROAD, SUITE A
ROCKY MOUNT, NORTH CAROLINA 27804
Telephone: 252-451-4055
Fax: 252-451-4088
Email: marsiglilaw@earthlink.net
URL: http://www.lawyers.com/marsiglilaw

Mailing Address: P.O. Box 8574, Rocky Mount, NC 27804

Roanoke Rapids Office: 500 Jackson Street, 27870. Telephone: 252-535-4477. Fax: 252-537-8060.

Criminal Defense, Drug Crimes, Felonies, Misdemeanors, Traffic Violations, Driving While Intoxicated, Personal Injury, Automobile Accidents, Slip and Falls, Worker's Compensation, Wrongful Death, General Practice.

FIRM PROFILE: Serving clients for nearly 30 years, Chichester & Walker offers a variety of legal services with the professionalism and courtesy that one should expect from his or her attorney. Our attorneys strive to protect your interests and help you through almost any legal issue. Contact one of our offices today to have a free consultation with one of our attorneys.

JEFFREY A. MARSIGLI, born Chicago, Illinois, June 1, 1974; admitted to bar, 2003, North Carolina. *Education:* North Carolina State University (B.A., 1997); Campbell University School of Law (J.D., 2002). Phi Alpha Delta. *Member:* North Carolina State Bar; American Bar Association. ***PRACTICE AREAS:*** Criminal Defense; Drug Crimes; Sexual Abuse; Juvenile Criminal Law; Parole and Probation; Traffic Violations; Driving While Intoxicated; Personal Injury; Automobile Accidents and Injuries; Wrongful Death; Estate Planning. ***Email:*** marsiglilaw@earthlink.net

---

HAROLD D. COLSTON, P.A.

1701 SUNSET AVENUE
P.O. BOX 8446
ROCKY MOUNT, NORTH CAROLINA 27804-1446
Telephone: 252-985-1701
Fax: 252-985-1800
Email: hcolston@coastalnet.com

Practice limited to Real Property, Business and Commercial Law, Trusts and Estates, Wills and Probate.

HAROLD D. COLSTON, born Nashville, North Carolina, January 10, 1937; admitted to bar, 1967, North Carolina. *Education:* North Carolina State University (B.S.C.E., 1960); University of North Carolina (J.D., 1967). Delta Theta Phi. Member, University of North

(This Listing Continued)

Carolina Law Review, 1966. Registered Land Surveyor, North Carolina, 1963. Registered Professional Engineer, North Carolina, 1965. *Member:* North Carolina Bar Association.

JANET B. DUDLEY
ATTORNEY AT LAW
ROCKY MOUNT, NORTH CAROLINA

(See Scotland Neck)

Family Law, Divorce, Adoption Law, Child Custody, Child Support, Domestic Violence, Visitation Rights, Traffic Violations, Consumer Fraud, Warranties.

NILE K. "NICK" FALK

Established in 1983

SUITE 143, STATION SQUARE
ROCKY MOUNT, NORTH CAROLINA 27804
Telephone: 252-977-3577
Fax: 252-977-0762
Email: nkfalk@earthlink.net
URL: http://www.nickfalk.com

General Civil and Criminal Practice. Social Security Disability, Criminal Trials, DWI, Traffic Offenses, Personal Injury, Automobile Accidents.

NILE K. "NICK" FALK, born Des Moines, Iowa, July 31, 1947; admitted to bar, 1977, North Carolina; U.S. District Court, Eastern District of North Carolina. *Education:* University of Iowa (B.A., 1969); University of Richmond (J.D., 1977). Omicron Delta Kappa; Phi Delta Phi. *Member:* Nash-Edgecombe County, North Carolina and 7th District Bar Associations; North Carolina State Bar; Christian Legal Society; North Carolina Academy of Trial Lawyers. [Capt., USNR, active duty, 1969-1974; USNR-R, 1974-1994.]

REPRESENTATIVE CLIENTS: Standard Electric Co.; SE&M Constructors, Inc., Tharrington Industries, Inc.; Golden East Crossing; Westgate and Carrolton Nursing Centers; House of Lights, Inc.
REFERENCES: RBC Centura Bank; BB&T.

FIELDS & COOPER, PLLC

Established in 1959

422 SUNSET AVENUE
P.O. BOX 4538
ROCKY MOUNT, NORTH CAROLINA 27803-0538
Telephone: 252-442-3115
Fax: 252-442-4170

Nashville, North Carolina Office: 113 Court Street, P.O. Box 757, 27856. Telephone: 252-459-2121. Fax: 252-459-2123.

General Civil and Trial Practice in State and Federal Courts. Personal Injury, Creditor Bankruptcy and Collections, Construction, Corporate, Business Law, Contracts, Trusts, Estates, Wills, Probate, Real Estate, Commercial and Residential, Municipal, Land Use, Zoning, Traffic and Elder Law.

MILTON P. FIELDS (Retired)

ROY A. COOPER, JR. (Retired)

JOHN S. WILLIFORD, JR., born Kinston, North Carolina, June 4, 1948; admitted to bar, 1976, North Carolina. *Education:* University of North Carolina at Chapel Hill (B.A. with highest honors, 1970; J.D., 1976). Phi Beta Kappa; Phi Eta Sigma. Morehead Fellow. *Member:* North Carolina Bar Association; North Carolina State Bar; North Carolina Academy of Trial Lawyers. [Lieutenant, U.S. Navy Reserves, 1970-1973]. (Board Certified Specialist in Bankruptcy Law, North Carolina State Board of Legal Specialization). ***PRACTICE AREAS:*** Creditor Bankruptcy; Corporate Law; Construction Law; Commercial Law.

ELIZABETH H. FAIRMAN, born Raleigh, North Carolina, June 23, 1961; admitted to bar, 1986, North Carolina. *Education:* University of North Carolina at Chapel Hill (B.A., 1983); Campbell University (J.D., 1986). *Member:* North Carolina Bar Association; North Carolina State Bar; Commercial Law League of America. ***PRACTICE AREAS:*** Collections; Creditor Bankruptcy; Municipal Law.

MARK E. EDWARDS, born Greensboro, North Carolina, November 12, 1971; admitted to bar, 1997, North Carolina. *Education:* Wake Forest University (B.A., 1994; J.D., 1997). Omicron Delta Kappa; Phi Alpha Theta (President). Member: Student Government; Executive Council, Moot Court Board. *Member:* North Carolina and American Bar Associations; North Carolina State Bar; National Academy of Elder Law Attorneys. (Resident, Nashville Office). ***PRACTICE AREAS:*** Estate Planning; Estate Administration; Real Estate; Elder Law.

MARK C. OSTERHOUT, born Durham, North Carolina, September 8, 1961; admitted to bar, 1988, North Carolina. *Education:* Belmont Abbey College (B.A., 1985); Campbell University (J.D., 1988). Licensed Real Estate Broker, North Carolina, 1994. Former Assistant District Attorney. *Member:* North Carolina Bar Association; North Carolina State Bar; North Carolina Academy of Trial Lawyers. ***PRACTICE AREAS:*** Creditor Bankruptcy; Construction Law; Collections; Traffic Violations; Personal Injury.

MICHAEL D. GAYNOR, born Wilson, North Carolina, April 26, 1976; admitted to bar, 2002, North Carolina. *Education:* Campbell University (B.B.A., 1998; J.D., 2001). Phi Alpha Delta (Treasurer, 2000-2001).*Member:* North Carolina State Bar. (Resident, Nashville Office)

(This Listing Continued)

REPRESENTATIVE CLIENTS: RBC Centura Bank; U.S. Foodservice, Inc.; PYA/Monarch, LLC; Bennette Paint Mfg. Co.; Ihrie Supply Company, Inc.; Peoples Building Supply Co.; L&L Stores, Inc.; Barnes Farming Corp.; Dale Bone Farms, Inc.; Southern Loans, Inc.; Century Finance, Inc.; American General Finance; V.I.P. Management, Inc.; Barnette Properties, Inc.; Eastern Log Sales, Inc.; J&B Logging, Inc.; Towns of Bailey, Castalia, Middlesex, Nashville and Spring Hope.

HENSON & FUERST, P.A.

Established in 1971

2317 SUNSET AVENUE
P.O. BOX 7008
ROCKY MOUNT, NORTH CAROLINA 27804-2529
Telephone: 252-443-2111
Fax: 252-443-9429
Email: henson-fuerst@lawmed.com
URL: http://www.lawmed.com

Raleigh Office: 2501 Blue Ridge Road, Suite 390, 27607. Telephone: 919-781-1107. Fax: 919-781-8048.

Civil Trial Practice, Medical Malpractice Nursing Home Liability, Nursing Home Abuse and Neglect, Personal Injury, Automobile Accidents, Wrongful Death, Social Security Disability and Worker's Compensation.

FIRM PROFILE: Henson & Fuerst, P.A., since 1972 is a North Carolina law firm with principal offices in Raleigh and Rocky Mount. We limit our practice to nursing home abuse and neglect, health care negligence, personal injury, social security disability and worker's compensation. All of our lawyers are licensed to practice in North Carolina and are dedicated to helping injured people.

THOMAS W. HENSON, born Roanoke, Virginia, October 2, 1942; admitted to bar, 1967, North Carolina and U.S. District Court, Eastern District of North Carolina; 1972, U.S. District Court, Middle District of North Carolina and U.S. Supreme Court. *Education:* University of North Carolina (B.S.B.A., 1964; J.D., 1967). Phi Delta Phi. *Member:* North Carolina State Bar; The Association of Trial Lawyers of America; North Carolina Academy of Trial Lawyers. (Resident, Raleigh Office). ***PRACTICE AREAS:*** Medical Malpractice; Nursing Home Abuse and Neglect. ***Email:*** twh@lawmed.com

ROBERT L. FUERST, born New York, N.Y., July 22, 1948; admitted to bar, 1973, North Carolina; 1975, U.S. District Court, Eastern District of North Carolina; 1977, U.S. Supreme Court. *Education:* University of North Carolina (B.A., 1969; J.D., 1973); University of Wisconsin (M.A., 1970); University of Brussels, Brussels, Belgium (LL.M., magna cum laude, 1974). Author, "The Brazilian Territorial Sea," University of North Carolina, Sea Grant Foundation, N.O.A.A., U.S. Department of Commerce, 1972. Co-Author, "The Latin American Approach to the Law of the Sea," University of North Carolina, Sea Grant Foundation, N.O.A.A., U.S. Department of Commerce, 1973. *Member:* North Carolina State Bar; The Association of Trial Lawyers of America; North Carolina Academy of Trial Lawyers. (Board Certified Specialist in Family Law, North Carolina State Board of Legal Specialization) (Also at Raleigh Office). ***LANGUAGES:*** Spanish. ***PRACTICE AREAS:*** Nursing Home Abuse and Neglect. ***Email:*** bfuerst@lawmed.com

THOMAS W. HENSON, JR., born Chapel Hill, North Carolina, January 15, 1965; admitted to bar, 1989, North Carolina. *Education:* University of North Carolina (B.S.B.A., 1986; J.D., 1989). *Member:* North Carolina State Bar; The Association of Trial Lawyers of America; North Carolina Academy of Trial Lawyers. (Also at Raleigh Office) (Also Member, Grimes & Teich, Asheville). ***PRACTICE AREAS:*** Nursing Home Abuse and Neglect; Personal Injury; Wrongful Death. ***Email:*** thomashenson@lawmed.com

DAVID S. HENSON, born Rocky Mount, North Carolina, January 4, 1973; admitted to bar, 1998, North Carolina. *Education:* University of North Carolina (B.A., Economics, with distinction, 1995; J.D., 1998). Phi Alpha Delta. *Member:* North Carolina State Bar; The Association of Trial Lawyers of America; North Carolina Academy of Trial Lawyers. (Also at Raleigh Office). ***LANGUAGES:*** Spanish. ***PRACTICE AREAS:*** Personal Injury; Wrongful Death; Automobile Accidents and Injuries; Social Security Disability. ***Email:*** dhenson@lawmed.com

---

CARMALETTA L. HENSON, born Raleigh, North Carolina, January 24, 1974; admitted to bar, 1999, North Carolina. *Education:* University of North Carolina-Chapel Hill (B.A., Psychology, 1996); University of North Carolina School of Law (J.D., 1999). Phi Alpha Delta (Chapter Justice, 1998-1999). Member, North Carolina Journal of International Law & Commercial Regulation, 1997-1999. *Member:* North Carolina State Bar; North Carolina Academy of Trial Lawyers. (Also at Raleigh Office). ***PRACTICE AREAS:*** Personal Injury; Wrongful Death; Automobile Accidents and Injuries; Nursing Home Abuse and Neglect. ***Email:*** carma@lawmed.com

JOSEPH S. HODGIN, born Raleigh, North Carolina, October 31, 1976; admitted to bar, 2002, North Carolina and U.S. District Court, Eastern District of North Carolina. *Education:* Campbell University (B.A., 1999); Ohio Northern University (J.D., 2002). Member, Ohio Northern University Law Review. *Member:* North Carolina Academy of Trial Lawyers. (Also at Raleigh Office). ***PRACTICE AREAS:*** Personal Injury; Automobile Accidents and Injuries; Workers Compensation; Wrongful Death. ***Email:*** jhodgin@lawmed.com

OF COUNSEL

ANNE DUVOISIN, born 1951; admitted to bar, 1978, North Carolina. *Education:* Duke University (B.A., 1973); University of North Carolina at Chapel Hill (J.D., 1978). Formerly with Nursing Home Abuse Law Center. ***PRACTICE AREAS:*** Nursing Home Abuse and Neglect; Personal Injury; Automobile Accidents and Injuries; Wrongful Death. ***Email:*** duvoisin@lawmed.com

KELLUM LAW FIRM

3250 ZEBULON ROAD
ROCKY MOUNT, NORTH CAROLINA 27804
Telephone: 252-442-3975
Fax: 252-442-7309
Email: ckeenhold@kellumlawfirm.com
URL: http://www.lawyers.com/kellumlawfirm

State and Federal Civil Trial Practice, Personal Injury Law, Wrongful Death, Workers' Compensation, Social Security, Defective Products, Mass Torts and Insurance Law.

(For complete biographical data on all personnel, see Professional Biographies at New Bern, North Carolina)

KNOX, KORNEGAY & BENNETT, L.L.P.

Established in 1962
531 SUNSET AVENUE
ROCKY MOUNT, NORTH CAROLINA 27804
Telephone: 252-442-8037
Fax: 252-442-0052; 252-442-1540
Email: kkblaw@earthlink.net
URL: http://www.lawyers.com/kkblawoffice

Mailing Address: P.O. Drawer 7666, Rocky Mount, NC 27804-7666

General Civil and Criminal Trial Practice. Personal Injury, Wrongful Death, Family/Domestic, DWI and Traffic Offenses, Corporate and Business Law, Probate Law and Mediation.

HOWARD A. KNOX, JR., born Pittsburgh, Pennsylvania, November 8, 1936; admitted to bar, 1961, North Carolina. *Education:* University of North Carolina (B.A., 1958; J.D., 1961). Delta Theta Phi. Student Editor, North Carolina Law Review, 1959-1961. Member, National Directory of Who's Who in Executives and Professional. President, Seventh Judicial Bar Association (Nash, Edgecombe and Wilson Counties), 2004. *Member:* Nash-Edgecombe (President, 2005—) and North Carolina Bar Associations; Seventh Judicial District and The North Carolina State Bars; North Carolina Academy of Trial Lawyers; National Association of Criminal Defense Lawyers. ***PRACTICE AREAS:*** Personal Injury; Wrongful Death; Criminal Practice; Misdemeanors; Felonies; DWI; Traffic Violations; Contract Litigation. ***Email:*** kkblaw@earthlink.net

ROBERT D. KORNEGAY, JR., born Rocky Mount, North Carolina, January 13, 1948; admitted to bar, 1973, North Carolina. *Education:* Wake Forest University (B.A., 1970); University of Louisville (J.D., 1973). Delta Theta Phi. Research Assistant to Justice I. Beverly Lake, North Carolina Supreme Court, 1973-1974. Certified Mediator, North Carolina, 1995. Board Certified Mediator. *Member:* Nash-Edgecombe and North Carolina Bar Associations; Seventh Judicial District and The North Carolina State Bars; North Carolina Academy of Trial Lawyers. ***PRACTICE AREAS:*** Domestic; Civil Litigation; Business Law; Estates and Probate; Real Estate Law; Mediation; Personal Injury. ***Email:*** kkblaw@earthlink.net

SPIER L. (BUDDY) BENNETT, III, born Rocky Mount, North Carolina, November 26, 1953; admitted to bar, 1979, North Carolina. *Education:* University of North Carolina (B.A., 1976); Campbell University (J.D., 1979). Assistant District Attorney, Seventh Judicial District, North Carolina, 1979-1984. Member, Board of Directors, Triangle East Community Penalties, 1993—. *Member:* Nash-Edgecombe and North Carolina Bar Associations; Seventh Judicial District Bar; North Carolina State Bar; North Carolina Academy of Trial Lawyers. ***PRACTICE AREAS:*** Criminal Law; Driving While Intoxicated; Traffic Violations; Juvenile Criminal Law; Expungement; Personal Injury. ***Email:*** kkblaw@earthlink.net

MORRISON LAW FIRM, P.L.L.C.

ROCKY MOUNT, NORTH CAROLINA

(See Wilson)

Litigation, Collections, Workers Compensation, Personal Injury Law, Creditor Rights and Bankruptcy.

MICHAEL P. MURPHY, P.A.

Established in 2000
3072 - C SUNSET AVENUE
P.O. BOX 8738
ROCKY MOUNT, NORTH CAROLINA 27804
Telephone: 252-451-1200
Fax: 252-451-1201
Email: murphylawoffice@aol.com
URL: http://www.rockymountattorney.com

Commercial Collections, Wills, Trust Law, Estate Planning, Personal Injury, Automobile Accidents and Injuries, Truck Accidents, Bankruptcy Chapter 7, Bankruptcy Chapter 13, Corporate Law, Limited Liability Company Law, Business Law, Criminal Law, Traffic Violations.

MICHAEL P. MURPHY, born Lenoir, North Carolina, March 4, 1958; admitted to bar, 1991, North Carolina; 1992, U.S. District Court, Middle and Eastern Districts of North Carolina. *Education:* University of North Carolina at Chapel Hill (B.S., 1979); North Carolina Central University (J.D., 1989). *Member:* Nash/Edgecombe County and North Carolina Bar Associations; North Carolina State Bar. ***Email:*** murphylawoffice@aol.com

O'GARRO-MOORE LAW OFFICE

SUNSET TOWERS
164 ROUNDABOUT COURT
ROCKY MOUNT, NORTH CAROLINA 27804
Telephone: 252-443-1419
Fax: 252-443-1493
Email: ogarromoore@earthlink.net
URL: http://www.lawyers.com/ogarro-moore

Immigration Law, Criminal Law, Family Law.

MEMBER OF FIRM

CAROLYN O'GARRO-MOORE, born Curacao, Netherlands Antilles, November 2, 1956; admitted to bar, 1987, Pennsylvania; 2002, North Carolina and U.S. District Court, Eastern District of North Carolina. *Education:* Georgetown University (A.B., 1979); North Carolina Central University (J.D., 1987). *Member:* North Carolina Bar Association (Member, Family Law Section); American Immigration Lawyers Association. ***PRACTICE AREAS:*** Immigration Law; Criminal Law; Family Law. ***Email:*** ogarromoore@earthlink.net

POYNER & SPRUILL LLP

130 S. FRANKLIN STREET
P.O. BOX 353
ROCKY MOUNT, NORTH CAROLINA 27802-0353
Telephone: 252-446-2341
Telecopier: 252-972-7045
URL: http://www.poynerspruill.com

Raleigh, North Carolina Office: 3600 Glenwood Avenue, P.O. Box 10096, 27605-0096. Telephone: 919-783-6400. Telecopier: 919-783-1075.
Charlotte, North Carolina Office: One Wachovia Center, 301 South College Street, Suite 2300, 28202. Telephone: 704-342-5250. Telecopier: 704-342-5264.
Southern Pines, North Carolina Office: 135 West New Hampshire Avenue, 28388-0371. Telephone: 910-692-6866. Telecopier: 910-695-3036.

Comprehensive business and litigation practice including: Appellate, Arbitration, Banking, Bankruptcy/Creditors' Rights, Complex Business Litigation, Construction, Credit and Financial Services, Eminent Domain/Condemnation, Employment Benefits, Employment Practices, Entertainment Law, Environmental, Estate, Exempt Organizations, General Corporate, Governmental Relations, Health Care, Intellectual Property Law, International, Land Use and Zoning, Limited Liability Companies, Local Government, Mediation, Partnerships, Personal and Financial Planning, Probate, Product Liability, Professional Liability, Railroad, Real Estate, Regulatory and Municipal, Securities, Sports Law, Tax, Technology and Emerging Business, Tort Litigation and Insurance Defense, Transactional including Mergers and Acquisitions, Transportation, Utilities, White Collar Criminal Defense.

MEMBERS OF FIRM

MICHAEL S. COLO, born Chicago, Illinois, November 4, 1945; admitted to bar, 1970, Virginia; 1971, North Carolina. *Education:* University of North Carolina (A.B., 1967); Washington & Lee University (J.D., 1970). ***PRACTICE AREAS:*** Municipal Law (40%); Corporate Law (30%); Public and Corporate Financing Law (20%); Securities Regulation Law (10%). ***Email:*** mscolo@poynerspruill.com

RICHARD J. ROSE, born Rocky Mount, North Carolina, January 10, 1946; admitted to bar, 1972, North Carolina. *Education:* Davidson College (A.B., 1969); University of North Carolina (J.D., 1972). [1st Lieut., USAR, 1973]. ***PRACTICE AREAS:*** Municipal Law; Electric Utilities; Zoning, Planning and Land Use. ***Email:*** jrose@poynerspruill.com

SAMUEL W. JOHNSON, born Hamilton, North Carolina, September 9, 1947; admitted to bar, 1972, North Carolina. *Education:* Duke University (B.A., 1969; J.D., 1972). ***PRACTICE AREAS:*** Corporate Law; Business Law; Real Estate Law; Mergers and Acquisitions. ***Email:*** swjohnson@poynerspruill.com

KIM L. BAYLESS, born Painesville, Ohio, June 20, 1952; admitted to bar, 1977, North Carolina; 1978, Ohio. *Education:* Ohio University (B.B.A., cum laude, 1974); University of Toledo College of Law (J.D., 1977). ***PRACTICE AREAS:*** Business Law; Mergers and Acquisitions Law; Franchise Law. ***Email:*** klbayless@poynerspruill.com

DAVID M. WARREN, born Rocky Mount, North Carolina, August 1, 1959; admitted to bar, 1984, North Carolina; 2001, U.S. Supreme Court. *Education:* Wake Forest University (B.A., cum laude, 1981; J.D., 1984). ***PRACTICE AREAS:*** Bankruptcy Law; Commercial Law. ***Email:*** dmwarren@poynerspruill.com

RANDALL R. ADAMS, born Hamilton, Ohio, September 4, 1959; admitted to bar, 1985, Michigan; 1990, North Carolina. *Education:* Miami University (B.A., 1981); Wayne State University (J.D., 1984). ***PRACTICE AREAS:*** General Civil Litigation. ***Email:*** rradams@poynerspruill.com

J. NICHOLAS ELLIS, born Newport News, Virginia, April 3, 1960; admitted to bar, 1986, North Carolina. *Education:* Virginia Polytechnic Institute and State University (B.S., 1982); Wake Forest University (J.D., 1986). Certified Mediator, North Carolina. *Member:* North Carolina Association of Defense Attorneys (President, 2004-2005); Eastern North Carolina Inn of Court (President, 2005-2006). ***PRACTICE AREAS:*** Tort Litigation; Commercial Litigation. ***Email:*** jnellis@poynerspruill.com

STEVEN A. ROWE, born Bethesda, Maryland, November 10, 1962; admitted to bar, 1988, North Carolina. *Education:* Wake Forest University (B.A., 1985; J.D., 1988). ***PRACTICE AREAS:*** General Civil Litigation; Insurance Law; Employment Law; Workers Compensation; Housing Law. ***Email:*** srowe@poynerspruill.com

BRADLEY J. HERRING, born Tacoma, Washington, May 21, 1964; admitted to bar, 1989, North Carolina. *Education:* University of North Carolina (B.A., 1986); Wake Forest University (J.D., 1989). ***PRACTICE AREAS:*** Real Estate Law; Banking Law; Commercial Law. ***Email:*** bjherring@poynerspruill.com

(This Listing Continued)

GREGORY S. CAMP, born Charleston, South Carolina, September 15, 1966; admitted to bar, 1994, North Carolina; 1995, Florida. *Education:* University of North Carolina, Chapel Hill (B.A., cum laude, 1989); Duke University (J.D., L.L.M., with honors, 1994). ***PRACTICE AREAS:*** General Corporate Law; Mergers and Acquisitions; Appellate Litigation. ***Email:*** gscamp@poynerspruill.com

TIMOTHY WOOD WILSON, born Raleigh, North Carolina, March 18, 1968; admitted to bar, 1995, North Carolina and Georgia. *Education:* Duke University (B.S., 1990); University of Georgia (J.D., cum laude, 1995). ***PRACTICE AREAS:*** Civil Litigation; Insurance Defense; Eminent Domain; Products Liability; Personal Injury. ***Email:*** twilson@poynerspruill.com

RESIDENT ASSOCIATES

DEBORAH E. SPERATI, born Greenville, North Carolina, March 12, 1974; admitted to bar, 1999, North Carolina. *Education:* University of North Carolina at Chapel Hill (B.A., cum laude, 1996; J.D., 1999). ***PRACTICE AREAS:*** Civil Litigation; Commercial Workouts; Creditor Bankruptcy; Insurance Defense; Banking Litigation. ***Email:*** dsperati@poynerspruill.com

JAMES SHIELDS LIVERMON, III, born Rocky Mount, North Carolina, March 27, 1969; admitted to bar, 1999, North Carolina. *Education:* Hampden-Sydney College (B.A., 1991); Campbell University (J.D., 1999). ***PRACTICE AREAS:*** Bankruptcy; Creditors Rights. ***Email:*** jlivermon@poynerspruill.com

JENNY L. MATTHEWS, born Ahoskie, North Carolina, November 14, 1979; admitted to bar, 2005, North Carolina. *Education:* University of North Carolina at Chapel Hill (B.A., with highest distinction, 2002; J.D., with high honors, 2005). ***PRACTICE AREAS:*** Bankruptcy; Litigation. ***Email:*** jmatthews@poynerspruill.com

RESIDENT OF COUNSEL

FRANK P. MEADOWS, JR., born Macon, Georgia, December 20, 1927; admitted to bar, 1956, North Carolina. *Education:* University of North Carolina (B.S., 1949); University of Pennsylvania (M.B.A., 1951); Wake Forest College (J.D., 1956). Certified Public Accountant, North Carolina, 1950. ***PRACTICE AREAS:*** Taxation Law (40%); Estate Planning (30%); Corporate Law (20%); Probate Law (10%).

CHARLES T. LANE, born Bertie County, North Carolina, December 20, 1931; admitted to bar, 1956, North Carolina. *Education:* Wake Forest University (B.A., 1954); Wake Forest Law School (J.D., 1956). Certified Mediator, North Carolina. ***PRACTICE AREAS:*** Eminent Domain/Condemnation Law; Real Estate Law; Land Use Law; Arbitration and Mediation; Business and Banking Law. ***Email:*** ctlane@poynerspruill.com

JAMES T. MARTIN, born Greensboro, North Carolina, March 23, 1942; admitted to bar, 1967, North Carolina; 1970, Virginia. *Education:* Wake Forest University (B.A., 1964; J.D., 1967). ***PRACTICE AREAS:*** Foreclosures. ***Email:*** jmartin@poynerspruill.com

All Attorneys are Members of The North Carolina State Bar and North Carolina Bar Association.

REPRESENTATIVE CLIENTS: American Airlines; Alliance One International; BB&T; Boddie-Noell Enterprises, Inc.; The Body Shop, Inc.; Browning-Ferris Industries; CSX Transportations, Inc.; Data General Corp.; Electricities of North Carolina, Inc.; Farm Bureau Mutual Insurance Co.; Food Lion, Inc.; General Electric Capital Corp.; General Electric Company; General Electric Mortgage Insurance Company; General Motors, Inc.; Granutec, Inc.; Guardian Corporation, Inc.; H&R Block, Inc.; Investors Holding Company (Golden Corral and affiliates); LSB Bancshares, Inc.; Martin Marietta Materials; Mitsubishi Semiconductor America, Inc.; Nomaco, Inc.; N.C. Eastern Municipal Power Agency; North Carolina Enterprise Corporation; N.C. Housing Finance Agency; North Carolina Municipal Power Agency; Pepsico, Inc.; PF Properties; Pitt County Memorial Hospital; Premium Standard Farms, Inc.; Purdue Pharmaceuticals, L.P.; RBC Centura Banks, Inc.; Research Triangle Foundation; Richardson Sports (Carolina Panthers); Roses Stores, Inc.; R.J. Reynolds Tobacco Co.; Schwarz Biosciences, Inc.; Semi-Conductor Research Corp.; T.A. Loving Company; WakeMed.

(For additional personnel and biographical data see listings at Raleigh, Charlotte and Southern Pines)

ROSE RAND ATTORNEYS, P.A.

ROCKY MOUNT, NORTH CAROLINA

(See Wilson)

General Practice, all Courts. Corporation, Labor and Insurance Law. Trials, including Personal Injury, Wrongful Death and Workers Compensation, Eminent Domain, Tax, Estate Planning and Administration, Municipal, Environmental, Real Estate, Bankruptcy.

RALPH G. WILLEY, P.A.

Established in 1987

3202 SUNSET AVENUE, SUITE A
P.O. BOX 7846
ROCKY MOUNT, NORTH CAROLINA 27804
Telephone: 252-443-1117
Fax: 252-443-5812

Workers Compensation, Board Certified, Personal Injury, Civil and Criminal Trial Practice in all Courts, Traffic, Mediation, Arbitration.

RALPH G. WILLEY, III, born Halifax County, North Carolina, August 28, 1949; admitted to bar, 1974, North Carolina; 1976, U.S. District Court, Eastern District of North Carolina. *Education:* North Carolina State University (B.A., 1971); University of North Carolina (J.D., 1974). Certified Mediator. *Member:* Edgecombe-Nash and North Carolina Bar Associations; Seventh Judicial District and North Carolina State Bars; North Carolina Academy of Trial Lawyers (Workers' Rights Committee); The Association of Trial Lawyers of America. (Board Certified Specialist in Workers' Compensation, North Carolina State Board of Legal Specialization)

GEORGE B. DANIEL, P.A.

ROXBORO, NORTH CAROLINA

(See Yanceyville)

Criminal Law, Felonies, Misdemeanors, Traffic Violations, Driving While Intoxicated, Automobile Accidents, Truck Accidents, Personal Injury, Wrongful Death, Civil Litigation, Real Estate, Residential Real Estate, Commercial Real Estate, Real Estate Litigation, Workers Compensation, Estate Planning, Estate Administration, Drug Crimes.

WILLIAM H. DANIEL, P.A.

ROXBORO, NORTH CAROLINA

(See Yanceyville)

Criminal Law, Felonies, Misdemeanors, Traffic Violations, Driving While Intoxicated, Drug Crimes, Personal Injury, Automobile Accidents, Truck Accidents, Motorcycle Accidents, Wrongful Death, Workers Compensation, Real Estate, Wills, Estate Administration.

ALAN S. HICKS, P.A.

3 UNION PLAZA
205 NORTH MAIN STREET
ROXBORO, NORTH CAROLINA 27573
Telephone: 336-599-4032
Fax: 336-599-3656
Email: ash@roxboro.net
URL: http://www.alanhicksattorney.com

Business, Probate, Trusts and Estates, Personal Injury, Civil Trials, Real Estate and Commercial Law.

FIRM PROFILE: Alan S. Hicks started as a solo practitioner in 1995 and prior to that he practiced for 22 years with 2 other firms in the area. His practice focuses on real estate, estate planning and business. He primarily represents small businesses, individuals and industries throughout the state of North Carolina. He is also certified as a Superior Court Mediator by the North Carolina Dispute Resolution Commission.

ALAN S. HICKS, born Goldsboro, North Carolina, July 20, 1947; admitted to bar, 1973, North Carolina; 1976, U.S. District Court, Middle District of North Carolina; 1977, U.S. District Court, Eastern District of North Carolina. *Education:* University of North Carolina (B.A., 1969; J.D., 1973). Member, Board of Commissioners, Person County Industrial Facilities & Pollution Control Financing Authority 1976—. Member, 1994-2004 and Chairman, 1998-2004, Person County Economic Development Commission. Member, Board of Directors, Roxboro Uptown Development Corp., 1995—. Member, 1982-1994; Chairman, 1990-1994, Person County Board of Education, 1982-1994. Superior Court Mediator, North Carolina Dispute Resolution Commission, 2002—. Member, Board of Trustees, North Carolina School of Science & Mathematics, 2003—. *Member:* Person County (President, 1977-1978), Judicial District 9A, North Carolina (Chairman, Small Business Committee, Business Law Section, 1987-1989) and American Bar Associations; The North Carolina State Bar; North Carolina Academy of Trial Lawyers. ***PRACTICE AREAS:*** Business Law; Trusts and Estates; Civil Litigation; Commercial Law; Real Estate Law. ***Email:*** ash@roxboro.net

REPRESENTATIVE CLIENTS: *Industrial:* Georgia-Pacific, Inc.; Design Works Inc.; Aluminum Casting Technology, LLC; Republic Services of NC, LLC. *Financial:* Roxboro Savings Bank SSB. *Development:* Person County Business and Industrial Center, Inc.; JES Properties. *Institutional:* Piedmont Community College; Person County Board of Education. *Automotive:* Carolina Chrysler-Plymouth-Jeep Dealer Advertising Assoc., Inc.; Boyette Automotive, Inc.; D&L Equipment Inc. *Services:* Thompson-Allen, Inc.; Convenience Corner 501, Inc.; Carver Agency Inc.; Metals Recycling Corp.; Horizontech, Inc. *Telecommunications:* Atcom, Inc.
APPROVED ATTORNEY FOR: United Title Company; Investors Title Insurance Co.; Lawyers Title Insurance Co.; First Title Insurance Co.; Federal Land Bank of Columbia.
REFERENCES: Wachovia Bank; Central Carolina Bank & Trust Co.; Branch Banking and Trust Co.; Roxboro Savings Bank, SSB.

HUBBARD & CATES

Established in 1967

36 COURT STREET
P.O. BOX 679
ROXBORO, NORTH CAROLINA 27573
Telephone: 336-597-2251; 599-2443
Fax: 336-597-3042

General Civil, Criminal Trial and Appellate Practice in all Courts. Corporate, Real Estate, Tort, Probate, Estate Planning, Administrative, Commercial, Family, Bankruptcy, Personal Injury, Automobile Accidents, Traffic Violations.

MEMBERS OF FIRM

CHARLES E. HUBBARD, born Danville, Virginia, April 8, 1936; admitted to bar, 1966, North Carolina. *Education:* Hampden-Sydney College and University of North Carolina (A.B., 1963); Washington & Lee University (LL.B., 1966). Phi Alpha Delta. Member, Board of Trustees, Person County Memorial Hospital, 1974—. Law Council of Law School Association, Washington & Lee University, 1981-1985. Member, North Carolina Capital Building Authority of the State Department of Administration, 1982-1986. *Member:* Person County, North Carolina and American Bar Associations; 9A Judicial District and North Carolina State Bars; North Carolina Academy of Trial Lawyers. [With U.S. Navy, active duty, 1956-1958]

WALTER BRADSHER CATES, born Person County, North Carolina, September 22, 1950; admitted to bar, 1979, North Carolina. *Education:* East Carolina University (B.S., B.A. in Accounting, 1972); Campbell University (J.D., 1979). Member, North Carolina Commission on the Superconducting Super Collider, 1988-1989. *Member:* Person County,

(This Listing Continued)

HUBBARD & CATES, Roxboro—Continued

North Carolina and American Bar Associations; 9A Judicial District (President, 1989) and North Carolina State Bars; North Carolina Academy of Trial Lawyers. ***Email:*** wbcates@roxboro.net

J. LINWOOD CATES, born Roxboro, North Carolina, May 21, 1974; admitted to bar, 1999, North Carolina. *Education:* University of North Carolina at Chapel Hill (B.A., 1996); Wake Forest University (J.D., 1999). Phi Alpha Delta. *Member:* Person County and North Carolina Bar Associations; North Carolina State Bar: North Carolina Academy of Trial Lawyers. ***Email:*** LinCates@yahoo.com

REPRESENTATIVE CLIENTS: Person Memorial Hospital; Camp Chemical Corp.; Person-Caswell Lake Authority; Cole's Pharmacy; Person County Board of Alcoholic Beverage Control; Piedmont Maintenance & Services, Inc.; Joe Wright Memorial Scholarship Fund Inc.; North State Medical Group; Roxboro Medical Associates; Roxboro American Legion Baseball, Inc.
APPROVED ATTORNEYS FOR: Investors Title Insurance Co.; Lawyers Title Insurance Corp.; The Title Guaranty Co.; Federal Land Bank of Columbia; American Title Insurance Co.; First Title Co.; Chicago Title Insurance; TransAmerican Title Insurance Co.; United Title Insurance Co.; Roxboro Savings Bank, SSB; Branch Banking and Trust Co.; First Union National Bank of North Carolina; Wachovia Bank and Trust Co.; North Central Farm Credit, ACA; Farmers Home Administration of U.S. Department of Agriculture; North Carolina Department of Transportation.
REFERENCES: Wachovia Bank; Roxboro Savings Bank, SSB; Branch Banking and Trust Co.; Central Carolina Bank and Trust Co., N.A.; The Fidelity Bank.

BYERS, MARTELLE & WILLIAMS, P.L.L.C.

226 NORTH MAIN STREET, SUITE 2
P.O. BOX 550
RUTHERFORDTON, NORTH CAROLINA 28139
Telephone: 828-288-1844
Fax: 828-288-1840
URL: http://www.williamsandmartellelawfirm.com
URL: http://www.gbyerslaw.com

General Civil and Criminal Trial Practice in all courts, Family Law, Real Property Law, Elder Law, Wills, Trusts and Estates, Corporate Law, and Municipal Law.

FIRM PROFILE: Byers, Martelle & Williams, P.L.L.C., is a full service law firm whose primary goal is the swift resolution of cases with the most favorable outcome possible for our clients. We pride ourselves on our attention to detail and on the personal attention given to every case.

MEMBERS OF FIRM

GARLAND F. BYERS, JR., born Rutherfordton, North Carolina, January 11, 1968; admitted to bar, 2000, North Carolina, U.S. District Court, Western District of North Carolina; 2001, U.S. Court of Appeals, Fourth Circuit; 2003, U.S. District Court, Middle District of North Carolina. *Education:* Isothermal Community College (A.A.S., Criminal Justice, Protective Service Technology, 1991); University of South Carolina (B.S., Criminal Justice, 1993); North Carolina Central University School of Law (J.D., 1999). Member, Who's Who in American Law, 1998—. Recipient, Isothemal Community College Criminal Justice Award, 1991; North Carolina Basic Law Enforcement Training Top Student Award, I.C.C., 1988; North Carolina Basic Law Enforcement Training Top Marksman Award I.C.C., 1988; North Carolina Department of Justice - Basic Law Enforcement Certificate, 1995; North Carolina Department of Justice - Intermediate Law Enforcement Certificate, 1995; North Carolina Department of Justice - Advanced Professional Law Enforcment Certificate, 1995. *Member:* North Carolina, Federal and American Bar Associations; North Carolina State Bar; North Carolina Academy of Trial Lawyers; The Association of Trial Lawyers of America; National Association of Criminal Defense Lawyers. ***PRACTICE AREAS:*** Accidents; Personal Injury; Litigation; Civil Practice; Trial Practice; Criminal Law; Automobile Accidents and Injuries; Wrongful Death; Civil Litigation; Commercial Litigation; Construction Litigation; Construction Law; Environmental Litigation; Criminal Defense; Tort Litigation; Products Liability; Medical Malpractice; Toxic Torts; Felonies; Federal Criminal Law; Municipal Law; Constitutional Law; Federal Civil Litigation.

ROBERT KENNETH MARTELLE, born Nantucket, Massachusetts, May 24, 1969; admitted to bar, 1995, North Carolina; 2004, U.S. District Court, Western District of North Carolina. *Education:* University of North Carolina at Charlotte (B.A., cum laude, 1991); Campbell University, Norman A. Wiggins School of Law (J.D., 1995). Phi Alpha Delta. *Member:* North Carolina Bar Associations; North Carolina State Bar. ***PRACTICE AREAS:*** Domestic Law; Family Law; Divorce; Adoption Law; Child Custody; Child Support; Equitable Distribution; Premarital Agreements; Criminal Law; Driving While Intoxicated; Traffic Violations; Municipal Law; Bankruptcy; Incompetency Proceedings.

RICHARD PRESTON WILLIAMS, born Charlotte, North Carolina, January 28, 1969; admitted to bar, 1994, North Carolina. *Education:* University of North Carolina (A.B., 1991; J.D., 1994). Phi Delta Phi. Recipient, James M. Johnston Scholarship, 1987-1991. *Member:* North Carolina Bar Associations; North Carolina State Bar. ***PRACTICE AREAS:*** Real Property; Real Estate; Wills; Estate Planning; Probate; Business Law; Corporate Law; Trusts and Estates; Estate Administration; Elder Law; Zoning, Planning and Land Use; Commercial Real Estate; Commercial Law; Industrial Property.

DEATON, BIGGERS & GULDEN, P.L.L.C.

RUTHERFORDTON, NORTH CAROLINA

(See Shelby)

General Civil Practice. Trials. Practice before all State and Federal Courts and Administrative Agencies, Real Estate, Business Law, Wills and Estates, Estate Planning, Personal Injury, Workers Compensation, Criminal Law.

ELKINS & ELKINS

RUTHERFORDTON, NORTH CAROLINA

(See Hendersonville)

Bankruptcy, Real Estate, Residential Real Estate, Buying and Selling a Home, Probate, Corporation, Civil Trial Practice, Out of Court Debt Restructuring.

HAMRICK, BOWEN, MEBANE, GREENWAY & LLOYD, L.L.P.

Established in 1946
153 WEST COURT STREET
P.O. DRAWER 790
RUTHERFORDTON, NORTH CAROLINA 28139
Telephone: 828-286-9152
Fax: 828-287-9101
Email: hbmg@rfci.net

General Trial and Appellate Practice in all State and Federal Courts, Business, Collections and Creditor's Rights, Commercial, Construction, Corporations, DWI, Traffic Offenses, Criminal, Family, Divorce, Equitable Distribution, Child Custody, Child Support, Domestic, Employment, Insurance, Personal Injury, Real Estate, Social Security, Trusts and Estates and Workers Compensation.

FIRM PROFILE: This well respected and established firm has been in Rutherfordton since 1946. The firm practices in all State and Federal Courts. They have earned a reputation for professional excellence and client service.

MEMBERS OF FIRM

FRED DELMAR HAMRICK, JR. (1908-1982)

ROBERT L. MEBANE, born Spartanburg, South Carolina, September 12, 1952; admitted to bar, 1980, North Carolina. *Education:* University of North Carolina (B.A., 1974); Cumberland Law School, Samford University (J.D., 1979). Delta Theta Phi. Law Clerk for Hon. Woodrow W. Jones, U.S. District Judge, Western District of North Carolina, 1979-1981. *Member:* North Carolina State Bar; North Carolina Bar Association. ***PRACTICE AREAS:*** Real Estate; Workers Compensation; Social Security Disability; Wills; Estates; General Civil Practice. ***Email:*** rmebane@rcfi.net

BRADLEY K. GREENWAY, born Baltimore, Maryland, September 30, 1952; admitted to bar, 1983, North Carolina. *Education:* University of North Carolina (B.A., 1974); Campbell University (J.D., 1983). Phi Kappa Phi; Omicron Delta Kappa; Delta Theta Phi. Recipient, American Jurisprudence Awards in Civil Procedure, Labor Law, Real Property. Law Clerk for Honorable Woodrow W. Jones, U.S. District Judge, Western District of North Carolina, 1983-1986. *Member:* North Carolina Bar Association; North Carolina State Bar. [United States Navy Reserve, Retired]. ***PRACTICE AREAS:*** DWI; Traffic Offenses; Criminal Trial Practice; Family Law; Divorce; Equitable Distribution; Child Custody; Child Support; Personal Injury Law; Automobile Accidents and Injuries; Wrongful Death; Real Estate; Juvenile Law. ***Email:*** bkgreenway@rfci.net

DAVID A. LLOYD, born Charlotte, North Carolina, May 29, 1965; admitted to bar, 1990, North Carolina. *Education:* Davidson College (A.B., 1987); University of North Carolina (J.D., 1990). Member, National Moot Court Team. Recipient, American Jurisprudence Award in Trial Advocacy. *Member:* North Carolina Bar Association; North Carolina State Bar. ***PRACTICE AREAS:*** Civil Litigation; Commercial Litigation; Construction; Business; Corporate Law; Wills; Estates. ***Email:*** dlloyd@rfci.net

OF COUNSEL

JAMES M. BOWEN, born Greenwood, Mississippi, October 15, 1942; admitted to bar, 1967, North Carolina. *Education:* Wake Forest University (B.A., 1964; J.D., 1967). Phi Delta Phi. Law Clerk for Hon. Woodrow W. Jones, U.S. District Judge, Western District of North Carolina, 1967-1968. *Member:* The North Carolina State Bar; North Carolina Bar Association. ***PRACTICE AREAS:*** Accident and Personal Injury; Litigation. ***Email:*** hbmg@rcfi.net

GENERAL COUNSEL FOR: Rutherford Railroad Development Corp.; American Water Graphics, Inc.; Thompson Contractors, Inc.; Parton Lumber Company, Inc.
REPRESENTATIVE CLIENTS: Bank One Corporation; Bell South Telecommunications, Inc.; Branch Banking & Trust Co.; Centura Bank; First USA Bank; Foothills Rebar, Inc.; Rutherford County Internet, Inc.; R & R Plastics Inc.
APPROVED ATTORNEYS FOR: Lawyers Title Insurance Corp.; Commonwealth Land Title Company of North Carolina; Pioneer National Title Insurance Co.; First Title Insurance Co.; Stewart Title Insurance Co.; Statewide Title Insurance Co.

NANNEY, DALTON & MILLER, L.L.P.

346 NORTH MAIN STREET
P.O. BOX 800
RUTHERFORDTON, NORTH CAROLINA 28139
Telephone: 828-286-8222
Fax: 828-286-8229
Email: bmiller@ndmlaw.com

General Practice in all Federal and State Courts, Trials, Business Law, Real Estate, Probate, Insurance Law, Personal Injury, Auto Accidents, Wrongful Death, Trusts and Estates.

MEMBERS OF FIRM

LOUIS W. NANNEY, JR., born Rutherfordton, North Carolina, January 10, 1948; admitted to bar, 1973, North Carolina. *Education:* University of North Carolina (A.B., 1970; J.D., 1973). Recipient, John Motley Morehead Scholarship, 1966-1970. Town Attorney,

(This Listing Continued)

Town of Rutherfordton, 1981—. Certified mediator. *Member:* North Carolina and American Bar Associations; North Carolina State Bar. ***PRACTICE AREAS:*** Business Law; Municipal Law; Health Care Law. ***Email:*** lwnanney@ndmlaw.com

WALTER H. DALTON, born Rutherfordton, North Carolina, May 21, 1949; admitted to bar, 1975, North Carolina; 1995, South Carolina. *Education:* University of North Carolina (B.S., 1971; J.D., 1975). Law Clerk for Hon. Woodrow W. Jones, U.S. District Judge, Western District of North Carolina, 1975-1977. Rutherford County Attorney, 1986-1996 and 1998—. U.S. Fourth Circuit Judicial Conference. North Carolina Senate, 1997—. *Member:* Rutherford County (President, 1984) and North Carolina Bar Associations; North Carolina State Bar. ***PRACTICE AREAS:*** Litigation; Probate Law; Estates; Real Estate; Personal Injury Law; Automobile Accidents and Injuries; Business Law; Wrongful Death. ***Email:*** wdalton@ndmlaw.com

ELIZABETH T. MILLER, born Laurinburg, North Carolina, July 23, 1963; admitted to bar, 1988, North Carolina. *Education:* University of North Carolina at Chapel Hill (B.A., 1984; J.D., 1988). Assistant District Attorney, 29th Judicial District, Rutherford County, November 1988-December 1991. *Member:* Rutherford County and North Carolina Bar Association (Vice President, 1989); North Carolina State Bar. ***PRACTICE AREAS:*** General Civil Practice; Real Estate; Wills; Business Law. ***Email:*** bmiller@ndmlaw.com

GENERAL COUNSEL FOR: Rutherford Electric Membership Corp.; Rutherford Hospital, Inc.; Rutherford Internal Medicine Associates, P.A.; County of Rutherford; Town of Rutherfordton; Town of Ellenboro; Broad River Water Authority; Gilkey Lumber Company, Inc.; Robbins Oil Co.; American Dairy Goat Association.
REPRESENTATIVE CLIENTS: Stonecutter Mills Corporation; Tanner Companies LLC; Centura Bank.

THE ROBERTS LAW FIRM, P.A.

RUTHERFORDTON, NORTH CAROLINA

(See Gastonia)

Trial Practice. Personal Injury, Workers Compensation, Social Security Disability, Medical Malpractice, Nursing home Litigation, Products Liability and Wrongful Death.

YELTON, FARFOUR, McCARTNEY, LUTZ & CRAIG, P.A.

RUTHERFORDTON, NORTH CAROLINA

(See Shelby)

General Practice. Corporation, Estate Planning, and Personal Injury Law. Trial and appellate practice in all courts. Creditors" Rights and Bankruptcy law. Domestic and Family Law.

JOHN A. BASINGER
ATTORNEY AT LAW

113-A EAST COUNCIL STREET
SALISBURY, NORTH CAROLINA 28144
Telephone: 704-637-0094
Fax: 704-637-0106
Email: johnbasinger2003@yahoo.com
URL: http://www.johnbasingerlaw.com

Criminal Law, Felonies, Misdemeanors, Drug Crimes, Driving While Intoxicated, DUI, Juvenile Criminal Law, Family Law, Divorce, Child Custody, Child Support, Adoption Law, Domestic Violence, Visitation Rights, Premarital Agreements, Personal Injury, White Collar Crime, Parole and Probation.

JOHN A. BASINGER, born January 30, 1978; admitted to bar, 2004, North Carolina. *Education:* Catawba College (B.A., 2000); Campbell University (J.D., 2003). *Member:* North Carolina State Bar; North Carolina Bar Association; North Carolina Academy of Trial Lawyers. ***PRACTICE AREAS:*** Criminal Law; Felonies; Misdemeanors; Drug Crimes; Driving While Intoxicated; Juvenile Criminal Law; Family Law; Divorce; Adoption Law; Child Custody; Child Support; Domestic Violence; Visitation Rights; Premarital Agreements; Personal Injury; White Collar Crime; Parole and Probation.

BLANTON LAW FIRM, P.A.

Established in 1990

228 WEST COUNCIL STREET
P.O. BOX 2327
SALISBURY, NORTH CAROLINA 28145-2327
Telephone: 704-637-1100
Fax: 704-637-1500
Email: mrb@blantonlawfirm.com
URL: http://www.blantonlawoffice.com

Family Law, Divorce, Collaborative Law, Child Custody, Child Support, Spousal Support, Criminal Law, Driving While Intoxicated (DWI), Drug Crimes, Felonies, Parole and Probation, Misdemeanors, Traffic Violations, Wrongful Death, Personal Injury, Real Estate, Civil Litigation, Contracts, Family Financial Mediation.

MARY R. BLANTON, born Alexandria, Virginia, July 4, 1950; admitted to bar, 1981, Virginia and U.S. Court of Appeals, Fourth Circuit; 1985, North Carolina. *Education:* Wake Forest University (B.A., magna cum laude, 1972); St. John's College, Graduate Institute (1973); Georgetown University (J.D., cum laude, 1981). Phi Beta Kappa. President, North Carolina District 19-C Bar, 1998-1999. North Carolina Certified Family Mediator. Member, Rowan Collaborative Family Law Group. *Member:* Rowan County and North Carolina Bar Associations; North Carolina State Bar; Virginia State Bar; International Association of Collaborative Practitioners; Association for Conflict Resolution. (Board Certified Specialist in Family Law, North Carolina State Board of Legal Specialization). ***PRACTICE AREAS:*** Family Law; Wills; Collaborative Law; Family Mediation; Real Estate. ***Email:*** mrb@blantonlawfirm.com

THEODORE A. (TED) BLANTON, born Albemarle, North Carolina, January 11, 1950; admitted to bar, 1984, North Carolina, U.S. District Court, Middle District of North Carolina and U.S. Court of Appeals, Fourth Circuit. *Education:* Wake Forest University; St. John's College, Annapolis (B.A., cum laude, 1975); Georgetown University (J.D., 1981). Legislative Assistant, Staff of the U.S. Senate, 1977-1983. District Court Judge, North Carolina District 19C, 1994-2002. *Member:* Rowan County and North Carolina Bar Associations (Board Member, Criminal Justice Section, 2001-2004); North Carolina State Bar; North Carolina Academy of Trial Lawyers. ***PRACTICE AREAS:*** Criminal Law; Traffic Violations; Family Law; Personal Injury; Civil Litigation. ***Email:*** tab@blantonlawfirm.com

(This Listing Continued)

BRIDGES LAW FIRM

SALISBURY PROFESSIONAL CENTER
1809 BRENNER AVENUE, SUITE 203
SALISBURY, NORTH CAROLINA 28144
Telephone: 704-633-6693
Telecopier: 704-633-6889
Email: bbridges@bridgeslawfirm.com
URL: http://www.bbridgeslaw.com

Real Estate Law, Mortgages, Business Law, Contract Law, General Civil Practice, Estate Planning, Probate and Wills.

BENJAMIN H. BRIDGES, III, born Salisbury, North Carolina, December 10, 1947; admitted to bar, 1973, North Carolina. *Education:* Catawba College (A.B., 1970); Wake Forest University (J.D., 1973). Phi Alpha Delta. Recipient: Student Advocacy Award; American Jurisprudence Award in Debtor's and Creditor's Rights. *Member:* Rowan County and 19A Judicial Districts, North Carolina and American Bar Associations; North Carolina State Bar. ***PRACTICE AREAS:*** Real Estate Law; Contract Law; General Civil Practice; Estate Planning; Probate; Wills.

SPECIAL COUNSEL FOR: Ryan's Restaurant Group, Inc.; Fire Mountain Restaurants, Inc.

JAMES L. CARTER, JR.

625 W. INNES STREET
SALISBURY, NORTH CAROLINA 28144
Telephone: 704-633-8857
Fax: 704-633-8620
Email: jlcarter@salisbury.net
URL: http://www.jcarter-law.com

Real Estate, Corporate, Business Law, Small Business, Limited Liability, Traffic, Insurance, Trust and Estates, Wills, Probate, Estate Planning, Contract, Civil Litigation.

JAMES L. CARTER, JR., born Salisbury, North Carolina, October 24, 1970; admitted to bar, 1998, North Carolina. *Education:* University of North Carolina at Charlotte (B.A., magna cum laude, 1993); University of Kentucky (J.D., cum laude, 1998). Rowan County Public Guardian, 1999—. *Member:* North Carolina and American Bar Associations.

AMY S. DAVIS

SALISBURY, NORTH CAROLINA

(See Concord)

Personal Bankruptcy, Business Bankruptcy, Foreclosures, Adoptions, Child Custody, Child Support.

HANCOCK, FAUST AND NANCE, P.L.L.C.

316 NORTH MAIN STREET
SALISBURY, NORTH CAROLINA 28144
Telephone: 704-636-2080
Fax: 704-637-7991
URL: http://www.hfn-law.com

Real Estate, Probate, Estate Planning, Wills, Personal Injury, Traffic Violations, Civil Litigation, Corporate Law and Bankruptcy.

MEMBERS OF FIRM

R. DARRELL HANCOCK, born Salisbury, North Carolina, May 15, 1953; admitted to bar, 1978, North Carolina. *Education:* University of North Carolina at Chapel Hill (A.B., Journalism, 1975; J.D., 1978). General Counsel, Hood Theological Seminary. Director, Rowan Regional Medical Center. Trustee, Z Smith Reynolds Foundation. *Member:* Rowan County (Member, Sections on: Probate Law; Residential Real Estate Law), North Carolina and National Bar Associations; North Carolina State Bar; North Carolina Association of Black Lawyers. ***PRACTICE AREAS:*** Real Estate; Probate; Traffic Violations; Personal Injury; Civil Litigation; Corporate Law. ***Email:*** rdh@hfn-law.com

GEORGE R. HUNDLEY (1952-2003)

JAMES Y. FAUST, born Pusan, South Korea, February 25, 1977; admitted to bar, 2004, North Carolina. *Education:* Bucknell University (B.A., 1999); Case Western Reserve University (J.D., 2002). *Member:* Rowan County and North Carolina Bar Associations; North Carolina State Bar. ***Email:*** jyf@hfn-law.com

(This Listing Continued)

HANCOCK, FAUST AND NANCE, P.L.L.C., Salisbury—Continued

BRADLEY J. NANCE, born Salisbury, North Carolina, March 11, 1977; admitted to bar, 2003, North Carolina. *Education:* Catawba College (B.A., 1999); Ohio Northern University (J.D., 2003). *Member:* Rowan County and North Carolina Bar Associations; North Carolina State Bar. ***Email:*** bjn@hfn-law.com

Representative Clients will be furnished upon request.

HARTSELL & WILLIAMS, P.A.

SALISBURY, NORTH CAROLINA

(See Concord)

General Civil and Criminal Practice in all Courts. Workers Compensation, Corporation, Insurance, Real Estate, Taxation, Probate Law, Estate Planning, Family Law and Motor Sports (Racing).

JOHN L. HOLSHOUSER, JR.

309 NORTH MAIN STREET, SUITE 1
SALISBURY, NORTH CAROLINA 28144
Telephone: 704-637-7700
FAX: 704-633-8617
Email: john@salisbury.net
URL: http://www.jholshouserlaw.com

General Civil Trial Practice in State and Federal Courts, County and Local Municipal Law, Real Estate and Business Litigation, Wills, Probate and Estates Administration.

JOHN L. HOLSHOUSER, JR., born Durham, North Carolina, August 28, 1938; admitted to bar, 1963, North Carolina. *Education:* University of North Carolina (A.B., 1961; LL.B., 1963). Delta Theta Phi. Special Agent, FBI, 1963-1966. U.S. Commissioner, Middle District of North Carolina, 1967-1968. Trial Judge, Rowan County Court, 1968-1970. Member, North Carolina Savings & Loan Commission, 1974-1977. County Attorney, Rowan County, 1989—. Arbitrator, District Court. Certified Superior Court Mediator. *Member:* Rowan County (Secretary-Treasurer, 1971-1972; President, 1972-1974) and North Carolina Bar Associations; 19th Judicial District (President, 1971-1972; Chairman, Bar Candidate Committee, 1976—; State Bar Councilor, District 19C, 1994-2001) and North Carolina State Bars; North Carolina Academy of Trial Lawyers. ***PRACTICE AREAS:*** County/Municipal Law; Real Estate Law; Wills and Estate Administration; Civil Litigation; Banking; Commercial Law.

REPRESENTATIVE CLIENTS: Rowan County; Farmers & Merchants Bank; Falcon Development Group, Inc.; Hammill Construction Co; Rouzer Motor Parts Co., Inc.; Rives Motor Co. APPROVED ATTORNEY FOR: Investors Title Insurance Co.; Statewide Title Insurance Co.; First American Title Insurance Co.; Lawyers Title Insurance Co.; Chicago Title Insurance Co.

KETNER & DEES, P.A.

Established in 1972
121 EAST KERR STREET
P.O. BOX 1308
SALISBURY, NORTH CAROLINA 28144
Telephone: 704-637-3434
Fax: 704-637-3449
Email: glenn@ketnerlaw.com
URL: http://www.ketner-law.com

General Civil Practice State and Federal Courts, Real Estate, Zoning, Planning and Land Use, Corporate and Business Law, Elder Law, Trusts and Estates, Estate Planning, Probate, Wills, Health Care Law.

FIRM PROFILE: The firm was founded in 1972 by Glenn E. Ketner, Jr. after serving three years as a Judge Advocate in the U.S. Air Force, two years in private practice and three years as Counsel to the U.S. Senate Subcommittee on Constitutional Rights chaired by the Honorable Sam J. Ervin. The firm employs highly qualified and experienced assistants, one of whom has worked with the firm for more than 28 years and another of whom has been with the firm for more than 22 years. The firm emphasizes continuing education and professional development and encourages participation in civic, charitable and professional activities.

GLENN E. KETNER, JR., born Salisbury, North Carolina, October 17, 1938; admitted to bar, 1963, North Carolina; 1964, U.S. District Court, Middle District of North Carolina; 1965, U.S. Court of Military Appeals; 1967, U.S. Supreme Court; 1975, U.S. Tax Court. *Education:* Duke University (A.B., 1960; J.D., 1963). Law Clerk to Honorable L. Richardson Preyer and Honorable Edwin S. Stanley, 1963-1964. Counsel, Subcommittee on Constitutional Rights, Committee on the Judiciary, U.S. Senate, 1969-1972. Trustee, Catawba College, 1975-1985, 1987—. Chairman, Catawba College Planned Giving Advisory Board. Trustee, Rowan Cabarrus Community College, 1994—. Member, Board of Directors, North Carolina Citizens for Business & Industry, 1998—. Member, Duke University Estate Planning Council, 1989—. Vice Chair, Rowan Regional Medical Center. Member, Board of Visitors, Duke University Law School. *Member:* Rowan County, North Carolina (Member, Sections on: Real Property; General Practice; Estate Planning and Fiduciary Law; Business Law; Tax Law; Bankruptcy Law; Environmental and Natural Resources Law; Health Law; Construction Law), Federal and American (Member, Sections on: Taxation; Corporation, Banking and Business Law; Real Property, Probate and Trust Law) Bar Associations; North Carolina State Bar; American Judicature Society. [Capt., Judge Advocate, U.S. Air Force, 1964-1967]. ***PRACTICE AREAS:*** Real Estate; Zoning, Planning and Land Use; Leases and Leasing; Wills; Trusts and Estates; Corporate Law; Business Law; Health Care.

JOHN W. (JAY) DEES, II, born Chapel Hill, North Carolina, May 13, 1966; admitted to bar, 1998, North Carolina. *Education:* University of North Carolina (B.A., 1992); Campbell University (J.D., 1998). *Member:* Rowan County, North Carolina and American Bar Associations; North Carolina State Bar. ***PRACTICE AREAS:*** Real Estate; Zoning, Planning and Land Use; Corporate Law; Business Law; Historic Preservation. ***Email:*** jay@ketnerlaw.com

REPRESENTATIVE CLIENTS: Rowan Investment Co., Inc.; Goodman Millwork, Inc.; Ketner Center, Inc.; Lutheran Services for the Aging, Inc.; Salisbury Mall Limited; Parkdale Mills, Inc.; KOSA; Hoechst-Celanese, Inc.; Trexler Construction, Inc.; Leatherman Associates; Sharonview Federal Credit Union; Textile Products, Inc.
APPROVED ATTORNEYS FOR: Investors Title Insurance Co.; First American Title Insurance Co.; Lawyers Title Insurance Co.; Chicago Title Insurance Co.; Commonwealth Land Title Insurance Co.; Stewart Title Co.
REFERENCES: Wachovia Bank & Trust Company, N.A.; Citizens Bank, FSB.

KLUTTZ, REAMER, HAYES, RANDOLPH & ADKINS, L.L.P.

Established in 1954
131 NORTH MAIN STREET
P.O. DRAWER 1617
SALISBURY, NORTH CAROLINA 28145-1617
Telephone: 704-636-7100
Telecopier: 704-636-2284
Email: office@rowanlawyer.com
URL: http://www.rowanlawyer.com

General Civil Practice. Trials. Employment Law, Corporation, Taxation, Real Estate, Estate Planning, Probate and Trusts, Traffic, Criminal Law, Mediation, Personal Injury, Driving While Impaired, Workers Compensation.

FIRM PROFILE: Established in 1954. The firm of Kluttz, Reamer, Hayes, Randolph & Adkins, L.L.P. has been serving the people of North Carolina for well over 50 years. Since that time the firm has achieved and maintained Martindale-Hubbell's highest rating for legal ability and ethical conduct. The focus of the firm is providing its clients with legal representation of the highest quality.

WM. CLARENCE KLUTTZ (1917-1996)

LEWIS P. HAMLIN, JR. (1919-1988)

RICHARD R. REAMER, born Dayton, Ohio, July 3, 1945; admitted to bar, 1971, North Carolina. *Education:* Duke University (A.B., 1967); University of North Carolina (J.D., 1971). Research Assistant, North Carolina Supreme Court, 1971-1972. Phi Delta Phi. *Member:* Rowan County, North Carolina and American (Member, Litigation Section) Bar Associations; North Carolina State Bar; North Carolina Association of Defense Attorneys (Board of Directors, 1993); Defense Research Institute. ***PRACTICE AREAS:*** Civil Litigation. ***Email:*** rrr@rowanlawyer.com

GLENN S. HAYES, born Camden, New Jersey, November 25, 1953; admitted to bar, 1980, Virginia; 1986, North Carolina. *Education:* College of William & Mary (B.A., with honors, 1976; J.D., 1980; M.L.T., 1986). Virginia Division Counsel, United Coal Company, 1981-1985. *Member:* North Carolina and American Bar Associations; Virginia State Bar; North Carolina State Bar. ***PRACTICE AREAS:*** Civil Litigation; Estates; Corporations; Partnerships; Taxation; General Business. ***Email:*** gsh@rowanlawyer.com

JAMES D.K.F. RANDOLPH, born Birmingham, Alabama, April 30, 1961; admitted to bar, 1990, North Carolina and U.S. District Court, Middle District of North Carolina. *Education:* North Carolina State University (B.A., 1985); Cumberland School of Law (J.D., 1989). Phi Alpha Delta (Sergeant at Arms, 1989). Recipient, American Jurisprudence Award for Torts. Certified Superior Court Mediator. *Member:* Rowan County, 19-C Judicial District (President, 1998-1999); North Carolina State Bar. ***PRACTICE AREAS:*** Civil Litigation; Traffic Violations; Criminal Law; Mediation. ***Email:*** jfr@rowanlawyer.com

MICHAEL S. ADKINS, born South Williamson, Kentucky, July 14, 1962; admitted to bar, 1987, West Virginia and U.S. District Court, Southern District of West Virginia; 1988, Kentucky and North Carolina; 1990, U.S. District Court, Middle District of North Carolina. *Education:* Berea College (B.A., 1984); Wake Forest University (J.D., 1987). *Member:* Rowan County (Past President), West Virginia, Kentucky and American Bar Associations; North Carolina State Bar; West Virginia State Bar; 19-C Judicial District Bar; North Carolina Academy of Trial Lawyers; Rowan County Criminal Defense Lawyers Association. ***PRACTICE AREAS:*** Civil Litigation; Criminal Litigation; Personal Injury; Wrongful Death; Driving While Impaired. ***Email:*** msadkins@rowanlawyer.com

ASSOCIATES

NATHAN C. PRATER, born Chattanooga, Tennessee, August 3, 1970; admitted to bar, 1996, Alabama and U.S. District Court, Middle District of Alabama; 1998, U.S. Court of Appeals, Eleventh Circuit; 2005, North Carolina, U.S. District Court, Middle and Western Districts of North Carolina. *Education:* Pensacola Christian College (B.A., 1991); Cumberland School of Law of Samford University (J.D., 1996). Comment Editor, Cumberland Law Review. Author: "Punitive Damages in Alabama: A Proposal for Reform," 26 Cumb. L. Rev., 1005 (1996). *Member:* Rowan County Bar Association; Alabama State Bar; North Carolina State Bar. ***PRACTICE AREAS:*** General Civil Litigation; Insurance Defense Law; Employment Law; Worker's Compensation Law. ***Email:*** prater@rowanlawyer.com

JENNIFER B. FLYNN, born Charlotte, North Carolina, December 29, 1963; admitted to bar, 1989, North Carolina and U.S. District Court, Western and Middle Districts of North Carolina. *Education:* Wake Forest University (B.A., 1986; J.D., 1989). Phi Delta Phi. Recipient, American Jurisprudence Award, Juvenile Law, Spring, 1988. Member and on Executive Board, Moot Court Board, 1987-1989. *Member:* Rowan County North Carolina and North Carolina State Bar Associations. ***PRACTICE AREAS:*** Real Estate; Wills; Estates; Litigation. ***Email:*** jbf@rowanlawyer.com

REPRESENTATIVE CLIENTS: Duke Power Co.; Carolina Power and Light; North Carolina Farm Bureau Mutual Insurance Co.; Virginia Mutual Insurance Co.; Johnson Concrete Co.; C.M. Black Construction; Power Curbers, Inc.; Rowan Business Forms, Inc.; GerryWood Automotive, L.L.C.; Rowan Regional Medical Center Inc.; The Papco Group, Inc.; Rowan-

(This Listing Continued)

Cabarrus Community College; Freightliner Corp.; R-Anell Housing Group, LLC; Salisbury Lumber, Inc.; Lawyers Mutual Liability Ins.Co.; The Salisbury Post; Cloninger Ford - Toyota.

McKENY, WILLIAM TRIPPE

116 NORTH MAIN STREET
SALISBURY, NORTH CAROLINA 28144
Telephone: 704-636-3700
Fax: 704-636-8060
URL: http://www.trippemckeny.com

Bankruptcy, Criminal Law, Traffic Violations, Family Law, Personal Injury, Automobile Accidents.

MEMBER OF FIRM

TRIPPE McKENY, born South Charleston, West Virginia, April 1, 1970; admitted to bar, 2003, North Carolina. *Education:* Marshall University (B.A., 1999); University of Toledo (J.D., 2001). Graduated in top of class, University of Toledo. *Member:* Rowan County, North Carolina and American Bar Associations; North Carolina Lawyers Association. ***PRACTICE AREAS:*** Bankruptcy; Criminal Law; Traffic Violations; Family Law; Personal Injury; Automobile Accidents.

ROBERT A. MONATH

213 SOUTH MAIN STREET, SUITE 201
SALISBURY, NORTH CAROLINA 28144
Telephone: 704-645-0630
Fax: 704-645-0790
Email: rob@robmonath.com

Mailing Address: P.O. Box 4506, Salisbury, NC 28145-4506
Copyright, Trademark, Entertainment and Business Law.

ROBERT A. MONATH, born New York, N.Y., July 21, 1960; admitted to bar, 1985, North Carolina. *Education:* University of North Carolina (A.B., 1982; J.D., 1985). Phi Beta Kappa. Clerk, North Carolina Court of Appeals, 1985-1987. Adjunct Professor, Business Law, North Carolina State University, 1988. Member, Rowan Rotary. *Member:* North Carolina Bar Association (Intellectual Property Section); Carolina Patent, Trademark and Copyright Law Association. ***LANGUAGES:*** Spanish. ***PRACTICE AREAS:*** Intellectual Property; Business Law.

REPRESENTATIVE CLIENTS: Wachovia Corporation (Legal Division); Catawba College; Pain Relief Centers, P.A.; That's Music to My Ears, LTD; Hinshaw Music.

JAMES T. OXENDINE

111 WEST COUNCIL STREET
SALISBURY, NORTH CAROLINA 28144
Telephone: 704-636-1862; Toll Free: 877-367-0296
Fax: 704-636-3175
Email: oxendinelaw@velocenet.net
URL: http://www.oxendine-law.com

Criminal Law, Driving While Intoxicated (DWI), Traffic Violations, Family Law, Separation, Divorce, Juvenile, Personal Injury, Auto Accidents, Business, Estate Administration and Guardianships.

JAMES T. OXENDINE, born Philadelphia, Pennsylvania, November 16, 1965; admitted to bar, 1994, North Carolina; 1995, South Carolina; 1999, U.S. Supreme Court. *Education:* Temple University (B.A., 1988); Syracuse University (J.D., 1992). *Member:* Rowan County Bar Association; North Carolina State Bar (Member, Family Law Section); South Carolina Bar. ***PRACTICE AREAS:*** Criminal Law; Driving While Intoxicated; Traffic Violations; Family Law; Separation Agreements; Divorce; Juvenile Law; Personal Injury; Automobile Accidents and Injuries; Business Law; Estate Litigation.

PATTERSON AND ADAMS PLLC

710 NORTH MAIN STREET
SALISBURY, NORTH CAROLINA 28144
Telephone: 704-795-4317
URL: http://www.patterson-adams.com
URL: http://www.pattersonadamslawoffice.com

Concord, North Carolina Office: 433 Church Street North, 28025. Telephone: 704-795-4317. Fax: 704-795-5738.
Gastonia, North Carolina Office: 1305 East Garrison Boulevard, 28054. Telephone: 704-867-1955. Fax: 704-853-1875.

Personal Injury, Automobile Accidents, Wrongful Deaths, Workers Compensation, Medical Malpractice.

(For complete biographical data on all personnel, see Professional Biographies at Concord, North Carolina)

MARK E. SHELLEY

SALISBURY, NORTH CAROLINA

(See Concord)

Tax, IRS Audits, Property Tax, Tax Planning, Trust and Estates, Asset Protection, Estate Planning, Wills and Probate.

SHERRILL & CAMERON

117 WEST COUNCIL STREET
SALISBURY, NORTH CAROLINA 28144
Telephone: 704-633-5723
FAX: 704-633-0150
URL: http://www.sherrillcameron.com

Criminal Trial Practice State and Federal Courts, Driving While Intoxicated, Drug Crimes, Juvenile Crimes, Traffic Violations, Family Law, Divorce, Child Custody, Child Support, Visitation Rights, Personal Injury, Automobile Accidents, Wrongful Death, Real Estate, Construction, Environmental, Landlord and Tenant, Bankruptcy, Debt and Credit, Collections, Wills and Probate.

CARLYLE SHERRILL, born Salisbury, North Carolina, November 1, 1953; admitted to bar, 1981, North Carolina; U.S. District Court, Middle and Western Districts of North Carolina and U.S. Court of Appeals, Fourth Circuit. *Education:* Davidson College (B.A., 1976); University of Baltimore (J.D., 1981). Member, Law Review, 1979-1981 and Legislative Editor, 1980-1981. Law Clerk to the Honorable Sam J. Ervin, III, U.S. Fourth Circuit Court of Appeals, 1981-1982. Legislative Assistant to Representative W.G. (Bill Hefner), United States Congress, 1975-1985. *Member:* Rowan County and North Carolina Bar Associations; North Carolina State Bar; North Carolina Academy of Trial Lawyers. ***Email:*** Carlyle@sherrillcameron.com

WILLIAM (BILL) W. CAMERON, III, born Fayetteville, North Carolina, August 17, 1975; admitted to bar, 2004, North Carolina. *Education:* Davidson College (B.A., 1998); University of Alabama, Tuscaloosa (J.D., 2001). Member, Trial Team. *Member:* Rowan County Bar Association; North Carolina State Bar. ***PRACTICE AREAS:*** Criminal Law; Traffic Violations; Real Estate; Civil Litigation; Family Law; Juvenile Law. ***Email:*** bill@sherrillcameron.com

REPRESENTATIVE CLIENTS: Shoemaker Racing, Inc.; Roberts Racing Engines.
APPROVED ATTORNEY FOR: Statewide Title Insurance Co.; First American Title Insurance Co.; TransAmerica Title Insurance Co.
REFERENCE: Wachovia Bank.

SHUFORD, CADDELL & FRALEY

Established in 1974
205 WACHOVIA BANK BUILDING
130 SOUTH MAIN STREET
SALISBURY, NORTH CAROLINA 28144
Telephone: 704-636-8050

Corporation, Taxation, Real Estate, Estate Planning, Trusts and Estates, Wills and Probate, Business Law.

MEMBERS OF FIRM

W. T. SHUFORD (1905-1990)

THOMAS M. CADDELL, born Maxton, North Carolina, October 6, 1935; admitted to bar, 1973, New York; 1974, North Carolina. *Education:* University of North Carolina (B.S., 1961; M.B.A., 1964); Fordham University (J.D., cum laude, 1972); New York University (LL.M. in Taxation, 1977). Certified Public Accountant: North Carolina, 1963; New York, 1966. *Member:* New York State, North Carolina and American Bar Associations; North Carolina State Bar; American Institute of Certified Public Accountants; New York State Society of Certified Public Accountants; North Carolina Association of Certified Public Accountants. (Board Certified Specialist in Estate Planning and Probate Law). ***Email:*** tcaddell@scflegal.com

LUCINDA L. FRALEY, born Faith, North Carolina, December 28, 1968; admitted to bar, 1995, North Carolina. *Education:* Catawba College (B.A., magna cum laude, 1991); Campbell University School of Law (J.D., cum laude, 1995). Campbell Law Review Notes and Comments Editor, 1994-1995. Certified Public Accountant, North Carolina, 1997. *Member:* North Carolina State Bar; North Carolina and American Bar Associations; American Institute of Certified Public Accountants; North Carolina Association of Certified Public Accountants. ***Email:*** lfraley@scflegal.com

REPRESENTATIVE CLIENTS: Wachovia Bank, N.A.; Taylor Clay Products; Premtec, Inc.; Rockwell Farms; Rowan Corp.; J. H. Cook & Sons, Inc.; Central Carolina Insurance Agency, Inc.; Gardner Glass Products, Inc.; Piedmont Farm & Yard Equipment, Inc.; Power Curbers Distributors, Inc.

DOUGLAS A. SMITH

Established in 2000
216 NORTH JACKSON STREET
SALISBURY, NORTH CAROLINA 28144
Telephone: 704-633-9000
Fax: 704-636-3000
Email: attorneysmith@bellsouth.net
URL: http://www.lawyers.com/dougsmith

Criminal Law, Felonies, Misdemeanors, Family Law, Divorce, Child Custody, Child Support, Separation, Traffic Violations, Driving While Intoxicated, Construction Law, Children, Child Abuse and Neglect, Child Care, Grandparents Custody, Grandparents Visitation Rights, Juvenile Criminal Law, Step Parent Adoptions, Criminal Defense, Drivers License Suspension, Theft, Weapons Charges, Drug Crimes, Alimony, Domestic Violence, Equitable Distribution, Military Divorce, Name Changes, Paternity, Qualified Domestic Relations Orders, Separation Agreements, Spousal Support, Uncontested Divorce, Guardianship and Conservatorship, Guardian Ad Litem, Incompetency Proceedings, Personal Injury, Accidents, Automobile Accidents and Injuries, Motor Vehicle Accidents and Injuries, Pedestrian Injuries.

DOUGLAS A. SMITH, born Atlanta, Georgia, May 14, 1967; admitted to bar, 1997, North Carolina. *Education:* Georgia Southern College (B.A., 1992); Mercer University

(This Listing Continued)

DOUGLAS A. SMITH, Salisbury—Continued

(M.B.A., 1994); University of South Dakota (J.D., 1997). Assistant District Attorney, Rowan County, North Carolina, 1997-2000. *Member:* Rowan County and North Carolina Bar Associations.

LEGAL SUPPORT PERSONNEL

MELISSA J. OLEEN. *Education:* Bethany College (B.A., 1992); Indiana University (M.L.S., cum laude, 1993). (Office Manager). ***Email:*** attorneysmith@bellsouth.net

WHITLEY, CASTOR & JORDAN

305 NORTH MAIN STREET
SALISBURY, NORTH CAROLINA 28144
Telephone: 704-637-1111
Fax: 704-642-0672

Criminal Law, Domestic Law, Personal Injury, Traffic.

MEMBERS OF FIRM

CECIL L. WHITLEY, born Monroe, North Carolina, March 3, 1944; admitted to bar, 1973, North Carolina. *Education:* Catawba College (B.A., 1966); Wake Forest University (J.D., 1973). *Member:* North Carolina State Bar. ***PRACTICE AREAS:*** Criminal Law; Domestic Law.

ANDREA BRYANT CASTOR, born Forsyth County, North Carolina, November 20, 1972; admitted to bar, 1999, North Carolina. *Education:* Catawba College (B.A., 1995); Ohio Northern University (J.D., 1999). Member, Moot Court, 1996-1998. Vice President, Legal Association for Women, 1996-1999. *Rowan County (Member, Family Law Section) and North Carolina Bar Associations.* ***PRACTICE AREAS:*** Family Law; Divorce; Child Custody; Criminal Defense; Traffic Violations.

DARRIN D. JORDAN, born Newport News, Virginia, October 26, 1965; admitted to bar, 1990, North Carolina. *Education:* Catawba College (B.A., 1987); Campbell University (J.D., 1990). Formerly Assistant District Attorney, Rown/Cabarrus Counties, North Carolina. *Member:* North Carolina State Bar. ***PRACTICE AREAS:*** Criminal Defense; Domestic Relations. ***Email:*** djordan@wcjlaw.com

WOODSON, SAYERS, LAWTHER, SHORT, PARROTT & WALKER, LLP

Established in 1899
225 NORTH MAIN STREET, SUITE 200
P.O. BOX 829
SALISBURY, NORTH CAROLINA 28145-0829
Telephone: 704-633-5000
Fax: 704-637-2388
Email: woodlaw@carolina.rr.com

General Practice. Trials in all State and Federal Courts. Estate Planning, Probate and Taxation, Corporate, Municipal and Real Estate Law. Criminal, Family and Domestic Relations Law. Personal Injury.

FIRM PROFILE: Established in 1899, the firm of Woodson, Sayers, Lawther, Short, Parrott & Walker, LLP, is the oldest firm in Rowan County. Since that time, the firm has achieved and maintained Martindale-Hubbell's highest rating for legal ability and ethical conduct. The firm is committed to providing the highest quality legal representation, and our practice reflects high standards, diligence, experience and integrity.

MEMBERS OF FIRM

Walter H. Woodson (1875-1964) ***James L. Woodson*** (1916-1992)
J. Giles Hudson (1890-1973) ***James G. Hudson, Jr.*** (1921-1996)

DONALD D. SAYERS, born Greenville, South Carolina, February 15, 1943; admitted to bar, 1968, North Carolina. *Education:* University of North Carolina (A.B., 1965; J.D., 1968). Phi Delta Phi. Law Clerk to Chief U.S. District Judge, Eastern District of North Carolina, 1968-1969. United States Magistrate, 1971-1976. ***PRACTICE AREAS:*** Civil Litigation; Education Law; Real Estate. ***Email:*** dsay@carolina.rr.com

FRANCIS RIVERS LAWTHER, JR., born Charleston, South Carolina, August 8, 1942; admitted to bar, 1972, North Carolina. *Education:* University of North Carolina (A.B., 1964; J.D., 1972). Phi Delta Phi. President, Rowan County Bar Association, 1977. [Capt., USAF, 1964-1969]. ***PRACTICE AREAS:*** Corporate Law; Real Estate Law; Municipal Law. ***Email:*** rlawther@carolina.rr.com

CARL M. SHORT, JR., born High Point, North Carolina, February 23, 1950; admitted to bar, 1976, North Carolina. *Education:* University North Carolina (A.B., 1972; J.D., 1976). Phi Delta Phi. President, Rowan County Bar Association, 1990, 1991. ***PRACTICE AREAS:*** Real Estate Law; Banking Law; Corporate Law; Wills. ***Email:*** cshort@carolina.rr.com

S. EDWARD PARROTT, born Lexington, North Carolina, December 18, 1952; admitted to bar, 1978, North Carolina; 1979, U.S. District Court, Middle District of North Carolina. *Education:* University of North Carolina (B.S.B.A., 1975; J.D., 1978). Phi Beta Kappa. President, Rowan County Bar Association, 1995-1996. ***PRACTICE AREAS:*** Real Estate Law; Estate Planning and Probate Law. ***Email:*** separrott@carolina.rr.com

SEAN C. WALKER, born Colorado Springs, Colorado, June 27, 1971; admitted to bar, 1997, North Carolina. *Education:* University of North Carolina at Chapel Hill (A.B., 1994); Norman Wiggins School of Law, Campbell University (J.D., 1997). Phi Beta Kappa. Phi Alpha Delta. President, Rowan County Bar Association. ***PRACTICE AREAS:*** Criminal; Domestic Relations; Civil Litigation; Appellate Practice; Traffic Law; Real Estate Litigation; Real Estate Law; Business Transactions; Corporate Law. ***Email:*** swalk@carolina.rr.com

ASSOCIATE

ANDREW J. ABRAMSON, born Miami Beach, Florida, August 30, 1970; admitted to bar, 1997, Florida; 2004, North Carolina. *Education:* University of Miami (B.A., 1993); Nova Southeastern University (J.D., 1997). Member, Law Review. ***LANGUAGES:*** Spanish. ***PRACTICE AREAS:*** Civil Litigation; Land Use-Environmental; Real Estate; Personal Injury. ***Email:*** ajabramson@carolina.rr.com

GENERAL COUNSEL FOR: *Financial Institutions:* First National Bank and Trust Co.; Salisbury Pediatric Investments, LLC.; Central Carolina Neurology & Sleep, P.A. *Municipalities:* City of Salisbury, N.C.; Town of Spencer, N.C.; Town of Granite Quarry, N.C. *Educational Institutions:* Catawba College; Rowan-Salisbury Board of Education. *Charitable Foundations:* Margaret C. Woodson Foundation; Proctor Foundation; Preserve America Educational Foundation, Inc. *General Business:* Piedmont Cheerwine Bottling Co.; Wayne Bost Trucking Company, Inc.; Salisbury Orthopaedic Association, P.A.; Williams Development Co.; Salisbury Community Development, Inc.
LOCAL COUNSEL FOR: Carolina Farm Credit, ACA; Freirich Foods, Inc.; SunTrust Bank; Cincinnati Ins. Co.; Imperial, Inc.
APPROVED ATTORNEYS FOR: Lawyers Title Insurance Corp.; First American Title Insurance Co. Stewart Title Ins. Co.; Chicago Title Insurance Co.
REPRESENTATIVE CLIENTS: Comfort Contractors, Inc.; Investors Title Insurance Co.; Jim L. Bost Construction Co.; Country Club of Salisbury.
REFERENCES: Wachovia Bank and Trust Co.; First Union National Bank; Farmers & Merchants Bank; SunTrust Bank.

BAIN, BUZZARD & McRAE, LLP

SANFORD, NORTH CAROLINA

(See Lillington)

General Civil and Criminal Practice. Trials in all State and Federal Courts. Real Estate, Trusts and Estates, Wills and Probate, Medicaid Planning, Elder Law, Business and Corporate Law, Taxation, Tax Planning, Personal Injury, Automobile Accidents, Wrongful Death, Medical Malpractice, Criminal Law, DWI, Traffic Offenses.

G. HUGH MOORE

1401 WOODLAND AVENUE
P.O. BOX 194
SANFORD, NORTH CAROLINA 27330
Telephone: 919-774-9536
Facsimile: 919-775-4098
Email: ghmoore05@alltel.net

General Civil, Traffic and Criminal Trial Practice in all Courts. Personal Injury, Workers Compensation, Family and Commercial Law.

G. HUGH MOORE, born Hampton, Virginia, February 4, 1953; admitted to bar, 1978, North Carolina; 1980, U.S. District Court, Middle District of North Carolina. *Education:* Guilford College; Davidson College (B.A., honors in English, 1974); University of North Carolina (J.D., 1978). *Member:* Lee County (President, 1984-1985, 1989-1990) and North Carolina Bar Associations; North Carolina State Bar.

REFERENCE: First Citizens Bank & Trust Co.
APPROVED ATTORNEY FOR: Investors Title Insurance Co.

JANET B. DUDLEY
ATTORNEY AT LAW

140 E. 10TH STREET
P.O. BOX 280
SCOTLAND NECK, NORTH CAROLINA 27874
Telephone: 252-826-5124
Fax: 252-826-5056
Email: jdudley83@aol.com
URL: http://www.dudleyfamilylaw.com

Family Law, Divorce, Adoption Law, Child Custody, Child Support, Domestic Violence, Visitation Rights, Traffic Violations, Consumer Fraud, Warranties.

JANET B. DUDLEY, born Charlotte, North Carolina, June 8, 1951; admitted to bar, 2000, North Carolina. *Education:* Duke University (B.A., 1973); North Carolina Central University (J.D., 2000). *Member:* North Carolina and American Bar Associations; North Carolina Association of Trial Lawyers. ***PRACTICE AREAS:*** Family Law; Divorce; Adoption Law; Child Custody; Child Support; Domestic Violence; Visitation Rights; Traffic Violations; Consumer Fraud; Warranty Law.

DOUGLAS W. BAXLEY

Established in 1985
114 CHEERS STREET
P.O. BOX 36
SHALLOTTE, NORTH CAROLINA 28459
Telephone: 910-754-6582
Fax: 910-754-9272
Email: dwbaxley@shallotte.net

Calabash Office: 10164 Beach Drive, SW, 28467. Telephone: 910-575-6884. Fax: 910-575-6885.

Real Estate, Probate, Corporate, Estate Planning, Civil Practice.

(This Listing Continued)

DOUGLAS W. BAXLEY, born Durham, North Carolina, July 6, 1946; admitted to bar, 1975, North Carolina; 1977, U.S. District Court, Eastern District of North Carolina. *Education:* University of North Carolina (A.B., 1968; J.D., 1975). *Member:* Brunswick County (President, 1982), North Carolina (Member, Sections on: Real Estate; Probate; Fiduciary Law) and American Bar Associations; 13th Judicial District and North Carolina State Bars. [Capt., USAF, 1969-1972]. (Board Certified Specialist in Real Property Law: Residential Transactions, North Carolina State Board of Legal Specialization). ***LANGUAGES:*** Spanish.

BRUMBAUGH, MU & KING, P.A.

Established in 1978

143 HOLDEN BEACH ROAD
SUITE #6-A
SHALLOTTE, NORTH CAROLINA 28459
Telephone: 910-754-3660
URL: http://www.bmklaw.net

Practice Limited to Injury Cases. Automobile, Wrongful Death, Medical Malpractice, Workers' Compensation, Products Liability and Social Security Claims.

(For complete biographical data on all personnel, see professional biographies, Jacksonville, North Carolina)

FRINK, FOY & YOUNT, P.A.

4646 MAIN STREET
P.O. BOX 3207
SHALLOTTE, NORTH CAROLINA 28459
Telephone: 910-754-6934
Fax: 910-754-9224
Email: frinkfoy@infoave.net

General Civil and Criminal Practice in State and Federal Courts. Family Law, Trials, Trusts, Personal Injury, Real Estate, Corporate and Admiralty Law.

S. BUNN FRINK (1899-1989)

HENRY G. FOY, born High Point, North Carolina, February 6, 1942; admitted to bar, 1968, North Carolina; 1973, U.S. District Court, Eastern District of North Carolina; 1980, U.S. Court of Appeals, Fourth Circuit. *Education:* University of North Carolina (A.B., 1964; J.D., 1968). *Member:* Brunswick County (Secretary, 1968-1973), North Carolina and American Bar Associations; Thirteenth Judicial District (President, 1973-1974) and The North Carolina State Bars. [With USAR, 1964-1970]. (Retired)

STEPHEN B. YOUNT, born Atlanta, Georgia, April 23, 1952; admitted to bar, 1980, North Carolina; U.S. District Court, Eastern District of North Carolina. *Education:* East Carolina University (B.A., 1974); North Carolina Central University (J.D., 1979). Phi Delta Phi. Member, North Carolina Central University Law Review, 1978-1979. *Member:* Brunswick County, North Carolina and American Bar Associations; Thirteenth Judicial District and The North Carolina State Bars; North Carolina Academy of Trial Lawyers.

LOCAL COUNSEL FOR: Seaboard Coastline Railroad Co.; Reeves Telecom, Limited Partnership.
APPROVED ATTORNEYS FOR: Lawyers Title Insurance Corp.; Commercial Standard Ins.; Title Guaranty Co.; Federal Land Bank of Columbia; First Title Insurance Co.; American Title Insurance Co.
REPRESENTATIVE CLIENTS: Branch Bank & Trust Co.; Brunswick County, N.C.; Jefferson Pilot Insurance Companies Greensboro, N.C.; Security Savings Bank S.S.B., Southport, Shallotte and Leland, N.C.; Southport Fisheries, Inc., Southport, N.C.; Nationwide Insurance Cos., Raleigh, N.C.; Veterans Administration, Winston-Salem, N.C.; Seaside Properties, Inc, Southport, N.C.; Northwestern Insurance Co.; Cameron Brown Co.; Martin Marietta Materials, Inc.; South Brunswick Water and Sewer Authority; Maintenance Inc.; Leland, N.C.; International Paper Company.
REFERENCES: Branch Bank and Trust Co.; Southport and Shallotte, N.C.; Security Savings Bank S.S.B., Southport and Shallotte, N.C.

GREG JONES & ASSOCIATES, P.A.

SHALLOTTE, NORTH CAROLINA

(See Wilmington)

Personal Injury, Automobile Accidents, Brain Injury, Motorcycle Accidents, Wrongful Death, Medical Malpractice, Spinal Cord Injuries, Drug and Medical Device Litigation, Pharmacists Liability, Head Injuries, Products Liability, Medical and Nursing Home Negligence, Workers Compensation, Toxic Torts, Nursing Home Abuse, Stock Fraud.

RAMOS & LEWIS, L.L.P.

Established in 1986

5101-4 SELLERS STREET, MEADOW SQUARE
P.O. BOX 2019
SHALLOTTE, NORTH CAROLINA 28459
Telephone: 910-754-7557; 754-7447
Fax: 910-754-6229
Email: ramoslewis@infoave.net

Real Property, Wills, Trusts and Estates, Corporations, Domestic, Hospital, Criminal Defense, Municipal, Personal Injury, Administrative Law, Criminal and Civil Litigation in State and Federal Courts.

MICHAEL R. RAMOS, born Hartford, Connecticut, January 1, 1950; admitted to bar, 1982, North Carolina; 1983, U.S. Federal Court, Eastern District of North Carolina; 1995, U.S. Court of Appeals, Fourth Circuit; 1998, U.S. Federal Court, Middle District of North Carolina. *Education:* University of Georgia; Pembroke State University (B.A. in History, 1979); Mercer University; Campbell University (J.D., 1982). Delta Theta Phi. Weinstein History Scholar. Instructor, Brunswick Community College, 1983-1987. County Attorney, Brunswick County, 1993-1996. Chairman, Brunswick County Indigent Appointment Committee. Certified Capital Defense Counsel, North Carolina Indigent Defense Services Commission. Member, Criminal Justice Act Panel, Eastern District of North Carolina. *Member:* North Carolina Bar Association (Member, Criminal Law Section); North Carolina State Bar; North Carolina Academy of Trial Lawyers (Member, Criminal Law Section); National Association of Criminal Defense Lawyers. [U.S. Army, 1972-1975]. (Board Certified Specialist in Criminal Law, North Carolina State Bar of Legal Specialization). ***PRACTICE AREAS:*** Criminal Law; Driving While Intoxicated; Felonies; Drugs and Narcotics; Federal Criminal Law; White Collar Crime; Administrative Law; Local Government Law; Criminal Appeals. ***Email:*** ramoslewis@infoave.net

MARK A. LEWIS, born Denver, Colorado, April 22, 1956; admitted to bar, 1981, Colorado and U.S. District Court, District of Colorado; 1982, North Carolina; 1983, U.S. District Court, Eastern District of North Carolina; 1985, U.S. Court of Appeals, Fourth Circuit and U.S. Supreme Court. *Education:* University of Southern California; Georgetown University (A.B., 1978); Duke University (J.D., 1981). Phi Beta Kappa. Recipient, American Jurisprudence Award for Labor Law, Duke University School of Law, 1980. *Member:* Brunswick County (Treasurer, 1982-1986; President, 1984-1986) and North Carolina Bar Associations; North Carolina State Bar; North Carolina Academy of Trial Lawyers. ***LANGUAGES:*** Spanish. ***PRACTICE AREAS:*** Personal and Commercial Real Estate Transactions; Civil Litigation; Wills, Trusts and Estates; Municipal Law; Family Law; Divorce; Personal Injury; Professional Malpractice; Corporate Law. ***Email:*** ramoslewis@infoave.net

COUNSEL FOR: Town of Calabash; BB&T; Brunswick Community Hospital; Security Savings Bank; Bank of America; First Citizens Bank; UAW-Legal Services Plan; Farmers Home Administration.
REPRESENTATIVE CLIENTS: BB&T; Security Savings Bank; Columbia-Brunswick Hospital; Brunswick County.

H. MAC TYSON, II

Established in 1977

4647 MAIN STREET, SUITE 11
SHALLOTTE, NORTH CAROLINA 28470
Telephone: 910-755-6600
Fax: 910-754-3800
Email: hmactyson2@atmc.net
URL: http://www.lawyers.com/mactysonii

General Practice including General Civil Trial, Traffic Violations, Criminal Defense, Personal Injury, Corporate, Municipal, Military Law, Equitable Distribution, Domestic Law, Workers Compensation, Real Estate (Commercial and Residential), Probate, Wills and Estates, Taxation, Business Litigation, Zoning Law, Governmental Law and Ethics.

FIRM PROFILE: H. Mac Tyson, II has been serving clients for over twenty-two years throughout the east coast with emphasis in North Carolina. The firm engages in general practice with a focus on trial, business, tax and real estate work.

H. MAC TYSON, II, born 1951; admitted to bar, 1977, North Carolina; U.S. District Court, Eastern District of North Carolina; U.S. Court of Appeals, Fourth Circuit. *Education:* University of North Carolina at Chapel Hill (B.A., 1972); North Carolina Central University (J.D., 1976). Town Attorney, Town of Hope Mills, North Carolina, 1984-1986. State Certified District Court Arbitrator. *Member:* North Carolina State Bar. ***PRACTICE AREAS:*** Personal Injury; Commercial Litigation; Business Litigation; Criminal Law; Tax Law; Trusts and Estates; Probate; Real Estate; Domestic Relations.

APPROVED ATTORNEY FOR: Lawyers Title Insurance Co.; Chicago Title Insurance Co.; Investor's Title Insurance Corp.
REPRESENTATIVE CLIENTS: Systel Office Automation; Tire King of Jacksonville, Inc.; Chrysler Motor Co.
REFERENCES: First Citizens Bank & Trust Co.; Branch Bank & Trust.

BOGLE, ANTHONY & LEACH, P.A.

SHELBY, NORTH CAROLINA

(See Gastonia)

Workers Compensation, Personal Injury, Wrongful Death, Criminal Defense, Traffic Violations, Driving While Intoxicated, Corporate Law, Wills, Trust Law, Family Law/Domestic, Divorce, Child Custody, Child Support.

DON H. BUMGARDNER

SHELBY, NORTH CAROLINA

(See Gastonia)

General Civil and Appellate Practice in all State and Federal Courts. Personal Injury, Products Liability, Workers Compensation and Medical Malpractice.

CERWIN LAW FIRM

522 S. DEKALB STREET
SHELBY, NORTH CAROLINA 28150
Telephone: 704-471-0808
Fax: 704-471-0878
Email: t_cerwin@bellsouth.net

Personal Injury, Workers Compensation, Social Security, Criminal, Traffic, Automobile Accidents, Family Law, Child Custody, Estate Contested.

MEMBER OF FIRM

TODD R. CERWIN, born Milwaukee, Wisconsin, November 3, 1958; admitted to bar, 1984, North Carolina. *Education:* University of Wisconsin-Madison (B.S., Economics, 1981); Campbell University Law School (J.D., 1984). Member, Shelby Rescue Squad.

(This Listing Continued)

CERWIN LAW FIRM, Shelby—Continued

Member: North Carolina Bar Association; North Carolina Academy of Trial Lawyers. **PRACTICE AREAS:** Personal Injury; Workers Compensation; Social Security; Criminal Law; Traffic Violations; Automobile Accidents and Injuries; Family Law; Child Custody; Contested Trusts and Estates. ***Email:*** t_cerwin@bellsouth.net

ASSOCIATE

MICHAEL W. MILLER, born Waynesboro, Virginia, January 26, 1965; admitted to bar, 1997, North Carolina and South Carolina; 2004, U.S. Supreme Court. *Education:* James Madison University (B.A., 1987); Regent University School of Law (J.D., 1997). *Member:* North Carolina State Bar; South Carolina Bar. ***PRACTICE AREAS:*** Criminal Law; Traffic Violations; Social Security; Personal Injury; Automobile Accidents and Injuries; Workers Compensation; Family Law; Child Custody; Contested Trusts and Estates.

DEATON, BIGGERS & GULDEN, P.L.L.C.

Established in 1989

402 EAST GRAHAM STREET
P.O. BOX 458
SHELBY, NORTH CAROLINA 28150
Telephone: 704-482-7300
Fax: 704-481-9562
Email: robdeaton@bellsouth.net
URL: http://www.lawyers.com/shelbylaw

General Civil Practice. Trials. Practice before all State and Federal Courts and Administrative Agencies, Real Estate, Business Law, Wills and Estates, Estate Planning, Personal Injury, Workers Compensation, Criminal Law.

FIRM PROFILE: The firm of Deaton, Biggers & Gulden, P.L.L.C. was founded in 1989 by W. Robinson Deaton, Jr., who was joined by A. Susan Biggers in 1991 and Brian Donald Gulden in 2004. They cover primarily Cleveland, Gaston and Rutherford counties, and practice in all areas of the law, with emphasis toward personal injury, workers compensation and civil litigation. The firm also handles some complex litigation including medical malpractice, contract matters and product liability. Mr. Deaton practiced law with two other law partnerships prior to 1989.

W. ROBINSON DEATON, JR., born Shelby, North Carolina, October 23, 1951; admitted to bar, 1976, North Carolina; 1979, U.S. District Court, Western District of North Carolina and U.S. Court of Appeals, Fourth Circuit; 1983, U.S. Court of Federal Claims. *Education:* University of Tennessee (B.S., with honors, 1973); Duke University (J.D., 1976). Editorial Assistant, Law & Contemporary Problems, Duke University, 1974-1975. Chairman, Cleveland County Board of Elections, 1982-1985; 1993-1998. President, Judicial District 27-B Bar Association, 1992-1993. *Member:* Cleveland County and North Carolina Bar Associations; 27th Judicial District and The North Carolina State Bar. ***PRACTICE AREAS:*** Civil Litigation; Personal Injury; Automobile Accidents and Injuries; Wrongful Death; Workers Compensation; Municipal Law; Complex Civil Trials; Criminal Trials; Business Law; Family Law; Equitable Distribution; Wills; Estates. ***Email:*** robdeaton@bellsouth.net

A. SUSAN BIGGERS, born Shelby, North Carolina, April 1, 1966; admitted to bar, 1991, North Carolina. *Education:* Wake Forest University (B.A., magna cum laude, 1988); University of North Carolina (J.D., with honors, 1991). Member, North Carolina Journal of International Law, 1990-1991. Recipient, American Legal Jurisprudence Awards in Legal Research and Writing and Professional Responsibility. *Member:* Cleveland County and North Carolina Bar Associations; North Carolina State Bar. ***PRACTICE AREAS:*** Real Estate; Social Security Disability; Personal Injury; Automobile Accidents and Injuries; Wrongful Death; Workers Compensation; Probate; Estate Planning; Domestic Violence; Misdemeanors; Family Law; Divorce; Equitable Distribution; Adoption Law; Child Support; Child Custody; Wills; Estates. ***Email:*** susanbiggers@bellsouth.net

BRIAN DONALD GULDEN, admitted to bar, 2000, North Carolina. *Education:* University of North Carolina at Asheville (B.S., 1993); Southern Illinois University at Carbondale School of Law (J.D., 1999). National Health Law Moot Court Competitor, 1997-1998. Recipient: Hiram and Rosa Lee Lesar Scholarship, 1996-1997; Edgar and Bonnie Zimmer Scholarship, 1997-1998. Co-Winner of Intra-Collegiate ABA Client Counseling Competition. Listed On: National Dean's List, 1990; UNCA Dean's List, 1990, 1992. Staff Attorney, Cobourn and Saleeby, L.L.P., 1999. Ordinance Administrator, Henderson County Planning Department, 1999—. ***PRACTICE AREAS:*** Civil Litigation; Personal Injury; Automobile Accidents and Injuries; Wrongful Death; Workers Compensation; Municipal Law; Complex Civil Trials; Criminal Trials; Driving While Intoxicated; Traffic Violations; Drug Crimes; Business Law; Family Law; Divorce; Equitable Distribution; Adoption Law; Child Support; Child Custody; Wills; Estates. ***Email:*** briangulden@bellsouth.net

APPROVED ATTORNEYS FOR: Investors Title Insurance Co.; Lawyers Title Insurance Co.; Chicago Title Insurance Co.
List of Clients furnished upon request.

FLOWERS, MARTIN, MOORE & DITZ, P.A.

Established in 1939

212 SOUTH DEKALB STREET
SHELBY, NORTH CAROLINA 28150
Telephone: 704-482-4441
Fax: 704-482-4872
Email: lawyers@flowersmartinmoore.com

Transaction and Litigation Practice. Civil and Criminal Trial Practice in State and Federal Courts. Banking, Business/Corporate Law, Entertainment Law, Real Estate, Estate Planning, Probate and Trusts, Family Law, Governmental Law, Education Law, Personal Injury, Social Security Disability, Workers Compensation, Traffic.

(This Listing Continued)

L. T. HAMRICK (1911-1989)

JOE MAUNEY (Retired)

FRED A. FLOWERS, born Red Oak, North Carolina, May 14, 1939; admitted to bar, 1963, North Carolina and U.S. District Court, Western District of North Carolina; 1980, U.S. Court of Appeals, Fourth Circuit. *Education:* Mars Hill College (A.A., 1959); Wake Forest University (B.A., 1961; J.D., 1963). Phi Alpha Delta. General Counsel, Gardner Webb University. *Member:* Cleveland County (Past President and Member, 27B Judicial District) and North Carolina Bar Associations; North Carolina State Bar; North Carolina Academy of Trial Lawyers. ***Email:*** fred@flowersmartinmoore.com

THOMAS W. MARTIN, JR., born Shelby, North Carolina, June 15, 1951; admitted to bar, 1976, North Carolina; 1983, U.S. District Court, Western District of North Carolina. *Education:* Wake Forest University (B.A., cum laude, 1973; J.D., 1976). Phi Delta Phi. General Counsel to: Town of Lattimore, Town of Lawndale and Town of Belwood; Cleveland County Association of Realtors. *Member:* Cleveland County and North Carolina Bar Associations; North Carolina State Bar. ***PRACTICE AREAS:*** Real Property; Municipal Law; Corporate Law. ***Email:*** tom@flowersmartinmoore.com

TIMOTHY K. MOORE, born Kings Mountain, North Carolina, October 2, 1970; admitted to bar, 1995, North Carolina; 1996, U.S. District Court, Eastern, Western and Middle Districts of North Carolina and U.S. Court of Appeals, Fourth Circuit; 1997, District of Columbia. *Education:* Campbell University; University of North Carolina (B.A., 1992); Oklahoma City University School of Law (J.D., 1995). Member: North Carolina House of Representatives, 2003—; Board of Governors, University of North Carolina, 1997-2001. *Member:* North Carolina State Bar; District of Columbia Bar. ***Email:*** tim@flowersmartinmoore.com

PAUL J. DITZ, born Syracuse, New York, January 11, 1971; admitted to bar, 1997, North Carolina and U.S. District Court, Western District of North Carolina. *Education:* Syracuse University (B.A., 1992); Wake Forest University (J.D., 1997). *Member:* Cleveland County and North Carolina Bar Associations; North Carolina State Bar. ***Email:*** paul@flowersmartinmoore.com

REPRESENTATIVE CLIENTS: Gardner-Webb University; Earl Owensby Studios; Moore Furniture Co., Inc.; Stitzel Construction, Inc.; Wade Ford, Inc.; Genesys Network Systems, Inc.; Southern Real Estate Group, Inc.
APPROVED ATTORNEYS FOR: Lawyers Title Insurance Corp.; AMI Title Insurance Co.; Jefferson-Pilot Title Insurance Co.; Chicago Title Insurance Co.; Investors Title Insurance Co.; Stewart Title Co.; First American Title Insurance Co.; First National Bank of Shelby; Shelby Savings Bank; Piedmont Farm Credit; B B & T.

J. BOYCE GARLAND, JR.

SHELBY, NORTH CAROLINA

(See Gastonia)

General Civil and Criminal Practice in all Courts. Corporations, Business, Estate Planning and Administration, Probate, Real Estate, Personal Injury, Automobile Accidents, and Criminal.

GRAY, LAYTON, KERSH, SOLOMON, SIGMON, FURR & SMITH, P.A.

SHELBY, NORTH CAROLINA

(See Gastonia)

General Civil Trial Practice, Arbitration, Corporation Law, Construction Law, Real Estate Law, Mediation, Municipal and Zoning Law, Mergers and Acquisitions, Bankruptcy, Family, Tax, Estate Planning and Probate Law, Personal Injury Law, Traffic, Professional Sports Representation, Community Association Law.

DAVID MARK HULLENDER

SHELBY, NORTH CAROLINA

(See Kings Mountain)

General Practice, Traffic Violations, Driving While Intoxicated, Real Estate, Family Law, Divorce, Wills, Probate.

LACKEY & LACKEY

400 WEST WARREN STREET
P.O. BOX 2544
SHELBY, NORTH CAROLINA 28150
Telephone: 704-487-4511
Fax: 704-487-4222
Email: lackeyandlackey@aol.com

General Practice. Trials in State and Federal Courts. Corporate, Personal Injury, Estates, Wills, Trusts and Real Property.

MEMBERS OF FIRM

MARK D. LACKEY, born Fort Knox, Kentucky, May 7, 1958; admitted to bar, 1983, North Carolina. *Education:* University of North Carolina, Chapel Hill, North Carolina (A.B., 1980; J.D., 1983). *Member:* Cleveland County and North Carolina Bar Associations; 27B Judicial District and North Carolina State Bars. ***PRACTICE AREAS:*** Real Estate; Corporate Law; Personal Injury.

SETH N. LACKEY, born Shelby, North Carolina, July 5, 1965; admitted to bar, 1993, North Carolina. *Education:* University of North Carolina at Charlotte; University of North Carolina at Chapel Hill (B.A., 1988); Campbell University (J.D., 1993). *Member:* North Carolina and American Bar Associations. ***PRACTICE AREAS:*** Criminal Litigation; Civil Litigation; Personal Injury.

(This Listing Continued)

REPRESENTATIVE CLIENTS: Shelby Federal Savings and Loan Assn.; Duke University; Cleveland Community College; Doran Textiles, Inc.; Belding-Heminway Co.; Duke Power Co.; United States Fidelity & Guaranty Co.; PPG Industries, Inc.; Hoechst Celanese Corp.; J.P. Stevens Co.; Martin-Marietta Corp.; Cleveland Mills Co.; Jefferson-Pilot Life Insurance Co.; Integon Life Insurance Corp.; Williams Oil Company of Shelby, Inc.; A.V. Dedmon Trucking, Inc.; NationsBank; State Employees' Credit Union; Old Stone Bank of North Carolina; BB&T Grover Industries Inc.
APPROVED ATTORNEYS FOR: Lawyers Title Insurance Corp.; Investors Title Insurance Co.; Ticor Title Insurance Co.; Chicago Title Insurance Co.; First Title Insurance Co.
REFERENCES: Shelby Savings and Loan Assn.; First National Bank of Shelby, N.C.; Shelby Savings Bank; Bryt First Charter Bank.

MULLEN HOLLAND & COOPER P.A.

SHELBY, NORTH CAROLINA

(See Gastonia)

General Civil Trial and Appellate Practice, all Federal and State Courts. Banking, Bankruptcy and Reorganization, Construction, Corporate and Commercial, Employment Discrimination, Estate Planning and Administration, Health Care, Insurance, Mergers and Acquisitions, Negligence, Personal Injury, Professional Malpractice, Real Estate, Workers' Compensation.

THE ROBERTS LAW FIRM, P.A.

SHELBY, NORTH CAROLINA

(See Gastonia)

Trial Practice. Personal Injury, Workers Compensation, Social Security Disability, Medical Malpractice, Nursing home Litigation, Products Liability and Wrongful Death.

LAW OFFICE OF LYNN BROADWAY WILKIE

SHELBY, NORTH CAROLINA

(See Lincolnton)

YELTON, FARFOUR, McCARTNEY, LUTZ & CRAIG, P.A.

Established in 1968

PROFESSIONAL MALL
211 SOUTH WASHINGTON STREET
P.O. BOX 1329
SHELBY, NORTH CAROLINA 28150
Telephone: 704-482-7718
Fax: 704-482-6747
Email: yeltonr@bellsouth.net
URL: http://www.ymflawfirm.com

General Practice. Corporation, Estate Planning, and Personal Injury Law. Trial and appellate practice in all courts. Creditors" Rights and Bankruptcy law. Domestic and Family Law.

FIRM PROFILE: Since 1968, when Robert W. Yelton opened his practice in Shelby, the firm which is now Yelton, Farfour, McCartney, Lutz & Craig, P.A., has continuously served the legal needs of Cleveland County, North Carolina and its surrounding counties. Leslie A. Farfour, Jr. and Charles E. McCartney, Jr., joined the firm in 1972, Robert H. Lutz joined in 1990, and Sam Craig in 2000. Each of our attorneys has special talents and interests that we draw upon to solve the legal concerns of our clients. Our goal is to provide high quality, client oriented legal services in a professional, ethical and economic manner. At Yelton, Farfour, McCartney, Lutz & Craig, P.A., we maintain a strong belief that preventive law is the best way to represent our clients. We take great pride in representing our clients today while preparing them for tomorrow.

ROBERT W. YELTON, born Charlotte, North Carolina, August 14, 1942; admitted to bar, 1967, North Carolina. *Education:* Wake Forest University (B.A., cum laude, 1964; J.D., 1967); Columbia University (LL.M., 1968). Phi Beta Kappa; Omicron Delta Kappa; Phi Delta Phi. Cleveland County Attorney, 1976-1993 . President, North Carolina County Attorneys Association, 1982-1983. Legal Officer, North Carolina Wing, Civil Air Patrol, 1989-1993. *Member:* Cleveland County (Treasurer, 1968; President, 1974) and North Carolina Bar Associations; 27th Judicial District; North Carolina State Bar. ***PRACTICE AREAS:*** Corporate; Estate Planning; Real Estate; Tax; Municipal. ***Email:*** yeltonr@bellsouth.net

LESLIE A. FARFOUR, JR., born Morganton, North Carolina, December 28, 1946; admitted to bar, 1972, North Carolina. *Education:* University of North Carolina (A.B., 1969; J.D., 1972). Phi Delta Phi. *Member:* Cleveland County (President, 1978), 27th Judicial District, North Carolina Bar Association; North Carolina State Bar; North Carolina Academy of Trial Lawyers. ***PRACTICE AREAS:*** Litigation; Personal Injury; Automobile Accidents and Injuries; Wrongful Death; Domestic Violence; Family Law; Divorce; Child Support; Child Custody; Equitable Distribution; Criminal Law; Driving While Impaired; Traffic Violations. ***Email:*** lafjr@bellsouth.net

ROBERT HOWARD LUTZ, born Kings Mountain, North Carolina, February 19, 1963; admitted to bar, 1989, Georgia and North Carolina; 1991, South Carolina. *Education:* Lenoir-Rhyne College (B.A., 1985); Georgia State University (J.D., 1988). Delta Theta Phi. *Member:* Cleveland County and North Carolina Bar Associations; North Carolina State Bar; South Carolina Bar; State Bar of Georgia; North Carolina Academy of Trial Lawyers; 27th Judicial District (President, 1994-1995). ***PRACTICE AREAS:*** Litigation; Criminal Law; Driving While Impaired; Traffic Violations; Bankruptcy; Creditors Rights. ***Email:*** robtlutz@bellsouth.net

SAM B. CRAIG, born Easley, South Carolina, August 5, 1958; admitted to bar, 2000, North Carolina; 2001, South Carolina and U.S. District Court, Western District of North Carolina; 2002, U.S. Court of Appeals, Fourth Circuit. *Education:* Clemson University (B.A., Forest Management, 1980); University of South Carolina School of Law (J.D., 2000, cum laude). Order of the Wig and Robe. Associate Articles Editor, South Carolina Law Review, 2000. Registered Forester, North Carolina, 1985-2005, and South Carolina, 1984-2005. *Member:* Cleveland County (President, 2003) and North Carolina Bar Associations (27B Secretary/Treasurer 2001); North Carolina Academy of Trial Lawyers. ***PRACTICE AREAS:*** Civil Litigation; Commercial Law; Real Estate; Criminal Law; Driving While Impaired; Traffic Violations; Automobile Accidents and Injuries; Wrongful Death; Personal Injury. ***Email:*** samcraig@bellsouth.net

OF COUNSEL

CHARLES E. McCARTNEY, JR., born Tampa, Florida, September 9, 1947; admitted to bar, 1972, North Carolina. *Education:* Wake Forest University (B.A., 1969; J.D., 1972). Phi Delta Phi. Associate Editor, Wake Forest Law Review, 1971-1972. Author: "The Limited Application of the Eighth Amendment's Cruel and Unusual Punishment Clause to the Death Penalty," Wake Forest Law Review, June, 1971. Member, Cleveland County Board of Elections, 1974-1975. President, Western Piedmont Estate Planning Council, 1979-1981. *Member:* Cleveland County (President, 1980-1981), 27th Judicial District, North Carolina Bar Association; North Carolina State Bar. [Colonel U.S. Army Reserve, 1972—]. ***PRACTICE AREAS:*** Commercial; Real Estate; Creditor; Corporate. ***Email:*** cemadc@bellsouth.net

REPRESENTATIVE CLIENTS: AIG Aviation; Arnold & Powers; Associates Financial Services; Avco Financial Services; Badcock Home Furnishings; Ballinger Corporation; Balsam Acres, Inc.; BB & T Company; Beam Structural Movers, Inc.; Burch Electric, Inc.; C & R Properties; Carolina Family Care, P.A.; Carter Chevrolet Oldsmobile-Geo, Inc.; Challenger Three Golf Club, Inc.; Cleveland County government; Cleveland Country Club; Cleveland Community College; Cleveland Progress, LLC; Copeland Corporation; Costner Motors Company, Inc.; Duke Power Company; Employment Staffing; First Charter Bank; First National Bank of Shelby; Fleet Finance; Fox Mountain Weavers, Inc.; H & H Pest Control, Inc.; Hanna Industries; Harrill Chemical and Paper Supply, Inc.; Icabod's Eatery of N.C., Inc.; Imperial Insurance & Finance Company; Iron Bar Gym; Isothermal Community College; Kentucky Finance Company; Marion Credit Company; Melton's Nissan; Minette Mills; Peeler Properties, Inc.; Pine Grove Golf Club, Inc.; The Prudential Carolinas Realty; Shelby Alarm Co., Inc.; Shelby Anesthesiology Associates, P.A.; Shelby Dyeing & Finishing, Inc.; The Shelby Shopper; Shoco, Inc.; Sluder Floral Co., Inc.; Southern Sunrise Foods; Tact Plastics, Inc.; Yelton Data Systems, Inc.; Young Motor Sales & Leasing.
REFERENCE: The First National Bank of Shelby, Inc.

(This Listing Continued)

JONATHAN D. BREEDEN

SMITHFIELD, NORTH CAROLINA

(See Garner)

Criminal Law, Driving While Intoxicated (DWI), Drug Crimes, Traffic Violations, Family Law, Child Custody, Child Support, Divorce, Education Law, Contracts, Wills.

THE LAW OFFICES OF HALES & CONAWAY, PLLC

SMITHFIELD, NORTH CAROLINA

(See Clinton)

Family Law, Divorce, Adoption, Custody, Child Support, Premarital Agreements, Separation Agreements, Criminal Defense, Social Security Disability, Collections, Debtor, Creditor, Juvenile Law, Estate Administration and Estate Planning, Civil Litigation, Workers Compensation, Personal Injury, Traffic, DWI.

JESSE W. JONES

SMITHFIELD, NORTH CAROLINA

(See Lillington)

Criminal Law, Felonies, Misdemeanors, Murder, Manslaughter, Parole and Probation, Sex Crimes, Capital Offenses, Personal Injury, Automobile Accidents and Injuries, Wrongful Death, Family Law, Child Custody, Divorce, Alimony, Spousal Support, Traffic Violations, Driving While Intoxicated.

NARRON, O'HALE & WHITTINGTON, P.A.

Established in 1975

102 SOUTH THIRD STREET
P.O. BOX 1567
SMITHFIELD, NORTH CAROLINA 27577
Telephone: 919-934-6021
Fax: 919-934-6280
URL: http://www.nowlaw.com

Benson, North Carolina Office: 207 East Main Street, P.O. Box 457. Telephone: 919-894-8565. Fax: 919-894-1198.

Alternative Dispute Resolution, Asset Acquisition, Mergers, and Divestitures, Automobile Accidents and Injuries, Civil Litigation, Corporate Law, Criminal Law, Trial and Appeals in State and Federal Courts, DWI, Elder Law, Estate Planning, Estate and Trusts, Family Law, Personal Injury, Taxation, Real Property Law, Commercial and Residential Real Estate, Workers Compensation, Wrongful Death.

JAMES W. NARRON, born Washington, D.C., January 18, 1948; admitted to bar, 1975, North Carolina and U.S. District Court, Eastern District of North Carolina; 1983, U.S. Tax Court and U.S. Court of Federal Claims. *Education:* University of North Carolina (A.B., 1970); Wake Forest University (J.D., cum laude, 1975); New York University (LL.M. in Taxation, 1983). Phi Delta Phi. Associate Editor, Wake Forest Law Review, 1974-1975.

(This Listing Continued)

NARRON, O'HALE & WHITTINGTON, P.A., Smithfield—Continued

Adjunct Professor, Campbell University School of Law, 1984-1996. *Member:* Johnston County, North Carolina and American Bar Associations; North Carolina State Bar (Councilor, 1995-1998). Fellow, American College of Trust and Estate Counsel. [Lt., U.S. Navy, 1970-1972]. (Board Certified Specialist in Estate Planning and Probate Law). ***PRACTICE AREAS:*** Mergers, Acquisitions and Divestitures; Corporate Law; Estate Planning; Trusts and Estates; Real Estate; Commercial Real Estate; Residential Real Estate; Taxation. ***Email:*** jwnarron@nowlaw.com

JOHN P. O'HALE, born Cleveland, Ohio, June 6, 1950; admitted to bar, 1975, North Carolina, U.S. District Court, Eastern District of North Carolina, U.S. Court of Appeals, Fourth Circuit and U.S. Supreme Court. *Education:* University of North Carolina (A.B., 1972; J.D., 1975). Phi Beta Kappa. Assistant District Attorney, Superior Court, Eleventh Judicial District, 1976-1979. Member: Johnston County Board of Education, 2000—; University of North Carolina, Board of Directors Law Alumni Association, 2000. *Member:* Johnston County (President, 1996-1997), North Carolina (Member, Criminal Justice Section, 2000-2004) and American Bar Associations; Eleventh Judicial District (President, 1994-1995) and North Carolina State Bars; North Carolina Academy of Trial Lawyers; Association of Trial Lawyers of America; National Association of Criminal Defense Lawyers. (Board Certified Specialist in Criminal Law). ***PRACTICE AREAS:*** Criminal Law; Civil Litigation.

O. HAMPTON WHITTINGTON, JR., born Benson, North Carolina, February 25, 1949; admitted to bar, 1975, North Carolina and U.S. District Court, Middle District of North Carolina; 1981, U.S. District Court, Eastern District of North Carolina. *Education:* Davidson College (B.A., 1971); University of North Carolina (J.D., with honors, 1975). Member, Holderness Moot Court Bench, 1974-1975. Assistant District Attorney, Superior Court Division, 11th Judicial District, 1979-1981. Certified Mediator, 1996—. Member, 1984-2002, Chairman, 1997-2002, Johnston County Planning Board. Member, Johnston County Economic Development Commission, 2004—. *Member:* Johnston County (President, 1998), Eleventh Judicial District (President, 2000), North Carolina and American Bar Associations; North Carolina State Bar; North Carolina Academy of Trial Lawyers; The Association of Trial Lawyers of America. (Resident, Benson Office). ***PRACTICE AREAS:*** Personal Injury Law; Workers Compensation; Wrongful Death; Civil Litigation; Alternative Dispute Resolution. ***Email:*** ohw@nowlaw.com

ASSOCIATES

JASON W. WENZEL, born September 15, 1976; admitted to bar, 2002, North Carolina. *Education:* Albion College (B.A., magna cum laude, 1999); Wake Forest University (J.D., 2002). Phi Beta Kappa. Author: "An Analysis of the Origins of the Federal Trademark Patent Law," Wake Forest Intell. Prop. L. J. 4 (2002). *Member:* Johnson County (Secretary and Treasurer, 2003), North Carolina, American (Member, Business Law Section) and Eleventh Judicial Circuit (Secretary and Treasurer, 2003) Bar Associations. ***PRACTICE AREAS:*** Corporate Law; Tax Law; Estate Planning; Elder Law; Estate Administration; Real Property; Civil Litigation; Criminal Law; Commercial Real Estate; Residential Real Estate. ***Email:*** jwenzel@nowlaw.com

JOY A. JONES, born Raleigh, North Carolina, January 12, 1958; admitted to bar, 1989, Indiana and U.S. District Court, Southern and Northern Districts of Indiana; 1990, California, U.S. District Court, Southern District of California and U.S. Court of Appeals, Ninth Circuit; 1998, North Carolina; 2002, U.S. District Court, Eastern District of North Carolina. *Education:* University of North Carolina (B.S., Administration of Criminal Justice/Political Science, 1980); Indiana University at Indianapolis (J.D., 1989). Member: California Narcotics Officers Association, 1991-1997; California District Attorneys Association, 1990-1998. *Member:* Johnson County, Indiana State, North Carolina, American and Eleventh Judicial District Bar Associations; State Bar of California; North Carolina State Bar. ***PRACTICE AREAS:*** Criminal Defense; State Government Law; Federal Government Law; Traffic Law. ***Email:*** jjones@nowlaw.com

E. SCOTT TART, born Smithfield, North Carolina, July 27, 1976; admitted to bar, 2001, North Carolina. *Education:* Campbell University (B.A., summa cum laude, 1998); University of North Carolina (J.D., 2001). *Member:* Johnson County (Secretary and Treasurer, 2002), North Carolina, American and Eleventh Judicial District Bar Associations; North Carolina State Bar; North Carolina Academy of Trial Lawyers. ***PRACTICE AREAS:*** Civil Litigation; Criminal Law; Traffic Law; Estate Administration; Real Property; Residential Real Estate; Personal Injury; Workers Compensation; Family Law. ***Email:*** start@nowlaw.com

REPRESENTATIVE CLIENTS: Wachovia Bank, N.A.; First Citizens Bank and Trust; E.D. Parker Corp.; Benson Auto Supply, Inc.; Carroll's Plant Center; Etheridge Oil Co.
APPROVED ATTORNEYS FOR: Lawyers Title Insurance Corp.; Key Title Insurance Co.; Fidelity National Title Insurance Co.; Investors Title Insurance Co.
REFERENCES: First Citizen's Bank & Trust Co.; Investors Title Ins. Co.

ROSE RAND ATTORNEYS, P.A.

SMITHFIELD, NORTH CAROLINA

(See Wilson)

General Practice, all Courts. Corporation, Labor and Insurance Law. Trials, including Personal Injury, Wrongful Death and Workers Compensation, Eminent Domain, Tax, Estate Planning and Administration, Municipal, Environmental, Real Estate, Bankruptcy.

SMITH AND STRICKLAND, PLLC

SMITHFIELD, NORTH CAROLINA

(See Goldsboro)

Criminal Defense, Driving While Impaired, DUI, DWI, Traffic Violations, Parole and Probation, Drug Crimes, White Collar Crimes, Juvenile Crimes, Personal Injury, Military Law.

SPENCE & SPENCE, P.A.

212 SOUTH SECOND STREET
P.O. BOX 1335
SMITHFIELD, NORTH CAROLINA 27577
Telephone: 919-934-1149
Fax: 919-934-3635
Email: spence@sst-law.com
URL: http://www.sstlaw.com

Civil Trial Practice, Insurance Litigation, Real Property and Business Litigation Transactions, Personal Injury, Construction and Business Litigation, Municipal Law, Planning Litigation, Corporation, Real Estate, Family Law, Juvenile, Domestic Relations, Traffic Tickets.

ROBERT A. SPENCE, JR., born Raleigh, North Carolina, September 29, 1949; admitted to bar, 1975, North Carolina. *Education:* Woodberry Forest School; Wesleyan University (A.B., 1972); University of North Carolina (J.D., 1975). Town Attorney, Town of Pine Level, 1977-2001; Town of Smithfield, 1996—Town of Princeton, 1995—. Past Board Director: Farm Workers Legal Services; East Central Community Legal Services. *Member:* Johnston County Bar Association (President, 1991); North Carolina State Bar (Counselor, 1998—); Eleventh Judicial District (Secretary-Treasurer, 1976; President, 2003); North Carolina Academy of Trial Lawyers. (Board Certified Specialist in Real Property Law, Residential Transactions, North Carolina State Board of Legal Specialization). ***PRACTICE AREAS:*** Civil Litigation; Insurance Defense; Real Property Litigation; Commercial Law; Construction Litigation; Real Property Transactions; Zoning, Planning and Land Use; Municipal Law; Domestic Relations; Family Law; Business Transactions. ***Email:*** spence@sst-law.com

---

BRIAN R. KNOTT, born Flint, Michigan, May 8, 1968; admitted to bar, 1995, North Carolina. *Education:* Michigan State University (B.S., 1990); University of Arkansas (J.D., 1993). *Member:* Johnston County Bar Association, North Carolina State Bar; Eleventh Judicial District Bar. ***PRACTICE AREAS:*** Civil Litigation; Criminal Law; Family Law; Business Transactions; Bankruptcy; Personal Injury; Traffic Violations. ***Email:*** bknott@sst-law.com

REPRESENTATIVE CLIENTS: North Carolina Farm Bureau Insurance Co.; Town of Smithfield; Safeway Finance Corp. of North Carolina; Town of Princeton; Independent Builders Supply Assn., Inc.; Williamsburg Woodcraft Inc.; First Citizens Bank; Heritage Bank; KS Bank, Inc.; Four Oaks Bank & Trust.
APPROVED ATTORNEY FOR: Chicago Title Insurance Company; Lawyers Title Insurance Corp.; Investors Title Insurance Co.; Fidelity National Title; First Citizens Bank & Trust Company and Four Oaks Bank and Trust Company; Key Title.
REFERENCE: First Citizens Bank & Trust Co.

WILKINS & WELLONS

141 EAST MARKET STREET
SMITHFIELD, NORTH CAROLINA 27577
Telephone: 919-934-0553
Fax: 919-934-4613

Personal Injury, Workers Compensation, Real Estate, Traffic Violations, Driving While Intoxicated, Corporate, Civil Litigation, Business Transactions, Automobile Accidents, Truck Accidents, Wrongful Death.

ALLEN H. WELLONS, born Smithfield, North Carolina, March 12, 1949; admitted to bar, 1975, North Carolina. *Education:* University of North Carolina at Chapel Hill (B.A., 1971); North Carolina Central University (J.D., 1975). ***PRACTICE AREAS:*** Personal Injury; Workers Compensation; Real Estate; Traffic Violations; Corporate Law. ***Email:*** allen@wilkinswellons.com

ASSOCIATE

JASON H. COATS, born Smithfield, North Carolina, April 29, 1977; admitted to bar, 2003, North Carolina. *Education:* Campbell University (B.B.A., M.B.A., 2000; J.D., 2003). *Member:* North Carolina State Bar; North Carolina Bar Association; Johnston County Bar Association; American Bar Association; Association of Trial Lawyers of America. ***PRACTICE AREAS:*** Trusts and Estates; Wills; Probate; Traffic Violations; Real Estate; Corporate Law; Guardianship; Collections; Driving While Intoxicated; Misdemeanors; Materialmens Liens; Mechanics Liens; Construction Law; Easements; Real Estate Title Examination; Residential Real Estate. ***Email:*** jason@wilkinswellons.com

---

LAW OFFICES OF ROBERT J. WILLIS

SMITHFIELD, NORTH CAROLINA

(See Raleigh)

Workers Compensation, Criminal Defense, Driving While Intoxicated, Traffic Violations, Automobile Accidents, Wage and Hour Disputes.

WOODRUFF, REECE & FORTNER

1023 B WEST MARKET STREET
P.O. BOX 708
SMITHFIELD, NORTH CAROLINA 27577
Telephone: 919-934-4000
Fax: 919-934-5884
URL: http://www.wrflaw.com
URL: http://www.lawyers.com/reecelawfirm

General Practice, Civil Trial Practice, Criminal, Driving While Intoxicated, Traffic Violations, Personal Injury, Domestic Relations, Family Law, Bankruptcy.

(This Listing Continued)

GORDON C. WOODRUFF, born Raleigh, North Carolina, December 29, 1951; admitted to bar, 1976, North Carolina. *Education:* University of North Carolina (B.A., 1973); Wake Forest University (J.D., 1976). Phi Delta Phi. Morehead Scholar. Member, Wake Forest Law Review, 1975-1976. Author: Note, 11 Wake Forest Law Review 473, 1975. Research Assistant to Judge Naomi E. Morris, North Carolina Court of Appeals, 1976-1977. Member, Johnston County Board of Education, 1988-1994; Chairman, 1992-1994. Chairman, Johnston County Board of Elections, 2003—. Member, Board of Directors, KS Bank. Dispute Resolution Commission, Certified Mediator. *Member:* Johnston County, North Carolina and American Bar Associations; North Carolina State Bar; North Carolina Academy of Trial Lawyers. ***PRACTICE AREAS:*** General Civil Litigation; Debtor/Creditors Rights Law; Bankruptcy Law; Corporate Law; Real Estate Law. ***Email:*** gwoodruff@wrflaw.com

MICHAEL J. REECE, born Winston-Salem, North Carolina, October 19, 1968; admitted to bar, 1994, North Carolina. *Education:* North Carolina State University (B.S., 1991); University of North Carolina at Chapel Hill (J.D., 1994). Chancellors Scholar. Member, Holderness Moot Court Invitational Team. *Member:* Johnston County and North Carolina Bar Associations; North Carolina State Bar; North Carolina Academy of Trial Lawyers. ***PRACTICE AREAS:*** Criminal Law. ***Email:*** mikereece@wrflaw.com

MARY M. REECE, born Bremerton, Washington, March 30, 1969; admitted to bar, 1994, North Carolina. *Education:* Duke University (B.A., 1991); University of North Carolina (J.D., 1994). Note and Comment Editor, North Carolina Journal of International Law & Commercial Regulation, 1993-1994. Certified Family Law Mediator, Dispute Resolution Commission. *Member:* Johnston County and North Carolina Bar Associations; North Carolina State Bar. ***PRACTICE AREAS:*** Family Law Mediation; Family Law. ***Email:*** maryreece@wrflaw.com

DIONNE LOY FORTNER, born Asheboro, North Carolina, December 14, 1969; admitted to bar, 1995, North Carolina. *Education:* University of North Carolina (B.A., 1992; J.D., 1995). Phi Beta Kappa. *Member:* Johnston County and North Carolina Bar Associations; North Carolina State Bar. ***PRACTICE AREAS:*** Family Law; Civil Litigation. ***Email:*** dfortner@wrflaw.com

WILLIAM E. CLARK

SOUTHERN PINES, NORTH CAROLINA

(See Fayetteville)

General Civil Practice. Wills, Estate Planning and Probate. Corporate and Business Law. Real Estate Closings and Development.

CLARKE & PHIFER, LLP

SOUTHERN PINES, NORTH CAROLINA

(See Pinehurst)

Family Law including: Alimony, Divorce, and Equitable Distribution, Adoptions, Personal Injury, Automobile Accidents, Wrongful Death, Traffic Violations, Commercial and Residential Real Property Transactions, Real Property Law and Litigation, Corporate and Small Business Formations, Transactions, and Planning, Asset Protection, Wills, Estate Planning, and Probate/Estate Administration.

MORRIS LAW OFFICE

SOUTHERN PINES, NORTH CAROLINA

(See Whispering Pines)

Criminal Law, Felonies and Misdemeanors, Traffic Violations and Tickets, Trucks, Motorcycles, Driving While Intoxicated, DUI, Animal Law, Equine, Horse Rights and Trusts, Veterans Benefits and Appeals.

POYNER & SPRUILL LLP

135 WEST NEW HAMPSHIRE AVENUE
P.O. BOX 371
SOUTHERN PINES, NORTH CAROLINA 28388
Telephone: 910-692-6866
Telecopier: 910-695-3036
URL: http://www.poynerspruill.com

Raleigh, North Carolina Office: 3600 Glenwood Avenue, P.O. Box 10096, 27605-0096. Telephone: 919-783-6400. Telecopier: 919-783-1075.

Rocky Mount, North Carolina Office: 130 S. Franklin Street, P.O. Box 353, 27802-0353. Telephone: 252-446-2341. Telecopier: 252-972-7045.

Charlotte, North Carolina Office: One Wachovia Center, 301 South College Street, Suite 2300, 28202. Telephone: 704-342-5250. Telecopier: 704-342-5264.

Comprehensive business and litigation practice including: Appellate, Arbitration, Banking, Bankruptcy/Creditors' Rights, Complex Business Litigation, Construction, Credit and Financial Services, Eminent Domain/Condemnation, Employment Benefits, Employment Practices, Entertainment Law, Environmental, Estate, Exempt Organizations, General Corporate, Governmental Relations, Health Care, Intellectual Property Law, International, Land Use and Zoning, Limited Liability Companies, Local Government, Mediation, Partnerships, Personal and Financial Planning, Probate, Product Liability, Professional Liability, Railroad, Real Estate, Regulatory and Municipal, Securities, Sports Law, Tax, Technology and Emerging Business, Tort Litigation and Insurance Defense, Transactional including Mergers and Acquisitions, Transportation, Utilities, White Collar Criminal Defense.

MEMBER

H. CHALK BROUGHTON, JR., born Pinehurst, North Carolina, April 19, 1961; admitted to bar, 1988, North Carolina; 2001, U.S. Supreme Court. *Education:* University of North Carolina at Chapel Hill (B.A., 1983; J.D., 1988); University of Florida (LL.M., Taxation, 1990). (Board Certified Specialist in Estate Planning and Probate, North Carolina State Board of Legal Specialization). ***PRACTICE AREAS:*** Estate Planning; Taxation; Business Law; Real Estate. ***Email:*** cbroughton@poynerspruill.com

(This Listing Continued)

RESIDENT OF COUNSEL

HOWARD C. BROUGHTON, born Hertford, North Carolina, May 24, 1930; admitted to bar, 1958, North Carolina. *Education:* University of North Carolina at Chapel Hill (B.S., 1952; LL.B., 1958). ***PRACTICE AREAS:*** Estate Planning; Real Estate; Probate. ***Email:*** hbroughton@poynerspruill.com

All Attorneys are Members of The North Carolina State Bar and North Carolina Bar Association.

REPRESENTATIVE CLIENTS: American Airlines; Alliance One International; BB&T; Boddie-Noell Enterprises, Inc.; The Body Shop, Inc.; Browning-Ferris Industries; CSX Transportations, Inc.; Data General Corp.; Electricities of North Carolina, Inc.; Farm Bureau Mutual Insurance Co.; Food Lion, Inc.; General Electric Capital Corp.; General Electric Company; General Electric Mortgage Insurance Company; General Motors, Inc.; Granutec, Inc.; Guardian Corporation, Inc.; H&R Block, Inc.; Investors Holding Company (Golden Corral and affiliates); LSB Bancshares, Inc.; Martin Marietta Materials; Mitsubishi Semiconductor America, Inc.; Nomaco, Inc.; N.C. Eastern Municipal Power Agency; North Carolina Enterprise Corporation; N.C. Housing Finance Agency; North Carolina Municipal Power Agency; Pepsico, Inc.; PF Properties; Pitt County Memorial Hospital; Premium Standard Farms, Inc.; Purdue Pharmaceuticals, L.P.; RBC Centura Banks, Inc.; Research Triangle Foundation; Richardson Sports (Carolina Panthers); Roses Stores, Inc.; R.J. Reynolds Tobacco Co.; Schwarz Biosciences, Inc.; Semi-Conductor Research Corp.; T.A. Loving Company; WakeMed.

(For additional Personnel and Biographical data see listings at Raleigh, Rocky Mount and Charlotte)

ROBBINS MAY & RICH LLP

SOUTHERN PINES, NORTH CAROLINA

(See Pinehurst)

General Civil and Criminal Litigation in all Courts. Traffic Violations, Real Property, Trust and Estate Planning and Administration, Commercial and Residential Real Estate Transactions, Banking, Taxation, Personal Injury, Family Law, Divorce, Worker's Compensation, Business Formations and Transactions and Social Security Disability.

HURLEY E. THOMPSON, JR.

SOUTHERN PINES, NORTH CAROLINA

(See Carthage)

Residential Real Property, Foreclosure, Traffic Offenses, Wills, Estates, Personal Injury.

ROBERT S. THOMPSON, P.A.

325 WEST PENNSYLVANIA, SUITE E
SOUTHERN PINES, NORTH CAROLINA 28387
Telephone: 910-692-2244
Fax: 910-692-3080
Email: rthompson@pinehurst.net
URL: http://www.lawyers.com/rthompson

Estate Planning Law, Business Law, Corporate Law, Probate Law, Wills, Trusts and Estates, Commercial and Residential Real Estate Law.

ROBERT S. THOMPSON, born Philadelphia, Pennsylvania, 1948; admitted to bar, 1983, North Carolina. *Education:* Ohio Wesleyan University (B.A., 1971); University of North Carolina (M.B.A., 1973); Wake Forest University (J.D., 1983). Omicron Delta Epsilon. Member, Wake Forest Law Review, 1981-1983. Author: Comment, "Landlord Eviction Remedies Act," 18 Wake Forest Law Review 25, 1982; Note, "Per Diem Damages in North Carolina - Weeks v. Holsclaw," 19 Wake Forest Law Review 645, 1983. *Member:* Moore County (Chairman, Office Practice Section) and North Carolina (Member: Real Property Section Council, 1993-1996; Real Property Task Force,1993-1996) Bar Associations; North Carolina State Bar (Member, Board of Legal Specialization, Real Property Law Specialty Committee). Fellow, Business Foundation, University of North Carolina. (Board Certified Specialist in Estate Planning and Probate Law, Real Property Law-Residential, Business, Commercial and Industrial Transactions, North Carolina State Board of Legal Specialization). ***PRACTICE AREAS:*** Estate Planning; Estate Administration; Corporate Law; Probate; Commercial Real Estate; Residential Real Estate.

VAN CAMP, MEACHAM & NEWMAN, PLLC

SOUTHERN PINES, NORTH CAROLINA

(See Pinehurst)

General Civil and Criminal Litigation and Appellate Practice in State and Federal Courts. Personal Injury, Commercial, Medical Malpractice, Wrongful Death, Worker's Compensation, Insurance, Land Condemnation, Constitutional and Civil Rights, Family, Corporate, Real Estate, Administrative, Social Security Disability, Construction Law, Labor and Employment, Wills, Estate Planning and Probate Law.

WEST & SMITH, L.L.P.

Established in 1997
140 WEST VERMONT AVENUE
P.O. BOX 1140
SOUTHERN PINES, NORTH CAROLINA 28388
Telephone: 910-693-3411
Fax: 910-693-7727
Email: ws@westandsmith.com
URL: http://www.lawyers.com/west&smith

Personal Injury, Wrongful Death, Civil Litigation, Insurance Litigation, Contested Wills, Worker's Compensation, Social Security Disability, Land Condemnation, Commercial Litigation, Construction Litigation, Mediation and Arbitration.

FIRM PROFILE: The partners of West & Smith, L.L.P. both practicing law since 1975, left a larger firm in 1997 to start their own firm dedicated to providing civil litigation services to clients located primarily within Moore County and the South Central Piedmont Region of North Carolina, although major cases can be handled statewide. They concentrate on personal injury and wrongful death, insurance litigation, contested wills, civil litigation, workers compensation, social security disability and mediation/arbitration.

STANLEY W. WEST, born Greensboro, North Carolina, August 25, 1950; admitted to bar, 1975, North Carolina, U.S. District Court, Middle District of North Carolina. *Education:* University of North Carolina (B.S. in Bus. Adm., 1971); Wake Forest University (J.D., cum laude, 1975). Phi Delta Phi. Special Editor, Wake Forest Law Review, 1974-1975. Contributing Author: "Independent Contractor Status, a State By State Legal Guide," Wiley Law Publications, 1993. *Member:* Moore County and North Carolina (Member, Sections on: Litigation; Workers Compensation) Bar Association; North Carolina Academy of Trial Lawyers (Member, Workers' Compensation Section). ***PRACTICE AREAS:*** Personal Injury; Workers Compensation; Head Injury; Contested Wills; Commercial Litigation; Condemnation; Wrongful Death; Insurance Litigation; Construction Litigation. **Email:** stan@westandsmith.com

S. KENT SMITH, born Durham, North Carolina, July 24, 1950; admitted to bar, 1975, North Carolina; 1976, U.S. Court of Military Appeals; 1985, U.S. District Court, Eastern District of North Carolina; 1989, U.S. District Court, Middle District of North Carolina. *Education:* University of North Carolina (B.A., 1972; J.D., 1975). Contributing Author: "Independent Contractor Status, a State by State Legal Guide," Wiley Law Publications, 1993. Assistant Public Defender, Greensboro, North Carolina, 1979-1982. Assistant District Attorney, Greensboro, North Carolina, 1983. Special Assistant U.S. Attorney, Eastern District of North Carolina, 1985-1986. Certified Superior Court Mediator. Certified Family Financial Mediator. *Member:* Moore County and North Carolina (Member, Sections on: Litigation and Dispute Resolution) Bar Associations; North Carolina Academy of Trial Lawyers (Member, Disability Advocacy Section); National Organization of Social Security Claimants Representatives. [Major, Judge Advocate, U.S. Marine Corps, 1975-1979 & 1983-1989]. ***PRACTICE AREAS:*** Personal Injury; Wrongful Death; Social Security Disability; Contested Wills; Mediation; Arbitration; Civil Litigation; Construction Litigation. **Email:** kent@westandsmith.com

---

ROY A. ARCHBELL, JR.

SOUTHERN SHORES, NORTH CAROLINA

(See Kitty Hawk)

General Civil Trial Practice in State and Federal Courts. Family, Personal Injury, Collection, Corporate, Construction, Insurance, Real Estate, Domestic Relations, Divorce.

HORNTHAL, RILEY, ELLIS & MALAND, L.L.P.

SOUTHERN SHORES, NORTH CAROLINA

(See Elizabeth City)

General Trial and Appellate Practice in all Courts. Personal Injury, Products Liability, Professional Malpractice, Corporate, Tax, Bankruptcy, Employment, Education, Criminal, Insurance, Construction, Real Estate, Environmental, Elder, Local Government, Wills and Trusts, Probate and Admiralty Law.

THE VINCENT LAW FIRM, PC

8 JUNIPER TRAIL
SOUTHERN SHORES, NORTH CAROLINA 27949
Telephone: 252-261-5477
Fax: 252-261-1828
Email: bwvincent2@earthlink.net
URL: http://www.ncworkerscompensationlaw.com

Workers Compensation, Personal Injury, Auto Accidents, Social Security Disability, Wrongful Death and Admiralty Longshores.

BRANCH W. "CHIP" VINCENT, born Richmond, Virginia, April 23, 1961; admitted to bar, 1986, North Carolina. *Education:* Hampden-Sydney College (B.A., 1983); Campbell University (J.D., 1986). *Member:* First Judicial District, North Carolina and American Bar Associations; North Carolina State Bar; North Carolina Academy of Trial Lawyers. (Board Certified Specialist in Worker's Compensation, North Carolina State Board of Legal Specialization). ***PRACTICE AREAS:*** Workers Compensation; Social Security Disability; Personal Injury; Wrongful Death; Admiralty Law.

DAVID AND ASSOCIATES, PLLC

SOUTHPORT, NORTH CAROLINA

(See Wilmington)

Personal Injury, Medical Malpractice, Wrongful Death, Products Liability, Workers Compensation, Aviation, Airplane Crashes, Negligence, Class Actions, Maritime Accidents, Boating Accidents, Bicycle Accidents, Motorcycle Accidents, Truck Accidents, School Bus Accidents, Railroad Accidents, Dog Bites, Slip and Fall, Birth Trauma, Brain Injury, Spinal Injury, Head Injury, Catastrophic Injury, Vehicular Homicide, Personal Injury Mediation, Products Liability, Drug and Medical Device Litigation, Product Defects, Automobile Liability, Motorcycle Products Liability, Amusement Park Liability, Hotel Liability, Marina Liability, Sports Injury.

JACKSON & ASSOCIATES

SOUTHPORT, NORTH CAROLINA

(See Wilmington)

Personal Injury, Wrongful Death, Automobile Accidents and Injuries, Medical Malpractice, Worker's Compensation, Criminal Law, Driving While Intoxicated, Misdemeanors, Felonies, Traffic Violations.

JOHNSON & MOORE, P.A.

1424 N. HOWE STREET
SOUTHPORT, NORTH CAROLINA 28461
Telephone: 910-457-6115
Fax: 910-457-6266
URL: http://www.johnsonmoore.com

Real Estate, Corporate Law, Estate Planning, Civil Litigation, Business Law, Commercial Litigation, Construction Law.

EDWARD A. JOHNSON, II, born High Point, North Carolina, May 10, 1970; admitted to bar, 1996, Georgia (inactive) and North Carolina. *Education:* Appalachian State University (B.S., 1992); Mercer University School of Law (J.D., 1996). *Member:* Brunswick County and North Carolina (Member, Real Property Section) Bar Associations. ***PRACTICE AREAS:*** Real Estate; Corporate Law; Estate Planning.

KIMBERLY L. MOORE, born Charlottesville, Virginia, June 14, 1967; admitted to bar, 1995, Georgia (inactive) and Indiana; 1996, U.S. Court of Appeals, Fourth Circuit; 1998, Nevada (inactive); 2001, North Carolina; 2003, U.S. District Court, Eastern District of North Carolina. *Education:* The Hotchkiss School, 1985; McIntire School of Commerce, University of Virginia (B.S., 1989); Walter F. George School of Law, Mercer University (J.D., cum laude, 1995). Brainerd Currie Honor Society. Order of Barristers. Mercer Law Review, Member, 1993-1994, Student Writing Editor, 1994-1995, Spring Competition Editor, 1995. Member, Moot Court Board, 1994-1995. Recipient: Best Brief for the Respondent, Gibbons National Criminal Procedure Moot Court Competition, April 1994; Faculty Award for Outstanding Achievement in Legal Writing, 1993; American Jurisprudence Awards in Legal Writing I, Real Estate Transactions, and Business Associations. Author: Publication: Casenote, United States v. Irvine: The Disclaimer of an Interest Created Before Enactment of the Federal Gift Tax Is Taxable, 45 Mercer L. Rev. 897 (1994). *Member:* Brunswick County and North Carolina Bar Associations. (Also Of Counsel to Fletcher Ray & Satterfield, L.L.P., Wilmington). ***PRACTICE AREAS:*** Civil Litigation; Business Law; Commercial Litigation; Construction Law.

BRUCE H. ROBINSON, JR

SOUTHPORT, NORTH CAROLINA

(See Wilmington)

SHIPMAN, MASON & WRIGHT, L.L.P.

SOUTHPORT, NORTH CAROLINA

(See Wilmington)

Focused Trial Practice in all Federal and State Courts. Complex Commercial Litigation, Product Liability, EIFS Litigation, Medical Devices, Medical Malpractice, Catastrophic Personal Injury and Wrongful Death, Nursing Home Litigation, Toxic Torts, Mold Litigation, Construction Litigation, and Consumer Class Actions.

CHARLES M. TIGHE

SOUTHPORT, NORTH CAROLINA

(See Wilmington)

General Practice, Civil Trials in all Courts, Corporate, Business Law, Intellectual Property, Commercial and Construction Law, Employment Law Discrimination, Employee Benefits, Sexual Harassment, Wrongful Termination, Civil Rights Discrimination, Land Use, Zoning, and Environmental Law, Decedents Estates, Wills, and Estate Planning.

VANNOY & REEVES, PLLC

A Professional Limited Liability Company

Established in 1975

112 SOUTH MAIN STREET

P.O. BOX 249

SPARTA, NORTH CAROLINA 28675

Telephone: 336-372-8740

Fax: 336-372-6114

Email: jim@vannoyandreeves.com

Email: alex@vannoyandreeves.com

Email: garland@vannoyandreeves.com

Email: jak@vannoyandreeves.com

Email: garland@vannoyandreeves.com

URL: http://www.vannoyandreeves.com

West Jefferson, North Carolina Office: 202 East Main Street, P.O.Drawer 67, 28694. Telephone: 336-246-7172. Fax: 336-246-5966.

General Civil and Criminal Trial Practice in State and Federal Courts, Real Property, Estate Planning, Probate, Business and Corporate Law, Traffic, Family Law, Plaintiff's Personal Injury Matters and Collections.

FIRM PROFILE: VANNOY & REEVES was organized in 1975 by Wade E. Vannoy, Jr. and Jimmy D. Reeves and has continued with the same name since Mr. Vannoy's death in 1991. Garland B. Baker, with extensive experience in criminal practice, joined the firm in 1998. M. Alexandra Reeves joined the firm in 2001, and John B. Reeves began his practice with the firm in 2004. The attorneys' concentration is upon civil and criminal trial practice in state and federal courts, and in corporate, commercial and municipal law. They and their staff have a complete real estate practice handling closings, real estate-related litigation, and representing creditors and lending institutions in bankruptcy matters.

APPROVED ATTORNEYS FOR: Investors Title Insurance Co.; LandAmerica Lawyers Title Insurance Corporation; First American Title Insurance Co.; Chicago Title Insurance Co.; Commonwealth Land Title Co.; United Title Insurance Co.; United States Department of Agriculture-Rural Development; Mountain Farm Credit/PCA; Fidelity National Title Insurance Co.; Southern Title Insurance; Old Republic National Title Insurance Company; Stewart Title Guaranty Company.
REPRESENTATIVE CLIENTS: AF Bank; Ashe Services for the Aging, Inc.; Town of West Jefferson; Parker-Tie Company, Inc.; Yadkin Valley Pontiac, Buick, Oldsmobile, GMC, Inc.
REFERENCES: First Citizens Bank & Trust Co.; Yadkin Valley Bank & Trust Co.; First Union National Bank; Centura Bank; BB&T; Northwestern Bank; High Country Bank.

(See West Jefferson, North Carolina)

CARL L. BRITT, JR., ATTORNEY AT LAW

SPRING LAKE, NORTH CAROLINA

(See Fayetteville)

Personal Injury, Wrongful Death, Traffic Violations, Driving While Intoxicated, Driving Under the Influence, Criminal Law.

MAXWELL & MELVIN

SPRING LAKE, NORTH CAROLINA

(See Fayetteville)

General Practice, Personal Injury, Wrongful Death, Medical Malpractice, Real Estate, Workers Compensation, Collections, Bankruptcy, Criminal, Traffic, Corporations, Elder Law, Wills and Estates.

THE BOLDUC LAW FIRM, PLLC

STATESVILLE, NORTH CAROLINA

(See Charlotte)

NASD Arbitration, Business Litigation, Securities Fraud, Corporate Malfeasance, Mutual Fund Disputes, Wrongful Termination, Banking and Finance Law, and Accounting.

ALAN G. CARPENTER, P.A.

1318 DAVIE AVENUE, SUITE C

STATESVILLE, NORTH CAROLINA 28677

Telephone: 704-872-6242

Fax: 704-872-6246

URL: http://www.alancarpenter.com

Email: statesville@bellsouth.net

URL: http://www.tandclaw.com

Residential Real Estate, Commercial Real Estate, Construction, Business Law, Limited Liability, Partnerships, Corporate, Wills and Estates.

FIRM PROFILE: Mr. Carpenter is a Board Certified Specialist in Real Property Law- Residential Transactions.

ALAN G. CARPENTER, born Knoxville, Tennessee, November 18, 1957; admitted to bar, 1983, North Carolina. *Education:* University of North Carolina (B.S., 1980; J.D., 1983). Chairman, Iredell County Board of Elections, 1993-2004. *Member:* Iredell County and North Carolina Bar Associations; North Carolina State Bar. (Board Certified Specialist in Real Property Law - Residential Transactions, North Carolina State Board of Legal Specialization). ***PRACTICE AREAS:*** Real Estate; Business Law; Corporate Law. ***Email:*** statesville@bellsouth.net

LAW OFFICE OF WILLIAM T. CORBETT, JR.

STATESVILLE, NORTH CAROLINA

(See Mooresville)

Insurance Defense, Wills and Probate, Estates, Criminal Law, Traffic Violations, General Civil Litigation.

JUDY DALTON

STATESVILLE, NORTH CAROLINA

(See Troutman)

Family Law, Child Custody, Child Support, Visitation Rights, Divorce, Property Distribution, Restraining Orders, Adoptions, Criminal Defense, Felonies and Misdemeanors, DWI, Traffic Violations, Drug Crimes, Probation Violations, Civil Litigation, Wills, Debt Collections.

LAW OFFICE OF DARYL G. DAVIDSON, SR., PC

210 EAST WATER STREET

STATESVILLE, NORTH CAROLINA 28677

Telephone: 704-871-2213; 871-2214

Fax: 704-871-2215

Email: darylgdavidson@bellsouth.net

URL: http://www.darylgdavidson.com

Family Law, Child Support, Child Custody, Divorce, Domestic Violence, Visitation Rights, Criminal Law, Driving While Intoxicated (DWI); Drug Crimes, Traffic Violations, Immigration, Automobile Accidents.

DARYL G. DAVIDSON, SR., born Statesville, North Carolina, August 28, 1969; admitted to bar, 1999, North Carolina and U.S. District Court, Western District of North Carolina. *Education:* Howard University (B.A., magna cum laude, 1990); University of Iowa (J.D., 1998). Member, University of Iowa Law Review, 1997-1998. *Member:* North Carolina State Bar. ***LANGUAGES:*** Spanish. ***Email:*** darylgdavidson@bellsouth.net

EISELE, ASHBURN, GREENE & CHAPMAN, P.A.

Established in 1986

320 WEST BROAD STREET

P.O. BOX 1108

STATESVILLE, NORTH CAROLINA 28687-1108

Telephone: 704-878-6400

Fax: 704-871-2039; 704-924-9727

URL: http://www.lawyers.com/eagandclaw

General Civil Practice in State and Federal Courts. Real Property, Estate Planning, Taxation, Corporation and Construction Law.

DOUGLAS G. EISELE, born Huntington, Indiana, April 24, 1936; admitted to bar, 1965, North Carolina. *Education:* University of North Carolina at Chapel Hill (LL.B., 1965). Phi Delta Phi. Author: Note, "Bankruptcy—Factors to Consider in Choosing Between Chapter X and Chapter XI for the Adjustment of Unsecured Debts," North Carolina Law Review, Vol. 43, p. 950, 1965. Member, Federal Bar Advisory Council, Western District of North Carolina, 1987-1994. Chairman, Civil Justice Reform Act Committee, Western District of North Carolina, 1997—. *Member:* Iredell County and North Carolina Bar Associations; The Association of Trial Lawyers of America. ***REPORTED CASES:*** Union Grove Milling and Manufacturing Company, Inc. v. Faw, 103 N.C. App. 166, 404 S.E. 2d 508 (1991); Stimpson Hosiery Mills v. PAM Trading Corp., 98 N.C. App 543, 392 S.E. 2d 128 (1990); Gilbert Engineering Co. v. City of Asheville, 74 N.D. App. 350, 328 S.E. 2d 849 (1985); NCNB v. McKee, 63 N.C. App. 58, 303 S.E. 2d 842 (1983); Threatte v. Threatte, 308 N.C. 384, 302 S.E. 2d 226 (1983); Stillwell Enterprises v. Interstate Equipment Co., 300 N.C. 286, 266 S.E. 2d 812 (1980); Interstate Equipment Co. v. Smith, 292 N.C. 592, 234 S.E. 2d 599 (1977); Mills v. Koscot Interplanetary, 13 N.C. App. 681, 187 S.E. 2d 372 (1972); Pine State Yarn Mills v. Troutman Foundry, Inc., 8 N.C. App. 521, 174 S.E. 2d 706 (1970); Board of Education v. Construction Corp., 304 N.C. 187, 282 S.E. 2d 778 (1981); Martin v. Ray Lackey Enterprises, 100 N.C. App. 349, 396 S.E. 2d 327 (1990); New England Leather Co. v. Feuer Leather Corp., 942 F. 2d 253 (4 Cir. 1991); Statesville Roofing and Heating Co. v. Duncan, 702 F. Supp. 118 (W.D. N.C. 1988); Rigby v. Clayton, CVMR of Revenue, 274 N.C. 465, 164 S.E. 2d (1968); numerous others. ***PRACTICE AREAS:*** Civil Law; State and Federal Civil Litigation; Corporate Law; Collections; Construction Law. ***Email:*** qblee@statesville.net

JAMES P. ASHBURN, born Statesville, North Carolina, March 14, 1942; admitted to bar, 1967, North Carolina. *Education:* Erskine College (A.B., 1964); Wake Forest University (J.D., 1967); Georgetown University (LL.M., in Taxation, 1973). Omicron Delta Kappa; Phi Alpha Delta. Member, Statesville City Board of Education, 1984-1992. *Member:* Iredell County, North Carolina and American Bar Associations. [Capt., JAGC, U.S. Army, 1968-1972]. ***PRACTICE AREAS:*** Taxation Law; Corporate and Estate Planning; Real Property Law. ***Email:*** jashburn@statesville.net

JOHN D. GREENE, born Lenoir, North Carolina, April 28, 1947; admitted to bar, 1989, North Carolina. *Education:* North Carolina State University (B.S., Civil Engineering, 1972); Wake Forest University (J.D., 1989). *Member:* Iredell County, North Carolina and American Bar Associations. ***PRACTICE AREAS:*** State and Federal Civil Litigation; Construction Law; Employment Law; Business Law; Real Property Law; Collections. ***Email:*** jdg@statesville.net

RUSSELL W. CHAPMAN, JR., born Bay St. Louis, Mississippi, October 31, 1954; admitted to bar, 1991, North Carolina. *Education:* University of Southern Mississippi

(This Listing Continued)

EISELE, ASHBURN, GREENE & CHAPMAN, P.A., Statesville—Continued

(B.S., with highest honors, 1976); Wake Forest University (J.D., cum laude, 1991). Member, Wake Forest University School of Law Moot Court Board (1989-1991). Editor-in-Chief, Wake Forest University Law Review (1990-1991). *Member:* Iredell County, North Carolina and American Bar Associations. ***PRACTICE AREAS:*** Real Property Law; Corporate; Social Security. ***Email:*** rwchapman@statesville.net

REPRESENTATIVE CLIENTS: Auto Equipment, Inc. Epperson Lumber Sales, Inc.; Bruning & Federle Mfg. Co.; Raymer Oil Co.; Interstate Equipment Co.; Statesville Roofing & Heating Co.; Davis Oil Co.; Ray Lackey Enterprises, Inc.; New Telephone Co.; Cline & Co., CPA's; P.A.; Iredell Eye Clinic, P.A.; Union Grove Milling Co.; Star Milling; Bell Construction Co.; Mocaro Dyeing & Finishing, Inc.; Toyota West; Bec Car Printing, Inc.; Piedmont Tile & Marble, Inc.; Piedmont Drilling & Blasting, Inc.; Finish Line Ford; Finish Line Dodge; Acme Metal Slides, Inc.; New South Electrical Contractors, Inc.; Toyota West; ABC Investments & Management Co.; tube-tec; D & D Enterprises of Irodell, LLC; Chris A. Davidson Contracting.
REFERENCES: Piedmont Bank; Title Company of North Carolina.

RAY A. HAYES II P.A.

STATESVILLE, NORTH CAROLINA

(See Cornelius)

Business Transactions, Business Litigation, Corporate Law, Business Planning, Buying or Selling a Business, Securities, Contracts, Trusts and Estates, Wills and Probate, Bankruptcy, Consumer Bankruptcy, Traffic Violations.

HOMESLEY, JONES, GAINES, DUDLEY, McLURKIN & DONALDSON, PLLC

Established in 1976

316 EAST BROAD STREET
P.O. BOX 149
STATESVILLE, NORTH CAROLINA 28677
Telephone: 704-873-2172
Fax: 704-924-2103; 704-873-5908
Real Estate Email: realestate@statesville.net
Email: hjgd@statesville.net
URL: http://www.iredell-law.com

Mooresville, North Carolina Office: 236 Raceway Drive, Suite 7, Lakeside Business Park, 28117. Telephone: 704-664-1127. Real Estate Telephone: 704-664-2145. Fax: 704-663-0939; 704-664-6596. URL: http://www.mooresvillelakelaw.com

General Civil and Criminal Practice in all Domestic and Federal Courts. Probate, Real Estate, Personal Injury, Family, Corporation, Insurance, Negligence, Workers Compensation, Social Security and Appeals.

MEMBERS OF FIRM

TROY C. HOMESLEY, JR., born Cherryville, North Carolina, December 22, 1934; admitted to bar, 1958, North Carolina; 1959, U.S. Court of Military Appeals. *Education:* University of North Carolina (B.S., 1956; J.D., 1958). Phi Delta Phi. Solicitor, Mooresville Recorder's Court, 1963. *Member:* Iredell County, North Carolina and American Bar Associations; 22nd Judicial District and North Carolina State Bars; North Carolina Academy of Trial Lawyers; The Association of Trial Lawyers of America; American Judicature Society. [Capt. JAGC, U.S. Army, 1958-1962]. ***PRACTICE AREAS:*** Criminal Law; Domestic Law; Personal Injury Law; Civil Litigation.

EDMUND L. GAINES, born Fayetteville, North Carolina, February 28, 1946; admitted to bar, 1971, North Carolina; 1999, U.S. Supreme Court. *Education:* University of North Carolina (B.A., 1968; J.D., 1971). Member, Moot Court Bench. City Attorney, Statesville, North Carolina, 1987—. *Member:* Iredell County, North Carolina and American Bar Associations; 22nd Judicial District and North Carolina State Bars; North Carolina Academy of Trial Lawyers; The Association of Trial Lawyers of America; North Carolina Municipal Attorney's Association. ***PRACTICE AREAS:*** Personal Injury Law; Negligence Law; Civil Litigation; Probate Law; Domestic Law; Municipal Law. ***Email:*** gaines@statesville.net

L. RAGAN DUDLEY, born Gastonia, North Carolina, October 9, 1966; admitted to bar, 1992, North Carolina. *Education:* University of North Carolina (B.A., 1989); Wake Forest University School of Law (J.D., 1992). *Member:* North Carolina Bar Association (General Practice Section Counsel) and American Bar Association; North Carolina Academy of Trial Lawyers. ***PRACTICE AREAS:*** Real Estate; Construction Law; Personal Injury; Workers Compensation; Social Security; Civil Litigation; Criminal Law; Appellate Practice. ***Email:*** dudley@statesville.net

---

MITCHELL P. JOHNSON, born Statesville, North Carolina, September 11, 1975; admitted to bar, 2000, North Carolina. *Education:* Duke University (A.B., 1997); University of North Carolina at Chapel Hill (J.D., with honors, 2000). Member, National Moot Court Team. Member, Banking Institute. Adjunct Professor, Business Law, Johnson C. Smith University, 2001. ***PRACTICE AREAS:*** Personal Injury; Negligence; Civil Litigation; Probate; Criminal Law; Real Estate. ***Email:*** mitchjohnson@statesville.net

REPRESENTATIVE CLIENTS: Branch Bank and Trust Co.; Wooten's Jewelers; City of Statesville; JMS Southeast, Inc.; Statesville Process Instruments; NGK Ceramics; Mooresville Savings Bank; Best Sweets, Inc; Crescent Resources; Custom Products, Inc.; Mooresville Graded School District; Northlake Lumber Company, Inc.; J.T. Alexander & Son, Inc.; Piedmont Investors, Inc.; Spectrum Financial Systems, Inc; Southern Container, Inc.; Bob Rudisill Homes, Inc.; Bay State Milling Company, Inc.; Cavin Funeral Home; Neill Funeral Home; First Charter National Bank; Southern Door of Mooresville; Hicks Companies, L.L.C.; Dane Construction, Inc; Lake Norman Regional Medical Center; Mooresville Foundation for Excellence in Education; Piedmont Pacific Industries, Inc.; The Point on Norman, LLC; Don Allen Surveyors; Crosslake Park Property Owners Association, Inc.; ET Homes, Inc.; G.D. Smith Development Group, Inc.; Realticorp, Inc.; Plaza Lake, LLC; Callaway Service Company, Inc; Aldelphia Business Solutions; Fox Den Country Club; Genesis Eldercare; Piedmont Fiberglass, Inc.; Bonanza Development Company, Inc.; Profit Technologies Corporation; Sponsorlogic, Inc.; Piedmont Bank; Carter County Bank; Consolidated Financial Resources; Amity Development and Realty Services; Fox Den Development, LLC; Collier Properties, Inc.
REFERENCES: Branch Bank and Trust Co., Statesville, North Carolina; Piedmont Bank, Mooresville, North Carolina.
APPROVED ATTORNEYS FOR: Chicago Title Insurance Company; Investors Title Insurance Company; Lawyers Title Insurance Company; Fidelity National Title Insurance Company; Colonial Insurance Company; Commonwealth Land Title Insurance Company; Stewart Title Insurance Company; First American Title Insurance Company; Old Republic Title Insurance Company; Statewide Title Insurance Company.

(For Other Biographical Information, see Professional Biographies at Mooresville, North Carolina)

MASSEY, CANNON & GRIFFIN, PLLC

140 EAST WATER STREET
STATESVILLE, NORTH CAROLINA 28677-5228
Telephone: 704-872-7438
Fax: 704-872-0108
URL: http://www.lawyers.com/ebedfordcannon

Civil Litigation, Corporation, Real Estate, Wills, Estate Planning, Probate, Business Law, Contracts, Personal Injury, Automobile Accidents, Family Law.

E. BEDFORD CANNON, born Winston-Salem, North Carolina, March 19, 1946; admitted to bar, 1971, North Carolina. *Education:* Duke University (B.A., 1968); University of North Carolina (J.D., 1971). Phi Delta Phi. *Member:* North Carolina Bar Association; North Carolina State Bar. [Capt., USMCR, 1971-1974]

JONATHAN DEAN GRIFFIN, admitted to bar, 2001, North Carolina. *Education:* University of Texas at Tyler (B.S., 1994); North Carolina Central College (J.D., cum laude, 2001). *Member:* North Carolina State Bar; North Carolina Bar Association.

JOHN M. MASSEY, born Statesville, North Carolina, December 18, 1943; admitted to bar, 1968, North Carolina. *Education:* University of North Carolina, Chapel Hill (B.A., 1965; J.D., with honors, 1968). Order of the Coif. Member, University of North Carolina Law Review. *Member:* Iredell County (President, 1987) and North Carolina Bar Associations; North Carolina State Bar. [Capt., U.S. Army, 1969-1973]. ***PRACTICE AREAS:*** Banking; Business Law; Corporate Law; Residential Real Estate; Commercial Real Estate; Estates and Wills; Municipal Law.

THE LAW OFFICE OF J. PRESSLY MATTOX, P.C.

Established in 1985

102 WEST BROAD STREET
STATESVILLE, NORTH CAROLINA 28687
Telephone: 704-872-8189
Fax: 704-873-1687
URL: http://www.mattoxlaw.net

Personal Injury, Auto Accidents, Workers Compensation, Real Estate, Business, Traffic.

MEMBER OF FIRM

J. PRESSLY MATTOX, born Lubbock, Texas, January 29, 1958; admitted to bar, 1983, North Carolina. *Education:* University of North Carolina (B.A., 1980); Pepperdine University (J.D., 1983). *Member:* North Carolina Bar Association; North Carolina State Bar; North Carolina Academy of Trial Lawyers. ***SPECIAL AGENCIES:*** Member, Iredell County Board of Election. ***PRACTICE AREAS:*** Real Estate; Traffic; Personal Injury; Workers Compensation. ***Email:*** mattox@mattoxlaw.net

POPE, McMILLAN, KUTTEH, SIMON & PRIVETTE, P.A.

Established in 1915

113 NORTH CENTER STREET, SUITE 200
P.O. DRAWER 1776
STATESVILLE, NORTH CAROLINA 28687-1776
Telephone: 704-873-2131
Fax: 704-872-7629
URL: http://www.popemcmillan.com

General Civil and Criminal Trial Practice in State and Federal Courts. Real Estate, Personal Injury, Probate, Corporation, Taxation, Estate Planning, Administrative Law, Domestic and Family Law, Zoning.

WILLIAM P. POPE, born Dunn, NC, 1942; admitted to bar, 1968, North Carolina. *Education:* University of North Carolina (B.S., 1965; J.D., 1968). Phi Alpha Delta. Iredell County Attorney, 1984—. Member, North Carolina State Banking Commission, 1985-1992. *Member:* Iredell County (President, 1982) and American Bar Associations; The Association of Trial Lawyers of America; Defense Research Institute. [With USAR, 1968-1974]. ***PRACTICE AREAS:*** Corporate; Civil Trial. ***Email:*** wpope@popemcmillan.com

WILLIAM H. McMILLAN, born Gaffney, SC, 1938; admitted to bar, 1968, North Carolina. *Education:* University of North Carolina (B.S., 1960; J.D., 1968). Phi Delta Phi. U.S. Magistrate, 1970-1973. Member, North Carolina House of Representatives, 1974-1980. Permanent Member, Fourth Circuit Judicial Conference. *Member:* Iredell County (President, 1981) and North Carolina (Member, Board of Governors, 1979-1982; Chairman, Administrative Law Committee, 1983-1986) Bar Associations. [First Lieut., USAF, 1961-1965]. ***PRACTICE AREAS:*** Civil Trial; Administrative; Real Estate. ***Email:*** mac@popemcmillan.com

(This Listing Continued)

CONSTANTINE H. KUTTEH, II, born Statesville, NC, 1952; admitted to bar, 1976, North Carolina. *Education:* Wake Forest University (B.A., magna cum laude, 1973); Duke University (J.D., 1976); Emory University (LL.M. in Taxation, 1982). Phi Beta Kappa; Omicron Delta Kappa. Member, Statesville City Council, 1989—. Certified Superior Court Mediator. *Member:* Iredell County (President, 1991) and North Carolina Bar Associations; North Carolina Academy of Trial Lawyers. ***PRACTICE AREAS:*** Estate Planning and Administration; Corporate Law; Real Estate; Personal Injury; Tax Law; Collections. ***Email:*** ckutteh@popemcmillan.com

PAMELA H. SIMON, born Baltimore, MD, 1945; admitted to bar, 1984, North Carolina. *Education:* Swarthmore College; University of California at Berkeley (B.A., 1968); University of North Carolina (J.D., 1984). Phi Beta Kappa; Order of the Coif. Morehead Fellow. Lecturer, Collaborative Law. Certified Family Financial Case Mediator. Certified Family Law Arbitrator. *Member:* North Carolina Bar Association (Chair, Family Law Section; Collaborative Law Committee). Fellow, American Academy of Matrimonial Lawyers. (Board Certified Specialist in Family Law, North Carolina State Board of Legal Specialization). ***PRACTICE AREAS:*** Family Law. ***Email:*** psimon@popemcmillan.com

ANTHONY S. PRIVETTE, born Greensboro, NC, 1970; admitted to bar, 1997, North Carolina. *Education:* University of North Carolina (B.S., 1992); Campbell University (J.D., summa cum laude, 1997). Phi Kappa Phi. Editor-at-large, Law Review. ***PRACTICE AREAS:*** Real Estate; Personal Injury; Civil Trial; Estate Planning; Estate Administration; Corporate; Employment; Workers Compensation. ***Email:*** aprivette@popemcmillan.com

---

CHARLES ARTHUR SCHIECK, born Mineola, NY, 1970; admitted to bar, 2001, North Carolina. *Education:* Southern Illinois University (B.S., 1998); Campbell University (J.D., 2001). *Member:* Iredell County and North Carolina Bar Associations; North Carolina State Bar. [Sgt., USMC, 1990-1998]. ***PRACTICE AREAS:*** Family Law; Civil Litigation; Personal Injury. ***Email:*** cschieck@popemcmillan.com

JUSTIN P. MOYER, born Tiffin, OH, 1979; admitted to bar, 2005, North Carolina. *Education:* Pensacola Christian College (B.A., 2001); Campbell University (J.D., 2005). *Member:* Iredell County and North Carolina Bar Associations; North Carolina State Bar. ***PRACTICE AREAS:*** Civil Litigation; Criminal Law; Personal Injury. ***Email:*** jmoyer@popemcmillan.com

REPRESENTATIVE CLIENTS: Nationwide Insurance Co.; Aetna Life & Casualty Insurance Co.; NationsBank; Barium Springs Home for Children; Piedmont Bank Carolina Farm Credit Assn.; Allstate Insurance Co.; Travelers Insurance Co.; Iredell County; Iredell-Statesville Schools.
APPROVED ATTORNEYS FOR: Lawyers Title Insurance Corp.; Farmers Home and Federal Land Bank Assn.

SCHWARTZ LAW FIRM, P.C.

STATESVILLE, NORTH CAROLINA

(See Charlotte)

Patents, Trademarks, Copyrights, Intellectual Property.

DOUGLAS A. SMITH

STATESVILLE, NORTH CAROLINA

(See Salisbury)

Criminal Law, Felonies, Misdemeanors, Family Law, Divorce, Child Custody, Child Support, Separation, Traffic Violations, Driving While Intoxicated, Construction Law, Children, Child Abuse and Neglect, Child Care, Grandparents Custody, Grandparents Visitation Rights, Juvenile Criminal Law, Step Parent Adoptions, Criminal Defense, Drivers License Suspension, Theft, Weapons Charges, Drug Crimes, Alimony, Domestic Violence, Equitable Distribution, Military Divorce, Name Changes, Paternity, Qualified Domestic Relations Orders, Separation Agreements, Spousal Support, Uncontested Divorce, Guardianship and Conservatorship, Guardian Ad Litem, Incompetency Proceedings, Personal Injury, Accidents, Automobile Accidents and Injuries, Motor Vehicle Accidents and Injuries, Pedestrian Injuries.

WILLIAM M. WILLIS IV
ATTORNEY AT LAW

STATESVILLE, NORTH CAROLINA

(See Mooresville)

Criminal Law, Traffic Violations, Drug Crimes, Personal Injury, Automobile Accidents, Family Law, Workers Compensation.

DAVID AND ASSOCIATES, PLLC

HIGHWAY 17
SUPPLY, NORTH CAROLINA 28462
Telephone: 910-754-8465
Toll Free: 1-800-856-9927
Email: aeverhart@davidandassociates.com
URL: http://www.wilmingtonpiattorneys.com

Jacksonville, North Carolina Office: 405-B Western Boulevard. 28546. Telephone: 910-219-4878.
Wilmington, North Carolina Office: 1516 Dawson Street. 28401. Telephone: 910-251-8088.
Wallace, North Carolina Office: 107 North Norwood Street. 28466. Telephone: 910-285-8777.
Clinton, North Carolina Office: 610 Beaman Street. 28328. Telephone: 910-592-8400.
Winston-Salem, North Carolina Office: 1100-A South Stratford Road. 27103. Telephone: 336-354-1040.

(This Listing Continued)

Greensboro, North Carolina Office: 529 College Road. Suite G. 27410. Telephone: 336-354-1040.

Personal Injury, Medical Malpractice, Wrongful Death, Products Liability, Workers Compensation, Aviation, Airplane Crashes, Negligence, Class Actions, Maritime Accidents, Boating Accidents, Bicycle Accidents, Motorcycle Accidents, Truck Accidents, School Bus Accidents, Railroad Accidents, Dog Bites, Slip and Fall, Birth Trauma, Brain Injury, Spinal Injury, Head Injury, Catastrophic Injury, Vehicular Homicide, Personal Injury Mediation, Products Liability, Drug and Medical Device Litigation, Product Defects, Automobile Liability, Motorcycle Products Liability, Amusement Park Liability, Hotel Liability, Marina Liability, Sports Injury.

(For complete biographical data on all personnel, see Professional Biographies, Wilmington, North Carolina)

WILLIAM J. MORGAN, P.A.

SWANSBORO, NORTH CAROLINA

(See Jacksonville)

Personal Injury Law, General Civil Litigation, Medical Negligence Law, Major Criminal Defense.

COWARD, HICKS & SILER, P.A.

Established in 1951

705 WEST MAIN STREET
SYLVA, NORTH CAROLINA 28779
Telephone: 828-586-2147
Fax: 828-586-2605

Franklin, North Carolina Office: 43 West Main Street, 28734. Telephone: 828-524-6475. Fax: 828-524-9833.
Cashiers, North Carolina Office: 211 Cashiers School Road, P.O. Box 1918, 28717. Telephone: 828-743-2401. Fax: 828-743-2403.

General Practice in all Courts. Trials, Eminent Domain, Personal Injury and Workers Compensation, Probate, Estate Planning, Real Estate, Corporations, Family Law.

FIRM PROFILE: Coward, Hicks & Siler has been a well respected law firm in Western North Carolina since 1951. This firm has three locations in the area to provide dependable client services. It offers knowledge and professionalism in numerous practice areas.

JAMES KENT COWARD (1929-1989)

ORVILLE D. COWARD, born Sylva, North Carolina, October 30, 1925; admitted to bar, 1951, North Carolina; 1974, U.S. Court of Appeals, Fourth Circuit. *Education:* Western Carolina University and University of North Carolina (A.B., 1949). President, 30th Judicial District of the North Carolina State Bar, 1961-1962. Attorney for Jackson County, 1970-1974. Member, Western Carolina University Board of Trustees, 1973-1978, 1985-1993. Member, University of North Carolina Board of Governors, 1995-1999. ***PRACTICE AREAS:*** Trials; Personal Injury; Automobile Accidents; Wrongful Death; Workers Compensation; Social Security.

RALPH L. HICKS, born Belmont, Mississippi, April 1, 1924; admitted to bar, 1981, North Carolina. *Education:* Mississippi State University (B.S., with special honors, 1947); Wake Forest University (J.D., cum laude, 1981). Research Editor, Wake Forest Law Review, 1980-1981. (Resident, Cashiers Office). ***PRACTICE AREAS:*** Real Property; Corporations; Probate. ***Email:*** rlhicks@cashierslaw.com

ROBERT F. SILER, born Asheville, North Carolina, June 28, 1937; admitted to bar, 1975, North Carolina. *Education:* Duke University (A.B., 1959); Wake Forest University (J.D., cum laude, 1975). Associate Editor, Wake Forest Law Review, 1974-1975. President, 30th Judicial District of North Carolina State Bar, 1990. Chairman, Bar Candidate Review Committee, 30th Judicial District, 1985-1994. Councilor to North Carolina State Bar, 1994-2002. President, North Carolina State Bar, 2004-2005. [Lt.Jg., USNR, 1960-1964]. (Resident, Franklin Office). ***PRACTICE AREAS:*** Estate Administration; Wills; Probate; Guardianship; Real Property; Elder Law. ***Email:*** rsiler@chspa.com

THOMAS R. CRAWFORD, born Franklin, North Carolina, January 11, 1947; admitted to bar, 1972, North Carolina; 1975, U.S. District Court, Middle and Eastern Districts of North Carolina; 1981, U.S. Tax Court. *Education:* Davidson College (B.A., 1969); University of North Carolina (J.D., with honors, 1972). Order of the Coif. Member, Board of Editors, North Carolina Law Review, 1971-1972. Research Assistant, Chief Justice William H. Bobbitt, North Carolina Supreme Court, 1972-1973. *Member:* North Carolina (Chair, Estate Planning and Fiduciary Law Section, 1998-1999) and American Bar Associations. Fellow, American College of Trust and Estate Counsel. (Board Certified Specialist in Estate Planning and Probate Law, North Carolina State Board of Legal Specialization). ***PRACTICE AREAS:*** Estate Planning; Trusts; Taxation; Gift and Estate Taxation; Trust and Estate Administration; Elder Law; Medicaid. ***Email:*** trcrawford@chspa.com

ORVILLE D. COWARD, JR., born Sylva, North Carolina, December 22, 1953; admitted to bar, 1979, North Carolina; 1985, U.S. Court of Appeals, Fourth Circuit. *Education:* Yale University (B.A., cum laude, 1976); University of North Carolina (J.D., 1979). Member, Southwestern Community College Board of Trustees, 1991-1995. *Member:* 30th Judicial District Bar Association (President, 2001-2002). (Resident, Franklin Office). ***PRACTICE AREAS:*** Real Property; Business Organization; Eminent Domain; Civil Litigation. ***Email:*** ocowardjr@chspa.com

J. K. COWARD, JR., born Chapel Hill, North Carolina, October 19, 1955; admitted to bar, 1984, North Carolina; 1986, U.S. District Court, Western District of North Carolina; 1987, U.S. Supreme Court. *Education:* University of East Anglia, Norwich, England; Davidson College (B.A., with honors in English, 1977); Campbell University (J.D., 1984). Member, Campbell Law Observer, 1983-1984. Member, Jackson County Board of Commissioners, 1994-1998. ***PRACTICE AREAS:*** Real Property; Eminent Domain; Civil Litigation. ***Email:*** jkcoward@chspa.com

WILLIAM H. COWARD, born Sylva, North Carolina, August 4, 1958; admitted to bar, 1987, North Carolina; 1988, U.S. District Court, Western District of North Carolina.

(This Listing Continued)

COWARD, HICKS & SILER, P.A., Sylva—Continued

Education: Davidson College (B.A., 1981); University of North Carolina (J.D., 1987). (Resident, Cashiers Office). ***LANGUAGES:*** Spanish. ***PRACTICE AREAS:*** Trials; Eminent Domain; Municipal Law; Personal Injury; Automobile Accidents; Wrongful Death; Family Law; Divorce. ***Email:*** bcoward@cashierslaw.com

KIMBERLY R. COWARD, born Council Bluffs, Iowa, November 25, 1962; admitted to bar, 1988, North Carolina. *Education:* Iowa State University (B.A., summa cum laude, 1985); University of North Carolina (J.D., 1988). Phi Beta Kappa. Member, North Carolina Law Review, 1986-1987. (Resident, Cashiers Office). ***PRACTICE AREAS:*** Real Property; Corporations; Probate. ***Email:*** kcoward@cashierslaw.com

MONTY C. BECK, born Lexington, North Carolina, December 4, 1958; admitted to bar, 1984, North Carolina and U.S. District Court, Western District of North Carolina; 1985, U.S. Court of Appeals, Fourth Circuit. *Education:* University of North Carolina at Chapel Hill (B.S., 1981); Campbell University (J.D., cum laude, 1984). Editor-in-Chief, Campbell Law Review, 1983-1984. *Member:* North Carolina Bar Association (Family Law Section Council, 2000-2003); North Carolina Academy of Trial Lawyers. (Board Certified Specialist in Family Law, North Carolina State Board of Legal Specialization) (Resident, Franklin Office). ***PRACTICE AREAS:*** Family Law; Divorce; Child Support; Equitable Distribution; Civil Litigation; Personal Injury Law. ***Email:*** mbeck@chspa.com

RICHARD K. WALKER, born Tryon, North Carolina, April 6, 1950; admitted to bar, 1987, North Carolina. *Education:* University of South Carolina (B.S., 1979); University of North Carolina (J.D., 1987). *Member:* North Carolina State Bar. [With U.S. Air Force, 1970-1977]. (Resident, Franklin Office). ***PRACTICE AREAS:*** Criminal Litigation; Driving While Intoxicated; Traffic Violations; Family Law; Civil Litigation. ***Email:*** rwalker@chspa.com

HEATHER C. BAKER, born Brunswick, Maine, September 21, 1968; admitted to bar, 1994, North Dakota; 1996, North Carolina. *Education:* Oxford College of Emory University (A.A., 1988); University of North Carolina at Chapel Hill (B.A., 1990; J.D., 1993). Assistant District Attorney, 30th Judicial District, 1997-2000. ***PRACTICE AREAS:*** Real Property; Corporate Law; Driving While Intoxicated; Traffic Violations. ***Email:*** hbaker@chspa.com

---

DAVID D. MOORE, born Sylva, North Carolina, June 20, 1972; admitted to bar, 2000, Tennessee; 2001, U.S. District Court, Eastern District of Tennessee; 2005, North Carolina. *Education:* Appalachian State University (B.A., 1994); University of Memphis (J.D., 2000). Phi Alpha Delta. *Member:* Chattanooga, Tennessee and American Bar Associations. ***PRACTICE AREAS:*** Workers Compensation; Civil Litigation; Real Estate Litigation; Consumer Protection. ***Email:*** dmoore@chspa.com

COUNSEL FOR: Cullasaja Club; Highlands Country Club; Fairfield Communities Inc.; Country Club of Sapphire Valley, Inc.; Highlands Falls Country Club, Inc.; Mill Creek Golf Club of Franklin, Inc.; Smoky Mountain Area Mental Health; Zickgrat Enterprises, Inc.; Nantahala Lumber Co.; Golf Properties, Inc.; Franklin Board of Realtors, Inc.; Highland-Cashiers Board of Realtors, Inc.; Trillium Links and Village; Centex Homes; Town of Highlands; Village of Forest Hills; Angel Medical Center.
REPRESENTATIVE CLIENTS: Wachovia Bank; TransAmerica Title Insurance Co.; Stewart Title Insurance Co.; Fidelity National Title Insurance Co.
APPROVED ATTORNEYS FOR: Lawyers Title Insurance Corp.; Federal Land Bank of Columbia; Farmers Home Administration; Fidelity National Title Insurance Co.; Stewart Title Insurance Co.; National Title Insurance Co.; Safeco Title Insurance Co.; Investors Title Insurance Co.; Title Insurance Company of Minnesota; American Title Insurance Co.; Chicago Title Insurance Co.; TransAmerica Title Insurance Co.; Wachovia Bank; First Citizens Bank and Trust Co.; Macon Bank, Inc.; Nantabala Bank and Trust Company; BBC Centura Bank; Rabun County Bank.
REFERENCES: First Citizens Bank and Trust Co.; Macon Bank, Inc.; Wachovia Bank.

WENZEL & WENZEL, PLLC

SYLVA, NORTH CAROLINA

(See Waynesville)

Wills and Probate, Trusts and Estates, Business, Bankruptcy, Real Estate, Buying or Selling a Home, Residential Real Estate, Real Estate Construction, Eminent Domain, Landlord Tenant Law, Civil Litigation, Workers Compensation, General Practice.

LAW OFFICE OF DAVID WIJEWICKRAMA

SYLVA, NORTH CAROLINA

(See Waynesville)

Personal Injury, Family Law, Civil Litigation, Bankruptcy, Real Estate.

SOLES, PHIPPS, RAY & PRINCE

Established in 1959

108 LIVE OAK STREET
P.O. BOX 6
TABOR CITY, NORTH CAROLINA 28463
Telephone: 910-653-2015
Fax: 910-653-4371
URL: http://www.lawyers.com/vaida

General Civil, Domestic and Criminal Practice. Real Estate, Probate and Personal Injury Law. Litigation.

ROBERT C. SOLES, JR., born Tabor City, North Carolina, December 17, 1934; admitted to bar, 1959, North Carolina. *Education:* Wake Forest University (B.S., 1956); University of North Carolina at Chapel Hill (J.D., 1959). Member, North Carolina Law Review, 1958-1959. Town Attorney, Tabor City, 1965. County Attorney, Columbus County, 1966-1972. Member: North Carolina House of Representatives, 1969-1976; North Carolina Senate, 1977—. Member, Board of Trustees, University of North Carolina, 1969-1973. President, Southeastern Community College Foundation, 1969-1976. *Member:* North Carolina Trial Lawyers Association; The Association of Trial Lawyers of America. [Capt., USAR, 1956-1967]. ***PRACTICE AREAS:*** Personal Injury; Criminal Law.

WILLIAM WINSLOW PHIPPS, born June 14, 1952; admitted to bar, 1978, North Carolina and South Carolina. *Education:* East Carolina University (B.A., 1974); University of South Carolina (J.D., 1978). Recipient, Outstanding Alumnus Award, 1984. Chairman, Columbus County Democratic Party, 1989-1993. Member, Southeastern North Carolina Regional Economic Development Commission, 1993—. *Member:* 13th Judicial District (Secretary-Treasurer, 1987-1989; President, 1991-1992); North Carolina State Bar; South Carolina Bar; Columbus County Board of Education Attorney. ***PRACTICE AREAS:*** Personal Injury; Criminal Law; Real Estate; Probate.

JOSEPH LANE RAY, born Loris, South Carolina, October 17, 1960; admitted to bar, 1987, North Carolina. *Education:* University of North Carolina (B.A., 1983); Campbell University (J.D., 1987). Member: Moot Court Association, 1985-1987. Columnist, Campbell Law Observer, 1984-1986. North Carolina Resolution Commission. *Member:* Columbus County (Past President), 13th Judicial District (Secretary-Treasurer, 1995-1996) and North Carolina Bar Associations; North Carolina State Bar. North Carolina Academy of Trial Lawyers; Association of Trial Lawyers of America. ***PRACTICE AREAS:*** Personal Injury; Criminal Law; Family Law; Real Estate; Probate.

SHERRY DEW PRINCE, admitted to bar, 1987, North Carolina and U.S. District Court, Eastern District of North Carolina. *Education:* Pembroke State University (B.S., 1976; M.A., 1981); Campbell University (J.D., 1987). *Member:* Columbus County, North Carolina, 13th Judicial District and American Bar Associations; North Carolina State Bar; North Carolina Academy of Trial Lawyers. ***PRACTICE AREAS:*** Personal Injury; Civil Law; Family Law; Criminal Law.

REPRESENTATIVE CLIENTS: BB & T; Cooperative Savings & Loan Assn.; Waccamaw Bank; First Investors Savings & Loan, Inc.
APPROVED ATTORNEYS FOR: Lawyers Title Insurance Corp.; Veterans Administration; Farmers Home Administration; Federal Land Bank; First Title Insurance Co.; United Title Insurance Co.; Investors, Title Insurance Co.

CHICHESTER & WALKER

TARBORO, NORTH CAROLINA

(See Roanoke Rapids)

Criminal Defense, Drug Crimes, Felonies, Misdemeanors, Traffic Violations, Driving While Intoxicated, Personal Injury, Automobile Accidents, Slip and Falls, Worker's Compensation, Wrongful Death, General Practice.

MICHAEL P. MURPHY, P.A.

TARBORO, NORTH CAROLINA

(See Rocky Mount)

Commercial Collections, Wills, Trust Law, Estate Planning, Personal Injury, Automobile Accidents and Injuries, Truck Accidents, Bankruptcy Chapter 7, Bankruptcy Chapter 13, Corporate Law, Limited Liability Company Law, Business Law, Criminal Law, Traffic Violations.

ROSE RAND ATTORNEYS, P.A.

TARBORO, NORTH CAROLINA

(See Wilson)

General Practice, all Courts. Corporation, Labor and Insurance Law. Trials, including Personal Injury, Wrongful Death and Workers Compensation, Eminent Domain, Tax, Estate Planning and Administration, Municipal, Environmental, Real Estate, Bankruptcy.

J. BRYAN ELLIOTT

TAYLORSVILLE, NORTH CAROLINA

(See Hickory)

Bankruptcy, Social Security Disability.

JOEL C. HARBINSON

Established in 1979

70 EAST MAIN AVENUE
P.O. BOX 400
TAYLORSVILLE, NORTH CAROLINA 28681-0400
Telephone: 828-632-4264
Telefax: 828-632-8927
Email: jharbinson@charter.net
URL: http://www.joelharbinson.com

Auto Accidents, Child Custody, Child Support, Criminal Law, Divorce, DWI, Family Law, Medical Malpractice, Personal Injury, Social Security, Traffic, and Workers Compensation.

JOEL C. HARBINSON, born Hickory, North Carolina, February 18, 1954; admitted to bar, 1979, North Carolina; 1982, U.S. District Court, Western District of North Carolina. *Education:* University of North Carolina at Chapel Hill (B.A., 1977; J.D., 1979). Phi Delta Phi. County Attorney, Alexander County Board of County Commissioners, 1982-1986, 1992-1994. School Board Attorney, Alexander County Board of Education, 1981-1998. Town Attorney, Town of Taylorsville, 1987-1989. Member: North Carolina Dispute Resolution Commission, Certified Mediator, 1998—. Elected Office: Alexander County Board of Commissioners, 1998-2002, 2003-2004 (Chairman, 1998-1999, 2001-2002). *Member:* North Carolina and American Bar Associations; Twenty-Second Judicial District (Presi-

(This Listing Continued)

dent, 1987-1988, 1999-2000) and North Carolina State Bars; North Carolina Academy of Trial Lawyers (County Captain). ***PRACTICE AREAS:*** Auto Accidents; Child Custody; Child Support; Criminal Law; Divorce; DWI; Family Law; Medical Malpractice; Personal Injury; Social Security; Traffic; Workers Compensation.

RON BUTLER

THOMASVILLE, NORTH CAROLINA

(See High Point)

Traffic Violations, Criminal Law, Driving While Intoxicated, Family Law, Divorce and Juvenile Law. Wills.

SCHELL BRAY AYCOCK ABEL & LIVINGSTON P.L.L.C.

THOMASVILLE, NORTH CAROLINA

(See Greensboro)

Corporate, Taxation, Securities Regulation, Venture Capital, Real Estate and Real Estate Finance, Mergers and Acquisitions, Health Care, Antitrust and Trade Regulation, Banking, Commercial, Employee Benefits, Estate Planning and Administration.

WYATT EARLY HARRIS WHEELER L.L.P.

THOMASVILLE, NORTH CAROLINA

(See High Point)

Litigation, Legal and Regulatory matters in Furniture/Home Furnishings Industries, General Civil, Insurance, Business, Securities, Taxation and Criminal Practice. Trials and Appeals in all State and Federal Courts. Probate and Estate Planning, Real Estate, Bankruptcy, Corporation, Banking, Negligence, Workers Compensation and Family Law.

JUDY DALTON

Established in 1994

403 N. MAIN STREET
TROUTMAN, NORTH CAROLINA 28166
Telephone: 704-528-7788
Fax: 704-528-7373
Email: judydalton_86@msn.com
URL: http://www.judydaltonlawfirm.com

Family Law, Child Custody, Child Support, Visitation Rights, Divorce, Property Distribution, Restraining Orders, Adoptions, Criminal Defense, Felonies and Misdemeanors, DWI, Traffic Violations, Drug Crimes, Probation Violations, Civil Litigation, Wills, Debt Collections.

JUDY DALTON, born Charlotte, North Carolina, August 8, 1964; admitted to bar, 1991, North Carolina. *Education:* Davidson College (B.A., Political Science, 1986); Campbell University School of Law (J.D., 1991). Certified Family Law Mediator. *Member:* Iredell County and North Carolina Bar Associations. ***PRACTICE AREAS:*** Family Law; Child Custody; Visitation Rights; Child Support; Alimony; Adoptions; Criminal Defense; Driving While Intoxicated; Misdemeanors; Felonies; Probation Violations; Civil Litigation; Wills; Debt Collections.

HOLLERS & ATKINSON

Established in 1978

110 NORTH MAIN STREET
P.O. BOX 567
TROY, NORTH CAROLINA 27371
Telephone: 910-572-3638
Fax: 910-576-1577
Email: hollers-atkinson@carolina.net

General Practice. Real Property and Estate Planning Law. Criminal Law. Traffic Court.

RUSSELL J. HOLLERS, born Durham, North Carolina, March 23, 1939; admitted to bar, 1963, North Carolina. *Education:* University of North Carolina (A.B., 1961; LL.B., 1963). Phi Delta Phi. Morehead Scholar. *Member:* Montgomery County, 19B Judicial District and North Carolina Bar Associations; North Carolina State Bar. [Capt., J.A.G.C., U.S. Army, 1963-1967]. ***PRACTICE AREAS:*** Real Estate; Business; Government Law.

CARL W. ATKINSON, JR., born Lilesville, North Carolina, August 25, 1944; admitted to bar, 1973, North Carolina. *Education:* Wingate College (A.A., 1964); University of North Carolina (B.A., 1966); Wake Forest University (J.D., 1973). Phi Delta Phi. *Member:* Montgomery County (President, 1978), 19B Judicial District and North Carolina Bar Associations; North Carolina State Bar. [1st Lieut., USMC, 1966-1969]. ***PRACTICE AREAS:*** Criminal; Family and Civil Litigation; Traffic Court.

REPRESENTATIVE CLIENTS: First Bank, Troy, North Carolina; Town of Troy, Candor and Mount Gilead; Jordan Lumber & Supply, Inc.; Montgomery County; Myrick Construction Inc.; Quik-Chek, Inc.; Alandale Knitting, Inc.; Capel, Incorporated; Troy Lumber; DeBerry Land & Timber.

BYERS, MARTELLE & WILLIAMS, P.L.L.C.

TRYON, NORTH CAROLINA

(See Rutherfordton)

General Civil and Criminal Trial Practice in all courts, Family Law, Real Property Law, Elder Law, Wills, Trusts and Estates, Corporate Law, and Municipal Law.

ROBERT J. DEUTSCH, P.A.

TRYON, NORTH CAROLINA

(See Asheville)

General Civil Trial Practice. Wills and Probate, Business, Family Law, Equitable Distribution, Real Estate, Corporate Law, Zoning, Personal Injury, Products Liability, Wrongful Death, Computer Law.

ELKINS & ELKINS

TRYON, NORTH CAROLINA

(See Hendersonville)

Bankruptcy, Real Estate, Residential Real Estate, Buying and Selling a Home, Probate, Corporation, Civil Trial Practice, Out of Court Debt Restructuring.

R. ANDERSON HAYNES

Established in 1973

78 PACOLET STREET
P.O. BOX 100
TRYON, NORTH CAROLINA 28782
Telephone: 828-859-9145
Fax: 828-859-2252

Estate Planning, Elder Law, Estate Administration, Probate, Real Estate, Corporate Law.

R. ANDERSON HAYNES, born Tryon, North Carolina, April 24, 1947; admitted to bar, 1973, North Carolina. *Education:* Trinity College (B.A., 1969); University of North Carolina (J.D., 1973). *Member:* Polk County (President, 1985-1988), North Carolina and American Bar Associations; North Carolina State Bar. ***PRACTICE AREAS:*** Estate Planning; Elder Law; Estate Administration; Probate; Real Estate; Corporate Law.

APPROVED ATTORNEY FOR: Lawyer's Title Land America; Investor's Title; Chicago Title; Wachovia Bank; First Citizens Bank; Bank of America; Tryon Federal/HomeTrust; Mountain 1st; Carolina 1st; BB&T.
REFERENCE: Bank of America, N.A., Tryon, NC.

RICHARD L. BROWN, JR.

WADESBORO, NORTH CAROLINA

(See Monroe)

Real Estate-Buying and Selling, Landlord and Tenant, Personal Injury, Automobile Accidents, Dog Bites, Criminal Law, White Collar Crime, Traffic Violations, Driving While Intoxicated, Employment Law, Wrongful Terminations, Bankruptcy, Civil Rights, Health Care, Nursing Home Issues.

CLODFELTER LAW OFFICE

202 EAST WADE STREET
P.O. BOX 754
WADESBORO, NORTH CAROLINA 28170
Telephone: 704-694-0195
Fax: 704-694-0182
Email: lynn_tlclaw@alltel.net
URL: http://www.tlclawfirm.com

Criminal Law, Domestic, Family Law, Child Custody, Divorce, Personal Injury, Wrongful Death, Traffic Violations, Driving While Intoxicated.

T. LYNN CLODFELTER, born Winston-Salem, North Carolina, September 16, 1968; admitted to bar, 1993, North Carolina. *Education:* University of North Carolina (A.B., 1990); Campbell University (J.D., 1993). Phi Alpha Delta. *Member:* Anson County Bar Association; North Carolina State Bar; North Carolina Academy of Trial Lawyers.

CHARLES WEAVER COLLINI

Established in 1984

ANSON PROFESSIONAL BUILDING
115 EAST WADE STREET
P.O. BOX 1039
WADESBORO, NORTH CAROLINA 28170
Telephone: 704-694-9311
Fax: 704-694-9312
Email:ccollini@carolina.rr.com
Email: ccollini@alltel.net
URL: http://www.lawyers.com/collinilaw

General Trial Practice. Personal Injury, Wrongful Death, Criminal Law, and Family Law.

FIRM PROFILE: Solo Practice established in 1984. Firm specializes in criminal defense litigation and plaintiff's personal injury litigation. Extensive DWI defense experience and practice handles traffic matters.

CHARLES WEAVER COLLINI, born North Carolina, July 30, 1948; admitted to bar, 1974, North Carolina and U.S. District Court, Eastern District of North Carolina. *Education:* Trinity School; University of North Carolina (B.A., 1970; J.D., 1974). Phi Delta Phi. Law Clerk to the Hon. Algernon L. Butler, Chief Judge, U.S. District Court, Eastern District of North Carolina, 1974-1976. Assistant District Attorney, 20th Judicial District of North Carolina, 1978-1984. Attorney, Anson/Richmond Child Support Enforcement Agency, 1989-1992. *Member:* Anson County (Secretary, 1984-1996), 20th Judicial District (Vice-

(This Listing Continued)

CHARLES WEAVER COLLINI, Wadesboro—Continued

President, 1984-1985, 1991-1992, 1995-1996; President, 1996-1997, 2000-2001) and North Carolina State Bars; North Carolina Academy of Trial Lawyers (Sustaining Patron-NCATL). ***LANGUAGES:*** French.

REFERENCES: BB&T; Centuraa Bank.

LAW OFFICE OF JOHN R. DANIEL

WADESBORO, NORTH CAROLINA

(See Rockingham)

General Civil Trial Practice in all State and Federal Courts and Administrative Agencies. Personal Injury, Workers Compensation, Social Security Disability, Real Estate and Traffic.

POISSON POISSON & BOWER, PLLC

Established in 1976

THE WYATT HOUSE
300 EAST WADE STREET
WADESBORO, NORTH CAROLINA 28170
Telephone: 704-694-5515
Fax: 704-694-9645
URL: http://www.poissonpoissonbowerlaw.com
Email: info@poissonlaw.com
URL: http://www.poissonlaw.com

Personal Injury, Wrongful Death, Workers' Compensation, Social Security, Real Estate, Probate, Corporate Law and Traffic Cases.

FIRM PROFILE: Poisson, Poisson & Bower, PLLC is a service-oriented law firm located in Wadesboro, North Carolina. The firm protects the rights of citizens throughout the communities of southern North Carolina.

Poisson, Poisson & Bower, PLLC enjoys the highest rating for excellence and integrity under the Martindale-Hubbell guidelines for the practice of law.

Mr. Poisson, Jr. is board certified as a specialist in workers' compensation law.

FRED D. POISSON, SR., born Wilmington, North Carolina, September 11, 1926; admitted to bar, 1966, North Carolina and U.S. District Court, Western District of North Carolina; 1974, U.S. District Court, Eastern District of North Carolina; 1976, U.S. Court of Appeals, Fourth Circuit; 1982, U.S. District Court, Middle District of North Carolina. *Education:* Pennsylvania State University; University of North Carolina (B.A., 1947; LL.B., 1966); University of Pennsylvania (M.B.A., 1950). Delta Theta Phi.

FRED D. POISSON, JR., born Raleigh, North Carolina, August 18, 1951; admitted to bar, 1976, North Carolina; 1978, U.S. District Court, Western District of North Carolina. *Education:* Davidson College; University of North Carolina-Asheville (B.A., 1973); Wake Forest University (J.D., 1976). Phi Delta Phi. Member, Wake Forest Law Review, 1973-1976. (Board Certified Specialist in Workers' Compensation, North Carolina State Board of Legal Specialization). ***Email:*** FDP@poissonlaw.com

GEORGE C. BOWER, JR., born Monroe, North Carolina, March 21, 1951; admitted to bar, 1978, North Carolina. *Education:* University of North Carolina (A.B., 1973); Mercer University and Wake Forest University (J.D., 1978). Phi Alpha Delta. ***Email:*** GCB@poissonlaw.com

---

E. STEWART POISSON, born Wadesboro, North Carolina, September 27, 1978; admitted to bar, 2004, North Carolina. *Education:* University of North Carolina (B.A., 2001; J.D., with honors, 2004). Member, 2002-2003 and Special Projects Editor, 2003-2004, North Carolina Law Review. ***Email:*** ESP@poissonlaw.com

DEWEY P. BRINKLEY

WAKE FOREST, NORTH CAROLINA

(See Raleigh)

Criminal Law, Driving While Intoxicated, DWI, Traffic Violations, Drug Crimes, Parole and Probation, Juvenile Crimes, White Collar Crimes.

MALCOLM E. HARRIS, P.A.

822 SOUTH WHITE STREET, 27587
P.O. BOX 1100
WAKE FOREST, NORTH CAROLINA 27588-1100
Telephone: 919-554-0700
Facsimile: 919-554-8052
Email: malcolmharris@nc.rr.com

Commercial and Residential Real Estate, Wills and Estates, Business Formation Law.

MALCOLM E. HARRIS, born Raleigh, North Carolina, April 25, 1948; admitted to bar, 1975, North Carolina. *Education:* University of North Carolina (B.A., 1970); North Carolina Central University School of Law (J.D., with honors, 1975). *Member:* Wake County, North Carolina and American Bar Associations; North Carolina State Bar. ***PRACTICE AREAS:*** Commercial Real Estate; Residential Real Estate; Wills and Estates; Business Formation Law.

APPROVED ATTORNEY FOR: Fidelity National Title Insurance Company of Pennsylvania; Investors Title Insurance Co.; The Title Insurance Company of North Carolina; Chicago Title Insurance Co.; Commonwealth Land Title Insurance Co.; Lawyers Title Insurance Co.

HOPPER LAW FIRM

WAKE FOREST, NORTH CAROLINA

(See Raleigh)

Family Law, Business Litigation, Construction Law, Child Custody, Divorce, Criminal Law, Traffic Violations, DWI, Commercial Litigation, Alimony and Misdemeanors.

TENNEY & TENNEY, LLP

WAKE FOREST, NORTH CAROLINA

(See Raleigh)

Wills, Estates, Probate, Trusts, Living Trusts, Business Law, Corporate Law, Small Business, Intellectual Property, Contracts, Personal Injury, Automobile Accidents, Slip and Fall, Civil Litigation, Real Estate, Residential Real Estate, Real Estate Closings, Family Law.

DAVID AND ASSOCIATES, PLLC

107 NORTH NORWOOD STREET
WALLACE, NORTH CAROLINA 28466
Telephone: 910-285-8777
Toll Free: 1-800-856-9927
Email: aeverhart@davidandassociates.com
URL: http://www.wilmingtonpiattorneys.com

Jacksonville, North Carolina Office: 405-B Western Boulevard. 28546. Telephone: 910-219-4878.

Supply, North Carolina Office: Highway 17. 28462. Telephone: 910-754-8465.

Wilmington, North Carolina Office: 1516 Dawson Street. 28401. Telephone: 910-251-8088.

Clinton, North Carolina Office: 610 Beaman Street. 28328. Telephone: 910-592-8400.

Winston-Salem, North Carolina Office: 1100-A South Stratford Road. 27103. Telephone: 336-354-1040.

Greensboro, North Carolina Office: 529 College Road. Suite G. 27410. Telephone: 336-354-1040.

Personal Injury, Medical Malpractice, Wrongful Death, Products Liability, Workers Compensation, Aviation, Airplane Crashes, Negligence, Class Actions, Maritime Accidents, Boating Accidents, Bicycle Accidents, Motorcycle Accidents, Truck Accidents, School Bus Accidents, Railroad Accidents, Dog Bites, Slip and Fall, Birth Trauma, Brain Injury, Spinal Injury, Head Injury, Catastrophic Injury, Vehicular Homicide, Personal Injury Mediation, Products Liability, Drug and Medical Device Litigation, Product Defects, Automobile Liability, Motorcycle Products Liability, Amusement Park Liability, Hotel Liability, Marina Liability, Sports Injury.

(For complete biographical data on all personnel, see Professional Biographies, Wilmington, North Carolina)

BANZET, BANZET & THOMPSON, P.L.L.C.

COURT HOUSE SQUARE
101 NORTH FRONT STREET
P.O. BOX 535
WARRENTON, NORTH CAROLINA 27589
Telephone: 252-257-3166
Fax: 252-257-2053
Email: bbanzet@nc.rr.com

General Civil and Criminal Trial Practice. State and Federal Criminal Defense, Traffic, Personal Injury Litigation, Workers Compensation, Medical Malpractice, Probate, Wills and Estates, Real Estate and Title Searches.

FIRM PROFILE: The firm has been in existence in the area for over seventy years. It is a continuance of the original firm, Williams & Banzet. The firm represents corporations, small businesses and individuals throughout the northeastern areas of North Carolina. The firm maintains a general civil and criminal trial practice with an emphasis on litigation and real property. The firm is listed in the Bar Register of Preeminent Lawyers.

MEMBERS OF FIRM

JULIUS BANZET, III, born Rocky Mount, North Carolina, January 26, 1937; admitted to bar, 1962, North Carolina and U.S. District Court, Eastern District of North Carolina. *Education:* University of North Carolina (A.B., 1960; LL.B., 1962). Phi Delta Phi. North Carolina State Bar Councilor, Ninth Judicial District. *Member:* Ninth Judicial District and North Carolina Bar Associations; North Carolina State Bar. ***Email:*** jbanzet@nc.rr.com

LEWIS A. THOMPSON, III, born Raleigh, North Carolina, January 5, 1952; admitted to bar, 1977, North Carolina; 1979, U.S. District Court, Eastern District of North Carolina; 1983, U.S. Court of Appeals, 4th Circuit. *Education:* University of North Carolina at Chapel Hill (B.A., 1974); Wake Forest University (J.D., 1977). *Member:* Ninth Judicial District Bar Association; North Carolina State Bar; North Carolina Academy of Trial Lawyers. ***Email:*** lat-banzet@nc.rr.com

MITCHELL G. STYERS, born Winston-Salem, North Carolina, December 31, 1969; admitted to bar, 1997, North Carolina; U.S. District Court, Eastern District of North Carolina. *Education:* North Carolina State University (B.A., 1992); North Carolina Central University (J.D., 1997). Law Clerk to the Honorable Chief Justice Burley B. Mitchell, Jr., North Carolina Supreme Court, 1997-1998). *Member:* Ninth Judicial District and North Carolina Bar Associations. ***Email:*** bbanzet@nc.rr.com

REPRESENTATIVE CLIENTS: The Town of Norlina; Branch Banking & Trust Co.; Warren County Board of Education; Town of Warrenton.
APPROVED ATTORNEYS FOR: Federal Land Bank of Columbia; Lawyers Title Insurance Corp.; Chicago Title Insurance Co.; Commonwealth Land Title Insurance Co.; AMI Title Insurance Co.; Farmers Home Administration; Fidelity National Title Insurance Corp; Investors Tirle Insurance Co.

DAVIS, STURGES & TOMLINSON

WARRENTON, NORTH CAROLINA

(See Louisburg)

General Civil and Criminal Trial Practice in State and Federal Courts. Estate and Probate, Real Estate and Corporation Law. Personal Injury, Automobile Accidents, Truck Accidents, Wrongful Death, Traffic Violations, DWI, Litigation, Land Condemnation.

HARVEY D. JACKSON ATTORNEY AT LAW

WARRENTON, NORTH CAROLINA

(See Henderson)

Worker's Compensation, Personal Injury, Auto Accident and Insurance Claims, Wrongful Death, Traffic Violations.

LUDLUM LAW FIRM

Established in 1994

404 NORTH PINE STREET
P.O. BOX 711
WARSAW, NORTH CAROLINA 28398-0711
Telephone: 910-293-2000
Facsimile: 910-293-2200
Email: gludlum@ludlumlawfirm.com
URL: http://www.lawyers.com/ludlaw-nc

Driving While Intoxicated and Traffic Violations. Criminal Defense, Real Estate, Divorce and Family Law, Accidents and Personal Injury, Litigation, Wills, Commercial Transactions.

J. GARRETT LUDLUM, born Wilmington, North Carolina, October 2, 1947; admitted to bar, 1981, North Carolina. *Education:* Campbell University (B.S., 1969; J.D., 1979). Delta Theta Phi. *Member:* Duplin County, Fourth Judicial District (Secretary-Treasurer, 1982-1985; Vice-President, 1992-1993; President, 1993-1994), North Carolina and American Bar Associations; North Carolina State Bar; North Carolina Academy of Trial Lawyers; The Association of North Carolina Municipal Attorneys (Member, Board of Directors, 1985-1986). ***PRACTICE AREAS:*** Driving While Intoxicated; Traffic Violations; Criminal Defense; Real Estate; Family Law; Accidents; Personal Injury.

HAYES S. LUDLUM, born Wilmington, North Carolina February 6, 1980; admitted to bar, 2005, North Carolina. *Education:* Hampden-Sydney College (B.A., History 2002); Campbell University (J.D., 2005). *Member:* Duplin County, 4th Judicial District and North Carolina Bar Associations; North Carolina State Bar; North Carolina Academy of Trial Lawyers; Association of North Carolina Municipal Attorneys. ***PRACTICE AREAS:*** Commercial Transactions; Criminal Law; Driving While Intoxicated; Traffic Violations; Family Law; Divorce; Local Government Law; Civil Litigation; Medical Malpractice; Personal Injury; Accidents; Real Estate; Wills.

THOMPSON & THOMPSON, P.C.

Established in 1966

114 W. HILL STREET
P.O. BOX 901
WARSAW, NORTH CAROLINA 28398
Telephone: 910-293-3124
Fax: 910-293-7171
Email: kennedythompson@yahoo.com
URL: http://www.thompsonandthompsonlaw.com

Criminal Law, Driving While Intoxicated, Traffic Violations, Civil Litigation, Medical Malpractice, Real Estate.

FIRM PROFILE: Our firm specializes in criminal law, driving while impaired, traffic violations, civil litigation, medical malpractice and real estate transactions.

KENNEDY L. THOMPSON, born Clinton, North Carolina, April 16, 1975; admitted to bar, 2001, North Carolina. *Education:* University of North Carolina at Chapel Hill (B.A., 1997); University of Baltimore School of Law (J.D., 2001). Phi Delta Phi. Assistant District Attorney, 2001-2003. *Member:* Duplin County and North Carolina Bar Associations; North Carolina State Bar; North Carolina Academy of Trial Lawyers; Fourth Judicial District Bar Association. ***PRACTICE AREAS:*** Criminal Litigation; Civil Litigation; Medical Malpractice; Real Estate; Criminal Law; Traffic Violations; Driving While Intoxicated. **Email:** kennedythompson@yahoo.com

E. C. THOMPSON, III, born Warsaw, North Carolina, February 15, 1936; admitted to bar, 1966, North Carolina and U.S. District Court, Eastern District of North Carolina. *Education:* University of North Carolina at Chapel Hill (B.A., 1959); Wake Forest University Law School (J.D., 1966). Member, Board of Directors, 1971-1976, Farm Workers Legal Services. *Member:* Duplin County (Vice President, 1969-2004; President, 2004—), North Carolina, Fourth Judicial District (Secretary-Treasurer, 1970-1971; President, 1990-1991) and American Bar Associations; North Carolina State Bar; North Carolina Academy of Trial Lawyers; The Association of Trial Lawyers of America; The Association of North Carolina Municipal Attorneys (Member, Board of Directors, 1973-1975; Vice President, 1976; President, 1977). ***LANGUAGES:*** Spanish. ***PRACTICE AREAS:*** Medical Malpractice; Criminal Law; Civil Litigation; Real Estate; Wills; Trusts and Estates. **Email:** kennedythompson@yahoo.com

Language: Spanish.

RODDEY M. BROWN III & ANGELA H. BROWN, P.A.

WASHINGTON, NORTH CAROLINA

(See Greenville)

Criminal Law, DWI, Drug Crimes, Juvenile Crimes, Parole and Probation, Traffic Violations, White Collar Crime, Education, Elder Law, Nursing Home Abuse, Workers Compensation, Medical Malpractice, Personal Injury, Automobile Accidents, Sexual Abuse, Slip and Fall, Wrongfull Death and Appellate Practice.

BRUMBAUGH, MU & KING, P.A.

Established in 1978

110 WEST THIRD STREET
P.O. BOX 338
WASHINGTON, NORTH CAROLINA 27889
Telephone: 252-946-0793
URL: http://www.bmklaw.net

Practice Limited to Injury Cases. Automobile, Wrongful Death, Medical Malpractice, Workers' Compensation, Products Liability and Social Security Claims.

(For complete biographical data on all personnel, see professional biographies, Jacksonville, North Carolina)

BURCH LAW OFFICE

WASHINGTON, NORTH CAROLINA

(See Greenville)

Personal Injury, Automobile Accidents, Wrongful Death, Medical Malpractice, Criminal Law, Driving While Intoxicated, Drug Crimes, Traffic Violations, White Collar Crime, Worker Compensation, Adoptions, Child Custody, Child Support, Divorce, Visitation Rights, Wills and Probate, Trust and Estates, Estate Planning, Social Security Disability, Eminent Domain, Zoning and Planning, Traumatic Brain Injury, Corporate-Business Formation.

GRAY LEGAL GROUP

WASHINGTON, NORTH CAROLINA

(See Greensboro)

Workers Compensation, Injuries, Wrongful Death, Life and Disability Insurance Claims, Auto Accidents.

The LeonLaw Firm

WASHINGTON, NORTH CAROLINA

(See Greenville)

Employment Law, Personal Injury, Workers Compensation, Contracts.

RODMAN, HOLSCHER, FRANCISCO & PECK, P.A.

Established in 1914

320 NORTH MARKET STREET
P.O. DRAWER 1747
WASHINGTON, NORTH CAROLINA 27889
Telephone: 252-946-3122
Fax: 252-946-3125
URL: http://www.rhfp.net

General Civil Practice, Insurance Defense, Personal Injury, Social Security, Family Law, Corporate, Trusts and Estates, Probate, Real Property, Municipal Law, Criminal Law and Defense.

FIRM PROFILE: The firm traces its roots to the late 1800's and has members who have served at the highest levels of the state judiciary and government and as leaders in the North Carolina Bar Association. The firm represents both plaintiffs and defendants in civil trials and proceedings, family law matters and personal injury suits; defendants in criminal proceedings; and those seeking social security disability benefits. In addition, the firm performs estate planning, assists in the estate administration process and is involved in residential and commercial real estate development projects and loan closings. The firm represents several local government units.

FREDERICK NORMAN HOLSCHER, born Rocky Mount, North Carolina, February 5, 1948; admitted to bar, 1973, North Carolina and U.S. District Court, Eastern District of North Carolina. *Education:* University of North Carolina (A.B., 1969; J.D., 1973). *Member:* Second Judicial District, Beaufort County and North Carolina Bar Associations; North Carolina State Bar. [With U.S. Army Reserve, 1970-1976]. ***PRACTICE AREAS:*** Real Estate Law; Corporate Law; Business Law; Municipal Law. **Email:** fnh@rhfp.net

DAVID C. FRANCISCO, born Roanoke, Virginia, June 29, 1944; admitted to bar, 1975, North Carolina and U.S. District Court, Eastern District of North Carolina; 2001, U.S. Supreme Court. *Education:* Virginia Commonwealth University (B.S., 1968); Wake Forest University (J.D., 1975). Public Administrator, Beaufort County, 1975-1982. *Member:* Second Judicial District, Beaufort County and North Carolina Bar Associations; North Carolina State Bar. [Capt., U.S. Army, 1968-1972]. ***PRACTICE AREAS:*** Probate; Trusts; Wills; Estates; Contested Wills; Municipal Law; Civil Law; Corporate Law. **Email:** dcf@rhfp.net

(This Listing Continued)

RODMAN, HOLSCHER, FRANCISCO & PECK, P.A., Washington—Continued

R. BRANTLEY PECK, JR., born Chapel Hill, North Carolina, January 28, 1957; admitted to bar, 1983, North Carolina and U.S. District Court, Eastern District of North Carolina. *Education:* University of North Carolina at Chapel Hill (B.S., 1979); Wake Forest University (J.D., 1983). Member, North Carolina Christian Legal Society. *Member:* Second Judicial District, Beaufort County (Past President) and North Carolina Bar Associations; North Carolina State Bar. ***PRACTICE AREAS:*** General Civil Practice; Family Law; Insurance Defense; Social Security Disability; Municipal Law; Creditor Law; Collections. ***Email:*** rbp@rhfp.net

FRANZ F. HOLSCHER, born Chapel Hill, North Carolina, August 5, 1970; admitted to bar, 1997, North Carolina and U.S. District Court, Eastern District of North Carolina. *Education:* University of North Carolina at Chapel Hill (B.S. in Business, 1992); Campbell University (J.D., 1997). Notes and Comments Editor, Campbell Law Review, 1996-1997. *Member:* Beaufort County (President, 1998-2000), Second Judicial District (Secretary-Treasurer, 2000-2004) and North Carolina Bar Associations; North Carolina State Bar; North Carolina Academy of Trial Lawyers. ***PRACTICE AREAS:*** Municipal Law; Criminal Law; Traffic Violations; Civil Litigation; Collections; Workers Compensation. ***Email:*** ffh@rhfp.net

RETIRED

EDWARD N. RODMAN, born Washington, North Carolina, October 20, 1926; admitted to bar, 1955, North Carolina. *Education:* North Carolina State College (B.S.Engr., 1950); University of North Carolina (LL.B., 1955).

GENERAL COUNSEL FOR: First South Bank; Mid-East Commission; Lee Chevrolet, Inc.
REPRESENTATIVE CLIENTS: Bank of America; Sprint; Government Employees Insurance Company (GEICO); Belhaven Cable TV; Carolina Power and Light, Rich Real Estate Co.; Lawyers Mutual Liability Co.; Gillko, Inc.; PCS Phosphate Company Inc.; Pamlico Timber Co.; Coastal Carolina Cotton Gin.
CITY ATTORNEYS FOR: City of Washington; Town of Plymouth.
APPROVED ATTORNEYS FOR: Lawyers Title Insurance Corp.; Chicago Title; Commonwealth Land Title Insurance Co.; Statewide Title Co.; Investors Title.
REFERENCES: First South Bank; Wachovia Bank, N.A.

BLANCHARD, NEWMAN & HAYES

WAYNESVILLE, NORTH CAROLINA

(See Hendersonville)

General Civil Litigation, Family Law, Divorce, Criminal in all State and Federal Courts, Traffic, DWI.

BROWN, WARD & HAYNES, P.A.

SUITE 300
370 NORTH MAIN STREET
P.O. DRAWER 928
WAYNESVILLE, NORTH CAROLINA 28786-0928
Telephone: 828-456-9436
Fax: 828-456-4069

General Practice in all Courts. Trials. Probate, Corporation, Real Estate, Business Law, Utility Law, Domestic Relations, Criminal, Traffic Offenses, Civil Litigation, Estate Planning, Appellate Practice.

FIRM PROFILE: The firm of Brown, Ward & Haynes, P.A., has been practicing in Waynesville, North Carolina for over 90 years.

GLENN W. BROWN (Retired)

H.S. WARD, JR. (Retired)

WOODROW H. GRIFFIN, born Greensboro, North Carolina, November 19, 1948; admitted to bar, 1974, North Carolina. *Education:* High Point College (B.A., 1971); Wake Forest University (J.D., 1974). Phi Alpha Delta. Recipient, American Jurisprudence Award, Future Interests. *Member:* Haywood County and North Carolina (Member, Sections on: Real Property and Estate Planning and Fiduciary Law Sections) Bar Associations; The North Carolina State Bar. ***PRACTICE AREAS:*** Real Estate; Probate; Business Law; Mediation; Estate Planning. ***Email:*** whgriffinbwh@yahoo.com

STEPHEN G. ELLIS, born Waynesville, North Carolina, August 3, 1949; admitted to bar, 1984, North Carolina; 1994, U.S. District Court, Western and Middle Districts of North Carolina. *Education:* North Carolina State University and University of North Carolina (B.A., 1971); University of North Carolina School of Law (J.D., 1984). Assistant District Attorney, North Carolina, 30th District, 1985-1988. *Member:* Haywood County (President, 1996) and North Carolina Bar Associations; North Carolina Academy of Trial Lawyers; 30th District Bar Association. ***PRACTICE AREAS:*** Family Law; Criminal Law; Civil Litigation; Divorce; Equitable Distribution; Adoption Law; Child Support; Child Custody. ***Email:*** ellis849@bellsouth.net

FRANK G. QUEEN, born Waynesville, North Carolina, December 1, 1951; admitted to bar, 1976, North Carolina; 1982, U.S. District Court, Western and Middle Districts of North Carolina; 1985, U.S. Court of Appeals, 4th Circuit. *Education:* University of North Carolina (A.B., 1974; J.D., 1976). Instructor, Real Estate Law, Haywood Technical College, 1983-1985. Member, Haywood County Election Board, 1981-1983. Town Attorney, Waynesville, 1987-1989. Director, Legal Aid of North Carolina, 1999—. *Member:* North Carolina (Member, Appellate Rules Study Committee, 1996—) and American (Member, Real Property, Probate and Trust Law Section; Reporter for North Carolina, Committee on Significant Decisions, 1984-1988) Bar Associations. ***PRACTICE AREAS:*** Real Property; Appellate Practice. ***Email:*** frankgqueen@cs.com

WILLIAM E. CANNON, JR., born Albany, Georgia, November 22, 1952; admitted to bar, 1977, Georgia and U.S. District Court, Middle District of Georgia; 1981, U.S. Court of Appeals, Eleventh Circuit; 1992, U.S. Supreme Court; 2001, U.S. Court of Appeals, Federal Circuit; 2004, North Carolina, U.S. Court of Appeals, Fourth Circuit and U.S. District Court, Western District of North Carolina; U.S. Supreme Court. *Education:* Emory University (A.B., 1974); University of Georgia (J.D., 1977). Author: "Celebrate Your Freedom", 1999 Judge Edward R. Finch Law Day Speech Award, American Bar Association; "Product Liability Law Update Annual Caribbean Seminar", The Institute of Continuing Legal Education in Georgia, 1999; "Analyzing Plaintiff Cases: How to Know If You Got a Dog or Not?", Georgia Tort Law, The Institute of Continuing Legal Education in Georgia, 1998; "The Evolution of Mandatory Interrogatories and Their Impact on Discovery in the District Courts," Verdict, Vol. 22, No. 2, 1997; "Trying the Automobile Injury Case in Georgia," National Business Institute, Inc., 1992; "Obtaining Better Settlements by Understanding and Using the Way Insurance Companies Evaluate Cases and Conduct Negotiations," Georgia Trial Lawyers Association Annual Seminar and Convention, 1986. City Attorney, Leesburg, Georgia, 1980—. County Attorney, Lee County, Georgia, 1982-1994. *Member:* State Bar of Georgia (President, 1998-1999); North Carolina State Bar; North Carolina Bar Association; North Carolina Academy of Trial Lawyers. Fellow: Georgia Bar Foundation; Lawyers Foundation of Georgia. ***PRACTICE AREAS:*** Civil Practice; Trial Practice; Personal Injury; Commercial Litigation; Products Liability.

(This Listing Continued)

OF COUNSEL

DAVID J. HAYNES, born Asheville, North Carolina, August 22, 1939; admitted to bar, 1962, North Carolina. *Education:* Mars Hill College (A.A., 1958); Rollins College; Wake Forest University (LL.B., 1962). Phi Delta Phi. Haywood County Attorney, 1970-1971. *Member:* Haywood County and North Carolina Bar Associations; The North Carolina State Bar. [Lt., USNR, 1962-1967]. ***PRACTICE AREAS:*** Utility Law.

GENERAL COUNSEL FOR: West I CATV; Junaluska Sanitary District; Town of Waynesville, N.C.; Haywood Electric Membership Corporation.
LOCAL COUNSEL FOR: Haywood Electric Membership Corporation.
APPROVED ATTORNEYS FOR: Lawyers Title Insurance Corp.; Commercial Standard Insurance Co.; Chicago Title Insurance Co.; Federal Land Bank of Columbia; Lawyers Title of North Carolina; Investors Title Co.; Commonwealth Land Title Insurance Co.; Fidelity National Title Insurance.

FERIKES & BLEYNAT, PLLC

WAYNESVILLE, NORTH CAROLINA

(See Asheville)

Business Litigation, Business Torts, Construction Litigation, Appellate Practice, Property Law and Litigation; Personal Injury and Medical Malpractice, Automobile Accidents, Wrongful Death, Brain Injury, Torts, Commercial Liability, Commercial Real Estate Litigation, Construction Defects and Liens, Contract Litigation, Corporate Litigation, Workers Compensation.

KERSTEN & DAVIS, P.A.

95 DEPOT STREET
P.O. DRAWER 1260
WAYNESVILLE, NORTH CAROLINA 28786
Telephone: 828-452-5801
Fax: 828-456-4917
Email: attorneys@kdlawfirm.com

Real Estate, Corporate Law, Probate, Trusts and Estates, Litigation, Personal Injury, Criminal Law, Local Government Law, Securities.

JOHN C. KERSTEN, born Richmond, Virginia, December 14, 1940; admitted to bar, 1965, Florida and U.S. District Court, Southern District of Florida; 1971, U.S. Supreme Court; 1982, North Carolina. *Education:* Duke University; University of Miami (B.A., 1962; J.D., 1965). Phi Delta Phi. Teaching Assistant, University of Miami School of Law, 1965. Assistant City Attorney, Fort Lauderdale, Florida, 1967. Member, Panel of Arbitrators, American Arbitration Association, 1968-1996. *Member:* Broward County (Member, Committees on: Public Relations, 1969-1971 and Professional Ethics, 1973-1974; Lawyers Title Guaranty Fund, 1973-1974), Haywood County (President, 1993) and American Bar Associations; North Carolina State Bar (Member, Condominium Committee, Real Property Section, 1983-1985); The Florida Bar. ***PRACTICE AREAS:*** Commercial Real Estate; Residential Real Estate; Corporate Law; Ad Valorem Tax; Golf Course Development; Condominium Law. ***Email:*** Kersten@kdlawfirm.com

ANN HINES DAVIS, born Asheville, North Carolina, June 19, 1955; admitted to bar, 1979, North Carolina. *Education:* Western Carolina University (B.S., magna cum laude, 1976); University of North Carolina (J.D., 1979). *Member:* 30th Judicial Bar; North Carolina State Bar; North Carolina Bar Association. ***PRACTICE AREAS:*** Residential Real Estate; Probate; Trusts and Estates; Corporate Law; Juvenile Law. ***Email:*** davisa@kdlawfirm.com

GENERAL COUNSEL FOR: Waynesville Country Club Inn; The Greens Condominium; Maggie Valley Country Club and Resort; Country Club Real Estate of WNC, Inc.; Laurel Ridge Country Club; Mountain View Housing; WNC Community Credit Union; Mountain Projects, Inc.; Carolina Log Homes, Inc.; Distinctive Building & Design, Inc.; Smoky Mountain Sanctuary; Whispering Woods; Brannon Forest; Masters Pointe; Soco Falls, Country Place; Rolling Hills Estates; Glen Meadows; Smoky Mountain Retreat Communities; Cherokee Tribal Casino Gaming Enterprise; WNC Community Credit Union.
APPROVED ATTORNEYS FOR: Lawyer's Title Insurance Corp.; Chicago Title Insurance Co.; Commonwealth Land Title Insurance Co.; Investors Title Insurance Co.; Stewart Title; Home Trust Bank; B. B. & T.; Asheville Federal Savings and Loan Assn.; PHH U.S. Mortgage Corporation; First Citizens Bank; Wachovia Bank & Trust Co. N.A.; Carolina Community Bank; Mountain Bank.

JAMES WEAVER KIRKPATRICK, III, P.A.

95 DEPOT STREET
P.O. DRAWER 1260
WAYNESVILLE, NORTH CAROLINA 28786
Telephone: 828-452-0801
Fax: 828-456-4917
Email: kirk@jwklaw.net
URL: http://www.kirkpatricklawfirm.com

Residential Real Estate, Criminal Law, DWI, Drug Offenses, Personal Injury, Auto Accidents, Wrongful Death, Traffic Violations.

JAMES WEAVER KIRKPATRICK, III, born Chapel Hill, North Carolina, December 7, 1968; admitted to bar, 1995, North Carolina and U.S. Court of Appeals, Fourth Circuit. *Education:* University of North Carolina; Catawba College (B.A., 1992); Regent University (J.D., 1994). Instructor, Real Estate, Haywood Community College, 1996-1997. Prosecutor, Eastern Bank of Cherokee Indians, 1998-2001. *Member:* Haywood County Bar Association (President, 1998, 1999; Vice President, 1997); North Carolina State Bar; North Carolina Academy of Trial Lawyers. ***PRACTICE AREAS:*** Criminal Law; Driving While Intoxicated; Drug Crimes; Personal Injury; Automobile Accidents; Wrongful Death; Traffic Violations; Residential Real Estate; Medical Malpractice.

GENERAL COUNSEL FOR: Waynesville Housing Authority; Mountain View Housing; Maggie Valley Sanitary District.
APPROVED ATTORNEY FOR: Lawyer's Title Insurance Corp.; Chicago Title Insurance Co.; Commonwealth Land Title Insurance Co.; Investors Title Insurance Co.; Stewart Title; Clyde Savings Bank; B. B. & T.; Ashville Federal Savings and Loan Assn.; PHH U.S. Mortgage Corporation; First Citizens Bank; Wachovia; Mountain Bank; RBC Centra; United Community Bank; Central Carolina Bank; State Employees Credit Union; Champion Credit Union; Blue Ridge Savings Bank; ABN Amro; Wells Fargo; Merril Lynch.

THE MOORE LAW FIRM

WAYNESVILLE, NORTH CAROLINA

(See Asheville)

Personal Injury, Medical Malpractice, Family Law, Child Custody, Child Support, Adoptions, Automobile Accidents, Divorce, Equitable Distribution, Workers' Compensation, Labor and Employment, Nursing Home Litigation..

LAW OFFICES OF E.K. MORLEY, PLLC

WAYNESVILLE, NORTH CAROLINA

(See Hendersonville)

Contested Wills, Will Contests, Estate Litigation, Decedents Estates, Inheritance, Successions, Trusts and Estates, Surrogates Court Practice, Contested Trusts and Estates, Estate Administration, Estate Settlements, Fiduciary Law, Fiduciary Liability, Fiduciary Litigation, Trust Law, Trust Litigation, Ancillary Probate, Probate Litigation.

JEFFREY W. NORRIS & ASSOCIATES, PLLC

NORRIS PROFESSIONAL BUILDING
177 NORTH MAIN STREET
WAYNESVILLE, NORTH CAROLINA 28786
Telephone: 828-452-2221
Toll Free: 1-800-410-0380
Fax: 828-452-3534
URL: http://www.norrisandassoc.com

Commercial Litigation, Real Estate, Business Transactions, Local Government Law, Estate Planning and Family Law, IRC Exchanges.

JEFFREY W. NORRIS, born Groves, Texas, March 7, 1964; admitted to bar, 1993, Georgia, Pennsylvania; 1994, U.S. District Court, Eastern District of Pennsylvania; 2000, North Carolina; 2001, U.S. District Court, Western District of North Carolina; U.S. Court of Appeals, Third and Fourth Circuits and U.S. Supreme Court. *Education:* Wake Forest University (B.A., 1986); Southeastern Baptist Theological Seminary (M.Div., 1989); Temple University School of Law (J.D., cum laude, 1992). Research Editor, Temple Law Review, 1991-1992. Law Clerk, Hon. Clarence C. Newcomer, U.S. District Court for the Eastern District of Pennsylvania. Author: "Reasonable Versus Intermediate Standard: Reviewing Prisoners' Constitutional Claims," 64 Temple L. Rev. 1109 (1991). Legal Writing Instructor, Temple University School of Law, 1997. Chairman 2003, Vice Chairman 2002, Haywood County Republican Party. *Member:* North Carolina, Pennsylvania and American Bar Associations; State Bar of Georgia. ***PRACTICE AREAS:*** Commercial Litigation; Commercial Real Estate; Residential Real Estate; Business Transactions; Wills; Estate Planning. ***Email:*** jnorris@norrisandassoc.com

OF COUNSEL

LARRY T. REIDA, born September 18, 1935; admitted to bar, 1960, Iowa and Nebraska; 1977, Maryland; 1979, District of Columbia; 1996, North Carolina. *Education:* State University of Iowa (B.S.C., 1958); Iowa College of Law (J.D., 1960). Recipient, Distinguished Service Award, U.S. Department of Justice, 1972. Associate Chief Counsel, House Select Committee on Crime, U.S. House of Representative, 1969-1970. Associate General Counsel, Interstate Commerce Commission, 1971-1974; Deputy, 1975-1976. Chief Minority Counsel, House Public Works and Transportation Committee, U.S. House of Representative, 1977-1982. Special Assistant to Special Attorney General for O.D.A.L.E., 1972. ***PRACTICE AREAS:*** Civil Litigation; Real Estate Litigation; Mediation; Tax Deferred Exchanges.

CURTIS ALAN SLUDER

WAYNESVILLE, NORTH CAROLINA

(See Asheville)

Criminal Law, Traffic Violations, Driving While Intoxicated, Expunction.

WENZEL & WENZEL, PLLC

160 NORTH MAIN STREET, SUITE 12
WAYNESVILLE, NORTH CAROLINA 28786
Telephone: 828-452-9099
Fax: 828-452-9059
URL: http://www.wenzellawfirm.com

Wills and Probate, Trusts and Estates, Business, Bankruptcy, Real Estate, Buying or Selling a Home, Residential Real Estate, Real Estate Construction, Eminent Domain, Landlord Tenant Law, Civil Litigation, Workers Compensation, General Practice.

FIRM PROFILE: The firm of Wenzel & Wenzel is committed to serving our community and providing our clients with superior service. Appointments are also available in Sylva.

DEREK M. WENZEL, born Asheville, North Carolina, December 12, 1976; admitted to bar, 2002, North Carolina. *Education:* Davidson College (B.A., with honors, 1999); Washington College of Law, American University (J.D., 2002). ***LANGUAGES:*** Spanish. ***PRACTICE AREAS:*** Real Estate; Homeowners Association Law; Civil Litigation; Construction Law; Real Estate Litigation; Business Law; Workers Compensation. ***Email:*** derek@wenzellawfirm.com

SARAH P. WENZEL, born Waterbury, Connecticut, February 23, 1978; admitted to bar, 2003, North Carolina. *Education:* Georgetown University McDonough School of Business (B.S.B.A., cum laude, 2000); American University Washington College of Law (J.D., cum laude, 2003). Note and Comment Editor, American University International Law Review, 2002-2003. ***LANGUAGES:*** French. ***PRACTICE AREAS:*** Wills; Trusts and Estates; Bankruptcy; Probate; Business Law; Contracts. ***Email:*** sarah@wenzellawfirm.com

---

LAW OFFICE OF DAVID WIJEWICKRAMA

160 NORTH MAIN STREET, SUITE 11
WAYNESVILLE, NORTH CAROLINA 28786
Telephone: 828-454-1999
Fax: 828-454-1990
Email: davidwije17@yahoo.com
URL: http://www.dwlawpractice.com

Personal Injury, Family Law, Civil Litigation, Bankruptcy, Real Estate.

DAVID WIJEWICKRAMA, born Kingston, Jamaica, March 17, 1969; admitted to bar, 2003, North Carolina, U.S. District Court, Western District of North Carolina and Cherokee Tribal Court. *Education:* University of South Carolina (B.S., 1991); Washburn University (J.D., 2000). ***PRACTICE AREAS:*** Personal Injury; Family Law; Civil Litigation; Bankruptcy; Real Estate.

ROBINSON LAW OFFICE

WEDDINGTON, NORTH CAROLINA

(See Charlotte)

Civil Practice, Appellate Practice, Commercial Litigation, Complex Litigation, Business Litigation, Products Liability, Estate Litigation, Trust Litigation, Personal Injury, Construction Litigation, Professional Liability, Banking Litigation, Insurance Litigation, Federal Indian Law.

R. L. ADAMS, PLLC

WENDELL, NORTH CAROLINA

(See Wendell)

Equine Law, Civil Litigation, Real Estate Litigation, Business Torts, Products Liability.

GEORGE B. DANIEL, P.A.

WENTWORTH, NORTH CAROLINA

(See Yanceyville)

Criminal Law, Felonies, Misdemeanors, Traffic Violations, Driving While Intoxicated, Automobile Accidents, Truck Accidents, Personal Injury, Wrongful Death, Civil Litigation, Real Estate, Residential Real Estate, Commercial Real Estate, Real Estate Litigation, Workers Compensation, Estate Planning, Estate Administration, Drug Crimes.

WILLIAM H. DANIEL, P.A.

WENTWORTH, NORTH CAROLINA

(See Yanceyville)

Criminal Law, Felonies, Misdemeanors, Traffic Violations, Driving While Intoxicated, Drug Crimes, Personal Injury, Automobile Accidents, Truck Accidents, Motorcycle Accidents, Wrongful Death, Workers Compensation, Real Estate, Wills, Estate Administration.

FOLGER & TUCKER, P.A.

WENTWORTH, NORTH CAROLINA

(See Madison)

General Civil and Criminal Practice in State Courts. Personal Injury, Automobile Accidents, Wrongful Death, Workers Compensation, Real Estate, Family Law, Divorce, Child Custody, Traffic Violations, Corporations and Probate Law.

MADDREY ETRINGER & SMITH, L.L.P.

WENTWORTH, NORTH CAROLINA

(See Eden)

General Trial Practice in all State and Federal Courts. Personal Injury, Automobile Accidents, Wrongful Death, Real Estate, Banking, Business and Corporate Law, Probate Law, Family Law, Divorce, Child Custody, Bankruptcy, Collections, Criminal, DWI, Traffic, Zoning, Planning and Land Use Law, Construction Law, Foreclosures.

WALKER & MELVIN, LLP

WENTWORTH, NORTH CAROLINA

(See Eden)

Civil Practice, Criminal Law, Driving While Intoxicated, Traffic Violations, Wrongful Death, Probate, Real Estate, Personal Injury, Automobile Accidents, Corporate Law, Family Law, Divorce, Child Custody, Adoptions.

VANNOY & REEVES, PLLC

A Professional Limited Liability Company

Established in 1975

202 EAST MAIN STREET

P.O. DRAWER 67

WEST JEFFERSON, NORTH CAROLINA 28694

Telephone: 336-246-7172

Fax: 336-246-5966

Email: jim@vannoyandreeves.com

Email: garland@vannoyandreeves.com

Email: alex@vannoyandreeves.com

Email: jak@vannoyandreeves.com

URL: http://www.lawyers.com/vannoyandreeves

URL: http://www.vannoyandreeves.com

Sparta, North Carolina Office: 112 South Main Street, P.O.Box 249, 28675. Telephone: 336-372-8740. Fax: 336-372-6114.

General Civil and Criminal Trial Practice in State and Federal Courts, Real Property, Estate Planning, Probate, Business and Corporate Law, Traffic, Family Law, Plaintiff's Personal Injury Matters and Collections.

FIRM PROFILE: VANNOY & REEVES was organized in 1975 by Wade E. Vannoy, Jr. and Jimmy D. Reeves and has continued with the same name since Mr. Vannoy's death in 1991. Garland B. Baker, with extensive experience in criminal practice, joined the firm in 1998. M. Alexandra Reeves joined the firm in 2001, and John B. Reeves began his practice with the firm in 2004. The attorneys' concentration is upon civil and criminal trial practice in state and federal courts, and in corporate, commercial and municipal law. They and their staff have a complete real estate practice handling closings, real estate-related litigation, and representing creditors and lending institutions in bankruptcy matters.

MEMBERS OF FIRM

WADE E. VANNOY, JR. (1927-1991)

JIMMY D. REEVES, born Jefferson, North Carolina, July 23, 1948; admitted to bar, 1973, North Carolina; 1978, U.S. District Court, Middle District of North Carolina and U.S. Supreme Court; 1982, U.S. District Court, Western District of North Carolina. *Education:* Wake Forest University (B.A., 1970; J.D., 1973). Attorney, Town of West Jefferson, 1978—. General Counsel, AF Bank. *Member:* Ashe County, Twenty-Third Judicial District (President, 1975-1976; 1985-1986) and North Carolina Bar Associations; North Carolina State Bar; North Carolina Academy of Trial Lawyers; The Association of Trial Lawyers of America; Outstanding Lawyers of America. ***PRACTICE AREAS:*** Civil Litigation; Real Property; Family Law; Divorce; Adoption Law; Child Support; Child Custody; Equitable Distribution; Premarital Agreements; Wills; Probate; Business; Corporate. ***Email:*** jim@vannoyandreeves.com

GARLAND B. BAKER, born Marion, Virginia, February 13, 1957; admitted to bar, 1986, North Carolina; 2002, U.S. Supreme Court. *Education:* University of Mississippi (B.A., magna cum laude, 1978; M.B.A., 1981); University of North Carolina (J.D., 1986). Assistant District Attorney: First Judicial District, 1986-1991; Twenty-Third Judicial District, 1994-1998. *Member:* Ashe County and Twenty-Third Judicial Bar Associations. ***PRACTICE AREAS:*** Criminal Defense; Driving While Intoxicated; Traffic Violations; Drug Crimes; Civil Litigation; Family Law; Divorce. ***Email:*** garland@vannoyandreeves.com

M. ALEXANDRA REEVES, born Boone, North Carolina, March 21, 1976; admitted to bar, 2001, North Carolina; 2002, Virginia and U.S. Court of Appeals, Fourth Circuit. *Education:* University of North Carolina at Chapel Hill (B.A., 1998); Wake Forest University (J.D., 2001). *Member:* North Carolina State Bar; Virginia State Bar; Twenty-Third Judicial District Bar Association (Secretary/Treasurer, 2002; Vice President, 2003; President, 2004); North Carolina Bar Association; North Carolina Academy of Trial Lawyers; North

(This Listing Continued)

Carolina Association of Women Attorneys; The Association of Trial Lawyers of America. ***PRACTICE AREAS:*** Real Property; Trusts and Estates; Business Law; Family Law; Civil Litigation. ***Email:*** alex@vannoyandreeves.com

ASSOCIATE

JOHN "JAK" B. REEVES, born Boone, North Carolina, January 13, 1979; admitted to bar, 2004, North Carolina. *Education:* University of North Carolina at Chapel Hill (B.A., 2001); Campbell University (J.D., 2004). *Member:* North Carolina State Bar; Twenty-Third Judicial District Bar Association (Secretary/Treasurer, 2005); North Carolina and American Bar Associations; North Carolina Academy of Trial Lawyers; The Association of Trial Lawyers of America. ***PRACTICE AREAS:*** Criminal Law (20%); Family Law (20%); Civil Litigation (20%); Personal Injury (20%); General Practice (20%). ***Email:*** jak@vannoyandreeves.com

APPROVED ATTORNEYS FOR: Investors Title Insurance Co.; Lawyers Title Insurance Corp.; First Title Insurance Co.; Chicago Title Insurance Co.; American Title Insurance Co.; Commonwealth Land Title Co.; United Title Insurance Co.; United States Department of Agriculture-Rural Development; Mountain Farm Credit/PCA; Old Republic National Title Insurance Company; Stewart Title Guaranty Company.
REPRESENTATIVE CLIENTS: AF Bank; Ashe County Motors, Inc.; Ashe Services for the Aging, Inc.; Town of West Jefferson; Parker-Tie Company, Inc.; Mack Brown, Inc.; AF Insurance Services; AF Brokerage, Inc.; Yadkin Valley Pontiac Buick, GMC, Inc.
REFERENCES: First Citizens Bank & Trust Co.; Yadkin Valley Bank & Trust Co.; Centura Bank; BB&T; The Northwestern Bank; High Country Bank; State Employees Credit Union.

MORRIS LAW OFFICE

7451 SUITE C, NC HWY 22

WHISPERING PINES, NORTH CAROLINA 28327

Telephone: 910-690-4595

Fax: 910-949-5587

Email: morrislawoffice@charter.net

URL: http://www.gmorrislaw.com

Criminal Law, Felonies and Misdemeanors, Traffic Violations and Tickets, Trucks, Motorcycles, Driving While Intoxicated, DUI, Animal Law, Equine, Horse Rights and Trusts, Veterans Benefits and Appeals.

GARY MORRIS, born Plainwell, Michigan, September 18, 1946; admitted to bar, 2000, California; 2004, North Carolina. *Education:* Adrian College (B.A., 1974); Central Michigan University (M.A. in Business Management, 1978); Thomas Jefferson School of Law (J.D., 1999). *Member:* Moore County Bar Association; North Carolina State Bar. ***PRACTICE AREAS:*** Criminal Law; Felonies; Misdemeanors; Traffic Violations; Traffic Tickets; Trucks; Motorcycles; Driving While Intoxicated; DUI; Child Support; Animal Law; Animal Cruelty; Equine Law; Horse Rights; Trusts; Veterans Benefits; Veterans Appeals; Soldiers and Sailors Civil Relief Act; Servicepersons Civil Relief Act.

HEATHER D. MILLER NICHOLS

WHITE LAKE, NORTH CAROLINA

(See Fayetteville)

Family Law, Civil Litigation, Real Estate Litigation, Wills, Estates.

HILL & HIGH, L.L.P.

Established in 1973

COURTHOUSE SQUARE

WHITEVILLE, NORTH CAROLINA 28472

Telephone: 910-642-8136

Fax: 910-640-2101

Email: hillandhigh@whitevillenc.net

URL: http://www.lawyers.com/hillandhigh

Personal Injury, Medical Malpractice, Automobile Accidents, Criminal Law, Driving While Intoxicated, Traffic Violations, Family Law, Divorce, Real Estate, Estate Planning, Wills, Trusts, Social Security and Disability Law.

MEMBERS OF THE FIRM

JAMES E. HILL, JR., born Whiteville, North Carolina, September 15, 1946; admitted to bar, 1973, North Carolina. *Education:* Wake Forest University (B.A., 1968); University of South Carolina (J.D., 1973). Columbus County Attorney, 1976—. *Member:* Columbus County, North Carolina, 13th Judicial District (Secretary-Treasurer, 1976-1978) and American Bar Associations; North Carolina State Bar; North Carolina Academy of Trial Lawyers. ***PRACTICE AREAS:*** Civil Practice; Real Estate; Criminal Law; Traffic Violations; Family Law; Divorce; Child Custody; Child Support; Spousal Support; Alimony; Probate; Wills; Trusts and Estates; Estate Planning. ***Email:*** hillandhigh@whitevillenc.net

JOHN ALAN HIGH, born Lumberton, North Carolina, November 4, 1966; admitted to bar, 1992, North Carolina and U.S. District Court, Eastern District of North Carolina. *Education:* University of North Carolina at Chapel Hill (B.S., 1989); Campbell University (J.D., 1992). *Member:* Columbus County and North Carolina Bar Associations; North Carolina State Bar; North Carolina Academy of Trial Lawyers. ***PRACTICE AREAS:*** Personal Injury; Criminal Law; Real Estate; Government; Medical Malpractice; Automobile Accidents and Injuries; Truck Accidents; Motorcycle Accidents; Wrongful Death; Dog Bites; Driving While Intoxicated; Traffic Violations; Misdemeanors; Felonies; Assault and Battery; Sexual Assault; Residential Real Estate; Real Estate Closings; Social Security; Disabilities Law; Insurance; Workers Compensation. ***Email:*** hillandhigh@whitevillenc.net

REPRESENTATIVE CLIENTS: Columbus Country; Waccamaw Bank; Hillcrest Corporation; Hills Food Stores, Inc.; Wells-Powell Enterprises; Boys and Girls Home of North Carolina, Inc.

GREG JONES & ASSOCIATES, P.A.

WHITEVILLE, NORTH CAROLINA

(See Wilmington)

Personal Injury, Automobile Accidents, Brain Injury, Motorcycle Accidents, Wrongful Death, Medical Malpractice, Spinal Cord Injuries, Drug and Medical Device Litigation, Pharmacists Liability, Head Injuries, Products Liability, Medical and Nursing Home Negligence, Workers Compensation, Toxic Torts, Nursing Home Abuse, Stock Fraud.

LEE & LEE

812 PINCKNEY STREET
WHITEVILLE, NORTH CAROLINA 28472
Telephone: 910-642-3708
Fax: 910-642-9058
Email: llg@weblnk.net

Business and Corporations, Business Formation, Corporation Formation, Criminal, Driving While Intoxicated, Traffic Violations, White Collar Crime, Personal Injury, Automobile Accidents, Employment Law, Workers Compensation, Social Security, Wills, Trusts and Estates, Real Estate, Family Law.

MEMBER OF FIRM

JUNIUS BRIGHT LEE, III, born Whiteville, North Carolina, December 12, 1953; admitted to bar, 1979, North Carolina; 1987, U.S. District Court, Eastern District of North Carolina; 1991, U.S. Court of Appeals, 4th Circuit. *Education:* University of North Carolina at Chapel Hill (B.S., 1976; J.D., 1979). *Member:* North Carolina State Bar. ***PRACTICE AREAS:*** Business Law; Corporate Law; Business Formation; Corporate Formation; Criminal Law; Driving While Intoxicated; Traffic Violations; White Collar Crime; Personal Injury; Automobile Accidents and Injuries; Employment Law; Workers Compensation; Social Security; Wills; Trusts and Estates; Real Estate; Family Law. ***Email:*** llg@weblnk.net

---

CUNNINGHAM & GRAY, P.A.

Established in 1974
105 WEST MAIN STREET
P.O. DRAWER 520
WILKESBORO, NORTH CAROLINA 28697-0520
Telephone: 336-838-7500
Fax: 336-838-7700

Trials-Criminal, Traffic Court, DWI Defense, Family Law, Divorce, Personal Injury, Probate and Estate Planning, Corporate.

GEORGE G. CUNNINGHAM, born Franklin, North Carolina, July 15, 1951; admitted to bar, 1975, North Carolina; 1980, U.S. Supreme Court; U.S. Court of Appeals, Fourth Circuit and U.S. District Court, Eastern, Middle and Western Districts of North Carolina. *Education:* Wake Forest University (B.A., 1973; J.D., 1975). Phi Delta Phi. Member, Fourth Circuit Judicial Conference. Chairman, 1993-1995 and Vice-Chairman, 1991-1993, North Carolina Property Tax Commission. Member, North Carolina Dispute Resolution Commission, 1999-2004. Vice-Chairman, North Carolina Indian Gaming Certification Commission, 1994—. Member, North Carolina Judicial Selection Study Commission, 1987-1989. Commissioner, Northwestern Regional Housing Authority, 1984-1990. Attorney, Wilkes County, 1982-1984. Chairman, Wilkes County Board of Elections, 1977-1982. Certified Civil Mediator. Certified Family Financial Mediator. *Member:* Wilkes County (President, 1982) and North Carolina Bar Associations; Twenty-Third Judicial District and North Carolina State Bars; North Carolina Academy of Trial Lawyers. (Board Certified Specialist in Family Law, North Carolina State Board of Legal Specialization). ***PRACTICE AREAS:*** Civil Litigation; Family Law; Divorce; Equitable Distribution; Probate Law; Estate Law; Personal Injury.

WILLIAM C. GRAY, JR., born Wilkes County, North Carolina, March 3, 1951; admitted to bar, 1976, North Carolina; 1977, U.S. District Court, Middle and Western Districts of North Carolina and U.S. Court of Appeals, Fourth Circuit; 1980, U.S. Supreme Court; 1981, U.S. Court of Appeals, Fifth and Eleventh Circuits. *Education:* University of North Carolina (A.B., 1973); Wake Forest University (J.D., 1976). Phi Delta Phi. Attorney, Town of Wilkesboro, 1988—. *Member:* Wilkes County (President, 1985), Twenty-Third Judicial District (President, 1987; Chairman, Bar Candidate Committee, 1991—) and North Carolina Bar Associations; North Carolina State Bar; North Carolina Academy of Trial Lawyers. ***PRACTICE AREAS:*** Criminal Defense; Criminal Appeals; DWI Defense; Traffic Violations.

REPRESENTATIVE CLIENT: Town of Wilkesboro.
REFERENCES: First Citizens Bank and Trust; First Union National Bank; Yadkin Valley Bank & Trust; Wachovia Bank & Trust; BB&T Piedmont Fed. S & L; Mountain Farm Credit, ACA; Wilkes National Bank.

DAVIS ELDER & DISABILITY LAW

WILKESBORO, NORTH CAROLINA

(See Lewisville)

Elder Law.

MAX F. FERREE

Established in 1949
COURT SQUARE
P.O. DRAWER 979
WILKESBORO, NORTH CAROLINA 28697
Telephone: 336-667-9500; 667-5557
Fax: 336-667-8050
Email: maxferreelaw@aol.com

General Civil and Criminal Trial Practice. Probate, Real Estate, Personal Injury Law, Products Liability, Construction Law, Insurance Law, Automobile Accidents, Wrongful Death.

MAX F. FERREE, born Burke County, North Carolina, April 27, 1924; admitted to bar, 1949, North Carolina; 1967, U.S. Supreme Court. *Education:* Duke University (A.B., 1945; LL.B., 1948). District Court Judge, 1981-1986. *Member:* North Carolina State Bar (Councillor, 1974-1977); North Carolina Academy of Trial Lawyers (Member, Board of Governors, 1968-1977); The Association of Trial Lawyers of America (State Committeeman, 1975-1977).

REFERENCES: Bank of America; Wachovia Bank; Integrity Financial; First Citizens Bank & Trust.

VANNOY, COLVARD, TRIPLETT & VANNOY, P.L.L.C.

WILKESBORO, NORTH CAROLINA

(See North Wilkesboro)

Civil and Criminal Litigation, Corporations, Personal Injury, Automobile Accidents, Traffic, Driving While Intoxicated, DWI, Real Estate, Wills, Trusts and Estates, Workers' Compensation, Social Security Disability.

ALLEN, MACDONALD & DAVIS, PLLC

1508 MILITARY CUTOFF ROAD
SUITE 102
WILMINGTON, NORTH CAROLINA 28403
Telephone: 910-256-6558
Fax: 910-256-6538
Email: allenmac@bellsouth.net
URL: http://www.macdonald-law.com

Real Estate, Residential Real Estate, Real Estate Closings, Commercial Real Estate, Estate Planning, Wills and Trusts, Probate, Collections, Creditors Rights, Commercial Law..

MEMBERS OF FIRM

L. GLEASON ALLEN (Retired)

JAMES A. MACDONALD, born Winston-Salem, North Carolina, May 6, 1949; admitted to bar, 1974, North Carolina and U.S. District Court, Eastern District of North Carolina. *Education:* Duke University (B.A., 1971); University of North Carolina (J.D., 1973). *Member:* New Hanover County Bar Association (Member, President, 2000; Board of Directors, 1995 -1997); North Carolina State Bar. ***PRACTICE AREAS:*** Commercial Real Estate; Residential Real Estate; Corporate; Estate Planning; Wills; Trusts and Estates; Probate; Foreclosures. ***Email:*** james.macdonald@macdonald-law.com

DEAN R. DAVIS, born Wabash, Indiana, April 1, 1944; admitted to bar, 1975, Georgia; 1980, North Carolina, U.S. District Court, Eastern District of North Carolina, U.S. Court of Appeals, Fourth Circuit and U.S. Supreme Court. *Education:* Wabash College (A.B., 1966); Georgia State University; Emory University (J.D., 1975). *Member:* New Hanover County, North Carolina and American Bar Associations; North Carolina State Bar; State Bar of Georgia. ***PRACTICE AREAS:*** Bankruptcy; Real Estate; Estate Planning; Trial Practice; Probate; Corporate Law; Elder Law; Tax Law; Family Law. ***Email:*** dean.davis@macdonald-law.com

---

ANDERSON, DANIEL & ASSOCIATES

WILMINGTON, NORTH CAROLINA

(See Wrightsville Beach)

Medical Malpractice, Birth Injury, Cerebral Palsy, Personal Injury, Nursing Home Neglect, Products Liability, Professional Misconduct, Legal Malpractice, Complex Civil Litigation.

AUSTIN & COOKE, PLLC

Established in 2004
5725 OLEANDER DRIVE
SUITE C-3
WILMINGTON, NORTH CAROLINA 28403
Telephone: 910-332-4104
Fax: 910-332-4124
URL: http://www.austinprice.com
Email: info@austincooke.com
URL: http://www.austincooke.com

Estate Planning, Wills, Trusts and Estates, Real Estates, Residential Real Estate, Business Law, Limited Liability Company Law, Family Law, Divorce, Custody, Adoption, Juvenile, Criminal, Tickets, DWI, Contracts.

JEFFERY W. AUSTIN, born Concord, North Carolina, May 16, 1965; admitted to bar, 2004, North Carolina. *Education:* University of North Carolina at Wilmington (B.A.,

(This Listing Continued)

AUSTIN & COOKE, PLLC, Wilmington—Continued

1995); Campbell University School of Law (J.D., 2003). *Member:* New Hanover County, North Carolina and American Bar Associations; North Carolina State Bar. ***LANGUAGES:*** English and Spanish. ***PRACTICE AREAS:*** Estate Planning; Wills; Trusts and Estates; Real Estate; Commercial Real Estate; Residential Real Estate; Business Law; Limited Liability Company Law; Employee Benefits. ***Email:*** jeff@austincooke.com

JENNIFER G. COOKE, born Smithfield, North Carolina, November 22, 1975; admitted to bar, 2003, North Carolina. *Education:* University of North Carolina at Chapel Hill (B.A., 1998); Campbell University School of Law (J.D., 2003). *Member:* North Carolina Bar Association; North Carolina State Bar. ***LANGUAGES:*** English. ***PRACTICE AREAS:*** Family Law; Child Custody; Child Support; Premarital Agreements; Adoption Law; Juvenile Law. ***Email:*** jgcooke@austincooke.com

LEGAL SUPPORT PERSONNEL

JENNIFER MERCER, (Paralegal)

JULIANNE M. AUSTIN, (Business Manager)

Languages: English and Spanish.

BLOCK, CROUCH & KEETER, L.L.P.

Established in 1996
310 NORTH FRONT STREET
P.O. BOX 4
WILMINGTON, NORTH CAROLINA 28402
Telephone: 910-763-2727
Fax: 910-762-6429
URL: http://www.bcklawfirm.com

General Practice.

FIRM PROFILE: Block, Crouch & Keeter, LLP was founded in 1996 by the merger of Block & Huffman with Crouch & Keeter. Each member of the firm brings a diverse base of knowledge and expertise to this firm, gained from experience at other North Carolina law firms.

Together with our dedicated staff, we are committed to delivering the highest quality legal services and work product in a timely, ethical, and professional manner. Our attorneys are active in the community, including service in leadership positions and on boards of directors, in many of Wilmington's civic organizations such as the Wilmington Family YMCA, Yahweh Center, Wilmington Rotary Club, Wilmington Jaycees, and The Child Development Center.

Block, Crouch & Keeter is a full service law firm emphasizing construction law, business organizations, federal and state civil litigation, real estate transactions, condemnation, criminal law, personal injury and products liability, estate planning and estate administration, and domestic relations.

FRANKLIN L. BLOCK (Retired)

AULEY M. CROUCH, III, born Wilmington, North Carolina, November 4, 1944; admitted to bar, 1976, North Carolina. *Education:* The Citadel (B.S., 1966); John Marshall Law School (J.D., with distinction, 1976). Associate Editor, The John Marshall Journal, 1975-1976. President, Fifth District Bar, 1995. Certified Mediator and Arbitrator. *Member:* North Carolina Bar Association; North Carolina State Bar; North Carolina Academy of Trial Lawyers; The Arbitration Group. ***PRACTICE AREAS:*** Federal Civil Litigation; Construction Litigation; Condemnation; Eminent Domain.

JEFFREY P. KEETER, born Elizabeth City, North Carolina, July 30, 1959; admitted to bar, 1985, North Carolina. *Education:* Campbell University (B.S., cum laude, 1981; J.D., 1984). Omicron Delta Kappa. Epsilon Pi Eta. Phi Alpha Delta. *Member:* New Hanover County Bar; Fifth Judicial District Bar; North Carolina Bar Association (Member, Sections on: Real Property; Business; Law Practice Management; Member, Law Practice Management Section Council, 2002-2005; Treasurer, 2004); North Carolina State Bar. ***PRACTICE AREAS:*** Corporate Law; Commercial Real Estate; Residential Real Estate; Buying and Selling of Businesses and Homes; Commercial Law; Wills; Trust Law; Probate; Zoning and Land Use Law. ***Email:*** jpkeeter@bcklawfirm.com

---

CHRISTOPHER K. BEHM, born Greensboro, North Carolina, March 8, 1973; admitted to bar, 1998, North Carolina. *Education:* Guilford College (A.B., with high honors, 1995); Wake Forest University School of Law (J.D., 1998). Phi Delta Phi. Research Editor, Wake Forest Law Review, 1997-1998. Member, Wake Forest Law Review, 1996-1997. Recipient: Corpus Juris Secundum Award in Civil Procedure I, CALI Award in National Security Law. *Member:* North Carolina Bar Association; North Carolina State Bar; North Carolina Academy of Trial Lawyers. ***PRACTICE AREAS:*** Civil Litigation; Commercial Litigation; Construction Litigation; Estate Litigation. ***Email:*** cbehm@bcklawfirm.com

LINDA B. SAYED, born Panama Canal Zone, November 18, 1957; admitted to bar, 1998, North Carolina. *Education:* University of North Carolina at Wilmington (B.A., Chemistry, cum laude, 1978; M.Ed., 1985); Campbell University, Norman Adrian Wiggins School of Law (J.D., cum laude, 1998). Omicron Delta Kappa; Order of the Barristers. Member, Association of Trial Lawyers of America Trial Team, 1998. Editor-At-Large, Campbell Law Review, 1996-1998. *Member:* North Carolina and American Bar Associations; North Carolina State Bar; North Carolina Academy of Trial Lawyers. ***PRACTICE AREAS:*** Civil Litigation; Family Law; Divorce; Child Custody; Child Support; Domestic Violence; Visitation Rights; Equitable Distribution; Alimony; Post Divorce Modification; Traffic Violations; Juvenile Law; Wills; Guardianship; Personal Injury; Automobile Accidents. ***Email:*** lsayed@bcklawfirm.com

(This Listing Continued)

REPRESENTATIVE CLIENTS: American Distillation, Inc.; Corning, Inc.; Waste Management of Wilmington; Investors Title Insurance Co.; Martin Self Storage, Inc.; WHQR-FM; Parham Properties, Inc.; Port Cape Fear Associates; Bald Head Island Club; High Rise Service Co., Inc.; Intracoastal Realty, Inc.; Logan Construction Co.; Landfall Council of Associations; HRS Terminals, Inc.
APPROVED ATTORNEYS: Lawyers Title Insurance Corp.; Commonwealth Land Title Insurance Co.; Chicago Title Insurance Co.; Security Union Title Co.; First Title Insurance Co.; Old Republic Title Insurance Co.
REFERENCES: Wachovia Bank & Trust; Branch Bank & Trust Co.

WILLIAM J. BONEY, JR.

Established in 1983
406 MARKET STREET
P.O. BOX 1301
WILMINGTON, NORTH CAROLINA 28402
Telephone: 910-762-4403
Fax: 910-762-0499
Email: bboney@bizec.rr.com

Civil and Criminal Trials, Criminal Law, DWI, Traffic Offenses, Personal Injury, Automobile Accidents, Wrongful Death, Domestic Law, Family Law, Divorce, Separation Agreements, Child Custody, Child Support, Alimony, Equitable Distribution.

WILLIAM J. BONEY, JR., born Wilmington, North Carolina, September 4, 1950; admitted to bar, 1976, North Carolina; 1983, U.S. District Court, Eastern District of North Carolina. *Education:* North Carolina State University (B.A., 1972); Wake Forest University (J.D., 1976). Assistant District Attorney, 5th Judicial District, North Carolina, 1976-1982. Chairman, Fifth Judicial Indigent Committee, 1988-1990. Member, Wilmington Community Development Commission, 1978-1979. Former Chairman, 5th District Bar Fee Grievance Committee. President, 5th Judicial District Bar, 1998. Member, Wilmington Civil Service Commission, 1995-2004. *Member:* North Carolina Bar Association (Member, Criminal Justice Council 1989-1991); North Carolina State Bar; North Carolina Academy of Trial Lawyers. ***PRACTICE AREAS:*** Criminal Law; Personal Injury Law; Domestic Law.

REFERENCE: Bank of America.

BOSEMAN & ASSOCIATES, LLP

115 NORTH 6TH STREET
WILMINGTON, NORTH CAROLINA 28401
Telephone: 910-251-6975
Fax: 910-251-6976
URL: http://www.bosemanandassociateslaw.com

Criminal Law, Misdemeanors, Traffic Violations, Driving While Intoxicated, Felonies, Family Law, Real Estate, Buying and Selling a Home.

MEMBER OF FIRM

JULIA BOSEMAN, born Wilmington, North Carolina, August 20, 1966; admitted to bar, 1993, North Carolina and U.S. District Court, Eastern and Middle Districts of North Carolina; 1998, U.S. Supreme Court. *Education:* University of North Carolina at Wilmington (B.S., Finance, 1989); North Carolina Central University School of Law (J.D., 1992). *Member:* North Carolina (Member, Real Property Section) and American (Member, Real Property Section) Bar Associations. ***PRACTICE AREAS:*** Real Estate. ***Email:*** julia@boseman-boyette.com

ASSOCIATE

BREANNA W. RUTLEDGE, born Pasadena, California, October 28, 1975; admitted to bar, 2001, Oregon; 2002, North Carolina. *Education:* Purdue University (B.A., with highest distinction, 1998); Washington University, St. Louis (J.D., 2001). Phi Beta Kappa. *Member:* Durham County and North Carolina Bar Associations. ***PRACTICE AREAS:*** Family Law; Divorce; Child Custody; Child Support; Equitable Distribution.

THE BOYETTE LAW FIRM

401 CHESTNUT STREET, SUITE H
WILMINGTON, NORTH CAROLINA 28401
Telephone: 910-251-9213
Fax: 910-251-8880
URL: http://www.boyettelawfirm.com

Family Law, Divorce, Custody, Visitation, Child Support, Adoption, Criminal Law, Traffic, DUI, White Collar Crimes.

GEANNINE M. BOYETTE, born Wilson, North Carolina, October 25, 1968; admitted to bar, 1998, North Carolina. *Education:* University of North Carolina at Wilmington (B.A., Criminal Justice and Sociology, 1991); North Carolina Central University School of Law (J.D., magna cum laude, 1998). *Member:* New Hanover County and North Carolina Bar Associations; North Carolina Academy of Trial Attorneys; Sentencing Services (Board Member, 2002—). ***PRACTICE AREAS:*** Family Law; Divorce; Child Custody; Visitation Rights; Child Support; Adoption Law; Criminal Law; Traffic Violations; Driving While Intoxicated; White Collar Crime. ***Email:*** gboyette@boyettelaw.com

ASSOCIATE

TRACY W. WILKINSON, born Honolulu, Hawaii, August 28, 1969; admitted to bar, 2001, North Carolina, U.S. Court of Appeals, Fourth Circuit and U.S. District Court, Eastern District of North Carolina; 2002, U.S. District Court, Middle and Western Districts of North Carolina. *Education:* University of North Carolina (B.A., 1993); Southern Illinois University School of Law (J.D., 2000). *Member:* New Hanover County and North Carolina Bar Associations; North Carolina Association of Women Attorneys; North Carolina Acad-

(This Listing Continued)

emy of Trial Lawyers. ***PRACTICE AREAS:*** Litigation; Appellate Practice. ***Email:*** twilkinson@boyettelaw.com

BRITT LAW FIRM

THE PROMENADE
720 NORTH THIRD STREET
SUITE 401
WILMINGTON, NORTH CAROLINA 28401
Telephone: 910-762-2697
Facsimile: 910-762-0231
Email: donbritt@brittlawfirm.com

General Civil, Asbestos Product Liability, Corporate, Real Estate, Estate Administration, Personal Injury, Wills & Trusts. North Carolina Certified Mediator.

DONALD E. BRITT, JR., born Winston-Salem, North Carolina, February 23, 1946; admitted to bar, 1971, North Carolina. *Education:* Wake Forest University (B.A., 1968; J.D., 1971). Phi Delta Phi. Law Clerk to Chief Judge Algernon L. Butler, U.S. District Court, Eastern District of North Carolina, 1971-1973. Life Member, Fourth Circuit Judicial Conference. North Carolina Certified Mediator. *Member:* New Hanover County and North Carolina Bar Associations; North Carolina State Bar; North Carolina Association of Defense Attorneys; Defense Research and Trial Lawyers Association.

APPROVED ATTORNEY FOR: Commonwealth Title Insurance Co.; The Title Company of North Carolina; Investors Title Insurance Co.
REFERENCE: Branch Banking & Trust Co.

BRUMBAUGH, MU & KING, P.A.

Established in 1978
2018 SOUTH 16TH STREET
WILMINGTON, NORTH CAROLINA 28401
Telephone: 910-763-2111
URL: http://www.bmklaw.net

Practice Limited to Injury Cases. Automobile, Wrongful Death, Medical Malpractice, Workers' Compensation, Products Liability and Social Security Claims.

(For complete biographical data on all personnel, see professional biographies, Jacksonville, North Carolina)

JOHN K. BURNS

208 PRINCESS STREET
WILMINGTON, NORTH CAROLINA 28401
Telephone: 910-343-8776
Fax: 910-343-8832
Email: johnkburnsatty@bellsouth.net
URL: http://www.johnkburns.com

Domestic Relations Law, Family Law, Divorce, Adoptions, Child Custody Agreements, Child Support, Personal Injury Law, Automobile Accidents, Truck Accidents, Wrongful Death, Slip and Fall, Workers Compensation Law, Employment Law, Wrongful Termination, Sexual Harassment, Criminal Law, DWI, Traffic Violations, Drug Crimes, Parole and Probation.

JOHN K. BURNS, born Whiteville, North Carolina, August 24, 1946; admitted to bar, 1984, North Carolina. *Education:* University of North Carolina at Chapel Hill (A.B., 1969); Wake Forest University (J.D., 1983). ***PRACTICE AREAS:*** Domestic Relations Law; Personal Injury Law; Workers Compensation Law.

CALDER & CALDER

611 PRINCESS STREET
WILMINGTON, NORTH CAROLINA 28401-4153
Telephone: 910-763-1683
Fax: 910-343-9444
URL: http://www.calderlawfirm.com
URL: http://www.calderlaw.com

General Civil Practice. Real Estate Law, Commercial Real Estate, Buying and Selling a Home, Title Examinations, Closings, Foreclosures, Zoning and Land Use, Estate Planning and Wills.

MEMBERS OF FIRM

ROBERT CALDER (Retired)

ROBERT CALDER, JR., born Wilmington, North Carolina, July 29, 1950; admitted to bar, 1984, North Carolina. *Education:* University of North Carolina at Wilmington (B.A., 1981); University of North Carolina at Chapel Hill (J.D., 1984). Phi Kappa Phi. *Member:* New Hanover County; North Carolina State Bar. (Also at Carolina Beach Office). ***Email:*** Robert@calderlaw.com

J. KEITH CALDER, born Wilmington, North Carolina, May 21, 1954; admitted to bar, 1988, North Carolina. *Education:* University of North Carolina at Wilmington (B.A., 1977); North Carolina Central University (J.D., cum laude, 1988). *Member:* New Hanover County Bar Association; North Carolina State Bar. ***Email:*** Keith@calderlaw.com

ASSOCIATE

MATTHEW PETER DOYLE, born San Francisco, California, May 9, 1969; admitted to bar, 2001, North Carolina. *Education:* Vanderbilt University (B.A., 1991); Wake Forest University (J.D., 1999). ***Email:*** matt@calderlaw.com

CARTER & HUFFINE, P.A.

408 MARKET STREET
P.O. BOX 2154
WILMINGTON, NORTH CAROLINA 28402-2154
Telephone: 910-763-3626; 910-251-1954
Fax: 910-343-8966
Fax: 910-251-8590
Email: joccl@bellsouth.net
Email: dhuffine@bizec.rr.com

Commercial and Residential Real Estate, Corporate, Business Law, Medical Business Practice, Business and Real Estate Litigation, Mediation, Bankruptcy and Creditors Rights.

JAMES OLIVER CARTER, born Washington, D.C., September 22, 1949; admitted to bar, 1974, North Carolina and U.S. District Court, Eastern District of North Carolina. *Education:* University of North Carolina at Wilmington and Wake Forest University (A.B., 1971); Wake Forest University (J.D., 1974). Member, Wake Forest Law Review, 1972-1974. Trustee in Bankruptcy, U.S. Bankruptcy Court, Eastern District of North Carolina, 1976-2000. *Member:* New Hanover County and North Carolina Bar Associations; The North Carolina State Bar. ***PRACTICE AREAS:*** Commercial Law; Bankruptcy; Corporate Law; Business Law; Debtor and Creditor; Trusts and Estates. ***Email:*** joccl@bellsouth.net

DAVID E. HUFFINE, born Goldsboro, North Carolina, December 16, 1951; admitted to bar, 1977, North Carolina. *Education:* Davidson College (B.A., cum laude, 1974); Phi Beta Kappa; University of North Carolina (J.D., 1977). Certified Mediator. *Member:* New Hanover County (President, 1987-1988) and North Carolina (Member, Sections on: Real Property and Business Law) Bar Associations; North Carolina State Bar. ***PRACTICE AREAS:*** Residential Real Estate; Commercial Real Estate; Corporate Law; Business Law; Health Care; Mediation. ***Email:*** dhuffine@bizec.rr.com

REPRESENTATIVE CLIENTS: Emrose Corp.; The Rosemyer Corporation; Nags Head Company, L.L.C.; Carolina Arthritis Associates P.A.; Coastal Carolina Surgical Associates; Moore Orthopaedics, Inc.; Coastal Thoracic Surgery, L.L.C.; Wilmington Plastic Surgery Specialists, P.A.; Coastal Pulmonary Medicine, P.A.

CLARK, CLARKE AND ASSOCIATES, L.L.P.

265 RACINE DRIVE, SUITE 101
WILMINGTON, NORTH CAROLINA 28403
Telephone: 910-452-3333
Fax: 910-452-4890
URL: http://www.wilmingtonnclawyers.com

Real Estate, Buying or Selling a Home, Construction, Business Law, LLC Formation, Trusts and Estates, Wills and Probate, Family Law, Divorce, Child Custody and Support, Equitable Distribution, Criminal Law, Traffic, DWI, DUI, Drug Crimes, Domestic Violence, Personal Injury, Automobile Accidents, Wrongful Death.

LINDA A. CLARK, born North Platte, Nebraska, October 27, 1948; admitted to bar, 1997, North Carolina. *Education:* University of North Carolina at Wilmington (B.A., 1994); North Carolina Central University (J.D., 1997). Phi Kappa Phi. Previously with District Attorney's Office. *Member:* North Carolina Bar Association. ***PRACTICE AREAS:*** Real Estate; Wills. ***Email:*** linaclarkatty@msn.com

SUSAN E. CLARKE, born 1953; admitted to bar, 1980, California; 1982, Missouri; 2004, North Carolina. *Education:* University of South Florida (B.A., 1974); Pepperdine University (J.D., 1979). Recipient, American Jurisprudence Award, Real Estate and Criminal Law. Adjunct Professor, St. Louis University School of Law, 1986-1994. Previously with The Spaulding Partnership LLP. Chesterfield Prosecuting Attorney, 1994-1998 and Missouri Council Member, 1991-1994, City of Chesterfield. *Member:* State Bar of California; North Carolina State Bar; The Missouri Bar. ***PRACTICE AREAS:*** Real Estate (69%); Family Law (11%); Criminal Law (20%).

CLARK, NEWTON, EVANS & BRYAN, L.L.P.

509 PRINCESS STREET
WILMINGTON, NORTH CAROLINA 28401
Telephone: 910-762-8743
Facsimile: 910-762-6206
Email: cneclaw@netscape.net
URL: http://www.lawyers.com/lawyerscomcneclaw

General Trial and Appellate Practice in all State and Federal Courts, Admiralty, Business Transactions, Real Estate and Corporate Law, Estate Planning and Estate Administration.

GEORGE T. CLARK, JR. (Retired)

JOHN RICHARD NEWTON, born Southport, North Carolina, June 4, 1932; admitted to bar, 1965, North Carolina; 1971, U.S. Supreme Court; U.S. Court of Appeals, Fourth Circuit; U.S. District Court, Eastern District of North Carolina. *Education:* University of North Carolina (A.B., 1957; LL.B., 1965). Certified Mediator and Arbitrator. *Member:* New Hanover County Bar Association; North Carolina State Bar; Maritime Law Association of the United States; Southeastern Admiralty Law Institute. ***PRACTICE AREAS:*** Admiralty Law; Civil Litigation.

DON T. EVANS, JR., born Rocky Mount, North Carolina, February 8, 1965; admitted to bar, 1992, North Carolina; 1993, U.S. Court of Military Appeals; 1998, U.S. District Court, Eastern District of North Carolina. *Education:* University of North Carolina (B.A., English, Psychology, 1987); Norman A. Wiggins School of Law (J.D., 1992). Omicron Delta Kappa. Articles Editor, Campbell Law Review. Member, Eastern District Admiralty Rules Committee. Port Director, Southeastern Admiralty Law Institute. Fellow, Nambu Foundation. [USNR]. ***LANGUAGES:*** Japanese. ***SPECIAL AGENCIES:*** U.S. Government Foreign Trial Observer. ***PRACTICE AREAS:*** Condemnation; Admiralty Law; Civil Litigation; Real Estate; Wrongful Death.

(This Listing Continued)

CLARK, NEWTON, EVANS & BRYAN, L.L.P., Wilmington—Continued

RUSS C. BRYAN, born Fayetteville, North Carolina, March 8, 1972; admitted to bar, 1997, North Carolina; 2000, District of Columbia. *Education:* University College of Wales Swansea, UK; University of North Carolina at Wilmington (B.A., 1994); Norman A. Wiggins School of Law (J.D., 1997). Phi Alpha Delta. Moot Court Association Board, Student Bar Representative. Formerly with Stevens, McGhee, Morgan, Lennon & Toll LLP. *Member:* New Hanover County and 5th Judicial District Bars; North Carolina State Bar; District of Columbia Bar; North Carolina Association of Defense Attorneys. ***PRACTICE AREAS:*** Insurance Defense; Workers Compensation Defense; Commercial Real Estate; Residential Real Estate.

REPRESENTATIVE CLIENTS: North Carolina Natural Gas; North Carolina Shipping Assn. P&I CLUBS: The Britannia Club; Liverpool & London P&I Club; London Steamship Mutual P&I; Standard Steamship P&I; The Swedish Club; The Gard; United Kingdom Club.

J. ALBERT CLYBURN, P.L.L.C.

502 MARKET STREET
WILMINGTON, NORTH CAROLINA 28401
Telephone: 910-202-1077
Fax: 910-202-1075
Email: clyburn@clyburnlaw.com

Family Law, Child Custody, Child Support, Divorce, Visitation Rights, Equitable Distribution.

JAMES ALBERT CLYBURN, born Raleigh, North Carolina, December 25, 1963; admitted to bar, 1990, North Carolina and U.S. District Court, Eastern District of North Carolina. *Education:* North Carolina State University (B.A., summa cum laude, 1986); University of North Carolina at Chapel Hill (J.D., 1990). Member, Holderness Moot Court National Team. *Member:* New Hanover and North Carolina (Member, Family Law Council) Bar Associations; North Carolina State Bar; North Carolina Academy of Trial Lawyers. ***PRACTICE AREAS:*** Family Law; Child Custody; Child Support; Divorce; Visitation Rights; Equitable Distribution.

LAWRENCE S. CRAIGE & ASSOCIATES, P.A.

701 MARKET STREET
WILMINGTON, NORTH CAROLINA 28401
Telephone: 910-815-0085
Fax: 910-815-1095
Email: mail@lsclawfirm.com
URL: http://www.lawrencecraige.com

Estate Planning, Wills and Probate, Trusts, Estate Administration, Construction Law, Civil Litigation, Juvenile Law, Real Estate, Buying and Selling a Home, Zoning and Land Use, Commercial Real Estate, Eminent Domain, Corporate Law, Business Law.

LAWRENCE S. CRAIGE & ASSOCIATES, P.A., born New Orleans, Louisiana, December 14, 1966; admitted to bar, 1998, North Carolina. *Education:* College of William & Mary (B.A., 1989); University of Alabama (M.A., 1993); University of North Carolina (J.D., 1997). President, Wilmington Downtown, Inc. Board of Directors, Wilmington Chamber of Commerce. *Member:* New Hanover County and American Bar Associations; North Carolina State Bar; New Hanover County Estate Planning Council. ***PRACTICE AREAS:*** Estate Planning; Wills; Probate; Trusts; Estate Administration; Construction Law; Civil Litigation; Juvenile Law; Real Estate; Buying and Selling a Home; Zoning, Planning and Land Use; Commercial Real Estate; Eminent Domain; Corporate Law; Business Law. ***Email:*** mail@lsclawfirm.com

ASSOCIATE

CHARLOTTE NOEL FOX, born Fayetteville, North Carolina, April 3, 1975; admitted to bar, 2004, North Carolina. *Education:* Wake Forest University (B.A., 1998); University of Georgia (M.E.D., 2000); Campbell University (J.D., 2004). Order of Old Kivet; Environmental Law Society (Trial Team). Defense Counsel, Honor Court. Recipient, Advocacy Award, North Carolina Academy of Trial Lawyers, 2004. "Williston on Contract", Research Assistant for Editor Richard A. Lord. *Member:* New Hanover County Bar Association; North Carolina State Bar. ***PRACTICE AREAS:*** Criminal Law; Real Estate; Buying and Selling a Home; Corporate Law; Wills; Trusts and Estates; Probate; Juvenile Law. ***Email:*** mail@lsclawfirm.com

REPRESENTATIVE CLIENTS: Urban Building Development, Inc.; Maximum Design and Advertising, Inc.; Taylor Custom Homes, LLC; Lower Cape Fear Hospice.

CRANFILL, SUMNER & HARTZOG, L.L.P.

1209 CULBRETH DRIVE, SUITE 200
WILMINGTON, NORTH CAROLINA 28405
Telephone: 910-509-9778
Fax: 910-509-9676
URL: http://www.cshlaw.com

Raleigh, North Carolina Office: Hillsborough Place, 225 Hillsborough Street, Suite 300, P.O. Box 27808. Telephone: 919-828-5100. Fax: 919-828-2277.
Charlotte, North Carolina Office: 227 West Trade Street, Suite 600. Telephone: 704-332-8300. Fax: 704-332-9994.

General Trial and Appellate Practice before all State and Federal Courts. Litigation of Insurance Law, Personal Injury, Medical Malpractice, Nursing Home Negligence, Professional Malpractice, Products Liability, Premises Liability, Municipal and Police Liability, Intentional Torts, Commercial Litigation, Workers' Compensation, Employment, Education, Construction and Land Condemnation Law.

(This Listing Continued)

MEMBERS OF THE FIRM

JOHN DEARMAN MARTIN, admitted to bar, 1985, North Carolina. *Education:* Wake Forest University (B.A., 1981); Campbell University (J.D., 1985).

COLLEEN SHEA COLLIS, admitted to bar, 1997, North Carolina. *Education:* University of North Carolina at Charlotte (B.A., 1993); Campbell University (J.D., 1997).

NORWOOD P. BLANCHARD, III, admitted to bar, 1999, North Carolina. *Education:* East Carolina University (B.S.B.A., 1993); Duke University (J.D., 1999).

REGAN S. TOUPS, admitted to bar, 2000, North Carolina. *Education:* North Carolina State University (B.S., 1996); Louisiana State University (J.D., 2000).

CAMERON D. SIMMONS, admitted to bar, 1999, North Carolina. *Education:* West Virginia University Institute of Technology (B.S., 1995); West Virginia University (M.S., 1996; J.D., 1999).

ROBERT B. JONES, JR., admitted to bar, 1997, North Carolina. *Education:* Davidson College (B.A., 1991); Campbell University (J.D., 1997).

NICOLE B. SLAUGHTER, admitted to bar, 1994, Tennessee; 1995, Georgia and North Carolina. *Education:* University of Memphis (B.B.A., 1991); University of Tennessee (J.D., 1994).

JENNIFER D. RAY, admitted to bar, 2003, North Carolina. *Education:* Davidson College (B.S., 1996); University of South Carolina (J.D., 2002).

MARGARET S. BENNINGTON, admitted to bar, 2002, North Carolina. *Education:* University of North Carolina at Chapel Hill (B.A., 1999); Wake Forest University (J.D., 2002).

JESSE J. BLYTHE, admitted to bar, 2005, North Carolina. *Education:* University of California at Santa Barbara (B.A., 1992); University of San Diego (J.D., 1996). *Member:* North Carolina State Bar.

(For complete biographical data on all personnel, see Professional Biographies at Raleigh and Charlotte, North Carolina)

CROSSLEY McINTOSH PRIOR & COLLIER

Established in 1949
2451 SOUTH COLLEGE ROAD
WILMINGTON, NORTH CAROLINA 28412
Telephone: 910-762-9711
Fax: 910-251-0446/ 1-800-499-9711
URL: http://www.cmpc-law.com

General Civil Trial Practice, Insurance Defense, Personal Injury, Workers Compensation, Admiralty, Longshore and Maritime Law, Professional Liability, Premises Liability, Products Liability, Municipal Litigation, Commercial/Business Transactions and Litigation, Criminal Defense, Construction Litigation, Labor and Employment Law, Sexual Harassment, Title VII Discrimination, Family and Medical Leave Act, Americans with Disabilities Act.

MEMBERS OF FIRM

DOUGLAS F. McINTOSH, born Royal Oak, Michigan, July 2, 1959; admitted to bar, 1984, North Carolina; 1987, Eastern District of North Carolina; 1990, U.S. Court of Appeals, Fourth Circuit; 1991, U.S. Supreme Court; 1996, U.S. District Court, Western and Middle Districts of North Carolina. *Education:* Oakland University (B.S., 1981); Campbell University (J.D., 1984). Member, Board of Directors, Southeastern Admiralty Law Institute. *Member:* New Hanover County and North Carolina Bar Associations; North Carolina State Bar; North Carolina Association of Defense Attorneys; Defense Research Institute. ***PRACTICE AREAS:*** Insurance Defense; Professional Liability; Premises Liability; Contractors Liability; Products Liability Defense; Personal Injury; Admiralty and Maritime Law. ***Email:*** douglasm@cmpc-law.com

FRANCIS B. PRIOR, born Trenton, New Jersey, June 2, 1957; admitted to bar, 1983, North Carolina; 1984, U.S. District Court, Western District of North Carolina; 1986, U.S. District Court, Eastern District of North Carolina; 1990, U.S. Court of Appeals, Fourth Circuit; 1991, U.S. Supreme Court. *Education:* North Carolina State University (B.A., Econ. and B.A., Bus.Mgt., 1980); Campbell University (J.D., 1983). Member, Campbell University Law Review, 1982-1983. *Member:* New Hanover County and North Carolina Bar Associations; North Carolina State Bar. ***PRACTICE AREAS:*** Civil Litigation; Mediation; Arbitration; Workers Compensation; Personal Injury. ***Email:*** frankp@cmpc-law.com

CLAY ALLEN COLLIER, born Fayetteville, North Carolina, December 20, 1959; admitted to bar, 1986, North Carolina, U.S. District Court, Eastern Division of North Carolina and U.S. Court of Appeals, Fourth Circuit. *Education:* University of North Carolina-Chapel Hill (A.B., 1982); Campbell University (J.D., 1985); IADC Defense Counsel National Trial Academy (1990). Delta Theta Phi. *Member:* New Hanover County, North Carolina and American Bar Associations; North Carolina State Bar; North Carolina Association of Defense Attorneys (Board of Directors, 2001-2003; Treasurer, 2004—); Defense Research Institute; North Carolina Adjuster's Association (General Counsel). ***PRACTICE AREAS:*** Professional Liability; Professional Negligence; Insurance Defense; Municipal Defense; Products Liability Defense; Personal Injury; Insurance Coverage. ***Email:*** clayc@cmpc-law.com

H. MARK HAMLET, born Martinsville, Virginia, February 21, 1966; admitted to bar, 1993, North Carolina, U.S. District Court, Eastern District of North Carolina and U.S. Court of Appeals, Fourth Circuit; 2005, South Carolina. *Education:* Wake Forest University (B.A., 1988); Campbell University (J.D., 1993). Order of the Barristers. *Member:* New Hanover County and North Carolina Bar Associations; North Carolina State Bar; South Carolina Bar. ***PRACTICE AREAS:*** Construction Litigation; Insurance Defense; Products Liability Defense; Personal Injury. ***Email:*** markh@cmpc-law.com

SAMUEL H. MACRAE, born Fayetteville, North Carolina, March 21, 1965; admitted to bar, 1991, North Carolina; 1995, U.S. District Court, Eastern District of North Carolina. *Education:* University of North Carolina (B.A., 1987); North Carolina Central University (J.D., 1991). Assistant District Attorney, 12th Prosecutorial District, 1991-1994. *Member:*

(This Listing Continued)

New Hanover County and North Carolina Bar Associations; North Carolina State Bar. **PRACTICE AREAS:** Criminal Defense; Civil Litigation; Insurance Defense; Personal Injury. **Email:** samuelm@cmpc-law.com

ANDREW HANLEY, born Cleveland, Ohio, July 22, 1963; admitted to bar, 1991, Texas; 1997, North Carolina; U.S. District Court, Eastern and Western Districts of North Carolina, U.S. District Court, Southern District of Texas, U.S. Court of Appeals, Fourth and Fifth Circuits and U.S. Supreme Court. *Education:* Cornell University (B.A., 1985); Tulane University (J.D., cum laude, 1991). Notes and Comment Editor, Tulane Maritime Law Journal. *Member:* North Carolina Bar Association; State Bar of Texas; Southeastern Admiralty Law Institute; Maritime Law Association. **PRACTICE AREAS:** Insurance Defense; Insurance Coverage; Civil Litigation; Maritime Law; Employment Law. **Email:** andrewh@cmpc-law.com

ASHLEY M. EDWARDS, born Jacksonville, Florida, October 2, 1972; admitted to bar, 1998, North Carolina. *Education:* University of North Carolina at Wilmington (B.S., 1993); University of Tennessee (J.D., 1998). Academic Honors Advanced Trial Practice and Commercial Law. *Member:* New Hanover County Bar; North Carolina State Bar; American Bar Association. **PRACTICE AREAS:** Mediation; Workers' Compensation; Personal Injury; Civil Litigation; Insurance Litigation; Social Security. **Email:** ashleye@cmpc-law.com

BRIAN E. EDES, born Jacksonville, North Carolina, June 9, 1971; admitted to bar, 1998, North Carolina. *Education:* University of North Carolina at Wilmington (B.A., 1995); Campbell University (J.D., 1998). Notes and Comments Editor, Campbell University Law Review. *Member:* New Hanover County Bar; North Carolina State Bar; North Carolina Bar Association; North Carolina Association of Defense Attorneys. **PRACTICE AREAS:** Municipal Law; Commercial Transactions; Commercial Litigation; Business Transactions; Business Litigation; Insurance Defense; Civil Litigation. **Email:** briane@cmpc-law.com

ASSOCIATE

CHRISTOPHER J. SKINNER, born Wilson, North Carolina, April 6, 1980; admitted to bar, 2005, North Carolina. *Education:* North Carolina State University (B.S., 2002); Campbell University (J.D., 2005). **Email:** chriss@cmpc-law.com

REPRESENTATIVE CLIENTS: AIG Aviation; Allstate Insurance Co.; American International Group; CNA; Builders Mutual Insurance Co.; Farm Bureau; State Farm Insurance Co.; Lloyds London (Certain underwriters); North Carolina League of Municipalities; First Trust Mortgage; GAB; Georgia Casualty Insurance Co.; Golden Corral; Great American Insurance Co.; Harleysville Insurance Co.; Horace Mann Insurance Co.; Lawyers Mutual Insurance Co.; Metropolitan Property and Casualty Insurance Co.; Monticello Insurance Co.; Lowes Home Improvement; Progressive Insurance Co.; Liberty Mutual; Ranger Insurance Co.; Ruby Tuesday; Seibels Bruce Insurance Co.; State Auto Insurance Co.; The St. Paul Insurance Co.; St. Paul Marine; Utica Mutual Insurance Co.; USAA.

CULBRETH LAW FIRM, L.L.P.

514 CHESTNUT STREET
P.O. BOX 446
WILMINGTON, NORTH CAROLINA 28402
Telephone: 910-763-3416
Facsimile: 910-763-9975
Email: culbrethlaw@juno.com
URL: http://www.culbrethlawfirm.com

General Civil and Criminal Trial Practice in all State and Federal Courts, Personal Injury, Automobile Accidents, Trucking Accidents, Construction Accidents, Probate, Wrongful Death, Workers Compensation, Appellate Work and Insurance Litigation, Collections, Mediation.

MEMBERS OF FIRM

STEPHEN E. CULBRETH, born Wilmington, North Carolina, January 10, 1943; admitted to bar, 1968, North Carolina, U.S. District Court, Eastern and Western Districts of North Carolina and U.S. Court of Appeals, Fourth Circuit. *Education:* Wilmington College (B.A., 1965); University of North Carolina at Chapel Hill (J.D., 1968). Inductee, General Practice Hall of Fame, North Carolina Bar Association, 2005. Member, Board of Editors, North Carolina Law Review, 1968. Certified Superior Court Mediator. *Member:* New Hanover County (Member, Executive Board, 1978-1981), Pender County and North Carolina Bar Associations; 5th Judicial District (President, 1979-1980) and North Carolina State Bars (5th District Councilor, 1990-1998); North Carolina Academy of Trial Lawyers. **REPORTED CASES:** Sutton v. Aetna, 325 NC 259 382S.E.2d 759 (1989); New South Ins. v. Kidd, 114 NC App. 749 443 S.E. 2nd 85 (1994); Pearce vs. Southern Bell Telephone & Telegraph, 299 NC 64, 261 SE 2nd 176 (1980); Nationwide vs. Edwards, 67 NC App 1, 312 SE 2nd 656 (1984); Newber vs. City of Wilmington, 82 NC App 90, 345 SE 2nd 444 (1986); Simmons v. N.C. Dept of Transportation 496 S.E.2d 790 128 NC App. 402 (1998). **Email:** culbrethlaw@juno.com

ASHLEY C. COUNCIL, born Wilmington, North Carolina, June 5, 1973; admitted to bar, 2001, North Carolina and U.S. District Court, Eastern District of North Carolina. *Education:* University of North Carolina at Chapel Hill (B.A., 1995); Campbell University (J.D., 2001). *Member:* New Hanover County, Pender County and North Carolina Bar Associations; North Carolina State Bar; North Carolina Academy of Trial Lawyers. **PRACTICE AREAS:** Criminal Law; Workers Compensation; Personal Injury; Wrongful Death; Traffic Court; Driving While Intoxicated. **Email:** ashleycouncil@juno.com

REPRESENTATIVE CLIENTS: Azalea Insurance Company, Inc.; DÆ Car Exchange, Inc.; Sylvia's Pet Care; Soil Recovery, Inc.; GLN Farms; Kinlaw's Wrecker Service; Suttons Rugs and Carpets; A & N Roofing.
APPROVED ATTORNEYS FOR: The Title Company of North Carolina.
REFERENCES: Branch Banking & Trust Company; Carolina First Bank.

CURRIN LAW FIRM, PLLC

GOOLSBY LAW BUILDING
620 MARKET STREET
WILMINGTON, NORTH CAROLINA 28401
Telephone: 910-763-3339
Fax: 910-763-1720
URL: http://www.currinlaw.com
URL: http://www.lawyers.com/currinlaw

Raleigh, North Carolina Office: Currin Law Building, 20 Market Plaza, P.O. Box 269, 27602-0269. Telephone: 919-833-0888. Facsimile: 919-833-8171.

Federal and State Criminal Defense, Civil and Criminal Forfeitures, Serious Personal Injury/ Wrongful Death, Medical Malpractice, Government Relations.

SAMUEL T. CURRIN, born Oxford, North Carolina, December 13, 1948; admitted to bar, 1974, North Carolina; 1975, U.S. District Court, Eastern, Middle and Western Districts of North Carolina and U.S. Court of Appeals, Fourth Circuit; 1980, U.S. Supreme Court. *Education:* Wake Forest University (B.A., cum laude, 1971); University of North Carolina (J.D., 1974). National Judicial College, 1988. Adjunct Professor of Law, Campbell University School of Law. Co-Author: "Regulation of Pornography-The North Carolina Approach," 21 Wake Forest Law Review 263, 1986. Superior Court Judge, 1987-1990. U.S. Attorney, Eastern District of North Carolina, 1981-1987. Assistant U.S. Attorney, Eastern District of North Carolina, 1976-1978. Legislative Counsel, U.S. Senate, 1978-1981. Presidential Elector, 1972, 2000. Chairman, North Carolina Republican Party, 1996-1999. *Member:* International Bar Association; North Carolina Academy of Trial Lawyers; National Association of Criminal Defense Lawyers; Association Internationale De Droit Penal; National Association of Former United States Attorneys. **PRACTICE AREAS:** Federal Criminal Law; Criminal Defense; Criminal Forfeiture; Wrongful Death; Personal Injury; Medical Malpractice; Government Relations. **Email:** sam@currinlaw.com

THOMAS C. GOOLSBY, born Dothan, Alabama, September 11, 1961; admitted to bar, 1992, North Carolina. *Education:* The Citadel (B.S., cum laude, with honors, 1984); Golden Gate University (M.B.A., 1987); University of North Carolina at Chapel Hill (J.D., 1991). Davis Honor Society. Air Traffic Control FAA Certified Tower Operator, 1985. Author: "Le Rôle Du Minist ère Public Am éricain, Revue Internationale De Droit Penal, 3 et 4 Trimestres 1992. Adjunct Professor of Law, Campbell University School of Law. Former Legal Counsel, North Carolina Governor's Crime Commission, 1992-1993. *Member:* North Carolina and International Bar Associations; North Carolina State Bar; Million Dollar Advocates Forum (Life Member); Association Internationale De Droit Penal. [USMC, 1984-1988, Recalled For Gulf War, Capt.]. **PRACTICE AREAS:** Federal Criminal Law; Criminal Defense; Personal Injury; Wrongful Death; Medical Malpractice. **Email:** thom@currinlaw.com

DAVID AND ASSOCIATES, PLLC

1516 DAWSON STREET
WILMINGTON, NORTH CAROLINA 28401
Telephone: 910-251-8088
Toll Free: 1-800-856-9927
Fax: 910-251-8430
Email: aeverhart@davidandassociates.com
URL: http://www.wilmingtonpiattorneys.com

Jacksonville, North Carolina Office: 405-B Western Boulevard. 28546. Telephone: 910-219-4878.
Supply, North Carolina Office: Highway 17. 28462. Telephone: 910-754-8465.
Wallace, North Carolina Office: 107 North Norwood Street. 28466. Telephone: 910-285-8777.
Clinton, North Carolina Office: 610 Beaman Street. 28328. Telephone: 910-592-8400.
Winston-Salem, North Carolina Office: 1100-A South Stratford Road. 27103. Telephone: 336-354-1040.
Greensboro, North Carolina Office: 529 College Road. Suite G. 27410. Telephone: 336-354-1040.

Personal Injury, Medical Malpractice, Wrongful Death, Products Liability, Workers Compensation, Aviation, Airplane Crashes, Negligence, Class Actions, Maritime Accidents, Boating Accidents, Bicycle Accidents, Motorcycle Accidents, Truck Accidents, School Bus Accidents, Railroad Accidents, Dog Bites, Slip and Fall, Birth Trauma, Brain Injury, Spinal Injury, Head Injury, Catastrophic Injury, Vehicular Homicide, Personal Injury Mediation, Products Liability, Drug and Medical Device Litigation, Product Defects, Automobile Liability, Motorcycle Products Liability, Amusement Park Liability, Hotel Liability, Marina Liability, Sports Injury.

G. PHILLIP DAVID, born Whiteville, North Carolina, September 29, 1959; admitted to bar, 1988, North Carolina. *Education:* East Carolina University (B.S.B.A., 1981); North Carolina Central University (J.D., 1988). *Member:* North Carolina State Bar.

ASSOCIATES

MICHAEL J. RIZZI, born Redding, Connecticut, May 27, 1969; admitted to bar, 1994, North Carolina. *Education:* Bucknell University (B.A., 1991); Campbell University (J.D., 1994). *Member:* Pitt County and North Carolina Bar Associations; The Association of Trial Lawyers of America.

DAVID F. TURLINGTON, born Rocky Mount, North Carolina, July 29, 1968; admitted to bar, 1993, North Carolina. *Education:* University of North Carolina at Chapel Hill (B.A., with honors and distinction, 1990; J.D., 1993). Phi Beta Kappa. *Member:* Lenoir County and North Carolina Bar Associations; North Carolina State Bar.

G. ANDREW EVERHART, born North Carolina, 1977; admitted to bar, 2004, North Carolina. *Education:* Wake Forest University (1999); University of Denver (J.D., 2004).

ANN M. DAVID, born Roxboro, North Carolina, March 14, 1962; admitted to bar, 1993, North Carolina. *Education:* Meredith College (B.A., 1984); North Carolina Central University (J.D., 1988). **PRACTICE AREAS:** Personal Injury.

R. THEODORE DAVIS, JR.

Established in 1984
8 SOUTH SIXTH STREET
P.O. BOX 2535
WILMINGTON, NORTH CAROLINA 28402
Telephone: 910-763-6249
Fax: 910-762-5175
Email: tdavjr@bellsouth.net
URL: http://www.tdavisjrlaw.com

Family Law including Adoptions, Domestic Violence, Separation Agreements, Divorce, Child Custody, Child Support, Spousal Support and Property Division. General Civil and Criminal Practice including Civil Litigation, Misdemeanor and Felony Criminal Violations, DWI and Traffic Offenses.

R. THEODORE DAVIS, JR., born Wilmington, North Carolina, January 23, 1950; admitted to bar, 1977, North Carolina; 1980, U.S. District Court, Eastern District of North Carolina and U.S. Court of Appeals, Fourth Circuit; 1982, U.S. Supreme Court. *Education:* University of North Carolina (B.A., 1972); Wake Forest University (J.D., 1976). Phi Delta Phi. Assistant District Attorney, 13th Judicial District of North Carolina, 1977-1980. Assistant U.S. Attorney, Eastern District of North Carolina, 1980-1982. Assistant New Hanover County Attorney, 1982-1984. New Hanover County Commissioner, 1996— and Chairman, 2000-2003. Cape Fear Community College Board of Trustees, 1997—. UNCW Seahawk Club Board of Directors, 1997—. *Member:* New Hanover County, North Carolina and American Bar Associations; North Carolina Academy of Trial Lawyers; The Association of Trial Lawyers of America.

MATTHEW T. DILL, P.L.L.C.

Attorney and Counsellor at Law
Established in 1989
1430 COMMONWEALTH DRIVE, SUITE 206
WILMINGTON, NORTH CAROLINA 28403
Telephone: 910-256-9700
Telecopier: 910-256-2529
Email: mtd@matthewtdill.com
Mailing Address: P.O. Box 1226, Wrightsville Beach, NC 28480

Wills, Estates and Estate Planning, Federal Income, Estate and Gift Taxation Law, Probate Law and Trust Administration.

MATTHEW T. DILL, born New York, N.Y., April 20, 1961; admitted to bar, 1986, North Carolina. *Education:* Hampden-Sydney College (B.A., 1983); Campbell University School of Law (J.D., 1986); University of Miami (LL.M. in Estate Planning, 1987). Delta Theta Phi. Recipient, BB&T Estate Planning Award, 1986. *Member:* New Hanover County, North Carolina (Member, Sections on: Estate Planning and Fiduciary Law; Taxation) and American (Member, Sections on: Real Property, Probate and Trust Law; Taxation; Law Practice Management) Bar Associations; North Carolina State Bar; New Hanover County Estate Planning Council (President, 1995-1996); Onslow County Estate Planning Council. (Board Certified Specialist in Estate Planning and Probate Law, North Carolina State Board of Legal Specialization). ***PRACTICE AREAS:*** Estate Planning and Administration; Trusts; Probate; Taxation.

REFERENCES: Centura Bank; First Citizens Bank; First Union National Bank of North Carolina; Bank of America; N.A.; Wachovia Bank of North Carolina, N.A.

ENNIS, NEWTON & BAYNARD, P.A.

Established in 1999
105 BURKE AVENUE, SUITE E
WILMINGTON, NORTH CAROLINA 28403
Telephone: 910-256-3992
Fax: 910-256-3578
Email: enb@enblaw.net
Mailing Address: P.O. Box 1327, Wrightsville Beach, NC 28480

General Insurance and Self Insured Defense Litigation, including Property, Casualty, Automobile, Personal Injury, Premises Liability, Coverage Opinions, Subrogation, Products Liability, Workers Compensation. Trials in all State and Federal Courts.

DONALD W. ENNIS, born Harnett County, North Carolina, August 17, 1960; admitted to bar, 1986, North Carolina. *Education:* North Carolina State University (B.S., 1982); Campbell University (J.D., 1986). Phi Alpha Delta. Member: Trial Advocacy Team; The Association of Trial Lawyers of America Team. *Member:* New Hanover County, North Carolina and American (Member, Sections on: Litigation; Tort and Insurance Law) Bar Associations; North Carolina State Bar; North Carolina Association of Defense Attorneys; Defense Research Institute. ***REPORTED CASES:*** Jansen vs. Collins 92 N.C. App. 516 (1988); Petteway vs. South Carolina Insurance Co., 93 N.C. App. 776 (1989); Hale vs. Leisure, 100 N.C. App. 163 (1990); Worrells vs. N.C. Farm Bureau Mutual Insurance Co., 103 N.C. App. 69 (1991). ***PRACTICE AREAS:*** Defense Litigation. ***Email:*** dennis@enblaw.net

JACQUELINE A. NEWTON, born Bryan, Texas, June 7, 1957; admitted to bar, 1991, North Carolina. *Education:* Western Carolina University (B.S.B.A., 1979); Campbell University (J.D., 1991). Delta Theta Phi. *Member:* North Carolina and American Bar Associations; North Carolina State Bar; North Carolina Association of Defense Attorneys (Member, Regional Meetings Committee); Defense Research Institute. ***PRACTICE AREAS:*** General Liability Defense; Casualty Insurance Defense; Workers Compensation Defense; Premises Liability. ***Email:*** jnewton@enblaw.net

STEPHEN C. BAYNARD, born Saint Louis, Missouri, July 26, 1968; admitted to bar, 1993, North Carolina. *Education:* University of North Carolina (B.A., 1990); Campbell University School of Law (J.D., 1993). Phi Alpha Delta (Justice, 1993). Vice-President, Student Bar Association, 1993. *Member:* New Hanover County, Fifth Judicial District (President), North Carolina and American Bar Associations; North Carolina State Bar; Defense Research Institute; North Carolina Association of Defense Attorneys (Chair, Young Lawyers Executive Committee). ***REPORTED CASES:*** Moore v. Cincinnati Ins., 556 SE 2d 682 (2001); Robinson v. Leach, 514 S.E.2d 567 (1999); Wolfson v. Cox, 2004 WL1191736, N.C. App., June 1, 2004; Parker v. Willis, 606 S.E.2d 184, N.C. App., 2004; Smith v. Murrell, 605, S.E.2d 742, 2004. ***PRACTICE AREAS:*** General Liability Defense; Casualty Insurance Defense; Premises Liability; Products Liability. ***Email:*** sbaynard@enblaw.net

REPRESENTATIVE CLIENTS: Allstate Insurance Co.; American Empire; Arbitration Forums, Inc.; Bankers Ins. Co. (Insurance Management Solutions); Brownyard Group; Cardinal Freight Carriers, Inc.; Essex Insurance Co.; Fleetwood Enterprises, Inc.; Liberty Mutual; Midlands Claims Administrators, Inc.; North Carolina Farm Bureau Mutual Insurance Co.; Penn-American Ins. Co.; Sears, Roebuck & Co.; Selective Insurance; Siebels Bruce Universal Insurance Co.; State Farm Insurance Co.; The Horace Mann Cos.; Montgomery Mutual Insurance Co.; Progressive Insurance; Providence Washington Insurance Co.; Viking Insurance; ARCH Insurance Co.; Esurance.

FLETCHER RAY & SATTERFIELD, L.L.P.

131 RACINE DRIVE, SUITE 201
WILMINGTON, NORTH CAROLINA 28403
Telephone: 910-251-9900
Fax: 910-251-9667
URL: http://www.fletcherlaw.com

General Practice in all State and Federal Courts, Trials, Banking, Insurance, Negligence, Health Law, Medical Malpractice, Bankruptcy, Construction, Creditors Rights, Lender Liability, Collections, Municipal and Land Use Law, Employment Law and Administrative Law.

MEMBERS OF FIRM

GEORGE L. FLETCHER, born Lake City, Florida, June 14, 1947; admitted to bar, 1978, North Carolina and U.S. District Court, Middle and Eastern Districts of North Carolina; U.S. Court of Appeals, Fourth Circuit. *Education:* University of Florida (B.A., with honors, 1976; J.D., 1978). *Member:* New Hanover County, North Carolina (Member, Sections on: Construction Law; Employment Law; Real Property) Bar Associations; North Carolina State Bar. ***PRACTICE AREAS:*** Commercial Litigation; Employment Law; Construction Litigation. ***Email:*** gfletch@fletcherlaw.com

DAVID L. RAY, born Alexandria, Virginia, May 14, 1966; admitted to bar, 1991, North Carolina; U.S. District Court, Eastern and Middle Districts of North Carolina and U.S. Court of Appeals, Fourth Circuit. *Education:* University of North Carolina at Chapel Hill (B.A., 1988; J.D., 1991). *Member:* New Hanover County and North Carolina (Member, Bankruptcy Law Section) Bar Associations; North Carolina State Bar; American Bankruptcy Institute. ***PRACTICE AREAS:*** Bankruptcy Law; Creditors Rights; Business Law; Collections; Commercial Litigation; Construction Law. ***Email:*** dray@fletcherlaw.com

T. MICHAEL SATTERFIELD, born High Point, North Carolina, March 17, 1959; admitted to bar, 1985, North Carolina; 1987, U.S. District Court, Eastern District of North Carolina. *Education:* University of North Carolina-Wilmington (B.A., cum laude, 1982); University of North Carolina-Chapel Hill (J.D., 1985). Phi Kappa Phi. *Member:* New Hanover County and North Carolina (Member, Sections on: Real Property; Environmental Law) Bar Associations. ***PRACTICE AREAS:*** Real Estate; Environmental; Land Use. ***Email:*** msatter@fletcherlaw.com

R. JAY SHORT, JR., born Chapel Hill, North Carolina, May 17, 1969; admitted to bar, 1995, North Carolina and U.S. District Court, Middle District of North Carolina; 1998, U.S. District Court, Eastern District of North Carolina. *Education:* University of North Carolina (B.A., 1991); Wake Forest University (J.D., 1995). *Member:* New Hanover County, North Carolina and American Bar Associations; North Carolina State Bar; Association of Trial Lawyers of America; North Carolina Academy of Trial Lawyers. ***PRACTICE AREAS:*** Civil Litigation; Personal Injury; Construction Law; Commercial Litigation. ***Email:*** jshort@fletcherlaw.com

---

KIERSTEN M. GORDON, admitted to bar, 1995, Pennsylvania; 1996, New Jersey; 1998, U.S. District Court, Eastern District of Pennsylvania; 1999, US. Court of Appeals, Third Circuit; 2004 North Carolina. *Education:* Oglethorpe University (B.A., Political Science, 1992); Villanova University School of Law (J.D., 1995). Recipient: James Edward Oglethorpe Scholarship; Robert Byrd Congressional Scholarship. Member, Environmental Law Journal, 1994-1995. *Member:* Montgomery, Brunswick County, Pennsylvania and American Bar Associations; North Carolina State Bar. ***PRACTICE AREAS:*** Civil Litigation; Personal Injury; Wrongful Death; Real Estate; Real Estate Foreclosure. ***Email:*** kgordon@jeffcoatlaw.com

ELIZABETH WRIGHT EMBREY, born Tabor City, North Carolina, September 18, 1978; admitted to bar, 2004, North Carolina and U.S. Court of Appeals, Fourth Circuit. *Education:* University of North Carolina at Chapel Hill (B.A., with distinction, 2001; J.D., 2004). Holderness Moot Court. Member, Executive Board, Environmental Appellate Advocacy Team. Recognition, North Carolina Bar Association, Pro Bono Service as a law student. *Member:* New Hanover County, North Carolina and American Bar Associations; North Carolina State Bar. ***PRACTICE AREAS:*** Real Estate Litigation; Civil Litigation; Creditors Rights; Land Use. ***Email:*** ewright@fletcherlaw.com

OF COUNSEL

KIMBERLY L. MOORE, born Charlottesville, Virginia, June 14, 1967; admitted to bar, 1995, Georgia (inactive) and Indiana; 1996, U.S. Court of Appeals, Fourth Circuit; 1998, Nevada (inactive); 2001, North Carolina; 2003, U.S. District Court, Eastern District of North Carolina. *Education:* The Hotchkiss School, 1985; McIntire School of Commerce, University of Virginia (B.S., 1989); Walter F. George School of Law, Mercer University (J.D., cum laude, 1995). Brainerd Currie Honor Society. Order of Barristers. Mercer Law Review, Member, 1993-1994, Student Writing Editor, 1994-1995, Spring Competition Editor, 1995. Member, Moot Court Board, 1994-1995. Recipient: Best Brief for the Re-

(This Listing Continued)

spondent, Gibbons National Criminal Procedure Moot Court Competition, April 1994; Faculty Award for Outstanding Achievement in Legal Writing, 1993; American Jurisprudence Awards in Legal Writing I, Real Estate Transactions, and Business Associations. Author: Publication: Casenote, United States v. Irvine: The Disclaimer of an Interest Created Before Enactment of the Federal Gift Tax Is Taxable, 45 Mercer L. Rev. 897 (1994). *Member:* New Hanover County and North Carolina Bar Associations. (Also Member, Johnson & Moore, P.A., Southport). ***PRACTICE AREAS:*** Civil Litigation; Business Law; Commercial Litigation; Construction Law. ***Email:*** kmoore@fletcherlaw.com

COUNSEL FOR: Chloride Power Electronics; Bedford Fair Industries; Wieland, Inc.; Miller Building Corporation; Applied Analytical Industries; Wright Chemical Company; Commonwealth Land Title Insurance Co.; Block Industries; Bald Head Island; Alliance Federal Credit Union; Corning Federal Credit Union; Civic Development Group; DBC, Inc.; S & L Properties; Achemco, Inc.; Coverbind Corporation; DeCarol Williamson Enterprises; LaDane Williamson Enterprises; 2M Development Company; Atlantic Quest Corporation; Hextek Technologies; Porter's Neck Plantation.
APPROVED ATTORNEYS FOR: Investors Title Insurance Co.; Lawyers Title Insurance Co.; Chicago Title Insurance Co.; First Title Insurance Co.; Commonwealth Land Title Co. of North Carolina; The Title Company of North Carolina.
REFERENCES: Centura Bank; Branch Banking and Trust Company; Wachovia Bank of North Carolina, N.A.

GODWIN LAW FIRM

130 N. FRONT STREET, SUITE 201
WILMINGTON, NORTH CAROLINA 28401
Telephone: 910-762-0410
Fax: 910-762-2591
Email: davidg@davidmgodwinlaw.com
URL: http://www.davidgodwinlaw.com

Family Law, Divorce, Property Settlements, Child Custody, Child Support, Adoptions, Alimony, Spousal Support, Personal Injury, Workers Compensation, Social Security Disability, Civil Litigation.

MEMBER

DAVID M. GODWIN, born Erwin, North Carolina, September 6, 1956; admitted to bar, 1988, North Carolina and U.S. District Court, Eastern District of North Carolina. *Education:* Campbell University (B.S.B.A., 1986; J.D., 1988). *Member:* North Carolina Bar Association; North Carolina Association of Trial Lawyers. ***PRACTICE AREAS:*** Family Law; Divorce; Marital Property Settlements; Child Custody; Child Support; Adoption Law; Alimony; Spousal Support; Personal Injury; Workers Compensation; Social Security Disability; Civil Litigation. ***Email:*** davidg@davidmgodwinlaw.com

MICHAEL A. GREEN, P.C.

1908 EASTWOOD ROAD, SUITE 217
WILMINGTON, NORTH CAROLINA 28403
Telephone: 910-509-9966
Fax: 910-509-0707
Email: mgreen@mgreenlaw.com
URL: http://www.mgreenlaw.com

Business Law, Health Care, Commercial Law, Banking Law, Construction Law, Corporate Law, Local Government Law, Entertainment Law; Contracts; Zoning and Land Use, Admiralty and Maritime Law.

FIRM PROFILE: The firm concentrates on strategic planning and efficient business organization, infrastructure and governance. Mr. Green has considerable experience in corporate start-up, mergers and acquisitions, business transactions, commercial litigation and the interface of business and local government.

MICHAEL A. GREEN, born Columbus, Ohio, August 30, 1946; admitted to bar, 1991, North Carolina and District of Columbia; 1995, U.S. Supreme Court. *Education:* Jacksonville University (B.A., summa cum laude, 1975); University of Chicago (A.M., cum laude, 1980); Campbell University (J.D., 1991). Research Editor, Campbell University Law Review. *Member:* New Hanover County, Fifth Judicial District, North Carolina (Member, Business Law Section) and American (Member, Sections on Litigation and Business Law) Bar Associations; District of Columbia Bar; Wilmington Inns of Court; Admiralty Law Association of the U.S. [Lt. Col., U.S. Army, 1966-1988, Retired]. ***PRACTICE AREAS:*** Business Law; Commercial Litigation; Mergers and Acquisitions; Government; Strategic Alliances; Corporate Law; Contracts; Health Care; Zoning; Land Use; Admiralty and Maritime Law. ***Email:*** mgreen@mgreenlaw.com

REPRESENTATIVE CLIENTS: Carolina Dermatology; Fisher & Co. CPA's; MasterCraftsman, Inc.; Good Shephard Ministries; Roge Pharmaceuticals; Wrightsville Builders, Inc.; NICO, Inc.; Brightstone Corp.; SitoChiropractic; Jericho Engineering, PA; SRS Development; Leinwand Properties; Atlantic Dermatology Associates; Blockade Runner Resort.

NANCY M. GUYTON

321 NORTH FRONT STREET
WILMINGTON, NORTH CAROLINA 28401
Telephone: 910-251-2190
Fax: 910-251-2191
Email: nancyguyton@guyton-law.com
URL: http://www.lawyers.com/nancyguyton

Commercial Real Estate, Corporate, Small Business, Community Associations, Real Estate, Limited Liability Companies, Partnerships, Corporations, Buying and Selling of Businesses, Commercial Law, Joint Ventures, Real Estate Development.

NANCY M. GUYTON, born Montgomery, Alabama, January 7, 1959; admitted to bar, 1985, North Carolina and U.S. District Court, Eastern District of North Carolina; 1990, U.S. Court of Appeals, Fourth Circuit. *Education:* Smith College (A.B., 1981); University of North Carolina at Chapel Hill (J.D., 1985). Member: Order of Barristers; Holderness Moot Court Society. *Member:* New Hanover County, North Carolina (Member, Sections on: Business; Environmental; Construction Law; Section Counsel Member, Real Property Section, 2000-2002) and American (Member, Sections on: Real Property, Trust and Probate; Business Law) Bar Associations; Fifth Judicial District and North Carolina State Bars; North Carolina Association of Women Attorneys; International Counsel of Shipping Centers. (Board Certified Specialist in Real Estate Law; Residential, Business, Commercial and Industrial Transactions, North Carolina State Board of Legal Specialization)

VIRGINIA R. HAGER

Established in 2005
3808-B PARK AVENUE
P.O. BOX 2184
WILMINGTON, NORTH CAROLINA 28402-2184
Telephone: 910-796-2044
Fax: 910-796-2041
URL: http://hager.lawoffice.com
Email: VRHager@aol.com
URL: http://www.lawyers.com/hagerlaw

Practice limited to Domestic Relations Litigation (Divorce, Child Custody, Child and Spousal Support and Domestic Violence) and Negotiation (Separation Agreements, Relationship Contracts), Family Mediation, Wills, Simple Estate Planning.

VIRGINIA R. HAGER, born Newport News, Virginia, July 9, 1955; admitted to bar, 1984, Ohio; 1987, Kentucky; 1990, North Carolina. *Education:* Allegheny College (B.A., 1977) Phi Beta Kappa; College of William & Mary (J.D., 1984). Certified Family Financial Issues Mediator, State of North Carolina, 2001. *Member:* New Hanover County, Fifth Judicial District, North Carolina (Member, Family Law Section) and American (Member, Family Law Section) Bar Associations; North Carolina Academy of Trial Lawyers.

KAREN L. SIMMONS, admitted to bar, 1996, Massachusetts (Not admitted in North Carolina). *Education:* Smith College (B.A., 1993); Western New England College (J.D., 1996). ***PRACTICE AREAS:*** Wills; Trusts and Estates; Estate Planning; Family Law; Divorce. ***Email:*** ksimmonsatty@yahoo.com

HALL & HORNE, L.L.P.

Established in 1983
718 MARKET STREET
WILMINGTON, NORTH CAROLINA 28401
Telephone: 910-343-8433
Fax: 910-343-8165
Email: ahall@hallandhorne.com

Personal Injury, Professional Negligence, Toxic Tort, Wrongful Death, Land Condemnation, Workers Compensation, Social Security, General Civil and Criminal Practice, Felonies, Drug Offenses, Driving While Impaired.

ALEXANDER M. HALL, born Wilmington, North Carolina, July 20, 1948; admitted to bar, 1978, Texas and North Carolina. *Education:* University of South Carolina; University of North Carolina (B.A., Zoology, 1971); South Texas College of Law (J.D., magna cum laude, 1977). Delta Theta Phi. Member of Staff, South Texas Law Journal. Member, 1985-1990 and Chairman, Finance Committee, 1989-1990, North Carolina House of Representatives. *Member:* North Carolina Academy of Trial Lawyers (Vice President, Legislation, 1995-1997; Member, Board of Governors, 1992-2002; Member, Board of Trustees, Political Action Committee, 1982-1985, and 1995—; Contributing Editor, North Carolina Prima Facie Tort Manual; Chair, Closed Head Injuries Seminar, 1994; Speaker, Wrongful Death Seminar, 1995 and 2005); Association of Trial Lawyers of America (Member, State Legislation Liaison Committee, 1996-1998); North Carolina General Statutes Commission, 1986-1989; New Hanover Bar Association; Fifth Judicial District Bar Association (President, 1983-1986); North Carolina State Bar. ***LANGUAGES:*** Spanish. ***PRACTICE AREAS:*** Trial Practice; Personal Injury Law; Wrongful Death; Criminal Law; Driving While Intoxicated; Felonies; Misdemeanors; Automobile Accidents and Injuries; Toxic Torts; Brain Injury; Head Injury. ***Email:*** ahall@hallandhorne.com

ROSEANNA C. HORNE, born Shelbyville, Kentucky, January 27, 1967; admitted to bar, 1992, North Carolina and U.S. District Court, Eastern District of North Carolina. *Education:* University of North Carolina at Wilmington (B.A., summa cum laude, 1989); University of North Carolina School of Law (J.D., 1992). Phi Eta Sigma; Phi Kappa Phi. Author: Wrongful Death Seminar Manuscript, 1995 and 2005. Speaker, Auto-Torts Law Update, 2001. Chair, Disbursements Seminar, 2004. *Member:* New Hanover County, Fifth Judicial District, North Carolina and American Bar Associations; North Carolina State Bar; North Carolina Academy of Trial Lawyers (Membership Chair, Auto-Torts Section, 2003-2004). ***PRACTICE AREAS:*** Personal Injury; Automobile Accidents and Injuries; Catastrophic Injury; Head Injury; Motorcycle Accidents; Wrongful Death; Chemical Exposure; Toxic Exposure; Medical Negligence; Nursing Home Negligence; Family Law. ***Email:*** rhorne@hallandhorne.com

JOHN FELIX GREEN, II, born Raleigh, North Carolina, December 2, 1965; admitted to bar, 1998, North Carolina. *Education:* North Carolina State University (B.A., 1989); University of Richmond School of Law (J.D., 1997); University of North Carolina School of Law (visiting, 1996-1997). Moot Court Board, Honor Court Justice. *Member:* New Hanover County, Fifth Judicial District, North Carolina and American Bar Associations; North Carolina State Bar; North Carolina Academy of Trial Lawyers. ***PRACTICE AREAS:*** Civil Litigation; Worker's Compensation; Social Security Disability; Construction Litigation; Wrongful Death; Insurance Bad Faith; Business Litigation. ***Email:*** jgreen@hallandhorne.com

WILLIAM R. SHELL, born Lenoir, North Carolina, June 5, 1943; admitted to bar, 1973, North Carolina and U.S. District Court, Eastern District of North Carolina; 1975,

(This Listing Continued)

HALL & HORNE, L.L.P., Wilmington—Continued

U.S. Court of Appeals, Fourth Circuit; 1978, U.S. Supreme Court; 1984, U.S. Tax Court; 1990, U.S. District Court, Middle District of North Carolina; U.S. Court of Federal Claims; U.S. District Court, Western District of North Carolina. *Education:* University of North Carolina at Chapel Hill (A.B., 1965; J.D., 1973). Member: North Carolina Federal Bar Advisory Council, 1988—; South Atlantic Fishery Management Council, 1986-1988. Trustee, Lutheran Services for the Aging, Inc., 1986—. *Member:* New Hanover County and North Carolina Bar Associations; Fifth Judicial District and The North Carolina State Bars; North Carolina Academy of Trial Lawyers; National Association of Criminal Defense Lawyers. [Capt., USAF, 1965-1970]. ***PRACTICE AREAS:*** Civil Litigation; Family Law; Federal Criminal Law. **Email:** bshell@hallandhorne.com

HEDRICK EATMAN GARDNER & KINCHELOE, L.L.P.

Established in 1956

1508 MILITARY CUTOFF ROAD, SUITE 202
WILMINGTON, NORTH CAROLINA 28403
Telephone: 910-509-9664
Fax: 910-509-9630
URL: http://www.hedrickeatman.com

Charlotte, North Carolina Office: 6000 Fairview Road, Suite 1000, 28210. Mailing Address: P.O. Box 30397, 28230. Telephone: 704-366-1101. Fax: 704-366-6181.
Raleigh, North Carolina Office: 4011 Westchase Boulevard, Suite 300, 27607. Telephone: 919-832-9424. Fax: 919-832-9425.
Columbia, South Carolina Office: 1201 Main Street, Suite 1200, 29201. Mailing Address: P.O. Box 11267, 29211. Telephone: 803-727-1200. Fax: 803-727-1259.

General Civil Litigation and Insurance Defense, Legal and Professional Malpractice, Motor Vehicle Negligence, Premises Liability, Product Liability, Construction, Insurance Coverage Disputes, Arson and Fraud, Employment Law, Trucking and Transportation and Worker's Compensation.

FIRM PROFILE: Hedrick Eatman Gardner & Kincheloe, L.L.P. is a full-service litigation defense firm which serves insurance and business clients. Founded in North Carolina in 1956, the firm's four offices allow us to provide cost-effective representation throughout North and South Carolina. Our attorneys have superior litigation and dispute resolution skills. We zealously represent our loyal client base, while maintaining a high degree of ethics and professionalism. Client satisfaction is a priority, which is how we preserve long-term relationships. We strive for continued growth while maintaining our solid reputation before the bench and the Bar, our focus on client service, and qualifty of life for our attorneys and staff.

PARTNERS

ERICA B. LEWIS, admitted to bar, 1995, North Carolina and U.S. District Court, Western and Eastern Districts of North Carolina. *Education:* University of California, Davis (B.A., with honors, 1991); Wake Forest University (J.D., 1995). (Resident). ***PRACTICE AREAS:*** Civil Litigation; Workers Compensation Defense; Insurance Defense; Products Liability Defense; Construction Law; Employment Law. **Email:** elewis@hedrickeatman.com

JEFFREY H. BLACKWELL, admitted to bar, 1986, North Carolina; 1990, U.S. District Court, Eastern, Middle and Western Districts of North Carolina. *Education:* University of North Carolina at Chapel Hill (B.S., with honors, 1981; J.D., 1986). ***PRACTICE AREAS:*** Construction Litigation; Civil Litigation; Motor Vehicle Negligence; Premises Liability; Products Liability; Public Entities; Public Municipal Law. **Email:** jblackwell@hedrickeatman.com

ASSOCIATES

TRACIE H. BRISSON, admitted to bar, 1998, North Carolina. *Education:* University of North Carolina at Chapel Hill (B.A., 1995); Campbell University (J.D., 1998).

WILLIAM B. DULANEY, admitted to bar, 2004, North Carolina. *Education:* Swarthmore College (B.A., 1997); Temple University (J.D., 2003).

MEREDITH T. EVERHART, admitted to bar, 1999, North Carolina. *Education:* North Carolina State University (B.A., 1995); University of North Carolina at Chapel Hill (J.D., 1999).

BENTON L. TOUPS, admitted to bar, 2000, Louisiana; 2002, North Carolina. *Education:* Louisiana State University (B.A., 1997; J.D., 2000). ***PRACTICE AREAS:*** Employment Law.

TOBIAS J. WEYER, admitted to bar, 2005, North Carolina. *Education:* Wake Forest University (B.A., 1996); The Ohio University (M.A., 1997); Catholic University (J.D., 2002).

REPRESENTATIVE CLIENTS: Ace-USA; Food Lion; Great American Insurance Co.; PMA Group; St. Paul Travelers Insurance Co.; Waffle House.
REFERENCE: Bank of America.

(For Complete biographical data on all personnel, see Professional Biographies at Charlotte)

HEDRICK & MORTON, L.L.P.

6317 OLEANDER DRIVE, SUITE C
WILMINGTON, NORTH CAROLINA 28403
Telephone: 910-343-1432
Fax: 910-762-3132
Email: info@Hedricklaw.com
URL: http://www.hedricklaw.com

General Civil Practice. Negligence, Insurance, Insurance Defense, Products Liability, Malpractice, Workers' Compensation, Construction, Employment, Corporation, Admiralty and Maritime Law, Alternative Dispute Resolution, Real Estate Litigation, Mediation and Arbitration. Trials in all Courts.

P. SCOTT HEDRICK, born Charlotte, North Carolina, July 1, 1956; admitted to bar, 1981, North Carolina; 1985, U.S. Supreme Court. *Education:* Wofford College (B.A., 1978); Campbell University (J.D., 1981). Phi Alpha Delta. *Member:* New Hanover County, North Carolina and American Bar Associations; The North Carolina State Bar; North Carolina Association of Defense Attorneys; Defense Research Institute. (Board Certified Specialist in Workers Compensation, North Carolina State Board of Legal Specialization). ***PRACTICE AREAS:*** Workers Compensation; Insurance Defense; Civil Litigation. **Email:** shedrick@hedricklaw.com

B. DANFORTH MORTON, born Brevard, North Carolina, February 25, 1960; admitted to bar, 1985, North Carolina. *Education:* Duke University (B.A., 1982); University of North Carolina (J.D., 1985). *Member:* New Hanover and North Carolina Bar Associations; North Carolina Defense Lawyers Association. ***REPORTED CASES:*** Pyco Supply Co. v. American Centennial Insurance, 85 N.C. App. 114, 354 S.E.2d 360 (1987), reversed 321 N.C. 435, 364 S.E.2d 380 (1988); Bailey v. LeBeau, 79 N.C. App. 345, 339 S.E. 2d 460, reversed, 318 N.C. 411, 348 S.E. 2d 524 (1986); Maring v. Hartford Cas. Ins. Co., 126 N.C. App. 201, 484 S.E.2d 417 (1997). ***PRACTICE AREAS:*** Insurance Defense; Insurance Coverage Defense; Litigation; Employment Law; Construction Law. **Email:** dmorton@hedricklaw.com

G. GRADY RICHARDSON, JR., born Wilmington, North Carolina, January 28, 1972; admitted to bar, 1998, North Carolina. *Education:* University of North Carolina at Wilmington (B.A., cum laude, 1994); Norman A. Wiggins School of Law (J.D., 1998). Phi Alpha Delta. Recipient, NCATL Advocacy Award, 1998. *Member:* North Carolina State Bar. ***PRACTICE AREAS:*** Civil Litigation; Business Transactions; Commercial Transactions; Workers Compensation; Real Property. **Email:** grichardson@hedricklaw.com

ASSOCIATE

STEPHEN E. COBLE, born Burlington, North Carolina, December 20, 1972; admitted to bar, 2004, North Carolina. *Education:* Elon College (B.A., 1995); Appalachian State University (M.P.A., 1997); University of Dayton School of Law (J.D., 2003). *Member:* New Hanover County, North Carolina and American Bar Association; North Carolina State Bar. ***PRACTICE AREAS:*** Civil Litigation; Insurance Defense; Workers Compensation; Real Estate; Real Estate Litigation; Real Estate Contracts; Negligence. **Email:** scoble@hedricklaw.com

REPRESENTATIVE CLIENTS: Allied Claims Administration, Inc.; Allianz Insurance Company; Allstate Insurance Company; Anthem Casualty Insurance Group; Atlanta Casualty Companies; Atlantic Mutual Insurance Companies; Bituminous Insurance Companies; CNA Insurance Companies; Chubb Group of Insurance Companies; City of Wilmington; Commercial Union Insurance Company; Crawford and Company; Crum & Forster Insurance Company; Fireman's Fund Insurance Company; First Financial Insurance Company; Food Lion, Inc.; GAB Robbins North America, Inc.; Gallagher Bassett Services, Inc.; Georgia-Pacific Corporation; Harleysville Insurance Companies; InServices, Inc.; Insura Property and Casualty Insurance Company; J.B. Hunt Transport Services, Inc.; Key Risk Management Services, Inc.; Life Insurance Company of Georgia; Metropolitan Property and Casualty Insurance Company; Met Life Auto; National Comp Administrators; North Carolina League of Municipalities; Ohio Casualty Group; Omni/Hartford; Penn-America Group; Penn National Insurance Companies; PMA Management Corporation; Providence Washington Insurance Company; Risk Enterprise Management Services; Risk Management Services, Inc.; Royal & Sun Alliance Insurance Company; RSKCo Insurance Company; SAFECO Insurance Companies; Shelby/Vesta Insurance Companies; Southern Guarantee Insurance Companies; St. Paul Companies, The; Staff America; Unisun Insurance Company; United Services Automobile Association; United States Liability Insurance Group; Utica National Insurance Group; Wausau Insurance Companies; Wilmington Transit Authority; Windsor Group; Zurich-American Insurance Group.

HELMS MULLISS & WICKER, PLLC

Established in 1922

127 GRACE STREET
P.O. BOX 599 (28402)
WILMINGTON, NORTH CAROLINA 28401
Telephone: 910-254-3800
Fax: 910-254-3900
URL: http://www.hmw.com

Charlotte, North Carolina Office: 201 North Tryon Street, P.O. Box 31247 (28231). Telephone: 704-343-2000. Fax: 704-343-2300. Telex: 572460.
Raleigh, North Carolina Office: 2600 Two Hannover Square, P.O. Box 27507. Telephone: 919-755-6600. Fax: 919-755-6699.

Banking, Finance, Corporate, Government Relations, Business Litigation, Tax, Securities, Real Property and Finance, Labor and Employment (Management) Law, Employee Benefits, International, Technology, Insurance Coverage, Media, Commercial Bankruptcy, Environmental, Public Finance, ERISA, Estate Planning and Administration, Education, Venture Capital, Intellectual Property.

MEMBER OF FIRM

J. DICKSON McLEAN, born Lumberton, North Carolina, April 17, 1963; admitted to bar, 1989, North Carolina; 1992, U.S. District Court, Western District of North Carolina; 1999, U.S. District Court, Eastern District of North Carolina. *Education:* Davidson College (B.A., 1985); University of North Carolina (J.D., 1989; M.B.A., 1989). Senior Staff Mem-

(This Listing Continued)

ber, North Carolina Journal of International Law and Commercial Regulation, 1988-1989. *Member:* New Hanover County, North Carolina (Member: Business Law, Real Property and Tax Sections) and American (Member, Business Law, Real Property, Probate and Trust Law and Taxation Sections) Bar Associations; North Carolina State Bar. (Resident). ***PRACTICE AREAS:*** Corporate; Mergers and Acquisitions; Real Property; Securities; Taxation. ***Email:*** Dickson.Mclean@hmw.com

ASSOCIATES

Mark S. Hartman
Henry L. Kitchin, Jr.

REPRESENTATIVE CLIENTS: Bank of America; Branch Banking and Trust Co.; Digital Optics; Freedom Communications, Inc.; General Electric Co.; General Motors Corp.; Kitty Hawk Capital; Osprey Systems; Royal & SunAlliance; The Coca-Cola Co.; Unifi, Inc.

(For complete biographical data on all personnel, see Professional Biographies at Charlotte and Raleigh, North Carolina)

HEWLETT, COLLINS AND ALLARD

515 PRINCESS STREET
P.O. BOX 121
WILMINGTON, NORTH CAROLINA 28402
Telephone: 910-763-0156
Fax: 910-763-9998

Trials in all Federal & State Courts, Criminal Defense, Trials, Traffic Law, DWI Defense, Sexual Assaults, Drug Offenses, Misdemeanors, Felonies, Federal Criminal Law, White Collar Crime.

MEMBERS OF FIRM

ADDISON HEWLETT, JR. (1912-1989)

JOHN C. COLLINS, born New York, N.Y., September 18, 1950; admitted to bar, 1976 North Carolina and U.S. District Court, Eastern District of North Carolina. *Education:* Duke University (B.A., 1972); Wake Forest University (J.D., 1976). Instructor: Business Law, Cape Fear Community College, 1980-1982; Traffic Offenses and Misdemeanors, Practical Skills Course, North Carolina Bar Association, 1981-1990 and 2000—. Assistant District Attorney, Fifth Judicial District, 1979-1982. *Member:* New Hanover County (President, 1989-1990) and North Carolina (Member, Practical Training Committee, 1984-1990) Bar Associations; Fifth Judicial District (President, 1987-1989; Chairman, Grievance Committee, 1990-1992) and North Carolina State Bars; North Carolina Academy of Trial Lawyers. ***PRACTICE AREAS:*** Criminal Law; Traffic Law; DWI Defense; Felonies; Misdemeanors.

JAMES L. ALLARD, JR., born Wilmington, North Carolina, June 25, 1960; admitted to bar, 1986, North Carolina. *Education:* University of North Carolina at Wilmington (B.A., 1982); Campbell University (J.D., 1985). Delta Theta Phi; Order of Barristers. Lecturer: Traffic Offenses, Practical Skills Course, North Carolina Bar Association, 1991-1999. *Member:* Fifth Judicial District (Member, Grievance Committee, 1990-1992) and North Carolina State Bars; North Carolina Academy of Trial Lawyers; The Association of Trial Lawyers of America. ***PRACTICE AREAS:*** Criminal Law; Traffic Law; DWI Defense; Felonies; Misdemeanors.

REFERENCES: Centura Bank; North Carolina Troopers Assn. Inc.; North Carolina Police Benevolent Assn. Inc., Fraternal Order of Police.

THOMAS S. HICKS, PLLC

Established in 1997

419 GRACE STREET
WILMINGTON, NORTH CAROLINA 28401
Telephone: 910-762-1202
Fax: 910-762-1108
Email: thomas.hicks@wilmingtonlaws.com
URL: http://www.wilmingtonlaws.com

Family Law, Divorce, Child Custody and Support, Domestic Violence, Pre and Postmarital Agreements, Spousal Support, Personal Injury, Auto Accidents, Wrongful Death, Slip and Fall, DWI, Criminal Law, Drug Crimes, Homicide, Misdemeanors, Felonies, Juvenile Law, Sexual Assault, Sexual Abuse, Parole and Probation, Traffic Violations, Divorce.

FIRM PROFILE: Thomas S. Hicks, PLLC was founded in 1997 by Thomas S. Hicks after having spent 17 years as a government attorney. The firm specializes in general trial practice with an emphasis on criminal defense, family law, and civil litigation as well as appellate practice.

THOMAS S. HICKS, born Philadelphia, Pennsylvania, May 16, 1952; admitted to bar, 1980, North Carolina; 1996, U.S. District Court, Eastern District of North Carolina and U.S. Supreme Court; 1997, U.S. Court of Appeals, Fourth Circuit; 2001, U.S. District Court, Western District of North Carolina. *Education:* University of North Carolina-Chapel Hill (B.A., 1973); Wake Forest University (J.D., 1980). Assistant Attorney General, 1993-1997. Assistant District Attorney, 1980-1993. *Member:* New Hanover County and North Carolina Bar Associations; North Carolina State Bar. ***REPORTED CASES:*** Skipper v. French, 130 F.3d 603 (4th Cir. 1997); State v. Ball, 344 N.C. 290, 474 S.E. 2d 345 (1996) cert. denied, 520 U.S. 1180, 137 L. Ed.2d 561 (1997); State v. Best, 342 N.C. 502, 467 S.E.2d 45, cert. denied, 519 U.S. 878, 136 L. Ed. 2d 139 (1996); State v. Billings, 348 N.C. 169, 500 S.E. 2d 423 (1998); State v. Billups, 151 N.C. App. 749, 567 S.E. 2d 467 (2002); State v. Brown, 335 N.C. 477, 439 S.E. 2d 589 (1994); State v. Clapp, 135 N.C. App. 52, 519 S.E. 2d 90 (1999); State v. Cummings, 346 N.C. 291, 488 S.E. 2d 550 (1997), cert. denied, 522 U.S. 1092, 139 L. Ed. 2d 873 (1998); State v. Gahren, 116 N.C. App. 361, 448 S.E. 2d 150, disc. rev. denied, 338 N.C. 312, 452 S.E. 2d 313 (1994); State v. Galloway, 145 N.C. App. 555, 551 S.E. 2d 525 (2001); State v. Gregory, 342 N.C. 580, 467 S.E. 2d 28 (1996); State v. McDougald, 336 N.C. 451, 444 S.E. 2d 211 (1994); State v. Sidden, 347 N.C. 218, 491 S.E. 2d 225 (1997), cert. denied, 523 U.S. 1097, 140 L. Ed. 2d 797 (1998); State v. Swindler, 339 N.C. 469, 450 S.E. 2d 907 (1994); State v. Vick, 341 N.C. 569, 461 S.E. 2d 655 (1995); U.S. v. Bowe, 257 F.3d 336 (4th Cir. 2001); U.S. v. Bowe, 309 F.3d 234, 60 Fed. R. Evid. Serv. 512 (4th Cir. 2002). ***PRACTICE AREAS:*** Criminal Law; Criminal Appeals; Family Law; Divorce; Personal Injury. ***Email:*** thomas.hicks@wilmingtonlaws.com

WILLIAM F. HILL, P.A.

WILMINGTON, NORTH CAROLINA

(See Greenville)

Creditor's Rights, Collections, Small Business, Buying or Selling a Business, Employment Contracts, General Business, Contracts, Starting a Business, Corporate Law, Family Law, Divorce.

HOGUE, HILL, JONES, NASH & LYNCH, L.L.P.

Established in 1913

101 S. THIRD STREET
P.O. DRAWER 2178
WILMINGTON, NORTH CAROLINA 28402
Telephone: 910-763-4565
Telecopier: 910-762-6687
Email: hhjnlllp@hoguehill.com

General Practice. Trials in all State and Federal Courts. Insurance, Corporations, Taxation, Probate, Real Estate, Personal Injury, Admiralty and Environmental Law, Education Law, Family Law.

FIRM PROFILE: Hogue, Hill, Jones, Nash & Lynch, L.L.P. was founded in 1913 by Cyrus D. Hogue, the father of Cyrus D. Hogue, Jr. The firm is a full-service law firm which provides a wide range of legal services. The firm requires continuing professional development for attorneys and staff, and encourages all partners and associates to participate in community and professional activities.

MEMBERS OF FIRM

CYRUS D. HOGUE (1888-1960)

WILLIAM L. HILL, II (1931-2001)

W. TALMAGE JONES, born Kinston, North Carolina, January 14, 1940; admitted to bar, 1966, North Carolina; 1967, U.S. District Court, Eastern District of North Carolina; 1970, U.S. Tax Court. *Education:* University of North Carolina at Chapel Hill (B.A., 1964; LL.B., 1966); Boston University (LL.M., 1967). *Member:* New Hanover County Bar Association; The North Carolina State Bar. ***PRACTICE AREAS:*** Commercial Real Estate; Residential Real Estate; Business Law; Corporate Law; Estate Planning. ***Email:*** wtaljo@hoguehill.com

DAVID A. NASH, born Charlotte, North Carolina, August 22, 1945; admitted to bar, 1970, North Carolina; 1971, U.S. District Court, Middle District of North Carolina; 1972, U.S. District Court, Eastern District of North Carolina; 1973, U.S. Court of Appeals, 4th Circuit; 1974, U.S. Supreme Court; 1990, U.S. Court of Federal Claims; 1998, U.S. District Court, Western District of North Carolina. *Education:* University of North Carolina at Chapel Hill (A.B., 1967; J.D., 1970). Law Clerk to U.S. District Judge, Edwin M. Stanley, Middle District of North Carolina, 1970-1971. *Member:* New Hanover County and North Carolina Bar Associations; The North Carolina State Bar; North Carolina Association of Defense Attorneys; Defense Research Institute; Southeastern Admiralty Law Institute. ***PRACTICE AREAS:*** Litigation; Commercial Law; Insurance; Banks and Banking; Torts; Personal Injury. ***Email:*** dnash@hoguehill.com

WILLIAM O. J. LYNCH, born Raleigh, North Carolina, December 26, 1945; admitted to bar, 1972, North Carolina and U.S. District Court, Eastern District of North Carolina. *Education:* Wilmington College (B.A., 1968); Wake Forest University (J.D., 1972). *Member:* New Hanover County and North Carolina Bar Associations; The North Carolina State Bar. [With U.S. Army Reserves, 1968-1974]. ***PRACTICE AREAS:*** Business Law; Commercial Real Estate; Real Estate; Municipal Law; Eminent Domain; Trusts and Estates. ***Email:*** wojl@hoguehill.com

JAMES B. SNOW III, born Baltimore, Maryland, December 27, 1956; admitted to bar, 1982, North Carolina; 1984, Virgin Islands and U.S. District Court, Eastern District of North Carolina. *Education:* University of Pennsylvania (B.A., 1979); University of North Carolina at Chapel Hill (J.D., 1982). Member: Board of Trustees, The Historic Wilmington Foundation, Inc., 1991—; Secretary, 1995-1998 and 2003—; Executive Committee, 1991-2000 and 2003—. Member, Board of Directors, Legal Services of the Lower Cape Fear, Inc., 1992-1998; Treasurer, 1995-1996; President, 1996-1997. *Member:* New Hanover County (Member, Executive Committee, 1990-1994) and North Carolina (Member: Business Law Section Council, 2004—; Business Law and Real Property Law Sections) Bar Associations; The North Carolina State Bar (Fifth Judicial District, Secretary-Treasurer, 1989-1990, Chairman, Fifth Judicial District Young Lawyers Division, 1990-1992). ***PRACTICE AREAS:*** Business Law; Commercial Law; Real Estate. ***Email:*** jsnow@hoguehill.com

WAYNE A. BULLARD, born Wilmington, North Carolina, July 20, 1961; admitted to bar, 1987, Tennessee and U.S. District Court, Middle District of Tennessee; 1990, North Carolina and U.S. District Court, Eastern District of North Carolina; 1994, U.S. Court of Federal Claims; 2002, U.S. Court of Appeals, Fourth Circuit. *Education:* University of North Carolina at Chapel Hill (B.S., 1983; J.D., 1986). Beta Gamma Sigma; Phi Delta Phi. Member, Holderness Moot Court Bench. *Member:* New Hanover County and North Carolina (Member, Sections on: Litigation; Construction Law; Education Law) Bar Associations; North Carolina State Bar; North Carolina Association of Defense Attorneys; North Carolina Council of School Attorneys. ***PRACTICE AREAS:*** Civil Litigation; Construction Litigation; Bankruptcy Litigation; Admiralty and Maritime Law; Public School Law; Labor and Employment. ***Email:*** wbullard@hoguehill.com

(This Listing Continued)

HOGUE, HILL, JONES, NASH & LYNCH, L.L.P., Wilmington—Continued

G. EDWARD COLEMAN, III, born Memphis, Tennessee, January 26, 1969; admitted to bar, 1994, Tennessee and U.S. District Court, Western District of Tennessee; 1998, U.S. Court of Appeals, Sixth Circuit; 2001, North Carolina, U.S. District Court, Eastern District of North Carolina and U.S. Court of Federal Claims. *Education:* University of Memphis (B.A., 1991; J.D., 1994). *Member:* New Hanover County and North Carolina State Bar Associations. ***PRACTICE AREAS:*** Insurance Defense; Civil Litigation; Commercial Law; Products Liability; Construction Law. ***Email:*** ecoleman@hoguehill.com

OF COUNSEL

CYRUS D. HOGUE, JR., born Wilmington, North Carolina, October 4, 1921; admitted to bar, 1947, North Carolina and U.S. District Court, Eastern District of North Carolina; 1955, U.S. Tax Court; 1958, U.S. Court of Appeals, 4th Circuit; 1964, U.S. Supreme Court. *Education:* University of North Carolina (B.S., 1942; LL.B., 1947). Phi Beta Kappa. Associate Editor, University of North Carolina Law Review, 1947. *Member:* New Hanover County Bar Association; The North Carolina State Bar. Fellow, American College of Trial Lawyers. ***Email:*** hdcj@earthlink.net

REPRESENTATIVE CLIENTS: Wilmington Shipping Co.; Cooperative Bank for Savings; Grandfather Mountain, Inc.; Trustees of Champion McDowell Davis Charitable Foundation; Cos.; Wachovia Bank; New Hanover County Board of Education; Becker Builders Supply Co.; Kaiser Aluminum & Chemical Corp.; Lower Cape Fear Water & Sewer Authority; CNA Insurance Co.; Pender County Board of Education; Clancy and Theys Construction Co.; Independence Mall Associates; International Paper Co.; International Paper Realty Co.; Plantation Village, Inc.; Miller-Mott Business College; The Oleander Co.; Canal Insurance Co.; Concepts Unlimited, Inc.; Martin Marietta Aggregates; Cape Fear Memorial Foundation; Cigna Insurance Co.; Eastwood Developers, Inc.; Eastland Developers, Inc.; Bank of America, N.A.; Biltmark Corp.; Bradley Barnes Const. Co.; Centex Home Equity Corp.; Child Advocacy Comm. of the Lower Cape Fear, Inc.; Empire Fire and Marine Ins. Co.; Fireman's Fund Ins. Co.; Lancer Claims Service; N.C. School Boards Trust; North Brunswick Sanitary District; Stevens Bldg. Co.; TFT & Co., Inc.; Nautilus Ins. Co.
APPROVED ATTORNEYS FOR: Lawyers Title Insurance Corp.; Title Guarantee Co.; Commonwealth Land Title Insurance Co.; Investors Title Insurance Co.; The Title Company of North Carolina, Inc.; First Title Insurance Co.; Statewide Title Insurance Company.
REFERENCES: RBC Centura Bank; Wachovia Bank.

THE LAW FIRM OF HUTCHENS, SENTER & BRITTON, P.A.

SUITE 210
1437 MILITARY CUTOFF ROAD
WILMINGTON, NORTH CAROLINA 28403
Telephone: 910-509-7480
Facsimile: 910-509-7448
Email: lawfirm@hutchensandsenter.com
URL: http://www.hutchensandsenter.com

Mailing Address: P.O. Box 12969, Wilmington, NC 28405

Fayetteville, North Carolina Office: 4317 Ramsey Street, P.O. Box 2505. Telephone: 910-864-6888. Fax: 910-864-6848.
Raleigh, North Carolina Office: Suite 1540, Two Hanover Square. Telephone: 919-834-2688. Fax: 919-834-3373.

General Civil Practice, Trials in all State and Federal Courts, Creditor Bankruptcy, Foreclosures and Collection, Personal Injury, Wrongful Death, Worker's Compensation, Insurance Law, Corporation, Business and Real Estate.

ASSOCIATES

ERIK T. BENNINGTON, born Wheeling, West Virginia, January 2, 1978; admitted to bar, 2003, North Carolina and U.S. District Court, Eastern and Western Districts of North Carolina. *Education:* Campbell University (B.B.A., 2000); Wake Forest University (J.D., 2003). *Member:* North Carolina Bar Association (Real Property and Young Lawyers Sections); New Hanover County Bar Association. (Also at Fayetteville, North Carolina Office). ***PRACTICE AREAS:*** Civil Litigation; Foreclosures; Real Estate. ***Email:*** erik.bennington@hutchensandsenter.com

STEPHEN BAILEY, born Eden, North Carolina, February 4, 1975; admitted to bar, 2003, North Carolina. *Education:* Appalachian State University (B.S., 1997); Mercer University (J.D., 2003). *Member:* Hanover County and North Carolina Bar Associations. (Also at Fayetteville, North Carolina Office). ***PRACTICE AREAS:*** Real Estate.

REPRESENTATIVE CLIENTS: Available Upon Request.

(For complete biographical data on all personnel, see Professional Biographies at Fayetteville, North Carolina)

JACKSON & ASSOCIATES

615 PRINCESS STREET
P.O. BOX 1407
WILMINGTON, NORTH CAROLINA 28402-1407
Telephone: 910-763-1041
Facsimile: 910-763-9375
URL: http://www.jacksonandassociates.com
URL: http://www.attorneysyoucancounton.com

Personal Injury, Wrongful Death, Automobile Accidents and Injuries, Medical Malpractice, Worker's Compensation, Criminal Law, Driving While Intoxicated, Misdemeanors, Felonies, Traffic Violations.

BRUCE H. JACKSON, JR., born Spiveys Corner, North Carolina, January 17, 1947; admitted to bar, 1979, North Carolina. *Education:* University of North Carolina (B.A., 1976); Campbell University (J.D., 1979). *Member:* New Hanover County and North Carolina Bar Associations; The North Carolina State Bar; North Carolina Academy of Trial

(This Listing Continued)

Lawyers. ***PRACTICE AREAS:*** Personal Injury Law; Wrongful Death; Automobile Accidents and Injuries; Medical Malpractice; Worker's Compensation; Criminal Law; Driving While Intoxicated; Misdemeanors; Felonies; Traffic Violations.

JOHNSON, LAMBETH & BROWN

Established in 1984
232 PRINCESS STREET
P.O. BOX 660
WILMINGTON, NORTH CAROLINA 28402
Telephone: 910-763-0481
Fax: 910-251-1276

Civil and Criminal Trials in all Courts. Insurance, Municipal Corporations, Estates, Family Law, Corporate Law, General Practice, Admiralty and Appellate Practice.

MEMBERS OF FIRM

ROBERT WHITE JOHNSON, born Raleigh, North Carolina, March 18, 1940; admitted to bar, 1966, North Carolina; 1970, U.S. District Court, Eastern District of North Carolina; 1973, U.S. District Court, Middle District of North Carolina; 1978, U.S. Court of Appeals, Fourth Circuit; 1991, U.S. Supreme Court. *Education:* University of Georgia (B.B.A., 1963); University of North Carolina (J.D., 1966). Phi Delta Phi. U.S. Magistrate, Eastern District of North Carolina, 1970-1972. Bar Councilor, Fifth Judicial District (1999—). *Member:* North Carolina Bar Association (Member, Litigation Section); North Carolina Association of Defense Attorneys; Defense Research and Trial Lawyers Association. ***PRACTICE AREAS:*** Insurance Law; Admiralty; Personal Injury Law; Commercial Litigation; Aviation Law. ***Email:*** rwj@johnsonandlambeth.com

CARTER TATE LAMBETH, born Durham, North Carolina, June 3, 1946; admitted to bar, 1971, North Carolina, U.S. District Court, Eastern, Middle and Western District of North Carolina and U.S. Court of Appeals, Fourth Circuit; 1978, U.S. Supreme Court. *Education:* University of the South (B.A., 1968); University of North Carolina (J.D., 1971). Omicrom Delta Kappa; Blue Key; Phi Delta Phi. City Attorney for Southport, 1973-1979. Brunswick County Social Services Attorney, 1974-1979. District Court Judge, Fifth Judicial District, North Carolina, 1979-1983. Town Attorney, Town of Carolina Beach, 1987-1994. Contract Attorney, Child Support Services for Hanover County DSS, 1988—. Certified Superior Court Mediator, 1996—. Certified Arbitrator, 1993—. Certified Family Law Mediator, 1999—. *Member:* New Hanover County, North Carolina and American Bar Associations; Fifth Judicial District and North Carolina State Bars; North Carolina Academy of Trial Lawyers. ***PRACTICE AREAS:*** Family Law; Criminal Law; Civil Litigation. ***Email:*** ctl@johnsonandlambeth.com

MAYNARD M. BROWN, born Saskatoon, Saskatchewan, Canada, March 2, 1957; admitted to bar, 1987, North Carolina and U.S. District, Eastern District of North Carolina; 1991, U.S. Supreme Court. *Education:* University of North Carolina (B.A., 1979); Wake Forest University (J.D., 1987). Delta Theta Phi. *Member:* North Carolina State Bar; North Carolina Association of Defense Attorneys. ***PRACTICE AREAS:*** Insurance; Civil Litigation; Personal Injury; Appellate Practice. ***Email:*** mbrown@johnsonandlambeth.com

ASSOCIATES

ANNA JOHNSON AVERITT, born Wilmington, North Carolina, October 13, 1972; admitted to bar, 2000, North Carolina; 2001, U.S. District Court, Eastern District of North Carolina. *Education:* Rhodes College (B.A., 1994); Campbell University (J.D., 2000). Order of the Barrister. Omicron Delta Kappa. Law Clerk, Hon. Sidney S. Eagles, Jr., Chief Judge, North Carolina Court of Appeals, 2000-2001. ***PRACTICE AREAS:*** Business Litigation; Insurance Defense; Construction Law; Personal Injury; Appellate Practice. ***Email:*** aja@johnsonandlambeth.com

MELISSA E. JOHNSON, born Raleigh, North Carolina, August 1, 1979; admitted to bar, 2004, North Carolina. *Education:* University of North Carolina at Wilmington (B.A., 2001); Campbell University (J.D., 2004). *Member:* North Carolina State Bar. ***PRACTICE AREAS:*** Civil Litigation; Insurance Defense. ***Email:*** melissa@johnsonandlambeth.com

REPRESENTATIVE CLIENTS: Cape Fear Bonded Warehouse, Inc.; St. Paul Travelers Insurance Co.; Burton Steel Co.; Nationwide; Self Insured Claims Service; Utica Mutual Insurance Co.; State Farm Insurance Co.; Hertz; Orion Auto, Seibels Bruce Cos.; Waste Industries, Inc.; GMAC Insurance Companies; Royal & Sunalliance DPIC; Lawyer's Mutual Insurance Company.
REFERENCES: B.B. & T.; Bank of America.

JOHNSON & MOORE, P.A.

WILMINGTON, NORTH CAROLINA

(See Southport)

Real Estate, Corporate Law, Estate Planning, Civil Litigation, Business Law, Commercial Litigation, Construction Law.

GREG JONES & ASSOCIATES, P.A.

3015 MARKET STREET
WILMINGTON, NORTH CAROLINA 28403
Telephone: 910-251-2240
Fax: 910-251-1520
URL: http://www.gregjoneslaw.com
Email: greg@gregjoneslaw.com
URL: http://www.lawyers.com/gregoryjones&associates

Personal Injury, Automobile Accidents, Brain Injury, Motorcycle Accidents, Wrongful Death, Medical Malpractice, Spinal Cord Injuries, Drug and Medical Device Litigation, Pharmacists Liability, Head Injuries, Products Liability, Medical and Nursing Home Negligence, Workers Compensation, Toxic Torts, Nursing Home Abuse, Stock Fraud.

(This Listing Continued)

GREGORY LAWING JONES, born Charlotte, North Carolina, August 27, 1960; admitted to bar, 1985, North Carolina and U.S. District Court, Eastern District of North Carolina; 2000, U.S. District Court, Middle District of North Carolina; 2001, South Carolina and U.S. District Court, District of South Carolina; 2002, Georgia. *Education:* Wingate College (A.A., 1980; B.A., cum laude, 1982); University of North Carolina at Chapel Hill (J.D., 1985). Alpha Chi; Alpha Mu Gamma; Phi Delta Phi (Lifetime Member). Listed in Who's Who in American Law, 1992-1993. Member, National Registry of Who's Who, 1997. *Member:* North Carolina and American Bar Associations; North Carolina State Bar; North Carolina Academy of Trial Lawyers (Benefactor; Member, Sections on: Products Liability; Auto Torts; Workers Compensation); The Association of Trial Lawyers of America (Sustaining Member, Leaders Forum, Lawyer Marketing Committee); Southern Trial Lawyers Association; South Carolina Trial Lawyers Association; Roscoe Pound Foundation; Trial Lawyers for Public Justice. **PRACTICE AREAS:** Personal Injury; Automobile Accidents; Brain Injury; Motorcycle Accidents; Wrongful Death; Medical Malpractice; Spinal Injury; Drug and Medical Device Litigation; Pharmacists Liability; Head Injury; Products Liability; Medical Negligence; Nursing Home Negligence; Workers Compensation. **Email:** greg@gregjoneslaw.com

---

RUSSELL D. NUGENT, born Sayre, Pennsylvania, September, 3 1976; admitted to bar, 2004, North Carolina. *Education:* University of North Carolina (B.A.,B.S., 1998); Georgetown University (J.D., 2004). *Member:* North Carolina State Bar; North Carolina Academy of Trial Lawyers. **PRACTICE AREAS:** Personal Injury. **Email:** russell@gregjoneslaw.com

MARLO L. THAGGARD, born 1980; admitted to bar, 2005, North Carolina. *Education:* Campbell University (B.A., summa cum laude, 2002); Campbell University (J.D., 2005).

OF COUNSEL

FRANKLIN D. POPE, admitted to bar, 1988, North Carolina. *Education:* University of North Carolina at Wilmington (B.A., 1985); University of North Carolina at Chapel Hill (J.D., 1988). *Member:* North Carolina and American Bar Associations; North Carolina Academy of Trial Lawyers (Education Committee, 2002-2003; Secretary, Auto Tort Section, 1999-2000; featured speaker at seminars); The Association of Trial Lawyers of America. (Also practicing individually, Jacksonville, North Carolina). **PRACTICE AREAS:** Personal Injury; Automobile Accidents and Injuries; Wrongful Death; Medical Malpractice; Workers Compensation.

VAIDEN P. KENDRICK

310 NORTH FRONT STREET, SUITE 250
WILMINGTON, NORTH CAROLINA 28401
Telephone: 910-343-9742
Fax: 910-343-9744
Email: vpklaw@bellsouth.net

Civil Litigation, Insurance Defense, Construction Litigation, Commercial Litigation, Legal Malpractice Defense, Appellate Practice.

VAIDEN P. KENDRICK, born Orlando, Florida, September 20, 1944; admitted to bar, 1969, North Carolina; 1975, U.S. District Court, Eastern District of North Carolina; 1976, U.S. Court of Appeals, Fourth Circuit. *Education:* The Citadel (B.A., 1966); University of North Carolina at Chapel Hill (J.D., 1969). Research Assistant, North Carolina Court of Appeals, 1971-1972. Certified Superior Court Mediator. *Member:* New Hanover County, North Carolina and American Bar Associations; Fifth Judicial District and North Carolina State Bars; North Carolina Association of Defense Attorneys. [Capt., U.S. Army, 1969-1971]. **PRACTICE AREAS:** Civil Litigation; Construction Litigation; Commercial Litigation; Insurance Defense; Legal Malpractice Defense; Appellate Practice.

LAW OFFICES OF THOMAS J. LAMB, P.A.

1908 EASTWOOD ROAD, SUITE 225
WILMINGTON, NORTH CAROLINA 28403
Telephone: 910-256-2971
Facsimile: 910-256-2972
Email: Info@LambLawOffice.com
URL: http://www.LambLawOffice.com

Drug and Medical Device Litigation, Toxic Torts, Asbestos Litigation, Chemical Exposure, Occupational Cancer, Workers Compensation, Products Liability, Welding Products Liability, Medical Malpractice, Hospital Negligence, Pharmacists Liability, Personal Injury and Wrongful Death.

THOMAS J. LAMB, born Washington, D.C., March 29, 1961; admitted to bar, 1988, California; 1990, District of Columbia; 1992, North Carolina. *Education:* College of William & Mary (B.A., 1983); George Washington University (J.D., 1988). *Member:* North Carolina Academy of Trial Lawyers; Association of Trial Lawyers of America. **PRACTICE AREAS:** Personal Injury; Products Liability; Toxic Torts; Medical Malpractice; Workers Compensation. **Email:** TJL@LambLawOffice.com

LEA, RHINE, ROSBRUGH & CHLEBOROWICZ, P.L.L.C.

314 WALNUT STREET, SUITE 1000 AND 2000
NEW HANOVER COUNTY
WILMINGTON, NORTH CAROLINA 28401
Telephone: 910-772-9960
Fax: 910-772-9062
Email: lrattorneys@lrlawfirm.com

General Trial Practice in all Federal and State Courts. Personal Injury including Wrongful Death, Construction Law, Stucco Litigation, Mold Litigation, Civil Litigation and Family Law. Complex Commercial Litigation including Class Actions, Securities Arbitrations.

JAMES W. LEA, III, born Atlanta, Georgia, November 3, 1954; admitted to bar, 1980, North Carolina; 1981, U.S. District Court, Eastern District of North Carolina and U.S. Court of Appeals, Fourth Circuit. *Education:* University of North Carolina at Chapel Hill (B.A., 1976); Campbell University (J.D., 1980). *Member:* New Hanover County (Secretary-Treasurer, 1987; President Elect, 1991; President, 1992) and North Carolina (Member, Family Law Council) Bar Associations; North Carolina State Bar (Member, Family Law Council); North Carolina Academy of Trial Lawyers (Member, Political Action Committee, 1987-1988); National Academy of Trial Lawyers. **PRACTICE AREAS:** Family Law; Divorce; Equitable Distribution; Civil Litigation; Marital Agreements. **Email:** jwl@lrlawfirm.com

JOEL R. RHINE, born New York, New York, November 13, 1962; admitted to bar, 1988, North Carolina. *Education:* University of Tampa (B.A., cum laude, 1985); Wake Forest University (J.D., 1988). Staff Member, Wake Forest University Law Review, 1986-1988. Recipient, Wake Forest Law Review Award, 1988. Author: Note, "Employment Discrimination - The Fourth Circuit Court of Appeals Finds Title VII Not to be the Exclusive Remedy Available to State and Local Government Employees, - *Keller v. Prince George's County Department of Social Services,*" 23 Wake Forest Law Review 343, 1988; Note, "Domestic Relations - The North Carolina Supreme Court Revokes the Marital Presumption and Adopts the Analytic Approach to the Classification of Personal Injury Settlements - *Johnson and Johnson,*" 22 Wake Forest Law Review 931, 1987. Contributor, Douglas' Forms, Civil Litigation, 4th ed., 1989. Former Town Attorney, Carolina Beach. Member, Wake Forest Law Alumni Council. *Member:* New Hanover County (President, 1997-1998; Vice President, 1996-1997; Secretary-Treasurer, 1995-1996), North Carolina (Member, Sections on: Litigation; Construction Law (Executive Board); and American (Member, Sections on: Litigation; Tort; Insurance; Construction) Bar Associations; North Carolina State Bar; North Carolina Academy of Trial Attorneys. **PRACTICE AREAS:** Civil Litigation; Construction Law; Mold Litigation; Wrongful Death; Personal Injury; Product Liability; Class Actions; Arbitration; Securities Arbitration; Drug and Medical Device Litigation. **Email:** jrr@lrlawfirm.com

LORI WIGGINS ROSBRUGH, born Florence, South Carolina, November 5, 1965; admitted to bar, 1996, Florida; 1998, North Carolina and U.S. District Court, Eastern District of North Carolina. *Education:* University of South Carolina (B.A., 1989); University of Florida College of Law (J.D., 1996). *Member:* North Carolina and American Bar Associations; North Carolina State Bar; The Florida Bar; North Carolina Academy of Trial Lawyers. **PRACTICE AREAS:** Civil Litigation; Family Law; Divorce; Premarital Agreements; Separation Agreements; Marital Property Distribution. **Email:** lwr@lrlawfirm.com

CHRISTOPHER A. CHLEBOROWICZ, born Bayshore, New York, December 16, 1971; admitted to bar, 1998, North Carolina and U.S. District Court, Eastern District of North Carolina; 2003, South Carolina. *Education:* Wake Forest University (B.S./B.A., magna cum laude, 1994; J.D., 1998); Albert Lüdwigs University Germany (1994-1995). Golden Key; German Honor Society; International Law Society; Tri Beta Biology Society; Political Science Honor Society; International Law Society; PAD Law Society. Carswell Scholar. Rotary Ambassador Scholar, 1994-1995. *Member:* North Carolina, South Carolina State and American Bar Associations; North Carolina State Bar; North Carolina Academy of Trial Lawyers. **LANGUAGES:** German. **PRACTICE AREAS:** Civil Litigation (20%); Construction Litigation (20%); Personal Injury (15%); Medical Malpractice; Insurance Litigation (10%); Contract Litigation (5%); Automobile Negligence (10%); Drug and Medical Device Litigation; Construction Defects (20%). **Email:** cac@lrlawfirm.com

ASSOCIATE

CARRIE A. ORLIKOWSKI, born High Point, North Carolina, August 19, 1978; admitted to bar, 2003, North Carolina, U.S. District Court, Eastern District of North Carolina and U.S. District Court, Western District of North Carolina. *Education:* Duke University (B.A., cum laude, 2000); University of North Carolina at Chapel Hill (J.D., 2003). *Member:* New Hanover County and North Carolina Bar Associations. **PRACTICE AREAS:** Civil Litigation; Construction Law; Wrongful Death; Personal Injury; Securities Arbitration; Securities Fraud. **Email:** cao@lrlawfirm.com

---

MACCORD MASON PLLC

Established in 1987
1209 CULBRETH DRIVE, SUITE 103
WILMINGTON, NORTH CAROLINA 28405
Telephone: 910-256-3557
Fax: 910-256-0523
Email: wmason@mmpatent.com
URL: http://www.maccordmason.com

Greensboro, North Carolina Office: 300 North Greene Street, Suite 1600, P.O. Box 2974. Telephone: 336-273-4422. Fax: 336-271-2830.
Raleigh, North Carolina Office: 510 Glenwood Avenue, Suite 321, 27611. Telephone: 919-664-8624. Fax: 919-664-8625.

(This Listing Continued)

MACCORD MASON PLLC, Wilmington—Continued

Patent, Trademark, Copyright and Unfair Competition. Trade Secret Practice before all Courts. Intellectual Property Law, Litigation.

(For complete biographical data on all personnel, see Professional Biographies at Greensboro, North Carolina)

MAKO & ASSOCIATES, P.A.

3208 OLEANDER DRIVE
WILMINGTON, NORTH CAROLINA 28403
Telephone: 910-343-9920
Fax: 910-343-9921
Email: smako@makoandasociates.com
URL: http://www.makoandrobinson.net

Personal Injury, Automobile Accidents, Wrongful Death, Trucking Accidents, Head Trauma, Spinal Cord Injuries, Motorcycle Accidents, Workers Compensation, Mediation and Arbitration, Birth Trauma, Medical Malpractice, Construction Accidents, Nursing Home Negligence, Nursing Home Abuse and Neglect and Dog Bites.

MEMBERS OF FIRM

SUE ELAINE MAKO, born Findlay, Ohio, October 26, 1944; admitted to bar, 1973, Ohio; 1976, Michigan; 1988, North Carolina. *Education:* Bowling Green University (B.S.Ed., 1966); University of Toledo (J.D., 1973). Instructor, University of North Carolina at Wilmington, 1989-1992. Listed in Who's Who American Law, 1985-1986. Deputy Director, Ohio Supreme Court, 1983-1986. Certified Mediator. *Member:* North Carolina State Bar; North Carolina Academy of Trial Lawyers; The Association of Trial Lawyers of America. ***PRACTICE AREAS:*** Personal Injury; Automobile Accidents and Injuries; Wrongful Death; Truck Accidents; Head Injury; Spinal Injury; Motorcycle Accidents; Bicycle Accidents; Birth Trauma; Workers Compensation; Mediation; Arbitration; Construction Accidents; Nursing Home Negligence; Nursing Home Abuse and Neglect; Medical Malpractice. ***Email:*** smako@makoandassociates.com

RICHARD SCOTT GIRDWOOD, born Fayetteville, North Carolina, 1978; admitted to bar, 2004, North Carolina. *Education:* North Carolina State University (B.A., magna cum laude, 2001); Campbell University (J.D., 2004). ***LANGUAGES:*** Spanish. ***PRACTICE AREAS:*** Personal Injury; Automobile Accidents and Injuries; Truck Accidents; Construction Accidents; Boating Accidents; Wrongful Death; Medical Malpractice; Criminal Law; DWI; DUI; Traffic Violations. ***Email:*** sgirwood@makoandassociates.com

MARSHALL, WILLIAMS & GORHAM, L.L.P.

Established in 1963
14 SOUTH FIFTH STREET
P.O. DRAWER 2088
WILMINGTON, NORTH CAROLINA 28402-2088
Telephone: 910-763-9891
Telecopier: 910-343-8604
Email: attorneys@mwglaw.com
URL: http://www.mwglaw.com

Civil Practice. Trials in all State and Federal Courts. Civil Litigation, Arbitration, Construction Law, Professional Liability, Insurance Defense, Personal Injury, Insurance, Banking Law, Business Law, Mergers and Acquisitions, Corporate Law, Commercial Law, Contracts, Collections, Debtor and Creditor, Health Care, Hospital Law, Estate Planning, Probate, Wills and Real Estate Law.

FIRM PROFILE: Marshall, Williams & Gorham, L.L.P. was formed in 1963 by Alan A. Marshall and Lonnie B. Williams. The firm emphasizes litigation and commercial/business practice. Marshall, Williams & Gorham L.L.P. has distinguished itself in litigation in both State and Federal Courts in the areas of insurance defense, personal injury, professional malpractice, construction and commercial litigation. The firm also provides services to clients in the area of banking, corporate, real estate, health care and estate planning and estate administration.

MEMBERS OF FIRM

ALAN A. MARSHALL (1908-1979)

LONNIE B. WILLIAMS, born Wilmington, North Carolina, July 19, 1928; admitted to bar, 1953, North Carolina. *Education:* Wake Forest University (B.S., summa cum laude, 1951; LL.B., magna cum laude, 1953). Phi Beta Kappa; Omicron Delta Kappa; Phi Delta Phi. Law Clerk, Supreme Court of North Carolina, 1953-1954. *Member:* New Hanover County (President, 1969), North Carolina and American Bar Associations; North Carolina State Bar; North Carolina Association of Defense Attorneys (President, 1988). Fellow, American College of Trial Lawyers. ***PRACTICE AREAS:*** Civil Litigation; Construction Law; Contracts; Estate Planning; Probate. ***Email:*** lbw@mwglaw.com

A. DUMAY GORHAM, JR., born Waynesboro, Mississippi, April 3, 1937; admitted to bar, 1965, North Carolina. *Education:* Wilmington Junior College (A.A., 1958); University of North Carolina (B.A., 1962; LL.B., 1965). *Member:* New Hanover County (President, 1975), North Carolina and American Bar Associations; North Carolina State Bar; American Health Lawyers Association; North Carolina Society of Health Care Attorneys. ***PRACTICE AREAS:*** Health Care; Hospital Law; Estate Planning; Probate. ***Email:*** adg@mwglaw.com

JERRY C. WOODELL, born Whiteville, North Carolina, September 20, 1944; admitted to bar, 1973, North Carolina. *Education:* University of North Carolina (B.A., 1967; J.D., 1973). *Member:* New Hanover County and North Carolina Bar Associations; North Carolina State Bar. ***PRACTICE AREAS:*** Business Law; Real Estate; Corporate Law; Mergers and Acquisitions. ***Email:*** jcw@mwglaw.com

(This Listing Continued)

WILLIAM ROBERT CHERRY, JR., born Raleigh, North Carolina, May 31, 1951; admitted to bar, 1977, North Carolina. *Education:* University of North Carolina (B.A., 1973; J.D., with honors, 1977). Phi Beta Kappa; Order of the Coif. Staff Member, North Carolina Law Review, 1976-1977. Author: "Mortgages-Use of Due on Sale Clause by a Lender is not a Restraint on Alienation in North Carolina," Vol. 55, p. 310, North Carolina Law Review, Jan., 1977. *Member:* New Hanover County, North Carolina and American Bar Associations; North Carolina State Bar; North Carolina Association of Defense Attorneys. ***PRACTICE AREAS:*** Civil Litigation; Commercial Litigation; Insurance Litigation; Insurance Defense. ***Email:*** wrc@mwglaw.com

RONALD H. WOODRUFF, born Kansas City, Missouri, November 22, 1952; admitted to bar, 1977, North Carolina. *Education:* Purdue University (B.A., 1974); Wake Forest University (J.D., 1977). Phi Delta Phi. *Member:* New Hanover County (President, 1990), North Carolina and American Bar Associations; North Carolina State Bar; Defense Research Institute; North Carolina Association of Defense Attorneys. (Board Certified Specialist in Workers Compensation Law, North Carolina State Board of Legal Specialization). ***PRACTICE AREAS:*** Civil Litigation; Construction Litigation; Insurance Defense; Workers Compensation. ***Email:*** rhw@mwglaw.com

LONNIE B. WILLIAMS, JR., born Wilmington, North Carolina, August 29, 1956; admitted to bar, 1981, North Carolina. *Education:* Wake Forest University (B.A., cum laude, 1978; J.D., cum laude, 1981). Author: Note, "Unemployment Compensation—The Labor Dispute Disqualification—Compensation of Replaced Strikers, State Policy of Neutrality and the Federal Labor Preemption," 16 Wake Forest Law Review 472, 1980. *Member:* New Hanover County, North Carolina and American Bar Associations; North Carolina State Bar. ***PRACTICE AREAS:*** Real Estate; Business Law; Wills; Probate. ***Email:*** lwj@mwglaw.com

CHARLES D. MEIER, born Richmond, Virginia, March 10, 1959; admitted to bar, 1985, North Carolina; 1987, U.S. District Court, Eastern District of North Carolina; 1997, U.S. Court of Appeals, Fourth Circuit and U.S. Supreme Court. *Education:* University of North Carolina at Chapel Hill (B.A., 1981; J.D., 1985). Member: Holderness Moot Court Bench, 1984-1985. Author: "Defenses Available to Guarantors," Notes Bearing Interest, Vol. 16, No. 1, 1995; "Environmental Concerns Plague Property Purchases," The Campbell Law Observer, Vol. 10, No. 7, 1989. *Member:* New Hanover County, North Carolina (Member, Sections on: Litigation, Construction, Real Estate and Business Law) and American Bar Associations; North Carolina State Bar. ***PRACTICE AREAS:*** Commercial Litigation; Construction Law; Construction Liens; Debtor and Creditor; Collections; Business Law; Corporate Law; Real Estate; Homeowners Association Law. ***Email:*** cdm@mwglaw.com

JOHN L. COBLE, born High Point, North Carolina, July 29, 1957; admitted to bar, 1985, North Carolina; 1987, U.S. District Court, Eastern District of North Carolina and U.S. Court of Appeals, Fourth Circuit; 1988, U.S. Supreme Court; 1998, U.S. District Court, Middle District of North Carolina; 2002, U.S. District Court, Western District of North Carolina. *Education:* North Carolina State University (B.A., cum laude, 1980); Campbell University (J.D., cum laude, 1985). Phi Kappa Phi; Delta Theta Phi. Recipient, Corpus Juris Secundum Award for Significant Legal Scholarship, 1983-1984; 1984-1985. Member, Campbell Law Review, 1983-1985. Articles Editor, Campbell Law Review, 1984-1985. Author: Note, "Edwards v. Arizona is Alive But Not Well in North Carolina," 7 Campbell Law Review 51 (1984). Law Clerk to U.S. District Court Judge James C. Fox, Eastern District of North Carolina, 1985-1987. Research Assistant, North Carolina Pattern Jury Instructions Committee-Criminal, 1983-1985. *Member:* New Hanover County, North Carolina and American Bar Associations; North Carolina State Bar; North Carolina Association for Defense Attorneys; Defense Research Institute. ***PRACTICE AREAS:*** Civil Litigation; Insurance Defense; Construction Litigation; Commercial Litigation; Products Liability. ***Email:*** jlc@mwglaw.com

F. MURPHY AVERITT, III, born Lumberton, North Carolina, August 31, 1972; admitted to bar, 1999, North Carolina, U.S. District Court, Eastern and Western Districts of North Carolina. *Education:* University of North Carolina at Chapel Hill (B.A., 1995); Campbell University (J.D., 1999). *Member:* New Hanover County and North Carolina (Member, Section on: Construction Law) Bar Associations; North Carolina State Bar; North Carolina Association for Defense Attorneys; Defense Research Institute. ***PRACTICE AREAS:*** Civil Litigation; Insurance Defense; Construction Litigation; Commercial Litigation. ***Email:*** fma@mwglaw.com

REPRESENTATIVE CLIENTS: State Farm Insurance Co.; Unitrin Ins. Co.; CNA Insurance Co.; Guaranty National Insurance Co.; Florists Mutual Insurance Co.; Government Employees insurance Co.; St. Paul Travelers Ins. Co.; Interstate Insurance Group; State Capital Insurance Co.; Grange Mutual Insurance Co.; N.C. Grange Mutual Insurance Co.; One Beacon Insurance; First of Georgia Insurance Co.; Integon Insurance Co.; Broadspire Insurance Co.; N.C. Insurance Guarantee Association; Nationwide Ins. Co.; Centura Bank; New Hanover Regional Medical Center; Air Wilmington, Inc.; American Crane Corp.; Lowe's Companies, Inc.; The Contractor Yard, Inc.; Builder's First Source, Inc.; H.W. Williams Lumber Co.; Stock Building Supply; Capital Hotel Associates, Inc.; MHI Hotels, LLC; Hanover Medical Specialists, P.A.; Southeastern Nephrology Associates, PLLC; Community Association Management Specialists, Inc.; Consolidated Estate and Property Control Corp.; Hale Building Co.; Oleander Co.; Almont Shipping Company; RSM McGladrey, LLP; LS3P Associates Ltd.; Ballard Architects, Inc.; Ballard Therapy Services, Inc.; Harold W. Wells & Son Insurance; Bayer Corp.; Brownyard Claims Management; Prudential Property & Casualty Insurance Co.; Orion Auto, Inc.; Unison Insurance Co.
APPROVED ATTORNEYS FOR: Lawyers Title Insurance Corp.; Commonwealth Land Title Co.; Attorney's Title; The Title Co. of N.C., Inc.; Investors Title Insurance Co.; Chicago Title; Old Republic Title Insurance Co.

MARTIN & JONES

1213 CULBRETH DRIVE, SUITE 121
WILMINGTON, NORTH CAROLINA 28405
Telephone: 910-256-4005
URL: http://www.MartinandJones.com

Raleigh, North Carolina Office: 410 Glenwood Avenue, 27603. Telephone: 919-821-0005.
Durham, North Carolina Office: University Towers, Suite 526, 3100 Tower Boulevard, 27707. Telephone: 919-544-3000.
Atlanta, Georgia Office: 3353 Peachtree Road, NE, Suite 510, 30326. Telephone: 404-257-1117.

(This Listing Continued)

Asbestos Litigation, Bad Faith and Unfair Competition, Business Litigation, Construction Site Injuries, Inadequate Security, Medical Malpractice, Nursing/Rest Home Negligence, Personal Injury, Pharmaceutical and Medical Device Litigation, Product Liability, Social Security Disability, Toxic Torts, Trucking Accidents, Workers' Compensation and Wrongful Death, Land Condemnation, FELA (Federal Employers' Liability Act), Securities Fraud.

JOHN ALAN JONES, born Pine Level, North Carolina, November 17, 1956; admitted to bar, 1982, North Carolina, U.S. District Court, Eastern, Middle and Western Districts of North Carolina and U.S Court of Appeals, 4th Circuit. *Education:* University of North Carolina at Chapel Hill (B.A., 1979; J.D., 1982). Phi Eta Sigma; Phi Beta Kappa; Holderness Moot Court Member. *Member:* Wake County, North Carolina and American Bar Associations; North Carolina State Bar; Association of Trial Lawyers of America; North Carolina Academy of Trial Lawyers. ***PRACTICE AREAS:*** Medical Malpractice; Obstetric Malpractice; Drug and Medical Device Litigation; Pediatric Malpractice; Products Liability; Surgeons Liability; Hospital Liability. ***Email:*** JAJ@M-J.COM

(For complete biographical data on other personnel, see Professional Biographies at Raleigh, North Carolina)

MAUPIN TAYLOR, P.A.

Established in 1870

LANDFALL PARK NORTH
1985 EASTWOOD ROAD, SUITE 200
WILMINGTON, NORTH CAROLINA 28403
Telephone: 910-256-5135
Telecopier: 910-256-6451
URL: http://www.maupintaylor.com

Raleigh, North Carolina: Highwoods Tower One, Suite 500, 3200 Beechleaf Court, P.O. Drawer 19764. Telephone: 919-981-4000. Telecopier: 919-981-4300.
Research Triangle Park, North Carolina Office: 480 Beta Building, Headquarters Park, Post Office Box 13646, 27709-3646. Telephone: 919-361-4900. Telecopier: 919-361-2262.

Agribusiness, Administrative, Alcoholic Beverages, Alternative Dispute Resolution, Antitrust and Trade Regulation, Aviation Law, Bankruptcy, Banking Law, Business Litigation, Charitable Organizations, Collective Bargaining, Commercial Leases, Commercial Real Estate, Computers and Software, Construction Law, Copyrights, Corporate Finance, Corporate Law, Creditors' Rights, Employee Benefits, Employer Liability, Employment Discrimination, Employment Law, Employment Litigation, Environmental Law, Franchises and Franchising, Government Contracts, Governmental (State and Local) Law, Health Law, Hospital Law, Immigration and Naturalization, Industrial Accidents, Industrial Relations, Intellectual Property, Labor Arbitration, Labor Law, Labor Legislation, Labor Relations, Management Labor Law, Medical Malpractice Defense, Mergers and Acquisitions, Occupational Health and Safety, Patent Litigation, Products Liability, Real Estate Finance, Secured Lending, Securities Regulation, Sports Law, Taxation, Technology Law, Trademark, Trusts and Estates, Venture Capital, Zoning Law.

FIRM PROFILE: The law firm of Maupin Taylor, P.A., embodies a legacy of leadership and legal excellence that dates back to 1870. The firm has a long history of serving its clients, large and small, with integrity and success. To better serve its clients it maintains offices in Raleigh, Research Triangle Park and Wilmington. It is one of the largest firms in the area. From start-up companies cultivating new ideas and technologies to venerable companies whose roots are embedded in North Carolina history, Maupin Taylor provides the experience, depth and diversity to help them all thrive.

Maupin Taylor is a full service corporate law firm that concentrates in business law, litigation, labor and employment matters, health law, environmental, commercial real estate, trusts and estates, and banking law. The firm takes great pride in its rich history and its ability to apply the practice of law to the technological demands of 21st century business.

GILBERT C. LAITE, III, born Camden, ME, October 28, 1957; admitted to bar, 1984, NC; 1986, ME. *Education:* Univ. of Southern Maine (B.S., Business Adm., 1980); Wake Forest Univ. (J.D., cum laude, 1984). Real Estate Broker, 1977-1981. Co-Author: "Real Estate Litigation in North Carolina, 1990; "Construction Lien Law in North Carolina," 1994, 1996; "Trial Book-Civil," Wake Forest Univ., 1994. Law Clerk to the Honorable Russell A. Eliason, U.S. Magistrate Judge, Middle District of NC, 1984-1986. *Member:* NC and American Bar Associations. ***PRACTICE AREAS:*** Commercial Litigation; Contracts; Sales; Lender Liability; Uniform Commercial Code; Products Liability; Construction; Railroad Real Property; Eminent Domain; Landlord and Tenant; Title and Boundary Disputes. ***Email:*** glaite@maupintaylor.com

OF COUNSEL

DANIEL LEE BRAWLEY, born Greensboro, NC, March 31, 1942; admitted to bar, 1967, NC. *Education:* University of North Carolina (A.B., 1964; J.D., 1967). Listed in *The Best Lawyers in America (Business Litigation, Maritime Law, Personal Injury and Civil Litigation).* Member, National Panel of Arbitrators, American Arbitration Association. *Member:* North Carolina and American Bar Associations; Southeastern Admiralty Law Institute (Member, Board of Governors, 1972-1974, 1988-1990, 1994, 1996, 1998-1999; Treasurer, 1975; Secretary, 1976; Vice Chairman, 1977; Chairman, 1978); Maritime Law Association of the United States (Proctor); North Carolina Association of Defense Attorneys (Member, Board of Directors, 1992-1995). ***PRACTICE AREAS:*** Construction Law; Commercial Litigation; Business Litigation; Admiralty Law; Personal Injury. ***Email:*** dbrawley@maupintaylor.com

REPRESENTATIVE CLIENTS: A I G Aviation, Inc.; Ajinomoto USA, Inc.; Alcoa, Inc.; Bandag Incorporated; Blue Cross/Blue Shield of North Carolina; City of Durham; City of Raleigh; Cornerstone Health Care, P.A.; CSX Transportation; DaimlerChrysler Corporation; Duke University; E & J Gallo Winery; Eastman Kodak Company; Ford Motor Company; GlaxoSmithKline; HealthSouth Corporation; Hog Slat, Inc.; McDonald's Corporation; Nash Finch Company, Inc.; North Carolina Hospital Association; North Carolina Housing Finance Agency; North Carolina Museum of Life and Science; Nortel; Reichhold Chemical Co., Inc.;

(This Listing Continued)

Sampson Regional Medical Center; Seaboard Group II; SouthTrust Bank; SpectraSite Communications, Inc.; The New Kerr Drugs; J. M. Thompson Company.

TODD E. McCURRY, P.A.
ATTORNEY AT LAW

207 1/2 PRINCESS STREET
WILMINGTON, NORTH CAROLINA 28401
Telephone: 910-772-1254
Fax: 910-772-1274
Email: lawyertm@bellsouth.net
URL: http://www.lawyers.com/toddmccurry

Mailing Address: P.O. Box 1443, Wilmington, NC 28402

Workers Compensation; On-the-Job Injuries; Personal Injury; Automobile Accidents; Wrongful Death; Family Law; Divorce; Child Custody; Child Support; Spousal Support; Premarital Agreements.

FIRM PROFILE: A North Carolina native, Todd McCurry has served the citizens of North Carolina for over 18 years. It is with attention to detail and compassion that we have built our reputation and relationships with a wide variety of clients. From simple divorces to catastrophic injuries, we are equipped with the expertise to successfully resolve your case. We cover all aspects of your divorce and worker's compensation claim with complete dedication to your needs and our personal commitment to legal excellence, aggressive representation, honesty and integrity, innovation, client service, responsiveness, quality and results.

TODD E. McCURRY, born Rutherfordton, North Carolina; admitted to bar, 1987, North Carolina; 1988, U.S. District Court, Middle District of North Carolina; 1991, U.S. District Court, Eastern District of North Carolina; 1992, U.S. Court of Appeals; 1996, U.S. District Court, Western District of North Carolina. *Education:* Limestone College (B.S., Business, 1983); North Carolina Central University (J.D., magna cum laude, 1987). Phi Delta Phi. Member, Board of Editors, North Carolina Central University Law Journal. *Member:* New Hanover County Bar Association; North Carolina State Bar; North Carolina Academy of Trial Lawyers; North Carolina Bar Association; The Association of Trial Lawyers of America (Graduate); National Institute of Trial Advocacy. ***PRACTICE AREAS:*** Workers Compensation; Personal Injury; Automobile Accidents and Injuries; Divorce; Child Custody; Child Support; Spousal Support; Premarital Agreements.

MURCHISON, TAYLOR & GIBSON, PLLC

Established in 1955

16 NORTH FIFTH AVENUE
WILMINGTON, NORTH CAROLINA 28401-4593
Telephone: 910-763-2426
Fax: 910-763-6561

General Practice: Trials in State and Federal Courts. Corporation and Business, Mergers and Acquisitions, Real Estate, Buying and Selling a Home, Commercial Real Estate, Commercial Finance, Taxation, Estate Planning and Administration, Elder Law, Healthcare, Employment Law, Intellectual Property, Administrative, Environmental, Labor Law and Creditor and Bankruptcy Law, Zoning and Land Use.

FIRM PROFILE: Murchison, Taylor & Gibson, PLLC is a full service law firm providing a wide range of legal services. The attorneys in the firm concentrate their practice in specific areas to offer high quality and more efficient service to clients. The firm requires continuing professional development for attorneys and staff and encourages active participation in community and professional activities.

MEMBERS OF FIRM

WALLACE C. MURCHISON (Retired)

JOSEPH O. TAYLOR, JR., born Sanford, North Carolina, March 25, 1946; admitted to bar, 1971, North Carolina; 1972, U.S. District Court, Eastern District of North Carolina; 1978, U.S. Supreme Court and U.S. Claims Court; 1979, U.S. District Court, Middle District of North Carolina; 1985, U.S. Court of Appeals, Fourth Circuit. *Education:* University of North Carolina at Chapel Hill (A.B., cum laude, 1968; J.D., 1971). Omicron Delta Epsilon; Phi Delta Phi. Alderman, Town of Wrightsville Beach, North Carolina, 1973-1977. Mayor, Pro-Tem, 1975-1977. *Member:* New Hanover County, North Carolina and American Bar Associations; Fifth Judicial District and North Carolina State Bars; North Carolina Academy of Trial Lawyers. ***PRACTICE AREAS:*** Real Estate; Commercial Law; Corporations Law. ***Email:*** jtaylor@murchisontaylor.com

FRANK B. GIBSON, JR., born Wilson, North Carolina, September 9, 1945; admitted to bar, 1975, North Carolina; 1976, U.S. District Court, Eastern District of North Carolina and U.S. Bankruptcy Court; 1978, U.S. Supreme Court; 1979, U.S. Court of Appeals, Fourth Circuit. *Education:* Dartmouth College (B.A., 1967); Vanderbilt Law School (J.D., 1975). Phi Alpha Delta; Dragon Senior Society. Recipient, American Jurisprudence Award-Evidence. Member, Editorial Board and Contributing Writer, "The Southern Aviator," 1988-1999. President, Greater Wilmington Chamber of Commerce, 1994-1995. *Member:* New Hanover County, North Carolina (Member, Sections: Estate Planning and Fiduciary Law, Business Law) and American (Member, Sections: Business Law, Real Property, Probate and Trust Law) Bar Associations; Fifth Judicial District and North Carolina State Bars; 4th Circuit Judicial Conference. [Capt., USMC, 1968-1973]. ***PRACTICE AREAS:*** Commercial Law; Corporate Law; Estate Planning; Probate; Intellectual Property. ***Email:*** fgibson@murchisontaylor.com

MICHAEL MURCHISON, born Wilmington, North Carolina, May 21, 1949; admitted to bar, 1975, District of Columbia; 1978, U.S. Court of Appeals, Fourth Circuit; 1983, North Carolina and U.S. District Court, Eastern District of North Carolina; 1991, U.S. Supreme Court. *Education:* Amherst College (B.A., 1971); Cornell University (J.D., magna cum laude, 1975). Order of the Coif. Attorney: National Labor Relations Board, 1975-1979; U.S. Environmental Protection Agency, 1979-1982. *Member:* New Hanover County,

(This Listing Continued)

MURCHISON, TAYLOR & GIBSON, PLLC, Wilmington—Continued

Fifth Judicial District and North Carolina (Council Member, Labor and Employment Law Section) Bar Associations; The District of Columbia Bar; North Carolina State Bar; North Carolina Association of Defense Attorneys. ***PRACTICE AREAS:*** Civil Litigation; Employment Law; Health Law; Environmental Law. ***Email:*** mmurchison@murchisontaylor.com

W. BERRY TRICE, born Shelby, North Carolina, March 27, 1960; admitted to bar, 1987, North Carolina. *Education:* North Carolina State University (B.A., Accounting, 1983); Campbell University (J.D., 1987). Certified Public Accountant, North Carolina, 1988. *Member:* New Hanover County, North Carolina and American Bar Associations; North Carolina State Bar; American Institute of Certified Public Accountants; North Carolina Association of Certified Public Accountants. ***PRACTICE AREAS:*** Estate Planning; Probate; Corporation Law; Taxation; Foreclosures. ***Email:*** btrice@murchisontaylor.com

G. STEPHEN DIAB, born Martins Ferry, Ohio, May 4, 1964; admitted to bar, 1990, North Carolina. *Education:* University of North Carolina, Chapel Hill (B.S., 1986; J.D. with high honors, 1990). Phi Beta Kappa; Order of the Coif. Articles Editor, University of North Carolina Law Review, 1989-1990. *Member:* North Carolina and American Bar Associations; American Institute of Certified Public Accountants; North Carolina Association of Certified Public Accountants. ***PRACTICE AREAS:*** Corporate and Tax; Trusts and Estates; Mergers and Acquisitions. ***Email:*** sdiab@murchisontaylor.com

JAMES W. LATSHAW, born Melrose, Massachusetts, April 27, 1960; admitted to bar, 1985, New Hampshire; 1997, North Carolina. *Education:* Cornell University (B.A., with distinction, 1982); University of Michigan (J.D., 1985). *Member:* North Carolina (Member, Sections on: Business, Tax and Estate Planning) and American (Member, Sections on: Business Law; Real Property, Probate and Trust Law) Bar Associations. ***PRACTICE AREAS:*** Corporate Law; Trusts and Estates; Business Law; Commercial Finance Law. ***Email:*** jlatshaw@murchisontaylor.com

ANDREW K. McVEY, born St. Louis, Missouri, March 14, 1968; admitted to bar, 1993, North Carolina; 1994, U.S. District Court, Middle District of North Carolina; 1999, U.S. District Court, Eastern District of North Carolina; 2000, U.S. Court of Appeals, Fourth Circuit. *Education:* Wake Forest University (B.A., summa cum laude, 1990); Wake Forest University School of Law (J.D., 1993). Phi Beta Kappa. Pi Sigma Alpha. Alpha Kappa Delta. Carswell Scholar. Certified Superior Court Mediator. Board of Directors, National High School Mock Trial Championship. *Member:* New Hanover County and North Carolina (Member, Litigation Section) Bar Associations; North Carolina Academy of Trial Lawyers. ***PRACTICE AREAS:*** Civil Litigation. ***Email:*** amcvey@murchisontaylor.com

PETER A. BYNUM, born Chapel Hill, North Carolina, November 16, 1968; admitted to bar, 1996, North Carolina. *Education:* Davidson College (B.A., magna cum laude, 1991); University of Virginia (J.D., 1996). Phi Beta Kappa; Omicron Delta Kappa. ***PRACTICE AREAS:*** Real Estate Leasing; Real Estate Development; Land Use. ***Email:*** pbynum@murchisontaylor.com

CHRISTOPHER J. LEONARD, born Wilmington, North Carolina, November 8, 1974; admitted to bar, 1999, North Carolina and United States Tax Court. *Education:* Wake Forest University (B.A., cum laude, 1996); Wake Forest University (J.D., 1999). Theta Alpha Kappa. Wake Forest Honor Scholar, Wake Forest University. James A. Webster, Jr. Faculty Award, Wake Forest University. Moot Court Board. Author: "Medicaid Estate Recovery: Law and Practice in North Carolina," *Elder Law,* Vol. 7, No. 3 and *The Will and the Way,* Vol. 23, No. 1. *Member:* New Hanover County, North Carolina (Member, Sections on: Estate Planning and Fiduciary Law; Council Member, Elder Law) and American Bar Associations; National Academy of Elder Law Attorneys. ***PRACTICE AREAS:*** Estate Planning; Business Law; Taxation; Elder Law. ***Email:*** cjleonard@murchisontaylor.com

ASSOCIATES

FRANCES YOUNGBLOOD TRASK, born Wilmington, North Carolina, June 9, 1937; admitted to bar, 1983, North Carolina. *Education:* Wake Forest University (B.S., magna cum laude, 1959); University of North Carolina at Chapel Hill (J.D., 1983). Phi Beta Kappa. *Member:* New Hanover County, North Carolina (Member, Real Property Section) and American Bar Associations; North Carolina State Bar. ***PRACTICE AREAS:*** Real Estate Law; Commercial Law. ***Email:*** ftrask@murchisontaylor.com

FAISON GIBSON SUTTON, born June 25, 1978; admitted to bar, 2004, North Carolina. *Education:* Duke University (B.A., 2000); University of North Carolina at Chapel Hill (J.D., 2003). *Member:* New Hanover County, North Carolina (Member, Real Property Section, Young Lawyers Division; Lawyer Effectivness Committee) and American Bar Associations. ***PRACTICE AREAS:*** Real Estate; Corporate Law. ***Email:*** faison@murchisontaylor.com

REPRESENTATIVE CLIENTS: Atlantic Corp.; Bald Head Association; Bellamy Drug Company; BellSouth; Branch Banking and Trust Co.; Coastal Beverage Co., Inc.; Coastal Communities at Ocean Ridge Plantation; ePlus Technology of North Carolina, Inc.; J. Arthur Dosher Memorial Hospital; First National Bank Southeast; General Electric Co.; Great West Property & Casualty; Greater Wilmington Chamber of Commerce; Image Products, Inc.; Interroll Corp.; Landfall Associates; Landmark Organization, Inc.; Lumina Station, LLC; Mayfaire I, LLC; MCO Transport, Inc.; MEDAC; Ocean Ridge Golf, Inc.; New Hanover Medical Group, PA; North Carolina Aviation Museum; Ocean Ridge Farms, Inc.; Pharmaceutical Product Development, Inc.; Porters Neck Co., Inc.; Sea Trail Corp.; Signature Homes; Southeastern Mental Health Center; Southern Lifestyles, LLC; Springer-Eubank Co.; Sunrise Homes; Technical Coating International, Inc.; Triple T Parts & Equipment Co.; Trustees, Employers-ILA Pension, Waccamaw Bank; Welfare & Vacation Fund; Wilmington Children's Museum, Inc.; Wilmington Health Associates; Wilmington Materials, Inc.; Wilmington Nissan; Wilmington Orthopedic Group, PA; Worsley Cos; W. K. Hobbs, Inc.
APPROVED ATTORNEYS FOR: Bank of America; Branch Banking & Trust Co.; Central Carolina Bank; Commonwealth Title Insurance Co.; Cooperative Bank for Savings; First Citizens Bank; First Title Insurance Company; Investors Title Insurance Company; Lawyers Title Insurance Corp.; Security Savings & Loan Assn.; Title Insurance Company of N.C.; Wachovia Bank; RBC Centura.
REFERENCE: Branch Banking & Trust Co.

PATTERSON, DILTHEY, CLAY, BRYSON & ANDERSON, L.L.P.

2516 INDEPENDENCE BOULEVARD, SUITE 200
P.O. BOX 2258
WILMINGTON, NORTH CAROLINA 28412
Telephone: 910-452-2797; Toll Free: 877-731-5007
Facsimile: 910-452-4151
URL: http://www.pattersondilthey.com

Raleigh, North Carolina Office: 4020 WestChase Boulevard, Suite 550. Telephone: 919-821-4020. FAX: 919-829-0055.

Civil Trial Practice. Trials in all State and Federal Courts. Workers Compensation, Products Liability, Medical Malpractice, Premises Liability, Automobile Liability and Insurance Law.

FIRM PROFILE: This firm is comprised of trial lawyers who actively engage in the defense of civil litigation throughout the state of North Carolina.

PARTNER

J. SCOTT LEWIS, born Brevard, North Carolina, March 7, 1970; admitted to bar, 1995, North Carolina and U.S. District Court, Western District of North Carolina; 1999, U.S. District Court, Eastern District of North Carolina. *Education:* University of North Carolina at Chapel Hill (B.A., 1992); Wake Forest University (J.D., 1995). Phi Alpha Delta (Co-Treasurer). Member: Wake Forest Moot Court Board. Morehead Scholar. *Member:* New Hanover County, North Carolina and American Bar Associations; North Carolina State Bar; North Carolina Association of Defense Attorneys; Defense Research Institute. ***PRACTICE AREAS:*** Civil Litigation; Insurance Defense; Commercial Litigation; Coverage Disputes; Medical Malpractice; Contract Litigation; Construction Defects; Construction Litigation. ***Email:*** SLewis@pattersondilthey.com

ASSOCIATES

TYLER PAIGE BAUCOM, born Raleigh, North Carolina, June 19, 1974; admitted to bar, 2000, North Carolina. *Education:* University of North Carolina at Chapel Hill (B.S.N., with honors, 1996; J.D., 2000). Sigma Theta Tau; Golden Key. Registered Nurse, 1996. *Member:* New Hanover County Bar Association; North Carolina State Bar; Defense Research Institute; North Carolina Association of Defense Attorneys. ***PRACTICE AREAS:*** Insurance Defense; Medical Malpractice Defense. ***Email:*** TBaucom@pattersondilthey.com

ELLEN J. PERSECHINI, born Newport News, Virginia, February 5, 1978; admitted to bar, 2002, North Carolina. *Education:* University of Tennessee at Knoxville (B.A., magna cum laude, 1999); Wake Forest University School of Law (J.D., 2002). Phi Beta Kappa; Phi Kappa Phi; Law Faculty Scholar. *Member:* New Hanover County and North Carolina Bar Associations; North Carolina Association of Defense Attorneys; Defense Research Institute. ***PRACTICE AREAS:*** Civil Litigation; Insurance Defense; Commercial Litigation. ***Email:*** EllenP@pattersondilthey.com

JUSTIN D. ROBERTSON, born Charlotte, North Carolina, July 7, 1972; admitted to bar, 1998, North Carolina. *Education:* University of North Carolina (B.A., Psychology and Sociology, 1994); Campbell University (J.D., 1998). *Member:* New Hanover County and American Bar Associations; North Carolina State Bar; North Carolina Academy of Defense Attorneys. ***PRACTICE AREAS:*** Workers Compensation; Employment Law. ***Email:*** JRobertson@pattersondilthey.com

JERRY L. WILKINS, born Fayetteville, North Carolina, December 18, 1973; admitted to bar, 2000, North Carolina. *Education:* University of North Carolina at Chapel Hill (B.A., English, 1995); Campbell University (J.D., 2000). Formerly with Hedrick & Morton. *Member:* North Carolina State Bar. (Resident). ***PRACTICE AREAS:*** Workers Compensation; Medical Malpractice; General Liability. ***Email:*** JWilkins@pattersondilthey.com

W. WALTER RAPP, born Winston-Salem, North Carolina, July 5, 1975; admitted to bar, 2003, North Carolina. *Education:* University of North Carolina at Chapel Hill (B.A., Economics, 1997); Wake Forest University (J.D., 2003). *Member:* North Carolina State Bar. ***PRACTICE AREAS:*** Civil Litigation; Workers Compensation. ***Email:*** WRapp@pattersondilthey.com

KARI A. LEE, born Glen Cove, New York, April 26, 1978; admitted to bar, 2003, North Carolina. *Education:* Mary Washington College (B.A., cum laude, 2000); Wake Forest University (J.D., 2003). *Member:* Forsyth County and North Carolina Bar Associations; North Carolina Association of Defense Attorneys. ***PRACTICE AREAS:*** Workers Compensation Defense. ***Email:*** KLee@PattersonDilthey.com

BRIAN J. KROMKE, born Buffalo, New York, July 13, 1973; admitted to bar, 2001, North Carolina. *Education:* State University of New York College at Geneseo (B.A., Biology, 1995); North Carolina Central University (J.D., 2001). *Member:* North Carolina Association of Defense Attorneys. [With U.S. Army Reserve, 1995-2003]. ***PRACTICE AREAS:*** Workers Compensation Defense. ***Email:*** BKromke@pattersondilthey.com

JENNIFER L. MORRIS, born San Juan, Puerto Rico, October 24, 1979; admitted to bar, 2005, North Carolina. *Education:* Salem College (B.A., cum laude, 2001); Campbell University, Adrian Wiggins School of Law (J.D., cum laude, 2005). Notes and Comments Editor, Campbell Law Review. Participant: William E. McGee Civil Rights Moot Court Competition; National Moot Court Competition (Selected as one of the Top Ten Best Overall Oral Advocates for the Competition). Recipient, Calhoun Advocacy Award. *Member:* North Carolina Bar Association.

JEREMY S. PAGE, born Omaha, Nebraska, February 20, 1978; admitted to bar, 2005, North Carolina. *Education:* University of North Carolina at Wilmington (B.A., 2000); Wake Forest University (J.D., 2005). Member, Political Science and Spanish Honor Societies. Member: Moot Court Board; Craven Constitutional Law Team; Trial Bar. *Member:* North Carolina Bar Association. ***PRACTICE AREAS:*** Workers Compensation; Defense Litigation.

(This Listing Continued)

REPRESENTATIVE CLIENTS: Amica Mutual Insurance Company; Carolina Casualty Insurance Co.; Carolina Power and Light; CIGNA; Cincinnati Insurance Cos.; Connecticut Specialty Insurance Group; Employers Mutual Casualty Co.; Fireman's Fund Insurance Co.; Gallagher Bassett Services, Inc.; Ohio Casualty Group; Hartford Accident & Indemnity Co.; Horace Mann Insurance Cos.; Kemper Insurance Group; Liberty Mutual Insurance Co.; Medical Protective Insurance Co.; National Benefits America, Inc.; North Carolina Farm Bureau; North Carolina Insurance Guaranty Associates; Safeco Insurance Co.; Sentry Insurance Group; St. Paul Insurance Co.; Universal Underwriters Insurance Group; Utica National Insurance; The Virginia Insurance Reciprocal; Zenith Insurance Company.

(For complete biographical data on all personnel, see Professional Biographies at Raleigh, North Carolina)

PENNINGTON & SMITH

107 NORTH SIXTH STREET
WILMINGTON, NORTH CAROLINA 28401
Telephone: 910-763-3340
Fax: 910-763-8034

Family Law, Divorce, Child Custody, Child Support, Alimony, Equitable Distribution, Civil Litigation.

MEMBERS OF FIRM

RALPH S. PENNINGTON, born Heidelberg, West Germany, June 13, 1954; admitted to bar, 1984, North Carolina; U.S. District Court, Eastern District of North Carolina. *Education:* University of North Carolina at Wilmington (B.A., with honors, magna cum laude, 1981); University of North Carolina at Chapel Hill (J.D., 1984). Phi Eta Sigma; Phi Kappa Phi. *Member:* New Hanover County and North Carolina (Member, Family Law Section) Bar Associations; Fifth Judicial District Bar; North Carolina State Bar; North Carolina Academy of Trial Lawyers. ***Email:*** rpennatt@bellsouth.net

TAMARA AVIS SMITH, born Roanoke, Virginia, October 24, 1974; admitted to bar, 2001, North Carolina. *Education:* Mary Baldwin College (B.A., 1996); Cumberland School of Law, Samford University (J.D., 2000). *Member:* New Hanover County and North Carolina (Member, Family Law Section) Bar Associations; North Carolina State Bar; North Carolina Academy of Trial Lawyers; Fifth Judicial District Bar. ***PRACTICE AREAS:*** Family Law; Divorce. ***Email:*** tamarasm@bellsouth.net

JAMES S. PRICE

4018 B SHIPYARD BOULEVARD, SUITE 3
WILMINGTON, NORTH CAROLINA 28406
Telephone: 910-791-9422
Fax: 910-791-0432
Email: jamespriceatty@bellsouth.net
URL: http://www.jamessprice.com

Real Estate.

JAMES S. PRICE, born Hickory, North Carolina, 1970; admitted to bar, 2004, North Carolina. *Education:* University of North Carolina at Chapel Hill (B.A., 1999); Campbell University (J.D., 2003). *Member:* New Hanover County and North Carolina Bar Associations. ***PRACTICE AREAS:*** Real Estate (100%).

STEPHANIE MICHELLE AKIN, born Tampa, Florida, June 23, 1975; admitted to bar, 2005, North Carolina. *Education:* Indiana University (B.A., Journalism, Political Science, 2001); Indiana University School of Law (J.D., 2004). *Member:* New Hanover County, North Carolina and American (Member, Sections on: International Law; Criminal Defense) Bar Associations; North Carolina Association of Trial Lawyers. ***PRACTICE AREAS:*** Immigration; Wills; Trusts and Estates; Criminal; Misdemeanors; Traffic Violations; Juvenile; Family Law. ***Email:*** stephanie@jamesspricelaw.com

WESLEY SHEFFIELD, born Austin, Texas, July 29, 1978; admitted to bar, 2004, North Carolina. *Education:* The Johns Hopkins University (B.S.E.E., 2000); Wake Forest University (J.D., 2004). *Member:* North Carolina (Member, Intellectual Property Section) and American (Member, Intellectual Property Section) Bar Associations. ***PRACTICE AREAS:*** Bankruptcy; Intellectual Property; Criminal. ***Email:*** wesleysheffield@mailsnare.net

TERRY B. RICHARDSON

209 PRINCESS STREET
WILMINGTON, NORTH CAROLINA 28402
Telephone: 910-763-7420
Fax: 910-762-4176

Personal Injury, Wrongful Death, Automobile Accidents, Truck Accidents, Criminal Cases, Traffic Offenses, DWIs, Estates and Wills. Trials in all Courts.

TERRY B. RICHARDSON, admitted to bar, 1981, North Carolina. *Education:* North Carolina Central University (B.A.); University of North Carolina at Chapel Hill (J.D.).

CHRISTINA RIVENBARK & ASSOCIATES

4009 OLEANDER DRIVE
WILMINGTON, NORTH CAROLINA 28403
Telephone: 910-251-8080
Facsimile: 910-395-8391
Email: cr@christinarivenbark.com
URL: http://www.christinarivenbarklaw.com/

Clinton, North Carolina Office: 603A Northeast Boulevard, 28328. Telephone: 1-800-777-5159.

(This Listing Continued)

Garner, North Carolina Office: 5533 NC Highway 42 West, 27529. Telephone: 1-800-561-9221.

Personal Injury, Automobile Accidents, Workers Compensation, Wrongful Death, Medical Malpractice, Slip and Fall, Criminal Law, Driving While Intoxicated, Traffic Violations, Drug Offenses, Misdemeanors, Felonies, Sexual Assaults, Assaults, Burglary, Motorcycle Accidents, Head Injuries.

CHRISTINA RIVENBARK, born Goldsboro, North Carolina, December 26, 1962; admitted to bar, 1987, North Carolina. *Education:* University of North Carolina at Chapel Hill (B.A., 1984; J.D., 1987). *Member:* North Carolina and American Bar Associations; North Carolina Academy of Trial Lawyers (Board of Directors, The Hispanic Committee of Southeastern; Member, Latino, Hispanic, Personal Injury and Workers Compensation Sections). ***PRACTICE AREAS:*** Personal Injury; Workers Compensation; Head Injury; Slip and Fall; Medical Malpractice; Automobile Accidents and Injuries; Truck Accidents; Boating Accidents; Wrongful Death; Construction Accidents; Social Security; Social Security Disability; Criminal Law; Traffic Violations; Driving While Intoxicated; Sexual Assault; Burglary.

BRUCE H. ROBINSON, JR.

401 CHESTNUT STREET, SUITE D
WILMINGTON, NORTH CAROLINA 28401
Telephone: 910-763-7446
Fax: 910-763-7466
Email: brucerobinsonjr@aol.com

Personal Injury, Medical Malpractice, Hospital Negligence, Nursing Home Abuse and Neglect, Spinal Injuries, Brain Injury, Birth Trauma, Wrongful Death, Automobile Accidents, Truck Accidents, Motorcycle Accidents, DWI, DUI, Workers Compensation, Misdiagnosis of Heart Condition, Negligence, Surgeons Liability, Domestic Relations, Family Law, Divorce, Interstate Child Custody, Commercial Litigation, Real Estate Litigation, General Civil Litigation, Criminal Law, Criminal Defense and Felonies in all State and Federal Courts.

BRUCE H. ROBINSON, JR., born San Diego, California, February 11, 1944; admitted to bar, 1969, North Carolina, U.S. Court of Appeals, Fourth Circuit and U.S. Tax Court. *Education:* Western Maryland College (B.A., Political Science, 1966); Wake Forest University (J.D., 1969). *Member:* North Carolina State Bar.

ROBIN WICKS ROBINSON, P.C.

701 MARKET STREET
P.O. BOX 135
WILMINGTON, NORTH CAROLINA 28402
Telephone: 910-763-3374
Fax: 910-763-4004
Email: rrspc@bellsouth.net

Family Law, Civil Litigation and Mediation.

ROBIN WICKS ROBINSON, born Roanoke Rapids, North Carolina, June 5, 1961; admitted to bar, 1986, North Carolina; 1987, U.S. District Court, Eastern District of North Carolina; 1997, U.S. District Court, Western District of North Carolina. *Education:* Converse College (B.A., Politics, with honors, 1982); University of North Carolina (J.D., 1985). Mortar Board; Pi Gamma Mu; Phi Sigma Iota; Phi Delta Phi. Certified Mediator and Arbitrator. *Member:* New Hanover County, North Carolina and American Bar Associations; North Carolina Academy of Trial Lawyers; Fifth Judicial District Bar (President, 2004); North Carolina State Bar. (Board Certified Specialist in Family Law, North Carolina State Board of Legal Specialization). ***PRACTICE AREAS:*** Family Law; Civil Litigation; Mediation.

ROUNTREE, LOSEE & BALDWIN, L.L.P.

Established in 1896
2419 MARKET STREET
P.O. BOX 1409
WILMINGTON, NORTH CAROLINA 28403
Telephone: 910-763-3404
Telecopier: 910-763-0320
URL: http://www.rlblawfirm.com

General Practice in all Courts. Civil Litigation, Business/Corporation, Admiralty, Environmental Law Litigation, Insurance, International, Estate Planning and Real Estate Law.

FIRM PROFILE: Among the oldest law firms in North Carolina, Rountree Losee & Baldwin was founded in 1896 by George Rountree, the grandfather of George Rountree, III. The firm today takes pride in representing local individuals and businesses, and also in its expanding regional and national business and litigation practices. The firm uses state-of-the-art technology to further its capabilities in providing high-quality, efficient legal services. The firm encourages its attorneys to participate in professional associations, politics, and civic affairs.

MEMBERS OF FIRM

GEORGE ROUNTREE, JR. (1904-1979)

GEORGE ROUNTREE, III, born Wilmington, North Carolina, August 10, 1933; admitted to bar, 1960, Arizona; 1962, North Carolina; 1969, U.S. Court of International Trade. *Education:* University of Arizona (B.A., cum laude, 1955; LL.B., 1960). Admitted to North Carolina Bar Association General Practice Hall of Fame, June 2004. Associate Editor, American Maritime Cases, 1969—. Member: North Carolina House of Representatives, 1971-1972; North Carolina Senate, 1972-1974. Listed in The Best Lawyers in America. *Member:* New Hanover County Bar Association (President, 1970-1971); State Bar of Arizona; North Carolina State Bar; Proctor in Admiralty, Maritime Law Association of the

(This Listing Continued)

ROUNTREE, LOSEE & BALDWIN, L.L.P., Wilmington—Continued

United States; Southeastern Admiralty Law Institute (Chairman, 1990); North Carolina Bar Association (Member, General Practice Hall of Fame, June 2004). ***PRACTICE AREAS:*** Admiralty; Commercial Law and Transactions; Civil Litigation. ***Email:*** grountree@rlblawfirm.com

GEOFFREY A. LOSEE, born Mineola, New York, November 24, 1963; admitted to bar, 1994, North Carolina and U.S. District Court, Eastern, Middle and Western Districts of North Carolina; U.S. Court of Appeals, Fourth Circuit. *Education:* U.S. Naval Academy (B.S., 1985); Campbell University (J.D. cum laude, 1994). Delta Theta Phi. Authorship: "Recent Developments in Admiralty Law in the Fourth and Other Circuits," 1994 Southeaster Admiralty Law Institute Annual Seminar Materials; "Recent Developments in Admiralty Law in the Fourth Circuit and Other Circuits," 1997 Southeastern Admiralty Law Institute Annual Seminar Materials. *Member:* New Hanover County and North Carolina Bar Associations; North Carolina State Bar; North Carolina Association of Trial Lawyers; Southeastern Admiralty Law Institute (Board of Directors, 1997-1998); Maritime Law Association. [U.S., Navy, Active, 1985-1991, Reserve 1991—; Rank CDR]. ***PRACTICE AREAS:*** Admiralty; Civil Litigation; Real Estate; Commercial Law; Commercial Transactions. ***Email:*** glosee@rlblawfirm.com

CHARLES S. BALDWIN, IV, born Winston-Salem, North Carolina, May 30, 1968; admitted to bar, 1993, North Carolina; 1994, District of Columbia; 1997, U.S. District Court, Eastern, Middle and Western Districts of North Carolina and U.S. Court of Appeals, Fourth Circuit. *Education:* University of North Carolina at Chapel Hill (B.A., 1990); American University (J.D., 1993; M.A., 1994); Georgetown University (LL.M., with distinction, 1996). Note and Comment Editor, Law Review. Author: "International Civil Dispute Resolution," West Publishing, 2000; "International Litigation: A Guide to Jurisdiction, Practice & Strategy," Transnational Publishers, 1998; "Protecting Confidential & Proprietary Commercial Information in International Arbitration," 31 Tex. Int'l L.J. 451, 1996. *Member:* New Hanover County Bar Association; North Carolina Bar Association (Member, International Law Section; Council Member, General Practice Section). ***PRACTICE AREAS:*** Litigation; Corporate Law; International. ***Email:*** cbaldwin@rlblawfirm.com

STEPHEN D. COGGINS, born Picayune, Mississippi, January 31, 1952; admitted to bar, 1978, North Carolina. *Education:* University of North Carolina at Chapel Hill (A.B., 1974); Wake Forest University (J.D., 1978). Recipient: North Carolina Bar Association Pro Bono Attorney of the Year, 2000; President's Award, Wake County Bar Association, 1997 and 1999. Member, Wake Forest Law Review. Law Clerk to the Honorable Franklin T. Dupree, Jr., U.S. District Judge, Eastern District of North Carolina, 1978-1980. Author: "NC Insurance Coverage Law," National Business Institute Seminar, 1997 and 1999; "Choice of Law and Insurance Coverage Matters and 50-State Survey;" "Liability Coverage for Intellectual Property Disputes: An Introductory Overview," The Defender, Vol. V, #7, Nov. 1995. Vice President: BarCARES of N.C., 1995—; Council for Entrepreneurial Development, 1988-1995. *Member:* Wake County, New Hanover County, North Carolina and American Bar Associations; North Carolina Association of Defense Attorneys; Defense Research Institute. ***PRACTICE AREAS:*** Commercial Litigation; Torts; Insurance Coverage; Environmental Law. ***Email:*** scoggins@rlblawfirm.com

JASON R. HARRIS, born Bronxville, New York, July 22, 1976; admitted to bar, 2001, North Carolina. *Education:* Auburn University (B.A., 1997); Wake Forest University (J.D., 2000); University of Miami School of Law (LL.M., Ocean and Coastal Law, 2001). Phi Kappa Phi; Pi Sigma Alpha; Golden Key. Author: "The Protection of Sunken Warships as Gravesites at Sea," 7 O. & C. L.J. 75 (2001); "The Protection of Sunken Warships as Objects Entitled to Sovereign Immunity," U. Miami Inter-Am L. Rev. 101 (2002). "Recent Development in Admiralty Law in the United States Supreme Court and the First, Second, Third and Fourth Circuits," Southeastern Admiralty Law Institute Program Materials, 2004. Instructor: Civil Litigation, Cape Fear Community College, Fall 2002; Criminal Law & Procedure, Cape Fear Community College, Spring 2003; Ocean & Coastal Law, Masters of Arts and Liberal Science Program, University of North Carolina at Wilmington, Fall 2003. Commercial Law, Cape Fear Community College, Spring 2004. Member: S.E. Admiralty Law Institute, 2001; Maritime Law Association, 2002; Member, 2002 and Board of Directors 2003-2004, Kiwani's Club; President, Cape Fear Auburn Club. *Member:* New Hanover County and North Carolina Bar Associations; North Carolina State Bar. [Army National Guard, Spec., E-4, 1994-2000; HHC 30th Engineer Brigade, Judge Advocate General Assistant, 71D slot, 214th Military Policy Company, 95B]. ***PRACTICE AREAS:*** Admiralty and Maritime Law; Criminal Law; Environmental Law; General Practice. ***Email:*** jharris@rlblawfirm.com

REPRESENTATIVE CLIENTS: American International Marine Agency; Answerthink, Inc.; Fireman's Fund Insurance Cos.; The Japan Shipowners' Mutual Protection & Indemnity Assn., Ltd.; Metropolitan Life Insurance Co.; MCO Industries, Inc.; MCO Transport, Inc.; The Travelers Insurance Co. (Marine Claims); Royal Insurance Co.; The Hartford; Bayliner Marine Corp.; Time Warner Entertainment; Del Laboratories; Stevedoring Services of America; Dean Hardwoods, Inc.; Bob King Pontiac - GMC, Inc.; Jerry Porters Motors Inc.; Coastal Carolina Yacht Yard Inc.; Baker Marine Corporation; Atlantic Diving & Marine Contractors, Inc.; Carolina Marine Terminal, Inc.; Fay Block Co.; Wilmington Pathology Associates, P.A.; Britthaven, Inc.; Barnes & Sons Masonry, LLC.
APPROVED ATTORNEYS FOR: Chicago Title Insurance Co.; Commonwealth Land Insurance Co.; Investors Title Insurance Co.; Lawyers Title Insurance Corp.; North Carolina Title Co.; Security Union Title Insurance Co.; The Title Guarantee Co.; United Title Insurance Co.
REFERENCES: Wachovia Bank; Bank of America; First Citizens Bank.

SAFFO LAW FIRM, P.C.

1508 MILITARY CUTOFF ROAD, SUITE 203
WILMINGTON, NORTH CAROLINA 28403
Telephone: 910-256-3364
Fax: 910-256-3301
URL: http://www.lawyers.com/saffolaw

Trusts and Estates, Estate Planning, Asset Protection, Estate Administration, Taxation, Tax Planning, Real Estate, Buying or Selling a Home, Zoning and Land Use, Business Transactions.

(This Listing Continued)

ANTHONY A. SAFFO, born 1961; admitted to bar, 1987, North Carolina; 1992, U.S. Tax Court; 1993, U.S. District Court, Eastern District of North Carolina. *Education:* University of North Carolina, Chapel Hill (B.A., 1983); Campbell University (J.D., 1987); Emory University (LL.M. in Taxation, 1988). *Member:* North Carolina State Bar. (Board Certified Specialist in Estate Planning and Probate Law, North Carolina State Board of Legal Specialization). ***PRACTICE AREAS:*** Trusts and Estates; Estate Planning; Asset Protection; Estate Administration; Taxation; Tax Planning; Real Estate; Residential Real Estate Sales; Zoning Law; Land Use; Business Transactions.

SEAY AND ALLEN
ATTORNEYS AND COUNSELORS AT LAW

519 MARKET STREET
WILMINGTON, NORTH CAROLINA 28401
Telephone: 910-763-2525
Fax: 910-251-7878

General Civil Practice. Trials in all State and Federal Courts. Corporation, Business Law, Insurance, Probate, Real Estate, Buying and Selling Homes, Criminal Defense, Traffic Violations, Driving While Intoxicated, Drug Crimes, Collections, Creditors Rights, Personal Injury, Automobile Accidents and Wrongful Death.

MEMBERS OF FIRM

JAMES L. SEAY, JR., born Raleigh, North Carolina, August 23, 1956; admitted to bar, 1982, North Carolina. *Education:* University of North Carolina at Chapel Hill (A.B., 1979); Campbell University (J.D., 1982). Member, Campbell University Law Review, 1982. *Member:* New Hanover County and North Carolina Bar Associations; North Carolina State Bar. [Retired, CDR, JAGC, USNR]

CHARLTON LARAMIE ALLEN, born Columbia, South Carolina, December 4, 1970; admitted to bar, 1997, North Carolina; 1998, U.S. District Court, Eastern District of North Carolina. *Education:* University of North Carolina at Chapel Hill (B.A., 1993; J.D., 1996). *Member:* New Hanover County, Fifth District, North Carolina and American Bar Associations; North Carolina State Bar; North Carolina Academy of Trial Lawyers.

SHANKLIN & NICHOLS, LLP

Established in 1988
214 MARKET STREET
P.O. BOX 1347
WILMINGTON, NORTH CAROLINA 28402-1347
Telephone: 910-762-9400
Fax: 910-251-1773
Email: shanklaw@earthlink.net
URL: http://www.shanklaw.com

Trial Practice in all Courts. Corporation, Real Estate, Appeals, Utilities, Condominium, Construction, Bankruptcy, Insurance, Municipal, Probate, zoning, Land Use, Estate Planning, Environmental, Personal Injury, Leasing and Admiralty.

FIRM PROFILE: Founded by Ken Shanklin in 1988, the firm represents a variety of corporate and commercial interests with principal emphasis on commercial and general real estate law. Mr. Shanklin has been a Board Certified Real Estate Specialist since 1991. Other areas of specific interest include bankruptcy, municipal, probate and utilities law, as well as commercial and civil litigation. Firm members are actively involved in the local community. Mr. Shanklin was on the county planning board for seven years and served as the chairman for five years. The firm primarily serves clients from southeast North Carolina as well as clients throughout the United States.

KENNETH A. SHANKLIN, born Mebane, North Carolina, May 25, 1948; admitted to bar, 1973, North Carolina and U.S. District Court, Eastern District of North Carolina; 1977, U.S. Court of Appeals, 4th Circuit; 1984, U.S. District Court, Middle District of North Carolina; 1985, U.S. District Court, Middle District of Georgia. *Education:* Appalachian State University (B.A., cum laude, 1970); University of North Carolina (J.D., 1973). Commissioner on Board of Commissioners of Navigation and Pilotage of the Cape Fear River, 1982-1985. Member and Chairman, New Hanover Planning Board, 1991-1998. *Member:* New Hanover County, North Carolina (Member, Committee on Law Office Economics, 1980-1984), Fifth Judicial District and American (Member, Sections on: Business; Real Property and Probate; Construction Law and Litigation) Bar Associations; The North Carolina State Bar; North Carolina Academy of Trial Lawyers; North Carolina Land Title Association. (Board Certified Specialist in Real Property Law - Residential, Business, Commercial and Industrial Transactions). ***PRACTICE AREAS:*** Real Estate Law; Commercial Law; Commercial Litigation; Municipal Law; Probate Law; Utility Law; Land Use Law; Estate Planning; Zoning Law; Environmental Law.

MATTHEW A. NICHOLS, born Morgantown, West Virginia, October 28, 1971; admitted to bar, 1996, North Carolina; 1998, New York; 2000, U.S. District Court, Eastern District of North Carolina. *Education:* University of Kentucky (B.A., With High Distinction, Dept. Honors in English, 1993); University of North Carolina at Chapel Hill (J.D., with Honors, 1996). Phi Beta Kappa. Recipient: O.J. & Ruby M. Wilson Award, University of Kentucky. Note Editor, North Carolina Law Review, 1995-1996; Staff Member, 1994-1995. Author: "Victor v. Nebraska: The Reasonable Doubt Dilemma," 79 N.C. L. Rev. 1709, 1995. Planning Board, Town of Wrightsville Beach, 2001—. Law Clerk to the Honorable William Norton Mason, U.S. Magistrate Judge, Eastern District of North Carolina, 1998-2000. *Member:* New Hanover County, New York State and American Bar Associations; North Carolina State Bar; North Carolina Academy of Trial Lawyers. ***PRACTICE AREAS:*** Civil Litigation; Land Use; Real Estate; Title Insurance; Administrative Law; Municipal Law; Zoning Law. ***Email:*** shanklaw@wilmington.net

(This Listing Continued)

STEPHANIE L. KIMBRO, born Nashville, Tennessee; admitted to bar, 2004, North Carolina. *Education:* Centre College of Kentucky (B.A., 1998); Miami University (M.A., 2000); University of Dayton School of Law (J.D., 2003). Omicron Delta Kappa, Phi Alpha Theta, Phi Sigma Iota. Law Review, Staff 2001-2002, Managing Editor 2002-2003, University of Dayton School of Law. Editor-in-Chief of Equitable Relief, University of Dayton School of Law Student Newspaper, 2001-2002. Editor-in-Chief of Centre College Cento, 1997-1998. *Member:* North Carolina Bar Association. ***LANGUAGES:*** French. ***PRACTICE AREAS:*** General Practice; Real Estate.

REPRESENTATIVE CLIENTS: Cabana de Mar Association, Inc.; Figure Eight Yacht Club, Inc.; J. Michael's Philly Deli; Ogden Construction Co.; Commonwealth Land Title Ins. Co.; The Bullock Company (Shopping Centers); Shell Island Resort Hotel HOA, Inc.; Central Carolina Bank; Federal Deposit Insurance Corp.; Small Business Adm.; Olde Point Property Owners Association; Wilmington Shipyard, Inc.; Coastal Carolina Developers; Mishra, Inc. (Hotels); Johnson Marine; Zimmer Development Co.; City National Bank of PA; Harbour Oaks HOA; Heron Run HOA; Ocean Dunes HOA.
APPROVED ATTORNEYS FOR: Commonwealth Land Title Ins. Co.; Investors Title Ins. Co.; Farmers Home Administration; Wachovia Mortgage Co.; Security Union Title Ins. Co.; Chicago Title Ins. Co.; The Title Co. of N.C.; Atlantic Land Title Agency.
SPECIAL COUNSEL FOR: Cape Fear River Navigation and Pilotage Commission; Board of Adjustment of the City of Wilmington; Town of Wrightsville Beach.

SHIPMAN, MASON & WRIGHT, L.L.P.

11 SOUTH FIFTH AVENUE
WILMINGTON, NORTH CAROLINA 28401
Telephone: 910-762-1990; 800-762-1990
Fax: 910-762-6752
URL: http://www.shipmanlaw.com

Focused Trial Practice in all Federal and State Courts. Complex Commercial Litigation, Product Liability, EIFS Litigation, Medical Devices, Medical Malpractice, Catastrophic Personal Injury and Wrongful Death, Nursing Home Litigation, Toxic Torts, Mold Litigation, Construction Litigation, and Consumer Class Actions.

FIRM PROFILE: Since 1980, we have been dedicated to the practice of complex litigation, focusing on the areas of corporate, commercial, personal injury and products liability. Shipman & Associates, L.L.P. possesses the technological capability, staff and library to effectively protect clients' interests. Whether negotiating a settlement, reaching agreement through arbitration, or trying cases, Shipman & Associates, L.L.P. is prepared to represent each client with unsurpassed legal expertise.

MEMBERS

GARY K. SHIPMAN, born Daytona Beach, Florida, July 30, 1956; admitted to bar, 1980, North Carolina and U.S. District Court, Eastern District of North Carolina. *Education:* University of North Carolina at Wilmington (B.A., cum laude, 1977); Campbell University (J.D., 1980). Delta Theta Phi. Author: "North Carolina's Unfair Trade Practices Act: A Port in the Storm of Tort Reform," Trial Briefs, Winter 1997; "The Economic Loss Rule in Products Liability Cases: How Far if Too Far?" Trial Briefs, November 2000. *Member:* New Hanover County (President, Young Lawyers Division, 1983-1986), North Carolina and American Bar Associations; North Carolina State Bar; North Carolina Academy of Trial Lawyers (Presidents Club); (Member: Medical Malpractice Subcommittee; Education Committee); The Association of Trial Lawyers of America; Southern Trial Lawyers Association. (Certified as a Civil Trial Specialist by the National Board of Trial Advocacy). ***PRACTICE AREAS:*** Catastrophic Injury; Wrongful Death; Medical Malpractice; Nursing Home Litigation; Products Liability; EIFS/Construction Litigation; Toxic Torts; Mold Litigation; Unfair Trade; Consumer Class Actions; Medical Devices; Tractor Trailer Accidents. ***Email:*** gshipman@shipmanlaw.com

WILLIAM NORTON MASON, born Winston-Salem, North Carolina, August 31, 1951; admitted to bar, 1977, North Carolina; 1985, U.S. District Court, Eastern District of North Carolina. *Education:* University of North Carolina at Chapel Hill (B.A., Anthropology, 1973); Wake Forest University (J.D., 1977). Assistant District Attorney, Fifth Judicial District, North Carolina, 1977-1981. Sole Practitioner, 1987-1983. Partner, Mason and Boney, 1984-1995. Part-Time U.S. Magistrate Judge, 1990-1995. Full-time U.S. Magistrate Judge, 1995-2003. Member, North Carolina Association of Trial Lawyers, 1995. *Member:* New Hanover County and North Carolina Bar Associations; North Carolina State Bar; Fifth Judicial Bar (Vice-President, 1982; President, 1983; Executive Committee Member, 1983). ***PRACTICE AREAS:*** Civil Litigation; Personal Injury; Wrongful Death; Criminal Defense; Mediation. ***Email:*** bmason@shipmanlaw.com

WILLIAM G. WRIGHT, born Wilmington, North Carolina, November 26, 1969; admitted to bar, 1999, North Carolina. *Education:* University of North Carolina at Wilmington (B.A., 1993); Campbell University (J.D., cum laude, 1999). Phi Alpha Theta; Omicron Delta Kappa; Phi Kappa Phi. Member, 1997-1999 and Articles Editor, 1998-1999, Campbell Law Review. Recipient, Corpus Juris Secundum Award, Criminal Law. Listed in Who's Who Among American Law Students, 1997-1999. Research Assistant: N.C. Court of Appeals, Hon. K. Edward Greene, 1999-2000; N.C. Superior Court Pattern Jury Instruction Committee-Criminal Subcommittee, 1997-1999. *Member:* North Carolina and American Bar Associations; North Carolina Academy of Trial Attorneys. ***LANGUAGES:*** Spanish. ***PRACTICE AREAS:*** Complex Commercial Litigation; Medical Malpractice; Nursing Home Abuse and Neglect; Catastrophic Injury; Wrongful Death; Products Liability; Construction Litigation; Truck Accidents; Consumer Class Actions; Appellate Practice; Unfair Trade. ***Email:*** wwright@shipmanlaw.com

ASSOCIATES

NICOLE JO MOSS, born Detroit, Michigan; admitted to bar, 2000, Maryland; 2001, District of Columbia; 2003, North Carolina. *Education:* Hawaii Pacific University (B.A., summa cum laude, 1996); Harvard University Law School (J.D., cum laude, 2000). Phi Sigma Alpha and Alpha Chi. Articles Editor, Harvard Journal of Law & Public Policy. President, Harvard Federalist Society for Law & Public Policy. Formerly with Covington & Burling. ***LANGUAGES:*** French and Spanish. ***PRACTICE AREAS:*** Complex Commercial Litigation; Products Liability; Medical Devices; Mass Torts; Unfair Trade; Consumer Class Actions; Appellate Practice. ***Email:*** nmoss@shipmanlaw.com

BRIAN ANDREW GESCHICKTER, born Washington, D.C., April 6, 1966; admitted to bar, 1992, Virginia; 1993, U.S District Court, Eastern District of Virginia; 1994, U.S. Court of Appeals, Fourth Circuit; 2004, North Carolina. *Education:* University of Virginia (B.A., history, 1989); George Mason University School of Law (J.D., 1992). Law Clerk: Chief Judge Richard J. Jamborsky and the Honorable Stanley P. Klein, Fairfax County Circuit Court, 1992-1993; National Moot Court Competition Region IV Committee Member, 1994-1999. Co-Chair, 1996-1998. *Member:* Fairfax County Bar Association; Virginia State Bar; North Carolina Bar. ***PRACTICE AREAS:*** Civil Litigation; Personal Injury; Wrongful Death; Medical Malpractice; Contracts; Workers Compensation. ***Email:*** bgeschickter@shipmanlaw.com

SMITH MOORE LLP

Established in 1919
300 NORTH THIRD STREET, SUITE 301
WILMINGTON, NORTH CAROLINA 28401
Telephone: 910-251-7001
Fax: 910-251-7007
Email: smith.moore@smithmoorelaw.com
URL: http://www.smithmoorelaw.com

Greensboro, North Carolina Office: Wachovia Tower, 300 North Greene Street, Suite 1400, P.O. Box 21927. Telephone: 336-378-5200. Fax: 336-378-5400.
Raleigh, North Carolina Office: 2800 Two Hannover Square, P.O. Box 27525. Telephone: 919-755-8700. Fax: 919-755-8800.
Atlanta, Georgia Office: One Atlantic Center, Suite 3700, 1201 West Peachtree Street. Telephone: 404-962-1000. Fax: 404-962-1200.

General, Trial and Appellate Practice in All State and Federal Courts, Dispute Resolution, Corporate, Taxation, Securities Regulation, Real Property and Finance, Labor and Employment (Management) Law, Employee Benefits, International and Immigration, Antitrust and Trade Regulation, Negligence, Products Liability, Insurance Coverage, Media, Banking, Commercial, Bankruptcy, Administrative, Environmental, Hospital and Health Care, Public Authority and Public Finance, Estate Planning and Administration, Probate, Legislative, Intellectual Property, Education, and Sports Law.

LAW FIRM ALLIANCES/ASSOCIATIONS: **TERRALEX, THE WORLDWIDE NETWORK OF INDEPENDENT LAW FIRMS**

PARTNER

MICHAEL V. LEE, admitted to bar, 1997, South Carolina; 1998, North Carolina. *Education:* University of North Carolina at Chapel Hill (B.A., 1991); Wake Forest University (J.D., cum laude, 1997). ***PRACTICE AREAS:*** Business; Real Estate Development. ***Email:*** michael.lee@smithmoorelaw.com

REPRESENTATIVE CLIENTS: AIG Insurance Group; Atlantic Coast Conference; Branch Banking and Trust Co.; Board of Commissioners of Douglas County; Board of Commissioners of Georgia County; Digital Optics; Dixon Hughes LLP; Eli Lilly and Co.; General Electric Co.; General Motors Corp.; Greensboro News & Record Co.; Miller Brewing Co.; North Carolina Hospital Association; Penn Western Benefits; Prime Care Health Networks; Royal & SunAlliance; Stafford Development Company; Stockhausen, Inc.; The Coca-Cola Co.; The Moses H. Cone Memorial Hospital; The Procter & Gamble Co.; United Dominion Industries, Inc.; Warner-Lambert Co.; Watauga Medical Center; Wayne Memorial Hospital.

(For complete biographical data on all personnel, see Professional Biographies at Greensboro, North Carolina)

STEVENS, McGHEE, MORGAN, LENNON & TOLL, L.L.P.

Established in 1917
602 MARKET STREET
P.O. DRAWER 59
WILMINGTON, NORTH CAROLINA 28402
Telephone: 910-763-3666
Fax: 910-251-9562

General Practice, Trials in all State and Federal Courts, Commercial Litigation, Eminent Domain, Corporation, Real Estate, Probate, Land Use and Zoning, Insurance, and Utilities.

MEMBERS OF FIRM

JOHN A. STEVENS (1895-1990)

KARL W. McGHEE (1923-1981)

RICHARD M. MORGAN, born Hamlet, North Carolina, July 18, 1940; admitted to bar, 1965, North Carolina. *Education:* Davidson College (A.B., 1962); Duke University (J.D., 1965). Phi Alpha Delta. *Member:* New Hanover County, 5th Judicial District and North Carolina Associations; North Carolina State Bar. ***PRACTICE AREAS:*** Business Law; Commercial Litigation; Eminent Domain; Estate Planning; Probate.

ALTON Y. LENNON, born Wilmington, North Carolina, December 27, 1942; admitted to bar, 1968, North Carolina. *Education:* Wake Forest University (B.A., 1965; J.D., 1968). Phi Delta Phi; Omicron Delta Kappa; Phi Alpha Theta. *Member:* New Hanover County, 5th Judicial District and North Carolina Bar Associations; North Carolina State Bar. ***PRACTICE AREAS:*** Commercial Transactions; Land Use and Zoning Litigation; Probate.

ALAN E. TOLL, born South Bend, Indiana, December 27, 1954; admitted to bar, 1984, North Carolina. *Education:* University of North Carolina (B.A., 1977); Wake Forest University (J.D., 1984). Member, Order of the Grail; Holderness; Moot Court Board. *Member:* New Hanover County, Fifth Judicial District and North Carolina Bar Associations; North

(This Listing Continued)

STEVENS, McGHEE, MORGAN, LENNON & TOLL, L.L.P., Wilmington—Continued

Carolina State Bar; North Carolina Academy of Trial Lawyers. ***PRACTICE AREAS:*** Civil Litigation; Banking; Creditors Rights; Business Law; Corporate Law; Construction Law; Employment; Eminent Domain.

MARK F. CARTER, born Savannah, Georgia, February 15, 1967; admitted to bar, 1992, North Carolina. *Education:* University of North Carolina, Chapel Hill (B.S., Business Administration, 1989); Campbell University (J.D., cum laude, 1992). Delta Sigma Pi. *Member:* New Hanover County, North Carolina and 5th Judicial District Bar Associations; North Carolina State Bar. ***PRACTICE AREAS:*** Real Estate; Civil Litigation; Corporate; Business.

ASSOCIATE

KURT B. FRYAR, born Bethesda, Maryland, May 16, 1975; admitted to bar, 2002, North Carolina. *Education:* University of North Carolina at Wilmington (B.S., 1998; M.S., 1999); University of North Carolina at Chapel Hill (J.D., 2002). Beta Alpha Psi; Beta Gamma Sigma Honorary Business Fraternity. Recipient: J.W. Jackson Scholarship. Staff Member, North Carolina Banking Institute, 2000-2001. *Member:* New Hanover County and Fifth Judicial District Bar Associations; North Carolina State Bar.

REPRESENTATIVE CLIENTS: aaiPharma, Inc.; Archmill Place, Inc.; Automatic Data Processing; Bank of America, N.A.; Bayshore Estates, Inc.; Beau Rivage Homeowners Association; Belvedere Plantation, LLC; Biltwell, Inc.; B.R. Dorsett Construction Company; Cameron Company L.L.C.; Carolina Orthopedics and Sports Medicine, PLLC; Cape Fear Bonded Warehouse, Inc.; Cape Homeowners Association; Carolian Pediatrics of Wilmington, P.A.; Coastal Water Systems, Inc; Cooperative Bank; Corbett Farming Company; Hanover Iron Works, Inc.; HCD Contractors; Jackson Beverage Company; JBR Enterprises of Winnabow; JDC America; Leland Development Company, LLC; Longley Supply Co.; Marvil Package Company; Monkey Junction Self-Storage, Inc.; New Bern Fitness, Inc.; New Hanover Associates; Osprey Point Homeowners Association; Pilot's Ridge HOA, Inc.; Point Associates, L.L.C.; Porter's Neck Fitness, Inc.; Rare Cargo, Inc.; Roy's Riverboat Landing, Inc.; Ryan Walsh; S & G Prestress Company; SHV Golf Course, L.L.C.; South Harbor Village Associates, L.L.C.; Wheel Estates, Inc.; Wrightsville Dunes Homeowners Association; Viable Corp.; Wachovia Bank, N.A.; W.H. McEachern's Sons, Inc; Westport HOA, Inc.; Wilmington Holding Corp.; Z.A. Sneeden's Sons, Inc.
APPROVED ATTORNEYS FOR: Chicago Title Insurance Co.; Commonwealth Land Title Insurance Co.; Investors Title Insurance Co.; Old Republic Title Insurance Co.; Lawyers Title Insurance Co.

THE SULLIVAN LAW FIRM, P.C.

29 NORTH THIRD STREET
WILMINGTON, NORTH CAROLINA 28401
Telephone: 910-362-1809
Fax: 910-362-9925
Email: sullivan-law@bizec.rr.com
URL: http://www.sullivantriallaw.com

Criminal Law, Criminal Defense, White Collar Crime, Fraud, DWI, Drug Crimes, Felonies and Misdemeanors, Homicide, Sexual Assault, Parole and Probation, Traffic Violations, Personal Injury, Automobile Accidents, Wrongful Death.

DENNIS H. SULLIVAN, JR., born Chapel Hill, North Carolina, August 17, 1968; admitted to bar, 1994, North Carolina and U.S. District Court, Eastern District of North Carolina; 2003, U.S. Supreme Court and U.S. Court of Appeals, 4th Circuit. *Education:* North Carolina State University (B.A., 1990); Campbell University (J.D., 1994). Phi Alpha Delta. Federalist Society. *Member:* 5th Judicial District, North Carolina (Former 5th Judicial District Representative, Young Lawyers Division) and American Bar Associations; North Carolina State Bar; North Carolina Academy of Trial Lawyers; New Hanover County Trial Lawyers Association (Founder and President); National Association of Criminal Defense Lawyers; North Carolina Academy of Trial Lawyers (Member, Board of Governors; Co-Chair, Criminal Law Section CLE, 2004—);. (Board Certified Specialist in State and Federal Criminal Law, North Carolina State Board of Legal Specialization). ***PRACTICE AREAS:*** Criminal Law; Driving While Intoxicated; Traffic Violations; White Collar Crime; Drug Crimes; Violent Crimes; Sex Crimes; Sex Offenses; Fraud; Criminal Defense of Immigrants. ***Email:*** sullivan-law@bizec.rr.com

---

CHARLES M. TIGHE

5725 OLEANDER DRIVE, SUITE E-3
WILMINGTON, NORTH CAROLINA 28403
Telephone: 910-794-4444
Fax: 910-794-4244
URL: http://www.tighelex.com
URL: http://www.charlestighe.com

General Practice, Civil Trials in all Courts, Corporate, Business Law, Intellectual Property, Commercial and Construction Law, Employment Law Discrimination, Employee Benefits, Sexual Harassment, Wrongful Termination, Civil Rights Discrimination, Land Use, Zoning, and Environmental Law, Decedents Estates, Wills, and Estate Planning.

CHARLES M. TIGHE, born Bronxville, New York, September 29, 1934; admitted to bar, 1960, Connecticut; 1969, U.S. Court of Appeals, Second Circuit; 1970, U.S. District Court, District of Connecticut; 1992, North Carolina; 1994, U.S. District Court, Eastern District of North Carolina; 1999, U.S. Court of Appeals, Fourth Circuit. *Education:* Harvard University (A.B., 1957; J.D., 1960). *Member:* New Hanover County, Connecticut (Member, Municipal Law and Governmental Services Committee, 1975-1993; Member, 1976-1993, and Chairman, 1986-1988, Executive Committee, Planning and Zoning Section) and North Carolina Bar Associations; North Carolina State Bar.

EDWIN J. TISDALE, ATTORNEY AT LAW PLLC

609-A PINER ROAD
P.O. BOX 323
WILMINGTON, NORTH CAROLINA 28409
Telephone: 910-343-4992
Fax: 910-343-4101
Email: edtisdale@yahoo.com
URL: http://www.edwintisdale.com

Family Law, Divorce, Child Support, Business Law, Copyrights and Trademarks, Estate Planning, Trusts and Estates, Wills, Probate, Real Estate, Environmental Law.

EDWIN J. TISDALE, born Norfolk, Virginia, December 7, 1962; admitted to bar, 1992, North Carolina. *Education:* Virginia Commonwealth University (B.S., 1985); University of North Carolina at Chapel Hill (J.D., 1991). *Member:* New Hanover County and North Carolina Bar Associations; North Carolina State Bar; 5th Judicial District Bar. ***PRACTICE AREAS:*** Family Law; Business Law; Small Business Law; Closely Held Business Law; Wills; Trusts and Estates; Probate; Real Estate. ***Email:*** edtisdale@yahoo.com

---

WARD AND SMITH, P.A.

Established in 1895
UNIVERSITY CORPORATE CENTER
127 RACINE DRIVE
P.O. BOX 7068
WILMINGTON, NORTH CAROLINA 28406-7068
Telephone: 910-794-4800
Facsimile: 910-794-4877
Email: wardsmith@wardandsmith.com
URL: http://www.wardandsmith.com

New Bern, North Carolina Office: 1001 College Court. P.O. Box 867. Telephone: 252-672-5400. Facsimile: 252-672-5477.
Greenville, North Carolina Office: 120 West Fire Tower Road, P.O. Box 8088. Telephone: 252-215-4000. Facsimile: 252-215-4077.
Raleigh, North Carolina Office: Suite 2400, Two Hannover Square, Fayetteville Street Mall, P.O. Box 2091. Telephone: 919-836-4260. Facsimile: 919-836-4277.

General and Trial Practice. Admiralty Law; Bankruptcy; Banks and Banking; Business Law; Civil Rights; Commercial Law; Construction Law; Contracts; Copyrights; Corporate Law; Debtor and Creditor; Elder Law; Eminent Domain; Employee Benefits; Environmental Law; Family Law including Divorce; Finance; Franchise Law; Government; Government Contracts; Health Care Law; Immigration and Naturalization; Insurance; International Law; International Trade; Investments; Labor and Employment including Discrimination, Sexual Harassment, and Workers' Compensation; Landlord and Tenant; Litigation; Personal Injury including Automobile Accidents, Legal Malpractice and Medical Malpractice; Products Liability; Real Estate; Securities; Taxation; Technology and Science including Internet Law, Trademarks, and Patents; Trusts and Estates including Estate Planning and Wills and Probate; Zoning and Land Use.

FIRM PROFILE: Located in Greenville, New Bern, Raleigh, and Wilmington, we are successor to a practice founded in New Bern, North Carolina in 1895. Our firm has grown to over 60 attorneys and more than 160 support staff members who are committed to quality and responsiveness. We strive to deliver a product that is tailored to our clients' unique needs wherever and whenever the need should arise. Our attorneys may be contacted by either a phone call or a confidential email, in or out of the office and at home. Attorney availability reinforces our commitment to a strong attorney-client relationship and a proactive and preventive approach to our clients' legal issues. Our philosophy is to utilize other attorneys in the firm whose knowledge and expertise allows a more efficient and timely delivery of our clients' legal services. In summary, the collective mission of our attorneys, legal assistants, and administrative staff is to provide our clients with the highest quality legal service at an affordable cost.

ADAM M. BEAUDOIN, admitted to bar, 2001, North Carolina. *Education:* James Madison University (B.A., magna cum laude, 1998); University of Richmond (J.D., cum laude, 2001). *Member:* Craven County (President, 2004-2005), North Carolina and American Bar Associations; North Carolina State Bar. ***PRACTICE AREAS:*** Business Law; Corporate Law; Nonprofit Organizations Law; Limited Liability Company Law; Real Estate - Community Associations; Dealer/Distributor and Franchising. ***Email:*** amb@wardandsmith.com

JENNA FRUECHTENICHT BUTLER, admitted to bar, 1996, North Carolina and Georgia. *Education:* Wake Forest University (B.A., magna cum laude, 1992); Wake Forest University School of Law (J.D., cum laude, 1995). Member, Moot Court Board. Notes and Comments Editor, Wake Forest Law Review. Law Clerk to the Honorable Malcolm J. Howard, U.S. District Judge, Eastern District of North Carolina, 1995-1996. *Member:* North Carolina Bar Association; North Carolina State Bar; State Bar of Georgia; North Carolina Association of Defense Attorneys; National Association of Women in Construction. ***PRACTICE AREAS:*** Business Litigation; Construction Law; Contract Litigation; Community Associations; Civil Litigation; Family Law. ***Email:*** jfb@wardandsmith.com

ALEXANDER C. DALE, admitted to bar, 2001, North Carolina. *Education:* University of North Carolina (B.A., 1998; M.A., 2001); Duke University School of Law (J.D., 2001). Phi Beta Kappa. Research Editor, Duke Journal of Comparative and International Law. *Member:* North Carolina and American Bar Associations; North Carolina State Bar; North Carolina Academy of Trial Lawyers. ***PRACTICE AREAS:*** Litigation; Business; Technology; Intellectual Property; Civil Litigation; Administrative Law; Alternative Dispute Resolution; Appellate Practice; Communications and Media; Computers and Software; Copyrights; Investments; Libel, Slander and Defamation; Media Law; Privacy Law;

(This Listing Continued)

Trademarks; Unfair Competition; Trusts and Estates Litigation; Securities Litigation; Business Disolution Litigation; Community Associations. ***Email:*** acd@wardandsmith.com

GEORGE K. FREEMAN, JR., admitted to bar, 1955, North Carolina. *Education:* University of North Carolina (B.S.B.A., 1952); Harvard University (J.D., cum laude, 1955). *Member:* North Carolina and American Bar Associations; North Carolina State Bar; American Arbitration Association; National Panel of Arbitrators. ***PRACTICE AREAS:*** Construction Law; Litigation; Family Law; Civil Litigation. ***Email:*** gkf@wardandsmith.com

CONSTANTINE C. HINGSON, admitted to bar, 2004, North Carolina. *Education:* University of North Carolina (B.A., 1998); Campbell University (J.D., 2004). *Member:* North Carolina State Bar. ***PRACTICE AREAS:*** Litigation. ***Email:*** cch@wardandsmith.com

THOMAS H. JOHNSON, JR., admitted to bar, 1985, North Carolina; 1988, U.S. District Court, Eastern District of North Carolina; 1993, U.S. Court of Appeals, Fourth Circuit; 1995, U.S. Court of Appeals for Veteran's Claims. *Education:* University of North Carolina at Chapel Hill (B.S., 1982; J.D., 1985). Phi Beta Kappa. *Member:* Pitt County (President, 1994-1995), North Carolina (Member: Business Law Section; Real Property Law Section; Estate Planning and Fiduciary Law Section; Law Practice Management Section; Zoning, Planning and Land Use Section) and American (Member: Business Law Section; Real Property and Probate Law Section; General Practice, Solo, and Small Firm Section) Bar Associations; North Carolina State Bar. ***PRACTICE AREAS:*** Real Estate. ***Email:*** thj@wardandsmith.com

W. DANIEL MARTIN, III, admitted to bar, 1973, North Carolina. *Education:* North Carolina State University (B.A., 1969); University of North Carolina (J.D., 1973). *Member:* North Carolina (Member, Real Property Section Council, 1984-1987) and American Bar Associations; North Carolina State Bar; Community Associations Institute; North Carolina Land Title Association. ***PRACTICE AREAS:*** Business Law; Community Associations; Real Estate; Commercial Real Estate; Planning and Land Use. ***Email:*** wdm@wardandsmith.com

JOHN REEVES SLOAN, admitted to bar, 1990, Virginia; 1994, North Carolina. *Education:* University of North Carolina (A.B., 1987; J.D., with honors, 1990). National Moot Court Team; Holderness Moot Court Bench. *Member:* North Carolina, Virginia and American Bar Associations; Virginia State Bar; North Carolina State Bar. (Board Certified Specialist in Estate Planning and Probate Law, North Carolina State Board of Legal Specialization). ***PRACTICE AREAS:*** Trusts and Estates; Wills and Probate; Taxation. ***Email:*** jrs@wardandsmith.com

JOHN P. SWART, admitted to bar, 1981, North Carolina. *Education:* East Tennessee State University (B.S., magna cum laude, 1974); University of Tennessee (J.D., 1980). Order of the Coif. *Member:* North Carolina State Bar. ***PRACTICE AREAS:*** Litigation; Personal Injury; Wrongful Death; Civil Litigation. ***Email:*** jps@wardandsmith.com

RYAL W. TAYLOE, admitted to bar, 1982, North Carolina. *Education:* University of North Carolina (B.A., 1979); Wake Forest University (J.D., 1982). *Member:* North Carolina and American Bar Associations; North Carolina State Bar; North Carolina Academy of Trial Lawyers; The Association of Trial Lawyers of America. ***PRACTICE AREAS:*** Construction Law; Eminent Domain; Litigation; Real Estate. ***Email:*** rwt@wardandsmith.com

MATTHEW W. THOMPSON, admitted to bar, 2004, North Carolina. *Education:* University of Delaware (B.A., 2000); William and Mary School of Law (J.D., 2004). Phi Beta Kappa. *Member:* North Carolina State Bar. ***PRACTICE AREAS:*** Trusts and Estates. ***Email:*** mwt@wardandsmith.com

A. REXFORD WILLIS, III, admitted to bar, 1980, North Carolina; 1986, U.S. Tax Court. *Education:* University of North Carolina (B.S., 1977; J.D., 1980). Certified Public Accountant, North Carolina, 1982. *Member:* North Carolina and American Bar Associations; North Carolina State Bar; North Carolina Association of Certified Public Accountants. ***PRACTICE AREAS:*** Business Law; Trusts and Estates; Corporate Law; Tax Law. ***Email:*** arw@wardandsmith.com

REPRESENTATIVE CLIENTS: Amital Spinning Corp.; Atlantic Coast Contracting; Atlantic States Bank; Barnhill Contracting Company; Cape Fear Community College; Central Carolina Bank and Trust Co.; Chubb Insurance; City of Havelock; Craven Community College; Daedong- USA, Inc.; East Carolina Bank; Eastern Carolina Regional Housing Authority; Eastern Radiologists, Inc.; First-Citizens Bank & Trust Company; First Flight Federal Credit Union; Fountain Powerboats, Inc.; Hatteras Yachts; Ironstone Bank; Janus Development Group; Mountainbank Financial Corp.; NC State Firemen's Association; Neuse Regional Water & Sewer; Physicians East, P.A.; Potash Corp.; Southern Banc & Trust Co.; State of North Carolina; Weyerhaeuser Co.; Wilmington Cardiology, PLLC.

(For complete biographical data on all personnel, see professional biographies at New Bern, North Carolina)

WESSELL & RANEY, L.L.P.

107-B NORTH 2ND STREET
P.O. BOX 1049
WILMINGTON, NORTH CAROLINA 28402
Telephone: 910-762-7475
Facsimile: 910-762-7557
Email: wrlaw@bellsouth.net

General Civil Practice in all Courts. Corporation, Real Estate, Probate, Municipal, Environmental, Commercial, Collection Law and Zoning, Planning and Land Use Law.

MEMBERS OF FIRM

JOHN C. WESSELL, III, born Wilmington, North Carolina, October 20, 1946; admitted to bar, 1976, North Carolina and U.S. District Court, Eastern District of North Carolina. *Education:* Davidson College; University of North Carolina (B.A., 1968); Wake Forest University (J.D., 1976). Phi Delta Phi. Member, Wake Forest Law Review, 1975-1976. *Member:* New Hanover County, Fifth Judicial District and North Carolina Bar Associations; North Carolina State Bar. [CDR, USNR-R]. ***PRACTICE AREAS:*** Collections; Commercial Law; Municipal Law; Corporate Law; Civil Litigation; Real Estate; Zoning, Planning and Land Use; Probate. ***Email:*** wessell@bellsouth.net

(This Listing Continued)

WILLIAM A. RANEY, JR., born Wilmington, North Carolina, February 16, 1947; admitted to bar, 1973, North Carolina; 1975, U.S. District Court, Eastern District of North Carolina; 1978, U.S. Supreme Court; 1982, U.S. Court of Appeals, Fourth Circuit. *Education:* University of North Carolina (B.A., 1969; J.D., 1973). Head of Environmental Protection Section, North Carolina Attorney General's Office, 1976-1982. *Member:* New Hanover County (Past President) and North Carolina (Past Chairman, Environmental and Natural Resources Law Section) Bar Associations; North Carolina State Bar. ***PRACTICE AREAS:*** Environmental Law; Real Estate Law; Corporate Law; Civil Litigation. ***Email:*** waraney@bellsouth.net

REPRESENTATIVE CLIENTS: Town of Wrightsville Beach; Town of Leland; City of Northwest; Wilmington Industrial Development, Inc.; Figure 8 Beach Homeowners Assn.; Brick Landing Plantation Homeowners Assn.; Shinn Point Homeowners Assn.; CEWD Credit Union; Hanover Federal Credit Union; Butler's Wholesale Electric; M & M Plumbing Company, Inc.; Tinney Painting, Inc.; Land Management Group, Inc.; Remote Data Systems, Inc.; Wilmington Housing Fincnce & Development, Inc.
APPROVED ATTORNEYS FOR: The Title Company of North Carolina, Inc.; Lawyers Title Insurance Corp.; Chicago Title Insurance Co.; Commonwealth Land Title Insurance Co.; Investors Title Insurance Co.; American Title Insurance Co.; First Title Insurance Corp.; Jefferson-Pilot Title Insurance Co.; United Title Insurance Co.
REFERENCE: Branch Banking and Trust Co.

WHITE & HEARNE, L.L.P.

265 RACINE DRIVE, UNIT 104
WILMINGTON, NORTH CAROLINA 28403
Telephone: 910-313-3336
Toll Free: 800-807-4783
Facsimile: 910-798-9294
URL: http://www.woodywhite.com
URL: http://www.whiteandhearne.com

General Practice in all Courts concentrating in Federal and State Criminal Law, Residential and Commercial Real Estate, Zoning and Land Use, DWI, Traffic Violations, Wills, Business Law, Misdemeaners, Felonies, Assaults, Personal Injury, Automobile Accidents, Wrongful Death, Medical Malpractice, Insurance and Civil Litigation.

WOODY WHITE, born Kinston, North Carolina, August 4, 1969; admitted to bar, 1994, North Carolina. *Education:* Southern College (B.A., 1991); University of Nebraska (J.D., 1994). President, Southern College Student Body, 1990-1991. Chairman, New Hanover County Republican Party, 1997-2001. Member, Federal Criminal Justice Act Panel Attorney. Trustee, New Hanover Regional Medical Center, 1999-2002; Chief Legal Counsel, NC Republican Party, 2002-2004. Senator, North Carolina, 2004. Board Member, Coastal Horizons of North Carolina, 2003-2004. *Member:* New Hanover County and North Carolina Bar Associations; North Carolina State Bar. ***PRACTICE AREAS:*** Criminal Law; Civil Litigation; Criminal Defense; Traffic Violations; Personal Injury; Wrongful Death; Business Law; Wills; Estate Planning. ***Email:*** woodyw7@aol.com

JOSEPH C. HEARNE, II, born Cherry Point, North Carolina, September 8, 1964; admitted to bar, 1991, North Carolina and U.S. District Court, Eastern District of North Carolina. *Education:* North Carolina State University; University of North Carolina at Chapel Hill (B.A., 1986); Wake Forest University (J.D., 1990). Member, Phi Delta Phi, Environmental Law Society. Member, Wilmington City Council, 1997-2001. Trustee, Wilmington-Cape Fear Homebuilders Association.*Member:* New Hanover County and North Carolina Bar Associations; North Carolina State Bar; Fifth Judicial Bar Association. ***PRACTICE AREAS:*** Residential Real Estate; Commercial Real Estate; Business Law; Wills; Zoning, Planning and Land Use. ***Email:*** jchearne2@aol.com

THE WORKERS COMPENSATION LAW FIRM

Established in 2002
508 MARKET STREET
WILMINGTON, NORTH CAROLINA 28401
Telephone: 910-251-0004
Fax: 910-251-0005
Email: scriner@twclf.com
URL: http://www.twclf.com
Mailing Address: P.O. Box 7275, Wilmington, NC 28406
Workers Compensation, Alternative Dispute Resolution.

FIRM PROFILE: Cary Office: 1120 Southeast Cary Parkway, Suite 201, 27511. Telephone: 919-852-0003.

MR. SHERMAN LEE CRINER, born Raleigh, North Carolina, May 10, 1966; admitted to bar, 1994, North Carolina; 1995, U.S. District Court, Eastern District of North Carolina; 1998, U.S. Court of Appeals, Fourth Circuit and U.S. Supreme Court; 2001, South Carolina. *Education:* North Carolina State University (B.A., Political Science, 1988); Campbell University (M.B.A., J.D., 1993). Certified Mediator, North Carolina Dispute Resolution Commission; D.R.C. Superior Court Mediator; D.R.C. Equitable Distribution and Other Family Financial Cases Mediator; N.C.I.C. Mediator; Arbitrator. *Member:* New Hanover County, North Carolina (Member, Dispute Resolution Commission, 2002-2005; Chairman, Mediation Committee, Workers Compensation Section, 2001-2003; Hispanic and Latino Committee; Section Counsel, Dispute Resolution Section, 2000-2003 and Membership Committee Chairman, 1999-2002) and American (Member, Dispute Resolution Section) Bar Associations. (Board Certified Specialist in Workers' Compensation, North Carolina State Board of Legal Specialization). ***PRACTICE AREAS:*** Workers Compensation; Alternative Dispute Resolution; Civil Litigation; Mediation. ***Email:*** scriner@twclf.com

YOW, FOX & MANNEN, L.L.P.

Established in 1933

102 NORTH FIFTH AVENUE

P.O. DRAWER 479

WILMINGTON, NORTH CAROLINA 28401

Telephone: 910-762-2421

Fax: 910-251-9247

General Civil and Criminal Trial Practice in all State and Federal Courts. Personal Injury, Automobile Accidents, Wrongful Death, Probate, Estate Planning, Administration, Corporation and Business Law, Real Estate Law, Buying or Selling a Home, Landlord and Tenant, Zoning and Land Use, Workers Compensation, Appellate Work, Commercial Litigation, Collections, Construction Law.

FIRM PROFILE: Founded in 1933, Yow, Fox & Mannen, L.L.P. has its origins in the practice founded by Edgar L. and Cicero P. Yow, in Wilmington, North Carolina. Today, the firm consists of 3 lawyers, with a total of more than 84 years of combined legal experience, and a comprehensive support staff with a General Civil and Criminal Trial Practice in all State and Federal Courts. For a complete picture of all the areas of law that the firm is involved, see our statement of practice listed above. Yow, Fox & Mannen, L.L.P.'s goal is to combine the accessibility and attentiveness of a small firm with the skills, experience and resources commonly associated with a large law firm. The firm also strives to offer cost-effective representation while providing high-quality, aggressive defense for its diverse clientele, ranging from individuals to corporations with local, national or international needs.

MEMBERS OF FIRM

EDGAR L. YOW (1902-1983)

CICERO P. YOW (1914-1990)

WILLIAM ALLEN COBB (1917-1999)

DOUGLAS A. FOX, born Newark, New Jersey, March 23, 1948; admitted to bar, 1974, North Carolina; 1976, U.S. District Court, Eastern District of North Carolina; 1978, U.S. District Court, Middle District of North Carolina; 1983, U.S. Court of Appeals, Fourth Circuit. *Education:* Guilford College (B.A., 1970); Cumberland School of Law of Samford University (J.D., 1973). Delta Theta Phi. *Member:* New Hanover County (President, 1986-1987) and North Carolina Bar Associations; The North Carolina State Bar; North Carolina Academy of Trial Lawyers; North Carolina Alcohol Beverage Control Commission (Chairman). ***PRACTICE AREAS:*** Real Estate Law; Business Law; Collections; Personal Injury. ***Email:*** dfox@yfmlaw.com

JERRY A. MANNEN, JR., born Kinston, North Carolina, December 9, 1961; admitted to bar, 1990, North Carolina; 1991, U.S. District Court, Eastern District of North Carolina; 1993, U.S. District Court, Middle and Western Districts of North Carolina and U.S. Court of Appeals, Fourth Circuit. *Education:* North Carolina State University (B.A., Business Management and Economics, 1985); Campbell University (J.D., 1990). Phi Alpha Delta. Treasurer, Federalist Society, 1989-1990. *Member:* New Hanover County and American Bar Associations; North Carolina State Bar; North Carolina Academy of Trial Lawyers; North Carolina Real Estate Commission. ***PRACTICE AREAS:*** Civil Litigation; Criminal Litigation; Debtor/Creditor; Appeals; Personal Injury; Business Law; Construction Law. ***Email:*** jmannen@yfmlaw.com

OF COUNSEL

LIONEL L. YOW, born Wallace, North Carolina, February 9, 1943; admitted to bar, 1968, North Carolina. *Education:* Wilmington College (B.A., 1965); University of South Carolina (J.D., 1968). Phi Delta Phi. *Member:* New Hanover County (Member, Executive Board, 1978-1981), North Carolina and American Bar Associations; The North Carolina State Bar; North Carolina Academy of Trial Lawyers. ***PRACTICE AREAS:*** Real Estate Development Law; Litigation; Employment Law; Workers Compensation Law.

REPRESENTATIVE CLIENTS: EBCO Inc.; General Motors Acceptance Corp.; New Hanover County ABC Board; Porters Neck Co., Inc.; Windham Distributing Co., Inc.; Azalea Insurance Co., Inc.; A & N Roofing, Inc.; Masonboro Forest, Inc.; Xanadu Associates; Racine LLC; North Shore Golf & Country Club; Ocean Club Village; Holly Ridge Association; Haverty's, J.G.A. Corporation; Hardison Building, Inc.; Green With Envy Irrigation & Landscape, Inc.; Southland Amusements & Venting, Inc.; P. Robertson Building Corp.; Greenhouse Properties, LLC; Melvin Building, Inc.; YEM Hollyridge, LLC; The Cove at Boca Bay, LLC.; Yow's Highway 50 Investments, LLC; Forest Creek Ventures, Inc.; LJM Ventures, LLC.; McKinley Building, Inc.; Cape Fear Marble & Tile; Fields Movers Services Worldwide, Inc.; The Cadle Company; Central Carolina Bank; M & N Equipment Rentals, Inc.; Davis Lancastor Builders Inc; Premier Spirits; American Heritrade; Action Freight Forwarding, Inc.
APPROVED ATTORNEYS FOR: AMI Title Insurance Co.; Chicago Title Insurance Co.; First Title Insurance Co.; Investors Title Insurance Co.; Lawyers Title Insurance Company of North Carolina Inc.; Safeco Title Insurance Co.; Wachovia Mortgage Co.
REFERENCES: Central Carolina Bank; Branch Banking & Trust Company.

LAW OFFICES OF W. THOMAS BOYD, JR., P.A.

2536 WARD BOULEVARD

WILSON, NORTH CAROLINA 27893

Telephone: 252-243-8400

Fax: 252-243-5017

Email: tom@boydlawfirm.com

URL: http://www.wthomasboyd.com

Mailing Address: P.O. Box 66, Wilson, NC 27894-0066

Commercial Real Estate, Real Estate, Corporate Law, Business Law.

W. THOMAS BOYD, JR., born May 23, 1949; admitted to bar, 1974, North Carolina. *Education:* University of North Carolina (A.B., 1971; J.D., 1974).

LAW OFFICE OF DEREK R. CALDWELL, P.A.

WILSON, NORTH CAROLINA

(See Raleigh)

Bankruptcy, Personal Bankruptcy, Chapter 7, Chapter 13, Consumer and Business Bankruptcy, Personal Injury, Automobile Accidents, Wrongful Death, Mediation, Business Law, Consumer Law, Lemon Law, Fair Debt Collection Practices.

CHICHESTER & WALKER

WILSON, NORTH CAROLINA

(See Roanoke Rapids)

Criminal Defense, Drug Crimes, Felonies, Misdemeanors, Traffic Violations, Driving While Intoxicated, Personal Injury, Automobile Accidents, Slip and Falls, Worker's Compensation, Wrongful Death, General Practice.

CONNOR, BUNN, ROGERSON & WOODARD, P.L.L.C.

Established in 1881

P.O. BOX 3299

WILSON, NORTH CAROLINA 27895-3299

Telephone: 252-243-3136

Fax: 252-243-8293; 252-243-2558

Email: kjr@nc.rr.com

General Trial and Appellate Practice in all State and Federal Courts. Corporate, Business and Limited Liability Company Law. Federal, State and Local Taxation. Tax Exempt Financing. Probate and Estate Planning. Commercial and Business Litigation. Personal Injury. Commercial and Residential Real Estate. Family and Domestic Law. Zoning.

FIRM PROFILE: Connor, Bunn, Rogerson & Woodard, P.L.L.C. is a law firm providing legal services throughout the state of North Carolina and in other states, with a principal service area of eastern North Carolina. The Firm is diverse and provides legal services in virtually every aspect of the law. The present Firm is the outgrowth of a legal practice that began in Wilson over a century ago. The Firm continues to grow in its expertise and its commitment to quality service for its clients.

HENRY GROVES CONNOR (1911-1989)

DAVID M. CONNOR (1935-1994)

TURNER B. BUNN, III, born Wilson, North Carolina, September 28, 1940; admitted to bar, 1967, North Carolina. *Education:* University of North Carolina (B.S., 1963; J.D., 1967). Phi Delta Phi. *Member:* Wilson County, North Carolina (Member, Real Property Section) and American Bar Associations; Seventh Judicial District Bar. ***PRACTICE AREAS:*** Commercial and Residential Real Estate. ***Email:*** tbb3@nc.rr.com

JAMES F. ROGERSON, born Martin County, North Carolina, October 2, 1945; admitted to bar, 1973, North Carolina. *Education:* University of North Carolina (B.A., 1967; J.D., 1973). *Member:* Wilson County, North Carolina and American Bar Associations; Seventh Judicial District Bar; North Carolina Academy of Trial Lawyers; The Association of Trial Lawyers of America. ***PRACTICE AREAS:*** Litigation; Condemnation; Personal Injury; Wrongful Death.

DAVID W. WOODARD, born Wilson, North Carolina, November 6, 1949; admitted to bar, 1976, North Carolina. *Education:* University of North Carolina (B.A., 1971; J.D., 1976); New York University (LL.M., in Taxation, 1979). Phi Delta Phi. *Member:* Wilson County, North Carolina (Member, Taxation Section) and American (Member, Taxation Section) Bar Associations; Seventh Judicial District Bar. ***PRACTICE AREAS:*** Probate; Estate Planning; Tax; Corporate Law; Limited Liability Companies; Partnership Law.

L. PATRICK FLEMING, JR., born Wilson, North Carolina, June 28, 1955; admitted to bar, 1980, North Carolina. *Education:* University of North Carolina at Chapel Hill (B.A., 1977); Wake Forest University (J.D., 1980); Georgetown University (LL.M., taxation, 1983). Phi Delta Phi. Clerk, Honorable Naomi E. Morris, Chief Judge, N.C. Court of Appeals, 1980-1981. *Member:* Wilson County, Seventh Judicial District, North Carolina and American Bar Associations. ***PRACTICE AREAS:*** Tax; Corporate; Business; Estate Planning; Probate; Banking Law.

STANLEY GLENN ABRAMS, born Smithfield, North Carolina; admitted to bar, 1994, North Carolina. *Education:* Bob Jones University (B.A., Pre-Law, 1991); University of North Carolina at Chapel Hill (J.D., 1994). Articles Editor, North Carolina Journal of International Law and Commercial, 1993-1994. Attorney for the City of Wilson Board of Adjustment. *Member:* North Carolina State Bar. ***PRACTICE AREAS:*** Family Law; Domestic Relations; Criminal Law; Personal Injury; Civil Litigation.

WILLIAM H. BOYETTE, born 1953; admitted to bar, 1980, North Carolina. *Education:* North Carolina State University (B.S.); Campbell University (J.D.). *Member:* Wilson County Seventh Judicial District and North Carolina Bar Associations. ***PRACTICE AREAS:*** Real Estate; Estate Planning; Probate; General Practice.

GENERAL COUNSEL FOR: The Wilson Daily Times, Inc.; New Hope Development Corp.; Bunn & Co.; Southern Piping Co.; Nash Realty Co.; Williamson Thermo King Dealerships, Inc.; Boone's Antiques. Inc.; Southern Testing & Research Laboratories, Inc.; Cordina Office Products, Inc.
LOCAL COUNSEL FOR: N.C. Chip Company; The Firestone Tire & Rubber Co.; Centura Bank.
REPRESENTATIVE CLIENTS: Brown Oil Co., Inc.; Bank of America; Wilson Orthopaedic Surgery and Neurology, P.A.; Eastern Carolina Pediatrics, P.A.; Wilson Urology, P.A.; Bowers Ophthalmology Services, Inc.; Wilson-Carolina Eye Center, P.A.

(This Listing Continued)

APPROVED ATTORNEYS FOR: Lawyers Title Insurance Corp.; First Title Insurance Co.; SAFECO Title Insurance Co.; Jefferson-Pilot Title Insurance Co.; Investors Title Insurance Co.; First Union National Bank; The Federal Land Bank of Columbia; Wachovia Bank & Trust Co., N.A.; First Citizens Bank & Trust Co.; Farmers Home Administration; Branch Banking & Trust Co.; The Title Company of North Carolina; Commonwealth Title Insurance Co.; Statewide Title Co.

WILLIAM F. HILL, P.A.

WILSON, NORTH CAROLINA

(See Greenville)

Creditor's Rights, Collections, Small Business, Buying or Selling a Business, Employment Contracts, General Business, Contracts, Starting a Business, Corporate Law, Family Law, Divorce.

HINSON & RHYNE, P.A.

2401-G WOOTEN BOULEVARD
P.O. BOX 7479
WILSON, NORTH CAROLINA 27895-7479
Telephone: 252-291-1746
Facsimile: 252-291-2521
Email: walterhinson@nc.rr.com
Email: johnrhyne@nc.rr.com

Bankruptcy and Debtor Creditor Rights Law, Corporate Law, Uniform Commercial Code Law, Agribusiness Law, Civil Litigation, Perishable Agricultural Commodities Act Claims.

WALTER L. HINSON, born Lenoir County, North Carolina, September 20, 1947; admitted to bar, 1973, North Carolina. *Education:* East Carolina University (B.S., 1969); Wake Forest University (J.D., 1973). Phi Alpha Delta. Member, Moot Court Board. Trustee, Bankruptcy Court, Eastern District of North Carolina, 1979—. Member, Agribusiness Committee, Wilson Chambers of Commerce. *Member:* Wilson County and North Carolina (Councillor, Bankruptcy Section) Bar Associations; North Carolina State Bar; Eastern Bankruptcy Institute (Board Director). (Board Certified Specialist in Bankruptcy Law, North Carolina State Board of Legal Specialization). ***PRACTICE AREAS:*** Bankruptcy Law; Debtor Creditor Rights Law; Corporate Law; Uniform Commercial Code Law; Agribusiness Law. ***Email:*** walterhinson@nc.rr.com

JOHN G. RHYNE, born Chapel Hill, North Carolina, November 13, 1964; admitted to bar, 1990, North Carolina and U.S. District Court, Eastern and Middle Districts of North Carolina. *Education:* Dickinson College (B.A., 1986); Wake Forest University (J.D., 1990). Bankruptcy Section Councilor. *Member:* Wilson County Bar Association; North Carolina State Bar. ***PRACTICE AREAS:*** Bankruptcy; Debtor and Creditor Law; Civil Litigation. ***Email:*** johnrhyne@nc.rr.com

The LeonLaw Firm

WILSON, NORTH CAROLINA

(See Greenville)

Employment Law, Personal Injury, Workers Compensation, Contracts.

MORRISON LAW FIRM, P.L.L.C.

Established in 2004

4612 W. NASH STREET
WILSON, NORTH CAROLINA 27894-2046
Telephone: 252-243-1003
Fax: 252-243-1004
Email: pmorrison@nccomplaw.com
URL: http://www.nccomplaw.com
Mailing Address: P.O. Box 2046, Wilson, NC 27894

Litigation, Collections, Workers Compensation, Personal Injury Law, Creditor Rights and Bankruptcy.

FIRM PROFILE: B. Perry Morrison, Jr. established the Morrison Law Firm, P.L.L.C. after 15 years with two other firms in Raleigh and Wilson. Morrison represents plaintiffs in state and federal courts, including representing creditors in the U.S. Bankruptcy Court. The firm further represents a large number of injured workers before the N.C. Industrial Commission and also handles social security disability claims.

B. PERRY MORRISON, JR., born Wilson, North Carolina, July 3, 1962; admitted to bar, 1989, North Carolina. *Education:* University of North Carolina at Chapel Hill (A.B., 1984; J.D., 1988). Phi Delta Phi (President, 1987-1988). Member, Order of the Grail. *Member:* Wilson County (President, Young Lawyers Division, 1991) and North Carolina Bar Associations; North Carolina Academy of Trial Lawyers. ***PRACTICE AREAS:*** Litigation; Collections; Workers Compensation; Personal Injury Law; Creditor Rights and Bankruptcy. ***Email:*** pmorrison@nccomplaw.com

LEGAL SUPPORT PERSONNEL

COURTNEY BARNES

BEVERLY DURRER

NANCY MORRISON

REPRESENTATIVE CLIENTS: Cargill, Inc.; State Employees Credit Union; Cornerstone Bank; Tidewater Finance; BB&T Leasing Corporation; Chase Manhattan; SunTrust; American Express; MBNA America.

MICHAEL P. MURPHY, P.A.

WILSON, NORTH CAROLINA

(See Rocky Mount)

Commercial Collections, Wills, Trust Law, Estate Planning, Personal Injury, Automobile Accidents and Injuries, Truck Accidents, Bankruptcy Chapter 7, Bankruptcy Chapter 13, Corporate Law, Limited Liability Company Law, Business Law, Criminal Law, Traffic Violations.

NARRON & HOLDFORD, P.A.

Established in 1950

204 NORTH TARBORO STREET
P.O. DRAWER 279
WILSON, NORTH CAROLINA 27894-0279
Telephone: 252-237-3153
Telecopier: 252-243-1733

Civil and Criminal Trial and Appellate Practice. Personal Injury, Wrongful Death, Products Liability, Professional Liability, Construction Law, Business, Commercial and Corporate Law, Individual and Corporate Taxation, Limited Liability Companies and Partnerships, Employment Law, Tax Exempt Organizations, Estate Planning and Administration, Real Estate, Land Use and Zoning, Family Law, Creditor Rights and Bankruptcy.

FIRM PROFILE: Narron & Holdford, P.A. and its predecessors have been providing legal services to clients throughout eastern North Carolina for over 50 years. Members of the firm are active in both state and local bar activities, and have taken on leadership roles in a multitude of professional, community and civic organizations. Narron & Holdford's clients range from individuals and small businesses to large public and privately held corporations. Divided into practice groups to enhance specialization and efficiency, the firm offers a wide range of corporate, business, tax and estate planning services in its Business Section; personal injury, products liability, professional malpractice, commercial and construction litigation services in its Trial Section; and full commercial and residential real estate services in its Real Property Section. By specializing in particular areas of law, our lawyers are able to meet the needs of our diverse clientele with outstanding legal services and experience.

TALMADGE L. NARRON (1925-1976)

WILLIAM H. HOLDFORD, born Wilson, North Carolina, October 17, 1932; admitted to bar, 1960, North Carolina. *Education:* University of North Carolina (B.A., 1958; LL.B., 1960). Phi Delta Phi. Solicitor, Wilson County Recorders Court, 1961-1965. *Member:* Wilson County (President, 1968-1970) and North Carolina Bar Associations; 7th Judicial District and The North Carolina State Bars; North Carolina Academy of Trial Lawyers (Member, Board of Governors, 1974-1977; President, 1978-1979); The Association of Trial Lawyers of America. Fellow, American College of Trial Lawyers. ***PRACTICE AREAS:*** Medical Negligence Law; Major Personal Injuries Law; Wrongful Death Law; Civil Litigation; Will Contests. ***Email:*** whh@narronholdford.com

REGINALD W. HARRISON, JR., born Washington, D.C., December 12, 1942; admitted to bar, 1967, North Carolina. *Education:* University of North Carolina (A.B., 1964; J.D., 1967). Delta Theta Phi. *Member:* North Carolina (Member, Board of Governors, 1987-1990; Chairman, Real Property Section, 1984-1985) and American (Member, Real Property, Probate and Trust Law Section) Bar Associations; North Carolina State Bar. [CDR, USNR-R, active duty, 1967-1972, Reserves 1972-1990]. (Board Certified Specialist in Real Property Law - Residential Transactions). ***PRACTICE AREAS:*** Real Estate Law; Estate Administration Law. ***Email:*** realestate@narronholdford.com

THOMAS J. RHODES, born Washington, North Carolina, May 7, 1947; admitted to bar, 1973, North Carolina. *Education:* University of North Carolina (B.A., 1970; B.S., 1970; J.D., 1973); Morehead Scholar. Certified Public Accountant, 1975. *Member:* North Carolina and American Bar Associations; North Carolina State Bar. ***PRACTICE AREAS:*** Taxation; Individual and Corporate Tax Planning; Estate Planning; Wills and Probate Law; Business and Corporate Law.

C. DAVID WILLIAMS, JR., born Asheville, North Carolina, June 23, 1947; admitted to bar, 1971, North Carolina. *Education:* University of North Carolina, Asheville (B.A., 1968); University of North Carolina, Chapel Hill (J.D., 1971). Phi Alpha Delta. Assistant District Attorney, 7th Judicial District, State of North Carolina, 1971-1979. Legal Counsel, North Carolina Jaycees, 1983-1984. *Member:* Wilson County (President, 1992-1993) Bar Association; North Carolina State Bar; North Carolina Academy of Trial Lawyers; The Association of Trial Lawyers of America. ***PRACTICE AREAS:*** Civil and Criminal Trial Practice. ***Email:*** dwilliams@narronholdford.com

IVAN JOE IVEY, born Lumberton, North Carolina, October 15, 1951; admitted to bar, 1977, North Carolina. *Education:* University of North Carolina (A.B., 1973; J.D., 1977). Assistant District Attorney, Seventh Judicial District, 1977-1982. *Member:* Wilson County, North Carolina and American Bar Associations; Seventh Judicial District Bar; North Carolina Academy of Trial Lawyers. ***PRACTICE AREAS:*** Personal Injury Law; Criminal Law; Foreclosures; Civil Trial Practice; Collections.

WILLIAM L. O'QUINN, JR., born Denver, Colorado, September 21, 1968; admitted to bar, 1994, North Carolina. *Education:* Duke University (A.B., cum laude, 1990); University of North Carolina at Chapel Hill (J.D., with honors, 1994). Staff Member, 1992-1993 and Articles Editor, 1993-1994, North Carolina Law Review. Author: Note, "Village of Pinehurst v. Regional Investments of Moore: Perpetuating the Rule Against Perpetuities in the Realm of Preemptive Rights-North Carolina Refuses to Accept an Exception to the Rule," 71 N.C.L.Rev. 2115 (1993). *Member:* Wilson County, North Carolina (Member, Business Law Section) and American (Member, Sections on: Business and International Law) Bar Associations; North Carolina State Bar. ***PRACTICE AREAS:*** Business and Corporate Law; Commercial Transactions.

BENJAMIN L. EAGLES, born Wilson, North Carolina, December 5, 1970; admitted to bar, 1999, North Carolina and U.S. District Court, Eastern District of North Carolina. *Education:* University of North Carolina at Chapel Hill (B.A., 1993); Campbell University Law School (J.D., 1999). Thomas T. Lanier Memorial Scholar. Listed Who's Who Among

(This Listing Continued)

NARRON & HOLDFORD, P.A., Wilson—Continued

Universities & Colleges. *Member:* North Carolina Bar Association; North Carolina Association of Trial Lawyers. ***PRACTICE AREAS:*** Personal Injury; Workers Compensation. ***Email:*** ble@narronholdford.com

---

THOMAS J. RHODES, JR., born Durham, North Carolina, May 14, 1972; admitted to bar, 1997, North Carolina. *Education:* Wake Forest University (B.S., in Accounting, 1994; J.D., 1997). Certified Public Accountant, North Carolina, 1999. ***PRACTICE AREAS:*** Corporate Taxation; Individual Taxation; Estate Planning; Wills; Probate; Business Law; Corporate Law; Tax Exempt Organizations. ***Email:*** tad@narronholdford.com

JONATHAN M. VANDEN BOSCH, born Dearborn, Michigan, August 14, 1974; admitted to bar, 1999, North Carolina. *Education:* University of North Carolina at Chapel Hill (B.A., with distinction, 1996); Duke University School of Law (J.D./M.A., magna cum laude, 1999). Phi Beta Kappa. ***PRACTICE AREAS:*** Business Law; Corporate Law; Taxation; Estate Planning; Estate Administration; Individual Taxation; Corporate Tax Planning; Commercial Real Estate.

REPRESENTATIVE CLIENTS: NationsBank, N.A.,; Standard Commercial Corp.; Parkwood Development Co.; Tarboro Clinic, Inc.; Landmark Development Co.; Imperial Tobacco Leaf Services, Inc.; Merck & Company, Inc.; Watson Electrical Construction Co.; Cargill, Inc.; S.T. Wooten Corp.; Nordic Refrigerated Services, Inc.
APPROVED ATTORNEYS FOR: Lawyers Title Insurance Corp.; Chicago Title Insurance Co.; Commonwealth Land Title Insurance Co.; Investors Title Insurance Co.; United Title Insurance Co.; Farm Credit Bank of Columbia; Title Company of North Carolina; First American Title Insurance Co.

O'GARRO-MOORE LAW OFFICE

WILSON, NORTH CAROLINA

(See Rocky Mount)

Immigration Law, Criminal Law, Family Law.

ROSE RAND ATTORNEYS, P.A.

Established in 1944

2500 WEST NASH STREET, UNIT C
P.O. DRAWER 2367
WILSON, NORTH CAROLINA 27894-2367
Telephone: 252-291-3848
Telecopier: 252-291-9555

Raleigh, North Carolina Office: Corporate Plaza Building, Suite 1508 333 Fayetteville Street, 27601. Telephone: 919-832-4040. Fax: 919-832-4050.

General Practice, all Courts. Corporation, Labor and Insurance Law. Trials, including Personal Injury, Wrongful Death and Workers Compensation, Eminent Domain, Tax, Estate Planning and Administration, Municipal, Environmental, Real Estate, Bankruptcy.

WILLIAM A. LUCAS (1881-1967)

OLIVER G. RAND (1895-1967)

NAOMI E. MORRIS (1921-1986)

Z. HARDY ROSE (1913-1999)

WILLIAM R. RAND (Retired)

JAMES P. CAULEY, III, born Munich, Germany, October 21, 1959; admitted to bar, 1987, North Carolina; 1989, U.S. District Court, Eastern District of North Carolina; 1992, U.S. Supreme Court. *Education:* Campbell University (B.B.A., 1984; J.D., 1987). Delta Theta Phi; Omicron Delta Kappa. Member, National Moot Court Team. Member, Board of Editors, Campbell Law Review, 1986-1987. Instructor, Legal Research and Appellate Advocacy, Campbell University School of Law, 1985-1987. Instructor, Real Estate Law, Wilson County Technical College, 1988-1989. Instructor, Business Law, Barton College, 1990-1991. Certified Superior Court Mediator, 2000. *Member:* Wilson County, North Carolina and American Bar Associations; Seventh Judicial District and The North Carolina State Bars; Eastern North Carolina Inn of Court (Member, 1994—). Global Transpark, Environment and Transportation Committee (Member, 1994-1997). North Carolina League of Municipalities (Member, Energy, Environment and Natural Resources Policy Committee, 1993-1996); North Carolina Association of Municipal Attorneys (Member, Board of Directors, 1994-1996); North Carolina Association of Defense Attorneys. ***PRACTICE AREAS:*** Civil Trial Practice; Municipal and Administrative Law; Business Law; Real Estate; Eminent Domain. ***Email:*** jcauley@rose-randlaw.com

PAUL N. BLAKE, III, born Wilson, North Carolina, November 1, 1960; admitted to bar, 1990, North Carolina and U.S. District Court, Eastern and Middle Districts of North Carolina. *Education:* Atlantic Christian College (B.S., 1984); East Carolina University (M.B.A., 1987); Notre Dame/London Law Center, London, England; Campbell University (J.D., 1990). Delta Theta Phi. Instructor, Business Law, Barton College, 1991-1992. Member, Campbell Law Observer, 1989-1990. Certified Superior Court Mediator. Certified North Carolina Industrial Commission Mediator. Chairman Wilson Chamber of Commerce, 2005-2006. *Member:* Wilson County and Seventh Judicial District Bar Associations; North Carolina State Bar; North Carolina Academy of Trial Lawyers. ***PRACTICE AREAS:*** Workers Compensation; Civil Trial Practice; Administrative Law; Business Law. ***Email:*** pblake@rose-randlaw.com

T. SLADE RAND, JR., born Chapel Hill, North Carolina, June 27, 1961; admitted to bar, 1998, North Carolina. *Education:* University of North Carolina at Chapel Hill (B.A., 1987); Babcock Graduate School of Management, Wake Forest University (M.B.A., 1988); Campbell University (J.D., 1998). *Member:* Wilson County, Seventh Judicial District, North Carolina and American Bar Associations; North Carolina Association of Defense Attorneys; North Carolina Association of Municipal Attorneys. ***PRACTICE AREAS:*** Municipal Law; Administrative Law; Eminent Domain; Business Law. ***Email:*** srand@rose-randlaw.com

(This Listing Continued)

SUSAN K. ELLIS, born High Point, North Carolina, November 25, 1958; admitted to bar, 1987, North Carolina. *Education:* University of North Carolina (B.S.B.A., 1980); Wake Forest University (J.D., cum laude, 1987). Staff Member, Wake Forest Law Review, 1985-1987. Member, AICPA, 1983-1984. Certified Public Accountant, Virginia, 1983. Staff Accountant, Seidman and Seidman, Greensboro, North Carolina, 1981-1982. Senior Tax Accountant, Hantzmon, Wiebel and Co., Charlottesville, Virginia, 1982-1984. *Member:* Wilson County, Seventh Judicial District and North Carolina Bar Associations; North Carolina State Bar (General Statutes Commission Commissioner, 2000-2004). ***PRACTICE AREAS:*** Estate Planning; Probate Law; Tax Law; Business Law. ***Email:*** sellis@rose-randlaw.com

J. YANCEY WASHINGTON, born Oxford, North Carolina, June 11, 1976; admitted to bar, 2001, North Carolina. *Education:* Hampden-Sydney College (B.A., History, cum laude, 1998); Virginia Programmee at Oxford, Oxford, England (1998); Campbell University (J.D., 2001). Phi Alpha Delta (Clerk, Iredell Chapter). *Member:* Wilson County, North Carolina, Seventh and Tenth Judicial District Bar Associations; North Carolina State Bar; Eastern North Carolina Inn of Court. ***PRACTICE AREAS:*** Bankruptcy; Municipal Law; General Practice. ***Email:*** ywashington@rose-randlaw.com

J. BRIAN PRIDGEN, born Wilson, North Carolina, December 23, 1977; admitted to bar, 2003, North Carolina. *Education:* University of North Carolina at Chapel Hill (B.A., in English, 2000); University of North Carolina School of Law (J.D., 2003). *Member:* Wilson County Bar Association; North Carolina State Bar; North Carolina Academy of Trial Lawyers. ***PRACTICE AREAS:*** Workers Compensation; Real Estate; Municipal Law; General Practice. ***Email:*** bpridgen@rose-randlaw.com

JASON R. PAGE, born Orangeburg, South Carolina, May 11, 1973; admitted to bar, 2005, North Carolina. *Education:* North Carolina State University (B.S., 1995; M.F., 1998); Campbell University (J.D., 2005). N.C. Registered Forester, 2000. Member, Society of American Foresters. ***PRACTICE AREAS:*** General Practice. ***Email:*** jpage@rose-randlaw.com

LOCAL COUNSEL FOR: Carol Wright Promotions; International Paper Company; Progress Energy, Inc.
ATTORNEYS FOR: Belle Meade, Inc.; City of Wilson; Town of Hookerton; Town of Scotland Neck; Town of Snow Hill; Upper Coastal Plain Council of Governments; Barton College; Wilson-Green Mental Health Association; Paxton Bonded Storage, Inc.; Triangle East Bonded Storages; Exclusive Cleaners, Inc.; Parker's Barbecue, Inc.; N.C. Global TransPark Development Commission; Eatmon Racing Engines, Inc.; Atlantic Hospitality Supply, LLC; Evans Machinery, Inc.
SPECIAL COUNSEL FOR: Town of Kenly; Town of Fremont; County of Lenoir.

WALLACE, MORRIS, BARWICK, LANDIS & STROUD, P.A.

WILSON, NORTH CAROLINA

(See Kinston)

General Civil and Trial Practice in all State and Federal Courts. Aviation, Banking, Corporate Law, Insurance, Personal Injury, Probate, Product Liability, Real Estate and Taxation.

GILLAM AND GILLAM

Established in 1946

201 DUNDEE STREET
P.O. BOX 547
WINDSOR, NORTH CAROLINA 27983
Telephone: 252-794-2233
Fax: 252-794-5007
Email: gillamandgillam@coastalnet.com

General Civil and Criminal Practice. Probate, Real Estate and Corporation Law. Trials.

MEMBERS OF FIRM

SARAH STARR GILLAM (1912-1996)

MOSES B. GILLAM, JR., born Windsor, North Carolina, October 2, 1916; admitted to bar, 1939, North Carolina. *Education:* University of North Carolina (A.B., 1937; J.D., 1939). Phi Beta Kappa; Order of the Coif. Member, Board of Editors, 1937-1938; Associate Editor-in-Chief, 1938-1939, North Carolina Law Review. Attorney: Town of Windsor, 1971—; Town of Roxobel, 1984—. *Member:* Bertie County and 6B Judicial District (President, 1956; Member, Candidate Committee, 1968) Bar Associations; North Carolina State Bar. ***PRACTICE AREAS:*** General Practice; Probate; Real Estate; Corporate Law; Domestic Relations; Civil Litigation. ***Email:*** gillamandgillam@coastalnet.com

M. BRAXTON GILLAM, III, born Windsor, North Carolina, September 15, 1952; admitted to bar, 1984, North Carolina. *Education:* University of North Carolina (B.A., 1974); Appalachian State University (M.A., 1980); Campbell University (J.D., 1984). Member, Campbell Law Review, 1983-1984. Attorney: Town of Windsor and Town of Roxobel, 1984—; Bertie County Department of Social Services, 1990—. *Member:* Bertie County, 6B Judicial District (President, 1996) and North Carolina Bar Associations. ***PRACTICE AREAS:*** General Practice; Real Estate; Business Law; Probate; Estate Planning; Domestic Relations; Civil Litigation. ***Email:*** gillamandgillam@coastalnet.com

REFERENCES: Southern Bank & Trust Co.; Wachovia.

ALLMAN SPRY LEGGETT & CRUMPLER, P.A.

Established in 1962

SUITE 700
380 KNOLLWOOD STREET
DRAWER 5129
WINSTON-SALEM, NORTH CAROLINA 27113-5129
Telephone: 336-722-2300
Telecopier: 336-721-0414

General Civil Practice, Litigation in all State and Federal Courts. Tax, Probate, Trust, Estate Planning, Corporation, Partnership, Bankruptcy and Creditors Rights, Real Estate, Securities and Insurance Law.

FIRM PROFILE: The firm is a Meritas member providing business clients legal services nationally and internationally through independent affiliated firms.

C. EDWIN ALLMAN (1926-1991)

W. DENNIE SPRY (1912-2000)

R. BRADFORD LEGGETT, born Fort Smith, Arkansas, July 19, 1944; admitted to bar, 1969, North Carolina. *Education:* Wake Forest University (B.A., 1966; J.D., cum laude, 1969). Phi Delta Phi. Legal Assistant to the Honorable Eugene A. Gordon, U.S. District Judge, Middle District of North Carolina, 1969-1971. Adjunct Professor, Wake Forest University School of Law, 1982-1988. *Member:* Forsyth County and North Carolina (Council, 1979-1982, Chairman, 1986-1987 and Member, Bankruptcy Section) Bar Associations; North Carolina State Bar. Fellow, American College of Bankruptcy. ***PRACTICE AREAS:*** Debtor and Creditor Rights; Corporate Reorganization; Commercial Litigation. ***Email:*** rbleggett@allmanspry.com

DONALD M. VONCANNON, born Greensboro, North Carolina, October 9, 1944; admitted to bar, 1971, North Carolina; 1996, U.S. Supreme Court. *Education:* Wake Forest University (B.A., 1967; J.D., 1971). Phi Delta Phi. Law Clerk to: Honorable Edwin M. Stanley, U.S. District Judge, Middle District of North Carolina, 1971; Honorable Eugene A. Gordon, U.S. District Judge, Middle District of North Carolina, 1972-1973. *Member:* Forsyth County and North Carolina (Member, Real Property Section) Bar Associations; North Carolina State Bar. [Capt., USMCR, 1969-1975]. (Board Certified Specialist in Real Property Law-Residential, Business, Commercial, and Industrial Transactions, North Carolina State Board of Legal Specialization). ***PRACTICE AREAS:*** Real Property. ***Email:*** dvoncannon@allmanspry.com

C. EDWIN ALLMAN, III, born Bat Cave, North Carolina, February 24, 1953; admitted to bar, 1979, North Carolina. *Education:* University of North Carolina at Charlotte (B.A., cum laude, 1976); Wake Forest University (J.D., 1979). Phi Delta Phi. Adjunct Professor, Wake Forest University School of Law, 1982-1986. *Member:* Forsyth County (Treasurer, 1981-1982) and North Carolina (Member: Bankruptcy Section; Council Member, 1993-1996; Real Property Section) Bar Associations; North Carolina State Bar. (Board Certified Specialist in Bankruptcy Law, North Carolina State Board of Legal Specialization). ***PRACTICE AREAS:*** Bankruptcy; Commercial Litigation; Reorganizations and Workouts; Unfair Trade. ***Email:*** ceallman@allmanspry.com

THOMAS T. CRUMPLER, born Reidsville, North Carolina, August 4, 1950; admitted to bar, 1975, North Carolina. *Education:* University of North Carolina (B.S., 1972); Wake Forest University (J.D., 19 75). Phi Delta Phi. *Member:* Forsyth County, North Carolina and American Bar Associations; North Carolina State Bar. ***PRACTICE AREAS:*** Mergers and Acquisitions; Securities; Commercial Real Estate; Corporate Law. ***Email:*** tcrumpler@allmanspry.com

EDWARD E. RAYMER, JR., born Winston-Salem, North Carolina, June 9, 1947; admitted to bar, 1974, North Carolina; 1977, U.S. Tax Court; 1979, U.S. Supreme Court. *Education:* University of North Carolina (B.S., Accounting, 1969); Wake Forest University (J.D., 1974). *Member:* Forsyth County and North Carolina (Member: Legislative Committee, Probate Section, 1979-1995; Legislative Committee, Tax Section, 1981-1982) Bar Associations; North Carolina State Bar; Winston-Salem Estate Planning Council (Secretary, 1990-1991; Treasurer, 2000-2002). (Board Certified Specialist in Estate Planning and Probate Law, North Carolina State Bar Board of Legal Specialization). ***PRACTICE AREAS:*** Estate Planning; Estate Administration; Probate; Taxation; Corporate Law. ***Email:*** eraymer@allmanspry.com

M. JOSEPH ALLMAN, born Chapel Hill, North Carolina, March 30, 1960; admitted to bar, 1986, North Carolina. *Education:* Wake Forest University (B.A., 1982; J.D., cum laude, 1986). Pi Sigma Alpha; Phi Delta Phi. *Member:* Forsyth County and North Carolina (Member, Sections on: Bankruptcy and Real Property; Council Member, 1998-2000) Bar Associations; North Carolina State Bar. ***PRACTICE AREAS:*** Commercial Leasing; Bankruptcy. ***Email:*** mjallman@allmanspry.com

WALTER R. HINNANT, born Charlotte, North Carolina, April 9, 1961; admitted to bar, 1989, North Carolina. *Education:* Wake Forest University (B.A., 1983; J.D., 1988). Member, Moot Court Board, 1986-1988. Member, Wake Forest University Law Review, 1986-1988. Author, "Fiduciary Duties of Officers and Directors: How Far Do They Go?" 23 Wake Forest University Law Review 163, 1988. *Member:* Forsyth County, North Carolina (Member, Litigation and Business Sections) and American Bar Associations; North Carolina State Bar. ***PRACTICE AREAS:*** Civil Litigation. ***Email:*** rhinnant@allmanspry.com

GEORGE T. "TED" MANN, born Boston, Massachusetts, July 14, 1949; admitted to bar, 1974, Tennessee; 1978, North Carolina. *Education:* University of Virginia (B.A., With High Distinction, 1971); Vanderbilt University (J.D., 1974). Phi Beta Kappa; Phi Eta Sigma. Administrator, North Carolina Credit Union Division, 1993-1996. Member, Board of Directors, National Association State Credit Union Supervisors, 1995-1996. Chairman, North Carolina Credit Union Commission, 1996-1998. *Member:* North Carolina State Bar; North Carolina Bar Association. ***PRACTICE AREAS:*** Corporate Law; Commercial Transactions; State Legislative Practice; Federal Legislative Practice; Administrative Law; Financial Institutions Law; Trademark Licensing. ***Email:*** tmann@allmanspry.com

SCOTT THOMAS HORN, born Winston-Salem, North Carolina, September 5, 1964; admitted to bar, 2000, North Carolina. *Education:* Salem College, Winston-Salem, NC (B.S.B.A., magna cum laude, 1997); Wake Forest School of Law (J.D., 2000). *Member:*

(This Listing Continued)

Forsyth County and North Carolina (Member, Real Property and Construction Law Sections) Bar Associations; North Carolina State Bar Association. ***PRACTICE AREAS:*** Commercial Real Estate; Corporate Law; Business Transactions; Construction Law; Commercial Leasing. ***Email:*** shorn@allmanspry.com

JEFFREY B. WATSON, born Durham, North Carolina, December 14, 1966; admitted to bar, 1998, North Carolina and U.S. District Court, Middle District of North Carolina; 2000, U.S. District Court, Western and Eastern Districts of North Carolina. *Education:* University of North Carolina-Greensboro (B.A., 1989); Regent University (M.A., 1995); Campbell University (J.D., 1998). National Moot Court Team, 1997-1998. *Member:* Forsyth County and North Carolina Bar Associations; North Carolina State Bar. ***PRACTICE AREAS:*** Civil Litigation; Commercial Litigation; Insurance Law; Collections; Personal Injury; Securities Litigation. ***Email:*** jwatson@allmanspry.com

HEATHER J. BOWEN, born Belleville, New Jersey, November 12, 1973; admitted to bar, 1999, North Carolina. *Education:* Duke University (B.A., 1995); Mercer University (J.D., 1998). *Member:* Forsyth County and American Bar Associations. ***PRACTICE AREAS:*** Commercial Transactions; Commercial Litigation; Equitable Distribution. ***Email:*** hbowen@allmanspry.com

KAREN B. MALAY, born Oak Hill, West Virginia, May 23, 1980; admitted to bar, 2005, North Carolina. *Education:* Campbell University (B.A., 2002; J.D., 2005). *Member:* Forsyth County and North Carolina (Member, Sections on: Bankruptcy and Young Lawyers Division) Bar Associations. ***PRACTICE AREAS:*** Bankruptcy; Debtor and Creditor. ***Email:*** kmalay@allmanspry.com

KAREN H. CHAPMAN, born Washington, North Carolina, July 11, 1977; admitted to bar, 2005, North Carolina. *Education:* University of North Carolina at Chapel Hill (B.A., with honors, 1999; J.D., 2005). *Member:* Forsyth County and North Carolina Bar Associations; North Carolina State Bar. ***PRACTICE AREAS:*** Civil Litigation.

REPRESENTATIVE CLIENTS: Highwoods Properties, Inc.; Krispy Kreme Doughnut Corporation; Malayan United Industries Behrad; Regent Carolina Corporation; Laura Ashley, Inc.; Adams Egloff & Avant Properties, LLC; The Shelton Companies; Forsyth Technical Community College; Candor Hosiery Mills, Inc.; E.G. Forrest Co., Inc.; Murray Supply Company, Inc.; First Carolina Corporate Credit Union; Sara Lee Credit Union; Triad Postal Credit Union; Carolina Mountains Credit Union; AT&T Family Federal Credit Union; Northwest Piedmont Development Corp.; The Bob Timberlake Collection, Inc.; Magnolia Partners, L.L.C.; The Burris Agency; Bob Neill Pontiac, Inc.; Bob Neill Mercedes of Winston-Salem, Inc.; North Point Chrysler Plymouth Jeep Eagle, Inc.; Carolina Investment Properties, Inc.; First Winston Securities, Inc.; Kallam Oil Company; American Blending Services, Inc.; Specialty Tobacco Products, Inc.; Summit Sleep Disorder Center, P.A.; Re: Source NC, SC, & GA.

ANDERSON KORZEN & ASSOCIATES, P.C.

WINSTON-SALEM, NORTH CAROLINA

(See Kernersville)

Complex Litigation and Trials, Long Term Care and Nursing Home Abuse and Neglect, Serious Personal Injuries, Wrongful Death, Medical Malpractice, Aviation Torts and Air Crash Disasters, Serious Professional Negligence, Tractor Trailer Collisions, Product Liability.

THE LAW PRACTICE OF DANIEL B. ANTHONY PC

1416 W. 4TH STREET, SUITE B
WINSTON-SALEM, NORTH CAROLINA 27101
Telephone: 336-917-0037
Fax: 336-917-0038
Email: daniel-b-anthony@bellsouth.net
URL: http://www.dananthonylaw.com
Mailing Address: P.O. Box 20517, Winston-Salem, NC 27120-0517

Workers Compensation, Personal Injury, Criminal Defense, Disability Claims, Civil Litigation.

DANIEL B. ANTHONY, born Akron, Ohio; admitted to bar, 1994, North Carolina. *Education:* Miami University of Ohio (B.A., 1984); University of North Carolina at Chapel Hill (J.D., 1994). *Member:* North Carolina and American Bar Associations; North Carolina Association of Trial Lawyers (Member, Workers Compensation Section). ***PRACTICE AREAS:*** Workers Compensation (55%); Personal Injury (15%); Criminal Defense (20%); Disability Benefits (5%); Civil Litigation (5%). ***Email:*** daniel-b-anthony@hotmail.com

---

GAIL C. ARNEKE

301 N. MAIN STREET, SUITE 2455
WINSTON-SALEM, NORTH CAROLINA 27101
Telephone: 336-760-1434
Fax: 336-760-6149
Email: garneke@garneke.com
URL: http://www.newsouthlaw.net

Bankruptcy, Consumer Bankruptcy, Business Bankruptcy, Foreclosures.

GAIL C. ARNEKE, born Binghamton, New York, May 19, 1950; admitted to bar, 1975, North Carolina and U.S. District Court, Eastern District of North Carolina; 1983, Georgia and U.S. District Court, Southern District of Georgia; 1987, U.S. District Court, Southern District of Texas. *Education:* Duke University (B.A., cum laude, 1972); University of North Carolina (J.D., 1975). Member, North Carolina Board of Law Examiners. *Member:* North Carolina Bar Association; State Bar of Georgia; North Carolina State Bar. ***PRACTICE AREAS:*** Bankruptcy.

BAILEY & THOMAS, P.A.

Established in 1955

3069 TRENWEST DRIVE, SUITE 100
P.O. BOX 52
WINSTON-SALEM, NORTH CAROLINA 27102-0052
Telephone: 336-725-8366
Fax: 336-725-9206
Email: bailey1law@aol.com

General Civil and Criminal Practice. Trials in all State and Federal Courts. Probate, Real Estate and Property Law. Wills, Trust and Estate Planning, Corporation, Insurance Law and Personal Injury Law.

FIRM PROFILE: The firm of Bailey & Thomas, P.A. was founded by Wesley Bailey in 1955. The firm consists of five attorneys, serving Winston-Salem, N.C. and surrounding counties.

WESLEY BAILEY, born Winston-Salem, North Carolina, June 20, 1931; admitted to bar, 1955, North Carolina. *Education:* Wake Forest University (B.S., 1954; LL.B., 1955). Former Member, North Carolina House of Representatives. Member, Judicial Council (Supreme Court), The United Methodist Church, 1992-2000. *Member:* North Carolina (Member, Estate Planning and Fiduciary Law Section) and American (Member, Probate, Trust and Real Property Law Section) Bar Associations; North Carolina State Bar; The Estate Planning Council of Winston-Salem. ***PRACTICE AREAS:*** Probate; Wills; Trust Planning; Trust Law; Estate Planning; Estate Administration; Litigation; Taxation; Real Estate; Contested Wills. ***Email:*** Bailey1law@aol.com

GEORGE S. THOMAS, born Farmville, North Carolina, June 19, 1941; admitted to bar, 1966, North Carolina. *Education:* University of North Carolina at Chapel Hill (B.S., 1963; J.D., 1966). *Member:* North Carolina State Bar; North Carolina Bar Association (Member, Real Property Law Section); North Carolina Academy of Trial Lawyers. ***PRACTICE AREAS:*** Real Estate; Bankruptcy; Foreclosures; Collections. ***Email:*** Bailey1law@aol.com

DAVID W. BAILEY, JR., born Winston-Salem, North Carolina, March 13, 1957; admitted to bar, 1982, North Carolina. *Education:* Duke University (B.A., magna cum laude, 1979); University of North Carolina at Chapel Hill (J.D., 1982). Recipient, American Jurisprudence Award for Civil Procedure. *Member:* Forsyth County, North Carolina (Member, Litigation Section) and American Bar Associations; North Carolina State Bar; North Carolina Association of Defense Attorneys; Defense Research Institute; North Carolina Insurance Crime Information Exchange; International Association of Arson Investigations (North Chapter). ***PRACTICE AREAS:*** Insurance Law; Corporate; Wills; Contested Wills; Estate Litigation. ***Email:*** Bailey1law@aol.com

JOHN R. FONDA, born Lowell, Massachusetts, October 29, 1961; admitted to bar, 1987, North Carolina. *Education:* University of North Carolina at Chapel Hill (B.A., 1984); Wake Forest University (J.D., 1987). *Member:* Forsyth County and North Carolina (Member, Litigation Section) Bar Associations; North Carolina State Bar; North Carolina Association of Defense Attorneys; Defense Research Institute. ***PRACTICE AREAS:*** Insurance Law; Traffic Violations; Real Estate Leasing. ***Email:*** Bailey1law@aol.com

REPRESENTATIVE CLIENTS: Montgomery Insurance Companies; Erie Insurance Group; Lititz Mutual Insurance Company; Progressive Insurance Co.; Harford Mutual Insurance Co.; The St. Paul Cos.; Essex Insurance Co.; State Farm Fire and Casualty Company; L.E. Pope Building Co., Inc.; Yarbrough Transfer Co.; Covington-Wilson, Inc.
APPROVED ATTORNEYS FOR: Piedmont Federal Savings & Loan Association; The Pfefferkorn Co.; Wachovia Mortgage Co.; Branch Banking & Trust Co.; CCB.
REFERENCES: Central Carolina Bank (Salem Group); Winston-Salem, N.C.

BELL, DAVIS & PITT, P.A.

Established in 1980

CENTURY PLAZA, SUITE 600
100 NORTH CHERRY STREET
WINSTON-SALEM, NORTH CAROLINA 27101
Telephone: 336-722-3700
Fax: 336-748-5890
URL: http://www.belldavispitt.com

Mailing Address: P.O. Box 21029, Winston-Salem, NC 27120

Charlotte, North Carolina Office: Carillon Building, Suite 2160, 227 West Trade Street, 28202. Telephone: 704-227-0400. Fax: 704-227-0178.

General Practice in State and Federal Court Trials. Banking and Commercial Law. Corporation and Labor Law, Federal, State and Local Taxation, Estate Planning, Probate and Real Estate Law.

FIRM PROFILE: Bell, Davis & Pitt, P.A. was founded in 1980. The firm provides a full range of legal services to corporations, individuals and organizations in North Carolina and other states in the southeast.

WILLIAM D. HARPER (1943-1995)

FRANK M. BELL, JR., born Charlotte, North Carolina, 1937; admitted to bar, 1963, North Carolina; U.S. District Court, Middle and Western Districts of North Carolina; U.S. Court of Claims. *Education:* Duke University (A.B., 1959); University of North Carolina (LL.B., 1963). Listed: The Best Lawyers in America, 1990—; Business North Carolina's Legal Elite, January 2002. *Member:* Forsyth County, North Carolina and American Bar Associations. ***PRACTICE AREAS:*** Real Property Law; Commercial Law; Corporation Law; Securities Law. ***Email:*** fbell@belldavispitt.com

WILLIAM K. DAVIS, born Raleigh, North Carolina, 1939; admitted to bar, 1966, North Carolina; U.S. District Court, Eastern, Middle and Western Districts of North Carolina; U.S. Court of Appeals, Fourth Circuit; U.S. Supreme Court. *Education:* Davidson College (A.B., 1960); University of North Carolina (M.B.A., 1961); Wake Forest College (LL.B., 1966). Editor-in-Chief, Wake Forest Law Review, 1965-1966. Permanent Member, Judicial Conference of the United States Court of Appeals for the Fourth Circuit. North Carolina Courts Commission (1982-1985). North Carolina Legal Services Corporation, Board of Directors (1981-1984). North Carolina Prepaid Legal Services Corporation, Board of Directors, (1984-1987). North Carolina State Bar Board of Continuing Legal Education (Chair, 1987-1990). North Carolina Judicial Standards Commission (Vice Chair, 1990-1996). Civil Justice Reform Act Advisory Group form the United States District Court, for the Middle District of North Carolina (Chair, 1991-1994). Founding Member, Chief Justice Joseph Branch Inns of Court, Business and Personal Injury Listing. Listed: Best Lawyer in America, 1991—; Business North Carolina's Legal Elite, 2002—. *Member:* Forsyth County, North Carolina (Member, Board of Governors, 1997—) and American (House of Delegates, 1988-1992) Bar Associations; North Carolina State Bar (Councilor, 1980-1984; Vice President, 1984-1985; President-Elect, 1985-1986; President, 1986-1987); North Carolina Association of Defense Attorneys (President, 1978-1979). Fellow: American Bar Foundation; American College of Trial Lawyers (State Chair, 1993-1994). ***PRACTICE AREAS:*** Business Litigation; Banking; Securities; Business Torts; Legal Malpractice; Personal Injury Litigation. ***Email:*** wdavis@belldavispitt.com

WALTER W. PITT, JR., born Rocky Mount, North Carolina, 1945; admitted to bar, 1971, North Carolina; U.S. District Court, Eastern, Middle and Western Districts of North Carolina; U.S. Court of Appeals, Fourth Circuit. *Education:* University of North Carolina (A.B., 1967); Wake Forest University (J.D., 1971). Phi Alpha Delta. Member, Wake Forest Law Review, 1970-1971. Adjunct Law Professor, Debtor-Creditor Relations, Wake Forest University School of Law (1990-1995). Bankruptcy Law Listing, The Best Lawyers in America (1994—). Listed: Who's Who in American Law; Business North Carolina's Legal Elite, 2002—. *Member:* Forsyth County and North Carolina (Member, Bankruptcy Section; Vice Chair, 1997-1998; Chair, 1998-1999) Bar Associations; North Carolina Association of Defense Attorneys; Commercial Law League of America (1986—). ***PRACTICE AREAS:*** Commercial Transactions; Banking Law; Bankruptcy Law; Municipal Corporations. ***Email:*** wpitt@belldavispitt.com

JAMES R. FOX, born Bethlehem, North Carolina, 1946; admitted to bar, 1971, District of Columbia; 1984, North Carolina; U.S. District Court, Eastern, Middle and Western Districts of North Carolina; U.S. Court of Appeals, Fourth, Ninth, Eleventh and District of Columbia Circuits; U.S. Supreme Court. *Education:* Duke University (A.B., 1968; J.D., 1971). Member, Editorial Board, Duke Law Journal, 1970-1971. Partner, Howrey & Simon, Washington, D.C., (1977-1984). Arbitrator, Court Annexed Arbitration Program of the United States District Court for the Middle District of North Carolina (1988-1994). Private Judge, Duke University Private Adjudication Center (1988—). Certified Mediator, all North Carolina Courts and United States. District Court Middle District of North Carolina, (1993—). Listed in: Best Lawyers in America, Civil Business Litigation, 1994—. *Member:* Forsyth County (Executive Committee, 1995; Vice-President, 1996) North Carolina (Appellate Rules Study Committee, 1990-1993; Continuing Legal Education Committee, 1995-2000; Trial Practice Curriculum Committee, 1991-1997, Chair, 1995-1997; Technology Advisory Committee, 1997—; Long Range Planning Implementation Committee, 1997-1999; AOC Liaison Committee, 1999—; Litigation Section Council Executive Committee; Strategic Planning/Emerging Trends Committee, 2001—), District of Columbia and American Bar Associations; North Carolina State Bar (Ethics Committee, 1992-1994; Disciplinary Hearing Commission, Vice Chairman, 1995-1999, Chair, 1999-2002; Twenty-First Judicial District Bar Councilor, 2002—); American Board of Trial Advocates; North Carolina Academy of Trial Lawyers; Association of Trial Lawyers of America. [Capt., U.S.A.R., Judge Advocate General Corps., 1972-1978]. ***PRACTICE AREAS:*** Complex Business Litigation; Counseling; Business Torts; Contracts; Corporate Disputes; Antitrust; Intellectual Property; Lender Liability; Administrative Law; Mediation. ***Email:*** jfox@belldavispitt.com

STEPHEN M. RUSSELL, born Salisbury, North Carolina, 1950; admitted to bar, 1980, North Carolina; U.S. District Court, Eastern, Middle and Western Districts of North Carolina; U.S. Court of Appeals, Fourth Circuit. *Education:* East Carolina University (B.S., with honors, 1972; M.A. Ed., 1977); Wake Forest University (J.D., cum laude, 1980). Member, Wake Forest Law Review, 1979-1980. Clerkships: Honorable Hiram H. Ward, U.S. District Judge, Middle District of North Carolina, 1981-1984; Honorable Russell A. Eliason, U.S. Magistrate Judge, District of North Carolina (1980-1981). *Member:* Forsyth County and North Carolina Bar Associations; 21st Judicial District Bar Ethics and Grievance Committee. [With U.S. Army, 1972-1975]. ***PRACTICE AREAS:*** Civil Litigation; Legal Malpractice; Insurance Litigation; Condemnation Law. ***Email:*** srussell@belldavispitt.com

D. ANDERSON CARMEN, born Greensboro, North Carolina, 1957; admitted to bar, 1982, North Carolina; U.S. District Court, Middle and Western Districts of North Carolina; U.S. Court of Appeals, Fourth Circuit; U.S. Tax Court. *Education:* North Carolina State University (B.A., magna cum laude, 1979); Wake Forest University (J.D., 1982). Former Chapter 7 Panel Trustee, United States Bankruptcy Court for the Middle District of North Carolina, 1986-1989. Certified Mediator, All North Carolina Courts and U.S. District Court, Middle District of North Carolina (1993—). Arbitrator in Forsyth County District Court. Clerkship: Honorable Hiram H. Ward, United States District Judge, Middle District of North Carolina, (1983-1985); Honorable Russell A. Eliason, United States Magistrate, Middle District of North Carolina, (1982-1983). Listed, Business North Carolina's Legal Elite, January 2002, 2004. *Member:* Forsyth County and North Carolina (Construction Law Council, 1997-2000) Bar Associations; American Arbitration Association. ***PRACTICE AREAS:*** Commercial Litigation; Bankruptcy Law; Civil Litigation; Construction Law; Arbitration; Mediation; Tax Litigation; Employment Litigation. ***Email:*** acarmen@belldavispitt.com

JOHN W. BABCOCK, born Detroit, Michigan, 1959; admitted to bar, 1986, North Carolina; U.S. District Court, Middle and Western Districts of North Carolina; U.S. Tax Court. *Education:* University of Michigan-Dearborn (B.S.A., with distinction, 1982); Wake Forest University (J.D., magna cum laude, 1985); New York University (LL.M., in Taxation, 1987). Adjunct Professor of Law, Business Planning, Partnership Taxation, Wake Forest University School of Law. (1985-1995—). Partnership Taxation, Wake Forest University School of Law, 1996—. *Member:* Forsyth County, North Carolina and American (Subcommittee on S Corporations, 1989-1995) Bar Associations. ***PRACTICE AREAS:*** Tax Law; Corporate Law; Securities Law. ***Email:*** jbabcock@belldavispitt.com

STEPHEN D. POE, born Durham, North Carolina, 1951; admitted to bar, 1976, North Carolina; U.S. District Court, Eastern, Middle and Western Districts of North Carolina; U.S. Court of Appeals, Fourth Circuit; U.S. Supreme Court. *Education:* Wake Forest University (A.B., cum laude, 1973); University of North Carolina (J.D., 1976). Vice President and Associate Legal Counsel, NCNB Corporation, 1979-1988. *Member:* Forsyth County,

(This Listing Continued)

North Carolina (Member, Business Law Section Council, 1987-1990, 1995—; Vice Chair, 1997-1999; Chair, 2000-2001; Continuing Legal Education Chair, 1995-1996; Business Law Curriculum Committee, 1994-1995; Financial Institutions Committee Chair, 1989-1991; Ad Hoc Committee on Proposed Revisions to Uniform Commercial Code, 1991-1992) and American (Business Law Section) Bar Associations; North Carolina Bankers Association (Bank Counsel Committee Chair, 1985). ***PRACTICE AREAS:*** Business Law; Commercial Law; Creditors' Rights Law; Consumer Credit; Banking Law. ***Email:*** spoe@belldavispitt.com

AMY K. SMITH, born North Palm Beach, Florida, 1963; admitted to bar, 1988, North Carolina; U.S. District Court, Middle and Western Districts of North Carolina. *Education:* Western Carolina University (B.S., summa cum laude, 1984); Wake Forest University (J.D., magna cum laude, 1988). Phi Kappa Phi. Member, Articles Editor, Wake Forest University Law Review, 1987-1988. Certified Public Accountant, North Carolina, 1990—. Wake Forest University Planned Giving Council, (1997-1999, 2004—). Board Member, The Hospice Foundation of Winston-Salem/Forsyth County, Inc., 2004—. Tax Accountant, Ernst & Young (1988-1989). Listed, Business North Carolina's Legal Elite, 2002. *Member:* Forsyth County and North Carolina (Member, Sections on: Estate Planning and Fiduciary Law; Taxation) Bar Associations; Winston Salem Estate Planning Council (Secretary, 1998-1999; Board Member, 2004—). ***PRACTICE AREAS:*** Estate Planning; Probate Law; Tax Law. ***Email:*** asmith@belldavispitt.com

CHARLOT F. WOOD, born Galax, Virginia, 1955; admitted to bar, 1989, North Carolina; U.S. District Court, Middle and Western Districts of North Carolina; U.S. Court of Appeals, Fourth Circuit. *Education:* Meredith College (B.A., magna cum Laude, 1976); Wake Forest University (J.D., magna cum laude, 1989). Research Editor, Wake Forest Law Review, 1988-1989. *Member:* Forsyth County and North Carolina (Member, Sections on: Litigation; Workers' Compensation; Labor Law) Bar Associations. ***PRACTICE AREAS:*** Civil Litigation; Workers' Compensation; Insurance Defense Litigation; Premises Liability; Personal Injury Law; Products Liability; Labor Law. ***Email:*** cwood@belldavispitt.com

ELIZABETH M. REPETTI, born Colorado Springs, Colorado, 1955; admitted to bar, 1986, North Carolina; 1987, District of Columbia; U.S. District Court, Eastern, Middle and Western Districts of North Carolina. *Education:* University of Colorado (B.S., 1978); Wake Forest University (J.D., cum laude, 1986). Articles Editor, Wake Forest University Law Review, 1985-1986. Former Chapter 7 Panel Trustee, United States Bankruptcy Court for the Middle District of North Carolina. *Member:* Forsyth County and North Carolina Bar Associations; The District of Columbia Bar. ***PRACTICE AREAS:*** Bankruptcy Law; Creditors Rights; Foreclosure Law. ***Email:*** erepetti@belldavispitt.com

ALAN M. RULEY, born Parkersburg, West Virginia, 1959; admitted to bar, 1987, West Virginia; 1989, North Carolina; U.S. District court, Eastern, Middle and Western Districts of North Carolina; U.S. District Court, Southern District of Virginia; U.S. Court of Appeals, Fourth Circuit; U.S. Supreme Court. *Education:* Duke University (B.A., summa cum laude, 1982); Stanford University (J.D., 1986). Phi Beta Kappa; Pi Sigma Alpha. Clerkship: Hon. John T. Copenhaver, Jr., United States District Judge, Southern District of West Virginia, 1986-1988. *Member:* Forsyth County and North Carolina Bar Associations; West Virginia State Bar. ***PRACTICE AREAS:*** Civil Litigation; Complex Business Litigation; Business Torts; Securities Litigation; Intellectual Property; Employment Law. ***Email:*** aruley@belldavispitt.com

MALLORY M. OLDHAM, born Winston-Salem, North Carolina, 1957; admitted to bar, 1981, North Carolina; U.S. District Court, Middle District of North Carolina. *Education:* University of North Carolina at Greensboro (B.A., magna cum laude, 1978); Wake Forest University School of Law (J.D., 1981). *Member:* Forsyth County and North Carolina (Member, Real Estate Section) Bar Associations. ***PRACTICE AREAS:*** Real Estate Law; Corporate Law. ***Email:*** moldham@belldavispitt.com

ROBIN J. STINSON, born Winston-Salem, North Carolina, 1959; admitted to bar, 1984, North Carolina; U.S. District Court, Middle District of North Carolina; 1986, U.S. Court of Appeals, Fourth Circuit; U.S. Supreme Court. *Education:* Duke University (A.B., cum laude, 1981); University of North Carolina (J.D., 1984). *Member:* Forsyth County (President, 2001-2002, President-Elect, 2000-2001, Vice President, 1999-2000, Treasurer, 1998-1999 and Secretary, 1997-1998), North Carolina (Member, Board of Governors, 2004—; Family Law Section, Chair, 1998-1999, Vice Chair, 1997-1998, Family Law Council, 1993-1996; Family Forum, Editor, 1995-1997) and American Bar Associations; 21st Judicial Bar Association (Member, Ethics and Grievance Committee, 1994-1997; Chair, 1996-1997). Fellow, American Academy of Matrimonial Lawyers. (Board Certified Specialist in Family Law, North Carolina State Board of Legal Specialization). ***PRACTICE AREAS:*** Family Law. ***Email:*** rstinson@belldavispitt.com

JOHN A. COCKLEREECE, JR., born Greensboro, North Carolina, 1954; admitted to bar, 1979, North Carolina; U.S. Supreme Court; U.S. Court of Appeals, Fourth Circuit; U.S. District Court, Middle and Eastern Districts of North Carolina; U.S. Tax Court; U.S. Claims Court. *Education:* Washington & Lee University (B.A., summa cum laude, 1976; J.D., magna cum laude, 1979). Winston-Salem Chamber of Commerce, Board of Directors, 1999-2000. Chair, Small Business Council, 1999. Winston-Salem Industries for the Blind, Inc., Board of Directors, 1998—; Chair, 2002. North Carolina Eye Bank, Inc., Board of Directors, 1994-2004, Vice Chair, 1998-2002, Chair, 2002-2004. Winston-Salem Coliseum and Convention Center Commission, Board of Directors, 1998-2002, Chair, 2001-2002. Winston-Salem Public Assembly Facilities Commission, Board of Directors, 2002—. Westwood Club, Board of Directors, 2002-2004, Chair, 2003-2004. North Carolina Property Tax Commission, 1990-1993, Chair, 1991-1993. *Member:* Forsyth County and North Carolina (Member, Tax Section Council, 1993-1996, 2000—, Chair, 1995-1996) Bar Associations. ***PRACTICE AREAS:*** Business Representation; Property Tax Appeals; Estate Planning; Estate Administration. ***Email:*** jcocklereece@belldavispitt.com

DANIEL C. BRUTON, born Andrews Air Force Base, Maryland, 1969; admitted to bar, 1995, North Carolina; U.S. District Court, Eastern, Middle and Western Districts of North Carolina. *Education:* Davidson College (B.A., 1991); Wake Forest University (J.D., 1995). Member, Wake Forest University Law Review, 1993-1995. Clerkship: Honorable Catherine R. Carruthers, United States Bankruptcy Judge, Middle District of North Carolina (1995-1997). *Member:* Forsyth County and North Carolina (Bankruptcy Section Council, 2000—) Bar Associations. ***PRACTICE AREAS:*** Bankruptcy Law; Commercial Law; General Litigation. ***Email:*** dbruton@belldavispitt.com

G. EMMETT McCALL, born Atlanta, Georgia, June 15, 1943; admitted to bar, 1969, Florida; 1973, North Carolina; 1976, U.S. District Court, Middle District of North Carolina. *Education:* University of Kentucky (B.A., 1966; J.D., 1969). *Member:* Forsyth County Bar Association; North Carolina State Bar; The Florida Bar. [Capt., U.S. Army, 1969-1971]. ***PRACTICE AREAS:*** Business; Commercial Real Estate; Construction Law; Estate Planning; Mediation; Arbitration.

DONALD M. NIELSEN, admitted to bar, 1990, North Carolina. *Education:* Hamilton College (A.B., cum laude, 1979); Duke University (J.D., with honors, 1990). Technical Editor, Law and Contemporary Problems, 1988-1990. Chair, Forsyth County Historic Resources Commission, 1992-2004. Board Member, Liberty Community Development Corporation, 2000—. President, Forsyth County Genealogical Society, 2000-2001. Co-Chair, Complete Count Committee, Winston-Salem/Forsyth County Census, 2000. Member: Governmental Affairs Committee; Environmental Issues Committee; Chamber of Commerce; Preservation North Carolina; Twin City Kiwanis Club. ***PRACTICE AREAS:*** Environmental; Zoning, Planning and Land Use; Municipal Law.

KEVIN G. WILLIAMS, born Honolulu, Hawaii, 1971; admitted to bar, 1998, North Carolina; U.S. District Court, Eastern, Middle and Western Districts of North Carolina; U.S. Court of Appeals, Fourth Circuit. *Education:* University of North Carolina (B.S., 1993); Wake Forest University (J.D., cum laude, 1998). Wake Forest Law Review (1996-1990). Editorial Staff (1997-1998). Moot Court Board (1996-1998). *Member:* Forsyth County, North Carolina and American Bar Associations; North Carolina Association of Defense Attorneys. ***PRACTICE AREAS:*** Business Litigation; Insurance Law; Products Liability. ***Email:*** kwilliams@belldavispitt.com

ANNE H. SHELBURNE, born Lexington, Kentucky, November 27, 1958; admitted to bar, 1984, Kentucky; 2003, North Carolina. *Education:* Centre College of Kentucky (B.A., 1980); University of Louisville (J.D., cum laude, 1984). Omicron Delta Kappa. Brandeis Honor Society. Editor, Journal of Family Law, 1983-1984. *Member:* Forsyth County, North Carolina and Kentucky Bar Associations. ***PRACTICE AREAS:*** Corporate Law; Commercial Real Estate.

GALEN G. CRAUN, III, born Staunton, Virginia, 1968; admitted to bar, 1999, North Carolina, U.S. District Court, Middle District of North Carolina. *Education:* Randolph-Macon College (B.A., Economics, 1990); Virginia Polytechnic Institute and State University (Master of Accountancy, 1993); Wake Forest University School of Law (J.D., 1999). Tax Consultant, Ernst & Young, LLP, 1994-1997. *Member:* Forsyth County, North Carolina (Member, Tax Business Section, 2000—) and American Bar Associations; North Carolina Association of Certified Public Accountants. ***PRACTICE AREAS:*** Tax Law; Corporate Law; Securities Law; Business Representation. ***Email:*** gcraun@belldavispitt.com

JENNA B. THOMAS, born Winston-Salem, North Carolina, 1970; admitted to bar, 1996, North Carolina; 1998, U.S. District Court, Eastern, Middle and Western Districts of North Carolina. *Education:* University of North Carolina at Chapel Hill (B.S., 1992); Wake Forest University School of Law (J.D., 1996). Clerkship: Honorable Ralph A. Walker, North Carolina Court of Appeals (1996-1998). *Member:* Forsyth County and North Carolina Bar Associations. ***PRACTICE AREAS:*** Collections; Foreclosures; Bankruptcy. ***Email:*** jthomas@belldavispitt.com

DANIEL P. QUESNEL, born 1973; admitted to bar, 1999, North Carolina. *Education:* University of North Carolina, Asheville (B.A., cum laude, 1996); Wake Forest University (J.D., 1999). ***PRACTICE AREAS:*** Commercial Transactions; Banking Law; Corporate Law; Employee Benefits.

JENNIFER I. OAKES, born South Boston, Virginia, 1977; admitted to bar, 2002, North Carolina and U.S. District Court, Middle and Western Districts of North Carolina. *Education:* Duke University (A.B., 1999); Campbell University School of Law (J.D., magna cum laude, 2002). Managing Editor, Campbell Law Review, 2001-2002. *Member:* Forsyth County and North Carolina Bar Associations. ***PRACTICE AREAS:*** Corporate Law; Real Estate; Estate Planning.

BRADLEY C. FRIESEN, born Kansas City, Kansas, 1977; admitted to bar, 2002, North Carolina; U.S. District Court, Middle District of North Carolina. *Education:* Wheaton College (B.A., 1999); University of Kansas (J.D., 2002). *Member:* North Carolina and American Bar Associations; Forsyth County Young Lawyers Association (Treasurer). ***PRACTICE AREAS:*** Business; Commercial Law; Civil Litigation; Eminent Domain; Family Law. ***Email:*** bfriesen@belldavispitt.com

ALEXANDER P. RYAN, born Elmira, New York, October 31, 1973; admitted to bar, 2001, North Carolina. *Education:* St. John Fisher College (B.A., summa cum laude, 1996); Wake Forest University (J.D., 2001). Delta Epsilon Sigma. *Member:* Forsyth County and North Carolina (Member, Legislative and Leadership Committees; Co-Chair, Internet Communications Committee) Bar Associations. ***PRACTICE AREAS:*** Civil Litigation; Business Litigation; Workers Compensation; Products Liability; Intellectual Property Litigation. ***Email:*** aryan@belldavispitt.com

MONICA R. GUY, born Tallahassee, Florida, 1977; admitted to bar, 2003, North Carolina. *Education:* Florida State University (B.S., Communication, 1998); Wake Forest University (J.D., cum laude, 2003). Member, Wake Forest Law Review, 2001-2003. *Member:* Forsyth County and North Carolina Bar Associations; Forsyth County Young Lawyers Association (Board Member, 2004-2005). ***PRACTICE AREAS:*** Family Law. ***Email:*** mguy@belldavispitt.com

EDWARD B. DAVIS, born Winston-Salem, North Carolina, May 9, 1972; admitted to bar, 1999, South Carolina; 2001, North Carolina. *Education:* Davidson College (B.A., 1994); University of North Carolina, Chapel Hill (J.D., 1999). Recipient, Pro Bono Certificate of Achievement. *Member:* South Carolina and American Bar Associations. (Resident, Charlotte Office). ***PRACTICE AREAS:*** Litigation. ***Email:*** ward.davis@belldavispitt.com

(This Listing Continued)

BELL, DAVIS & PITT, P.A., Winston-Salem—Continued

MATTHEW F. ARUNDALE, born Warwick, Rhode Island, April 30, 1977; admitted to bar, 2004, North Carolina. *Education:* Marymount University (B.A., 1999); Wake Forest University (J.D., 2004). ***PRACTICE AREAS:*** Corporate Law. ***Email:*** marundale@belldavispitt.com

MICHAEL D. PHILLIPS, born Scottsdale, Arizona, January 30, 1968; admitted to bar, 2003, North Carolina and U.S. District Court, Eastern District of North Carolina; 2004, U.S. District Court, Middle and Western Districts of North Carolina and U.S. Court of Appeals, Fourth Circuit. *Education:* University of Redlands (B.A., 1990); University of Cincinnati (M.A., 1999); Wake Forest University (J.D., 2003). Member: Wake Forest Law Review, 2002-2003; National Trial Team, 2002-2003. Law Clerk, Justice George Wainwright, Supreme Court of North Carolina. *Member:* Forsyth County and North Carolina Bar Associations. ***PRACTICE AREAS:*** Civil Litigation. ***Email:*** mphillips@belldavispitt.com

OF COUNSEL

JAMES T. LAMBIE, born Harrisburg, Pennsylvania, 1942; admitted to bar, 1970, North Carolina. *Education:* Carson-Newman College (B.S., 1964); George Washington University (J.D., 1967). Certified Mediator. *Member:* Forsyth County and North Carolina Bar Associations. ***PRACTICE AREAS:*** Corporate Law; Real Estate; Insurance Regulation; Government Relations. ***Email:*** jlambie@belldavispitt.com

BENNETT & GUTHRIE PLLC

Established in 1995

1560 WESTBROOK PLAZA DRIVE
WINSTON-SALEM, NORTH CAROLINA 27103-1328
Telephone: 336-765-3121
Fax: 336-765-8622
URL: http://www.bennett-guthrie.com

Civil Litigation in State and Federal Courts, Medical Malpractice (Defense), Employment Law, Personal Injury, Construction Litigation, Commercial Litigation, Insurance Defense, Business Law.

FIRM PROFILE: Bennett & Guthrie PLLC is a law firm in Winston-Salem, North Carolina, concentrating in civil litigation, primarily representing businesses and insurance companies in defending actions involving commercial disputes, medical malpractice, personal injury claims of all types, insurance coverage, general liability, employment issues and workers compensation.

The firm's attorneys are experienced in alternative dispute resolution and take an active role in assisting clients in avoiding litigation whenever possible.

The firm's attorneys practice in the North Carolina state and federal courts at both the trial and appellate levels and are frequently called upon by attorneys from other states to serve as local counsel for their clients.

RICHARD V. BENNETT, born Winston-Salem, North Carolina, July 19, 1945; admitted to bar, 1974, North Carolina. *Education:* Wake Forest University (B.A., 1968; J.D., cum laude, 1974). Member, Board of Editors, Wake Forest Law Review, 1973-1974. Law Clerk to the Honorable Hiram H. Ward, U.S. District Judge, Middle District of North Carolina, 1974-1976. *Member:* Forsyth County, 21st Judicial District and North Carolina Bar Associations; North Carolina State Bar (21st Judicial District Councilor, 1995-2001); North Carolina Association of Defense Attorneys (Member, Board of Directors, 1991-2001; Secretary-Treasurer, 1992-1994; Secretary, 1995-1997; Executive Vice President, 1997-1998; President-Elect, 1998-1999; President, 1999-2000); Defense Research Institute (North Carolina State Representative, 2002-2004); Branch Inn of Court, 2001—; Fourth Circuit Judicial Conference (Permanent Member). ***PRACTICE AREAS:*** Medical Malpractice Defense; Defense Litigation; Insurance Coverage; Products Liability Defense; Insurance Defense; Employment Defense; Commercial Litigation. ***Email:*** rbennett@bennett-guthrie.com

RODNEY A. GUTHRIE, born Sebring, Florida, September 22, 1952; admitted to bar, 1980, North Carolina. *Education:* Stetson University (B.A., 1974); University of Madrid, Madrid, Spain; Stetson University; Wake Forest University (J.D., 1980). Omicron Delta Kappa. Author, "Declarations Against Penal Interests: New Standard for Admissibility in North Carolina," 15 Wake Forest Law Review 375 (1979). *Member:* Forsyth County and North Carolina (Member, Sections on: Litigation; Construction) Bar Associations; North Carolina State Bar; North Carolina Association of Defense Attorneys; Defense Research Institute. [Capt., USAR, 1978-1987]. ***LANGUAGES:*** Spanish. ***PRACTICE AREAS:*** Medical Malpractice Defense; Professional Liability Defense; Commercial Litigation; Insurance Coverage; Construction Litigation; Workers Compensation; Insurance Defense. ***Email:*** rguthrie@bennett-guthrie.com

FRANKLIN SCOTT TEMPLETON, born May 1, 1961; admitted to bar, 1989, North Carolina. *Education:* University of North Carolina (B.S.B.A., 1983); Wake Forest University (J.D., 1989). Member, Trial Team. Recipient, Goldberg Award. Member, Wake Forest Law Review; National Trial Team. Regional Champion, National Trial Competition, 1989. Recipient, Robert Goldberg Award in Trial Advocacy; ACTL Powell Medallion in Advocacy. Member, Student Trial Bar; Honor Council. Law Clerk to Hon. Burley B. Mitchell, Jr., Supreme Court of North Carolina, 1989-1990. North Carolina Deputy Secretary of State, 1997-2004. Legal Counsel, North Carolina Commissioner of Labor, 1993-1997; Division of Occupational Safety & Health, 1991-1992. Associate Attorney General, Labor Section, 1992-1993. Member, Tenth Judicial District Bar Grievance Committee, 1998-2001. *Member:* Forsyth County Bar Association; North Carolina State Bar (Member: Business Law Section Council, 2004—; Government Section Council, 2002-2004); Order of Barristers. ***PRACTICE AREAS:*** Business Law; Commercial Litigation. ***Email:*** fstempleton@bennett-guthrie.com

ROBERTA B. KING, born February 2, 1975; admitted to bar, 2003, North Carolina and U.S. District Court, Western District of North Carolina; 2004, U.S. District Court, Middle District of North Carolina. *Education:* Wake Forest University (B.A., cum laude, 1997); Wake Forest University (J.D., 2002). Pi Sigma Alpha; Golden Key. Member, Wake Forest Moot Court Board. Recipient, CALI Excellence for the Future Award in Legal Research and Writing. Member, Wake Forest Law Review. *Member:* Forsyth County and North Carolina Bar Associations; North Carolina State Bar; North Carolina Association of Defense Attorneys (Young Lawyers' Committee); Defense Research Institute. ***PRACTICE AREAS:*** Medical Malpractice Defense; Insurance Coverage; Defense Litigation. ***Email:*** rking@bennett-guthrie.com

JOSHUA H. BENNETT, born Winston-Salem, North Carolina, September 29, 1977; admitted to bar, 2004, North Carolina and U.S. District Court, Middle District of North Carolina. *Education:* Davidson College (B.A., Political Science, 2000); University of North Carolina (J.D., 2004). *Member:* Forsyth County and North Carolina Bar Associations; Defense Research Institute; North Carolina Association of Defense Attorneys. ***PRACTICE AREAS:*** Medical Malpractice Defense; Insurance Coverage; Business Law; Criminal Defense.

REPRESENTATIVE CLIENTS: American Home Assurance Company; GMAC Insurance; Hospice and Palliative CareCenter; Medtronic, Inc.; Novant Health, Inc.; St. Paul Fire and Marine Insurance Co.; Utica Insurance Co.; North American Risk Services; CNA Health Pro; Colony Insurance Company; First Colonial Insurance Company; Great West Casualty Company; Western Heritage Insurance Company; Universal Underwriters; Mag Mutual Insurance Co.; Atlantic Mutual Companies; State Farm Ins. Co.; American National Can Company; Atlantic Risk Management; Farmer's Insurance Group; Western Litigation Specialists; Farmers Insurance Exchange; N.C. Farm Bureau Insurance Companies; U.S. Liability Insurance Group; Royal Sun Alliance.

BENSON & MARSHALL, L.L.P.

WINSTON-SALEM, NORTH CAROLINA

(See Greensboro)

General Civil Practice, Corporation, Commercial, Personal Injury and Insurance, Real Estate, Business Acquisitions, Probate, Wills and Estate Planning, Elder Law, Business, Contracts, Collections, Civil Litigation, Domestic Relations, Family Law, Divorce, Adoptions, Foreclosures, General Practice.

BLANCATO, DOUGHTON & HART, PLLC

SUITE 150, 633 WEST FOURTH STREET
WINSTON-SALEM, NORTH CAROLINA 27101
Telephone: 336-725-9416
Fax: 336-725-5129

General Civil Practice. Corporate and Limited Liability Company Law, Real Estate, Wills, Estates and Probate, Commercial and Business Transactions, Litigation (Trials and Appeals in State and Federal Court), Insurance, Professional Liability, Governmental Liability, Construction Law, Mediation, Arbitration.

WILLIAM A. BLANCATO, born Queens, New York, September 16, 1957; admitted to bar, 1983, District of Columbia; 1984, U.S. Claims Court; 1985, North Carolina; 1992, U.S. Supreme Court. *Education:* Queens College (B.A., cum laude, 1980); Duke University (J.D., with high honors, 1983). Order of the Coif. Senior Editor, Law & Contemporary Problems, 1982-1983. Certified Mediator, North Carolina. Law Clerk to Honorable Alex Kozinski, Chief Judge U.S. Claims Court, 1983-1984. *Member:* Forsyth County, North Carolina (Member, Sections on: Litigation; Construction, Dispute Resolution) and American (Member, Sections on: Litigation; Construction Industry) Bar Associations. ***REPORTED CASES:*** Tarantino v. Baker, 825 F.2d 772 (4th Cir. 1987); Jackson v. Long, 102 F.3d 722 (1996); Jenkins v. Medford, 119 F.3d 1156 (4th Cir. 1997) (en banc). ***PRACTICE AREAS:*** Litigation; Insurance; Governmental Liability; Aviation Litigation; Business Litigation; Construction Law; Mediation; Arbitration. ***Email:*** blancato@bdh-law.com

THOMAS J. DOUGHTON, born Winston-Salem, North Carolina, October 20, 1961; admitted to bar, 1989, North Carolina. *Education:* Furman University (B.A., 1984); Wake Forest University (J.D., 1989). *Member:* Forsyth County and North Carolina Bar Associations; North Carolina State Bar. ***PRACTICE AREAS:*** Insurance Law; Collections Law; Civil Trials and Appeals; Workers Compensation Law; Construction Law; Estate Planning; Estate Administration. ***Email:*** doughton@bdh-law.com

ANDREW D. HART, born Greensboro, North Carolina, September 8, 1969; admitted to bar, 1997, North Carolina and U.S. District Court, Middle District of North Carolina. *Education:* North Carolina State University (B.A., 1992); Wake Forest University (J.D., cum laude, 1997). Order of the Coif. Member, Wake Forest Law Review. *Member:* Forsyth County and North Carolina (Member, Sections on: Real Estate, Business) Bar Associations; North Carolina State Bar. ***PRACTICE AREAS:*** Commercial Real Estate; Residential Real Estate; Commercial Transactions; Business Law; Foreclosures. ***Email:*** ahart@bdh-law.com

REPRESENTATIVE CLIENTS: A. Watts Inc.; I.L. Long Construction Co.; P.F. Plumbing, Inc.; Lyon Construction, Inc.; John S. Clark Company; Utica National Insurance Group; North Carolina League of Municipalities; Regal Ford, Inc.; Rymco Inc.; American International Group; National Loan Investors, L.P.; Crowne Partners; Omega Construction, Inc.; Piedmont Aviation Component Services, LLC; AIG Aviation; One Source Communications, Inc.; LPT Development Company, Inc.; Wilco Hess, LLC; Chicago Title Insurance Company.
REFERENCES: RBC; Centura Bank.
APPROVED ATTORNEYS FOR: Chicago Title Insurance Company; Commonwealth Land Title Company; Investors Title Insurance Company; Lawyers Title Insurance Company.

BLANCO TACKABERY COMBS & MATAMOROS, P.A.

Established in 1973
110 SOUTH STRATFORD ROAD, 5TH FLOOR
P.O. DRAWER 25008
WINSTON-SALEM, NORTH CAROLINA 27114-5008
Telephone: 336-293-9000
Facsimile: 336-293-9030
URL: http://www.btcmlaw.com

General, Trial and Appellate Practice in all State and Federal Courts. Corporation, Partnership, Taxation, Commercial, Real Estate, Probate, Securities, Intellectual Property Registration, Intellectual Property Licensing, Intellectual Property Protection, Employment, Environmental, Bankruptcy and White Collar Crime.

FIRM PROFILE: Blanco Tackabery Combs & Matamoros, P.A. was founded in 1973. Since that time the firm has represented businesses and their owners and managers, and individuals, providing a broad range of legal services for these clients. Our mission is to provide high-quality, cost-effective legal services for our clients in those practice areas in which Blanco Tackabery Combs & Matamoros can offer significant value. Blanco Tackabery Combs & Matamoros is organized into a number of practice groups. This allows our attorneys to develop specialized skills to meet the changing needs of our clients.

DAVID B. BLANCO, born Peoria, Illinois, March 23, 1941; admitted to bar, 1966, North Carolina. *Education:* Duke University (A.B., 1963; J.D., 1966). Phi Delta Phi. Legal Assistant to the Honorable Eugene A. Gordon, Chief Judge, U.S. District Court for the Middle District of North Carolina, 1966-1968. *Member:* Forsyth County, North Carolina (Member, Business Law Section) and American (Member, Business Law Section) Bar Associations; North Carolina State Bar. ***PRACTICE AREAS:*** Corporate Law; Mergers and Acquisitions; Estate Planning; Estate Administration. ***Email:*** dbb@btcmlaw.com

NEAL E. TACKABERY, born Atlanta, Georgia, October 2, 1949; admitted to bar, 1976, North Carolina. *Education:* Northwestern University (B.S., 1972); Duke University (J.D., 1975). Member, Editorial Board, Duke Law Journal, 1974-1975. *Member:* Forsyth County, North Carolina (Member, Tax and Estate Planning and Fiduciary Law Sections) and American Bar Associations; North Carolina State Bar. ***PRACTICE AREAS:*** Estate Planning and Administration; Employee Benefits; Corporate Law. ***Email:*** net@btcmlaw.com

REGINALD F. COMBS, born Winston-Salem, North Carolina, November 19, 1953; admitted to bar, 1978, North Carolina and U.S. District Court, Middle and Western Districts of North Carolina; U.S. Court of Appeals, Fourth Circuit. *Education:* Wake Forest University (B.A., magna cum laude, 1976; J.D., 1978). Phi Beta Kappa; Phi Alpha Delta. Member, Order of Barristers. Member, Wake Forest Law Review, 1977-1978. Author: "Tolled Statute of Limitations v. Long Arm Statute Amenability," 12 Wake Forest Law Review 1041, 1976; "The Scope of Discovery in North Carolina Under Amended Rule 26," 13 Wake Forest Law Review 640, 1977. Lecturer in Law, Wake Forest University School of Law, 1980-1981, 1990-1998. Certified Mediator, Federal and State Court. *Member:* Forsyth County (Secretary, 1991-1992 and Vice President, 1992-1993; Chairman, Ethics and Grievance Committee, 1995-1996; President, 1998-1999), North Carolina and American Bar Associations; North Carolina State Bar; The Association of Trial Lawyers of America; North Carolina Academy of Trial Lawyers; North Carolina College of Advocacy. ***PRACTICE AREAS:*** Civil Litigation; Commercial Litigation; Intellectual Property Litigation; Securities Litigation. ***Email:*** rfc@btcmlaw.com

RONALD A. MATAMOROS, born New York, N.Y., February 15, 1950; admitted to bar, 1975, Georgia; 1978, North Carolina. *Education:* Emory University (B.A., 1972; J.D., 1975). Phi Delta Phi. *Member:* North Carolina (Member, Real Property and Environmental Law Sections; Real Property Law Section Council, 1991-1994) and American (Member, Real Property, Probate and Trust Law Sections) Bar Associations; State Bar of Georgia; North Carolina State Bar. ***PRACTICE AREAS:*** Commercial Real Estate Law; Environmental Law; Real Estate Finance Law. ***Email:*** ram@btcmlaw.com

GENE B. TARR, born Stroudsburg, Pennsylvania, July 8, 1951; admitted to bar, 1983, North Carolina; 1984, U.S. District Court, Eastern, Middle and Western Districts of North Carolina. *Education:* Southern College (B.A., 1972); Campbell University (J.D., cum laude, 1983). Phi Kappa Phi; Omicron Delta Kappa; Phi Alpha Delta. Editor, Campbell Law Review, 1982-1983. Member, Moot Court Board, 1981-1982. Recipient, Phi Alpha Delta Award for Scholastic Excellence, 1983. Editor, Campbell Law Review, 1982-1983. North Carolina Board of Examiners for Nursing Home Administrators, 1992-1994. Lecturer: Bankruptcy Law, 1996, 1997, 2002, 2004. *Member:* Forsyth County, Yadkin County and North Carolina (Member, Bankruptcy Section) Bar Associations; North Carolina State Bar; American Bankruptcy Institute (Treasurer, North Carolina Bankruptcy Section Council, 1993-1995; Council Member, 1996-1999). ***PRACTICE AREAS:*** Bankruptcy Law; Creditors Rights; Business Debtor-Creator Relations. ***Email:*** gbt@btcmlaw.com

STEVEN C. GARLAND, born Trenton, New Jersey, November 9, 1953; admitted to bar, 1980, North Carolina. *Education:* Duke University (B.A., magna cum laude, 1975); Wake Forest University (J.D., magna cum laude, 1980). Editor-in-chief, Wake Forest Law Review, 1979-1980. Law Clerk to Hon. Joseph Branch, Chief Justice, North Carolina Supreme Court, 1980-1981. Lecturer: Wake Forest University School of Law, CLE, Practical Skills, 1988—. Town Attorney, Town of Lewisville, 1991—; Village Attorney, Village of Tobaccoville, 1991—. *Member:* Forsyth County, North Carolina (Member, Real Property Section) and American Bar Associations; North Carolina State Bar. ***PRACTICE AREAS:*** Commercial Real Estate Law; Real Estate Finance Law; Municipal Law. ***Email:*** scg@btcmlaw.com

PETER J. JURAN, born Redlands, California, July 3, 1961; admitted to bar, 1986, North Carolina, U.S. District Court, Eastern, Middle and Western Districts of North Carolina, U.S. Court of Appeals, Fourth and Federal Circuits and U.S. Tax Court. *Education:* Colgate University (B.A., cum laude, 1983); Duke University (M.A., philosophy, 1986; J.D., 1986). *Member:* Forsyth County and North Carolina Bar Associations; North Carolina State Bar. ***REPORTED CASES:*** Cooke v. Manufactured Homes, 998 F2d 1256 (4th Cir. 1993); Devan Designs Inc. v. Palliser Furniture Co., 25 USPQ 2d 1991 (MDNC 1992); O'Connor v. Booker, 165 B.R. 164 (BKRPTCY, MDNC 1994); Magnussen Presidential v. Collezione Europa USA Inc., 116 F3d 472 (1997). ***PRACTICE AREAS:*** Intellectual Property Litigation; Construction Law; Commercial Litigation; Employment Litigation; General Civil Litigation. ***Email:*** pjj@btcmlaw.com

BRIAN L. HERNDON, born High Point, North Carolina, October 18, 1958; admitted to bar, 1986, North Carolina and U.S. Tax Court. *Education:* North Carolina State University (B.A., 1981); Cumberland School of Law of Samford University (J.D., magna cum laude, 1986). Member, Cumberland Law Review, 1984-1986. *Member:* Forsyth County, North Carolina (Member, Business Law Section) and American (Member, Taxation, Business Law and Real Property Sections; Forum on Franchising) Bar Associations; North Carolina State Bar. ***PRACTICE AREAS:*** Corporate Law; Corporate Finance; Commercial Finance; Mergers and Acquisitions; Commercial Real Estate Law; Intellectual Property Law; Franchise Law. ***Email:*** blh@btcmlaw.com

BOWEN C. HOUFF, born Santa Ana, California, November 3, 1957; admitted to bar, 1988, North Carolina and U.S. District Court, Middle District of North Carolina; 1992, U.S. Court of Appeals, Fourth Circuit. *Education:* University of North Carolina (B.A., 1980; J.D., 1988); Université de Pau, France. *Member:* Forsyth County, North Carolina and American Bar Associations; North Carolina State Bar. ***LANGUAGES:*** French. ***PRACTICE AREAS:*** Civil Litigation; Bankruptcy Law; Municipal Law; Creditors Rights; Zoning Law. ***Email:*** bch@btcmlaw.com

GEORGE E. HOLLODICK, born Hazelton, Pennsylvania, April 14, 1959; admitted to bar, 1989, North Carolina and U.S. District Court, Middle District of North Carolina; 1990, District of Columbia. *Education:* University of North Carolina (B.A., 1981); Wake Forest University (J.D., magna cum laude, 1989). Member: Order of Barristers; Moot Court; National Moot Court Team; Wake Forest Law Review, 1987-1989. Author: Note, "Real Estate Finance - Subordination Clauses: North Carolina Subordinates Substance to Form," 23 Wake Forest Law Review 575 (1988). *Member:* Forsyth County and North Carolina (Member, Real Property Section; Council Member, 2001-2004) Bar Associations; North Carolina State Bar; District of Columbia Bar; American Health Lawyers Association. ***PRACTICE AREAS:*** Banking Law; Commercial Real Estate; Business Transactions; Commercial Finance; Bankruptcy Law; Long Term Health Care. ***Email:*** geh@btcmlaw.com

CHARLES D. LUCKEY, born Cleveland, Ohio, January 1, 1955; admitted to bar, 1985, Wisconsin, Connecticut and U.S. Army Court of Military Review; 1990, North Carolina; 1991, U.S. District Court, Middle, Eastern and Western Districts of North Carolina; 1994, U.S. Court of Appeals, Fourth Circuit; 1996, U.S. Supreme Court. *Education:* University of Virginia (B.A., with distinction, 1977); University of Connecticut (J.D., with honors, 1985); U.S. Army War College (Masters, Strategic Studies, 2001). Member, 1983-1985; Administrative Editor, 1984-1985, Connecticut Law Review. Author: "*Chappell v. Wallace:* Drawing the Line on Constitutional Torts," 17 Connecticut Law Review, 221 (1984). Adjunct Instructor, Wake Forest University. Certified Mediator, North Carolina Superior Court and U.S. District Court. *Member:* Forsyth County, North Carolina and American Bar Associations; North Carolina State Bar; State Bar of Wisconsin. [Commander, 1st BDE, 108th Division (IT); Colonel, Infantry, USAR]. ***PRACTICE AREAS:*** Civil and Environmental Litigation; Family Law; Criminal Defense. ***Email:*** cdl@btcmlaw.com

MARY MARGARET OGBURN, born Winston-Salem, North Carolina, July 13, 1951; admitted to bar, 1994, North Carolina. *Education:* North Carolina State University (B.S., 1973); Duke University (M.S., 1977; J.D., 1993). Phi Kappa Phi. Formerly Corporate Systems Director, Waccamaw Corporation. *Member:* Forsyth County and North Carolina (Member, Sections on: Real Property; Business Law; Intellectual Property) Bar Associations; North Carolina State Bar. ***PRACTICE AREAS:*** Corporate Law; Commercial Law; Intellectual Property Law; Nonprofit Corporation Law. ***Email:*** mmo@btcmlaw.com

JEFFREY D. PATTON, born Washington, D.C., July 3, 1969; admitted to bar, 1994, North Carolina; 1996, U.S. District Court, Middle, Eastern and Western Districts of North Carolina. *Education:* College of William & Mary (B.A., 1991); Wake Forest University (J.D., 1994). Phi Alpha Delta. Member, Moot Court Board. Member, Wagner Labor Law Team, 1994. Law Clerk to Honorable Russell A. Eliason, U.S. Magistrate Judge, Middle District of North Carolina. *Member:* Forsyth County, North Carolina (Member, Labor and Employment Law Section) and American (Member: Labor and Employment Law Section; Federal Labor Standard Legislation Committee; Employment Rights and Responsibilities Committee) Bar Associations; North Carolina State Bar. ***PRACTICE AREAS:*** Labor and Employment Law; Civil Litigation; Commercial Litigation. ***Email:*** jdp@btcmlaw.com

DEBORAH L. McKENNEY, born Royal Oak, Michigan, January 29, 1970; admitted to bar, 1995, Michigan; 1997, North Carolina; 2000, South Carolina. *Education:* University of Michigan (A.B., 1992; J.D., 1995). *Member:* Forsyth County, North Carolina and American Bar Associations; State Bar of Michigan; North Carolina State Bar; South Carolina State Bar. ***PRACTICE AREAS:*** Corporate Law; Commercial Law; Affordable Housing Law. ***Email:*** dlm@btcmlaw.com

ASHLEY S. RUSHER, born Hopkinsville, Kentucky, August 26, 1962; admitted to bar, 1987, North Carolina; 1993, Georgia. *Education:* University of Kentucky (B.A., Economics, 1984; J.D., 1987). Member, Moot Court Board. Visiting Student, Wake Forest University School of Law, 1987-1987. Law Clerk: Hon. Jerry G. Tart, United States Bankruptcy Judge, Middle District of North Carolina, 1987-1989; Hon. James E. Massey, U.S. Bankruptcy Judge, Northern District of Georgia, 1993-1995; Hon. Margaret H. Murphy, U.S. Bankruptcy Judge, Northern District of Georgia, 1993. Lecturer: Bankruptcy Law, 1990-1991, North Carolina Bar Foundation; National Business Institute, 1991. *Member:* American Bankruptcy Institute; North Carolina Bar Association (Member, Bankruptcy Section, Executive Council, 1992-1993 and 2001-2005); State Bar of Georgia (Member, Bankruptcy Section); Forsyth County Bar Association (Young Lawyers Division Vice President, 1991 and President Elect, 1992); International Women's Insolvency and Restructuring Confederation - Carolinas Network. ***PRACTICE AREAS:*** Bankruptcy Law; Creditors Rights; Commercial Litigation. ***Email:*** asr@btcmlaw.com

---

STEPHEN C. MINNICH, born Chambersburg, Pennsylvania, March 29, 1970; admitted to bar, 1996, North Carolina. *Education:* Grove City College (B.A., cum laude, 1992);

(This Listing Continued)

BLANCO TACKABERY COMBS & MATAMOROS, P.A.,
Winston-Salem—Continued

Case Western Reserve University (J.D., magna cum laude, 1996). Order of the Coif. Associate Editor and Contributing Editor, 1994-1996, Case Western Reserve University Law Review. Author: "Adarand Constructors, Inc. v. Pena: A Strict Scrutiny of Affirmative Action," 46 Case W. Res. L. Rev. 271 (1995). *Member:* North Carolina Bar Association (Member, Business Law and Tax Sections); North Carolina State Bar. [U.S. Army Reserve, 1989-1997; U.S. Army Active Duty, 1991]. ***PRACTICE AREAS:*** Corporate Law; Commercial Law; Commercial Real Estate; Mergers and Acquisitions; Tax Law. ***Email:*** scm@btcmlaw.com

JAMES E. CREAMER, JR., born Salisbury, Maryland, February 11, 1967; admitted to bar, 1997, North Carolina. *Education:* University of Virginia (B.A., 1989); Virginia Commonwealth University (M.P.A., 1992); Wake Forest University (J.D., 1997). Law Clerk, Honorable Ben F. Tennille, Special Superior Court Judge for Complex Business Cases. *Member:* Forsyth County, North Carolina (Member, Estate Planning Section) and American Bar Associations; North Carolina State Bar. ***PRACTICE AREAS:*** Estate Planning and Administration. ***Email:*** jec@btcmlaw.com

CAROLYN W. SCOGIN, born Syracuse, New York, September 25, 1974; admitted to bar, 1999, North Carolina. *Education:* University of Georgia (B.A., 1996); Wake Forest University (J.D., 1999). Editor, Wake Forest Law Review. Law Clerk, Hon. K. Edward Greene, North Carolina Court of Appeals, 1999-2001. *Member:* North Carolina Bar Association; North Carolina Association of Women Attorneys; Forsyth County Women Attorneys Association; American Health Lawyers Association. ***PRACTICE AREAS:*** Corporate Transactions; Commercial Transactions; Health Insurance Portability and Accountability Act (HIPAA). ***Email:*** cws@btcmlaw.com

NATHAN B. ATKINSON, born Birmingham, Alabama, December 12, 1975; admitted to bar, 2001, North Carolina. *Education:* Wake Forest University (B.A., 1998); Mercer University Law School (J.D., 2001). *Member:* Forsyth County, North Carolina (Member, Labor and Employment Law Section) and American (Member, Labor and Employment Law Section, Employment Rights and Responsibilities Committee) Bar Associations. ***PRACTICE AREAS:*** Employment Law; Civil Litigation; Commercial Litigation. ***Email:*** nba@btcmlaw.com

JEANETTE M. STARK, born Glen Ridge, New Jersey, September 4, 1977; admitted to bar, 2003, North Carolina. *Education:* College of William & Mary (B.B.A., 2000); Wake Forest University (J.D., 2003). ***PRACTICE AREAS:*** Bankruptcy; Business Transactions. ***Email:*** jbs@btcmlaw.com

AMY C. LANNING, born Winston-Salem, North Carolina, March 15, 1975; admitted to bar, 2004, North Carolina. *Education:* University of North Carolina at Charlotte (B.A., 1997); Wake Forest University School of Law (J.D., 2004). Member, Wake Forest University Law Review. ***PRACTICE AREAS:*** Real Estate; Business Transactions. ***Email:*** acl@btcmlaw.com

MELYNDA G. BROOMFIELD, born Richester, New York, July 15, 1970; admitted to bar, 1996, Massachusetts; 1997, New York; 2005, North Carolina. *Education:* Hobart and William Smith Colleges (B.A., 1992); Boston College Law School (J.D., 1996). ***PRACTICE AREAS:*** Civil Litigation; Labor and Employment. ***Email:*** mgb@btcmlaw.com

LINDA L. McCARTY, born Eskilstuna, Sweden, September 9, 1972; admitted to bar, 2002, Massachusetts; 2004, North Carolina. *Education:* San Diego State University (B.A., 1998); New England School of Law (J.D., 2001); Boston University School of Law (LL.M., Taxation, 2002). ***LANGUAGES:*** Swedish, Norwegian, Danish, German. ***PRACTICE AREAS:*** Business Transactions; Taxation. ***Email:*** llm@btcmlaw.com

SUSAN M. CLAPP, born Frankfort, Kentucky, September 29, 1979; admitted to bar, 2004, North Carolina. *Education:* Wake Forest University (B.A., cum laude, 2001; J.D., 2004). *Member:* Forsyth County and North Carolina (Member, Litigation Section) Bar Associations. ***PRACTICE AREAS:*** Litigation. ***Email:*** smc@btcmlaw.com

REPRESENTATIVE CLIENTS: Allegacy Federal Credit Union; Amarr Co.; American Sugar Refining, Inc.; Angell Group Incorporated; Bank of North Carolina; Bermuda Run Country Club; Bermuda Village Retirement Center; Branch Banking and Trust Company; C.B. Development Co.; Carolina Medical, Inc.; Chase Manhattan Bank USA; Choice Community Credit Union; City of Winston-Salem; Collezione Europe U.S.A.; Commodore Corporation; D.L. Davis & Co., Inc.; Davis Insurance Service, Inc.; Debbie's Staffing Services, Inc.; Domino Foods, Inc.; Douglas Company; Eagan Associates; First American Title Insurance Company; Fleet Finance, Inc.; Foils, Inc.; Forsyth Memorial Hospital, Inc.; G & B Energy; G.E. Capital Corp.; HHHunt Corporation; Installment Discount Corp.; Kaplan Companies, Inc.; Landura Cos.; Lawyers Title Insurance Corporation; Meadowbrook of North Carolina; Michael Waltrip Racing, Inc.; Novant Health, Inc.; Old Town Club, Incorporated; The Orr Group, LLC; Palliser Furniture Corp.; Premier Federal Credit Union; Progressive Technologies, Inc.; Protective Life Insurance Co.; Prudential Carolinas Realty; Regency Development Associates, Inc.; Salem Leasing Corp.; Shugart Enterprises; Southeastern Hospitality; Southern Community Bank and Trust; The Town of Lewisville; The Village Tavern, Inc.; Transom Development, Inc.; Village of Tobaccoville; Waltrip Racing, Inc.; Winston Printing Co.; Yadkin Valley Telephone Membership Corp.
APPROVED ATTORNEYS FOR: Chicago Title Insurance Co.; Farmers Home Administration; First American Title Insurance Company; Lawyers Title Insurance Corp.; Commonwealth Land Title Insurance Company; Stewart Title.
REFERENCES: Branch Banking and Trust Company, Winston-Salem, North Carolina Southern Community; Bank and Trust, Winston-Salem, North Carolina.

BROTHERTON FORD YEOMAN & WORLEY, PLLC

WINSTON-SALEM, NORTH CAROLINA

(See Greensboro)

Employment Litigation, Medical Malpractice, Commercial Claims, Business Torts, General Liability Claims, Insurance Defense, Workers Compensation, Insurance Coverage, Business Litigation, Commercial Litigation, Professional Malpractice.

DONALD R. BUIE

8 WEST 3RD STREET, SUITE 100
WINSTON-SALEM, NORTH CAROLINA 27101
Telephone: 336-773-1398
Fax: 336-773-1505
URL: http://www.donald-buielaw.com
Email: drbuie@bellsouth.net
URL: http://www.donaldrbuie.com
Mailing Address: P.O. Box 20031, Winston-Salem, NC 27120

Serious Automobile Accidents, Tractor Trailer Accidents, Wrongful Death, Personal Injury, Consumer Bankruptcy, Driving Under the Influence, Traffic, Wills and Estates.

FIRM PROFILE: Mr. Buie has been practicing in Winston-Salem, N.C. since 1981.

DONALD R. BUIE, born North Carolina, February 4, 1956; admitted to bar, 1981, North Carolina. *Education:* Wingate College (A.A., 1976); Elon College (B.A., 1978); North Carolina Central University (J.D., 1981). *Member:* North Carolina State Bar; Forsyth County and North Carolina Bar Associations. ***PRACTICE AREAS:*** Personal Injury Law (25%); Criminal Law; Domestic Law; Bankruptcy Law (50%).

STEPHEN G. CALAWAY

1330 ASHLEY SQUARE
ASHLEYBROOK LANE
WINSTON-SALEM, NORTH CAROLINA 27103
Telephone: 336-760-6420
Fax: 336-760-8811
Email: SCalawayAtty@aol.com

General Civil Practice, Residential Real Estate, Commercial Real Estate, Zoning and Land Use, Commercial Leasing, Construction.

STEPHEN G. CALAWAY, born Forsyth County, North Carolina, February 19, 1940; admitted to bar, 1964, North Carolina; 1969, U.S. District Court, Middle District of North Carolina. *Education:* Wake Forest University (B.A., 1962; LL.B., 1964). Phi Delta Phi. *Member:* Forsyth County and North Carolina Bar Associations; The North Carolina State Bar. [1st Lieut., U.S. Army, 1964-1966]

APPROVED ATTORNEYS FOR: Chicago Title Insurance Corp.; Commonwealth Title Insurance Corp.; Wachovia; Wachovia Mortgage Corp.; Lawyers Title Insurance Corp.; Bank of America; Federal Land Bank; Wachovia Bank & Trust Co., N.A.; Investors Title Co.; Branch Bank & Trust Co.
REFERENCE: Branch Bank and Trust Co.

CARRUTHERS & BAILEY, P.A.

Established in 2001
155 SUNNYNOLL COURT, SUITE 102
WINSTON-SALEM, NORTH CAROLINA 27106
Telephone: 336-714-1220
Facsimile: 336-722-1993
Email: jcarruthers@carruthersbailey.com
URL: http://www.lawyers.com/carruthers&bailey

Medical Malpractice, Products Liability, Personal Injury, Wrongful Death, Insurance Law, Premises Liability, Corporate Law, Employment Law.

FIRM PROFILE: The firm handles all types of civil litigation, including wrongful death, personal injury, products liability and medical malpractice.

JOSEPH T. CARRUTHERS, born Greensboro, North Carolina, August 31, 1952; admitted to bar, 1977, North Carolina. *Education:* Duke University (B.A., 1974); Wake Forest University (J.D., cum laude, 1977). Member, Board of Editors, Wake Forest Law Review, 1976-1977. Listed in Best Lawyers in America, 1996-2005. *Member:* Forsyth County and North Carolina (Member, Litigation Section Council, 1990-1993) Bar Associations; North Carolina State Bar; North Carolina Association of Defense Attorneys. Fellow, American College of Trial Attorneys. ***PRACTICE AREAS:*** Medical Malpractice; Products Liability; Personal Injury; Insurance Law; Premises Liability. ***Email:*** jcarruthers@carruthersbailey.com

J. DENNIS BAILEY, born Danville, Virginia, September 6, 1960; admitted to bar, 1985, North Carolina. *Education:* Elon College (B.A., magna cum laude, 1982); Wake Forest University (J.D., 1985). Law Clerk to Honorable Frank W. Bullock, Jr., U.S. District Judge, Middle District of North Carolina, 1985-1986. *Member:* Forsyth County and North Carolina Bar Associations; North Carolina State Bar. ***PRACTICE AREAS:*** Medical Malpractice; Personal Injury Litigation; Premises Liability; Insurance Law. ***Email:*** dbailey@carruthersbailey.com

COMERFORD & BRITT, L.L.P.

250 WEST FIRST STREET
SUITE 300
WINSTON-SALEM, NORTH CAROLINA 27101
Telephone: 336-631-8510
Fax: 336-631-8228
Email: @comerfordbritt.com
URL: http://www.comerfordbritt.com

Aviation, Medical Malpractice, Products Liability, Personal Injury, Wrongful Death, Complex Civil Litigation.

(This Listing Continued)

MEMBERS OF FIRM

W. THOMPSON COMERFORD, JR., born Bristol, Virginia, 1949; admitted to bar, 1974, North Carolina; U.S. District Court, Middle, Eastern and Western District of North Carolina; U.S. Court of Appeals, Fourth, Fifth and Eleventh Circuits; U.S. Supreme Court. *Education:* University of Tennessee and Wake Forest University (A.B., magna cum laude, 1972); Wake Forest University (J.D., cum laude, 1974). Editor, Wake Forest Law Review, 1973-1974. Permanent Member, Fourth Circuit Judicial Conference. Member, Wake Forest University School of Law Board of Visitors. Wake Forest University School of Law Alumni Council (President, 2001-2002). North Carolina Aeronautical Council (Jan. 2004 - June 2008). *Member:* Forsyth County, North Carolina and American Bar Associations; The Association of Trial Lawyers of America; North Carolina Academy of Trial Lawyers; Joseph Branch Inn of Court; Lawyer Pilots Bar Association; American Board of Trial Advocates. American Bar Foundation. ***PRACTICE AREAS:*** Civil Litigation; Aviation; Product Liability; Medical Malpractice. ***Email:*** WTC@comerfordbritt.com

CLIFFORD BRITT, born Lumberton, North Carolina, 1960; admitted to bar, 1986, North Carolina; 1987, U.S. District Court, Middle District of North Carolina; 1988, U.S. District Court, Eastern District of North Carolina; 1993, U.S. District Court, Western District of North Carolina. *Education:* Wake Forest University (B.A., 1982; M.B.A., 1986; J.D., 1986). Articles Editor, Wake Forest Law Review, 1985-1986. Permanent Member, Fourth Circuit Judicial Conference. *Member:* Forsyth County and North Carolina (Member, Litigation Section Council, 2000—; Secretary, 2002-2003; Chair-elect, 2003-2004; Chair, 2004-2005) Bar Associations; North Carolina Academy of Trial Lawyers (President-Elect, 2004-2005, Vice President, Education, 2001-2003; Vice President Legislative Affairs, 2003-2004; Board of Governors, 1999—; Executive Committee, 2001—; Chair, Professional Negligence Section, 2000-2001 and Vice-Chair, 1999-2000; Chair, Editorial Board, 1999-2001); The Association of Trial Lawyers of America; Joseph Branch Inn of Court; Wake Forest Law Alumni Council (President-elect, 2004-2005). ***PRACTICE AREAS:*** Medical Malpractice; Truck Accidents; General Civil Litigation; Aviation; Defective Products; Catastrophic Injury; Personal Injury; Wrongful Death. ***Email:*** Britt@comerfordbritt.com

ASSOCIATES

TERRE THOMAS YDE, born New Orleans, Louisiana, June 16, 1969; admitted to bar, 2000, North Carolina and U.S. District Court, Middle, Eastern and Western Districts of North Carolina. *Education:* University of South Florida (B.A., 1996); West Virginia University (J.D., 1999). Member: Order of the Coif; The Order of Barristers; National Moot Court Team; International Moot Court Team; Law Review. *Member:* North Carolina Bar Association; North Carolina Academy of Trial Lawyers (Publications Chair, YLD, 2003-2006; Vice-Chair, Professional Negligence Section, 2004-2005; Chair, Professional Negligence Section, 2005-2006); Forsyth County Women Attorneys Association (Treasurer, 2000-2001; President, 2001-2002); The Association of Trial Lawyers of America. ***PRACTICE AREAS:*** Civil Litigation; Medical Malpractice; Wrongful Death; Personal Injury. ***Email:*** ydet@comerfordbritt.com

KEVIN J. WILLIAMS, born Skaelskør, Denmark, February 16, 1971; admitted to bar, 1996, North Carolina and U.S. District Court, Middle District of North Carolina; 2000, U.S. District Court, Eastern and Western Districts of North Carolina; 2001, U.S. Court of Appeals, Fourth Circuit. *Education:* Duke University (A.B., 1993); Wake Forest University School of Law (J.D., 1996). *Member:* Forsyth County and North Carolina Bar Associations; North Carolina State Bar; North Carolina Academy of Trial Lawyers; Forsyth County Young Lawyers Division (Treasurer, 2002-2003; Vice President, 2003-2004; President-Elect, 2004-2005); The Association of Trial Lawyers of America. ***PRACTICE AREAS:*** Medical Malpractice; Civil Litigation; Personal Injury; Wrongful Death. ***Email:*** williamsk@comerfordbritt.com

BRIAN T. BAKER, born Lisle, Illinois, 1975; admitted to bar, 2000, North Carolina; U.S. District Court, Western and Middle Districts of North Carolina. *Education:* Wake Forest University (B.A., cum laude, 1997; J.D., 2000). Recipient, Junius C. Brown Scholarship. Member: Moot Court Board; Constitutional Law Moot Court Team. *Member:* North Carolina State Bar; Forsyth County and North Carolina Bar Associations; North Carolina Academy of Trial Lawyers; Association of Trial Lawyers of America. ***PRACTICE AREAS:*** Medical Malpractice; Civil Litigation; Wrongful Death; Personal Injury. ***Email:*** bakerb@comerfordbritt.com

ALAN RONALD DICKINSON, born Brooklyn, New York, 1976; admitted to bar, 2001, North Carolina; U.S. District Court, Western District of North Carolina. *Education:* Wake Forest University (B.A., magna cum laude, 1998); Duke University (J.D., magna cum laude, 2001). Phi Beta Kappa; Omicron Delta Kappa; Order of the Coif. Recipient, T.K. Hearn Scholarship for Excellence in Leadership & Service. *Member:* North Carolina State Bar; Mecklenburg County and North Carolina Bar Associations; North Carolina Academy of Trial Lawyers. ***PRACTICE AREAS:*** Medical Malpractice; Civil Litigation; Wrongful Death; Personal Injury. ***Email:*** dickinson@comerfordbritt.com

CONSTANGY, BROOKS & SMITH, LLC

100 NORTH CHERRY STREET, SUITE 300
WINSTON-SALEM, NORTH CAROLINA 27101
Telephone: 336-721-1001 Charlotte Telephone: 704-344-1040
Fax: 336-748-9112
URL: http://www.constangy.com

Asheville, North Carolina Office: 80 Peachtree Road, Suite 208. Telephone: 828-277-5137. Fax: 828-277-5138.

Atlanta, Georgia Office: 230 Peachtree Street, N.W., Suite 2400. Telephone: 404-525-8622. Fax: 404-525-6955.

Austin, Texas Office: 111 Congress Avenue, Fourth Floor. Telephone: 512-391-4989. Fax: 512-391-6821.

Birmingham, Alabama Office: 1901 Sixth Avenue North, Suite 1410. Telephone: 205-252-9321. Fax: 205-323-7674.

Columbia, South Carolina Office: 1301 Gervais Street, NationsBank Tower, Suite 810. Telephone: 803-256-3200. Fax: 803-256-6277.

(This Listing Continued)

Fairfax, Virginia Office: 4100 Monument Corner Drive, Suite 520. Telephone: 571-522-6100. Fax: 571-522-6101.

Jacksonville, Florida Office: 200 West Forsyth Street, Suite 1610. Telephone: 904-356-8900. Fax: 904-356-8200.

Kansas City, Missouri Office: 2600 Grand Avenue, Suite 300. Telephone: 816-472-6400. Fax: 816-472-6401.

Macon, Georgia Office: 577 Mulberry Street, Suite 710. Telephone: 478-750-8600. Fax: 478-750-8686.

Nashville, Tennessee Office: Vanderbilt Plaza, Suite 925, 2100 West End Avenue. Telephone: 615-320-5200. Fax: 615-321-5891.

San Antonio, Texas Office: The Forum, 8000 IH 10 West, Suite 600. Telephone: 210-525-7977. Fax: 210-525-7978.

Tampa, Florida Office: 100 North Tampa Street, Suite 3350. Telephone: 813-223-7166. Fax: 813-223-2515.

Labor Relations, Employment Litigation, Employee Benefits Law, Wage and Hour, OSHA Law, Business Immigration, Affirmative Action.

MEMBERS

PENNI P. BRADSHAW, born Bradenton, Florida, October 14, 1954; admitted to bar, 1980, North Carolina; 1985, U.S. Supreme Court. *Education:* Randolph-Macon Woman's College (A.B., magna cum laude, 1977); University of North Carolina (J.D., with honors, 1980). ***PRACTICE AREAS:*** Immigration Law. ***Email:*** pbradshaw@constangy.com

KENNETH P. CARLSON, JR., born Atlanta, Georgia, November 22, 1954; admitted to bar, 1990, North Carolina. *Education:* University of North Carolina, Chapel Hill (B.A., English Literature, 1976); Yale University (M.Div., 1981); Wake Forest University (J.D., 1990). ***PRACTICE AREAS:*** Labor and Employment; Employment Litigation; Trade Secret and Noncompetition Litigation; Wage and Hour Law. ***Email:*** kcarlson@constangy.com

TERRY A. CLARK, born Atlanta, Georgia, May 27, 1960; admitted to bar, 1986, Alabama; 1987, South Carolina and U.S. District Court, District of South Carolina; U.S. District Court, Western, Middle and Eastern Districts of North Carolina; 1994, North Carolina; 1990, U.S. Court of Appeals, Fourth Circuit. *Education:* Furman University (B.A., in History, 1982); Cumberland School of Law of Samford University (J.D., 1986). ***PRACTICE AREAS:*** Labor Law; Employment Law; Affirmative Action. ***Email:*** tclark@constangy.com

JILL S. COX, born Royal Oak, Michigan, June 6, 1968; admitted to bar, 1993, North Carolina. *Education:* St. Andrews Presbyterian College (B.A., cum laude, 1990); Wake Forest University (J.D., 1993). ***PRACTICE AREAS:*** Labor and Employment; Employment Litigation. ***Email:*** jcox@constangy.com

JOHN J. DOYLE, JR., born Doylestown, Pennsylvania, June 12, 1942; admitted to bar, 1966, North Carolina; 1974, U.S. Supreme Court. *Education:* University of North Carolina at Chapel Hill (A.B., 1964; LL.B., 1966). ***PRACTICE AREAS:*** Labor and Employment. ***Email:*** jdoyle@constangy.com

W. RANDOLPH LOFTIS, JR., born Hickory, North Carolina, June 24, 1947; admitted to bar, 1971, North Carolina; U.S. District Courts, Middle, Western and Northern Districts of North Carolina; U.S. Court of Appeals, Fourth Circuit; U.S. District Court, Eastern District of Michigan and U.S. Court of Appeals, Sixth Circuit; U.S. Supreme Court. *Education:* Wofford College (B.A., Political Science, 1968); Wake Forest University (J.D., cum laude, 1971). ***PRACTICE AREAS:*** Labor and Employment; Employment Litigation; Agricultural Labor. ***Email:*** rloftis@constangy.com

CHARLES P. ROBERTS III, born Shelby, North Carolina, October 1, 1953; admitted to bar, 1979, North Carolina; 1980, South Carolina; 1985, U.S. District Court, District of South Carolina; 1984, U.S. District Courts, Western and Eastern Districts of North Carolina and U.S. Court of Appeals, Fourth Circuit; 1986, U.S. District Court, Middle District of North Carolina and U.S. Court of Appeals, District of Columbia Circuit; 1990, U.S. Supreme Court; 1991, U.S. Court of Appeals, Seventh Circuit; 1995, U.S. Court of Appeals, Eleventh Circuit; 1998, U.S. Court of Appeals, First Circuit; 2003, U.S. Court of Appeals, Eighth Circuit. *Education:* North Carolina State University (B.S., Textile Technology, high honors, 1975); University of North Carolina (M.B.A., 1979; J.D., 1979). ***PRACTICE AREAS:*** Labor and Employment. ***Email:*** croberts@constangy.com

ROBIN E. SHEA, born San Antonio, Texas, August 12, 1955; admitted to bar, 1988, North Carolina; U.S. District Courts, Eastern, Middle and Western Districts of North Carolina; U.S. Court of Appeals, Fourth Circuit; U.S. Supreme Court. *Education:* University of North Carolina at Chapel Hill (B.A., English, 1977); Wake Forest University (J.D., cum laude, 1988). ***PRACTICE AREAS:*** Labor and Employment; Employment Litigation; Affirmative Action Law; Agricultural Labor; Wage-Hour Litigation. ***Email:*** rshea@constangy.com

ASSOCIATES

KRISTINE M. HOWARD, born South River, New Jersey, July 23, 1973; admitted to bar, 1998, West Virginia; 1999, North Carolina; U.S. District Court, Northern and Southern Districts of West Virginia and U.S. District Court, Eastern, Middle, and Western Districts of North Carolina; U.S. Court of Appeals, Fourth Circuit; U.S. Supreme Court. *Education:* University of Virginia (B.A., 1995); University of Richmond (J.D., 1998). ***PRACTICE AREAS:*** Labor and Employment; Employment Litigation. ***Email:*** khoward@constangy.com

JEANETTE K. PHELAN, born Long Beach, California, February 4, 1963; admitted to bar, 1994, Florida; 2000, Kentucky; 2004, North Carolina. *Education:* University of South Florida (B.A., Political Science, 1990); Stetson University College of Law (J.D., cum laude, 1994). ***PRACTICE AREAS:*** Immigration. ***Email:*** jphelan@constangy.com

CANDICE SYLVETTE WOOTEN, born Winston-Salem, North Carolina, December 8, 1976; admitted to bar, 2001, North Carolina; 2001, U.S. District Courts, Eastern, Middle, Western Districts of North Carolina and U.S. Court of Appeals, Fourth Circuit. *Education:* University of North Carolina (B.A., American History, 1997; J.D., 2001). ***PRACTICE AREAS:*** Labor and Employment; Employment Litigation. ***Email:*** cwooten@constangy.com

(This Listing Continued)

CONSTANGY, BROOKS & SMITH, LLC, Winston-Salem—Continued

REPRESENTATIVE CLIENTS: Allergy Partners; Asheville Savings Bank; Carolina Day School; Charles Stewart Company; Community Management Corporation; Macon Program for Progress; McDowell Hospital; Mind Your Business, Inc.; Mission Hospitals; PrintPack, Inc.; Renaissance Stone and Biltmore Tile, Inc.; Rich Mount, Inc.; Shogren Industries; The Sway Inn; Trader Construction Company; W.P. Hickman Company; YMCA of Western North Carolina.

CRAIGE BRAWLEY LIIPFERT & WALKER LLP

Established in 1832

110 OAKWOOD DRIVE, SUITE 300
WINSTON-SALEM, NORTH CAROLINA 27103-1958
Telephone: 336-725-0583
Fax: 336-725-4677
URL: http://www.craigebrawley.com

General Practice in State and Federal Courts. Taxation, Estate and Trust Administration, Estate Planning, Fiduciary Law, Guardianships, Elder Law, Long Term Care Planning, Special Needs Trust Planning and Administration, Real Property, Corporation, Commercial, Domestic, Collections and Personal Injury Law.

FIRM PROFILE: Established in 1832, Craige Brawley Liipfert & Walker LLP is the oldest law firm in North Carolina. The firm is engaged in the general practice of law and provides a broad range of legal services to individual and business clients. The firm provides sophisticated legal expertise in the areas of estate planning, elder law, long term care planning, special needs trust planning and administration, probate, estate administration, trust administration and guardianships. The firm also provides extensive experience in corporate, litigation and real estate matters. Several attorneys are board certified specialists in their particular areas of practice.

MEMBERS OF FIRM

COWLES LIIPFERT, born Winston-Salem, North Carolina, May 9, 1938; admitted to bar, 1964, North Carolina. *Education:* University of North Carolina (A.B., 1960; LL.B., 1964). Member, Board of Editors, North Carolina Law Review, 1962-1964. *Member:* North Carolina State Bar; National Academy of Elder Law Attorneys. (Board Certified Specialist in Estate Planning and Probate Law, North Carolina State Board of Legal Specialization). ***PRACTICE AREAS:*** Probate and Estate Planning; Taxation; Corporate; Business. ***Email:*** cliipfert@craigebrawley.com

WILLIAM W. WALKER, born Bethesda, Maryland, October 19, 1948; admitted to bar, 1977, North Carolina. *Education:* Gettysburg College (A.B., 1970); Wake Forest University (J.D., 1977). Law Clerk to: Honorable Russell A. Eliason, U.S. Magistrate, Middle District of North Carolina, 1977-1978; Honorable Hiram H. Ward, U.S. District Judge, Middle District of North Carolina, 1978-1980. Adjunct Clinical Professor, Wake Forest University School of Law, 1984—. Certified Mediator, North Carolina Superior Courts, 1992—. *Member:* North Carolina State Bar. [1st Lt., U.S. Marine Corps, 1970-1974]. ***PRACTICE AREAS:*** Civil Litigation; Estates; Fiduciary Law; Personal Injury; Railroad; Domestic Relations; Collection Law. ***Email:*** wwalker@craigebrawley.com

B. BAILEY LIIPFERT, III, born Chapel Hill, North Carolina, October 28, 1961; admitted to bar, 1991, North Carolina. *Education:* University of North Carolina at Chapel Hill (A.B., 1984); Campbell University (J.D., cum laude, 1991). Campbell University Law Review, 1989-1991; Research Editor, 1990-1991. Certified Elder Law Attorney as Certified by the National Elder Law Foundation. Charter Member, Special Needs Trust Alliance. *Member:* North Carolina State Bar; National Academy of Elder Law Attorneys; North Carolina Association of Trial Lawyers. ***PRACTICE AREAS:*** Elder Law; Estate Planning; Long Term Care Planning; Medicaid Planning; Special Needs Trusts. ***Email:*** bbliipfert@craigebrawley.com

JOHN A. KEIGER, born Winston Salem, North Carolina, August 4, 1960; admitted to bar, 1989, North Carolina. *Education:* University of North Carolina at Chapel Hill (B.A., 1982; M.B.A., J.D., 1986). *Member:* North Carolina State Bar. (Board Certified Specialist in Estate Planning and Probate Law, North Carolina State Bar Board of Legal Specialization). ***PRACTICE AREAS:*** Estate Planning; Estate Administration; Trust Administration; Corporate; Business Law. ***Email:*** jkeiger@craigebrawley.com

BRENT W. STEPHENS, born Hillsborough, North Carolina, March 15, 1970; admitted to bar, 1996, North Carolina. *Education:* University of North Carolina at Chapel Hill (B.A., 1992); Campbell University (J.D., summa cum laude, 1996). Campbell Law Review, 1994-1996. *Member:* North Carolina State Bar; National Academy of Elder Law Attorneys. ***PRACTICE AREAS:*** Estate Planning; Estate Administration; Trust Administration; Elder Law; Long Term Care; Special Needs Trusts. ***Email:*** bstephens@craigebrawley.com

ROBERT MARTIN ADDISON, born Spartanburg, South Carolina, February 22, 1968; admitted to bar, 1998, North Carolina and South Carolina. *Education:* Southern College (B.S., 1991) Wake Forest University (J.D., 1998). *Member:* North Carolina State Bar; South Carolina Bar; National Academy of Elder Law Attorneys; American Bar Association. ***PRACTICE AREAS:*** Estate Planning; Estate Administration; Trust Administration; Probate; Elder Law; Taxation; Guardianships. ***Email:*** maddison@craigebrawley.com

ASSOCIATES

AIMEE L. SMITH, born Albemarle, North Carolina, July 15, 1972; admitted to bar, 2002, North Carolina. *Education:* University of North Carolina, Greensboro, N.C. (B.A., 1995); Wake Forest University (J.D., 2002). *Member:* North Carolina State Bar. ***PRACTICE AREAS:*** Elder Law; Estate Planning. ***Email:*** asmith@craigebrawley.com

REBECCA L. SMITHERMAN, born Richmond, Virginia, July 21, 1976; admitted to bar, 2002, North Carolina. *Education:* University of North Carolina, Chapel Hill (B.A., 1998); Wake Forest University (J.D., cum laude, 2002). *Member:* North Carolina State Bar. ***PRACTICE AREAS:*** Estate Planning; Corporate Law; Civil Litigation. ***Email:*** rsmitherman@craigebrawley.com

(This Listing Continued)

SUSAN J. RYAN, born Danville, Virginia, November 21, 1954; admitted to bar, 2005, North Carolina. *Education:* College of William & Mary (B.A., 1976); Wake Forest University (J.D., 2005). *Member:* North Carolina State Bar; American Bar Association; National Association of Women Lawyers. ***PRACTICE AREAS:*** Civil Litigation; Fiduciary Liability; Domestic Relations. ***Email:*** sryan@craigebrawley.com

JULIAN P. ROBB, born Roodepoort, South Africa, December 29, 1972; admitted to bar, 1998, North Carolina. *Education:* University of North Carolina (B.A., with distinction, 1995); Wake Forest University School of Law (J.D., 1998). *Member:* North Carolina State Bar; North Carolina Bar Association. ***PRACTICE AREAS:*** Residential Real Estate; Commercial Real Estate. ***Email:*** jrobb@craigebrawley.com

OF COUNSEL

H. DAVID NIBLOCK, born Winston-Salem, North Carolina, July 13, 1954; admitted to bar, 1981, North Carolina. *Education:* St. Andrews Presbyterian College (B.A., 1977); Campbell University School of Law (J.D, 1981). *Member:* North Carolina State Bar (DRC Certified Mediator). (Also Member, Nelson, Boyles, Niblock and Green). ***PRACTICE AREAS:*** Domestic Relations; Personal Injury; Civil Litigation; Real Estate; Estate Planning; Estate Administration; Traffic Violations; Criminal Law. ***Email:*** dniblock@craigebrawley.com

DAVID AND ASSOCIATES, PLLC

1100-A SOUTH STRATFORD ROAD
WINSTON-SALEM, NORTH CAROLINA 27103
Telephone: 336-354-1040
Toll Free: 1-800-856-9927
Email: aeverhart@davidandassociates.com
URL: http://www.wilmingtonpiattorneys.com

Jacksonville, North Carolina Office: 405-B Western Boulevard. 28546. Telephone: 910-219-4878.
Supply, North Carolina Office: Highway 17. 28462. Telephone: 910-754-8465.
Wallace, North Carolina Office: 107 North Norwood Street. 28466. Telephone: 910-285-8777.
Clinton, North Carolina Office: 610 Beaman Street. 28328. Telephone: 910-592-8400.
Wilmington, North Carolina Office: 1516 Dawson Street. 28401: Telephone: 910-251-8088.
Greensboro, North Carolina Office: 529 College Road. Suite G. 27410. Telephone: 336-354-1040.

Personal Injury, Medical Malpractice, Wrongful Death, Products Liability, Workers Compensation, Aviation, Airplane Crashes, Negligence, Class Actions, Maritime Accidents, Boating Accidents, Bicycle Accidents, Motorcycle Accidents, Truck Accidents, School Bus Accidents, Railroad Accidents, Dog Bites, Slip and Fall, Birth Trauma, Brain Injury, Spinal Injury, Head Injury, Catastrophic Injury, Vehicular Homicide, Personal Injury Mediation, Products Liability, Drug and Medical Device Litigation, Product Defects, Automobile Liability, Motorcycle Products Liability, Amusement Park Liability, Hotel Liability, Marina Liability, Sports Injury.

(For complete biographical data on all personnel, see Professional Biographies, Wilmington, North Carolina)

DAVIS ELDER & DISABILITY LAW

WINSTON-SALEM, NORTH CAROLINA

(See Lewisville)

Elder Law.

DAVIS & HAMRICK, L.L.P.

Established in 1946

635 WEST FOURTH STREET
P.O. DRAWER 20039
WINSTON-SALEM, NORTH CAROLINA 27120-0039
Telephone: 336-725-8385
Telecopier: 336-723-8838
Email: info@davisandhamrick.com
URL: http://www.davisandhamrick.com

General Civil Practice in North Carolina and Federal Courts. Insurance Defense, Labor and Employment Law, Personal Injury, Workers' Compensation, Trucking, Real Estate, Traffic and Transportation Law.

MEMBERS OF FIRM

H. LEE DAVIS, JR., born Greenville, North Carolina, March 5, 1952; admitted to bar, 1977, North Carolina and U.S. District Court, Eastern, Middle and Western Districts of North Carolina; 1982, U.S. Court of Appeals, Fourth Circuit and U.S. Supreme Court. *Education:* North Carolina State University (B.S., 1974); Wake Forest University (J.D., 1977). Adjunct Professor of Law, Wake Forest University School of Law, 1995—. Faculty Member, Southeast Region N.I.T.A. Member, Board of Visitors, Wake Forest University School of Law. Certified Mediator in North Carolina. *Member:* Forsyth County and North Carolina Bar Associations; North Carolina State Bar; Trucking Industry Defense Association (TIDA); Defense Research Institute; North Carolina Association of Defense Attorneys; Federation of Defense and Corporate Counsel. ***PRACTICE AREAS:*** Insurance Defense; Employment Law; Products Liability; Asbestos Defense; Trucking Law. ***Email:*** ldavis@davisandhamrick.com

KENT L. HAMRICK, born Winston-Salem, North Carolina, August 12, 1958; admitted to bar, 1983, North Carolina and U.S. District Court, Middle District of North Carolina; 1988, U.S. Court of Appeals, Fourth Circuit. *Education:* Wake Forest University (B.A., magna cum laude, 1980); University of North Carolina at Chapel Hill (J.D., 1983). Phi Delta

(This Listing Continued)

Phi. *Member:* Forsyth County and North Carolina Bar Associations; North Carolina Association of Defense Attorneys; Defense Research Institute; North Carolina Chapter International Association of Arson Investigators. ***PRACTICE AREAS:*** Insurance Defense; Civil Litigation; Personal Injury; Wrongful Death; Arson; Insurance Fraud; Real Estate Brokers and Agents Liability; Property Damage; Construction Law. ***Email:*** klhamrick@davisandhamrick.com

SHANNON WARF BEACH, born Winston-Salem, North Carolina, November 19, 1966; admitted to bar, 1992, North Carolina and U.S. District Court, Middle District of North Carolina. *Education:* Davidson County Community College (A.S., with honors, 1987); Greensboro College (B.S., cum laude, 1989); Campbell University School of Law (J.D., 1992). *Member:* Forsyth County and North Carolina Bar Associations; North Carolina State Bar; North Carolina Association of Defense Attorneys; Defense Research Institute. (Board Certified Specialist in Workers' Compensation, North Carolina State Board of Legal Specialization). ***PRACTICE AREAS:*** Civil Litigation; Workers' Compensation; Insurance Defense; Real Estate. ***Email:*** shannonbeach@davisandhamrick.com

JAMES G. WELSH, JR., born Washington, D.C., February 11, 1965; admitted to bar, 1997, North Carolina and U.S. District Court, Middle District of North Carolina; U.S. Supreme Court. *Education:* Wake Forest University (B.A., 1987; J.D., 1997). Member: Moot Court; Chief Justice Moot Court; Order of Barristers. Recipient, Dean's Leadership Award. *Member:* North Carolina State Bar; North Carolina Bar Association; North Carolina Association of Defense Attorneys; Defense Research Institute. ***PRACTICE AREAS:*** Insurance Defense; Trucking Defense; Civil Litigation; Traffic; Subrogation. ***Email:*** jwelsh@davisandhamrick.com

---

ANN C. ROWE, born Lexington, North Carolina, August 14, 1974; admitted to bar, 1999, North Carolina and U.S. District Court, Middle District of North Carolina; 2001, U.S. Court of Appeals, Fourth Circuit. *Education:* Duke University (A.B., magna cum laude, 1996); University of North Carolina at Chapel Hill (J.D., 1999). *Member:* Forsyth County and North Carolina Bar Association; North Carolina State Bar; North Carolina Association of Defense Attorneys. ***PRACTICE AREAS:*** Insurance Defense; Civil Litigation; Workers' Compensation; Subrogation. ***Email:*** arowe@davisandhamrick.com

R. ANDREW KEEVER, born Lynchburg, Virginia, December 30, 1973; admitted to bar, 2004, North Carolina and U.S. District Court, Middle District of North Carolina. *Education:* University of North Carolina at Chapel Hill (B.A., 1996); Campbell University Norman Adrian Wiggins School of Law (J.D., 2004). *Member:* Forsyth County and North Carolina Bar Association; North Carolina State Bar. ***PRACTICE AREAS:*** Insurance Defense; Subrogation; Collections; District Court Criminal; Traffic Violations; Personal Injury. ***Email:*** akeever@davisandhamrick.com

LOCAL COUNSEL FOR: State Farm Mutual Automobile Insurance Co.; State Farm Fire & Casualty; Philadelphia Insurance Group; Safeco Insurance Co.; Lawyers Mutual; A.M.I.C.A.; Liberty Mutual Insurance Co.; RBC/Centura Bank; Colonial Insurance; Motorists Insurance Companies; Coachman Industries; St. Paul Insurance Companies; Metlife Property and Casualty Company; J.C. Penney Life Insurance Company; American Family Life Assurance Co. (AFLAC); Swift Transportation; ABF Freight; National Claims Management; Allstate Ins. Co.; Dresser Industries; Halliburton; Kellogg, Brown and Root; Lawyers Title Insurance Co.; United Parcel (UPS); Colony Group; National Interstate; Kemper Professional; Pennsylvania's Lumbermans Mutual; Philadelphia Ins. Co.; Hartford.
APPROVED ATTORNEYS FOR: Lawyers Title Insurance Corp.; Commonwealth Land Title Ins. Co.; Stewart Title Co.; Chicago Title Insurance.
REFERENCES: Wachovia Bank and Trust Co., N.A.; First Citizens Bank and Trust Co.; NationsBank of North Carolina; RBC/Centura Bank.

DAVIS & HARWELL, P.A.

Established in 1980

101 SOUTH STRATFORD ROAD
SUITE 200
WINSTON-SALEM, NORTH CAROLINA 27104-4224
Telephone: 336-722-1534
Fax: 336-722-2382
Email: info@davisharwell.com
URL: http://www.davisharwell.com

General Civil and Criminal Trial Practice in State and Federal Courts. Commercial, Business and Corporate, Personal Injury and Tort Litigation, Family Law, Wills and Estate Planning, and Employment Law.

FIRM PROFILE: Davis & Harwell, P.A., was formed in 1980 with emphasis on business and commercial litigation, family law, criminal defense, serious torts and estate planning. Organized as an interactive combination of attorneys and other legal professionals with diverse skills and interests, the firm offers a wide range of specialized legal services and strives to maintain close client contact. Attorneys and paralegals are encouraged to employ innovative practice techniques and to maintain high standards of professionalism and competence through frequent participation in continuing legal education activities.

FRED R. HARWELL, JR., born Washington, North Carolina, March 3, 1944; admitted to bar, 1973, New York; 1980, North Carolina, U.S. District Court, Eastern, Middle and Western Districts of North Carolina, U.S. Court of Appeals, Fourth Circuit and U.S. Tax Court. *Education:* University of North Carolina (A.B., 1966; J.D., 1972). Named in, "The Best Lawyers in America," Woodward/White, Inc. ***PRACTICE AREAS:*** Civil Litigation; White Collar Criminal Defense; Business Law; Corporate Law; Commercial Law; Contract Law; Creditors Rights in Bankruptcy; Professional Malpractice. ***Email:*** fharwell@davisharwell.com

JOSLIN DAVIS, born Raleigh, North Carolina, December 30, 1951; admitted to bar, 1977, North Carolina; 1978, District of Columbia and Florida; 1980, U.S. District Court, Eastern District of North Carolina; 1981, U.S. District Court, Middle District of North Carolina. *Education:* University of Georgia (B.A., 1974); Wake Forest University (J.D., 1977). Named in: The Best Lawyers in America, Woodward/White, Inc., 1993—. Adjunct Professor, Family Law, Wake Forest University Law School, 2000—. American Academy of Matrimonial Lawyers, 1993—. American Board of Trial Advocates, 1995—. (Board

(This Listing Continued)

Certified Specialist in Family Law, North Carolina State Board of Legal Specialization). ***PRACTICE AREAS:*** Complex Family Law; Civil Litigation; Family Law; Arbitration; Mediation. ***Email:*** jdavis@davisharwell.com

LORETTA C. BIGGS, born Atlanta, Georgia, March 6, 1954; admitted to bar, 1979, Georgia; 1984, North Carolina. *Education:* Spelman College (B.A., cum laude, 1976); Howard University School of Law (J.D., with honors, 1979). Named in "The Best Lawyers in America," Woodward/White, Inc., Adjunct Professor, Wake Forest University School of Law, 1984-1987. Associate Judge, North Carolina Court of Appeals, Raleigh, North Carolina, 2001-2002. State District Court Judge, 21st Judicial District, Forsyth County, Winston-Salem, North Carolina, 1987-1994. ***PRACTICE AREAS:*** Family Law; Appellate Practice; Civil Litigation. ***Email:*** lbiggs@davisharwell.com

MARK H. HOPPE, born Bryan, Texas, October 16, 1957; admitted to bar, 1983, Texas; 1987, North Carolina and U.S. District Court, Northern District of Texas; 1990, U.S. District Court, Western District of Texas and U.S. Court of Appeals, Fifth Circuit; 1997, U.S. District Court, Middle District of North Carolina. *Education:* Duke University (B.S., magna cum laude, 1980); Southern Methodist University (J.D., 1983). ***PRACTICE AREAS:*** Civil Litigation; Employment Law; Employment Discrimination; Commercial and Tort Litigation. ***Email:*** mhoppe@davisharwell.com

JOHN A. McMILLEN, born New York, New York, April 5, 1963; admitted to bar, 1991, North Carolina and U.S. District Court, Middle District of North Carolina; 1992, New York; 2001, U.S. Tax Court. *Education:* University of Pennsylvania (B.A., 1985); Washington University (J.D., 1990). ***PRACTICE AREAS:*** Trusts and Estates; Taxation; Probate; Wills; Business Law. ***Email:*** jmcmillen@davisharwell.com

DEBORAH S. HALVORSEN, born Dunkirk, New York, July 2, 1973; admitted to bar, 1998, North Carolina and U.S. District Court, Middle District of North Carolina. *Education:* St. Mary's College (B.A., cum laude, 1995); Wake Forest University (J.D., 1998). (Board Certified Specialist in Family Law, North Carolina State Board of Legal Specialization). ***PRACTICE AREAS:*** Family Law; Criminal Defense; Civil Litigation. ***Email:*** dhalvorsen@davisharwell.com

CALEIGH H. EVANS, born Mission Viejo, California, May 28, 1974; admitted to bar, 2001, North Carolina and U.S. District Court, Middle District of North Carolina. *Education:* Appalachian State University (B.S., cum laude, 1996); University of Georgia (J.D., cum laude, 2001). ***PRACTICE AREAS:*** Family Law; Criminal Defense; Civil Litigation. ***Email:*** cevans@davisharwell.com

APPROVED ATTORNEYS FOR: Commonwealth Land Title Co.; First American Title Co.; First Title Insurance Co.; Lawyers Title Insurance Co.

THE DEUTERMAN LAW GROUP, P.A.

WINSTON-SALEM, NORTH CAROLINA

(See Greensboro)

Workers Compensation, Auto Accidents, Social Security Disability, Wrongful Death, Nursing Home Neglect, Slip and Fall, Products Liability.

JAMES H. EARLY, JR.

1320 WESTGATE CENTER DRIVE
WINSTON-SALEM, NORTH CAROLINA 27103-2933
Telephone: 336-768-2546
Fax: 336-765-9193
Email: jim@jimearly.com

Limited Civil Practice, Personal Injury, Malpractice, Employment Claims, Corporate and Business Law and Family Law. Trials in all Courts.

JAMES H. EARLY, JR., born Henderson, North Carolina, May 6, 1939; admitted to bar, 1964, North Carolina. *Education:* Mars Hill College (A.A., 1960); Wake Forest University (B.A., 1962; J.D., 1964).

ELLIOT PISHKO MORGAN, P.A.

Established in 1988

426 OLD SALEM ROAD
WINSTON-SALEM, NORTH CAROLINA 27101-5283
Telephone: 336-724-2828
Fax: 336-724-3335
Email: jgmorgan@epmlaw.com
URL: http://www.epmlaw.com

Civil Practice in State and Federal Courts. Negligence, Civil Rights, Family, Labor, Employment, Workers' Compensation and Commercial Litigation.

FIRM PROFILE: Elliot Pishko Morgan, P.A. emphasizes the representation of individuals and businesses in the resolution of civil disputes through litigation and negotiation. The firm endeavors to handle each matter with excellence, integrity and zeal. Each of its attorneys has extensive experience in state and federal courts, at both the trial and appellate levels and maintains a high level of competence through continuing education and training. The firm's attorneys regularly lecture and publish articles in the areas of trial practice and evidence, personal injury, employment, worker's compensation and family law. Members of the firm share a commitment to the protection of individual rights and the improvement of community relations and are energetically involved in trial lawyer groups, civil rights organizations and other public service activities.

DAVID C. PISHKO, born 1950; admitted to bar, 1977, North Carolina. *Education:* Duke University (B.A., cum laude, 1972; J.D., with distinction, 1977). (Board Certified Specialist in Family Law, North Carolina State Board of Legal Specialization). ***PRACTICE AREAS:*** Medical Malpractice; Professional Liability; Securities; Family Law. ***Email:*** dcpishko@epmlaw.com

(This Listing Continued)

ELLIOT PISHKO MORGAN, P.A., Winston-Salem—Continued

ROBERT M. ELLIOT, admitted to bar, 1977, North Carolina. *Education:* University of North Carolina (B.A., 1973); Wake Forest University (J.D., cum laude, 1977). ***PRACTICE AREAS:*** Labor and Employment; Civil Rights; ERISA; Personal Injury. ***Email:*** rmelliot@epmlaw.com

J. GRIFFIN MORGAN, born Springfield, Massachusetts, 1950; admitted to bar, 1976, North Carolina. *Education:* Denison University (B.A., 1972); Antioch School of Law (J.D., 1975). (Board Certified Specialist in Workers' Compensation, North Carolina State Board of Legal Specialization). ***PRACTICE AREAS:*** Workers Compensation; Labor and Employment; Personal Injury. ***Email:*** jgmorgan@epmlaw.com

THE ELLISON LAW FIRM

515 W. 2ND STREET
WINSTON-SALEM, NORTH CAROLINA 27101
Telephone: 336-723-7370
Fax: 336-723-7372
Email: ellison@earthlink.net

Real Estate, Landlord Tenant, Criminal Law, Traffic Violations, Divorce.

ERIC ELLISON, born Detroit, Michigan, June 9, 1970; admitted to bar, 1999, North Carolina. *Education:* Michigan State University (B.S., 1993); Thomas M. Cooley Law School (J.D, 1999). *Member:* Forsyth County (Secretary; Former Member, Ethics and Grievance Committee), Winston-Salem, North Carolina State Bar Associations.

ENNS & ARCHER LLP

Established in 2001
939 BURKE STREET
WINSTON-SALEM, NORTH CAROLINA 27101
Telephone: 336-723-5180
Fax: 336-723-5181
URL: http://www.ennsandarcher.com

Trademarks, Advertising and Marketing, Promotion Law and Sweepstakes, Copyrights, Trade Secrets, Intellectual Property Licensing, Intellectual Property Litigation, Antitrust and Trade Regulation, Commercial Law, Distribution Agreements, Dealer and Distributor Termination, Computers and Software, Internet Law, Federal Civil Litigation, Appellate Practice.

FIRM PROFILE: Enns & Archer LLP was formed in February 2001 by Rodrick J. Enns and Julia C. Archer.

After many years in a sophisticated intellectual property practice with a large first-tier law firm, we wished to create an informal and flexible environment in which we can focus on what we enjoy: providing legal advice and support to those who market branded products and services. We assist regional, national and international companies in obtaining, licensing and maintaining rights in trademarks, copyrights, and related intellectual property; formulating and executing branding, advertising and marketing strategies; establishing and protecting channels of distribution; and avoiding, resolving, and, when necessary, litigating disputes relating to activities in the marketplace.

Our philosophy is simple: We strive to deliver superior value in the fields in which we practice, and we rely completely on our clients to decide if we have succeeded.

PARTNERS

RODRICK J. ENNS, born Wichita, Kansas, May 28, 1955; admitted to bar, 1979, Colorado; 1984, North Carolina. *Education:* University of Washington (B.A., magna cum laude, with distinction, 1976); Harvard University (J.D., cum laude, 1979). Phi Beta Kappa. *Member:* Forsyth County and North Carolina (Founding Member, Antitrust and Trade Regulation Law Section; Section Council, 1987—; Section Chair, 1991-1992; Member, Intellectual Property Section) Bar Associations; International Trademark Association (Vice Chair, Legislation and Regulatory Analysis Committee, 2006—; Member, Select Committee on Federal Trademark Dilution Act, 2003; Member, U.S. Legislation Subcommittee, 2002-2005; Chair, Emerging Issues Subcommittee, 1997-2001; Chair, Model State Trademark Bill Subcommittee, 1994-1997). ***REPORTED CASES:*** National Ass'n For Stock Car Auto Racing, Inc. v. Scharle, 356 F.Supp.2d 515 (E.D.Pa. 2005); Brown & Williamson Tobacco Corp. v. Pataki, 320 F.3d 200 (2d Cir. 2003); Kidd v. Bass Hotels & Resorts, Inc., 136 F.Supp.2d 965 (E.D.Ark. 2000); Resorts of Pinehurst, Inc. v. Pinehurst National Corp., 148 F.3d 417, 47 U.S.P.Q.2d 1465 (4th Cir. 1998); Santa Fe Natural Tobacco Co., Inc. v. Judge, 63 F.Supp. 437 (M.D.Pa. 1997); Sara Lee Corp. v. Kayser-Roth Corp., 81 F.3d 455, (4th Cir. 1996); Pinkham v. Camex, Inc., 84 F.3d 292 (8th Cir. 1996); Mirafi, Inc. v. Murphy, 928 F.2d 410 (Fed. Cir. 1991). ***PRACTICE AREAS:*** Trademarks; Advertising and Marketing; Copyrights; Trade Secrets; Intellectual Property Licensing; Intellectual Property Litigation; Antitrust and Trade Regulation; Commercial Contracts; Distribution Agreements; Dealer and Distributor Termination; Computers and Software; Internet Law; Federal Civil Litigation; Appellate Practice. ***Email:*** renns@ennsandarcher.com

JULIA C. ARCHER, born Danville, Kentucky, December 18, 1966; admitted to bar, 1992, North Carolina and South Carolina. *Education:* Davidson College (B.A., cum laude, 1988); University of South Carolina (J.D., cum laude, 1992). South Carolina Law Review. *Member:* North Carolina Bar Association (Member, Intellectual Property Section); South Carolina Bar; International Trademark Association (Member, Trademark Office Practices Committee and Classification Subcommittee, 2004—; Chair, Special Projects Subcommittee of Trademark Administrators Committee, 2002-2003; Member, Trademark Management Committee, 1999-2001); Promotion Marketing Association. ***PRACTICE AREAS:*** Trademark Registration; Trademark Licensing; International Trademarks; Advertising and Marketing; Domain Names; Promotion Law; Sweepstakes; Intellectual Property Portfolio Management. ***Email:*** jarcher@ennsandarcher.com

(This Listing Continued)

REPRESENTATIVE CLIENTS: NASCAR, Inc.; Wal-Mart Stores, Inc.; International Textile Group (Burlington Industries); Santa Fe Natural Tobacco Company, Inc.; Lance, Inc.; Lowes Companies, Inc.
REFERENCE: Wachovia Bank.

LAW OFFICE OF JODI A. ERNEST

WINSTON-SALEM, NORTH CAROLINA

(See Greensboro)

Real Estate, Residential, Buying or Selling Home, Commercial Real Estate, Conveyancing, Living Wills, Wills.

FITZGERALD & HUNTER

114 SOUTH SPRUCE STREET
WINSTON-SALEM, NORTH CAROLINA 27101
Telephone: 336-777-1090
Fax: 336-723-8433
URL: http://www.fitzgeraldhunterlaw.com

Criminal Law, Driving While Intoxicated (DWI), Drug Crimes, Parole and Probation, Traffic Violations, White Collar Crimes.

MEMBERS OF FIRM

JOHN E. FITZGERALD, born Grosse Pointe, Michigan, May 4, 1965; admitted to bar, 1990, North Carolina. *Education:* Wake Forest University (B.A., 1987; J.D., 1990). ***LANGUAGES:*** French. ***PRACTICE AREAS:*** Criminal Defense; Driving While Intoxicated; Traffic Violations.

ROBERT C. HUNTER, born Chicago, Illinois, August 3, 1960; admitted to bar, 1986, Arizona; 1988, North Carolina. *Education:* Northwestern University (B.A., 1982); Duke University (J.D., 1986). *Member:* Forsyth County Bar Association; North Carolina State Bar. ***PRACTICE AREAS:*** Traffic Violations; Driving While Intoxicated; Criminal Law; Drug Crimes.

GEORGE FRANCISCO, PC

2000 WEST FIRST STREET, SUITE 501
WINSTON-SALEM, NORTH CAROLINA 27104
Telephone: 336-722-5088
Fax: 336-722-5118
Email: George@GeorgeFranciscoLaw.com
URL: http://www.GeorgeFranciscoLaw.com

Civil Trial Practice including Personal Injury, Workers' Compensation, Insurance Claims, Business Torts, Investment Losses.

GEORGE FRANCISCO, born Mount Airy, North Carolina, December 7, 1949; admitted to bar, 1983, North Carolina; 1987, U.S. District Court, Middle and Western Districts of North Carolina. *Education:* Duke University; Appalachian State University (B.A., magna cum laude, 1976); Campbell University School of Law (J.D., 1982). Commendation, International Academy of Trial Lawyers for Distinguished Achievement in Advocacy. *Member:* Forsyth County, North Carolina and American (Member, Litigation Section) Bar Associations; North Carolina Academy of Trial Lawyers; The Association of Trial Lawyers of America. [With U.S. Army, 1972-1974]. (Board Certified Specialist in Workers Compensation Law, North Carolina State Board of Legal Specialization) (Board Certified Civil Trial Advocacy Specialist by the National Board of Trial Advocacy). ***Email:*** george@georgefranciscolaw.com

GATTO LAW OFFICES, P.A.

501 HARVEY STREET
WINSTON-SALEM, NORTH CAROLINA 27103
Telephone: 336-768-2345
Telecopier: 336-768-2622
Email: jgatto@triad.rr.com
URL: http://www.gattolawoffices.com

Family Law, Domestic Relations, Divorce, Equitable Distribution, Child Custody, Child Support, Premarital Agreements, Spousal Agreements.

FIRM PROFILE: Mr. Gatto is Board Certified Specialist in Family Law since 1989.

JOSEPH J. GATTO, born Elizabeth, New Jersey, June 26, 1953; admitted to bar, 1979, North Carolina and U.S. District Court, Middle District of North Carolina. *Education:* Ursinus College (B.A., 1975); Wake Forest University (J.D., 1979). Phi Delta Phi. Recipient, International Academy of Trial Lawyers Moot Court Award, 1979. Author: "Judgments In Equitable Distribution Cases," North Carolina Bar Foundation CLE Seminar, Nov. 1985; "Alimony & Divorce from Bed and Board," North Carolina Bar Foundation CLE Seminar, November 1986, November 1988; "Valuation of Closely Held Businesses & Professional Practices," Professional Education Systems, Inc. Seminar, July 1988; "Discovery and Pre-Trial Matters," WFU, CLE, 1994 Equitable Distribution Seminar. Lecturer, North Carolina Bar Association, Family Law Seminar, 1985, 1986. Clinical Adjunct Professor, Wake Forest University, 1981-1983. Assistant District Attorney, 21st Judicial District, 1980-1983. District Court Judge, 21st. Judicial District, 1983-1986. *Member:* Forsyth County and North Carolina (Member, Family Law Section) Bar Associations; North Carolina State Bar; North Carolina Trial Lawyers Association (Member, Family Law Section); Advisory Committee for N.C. Practical Skills Course, 1984-1986); American Adjudication Society; North Carolina Academy of Trial Lawyers of America. (Board Certified Specialist in Family Law, North Carolina State Board of Legal Specialization). ***PRACTICE AREAS:*** Family Law.

DENISE M. GOLD

1404 W. FIRST STREET
WINSTON-SALEM, NORTH CAROLINA 27101
Telephone: 336-722-5950
Fax: 336-722-5951
Email: dmgoldattorney@aol.com
URL: http://www.dmgoldattorney.com

General Civil Litigation, Criminal Law, DWI, Drug Crimes, Misdemeanors, Child Custody, Child Support, Divorce, Personal Injury, Adoption Law, Juvenile Law.

DENISE M. GOLD, born St. Louis, Missouri, March 27, 1968; admitted to bar, 1999, North Carolina. *Education:* Lenoir Rhyne College (B.A., 1990); Wake Forest University (J.D., 1999). Phi Alpha Delta; Omicron Delta Epsilon; Mu Sigma Epsilon. *Member:* American Bar Association; Forsyth County Women Attorney Association; Forsyth County Criminal Defense Attorneys (Treasurer, 2002); North Carolina Association of Trial Lawyers; North Carolina Junior Chamber of Commerce (Past President); United States Junior Chamber of Commerce (Metro Conference Legal Counsel).

GOULDER IMMIGRATION LAW FIRM

WINSTON-SALEM, NORTH CAROLINA

(See Greensboro)

Immigration and Naturalization, Visas, U.S. Citizenship, Student Visa, HI-B, L Visas, E Visas, Employment Visa, J-Visa, Fiancée Visas, all Family-Based Immigration Visas and Adjustments of Status.

GRACE HOLTON TISDALE & CLIFTON P.A.

301 N. MAIN STREET, SUITE 100
WINSTON-SALEM, NORTH CAROLINA 27101
Telephone: 336-725-9428
Fax: 336-721-1176
URL: http://www.graceholtontisdalecliftonlaw.com

Criminal Law in all State and Federal Courts. Traffic Violations, White Collar Crime.

MICHAEL A. GRACE, admitted to bar, 1977, North Carolina; U.S. District Court, Middle and Western Districts of North Carolina and U.S. Court of Appeals, Fourth Circuit. *Education:* University of North Carolina, Asheville (B.A., 1974); Wake Forest University Law School (J.D., 1977). *Member:* Forsyth County and North Carolina (Member, Disciplinary Committee) Bar Associations; North Carolina Academy of Trial Lawyers; Forsyth County Criminal Defense Attorneys. ***PRACTICE AREAS:*** Criminal Law; Traffic Violations. ***Email:*** mgrace@ghtclaw.com

WALTER C. HOLTON, JR., born Winston-Salem, North Carolina, September 27, 1955; admitted to bar, 1984, North Carolina; 1985, U.S. District Court, Middle District of North Carolina; 1991, U.S. Court of Appeals, Fourth Circuit. *Education:* University of North Carolina at Chapel Hill (B.A., 1977); Wake Forest University Law School (J.D., 1984). *Member:* Forsyth County and North Carolina Bar Associations; American Inns of Court; National Association of Former U.S. Attorneys; North Carolina Academy of Trial Lawyers. ***PRACTICE AREAS:*** Civil Litigation; White Collar Crime. ***Email:*** wholton@ghtclaw.com

DONALD K. TISDALE, SR., born LaGrange, Georgia, November 25, 1942; admitted to bar, 1968, North Carolina; U.S. District Court, Western and Middle Districts of North Carolina and U.S. Court of Appeals, Fourth Circuit. *Education:* Wake Forest University (B.A., 1965; J.D., 1968). *Member:* Forsyth County Bar Association; North Carolina State Bar; Forsyth County Criminal Defense Attorneys. ***PRACTICE AREAS:*** Criminal Law; Traffic Violations. ***Email:*** dtisdale@ghtclaw.com

CHRISTOPHER R. CLIFTON, born 1970; admitted to bar, 1995, North Carolina. *Education:* North Carolina State University (B.A., 1992); Wake Forest University Law School (J.D., 1995). *Member:* Forsyth County and North Carolina (Chair, Criminal Justice Section, 2005—) Bar Association; National Association of Criminal Defense Lawyers; North Carolina Academy of Trial Lawyers; Forsyth County Criminal Defense Attorneys; American Inns of Court. ***PRACTICE AREAS:*** Criminal Law; Personal Injury. ***Email:*** cclifton@ghtclaw.com

D. KENNETH TISDALE, JR., born 1970; admitted to bar, 1997, North Carolina. *Education:* North Carolina State University (B.A., 1993); Wake Forest University Law School (J.D., 1997). *Member:* Forsyth County and North Carolina Bar Associations; North Carolina Academy of Trial Lawyers; Forsyth County Criminal Defense Attorneys. ***PRACTICE AREAS:*** Criminal Law; Traffic Violations. ***Email:*** ktisdale@ghtclaw.com

MIRIELLE P. CLOUGH, admitted to bar, 2001, North Carolina. *Education:* Duke University (B.A., 1999); Wake Forest University Law School (J.D, 2001). ***PRACTICE AREAS:*** Criminal Law; Traffic Violations. ***Email:*** mclough@ghtclaw.com

OF COUNSEL

MICHELLE B. CLIFTON, admitted to bar, 1995, North Carolina. *Education:* North Carolina State University (B.A., 1992); Wake Forest University (J.D., 1995). *Member:* Forsyth County and North Carolina (Member, Litigation Section) Bar Associations. ***PRACTICE AREAS:*** Corporate Law; Employment Law; Medical Malpractice; Civil Litigation. ***Email:*** mclifton@ghtclaw.com

LEGAL SUPPORT PERSONNEL

LEE HENDRIX, (Paralegal)

GRIMES & GRIMES OF NORTH CAROLINA, P.A.

WINSTON-SALEM, NORTH CAROLINA

(See Greensboro)

Entertainment Law, Entertainment Litigation, Business and Commercial Litigation, Administrative Agency Practice, Construction Law and Collections and Business Law.

HANDLER & BROWN, P.L.L.C.

1014 WEST FIFTH STREET
WINSTON-SALEM, NORTH CAROLINA 27101-2522
Telephone: 336-723-7966
Fax: 336-723-1035

Business Law, Commercial Law, Insurance Premium Finance Law, Factoring, Leasing, Licensing, Franchise Law, Intellectual Property Law, Trademarks, Copyrights, Unfair Competition, Real Estate, Condominium Law, Association Law, Land Use, Environmental Law, Commercial Litigation, Unfair Trade Practice Law, Creditors Rights, Civil Trial Practice, Appellate Practice, Arbitration, Class Actions, Constitutional Law, Professional Liability, Medical Malpractice, Products Liability, Personal Injury, Civil Rights, Labor and Employment, Wrongful Discharge and Discrimination Law.

MEMBERS OF FIRM

ERIC P. HANDLER, born Durham, North Carolina, July 4, 1946; admitted to bar, 1973, North Carolina; 1974, U.S. Court of Appeals, Fourth Circuit. *Education:* Duke University (A.B., 1968; J.D., 1973). Member, Editorial Board, Duke Law Journal, 1971-1973. Senior Member, National Panel of Consumer Arbitrators, Council of Better Business Bureaus, 1988—. Associate Member, North Carolina Association of Premium Finance Companies, 2000—. *Member:* American Bar Association (Business Law Section); North Carolina Bar Association (Member, Sections on: Bankruptcy; Litigation); North Carolina State Bar (Chair, 18th Judicial District Committee on Fee Dispute Resolution, 1998-2002). ***PRACTICE AREAS:*** Business Law; Commercial Law; Commercial Litigation; Commercial Real Estate; Creditors Rights; Intellectual Property; Franchise Law; Intellectual Property Law; Land Use; Condominium Law. ***Email:*** eph@hb-law.us

B. ERVIN BROWN, II, born Greensboro, North Carolina, October 12, 1944; admitted to bar, 1971, North Carolina; 1972, Kentucky; 1973, U.S. Court of Appeals, Sixth Circuit; 1975, U.S. Supreme Court; 1976, U.S. Court of Appeals, Fourth Circuit. *Education:* University of North Carolina-Chapel Hill (B.A., 1968; J.D., 1971). Author: "Unfair Trade Practices-Caveats," North Carolina Business Practice Handbook, Rev. Ed., 1985; "Unfair Trade Practice and RICO Claims Under State and Federal Law," North Carolina Corporation and Partnership Law, 1990; "Business Torts," Representing the Small Business Handbook, 1995. *Member:* North Carolina and American Bar Associations, Member, Civil Justice Reform Act Committee (1993-1995), Middle District of North Carolina. ***REPORTED CASES:*** Erler v. Aon Risks 540 S.E. 2d 65 (2000); Wilson Realty v. Asheboro Bd. of Realtors, 518 S.E.2d 28 (1999); Baker Construction Co. v. Phillips 426 S.E. 2d 679 (1993). ***PRACTICE AREAS:*** Complex Litigation; Unfair Trade; Professional Malpractice; Antitrust; Employment Law; Personal Injury; Products Liability; Civil Rights; Commercial Litigation; Class Actions; RICCO. ***Email:*** beb@hb-law.us

REPRESENTATIVE LITIGATION CLIENTS: Klaussner Furniture Industry, Inc.; Morgan Stanley Asset Funding, Inc.; Cananwill, Inc.; Prime Rate Premium Finance Co.; Hewlett Packard Company; Brookline Furniture Company, L.L.C.; iconnectv.com, Inc.; W.C. Bradley Co.; Forsyth Gastroenterology Assoc., P.A.; Chesapeake Microfilm, Inc.; Piedmont Medical Imaging, P.S.; Associated Nail Co.; Baker Construction Company; Insul Industries; Hunter Textbooks; Forsyth Neurosurgery, Inc.; Wallace Electronics; Communications Technology, Inc., d/b/a DILAN; Ferrari America, Inc.; Southpark Homes, LLC; ACS Benefit Services, Inc.; Provident Bank; Electronic Information Systems, Inc.; Riverfront Acres Homeowners Association; Sony Pictures Entertainment, Inc.; Elkes Carpet Outlets, Inc.; T-N-T Carports, Inc.; American Steel Company, Inc.

HATFIELD, MOUNTCASTLE, DEAL, VAN ZANDT & MANN, L.L.P.

SUITE 605, BETHESDA OAKS
2990 BETHESDA PLACE
WINSTON-SALEM, NORTH CAROLINA 27103
Telephone: 336-768-1842
Fax: 336-768-1773; 336-768-5051
URL: http://www.h-mlawyers.com

General Civil Practice in all State and Federal Courts, Real Estate, Estate Planning, Probate, Taxation, Corporation and Estate Law.

MEMBERS OF FIRM

WESTON P. HATFIELD, born Hickory, North Carolina, July 5, 1920; admitted to bar, 1947, North Carolina. *Education:* Wake Forest College (B.A., 1941); Harvard University Law School (LL.B., 1947). Member, North Carolina State Bar Council, 1976-1985. *Member:* Forsyth County (President, 1963-1964), North Carolina and American (Member, Standing Committee on Professional Discipline, 1985-1988) Bar Associations; North Carolina State Bar (Chairman, Ethics Committee, 1982-1985); American Judicature Society. Life Fellow, American Bar Association. [A.U.S., active duty, 1943-1946]. ***Email:*** wphatfield@aol.com

GEORGE C. MOUNTCASTLE, born Winston-Salem, North Carolina, April 4, 1932; admitted to bar, 1961, North Carolina. *Education:* Woodberry Forest School; University of North Carolina (A.B., 1954); Wake Forest University (J.D., 1960). *Member:* Forsyth County, North Carolina and American Bar Associations; North Carolina State Bar. ***PRACTICE AREAS:*** Tax; Estates; Estate Planning. ***Email:*** gcmpa@aol.com

R. BRANDT DEAL, born Norfolk, Virginia, June 23, 1948; admitted to bar, 1973, North Carolina. *Education:* Hampden-Sydney College (B.S., 1970); Wake Forest University (J.D., 1973). Phi Delta Phi (President, 1972-1973). *Member:* Forsyth County (Trea-

(This Listing Continued)

HATFIELD, MOUNTCASTLE, DEAL, VAN ZANDT & MANN, L.L.P., Winston-Salem—Continued

surer, 1980-1981; Member, Real Estate Section), North Carolina (Member, Real Estate Section) Bar Associations. ***PRACTICE AREAS:*** Commercial Real Estate; Residential Real Estate; Real Estate Law. ***Email:*** rbdeal@bellsouth.net

JOHN P. VAN ZANDT, III, born Ithaca, New York, May 6, 1948; admitted to bar, 1973, North Carolina and U.S. Court of Military Appeals. *Education:* Wake Forest University (B.A., 1970; J.D., 1973). Phi Delta Phi; The Order of Barristers. Member, Moot Court Board. *Member:* Forsyth County and North Carolina Bar Associations; North Carolina State Bar; North Carolina Academy of Trial Lawyers; American Board of Trial Advocates. [Capt., U.S. Army, JAGC, 1973-1976]. ***PRACTICE AREAS:*** Litigation. ***Email:*** jpvz@bellsouth.net

JOHN R. MANN, born Winston-Salem, North Carolina, June 19, 1954; admitted to bar, 1981, North Carolina. *Education:* University of North Carolina at Chapel Hill (B.S., 1976; M.B.A., 1978); Wake Forest University (J.D., 1981). Certified Public Accountant, North Carolina, 1986. *Member:* Forsyth County, North Carolina (Member, Section of Taxation) and American Bar Associations; North Carolina State Bar. ***PRACTICE AREAS:*** Tax Law; Tax Litigation; Estate Planning. ***Email:*** johnrandolphmann@msn.com

ASSOCIATE

MARC HUNTER EPPLEY, born Greensboro, North Carolina, January 9, 1954; admitted to bar, 2001, North Carolina and U.S. District Court, Middle District of North Carolina. *Education:* University of North Carolina at Chapel Hill (B.A., 1988); University of North Florida (M.P.A., 1991); Wake Forest University Law School (J.D., 1995). Member, Wake Forest Law Review, 1993-1994. ***LANGUAGES:*** Russian, German and Spanish. ***PRACTICE AREAS:*** Corporate Law; Litigation; Real Estate; Commercial Real Estate; Real Property. ***Email:*** mhepp@bellsouth.net

REPRESENTATIVE CLIENTS: Forsyth County Bond Authority; Time Warner, Inc.; Topsider Building Systems, Inc.; Foodcraft Equipment Company; Modern Chevrolet; Wake Forest University; Bassett-Walker, Inc.; Johnston Mills Co.; Benton Investment Co.; Vulcan Materials Co.; Bank of America; Anderson Development Co.; Young Phillips Sales Co.; Community Management Co.; Pike & Cassels, Inc.; LandAmerica/Lawyers Title/Commonwealth Land Title; Chicago Title, Business Loan Center/Business Loan Express.
APPROVED ATTORNEYS FOR: Real Estate Titles, Inc.; Chicago Title Insurance Company; Commonwealth Land Title; Investors Title Agencies/Winston-Salem; Lawyers Title of North Carolina, Inc.; Safeco Title of Charlotte, N.C.; Hubbard Realty; Coldwell Banker - Triad Realtor.
BANK REFERENCES: Furnished upon request.

HENDRICK & BRYANT, L.L.P.

Established in 1977
723 COLISEUM DRIVE
SUITE 101
WINSTON-SALEM, NORTH CAROLINA 27106-5326
Telephone: 336-723-7200
Fax: 336-723-7201
URL: http://www.hendricklawfirm.com

General Business and Corporation Practice including Civil Trial and Appellate Practice. Business Start-Ups, Business Transactions, Closely Held Business Law, Professional Sports Law, Corporate Commercial Law, Corporate Litigation, Real Estate and Banking, Merger and Acquisition, Sports, Automotive, Unfair Competition, Federal, State and Local Taxation, Construction, Insurance, Estate Planning and Bankruptcy.

FIRM PROFILE: The firm represents businesses and their owners in connection with their personal and commercial transactions. The firm prides itself in its ability to offer complete counseling in business planning. This planning includes choosing the most effective business structure, financing and capitalization issues, tax considerations, business asset and land transfers. The firm has experience in sports law, construction litigation and automotive law.

T. PAUL HENDRICK, born Fort Worth, Texas, May 11, 1948; admitted to bar, 1973, North Carolina, U.S. Court of Appeals, Fourth Circuit and U.S. Supreme Court. *Education:* Pfeiffer College (B.A., 1970); Wake Forest University School of Law (J.D., 1973). Phi Alpha Delta (Justice, Timberlake Chapter, 1973). Babcock Scholar. Clinical Adjunct Professor, Wake Forest University School of Law, 1982-1984. Law Clerk to Judge Hiram H. Ward, U.S. District Judge, Middle District of North Carolina, 1973-1975. Author: Comment, "Constitutionality of North Carolina Statute Concerning Possessory Liens on Personal Property," 9 Wake Forest Law Review 97, 1972; Note, "The Burden of Establishing Signature, Defenses, and Due Course," 8 Wake Forest Law Review 119, 1972. *Member:* Forsyth County, North Carolina (Officer in Sports and Entertainment Section) and American Bar Associations. Permanent Member of the Fourth Circuit Judicial Conference. ***PRACTICE AREAS:*** Commercial and Construction Litigation; General Corporate; Merger and Acquisition; Sports; Real Estate and Commercial Financing; Estate Planning; Labor Law. ***Email:*** phendrick@hendricklawfirm.com

MATTHEW H. BRYANT, born Anderson, South Carolina, May 18, 1963; admitted to bar, 1995, North Carolina and U.S. District Court, Middle District of North Carolina. *Education:* University of North Carolina (B.A., 1985) Wake Forest School of Law (J.D., 1995). Moot Court Board. *Member:* Forsyth County, North Carolina and American Bar Associations. [Lt. U.S. Navy, 1985-1992]. ***PRACTICE AREAS:*** General Corporate; Commercial Real Estate; Commercial Litigation; Civil Litigation; Sports Law; Property Law; Trademarks; Employment Law; Administrative Agency Practice; Outdoor Advertising. ***Email:*** mbryant@hendricklawfirm.com

PHYLLIS E. MENDEL, born Danbury, Connecticut, August 10, 1955; admitted to bar, 1995, North Carolina, U.S. District Court, Middle District of North Carolina and Bankruptcy Court, Middle District of North Carolina. *Education:* University of North Carolina, Greensboro, N.C. (B.S., summa cum laude, 1991); Wake Forest University (J.D., 1994).

(This Listing Continued)

Member: Forsyth County and North Carolina Bar Associations. ***PRACTICE AREAS:*** Residential Real Estate; Commercial Real Estate; Corporate; Bankruptcy; Estate Planning. ***Email:*** pmendel@hendricklawfirm.com

TIMOTHY NERHOOD, born Morgantown, West Virginia, October 9, 1972; admitted to bar, 1998, North Carolina. *Education:* University of North Carolina at Chapel Hill (B.S.B.A., 1994; J.D., 1998). ***PRACTICE AREAS:*** Corporate Law; Civil Litigation; Employment Law. ***Email:*** tnerhood@hendricklawfirm.com

KELLY E. MOTYCKA, born Kalamazoo, Michigan, May 28, 1977; admitted to bar, 2002, North Carolina. *Education:* Purdue University (B.A., 1998); Wake Forest University (J.D., 2002). Purdue University Sophomore of the Year. Member, Mortar Board. Editor-In-Chief, Wake Forest Intellectual Property Law Journal, 2001-2002. Author: "Napster Makes Another Comeback," North Carolina Bar Association Sports & Entertainment Newsletter, Vol. 2, No. 1 (September 2001). *Member:* North Carolina Bar Association. ***PRACTICE AREAS:*** Real Property; Commercial Law; Corporate Law; Intellectual Property; Trusts and Estates; Foreclosures; Wills; Land Use. ***Email:*** kmotycka@hendricklawfirm.com

KENNETH C. OTIS, III (CASEY), born Stamford, Connecticut, November 16, 1972; admitted to bar, 2001, North Carolina. *Education:* Davidson College (B.A., 1995); Wake Forest University (J.D., 2001). Aide to Senator Connie Mack, 1995-1998. ***PRACTICE AREAS:*** Civil Litigation; Corporate Law; Copyrights; Trademarks. ***Email:*** cotis@hendricklawfirm.com

REPRESENTATIVE CLIENTS: Anchor Industrial Sales, Inc.; Beroth Oil Co.; Broyhill Group, LLC.; Cahill & Swain; Capcare Group, Inc.; Centura Bank; Classic Packaging Company; CoPak Solutions, Inc.; ECHL, Inc.; ECHL Properties, LLC; Flex-Pay Business Services, LLC; Nationwide Marketing Group; OPC Packaging Corporation; Pellcare Corp.; RBC Sports I, LLC; Ronco Communications, Inc.; Secure One, Inc.; Sharpe Company; Shields, Inc.; Southeastern Employee Benefit Services; T.I. Industries, Inc.; Tribuzio-Hilliard Studio, Inc.; Belle Meade Residents Association; Bank of the Carolinas; BF Saul, LTD; Bank of America; Audio Video Repair Center, Inc.
APPROVED ATTORNEYS FOR: Lawyers Mutual; Commonwealth Land Title Co. of North Carolina; Chicago Title Co.; Investors Title Co.; Real Estate Titles, Inc.
REFERENCES: BBT; RBC Centura Bank; Bank of America; Bank of the Carolinas.

DAVID B. HOUGH

301 NORTH MAIN STREET, SUITE 2303
WINSTON-SALEM, NORTH CAROLINA 27101
Telephone: 336-724-5987
Fax: 336-724-3980
Email: dhough@triad.rr.com
URL: http://www.dhoughlaw.com

Divorce, Family Law, Personal Injury, Breach of Contract, Jury Trials, Prenuptial Agreements, Construction Law, Spousal Support, Premarital Agreements, Mediation, Lemon Law, Unfair Trade Practice, Child Custody, Traffic Violations, Consumer Law.

DAVID B. HOUGH, born 1944; admitted to bar, 1970, North Carolina; 1973, District of Columbia. *Education:* Dartmouth College (A.B., 1967); Duke University (J.D., 1970). Certified Mediator, Superior Court and Family Financial, North Carolina. *Member:* North Carolina State Bar; Forsyth County and North Carolina Bar Associations. ***LANGUAGES:*** Spanish.

HOUSE & TIPPETT, PLLC

3325 HEALY DRIVE
WINSTON-SALEM, NORTH CAROLINA 27103
Telephone: 336-768-2225
Fax: 336-768-3369
URL: http://www.lawyers.com/houseandtippett
Email: info@housetippett.com
URL: http://www.housetippett.com

Practice limited to Business Law, Taxation, Securities, Wills, Trusts, Probate and Commercial Real Estate.

DON R. HOUSE, born Monroe, North Carolina, April 12, 1941; admitted to bar, 1966, North Carolina. *Education:* Duke University (A.B., Accounting, 1963; LL.B., 1966). ***PRACTICE AREAS:*** Business Law; Tax Law; Securities; Commercial Real Estate; Trusts and Estates; Wills; Probate. ***Email:*** don@housetippett.com

SCOTT K. TIPPETT, born Greensboro, North Carolina, November 5, 1961; admitted to bar, 1987, Georgia; 1995, North Carolina. *Education:* Duke University (B.A., cum laude, 1984); University of North Carolina at Chapel Hill (J.D., 1987). Member: Holderness Moot Court Bench; Jessup Cup International Moot Court Team. Member, Executive Editor, The North Carolina Journal of International Law and Commercial Regulation, 1985-1987. *Member:* State Bar of Georgia. ***PRACTICE AREAS:*** Business Law; Corporate Law; Entertainment Law; Commercial Real Estate; Trusts and Estates; Wills; Probate; Tax Law; Civil Litigation. ***Email:*** scott@housetippett.com

H. MARIE HUTTO, P.C.

8 WEST THIRD STREET, SUITE 500
WINSTON-SALEM, NORTH CAROLINA 27101
Telephone: 336-721-1060
Fax: 336-721-9102
Email: huttolaw2@hotmail.com
URL: http://www.huttolawyer.com

Criminal Law, Driving While Intoxicated, Drug Crimes, Felonies, Misdemeanors, Traffic Violations, Family Law, Separation Agreements, Collaborative Law, Divorce, Child Custody and Child Support, Spousal Support, Adoptions, Personal Injury.

(This Listing Continued)

H. MARIE HUTTO, born Charleston, South Carolina, November 26, 1967; admitted to bar, 1997, North Carolina. *Education:* Salisbury State University (B.A., summa cum laude, 1994); Campbell University School of Law (J.D., 1996). *Member:* Forsyth County, North Carolina (Member, Family Law Section) and American Bar Associations; Triad Collaborative Law Practice Group; Forsyth County Criminal Defense Trial Lawyers Association; Association of Trial Lawyers of America. ***PRACTICE AREAS:*** Family Law; Criminal Law; Personal Injury.

INGERSOLL & ASSOCIATES, PLLC

1590 WESTBROOK PLAZA DRIVE, SUITE 203
WINSTON-SALEM, NORTH CAROLINA 27103
Telephone: 336-794-2278
Fax: 336-794-2281
URL: http://www.ingersollfirm.com

Wills, Estate Planning, Trusts and Estates, Probate, Elder Law, Business Law, Corporate Law, Commercial Real Estate, Tax Law, Collections.

MARC W. INGERSOLL, born Columbus, Ohio, April 10, 1964; admitted to bar, 1991, North Carolina. *Education:* Bob Jones University (B.S., in Accounting, 1986); Wake Forest University (J.D., 1990). Phi Alpha Delta. Recipient, Bureau of National Affairs Law Award, Wake Forest University, 1990. Co-Author: "Noncompete Clauses v. Public Policy," Health Law Notes, Campbell Law Observer (August 1991). Adjunct Professor, Estates, Trusts and Probate, St. Mary's College, 1990-1993. *Member:* Forsyth County (Member, Legal Education Partnership Committee, 1992-1995) and North Carolina (Member: Business, Tax, Wills and Trusts, Elder Law Sections; Young Lawyers Division Professionalism Committee, 1992-1995) Bar Associations; Winston-Salem Estate Plan Council, 1995—; North Carolina State Bar. ***PRACTICE AREAS:*** Wills; Trusts and Estates; Probate; Elder Law; Business Law; Corporate Law; Commercial Real Estate; Tax Law. ***Email:*** marc@ingersollfirm.com

JOEL M. WILLIAMS, born Carroll, Iowa; admitted to bar, 2004, North Carolina. *Education:* University of Iowa (B.B.A., Finance, 2001; B.A., Psychology, 2001; J.D., 2004). Golden Key. *Member:* North Carolina (Member, Young Lawyers Division, Estate Planning & Fiduciary Law, Business Law, Real Property) and American Bar Associations; North Carolina State Bar. ***PRACTICE AREAS:*** Wills; Trusts and Estates; Probate; Elder Law; Business Law; Real Estate. ***Email:*** joel@ingersollfirm.com

LEGAL SUPPORT PERSONNEL

AMY MOOREFIELD, born High Point, North Carolina, May 23, 1967. *Education:* University of North Carolina at Chapel Hill (1985-1988). Recipient: North Carolina National Guard Civilian Commendation Medal, 1999. Member, Legal Support Staff of North Carolina. (Senior Paralegal). ***Email:*** amy@ingersollfirm.com

RANDOLPH M. JAMES, P.C.

116 NORTH SPRUCE STREET
P.O. BOX 20069
WINSTON-SALEM, NORTH CAROLINA 27101
Telephone: 336-724-7707
Fax: 336-724-9722
Email: rmjames@rmjameslaw.com
URL: http://www.rmjameslaw.com

Civil Litigation Practice in State and Federal Courts. Personal Injury, Workers Compensation, Employment, Products Liability, Professional Malpractice, Medical Malpractice, Legal Malpractice, Commercial and Construction Litigation, Unfair and Deceptive Trade Practices, Class Actions, Discrimination, Sexual Harassment, Automobile Accidents, Dog Bites, Sexual Abuse, Slip and Fall, Wrongful Death.

RANDOLPH M. JAMES, born Denver, Colorado, January 23, 1953; admitted to bar, 1981, North Carolina; 1985, U.S. District Court, Middle, Eastern and Western Districts of North Carolina; 1991, U.S. Court of Appeals, Fourth and Fifth Circuits; 1993, U.S. District Court, Western District of Texas; 1994, U.S. Supreme Court. *Education:* North Carolina State University (B.A. of Environmental Design in Architecture, with honors, 1976); Wake Forest University School of Law (J.D., 1981). Member, North Carolina State Bar Committee on Personal Injury Trial Law Specialization, 1994-1997. *Member:* North Carolina Bar Association; North Carolina State Bar; North Carolina Academy of Trial Lawyers; The Association of Trial Lawyers of America. ***PRACTICE AREAS:*** Personal Injury; Workers Compensation; Business Litigation; Construction Law; Products Liability; Class Actions; Complex Business Litigation; Professional Malpractice. ***Email:*** rmjames@rmjameslaw.com

REPRESENTATIVE CLIENT: K & W Restaurants, Inc.
REFERENCE: Branch Banking & Trust.

LAW OFFICES OF EDWARD JENNINGS

Established in 1973

3333 BROOKVIEW HILLS BOULEVARD, SUITE 206
WINSTON-SALEM, NORTH CAROLINA 27103-5661
Telephone: 336-760-3421
Fax: 336-659-6048
Email: lawyeroncall@aol.com
URL: http://www.edwardjenningslaw.com

Taylorsville, North Carolina Office: 83 South Center Street, 28681. Telephone: 828-632-5869. Facsimile: 828-632-5764.

(This Listing Continued)

Civil and Criminal Trials and Appeals in all State and Federal Courts. Personal Injury, Family Law, Divorce, Child Custody, Estates, Real Estate, Workers Compensation, Social Security.

EDWARD JENNINGS, born Harmony, Iredell County, North Carolina, April 17, 1948; admitted to bar, 1973, North Carolina and U.S. District Court, Middle and Western Districts of North Carolina; 1974, U.S. Court of Appeals, 4th Circuit; 1980, U.S. Supreme Court. *Education:* Wake Forest University (B.A., cum laude, 1970; J.D., 1973). Phi Delta Phi. Assistant U.S. Attorney, Middle District of North Carolina, 1974-1978. Assistant State District Attorney, 23rd Judicial District of North Carolina, 1973-1974. *Member:* Forsyth County, Alexander County, North Carolina and American Bar Associations; North Carolina State Bar; North Carolina Academy of Trial Lawyers; The Association of Trial Lawyers of America. (Also Associated with Kirschbaum, Nanney & Brown, P.A., Raleigh). ***LANGUAGES:*** English.

Languages: English.

JERRY D. JORDAN

8 W. THIRD STREET, SUITE 610
WINSTON-SALEM, NORTH CAROLINA 27101
Telephone: 336-725-5656
Fax: 336-725-5657
Email: JdjLaw@aol.com
URL: http://www.jerryjordanlaw.com

Criminal, Drug Crimes, DWI, Traffic Violations, Family Law, Child Custody, Child Support.

JERRY D. JORDAN, born Poplar Bluff, Missouri, August 17, 1965; admitted to bar, 1997, North Carolina; U.S. District Court, Western District of North Carolina; 1999, U.S. District Court Middle District of North Carolina. *Education:* Arkansas State University (B.S., 1992); Thomas M. Cooley Law School (J.D., 1997). ***PRACTICE AREAS:*** Criminal Law; Drug Crimes; Driving While Intoxicated; Traffic Violations; Family Law; Child Custody; Child Support.

KILPATRICK STOCKTON LLP

1001 WEST FOURTH STREET
WINSTON-SALEM, NORTH CAROLINA 27101-2400
Telephone: 336-607-7300
Facsimile: 336-607-7500
Email: info@KilpatrickStockton.com
URL: http://www.KilpatrickStockton.com

Atlanta, Georgia Office: Suite 2800, 1100 Peachtree Street. Telephone: 404-815-6500. Facsimile: 404-815-6555. Telex: 54-2307.
Augusta, Georgia Office: 699 Broad Street, Suite 1400, 30903-2043. Telephone: 706-724-2622. Facsimile: 706-722-0219.
Charlotte, North Carolina Office: Suite 2500, 214 North Tryon Street, 28202. Telephone: 704-338-5000. Facsimile: 704-338-5125.
London, England Office: 39th Floor, One Canada Square, London E145 NZ. Telephone: 44 (0)20 7154 6000. Facsimile: 44 (0)20 7154 6100.
New York, New York Office: 805 Third Avenue, 20th Floor, 10022. Telephone: 212-912-3527.
Raleigh, North Carolina Office: Suite 400, 3737 Glenwood Avenue, 27612. Telephone: 919-420-1700. Facsimile: 919-420-1800.
Stockholm, Sweden Office: Box 5421, SE-114 84. Telephone: 46-8-505-646-00. Facsimile: 46-8-505-646-99.
Washington, D.C. Office: Suite 900, 607 14th Street, N.W., 20005-2018. Telephone: 202-508-5800. Facsimile: 202-508-5858.

Civil Trial and Appellate Practice in all State and Federal Courts, Federal State and Local Taxation, Probate, Trust and Estate Planning, Real Estate, Environmental, Corporate, Corporate Reorganization, Securities, Banking Commercial, Antitrust, Labor, Employment, Administrative, Bankruptcy, Construction, Healthcare, Intellectual Property, Professional Malpractice, Products Liability and Negligence Law, Domestic Law and Equitable Distribution, Employee Benefits and Executive Compensation, Entrepreneurial Development, Franchising, Insurance Defense, Sports and Entertainment, State Agency and Lobbying Practice.

FIRM PROFILE: Kilpatrick Stockton LLP is a full-service international law firm with more than 470 attorneys in nine offices across the globe: Atlanta and Augusta, GA; Charlotte, Raleigh and Winston-Salem, NC; New York, NY; Washington, DC; London, England; and Stockholm, Sweden. Kilpatrick Stockton's delivery of innovative business solutions provides results-oriented counsel for corporations, from the challenging demands of financial transactions and securities to the disciplines of intellectual property management. Collaboration among Kilpatrick Stockton's corporate, tax, employment and employee benefit attorneys provides knowledgeable and proactive guidance for companies at every stage of the business life cycle.

MEMBERS OF FIRM

STEPHEN R. BERLIN, admitted to bar, 1984, North Carolina. *Education:* Wake Forest University (B.A., magna cum laude, 1981; J.D., cum laude, 1984). (Resident). ***PRACTICE AREAS:*** Environmental; Zoning, Planning and Land Use. ***Email:*** SBerlin@KilpatrickStockton.com

SUSAN HOLDSCLAW BOYLES, admitted to bar, 1994, North Carolina and U.S. District Court, Middle and Western Districts of North Carolina. *Education:* University of North Carolina (B.A., with highest distinction, 1990; J.D., with honors, 1994), Order of the Coif. ***PRACTICE AREAS:*** Litigation; Appellate Practice. ***Email:*** SBoyles@KilpatrickStockton.com

PETER S. BRUNSTETTER, admitted to bar, 1984, Virginia; 1985, District of Columbia; 1986, North Carolina. *Education:* Tulane University of Louisiana (B.A., 1977); University of Virginia (J.D., 1984). (Resident). ***PRACTICE AREAS:*** Health; Hospital Law; Business Law. ***Email:*** PBrunstetter@KilpatrickStockton.com

(This Listing Continued)

KILPATRICK STOCKTON LLP, Winston-Salem—Continued

CHARLES W. CALKINS, admitted to bar, 1985, Massachusetts; 1989, District of Columbia; 1995, North Carolina; registered to practice before U.S. Patent and Trademark Office. *Education:* Massachusetts Institute of Technology (S.B.Ch.E., 1981); Boston University (J.D., 1984). (Resident). ***PRACTICE AREAS:*** Intellectual Property; Technology and Science. ***Email:*** CCalkins@KilpatrickStockton.com

ADAM H. CHARNES, admitted to bar, 1993, Pennsylvania (inactive); 1994, District of Columbia and U.S. Court of Appeals, District of Columbia and Fourth Circuits; 1995, U.S. District Court, District of Maryland; 1997, U.S. Supreme Court; 1998, U.S. District Court, Western District of Michigan and District of Columbia and U.S. Court of Appeals, First Circuit; 1999, U.S. Court of Appeals, Eleventh Circuit; 2000, U.S. Court of Appeals, Sixth Circuit; 2003, North Carolina. *Education:* Princeton University (A.B., summa cum laude, 1988); Harvard Law School (J.D., magna cum laude, 1991). *Member:* Chief Justice Joseph Branch Inn of Court (Barrister, 2003—); Federal Communications Bar Association; Federal Bar Association. (Resident). ***PRACTICE AREAS:*** Litigation. ***Email:*** ACharnes@KilpatrickStockton.com

W. MARK CONGER, admitted to bar, 1991, North Carolina. *Education:* Hampden-Sydney College (B.A., 1985); Wake Forest University (M.B.A., 1991; J.D., cum laude 1991). (Resident). ***PRACTICE AREAS:*** Business; Securities. ***Email:*** MConger@KilpatrickStockton.com

C. PENN CRAVER, JR., admitted to bar, 1966, North Carolina. *Education:* Davidson College (A.B., 1963); University of North Carolina (J.D., with honors, 1966). (Resident). ***PRACTICE AREAS:*** Taxation; Probate; Trusts and Estates; Business. ***Email:*** PCraver@KilpatrickStockton.com

TONYA R. DEEM, admitted to bar, 1996, North Carolina. *Education:* Wake Forest University (B.A., magna cum laude, 1993); University of North Carolina at Chapel Hill (J.D., with honors, 1996). ***PRACTICE AREAS:*** Litigation. ***Email:*** TDeem@KilpatrickStockton.com

LOUIS W. DOHERTY, admitted to bar, 1990, North Carolina. *Education:* Duke University (B.A., magna cum laude, 1984); University of North Carolina at Chapel Hill (J.D., with high honors, 1990). (Resident). ***PRACTICE AREAS:*** Labor and Employment; Employee Benefits. ***Email:*** LDoherty@KilpatrickStockton.com

MICHAEL L. DRYE, admitted to bar, 1990, North Carolina. *Education:* University of Central Florida (B.S.B.A., 1978); University of North Carolina at Chapel Hill (J.D., 1990). (Resident). ***PRACTICE AREAS:*** Mergers and Acquisitions; Securities. ***Email:*** MDrye@KilpatrickStockton.com

ROBERT L. EDWARDS, admitted to bar, 1965, North Carolina. *Education:* East Carolina College (A.B., 1962); University of North Carolina (LL.B., 1965). (Resident). ***PRACTICE AREAS:*** Taxation; Trusts and Estates. ***Email:*** BEdwards@KilpatrickStockton.com

J. ROBERT ELSTER, admitted to bar, 1964, North Carolina; 1973, U.S. Supreme Court. *Education:* Rice University (A.B., 1959); Duke Law School (J.D., 1964). (Resident). ***PRACTICE AREAS:*** Corporate; Commercial Litigation; Complex Litigation. ***Email:*** BEbelster@KilpatrickStockton.com

STEVEN GARDNER, admitted to bar, 1994, North Carolina; registered to practice before U.S. Patent and Trademark Office. *Education:* University of North Carolina at Charlotte (B.S.E.E., 1990; M.S.E.E., 1992); Wake Forest University (J.D., cum laude, 1994). (Resident). ***PRACTICE AREAS:*** Patents; Litigation; Intellectual Property. ***Email:*** SGardner@KilpatrickStockton.com

RICHARD S. GOTTLIEB, admitted to bar, 1996, North Carolina. *Education:* Emory University (B.A., 1992); University of North Carolina (J.D., with honors, 1996). ***PRACTICE AREAS:*** Trade Secrets; Class Action; Business Litigation. ***Email:*** RGottlieb@KilpatrickStockton.com

JOHN M. HARRINGTON, admitted to bar, 1968, North Carolina; registered to practice before U.S. Patent and Trademark Office. *Education:* North Carolina State University (B.S.Chem.E., 1962); University of South Carolina (J.D., cum laude, 1968). (Resident). ***PRACTICE AREAS:*** Intellectual Property; Patents. ***Email:*** JHarrington@KilpatrickStockton.com

DUDLEY HUMPHREY, admitted to bar, 1961, North Carolina. *Education:* Duke University (A.B., 1955); University of North Carolina (J.D., with honors, 1961). (Resident). ***PRACTICE AREAS:*** Construction; Probate; Trusts and Estates. ***Email:*** DHumphrey@KilpatrickStockton.com

JAMES H. KELLY, JR., admitted to bar, 1968, North Carolina; 1973, U.S. Supreme Court. *Education:* Davidson College (A.B., 1965); Duke University (J.D., 1968). (Resident). ***PRACTICE AREAS:*** Business; Personal Injury; Torts. ***Email:*** JKelly@KilpatrickStockton.com

RICHARD J. KESHIAN, admitted to bar, 1983, North Carolina. *Education:* Duke University (A.B., magna cum laude, 1979); Vanderbilt University (J.D., 1982). (Resident). ***PRACTICE AREAS:*** Civil Litigation; Products Liability. ***Email:*** RKeshian@KilpatrickStockton.com

JEFFREY T. LAWYER, admitted to bar, 1986, North Carolina. *Education:* Florida State University (B.S., 1977); Duke University (J.D., with highest honors, 1986). (Resident). ***PRACTICE AREAS:*** Taxation Law. ***Email:*** JLawyer@KilpatrickStockton.com

GEORGE L. LITTLE, JR., admitted to bar, 1967, North Carolina. *Education:* Davidson College (A.B., 1964); University of North Carolina (J.D., with honors, 1967). (Resident). ***PRACTICE AREAS:*** Antitrust and Trade Regulation; Intellectual Property. ***Email:*** GLittle@KilpatrickStockton.com

DAVID C. SMITH, admitted to bar, 1984, North Carolina; 1986, Maine. *Education:* Wake Forest University (B.A., cum laude, 1981; J.D., cum laude, 1984). (Resident). ***PRACTICE AREAS:*** Commercial Litigation; Construction Litigation. ***Email:*** DCsmith@KilpatrickStockton.com

DANIEL R. TAYLOR, JR., admitted to bar, 1976, North Carolina. *Education:* United States Military Academy (B.S., 1968); George Washington University, Graduate School of Government and Business Administration (1971-1973); Wake Forest University (J.D., cum laude, 1976). (Resident). ***PRACTICE AREAS:*** Corporate Litigation; Securities Litigation; Shareholder Litigation. ***Email:*** DTaylor@KilpatrickStockton.com

DANIELLE THOMPSON WILLIAMS, admitted to bar, 1996, North Carolina. *Education:* University of North Carolina at Chapel Hill (B.A., 1992); Wake Forest University (J.D.,M.B.A., 1996). ***PRACTICE AREAS:*** Commercial Litigation. ***Email:*** DTWilliams@KilpatrickStockton.com

WILLIAM E. WRIGHT, admitted to bar, 1984, North Carolina. *Education:* Trinity College (B.A., 1974); American Christian Theological Seminary (M.Div., 1979); Duke University (J.D., with high honors, 1984). (Resident). ***PRACTICE AREAS:*** Employee Benefits; Executive Compensation. ***Email:*** BWright@KilpatrickStockton.com

RESIDENT ASSOCIATES

JOHN C. ALEMANNI, admitted to bar, 1996, North Carolina; registered to practice before U.S. Patent and Trademark Office. *Education:* University of North Carolina, Greensboro (B.S., 1990); Wake Forest University (J.D., 1996). ***PRACTICE AREAS:*** Patents; Intellectual Property. ***Email:*** JAlemanni@KilpatrickStockton.com

JAMES M. BOGGS, admitted to bar, 1999, North Carolina. *Education:* Clemson University (B.S., 1977); Franklin Pierce Law Center (J.D., 1999). ***PRACTICE AREAS:*** Intellectual Property. ***Email:*** MBoggs@KilpatrickStockton.com

DAVID POPHAM BROUGHTON, admitted to bar, 1997, North Carolina. *Education:* University of North Carolina at Chapel Hill (B.A., 1990; J.D., 1997). ***PRACTICE AREAS:*** Corporate and Business; Mergers and Acquisitions; Corporate Finance; Securities Regulation. ***Email:*** DBroughton@KilpatrickStockton.com

WILLIAM M. BRYNER, admitted to bar, 1996, North Carolina. *Education:* Brigham Young University (B.A., Political Science, summa cum laude, 1993); Duke University (J.D., with honors, 1996). ***PRACTICE AREAS:*** Intellectual Property; Litigation. ***Email:*** BBryner@KilpatrickStockton.com

JAMES CALVIN (CAL) CUNNINGHAM, III, admitted to bar, 2000, North Carolina. *Education:* University of North Carolina at Chapel Hill (B.A., 1996); London School of Economics (M.Sc., 1997), University of North Carolina at Chapel Hill (J.D., 1999). Member, Board of Trustees, Davidson County Community College. *Member:* North Carolina and American Bar Associations; North Carolina Academy of Trial Lawyers. ***Email:*** CCunningham@KilpatrickStockton.com

DANIEL P. EBERSOLE, admitted to bar, 2004, North Carolina. *Education:* University of Maryland (B.S.M.E., 1999); University of North Carolina (J.D., 2004). ***PRACTICE AREAS:*** Intellectual Property. ***Email:*** DEbersole@KilpatrickStockton.com

ELLIOT ALEXANDER FUS, admitted to bar, 1997, North Carolina; 1999, U.S. District Court, Middle District of North Carolina; 2000, U.S. District Court, Eastern and Western Districts of North Carolina. *Education:* University of North Carolina (A.B., 1991); Wake Forest University (J.D., 1997). ***PRACTICE AREAS:*** Civil Litigation. ***Email:*** EFus@KilpatrickStockton.com

TODD W. GALINSKI, admitted to bar, 2001, North Carolina. *Education:* University of Arizona (B.S., 1997); Wake Forest University Law School (J.D., 2001). ***PRACTICE AREAS:*** Patents; Trademarks. ***Email:*** TGalinski@KilpatrickStockton.com

LAURA A. GREER, admitted to bar, 2003, North Carolina. *Education:* Marshall University (B.S, Biology, summa cum laude, 1999); Wake Forest University (J.D., cum laude, 2003). ***PRACTICE AREAS:*** Litigation. ***Email:*** LGreer@KilpatrickStockton.com

JESSICA R. HARRIS, admitted to bar, 2004, North Carolina. *Education:* Belmont University (B.A., Political Science, magna cum laude, 2001); Vanderbilt University Law School (J.D., 2004). ***PRACTICE AREAS:*** Litigation. ***Email:*** JHarris@KilpatrickStockton.com

JAMES J. HEFFERAN, JR., admitted to bar, 2003, North Carolina. *Education:* University of Michigan (B.A., Political Science, with highest distinction, 1999); Wake Forest University (J.D., magna cum laude, 2003). ***PRACTICE AREAS:*** Litigation. ***Email:*** JHefferan@KilpatrickStockton.com

STEPHEN T. INMAN, admitted to bar, 1999, North Carolina; 2003, District of Columbia. *Education:* Washington & Lee University (B.A., German and History, magna cum laude, 1996); Vanderbilt University (J.D., 1999). ***LANGUAGES:*** German. ***PRACTICE AREAS:*** Commercial Litigation; Intellectual Property; Antitrust. ***Email:*** SInman@KilpatrickStockton.com

J. JASON LINK, admitted to bar, 1998, North Carolina. *Education:* North Carolina State University (B.S., Chemical Engineering, summa cum laude, 1995); University of North Carolina (J.D., with honors, 1998). ***PRACTICE AREAS:*** Intellectual Property; Patents. ***Email:*** JLink@KilpatrickStockton.com

CORENA A. NORRIS-McCLUNEY, admitted to bar, 2000, North Carolina. *Education:* North Carolina State University (B.A., 1997); Wake Forest University (J.D., 2000). Law Clerk to the Honorable K. Edward Greene, Senior Associate Judge, North Carolina Court of Appeals. *Member:* American Bar Association. ***PRACTICE AREAS:*** Labor and Employment; Environmental; Litigation. ***Email:*** cnorris-mccluney@kilpatrickstockton.com

RYAN B. OPEL, admitted to bar, 2002, North Carolina. *Education:* Wake Forest University (B.A., 1999); Duke University (M.A., 2002; J.D., 2002). ***PRACTICE AREAS:*** Business Transactions; Corporate Finance; Securities; Corporate Law; Mergers and Acquisitions. ***Email:*** Ropel@KilpatrickStockton.com

ANDREW A. ROPPEL, admitted to bar, 1995, Virginia (Not admitted in North Carolina). *Education:* Georgetown University (B.S.B.A., cum laude, 1990); George Mason University School of Law (J.D., 1995). ***PRACTICE AREAS:*** Intellectual Property; Trademarks. ***Email:*** ARoppel@KilpatrickStockton.com

CYNTHIA B. ROTHSCHILD, admitted to bar, 1999, North Carolina. *Education:* University of Virginia (B.A., 1978); Wake Forest University (J.D., 1999). ***PRACTICE AREAS:*** Patents. ***Email:*** CRothschild@KilpatrickStockton.com

(This Listing Continued)

T. BENJAMIN SCHROEDER, admitted to bar, 2002, Virginia; registered to practice before U.S. Patent and Trademark Office (Not admitted in North Carolina). *Education:* University of Wisconsin-Madison (B.S., Biochemistry and Molecular Biology, 1986); University of Arizona (Ph.D., Chemistry, 1997); George Mason University School of Law (J.D., 2001). ***LANGUAGES:*** French and Sango. ***Email:*** BSchroeder@KilpatrickStockton.com

C. EDWARD TEAGUE, III, admitted to bar, 2002, North Carolina; 2003, U.S. District Court, Middle District of North Carolina; 2004, U.S. District Court, Western and Eastern Districts of North Carolina; 2005, U.S. Court of Appeals, Fourth Circuit. *Education:* University of North Carolina at Chapel Hill (B.A., 1995); Wake Forest University (M.B.A., 2002); Wake Forest University School of Law (J.D., 2002). *Member:* Forsyth County, North Carolina (Member, Real Property Section) and American Bar Associations; American Health Lawyers Association. ***PRACTICE AREAS:*** Real Estate. ***Email:*** TTeague@KilpatrickStockton.com

MARK D. TOLMAN, admitted to bar, 2004, North Carolina. *Education:* Weber State University (B.S., Economics, summa cum laude, 2001); University of North Carolina School of Law (J.D., 2004). ***PRACTICE AREAS:*** Litigation. ***Email:*** MTolman@KilpatrickStockton.com

ANDREW H. VEACH, admitted to bar, 1999, North Carolina. *Education:* Davidson College (B.A., 1996); Wake Forest University (J.D., 1999). ***PRACTICE AREAS:*** Trusts and Estates; Tax. ***Email:*** DVeach@KilpatrickStockton.com

J. CLINTON WIMBISH, admitted to bar, 2003, North Carolina and U.S. District Court, Middle District of North Carolina; registered to practice before U.S. Patent and Trademark Office. *Education:* University of North Carolina at Chapel Hill (B.S., 1998; J.D., 2003); Princeton University (M.A., 2000). ***PRACTICE AREAS:*** Intellectual Property; Patents. ***Email:*** CWimbish@KilpatrickStockton.com

BRET T. WINTERLE, admitted to bar, 2003, North Carolina; registered to practice before U.S. Patent and Trademark Office. *Education:* Iowa State University (B.S., Mechanical Engineering, with distinction, 2000); University of Virginia (J.D., 2003). ***PRACTICE AREAS:*** Intellectual Property; Patents. ***Email:*** BWinterle@KilpatrickStockton.com

(For complete biographical data on all personnel, see Professional Biographies at Atlanta and Augusta, Georgia; Washington, D.C.; Charlotte and Raleigh, North Carolina; Stockholm, Sweden and London, England).

C. R. "SKIP" LONG, JR.

2000 FRONTIS PLAZA BOULEVARD, SUITE 100
WINSTON-SALEM, NORTH CAROLINA 27103
Telephone: 336-768-7772
Fax: 336-774-9914
Email: skiplong@triad.rr.com
URL: http://www.lawyers.com/skiplong

Board Certified Specialist in Family Law; Certified Equitable Distribution Mediator, Equitable Distribution, Child Custody and Support, Alimony, Divorce, Personal Injury and Major Insurance Claims, Domestic and other Civil Appeals, Mediation and Arbitration.

C. R. "SKIP" LONG, JR., born 1950; admitted to bar, 1982, North Carolina. *Education:* East Carolina University (B.A., 1972); Appalachian State University (M.A., 1978); Wake Forest University (J.D., 1982). Certified Family Law Mediator. Certified Equitable Distribution Mediator. *Member:* Forsyth County and North Carolina Bar Associations; North Carolina State Bar; North Carolina Academy of Trial Lawyers. (Board Certified Specialist in Family Law, North Carolina State Board of Legal Specialization). ***PRACTICE AREAS:*** Family Law; Equitable Distribution; Child Custody; Child Support; Alimony; Divorce; Personal Injury; Insurance Claims; Domestic Relations; Civil Appeals; Mediation; Arbitration.

MAYNARD & HARRIS
ATTORNEYS AT LAW, PLLC

514 SOUTH STRATFORD ROAD, SUITE 321
WINSTON-SALEM, NORTH CAROLINA 27103
Telephone: 336-777-1411
Facsimile: 336-777-8882
URL: http://www.maynardharris.com
Email: maynlaw@aol.com
URL: http://www.lawyers.com/maynard&harris

Plaintiff Trial Practice, Personal Injury, Automobile and Tractor Trailer Accidents, Workers Compensation, Social Security, Wrongful Death, Nursing Home Liability, Insurance Claims.

FIRM PROFILE: Mr. Maynard is a former Insurance Adjuster. Ms. Harris is a former Registered Nurse and is a Board Certified Specialist in Workers Compensation.

C. DOUGLAS MAYNARD, JR., born Fayetteville, North Carolina, February 19, 1963; admitted to bar, 1992, North Carolina; U.S. District Court, Middle District of North Carolina. *Education:* Duke University (B.A., 1985, Sigma Phi Epsilon); Wake Forest University (J.D., 1988). Phi Delta Phi. Former State Farm Insurance Adjuster. *Member:* Forsyth County Bar Association (Ethics and Grievance Committee, 1999-2002; Secretary, 1998-1999; President, Young Lawyers Division, 1996-1997); North Carolina Bar Association (Litigation Section: Board of Directors, 2002-2005; Treasurer); American Bar Association; North Carolina Academy of Trial Lawyers (Committees: Legislative and Legal Affairs; Chair, Auto Torts Section, 2001-2002); Association of Trial Lawyers of America. ***PRACTICE AREAS:*** Automobile Accidents and Injuries; Personal Injury; Workers Compensation; Insurance Coverage; Civil Litigation. ***Email:*** MaynLaw@aol.com

CELESTE M. HARRIS, born Minneapolis, Minnesota, December 15, 1959; admitted to bar, 1991, North Carolina. *Education:* University of Missouri at Columbia (B.S.N., 1983); St. Louis University (J.D., 1991). Member, St. Louis University Law Review, 1990-1991. *Member:* Forsyth County Bar Association (Member, Ethics and Grievance Committee, 2002-2005); Forsyth County Women Attorneys Association (President 1998-1999);

(This Listing Continued)

North Carolina Academy of Trial Lawyers (Member, Board of Governors, 2000-2006); Association of Trial Lawyers of America; Legal Aid Society of North Carolina, Inc. (Chair, Local Advisory Council, 2004—). (Board Certified Specialist in Workers Compensation Law, North Carolina State Board of Legal Specialization). ***REPORTED CASES:*** Rogers v. Lowe's Home Improvement, — N.C. App. —, 612 S.E. 2d 143 (2005), Hooker v. Stokes-Reynolds Hospital/North Carolina Baptist Hosp., Inc., 161 N.C. App. 111, 587 S.E.2d 440 (2003), Irby v. New Telephone Co., N.C. Ct. App. Sept. 16, 2003, unpublished. ***PRACTICE AREAS:*** Workers Compensation; Personal Injury; Social Security; Wrongful Death; Nursing Home Liability. ***Email:*** charris@maynardharris.com

Spanish speaking Legal Assistant on staff

METCALF & BEAL, L.L.P.

380 KNOLLWOOD STREET, SUITE 450
WINSTON-SALEM, NORTH CAROLINA 27103
Telephone: 336-777-0067
Fax: 336-748-0375
Email: metcalf@metcalfandbeal.com
URL: http://www.metcalfandbeal.com

General Civil and Criminal Practice in State and Federal Courts. Family Law, Adoptions, Child Custody, Child Support, Divorce, Equitable Distribution, Visitation Rights, Criminal Law, Driving While Intoxicated (DUI), Drug Crimes, Parole and Probation, White Collar Crime, Traffic Violations, Personal Injury, Automobile Accidents, Slip and Fall, Wrongful Death, Medical Malpractice, Nursing Home Abuse, Workers Compensation, Real Estate, Eminent Domain, Employment, Wrongful Termination, Trust and Estates, Wills, Probate.

W. EUGENE METCALF, born Asheville, North Carolina, August 24, 1954; admitted to bar, 1981, North Carolina. *Education:* University of North Carolina at Asheville (B.S., Business Administration, with honors, 1978); Wake Forest University School of Law (J.D., 1981). Adjunct Professor of Law, 1983—, Wake Forest University School of Law. *Member:* Forsyth County, North Carolina and American Bar Associations; The Association of Trial Lawyers of America; North Carolina Academy of Trial Lawyers. ***PRACTICE AREAS:*** Divorce; Family Law; Criminal Law; Personal Injury; Child Custody; Wills; Probate; Traffic Violations. ***Email:*** metcalf@metcalfandbeal.com

CHRISTOPHER L. BEAL, born Vass, North Carolina, September 3, 1953; admitted to bar, 1982, North Carolina. *Education:* Campbell College (B.S., 1975; J.D., 1982). *Member:* Forsyth County, North Carolina and American Bar Associations; North Carolina Academy of Trial Lawyers. (Board Certified Specialist in Family Law, North Carolina State Board of Legal Specialization). ***PRACTICE AREAS:*** Divorce; Family Law; Personal Injury; Medical Malpractice; Traffic Violations; Wills; Probate. ***Email:*** cbeal@metcalfandbeal.com

---

EDDIE C. MITCHELL, P.A.

110 OAKWOOD DRIVE, SUITE 410
WINSTON-SALEM, NORTH CAROLINA 27103
Telephone: 336-725-9597
Fax: 336-725-6662

Civil and Criminal Practice in all State Courts. Family Law, Divorce, Traffic, Driving While Impaired (DWI), Personal Injury, Mediation, Family Financial and Superior Court Mediation.

EDDIE C. MITCHELL, born Danville, Virginia, March 1, 1941; admitted to bar, 1968, North Carolina; 1969, U.S. District Court, Middle and Western Districts of North Carolina; 1973, U.S. Court of Appeals, Fourth Circuit. *Education:* East Carolina University (B.A., 1965); University of North Carolina (J.D., 1968). Delta Theta Phi. Order of the Coif. Law Clerk to Judge Eugene A. Gordon, U.S. District Court, Middle District of North Carolina, 1968-1969; Certified Family Financial Mediator, Certified Superior Court Mediator. *Member:* Forsyth County Bar Association (President, 1992-1993); North Carolina Bar Association; North Carolina State Bar; Forsyth County Criminal Defense Trial Lawyers Association (President, 1983-1984).

REFERENCES: Wachovia Bank & Trust Co., N.A.; First Citizens Bank and Trust Company.

MORGAN, HERRING, MORGAN, GREEN, ROSENBLUTT & GILL, LLP

WINSTON-SALEM, NORTH CAROLINA

(See High Point)

General Civil and Criminal Trial Practice in all State and Federal Courts. Interstate Commerce, Probate, Real Estate, Corporation and Tax Law. Torts. Traffic Violations and Driving Under the Influence, Personal Injury, Auto Accidents, Wills and Estates, Family Law, Divorce, Custody, Support, Adoption, Workers Compensation, Bankruptcy, Social Security, Employment Discrimination.

MORRIS YORK WILLIAMS SURLES & BARRINGER, L.L.P.

WINSTON-SALEM, NORTH CAROLINA

(See Charlotte)

Civil, Business and Commercial Litigation. Insurance Defense Litigation, Insurance Coverage and Workers Compensation. Medical and Professional Malpractice Defense. Land Condemnation and Alternative Dispute Resolution Services.

MORROW ALEXANDER & PORTER, PLLC

3890 VEST MILL ROAD
WINSTON-SALEM, NORTH CAROLINA 27103-1302
Telephone: 336-760-1400
Fax: 336-760-4520
Email: info@morrowalexander.com
URL: http://www.morrowalexander.com
Mailing Address: P.O. Box 25226, Winston-Salem, NC 27114-5226

Personal Injury, Domestic Relations, Equitable Distribution, Custody, Criminal Defense, Federal Criminal Law, DWI, Drug Crimes, Traffic, Mediation, Arbitration.

FIRM PROFILE: The firm's principal focus is the representation of clients in Personal Injury, Family Law, Criminal Law and Civil Litigation. All of our attorneys are Board Certified Specialists in either Family Law or Criminal Law.

JOHN F. MORROW, born 1940; admitted to bar, 1965, North Carolina. *Education:* Wake Forest University (B.B.A.; J.D., cum laude). Listed in, The Best Lawyers in America (Family Law). *Certified Mediator and Arbitrator. Member:* Forsyth County and North Carolina Bar Associations; North Carolina State Bar; North Carolina Academy of Trial Lawyers; American Academy of Matrimonial Lawyers. (Board Certified Specialist in Family Law, North Carolina State Board of Legal Specialization). ***PRACTICE AREAS:*** Personal Injury; Domestic Relations; Equitable Distribution; Child Custody; Alimony; Mediation; Arbitration. ***Email:*** jmorrow@morrowalexander.com

CHARLES J. ALEXANDER, II, born November 20, 1946; admitted to bar, 1972, North Carolina. *Education:* Wake Forest University (B.A., 1969; J.D., 1972). Listed in, The Best Lawyers in America (Criminal Law); Most Outstanding Lawyers in America. *Member:* Forsyth County and North Carolina Bar Associations; North Carolina State Bar; North Carolina Academy of Trial Lawyers; National Association of Criminal Defense Lawyers; National College of DUI Defense. (Board Certified Specialist in Criminal Law, North Carolina State Board of Legal Specialization). ***PRACTICE AREAS:*** Criminal Law; Federal Criminal Law; DWI; Traffic. ***Email:*** calexander@morrowalexander.com

BENJAMIN D. PORTER, born Akron, Ohio, April 27, 1970; admitted to bar, 1995, North Carolina. *Education:* Miami University at Ohio (B.S., 1992); Wake Forest University (J.D., 1995). Author: "Defending Traffic Cases" - 1998 North Carolina General Practice Deskbook. *Member:* Forsyth County and North Carolina Bar Associations; North Carolina State Bar; North Carolina Academy of Trial Lawyers; North Carolina Criminal Defense Lawyers Association; National Association of Criminal Defense Lawyers. (Board Certified Specialist in Criminal Law, North Carolina State Board of Legal Specialization). ***PRACTICE AREAS:*** Criminal/Traffic Defense. ***Email:*** bporter@morrowalexander.com

NAGLE & ASSOCIATES, P.A.

380 KNOLLWOOD STREET
SUITE 320
WINSTON-SALEM, NORTH CAROLINA 27103
Telephone: 336-723-4500
Fax: 336-723-1219
URL: http://www.lawyers.com/nagleandassociates

Plaintiff Personal Injury.

CARL B. NAGLE, born Atlanta, Georgia, January 31, 1965; admitted to bar, 1993, Georgia; 1996, North Carolina. *Education:* University of Georgia (B.B.A., 1987; J.D., 1993). *Member:* North Carolina and American Bar Associations. ***PRACTICE AREAS:*** Personal Injury. ***Email:*** carlbnagle@aol.com

NELSON MULLINS RILEY & SCARBOROUGH LLP

THE KNOLLWOOD
380 KNOLLWOOD STREET, SUITE 530
WINSTON-SALEM, NORTH CAROLINA 27103
Telephone: 336-774-3300
Fax: 336-774-3299
URL: http://www.nelsonmullins.com

Atlanta, Georgia Office: 999 Peachtree Street, N.E., Suite 1400, 30309-3964. P.O. Box 77707, 30357-0707. Telephone: 404-817-6000. Telecopy: 404-817-6050.
Charleston, South Carolina Office: Liberty Center, Suite 600, 151 Meeting Street, 29401-2239. P.O. Box 1806, 29402-1806. Telephone: 843-853-5200. Telecopy: 843-722-8700.
Charlotte, North Carolina Office: Bank of America Corporate Center, Suite 2400, 100 North Tryon Street, 28202-4007. Telephone: 704-417-3000. Telecopy: 704-377-4814.
Columbia, South Carolina Office: Meridian, 17th Floor, 1320 Main Street, 29201, P.O. Box 11070, 29211-1070. Telephone: 803-799-2000. Telecopy: 803-256-7500.
Greenville, South Carolina Office: Poinsett Plaza, 104 South Main Street, Suite 900, 29601. P.O. Box 10084, 29603-0084. Telephone: 864-250-2300. Telecopy: 864-232-2925.
Myrtle Beach, South Carolina Office: Founders Centre, Suite 301, 2411 North Oak Street, 29577-3165. P.O. Box 3939, 29578-3939. Telephone: 843-448-3500. Telecopy: 843-448-3437.
Raleigh, North Carolina Office: GlenLake One, Suite 200, 4140 Parklake Avenue, 27612. Telephone: 919-877-3800. Telecopy: 919-877-3799.
Washington, D.C. Office: 101 Constitution Avenue, NW, Suite 900, 20001. Telephone: 202-712-2800. Fax: 202-712-2860.

Health Care.

PARTNERS

DENISE M. GUNTER, born Englewood, New Jersey, 1964; admitted to bar, 1989, North Carolina. *Education:* Northwestern University (B.A., 1986); George Washington

(This Listing Continued)

University (J.D., 1989). Member: George Washington University Moot Court Board; National Moot Court Team. *Member:* North Carolina (Member, 1996— and Chair, 2002-2003, Antitrust and Trade Regulation Section Council; Member, Health Law Section) and American (Member, Antitrust and Litigation Sections) Bar Associations; American Health Lawyers Association. ***PRACTICE AREAS:*** Antitrust and Trade Regulation; Health Care; Civil Litigation. ***Email:*** denise.gunter@nelsonmullins.com

MARK A. STAFFORD, born Kernersville, North Carolina, December 14, 1962; admitted to bar, 1989, North Carolina, U.S. District Court, Western, Eastern, and Middle Districts of North Carolina; 1994, U.S. Court of Appeals, Fourth Circuit; 1997, U.S. Tax Court; 1999, U.S. Supreme Court. *Education:* University of North Carolina at Chapel Hill (A.B., with honors, Economics, 1985; J.D., with honors, 1989). Board of Editors, North Carolina Law Review, 1988-1989. Order of the Coif, 1989. Editorial Board for the American Bar Association's Computer and Internet Litigation Journal, 2000-2002. Cubmaster, Pack 910 of the Boy Scouts of America (Old Hickory Council), 2000-2003. President, Board of Directors, Association for the Benefit of Child Development, Inc., 1998. Member, Rotary Club of Winston-Salem. Coach, Winston-Salem Nationals Little League. Vestryman and Parish Legal Counsel, St. Paul's Episcopal Church, Winston-Salem, N.C. *Member:* North Carolina (Member, Sections on: Litigation; Construction; Employment Law) and American (Member, Committees on: Commercial and Business; Computer and Internet/Intellectual Property; Business Tort) Bar Associations; North Carolina Association of Defense Attorneys. ***PRACTICE AREAS:*** Litigation; Mortgages; Construction Law; Computers and Software; Banks and Banking. ***Email:*** mark.stafford@nelsonmullins.com

RICHARD B. HOWINGTON, born Shelby, North Carolina, May 24, 1944; admitted to bar, 1969, North Carolina. *Education:* Wake Forest University (B.S., 1966; J.D., cum laude, 1969). Phi Delta Phi. Member, Wake Forest Law Review, 1968-1969. Co-Author: "Physician Group Practices," Aspen Publishing's Health Care Corporate Law Series, 1996. Listed in The Best Lawyers in America, 1995-2006 editions. *Member:* Forsyth County, North Carolina (Member, Sections on: Business; Health Law) and American Bar Associations; American Health Lawyers Association. [Captain, JAGC, U.S. Army, 1969-1973]. ***PRACTICE AREAS:*** Corporate; Health; Hospital Law. ***Email:*** richard.howington@nelsonmullins.com

ASSOCIATES

CRYSTAL B. BAKER, born LaPlata, Maryland, December 9, 1974; admitted to bar, 2002, North Carolina. *Education:* Wake Forest University (B.A., 1996; J.D., 2002). *Member:* North Carolina Bar Association (Health Law Section); American Bar Association (Health Law Section); American Health Lawyers Association. ***PRACTICE AREAS:*** Products Liability Litigation; Pharmaceutical Liability Litigation; Business Litigation; Health Care. ***Email:*** crystal.baker@nelsonmullins.com

DONALD R. POCOCK, born Chapel Hill, North Carolina, 1974; admitted to bar, 2000, North Carolina. *Education:* Wake Forest University (B.A., cum laude, 1997; J.D., 2000). Order of Barristers. Moot Court Board, 1998-2000; National Trial Team, 1998-2000; Regional Champion, National Trial Competition, 1999. Recipient, Robert Goldberg Award for Excellence in Trial Advocacy, 2000. *Member:* Forsyth County, North Carolina (Member: Law School Liaison Committee; Construction Law Section) and American (Member, Litigation Section) Bar Associations. ***PRACTICE AREAS:*** Construction Law; Litigation; Professional Liability; Products Liability.

OF COUNSEL

GORAN P. STOJKOVICH, born Chicago, Illinois, December 18, 1965; admitted to bar, 1997, Illinois; 1998, District of Columbia; 2003, North Carolina; registered to practice before U.S. Patent and Trademark Office. *Education:* University of Illinois (B.S., 1989); Chicago-Kent College of Law, Illinois Institute of Technology (J.D., with honors, 1997). *Member:* American Bar Association (Member, Intellectual Property Law Section); American Intellectual Property Law Association. ***LANGUAGES:*** Serbo-Croatian. ***PRACTICE AREAS:*** Intellectual Property; Patents; Litigation. ***Email:*** goran.stojkovich@nelsonmullins.com

All Winston-Salem Attorneys are Members of the North Carolina State Bar unless indicated otherwise.

(For biographical data on Atlanta, Georgia, Charleston, South Carolina, Columbia, South Carolina, Greenville, South Carolina, Myrtle Beach, South Carolina, Charlotte, North Carolina, Raleigh, North Carolina and Washington, D.C., see Professional Biographies of those cities)

GUY B. OLDAKER III

Established in 1997

3410 HEALY DRIVE, SUITE 115
WINSTON-SALEM, NORTH CAROLINA 27103-1403
Telephone: 336-725-2346
Facsimile: 336-760-0922
Email: oldakerg@bellsouth.net
URL: http://www.oldakerlaw.com

Family Law, Child Custody, Child Support, Divorce, Separation Agreements, Visitation Rights, Criminal Law, Driving While Intoxicated, (DWI), Drug Crimes, Traffic Violations, Personal Injury, Automobile Accidents and Injuries, Wrongful Death, Lemon Law, Toxic Torts.

GUY B. OLDAKER, III, born 1950; admitted to bar, 1996, North Carolina. *Education:* University of Virginia (B.A., Chemistry, 1972); Virginia Polytechnic Institute and State University (Ph.D., Chemistry, 1979); West Virginia University (J.D., 1995). Instructor, Virginia Polytechnic Institute and State University, 1977-1978. *Member:* Forsyth County Bar Association; North Carolina State Bar; North Carolina Academy of Trial Lawyers. ***REPORTED CASES:*** State v. Jackson, 348 N.C. 644, 503 S.E. 2d 101 (1998).

ORBOCK RUARK & DILLARD, PC

1590 WESTBROOK PLAZA DRIVE, SUITE 102
WINSTON-SALEM, NORTH CAROLINA 27103
Telephone: 336-760-8848
Fax: 336-760-5903
Email: thomaslaw@triad.rr.com
URL: http://www.ordlawfirm.com

Workers Compensation, Personal Injury Defense.

MAUREEN TIERNEY ORBOCK, born Shenandoah, Pennsylvania, February 13, 1944; admitted to bar, 1987, North Carolina. *Education:* Pottsville Hospital School of Nursing (R.N., 1964); Salem College (B.A., magna cum laude, 1983); Wake Forest University (J.D., 1987). Registered Nurse, North Carolina, 1964. *Member:* Forsyth County (Member, Executive Committee, 1992; Member, 21st Judicial District Bar Ethics and Grievance Committee, 1993—), North Carolina (Member, Workers Compensation Committee of Litigation Section) and American Bar Associations; North Carolina State Bar; North Carolina Association of Defense Attorneys. ***PRACTICE AREAS:*** Workers Compensation.

ROGER LEE DILLARD, JR., born Asheville, North Carolina, January 3, 1945; admitted to bar, 1972, North Carolina; 1974, U.S. Court of Appeals, Fourth Circuit. *Education:* University of North Carolina at Chapel Hill (A.B., 1967); Samford University (J.D., 1972). Phi Delta Phi. Attorney: Swain County, 1975-1978; Graham County, 1979-1982. Member, North Carolina Banking Commission, 1975-1979. Former Deputy Commissioner, North Carolina Industrial Commission. *Member:* North Carolina and American (Member, General Practice Section) Bar Associations; North Carolina State Bar. ***PRACTICE AREAS:*** Workers Compensation Defense.

BARBARA E. RUARK, born Mount Gilead, North Carolina, February 5, 1962; admitted to bar, 1987, North Carolina. *Education:* Wake Forest University (B.A., cum laude, 1984; J.D., magna cum laude, 1987). Notes and Comments Editor, Wake Forest Law Review, 1986-1987. *Member:* Forsyth County, North Carolina and American Bar Associations. ***PRACTICE AREAS:*** Workers Compensation; Insurance Litigation.

KENT CONRAD FORD, born Johnstown, Pennsylvania, August 7, 1967; admitted to bar, 1992, North Carolina. *Education:* University of North Carolina at Charlotte (B.A., 1989); Wake Forest University (J.D., 1992). Associate Chief Justice, Moot Court Board, 1991-1992. ***PRACTICE AREAS:*** Workers Compensation; Employment Law.

MARK A. LEACH, born 1971; admitted to bar, 1996, North Carolina and U.S. District Court, Middle District of North Carolina. *Education:* State University of New York at Binghamton (B.A., 1993); Wake Forest University (J.D., 1996). ***PRACTICE AREAS:*** Workers Compensation; Civil Liability; Subrogation.

STACEY DAWN RUBAIN, born 1975; admitted to bar, 1999, North Carolina. *Education:* Syracuse University (B.A., 1996); Wake Forest University (J.D., 1999). ***PRACTICE AREAS:*** Civil Liability; Subrogation.

REPRESENTATIVE CLIENTS: AIG; AmComp; Amerisure; Bank of America; Bellsouth Telecommunications; Broadspire; Burlington Industries; Cincinnati Insurance Companies; CNA/RSKCo; Crawford and Company; Creative Risk Solutions; Exxon; Federal Express; Hewitt, Coleman and Associates; International Paper; iSurity Insurance Services/NCME Fund; Liberty Mutual Insurance Company; Lumberman's Underwriting Alliance; North Carolina Insurance Guaranty Association; Novantl-Health; Sara Lee Corporation; Scott Insurance; Specialty Risk; SPX Corporation; St. Paul Travelers; The Schaffer Companies, Ltd.; Thomasville Furniture Industries, Inc.; Tyson Foods, Inc.; Universal Underwriter's Insurance Group; Wausau Insurance Company.

THE LAW OFFICES OF JEFFREY K. PERALDO, P.A.

WINSTON-SALEM, NORTH CAROLINA

(See Greensboro)

Serious Personal Injury, Wrongful Death, Automobile Accidents, Trucking Accidents, Medical Malpractice, Hospital Malpractice, Nursing Home Neglect and Abuse, Product Liability, Construction Accidents, Consumer Fraud, Land Condemnation, Negligent Security.

PHARR & BOYNTON, PLLC

Established in 2000

2720 GEORGETOWN DRIVE
WINSTON-SALEM, NORTH CAROLINA 27106
Telephone: 336-721-2400
Fax: 336-721-0039
Email: lwray@pharrlaw.com
URL: http://www.lawyers.com/pharr&boynton

Litigation, Construction, Products Liability, Professional Liability, Real Estate Litigation in State and Federal Courts.

STEVE M. PHARR, born Richmond, Virginia, 1953; admitted to bar, 1985, North Carolina. *Education:* Davidson College (A.B., cum laude, 1975); University of Montpellier, France; Union Theological Seminary in Virginia (M.Div., 1979; Th.M., 1980); University of Virginia (J.D., 1985). *Member:* Forsyth County, North Carolina (Chairman, Construction Law Section) and American Bar Associations; Forum on Construction Law; American Institute of Architects (Allied Individual Member). ***PRACTICE AREAS:*** Litigation; Construction Law; Products Liability; Professional Liability. ***Email:*** spharr@pharrlaw.com

MARK D. BOYNTON, born Burlington County, New Jersey, 1968; admitted to bar, 1997, Georgia; 1998, North Carolina. *Education:* University of Virginia (B.A., 1991); Wake Forest University (J.D., 1997). Phi Delta Phi. Order of the Barristers. Author: The Wild West Down East," Change Order, NC Lawyers Weekly, August 2003. *Member:* Forsyth County, North Carolina (Chairman, Litigation Section Council; Past Chair, Civil Rules and Practice Committee), Georgia and American Bar Associations. ***REPORTED CASES:*** Kaleel Builders, Inc. v. Ashby (2003). ***PRACTICE AREAS:*** Litigation; Construction Law; Products Liability. ***Email:*** mboynton@pharrlaw.com

ASSOCIATES

STACEY D. BAILEY, born Hampton, Virginia, 1970; admitted to bar, 2001, North Carolina; 2003, South Carolina. *Education:* University of Virginia (B.A., 1992; Echols Scholar, Jefferson Society); Wake Forest University (J.D., 2001). Author: "Impact of Creek Pointe," Change Order, March 2002. *Member:* Forsyth County, North Carolina and American Bar Associations. ***PRACTICE AREAS:*** Litigation; Construction Law; Professional Liability; Products Liability. ***Email:*** sbailey@pharrlaw.com

KENNETH E. MENZEL, born 1979; admitted to bar, 2005, North Carolina. *Education:* Gettysburg College (B.A., Political Science, magna cum laude, 2002); Wake Forest University (J.D., 2005). *Member:* North Carolina State Bar. ***PRACTICE AREAS:*** Construction Law.

REPRESENTATIVE CLIENTS: St. Paul Travelers Insurance Companies; CNA Insurance Companies; The Cincinnati Insurance Companies; Montreat College; MW Manufacturers, Inc.; ECMD, Inc.; Thomas Harris Building & Design, Inc.; Prudential Carolinas Realty; Coldwell Banker Triad Realtors; Essex Insurance Company; Kemper Insurance Companies.

PRICE LAW OFFICE

1144 WEST FOURTH STREET
WINSTON-SALEM, NORTH CAROLINA 27101
Telephone: 336-724-7030
Facsimile: 336-724-7047
Email: info@replegal.com
URL: http://www.repcollect.com

Bankruptcy, Creditors Rights, Collections, Debtor/Creditor, Commercial Litigation.

ROBERT E. PRICE, JR., born Boston, Massachusetts, April 27, 1956; admitted to bar, 1980, North Carolina, Virginia and U.S. District Court, Middle District of North Carolina; 1989, U.S. Court of Appeals, Fourth Circuit. *Education:* Dartmouth College (A.B., summa cum laude, 1977); University of Virginia (J.D., 1980). Phi Beta Kappa. Lecturer, Wake Forest University, Continuing Legal Education, 1993, 1997, 2001. Davie County Attorney, 1993—. *Member:* Forsyth County and North Carolina Bar Associations; North Carolina State Bar; Virginia State Bar; Commercial Law League of America. (Board Certified Specialist in Bankruptcy Law, North Carolina State Board of Legal Specialization). ***PRACTICE AREAS:*** Bankruptcy; Creditors Rights; Commercial Litigation; Collections; Secured Collections. ***Email:*** rprice@replegal.com

---

HOLLY GROCE, born Landstuhl, Germany, May 8, 1970; admitted to bar, 1995, North Carolina. *Education:* University of North Carolina at Chapel Hill (B.S.B.A., 1992); Campbell University (J.D., 1995). Phi Alpha Delta. Order of the Barristers. Member, National Trial Advocacy Team. Teaching Assistant, Campbell University Law School, 1994-1995. *Member:* Forsyth County Bar Association; North Carolina State Bar. ***PRACTICE AREAS:*** Creditors Rights; Real Estate. ***Email:*** hgroce@replegal.com

JULIE M. LUCKEY, born Decatur, Illinois, January 18, 1963; admitted to bar, 1990, North Carolina. *Education:* University of North Carolina at Chapel Hill (B.A., 1985; J.D., 1990). *Member:* North Carolina Bar Association (Bankruptcy Section). ***PRACTICE AREAS:*** Bankruptcy; Foreclosures; Collections. ***Email:*** jluckey@replegal.com

RANDOLPH & FISCHER

Established in 1992

200 BROOKSTOWN AVENUE, SUITE 304
WINSTON-SALEM, NORTH CAROLINA 27101
Telephone: 336-724-3513
Fax: 336-725-6330
Email: clarkf@randolphfischerlaw.com
URL: http://www.randolphfischerlaw.com

Criminal Trials, Felonies, Homicide, Drug Crimes, Appellate Practice, Family Law, Divorce, Custody, Litigation.

FIRM PROFILE: Criminal Trials including Capital, Appeals, Family Law, Personal Injury.

J. CLARK FISCHER, born Memphis, Tennessee, June 22, 1955; admitted to bar, 1980, North Carolina; 1981, U.S. District Court, Middle District of North Carolina; 1983, Virginia. *Education:* Vanderbilt University (B.A., cum laude, 1977); Wake Forest University (J.D., 1980). *Member:* Forsyth County Bar Association; North Carolina State Bar; North Carolina Academy of Trial Lawyers; Forsyth County Criminal Defense Trial Lawyer's Association (President, 1995). [Capt., USAF, JAG, 1984-1988]. (Board Certified Specialist in Criminal Law including Appellate Practice, North Carolina State Board of Legal Specialization). ***REPORTED CASES:*** State v. Rivera, 350 N.C. 285, 514 S.E. 2d 720 (1999); State v. Jones, 355 N.C. 117, 558 S.E. 2d, 97 (2002). ***PRACTICE AREAS:*** Criminal Defense; Criminal Appeals; Federal Criminal Law; Civil Appeals; Personal Injury; Domestic Appeals. ***Email:*** clarkf@randolphandfischer.com

ROBINSON & LAWING, L.L.P.

Established in 1992

370 KNOLLWOOD STREET, SUITE 600
WINSTON-SALEM, NORTH CAROLINA 27103-1835
Telephone: 336-631-8500
Fax: 336-631-6999
URL: http://www.robinson-lawing.com

General Civil and Complex Litigation in All Courts. Business, Corporate, Antitrust and Trade, Intellectual Property, Products Liability, Personal Injury, Professional Malpractice, Workers Compensation, Bankruptcy, Family Law, Wrongful Death, Insurance, Employee Benefits Law, Employment and Labor Law, Business Law, Estate and Tax Law.

FIRM PROFILE: The firm consists of a group of experienced and highly skilled lawyers who have been widely recognized for their accomplishments in the practice of law. The firm has an active litigation practice in the State and Federal courts throughout North Carolina. The firm's trial and litigation practice includes antitrust and business law disputes, intellectual property, insurance litigation, products liability, personal injury, professional malpractice, employment litigation, workers' compensation, and equitable distribution.

MEMBERS OF FIRM

NORWOOD ROBINSON, born Roseboro, North Carolina, June 18, 1925; admitted to bar, 1952, North Carolina. *Education:* United States Military Academy (B.S., 1945); Duke University (J.D., 1952). Order of the Coif. Recipient, Charles S. Rhyne Award, Duke University, in recognition of accomplishment in private practice and contribution to public service. Listed, The Best Lawyers in America. Associate Editor, Duke Bar Journal, 1951-1952. Permanent Member, Fourth Circuit Judicial Conference. Member, Board of Visitors of Duke University School of Law, Duke University Divinity School. Past Member, Board of Visitors of Wake Forest University School of Law. Past Chairman of Board, Private Adjudication Center, Duke University. Member, Board of Trustees, Association of Graduates, United States Military Academy. North Carolina Civilian Aide to the Secretary of the Army, 1996-2001. *Member:* Forsyth County (President), North Carolina (Member, Board of Governors) and American Bar Associations. Fellow: American College of Trial Lawyers. Fellow: American Bar Foundation; Inn of Court Emeritus. ***PRACTICE AREAS:*** General Litigation; Antitrust; Trade; Corporate. ***Email:*** nrobinson@robinson-lawing.com

ROBERT J. LAWING, born Charlotte, North Carolina, December 14, 1946; admitted to bar, 1973, North Carolina. *Education:* East Carolina University (A.B., 1969); Wake Forest University (J.D., magna cum laude, 1973). Member, Board of Editors, Wake Forest Law Review, 1972-1973. Member, Board of Visitors of Wake Forest Law School. Listed in "Best Lawyers in America." *Member:* Forsyth County, North Carolina and American Bar Associations; International Association of Defense Counsel; North Carolina Association of Defense Counsel; American Board of Trial Advocates. ***PRACTICE AREAS:*** General Civil Litigation; Insurance; Personal Injury; Corporate Litigation; Business Litigation; Employment Litigation. ***Email:*** blawing@robinson-lawing.com

MICHAEL L. ROBINSON, born Winston-Salem, North Carolina, September 21, 1955; admitted to bar, 1980, North Carolina. *Education:* Woodberry Forrest School (1973); Davidson College (B.A., 1977); University of North Carolina (J.D., with honors, 1980). Order of the Coif. *Member:* Forsyth County, North Carolina and American Bar Associations. ***PRACTICE AREAS:*** General Civil; Antitrust; Business; Domestic Litigation. ***Email:*** mrobinson@robinson-lawing.com

JANE C. JACKSON, born Washington, D.C., August 2, 1958; admitted to bar, 1983, North Carolina. *Education:* Wake Forest University (B.S., summa cum laude, 1980); University of Virginia (J.D., 1983). Phi Beta Kappa; Order of the Coif. Listed in "Best Lawyers in America." *Member:* Forsyth County, North Carolina (Member: Litigation Section; Member, Section Council, 2001-2002; Chair, Workers Compensation Section) and American Bar Associations; North Carolina Association of Defense Attorneys. ***PRACTICE AREAS:*** Workers Compensation Litigation; Employment Litigation; Civil Litigation. ***Email:*** jjackson@robinson-lawing.com

KEVIN L. MILLER, born Charlotte, North Carolina, May 13, 1959; admitted to bar, 1984, North Carolina. *Education:* Duke University (A.B., cum laude, 1981); University of North Carolina (J.D., 1984). Order of the Coif. Lecturer, various CLE Programs. *Member:* Forsyth County and North Carolina Bar Associations. ***PRACTICE AREAS:*** General Civil Litigation; Antitrust; Medical Malpractice Litigation; Broker-Dealer Arbitration; Corporate Law; Complex Equitable Distribution. ***Email:*** kmiller@robinson-lawing.com

C. RAY GRANTHAM, JR., born Fort Rucker, Alabama, February 8, 1957; admitted to bar, 1988, North Carolina; 1994, U.S. District Court, Eastern, Middle and Western Districts of North Carolina; 1996, U.S. Court of Appeals, Fourth Circuit. *Education:* U.S. Military Academy (B.S., 1979); University of North Carolina (J.D., with honors, 1988). Order of the Coif. Member, North Carolina Law Review. *Member:* Forsyth County and North Carolina (Member, Sections on: Employment; Construction and Family Law) Bar Associations. [U.S. Army, Infantry and Special Forces, 1979-1988; JAGC, 1988-1992]. (Board Certified Specialist in Family Law, North Carolina State Board of Legal Specialization). ***PRACTICE AREAS:*** Civil Litigation; Employment Law; Complex Equitable Distribution; Commercial Litigation; Construction Law. ***Email:*** rgrantham@robinson-lawing.com

JOHN N. TAYLOR, JR., born Rocky Mount, North Carolina, April 2, 1963; admitted to bar, 1988, North Carolina. *Education:* Wake Forest University (B.A., magna cum laude, 1985; J.D., 1988). Phi Beta Kappa; Eta Sigma Phi; Phi Alpha Delta. Law Clerk to Honorable Hiram H. Ward, United States District Judge, Middle District of North Carolina, 1988-1990. Treasurer, Legal Aid Society of Northwest North Carolina, 1996-1999. *Member:* Forsyth County and North Carolina Bar Associations; North Carolina State Bar. ***PRACTICE AREAS:*** Civil Litigation; Products Liability; Administrative Law; Commercial Litigation; Intellectual Property; Employment Discrimination. ***Email:*** jtaylor@robinson-lawing.com

JOLINDA J. BABCOCK, born Williamsport, Pennsylvania, November 11, 1967; admitted to bar, 1992, North Carolina. *Education:* University of Scranton (B.S., summa cum laude, 1989); University of North Carolina (J.D., 1992). Alpha Sigma Nu; Delta Mu Delta; Omega Beta Sigma; Phi Alpha Delta. Certified Mediator. *Member:* Forsyth County and North Carolina (Member, Sections on: Dispute Resolution; Workers Compensation; Section Council Member, 2004-2007) Bar Associations. ***PRACTICE AREAS:*** General Civil Litigation; Workers Compensation Litigation. ***Email:*** jbabcock@robinson-lawing.com

KAREN M. WILSON, born Lenoir, North Carolina, April 1, 1960; admitted to bar, 1985, North Carolina. *Education:* Wake Forest University (B.S., 1982; J.D., cum laude, 1985). Member, Moot Court Board. Member, Wake Forest Law Review. Certified Public Accountant, North Carolina, 1988. Author: "North Carolina Limited Liability Company Forms and Practice Manual," Data Trace Legal Publishers, 1995; "Corporate and Income Tax and Franchise Tax Summaries," Prentice Hall's North Carolina State and Local Tax Service, 1992 ed.; "Who May Sign Individual Tax Returns," 4 No. 2 Probate and Property 11, 1990. *Member:* Forsyth County, North Carolina (Member, Tax Section, Estate Planning and Fiduciary Law Section) and American (Member, Section on Taxation) Bar Associations. ***PRACTICE AREAS:*** Taxation Law; Estate Planning; Corporate Law; Partnership Law. ***Email:*** kwilson@robinson-lawing.com

HOWARD BRENT HELMS, born Raleigh, North Carolina, December 30, 1966; admitted to bar, 1992, North Carolina. *Education:* Wake Forest University (B.S., cum laude, 1989; J.D., cum laude, 1992). Beta Gamma Sigma; Phi Delta Phi. Member, Wake Forest University Moot Court Board. Member, Wake Forest University Law Review, 1991-1992. Law Clerk to Honorable John B. Lewis, North Carolina Court of Appeals, 1993. Author: Comment, "Financial Institutions Reform, Regulatory and Enforcement Act,: An Ethical Quagmire for Attorneys Representing Financial Institutions," 27 Wake Forest Law Review 277, 1992. *Member:* North Carolina and American Bar Associations; North Carolina State Bar. ***PRACTICE AREAS:*** Civil Litigation; Insurance Litigation; Personal Injury; Business Litigation. ***Email:*** bhelms@robinson-lawing.com

KURT A. SEEBER, born Durham, North Carolina, January 1, 1966; admitted to bar, 1993, North Carolina and U.S. District Court, Middle District of North Carolina; 1994, U.S. District Court, Eastern District of North Carolina and U.S. Court of Appeals, Fourth Circuit. *Education:* North Carolina State University (B.A., 1989); Wake Forest University (J.D., 1993). Law Clerk to Honorable Jack L. Cozort, Sydnor Thompson and Mark D. Martin, 1994-1995. *Member:* Forsyth County and North Carolina Bar Associations; North Carolina State Bar; North Carolina Association of Defense Attorneys. ***PRACTICE AREAS:*** Workers Compensation; Insurance Defense; Civil Litigation; Personal Injury; Business Litigation. ***Email:*** kseeber@robinson-lawing.com

ASSOCIATES

STEPHEN ROBINSON, born Berea, Kentucky, April 18, 1962; admitted to bar, 1991, North Carolina. *Education:* Berea College (B.A., 1984); University of North Carolina (J.D., 1991). Recipient: Louis C. Smith Scholarship; Louise Veltin Prize. *Member:* Forsyth County, North Carolina and American Bar Associations; North Carolina State Bar. ***PRACTICE AREAS:*** General Civil Litigation; Intellectual Property Litigation; Business Litigation. ***Email:*** srobinson@robinson-lawing.com

OLIVER M. READ IV, born New York, New York, November 16, 1955; admitted to bar, 2000, North Carolina; U.S. District Court, Western and Middle Districts of North Carolina. *Education:* United States Naval Academy (B.S., 1977); University of Southern California (M.S., 1985); Wake Forest University (J.D., 2000). *Member:* Forsyth County and North Carolina Bar Associations. [U.S. Navy, 1977-1997]. ***PRACTICE AREAS:*** Insurance; Governmental; Tort Litigation; Civil Litigation; Business Litigation; Commercial Litigation. ***Email:*** oread@robinson-lawing.com

W. MARK PECK, born Honolulu, Hawaii, December 6, 1968; admitted to bar, 2001, North Carolina. *Education:* University of Delaware (B.A., 1990); Wake Forest University (M.S., 1998; J.D., 2001). Member, Order of the Barristers. Law Clerk, The Honorable Ralph A. Walker, North Carolina Court of Appeals, 2001-2002. ***PRACTICE AREAS:*** Workers Compensation Defense; Insurance Litigation; Civil Litigation. ***Email:*** Mpeck@robinson-lawing.com

REBECCA H. MILLER, born Atlanta, Georgia, December 18, 1974; admitted to bar, 2000, Georgia; 2003, North Carolina. *Education:* Oglethorpe University (B.A., magna cum laude, 1997); University of Georgia School of Law (J.D., cum laude, 2000). Articles Editor, 1999-2000 and Editorial Board, 1998-1999, Georgia Law Review. Law Clerk to Honorable Richard W. Story, U.S. District Court, Northern District of Georgia. *Member:* State Bar of Georgia; North Carolina State Bar. ***Email:*** rmiller@robinson-lawing.com

ADAM R. SMART, born Petersburg, Virginia, March 30, 1977; admitted to bar, 2003, North Carolina; 2004, U.S. District Court, Middle District of North Carolina and U.S. Court of Appeals, Fourth Circuit. *Education:* University of North Carolina (B.A., cum laude, distinction, 1999; J.D., magna cum laude, 2002). Order of the Coif. Morehead Scholar. Law Clerk: Judge Linda McGee, North Carolina Court of Appeals, 2002-2003; Judge R. Lanier Anderson, III, U.S. Court of Appeals, 11th Circuit, 2003-2004. Member, 200-2001 and Executive Editor, 2001-2002 North Carolina Banking Institute. Author: "E-Sign vs. State Electronic Signature Laws: The Electronic Statutory Battleground," 5 N.C. Banking Institute 485 (2001). *Member:* Forsyth County and North Carolina Bar Associations. ***PRACTICE AREAS:*** Civil Litigation; Insurance Litigation; Commercial Litigation. ***Email:*** asmart@robinson-lawing.com

REPRESENTATIVE CLIENTS: American Furniture Manufacturers Association; Amoco Corp.; Bernhardt Furniture Industries; Brown & Williamson Tobacco Corp.; Pine State Knitwear Co.; Rage, Inc.; Vaughan Furniture Co., Inc.; ACE Insurance Cos.; Ohio Casualty Group; The Stanley Works; Liberty Corp.; Champion International; Cross Creek Apparel, Inc.; Hooker; Aramark; Food Lion; Forsyth County; Piedmont Natural Gas; Dana Corporation.

DEAN B. RUTLEDGE

1 NORTH MARSHALL STREET
SUITE 101
WINSTON-SALEM, NORTH CAROLINA 27101
Telephone: 336-722-7000
Fax: 336-722-9011
Email: dbrutledge@aol.com
URL: http://www.deanrutledge.com

Family Law, Adoptions, Child Custody, Child Support, Divorce, Equitable Distribution, Premarital Agreements, Spousal Support, Mediation, Felonies, Misdemeanors, Drug Crimes, Traffic Violations.

(This Listing Continued)

FIRM PROFILE: Mr. Rutledge is board certified specialist in Family Law.

DEAN B. RUTLEDGE, born Charlotte, North Carolina, February 28, 1954; admitted to bar, 1982, North Carolina. *Education:* University of North Carolina (B.A., 1977); Wake Forest University (J.D., 1982). Certified Family Financial Mediator. *Member:* North Carolina Bar Association; North Carolina State Bar; Forsyth County Criminal Defense Trial Lawyers Association. (Board Certified Specialist in Family Law, North Carolina State Board of Legal Specialization). ***PRACTICE AREAS:*** Family Law; Criminal Law.

SCHELL BRAY AYCOCK ABEL & LIVINGSTON P.L.L.C.

WINSTON-SALEM, NORTH CAROLINA

(See Greensboro)

Corporate, Taxation, Securities Regulation, Venture Capital, Real Estate and Real Estate Finance, Mergers and Acquisitions, Health Care, Antitrust and Trade Regulation, Banking, Commercial, Employee Benefits, Estate Planning and Administration.

PAUL C. SHEPARD

8 WEST THIRD STREET, SUITE 245
WINSTON-SALEM, NORTH CAROLINA 27101
Telephone: 336-727-1364
Fax: 336-727-1365
Email: PaulCShepard@abanet.org
URL: http://www.lawyers.com/paulcshepardattorney

Child Custody, Divorce, Family Law, Social Security Disability, Automobile Accidents and Personal Injury, Wills and Probate, Workers Compensation, Real Estate, Zoning and Land Use, Traffic Violations.

FIRM PROFILE: A solo general practice focusing on both family needs and disability and personal injury as set forth in the specific practice areas described above, founded in 1985 and located in the historic Eight West Third Street Building in downtown Winston-Salem.

PAUL C. SHEPARD, born April 28, 1948; admitted to bar, 1976, North Carolina. *Education:* Vassar College (B.A., 1970); Wake Forest University (J.D., with honors, 1976). Presenter: Family Law CLE programs at Equal Justice Conferences, 2001 and 2004; Social Security CLE Program, 2002; Zoning and Land Use Seminar, 2005. *Member:* Forsyth County, North Carolina and American Bar Associations; North Carolina Academy of Trial Lawyers; The Association of Trial Lawyers of America. (Board Certified Specialist in Family Law, North Carolina State Board of Legal Specialization)

CHRISTOPHER J. SMALL

1078 WEST FOURTH STREET
WINSTON-SALEM, NORTH CAROLINA 27101
Telephone: 336-722-0333
Fax: 336-722-0334
Email: cjsmall@cjsmallatty.com
URL: http://www.cjsmallatty.com

Collections and Creditors' Rights enforced in all Courts.

CHRISTOPHER J. SMALL, born Camden, New Jersey, March 15, 1953; admitted to bar, 1978, North Carolina. *Education:* Catawba College (B.A., magna cum laude, 1975); Wake Forest University (J.D., 1978). Phi Alpha Delta. Lecturer, on CLE Seminar on "Collection and Enforcement of Judgments," Wake Forest University School of Law, 2001. *Member:* Forsyth County and North Carolina Bar Associations; The North Carolina State Bar; Commercial Law League of America. (Certified in Creditor's Rights Law by the American Board of Certification). ***PRACTICE AREAS:*** Collections; Creditor's Rights.

REFERENCE: Wachovia Bank and Trust Co.

ROBERT G. SPAUGH

1352 ASHLEY BROOK LANE
WINSTON-SALEM, NORTH CAROLINA 27103
Telephone: 336-659-9450
Fax: 336-659-4570
Email: Spaughlaw@aol.com
URL: http://www.rspaughlaw.com

Family Law, Child Support, Child Custody, Separation, Separation Agreements, Divorce, Visitation Rights, Domestic Violence, Marital Property, Equitable Distribution, Pre-Marital Agreements, Spousal Support, Workers Compensation, On the Job Injuries, Personal Injury, Automobile Accidents, Traffic Violations, Trusts and Estates, Wills and Probate.

ROBERT G. SPAUGH, born Winston-Salem, North Carolina, June 24, 1962; admitted to bar, 1990, North Carolina and U.S. District Court, Middle District of North Carolina. *Education:* Cambridge University; Davidson College (A.B., 1984); Wake Forest University (J.D., 1990). Phi Delta Phi. *Member:* Forsyth County, North Carolina and American (Member, Family Law Section) Bar Associations; North Carolina State Bar; Forsyth County Young Lawyers Association (Past President); 21st Judicial District Bar (President, 2005-2006); North Carolina Academy of Trial Lawyers; The Association of Trial Lawyers of America.

HERMAN L. STEPHENS

200 WEST FIRST STREET
WINSTON-SALEM, NORTH CAROLINA 27101
Telephone: 336-722-7126
Fax: 336-631-8702
Email: lawstephens@bellsouth.net
URL: http://www.lawstephens.com

Civil Litigation in all State and Federal Courts, Unfair Business Practice, Business Lawsuits, Workers Compensation, Personal Injury, Automobile Accidents, Consumer Protection, Lemon Law, Consumer Fraud.

FIRM PROFILE: Mr. Stephens has been a trial attorney in Winston-Salem, North Carolina since 1970.

HERMAN L. STEPHENS, born Winston-Salem, North Carolina, August 21, 1945; admitted to bar, 1970, North Carolina; 1971, U.S. District Court, Middle District of North Carolina; 1972, U.S. Court of Appeals, Fourth Circuit. *Education:* University of North Carolina (A.B., 1967; J.D., 1970). *Member:* Forsyth County and North Carolina (Member: Appellate Rules Study Committee, 1992-1996; Civil Litigation Committee, 1978; Employment and Labor Law Section; Council, 1986-1990) Bar Associations; North Carolina State Bar; North Carolina Academy of Trial Lawyers.

A List of Clients furnished upon request.

STROUD AND PANETTI, P.C.

Established in 1998
102 WEST THIRD STREET, SUITE 650
WINSTON-SALEM, NORTH CAROLINA 27101
Telephone: 336-724-2600
Telecopier: 336-724-6950
URL: http://www.stroudandpanetti.com

Business Law, Business Litigation, Planning, Buying and Selling of Businesses, Limited Liability Company Law, Family Law, Adoptions, Child Custody, Child Support, Divorce, Domestic Violence, Premarital Agreements, Visitation Rights, Criminal Law, Driving While Intoxicated, (DWI), Drug Crimes, Felonies, Misdemeanors, Traffic Violations, Personal Injury, Automobile Accidents, Slip and Fall, Wrongful Death, Real Estate, Mortgages, Bankruptcy, Elder Law.

FIRM PROFILE: Stroud and Panetti, P.C. was formed in 1998 by Keith Stroud and Eleanor Panetti after having spent years in other law practices. Their goal was to create a firm where each attorney gives each client practical, resourceful and valuable advice to help guide them through their personal and professional lives. Our mission is to provide services that help clients through the good time and the bad, during the planning, performance and inevitable mishaps that happen during business and life.

J. KEITH STROUD, born Statesville, North Carolina, February 12, 1955; admitted to bar, 1981, North Carolina. *Education:* University of North Carolina (B.A., 1977); Wake Forest University (J.D., 1981). Phi Alpha Delta. Recipient, North Carolina Academy of Trial Lawyers Award. *Member:* Forsyth County Bar Association; North Carolina State Bar (Member, Sections on: Business Law and Family Law); Forsyth County Criminal Defense Trial Lawyers Association; North Carolina Academy of Trial Lawyers. ***REPORTED CASES:*** State v. Aguallo, 318 NC 590 (1986). ***PRACTICE AREAS:*** Business Law; Family Law; Criminal Law. ***Email:*** keithstroud@bellsouth.net

ELEANOR PANETTI, born Charlotte, North Carolina, 1964; admitted to bar, 1989, North Carolina. *Education:* University of North Carolina, Chapel Hill (B.A., 1986; J.D., 1989). *Member:* Forsyth County Bar Association; North Carolina State Bar (Member, Sections on: Litigation; Family Law); Forsyth County Criminal Defense Trial Lawyers Association. ***REPORTED CASES:*** Burgess v. JimWalter Home, Inc. et al, 161 NC App. 488 (2003), 58S SE2d 575. ***PRACTICE AREAS:*** Business Law; Family Law; Criminal Law. ***Email:*** eleanorpanetti@bellsouth.net

APPROVED ATTORNEYS FOR: Investors Title Insurance Company; Lawyers Title Insurance Corp.; Wachovia Bank and Trust Co., N.A.; Piedmont Federal Savings and Loan Association; First American Title Insurance Company; Chicago Title Insurance Company; Bankers Mortgage Company; Branch Banking and Trust Company; Colonial Mortgage Company; Wachovia Mortgage Co.
REPRESENTATIVE CLIENTS: Provided Upon Request.
REFERENCE: Branch Banking and Trust Company.

SURRATT & THOMPSON, PLLC

Established in 1932
WACHOVIA CENTER
100 N. MAIN STREET, SUITE 1500
WINSTON-SALEM, NORTH CAROLINA 27101
Telephone: 336-725-8323
Facsimile: 336-722-5218
Email: firm@sandtpllc.com

General Civil Practice in all State and Federal Courts. Corporate Law, Business Law, Collections, Wills, Probate, Trusts and Estates, Taxation, Real Estate, Commercial Law, Bankruptcy, Family Law and Litigation.

FIRM PROFILE: John R. Surratt, P.A. was founded in 1932 by Benet Polikof and Dallace McLennan as Polikof and McLennan. In 1951 John R. Surratt joined the firm and the name was subsequently changed to McLennan & Surratt, and thereafter to its present name. Since its origin, the firm has continuously conducted a general civil practice with concentrations in corporate and commercial law, estate planning and administration, real estate and family law. The firm is proud of its ability to deliver quality legal services, utilizing state of the art systems,

(This Listing Continued)

SURRATT & THOMPSON, PLLC, Winston-Salem—Continued

while maintaining a close and personal relationship with clients. The firm encourages continuing professional development and all attorneys participate in continuing legal education seminars, professional associations and civic affairs.

JOHN R. SURRATT, born Winston-Salem, North Carolina, August 7, 1928; admitted to bar, 1951, North Carolina. *Education:* University of North Carolina (B.S., 1948); Duke University (J.D., 1951). Phi Delta Phi. Associate Judge, Municipal Court, Winston-Salem, North Carolina, 1958-1961. Mayor, City of Winston-Salem, 1961-1963. *Member:* Forsyth County (President, 1983-1984), North Carolina and American Bar Associations; The North Carolina State Bar. ***PRACTICE AREAS:*** Corporate Law; Commercial Law; Trusts and Estates; Wills; Probate; Real Estate; Property Law; Environmental Law; Litigation. ***Email:*** jsurratt@sandtpllc.com

BRYAN C. THOMPSON, born Winston-Salem, North Carolina, September 6, 1975; admitted to bar, 1999, North Carolina. *Education:* Appalachian State University (B.S., 1995); Campbell University (J.D., cum laude, 1999). ***PRACTICE AREAS:*** Corporate Law; Collections; Taxation; Family Law; Consumer; Wills; Trusts and Estates; Real Estate; Property; Commercial Real Estate. ***Email:*** bthompson@sandtpllc.com

REPRESENTATIVE CLIENTS: Names furnished upon request.
APPROVED ATTORNEYS FOR: Commonwealth Land Title Insurance Company; Lawyers Title Insurance Company; Most other title insurance companies insuring real estate titles in the area of the firm's practice.
REFERENCES: Bank of America; Winston-Salem, N.C.

TASH & KURTZ, PLLC

3305 HEALY DRIVE
WINSTON-SALEM, NORTH CAROLINA 27103
Telephone: 336-768-1515
Fax: 336-768-1550
URL: http://www.lawyers.com/tashkurft

Family Law, Divorce, Equitable Distribution, Child Custody, Child Support, Alimony, Domestic Violence, Visitation Rights, Appellate Practice, Mediation, Estate Planning.

GARY B. TASH, born 1946; admitted to bar, 1971, North Carolina. *Education:* University of Virginia (B.A., 1968); Wake Forest University (J.D., 1971). Phi Alpha Delta. Certified Mediator and Arbitrator. Listed in, The Best Lawyers in America (Family Law), Woodward/White, Inc., 1995—. Adjunct Professor, Wake Forest University School of Law, 1987-1997. State District Court Judge, 21st Judicial District, Forsyth County, North Carolina, 1976-1983. *Member:* Forsyth County and North Carolina Bar Associations; North Carolina State Bar. Fellow, American Academy of Matrimonial Lawyers. (Board Certified Specialist in Family Law, North Carolina State Board of Legal Specialization). ***PRACTICE AREAS:*** Family Law; Equitable Distribution; Child Custody; Child Support; Alimony; Mediation; Arbitration. ***Email:*** gtash@tashkurtzlaw.com

JON BRENNER KURTZ, born Winston-Salem, North Carolina, August 23, 1968; admitted to bar, 1994, North Carolina. *Education:* University of Alabama (B.A., magna cum laude, 1991) Phi Beta Kappa; University of North Carolina (J.D., 1994). Past-Chair, Ethics and Grievance Committee, Twenty First Judicial District, 2002-2003. Chair, Alimony Legislative Committee, North Carolina Bar Association, Family Law Council, 2003—. *Member:* Forsyth County and North Carolina Bar Associations; North Carolina State Bar. (Board Certified Specialist in Family Law, North Carolina State Board of Legal Specialization). ***PRACTICE AREAS:*** Family Law; Equitable Distribution; Child Custody; Child Support; Alimony; Appellate Practice. ***Email:*** jkurtz@tashkurtzlaw.com

---

AMANDA H. CREAMER, born Richmond, Virginia, July 31, 1970; admitted to bar, 1997, North Carolina. *Education:* James Madison University (B.A., cum laude, 1992); Wake Forest University (J.D., 1997). *Member:* Forsyth County and North Carolina (Member, Family Law Section) Bar Associations. ***PRACTICE AREAS:*** Family Law; Equitable Distribution; Child Support; Child Custody; Alimony; Appellate Practice; Estate Planning. ***Email:*** acreamer@tashkurtzlaw.com

TEETER LAW FIRM

315 N. SPRUCE STREET, SUITE 275
WINSTON-SALEM, NORTH CAROLINA 27101
Telephone: 336-725-8376
Fax: 336-722-5680
URL: http://www.teeterlawfirm.com

Appellate Practice, Criminal Law, Civil Litigation, Domestic Relations, Personal Injury, Trusts and Estates and Wills.

MEMBERS OF FIRM

CARROLL L. TEETER, born Oakboro, North Carolina, July 15, 1933; admitted to bar, 1960, North Carolina. *Education:* Wake Forest University (B.A., 1955; J.D., 1959). *Member:* Forsyth County and North Carolina Bar Associations; North Carolina State Bar; 21st Judicial Bar Association. ***PRACTICE AREAS:*** Criminal Law; Domestic Relations; Trusts and Estates; Wills.

STUART L. TEETER, born Winston-Salem, North Carolina, January 26, 1963; admitted to bar, 1989, North Carolina. *Education:* East Carolina University (B.A., History, 1985); Wake Forest University (J.D., 1989). *Member:* North Carolina State Bar. ***PRACTICE AREAS:*** Criminal Law; Domestic Relations; Personal Injury; General Practice. ***Email:*** steeter@triad.rr.com

KELLY SCOTT LEE, born Monroe, Michigan, February 13, 1962; admitted to bar, 1998, North Carolina. *Education:* California State University, Los Angeles (B.A., 1996); Wake Forest University (J.D., 1998). *Member:* North Carolina Bar Association; North Carolina State Bar. ***PRACTICE AREAS:*** Criminal Law; Civil Litigation; Domestic Relations; Appellate Practice.

TEMPLE LAW FIRM, PLLC

WINSTON-SALEM, NORTH CAROLINA

(See Raleigh)

Pharmaceutical and Defective Medical Devices (Fen-hen, Vioxx, Celebrex & Bextra), Environmental and Toxic Torts, Personal Injury, Products Liability, Wrongful Death, Civil Litigation.

TUGGLE DUGGINS & MESCHAN, P.A.

WINSTON-SALEM, NORTH CAROLINA

(See Greensboro)

General Civil Practice. Corporation, Tax, Insurance, Banking, Pension and Profit Sharing, Bankruptcy and Creditors' Rights, Trust and Estate, Construction and Real Estate Law. Trials and Appeals in all State and Federal Courts.

JAMES E. VAUGHAN, ATTORNEY AT LAW, P.C.

206 NORTH SPRUCE STREET, SUITE 2A
WINSTON-SALEM, NORTH CAROLINA 27101
Telephone: 336-725-7772
Telecopier: 336-725-7737
Email: jvaughanlaw@earthlink.net
URL: http://www.lawyers.com/jvaughan

Creditors Rights, Commercial Bankruptcy, Consumer Bankruptcy, Business Litigation, Commercial Litigation, Collections.

JAMES E. VAUGHAN, born Detroit, Michigan, May 28, 1959; admitted to bar, 1984, North Carolina; U.S. District Court, Middle, Western and Eastern Districts of North Carolina. *Education:* Bowling Green State University (B.S., 1981); Ohio Northern University (J.D., with distinction, 1984). Phi Kappa Phi. Willis Scholar. Formerly with Bankruptcy & Creditors' Rights Practice Group, Womble Carlyle Sandridge & Rice, PLLC, 1984-1999. *Member:* Forsyth County and North Carolina (Member: Bankruptcy Law Section) Bar Associations; North Carolina State Bar.

VAUGHN PERKINSON EHLINGER MOXLEY & STOGNER

4505 COUNTRY CLUB ROAD
P.O. BOX 25715
WINSTON-SALEM, NORTH CAROLINA 27114
Telephone: 336-794-6000
Fax: 336-760-1625

Probate, Trusts and Estates, Taxation, Estate Planning, Wills.

MEMBERS OF THE FIRM

ROBERT C. VAUGHN, JR., admitted to bar, 1955, North Carolina. *Education:* University of North Carolina (B.S., 1953; J.D., 1955). Order of the Coif; Phi Beta Kappa; Beta Gamma Sigma. Listed in Who's Who in American Law. Member of Board of Editors and Business Manager, North Carolina Law Review, 1954-1955. Adjunct Lecturer, Estate Planning, University of North Carolina Law School, 1983. Member, Board of Advisors, UNC Tax Institute, 1982-1996. Former Chairman, Board of Directors, Winston-Salem Foundation, 2003. Former Chairman, Board of Directors, Forsyth Medical Center Foundation. Past President, Winston-Salem Estate Planning Council. Listed in Best Lawyers in America, Trusts and Estates, 1983— and Taxation, 1987—. *Member:* Forsyth County (President, 1981-1982), North Carolina (Chairman, Probate and Fiduciary Law Section, 1979-1980; Member, Board of Governors, 1981-1984; President, 1985-1986) and American Bar Associations. Fellow: American College of Trusts and Estates Counsel (North Carolina State Chairman, 1990-1995); American Bar Foundation; American College of Tax Counsel. ***PRACTICE AREAS:*** Probate; Trusts and Estates; Taxation. ***Email:*** bob.vaughn@vpems.com

JOHN R. PERKINSON, JR., admitted to bar, 1981, North Carolina. *Education:* Wake Forest University (B.A., 1971; J.D., 1981). Certified Public Accountant, North Carolina, 1981. *Member:* North Carolina Bar Association; American Institute of Certified Public Accountants; North Carolina Association of Certified Public Accountants. ***PRACTICE AREAS:*** Probate; Trusts and Estates; Taxation. ***Email:*** jay.perkinson@vpems.com

TIMOTHY J. EHLINGER, admitted to bar, 1985, North Carolina and New York; 1986, U.S. Tax Court. *Education:* State University of New York at Albany (B.S. in Accounting, cum laude, 1981); University of North Carolina (J.D., cum laude, 1984). Member, Forsyth Medical Center Foundation Planned Giving Committee. Immediate Past President, Winston-Salem Estate Planning Council. *Member:* Forsyth County and North Carolina (Member, Estate Planning and Fiduciary Law Legislative Committee, 1997— Tax Section, Business Law Sections) Bar Associations; North Carolina Citizens for Business and Industry (Member, Tax and Fiscal Policy Committee, 1996—). ***PRACTICE AREAS:*** Taxation; Probate; Trusts and Estates. ***Email:*** tim.ehlinger@vpems.com

MARCUS L. MOXLEY, admitted to bar, 1989, North Carolina. *Education:* University of North Carolina (B.S., 1984; J.D., with honors, 1989). Phi Beta Kappa; Order of the Coif. Member, North Carolina Law Review, 1987-1988. Certified Public Accountant, North Carolina, 1992. *Member:* Forsyth County and North Carolina (Tax and Fiduciary Law Sec-

(This Listing Continued)

tions) Bar Associations. (Board Certified Specialist in Estate Planning and Probate Law, North Carolina State Board of Legal Specialization). ***PRACTICE AREAS:*** Taxation; Trusts and Estates; Probate. ***Email:*** marc.moxley@vpems.com

KIMBERLY H. STOGNER, admitted to bar, 1994, North Carolina. *Education:* Wake Forest University (B.A., 1986; J.D., cum laude, 1994). Member, Order of Barristers. Member, Moot Court Board, 1992-1994. Editor, Wake Forest Law Review, 1993-1994. *Member:* Forsyth County and North Carolina (Council Member, Fiduciary Law Section; Trustee, Lisatat Benefit Trust; Chair, Wake Forest Planned Giving Advisory Council; Member, Winston Society Estate Planning Council) Bar Associations. ***PRACTICE AREAS:*** Probate; Trusts and Estates; Taxation. ***Email:*** kim.stogner@vpems.com

WALL LAW FIRM, P.C.

1076 WEST FOURTH STREET, SUITE 100
WINSTON-SALEM, NORTH CAROLINA 27101
Telephone: 336-722-2900
Fax: 336-722-2906
URL: http://www.walllawoffice.com
Email: jwall@wallfirm.com
URL: http://www.wallfirm.com

Health Care, Corporate Law, Commercial Transactions, Bankruptcy, Mediation.

JAMES DAVID WALL, born Radford, Virginia, 1963; admitted to bar, 1989, Georgia; 1991, North Carolina. *Education:* College of William & Mary (B.B.A., 1986); University of Virginia (J.D., 1989). Beta Gamma Sigma. Certified Mediator. *Member:* Forsyth County and North Carolina (Bankruptcy Section Council, 1995-1998; Treasurer, 1996-1997; Young Lawyers Division, Silent Partners Program, Chair, 1995-1997, Executive Council, 1995-1997) and Georgia Bar Associations; American Health Lawyers Association. ***PRACTICE AREAS:*** Health Care; Corporate; Commercial Transactions; Bankruptcy; Mediation.

WEIDEMANN LAW FIRM, P.C.

102 WEST 3RD STREET, SUITE 485
WINSTON-SALEM, NORTH CAROLINA 27101
Telephone: 336-725-8557
Fax: 336-725-8571
URL: http://triadlawyer.com

Criminal Law, Driving While Intoxicated (DWI), Drug Crimes, Felonies, Juvenile Law, Misdemeanors, Parole and Probation, Traffic Violations, Family Law, Adoptions, Child Custody, Child Support, Divorce, Premarital Agreements, Spousal Support, Visitation Rights, Collections, Estate Planning, Wills and Probate.

BRADLEY J. WEIDEMANN, born 1972; admitted to bar, 1996, North Carolina. *Education:* Alma College (B.A., 1993); Wake Forest University (J.D., 1996). *Member:* Forsyth County and North Carolina Bar Association; North Carolina State Bar; Forsyth County Criminal Defense Attorneys.

WELLS, JENKINS, LUCAS & JENKINS PLLC

155 SUNNYNOLL COURT, SUITE 200
WINSTON-SALEM, NORTH CAROLINA 27106
Telephone: 336-725-2900
Fax: 336-724-1226
Email: youlaw.com
URL: http://www.wellsjenkins.com

Business Transactions, Mergers and Acquisitions, Nursing Home Litigation, Elder Law, Medicaid Planning, Business Transactions, Corporate Law, Limited Liability Company Law, Franchise Law, Commercial, Construction and Civil Litigation, Residential Real Estate, Commercial Real Estate, Personal Injury, Workers Compensation, Wills, Trusts, Estates, Bankruptcy, Traffic, Family Law, Equitable Distribution, Alimony, Child Support.

FIRM PROFILE: Wells, Jenkins, Lucas & Jenkins PLLC is a full service law firm with a staff of twenty four (24), including nine (10) attorneys.

R. MICHAEL WELLS, born Charleston, West Virginia, September 16, 1949; admitted to bar, 1974, North Carolina and U.S. District Court, Eastern District of North Carolina; 1975, West Virginia and U.S. District Court, Southern District of West Virginia; 1977, U.S. District Court, Middle District of North Carolina; 1978, U.S. Court of Appeals, Fourth Circuit; 1980, U.S. Supreme Court. *Education:* University of Virginia (B.A., 1971); Wake Forest University (J.D., 1974). Law Clerk, Supreme Court of North Carolina, 1974-1975. Certified Superior Court Domestic and Workers' Compensation Mediator. Member, Board of Directors, Greater Winston-Salem Chamber of Commerce and Chairman, 2004. Member, Board of Trustees: North Carolina Hospital, 2005; Forsyth Technical Community College, 1994. *Member:* North Carolina Bar Association (Member, Estate Planning and Fiduciary Law Section; Member, Communications Committee; Chairman, 2004-2005); National Association of Elder Law Attorneys; Estate Planning Council of Winston-Salem. ***PRACTICE AREAS:*** Estate Planning; Elder Law; Medicaid Planning. ***Email:*** mikew@wellsjenkins.com

GORDON W. JENKINS, born Winston-Salem, North Carolina, November 20, 1945; admitted to bar, 1974, North Carolina and U.S. District Court, Middle District of North Carolina. *Education:* Duke University (B.A., 1968); University of North Carolina at Chapel Hill (J.D., 1973). *Member:* Forsyth County (President; Secretary; Treasurer; Program Chairman; Ethics Committee) and North Carolina (Member: Development Committee; Estate Planning, Fiduciary Law and Elder Law Sections; Member, Elder Law Council) Bar Associations; Estate Planning Council of Winston-Salem (President, 1997-1998); National Association of Elder Law Attorneys; Forsyth Technical College Planned Giving Advisory Board. [1st Lt., USAR, Military Intelligence, 1969-1972]. (Board Certified Specialist in

(This Listing Continued)

Estate Planning and Probate Law, North Carolina State Board of Legal Specialization). ***PRACTICE AREAS:*** Estate Planning; Estate Administration; Business Law; Elder Law; Medicaid Planning. ***Email:*** gordonj@wellsjenkins.com

JOHN L. BARBER, born Charlotte, North Carolina, September 14, 1946; admitted to bar, 1972, North Carolina and U.S. District Court, Middle District of North Carolina. *Education:* University of North Carolina at Chapel Hill (B.A., 1968); Wake Forest University (J.D., cum laude, 1972). Phi Eta Sigma. Mary Reynolds Babcock Scholar. Editor, Wake Forest Law Review, 1971-1972. General Counsel, Krispy Kreme Doughnut Corporation, Winston-Salem, North Carolina, 1993-1995. *Member:* North Carolina (Member, Business Law and Intellectual Property Law Sections) and American (Member, Forum on Franchising) Bar Associations. ***PRACTICE AREAS:*** Business Transactions; Corporate Law; Limited Liability Company Law; Mergers and Acquisitions; Franchise Law. ***Email:*** johnb@wellsjenkins.com

CLYDE R. CASH, born Shelby, North Carolina, December 17, 1958; admitted to bar, 1985, North Carolina. *Education:* Wake Forest University (B.A., 1981; J.D., 1984). Assistant District Attorney, 22nd Judicial District, 1987-1991. *Member:* Forsyth County and North Carolina Bar Associations; North Carolina State Bar; North Carolina Academy of Trial Lawyers. ***PRACTICE AREAS:*** Civil Litigation; Criminal Law; Traffic Violations; Real Estate; Bankruptcy. ***Email:*** clydec@wellsjenkins.com

ELLIS B. DREW, III, born Anderson, South Carolina, March 1, 1959; admitted to bar, 1984, South Carolina; 1985, North Carolina. *Education:* Wake Forest University (B.A., cum laude, 1981); Washington & Lee University (J.D., 1984). Law Clerk, Honorable G. Ross Anderson, Jr., U.S. District Court, District of South Carolina. *Member:* North Carolina and South Carolina State Bars; Forsyth County Bar Association; North Carolina Association of Trial Lawyers. ***PRACTICE AREAS:*** Commercial Litigation; Personal Injury; Construction Litigation. ***Email:*** bod@wellsjenkins.com

PHILIP E. SEARCY, born Johnson City, Tennessee, October 20, 1955; admitted to bar, 1981, North Carolina. *Education:* University of North Carolina at Chapel Hill (B.S., 1978); Wake Forest University School of Law (J.D., 1981). Assistant District Attorney, 22nd Judicial District, 1981-1983. *Member:* Forsyth County and North Carolina Bar Associations; North Carolina State Bar (Member, Real Property Section). (Board Certified Specialist in Real Property Law, Residential, Business, Commercial and Industrial Transactions, North Carolina State Board of Legal Specialization). ***PRACTICE AREAS:*** Residential Real Estate; Commercial Real Estate; Foreclosure; Corporate Law; Business Law. ***Email:*** phils@wellsjenkins.com

SUSAN H. GRAY, born Asheville, North Carolina, June 9, 1953; admitted to bar, 1978, North Carolina and U.S. District Court, Eastern District of North Carolina; 1983, U.S. District Court, Middle District of North Carolina. *Education:* Vanderbilt University (B.A., 1975); University of Tennessee at Knoxville (J.D., 1977). Clerk for Judge J. Phil Carlton, North Carolina Court of Appeals, 1979. *Member:* Forsyth County and North Carolina (Member, Family Law Section) Bar Associations; North Carolina State Bar. (Board Certified Specialist in Family Law, North Carolina State Board of Legal Specialization). ***PRACTICE AREAS:*** Family Law; Alimony; Equitable Distribution; Child Support; Child Custody. ***Email:*** susang@wellsjenkins.com

T. LAWSON NEWTON, born Baltimore, Maryland, December 10, 1954; admitted to bar, 1981, North Carolina. *Education:* Wake Forest University (B.S., 1976; J.D., 1981). Certified Superior Court Mediator. *Member:* North Carolina State Bar; North Carolina Bar Association (Member, Real Property Section). ***PRACTICE AREAS:*** Real Estate; Residential Real Estate; Commercial Real Estate; Business Law; Wills; Business Litigation; Real Estate Litigation. ***Email:*** lawsonn@wellsjenkins.com

ROBERT W. PORTER, born Galax, Virginia, January 31, 1940; admitted to bar, 1966, Virginia; 1971, North Carolina; 1975, U.S. District Court, Middle District of North Carolina. *Education:* Davidson College (B.A., 1962); Wake Forest University (LL.B., 1965). Phi Alpha Delta. *Member:* Forsyth County, Virginia, North Carolina (Member, Real Estate Section, 1980-2005) and American Bar Associations; North Carolina State Bar; North Carolina Land Title Association. [Capt., U.S. Army Adjutant General Corps, 1966-1969]. ***PRACTICE AREAS:*** Real Estate. ***Email:*** bobp@wellsjenkins.com

R. MICHAEL WELLS, JR., admitted to bar, 2005, North Carolina. *Education:* University of Virginia (B.A., 2001); Wake Forest University (J.D., 2004). *Member:* North Carolina Bar Association; North Carolina Academy of Trial Lawyers. ***PRACTICE AREAS:*** Bankruptcy Chapter 7; Bankruptcy Chapter 13; Medical Malpractice; Personal Injury; Real Estate; Social Security Disability; Workers Compensation.

MITRA SANAI, born 1976; admitted to bar, 2001, North Carolina. *Education:* University of California, Berkeley (B.A., 1997); Wake Forest University (J.D., 2001). *Member:* North Carolina State Bar (Member and Secretary of Elder Law Section); North Carolina Academy of Trial Lawyers; National Academy of Elder Law Attorneys. ***PRACTICE AREAS:*** Elder Law; Medicaid Planning; Estate Planning. ***Email:*** mitras@wellsjenkins.com

OF COUNSEL

ANN G. SUGG, born Trenton, New Jersey, November 30, 1955; admitted to bar, 1980, New Jersey, Pennsylvania; 1982, District of Columbia and U.S. Court of Appeals, Fourth Circuit; 1983, North Carolina. *Education:* Cornell University (B.S., 1977); Dickinson School of Law (J.D., 1980). Articles Editor, The Dickinson Law Review, 1979-1980. Staff Clerk, U.S. Court of Appeals, Fourth Circuit, 1980-1982. *Member:* Forsyth County, New Jersey State, Pennsylvania, North Carolina and American Bar Associations; The District of Columbia Bar. ***PRACTICE AREAS:*** Personal Injury. ***Email:*** anns@wellsjenkins.com

F. GAITHER JENKINS (1910-2001)

PHILIP E. LUCAS (Retired)

WHITE AND CRUMPLER

301 N. MAIN STREET, SUITE 1100
WINSTON-SALEM, NORTH CAROLINA 27101
Telephone: 336-725-1304
Fax: 336-761-8845
URL: http://www.whiteandcrumpler.com

General Civil and Criminal Practice. Trials in State and Federal Courts. Domestic Relations, Family Law, Equitable Distribution, Divorce, Complex Civil Law, Complex Business Law, Medical Malpractice, Personal Injury, White Collar Criminal Defense, Appellate Practice.

FIRM PROFILE: The firm has been representing individuals and businesses for nearly half a century in all courts throughout North Carolina and Federal Courts along the eastern seaboard. Our attorneys have been associated by lawyers in other states in complex civil and criminal litigation. We are actively involved in every stage of the legal process from negotiating settlements to mediation and arbitration to litigating in the courtroom and all the way to the North Carolina Court of Appeals and Supreme Court.

MEMBERS OF FIRM

JAMES G. WHITE (1924-1974)

FRANK M. ARMSTRONG (1900-1979)

CLYDE C. RANDOLPH, JR. (1928-1995)

BARBARA C. WESTMORELAND (1929-2000)

FRED G. CRUMPLER, JR., born Danville, Virginia, January 8, 1931; admitted to bar, 1957, North Carolina; 1958, U.S. District Court, Middle District of North Carolina; 1974, U.S. Supreme Court. *Education:* Appalachian State University; Guilford College (B.A.); Wake Forest University (J.D., 1957). Phi Delta Phi. Listed in the Best Lawyers in America, Criminal, Family Law Sections. Assistant Director, Institute of Government, University of North Carolina, 1957-1958. *Member:* Forsyth County, North Carolina and American Bar Associations; North Carolina State Bar; The Association of Trial Lawyers of America; Lawyer-Pilot Bar Association; North Carolina Defense Lawyers Association; North Carolina Academy of Trial Lawyers; American College of Trial Lawyers; American Board of Trial Advocates. [USAF, 1950-1952]. (Board Certified Specialist in Family Law, North Carolina State Board of Legal Specialization). ***PRACTICE AREAS:*** Federal and State Civil and Criminal Law; Personal Injury Law; Domestic Relations Law.

G. EDGAR PARKER, born Raleigh, North Carolina, November 2, 1946; admitted to bar, 1971, North Carolina; 1972, U.S. District Court, Middle District of North Carolina; U.S. Supreme Court. *Education:* Wake Forest University (B.A., 1968; J.D., 1971). Member, Wake Forest University Intramural Law Review. Listed in The Best Lawyers of America, Family Law Section. *Member:* Forsyth County, North Carolina and American Bar Associations; North Carolina State Bar; North Carolina Academy of Trial Lawyers (Patron Member); The Association of Trial Lawyers of America. [Capt., USA, 1972]. (Board Certified Specialist in Family Law). ***PRACTICE AREAS:*** Domestic Relations; Family Law; Equitable Distribution; Divorce; General Civil Litigation.

DAVID B. FREEDMAN, born Philadelphia, Pennsylvania, December 1, 1956; admitted to bar, 1982, North Carolina; U.S. Court of Appeals, Fourth Circuit; U.S. District Court, Eastern, Western and Middle Districts of North Carolina. *Education:* University of North Carolina at Chapel Hill (B.A., 1979; J.D., 1982). Listed in The Best Lawyers of America, Criminal Law Section. Adjunct Professor, Wake Forest University, School of Law. *Member:* Forsyth County and North Carolina Bar Associations; North Carolina State Bar; North Carolina Academy of Trial Lawyers. (Board Certified Specialist in Federal and State Criminal Law). ***PRACTICE AREAS:*** Federal and State Criminal Law; Personal Injury Law.

DUDLEY A. WITT, born Napoleon, Ohio, March 11, 1958; admitted to bar, 1983, North Carolina; U.S. District Court, Eastern and Middle Districts of North Carolina. *Education:* Wake Forest University (B.A., 1980; J.D., 1983). Phi Alpha Theta. *Member:* Forsyth County and North Carolina Bar Associations; North Carolina State Bar; North Carolina Academy of Trial Lawyers. ***PRACTICE AREAS:*** Complex Civil Law; Business Litigation; Personal Injury Law; Domestic Relations Law.

LAURIE SCHLOSSBERG KELLY, born Kitchener, Ontario, Canada, September 24, 1966; admitted to bar, 1995, North Carolina and U.S. District Court, Eastern and Middle Districts of North Carolina. *Education:* Whitworth College (B.A., 1988); Seattle University (J.D., cum laude, 1995). *Member:* Forsyth County and North Carolina Bar Associations; Forsyth County Criminal Defense Attorneys; North Carolina Academy of Trial Lawyers. ***PRACTICE AREAS:*** Family Law; Criminal Law.

ASSOCIATE

JONES P. BYRD JR., born Asheville, North Carolina, November 12, 1976; admitted to bar, 2002, North Carolina and U.S. District Court, Middle District of North Carolina. *Education:* Wake Forest University (B.A., cum laude, 1999; J.D., 2002). *Member:* Forsyth County and North Carolina Bar Associations. ***PRACTICE AREAS:*** Criminal Law; Personal Injury; Family Law; Traffic Violations. ***Email:*** jones@whiteandcrumpler.com

OF COUNSEL

FRED S. HUTCHINS, JR., born Winston-Salem, North Carolina, August 31, 1932; admitted to bar, 1959, North Carolina. *Education:* Episcopal High School, Alexandria, Virginia; University of North Carolina (B.S., 1954); Wake Forest College (LL.B., cum laude, 1959). Phi Delta Phi. Member, North Carolina House of Representatives, 1972-1976. *Member:* Forsyth County and North Carolina Bar Association; North Carolina State Bar; North Carolina Association of Defense Attorneys. ***PRACTICE AREAS:*** Family Law; Estates; Civil Litigation.

WILSON & ISEMAN, L.L.P.

Established in 1992
110 OAKWOOD DRIVE, SUITE 400
WINSTON-SALEM, NORTH CAROLINA 27103
Telephone: 336-631-8866
Telefax: 336-631-9770
URL: http://www.wilsonandiseman.com

Charlotte Office: 435 East Morehead Street, 28202. Telephone: 704-331-9585. Fax: 704-331-0773.

General Civil Practice, including Civil Trial and Appellate Work in all State and Federal Courts, Administrative, Aviation, Commercial, Construction, Corporate, Employee Benefits and Executive Compensation, Employment, Criminal, Federal, State and Local Taxation, Insurance Defense, Personal Injury, Probate, Wills, Trusts and Estate Planning, Products Liability and Negligence Law, Professional Malpractice and Real Estate.

FIRM PROFILE: Wilson & Iseman was established in April 1992 by four attorneys formerly with a large local law firm. G. Gray Wilson has been practicing for over twenty-nine years in the area of insurance defense litigation, with concentration in the specialties of professional malpractice and product liability defense. His partner, James M. Iseman, Jr., has been in practice for over twenty-eight years and is a business and tax specialist who also practices in the areas of probate and estate work and corporate planning. Tamura D. Coffey joined the firm in 1994 and became a partner in January 2000. S. Ranchor Harris, III, a partner, joined the firm in 1998 and became a partner in January 2001. Linda L. Helms, a partner, joined the firm in 1999 and became a partner in January 2002. Kevin B. Cartledge, joined the firm in 1998 and became a partner in 2004. Associate Maria C. Papoulias joined the firm in 2001, associate J. Chad Bomar joined the firm in 2002, associate David M. Fothergill joined the firm in 2003 and associate Edward T. Shipley III joined the firm in 2004.

MEMBERS OF FIRM

G. GRAY WILSON, born Louisville, Kentucky, April 1, 1951; admitted to bar, 1976, North Carolina. *Education:* Davidson College (B.A., 1973); Duke University (J.D., 1976). Phi Beta Kappa. Listed, Best Lawyers in America. Author: "North Carolina Civil Procedure." *Member:* Forsyth County and North Carolina Bar Associations (President-Elect, 2003-2004; President, 2004-2005); North Carolina Association of Defense Attorneys; American College of Trial Lawyers; American Board of Trial Advocates; American Bar Association. Fellow, American College of Trial Lawyers. ***PRACTICE AREAS:*** Professional Malpractice; Insurance Litigation; Commercial Litigation; Tax Litigation. ***Email:*** gwilson@wilsonandiseman.com

JAMES M. ISEMAN, JR., born Florence, South Carolina, December 5, 1951; admitted to bar, 1977, North Carolina. *Education:* Duke University (A.B., summa cum laude, 1974); University of North Carolina (J.D., with honors, 1977). Phi Beta Kappa; Order of the Coif. Member, Board of Editors, North Carolina Law Review, 1975-1976. Adjunct Professor, Taxation, Babcock School of Management, Winston-Salem, North Carolina. *Member:* Forsyth County and North Carolina Bar Associations. ***PRACTICE AREAS:*** Corporate Law; Commercial law; Tax Law; Probate; Wills; Trusts and Estates. ***Email:*** jiseman@wilsonandiseman.com

TAMURA D. COFFEY, born Lenoir, North Carolina, March 22, 1968; admitted to bar, 1993, North Carolina. *Education:* Wake Forest University (B.A. magna cum laude, 1990; J.D. cum laude, 1993). Phi Beta Kappa. Member, Moot Court Board. Articles Editor, Wake Forest Law Review. Law Clerk, U.S. District Judge William L. Osteen, Sr., Middle District of North Carolina. Adjunct Professor, Wake Forest University School of Law. *Member:* Forsyth County and North Carolina (Member, Litigation Counsel) Bar Associations; North Carolina Association of Defense Attorneys. ***PRACTICE AREAS:*** Professional Malpractice; Commercial Litigation; Insurance Litigation. ***Email:*** tcoffey@wilsonandiseman.com

S. RANCHOR HARRIS, III, born Gainesville, Florida, August 21, 1968; admitted to bar, 1994, North Carolina and U.S. District Court, Middle, Western and Eastern Districts of North Carolina and U.S. Court of Appeals, Fourth Circuit. *Education:* University of North Carolina at Chapel Hill (B.A., 1990); Whittier College School of Law (J.D., cum laude, 1994). Recipient, American Jurisprudence Award for Professional Responsibility. Research Editor, Whittier Law Review, 1993-1994. *Member:* Forsyth County and North Carolina Bar Associations; North Carolina State Bar; Public Investors Arbitration Bar Association; American Board of Trial Advocacy; North Carolina Association of Defense Attorneys. ***PRACTICE AREAS:*** Professional Malpractice; Civil Litigation; Insurance Litigation. ***Email:*** rharris@wilsonandiseman.com

LINDA L. HELMS, born Martinsville, Virginia, March 19, 1967; admitted to bar, 1992, North Carolina. *Education:* High Point University (B.A., summa cum laude, 1989); Wake Forest University (J.D., cum laude, 1992). Order of Barristers. Member, Moot Court Board and National Moot Court Team. Research Editor, Wake Forest Law Review. *Member:* Forsyth County and North Carolina Bar Associations; American Bar Association; North Carolina Association of Defense Attorneys. ***PRACTICE AREAS:*** Professional Malpractice; Commercial Litigation; Insurance Litigation; Civil Litigation. ***Email:*** lhelms@wilsonandiseman.com

KEVIN B. CARTLEDGE, born Conover, North Carolina, November 13, 1971; admitted to bar, 1997, North Carolina. *Education:* University of North Carolina at Chapel Hill (B.A., 1994); Wake Forest University (J.D., 1997). Member, Moot Court Board, 1995-1997. Craven Constitutional Team, 1996. *Member:* Forsyth County and North Carolina Bar Associations; North Carolina Association of Defense Attorneys. ***PRACTICE AREAS:*** Professional Malpractice; Insurance Litigation; Commercial Litigation. ***Email:*** kcartledge@wilsonandiseman.com

ASSOCIATES

J. CHAD BOMAR, born Lynchburg, Virginia, May 31, 1975; admitted to bar, 1999, North Carolina; 2000, South Carolina. *Education:* Liberty University (B.S., cum laude, 1996); Campbell University (J.D., 1999). *Member:* Forsyth County and North Carolina As-

(This Listing Continued)

sociations; South Carolina Bar; North Carolina State Bar; North Carolina Association of Defense Attorneys. **PRACTICE AREAS:** Professional Malpractice; Insurance Litigation; Commercial Litigation; Civil Litigation. **Email:** cbomar@wilsonandiseman.com

MARIA C. PAPOULIAS, born Silver Spring, Maryland, February 28, 1976; admitted to bar, 2001, North Carolina. *Education:* University of North Carolina at Chapel Hill (B.A., with honors, 1998); Wake Forest University (J.D., 2001). Member, Moot Court Board, 1999-2001. Member, Jessup International Law Team, 2000. *Member:* Forsyth County and North Carolina Bar Associations. **PRACTICE AREAS:** Commercial Litigation; Civil Litigation; Insurance Litigation. **Email:** mpapoulias@wilsonandiseman.com

DAVID M. FOTHERGILL, born Kingston, Ontario, Canada, July 1, 1977; admitted to bar, 2003, North Carolina; U.S. District Court, Middle District of North Carolina. *Education:* University of North Carolina at Wilmington (B.A., 2000); Wake Forest University (J.D., 2003). Member, Moot Court Board, 2002-2003; Kauffman National Securities Law Team, 2002. Associate Chief Justice, Moot Court Executive Board, 2003. *Member:* Forsyth County and North Carolina Bar Associations. **PRACTICE AREAS:** Commercial Litigation; Civil Litigation; Insurance Litigation. **Email:** dfothergill@wilsonandiseman.com

EDWARD T. SHIPLEY, III, born Winston-Salem, North Carolina, November 26, 1977; admitted to bar, 2004, North Carolina and U.S. District Court, Middle District of North Carolina. *Education:* University of North Carolina at Chapel Hill (B.S., Business Administration); Wake Forest University (J.D., 2004). Moot Court Board, 2002-2004. *Member:* Forsyth County and North Carolina Bar Associations. **PRACTICE AREAS:** Corporate Law; Commercial Law; Professional Malpractice; Commercial Litigation; Civil Litigation; Insurance Litigation.

REPRESENTATIVE CLIENTS: St. Paul Insurance Co.; Novant Health, Inc.; Wake-Forest University Baptist Medical Center; Allstate Insurance Company; CNA Insurance Company; Pennsylvania National Insurance Co.; Lawyers Mutual Insurance Company; Medical Mutual Insurance Company of North Carolina; MAG Mutual Insurance Company; Scottsdale Insurance Company; Nationwide Insurance Company; USF&G; Elk River Club; Senator Pen Corporation; Merz Pharmaceuticals; South Atlantic Galvanizing; Spevco; Winston-Salem Housing Foundation, Inc.; Luwa; Tyson Foods; International Legwear Group; Zellweger Analytics; First Community Bank; Senator USA; North Carolina Housing Foundation.

WOMBLE CARLYLE SANDRIDGE & RICE

A Professional Limited Liability Company

ONE WEST FOURTH STREET

WINSTON-SALEM, NORTH CAROLINA 27101

Telephone: 336-721-3600
Fax: 336-721-3660
Email: lawyers@wcsr.com
URL: http://www.wcsr.com

REVISER OF THE NORTH CAROLINA LAW DIGEST FOR THIS DIRECTORY.

Charlotte, North Carolina Office: 3500 One Wachovia Center, 301 South College Street. Telephone: 704-331-4900. Fax: 704-331-4955.

Raleigh, North Carolina Office: 2100 First Union Capitol Center, 150 Fayetteville Street Mall, P.O. Box 831. Telephone: 919-755-2100. Fax: 919-755-2150.

Research Triangle Park, North Carolina Office: 2530 Meridian Parkway, Suite 400 (Durham), 27713, P.O. Box 13069, Research Triangle Park, 27709. Telephone: 919-484-2300. Fax: 919-484-2340.

Greensboro, North Carolina Office: 300 North Greene Street. Telephone: 336-574-8030. Fax: 336-574-4520.

Atlanta, Georgia Office: One Atlantic Center, 1201 West Peachtree Street, Suite 3500. Telephone: 404-872-7000. Fax: 404-888-7490.

Other Atlanta, Georgia Office: Suite 404, 2296 Henderson Mill Road, N.E. Telephone: 770-492-9030. Fax: 770-492-9609.

Washington, D.C. Office: Suite 700, 1401 Eye Street. Telephone: 202-857-4400. Fax: 202-467-6910.

Greenville, South Carolina Office: 700 Poinsett Plaza, 104 South Main Street, P.O. Box 10208. Telephone: 864-255-5400. Fax: 864-255-5440.

Tysons Corner, Virginia Office: 8065 Leesburg Pike, Fourth Floor. Telephone: 703-790-3310. Fax: 703-790-2623.

General Civil Practice, Trial and Appellate Litigation. Administrative, Antitrust, Aviation, Banking, Bankruptcy and Creditor's Rights, Bond Financing, Civil Rights, Commercial, Construction, Consumer Lending, Corporate, E-Commerce, Employee Benefits, Environmental, Estate Planning, Family, Government Relations, Health Care, Insurance, Intellectual Property, International, Labor and Employment, Municipal, Negligence, Probate, Product Liability, Real Estate, Retirement Plans, Securities, Taxation, Toxic Tort, Wills and Trusts Law.

FIRM PROFILE: Womble Carlyle Sandridge & Rice, PLLC, which traces its history to 1876, is a full-service law firm that delivers sophisticated and innovative legal services to a wide spectrum of business clients in industries that include information technology, health care, manufacturing, telecommunications and financial services. The Firm also represents a variety of governmental units and agencies.

Womble Carlyle's mission is to provide value to clients by combining professional skill, technology and a thorough understanding of clients' needs to deliver high quality, cost-effective and responsive service. The firm is comprised of approximately 470 lawyers and 838 staff members operating from offices in Atlanta, GA; Greenville, SC; Charlotte, Winston-Salem, Research Triangle Park, Raleigh and Greensboro, NC; Tysons Corner, VA; and Washington, DC.

The Firm considers technology and the benefits it offers an integral part of the legal services it provides. All of the Firm's offices are linked for full communications by telephone, fax, electronic mail and video conference over a wide area network. The Firm takes full advantage of its sophisticated computer technology for support in large-case litigation, as well as management of complex transactions. The Director of Technology is responsible for implementing existing systems, and in some instances, developing new software applications to meet specific client needs. The firm-wide communications and computer network permit the Firm to allocate resources from all offices, as needed, as well as to establish direct, secure links with clients and their legal departments, thus enhancing the responsiveness and efficiency of the Firm's lawyers.

The lawyers of Womble Carlyle have traditionally been active in community affairs, in Bar and other professional activities, and in state government. Many lawyers assume leading roles in civic and professional organizations, and several have served the government in elected or appointed positions.

LAW FIRM ALLIANCES/ASSOCIATIONS: **TOLEDO CONFERENCE GROUP**

LEX MUNDI

RESIDENT MEMBERS

B. S. WOMBLE (1882-1976)

IRVING E. CARLYLE (1896-1971)

W. PENDLETON SANDRIDGE (1904-1982)

LEON L. RICE JR. (1912-1987)

ALFRED G. ADAMS, born Winston-Salem, North Carolina, February 28, 1942; admitted to bar, 1973, North Carolina. *Education:* Wake Forest University (B.A., 1968; J.D., 1973). Phi Delta Phi. Member, Wake Forest Law Review, 1972-1973. Listed in Best Lawyers in America, 1992—. Author, "Proposals for Statewide Land Planning," Wake Forest University Law Review, Volume 18, Number 3. Adjunct Professor of Law, Wake Forest University School of Law, 1995—. *Member:* North Carolina (Board of Governors, 1987-1990; Chair, Real Property Section, 1983-1984; Chair, Continuing Education Committee, 1992-1994) and American Bar Associations; The North Carolina State Bar; American College of Mortgage Attorneys (Board of Regents, 1996-1999; President, 2001); American College of Real Estate Lawyers. (Board Certified Specialist in Real Property Law, Residential, Business, Commercial and Industrial Transactions, North Carolina State Board of Legal Specialization). **PRACTICE AREAS:** Commercial Real Estate Transactions; Real Estate Lending. **Email:** aadams@wcsr.com

JEAN TAYLOR ADAMS, born Newport News, Virginia, July 31, 1950; admitted to bar, 1985, Georgia; 1992, North Carolina. *Education:* Duke University (B.A., summa cum laude, 1972; M.Ed., 1975; J.D., 1979). Phi Beta Kappa; Order of the Coif. Author: "Reconciling Family Law with Tax Policy: Untangling the Tax Treatment of Parental Trusts," 46 Tax Law Review 107 (1990). Adjunct Professor, Wake Forest University School of Law, 1991-1992. Senior Lecturer, Duke University School of Law, 1984-1990. Assistant Professor, Duke University School of Law, 1980-1984. Fellow, The American College of Trust and Estate Counsel. Member, Planning Giving Councils of: Wake Forest University, 1995-1997; Duke University, 1996—; Summit School, 1995—. **PRACTICE AREAS:** Estate Planning; Estate Administration; Charitable Planned Giving; Probate. **Email:** jadams@wcsr.com

REID C. ADAMS, JR., born Kinston, North Carolina, June 26, 1956; admitted to bar, 1981, North Carolina and U.S. District Court, Middle District of North Carolina; 1990, U.S. District Court, Western District of North Carolina and U.S. Court of Appeals, Fourth Circuit. *Education:* Wake Forest University (B.A., cum laude, 1978; J.D., cum laude, 1981). Chairman, Forsyth County Pro Bono Committee; President, Legal Aid Society of Northwest North Carolina. *Member:* Forsyth County and North Carolina Bar Associations. **PRACTICE AREAS:** Insurance Coverage; Litigation; Tort; Products Liability Law. **Email:** cadams@wcsr.com

PATRICK M. ALLEN, born Kernersville, North Carolina, June 4, 1969; admitted to bar, 1993, North Carolina. *Education:* Duke University (B.A., cum laude, 1989); University of North Carolina, Chapel Hill (J.D., with honors, 1993). Member, Holderness Moot Court Bench. President, Christian Legal Society, 1992-1993. *Member:* Forsyth County, North Carolina and American Bar Associations. **PRACTICE AREAS:** Employee Benefits; ERISA. **Email:** pallen@wcsr.com

JANICE C. BALDWIN, born Washington, D.C., October 6, 1960; admitted to bar, 1985, North Carolina. *Education:* James Madison University (B.A., summa cum laude, 1982); Wake Forest University (J.D., cum laude, 1985). Member, Moot Court Board, 1983-1985. Articles Editor, Wake Forest Law Review, 1983-1985. *Member:* Forsyth County and North Carolina Bar Associations. **PRACTICE AREAS:** Employee Benefits; Executive Compensation; Tax. **Email:** jbaldwin@wcsr.com

H. GRADY BARNHILL, JR., born Buena Vista, Georgia, August 24, 1930; admitted to bar, 1958, North Carolina. *Education:* Atlantic Christian College; Wake Forest University (LL.B., cum laude, 1958). Phi Alpha Delta. Listed in Best Lawyers in America (Business Litigation; Personal Injury). *Member:* Forsyth County (President, 1979-1980), North Carolina and American Bar Associations; U.S. Fourth Circuit Judicial Conference (Permanent Member); American Board of Trial Advocates (Advocate). Fellow: American College of Trial Lawyers; American Bar Foundation; Chief Justice Joseph Branch Inn of Court (Founding Director); North Carolina Association of Defense Attorneys; Defense Research Institute. [1st Lt., USAF, 1951-1955]. **PRACTICE AREAS:** Complex and Multidistrict Litigation; Aviation Law; Litigation. **Email:** gbarnhill@wcsr.com

JIMMY H. BARNHILL, born Rocky Mount, North Carolina, September 15, 1940; admitted to bar, 1965, North Carolina. *Education:* Wake Forest University (A.B., 1962; LL.B., 1965). Phi Alpha Delta. Listed in The Best Lawyers in America, Family Law Section. *Member:* North Carolina and American Bar Associations; North Carolina Academy of Trial Lawyers. **PRACTICE AREAS:** Domestic Relations Law. **Email:** jbarnhill@wcsr.com

AMY L. BIRCHER, born Winston-Salem, North Carolina, July 31, 1962; admitted to bar, 1995, North Carolina. *Education:* University of North Carolina at Charlotte (B.S., Biology, 1983); Wake Forest University (J.D., 1995). Member, Moot Court Board. Articles Editor, Wake Forest University Law Review. *Member:* Forsyth County, North Carolina and American Bar Associations. **PRACTICE AREAS:** Litigation; Environmental; Toxic Torts. **Email:** abircher@wcsr.com

S. FRALEY BOST, born Erwin, North Carolina, April 3, 1947; admitted to bar, 1979, North Carolina. *Education:* Hampden-Sydney College (B.S., 1969); Old Dominion University (M.B.A., with honors, 1976); Wake Forest University (J.D., 1979). Staff Member,

(This Listing Continued)

WOMBLE CARLYLE SANDRIDGE & RICE, Winston-Salem—Continued

Wake Forest Law Review, 1978-1979. *Member:* Forsyth County, North Carolina and American Bar Associations; North Carolina Association of Defense Attorneys; Defense Research Institute; Aviation Insurance Association. ***PRACTICE AREAS:*** Aviation; Commercial Litigation; Product Liability; Insurance Defense. ***Email:*** sbost@wcsr.com

ANTHONY H. BRETT, born Ahoskie, North Carolina, October 11, 1953; admitted to bar, 1979, North Carolina; 1983, U.S. Supreme Court. *Education:* Yale University (B.A., 1975); Institute of Policy Sciences and Public Affairs, Duke University (1976-1977); Duke University (J.D., 1979). Listed in The Best Lawyers in America. *Member:* Forsyth County and North Carolina (Member, Health Care Section Council, 1988-1991) Bar Associations; American Health Lawyers Association; North Carolina Society of Health Care Attorneys; North Carolina Municipal Attorneys Association. ***PRACTICE AREAS:*** Health Care Law; Municipal Law. ***Email:*** abrett@wcsr.com

CHARLES A. BURKE, born Charleston, West Virginia, February 18, 1962; admitted to bar, 1987, California; 1992, North Carolina. *Education:* University of North Carolina (B.A., with honors, 1984; J.D., with honors, 1987). Research Editor, University of North Carolina Law Review, 1986-1987. *Member:* Forsyth County, North Carolina (Member, Litigation Section) and American (Member, Litigation Section) Bar Associations. ***PRACTICE AREAS:*** Intellectual Property Litigation. ***Email:*** cburke@wcsr.com

KAREN ESTELLE CAREY, born Longview, Texas, June 8, 1943; admitted to bar, 1981, North Carolina; 1982, U.S. District Court, Middle District of North Carolina; 1983, U.S. District Court, Eastern District of North Carolina; 1985, U.S. Court of Appeals, 4th Circuit. *Education:* Wartburg College (B.M.E., magna cum laude, 1964); Duke University (J.D., 1981). Member, National Panel of Construction Arbitrators, American Arbitration Association. North Carolina Court-Certified Mediator. *Member:* North Carolina (Member, Construction Section) and American (Member, Forum Committee on the Construction Industry) Bar Associations. ***PRACTICE AREAS:*** Construction Law; Commercial Contracts; Technology; Commerce; International Law. ***Email:*** kcarey@wcsr.com

KEITH A. CLINARD, born High Point, North Carolina, February 25, 1954; admitted to bar, 1979, North Carolina. *Education:* Wake Forest University (B.A., cum laude, 1976; J.D., cum laude, 1979). Staff Member, 1977-1979 and Notes and Comments Editor, 1978-1979, Wake Forest Law Review. *Member:* Forsyth County, North Carolina and American Bar Associations; North Carolina Association of Defense Attorneys (Board of Directors, 1989-1992). ***PRACTICE AREAS:*** Civil Litigation; Product Liability Law; Construction Law; Federal Practice. ***Email:*** kclinard@wcsr.com

W. ANDREW COPENHAVER, born November 10, 1946; admitted to bar, 1972, North Carolina; 1980, U.S. Supreme Court; U.S. District Court, Middle, Eastern and Western Districts of North Carolina; U.S. Court of Appeals, 4th and 5th Circuits. *Education:* Duke University (A.B., 1969); University of North Carolina (J.D., 1972). Listed in Best Lawyers in America, Business Litigation and First Amendment Rights. *Member:* Forsyth County, North Carolina and American Bar Associations; North Carolina Federal Bar Advisory Council. ***PRACTICE AREAS:*** Antitrust Law; Unfair Trade Practices; Defamation; Intellectual Property Litigation. ***Email:*** acopenhaver@wcsr.com

LINWOOD L. DAVIS, born Winston-Salem, North Carolina, January 24, 1940; admitted to bar, 1967, North Carolina. *Education:* Princeton University (A.B., cum laude, 1962); Duke University (J.D., 1967). Member, Editorial Board, Duke Law Journal, 1966-1967. Listed in The Best Lawyers in America, Corporate Law Section. Member, Revenue Laws Study Committee of North Carolina Legislative Research Commission, 1979-1981. *Member:* Forsyth County (President, 1997-1998), North Carolina and American Bar Associations. Fellow, American College of Trust and Estate Counsel. ***PRACTICE AREAS:*** Corporate Law; Exempt Organizations. ***Email:*** lldavis@wcsr.com

RONALD R. DAVIS, born Abington, Pennsylvania, December 6, 1958; admitted to bar, 1987, Texas; 1993, North Carolina; U.S. District Court, Middle and Western Districts of North Carolina, U.S. Court of Appeals, Fourth and Fifth Circuits and U.S. Supreme Court. *Education:* Davidson College (B.A., 1981); University of North Carolina at Chapel Hill (M.B.A., 1986; J.D., 1986). Phi Delta Phi. Kenan Scholar. Member, Holderness Moot Court Bench. Author, "Forged Endorsements on Checks: A Primer," 59 Tex. B.J. 30 (1996). *Member:* Forsyth County, North Carolina and American Bar Associations; North Carolina State Bar (Member, Ethics Committee); North Carolina Association of Defense Attorneys (Member, Commercial Litigation Committee); Defense Research Institute. (Also at Greensboro Office). ***PRACTICE AREAS:*** Business Litigation; Trial Practice; Appellate Practice. ***Email:*** rdavis@wcsr.com

BONNIE KAY DONAHUE, born Jennings, Florida, August 24, 1951; admitted to bar, 1979, North Carolina. *Education:* Florida State University (B.A., cum laude, 1973; M.A., 1974); Wake Forest University (J.D., 1979). Member, Order of Barristers. Law Clerk: Bankruptcy Court for the Middle District of North Carolina, 1979-1980; Chapter 13 Standing Trustee for the Middle District of North Carolina, 1980-1981. Candidate, Leadership America, 1999. *Member:* Greensboro, Forsyth County, Guilford County, North Carolina (Editor, Bankruptcy Lawyer, 1980-1992; Counsel Member, Bankruptcy Section, 1981-1983; 1984-1986; Treasurer, 1990-1991) and American (Member, Business Bankruptcy Committee; Chair, Bankruptcy Avoiding Powers Subcommittee; Member, Chapter 11 Subcommittee; Consumer Financial Services Committee) Bar Associations; North Carolina State Bar. Fellow: American College of Bankruptcy; American Bar Foundation. ***PRACTICE AREAS:*** Bankruptcy, Workouts and Commercial Litigation. ***Email:*** kdonahue@wcsr.com

CHRISTINA U. DOUGLAS, born Milwaukee, Wisconsin, November 19, 1968; admitted to bar, 1993, Tennessee; 1994, U.S. District Court, Western District of Tennessee; 1995, U.S. District Court, Middle District of Tennessee; 1998, North Carolina; 2001, U.S. District Court, Eastern, Western and Middle Districts of North Carolina; 2002, U.S. Supreme Court. *Education:* University of Mississippi (B.A., cum laude, 1989); University of Memphis (J.D., 1993). Member, University of Memphis Law Review, 1991-1992. Recipient: American Jurisprudence Award in Trial Advocacy; A Kemp Stallings Scholarship at University of Memphis. Author: Jones v. Jones: Overcoming the Presumption of Delivery, 22 Mem. St.. L. Rev. 187 (1991). *Member:* Forsyth County, North Carolina, Tennessee and American (Member, Sections on: Litigation: Tort and Insurance Practice, Medicine and Law Committee) Bar Associations; North Carolina Association of Defense Attorneys; Defense Research Institute (Member, Products Liability Committee). ***PRACTICE AREAS:*** Products Liability; Litigation. ***Email:*** cdouglas@wcsr.com

W. DAVID EDWARDS, born Winston-Salem, North Carolina, June 15, 1957; admitted to bar, 1982, North Carolina and U.S. District Court, Western, Middle and Eastern Districts of North Carolina; U.S. Court of Appeals, Fourth Circuit. *Education:* University of North Carolina at Chapel Hill (B.S.B.A., 1979); Duke University (J.D., 1982). Contributing Editor, "Norton Bankruptcy Law & Practice 2d" (Clark Boardman & Callaghan). Contributor: "Chapter 11 Theory and Practice" (LRP Publications). Author: "The Treatment of Assignments of Rent in Bankruptcy," 48 *Business Lawyer* 633 (1993); "Molding the Successful Workout with Pre-Workout Agreements," 7(5) *Probate & Property* 7 (1993). ***PRACTICE AREAS:*** Litigation; Class Actions; Constitutional Law. ***Email:*** dedwards@wcsr.com

JONATHAN M. ENGRAM, born Lynn, Massachusetts, March 25, 1957; admitted to bar, 1983, Georgia; 1996, North Carolina; 2004, Florida. *Education:* University of the South (B.A., cum laude, 1978); University of Georgia (J.D., cum laude, 1983). Recipient, Henry B. Shinn Award in Legal Writing. Editor in Chief, Georgia Journal of International and Comparative Law, 1982-1983. *Member:* Atlanta, Forsyth County (Member, Section on Litigation), North Carolina and American (Member, Sections on: Litigation; Tort and Insurance Practice) Bar Associations; State Bar of Georgia (Member, Products Liability and Insurance Law Sections); Defense Research Institute; Lawyers Club of Atlanta; North Carolina Association of Defense Attorneys. ***PRACTICE AREAS:*** Litigation; Products Liability Law; Insurance Coverage Law. ***Email:*** jengram@wcsr.com

GUSTI W. FRANKEL, born Los Angeles, California, February 8, 1946; admitted to bar, 1984, North Carolina; U.S. Court of Appeals, Fourth Circuit; U.S. District Court, Middle, Western and Eastern Districts of North Carolina. *Education:* University of California at Berkeley (B.A., 1967); University of Minnesota (Ph.D., 1977); Duke University (J.D., with high honors, 1984). Staff Member, 1982-1983 and Member, Editorial Board, 1983-1984, Duke Law Journal. Author/Speaker: "Employment Law Update," North Carolina Association of Police Attorneys Conference 2001; "Impact of the Americans With Disabilities Act on the Employment of Police Officers," International Association of Police Chiefs Annual Meeting, 1999. *Member:* Forsyth County and North Carolina Bar Associations. ***PRACTICE AREAS:*** Litigation; Employment. ***Email:*** gfrankel@wcsr.com

JEFFREY L. FURR, born Morgantown, West Virginia, November 1, 1956; admitted to bar, 1987, North Carolina; 1988, District of Columbia. *Education:* West Virginia University (B.S., cum laude, 1981); Resident, Rush-Presbyterian - St. Lukes Medical Center; Wake Forest University (J.D., cum laude, 1987). Editor-in-Chief, Wake Forest Law Review, 1986-1987. Associate, Hunton and Williams, 1987-1988 (Resident, Washington, D.C. Office). *Member:* Forsyth County, North Carolina and American Bar Associations. ***PRACTICE AREAS:*** Litigation. ***Email:*** jfurr@wcsr.com

ALLAN R. GITTER, born Yonkers, New York, August 26, 1936; admitted to bar, 1963, North Carolina. *Education:* Washington & Lee University (A.B., 1958); University of Michigan (J.D., 1961). Listed in: Who's Who in America; The Best Lawyers in America, Personal Injury Litigation Section. *Member:* Forsyth County and North Carolina Bar Associations; International Association of Insurance Counsel; American Board of Trial Advocates. Fellow, American College of Trial Lawyers. ***PRACTICE AREAS:*** Insurance Defense Law; General Negligence Trials and Appeals; Accident Law; Health Insurance Law; Defense of Civil Rights Actions. ***Email:*** agitter@wcsr.com

MURRAY C. GREASON, JR., born Wake Forest, North Carolina, December 12, 1936; admitted to bar, 1962, North Carolina. *Education:* Wake Forest University (B.S., magna cum laude, 1959; J.D., magna cum laude, 1962). Phi Delta Phi; Phi Beta Kappa; Omicron Delta Kappa. Listed in: The Best Lawyers in America; Who's Who in America. *Member:* Forsyth County (President, 1986-1987), North Carolina and American Bar Associations. Fellow, American College of Tax Counsel, 1983—. [Capt., U.S. Army, active duty, 1962-1965]. ***PRACTICE AREAS:*** Acquisitions, Divestitures and Mergers Law; Charitable Entities; Corporate Law. ***Email:*** mgreason@wcsr.com

ELLEN M. GREGG, born Elkton, Maryland, July 9, 1961; admitted to bar, 1986, North Carolina; 1987, U.S. District Court, Middle, Eastern and Western Districts of North Carolina; U.S. Court of Appeals, Fourth Circuit. *Education:* Campbell University (B.A., summa cum laude, 1983; J.D., cum laude, 1986). Phi Kappa Phi; Omicron Delta Kappa; Delta Theta Phi. Member, National Trial Team. Member, Campbell Law Review, 1984-1986. Membership Editor, Campbell Law Review, 1985-1986. *Member:* Forsyth County (Member, Young Lawyers Section), North Carolina (Member: Young Lawyers Division; Litigation Section) and American (Member, Litigation Section) Bar Associations; Chief Justice Joseph Branch Inn of Court (1992-1993). ***PRACTICE AREAS:*** Municipal/Public Officials/Government Litigation; Insurance Coverage and Defense; Personal Injury; Tort; Civil Rights Litigation; Environmental and Toxic Tort Law. ***Email:*** egregg@wcsr.com

MICHAEL D. GUNTER, born Gastonia, North Carolina, March 26, 1947; admitted to bar, 1972, North Carolina. *Education:* Wake Forest University (B.A., with honors, 1969); University of Pennsylvania (M.B.A., with honors, 1973); University of North Carolina (J.D., with honors, 1972). Phi Alpha Theta; Eta Sigma Phi; Order of the Coif; Phi Delta Phi. Staff Member, University of North Carolina Law Review, 1971-1972. Recipient: Walter Clark Award; William E. Newcombe Scholarship. Listed in: The Best Lawyers in America; Who's Who in American Law; Who's Who in the South and Southwest; Who's Who in America; International Who's Who of Professionals; Sterling's Who's Who; Strathmore's Who's Who. *Member:* Forsyth County, North Carolina and American Bar Associations; Southern Employee Benefits Conference, The ESOP Association, Profit-Sharing Council of America; Association of Private Pension and Welfare Plans. (Leader, Employee Benefits Practice Group). ***PRACTICE AREAS:*** Employee Benefits Law; Executive Compensation; Qualified and Non-Qualified Retirement Plans; Professional Corporations Law; Taxation (Federal) Law. ***Email:*** mgunter@wcsr.com

HARDIN G. HALSEY, born Mouth of Wilson, Virginia, April 21, 1955; admitted to bar, 1983, North Carolina. *Education:* Virginia Polytechnic Institute and State University (B.S., with distinction, 1977); University of Kentucky School of Law (J.D., with high distinction, 1983). Pi Tau Sigma Mechanical Engineering Honor Fraternity, Vice President; Tau Beta Pi Engineering Fraternity; Phi Eta Sigma Honor Fraternity; Order of the Coif; Phi Delta Phi. Member, Kentucky Law Journal, 1981-1983. Co-author: "North Carolina Real

(This Listing Continued)

Estate Forms - Practice and North Carolina Commercial Finance Forms - Practice," (1992, Lawyers Cooperative Publishing, Rochester, New York). Listed in "The Best Lawyers in America". *Member:* Forsyth County, North Carolina (Member, Business Law Section) and American Bar Associations. (Also at Greensboro Office). ***PRACTICE AREAS:*** Real Estate Finance; Commercial Finance; Secured Transactions; Commercial Law; Troubled Loans and Workouts. ***Email:*** hhalsey@wcsr.com

HADA V. HAULSEE, born Havana, Cuba, February 20, 1950; admitted to bar, 1981, North Carolina. *Education:* College of William and Mary (B.A., 1970); Virginia Polytechnic Institute and State University (M.S., 1973); University of North Carolina at Chapel Hill (J.D., with high honors, 1981). Order of the Coif. Staff Member, North Carolina Law Review, 1979-1981; Novant Health Triad Region Board of Trustees; Past Member, Chief Justice's Commision on the Future of the North Carolina Business Court. *Member:* Forsyth County and North Carolina Bar Associations; Hispanic National Bar Association; Defense Research Institute. ***REPORTED CASES:*** Land v. Tall House Bldg. Co., 165 N.C. (App. 880, 602 S.E.2d 1, 2004); Skinner V. Preferred Credit, --S.E.2d--, 2005 WL 1949532 (N.C. App. 2005); Street v. Smart Corp., 157 N.C. (App. 303, 578 S.E.2d 695, 2003); Faircloth v. Financial Asset Securities Corporation Mego Mortgage Homeowner Loan, 87 Fed.Appx. 314 (4th Cir. 2004). ***PRACTICE AREAS:*** Product Liability Litigation; Class Action Defense; Business Litigation; Unfair and Deceptive Trade Practices; Lending and Financial Services Litigation. ***Email:*** hhaulsee@wcsr.com

URSULA M. HENNINGER, born Princeton, New Jersey, January 21, 1967; admitted to bar, 1992, North Carolina; 2004, Florida. *Education:* Appalachian State University (B.A., cum laude, 1989); Wake Forest School of Law (J.D., cum laude, 1992). Member: Wake Forest Law Review; Moot Court Board; National Moot Court Team. First Year Moot Court Competition Winner and Award for Best Brief. Listed in Who's Who in American Law Schools; Who's Who in American Colleges and Universities. Author: "Choice of Law-The Plaintiff's Forum Shopping Gold Card: Choice of Law in Federal Courts After Transfer of Venue Under §1404(a)-Ferens v. John Deere Co." 26 Wake Forest L. Rev. 809 (1991). *Member:* Forsyth County, North Carolina and American Bar Associations; Forsyth County Young Lawyers (President). ***PRACTICE AREAS:*** Environmental; Toxic Tort Litigation; Public Official and Insurance Defense. ***Email:*** uhenninger@wcsr.com

LORI PRIVETTE HINNANT, born Rockingham, North Carolina, June 25, 1961; admitted to bar, 1987, North Carolina and U.S. District Court, Middle District of North Carolina; U.S. Court of Appeals, Fourth Circuit. *Education:* Wake Forest University (B.A., cum laude, 1983; J.D., cum laude, 1987). Phi Alpha Theta. Member, Order of Barrister. Member: National Moot Court Team; International Moot Court Team. Member, Wake Forest Law Review, 1986-1987. *Member:* Forsyth County, North Carolina (Environmental and Natural Resource Section) and American (Member: Litigation Section; Natural Resources, Energy and Environmental Law Section) Bar Associations. ***PRACTICE AREAS:*** Environmental Law. ***Email:*** lhinnant@wcsr.com

JEFFREY C. HOWLAND, born Red Bank, New Jersey, June 30, 1958; admitted to bar, 1982, Texas; 1987, North Carolina. *Education:* Tulane University; Wake Forest University (B.A., 1979); University of South Carolina (J.D., cum laude, 1982). Member: Order of the Coif; Order of the Wig and Robe. Articles Editor, Member, South Carolina Law Review, 1981-1982. *Member:* Forsyth County, North Carolina (Member, Business Law Section) and American (Member: Business Law Section; Small Business Committee; Emerging Growth Ventures Subcommittee; Securities Regulation Subcommittee) Bar Associations. (Practice Group Leader, Corporate and Securities). ***PRACTICE AREAS:*** Securities Regulation; Corporate Law; Technology Law; Venture Capital; Mergers and Acquisitions. ***Email:*** jhowland@wcsr.com

DAVID A. IRVIN, born Winston-Salem, North Carolina, September 15, 1939; admitted to bar, 1966, North Carolina. *Education:* Davidson College (B.A., 1961); University of North Carolina (LL.B., 1966). Phi Delta Phi. Member, Board of Editors, North Carolina Law Review, 1965-1966. Listed in The Best Lawyers in America, Labor and Employment Discrimination Section. North Carolina Certified Mediator. *Member:* Forsyth County, North Carolina (Member, Labor and Employment Section) and American (Member, Labor and Employment Section) Bar Associations. [1st Lt., U.S. Army, 1961-1963]. ***PRACTICE AREAS:*** Labor and Employment Law (Management). ***Email:*** dirvin@wcsr.com

GEORGE WILLIAM JOYNER, III, born Asheboro, North Carolina, November 21, 1969; admitted to bar, 1996, North Carolina. *Education:* Princeton University (A.B., 1992); Wake Forest University (J.D., cum laude, 1996; M.B.A., 1996). Order of the Coif. Executive Editor, Wake Forest Law Review. Author: "Beyond Budd Tire: Examining Corporate Successor Liability in North Carolina," 30 Wake Forest Law Review 889, 1995. *Member:* North Carolina (Member, Business Law Section) and American (Member, Business Law Section) Bar Associations. ***Email:*** wjoyner@wcsr.com

CHRISTOPHER A. KREINER, born Baltimore, Maryland, April 16, 1969; admitted to bar, 1994, North Carolina. *Education:* University of North Carolina at Chapel Hill (B.S., Business Administration, 1991; J.D., 1994). *Member:* Forsyth County and North Carolina Bar Associations. ***PRACTICE AREAS:*** Products Liability Litigation. ***Email:*** ckreiner@wcsr.com

WILLIAM E. LATHAM II, born Travis AFB, California, June 2, 1968; admitted to bar, 1993, Louisiana; 1996, North Carolina. *Education:* Duke University (A.B., 1990); Louisiana State University (J.D., 1993). Order of the Coif; Phi Kappa Phi. *Member:* Louisiana State, North Carolina and American Bar Associations; North Carolina State Bar. ***PRACTICE AREAS:*** Environmental; Toxic Torts; Litigation. ***Email:*** wlatham@wcsr.com

CHRISTOPHER E. LEON, born Evanston, Illinois, July 1, 1958; admitted to bar, 1984, District of Columbia; 1988, North Carolina; 1994, Georgia. *Education:* Northwestern University (B.S.I.E., with distinction, 1980); Wake Forest University (J.D., cum laude, 1983). Member: Editorial Staff, Wake Forest Law Review, 1982-1983; Editorial Staff, American Society of International Law Proceedings, 1982. Co-Author: *North Carolina Real Estate Forms,* Lawyers Cooperative Publishing, 1995; *North Carolina Commercial Financing Forms,* Lawyers Cooperative Publishing, 1995. Author: "The Lead Lender's Liability to its Participant," Banking Law Journal 1992; "Letters of Credit: A North Carolina Primer," Wake Forest Law Review, 1989. *Member:* North Carolina and American Bar Associations; State Bar of Georgia. ***PRACTICE AREAS:*** Corporate Law; Mergers and Acquisitions; Corporate Finance; Real Estate Finance Law; Creditor's Rights Law. ***Email:*** cleon@wcsr.com

R. MICHAEL LEONARD, born Atlanta, Georgia, February 27, 1953; admitted to bar, 1978, Alabama; 1987, North Carolina. *Education:* University of North Carolina at Chapel Hill (A.B., 1975); University of North Carolina (J.D., cum laude, 1978). Phi Eta Sigma; Phi Beta Kappa; Order of the Coif. Member, North Carolina Law Review, 1977-1978. *Member:* Birmingham, Forsyth County, North Carolina and American Bar Associations; Alabama State Bar. ***PRACTICE AREAS:*** Products Liability. ***Email:*** mleonard@wcsr.com

RODDEY M. LIGON, JR., born Rock Hill, South Carolina, September 21, 1924; admitted to bar, 1951, North Carolina. *Education:* University of North Carolina (B.S., 1948; J.D., 1951). Order of the Coif; Phi Delta Phi. Author: "North Carolina Hospital Law," Institute of Government, The University of North Carolina at Chapel Hill, 1964. Member, Editorial Board, North Carolina Law Review, 1949-1950. Professor of Public Law and Government and Assistant Director, Institute of Government, University of North Carolina, 1953-1964. Forsyth County Attorney, 1964-1970. *Member:* Forsyth County, North Carolina and American Bar Associations; American Judicature Society; American Health Lawyers Association; North Carolina Society of Health Care Attorneys; Municipal Attorneys Association. [Major, USAF, 1942-1945; 1951-1953]. ***PRACTICE AREAS:*** Health Care Law; Hospital Law; Municipal Law; Litigation. ***Email:*** rligon@wcsr.com

KIM KELLY MANN, born Statesville, North Carolina, January 23, 1958; admitted to bar, 1985, North Carolina. *Education:* University of North Carolina at Greensboro (B.A., 1979); Campbell University (J.D., cum laude, 1985). Omicron Delta Kappa; Phi Kappa Phi. Staff Member, 1983-1984 and Notes and Comments Editor, 1984-1985, Campbell Law Review. *Member:* Forsyth County, North Carolina and American Bar Associations. ***PRACTICE AREAS:*** Real Estate; Finance; Mortgage Law; Corporate Finance; Secured Lending; Commercial Law; Real Property Law. ***Email:*** kmann@wcsr.com

JEFFREY R. McFADDEN, born Minneapolis, Minnesota, August 11, 1958; admitted to bar, 1985, District of Columbia; 1987, U.S. District Court for the District of Columbia and U.S. Court of Appeals, District of Columbia Circuit; 1989, North Carolina; 1990, U.S. District Court, Middle District of North Carolina and U.S. Court of Appeals, Fourth Circuit; 1992, U.S. District Court, Western District of North Carolina; 1995, U.S. District Court, Eastern District of North Carolina; registered to practice before U.S. Patent and Trademark Office. *Education:* Wake Forest University (B.S., 1980); Catholic University of America (J.D., 1985). Trustee, Forsyth Technical Community College, 1995—. *Member:* Forsyth County and North Carolina (Intellectual Property Law Section, Council Member, 1994-1997; Chair, Trademark Committee, 1994—) Bar Associations. ***PRACTICE AREAS:*** Patent; Trademark; Copyright; Computer Law; Entertainment Law; Antitrust. ***Email:*** jmcfadden@wcsr.com

DENNIS W. McNAMES, born Memphis, Tennessee, September 29, 1947; admitted to bar, 1972, North Carolina. *Education:* University of North Carolina (B.S. in B.A., 1969); Wake Forest University (J.D., 1972). Phi Alpha Delta. *Member:* Forsyth County, North Carolina (Member, Real Property Section Council, 1986-1988; Secretary, 1988-1989) and American Bar Associations. ***PRACTICE AREAS:*** Real Estate Law; Finance; Foreclosure Law. ***Email:*** dmcnames@wcsr.com

KENNETH R. MICHAEL, born St. Petersburg, Florida, May 17, 1957; admitted to bar, 1994, Florida; 1995, North Carolina. *Education:* University of Florida (B.Design, with high honors, 1980); Virginia Polytechnic Institute and State University (M.Arch., 1983); University of Florida (J.D., with honors, 1994). Tau Sigma Delta; Alpha Phi Alpha. Associate Editor, Florida Law Review, 1993-1994. Registered Architect, Florida, 1989; Certified Construction Specifier, The Construction Specifications Institute, 1991. Author: "Design Professional Liability: Third-Party Actions by Tenants and Users," The Construction Lawyer, Vol. 14, No. 3 (Aug. 1994). *Member:* North Carolina and American (Forum on the Construction Industry, 1992—) Bar Associations; American Institute of Architects; National Council of Architectural Registration Boards. ***PRACTICE AREAS:*** Construction. ***Email:*** kmichael@wcsr.com

JAMES R. MORGAN, JR., born Winston-Salem, North Carolina, June 4, 1958; admitted to bar, 1984, North Carolina, U.S. District Court, Eastern, Western and Middle Districts of North Carolina and U.S. Court of Appeals, Fourth Circuit, 1985, Georgia, Georgia Court of Appeals, U.S. District Court, Middle District of Georgia; U.S. District Court, Northern District of Georgia; U.S. Court of Appeals, Eleventh Circuit. *Education:* Wake Forest University (B.S., cum laude, 1980; J.D., 1984). *Member:* State Bar of Georgia; North Carolina Bar Association; American Judicature Society. ***PRACTICE AREAS:*** Public Official Defense; Civil Rights; Employment Law; Litigation. ***Email:*** jmorgan@wcsr.com

KENNETH A. MOSER, born Rowan County, North Carolina, September 8, 1942; admitted to bar, 1968, North Carolina. *Education:* Wake Forest University (B.A., 1965); Wake Forest University (J.D., cum laude, 1968). Phi Delta Phi (President); Omicron Delta Kappa. Associate Editor, Wake Forest Law Review, 1967-1968. Member of Faculty, Graduate School of Banking of the South, Baton Rouge, Louisiana, 1987-1989. Listed in: Who's Who in American Law; The Best Lawyers in America, Banking Law and Real Estate Law Section. *Member:* Forsyth County, North Carolina and American (Member, Sections on: Business Law; Real Property, Probate and Trust Law; Chair, Loan Practices and Lender Liability Committee, 1988-1993; Member, Books and Media Committee, 1995— and Committee on Committees, 1993-1997) Bar Associations; Member, American College of Real Estate Lawyers. Fellow, American College of Mortgage Attorneys. (Managing Member of the Winston Office). ***PRACTICE AREAS:*** Banking Law; Commercial Law; Mortgage Law; Real Estate. ***Email:*** kmoser@wcsr.com

JAMES K. PHILLIPS, born Lexington, North Carolina, October 22, 1951; admitted to bar, 1977, North Carolina. *Education:* Wake Forest University (B.S., cum laude, 1974; J.D., 1977). Member, Wake Forest Law Review, 1975-1977. Law Clerk, Judge Robert M. Martin, North Carolina Court of Appeals, 1977-1978. Assistant Secretary and Assistant General Counsel, Fieldcrest Mills, Inc., 1978-1985. Member: North Carolina World Trade Association; North Carolina Global Partnership. *Member:* Forsyth County, North Carolina (Member: Council, International Law and Practice Section, 1995—), American and International Bar Associations. ***PRACTICE AREAS:*** Antitrust and Trade Regulation; International Trade and Investment; Intellectual Property. ***Email:*** jphillips@wcsr.com

(This Listing Continued)

WOMBLE CARLYLE SANDRIDGE & RICE, Winston-Salem— Continued

ROBERT S. PIERCE, born Gloucester, Massachusetts, October 29, 1950; admitted to bar, 1980, New York; 1981, U.S. District Court, Southern and Eastern Districts of New York; 1987, North Carolina; 1989, U.S. District Court, Eastern and Middle Districts of North Carolina; 1990, U.S. Court of Appeals, Fourth Circuit; 1992, U.S. District Court, Western District of North Carolina. *Education:* University of Massachusetts (B.A., magna cum laude, 1972); University of North Carolina (M.A., 1974; J.D., cum laude, 1979). Phi Beta Kappa. *Member:* Forsyth County, North Carolina, New York State and American Bar Associations. ***PRACTICE AREAS:*** Civil Litigation; Public Official Defense; Insurance Defense. ***Email:*** rpierce@wcsr.com

MARK N. POOVEY, born Durham, North Carolina, August 11, 1956; admitted to bar, 1980, North Carolina and U.S. District Court, Middle, Western and Eastern Districts of North Carolina and U.S. Court of Appeals, Fourth Circuit. *Education:* Wake Forest University (B.A., cum laude, 1978; J.D., cum laude, 1980). Carswell Scholarship. Notes and Comments Editor, Wake Forest Law Review, 1979-1980. *Member:* Forsyth County, North Carolina (Antitrust Section) and American (Member, Sections on: Antitrust; Litigation) Bar Associations; International Association of Gaming Attorneys. (Leader, Technology and Commercial Practice Group). ***PRACTICE AREAS:*** Technology Law; Commerce; Antitrust Law; Business Litigation; Gaming Law. ***Email:*** mpoovey@wcsr.com

ELIZABETH L. QUICK, born Izmir, Turkey, May 22, 1948; admitted to bar, 1974, North Carolina. *Education:* Duke University (A.B., 1970); University of North Carolina (J.D., with honors, 1974). Order of the Coif. Staff Member, University of North Carolina Law Review, 1973-1974. Author and Principal Editor, North Carolina Estate Administration Manual. Visiting Lecturer, University of North Carolina, School of Law, 1977. Listed in The Best Lawyers in America, Probate and Estate Planning Section. Member: Board of Directors, The Cannon Foundation, Inc.; Board of Directors, Reynolda House, Inc.; Board of Trustees, Salem College and Academy. *Member:* Forsyth County, North Carolina (President, 1997-1998) and American Bar Associations. Fellow, American College of Trust and Estate Counsel. ***PRACTICE AREAS:*** Estate Planning Law; Probate Law; Charitable Trusts and Foundations Law. ***Email:*** equick@wcsr.com

ROBERT L. QUICK, born Saginaw, Michigan, October 10, 1946; admitted to bar, 1974, North Carolina. *Education:* Oakland University (B.A., 1968); Boston University (Th.M., 1971); University of North Carolina (J.D., 1974). Associate Editor, North Carolina Law Review, 1973-1974. *Member:* Forsyth County, North Carolina and American Bar Associations; National Association of Bond Lawyers. ***PRACTICE AREAS:*** Bond Law; Corporate Financing Law; Secured Transactions Law; Public Finance; Tax Exempt Finance; Commercial Law. ***Email:*** rquick@wcsr.com

GEORGE A. RAGLAND, born Charleston, West Virginia, May 14, 1943; admitted to bar, 1978, North Carolina. *Education:* University of Virginia (B.S., 1965); Washington and Lee University (LL.B., cum laude, 1968). Law Review; Officer/Director, Estate Planning Council of Winston-Salem; Listed in Best Lawyers in America, Trusts and Estates Section; Business North Carolina as one of its Legal Elite in both Tax and Estate Planning. *Member:* Forsyth County, North Carolina (Past Chair, Estate Planning and Fiduciary Law Section) and American (Real Property, Probate and Trust Law Section) Bar Associations. Fellow, American College of Trust and Estate Counsel. (Practice Group Leader, Trusts and Estates). ***PRACTICE AREAS:*** Estate Planning Law; Estate Administration; Charitable Gift Planning; Trust Administration; Estate Settlement; Probate. ***Email:*** gragland@wcsr.com

MICHAEL E. RAY, born Charlotte, North Carolina, December 13, 1949; admitted to bar, 1978, North Carolina and South Carolina. *Education:* Furman University (B.A., 1972); University of South Carolina (J.D., 1978). Recipient, Algernon Sidney Sullivan Award. Editor in Chief, South Carolina Law Review, 1977-1978. Member, Board of Governors, Federal Circuit Bar Association, 1994-1997. Member, Board of Directors, Furman University Alumni Association, 1995-2000. Member, Board of Directors, Lex Mundi, Ltd., 1995-1999; Secretary, 1996-1997; Chairman-Elect, 1997-1998; Chairman, 1998-1999. Member, Editorial Board, Journal of College and University Law, 1984-1986. *Member:* North Carolina, Federal Circuit and American Bar Associations; South Carolina Bar; North Carolina Association of Defense Attorneys; American Intellectual Property Law Association. (Practice Group Co-Chair, Intellectual Property). ***PRACTICE AREAS:*** Intellectual Property Litigation; International Litigation; Alternative Dispute Resolution. ***Email:*** mray@wcsr.com

RICHARD T. RICE, born Winston-Salem, North Carolina, August 21, 1951; admitted to bar, 1977, North Carolina. *Education:* Duke University (B.A., 1973); Wake Forest University (J.D., 1977). Member, Wake Forest Law Review, 1975-1977. *Member:* Forsyth County (Secretary, 1982-1983), North Carolina and American Bar Associations; Forsyth County Young Lawyers (Secretary, 1978-1979); North Carolina Association of Defense Attorneys; Defense Research Institute; Central Winston-Salem Association (President, 1993-1995). (Practice Group Leader, Insurance, Governmental and Tort Litigation). ***PRACTICE AREAS:*** Insurance Coverage Litigation; General Negligence Trials and Appeals; Insurance Defense Law. ***Email:*** rrice@wcsr.com

W. P. SANDRIDGE, JR., born Winston-Salem, North Carolina, January 27, 1934; admitted to bar, 1961, North Carolina. *Education:* University of North Carolina (A.B., 1956); University of Virginia (LL.B., 1961). Phi Alpha Delta. *Member:* Forsyth County, North Carolina and American Bar Associations. [Lt., (j.g.), U.S. Navy, 1956-1958]. ***PRACTICE AREAS:*** Finance Law; Commercial Law; Contract Law; Creditors Rights. ***Email:*** psandridge@wcsr.com

THOMAS D. SCHROEDER, born Atlanta, Georgia, May 26, 1959; admitted to bar, 1984, North Carolina. *Education:* University of Kansas (B.S., 1981); University of Notre Dame (J.D., 1984). Phi Alpha Delta. Editor-in-Chief, Notre Dame Law Review, 1983-1984. Law Clerk, Judge George E. MacKinnon, U.S. Court of Appeals for the District of Columbia Circuit, 1984-1985. *Member:* Forsyth County, North Carolina and American (Member: Litigation Section; Appellate Practice, Federal Procedure and Products Liability Committees) Bar Associations; North Carolina Association of Defense Attorneys (Member, Board of Directors, 1997-1999; Secretary, 1999-2000); International Association of Defense Counsel; Defense Research Institute. (Practice Group Leader, Product Liability). ***PRACTICE AREAS:*** Litigation; Products Liability Litigation; Promotion Law and Litigation. ***Email:*** tschroeder@wcsr.com

(This Listing Continued)

DAVID A. SHIRLEN, born Charlotte, North Carolina, October 9, 1961; admitted to bar, 1986, Georgia and North Carolina. *Education:* Guilford College (B.A., with honors, 1983); University of Georgia (J.D., magna cum laude, 1986). Order of the Coif. Member, Editorial Board, University of Georgia Law Review, 1984-1985. Law Clerk for The Honorable Eugene A. Gordon, U.S. District Judge, Middle District of North Carolina, 1986-1988. *Member:* Forsyth County, North Carolina (Member, Antitrust Section) and American (Member, Antitrust Section) Bar Associations. ***PRACTICE AREAS:*** Business Litigation; Antitrust and Trade Regulation; Commercial Torts; Intellectual Property; Trade Secrets; Covenants Not To Compete. ***Email:*** dshirlen@wcsr.com

GREG L. SMITH, born McComb, Mississippi, July 12, 1956; admitted to bar, 1982, North Carolina. *Education:* Brown University (A.B., magna cum laude, 1979); Cornell University (J.D., cum laude, 1982). *Member:* North Carolina and American (Member, Tax Section) Bar Associations. ***PRACTICE AREAS:*** Health Care; Taxation; Partnerships, S Corporations; Limited Liability Companies; Real Estate Development; Syndications Law; International Law. ***Email:*** gsmith@wcsr.com

RANDEL S. SPRINGER, born East St. Louis, Illinois, November 9, 1962; admitted to bar, 1990, Ohio; 1991, U.S. District Court, Southern District of Ohio; 1999, North Carolina. *Education:* Indiana University (B.A., 1984); University of Iowa (M.A., 1986); Marshall-Wythe School of Law, College of William and Mary (J.D., 1990). Member, Board of Editors: William and Mary Law Review, 1989-1990; The Trademark Reporter. *Member:* Cincinnati, Ohio State and American Bar Associations; Cincinnati Intellectual Property Law Association; International Trademark Association. ***PRACTICE AREAS:*** Trademarks; Intellectual Property Law; General Litigation; Copyrights. ***Email:*** rspringer@wcsr.com

WILLIAM B. SULLIVAN, born Kansas City, Missouri, May 12, 1945; admitted to bar, 1970, District of Columbia and U.S. Court of Appeals for the District of Columbia Circuit; 1971, U.S. District Court, District of Maryland; 1974, U.S. Supreme Court; 1979, U.S. Court of Appeals, Fifth Circuit; 1981, U.S. Court of Appeals, Eleventh Circuit; 1989, U.S. District Court, District of Hawaii; 1990, North Carolina and U.S. District Court, Middle and Eastern Districts of North Carolina; 1992, U.S. Court of Appeals, Fourth Circuit. *Education:* University of Virginia (B.A., magna cum laude, 1967); Harvard Law School (J.D., cum laude, 1970). Phi Eta Sigma; Phi Beta Kappa. Member: Raven Society; Walter Chandler Inn of Court. Member, Board of Editors, Harvard Legal Commentary, 1969-1970. Listed in The Best Lawyers in America. Member: National Institute of Trial Advocacy, Georgetown University Law School, 1980; Panel of Chapter 7 Trustees, District of Maryland, 1988-1990. Member, Commercial Finance Dispute Panel, American Arbitration Association. *Member:* Forsyth County, North Carolina (Bankruptcy Law Section) and American (Business Bankruptcy Committee, Subcommittee of Chapter 11) Bar Associations; District of Columbia Bar; Turnaround Management Association; Commercial Law League of America. Fellow: American Bar Foundation; American College of Bankruptcy; American Bankruptcy Institute. (Practice Group Leader, Bankruptcy and Creditor's Rights). ***PRACTICE AREAS:*** Bankruptcy; Creditors' Rights; Commercial Litigation. ***Email:*** wsullivan@wcsr.com

ASHLEY O. THRIFT, born Charlotte, North Carolina, 1946; admitted to bar, 1973, North Carolina; 1974, U.S. District Court, Western District of North Carolina and U.S. Court of Appeals, Fourth Circuit; 1975, South Carolina; 1977, U.S. Tax Court; 1978; District of Columbia Court of Appeals; 1979, District of Columbia; U.S. Supreme Court; U.S. District Court for the District of Columbia; U.S. Court of Appeals for the District of Columbia Circuit. *Education:* University of North Carolina at Chapel Hill (A.B., 1968); University of South Carolina School of Law (J.D., 1972). Recipient, Holderness-Weaver Award (UNC-G) for distinguished service to North Carolina. Listed in: Who's Who in America; Who's Who in the World. Assistant Dean, University of South Carolina School of Law, 1972-1974. Associate University Counsel, University of South Carolina, 1974-1975. Legislative Counsel, S.C. Representative James R. Mann, 1976. Assistant Counsel, Committee on Judiciary U.S. House of Representatives, 1976-1977. Legislative Director and General Counsel, 1977-1984 and Administrative Assistant, Legislative Director and Counsel, 1984-1987 and Chief of Staff and Counsel, 1987-1992 to South Carolina Senator Ernest F. Hollings. Member, Board of Trustees, U.N.C. Center for Public TV. Member: Winston-Salem State University Board of Visitors. Chair, Government Affairs Committee, Lex Mundi, 1999—. Chairman and Recipient of Order of the Long Leaf Pine, North Carolina Partnership for Children. *Member:* Forsyth County and North Carolina Bar Association; The District of Columbia Bar; North Carolina State Bar; South Carolina Bar; Society of International Business Fellows. ***PRACTICE AREAS:*** Legislative Practice; Regulatory Law; Administrative Law; International Law; Business Development. ***Email:*** athrift@wcsr.com

KEITH W. VAUGHAN, born Bluefield, West Virginia, October 1, 1950; admitted to bar, 1975, Georgia and North Carolina. *Education:* Wake Forest University (B.A., cum laude, 1972); University of Georgia (J.D., cum laude, 1975). Omicron Delta Kappa; Delta Sigma Rho; Tau Kappa Alpha. Editor in Chief, Georgia Law Review, 1974-1975. *Member:* Forsyth County, North Carolina and American Bar Associations; State Bar of Georgia; North Carolina Association of Defense Attorneys; American Inns of Court. ***PRACTICE AREAS:*** Litigation. ***Email:*** kvaughan@wcsr.com

WILLIAM R. WHITEHURST, born December 19, 1956; admitted to bar, 1982, Georgia; 1984, North Carolina; U.S. District Court, Northern District of Georgia and U.S. Court of Appeals, 11th and 5th Circuits. *Education:* Wake Forest University (B.A., cum laude, 1978); University of North Carolina (M.B.A., 1982; J.D., with honors, 1982). Order of the Coif; Beta Gamma Sigma. Member, North Carolina Law Review, 1981-1982. *Member:* Forsyth County, North Carolina and American Bar Associations; State Bar of Georgia. (Also at Charlotte, North Carolina Office). ***PRACTICE AREAS:*** Executive Compensation Law; Employee Benefits Law. ***Email:*** wwhitehurst@wcsr.com

C. MARK WILEY, born High Point, North Carolina, October 9, 1963; admitted to bar, 1988, North Carolina; 1989, U.S. Tax Court; 1990, U.S. Court of Federal Claims. *Education:* Wake Forest University (B.S., cum laude, 1985; J.D., cum laude, 1988); New York University (LL.M. in Taxation, 1989). Law Faculty Scholar, 1988. Member, Wake Forest Law Review, 1987-1988. I Beverly Lake Award Recipient, 1988. Recipient: Corpus Juris Secundum Award, 1987; American Jurisprudence Awards in Corporate Taxation, State and

(This Listing Continued)

Local Taxation, Corporate Finance, Constitutional Law, Debtor-Creditor Law. Member, Honor Council, 1987-1988. Certified Public Accountant, North Carolina, 1988. Member, Firm Management Committee. Former Leader, Tax Practice Group, 1998-2002. *Member:* Forsyth County, North Carolina (Member, Tax Council) and American Bar Associations; North Carolina State Bar; North Carolina Association of Certified Public Accountants; American Institute of Certified Public Accountants. ***PRACTICE AREAS:*** Tax Planning; Tax Litigation. ***Email:*** mwiley@wcsr.com

G. CRISTON WINDHAM, born Washington, D.C., December 10, 1950; admitted to bar, 1976, North Carolina; 1978, District of Columbia. *Education:* Wake Forest University (B.A., 1972; J.D., 1976). Assistant Attorney General, State of North Carolina, 1981-1985. *Member:* Forsyth County and North Carolina Bar Associations. (Leader, Litigation Resources Team). ***PRACTICE AREAS:*** Environmental Law; Litigation. ***Email:*** cwindham@wcsr.com

CALDER W. WOMBLE, born Winston-Salem, N.C., June 25, 1922; admitted to bar, 1947, North Carolina. *Education:* Duke University (A.B., 1943; LL.B., 1947). Phi Delta Phi. Junior Assistant Attorney General, North Carolina, 1947-1948. *Member:* Forsyth County, North Carolina and American Bar Associations. Fellow: American Bar Foundation; American Judicature Society; American College of Real Estate Lawyers. [With U.S. Navy Air Force, 1943-46; Lt. (j.g.), 1945-46]. ***PRACTICE AREAS:*** Corporate Law; Corporate Financing Law; Federal Income, Estate and Gift Taxation Law. ***Email:*** cwomble@wcsr.com

ERNA A. P. WOMBLE, born March 25, 1955; admitted to bar, 1986, North Carolina; U.S. District Court, Eastern, Middle and Western Districts of North Carolina; U.S. Court of Appeals, Fourth Circuit; U.S. Supreme Court. *Education:* College of Charleston (B.A., 1978; M.Ed., 1981); University of South Carolina (J.D., 1986). Federal Law Clerk, Hon. Judge Matthew J. Perry, U.S. District Court of South Carolina, 1986-1987. *Member:* Forsyth County, North Carolina (Professionalism Committee, 1997—; Member, Litigation Section) and American (Member: Litigation, Torts and Insurance Practice) Bar Associations; North Carolina Association of Defense Attorneys (Member, Board of Directors, 1998—); Defense Research Institute (Member: Life, Health and Disability Law Committee; Product Liability Committee); Product Liability Advisory Council (Board of Directors, 1996—; Executive Committee, 1997—). ***PRACTICE AREAS:*** Litigation; Products Liability; Life, Health and Disability Insurance Litigation; Neuro/Psychological Damages; Federal Multi-District Litigation. ***Email:*** ewomble@wcsr.com

WILLIAM F. WOMBLE, born Winston-Salem, North Carolina, Oct. 29, 1916; admitted to bar, 1939, North Carolina; 1950, U.S. Supreme Court. *Education:* Duke University (A.B., 1937; J.D., 1939). Phi Delta Phi. Member, State Legislature, 1953-1955-1957. Member, N.C. General Statutes Commission, 1953-1955. *Member:* Forsyth County (President, 1962), North Carolina (President, 1966) and American (Member: House of Delegates, 1978-1987; Board of Governors, 1982-1985; Member: Standing Committee on Ethics and Professional Responsibility, 1985-1991; Resource Development Council, 1986-1992; Executive Council, National Conference of Bar Presidents, 1985-1988)Bar Associations; American Counsel Association; U.S. Fourth Circuit Judicial Conference (Permanent Member). Life Fellow: American Bar Foundation (Recipient, Fifty-Year Award, 1995); American Judicature Society. [With Armed Forces, 1941-1946; Major, 1945-1946]. ***PRACTICE AREAS:*** General Practice; Consulting Partner. ***Email:*** wwomble@wcsr.com

WILLIAM F. WOMBLE, JR., born Oakland, California, September 21, 1942; admitted to bar, 1967, North Carolina; 1987, U.S. Supreme Court. *Education:* Duke University (B.A., 1964; J.D., 1967). Listed in The Best Lawyers in America, Business Litigation and Personal Injury Sections. *Member:* Forsyth County, North Carolina (Chairman, Practical Training Committee, 1982-1983) and American Bar Associations; International Association of Defense Counsel; North Carolina Association of Defense Attorneys (Director, 1982-1984; President, 1987-1988); Product Liability Advisory Council; Propane Gas Defense Association; Defense Research Institute (Regional Vice-President, 1992-1993; State Representative, 1985-1992); The Association of Trial Lawyers of America (Associate); American Board of Trial Advocates (Advocate); U.S. Fourth Circuit Judicial Conference (Permanent Member). Fellow, American College of Trial Lawyers. [Lt., U.S. Navy, 1967-1971]. ***PRACTICE AREAS:*** Products Liability Law; Aviation Law; Drug and Medical Device Law; Commercial and Complex Litigation. ***Email:*** bwomble@wcsr.com

RESIDENT ASSOCIATES

ELIZABETH K. ARIAS, born Bethesda, Maryland, April 5, 1974; admitted to bar, 2000, North Carolina. *Education:* University of North Carolina at Chapel Hill (B.A., 1995); Campbell University (J.D., summa cum laude, 2000). Articles Editor, 1999-2000, Law Review, 1998-2000. Author: Batch v. Town of Chapel Hill, Takings Law & Exactions: Where Should North Carolina Stand? Campbell Law Review, Winter 1998. *Member:* American Bar Association. ***PRACTICE AREAS:*** Trusts and Estates. ***Email:*** earias@wcsr.com

ALISON Y. ASHE-CARD, born Camden, New Jersey, June 21, 1967; admitted to bar, 1992, Illinois; 1993, U.S. District Court, Northern District of Illinois; 2000, North Carolina. *Education:* Spelman College (B.A., 1989); American University Washington College of Law (J.D., 1992). Pi Sigma Alpha. *Member:* Winston-Salem Bar Association. ***PRACTICE AREAS:*** Products Liability; Litigation. ***Email:*** aacard@wcsr.com

KENNETH R. ASHFORD, born Omaha, Nebraska, September 27, 1962; admitted to bar, 1994, New York and New Jersey; 1997, North Carolina. *Education:* Tufts University (B.A./B.S., 1985); New York University (J.D., 1993). *Member:* American Bar Association (Young Lawyers Division). ***PRACTICE AREAS:*** General Litigation; Products Liability. ***Email:*** kashford@wcsr.com

THOMAS A. BISSETTE, born Charlotte, North Carolina, 1972; admitted to bar, 1997, North Carolina and South Carolina. *Education:* Wake Forest University (B.A., 1994; J.D., 1997); University of Miami (LL.M., in Real Property Development, 2002). *Member:* North Carolina State Bar; South Carolina Bar. ***PRACTICE AREAS:*** Real Estate Development; Capital Markets. ***Email:*** tbissette@wcsr.com

ALISON R. BOST, born Durham, North Carolina, March 24, 1970; admitted to bar, 1997, North Carolina. *Education:* Guilford College (B.S., 1992); Wake Forest University (J.D., 1997). Author: Stacy v. Jedco Construction Inc: North Carolina Adopts a Diminished Capacity Standard for Contributory Negligence, 31 Wake Forest L. Rev. 1215 (1996). *Member:* North Carolina Bar Association. ***PRACTICE AREAS:*** Labor and Employment. ***Email:*** abost@wcsr.com

JULIE B. BRADBURN, born Charlotte, North Carolina, October 1, 1974; admitted to bar, 2003, North Carolina. *Education:* North Carolina State University (B.A., summa cum laude, 1996); Campbell University (J.D., cum laude, 2003). Phi Beta Kappa; Order of the Barristers. Recipient: Book Awards: Contract I, Torts II, Constitutional Law; 1st Amendment; 1983 Civil Rights Litigation; Trial Advocacy; F. Leary Davis Scholarship, 2001-2003. Member, Campbell Law Review, 2001-2003. Finalist, John Marshall School of Law Moot Court Competition; Trial Team. *Member:* Forsyth County Women Attorney's Association; North Carolina Bar Association. ***PRACTICE AREAS:*** Insurance Defense. ***Email:*** jbradburn@wcsr.com

STUART A. BROCK, born Whiteville, North Carolina, October 26, 1967; admitted to bar, 2000, North Carolina. *Education:* Wake Forest University (B.S., Biology, cum laude, 1990); Bowman Gray School of Medicine, Wake Forest University (Clinical Studies, 1992); North Carolina Central University School of Law (J.D., cum laude, 2000). CCM Certified Case Manager, 1995; Certification of Insurance Rehabilitation Specialists Commission. Managed Care Consultant, Winston-Salem, NC, 1994-2000; Case Manager, Qual-Choice of North Carolina, Inc., Winston-Salem, NC, 1995-1997; Case Management Specialist, MedCost, Inc., Winston-Salem, NC, 1994-1995; Manager ACS Medical Services, ACS Group, Inc., Winston-Salem, NC, 1992-1994. *Member:* Forsyth County and North Carolina (Member, Sections on: Litigation; Labor and Employment; Health Law) Bar Associations; Forsyth County Young Lawyers' Association; Case Management Society of America (North Carolina Chapter); American Society of Law, Medicine & Ethics; Health Insurance Association of America. (Also at Winston-Salem, North Carolina Office). ***PRACTICE AREAS:*** Labor and Employment; Pharmaceutical Patent Prosecution; Workers Compensation; Governmental Litigation; Tort Litigation. ***Email:*** sbrock@wcsr.com

JASON B. BUCKLAND, born Pearisburg, Virginia, 1977; admitted to bar, 2002, North Carolina; U.S. District Court, Middle District of North Carolina. *Education:* Virginia Polytechnic Institute and State University (B.S., Finance, 1999); Wake Forest University School of Law (J.D., 2002). Phi Alpha Delta. Member: Law Student Division, American Bar Association; Wake Forest Legal Clinic Program. *Member:* Forsyth County Bar Association; North Carolina State Bar. ***PRACTICE AREAS:*** Products Liability Litigation. ***Email:*** jbuckland@wcsr.com

CRAIG D. CANNON, born Sioux City, Iowa, July 9, 1974; admitted to bar, 2001, North Carolina. *Education:* University of Iowa (B.A., 1997; J.D., 2000). *Member:* Forsyth County, North Carolina and American Bar Assocations. ***PRACTICE AREAS:*** Products Liability Litigation; Tort Litigation; Insurance Litigation; Class Action Litigation; Complex Business Litigation; Alcoholic Beverage Regulation; Firearms Regulation; Personal Injury Litigation. ***Email:*** ccannon@wcsr.com

MARY NELL CRAVEN, born Anderson, South Carolina, June 21, 1971; admitted to bar, 1996, North Carolina; U.S. District Court, Middle District of North Carolina. *Education:* University of North Carolina at Chapel Hill (B.A., 1993); Wake Forest University (J.D., 1996). Recipient, American Jurisprudence Award in Civil Procedure. *Member:* North Carolina Bar Association. ***PRACTICE AREAS:*** Domestic Relations; Business Litigation. ***Email:*** mcraven@wcsr.com

RACHEL E. DALY, born Fredericksburg, Virginia, December 6, 1974; admitted to bar, 2001, North Carolina. *Education:* Mary Washington College (B.A., 1996); Wake Forest University (J.D., cum laude, 2001). Order of the Coif; Order of the Barristers; Moot Court Board; Member, National Trial Team. Member, Wake Forest Law Review. ***PRACTICE AREAS:*** Litigation. ***Email:*** rdaly@wcsr.com

CHRISTOPHER G. DANIEL, born Atlanta, Georgia, July 8, 1966; admitted to bar, 1992, California; 1993, U.S. District Court, Eastern and Northern Districts of California; 1997, North Carolina and U.S. District Court, Middle District of North Carolina; registered to practice before U.S. Patent and Trademark Office. *Education:* University of California at Berkeley (B.S.M.E., 1989); Tulane Law School (J.D., cum laude, 1992). Order of the Coif. Recipient, American Jurisprudence Awards: Antitrust; Uniform Commercial Code; Mergers and Acquisitions. Junior Appellate Moot Court Champion; Oralist, National Appellate Moot Court Team, 1991. Extern, Honorable Martin L.C. Feldman, U.S. District Court, Eastern District of Louisiana, 1991-1992. *Member:* Forsyth County and American Bar Associations; State Bar of California; North Carolina State Bar. ***PRACTICE AREAS:*** Intellectual Property Litigation; Antitrust; Trade Regulation. ***Email:*** cdaniel@wcsr.com

ANDREW FITZGERALD, born Nashville, Tennessee, 1977; admitted to bar, 2002, Virginia; 2003, North Carolina; U.S. District Court, Middle District of North Carolina. *Education:* Wake Forest University (B.A., 1999); University of Virginia (J.D., 2002). ***PRACTICE AREAS:*** Bankruptcy Litigation. ***Email:*** afitzgerald@wcsr.com

ANNE FLEESON, admitted to bar, 2002, North Carolina. *Education:* Duke University (B.A., Biology, with distinction, 1995); Wake Forest University (M.S., Cell and Molecular Biology, 1998; J.D., 2001). *Member:* North Carlina State Bar; American Bar Association (Member, Intellectual Property Section); International Trademark Association. ***PRACTICE AREAS:*** Intellectual Property. ***Email:*** afleeson@wcsr.com

CHRISTOPHER J. GEIS, born Queens, New York, 1966; admitted to bar, 1998, North Carolina, U.S. District Court, Middle District of North Carolina and Navy-Marine Corps Trial Judiciary; 2002, U.S. Navy-Marine Corps Court of Criminal Appeals and U.S. Court of Appeals for Armed Forces. *Education:* Western Carolina University (B.A., 1988); Wake Forest University School of Law (J.D., 1998). [Lieutenant, U.S. Navy, 1998-2003]. ***PRACTICE AREAS:*** Insurance; Torts; Government Defense. ***Email:*** cgeis@wcsr.com

JACQUELINE M. GOBLE, born Lenior, North Carolina, July 25, 1970; admitted to bar, 1996, North Carolina. *Education:* Campbell University (B.A., cum laude, 1991; M.B.A., with distinction, 1993; J.D., 1996). Phi Kappa Phi; Delta Theta Phi. Listed in Who's Who in American Law Students. *Member:* Guilford County, North Carolina and American Bar Associations. ***LANGUAGES:*** Spanish. ***PRACTICE AREAS:*** Products Liability; Commercial Litigation. ***Email:*** jgoble@wcsr.com

MURRAY C. GREASON, III, born Charlottesville, Virginia, January 17, 1963; admitted to bar, 1997, Montana; 2000, North Carolina; 2002, New York. *Education:* University of Colorado (B.A., 1990); University of Montana (J.D., 1997). International Law Stu-

(This Listing Continued)

WOMBLE CARLYLE SANDRIDGE & RICE, Winston-Salem—Continued

dent Association; Jessup International Law; Moot Court Team. *Member:* State Bar of Montana; North Carolina, New York State and American Bar Associations. ***LANGUAGES:*** German and Italian. ***PRACTICE AREAS:*** Environmental Litigation; Toxic Tort Litigation. ***Email:*** tgreason@wcsr.com

STANLEY B. GREEN, born Macon, Georgia, February 28, 1970; admitted to bar, 1998, North Carolina. *Education:* University of North Carolina at Chapel Hill (B.A., 1993); Vermont Law School (M.S. in Environmental Law, magna cum laude, 1998; J.D., magna cum laude, 1998). Note Editor, Vermont Law Review. *Member:* North Carolina Bar Association. (Also at Charlotte, North Carolina Office). ***PRACTICE AREAS:*** Environmental; Toxic Tort. ***Email:*** sgreen@wcsr.com

EDWARD GRIGGS, born Cheraw, South Carolina, July 16, 1977; admitted to bar, 2003, North Carolina; U.S. District Court, Middle District of North Carolina. *Education:* Wake Forest University (B.S., 2000); University of South Carolina (J.D., 2003). Phi Delta Phi; Order of the Wig and Robe. Member, University of South Carolina School of Law Pro Bono Board. Member, Southeastern Environmental Law Journal. *Member:* Forsyth County and North Carolina Bar Associations. ***PRACTICE AREAS:*** Trusts and Estates. ***Email:*** egriggs@wcsr.com

CHRISTOPHER J. GYVES, born Milwaukee, Wisconsin, June 14, 1977; admitted to bar, 2004, North Carolina. *Education:* Davidson College (B.S., Biology, Philosophy, 2000); Wake Forest University Law School (J.D., 2004); Wake Forest University, Babcock Graduate School of Management (M.B.A., 2004). Harper Music Scholar. Concertmaster, Davidson College Symphony. Symposium Editor, Wake Forest Law Review. *Member:* North Carolina State Bar. ***PRACTICE AREAS:*** Corporate; Securities. ***Email:*** cgyves@wcsr.com

JERRY CARLYLE "CARL" HEARN, III, born Munich Bavaria, Germany, 1967; admitted to bar, 2000, Illinois; 2001, North Carolina. *Education:* Lenoir-Rhyne College (B.A., Political Science, 1989); DePaul University (J.D., with honors, 2000). Pi Sigma Alpha. Order of the Coif. Robson Scholar. Recipient, CALI Awards in Contracts, Civil Procedure, Torts and Legal Writing. *Member:* Mecklenburg County, Illinois State and American (Member, Sections on: Litigation; Torts; Insurance Practice) Bar Associations; North Carolina Association of Defense Attorneys; Defense Research Institute. ***PRACTICE AREAS:*** Products Liability; Civil Litigation. ***Email:*** chearn@wcsr.com

JASON C. HICKS, born Lynchburg, Virginia, July 16, 1975; admitted to bar, 2001, Virginia (Not admitted in North Carolina). *Education:* University of Virginia (B.A., 1996); Wake Forest University School of Law (J.D., magna cum laude, 2001). Order of the Coif. *Member:* Virginia State Bar. ***PRACTICE AREAS:*** Commercial Litigation; Local Government Law. ***Email:*** jhicks@wcsr.com

TRENT E. JERNIGAN, born Raleigh, North Carolina, February 26, 1975; admitted to bar, 2000, North Carolina. *Education:* University of North Carolina at Chapel Hill (B.A., 1997); Wake Forest University (J.D., 2000). *Member:* Forsyth County and North Carolina Bar Associations. ***PRACTICE AREAS:*** Commercial Real Estate; Property Law. ***Email:*** tjernigan@wcsr.com

ANA DAVIS JOHNSON, born Coral Gables, Florida, January 15, 1972; admitted to bar, 1997, New York and Florida; 1999, Georgia (Not admitted in North Carolina). *Education:* University of Miami (B.B.A., with honors, 1992); New York University School of Law (J.D., 1996). Member, Order of the Barristers. *Member:* Atlanta and American Bar Associations; State Bar of Georgia; The Florida Bar. ***PRACTICE AREAS:*** Litigation; Intellectual Property. ***Email:*** adavis@wcsr.com

BRADLEY R. JOHNSON, born Anoka, Minnesota, 1970; admitted to bar, 1998, Minnesota; 2001, Montana; 2003, North Carolina; U.S. District Court, District of Minnesota and Middle District of North Carolina; U.S.Court of Appeals, Fourth Circuit. *Education:* Montana State University (B.A., History, highest honors, 1992); William Mitchell College of Law (J.D., summa cum laude, 1998). *Member:* North Carolina State Bar; State Bar of Montana; American Bar Association. ***REPORTED CASES:*** Skinner v. Preferred Credit, S.E.2d, 2005 WL 1949532 (N.C. App. 2005); Hicks v. MidCarolina Bank, Civil Action No. 1:05CV00145 (M.D.N.C. 2005); Faircloth v. Financial Asset Securities Corporation Mego Mortgage Homeowner Loan Trust, 87 Fed.Appx. 314 (4th Cir. 2004). ***PRACTICE AREAS:*** Business Litigation. ***Email:*** brjohnson@wcsr.com

G. WRISTON MARSHBURN, JR, born Chapel Hill, North Carolina, May 22, 1967; admitted to bar, 1997, North Carolina and South Carolina. *Education:* Furman University (B.A., 1989); Cumberland School of Law of Samford University (J.D., 1997). *Member:* Forsyth County and North Carolina Bar Associations. ***PRACTICE AREAS:*** Environmental; Toxic Torts; Litigation. ***Email:*** wmarshburn@wcsr.com

ROBERT D. MASON, JR., born Durham, North Carolina, October 18, 1974; admitted to bar, 2000, North Carolina. *Education:* Duke University (A.B., Political Science and History, cum laude, 1997); Washington & Lee University (J.D., cum laude, 2000). Pi Sigma Alpha; Phi Eta Sigma; Phi Delta Phi; Golden Key. Editor-in-Chief, Environmental Law Digest, 1999-2000; Review Editor, 1998-1999, Staff Writer, 1997-1998; Vice-President, Environmental Law Society, 1998-1999. *Member:* Forsyth County, North Carolina and American (Member, Sections on: Intellectual Property; Litigation) Bar Associations; American Intellectual Property Law Association. ***PRACTICE AREAS:*** Intellectual Property Litigation; Commerce. ***Email:*** rmason@wcsr.com

CARL B. MASSEY, JR., born Jefferson, North Carolina, July 5, 1964; admitted to bar, 1997, Virginia; 1999, North Carolina; U.S. Court of Appeals, Fourth Circuit; registered to practice before U.S. Patent and Trademark Office. *Education:* Wake Forest University (B.S., cum laude, 1986); University of Alabama at Birmingham (M.S., Biology, 1990); Duke University (M.S., Biochemistry, 1994); Boston University (J.D., cum laude, 1997). ***PRACTICE AREAS:*** Technology Law; Commerce; Patent Applications; Patent Prosecution; Intellectual Property. ***Email:*** cmassey@wcsr.com

DAVID J. MAZZA, born Chicago, Illinois, July 14, 1962; admitted to bar, 1995, Missouri; 1996, U.S. District Court, Eastern District of Missouri; 1997, Illinois; 1999, North Carolina. *Education:* St. John's University (B.S., 1984); St. Louis University (J.D., cum

(This Listing Continued)

laude, 1995). *Member:* Bar Association of Metropolitan St. Louis; The Missouri Bar; American Bar Association. ***PRACTICE AREAS:*** Products Liability. ***Email:*** dmazza@wcsr.com

PHILIP J. MOHR, born Atlanta, Georgia, October 5, 1970; admitted to bar, 1997, Missouri and North Carolina. *Education:* University of Notre Dame (B.A., magna cum laude, 1993; J.D., cum laude, 1996). Phi Beta Kappa. *Member:* American Bar Association. ***PRACTICE AREAS:*** Workers Compensation; Insurance Defense. ***Email:*** pmohr@wcsr.com

MICHAEL MONTECALVO, born Worcester, Massachusetts, September 7, 1969; admitted to bar, 1994, Connecticut; 1998, North Carolina. *Education:* University of Vermont (B.A., cum laude, 1990); Duke University (J.D., 1994). Phi Beta Kappa. *Member:* Stamford/Norwalk Regional, Connecticut and American Bar Associations. ***PRACTICE AREAS:*** Products Liability; Commercial Litigation. ***Email:*** mmontecalvo@wcsr.com

JOHN F. MORROW, JR., born Winston-Salem, North Carolina, December 9, 1970; admitted to bar, 1996, North Carolina; U.S. District Court, Western, Middle and Eastern Districts of North Carolina; U.S. Court of Appeals, Federal and Fourth Circuits. *Education:* University of North Carolina at Chapel Hill (B.S., 1993); Wake Forest University School of Law (J.D., 1996). *Member:* Forsyth County (Vice President, Young Lawyers Division, 2001), North Carolina and Federal Circuit Bar Associations; American Intellectual Property Law Association. ***PRACTICE AREAS:*** Intellectual Property Litigation. ***Email:*** jmorrow@wcsr.com

CHRISTOPHER H. OLDHAM, born Port Jefferson, New York, August 8, 1966; admitted to bar, 1995, Colorado, U.S. District Court, District of Colorado and U.S. Court of Appeals, Tenth Circuit; 2000, North Carolina. *Education:* Williams College (B.A., 1988); University of Colorado (J.D., 1994). *Member:* Forsyth County, North Carolina and American Bar Associations. ***LANGUAGES:*** French. ***REPORTED CASES:*** United States v. Holdsworth, 990 F. Supp 1274. ***PRACTICE AREAS:*** Banking; Finance; Property. ***Email:*** coldham@wcsr.com

JULIE BARKER PAPE, born Cincinnati, Ohio, August 11, 1972; admitted to bar, 1999, New York; 2001, North Carolina. *Education:* Vanderbilt University (B.A., 1993); Fordham University School of Law (J.D., 1998). *Member:* New York State and American Bar Associations. ***PRACTICE AREAS:*** Bankruptcy. ***Email:*** jpape@wcsr.com

DAVID V. PATTON, born Cleveland, Ohio, August 12, 1969; admitted to bar, 1999, Ohio; 2000, U.S. District Court, Northern and Southern Districts of Ohio and U.S. Court of Appeals, Sixth Circuit; 2001, North Carolina and U.S. District Court, Middle District of North Carolina. *Education:* Ohio State University (B.S., 1996; J.D., 1999). Assistant State Solicitor and Assistant Attorney General, State of Ohio, 1999-2001. [U.S. Army, 1987-1992]. ***REPORTED CASES:*** Edwards v. Carpenter, 529 U.S. 446(2000). Combs v. Coyle, 205 F.3d 269(6th cir.), cert. denied, 528 U.S. 1189(2000). State v. Orr, 745 N.E.2d 1036(Ohio 2001). State v. Nasrallah, 745 N.E. 2d 511 (Ohio Ct. app. 2000). Chirila v. Ohio State Chiropractice Board, 763 N.E. 2d 1192 (Ohio Ct. App. 2001). ***PRACTICE AREAS:*** Product Liability Litigation. ***Email:*** dpatton@wcsr.com

MATTHEW D. PIPES, born Charlotte, North Carolina, February 3, 1974; admitted to bar, 1999, Texas (Not admitted in North Carolina). *Education:* University of Florida (B.S., 1995); Duke University School of Law (J.D., 1999). Associate, Fulbright and Jaworski LLP, Dallas, TX, August 1999 to June 2003. ***PRACTICE AREAS:*** Corporate and Securities; Health Care.

PATRICIA F. POOLE, born Charlotte, North Carolina, May 28, 1959; admitted to bar, 1986, North Carolina. *Education:* Guilford College (B.S., 1981); University of North Carolina at Greensboro (M.Ed., 1984); Wake Forest University (J.D., 1986). Phi Alpha Delta. *Member:* Forsyth County, North Carolina and American Bar Associations; North Carolina State Bar; Student Trial Bar. ***PRACTICE AREAS:*** Litigation; Products Liability. ***Email:*** ppoole@wcsr.com

JOHN E. PUESCHEL, born Winston-Salem, North Carolina, 1970; admitted to bar, 2001, North Carolina. *Education:* University of North Carolina at Chapel Hill (B.A., 1992); Wake Forest University (J.D., cum laude, 2001). Order of the Coif. Moot Court Board. Moot Court Board. Editor-in-Chief, Wake Forest Law Review, 1999-2000. *Member:* North Carolina Bar Association. ***PRACTICE AREAS:*** Labor and Employment. ***Email:*** jpueschel@wcsr.com

I'ANS REEDER, born Raleigh, North Carolina, September 27, 1962; admitted to bar, 1988, North Carolina. *Education:* University of North Carolina at Chapel Hill (B.S., 1984); Wake Forest University (J.D., 1988). *Member:* Forsyth County Bar Association. ***PRACTICE AREAS:*** Products Liability. ***Email:*** ireeder@wcsr.com

STEPHANIE U. ROBERTS, born Atlanta, Georgia, November 16, 1970; admitted to bar, 1998, North Carolina; 1999, Florida. *Education:* Emory University (B.A., summa cum laude, 1993); University of Florida (J.D., 1996). Senior Research Editor, Florida Journal of International Law, 1995-1996. *Member:* Forsyth County, North Carolina and American Bar Associations; The Florida Bar; Forsyth County Women Attorneys Association. ***LANGUAGES:*** French. ***PRACTICE AREAS:*** Products Liability; Toxic Torts; Environmental Law. ***Email:*** suroberts@wcsr.com

DONALD J. SCALES, born Winston-Salem, North Carolina, January 23, 1953; admitted to bar, 1981, North Carolina; 1984, U.S. District Court, Middle District of North Carolina. *Education:* Guilford College (B.A., 1975); Campbell University School of Law (J.D., 1981). Member, Campbell University Law Review, 1979-1981. *Member:* Forsyth County Bar Association. ***PRACTICE AREAS:*** Products Liability; Litigation. ***Email:*** dscales@wcsr.com

CYNTHIA G. SPIVEY, born Charlotte, North Carolina, December 5, 1959; admitted to bar, 1985, North Carolina and U.S. District Court, Western District of North Carolina. *Education:* University of North Carolina, Chapel Hill (B.S., 1982); DePaul University; Wake Forest University (J.D., 1985). *Member:* Forsyth County and North Carolina Bar Associations. ***PRACTICE AREAS:*** Civil Litigation.

ERIN S. STATON, born Winston-Salem, North Carolina, November 26, 1978; admitted to bar, 2004, North Carolina. *Education:* University of North Carolina at Chapel Hill

(This Listing Continued)

(B.A., 2001); Georgetown University (J.D., cum laude, 2004). Phi Beta Kappa, The Tax Lawyer. *Member:* North Carolina State Bar. ***LANGUAGES:*** French. ***PRACTICE AREAS:*** Real Estate. ***Email:*** estaton@wcsr.com

JOHN R. STILL, born Winston-Salem, North Carolina, September 22, 1961; admitted to bar, 1993, Georgia; 1994, North Carolina. *Education:* University of North Carolina, Greensboro (B.S., 1983); Mississippi College School of Law (J.D., 1993). Phi Delta Phi. *Member:* Forsyth County, North Carolina and American Bar Associations; State Bar of Georgia. ***PRACTICE AREAS:*** Environmental Law; Toxic Tort Litigation. ***Email:*** jstill@wcsr.com

JACK M. STRAUCH, born Cleveland, Ohio, December 14, 1966; admitted to bar, 1995, North Carolina. *Education:* Dartmouth College (B.A., 1995); University of Notre Dame Law School (J.D., magna cum laude, 1995). Member, Barristers Team. Recipient: Arthur A. May Award for Trial Advocacy; Edward F. Barrett Award for Trial Advocacy. *Member:* Forsyth County and North Carolina Bar Associations. ***PRACTICE AREAS:*** Public Officials Liability; Products Liability. ***Email:*** jstrauch@wcsr.com

ELIZABETH D. TUCKER, born Winston-Salem, North Carolina, September 27, 1973; admitted to bar, 2004, North Carolina. *Education:* University of Pennsylvania (B.A., cum laude, 1996); Duke University (J.D., 2004). Executive Editor, Duke Environmental Law and Policy Forum. *Member:* North Carolina State Bar. ***PRACTICE AREAS:*** Insurance; Governmental Law; Torts. ***Email:*** betucker@wcsr.com

SHANNON L. VANDIVER, born Charlotte, North Carolina, September 14, 1975; admitted to bar, 2000, North Carolina. *Education:* University of North Carolina at Chapel Hill (B.A., 1997); Campbell University (J.D., cum laude, 2000). Omicron Delta Kappa. Order of the Barristers. Recipient, I. Beverly Lake Constitutional Law Award, Moot Court Board. Listed in, "Who's Who Among American Law Students." Notes and Comment Editor, Campbell Law Review, 1999-2000. Editor-in-Chief, Campbell Law Observer. Member, The Association of Trial Lawyers of America Trial Team. ***PRACTICE AREAS:*** Products Liability Litigation. ***Email:*** svandiver@wcsr.com

DOUGLAS R. VREELAND, born Winston-Salem, North Carolina, September 12, 1970; admitted to bar, 1998, North Carolina and Tennessee. *Education:* North Carolina State University (B.A., cum laude, 1992); Waker Forest University (J.D., 1997). Pi Sigma Alpha. Teaching Assistant, Legal Research & Writing WFU School of Law, 1996. Assistant District Attorney, 22nd Pros. Dist. of North Carolina, 1998-2000. *Member:* North Carolina State Bar. ***LANGUAGES:*** Spanish. ***PRACTICE AREAS:*** Litigation; Insurance Defense. ***Email:*** dvreeland@wcsr.com

JOANN A. WATERS, born Jacksonville, North Carolina, August 7, 1972; admitted to bar, 2000, North Carolina. *Education:* Campbell University (B.A., magna cum laude, 1994; J.D., 2000). Omicron Delta Kappa; Epsilon Pi Eta; Alpha Phi Omega; Phi Alpha Delta; Habitat for Humanity Volunteer. Listed in Who's Who Among American Colleges and Universities. Case Summary Writer, Campbell Law Observer. Vice President, Christian Legal Society; Treasurer, Law Students Civil Rights Research Council. Teacher's Assistant - Legal Research Writing, Norman Adrian Wiggins School of Law, Campbell University, 1998-2000. ***PRACTICE AREAS:*** Environmental; Toxic Tort; Litigation. ***Email:*** jwaters@wcsr.com

RANDI B. WEISS, born Philadelphia, Pennsylvania, February 14, 1958; admitted to bar, 2000, North Carolina. *Education:* University of Pennsylvania (B.A., Biology and Psychology, 1980); Temple University School of Medicine (M.S., Microbiology and Immunology, 1983; Ph.D., Molecular and Cellular Pathology, 1987); Wake Forest University (J.D., 2000). Research Assistant Professor, Department of Biology, West Virginia University, Morgantown, West Virginia, 1989-1994; Postdoctoral Fellow, Department of Biology, West Virginia University, Morgantown, West Virginia, 1987-1989; Research Scientist, Department of Molecular Genetics, Smith Kline, and French Laboratories, Swedeland, Pennsylvania, 1983-1985; Laboratory Assistant, Department of Human Genetics, Children's Hospital of Philadelphia, Philadelphia, Pennsylvania, 1978-1979. Lecturer: "Molecular Cell Biology," Department of Biology, West Virginia University, 1994; "The Living Cell," Department of Biology, West Virginia University, 1993, 1992; "General Biology," Department of Biology, West Virginia University, 1993, 1992. Manuscript Reviewer, Photochemistry and Photobiology, 1991-1997; Manuscript Reviewer, Hypertension, 1994-1997; Member, Undergraduate Curriculum Committee, Department of Biology, West Virginia University, 1991-1994; Member, West Virginia, Legislative Committee, American Association for Cancer Research, 1991-1994. Author: Randi B. Weiss, G. Criston Windham, Patricia G. Scales, Brandy K. Gillenwater, Drew H. McNeil. The Use of Genetic Testing in the Courtroom. Wake Forest Law Review(1999) Volume 34 pp. 889-913; Tallant EA, Lu ZX, Weiss RB, Chappell MC, Ferrario CM. Bovine Aortic Endothelial Cells Contain an Angiotensin-(1-7). *Hypertension* 1997;29 (pt.2):388-393; Weiss RB, Gallagher PE. In Vivo Repair of Cytosine Hydrates in Cultured Human Lymphoblasts. *Photochem Photobiol* 1993;58:219-225; Gallagher PE, Weiss RB, Brent TP, Duker NJ. A Human Endonuclease Incises Ultraviolet-Irradiated DNA at Cytosines and Oxidized DNA at Thymines. *Molecular Carcinogenesis* 1989;2:188-1991; Gallagher PE, Weiss RB, Brent TP, Duker NJ. Wavelength Dependence of DNA Incision by a Human Ultraviolet Endonuclease. *Photochem Photobiol* 1989;49:363-367; Weiss RB, Gallagher PE, Brent TP, Duker NJ. Cytosine Photoproduct-DNA Glycosylase in Escherichia coli and Cultured Human Cells. *Biochemistry* 1989;28:1488-1492. Weiss RB, Duker NJ. Endonucleolytic Incision of UVB-Irradiated DNA. *Photochem Photobiol* 1987;45:763-768; Weiss RB, Duker NJ. Photoalkylated DNA and Ultraviolet-Irradiated DNA are Incised at Cytosines by Endonuclease III. *Nucl. Acids Res.* 1986;14:6621-6631; Weiss RB, Mineura K. Henderson EE, Duker NJ, deRiel JK. Enzymic Detection of Uracil in a Cloned and Sequenced Deoxyribonucleic Acid Segment. *Biochemsitry* 1983;22:4501-4507. ***Email:*** rweiss@wcsr.com

BRADLEY O. WOOD, born Fort Bragg, North Carolina, May 24, 1970; admitted to bar, 1995, North Carolina. *Education:* Wake Forest University (B.A., magna cum laude, 1992); University of North Carolina-Chapel Hill (J.D., with honors, 1995). Phi Beta Kappa. Articles Editor, North Carolina Journal of International Law and Commercial Regulation, 1994-1995. Legal Assistance Attorney, Task Force Judge Advocate, Trial Counsel, 1st Infantry Division, Kitzingen, Germany, 1996-1998. Administrative and Operational Law Attorney, Headquarters, U.S. Army Forces Command, Fort McPherson, Georgia, 1999-2000. 2nd Brigade Command Judge Advocate, 108th Division (IT), U.S. Army Reserve, Charlotte, North Carolina, 2002—. *Member:* North Carolina State Bar; American Bar Association. [With U.S. Army Judge Advocate General's Corps., 1995-2000]. ***PRACTICE AREAS:*** Insurance Defense. ***Email:*** bwood@wcsr.com

MEMBERS OF COUNSEL

H. JESSE ARNELLE, born New Rochelle, New York, December 30, 1933; admitted to bar, 1968, Pennsylvania and U.S. District Court, Eastern District of Pennsylvania; 1971, California, U.S. District Court, Northern District of California and U.S. Court of Appeals, Ninth Circuit; 1977, U.S. Supreme Court (Not admitted in North Carolina). *Education:* Pennsylvania State University (B.A., 1955); The Dickinson School of Law (LL.B., 1962). Deputy U.S. Public Defender, Northern District of California, 1973-1975. Adjunct Professor, College of Advocacy, Hastings College of the Law, 1980-1984. Member: Federal Practice Panel, California Continuing Education of the Bar, 1979-1980; Magistrates Selection Committee, U.S. District Court, Northern District of California, 1981-1982. Member, American Inns of Court, U.S. District Court of Northern California, 1990—. Vice-President, 1969-1988 and Chairman, 1996—, Board of Trustees, Penn State University. Member, Corporate Board of Directors: Eastman Chemical Corp.; Textron Corporation; WMK Technologies, Inc.; FPL Group, Inc.; Wells Fargo & Co., Inc. and Wells Fargo Bank, N.A.; Union Pacific Resources; Armstrong World Industries. Commissioner, San Francisco Redevelopment Agency, 1980-1990. Member, Board of Directors, 1983—, President and Director, 1989—, World Affairs Council. Member, Board of Directors, World Center, 1986—. Director: San Francisco Commonwealth Club, 1989—; San Francisco Opera, 1990—. Recipient, Bay Area UNICEF Award. Member, Panel of Arbitrators, American Arbitration Association. *Member:* Bar Association of San Francisco (Member, Judicial Review Committee, 1981-1983); Pennsylvania and American Bar Associations; State Bar of California; National Bar Association; American Board of Criminal Trial Lawyers. [With USAF, 1955-1957]. ***LANGUAGES:*** Spanish and Turkish. ***PRACTICE AREAS:*** Litigation; Products Liability Law; Commercial Law; Environmental Law; Public Utility; White Collar Crime Law; Banking Law.

RANLET S. BELL, born Detroit, Michigan, July 26, 1948; admitted to bar, 1989, North Carolina and U.S. District Court, Middle District of North Carolina. *Education:* Vassar College (A.B., 1970); Wake Forest University (J.D., cum laude, 1989). Phi Alpha Delta; The Order of Barristers. Member, Moot Court Board. Staff Member, Wake Forest University Law Review, 1988-1989. *Member:* Forsyth County, North Carolina (Member, Sections on: Business Law; Taxation) and American (Member, Sections on: Business Law; Taxation) Bar Associations. ***PRACTICE AREAS:*** Tax-Exempt Organizations; Charitable Giving; Corporate Law. ***Email:*** rbell@wcsr.com

IAN A. CALVERT, born Point-A-Pierre, Trinidad, May 22, 1939; admitted to bar, 1962, Texas; 1999, North Carolina; registered to practice before the U.S. Patent and Trademark Office. *Education:* Rice University (B.A., 1959); University of Houston (LL.B., cum laude, 1962); George Washington University (LL.M., 1963). Author: "Recent Developments in Patent Interference Procedure, " Southwest Legal Foundation Patent Law Annual, 1976; "An Overview of Interference Practice," Journal of the Patent Office Society, May, 1980; "Three Years of Interference Statistics," Journal of the Patent Office Society, Dec., 1982, Aug., 1986, May, 1989, Nov., 1992, May, 1995. Member, Patent and Trademark Office Society, 1966-2002. Administrative Patent Judge, U.S. Patent and Trademark Office, 1985-2001. *Member:* American Bar Association. ***PRACTICE AREAS:*** Patent Law. ***Email:*** icalvert@wcsr.com

GEORGE K. EVANS, JR., born Sewanee, Tennessee, November 17, 1946; admitted to bar, 1971, North Carolina, U.S. District Court, Western, Middle and Eastern Districts of North Carolina and U.S. Court of Appeals, Fourth Circuit. *Education:* University of the South (B.A., 1968); University of Virginia (J.D., 1971). Phi Beta Kappa. *Member:* North Carolina Association of Defense Attorneys; Defense Research Institute. [Lieut., JAGC, USNR, 1971-1975]. ***PRACTICE AREAS:*** Insurance Defense; ERISA; Employment Law; Life and Disability Insurance Law; Products Liability. ***Email:*** gevans@wcsr.com

LUCRETIA D. GUIA, born Fort Knox, Kentucky, January 12, 1963; admitted to bar, 1989, Georgia; 1991, North Carolina; U.S. District Court, Eastern, Middle and Western Districts of North Carolina; U.S. District Court, Northern Districts of Georgia; U.S. Court of Appeals, First and Fourth Circuits; U.S. Supreme Court. *Education:* University of Virginia (B.S., 1986); Wake Forest University (J.D., cum laude, 1989). Member, Wake Forest Law Review. *Member:* Greensboro Bar Association. ***PRACTICE AREAS:*** Labor and Employment. ***Email:*** lguia@wcsr.com

KURT C. STAKEMAN, born Washington, D.C., September 27, 1949; admitted to bar, 1974, North Carolina; 1975, U.S. District Court, Eastern and Middle Districts of North Carolina; 1986, U.S. Court of Appeals, 4th Circuit. *Education:* Furman University (B.A., 1971); University of North Carolina (J.D., 1974). Police Legal Advisor, Raleigh, North Carolina, 1974-1981. Assistant District Attorney, Raleigh, North Carolina, 1981-1985. *Member:* Forsyth County, North Carolina (Member: Litigation Section; Criminal Justice Section) and American (Member: Litigation Section; Criminal Justice Section) Bar Associations; North Carolina Association of Law Enforcement Legal Advisors (President, 1979-1980). ***PRACTICE AREAS:*** Litigation; White Collar Crime; Criminal Law; Animal Issues. ***Email:*** kstakeman@wcsr.com

DEWEY W. WELLS, born Raleigh, North Carolina, October 14, 1929; admitted to bar, 1954, North Carolina; 1962, U.S. Court of Appeals, 4th Circuit. *Education:* Mars Hill College; Wake Forest University (B.S., 1952; LL.B., 1954). Phi Delta Phi. Secretary, North Carolina Judicial Council, 1954-1955. Judge of Superior Court, 1974. Member: North Carolina Board of Conservation and Development, 1973-1974; North Carolina Wildlife Resources Commission, 1975-1981; North Carolina Judicial Nominating Committee, 1977-1984; Chairman, Board of Trustees, N.C. Natural Heritage Trust, 1990—; Permanent Member, 4th Circuit Judicial Conference; Certified Mediator, North Carolina Superior Courts. *Member:* North Carolina (Member, Board of Governors, 1975-1978; President, 1980-1981) and American Bar Associations. Fellow, American College of Trial Lawyers. ***PRACTICE AREAS:*** Litigation; Products Liability Law; Personal Injury Law; Eminent Domain. ***Email:*** dwells@wcsr.com

SENIOR COUNSEL

SCOTT A. WELTZ, born Bowman, North Dakota, May 8, 1960; admitted to bar, 1994, North Carolina. *Education:* University of North Dakota (B.A. in Russian Studies, cum

(This Listing Continued)

WOMBLE CARLYLE SANDRIDGE & RICE, Winston-Salem—Continued

laude, 1984); Boston University (M.A. in International Relations, with distinction, 1989); Wake Forest University (J.D., 1994). Author: "Military Courts in the Russian Federation," American Bar Association Reviewer, 1997. Member, American Translators Association. *Member:* Forsyth County and American (Member, International Law Section) Bar Associations; North Carolina State Bar (Member, International Law Section). ***LANGUAGES:*** Russian. ***PRACTICE AREAS:*** Business Litigation; Intellectual Property Litigation. ***Email:*** sweltz@wcsr.com

COUNSEL

SARAH M. JOHNSON, born Winston-Salem, North Carolina, October 16, 1945; admitted to bar, 1979, North Carolina. *Education:* Wake Forest University (B.A., 1967; J.D., 1979). Phi Alpha Delta; Phi Delta Kappa. Instructor, Forsyth Technical Community College, 1997-1998. *Member:* Forsyth County, North Carolina and American Bar Associations; North Carolina State Bar. ***PRACTICE AREAS:*** Products Liability Litigation. ***Email:*** smjohnson@wcsr.com

MARGARET L. LEFEVRE, born Waynesboro, Virginia, October 11, 1973; admitted to bar, 2000, North Carolina; U.S. District Court, Middle District of North Carolina. *Education:* Washington & Lee University (B.A., cum laude, 1996); Wake Forest University (J.D., 2000). *Member:* Mecklenburg County Bar Association (Member, Young Lawyers Division); North Carolina State Bar. ***LANGUAGES:*** Spanish. ***PRACTICE AREAS:*** Products Liability. ***Email:*** mlefevre@wcsr.com

DANNIELLE D. WILLIARD, born Tampa, Florida, September 21, 1968; admitted to bar, 2000, North Carolina. *Education:* Ambassador College (B.A., with distinction, 1991); University of South Florida (B.A., 1996); Wake Forest University (J.D., 2000). Phi Alpha Delta (Chapter Justice). Tutor, Academic Success Program. *Member:* North Carolina State Bar. ***PRACTICE AREAS:*** Products Liability Litigation. ***Email:*** dwilliard@wcsr.com

STAFF ATTORNEYS

ROBERT J. JOLLY, born Fullerton, California, May 30, 1957; admitted to bar, 1984, North Carolina. *Education:* Wake Forest University (B.A., Romance Languages, cum laude, 1980); University of North Carolina at Chapel Hill (J.D., 1983). Recipient, Harold Dawes Parcell Award. *Member:* North Carolina Bar Association; North Carolina State Bar. ***LANGUAGES:*** French, Spanish and Portuguese. ***PRACTICE AREAS:*** Civil Litigation.

HANNAH C.E. YONAN TALLEY, born Montgomery County, Pennsylvania, 1958; admitted to bar, 1986, North Carolina. *Education:* Grove City College (B.A., Political Science and French, summa cum laude, 1980); Wake Forest University (J.D., 1985). Recipient, Am Jur Award, Administrative Law. *Member:* North Carolina State Bar; North Carolina Bar Association. ***PRACTICE AREAS:*** Products Liability.

JAMES J. FRADENBURG, born Oswego, New York, 1968; admitted to bar, 1993, North Carolina. *Education:* State University of New York College at Brockport (B.S., History/Political Science, 1990); Wake Forest University (J.D., 1993). *Member:* North Carolina Bar Association. ***PRACTICE AREAS:*** Products Liability Litigation.

RANDY G. VESTAL, born Winston-Salem, North Carolina, 1960; admitted to bar, 1986, North Carolina. *Education:* North Carolina Central University (B.A., 1983); University of North Carolina, Chapel Hill (J.D., 1986). ***PRACTICE AREAS:*** Products Liability; Corporate Defense; Antitrust. ***Email:*** rvestal@wcsr.com

LEGAL SUPPORT PERSONNEL

Terry Michael Wiley (Executive Director)
Susan DeVore (Office Administrator - Atlanta)
Keith Tedrow (Office Administrator - Winston-Salem)
John E. Turlington (Office Administrator - Research Triangle Park and Raleigh)
Cheri Edwards (Office Administrator, Tysons Corner - VA)
Patricia A. Kight (Director of Human Resources)
Charles R. Allison, III (Office Administrator - Charlotte)
John T. Boyer (Office Administrator - Washington, DC)
Hails Foster (Director of Finance and Systems)
Mark Whitley (Director, Strategic Planning and Marketing)
Julie D. Beavers (Professional Development/Recruiting Administrator - Research Triangle Park and Raleigh)
Cynthia K. Pruitt (Professional Development/Recruiting Administrator - Winston-Salem and Greensboro)
Kristin F. Carretta (Director of Professional Development and Recruiting)
Elizabeth P. Keasler (Professional Development/Recruiting Administrator - Charlotte and Greenville, SC)
Stacy H. Stephens (Professional Development/Recruiting Administrator - Atlanta)
Barbara Fountain (Office Manager - Greenville)
Melissa B. Weaver (Office Manager/Billing Coordinator - Greensboro)

GENERAL COUNSEL FOR: Brenner Companies; Charles & Colvard, Ltd.; Inmar Enterprises, Inc.; NC Biosciences Industry Organization; Piedmont Federal Savings & Loan Assn.; RF Micro Devices, Inc.; Venture First Associates.
REPRESENTATIVE CLIENTS: ALLTEL Corp.; Armstrong World IndustriesAndersen Corporation; Armtex, Inc.; Associated Aviation Underwriters; Bank of America; BB&T Corporation; Brad Ragan, Inc.; Brenner Companies; Budd Services, Inc.; Carolina Beverage Corporation; Carolina Biological Supply Company; Carolinas Medical; Carolina Mills, Inc.; Charles & Colvard, Ltd.; Childress Klein Properties, Inc.; Cisco Systems, Inc.; City of Charlotte, North Carolina; The Crosland Group, Inc.; Dell Inc.; Duke University; First Factors, Inc.; GlaxoSmithKline; The Harris Group; Inmar Enterprises, Inc.; Jefferson-Pilot Life Insurance Company; John Hancock Mutual Life Insurance Co.; Klaussner Furniture Industries, Inc.; Lowes Companies, Inc.; Magneti Marelli USA, Inc.; Metropolitan Life Insurance Co.; NC Biosciences Industry Organization; North Carolina Association of County Commissioners; Novant Health, Inc.; Novartis Pharmaceutical Corporation; Old Dominion Freight Lines, Inc.; Piedmont Federal Savings & Loan Assn.; Phillips Industries, Inc.; RegO Claimants Trust; Remington Arms Company, Inc.; RF Micro Devices, Inc.; RJ Reynolds Tobacco Company; Sedgwick James; Sentry Insurance, a Mutual Company; Spectrum Properties; SQL Financials International, Inc.; Talecris Biotherapeutics; Thomas Built Buses, Inc.; The Travelers Insurance Companies; Vulcan Materials Company; Wachovia Bank, N.A.; Wake Forest University; Wake Forest University Baptist Regional Medical Center; Zemex Industrial Minerals.

(This Listing Continued)

REVISER OF THE NORTH CAROLINA LAW DIGEST FOR THIS DIRECTORY.

(For Biographical Data of other Personnel, see Professional Biographies at Charlotte, Raleigh, Research Triangle Park, North Carolina, Atlanta, Georgia, Washington, D.C., Greenville, South Carolina and Tysons Corner, Virginia)

D. BLAKE YOKLEY, P.A.

230 TOWN RUN LANE
WINSTON-SALEM, NORTH CAROLINA 27101
Telephone: 336-721-4772
Fax: 336-722-8589
Email: d105@bellsouth.net
URL: http://www.dbyokley-law.com

General Civil and Criminal Trial Practice in all State and Federal Courts. Personal Injury, Automobile Accidents, Workers Compensation, Domestic/Family Law, Divorce, Child Custody, Child Support, Real Estate, Probate and Estates, Criminal Defense, Traffic and DWI/DUI Defense.

D. BLAKE YOKLEY, born 1938; admitted to bar, 1963, North Carolina. *Education:* Wake Forest University (A.B.; LL.B.). *Member:* Forsyth County and North Carolina (Member, Sections On: Litigation, Family/Domestic and Criminal Law) Bar Associations; North Carolina State Bar; North Carolina Academy of Trial Lawyers.

ANDERSON, DANIEL & ASSOCIATES

232 CAUSEWAY DRIVE
P.O. BOX 1309
WRIGHTSVILLE BEACH, NORTH CAROLINA 28480
Telephone: 910-256-6896
Fax: 910-256-3472
Email: janderson@attorneysada.com
URL: http://www.attorneysada.com

Medical Malpractice, Birth Injury, Cerebral Palsy, Personal Injury, Nursing Home Neglect, Products Liability, Professional Misconduct, Legal Malpractice, Complex Civil Litigation.

FIRM PROFILE: Anderson, Daniel & Associates are experienced trial lawyers with decades of experience in civil litigation. Our team has successfully prosecuted civil cases throughout North Carolina and the East Coast.

We accept only a small number of cases per year and meticulously analyze each case with the input of specialists and multiple disciplines, formulating the best possible legal and factual strategy. The firm takes a team approach with every case as we aggressively pursue our clients' interests.

HENRY L. ANDERSON, JR., born Charleston, South Carolina, November 11, 1943; admitted to bar, 1968, North Carolina. *Education:* University of North Carolina (A.B., 1965; J.D., 1968). Assistant District Attorney, General Court of Justice, 12th Judicial District, State of North Carolina, 1968-1969. *Member:* New Hanover County, North Carolina, Federal and American Bar Associations; The North Carolina State Bar; North Carolina Association of Defense Attorneys (President, 1982-1983); 4th Circuit Judicial Conference (permanent member). ***PRACTICE AREAS:*** Civil Litigation; Medical Malpractice; Personal Injury; Wrongful Death.

A. L. BUTLER DANIEL, born Pinehurst, North Carolina, September 26, 1965; admitted to bar, 1993, North Carolina. *Education:* East Carolina University (B.S., Political Science, 1989); Campbell University (J.D., 1993). Delta Theta Phi. *Member:* North Carolina State Bar; New Hanover County, North Carolina and American Bar Associations; Association of Trial Lawyers of America. ***PRACTICE AREAS:*** Civil Litigation; Medical Malpractice; Personal Injury; Wrongful Death. ***Email:*** bdaniel@attorneysada.com

D. STUART SMITH, born Warsaw, North Carolina, August 14, 1975; admitted to bar, 2001, North Carolina. *Education:* University of North Carolina at Chapel Hill (B.A., 1997); Campbell University (J.D., 2001). *Member:* New Han Hanover County, North Carolina and American Bar Associations; North Carolina State Bar; Association of Trial Lawyers of America; North Carolina Academy Trial Lawyers. ***PRACTICE AREAS:*** Personal Injury; Medical Malpractice; Products Liability; Construction Litigation; Automobile Accidents. ***Email:*** dsmith@attorneysada.com

JOHN H. ANDERSON, JR., born Fayetteville, North Carolina, September 22, 1975; admitted to bar, 2002, North Carolina. *Education:* North Carolina State University (B.S., magna cum laude, 1998); University of North Carolina at Chapel Hill (J.D., with honors, 2002). Phi Delta Phi. Member: Golden Key Honor Society; North Carolina Law Review. Author, "Brisson v. Santoriello and Rule 9: A Step Backward in the Pursuit to Prevent Frivolous Medical Malpractice Actions in North Carolina," 79 North Carolina Law Review, 855, 2002. *Member:* New Hanover County, North Carolina and American Bar Associations; North Carolina State Bar; Association of Trial Lawyers of America; North Carolina Academy of Trial Lawyers. ***PRACTICE AREAS:*** Medical Malpractice; Personal Injury; Wrongful Death; Civil Litigation. ***Email:*** janderson@attorneysada.com

ENNIS, NEWTON & BAYNARD, P.A.

WRIGHTSVILLE BEACH, NORTH CAROLINA

(See Wilmington)

General Insurance and Self Insured Defense Litigation, including Property, Casualty, Automobile, Personal Injury, Premises Liability, Coverage Opinions, Subrogation, Products Liability, Workers Compensation. Trials in all State and Federal Courts.

JAMES S. PRICE

WRIGHTSVILLE BEACH, NORTH CAROLINA

(See Wilmington)

Real Estate.

TEETER LAW FIRM

YADKINVILLE, NORTH CAROLINA

(See Winston-Salem)

Appellate Practice, Criminal Law, Civil Litigation, Domestic Relations, Personal Injury, Trusts and Estates and Wills.

GEORGE B. DANIEL, P.A.

139 EAST MAIN STREET
P.O. BOX 999
YANCEYVILLE, NORTH CAROLINA 27379
Telephone: 336-694-4363
Fax: 336-694-6601
URL: http://www.danielthomaslaw.com

Criminal Law, Felonies, Misdemeanors, Traffic Violations, Driving While Intoxicated, Automobile Accidents, Truck Accidents, Personal Injury, Wrongful Death, Civil Litigation, Real Estate, Residential Real Estate, Commercial Real Estate, Real Estate Litigation, Workers Compensation, Estate Planning, Estate Administration, Drug Crimes.

GEORGE B. DANIEL, born Raleigh, North Carolina, April 1, 1951; admitted to bar, 1976, North Carolina. *Education:* North Carolina State University (B.S., 1973); Wake Forest University (J.D., 1976). Pi Sigma Alpha. *Member:* Caswell County, North Carolina, 9A Judicial District and American Bar Associations; North Carolina State Bar; North Carolina Academy of Trial Lawyers. ***PRACTICE AREAS:*** Criminal Law; Felonies; Misdemeanors; Traffic Violations; Driving While Intoxicated; Automobile Accidents and Injuries; Truck Accidents; Personal Injury; Wrongful Death; Civil Litigation. ***Email:*** gbdaniel22@aldelphia.net

JOHN M. THOMAS, born Danville, Virginia, September 21, 1955; admitted to bar, 1989, North Carolina. *Education:* Brevard College (A.A., 1975); East Carolina University (B.F.A., 1978); North Carolina Central University (J.D., 1989). *Member:* North Carolina and American Bar Associations; North Carolina State Bar. ***PRACTICE AREAS:*** Real Estate; Residential Real Estate; Commercial Real Estate; Real Estate Litigation; Workers Compensation; Estate Planning; Estate Administration; Criminal Law; Drug Crimes; Driving While Intoxicated; Traffic Violations. ***Email:*** jthomas19@adelphia.net

WILLIAM H. DANIEL, P.A.

118 WEST MAIN STREET
YANCEYVILLE, NORTH CAROLINA 27379
Telephone: 336-694-5882
Fax: 336-694-4888
Email: attorney@williamhdaniel.com
URL: http://www.williamdaniellaw.com

Criminal Law, Felonies, Misdemeanors, Traffic Violations, Driving While Intoxicated, Drug Crimes, Personal Injury, Automobile Accidents, Truck Accidents, Motorcycle Accidents, Wrongful Death, Workers Compensation, Real Estate, Wills, Estate Administration.

WILLIAM H. DANIEL, born Danville, Virginia, January 7, 1953; admitted to bar, 1985, North Carolina and U.S. District Court, Middle and Western Districts of North Carolina. *Education:* University of Richmond (B.S., 1975; M.B.A., 1982); Mississippi College School of Law (J.D., 1984). President, 9-A Judicial District, 2005. *Member:* North Carolina State Bar; American Bar Association; North Carolina Academy of Trial Lawyers. ***PRACTICE AREAS:*** Criminal Law; Felonies; Misdemeanors; Traffic Violations; Driving While Intoxicated; Drug Crimes; Personal Injury; Automobile Accidents; Truck Accidents; Motorcycle Accidents; Wrongful Death; Workers Compensation; Real Estate; Wills; Estate Administration.

LAW OFFICES OF
R. LEE FARMER, P.L.L.C.

Established in 1915

21 MAIN STREET WEST
P.O. BOX 1600
YANCEYVILLE, NORTH CAROLINA 27379-1600
Telephone: 336-694-4361; 694-6549
FAX: 336-694-5448
Email: caswelllaw@adelphia.net

Bald Head Island, North Carolina Office: 19 Ibis Roost, 28461.
Granite City, Illinois Office: 3388-B Maryville Road, 62040.

General Civil and Criminal Practice in all State and Federal Courts. Probate, Real Estate, Personal Injury, Commercial, Construction, Administrative and Corporation Law.

FIRM PROFILE: The Law Offices of R. Lee Farmer, P.L.L.C. is the oldest established law firm in Caswell County, North Carolina, being the successor to the R.T. Wilson Law Office founded in 1915. Established as a local general practice, the firm now serves the Southeastern United States offering a wide range of legal services. The firm encourages continuing professional development and all members participate in continuing legal education programs, professional association activities and civic affairs.

(This Listing Continued)

R. LEE FARMER, born Hagerstown, Maryland, May 5, 1948; admitted to bar, 1973, North Carolina; 1974, District of Columbia, U.S. District Court, Middle District of North Carolina and U.S. Court of Appeals, 4th Circuit; 1975, U.S. District Court, Eastern District of North Carolina; 1976, U.S. Tax Court; 1982, U.S. District Court, Western District of North Carolina; 1985, U.S. Court of Military Appeals; 1986, U.S. Supreme Court; 1993, U.S. Court of Veterans Appeals; 2002, U.S. District Court, Eastern and Western Districts of Arkansas; 2004, U.S. Court of Appeals, Seventh Circuit. *Education:* Elon University (B.A., 1970); Wake Forest University (J.D., 1973). Phi Delta Phi. County Attorney, Caswell County, 1973-1991 and 2000-2002. Town Attorney, Town of Yanceyville, 1986—. Member: North Carolina Criminal Code Commission, 1979-1985; State Judicial Nominating Committee, 1981-1985; North Carolina Business Advisory Council, 1989-1996; North Carolina Criminal Justice Education and Training Standards Commission, 1993-1997. Certified Court Mediator, North Carolina Dispute Resolution Commission, 1997—. Certified Court Arbitrator, Administrative Office of the Courts, 1998—. *Member:* Caswell County, 9-A Judicial District and North Carolina Bar Associations; North Carolina State Bar (Member, District Bar Applicant Committee, 1978-1996 and State Bar Councilor, 2005—); District of Columbia Bar; North Carolina Academy of Trial Lawyers; North Carolina County Attorneys Association (President, 1986-1987); North Carolina Municipal Attorneys Association (President, 2003-2004). ***REPORTED CASES:*** Geneva P. Gammon v. William Jackson Clark, 25 N.C. App. 670 (1975); Alex Hensley, etals v. Caswell Action Committee, Inc., etals, 296 N.C. 527 (1979); William Lee Dunevant v. Elizabeth Ann Lewis Dunevant, 142 N.C. App. 169 (2001); Whitacre Partnership v. Bio Signia, Inc., etals 153 N.C. App. 608 (2002); Whitacre Partnership v. Bio Signia, Inc., etals 358 N.C. (2004); Caswell County v/ town of Yanceyville, et als, 170 N.C. App. ___ (2005). ***PRACTICE AREAS:*** Civil and Criminal Litigation; Real Estate Law; Probate Law; Local Government Law; Corporation Law; Construction Law; Government Relations; Alternative Dispute Resolution.

OF COUNSEL

BILL T. WALKER, born Atlanta, Georgia, January 15, 1948; admitted to bar, 1978, Illinois and U.S. District Court, Southern District of Illinois; 1981, U.S. Tax Court, U.S. Court of International Trade, U.S. Court of Appeals, Seventh Circuit and U.S. Supreme Court; 1982, U.S Court of Military Appeals; 1983, Missouri; 1985, U.S. District Court, Eastern and Western Districts of Arkansas; 2000, U.S. Court of Appeals, 8th Circuit (Not admitted in North Carolina). *Education:* Elon College (A.B., 1970); Vermont Law School (J.D., 1976); Washington University (LL.M., 1977). *Member:* Illinois State Bar Association; The Missouri Bar. ***PRACTICE AREAS:*** Civil Litigation; Criminal Litigation; Administrative Law.

SANDRA S. PUGH, born Roxboro, North Carolina, October 14, 1944; admitted to bar, 1983, North Carolina. *Education:* Stratford College (A.A., 1965); University of North Carolina at Chapel Hill (B.A., 1967); Campbell University (J.D., 1983). Probation-Parole Officer, N.C. Department of Correction, 1967-1978. Administrative Assistant, Office of the District Attorney, 19A District, 1978-1980. Assistant District Attorney: 29 District, 1984-1988; 17A District, 1988-1996 and 1998-2003. *Member:* 17 Judicial District Bar; 9th Judicial District Bar; North Carolina State Bar. ***PRACTICE AREAS:*** Civil Litigation; Criminal Litigation.

GENERAL COUNSEL FOR: The Gatewood Co.; Town of Yanceyville; C.B. Rowland Co., Inc.; Seven Maples Farms; Ronco, Inc.; A.D. Swann Trucking Co., Inc.; Yanceyville Drug Co.; Gregory Pallet Co.; Marley Funeral Home, Inc.; South Park Enterprises, Inc.; The Forest Home Trust.
LOCAL COUNSEL FOR: Federal Land Bank Assn.; Carolina Farm Credit, ACA.
REPRESENTATIVE CLIENTS: Fidelity Bank; Bank of America; Branch Banking and Trust Co.; Duke Power Co.; Peoples Bank of Danville; State Employers' Credit Union; Caswell Insurance Services, Inc.; Wachovia Bank of North Carolina, N.A.; Shields Auction and Realty Co., Inc.; Virginia Bank & Trust Co.; American National Bank and Trust Co.; Progress Energy Carolinas, Inc.
APPROVED ATTORNEYS FOR: Lawyers Title Insurance Corp.; Chicago Title Insurance Co.; Investors Title Insurance Co.; Federal Land Bank Assn.; Rural Development, U.S.D.A.
REFERENCES: Fidelity Bank; American National Bank and Trust Co.

STUART N. WATLINGTON

114 COURT SQUARE
YANCEYVILLE, NORTH CAROLINA 27379
Telephone: 336-694-1155
Fax: 336-694-1057
Email: snwatlaw@earthlink.net
URL: http://www.swatlingtonlaw.com
Mailing Address: P.O. Box 1776, Yanceyville, NC 27379

General Civil and Criminal Practice in all State and Federal Courts. DWI, Traffic Violations, Personal Injury, Wrongful Death, Probate, Real Estate.

STUART N. WATLINGTON, born Danville, Virginia, June 15, 1954; admitted to bar, 1981, North Carolina; 1982, U.S. District Court, Middle and Western Districts of North Carolina. *Education:* University of North Carolina (A.B., 1976); Campbell University (J.D., 1979). Delta Theta Phi. Morehead Scholar. Campbell Merit Scholar. Public Administrator, Caswell County, 1981-1995. Chairman, Lake Farmer Advisory Board, 1986—. *Member:* Caswell County (President, 1989-1990), North Carolina (Young Lawyers Division Judicial District Representative, 1982-1988) and 9-A Judicial District Bar Associations; North Carolina State Bar; North Carolina Academy of Trial Lawyers; Greensboro Criminal Defense Lawyers Association. ***PRACTICE AREAS:*** Civil and Criminal Litigation; Probate Law; Real Estate Law.

MALCOLM H. BROWN, P.C.

209 EAST BROADWAY AVENUE
P.O. BOX 2692
BISMARCK, NORTH DAKOTA 58502-2692
Telephone: 701-224-8825
Fax: 701-224-8820
Email: mhblaw@btinet.net

Business Law, Real Estate, Commercial Law, Estate Planning, Probate, Condemnation, Eminent Domain, Bankruptcy, General Civil Trial before all State and Federal Courts.

MALCOLM H. BROWN, born Duluth, Minnesota, May 11, 1940; admitted to bar, 1967, North Dakota; 1974, U.S. Court of Appeals, 8th Circuit and U.S. Supreme Court. *Education:* University of North Dakota (Ph.B., 1964; J.D., 1967). Legal Officer, North Dakota Wing, Civil Air Patrol, 1991—. *Member:* Big Muddy Bar Association; State Bar Association of North Dakota; Lawyer-Pilots Bar Association.

REPRESENTATIVE CLIENTS: Basin Electric Power Cooperative; Dakota Gasification Company; North Dakota Guaranty & Title Co.; Starion Financial; Heartview Foundation; The Mandan Title Company; City of Mandan, N.D.

BUCKLIN, KLEMIN & McBRIDE, P.C.

Established in 1982
WELLS FARGO BANK BUILDING, SUITE 500
400 EAST BROADWAY AVENUE
BISMARCK, NORTH DAKOTA 58502-0955
Telephone: 701-258-8988
Fax: 701-258-8486
Email: lawyers@bkmpc.com
URL: http://www.bkmpc.com

Products Liability, Environmental Law, Asbestos, Insurance Defense, Personal Injury, Natural Resources, Commercial Law, Civil Litigation, Corporate, Bankruptcy, Real Estate, Family Law, Domestic Relations, Divorce, Child Custody, Adoptions, Workers Compensation, Social Security, Health Law, Commercial Litigation, Administrative Law, Insurance Law, Estate Planning, Probate, Wills, Business Law.

FIRM PROFILE: Bucklin, Klemin & McBride, P.C. is a regional law firm specializing in litigation. The firm handles a wide variety of litigation for individuals, businesses, other attorneys and insurance companies throughout North Dakota, South Dakota and Montana. Bucklin, Klemin & McBride, P.C. is committed to providing the highest quality of legal services and utilizes state of the art research and other computer services. Members of the firm are also actively engaged in community service and are involved in numerous state and local committees and advisory boards.

LAWRENCE R. KLEMIN, born New Rockford, North Dakota, March 31, 1945; admitted to bar, 1978, North Dakota and U.S. District Court, District of North Dakota; 1987, U.S. Court of Appeals, Eighth Circuit; 1988, U.S. Supreme Court. *Education:* University of North Dakota (B.A., 1967; J.D., with distinction, 1978). Research Editor, North Dakota Law Review, 1977-1978. Author: Civil Practice of North Dakota, Second Edition. President, Litigation Services, Inc. Appeals Referee, North Dakota Employment Security Bureau, 1970-1975. Member, North Dakota House of Representatives; Commissioner, National Conference of Commissioners on Uniform State Laws. Member, National Arbitration Forum. Member, State Advisory Council for North Dakota Office of Administrative Hearings, 1993-1998. *Member:* Big Muddy and American Bar Associations; State Bar Association of North Dakota (Chair, Administrative Law Committee, 1996-1998); The Association of Trial Lawyers of America. [With U.S. Army, 1967-1970]. ***PRACTICE AREAS:*** Products Liability; Insurance Defense; Environmental Law; Commercial Law; Corporate Law; Real Estate Law; Natural Resources; Asbestos Litigation. ***Email:*** lklemin@bkmpc.com

KAREN L. McBRIDE, born Minot, North Dakota, November 10, 1945; admitted to bar, 1984, North Dakota and Minnesota; 1985, U.S. District Court, District of North Dakota and U.S. Court of Appeals, Eighth Circuit. *Education:* Minot State College (B.S., 1969); University of North Dakota (J.D., with distinction, 1984). Order of the Coif. *Member:* Big Muddy and Minnesota State Bar Associations; State Bar Association of North Dakota; Defense Research Institute. ***PRACTICE AREAS:*** Domestic Relations Law; Family Law; Probate Law; Real Estate; Business Law; Estate Planning; Litigation. ***Email:*** kmcbride@bkmpc.com

DAVID SCHWEIGERT, born Baker, Montana, November 7, 1967; admitted to bar, 1993, North Dakota, South Dakota; 1994, Montana, U.S. District Court, Districts of North Dakota, South Dakota and Montana and U.S. Court of Appeals, Eighth Circuit. *Education:* Jamestown College (B.A., cum laude, 1990); University of North Dakota (J.D., with distinction, 1993). Phi Alpha Delta. *Member:* State Bar Association of North Dakota; Big Muddy Bar Association; The State Bar of South Dakota; State Bar Association of Montana; The Association of Trial Lawyers of America. ***PRACTICE AREAS:*** Personal Injury Law; Product Liability Law; Insurance Defense Law; Litigation. ***Email:*** dschweigert@bkmpc.com

ASSOCIATE

STEVEN M. BITZ, born Bismarck, North Dakota, November 10, 1976; admitted to bar, 2003, North Dakota. *Education:* Bismarck State College (A.A., 1997; A.S., 1997) University of Mary (B.A., Accounting, 1999); Bismarck State College (A.A.S., Residential Carpentry, 2000); University of North Dakota School of Law (J.D., 2003). Real Estate Broker, North Dakota, 2002. Certified Abstracter of Title, North Dakota, 2002. *Member:* State Bar Association of North Dakota; North Dakota Association of Realtors; National Association of Realtors. ***PRACTICE AREAS:*** Personal Injury; Products Liability; Real Estate; Probate; Estate Planning; Domestic Relations; Civil Litigation. ***Email:*** sbitz@bkmpc.com

(This Listing Continued)

OF COUNSEL

LEONARD H. BUCKLIN, born Minneapolis, Minnesota, April 17, 1933; admitted to bar, 1957, Minnesota; 1958, U.S. District Court, District of Minnesota; 1960, North Dakota and U.S. District Court, District of North Dakota; 1973, U.S. Court of Appeals, Eighth Circuit and U.S. Supreme Court; 1988, Colorado; 1992, Texas. *Education:* University of Minnesota (B.S.L., 1954; J.D., 1956). Order of the Coif; Phi Delta Phi; Delta Sigma Rho. *Member:* State Bar Association of North Dakota; State Bar of Texas; American Bar Association. Fellow, International Academy of Trial Lawyers (Director, 1990-1996). ***PRACTICE AREAS:*** Personal Injury Law; Complex Commercial Litigation; Insurance Coverage Litigation. ***Email:*** Leonard@bucklin.org

REPRESENTATIVE CLIENTS: Adams Farm Mutual Insurance Co.; Alexsis; American Bankers Insurance Co.; American Reliable Insurance Co.; Avco Financial Services; Bank of North Dakota; Basin Electric Power Cooperative; Bismarck-Mandan Development Association; Center Mutual Insurance Co.; Chubb Group of Insurance Cos.; Central National Insurance Co.; Cooper Industries, Inc.; Crum and Forster Group; Electric Insurance; Electric Mutual Insurance Co.; Empire Fire & Marine Insurance Co.; Eye Clinic of North Dakota; Farmers Alliance Mutual Insurance; Farmers Union Mutual Insurance Co.; Forum Insurance; Gardner Denver, Inc.; General Accident Insurance Co.; General Casualty Cos.; General Electric Company; Globe Life Insurance Co.; Hawkeye Security Insurance Co.; GMAC Mortgage Corporation of Iowa; Hartford Insurance Group; Kmart; LeMars Mutual Insurance Co.; Montgomery Ward & Co.; Mutual of Omaha; National Farmers Union Property and Casualty Co.; Nodak Mutual Insurance Co.; North Dakota Guaranty and Title Company; Wells Fargo Bank North Dakota; Wells Fargo Bank Minnesota; Wells Fargo Home Mortgage, Inc.; Principal Mutual Life Insurance Co.; Prudential; Regional Neurological Center; Reliance Insurance Co.; Sedgwick James of Illinois; Southwest Water Authority; US Bank; Waste Management Co.
REFERENCE: Wells Fargo Bank North Dakota.

JOSEPH J. CICHY, P.C.

115 NORTH 4TH STREET, SUITE 2
BISMARCK, NORTH DAKOTA 58501
Telephone: 701-223-4524
Fax: 701-223-0855
Email: jcichy@midconetwork.com

Real Estate, Business Law, Corporate Law, Administrative Law, Association Management, Water Law, Lobbying, Family Law, Personal Injury.

JOSEPH J. CICHY, born Fargo, North Dakota, May 12, 1949; admitted to bar, 1981, North Dakota and U.S. District Court, District of North Dakota; 1984, U.S. Court of Appeals, Ninth Circuit. *Education:* North Dakota State University (B.A., 1971; M.Ed., 1981); University of North Dakota (J.D., 1981). Delta Theta Phi. North Dakota Assistant Attorney General, 1981-1985. Director, Legal Services, North Dakota Water Commission, 1983-1985. *Member:* Burleigh County Bar Association; State Bar Association of North Dakota. ***PRACTICE AREAS:*** Real Estate (25%); Business Law (20%); Administrative Law (10%); Water Law (15%); Family Law (20%); Government Relations (10%). ***Email:*** jcichy@midconetwork.com

DYER & SUMMERS, P.C.

Established in 1985
418 EAST BROADWAY, SUITE 246
P.O. BOX 2261
BISMARCK, NORTH DAKOTA 58502
Telephone: 701-223-2099
Fax: 701-223-4889
Email: dyersums@gcentral.com
URL: http://www.lawyers.com/dyersums

General Civil Practice in State, Federal, and Tribal Courts, Divorce and other Family Law, Consumer Bankruptcy, and Social Security Disability.

FIRM PROFILE: Dyer & Summers, P.C. was founded by Edwin W.F. Dyer III in 1985 after eleven years of practice in the legal services area. He was joined by Anne E. Summers, who then had four years of experience, in 1986. The firm provides a range of civil legal services to clients, both in the Bismarck-Mandan area and in other parts of North Dakota.

EDWIN W. F. DYER, III, born Greenfield, Massachusetts, October 14, 1946; admitted to bar, 1974, Massachusetts; 1975, Montana; 1978, South Dakota and U.S. District Court, District of North Dakota; 1979, U.S. Court of Appeals, Eighth Circuit; 1980, North Dakota; 1991, Standing Rock Sioux Tribal Court. *Education:* University of Massachusetts (B.A., 1968); Boston University (J.D., 1973). Former Temporary Administrative Law Judge, North Dakota Office of Administrative Hearings, 1995-2003. Former Chief Judge, Standing Rock Sioux Tribal Court, 1989-1991. *Member:* Big Muddy Bar Association; State Bar Association of North Dakota. ***PRACTICE AREAS:*** Consumer Bankruptcy; Social Security Disability; Administrative Law; Family Law; Indian Law. ***Email:*** dyersums@gcentral.com

ANNE E. SUMMERS, born Boone, Iowa, December 21, 1947; admitted to bar, 1982, North Dakota; 1983, U.S. District Court, District of North Dakota. *Education:* University of North Dakota (B.A., 1970; J.D., 1982). *Member:* Big Muddy Bar Association; State Bar Association of North Dakota (Sections on: Family Law; Women Lawyers). ***LANGUAGES:*** French. ***PRACTICE AREAS:*** Family Law; Child Custody; Guardian Ad Litem; Juvenile Law; Social Security Disability; General Practice. ***Email:*** ladystar@gcentral.com

LEGAL SUPPORT PERSONNEL

STACY KUNTZ, born Grand Forks, North Dakota, October 3, 1978. *Education:* North Dakota State University (B.S., 2001). (Certified Legal Assistant)

FLECK LAW OFFICE

314 EAST THAYER AVENUE, SUITE 220
P.O. BOX 6178
BISMARCK, NORTH DAKOTA 58506-6178
Telephone: 701-258-5256
Fax: 701-258-5626
Email: arnfleck@usa.net

Personal Injury, Automobile Accidents, Wrongful Death, Medical Malpractice, Family Law, Divorce, Collections, Estate Planning, Probate, Civil Litigation.

ARNOLD V. FLECK, born Mandan, North Dakota, March 14, 1958; admitted to bar, 1983, North Dakota; 1984, U.S. District Court, District of North Dakota; 1985, Minnesota; 1991, U.S. Court of Appeals, Eighth Circuit. *Education:* North Dakota State University (B.S., cum laude, 1980); University of North Dakota (J.D., 1983). *Member:* American Bar Association (Member: Family Law Section; Tort & Insurance Practice Section); State Bar Association of North Dakota; Bid Muddy Bar Association; North Dakota Trial Lawyers Association; The Association of Trial Lawyers of America. ***PRACTICE AREAS:*** Civil Litigation.

FLECK, MATHER & STRUTZ, LTD.

Established in 1945
SIXTH FLOOR, WELLS FARGO BANK BUILDING
400 EAST BROADWAY, SUITE 600
P.O. BOX 2798
BISMARCK, NORTH DAKOTA 58502-2798
Telephone: 701-223-6585
Facsimile: 701-222-4853
Email: fms@flecklaw.com
URL: http://www.flecklaw.com

Corporation, Real Estate, Labor and Employment Relations, Insurance, Legal Malpractice Litigation, Defense Litigation, Dental Malpractice, Medical Devices, Medical Malpractice, Oil and Gas and Mining Law, Trials and Appeals. General Civil Practice before all Courts and Administrative Boards.

FIRM PROFILE: Fleck, Mather & Strutz, Ltd. has engaged in the general practice of law since its founding in 1945. The firm offers a wide variety of legal services and serves the entire state of North Dakota and has attorneys licensed in Minnesota, Montana, Iowa and Wyoming and Nebraska.

ERNEST R. FLECK (1921-1995)

RUSSELL R. MATHER (Retired)

WILLIAM A. STRUTZ (Retired)

GARY R. WOLBERG, born Dickinson, North Dakota, October 23, 1947; admitted to bar, 1976, North Dakota and Iowa. *Education:* Dickinson State College (B.A., 1969); Iowa State University (M.A., 1971); University of North Dakota (J.D., 1975). Author: Note, "Long Arm Jurisdiction in North Dakota," 52 North Dakota Law Review 183, 1975. Lecturer: "Tackling Environmental Issues in North Dakota," The Cambridge Institute, June, 1991, May, 1992, Nov., 1993; "Avoiding Environmental Liability in North Dakota," National Business Institute, Sept., 1991, Dec., 1992; "Advanced Real Estate Law," National Business Institute, Sept., 1992; "North Dakota Water Law," Law Seminars International, May, 1995, Sept., 1996. *Member:* State Bar Association of North Dakota (Member, Sections of: Insurance Negligence and Compensation Law; Natural Resources Law); Iowa State (Member, Environmental and Natural Resources Section) and American (Member, Sections of: Tort and Insurance Practice Law; Natural Resources Law) Bar Associations; American Agricultural Law Association. ***PRACTICE AREAS:*** Insurance Defense; Litigation; Employment Law; Environmental Law; Oil and Gas Law; Products Liability. ***Email:*** gwolberg@flecklaw.com

PAUL W. SUMMERS, born Fargo, North Dakota, July 13, 1952; admitted to bar, 1978, North Dakota. *Education:* Concordia College and Jamestown College (B.A., 1974); Pepperdine University (J.D., 1978). *Member:* State Bar Association of North Dakota (Member: Section of Real Property, Probate and Trust Law; Mineral Title Standards Committee); American Bar Association (Member, Sections of: Natural Resources Law; Real Property, Probate and Trust Law). ***PRACTICE AREAS:*** Oil and Gas Law; Mining Law; Real Property Law; Probate. ***Email:*** psummers@flecklaw.com

BRIAN R. BJELLA, born Williston, North Dakota, March 24, 1952; admitted to bar, 1979, North Dakota; 1997, Montana; 2000, Minnesota. *Education:* University of North Dakota (B.A., cum laude, 1975; J.D., 1979). Program Vice-Chair, "Mineral Title Examination III," Rocky Mt. Min. L. Fdn. 1992; Program Chair, "Oil & Natural Gas Pipelines," Rocky Mt. Min. L. Fdn. 1995; Program Committee, "The Electric Industry," Rocky Mt. Min. L. Fdn., 1997. Author, "Removing the Operator Under the Joint Operating Agreement," 45 Rocky Mtn. Min. L. Fdn. 1999; Program Chair, "Water Quality and Wetlands," Rocky Mtn. Min. L. Fdn. 2002. *Member:* American Bar Association (Member, Sections on: Real Property; Environment and Energy); Rocky Mountain Mineral Law Foundation (Trustee, 2002-2004); Lignite Energy Council (Secretary/Treasurer). ***PRACTICE AREAS:*** Real Property Law; Oil and Gas Law; Mining Law; Environmental Law; Public Utilities Law; Government Relations. ***Email:*** brbjella@flecklaw.com

JOHN W. MORRISON, JR., born Independence, Missouri, October 11, 1954; admitted to bar, 1978, North Dakota. *Education:* Mary College (B.S., 1975); University of North Dakota (J.D., 1978). Author: "Horizontal Drilling-The Changing Role of Conservation Principles," Federal Onshore Pooling and Unitization II, Rocky Mt. Mineral Law Inst (1990); "Regulation of Gas Gathering Systems," 39 Rocky Mt. Law Inst. (1993). *Member:* State Bar Association of North Dakota (Member, Section of Real Property, Probate and Trust Law); American Bar Association (Member, Sections of: Natural Resources Law; Real Property, Probate and Trust Law; Administrative Law). ***PRACTICE AREAS:*** Oil and Gas Law; Utilities Law; Real Property Law; Corporate Financing Law; Communications Law. ***Email:*** jwmorris@flecklaw.com

CURTIS L. WIKE, admitted to bar, 1985, North Dakota; 1986, Minnesota; 1997, Montana. *Education:* University of North Dakota (B.A., cum laude, 1982; J.D., with distinction, 1985). *Member:* State Bar Association of North Dakota; American Bar Association (Member, Sections on Tort and Insurance Practice, Litigation); Defense Research Institute; North Dakota Defense Lawyers Association. ***PRACTICE AREAS:*** Insurance Defense Law; Insurance; General Litigation. ***Email:*** cwike@flecklaw.com

CRAIG CORDELL SMITH, born Williston, North Dakota, July 27, 1963; admitted to bar, 1988, North Dakota; 1989, Montana; 1990, U.S. District Court, District of North Dakota and U.S. Court of Appeals, Eighth Circuit; 2002, Wyoming. *Education:* University of North Dakota (B.A., cum laude, 1985); University of Tulsa (J.D., 1988). Editor, Notes & Comments, Energy Law Journal, 1987-1988. Student Editor, American Bar Association Natural Resource Law Monograph Series, 1987-1988. *Member:* State Bar of Montana (Member, Section on Natural Resources); State Bar Association of North Dakota (Member, Section on Natural Resources); American Bar Association (Member, Section on Natural Resources). ***PRACTICE AREAS:*** Oil and Gas Law; Real Property; Commercial Law. ***Email:*** ccsmith@flecklaw.com

SHANE A. HANSON, born Finley, North Dakota, June 6, 1970; admitted to bar, 1996, North Dakota. *Education:* Jamestown College (B.A., magna cum laude, 1991); University of North Dakota (J.D., with distinction, 1996). Delta Theta Phi. *Member:* North Dakota State and American Bar Association (Member, Section on Natural Resources and Real Property). ***PRACTICE AREAS:*** Oil and Gas Law; Real Property; Commercial Law; Debtor/Creditor Law; Insurance Defense. ***Email:*** sahanson@flecklaw.com

MICHAEL C. WALLER, born Helena, Montana, October 22, 1957; admitted to bar, 1985, Montana; 1986, U.S. District Court, District of Montana; 1987, U.S. Court of Appeals, Eighth Circuit; 1991, North Dakota and U.S. District Court, District of North Dakota. *Education:* University of North Dakota (B.S., cum laude, in Ed., 1980); University of Idaho College of Law (J.D., cum laude, 1985). Member, 1983-1985 and Executive Editor, 1984-1985, Idaho Law Review. *Member:* State Bar of Montana; State Bar Association of North Dakota (Member: Inquiry Committee West; Fee Arbitration Panel); American Bar Association (Member: Sections on: Health Law; Litigation); North Dakota Defense Lawyers Association (President, 2003; Vice President, 2002); Defense Research Institute (Member, Medical Liability Section). ***PRACTICE AREAS:*** Medical Law; Professional Malpractice Defense; Health Care Law; Medical Malpractice Defense; Dental Malpractice Defense. ***Email:*** mwaller@flecklaw.com

ASSOCIATE

PETRA H. MANDIGO, born Hartford, Connecticut, April 2, 1976; admitted to bar, 2003, Nebraska; 2004, North Dakota. *Education:* Ripon College (B.A., 1998); Creighton University (J.D., magna cum laude, 2003). Phi Delta Phi. Member, North Dakota Supreme Court Joint Committee on Attorney Standards, 2005—. *Member:* Big Muddy, Nebraska State and American (Member, Sections on: Torts; Insurance Practice) Bar Associations; State Bar Association of North Dakota; Defense Research Institute; Inns of Court. ***PRACTICE AREAS:*** Medical Malpractice Defense; Dental Malpractice Defense; Professional Malpractice Defense; Health Care Law; Insurance Defense. ***Email:*** pmandigo@flecklaw.com

All Attorneys are Members of the State Capital Law Firm Group. (Member firms of the State Capital Law Firm Group practice independently and not in a relationship for the joint practice of law).

REPRESENTATIVE CLIENTS: Amerada Hess Corp.; Basin Electric Power Cooperative; Burlington Resources Oil & Gas Company; Exxon Company; Great River Energy; Koch Industries, Inc.; Lignite Energy Council; The North American Coal Corporation; Petro-Hunt LLC; American International Group; CNA Insurance; Dakota Fire Insurance Company; The Doctors' Company; The Hartford; Medical Protective Company; Mid Dakota Clinic, Inc.; National Farmers Union Insurance Cos.; North Dakota Insurance Reserve Fund; State Farm; Wells Fargo Bank.

GERMOLUS LAW OFFICE

Established in 2005
REGENCY BUSINESS CENTER
3333 E. BROADWAY AVENUE, SUITE 1215
BISMARCK, NORTH DAKOTA 58501-3395
Telephone: 701-255-2010
Fax: 701-255-1980
Email: germoluslaw@bis.midco.net
URL: http://www.lawyers.com/germoluslaw

Natural Resources Law, Agricultural Law, Fish and Wildlife Law, Real Property Law, Administrative Law.

MEMBER OF FIRM

PAUL C. GERMOLUS, born Ada, Minnesota, February 27, 1967; admitted to bar, 1997, North Dakota and Minnesota; 1999, U.S. District Court, District of North Dakota. *Education:* North Dakota State University (B.S., 1989); University of North Dakota (J.D., 1997). *Member:* Burleigh County Bar Association; State Bar Association of North Dakota; American Agricultural Law Association. ***PRACTICE AREAS:*** Natural Resources; Fisheries Law; Wildlife Law; Agricultural Law; Real Property; Administrative Law. ***Email:*** germoluslaw@bis.midco.net

REPRESENTATIVE CLIENTS: International Association of Fish and Wildlife Agencies; Independent Beef Association of North Dakota; ND Dry Pea & Lentil Association; Gartner Seed Farm; Keller Broken Heart Ranch.

(This Listing Continued)

JEFFRIES, OLSON & FLOM, P.A.

BISMARCK, NORTH DAKOTA

(See Fargo)

General Insurance Defense, Trial and Appellate Practice in Minnesota and North Dakota State and Federal Courts. Medical and other Professional Malpractice, Civil Rights, Construction, Products Liability, Fire, Government and Municipalities, Errors & Omissions, Environmental Law, Health Law, Casualty, Negligence, Asbestos Litigation, Hazardous Waste, Toxic Substances, Pollution, No-Fault, Insurance Coverages, Employment, Liquor Liability, Automobile, Premises Liability, Commercial Litigation, Subrogation.

KELSCH KELSCH RUFF & KRANDA

BISMARCK, NORTH DAKOTA

(See Mandan)

Estate Planning, Probate, Wills, Real Estate, Family Law, Divorce, Adoptions, Commercial Litigation, Personal Injury, Products Liability, Administrative Law, Environmental Law, Lobbying, Banking, Business Law, Bankruptcy, Corporate Law, Collections, Civil Litigation.

LINDELL LAW OFFICE

BISMARCK, NORTH DAKOTA

(See Washburn)

Estate Planning, Wills, Trusts, Probate, Real Estate, Business Law, Taxation, Collections, Commercial Litigation, Civil Practice in all State and Federal Courts.

MARING WILLIAMS LAW OFFICE, P.C.

400 EAST BROADWAY
SUITE 307
BISMARCK, NORTH DAKOTA 58501
Telephone: 701-224-0430
Fax: 701-224-0454
Email: mwlo@maringlaw.com
URL: http://www.maringlaw.com

Fargo, North Dakota Office: 1220 Main Avenue, Suite 105, P.O. Box 2103. 58107-2103. Telephone: 701-241-4141. Fax: 701-235-2268.
Detroit Lakes, Minnesota Office: 714 Lake Avenue, Suite 101. 56501. Telephone: 218-847-2257.

Automobile Accidents, Wrongful Death, Personal Injury, NeuroLaw, Commercial Litigation, Professional Liability, Products Liability, Negligence, Civil Rights and Torts, Family Law, Civil Litigation. Trial Practice in all Courts.

(For Complete Biographical Data on all Personnel, see Professional Biographies at Fargo, North Dakota)

MAXSON LAW OFFICE, P.C.

BISMARCK, NORTH DAKOTA

(See Minot)

Estate Planning, Probate, Trusts, Wills, Business Planning, Corporate Law, Real Estate, Commercial Litigation, Civil Litigation.

MORLEY LAW FIRM, LTD.

BISMARCK, NORTH DAKOTA

(See Grand Forks)

Insurance Defense, Negligence, Personal Injury, Governmental Defense, Products Liability, Toxic Torts Defense, Insurance Coverage, Legal Malpractice, Dram Shop, Construction Litigation, Communications Law, Medical Malpractice, Complex Business Litigation, Complex Commercial Litigation, Civil Trial Practice in all Courts.

PEARCE & DURICK

Established in 1919

314 EAST THAYER AVENUE
P.O. BOX 400
BISMARCK, NORTH DAKOTA 58502
Telephone: 701-223-2890
Fax: 701-223-7865
Email: law.office@pearce-durick.com
URL: http://www.pearce-durick.com

Products Liability Defense, Oil and Gas, Mining, Insurance Defense, Negligence, Real Estate, Corporate Law, Taxation, Business Law, Commercial Law, Banking, Estate Planning, Probate, Wills, Public Utilities, Education Law, Intellectual Property, Employment Law, Appeals, Civil Litigation before all Courts and Administrative Agencies.

FIRM PROFILE: Pearce & Durick traces its roots back to 1919, when Edward Cox joined Herbert O'Hare in the practice of law in Bismarck, North Dakota. The firm offers a wide range of legal services throughout North Dakota and the Midwestern and Western states and specializes in products liability law, insurance defense law, natural resources law, employment law, and education law. All attorneys and professional support staff regularly participate in continuing education seminars and professional association activities.

(This Listing Continued)

MEMBERS OF FIRM

WILLIAM R. PEARCE (1910-1978)

WILLIAM P. PEARCE, born Valley City, North Dakota, August 17, 1940; admitted to bar, 1971, North Dakota; 1974, U.S. Supreme Court. *Education:* Purdue University and Northwestern University (B.A., 1962; M.S., 1964; Ph.D., 1967); Northwestern University (J.D., 1971). Phi Beta Kappa; Order of the Coif; Sigma Xi. Articles Editor, Northwestern University Law Review, 1970-1971. Author: "Surface Damages and the Oil and Gas Operator in North Dakota," 58 North Dakota Law Review 457, 1982; "Keeping Oil and Gas Leases Alive," Rocky Mountain Min. Law Foundation Institute on Problems and Opportunities During Hard Times in the Minerals Industry, May, 1986; "The Basis of the Implied Covenants," Rocky Mountain Min. Law Foundation Workshop, November, 1986; "Methodology of Reviewing Title Data and Preparing the Title Opinion," Rocky Mountain Min. Law Foundation Institute, "Mineral Title Examination III," February 1992; "Acquiring Mineral Rights of Unknown or Unlocatable Heirs," Rocky Mountain Min. Law Foundation 1994 Annual Institute; "Dormant Minerals and Reunification of Estates," Rocky Mountain Mineral Law Foundation Institute on Severed Minerals, Split Estates, Rights of Access, and Surface Use in Mineral Extraction Operations, February 2005. Co-Author: "North Dakota Mineral Title Standards," State Bar Association of North Dakota, 1989. Adjunct Professor, Oil and Gas Law, University of North Dakota School of Law, 1983-1989. Adjunct Professor, Astronomy and Meteorology, Bismarck State College, 1995—. Member, Board of Directors and Legal Committee of Rocky Mountain Oil and Gas Association, 1984-1999. Member, Grants Committee of Rocky Mountain Mineral Law Foundation. *Member:* Burleigh County and American Bar Associations; State Bar Association of North Dakota. ***LANGUAGES:*** French. ***PRACTICE AREAS:*** Oil and Gas Law; Public Utility Law; Taxation Law; Real Estate; Probate Law. **Email:** wpp@pearce-durick.com

PATRICK W. DURICK, born Powers Lake, North Dakota, December 12, 1940; admitted to bar, 1973, Nebraska; 1974, North Dakota; 1975, U.S. Court of Appeals, Eighth Circuit. *Education:* United States Air Force Academy (B.S., 1964); Creighton University (J.D., 1972). Law Clerk to the Honorable Robert Denney, U.S. District Judge, District of Nebraska, 1973-1974. Member, 1981-1992 and Chairman, 1989-1991, U.S. District Court of North Dakota Federal Practice Committee. Chairman, Board of Trustees, Medcenter One, 1991—. Member: North Dakota Supreme Court, Commission on Gender Fairness in the Courts, 1994-1996; Gender Fairness Implementation Committee, 1997—; Member, 1991-1997 and Chairman, 1996-1997, North Dakota Pattern Jury Instruction Committee; U.S. District Court, District of North Dakota, Civil Justice Reform Act Advisory Group, 1990-1997. *Member:* Burleigh County and American Bar Associations; State Bar Association of North Dakota. [Capt., USAF, 1964-1970]. ***PRACTICE AREAS:*** Products Liability Law; Communications Law; Insurance Defense Law; Commercial Law; Professional Malpractice. **Email:** pwd@pearce-durick.com

B. TIMOTHY DURICK, born Crosby, North Dakota, March 31, 1945; admitted to bar, 1971, North Dakota. *Education:* University of Notre Dame (B.A., 1967); University of Minnesota (J.D., 1971). Legal Counsel and Special Assistant Attorney General, North Dakota Tax Department, 1971-1972. *Member:* Burleigh County Bar Association; State Bar Association of North Dakota; Defense Research Institute. ***PRACTICE AREAS:*** General Negligence Trials and Appeals; Insurance Defense Law; Products Liability Defense. **Email:** btd@pearce-durick.com

GARY R. THUNE, born Williston, North Dakota, May 18, 1942; admitted to bar, 1974, North Dakota and U.S. District Court, District of North Dakota; 1978, U.S. Court of Appeals, Eighth Circuit; 1979, U.S. Supreme Court; 1980, Minnesota. *Education:* Minot State College (B.S., 1964); University of North Dakota (M.Ed., 1967; J.D., 1974). Order of the Coif. Member, Editorial Staff, North Dakota Law Review, 1973-1974. *Member:* Burleigh County and American Bar Associations; State Bar Association of North Dakota; North Dakota Council of School Attorneys; National School Boards Association Council of School Attorneys (Chairman). ***PRACTICE AREAS:*** Education Law; Litigation; Employment Law. **Email:** grt@pearce-durick.com

DAVID E. REICH, born Medina, North Dakota, December 29, 1956; admitted to bar, 1982, North Dakota. *Education:* University of North Dakota (B.A., summa cum laude, 1979; J.D., with distinction, 1982). Phi Delta Phi. Law Clerk, North Dakota Supreme Court, 1982-1983. *Member:* Burleigh County and American (Member, Sections on: Tort and Insurance Practice; Labor and Employment) Bar Associations; State Bar Association of North Dakota; Defense Research Institute; North Dakota Defense Lawyers Association; North Dakota Council of School Attorneys; National School Boards Association Council of School Attorneys. ***PRACTICE AREAS:*** General Negligence Trials and Appeals; Education Law; Insurance Defense Law; Employment Law; Alternative Dispute Resolution; Administrative Law. **Email:** der@pearce-durick.com

JEROME C. KETTLESON, born Bismarck, North Dakota, December 2, 1946; admitted to bar, 1973, North Dakota and U.S. District Court, District of North Dakota; U.S. Court of Appeals, Eighth Circuit. *Education:* St. John University (B.A., 1967); University of North Dakota (J.D., 1973). Phi Delta Phi. Member, 1976-1981 and President, 1978, Lisbon, North Dakota Public School District School Board. Assistant U.S. Attorney, Bismarck, North Dakota, 1981-1986. Member: U.S. District Court Federal Practice Committee, 1993—; Civil Justice Reform Act Advisory Group, 1993-1997; Disciplinary Board of the North Dakota Supreme Court, 1997-2003. *Member:* Burleigh County Bar Association; State Bar Association of North Dakota (Commission on Continuing Legal Education, 1992-1996). [1st Lt. U.S. Army Infantry, 1968-1970]. (Certified as a Civil Trial Advocate by the National Board of Trial Advocacy). ***PRACTICE AREAS:*** General Negligence Trials and Appeals; Insurance Defense Law; Products Liability Defense. **Email:** jck@pearce-durick.com

LARRY L. BOSCHEE, born Wishek, North Dakota, April 18, 1960; admitted to bar, 1985, North Dakota and Minnesota; 1987, U.S. District Court, District of North Dakota; 1988, U.S. Court of Appeals, Eighth Circuit; 1991, South Dakota; 1992, U.S. District Court, District of South Dakota; 2005, Montana and U.S. Supreme Court. *Education:* Valley City State University (B.S., summa cum laude, 1982); University of North Dakota (J.D., with distinction, 1985). Contributing Author: "Product Liability Desk Reference, A Fifty State Compendium," (M. Daller, 2005). Law Clerk to the Honorable Paul Benson, United States District Court, District of North Dakota, 1985-1987. *Member:* State Bar Association of North Dakota; The State Bar of South Dakota; Product Liability Advisory Council; Defense

(This Listing Continued)

PEARCE & DURICK, Bismarck—Continued

Research Institute (Member, Product Liability Committee); North Dakota Defense Lawyers Association; South Dakota Defense Lawyers Association; North Dakota Pattern Jury Instruction Committee, 2002—; Judge Bruce Van Sickle American Inn of Court (President, 2005). ***PRACTICE AREAS:*** Products Liability Defense; Insurance Defense; Commercial Litigation. ***Email:*** llb@pearce-durick.com

LAWRENCE BENDER, (P.C.), born Streeter, North Dakota; admitted to bar, 1982, North Dakota; 1983, Minnesota; 2004, South Dakota. *Education:* North Dakota State University (B.A., 1976; M.A., 1981); University of North Dakota (J.D., 1982). Phi Delta Phi. Assistant Attorney General of the State of North Dakota, 1982-1987. Counsel for North Dakota Industrial Commission, Oil and Gas Division, Board of University and School Lands, 1982-1987. Governor's Representative, Interstate Oil Compact Commission, 1985-1987. Recipient, North Dakota's Attorney General's Office Lawyer of the Year Award, 1985. *Member:* Burleigh County Bar Association; State Bar Association of North Dakota; Minnesota State Bar Association. ***PRACTICE AREAS:*** Oil and Gas Law; Real Property Law; Environmental Law; Governmental Relations Law. ***Email:*** lxb@pearce-durick.com

JONATHAN P. SANSTEAD, born Fargo, North Dakota; admitted to bar, 1995, North Dakota; 1996, U.S. District Court, District of North Dakota; 1998, U.S. Court of Appeals, Eighth Circuit; 2002, U.S. Supreme Court. *Education:* St. Cloud State University (B.A., 1992); William Mitchell College of Law (J.D., cum laude, 1995). Law Clerk to The Honorable Patrick A. Conmy, U.S. District Court, District of North Dakota, 1995-1996. *Member:* State Bar Association of North Dakota; American Bar Association. ***PRACTICE AREAS:*** Commercial Law; Employment Law; Intellectual Property Law; Business Law; Banks and Banking; Financial Law. ***Email:*** jps@pearce-durick.com

---

TIFFANY L. JOHNSON, born Williston, North Dakota, June 9, 1977; admitted to bar, 2005, North Dakota. *Education:* Moorhead State University (B.A., 2000); University of North Dakota (J.D., with distinction, 2005). Order of the Barristers. Symposium Editor, North Dakota Law Review, 2004-2005. Author, "Mental Health Crimes: United States Supreme Court Sets Guidelines for Forcibly Medicating Pre-Trial Detainees Solely for Prosecutorial Purposes, Sell v. United States, 539 U.S. 166 (2003)," 80 North Dakota Law Review 355, 2004. *Member:* State Bar Association of North Dakota. ***PRACTICE AREAS:*** General Practice.

LEGAL SUPPORT PERSONNEL

SUZANNE CAHILL, born Bismarck, North Dakota, March 13, 1961. *Education:* National Academy for Paralegal Studies, University of Mary (Certificate, 1992). Outstanding Scholastic Achievement Award, 1992. (Paralegal). ***PRACTICE AREAS:*** Litigation Support; Products Liability Defense; Asbestos; Insurance Defense. ***Email:*** sue@pearce-durick.com

REPRESENTATIVE CLIENTS: AGCO Corporation; Alliance Pipeline, Ltd.; Attorneys Liability Protection Society; Bank Center First; Bear Paw Energy, Inc.; BNC National Bank; BP Amoco Corp.; Bombardier Inc.; Bridgestone Firestone, Inc.; Brown & Brown, Inc.; Chevron U.S.A. Inc.; Chubb Group of Insurance Cos.; Cincinnati Insurance Cos.; CNH Global N.V.; Conoco Inc.; Continental Resources, Inc.; Continental Western Insurance Co.; Cooper Tire & Rubber Co.; Crum & Forster Insurance Co.; DaimlerChrysler Corp.; Dawes Rigging & Crane Rental, Inc.; Deere & Co.; Emerson Electric Co.; Enron Oil & Gas Co.; Ford Motor Co.; Ford Motor Credit Co.; Freightliner LLC; Gallagher Basset Services, Inc.; General Motors Corp.; Grupo IMSA, S.A. de C.V.; Interstate Insurance Group; Kawasaki Motor Corp., USA; Kemper Insurance Cos.; Lakehead Pipe Line Co.; Merrill-Lynch, Inc.; Midwest Casualty Insurance Co.; Minnesota Mining and Manufacturing Co.; MDU Resources Group, Inc.; Motorists Insurance Cos.; National Indemnity Insurance Co.; Nexen Oil & gas U.S.A., Inc.; North Dakota Association of Builders; North Dakota Board of Dental Examiners; North Dakota Development Fund; North Dakota High School Activities Assn.; North Dakota Insurance Reserve Fund; North Dakota Real Estate Commission; North Dakota School Boards Assn.; North Dakota State Board of Architecture; Penn-American Group; Pharmacists Mutual Cos.; Phelps Dodge Industries, inc.; Phoenix Aviation Managers, Inc.; Sears Roebuck & Co.; Sentry Claims Service; Sentry Insurance Co.; Shell Oil Co.; St. Paul Travelers; Summit Resources Inc.; Texaco Inc.; The Goodyear Tire & Rubber Co.; U.S. Bancorp; Vanliner Insurance Co.; Wausau Insurance Cos.; Westmoreland Coal Co.; North Dakota Workforce Safety & Insurance; Zurich North America.

STORSLEE LAW FIRM, P.C.

P.O. BOX 4007
P.O. BOX 1802 ALLISON DRIVE
BISMARCK, NORTH DAKOTA 58502-4007
Telephone: 701-222-1315
Fax: 701-222-1373
Email: sstorslee@storsleelaw.com
URL: http://www.lawyers.com/storsleelaw

Insurance Defense, Products Liability, Professional Liability Defense, Insurance Coverage, Property Damage Subrogation.

STEVEN A. STORSLEE, born Ada, Minnesota, May 1, 1951; admitted to bar, 1976, North Dakota and Minnesota. *Education:* Concordia College (B.A., 1973); University of North Dakota (J.D., 1976). Order of the Coif. *Member:* State Bar Association of North Dakota; Minnesota State Bar Association; North Dakota Trial Lawyers Association; North Dakota Defense Lawyers Association. ***PRACTICE AREAS:*** General Insurance Defense Law; Products Liability; Professional Liability Defense; Insurance Coverage; Property Damage Subrogation. ***Email:*** sstorslee@storsleelaw.com

CHRIS A. EDISON, born Lisbon, North Dakota, January 16, 1966; admitted to bar, 1995, North Dakota; 1997, Minnesota. *Education:* Moorhead State University (B.S., 1992); University of North Dakota (J.D., 1995). Special Assistant Attorney General, 1995-1999. General Counsel, North Dakota Commissioner of Insurance, 1998-1999. *Member:* State Bar Association of North Dakota; Minnesota State Bar Association. ***PRACTICE AREAS:*** Insurance; Regulatory; General Practice. ***Email:*** cedison@storslee.com

REPRESENTATIVE CLIENTS: Employers Mutual Companies; State Farm Fire & Casualty; National Farmers Union Companies; Farmers Insurance Group; Crum & Forster; Safeco.

TSCHIDER & SMITH

A Partnership including Professional Corporations
Established in 1962
PROFESSIONAL BUILDING - SUITE 200
418 EAST ROSSER AVENUE
BISMARCK, NORTH DAKOTA 58501
Telephone: 701-258-4000
Fax: 701-258-4001
Email: ssmith@tschider-smithlaw.com

General Civil Practice before all State and Federal Courts. Litigation, Real Estate, Taxation, Banking, Commercial, Partnership, Corporation, Bankruptcy, Personal Injury, Estate Planning and Probate Law, Health Care Law.

MEMBERS OF FIRM

MORRIS A. TSCHIDER, (P.C.), born Bismarck, North Dakota, April 6, 1933; admitted to bar, 1958, North Dakota and U.S. District Court, District of North Dakota. *Education:* University of North Dakota (B.S., 1954; M.A. Accounting, 1960; J.D., 1958). Certified Public Accountant, North Dakota, 1960. *Member:* State Bar Association of North Dakota; American Bar Association; North Dakota Society of Certified Public Accountants. [With U.S. Army, 1954-1955]. ***PRACTICE AREAS:*** Tax Law; Probate; Estate Planning; Real Estate; Commercial.

SEAN O. SMITH, (P.C.), born Sioux Falls, South Dakota, June 3, 1957; admitted to bar, 1981, North Dakota and U.S. District Court, District of North Dakota; 1986, U.S. Court of Appeals, Eighth Circuit; 1992, U.S. Supreme Court. *Education:* University of North Dakota (B.S.B.A., cum laude, 1978; J.D., with distinction, 1981). Order of the Coif; Delta Theta Phi. Certified Public Accountant, North Dakota, 1980. *Member:* Burleigh County and American Bar Associations; State Bar Association of North Dakota (Member, Fee Arbitration Committee, 1987-1990, Chair, Continuing Legal Education Committee, 1991-1994); North Dakota Society of Certified Public Accountants; American Institute of Certified Public Accountants. ***PRACTICE AREAS:*** Real Estate Law; Corporate Business Law; Bankruptcy Law; Health Care Law. ***Email:*** ssmith@tschider-smithlaw.com

DAVID A. TSCHIDER, born Grand Forks, North Dakota, May 21, 1959; admitted to bar, 1984, North Dakota, Colorado and U.S. District Court, District of North Dakota. *Education:* University of North Dakota (B.S.B.A., Accounting, summa cum laude, 1980; J.D., with distinction, 1984). Certified Public Accountant, North Dakota, 1981. *Member:* State Bar Association of North Dakota; American Bar Association; North Dakota Society of Certified Public Accountants; American Institute of Certified Public Accountants. ***PRACTICE AREAS:*** Probate; Estate Planning; Real Estate; Commercial; Personal Injury; Tax Law. ***Email:*** dtschider@tschider-smithlaw.com

ASSOCIATE

AMBER L. SMITH-HEINERT, born Grand Forks, North Dakota, December 11, 1977; admitted to bar, 2002, North Dakota. *Education:* University of North Dakota (B.A., 1999; J.D., 2002). ***PRACTICE AREAS:*** Real Estate; Bankruptcy; Corporate Law; Business Law; Health Care; Estate Planning. ***Email:*** asmith-heinert@tschider-smithlaw.com

REPRESENTATIVE CLIENTS: Agri Bank, FCB; Farm Credit Services of Mandan, FLCA; Farm Credit Services of Mandan, P.C.A.; Twin City Implement, Inc.; First Bank Bismarck; Independent Insurance Agents; Western Steel & Plumbing; Froelich Oil Co.; Tucker Sales, Inc.; Comfort Inn, Bismarck, N.D.; Saint Alexius Medical Center, Bismarck, N.D.; Bismarck Eagles; Jamestown Hospital; Garrison Memorial Hospital.

VOGEL LAW FIRM

U.S. BANK BUILDING
200 N. 3RD STREET, SUITE 201
P.O. BOX 2097
BISMARCK, NORTH DAKOTA 58502-2097
Telephone: 701-258-7899
URL: http://www.vogellaw.com

Fargo, North Dakota Office: 218 N.P. Avenue, 58107. Telephone: 701-237-6983. Fax: 701-356-6395.
Moorhead, Minnesota Office: 215 North 30th Street, P.O. Box 1977, 56561-1077. Telephone: 218-236-6462. Fax: 218-236-9873.

Insurance Defense, Personal Injury, Products Liability, Professional Malpractice, Corporate, Labor and Employment, Probate, Tax Law, Health Law, Real Estate, Bankruptcy, Construction Law, Public Utilities, Securities and Antitrust, Arbitration and Mediation. Family Law, Criminal Law, Environmental Law, Intellectual Property, Ecommerce. Trials and Appeals in all Courts.

FIRM PROFILE: Vogel, Weir, Hunke & McCormick, Ltd. also known as the Vogel Law Firm, with offices in Fargo and Bismarck, North Dakota, is a general practice firm dating back to 1882, when William Huntley Barnett set up his own office in Fargo, later adding Seth W. Richardson in 1905, to form Barnett & Richardson. The Firm has traditionally been the largest in North Dakota and Western Minnesota, providing a broad spectrum of legal services in North Dakota, Minnesota, South Dakota and Montana. The Firm is a member of the American Law Firm Association (ALFA) which provides access to national and world wide legal services of all types.

H. PATRICK WEIR, born Dickinson, North Dakota, November 4, 1939; admitted to bar, 1964, North Dakota; 1990, Minnesota. *Education:* St. John's University (B.S., cum laude, 1961); University of Notre Dame (LL.B., 1964). Member, Editorial Board, Notre Dame Law Review, 1963-1964. Law Clerk to Charles J. Vogel, Chief Judge, U.S. Court of Appeals, Eighth Circuit, 1964-1965. *Member:* Cass County, Minnesota State and American Bar Associations; State Bar Association of North Dakota; North Dakota Defense Lawyers Association; North Dakota Trial Lawyers Association; International Academy of Trial Law-

(This Listing Continued)

yers; American Judicature Society. Advocate, American Board of Trial Advocates. Fellow, International Society of Barristers. ***PRACTICE AREAS:*** Malpractice Defense; Insurance Defense; Corporate Law. ***Email:*** pweir@vogellaw.com

JOHN C. KAPSNER, born Bismarck, North Dakota, June 1, 1947; admitted to bar, 1973, North Dakota, U. S. District Court, District of North Dakota; 1976, U.S. Court of Appeals, Eighth Circuit; 1985, U.S. Supreme Court. *Education:* Saint John's University of Minnesota (B.A., 1969); Indiana University (J.D., 1973). Enforcement Division, U.S. Environmental Protection Agency, Denver, Colorado, 1974-1977. President, Bruce M. Van Sickle American Inns of Court, 1997-1999. *Member:* Big Muddy Bar Association; State Bar Association of North Dakota (Member, Supreme Court Joint Procedure Committee, 1988—); Defense Research Institute. ***PRACTICE AREAS:*** Professional Malpractice; Insurance Defense Law; Employment Discrimination Law. ***Email:*** jkapsner@vogellaw.com

JOHN J. PETRIK, born Yankton, South Dakota, March 2, 1954; admitted to bar, 1982, North Dakota; 1983, U.S. District Court, District of North Dakota; 1991, Montana. *Education:* Michigan State University (B.A., with honors, 1977); University of Minnesota (J.D., with honors, 1982). *Member:* Burleigh County and American Bar Associations; State Bar Association of North Dakota (Board of Governors, 1997-1999), (Ward County President, 1987-1988); State Bar of Montana. ***REPORTED CASES:*** H & F Hogs v. Howe, 368 N.W. 2d 553, (N.D. 1985); Allen v. City of Minot, 363 N.W. 2d 553 (N.D. 1985); PCA of Minot v. Klein, 385 N.W. 2d 485 (N.D. 1986); Timm v. Shoenwald, 400 N.W. 2d 263 (N.D. 1986); Eckert v. Ectert, 425 N.W. 2d 914 (N.D. 1988); Haider v. Montgomary, 423 N.W. 2d 494 (N.D. 1988); FDIC v. McCawley, 438 N.W. 2d 198 (N.D. 1989); Huntley v. Timm, 435 N.W. 2d 683 (N.D. 1989); Miles Homes v. City of Westhope, 458 N.W. 2d 321 (N.D. 1990); Rolla Farmers Oil v. White Farm Equipment, 162 BR 834 (D.N.D. 1994). ***PRACTICE AREAS:*** Commercial Transactions; Business Transactions; Litigation; Health Care; Cooperative Association Law. ***Email:*** jpetrik@vogellaw.com

BRENDA L. BLAZER, born Grand Forks, North Dakota, June 28, 1952; admitted to bar, 1984, North Dakota, U.S. District Court, District of North Dakota. *Education:* University of North Dakota (B.A., 1981; J.D., 1984). Delta Theta Phi. Order of the Barristers. Member, Moot Court Board. Member, Mortar Board. Recipient: Outstanding Service Award, Legal Aid Association; Burtness Scholarship. Nationally Registered Emergency Medical Technician-Paramedic, 1980-1982. *Member:* Big Muddy and American (Member: Sections on: Litigation; Health Law) Bar Associations; State Bar Association of North Dakota (Chair, Alternate Dispute Resolution Committee, 1992-1994; Group Insurance Committee, 1995-1997); North Dakota Defense Lawyers Association; American Society of Law and Medicine; North Dakota Pattern Jury Instruction Commission (1996—); American Health Lawyers Association; Defense Research Institute; Judge Bruce M. Van Sickle American Inn of Court. ***REPORTED CASES:*** Michael Fastow v. Burleigh County Water Resource Dist. 415 N.W. 2d 505 (ND 1987); Trinity Medical Center, Inc. v. Holum, 544 N.W. 2d 148 (N.D. 1996). ***PRACTICE AREAS:*** Medical Malpractice Defense Law; Personal Injury Litigation; Health Law; Government Relations. ***Email:*** bblazer@vogellaw.com

LESLIE BAKKEN OLIVER, born Phoenix, Arizona, December 6, 1952; admitted to bar, 1991, North Dakota; 1992, U.S. District Court, District of North Dakota; 1994, U.S. Court of Appeals, Eighth Circuit. *Education:* Denison University (B.A., 1974); University of North Dakota (J.D., with distinction, 1991). Senior Editor, North Dakota Law Review, 1990-1991. Law Clerk to the Honorable Herbert L. Meschke, North Dakota Supreme Court, 1991-1992. Author: "The Right To Die in North Dakota: The North Dakota Living Will Act," 66 N.D.L.Rev. 495, 1990. *Member:* Big Muddy and American Bar Associations; State Bar Association of North Dakota. ***PRACTICE AREAS:*** Litigation. ***Email:*** loliver@vogellaw.com

MONTE L. ROGNEBY, born Bismarck, North Dakota, October 5, 1966; admitted to bar, 1992, North Dakota and Minnesota; 1995, U.S. District Court, District of North Dakota; 1998, U.S. Court of Appeals, Eighth Circuit; 2000, Montana. *Education:* Moorhead State University (B.A., summa cum laude, 1989); University of Minnesota (J.D., cum laude, 1992). Phi Kappa Phi. Truman Scholar, 1997. Law Clerk to the Honorable Thomas Stringer, Minnesota District Court, 1992-1993. Law Clerk to the Honorable Dale V. Sandstrom, North Dakota Supreme Court, 1993-1994. Assistant Attorney General, Civil Litigation Division, State of North Dakota, 1994-1996. Member, Standing Rock Sioux Tribal Court, 1998. *Member:* State Bar Association of North Dakota; Minnesota State Bar Association. ***PRACTICE AREAS:*** Commercial Law; Litigation. ***Email:*** mrogneby@vogellaw.com

MICHAEL T. ANDREWS, born Rochester, Minnesota, July 4, 1966; admitted to bar, 1998, North Dakota; 2000, Minnesota and South Dakota. *Education:* North Dakota State University (B.A., 1994); University of North Dakota (J.D. with distinction, 1998). Order of the Coif. Case Comment Editor, North Dakota Law Review. Law Clerk to the Honorable Rodney Webb, Chief Judge, United States District Court, District of North Dakota. Author: "Constitutional Law-Punitive Damages: The U.S. Supreme Court Uses the Due Process Clause of the Fourteenth Amendment to Strike Down a Two Million Dollar Punitive Damage Award," 73 N.D.L.Rev. 299 (1997). *Member:* Burleigh County and American Bar Associations; State Bar Association of North Dakota; North Dakota State Bar Foundation. ***PRACTICE AREAS:*** Litigation. ***Email:*** mandrews@vogellaw.com

JOEL W. GILBERTSON, born Valley City, North Dakota, November 9, 1949; admitted to bar, 1976, North Dakota; 1978, U.S. District Court, District of North Dakota; 1989, U.S. Court of Appeals, Eighth Circuit. *Education:* Concordia College (B.A., cum laude, 1972); University of North Dakota (J.D., 1975). Phi Delta Phi. Listed in Best Lawyers in America. Co-Author: "The Changing Insurance Market-Who Will Bear the Risks?" 32 Rocky Mountain Mineral Law Institute 17-1, 1986. Staff Attorney, North Dakota Supreme Court, 1976-1978. Executive Director, State Bar Association of North Dakota, 1978-1981. Member, Board of Directors, Independent Bankers Association of America, 2001-2002. President-Elect, Council of Community Banking Association, 2001-2002. Certified Neutral Arbitrator. *Member:* Big Muddy and South Central District (President, 1989-1991; Vice-President, 1987-1989; Secretary-Treasurer, 1983-1987) Bar Associations; State Bar Association of North Dakota (President, 1992-1993; President-Elect, 1991-1992; Member, Board of Governors, 1989-1994; School Committee, 1982-1993; Member, Legislative Committee, 1978-1986); Law North Dakota Bar Foundation (Chairman, 1986-1989; Vice-Chairman, 1981-1986); Product Liability Advisory Council; Defense Research Association; North Dakota Defense Lawyers Association; National Conference of Bar Presidents. [U.S. National Guard and U.S. Army Reserve, 1972-1978]. ***REPORTED CASES:*** Jacobs

(This Listing Continued)

v. Anderson Bldg. Co., 430 NW2d 558 (ND 1988); Castow v. Burleigh County Water Resource District, 415 NW2d 505 (ND 1987); Downtowner, Inc. v. Acrometal Products, Inc., 347 NW2d 118 (ND 1984); Carlson v. Dickson Gross, Inc., 372 NW2d 902 (ND 1985). ***PRACTICE AREAS:*** Government Relations; Mediation; Arbitration; Commercial Law; Litigation. ***Email:*** jgilbertson@vogellaw.com

---

MANDY R. MAXON, born Mobridge, South Dakota, May 6, 1977; admitted to bar, 2002, North Dakota. *Education:* Moorhead State University; Minot State University (B.S., summa cum laude, 1999); University of North Dakota (J.D., with distinction, 2002). Member, Law Women's Caucus, 2000-2001. President, Public Interest Law Student Association, 2001-2002. *Member:* State Bar Association of North Dakota. ***LANGUAGES:*** English. ***PRACTICE AREAS:*** Family Law; Criminal Law; General Practice. ***Email:*** mmaxon@vogellaw.com

ATTORNEYS FOR: *General Clients:* Associated General Contractors of North Dakota; Bobcat Co.; Cable One, Inc.; Case Corporations; Cass County Electric Cooperative, Inc.; Clark Equipment Co.; Forum Communications Company; Harleysville Companies; Merit Care Medical Group; New Holland North America, Inc.; Northern Improvement Co.; Dakota Clinic Ltd.; United Parcel Service; Gateway Chevrolet, Inc.; Fargo Tank Company; Fargo Culvert Company; Meinecke-Johnson Construction Co.; Border States Paving, Inc.; Wanzek Construction, Inc.; Tri State Auction Company, Inc.; West Acres Development; Transystems, Inc.; Matrix Properities Corporation; Fargo Glass & Paint Company; Northern Bottling Company; National Sun Industries. Able, Inc.; Heart-Lung Clinic; North Dakota Healthcare Association; North Dakota Long Term Care Association; Health Insurance of America; Brown & Williamson Tobacco Corp.; Med Center One Health Systems; West River Health Services; Johns Manville Corporation; Archer Daniels S. Midland Co.; S.C. Johnson & Son, Inc.; Werner Co.; Magnum, Ltd.; Waste Management of North Dakota, Inc.
FINANCIAL INSTITUTIONS: Community First National Bank of Fargo; Ramsey National Bank & Trust Co.; Northern Capital Management Co.; Farmers & Merchants Bank of Valley City; First Trust Company of North Dakota; First International Bank & Trust, Fargo; Bremer Financial Corporation; AgriBank, FCB; Ag Services of America, Inc.; St. Alexius Credit Union.
INSURANCE CLIENTS: Acceptance Insurance Company; All Nation Insurance Company; American Family Insurance Group; American Life & Casualty Company; Auto Owners Insurance; Automobile Club Insurance Company; Center Mutual Insurance Co.; Chubb Group of Insurance Companies; CIGNA Companies; CNA Insurance Company; Continental Insurance Companies; Dakota Fire Insurance Company; Employers Mutual Insurance Company; Farmers Alliance Mutual Insurance Company; General Casualty Companies; Great West Casualty Company; Grinnell Mutual Reinsurance Co.; Home Insurance Company; Horace Mann Insurance Company; Kemper Group; Midwest Medical Insurance Company; Milbank Mutual Insurance Company; Minnesota Fire & Casualty; National Farmers Union Insurance Company; North Dakota Insurance Reserve Fund; Northstar Mutual Insurance Company; Northwestern National; Ohio Casualty Group; Old Republic Insurance Company; Orion Auto, Inc.; Preferred Physicians Medical; Nationwide Insurance; Royal Insurance Company; Saskatchewan Government Insurance; Scottsdale Insurance Company; St. Paul Insurance Companies; Travelers Insurance Companies; Unitrin Property & Casualty Insurance Group; One Beacon Insurance Company.

(For Complete Personnel and Biographical Data, see Professional Biographies at Fargo, North Dakota)

WHEELER WOLF LAW FIRM

220 NORTH 4TH STREET
P.O. BOX 2056
BISMARCK, NORTH DAKOTA 58502-2056
Telephone: 701-223-5300
Fax: 701-223-5366

Civil Trial Practice in all Courts and Administrative Agencies, Corporate Law, Administrative Law, Public Utilities, Taxation, Estate Planning, Probate, Wills, Elder Law, Banking, Real Estate, Commercial Law, Lobbying, Communications Law, Construction Law, Labor Relations, Collections, Personal Injury, Negligence, Workers Compensation, Social Security, Criminal Law, Bankruptcy, Agricultural Law.

FIRM PROFILE: The Wheeler Wolf Law Firm continues to grow and expand as it follows its philosophy of striving to provide the best legal services possible to meet the diverse interests and needs of its clients. The firm's seven attorneys have an average of 25 years of practice experience ranging from 49 years to 8 years and have a reputation of being some of the top plaintiff and defense trial lawyers in the state. The firm's practice extends throughout North Dakota and adjacent states. In addition to its strong team of attorneys, Wheeler Wolf has three legal assistants, an office support staff of eight and state of the art computer information systems.

ALBERT A. WOLF, born Bismarck, North Dakota, April 27, 1931; admitted to bar, 1956, Minnesota; 1957, North Dakota and U.S. Court of Military Appeals; 1971, U.S. Supreme Court. *Education:* University of St. Thomas (B.A., 1952); University of Minnesota and William Mitchell College of Law (LL.B., 1956). Delta Theta Phi. Special Assistant Attorney General, North Dakota, 1961—. State Attorney, Burleigh County, 1964-1966. Chairman, North Dakota Judicial Nominating Committee, 1979-1981. Member, Eighth Circuit U.S. Circuit Judge Nominating Commission, 1979-1981. *Member:* Burleigh County and American (Member, Insurance, Negligence and Compensation Law Section) Bar Associations; State Bar Association of North Dakota (Member, Ethics Committee, 1989-1998); North Dakota Trial Lawyers Association; The Association of Trial Lawyers of America; Defense Research and Trial Lawyers Association; ABOTA (Past President, North Dakota Chapter). [With JAGC, U.S. Army Reserve, active duty, 1957-1960]. ***LANGUAGES:*** German. ***SPECIAL AGENCIES:*** North Dakota Legislative Assembly; North Dakota State Banking Board; North Dakota State Insurance Department; North Dakota State Electrical Board; North Dakota Workers' Compensation Bureau; North Dakota Department of Transportation; North Dakota Department of Human Services. ***REPORTED CASES:*** Newman Signs v. Hjelle, 281 NW2d 794 (1979); Krueger v. St. Joseph's Hospital, 305 NW2d 18 (1981); Hodek v. Nelson Schools, 531 NW2d 280 (1995); 1st National Bank v. Scherr, 467 NW2d 427 (1991). ***PRACTICE AREAS:*** Personal Injury Law; Construction Law; Banking Law; Legislative Law. ***Email:*** aawolf@wheelerwolf.com

JACK McDONALD, born Bismarck, North Dakota, September 21, 1940; admitted to bar, 1970, North Dakota and U.S. District Court, District of North Dakota. *Education:* University of North Dakota (B.A., 1962; J.D., 1970); Southern Illinois University and American University (M.A., 1967). Phi Delta Phi (Secretary, 1963). Author: "Government in the

(This Listing Continued)

WHEELER WOLF LAW FIRM, Bismarck—Continued

Sunshine," North Dakota Law Review, Vol. 53, No. 1, 1976. President, Bismarck YMCA, 1979-1980. President, Bismark Public Access TV Corporation, 1987—. *Member:* State Bar Association of North Dakota; American Bar Association (Member: Economics of Law Practice Section; Communications Law Forum Committee, 1981—); The North Dakota Association of Trial Lawyers (Executive Secretary, 1982-1984). ***SPECIAL AGENCIES:*** North Dakota Legislative Assembly (Lobbyist, 1976—); North Dakota Public Service Commission; North Dakota Board of Physical Therapy Examiners. ***REPORTED CASES:*** Minot Daily News, et al vs. Holum, et al, 1986, 380 NW2347; Mees vs. Ereth, 1991, 466 NW2135; Wolf vs. Anderson, et al, 1983, 334 NW2212. ***PRACTICE AREAS:*** Communications Law; Bankruptcy Law; Legislation. ***Email:*** jackmcdonald@wheelerwolf.com

GREGORY C. LARSON, born Malta, Montana, November 30, 1952; admitted to bar, 1980, North Dakota and U.S. District Court, District of North Dakota; 1984, U.S. Tax Court and U.S. Court of Appeals, Eighth Circuit; 1995, U.S Court of Federal Claims and U.S. Supreme Court. *Education:* University of North Dakota (B.S., 1974); Gonzaga University (J.D., 1978); University of Miami (LL.M. in Taxation, 1979). Member, Medcenter One Foundation Advisory Board, 1986—. *Member:* Burleigh County and American (Member, Taxation Section) Bar Associations; State Bar Association of North Dakota (Member, Section of Real Property, Probate and Trust Law; Probate and Trust Law Committee); International Association of Financial Planning, Inc., North Dakota Chapter (Member, Board of Directors, 1984-1990; Regulatory Coordinator, 1984-1990); Western Dakota Estate Planning Council (President, 1983-1984; Member, Board of Directors, 1982-1995); Christian Legal Society (Member and State Director); National Academy of Elder Law Attorneys (Member and State Director). ***REPORTED CASES:*** Ketterling v. Gonzales, 515 NW2d 158 (1994); State v. Brewer, 444 NW2d 923 (1989); Gustafson v. Gustafson, 381 NW2d 208 (1986); Bendickson v. Sunduist, 353 NW2d 320 (1984). ***PRACTICE AREAS:*** Tax and Probate Law; Estate Law; Elder Law; Business Planning Law. ***Email:*** glarson@wheelerwolf.com

STEVEN L. LATHAM, born Fort Rucker, Alabama, June 7, 1951; admitted to bar, 1976, North Dakota, U.S. District Court, District of North Dakota and U.S. Court of Appeals, Tenth Circuit. *Education:* University of North Dakota (B.A., 1973; J.D., 1976). Special Assistant Attorney General, North Dakota and Trial Counsel North Dakota Highway Department, 1978-1981. *Member:* Burleigh County and American Bar Associations; State Bar Association of North Dakota; The Association of Trial Lawyers of America; North Dakota Trial Lawyers Association. ***REPORTED CASES:*** Spangler v. ND Workers Compensation Bureau, 519 NW2d 576 (1994); Devils Lake v. Davis, 480 NW2d 720 (1992); Hartlieb v. Sawyer Township, 366 NW2d 486 (1985). ***PRACTICE AREAS:*** Litigation; Personal Injury Law; Workers Compensation Law. ***Email:*** slatham@wheelerwolf.com

MICHAEL F. DALEY, born Grafton, North Dakota, September 21, 1956; admitted to bar, 1980, North Dakota; 1982, Minnesota. *Education:* University of North Dakota (B.A., 1977; J.D., 1980). Phi Beta Kappa; Order of the Coif. Special Assistant Attorney General, 1983. Member: Board of Directors, Legal Assistance of North Dakota, Inc., 1992—; North Dakota Judicial Conference, 2000—. *Member:* Big Muddy Bar Association; State Bar Association of North Dakota (Member, Board of Governors, 1995-1999); The Association of Trial Lawyers of America; North Dakota Trial Lawyers Association. ***PRACTICE AREAS:*** Litigation; Real Estate Law; Personal Injury. ***Email:*** mfdaley@wheelerwolf.com

COURTNEY M. KOEBELE, born Washington, D.C., September 28, 1966; admitted to bar, 1991, North Dakota; 1992, Minnesota; 1993, U.S. District Court, District of North Dakota. *Education:* University of North Dakota (B.S., summa cum laude, 1988; J.D., with distinction, 1991). Law Clerk: U.S. District Judge, Pat Conmy, 1991-1993; U.S. Magistrate Dewey Kautzmann, 1994-1995. ***PRACTICE AREAS:*** Real Estate; Domestic Relations; Probate; Bankruptcy; General Practice. ***Email:*** cmkoebele@wheelerwolf.com

DAMIAN J. HUETTL, born Garrison, North Dakota, April 26, 1972; admitted to bar, 1997, North Dakota; 1999, U.S. District Court, District of North Dakota. *Education:* Moorhead State University (B.A., 1994); University of North Dakota (J.D., 1997). Member, 1994-1997 and Vice President, 1998-1999, Phi Alpha Delta. Recipient, Academic Excellence Award, Criminal Procedure, 1996. Assistant State's Attorney, Grant County, North Dakota, 1999. *Member:* State Bar Association of North Dakota; Muddy Bar Association; North Dakota State's Attorney's Association; Association of Certified Fraud Examiners. ***PRACTICE AREAS:*** Litigation; Criminal Defense; Elder Law; Trusts and Estates. ***Email:*** djhuettl@wheelerwolf.com

LEGAL SUPPORT PERSONNEL

DIANNE M. TAIX, *Member:* Western Dakota Association of Legal Assistant and National Association of Legal Assistant; Big Muddy Bar Association (Associate Member). (Certified Legal Assistant Specialist; Certified Civil Litigation Specialist; Certified Real Estate Specialist). ***Email:*** dtaix@wheelerwolf.com

CHAR J. JACOBER, *Member:* Western Dakota Association of Legal Assistant and National Association of Legal Assistant; Big Muddy Bar Association (Associate Member). (Certified Legal Assistant). ***Email:*** seejay@wheelerwolf.com

SHARON R. CAVENDER, born Thief River Falls, Minnesota. *Education:* University of North Dakota (B.S., 1987). *Member:* Big Muddy Bar Association (Associate Member). (Certified Legal Assistant)

COUNSEL FOR: North Dakota Newspaper Assn.; N.D. Physical Therapy Assn.; N.D. Electrical Board.
REPRESENTATIVE CLIENTS: Bank Center First; Continental Western Insurance Co.; John Deere Co.; AVCO Finance; Beneficial Finance; The Associated Press; The Bismarck Tribune; Commercial Credit Equipment Corp.; Agway, Inc.; Associates Commercial Corp.; Household Finance; Greyhound Lines, Inc.; McQuade Distributing Co.; N.D. Cable Television Association; Chrysler Credit Corp.; Great Global Assurance Co.; Rain and Hail Insurance Service, Inc.; Kirkwood Mall Shopping Center; Scherr Plastering & Drywall.

ZUGER KIRMIS & SMITH

A Partnership including Professional Corporations

316 NORTH FIFTH STREET
P.O. BOX 1695
BISMARCK, NORTH DAKOTA 58502-1695
Telephone: 701-223-2711
Fax: 701-223-7387; 701-223-9619
Email: zkslaw@zkslaw.com
URL: http://www.zkslaw.com

Tort and Commercial Litigation. Insurance, Products Liability, Corporation, Malpractice, Real Estate, Labor Law, Public Utilities and Administrative Law, Probate, Natural Resources.

FIRM PROFILE: Zuger Kirmis & Smith was founded at about the same time the State of North Dakota was formed, and possesses an especially broad base of litigation and other legal experience. The firm serves the entire state and has attorneys licensed in North Dakota, Minnesota, Illinois, Montana and Missouri, offering a wide range of legal services. The firm is actively involved in the North Dakota State Bar Association, continuing legal education seminars, civil affairs and other professional associations. Zuger Kirmis & Smith has a support staff composed of highly trained paralegals and nurse consultants.

THOMAS O. SMITH (1944-2001)

LYLE W. KIRMIS, born Bismarck, North Dakota, November 6, 1949; admitted to bar, 1974, North Dakota and U.S. District Court of North Dakota. *Education:* North Dakota State University and University of Minnesota (B.Ch.E., 1971); University of Minnesota (J.D., 1974). Phi Eta Sigma. Member, Minnesota Law Review, 1972-1973. *Member:* Big Muddy Bar Association; State Bar Association of North Dakota (Member: Committee on Ethics and Internal Affairs, 1977-1978; Committee on Pattern Jury Instructions, 1979-1981); Commercial Law League of America; Trial Attorneys of America; Defense Research Institute. ***REPORTED CASES:*** Scherbenske Excavating, Inc. v. North Dakota State Highway Department, 365 N.W. 2d 485 North Dakota Supreme Court 1985; Thoring v. Bottensek, 350 N.W. 2d 586, North Dakota Supreme Court 1984; Sorlie v. Ness, 323 N.W. 2d 841, North Dakota Supreme Court 1982; Soentgen v. Quain & Ramstad Clinic, P.C. et al., 467 N.W. 2d 73, North Dakota Supreme Court, 1991; Jacobsen v. Haugen, 529 N.W. 2d 882, North Dakota Supreme Court 1995; Hamilton v. Oppen 653 NW 2d 678, North Dakota Supreme Court 2002. ***PRACTICE AREAS:*** Commercial and Construction Litigation; Personal Injury Litigation; Professional Malpractice Defense; Corporate Law; Insurance; Real Property. ***Email:*** lkirmis@zkslaw.com

LANCE D. SCHREINER, P.C., born Grand Forks, North Dakota, June 25, 1950; admitted to bar, 1979, North Dakota, U.S. District Court, District of North Dakota, U.S. Court of Appeals, Eighth Circuit and U.S. Supreme Court. *Education:* University of Texas at Arlington (B.A., 1972); University of North Dakota (J.D., with distinction, 1979). Senior Editor, North Dakota Law Review, 1978-1979. Law Clerk to Judge Bruce M Van Sickle, U.S. District Court, District of North Dakota, 1979-1981. *Member:* American Bar Association (Member, Section on Litigation); State Bar Association of North Dakota; Defense Research Institute (Member, Medical-Legal Committee); North Dakota Defense Lawyers Association (President, 2001). ***PRACTICE AREAS:*** Medical Malpractice Defense Law; Medical Device Products Liability. ***Email:*** lschreiner@zkslaw.com

JAMES S. HILL, P.C., born Grand Forks, North Dakota, September 20, 1949; admitted to bar, 1974, North Dakota, Minnesota, U.S. District Court, District of North Dakota, U.S. District Court, District of Minnesota, U.S. District Court, District of Wyoming, U.S. Court of Appeals, Eighth and Tenth Circuits and U.S. Supreme Court. *Education:* University of North Dakota (B.A., 1971; J.D., 1974). Phi Alpha Delta. Development Editor, North Dakota Law Review, 1973-1974. Law Clerk to Judge Paul Benson, U.S. District Court, District of North Dakota, 1974-1976. Assistant U.S. Attorney, North Dakota, 1976-1981. Special Assistant U.S. Attorney, North Dakota, 1981-1983. Special Assistant Attorney General, 1988-1989, 1991-1993, 1996-2001. President, South Central Judicial District Bar Association, 1987-1989. Member, 1990— and Board of Directors, North Dakota Bar Foundation, 1990-1992. *Member:* Big Muddy and American (Member: Litigation Section; Torts and Insurance Practice Section; Standing Committee on Client Protection) Bar Associations; State Bar Association of North Dakota (President, 1991-1992; Member, 1980-1997, and Chairman, 1986-1989, Federal Practice Committee; Member, 1983-1989, and Chairman, 1985-1989, North Dakota Commission for Continuing Legal Education; Chairman, 1985-1989, Inquiry Committee West; Member, Board of Governors, 1987-1989, 1991—; Member, Client Security Fund Committee, 1987-1989, 1990-1992); North Dakota Defense Lawyers Association (President, 1992-1994); Recipient, 1997 State Bar Association of North Dakota Distinguished Service Award; Member, North Dakota Judicial Conduct Commission; Member, North Dakota Judicial Conference; Member, Judge Bruce M. Van Sickle, American Inn of Court (President, 1992-1995); National Association of Railroad Trial Counsel; Board Certified Civil Litigation, National Board of Trial Advocacy; Delegate to American Bar Association from State Bar Association of North Dakota; American College of Barristers; International Association of Defense Counsel; Association of Defense Trial Counsel. Life Fellow: American Bar Foundation. ***REPORTED CASES:*** Mr. G's Turtle Mountain Lodge v. Roland Township, 2002 ND 140, 651 NW 2d 625; Estate of Murphy v. Maus 2001 ND 87, 626 NW2d 281; Belisle v. Gibson 2000 ND 191, 622 NW2d 432; Estate of Lutz 1999 ND 191, 595 NW2d 590; Gottbrecht v. State of North Dakota 1999 ND 159, 598 NW2d 794; Toth v. Disciplinary Board 1997 ND 75, 562 NW2d 744; Dan Nelson Construction v. Nodland & Dickson 2000 ND 61, 608 NW2d 267. ***PRACTICE AREAS:*** Civil Litigation; Professional Malpractice Defense Law; Trial Practice; Insurance Defense Law. ***Email:*** jhill@zkslaw.com

PATRICK J. WARD, born Chicago, Illinois, September 13, 1952; admitted to bar, 1979, North Dakota and U.S. District Court, District of North Dakota; 1980, Illinois, U.S. District Court, Northern District of Illinois; 1981, U.S. Court of Appeals, Seventh Circuit; 1984, U.S. Court of Appeals, Eighth Circuit; 1991, Montana; 1996, U.S. Supreme Court. *Education:* Elmhurst College (B.A., with honors, 1976); University of North Dakota (J.D., with distinction, 1979). Order of the Coif. Editor-in-Chief, North Dakota Law Review, 1978-1979. Law Clerk to Associate Justice William L. Paulson, North Dakota Supreme Court, 1979-1980. Associate, Schiff Hardin & Waite, Chicago, Illinois, 1980-1982. *Mem-*

(This Listing Continued)

ber: State Bar Association of North Dakota (Member, Ethics Committee, 1983-1990; Chairman, 1985-1989); Defense Research Institute; American Employment Law Council; National Institute for Farm Safety. ***REPORTED CASES:*** Strate v. A-1 Contractors, U.S. 520 U.S. 438, 117 S.Ct. 1404, 137 L.Ed. 2d. 661 (1997), 1997 U.S. Lexis 2795, 1997 WL 202022; Source One Mgmt. Co. Inc., 591 NW2d 101 (ND 1999); Moritz v. Frontier Airlines, 147 F. 3d 784 (8th Cir. 1998); Schweigert v. Provident Life Ins. Co., 503 N.W.2d 225; Johnson v. Kennedy, 453 N.W.2d 830 (N.D., Mar 01, 1990) (NO. CIVIL 890341); Thoring v. Bottonsek, 350 N.W.2d 586 (N.D., May 23, 1984) (NO. CIV. 10555); Murphy v. Tivoli Enterprises, 953 F.2d 354, 60 USLW 2527, 21 Fed.R.Serv. 3d 579 (8th Cir. (N.D.), Jan 06, 1992) (NO. 91-2207). ***PRACTICE AREAS:*** Civil Litigation; Insurance; Antitrust; Labor Law; Automobile Law; Indian Law. ***Email:*** pward@zkslaw.com

REBECCA S. THIEM, P.C., born Grand Forks, North Dakota, November 12, 1950; admitted to bar, 1980, North Dakota; 1981, U.S. Court of Appeals, Eighth Circuit and U.S. District Court, District of North Dakota; 1983, Minnesota. *Education:* Valparaiso University (B.A., 1972); University of North Dakota (J.D., 1980). Order of the Coif. Member, Board of Editors, North Dakota Law Review, 1979-1980. Law Clerk to Judge Myron H. Bright, U.S. Court of Appeals for the Eighth Circuit, 1980-1981. *Member:* State Bar Association of North Dakota (President, 1996-1997; Secretary-Treasurer and Member, Board of Governors, 1988-1990; Recipient, Distinguished Service Award, 2000; Member, State Board of Bar Examiners, 1991—; Chair, 1996—; Chair, Alternative Dispute Resolution Committee, 2001—; Member, Supreme Court Judicial Planning Committee, 2001—); American Bar Association (Member, Bar Admissions Committee of Section on Legal Education and Bar Admissions). ***PRACTICE AREAS:*** Commercial Law; Commercial Litigation; Appellate Practice; Commercial Transactions; Employment Law; Employment Litigation; Mediation; Professional Errors and Omissions. ***Email:*** rthiem@zkslaw.com

JERRY W. EVENSON, P.C., born Wahpeton, North Dakota, April 1, 1949; admitted to bar, 1980, North Dakota and U.S. District Court, District of North Dakota; 1988, U.S. Court of Appeals, Eighth Circuit. *Education:* University of North Dakota (B.A., 1971; J.D., 1980). Recipient: Outstanding Service Award, Legal Aid Association; Burtness Scholarship. President, Legal Aid Association, 1979-1980. Law Clerk to the Hon. Justice Gerald Vande Walle, North Dakota Supreme Court, 1980-1981. Senior Counsel, American College of Barristers. *Member:* Big Muddy Bar Association (Member, Executive Committee, 1988—; President, 1991); State Bar Association of North Dakota; Defense Research Institute; North Dakota Defense Lawyers Association; Board Certified Civil Litigation, National Board of Trial Advocacy. ***PRACTICE AREAS:*** Personal Injury Litigation; Insurance Litigation. ***Email:*** jevenson@zkslaw.com

LAWRENCE A. DOPSON, born Columbia, Missouri, March 16, 1949; admitted to bar, 1975, North Dakota, U.S. District Court, District of North Dakota; U.S. Court of Appeals, Eighth Circuit. *Education:* Jamestown College (B.S., magna cum laude, 1971); Northwestern University (J.D., 1975). Law Clerk, North Dakota Supreme Court, 1975-1976. *Member:* State Bar Association of North Dakota; Defense Research Institute; North Dakota Defense Lawyers Association. ***PRACTICE AREAS:*** Commercial Litigation; Banking Law; Real Estate Law; Insurance Defense Litigation. ***Email:*** ldopson@zkslaw.com

LAWRENCE E. KING, P.C., born Fairbanks, Alaska, September 16, 1965; admitted to bar, 1992, North Dakota and U.S. District Court, District of North Dakota; 1995, Minnesota. *Education:* University of North Dakota (B.A., 1989); University of North Dakota Law School (J.D., with distinction, 1992). Managing Research Editor, North Dakota Law Review, 1991-1992. Recipient: William DePuy Memorial Scholarship; William Holland Memorial Scholarship. Author: "Strate v. A-1 Contractors: A Perspective," Vol. 75, No. 1, North Dakota Law Review, 1999; "Intoxilyzer Tests Held Admissible Even if 'Qualified Right' to Counsel was Denied," Vol. 67, No. 1, North Dakota Law Review, 1991. *Member:* Big Muddy (President, 1999) and American (Member, Tort and Insurance Practice, Young Lawyers Division-District Representative to Executive Council, 1994) Bar Associations; State Bar Association of North Dakota (President, Young Lawyers Section, 1993-1995; Board of Governors, 2001—). ***REPORTED CASES:*** Imperial Oil of North Dakota, Inc. v. Robert E. Hanson and Investors Oil, Inc., 510 N.W. 2d 598 (N.D. 1994); Hausauer v. North Dakota Workers Compensation Bureau, 1997 ND 243, 572 N.W. 2d 426; Unser v. North Dakota Workers Compensation Bureau, 1999 ND 129, 598 N.W. 2d 89; Snyder v. North Dakota Workers Compensation Bureau, 2001 ND 38, 622 N.W. 2d 712; Grand Forks Professional Baseball, Inc. et al. v. North Dakota Workers Compensation Bureau, 2002 ND 204, 654 N.W. 2d 426. ***PRACTICE AREAS:*** Civil Litigation; Indian Law; Tribal Jurisdiction; Workers Compensation Law; Bankruptcy Law. ***Email:*** lking@wcb.state.nd.us

TRACY VIGNESS KOLB, P.C., born Bottineau, North Dakota, April 18, 1963; admitted to bar, 1995, North Dakota. *Education:* Minot State University (B.A., 1992); University of North Dakota (J.D., with distinction, 1995). Order of the Coif. Articles Editor, North Dakota Law Review. Law Clerk, Hon. William Newmann, North Dakota Supreme Court. *Member:* American Bar Association; State Bar Association of North Dakota; Defense Research Institute; Judge Bruce M. Van Sickle American Inn of Court. ***PRACTICE AREAS:*** Civil Litigation; Insurance; Medical Malpractice; Personal Injury. ***Email:*** tkolb@zkslaw.com

ASSOCIATES

SHAWNDA R. REID, born Miles City, Montana, February 4, 1974; admitted to bar, 1999, North Dakota. *Education:* University of North Dakota (B.A., 1995); University of Nebraska at Lincoln (J.D., with distinction, 1999). *Member:* Big Muddy and American Bar Association; State Bar Association of North Dakota; Defense Research Institute. ***PRACTICE AREAS:*** Civil Litigation; Workers Compensation. ***Email:*** sreid@zkslaw.com

CONSTANCE N. HOFLAND, born Bottineau, North Dakota, March 10, 1958; admitted to bar, 2000, North Dakota. *Education:* University of North Dakota (B.S., 1980); University of Minnesota (M.S., 1982); University of North Dakota (J.D., with distinction, 2000). Order of the Coif, 2000. Editor, North Dakota Law Review. Law Clerk to Chief Justice Vande Walle, North Dakota Supreme Court. *Member:* Big Muddy (Vice President, 2004) and American Bar Associations; State Bar Association of North Dakota. ***PRACTICE AREAS:*** General Practice. ***Email:*** chofland@zkslaw.com

PAUL R. SANDERSON, born Bottineau, North Dakota, May 23, 1974; admitted to bar, 2001, North Dakota. *Education:* University of North Dakota (B.B.A., magna cum laude, 1997; J.D., with distinction, 2001). Law Clerk, Justice William A. Newmann, North Dakota Supreme Court. *Member:* State Bar Association of North Dakota, American Bar Association; Defense Research Institute. ***PRACTICE AREAS:*** General Practice. ***Email:*** psanderson@zkslaw.com

AARON K. WEBB, born Winnipeg, Canada, April 25, 1977; admitted to bar, 2003, North Dakota; 2004, Minnesota. *Education:* University of Mary (B.S., 1999); University of North Dakota (J.D., with distinction, 2003). *Member:* State Bar Association of North Dakota; American Bar Association. ***PRACTICE AREAS:*** General Practice. ***Email:*** awebb@zkslaw.com

OF COUNSEL

JOHN A. ZUGER, P.C., born Bismarck, North Dakota, October 26, 1940; admitted to bar, 1967, North Dakota. *Education:* University of Minnesota (B.A., 1962; J.D., 1967).

COUNSEL FOR: BNI Coal; Burlington Northern Santa Fe Railway Co.; Dan's Supermarket, Inc.; Frontier Airlines, Inc.; Medcenter One Health Systems; Microsoft Corporation; Mobil Oil Corp.; Montana-Dakota Utilities Co., A Division of MDU Resources Group, Inc.; Mor-Gran-Sou Electric Cooperative, Inc.; National Association of Independent Insurers; North Dakota Healthcare Association; North Dakota Insurance Reserve Fund; North Dakota Workers Compensation Bureau; Oryx Energy Co.; Philip Morris Companies; Qwest; R.J. Reynolds Tobacco Companies; Smith & Nephew Richards, Inc.; Washington Energy Exploration, Inc.; Williston Basin Interstate Pipeline Company, a wholly-owned subsidiary of MDU Resources Group, Inc.; Xcel Energy. *Financial Institutions:* Dakota Community Bank; First National Bank of McClusky; 1st National Bank of Minneapolis; First Security Bank of Underwood; Investment Centers of America; National Bank of Harvey. *Insurance Corporations:* Acceptance Insurance Companies; Acuity; AFLAC; AID Insurance Group; American Continental Insurance Company; American Equity Insurance Company; American Family Ins. Co.; American Travelers Life Insurance Company; Auto Owners Insurance; Citizens Security Group; Continental Western Insurance Company; Coregis, Inc.; Dominion Insurance Company of Canada; Farmers Group, Inc.; Fireman's Fund Insurance Company; Great American Insurance Co.; Great West Casualty Company; Guaranty National Insurance Cos.; Grinnell Mutual Reinsurance Company; Home Insurance; INA/AETNA Insurance Co.; LeMars Mutual Insurance Company; Mutual of Omaha Insurance Company; Nodak Mutual Farm Bureau; Northwestern National Life Insurance Co.; Northwest G.F. Mutual Company; Ohio Casualty Insurance Companies; Pioneer Life Insurance Company; Republic Western Ins. Co.; Royal Insurance-Milbank Insurance; St. Paul Cos.; State Farm Ins. Co.; The Doctors' Company; United Fire & Casualty Company; Western World Insurance Co.; Westfield Cos. *Manufacturers:* Bridgestone-Firestone, Inc.; Bucyrus International; Carlisle Syntec Incorporated; Ceco Friction Products Company; Siemens, Hirschfeld Steel Co, Inc.; Stromberg-Carlson; United Dominion Inc.; Wedgcor Steel Inc.; Yamaha Motor Corporation, USA.

MOOSBRUGGER, CARTER & McDONAGH, P.L.L.P.

DEVILS LAKE, NORTH DAKOTA

(See Grand Forks)

Business Law, Real Estate, Banking, Corporate Law, Commercial Litigation, Personal Injury, Automobile Accidents, Wrongful Death, Medical Malpractice, Family Law, Divorce, Criminal Law, Civil Litigation.

PEARSON CHRISTENSEN CAHILL & CLAPP, PLLP

DEVILS LAKE, NORTH DAKOTA

(See Grand Forks)

Insurance Defense, Construction Litigation, Products Liability, Tax Litigation, Commercial Litigation, Criminal Defense, Family Law, Appeals.

TRAYNOR LAW FIRM, P.C.

Established in 1897

Attorneys at Law since 1897

509 5TH STREET NE, SUITE 1
P.O. BOX 838
DEVILS LAKE, NORTH DAKOTA 58301
Telephone: 701-662-4077
Fax: 701-662-7537
Toll Free: 877-872-9667
URL: http://www.traynorlawoffice.com
Email: dantraynor@traynorlaw.com
URL: http://www.traynorlaw.com

Insurance Defense, Insurance Coverage, Insurance Bad Faith, Personal Injury, Wrongful Death, Real Estate, Corporate Law, Banking, Estate Planning, Probate and Trusts, Collections, Subrogation, Title Insurance, Tribal Law, Civil Trial Practice before all State and Federal Courts.

FIRM PROFILE: Traynor Law Firm, P.C. is one of North Dakota's most established and respected law firms. Our clients have come to expect prompt, experienced, and professional service. All with the personal attention and trust of a small-town law practice. We are the only area law firm included in the Bar Register of Preeminent Lawyers.

MEMBERS OF FIRM

JOHN T. TRAYNOR, born Devils Lake, North Dakota, November 19, 1926; admitted to bar, 1951, North Dakota. *Education:* United States Naval Academy and University of North Dakota (B.A., 1949); University of North Dakota (J.D., 1951). Phi Beta Kappa; Phi Alpha Delta; Order of the Coif. Member, Grievance Committee, State Supreme Court, 1966-1967. State Senator, 1990 (re-elected 1994, 1998 and 2002). *Member:* Devils Lake Bar Association; State Bar Association of North Dakota. Fellow: American College of Trust and Estate Counsel. (Retired). ***PRACTICE AREAS:*** Estate Planning Law; Probate Law; Trust Administration Law; Landlord and Tenant Law; Wills Law; Contracts Law; Lease Law. ***Email:*** jacktraynor@traynorlaw.com

J. THOMAS TRAYNOR, JR., born Devils Lake, North Dakota, June 14, 1955; admitted to bar, 1980, North Dakota. *Education:* University of North Dakota (B.A., 1977; J.D., 1980). Phi Delta Phi. Case Comment Editor, University of North Dakota Law Review,

(This Listing Continued)

TRAYNOR LAW FIRM, P.C., Devils Lake—Continued

1979-1980. Municipal Judge, 1983-1984. Devils Lake City Attorney, 1993—. *Member:* Lake Region (President, 1980-1983) and Northeast Judicial District Bar Associations; State Bar Association of North Dakota. ***PRACTICE AREAS:*** Real Estate Law; Debtor Creditor Law; Real Estate Title Insurance (Licensed Agent) Law; General Practice; Estate Planning; Probate; Wills and Trusts; Municipal Law; Loans. ***Email:*** tomtraynor@traynorlaw.com

DANIEL M. TRAYNOR, born Devils Lake, North Dakota, May 22, 1970; admitted to bar, 1997, North Dakota, Minnesota and U.S. District Court, District of North Dakota; Spirit Lake Sioux Tribal Court; Turtle Mountain Band of Chippewa Tribal Court. *Education:* University of North Dakota (B.A., 1994; J.D., with distinction, 1997). Delta Theta Phi. Order of the Coif. Associate Editor, North Dakota Law Review, 1996-1997. Law Clerk, Hon. Gerald W. Vande Walle, Chief Justice, North Dakota Supreme Court, 1997-1998. Extern, Hon. Patrick A. Conmy, U.S. District Court, District of North Dakota, 1995. Author: North Dakota Law Review, 72 N.D. L. Rev. 745, 1996. Republican National Committee, 2001-2003. City Prosecutor, City of Devils Lake, North Dakota, 1998—. *Member:* Lake Region, Northeast Judicial District, Minnesota State and American Bar Associations; State Bar of North Dakota; Defense Research Institute; North Dakota Defense Lawyers Association; Republican National Lawyers Association; American Law Institute. ***PRACTICE AREAS:*** Insurance Defense; Personal Injury; Coverage; Insurance Bad Faith; Business Litigation. ***Email:*** dantraynor@traynorlaw.com

REPRESENTATIVE CLIENTS: Farm Credit Services of Grand Forks FLCA; Brunswick Corp; City of Devils Lake; Devils Lake Airport Authority; Ramsey County Water Resource District; Alexis, Inc.; Allied Group Insurance; Allstate Insurance Company; American Hardware Mutual Ins. Co.; American West Ins. Co.; Austin Mutual Ins. Co.; Aviation Adjustment Bureau; Bituminous Casualty Co.; Capitol Indemnity Corp.; Casualty & Indemnity Ins. Co.; Casualty Underwriters, Inc.; Cimarron Ins. Co.; Dairyland Mutual; Dakota Fire Insurance Company; Dundee Mutual Insurance Co.; Employers Reinsurance Corporation; Farmers Union Natl. Ins. Co.; Federated Ins. Co.; Firemen"s Fund Ins. Co.; Great Amer. Ins. Co.; Great Central Ins. Co.; Great West Casualty Co.; Grinnell Mutual Reinsurance Group; Guaranty National Companies; Hardware Mut. Cas. Co.; Horace Mann Ins. Co.; Iowa National Mutual Ins. Co.; Ladder Management Service; Liberty Mut. Ins. Co.; Metropolitan Property & Casualty; Milbank Mutual Ins. Co.; Minnesota Ins. Guaranty Co.; Mutual Service Insurance Company; National Indemnity Insurance; Nodak Mutual Insurance Co.; North American Dealer Group; QBE Insurance Corporation; Preferred Risk Insurance Co.; Ranger Ins. Co.; Redland Ins. Co.; Reliance Ins. Co.; Sentry Insurance; Service Fire Ins. Co.; State Farm Ins. Co.; TCO Insurance Services; Underwriters Adjusting Co.; U.S.F. & G. Co.; Universal Underwriters Ins. Co.; Viking Insurance Co.; Western Ins. Cos.; Aetna Life Ins. Co.; Great-West Life Assurance Co.; Mutual of Omaha; Mutual Trust Life Ins. Co.; New York Life Ins. Co.; Northwestern National Life Ins. Co.; Union Central Life Ins. Co.; Bremer Bank of Devils Lake, North Dakota; Leevers Foods, Inc.; Western State Bank, Devils Lake, North Dakota; Ramsey National Bank & Trust Co., Devils Lake, ND; Western Finance and Lease, Inc.; Classic Motorworks, Ltd.; Chicago Insurance Co.; Atlantic Mutual Companies; United Community Bank of North Dakota, Leeds, North Dakota.

DYER & SUMMERS, P.C.

DICKINSON, NORTH DAKOTA

(See Bismarck)

General Civil Practice in State, Federal, and Tribal Courts, Divorce and other Family Law, Consumer Bankruptcy, and Social Security Disability.

MARK GREENWOOD LAW OFFICE

30 FIRST AVENUE EAST
P.O. BOX 327
DICKINSON, NORTH DAKOTA 58602-0327
Telephone: 701-227-3607
Fax: 701-483-3631
Email: mlglaw@ndsupernet.com
URL: http://www.lawyers.com/mgreenwood

Criminal Defense, Felonies, Misdemeanors, Homicides, Sex Crimes, DUI, Family Law, Divorce, Support, Custody, Adoptions.

MARK L. GREENWOOD, born Fargo, North Dakota, September 14, 1951; admitted to bar, 1976, North Dakota and U.S. District Court, District of North Dakota. *Education:* Dickinson State University (B.A., 1973); University of North Dakota (J.D., 1976). District 37 Democrats/NPL (Chairman, 1988-1992; Treasurer, 1986-1988); North Dakota Democrats/NPL (Rules Committee, 1972—). *Member:* Stark, Dunn and Slope Counties Bar Association (President, 2000-2002); State Bar Association of North Dakota; Southwest Judicial District Bar Association (President, 1984-1986); North Dakota Trial Lawyers Association; National Association of Criminal Defense Lawyers. ***PRACTICE AREAS:*** Criminal Defense; Family Law.

GREENWOOD & RAMSEY, P.L.L.P.

30 FIRST AVENUE EAST
P.O. BOX 1157
DICKINSON, NORTH DAKOTA 58602-1157
Telephone: 701-225-6074
Fax: 701-225-0492
URL: http://www.greenwoodramseylaw.com
URL: http://www.lawyers.com/greenwood&ramsey

Personal Injury, Auto Accidents, Family Law, Divorce, Adoptions, Probate, Bankruptcy, Creditors Rights, Collections, Real Estate, Criminal Defense, Civil Litigation.

DANN E. GREENWOOD, born Dickinson, North Dakota, September 21, 1952; admitted to bar, 1977, North Dakota; 1980, U.S. District Court, District of North Dakota. *Education:* Dickinson State College; University of North Dakota (B.S.B.A., magna cum laude, 1974); University of North Dakota (J.D., 1977). *Member:* State Bar Association of North Dakota (President, 1998-1999); North Dakota Trial Lawyers Association (President, 1987-1988). ***PRACTICE AREAS:*** Personal Injury; Family Law; Wrongful Death; General Litigation. ***Email:*** grlawdg@ndsupernet.com

GARY D. RAMSEY, born Grand Forks, North Dakota, July 30, 1954; admitted to bar, 1985, North Dakota and U.S. District Court, District of North Dakota. *Education:* University of North Dakota (B.S.B.A., cum laude, 1982; J.D., with distinction, 1985). President, Legal Assistance of North Dakota, 1998-2001. *Member:* North Dakota Trial Lawyers Association. [With U.S. Navy, 1972-1976]. ***PRACTICE AREAS:*** Bankruptcy; Debtor-Creditor; Criminal Law; Business Law; Family Law; General Litigation. ***Email:*** grlawgdr@ndsupernet.com

BRENDA L. SELINGER

MACKOFF KELLOGG LAW FIRM

(Mackoff, Kellogg, Kirby & Kloster, P.C.)
Established in 1889
46 WEST SECOND STREET
P.O. BOX 1097
DICKINSON, NORTH DAKOTA 58601
Telephone: 701-227-1841
Fax: 701-227-4739
Email: firm@mackoff.com
URL: http://www.mackoff.com

Beach, North Dakota Office: 41 Central Avenue, South. Telephone: 701-872-3731. Fax: 701-872-4695.

Estate Planning, Probate, Wills, Trusts, Real Estate, Foreclosures, Insurance Defense, Corporate Law, Personal Injury, Oil and Gas, Natural Resources, Environmental Law, Business Law, Creditor Bankruptcy, Banking, Contracts, Municipal Law, Administrative Law, Health Care, Taxation, Employee Benefits, Employment Law, Commercial Litigation, Medical Malpractice, Workers Compensation, Family Law, Mediation, Arbitration, Appeals, Civil Litigation in all State and Federal Courts.

FIRM PROFILE: Mackoff Kellogg provides its clients with the personal attention of a small law firm and the depth of legal experience usually associated with larger firms. The firm has built its reputation on trust, integrity, and results for more than a century.

H. A. MACKOFF (1888-1963)
THEODORE KELLOGG (1904-1990)
WARD M. KIRBY (1922-1993)
PAUL G. KLOSTER (Retired)
JOHN L. SHERMAN (Retired)

GORDON W. SCHNELL, born Dickinson, North Dakota, July 6, 1940; admitted to bar, 1965, North Dakota and U.S. District Court, District of North Dakota. *Education:* St. Louis University and University of North Dakota (B.S.L., 1965); University of North Dakota (LL.B., 1965). *Member:* American Bar Association (Member, Real Property, Probate and Trust Law Section and Business Law Section); State Bar Association of North Dakota (President, 1993-1994; Member, Real Property, Probate and Trust Section and Business Law Section). ***PRACTICE AREAS:*** Estate Planning and Probate Law; Corporate Law; Business Enterprises; Real Estate; Mineral Law; Employee Benefits; Tax Law. ***Email:*** gschnell@mackoff.com

PAUL F. EBELTOFT, JR., born Dickinson, North Dakota, March 30, 1949; admitted to bar, 1976, North Dakota; 1977, U.S. District Court, District of North Dakota; 1990, U.S. Court of Appeals, Eighth Circuit. *Education:* Gonzaga University (A.B., with honors, 1971); George Washington University (J.D., 1976); Mediation Center for Dispute Resolution, Hamline University Law and Graduate School (General Mediation, 2002). Legislative Assistant to U.S. Senator, Quentin N. Burdick, 1971-1973. Member, Professional Staff, U.S. Senate Committee on Public Works, 1973-1976; North Dakota State Board of Higher Education, 1992-1999. President, 1997-1998. Adjunct Assistant Professor of Business Administration and Political Science, Dickinson State University, 2001— *Member:* State Bar Association of North Dakota (Chairman, Attorney Standards Committee, 1991-1995); International Association of Defense Counsel; North Dakota Defense Lawyers Association (President, 1994-1999); Defense Research Institute. ***PRACTICE AREAS:*** Insurance Defense Law; Personal Injury Law; Environmental Law; Alternative Dispute Resolution; Health Law; Employment Law. ***Email:*** pebeltoft@mackoff.com

TIMOTHY A. PRIEBE, born Powers Lake, North Dakota, August 3, 1961; admitted to bar, 1986, North Dakota, U.S. District Court, District of North Dakota and U.S. Court of Appeals, Eighth Circuit. *Education:* North Dakota State University (B.S., 1983); University of North Dakota School of Law (J.D., with distinction, 1986). City Attorney, City of Dickinson, Beach and Hettinger. *Member:* Southwest Judicial District (President, 1998-2000) and American Bar Associations; State Bar Association of North Dakota (President, Young Lawyers Division, 1989-1990; Member, Board of Governors, 1998-2000); American Agricultural Law Association; North Dakota Municipal Attorneys Association; National Academy of Elder Law Attorneys. ***PRACTICE AREAS:*** Commercial Law; Estate Planning & Probate Law; Real Property Law; Oil & Gas Law; Corporate Law; Banking Law. ***Email:*** tpriebe@mackoff.com

CHARLES J. PETERSON, born Elgin, North Dakota, September 26, 1958; admitted to bar, 1983, North Dakota, Montana, U.S. District Court, District of North Dakota and U.S. District Court, District of Montana. *Education:* Dickinson State College (B.A., 1979); University of Montana (J.D., 1983). Phi Beta Lambda; Phi Delta Phi. Golden Valley County States Attorney, 1987—. Member, USFN.*Member:* State Bar Association of North Dakota; State Bar of Montana; American Bar Association. ***PRACTICE AREAS:*** Foreclosures; Bankruptcy; Creditors Rights; Real Property Law; Commercial Law; Estate Planning & Probate Law. ***Email:*** cpeterson@mackoff.com

GLEN R. BRUHSCHWEIN, born Valley City, North Dakota, October 29, 1961; admitted to bar, 1987, North Dakota; 1988, U.S. District Court, District of North Dakota;

(This Listing Continued)

2000, South Dakota and U.S. District Court, District of South Dakota. *Education:* University of North Dakota (B.A., 1984); University of North Dakota School of Law (J.D., 1987). Student Director, Legal Aid Association, Grand Forks, North Dakota. Southwest District Representative of Young Lawyers Division, 1988-1989. Golden Valley County Assistant States Attorney, 1990—. Member: U.S. Foreclosure Network; American Foreclosure Network. *Member:* State Bar Association of North Dakota; State Bar of South Dakota. ***PRACTICE AREAS:*** Foreclosures; Insurance Defense Law; Workers Compensation; Environmental Law; Personal Injury Law; Employment Law. ***Email:*** gbruhschwein@mackoff.com

RANDALL N. SICKLER, born Dickinson, North Dakota, December 1, 1963; admitted to bar, 1989, Colorado and U.S. District Court, District of Colorado; 1993, North Dakota and U.S. District Court, District of North Dakota; U.S. Court of Appeals, Eighth Circuit. *Education:* University of North Dakota (B.S., magna cum laude, 1986); University of North Dakota School of Law (J.D., 1989). *Member:* State Bar Association of North Dakota (Board of Governors, 2002-2004); Southwest District Bar Association (Treasurer and Secretary, 2000-2002; President, 2002-2004); North Dakota Defense Lawyers Association (Treasurer, 1998-2003; Vice President, 2003-2004; President, 2004-2005); Defense Research Institute (State Representative, 2001-2004). ***PRACTICE AREAS:*** Insurance Defense; Commercial Law; Personal Injury Law; Creditors Rights. ***Email:*** rsickler@mackoff.com

SANDRA K. KUNTZ, born Bowman, North Dakota, April 10, 1969; admitted to bar, 1994, North Dakota; 1995, Montana; 1998, U.S. District Court, District of North Dakota; 2000, U.S. District Court, District of Montana; 2004, South Dakota. *Education:* University of North Dakota (B.S.P.A., summa cum laude, 1991); University of North Dakota School of Law (J.D., with distinction, 1994). *Member:* State Bar Association of North Dakota; State Bar of Montana; State Bar of South Dakota; American Bar Association. ***PRACTICE AREAS:*** Foreclosures; Family Law; Juvenile Law. ***Email:*** skuntz@mackoff.com

ASSOCIATES

MATTHEW R. KOLLING, born Dickinson, North Dakota, October 4, 1975; admitted to bar, 2001, Minnesota; 2003, North Dakota; 2004, Montana. *Education:* University of North Dakota (B.A., summa cum laude, 1998); University of Minnesota (J.D., cum laude, 2001). Phi Beta Kappa. ***PRACTICE AREAS:*** Real Property; Creditor Bankruptcy; Commercial Litigation; Insurance Defense; Creditors Rights. ***Email:*** mkolling@mackoff.com

N. BOB PESALL, born Brookings, South Dakota, October 31, 1975; admitted to bar, 2004, North Dakota; 2005, South Dakota, U.S. District Court, District of South Dakota. *Education:* South Dakota State University (B.S., 1998); University of South Dakta School of Law (J.D., 2004). Editor, Great Plains Natural Resources Journal. Case Note, Sinkhole in Swampduster, Great Plains Natural Resources Journal, 2003, ed. ***PRACTICE AREAS:*** Personal Injury; Real Property Litigation; Constitutional Law; Election Law; Family Law. ***Email:*** npesall@mackoff.com

JESSICA L.Z. PESALL, born Scottsbluff, Nebraska, July 31, 1979; admitted to bar, 2004, North Dakota. *Education:* University of South Dakota (B.A., English, B.A., Spanish, minor Theatre, 2001; J.D., 2004). Golden Key National Honor Society. Recipient: Sanger Award for Writing; Alex Wartman Award for Modern Foreign Languages; Talent Award for Creative Playwriting. Member: National Forensics League, 1995—; Thespian Society, 1996—. ***LANGUAGES:*** Spanish. ***PRACTICE AREAS:*** Foreclosures; Personal Injury; General Practice. ***Email:*** jpesall@mackoff.com

REPRESENTATIVE CLIENTS: *Insurance:* Atlantic Mutual Insurance Company; Employers Mutual Cos.; Farmland Insurance; Federated Insurance; Fireman's Fund; Grinnell Mutual Reinsurance; Center Mutual Insurance Company; Nationwide Group; Nodak Mutual Insurance Company; North Dakota Insurance Reserve Fund; Catholic Health Initiatives; St. Paul Companies; State Farm Group; Westfield Cos. *Banks:* AgriBank, FCB; Wells Fargo Bank, North Dakota, N.A.; American State Bank and Trust, Dickinson, Killdeer and New England, North Dakota; Union State Bank of Halliday; First National Bank of Bowman, Bowman, N.D.; Great Plains National Bank of Belfield and Dickinson, N.D.; Community First National Bank of Dickinson and Beach, N.D. *Oil Related:* Halliburton Services; High Plains, Inc.; WellPro, Inc.; Armstrong Operating, Inc.; Bob's Oil Field Service, Inc.; Armstrong Corporation; M-I Corporation. *Manufacturing:* Baker Boy Bake Shop, Inc.; Royal Oak Industries; TMI Corporation; Steffes, Inc.; Fisher Industries, Inc.; Dakota Church Furniture Mfg.; Industrial Electric. *Health Related:* St. Joseph's Hospital & Health Care Center; St. Luke's Nursing Home; Western Eye Clinic, Ltd.; St. Luke's Tri-State Hospital. *Power Suppliers:* West Plains Electric Cooperative; MDU Resources Group.*Schools:* Dickinson Catholic Schools of Dickinson; Killdeer Public School District; Scranton Public School District; Regent Public School District; South Heart Public School District. *Others:* The Equitable Life Assurance Society of the United States (Loan Department); North Dakota Stockmen's Assn.; Dakota Dinosaur Museum, Inc.; Assumption Abbey; Dan Porter Motors, Inc.; King Realty, Inc.; Medora Grazing Associtionn; Berger Electric, Inc.; Southwest Multi-County Correction Center; ESP Computers and Sofware, Inc.; Kadrmas, Lee & Jackson, Inc. *Foreclosure Clients:* ABN AMRO Mortgage Group; Aames Home Loans; Alegis Group; Ameriquest Mortgage Co.; Atlantic Mortgage and Investment Corp.; Aurora Loan Financing; Bank of America; Banc One Mortgage Corp.; Bank of Oklahoma; Bank of United Texas; Beal Bank; CUNA Mutual Mortgage; Cendant Mortgage; Chase Manhattan Mortgage Corp.; Chase Mortgage West; CitiFinancial, Inc.; CitiMortgage, Inc.; Dovenmuehle Mortgage, Inc.; EMC Mortgage; Eastern Savings Bank; EquiCredit Corp. of America; Fairbanks Capital Corp.; Fidelity National Foreclosure Solutions; First Nationwide Mortgage Corp.; GMAC Mortgage Corp.; GreenPoint Mortgage; Guaranty National; HomeComings Financial Network; Homeside Lending, Inc.; Indymac Bank; Interbay Funding; Irwin Mortgage Group; Litton Loan Servicing, LP; Nationawide Default; Nationawide Home Mortgage; North American Mortgage Co.; Ocwen Federal Bank, FSB; Olympic Calmco; Option One; Provident Consumer Financial; RBMG, Inc.; Saxon Mortgage, Inc.; Suntrust Mortgage, Inc.; U.S. Bank Natioanl Association; Washington Mutual Bank; Wells Fargo Bank. ATTORNEYS FOR: City of Dickinson; Golden Valley County; City of Beach; Dickinson Municipal Airport Authority; Dry Prairie Rural Water Authority; City of Hettinger. APPROVED ATTORNEYS FOR: Bank of North Dakota and FDIC.

WHEELER WOLF LAW FIRM

DICKINSON, NORTH DAKOTA

(See Bismarck)

Civil Trial Practice in all Courts and Administrative Agencies, Corporate Law, Administrative Law, Public Utilities, Taxation, Estate Planning, Probate, Wills, Elder Law, Banking, Real Estate, Commercial Law, Lobbying, Communications Law, Construction Law, Labor Relations, Collections, Personal Injury, Negligence, Workers Compensation, Social Security, Criminal Law, Bankruptcy, Agricultural Law.

DAVID R. BOSSART

1220 MAIN AVENUE, SUITE 105

FARGO, NORTH DAKOTA 58103

Telephone: 701-271-8030

Fax: 701-271-6849

Email: david@bossartlaw.com

URL: http://www.bossartlaw.com

Personal Injury Law, Wrongful Death, General Litigation.

DAVID R. BOSSART, born Fargo, North Dakota, March 13, 1942; admitted to bar, 1965, North Dakota; 1966, U.S. District Court, District of North Dakota; 1968, U.S. Court of Appeals, Eighth Circuit; 1989, U.S. Supreme Court. *Education:* University of North Dakota (B.A., 1963; J.D., 1965). Phi Alpha Delta. Member, Board of Directors, North Dakota Law Review, 1964-1965. Listed in, Best Lawyers in America, 1990—. Assistant City Attorney, Fargo, ND, 1967-1968. Assistant States Attorney, Cass County, 1971-1975. Recipient: Wiedemann-Wysocki Citation of Excellence given by The Association of Trial Lawyers in America, 1991-1992, 1994-1998 and 2002; Diplomate in Trial Advocacy 1994, awarded by National College of Advocacy for The Association of Trial Lawyers of America. Faculty Instructor, National College of Advocacy, The Association of Trial Lawyers of America, 1989—. Member of Faculty: Basic College of Trial Advocacy, The Association of Trial Lawyers of America, Scottsdale, AZ, 1990; Princeton, NJ, 1990; Hastings School of Law, San Francisco, CA, 1991; University of Alabama Law School, Tuscaloosa, 1993; University of New Mexico School of Law, Albuquerque, New Mexico, 1997; Ultimate Course in Trial Advocacy, Harvard Law School, 1993, 1998, 2000 and 2002; Ultimate Trial Advocacy Course, Stanford University Law School, 1995; U.C. Berkley, 1997; Overcoming Juror Bias College, 2001, 2002, 2003 and 2004; and Chairman, Civil Service Commission, Fargo, North Dakota, 1976-1979. *Member:* Cass County (President, 1977-1978) and American (Member, Torts and Insurance Practice Section) Bar Associations; State Bar Association of North Dakota (Member, Attorney Standards Committee, 1986-1999; Chairman, Drug and Alcohol Abuse Committee, 1986-1988); North Dakota Trial Lawyers Association (Founding Member, 1975; President, 1986-1987; Member: Board of Directors, 1984—; State Key Person Committee, 1987—); The Association of Trial Lawyers of America (President's Council, 1986-1988; Board of Governors, 1989—; Key Person Committee, 1986—; Co-chair, Quality of Life and Substance Abuse Committee, 1996—; Budget Committee, 1997-1998; Trial Lawyers for Public Justice (State Captain, Board of Directors, 1988-1996); Fellow, International Academy of Trial Lawyers. Fellow, American College of Trial Lawyers; Roscoe Pound Foundation; Civil Justice Foundation; Minnesota Trial Lawyers Association; Consumer Attorney's of California; Texas Trial Lawyers Association; Arizona Trial Lawyers Association. ***PRACTICE AREAS:*** Personal Injury; Wrongful Death.

CAMRUD, MADDOCK, OLSON & LARSON, LTD.

FARGO, NORTH DAKOTA

(See Grand Forks)

Insurance, Insurance Defense, Healthcare, Hospital Law, Probate, Trusts, Estates, Labor, Employment, Taxation, Real Estate, Corporate Law, Mediation. General Civil and Appellate Practice in North Dakota and Minnesota State and Federal Courts.

CONMY FESTE LTD.

Established in 1879

200 WELLS FARGO CENTER

406 MAIN AVENUE

P.O. BOX 2686

FARGO, NORTH DAKOTA 58108-2686

Telephone: 701-293-9911

Fax: 701-293-3133

Email: firm@conmylaw.com

URL: http://www.conmylaw.com

General Civil Practice in State and Federal Courts. Banking, Creditor Bankruptcy, Commercial, Corporate, Insurance Defense, Insurance, Personal Injury, Wrongful Death, Products Liability, Trusts and Estates, Estate Planning, Title Insurance, Employment Law and Family Law.

PAUL M. HUBBARD, born Omaha, Nebraska, 1945; admitted to bar, 1973, North Dakota and U.S. District Court, District of North Dakota; 1985, Minnesota and U.S. District Court, District of Minnesota. *Education:* Moorhead State University (B.A., 1966); University of South Dakota (J.D., cum laude, 1973). Member, Thomas Sterling Scholastic Honor Society (University of South Dakota - Law). Board of Editors, South Dakota Law Review, 1972-1973. Listed in: Best Lawyers in America and Chambers USA, (Real Property). Licensed Title Insurance Agent: North Dakota; Minnesota. Instructor, North Dakota State Bar C.L.E. (Real Property). Member: North Dakota Land Titles Association; U.S. Foreclosure Network. *Member:* Cass County (President, 1981-1982), Minnesota State and American Bar Associations; State Bar Association of North Dakota (Member, Real Property, Probate and Trust Law Section, Chairman, 1985-1988, Vice Chairman, 1989—; Chairman, Liens and Foreclosure Committee; Title Standards Committee, 1976-1987). (Real Property Specialist Certified by the Real Property Section, Minnesota State Bar Association). ***PRACTICE AREAS:*** Real Estate Law; Commercial Law; Creditors' Law. ***Email:*** phubbard@conmylaw.com

WICKHAM CORWIN, born Fargo, North Dakota, July 25, 1950; admitted to bar, 1976, North Dakota and U.S. District Court, District of North Dakota; 1982, Minnesota; 1983, U.S. Court of Appeals, Eighth Circuit; 1991, U.S. District Court, District of Minnesota. *Education:* University of Utah (B.S., 1972); University of North Dakota (J.D., 1976). Member, Board of Editors, North Dakota Law Review, 1975-1976. *Member:* Cass County, Clay County and Minnesota State Bar Associations; State Bar Association of North Dakota.

(This Listing Continued)

CONMY FESTE LTD., Fargo—Continued

Certified as a Civil Trial Specialist by the National Board of Trial Advocacy and the Minnesota State Bar Association. ***PRACTICE AREAS:*** Commercial Litigation; Civil Trial Practice; Personal Injury. ***Email:*** wcorwin@conmylaw.com

KIM E. BRUST, born Fargo, North Dakota, May 26, 1954; admitted to bar, 1979, North Dakota; U.S. District Court, District of North Dakota; 1991, Minnesota and U.S. District Court, District of Minnesota. *Education:* North Dakota State University (B.A., 1976); University of North Dakota (J.D., with distinction, 1979). Order of the Coif; Phi Delta Phi. *Member:* Cass County Bar Association (President, 1994-1995); State Bar Association of North Dakota; North Dakota Trial Lawyers Association (Member, Board of Governors, 1990—; Vice-President, 1994-1995, President-Elect, 1995-1996, President, 1996-1997); The Association of Trial Lawyers of America (President's Council, 1996). (Certified as a Civil Trial Specialist by the National Board of Trial Advocacy). ***PRACTICE AREAS:*** Personal Injury Law; Trial Practice. ***Email:*** kbrust@conmylaw.com

MICHAEL M. THOMAS, born Duluth, Minnesota, May 1, 1959; admitted to bar, 1984, North Dakota; 1985, Minnesota; U.S. District Court, District of North Dakota and District of Minnesota. *Education:* University of North Dakota (B.S.B.A., summa cum laude, 1981; J.D., with distinction, 1984). Phi Eta Sigma; Phi Alpha Delta; Order of the Coif. Listed in: Best Lawyers of America; Chambers U.S.A. Extern to Honorable Myron H. Bright, Judge, U.S. Court of Appeals, Eighth Circuit, 1983. *Member:* Cass County, Minnesota State and American Bar Associations; State Bar Association of North Dakota. ***PRACTICE AREAS:*** Creditors' Rights; Banking Law; Commercial Law; Mergers and Acquisitions. ***Email:*** mthomas@conmylaw.com

ROBERT J. SCHULTZ, born Wisconsin Rapids, Wisconsin, March 31, 1955; admitted to bar, 1987, North Dakota, Minnesota and U.S. District Court, District of North Dakota. *Education:* University of Wisconsin, Stevens Point (B.S., 1977); University of North Dakota (J.D., with distinction, 1987). Order of the Coif. Member, North Dakota Law Review, 1985-1987. *Member:* Cass County and Minnesota State Bar Associations; State Bar Association of North Dakota. ***PRACTICE AREAS:*** Domestic Relations; Employment Law; Civil Litigation. ***Email:*** rschultz@conmylaw.com

ASSOCIATES

JEREMY D. HOLMES, born Rugby, North Dakota, July 12, 1974; admitted to bar, 2000, North Dakota, Minnesota and U.S. District Court, District of North Dakota. *Education:* North Dakota State University (B.S., 1997); University of Iowa College of Law (J.D., 2000). Phi Delta Phi. Member, Journal of Corporation Law, 1998-2000. *Member:* Cass County Bar Association; State Bar Association of North Dakota. ***PRACTICE AREAS:*** Real Estate Law; Commercial Law; Creditors' Rights. ***Email:*** jholmes@conmylaw.com

STEPHANNIE N. STIEL, born Aberdeen, South Dakota, June 25, 1978; admitted to bar, 2003, North Dakota; 2004, Minnesota. *Education:* Minnesota State University Moorhead (B.A., cum laude, 2000); University of North Dakota (J.D., with distinction, 2003). Delta Theta Phi. Member, National Order of Barristers, 2003—. Member, Board of Editors and Outside Articles Editor, North Dakota Law Review, 2002-2003. *Member:* State Bar Association of North Dakota; American Bar Association. ***Email:*** sstiel@conmylaw.com

RETIRED

E. T. CONMY, JR., born Fargo, North Dakota, October 12, 1912; admitted to bar, 1935, North Dakota. *Education:* University of Southern California and University of North Dakota (A.B.); University of North Dakota (LL.B., 1935). Phi Delta Phi. City Attorney, 1947-1968. *Fellow:* American College of Trial Lawyers; International Society of Barristers. [Lieut., U.S. Naval Reserve, 1944-1946]

CHARLES A. FESTE, born Fargo, North Dakota, October 27, 1928; admitted to bar, 1956, North Dakota and U.S. District Court, District of North Dakota; 1959, U.S. Court of Appeals, Eighth Circuit; 1977, U.S. Supreme Court. *Education:* Concordia College (B.A., 1950); University of North Dakota (J.D., 1956). Phi Alpha Delta. Member, Editorial Board, North Dakota Law Review, 1955-1956. Assistant City Attorney, Fargo, North Dakota, 1956-1968. *Fellow:* American College of Trust and Estate Counsel. [1st Lieut., U.S. Army, active duty, 1951-1953]

STATE COUNSEL FOR: Metropolitan Life Insurance Company; Citicorp Mortgage, Inc.; Nissan Motors Acceptance Corp.; New Holland Credit Co.; Wells Fargo Home Mortgage; Bank of America; Atlantic Mortgage; Western Finance and Lease; Ford Motor Credit Co.
REPRESENTATIVE CLIENTS: Border State Industries, Inc.; UNISYS Corp.; TRW; Wells Fargo Corporation; Wells Fargo Bank, N.A.; U.S. Bank, N.A.; Bremer Bank, N.A.; Bank of the West, NA; Ticor Title Insurance; U.S. Gypsum Co.; GMAC Mortgage Corp.; Wendover Funding, Inc.; Chase Mortgage Services; Bankers Trust of California; First Nationwide Bank; Midland Mortgage Co.; Mortgage Investment Corporation; Wells Fargo Mortgage, Inc.; The Prudential Home Mortgage Company; Homeside Lending, Inc.; Nationsbanc Mortgage Corp.; Union Planters Mortgage Services Group; Wells Fargo Equipment Finance, Inc.; Fidelity Savings Bank, Green Tree Financial; FT Mortgage; Banc One Mortgage; Conti Mortgage. *Insurance:* Motorists Insurance Companies; G.E. Auto Insurance Program; Bituminous Insurance Co.; Colonial Penn; Great American Insurance Co.; Imperial Casualty Co.; The Mill Mutuals; Bank of America; TMG Life Insurance Company; Old Republic Title Insurance Company; Commonwealth Title Insurance Company; Kemper National Insurance Company; Zurich Commercial.

DEMARS & TURMAN, LTD.

Established in 1978

15 BROADWAY, SUITE 510

P.O. BOX 110

FARGO, NORTH DAKOTA 58107

Telephone: 701-293-5592

Fax: 701-293-8837

URL: http://www.demarsandturmanlaw.com

General Civil and Criminal Practice, Trials in State and Federal Courts, Business Bankruptcy, Business Reorganization, Commercial Law, Partnerships, Corporate, Banks and Banking, Agribusiness, Collections, Real Estate, Probate, Personal Injury, Family Law, Mediation and Arbitration.

(This Listing Continued)

FIRM PROFILE: DeMars & Turman, Ltd. was incorporated 1978. For over 30 years the firm has provided high quality, efficient, cost effective, personalized and successful representation to a broad range of clients in North Dakota and northwestern Minnesota, including financial institutions, large and small commercial and agricultural entities of all kinds. The firm provides experienced legal service in its principal areas of practice, including commercial transactions and litigation, bankruptcy, reorganization, foreclosure, collection, real estate, construction litigation, and estate planning.

DAVID T. DEMARS, born Westhope, North Dakota, October 7, 1941; admitted to bar, 1965, North Dakota; 1982, Minnesota. *Education:* University of North Dakota (B.S.B.A., 1963; J.D., 1965). Phi Delta Phi; Order of the Coif. Author: "Artificial Insemination: Problem Child of the Law," 40 N.D.L. Rev. 89, 1964. Editor-in-Chief, North Dakota Law Review, 1964-1965. Member, 1970-1974 and Chairman, 1973-1974, City of Fargo Zoning Commission. Member, 1974-1983 and Chairman, 1978-1980, City of Fargo Planning Commission. Assistant City attorney, Fargo, North Dakota, 1966-1968. Listed in: Best Lawyers in America. *Member:* Cass County, Becker County, North Dakota State, Minnesota State and American (Sections on: Corporation, Banking and Business Law; Economics of Law Practice) Bar Associations; American Bankruptcy Institute. ***PRACTICE AREAS:*** Commercial Law; Commercial Litigation; Business Reorganization; Workouts; Real Estate; Wills; Trusts and Estates; Civil Litigation; Zoning; Planning; Land Use; Mediation; Arbitration; Commercial Bankruptcy; Commercial Workouts; Creditor Bankruptcy. ***Email:*** daviddemars@demarsandturmanlaw.com

JOSEPH A. TURMAN, born Fargo, North Dakota, July 20, 1948; admitted to bar, 1973, North Dakota; 1996, Minnesota. *Education:* University of North Dakota (B.S., 1970; J.D., 1973). Phi Delta Phi. Member, Governor's Juvenile Justice Advisory Committee, 1976. *Member:* Cass County (President, 1988-1989) and Minnesota Bar Associations; State Bar Association of North Dakota; The Association of Trial Lawyers of America; North Dakota Trial Lawyers Association. ***REPORTED CASES:*** Lenthe Investment's, Inc. v. Service Oil, Inc. (ND 2001) 636 NW2d 189; Union State Bank v. Woell, (N.D. 1984) 357, N.W.2d 234; Gust v. Peoples and Enderlin State Bank, (N.D. 1989) 447, N.W.2d 914; First Bank South Dakota v. Asbridge, (Bkrptcy. N.D. 1984) 45 B.R. 564. ***PRACTICE AREAS:*** Loan Workouts; Complex Business Litigation; Creditor Rights in Bankruptcy; Business Organization; Real Estate; Employee Benefits; Mortgages; Estate Planning; Construction Litigation. ***Email:*** joeturman@demarsandturmanlaw.com

KATRINA A. TURMAN, born Fargo, North Dakota, November 18, 1977; admitted to bar, 2005, North Dakota. *Education:* University of Minnesota (B.S., Retail Merchandising, 2002); University of North Dakota (J.D., with distinction, 2005). Research Editor, North Dakota Law Review 2004-2005, Member, 2003-2004. Internship with Judge Kermit Bye, Eighth Circuit Court of Appeals, Summer of 2004. *Member:* Cass County Bar Association; State Bar Association of North Dakota. ***REPORTED CASES:*** Smith Enterprises, Inc. v. In-Touch Phone Cards, Inc., 685 NW2d 741 (2004). ***PRACTICE AREAS:*** Commercial Law; Debtor and Creditor. ***Email:*** katrinaturman@demarsandturmanlaw.com

LEGAL SUPPORT PERSONNEL

JANELLE ALBRECHT

KIM JOHNSON

REPRESENTATIVE CLIENTS: Ramsey National Bank & Trust Co., Devils Lake, North Dakota; First Community Credit Union, Jamestown, N.D.; Heyer Engineering, Inc.; IDA of Moorhead Corporation; Pierce Roofing & Sheet Metal, Inc.; City of Oxbow; Builders Management & Investment, Co.; PRACS Institute, Ltd.; Twin Valley State Bank; Service Oil, Inc.; American State Bank of Erskine; Kindred State Bank; Pearle Vision Center; Northland Truss Systems, Inc.; Alerus Financial f/k/a First National Bank North Dakota; Bremer Bank; Mid-America Aviation, Inc.; Bank of The West; Dakota Underground, Inc.; Heartland Trust Company; SuperValu, Inc.
REFERENCES: Bank of the West; Ramsey National Bank & Trust Co., Devils Lake, North Dakota.

DORSEY & WHITNEY LLP

51 NORTH BROADWAY, SUITE 402

P.O. BOX 1344

FARGO, NORTH DAKOTA 58107-1344

Telephone: 701-235-6000

Facsimile: 701-235-9969

URL: http://www.dorsey.com

Minneapolis, Minnesota Office: Suite 1500, 50 South Sixth Street, 55402-1498. Telephone: 612-340-2600.

Seattle, Washington Office: U.S. Bank Centre, 1420 Fifth Avenue, Suite 3400, 98101. Telephone: 206-903-8800.

New York, New York Office: 250 Park Avenue, 10177. Telephone: 212-415-9200.

Washington, D.C. Office: 1001 Pennsylvania Avenue, N.W., Suite 400 South, 20004. Telephone: 202-442-3000.

Denver, Colorado Office: 370 Seventeenth Street, Republic Plaza Building, Suite 4700, 80202-5647. Telephone: 303-629-3400.

London, England Office: 21 Wilson Street, EC2M 2TD. Telephone: 011-44-207-588-0800.

Hong Kong Office: Suite 3008, One Pacific Place, 88 Queensway. Hong Kong. Telephone: 011-852-252-65000. Fax: 011-852-252-43000.

Shanghai, China Office: Suite 6211-12, Plaza 66, No. 1266 Nanjing Xi Lu, Shanghai, 200040. Telephone: 86-21-6288-2323. Fax: 86-21-6288-3222.

Toronto, Ontario Office: BCE Place, 161 Bay Street, Suite 4310, P.O. Box 512, M5J 2S1. Telephone: 416-367-7370. Fax: 416-367-7371.

Vancouver, British Columbia Office: 666 Burrard Street, Suite 500, V6C 3P6. Telephone: 604-687-5151.

Anchorage, Alaska Office: 1031 West 4th Avenue, Suite 600, 99501-5907. Telephone: 907-276-4557.

Des Moines, Iowa Office: 801 Grand, Suite 3900, 50309. Telephone: 515-283-1000.

(This Listing Continued)

Salt Lake City, Utah Office: Wells Fargo Plaza, 170 South Main Street, Suite 900, 84101. Telephone: 801-933-7360.

Southern California Office: 38 Technology Drive, Irvine, 92618-5310. Telephone: 949-932-3600.

Great Falls, Montana Office: 507 Davidson Building, 8 Third Street North, P.O. Box 1566, 59401. Telephone: 406-727-3632.

Missoula, Montana Office: 125 Bank Street, Suite 600, 59802-4407. Telephone: 406-721-6025. Fax: 406-543-0863.

Paramus, New Jersey Office: 95 Route 17 South, Suite 203, 07652. Telephone: 201-291-8904. Fax: 201-712-9444.

Palo Alto, California Office: 1717 Embarcadero Road, 94303. Telephone: 650-857-1717.

San Francisco, California Office: 555 California Street, Suite 1000, 94104-1513. Telephone: 415-781-1989.

Administrative Law, Antitrust and Trade Regulation, Business, Banking, Bankruptcy, Civil Litigation, Construction Law, Contracts, Labor and Employment Law, Health Law, Railroad Law, Real Estate, Structured Finance, Toxic Tort Law and Trade Secrets, Tax, Employee Benefits, Mergers and Acquisitions, Corporate, Securities.

FIRM PROFILE: Clients have relied on Dorsey since 1912 as a valued, cutting-edge business partner. With over 700 lawyers in 20 locations in the USA, Canada, Europe and Asia, we provide an integrated, proactive approach to our clients' legal and business needs. Dorsey represents a number of the world's most successful Fortune 500 companies from a variety of industries including leaders in the financial services, investment banking, life sciences, securities, technology and energy sectors as well as nonprofit and government entities.

MEMBERS OF FIRM

SARAH ANDREWS HERMAN, born 1952; admitted to bar, 1977, North Dakota. *Education:* University of North Dakota (B.A., magna cum laude, 1974); University of Michigan (J.D, 1977); University of Oklahoma. Member, North Dakota Federal Practice Committee. Member (N.D. Co-Chair) Eighth Circuit Gender Fairness Task Force. N.D. Judicial Evaluation Committee. *Member:* North Dakota State (President, 1997-1998) and American (Member, Employment and Labor Section) Bar Associations. (Resident). ***LANGUAGES:*** French. ***PRACTICE AREAS:*** Employment Law; Labor Law; Civil Litigation; Commercial Litigation; Medical Products Litigation; Franchise; Antitrust and Trade Regulation. **Email:** herman.sarah@dorsey.com

JON E. STRINDEN, born 1957; admitted to bar, 1982, North Dakota; 1983, Minnesota, U.S. District Court, District of North Dakota, U.S. Court of Appeals, Eighth Circuit and U.S. Tax Court. *Education:* University of North Dakota (B.S.B.A., Accounting, 1979; J.D., 1982). Beta Alpha Psi; Blue Key. Certified Public Accountant, North Dakota, 1980. Member: Advisory Committee, College for Financial Planning, Denver, Colorado, 1984-1990; International Association of Financial Planners, 1986-1990. *Member:* Clay County, Cass County, Seventh Judicial District, Minnesota State and American Bar Associations; State Bar Association of North Dakota (Member, Drafting Committee, North Dakota Limited Liability Company Act; Limited Liability Partnership Act); North Dakota Society of Certified Public Accountants (Chairman, Legislative Committee). ***PRACTICE AREAS:*** Corporate; Tax; Banking; Real Estate. **Email:** strinden.jon@dorsey.com

TODD E. ZIMMERMAN, born 1965; admitted to bar, 1990, Minnesota; 1996, North Dakota. *Education:* University of North Dakota (B.B.A., summa cum laude, 1987); University of Minnesota (J.D., magna cum laude, 1990). Order of the Coif. *Member:* Minnesota, North Dakota and American (Member, Litigation Section) Bar Associations; North Dakota Society of Certified Public Accountants. ***PRACTICE AREAS:*** Commercial and Business Litigation; Banking; Corporate; Real Estate. **Email:** zimmerman.todd@dorsey.com

KRISTY L. ALBRECHT, born 1961; admitted to bar, 1995, Iowa; 1997, North Dakota and Minnesota. *Education:* Jamestown College (B.A., summa cum laude, 1983); University of Iowa College of Law (J.D., with high honors, 1995). Order of the Coif. Editor in Chief of the Iowa Law Review. Recipient of the Hancher Finkbine Medallion, University of Iowa. Law Clerk for the Honorable David R. Hansen, U.S. Eighth Circuit Court of Appeals, 1995-1997. *Member:* Iowa State, North Dakota State, Minnesota State and American Bar Associations. ***PRACTICE AREAS:*** Commercial Litigation; Civil Rights; Employment Law; Telecommunications Law. **Email:** albrecht.kristy@dorsey.com

RESIDENT ASSOCIATES

MATTHEW GREENLEY, born 1977; admitted to bar, 2003, North Dakota. *Education:* Iowa State University (B.S., 2000); Duke University School of Law (J.D., 2003). **Email:** greenley.matthew@dorsey.com

NOLA A. McNEALLY, born 1968; admitted to bar, 2000, Minnesota; 2001, North Dakota. *Education:* Moorhead State University (B.S., 1991); University of North Dakota (J.D., with distinction, 2000). Order of the Coif. Note Editor, North Dakota Law Review, 1999-2000. *Member:* Minnesota State Bar Association; State Bar Association of North Dakota. ***PRACTICE AREAS:*** Corporate; Securities; Business Planning; Banking. **Email:** mcneally.nola@dorsey.com

OF COUNSEL

BRADLEY J. SWENSON, born 1965; admitted to bar, 1992, Missouri and U.S. District Court, Eastern and Western Districts of Missouri, U.S. Court of Appeals, Eighth Circuit; 1994, U.S. Court of International Trade Law, U.S. Court of Appeals for the Federal Circuit; 1997, U.S. Court of Appeals, Eleventh Circuit and U.S. Tax Court; 1998, Minnesota and U.S. District Court of Minnesota; 1999, North Dakota. *Education:* North Dakota State University (B.A., with honors, 1989); University of Denver, College of Law (J.D., with highest honors, 1992); The Hague Academy of International Law, The Hague, Netherlands (1993). Ford Foundation Fellow. International Protection of Intellectual Property Rights, 1992. Assistant Special Counsel, Office of Special Counsel, Waco Investigation, 1999-2001. *Member:* Bar Association of Metropolitan St. Louis; Cass County, Hennepin County, Minnesota State, North Dakota, and American Bar Associations; Missouri Bar. ***PRACTICE AREAS:*** Business Law; Intellectual Property; Technology Licensing; Commercial Litigation.

(This Listing Continued)

ATTORNEY

LYNN BLOCK, born 1957; admitted to bar, 1996, North Dakota. *Education:* North Dakota State University (B.A., 1991); University of North Dakota School of Law (J.D., with distinction, 1996). ***LANGUAGES:*** Spanish. ***PRACTICE AREAS:*** Civil Litigation; Employment Law. **Email:** block.lynn@dorsey.com

FARGO OFFICE IS COUNSEL FOR: US Bank; CNH Global; Blue Cross and Blue Shield of NorthDakota; Nodak Mutual Insurane Company; Dakota Medical Foundation; Montana Dakota UtilitiesResource Group; Knife River Coal Co.; Friendship; Northwest Professional Color; St. Joseph'sHospital Dickinson; New Flyer Industries; NDSU Research Foundation; Ag Country Farm CreditServices; Stearns County National Bank.

(For personnel and biographical data on Dorsey & Whitney's other offices, see that specific city and state listing)

GARY A. FICEK

ALERUS FINANCIAL BUILDING, SUITE 505
15 BROADWAY
FARGO, NORTH DAKOTA 58102-4907
Telephone: 701-241-8525
Fax: 701-241-8443. Toll Free: 1-800-786-8525
Email: ficeklaw@mcleodusa.net
URL: http://www.ficeklaw.com

Social Security Disability, Social Security Appeals, Supplemental Security Income Disability, Administrative Hearings and Appeals, Workers' Compensation, Federal Employees Liability Act (FELA), Railroad Retirement Board, Federal Workers Compensation Appeals, Accidents and Civil Litigation.

GARY A. FICEK, born Waukesha, Wisconsin, October 23, 1956; admitted to bar, 1981, North Dakota; 1990, Minnesota. *Education:* University of North Dakota (B.A., summa cum laude, 1978; J.D., 1981). Phi Beta Kappa; Delta Theta Phi; Blue Key. Member, National Moot Court. Senior Editor, North Dakota Law Review, 1980-1981. *Member:* State Bar Association of North Dakota; Minnesota State Bar Association; The Association of Trial Lawyers of America. ***REPORTED CASES:*** 326 N.W. 2d 203; 377 N.W. 2d 560; 386 N.W. 2d 918; and 952 F. Supp. 659. ***PRACTICE AREAS:*** Social Security Disability Law; Workers Compensation Law; Civil Litigation Law.

JEFFRIES, OLSON & FLOM, P.A.

Established in 1986
1325 23RD STREET S.W.
FARGO, NORTH DAKOTA 58103
Telephone: 701-280-2300
Fax: 701-280-1880
URL: http://www.jeffrieslaw.com

General Insurance Defense, Trial and Appellate Practice in Minnesota and North Dakota State and Federal Courts. Medical and other Professional Malpractice, Civil Rights, Construction, Products Liability, Fire, Government and Municipalities, Errors & Omissions, Environmental Law, Health Law, Casualty, Negligence, Asbestos Litigation, Hazardous Waste, Toxic Substances, Pollution, No-Fault, Insurance Coverages, Employment, Liquor Liability, Automobile, Premises Liability, Commercial Litigation, Subrogation.

FIRM PROFILE: Jeffries, Olson & Flom, P.A., was established for the purpose of concentrating in civil litigation. The firm's primary emphasis is representing insurance companies and their insureds in all areas of modern day tort and contract claims. With 80 years of collective experience in insurance defense, the firm does trial and appellate work in both Minnesota and North Dakota. The firm also handles commercial, real estate and business matters for select clients.

RICHARD N. JEFFRIES, born Hastings, Nebraska, October 20, 1942; admitted to bar, 1970, Minnesota; 1981, North Dakota and Florida; U.S. District Court, District of Minnesota; U.S. District Court, District of North Dakota; 1991, U.S. Court of Appeals, Eighth Circuit. *Education:* Moorhead State University (B.A., 1965); University of North Dakota (J.D., with distinction, 1970). Phi Alpha Delta; Order of the Coif. Articles Editor, North Dakota Law Review, 1969-1970. Author: "Damages-Aggravation, Mitigation and Reduction of Loss," 45 N.D. Law Review 528, 1969; "Automobiles-Liability of Manufacturers or Sellers-Automobile Manufacturer's Liability for Negligent Design," 45 N.D. Law Review 100, 1968; "Using the Structured Settlement Annuity Expert to Combat the Plaintiff's Economist in Catastrophic Injury Cases," Minnesota Defense, Spring, 1984; "Enforcement of Settlement Agreements," Minnesota Defense, Spring, 1986; "Statutes of Limitation-An Overview," 1988, revised 2001; "A Comparison of Duty to Defend and Insurance Coverage Issues in Minnesota and North Dakota," 1991. Selected as "Super Lawyer," Minnesota Law & Leading Attorney, 1995-2002. *Member:* Clay County, Minnesota State and American Bar Associations; State Bar Association of North Dakota; The Florida Bar; American Arbitration Association (Arbitrator). ***REPORTED CASES:*** DeCoteau v. Nodak Mut. Ins. Co., 2001 ND 182, 636 NW2d 432; First Natl. Bank and Trust Co. of Williston v. St. Paul Fire & Marine Ins. Co., 971 F.2d 142 (8th Cir. 1992). ***PRACTICE AREAS:*** Products Liability Law; Professional Liability Law; Insurance Coverage Law; Medical Malpractice; Alternative Dispute Resolution. **Email:** Richard@Jeffrieslaw.com

THOMAS R. OLSON, born Spokane, Washington, 1952; admitted to bar, 1981, Minnesota and North Dakota; U.S. District Court, District of Minnesota; U.S. District Court, District of North Dakota; 1986, U.S. Court of Appeals, Eighth Circuit. *Education:* Augsburg College (B.A., 1976); William Mitchell College of Law (J.D., 1981). Author: "Defending the Mild Brain Injury Case," 1996. *Member:* Clay County, Cass County, Seventh District, Minnesota State and American Bar Associations; State Bar Association of North Dakota; Defense Research Institute; Minnesota Defense Lawyers Association; North Dakota Defense Lawyers Association. (Civil Trial Specialist Certified by the Civil Litigation

(This Listing Continued)

JEFFRIES, OLSON & FLOM, P.A., Fargo—Continued

Section, Minnesota State Bar Association). ***PRACTICE AREAS:*** Professional Liability; Automobile Law; Premises Liability Law; Products Liability Law. ***Email:*** Tom@Jeffrieslaw.com

JOEL A. FLOM, born Redwood Falls, Minnesota, 1953; admitted to bar, 1981, Minnesota; 1986, North Dakota; U.S. District Court, District of Minnesota; U.S. District Court, District of North Dakota; U.S. Court of Appeals, Eighth Circuit. *Education:* University of Minnesota (B.A., 1975); William Mitchell College of Law (J.D., 1981). *Member:* Clay County, Cass County, Seventh District and Minnesota State Bar Associations; State Bar Association of North Dakota; Defense Research Institute; Minnesota Defense Lawyers Association; North Dakota Defense Lawyers Association. (Civil Trial Specialist Certified by the Civil Litigation Section, Minnesota State Bar Association). ***REPORTED CASES:*** Horvath v. Liquid Controls Corp., 455 N.W.2d 60 (Minn. App. 1990); Target Stores v. Automated Maintenance Services, Inc., 492 N.W.2d 899 (N.D. 1992); Black v. Abex Corp., 1999 ND 236, 603 N.W.2d 182; Greenwood v. Paracelsus Health Care Corp., 2001 N.D. 28, 622 N.W.2d 195. ***PRACTICE AREAS:*** Products Liability Law; Medical Malpractice; Insurance Defense; Personal Injury. ***Email:*** Joel@Jeffrieslaw.com

---

ERIN M. CONROY, born Grand Forks, North Dakota, July 25, 1974; admitted to bar, 2003, North Dakota; 2004, Minnesota. *Education:* Concordia College (B.A., 1996); University of North Dakota (J.D., 2003). Moot Court. Member, Law Review. ***LANGUAGES:*** American Sign Language. ***PRACTICE AREAS:*** Insurance Defense; Appellate Practice; Asbestos Litigation; Construction Law; Subrogation. ***Email:*** erin@jeffrieslaw.com

INSURANCE CLIENTS: ACUITY; Adjusting Services, Unlimited, Inc.; Adjustment Services, Inc.; Aetna; Aid Association for Lutherans; All Nation Ins. Co.; Allied Mutual Insurance Co.; American Hardware Insurance Co.; American International Adjustment Co.; American Reliable Insurance Company; Atlantic Mutual Insurance Co.; ATT Central National Insurance Co.; Charter Insurance Co.; Citizens Security Insurance Co.; CNA Insurance Co.; Commercial Union Insurance Co.; Continental Insurance Co.; Crawford & Co.; Diamond States Insurance Co.; Essex Insurance Co.; Farmers Home Group; Farmers Insurance Group; Federated Mutual Insurance Co.; GAB Business Services; Gallagher Bassett Services, Inc.; General Casualty Insurance Company; Grinnell Mutual Group; Hartford Insurance Co.; Imperial Casualty & Indemnity Co.; Indiana Lumberman's Mutual Insurance Co.; Insurance Corp. of B.C.; John Deere Insurance Co.; Kemper Insurance Co.; Liberty Mutual Group; Meadowbrook Insurance Group; Media Professional Insurance; Medical Protective Co.; Meridian Ins. Co.; Midwest Medical Insurance Co.; Minnesota Counties Insurance Trust; Minnesota Mining and Manufacturing; Mutual Service Insurance Co.; National Farmers Union Insurance Co.; Nodak Mutual Insurance Co.; North American Specialty Insurance Co.; Northwestern National Insurance Co.; One Beacon Insurance; Phico Insurance Co.; Phoenix Aviation Managers, Inc.; Preferred Risk Group; Principal Casualty Co.; Prudential Insurance Co.; Reliance Insurance Co.; Rockwood Insurance Co.; Safeco Insurance Co.; Scottsdale Insurance Co.; Shand, Morahan & Assoc., Inc.; State Auto Insurance Company; St. Paul Fire & Marine Insurance Co.; Transco Insurance Co.; Travelers Insurance Co.; Tri-State Insurance Company; U.S.F.G United National Insurance Co.; Zurich Insurance Co.
REPRESENTATIVE CLIENTS: AG Capital Co.; Borg-Warner Corporation; First International Bank & Trust; Hydraulic Machines Corporation; Johnson Controls, Inc.; Land O'Lakes, Inc.; Lear Siegler Holdings Corp.; Northern Power Systems, Inc.; R.D. Offutt Co.; Sepco Corporation; Silver Engineering Inc.; Westinghouse Electric Corporation; White Consolidated Industries, Inc.

JOHNSON, RAMSTAD & MOTTINGER

15 9TH STREET
FARGO, NORTH DAKOTA 58103-1830
Telephone: 701-235-7501
Fax: 701-235-8906

General Practice in all Courts. Probate, Real Estate, Corporate, Commercial, Personal Injury and Negligence Law. Products Liability and Criminal Law.

MEMBERS OF FIRM

CRAIG E. JOHNSON, born Fargo, North Dakota, January 8, 1953; admitted to bar, 1980, North Dakota; 1982, Minnesota. *Education:* North Dakota State University (B.S., 1977); University of North Dakota (J.D., 1980). Phi Delta Phi. *Member:* Cass County, Clay County and Minnesota State Bar Associations; State Bar Association of North Dakota. ***PRACTICE AREAS:*** Personal Injury; Probate; Business Law; Civil Litigation. ***Email:*** cjohnson@jrmlawfirm.com

DAYLEN D. RAMSTAD, born Fargo, North Dakota, February 10, 1955; admitted to bar, 1979, North Dakota. *Education:* North Dakota State University (B.S., 1976); University of North Dakota (J.D., 1979). Phi Delta Phi. *Member:* Cass County Bar Association; State Bar Association of North Dakota; North Dakota School Board Attorney Association. ***PRACTICE AREAS:*** Family Law; Divorce; Personal Injury; Business Organization; Probate; Civil Practice. ***Email:*** dramstad@jrmlawfirm.com

STEVEN D. MOTTINGER, born Shelby, Iowa, April 5, 1952; admitted to bar, 1979, North Dakota. *Education:* St. John University (B.A., 1974); William Mitchell College of Law (J.D., 1979). *Member:* American Bar Association. ***PRACTICE AREAS:*** Criminal Law (75%, 200); Felonies; Misdemeanors; DUI/DWI. ***Email:*** smottinger@jrmlawfirm.com

REFERENCE: State Bank of Fargo.

JOHNSON, RODENBURG & LAUINGER

107 ROBERTS STREET
P.O. BOX 2427
FARGO, NORTH DAKOTA 58108
Telephone: 701-235-6411
Fax: 701-235-6678
URL: http://www.jrllawfirm.com

Creditors Rights, Commercial Law, Creditor Bankruptcy, Real Estate, Business Law, Corporate Law, Probate, Wills, Elder Law, Trusts, Estate Planning, Collections.

(This Listing Continued)

MEMBERS OF FIRM

BRUCE D. JOHNSON, born Fargo, North Dakota, October 19, 1945; admitted to bar, 1973, North Dakota. *Education:* Concordia College (B.A., 1967); University of North Dakota (J.D., 1973). Phi Alpha Delta. *Member:* Cass County and American Bar Associations; State Bar Association of North Dakota; National Academy of Elder Law Attorneys. [1st Lt., U.S. Army, Military Intelligence, 1968-1971]. ***LANGUAGES:*** Vietnamese. ***PRACTICE AREAS:*** Real Estate Law; Probate; Estate Planning; Elder Law; Business Law. ***Email:*** johnson@jrllawoffice.com

CLIFTON G. RODENBURG, born Jamestown, North Dakota, April 5, 1949; admitted to bar, 1974, North Dakota; 1980, Minnesota; 1983, South Dakota; 1984, Nebraska; 1985, Wisconsin; 1986, Montana. *Education:* North Dakota State University (B.S., 1971); Michigan State University (M.L.I.R., 1976); University of North Dakota (J.D., 1974). *Member:* Cass County, Nebraska State, Minnesota State and American Bar Associations; State Bar Association of North Dakota; State Bar of South Dakota; State Bar of Wisconsin; State Bar of Montana; Commercial Law League of America. (Certified in Creditors' Rights Law by the American Board of Certification). ***PRACTICE AREAS:*** Creditors Rights; Commercial Law; Collection Law. ***Email:*** rodenburg@jrllawoffice.com

LISA DAWN LAUINGER, born Linton, North Dakota, February 6, 1971; admitted to bar, 1996, North Dakota and Minnesota; 1998, South Dakota and Montana. *Education:* North Dakota State University (B.S., 1993); University of North Dakota (J.D., 1996). *Member:* Big Muddy Bar Association; State Bar Association of North Dakota; State Bar of South Dakota; State Bar of Montana. ***PRACTICE AREAS:*** Commercial Law; Bankruptcy; Collections. ***Email:*** lisa@jrllawoffice.com

CHARLES L. DENDY, born Shreveport, Louisiana, February 27, 1976; admitted to bar, 2002, North Dakota. *Education:* University of North Dakota (J.D., 2002). *Member:* Big Muddy Bar Association; State Bar Association of North Dakota. ***PRACTICE AREAS:*** Commercial Law; Bankruptcy; Collections. ***Email:*** charles@jrllawoffice.com

ASSOCIATE

ERIN P.B. ZASADA, born Winnipeg, Manitoba, June 7, 1977; admitted to bar, 2003, Minnesota; 2005, North Dakota. *Education:* University of Manitoba (B.A., 1999); University of North Dakota School of Law (J.D., with distinction, 2003). Member, University of North Dakota Law Review, 2002-2003. Author: Case Comment, "Civil Rights: Rights Protected Discrimination Prohibited: Living in Sin in North Dakota? Not Under My Lease," 78 N.D. L. Rev. 539 (2002). *Member:* Cass county and American Bar Associations; Minnesota State Bar Association, State Bar Association of North Dakota. ***LANGUAGES:*** French. ***PRACTICE AREAS:*** Commercial Collections; Retail Collections. ***Email:*** erin@jrllawoffice.com

REPRESENTATIVE CLIENTS: West Publishing Corp.; Sears; Horace Mann Cos.; General Motors Acceptance Corp.; Montana State University; United Savings Credit Union; Dakota Clinic, Ltd.

KENNELLY & O'KEEFFE LTD.

ALERUS FINANCIAL BUILDING
15 BROADWAY, SUITE 604
FARGO, NORTH DAKOTA 58102
Telephone: 701-235-8000
Fax: 701-235-8023
URL: http://www.kennellylaw.com

Business Law, Real Estate, Corporate Law, Estate Planning, Probate, Wills, Trusts, Elder Law, Commercial Litigation, Personal Injury, Automobile Accidents, Wrongful Death, Premises Liability, Bankruptcy, Municipal Law, Zoning, Planning, Land Use, Civil Litigation.

CHRISTOPHER M. KENNELLY, born Philadelphia, Pennsylvania, December 1, 1971; admitted to bar, 1997, North Dakota; 1998, U.S. District Court, District of North Dakota. *Education:* University of North Dakota (B. Acc., cum laude, 1994); Gonzaga University (J.D., 1997). *Member:* Cass County and Clay County Bar Associations; State Bar Association of North Dakota; North Dakota Society of Certified Public Accountants; American Association of Attorney-Certified Public Accountants. ***PRACTICE AREAS:*** Business Law; Estate Planning; Probate; Real Estate; Taxation. ***Email:*** cmk@kennellylaw.com

TIMOTHY M. O'KEEFFE, born Breckenridge, Minnesota, July 15, 1973; admitted to bar, 1998, North Dakota and Minnesota; 2000, U.S. District Court, District of North Dakota; 2001, U.S. District Court, District of Minnesota. *Education:* Jamestown College (B.A., cum laude, 1995); Hamline University (J.D., 1998). *Member:* Cass County, Clay County, Minnesota State and American Bar Associations; State Bar Association of North Dakota; North Dakota Trial Lawyers Association; Minnesota Trial Lawyers Association. ***PRACTICE AREAS:*** Personal Injury; Commercial Litigation; Municipal Law. ***Email:*** tmo@kennellylaw.com

OF COUNSEL

MAX D. ROSENBERG, born Grand Forks, North Dakota, October 8, 1930; admitted to bar, 1957, North Dakota, U.S. District Court, District of North Dakota, U.S. Court of Appeals, Eighth Circuit and U.S. Supreme Court. *Education:* University of North Dakota (B.Sc., 1952; J.D., 1957). *Member:* State Bar Association of North Dakota (Member, Special Committee on Local Bankruptcy Rules, 1983-1988). ***PRACTICE AREAS:*** Bankruptcy Law; Debtor and Creditor Rights; General Practice. ***Email:*** mdr@kennellylaw.com

REPRESENTATIVE CLIENTS: Wanzek Construction; Wrigley Mechanical; ND Soybean Council; City of Northwood; All American Title and Escrow; Red River Collections, Inc.; Bledsoe Rail Services, Inc.; Professional Rehabilitation Center, Inc.; CF Financial Management; Pifer Group, LLC; Bremer Bank; Advanced Corporate Services, Inc.; D&M Industries Inc.; Landu & York Inc.; Option One Mortgage; Skin & Laser LLC; Mechtel Farms; City of West Fargo, S.D.; Preservation Insurance Co.; Laughlin Electric; Hubert Oge & Sons Inc.; Howard, Inc.

LETNES, MARSHALL, SWANSON & WARCUP, LTD.

FARGO, NORTH DAKOTA

(See Grand Forks)

Insurance Defense, Municipal Law, Real Estate, Casualty, Fire, Auto, Products Liability, Professional Liability, Negligence, Employment Law, Environmental Law, Dramshop, Subrogation, Estate Planning, Probate, Arbitration, Civil Litigation in all state and federal courts.

MARING WILLIAMS LAW OFFICE, P.C.

1220 MAIN AVENUE, SUITE 105
P.O. BOX 2103
FARGO, NORTH DAKOTA 58107-2103
Telephone: 701-241-4141
Fax: 701-235-2268
Email: mwlo@maringlaw.com
URL: http://www.maringlaw.com

Detroit Lakes, Minnesota Office: 714 Lake Avenue, Suite 101. 56501. Telephone: 218-847-2257.
Bismarck, North Dakota Office: 400 East Broadway, Suite 307. 58501. Telephone: 701-224-0430. Fax: 701-224-0454.

Automobile Accidents, Wrongful Death, Personal Injury, NeuroLaw, Commercial Litigation, Professional Liability, Products Liability, Negligence, Civil Rights and Torts, Family Law, Civil Litigation. Trial Practice in all Courts.

DAVID S. MARING, born Fargo, North Dakota, June 13, 1949; admitted to bar, 1974, North Dakota; 1975, Minnesota. *Education:* North Dakota State University (B.S., 1971); University of North Dakota (J.D., with distinction, 1974). Note Editor, Law Review Board of Editors, 1973-1974. Law Clerk to U.S. District Court Judge, Donald D. Alsop, 1975-1976. *Member:* Association of Trial Lawyers of America. Fellow, American College of Trial Lawyers; Fellow, The International Society of Barristers. (Board Certified Civil Trial Advocacy Specialist by the National Board of Trial Advocacy). ***PRACTICE AREAS:*** Personal Injury; Commercial Litigation; Professional Liability Law. ***Email:*** dmaring@maringlaw.com

MICHAEL J. WILLIAMS, born Breckenridge, Minnesota, July 13, 1954; admitted to bar, 1979, North Dakota; 1985, Minnesota; U.S. District Court, District of Minnesota; U.S. District Court, District of North Dakota. *Education:* North Dakota State School of Science (A.A., 1974); University of North Dakota (B.S., with honors, 1976; J.D., 1979). *Member:* Minnesota State and American Bar Associations; State Bar Association of North Dakota (President-Elect, 2004-2005); North Dakota Trial Lawyers Association (President, 2004); North Dakota Bar Foundation Board; Minnesota Trial Lawyers Association; The Association of Trial Lawyers of America; Ronald A. Davies Inns of Court. ***REPORTED CASES:*** Association for Retarded Citizens of North Dakota v. Olson, 561 F.Supp. 495 (D.N.D. 1982), Affirmed 713 F.2d 1384 (8th Cir. 1983). ***Email:*** mwilliams@maringlaw.com

DANIEL J. DUNN, born Fargo, North Dakota, June 2, 1965; admitted to bar, 1991, North Dakota and Minnesota; 1999, U.S. Supreme Court. *Education:* Moorhead State University; North Dakota State University (B.S., 1988); University of North Dakota (J.D., with distinction, 1991). *Member:* Minnesota State Bar Association; State Bar Association of North Dakota; Minnesota Trial Lawyers Association; North Dakota Trial Lawyers Association. (Board Certified Civil Trial Advocacy Specialist by the National Board of Trial Advocacy) (Civil Trial Specialist Certified by the Civil Litigation Section, Minnesota State Bar Association). ***REPORTED CASES:*** Liliam Gonzalez v. Jessica Tounjian and Dolund Partnership, 2003 ND 121; Liliam Gonzalez v. Jessica Tounjian and Dolund Partnership, 2004 ND 156. ***Email:*** ddunn@maringlaw.com

DeANN M. PLADSON, born Duluth, Minnesota, March 23, 1967; admitted to bar, 1992, North Dakota; 1993, Minnesota. *Education:* Moorhead State University (B.A., 1989); University of North Dakota (J.D., 1992). *Member:* State Bar Association of North Dakota (Member, Family Law Section); Cass County, Clay County and Minnesota State (Member, Family Law Section) Bar Associations; North Dakota Trial Lawyers Association (Board of Governors). ***REPORTED CASES:*** J.W., a minor, by and through his mother D.W. v. C.M., a minor and A.K.M., and infant child of C.M. and Terry Braun, et al, 627 N.W. 2d 687 (Minn. App., 2001). ***Email:*** dpladson@maringlaw.com

---

DUANE A. LILLEHAUG, born Hettinger, North Dakota, July 31, 1950; admitted to bar, 1975, North Dakota; 1976, Minnesota. *Education:* North Dakota State University (B.A., 1971); University of North Dakota (J.D., 1975). Order of the Coif. *Member:* Minnesota State Bar Association (Member, Civil Litigation Section); Minnesota Trial Lawyers Association (President, 2002-2003); The Association of Trial Lawyers of America; Academy of Certified Trial Lawyers of Minnesota. (Certified as a Civil Trial Advocate by the National Board of Trial Advocacy). ***Email:*** dlillehaug@maringlaw.com

ANTHONY J. WEILER, born Bismarck, North Dakota, October 25, 1969; admitted to bar, 1998, North Dakota. *Education:* University of North Dakota (B.A., 1992; J.D., with distinction, 1998). Articles Editor, North Dakota Law Review. Law Clerk, Hon. Dale V. Sandstrom, North Dakota Supreme Court, 1998-1999. *Member:* Association of Trial Lawyers of America; North Dakota Trial Lawyers Association. ***Email:*** tweiler@maringlaw.com

MARSH FISCHMANN & BREYFOGLE LLP

51 BROADWAY, SUITE 502
FARGO, NORTH DAKOTA 58102
Telephone: 701-293-0301
Fax: 701-293-0286
URL: http://www.mfblaw.com

Aurora, Colorado Office: 3151 South Vaughn Way, Suite 411, 80014. Telephone: 303-338-0997. Fax: 303-338-1514.
Boulder, Colorado Office: 507 Canyon Boulevard, Suite 201, 80302. Telephone: 720-406-0506. Fax: 720-406-0520.

Intellectual Property Law, Patent and Trademark Prosecution, Technology Transfer, Licensing and Due Diligence.

JAMES L. JOHNSON, admitted to bar, 1989, Colorado; 1991, Minnesota (inactive); 1998, North Dakota; registered to practice before U.S. Patent and Trademark Office. *Education:* University of North Dakota (B.S.M.E., 1984; J.D., with distinction, 1989). Order of the Coif. Editor-in-Chief, North Dakota Law Review. *Member:* Colorado Bar Association; State Bar Association of North Dakota.

MILLER, NORMAN & ASSOCIATES, LTD.

FARGO, NORTH DAKOTA

(See Moorhead, Minnesota)

Real Estate, Estate Planning, Probate, Wills, Medical Malpractice, Personal Injury, Automobile Accidents, Wrongful Death, Products Liability, Business Law, Commercial Law, Civil Litigation.

MORLEY LAW FIRM, LTD.

FARGO, NORTH DAKOTA

(See Grand Forks)

Insurance Defense, Negligence, Personal Injury, Governmental Defense, Products Liability, Toxic Torts Defense, Insurance Coverage, Legal Malpractice, Dram Shop, Construction Litigation, Communications Law, Medical Malpractice, Complex Business Litigation, Complex Commercial Litigation, Civil Trial Practice in all Courts.

NILLES, ILVEDSON, STROUP, PLAMBECK & SELBO, LTD.

1800 RADISSON TOWER
201 NORTH 5TH STREET
P.O. BOX 2626
FARGO, NORTH DAKOTA 58108
Telephone: 701-237-5544
Facsimile: 701-280-0762
URL: http://www.nilleslaw.com

REVISER OF THE NORTH DAKOTA LAW DIGEST FOR THIS DIRECTORY.

Williston, North Dakota Office: 3-4th Street East, Suite 206, Plainsman Building, P.O. Box 1525. Telephone: 701-572-5544. Fax: 701-572-5561.
Moorhead, Minnesota Office: 1401 South 8th Street. Telephone: 218-233-7407. Fax: 218-233-5133.

Civil Litigation, Commercial Litigation, Insurance Law, Errors and Omissions Litigation, Tort, Product Liability, Personal Injury, Railroad, Construction Litigation, Appeals, Professional Liability, Business Law, Probate, Estate Planning, Real Estate, Commercial Law, Banking, Bankruptcy, Employment Law and Worker's Compensation.

FIRM PROFILE: The firm of Nilles, Ilvedson, Stroup, Plambeck & Selbo, Ltd. dates from the 1920's. When Daniel B. Holt of Holt & Nilles was appointed as a District Court Judge in 1932, the remaining partner, Herbert G. Nilles, together with Lewis H. Oehlert and John J. Nilles, formed the partnership known as Nilles, Oehlert and Nilles. The firm began expanding rapidly in 1949 and was incorporated in 1971 under the name of Nilles, Hansen, Selbo, Magill & Davies, Ltd. The firm now consists of 23 lawyers and over 30 support personnel.

LAW FIRM ALLIANCES/ASSOCIATIONS: ***LEX MUNDI:*** *North Dakota's Lex Mundi Member.*

J. GERALD NILLES (1922-1990)
LYLE W. SELBO (1926-1988)
DONALD R. HANSEN (1922-2001)

RUSSELL F. FREEMAN, admitted to bar, 1964, North Dakota. (Retired 2001, Accepting appointment as U.S. Ambassador to Belize)

DUANE H. ILVEDSON, born Minot, North Dakota, June 17, 1940; admitted to bar, 1966, North Dakota. *Education:* Jamestown College; George Washington University (B.A., 1963); University of Michigan (J.D., 1966). Phi Delta Phi. President, Cass County Bar Association, 1983. President, North Dakota Defense Lawyers Association, 1987. Member, Sections of Tort and Insurance Practice, American Bar Associations; *Member:* International Association of Defense Counsel; Defense Research Institute; American Board of Trial Advocates. ***PRACTICE AREAS:*** Insurance Defense; Insurance Coverage; Civil Litigation. ***Email:*** dilvedson@nilleslaw.com

ROBERT L. STROUP, II, born Hazen, North Dakota, May 30, 1941; admitted to bar, 1967, North Dakota. *Education:* North Dakota State University; University of North Dakota (B.A., 1965; J.D. with distinction, 1967). Phi Alpha Delta. Associate Editor, North Dakota Law Review, 1966-1967. Member, Real Property Section, North Dakota and American Bar Associations. Chairman, Title Standards Committee, Real Property Section,

(This Listing Continued)

NILLES, ILVEDSON, STROUP, PLAMBECK & SELBO, LTD., Fargo—Continued

State Bar Association of North Dakota. *Member:* The American College of Real Estate Lawyers; Lex Mundi College of Mediators. ***PRACTICE AREAS:*** Real Estate; Commercial Law; Bankruptcy. ***Email:*** rstroup@nilleslaw.com

E. THOMAS CONMY, III, born Fargo, North Dakota, September 9, 1937; admitted to bar, 1973, North Dakota. *Education:* North Dakota State University (B.S., 1964; M.S., 1968); University of North Dakota (J.D., 1973). ***PRACTICE AREAS:*** Civil Litigation; Insurance Law; Tort; Products Liability; Errors and Omissions Litigation. ***Email:*** econmy@nilleslaw.com

STEPHEN W. PLAMBECK, born Sioux City, Iowa, January 22, 1950; admitted to bar, 1975, North Dakota. *Education:* George Washington University (B.A., 1972; J.D., with honors, 1975). Member, George Washington University Law Review, 1973-1975. Author: "Class Action Judgements and Mutuality of Estoppel," 43 George Washington Law Review 814. Member: Sections on Public Utility Law and Litigation, American Bar Association; Federal Advisory Committee, Eighth Circuit; North Dakota Commission on Pattern Jury Instructions; North Dakota Joint Procedures Committee. *Member:* National Association of Railroad Trial Counsel; Defense Research Institute; North Dakota Defense Lawyers Association. Fellow: International Society of Barristers; American College of Trial Lawyers. ***PRACTICE AREAS:*** Civil Litigation; Railroad; Product Liability; Professional Liability; Construction; Commercial; Class Actions. ***Email:*** splambeck@nilleslaw.com

GREGORY B. SELBO, born Fargo, North Dakota, September 6, 1950; admitted to bar, 1975, North Dakota and U.S. Court of Military Appeals. *Education:* Southern Methodist University (B.B.A., 1972); University of North Dakota (J.D., 1975). Chairman, Consumer Protection Committee, State Bar Association of North Dakota, 1992—. [Judge Advocate, U.S. Air Force, 1975-1979]. ***PRACTICE AREAS:*** Business Law; Contracts; Real Estate Law; Probate; Estate Planning. ***Email:*** gselbo@nilleslaw.com

LEO F. J. WILKING, born New York, N.Y., January 28, 1953; admitted to bar, 1978, New York; 1979, North Dakota. *Education:* Harvard University (A.B., 1974); Fordham University (J.D., 1978). Assistant Attorney General, North Dakota Tax Department, 1979-1981. Staff Attorney for U.S. Senator Quentin N. Burdick, 1981-1982. Special Assistant Attorney General, North Dakota Workers Compensation, 1995—. ***PRACTICE AREAS:*** Civil Litigation; Personal Injury Law; Workers Compensation. ***Email:*** lwilking@nilleslaw.com

RICHARD HENDERSON, born Waukegan, Illinois, December 13, 1952; admitted to bar, 1983, Minnesota; 1985, North Dakota. *Education:* Moorhead State University (B.A., 1975); University of Chicago (J.D., 1983). Law Clerk To: Lawrence R. Yetka, Minnesota Supreme Court, 1983-1984; Myron H. Bright, U.S. Court of Appeals, Eighth Circuit, 1984-1985. (Resident, Moorhead, Minnesota Office). ***PRACTICE AREAS:*** Construction Law; Employment Law; Commercial Litigation. ***Email:*** rhenderson@nilleslaw.com

DANIEL J. CROTHERS, born Fargo, North Dakota, January 3, 1957; admitted to bar, 1982, New Mexico; 1983, North Dakota; U.S. Court of Appeals, Eighth and Tenth Circuits; U.S. District Court, District of North Dakota; U.S. District Court, District of New Mexico; U.S. District Court, District of Minnesota. *Education:* University of North Dakota (B.A., 1979; J.D., 1982). Member, University of North Dakota Law Review, 1980-1982. Author: "The Constitutional Dimension of Discovery in DWI Cases," 59 North Dakota Law Review 369, 1983. Co-Author, "A Proposal for Presumed Consent Organ Donation Policy in North Dakota," 68 North Dakota Law Review, 637, 1992. Law Clerk, New Mexico Court of Appeals, 1982-1983. Assistant Walsh County States Attorney, 1983. Adjunct Professor, Real Estate Law 1986-1989 and Natural Resources Law, 1988, Moorhead State University. President, State Bar Association of North Dakota, 2001. Immediate Past-President and Member, Board of Governors, State Bar Association of North Dakota. ***PRACTICE AREAS:*** Commercial Litigation; Class Actions; Railroad Law; Appeals. ***Email:*** dcrothers@nilleslaw.com

WILLIAM P. HARRIE, born Grand Forks, North Dakota, April 10, 1960; admitted to bar, 1986, North Dakota and Minnesota. *Education:* University of North Dakota (B.S.B.A., 1982; J.D., with distinction, 1986). Order of the Coif; Order of the Barrister. Articles Editor, North Dakota Law Review, 1985-1986. *Member:* Minnesota State Bar Association. ***PRACTICE AREAS:*** Civil Litigation; Insurance Law; Tort and Personal Injury. ***Email:*** wharrie@nilleslaw.com

MARK R. HANSON, born Valley City, North Dakota, June 12, 1964; admitted to bar, 1989, North Dakota and South Dakota; U.S. Court of Federal Claims; U.S. District Court, District of North Dakota; U.S. Court of Appeals, Eighth Circuit. *Education:* Valley City State University (B.S., cum laude, 1986); University of North Dakota (J.D., with distinction, 1989). Author: Case Comment, "Negligence—The Unit Rule and North Dakota's Comparative Negligence Statute," 64 N.D. L. Rev. 135 (1988). Managing Research Editor, North Dakota Law Review, 1988-1989. *Member:* State Bar of South Dakota. ***PRACTICE AREAS:*** Civil Litigation; Commercial Law; Commercial Litigation; Insurance; Railroad Defense Law. ***Email:*** mhanson@nilleslaw.com

H. MALCOLM PIPPIN, born Williston, North Dakota, April 17, 1963; admitted to bar, 1989, North Dakota; 1990, Minnesota; 1999, Montana. *Education:* University of North Dakota (B.B.A., 1985; J.D., with distinction, 1989). Phi Alpha Delta. Senior Editor, 1988-1989, North Dakota Law Review. Certified Public Accountant, North Dakota, 1987. Law Clerk to the Hon. H.F. Gierke III, Supreme Court of North Dakota, 1989-1990. Special Assistant Attorney General, 1995—. *Member:* Minnesota State Bar Association; State Bar of Montana; American Institute of Certified Public Accountants; North Dakota Society of Certified Public Accountants. (Resident, Williston Office). ***PRACTICE AREAS:*** Civil Litigation; Insurance; Family Law; Estate Planning. ***Email:*** mpippin@nilleslaw.com

DOUGLAS W. GIGLER, born Ada, Minnesota, February 3, 1959; admitted to bar, 1992, Minnesota and North Dakota. *Education:* Mayville State University (B.S., 1988); University of North Dakota (J.D., with distinction, 1992). Member, North Dakota Law Review, 1991-1992. ***Email:*** dgigler@nilleslaw.com

ANDREW L. B. NOAH, born Fargo, North Dakota, August 2, 1967; admitted to bar, 1993, North Dakota. *Education:* University of North Dakota (B.B.A., 1989; J.D., with distinction, 1993). Order of the Coif; Beta Gamma Sigma. Articles Editor, North Dakota Law Review, 1991-1992. Author, "The Family Purpose Doctrine - Just What Is Its Purpose in North Dakota?" 68 N.D.L. Rev. 209, 1992. ***PRACTICE AREAS:*** Business Law; Real Estate. ***Email:*** anoah@nilleslaw.com

(This Listing Continued)

JACQUELINE S. ANDERSON, born Moorhead, Minnesota, August 31, 1962; admitted to bar, 1995, North Dakota and Minnesota; 1996, U.S. District Court, District of North Dakota; 2001, U.S. District Court, District of Minnesota. *Education:* Moorhead State University (B.A., summa cum laude, 1992); University of North Dakota (J.D., with distinction, 1995). Member, Order of the Coif. Research Editor, North Dakota Law Review, 1994-1995. Author: "Changing Venue to Obtain a Fair and Impartial Trial: Trial Court Discretion or Subject of Evaluation? Is This The End of Trials in Rural North Dakota Counties?" 70 NDL Review 675, 1994. *Member:* Minnesota State Bar Association. (Also at Moorhead, Minnesota Office). ***PRACTICE AREAS:*** Civil Litigation; Workers Compensation; Labor and Employment. ***Email:*** janderson@nilleslaw.com

JOEL M. FREMSTAD, born Thief River Falls, Minnesota, April 30, 1973; admitted to bar, 1997, North Dakota and Minnesota. *Education:* Jamestown College (B.A., magna cum laude, 1994); University of North Dakota (J.D., with distinction, 1997). Order of the Coif. Order of the Barristers. Delta Theta Phi. Law Clerk, Justice Dale Sandstrom, North Dakota Supreme Court. Research Editor, North Dakota Law Review, 1996- 1997. Case Comment, North Dakota Rule of Civil Procedure 54 (b): Looking for the Storied "Infrequent Harsh Case," 70 N.D.L. Review 731, 1996. Seminar Presentations on: Employment Law, Legal Technology and Research; Litigation Issues. *Member:* Fargo Inn of Court. ***REPORTED CASES:*** Ziegelmann v. DaimlerChrysler Corp., 2002 ND 134; Rodenburg v. Fargo-Moorhead Y.M.C.A., 2001 ND 139, 632 N.W.2d 407; Praus v. Mack, 2001 ND 80, 626 N.W.2d 239. ***PRACTICE AREAS:*** General Litigation; Commercial Litigation; Debtor and Creditor; Bankruptcy; Employment Law. ***Email:*** jfremstad@nilleslaw.com

KIRSTI BROEDER HOURIGAN, born Breckenridge, Minnesota, September 22, 1972; admitted to bar, 2000, North Dakota. *Education:* Cornell University (B.S., 1995); Wake Forest University School of Law (J.D., 2000). Phi Delta Phi. ***PRACTICE AREAS:*** Civil Litigation. ***Email:*** khourigan@nilleslaw.com

SHANON MARIE GREGOR, born Britton, South Dakota, April 11, 1970; admitted to bar, 1999, Minnesota; 2001, North Dakota. *Education:* North Dakota State University (B.A., with honors, 1992); University of North Dakota (J.D., with distinction, 1998). Phi Kappa Phi. Order of the Coif. Listed, National Dean's List, 1998-1999. Recipient, North Dakota Bar Foundation Award, 1995-1996. Law Clerk, Rodney S. Webb, Chief Judge, United States District Court, District of North Dakota, 1999-2001. Author, Case Comment, "The Virginia Military Institute is Given the Opportunity to Create 'Citizen-Soldiers' Out of Qualified Women," 73 N.D. L. Rev. 323, 1997. *Member:* Minnesota State Bar Association; State Bar Association of North Dakota. (Resident, Moorhead, Minnesota Office). ***PRACTICE AREAS:*** Civil Litigation; Criminal Law.

PATRICIA R. ELLINGSON MONSON, born Jamestown, North Dakota, July 16, 1951; admitted to bar, 1979, North Dakota; 1980, Minnesota. *Education:* University of North Dakota (B.A., 1972; J.D., 1979). Phi Delta Phi. Articles Editor, North Dakota Law Review, 1978-1979. Member, Federal Practice Committee. Member, Litigation, Employment, Labor Law and Construction Law Section, American Bar Association. Past President, Cass County Bar Association. Treasurer, American Inns of Court. *Member:* Minnesota State Bar Association; State Bar Association of North Dakota (Judicial Nominating Committee; Inquiry Committee Southeast); American Health Lawyers Association. ***LANGUAGES:*** German. ***PRACTICE AREAS:*** Civil Trial; Labor and Employment; Construction Law; Wrongful Death; Personal Injury. ***Email:*** pmonson@nilleslaw.com

TELLY J. MEIER, born March 7, 1977; admitted to bar, 2002, North Dakota. *Education:* University of North Dakota (B.A., 1999; J.D., 2002); University of Florida (LL.M., 2003). *Member:* Red River Valley Estate Planners. ***PRACTICE AREAS:*** Estate Planning; Taxation; Employee Benefits. ***Email:*** tmeier@nilleslaw.com

All Attorneys are Members of the Cass County and American Bar Associations and State Bar Association of North Dakota.

STATE COUNSEL: Burlington Northern; Santa Fe Railway.
COUNSEL FOR: Fargo Park District; National Railroad Passenger Corp. (Amtrak); Soo Line Railroad, North Dakota Commissioner for H.U.D. under federal foreclosure act; Banner Health Systems; U.S. Bank National Association; Northern Capital Trust; W.W. Wallwork, Inc.; Valley Imports, Inc.; Western Products, Inc.; Fargo Cass County Economic Development Corp.; Dakota Certified Development Co.; Daktech, Inc.; Bell Genetics, LLC; Immunotherapeutics, Inc.; ND Guarantee Assoc.; Weather Modification, Inc.; Fargo Jet Center, Inc.; Northern Title.
INSURANCE CLIENTS: Travelers-Aetna; Prudential Insurance Company of America; Continental National Insurance Group; Farmers Insurance Group; U.S. Insurance Group; Fireman's Fund Insurance Cos.; Nodak Mutual Insurance Company; CNA Insurance Companies; United Fire and Casualty; Atlantic Companies; USAA Group; Zurich-American Insurance Group; Continental Western Casualty Company; Crum & Foster Group; Blue Cross/Blue Shield of North Dakota; State Farm Insurance Companies; Heritage Ins. Cos.; St. Paul Cos.; Coregis Group; Employer Mutual Cos.; Catholic Mutual Relief Society.

REVISER OF THE NORTH DAKOTA LAW DIGEST FOR THIS DIRECTORY.

PAGE LAW FIRM LLC

118 BROADWAY, SUITE 200
P.O. BOX 2067
FARGO, NORTH DAKOTA 58107-2067
Telephone: 701-237-3423
Fax: 701-237-3426
URL: http://www.pagelf.com

Labor and Employment Law Representing Management.

ADELE PAGE, born 1956; admitted to bar, 1992, Minnesota; 1993, North Dakota. *Education:* Cornell University; State University of New York at Buffalo (B.S., Nursing, cum laude, 1979); Georgetown University Law Center (J.D., magna cum laude, 1992). Order of the Coif. Law Clerk for the Honorable Frank J. Magill, Judge, U.S. Eighth Circuit Court of Appeals, 1993-1994. *Member:* Minnesota, North Dakota (Ethics Committee) and American (Member, Labor and Employment Section) Bar Associations. ***PRACTICE AREAS:*** Labor and Employment.

PEARCE & DURICK

FARGO, NORTH DAKOTA

(See Bismarck)

Products Liability Defense, Oil and Gas, Mining, Insurance Defense, Negligence, Real Estate, Corporate Law, Taxation, Business Law, Commercial Law, Banking, Estate Planning, Probate, Wills, Public Utilities, Education Law, Intellectual Property, Employment Law, Appeals, Civil Litigation before all Courts and Administrative Agencies.

PEARSON CHRISTENSEN CAHILL & CLAPP, PLLP

FARGO, NORTH DAKOTA

(See Grand Forks)

Insurance Defense, Construction Litigation, Products Liability, Tax Litigation, Commercial Litigation, Criminal Defense, Family Law, Appeals.

SERKLAND LAW FIRM

A PROFESSIONAL CORPORATION

Established in 1888

10 ROBERTS STREET

P.O. BOX 6017

FARGO, NORTH DAKOTA 58108-6017

Telephone: 701-232-8957

Fax: 701-237-4049

Email: firm@serklandlaw.com

URL: http://www.serklandlaw.com

Insurance Defense, Banking, Estate Planning and Probate, Real Estate, Personal Injury, Commercial Litigation, Family, Health Care, Taxation, Employment, Transportation, Landlord/ Tenant, Agricultural, Product Liability, General Litigation, Construction, Creditors Rights in Bankruptcy, Secured Transaction, Loan Documentation, Workouts, Collections, Foreclosures, Medical Malpractice (Defense Law), Mediation/Arbitration and Alternative Dispute Resolution, Guardianships and Conservatorships, General Civil Practice in all State and Federal Courts, Trials and Appeals.

FIRM PROFILE: Serkland Law Firm was founded in 1888 by Mr. Edmund Pierce, who was admitted to the Bar of Dakota Territory in 1888. The firm has served North Dakota and Minnesota since that time, offering a full range of civil legal services.

CHESTER J. SERKLAND (1909-1996)

JACK G. MARCIL, born Garrison, North Dakota, February 20, 1941; admitted to bar, 1968, North Dakota; 1983, Minnesota. *Education:* University of North Dakota (B.S.B.A., 1963; J.D., 1968). Special Assistant Attorney General to the Attorney General of North Dakota, 1968-1969. Member, Board of Directors, North Dakota Council of School Attorneys. Arbitrator and Mediator, American Arbitration Association *Member:* Cass County (President, 1983-1984), Minnesota State and American Bar Associations; State Bar Association of North Dakota (President, 1989-1990); North Dakota Bar Foundation (President, 1992-1996); North Dakota Trial Lawyers Association (President, 1981-1982); Minnesota Trial Lawyers Association; The Association of Trial Lawyers of America. Fellow: International Society of Barristers; International Academy of Trial Lawyers; American Board of Trial Advocates. [Capt., U.S. Army, Active Duty, 1963-1965]. (Civil Trial Specialist Certified by the Civil Litigation Section, Minnesota State Bar Association; Certified as a Civil Trial Advocate by the National Board of Trial Advocacy). ***PRACTICE AREAS:*** Personal Injury; Products Liability; General Litigation; Construction Law; Commercial Litigation; Legal Malpractice Defense; Medical Malpractice Defense. ***Email:*** JMarcil@serklandlaw.com

RONALD H. McLEAN, born Fargo, North Dakota, February 8, 1950; admitted to bar, 1975, North Dakota; 1983, Minnesota. *Education:* University of Wisconsin (B.A., with honors, 1972); University of North Dakota (J.D., 1975). Senior Editor, University of North Dakota Law Review, 1974-1975. Author: "Admissibility of Polygraph Evidence," N.D. Law Review, 1975. *Member:* Cass County, Minnesota State and American (Member, Sections on: Litigation; Tort and Insurance Practice Law; Class Actions and Derivative Suits) Bar Associations; State Bar Association of North Dakota (Chairman, North Dakota Supreme Court, Pattern Jury Instruction Commission, 1991 and 1993; North Dakota Supreme Court Joint Procedures Committee, 1985—; Board of Directors, Legal Assistance for North Dakota, 1983-1990; President, 1989-1990); Defense Research Institute (State Chair, Business Litigation Section); Attorneys Liability Protection Society (ALPS) (Chairperson, Board of Directors, 1996—). Consul to Norway. ***PRACTICE AREAS:*** Litigation. ***Email:*** RMcLean@serklandlaw.com

ROGER J. MINCH, born Fargo, North Dakota, June 28, 1952; admitted to bar, 1978, North Dakota and Minnesota. *Education:* North Dakota State University (B.A., 1974); University of North Dakota (J.D., 1978). Adjunct Professor, Bankruptcy, Moorhead State University, 1984 and 1986. Bankruptcy Update, State Bar Association of North Dakota, Fargo, North Dakota, Spring 1988, 1989, 1990, 1991, 1992, 1993, 1994, 1995, 1996, 1997, 1999, 2000, 2001, 2002, 2003, 2004 and 2005. Frequent Lecturer, State Bar Association of North Dakota, Minnesota and Montana, as well as for Banking Associations and private promoters of CLE programs. Secretary and Director, University of North Dakota Legal Aid Association, 1976-1978. Certification, Creditors Rights Specialist, Certified by the American Board of Certification, Sponsored by the American Bankruptcy Institute and the Commercial Law League of America. *Member:* Cass County and Minnesota State (Member, Bankruptcy Section, 1981—) Bar Associations; State Bar Association of North Dakota (Chairman, CLE Committee, 1988-1992; Member: Local Bankruptcy Rules Committee, 1989—; CLE Commission, 2002; Mediation and Arbitration Committee, 1998-2001); American Bankruptcy Institute; Commercial Law League of America. ***PRACTICE AREAS:*** Creditors Rights in Bankruptcy; Agricultural Law; Commercial Litigation; Secured Transactions; Leasing; Loan Documentation; Workouts; Collections and Foreclosures. ***Email:*** RMinch@serklandlaw.com

(This Listing Continued)

STEVEN K. AAKRE, born Fargo, North Dakota, July 31, 1953; admitted to bar, 1981, North Dakota and Minnesota. *Education:* University of North Dakota (B.A., summa cum laude, 1975); University of Minnesota (J.D., cum laude, 1981). *Member:* Cass County, Clay County and Minnesota State (Member, Greater Minnesota Committee of Probate and Trust Section) Bar Associations; State Bar Association of North Dakota. ***PRACTICE AREAS:*** Estate Planning Law; Commercial Law; Corporate and Business Associations; Real Estate; Probate Law. ***Email:*** SAakre@serklandlaw.com

MAUREEN HOLMAN, born Minneapolis, Minnesota, January 30, 1952; admitted to bar, 1983, North Dakota and Minnesota. *Education:* University of Nebraska (B.A., 1973); University of North Dakota (J.D., 1983). Phi Beta Kappa; Phi Delta Phi; Order of the Coif. Articles Editor, University of North Dakota Law Review, 1982-1983. *Member:* Cass County, Minnesota State and American Bar Associations; State Bar Association of North Dakota (Board of Governors, 1995-1997; Member, Joint Task Force on Family Law, 1995-2002; Member, Disciplinary Board, Supreme Court, 1997-2002; President, 2003-2004). ***PRACTICE AREAS:*** Family Law. ***Email:*** MHolman@serklandlaw.com

BRAD A. SINCLAIR, born El Paso, Texas, October 30, 1958; admitted to bar, 1984, North Dakota and Minnesota. *Education:* Moorhead State University (B.S., cum laude, 1981); University of North Dakota (J.D., 1984). Adjunct Professor, Bankruptcy, Moorhead State University, 1987-1990. *Member:* Cass County Bar Association; State Bar Association of North Dakota; North Dakota Society of Certified Public Accountants. ***PRACTICE AREAS:*** Bankruptcy Law; Commercial Litigation; Secured Transactions; Real Estate; Transportation Law; Banking Law. ***Email:*** BSinclair@serklandlaw.com

JANE L. DYNES, born Dickinson, North Dakota, November 12, 1959; admitted to bar, 1987, North Dakota; 1990, Minnesota; U.S. District Court, District of North Dakota and District of Minnesota. *Education:* Concordia College (B.A., summa cum laude, 1982); University of North Dakota (J.D., 1987). Law Clerk to U.S. District Court Judge Rodney S. Webb, 1987-1990. *Member:* Cass County, Minnesota State and American Bar Associations; State Bar Association of North Dakota. ***PRACTICE AREAS:*** Litigation; Family Law; Insurance Defense. ***Email:*** JDynes@serklandlaw.com

---

BEVERLEY L. ADAMS, born Emerson, Manitoba, Canada, December 3, 1969; admitted to bar, 1995, North Dakota and Minnesota. *Education:* University of Manitoba (B.A., cum laude, 1990); University of North Dakota (J.D., with distinction, 1995). Order of the Barristers. Secretary/Vice President, Jan.-May 1994; President, Aug.-Dec. 1994, Moot Court Board. Law Clerk to Honorable Michael L. Kirk, Clay County District Court Judge, Clay County, Minnesota, Aug. 1995-Dec. 1995. Assistant Clay County Attorney, 1996-1998. *Member:* State Bar Association of North Dakota; Minnesota State Bar Association. ***LANGUAGES:*** English and French. ***PRACTICE AREAS:*** Labor and Employment Law; Litigation; Insurance Defense; Guardianship and Conservatorship. ***Email:*** badams@serklandlaw.com

TIMOTHY G. RICHARD, born Fargo, North Dakota, February 3, 1969; admitted to bar, 1997, North Dakota and Minnesota. *Education:* North Dakota State University (B.S., 1992); University of North Dakota (J.D., with distinction, 1997). Order of the Coif. Law Clerk to Honorable Karen K. Klein, U.S. District Court, District of North Dakota, 1997-1999; *Member:* State Bar Association of North Dakota; Minnesota State Bar Association. ***PRACTICE AREAS:*** Corporate Law; Estate Planning; Probate; Real Estate. ***Email:*** trichard@serklandlaw.com

JOSEPH A. WETCH, JR., born Bismarck, North Dakota, November 28, 1966; admitted to bar, 2001, North Dakota; 2002, Minnesota. *Education:* University of North Dakota (B.A., magna cum laude, 1998; J.D., with distinction, 2001). Delta Theta Phi. Author, "Constitutional Law First Amendment Commercial Speech: Broadcasters come up all 7's: Advertising of Casinos and Gambling, Greater New Orleans Broadcasters Association v. United States," North Dakota Law Review Vol. 76, No.1, pg. 161. *Member:* Cass County, Minnesota State and American Bar Associations; State Bar Association of North Dakota; The Association of Trial Lawyers of America; North Dakota Trial Lawyers Association. [Sergeant, U.S. Army, 1987-1995]. ***PRACTICE AREAS:*** Litigation; Medical Malpractice Defense; Insurance Law; Personal Injury; Products Liability. ***Email:*** jwetch@serklandlaw.com

BERLY D. NELSON, born November 2, 1978; admitted to bar, 2004, North Dakota; 2005, U.S. District Court, District of North Dakota. *Education:* University of North Dakota (B.A., 2001); University of North Dakota School of Law (J.D., 2004). Delta Theta Phi. *Member:* State Bar Association of North Dakota. ***LANGUAGES:*** English and Spanish. ***Email:*** bnelson@serklandlaw.com

REPRESENTATIVE CLIENTS: C.I.T. Group/Sales Financing, Inc.; Liberty Mutual Insurance Co.; Prudential Insurance Co. of America; New York Life Insurance Co.; Equitable Life Assurance Society of U.S.; Government Employees Insurance Co.; Fargo Board of Education; Cook Sign Co.; Stop-n-Go Food Stores; American Lutheran Homes, Inc.; Massachusetts Mutual Insurance Co.; Transamerica Insurance Services; Union Carbide; Certain Teed; Danna Corp; Maremont Corp; Quiqley Company; Pfizer Inc.; Ohio Casualty Insurance Co.; Loss Management Services; Harwood State Bank; State Bankshares, Inc.; Firemen's Insurance Co. of Newark, NJ; Healthcare Accessories, Inc.; American International Group; Citizens State Bank of Enderlin; First State Bank of LaMoure; American Federal Bank; State Bank & Trust of Fargo; American Bank & Trust of Williston; Sears, Roebuck and Company; Hartford Insurance Company; Heartland State Bank of Edgeley; Wheels Leasing Corporation; First State Bank of Hope; Security State Bank of Hunter; Lloyds of London; MeritCare Health System; Bankers Life; North Central Life; National AG Underwriters; Industrial Underwriters, Inc.; Presentation Health System; Community Credit Union of New Rockford; United Fidelity Insurance Company; Dalkon Shield Claimant's Trust; Guardian Life Insurance Company; Agri Bank, fsb as successor to Farm Credit Services; Chicago Title Insurance; Domeco Partnership; Island Mortgage; Bethany Homes; First International Bank; Anda Construction Company; CNA Insurance Company; Risk Enterprise Management; Butler Manufacturing Company; Safeco Insurance Company; J.C. Penney; AT&T; Monsanto; BNC Bank; Bergseth Bros. Co., Inc.; Mutual Insurance; Houston General; Union State Bank; Town & Country Credit Union; Bremer Bank; U.S. Bank; Chrysler Insurance; Wausau Insurance; State Bank of Buxton; Johnson & Johnson; Custom Marketing Company; Empire Insurance; Berlin Farmers Elevator; CoBank, ACB; Western State Bank; Citizens State Bank of Finley; Zurich Insurance Company; First National Insurance Company of America; Wyeth; Becton Dickinson; Catholic Health Initiatives; First State Bank Gackle; Farmers State Bank Elgin; State Bank of Moorhead; Associated Bank; Rabo Agrifinance, Inc.; United Valley Bank; United Rentals, Northwest; Alerus Financial; American Federal Bank; Vision Bank; Caterpillar Financial Services; Northland Educators Federal Credit Union; Diversified Financial Resources, Inc.; TransAmerican Financial Corp.; Educational Credit Management Corp.; Farm Pro Services, Inc.; Central Bank; Gobal Electric Motor Cars, Inc.; Central Cass Public

(This Listing Continued)

SERKLAND LAW FIRM, A PROFESSIONAL CORPORATION, Fargo—Continued

Schools; Pembilier Nursing Center; Specialized Contracting; Attorneys Liability Protection Society; Employers Reinsurance Company; Weyth Laboratories.

SMITH BAKKE OPPEGARD PORSBORG & WOLF

ALERUS BANK BUILDING
3137 32ND AVENUE SW, SUITE 212
FARGO, NORTH DAKOTA 58102
Telephone: 877-233-2336
Email: poppegard@sbolaw.com
URL: http://www.sbolaw.com

Moorhead, Minnesota Office: 1800 30th Avenue S., P.O. Box 657, 56561-0657. Telephone: 218-233-8105. Fax: 218-233-8620.
Bismarck, North Dakota Office: 116 N. 2nd Street, P.O. Box 460, 58502-0460. Telephone: 1-877-233-2336.

Products Liability Defense, Civil Litigation, Insurance Defense, Environmental Torts, Toxic Torts, Asbestos Personal Injury and Property Litigation, Medical Malpractice, Professional Liability, Personal Injury, Governmental and Municipal Liability, Fire Losses, Liquor and Dram Shop Liability, Labor and Employment Law, Insurance Coverage, Civil Trial Practice in all State and Federal Courts in Minnesota, North Dakota and South Dakota.

FIRM PROFILE: The firm specializes in defense of civil litigation. We are licensed to practice and defending cases throughout Minnesota, North Dakota and South Dakota. We have offices in Moorhead, Minnesota, Fargo and Bismarck, North Dakota. Our clients include the largest and most sophisticated consumers of legal services.

MEMBERS OF FIRM

PAUL R. OPPEGARD, born Wadena, Minnesota, January 28, 1954; admitted to bar, 1980, Minnesota and North Dakota, U.S. District Court, District of Minnesota, U.S. District Court, District of North Dakota, U.S. Court of Appeals, Eighth Circuit and U.S. Supreme Court. *Education:* Concordia College (B.A., summa cum laude, 1976); William Mitchell College of Law (J.D., 1980). *Member:* Clay County, Cass County, Minnesota State and American Bar Associations; State Bar Association of North Dakota; Minnesota Defense Lawyers Association; North Dakota Defense Lawyers Association Defense Research Institute. (Civil Trial Specialist Certified by the Civil Litigation Section, Minnesota State Bar Association) (Certified as a Civil Trial Advocate by the National Board of Trial Advocacy) (Also at Moorhead, Minnesota Office). ***PRACTICE AREAS:*** Insurance Defense; Products Liability; Asbestos Claims; Environmental. ***Email:*** poppegard@sbolaw.com

SHELDON A. SMITH, born Minot, North Dakota, May 6, 1958; admitted to bar, 1983, North Dakota and U.S. District Court, District of North Dakota; 1985, U.S. Tax Court; 1988, U.S. Court of Appeals, Eighth Circuit. *Education:* University of North Dakota (B.S.B.A., cum laude, 1979; J.D., with distinction, 1983). Order of the Coif. Senior Editor, North Dakota Law Review, 1982-1983. Certified Public Accountant, North Dakota, 1980. (Resident, Bismarck Office). ***PRACTICE AREAS:*** Taxation Law; Business Law.

RANDALL J. BAKKE, born Fargo, North Dakota, March 14, 1957; admitted to bar, 1982, North Dakota and Minnesota. *Education:* Universidad Del Carmen, Campeche, Mexico; University of North Dakota (B.A., summa cum laude, 1979; J.D., 1982). *Member:* Minnesota State Bar Association; State Bar Association of North Dakota; North Dakota Defense Lawyers Association; Defense Research Institute. (Resident, Bismarck Office). ***LANGUAGES:*** Spanish. ***PRACTICE AREAS:*** Personal Injury; Torts; Fire Loss; Property Loss.

SCOTT K. PORSBORG, born Mandan, North Dakota, January 9, 1966; admitted to bar, 1991, North Dakota; 1992, Minnesota, South Dakota and U.S. District Court, District of North Dakota. *Education:* University of North Dakota (B.A., 1988; J.D., with distinction, 1991). *Member:* Minnesota State and American Bar Associations; State Bar Association of North Dakota; State Bar of South Dakota. (Resident, Bismarck Office). ***PRACTICE AREAS:*** Litigation.

TROY A. WOLF, born March 25, 1961; admitted to bar, 1991, Minnesota and North Dakota; U.S. District Court, District of Minnesota; U.S. Court of Appeals, Eighth Circuit. *Education:* University of Iowa; Arizona State University (B.S., magna cum laude, 1983); William Mitchell College of Law (J.D., magna cum laude, 1991). *Member:* Minnesota State and American Bar Associations; State Bar Association of North Dakota. ***PRACTICE AREAS:*** Insurance Coverage; Civil Litigation. ***Email:*** twolf@sbolaw.com

SUZANNE M. SCHWEIGERT, born Watford City, North Dakota, December 12, 1969; admitted to bar, 1996, North Dakota; 1997, U.S. District Court, District of North Dakota; 1998, U.S. Court of Appeals, Eighth Circuit. *Education:* Jamestown College (B.A., 1992); University of North Dakota (J.D., 1995). *Member:* State Bar Association of North Dakota. (Resident, Bismarck Office). ***PRACTICE AREAS:*** Business Law.

COREY J. QUINTON, born Rapid City, South Dakota, September 3, 1969; admitted to bar, 1995, Minnesota and North Dakota. *Education:* Northern State College (B.S., 1992); University of North Dakota (J.D., with distinction, 1995). *Member:* Cass County, Clay County and Minnesota State Bar Associations; State Bar Association of North Dakota. ***PRACTICE AREAS:*** Insurance Defense; Personal Injury. ***Email:*** cquinton@sbolaw.com

BARBARA ANDERSON LEWIS, born Rapid City, South Dakota, April 9, 1956; admitted to bar, 1984, South Dakota; U.S. District Court, District of South Dakota; U.S. Court of Appeals, Eighth Circuit; 1996, North Dakota; 1997, Sisseton-Wahpeton Tribal Court and Standing Rock Sioux Tribal Court; 2001, Minnesota. *Education:* Black Hills State College (B.S., 1978); University of South Dakota (J.D., 1984). *Member:* Minnesota State Bar Association; State Bar Association of North Dakota; State Bar of South Dakota; South Dakota Defense Bar; North Dakota Defense Bar; International Association of Defense Counsel; Defense Research Institute. ***PRACTICE AREAS:*** Trial Practice; Insurance Defense. ***Email:*** blewis@sbolaw.com

SHAWN ARLIN GRINOLDS, born Grand Forks, North Dakota, July 17, 1967; admitted to bar, 1996, Minnesota, North Dakota and U.S. District Court, District of North Dakota. *Education:* University of North Dakota (B.A., 1991; B.B.A., 1992; J.D., 1996). *Member:* State Bar Association of North Dakota; Minnesota State Bar Association. (Resident, Bismarck Office). ***PRACTICE AREAS:*** Civil Litigation.

MITCHELL ARMSTRONG, admitted to bar, 2003, North Dakota. *Education:* University of North Dakota (B.B.A., summa cum laude, 2000; J.D., with distinction, 2003). Order of the Coif. Editor and Chief, North Dakota Law Review, 2002-2003. Law Clerk, Chief Justice Vande Walle, North Dakota Supreme Court, 2003-2004. (Resident, Bismarck Office). ***PRACTICE AREAS:*** Civil Litigation.

REPRESENTATIVE CLIENTS: Deere & Co.; Tyco,Uniroyal Inc., Graybar Electric Co.; Goodrich, Kelsey-Hayes & TRW; Crouse-Hinds Division of Cooper Industries; BOC Group; Hobart Brothers; Lincoln Electric Co.; Illinois Tool Works; Praxair Companies and Praxair Distribution Inc.; Western Steel & Plumbing; National Car Rental; Conoco Inc.; Pennzoil Exploration and Production Co.; and representation of various state agencies as Assistant Attorney General for the State of North Dakota; Starwood Hotels and Resorts Worldwide Inc.; Swift Transportation Companies. *Insurance Defense*: Allied Group; Nationwide Insurance; Austin Mutual Insurance; Dakota Fire; Employers' Mutual; General Casualty Insurance; Great American; Great West Casualty; Hartford; Hawkeye Security Insurance; Milbank Insurance Co.; State Auto; The Mills Mutual; National Farmers Union; North Dakota Insurance Reserve Fund (NDIRF); Ohio Casualty; PHICO; Podiatry Insurance Co.; Royal Sun; St. Paul Travelers; Westfield; Cincinnati Insurance Co.; Commercial Union; Liberty Mutual; Yasuda Fire and Marine; American International Group Inc.; CNA; Acuity; Alpha Property and Casualty; Chubb Group; Harleysville; Old Republic; Meridian Insurance; Metlife Auto and Home; Zurich; Gates McDonald. *Misc. Litigation*: United Agri-Products; Ground Round Restaurants; ANR Freight Systems; ANR Pipeline; the City of Bismarck; Melrose Division of Clark Equipment.

STEFANSON LAW

A Professional Limited Liability Partnership
606 1ST AVENUE NORTH
FARGO, NORTH DAKOTA 58102
Telephone: 701-280-0015
Email: spff@stefansonlaw.com.
URL: http://www.stefansonlaw.com

Moorhead, Minnesota Office: 302 First Bank Building, 403 Center Avenue, PO Box 1287, 56561-1287. Telephone: 218-236-1925. Fax: 218-236-6697.

Real Estate, Family Law, Divorce, Criminal Defense, Estate Planning, Probate, Wills, Business Law, Employment Law, Personal Injury, Automobile Accidents, Wrongful Death, Health and Hospital Law, Mediation, Arbitration, Civil Litigation.

(For complete biographical data on all personnel, see Professional Biographies at Moorhead, Minnesota)

DAVID C. THOMPSON ATTORNEY AT LAW, P.C.

FARGO, NORTH DAKOTA
(See Grand Forks)
Personal Injury.

VOGEL LAW FIRM

218 N.P. AVENUE
FARGO, NORTH DAKOTA 58107
Telephone: 701-237-6983
Facsimile: 701-356-6395
Email: vogellaw@vogellaw.com
URL: http://www.vogellaw.com

Bismarck, North Dakota Office: U.S. Bank Building, 200 N. 3rd Street, Suite 201, PO Box 2097, 58502-2097. Telephone: 701-258-7899.
Moorhead, Minnesota Office: 215 North 30th Street, P.O. Box 1077, 56561-1077. Telephone: 218-236-6462. Fax: 218-236-9873.

Insurance Defense, Personal Injury, Products Liability, Professional Malpractice, Corporate, Labor and Employment, Probate, Tax Law, Health Law, Real Estate, Bankruptcy, Construction Law, Public Utilities, Securities and Antitrust, Arbitration and Mediation. Family Law, Criminal Law, Environmental Law, Intellectual Property, Ecommerce. Trials and Appeals in all Courts.

FIRM PROFILE: Vogel Law Firm, with offices in Fargo and Bismarck, North Dakota, is a general practice firm dating back to 1882, when William Huntley Barnett set up his own office in Fargo, later adding Seth W. Richardson in 1905, to form Barnett & Richardson. The Firm has traditionally been the largest in North Dakota and Western Minnesota, providing a broad spectrum of legal services in North Dakota, Minnesota, South Dakota and Montana. The Firm is a member of the American Law Firm Association (ALFA) which provides Laccess to national and world wide legal services of all types.

CARLTON J. HUNKE, born Richardton, North Dakota, May 26, 1943; admitted to bar, 1967, North Dakota; 1968, Colorado; 1981, Minnesota. *Education:* United States Air Force Academy; University of North Dakota (Ph.B., 1965; J.D., cum laude, 1967). Order of the Coif; Phi Alpha Delta. Editor-in-Chief, North Dakota Law Review, 1966-1967. Law Clerk to Charles J. Vogel, Chief Judge, U.S. Court of Appeals, Eighth Circuit, 1967-1968. *Member:* Cass County and Minnesota State Bar Associations; State Bar Association of North Dakota; Minnesota Association of Insurance Attorneys; Minnesota Defense Lawyers Association; North Dakota Defense Lawyers Association; Association of Insurance Attorneys; Defense Research and Trial Lawyers Association. ***REPORTED CASES:*** National Farmers Union Property & Casualty Co. v. Dairyland Insurance Co., 485 F.Supp. 1009

(This Listing Continued)

(D.N.D. 1980); U.S. v. Dairyland Insurance Co., 674 F.2d 750 (8th Cir. 1982); Steenson v. General Casualty Co., 397 N.W.2d 461 (N.D. 1986); Kohoutek v. Haffner, 383N.W.2d 295 (Minn. 1986); Bennedict v. St. Luke's Hospitals, 365 N.W.2d 499 (N.D. 1985); Marohl v. Osmundson, 462 N.W.2d 145 (N.D. 1990). ***PRACTICE AREAS:*** Insurance Defense; Malpractice; Litigation; Arbitration; Mediation. ***Email:*** chunke@vogellaw.com

C. NICHOLAS VOGEL, born Fargo, North Dakota, March 13, 1943; admitted to bar, 1968, North Dakota; 1969, U.S. District Court, District of North Dakota; 1988, U.S. Court of Appeals, Eighth Circuit. *Education:* Lawrence College (A.B., summa cum laude, 1965); University of Chicago (J.D., with honors, 1968). Order of the Coif. Member, Board of Editors, University of Chicago Law Review, 1967-1968. Instructor, Stanford University Law School, 1968-1969. *Member:* Cass County Bar Association; State Bar Association of North Dakota; American College of Trust and Estate Counsel. ***PRACTICE AREAS:*** Estate Planning; Pension and Profit Sharing; Taxation. ***Email:*** nvogel@vogellaw.com

MAURICE G. McCORMICK, born Fargo, North Dakota, October 23, 1946; admitted to bar, 1971, Wisconsin and North Dakota. *Education:* Marquette University (B.S., 1968; J.D., 1971). Instructor, Construction Law, Minnesota State University Moorhead, 2000—. *Member:* Cass County Bar Association; State Bar Association of North Dakota. ***PRACTICE AREAS:*** Litigation; Construction Law; Corporate Law. ***Email:*** mmccormick@vogellaw.com

MART DANIEL VOGEL, born Fargo, North Dakota, January 25, 1948; admitted to bar, 1974, North Dakota; 1981, Minnesota. *Education:* University of the Americas, Mexico City, Mexico; University of California at Berkeley; Lawrence University (A.B., 1970); University of Wisconsin (J.D., 1974). Recipient, Fred Sievert Award, Defense Research Institute, 1993. *Member:* Cass County and Minnesota State Bar Associations; State Bar Association of North Dakota; American Law Firm Association (Firm Representative, 1981—); North Dakota Defense Lawyers Association (President, 1988-1992); International Association of Defense Counsel; Federation of Insurance and Corporate Counsel; Minnesota Defense Lawyers Association; Defense Research Institute (Former State Representative and Diplomat); American Board of Professional Liability Attorneys; American Arbitration Association. (Certified as a Civil Trial Advocacy Specialist by the National Board of Trial Advocacy)(Civil Trial Specialist Certified by the Civil Litigation Section, Minnesota State Bar Association). ***LANGUAGES:*** Spanish and French. ***PRACTICE AREAS:*** Trial Practice; Products Liability; Insurance Defense; Alternative Dispute Resolution. ***Email:*** dvogel@vogellaw.com

WILLIAM A. SCHLOSSMAN, JR., born Fargo, North Dakota, January 8, 1951; admitted to bar, 1976, Minnesota; 1977, North Dakota. *Education:* Northwestern University (B.A., 1973); University of Minnesota (J.D., cum laude, 1976). *Member:* Cass County Bar Association; State Bar Association of North Dakota. ***PRACTICE AREAS:*** Commercial Law; Corporate Law. ***Email:*** wschlossman@vogellaw.com

JON R. BRAKKE, born Barnesville, Minnesota, June 1, 1954; admitted to bar, 1979, Minnesota, North Dakota and U.S. District Court, District of North Dakota; 1981, U.S. District Court, District of Minnesota and U.S. Court of Appeals, Eighth Circuit; 1990, U.S. Supreme Court. *Education:* Northwestern University (B.A., 1976); University of Minnesota (J.D., cum laude, 1979). *Member:* Cass County, Minnesota State and American Bar Associations; State Bar Association of North Dakota. ***PRACTICE AREAS:*** Bankruptcy; Commercial Law; Business Law. ***Email:*** jbrakke@vogellaw.com

W. TODD HAGGART, born Fargo, North Dakota, July 8, 1950; admitted to bar, 1975, Minnesota; 1976, U.S. District Court, District of Minnesota; 1979, North Dakota and U.S. District Court, District of North Dakota; 1984, U.S. Court of Appeals, Eighth Circuit. *Education:* University of Utah (B.A., 1972; J.D., cum laude, 1975); Northwestern University; University of North Dakota. *Member:* Cass County Bar Association; State Bar Association of North Dakota; Defense Research Institute. (Certified as a Civil Trial Advocate by the National Board of Trial Advocacy). ***PRACTICE AREAS:*** Trial Practice; Insurance Defense; Commercial Litigation. ***Email:*** thaggart@vogellaw.com

FRANK G. GOKEY, born Fargo, North Dakota, July 2, 1957; admitted to bar, 1982, Minnesota; 1983, North Dakota, U.S. District Court, District of North Dakota and U.S. District Court, District of Minnesota. *Education:* University of Michigan (B.B.A., 1979); University of North Dakota (J.D., 1982). Order of the Coif. Member, University of North Dakota Law Review, 1981-1982. Certified Public Accountant, North Dakota, 1983. Trial Attorney, U.S. Department of Justice Tax Division, 1982-1986. *Member:* State Bar Association of North Dakota; North Dakota Society of Certified Public Accountants; American Health Lawyers Association. ***PRACTICE AREAS:*** Commercial Law; Health Law; Contracts; Corporate Law. ***Email:*** sgokey@vogellaw.com

STEVEN A. JOHNSON, born Moorhead, Minnesota, October 11, 1961; admitted to bar, 1988, North Dakota and Minnesota. *Education:* Moorhead State University (B.S., 1985); University of North Dakota (J.D., with distinction, 1988). Order of the Coif; Order of the Barristers. Certified Public Accountant, North Dakota, 1985. *Member:* State Bar Association of North Dakota; North Dakota Society of Certified Public Accountants. ***PRACTICE AREAS:*** Corporate Law; Commercial Litigation. ***Email:*** sjohnson@vogellaw.com

BRUCE D. QUICK, born Devils Lake, North Dakota, July 23, 1952; admitted to bar, 1978, North Dakota; 1985, U.S. District Court, District of North Dakota; 1993, U.S. District Court of Appeals, Eighth Circuit; 1994, Minnesota. *Education:* North Dakota State University (B.A., 1975); University of North Dakota (J.D., with distinction, 1978). Phi Delta Phi. Special Projects Editor, North Dakota Law Review, 1977-1978. Law Clerk to the Hon. Chief Justice Ralph Erickstad, North Dakota Supreme Court, 1978-1979. Author: "If Defendant is Predisposed to Commit the Offense, No Defense of Entrapment Exists, Even if Government Agent Supplies the Contraband," 53 North Dakota Law Review p. 284 (1976); "Reflections on State v. Nagel: The State's Perspective," 50 North Dakota Law Review, p. 745 (1982); "I Only Had 2 Beers! A North Dakota Prosecutor's Manual for DUI Cases" (1989); "The Polygraph in 1995: Progress in Science and the Law," 71 North Dakota Law Review, p. 987 (1995). Instructor: Criminal Justice, North Dakota State University, 1981-1983; Criminal Advocacy, University of North Dakota, School of Law, 1992—. Prosecutor, Cass County, North Dakota, 1979-1985. Executive Director, North Dakota State's Attorney's Association, 1983-1985. First Assistant Attorney General, North Dakota Attorney General's Office, 1985-1989. *Member:* Cass County and Minnesota State Bar Associations; State Bar Association of North Dakota. ***PRACTICE AREAS:*** Criminal Defense; Trial Practice. ***Email:*** bquick@vogellaw.com

(This Listing Continued)

ROBERT J. UDLAND, born Williston, North Dakota, November 18, 1948; admitted to bar, 1976, Minnesota, Montana, North Dakota and U.S. Court of Military Appeals; 1983, U.S. Court of Appeals, Eighth Circuit and U.S. Supreme Court. *Education:* University of North Dakota (B.S., 1970; J.D., 1976). Articles Editor, North Dakota Law Review. Assistant Attorney General, State of North Dakota, 1982-1985. *Member:* State Bar Association of North Dakota (Member, Joint Attorney Standards Committee, 2002); State Bar of Montana; Minnesota State and American (Member: Litigation Section; Labor and Employment Law; Health Care Committee) Bar Associations; American Health Lawyer's Association; Defense Research Institute. [Colonel, JAGC, ND Army National Guard]. ***PRACTICE AREAS:*** Employment Law; Health Care Law; Medical Malpractice Defense; Insurance Defense; General Litigation. ***Email:*** rudland@vogellaw.com

WAYNE W. CARLSON, born Montevideo, Minnesota, November 7, 1965; admitted to bar, 1991, Minnesota and North Dakota; 1992, U.S. District Court, District of Minnesota, U.S. District Court, District of North Dakota, and U.S. Court of Appeals, Eighth Circuit. *Education:* North Dakota State University (B.S., with honors, 1988); University of Minnesota (J.D., cum laude, 1991). *Member:* Cass County and Minnesota State Bar Associations; State Bar Association of North Dakota. ***PRACTICE AREAS:*** Business Litigation; Medical Malpractice Defense; Health Care; Agricultural Litigation. ***Email:*** wcarlson@vogellaw.com

DANIEL A. BUEIDE, born St. Paul, Minnesota, March 18, 1965; admitted to bar, 1990, Wisconsin; 1991, Minnesota; 1993, North Dakota. *Education:* University of North Dakota (B.B.A., summa cum laude, 1987; J.D., with distinction, 1990). Order of the Coif; Phi Alpha Delta. Certified Public Accountant, North Dakota, 1988. ***PRACTICE AREAS:*** Real Estate; Estate Planning; Business Transactions. ***Email:*** dbueide@vogellaw.com

SIDNEY J. SPAETH, born Moorhead, Minnesota, November 4, 1960; admitted to bar, 1991, Minnesota; 1992, North Dakota. *Education:* Stanford University (B.A., 1983); University of California at Berkeley (J.D., 1991). Member, California Law Review, 1990-1991. Law Clerk to Honorable Frank J. Magill, Judge, U.S. Court of Appeals, Eighth Circuit, 1991-1992. ***PRACTICE AREAS:*** Business Litigation; Intellectual Property; Securities Law. ***Email:*** sspaeth@vogellaw.com

JERILYNN BRANTNER ADAMS, born Fargo, North Dakota, March 14, 1968; admitted to bar, 1993, North Dakota. *Education:* Concordia College (B.A., magna cum laude, 1990); University of North Dakota (J.D., with distinction, 1993). Order of Barristers. Vice President, Spring 1992 and President, Fall 1992, Moot Court Board. Law Clerk to Russell A. Anderson, Chief Judge, Ninth Judicial District, Minnesota, 1993-1995. *Member:* State Bar Association of North Dakota. ***PRACTICE AREAS:*** Family Law; Civil Litigation. ***Email:*** jadams@vogellaw.com

LISA KAY EDISON-SMITH, born Lisbon, North Dakota, November 7, 1959; admitted to bar, 1996, Minnesota; 1997, North Dakota. *Education:* North Dakota State University (B.S., 1982); Hamline University (J.D., 1996). Law Clerk to Justice A. M. Keith, Minnesota Supreme Court, 1996-1997. *Member:* Minnesota State (Member, Labor and Employment Section) and American (Member, Labor and Employment Section) Bar Associations; State Bar Association of North Dakota. ***PRACTICE AREAS:*** Employment Law. ***Email:*** ledison-smith@vogellaw.com

ANGELA ELSPERGER LORD, born Grand Forks, North Dakota, July 9, 1970; admitted to bar, 1995, North Dakota; 1997, Minnesota. *Education:* University of North Dakota (B.A., summa cum laude, 1992; J.D., with distinction, 1995). Phi Beta Kappa. Order of the Coif. Order of Barristers. Symposium Editor, North Dakota Law Review, 1994-1995. Law Clerk to: Chief Justice Gerald W. VandeWalle, North Dakota Supreme Court, 1995-1996; Judge David S. Doty, U.S. District Court, District of Minnesota, 1996-1998. Author: Case Comment, "Damages - Intentional Infliction of Emotional Distress in the Workplace: Defining Extreme and Outrageous Conduct in North Dakota's Job Description," 70 N.D.L. Rev. 185 (1994); "Florida's Battle with the Federal Government Over Immigration Policy Holds Children Hostage: They Are Not Our Children!" 13 Law & Ineq. J. 141 (1994). *Member:* State Bar Association of North Dakota; American Bar Association; Association of Defense Trial Lawyers. ***PRACTICE AREAS:*** Civil Litigation; Health Law. ***Email:*** alord@vogellaw.com

TAMI L. NORGARD, born Minot, North Dakota, February 5, 1970; admitted to bar, 1995, Minnesota; 1996, North Dakota and U.S. District Court, District of Minnesota. *Education:* University of North Dakota (B.A., 1992); Vermont Law School (J.D., 1995; M.L.S., Masters of Environmental Law & Policy, 1995). Adjunct Professor: Environmental Moot Court; University of Minnesota Law School, 1998-1999; Civil Rights Moot Court University of Minnesota, 1997-1999; Environmental Law, University of North Dakota Law School, 2003; Environmental Law and Policy, North Dakota State University, 2003. Council Member, Woodbury City Council Environmental Advisory Board, 1999. Judge, Cass County Youth Court. *Member:* Minnesota State Bar Association (Member, Environment and Natural Resource Governing Board, 1997-1999, 2002-2004); American Bar Association; State Bar Association of North Dakota. ***LANGUAGES:*** Spanish. ***REPORTED CASES:*** ABB Idus. Sys. Inc. V. Prime Technology, Inc. 120 F3d 351 (2d Cir 1997); State v. Kalman Abrams Metals, 155 F3d 1019 (8th Cir., 1998); City of West Fargo v. Hawkins, 616 NW2d 856 (ND 2000); Hoffner v. N.D. Workers Compensation Bureau, 612 NW2d 270 (ND 2000); Douville v. Pembina County Water Resource District, 612 NW2d 270 (ND 2000); In re: Disciplinary Action v. Dvorak, 611 NW2d 147 (ND 2000). ***PRACTICE AREAS:*** Environmental Law; Water Law; Litigation; Land Use; Criminal Law. ***Email:*** tnorgard@vogellaw.com

STEVEN E. NOACK, born Carrington, North Dakota, April 10, 1960; admitted to bar, 1985, North Dakota; 1987, Minnesota; 1990, Arizona. *Education:* University of Notre Dame (B.B.A., with honors, 1982); Cornell Law School (J.D., 1985). Certified Public Accountant, North Dakota, 1983. *Member:* Minnesota State Bar Association; State Bar Association of North Dakota; State Bar of Arizona. ***PRACTICE AREAS:*** Business Law; Securities Law; Telecommunications Law; Business Cooperatives. ***Email:*** snoack@vogellaw.com

---

MARK A. FRIESE, born Minot, North Dakota, November 18, 1969; admitted to bar, 2000, North Dakota; 2001, Minnesota. *Education:* University of Mary (B.S., 1995); University of North Dakota (J.D., with distinction, 2000). Order of the Coif. Law Clerk to Jus-

(This Listing Continued)

VOGEL LAW FIRM, Fargo—Continued

tice Dale V. Sandstrom, North Dakota Supreme Court, 2000-2001. Licensed Law Enforcement Officer, 1992-1997. [Capt., Army-National Guard, 1986—.]. ***PRACTICE AREAS:*** Criminal Law; Personal Injury; Litigation. ***Email:*** mfriese@vogellaw.com

LEAH M. WARNER, born Winger, Minnesota, March 24, 1976; admitted to bar, 2001, Minnesota; 2002, North Dakota. *Education:* Concordia College (B.A., cum laude, 1998); William Mitchell College of Law, St. Paul (J.D., cum laude, 2001). Member, Rosalie E. Wahl Moot Court. ***PRACTICE AREAS:*** Civil Litigation. ***Email:*** lwarner@vogellaw.com

MART R. VOGEL (Retired)

JERRY O. BRANTNER (Retired)

DANIEL R. CONRAD, born Fargo, North Dakota, August 11, 1970; admitted to bar, 1996, North Dakota; 1997, Minnesota; 2002, U.S. District Court, District of North Dakota; U.S. Supreme Court. *Education:* Moorhead State University (B.A., 1993); University of North Dakota (J.D., 1996). Member, Editorial Board, North Dakota Law Review. Order of the Coif. Law Clerk to the Honorable Rodney S. Webb, Chief Judge, U.S. District Court, District of North Dakota, 1996-1998. Author: "Intoxicating Liquors-Persons Liable: North Dakota Extends Statutory Dram Shop Liability to Social Hosts", Born v. Mayers, 514 N.W.2d 687 (N.D. 1994), 71 N.D. Law Review 743 (Sept. 1995); Trial Attorney, U.S. Department of Justice, Tax Division, 1998-2002. "Confidentiality Protection in Mediation: Methods and Potential Problems in North Dakota," 74 N.D. Law Review 45 (March 1998). ***PRACTICE AREAS:*** Corporate Law; Commercial Law; Commercial Litigation. ***Email:*** dconrad@vogellaw.com

KARI R. REICHERT, born Bismarck, North Dakota; admitted to bar, 2004, North Dakota. *Education:* University of Minnesota, Minneapolis (B.A., 2001); Yale University Law School (J.D., 2004). ***Email:*** kreichert@vogellaw.com

CAREN L. STANLEY, born Fargo, North Dakota, April 23, 1975; admitted to bar, 2004, Minnesota; 2005, North Dakota. *Education:* Carleton College (B.A., 1997); Hamline University School of Law (J.D., 2004). ***PRACTICE AREAS:*** Business Law; Commercial Litigation; Employment Law; Real Estate. ***Email:*** cstanley@vogellaw.com

ATTORNEYS FOR: *General Clients:* Associated General Contractors of North Dakota; Bobcat Co.; Cable One, Inc.; Case Corporations; Cass County Electric Cooperative, Inc.; Clark Equipment Co.; Forum Communications Company; Harleysville Companies; Merit Care Medical Group; New Holland North America, Inc.; Northern Improvement Co.; Dakota Clinic Ltd.; United Parcel Service; Gateway Chevrolet, Inc.; Fargo Tank Company; Fargo Culvert Company; Meinecke-Johnson Construction Co.; Border States Paving, Inc.; Wanzek Construction, Inc.; Tri State Auction Company, Inc.; West Acres Development; Transystems, Inc.; Matrix Properties Corporation; Fargo Glass & Paint Company; Northern Bottling Company; National Sun Industries. Able, Inc.; Heart-Lung Clinic; North Dakota Healthcare Association; North Dakota Long Term Care Association; Health Insurance of America; Brown & Williamson Tobacco Corp.; Med Center One Health Systems; West River Health Services; Johns Manville Corporation; Archer Daniels S. Midland Co.; S.C. Johnson & Son, Inc.; Werner Co.; Magnum, Ltd.; Waste Management of North Dakota, Inc.
FINANCIAL INSTITUTIONS: Community First National Bank of Fargo; Ramsey National Bank & Trust Co.; Northern Capital Management Co.; Farmers & Merchants Bank of Valley City; First Trust Company of North Dakota; First International Bank & Trust, Fargo; Bremer Financial Corporation; AgriBank, FCB; Ag Services of America, Inc.; St. Alexius Credit Union.
INSURANCE CLIENTS: Acceptance Insurance Company; All Nation Insurance Company; American Family Insurance Group; American Life & Casualty Company; Auto Owners Insurance; Automobile Club Insurance Company; Center Mutual Insurance Co.; Chubb Group of Insurance Companies; CIGNA Companies; CNA Insurance Company; Continental Insurance Companies; Dakota Fire Insurance Company; Employers Mutual Insurance Company; Farmers Alliance Mutual Insurance Company; General Casualty Companies; Great West Casualty Company; Grinnell Mutual Reinsurance Co.; Home Insurance Company; Horace Mann Insurance Company; Kemper Group; Midwest Medical Insurance Company; Milbank Mutual Insurance Company; Minnesota Fire & Casualty; National Farmers Union Insurance Company; North Dakota Insurance Reserve Fund; Northstar Mutual Insurance Company; Northwestern National; Ohio Casualty Group; Old Republic Insurance Company; Orion Auto, Inc.; Preferred Physicians Medical; Nationwide Insurance; Royal Insurance Company; Saskatchewan Government Insurance; Scottsdale Insurance Company; St. Paul Insurance Companies; Travelers Insurance Companies; Unitrin Property & Casualty Insurance Group; One Beacon Insurance Company.

VOGEL, WEIR, HUNKE & McCORMICK, LTD.

FARGO, NORTH DAKOTA

(See Vogel Law Firm)

WOLD JOHNSON, P.C.

400 GATE CITY BUILDING
P.O. BOX 1680
FARGO, NORTH DAKOTA 58107
Telephone: 701-235-5515
Fax: 701-232-2585
Email: office@woldlaw.com
URL: http://www.woldlaw.com

Real Estate, Estate Planning, Wills and Trusts, Probate, Corporations, Limited Liability Companies, Employment Law, Wrongful Termination, Business Law, Commercial Litigation, Personal Injury, Car Accidents, Wrongful Death, Family Law, Divorce, Child Custody, Guardianships, Juvenile Law, Hospital Law, Land Use, Criminal Defense, DWI, Civil Litigation.

THOMAS C. WOLD, born Rugby, North Dakota, June 24, 1937; admitted to bar, 1962, North Dakota. *Education:* University of North Dakota (Ph.B., 1960; LL.B., 1962). *Member:* State Bar Association of North Dakota; American Bar Association. ***PRACTICE AREAS:*** Business; Real Estate; Probate. ***Email:*** twold@woldlaw.com

J. PHILIP JOHNSON, born Minot, North Dakota, March 28, 1938; admitted to bar, 1962, North Dakota. *Education:* Minot State College and University of North Dakota (Ph.B., 1961); University of North Dakota (J.D., 1962); Georgetown University. Justice, North Dakota Supreme Court, 1974-1975, 1992-1993. Member, House of Delegates, American Bar Association, 1983-1991. *Member:* State Bar Association of North Dakota (Secretary-Treasurer, 1968-1969; President, 1980-1981; Chairman, Real Property, Probate and Trust Law Section, 1977-1979). ***PRACTICE AREAS:*** Real Estate; Banking; Probate; Civil Appeals. ***Email:*** pjohnson@woldlaw.com

JOHN V. BOULGER, born Fargo, North Dakota, March 31, 1949; admitted to bar, 1974, North Dakota. *Education:* St. John's University; Moorhead State University (B.A., 1971); University of North Dakota (J.D., 1974). Assistant City Attorney, 1978-1993. *Member:* State Bar Association of North Dakota. ***PRACTICE AREAS:*** Business Law; Real Estate; Probate; Wills; Trust Law; Corporate Law; Limited Liability Company Law. ***Email:*** jboulger@woldlaw.com

JAMES R. BROTHERS, born Fargo, North Dakota, August 15, 1950; admitted to bar, 1975, North Dakota; 1985, Minnesota. *Education:* North Dakota State University (B.A., 1972); University of North Dakota (J.D., 1975). Assistant State's Attorney, Richland County, 1975-1977. Cass County Domestic Relations Referee, 1977-1978. Cass County Small Claims Court Referee, 1979-1982. *Member:* State Bar Association of North Dakota; North Dakota Trial Lawyers Association. ***PRACTICE AREAS:*** Divorce; Child Custody; Family Law; Torts; Trial Practice. ***Email:*** jbrothers@woldlaw.com

MARK A. BEAUCHENE, born Crookston, Minnesota, May 21, 1954; admitted to bar, 1979, North Dakota. *Education:* North Dakota State University (B.S., 1976); University of North Dakota (J.D., 1979). *Member:* State Bar Association of North Dakota; North Dakota Trial Lawyers Association. ***PRACTICE AREAS:*** Criminal Law; Driving While Intoxicated; Personal Injury. ***Email:*** mbeauchene@woldlaw.com

BENJAMIN E. THOMAS, born Minot, North Dakota, February 22, 1964; admitted to bar, 1989, North Dakota and Minnesota. *Education:* University of North Dakota (B.S., 1986; J.D., 1989). Phi Delta Phi. *Member:* State Bar of North Dakota; Minnesota State Bar Association; North Dakota Trial Lawyers Association. ***PRACTICE AREAS:*** Employment; Family Law; Juvenile; Commercial Litigation. ***Email:*** bthomas@woldlaw.com

REPRESENTATIVE CLIENTS: Gate City Bank; Moorhead Public Service; Community First Bank; Union State Bank; U.S. Bank; Lawyers Title Insurance Corporation; Western Surety Company; CUMIS Insurance; North Dakota Insurance Reserve Fund; Fargo-Moorhead Area Association of Realtors; Holiday Inn of Fargo; Red River Commodities, Inc.; Custom Graphics, Inc.; Voyager Aluminum, Inc.; CIGNA Investments, Inc.; IDS Financial Corporation; Teachers Insurance and Annuity Association of America; The Mutual Group (U.S.), Inc.; Van Raden Properties, Inc.; Plaza Development Company; Midwest Community Developers, Inc.; Grants Mechanical, Inc.; Laney's Inc.; Holland Enterprises, Inc.; West River Regional Medical Center; United Clinics, P.C.; Carrington Health Center; Oakes Community Hospital; Presentation Medical Center.

MOOSBRUGGER, CARTER & McDONAGH, P.L.L.P.

GRAFTON, NORTH DAKOTA

(See Grand Forks)

Business Law, Real Estate, Banking, Corporate Law, Commercial Litigation, Personal Injury, Automobile Accidents, Wrongful Death, Medical Malpractice, Family Law, Divorce, Criminal Law, Civil Litigation.

CAMRUD, MADDOCK, OLSON & LARSON, LTD.

Established in 1932
401 DEMERS AVENUE, SUITE 500
P.O. BOX 5849
GRAND FORKS, NORTH DAKOTA 58206-5849
Telephone: 701-775-5595
Fax: 701-772-3743
URL: http://www.camrudlaw.com

Insurance, Insurance Defense, Healthcare, Hospital Law, Probate, Trusts, Estates, Labor, Employment, Taxation, Real Estate, Corporate Law, Mediation. General Civil and Appellate Practice in North Dakota and Minnesota State and Federal Courts.

FIRM PROFILE: Camrud, Maddock, Olson & Larson, Ltd. conducts a diversified general practice with particular emphasis on insurance defense, healthcare and hospital law and corporate and business planning.

PATRICK J. MADDOCK, born Devils Lake, N.D., September 19, 1938; admitted to bar, 1964, North Dakota. *Education:* University of North Dakota (B.S. and B.A., 1962; LL.B., 1964). Member, National Board of Trial Advocacy. *Member:* State Bar Association of North Dakota; American Bar Association; North Dakota Defense Lawyers Association; Association of Defense Trial Lawyers; Defense Research Institute; International Academy of Dispute Resolution. (Certified as a Civil Trial Advocacy Specialist by the National Board of Trial Advocacy). ***PRACTICE AREAS:*** Insurance; Health; Malpractice; Professional Liability; Trials; Mediation; Arbitration. ***Email:*** pmaddock@camrudlaw.com

GORDON W. MYERCHIN, born Crookston, Minn., March 22, 1947; admitted to bar, 1975, Minnesota and North Dakota. *Education:* Minnesota State University-Moorhead (B.A., 1969); University of North Dakota (J.D., 1975). *Member:* Grand Forks County, Minnesota State and American (Member, Construction Law Section) Bar Associations; State Bar Association of North Dakota (Member, Board of Governors, 1991-1995); American Health Lawyers Association (Long-Term Care Practice Group); Minnesota Defense Lawyers Association. ***PRACTICE AREAS:*** Mediation; Insurance; Commercial Litigation; Personal Injury; Construction Law; Health Care Law. ***Email:*** gmyerchin@camrudlaw.com

DARRELL E. LARSON, born Grand Forks, N.D., June 2, 1952; admitted to bar, 1977, Minnesota; 1978, North Dakota. *Education:* Moorhead State University (B.A., 1974); Gonzaga University (J.D., 1977); New York University (LL.M., in Taxation, 1978). *Member:* Grand Forks County, Minnesota State (Member, Taxation Section) and American Bar Associations (Member, Taxation Section); State Bar Association of North Dakota (Member, Taxation Section). ***PRACTICE AREAS:*** Tax; Corporate; Estates; Trusts; Wills. ***Email:*** dlarson@camrudlaw.com

SCOTT D. JENSEN, born Minneapolis, Minn., June 15, 1961; admitted to bar, 1985, North Dakota; 1986, Minnesota. *Education:* University of North Dakota (B.A., 1982; J.D., 1985). *Member:* Grand Forks County Bar Association (Past President); State Bar Associa-

(This Listing Continued)

tion of North Dakota; Minnesota Defense Lawyers Association. ***PRACTICE AREAS:*** Insurance Defense; Personal Injury; Commercial Litigation. ***Email:*** sjensen@camrudlaw.com

TIMOTHY R. DITTUS, born Valley City, N.D., September 12, 1959; admitted to bar, 1986, North Dakota and Minnesota. *Education:* Jamestown College; Arizona State University (B.S., 1981); University of North Dakota (J.D., 1986). *Member:* Grand Forks County, Minnesota State and American Bar Associations; State Bar Association of North Dakota; American Health Lawyers Association. ***PRACTICE AREAS:*** Real Estate; Title Insurance; Mortgages; Debtor and Creditor Law; Health Law; Commercial Law. ***Email:*** tdittus@camrudlaw.com

RANDALL S. HANSON, born McVille, N.D., July 28, 1966; admitted to bar, 1991, North Dakota and Minnesota. *Education:* University of North Dakota (B.S.Ed, magna cum laude, 1988; J.D. with distinction, 1991). Order of the Coif. *Member:* Grand Forks County and Minnesota State Bar Associations; State Bar Association of North Dakota; Defense Research Institute. ***PRACTICE AREAS:*** Hospital Law; Health Care Law; Medical Malpractice; Insurance Defense; Civil Litigation; Appellate Practice. ***Email:*** rhanson@camrudlaw.com

RUSS J. MELLAND, born Jamestown, N.D., January 18, 1957; admitted to bar, 1991, North Dakota and Minnesota. *Education:* Jamestown College (B.Ad & Econ., 1983); University of North Dakota (J.D., with distinction, 1991). *Member:* Grand Forks County and Minnesota State Bar Associations; State Bar Association of North Dakota. ***PRACTICE AREAS:*** Real Property; Commercial; Tax; Trusts and Estates; Wills; Probate; Commercial Transactions. ***Email:*** rmelland@camrudlaw.com

GERAD C. PAUL, born Devils Lake, N.D., March 11, 1970; admitted to bar, 1995, North Dakota and Minnesota. *Education:* Concordia College (B.A., magna cum laude, 1992); University of North Dakota (J.D., with distinction, 1995). *Member:* Grand Forks County and Minnesota State Bar Associations; State Bar Association of North Dakota. ***PRACTICE AREAS:*** Commercial Transactions; Commercial Litigation; Civil Motion Practice; Credit Law; Collections; Business Entity Formation. ***Email:*** gpaul@camrudlaw.com

JANEL C. FRANK, born Dickinson, N.D., April 20, 1960; admitted to bar, 2003, North Dakota; 2004, Minnesota. *Education:* Dickinson State University (B.S., summa cum laude, Accounting, 2000); University of North Dakota (J.D., with distinction, 2003). Certified Public Accountant. *Member:* Grand Forks County and Minnesota State Bar Associations; State Bar Association of North Dakota. ***PRACTICE AREAS:*** Tax Law; Elder Law; Estate Planning; Probate; Commercial Law. ***Email:*** jfrank@camrudlaw.com

---

JODI NELSON MEYER, born Minot, N.D., July 11, 1974; admitted to bar, 2000, North Dakota; 2002, Minnesota. *Education:* University of North Dakota; University of North Dakota School of Law (J.D., with distinction, 2000). Law Clerk, U.S. District Court, District of North Dakota, 2000-2002. *Member:* Grand Forks County Bar Association; State Bar Association of North Dakota; Minnesota State Bar Association. ***PRACTICE AREAS:*** Insurance Defense; Labor and Employment; Litigation; Commercial Litigation; Personal Injury. ***Email:*** jmeyer@camrudlaw.com

JANEL C. FRANK, born Dickinson, N.D., April 20, 1960; admitted to bar, 2003, North Dakota; 2004, Minnesota. *Education:* Dickinson State University (B.S., summa cum laude, Accounting, 2000); University of North Dakota (J.D., with distinction, 2003). Certified Public Accountant. *Member:* Grand Forks County and Minnesota State Bar Associations; State Bar Association of North Dakota. ***PRACTICE AREAS:*** Tax Law; Elder Law; Estate Planning; Probate; Commercial Law. ***Email:*** jfrank@camrudlaw.com

TARA L. TROGE, born St. Paul, Minnesota, October 8, 1974; admitted to bar, 2005, North Dakota. *Education:* Minnesota State University (B.S., 2002); University of North Dakota School of Law (J.D., with distinction, 2005). *Member:* State Bar Association of North Dakota. ***PRACTICE AREAS:*** Family Law. ***Email:*** ttroge@camrudlaw.com

REPRESENTATIVE CLIENTS: Advanced Engineering and Environmental Services, Inc.; Alerus Financial; Community Bank of the Red River Valley; City of Michigan; Altru Hospital; Altru Clinic; Union Hospital, Mayville, ND; Valley Memorial Homes; Peterson Construction, Co.; Concrete, Inc.; Pro-Ag, Inc.; Brady, Martz & Assoc., P.C.; U.S. Bank of North Dakota, N.A.; U.S. Bank National Association; Farm Credit Services of Grand Forks; Grand Forks Regional Airport Authority; Grand Forks Housing Authority; Grand Forks Homes, Inc.; Grand Forks Regional Economic Development Corporation; Associated Potato Growers; Altru Health Plan; Tel Pro, Inc.; Webster, Foster & Weston; Valley Growers Grain Company, LLC.
INSURANCE CLIENTS: Aetna Insurance Cos.; The Hartford; St. Paul Cos.; Liberty Mutual; Kemper Insurance; Great American Cos.; Balboa Insurance Cos.; Ohio Casualty; GE-Medical Protective Insurance Company; Argonaut Insurance Co.; Minnesota Lawyers Mutual Insurance Co; The Doctor's Company, Midwest Medical Ins., Co.; Banc Insure; United Fire and Casualty; American Family Insurance Co.; DPIC Companies.
REFERENCE: Alerus Financial.

FISHER, OLSON & JUNTUNEN, LTD.

Established in 1898

315 FIRST AVENUE NORTH
P.O. BOX 5788
GRAND FORKS, NORTH DAKOTA 58206-5788
Telephone: 701-775-4688
Fax: 701-775-2440
Email: pfisher@rrv.net
URL: http://www.lawyers.com/f&olaw

Insurance Defense, Property Damage, Personal Injury, Products Liability, Wrongful Death, Agricultural, Banking, Corporate, Estate Planning, and Probate, Taxation, Collections, Education and School Law, Negligence, Tort and Commercial Litigation, Real Estate, Wills and Trusts, Elder Law, General Civil, Trial and Appellate Practice in North Dakota and Minnesota State and Federal Courts.

FIRM PROFILE: Fisher, Olson & Juntunen, LTD. was founded in 1898 and is dedicated to serving clients throughout North Dakota and western Minnesota. The firm engages in a General Practice with each lawyer focusing in specific areas of the law.

(This Listing Continued)

PATRICK W. FISHER, born Grafton, North Dakota, January 29, 1935; admitted to bar, 1968, North Dakota. *Education:* University of North Dakota (B.S., 1956; J.D., 1968). Order of the Coif; Phi Alpha Delta. Member, Board of Editors, North Dakota Law Review, 1967-1968. Special Assistant Attorney General. *Member:* State Bar Association of North Dakota; American Bar Association; Defense Research Institute. ***PRACTICE AREAS:*** Personal Injury Law; Insurance Defense; Products Liability Law; Malpractice Law; Agricultural Law; Litigation; Probate; School Law. ***Email:*** pfisher@rrv.net

RICHARD W. OLSON, born Northwood, North Dakota, July 25, 1944; admitted to bar, 1974, North Dakota; 1976, Minnesota. *Education:* North Dakota State University (B.S., 1966); Montana State University (M.Ed., 1971); University of North Dakota (J.D., 1974). Phi Alpha Delta (Marshall, 1972-1974). Member, Editorial Staff, North Dakota Law Review, 1973-1974. Clinical Instructor, Legal Aid Clinic, University of North Dakota Law School, 1974-1975. Assistant City Attorney, City of Grand Forks, 1975-1976. City Attorney, Cities of Thompson and Park, District of City of Grand Forks, North Dakota, 1984—. Special Assistant Attorney General. *Member:* Grand Forks County, Minnesota State and American Bar Associations; State Bar Association of North Dakota. [Capt., U.S. Air Force, 1967-1971]. ***PRACTICE AREAS:*** Personal Injury Law; Agricultural Law; Family Law; Estate Planning Law; Probate Law; Municipal Law; Real Estate. ***Email:*** rwolson@rrv.net

MICHAEL E. JUNTUNEN, born Grand Forks, North Dakota, October 29, 1951; admitted to bar, 1983, North Dakota. *Education:* North Dakota State School of Science (A.A., 1972); University of North Dakota (B.S.B.A., 1975; J.D., 1983). Member, Moot Court Association. Member, 1982-1983 and Business Manager, 1983, North Dakota Law Review. Certified Public Accountant, North Dakota, 1977. Special Assistant Attorney General, Real Estate Transactions, State of North Dakota. Author: "Secured Transactions - Notice, Deficiency and Personal Liability - Creditor Required to Furnish Debtor Notice of Repossession Sale," 58 North Dakota Law Review 313, 1982. *Member:* State Bar Association of North Dakota; Grand Forks County and American Bar Associations; North Dakota Society of Certified Public Accountants; American Institute of Certified Public Accountants. ***PRACTICE AREAS:*** Real Estate; Estate Planning; Probate; Trust Law; Guardian Ad Litem; Conservation Law; Income Tax; Bankruptcy.

REPRESENTATIVE CLIENTS: Alerus Financial; Gate City Federal Savings Bank; Grand Forks School District; UND Aerospace Foundation; Grand Forks Park District; City of Thompson, North Dakota; Grand Forks Herald; Knight-Ridder, Inc.; Morrison-Knudsen Co.; Gowan Construction Co.; Alvarado Bean Co.; Northern Valley Fertilizer Co.; CENEX-Harvest States; Frito-Lay, Inc.; Good Samaritan Homes; U.S. Wheat Assoc., Inc.
INSURANCE CLIENTS: CNA Insurance Cos.; Manitoba Public Insurance Co.; CHUBB Insurance; Kemper; The Prudential Insurance Company of America; Utica Mutual Insurance Co.; Minnesota Insurance Guaranty Assn.; United Fire & Casualty Co.; Midwest Family Mutual Insurance Co.; Mutual Service Corp.; Catholic Mutual Relief Society of America; Empire Fire and Marine Ins.; USAble Life; STAR Insurance Co.; Liberty International Underwriters.

HAMMARBACK DUSEK & ASSOCIATES, PLC

GRAND FORKS, NORTH DAKOTA

(See East Grand Forks, Minnesota)

Civil Practice, Criminal Defense, Personal Injury, Bankruptcy, Wills, Trusts and Estates, DUI.

JEFFRIES, OLSON & FLOM, P.A.

GRAND FORKS, NORTH DAKOTA

(See Fargo)

General Insurance Defense, Trial and Appellate Practice in Minnesota and North Dakota State and Federal Courts. Medical and other Professional Malpractice, Civil Rights, Construction, Products Liability, Fire, Government and Municipalities, Errors & Omissions, Environmental Law, Health Law, Casualty, Negligence, Asbestos Litigation, Hazardous Waste, Toxic Substances, Pollution, No-Fault, Insurance Coverages, Employment, Liquor Liability, Automobile, Premises Liability, Commercial Litigation, Subrogation.

LABINE LAW FIRM

Established in 1982

US BANK BUILDING, SUITE 202
600 DEMERS AVENUE
P.O. BOX 5010
GRAND FORKS, NORTH DAKOTA 58206-5010
Telephone: 701-746-7338
Toll Free: 800-762-4284
Fax: 701-746-8692
Email: rjlabine@rrv.net
URL: http://www.labinelaw.com

Personal Injury, Automobile Accidents, Premises Liability, Wrongful Death, Medical Malpractice and Criminal Defense, Civil Litigation.

ROBERT J. LABINE, born Warren, Minnesota, January 4, 1947; admitted to bar, 1974, Mississippi; 1980, New York; 1982, Minnesota and North Dakota. *Education:* University of Minnesota (B.A., 1968); Chapman College; University of Mississippi (J.D., 1974). *Member:* Grand Forks County, Minnesota State and New York State Bar Associations; State Bar Association of North Dakota; The Association of Trial Lawyers of America; North Dakota Trial Lawyers Association; American Judicature Society; International Bar Association; National Association of Criminal Defense Lawyers. ***PRACTICE AREAS:*** Personal Injury; Wrongful Death; Medical Malpractice; Criminal Defense; Civil Litigation.

LEGAL SUPPORT PERSONNEL

ANN M. STEPHENS
KELSEY MACINTOSH

(This Listing Continued)

LABINE LAW FIRM, Grand Forks—Continued

TYLER HART

JUSTIN BREITWIESER

LETNES, MARSHALL, SWANSON & WARCUP, LTD.

1397 LIBRARY CIRCLE, SUITE 202
P.O. BOX 12909
GRAND FORKS, NORTH DAKOTA 58208-2909
Telephone: 701-772-3407; 800-342-0139
Fax: 701-772-3833
Email: hswanson@letneslaw.com
URL: http://www.lawyers.com/letneslaw

Insurance Defense, Municipal Law, Real Estate, Casualty, Fire, Auto, Products Liability, Professional Liability, Negligence, Employment Law, Environmental Law, Dramshop, Subrogation, Estate Planning, Probate, Arbitration, Civil Litigation in all state and federal courts.

FIRM PROFILE: Letnes, Marshall, Swanson & Warcup, Ltd. dates back to the original firm founded in 1937 by Daniel S. Letnes. The firm has had a distinguished record in providing quality and professional legal services. The firm has built a highly successful practice in all areas of law, with an emphasis in civil litigation, insurance defense, and state and local government law. The entire resources of the firm are available to meet the needs of the firm's clients. The individual attorneys concentrate their practices in areas of specialty and collaborate on major cases and transactions. Legal services are provided in all State and Federal Courts throughout North Dakota and northern Minnesota.

The members of the firm are encouraged to pursue and have assumed leadership roles in numerous professional, community and civic affairs. The firm stresses consistent, professional representation of its clients with quality and efficiency. Letnes, Marshall, Swanson & Warcup, Ltd. has an experienced support staff which enables it to be responsive to the needs of its clients.

DANIEL S. LETNES, born Crookston, Minnesota, 1911; admitted to bar, 1937, North Dakota. *Education:* University of North Dakota (J.D., 1936). (Retired)

F. JOHN MARSHALL, born Oskaloosa, Iowa, April 13, 1937; admitted to bar, 1962, North Dakota. *Education:* University of North Dakota (Ph.B., 1959; J.D., 1962). Phi Delta Phi; Blue Key. First Assistant States Attorney, Grand Forks County, 1963-1966. City Attorney, 1976-1981. *Member:* Grand Forks County and American Bar Associations; Minnesota Defense Lawyers Association; North Dakota Defense Lawyers Association; American Board of Trial Advocates. ***PRACTICE AREAS:*** Civil Litigation; Products Liability Law; Insurance Defense Law.

HOWARD D. SWANSON, born Grand Forks, North Dakota, June 25, 1958; admitted to bar, 1983, North Dakota; 1984, Minnesota, U.S. Court of Appeals, Eighth Circuit and U.S. Supreme Court. *Education:* University of North Dakota (B.S./B.A., 1980); Hamline University School of Law (J.D., cum laude, 1983). Editor, "City Briefs." City Attorney, 1987—. Assistant City Attorney, 1984-1987. IMLA Municipal Law Fellow, 1999—. *Member:* State Bar Association of North Dakota (Member, Board of Governors, 1987-1991; President, 1994-1995); Grand Forks County, Hennepin County (Member, Sections on: Local Government Law; Litigation) and Minnesota State Bar Associations; North Dakota Municipal Attorneys Association (Secretary/Treasurer, 1989-1992; President Elect, 1992-1993; President, 1994-1995); National Institute of Municipal Law Officers (North Dakota State Chair, 1989-1995; Regional Vice President, 1995—); North Dakota Bar Foundation (Member, Board of Directors, 1991-1995). ***REPORTED CASES:*** Smith v. City of Grand Forks, 525 N.W.2d 251 (N.D. 1994); Rott v. Jaeger, et al., 510 N.W.2d 651 (N.D. 1994); Dale v. Cronquist, 493 N.W.2d 667 (N.D. 1992); Farmers Union Central Exchange, Inc. v. Grand Forks County, 443 N.W.2d 907 (N.D. 1989); Ulvedal v. Board of County Commissioners of Grand Forks County, 434 N.W.2d 707 (N.D. 1989); City of Grand Forks v. Mik-Lan Recreation Association, Inc., 421 N.W.2d 806 (N.D. 1988); Sunderland v. North Dakota Workmen's Compensation Bureau, 370 N.W.2d 549 (N.D. 1985); Heartview Foundation v. Glaser, 361 N.W.2d 232 (N.D. 1985). ***PRACTICE AREAS:*** Municipal Law; Commercial Law; Civil Litigation; Administrative Law; Appellate Law; Insurance Defense Law. ***Email:*** hswanson@letneslaw.com

JOHN ALAN WARCUP, born Grand Forks, North Dakota, September 11, 1967; admitted to bar, 1993, North Dakota and U.S. District Court, District of North Dakota. *Education:* University of North Dakota (B.B.A., 1990); University of North Dakota School of Law (J.D., with distinction, 1993). Assistant City Attorney, Grand Forks, 1997—. City Attorney, Emerado, 1997—. *Member:* Grand Forks County Bar Association; State Bar Association of North Dakota. ***PRACTICE AREAS:*** Estate and Probate Law; Tax Law; Litigation; Real Estate Law; Title Insurance Law; Municipal Law. ***Email:*** jwarcup@letneslaw.com

REPRESENTATIVE CLIENTS: American Family Insurance Group; AUSCO; Austin Mutual Insurance Co.; Certified Claims Corp.; City of Emerado, North Dakota; City of Grand Forks, North Dakota; Connecticut General Life Ins. Co.; Crum & Forster Insurance Cos.; Farmers Alliance Mutual Insurance Co.; Fireman's Fund Insurance Co.; Government Employees Insurance Co.; Great Central Insurance Co.; Great West Casualty Co.; The Hartford; Holmes & Narver; Iowa Mutual Insurance Co.; Mill Mutuals; Mutual Service Insurance Co.; Nodak Mutual Insurance Co.; North Dakota Insurance Reserve Fund; Prudential Property & Casualty Insurance Co.; Transamerica Insurance Services; U.S. Insurance Group; United Fire & Casualty Co.; United Services Automobile Assn.; United States Fidelity & Guaranty Co.

MOOSBRUGGER, CARTER & McDONAGH, P.L.L.P.

311 S. 4TH STREET, SUITE 101
GRAND FORKS, NORTH DAKOTA 58201-4782
Telephone: 701-775-8146
Fax: 701-780-9081
URL: http://www.gflawfirm.net

Business Law, Real Estate, Banking, Corporate Law, Commercial Litigation, Personal Injury, Automobile Accidents, Wrongful Death, Medical Malpractice, Family Law, Divorce, Criminal Law, Civil Litigation.

RALPH F. CARTER, born New Bedford, Massachusetts, September 12, 1946; admitted to bar, 1976, Arkansas; 1980, North Dakota; 1981, Minnesota. *Education:* University of Arkansas (B.A., 1968; J.D., 1976). *Member:* Arkansas and American Bar Associations; State Bar Association of North Dakota; The Association of Trial Lawyers of America; North Dakota Trial Lawyers Association. [Capt., JAG, USAF, 1976-1980]. ***PRACTICE AREAS:*** Personal Injury; Civil Litigation. ***Email:*** rfcarter@gflaw.com

ALAN M. McDONAGH, born Moorhead, Minnesota, May 7, 1972; admitted to bar, 1997, North Dakota and Minnesota. *Education:* University of North Dakota (B.A., 1994; J.D., 1997). *Member:* State Bar Association of North Dakota. ***PRACTICE AREAS:*** Family Law; Corporate Law. ***Email:*** amcdonagh@gflaw.com

OF COUNSEL

JOHN H. MOOSBRUGGER, born St. Paul, Minnesota, March 29, 1934; admitted to bar, 1965, North Dakota, U.S. Court of Appeals, Eighth Circuit and U.S. District Court, Northeast Central District of North Dakota. *Education:* St. John's University (B.A., 1962); University of North Dakota (LL.B., 1965). *Member:* Grand Forks County and American Bar Associations; State Bar Association of North Dakota; The Association of Trial Lawyers of America. ***PRACTICE AREAS:*** Corporate Law; Asbestos Defense; Litigation.

MORLEY LAW FIRM, LTD.

1697 SOUTH 42ND STREET, SUITE 200
P.O. BOX 14519
GRAND FORKS, NORTH DAKOTA 58208-4519
Telephone: 701-772-7266
Toll Free: 800-450-7266
Fax: 701-772-7269
Email: morley@morleylawfirm.com
URL: http://www.morleylawfirm.com

Insurance Defense, Negligence, Personal Injury, Governmental Defense, Products Liability, Toxic Torts Defense, Insurance Coverage, Legal Malpractice, Dram Shop, Construction Litigation, Communications Law, Medical Malpractice, Complex Business Litigation, Complex Commercial Litigation, Civil Trial Practice in all Courts.

PATRICK R. MORLEY, born Wausau, Wisconsin, December 28, 1950; admitted to bar, 1976, North Dakota and U.S. District Court, District of North Dakota; 1977, Minnesota. *Education:* University of North Dakota (B.S.B.A., 1972; J.D., with distinction, 1976). Phi Delta Phi. Senior Editor, University of North Dakota Law Review, 1975-1976. Recipient, American Jurisprudence Award for Evidence. Former Member, Federal Practice Committee, State of North Dakota. Former Member, North Dakota Pattern Jury Instruction Commission. *Member:* Greater Grand Forks County Bar Association (Former President); State Bar Association of North Dakota; American Arbitration Association. ***LANGUAGES:*** Sign Language. ***REPORTED CASES:*** Follman v. Upper Valley Special Education Unit, 609 NW 2d 90, 143 Ed. Law Rep. 623, 2000 ND 72 (N.D. 2000); Estate of Pascal v. Benson County, 1995 WL 394 3 72, 2 Wage & Hour Cas. 2d (BNA) 1117 (D.N.B. 1995); North Dakota Ins. Guar. Ass'n v. Agway, Inc., 462 NW 2d 142 (N.D. 1990); Butz v. Werner, 438 NW 2d 509, 77 A.L.P. 4th 1093, Prod. Lib. Rep. (CCH) p12, 083 (N.D. 1989); Morris v. Grand Forks Housing Authority, 436 NW 2d 221, Prod. Lib. Rep. (CCH) p12, 051 (N.D. 1989); Grand Forks Herald v. District Court in and for Grand Forks County, 322 NW 2d 850, 8 Media L. Rep. 2269 (N.D.1982). ***PRACTICE AREAS:*** Litigation; Governmental Defense; Insurance; Communications Law; Toxic Tort Defense; Commercial Litigation; Construction Litigation; Business Torts; Dram Shop Liability; Legal Malpractice; Medical Malpractice. ***Email:*** pmorley@morleylawfirm.com

MICHAEL J. MORLEY, born Grand Forks, North Dakota, October 13, 1953; admitted to bar, 1979, North Dakota and U.S. District Court, District of North Dakota; 1981, Minnesota, U.S. District Court, District of Minnesota and U.S. Court of Appeals, Eighth Circuit. *Education:* University of North Dakota (B.S.B.A., 1975; J.D., with distinction, 1979). Order of the Coif. Recipient, American Jurisprudence Award for Civil Procedure and Corporation Law. Certified Minnesota No-Fault Insurance Arbitrator. *Member:* State Bar Association of North Dakota; Minnesota State Bar Association. ***REPORTED CASES:*** Lemer v. Campbell, 602 NW 2d 686, 1999 ND 223; Ziegler v. Stalberger, 1996 WL 39113 (Minn. Ct. App. 1996); Stewart v. Ryan, 520 NW 2d 39 (ND 1994); Omlid v. Sweeney, 484 NW 2d 486 (ND 1992); Universal Underwriters Ins. Co. v. McMahon Chevrolet-Oldsmobile, Inc., 966 F2d 1060 (8th Cir. 1989); DeCoteau v. Sentry Ins. Co., 915 F.Supp. 155 (D.N.D. 1996); Glyten v. Swalboski, 246 F. 3d 1139 (8th Cir. 2001). ***PRACTICE AREAS:*** Insurance Defense; Insurance; Negligence; Litigation; Personal Injury; Real Estate; Torts; Premises Liability Defense; Civil Practice; Appellate Practice. ***Email:*** mmorley@morleylawfirm.com

BRADLEY J. BEEHLER, born Bismarck, North Dakota, December 31, 1962; admitted to bar, 1995, North Dakota, South Dakota, U.S. District Court, District of North Dakota and U.S. Court of Appeals, Eighth Circuit; 1997, Minnesota; 1999, U.S. District Court, District of Minnesota and U.S. Supreme Court. *Education:* University of North Dakota (B.B.A., 1985; J.D., with distinction, 1995). Order of Barristers. *Member:* Greater Grand Forks County and Minnesota State Bar Associations; State Bar Association of North Dakota (Member: Pattern Jury Instruction Commission; SBAND/ND Medical Association Committee; Continuing Legal Education Committee, 1997-2001; Past President, Young Lawyers Section, 1995-1997); State Bar of South Dakota; Defense Research Institute;

(This Listing Continued)

North Dakota Defense Lawyers Association (Vice-President, 2005—); Minnesota Defense Lawyers Association; International Association of Defense Counsel; National Association of Legal Assistants Certifying Board. ***REPORTED CASES:*** St. Yves v. DJ'S Dance & Arcade, Inc., 606 NW 2d 137 (ND 1999); Effeland v. Holte, 1998 WL 887480 (MN. Ct. App. 1998). ***PRACTICE AREAS:*** Products Liability Defense; Premises Liability Defense; Municipal Defense; Corporate Insurance Defense; Construction Insurance Defense; Insurance Defense; Negligence; Litigation; Personal Injury; Civil Practice. ***Email:*** bbeehler@morleylawfirm.com

LOLITA G. ROMANICK, born New Rockford, North Dakota, February 25, 1956; admitted to bar, 1984, North Dakota; 1986, U.S. District Court, District of North Dakota; 1987, U.S. Court of Appeals, Eighth Circuit; 1991, U.S. Supreme Court; 2001, Minnesota and U.S. District Court, District of Minnesota. *Education:* University of North Dakota (B.S., 1979; B.A., 1995); University of Idaho (J.D., 1983). Phi Alpha Delta (Vice-President, 1988-1989); Mortar Board. Former Member, Inquiry Committee East and Northeast. *Member:* Grand Forks County and Minnesota State Bar Associations; State Bar Association of North Dakota (President, Young Lawyers Division, 1990-1991; Chair, Womens Lawyers' Section, 1993-1994; Chair, Joint Committee on Civil Legal Services to the Poor, 1993-1994); North Dakota Bar Foundation (Director, 2001—); Commission for Continuing Legal Education (Chair, 2004—). ***LANGUAGES:*** French. ***REPORTED CASES:*** Freidt v. Moseanko, 459 NW 2d 240 (ND 1990); Jedco Development Co., Inc. v. Bertsch, 441 NW 2d 664 (ND 1989). ***PRACTICE AREAS:*** Accident Insurance; Automobile Liability; First and Third Party Insurance; Negligence Defense; Employment Law. ***Email:*** lromanick@morleylawfirm.com

KRAIG A. WILSON, born Scottsbluff, Nebraska, November 13, 1972; admitted to bar, 1999, North Dakota, U.S. District Court, District of North Dakota and U.S. Court of Appeals, Eighth Circuit; 2000, Minnesota and U.S. District Court, District of Minnesota; 2004, U.S. Supreme Court. *Education:* University of Wyoming (B.S., 1995); University of North Dakota (J.D., with distinction, 1999). Phi Alpha Delta. *Member:* Grand Forks County, Minnesota State and American Bar Associations; State Bar Association of North Dakota; The Association of Trial Lawyers of America. ***REPORTED CASES:*** Boser v. Hanson, 663 NW 2d 182 (ND 2003). ***PRACTICE AREAS:*** Insurance Defense; Negligence Defense; Personal Injury; Litigation; Civil Practice. ***Email:*** kwilson@morleylawfirm.com

---

TROY R. MORLEY, born Grand Forks, North Dakota, November 11, 1972; admitted to bar, 2005, North Dakota. *Education:* University of Nevada (B.A., 2002); University of North Dakota (J.D., with distinction, 2005). *Member:* State Bar Association of North Dakota. [U.S. Navy, 1991-1994]. ***LANGUAGES:*** American Sign Language.

LEGAL SUPPORT PERSONNEL

KRISTY L. SUMNER, born Mayville, North Dakota, March 24, 1970. *Education:* Community College of the Air Force (A.A.S., 1997); Kaplan University (Paralegal Certificate, 2003-2005). *Member:* Red River Valley Paralegal Association. [With USAF, 1989-1997]. ***Email:*** ksumner@morleylawfirm.com

TRACY L. DALSTED, born Cavalier, North Dakota, June 27, 1972. *Member:* Red River Valley Paralegal Association.

DENISE PIKER-GORDON, born 1966. Certified Paralegal, 1993.

REPRESENTATIVE CLIENTS: Insurance; Acceptance Insurance Company; Aetna Insurance Company; All National Family Insurance; Allied Insurance Group; Allstate Insurance Company; American Concept Insurance; American Family Insurance Company; American Modern Insurance; American National Property & Casualty Company; Austin Mutual Insurance Company; Auto Owners Insurance; Balboa Insurance Company; Bankers Standard Insurance; Capitol Indemnity Company; Center Mutual Insurance Company; Colonial Insurance Company of California; Colt/ Garlock; Continental Western Insurance Company; Crop Growers Insurance, Inc.; Economy Fire Insurance Company; Employers Mutual Insurance Companies; Farm Bureau Casualty; Farm & City Insurance Co.; Farmers Insurance Group; Farmers Union Mutual Insurance Company; Firemans Fund Agribusiness Insurance Co.; First Auto & Casualty Company; General Casualty Companies; Guaranty National Insurance Company; Jefferson Insurance Company of NY; Jersey International Group; Lancer Claims Services; Milwaukee Safeguard Insurance Company; National America Insurance Company; National Casualty Company; National Family Insurance Company; National Farmers Union Insurance Company; National States Insurance Company; North Dakota Insurance Reserve Fund; North Dakota Insurance Guaranty Association; Northbrook Property & Casualty Co.; Northwest GF Mutual Insurance Co.; Northwestern National Insurance Group; Reliance Insurance Company; Safeco Insurance Company; Scottsdale Insurance Company; Sentry Insurance Company; Travelers Insurance; United Equitable Insurance Company; United Services Auto Association; Universal Underwriters; Utica Mutual Insurance Company; Viking Insurance Company.
NON-INSURANCE CLIENTS: Aggregate Industries; Ralph Englestad Arena (REA, Inc.); Xcel Energy (f/k/a Northern States Power).

PEARSON CHRISTENSEN CAHILL & CLAPP, PLLP

Established in 1958

24 NORTH 4TH STREET
P.O. BOX 5758
GRAND FORKS, NORTH DAKOTA 58201
Telephone: 701-775-0521
Fax: 701-775-0524
Email: rclapp@grandforkslaw.com
URL: http://www.grandforkslaw.com

Moorhead, Minnesota Office: 403 Center Avenue, P.O. Box 1238, 56561. Telephone: 218-236-4900. Fax: 218-236-4909.

Insurance Defense, Construction Litigation, Products Liability, Tax Litigation, Commercial Litigation, Criminal Defense, Family Law, Appeals.

FIRM PROFILE: The law firm of Pearson Christensen Cahill & Clapp, PLLP provides professional legal services to people and businesses throughout North Dakota and Minnesota. This broadly based firm is engaged in civil trial practice in all courts with a primary emphasis on insurance defense and insurance related matters, tax litigation and complex commercial litigation. The firm also has a criminal law section and a domestic relations section. All attorneys are actual trial lawyers actively involved in all aspects of litigation.

LINDA E. BATA, admitted to bar, 1990, Minnesota and North Dakota. *Education:* Concordia College (B.A., summa cum laude, 1987); University of North Dakota Law School (J.D., with distinction, 1990). Order of the Coif. *Member:* Minnesota State and American Bar Associations; State Bar Association of North Dakota. ***PRACTICE AREAS:*** Litigation; Commercial Law; Collections; Employment Law; Estate Planning; Health Care Law. ***Email:*** lbata@grandforkslaw.com

DOUGLAS A. CHRISTENSEN, born Rugby, North Dakota, September 9, 1947; admitted to bar, 1971, North Dakota, U.S. District Court, District of North Dakota and U.S. Court of Appeals, Eighth and Eleventh Circuits; 1978, Minnesota. *Education:* Concordia College (B.A., 1968); University of North Dakota (J.D., 1971). *Member:* State Bar Association of North Dakota. ***PRACTICE AREAS:*** Commercial Litigation; Business Organization; Estate Planning; Tax Planning. ***Email:*** dougc@grandforkslaw.com

STEVEN J. CAHILL, born Minneapolis, Minnesota, May 24, 1948; admitted to bar, 1976, Minnesota; 1982, North Dakota. *Education:* Winona State College (B.A., 1972); Moorhead State College; William Mitchell College of Law (J.D., 1976). *Member:* State Bar Association of North Dakota; Minnesota Defense Lawyers Association (President, 1994-1995; Member, Board of Directors, 1987-1994); Advocate, American Board of Trial Advocates. ***PRACTICE AREAS:*** Civil Litigation; Insurance Defense; Personal Injury; Professional Liability; Product Liability; Premises Liability; Negligence.

RICHARD A. CLAPP, born Cincinnati, Ohio, March 20, 1948; admitted to bar, 1976, North Dakota, U.S. District Court, District of North Dakota and U.S. District Court, District of Minnesota; 1982, Minnesota and U.S. Court of Appeals, Eighth Circuit. *Education:* University of North Dakota (B.A., 1972; J.D., with distinction, 1976). *Member:* American Board of Trial Advocates; National Board of Trial Advocates; State Bar Association of North Dakota; Defense Research Institute; Minnesota Defense Lawyers Association. (Certified as a Civil Trial Advocacy Specialist by the National Board of Trial Advocacy). ***PRACTICE AREAS:*** Insurance Defense; Construction Litigation; Products Liability; Civil Litigation; Commercial Litigation; Asbestos. ***Email:*** rclapp@grandforkslaw.com

JAY H. FIEDLER (1952-2004)

RONALD F. FISCHER, born Bismarck, North Dakota, September 10, 1955; admitted to bar, 1980, North Dakota, U.S. District Court, District of North Dakota and U.S. Court of Appeals, Eighth Circuit; 1982, U.S. Claims Court; 1984, U.S. Tax Court; 1988, Minnesota and U.S. District Court, District of Minnesota. *Education:* Mary College (B.S., 1977); University of North Dakota (J.D., with distinction, 1980). Order of the Coif. *Member:* The Association of Trial Lawyers of America; North Dakota Trial Lawyers Association (Member, Board of Governors, 1989—). ***PRACTICE AREAS:*** Civil Litigation; Business Litigation; Insurance. ***Email:*** rfischer@grandforkslaw.com

DANIEL L. GAUSTAD, born Grafton, North Dakota, November 27, 1966; admitted to bar, 1994, Montana and U.S. District Court, District of Montana; 1995, North Dakota. *Education:* University of North Dakota (B.A., 1989; J.D., with distinction, 1994). Order of the Coif. Certified Public Accountant, North Dakota, 1990. *Member:* State Bar of North Dakota; State Bar of Montana; North Dakota Society of Certified Public Accountants. ***PRACTICE AREAS:*** Commercial Law; Estate Planning; Creditors Rights; Water Law. ***Email:*** dlglaw@polarcomm.com

JAMES D. HOVEY, born Grand Forks, North Dakota, April 26, 1964; admitted to bar, 1996, North Dakota and U.S. District Court, District of North Dakota; 1997, Minnesota and U.S. District Court, District of Minnesota. *Education:* University of North Dakota (B.A., 1987; J.D., with distinction, 1996). ***LANGUAGES:*** Russian. ***PRACTICE AREAS:*** Civil Litigation; Personal Injury; Insurance Defense; Contracts; Real Property; Domestic Relations; Criminal Defense. ***Email:*** jhovey@grandforkslaw.com

JON J. JENSEN, admitted to bar, 1990, North Dakota, Minnesota, U.S. District Court, Districts of North Dakota and Minnesota and U.S. Court of Appeals, Eighth Circuit. *Education:* Mankato State University (B.S., 1987); University of North Dakota (J.D., with distinction, 1990). *Member:* Grand Forks (President, 1999), Minnesota State and American Bar Associations; State Bar Association of North Dakota. ***PRACTICE AREAS:*** Civil Litigation; Commercial Transactions; Taxation. ***Email:*** jjensen@grandforkslaw.com

GARRY A. PEARSON, born Minot, North Dakota, August 27, 1934; admitted to bar, 1958, North Dakota, U.S. District Court, District of North Dakota, U.S. Court of Appeals, Eighth and Ninth Circuits, U.S. Supreme Court, U.S. Court of Federal Claims and U.S. Tax Court; 1988, Minnesota. *Education:* University of North Dakota (B.S.B.A., 1956); University of Wisconsin and University of North Dakota (J.D., 1958). Order of the Coif. ***PRACTICE AREAS:*** Income Tax; Federal Income Tax; Estate and Gift Taxation. ***Email:*** garrypearson@hotmail.com

BARTON J. CAHILL, born Moorhead, Minnesota, April 17, 1961; admitted to bar, 1986, Minnesota and North Dakota. *Education:* Winona State University; Concordia College (B.S., 1983); Hamline University (J.D., 1985). *Member:* Minnesota Defense Lawyers Association; Defense Research Institute; Academy of Defense Trial Attorneys. ***PRACTICE AREAS:*** Insurance Defense; Insurance Coverage; Personal Injury Defense; Professional Liability; Products Liability; Negligence Defense.

ASSOCIATES

SCOTT M. STRAND, born Fargo, North Dakota, October 3, 1976; admitted to bar, 2003, North Dakota; 2004, U.S. District Court, District of North Dakota. *Education:* University of North Dakota (B.B.A., 2000); University of North Dakota School of Law (J.D., 2003). Order of the Coif. *Member:* State Bar Association of North Dakota; American Bar Association. ***PRACTICE AREAS:*** Insurance Defense; Taxation; Criminal Defense; Personal Injury. ***Email:*** scott@grandforkslaw.com

SARAH SUSAN BARRON, born Billings, Montana, March 31, 1953; admitted to bar, 1995, North Dakota; 1996, Minnesota; 2001, U.S. District Court, District of North Dakota. *Education:* Antioch College (B.A., 1975); Cleveland Marshall College of Law (J.D., cum

(This Listing Continued)

PEARSON CHRISTENSEN CAHILL & CLAPP, PLLP, Grand Forks—Continued

laude, 1995). *Member:* Greater Grand Forks County and American Bar Associations; State Bar Association of North Dakota; Minnesota State Bar Association. ***PRACTICE AREAS:*** Criminal Defense; Domestic Relations. ***Email:*** sbarron@grandforkslaw.com

Language: Russian.

INSURANCE CLIENTS: American Universal Insurance Company; Austin Mutual Insurance Company; Auto Owners Insurance Company; Catholic Mutual Relief Society of America; Certified Claims Corporation; Cincinnati Insurance Company; CNA Insurance Company; Continental Western Insurance Company; Crum & Forster Insurance Company; Dakota Fire and EMC Insurance Company; Economy Companies; Elevators Mutual Insurance Company; Equitable Life Assurance Society of the United States; Farmers Alliance Mutual Insurance Company; GEICO; Government Employees Insurance Company; Great Central Insurance Company; Great West Casualty Company; Home Insurance Company; Iowa Mutual Insurance Company; John Deere Insurance Company; Manitoba Public Insurance Corporation; MN Fire & Casualty Company; Mutual Service Insurance Corporation; National American Insurance Company of New York; New Hampshire Insurance Company; North Dakota Insurance Reserve Fund (NDIRF); Safeco Insurance Companies; Seibels, Bruce & Company; The Atlantic Companies; The Hartford Companies; The Mill Mutuals; Tri-State Insurance Company of Minnesota; U.S. Insurance Group; United Fire and Casualty Company; United Services Auto Association; United States Fidelty and Guaranty Company; Westfield Companies; Rydells; Cloverdale Foods; Acme Electric Tool Crib of the North; University of North Dakota.
REFERENCE: Alerus Financial Services.

SHAFT, REIS & SHAFT, LTD.

Established in 1907

GATE CITY FEDERAL BUILDING
2850 24TH AVENUE SOUTH, SUITE 302
P.O. BOX 5116
GRAND FORKS, NORTH DAKOTA 58206-5116
Telephone: 701-772-8156
Fax: 701-772-9564
Email: shaftreis@gfwireless.com

Real Estate, Title Insurance Law, Business Law, Corporate Law, Estate Planning, Probate, General Practice.

FIRM PROFILE: Admitted before North Dakota, Minnesota, U.S. District Courts, U.S. Court of Appeals, Eighth Circuit, U.S. Supreme Court.

JOHN G. SHAFT (1927-1997)

SHARON M. REIS, admitted to bar, 1977, North Dakota and Minnesota. *Education:* Valley City State University (B.S., 1974); University of North Dakota (J.D., 1977). *Member:* State Bar Association of North Dakota (Chairperson, Probate and Trust Committee), Minnesota State Bar Association. ***PRACTICE AREAS:*** Commercial Real Estate; Residential Real Estate; Probate; Estate Planning; Title Insurance. ***Email:*** sreis@gfwireless.com

GRANT H. SHAFT, admitted to bar, 1986, North Dakota and Minnesota. *Education:* Arizona State University (B.S., 1983); University of North Dakota (J.D., 1986). Special Attorney General, North Dakota. *Member:* State Bar Association of North Dakota (Member, Title Standards Committee; Chairman, Real Property, Probate and Trust Section; Member, Board of Governors), American Bar Association; American College of Real Estate Lawyers. ***PRACTICE AREAS:*** Commercial Real Estate; Residential Real Estate; Title Insurance. ***Email:*** gshaft@gfwireless.com

SYLVIA N. KLOSTER, admitted to bar, 1988, North Dakota. *Education:* University of North Dakota (B.S., 1984; J.D., 1988). *Member:* State Bar Association of North Dakota, American Bar Association. ***PRACTICE AREAS:*** Business Organization; Probate; Real Estate. ***Email:*** skloster@gfwireless.com

REPRESENTATIVE CLIENTS: Chicago Title Insurance Co.; University of North Dakota; Alerus Financial, North Dakota; J.R. Simplot Co.; U.S. Bank; Gate City Savings Bank; Grand Forks County; Simonson Lumber; Simonson Station Stores; Greenberg Realty; Crary Homes and Real Estate; Grand Forks Board of Realtors; Fritz Building Co.; Innes Construction; First State Bank; Wells Fargo; United Bank Valley; Bremer Bank; Ralph Engelstad Arena, Inc.
REFERENCES: Gate City Savings Bank; Alerus Financial, N.A.; First State Bank.

DAVID C. THOMPSON ATTORNEY AT LAW, P.C.

321 KITTSON AVENUE
P.O. BOX 5235
GRAND FORKS, NORTH DAKOTA 58201
Telephone: 1-800-704-7012
Email: dct@rrv.net

Personal Injury.

DAVID C. THOMPSON, born Glen Ridge, New Jersey, July 18, 1953; admitted to bar, 1983, North Dakota; 1984, U.S. District Court, North Dakota; 1987, U.S. Tax Court and U.S. Court of Appeals, Eighth Circuit; 2001, U.S. District Court, Northern District of New York; 2005, U.S. Court of Appeals, Ninth Circuit. *Education:* University of Maine (B.A., 1975); Carleton University, Ottawa, Ontario, Canada (M.A., Journalism, 1978); University of North Dakota (J.D., 1982). Member, Board of Governors, North Dakota Trial Lawyers' Association. Commissioner, Grand Forks Historical Preservation Commission, 1989-1999. Legal Staff, North Dakota Legislative Assembly, 1982-1983. *Member:* Grand Forks County, North Dakota State and American Bar Associations; Association of Trial Lawyers of America; North Dakota Trial Lawyers' Association. ***REPORTED CASES:*** Black v. Abex Corp., 603 N.W.2d (N.D. 1999); Blikre v. Acands, Inc., 593 N.W.2d 775 (N.D. 1999); Thompson v. Peterson, 187 F.3d 643, 1999 Westlaw 332794 (8th Cir. 1999); Peterson v. Daugherty Dawkins, 583 N.W.2d 626 (N.D. 1998); United States v. Grey Bear, 116 F.3d 349 (8th Cir. 1997); Anderson v. A.P.I. Co. of Minnesota, 559 N.W.2d 204 (N.D. 1997); Thompson v. Peterson, 546 N.W.2d 856 (N.D. 1996); Myers v. Moore Engineering, 42 F.3d 452 (8th Cir. 1994); Fleck v. ANG Coal Gasification Co., 522 N.W.2d 445 (N.D. 1994); Evert v. Keene Corp., 19 F.3d 1437, 1994 Westlaw 108844 (8th Cir. 1994); Adams Public School Dist. v. Asbestos Corp. Ltd., 7 F.3d 717 (8th Cir. 1993); Fields v. Kelly, 986 F.2d 225 (8th Cir. 1993); Stanek v. A.P.I., Inc. 474 N.W.2d 829 (Minn.App., 1991), review denied, (Minn. 1991), certiorari denied, 503 U.S. 977 (1992), Justice While dissenting; United State v. Cavanaugh, 948 F.2d 405 (8th Cir. 1991); Iverson v. Meece, 1991 Westlaw 353879 (D.N.D. 1991); Biesterfeld v. Asbestos Corporation of America, 467 N.W.2d 730 (N.D. 1991); United State v. Lewis, 907 F.2d 773 (8th Cir. 1990); In re North Dakota Personal Injury Asbestos Litigation No. 1, 737 F.Supp. 1087 (D.N.D. 1990); MOrris v. Clifford, 903 F.2d 574 (8th Cir. 1990); Industrial Commission v. Wilber, 453 N.W.2d 824 (N.D. 1990); Production Credit Association v. Ista, 451 N.W.2d 118 (N.D. 1990); Puppe v. AcandS, Inc., 733 F.Supp. 1355 (D.N.D. 1990); Nogosek v. Asbestos Corp. of America, 129 F.R.D. 540 (D.N.D. 1989); Adolf v. A.P.I., Inc., 726 F.Supp. 764 (D.N.D. 1989); United State v. Grey Bear, 883 F.2d 1382 (8th Cir. 1989); Muchow v. Lindblad, 435 N.W. 2d 918 (N.D. 1989); Dakota Grain Systems, Inc. v. Rauser, 435 N.W.2d 205 (N.D. 1989); United States v. Grey Bear, 863 F.2d 572 (8th Cir. 1988); State v. Gelger, 430 N.W.2d 346 (N.D. 1988); Warner v. Graham, 845 F.2d 179 (8th Cir. 1988); Zajac v. Annear, 871 F.2d 1090 (8th Cir. 1988); State v. Ricehill, 415 N.W.2d 481 (N.D. 1987); City of Riverside v. Helenske, 413 N.W.2d 363 (N.D. 1987); Wamer v. Graham, 675 F.Supp. 1171 (D.N.D. 1987); United States v, Grey Bear, 828 F.2d 1286 (8th Cir. 1987); Bergstrom v. Buettner, 697 F.Supp. 1098 (D.N.D. 1987); United States v. Hintzman, 806 F.2d 840 (8th Cir. 1986); Blueshield v. Job Service North Dakota, 392 N.W.2d 70 (N.D. 1986); United States v. Grey Bear, 636 F.Supp. 1551 (D.N.D. 1986); State v. Solberg, 381 N.W.2d 197 (N.D. 1986); United States v. Warner, 595 F.Supp. 595 (D.N.D. 1984). ***PRACTICE AREAS:*** Personal Injury. ***Email:*** dct@rrv.net

(This Listing Continued)

TRAYNOR LAW FIRM, P.C.

GRAND FORKS, NORTH DAKOTA

(See Devils Lake)

Insurance Defense, Insurance Coverage, Insurance Bad Faith, Personal Injury, Wrongful Death, Real Estate, Corporate Law, Banking, Estate Planning, Probate and Trusts, Collections, Subrogation, Title Insurance, Tribal Law, Civil Trial Practice before all State and Federal Courts.

ROBERT VOGEL LAW OFFICE, P.C.

Established in 1981

106 NORTH 3RD STREET, SUITE 202
P.O. BOX 5576
GRAND FORKS, NORTH DAKOTA 58206
Telephone: 701-775-3117
Fax: 701-775-6274
Email: rvlo@prodigy.net

Civil Litigation, Personal Injury, Professional Malpractice, Workers Compensation, Employment Law, and Health Care Law.

ROBERT VOGEL (1918-2005)

ROGER R. SUNDLING, born Glendale, California, March 18, 1942; admitted to bar, 1983, North Dakota and U.S. District Court, District of North Dakota. *Education:* San Francisco State College (B.A., 1964; M.S., 1966); University of North Dakota (B.S., 1973); University of Minnesota (M.D., 1974); University of North Dakota (J.D., 1983); Harvard School of Public Health (M.S.P.H., 1989). *Member:* State Bar Association of North Dakota; American Bar Association; The Association of Trial Lawyers of America. ***PRACTICE AREAS:*** Medical Malpractice; Personal Injury; Health Care Law. ***Email:*** rrs1@prodigy.net

ALVIN O. BOUCHER, born Rolla, North Dakota, September 24, 1951; admitted to bar, 1984, Minnesota, North Dakota, U.S. District Courts, Districts of North Dakota and Minnesota and U.S. Court of Appeals, 8th Circuit. *Education:* University of North Dakota (B.A., summa cum laude, 1974); Mankato State University (M.A., 1977); University of New Mexico (J.D., 1984). Phi Beta Kappa. *Member:* State Bar Association of North Dakota; Minnesota State and American (Member: Tort and Insurance Practice Section; Health Law Forum) Bar Associations; North Dakota Trial Lawyers (Past Member, Board of Governors); The Association of Trial Lawyers of America. ***PRACTICE AREAS:*** Personal Injury; Health Care Law; Medical Malpractice; Legal Malpractice. ***Email:*** rvlo-aob@prodigy.net

ALICE R. SENECHAL, born Rugby, North Dakota, June 25, 1955; admitted to bar, 1984, Minnesota; 1985, North Dakota, U.S. District Courts, Districts of Minnesota and North Dakota and U.S. Court of Appeals, 8th Circuit. *Education:* North Dakota State University (B.S., 1977); University of Minnesota (J.D., cum laude, 1984). U.S. Magistrate Judge (part time), Grand Forks, North Dakota, 1990—. *Member:* State Bar Association of North Dakota; Minnesota State and American Bar Associations. ***PRACTICE AREAS:*** Professional Malpractice; Workers Compensation; Employment Law. ***Email:*** rvlo-ars@prodigy.net

ZIMNEY FOSTER P.C.

Established in 1932

BREMER FINANCIAL CENTER, SUITE 200
3100 SOUTH COLUMBIA ROAD
P.O. BOX 13417
GRAND FORKS, NORTH DAKOTA 58208-3417
Telephone: 701-772-8111
Fax: 701-772-7328
Email: firm@northdakotalaw.net
URL: http://www.northdakotalaw.net

Agricultural Law, Banking Law, Business Law, Commercial Law, Construction Law, Corporate Law, Debtor-Creditor Law, Eminent Domain, Employment Law, Family Law, Immigration Law, Indian Law and Tribal Financing, Insurance, Litigation, Mediation, Mergers and Acquisitions, Natural Resources, Personal Injury, Products Liability, Real Estate, Taxation, Toxic Torts, Trusts and Estates, Wills and Probate, and Zoning, Planning and Land Use.

FIRM PROFILE: Representing clients throughout ND and MN, Zimney Foster's reputation for prompt service, dedication to developing expertise, and maintaining long-term relationships with clients has been developed through effective advocacy on behalf of its clients, which include individuals as well as large national companies.

THOMAS L. ZIMNEY, admitted to bar, 1970, North Dakota and U.S. District Court, District of North Dakota; 1977, U.S. Court of Appeals, 8th Circuit; U.S. Supreme Court. *Education:* University of North Dakota (B.S.B.A., 1966; J.D., 1970). Qualified Mediator, ND ADR Neutral Roster. *Member:* National Arbitration Forum; Int' l. Assoc. of Defense Counsel; Defense Research Inst., Inc.; Federation of Insurance and Defense Counsel; ND Defense Lawyer Assoc. ***PRACTICE AREAS:*** Insurance Law; Automobile Law; Products Liability; Construction Law; Mediation. ***Email:*** thomaszimney@northdakotalaw.net

JOHN S. FOSTER, admitted to bar, 1976, North Dakota. *Education:* Marquette University and University of Wisconsin (B.A., cum laude, 1972); University of North Dakota (J.D., with distinction, 1976). Author: "Bankruptcy," "Debtor-Creditor Law," " Commercial Paper and Payment Systems" and "Advanced Commercial Transactions," Textbooks, Prof. of Creditor Rights, Bankruptcy, Comm. Paper and Comm. Transactions at Univ. of ND School of Law. Spec. Asst. Atty. Gen., 1989. Listed, Best Lawyers In America. ***PRACTICE AREAS:*** Banking Law; Commercial Law; Business Litigation; Creditors Rights in Bankruptcy Law; Debtor-Creditor Law.

CAROL E. JOHNSON, admitted to bar, 1983, North Dakota, Minnesota, U.S. District Court, District of North Dakota and U.S. District Court, District of Minnesota. *Education:* University of North Dakota (B.S., magna cum laude, 1980; J.D., with distinction, 1983). ***PRACTICE AREAS:*** Domestic Relations; Divorce; Mediation; Custody Investigations; Custody Disputes; Toxic Tort Litigation.

SANDRA B. DITTUS, admitted to bar, 1986, North Dakota, Minnesota and U.S. District Court, District of North Dakota. *Education:* Univ. of ND (B.S.B.A., cum laude, 1983; J.D., with distinction, 1986). Agent, Lawyers Title Insurance Company. Prof. of Agency, Partnership, and Corporations at Univ. of ND School of Law. ***PRACTICE AREAS:*** Real Estate Law; Trusts and Estates; Corporate Law; Tax Law; Natural Resources; Wills; Probate; Zoning, Planning and Land Use.

ALLEN J. FLATEN, admitted to bar, 1982, North Dakota and U.S. District Court, District of North Dakota; 1984, Minnesota and U.S. District Court, District of Minnesota; 1988, U.S. Supreme Court and U.S. Court of Appeals, 8th Circuit; U.S. Claims Court; U.S. Court of Appeals, 7th Circuit. *Education:* North Dakota State University (B.S., Pharmacy, with honors, 1973); University of North Dakota (J.D., 1982). *Member:* ND Defense Lawyer Assoc. ***PRACTICE AREAS:*** Federal Indian Law; Tribal Indian Law; Commercial Law; Employment Law; Defense Litigation; Business Litigation; Toxic Tort Litigation.

SCOTT J. LANDA, admitted to bar, 1990 North Dakota; U.S. District Court, District of North Dakota. *Education:* University of North Dakota (B.A., cum laude, 1987; J.D., 1990). Law Clerk, ND Sup. Ct., 1990-1991. ***PRACTICE AREAS:*** Insurance Defense; Commercial Litigation; Complex Civil Litigation; Toxic Tort Litigation.

TRACY A. KENNEDY, admitted to bar, 1999, North Dakota, Minnesota, U.S. District Court, District of North Dakota and U.S. Court of Appeals, 8th Circuit. *Education:* Minot St. Univ. (B.A., 1994); Univ. of ND (J.D., 1999). ***PRACTICE AREAS:*** Banking Law; Commercial Law; Agricultural Law; Business Law; Creditors Rights. ***Email:*** tracykennedy@northdakotalaw.net

WARREN J. ROEHL, admitted to bar, 2001, North Dakota and U.S. District Court, District of North Dakota; 2002, Minnesota. *Education:* University of North Dakota (B.A., cum laude, 1991; J.D., with distinction, 2001). ***PRACTICE AREAS:*** Commercial Law; Business Law; Real Estate; Creditors Rights.

BRADLEY A. MEYER, admitted to bar, 2001, North Dakota; 2002, Minnesota and U.S. District Court, District of North Dakota. *Education:* Jamestown College (B.A., magna cum laude, 1998); University of North Dakota (J.D., with distinction, 2001). Law Clerk, ND Sup. Ct., 2001-2002. Adjunct Prof. of Legal Process and Appellate Advocacy at Univ. of ND School of Law. ***PRACTICE AREAS:*** Insurance Law; Construction Law; Domestic Relations.

BRADLEY W. PARRISH, admitted to bar, 2005, North Dakota. *Education:* Washington State University (B.A., 1993); Oklahoma State University (M.S., 1997); University of North Dakota (J.D., with distinction, 2005). ***PRACTICE AREAS:*** Commercial Law; Contracts.

REPRESENTATIVE CLIENTS: Agri-Bank; Agsco, Inc.; Alerus Financial; Allied Van Lines, Inc.; Altendorf Trucking Inc.; American Federal Bank; Bremer Bank, N.A.; Community Bank of the Red River Valley; Dacotah Bank; Dakota Tribal Industries; Farm Credit Services; Federal Deposit Insurance Corp.; First State Bank; Lunseth Plumbing & Heating, Inc.; Mine Safety Appliances Co.; North Dakota State Mill and Elevator; Sears; Strata Corporation; The Okonite Co.; Wal-Mart; Wells Fargo Bank.
REPRESENTATIVE INSURANCE CLIENTS: ALLIED Group; American International Group, Inc.; Capitol Indemnity Corporation; CIGNA Group; Cincinnati Life Insurance Company; Farm and City Insurance Company; Farmers Mutual Hail Insurance Company of Iowa; Fireman's Fund Insurance Company; Grinnell Mutual Group; Horace Mann Insurance Company; Liberty Mutual Insurance Companies; Manitoba Public Insurance Corporation; Nationwide Group;

(This Listing Continued)

Nodak Mutual Insurance Company; Ohio Casualty Group; OneBeacon Insurance; State Farm Insurance Companies; Western Heritage Insurance Company.

TED D. SEIBEL

Established in 1982

708 LINCOLN AVENUE
P.O. BOX 186
HARVEY, NORTH DAKOTA 58341
Telephone: 701-324-4668
Fax: 701-324-4669
Email: tdseibel@gondtc.com
URL: http://www.seibellaw.com

Estate Planning, Wills, Probate, Trusts and Estates, Real Estate, Insurance, Business Law, Banking, Collections, Corporate Law, Municipal Law, Personal Injury, Criminal Defense, Family Law, Social Security, Civil Litigation.

FIRM PROFILE: Mr. Seibel began practicing law with the Wartner Law Firm in Harvey, North Dakota in 1977. In 1982 he purchased the firm where he has practiced continuously in the general practice of law, with emphasis in Real Estate, Probate, Estate Planning and Municipal Law.

TED D. SEIBEL, born Harvey, North Dakota, August 4, 1951; admitted to bar, 1977, North Dakota; 1987, U.S. District Court, Northern District of North Dakota. *Education:* University of North Dakota (B.A., 1973; J.D., 1977). *Member:* State Bar Association of North Dakota. ***LANGUAGES:*** English. ***PRACTICE AREAS:*** Estate Planning; Wills; Probate; Trusts and Estates; Real Estate; Insurance; Business Law; Banking Law; Collections; Municipal Law; Personal Injury; Criminal Defense; Family Law; Civil Litigation; General Practice; Social Security.

REPRESENTATIVE CLIENTS: Wells County Abstract Co.; City of Anamoose; City of Fessenden; First State Bank of Harvey; First International Bank & Trust; St. Aloisius Hospital.

JEFFRIES, OLSON & FLOM, P.A.

JAMESTOWN, NORTH DAKOTA

(See Fargo)

General Insurance Defense, Trial and Appellate Practice in Minnesota and North Dakota State and Federal Courts. Medical and other Professional Malpractice, Civil Rights, Construction, Products Liability, Fire, Government and Municipalities, Errors & Omissions, Environmental Law, Health Law, Casualty, Negligence, Asbestos Litigation, Hazardous Waste, Toxic Substances, Pollution, No-Fault, Insurance Coverages, Employment, Liquor Liability, Automobile, Premises Liability, Commercial Litigation, Subrogation.

OTTMAR & OTTMAR

Established in 1979

226 2ND AVENUE S.W.
P.O. BOX 1397
JAMESTOWN, NORTH DAKOTA 58402-1397
Telephone: 701-252-7229
Fax: 701-252-7461

Estate Planning, Probate, Wills and Trusts, Family Law, Divorce, Real Estate, Bankruptcy (Creditors), Personal Injury, Social Security Disability, Mediation, Civil Trial Practice.

MEMBERS OF FIRM

TIMOTHY J. OTTMAR, born Grand Forks, North Dakota, October 19, 1954; admitted to bar, 1979, North Dakota and U.S. District Court, District of North Dakota. *Education:* Jamestown College (B.A., 1976); University of North Dakota (J.D., 1979). Phi Delta Phi. Municipal Judge, Jamestown, 1982—. *Member:* State Bar Association of North Dakota. ***PRACTICE AREAS:*** Estate Planning; Real Estate; Collections; Wills; Trusts; Probate. ***Email:*** tottmar@csicable.net

JOANNE HAGER OTTMAR, born Grand Forks, North Dakota, March 15, 1954; admitted to bar, 1979, North Dakota and U.S. District Court, District of North Dakota. *Education:* University of North Dakota (B.A., 1976; J.D., 1979). Phi Delta Phi; Phi Beta Kappa; Blue Key. Member: Mortar Board; Order of the Barristers. *Member:* State Bar Association of North Dakota. ***LANGUAGES:*** Spanish and Norwegian. ***PRACTICE AREAS:*** Family Law; Divorce; Personal Injury; Social Security Disability; Mediation; Civil Trial Practice. ***Email:*** jottmar@csicable.net

REPRESENTATIVE CLIENTS: Jamestown College; Stutsman County State Bank; Hi-Acres Manor.

TRAYNOR LAW FIRM, P.C.

JAMESTOWN, NORTH DAKOTA

(See Devils Lake)

Insurance Defense, Insurance Coverage, Insurance Bad Faith, Personal Injury, Wrongful Death, Real Estate, Corporate Law, Banking, Estate Planning, Probate and Trusts, Collections, Subrogation, Title Insurance, Tribal Law, Civil Trial Practice before all State and Federal Courts.

JOHNSON & SUNDEEN, LTD.

KILLDEER, NORTH DAKOTA

(See Watford City)

Oil and Gas, Natural Resources, Probate, Real Estate, Collections, Personal Injury, Automobile Accidents, Professional Negligence, Wrongful Death, Medical Malpractice, Commercial Litigation, Corporate Law, Family Law, Estate Planning, Business Law, Wills and Probate, Tribal Law, Trials and Appeals.

KELSCH KELSCH RUFF & KRANDA

"A Partnership including Professional Corporations"

Established in 1918

103 COLLINS AVENUE
P.O. BOX 1266
MANDAN, NORTH DAKOTA 58554-7266
Telephone: 701-663-9818
Fax: 701-663-9810
URL: http://www.kelschlaw.com

Estate Planning, Probate, Wills, Real Estate, Family Law, Divorce, Adoptions, Commercial Litigation, Personal Injury, Products Liability, Administrative Law, Environmental Law, Lobbying, Banking, Business Law, Bankruptcy, Corporate Law, Collections, Civil Litigation.

FIRM PROFILE: Kelsch Kelsch Ruff & Kranda is presently a 7 member law firm serving central North Dakota. Its roots go back over 80 years, and it provides general legal and litigation services and specializes in tort actions, administrative law, environmental law, and contract lobbying services before the North Dakota Legislature.

LAW FIRM ALLIANCES/ASSOCIATIONS: ***MERITAS:*** *An affiliation of 202 medium sized law firms in 266 cities worldwide.*

MEMBERS OF FIRM

C. F. KELSCH (1890-1987)

WILLIAM C. KELSCH (Retired)

THOMAS F. KELSCH, admitted to bar, 1965, North Dakota; U.S. Court of Appeals, Eighth Circuit; U.S. District Court, District of North Dakota; U.S. District Court, District of Minnesota; U.S. Supreme Court. *Education:* St. John's University (B.A., 1958); University of North Dakota (J.D., with distinction, 1965). States Attorney, Burleigh County, 1970-1974. Deputy Attorney General, 1974-1975. [1st Lt., U.S. Army Intelligence, 1958-1961]. ***PRACTICE AREAS:*** Business Litigation; Environmental Law; Administrative Practice; Lobbying. ***Email:*** tfwk@kelschlaw.com

ARLEN M. RUFF, P.C., admitted to bar, 1979, North Dakota; 1980, U.S. District Court, District of North Dakota. *Education:* Jamestown College (B.A., magna cum laude, 1976); Drake University (J.D., 1979). ***PRACTICE AREAS:*** Commercial Litigation; Banking Law; Debtor Creditor Law; Real Estate Law; Probate Law. ***Email:*** arlenruff@kelschlaw.com

THOMAS D. KELSCH, P.C., admitted to bar, 1982, North Dakota and U.S. District Court, District of North Dakota. *Education:* University of North Dakota (B.A., 1979; J.D., with distinction, 1982). Phi Delta Phi; Order of Coif. ***PRACTICE AREAS:*** Personal Injury Law; Civil Trials; Commercial Litigation; Administrative Law; Domestic Relations Law. ***Email:*** tdkelsch@kelschlaw.com

TODD D. KRANDA, P.C., admitted to bar, 1987, North Dakota; 1989, Minnesota. *Education:* North Dakota State University (B.S., 1984); University of North Dakota (J.D., with distinction, 1987). Judicial Clerk, North Dakota Supreme Court, 1987-1989. ***PRACTICE AREAS:*** Business Litigation; Family Law; Probate Law; Bankruptcy; Real Estate Law; Contract Lobbying. ***Email:*** kranda@kelschlaw.com

WILLIAM J. DELMORE, admitted to bar, 1975, North Dakota; U.S. Supreme Court; U.S. Court of Appeals, Eighth Circuit; U.S. District Court, District of North Dakota. *Education:* University of North Dakota (B.A., 1970); Yale University (J.D., 1975); Harvard University. ***PRACTICE AREAS:*** Environmental Law; Administrative Law; Regulatory; Contract Litigation. ***Email:*** delmore@kelschlaw.com

ASSOCIATES

CYNTHIA WAGNER-GOULET, admitted to bar, 1985, North Dakota. *Education:* North Dakota State University (B.S., cum laude, 1979); University of North Dakota (J.D., 1985). ***PRACTICE AREAS:*** Environmental Law; Personal Injury; Family Law; Employment Law. ***Email:*** cgoulet@kelschlaw.com

DANIEL J. NAGLE, born Milwaukee, Wisconsin, October 8, 1976; admitted to bar, 2004, North Dakota. *Education:* University of North Dakota (B.B.A., 1999; J.D., with distinction, 2003). Delta Theta Phi. ***PRACTICE AREAS:*** Family Law; Labor and Employment; Debtor and Creditor; Bankruptcy; Criminal Law. ***Email:*** dnagle@kelschlaw.com

Member of Commercial Law Affiliates (CLA), an affiliation of 202 median sized law firms in 266 cities worldwide.

CONTRACT LOBBYIST FOR: Canadian Pacific Railway Co.; Charitable Gaming Association of North Dakota; Safety-Kleen Corp.; McDonald's Corp.; Alliance Pipeline, Inc.; North Dakota Consulting Engineers Council; North Dakota Society of Professional Engineers; North Dakota Manufactured Housing Association; Waste Management; Explore Information Services; AT&T; United States Tobacco; 3M Traffic Control Materials Division; Anheuser-Bush Co.; Verizon Wireless.
REPRESENTATIVE CLIENTS: BANKS: Wells Fargo; Bank of Steele, ND; Commercial Bank of Mott, ND; First Security Bank West of Robinson, ND; West River State Bank, Hettinger, ND; First Southwest Bank, Mandan, ND; Farmers Security Bank, Washburn, ND; Dakota Community Bank, Mandan, ND. SCHOOLS: Turtle Mountain Community College, Belcourt, ND; Belcourt School District, Belcourt, ND; Flasher School District, Flasher, ND; Roosevelt School District, Carson, ND.
GENERAL COUNSEL FOR: Cloverdale Foods Co.; L & H Manufacturing Co. OTHERS: North Country Thermal Line, Inc., Mandan, ND; Gateway Mall, Bismarck, ND; Rainbow Gas Co., Bismarck, ND; Bismarck, ND; Missouri Valley Petroleum, Mandan, ND; Flasher Community Credit Union, Flasher, ND; Logan Hill Realty, Bismarck, ND; Buehler-Larson Funeral Home, Mandan, ND; Weigel Funeral Home, Mandan, ND; Unicom, Bismarck, ND.

JOHNSON & SUNDEEN, LTD.

MEDORA, NORTH DAKOTA

(See Watford City)

Oil and Gas, Natural Resources, Probate, Real Estate, Collections, Personal Injury, Automobile Accidents, Professional Negligence, Wrongful Death, Medical Malpractice, Commercial Litigation, Corporate Law, Family Law, Estate Planning, Business Law, Wills and Probate, Tribal Law, Trials and Appeals.

MAXSON LAW OFFICE, P.C.

TOWN & COUNTRY CENTER
1015 S. BROADWAY, SUITE 15
MINOT, NORTH DAKOTA 58701
Telephone: 701-839-6704
Fax: 701-852-8782
Email: maxsonlaw@minot.com
URL: http://www.maxsonlaw.com

Estate Planning, Probate, Trusts, Wills, Business Planning, Corporate Law, Real Estate, Commercial Litigation, Civil Litigation.

R. JAMES MAXSON, born Thief River Falls, Minnesota, December 12, 1947; admitted to bar, 1973, North Dakota. *Education:* Moorhead State University (B.A., 1970); University of North Dakota (J.D., 1973). Assistant State's Attorney, Ward County, North Dakota, 1974-1976. North Dakota State Senator, 1986-1994. Democratic National Committeeman, North Dakota, 2000—. *Member:* Ward County Bar Association (President, 1980); State Bar Association of North Dakota; North Dakota Trial Lawyers Association (State President, 1984); The Association of Trial Lawyers of America (State Delegate, 1985-2000). ***LANGUAGES:*** Norwegian.

OF COUNSEL

ELIN S. ALM, born Hitra, Norway, December 30, 1975; admitted to bar, 2003, North Dakota and U.S. District Court, District of North Dakota. *Education:* University of Oslo, Norway (2001); University of North Dakota (J.D., 2003). *Member:* State Bar Association of North Dakota. ***LANGUAGES:*** Norwegian. ***PRACTICE AREAS:*** Estate Planning; Business Law; Real Estate.

McGEE, HANKLA, BACKES & DOBROVOLNY, P.C.

Established in 1901

SUITE 305 WELLS FARGO BANK CENTER
15 SECOND AVENUE SOUTHWEST
P.O. BOX 998
MINOT, NORTH DAKOTA 58702-0998
Telephone: 701-852-2544
Fax: 701-838-4724
URL: http://www.mcgeelaw.com

Personal Injury, Auto Accidents, Medical Malpractice, Wrongful Death, Products Liability, Insurance Defense, Business Law, Business Litigation, Immigration Law, Probate, Guardianships, Estate Planning, Wills, Trusts, Banking Law, Real Estate Law, Commercial Litigation, Agricultural Law, Cooperative Law, School Law, Employment Law, Healthcare Law, Family Law, Construction Law, Civil Trial Practice in all courts.

FIRM PROFILE: Since 1901, when George A. McGee set up practice in Minot, McGee, Hankla, Backes & Dobrovolny, P.C., has continuously served the legal needs of western North Dakota and beyond. Our operating philosophy is straight-forward: serve the client aggressively, professionally, ethically, effectively and economically. At McGee, Hankla, Backes & Dobrovolny, we maintain a strong commitment to preventive law as the best way to represent our clients.

RICHARD H. McGEE (1918-1992)

ORLIN W. BACKES, born Glenburn, North Dakota, May 11, 1935; admitted to bar, 1963, North Dakota. *Education:* Minot State University (B.S., 1958); University of North Dakota (J.D., 1963). Order of the Coif. *Member:* Ward County and American Bar Associations; State Bar Association of North Dakota (President, 1984-1985). Fellow: American College of Trial Lawyers (State Chair, 1994-1995 and 1998-1999). Advocate, The American Board of Trial Lawyers (Member, National Director, 1992-1995). ***PRACTICE AREAS:*** Business Law; Business Litigation; Real Estate Law; Estate Planning; Probate. ***Email:*** obackes@mcgeelaw.com

RICHARD H. McGEE, II, born Minot, North Dakota, June 19, 1950; admitted to bar, 1977, North Dakota. *Education:* Minot College (B.A., 1974); University of North Dakota (J.D., 1977). Phi Delta Phi. *Member:* Ward County (President, 1984) and American Bar Associations; State Bar Association of North Dakota; The Association of Defense Trial Attorneys; The American Board of Trial Advocates. Fellow, International Society of Barristers; Fellow, American College of Trial Lawyers. ***PRACTICE AREAS:*** Medical Malpractice; Insurance Defense; Personal Injury; Wrongful Death. ***Email:*** rmcgee@mcgeelaw.com

BRIAN W. HANKLA, born Bismarck, North Dakota, 1959; admitted to bar, 1986, Texas; 1989, North Dakota. *Education:* University of North Dakota (B.S., B.A., cum laude, 1981); Southern Methodist University (J.D., 1985). *Member:* Ward County (President, 1992) and American Bar Associations; State Bar Association of North Dakota. ***PRACTICE AREAS:*** Business Law; Business Litigation; Real Estate Law; School Law; Social Security Disability; Banking Law; Probate. ***Email:*** bhankla@mcgeelaw.com

COLLIN P. DOBROVOLNY, born Minot, North Dakota, April 13, 1950; admitted to bar, 1976, North Dakota. *Education:* Minot State University (B.S., 1973); University of North Dakota (J.D., 1976). Phi Sigma Pi. *Member:* Ward County and American Bar Associations; State Bar Association of North Dakota. [With U.S. Navy, 1969-1970]. ***PRACTICE AREAS:*** Personal Injury; Fires and Explosions; Automobile Accidents and Injuries; Products Liability; Wrongful Death; Insurance Defense. ***Email:*** cdobrovolny@mcgeelaw.com

JON W. BACKES, born Grand Forks, North Dakota, December 3, 1960; admitted to bar, 1990, Colorado; 1993, North Dakota. *Education:* Dakota Northwestern University (B.S., 1983); University of North Dakota (J.D., 1990). Order of the Coif. Author: "Mortgages: North Dakota's Anti-Deficiency Statute Defined," 56 North Dakota L. Rev. *Member:* Denver and Ward County (President, 1996) Bar Associations; The Colorado Bar Associa-

(This Listing Continued)

tion; State Bar Association of North Dakota; American Bar Association. ***PRACTICE AREAS:*** Business Litigation; Business Law; Real Estate Law; Estate Planning; Probate. ***Email:*** jbackes@mcgeelaw.com

PETER B. HANKLA, born Minot, North Dakota, January 11, 1965; admitted to bar, 1991, North Dakota and Minnesota. *Education:* University of North Dakota (B.B.A., 1987; J.D., 1991). Phi Alpha Delta. *Member:* American Immigration Lawyers Association (AILA); State Bar Association of North Dakota; Minnesota State and American Bar Associations. ***PRACTICE AREAS:*** Business Law; Estate Planning; Business Immigration Law; Business Litigation; Real Estate; Probate; Construction Law; Employment Law; Guardianship. ***Email:*** phankla@mcgeelaw.com

JASON R. VENDSEL, born Minot, North Dakota, September 19, 1965; admitted to bar, 1991, North Dakota; 1993, Minnesota. *Education:* University of North Dakota (B.S., B.A., 1987; J.D. with distinction, 1991). Phi Delta Phi. Member, Moot Court. Member, University of North Dakota, Law Review. *Member:* Ward County (Board of Governors, Northwest Judicial District; President) and Minnesota State Bar Associations; State Bar Association of North Dakota. ***PRACTICE AREAS:*** Insurance Defense; Personal Injury; Automobile Accidents and Injuries; Wrongful Death; Products Liability; Business Litigation; Criminal Defense. ***Email:*** jvendsel@mcgeelaw.com

BRYAN VAN GRINSVEN, born Minot, North Dakota, September 16, 1969; admitted to bar, 1995, North Dakota and Minnesota; U.S. District Court, District of North Dakota; U.S. District Court, District of Minnesota. *Education:* University of North Dakota (B.A., 1992); University of Minnesota (J.D., 1995). *Member:* Ward County and Minnesota State Bar Associations; State Bar Association of North Dakota; North Dakota Trial Lawyers Association. ***PRACTICE AREAS:*** Business Law; Business Litigation; Contracts; Probate; Real Property Law; Guardianship; Estate Planning; Criminal Defense. ***Email:*** bvangrinsven@mcgeelaw.com

---

JENNIFER M. STANLEY, born Bismarck, North Dakota, September 23, 1977; admitted to bar, 2003, North Dakota. *Education:* Minot State University (B.A., 2000); University of North Dakota School of Law (J.D., 2003). Delta Theta Phi. ***PRACTICE AREAS:*** Litigation; Criminal Defense; Family Law. ***Email:*** jstanley@mcgeelaw.com

REPRESENTATIVE CLIENTS: Attorneys Liability Protection Society, Inc.; CIGNA-CNA; Dakota Fire Insurance Co.; DPIC Cos., Inc.; Farmers Insurance Group; Grinnell Mutual Reinsurance Co.; Horace Mann Insurance Co.; Manitoba Public Ins. Co.; North Dakota Insurance Reserve Fund; PHH Homequity; Saskatchewan Government Insurance; State Farm Mutual Insurance Co.; Travelers Insurance Co.
LEGAL COUNSEL FOR: Dakota Drug, Inc.; First Western Bank & Trust; Medical Arts Clinic; Minot Public Schools; Wolverine Drilling, Inc.; Bushel 42 Pasta Co.; Northwestern Dairy, L.L.L.P.; Westlie Motor Co.; Minot Farmer's Elevator; Dakota Square Mall; Northern Tier Federal Credit Union; Norwest Wells Fargo Bank, North Dakota N.A.; Uni Med Medical Center.

PEARCE & DURICK

MINOT, NORTH DAKOTA

(See Bismarck)

Products Liability Defense, Oil and Gas, Mining, Insurance Defense, Negligence, Real Estate, Corporate Law, Taxation, Business Law, Commercial Law, Banking, Estate Planning, Probate, Wills, Public Utilities, Education Law, Intellectual Property, Employment Law, Appeals, Civil Litigation before all Courts and Administrative Agencies.

MICHAEL G. STURDEVANT, P.C.

SW PLAZA BUILDING
900 20TH AVENUE SW
P.O. BOX 970
MINOT, NORTH DAKOTA 58702
Telephone: 701-852-4118
Email: mgslaw@srt.com

Business Organizations, Corporate Law, Business Planning, Real Estate, Estate Planning, Probate, Commercial Litigation.

MICHAEL G. STURDEVANT, born Wahpeton, North Dakota, March 5, 1949; admitted to bar, 1974, North Dakota; 1983, U.S. Court of Appeals, Eighth Circuit. *Education:* University of Denver and Vanderbilt University (B.A., 1971); University of North Dakota (J.D., 1974). Member, North Dakota Judicial Conference, 1999—; Joint Procedure Committee, 2001—; Disciplinary Board of the Supreme Court, 2003—. Special Assistant Attorney General for North Dakota Housing Finance Agency, 1987—. *Member:* Ward County (President, 1978-1979), Northwest Judicial District Bar Association (President, 1983-1985); State Bar Association of North Dakota (Member, Board of Governors, 1979-1980; 1983-1985). ***PRACTICE AREAS:*** Estate Planning; Real Estate; Business Planning; Commercial Litigation. ***Email:*** mgslaw@srt.com

---

TRAYNOR LAW FIRM, P.C.

MINOT, NORTH DAKOTA

(See Devils Lake)

Insurance Defense, Insurance Coverage, Insurance Bad Faith, Personal Injury, Wrongful Death, Real Estate, Corporate Law, Banking, Estate Planning, Probate and Trusts, Collections, Subrogation, Title Insurance, Tribal Law, Civil Trial Practice before all State and Federal Courts.

WHEELER WOLF LAW FIRM

MINOT, NORTH DAKOTA

(See Bismarck)

Civil Trial Practice in all Courts and Administrative Agencies, Corporate Law, Administrative Law, Public Utilities, Taxation, Estate Planning, Probate, Wills, Elder Law, Banking, Real Estate, Commercial Law, Lobbying, Communications Law, Construction Law, Labor Relations, Collections, Personal Injury, Negligence, Workers Compensation, Social Security, Criminal Law, Bankruptcy, Agricultural Law.

LAW OFFICES OF JAMES G. WOLFF

Established in 2003

105 WEST MAIN
P.O. BOX 8
MOHALL, NORTH DAKOTA 58761
Telephone: 701-756-7199
Fax: 701-756-6882
Email: jamesgwolff@wolfflawoffices.com
URL: http://www.wolfflawoffices.com

General Practice.

FIRM PROFILE: The Law Offices of James G. Wolff is a solo practice founded upon principles of attentive service to, and results for, its clients.

Mr. Wolff began his legal career as an associate in a large law firm. He brings the knowledge and skill set acquired at that firm to his own practice, adding the additional benefits of flexibility and relative economy that a smaller office is able to provide.

The firm accepts only a limited number of clients in order to ensure timely and personal attention. Innovative and focused effort is applied to every matter, whether it consists of litigation, a business transaction, estate planning, probate, or another sort of legal service.

JAMES G. WOLFF, born Medford, Oregon, February 22, 1969; admitted to bar, 1997, Nevada and U.S. District Court, District of Nevada; 2003, U.S. District Court, District of North Dakota and U.S. Court of Appeals, 8th Circuit; 2004, North Dakota. *Education:* St. John's College (B.A., with honors, 1991); University of Oregon (J.D., 1996). Order of the Coif. Recipient, American Jurisprudence Award for Civil Procedure. University of Oregon. Law Clerk, Hon. Chief Justice Warren Matthews, Alaska Supreme Court, 1996-1997. *Member:* Federal and American Bar Associations; State Bar of Nevada; State Bar of North Dakota. ***REPORTED CASES:*** United States v. Parisien, 413 F.3d 924 (8th Cir. 2005), United States v. Azure, 279 F.Supp. 2d 1093 (D.N.D. 2003); United States v. LaFountain, 252 F.Supp. 2d 883 (D.N.D. 2003); United States v. Moser, 240 F.Supp. 2d 1058 (D.N.D. 2003); United States v. Sprinks, 339 F.Supp.2d 1070 (D.N.D. 2004); United States v. Bailey, 318 F.Supp.2d 839 (D.N.D. 2004); United States v. Serdahl, 316 F.Supp.2d 859 (D.N.D. 2004), State v. Bernstein, 697 N.W.2d 371 (N.D.App. 2005). ***PRACTICE AREAS:*** Litigation; Appellate Practice; Criminal Defense; Estate Planning; Probate; Business Law; Commercial Law; Real Estate Law; Agricultural Law.

REPRESENTATIVE CLIENTS: Citizen's State Bank; Gallery 18; North Central Good Samaritan Center; O'Keeffe's Oil Co.; Hett's Agri. Service, LLP; Precision Farm Parts, Inc; Propane Service, Inc., Norrie's Plumbing and Heating, Playhouse Daycare, Inc.

JEFFRIES, OLSON & FLOM, P.A.

WAHPETON, NORTH DAKOTA

(See Fargo)

General Insurance Defense, Trial and Appellate Practice in Minnesota and North Dakota State and Federal Courts. Medical and other Professional Malpractice, Civil Rights, Construction, Products Liability, Fire, Government and Municipalities, Errors & Omissions, Environmental Law, Health Law, Casualty, Negligence, Asbestos Litigation, Hazardous Waste, Toxic Substances, Pollution, No-Fault, Insurance Coverages, Employment, Liquor Liability, Automobile, Premises Liability, Commercial Litigation, Subrogation.

LIES & BULLIS

Established in 1983

610 SECOND AVENUE NORTH
P.O. BOX 275
WAHPETON, NORTH DAKOTA 58074
Telephone: 701-642-8055
Fax: 701-642-1449
URL: http://www.liesandbullislaw.com

Personal Injury, Insurance Defense, Civil Litigation, Toxic Torts, Products Liability, Real Estate, Wills, Estate Planning, Probate, Family Law, Business Law, Collections, Construction Law, Governmental, Municipal Law.

MEMBERS OF FIRM

STEVEN J. LIES, born Mitchell, South Dakota, April 4, 1947; admitted to bar, 1972, North Dakota and U.S. District Court, District of North Dakota; 1982, Minnesota. *Education:* University of North Dakota (B.A., 1969; J.D., 1972). North Dakota Deputy Secretary of State, 1972-1973. *Member:* Richland County (President, 1979-1982) and Minnesota State Bar Associations; State Bar Association of North Dakota; Minnesota and North Dakota Trial Lawyers Associations; The Association of Trial Lawyers of America; National Institute of Municipal Law Officers; North Dakota City Attorneys Association (President,

(This Listing Continued)

LIES & BULLIS, Wahpeton—Continued

1992-1993); North Dakota Judicial Conference. ***PRACTICE AREAS:*** Personal Injury; Civil Litigation; Insurance Defense; Municipal Law; Toxic Torts. ***Email:*** slies@liesandbullis.com

JOHN BULLIS, born Washington, D.C., September 20, 1957; admitted to bar, 1983, North Dakota; 1985, Minnesota and U.S. District Court, District of North Dakota. *Education:* North Dakota State University (B.S., 1980); University of North Dakota (J.D., 1982). *Member:* State Bar Association of North Dakota; North Dakota Trial Lawyers Association; The Association of Trial Lawyers of America. ***PRACTICE AREAS:*** Real Estate; Civil Litigation; Probate and Estate Planning; Business Law; Family Law. ***Email:*** jbullis@liesandbullis.com

REPRESENTATIVE CLIENTS: Wells Fargo Bank North Dakota, N.A., Wahpeton; American Federal Bank, Wahpeton; Gate City Federal Savings Bank, Wahpeton; First Community Credit Union, Wahpeton; Bremer Bank, Breckenridge, Minnesota; Peoples State Bank, Fairmount-Wahpeton; Community First National Bank, Lidgerwood; Action Realtors, Ltd.; Century 21-Executive Realtors; USDA Rural Development (FMHA); Southeast Water Users District; Cities of: Wahpeton, Hankinson, Fairmount, Great Bend, Mantador, Lidgerwood, Wyndmere, Abercrombie, Colfax, Dwight, Christine, Mooreton, Walcott and Davenport, North Dakota and Kent, Minnesota; St. Catherine's Living Center; Plains Truck & Trailer Service Center; North Dakota Insurance Reserve Fund; AgCountry-Farm Credit Services.

SMITH, STREGE & FREDERICKSEN, LTD.

Established in 1981

321 DAKOTA AVENUE
P.O. BOX 38
WAHPETON, NORTH DAKOTA 58074
Telephone: 701-642-2668
Fax: 701-642-4729
Email: fredstrege@smithstrege.com
URL: http://www.smithstrege.com

Personal Injury, Automobile Accidents, Wrongful Death, Business Law, Mergers and Acquisitions, Taxation, Real Estate, Collections, Commercial Litigation, Estate Planning, Wills, Trusts and Probate, Elder Law, Banking Law, Family Law, Divorce, Support, Custody, Adoptions, Criminal Defense, Felonies, Misdemeanors, DUI, Bankruptcy, Construction Law, Mediation, Arbitration, Civil Litigation in all State and Federal Courts.

RICHARD E. T. SMITH, born Breckenridge, Minnesota, March 19, 1952; admitted to bar, 1977, North Dakota and U.S. District Court, District of North Dakota; 1978, U.S. Tax Court; 1985, U.S. Supreme Court. *Education:* Creighton University (B.S.B.A., 1974; J.D., 1977). Phi Alpha Theta; Member of North Dakota State Board of Higher Education, 2005. *Member:* Richland County (President) and American Bar Associations; State Bar Association of North Dakota; North Dakota Council of School Attorneys (Past President); North Dakota Attorney Disciplinary Board (Past Chairman). ***PRACTICE AREAS:*** Business Planning; Estate Planning; Probate; Tax Law; Mergers and Acquisitions; School Law.

FRED STREGE, born Breckenridge, Minnesota, August 25, 1952; admitted to bar, 1977, North Dakota, Minnesota and U.S. District Court, Districts of North Dakota and Minnesota. *Education:* University of North Dakota (B.S.B.A., summa cum laude, 1974; J.D., with distinction, 1977). *Member:* Minnesota State and American Bar Associations; State Bar Association of North Dakota (Member, Board of Governors); North Dakota Association of Trial Lawyers; Minnesota Trial Lawyers Association; Association of Trial Lawyers of America; Southeast Judicial District Bar Association (President, 1995-1996). ***PRACTICE AREAS:*** Personal Injury; Wrongful Death; Automobile Accidents and Injuries; Commercial Law; Civil Practice; Trial Practice; Real Estate; Construction Law; Banking Law. ***Email:*** fredstrege@smithstrege.com

JANEL B. FREDERICKSEN, born Breckenridge, Minnesota, October 8, 1968; admitted to bar, 1995, North Dakota; 1996, U.S. District Court, District of North Dakota; 1997, U.S. Tax Court; 2005, Minnesota. *Education:* Concordia College (B.S.B.A., cum laude, 1991); University of North Dakota (J.D., 1994). Member: Ethics Committee, St. Catherine's Living Center Nursing Home; Three Rivers Crisis Center Board of Directors. *Member:* State Bar Association of North Dakota; American Bar Association. ***PRACTICE AREAS:*** Family Law; Divorce; Child Custody; Child Support; Adoption Law; Criminal Law; Collections; Estate Planning; Probate; Elder Law; Tax Law; Bankruptcy; Misdemeanors.

JASON R. BUTTS, born Aberdeen, Maryland, June 30, 1972; admitted to bar, 2003, North Dakota; 2004, U.S. District Court, District of North Dakota. *Education:* Jamestown College (B.A., 1994); University of North Dakota Law School (J.D., 2003). Phi Delta Phi (President, 2002-2003). *Member:* State Bar Association of North Dakota. ***PRACTICE AREAS:*** Family Law; Divorce; Child Custody; Child Support; Adoption Law; Criminal Law; Collections; Estate Planning; Bankruptcy.

REPRESENTATIVE CLIENTS: Bank of the West; Comstock Construction; PrimeBoard; Waste Management; Bremer Bank; Lincoln State Bank; Wahpeton Public School District; Richland 44 School District; Wyndmere School District; Titan Implement; Vertin Companies; Sigco Sun Products; Red River Valley and Western Railroad.

LINDELL LAW OFFICE

Established in 1915

709 MAIN STREET
P.O. BOX 427
WASHBURN, NORTH DAKOTA 58577
Telephone: 701-462-8566
Fax: 701-462-3761
Email: dlindell@westriv.com

Estate Planning, Wills, Trusts, Probate, Real Estate, Business Law, Taxation, Collections, Commercial Litigation, Civil Practice in all State and Federal Courts.

(This Listing Continued)

WILLIAM F. LINDELL, born Bismarck, North Dakota, March 19, 1934; admitted to bar, 1959, North Dakota. *Education:* University of Washington (B.A., 1956); University of North Dakota (J.D., 1959). States Attorney, 1962-1966. City Attorney, Washburn, North Dakota, 1979—. County Justice, 1960-1962; 1980-1982. *Member:* State Bar Association of North Dakota; American Bar Association. ***PRACTICE AREAS:*** Civil Trial; Probate; Real Estate; Negligence; Tax Law.

DAVID A. LINDELL, born Bismarck, North Dakota, March 25, 1966; admitted to bar, 1994, North Dakota and Minnesota. *Education:* University of North Dakota (B.B.A., 1989; J.D., with distinction, 1994). Phi Alpha Delta. Certified Public Accountant, North Dakota, 1991. *Member:* Minnesota State and American Bar Associations; State Bar Association of North Dakota; North Dakota Society of Certified Public Accountants.

JOHN E. WILLIAMS (1879-1973)

COUNSEL FOR: Farmers Security Bank of Washburn; Bank of Turtle Lake; McLean Electric Cooperative; City of Wilton; City of Turtle Lake; City of Washburn; City of Max; City of Underwood; North Dakota State Board of Pharmacy; North Dakota State Board of Water Well Contractors.

JOHNSON & SUNDEEN, LTD.

Established in 1980

Formerly, Dennis Edward Johnson, Ltd.

109 5TH STREET S.W.
P.O. BOX 1260
WATFORD CITY, NORTH DAKOTA 58854
Telephone: 701-444-2211
Toll Free: 888-783-8447
Fax: 701-842-2847
Email: jslo@ruggedwest.com
URL: http://www.johnsonandsundeen.com

Oil and Gas, Natural Resources, Probate, Real Estate, Collections, Personal Injury, Automobile Accidents, Professional Negligence, Wrongful Death, Medical Malpractice, Commercial Litigation, Corporate Law, Family Law, Estate Planning, Business Law, Wills and Probate, Tribal Law, Trials and Appeals.

DENNIS EDWARD JOHNSON, born Williston, North Dakota, April 4, 1956; admitted to bar, 1980, North Dakota; U.S. District Court, District of North Dakota; U.S Court of Appeals, 8th Circuit. *Education:* University of North Dakota (B.A., summa cum laude, 1976; J.D., with distinction, 1980). Phi Alpha Delta; Order of the Coif. Senior Member, Moot Court. Recipient, American Jurisprudence Award in Contracts. Staff Member, Student Editorial, North Dakota Law Review, 1979-1980. States Attorney, McKenzie County, North Dakota, 1982—. Registered Abstractor, 1985—. *Member:* Upper Missouri Valley Bar Association; State Bar Association of North Dakota (Member, Ethics Committee, 1983-1989; Judicial Conference Committee, 2004—); The Association of Trial Lawyers of America (State Delegate); North Dakota Trial Lawyers Association (Member, Board of Governors; Past President); North Dakota State's Attorneys Association. ***PRACTICE AREAS:*** Civil Litigation; Oil and Gas Law; Water Law; Products Liability; Trusts and Estates; Wills; Probate; Natural Resources.

ROSS L. SUNDEEN, born Grand Forks, North Dakota, December 18, 1964; admitted to bar, 1993, North Dakota and U.S. District Court, District of North Dakota; Tribal Court - Three Affiliated Tribes. *Education:* North Dakota State University (B.S., 1990); University of North Dakota (J.D., 1993). Student Researcher, Central Legal Research, University of North Dakota. Phi Delta Phi. Moot Court. Lecturer in Law, Business Law, Ft. Berthold Community College, 1996-1998. States Attorney, Dunn County, North Dakota, 1996—. Assistant State's Attorney, McKenzie County, North Dakota, 1993—; Special Assistant Attorney General, 1995—. Member, National Eagle Scout Association. *Member:* Upper Missouri Valley and American Bar Associations; State Bar Association of North Dakota (Member, Executive Council, Young Lawyers Section, 1995-1997; Member, Fee Arbitration Committee, NW Judicial District, 2002—); North Dakota Trial Lawyers Association; North Dakota States Attorneys Association. ***PRACTICE AREAS:*** Personal Injury; Family Law; Real Estate; Indian Law; Trusts and Estates; Wills; Probate.

REPRESENTATIVE CLIENTS: McKenzie County Bank, Watford City; Lakeside State Bank, New Town; McKenzie County Co-op Credit Union, Watford City; Union Bank, Halliday; First International Bank & Trust, Watford City; Northern States Tool Fishing Co., Inc.; McKenzie County Memorial Hospital; McKenzie Electric Cooperative, Inc.; McKenzie County; Slope County; Billings County; Golden Valley County; McKenzie County Grazing Association.
REFERENCES: McKenzie County Bank, Watford City, North Dakota; Lakeside State Bank, New Town, North Dakota; First International Bank & Trust, Watford City, ND.

CROWLEY, HAUGHEY, HANSON, TOOLE & DIETRICH P.L.L.P.

Established in 1895

111 EAST BROADWAY
P.O. BOX 1206
WILLISTON, NORTH DAKOTA 58801
Telephone: 701-572-2200
Fax: 701-752-7072
Email: crowley@crowleylaw.com
URL: http://www.crowleylaw.com

REVISER OF THE MONTANA LAW DIGEST FOR THIS DIRECTORY.

Billings, Montana Office: 500 Transwestern Plaza II, 490 North 31st Street, P.O. Box 2529, 59103-2529. Telephone: 406-252-3441. Fax: 406-259-4159.
Helena, Montana Office: IBM Building, 100 North Park Avenue, Suite 300, 59601. Telephone: 406-449-4165. Fax: 406-449-5149.
Kalispell, Montana Office: 431 1st Avenue West, 59901. Telephone: 406-752-6644. Fax: 406-752-5108.
Bozeman, Montana Office: 45 Discovery Drive, Suite 200, P.O. Box 10969, 59715. Telephone: 406-556-1430. Fax: 406-556-1433.

(This Listing Continued)

Missoula, Montana Office: 700 S.W. Higgins Avenue, Suite 200, 59803. Telephone: 406-829-2732. Fax: 406-829-2722.

General Civil Practice. Litigation, Insurance, Workers Compensation, Personal Injury, Products Liability, Malpractice, Bankruptcy, Financing Transactions, Administrative, Immigration, Antitrust, Banking, Corporate, Commercial, Real Estate, Public Utilities, Securities, Tax, Municipal and Tax Exempt Bonds, Entertainment, Health Care, Agricultural, Estate Planning, Probate, Pension and Profit Sharing, Natural Resources including Oil and Gas, Mining, Environmental and Water Law, Employment Law, Indian Law and Intellectual Property.

FIRM PROFILE: Crowley, Haughey, Hanson, Toole & Dietrich P.L.L.P. is the largest firm in Montana and its adjoining states. It provides a full range of legal services throughout the region, offering expertise in nearly all areas of law. Since its founding in 1895, the firm has continued in its tradition of exercising high ethical standards and leadership in community and professional affairs. The firm maintains six fully staffed offices, one in Billings, the largest city in Montana, one in Helena, the capital of Montana, as well as offices in Kalispell, Bozeman and Missoula, Montana and Williston, North Dakota. Crowley, Haughey, Hanson, Toole & Dietrich is the reviser of the Martindale- Hubbell Law Digest; please refer to the firm's complete profile therein.

PARTNERS

SHANE DOUGLAS PETERSON, born Williston, North Dakota, March 20, 1969; admitted to bar, 1995, North Dakota; 1996, Montana. *Education:* University of North Dakota (B.A., Psychology, summa cum laude, 1991; J.D. with distinction, 1994). *Member:* State Bar Association of North Dakota; Upper Missouri Bar Association. ***PRACTICE AREAS:*** Insurance Defense; General Civil Litigation; Family law; Criminal Defense; Probate. ***Email:*** speterson@crowleylaw.com

FRED C. RATHERT, born Wolf Point, Montana, July 8, 1940; admitted to bar, 1965, Montana and North Dakota. *Education:* St. Olaf College (B.A., 1962); Montana State University (LL.B., with honors, 1965). Listed in Best Lawyers in America (Oil and Gas), 1991—. Associate Editor, Montana Law Review, 1963-1965. Author, "Use of the Model Form Operating Agreement for the Creation and Enforcement of A Security Interest," 62 North Dakota Law Review, 1986. Co-Author, "North Dakota Mineral Title Standards," State Bar Association of North Dakota, 1989. *Member:* State Bar of Montana; State Bar Association of North Dakota (Member, Mineral Title Standards Committee); American Law Institute; Rocky Mountain Mineral Law Institute. ***PRACTICE AREAS:*** Natural Resources; Oil and Gas; Banking; Real Estate; Probate; Regulatory and Administrative Proceedings. ***Email:*** frathert@crowleylaw.com

GARTH H. SJUE, born Estevan, Saskatchewan, Canada, September 12, 1953; admitted to bar, 1982, North Dakota; 2002, Montana. *Education:* University of North Dakota (B.S.B.A., 1977; J.D., with distinction, 1982). Beta Alpha Psi. Certified Public Accountant, North Dakota, 1978. *Member:* Upper Missouri (President and Secretary) and American Bar Associations; State Bar Association of North Dakota (Former Member, Continuing Legal Education Committee); American Institute of Certified Public Accountants; North Dakota Society of Certified Public Accountants (Former Member, Taxation Committee). ***PRACTICE AREAS:*** Commercial Law; Commercial Litigation; Estate Planning; Estate Administration; Business Formation; Real Estate; Oil and Gas Law; Creditor Bankruptcy. ***Email:*** gsjue@crowleylaw.com

ASSOCIATES

KENNETH G. HEDGE, born Glendive, Montana, July 11, 1973; admitted to bar, 1999, North Dakota; 2001, Montana. *Education:* Montana State University (B.A., highest honors, 1995); University of Wyoming (J.D., with honors, 1999). Order of the Coif. Managing Editor, Land & Water Law Review (now Wyoming Law Review), 1999. *Member:* State Bar Association of North Dakota; State Bar of Montana; American Bar Association; Northwest Estate Planning Council. ***PRACTICE AREAS:*** Estate Planning; Business Law; Natural Resources; Real Estate; Commercial Law; Debtor and Creditor. ***Email:*** khedge@crowleylaw.com

JENNIFER NASNER, born 1978; (admission pending). *Education:* Jamestown College (B.A., summa cum laude, 2000); Gonzaga University (J.D., summa cum laude, 2005). ***PRACTICE AREAS:*** Commercial Law. ***Email:*** jnasner@crowleylaw.com

OF COUNSEL

BRUCE A. FREDRICKSON, born Williston, North Dakota, February 3, 1955; admitted to bar, 1986, Montana; 1987, North Dakota, U.S. District Court, District of Montana, U.S. District Court, District of North Dakota, U.S. District Court, District of Colorado, U.S. Court of Appeals, Ninth Circuit and U.S. Supreme Court. *Education:* North Dakota State University (B.S., Pharmacy, 1980); University of North Dakota (J.D., with high honors, 1986). Order of the Coif. Member, Moot Court Competition Team. Registered Pharmacist, North Dakota, 1980 and South Dakota, 1980. Member and Executive Secretary, Commission on Practice of the Supreme Court of the State of Montana. *Member:* Northwest Montana and American Bar Associations; State Bar of Montana; State Bar of North Dakota; American Pharmaceutical Association; North Dakota Pharmaceutical Association; South Dakota Pharmaceutical Association; Montana Pharmaceutical Association; American Society for Pharmacy Law. ***SPECIAL AGENCIES:*** Member and Executive Secretary, Commission on the Practice of the Supreme Court of the State of Montana. ***PRACTICE AREAS:*** Commercial Tort and Contract Litigation; Intellectual Property Litigation; Employment Litigation; Herbicide/Pesticide Litigation; Toxic Tort Litigation; Drug Products Liability Litigation; Chemical Products Liability Litigation; Pharmacy Law. ***Email:*** bfredrickson@crowleylaw.com

FRED E. WHISENAND, born Williston, North Dakota, February 11, 1929; admitted to bar, 1957, North Dakota; 1965, California; 1995, Montana. *Education:* University of North Dakota (Ph.B., 1956; J.D., with distinction, 1957). Phi Alpha Delta. Associate Editor, North Dakota Law Review, 1956-1957. Assistant States Attorney, Williams County, 1957-1959. Municipal Judge, Williston, 1961-1964. Member, Disciplinary Board of North Dakota Supreme Court, 1974-1980. Member, Judicial Conduct Commission of North Dakota Supreme Court, 1983-1989. *Member:* Upper Missouri and American Bar Associations; State Bar Association of North Dakota; The State Bar of California; State Bar of Montana; American Board of Trial Advocates (Chapter President, 1991; National Director, 1995-1996). ***PRACTICE AREAS:*** Insurance Defense; Commercial Litigation; Family Law; Real Estate; Natural Resources-Oil and Gas.

REPRESENTATIVE CLIENTS: First Interstate Bank of Commerce; General Motors Acceptance Corp.; Noranda Minerals Corp.; Montana Power Company; MDU Resources Group, Inc.; Chevron U.S.A., Inc.; Farm Credit Bank; Northwest Farm Credit Services, ACA; Conoco Inc.; Pegasus Gold Corp.; Mid-Rivers Telephone Cooperative; R.J. Reynolds Tobacco Co., Inc.; Norfolk Energy Inc.; United Parcel Service; Sinclair Oil Corp.; Deaconess Medical Center of Billings; Peabody Coal Co.; Billings Clinic; John Deere Co.; Decker Coal Co.; Kennecott Corporation; Manufacturer's Hanover Trust; General Electric Co.; AT&T; General Mills; Holly Sugar Corp.; The Western Sugar Co.; Grace Petroleum Corp.; Arch Minerals Corporation; Turner Enterprises, Inc.; Natural Gas Processing Company; Yellowstone Banks; American State Bank & Trust Co. of Williston; First National Bank & Trust Co. of Williston; Mercy Hospital; Triangle Electric, Inc.; Farmers Union Lumber Co.; Valley Chrysler & Marine, Inc. Coca Cola Bottling Co.; Black Hills Trucking Inc.; Northwest Grain Co-Op Terminal; Medical Center of Williston, ND; Source Energy, LLC; American State Bank & Trust Co. of Williston, ND; Craven-Hagan Clinic; Frontier Insurance Group; Millers First Insurance Co.
INSURANCE CLIENTS: Aetna; CNA Insurance; Connecticut Mutual Life; Crawford & Co.; Employers Casualty; Farmers Insurance Group; Fireman's Fund Insurance Co.; Kemper Insurance Group; Liberty Mutual Insurance Co.; Metropolitan Life Insurance Co.; Mutual Life Insurance Co., N.Y.; New York Life Insurance Co.; Prudential Insurance Co.; Federated Insurance Co.; Petroleum Casualty Co.; Washington National Insurance Aetna; St. Paul Insurance Cos.; The Doctor's Co.; The Home Insurance Cos.; The Travelers; Transamerica Insurance Co.; Underwriters Adjusting Co.; Montana State Compensation Insurance Fund; Equitable Life Assurance Society of the United States; Chubb Insurance; Nodak Mutual Insurance Co.; U.S.F.& G.; National Farmers Union Property and Casualty Co.

REVISER OF THE MONTANA LAW DIGEST FOR THIS DIRECTORY.

HENNESSY LAW OFFICE, P.C.

Established in 1993

417 1ST AVENUE EAST
DRAWER 756
WILLISTON, NORTH DAKOTA 58802-0756
Telephone: 701-572-8296
Fax: 701-572-9181
Email: integrated@nemontel.net
URL: http://www.lawyers.com/hennessylawoffice

Professional Malpractice, Oil and Gas, Personal Injury, Automobile Accidents, Wrongful Death, Employment Law, Child Custody for Husband, Civil Trial Practice, Alternative Dispute Resolution.

GREG W. HENNESSY, born Minot, North Dakota, April 8, 1952; admitted to bar, 1977, North Dakota and Montana. *Education:* University of North Dakota (B.A., 1974; J.D., 1977). Associate Editor, North Dakota Law Review, 1976-1977. Shareholder, Bjella Neff Rathert Wahl & Eiken P.C., 1977-1993. City Attorney, Culbertson, Montana, 1979—. Arbitrator, American Arbitration Association, 1993—. Title Insurance Agent. North Dakota Bar Examiner, 1994-1997. *Member:* State Bar Association of North Dakota (Investigator, Inquiry Committee West, 1994-2001); State Bar of Montana; Upper Missouri and American Bar Associations; American Trial Lawyers Association; Montana and North Dakota Trial Lawyers Associations. ***REPORTED CASES:*** Lynch v. Williston City Comm'n, 460 NW2d 136; Arbitrator, Prudential Ins. Co. Sales Practices Litigation (D.N.J.); L & L Sanitation v. Town of Culbertson 938 P2d 611; Moen v. Thomas, 2001 ND 110. ***PRACTICE AREAS:*** Natural Resources; Personal Injury; Commercial Litigation; Alternative Dispute Resolution; Child Custody. ***Email:*** integrated@nemontel.net

REPRESENTATIVE CLIENTS: Citation Oil & Gas; Enterra Petroleum; Yockim Resource Exploration Co.; Hickman Oilfield Sales & Service, Inc.; Bridge Oil (USA), Inc.; North Dakota Court Reporters Assoc.; American State Bank & Trust Co.; Heller Farms; Williston Convention & Visitors Bureau; North Star Caviar; Brew Real Estate & Development Corp.; Austin Mutual Insurance Co.

JOHNSON & SUNDEEN, LTD.

WILLISTON, NORTH DAKOTA

(See Watford City)

Oil and Gas, Natural Resources, Probate, Real Estate, Collections, Personal Injury, Automobile Accidents, Professional Negligence, Wrongful Death, Medical Malpractice, Commercial Litigation, Corporate Law, Family Law, Estate Planning, Business Law, Wills and Probate, Tribal Law, Trials and Appeals.

NILLES, ILVEDSON, STROUP, PLAMBECK & SELBO, LTD.

PLAINSMAN BUILDING
3 - 4TH STREET EAST, SUITE 206
P.O. BOX 1525
WILLISTON, NORTH DAKOTA 58802-1525
Telephone: 701-572-5544
Fax: 701-572-5561
URL: http://www.nilleslaw.com

REVISER OF THE NORTH DAKOTA LAW DIGEST FOR THIS DIRECTORY.

Fargo, North Dakota Office: 1800 Radisson Tower, 201 North 5th Street, P.O. Box 2626. Telephone: 701-237-5544. Fax: 701-280-0762.

Moorhead, Minnesota Office: 1401 South 8th Street. Telephone: 218-233-7407. Fax: 218-233-5133.

Civil Litigation, Commercial Litigation, Insurance Law, Errors and Omissions Litigation, Tort, Product Liability, Personal Injury, Railroad, Construction Litigation, Appeals, Professional Liability, Business Law, Probate, Estate Planning, Real Estate, Commercial Law, Banking, Bankruptcy, Employment Law and Worker's Compensation.

(This Listing Continued)

NILLES, ILVEDSON, STROUP, PLAMBECK & SELBO, LTD., Williston—Continued

FIRM PROFILE: The firm of Nilles, Ilvedson, Stroup, Plambeck & Selbo, Ltd. dates from the 1920's. When Daniel B. Holt of Holt & Nilles was appointed as a District Court Judge in 1932, the remaining partner, Herbert G. Nilles, together with Lewis H. Oehlert and John J. Nilles, formed the partnership known as Nilles, Oehlert and Nilles. The firm began expanding rapidly in 1949 and was incorporated in 1971 under the name of Nilles, Hansen, Selbo, Magill & Davies, Ltd. The firm now consists of 23 lawyers and over 30 support personnel.

H. MALCOLM PIPPIN, born Williston, North Dakota, April 17, 1963; admitted to bar, 1989, North Dakota; 1990, Minnesota. *Education:* University of North Dakota (B.B.A., 1985; J.D., with distinction, 1989). Phi Alpha Delta. Senior Editor, 1988-1989, North Dakota Law Review. Certified Public Accountant, North Dakota, 1987. Law Clerk to the Hon. H.F. Gierke III, Supreme Court of North Dakota, 1989-1990. *Member:* Minnesota State Bar Association; American Institute of Certified Public Accountants; North Dakota Society of Certified Public Accountants. ***PRACTICE AREAS:*** Civil Litigation; Insurance; Product Liability. ***Email:*** mpippin@nilleslaw.com

All Attorneys are Members of the Upper Missouri and American Bar Associations and State Bar Association of North Dakota.

(This Listing Continued)

STATE COUNSEL: Burlington Northern; Santa Fe Railway.

COUNSEL FOR: National Railroad Passenger Corp. (Amtrak); Soo Line Railroad; Christopherson's Plumbing and Heating; Gunderson Excavating; North Dakota Commissioner for H.U.D. under federal foreclosure act; Banner Health Systems; U.S. Bank National Association; Northern Capital Trust; W.W. Wallworks, Inc.; Valley Imports, Inc.; Western Products, Inc.; First International Bank and Trust; First National Bank and Trust; Triangle Electric; OK Tire; Selid Plumbing and Heating; Tofte Brothers Construction; Stockman Motors; Murphy Motors.

INSURANCE CLIENTS: Travelers Aetna; Prudential Insurance Company of America; Continental National Insurance Group; Farmers Insurance Group; U.S. Insurance Group; Fireman's Fund Insurance Co.; Nodak Mutual Insurance Company; CNA Insurance Companies; United Fire and Casualty; Atlantic Companies; USAA Group; Zurich-American Insurance Group; Continental Western Casualty Company; Crum & Forster Group; Blue Cross/Blue Shield of North Dakota; State Farm Insurance Companies; Catholic Mutual Relief Society; Atlantic Mutual Companies; Coregis.

REVISER OF THE NORTH DAKOTA LAW DIGEST FOR THIS DIRECTORY.

CHARLES VANDYNE

HUBER BUILDING
231 1/2 NORTH MAIN STREET
ADA, OHIO 45810
Telephone: 419-634-5791
Fax: 419-634-9242

General Practice in all Courts. Probate and Estate Planning, Corporation, Negligence, Real Estate Law, Banking and Insurance. Trials.

CHARLES VanDYNE, born Hardin County, Ohio, September 19, 1930; admitted to bar, 1954, Ohio. *Education:* Ohio Northern University (B.A., 1952; J.D., 1954).

ABERTH & CHAMPION CO., LPA

Established in 1995
3296 WEST MARKET STREET, SUITE D
AKRON, OHIO 44333-3355
Telephone: 330-865-7722
Fax: 330-865-9742
URL: http://www.aberth-champion.com
Email: thchampion@aberth-champion.com
URL: http://www.lawyers.com/aberth&championlaw

Trust Administration, Estate Administration, Estate Planning, Probate, Real Estate, Elder Law.

FIRM PROFILE: Aberth & Champion Co., LPA is a law firm dedicated to assisting clients in the avoidance of unnecessary costs and expense involved in the probate of persons or property. Our attorneys strive to deliver prompt and efficient legal services at reasonable costs.

JOEL R. ABERTH, born Akron, Ohio, August 6, 1942; admitted to bar, 1971, Ohio. *Education:* The Ohio State University (B.S., 1965); University of Akron (J.D., 1970). *Member:* Akron Bar Association (Member, Probate Law Section). ***PRACTICE AREAS:*** Corporate Law; Trust Law; Estate Administration; Estate Planning; Probate; Trust and Estate Taxation; Real Estate. ***Email:*** jraberth@aberth-champion.com

TIMOTHY H. CHAMPION, born Akron, Ohio, April 12, 1962; admitted to bar, 1988, Ohio; 1989, U.S. District Court, Northern District of Ohio. *Education:* Xavier University (A.B., 1984); University of Akron (J.D., 1988); McGill University Institute of Air and Space Law Masters Program (1988-1989). Delta Theta Phi. Sixth Circuit Governor, American Bar Association/Law Student Division, 1987-1988. Who's Who in American Law Students, 1987. *Member:* Akron Bar Association (Member, Probate Law Section); Ohio State Bar Association; Akron Tax and Estate Plan. ***LANGUAGES:*** French. ***PRACTICE AREAS:*** Corporate Law; Estate Planning; Probate; Real Estate; Trust Administration; Estate Administration; Trust and Estate Taxation. ***Email:*** thchampion@aberth-champion.com

AMER CUNNINGHAM CO., L.P.A.

KEY BUILDING
159 SOUTH MAIN STREET, SUITE 1100
AKRON, OHIO 44308-1322
Telephone: 330-762-2411
Telecopy: 330-762-9918
URL: http://www.amer-law.com

General Civil Trial and Appellate Practice. Real Estate, Zoning, Corporate, Taxation, Labor, Personal Injury, Public Law, Probate, Trust, Pension and Profit Sharing, Estate Planning Law and Workers' Compensation, Government, Municipal and Public Law, Health Care Law.

FIRM PROFILE: Over the years, the firm has carved a unique niche in the Akron area and in many states representing manufacturers, commercial enterprises and lending institutions, entrepreneurs, real estate developers, businesses and various governmental entities. A flourishing and successful trial department is an integral part of the firm.

Although the practice of law must always be of prime concern, the firm encourages its members to participate in both bar and civic activities. To date, five local bar presidents and one state bar president have come from its ranks.

Many community activities receive active support from members of the law firm.

Today the firm consists of thirty-five employees, including six partners, six associates, and a staff of paralegals, law clerks and support personnel.

BERNARD J. AMER (1896-1985)

ERNEST L. CUNNINGHAM (1897-1971)

JOSEPH F. COOK, JR., born Akron, Ohio, June 10, 1956; admitted to bar, 1982, Ohio. *Education:* Ohio State University (B.S.B.A., 1979); University of Akron (J.D., 1982). Certified Public Accountant, Ohio (inactive), 1986. Assistant Law Director, City of Akron, 1982-1984. Vice-President and Member, Board of Trustees, Mobile Meals Foundation. Member, Leadership Akron Class of 2001-2002. Member, United Way Professional Advisory Board. Member and Treasurer, Board of Trustees, Akron Rotary Club. Member and Treasurer, A.A.S.R. of Freemasonry, Valley of Akron. Member, American Cancer Society, Planned Giving Committee. *Member:* Akron (Member, Business and Corporate Law, Tax Law Committees), Ohio State and American Bar Associations; American Institute of Certified Public Accountants; Ohio Society of Certified Public Accountants; Institute of Business Appraisers. ***PRACTICE AREAS:*** Taxation; Business Law; Estate Planning; Probate. ***Email:*** jcookjr@amer-law.com

ANDREW R. DUFF, born Akron, Ohio, November 29, 1954; admitted to bar, 1979, Ohio. *Education:* Miami University (B.A., 1976); University of Akron (J.D., 1979). Leadership Akron, Class of 1987. Member, 1985-1994 and President, 1991-1994, Hudson Village Council. Member, Hudson Merger Commission, 1987, 1994. Member, Hudson Charter Commission, 1995. Member, Hudson School Board, 2001. *Member:* Akron, Ohio State (Member, Real Estate Law Committee) and American Bar Associations. ***PRACTICE AREAS:*** Real Estate; Construction Law; Business Law; Corporate Law; Municipal Law. ***Email:*** aduff@amer-law.com

JACK MORRISON, JR., born Mount Vernon, Ohio, October 25, 1952; admitted to bar, 1981, Ohio and U.S. Supreme Court. *Education:* University of Maryland (A.A., 1976); University of Akron (B.S.B.A., magna cum laude, 1977; J.D., 1981). Beta Gamma Sigma; Alpha Sigma Lambda (President, 1973-1975). Recipient, Outstanding Alumni Award, University of Akron School of Law, 1997. Leadership Akron, 1988-1989. Assistant Law Director (City of Akron), 1981-1982. Member, Federal ADR Mediation Panel, U.S. District Court, Northern District of Ohio, 1992—. Member, Advisory Board & Legal Counsel, Silver Lake Estates. Former Board of Trustees, Greater Akron Chamber. Board of Trustees, Akron-Summit County Public Library, 2001—. Secretary, Summit County Republican Party. Member, Former Board of Trustees and Executive Committee, Walsh Jesuit High School. Listed in Ohio Super Lawyer by Law & Politics Magazine, 2005 and 2006. Member Board of Trustees, The University of Akron. *Member:* Akron (Vice President, 2000; President, 2001; Member: Executive Committee, 1987-1990; Judicial Commission, 1990-1998; Finance; Professionalism; Continuing Legal Education; Grievance Committees), Ohio State (Member: Council of Delegates, 1990-1996; Board of Governors, Litigation Section, 1989—) and American Bar Associations; Ohio Academy of Trial Lawyers (Governing Trustee, 1994); Summit County Trial Lawyers Association (Governing Trustee and Treasurer, 1987-1990; President, 1990-1992); The Association of Trial Lawyers of America; American Inns of Court (Barrister). Fellow: American Bar Foundation; Akron Bar Foundation. [U.S. Air Force, 1970-1974]. ***PRACTICE AREAS:*** Products Liability; Medical Malpractice; Business Litigation; Personal Injury; Health Care Law; Government; Public Law; Municipal Law. ***Email:*** morrison@amer-law.com

MICHAEL S. URBAN, born Chicago, Illinois, September 5, 1957; admitted to bar, 1987, Ohio. *Education:* Kent State University (B.A., summa cum laude, 1979; M.A., 1984); Ohio State University (J.D., 1987). Phi Beta Kappa; Order of the Coif. Member, Policies and Procedures Committee, Service Review Team Committee, United Way of Summit County. *Member:* Akron, Ohio State and American Bar Associations. ***PRACTICE AREAS:*** Labor and Employment; Business Law; Corporate Law; Health Care Law. ***Email:*** murban@amer-law.com

JOSEPH F. COOK (1926-1998)

THOMAS M. SAXER, born Canton, Ohio, July 10, 1966; admitted to bar, 1991, Ohio; 1993, U.S. District Court, Northern District of Ohio; 2003, U.S. District Court, Southern District of Ohio; 2004, U.S. Court of Appeals, Sixth Circuit; 2005, U.S. District Court, Western District of Michigan and U.S. Supreme Court. *Education:* Kent State University (B.B.A., 1988); University of Akron (J.D., magna cum laude, 1991). Phi Alpha Delta. Member, Akron Law Review. Listed in Ohio Super Lawyer-Rising Star by Law & Politics Magazine, 2005. *Member:* Akron, Ohio State and American Bar Associations; The Association of Trial Lawyers of America; Ohio Academy of Trial Lawyers; Summit County Trial Lawyers Association. ***PRACTICE AREAS:*** Appellate Practice; Commercial Litigation; Products Liability; Personal Injury Litigation. ***Email:*** tsaxer@amer-law.com

THERESA A. TARCHINSKI, born Grand Rapids, Michigan, April 2, 1963; admitted to bar, 1989, Ohio; 1990, U.S. District Court, Northern District of Ohio; 1992, U.S. Court of Appeals, Sixth Circuit; 2004, U.S. Supreme Court. *Education:* University of Michigan (B.A., 1985); Case Western Reserve University (J.D., 1988). Member, Moot Court. Executive Research Editor, Journal of International Law, 1987-1988. *Member:* Akron (Member, Investigative Grievance Sub Committee; Mock Trial Chairperson, Lawyer Referral), Portage County (Leadership Portage County, 2003), Ohio State and American Bar Associations; Summit County Trial Lawyers Association (Member, Board of Trustees); Ohio Academy of Trial Lawyers; The Association of Trial Lawyers of America. ***PRACTICE AREAS:*** Personal Injury; Employment Law; Products Liability; Medical Malpractice; Civil Litigation; Professional Liability. ***Email:*** tarchinski@amer-law.com

---

THOMAS R. HOULIHAN, born Akron, Ohio, June 3, 1971; admitted to bar, 1998, Ohio and U.S. District Court, Northern District of Ohio; 1999, U.S. District Court, Southern District of Ohio; 2001, U.S. Supreme Court; 2003, U.S. District Court, Western District of Michigan; 2005, U.S. Court of Appeals, Sixth Circuit. *Education:* Mount Union College (B.A., 1993); University of Akron (J.D., 1998). *Member:* Akron (Fee Arbitration Committee), Ohio State (Antitrust Division) and American (Tort Trial and Insurance Practice Section) Bar Associations; The Association of Trial Lawyers of America; Ohio Academy of Trial Lawyers; Summit County Trial Lawyers Association. ***REPORTED CASES:*** Spencer v. Pugh, 543 U.S._, 125 S.Ct. 305, 160 L.Ed.2d 213 (2004); Summit County Democratic Central and Executive Committee v. Blackwell 388 F.3d 547 (6th Cir., 2004); Campus Bus Serv. v. Zaino (2003), 98 Ohio St.3d 463; Stewart v. Cleveland Clinic Foundation (1999), 136 Ohio App.3d. 244. ***PRACTICE AREAS:*** Appellate Practice; Complex Business Litigation; Complex Tort Litigation; Antitrust; Intellectual Property; Securities Litigation; Government Law; Election Law. ***Email:*** Houlihan@amer-law.com

J. FRANCIS MACKEY, born Akron, Ohio, May 22, 1970; admitted to bar, 1998, Ohio. *Education:* Miami University (B.S.Ed., cum laude, 1992); University of Akron (J.D., 1997). *Member:* Akron, Ohio State and American Bar Associations. ***PRACTICE AREAS:*** Civil Litigation; Appellate Practice; Personal Injury; Professional Liability; Criminal. ***Email:*** fmackey@amer-law.com

LISA A. FIKE, born Fort Wayne, Indiana, August 26, 1966; admitted to bar, 1991, Indiana; U.S. District Court, Northern and Southern Districts of Indiana; 1994, Ohio. *Education:* Manchester College (B.A., 1988); Indiana University School of Law (J.D., 1991). Phi Beta Phi. *Member:* Akron, Indiana State, Ohio State and American Bar Associations. ***PRACTICE AREAS:*** Workers' Compensation; Unemployment Law; Health Care Law; Government; Municipal Law; Complex Corporate Litigation. ***Email:*** lfike@amer-law.com

MARK GERALD STASITIS, born Akron, Ohio, June 22, 1974; admitted to bar, 2001, Ohio; 2003, U.S. District Court, Northern District of Ohio. *Education:* Kent State University (B.A., 1996); University of Akron Law School (J.D., 2001). Certified Mediator,

(This Listing Continued)

AMER CUNNINGHAM CO., L.P.A., Akron—Continued

Ohio State Supreme Court. *Member:* Akron, Ohio State, Federal and American Bar Associations. ***PRACTICE AREAS:*** Employment Law; Corporate Law; Consumer Law; Civil Litigation; Appellate Practice. ***Email:*** mstasitis@amer-law.com

DANIEL L. SILFANI, born Akron, Ohio, June 6, 1973; admitted to bar, 1999, Ohio; 2000, U.S. District Court, Northern District of Ohio; 2002, U.S. Tax Court. *Education:* University of Akron (B.S./B.A., magna cum laude, Finance, 1994); Case Western Reserve University (J.D., 1998); University of Akron (M.Tax, 2002). *Member:* Akron, Ohio State and American Bar Associations. (Resident Bath, Ohio). ***REPORTED CASES:*** Slack et al. v Cropper et al. (2001), 143 Ohio App.3d 74, 757 N.E.2d 404. ***PRACTICE AREAS:*** Estate Planning; Tax Law; Tax Planning; Business Planning; Individual Tax Law; Partnership Taxation; Nonprofit Tax Law; Corporate Tax Law; Probate; Real Estate Law. ***Email:*** dsilfani@amer-law.com

SERGIO A. CARANO, born Akron, Ohio, August 17, 1961; admitted to bar, 1989, Ohio; 1993, U.S. District Court, Northern District of Ohio. *Education:* University of Akron (B.S.L.E., 1986; J.D., 1989). Finalist, American Bar Association Appellate Advocacy National Competition. Judge W.E. Pardee Scholarship and Evan B. Brewster Scholarship. Judicial Internship, Late Hon. Leroy J. Contie, Jr., U.S. Court of Appeals, Sixth Circuit, 1988-1989. Law Clerk, Ohio Court of Appeals, Ninth Judicial District, 1989-1991. Instructor, University of Akron School of Law Moot Court Team, 1990-1991. *Member:* Akron, Cleveland, Ohio State and American Bar Associations. ***LANGUAGES:*** Italian. ***PRACTICE AREAS:*** Business Litigation. ***Email:*** scarano@amer-law.com

SUZANNE M. GRADISHER, born Barberton, Ohio, September 5, 1961; admitted to bar, 2004, Ohio. *Education:* University of Nevada, Las Vegas (B.S.B.A., Administration, 1989); Kent State University (M.B.A., 2004); University of Akron (J.D., M. Tax, 2004). CPA, Ohio, 2004. ***PRACTICE AREAS:*** Probate; Estate Planning; Taxation. ***Email:*** sgardisher@amer-law.com

---

DENNIS J. BARTEK

Established in 1973

2300 EAST MARKET STREET
SUITE E
AKRON, OHIO 44312
Telephone: 330-784-8580
Fax: 330-784-8434
Email: DJBARTEK@AOL.COM

Trial Litigation, Wrongful Death, Personal Injury, Medical Malpractice, Products Liability, Business Litigation, Insurance Law, Criminal Law.

FIRM PROFILE: Practice focus on litigation including wrongful death, medical negligence, products, automobile accidents, business litigation, complex litigation, insurance law litigation and criminal law defense.

Professional resume available upon request.

DENNIS J. BARTEK, born Akron, Ohio, July 31, 1946; admitted to bar, 1971, Ohio; 1973, U.S. District Court, Northern District of Ohio; 1986, U.S. Supreme Court; 1997, U.S. Court of Appeals, Sixth Circuit. *Education:* University of Akron (B.A., Political Science, 1968; J.D., 1971). Former Assistant Summit County Prosecutor. Acting Judge, Cuyahoga Falls, Ohio Municipal Court by Periodic Assignment, 1977-1991. Selected as a Leading Lawyer, Inside Business Magazine. Selected as one of Ohio's "Super Lawyers", Law and Politics Magazine. Member, Federal ADR Panel, Northern District of Ohio. *Member:* Akron (Past President) and Ohio State (Past Member, Council of Delegates) Bar Associations; Ohio Association of Trial Lawyers; Ohio Association of Civil Trial Attorneys; The Association of Trial Lawyers of America; National Association of Criminal Defense Lawyers; Summit County Trial Lawyers; Scanlon Inn of Court (Master of the Bench). ***REPORTED CASES:*** Hybud Equip. v. Sphere Drake Ins., 64 Ohio St.3d 657 (1992); Bailey v. Chu, 610 NE2d 531, 80 Ohio App.3d 627 (1992).

REPRESENTATIVE CLIENTS: Lloyds of London (London Market Companies); Temperture Control Company; Woodbine Management.

SHARON BERG CO., LPA

784 KENMORE BOULEVARD
AKRON, OHIO 44314
Telephone: 330-745-1000
Fax: 330-745-2661
Email: attyberg@sbcglobal.net
URL: http://www.sberglaw.com

Family Law, Divorce, Dissolution, Separation Agreements, Spousal Support, Premarital Agreements, Post Divorce Modification, Domestic Violence, Child Custody, Child Support, Visitation, Paternity, Grandparents' Rights, Collaborative Divorce, Juvenile Law.

MEMBER OF FIRM

SHARON BERG, born Akron, Ohio, February 22, 1945; admitted to bar, 1976, Ohio. *Education:* University of Akron (J.D., 1976). Former Summit County, Ohio Domestic Relations Referee. Chief Justice Warren Burger "Healer Award", National Council for Childrens Rights, Washington, D.C. Guest Speaker in Family Law, Ohio Academy of Trial Lawyers and Akron Bar Association. *Member:* Akron (Member, Family Law Section; Former Co-Chair and Chair, Family Law Committee, 1983-1985), Ohio State (Member, Family Law Section). ***Email:*** attyberg@sbcglobal.net

THE BERNARD LAW FIRM

AKRON, OHIO

(See Cleveland)

Complex Business Litigation, Accountants Malpractice, Stockbroker Malpractice, Banking Litigation, Employment Litigation, Personal Injury, Wrongful Termination, Employment Discrimination, Race Discrimination, Sex Discrimination, Sexual Harassment, Americans with Disabilities, Age Discrimination in Employment, Employment Termination, Family and Medical Leave Act, Breach of Contract, Contract Litigation, Insurance, Class Actions, Securities Litigation, Shareholder Derivative Actions, Lender Liability, Antitrust, Consumer Litigation, Consumer Fraud, Construction Defects, Construction Accidents, Construction Law, Automobile Accidents and Injuries, Wrongful Death, Dog Bites, Slip and Fall, Nursing Home Litigation, Products Liability.

BERNLOHR WERTZ, LLP

THE NANTUCKET BUILDING
23 SOUTH MAIN STREET, 3RD FLOOR
AKRON, OHIO 44308-1460
Telephone: 330-434-1000
Fax: 330-434-1001
Email: jack@b-wlaw.com
URL: http://www.b-wlaw.com

General Practice.

PARTNERS OF FIRM

MARK W. BERNLOHR, born Columbus, Ohio, March 25, 1962; admitted to bar, 1987, Ohio; 1988, U.S. District Court, Northern District of Ohio. *Education:* Pennsylvania State University (B.S., 1984); Capital University (J.D., 1987). Phi Alpha Delta. *Member:* Akron, Ohio State and American Bar Associations. ***PRACTICE AREAS:*** Commercial Litigation; Construction Litigation; Business Litigation. ***Email:*** mark@b-wlaw.com

GEORGE R. WERTZ, born Youngstown, Ohio, November 26, 1950; admitted to bar, 1979, Ohio; 1980, U.S. District Court, Northern District of Ohio. *Education:* Youngstown State University (B.S.Ed., 1975); University of Akron (J.D., 1979). Referee, Summit County Probate Court, 1979-1991. *Member:* Akron (Past President, Probate Section) and Ohio State Bar Associations; NAELA. ***REPORTED CASES:*** Waterman v. Elk & Elk Co., L.P.A. (1994), 96 Ohio App.3rd 772; In re Adoption of Baby Boy Dearing (1994), 98 Ohio App.3rd 197; In re Guardianship of Myers (1993), 62 Ohio Misc.2d. 763; Belsito v. Clark (1994), 67 Ohio Misc.2d 54; Matter of Thomas (1996), 1996 WL 27911; In re Guardianship of Standel (1995) 1995 WL 655934. ***PRACTICE AREAS:*** Probate; Estate Planning; Medicaid Planning; Probate Litigation; Adoptions. ***Email:*** george@b-wlaw.com

CHRISTOPHER J. NIEKAMP, born Akron, Ohio, August 27, 1965; admitted to bar, 1990, Ohio; 1991, U.S. District Court, Northern District of Ohio. *Education:* Miami University (B.S., Ed., 1987); Case Western Reserve University (J.D., 1990). Delta Theta Phi. Contributing Legal Author, Business Headlines, 1994-1995. *Member:* Akron (Member, Bankruptcy and Commercial Law Section; Real Property Law Committee), Ohio State (Corporate Section) and American Bar Associations; American Bankruptcy Institute; Commercial law League of America. ***LANGUAGES:*** Spanish. ***PRACTICE AREAS:*** Commercial Law; Bankruptcy; Corporate; Real Estate; Entertainment. ***Email:*** cjn@b-wlaw.com

JOHN C. WEISENSELL, born Cleveland, Ohio, December 16, 1958; admitted to bar, 1985, Ohio; 1986, Florida, U.S. District Court, Northern District of Ohio and U.S. Court of Appeals, Sixth Circuit; 1995, U.S. Supreme Court; 2001, U.S. District Court, Northern District of Illinois; 2002, U.S. District Court, Eastern District of Michigan. *Education:* College of Wooster (B.A., History, 1981); Ohio Northern University; Cleveland Marshall College of Law, Cleveland State University (J.D., 1985). Member, Charles Scanlon Inn of Court, 1989-1991. Recipient, Community Service Award, Ohio State Bar Foundation, 1999. Law Clerk to the Hon. Paul C. Weick, U.S. Court of Appeals, Sixth Circuit. Member, 1991-1996 and President, 1994-1996, College of Wooster "W" Association Board of Trustees. Trustee, YMCA, Cuyahoga Falls Branch, 1997-2002. Member, Summit County Court of Common Pleas Mediation Advisory Council. Certified as a Civil Trial Advocacy Specialist, National Board of Trial Advocacy. Board Member, Cuyahoga Falls Board of Zoning Appeals. Torch and Peer Committee, United Way. *Member:* Akron (Chairman, Federal Court Committee, 1993-1994; Member, Board of Trustees, 1995-1998) and Ohio State Bar Associations; The Florida Bar; Ohio Academy of Trial Lawyers (Board of Trustees, 2005— Leadership Council, 2005—); The Association of Trial Lawyers of America; Summit County Trial Lawyers Association (Treasurer, 1992-1993; Secretary, 1993-1996; Vice President, 1996-1997; President, 1997-1998); Trial Lawyers for Public Justice; Fellow, Akron Bar Association Foundation. ***REPORTED CASES:*** Things Remembered, Inc. v. Anthony A. Petrarca, 516 U.S. 124, 116 S.Ct. 494,133 L.Ed.2d 461 (1995); Stewart v. Cleveland Clinic Foundation (1999), 136 Ohio App. 3d 244; Turner Liquidating Co. v. St. Paul Surplus Lines Ins. Co. (1994), 93 Ohio App. 3d 292; Akron Bar Association v. Snyder (1999), 87 Ohio St. 3d 211; Akron Bar Association v. Snyder (1997), 78 Ohio St. 3d 47; Sanek v. Duracote Corporation (1989), 43 Ohio St. 3d 169; Rigby v. Fallsway Equipment Co., Inc. (2002) 150 Ohio App.3d 155; State ex rel. Beacon Journal Publ. Co. v. Bond (2002), 98 Ohio St. 3d 146 (Counsel for Amicus, Summit County Trial Lawyers Assn.). ***PRACTICE AREAS:*** Personal Injury; Medical Malpractice; Products Liability; Business Litigation; Contracts. ***Email:*** jack@b-wlaw.com

ASSOCIATES

JENNIFER J. JACQUEMAIN, born Parma, Ohio; admitted to bar, 1998, Ohio and U.S. District Court, Northern District of Ohio. *Education:* Cleveland State University (B.A., 1993); University of Akron School of Law (J.D., cum laude, 1998). *Member:* Akron and Ohio State Bar Associations; Ohio Woman's Bar Association. ***PRACTICE AREAS:*** Commercial Litigation; Construction; Mechanics Liens; Utilities; Corporate; Transactional; General Business; Foreclosures; Collections. ***Email:*** jennifer@b-wlaw.com

(This Listing Continued)

MELISSA R. COX, born Cleveland, Ohio, 1968; admitted to bar, 1999, Ohio. *Education:* State University of Buffalo (B.A., Political Science; Psychology, 1993); University of Akron (J.D., 1999; LL.M., 2001). *Member:* Akron and Ohio State Bar Associations. ***PRACTICE AREAS:*** Estate and Business Succession Planning; Estate Administration; Probate; Tax; Guardianships; General Business; Corporate. ***Email:*** mdelgros@b-wlaw.com

SARAH B. CAVANAUGH, born Barberton, Ohio, 1979; admitted to bar, 2004, Ohio. *Education:* Pennsylvania State University (Public Relations, 2001); Villanova University School of Law (J.D., 2004). ***PRACTICE AREAS:*** Business Litigation. ***Email:*** sarah@b-wlaw.com

REPRESENTATIVE CLIENTS: Sky Bank; North Akron Savings Bank; Harware Components, Inc.

PRAVIN S. BHAKUNI
ATTORNEY AT LAW
AKRON, OHIO

(See Medina)

Tax, Small Business, Estate Planning, Domestic Relations, Probate.

BLACK McCUSKEY SOUERS & ARBAUGH
A LEGAL PROFESSIONAL ASSOCIATION

AKRON, OHIO

(See Canton, Ohio)

General Civil Practice in all State and Federal Courts. Administrative, Acquisitions, Antitrust, Banking, Bankruptcy, Commercial, Construction, Corporate, Divorce, Environmental, Estate Planning and Trusts, Estate Administration, Family Law, Government, Health Care Law, Insurance, Labor, Litigation, Oil and Gas, Personal Injury, Real Estate, Securities, Taxation Law, Workers' Compensation and Wrongful Death and Zoning.

KEVIN J. BREEN
Established in 1996

THE HERMES BUILDING
43 E. MARKET STREET
SUITE 202
AKRON, OHIO 44308
Telephone: 330-374-9444
Fax: 330-762-2936
Email: kevin.j.breen@sbcglobal.net
URL: http://www.home.att.net/~kevin.j.breen

Trial Litigation, Contracts Law and Business Representation including Small Business Law, Noncompetition Agreements, Employment Law, Franchise Law, Construction, Product Liability, Appellate Practice.

FIRM PROFILE: Providing "big firm" quality services at an affordable rate to the business community.

KEVIN J. BREEN, born Cleveland, Ohio, September 25, 1958; admitted to bar, 1986, Ohio; U.S. District Court, Northern District of Ohio; U.S. Court of Appeals, Sixth Circuit. *Education:* Marietta College (B.A., 1980); Cleveland Marshall College of Law (J.D., 1986). Recipient: American Jurisprudence Award for Excellence in Law of Evidence. Judicial Externship, Hon. Alvin I. Krenzler, United States District Judge, Northern District of Ohio. Associate, Roetzel & Andress, 1986-1989; Thompson Hine & Flory, 1989-1994.

REPRESENTATIVE CLIENTS: Alco Industries, Inc.; Command Management Services, Inc.; Efco Corporation; Lafarge Corporation; Progressive Stamping & Fabrication; Ohio Gasket & Shim Co.; Edward Jones & Co; Fox Tool Company; Inter-Tel, Inc.; Kemper Insurance Company; Russell Standard Corporation; Echostar Communications; U.S. Coaters, LLC.

BRENNAN, MANNA & DIAMOND, LLC
Established in 2000

75 EAST MARKET STREET
AKRON, OHIO 44308
Telephone: 330-253-5060
Fax: 330-253-1977
Email: lswalko@bmdllc.com
URL: http://www.bmdllc.com

Jacksonville, Florida Office: 76 South Laura Street, Suite 2110, 32202. Telephone: 904-366-1500. Fax: 904-366-1501.

Bonita Springs Office: 3301 Bonita Beach Road Suite 202, 34134. Telephone: 239-992-6578 Fax: 239-992-9328

Corporate Law, Business Law, Business Litigation, Mergers and Acquisitions, Finance, Commercial Lending, Taxation, Real Estate.

DAVID L. BRENNAN, born Akron, Ohio, July 5, 1931; admitted to bar, 1957, Ohio. *Education:* Kent State University; The Ohio State University (B.Sc., 1953); Western Reserve University (J.D., 1957); University of Akron (Awarded LL.D., 1985). Member: Society of Benchers, 1983; Brennan, Manna & Diamond, LLC. Chairman, Board of Directors, The Brenlin Group, 1976—. Trustee: Case Western Reserve University, 1990—; Ohio State University, 1993—. *Member:* Akron (Secretary, 1970-1972; Trustee), Ohio State and American Bar Associations. ***PRACTICE AREAS:*** Mergers and Acquisitions; Taxation; Corporate Law. ***Email:*** BrenlinInc@aol.com

ANTHONY S. MANNA, born Yonkers, New York, December 11, 1960; admitted to bar, 1986, Ohio; 1987, U.S. District Court, Northern District of Ohio, U.S. Court of Appeals, Sixth Circuit and U.S. Tax Court. *Education:* The Ohio State University (B.A., Accounting, cum laude, 1983); Emory University (J.D., 1986). Alpha Lambda Delta; Psi Kappa Psi. Recipient: Pace Setter Award, Ohio State University; Dealmaker Award, Association for Corporate Growth, 1997. Chairman and CEO, Janna Enterprises, LLC. Chairman, Signet Development, Ltd. Leadership, Akron, Ohio, 1992. Leadership Ohio, 1994. Director, Summa Health Systems. Director, Westfield Bank. Chairman, Executive Board St. Vincent St Mary High School. *Member:* Akron, Ohio State and American Bar Associations. ***PRACTICE AREAS:*** Corporate Law; Real Estate; Finance. ***Email:*** asmanna@bmdllc.com

JACK T. DIAMOND, born Cleveland, Ohio, September 10, 1956; admitted to bar, 1983, Ohio. *Education:* Xavier University (B.S.B.A., magna cum laude, 1978); Case Western Reserve University (J.D., with honors, 1983). Law Review, Case Western Reserve University School of Law (1982, 1983). Teaching Fellow, Research, Advocacy and Writing. Faculty Member and National Speaker, Medical Management Development Associates, Inc., 1994-1998, Health Care Forum Governing Board. Listed: The Best Lawyers in America; Who's Who in American Law; and the National Registry of Who's Who, Life member. Member and Board of Trustees: Northern American Indian Cultural Center; Member, Board of Trustees, Senior Workers Action Program; Case Western Reserve University's Professional Advisory Committee to the Law-Medicine Center; Member, Medical Committee: National Health Lawyers Association; American Academy of Healthcare Attorneys; Member, Area Agency on Aging Board of Trustee; President, St. Hilary School Board; Member, Coming Together Board of Trustees; Chairman of Board of Directors, Surgical Development Partners; Chairman of Board of Directors, Carnegie Healthcare Consulting; President of Brennan, Manna & Diamond, LLC. ***Email:*** jtdiamond@bmdllc.com

LEE S. WALKO, born Bedford, Ohio, May 1, 1964; admitted to bar, 1993, Ohio; 1995, U.S. District Court, Northern District of Ohio. *Education:* Muskingum College (B.A., magna cum laude, 1985); Case Western Reserve School of Law (J.D., cum laude, 1993). Certified Public Accountant, Ohio, 1988. Member: American Institute of CPA's; Ohio Society of CPA's; The Greater Akron/Canton Area Agency on Aging Foundation. Trustee, Mature Service. Trustee, Akron Aeros Charities. *Member:* Akron, Ohio State and American Bar Associations. ***PRACTICE AREAS:*** Corporate Law; Business Law; Real Estate; Mergers and Acquisitions. ***Email:*** lswalko@bmdllc.com

MATTHEW A. HEINLE, born Cuyahoga Falls, Ohio, May 7, 1970; admitted to bar, 1995, Ohio. *Education:* Miami University (B.S., 1992); The Ohio State University College of Law (J.D., 1995). Chairman, Board of Directors, Cuyahoga Falls General Hospital. Director: Great Lakes Health Alliance; Summa Health System. ***PRACTICE AREAS:*** Corporate Law; Health Law; Hospital Law. ***Email:*** maheinle@bmdllc.com

JOHN B. SCHOMER, born Jackson, Michigan, March 29, 1966; admitted to bar, 1991, Ohio; U.S. District Court, Northern District of Ohio; U.S. Court of Appeals, Sixth Circuit; U.S. Court of Appeals, Federal Circuit; U.S. Court of Federal Claims; U.S. Tax Court. *Education:* Brown University (B.A., 1988); Case Western Reserve University (J.D., 1991). Recipient, American Jurisprudence Award in Civil Procedure. ***PRACTICE AREAS:*** Business Litigation; Commercial Litigation; Real Estate Law; Real Estate Litigation; Business Law; Corporate Law; Environmental Law; Environmental Litigation; Federal Practice; General Trial Practice. ***Email:*** jbschomer@bmdllc.com

JOHN F. MARTIN, born Akron, Ohio, January 23, 1959; admitted to bar, 1984, Ohio. *Education:* Miami University (B.A., cum laude, 1981); The Ohio State University (J.D., 1984). Law Clerk to the Hon. Edward J. Mahoney, Ninth District Court of Appeals of Ohio, 1984-1986. Trustee, Akron Cascade Capital Corporation. Former Trustee and Treasurer, Akron Rotary Camp for Special Children, Inc. Member, Copley-Fairlawn Kiwanis. *Member:* Akron, Ohio State and American Bar Associations; National Association of Bond Lawyers. ***PRACTICE AREAS:*** Business Law; Corporate Law; Real Estate. ***Email:*** jfmartin@bmdllc.com

RICHARD W. BURKE, born Canton, Ohio, April 17, 1958; admitted to bar, 1983, Ohio and U.S. District Court, Northern District of Ohio. *Education:* The Ohio State University (B.S., magna cum laude, 1980); University of Akron (J.D., cum laude, 1983). Adjunct Law Professor, University of Akron Law School, 1983. Adjunct Professor, Masters of Taxation, University of Akron, 1991—. *Member:* Akron, Ohio State and American Bar Associations. (Also Member, Stark & Knoll, Co., L.P.A.). ***PRACTICE AREAS:*** Corporate Law; Business Succession Planning; Healthcare; Estate Planning. ***Email:*** rwburke@bmdllc.com

FRANK THOMAS SOSSI, born Cleveland, Ohio, June 27, 1952; admitted to bar, 1978, Ohio. *Education:* John Carroll University (B.A., 1974); University of Toledo (J.D., 1978); Case Western Reserve University, College of Law (LL.M., Tax Program, 1995). Certified Public Accountant, Ohio, 1986. Instructor, Tax Exempt Organizations, University of Akron, Masters in Taxation Program, 1996—. Adjunct Professor, Tax Exempt Organizations, Case Western Reserve University, College of Law, 2000—. Adjunct Professor, Justice Studies Program, Kent State University, 2002—. ***PRACTICE AREAS:*** Tax Law; Healthcare Law. ***Email:*** ftsossi@bmdllc.com

JOHN N. CHILDS, born Akron, Ohio, April 5, 1946; admitted to bar, 1974, Ohio. *Education:* University of Akron (B.S., 1971; J.D., 1974). Member: Akron Law Review. *Member:* Akron and Ohio State Bar Associations; American Health Lawyers Association. ***PRACTICE AREAS:*** Healthcare Law; Labor and Employment Law; Workers Compensation Law; Litigation. ***Email:*** jnchilds@bmdllc.com

FRANK A. LETTIERI, born Bari, Italy, February 6, 1947; admitted to bar, 1974, Ohio and U.S. District Court, Northern District of Ohio. *Education:* University of Akron (B.S.A., cum laude, 1969; J.D., 1974); New York University (LL.M., Taxation, 1975). Beta Alpha Psi; Delta Theta Phi. Listed in Best Lawyers in America, 1989-1999. Certified Public Accountant, Ohio, 1972. Member: Board of Trustees, University of Akron College of Business Alumni Association, 1988-2003; Business Alumni Board, University of Akron College of Business Administration, 1990-1994; University of Akron College of Business Administration Advancement Council, 1990-1994. *Member:* Akron, Ohio State and American Bar Associations; Ohio Society of Certified Public Accountants; American Institute of Certified Public Accountants. ***PRACTICE AREAS:*** Taxation; Estate Planning; Pension and Profit Sharing Plans. ***Email:*** falettieri@bmdllc.com

(This Listing Continued)

BRENNAN, MANNA & DIAMOND, LLC, Akron—Continued

SCOTT P. SANDROCK, born Massillon, Ohio, April 11, 1953; admitted to bar, 1978, Ohio; U.S. District Court, Northern District and Southern Districts of Ohio; U.S. Court of Appeals, Sixth and Federal Circuits; U.S. Court of Federal Claims; U.S. Tax Court; U.S. Court of International Trade; U.S. Supreme Court. *Education:* University of Notre Dame (B.A., with high honors, 1975); The Ohio State University College of Law (J.D., with honors, 1978). Paul Harris Fellow. Recipient: Silver Beaver Award, Boy Scouts of America; Distinguished Service Award, Canton Jaycees. Contributing Author: "The Biggest Legal Mistakes That Physicians Make and How to Avoid Them," Seak Publications, 2005; "Ohio Taxation," Matthew Bender, 1985. Author: "Trade Secret Protection and the Terminated Franchisee," ABA Franchise Law Journal, Summer, 1988; "The Evolution and Moderate Application of the Shop Right Rule," 38 Business Lawyer 953, 1983; "Tort Liability of the Non-Manufacturing Franchisor for Acts of its Franchisee," 48 University of Cincinnati Law Review 699, 1979. Past President: Rotary Club of Canton; Community Services of Stark County, Inc. Past Chapter Chairman, American Red Cross. Member, Leadership Stark County. Cited as authority at Hebel v. Sherman Equipment 92 Ill 2d 368 (Ill Supreme Court 1982). Neutral, Panel of Alternate Dispute Resolution, Northern District of Ohio. Listed: Who's Who in American Law; Ohio Super Lawyer. Commercial Arbitrator, American Arbitration Association. *Member:* Stark County (Member Committees on: Corporate Law; Disputed Fee); Ohio State (Member, Healthcare Section); and American (Member, Franchise Forum and Sections on: Business Law; Healthcare) Bar Associations. Ohio State Bar Association Foundation. ***PRACTICE AREAS:*** Health Law; Corporate Law; Commercial Litigation; Trade Practice Law. ***Email:*** spsandrock@bmdllc.com

---

GEORGE F. VOINOVICH, born Cleveland, Ohio, November 1, 1963; admitted to bar, 1990, Ohio and U.S. District Court, Northern District of Ohio. *Education:* University of Cincinnati (B.A., Accounting, summa cum laude, 1987); Case Western Reserve University (J.D., cum laude, 1990). Delta Theta Phi; Beta Gamma Sigma. CWRU Law Review. *Member:* Cleveland (Member, Real Estate Section) and Ohio State Bar Associations. ***PRACTICE AREAS:*** Corporate Law; Real Estate Law; Mergers and Acquisitions; Finance. ***Email:*** gfvoinovich@bmdllc.com

MICHAEL P. MORLEY, born Youngstown, Ohio, March 13, 1961; admitted to bar, 1989, Ohio and U.S. District Court, Southern District of Ohio; U.S. Tax Court. *Education:* Miami University (B.S.Ed., cum laude, 1982); University of Cincinnati (J.D.,1989); Capital University (LL.M., 1992). ***PRACTICE AREAS:*** Estate Planning; Probate Administration. ***Email:*** mpmorley@bmdllc.com

JOSEPH A. SHOAFF, born New Castle, Pennsylvania, June 15, 1962; admitted to bar, 1999, Ohio. *Education:* Youngstown State University (B.S.A.S., 1992); University of Akron (J.D., summa cum laude, 1999). Registered Respiratory Therapist, 1986—. Author: "State v. Nemeth: Equal Protection for the Battered Child," Akron Law Review, 1997 Vol. 31. *Member:* Ohio State and American Bar Associations. ***PRACTICE AREAS:*** Healthcare Law. ***Email:*** jashoaff@bmdllc.com

DARRIN R. TONEY, born May 27, 1968; admitted to bar, 1995, Ohio. *Education:* Delta State University (B.S., Business Administration, 1991); University of Akron Law School (J.D., 1995). Member: Akron Summit Community Action Agency Board (Board of Trustees); Big Brothers & Big Sisters of Greater Akron; Boy Scouts of America (Pathfinder District); Head of BSLA Adopt-a-School Program, 1994. *Member:* Akron and Ohio State Bar Associations; Akron Barristers Association (Vice President). ***PRACTICE AREAS:*** Labor and Employment Law; Business Litigation; Public Sector Law. ***Email:*** drtoney@bmdllc.com

PRISCILLA A. GRANT, admitted to bar, 1997, Ohio; 1999, United States Tax Court. *Education:* Hiram College, (B.A., 1994); University of Akron School of Law (J.D., 1997). Certified Public Accountant, Ohio, 2002—. *Member:* Ohio State and American Bar Associations; American Institute of CPA's. ***PRACTICE AREAS:*** Tax Law; Probate; Estate Planning. ***Email:*** pagrant@bmdllc.com

ERIC J. STECZ, born Akron, Ohio, September 30, 1971; admitted to bar, 1996, Ohio. *Education:* Johnson Carroll University (B.A., 1993); Case Western Reserve University (J.D., 1996). *Member:* Akron and Trumbull County Bar Associations. ***REPORTED CASES:*** Shaker Heights v. Hunte; Pauer v. Ertel. ***PRACTICE AREAS:*** Litigation. ***Email:*** ejstecz@bmdllc.com

JASON A. BUTTERWORTH, born Lebanon, Ohio, August 8, 1974; admitted to bar, 2000, Ohio. *Education:* The Ohio State University (B.A., Finance, 1996); University of Akron (J.D., cum laude, 2000; M.B.A., Finance, 2000). *Member:* Akron, Ohio State and American (Member, Real Property Section) Bar Associations; American Health Lawyers Association. ***PRACTICE AREAS:*** Corporate Law; Health Law; Real Estate. ***Email:*** jabutterworth@bmdllc.com

LEIGH A. MAXA, born Canton, Ohio, June 1, 1978; admitted to bar, 2003, Ohio. *Education:* Bowling Green State University (B.S., Business Administration, 2000); University of Akron School of Law (J.D., 2003). *Member:* Akron and Ohio State Bar Associations. ***PRACTICE AREAS:*** Litigation. ***Email:*** lamaxa@bmdllc.com

LISA MARIE CLARK, born Cleveland, Ohio, April 20, 1959; admitted to bar, 1989, Ohio. *Education:* Kent State University (B.S.N., cum laude, 1983); University of Akron (J.D.,1989). Registered Nurse, Ohio, 1983. *Member:* Cleveland, Ohio State and American Bar Associations.

STEPHEN J. YEARGIN, born Akron, Ohio; admitted to bar, 2004, Ohio. *Education:* Malone University (B.A., English, 2001); University of Arkon (J.D., 2004). ***PRACTICE AREAS:*** Litigation; Business Law; Corporate Law. ***Email:*** siyeargin@bmdllc.com

OF COUNSEL

NICKOLAS P. ANDREEFF, born Akron, Ohio, October 17, 1931; admitted to bar, 1961, Ohio. *Education:* University of Akron (B.A., 1952; J.D., 1960); Syracuse University (M.P.A., 1953). Pi Sigma Alpha; Omicron Delta Kappa. President, Edwin Shaw Hospital Foundation. Executive Director, Tri-County Regional Planning Commission, 1958-1960. President, Board of Trustees, 1980-1982 and Former Chairman, Akron Regional Development Board. Former Trustee, Edwin Shaw Hospital. Chairman, Private Industry Council of Summit and Medina Counties and the City of Akron, Ohio, 1983-1984. Member, Metropolitan Human Services Commission. *Member:* Akron (Member, Executive Committee, 1977-1978; President, 1986-1987), Ohio State (Former Member, Board of Governors, Labor and Employment Law Section) and American Bar Associations; National Association of Bar Foundations (Board of Trustees, 2003-2006). ***PRACTICE AREAS:*** Municipal Finance; Labor Law; Employment Law; Corporate Law; Business Litigation. ***Email:*** npandreeff@bmdllc.com

---

JAMES E. BRIGHTBILL

Established in 1987

ONE CASCADE PLAZA, SUITE 710
AKRON, OHIO 44308
Telephone: 330-374-0300
Fax: 330-374-0433
Email: jebrightbill@brightbill.org
URL: http://www.brightbilllaw.com

Family Law, Domestic Law, Divorce, Dissolutions, Child Custody, Bankruptcy, Personal Injury, Child Support, Auto Accidents, DUI, Criminal Law.

FIRM PROFILE: A family law office specializing in the need of the average family including divorce, dissolution, custody, child support, bankruptcy, auto accidents, DUI and criminal law.

JAMES E. BRIGHTBILL, born Loudonville, Ohio, October 9, 1949; admitted to bar, 1987, Ohio. *Education:* Ohio State University (B.S., 1971); University of Akron (J.D., 1986). Member, The Better Business Bureau. *Member:* Akron and Ohio State Bar Associations. ***PRACTICE AREAS:*** Family Law; Bankruptcy.

BROUSE McDOWELL

A LEGAL PROFESSIONAL ASSOCIATION

Established in 1919

388 S. MAIN STREET
SUITE 500
AKRON, OHIO 44311
Telephone: 330-535-5711
Toll Free: 800-837-5711
Facsimile: 330-253-8601
URL: http://www.brouse.com

Cleveland, Ohio Office: 1001 Lakeside Avenue, Suite 1600. Telephone: 216-830-6830. Toll Free: 877-837-5711. Facsimile: 216-830-6807.

Administrative, Bankruptcy, Business, Business Litigation, Commercial, Corporation, Creative Technologies, Creditors' Rights, E-Commerce, Environmental, Estate Planning, Federal Securities, General Civil, Health Care, Immigration, Insurance, Intellectual Property, Labor and Employment, Litigation, Mediation, Mergers and Acquisitions, Municipal and Bond, OSHA Compliance, Probate, Real Estate, Succession Planning, Tax, Trademarks, Trial and Appellate Practice, Venture Capital.

FIRM PROFILE: Brouse McDowell is particularly noted for its experience in the areas of business, commercial law, insurance recovery litigation, and environmental compliance and litigation. The firm has a strong business practice, assisting clients with public and private debt, equity offerings, securities law compliance, venture capital arrangements, labor/employment, joint ventures and mergers, acquisitions and divestitures. The firm has an equally strong commercial law practice, including creditors' rights and debtors' protection issues, loan workouts, restructuring strategies, and the implications of creditors' rights issues in leveraged buy-outs. In addition, the firm has a national health care practice, representing hospitals, physician practice groups, and other health care providers.

SHAREHOLDERS

RAJESH BAGGA, born New Delhi, India, February 5, 1964; admitted to bar, 1997, Ohio; U.S. District Court, Northern District of Ohio. *Education:* University of Pennsylvania (B.S.E.E., 1986); Case Western Reserve University (J.D., magna cum laude, 1997). ***LANGUAGES:*** Hindi. ***PRACTICE AREAS:*** Litigation. ***Email:*** rbagga@brouse.com

RICHARD F. BATTAGLINE, born Bell Gardens, California, August 9, 1945; admitted to bar, 1970, Ohio; U.S. Tax Court; U.S. District Court, Northern District of Ohio. *Education:* Ohio University (B.B.A., 1967); University of Notre Dame (J.D., 1970); New York University (LL.M., Taxation, 1978). ***PRACTICE AREAS:*** Tax; Successions; Estate Planning; Estate Administration. ***Email:*** rbattagline@brouse.com

DANIEL L. BELL, born North Hollywood, California, December 27, 1963; admitted to bar, 1990, Ohio; 1992, Pennsylvania; U.S. Court of Appeals, Sixth Circuit. *Education:* University of Texas at Austin (B.A., 1985); The University of Akron (M.A., Psychology, 1987; J.D., summa cum laude, 1990). ***PRACTICE AREAS:*** Litigation; Labor and Employment. ***Email:*** dbell@brouse.com

LISA S. DELGROSSO, born Akron, Ohio, August 12, 1970; admitted to bar, 1995, Ohio; U.S. District Court, Northern District of Ohio. *Education:* University of Akron (B.A., summa cum laude, 1992; J.D., magna cum laude, 1995). ***PRACTICE AREAS:*** Litigation. ***Email:*** ldelgrosso@brouse.com

CLAIR E. DICKINSON, born Saxton, Pennsylvania, May 6, 1951; admitted to bar, 1977, Ohio. *Education:* University of Pittsburgh (B.A., 1973); Cleveland State University (J.D., cum laude, 1977). ***PRACTICE AREAS:*** Real Estate; Labor and Employment; Litigation; Mediation. ***Email:*** cdickinson@brouse.com

ROGER D. EMERSON, born Akron, Ohio, July 22, 1958; admitted to bar, 1987, Ohio; U.S. District Court, Northern District of Ohio; U.S. Court of Appeals for the Federal Cir-

(This Listing Continued)

cuit; registered to practice before the U.S. Patent and Trademark Office. *Education:* University of Akron (B.S., 1981; J.D., 1986). ***PRACTICE AREAS:*** Intellectual Property. ***Email:*** remerson@brouse.com

STANLEY E. EVERETT, born San Mateo, California, November 25, 1944; admitted to bar, 1981, Ohio; 1982, Utah; U.S. District Court, Northern District of Ohio; U.S. District Court, District of Utah; U.S. Supreme Court. *Education:* Brigham Young University (B.A., summa cum laude, 1972; J.D., cum laude, 1980). ***PRACTICE AREAS:*** Business; Corporate. ***Email:*** severett@brouse.com

JOHN C. FAIRWEATHER, born New York, New York, April 24, 1952; admitted to bar, 1977, Ohio; U.S. District Court, Northern District of Ohio; U.S. Court of Appeals, Sixth Circuit. *Education:* University of Colorado at Boulder (B.A., with distinction, 1974); Case Western Reserve University (J.D., 1977). ***PRACTICE AREAS:*** Business Litigation. ***Email:*** jfairweather@brouse.com

JOHN C. FICKES, born Akron, Ohio, March 7, 1955; admitted to bar, 1985, Ohio, U.S. District Court, Northern District of Ohio and U.S. Court of Appeals, Sixth and Eighth Circuits. *Education:* John Carroll University (B.A., cum laude, 1977); University of Detroit (M.A., 1981); Case Western Reserve University (J.D., 1985). ***PRACTICE AREAS:*** Litigation. ***Email:*** jfickes@brouse.com

RICHARD H. HARRIS III, born Akron, Ohio, August 14, 1954; admitted to bar, 1980, Ohio. *Education:* Kenyon College (B.A., cum laude, 1977); University of Akron (J.D., 1980). ***PRACTICE AREAS:*** Successions; Estate Planning; Estate Administration; Tax; Real Estate. ***Email:*** rharris@brouse.com

JEFFREY T. HEINTZ, born Akron, Ohio, November 9, 1949; admitted to bar, 1975, Ohio; U.S. District Court, Northern District of Ohio; U.S. Court of Appeals, Sixth Circuit. *Education:* Ohio University (B.A., summa cum laude, 1972); University of Akron (J.D., 1975). (Certified in Business Bankruptcy Law by the America Board of Certification). ***PRACTICE AREAS:*** Banking; Bankruptcy; Creditors Rights; Real Estate; Business; Corporate. ***Email:*** jheintz@brouse.com

DAVID M. HUNTER, born Akron, Ohio, May 9, 1950; admitted to bar, 1975, Ohio; U.S. District Court, Northern District of Ohio; U.S. Court of Appeals, Sixth Circuit. *Education:* Princeton University (A.B., 1972); University of Akron (J.D., 1975); New York University (LL.M., Corporation Law, 1976). ***PRACTICE AREAS:*** Banking; Bankruptcy; Creditors Rights; Business; Corporate; Real Estate. ***Email:*** dhunter@brouse.com

LINDA B. KERSKER, born Akron, Ohio, October 21, 1947; admitted to bar, 1972, Ohio; U.S. District Court, Northern District of Ohio; U.S. Court of Appeals, Sixth Circuit. *Education:* Denison University (B.A., 1969); University of Michigan (J.D., 1972). ***PRACTICE AREAS:*** Litigation; Environmental; Labor and Employment. ***Email:*** lkersker@brouse.com

SALLIE CONLEY LUX, born Cincinnati, Ohio, November 9, 1952; admitted to bar, 1981, Ohio; U.S. District Court, Northern and Southern Districts of Ohio; U.S. Court of Appeals, Sixth Circuit; U.S. Supreme Court. *Education:* University of Cincinnati (B.A., magna cum laude, 1974; J.D., 1981). ***PRACTICE AREAS:*** Litigation; Labor and Employment. ***Email:*** slux@brouse.com

SHAWN M. LYDEN, born Cleveland, Ohio, September 26, 1959; admitted to bar, 1984, Illinois; 1995, Ohio; U.S. District Court, Nothern District of Illinois. *Education:* Denison University (B.A., magna cum laude, 1981); Case Western Reserve University (J.D., 1984). ***PRACTICE AREAS:*** Health Care; Business; Corporate. ***Email:*** slyden@brouse.com

MARC B. MERKLIN, born Akron, Ohio, February 10, 1960; admitted to bar, 1984, Ohio; U.S. District Court, Northern District of Ohio; U.S. Court of Appeals, Sixth Circuit. *Education:* Case Western Reserve University (B.A., magna cum laude, 1981; J.D., 1984). ***PRACTICE AREAS:*** Banking; Bankruptcy; Creditors Rights; Litigation. ***Email:*** mmerklin@brouse.com

DAVID F. RAYNOR, born Oceanside, New York, March 17, 1950; admitted to bar, 1976, Ohio; U.S. District Court, Northern District of Ohio; U.S. Court of Appeals, Sixth Circuit. *Education:* Ohio Wesleyan University (B.A., cum laude, 1972); Case Western Reserve University (J.D., 1976). ***PRACTICE AREAS:*** Business; Corporate; Tax; Labor and Employment. ***Email:*** draynor@brouse.com

ROBERT P. REFFNER, born Akron, Ohio, June 30, 1950; admitted to bar, 1977, Ohio. *Education:* University of Akron (B.S.E.E., 1973); Case Western Reserve University (J.D., 1977). ***PRACTICE AREAS:*** Business; Corporate. ***Email:*** rreffner@brouse.com

PAUL A. ROSE, born Garfield Heights, Ohio, December 26, 1956; admitted to bar, 1982, Ohio; U.S. District Court, Northern District of Ohio; U.S. Court of Appeals, Sixth Circuit; U.S. Supreme Court. *Education:* University of Oklahoma (B.A., with special distinction, 1979); The Ohio State University (J.D., with honors, 1982). ***PRACTICE AREAS:*** Environmental; Litigation. ***Email:*** prose@brouse.com

JOHN M. SKERIOTIS, born Akron, Ohio, July 6, 1965; admitted to bar, 1997, Ohio; U.S. District Court, Northern District of Ohio; U.S. Court of Appeals for the Federal Circuit; registered to practice before U.S. Patent and Trademark Office. *Education:* University of Akron (B.S., 1990; J.D., 1997). ***PRACTICE AREAS:*** Intellectual Property. ***Email:*** jskeriotis@brouse.com

MICHAEL A. SWEENEY, born Cleveland, Ohio, December 7, 1947; admitted to bar, 1976, Ohio; U.S. District Court, Northern District of Ohio; U.S. Tax Court. *Education:* Cleveland State University (B.A., 1971); Cleveland-Marshall College of Law (J.D., cum laude, 1976). ***PRACTICE AREAS:*** Successions; Estate Planning; Estate Administration; Tax; Business; Corporate. ***Email:*** msweeney@brouse.com

CHRISTOPHER F. SWING, born Beech Grove, Indiana, May 13, 1965; admitted to bar, 1991, Ohio; 1993, Florida; U.S. District Court, Northern District of Ohio; U.S. Court of Appeals, Sixth Circuit. *Education:* Kent State University (B.B.A., Finance, cum laude, 1987); Case Western Reserve University (J.D., 1991). ***PRACTICE AREAS:*** Litigation; Real Estate. ***Email:*** cswing@brouse.com

JERRY F. WHITMER, born Wauseon, Ohio, September 19, 1935; admitted to bar, 1960, Ohio; U.S. District Court, Northern District of Ohio; U.S. Court of Appeals, Sixth Circuit. *Education:* Kent State University (B.A., 1957); Case Western Reserve University (J.D., 1960). ***PRACTICE AREAS:*** Banking; Bankruptcy; Creditors Rights; Business; Corporate. ***Email:*** jwhitmer@brouse.com

THOMAS J. WIENCEK, born Geddes, New York, April 22, 1956; admitted to bar, 1985, Michigan; 1986, Ohio, Florida; U.S. District Court, Northern and Southern Districts of Ohio; U.S. Court of Appeals, Sixth and Seventh Circuits. *Education:* Colgate University (B.A., Social Sciences, 1978); Michigan State University (M.I.L.R., 1979); Detroit College of Law at Michigan State University (J.D., cum laude, 1985). ***PRACTICE AREAS:*** Labor and Employment; Litigation. ***Email:*** twiencek@brouse.com

---

HEATHER M. BARNES, born Columbus, Ohio, October 16, 1972; admitted to bar, 1999, Ohio and U.S. District Court, Northern District of Ohio; admitted to practice before the U.S. Patent and Trademark Office. *Education:* University of Akron (B.S., 1996); Ohio Northern University (J.D., 1999). ***PRACTICE AREAS:*** Intellectual Property. ***Email:*** hbarnes@brouse.com

TIMOTHY D. BENNETT, born Akron, Ohio, April 3, 1960; admitted to bar, 2002, Ohio; registered to practice before the U.S. Patent Agent and Trademark Office. *Education:* University of Akron (B.S., 1984; J.D., 2002). ***PRACTICE AREAS:*** Intellectual Property. ***Email:*** tbennett@brouse.com

KATE M. BRADLEY, born Oxford, Ohio, August 8, 1975; admitted to bar, 2001, Ohio; 2002, U.S. District Court, Nothern District of Ohio. *Education:* University of Akron (B.A., magna cum laude, 1997); Case Western Reserve University (J.D., cum laude, 2001). ***PRACTICE AREAS:*** Commercial; Business; Corporate; Bankruptcy; Insolvency; Commercial Contract Preparation and Dispute; Commercial Litigation; Creditors' Rights and Collections; Real Estate. ***Email:*** kbradley@brouse.com

NICHOLAS P. CAPOTOSTO, born Akron, Ohio, August 14, 1972; admitted to bar, 2003, Ohio. *Education:* Western New England College (B.A., 1998); University of Akron (J.D., 2003). ***PRACTICE AREAS:*** Litigation. ***Email:*** ncapotosto@brouse.com

DERON A. COOK, born Greenville, North Carolina, July 17, 1974; admitted to bar, 2000, Ohio; U.S. District Court, Northern District of Ohio; registered to practice before the U.S. Patent and Trademark Office. *Education:* University of Michigan (B.S., 1996); University of Wisconsin (J.D., 2000). ***PRACTICE AREAS:*** Intellectual Property. ***Email:*** dacook@vssp.com

BRANDON L. FORD, admitted to bar, 2004, Ohio. *Education:* Case Western Reserve University (B.S.N., 2001); Akron University Law School (J.D., 2004). ***PRACTICE AREAS:*** Commercial Law; Health Care. ***Email:*** bford@brouse.com

JOY D. KOSIEWICZ, born Parma, Ohio, June 15, 1973; admitted to bar, 1998, Ohio. *Education:* Allegheny College (B.S., Psychology, magna cum laude, 1995); Case Western Reserve University (J.D., cum laude, 1998). ***PRACTICE AREAS:*** Health Care; Real Estate. ***Email:*** jkosiewicz@brouse.com

AMANDA M. LEFFLER, admitted to bar, 2002, Ohio, U.S. District Court, Northern District of Ohio. *Education:* University of Toledo (B.A., 1999); University of Akron School of Law (J.D., summa cum laude, 2002). ***PRACTICE AREAS:*** Litigation. ***Email:*** aleffler@brouse.com

JOY AMES MOXON, born Perrysburg, Ohio, April 4, 1973; admitted to bar, 1999, Ohio. *Education:* Miami University (B.A., magna cum laude, 1995); University of Akron (J.D., summa cum laude, 1999). ***PRACTICE AREAS:*** Business; Corporate. ***Email:*** jmoxon@brouse.com

HANS A. NILGES, born Hanover, New Hampshire, September 22, 1973; admitted to bar, 2002, Ohio. *Education:* University of Toledo (B.A., 1998; J.D., 2002). ***PRACTICE AREAS:*** Labor and Employment. ***Email:*** hnilges@brouse.com

NICOLE SWEARINGEN-HILKER, born Steubenville, Ohio, September 7, 1977; admitted to bar, 2003, Ohio. *Education:* University of Akron (B.A., summa cum laude, 2000; J.D., summa cum laude, 2003). ***PRACTICE AREAS:*** Estate; Succession Planning; Probate. ***Email:*** nhilker@brouse.com

DANIEL A. THOMSON, born Cincinnati, Ohio, June 3, 1971; admitted to bar, 1998, Ohio and U.S. Court of Appeals for the Federal Circuit; U.S. District Court, Northern District of Ohio; registered to practice before U.S. Patent and Trademark Office. *Education:* Florida State University (B.S., Chemistry, 1993); Ohio State University (J.D., 1998). ***PRACTICE AREAS:*** Intellectual Property. ***Email:*** dthomson@brouse.com

JENNIFER D. TOWELL, admitted to bar, 2000, Colorado; 2003, Ohio. *Education:* Miami University of Ohio (B.S., cum laude, 1997); Ohio State University College of Law (J.D., 2000). ***PRACTICE AREAS:*** Litigation. ***Email:*** jfreimuth@brouse.com

KAREN S. WALTER, born Cleveland, Ohio, December 19, 1966; admitted to bar, 1996, Ohio. *Education:* Case Western Reserve University (B.S.Ch.E., 1989); University of Akron (M.S., Civil Engineering, 1992; J.D., cum laude, 1995). ***PRACTICE AREAS:*** Environmental. ***Email:*** kwalter@brouse.com

NORA J. WHITTEN, born Akron, Ohio, February 12, 1956; admitted to bar, 2001, Ohio. *Education:* University of Akron (B.A./B.S., magna cum laude, 1997); Akron University Law School (J.D., summa cum laude, 2001). ***PRACTICE AREAS:*** Business; Corporate; Corporate Counseling; Mergers and Acquisitions. ***Email:*** nwhitten@brouse.com

OF COUNSEL

ROBERT S. BURNS, born Akron, Ohio, 1960; admitted to bar, 1985, Ohio. *Education:* University of Akron (B.A., summa cum laude, 1982; J.D., summa cum laude, 1985; M.B.A., 1988). ***PRACTICE AREAS:*** Business; Corporate Law; Mergers and Acquisitions; Real Estate; Employment. ***Email:*** rburns@brouse.com

RICHARD T. CUNNINGHAM, born Akron, Ohio, March 19, 1930; admitted to bar, 1953, Ohio, U.S. District Court, Northern District of Ohio, U.S. District Court, Eastern District of Michigan, U.S. Court of Appeals, Sixth and Eleventh Circuits, U.S. Court of Appeals for the District of Columbia Circuit and U.S. Supreme Court. *Education:* Western Reserve University; Columbia University; University of Illinois (LL.B., 1953). Phi Delta Phi. Legal Officer, U.S. Navy, 1953-1956. Assistant Attorney General, State of Ohio, 1956. Trustee,

(This Listing Continued)

BROUSE McDOWELL, A LEGAL PROFESSIONAL ASSOCIATION, Akron—Continued

1979-1987 and Chairman, 1984-1985, Kent State University. Trustee, 1990-1995 and Chairman, 1993, Kent State University Foundation. *Member:* Akron (President, 1976-1977), Ohio State (Delegate, 1978-1979; Member, Executive Committee, 1988-1991) and American Bar Associations; The Association of Trial Lawyers of America; The Ohio Academy of Trial Lawyers; The Summit County Trial Lawyers Association. Fellow: American College of Trial Lawyers; Ohio State Bar Foundation; American Bar Foundation. ***PRACTICE AREAS:*** Litigation; Appellate Practice. ***Email:*** rcunningham@brouse.com

FRANK H. HARVEY, JR., born Akron, Ohio, October 10, 1930; admitted to bar, 1955, Ohio. *Education:* Princeton University (A.B., cum laude, 1952); Western Reserve University (LL.B., 1955).

JOSEPH M. HOLDEN, born Akron, Ohio, December 5, 1927; admitted to bar, 1952, Ohio. *Education:* Harvard College (A.B., 1949); Western Reserve University (LL.B., 1952). Order of the Coif. Member, Editorial Board, Western Reserve Law Review, 1951-1952. ***PRACTICE AREAS:*** Business; Corporate; Real Estate; Health Care. ***Email:*** jholden@brouse.com

OSCAR A. HUNSICKER, JR., born Akron, Ohio, July 13, 1922; admitted to bar, 1948, Ohio. *Education:* University of Akron (A.B., 1943); Western Reserve University (J.D., 1948). ***PRACTICE AREAS:*** Business; Corporate; Real Estate; Probate; Estate Planning.

CHARLES R. IDEN, born Newton Falls, Ohio, February 25, 1914; admitted to bar, 1938, Ohio. *Education:* Western Reserve University (A.B., 1936; LL.B., 1938).

FREDERICK K. LACHER, born Chicago, Illinois, August 16, 1920; admitted to bar, 1950, Ohio, U.S. District Court, Northern District of Ohio and U.S. District Court for the District of Columbia. *Education:* Carnegie Mellon University (B.S., 1942); University of Akron (J.D., 1950). ***PRACTICE AREAS:*** Intellectual Property. ***Email:*** flacher@brouse.com

MARY T. LINK, born Milwaukee, Wisconsin, October 1, 1960; admitted to bar, 1990, Illinois; 1994, Wisconsin (Not admitted in Ohio). *Education:* Marquette University (B.S., Nursing, 1982); New York University (M.A., Nursing Eduation, 1987); Loyola University of Chicago (J.D., 1990). ***PRACTICE AREAS:*** Health Care. ***Email:*** mlink@brouse.com

M. TERRELL MENEFEE, born Cleveland, Ohio, July 11, 1968; admitted to bar, 1999, Ohio. *Education:* Grove City College (B.A., cum laude, 1991); Cleveland-Marshall College of Law (J.D., summa cum laude, 1999). ***PRACTICE AREAS:*** Immigration Law; Real Estate; Business and Corporate. ***Email:*** tmenefee@brouse.com

FRANK E. QUIRK, born Cambridge, Massachusetts, November 24, 1932; admitted to bar, 1959, Ohio; 1999, Colorado. *Education:* The Ohio State University (B.S., 1957; J.D., 1958). *Member:* Akron Bar Association (Treasurer, 1973-1975; President, 1983-1984); Akron Bar Association Foundation (President, 1989-1990). ***PRACTICE AREAS:*** Business; Corporate; Business Litigation. ***Email:*** fquirk@brouse.com

JAY G. VOLK, born Hartville, Ohio, 1968; admitted to bar, 1993, Pennsylvania; 1998, Ohio, U.S. District Court, Northern District of Ohio and U.S. Tax Court. *Education:* Miami University (B.A., summa cum laude, 1990); Duke University (M.A., 1993; J.D., with honors, 1993); New York University (LL.M., 1997). *Member:* Ohio State (Member, Legislative Screening Committee) and American (Member, Tax Sections. Sections: Affiliated and Regulated Corporations; Regulated Investment Companies). ***Email:*** jvolk@brouse.com

All Attorneys are Members of the Akron, Ohio State, and American Bar Associations.

COUNSEL FOR: A. Schulman, Inc.; Americhem, Inc.; Bekaert Corporation; Goodrich Company; BP Amoco Corporation; Centers for Dialysis Care; Children's Hospital Medical Center of Akron; Electrolux; FirstEnergy Corp.; The Goodyear Tire & Rubber Co.; The Lubrizol Corp.; Myers Industries, Inc.; Sterling Jewelers, Inc.

(For complete biographical data on Cleveland personnel, see Professional Biographies at Cleveland, Ohio)

ROBERT H. BROWN

407 QUAKER SQUARE
120 EAST MILL STREET
AKRON, OHIO 44308-1721
Telephone: 330-376-3000
Fax: 330-376-2906
Email: rhbrownlaw@yahoo.com
Family Law, Domestic Relations, Divorce.

ROBERT H. BROWN, born Akron, Ohio, April 19, 1940; admitted to bar, 1965, Ohio; 1967, U.S. District Court, Northern and Eastern Districts of Ohio; 1970, U.S. Supreme Court. *Education:* University of Akron (B.S., 1962); University of Cincinnati (J.D., 1965). *Member:* Akron and Ohio State Bar Associations; Ohio Academy of Trial Lawyers; American Academy of Matrimonial Lawyers. (Certified Specialist in Family Relations Law, Ohio State Bar Association). ***PRACTICE AREAS:*** Family Law; Domestic Relations; Divorce.

BUCKINGHAM, DOOLITTLE & BURROUGHS, LLP

Established in 1913
50 SOUTH MAIN STREET
P.O. BOX 1500
AKRON, OHIO 44309-1500
Telephone: 330-376-5300;
Toll Free: 1-800-686-2825
Fax: 330-258-6559
Email: bdb@bdblaw.com
URL: http://www.bdblaw.com

Canton, Ohio Office: 4518 Fulton Drive Northwest, P.O. Box 35548, 44735-5548. Telephone: 330-492-8717. Toll Free: 800-811-2825. Fax: 330-492-9625.

(This Listing Continued)

Cleveland, Ohio Office: 1375 East Ninth Street, Suite 1700, 44114. Telephone: 216-621-5300. Toll Free: 888-843-2825. Fax: 216-621-5440.
Columbus, Ohio Office: 191 West Nationwide Boulevard, 43215-3506. Telephone: 614-221-8448. Toll Free: 888-686-2825. Fax: 614-221-8590.
Boca Raton, Florida Office: 2500 North Military Trail, Suite 480, 33431. Telephone: 561-241-0414. Toll Free: 800-682-2825. Fax: 561-241-9766.

Appellate, Bankruptcy, Business Law, Closely Held Companies, Commercial Law, Complex Litigation, Computer Law, Construction Law, Copyrights, Corporate Law, Creditors Rights, White Collar Crime or White Collar Criminal Defense, Employee Benefits, Employment Law, Environmental Law, Estate Planning, Family Law, Finance Law, Franchise, Health Care, Immigration Law, Insurance Defense, Intellectual Property, Labor, Land Use, Medical Malpractice Defense, Mergers and Acquisitions, Nonprofit Organizations Law, Patents, Private Foundations, Probate, Public Law, Publicly Held Companies, Real Estate, School Law, Securities, Service Marks, Succession Planning, Taxation, Toxic Tort, Trademarks, Trade Secrets, Trial, Trusts, Workers' Compensation, Zoning Law.

FIRM PROFILE: Established in 1913, Buckingham, Doolittle & Burroughs, LLP is a full-service law firm representing clients from the sole proprietor to multinational corporations, tax-exempt organizations, governmental bodies, charities, foundations and public organizations.

Buckingham is committed to finding practical solutions to legal problems. The breadth of its practice in all forums often enables the firm to avoid disputes by providing legal guidance before problems arise. When necessary, Buckingham represents clients in complex litigation and arbitration matters before courts, administrative agencies and arbitration panels. The focus is on meeting client objectives, maximizing recovery and containing costs.

Most important, the firm's attorneys understand what it takes, not only to run a business but to make it grow and prosper.

Buckingham, Doolittle & Burroughs, LLP is dedicated to maintaining the trusting client relationships developed through the years by offering common-sense advice and legal services of the highest quality.

GILLUM H. DOOLITTLE (1883-1973)
EDMUND BURROUGHS (1890-1981)
CHARLES F. SCANLON (1906-1985)
LISLE M. BUCKINGHAM (1895-1992)
JAMES C. HERNDON (1918-1998)

MANAGING PARTNER

PATRICK J. KEATING, born Warren, Ohio, October 2, 1954; admitted to bar, 1983, Ohio; 1985, U.S. District Court, Northern District of Ohio and U.S. Court of Appeals, Sixth and Eleventh Circuits. *Education:* Saint Mary's College; Kent State University (B.A., Philosophy, magna cum laude, 1978); University of Akron (J.D., magna cum laude, 1983). Akron Law Review. Listed: The Best Lawyers in America (1997 through 2006). Recognized as one of Ohio's Super Lawyers in the 2004 and 2005 Cincinnati Magazine, as voted by his peers. Member, College of Arts and Sciences Advisory Board, Kent State University. Deacon, Hudson Community Chapel. Board Member, Central States Bankruptcy Workshop. *Member:* Akron Bar Association (Member, Sections on: Commercial Law; Bankruptcy Law); Ohio State Bar Association (Member, Sections on: Litigation; Bankruptcy; Commercial Law); American Bankruptcy Institute (Advisory Board Member); National Lawyers Association. ***PRACTICE AREAS:*** Commercial Litigation; Creditors Rights; Bankruptcy. ***Email:*** PKeating@bdblaw.com

SHAREHOLDERS

RONALD C. ALLAN, born Chicago, Illinois, October 5, 1937; admitted to bar, 1965, Illinois; 1966, Ohio. *Education:* University of Michigan (A.B., 1959; J.D., 1965). Editor, *Ohio Business Organization Laws and Rules*. Past Director and Member, Executive Committee, Akron General Medical Center. Director and Secretary: Banks Baldwin Foundation; Akron Rotary Foundation; Greater Akron Musical Association Foundation. President Elect and Director, Akron Roundtable. Member, Executive Committee and Member, Advisory Board, WKSU. Member, Advisory Board, Tuesday Musical Association. *Member:* Akron, Ohio State and American Bar Associations. [CAPT., SC, USNR-R, retired]. ***PRACTICE AREAS:*** Corporate Law; Business Law. ***Email:*** RAllan@bdblaw.com

DAVID P. BERTSCH, born Akron, Ohio, May 12, 1953; admitted to bar, 1978, Ohio; U.S. District Court, Northern and Southern Districts of Ohio; U.S. Court of Appeals, Sixth Circuit. *Education:* The Ohio State University (B.A., 1975); Stanford University (J.D., 1978). ***PRACTICE AREAS:*** Personal Injury; Product Liability; Commercial Law; Insurance; Trial Practice. ***Email:*** DBertsch@bdblaw.com

ROBERT W. (ROB) BRIGGS, ESQ., born Cincinnati, Ohio, May 18, 1941; admitted to bar, 1966, Ohio; 1984, New York. *Education:* Duke University (B.A., 1963); The Ohio State University (J.D., 1966). Speaker, "The Fund for Our Economic Future," Cleveland City Forum. Recipient: 1st Annual H. Peter Burg Regional Vision Award by Team NEO; Community Service Award from the Great Trail Council of the Boy Scouts and the Northwest Summit County Rotary; Honorary Alumni Award from the University of Akron. Co-Trustee and Executive Director, GAR Foundation, Akron, Ohio. Vice Chair, The John S. and James L. Knight Foundation, Miami, Florida. Member, Board of Directors, Credit Committee, and Risk Management Committee: FirstMerit Corp. Member, Board of Directors, Akron Porcelain & Plastics Co. Member, Board of Directors, Akron Neonatology, Inc. Member, Board of Directors, Buckeye Oil Producing Co. Member, Ohio Venture Capital Authority. Chair, Fund For Our Ecconomic Future (Northeast Ohio Funders Group). Trustee, Musical Arts Association (Cleveland Orchestra). Trustee, Catholic Diocese of Cleveland Foundation. Trustee, Northeast Ohio Technology Coalition. Member, Law Enforcement Foundation. Chairman of the Board, National Inventors Hall of Fame. *Member:* Akron, New York State, Ohio State and American Bar Associations. [United States Air Force JAG, 1967-1970]. ***PRACTICE AREAS:*** Business Law; Nonprofit and Charitable Organizations; Private Foundations. ***Email:*** RBriggs@bdblaw.com

(This Listing Continued)

EDWARD V. BUEHRLE, born Red Bank, New Jersey, July 24, 1964; admitted to bar, 1993, Ohio. *Education:* Hillsdale College (B.A., 1987); The University of Akron Law School and the School of Business Administration (J.D., 1992; M.B.A., 1992). Member: Board of Trustees, YMCA Foundation; Child Guidance and Family Solutions. Trustee and Secretary, Cascade Capital Corporation. Speaker: "Using Letters of Intent"; "Successful Real Estate Closings"; "Avoiding Common Causes of Litigation"; "Collaborating Among Attorneys and Brokers" (Akron Area Board of Realtors Commercial and Industrial Forum) May 2005; "Ground Leases" (Cleveland State Bar Association); "Recent Case Reports and Legislative Updates" (Buckingham Annual Real Estate & Construction Seminar) 2001; "Updates & Strategies: Choice of Entities" (Buckingham Annual Real Estate & Construction Seminar) 2000. *Member:* Akron, Ohio State and American Bar Associations. ***PRACTICE AREAS:*** Real Estate; Business Law. ***Email:*** EBuehrle@bdblaw.com

PETER T. CAHOON, born Nyack, New York, July 22, 1953; admitted to bar, 1977, Ohio; 1978, U.S. District Court, Northern District of Ohio; 1993, U.S. Court of Appeals, Sixth Circuit. *Education:* New York University (B.A., 1974); University of Akron (J.D., 1977). Listed in The Best Lawyers in America, 2003-2006. Recognized by "Inside Business Magazine" in 2001 through 2004 as a Leading Lawyer in Criminal Defense in Northeast Ohio, as voted by his peers. Adjunct Instructor, Trial Advocacy, University of Akron School of Law, 1994—. *Member:* Akron (President, 2004-2005), Ohio State (Elected Member, Council of Delegates, 2005-2006 term) and American Bar Associations. (Certified as a Criminal Trial Advocate by the National Board of Trial Advocacy). ***PRACTICE AREAS:*** Criminal Defense; Appellate Practice; Family Law. ***Email:*** PCahoon@bdblaw.com

WILLIAM L. CAPLAN, born Warren, Ohio, July 31, 1951; admitted to bar, 1980, Ohio; 1995, U.S. Court of International Trade. *Education:* The Ohio State University (B.S., 1973; M.B.A., 1976); University of Cincinnati (J.D., 1980). Order of the Barrister. Listed, Best Lawyers in America. Adjunct Professor, University of Akron College of Law. ***PRACTICE AREAS:*** Corporate Law; Business Law; Environmental Law. ***Email:*** BCaplan@bdblaw.com

STEVEN A. DIMENGO, born Akron, Ohio, June 12, 1961; admitted to bar, 1986, Ohio. *Education:* University of Akron (B.A., magna cum laude, 1983; M.A., Taxation, 1986; J.D., cum laude, 1986). Akron Law Review. Certified Public Accountant, Ohio, 1987. Listed in The Best Lawyers in America, 2003-2006. Recognized by "Inside Business Magazine" as a Leading Lawyer in Tax Law in Northeast Ohio, as voted by his peers, 2001-2005. Recognized as one of Ohio's Super Lawyers in the 2004 and 2005 Cincinnati Magazine, as voted by his peers. Adjunct Professor, University of Akron, Masters in Taxation, Tax Department Head. Member of Tax Commissioner Zaino's Advisory Council. Chair, Taxation Committee, Ohio State Bar Association. ***PRACTICE AREAS:*** Tax Law. ***Email:*** SDimengo@bdblaw.com

DAVID L. DRECHSLER, born Beachwood, Ohio, September 2, 1963; admitted to bar, 1989, Ohio. *Education:* Ohio State University (B.S., 1986); Case Western Reserve University (J.D., cum laude, 1989). *Member:* Cleveland, Akron, Ohio State and American Bar Associations. ***PRACTICE AREAS:*** Commercial Litigation; Probate Litigation; Intellectual Property Litigation; Federal Litigation; Complex Litigation; Employment Litigation. ***Email:*** DDrechsler@bdblaw.com

JAMES L. FISHER, born Akron, Ohio, April 10, 1944; admitted to bar, 1971, Ohio. *Education:* The University of Akron (B.S.C.E., 1968; J.D., 1971). Registered Professional Engineer, Ohio, 1972. Listed in the Best Lawyers in America, 1995-1996; 1997-1998; 1999-2006. Recognized as one of Ohio's Super Lawyers in the 2004 and 2005 Cincinnati Magazine, as voted by his peers. Co-Author: "Doing a Good Deed," (Properties Magazine, April 2003). ***PRACTICE AREAS:*** Property Rights; Real Estate and Construction; Business. ***Email:*** JFisher@bdblaw.com

NICHOLAS T. GEORGE, born Akron, Ohio, August 8, 1944; admitted to bar, 1970, Ohio; U.S. District Court, Northern District of Ohio; 1975, U.S. Supreme Court; 1989, U.S. Court of Appeals, 6th Circuit. *Education:* University of Akron (B.A., 1968; J.D., 1970). Akron Law Review. Listed in the Best Lawyers in America, 2001-2005. Recognized as one of Ohio's Super Lawyers in the 2004 and 2005 Cincinnati Magazine, as voted by his peers. Co-Chairman, American Heart Walk. Board Member, Heart-to-Heart Communications. Vice President, Board of Trustees, Creutzfeldt-Jakob Disease (CJD) Foundation. Member, The Rotary Club of Akron. Board Member, American Heart Association Summit County Chapter. Board Member, The Rotary Club of Akron Camp for Special Children. *Member:* American Arbitration Association (Arbitrator). CEO/President of Firm. ***PRACTICE AREAS:*** Business Law; Real Estate. ***Email:*** NGeorge@bdblaw.com

CATHY CARTER GODSHALL, born Akron, Ohio, November 17, 1951; admitted to bar, 1976, Ohio. *Education:* Smith College; Kenyon College (A.B., magna cum laude, 1973); Case Western Reserve University (J.D., 1976). Phi Beta Kappa. Editor, Case Western Reserve Law Review, 1975-1976. ***PRACTICE AREAS:*** Corporate Law; Business Law; Nonprofit Tax Law. ***Email:*** CGodshall@bdblaw.com

STEPHEN M. HAMMERSMITH, born Columbus, Ohio, February 4, 1956; admitted to bar, 1981, Ohio. *Education:* The Ohio State University (B.A., 1978; J.D., with honors, 1981). Kappa Tau Alpha. Listed in The Best Lawyers in America, 1995 through 2006. *Member:* Ohio State Bar Association; National Association of Bond Lawyers. ***PRACTICE AREAS:*** Finance; Municipal Bonds; Commercial Law. ***Email:*** SHammersmith@bdblaw.com

DAVID W. HILKERT, born Akron, Ohio, July 15, 1949; admitted to bar, 1974, Ohio. *Education:* The University of Akron (B.A., magna cum laude, 1971); The Ohio State University (J.D., cum laude, 1974). Omicron Delta Kappa. ***PRACTICE AREAS:*** Trial Practice; Insurance Law; Environmental Law; Products Liability; Taxation. ***Email:*** DHilkert@bdblaw.com

DAVID KERN, born Ohio, November 8, 1960; admitted to bar, 1990, Ohio; 1992, Pennsylvania (inactive); U.S. District Court, Western District of Pennsylvania and Northern District of Ohio. *Education:* Tulane University (B.S., 1983); The Ohio State University (B.S.B.A., 1990); Capital University Law School (J.D., with honors, 1990); Georgetown University (LL.M. in Taxation, 1992). Leadership Ohio, 1996. Listed in The Best Lawyers in America, 2003-2006 and Ohio Super Lawyer 2003-2006. *Member:* American Bar Association; Ohio State Bar Association. ***PRACTICE AREAS:*** Mergers and Acquisitions; Tax Law; Business Law; Business Succession Planning; Estate Planning; Tax Exempt Organizations; Employee Benefits. ***Email:*** DKern@bdblaw.com

(This Listing Continued)

JAMES D. KRAUS, born Akron, Ohio, September 17, 1956; admitted to bar, 1983, Ohio. *Education:* Ohio Wesleyan University; University of Akron (B.A., 1979; J.D., cum laude, 1983). ***PRACTICE AREAS:*** Corporate Law; Business Law; Securities; Real Estate. ***Email:*** JKraus@bdblaw.com

DAVID J. LEWIS, born June 18, 1957; admitted to bar, 1987, Ohio. *Education:* Kent State University (B.B.A., Accounting, 1979); Cleveland Marshall College of Law (J.D., cum laude, 1987). Certified Public Accountant, Ohio, 1987. President, Akron Tax Club. Adjunct Professor, Masters of Taxation, University of Akron, Tax Practice and Procedures. Listed: The Best Lawyers in America, 2006 edition. Recognized as one of Ohio's Super Lawyers, in the 2004 and 2005 Cincinnati Magazine, as voted by his peers. President and Trustee, St. Herman of Alaska Eastern Orthodox Christian Church. Past Trustee, St. Thomas Eastern Orthodox Church. Past Superintendent, St. Thomas Eastern Orthodox Church's Sunday School. Current Youth League baseball coach. *Member:* Akron (Past Chair: Tax Section; Business and Corporate Law Committee), Ohio State and American (Member, Tax Section) Bar Associations; Ohio Society of CPAs; American Institute of Certified Public Accountants. ***PRACTICE AREAS:*** Tax Law; Mergers and Acquisitions; Corporate Dissolutions; Corporate Law; Business Law; Shareholder Disputes; Disciplinary Proceedings for Licensed Professionals; Tax Practice and Procedures; License Agreements. ***Email:*** DLewis@bdblaw.com

FREDERICK M. LOMBARDI, born Akron, Ohio, April 1, 1937; admitted to bar, 1962, Ohio; U.S. District Court, Northern and Southern Districts of Ohio; U.S. Court of Appeals, 6th Circuit. *Education:* The University of Akron (B.A., 1960); Case Western Reserve Law School (J.D., 1962). Delta Theta Phi; Pi Sigma Alpha. Member, Society of Benchers, Case Western Reserve University School of Law, 1989. Board Member: Case Western Reserve Law Alumni Association (1995-1998; 2003-2006); Summa Health System Foundation. Lifetime Trustee, Akron Golf Charities. Board Member: Downtown Akron Partnership; St. Hilary Parish Foundation. Panel Member: Federal Panel of Alternate Dispute Resolution Neutrals; Ohio Arbitration & Mediation Center, Inc.. Listed in: Who's Who in America; Who's Who in American Law; Who's Who in the World; Ohio Super Lawyers 2004-2006. *Member:* Akron (President, 1998-1999; Board of Trustees 1991-1994, 1997-2000) and Ohio State Bar Associations. Fellow, Akron Bar Association Foundation. ***REPORTED CASES:*** The Wayne Building & Loan Co. v. Yarborough, 11 Ohio St. 2d 195 (1967); In Re: Freed, 534 F.2d. 1235 (6th Cir. 1976); Ott v. Lectromelt Casting Co., et al., C.A. Nos. 9293, 9295 (9th Jud. Dist., Dec. 5, 1979); Richard v. Stahle, 70 Ohio App. 2d 93 (1980); Reiter Foods, Inc. v. State of Ohio, Common Pleas Court of Franklin County, Case No. 80-CV-08-4631 Great Northern Savings v. Ingarra, 66 Ohio St.2d 503 (1981); Fairway Development Company v. Title Insurance Company of Minnesota, 621 F. Supp. 120 (N.D. Ohio 1985); Nagy v. DeLeone, 193 F.2d 1292 (6th Cir. 1986). ***PRACTICE AREAS:*** Business Litigation; Real Estate; Construction Law; Computer Law; Unfair Competition. ***Email:*** FLombardi@bdblaw.com

ROBERT W. MALONE, born Ohio, March 31, 1951; admitted to bar, 1976, Ohio. *Education:* Mount Union College (B.A., magna cum laude, 1973); The Ohio State University (J.D., summa cum laude, 1976). Listed in The Best Lawyers in America, as one of the best tax lawyers in the country, 1989-1990; 1995-1996; 1999-2006. Recognized as one of Ohio's Super Lawyers in the 2004 and 2005 Cincinnati Magazine, as voted by his peers. Adjunct Professor, University of Akron College of Law, MBA and Masters of Tax Program. *Member:* Ohio State Bar Association (Past Chair, Tax Committee; Member, Ohio Limited Liability Company Statute Subcommittee). ***PRACTICE AREAS:*** Federal Taxation; Local Taxation; Business Law; Mergers and Acquisitions. ***Email:*** RMalone@bdblaw.com

CRAIG S. MARSHALL, born Akron, Ohio, February 21, 1960; admitted to bar, 1986, Ohio. *Education:* University of Akron (B.S., Accounting, 1982; Masters of Taxation, 1986; J.D., 1986). ***PRACTICE AREAS:*** Mergers and Acquisitions; Business Transactions; Corporate Law; Real Estate Development; Construction Law; Tax Law; Business Succession Planning; Estate Planning; Zoning, Planning and Land Use. ***Email:*** CMarshall@bdblaw.com

PATRICIA A. PACENTA, born Ohio, October 17, 1946; admitted to bar, 1977, Wisconsin; 1981, Ohio. *Education:* Marquette University (B.A., 1968; J.D., magna cum laude, 1977); The Ohio State University (M.A., 1969). Listed in The Best Lawyers in America (1989-2006). Listed among the top 100 Ohio Super Lawyers and the Top 50 Female Super Lawyers in 2004 and 2005 by Law & Politics, Inc., as recognized by her peers. Member, Past President, Akron Tax and Estate Planning Council. Ohio Super Lawyer designated by Cincinnati Bar Association. *Member:* Akron (Member, Probate Law Section) and Ohio State (Member, Probate Section) and American Bar Associations. American College of Trust and Estate Counsel. ***PRACTICE AREAS:*** Estate Planning; Probate. ***Email:*** PPacenta@bdblaw.com

ORVILLE L. REED, III, born Akron, Ohio, June 18, 1947; admitted to bar, 1973, Ohio. *Education:* Borromeo Seminary College of Ohio (B.A., magna cum laude, 1969); University of Notre Dame (J.D., with distinction, 1973). Listed in The Best Lawyers in America, 1989-2006. Recognized by "Inside Business Magazine" in 2001 and 2002 and 2004 as a Leading Lawyer in Business Litigation in Northeast Ohio, as voted by his peers. Listed among the Top 100 Ohio Super Lawyers in 2004 and 2005 by Law & Politics, Inc., as recognized by his peers. *Member:* American College of Trial Lawyers; International Society of Barristers. ***PRACTICE AREAS:*** Trial Practice. ***Email:*** OReed@bdblaw.com

JOHN L. REYES, born Steubenville, Ohio, January 31, 1953; admitted to bar, 1978, Ohio. *Education:* Ashland College; University of Akron (B.S., summa cum laude, 1975); Vanderbilt University (J.D., 1978). Adjunct Professor, Department of Public Administration, University of Akron, 1996—. President, July 2005 and Member, Akron Rotary Club. Member, Board of Trustees: St. Luke Lutheran Community Foundation, 2004—; Pastoral Counseling Service, 2003—; Lawrence School, 1997-2004. Chair, Long Range Planning Sub-Committee (1984-1986). Chair, Rules Committee (2003-2005). Member, Summit County Planning Commission (1981-1990; 2000-2005). *Member:* Stark County (Past Chair, Federal Courts Committee), Akron (Member and Past Chair, Federal Courts Committee and Member, Commercial Bankruptcy Section), Ohio State (Member, Bankruptcy, Banking and Commercial Law Committees) and American Bar Associations; American Bankruptcy Institute. ***PRACTICE AREAS:*** Civil Rights; Bankruptcy; Creditor's Rights; Toxic Torts; Public Law. ***Email:*** JReyes@bdblaw.com

(This Listing Continued)

BUCKINGHAM, DOOLITTLE & BURROUGHS, LLP, Akron—Continued

SUSAN C. RODGERS, born Akron, Ohio, January 6, 1966; admitted to bar, 1991, Ohio; U.S. Court of Appeals, Sixth Circuit; U.S. District Court, Northern District of Ohio. *Education:* The Ohio State University (B.A., 1988); University of Cincinnati College of Law (J.D., 1991); University of Oxford - New College, Oxford England. Trustee, Former President, Board of the Domestic Violence Project. Trustee, Vice President, Hartville Homes, Inc. Member, 9th Class, Leadership Stark County. *Member:* Stark County and Ohio State Bar Associations. ***PRACTICE AREAS:*** Labor and Employment; Business Law. ***Email:*** srodgers@bdblaw.com

GEORGE H. ROSIN, born Plainfield, New Jersey, March 7, 1951; admitted to bar, 1976, Ohio. *Education:* Wittenberg University (B.A., 1973); The Ohio State University (J.D., 1976). Phi Eta Sigma; Phi Alpha Delta (President, 1975-1976). Executive Vice President, Greater Akron Musical Association (Akron Symphony Orchestra), 2004-2006. ***PRACTICE AREAS:*** Workers Compensation. ***Email:*** GRosin@bdblaw.com

MARK J. SKAKUN, III, born Canton, Ohio, January 29, 1950; admitted to bar, 1974, Ohio. *Education:* University of Notre Dame (B.A., 1971); Case Western Reserve University (J.D., 1974). Law Clerk to Hon. Leroy Contie, Jr., U.S. District Judge, Northern District of Ohio, 1974-1977. Listed in The Best Lawyers In America, 1995-2006. Recognized as one of Ohio's Super Lawyers in the 2004 and 2005 Cincinnati Magazine, as voted by his peers. Life Member, 6th Circuit Conference. Member, Scanlon Inn of Court. Edited, Banks Baldwin Annotated "Ohio Rules of Civil Procedure". Contributing Author, Inside the Minds, Developing an IP Strategy for Your Company, chapter entitled "Winning Legal Strategies," (Aspatore Books), 2005. *Member:* Akron, Stark County, Ohio State, Federal and American Bar Associations. ***PRACTICE AREAS:*** Federal Litigation; Business Litigation; Patent Litigation. ***Email:*** MSkakun@bdblaw.com

MICHELLE A. SMITHERN, born Akron, Ohio, March 31, 1959; admitted to bar, 1986, Ohio, U.S. District Court, Northern and Southern Districts of Ohio and U.S. Court of Appeals, Sixth Circuit. *Education:* University of Akron (B.S., Political Science/Criminal Justice, cum laude, 1982; J.D. 1985). *Member:* Akron, Ohio State and American Bar Associations. ***PRACTICE AREAS:*** Family Law; Trial Practice; Insurance Defense Law. ***Email:*** MSmithern@bdblaw.com

THOMAS R. TROTTER, born Ohio, April 11, 1949; admitted to bar, 1975, Ohio; 2000, District of Columbia. *Education:* Ohio University (B.A., 1971); Tulane University of Louisiana (J.D., 1975). Order of the Coif. Listed in The Best Lawyers in America, 1996-1997; 1999-2006. Recognized as one of Ohio's Super Lawyers, 2004, Cincinnati Magazine, as voted by his peers. Past Member, Executive Committee, Secretary, Cascade Capital Corporation. Past Trustee, Past Chair Taxation and Legislation Committee, Greater Akron Chamber. Past Member, Board of Trustees, Secretary, Greater Akron Musical Association. Past Member, Board of Trustees, President, Secretary, Weathervane Community Playhouse. Member, Leadership Akron. Member, Leadership Akron Alumni Association. Past Member, Summit County Social Services Advisory Board. Past Member, Draftsman, Summit County Charter Review Commission. Past Member, Summit/Akron Solid Waste Management Authority Board. Speaker: "The Vanilla Deal," Summit County Port Authority; "1986 Tax Reform Act," Certified Public Finance Officer Program, Kent State University; "Industrial Development Bonds," Ohio DOD Community Improvement Corporation Seminar; "More Money for Your School District," Ohio School Boards Association Capital Conference; "Port Authority Financing," Summit County Port Authority. *Member:* Akron, Ohio State and American Bar Associations; National Association of Bond Lawyers. ***PRACTICE AREAS:*** Municipal Finance; Municipal Law; Commercial Finance; Finance; Public Finance; Tax Exempt Securities. ***Email:*** TTrotter@bdblaw.com

ELEANOR J. TSCHUGUNOV, born Warren, Ohio, January 6, 1955; admitted to bar, 1979, Ohio. *Education:* Heidelberg College (B.A., 1976); Universitat Heidelberg, Heidelberg, Germany; University of Akron Law School (J.D., 1979). Assistant Attorney General, State of Ohio, 1980-1987. Member, 1999— and President, 2003-2005, International Institute of Akron. ***PRACTICE AREAS:*** Workers Compensation; Immigration Law. ***Email:*** ETschugunov@bdblaw.com

LOUIS F. WAGNER, born New York, March 11, 1952; admitted to bar, 1984, Ohio; 1991, Federal District Court, Northern District of Ohio; 1992, U.S. Court of Appeals, Federal Circuit; 1993, U.S. Supreme Court; 2002, U.S. District Court, Southern District of New York; U.S. District Court, Eastern District of New York; U.S. District Court, District of Colorado; registered to practice before U.S. Patent and Trademark Office. *Education:* Washington and Jefferson College (B.A., magna cum laude, 1974); University of Pittsburgh (M.S., 1977); University of Akron (J.D., 1983). Adjunct Professor: Intellectual Property, Kent State University; Adjunct Professor: Electronic Business - Legal Issues, University of Akron. Speaker: Intellectual Property Seminar, Akron Bar Association, November 16, 2000; "Protecting Your Intellectual Property at Home, Abroad and in Cyberspace," Kent State University, October 24, 2001; "One Strike and ... Y'er OUT," Price Waterhouse Coopers Corporate Business Forum, September 14, 2004. Contributing Author, Inside the Minds, Developing an IP Strategy for Your Company, chapter entitled "Winning Legal Strategies," (Aspatore Books), 2005. Author, "Patents, Balancing Acts, and Tightropes" (BioExecutive International) June 2005. Author, "Domestic Patents - Questions You Should Ask Your Patent Attorney" (BioPharm International) August 2005. *Member:* Ohio State Bar Association; American Intellectual Property Association; Cleveland Intellectual Property Association. ***REPORTED CASES:*** JRB Co. v. Pemberton, Inc., 4 Fed. Appx. 920, (Fed. Cir. 2001); JRB Co. v. Pemberton, Inc., 91 F. Supp. 2d 1112 (6th Cir. 2000); Aspex et al. v. Sears, Roebuck & Co., 01 CV 4050 (S.D.N.Y. 2001); Aspex et al. v. BJ's Wholesale Club, Inc., Case No. 01 CV 4062 (S.D.N.Y. 2001); Aspex et al. v. Global Optical Resources, Inc., 02 CV 4082 (S.D.N.Y. 2002); Marchon et al. v. Global Optical resources, Inc., 02 CV 5323 (E.D.N.Y. 2002). ***PRACTICE AREAS:*** Intellectual Property; Intellectual Property Litigation. ***Email:*** LWagner@bdblaw.com

PATRICK J. WESCHLER, born Pittsburgh, Pennsylvania, September 27, 1956; admitted to bar, 1981, Ohio; 1985, District of Columbia. *Education:* Mercyhurst College (B.A., 1978); University of Virginia (J.D., 1981). Order of the Coif. Member, University of Virginia Law Review. Listed in The Best Lawyers in America, 2003-2006. ***PRACTICE AREAS:*** Estate Planning; Probate; Charitable Organizations Law. ***Email:*** PWeschler@bdblaw.com

(This Listing Continued)

PHILIP R. WIESE, born Ohio, March 16, 1966; admitted to bar, 1996, Ohio; 1997, U.S. District Court, Northern District of Ohio; 1998, U.S. Court of Appeals, 6th Circuit; 2001, U.S. Supreme Court; 2003, U.S. Court of Appeals for the Federal Circuit; 2005, U.S. District Court, Southern District of Ohio and District of Colorado. *Education:* College of Wooster (B.A., 1988); Ohio Northern University (J.D., 1996). Law Clerk: Hon. James S. Gwin, U.S. District Court, Northern District of Ohio, 1997-1999 and Hon. William T. Bodoh, Chief Judge, U.S. Bankruptcy Court, Ohio, 1996-1997. Judicial Extern, Walter H. Rice, Chief Judge, U.S. District Court, Southern District of Ohio, 1993. Research Specialist, U.S. Securities and Exchange Commission, Office of General Counsel, 1995. Adjunct Professor of Law, University of Akron. Ass't Basketball Coach, Kiwanis Basketball Program, Hudson, Ohio. Assistant Scoutmaster, BSA Troop 333, Hudson, Ohio (Eagle Scout). Member, Bd. of Dir., St. Andrews Homeowners Assoc. *Member:* Akron, Ohio State, Federal and American Bar Associations; American Bankruptcy Institute. Barrister, Scanlon Inn of Court (Summit County, Ohio). ***PRACTICE AREAS:*** Federal Practice; Complex Litigation; Intellectual Property Litigation; Bankruptcy; Commercial Litigation. ***Email:*** PWiese@bdblaw.com

DAVID W. WOODBURN, born Sacramento, California, June 30, 1971; admitted to bar, 1997, Ohio. *Education:* Miami University (B.S., 1993); The University of Akron (M.B.A.; J.D., 1996). Author: "Energy Act Provides Tax Opportunities for Developers," (Properties Magazine, September 2005); "House Bill 175-A New Way for Residential Contractors and Remodelers to Deal with Clients," (Properties Magazine, June 2005); Contributing Author: "Legal Perspectives" articles, Properties Magazine; "Intentional Interference with an Inheritance - An Option Beyond a Will Contest," Elder Law Handbook, 3rd Edition, Ohio State Bar Association. Vice-President, Akron Tax and Estate Planning Council; President, Board of Trustees: Habitat for Humanity of Summit County; Board of Trustees: First United Methodist Church of Akron. Rockynol Local Board. Member, Akron Jaycees. Member and Rockynol Philanthropy Chair, Rockynol Marketing Committee; Member, Miami University Alumni Recruitment Network. Co-author: "Doing a Good Deed," Properties Magazine, April 2005. Speaker: "Top 10 Ways to Make the Board of Realtors Contract Buyer Friendly," and "Top 10 Pitfalls to Avoid in Commercial Leases" (Akron Area Board of Realtors Commercial and Industrial Forum) May 2005. *Member:* Akron, Ohio State and American Bar Associations; Akron Tax & Estate Planning Council. ***PRACTICE AREAS:*** Estate Planning; Estate Administration; Guardianship; Real Estate; Probate Litigation. ***Email:*** DWoodburn@bdblaw.com

PARTNER

RICHARD P. ROHRICH, born Akron, Ohio, May 7, 1949; admitted to bar, 1973, Ohio. *Education:* Wittenberg University (B.A., summa cum laude, 1970); Duke University (J.D., with distinction, 1973). ***PRACTICE AREAS:*** ERISA; Employee Benefits. ***Email:*** RRohrich@bdblaw.com

OF COUNSEL

RICHARD A. CHENOWETH, born Akron, Ohio, July 9, 1925; admitted to bar, 1948, Ohio. *Education:* Harvard University (A.B., 1944); Western Reserve University (LL.B., 1948). Phi Delta Phi; Order of the Coif. Society of Benchers. President, Akron Bar Association, 1968-1969. ***PRACTICE AREAS:*** Corporate Law; Business Law; Estate Planning Law; Charitable Trusts and Foundations. ***Email:*** RChenoweth@bdblaw.com

CHRISTINE AMER MAYER, born Akron, Ohio, July 12, 1971; admitted to bar, 1996, Ohio, U.S. District Court, Northern and Southern Districts of Ohio and U.S. Court of Appeals, Sixth Circuit. *Education:* Duke University (B.A., cum laude, 1993); The Ohio State University (J.D., with honors, 1996). *Member:* Cleveland and Ohio State Bar Associations. ***PRACTICE AREAS:*** Corporate Law; Securities; Tax Exempt Organizations. ***Email:*** CMayer@bdblaw.com

DUANE MORRIS, born Barberton, Ohio, March 12, 1927; admitted to bar, 1953, Ohio. *Education:* Amherst College (B.A., 1950); University of Michigan (J.D., with honors, 1953). Phi Beta Kappa. ***PRACTICE AREAS:*** Property Rights; Real Estate. ***Email:*** DMorris@bdblaw.com

JEAN VAN NESS, born Evanston, Illinois, November 18, 1953; admitted to bar, 1979, Ohio; 1995, District of Columbia. *Education:* Yale University (B.A., 1975); University of Virginia School of Law (J.D., 1979). ***LANGUAGES:*** French. ***PRACTICE AREAS:*** Nonprofit and Charitable Organizations. ***Email:*** jvanness@bdblaw.com

ASSOCIATES

PEGGY S. BEISTEL, born Canton, Ohio, October 30, 1966; admitted to bar, 1999, Ohio. *Education:* Walsh College (B.A., Accounting, summa cum laude, 1996); Case Western Reserve University (J.D., cum laude, 1999; LL.M. in Taxation, 2000). Recipient: Outstanding Student in Accounting Award; Conviser Duffy Accounting Award; Richard Collier Award for Outstanding Tax Student. *Member:* Cleveland and Ohio State Bar Associations. ***PRACTICE AREAS:*** Business Law; Taxation; Employee Benefits. ***Email:*** pbeistel@bdblaw.com

JOSHUA S. BERGER, born Baltimore, Maryland, December 24, 1970; admitted to bar, 1997, Ohio; 2002, District of Columbia. *Education:* University of Pennsylvania (B.A., 1993); Case Western Reserve University (M.B.A., 1997; J.D., summa cum laude, 1997). Recipient, Arthur E. Petersilge Award, Wills and Trusts. Articles Editor, Case Western Reserve Law Review. *Member:* Ohio State and American Bar Associations; District of Columbia Bar. ***PRACTICE AREAS:*** Litigation; Antitrust. ***Email:*** jberger@bdblaw.com

MATTHEW R. DUNCAN, born Highland Park, Illinois, October 28, 1975; admitted to bar, 2003, Ohio; 2003, U.S. District Court, Northern District of Ohio. *Education:* Wheaton College (B.A., Political Science and History, summa cum laude, 1998); Case Western Reserve University (J.D., cum laude, 2003). *Member:* Akron, Ohio State and American Bar Associations. ***PRACTICE AREAS:*** Litigation; Bankruptcy. ***Email:*** mduncan@bdblaw.com

CHRISTOPHER C. ESKER, born Ohio; admitted to bar, 1988, Ohio; 1996, U.S. District Court, Northern District of Ohio; 2003, U.S. District Court, Southern District of Ohio; 1997, U.S. Court of Appeals, Sixth Circuit; 2001, U.S. Supreme Court. *Education:* University of Akron (B.A., 1983; J.D., 1988). Phi Alpha Delta. Acting Case and Comment Editor,

(This Listing Continued)

Akron Law Review, 1988. Member, Community Advisors for the Reserve, Copley, Ohio, 1996-2000. Board Member, Copley Township Board of Zoning Appeals, 2002—. Member, Copley Township Audit Committee, 2001—. Board Member, St. Hilary School Board, 1999-2004. Board Member, 2003— and Second Vice President, 2005—, Weathervane Community Playhouse. Member, 1995— and President, 2003-2004, Summit County Farm Bureau Board of Trustees. *Member:* Akron, Ohio State (Member, Litigation Board of Governors, 1999-2004) and American Bar Associations. ***REPORTED CASES:*** Shealy v. Caldwell (C.A. 6, 2001), 2001 U.S. App. LEXIS 17181; Gottfried v. Medial Planning Services (C.A. 6, 1998), 1998 U.S. App. LEXIS 7483; Gunther v. Hilton (C.A. 6, 1997), 1997 U.S. App. LEXIS 40797; Ellwood Engineered Castings v. Zaino (2003), 98 Ohio St.3d 424, 2003-Ohio-1812; Shugarman Surgical Supply v. Zaino (2002), 97 Ohio St.3d 183, 2002-Ohio-5809; Selander v. Erie Ins. Co. (1999), 85 Ohio St.3d 541, 1999-Ohio-287; State ex rel. Beacon Journal Publ'g Co. v. Whitmore (1998), 83 Ohio St. 3d 61, 1998-Ohio-180; State ex rel. Hunter v. Summit County Human Resource Cmm'n (1998), 81 Ohio St. 3d 450, 1998-Ohio-614; State ex rel. Strategic Capital Investors v. McCarthy (1997), 126 Ohio App. 3d 237. ***PRACTICE AREAS:*** Trial Practice; Appellate Practice; Complex Litigation; Products Liability; Intentional Torts. ***Email:*** CEsker@bdblaw.com

DAVID J. HRINA, born Youngstown, Ohio, June 5, 1970; admitted to bar, 2000, Ohio; 2003, U.S. District Court, Northern District of Ohio; registered to practice before the U.S. Patent & Trademark Office. *Education:* Youngstown State University (B.E.C.E., 1993; M.S.C.E., 1995); University of Akron School of Law (J.D., magna cum laude, 2000). Author: "The Future of IOLTA: Has the Death Knell Been Sounded for Mandatory IOLTA Programs," 32 Akron Law Review 301, 1999. Licensed Patent Attorney; Recognized as one of Ohio's Super Lawyers - Rising Stars, in the 2005 CIncinnati Magazine, as voted by his peers. *Member:* Akron, Mahoning County, Ohio State and American Bar Associations. ***PRACTICE AREAS:*** Business Law; Intellectual Property; Environmental Law. ***Email:*** DHrina@bdblaw.com

CLAY KENNETH KELLER, born November 22, 1969; admitted to bar, 2000, Ohio; 2001, U.S. District Court, Northern and Southern Districts of Ohio; 2002, U.S. Court of Appeals, Sixth Circuit. *Education:* University of Wisconsin-LaCrosse (B.S., 1997); University of Notre Dame Law School (J.D., 2000). *Member:* Ohio State and American Bar Associations; American Bankruptcy Institute. ***PRACTICE AREAS:*** Commercial Litigation; Bankruptcy. ***Email:*** CKeller@bdblaw.com

MICHAEL J. MATASICH, born Tallmadge, Ohio; admitted to bar, 2004, Ohio; 2005, U.S. District Court, Northern District of Ohio. *Education:* University of Akron (B.A., Political Science, 2000); University of Akron School of Law (J.D., 2004). Recipient, CALI Excellence for the Future Award in Corporations. Served in many capacities in law school including: 2003 Saul Lefkowitz Intellectual Property Moot Court Regional Competition in Chicago; Member, Phi Delta Phi, International Legal Fraternity, Magister (2003-2004); Member, National Committee on Credentials, Rules, and Constitutional Amendments (2003); Member, Student Bar Association. *Member:* Akron, Ohio State and American Bar Associations. ***PRACTICE AREAS:*** Litigation. ***Email:*** mmatasich@bdblaw.com

HILLARY B. McLEAN, born Cleveland, Ohio, November 1, 1971; admitted to bar, 2004, Ohio. *Education:* John Carroll University (B.A., cum laude, 1995); The University of Akron (J.D., summa cum laude, 2004). Member, Law Review 2002-2004. Recipient: Magistrate Karam Award, 2001; Soroptimist Award, 2001; Akron Bar Foundation Scholarship, 2001-2004; American Association of University Women Career Development Grant, 2002-2003. Adjunct Professor, Legal Analysis, Research, and Writing, The University of Akron School of Law. Cuyahoga County Court of Common Pleas, Juvenile Division, Probation Deartment, 1995-2004. *Member:* Akron, Cleveland, Cuyahoga County, Ohio State and American Bar Associations. ***PRACTICE AREAS:*** Trusts and Estates. ***Email:*** hmclean@bdblaw.com

HENRY (HANK) F. MEYER, born 1962; admitted to bar, 1999, Ohio. *Education:* University of Akron (B.S., Political Science/Criminal Justice, 1985); Akron University Law School (J.D., 2000). Assistant Editor, Akron Law Review, 1999-2000. Former Prosecutor: City of New Philadelphia, Ohio; Village of Baltic, Ohio; Village of Sugarcreek, Ohio; Village of Barnhill, Ohio; Village of Parrel, Ohio; Village of Roswell, Ohio. Former Prosecutor and Former Law Director/Solicitor, Village of Zoar, Ohio. ***PRACTICE AREAS:*** Litigation; Family Law; Estate Planning; Probate; Juvenile Law; Consumer Law.

MARIETTA M. PAVLIDIS, born Warren, Ohio, July 31, 1971; admitted to bar, 1997, Ohio; 2001, U.S. District Court, Northern District of Ohio. *Education:* Kent State University (B.A., cum laude, 1994); Cleveland-Marshall College of Law, Cleveland State University (J.D., 1997). *Member:* Trumbull County, Akron and Ohio State Bar Associations. ***LANGUAGES:*** Greek. ***PRACTICE AREAS:*** Family Law; Workers Compensation. ***Email:*** mpavlidis@bdblaw.com

ADAM R. VAN REES, born Des Moines, Iowa, November 22, 1976; admitted to bar, 2002, Ohio; 2003, U.S. District Court, Northern District of Ohio. *Education:* Ohio University (B.B.A., Finance, cum laude, 1999); Case Western Reserve University School of Law (J.D., 2002). NFL Certified Contract Advisor. Ohio Certified Sports Agent. *Member:* Mahoning County, Akron and Ohio State Bar Associations. ***PRACTICE AREAS:*** Business Law; Entertainment Law; Sports Law. ***Email:*** avanrees@bdblaw.com

REPRESENTATIVE CLIENTS: Akron Metropolitan Housing Authority; Alpha Phi Alpha Homes, Inc.; Audio Technica US Inc.; ASB Industries, Inc.; City of Akron; Campbell and Associates, Inc.; Dellagnese Companies; Direct Healthcare Supply; FedEx Supply Chain Services, Inc.; Frontier Fruit & Nut/Cookie Express; GAR Foundation; Gemco Medical, Inc.; The Goodyear Tire & Rubber Company; Jeter Systems Corporation; The J.M. Smucker Company; Lexi-Comp, Inc.; Mercury Plastics; MetroParks Serving Summit County; Mosley Companies; The National Inventors Hall of Fame; Panther II Transportation; Seese/Sveda Construction Company; State Farm Mutual; Summa Health System; Summit County Port Authority; County of Summit; Testa Builders Inc.; Yellow Roadway Corporation; Yoder Brothers.

CALLAHAN, GREVEN, RILLEY AND SINN, LLC

7 WEST BOWERY STREET, SUITE 907
AKRON, OHIO 44308
Telephone: 330-376-9260
Fax: 330-376-9307
URL: http://www.cgrslaw.com

Criminal Law, DUI, Felonies, Driving While Intoxicated, Drug Crimes, Juvenile Crimes, Parole and Probation, Traffic Violations, Personal Injury, Domestic, Juvenile Law, Divorce, Family Law.

MICHAEL T. CALLAHAN, born December 16, 1957; admitted to bar, 1982, Ohio; 1983, U.S. District Court, Northern District of Ohio. *Education:* Grove City College (B.A., 1979); University of Akron (J.D., 1982). Recipient: First Place, University of Akron Mock Trial Competition, 1982; Captain, University of Akron National Mock Trial Team, 1982; Dennis & Co., Inc. Award, 1982. Adjunct Professor, Criminal Law for Police Officers, University of Akron, 1992-2000. Prosecuting Attorney, Summit County, 1999-2001. Judge: Summit County Common Pleas Court, 1995-1999; Akron Municipal Court, 1993-1995. Assistant Prosecuting Attorney, Summit County, 1986-1993. Court Administrator, Akron Municipal Court, 1983-1986. *Member:* Akron and Ohio State Bar Associations; American Judges Association; Akron Metropolitan Judges Association; Ohio Judicial Conference; Association of Municipal/County Judges of Ohio. ***PRACTICE AREAS:*** Criminal; Driving While Intoxicated; Litigation; Personal Injury; Probate; Business Law; Liquor Licensing; Administrative Law. ***Email:*** judgemtc@aol.com

JOHN WILLIAM GREVEN, born Elmira, New York, May 29, 1964; admitted to bar, 1994, Ohio; 2001, U.S. District Court, Northern District of Ohio. *Education:* State University of New York, Fredonia (B.S., 1986); Elmira College, New York (M.S.Ed., 1994); Cleveland-Marshall College of Law (J.D., cum laude, 1994). Assistant County Prosecutor, Summit County, OH, 1995-2001. *Member:* Akron and Ohio State Bar Associations. ***PRACTICE AREAS:*** Criminal Law; Driving While Intoxicated; Personal Injury. ***Email:*** greven214@aol.com

SCOTT A. RILLEY, born Akron, Ohio, September 30, 1966; admitted to bar, 1993, Ohio; 1995, U.S. District Court, Northern District of Ohio. *Education:* University of Akron (B.A., cum laude, 1990); Case Western Reserve University (J.D., 1993). Assistant Summit County Prosecutor, 1995-2001. *Member:* Akron and Ohio State Bar Associations; Ohio Academy of Trial Lawyers'; The Association of Trial Lawyers of America; Summit County Trial Lawyers Association. ***PRACTICE AREAS:*** Personal Injury; Criminal Law; Driving While Intoxicated. ***Email:*** rilley-law@hotmail.com

JONATHAN TODD SINN, born Youngstown, Ohio, September 11, 1968; admitted to bar, 1994, Ohio; 2000, U.S. District Court, Northern District of Ohio. *Education:* Youngstown State University (B.A., 1993); University of Akron (J.D., 1994). ***PRACTICE AREAS:*** Criminal Law; Driving While Intoxicated; Traffic Violations.

DAVIS & YOUNG

A Legal Professional Association
NATIONAL CITY CENTER
ONE CASCADE PLAZA, SUITE 800
AKRON, OHIO 44308
Telephone: 330-376-1717
Fax: 330-376-1797
URL: http://www.davisyoung.com

Cleveland, Ohio Office: 1700 Midland Building, Suite 1700, 44115. Telephone: 216-348-1700. Fax: 216-621-0602.
Youngstown, Ohio Office: The Commerce Building, 201 East Commerce Street, Suite 100, 44503. Telephone: 330-743-1717.
Warren, Ohio Office: 108 Main Street, SW, Suite 1000, 44481. Telephone: 330-373-1717. Fax: 330-395-0610.

General Trial and Appellate Practice, Products Liability, General Tort, Insurance Coverage, Personal Injury, Toxic Torts, Complex Mass Tort Claims, Legal and Medical Malpractice, Municipal Liability, Civil Rights, Employment Practices Liability, and Environmental and Commercial Liability.

FIRM PROFILE: Many of Davis & Young's attorneys are members of the following organizations: Akron, Portage County and Ohio State Bar Associations, Defense Research Institute (DRI), and Ohio Association of Civil Trial Attorneys (OACTA).

GREGORY H. COLLINS, admitted to bar, 1988, Ohio. *Education:* Hiram College (B.A., 1985); Case Western Reserve University (J.D., 1988). ***Email:*** greg@dyakron.com

DAVID G. UTLEY, admitted to bar, 1987, Ohio. *Education:* Kent State University (B.A., 1984); Case Western Reserve University (J.D., 1987). ***Email:*** david@dyakron.com

ANN MARIE O'BRIEN, admitted to bar, 1991, Ohio. *Education:* Hiram College (B.A., 1987); Kent State University (Honors College 1987); University of Akron (J.D., 1991). ***Email:*** annmarie@dyakron.com

JAMES PATRICK SALAMONE, admitted to bar, 2000, Ohio. *Education:* Mount Union College (B.A., 1995); John Marshall School of Law (J.D., 2000). Staff Attorney, Lake County Court of Common Pleas, 2000-2002. *Member:* Lake County Board of Arbitration. ***Email:*** jim@dyakron.com

DANIEL K. DISMUKE

P.O. BOX 995
AKRON, OHIO 44223
Telephone: 330-762-0080
Fax: 330-762-0720
Email: dismuke@attorneydismuke.com
URL: http://www.neohiorealestatelawyer.com

Real Estate, Business Law, Litigation, Trusts and Estates, Family Law.

DANIEL K. DISMUKE, born Akron, Ohio, August 24, 1977; admitted to bar, 2001, Ohio; 2004, U.S. District Court, Northern District of Ohio. *Education:* Pennsylvania State University (B.A., Political Science, 1998); University of Akron (J.D., 2001). Deputy Director of Law, City of Stow, Ohio, 2004-2005. Assistant Solicitor, Village of Mantua, Ohio, 2002-2004. *Member:* Akron and Ohio State Bar Associations. ***PRACTICE AREAS:*** Real Estate (50%); Business Law (20%); Litigation (10%); Trusts and Estates (10%); Family Law (10%).

JOHN M. DOHNER

407 QUAKER SQUARE
120 EAST MILL STREET
AKRON, OHIO 44308
Telephone: 330-376-6300
Fax: 330-376-2906
Email: dohnerlaw@aol.com
URL: http://www.lawyers.com/johndohnerlaw

Trial Practice, Divorce, Dissolution, Child Custody, Child Support, Business Valuation for Divorce, Adoption, Premarital Agreements, Special Education Law.

JOHN M. DOHNER, born Akron, Ohio, June 9, 1955; admitted to bar, 1986, Ohio and U.S. District Court, Northern District of Ohio; 1991, U.S. Court of Appeals, Sixth Circuit; 1997, U.S. Supreme Court. *Education:* University of Akron (B.S., 1980; J.D., 1986). Judicial Law Clerk, Hon. Judge Frank J. Bayer, 1984-1985. Fellow, American Academy of Matrimonial Lawyers. (Certified Specialist in Family Relations Law, Ohio State Bar Association). ***PRACTICE AREAS:*** Trial Practice; Divorce; Child Custody; Child Support; Business Valuation for Divorce; Adoption Law; Premarital Agreements; Special Education.

ELK & ELK CO., L.P.A.

AKRON, OHIO

(See Cleveland)

Automobile Accidents, Product Defects, Nursing Home Neglect, Medical Malpractice, Personal Injury.

FORTNEY & KLINGSHIRN

Established in 1993
4040 EMBASSY PARKWAY
SUITE 280
AKRON, OHIO 44333
Telephone: 330-665-5445
Telefax: 330-665-5446
Email: fortney@fklaborlaw.com
URL: http://www.fklaborlaw.com

Employment and Construction Law, Commercial Litigation. Trial and appellate practice in all state and federal courts. Construction practice includes claims and disputes, competitive bidding, and mechanics liens involving commercial projects. Employment practice includes discrimination, retaliation and harassment claims, Family Medical Leave Act, ERISA, Fair Labor Standard Act and non-competition litigation.

FIRM PROFILE: Fortney & Klingshirn was formed in 1993 with the mission of providing the highest caliber litigation, employment and construction practice to our clients with small firm efficiency and flexibility.

MEMBERS OF FIRM

MICHAEL L. FORTNEY, born Avon Lake, Ohio, 1955; admitted to bar, 1986, Ohio; U.S. District Court, Northern District of Ohio; U.S. Court of Appeals, Sixth and Federal Circuits. *Education:* Miami University; University of Tennessee (B.S., 1979); Cleveland State University (J.D., summa cum laude, 1985). Editor, Cleveland State Law Review. Member, ADR Panel of Neutrals for the Federal Court, Northern District of Ohio. *Member:* Medina, Ohio State and American Bar Associations; American Arbitration Association (Arbitrator, Employment and Construction Panel); NASD. ***PRACTICE AREAS:*** Construction Law; Labor and Employment Law; Alternative Dispute Resolution. ***Email:*** fortney@fklaborlaw.com

NEIL E. KLINGSHIRN, born Avon Lake, Ohio, 1961; admitted to bar, 1986, Ohio; U.S. District Courts, Northern and Southern Districts of Ohio; U.S. Court of Appeals, Sixth Circuit. *Education:* Kent State University (B.B.A., summa cum laude, in Accounting, 1983); Ohio State University (J.D, 1986). Order of the Coif. Articles Editor, Ohio State Law Journal, 1985. Editor, Employment Law Newsletter, Ohio State Bar Association. Chair, Hudson Personnel Advisory and Appeals Board. *Member:* Cleveland and Ohio State (Member, Board of Governors, Labor and Employment Law Section) Bar Associations; National Employment Lawyers Association; Ohio Employment Lawyers Association. (Certified Specialist, Labor and Employment Law, Ohio State Bar Association). ***PRACTICE AREAS:*** Employment Discrimination; Retaliatory Discharge; Non-Competition Agreements; Family and Medical Leave Act; ERISA; Fair Labor Standards. ***Email:*** neil@fklaborlaw.com

GOLDMAN & ROSEN, LTD.

Established in 1974
11 SOUTH FORGE STREET
AKRON, OHIO 44304
Telephone: 330-376-8336
Telecopier: 330-376-2522
Email: Goldman@Goldman-Rosen.com

Business Corporation, Bankruptcy, Civil Litigation, Criminal, Family Law, Divorce, Child Support, Visitation Rights, Adoption Law, Alimony, General Practice, Business, Civil Rights, Employment, Estate Planning, Probate, Commercial, Wills, Criminal Law, Driving While Intoxicated, Drug Crimes, Sexual Assault, Homicide, Inheritance, Bankruptcy Chapter 7, Bankruptcy Chapter 11, Bankruptcy Chapter 13, Insurance Defense, Zoning, Real Estate, Consumer Law, Appeals.

SAMUEL GOLDMAN (1948-2000)

BERNARD I. ROSEN, born Akron, Ohio, April 3, 1918; admitted to bar, 1947, Ohio; 1961, U.S. Supreme Court. *Education:* University of Akron (B.A., 1940); The Ohio State University; Case Western Reserve University (LL.B., 1947). Tau Epsilon Rho. Trustee, 1961-1967; 1971-1980; Chairman, Board of Trustees, 1977-1980, University of Akron. Assistant County Prosecutor, Summit County, 1952-1953. *Member:* Akron (Member, Executive Committee, 1966-1968), Ohio State (Member, Legal Ethics Committee, 1969-1972) and American Bar Associations; Ohio Academy of Trial Lawyers. ***PRACTICE AREAS:*** Family Law. ***Email:*** BRosen@Goldman-Rosen.com

GEORGE P. TSARNAS, born Akron, Ohio, January 29, 1938; admitted to bar, 1963, Ohio. *Education:* University of Akron (B.A., 1960); The Ohio State University (J.D., 1963). Assistant Law Director, City of Akron, 1966-1967. Assistant County Prosecutor, Summit County, 1968. *Member:* Akron, Cleveland, Ohio State and American Bar Associations. [Capt., U.S. Army, 1963-1965]. ***LANGUAGES:*** Greek. ***PRACTICE AREAS:*** Real Estate; Business Law; Estate Planning. ***Email:*** GTsarnas@Goldman-Rosen.com

MICHAEL B. HENDLER, born Akron, Ohio, April 13, 1938; admitted to bar, 1963, Ohio; 1964, U.S. Court of Military Appeals. *Education:* University of Akron (B.A., with distinction, 1960); The Ohio State University (J.D., 1963). Tau Epsilon Rho. Assistant City Prosecutor, City of Akron, 1967-1968. *Member:* Akron (President, 1989-1990) and Ohio State (Member, House of Delegates, 1990-1991; 1996-2003; Governor, 2003-2006) Bar Associations; American Bar Foundation; Akron Bar Foundation (Governor, 1996-2001; Chairman of the Board, 1997-2001). ***PRACTICE AREAS:*** Business Law; Family Law; Probate; Trusts and Estates; Real Estate. ***Email:*** MHendler@Goldman-Rosen.com

ROBERT M. GIPPIN, born Cleveland, Ohio, February 3, 1948; admitted to bar, 1973, Ohio. *Education:* Dartmouth College (A.B., magna cum laude, 1969); Harvard University (J.D., 1973). Phi Beta Kappa. Member, 1993—, President, 1996—, Project: LEARN. Trustee, 1996—, Community Support Services. Member, Magistrate Judge Merit Selection Panel, Northern District of Ohio. President, Summit County Council, 1982-1985. National Conference for Community and Justice, Cleveland Regional Board, 1996—. Executive Committee, 1996—, Central Committee, 1976-1992, Summit County Democratic Party. Board Member, Akron Jewish Community Federation, 1996-1998. Board Member, Akron Jewish Family Services, 1989-1993. *Member:* Akron (Chair, Alternative Dispute Resolution Committee, 1994-1996), Ohio State and American Bar Associations; Ohio School Boards Associations. ***LANGUAGES:*** French and German. ***PRACTICE AREAS:*** Complex Litigation; Administrative Law; School Law; Municipal Law; Health Law; Antitrust Law; Environmental Law.

MARC P. GERTZ, born Akron, Ohio, July 27, 1952; admitted to bar, 1977, Ohio; 1978, U.S. District Court, Northern District of Ohio. *Education:* The Ohio State University (B.S., cum laude, 1974; J.D., 1977). Beta Gamma Sigma. Member, Panel of Interim Trustees, United States Bankruptcy Court, Northern District of Ohio, Eastern Division. *Member:* Akron (Chairman, Municipal Court Committee, 1978-1986; Chair, Bankruptcy and Commercial Section, 1995-1996) and Ohio State Bar Associations; American Bankruptcy Law Institute; National Association of Bankruptcy Trustees. ***PRACTICE AREAS:*** Bankruptcy; Commercial Collections; Real Estate. ***Email:*** MPGertz@Goldman-Rosen.com

GARY M. ROSEN, born Akron, Ohio, March 26, 1953; admitted to bar, 1978, Ohio; 1979, U.S. District Court, Northern District of Ohio; 1981, U.S. Court of Appeals, Sixth Circuit. *Education:* Tufts University (B.A., magna cum laude, 1975); George Washington University (J.D., 1978). Author: "Practical and Ethical Considerations," Family Law Practice in Ohio, LPH 1996. Chief Prosecutor, City of Akron, 1984-1989. Coordinator, Mental Health Law Clinic, University of Akron, 1982. President, Akron Jewish community Federation, 1996-1998. President, Board of Trustees, Akron Summit County Library, 1998-2000. *Member:* Akron (Chairman, Family Law Committee, 2004), Ohio State and American (Member, Commission on Mentally Disabled, 1984-1985; Chairman, Young Lawyers Division, Committee on Delivery of Legal Services to the Disabled, 1983-1984) Bar Associations. ***PRACTICE AREAS:*** Family Law; Civil Litigation; Criminal Law; Collections. ***Email:*** GRosen@Goldman-Rosen.com

IRVING B. SUGERMAN, born Rapid City, South Dakota, August 14, 1956; admitted to bar, 1982, Ohio; 1984, U.S. District Court, Northern District of Ohio; 1985, U.S. Court of Appeals, Sixth Circuit. *Education:* Marietta College (B.A., 1978); University of Akron (J.D., 1982). Omicron Delta Kappa. Assistant County Prosecutor Summit County, 1982-1984. Law Director, Springfield Township, 1991—. Law Director, Copley Township, 2000—. Law Director, Coventry Township 1991—. *Member:* Akron (Member, Local Government Law Lawyers Assistance Committees) and Ohio State Bar Associations. ***PRACTICE AREAS:*** Municipal Zoning; Personal Injury; Real Estate; Litigation; Appeals. ***Email:*** IBS814@aol.com

MICHAEL A. STEEL, born Akron, Ohio, September 6, 1967; admitted to bar, 2000, Ohio; 2001, U.S. District Court, Northern Distrist of Ohio. *Education:* Miami University (B.S., Mass Communications, 1990); University of Akron (J.D., 2000). Member, Trial Team, N.I.T.A. Tournament of Champions, University of Akron, 1999. *Member:* Akron and Ohio State (Member, Real Property and Environmental Law Committees) Bar Associa-

(This Listing Continued)

tions. ***PRACTICE AREAS:*** Civil Litigation; Real Estate; Landlord and Tenant Law; Insurance; Business Law; Bankruptcy; Criminal Defense. ***Email:*** MASteel@Goldman-Rosen.com

STACEY TSARNAS HACKENBERG, born Akron, Ohio, May 18, 1971; admitted to bar, 1996, Ohio; U.S. District Court, Northern and Southern Districts of Ohio. *Education:* Miami University (B.A., cum laude, 1992); Capital University (J.D., 1996). Order of the Curia. *Member:* Akron, Cleveland and Ohio State Bar Associations. ***PRACTICE AREAS:*** Real Estate; Business Law; Employment Law. ***Email:*** STHackenberg@Goldman-Rosen.com

JOY CHICATELLI, born Millersburg, Ohio, December 26, 1967; admitted to bar, 2000, Ohio. *Education:* Malone College (B.A., 1996); Cleveland-Marshall College of Law (J.D., 2000). Assistant County Prosecutor, Civil Division, Portage County, Ohio, 1999-2000. Assistant City Prosecutor, Criminal Division, Akron, Ohio, 2000-2002. ***PRACTICE AREAS:*** Criminal Defense; Domestic Relations; Labor and Employment. ***Email:*** JChicatelli@Goldman-Rosen.com

OF COUNSEL

FRANK E. STEEL, JR., born Akron, Ohio, July 6, 1938; admitted to bar, 1963, Ohio; 1966, U.S. Supreme Court; 1967, U.S. District Court, Northern District of Ohio; 1970, U.S. Court of Appeals, Sixth Circuit. *Education:* St. Bonaventure University (B.B.A., 1960); The Ohio State University (J.D., 1963). *Member:* Akron and Ohio State Bar Associations; Defense Research Institute; American Financial Services Association. [With Judge Advocate General's Corps, U.S. Army, 1963-1966; Col., Judge Advocate General's Corps, U.S. Army Reserve]. ***PRACTICE AREAS:*** Insurance Defense; Consumer Law; Commercial; General Practice. ***Email:*** FESteel@Goldman-Rosen.com

REPRESENTATIVE CLIENTS: B.F. Goodrich Credit Union; Bank One; Cascade Group; First Merit Bank; State Farm Insurance; Summit Federal Credit Union; WBNX; Welty Building Corp.
REFERENCES: FirstMerit Bank; National City Bank, Akron.

MELISSA GRAHAM-HURD

Established in 1984

704 LANDMARK BUILDING
7 WEST BOWERY STREET
AKRON, OHIO 44308-1149
Telephone: 330-996-4099
Telecopier: 330-376-3291
330-643-0732
Email: GrahamHurd@aol.com
URL: http://www.ohiodrlaw.com

Family Law including Child Support, Custody, Visitation, Grandparent Rights, Paternity, Divorce, Spousal Support, Marital Property Settlements, Post Divorce Modification, Premarital Agreements, and Mediation.

MELISSA GRAHAM-HURD, born Akron, Ohio, September 18, 1956; admitted to bar, 1984, Ohio; 1985, U.S. District Court, Northern District of Ohio; 1990, U.S. Court of Appeals, Sixth Circuit; 1999, U.S. Supreme Court. *Education:* University of Akron (B.A., 1980); University of Akron School of Law (J.D., 1983). Member, Ohio Supreme Court Advisory Committee on Children, Families and the Courts. Author: Chapter 29: Governmental Retirement Benefits in "Sowald & Morganstern's Ohio Domestic Relations Law". *Member:* Akron (Past Chair, Family Law Section), Ohio State (Past Chair, Family Law Committee) and American (Family Law Section) Bar Associations. Ohio State Bar Foundation (Class of 2003). ***PRACTICE AREAS:*** Family Law; Divorce; Dissolution; Mediation; Custody; Child Support; Visitation Rights; Spousal Support; Juvenile; Wills; Trusts and Estates; Civil Rights.

GRISI & RIEGLER

Established in 1983

159 SOUTH MAIN STREET, SUITE 1030
AKRON, OHIO 44308
Telephone: 330-535-8171
Fax: 330-535-0106
Email: ejriegler@rieglerlaw.com
Email: grisi@nls.net

Personal Injury, Medical Malpractice, Divorce, Probate and Estates, Municipal Zoning, Corporate.

CHARLES E. GRISI, born Jersey City, New Jersey, August 26, 1945; admitted to bar, 1970, Ohio and U.S. District Court, Northern District of Ohio; 1980, U.S. Supreme Court. *Education:* University of Akron (B.S., 1967; J.D., 1970). Lecturer, "Tort Law", University of Akron School of Law, 1984. Assistant County Prosecuting Attorney, 1970-1972. Commissioner for Board of Character and Fitness for Lawyers and Judges for Supreme Court of Ohio, 1988-1994. *Member:* Akron and Ohio State Bar Associations; Ohio Academy of Trial Lawyers; The Association of Trial Lawyers of America; Summit County Trial Lawyers Association (President, 1986-1988); American Inns of Court (Bencher). ***PRACTICE AREAS:*** Plaintiff's Personal Injury; Medical Malpractice; Divorce. ***Email:*** cegrisi@grisilaw.com

EDWARD J. RIEGLER, admitted to bar, 1974, Ohio; 1976, U.S. District Court, Northern District of Ohio; 1978, U.S. Court of Appeals, 6th Circuit; 1979, U.S. Supreme Court; 1985, U.S. Court of Claims. *Education:* University of Akron (B.A., 1967; M.A., 1969; J.D., 1974). Omicron Delta Kappa. Law Director, City of Fairlawn, Ohio. *Member:* Akron, Ohio State and American Bar Associations. ***PRACTICE AREAS:*** Probate and Estates; Estate Planning and Administration; Municipal Law. ***Email:*** ejriegler@rieglerlaw.com

(This Listing Continued)

GUY, LAMMERT & TOWNE

Established in 1973

2210 FIRST NATIONAL TOWER
106 S. MAIN STREET
AKRON, OHIO 44308-1419
Telephone: 330-535-2151
Fax: 330-535-9048
Email: guylaw2210@aol.com
URL: http://www.glt-law.com

Canton, Ohio Office: P.O. Box 6426. Telephone: 330-452-1818 Fax: 330-535-9048

Bankruptcy, Banking, Business Torts, Corporation, Commercial Litigation, Creditors Rights and Reorganization Law. Employment Law, Probate, Personal Injury, Trial Practice, Malpractice and Products Liability Law. General Litigation.

MEMBERS OF FIRM

JOHN J. GUY, born Pittsburgh, Pennsylvania, January 10, 1942; admitted to bar, 1970, Ohio; 1971, U.S. District Court, Northern District of Ohio; 1974, U.S. Supreme Court; 1975, U.S. Court of Appeals, Sixth Circuit. *Education:* Kent State University (B.B.A., 1967); Akron University Law School (J.D., 1970). Listed in The Best Lawyers in America - Bankruptcy Law. *Member:* Akron (Chairman, Bankruptcy Law Section), Ohio State (Member, Commercial and Bankruptcy Law Committee) and American Bar Associations. ***PRACTICE AREAS:*** Bankruptcy Law; Commercial Litigation; Creditors Rights Law. ***Email:*** johnguy@neo.rr.com

THOMAS E. LAMMERT, born Pittsburgh, Pennsylvania, March 26, 1947; admitted to bar, 1976, Ohio and U.S. District Court, Northern District of Ohio; 1982, U.S. Supreme Court; 1983, Florida and U.S. Court of Appeals, Sixth Circuit. *Education:* College of Wooster; University of Pittsburgh (B.S., 1969); University of Akron (J.D., 1976). *Member:* Akron (Vice-Chairman, 1990-1991 and Chairman, 1991-1993, Law Office Management Committee), Stark County, Ohio State and American Bar Associations; The Florida Bar. [With U.S. Navy, 1971-1973]. (Resident, Canton, Ohio Office). ***PRACTICE AREAS:*** Bankruptcy Law; Commercial Litigation; Creditors Rights Law; Personal Injury Law. ***Email:*** Telammert@aol.com

RONALD N. TOWNE, born Youngstown, Ohio, September 19, 1944; admitted to bar, 1969, Ohio; 1971, U.S. District Court, Northern District of Ohio; 1974, U.S. Supreme Court; 1975, U.S. Court of Appeals, Sixth Circuit. *Education:* Youngstown State University (B.A., 1966); Akron University Law School (J.D., 1969). Phi Alpha Delta. The Best Lawyers in America-Bankruptcy Law. Assistant Law Director, City of Akron, 1970-1971. *Member:* Akron, Cleveland, Medina, Stark County and Ohio State (Member, Banking, Commercial & Bankruptcy Law Committee) Bar Associations. ***REPORTED CASES:*** Blon vs. Bank One, Akron, NA (1988), 35 Ohio St. 3d 98; Thompson Electric vs. Bank One, Akron, NA (1988) 37 Ohio St. 3d 259; Standard Oil v. Steele, 22 Ohio Mis. 2d 27 (1985); In re: Camillia Court Apts. Ltd, 117 Bankr. 316 (1990); Bank One, Akron, NA v. Nobil, 80 Ohio App. 3d 638 (1992); In re Kenneth R. Falkenberg, 136 Bankr. 481 (1992); BuyRite Lumber Co. v. Bank One, Akron, N.A., 81 Ohio App. 3d 74 (1991). ***PRACTICE AREAS:*** Banking Law; Commercial Litigation; Business Torts; Creditors Rights Law; Bankruptcy Law. ***Email:*** rntowne@neo.rr.com

E. JANE TAYLOR, born Niagara Falls, New York, December 16, 1954; admitted to bar, 1981, Ohio and U.S. District Court, Northern and Southern Districts of Ohio; U.S. Court of Appeals, Sixth Circuit. *Education:* Kent State University (B.A., cum laude, 1977); University of Akron (J.D., 1980). Staff Member, Akron Law Review, 1979-1980. Member, Board of Trustees, United Way of Summit County, 1995-2002. *Member:* Akron (President, 1994-1995; Vice-President, 1993-1994; Member, Board of Trustees, 1990-1993; Chair, Bar Applicants and Students Committee, 1988-1990; Member, Bankruptcy and Commercial Law Section, 1989—), Ohio State (Member, Board of Governors, 2000-2003; Council of Delegates, 1996-2003; President-Elect, 2004-2005; President, 2005-2006) and American Bar Associations; National Conference of Bar Presidents; Ohio Women's Bar Association; Commercial Law League of America. ***PRACTICE AREAS:*** Commercial Litigation; Creditors Rights Law; Bankruptcy Law. ***Email:*** guylaw2210@aol.com

DONALD W. DAVIS, JR., born Akron, Ohio, September 29, 1958; admitted to bar, 1985, Ohio; 1988, U.S. District Court, Northern District of Ohio; 1991, U.S. Court of Appeals, Sixth Circuit; 1992, U.S. Supreme Court. *Education:* Bowling Green State University (B.S., in Business Administration, 1982); University of Akron (J.D., 1985). Law Clerk to Hon. Frank J. Bayer, Summit County Court of Common Pleas, 1986-1988. *Member:* Akron, Ohio State and American Bar Associations. ***PRACTICE AREAS:*** Commercial Litigation; Commercial Leasing; Franchise Law; Business Tort Litigation; Injunctive Relief Litigation. ***Email:*** ddavis@rrbiznet.com

ASSOCIATES

ANN LYNN WEHENER, born Garland, Texas, March 26, 1968; admitted to bar, 1994, Ohio; 1997, U.S. District Court, Northern District of Ohio; U.S. Court of Appeals, Sixth Circuit. *Education:* Wright State University (B.S., summa cum laude, 1990); Capital University (J.D., summa cum laude, 1994). Member, Law Review, 1993-1994. Law Clerk to the Honorable Earl E. Stephenson, Fourth District Court of Appeals of Ohio, 1994-1996. *Member:* Akron and Ohio State Bar Associations. ***PRACTICE AREAS:*** Business Torts; Commercial Litigation; Banking Law; Creditors Rights; Bankruptcy. ***Email:*** awehener@neo.rr.com

DURIYA A. DHINOJWALA, born Bombay, India, May 3, 1968; admitted to bar, 2002, Ohio, U.S. District Court, Northern District of Ohio and U.S. Court of Appeals, Sixth Circuit. *Education:* Sophia College, Bombay, India (B.F.A., 1989); University of Akron (J.D., 2002). Recipient, CALI Award for Student Excellence, Commercial Law and Em-

(This Listing Continued)

GUY, LAMMERT & TOWNE, Akron—Continued

ployment Discrimination Law. *Member:* Akron, Ohio State and American Bar Associations. ***LANGUAGES:*** Hindi, Gujarati and Marathi. ***PRACTICE AREAS:*** Commercial Litigation; Bankruptcy; Commercial Law; Probate. ***Email:*** duriya@neo.rr.com

THOMAS R. BARTILSON, born Akron, Ohio, 1970; admitted to bar, 2004, Ohio; 2005, U.S. District Court, Northern District of Ohio. *Education:* University of Akron (B.S. Elementary Education, 1994); University of Akron, School of Law (J.D., 2004). *Member:* American and Akron Bar Associations. ***PRACTICE AREAS:*** Commercial Law; Bankruptcy; Franchise Law. ***Email:*** tbartilson@rrbiznet.com

REPRESENTATIVE CLIENTS: Bank One N.A.; Beacon Journal Publishing Company; CIT Financial Services; Charter Express, Inc.; Four Star Mortgage, Inc.; FCC National Bank; M&T Bank; Keybank National Association; First Energy; Second National Bank; Protection One; 84 Lumber Co.; G.E. Capital; Trumbull Supply Co.; WHBC Radio; Quaker Square.
REFERENCE: First Merit.

HAHN LOESER & PARKS LLP

ONE GOJO PLAZA
SUITE 300
AKRON, OHIO 44311-1076
Telephone: 330-864-5550; 1-877-HAHNLAW
Facsimile: 330-864-7986
Email: inquiry@hahnlaw.com
URL: http://www.hahnlaw.com

Cleveland, Ohio Office: 3300 BP Tower, 200 Public Square, 44114-2301. Telephone: 216-621-0150. Fax: 216-241-2824.
Columbus, Ohio Office: 65 East State Street, Suite 1400, 43215. Telephone: 614-221-0240. Fax: 614-221-5909.
Naples, Florida Office: 3301 Bonita Beach Road, Suite 308, Bonita Springs, 34134. Telephone: 239-949-6989. Fax: 239-949-6687.

Business, Corporate and Securities, Litigation, Taxation and Employee Benefits, Estate Planning, Probate, Real Estate, Labor, Creditors Rights, Reorganization and Bankruptcy, Intellectual Property and Technology, Environmental, Patent, Trademark and Copyright Law, Telecommunications Law, Government Relations, Public Utility and Regulatory Law, Health Care, Construction Law.

FIRM PROFILE: Hahn Loeser & Parks LLP . . . Dedicated, diverse legal counsel serving businesses, industries, institutions and individuals since 1920. We deliver sophisticated and innovative counseling to a wide spectrum of clients from our offices in Cleveland, Columbus and Akron, Ohio, and Bonita Springs and Naples, Florida.

RESIDENT MEMBERS

R. ERIC GAUM, born Cincinnati, Ohio, December 26, 1966; admitted to bar, 1996, Ohio; registered to practice before U.S. Patent and Trademark Office. *Education:* University of Cincinnati (B.S.E.E.T., 1989); University of Akron School of Law (J.D., 1996). Phi Alpha Delta. *Member:* Cleveland Intellectual Property Law Association; American Intellectual Property Law Association. ***PRACTICE AREAS:*** Intellectual Property Litigation; Patents; Trademarks; Copyrights. ***Email:*** regaum@hahnlaw.com

SCOTT M. OLDHAM, born Philadelphia, Pennsylvania, June 3, 1961; admitted to bar, 1991, Ohio; registered to practice before U.S. Patent and Trademark Office, Electrical Patent Examiner at U.S. Patent & Trademark Office, 1984-1987. *Education:* Colorado School of Mines (B.S., Geophysical Engineering, 1983); University of Akron (J.D., 1991). Adjunct Professor at University of Akron School of Law, Faculty Member, Ohio Aerospace Institute. *Member:* Cleveland Intellectual Property Law Association. ***PRACTICE AREAS:*** Patents; Trademarks; Copyrights; Intellectual Property; Technology Licensing; Intellectual Property Litigation; Unfair Competition; Trade Secrets. ***Email:*** smoldham@hahnlaw.com

MARK A. WATKINS, born Cleveland, Ohio, October 4, 1960; admitted to bar, 1988, Ohio; registered to practice before U.S. Patent and Trademark Office. *Education:* Ohio Northern University (B.S., in Pharmacy, 1983); University of Akron (J.D., 1988). *Member:* International Trademark Law Association; Cleveland Intellectual Property Law Association (Treasurer, 1995-1997; President, 1998-1999). ***PRACTICE AREAS:*** Patents; Trademarks; Licensing; Copyrights; Trade Secrets; Intellectual Property Litigation. ***Email:*** mawatkins@hahnlaw.com

RESIDENT OF COUNSEL

LOUIS F. KREEK, JR., born August 24, 1928; admitted to bar, 1952, District of Columbia; 1955, Ohio; 1964, New York; 1972, New Jersey; registered to practice before U.S. Patent and Trademark Office. *Education:* Massachusetts Institute of Technology (B.S., Chemical Engineering, 1948); George Washington University (J.D., 1952). Phi Alpha Delta. ***PRACTICE AREAS:*** Patents; Technology and Science. ***Email:*** lfkreek@hahnlaw.com

RESIDENT ASSOCIATES

ROBERT J. CLARK, born Barberton, Ohio, November 9, 1966; admitted to bar, 1996, Ohio; registered to practice before U.S. Patent and Trademark Office. *Education:* The Ohio State University (B.S.M.E., 1990); University of Akron (J.D., 1996). *Member:* American Intellectual Property Law Association; Cleveland Intellectual Property Law Association. ***PRACTICE AREAS:*** Patents; Intellectual Property. ***Email:*** rjclark@hahnlaw.com

W. EDWARD CROOKS, born Gallipolis, Ohio, December 10, 1971; admitted to bar, 2002, Ohio; U.S. Court of Appeals for the Federal Circuit; U.S. District Court, Northern District of Ohio; registered to practice before United States Patent and Trademark Office. *Education:* The Ohio State University (B.S., 1994); The University of Akron School of Law (J.D., cum laude, 2002). *Member:* Cleveland Intellectual Property Law Association. ***PRACTICE AREAS:*** Patents; Trademarks; Copyrights; Licensing. ***Email:*** wcrooks@hahnlaw.com

(This Listing Continued)

JOHN J. CUNNIFF, born New York, N.Y., February 28, 1962; admitted to bar, 1999, Ohio, U.S. District Court, Northern District of Ohio, U.S. District Court, District of Colorado and U.S. Court of Appeals, Sixth Circuit; registered to practice before U.S. Patent and Trademark Office. *Education:* Indiana University (B.S., with honors in Biology, 1984; M.A., Microbiology, 1988); Akron University Law School (J.D., 1999). *Member:* Cleveland Intellectual Property Law Association; American Intellectual Property Law Association. ***PRACTICE AREAS:*** Intellectual Property Law; Patent Law; Trademark Law; Copyrights. ***Email:*** jcunniff@hahnlaw.com

BRET A. HRIVNAK, born November 6, 1970; admitted to bar, 2004, Ohio; U.S. District Court, Northern District of Ohio; U.S. Court of Appeals for the Federal Circuit; registered to practice before U.S. Patent and Trademark Office, 2003. *Education:* University of Akron (B.S., Mechanical Engineering, 1994; M.S., Mechanical Engineering, 2001; J.D., 2004). *Member:* American Intellectual Property Law Association; Licensing Executives Society; Cleveland Intellectual Property Law Association. ***PRACTICE AREAS:*** Intellectual Property; Litigation; Technology Transfers. ***Email:*** bhrivnak@hahnlaw.com

MICHAEL H. MINNS, born Bay City, Michigan, August 7, 1950; admitted to bar, 1985, Ohio; registered to practice before U.S. Patent and Trademark Office. *Education:* University of Michigan (B.S.E., 1972; M.S.E., 1975); Cleveland Marshall College of Law (J.D., cum laude, 1985). *Member:* American Intellectual Property Law Association; Cleveland Intellectual Property Law Association. ***PRACTICE AREAS:*** Intellectual Property; Patents. ***Email:*** mhminns@hahnlaw.com

AMANDA H. WILCOX, born Cleveland, Ohio, December 20, 1976; admitted to bar, 2001, Ohio; 2002, U.S. District Court, Northern District of Ohio, U.S. Court of Appeals, Sixth Circuit and U.S. Court of Appeals for the Federal Circuit; registered to practice before U.S. Patent and Trademark Office. *Education:* Miami University (B.S., Biochemistry, 1998); University of Toledo (J.D., 2001). *Member:* International Trademark Association; American Chemical Society; Cleveland Intellectual Property Law Association. ***PRACTICE AREAS:*** Trademark Law; Patent Law. ***Email:*** awilcox@hahnlaw.com

REPRESENTATIVE CLIENTS: Crown North America, Division of Transpro, Inc.; Natural Golf Corp; Dana Corp; Myers Industries; Dover Chemical Corporation, a Subsidiary of ICC Industries Inc.; International Marketing, Inc.; Norco Industries, Inc.; Georgia Institute of Technology; The Step2 Company; East Manufacturing Co.; City of Akron; Allied Machine and Engineering; Paragon Vision Sciences; SmartDisk Corp.; Noven Pharmaceuticals, Inc.; OM Group, Inc.; Matco Tools; PlanSoft; Biotronik, Inc.; Legget & Platt Property Management Co.; Couer, Inc.; Grover Musical Co.; X2Y Attenuators, Inc.

HENNING & YOST, L.P.A.

AKRON, OHIO

(See Canton)

Employment Law, Human Resource Management, Civil Litigation.

HENRETTA LAW OFFICES

400 KEY BUILDING
159 S. MAIN STREET
AKRON, OHIO 44308
Telephone: 330-376-7800
Fax: 330-376-7854
Email: henrettalaw@neo.rr.com
URL: http://www.henrettalaw.com

Medical Malpractice, Legal Malpractice, Nursing Home Litigation, Insurance Litigation, Automobile Accidents and Injuries and Wrongful Death.

MEMBER OF FIRM

J. THOMAS HENRETTA, born Barberton, Ohio, April 25, 1945; admitted to bar, 1975, Ohio; 1976, U.S. District Court, Northern District of Ohio; 1986, U.S. Supreme Court; 1998, U.S. Court of Appeals, Sixth Circuit. *Education:* University of Akron (B.A., 1968); Akron University Law School (J.D., 1975). *Member:* Cuyahoga County, Akron and Ohio State Bar Associations; Ohio Academy of Trial Lawyers (Past-President); The Association of Trial Lawyers of America (Member, Board of Governors); Cleveland Academy for Trial Lawyers. (Certified as a Civil Trial Specialist by the National Board of Trial Advocacy). ***Email:*** henrettalaw@neo.rr.com

SHERI L. HOLDA

1699 KING DRIVE
P.O. BOX 308
AKRON, OHIO 44309-0308
Telephone: 330-607-0438
Fax: 330-896-6496
Email: attorneyholda@neo.rr.com

Divorce, Child Custody, Adoption, Bankruptcy, Personal Bankruptcy, Wills.

SHERI L. HOLDA, born Buffalo, New York, 1957; admitted to bar, 2001, Ohio. *Education:* University of Akron (L.P.N. Certificate, 1983; B.S., Natural Science, 1988; M.S., Molecular Biology, 1994; J.D., 2001). *Member:* Portage County and Ohio State Bar Associations; American Bar Association. ***PRACTICE AREAS:*** Estate Planning; Trust Planning; Personal Planning; Trusts and Estates; Family Trusts; Family Wealth Transfer; Wealth Preservation; Living Trusts; Wills; Powers of Attorney; Trust Law; Family Law; Child Custody.

THE HORWITZ GROUP, LLC

Established in 2005
130 SPRINGSIDE DRIVE
SUITE 106
AKRON, OHIO 44333
Telephone: 330-670-5300
Fax: 330-670-5355
URL: http://www.thehorwitzgroup.com

Federal, State and Local Taxation, Corporate Law, ERISA, Estate Planning.

FIRM PROFILE: The Horwitz Group, LLC is a cutting edge boutique law firm providing transactional services to mid-level companies and business owners across a variety of industry segments. Areas of practice include corporate, tax, estate planning, real estate, and mergers and acquisitions. The firm serves a broad base of clients within Northeast Ohio.

The Horwitz Group's mission is to provide the client with cutting-edge legal services in partnership with the client's other financial and operational partners and consultants. By adopting this unique cross discipline team approach, soliciting the advice of all parties, we are able to provide the client with a comprehensive legal framework that takes into consideration all aspects impacting the client's business, both professional and personal.

STUART M. HORWITZ, born Cincinnati, Ohio, April 6, 1959; admitted to bar, 1985, Ohio. *Education:* The Ohio State University (B.S., 1982; J.D., 1985); Georgetown University (LL.M., 1989). *Member:* Cleveland, Akron and Ohio State Bar Associations. ***PRACTICE AREAS:*** Federal, State and Local Taxation; Business Law; Estate Planning; Probate; ERISA. ***Email:*** shorwitz@thehorwitzgroup.com

ASSOCIATE

JAVAN A. KLINE, born Napoleon, Ohio, 1978; (admission pending). *Education:* University of Notre Dame (B.B.A., 2000); University of Cincinnati (J.D., 2005). ***PRACTICE AREAS:*** Federal Taxation; State Taxation; Local Taxation; Business Law; Estate Planning; Probate. ***Email:*** jkline@thehorwitzgroup.com

LEGAL SUPPORT PERSONNEL

ANGELA M. BARSTOW, born Ogdensburg, New York. *Education:* State University of New York at Plattsburgh (B.A., 2002); Syracuse University (M.A., 2003). ***PRACTICE AREAS:*** Estate Planning; Probate. ***Email:*** abarstow@thehorwitzgroup.com

TIMOTHY J. JEFFRIES

AKRON, OHIO

(See Canton)

Business Litigation, Real Estate, Commercial Real Estate, Landlord and Tenant Law, Residential Real Estate, Zoning Law, Land Use, Business Law, Business Acquisitions, Business Sales, Bankruptcy, Business Formation, Business Planning, Business Taxation, Collections, Contracts, Corporate, Partnership Law, Family Business Law, Franchise Law, Estate Planning.

DOUGLAS D. JONES CO., LPA

AKRON, OHIO

(See Canton)

Wills, Probate, Trusts and Estates, Family Law, Bankruptcy, Real Estate, Property Law, Personal Injury, Torts, Automobile Accidents, Adoptions, Divorce, Child Custody, Child Support, Debtor and Creditor, Estate Planning, Medical Malpractice and Products Liabilities.

JOONDEPH & BITTEL, LLP

Established in 1978
SUITE 700 AKRON CENTRE PLAZA
50 SOUTH MAIN STREET
AKRON, OHIO 44308-1881
Telephone: 330-762-2600
Facsimile: 330-762-2604
Cleveland Telephone: 216-348-1935
Email: JB1LAW@aol.com

Civil Trial and Appellate Practice in Federal and State Courts. Taxation, Corporate, Health Care, Administrative, Pension, Real Estate, Construction Litigation, Labor and Employment, Bankruptcy, Estate Planning, Probate Law and Boat Manufacturing Liability.

MEMBERS OF FIRM

JEROME J. JOONDEPH, born Brooklyn, New York, September 20, 1943; admitted to bar, 1968, Ohio; 1970, U.S. District Court, Northern District of Ohio and U.S. Tax Court; 1982, U.S. Claims Court; U.S. Court of Appeals, Sixth Circuit. *Education:* Rollins College; Temple University; Kent State University (B.A., 1965); The Ohio State University (J.D., cum laude, 1967). Trustee and President, Children's Hospital of Akron Foundation. Member, Akron Children's Hospital Board. *Member:* Akron, Ohio State and American Bar Associations. ***PRACTICE AREAS:*** Business Estate Planning; Business Succession Planning; Tax Planning; Tax Litigation; Real Estate; Taxation; Estate Planning; Probate. ***Email:*** jjoondeph@neo.rr.com

TIMOTHY M. BITTEL, born Cleveland, Ohio, September 10, 1945; admitted to bar, 1971, Ohio; 1974, Florida, U.S. Supreme Court, U.S. Court of Appeals, Sixth and Seventh Circuits, U.S. District Court, Northern District of Ohio and U.S. District Court, Southern and Middle Districts of Florida. *Education:* Case Institute of Technology (B.S., cum laude, 1967); Cleveland State University (J.D., magna cum laude, 1971). NBTA Examiner, 1995—. *Member:* Akron, Cleveland, Cuyahoga County and Ohio State Bar Associations; Cleveland Academy of Trial Lawyers; Academy of Florida Trial Lawyers; The Association of Trial Lawyers of America; Ohio Academy of Trial Lawyers. (Certified as a Civil Trial Advocate by the National Board of Trial Advocacy). ***REPORTED CASES:*** State, ex. rel. Pinzone v. Cleveland, 34 Ohio St.2d 26 (1973); Panther Pumps & Equip. v. Hydrocraft, Inc., 424 F.Supp. 815 (N.D. Ill. 1976), 566 F.2d 8 (7th cir. 1977), cert. denied; Clutter v. Johns-Manville Sales Corp., 646 F.2d 1151 (6th Cir. 1981); Cuyahoga Cty. Bar Association v. Curry, 79 Ohio St.3d 181 (1997); Driscoll v. NorProp, Inc. 129 Ohio App.3d 757 (1998); Markham v. Earle M. Jorgensen Co., 138 Ohio App.3d 484 (2000). ***PRACTICE AREAS:*** Civil Trials and Appeals; Labor and Employment Law; Recreational Boating Law; Construction Litigation. ***Email:*** TMBittel@aol.com

ASSOCIATES

DALE V. WILSON, born Akron, Ohio, October 25, 1945; admitted to bar, 1983, Ohio, U.S. District Court, Northern District of Ohio and U.S. Tax Court. *Education:* Kent State University (B.A., 1968); University of Akron (J.D., cum laude, 1983). Certified Public Accountant, Ohio, 1979. *Member:* Akron, Ohio State and American Bar Associations; Ohio Society of Certified Public Accountants. ***PRACTICE AREAS:*** Corporate; Pension; Real Estate; Bankruptcy.

KEVIN T. LYDEN, born Youngstown, Ohio, August 20, 1956; admitted to bar, 1987, Ohio and U.S. District Court, Northern District of Ohio; 1989, U.S. Court of Appeals, Sixth Circuit. *Education:* Youngstown State University (A.B., 1978); University of Akron (J.D., 1986). *Member:* Akron, Ohio State and American Bar Associations. ***PRACTICE AREAS:*** Administrative; Probate.

REFERENCES: First Merit Bank N.A.; Bank One, Akron, NA.; National City Bank, Northeast.

THOMAS N. JULIUS

265 STEEPLECHASE LANE
AKRON, OHIO 44262
Telephone: 330-283-6480
Fax: 330-633-5313
Email: tnjulius@aol.com
URL: http://www.lawyers.com/tjulius

Securities, Tax Law, Corporate Law, Business Law, Estate Planning, Mergers and Acquisitions.

THOMAS NORBERT JULIUS, born Erie, Pennsylvania, February 12, 1949; admitted to bar, 1973, Ohio and Pennsylvania; 1975, Florida. *Education:* Gannon College (B.S.B.A., cum laude, 1970); Akron University Law School (J.D., 1972). Phi Alpha Delta. Member, Akron Law Review, 1971-1972. ***PRACTICE AREAS:*** Securities; Tax Law; Corporate Law; Business Law; Estate Planning; Mergers and Acquisitions.

ELLEN C. KAFOREY

1024 KEY BUILDING
159 SOUTH MAIN STREET
AKRON, OHIO 44308
Telephone: 330-253-0719
Fax: 330-253-0722
Email: ekaforey@neo.rr.com

Estate Planning, Wills, Trust Law, Guardianship, Adoption Law.

ELLEN C. KAFOREY, born Akron, Ohio, October 21, 1953; admitted to bar, 1989, Ohio. *Education:* University of Akron (B.S.N., 1975; J.D., 1989). *Member:* Akron (Member, Probate Section) and Ohio State Bar Associations.

KASTNER WESTMAN & WILKINS, LLC

3480 WEST MARKET STREET, SUITE 300
AKRON, OHIO 44333
Telephone: 330-867-9998
Fax: 330-867-3786
Email: kww@kwwlaborlaw.com
URL: http://www.kwwlaborlaw.com

Employment Law, including Labor Relations, Equal Employment Opportunity, Public Sector Labor Law, OSHA, Arbitration, Wage and Hour, Workers Compensation Law, Claims Management, Affirmative Action, Employee Benefits, Human Resources Consulting, Site Selection Analysis.

HARLEY M. KASTNER, born Akron, Ohio, 1949; admitted to bar, 1973, Ohio; U.S. Supreme Court; U.S. Court of Appeals, Third, Fifth, Sixth, Eighth and Tenth Circuits. *Education:* Wake Forest University; University of Akron (B.A., 1970; J.D., 1973). Member, National Order of Barristers. *Member:* Akron, Ohio State (Member, Equal Employment Opportunity Subcommittee, Labor Law Section) and American (Member, Equal Employment Law Committee, Labor and Employment Law Section) Bar Associations. ***PRACTICE AREAS:*** Labor Management Law; Equal Employment Opportunity Law; Public Sector; Arbitration Law. ***Email:*** hkastner@kwwlaborlaw.com

DEAN E. WESTMAN, born Harvey, Illinois, 1953; admitted to bar, 1978, Tennessee; 1981, Ohio; U.S. District Court, Northern and Southern Districts of Ohio; U.S. District Court, Middle District of Tennessee; U.S. District Court, District of Arizona; U.S. Court of Appeals, Sixth, Eighth and Tenth Circuits; U.S. Supreme Court. *Education:* Duke University (B.A., magna cum laude, 1975); Vanderbilt University (J.D., 1978). *Member:* Akron and Ohio State Bar Associations. ***PRACTICE AREAS:*** Labor Management Law; Equal Employment Opportunity Law; Public Sector; Arbitration; Litigation. ***Email:*** dwestman@kwwlaborlaw.com

(This Listing Continued)

KASTNER WESTMAN & WILKINS, LLC, Akron—Continued

JAMES P. WILKINS, born Cleveland, Ohio, 1957; admitted to bar, 1983, Ohio; U.S. District Court, Northern and Southern Districts of Ohio; U.S. Court of Appeals, Sixth Circuit. *Education:* College of Wooster (B.A., with honors, 1979); George Washington University (J.D., with honors, 1983). *Member:* Akron and Ohio State (Member, Labor and Employment Law Section) Bar Associations. ***PRACTICE AREAS:*** Labor Management Law; Equal Employment Opportunity Law; Public Sector; Arbitration Law; Affirmative Action; Immigration Law. ***Email:*** jwilkins@kwwlaborlaw.com

KENNETH M. HANELINE, born Cleveland, Ohio, 1958; admitted to bar, 1986, Ohio. *Education:* Case Western Reserve University (B.S., 1980); Cleveland Marshall College of Law (J.D., 1986). Beta Alpha Psi. Certified Public Accountant, Ohio, 1980. *Member:* Ohio State Bar Association; Ohio Society of Certified Public Accountants (Member, Taxation Division). ***PRACTICE AREAS:*** Employee Benefits; Taxation; HIPAA Privacy. ***Email:*** khaneline@kwwlaborlaw.com

KEITH L. PRYATEL, born Cleveland, Ohio, 1961; admitted to bar, 1986, Ohio; U.S. District Court, Northern and Southern Districts of Ohio; U.S. Court of Appeals, First, Third, Sixth and Tenth Circuits; U.S. Supreme Court. *Education:* Xavier University (B.S.B.A., magna cum laude, 1983); Cleveland Marshall College of Law (J.D., magna cum laude, 1986). Recipient: Ralph K. Frew Labor Law Award; Charles Auerbach Evidence Award. *Member:* Ohio State and Federal Bar Associations. ***PRACTICE AREAS:*** Equal Employment Opportunity Law; Public Sector; OSHA Law; Arbitration Law; Employee Benefit Law; Litigation. ***Email:*** kpryatel@kwwlaborlaw.com

JOHN W. McKENZIE, born Akron, Ohio, 1962; admitted to bar, 1992, Ohio; U.S. District Court, Northern District of Ohio; U.S. Court of Appeals, Sixth Circuit; U.S. Supreme Court. *Education:* Wake Forest University (B.A., 1985); Case Western Reserve University (J.D., 1992). Recipient, CWRU "Outstanding Written Advocate" Award for Moot Court, 1991. Niagara International Moot Court Team, 1992. *Member:* Akron, Ohio State and Federal Bar Associations. ***PRACTICE AREAS:*** Management Labor Law; Equal Employment Opportunity Law; Wage and Hour Law; Arbitration; Litigation. ***Email:*** jmckenzie@kwwlaborlaw.com

LISA A. KAINEC, born Cleveland, Ohio, 1967; admitted to bar, 1993, Ohio; U.S. District Court, Northern and Southern Districts of Ohio; U.S. District Court, District of Arizona; U.S. District Court, Western District of Michigan; U.S. Court of Appeals, Fourth, Sixth, Eighth and Tenth Circuits; U.S. Supreme Court. *Education:* Cleveland State University (B.B.A., cum laude, 1990); Case Western Reserve University (J.D., magna cum laude, 1993). Order of the Coif. Recipient: Heiss Labor Law Award. Executive Editor, Case Western Reserve Law Review. *Member:* Cleveland, Ohio State and Federal Bar Associations. ***PRACTICE AREAS:*** Labor Management Law; Equal Employment Opportunity Law; Arbitration Law; Litigation. ***Email:*** lkainec@kwwlaborlaw.com

BRUCE H. FAHEY, born Steubenville, Ohio, 1955; admitted to bar, 1980, Ohio; U.S. District Court, Northern District of Ohio. *Education:* Bethany College (B.A., cum laude, 1977); University of Akron (J.D., 1980). *Member:* Akron (Member, Workers' Compensation Committee) and Ohio State (Member, Workers Compensation Committee) Bar Associations; Self-Insured Group of Ohio (Trustee, Secretary, 1992-1994). ***PRACTICE AREAS:*** Worker's Compensation Law. ***Email:*** bfahey@kwwlaborlaw.com

ASSOCIATES

THOMAS E. GREEN, born Warren, Ohio, 1970; admitted to bar, 2002, Ohio and U.S. District Court, Northern District of Ohio; 2004, U.S. Court of Appeals, Sixth Circuit. *Education:* Youngstown State University (B.S., Education, 1993); Cleveland-Marshall College of Law (J.D., magna cum laude, 2002). Editor-in-Chief, Journal of Law and Health, 2001-2002. *Member:* Cleveland, Ohio and American Bar Associations. ***PRACTICE AREAS:*** Litigation; Labor Law; Management Employment Law; Workers Compensation. ***Email:*** tgreen@kwwlaborlaw.com

RICHARD DAVIES, born Hamburg, West Germany, August 24, 1953; admitted to bar, 1980, Ohio; 1982, U.S. District Court, Northern District of Ohio. *Education:* College of Wooster (B.A., 1977); The Ohio State University (J.D., 1980). Phi Eta Sigma; Phi Delta Phi. Certified Specialist, Ohio Workers' Compensation Law. *Member:* Medina County and Ohio State Bar Associations; Self Insurers' Group of Northern Ohio. ***PRACTICE AREAS:*** Workers' Compensation Law; Litigation; Labor and Employment. ***Email:*** rdavies@kwwlaborlaw.com

OF COUNSEL

TED N. KAZAGLIS, born Warren, Ohio, 1962; admitted to bar, 1987, Michigan; 1988, Ohio; U.S. District Court, Eastern and Western Districts of Michigan; U.S. District Court, Northern District of Ohio; U.S. Court of Appeals, Sixth and Tenth Circuits. *Education:* Kent State University (B.B.A., cum laude, 1984); University of Akron (J.D., 1987). *Member:* Ohio State and American Bar Associations; National Association of Professional Employer Organizations. ***LANGUAGES:*** Greek. ***PRACTICE AREAS:*** Employment Law; Management Employment Law; Equal Employment Opportunity Law. ***Email:*** tkazaglis@kwwlaborlaw.com

LEGAL SUPPORT PERSONNEL

JAMES M. KITCHIN, born Appleton, Wisconsin, 1940. *Education:* University of Wisconsin (B.B.A., 1962). Director, Human Resources Consulting. ***PRACTICE AREAS:*** Employee Benefits; Labor and Employment; Employee Surveys; New Plant Site Selection; Management Training and Development; Labor Climate Analysis. ***Email:*** jkitchin@kwwlaborlaw.com

PARALEGALS

ANGELA M. BERTKA, born Akron, Ohio, 1954. *Education:* University of Akron (B.A., 1981); Denver Paralegal Institute (1984). ***PRACTICE AREAS:*** Labor & Employment Litigation. ***Email:*** abertka@kwwlaborlaw.com

(This Listing Continued)

GEORGETTA J. PURDY, born Barberton, Ohio, 1960. *Education:* Ohio Paralegal Institute (1980); University of Akron (B.S., magna cum laude, 1989). (Paralegal). ***PRACTICE AREAS:*** Labor and Employment. ***Email:*** gpurdy@kwwlaborlaw.com

REPRESENTATIVE CLIENTS: Anthony Allega Construction; Electrolux, Inc.; Elickem; Noveon; First Energy; Hendrickson Trailers; Home Care Network; Infocision Management Corp.; JoAnn Stores, Inc.; Metro Health; University Hospitals of Cleveland; Akron Children's Hospital; Lowe's; The Gertenslager Company; St. Gobain/Nor Pro; Parma Community General Hospital; Webster Industries; Werk Brau; Albrecht Grocery; Cuyahoga County Public Library.

KAUFMANN & KAUFMANN

1200 FIRST NATIONAL TOWER
AKRON, OHIO 44308-1460
Telephone: 330-762-7655
Telecopier: 330-762-7537

General Civil Practice in all Courts. Corporate Law, Real Estate, Probate, Federal Income, Estate and Gift Taxation, Estate Planning, Guardianships, Medicaid Planning, Elder Law, Estate Planning for the Disabled, Estate Planning for Parents of Disabled Children.

FIRM PROFILE: Founded in Akron, Ohio, Kaufmann & Kaufmann now serves the needs of individual clients, families, and businesses through its medium sized firm in Akron, Ohio. The firm currently has five attorneys providing a broad range of services focusing in the areas of estate planning, general probate and estate administration, probate litigation, Medicaid planning, personal injury settlement trusts/planning, guardianships, estate and gift taxation, elder law, estate planning for parents of a child with disabilities and people with disabilities, corporate law focusing on closely held corporations and limited liability entities, and general civil practice. Kaufmann & Kaufmann prides itself on blending years of tradition in the legal profession with new innovative ideas and solutions to assist individual clients, families and businesses in solving legal problems, while understanding the practical implications of each potential solution.

FRANK P. KAUFMANN (1908-1994)
FRANK P. DEVANY (1920-1980)
AMOS H. ENGLEBECK (1885-1952)

PHILIP S. KAUFMANN, born Akron, Ohio, July 18, 1946; admitted to bar, 1971, Ohio; 1975, U.S. District Court, Northern District of Ohio and U.S. Court of Appeals, Sixth Circuit; 1988, U.S. Tax Court; 1989, U.S. Supreme Court. *Education:* Loyola University (B.A., 1968); University of Akron (J.D., 1971). Phi Alpha Delta. Recipient, Outstanding Scholastic Achievement Award. Member, Summit County Board of Mental Retardation Developmental Disabilities, 1985—. Listed in The Best Lawyers of America, Trusts. *Member:* Akron (Section, Probate), Ohio State (Section, Probate) and American Bar Associations. Fellow, American College of Trust and Estate Counsel. ***PRACTICE AREAS:*** Estate Planning; Probate; Guardianship; Medicaid Planning; Corporate Law. ***Email:*** pkaufmann@kaufmannandkaufmann.com

ROY A. KRALL, born Buffalo, New York, October 12, 1962; admitted to bar, 1989, Ohio; 1993, U.S. District Court, Northern District of Ohio. *Education:* University of Pennsylvania (B.A., 1985); Case Western Reserve University (J.D., 1989). Past President and current member, Akron Tax and Estate Planning Council; Cleveland Estate Planning Council. Adjunct Professor, University of Akron, 1997—. *Member:* Cleveland, Akron, Ohio State (Member, Board of Governors) and American Bar Associations. ***PRACTICE AREAS:*** Estate Planning; Elder Law; Business Succession Planning. ***Email:*** rkrall@kaufmannandkaufmann.com

---

LOMA L. SWETT, born Hackensack, New Jersey, August 31, 1955; admitted to bar, 1980, Ohio; 1990, New Jersey. *Education:* Stetson University (B.A., 1977); Akron University Law School (J.D., 1980). Former Associate: Stark & Knoll; Matz Petersilge & Weimer. *Member:* Akron, Ohio and American Bar Associations. ***PRACTICE AREAS:*** Estate Planning and Trusts (50%); Estate Planning for Parents of Handicapped Children (20%); Estate Planning for the Elderly (20%); Estate Planning for the Disabled (10%). ***Email:*** lswett@kaufmannandkaufmann.com

STEVEN P. MUTERSBAUGH, born Akron, Ohio, November 19, 1971; admitted to bar, 2002, Ohio. *Education:* University of Findlay (B.A., 1994); University of Akron Law School (J.D., 2002). *Member:* Akron (Member, Probate Law Section), Ohio State (Member, Estate Planning Section) and American Bar Associations. ***PRACTICE AREAS:*** Estate Planning; Probate; Estate Planning for the Disabled; Elder Law; Corporate Law. ***Email:*** smutersbaugh@kaufmannandkaufmann.com

JULIE A. FARRIS, born Akron, Ohio, November 24, 1973; admitted to bar, 2001, Ohio. *Education:* Wheaton College (B.A., 1996); New England School of Law (J.D., 2001). Former Judicial Attorney, Ninth District Court of Appeals. *Member:* Akron (Member, Probate Section), Portage County and Ohio State (Member: Estate Planning, Trust and Probate Section; Elder Law Committee) Bar Associations; National Academy of Elder Law Attorneys. ***PRACTICE AREAS:*** Estate Planning; Estate Planning for the Disabled; Elder Law; Guardianship. ***Email:*** jfarris@kaufmannandkaufmann.com

REPRESENTATIVE CLIENTS: Miller's Rental and Sales Co., Inc.; The Village of St. Edward; Blind & Sons, Inc.; King Machine of Akron, Inc.; J. Parker & Sons, Inc.
REFERENCES: First National Bank of Akron; Bank One, Akron, NA.

KOVACH & FARLING CO., LPA

AKRON, OHIO

(See Cleveland)

Commercial Contract Disputes, Business Litigation, Trade Secret Litigation, Business Tort Litigation, Takeover Litigation, Class Action Litigation, Securities Litigation, Restrictive Covenant Litigation, Shareholder Derivative.

DANIEL J. LEFFLER
COUNSELOR AT LAW

UNION POINT
190 UNION STREET, SUITE 201
AKRON, OHIO 44304
Telephone: 330-253-5996
Fax: 330-762-9743
Email: danielleffler@sbcglobal.net
URL: http://www.djlnegotiations.com

Employment Law, Union Contract Negotiations, Union Labor Law, Civil Litigation.

DANIEL J. LEFFLER, born 1967; admitted to bar, 2003, Ohio. *Education:* University of Akron (B.S., Political Science, 1991; J.D., 2003). Phi Delta Phi (President, 2003). Firefighter, City of University Heights, 1990—. Appointed to State Fire Commission. *Member:* Akron and Ohio State Bar Associations; The Association of Trial Lawyers of America. ***PRACTICE AREAS:*** Employment Law; Union Contract Negotiations; Union Labor Law; Civil Litigation.

MARSHALL, DENNEHEY, WARNER, COLEMAN & GOGGIN

120 E. MILL STREET
SUITE 240
AKRON, OHIO 44308
Telephone: 330-255-0037
Fax: 330-255-0040
Email: marshalldennehey@mdwcg.com
URL: http://www.marshalldennehey.com

Bethlehem, Pennsylvania Office: 1200 Martin Tower. Telephone: 484-895-2300. Fax: 484-895-0208.

Doylestown, Pennsylvania Office: 10 North Main Street. Telephone: 267-880-2020. Fax: 215-348-5439.

Erie, Pennsylvania Office: Renaissance Centre, 1001 State Street, 14th Floor. Telephone: 814-461-7800. Fax: 814-461-7818.

Harrisburg, Pennsylvania Office: 4200 Crums Mill Road, Suite B. Telephone: 717-651-3500. Fax: 717-651-9630.

King Of Prussia, Pennsylvania Office: 620 Freedom Business Center, Suite 300. Telephone: 610-354-8250. Fax: 610-354-8299; 610-354-8499.

Pittsburgh, Pennsylvania Office: 600 Grant Street, US Steel Tower, Suite 2900. Telephone: 412-803-1140. Fax: 412-803-1188.

Scranton, Pennsylvania Office: 401 Adams Avenue, Suite 400. Telephone: 570-496-4600. Fax: 570-496-0567.

Williamsport, Pennsylvania Office: 33 W. Third Street, Suite 200. Telephone: 570-326-9091. Fax: 570-326-5507.

Cherry Hill, New Jersey Office: Woodland Falls Corporate Park, 200 Lake Drive East, Suite 300. Telephone: 856-414-6000. Fax: 856-414-6077.

Wilmington, Delaware Office: 1220 North Market Street, 5th Floor. Telephone: 302-552-4300. Fax: 302-651-7905.

Roseland, New Jersey Office: 425 Eagle Rock Avenue, Suite 302. Telephone: 973-618-4100. Fax: 973-618-0685.

Tampa, Florida Office: 201 E. Kennedy Boulevard, Suite 1100. Telephone: 813-472-7800. Fax: 813-472-7811.

Orlando, Florida Office: Landmark Center One, 315 East Robinson Street, Suite 475. Telephone: 407-246-0668. Fax: 407-839-3008.

Fort Lauderdale, Florida Office: One East Broward Boulevard, Suite 500. Telephone: 954-847-4920. Fax: 954-627-6640.

Jacksonville, Florida Office: 200 West Forsythe Street, Suite 1400. Telephone: 904-358-4200. Fax: 904-355-0018.

Defense Litigation Practice before all State and Federal Courts and Administrative Agencies. Appellate Advocacy; Arson; Fraud Litigation; Automobile Liability; Automotive Products Liability; Bad Faith; Employment Law; Commercial Litigation; Environmental and Toxic Torts; General Liability; Health Care Liability; Insurance Coverage; Insurance Law; Intellectual Property; Life, Health & Disability; Liquor Liability; Long-Term Care Liability; Municipal Liability and Civil Rights; Construction Litigation; Medical Device and Pharmaceutical; Medical Malpractice; Products Liability; Professional Malpractice; Property Damage; Railroad Litigation; Retail Liability; Special Investigations Litigation; Amusement Park, Sports and Entertainment; Securities & Investments; Transportation Litigation; Trucking Litigation; Workers' Compensation; Technology.

FIRM PROFILE: Marshall, Dennehey, Warner, Coleman and Goggin, founded in 1961, has realized substantial growth in response to our continually expanding client base.

We are exclusively a defense firm, and our professional practices encompass a wide spectrum of litigation matters.

We are over 300 attorneys strong and have seventeen offices strategically located in Pennsylvania, New Jersey, Delaware, Ohio and Florida.

This distribution of attorneys and offices provides our clients with access to state-wide or regional representation coupled with strong, accessible, and experienced centralized management.

We are proud of the remarkable level of our internal stability, ensuring file handling continuity.

Surveys of the nation's largest firms consistently show our firm to be a leader in minority hiring and advancement as measured by the number of African-American partners and associates in our ranks.

(This Listing Continued)

Our expertise is evidenced by the fact that many of our attorneys have had books, chapter contributions, monographs, and articles published in their practice areas.

Our firm members are quite active and play leadership roles in numerous professional, charitable, community and business associations.

We are on the cutting-edge of alternative billing arrangements.

Inquiries concerning our firm should be directed to our President and CEO, Thomas A. Brophy, Esq., whose number is (215) 575-2748. His fax number is (215) 575-0856 and his email address is tbrophy@mdwcg.com. His address is 1845 Walnut Street, Philadelphia, PA 19103.

SHAREHOLDER

SAMUEL G. CASOLARI, JR., born Coraopolis, Pennsylvania; admitted to bar, 1986, Ohio and U.S. District Court, Northern District of Ohio; 1987, U.S. Court of Appeals, Sixth Circuit; 2004, U.S. District Court, Southern District of Ohio. *Education:* Grove City College (B.A., cum laude, 1983); University of Akron (J.D., 1986). Omicron Delta Kappa; Phi Alpha Theta; Pi Gamma Mu; Beta Sigma. Trustee, Grove City College, 1998—. Trustee, Marva Collins Prep School, 1996—. Co-Author, Ohio - Chapter Contribution: Civil Rule 35 Examinations, Law Office Practice Series. *Member:* Ohio State Bar Association (Member, Judicial Administration and Legal Reform Committee). ***REPORTED CASES:*** Criss v. Springfield Tp., 538 N.E.2d 406 (Ohio 1989); Hunter v. Shenango Furnace Co., 527 N.E.2d 871 (Ohio 1988); Criss v. Springfield Township, 566 N.E.2d 1232 (Ohio 1991). ***PRACTICE AREAS:*** Insurance Defense; Auto Insurance Defense; Slip and Fall Defense; Appellate; Asbestos Litigation; Insurance Coverage. ***Email:*** scasolari@mdwcg.com

RESIDENT ASSOCIATES

JOHN CHRISTOPHER REECE, born Akron, Ohio; admitted to bar, 1989, Ohio; 1991, U.S. District Court, Northern District of Ohio and U.S. Court of Appeals, Sixth Circuit; 1993, U.S. Supreme Court; 2004, U.S. District Court, Southern District of Ohio. *Education:* University of Akron (B.S., 1985; J.D., 1989). Assistant Director of Law, Akron, Ohio, 1990-2003. *Member:* Akron Bar Association. ***REPORTED CASES:*** Bukowski v. City of Akron, 326 F.3d 702 (6th Cir. 2003); Feathers v. Aey, 319 F.3d 843 (6th Ciru. 2003); Lorenzo v. City of Akron, 9th Dist. No. 21085, 2002 Ohio 7.318, (2002 Ohio App. Lexis 7162). ***PRACTICE AREAS:*** Premises Liability Defense; Motor Vehicle Defense; Product Liability; Appellate. ***Email:*** creece@mdwcg.com

MARTIN H. SITLER, born Salem, Ohio; admitted to bar, 1992, South Dakota; 2004, Pennsylvania and Ohio; 2005, U.S. District Court, Southern District of Ohio. *Education:* The Ohio State University (B.S., 1983); University of South Dakota (J.D., 1992); Judge Advocate General School, U.S. Army (LL.M., 1997). Associate Professor, Criminal Law Department, The Judge Advocate General School, U.S. Army, Charlottesville, Virginia, 1997-2000. Deputy Circuit Military Judge, Piedmont Judicial Circuit, Navy-Marine Corps Trial Judiciary, 2000-2004. Scanlon Inn of Court, Akron, Ohio, 2005. Author: "A Hole in the Make-Whole Doctrine: The Ohio Supreme Court Approves an Insurance Contract that Avoids the Make-Whole Doctrine," Defense Digest, Vol. 11, No. 1, March 2005. [Lieut. Col., U.S. Marine Corps, retired, 1984-2004]. ***PRACTICE AREAS:*** Liability. ***Email:*** msitler@mdwcg.com

REPRESENTATIVE CLIENTS: Acceptance Insurance Company; Ace USA; Acme Markets, Inc.; Aegis Insurance Group; Allstate Insurance Company; American Honda Motor Company, Inc.; American International Group; American Reinsurance Company; Amerimar Realty Company; Amguard Insurance Company; Anheuser Busch Companies, Inc.; Aon Corporation; ARAMARK; Avis Rent-A-Car Systems, Inc.; Bayliner Marine Corporation; Bethlehem Steel Corporation; BIC Corporation; Bituminous Insurance Company; Bridgestone Tire; Britamco Underwriters, Inc.; Budget Rent-A-Car Corporation; Cambridge; Cameron-Cooper Corporation; Campbell Soup Company; Canal Insurance Company; Catholic Mutual Group; CDI Corporation; CGH Claims Services; Chubb Group of Insurance Companies; CIGNA Insurance Group Claims and Risk Control, Inc.; Cincinnati Insurance Company; Clarendon National Insurance Company; Claridge Casino Hotel; Claims Management Services; CNA Insurance Companies; Commonwealth of Pennsylvania; Conair Corporation; Consolidated Freightways; Countrywide Services Corp.; Crawford & Company; Crum & Forster; Cunningham Lindsey; VS; Daimler Chrysler Corporation; Denny's Restaurant; Dorney Park Coaster Co., Inc; Eastern Engineering and Elevator Company; Empire Insurance Company; Empire State Claims Service; Employers Insurance of Wausau; Employers Mutual Insurance Company; Encompass-NJ; Erie Insurance Company; Executive Risk; Federal Black Lung; Federated Department Stores, Inc.; Fireman's Fund Insurance Company; First Mercury Syndicate; First Union Corp.; GAB Robins/North America, Inc.; Gallagher Bassett Services, Inc.; General Electric Company; Georgia-Pacific Corporation; General Motors Corporation; General Star Indemnity Company; Gerling American Insurance Company; Getty Oil Company; Giles & Ransome; Gillians Wonderland Pier; Great American Insurance Cos.; Hardee's Food Systems, Inc.; Harleysville Insurance Co.; Honda Motor Company, Ltd.; Hyatt Hotels; Integon Insurance Company; INX International Ink Company; ITT Consumer Financial Corporation; J.B. Hunt Transportation, Inc.; J.C. Penney Financial Services & Insurance Company; K & K Insurance Group; Kemper National Insurance Company; Kmart Corporation; Liberty Mutual Insurance Company; Living Well Lady; Lloyds of London; Lumberman's Underwriting Alliance; Makita USA, Inc.; Marsh USA, Inc.; May Department Stores; Manville Personal Injury Settlement Trust; Marriott Corporation; Mazda Motor Corporation; McDonald's Corporation; Medical Cat Fund; Medical Inter-Insurance Exchange; Mellon Bank; Merck and Company, Inc.; Metropolitan Property & Casualty Company; Minnesota Mining & Manufacturing Co. (3M); Mitsubishi Heavy Industries; Mitsubishi Motors Corporation; National Interstate; National Railroad Passenger Corporation; Nationwide Group; Naughton Insurance; Nestle USA, Inc.; NJ Cure; Nordstrom, Inc.; Occidental; Orkin Exterminating Company; Overnite Transportation Company; Pennsylvania Insurance Guaranty Association; Pennsylvania Inter-Governmental Risk Management Association; Philadelphia Eagles; PNC Bank Corporation; Pret-Rubin, Inc.; Price America Financial Services; Princeton Insurance Company; Prudential Property & Casualty Insurance Company; Prudential Reinsurance Company; Quaker City Insurance Company; Ranger Insurance Company; Republic Insurance Company; Richard I. Rubin & Co., Inc.; Riddell, Inc.; Risk Enterprise Management; Risk Retention; Risk Services, Inc.; Rite-Aid Corporation; Roadway Services, Inc.; Royal Insurance Company; RSKco.; Safeco Insurance Companies; Sara Lee Corporation; Schindler Elevator Corporation; Scottsdale Insurance Company; Sears, Roebuck and Company; Sedgwick Claims Management Services Inc.; Selective Insurance Company; Selective Insurance Group; Shand Morahan Company; Sherwin Williams; Six Flags Great Adventure; SFK USA, Inc.; St. Paul Insurance Companies; Supervalu; Suzuki Motor Corporation; Target Stores; Temple University; The Boeing Company; The Carrier Corporation; The Coca-Cola Company; The Delaware Valley Insurance Trust; The Doctor's Company; The Goodyear Tire and Rubber Company; The Ohio Casualty Insurance Company; The Pep Boys - Manny, Moe and Jack; The Philadelphia Housing Authority; The PMA Group; The Shelby Insurance Company; The Stanley Works; The Travelers Insurance Companies; Thompson Consumer Electronics; TJ Maxx Company; Toplis & Harding, Inc.; TIG Insurance; Trek Bicycle Corporation; Tyco International; U-Haul Corporation; United Educators Insurance Risk Retention Group, Inc.; United Parcel Service; United Skates of America; United States Fidelity and Guaranty Company; University of

(This Listing Continued)

MARSHALL, DENNEHEY, WARNER, COLEMAN & GOGGIN, Akron—Continued

Pennsylvania; USAA; U.S. Steel Mining Company; Utica Mutual Insurance Company; VHA East, Inc.; Waste Management Systems, Inc.; Wawa, Inc.; Weichert Realtors; Wells Fargo Guard Service; Westinghouse Electric Corporation; Westport Insurance Company; Weyerhaeuser Company; Whirlpool Corporation; White Consolidated Industries, Inc.; Willis-Corroon Administrative Services; Yellow Freight System, Inc.; Young Men's Christian Association; Zurich-American Insurance Company.

JOHN J. McCARROLL

AKRON, OHIO

(See Cleveland)

Victims Rights, Personal Injury, Bankruptcy, Business Law, Probate, Criminal Defense, Immigration Law.

McKINZIE AND ASSOCIATES

529 WHITE POND
AKRON, OHIO 44320-1123
Telephone: 330-864-3100
Fax: 330-864-7753
Email: law@apk.net
URL: http://www.mckinzieandassociateslaw.com

Business Law, Criminal Law, Construction, Personal Injury, Family Law and Civil Practice.

TIMOTHY DALE McKINZIE, born 1954; admitted to bar, 1993, Ohio and Florida. *Education:* Indiana University (B.A., 1976); University of Akron (J.D., 1993). *Member:* The Florida Bar. ***LANGUAGES:*** Spanish. ***PRACTICE AREAS:*** Business Law; Criminal Law; Construction Law; Personal Injury; Family Law; Civil Practice.

LAW OFFICE OF WARNER MENDENHALL

Established in 1998

190 NORTH UNION STREET
AKRON, OHIO 44304
Telephone: 330-535-9160; 877-764-2219
Fax: 330-762-9743
Email: warnermendenhall@hotmail.com
URL: http://www.warnermendenhall.com

False Claims Act, Whistleblower Litigation, Qui Tam Litigation, Employment Law, Government, Municipal Law, Litigation, Bankruptcy.

FIRM PROFILE: Warner Mendenhall is a sole practitioner focused on representing whistleblowers, citizens enforcing their civil rights, employees wrongfully discharged, and debtors.

WARNER MENDENHALL, born Durham, North Carolina, February 24, 1962; admitted to bar, 1998, Ohio and U.S. District Court, Northern District of Ohio; 1999, U.S. Court of Appeals, Sixth Circuit. *Education:* University of Akron (B.A., 1985; J.D., 1998); Kent State University (M.A., Political Science, 1996). Member, Taxpayers Against Fraud Qui-Tam Attorney Network. Akron City Council, 1992-1995. *Member:* Akron, Ohio State and American Bar Associations; The Association of Trial Lawyers of America; Summit County Trial Lawyers Association; Ohio Association of Trial Lawyers; The Scanlon Inn of Court. ***LANGUAGES:*** Spanish. ***REPORTED CASES:*** State of Ohio Ex. Rel Gaydosh v. City of Twinsburg; Frank v. City of Akron; Hickory Street Coalition v. City of Akron; In re Hall. ***PRACTICE AREAS:*** False Claims Act; Whistleblower Litigation; Qui Tam Litigation; Government; Municipal Law; Litigation; Bankruptcy.

Language: Spanish.

THE LAW OFFICES OF MICHAEL MOTYLINSKI

AKRON, OHIO

(See Broadview Heights)

Business Law, Real Estate, Estate Planning, Collections, Criminal.

OLDHAM & DOWLING

Established in 1994

195 SOUTH MAIN STREET
SUITE 300
AKRON, OHIO 44308
Telephone: 330-762-7377
Telecopier: 330-762-7390
Email: wdowling@oldham-dowling.com
URL: http://www.lawyers.com/oldham&dowling

Civil Litigation, Insurance Defense, Personal Injury, Product Liability, Probate & Estate Planning, Administration, Family Law, Adoption.

PARTNERS

WILLIAM M. OLDHAM, born Youngstown, Ohio, January 5, 1942; admitted to bar, 1967, Ohio. *Education:* College of Wooster; University of Akron (B.A., 1964; J.D., 1967). Phi Alpha Delta. Distinguished Visiting Professor, University of Akron College of Law, 1991. Partner, Buckingham, Doolittle & Burroughs, A Legal Professional Association, 1974-1994 (Managing Partner, 1985-1990). *Member:* Akron Bar Association (Member, Executive Committee, 1981-1984; President, 1987-1988). ***PRACTICE AREAS:*** Trial Practice; Probate; Adoption Law. ***Email:*** wmo@oldham-dowling.com

WILLIAM D. DOWLING, JR., born Wausau, Wisconsin, 1953; admitted to bar, 1980, Ohio. *Education:* The Ohio State University (B.S., summa cum laude, 1974; M.A., 1977); Yale University (J.D., 1980). Partner, Buckingham, Doolittle & Burroughs, A Legal Professional Association, 1987-1994. Member, Board of Trustees: Summit County Children Services; Western Reserve Legal Services Board (President, 1990-1993; Treasurer, 1994-1996). *Member:* Akron (Chair, Common Pleas Court Committee, 1994-1996), Ohio State and American Bar Associations; Defense Research Institute; Ohio Association of Civil Trial Attorneys. ***PRACTICE AREAS:*** Litigation; Trial Practice; Insurance Defense; Employment Law. ***Email:*** wdowling@oldham-dowling.com

HAMILTON DeSAUSSURE, JR., born Wiesbaden, Germany, April 10, 1957; admitted to bar, 1983, Ohio and U.S. District Court, Northern District of Ohio. *Education:* Kenyon College (B.A., 1979); Wake Forest University (J.D., 1983). National Order of Barristers. *Member:* Akron, Ohio State and American Bar Associations. ***PRACTICE AREAS:*** Litigation; Trial Practice; Insurance Defense. ***Email:*** hd@oldham-dowling.com

REGINALD S. KRAMER, born Jersey City, New Jersey, April 21, 1952; admitted to bar, 1980, Ohio; 1990, U.S. District Court, Northern District of Ohio. *Education:* College of Wooster (B.A., 1974); University of Akron (J.D., 1980). Contributing Author: Chapter on Ohio's "Referee System," Ohio Domestic Relations Law, Baldwin's, 1984. Common Pleas Referee, Medina County, 1980-1983. Assistant Prosecutor, Medina County, 1985-1986. Trustee, Wayne County Public Library, 1998+13 . *Member:* Akron, Wayne County, Ohio State and American Bar Association. ***PRACTICE AREAS:*** Trial Practice; Environmental Litigation; Insurance Defense Law. ***Email:*** rkramer@oldham-dowling.com

MATTHEW W. OBY, born Canton, Ohio, July 13, 1955; admitted to bar, 1987, Ohio; 1989, U.S. District Court, Northern District of Ohio. *Education:* College of Wooster (B.A., 1977); University of Akron (J.D., cum laude, 1987). *Member:* Akron and Ohio State Bar Associations. ***PRACTICE AREAS:*** Tort Litigation; Commercial Litigation; Public Utility Litigation; Real Estate. ***Email:*** oby@oldham-dowling.com

JOSEPH K. OLDHAM, born Akron, Ohio, February 6, 1970; admitted to bar, 1995, Ohio and U.S. District Court, Northern District of Ohio. *Education:* Miami University (B.A., 1992); University of Akron (J.D., 1995). *Member:* Akron, Ohio State and American Bar Associations. ***PRACTICE AREAS:*** Trial Practice; Insurance Defense; Probate. ***Email:*** joldham@oldham-dowling.com

BLAKE R. GERNEY, born Abington, Pennsylvania, April 29, 1968; admitted to bar, 1995, Ohio and Pennsylvania; U.S. District Court, Northern District of Ohio. *Education:* Texas A&M University (B.S, 1990); University of Akron School of Law (J.D., 1995). Phi Delta Phi. *Member:* Akron, Ohio State, Pennsylvania and American Bar Associations. ***PRACTICE AREAS:*** Business Law; Corporate Law; Real Estate; Probate; Litigation. ***Email:*** bgerney@oldham-dowling.com

ASSOCIATES

RAYMOND C. MUELLER, born Pittsburgh, Pennsylvania, April 20, 1952; admitted to bar, 1988, Ohio and U.S. District Court, Northern District of Ohio. *Education:* Ohio University (B.A., cum laude, 1974); University of Akron (J.D., 1986). *Member:* Akron Bar Association; Canton Claims Association. ***PRACTICE AREAS:*** Litigation; Insurance Defense; Trial Practice. ***Email:*** rmueller@oldham-dowling.com

HALLE M. HEBERT, born Cleveland, Ohio, May 6, 1975; admitted to bar, 2000, Ohio. *Education:* Ohio State University (B.S., 1997); Cleveland State University (J.D., 2000). Phi Upsilon Omicron. *Member:* Akron, Ohio State (Member, Womens Section) and American Bar Associations. ***PRACTICE AREAS:*** Insurance Defense; Estate Planning; Adoption Law. ***Email:*** hhebert@oldham-dowling.com

COLIN G. SKINNER, born New Bethlehem, Pennsylvania, September 19, 1963; admitted to bar, 1995, Ohio. *Education:* The Pennsylvania State University (B.S.B.A., 1985); The University of Akron School of Law (J.D., magna cum laude, 1995). *Member:* Akron and Ohio State Bar Associations. ***PRACTICE AREAS:*** Litigation; Insurance Defense. ***Email:*** cskinner@oldham-dowling.com

JON A. OLDHAM, born Akron, Ohio, April 20. 1977; admitted to bar, 2002, Ohio. *Education:* Ohio University (B.S., cum laude, 1999); University of Akron School of Law (J.D., 2002). Magister, Phi Delta Phi. *Member:* Akron Bar Association. ***PRACTICE AREAS:*** Litigation; Business Law; Estate Planning. ***Email:*** jonoldham@oldham-dowling.com

MARK J. SCARPITTI, born Akron, Ohio, March 12, 1973; admitted to bar, 2002, Ohio. *Education:* Bowling Green State University (B.A., 1995); University of Akron School of Law (J.D., 2002). ***PRACTICE AREAS:*** Insurance Defense Litigation; Civil Litigation; Business Law; Estate Planning. ***Email:*** mscarpitti@oldham-dowling.com

CARA L. STALEY, born Bluffton, Ohio, April 15, 1979; admitted to bar, 2004, Ohio. *Education:* Bowling Green State University (B.A., summa cum laude, 2001); University of Akron School of Law (J.D., with honors, 2004). *Member:* Akron and Ohio State Bar Association; Ohio Women's Bar Association. ***LANGUAGES:*** Spanish. ***PRACTICE AREAS:*** Insurance Defense; Civil Litigation; Small Business Law. ***Email:*** cstaley@oldham-dowling.com

OF COUNSEL

DONALD S. VARIAN, JR., born Akron, Ohio, April 8, 1945; admitted to bar, 1970, Ohio. *Education:* University of Akron (B.A., 1967); American University (J.D., 1970). Pi Sigma Alpha; Omicron Delta Kappa; Phi Alpha Delta. Member, American University Law Review, 1969-1970. Assistant Director of Law, Akron, Ohio, 1971-1973. *Member:* Akron and Ohio State Bar Associations; Ohio Academy of Trial Lawyers; The Association of Trial Lawyers of America. ***PRACTICE AREAS:*** Personal Injury; Medical Malpractice; Civil Litigation; Criminal. ***Email:*** varianlaw@aol.com

REPRESENTATIVE CLIENTS: State Farm Mutual Automobile Insurance Co.; State Farm Fire & Casualty; Ohio Casualty Group Insurance Companies; The Step2 Company; SAFECO/American States Insurance Company; May Department Stores Company; National

(This Listing Continued)

City Bank; MASCO; Liberty Mutual; Kokosing Construction Company General Electric Co.; PPG Industries, Inc.; A.S. Automotive Systems; APA Transport Co.

PAGANO, WILSON, THOMARIOS, GILLISSIE & LENAHAN LLC

AKRON, OHIO

(See Cleveland)

Criminal Law, Employment Defense, Personal Injury, Workers Compensation, Social Security Disability, Probate, Estate Planning, Family Law, Business Law, Collections.

PARKER LEIBY HANNA & RASNICK, LLC

Established in 1988

388 S. MAIN STREET, SUITE 402
AKRON, OHIO 44311
Telephone: 330-253-2227
Fax: 330-253-1261
Email: main@neolaw.biz
URL: http://www.neolaw.biz

Civil Litigation, Civil Appeals, Toxic Torts Litigation, Products Liability Litigation, Real Estate Brokers and Agents Liability, Commercial Real Estate, Residential Real Estate, Personal Injury, Medical Malpractice, Insurance Liability, Estate Planning, Probate, Corporate Law and Family Law.

FIRM PROFILE: Parker Leiby Hanna & Rasnick, LLC serves clients across the nation and locally who demand a sophisticated approach to solving their problems. We focus on complex business, personal planning and litigation issues.

MEMBERS OF FIRM

THOMAS M. PARKER, born Cleveland, Ohio, February 10, 1954; admitted to bar, 1979, Ohio and U.S. District Court, Northern District of Ohio; 1982, U.S. Court of Appeals, Sixth Circuit; 1986, U.S. District Court, Eastern District of Michigan; 1996, U.S. Supreme Court; 2000, U.S. District Court, Southern District of Ohio; 2001, U.S. District Court, Northern District of Indiana. *Education:* Miami University (A.B., cum laude, 1976); Case Western Reserve University (J.D., 1979). Member, Akron Board of Education, 1990-1993. Member, Product Liability Advisory Council. *Member:* Defense Research Institute (Member, Committees on: Environmental Law; Toxic Torts; Medical Device Law). ***REPORTED CASES:*** Kemp v. Medtronic, Inc., 231 F.3d 216, (6th Cir 2000); Dunlap v. Medtronic, Inc., 47 F.Supp.2d 888, (N.D.Ohio 1999); Midwest Specialties, Inc. v. Crown Indus. Products Co., 940 F.Supp 1160, (N.D.Ohio 1996); Ditto v. Monsanto Co. 867 F.Supp. 585 (N.D.Ohio 1993); Sekeres v. Arbaugh, 31 Ohio St.3d 24 (1987). ***PRACTICE AREAS:*** Products Liability Litigation; Toxic Torts Litigation; Medical Device Litigation; General Civil Litigation. ***Email:*** tparker@neolaw.biz

STEPHEN P. LEIBY, born Oswego, New York, September 27, 1947; admitted to bar, 1973, Ohio; 1974, U.S. District Court, Northern District of Ohio; 1997, U.S. Tax Court; 2002, U.S. Court of Appeals, Sixth Circuit. *Education:* Wright State University (B.A., 1969); University of Akron (J.D., 1973). Chair, Common Pleas and Appellate Courts Committee, Akron Bar Association, 1998-2001. Outstanding Committee Chair, Akron Bar Association, 2001; Commission on Judicial Candidates, Akron Bar Association, 1998-2000. Lecturer, Real Estate Purchases, Sales, and Leases. *Member:* Ohio State Bar Association (Member, Sections on: Litigation and Real Estate); Fellow: Akron Bar Association Foundation. ***REPORTED CASES:*** Summit County Crisis Pregnancy Center, Inc. v. Fisher, 830 F.Supp.1029, (N.D.Ohio 1993); Maloney v. Patterson, 63 Ohio App.3d 405 (Ohio App. 9 Dist. 1989); Gathagan v. Firestone Tire & Rubber Co., 23 Ohio App. 3d 16 (Ohio App. 9 Dist. 1985). ***PRACTICE AREAS:*** Business Litigation; Franchise Litigation; Real Estate Litigation; Commercial Real Estate; Residential Real Estate; Real Estate Brokers and Agents Liability. ***Email:*** sleiby@neolaw.biz

TIMOTHY H. HANNA, born Barberton, Ohio, November 14, 1958; admitted to bar, 1985, Ohio, U.S. Court of Appeals, Sixth and Eleventh Circuits, U.S. District Court, Northern District of Ohio and U.S. District Court, Eastern District of Michigan. *Education:* University of Akron (B.S., 1981; J.D., 1985). *Member:* Akron, Ohio State and American Bar Associations; Ohio Academy of Trial Lawyers; The Association of Trial Lawyers of America. ***PRACTICE AREAS:*** Personal Injury; Medical Malpractice; Insurance; Products Liability. ***Email:*** thanna2074@aol.com

JOHN F. RASNICK, born Akron, Ohio, September 2, 1956; admitted to bar, 1982, Ohio. *Education:* Walsh College (B.A., 1979); University of Akron (J.D., 1982). *Member:* Akron and Ohio State Bar Associations. ***PRACTICE AREAS:*** Estate Planning; Probate; Corporate Law. ***Email:*** jrasnick@neolaw.biz

ASSOCIATES

DONALD S. PLUM, born Akron, Ohio, February 24, 1963; admitted to bar, 1988, Ohio; 1989, U.S. District Court, Northern District of Ohio; 1993, U.S. Tax Court. *Education:* University of Virginia (B.A., with honors, 1985); University of Michigan (J.D., cum laude, 1988). ***PRACTICE AREAS:*** Probate; Estate Planning; Corporate Law. ***Email:*** dplum@neolaw.biz

ROBERT ROE FOX, born York, Pennsylvania, January 14, 1964; admitted to bar, 1989, Ohio. *Education:* Denison University (B.A., 1986); University of Akron (J.D.,1989). *Member:* Akron and Ohio State Bar Associations. ***PRACTICE AREAS:*** General Practice; Products Liability; Family Law. ***Email:*** rfox@neolaw.biz

STEVEN R. HOBSON, II, born Alliance, Ohio, July 13, 1971; admitted to bar, 1998, Ohio; 1999, U.S. District Court, Northern District of Ohio; 2002, U.S. Court of Appeals, Sixth Circuit. *Education:* Kent State University (B.A., magna cum laude, 1993); University of Akron (J.D., magna cum laude, 1997). Phi Beta Kappa. Case and Comment Editor, Akron Law Review. *Member:* Akron (Member, Scholarship Chair, 2003-2004) and Ohio State Bar Associations. ***PRACTICE AREAS:*** Business Litigation; Civil Litigation; Real Estate Litigation. ***Email:*** shobson@neolaw.biz

(This Listing Continued)

ANDREW T. HAYES, born Springfield, Ohio, 1973; admitted to bar, 2002, Ohio; 2003, U.S. District Court, Northern District of Ohio. *Education:* Grace College (B.S., 1999); University of Akron (J.D., 2002). *Member:* Akron (Member, Scholarship Committee, 2003—), Ohio State and American Bar Associations. ***PRACTICE AREAS:*** Products Liability Litigation; General Civil Litigation. ***Email:*** ahayes@neolaw.biz

OF COUNSEL

CHERYL L. RAMSBURG, born Lorain, Ohio, February 2, 1958; admitted to bar, 1996, Ohio. *Education:* Malone College, Canton (B.A., cum laude, 1980); Kent State University (M.B.A., 1987); Akron University Law School (J.D., summa cum laude, 1996). Certified Public Accountant, Ohio, 1981. *Member:* Ohio State and American Bar Associations. ***PRACTICE AREAS:*** Estate Planning; Probate Administration; Business Law. ***Email:*** cheriramsburg@neo.rr.com

REPRESENTATIVE CLIENTS: Medtronic, Inc.; Shell Oil Co.; ChevronTexaco; PPG Industries, Inc.; Monsanto Co.; The Dow Chemical Co.

DENNIS E. PAUL

AKRON, OHIO

(See Medina)

Personal Injury, Divorce, Adoption Advocate.

PERANTINIDES & NOLAN CO., L.P.A.

Established in 1957

300 COURTYARD SQUARE
80 SOUTH SUMMIT STREET
AKRON, OHIO 44308-1736
Telephone: 330-253-5454
Telecopier: 330-253-6524
Email: pn@perantinides.com
URL: http://www.perantinides.com

General Civil Trial and Appellate Practice. Negligence, Products Liability, Medical Legal, Malpractice, Construction, Toxic Tort and Commercial Law. Insurance, Environmental, Aviation, Wrongful Death and Civil Rights.

PAUL G. PERANTINIDES, born Youngstown, Ohio, March 7, 1944; admitted to bar, 1969, Ohio. *Education:* Youngstown State University (B.A., 1966); The University of Akron (J.D., 1969). Listed in Best Lawyers in America, 1995-2000. Lecturer, Insurance Law, University of Akron School of Law, 1976-1979. *Member:* Akron (Member, Executive Committee, 1982-1985; Chairman, Common Pleas Court Committee, 1981-1982; President, Trial Section, 1985-1986), Ohio State and American Bar Associations; Illinois Trial Lawyers Association; Ohio Academy of Trial Lawyers; American College of Legal Medicine; Trial Lawyers for Public Justice; Illinois Trial Lawyers Association; Texas Trial Lawyers Association; The Association of Trial Lawyers of America. ***REPORTED CASES:*** Criss v. Springfield Township, 56 Oh St 3d 82, 564 NE2d, Pg 440, 10 ALR 5th 1064; Faruque, et al v. Provident Life and Accident Ins. Co. et al, 31 Oh St 3d, Pg 34; Hersberger v. Akron City Hospital, 34 Oh St 3d 1; Richards v. St. Thomas Hospital, 24 Oh 3d 27; Herr v. Robinson Memorial Hospital, 49 Oh St 3d 6; Beck v. Cianchetti, 1 Oh St 3 231; Stein v. Brown, 18 Oh St 3d 305; Bradford v. Zahn, 36 Oh St 3d 236, 522 N.E. 2d 1088; Preston v. Murty, 32 Oh St 3d 334, 512 N.E. 2d 1174; Unrue v. Akron City Hospital, Finegan v. Akron City Hospital and Keaton v. Coshocton Hospital, 28 Oh St 3d 743, 503 N.E. 2d 742. ***PRACTICE AREAS:*** Medical Malpractice; Personal Injury; Defective Products; Wrongful Death. ***Email:*** paul@perantinides.com

CHRIS T. NOLAN, born Skopia, Greece, August 18, 1947; admitted to bar, 1973, Ohio. *Education:* The Ohio State University (B.A., 1970); The University of Akron (J.D., 1973). Phi Alpha Delta. Author: Chapter for Personal Injury Litigation in Ohio, Legal Center Institute, 1985—. CLE Lecturer, Ohio Heights Center, Inc., 1982-1983 and 1986-1987. *Member:* Akron (Member, Executive Committee, 1988-1991; Common Pleas Court Committee; Federal Court Committee), Ohio State and American Bar Associations; Ohio Association of Civil Trial Attorneys; American Arbitration Association; Association of Trial Lawyers of America; Ohio Association of Trial Lawyers. ***PRACTICE AREAS:*** Civil Trial Litigation; Medical Malpractice; Personal Injury; Defective Products; Wrongful Death. ***Email:*** cnolan@perantinides.com

---

PETER D. JANOS, born Warren, Ohio, September 30, 1966; admitted to bar, 1992, Ohio. *Education:* University of Pittsburgh (B.A., cum laude, 1989); University of Akron (J.D., 1991). *Member:* Akron, Ohio State and American Bar Associations; Scanlon Inns of Court. ***LANGUAGES:*** Greek. ***PRACTICE AREAS:*** Trial Litigation; Insurance Defense; Personal Injury; Medical Malpractice. ***Email:*** peter@perantinides.com

ANTONIOS P. TSAROUHAS, born Altoona, Pennsylvania, September 4, 1967; admitted to bar, 1994, Ohio. *Education:* University of Pittsburgh (B.A., in Economics, 1989); Ohio Northern University (J.D., 1994). *Member:* Akron, Ohio State and American Bar Associations. ***PRACTICE AREAS:*** Medical Malpractice; Personal Injury; Product Defects; Wrongful Death. ***Email:*** tony@perantinides.com

MICHAEL J. MAILLIS, born Youngstown, Ohio, September 27, 1969; admitted to bar, 1995, Ohio. *Education:* Youngstown State University (B.A., 1990) Dean's List; University of Akron School of Law (J.D., 1995) Dean's List. Former Assistant Law Director,

(This Listing Continued)

PERANTINIDES & NOLAN CO., L.P.A., Akron—Continued

City of Youngstown. Former Assistant County Prosecutor, Mahoning County. ***PRACTICE AREAS:*** Personal Injury; Medical Malpractice; Trial Practice Litigation; Criminal Defense. ***Email:*** mmaillis@perantinides.com

REFERENCES: National City Bank, Akron; Charter One Bank.

PORTER WRIGHT MORRIS & ARTHUR LLP

AKRON, OHIO

(See Cleveland)

Alternative Dispute Resolution, Agricultural Law, Antitrust and Trade Regulation, Business and Corporate, Complex Litigation, Construction, Employee Benefits, Energy and Utilities, Environment, Federal Administrative Law, Federal Contracting and Procurement, Financial Institutions, General Practice, Governmental Affairs, Health Care, Insurance, Intellectual Property, International Business, Labor and Employment, Litigation, Public Law, Public Finance, Real Estate, Securities, Taxation, Technology, Trusts and Estates.

RENNER, KENNER, GREIVE, BOBAK, TAYLOR & WEBER

A LEGAL PROFESSIONAL ASSOCIATION

Established in 1917

4TH FLOOR, FIRST NATIONAL TOWER
AKRON, OHIO 44308-1456
Telephone: 330-376-1242
Facsimile: 330-376-9646
Email: patlaw@rennerkenner.com
URL: http://www.rennerkenner.com

U.S. and Foreign Patent, Trademark and Copyright Law and Licensing. Antitrust and Unfair Competition Law. Litigation.

FIRM PROFILE: Founded in 1917, the firm continues its 87 year tradition of a full range of services in the intellectual property field, including protecting and exploiting the intellectual property rights of its clients both in the United States and worldwide. The firm also has extensive experience in asserting and defending claims involving intellectual property rights for clients ranging from individuals to multinational companies.

PHILLIP L. KENNER, born Fort Wayne, Indiana, February 12, 1935; admitted to bar, 1965, Ohio; registered to practice before U.S. Patent and Trademark Office. *Education:* University of Illinois (B.S., 1958); University of Akron (J.D., 1965). ***PRACTICE AREAS:*** Intellectual Property Law. ***Email:*** plkenner@rennerkenner.com

EDWARD G. GREIVE, born Cleveland, Ohio, May 19, 1942; admitted to bar, 1967, Ohio; registered to practice before U.S. Patent and Trademark Office. *Education:* Valparaiso University (B.S.E.E., 1964); Western Reserve University (J.D., 1967). Order of the Coif. ***PRACTICE AREAS:*** Intellectual Property Law. ***Email:*** eggreive@rennerkenner.com

DONALD J. BOBAK, born Cleveland, Ohio, August 1, 1943; admitted to bar, 1973, Ohio; registered to practice before U.S. Patent and Trademark Office and Canadian Patent Office. *Education:* John Carroll University; University of Akron (B.S., 1968; J.D., 1973). ***PRACTICE AREAS:*** Intellectual Property Law. ***Email:*** bobak@rennerkenner.com

RAY L. WEBER, born Canton, Ohio, June 3, 1945; admitted to bar, 1972, Ohio; registered to practice before U.S. Patent and Trademark Office. *Education:* University of Akron (B.S.E.E., 1968; J.D., 1972). ***PRACTICE AREAS:*** Intellectual Property Law. ***Email:*** rlweber@rennerkenner.com

RODNEY LEE SKOGLUND, born Marietta, Ohio, December 14, 1965; admitted to bar, 1991, Ohio; registered to practice before U.S. Patent and Trademark Office. *Education:* Muskingum College (B.A., 1988); University of Akron (J.D., 1991). ***PRACTICE AREAS:*** Intellectual Property Law. ***Email:*** rlskoglund@rennerkenner.com

ANDREW B. MORTON, born Cincinnati, Ohio, October 9, 1962; admitted to bar, 1993, Ohio; registered to practice before U.S. Patent and Trademark Office. *Education:* Ohio Northern University (B.S.E.E., 1984); Valparaiso University (J.D., 1993). ***PRACTICE AREAS:*** Intellectual Property Law. ***Email:*** morton@rennerkenner.com

ARTHUR M. REGINELLI, born Cleveland, Ohio, September 27, 1969; admitted to bar, 1995, Ohio; registered to practice before U.S. Patent and Trademark Office. *Education:* John Carroll University (B.S., 1992); Cleveland Marshall College of Law (J.D., cum laude, 1995). ***PRACTICE AREAS:*** Intellectual Property Law. ***Email:*** reginelli@rennerkenner.com

LAURA J. GENTILCORE, born Cleveland Heights, Ohio, February 6, 1953; admitted to bar, 1986, Ohio; registered to practice before U.S. Patent and Trademark Office. *Education:* Case Western Reserve University (B.A., 1975); Cleveland Marshall College of Law (J.D., cum laude, 1986). ***PRACTICE AREAS:*** Intellectual Property Law; Litigation. ***Email:*** ljgentilcore@rennerkenner.com

SHANNON V. McCUE, born Painesville, Ohio, March 21, 1971; admitted to bar, 1998, Ohio; registered to practice before U.S. Patent and Trademark Office. *Education:* Ohio State University (B.S.M.E., 1994); University of Akron (J.D., 1998). ***PRACTICE AREAS:*** Intellectual Property. ***Email:*** svmccue@rennerkenner.com

MARK L. WEBER, born Akron, Ohio, May 25, 1974; admitted to bar, 1999, Ohio; registered to practice before U.S Patent and Trademark Office. *Education:* Syracuse University (B.S., Chemical Engineering, 1996); University of Akron (J.D., 1999). ***PRACTICE AREAS:*** Intellectual Property Law. ***Email:*** mlweber@rennerkenner.com

TAMA L. DRENSKI, born East Liverpool, Ohio, September 10, 1956; admitted to bar, 2003, Ohio; registered to practice before U.S. Patent and Trademark Office. *Education:* Ohio Northern University (B.A., high distinction, 1977); University of Akron (J.D., cum laude, 2003). ***PRACTICE AREAS:*** Intellectual Property. ***Email:*** tldrenski@rennerkenner.com

TIM A. HODGKISS, born Warren, Ohio, May 3, 1973; admitted to bar, 2003, Ohio; registered to practice before U.S. Patent and Trademark Office. *Education:* Ohio University (B.S.E.E., 1996); University of Akron School of Law (J.D., 2002); Youngstown State University (M.B.A., 1998). Delta Mu Delta Business Administration Honor Society. ***PRACTICE AREAS:*** Intellectual Property. ***Email:*** thodgkiss@rennerkenner.com

REFERENCE: Key Bank.

RODERICK LINTON, LLP

Established in 1885

ONE CASCADE PLAZA, 15TH FLOOR
AKRON, OHIO 44308
Telephone: 330-434-3000
Telecopier: 330-434-9220
Email: rodericklinton@neo.rr.com
URL: http://www.rodericklinton.com

General Civil Trial Practice. Banking, Business, Commercial, Corporate, Probate, Workers Compensation, Administrative, Taxation, Insurance, Real Estate, Bankruptcy and Securities Law, Estate Planning, Zoning.

MEMBERS OF FIRM

KURT R. WEITENDORF, born Lakewood, Ohio, June 15, 1955; admitted to bar, 1980, Ohio and U.S. District Court, Northern District of Ohio; 1981, U.S. Court of Appeals, Sixth Circuit. *Education:* University of Kentucky; The Ohio State University (B.A., 1977); University of Akron (J.D., 1980). *Member:* Akron, Ohio State and American Bar Associations. ***PRACTICE AREAS:*** Civil Litigation; Insurance Defense. ***Email:*** kweitendorf@rodericklinton.com

TIMOTHY J. TRUBY, born Akron, Ohio, June 17, 1946; admitted to bar, 1972, Ohio. *Education:* Kent State University (B.A., 1967); University of Akron (J.D., 1971). *Member:* Akron and Ohio State Bar Associations. ***Email:*** ttruby@rodericklinton.com

STEPHEN J. PRUNESKI, born Youngstown, Ohio, June 20, 1960; admitted to bar, 1985, Ohio, U.S. District Court, Northern District of Ohio and U.S. Court of Appeals, Sixth Circuit. *Education:* Youngstown State University (B.A., 1982); University of Akron (J.D., 1985). *Member:* Akron and Ohio State Bar Associations. ***PRACTICE AREAS:*** Business Law; Real Estate; Construction Law; Personal Injury. ***Email:*** spruneski@rodericklinton.com

WILLIAM J. DETWEILER, born Akron, Ohio, May 8, 1961; admitted to bar, 1987, Ohio. *Education:* University of Akron (B.A., magna cum laude); Case Western Reserve University (J.D.). *Member:* Akron, Ohio State and American Bar Associations. ***PRACTICE AREAS:*** Family Law. ***Email:*** wdetweiler@rodericklinton.com

MICHAEL DeCARLO, born Wooster, Ohio, October 6, 1960; admitted to bar, 1986, Ohio and U.S. District Court, Northern District of Ohio; 1989, U.S. Court of Appeals, Sixth Circuit. *Education:* Bowling Green State University (B.S., 1982); University of Akron (J.D., 1986). *Member:* Akron, Ohio State and American Bar Associations. ***PRACTICE AREAS:*** Estate Planning; Probate; Real Estate Law; Condominium Law; Business Law. ***Email:*** mdecarlo@rodericklinton.com

TAMARA A. O'BRIEN, born Cleveland, Ohio, October 22, 1966; admitted to bar, 1992, Ohio, U.S. District Court, Northern District of Ohio and U.S. Court of Appeals, Sixth Circuit. *Education:* University of Akron (B.A., Ed., magna cum laude, 1989); Cleveland State University (J.D., cum laude, 1992). Adjunct Professor of Law, University of Akron School of Law, 1992-1995. *Member:* Akron and Ohio State Bar Associations. ***PRACTICE AREAS:*** General Civil Trial Practice. ***Email:*** tobrien@rodericklinton.com

DUARD D. BRADSHAW, born Aguadulce, Panama, September 19, 1943; admitted to bar, 1973, Ohio, U.S. District Court, Northern District of Ohio and U.S. Court of Appeals, Sixth Circuit; 1984, U.S. Tax Court. *Education:* George Washington University; Kent State University (B.A., 1966); University of Akron (J.D., 1972). Phi Alpha Delta. Trustee: Edwin Shaw Hospital (1976-1982); Metropolitan Transit Authority (1982-1988)Member, Commission on Spanish Speaking Affairs (1982-1983. *Member:* Akron, Ohio, American and Inter-American Bar Association; National Hispanic Bar Association (Vice-President of Programs and Committees, 2000-2001); American Immigration Lawyers Association; Ohio Hispanic Bar Association (President, 1997-1999). [Lt. Col. USAFR., 1966-1992]. ***LANGUAGES:*** Spanish. ***PRACTICE AREAS:*** Corporate Law; Immigration and Naturalization Law; General Practice. ***Email:*** dbradshaw@rodericklinton.com

WILLIAM G. CHRIS, born Akron, Ohio, June 14, 1960; admitted to bar, 1985, Ohio and U.S. District Court, Northern District of Florida; 1986, Florida. *Education:* University of Akron (B.A., 1982); University of Toledo (J.D., 1984). National Executive Board Member for the National Society of Professional Insurance Investigators (NSPII).*Member:* Akron, Ohio State and American Bar Associations; The Florida Bar; Defense Research Institute. (Resident, Akron Office). ***PRACTICE AREAS:*** Insurance Defense; Real Estate; Collections; Corporate. ***Email:*** wchris@rodericklinton.com

LAWRENCE R. BACH, born Dayton, Ohio, May 7, 1954; admitted to bar, 1984, Ohio; 1985, U.S. District Court, Northern District of Ohio. *Education:* University of Dayton (A.B., 1978); Case Western Reserve University (J.D., 1984). ***PRACTICE AREAS:*** Commercial Litigation. ***Email:*** lbach@rodericklinton.com

RONALD K. LEMBRIGHT, born Cleveland, Ohio, October 25, 1939; admitted to bar, 1973, Ohio. *Education:* Ohio University (B.S.C., 1961); Cleveland State University (J.D., 1972). *Member:* Akron and Ohio State Bar Associations. [U.S. Coast Guard Reserve, 1961-1966]. ***PRACTICE AREAS:*** Securities; Corporate Organization; Business Transactions; Business Organization; Oil and Gas Law. ***Email:*** rlembright@rodericklainton.com

(This Listing Continued)

John K. Riemenschneider
David S. Nichol
Rodd A. Sanders
Steven W. Mastrantonio
Jason E. Hickman
Craig W. Beidler
Brian K. Harnak

OF COUNSEL

Robert F. Linton
Todd A. Mazzola
Howard L. Calhoun (Also Member, Calhoun, Waddell & Hunt)
Frederick S. Corns
James E. Davis
John J. Lynett

COUNSEL FOR: National City Bank; First Energy Co.; The Prudential Insurance Co. of America; John Hancock Mutual Life Insurance Co.; Summit County Medical Society; American General Life & Accident Insurance Co.; Great Lakes Truck Equipment Co.; Lawyers Title Insurance Corp.; Motorists Insurance Companies; Physicians Insurance Co. of Ohio; Federated Insurance Cos.; Akron Better Business Bureau; Summit Plastics; University of Akron; Kent State University; East Ohio Gas Co.

ROETZEL & ANDRESS

A LEGAL PROFESSIONAL ASSOCIATION

Established in 1876

222 SOUTH MAIN STREET
AKRON, OHIO 44308
Telephone: 330-376-2700
Telecopier: 330-376-4577
Email: inquiries@ralaw.com
URL: http://www.ralaw.com

Columbus, Ohio Office: National City Center, 155 E. Broad Street, 12th Floor. Telephone: 614-463-9770. Telecopier: 614-463-9792.

Naples, Florida Office: 850 Park Shore Drive, Trianon Centre, 3rd Floor. Telephones: 239-649-6200; 800-535-7239. Telecopier: 239-261-3659.

Cleveland, Ohio Office: One Cleveland Center, 1375 East Ninth Street, 9th Floor. Telephone: 216-623-0150. Telecopier: 216-623-0134.

Cincinnati, Ohio Office: 250 East Fifth Street, 310 Chiquita Center. Telephone: 513-361-0200. Telecopier: 513-361-0335.

Fort Myers, Florida Office: 2320 First Street, Suite 1000. Telephone: 239-337-3850. Telecopier: 239-337-0970.

Toledo, Ohio Office: One SeaGate, 9th Floor. Telephone: 419-242-7985. Facsimile: 419-242-0316.

Tallahassee, Florida Office: 225 South Adams Street, Suite 250, P.O. Box 10369. Telephone: 850-222-7718. Telecopier: 850-222-8222.

Washington, D.C. Office: 1025 Connecticut Avenue, NW, Suite 220. Telephone: 202-625-0600. Telecopier: 202-338-6340.

General Corporate and Business Law, Banking and Finance, Mergers, Acquisitions and Divestitures, Securities Law, Real Estate Law, Real Estate Development/Syndication/Condominium Law, Tax Law, Intellectual Property Law, Computer Law, Hospital and Health Care Law, Public Law and Finance, Governmental Relations, School Law, Commercial/Bankruptcy Law, Employment Law, Pension, Employee Benefits, Workers' Compensation, OSHA, Business and Commercial Litigation, Complex and Multidistrict Litigation, Antitrust Law, RICO, Federal Court Practice, Product Liability, Environmental Law/Toxic Torts, Insurance Law, Information Technology Law, Medical Malpractice Defense, Asbestos Litigation, Construction Law, 1st Amendment/Media Law, White Collar Criminal Defense, Railroad and FELA, Trucking and Transportation Law, Probate and Estate Planning, Utility Law, International Law, Trial and Appellate Practice.

FIRM PROFILE: Founded in 1876, Roetzel & Andress is one of the largest and fastest growing full-service, corporate law firms with nine offices throughout Ohio, Florida, and Washington, D.C. Roetzel & Andress represents a wide range of clients from individuals and closely-held businesses to multi-national corporations, financial institutions, and government entities. Our lawyers serve as general counsel to many clients, and many of those relationships have existed for much of our history. Our lawyers provide a broad range of legal services to clients on a local, national, and international basis.

PARTNERS

LEWIS W. ADKINS, JR., born Roosevelt, New York, March 8, 1964; admitted to bar, 1993, Ohio. *Education:* City College of the City University of New York (B.S., cum laude, 1988); University of Akron Law School (J.D., 1993). *Member:* Cleveland, Cuyahoga County and Ohio State Bar Associations. (Resident, Cleveland Office). ***PRACTICE AREAS:*** Labor and Employment Law; Public and School Law. ***Email:*** ladkins@ralaw.com

R. BRUCE ANDERSON, born Effingham, Illinois, February 4, 1956; admitted to bar, 1981, Illinois and Florida. *Education:* Illinois State University (B.S., 1977); Stetson University (J.D., 1981). Chief Assistant County Attorney and Utilities Counsel, Collier County, Florida, 1982-1988. Partner, Young, van Assenderp, Varnadoe & Anderson, 1988-2003. *Member:* Collier County Bar Association; The Florida Bar (Member, Sections on: Environmental and Land Use; Local Government); Urban Land Institute; National Institute of Municipal Law Officers (Chairman, Committee on Municipally Owned Utilities, 1984-1985; 1985-1986). (Resident, Naples, Florida Office). ***PRACTICE AREAS:*** Zoning, Planning and Land Use. ***Email:*** banderson@ralaw.com

JOHN W. BECKER, born Youngstown, Ohio, September 23, 1969; admitted to bar, 1995, Ohio; 1996, U.S. District Court, Northern District of Ohio; 2000, U.S. Court of Appeals, Sixth Circuit; 2003, U.S. District Court, Southern District of Ohio. *Education:* Alma College (B.A., cum laude, 1991); Case Western Reserve School of Law (J.D., cum laude, 1995). *Member:* Akron, Cleveland, Cuyahoga County and Ohio State Bar Associations. ***REPORTED CASES:*** Chitty v. Bank One, N.A., 42 UCC Rep. Serv.2d 799, 2000 WL 877822 (Ohio App. 9 Dist 2000). ***PRACTICE AREAS:*** Business Litigation; Banking Litigation; Commercial Real Estate Litigation; Leasing Litigation. ***Email:*** jbecker@ralaw.com

ARETTA K. BERNARD, born Akron, Ohio, June 27, 1962; admitted to bar, 1987, Ohio; 1989, U.S. District Court, Northern District of Ohio; 1993, U.S. Court of Appeals, Sixth Circuit. *Education:* Kenyon College (B.A., 1984); University of Akron School of Law (J.D., 1987). *Member:* Akron and Ohio State Bar Associations. ***LANGUAGES:*** Greek. ***PRACTICE AREAS:*** Employment Litigation; Age Discrimination; Sexual Discrimination; Wrongful Termination. ***Email:*** abernard@ralaw.com

ROBERT E. BLACKHAM, born Lorain, Ohio, January 14, 1959; admitted to bar, 1987, Ohio and U.S. District Court, Northern District of Ohio; 2001, Pennsylvania and U.S. Supreme Court; 2004, U.S District Court, Southern District of Ohio. *Education:* Ohio State University (B.A., 1984); Cleveland-Marshall College of Law (J.D., 1987). Phi Alpha Delta. Member, Moot Court Board. Member: Cleveland Advanced Manufacturing Program (CAMP); Disability Management Employers Coalition; Ohio Self-Insurers Association. Board Member: Cuyahoga County Public Library Foundation; Cleveland Marshall College of Law Visiting Committee. *Member:* Akron, Greater Cleveland, Cuyahoga County, Ohio State and Federal Bar Associations; Defense Research Institute. (Certified Specialist in Workers' Compensation Law, Ohio State Bar Association; Certified Civil Trial Advocate by the National Board of Trial Advocacy) (Resident Partner, Cleveland Office). ***LANGUAGES:*** Spanish. ***PRACTICE AREAS:*** Labor and Employment; Workers; OSHA; Emergency Medical Services Law; Environmental Health and Safety; General Liability Defense; Litigation. ***Email:*** rblackham@ralaw.com

JOHN T. BLAKELY, born Beloit, Wisconsin, May 26, 1944; admitted to bar, 1969, Wisconsin; 1970, Florida; 1971, U.S. District Court, Middle District of Florida; 1975, U.S. Supreme Court; 1978, U.S. Tax Court; 1981, U.S. Court of Appeals, Eleventh Circuit. *Education:* Duke University (B.A., with distinction in Economics, 1966); University of Michigan (J.D., with honors, 1969). Member, Barristers, University of Michigan. Instructor of Law, University of Wisconsin Law School, 1969-1970. Municipal Judge: Belleair, Florida, 1975; Belleair Beach, Florida, 1975-1976. (Board Certified Civil Trial Lawyer, Florida Bar Board of Legal Specialization and Education) (Resident, Naples, Florida Office). ***PRACTICE AREAS:*** Commercial Litigation; Personal Injury Law. ***Email:*** jblakely@ralaw.com

SUSAN S. BOX, born Defiance, Ohio, June 2, 1960; admitted to bar, 1985, Ohio, U.S. District Court, Southern and Northern Districts of Ohio and U.S. Court of Appeals, Sixth Circuit. *Education:* Ohio State University (B.S., summa cum laude, 1982); Ohio State University College of Law (J.D., 1985). *Member:* Akron, Ohio State and American Bar Associations. ***PRACTICE AREAS:*** Products Liability; Toxic Torts; Litigation. ***Email:*** sbox@ralaw.com

WILBUR E. BREWTON, born Ocala, Florida, March 14, 1941; admitted to bar, 1968, Florida. *Education:* Jacksonville University (B.S., 1964); Stetson University (J.D., 1968); University of Florida (LL.M., in Taxation, 1981). Phi Delta Phi. Florida Blue Key. Administrative Assistant and Counsel to Governor of Florida, 1968-1969. General Counsel, Department of Business Regulation, 1969-1971. *Member:* The Florida Bar (Member, Sections on: Corporate and Banking; Administrative Law; Tax); American Bar Association. (Resident, Tallahassee, Florida Office). ***PRACTICE AREAS:*** Administrative Law (50%); Appellate Practice (20%); Corporate Law (25%); Commercial Law (5%). ***Email:*** wbrewton@ralaw.com

ERIC G. BRUESTLE, born Cincinnati, Ohio, April 23, 1953; admitted to bar, 1977, Ohio. *Education:* University of Cincinnati (B.M., Conservatory of Music, 1974; J.D., 1977). *Member:* Cincinnati (Past Chair, Workers' Compensation Committee) and Ohio State (Member, Workers' Compensation Committee) Bar Associations. (Certified Specialist in Workers' Compensation Law, Ohio State Bar Association) (Managing Partner, Cincinnati Office). ***PRACTICE AREAS:*** Workers Compensation; Labor and Employment; Probate; Estate Planning. ***Email:*** ebruestle@ralaw.com

AMIE L. BRUGGEMAN, admitted to bar, 1982, Ohio; 1983, U.S. District Court, Northern District of Ohio; 1984, U.S. Court of Appeals, Sixth Circuit; 1993, U.S. Tax Court; 1995, U.S. Supreme Court. *Education:* University of Montana (B.A., 1969); University of Akron (J.D., 1982). *Member:* Akron and Ohio State Bar Associations. Federal Bar Association. ***PRACTICE AREAS:*** Land Use Law; Land Use Litigation; Municipal Law; Business Litigation. ***Email:*** abruggeman@ralaw.com

ANTHONY J. CALAMUNCI, SR., born Jamestown, New York, February 2, 1968; admitted to bar, 1994, Ohio; 1995, U.S. District Court, Northern District of Ohio; 1996, U.S. Court of Appeals, Sixth Circuit; 2002, U.S. Supreme Court. *Education:* Alfred University (B.A., 1990); Ohio Northern University (J.D., 1994). Former Assistant Lucas County Prosecuter. *Member:* Lucas County, Toledo, Ohio State and American Bar Associations. (Resident, Toledo Office). ***PRACTICE AREAS:*** Medical Law (10%); Health Care Law (5%); Civil Litigation (60%); Corporate Law (20%); Criminal Defense (5%). ***Email:*** acalamunci@ralaw.com

ANNA MOORE CARULAS, born Flint, Michigan, January 12, 1961; admitted to bar, 1986, Ohio; U.S. District Court, Northern District of Ohio. *Education:* Alma College (B.A., cum laude, 1983), Phi Beta Kappa; University of Notre Dame (J.D., 1986). *Member:* Cleveland, Cuyahoga County and Ohio State Bar Associations. (Board Certified Civil Trial Advocate by the National Board of Trial Advocacy) (Resident, Cleveland Office) (Practice Group Manager, Medical Defense). ***PRACTICE AREAS:*** Medical Defense. ***Email:*** acarulas@ralaw.com

ROBERT B. CASARONA, born Canton, Ohio, November 13, 1960; admitted to bar, 1986, Ohio; 1987, U.S. District Court, Northern and Southern Districts of Ohio; U.S. Court of Appeals, 6th and 8th Circuits. *Education:* Denison University; Arizona State University (B.S., cum laude, 1983); University of Cincinnati (J.D., 1986). Author: "Why Should We Care About Electronic Evidence," Cleveland Bar Journal; "Civil and Criminal Enforcement of Environmental Law in Ohio," Banks Baldwin Law Publishing (1992); "Private Enforcement Actions," Banks Baldwin Law Publishing (1993); "Environmental Criminal Liability," Banks Baldwin Law Publishing (Supplement, 1993); "Special Issues of Civil Li-

(This Listing Continued)

ROETZEL & ANDRESS, A LEGAL PROFESSIONAL ASSOCIATION, Akron—Continued

ability Under CERCLA," Banks Baldwin Law Publishing (Supplement, 1993); "Environmental Law Compliance: A Business Approach," Cleveland Professional Services Guide, Cleveland Growth Association. Member: The Geauga County Bluecoats; The Justinian Forum; Executive Committee, Geauga County Republican Party. Trustee, The Gathering Place. *Member:* Cleveland, Cuyahoga County, Federal and American (Member, Sections on: Natural Resources; Energy and Environmental Law; Litigation; Intellectual Property Law) Bar Associations; Ohio State Bar Association (Member, Environmental Law Committee; Litigation Section); Northern Ohio Italian American Association. (Resident, Cleveland Office). ***PRACTICE AREAS:*** Business Litigation; Environmental; Construction Law. ***Email:*** rcasarona@ralaw.com

JEFFREY J. CASTO, born Akron, Ohio, October 22, 1954; admitted to bar, 1981, Ohio and U.S. District Court, Northern District of Ohio; 1985, U.S. Court of Appeals, Sixth Circuit; 1990, U.S. Court of Appeals, Tenth Circuit; 2002, U.S. Court of Appeals, Eleventh Circuit. *Education:* The Ohio State University (B.A., 1976); Case Western Reserve University (J.D., 1981). *Member:* Akron, Ohio State and Federal Bar Associations; Federation of Defense and Corporate Counsel; Defense Research Institute; Ohio Association of Civil Trial Attorneys. (Certified Civil Trial Advocate by the National Board of Trial Advocacy). ***PRACTICE AREAS:*** Product Liability; Tire Litigation; Trust Litigation; Commercial Litigation. ***Email:*** jcasto@ralaw.com

M. BRIAN CHEFFER, born Normal, Illinois, September 24, 1964; admitted to bar, 1990, Florida and U.S. District Court, Middle District of Florida; 1993, U.S. District Court, Southern District of Florida; 2000, U.S. Supreme Court and U.S. Court of Appeals, Eleventh Circuit. *Education:* University of Florida (B.S., B.A., high honors in Finance, magna cum laude, 1986; J.D., cum laude, 1989). Golden Key; Alpha Lambda Delta. *Member:* Lee County and American Bar Associations; The Florida Bar; Association of Trial Lawyers of America. (Resident, Fort Myers, Florida Office). ***PRACTICE AREAS:*** Commercial Litigation; Restrictive Covenants; Civil Litigation; Contracts; Appellate Practice; Intellectual Property Litigation. ***Email:*** bcheffer@ralaw.com

STEVEN ST. LEGER COX, born Akron, Ohio, July 17, 1966; admitted to bar, 1994, Ohio, U.S. Court of Appeals, Sixth Circuit and U.S. Tax Court; 1995, U.S. District Court, Northern District of Ohio; 2003, U.S. District Court, Southern District of Ohio. *Education:* The Ohio State University (B.A., Economics, 1989); University of Akron College of Business Administration (Master of Taxation, 1995); University of Akron School of Law (J.D., 1994). Member, Board of Directors: Boys and Girls Clubs of Summit County; Akron Symphony; Stan Hywet Hall and Gardens Foundation; Children's Family Care; Tuscora Park Health and Wellness Foundation; Western Reserve Planned Giving Council. Member: Association for Corporate Growth; Akron Tax and Estate Planning Council; Cleveland Estate Planning Council; National Committee on Planned Giving; 2001-2002 Leadership Akron Class XVIII. *Member:* Akron (Member and Chair, 2000-2001, Corporate and Business Law Committee, Member: Taxation Committee, Probate Law Section and Grievance Committee), Ohio State and American Bar Associations. ***PRACTICE AREAS:*** Corporate Law; Business Law; Estate Planning; Business Succession Planning; Federal, State and Local Tax. ***Email:*** scox@ralaw.com

JOHN M. COYNE, III, born Cleveland, Ohio, August 16, 1968; admitted to bar, 1995, Ohio, U.S. District Court, Northern District of Ohio and U.S. Court of Appeals, Sixth Circuit. *Education:* University of Tennessee (B.S., magna cum laude, 1990); Cleveland State University (M.B.A., 1994); Cleveland-Marshall College of Law (J.D., magna cum laude, 1994). Licensed Title Insurance Agent. Council-at-Large, City of Medina. Member, Medina Area Chamber of Commerce, 2005 Super Lawyer Rising Star. *Member:* Akron and Ohio State Bar Associations. ***PRACTICE AREAS:*** Real Estate; Commercial Real Estate Law; Railroad Line Acquisition; Condominium Law; Real Estate Finance. ***Email:*** jcoyne@ralaw.com

CLAYTON W. CREVASSE, born Chattanooga, Tennessee, December 21, 1954; admitted to bar, 1980, Florida; 1981, U.S. District Court, Northern District of Florida; 1993, U.S. District Court, Middle District of Florida. *Education:* University of Florida (B.A., 1977; J.D., 1980). Phi Beta Kappa. *Member:* Lee County and American Bar Associations; The Florida Bar; Defense Research Institute; Lee County Personal Injury Association. (Resident, Fort Myers, Florida Office). ***PRACTICE AREAS:*** Commercial Litigation; Civil Practice; Insurance Defense; Personal Injury; Probate Litigation. ***Email:*** ccrevasse@ralaw.com

ELIZABETH N. DAVIS, born Youngstown, Ohio, March 2, 1953; admitted to bar, 1984, Ohio and U.S. District Court, Northern District of Ohio. *Education:* Youngstown State University (B.A., 1975); University of Akron (J.D., 1984). Delta Theta Phi; Bracton's Inn Oral Advocacy Honorary Society, 1982-1984; Mock Trial Team, 1982-1983. *Member:* Akron and Ohio State Bar Associations; Leadership Akron Alumni Association. (Board Certified Civil Trial Attorney by the National Board of Trial Advocacy). ***LANGUAGES:*** Italian. ***PRACTICE AREAS:*** Medical Defense; Products Liability; Medical Devices; Asbestos Litigation; Mold Litigation. ***Email:*** edavis@ralaw.com

DAVID J. DEMERS, born 1965; admitted to bar, 1991, Ohio; 1992, U.S. Court of Appeals, Sixth Circuit and U.S. District Court, Southern District of Ohio; 1994, Indiana and U.S. District Court, Northern District of Ohio; 2000, U.S. District Court, Northern District of Indiana; 2003, U.S. District Court, Western District of Pennsylvania; 2004, U.S. District Court, Southern District of Indiana. *Education:* Mount Union College (B.S., History and Political Science, cum laude, 1988); University of Toledo College of Law (J.D., 1991). Pi Gamma Mu. Recipient, Herschel Kreger Award. *Member:* Indiana State, Ohio State and American Bar Associations. (Resident, Columbus Office). ***PRACTICE AREAS:*** Bankruptcy; Defense Litigation; Products Liability; Risk Management. ***Email:*** ddemers@ralaw.com

GEORGE A. DIETRICH, born Akron, Ohio, August 2, 1943; admitted to bar, 1968, Ohio; 1976, U.S. District Court, Northern District of Ohio; 1980, U.S. Court of Appeals, Sixth Circuit. *Education:* Miami University (B.A., 1965); University of Michigan (J.D., 1968). *Member:* Akron and Ohio State Bar Associations. [With U.S. Army, 1968-1974]. ***PRACTICE AREAS:*** Mergers, Acquisitions and Divestitures; Finance; Capital Formation; Corporate Governance; International Transactions; Strategic Alliances. ***Email:*** gdietrich@ralaw.com

THOMAS A. DILLON, born Champaign, Illinois, November 4, 1945; admitted to bar, 1974, Ohio, U.S. District Court, Southern District of Ohio and U.S. Court of Appeals, Sixth Circuit. *Education:* Western Michigan University; Taylor University (B.S., 1968); The Ohio State University (J.D., 1973). Listed in Best Lawyers in America, 2006. Author: "Professional Liability Insurance: Is It for the Nurse?"; "The Good Samaritan Law and the Nurse"; "Standards of Liability"; "The Nurse in the Middle," Association of Nurses in Osteopathic Medicine Newsletters; "Insurance Law Section," Ohio Insurance Law Journal, 1993. Member, Board of Trustee, Taylor University, 1985-1990. *Member:* Columus and Ohio State Bar Associations; Federation of Defense and Corporate Counsel; American Board of Trial Advocates; Defense Research Institute; Columbus Bar Foundation. (Managing Partner, Columbus Office). ***PRACTICE AREAS:*** Medical and Legal Malpractice; Product Liability; Personal Injury; Insurance Coverage. ***Email:*** tdillon@ralaw.com

CARL J. DYCZEK, born November 22, 1954; admitted to bar, 1980, Ohio; 1980, U.S. District Court, Northern District of Ohio and 1980, U.S. Tax Court. *Education:* State University of New York at Buffalo (B.A.,1976); Cleveland State University (J.D., 1980); Case Western Reserve University (M.B.A., 1986). Member: American Land Title Association; Association for Corporate Growth; Estate Planning Council of Greater Cleveland; Greater Cleveland Mortgage Banker's Association; Growth Capital Corporation; Lawyer's Guild of the Catholic Diocese of Cleveland; Turnaround Management Association; Cleveland World Trade Center, Shoes and Clothes for Kids. *Member:* Ohio State Bar Association; Greater Cleveland Bar Association. (Resident, Cleveland Office). ***LANGUAGES:*** German. ***PRACTICE AREAS:*** Financial Transactions; Real Estate; Tax; Creditors Rights; Estate Planning; Banking. ***Email:*** cdyczek@ralaw.com

STEVEN M. FALK, born Hartford, Connecticut, August 4, 1963; admitted to bar, 1988, Connecticut; 1992, Florida; 1996, U.S. District Court, Middle District of Florida. *Education:* Brown University (B.A., 1985); Boston University School of Law (J.D., cum laude, 1988). .Instructor, Condominium Law, Collier County Chapter of Building Managers International; Community Associations Institute, South Gulf Coast Chapter. *Member:* Collier County Bar Association; The Florida Bar (Member, Real Property, Probate and Trust Law Section). (Resident, Naples, Florida Office). ***PRACTICE AREAS:*** Condominium and Community Association Law; Real Estate Law. ***Email:*** sfalk@ralaw.com

SHANE A. FAROLINO, born Welland, Ontario, Canada, February 16, 1962; admitted to bar, 1988, Ohio; 1990, U.S. District Court, Southern District of Ohio; 1991, U.S. District Court, Northern District of Ohio. *Education:* State University of New York at Buffalo (B.A., 1985); University of Toledo (J.D., 1988). *Member:* Akron (Member, Environmental Law Committee) and Ohio State (Member, Environmental Law Committee) Bar Associations. ***PRACTICE AREAS:*** Environmental Law; White Collar Criminal Defense. ***Email:*** sfarolino@ralaw.com

LAURA (MEGAN) FAUST, born Cleveland, Ohio, September 2, 1966; admitted to bar, 1992, Ohio, U.S. Court of Appeals, Sixth Circuit and U.S. District Court, Northern District of Ohio; 2001, U.S. District Court, Southern District of Ohio. *Education:* The College of Wooster (B.A., 1988); Cleveland-Marshall College of Law (J.D., 1992). Member, Federation of Defense and Corporate Counsel. Member, USLaw. *Member:* Akron and Ohio State Bar Associations; Ohio Women's Bar Association; Defense Research Institute. ***LANGUAGES:*** French. ***PRACTICE AREAS:*** Insurance Coverage; Appellate Practice; Product Liability; Transportation Law; Risk Management. ***Email:*** lfaust@ralaw.com

TERRENCE S. FINN, born Youngstown, Ohio, March 12, 1962; admitted to bar, 1987, Ohio; 1988, U.S. District Court, Southern District of Ohio and U.S. Court of Appeals, Sixth Circuit; 1991, U.S. Supreme Court; 1997, U.S. District Court, Northern District of Ohio. *Education:* Youngstown State University School of Engineering (B.E., 1984); University of Toledo College of Law (J.D., 1987). Assistant Attorney General, State of Ohio, 1987-1996. State of Ohio Engineer-In-Training Certification, 1984-1994. *Member:* Akron and Ohio State Bar Associations; Ohio Water and Environment Association; Air & Water Association (Member, Ohio Chapter); National Brownfields Association. ***REPORTED CASES:*** Hale v. Shank, 1988 Ohio Env Lexis 29 (November 8, 1988); Hale v. Shank, 1989 Ohio App. Lexis 1652 (Franklin Cty. Ct. of App., April 27, 1989); Ohio v. Department of Energy, 904 F.2d 1058 (1989); Lawrence County Bd. of Commissioners v. Shank, 1990 Ohio Env Lexis 9 (October 10, 1990); Department of Energy v. Ohio 503 U.S. 607 (1991); In re Application of Envirosafe, 1991 Ohio App. Lexis 6304 (Franklin Cty. Ct. of App., December 24, 1991); City of Oregon v. Schregardus, 1994 Ohio Env Lexis 4 (April 21, 1994); State of Ohio v. Allison, 1994 Ohio App. Lexis 6038 (Columbiana Cty Ct. of App., December 22, 1994); Bartholow Auto Wrecking v. Schregardus, 1995 Ohio Env Lexis 12 (August 22, 1995); Tekavec v. Van Waters & Rogers, 12 F.Supp 2d 672 (1998); State of Ohio ex rel. Montgomery v. City of Akron, (Summit Cty Ct. of App., February 13, 2002). ***PRACTICE AREAS:*** Environmental Law; Litigation. ***Email:*** tfinn@ralaw.com

JON D. FISHBANE, admitted to bar, 1988, Ohio and U.S. District Court, Northern District of Ohio; 1989, U.S. Court of Appeals, Sixth Circuit; 1995, Florida and U.S. District Court, Middle District of Florida; 1996, U.S. Court of Appeals, Eleventh Circuit; 1998, U.S. Court of Appeals, Fourth Circuit. *Education:* University of Massachusetts (B.A., cum laude, 1970; M.A., 1972); University of Michigan (Ph.D., 1981); Indiana University (J.D., 1988). Phi Beta Kappa; Phi Kappa Phi. Member, Indiana University Student Legal Services, 1986-1987. Author: "The Troubled Evolution of Energy Policy in the EEC," Akron Law Review, 1994; articles on civic responsibility for Naples Chamber of Commerce Leadership Link. Adjunct Professor, Florida Gulf Coast University. Member: Civic Engagement Foundation Board, Naples Chamber of Commerce; Florida Humanities Council Board; Leadership Collier, 2003. *Member:* Collier County, American and International Bar Associations; The Florida Bar. (Resident, Naples, Florida Office). ***LANGUAGES:*** French and German. ***PRACTICE AREAS:*** Labor and Employment; Immigration Law. ***Email:*** jfishbane@ralaw.com

JEFFREY E. FROMSON, born Boise, Idaho, July 24, 1944; admitted to bar, 1969, Ohio; 1984, Massachusetts. *Education:* Miami University (B.A., 1966); The Ohio State University (J.D., cum laude, 1969). Tau Epsilon Rho. Associate Editor, Ohio State Law

(This Listing Continued)

Journal, 1968-1969. *Member:* Columbus and Ohio State Bar Associations. (Resident, Columbus Office). ***PRACTICE AREAS:*** Corporate; Mergers and Acquisitions; Business; Securities; Franchising; International. ***Email:*** jfromson@ralaw.com

PATRICIA B. FUGÉE, born Oak Bluffs, Massachusetts, May 21, 1965; admitted to bar, 1991, New Jersey, New York and U.S. District Court, District of New Jersey; 1993, 1993, U.S. District Court, Southern and Eastern Districts of New York; 1998, U.S. Court of Appeals, Third Circuit; 1999, Ohio and U.S. District Court, Northern District of Ohio; 2000, Michigan and U.S. District Court, Southern District of Ohio. *Education:* Wellesley College (B.A., 1986); Rutgers University-Camden (J.D., high honors, 1990). Tax Honors Program. Member, Rutgers Law Journal, 1989-1990. Law Clerk to the Honorable John W. Bissell, U.S.D.J., Newark, New Jersey, 1990-1992. Member, New Jersey Bankruptcy Inn of Court, 1994-1998. *Member:* Toledo and Ohio State Bar Associations; State Bar of Michigan; American Bankruptcy Institute. (Resident, Toledo Office). ***PRACTICE AREAS:*** Bankruptcy; Commercial Litigation; Debtor and Creditor Law. ***Email:*** pfugee@ralaw.com

STEPHEN W. FUNK, born Le Mars, Iowa, August 25, 1966; admitted to bar, 1992, Ohio; 1994, District of Columbia; U.S. Supreme Court; U.S. Court of Appeals, Third, Fourth, Fifth, Sixth, Seventh, Ninth and Tenth Circuits; U.S. District Court, Northern and Southern Districts of Ohio. *Education:* Miami University (B.A., summa cum laude, 1988); Harvard Law School (J.D., cum laude, 1991). *Member:* Akron (Elected Member, Board of Trustees, Chair, Federal Courts Committee; former Chair, University of Akron Liason Committee, Member, Common Pleas Committee), Ohio State (Member, Antitrust Section, Appellate Courts Committee) and Federal (Member, Board of Directors for Northern District of Ohio Chapter) Bar Associations. ***PRACTICE AREAS:*** Business Litigation; Public Law Litigation; Land Use and Zoning Litigation; Constitutional Law. ***Email:*** sfunk@ralaw.com

STANLEY H. GOLDSCHMIDT, born Washington, D.C., July 30, 1953; admitted to bar, 1979, Maryland; 1983, District of Columbia. *Education:* Yeshiva University (B.A., magna cum laude, 1975); Georgetown University Law Center (J.D., cum laude, 1978). *Member:* The District of Columbia Bar. (Resident, Washington, DC Office). ***PRACTICE AREAS:*** Litigation; Complex Civil Litigation; Commercial Law; Business Litigation; Real Estate; Real Estate Acquisitions; Real Estate Brokerage Law; Real Estate Contracts; Real Estate Development; Real Estate Finance; Real Estate Leasing; Real Estate Litigation. ***Email:*** sgoldschmidt@ralaw.com

AMANDA E. GORDON, born Massillon, Ohio, July 9, 1965; admitted to bar, 1990, Ohio. *Education:* University of Akron (B.S., 1987); Case Western Reserve University (J.D., 1990). Order of the Coif. Member, Case Western Reserve University Law Review. *Member:* Akron, Cleveland, Ohio State and American Bar Associations; National Association of Bond Lawyers; Government Finance Officers Association; Municipal Finance Officers Association. ***PRACTICE AREAS:*** Public Finance; Public Law. ***Email:*** agordon@ralaw.com

BEVERLY GRADY, born Pittsburgh, Pennsylvania, September 1, 1949; admitted to bar, 1976, Ohio; 1977, Florida; 1979, U.S. District Court, Middle District of Florida. *Education:* Connecticut College (B.A., 1971); Case Western Reserve University (J.D., 1976). Member, Board of Governors, Student Bar Association, 1975-1976. Assistant County Attorney, Lee County Attorneys' Office, 1977-1980. *Member:* Lee County and Ohio State Bar Associations; The Florida Bar. (Board Certified City, County and Local Government Lawyer, Florida Bar Board of Legal Specialization and Education) (Resident, Fort Myers, Florida Office). ***PRACTICE AREAS:*** Land Use Law; Administrative Law; Public Law. ***Email:*** bgrady@ralaw.com

ROBERT B. GRAZIANO, born McKeesport, Pennsylvania, December 6, 1964; admitted to bar, 1991, Ohio. *Education:* Duquesne University (B.A., 1987); Case Western Reserve University (J.D., 1990). Kappa Tau Alpha; Delta Theta Phi. Member: Mock Trial Team; Moot Court Board, 1989-1990. *Member:* Columbus, Ohio State and American Bar Associations; Ohio Association of Civil Trial Attorneys; Defense Research Institute; Columbus Claims Association. (Resident, Columbus Office). ***PRACTICE AREAS:*** Litigation; Medical Malpractice; Personal Injury; Products Liability. ***Email:*** rgraziano@ralaw.com

C. NEIL GREGORY, born Waltham, Massachusetts, February 8, 1958; admitted to bar, 1984, Florida. *Education:* University of Florida (B.A., 1980); Stetson University (J.D., 1984). *Member:* Collier County and American (Member, Real Property, Probate and Trust Law Section) Bar Associations; The Florida Bar (Member, Real Property Section; Past Chair, General Practice Section). (Board Certified Real Estate Lawyer, Florida Bar Board of Legal Specialization and Education) (Resident, Naples, Florida Office). ***PRACTICE AREAS:*** Real Property; Title Insurance; Business Law; Contracts. ***Email:*** ngregory@ralaw.com

DAVID H. GUNNING II, born Cleveland, Ohio, June 8, 1967; admitted to bar, 1994, Ohio and U.S. District Court, Northern District of Ohio. *Education:* Lake Forest College (B.A., 1989); Cleveland Marshall School of Law (J.D., 1994). *Member:* Cleveland, Ohio State and American Bar Associations; American Institute of Constructers; Associated Builders and Contractors; Home Builders Association of Greater Cleveland; Association of General Contractors; International Council of Shopping Centers. (Resident, Cleveland Office). ***PRACTICE AREAS:*** Commercial Real Estate; Construction Law; Telecommunications Law; Commercial Litigation. ***Email:*** dgunning@ralaw.com

MICHAEL J. HAAS, born Cleveland, Ohio, September 21, 1968; admitted to bar, 1994, Ohio and U.S. District Court, Northern District of Ohio. *Education:* Syracuse University (B.A., 1991); Cleveland Marshall School of Law (J.D., 1994). Sigma Alpha Mu. *Member:* Cleveland, Cuyahoga County, Ohio State and American Bar Associations; International Council of Shopping Centers; National Association of Industrial and Office Properties. (Resident, Cleveland Office). ***LANGUAGES:*** Hebrew. ***PRACTICE AREAS:*** Real Estate; Finance. ***Email:*** mhaas@ralaw.com

DAVID R. HARBARGER, born Uniontown, Pennsylvania, March 4, 1945; admitted to bar, 1975, Ohio; 1977, U.S. District Court, Northern District of Ohio and U.S. Tax Court; 1980, U.S. Supreme Court; 1985, U.S. Court of Appeals, Sixth Circuit. *Education:* Wichita State University (B.A., 1969); Cleveland State University (J.D., 1975). Law Director: City of Westlake, 1998-2005; City of Lakewood, 1988-1991. Mayor, City of Lakewood, 1991-1995. Practice Group Manager, Public Law Group, 2003—. *Member:* Cleveland, Cuyahoga County, Ohio State and American Bar Associations; American Judicature Society; International Municipal Lawyers Association. [LTC, USAR Retired, 1997]. (At Washington, D.C. and Cleveland, Ohio Offices). ***PRACTICE AREAS:*** Public Law (25%); Real Estate Development (25%); Land Use (25%); Governmental Relations (25%). ***Email:*** dharbarger@ralaw.com

DENISE M. HASBROOK, born Livonia, Michigan, July 10, 1960; admitted to bar, 1984, Ohio and U.S. District Court, Northern District of Ohio; 1987, U.S. Court of Federal Claims; 1993, U.S. Court of Appeals, Sixth Circuit; Ohio Supreme Court. *Education:* University of Toledo (B.A., magna cum laude, 1981; J.D., 1984). *Member:* Toledo and Ohio State Bar Associations; Toledo Women's Bar Association. (Resident, Toledo Office). ***REPORTED CASES:*** Detzel v. Brush Wellman, Inc., 141 Ohio App.3d 474, 751 N.E.2d 1067 (2001); Sopkovich v. Ohio Edison Co., 81 Ohio St.3d 628, 693 N.E.2d 233, 1998-Ohio-341 (1998); International Brotherhood of Electrical Workers, AFL-CIO, Local Union No. 245 v. FirstEnergy Corp., 233 F.Supp.2d 913 (N.D. Ohio 2001); Brush Wellman, Inc. v. Montes, et al., 288 F.Supp.2d 860 (N.D. Ohio 2003); Brush Wellman, Inc. v. Montes, et al., 295 F.Supp.2d 785 (N.D. Ohio 2003); Fillmore v. Brush Wellman, Inc., 243 F.Supp.2d 758 (N.D. Ohio 2003); Grosjean v. FirstEnergy Corporation, 349 F.3d 332 (6th Cir. 2003); Tobias v. First Energy Nuclear Operating Company, et al., 302 F.Supp.2d 849 (N.D. Ohio 2004); Yuhasz v. Brush Wellman, Inc., 181 F.Supp.2d 785 (N.D. Ohio 2001); Yuhasz v. Brush Wellman, Inc., 341 F.3d 559 (6th Cir. 2003). ***PRACTICE AREAS:*** Civil Litigation (50%); Employment Law (50%). ***Email:*** dhasbrook@ralaw.com

ERIKA L. HAUPT, born Canton, Ohio, December 13, 1968; admitted to bar, 1994, Ohio; 1996, U.S. District Court, Northern District of Ohio; 1999, U.S. Tax Court. *Education:* Miami University, Oxford, Ohio (B.S.B., 1991); The Ohio State University College of Law (J.D., 1994). Recipient, Joseph J. Harter Memorial Award for Excellence in Trial Practice, 1994. Managing Editor, Ohio State Law Journal, 1993-1994. Author: "For Better, For Worse, For Richer, For Poorer: Premarital Agreement Case Studies," 37 Real Prop., Prob. & Tr. J. 29 (2002); "Brady v. Safety-Kleen Corp.: Tipping Ohio's Workers' Compensation Scale in Favor of the Employee," 54 Ohio St. L.J. 837 (1993). Greater Columbus Salvation Army Advisory Board: Member; Resource Development Chair, 2005—; Secretary, 2003-2005. Member: Leadership Columbus Class of 2000; Miami University Alumni Association Recruitment Network; Ohio Pet Fund Board of Directors. *Member:* Columbus (Member, Business Tax and Estate and Gift Tax Committees) and Ohio State (Member, Estate Planning, Trust and Probate Law Section) Bar Associations. (Resident, Columbus Office). ***PRACTICE AREAS:*** Estate Planning; Tax; Business Law; Charitable Organizations; Probate. ***Email:*** ehaupt@ralaw.com

JOSEPH E. HERBERT, born Cincinnati, Ohio, May 14, 1965; admitted to bar, 1992, Ohio; 1996, Missouri (inactive). *Education:* Miami University (B.A., 1987); University of Toledo (J.D., cum laude, 1992). Member, National Moot Court Team and Moot Court Board. *Member:* Cleveland, Cuyahoga County and Ohio State Bar Associations; Cleveland Association of Civil Trial Lawyers; Defense Research Institute. (Resident, Cleveland Office). ***PRACTICE AREAS:*** Medical Malpractice Defense. ***Email:*** jherbert@ralaw.com

EDWARD C. HERTENSTEIN, born Columbus, Ohio, August 25, 1951; admitted to bar, 1976, Ohio; 1978, U.S. District Court, Southern District of Ohio; 1979, U.S. Tax Court; 1980, U.S. Supreme Court. *Education:* Southern Methodist University (B.B.A., 1973; J.D., 1976). Phi Delta Phi. Editor, Journal of Air Law and Commerce, 1975-1976. Law Clerk to Associate Justice, Supreme Court of Ohio, 1976-1977. Commissioner, Supreme Court of Ohio, 1977-1978. Author: "Interest-Free Loans," 1983 Columbus Tax Conference Manual; "Estate Freezes: Maintaining After Tax Values," 1985 Columbus Tax Conference Manual; "Estate Planning Implications of The Tax Reform Act of 1986," 1986, Columbus Tax Conference Manual; "Life Insurance for the Business Owner: Income and Estate Tax Planning to Reduce Cost," 1987 Columbus Tax Conference Manual; "GRITs, GRATs and GRUTs, and How to Use Them," 1993 Columbus Tax Conference Manual and Passing the Buck! A Guide to Flow-Through Entities in the Context of Wealth Transfer for Families," 1995 Wealth Transfer Conference Reference Manual, Volume 95-07; "GRAT-itude: Effective Use of GRATs and Other Techniques — The Alchemy of Leveraged Giving," 1996 Wealth Transfer Conference Manual, Volume 1996—; "Some Thoughts on Installment Sales to Grantor Trusts: A GRAT Alternative," 2000 Wealth Transfer Conference Manual, Volume 2000—. *Member:* Columbus (Member, Committee on: Taxation, 1978—; Chairman, 1985-1986), Ohio State and American (Member, Section of Taxation) Bar Associations. The American College of Trust and Estate Counsel. (Certified Specialist in Federal Tax Law, Ohio State Bar Association) (Resident, Columbus Office). ***PRACTICE AREAS:*** Taxation Law (40%); Trusts and Estates (40%); Corporate Law (20%). ***Email:*** ehertenstein@ralaw.com

PAUL K. HEUERMAN, born Midland, Michigan, December 28, 1959; admitted to bar, 1985, Ohio, Florida and U.S. District Court, Southern District of Ohio; 1988, U.S. District Court, Middle District of Florida. *Education:* University of Michigan (B.A., with distinction, 1981); University of Florida (J.D., 1984). *Member:* Collier County Bar Association; The Florida Bar (Member, Sections: Business Law; Real Property, Probate and Trust Law). (Resident, Naples, Florida Office). ***PRACTICE AREAS:*** Real Estate; Banks and Banking; Business Law. ***Email:*** pheuerman@ralaw.com

DANIEL G. HILSON, born 1959; admitted to bar, 1986, Ohio; U.S. District Court, Northern District of Ohio. *Education:* Loyola University, Rome, Italy, 1981; John Carroll University (B.A., Political Science, 1982); Capital University Law School (J.D., with honors, 1986). Order of the Barrister. Order of the Curia. Recipient, Alumni Service Medal, John Carroll University, 2000. Recognized as a Ohio Super Lawyer by Law and Politics Magazine. Author: "Lobbying, PACS and Campaigning Finance," 50 State Handbook, Ohio Chapter, West Publishing Company, 1994-2004. Majority Legal Counsel to Ohio Senate, 1990-1993. *Member:* Columbus and American Bar Associations. Fellow, Columbus Bar Foundation. (Resident, Columbus Office). ***PRACTICE AREAS:*** Government Relations; Public Law and Finance; Health Care Facility Licensing; Health Care Legislation; Home Health Care; Pharmacy Law. ***Email:*** dhilson@ralaw.com

STEVEN W. HUBBARD, born Bonne Terre, Missouri, July 30, 1952; admitted to bar, 1982, Missouri; 1985, Florida. *Education:* Jefferson College; Central Missouri State University (B.S., cum laude, 1974); University of Missouri at Columbia (J.D., cum laude, 1982). Order of the Coif. Note and Comment Editor, Missouri Law Review, 1981-1982. *Member:* Lee County Bar Association; The Florida Bar; The Missouri Bar. (Resident Managing Partner, Fort Myers, Florida Office). ***PRACTICE AREAS:*** Real Estate Law; Banking Law; Business Law. ***Email:*** shubbard@ralaw.com

(This Listing Continued)

ROETZEL & ANDRESS, A LEGAL PROFESSIONAL ASSOCIATION, Akron—Continued

MICHAEL J. HUDAK, born Youngstown, Ohio; admitted to bar, 1987, Ohio; 1988, West Virginia; 1995, Pennsylvania; 1999, Virginia; U.S. District Court, Northern District of Ohio, Eastern and Western Districts of West Virginia, Western District of Pennsylvania and Eastern District of Virginia. *Education:* Youngstown State University (B.S., 1980); University of Akron School of Law (J.D., cum laude, 1987). Delta Theta Phi. Member, University of Akron Law Review, 1986-1987. Recipient, Judge Harold and Jeanette White Scholarship. *Member:* Akron, Cleveland and Ohio State Bar Associations; Ohio Association of Civil Trial Attorneys; Ohio Society of Hospital Attorneys; Defense Research Institute. ***PRACTICE AREAS:*** Medical Defense; Hospital Defense; Insurance Defense. ***Email:*** mhudak@ralaw.com

TIMOTHY C. IVEY, born Cleveland, Ohio, February 14, 1962; admitted to bar, 1987, Ohio and U.S. District Court, Northern District of Ohio. *Education:* University of Toledo (B.B.A., 1984); Case Western Reserve University (J.D., 1987). Alpha Phi Alpha; Blue Key. Member: Jessup Moot Court Team, 1986-1987; National Mock Trial Team, 1985-1987; American Inns of Court, 1987. Recipient: Dunmore Tournament Moot Court Award, 1986; International Academy of Trial Lawyers Award, 1987; Martin Luther King Award, 1987. *Member:* National Association of Criminal Defense Lawyers; The Ohio Association of Criminal Defense Lawyers. ***Email:*** tivey@ralaw.com

PAUL L. JACKSON, born Akron, Ohio, August 20, 1963; admitted to bar, 1988, Ohio and U.S. District Court, Northern District of Ohio; U.S. Court of Appeals, Sixth Circuit; U.S. District Court, Southern District of Ohio. *Education:* University of Akron (B.S., summa cum laude, 1985; J.D., summa cum laude, 1988). *Member:* Akron and Ohio State Bar Associations. (Certified Specialist in Labor & Employment Law, Ohio State Bar Association). ***LANGUAGES:*** French. ***PRACTICE AREAS:*** Employee Benefits Law; Employment Law; Pension Law. ***Email:*** pjackson@ralaw.com

KENNETH A. JONES, born Chicago, Illinois, September 9, 1947; admitted to bar, 1975, Florida. *Education:* Florida Atlantic University (B.S., 1972); Walter F. George School of Law, Mercer University (J.D., 1975). Phi Delta Phi. Member and Committee Chairman, City of Fort Myers Planning Board, 1990-1991. Vice-Chair, City of Fort Myers Downtown Redevelopment Agency, 1991-2004. Director, Downtown Management Corporation, 1996-2004. *Member:* Lee County Bar Association; The Florida Bar (Member, Committee on Eminent Domain); Association of Eminent Domain Professionals. (Resident, Fort Myers, Florida Office). ***PRACTICE AREAS:*** Eminent Domain Law; Land Use Law. ***Email:*** kjones@ralaw.com

PETER LAWSON JONES, born December 23, 1952; admitted to bar, 1980, Ohio; 1986, U.S. District Court, Northern District of Ohio. *Education:* Harvard University (A.B., magna cum laude, 1975; J.D., 1980). Law Clerk, Supreme Court of Ohio, 1992-1993. Commissioner, Cuyahoga County, Ohio, 2002—. Member, Ohio House of Representatives, 1997-2002. Councilman, Shaker Heights, Ohio, 1984-1991. Former Bar Examiner, Supreme Court of Ohio, Law Director, Woodmere Village, Ohio, and Special Counsel, Office of the Attorney General of Ohio. *Member:* Cleveland, Cuyahoga County and Ohio State Bar Associations; Norman S. Minor Bar Association. (Resident, Cleveland Office). ***PRACTICE AREAS:*** Public Law (40%); Criminal Defense (20%); Plaintiffs Personal Injury (40%). ***Email:*** pjones@ralaw.com

R. MARK JONES, born Painesville, Ohio, January 13, 1957; admitted to bar, 1983, Ohio and U.S. District Court, Northern District of Ohio. *Education:* University of Colorado at Boulder (B.A., 1979); Case Western Reserve School of Law (J.D., 1983). Member, Ohio Super Lawyers, 2004. *Member:* Cleveland and Ohio State Bar Associations; Defense Research Institute. (Resident, Cleveland Office)(Certified as a Civil Trial Advocacy Specialist by the National Board of Trial Advocacy). ***PRACTICE AREAS:*** Medical Malpractice Defense; Drug and Medical Device Defense. ***Email:*** mjones@ralaw.com

STEPHEN D. JONES, born Cincinnati, Ohio, June 5, 1953; admitted to bar, 1981, Ohio; U.S. Court of Appeals, Federal Circuit; U.S. Supreme Court. *Education:* Otterbein College (B.A., 1975); University of Michigan (M.S.W., 1977); Capital University (J.D., 1980). Frequent Lecturer throughout Ohio and the U.S. on Discovery of Electronic Evidence, Internet and e-Commerce issues. President, Franklin County Chapter, Mothers Against Drunk Driving. Public Policy Director, MADD Ohio. *Member:* Columbus and Ohio State (Chair, Computer Law Committee, 2001-2003) Bar Associations; Association of Defense Trial Attorneys. (Resident, Columbus Office). ***REPORTED CASES:*** CompuServe v. Patterson, 89 F.3d 1257 (1996); Ohio Edison v. Parrott, 73 O. St. 3d 70J (1995); Wheeling Corporation v. Columbus and Ohio River Railroad, et al., 147 Ohio App.3d 460 (2001). ***PRACTICE AREAS:*** Business Litigation; Medical Malpractice Defense; UCC Warranty Litigation; Government Contracts; Government Litigation; Real Estate Litigation; Technology Litigation; Employment Litigation. ***Email:*** sjones@ralaw.com

WAYNE M. JONES, born Akron, Ohio, July 28, 1954; admitted to bar, 1989, Ohio. *Education:* University of Akron (A.A.S., Criminal Justice, with distinction, 1982; B.S. cum laude, 1983); Capital University (J.D., 1988). . *Member:* Akron and Ohio State Bar Associations. ***PRACTICE AREAS:*** Public Law; Health Care Law. ***Email:*** wjones@ralaw.com

DOUGLAS M. KENNEDY, born Columbus, Ohio, October 11, 1954; admitted to bar, 1980, Ohio; 1981, U.S. District Court, Southern District of Ohio; 1993, U.S. Court of Appeals, Sixth Circuit. *Education:* Ohio Wesleyan University (B.A., 1977); University of Toledo (J.D., 1980). Member and Associate Editor, University of Toledo Law Review, 1979-1980. Speaker: Professional Educations Systems, Inc: "Ohio Uninsured and Underinsured Motorist Coverage Issues," 1990; "Orthopedics For Lawyers," 1991. Assistant Attorney General, State of Ohio, 1980-1985. *Member:* Columbus and Ohio State Bar Associations; Ohio Association of Civil Trial Attorneys; Defense Research Institute; Columbus Defense Association. (Resident, Columbus Office). ***PRACTICE AREAS:*** Employment Law; Workers Compensation; Litigation. ***Email:*** dkennedy@ralaw.com

INGRID A. KINKOPF-ZAJAC, born Cleveland, Ohio, November 12, 1961; admitted to bar, 1996, Ohio; 2003, U.S. District Court, Northern District of Ohio. *Education:* St. Vincent Charity Hospital School of Nursing (R.N. Diploma, 1982); Nazareth College of Rochester (B.A., 1993); Case Western Reserve University School of Law (J.D., 1996). *Member:* Cleveland, Cuyahoga County and Ohio State Bar Associations. (Resident, Cleveland Office). ***LANGUAGES:*** German. ***PRACTICE AREAS:*** Medical Defense. ***Email:*** ikinkopf-zajac@ralaw.com

RONALD S. KOPP, born Canton, Ohio, May 21, 1954; admitted to bar, 1979, Ohio and U.S. District Court, Northern District of Ohio; 2004, U.S. District Court, Southern District of Ohio, 1980, U.S. Court of Appeals, Sixth Circuit; 1995, U.S. Supreme Court. *Education:* Miami University (A.B., cum laude, 1976); The Ohio State University (J.D., 1979). *Member:* Akron Bar Association (President, 1996-1997; Trustee, 1989-1992 and 1995-1998); Ohio State Bar Association (Member, Council of Delegates, 1997-2003). Founding Fellow, Akron Bar Foundation, 1989; Board of Governors, Akron Bar Foundation, 2004 - present. (Certified Civil Trial Advocate by the National Board of Trial Advocacy) (Managing Partner, Akron Office) (Manager, Statewide Business Litigation Group, 1989-2003). ***REPORTED CASES:*** State ex. rel. Beacon Journal Publishing Co. v. Maurer, 91 Ohio St. 3d 54 (2001); Grendell v. Ohio Environmental Protection Agency, 146 Ohio App. 3d 1 (Ninth Dist. App. 2001); Irvine v. Akron Beacon Journal, 147 Ohio App. 428 (Ninth Dist. App. 2002); Bosley v. Wetwild.com, 2004 WL 216179, C.A. 6, April 21, 2004. ***PRACTICE AREAS:*** Business Litigation; Media Law. ***Email:*** rkopp@ralaw.com

PETER M. KOSTOFF, born Akron, Ohio, January 16, 1956; admitted to bar, 1982, Ohio; 1984, U.S. District Court, Northern District of Ohio and U.S. Court of Appeals, Sixth Circuit. *Education:* University of Akron (B.A., cum laude, 1978); Cleveland-Marshall College of Law (J.D., 1981). Law Director, Village of Mogadore, Ohio, 1999-2004. Former Mayor, City of Fairlawn, Ohio, 1984-1995. *Member:* Akron Bar Association; Ohio State Bar Association. ***PRACTICE AREAS:*** Public Law; State and Local Governmental Relations; Structuring Governmental Entities; Intergovernmental Agreements; Land Use and Zoning. ***Email:*** pkostoff@ralaw.com

JAMES D. KUREK, born Toledo, Ohio, November 2, 1955; admitted to bar, 1981, Ohio; 1982, U.S. District Court, Northern District of Ohio; 1983, U.S. Court of Appeals, Sixth Circuit; 1986, U.S. Supreme Court. *Education:* University of Toledo (B.B.A., magna cum laude, 1978); University of Michigan Law School (J.D., cum laude, 1981). *Member:* Akron, Ohio State and American Bar Associations. (Certified Specialist in Labor and Employment Law, Ohio State Bar Association). ***PRACTICE AREAS:*** Management Labor Law (40%); Employment Law (60%). ***Email:*** jkurek@ralaw.com

KENNETH M. LAPINE, born January 30, 1942; admitted to bar, 1967, Ohio and U.S. District Court, Northern District of Ohio; 1994, U.S. Supreme Court. *Education:* Dartmouth College (A.B., 1964); University of Michigan (J.D., 1967). Publications: *Consumer Credit: Law, Transactions and Forms,* (6 vols.), Matthew Bender & Co. (1984—); *Banking Law,* (multiple vols.), Matthew Bender & Co. (1979—); *Rabkin & Johnson, Current Legal Forms,* (Volume 8), Matthew Bender & Co. (1978—). *Member:* Cleveland, Toledo, Cuyahoga County, Ohio State and American Bar Associations. (Resident, Cleveland Office). ***PRACTICE AREAS:*** Real Estate (35%); Real Estate Finance (15%); Real Estate Syndication (20%); Banking Law (5%); Consumer Credit (15%); Business Law (10%). ***Email:*** klapine@ralaw.com

DOUGLAS G. LEAK, born Buffalo, New York, November 8, 1962; admitted to bar, 1988, New Jersey and Pennsylvania; 1989, Ohio; 1993, U.S. Court of Appeals, Sixth Circuit; 1998, U.S. District Court, Northern District of Ohio. *Education:* Boston University (B.A., cum laude, 1985); Cleveland Marshall College of Law (J.D., 1988). *Member:* Cleveland, Cuyahoga County, Lake County and Ohio State Bar Associations; Defense Research Institute. (Resident, Cleveland Office). ***REPORTED CASES:*** Heiner v. Moretuzzo (Ohio Supreme Court); Multiple Appellate decisions. ***PRACTICE AREAS:*** Medical Malpractice; Appellate Law. ***Email:*** dleak@ralaw.com

RONALD B. LEE, born Canton, Ohio, January 28, 1952; admitted to bar, 1978, Ohio; 1979, U.S. Tax Court and U.S. District Court, Northern District of Ohio; 1985, U.S. Court of Appeals, Sixth Circuit; 2003, U.S. District Court, Southern District of Ohio. *Education:* Kent State University; University of Akron (B.S., magna cum laude, 1974; J.D., 1978). Phi Alpha Delta. Editor, Akron Law Review, 1977-1978. *Member:* Akron and Ohio State Bar Associations; Ohio Association of Civil Trial Attorneys; Defense Research Institute. (Certified Civil Trial Advocate by the National Board of Trial Advocacy). ***PRACTICE AREAS:*** Products Liability; Personal Injury Defense; Business Insurance Litigation; Insurance Coverage Issues; Construction Litigation; Mold Litigation; Latex Allergy Litigation; Popcorn Litigation. ***Email:*** rlee@ralaw.com

FREDERICK W. LEFFLER, born Massillon, Ohio, December 27, 1964; admitted to bar, 1990, Ohio. *Education:* Grove City College (B.A., 1987); University of Akron (J.D., cum laude, 1990). Senior Staff, University of Akron Law Review. Member, Board of Governors, Boy Scouts of America, Great Trail Council. Member, Audit Review Committee, American Red Cross, Summit County Chapter. *Member:* Akron and Ohio State Bar Associations; Ohio Society of Certified Public Accountants. ***PRACTICE AREAS:*** Commercial Real Estate Finance. ***Email:*** fleffler@ralaw.com

JUDITH D. LEVINE, born New York, N.Y., September 2, 1950; admitted to bar, 1975, Colorado; 1979, Ohio; 1982, New York. *Education:* Kirkland College (B.A., 1972); University of Denver (J.D., 1975). Order of St. Ives. Editor, Denver Law Journal, 1974-1975. Member, Board of Directors, CREW Network, 2001-2002. Member, Board of Trustees, CREW Foundation, 2005. Chair, Subcommittee on Mortgage Loan Commitments for Lenders and Borrowers, American Bar Association, 1987-1991. (Resident, Columbus Office). ***PRACTICE AREAS:*** Real Estate; Financial Services; Restructuring; Commercial Law; Corporate. ***Email:*** jlevine@ralaw.com

G. CARSON McEACHERN, born New York, N.Y., November 19, 1946; admitted to bar, 1972, Florida; 1974, U.S. District Court, Northern District of Florida; 1975, U.S. District Court, Middle District of Florida. *Education:* Colgate University (A.B., 1968); University of Florida (J.D., 1972). *Member:* Collier County Bar Association; The Florida Bar (Member, Real Property, Probate and Trust Law Section); The Estate Planning Council of Naples. (Board Certified Real Estate and Wills, Trusts and Estates Lawyer, Florida Bar Board of Legal Specializations and Education) (Resident, Naples, Florida Office). ***PRACTICE AREAS:*** Estate Planning; Trust and Estate Administration; Real Estate Law; Business Law. ***Email:*** cmceachern@ralaw.com

MARK P. McGRIEVY, born March 10, 1963; admitted to bar, 1990, New Jersey; 1993, Ohio. *Education:* Muhlenberg College (B.A., 1985); Cleveland-Marshall College of Law (J.D., 1988). Law Clerk, Hon. Thomas Rumano, Superior Court of New Jersey, 1988-

(This Listing Continued)

1989. *Member:* American Health Lawyers Association. (Resident, Cleveland Office). ***PRACTICE AREAS:*** Health Care; Long Term Care; Business and Corporate Law. ***Email:*** mmcgrievy@ralaw.com

AARON E. McQUEEN, born Lorain, Ohio, April 3, 1971; admitted to bar, 1997, Ohio; 1998, U.S. District Court, Northern District of Ohio; 2001, U.S. Court of Appeals, Sixth Circuit. *Education:* Cleveland State University (B.B.A., magna cum laude, 1993); Case Western Reserve University (J.D., cum laude, 1997). *Member:* Akron and Ohio State Bar Associations. ***PRACTICE AREAS:*** Product Liability; Toxic Tort; Mold Defense. ***Email:*** amcqueen@ralaw.com

ROBERT G. MENZIES, born San Francisco, California, December 7, 1955; admitted to bar, 1982, Michigan; 1984, Florida; 1988, U.S. District Court, Middle District of Florida. *Education:* Northern Michigan University (B.S., magna cum laude, 1978); Thomas M. Cooley Law School (J.D., 1981). Editor-in-Chief, Thomas M. Cooley Law School Review, 1981. Member, Judicial Nominating Commission, 20th Judicial Circuit, 2000—. *Member:* Collier County Bar Association (Director, 1988-1991, 2000 and President, Trial Lawyers Section, 1991); The Florida Bar; State Bar of Michigan. (Resident, Naples, Florida Office). ***PRACTICE AREAS:*** Commercial Litigation; Real Estate Litigation; Trial Practice; Community Association Law. ***Email:*** rmenzies@ralaw.com

RUSSELL R. MILLER, born Athens, Ohio, December 7, 1949; admitted to bar, 1977, Ohio. *Education:* Ohio University (B.S.Ed., summa cum laude, 1972); Ohio Northern University (J.D., 1977). *Member:* Toledo and Ohio State Bar Associations; Toledo Estate Planning Council. [1st Lieut., U.S. Army, 1972-1975]. (Resident, Toledo Office). ***PRACTICE AREAS:*** Banking Law; Business Law; Commercial Law; Real Estate Law; Estate Planning. ***Email:*** rmiller@ralaw.com

RICHARD S. MITCHELL, born Cleveland, Ohio, June 3, 1959; admitted to bar, 1984, Ohio and U.S. District Court, Northern District of Ohio; 1987, U.S. Court of Appeals, Sixth Circuit; 2002, U.S. Supreme Court. *Education:* Tulane University of Louisiana (B.S., Business Management, 1981); Case Western Reserve University (J.D., 1984). *Member:* Cleveland, Ohio State and American Bar Associations. (Resident, Cleveland Office). ***REPORTED CASES:*** Telxon Corporation v. Symbol Technologies, 961 F. Supp. 1113 (N.D. Ohio 1996); Stavroff v. Meyo, 987 F.Supp 987 (N.D. Ohio 1995, aff'd, 129 F. 3d 1265 (6th Cir. 1997); Basicomputer v. Scott, 791 F. Supp 1280 (N.D. Ohio 1991), aff'd, 973 F2d 507 (6th Cir. 1992); Stern Enterprises v. Plaza Theatres I and II, Inc., 105 Ohio App 3d 601 (Portage Cty. 1995); Mor-Flo Industries, Inc. v. Board of Review, 817 P.2d 328 (Utah App. 1991). ***PRACTICE AREAS:*** Business and Complex Litigation; Securities Litigation; Class Actions; Emergency Injunctions in Non-Competes; Misappropriation of Trade Secrets; Lanham Act Violations. ***Email:*** rmitchell@ralaw.com

BRIAN J. MOORE, born Dunkirk, New York, November 1, 1958; admitted to bar, 1984, Ohio and U.S. District Court, Northern District of Ohio. *Education:* State University of New York at Fredonia (B.A., magna cum laude, 1980); University of Akron (J.D., cum laude, 1984). *Member:* Akron, Ohio State and American Bar Associations. ***PRACTICE AREAS:*** Real Estate Law; Finance Law; Construction Law; Title Services. ***Email:*** bmoore@ralaw.com

RANDALL J. MOORE, born Rome, New York, February 27, 1959; admitted to bar, 1984, Ohio; 1985, U.S. District Court, Northern District of Ohio; 1988, U.S. Court of Appeals, Sixth Circuit. *Education:* State University of New York College at Brockport (B.S., 1981); Ohio Northern University College of Law (J.D., 1984). Delta Theta Phi. Associate Editor, Ohio Northern University Law Review, 1983-1984. *Member:* Akron, Stark County, Ohio State and Federal Bar Associations; Ohio Manufacturers Association; Defense Research Institute; Ohio Association of Civil Trial Attorneys. ***PRACTICE AREAS:*** Product Liability and Personal Injury Defense; Insurance Litigation; Insurance Coverage Issues. ***Email:*** rmoore@ralaw.com

GEORGE W. MOXON, II, born Asheville, North Carolina, February 2, 1944; admitted to bar, 1972, Virginia; 1973, District of Columbia; 1975, Ohio; registered to practice before U.S. Patent and Trademark Office. *Education:* University of Maryland (B.S.Ch.E., 1966); Catholic University of America (J.D., 1972). Member, Catholic University Law Review, 1971-1972. Author: "Products of Nature: The New Criteria," 20 Cath. U. L.R. 783, 1971. *Member:* American Bar Association; American Intellectual Property Law Association; Cleveland Intellectual Property Law Association (Treasurer, 1989-1991; Director, 1995-1996); International Trademark Association; LES USA/Canada (Past Co-Chairman, Cleveland/Akron Chapter). ***PRACTICE AREAS:*** Intellectual Property; Patents; Trademarks; Copyrights; Trade Secrets; Technology and Science; Intellectual Property Licensing; Intellectual Property Disputes; Intellectual Property International Law. ***Email:*** gmoxon@ralaw.com

RICHARD S. MULLIGAN, born Yonkers, New York, April 18, 1951; admitted to bar, 1979, Ohio and U.S. District Court, Southern District of Ohio; 1983, U.S. Tax Court. *Education:* Kenyon College (A.B., cum laude, 1973); Capital University (J.D., cum laude, 1979). Order of the Curia. Law Clerk to Justice William B. Brown, Ohio Supreme Court, 1979-1981. *Member:* Columbus, Ohio State and American Bar Associations. (Resident, Columbus Office). ***PRACTICE AREAS:*** Corporate; Business; Mergers and Acquisitions; Real Estate; Franchising; Estate Planning; Probate. ***Email:*** rmulligan@ralaw.com

DOUGLAS S. MUSICK, born Cheverly, Maryland, July 11, 1967; admitted to bar, 1992, Ohio. *Education:* University of Michigan (B.A., 1989); Case Western Reserve School of Law (J.D., 1992). *Member:* Cleveland, Cuyahoga County and Ohio State Bar Associations; Self-Insured Employers Association. (Resident, Cleveland Office). ***PRACTICE AREAS:*** Workers' Compensation; General Civil Litigation; Employment Law. ***Email:*** dmusick@ralaw.com

BASIL J. MUSNUFF, born Philadelphia, Pennsylvania, January 23, 1964; admitted to bar, 1989, Ohio; 1994, U.S. Court of Appeals, Sixth Circuit; U.S. District Court, Northern and Southern Districts of Ohio. *Education:* Haverford College (B.A., with honors, 1986); Cornell Law School (J.D., magna cum laude, 1989). *Member:* Cleveland, Akron, Ohio State and Federal Bar Associations; Defense Research Institute. (Resident, Cleveland Office). ***PRACTICE AREAS:*** Product Liability; General Litigation; Insurance; Civil Litigation; Torts. ***Email:*** bmusnuff@ralaw.com

PETER K. NEWMAN, admitted to bar, 1980, Ohio and U.S. District Court, Southern District of Ohio; 1984, Illinois; 1988, U.S. Court of Appeals, Sixth Circuit; 1990, U.S. District Court, Northern District of Ohio and U.S. Court of Appeals, Ninth Circuit; 1998, U.S. District Court, Western District of Kentucky; 1999, Kentucky. *Education:* Miami University (B.A., Economics and Political Science, cum laude, 1977); Georgetown University Law Center (J.D., 1980). *Member:* Cincinnati, Kentucky, Ohio State and American Bar Associations. (Resident, Cincinnati Office). ***PRACTICE AREAS:*** Employment Litigation; Intellectual Property; Labor and Employment; Regulatory Compliance; Union Labor Law. ***Email:*** pnewman@ralaw.com

CHERYL A. O'BRIEN, born Cleveland, Ohio, June 15, 1959; admitted to bar, 1989, Ohio. *Education:* Ursuline College (B.S.N., 1981); Cleveland-Marshall College of Law (J.D., 1988). *Member:* Cleveland and Ohio State Bar Associations. (Resident, Cleveland Office). ***PRACTICE AREAS:*** Medical Defense. ***Email:*** cobrien@ralaw.com

TIMOTHY J. OCHSENHIRT, born Phoenix, Arizona, November 16, 1946; admitted to bar, 1971, Ohio; 1983, U.S. Court of Appeals, Sixth Circuit. *Education:* University of Akron (B.A., 1968); University of Virginia (J.D., 1971). Firm Chairman and CEO. *Member:* Akron and Ohio State Bar Associations. ***PRACTICE AREAS:*** Business Law. ***Email:*** tochsenhirt@ralaw.com

WILLIAM R. O'NEILL, born Rahway, New Jersey, August 8, 1950; admitted to bar, 1977, Connecticut; 1978, Florida; 1990, U.S. Tax Court. *Education:* Boston College (B.A., summa cum laude, 1972); University of Virginia (M.A., 1974; J.D., 1977); New York University (LL.M., Taxation, 1983). Phi Beta Kappa. Director, Neighborhood Health Clinic of Naples; President, Collier Athletic Club, 2002-2003; President, United Arts Council of Collier County, 2001-2003; Chairman, Tamiami Trail Scenic Highway Designation Committee, 1997-1999; Leadership Collier Class of 1997; National Multiple Sclerosis Society; Economic Development Council of Collier County; Big Cypress Wilderness Institute; Attorneys for Family-Held Enterprises. *Member:* Connecticut and American Bar Associations; The Florida Bar. (Resident, Naples, Florida Office). ***PRACTICE AREAS:*** Estate Planning (33%); Taxation (33%); Corporate Law (34%). ***Email:*** woneill@ralaw.com

KEVIN J. OSTERKAMP, born Anamosa, Iowa, January 29, 1949; admitted to bar, 1974, Ohio and U.S. District Court, Southern District of Ohio; 1985, U.S. Court of Appeals, Sixth Circuit; 2005, U.S. District Court, Northern District of Ohio. *Education:* University of Iowa (B.B.A., cum laude, 1971); The Ohio State University (J.D., cum laude, 1974). Beta Gamma Sigma; Phi Delta Phi. Administrative Law Judge, Rate Section, Public Utilities Commission of Ohio, 1974-1978. *Member:* Columbus (Member, Business and Administrative Law Section), Ohio State and American (Member, Business Law Section) Bar Associations. (Resident, Columbus Office). ***REPORTED CASES:*** Penn. Traffic v.AIU Ins. Co. et al 99 Ohio St.3rd 227, 203-3373. ***PRACTICE AREAS:*** Business Litigation (60%); Construction Litigation (20%); Administrative Law (20%). ***Email:*** kosterkamp@ralaw.com

KELLY B. PLANTE, born Daytona Beach, Florida, 1965; admitted to bar, 1990, Florida; U.S. District Court, Middle District of Florida; U.S. Court of Appeals, Eleventh Circuit; U.S. Supreme Court. *Education:* University of Florida (B.S.B.A., 1987); Stetson University (J.D., 1990). Phi Alpha Delta. Assistant General Counsel, Florida Department of Natural Resources, 1990-1991. *Member:* The Florida Bar (Member, Sections on: Administrative Law; Environmental and Land Use). (Resident, Tallahassee, Florida Office). ***PRACTICE AREAS:*** Administrative Law; Corporate Law; Environmental Law; Appellate Practice. ***Email:*** kbplante@ralaw.com

KENNETH J. PLANTE, born Manchester, New Hampshire, September 3, 1948; admitted to bar, 1983, Florida. *Education:* Cornell University (B.A., 1970); Florida State University (M.A., 1976; M.S.P., 1977; J.D., 1983). Co-Author: "Babbit v. Sweet Home Chapter of Communities for a Great Oregon: Preserving the 'Critical Link' between Habitat Modification and the 'Taking' of an Endangered Species," Nova Law Review, Vol. 20, No. 1 (1996). General Counsel, Florida Department of Natural Resources, 1988-1993. General Counsel, Florida Department of Environmental Protection, 1993-1996. *Member:* The Florida Bar (Member, Sections on: Environmental Law; Administrative Law). [Lt. U.S. Navy, 1970-1974]. (Resident, Tallahassee, Florida Office). ***PRACTICE AREAS:*** Environmental Law; Administrative Law; Governmental Law; Appellate Practice. ***Email:*** kplante@ralaw.com

RICHARD A. PLEWACKI, born Cleveland, Ohio, November 26, 1948; admitted to bar, 1980, Ohio. *Education:* Bowling Green State University (B.A., 1970); University of Akron School of Law (J.D., 1980). *Member:* Cleveland, Cuyahoga County, Ohio State and American Bar Associations; Transportation Lawyers Association; Canadian Transportation Lawyers Association; Association for Transportation Law, Logistics and Policy; Ohio Trucking Association; Truckload Carriers Association; American Arbitration Association. (Resident, Cleveland Office). ***PRACTICE AREAS:*** Transportation and Logistics Law; Corporate Law; Commercial Law; Mergers and Acquisitions. ***Email:*** rplewacki@ralaw.com

MICHAEL A. POE, born Greenville, Mississippi, October 26, 1953; admitted to bar, 1978, Mississippi and Ohio. *Education:* University of Mississippi (B.A., 1975; J.D., 1978). *Member:* Columbus and Ohio State Bar Associations. (Resident, Columbus Office). ***PRACTICE AREAS:*** Corporate Law; Personal Planning; Successions; Estate Planning Law; Probate Law. ***Email:*** mpoe@ralaw.com

MARK J. PRICE, born New York, New York, December 4, 1962; admitted to bar, 1988, Connecticut; 1990, Florida. *Education:* Florida State University (B.S., summa cum laude, 1985) Phi Kappa Phi, Omicron Delta Kappa; University of California at Los Angeles (J.D., 1988). Author: "International Copyright Protection, Licensing and the Collection and Distribution of Royalties in the Satellite Era," Fifth Biennial UCLA Communications Law Symposium Resource Book, 1987; "New Escrow Mandates for Builders and Developers Under the Homebuyer's Protection Act," Actionline - The Journal of the Real Property, Probate and Trust Law Section of the Florida Bar, April/May, 1996. Lecturer: Real Property Law, International College of Naples, 1993. General Counsel, Collier Building Industry Association, 2000—. *Member:* Collier County Bar Association (Chair, Real Estate Section, 1995-1996); The Florida Bar (Member, Real Property Section). (Board Certified Real Estate Lawyer, Florida Bar Board of Legal Specialization and Education) (Resident Managing Partner, Naples, Florida Office). ***PRACTICE AREAS:*** Real Estate Law; Business Law. ***Email:*** mprice@ralaw.com

ROBERT D. PRITT, admitted to bar, 1974, Ohio; 1975, Florida and U.S. District Court, Northern District of Ohio; 1980, U.S. Court of Appeals, Sixth Circuit; 1981, U.S.

(This Listing Continued)

ROETZEL & ANDRESS, A LEGAL PROFESSIONAL ASSOCIATION, Akron—Continued

Supreme Court; 1987, U.S. District Court, Middle District of Florida; 1987, U.S. Court of Appeals, Eleventh Circuit; 2004, U.S. Court of Appeals, D.C. Circuit. *Education:* Kent State University; University of Akron (B.A., 1969; J.D., 1974). Pi Sigma Alpha (Honorary); Delta Theta Phi. Licensed Real Estate Broker (Inactive) and Instructor. Recipient, Outstanding Alumni Award: University of Akron School of Law, 2004. Former Adjunct Professor, Federal Courts, University of Akron School of Law. Author, "Use of Videotape and Audiotape as Deposition Media," Ohio Legal Center Institute, 1979. Co-Author: "Municipal Antitrust: Evaluating the Effect of Boulder on a Municipal Recycle Energy System," Antitrust & Local Government, James Siena, Editor, 1982; "Takings Update," Florida Institute of Government, Fall, 1994 reprinted in The Florida Bar Local Government Section Newsletter, Spring 1995; "The Zoning Process After Passage of Property Rights Legislation," The Urban Lawyer Vol. 28, No.4 801 @808, 1996; "Florida Private Property Rights Legislation," American Bar Association, Land Use Section, 1996; "Gated Communities: Solution or Public Dilemma?" The Urban Lawyer, Vol. 29, No.3, Page 413 @421, 1997; "Medium Sized Bar Association" Bar Leaders Conference, The Florida Bar, 1998; "Coping With the Florida Government in the Sunshine & Public Records Laws," Florida City & County Clerks Association, 1999; "Fifty (Or So) Cases Every City Attorney Should Know," Florida Municipal Attorneys Association, 2002; "Television-Taking Cities to Court," MacNeil Lehrer Reports, 1982; "Avoiding the Pitfalls of Municipal Contracting," Florida Municipal Attorneys Association, 2005. Director of Law, City of Akron, Ohio, 1980-1983. General Counsel, Akron Metropolitan Housing Authority, 1985-1987. City Attorney, 1987-2000 and Acting City Manager, 1999, City of Sanibel, Florida. Acting City Attorney, City of Bonita Springs, Florida, 2000. City Attorney, City of Naples, Florida, 2002. Member, Lee County Land Development Code Advisory Committee, 2001-2002. Member, Lee County Local Planning Agency, 2004. *Member:* Akron (Executive Committee Member, 1979-1980), Lee County (President, 1994), Collier County and Ohio State Bar Associations; The Florida Bar (Chair, Voluntary Bar Liaison Committee, 2001; Chair, Certification Committee, 2002); Appellate Court Rules Committee (Chair, Administrative Practice Subcommittee, 2005); Ohio Municipal Attorneys Association (Secretary/Treasurer, 1982-1983); Florida Municipal Attorneys Association (President, 2000; Municipal Attorney of the Year, 2004); International Municipal Lawyers Association (Florida Chair, 1998-2000); Florida Council of Bar Association Presidents (Treasurer, 2005); American Inns of Court (Member, Calusa Chapter). [1969-1971; National Defense & Army Commendation Medal]. (Board Certified City, County and Local Government Lawyer, Florida Bar Board of Legal Specialization and Education) (Resident, Naples, Florida Office). ***LANGUAGES:*** Spanish. ***REPORTED CASES:*** Akron Center for Reproductive Health v. Akron, U.S. Supreme Court (1982); Hybud v. Akron, U.S. Supreme Court (1981) (remand to 6th Cir. Court of Appeals); King v. Williams, Ohio Supreme Court (1983); Coventry Township Trustees v. Akron, 6th Cir. Court of Appeals (1981). ***TRANSACTIONS:*** Municipal Bonding for Akron, Ohio; Sanibel, Florida; and Naples, Florida. ***PRACTICE AREAS:*** Public Law; Land Use; Real Estate; Municipal Finance. ***Email:*** rpritt@ralaw.com

STACY A. RAGON, born Kankakee, Illinois, June 6, 1969; admitted to bar, 1996, Ohio; 1999, U.S. District Court, Northern District of Ohio; U.S. District Court, Eastern District of Michigan; U.S. Court of Appeals, Sixth Circuit. *Education:* Malone College (B.A., magna cum laude, 1991); University of Dayton School of Law (J.D., magna cum laude, 1996). Phi Alpha Delta. Member, Moot Court, 1994-1995. Staff Member, University of Dayton Law Review, 1994-1995. Author: "A Doctor's Dilemma: Resolving the Conflict Between Physician Participation in Executions and the AMA's Code of Medical Ethics," Dayton L.Rev., Vol. 20, Issue 3, Spring 1995. Law Clerk to the Honorable Robert A. Nader, Ohio Court of Appeals, 11th District, 1996-1998. *Member:* Akron and Ohio State Bar Associations. ***PRACTICE AREAS:*** Medical Malpractice Defense. ***Email:*** sragon@ralaw.com

CATHY S. REIMAN, born St. Louis, Missouri, June 16, 1957; admitted to bar, 1985, Florida. *Education:* University of Missouri (B. Journalism, 1979); Stetson University (J.D., summa cum laude, 1985). *Member:* Collier County Bar Association (President, 1991-1992); Grievance Committee, 20th Circuit, 1993-1996 (Chairman, 1995-1996). (Board Certified Business Litigation Lawyer, Florida Bar Board of Legal Specialization and Education) (Resident, Naples, Florida Office). ***PRACTICE AREAS:*** Commercial Litigation; Probate Litigation; Estate Litigation; Guardianship. ***Email:*** creiman@ralaw.com

GEORGE W. ROONEY, JR., born Akron, Ohio, October 23, 1949; admitted to bar, 1974, Ohio and U.S. District Court, Northern District of Ohio; 1977, U.S. Court of Appeals, Sixth Circuit; 1980, U.S. Supreme Court; 1987, U.S. District Court, Southern District of Ohio; 1993, U.S. Tax Court; 1996, U.S. Court of International Trade; 2003, U.S. Court of Appeals, Federal Circuit; registered to practice before U.S. Patent and Trademark Office. *Education:* University of Virginia (B.S.M.E., 1971); The Ohio State University (J.D., cum laude, 1973). Life Member, Sixth Circuit Judicial Conference. Chairman, Federal Court Committee, Akron Bar Association, 1991-1993. Member, Federal Court Panel, Alternative Dispute Resolution, 1992—. Chairman, Technology Committee, Advisory Group of U.S. District Court, Northern District of Ohio, 1999-2002. President, Rotary Club of Akron, 1988-1989. Vice Chairman, Summit County Red Cross, 1988-1991. President, Akron Law Library Association, 1995-1997. President, Great Trail Council, B.S.A., 1996-1997. *Member:* Cleveland, Ohio State (Chairman, Uniform State Law Committee, 1989-1991; Chairman, Law Libraries Committee, 1993-1995) and Federal Bar Associations. (Board Certified Civil Trial Advocacy Specialist by the National Board of Trial Advocacy) (Resident, Cleveland Office). ***REPORTED CASES:*** Frankl v. Goodyear Tire and Rubber Company, 181 N.J. 1 (2004); Luntz Corp. v. Public Ulilities Comm., 79 Ohio St.3d 509 (1997); Ohio Edison Co. v. Public Utilities Comm., 78 Ohio St.3d 466 (1997); Bank One, Akron, N.A. v. Atwater Enterprises, Inc., 115 Ohio App.3d 461 (1996); R&R Plastics, Inc. v. F.E. Myers Co., 92 Ohio App.3d 789 (1993); Silver Cloud v. National Kitchen Products, 989 F.2d 501 (6th Cir. 1993); Bank One of Cleveland, N.A. v. Abbe, 916 F.2d 1067 (6th Cir. 1990); Van Fossen v. Babcock & Wilcox Company, 36 Ohio St.3d 100 (1988); Michaels Bldg. Co. v. Ameritrust Co., N.A., 848 F.2d 674 (6th Cir. 1988); XXTH Century Heating & Ventilating Co. v. Dept. of Energy, 618 F.2d 1 (6th Cir. 1980). ***PRACTICE AREAS:*** Complex Business Litigation (50%); Alternative Dispute Resolution (10%); Intellectual Property Litigation (40%). ***Email:*** grooney@ralaw.com

(This Listing Continued)

MARK A. ROPCHOCK, born Cleveland, Ohio, October 10, 1960; admitted to bar, 1985, Ohio; 1989, U.S. District Court, Northern District of Ohio; 2002, U.S. District Court Eastern District of Michigan; 2003, Southern District of Ohio; 2003, U.S. Court of Appeals, 6th Circuit. *Education:* Ohio Northern University (B.A., Political Science, with distinction, 1982); Case Western Reserve University (J.D., 1985). *Member:* Akron and Ohio State Bar Associations. ***PRACTICE AREAS:*** Insurance Defense; Complex and Multi-District Litigation; Mass Torts; Products Liability; Plaintiffs Personal Injury. ***Email:*** mropchock@ralaw.com

THOMAS L. ROSENBERG, born 1955; admitted to bar, 1983, Ohio; U.S. Court of Appeals, Sixth Circuit; U.S. District Court, Northern District of Ohio; U.S. District Court, Southern District of Ohio. *Education:* Ohio Wesleyan University (B.A., 1977); Capital University (J.D., 1983). *Member:* Columbus, Ohio State and American Bar Associations. (Resident, Columbus Office). ***PRACTICE AREAS:*** Business Litigation; Construction Law; Government Relations; Regulatory Compliance. ***Email:*** trosenberg@ralaw.com

ALBERT N. SALVATORE, born Cleveland, Ohio, 1954; admitted to bar, 1982, Ohio. *Education:* John Carroll University (B.S.B.A., cum laude, 1976); Cleveland-Marshall College of Law (J.D., 1982); New York University (LL.M., Taxation, 1983). *Member:* Cleveland, Ohio State and American (Member, Sections on: Corporations; Bank and Business Law; Taxation Law) Bar Associations. (Resident, Cleveland Office). ***PRACTICE AREAS:*** Taxation; Corporate Law; Partnership Law; Securities. ***Email:*** asalvatore@ralaw.com

BEVERLY A. SANDACZ, born Euclid, Ohio, August 9, 1960; admitted to bar, 1994, Ohio. *Education:* Ursuline College (B.S.N., magna cum laude, 1982); Cleveland-Marshall College of Law (J.D., summa cum laude, 1994). Law Clerk, Hon. Joseph Mahoney, 11th District Court of Appeals, 1993-1995. *Member:* Cuyahoga County, Lake County and Ohio State Bar Associations. (Resident, Cleveland Office). ***PRACTICE AREAS:*** Medical Malpractice; Health Care. ***Email:*** bsandacz@ralaw.com

GEORGE R. SARKIS, born Akron, Ohio, May 17, 1955; admitted to bar, 1980, Ohio and U.S. District Court, Northern District of Ohio. *Education:* Brown University (A.B., with honors, 1977); Case Western Reserve University (J.D., 1980). *Member:* Akron and Ohio State Bar Associations; National Association of Bond Lawyers. ***PRACTICE AREAS:*** Public Finance; Capital Markets; Economic Development. ***Email:*** gsarkis@ralaw.com

MARK L. SARLSON, born Akron, Ohio, April 20, 1961; admitted to bar, 1986, Ohio and U.S. District Court, Northern District of Ohio. *Education:* University of Virginia (B.A., 1983); Ohio State University (J.D., 1986). Chief Justice, Moot Court Governing Board. Article Editor, The Ohio State Journal on Dispute Resolution, 1985-1986. Member: ABA Appellate Advocacy Team, 1985-1986. *Member:* Cleveland and Ohio State Bar Associations. (Resident, Cleveland Office). ***PRACTICE AREAS:*** Corporate Law; Corporate Finance; Commercial Finance; Real Estate. ***Email:*** msarlson@ralaw.com

DONALD S. SCHERZER, born Brooklyn, New York, March 16, 1949; admitted to bar, 1975, Ohio and U.S. District Court, Northern District of Ohio; 1979, U.S. Court of Appeals, Sixth Circuit, U.S. Supreme Court and U.S. Tax Court. *Education:* Bowling Green State University (B.S., 1971); Case Western Reserve University (J.D., 1975). Trial Attorney, U.S. Dept. of Justice, Antitrust Div., 1975-1982. *Member:* Cleveland, Ohio State (Chairman, Antitrust Section, 1997-1998), Federal (President, Cleveland Chapter, 1984-1985; National Chairman Antitrust and Trade Regulation Section, 1985-1986) and American (Member, Antitrust, Litigation and Criminal Law Sections) Bar Associations; Sixth Circuit Judicial Conference (Life Member). (Resident, Cleveland Office). ***PRACTICE AREAS:*** Antitrust Law; Trade Regulation Law; Civil Litigation; Complex Litigation; Environmental Litigation; Securities Litigation; Criminal Law. ***Email:*** dscherzer@ralaw.com

BRUCE R. SCHRADER, II, born Orrville, Ohio, April 30, 1963; admitted to bar, 1987, Ohio; 1990, U.S. District Court, Northern and Southern Districts of Ohio; 1997, U.S. Court of Appeals, Sixth Circuit. *Education:* University of Akron (B.A., Certificate in Peace Studies, cum laude, 1984); University of Cincinnati (J.D., 1987). Law Clerk for Hon. James H. Williams, Chief Judge, U.S. Bankruptcy Court, Northern District of Ohio, 1987-1990. *Member:* Akron, Stark County and Ohio State Bar Associations; American Bankruptcy Institute. ***PRACTICE AREAS:*** Commercial Law; Bankruptcy Law; Creditors' Rights; Debtors' Protection; Business Reorganization. ***Email:*** bschrader@ralaw.com

JAMES C. SCOTT, born Lansing, Michigan, 1961; admitted to bar, 1991, Ohio; registered to practice before U.S. Patent and Trademark Office. *Education:* Hope College (B.S., 1983); Case Western Reserve University (J.D., 1989). *Member:* American Bar Association; Cleveland Intellectual Property Law Association; Lawyer-Pilot Bar Association. (Resident, Cleveland Office). ***PRACTICE AREAS:*** Patents; Trademarks; Copyright; Intellectual Property; Litigation and Licensing. ***Email:*** jscott@ralaw.com

JEFFREY S. SHOSKIN, born Pittsburgh, Pennsylvania, July 7, 1958; admitted to bar, 1983, Ohio and U.S. District Court, Southern District of Ohio; 1990, U.S. Court of Appeals, Sixth Circuit. *Education:* Grove City College (B.A., magna cum laude, 1980); Temple University (J.D., cum laude, 1983). Named an Ohio Super Lawyer. Co-Author, Chapter, "Defenses to Wrongful Termination Claims," Litigating Wrongful Discharge Claims, Clark Boardman Callaghan. Member, Inaugural Class, Cincinnati Academy of Leadership for Lawyers. *Member:* Cincinnati (Chair, Labor and Employment Committee, 2000-2004; Vice President, Board of Trustees; Former Secretary and Treasurer; Former Chair, Young Lawyers Section), Ohio State (Member, Labor & Employment Law Committee) and American (Member, Labor & Employment Law Committee) Bar Associations; Potter Stewart American Inn of Court (Member, Executive Committee). (Resident, Cincinnati Office). ***PRACTICE AREAS:*** Labor and Employment (95%); Alternative Dispute Resolution (5%). ***Email:*** jshoskin@ralaw.com

THOMAS M. SKOVE, born Cleveland, Ohio, June 29, 1951; admitted to bar, 1977, Ohio and U.S. District Court, Northern and Southern Districts of Ohio. *Education:* Amherst College (B.A., magna cum laude, 1973); Case Western Reserve University (J.D., 1977). Attorney and Associate Counsel, GenCorp Inc. and General Tire, Inc., 1984-1990. Senior Environmental Counsel, GenCorp Inc., 1991-1995. *Member:* Cleveland (Member, Environmental Section), Akron, Cuyahoga County, Ohio State (Member, Environmental Law Committee) and American (Member, Section on Natural Resources, Energy and Environmental Law; Vice Chair, Technology and Public Service, Ethics) Bar Associations.

(This Listing Continued)

REPORTED CASES: Grendell v. Ohio Environmental Protection Agency 146 Ohio App.3d. 34 (2001). ***PRACTICE AREAS:*** Environmental Law; Government Contracts. ***Email:*** tskove@ralaw.com

CHARLES D. SMITH, born New York, N.Y., July 24, 1958; admitted to bar, 1983, Ohio and U.S. District Court, Southern District of Ohio. *Education:* Ohio Wesleyan University (B.A., 1980); Capital University (J.D., 1983). Order of the Curia. Judicial Clerk to Judge Dean Strausbaugh, Tenth District Court of Appeals, Ohio, 1983-1984. *Member:* Columbus and Ohio State and American Bar Associations. (Resident, Columbus Office). ***PRACTICE AREAS:*** Civil Litigation; Workers' Compensation. ***Email:*** csmith@ralaw.com

BRADLEY L. SNYDER, born Shelby, Ohio, September 28, 1956; admitted to bar, 1981, Ohio; 1982, U.S. District Court, Southern District of Ohio and U.S. Court of Appeals, Sixth Circuit; 1983, Florida and U.S. District Court, Northern District of Ohio. *Education:* The Ohio State University (B.S., cum laude, 1978); Capital University (J.D., with honors, 1981). Order of the Curia. *Member:* Columbus and Ohio State Bar Associations; Defense Research Institute; Ohio Association of Civil Trial Attorneys; Transportation Lawyers Association; Central Ohio Civil War Roundtable. (Board Certified in Civil Trial Advocacy by the National Board of Trial Advocacy) (Resident, Columbus Office). ***PRACTICE AREAS:*** Trucking Litigation; Insurance Coverage Litigation; Product Liability and Personal Injury Defense; Employment Litigation; Civil Rights Litigation. ***Email:*** bsnyder@ralaw.com

DOUGLAS E. SPIKER, born Cadiz, Ohio, September 1, 1961; admitted to bar, 1986, Ohio and U.S. District Court, Southern District of Ohio. *Education:* Mount Union College (B.A., 1983); Ohio Northern University (J.D., 1986). *Member:* Toledo, Columbus and Ohio State (Member, Workers' Compensation Committee) Bar Associations. (Certified Specialist in Workers' Compensation, Ohio State Bar Association) (Resident, Toledo Office). ***PRACTICE AREAS:*** Workers; Litigation; Administrative Law; Workers Compensation; Workers Compensation Defense; Workers Compensation Self-Insurance; Workers Compensation Mediation; Workers Compensation Subrogation; Workers Compensation Appeals. ***Email:*** dspiker@ralaw.com

GARY W. SPRING, born New Philadelphia, Ohio, April 25, 1954; admitted to bar, 1979, Ohio; 1981, U.S. District Court, Northern and Southern Districts of Ohio; 1982, U.S. Court of Appeals, Sixth Circuit; 1992, U.S. Supreme Court. *Education:* Kent State University (A.A., 1974); University of Akron (B.A., 1976); The Ohio State University (J.D., with honors, 1979). Member, Ohio State Law Journal. Law Clerk for Justice Paul Brown, Ohio Supreme Court, 1979-1981. Listed in The Best Lawyers in America; Labor & Employment Law, 1995-2006 editions. Adjunct Professor, University of Akron School of Law, Labor Law and Employment Law. Recipient, Quine Award as Outstanding Adjunct Professor. *Member:* Akron, Ohio State and American Bar Associations. (Certified Specialist in Labor & Employment Law, Ohio State Bar Association). ***PRACTICE AREAS:*** Labor and Employment Law; Employment Litigation. ***Email:*** gspring@ralaw.com

ROGER J. STEVENSON, born Ashtabula, Ohio, December 9, 1952; admitted to bar, 1981, Ohio; 1982, U.S. District Court, Northern District of Ohio; 1985, U.S. Court of Appeals, Sixth Circuit. *Education:* Kent State University (B.A., magna cum laude, 1976; B.S.Ed., 1977); University of Akron (J.D., with highest honors, 1981). *Member:* Akron and Ohio State Bar Associations. ***PRACTICE AREAS:*** Bankruptcy Law; Creditors; Debtors; Business Reorganization. ***Email:*** rstevenson@ralaw.com

MARK C. TERZOLA, born South Bend, Indiana, December 25, 1970; admitted to bar, 1996, Ohio; U.S. District Court, Northern District of Ohio; U.S. Court of Appeals, Sixth Circuit; registered to practice before U.S. Patent and Trademark Office. *Education:* University of Notre Dame (B.S.Eng., 1993); The University of Akron (J.D., summa cum laude, 1996). *Member:* Akron and Ohio State Bar Associations. ***PRACTICE AREAS:*** Intellectual Property Law. ***Email:*** mterzola@ralaw.com

DIANA M. THIMMIG, born West Germany, May 5, 1959; admitted to bar, 1983, Ohio, U.S. District Court, Northern District of Ohio and U.S. Court of Appeals, Sixth Circuit; 1993, U.S. Supreme Court; 1996, U.S Court of Appeals, Third Circuit; 1998, U.S. District Court, Western District of Pennsylvania; 2002, U.S. District Court, Western District of Michigan. *Education:* John Carroll University (B.A., cum laude, 1980); Cleveland-Marshall College of Law (J.D., 1982). Bankruptcy Trustee, U.S. Bankruptcy Court, Northern District of Ohio, 1987-1991. Member, Civil Justice Reform Advisory Group, U.S. District Court, Northern District of Ohio, 1995-2003. Honorary Consul, Federal Republic of Germany, 1989—. President, Legal Aid Society of Cleveland, 2003—. Trustee, International Services Center, 1998-2004. *Member:* Cuyahoga County (President, 2005—) and Ohio State Bar Associations; Cuyahoga County Bar Foundation (Trustee, 2002—). (Certified Specialist, Consumer Bankruptcy Law and Business Bankruptcy Law, American Bankruptcy Board of Certification) (Resident, Cleveland Office). ***SPECIAL AGENCIES:*** Legal Aid Society of Cleveland (President, 2003- present); Honorary Consul, Federal Republic of Germany (1988-present). ***PRACTICE AREAS:*** Bankruptcy; Commercial Litigation; Commercial Transactions. ***Email:*** dthimmig@ralaw.com

STEPHEN E. THOMPSON, born Salt Lake City, Utah, November 27, 1953; admitted to bar, 1983, Ohio; 1984, Utah and Florida. *Education:* Florida International University (B.A., with honors, 1980); J. Reuben Clark Law School of Brigham Young University (J.D., cum laude, 1982). Author: "The Uniform Consumer Sales Practices Act," Brigham Young University Journal of Legal Studies, 1981 and Editor, 1982-1983. Special Counsel to the Attorney General of Ohio. *Member:* Collier County Bar Association (Chairman, Real Estate Section, 1990-1991); The Florida Bar (Member, Section on Real Property, Probate and Trust Law). Inactive Member: Ohio State Bar Association; Utah State Bar. [U.S. Army, 1972-1975]. (Board Certified Real Estate Lawyer, Florida Bar Board of Legal Specialization and Education) (Resident, Naples, Florida Office) (Managing Partner, Florida Offices). ***LANGUAGES:*** French. ***PRACTICE AREAS:*** Real Estate Law; Commercial Real Estate Development; Title Insurance Services; Residential Real Estate Development. ***Email:*** sthompson@ralaw.com

THOMAS A. TREADON, born Cleveland, Ohio, January 19, 1943; admitted to bar, 1975, Ohio; 1976, U.S. District Court, Northern District of Ohio; 1980, U.S. Court of Appeals, Sixth Circuit. *Education:* U.S. Air Force Academy (B.S., 1965); University of Akron (J.D., 1975). Editor, Akron Law Review, 1974-1975. Assistant Law Director, City of North Canton, Ohio, 1976-2003. Special Counsel, North Canton Charter Review Commission, 1977 and 1997. Trustee, North Canton Community Improvement Corporation, 1980—. Law Director, City of Louisville, 1989-1991. *Member:* Akron, Stark County and Ohio State Bar Associations; Ohio Association of Civil Trial Attorneys. [Captain, USAF]. ***PRACTICE AREAS:*** Medical Malpractice Defense (90%); Legal Malpractice Defense (10%). ***Email:*** ttreadon@ralaw.com

TIMOTHY J. WEBSTER, born Cleveland, Ohio, January 24, 1959; admitted to bar, 1987, Ohio. *Education:* University of Dayton (B.A., 1981); Cleveland-Marshall College of Law (J.D., 1987). *Member:* Akron and Ohio State Bar Associations; Ohio Self-Insured Group Association. (Certified Specialist in Workers' Compensation Law, Ohio State Bar Association). ***PRACTICE AREAS:*** Workers' Compensation. ***Email:*** twebster@ralaw.com

STEVEN I. WINER, born St. Paul, Minnesota, October 29, 1946; admitted to bar, 1973, Minnesota, U.S. District Court, District of Minnesota and U.S. Court of Appeals, Eighth Circuit; 1976, U.S. Supreme Court; 1985, Florida; 1986, U.S. District Court, Middle District of Florida. *Education:* University of Minnesota (B.A., 1968); John Marshall Law School (J.D., with honors, 1972). Editor, John Marshall Law Review, 1971-1972. Chairman, Camp Genesis Committee, Lee County, 1992-1996. Board of Directors, Jewish Federation of Lee and Charlotte Counties, 1992-2004. General Counsel, Sanibel/Captiva Board of Realtors, 1990-1996. *Member:* Lee County, Minnesota State and American Bar Associations; The Florida Bar; Fort Myers Board of Realtors (Associate); Community Association Institute (South Gulf Chapter); Real Estate Investment Society (Lee County). [U.S. Army Security Agency, 1968-1974]. (Resident, Fort Myers, Florida Office). ***PRACTICE AREAS:*** Real Estate; Corporate Law; Banking Law; Condominium and Homeowners Associations. ***Email:*** swiner@ralaw.com

ALISA LABUT WRIGHT, born Akron, Ohio, May 7, 1968; admitted to bar, 1993, Ohio. *Education:* University of Akron (B.A., summa cum laude, 1990); The Ohio State University (J.D., cum laude, 1993). *Member:* Akron and Ohio State Bar Associations; Ohio Women's Bar Association. ***REPORTED CASES:*** Strussion, et al. v. Akron Beacon Journal Publishing Co., et al. (June 26, 2002), 2002-Ohio-3200, Summit App. No. 20833, 2002 WL 1371166; Irvine, et al. v. Akron Beacon Journal, et al. (2002), 2002-Ohio-2204, 147 Ohio App.3d 428; Robinson, et al. v. Akron Metropolitan Housing Authority (2001), Summit App. No. 20405, 2001 WL 866275. ***PRACTICE AREAS:*** Business Litigation; Media Law; Probate Litigation; Appellate Practice; Complex Motion Practice. ***Email:*** awright@ralaw.com

BRADLEY A. WRIGHT, born Des Moines, Iowa, November 24, 1964; admitted to bar, 1990, Ohio; 1991, U.S. District Court, Northern District of Ohio; 1996, U.S. Court of Appeals, Sixth Circuit; U.S. District Court, Southern District of Ohio. *Education:* Miami University (B.A., 1987); The Ohio State University College of Law (J.D., 1990). *Member:* Akron and Ohio State Bar Associations; Transportation Lawyers Association; Trucking Industry Defense Association. ***PRACTICE AREAS:*** Insurance Litigation; Transportation Law; Trucking; Business Litigation; Tort Defense; Professional Liability. ***Email:*** bwright@ralaw.com

MICHAEL S. YASHKO, born Wintersville, Ohio, December 2, 1961; admitted to bar, 1987, Ohio; 2003, Florida; U.S. Court of Appeals, Sixth Circuit; U.S. District Court, Southern and Northern Districts of Ohio; U.S. Tax Court. *Education:* The Ohio State University (B.S.B.A., cum laude, 1984); Northwestern University (J.D., cum laude, 1987). Co-Author: "A Positive Theory of the Attorney-Client Privilege," The Journal of Legal Studies, June 1990. Member, Board of Directors, Accelerated Cure Project for Multiple Sclerosis. *Member:* Columbus, Lee County and Ohio State Bar Associations; The Florida Bar; Urban Land Institute; International Council of Shopping Centers; Associated General Contractors. (Chair of Real Estate, Construction and Environmental Law Group) (At Columbus, Ohio and Fort Myers, Florida Offices). ***PRACTICE AREAS:*** Real Estate; Construction; Business Law. ***Email:*** myashko@ralaw.com

JOSEPH D. ZAKS, admitted to bar, 1985, Massachusetts; 1986, U.S. Court of Appeals, First Circuit; 1990, U.S. Supreme Court; 1991, Florida; 1993, U.S. Tax Court. *Education:* University of Massachusetts (B.S., summa cum laude, 1982); Boston University (J.D., 1985; LL.M., 1989). Hennessey Scholar. Member, Advisory Board, Collier County, Florida Parks and Recreation, 1994-1999; Chairman, 1996-1999. Lieutenant Governor, Division 22, 2001-2002 and Chairman, Florida District of Kiwanis, Kiwanis International Foundation, 2005-2006. Director, Lee Memorial Health System Foundation, 2002-2004. Member, Advisory Board, Community Foundation of Collier County. *Member:* Lee County, Collier County and Massachusetts Bar Associations; The Florida Bar. [U.S. Air Force, 1968-1971]. (Board Certified Wills, Trusts and Estates Lawyer, Florida Bar Board of Legal Specialization and Education) (Resident, Naples, Florida Office). ***PRACTICE AREAS:*** Wills; Trusts and Estates; Tax Law; Corporate Law; Family Law. ***Email:*** jzaks@ralaw.com

THOMAS S. ZAREMBA, born Warren, Ohio, December 20, 1951; admitted to bar, 1977, Ohio. *Education:* Hillsdale College (A.B., summa cum laude, 1974); Case Western Reserve University (J.D., summa cum laude, 1977). Order of the Coif. Author: "The C-L Cartage and Deprizio Cases," Ohio Lawyer, January, 1991; "Environmental Risks in Bankruptcy," Ohio Lawyer, July, 1991; "The 'Fair Use' of Copyrighted Materials," Ohio Lawyer, November, 1995. Appointed to Board of Editors, *Ohio Lawyer,* 1994-1996. Appointed to Industry Advisory Committee of the International Building Code Council, 1996—. *Member:* Toledo and Ohio State Bar Associations. (Resident, Toledo Office). ***PRACTICE AREAS:*** Commercial; Litigation; Bankruptcy Law; Building Codes. ***Email:*** tzaremba@ralaw.com

OF COUNSEL

JANICE A. ISAKOFF, born Toledo, Ohio, February 22, 1960; admitted to bar, 1986, Ohio. *Education:* Findlay College (B.A., cum laude, 1982); University of Toledo (J.D., 1986). *Member:* Cleveland and Ohio State Bar Associations. (Resident, Cleveland Office). ***PRACTICE AREAS:*** Banking; Finance; Closely Held Business; Emerging Business Law; Condominium Association Law; Homeowners Law; Construction Law; Real Estate Law; Land Use Law; Residential Association Litigation; School Law. ***Email:*** jisakoff@ralaw.com

TERESA E. PURTIMAN, admitted to bar, 2001, Ohio. *Education:* The Ohio State University (B.A., Economics, summa cum laude, 1986); The University of Akron School of Law (J.D., magna cum laude, 2001). Phi Beta Kappa. *Member:* Ohio State and American

(This Listing Continued)

ROETZEL & ANDRESS, A LEGAL PROFESSIONAL ASSOCIATION, Akron—Continued

Bar Associations. (Resident, Cleveland Office). ***PRACTICE AREAS:*** Intellectual Property; Closely Held Business Law; Emerging Business Law. ***Email:*** tpurtiman@ralaw.com

GARY A. WEISS, born Cleveland, Ohio, November 6, 1963; admitted to bar, 1990, Ohio; 1992, U.S. District Court, Northern District of Ohio; 1995, U.S. District Court, Eastern District of Michigan; 2003, U.S. District Court, Southern District of Ohio and U.S. Court of Appeals, Sixth Circuit. *Education:* University of Akron (B.A., cum laude, 1986); University of Toledo (J.D., 1990). *Member:* Cleveland and Ohio State Bar Associations. (Resident, Cleveland Office). ***PRACTICE AREAS:*** Insurance Defense; Workers Compensation; Litigation. ***Email:*** gweiss@ralaw.com

CHARLES E. ZUMKEHR, born Canton, Ohio, 1938; admitted to bar, 1964, Ohio; 1968, U.S. District Court, Northern and Southern Districts of Ohio; 1975, U.S. Court of Appeals, Sixth Circuit; 1978, U.S. Supreme Court and U.S. Tax Court. *Education:* Ohio University (B.A., History and Government, 1961); Case Western Reserve University School of Law (J.D., 1964). *Member:* Akron, Ohio State, American and International Bar Associations. ***PRACTICE AREAS:*** International Law; Corporate and Business Services; Real Estate, Land Use, and Construction. ***Email:*** czumkehr@ralaw.com

---

KAREN D. ADINOLFI, born Cleveland, Ohio, October 13, 1969; admitted to bar, 2001, Ohio; 2002, U.S. District Court, Northern District of Ohio; 2003, U.S. Court of Appeals, Sixth Circuit; 2004, U.S. District Court, Southern District of Ohio. *Education:* University of Toledo (B.A., magna cum laude, 1992); Kent State University (M.A., 1995); University of Akron (J.D., summa cum laude, 2001). Member, 1999-2000 and Citations Editor, 2000-2001, Akron Law Review. Author, Note: "Genaro v. Central Transport: A New Direction in Ohio Regarding Employment Discrimination, 33 Akron Law Review 391, 2000. Adjunct Instructor, Legal Writing Program, University of Akron School of Law, 2001-2002. Judicial Attorney, The Honorable Deborah L. Cook, Supreme Court of Ohio, 2001. *Member:* Akron and Ohio State Bar Associations. ***PRACTICE AREAS:*** Labor and Employment Litigation; Regulatory Compliance; Union Relations. ***Email:*** kadinolfi@ralaw.com

CHAD ARFONS, born January 9, 1971; admitted to bar, 1997, Ohio; 2004, U.S. Tax Court. *Education:* Unversity of Akron (B.A., 1994); Tulane University Law School (J.D., 1997). Contributing Author, "Consumer Credit Law, Transactions and Forms," Matthews Bender & Co., 1999—. *Member:* Cleveland and Ohio State Bar Associations. (Resident, Cleveland Office). ***PRACTICE AREAS:*** Real Estate; Real Estate Finance; Real Estate Syndication; Banking Law; Consumer Credit; Corporate Law; Loan Syndication. ***Email:*** carfons@ralaw.com

CYNTHIA P. BAYER, born Cleveland, Ohio, February 15, 1979; (admission pending). *Education:* Miami University (B.S., 2001); Cleveland-Marshall College of Law (J.D., summa cum laude, 2004). ***PRACTICE AREAS:*** Corporate Law; Real Estate. ***Email:*** cbayer@ralaw.com

RYAN E. BONINA. *Education:* Oberlin College (B.A., 2000); University of Pittsburgh School of Law (J.D., 2005). (Resident, Columbus Office). ***PRACTICE AREAS:*** Labor and Employment. ***Email:*** rbonina@ralaw.com

JEFFREY S. BRAUN, born June 14, 1975; admitted to bar, 2002, Ohio. *Education:* Albion College (B.A., cum laude, 1997); The Ohio State University (J.D., 2002). *Member:* Columbus and Ohio State Bar Associations. (Resident, Columbus Office). ***PRACTICE AREAS:*** Corporate Law. ***Email:*** jbraun@ralaw.com

ERIC S. BRAVO, born Columbus, Ohio, April 12, 1965; admitted to bar, 1990, Ohio; 1991, U.S. District Court, Northern District of Ohio. *Education:* Northwestern University (B.A., 1987); Ohio State University (J.D., 1990). *Member:* Columbus and Ohio State Bar Associations. (Resident, Columbus Office). ***PRACTICE AREAS:*** Workers Compensation (100%). ***Email:*** ebravo@ralaw.com

AMY L. BUTLER, born Toledo, Ohio, 1972; admitted to bar, 2002, Ohio; 2004, U.S. District Court, Northern District of Ohio. *Education:* University of Toledo (B.A., 1995; J.D., 2002); Bowling Green State University (M.Ed., 1998). Member, University of Toledo Law Review. Law Clerk to the Honorable J. Ronald Bowman, Lucas County Common Pleas Court. *Member:* Toledo and Ohio State Bar Associations. (Resident, Toledo Office). ***PRACTICE AREAS:*** Litigation. ***Email:*** abutler@ralaw.com

RICARDO J. CARDENAS, born Cleveland, Ohio, May 8, 1968; admitted to bar, 1996, Ohio. *Education:* Cleveland State University (B.A., cum laude, 1993); Case Western Reserve (J.D., 1996). (Resident, Cleveland Office). ***Email:*** rcardenas@ralaw.com

TAMMI J. CARTER, born Geneva, New York, October 12, 1979; admitted to bar, 2004, Ohio; 2005, U.S. District Court, Northern District of Ohio. *Education:* Le Moyne College (B.A., summa cum laude, 2001); Case Western Reserve University (J.D., cum laude, 2004). Executive Contributing Editor, Case Western Reserve University Law Review, 2003-2004. Author, Note, "The Individual v. The Employer: Who Should Be Held Liable Under Employment Discrimination Law," 54 Case W. Res. L. Rev. 861 (2004). *Member:* Cleveland and Ohio State Bar Associations. (Resident, Cleveland Office). ***PRACTICE AREAS:*** Labor and Employment. ***Email:*** tcarter@ralaw.com

SHARON CASON-ADAMS, admitted to bar, 1997, Ohio; 1999, U.S. District Court, Southern District of Ohio; 2001, U.S. District Court, Northern District of Ohio; 2002, U.S. Supreme Court. *Education:* Franklin University (B.S., 1991); Capital University (J.D., 1997). *Member:* Columbus, Ohio State (Member, Labor and Employment Law Section) and American Bar Associations; Society of Human Resources Management. [With, Ohio Air National Guard, 1983-1991]. (Resident, Columbus Office). ***PRACTICE AREAS:*** Employment Litigation; Insurance Coverage; Labor and Employment; Risk Management; Workers Compensation. ***Email:*** sadams@ralaw.com

STEPHENIE L. CONDE, born Canton, Ohio; admitted to bar, 1994, Ohio. *Education:* Bowling Green State University (B.A., 1991); Cleveland-Marshall College of Law (J.D., 1994). Research Editor, Cleveland-Marshall Law Review. *Member:* Cuyahoga County and Ohio State Bar Associations. (Resident, Cleveland Office). ***PRACTICE AREAS:*** Workers; Workers Compensation Defense. ***Email:*** sconde@ralaw.com

JOSEPH J. CRIMALDI, admitted to bar, 1995, Ohio; 1996, U.S. District Court, Northern District of Ohio; registered to practice before U.S. Patent and Trademark Office, 1998. *Education:* Miami University (B.S., Chemistry, 1992); Cleveland-Marshall College of Law (J.D., 1995). ***PRACTICE AREAS:*** Biotechnology; Intellectual Property; Patent Prosecution; Patent Licensing. ***Email:*** jcrimaldi@ralaw.com

SCOT C. CROW, born Bergholz, Ohio, April 30, 1972; admitted to bar, 1997, Ohio; 1998, U.S. District Court, Southern District of Ohio; 1999, U.S. Tax Court. *Education:* Franciscan University of Steubenville (B.S., Business Administration, 1994); Capital University (J.D., 1997; LL.M., in Taxation, 1997). Order of the Curia. *Member:* Columbus (Member, Business Taxation and Estate and Gift Taxation Committees), Ohio State and American Bar Associations. (Resident, Columbus Office). ***PRACTICE AREAS:*** Taxation; Business Law; Estate and Gift Taxation; Trusts and Estates Taxation; Estate Planning. ***Email:*** scrow@ralaw.com

TAMIR D. DAMARI, admitted to bar, 1995, Maryland; 1997, District of Columbia. *Education:* State University of New York at Binghamton (B.A., 1992); George Washington University (J.D., cum laude, 1995). *Member:* Maryland State Bar Association; The District of Columbia Bar. (Resident, Washington, DC Office). ***PRACTICE AREAS:*** Litigation; Real Estate. ***Email:*** tdamari@ralaw.com

KIMBERLY A. DAVIS, born 1980; admitted to bar, 2005, Florida. *Education:* University of Florida (B.A., with honors, 2002); University of Florida, Levin College of Law (J.D., magna cum laude, 2005). Research Editor, Florida Law Review, 2004-2005. (Resident, Fort Myers, Florida Office). ***PRACTICE AREAS:*** Civil Law Litigation. ***Email:*** kdavis@ralaw.com

JULIE A. DOUGLAS, born Lima, Ohio, December 28, 1974; admitted to bar, 2001, Ohio. *Education:* University of Toledo (B.A., summa cum laude, 1997; J.D., cum laude, 2001). *Member:* Toledo and Ohio State Bar Associations. (Resident, Toledo Office). ***PRACTICE AREAS:*** Business Litigation. ***Email:*** jdouglas@ralaw.com

SEAN M. ELLIS, born Normal, Illinois, 1977; admitted to bar, 2002, Florida. *Education:* Florida State University (B.A., 1999; J.D., 2002). *Member:* Lee County Bar Association; The Florida Bar. (Resident, Fort Myers Office). ***PRACTICE AREAS:*** Real Estate; Banks and Banking. ***Email:*** sellis@ralaw.com

LAURA A. EPHLIN, born Akron, Ohio, February 10, 1964; admitted to bar, 1991, Ohio. *Education:* Purdue University (B.A., 1986); The Ohio State University (J.D., 1991). *Member:* Akron and Ohio State Bar Associations. ***Email:*** lephlin@ralaw.com

JAMES D. FOX, admitted to bar, 2003, Florida. *Education:* University of Science and Arts of Oklahoma (B.A., 1983); Georgetown University (M.A., 1987); Ave Maria School of Law (J.D., 2003). *Member:* Collier County Bar Association. (Resident, Naples, Florida Office). ***PRACTICE AREAS:*** Litigation; Real Estate; Commercial Relations; Municipal Law. ***Email:*** jfox@ralaw.com

DOMINIC A. FRISINA, born December 11, 1972; admitted to bar, 2004, Ohio; registered to practice before U.S. Patent and Trademark Office. *Education:* Gannon University (B.S., Chemistry, magna cum laude, 1995); Johns Hopkins University (M.A., Chemistry, 1997); Louis D. Brandeis School of Law, University of Louisville (J.D., 2004). American Chemical Society; Cleveland Intellectual Property Law Association; American Intellectual Property Law Association. *Member:* Ohio State and American Bar Associations. ***PRACTICE AREAS:*** Patents; Trademarks; Copyrights. ***Email:*** dfrisina@ralaw.com

MICHAEL J. FUCHS, born 1978; admitted to bar, 2003, Ohio. *Education:* Miami University (B.A., Political Science, 2000); The University of Akron School of Law (J.D., magna cum laude, 2003). *Member:* Akron and Ohio State Bar Associations. ***PRACTICE AREAS:*** Medical Malpractice Defense. ***Email:*** mfuchs@ralaw.com

LYNN A. GROSS, born Lansing, Michigan, December 3, 1974; admitted to bar, 2000, Ohio and U.S. District Court, Northern District of Ohio; 2001, U.S. Court of Appeals, Sixth Circuit; 2003, U.S. District Court, Southern District of Ohio. *Education:* Michigan State University (B.A., 1997); Case Western Reserve University (J.D., 2000). Recipient, Labor and Employment Law Award, 2000, and Legal Clinic Award, 2000, Case Western Reserve University School of Law. *Member:* Cleveland and Ohio State Bar Associations. (Resident, Cleveland Office). ***REPORTED CASES:*** Goins v. Cuyahoga Metropolitan Housing Authority, 2004 WL 63966, 20 IER 1449, 2004-Ohio-139, Ohio App. 8th Dist. (Jan. 15, 2004) McGowan v. Cuyahoga Metropolitan Housing Authority, 2004 WL 1752867, 2004-Ohio-4070, Ohio App. 8th Dist. (Aug. 5, 2004). ***PRACTICE AREAS:*** Employment Law; Labor Law; Civil Rights Law; Workers Compensation. ***Email:*** lgross@ralaw.com

TODD A. HARPST, born Greenville, Pennsylvania, November 26, 1969; admitted to bar, 1996, Ohio and U.S. District Court, Northern District of Ohio; 1997, Pennsylvania and U.S. Court of Appeals, Sixth Circuit; 1999, U.S. District Court, Western District of Pennsylvania. *Education:* Pennsylvania State University (B.A., 1992); University of Akron (J.D., cum laude, 1996). Articles Editor, Akron Law Review. *Member:* Pennsylvania and Ohio State Bar Associations. ***PRACTICE AREAS:*** Construction Law; Transportation Law; Products Liability; General Liability Defense. ***Email:*** tharpst@ralaw.com

MELISSA R. HOEFFEL, admitted to bar, 2003, Ohio. *Education:* The College of Wooster (B.A., 1995); Capital University Law School (J.D., 2003). Associate Editor, Capital University Law Review. *Member:* Columbus and Ohio State Bar Associations. (Resident, Columbus Office). ***PRACTICE AREAS:*** Government Relations; Public Law and Finance. ***Email:*** mhoeffel@ralaw.com

BRANDIE H. HOLLINGER PEEPLES, born Akron, Ohio; admitted to bar, 2003, Ohio. *Education:* Hampton University (B.A., 1998) University of Akron (J.D., 2003). *Member:* Akron and American Bar Associations. **PRACTICE AREAS:** Employment Law; Workers Compensation. ***Email:*** bpeeples@ralaw.com

PAM ELLEN HUDSON, admitted to bar, 2002, Georgia, Florida, U.S. District Court, Northern District of Georgia and Georgia Trial and Appellate Courts. *Education:* Auburn University (B.S., 1988); Florida State University (J.D. cum laude, 2002). *Member:* State

(This Listing Continued)

Bar of Georgia. (Resident, Naples, Florida Office). ***LANGUAGES:*** Spanish. ***PRACTICE AREAS:*** Litigation; Intellectual Property; Trademarks and Copyrights. ***Email:*** phudson@ralaw.com

MARC A. HULING, born Bridgeport, Connecticut, 1976; admitted to bar, 2002, Florida. *Education:* Emory University (B.A., 1998); Florida State University (J.D., 2002). Law Review Ausley Scholar, Journal of Land Use. *Member:* The Florida Bar. (Resident, Naples, Florida Office). ***PRACTICE AREAS:*** Business Law; Public Law; Employment Law. ***Email:*** mhuling@ralaw.com

CHRISTINE M. KATTOLA, born Flint, Michigan, December 16, 1979; admitted to bar, 2004, Ohio. *Education:* University of Michigan (B.A., Political Science, with distinction, 2001); The Ohio State University (J.D., 2004). (Resident, Cleveland Office). ***LANGUAGES:*** Arabric and Chaldean. ***PRACTICE AREAS:*** Business Litigation; Labor and Employment. ***Email:*** ckattola@ralaw.com

RYAN P. KENNEDY, born San Diego, California; admitted to bar, 2004, Ohio. *Education:* Wittenberg University (B.S., 2001); University of Akron (J.D., magna cum laude, 2004). ***PRACTICE AREAS:*** Risk Management; Insurance Defense; Products Liability. ***Email:*** rkennedy@ralaw.com

GREGORY S. KESSLER, born Cincinnati, Ohio, January 26, 1966; admitted to bar, 1996, Ohio; Kentucky; U.S. District Court, Northern District of Ohio; U.S. District Court, Southern District of Ohio; U.S. Court of Appeals, Sixth Circuit. *Education:* University of Cincinnati (B.S.A.E., 1988; J.D., 1996). Member: Law Review, 1994-1996; Moot Court, 1994-1996. *Member:* Cincinnati and Ohio State Bar Associations. (Resident, Cincinnati Office). ***PRACTICE AREAS:*** Civil Litigation; Commercial Law; Consumer Law; Insurance Defense; Personal Injury; Products Liability; Breach of Contract. ***Email:*** gkessler@ralaw.com

HUGH S. KINAST, born Cleveland, Ohio, August 8, 1977; admitted to bar, 2004, Ohio. *Education:* Indiana University (B.A., 2001); Case Western Reserve University (J.D., cum laude, 2004). *Member:* Cuyahoga County Bar Association; American Health Lawyers Association. (Resident, Cleveland Office). ***PRACTICE AREAS:*** Real Estate Leasing; Real Estate Banking Law; Real Estate Sales; Long Term Care; Health Care; Business Law. ***Email:*** hkinast@ralaw.com

LAUREN K. KINKOPF, born Cleveland, Ohio; admitted to bar, 1992, Ohio. *Education:* Medical College of Ohio (B.S. in Nursing, 1986); Cleveland-Marshall College of Law (J.D., 1992). *Member:* Cuyahoga County Bar Association; American Nurses Association; Ohio Nurses Association. (Resident, Cleveland Office). ***PRACTICE AREAS:*** Medical Defense. ***Email:*** lkinkopf@ralaw.com

DAVID A. KOTNIK, born 1969; admitted to bar, 2005, Ohio. *Education:* The Ohio State University (B.S., 1992); Cleveland-Marshall College of Law (J.D., 2004). *Member:* Cuyahoga County, Ohio State and American Bar Associations. (Resident, Cleveland Office). ***PRACTICE AREAS:*** Business Litigation; Construction Law; Corporate and Business Services; Public Law Litigation; Real Estate, Land Use, and Construction; Real Estate, Land Use, and Construction Litigation. ***Email:*** dkotnik@ralaw.com

DOUGLAS A. LEWIS, born Scottsdale, Arizona, July 5, 1968; admitted to bar, 1999, Florida. *Education:* Florida State University (B.A., Economics, cum laude, 1995); Brigham Young University, J. Rueben Clark Law School (J.D., cum laude, 1999). *Member:* Collier County Bar Association; The Florida Bar. (Resident, Naples, Florida Office). ***LANGUAGES:*** Spanish. ***PRACTICE AREAS:*** Commercial Real Estate; Construction Law; Land Use; Real Estate. ***Email:*** dlewis@ralaw.com

JOSEPH L. LINDSAY, admitted to bar, 1995, Nevada; 2000, District of Columbia. *Education:* Drake University Law School (J.D., cum laude, 1995); Georgetown University Law Center (LL.M., Securities Regulation, 1997). Finalist, Moot Court Competition, 1993. Member: National Insurance Moot Court Team, 1994; National Mock Trial Team, 1995. Editor, Drake Law School Constitutional Law Seminar Journal, 1994. Member, Editorial Board, Drake Law Review, 1995. Assistant to Professor Roberta Berry, 1994. Speaker, "Exclusion of Gain from Sale of Principal Residence," Oklahoma County Continuing Education Conference, 1997. (Resident, Naples, Florida Office). ***PRACTICE AREAS:*** Corporate and Business Services; Estate and Succession Planning. ***Email:*** jlindsay@ralaw.com

BRIAN H. LINICK, born Cleveland, Ohio; admitted to bar, 2005, Ohio. *Education:* The Ohio State University (B.S., 2002); Cleveland-Marshall College of Law (J.D., 2004). *Member:* Cleveland, Cuyahoga County, Ohio State and American Bar Associations. (Resident, Cleveland Office). ***LANGUAGES:*** Spanish. ***PRACTICE AREAS:*** Banking and Finance; Closely-Held and Emerging Businesses; Corporate and Business Services; Real Estate, Land Use, and Construction. ***Email:*** blinick@ralaw.com

TERRENCE H. LINK, II, born Akron, Ohio, March 1, 1973; admitted to bar, 1999, Ohio; 2000, U.S. District Court, Northern District of Ohio. *Education:* Miami University (B.S., Business, 1995); Case Western Reserve University (J.D., cum laude, 1999). *Member:* Akron and Ohio State Bar Associations. ***PRACTICE AREAS:*** Business Law; Commercial Law; Corporate Law; Contracts; Mergers, Acquisitions and Divestitures; Trademarks. ***Email:*** tlink@ralaw.com

PAUL W. LOMBARDI, (admission pending). *Education:* Ohio University (B.A., magna cum laude, 2002); The University of Akron School of Law (J.D., summa cum laude, 2005). ***PRACTICE AREAS:*** Business Litigation; Bank Foreclosures; Banking Litigation. ***Email:*** plombardi@ralaw.com

ASHLEY D. LUPO, born Birmingham, Alabama; admitted to bar, 1998, Florida; 1999, U.S. District Court, Middle District of Florida. *Education:* University of Miami (B.A., cum laude, 1995; J.D., cum laude, 1998). Director, Marco Island YMCA. Member, Rookery Bay Foundation. Past-President and Director: Friends of Rookery Bay; Marco Island Rotary. *Member:* Collier County Bar Association; The Florida Bar. (Resident, Naples, Florida Office). ***PRACTICE AREAS:*** Community Association Law; Condominium Association Law; Real Property; Land Use Law. ***Email:*** alupo@ralaw.com

RACHEL K. MATHOSLAH, admitted to bar, 2004, Ohio. *Education:* Boston University (B.A., 1999); Case Western Reserve University School of Law (J.D., 2004). *Member:* Cayahoga County and Ohio State Bar Associations. (Resident, Cleveland Office). ***PRACTICE AREAS:*** Real Estate; Real Estate Development; Real Estate Finance. ***Email:*** rmathoslah@ralaw.com

(This Listing Continued)

ADAM C. MILLER, born Columbus, Ohio, January 27, 1965; admitted to bar, 1994, Ohio. *Education:* The Ohio State University (B.A., English, 1988); Otterbein College (Ohio Teaching Certificate, 1989); Capital University (J.D., 1994). U.S. Army (JAG) Judge Advocate General's School Officer Basic Course (1998), Advanced Course (2002). Author: "OSBA's Sunshine Law Guide," The Ohio School Ethics Guide, Ohio School Records Guide and Managing Employee Leaves. Deputy Director of Legal Services, Ohio School Boards Association, Westerville, Oh., 1995-2000. Local School Superintendent, 2000-2002. Maguire & Schneider, L.L.P., 2002-2005. Ohio Director, Operation Homefront. *Member:* Columbus, Ohio State and American (Member, Legal Assistance to Military Personnel (LAMP) Committee) Bar Associations. [U.S. Army Reserve JAG Corps., 1996—; Commander, HHC, TF Victory, Bagram Air Field, Afghanistan]. (Resident, Cleveland Office). ***PRACTICE AREAS:*** Education Law; Special Education; Collective Bargaining; Military Law; Probate; Domestic Relations; Labor and Employment; Administrative Law; International Law; Constitutional Law; Civil Litigation. ***Email:*** amiller@ralaw.com

BRADEN MONTIERTH, born Provo, Utah, February 5, 1978; (admission pending). *Education:* Brigham Young University (B.A. History, Minor, Business Management, magna cum laude, 2002; J.D., magna cum laude, 2005). (Resident, Naples, Florida Office). ***PRACTICE AREAS:*** Real Estate; Land Use; Construction. ***Email:*** bmontierth@ralaw.com

LORI L. MOORE, born Oahu, Hawaii, October 14, 1973; admitted to bar, 2004, Florida and U.S. District Court, Southern District of Florida. *Education:* University of North Florida (B.A., summa cum laude, 1999); University of Florida College of Law (J.D., cum laude, 2003). *Member:* The Florida Bar Calusa Inns of Court. (Resident, Fort Myers Office). ***PRACTICE AREAS:*** Litigation. ***Email:*** lmoore@ralaw.com

CHAD L. MOWERY, born Zanesville, Ohio, April 2, 1975; admitted to bar, 2000, Ohio; 2001, U.S. District Court, Southern District of Ohio; 2004, U.S. District Court, Northern District of Ohio. *Education:* University of Notre Dame (B.A., 1997); Georgetown University (J.D., 2000). *Member:* Ohio State Bar Association. ***PRACTICE AREAS:*** Product Liability; Trust Litigation. ***Email:*** cmowery@ralaw.com

JAMES P. MYERS, born Cleveland, Ohio, September 28, 1976; admitted to bar, 2002, Ohio; 2003, U.S. District Court, Northern District of Ohio. *Education:* Wake Forest University (B.A., Political Science, 1999); Case Western Reserve University (J.D., 2002). *Member:* American, Cleveland, and Ohio State Bar Associations. (Resident, Cleveland Office). ***PRACTICE AREAS:*** Civil Litigation; Medical Malpractice Defense. ***Email:*** jmyers@ralaw.com

LISA PALM-KUEBLER, born October 11, 1973; admitted to bar, 2001, Ohio and U.S. District Court, Northern District of Ohio. *Education:* University of Toledo (B.A., 1997; J.D., 2000). *Member:* Toledo and Ohio State Bar Associations. (Resident, Toledo Office). ***PRACTICE AREAS:*** Workers Compensation; Insurance Defense; Business Litigation. ***Email:*** lpalm@ralaw.com

MOIRA H. PIETROWSKI, born Chicago, Illinois, July 4, 1972; admitted to bar, 1997, Illinois and U.S. District Court, Northern District of Illinois; 1998, Ohio; 1999, U.S. District Court, Northern District of Ohio. *Education:* Northwestern University (B.A., 1994); The John Marshall Law School (J.D., cum laude, 1997). *Member:* Akron and Ohio State Bar Associations. ***PRACTICE AREAS:*** Risk Management; Transportation; Product Liability; Toxic Torts. ***Email:*** mpietrowski@ralaw.com

MARSHAL M. PITCHFORD, born New York, N.Y., February 25, 1974; admitted to bar, 1999, Ohio; 2000, U.S. District Court, Northern District of Ohio; 2003, U.S. District Court, Southern District of Ohio; 2003, U.S. District Court, Eastern District of Michigan; 2002, U.S. Court of Appeals, Sixth Circuit. *Education:* Miami University (B.A., 1996); University of Akron School of Law (J.D., 1999). Member, Akron Law Review. Former Law Clerk for Judge Beth Whitmore, Ohio Court of Appeals, Ninth Judicial District. Member, Transportation Committee, USLAW Network; Kiwanis Club of Akron. *Member:* Akron and Ohio State Bar Associations; Transportation Lawyers Association; Defense Research Institute (Member, Transportation Committee); Ohio Trucking Association; Scanlon Inn of Court. ***PRACTICE AREAS:*** Business Torts; Contract Litigation; Appellate Practice; Risk Management; Litigation; Transportation. ***Email:*** mpitchford@ralaw.com

ERIC M. PIZZUTI, born 1980. *Education:* Miami University, Richard T. Farmer School of Business Administration (B.S., 2002); Catholic University of America, Columbus School of Law (J.D., 2005). (Resident, Cleveland Office). ***PRACTICE AREAS:*** Corporate Law. ***Email:*** epizzuti@ralaw.com

CAROLINE REGALLIS, born Ashland, Kentucky; admitted to bar, 2002, Ohio; 2003, U.S. District Court, Northern and Southern Districts of Ohio. *Education:* University of Akron (B.S., Accounting, 1999); Case Western Reserve University (J.D., cum laude, 2002). *Member:* Akron, Ohio State and American Bar Associations. ***PRACTICE AREAS:*** Trial Practice; Commercial Litigation; Business Law; Litigation; Contract Litigation; Federal Litigation; Real Estate Litigation; Real Estate Tax Appeals. ***Email:*** cregallis@ralaw.com

BRAD A. RIMMEL, born Canton, Ohio, April 19, 1970; admitted to bar, 1999, Ohio; 2000, Pennsylvania; 2001, U.S. District Court, Northern District of Ohio; 2004, U.S. District Court, Southern District of Ohio. *Education:* Kent State University (B.A., 1992); Shimane University, Japan (graduate research, 1992); University of Akron (J.D., 1999). *Member:* Summit County Bar Association Ohio State Bar Association Pennsylvania State Bar Association. ***PRACTICE AREAS:*** Products Liability; Toxic Tort Defense; Insurance Defense. ***Email:*** brimmel@ralaw.com

JOHN (JAY) RUTTER, born 1971; (admission pending). *Education:* The Pennsylvania State University (B.A., 1993); The University of Akron School of Law (J.D., summa cum laude, 2005). Assistant Editor, The University of Akron Law Review, 2003-2004. Author, case note, "Uncertain Terms: The Supreme Court's Failure to Address the Pre-Emptive Power of the Federal Arbitration Act in Green Tree v. Bazzle". Assistant Editor, 2004-2005. Member, Scanlon Inn of Court, 2002. *Member:* Akron and American Bar Associations. ***PRACTICE AREAS:*** Bankruptcy Trustee Rights; Bankruptcy Litigation; Bankruptcy Reorganization; Secured Transactions; Commercial Law; Uniform Commercial Code. ***Email:*** jrutter@ralaw.com

KYLE S. SCHEATZLE, born Akron, Ohio, 1976; admitted to bar, 2002, Ohio; U.S. District Court, Northern District of Ohio. *Education:* Kent State University (B.A., summa

(This Listing Continued)

ROETZEL & ANDRESS, A LEGAL PROFESSIONAL ASSOCIATION, Akron—Continued

cum laude Ohio, 1998); The Ohio State University (J.D., with honors, 2002). *Member:* Akron and Ohio State Bar Associations. ***PRACTICE AREAS:*** Labor and Employment; Labor and Employment Litigation; Union Matters. ***Email:*** kscheatzle@ralaw.com

BETH ANN SCHENZ, born Barberton, Ohio, November 30, 1970; admitted to bar, 2001, Ohio and U.S. District Court, Northern District of Ohio; 2003, U.S. Court of Appeals, Sixth Circuit. *Education:* Xavier University (B.S., 1992); Cleveland-Marshall College of Law (J.D., 2001). Member, Board of Governors, Moot Court, 2000-2001. *Member:* Cuyahoga County, Cleveland and Ohio State Bar Associations. (Resident, Cleveland Office). ***PRACTICE AREAS:*** Bankruptcy; Creditors Rights; Business Litigation. ***Email:*** bschenz@ralaw.com

JOHN J. SCHRINER, JR., born Cleveland, Ohio, December 19, 1973; admitted to bar, 1999, Ohio. *Education:* Northwestern University (B.A., 1996); Ohio State University College of Law (J.D., 1999). Law Clerk, U.S. Magistrate Judge George J. Limbert, Northern District of Ohio, 1999-2001. *Member:* Cleveland, Cuyahoga County and Ohio State Bar Associations. (Resident, Cleveland Office). ***PRACTICE AREAS:*** Business Litigation. ***Email:*** jschriner@ralaw.com

ELIZABETH SHAFFER, born 1978; admitted to bar, 2003, Ohio; 2004, Kentucky. *Education:* Centre College (B.A., 2000); University of Cincinnati College of Law (J.D., 2003). Order of the Coif. *Member:* Cincinnati, Ohio State and Kentucky Bar Associations. (Resident, Cincinnati Office). ***PRACTICE AREAS:*** Bankruptcy; Employment Litigation; Labor and Employment; Litigation; Products Liability; Regulatory Compliance; Union Labor Law. ***Email:*** lshaffer@ralaw.com

MARIAM ALIKHAN SHAH, born 1976; admitted to bar, 2002, New York; 2003, Ohio; U.S. District Court, Eastern District of New York; U.S. District Court, Northern District of Ohio; U.S. District Court, Southern District of New York. *Education:* University of Michigan (B.A., with high distinction, 1998); Georgetown University Law Center (J.D., 2001). *Member:* Cleveland Bar Association. ***LANGUAGES:*** Spanish. ***PRACTICE AREAS:*** Litigation; Civil Litigation; Complex Litigation; Federal Civil Litigation. ***Email:*** mshah@ralaw.com

JENNIFER L. SOUZA, born Akron, Ohio, February 29, 1972; admitted to bar, 1998, Ohio; 2000, U.S. District Court, Northern District of Ohio; 2003, U.S. District Court, Southern District of Ohio; 2004, United States Court of Appeals for the Sixth Circuit. *Education:* John Carroll University (B.A., magna cum laude, 1994); Case Western Reserve University (J.D., 1998). Alpha Sigma Nu. *Member:* Akron and Ohio State Bar Associations. Defense Research Institute. ***PRACTICE AREAS:*** Insurance Coverage; Insurance Bad Faith; Litigation. ***Email:*** jsouza@ralaw.com

JAMISON S. SPEIDEL, born 1970; admitted to bar, 2001, Ohio; 2002, District of Columbia; 2003, West Virginia and U.S. District Court, Northern and Southern Districts of West Virginia; 2005, U.S. Court of Appeals, Sixth and Fourth Circuits and U.S. District Court, Northern and Southern Districts of Ohio. *Education:* The Ohio State University (B.S.B.A., 1993); Wheeling Jesuit University (M.B.A., 1998); University of Dayton School of Law (J.D., 2001). Phi Delta Phi (Treasurer, 2000-2001). Member, MENSA 1997—. *Member:* Columbus, Ohio State, West Virginia and American Bar Associations; District of Columbia Bar. (Resident, Columbus Office). ***PRACTICE AREAS:*** Banking and Finance; Creditor Bankruptcy; Business Tort and Contract Litigation; Condominium, Associations, and Homeowners Law; Estate Planning; Probate and Estate Administration. ***Email:*** jspeidel@ralaw.com

VINCENT J. SQUILLACE, III, born Columbus, Ohio, July 10, 1975; admitted to bar, 2002, Ohio and District of Columbia. *Education:* University of Notre Dame (B.A., 1998); Capital University (J.D., 2002). *Member:* Columbus and Ohio State Bar Associations; Ohio Lobbying Association. (Resident, Columbus Office). ***PRACTICE AREAS:*** Government; Government Contracts; Federal Government Law; Federal Legislative Practice; Government Affairs; Government Agency Practice; Government Ethics; Government Relations; Governmental Law; Legislative Practice; Local Government Law; Local Government Relations; Public Policy; State Government Law; State Legislative Practice. ***Email:*** vsquillace@ralaw.com

TANA D. STOREY, born Tallahassee, Florida; admitted to bar, 2001, Florida. *Education:* Florida State University (B.S., 1994; J.D., cum laude, 2001). Member, Florida State Law Review. *Member:* The Florida Bar (Young Lawyers Division, Sections on: Administrative Law and Environmental and Land Use Law). (Resident, Tallahassee, Florida Office). ***PRACTICE AREAS:*** Administrative Law; Environmental Law; Transactional Practice; Appellate Practice. ***Email:*** tstorey@ralaw.com

NATHAN F. STUDENY, born Cleveland, Ohio, 1978; admitted to bar, 2004, Ohio. *Education:* Miami University (B.A., 2000); Cleveland-Marshall College of Law (J.D., summa cum laude, 2004). *Member:* Ohio State Bar Association. ***PRACTICE AREAS:*** Products Liability; Toxic Tort Defense; General Liability Defense and Litigation. ***Email:*** nstudeny@ralaw.com

BRIAN A. TARIAN, born Columbus, Ohio, July 31, 1955; admitted to bar, 1982, Ohio. *Education:* Georgetown University (B.A., 1977); University of Akron (J.D., 1982). *Member:* Columbus and Ohio State Bar Associations. (Resident, Columbus Office). ***PRACTICE AREAS:*** Workers Compensation. ***Email:*** btarian@ralaw.com

SEAN J. URVAN, born 1977; admitted to bar, 2003, Ohio. *Education:* Kent State University (B.S., cum laude, 1999); The University of Akron School of Law (J.D., 2003); University of Houston Law Center (LL.M. in Energy, Environment and Natural Resources Law). *Member:* Ohio State, Federal Energy and American Bar Associations. ***PRACTICE AREAS:*** Environmental, Health and Safety. ***Email:*** survan@ralaw.com

TARA L. VAN HO. *Education:* Marietta College (B.A., English); University of Cincinnati College of Law (J.D., 2005). Corporate Law Fellow, University of Cincinnati College of Law. (Resident, Columbus Office). ***PRACTICE AREAS:*** Corporate and Business Services. ***Email:*** tvanho@ralaw.com

DANIEL K. WEIDENBRUCH, born Cincinnati, Ohio, February 5, 1979; admitted to bar, 2005, Florida. *Education:* University of Florida (B.A., cum laude, 2001); University of

(This Listing Continued)

Florida, Levin College of Law (J.D., cum laude, 2004). Vice President, Ricky King Children's Fund of Southwest Florida. *Member:* Collier County Bar Association. (Resident, Naples, Florida Office). ***PRACTICE AREAS:*** Real Estate and Land Use Law. ***Email:*** dweidenbruch@ralaw.com

JEROME G. WYSS, born 1975; admitted to bar, 2001, Ohio; 2003, U.S. District Court, Northern District of Ohio. *Education:* University of Dallas (B.A., Politics, cum laude, 1997); Case Western Reserve University (J.D., cum laude, 2001). Law Clerk to Judge Beth Whitmore, Ohio Court of Appeals, Ninth Judicial District, 2001-2003. *Member:* Akron and Ohio State Bar Associations. ***PRACTICE AREAS:*** Litigation; Insurance Coverage. ***Email:*** jwyss@ralaw.com

E. MARK YOUNG, admitted to bar, 2001, Ohio. *Education:* Wake Forest University (B.A., Economics, 1996); University of Toledo (J.D., 2001). *Member:* Cleveland and Ohio State Bar Associations. (Resident, Cleveland Office). ***PRACTICE AREAS:*** Creditor Bankruptcy; Business Litigation. ***Email:*** myoung@ralaw.com

REPRESENTATIVE CLIENTS: Advanced Elastomer Systems, Inc.; Akron General Medical Center; Atlantic Tool & Die; Babcock & Wilcox, a McDermott Company; Bank One; Barberton Citizens Hospital; Beacon Journal Publishing Company; Burger Iron Company; Catholic Healthcare Partners; City of Akron; The Cleveland Clinic Foundation; CSX Transportation; Dart Industries, Inc.; Doctors Hospital; Edward J. Debartolo Corp.; F.E. Myers; FirstEnergy; Ford Motor Company; General Motors Corporation; Grant/Riverside Methodist Hospitals; Honeywell, Inc.; Lloyd's of London; Louisiana Pacific Corporation; Marathon Oil Company; Marriott Corporation; Medtronic, Inc.; MRK Technologies; National City Bank; National Railroad Passenger Corporation (AMTRAK); Norfolk Southern Corporation; Ohio Health Corporation; Ohio Rail Commission; Pentair, Inc.; PPG Industries, Inc.; Pulte Homes Corporation; Rite-Aid; Seaman Corporation; Sky Bank; State of Ohio; Summa Health System; Summit County; The Goodyear Tire & Rubber Company; The University of Akron; Waste Management, Inc.; Western Parcel Express.

RUPORT CO., L.P.A.

3700 EMBASSY PARKWAY, SUITE 200
AKRON, OHIO 44333
Telephone: 330-666-5555
Telecopier: 330-666-7272
URL: http://www.lawyers.com/ruportlaw

Complex Litigation. Civil Trial and Appellate Practice in Federal and State Courts. Construction, Banking, Commercial, Surety, Business, Corporate, Real Estate Law and Litigation.

FIRM PROFILE: Ruport Co., L.P.A. was formed in 1985 to provide the highest caliber litigation service to clients in the areas of construction, business, partnership, corporation and real estate. The firm's aggressive and proven trial experience allows early resolution of appropriate cases. If resolution is not possible, the service and efficiency of a small firm enhances the litigation process. Scott H. Ruport has thirty years of trial experience in Ohio and is a certified civil trial specialist by the National Board of Trial Advocacy.

SCOTT H. RUPORT, born Paterson, New Jersey, November 22, 1949; admitted to bar, 1974, Ohio and U.S. District Court, Northern District of Ohio; 1978, U.S. Supreme Court and U.S. Court of Appeals, Sixth Circuit; 1984, Pennsylvania; 2002, Florida. *Education:* Bowling Green State University (B.S. in B.A., 1971); University of Akron (J.D., 1974). Beta Gamma Sigma; Phi Alpha Delta. Adjunct Professor, Legal Aspects of Construction, University of Akron, College of Engineering, 1983. Lecturer, Ohio Academy of Trial Lawyers, "Filing of Mechanic Liens, Attested Accounts of Bond Claims", 1989*Member:* Akron, Ohio State and American Bar Associations; Ohio Academy of Trial Lawyers (Chairman, Civil and Business Litigation, 1989); The Association of Trial Lawyers of America. [Capt., Finance Corps, U.S. Army Reserve, 1971-1979]. (Board Certified, Civil Trial Specialist by the National Board of Trial Advocacy). ***REPORTED CASES:*** Sarbey v. National City Bank, 66 Ohio App. 3d 18 (1990); AFC Interiors v. DiCello, 46 Ohio St.3d 1 (1989); Brown-Graves Co. v. Obert, 98 Ohio App. 3d 517 (1994); Buy-Rite Lumber Co. v. Bank One, Akron, N.A., 81 Ohio App.3d 74 (1991); Hudson Local School Dist. Bd. of Education v. Hudson Park Estates, Inc.; Dubetz, et al., 64 Ohio App.3d 119 (1989); Kontos v. Luxmore, 65 Ohio App. 3d 148 (1989); Horning-Wright Company v. Great American Insurance Co., 27 Ohio App.3d 261 (1985); Gaal v. Mosher, et al., 16 Ohio App.3d 229 (1984); Welsh, et al. v. Brown-Graves Lumber Co., 58 Ohio App.2d 49 (1978); Homico Const. & Development Co. v. Ti-Bert Systems, Inc. 939 F.2d 392, 20 Fed. R. Serv. 3d 521, RICO Bud. Disp. Guide 7812 (6th Cir. (Ohio); Sadler-Cisar, Inc. v. Commercial Sales Network, Inc., 786 F.Supp. 1287 (1991); Commercial Sales Network v. Sadler-Cisar, Inc., 755 F.Supp. 756 (1991). ***PRACTICE AREAS:*** Construction; Business; Real Estate; Commercial; Appellate; Litigation. ***Email:*** sruport@ruportlaw.com

OF COUNSEL

LOUISE M. MAZUR, born Cleveland, Ohio, June 5, 1957; admitted to bar, 1982, Ohio, U. S. District Court, Northern District of Ohio and U.S. Court of Appeals, Sixth Circuit. *Education:* Kent State University (B.S., 1979); Akron University Law School (J.D., 1982). Phi Alpha Delta. Member, National Moot Court Team. Prosecuting Attorney, City of Cuyahoga Falls, Ohio, 1982-1983. Deputy Law Director, City of Cuyahoga Falls, Ohio, 1982-1984. *Member:* Akron and Ohio State Bar Associations. ***REPORTED CASES:*** Hershberger v Akron City Hospital, 34 Ohio St.3d 1 (1987); Lewis v Blair, 110 Ohio App.3d 342 (1996); Bentley v Cuy. Falls Bd. of Edn., 126 Ohio App.3d 186 (1998). ***PRACTICE AREAS:*** Business Litigation; Commercial Litigation; Negligence; Personal Injury; Insurance Defense. ***Email:*** lmazur@ruportlaw.com

REPRESENTATIVE CLIENTS: Halliburton Energy Serices; Edens & Avant; Graves Lumber Company; Ray Fogg Building Methods, Inc.; Empire Wholesale Lumber Co.; Dellagnese Companies; Marchetta Construction Co.

SCANLON & CO., L.L.C.

Established in 1984

159 SOUTH MAIN STREET, SUITE 400
KEY BUILDING
AKRON, OHIO 44308
Telephone: 330-376-1440
Telecopier: 330-376-0257
URL: http://www.scanlonco.com
Email: ljscanlon@scanlonco.com
URL: http://www.lawyers.com/scanlonco

Boca Raton, Florida Office; Scanlon & Croyle, LLP: 370 West Camino Gardens Boulevard, Suite 300. 33432-5817. Telephone: 561-368-4408. Fax: 561-368-4309.

Civil Trial and Appellate Advocacy, Products Liability, Professional Liability and Wrongful Death Law, Insurance Law Litigation, Aviation Law, Highway Design Law, Personal Injury, Airplane Crashes, Automobile Accidents, Construction Site Accidents, Medical Malpractice, Nursing Home Abuse and Neglect, Railroad Accidents and Injuries, Slip and Fall, Unsafe Products, Wrongful Death, Contested Wills, Investor and Securities Litigation.

LAWRENCE J. SCANLON, born Akron, Ohio, May 22, 1951; admitted to bar, 1978, Ohio; 1983, U.S. Court of Appeals, Sixth Circuit; 1986, U.S. Supreme Court; 1989, Florida; 1990, U.S. District Court, Southern District of Ohio; 1993, U.S. Court of Appeals, Eleventh Circuit; 2000, U.S. District Court, Middle District of Florida; 2002, U.S. District Court, Northern and Southern Districts of Florida. *Education:* University of Akron (B.A., 1974; J.D., 1978). Advocate, National College of Advocacy, 1992. Associate-of-Law, American College of Legal Medicine, 1992. President, University of Akron School of Law Alumni Association, 1997-1998 and Member, Board of Trustees, 1993—. *Member:* Akron (Member, Board of Trustees, 1994-1997; Treasurer, 1995-1997), Cuyahoga County, Palm Beach County, Ohio State and American Bar Associations; The Florida Bar; The Association of Trial Lawyers of America (Member, PAC Committee); Cleveland Academy of Trial Attorneys; Summit County Trial Lawyers Association (Member, Board of Trustees, 1995—; President, 2000-2001); Ohio Academy of Trial Lawyers (Member, Board of Trustees, 1994—); The Academy of Florida Trial Lawyers; The College of Master Advocates and Barristers (Senior Counsel, 2003). (Board Certified Civil Trial Advocacy Specialist by the National Board of Trial Advocacy) (Board Certified Civil Trial Lawyer, Florida Bar Board of Legal Specialization and Education). ***PRACTICE AREAS:*** Personal Injury; Product Liability; Professional Malpractice; Securities Fraud; Securities Litigation. ***Email:*** ljscanlon@scanlonco.com

REFERENCE: First Merit Bank.

SCANLON & GEARINGER CO., L.P.A.

Established in 1975

50 SOUTH MAIN STREET, SUITE 1200
AKRON, OHIO 44308
Telephone: 330-376-4558
Telecopier: 330-376-3550
URL: http://www.scangearlaw.com

General Civil Trial and Appellate Practice. Negligence, Personal Injury, Products Liability, Medical Malpractice, Legal Malpractice, Litigation.

OF COUNSEL

TIMOTHY F. SCANLON, born Akron, Ohio, December 21, 1937; admitted to bar, 1962, Ohio. *Education:* College of the Holy Cross (A.B., 1959); University of Michigan (J.D., 1961). Delta Theta Phi; Order of the Coif. Member, Board of Editors, Michigan Law Review, 1960-1961. *Member:* Akron (President, 1980-1981) and Ohio State Bar Associations. Fellow: American College of Trial Lawyers; International Academy of Trial Lawyers; International Society of Barristers. ***PRACTICE AREAS:*** Personal Injury; Medical Malpractice; Products Liability; Litigation.

BRADFORD M. GEARINGER, born Abington, Pennsylvania, November 17, 1940; admitted to bar, 1965, Tennessee; 1969, Ohio. *Education:* University of the South (B.A., 1962); Vanderbilt University (J.D., Phi Delta Phi, 1965). Phi Delta Phi. *Member:* Akron (President, 1988-1989), Ohio State and American Bar Associations. Fellow: International Society of Barristers; American Bar Foundation. [Major, USMCR, 1965-1968]. ***PRACTICE AREAS:*** Personal Injury; Medical Malpractice; Products Liability; Litigation.

PARTNERS

MICHAEL J. DEL MEDICO, born Akron, Ohio, January 7, 1955; admitted to bar, 1980, Ohio. *Education:* Brown University (A.B., 1977); University of Dayton (J.D., 1980). Adjunct Professor, University of Akron School of Law. *Member:* Akron and Ohio State Bar Associations; Ohio Academy of Trial Lawyers (Trustee, 1990-1991). ***PRACTICE AREAS:*** Personal Injury; Medical Malpractice; Products Liability; Litigation.

MARK HILKERT, born Akron, Ohio, August 4, 1950; admitted to bar, 1976, Ohio; 1984, U.S. District Court, Northern District of Ohio; 1989, U. S. Supreme Court; 1991, U.S. Court of Appeals, Sixth Circuit. *Education:* University of Akron (B.A., 1972); Case Western Reserve University (J.D., 1976). Omicron Delta Kappa. University of Akron Ambassador to Ghana, 1971-1972. *Member:* Akron Bar Association; Ohio Academy of Trial Lawyers. ***PRACTICE AREAS:*** Personal Injury; Medical Malpractice; Products Liability; Litigation.

PATRICK J. HART, born Akron, Ohio, December 13, 1950; admitted to bar, 1975, Ohio; 1978, U.S. District Court, Northern District of Ohio. *Education:* University of Akron (B.S., 1972; J.D., 1975). Phi Alpha Delta (Secretary, 1974-1975). Instructor, Real Estate Law, University of Akron and Malone College, 1979-1987. Assistant Law Director, Akron, Ohio, 1976-1980. *Member:* Akron Bar Association; Ohio Trial Lawyers Association. ***PRACTICE AREAS:*** Personal Injury; Medical Malpractice; Products Liability; Litigation.

(This Listing Continued)

ROBERT A. ROYER, born Havre de Grace, Maryland, June 29, 1959; admitted to bar, 1984, Ohio. *Education:* Allegheny College (B.A., honors in Political Science, 1981); Ohio State University (J.D., honors in Law, 1984). Phi Beta Kappa; Pi Gamma Mu. Alden Scholar. *Member:* Akron and Ohio State Bar Associations; Ohio Academy of Trial Lawyers; The Association of Trial Lawyers of America; Summit County Trial Lawyers Association. ***PRACTICE AREAS:*** Personal Injury; Medical Malpractice; Products Liability; Litigation.

KEVIN P. HARDMAN, born Akron, Ohio, May 10, 1960; admitted to bar, 1985, Ohio; 1986, U.S. District Court, Northern District of Ohio; 1990, U.S. Court of Appeals, Sixth Circuit. *Education:* Ohio State University (B.A., magna cum laude, 1982; J.D., honors in law, 1985). Phi Kappa Phi; Pi Sigma Alpha. *Member:* Akron and Ohio State Bar Associations; Ohio Academy of Trial Lawyers. ***PRACTICE AREAS:*** Personal Injury; Medical Malpractice; Products Liability; Litigation.

JOHN F. HILL, born Erie, Pennsylvania, April 5, 1962; admitted to bar, 1988, Ohio; 1989, U.S. District Court, Northern District of Ohio; 1991, U.S. Court of Appeals, Sixth Circuit; 1992, Pennsylvania. *Education:* Temple University; Gannon University (B.A., cum laude, 1984); Case Western Reserve Law School (J.D., 1987). *Member:* Akron and Ohio State Bar Associations; Ohio Academy of Trial Lawyers; Association of Trial Lawyers of America. ***PRACTICE AREAS:*** Personal Injury; Medical Malpractice; Products Liability; Litigation.

JOHN T. SCANLON, born Akron, Ohio, June 19, 1968; admitted to bar, 1994, Ohio. *Education:* University of Dayton (B.A., 1990); Cleveland Marshall College of Law (J.D., 1994). *Member:* Akron Bar Association; Ohio Academy of Trial Lawyers. ***PRACTICE AREAS:*** Personal Injury; Medical Malpractice; Products Liability; Litigation.

MAURA E. SCANLON, born Akron, Ohio, September 7, 1963; admitted to bar, 1988, Ohio; 1989, U.S. District Court, Northern District of Ohio; 1991, U.S. Court of Appeals, Sixth Circuit. *Education:* College of the Holy Cross (B.A., Economics, 1985); Case Western Reserve University (J.D., 1988). Delta Theta Phi. Member: The Order of the Barristers; The National Moot Court Team, 1987-1988. *Member:* Akron and Ohio State Bar Associations; Ohio Academy of Trial Lawyers. ***PRACTICE AREAS:*** Personal Injury; Medical Malpractice; Products Liability; Litigation.

MELINDA E. SMITH, born Bradford, Pennsylvania, May 21, 1974; admitted to bar, 1999, Ohio and U.S. District Court, Northern District of Ohio. *Education:* Grove City College (B.A., magna cum laude, Psychology/Spanish, 1996); University of Akron School of Law (J.D., magna cum laude, 1999). *Member:* Akron and Ohio State Bar Associations; Ohio Academy of Trial Lawyers. ***PRACTICE AREAS:*** Personal Injury; Medical Malpractice; Products Liability; Litigation.

JOY MALEK OLDFIELD, born Akron, Ohio, November 9, 1975; admitted to bar, 2000, Ohio and U.S. District Court, Northern District of Ohio. *Education:* John Carroll University (B.A., 1997); University of Akron School of Law (J.D., 2000). *Member:* Akron and Ohio State Bar Associations; Ohio Academy of Trial Lawyers; Ohio Women's Bar Association. ***PRACTICE AREAS:*** Personal Injury; Medical Malpractice; Products Liability; Litigation.

GREGORY J. LUCHT, born Erie, Pennsylvania, August 10, 1976; admitted to bar, 2002, Ohio and U.S. District Court, Northern District of Ohio. *Education:* Grove City College (B.A., 1999); Akron University Law School (J.D., magna cum laude, 2002). *Member:* Akron and Ohio State Bar Associations; Ohio Academy of Trial Lawyers; The Association of Trial Lawyers of America. ***PRACTICE AREAS:*** Personal Injury; Medical Malpractice; Products Liability; Litigation.

SKIDMORE & ASSOCIATES
A LEGAL PROFESSIONAL ASSOCIATION

Established in 1955

NATIONAL CITY CENTER
ONE CASCADE PLAZA, 12TH FLOOR
AKRON, OHIO 44308
Telephone: 330-253-1550
Medina: 330-721-4452
Telecopier: 330-253-9657
Email: info@skidmorelaw.com
URL: http://www.skidmorelaw.com

General Civil Practice in all State and Federal Courts. Complex Litigation, Business, Commercial, Real Estate, Condominium, Construction, Banking, Corporation, Domestic Relations, Probate, Savings and Loan, Personal Injury and Tort Law. Bankruptcy and Corporate Reorganization. Trials and Appeals.

FIRM PROFILE: Skidmore & Associates is a boutique law firm specializing in transactional and complex litigation in the areas of commercial, business, real property and construction law. The firm also provides services in the areas of probate and estate planning, employment and municipal corporation law.

ARCHIE W. SKIDMORE, born Tioga, West Virginia, October 6, 1926; admitted to bar, 1954, Ohio, U.S. District Court, Northern District of Ohio and U.S. Court of Appeals, Sixth Circuit; 1975, U.S. Supreme Court. *Education:* Kent State University; The University of Akron (LL.B., 1955). Presenter for Continuing Legal Education Programs. Lecturer to lay groups in Real Estate and Title Issues. *Member:* Akron, Medina County and Ohio State (Member, Corporate Counsel, Sections on: Estate Planning; Trust; Probate; Intellectual Property Law; Labor & Employment Law; Litigation; Real Property) Bar Associations. ***PRACTICE AREAS:*** Real Estate; Construction Law; Business and Corporate Law; Probate; Municipal Corporation Law; Business and Civil Litigation. ***Email:*** aws@skidmorelaw.com

SPIROS VASILATOS, JR., born Akron, Ohio, July 4, 1958; admitted to bar, 1984, Ohio and U.S. District Court, Northern District of Ohio; 2001, U.S. Court of Appeals, Sixth

(This Listing Continued)

SKIDMORE & ASSOCIATES A LEGAL PROFESSIONAL ASSOCIATION, Akron—Continued

Circuit; 2002, U.S. Supreme Court. *Education:* University of Akron (B.S., 1980; J.D., 1984). Participant, Mentor Program, University of Akron School of Law and Akron Bar Association. Counsel to Soldiers in Summit County. *Member:* Akron, Medina, Wayne County, Ohio State (Member, Real Property Law Section) and American (Member, Business Law Section) Bar Associations; Summit County Trial Lawyers Association. ***LANGUAGES:*** Greek. ***TRANSACTIONS:*** -Representation of U.S. Department of Housing and Urban Development in non-judicial foreclosures. ¶-Representation of Private Health Care facility interface with federal. state and local government entities. ¶-Representation of municipalities as special counsel. ¶-Representation of trusts, estates and guardianships. ¶-Representation of contractors, developers and claimants in residential and commercial construction issues. ¶-Representation of lenders, investors and individuals in state foreclosure proceedings. ¶-Representation of corporations in business and commercial transactions. ***PRACTICE AREAS:*** Real Estate; Construction Law; Probate; Business and Corporate Law; Municipal Corporation Law; Personal Injury; Business and Civil Litigation. ***Email:*** svjr@skidmorelaw.com

BRIAN K. SKIDMORE, born Akron, Ohio, April 5, 1957; admitted to bar, 1984, Ohio and U.S. District Court, Northern District of Ohio; 1989, U.S. Tax Court; 2001, U.S. Court of Appeals, Sixth Circuit; 2002, U.S. Supreme Court. *Education:* Mount Union College (B.A., 1979); University of Tennessee (M.A.C.C., 1981); Wake Forest University (J.D., 1984). *Member:* Akron (Member, Sections on: Bankruptcy; Commercial Law), Medina, Ohio State (Member, Sections on: Intellectual Property; Labor & Employment Law) and American Bar Associations; Ohio Trial Lawyers Association. ***PRACTICE AREAS:*** Real Estate; Probate; Employment Law; Construction Law; Business and Corporate Law; Civil Litigation; Appellate Practice. ***Email:*** bks@skidmorelaw.com

ERIC E. SKIDMORE, born Akron, Ohio, May 14, 1960; admitted to bar, 1989, Ohio, U.S. District Court, Northern District of Ohio and U.S. Court of Appeals, Sixth Circuit; U.S. Supreme Court. *Education:* Mt. Union College (B.A., 1982); Ohio State University (M.A., 1984); Ohio Northern University (J.D., 1987). Phi Alpha Delta. Recipient, U.S. Law Week Award, 1987. Author: "Ohio's New Seller Disclosure Law: O.R.C. §5302.30," Legal Perspective," June 1993; "Ohio Responds to the Threat of Terrorism," Ohio Lawyer, January/February 2003. *Member:* Akron, Medina and Ohio State (Member, Corporate Counsel, Sections on: Litigation; Real Property) Bar Associations; American Trial Lawyers Association (Member, Sections on: Commercial Litigation; Small Office Practice). ***TRANSACTIONS:*** -Representation of Texas-based venture capital developer in local commercial, real estate, planning, zoning, water acquisition and title matters concerning a proposed $1 billion development of a 2,700 mega watt compressed air electrical generation project. ¶-Representation of investor in commercial real estate in multi-million dollar workout of real estate mortgage investment conduit (REMIC). ¶-Representation of municipal corporation in water source and supply negotiator and transactions with other municipal and county government entities. ***PRACTICE AREAS:*** Banking; Real Estate; Bankruptcy; Municipal Corporation Law; Condominium Law; Construction Law; Business Litigation; Civil Litigation; Appellate Practice. ***Email:*** ees@skidmorelaw.com

REPRESENTATIVE CLIENTS: City of Akron; Haddington Ventures, L.L.C.; Norton Energy Storage, L.L.C.; BankOne, N.A.; Emerge Ministries; Continental Machinery Movers, Inc.; Kuhmo Tire Co.; Strongsville Family Medicine, Inc.; Humane Society of Greater Akron; Backus Custom Remodeling, Inc.; Mogadore Family Dentistry; Secret Ceramics, Inc.; Seal Construction Co.; Paragon Investments Co.; Bourgeois Excavating; Re/Max: Key Realty; Kruger Realty; Highpoint Furniture Co.; Ino's Fashions; H.U.D.; Hermitage Homes, Ltd.; Northcoast Builders, Inc.
REFERENCES: First National Bank of Akron; Charter One Bank, F.S.B.; Key Bank; North Akron Savings; National City Bank; Midland Commerce Title.

SLATER, ZURZ & GILBERT

ONE CASCADE PLAZA
AKRON, OHIO 44308-1135
Telephone: 330-762-0700
Toll Free: 800-297-9191
Fax: 330-762-3923
Email: s-z@ix.netcom.com
URL: http://www.slater-zurz-gilbert.com

Canton, Ohio Office: 4450 Belden Village Street, N.W., Suite 301, 44718. Telephone: 330-864-2999.

Personal Injury, Wrongful Death, Commercial Litigation, Corporate, Business, Real Estate, Business Organization, Domestic Relations, Construction Litigation.

JAMES W. SLATER, born Waterbury, Connecticut, October 5, 1943; admitted to bar, 1970, Ohio and U.S. District Court, Northern District of Ohio. *Education:* University of Connecticut (A.B., with honors, 1966); Georgetown University Law Center (J.D., 1969). *Member:* Akron, Ohio State and American Bar Associations; Ohio Academy of Trial Lawyers; The Association of Trial Lawyers of America. ***PRACTICE AREAS:*** Corporate Law; Business Litigation; Personal Injury; Wrongful Death; Products Liability; Medical Malpractice. ***Email:*** s-z@ix.netcom.com

RICHARD V. ZURZ, JR., born Akron, Ohio, June 30, 1957; admitted to bar, 1982, Ohio and U.S. District Court, Northern District of Ohio. *Education:* Bowling Green State University (B.S., 1979); University of Akron (M.T., 1982; J.D., 1982). *Member:* Akron, Ohio State and American Bar Associations; Ohio Academy of Trial Lawyers; The Association of Trial Lawyers of America. ***PRACTICE AREAS:*** Negligence; Personal Injury; Products Liability; Medical Malpractice; Commercial Litigation; Construction Litigation; Business Litigation. ***Email:*** s-z@ix.netcom.com

LOUIS J. GIGLIOTTI, JR., born Cleveland, Ohio, September 6, 1962; admitted to bar, 1991, Ohio. *Education:* Ohio University (B.B.A., 1984); Cleveland Marshall College of Law (J.D., 1991). *Member:* Akron and Ohio State Bar Associations; Ohio Association of Civil Trial Attorneys. ***PRACTICE AREAS:*** Insurance Coverage; Insurance Bad Faith; Automobile Insurance Defense; Casualty Insurance Defense; Property Insurance Defense; Toxic Defense; Personal Injury; Wrongful Death; Products Liability. ***Email:*** s-z@ix.netcom.com

EDWARD C. PULLEKINS, born Akron, Ohio, February 6, 1950; admitted to bar, 1975, Ohio and U.S. District Court, Northern District of Ohio; 1998, U.S. Court of Appeals, Sixth Circuit. *Education:* University of Akron (B.A., summa cum laude, 1972; J.D., 1975). Phi Eta Sigma; Phi Sigma Alpha; Omicron Delta Kappa. Watts Foundation Scholar. General Counsel for Community Hall Foundation, 1978-1986. Outstanding Young Man in America, 1979. *Member:* Akron (Member: Family Law Committee, 1976—; Common Pleas Court Committee, 1979—), Ohio State and American Bar Associations; Ohio Academy of Trial Lawyers; The Association of Trial Lawyers of America. ***REPORTED CASES:*** Conley v. Conley 612 N.E.2d 355; Kapsos v. Hammond 468 N.E.2d 325; Gollings v. National Life Insurance Co. 637 NE.2d 76. ***PRACTICE AREAS:*** Estate Planning and Probate (50%, 50); Small Business Real Estate; Municipal and Zoning; Domestic Relations; Civil Trial. ***Email:*** epullekins@slater-zurz.com

JOHN J. LYNETT, JR., born Frankfurt, Germany, January 21, 1956; admitted to bar, 1993, Ohio. *Education:* University of Akron (B.S.M.T., 1979); University of Akron Law School (J.D., cum laude, 1993). Member, American Society of Clinical Pathologists. Member, College of American Pathologists. *Member:* Akron, Ohio State and American Bar Associations. ***PRACTICE AREAS:*** Personal Injury; Medical Malpractice; Products Liability; Probate; Estate Planning; Corporate. ***Email:*** s-z@ix.netcom.com

GARY M. PETTI, born Cleveland, Ohio, July 24, 1968; admitted to bar, 1995, Ohio; 1996, U.S. District Court, Northern District of Ohio. *Education:* University of Akron (B.A., with honors, 1991); University of Akron School of Law (J.D., 1995). Member: National Moot Court Team; Defense Research Institute. *Member:* Akron and Ohio State Bar Associations; Ohio Association of Civil Trial Attorneys. ***PRACTICE AREAS:*** Personal Injury; Corporate; Business Litigation; Real Estate. ***Email:*** s-z@ix.netcom.com

EDWARD L. GILBERT, born Indianapolis, Indiana, January 20, 1951; admitted to bar, 1980, Ohio. *Education:* College of Wooster (B.S., 1973); Akron University Law School (J.D., 1976). ***PRACTICE AREAS:*** Civil Rights; Discrimination; General Practice. ***Email:*** egilbert8@sbcglogal.net

ASSOCIATES

E. LEE WAGONER, JR., born Norfolk, Virginia, December 30, 1952; admitted to bar, 1987, Ohio and Kentucky; 1989, U.S. District Court, Northern District of Ohio; 1999, U.S. Court of Appeals, Sixth Circuit. *Education:* Miami University (B.A., cum laude, 1975); Chase College of Law (J.D., cum laude, 1986). Phi Beta Kappa; Phi Kappa Phi. Associate Editor, Northern Kentucky Law Review, 1986. Order of the Curia, 1986. Magistrate, Village of Richfield, Ohio, 1999—. *Member:* Akron, Ohio State and American Bar Associations. ***PRACTICE AREAS:*** Business Litigation; Civil Litigation; Corporate Law; Criminal Law; Bankruptcy. ***Email:*** s-z@ix.netcom.com

JAMES E. BROWN, born Youngstown, Ohio, July 20, 1954; admitted to bar, 1983, Ohio; U.S. District Court, Northern District of Ohio and U.S. Court of Appeals, Sixth Circuit. *Education:* Kent State University (B.A., 1977; M.A., 1979); University of Akron School of Law (J.D., 1983). *Member:* Akron and Ohio State Bar Associations. ***PRACTICE AREAS:*** Civil Litigation; Real Estate; Domestic Relations; Probate. ***Email:*** s-z@ix.netcom.com

MICHAEL J. WRIGHT, born Salem, Ohio, June 22, 1977; admitted to bar, 2002, Ohio; 2003, U.S. District Court, Northern District of Ohio. *Education:* University of Dayton (B.A., 1999); Akron University Law School (J.D., 2002). ***PRACTICE AREAS:*** Civil Rights; Discrimination; Employment Law; Personal Injury. ***Email:*** egilbert@sbcglobal.net

OF COUNSEL

ELLEN M. BROOKS, born Shenandoah, Pennsylvania, August 15, 1947; admitted to bar, 1987, Ohio; U.S. District Court, Northern and Southern Districts of Ohio and U.S. Supreme Court. *Education:* University of Michigan, Ann Arbor (B.A., with honors, 1969); Cleveland-Marshall College of Law (J.D., summa cum laude, 1986). *Member:* Cleveland, Ohio State and Federal Bar Associations. ***PRACTICE AREAS:*** Business Litigation; Real Estate Litigation; Employment Litigation; Torts. ***Email:*** ebrooks@slater-zurz.gilbert.com

RUSSELL SMITH

ATTORNEY AT LAW
503 KEY BUILDING
159 SOUTH MAIN STREET
AKRON, OHIO 44308
Telephone: 330-434-7167; 877-434-7167
Fax: 330-434-7195
Email: smithar@bright.net
URL: http://www.russsmithlaw.com

Personal Injury, Products Liability, Malpractice and Civil Litigation.

FIRM PROFILE: Russell Smith has achieved Martindale-Hubbell's highest rating for ethics and legal ability.

RUSSELL SMITH, born Akron, Ohio, February 1, 1936; admitted to bar, 1961, Ohio. *Education:* The Ohio State University (B.A., 1959; J.D., 1961); East Tennessee State University (M.Ed., Storytelling Program, 1999). Phi Delta Phi. Co-Author: with Bob Gibbins, "Product Liability Litigation: Trial Strategy and Procedure," West Group, 1988 (updated 1999). Author: "Discovery Strategy and Privileges," Chapter 14, ATLA's Litigating Tort Cases, West Group, 2003. Author of other legal articles. Past President, WRAPPS (Storytelling Association). *Member:* Ohio Academy of Trial Lawyers (Past President); The Association of Trial Lawyers of America (Member, Board of Governors); Summit County Trial Lawyers (President); Akron Bar Association (Past Representative, OSBA Council of Delegates); The Roscoe Pound Foundation (Past Treasurer); Ohio State Bar Association (Past

(This Listing Continued)

Chairman, Negligence Law Committee; Past Member, Council of Delegates); American Board of Trial Advocates (Advocate, 1989—); Akron Law Library Association (Vice President); American Inns of Court (Master of the Bench, 1988—; President, Scanlon Chapter, 2004-2005). (Certified as a Civil Trial Advocacy Specialist by the National Board of Trial Advocacy). ***PRACTICE AREAS:*** Personal Injury Law; Product Liability Law; Malpractice Law; Civil Trial. ***Email:*** smithar@bright.net

JAMES T. STANCEU

AKRON, OHIO

(See Cleveland)

Personal Injury, Automobile Accidents and Injuries, Truck Accidents and Injuries, Wrongful Death, Medical Malpractice, Workers Compensation, Workers' Compensation Appeals.

STARK & KNOLL CO., L.P.A.

Established in 1985

76 SOUTH MAIN STREET, SUITE 1512
AKRON, OHIO 44308-1824
Telephone: 330-376-3300
Telecopier: 330-376-6237
URL: http://www.stark-knoll.com

Corporate Transactions, Real Estate and Commercial Leasing; Business Succession Planning, Taxation, Commercial Lending, Healthcare, Non-Profit Organizations, E-Commerce, Litigation, Labor and Employment, Estate Planning and Probate.

FIRM PROFILE: Stark & Knoll, founded in 1985, is a specialty law firm concentrating its practice in areas of relevance to small and medium-sized businesses and their owners and managers. The firm's objective emphasizes the delivery of timely and cost-effective legal services to business and entrepreneurs in a results-oriented environment.

MICHAEL L. STARK, born Watseka, Illinois, April 29, 1936; admitted to bar, 1961, Indiana; 1967, Ohio. *Education:* Miami University (B.S., cum laude, 1958); Indiana University (J.D., 1961). Beta Gamma Sigma; Phi Beta Kappa; Beta Alpha Psi; Omicron Delta Kappa. ***PRACTICE AREAS:*** Estate Planning; Corporate Transactions; Taxation; Healthcare; Nonprofit and Charitable Organizations. ***Email:*** MStark@Stark-Knoll.com

THOMAS G. KNOLL, born Flint, Michigan, November 5, 1939; admitted to bar, 1965, Ohio. *Education:* Cornell University; Miami University (B.A., 1962); The Ohio State University (J.D., 1965). ***PRACTICE AREAS:*** Corporate Law; Real Estate; Corporate Transactions; Business Succession Planning. ***Email:*** TKnoll@Stark-Knoll.com

JAMES L. RENCH, born Troy, Ohio, 1947; admitted to bar, 1974, Ohio. *Education:* Miami University (B.S., 1969); The Ohio State University (J.D., magna cum laude, 1973). Order of the Coif. ***PRACTICE AREAS:*** Corporate Law; Corporate Transactions; Commercial Lending. ***Email:*** JRench@Stark-Knoll.com

JOHN K. KRAJEWSKI, born Buffalo, New York, March 31, 1959; admitted to bar, 1985, Ohio and U.S. District Court, Northern District of Ohio; 1990, U.S. Tax Court. *Education:* Niagara University (B.B.A., cum laude, Accounting, 1981); Case Western Reserve University (J.D., 1985). Certified Public Accountant, 1987. ***PRACTICE AREAS:*** Corporate Law; Business Succession Planning; Taxation; Nonprofit and Charitable Organizations. ***Email:*** JKrajewski@Stark-Knoll.com

JOHN P. SUSANY, born Youngstown, Ohio, 1962; admitted to bar, 1987, Ohio; 1989, U.S. District Court, Northern District of Ohio; 1994, U.S. Court of Appeals, Seventh Circuit; 2003, U.S. Court of Appeals, Sixth Circuit. *Education:* Ohio University Honors Tutorial College (A.B., summa cum laude, 1983); University of Michigan (J.D., 1987). ***PRACTICE AREAS:*** Litigation; Labor and Employment. ***Email:*** JSusany@Stark-Knoll.com

JEFFREY T. KNOLL, born Akron, Ohio, July 26, 1966; admitted to bar, 1991, Ohio. *Education:* Virginia Polytechnic Institute & State University (B.S., 1988); Ohio State University (J.D., with honors, 1991). ***PRACTICE AREAS:*** Corporate Law; Real Estate; Commercial Leasing; Business Succession Planning; Commercial Lending. ***Email:*** JKnoll@Stark-Knoll.com

RONALD K. STARKEY, born Akron, Ohio, June 4, 1967; admitted to bar, 1992, Ohio and U.S. District Court, Northern District of Ohio; 1993, U.S. District Court, Southern District of Ohio and U.S. District Court, Northern District of Texas; 1995, District of Columbia and U.S. Court of Appeals, Sixth Circuit. *Education:* University of Akron (B.S., magna cum laude, 1989); Case Western Reserve University (J.D., cum laude, 1992). Phi Sigma Alpha. ***PRACTICE AREAS:*** Litigation; Employment Law. ***Email:*** RStarkey@Stark-Knoll.com

AARON G. LEPP, born Akron, Ohio, December 21, 1969; admitted to bar, 1995, Ohio. *Education:* Wake Forest University (B.A., Economics and History, 1992); The Ohio State University (J.D., 1995). ***PRACTICE AREAS:*** Corporate Transactions; Real Estate; Commercial Leasing; Healthcare. ***Email:*** ALepp@Stark-Knoll.com

MICHAEL L. WEAR, born Akron, Ohio, February 5, 1969; admitted to bar, 1995, Ohio. *Education:* University of Akron (B.S.B.A., 1991; M.B.A., 1994; J.D., cum laude, 1994). ***PRACTICE AREAS:*** Corporate Successions; Estate Planning; Estate Administration; Trust Planning; Trust Administration; Tax Law. ***Email:*** mwear@stark-knoll.com

MARY JO LOCKSHIN, born Neenah, Wisconsin, July 3, 1957; admitted to bar, 1981, Ohio. *Education:* Ohio Northern University (B.A., 1978; J.D., 1981). ***PRACTICE AREAS:*** Estate Planning; Probate; Corporate Law.

TERRENCE L. SEEBERGER, born Casper, Wyoming, 1954; admitted to bar, 1978, Illinois; 1979, Ohio; U.S. Court of Appeals, Sixth Circuit. *Education:* Grinnell College (B.A., 1975); Washington University (J.D., 1978). ***PRACTICE AREAS:*** Commercial Law; Construction Law; Environmental Law; Probate Litigation; Annexation Litigation; Governmental Law.

REFERENCES: Bank One; Key Bank National Association; First Merit Bank.

JOHN S. STEINHAUER

159 SOUTH MAIN STREET, SUITE 530
AKRON, OHIO 44308-1300
Telephone: 330-535-1010
Fax: 330-535-1531
Email: jss530@sbcglobal.net

Mergers and Acquisitions, Corporate Law, Real Estate, Finance, Commercial and Business Law.

JOHN S. STEINHAUER, born Columbus, Ohio, June 22, 1943; admitted to bar, 1969, Ohio; 1990, District of Columbia. *Education:* Muskingum College; The Ohio State University (B.A., 1965; J.D., 1969); University of Akron (Honorary LL.D., 1989). Assistant City Attorney, Columbus, 1969-1971. Trustee, 1979-1988, Vice Chairman, 1981-1984 and Chairman, 1984-1986, University of Akron. *Member:* Akron, Ohio State and American Bar Associations; The District of Columbia Bar.

REPRESENTATIVE CLIENTS: The Reserve Group; The Brenlin Group, LLC; The Cedarwood Companies; Seibert-Keck Insurance Agency, Inc.; Automotive Technologies, Inc.; The Kissel Group; Rotocast Technologies, Inc.

TIPPING CO., L.P.A.

A LEGAL PROFESSIONAL ASSOCIATION

SANCTUARY PROFESSIONAL BUILDING - SUITE 207
525 NORTH CLEVELAND-MASSILLON ROAD
AKRON, OHIO 44333
Telephone: 330-670-8400
Fax: 330-670-8454

General Civil Trial and Appellate Practice, Negligence, Personal Injury, Business, Commercial, Corporate, Probate, Workers Compensation, Administrative, Insurance, Real Estate, Bankruptcy, Estate Planning, Labor/Employment, Zoning, Municipal Law and Social Security Disability Law.

HARRY A. TIPPING, born Bainbridge, Maryland, November 2, 1944; admitted to bar, 1971, Ohio; 1972, U.S. District Court, Northern District of Ohio; 1976, U.S. Supreme Court; 1983, U.S. Court of Appeals, Sixth Circuit; 1984, U.S. District Court, Northern District of Illinois; 1996, U.S. Tax Court. *Education:* Gannon University (B.A., 1966); University of Akron (J.D., 1970). Phi Alpha Delta (Secretary, 1969-1970). Listed in Who's Who in American Law, 1985—, Who's Who in the Midwest, 1986— and National Registry of Who's Who, 1998—. Editor-in-Chief of Arete (Akron Law Paper), 1969-1970. Member, Panel of Arbitrators, American Arbitration Association. Assistant Law Director, 1971-1972, Chief Assistant Law Director, 1972-1974, City of Akron. *Member:* Akron, Ohio State and American Bar Associations; Federation of Insurance and Corporate Counsel; American Board of Trial Advocates; Defense Research Institute. Fellow, Akron Bar Foundation. ***REPORTED CASES:*** State ex rel. Mayle v. Industrial Commission, et al. (1999) 86 Ohio St. 3d 74; Bond v. Howard Corp., (1995), 72 Ohio St. 3d 332; Nuspl v. Akron, (1991), 61 Ohio St. 3rd 511; Vogel v. Wells, (1991), 57 Ohio St. 3d 91; State, ex rel. Wright v. Weyandt, (1977), 50 Ohio St. 2d 194; Civil Service Personnel Assn. v. Akron, (1976) 48 Ohio St. 2d 25; Romito Bros. v. Frank A. Flannery, Inc. (1974), 40 Ohio St. 2d 79. ***PRACTICE AREAS:*** General Civil Trial Practice; Insurance Defense; Negligence Law; Personal Injury Law; Business Law; Employment Law; Corporate Labor and Zoning Law. ***Email:*** htipping@tippinglaw.com

CHRISTOPHER A. TIPPING, born Akron, Ohio, July 23, 1970; admitted to bar, 1995, Ohio; 1996, U.S. District Court, Northern District of Ohio; 1998, District of Columbia; 2003, U.S. Court of Appeals, Sixth Circuit. *Education:* George Washington University (B.A., cum laude, 1992); Ohio State University Law School (J.D., 1995). Phi Beta Kappa. Recipient, Jessie Fant Evans Award in American History, 1992. Articles Editor, 1994-1995 and Staff Member, 1993-1994, Ohio State Law Journal. *Member:* Akron, Ohio State and American Bar Associations. ***PRACTICE AREAS:*** General Civil Trial Practice; Business Law; Negligence Law; Insurance Defense; Appellate Practice. ***Email:*** ctipping@tippinglaw.com

SOPHIE M. MILO, born Toronto, Canada, August 26, 1971; admitted to bar, 1997, Ohio. *Education:* University of Toronto (B.A., 1993); University of Akron (J.D., 1996). *Member:* Akron, Ohio State and American Bar Associations. ***LANGUAGES:*** Greek and French. ***PRACTICE AREAS:*** Insurance Defense Law; Civil Practice; Employment Law; Business Law; Personal Injury. ***Email:*** smilo@tippinglaw.com

MICHAEL J. ELLIOTT, born Akron, Ohio, September 26, 1968; admitted to bar, 1998, Ohio; 1999, U.S. District Court, Northern District of Ohio; 2002, U.S. Court of Appeals, Sixth Circuit. *Education:* Ohio University (B.A., 1991); Case Western Reserve University (J.D., 1998). *Member:* Akron, Ohio State and American Bar Associations; Ohio Academy of Trial Lawyers; The Association of Trial Lawyers of America. ***PRACTICE AREAS:*** Products Liability; Medical Malpractice; Premises Liability; Insurance; Automobile Accidents and Injuries; Securities Fraud; Securities Litigation. ***Email:*** melliot@tippinglaw.com

OF COUNSEL

DOMINIC A. OLIVO (1908-1997)

RICHARD L. GRANT, born Chicago, Illinois, August 23, 1941; admitted to bar, 1967, California; 1972, Ohio; 1974, U.S. District Court, Northern District of Ohio and U.S. Supreme Court; 1975, U.S. Court of Appeals, Sixth Circuit and U.S. Tax Court. *Education:* University of Pennsylvania (B.S., 1963); Stanford University (J.D., 1966); Georgetown University (LL.M. Taxation, 1967). Beta Gamma Sigma. Dean's Club Professorship, 1995-1996, Professor of Law, 1974-1996, Acting Associate Dean, 1984, Associate Professor of Law, 1970-1974, Assistant Professor of Law, 1967-1970, University of Akron School of

(This Listing Continued)

TIPPING CO., L.P.A., A LEGAL PROFESSIONAL ASSOCIATION, Akron—Continued

Law. Attorney, U.S. Securities and Exchange Commission, Division of Corporate Finance, 1966-1967. *Member:* Akron and Ohio State Bar Associations; State Bar of California. ***PRACTICE AREAS:*** Corporate; Probate; Real Estate.

REPRESENTATIVE CLIENTS: AIG National Insurance Co., Inc.; Alliance Hospitality, Inc.; Allied Group Insurance Co.; American National Property and Casualty Co.; American Select Risk Insurance Co.; Brott Mardis & Co.; Citizens Insurance Co.; CNA Insurance Co.; Community Drug Board, Inc.; Creative Pultrusions, Inc.; Cumis Insurance Society, Inc.; CUNA Mutual Insurance Co.; Dunn-Quigley-Ciriello & Carr Funeral Homes; Evans Insurance Agency, Inc.; FCCI Insurance Group; Great American Insurance Companies, Personal Lines Division; Great Oaks Insurance Co.; Great Midwest Insurance Co.; Great West Casualty Co.; Hanover Group of Insurance Cos.; Harleysville Insurance Group; Hastings Mutual Insurance Co.; Hydraulic Parts Store, Inc.; JWF Specialty, Inc.; City of Kent; McCann Plastics, Inc.; Monroe Guaranty Insurance Co.; Murdock Industrial, Inc.; Northeast Ohio Four County Regional Planning & Development Organization (NEFCO); Ohio Mutual Casualty Co.; Reinbolt, Evans & Mann, Inc.; Sentry Insurance Co.; Sherwin Williams; Summervilles', Inc.; Trans-Enviro, Inc.; Union Commerce Corp.; Unitrin Specialty Lines Insurance Co.; Westfield Insurance Group; Zurich American Insurance.

TRIVERS & DICKERSON, LLC

AKRON, OHIO

(See Cleveland)

Criminal Law, Family Law, Personal Injury, Divorce.

DAVID G. UMBAUGH

AKRON, OHIO

(See Hudson)

Estate Planning, Probate, Business Law, Business Law with Exit Planning, Elder Care, Trusts and Estates, Wills, Civil Practice.

VORYS, SATER, SEYMOUR AND PEASE LLP

Established in 1909

FIRST NATIONAL TOWER
106 SOUTH MAIN STREET, SUITE 1100
AKRON, OHIO 44308
Telephone: 330-208-1000
Fax: 330-208-1001
URL: http://www.vssp.com

Columbus, Ohio Office: 52 East Gay Street, P.O. Box 1008, 43216-1008. Telephone: 614-464-6400. Facsimile: 614-464-6350.

Washington, D.C. Office: 1828 L Street, N.W., 20036-5109. Telephone: 202-467-8800. Facsimile: 202-467-8900.

Cleveland, Ohio Office: 2100 One Cleveland Center, 1375 East Ninth Street, 44114-1724. Telephone: 216-479-6100. Facsimile: 216-479-6060.

Cincinnati, Ohio Office: Suite 2000, Atrium Two, 221 East Fourth Street, P.O. Box 0236, 45201-0236. Telephone: 513-723-4000. Facsimile: 513-723-4056.

Alexandria, Virginia Office: 277 South Washington Street, Suite 310, 22314. Telephone: 703-837-6999. Facsimile: 703-549-4492.

Alternative Dispute Resolution, Antitrust, Trade Regulation, Customs, Banks and Banking, Finance, Bankruptcy, Biotechnology, Business Law, Civil Rights, Debtors and Creditors Rights, Computers and Software, Congressional Investigations, Construction Law, Contracts, Copyrights, Disabilities, Election, Campaign and Political Law, Employee Benefits, Environmental Law, Probate, Guardianship and Conservatorship, General Practice, Health Care, Labor, Employment, Occupational Safety and Health, Workers Compensation, Corporate Law, Securities, Energy, Natural Resources, Franchises and Franchising, Government Contracts, Hospital Law, Immigration and Naturalization, Insurance, Intellectual Property, International Law, International Trade, Legal Ethics and Professional Responsibility, Litigation, Media Law, Medicare and Medicaid, Mergers, Acquisitions and Divestitures, Municipal Law, Telecommunications, Personal Injury, Products Liability, Railroad Law, Real Estate, RICO, Sports Law, Taxation, Technology and Science, Torts, Toxic Torts, Trade Secrets, Transportation, Trusts and Estates, Unfair Competition, Utility Law, White Collar Defense, Wills, Zoning, Planning and Land Use.

PARTNER

F. DANIEL BALMERT, born Portsmouth, Ohio, January 3, 1951; admitted to bar, 1976, Ohio; 1977, U.S. District Court, Southern District of Ohio; 1982, U.S. District Court, Northern District of Ohio; 1987, U.S. Court of Appeals, Sixth Circuit; 1993, U.S. Supreme Court. *Education:* University of Notre Dame (B.A., with honors, 1973); Capital University (J.D., magna cum laude, 1976). Member, Order of the Curia. Member, Panel of Arbitrators, Cuyahoga County Court Common Pleas Court. Member, Civil Justice Reform Act Advisory Group, United States District Court, The Northern District of Ohio; Life Member, Eighth Judicial District; Delegate, Sixth Circuit Judicial Conference. *Member:* Akron, Ohio State, Federal and American Bar Associations; Association of Defense Trial Attorneys. ***PRACTICE AREAS:*** Workers Compensation Law; Litigation; Employment Law. ***Email:*** fdbalmert@vssp.com

ASSOCIATES

ASHLEY M. MANFULL, born Harrisburg, Pennsylvania; admitted to bar, 1999, Ohio; 2000, U.S. District Court, Northern District of Ohio; 2001, U.S. Court of Appeals, Sixth Circuit. *Education:* Grove City College (B.A., 1996); University of Akron (J.D., summa cum laude, 1999). Member, Akron Law Review. *Member:* Akron (Member, Labor and Employment Law Section, 1999—), Ohio State and American Bar Associations. ***PRACTICE AREAS:*** Labor and Employment Law. ***Email:*** ammanfull@vssp.com

AARON S. BERKE, born Ann Arbor, Michigan; admitted to bar, 2000, Ohio. *Education:* University of Pennsylvania (B.A., cum laude, 1997); University of Michigan Law School (J.D., 2000). ***Email:*** asberke@vssp.com

PATRICIA M. OCHMANN, born Akron, Ohio, October 6, 1970; admitted to bar, 2001, Ohio. *Education:* Kent State University (B.S., 1994); University of Akron (J.D., magna cum laude, 2001). Associate Editor, Akron Law Review. Author: Article, "Managed Care Organizations Manage to Escape Liability: Why Issues of Quantity vs. Quality Lead to ERISA's Inequitable Preemption of Claims," 34 Akron Law Review 571, 2001; Article, "Heightened Scrutiny: Sarbanes-Oxley Implications Surface for Nonprofit Organizations," SmartBusiness Magazine, Akron/Canton, March, 2004. *Member:* Akron, Ohio State and American Bar Associations. ***PRACTICE AREAS:*** Health Law; Labor and Employment. ***Email:*** pmochmann@vssp.com

AMANDA J. ZAREMBA, born Chicago Heights, Illinois, January 24, 1979; admitted to bar, 2004, Ohio; U.S. District Court, Northern District of Ohio and U.S. Court of Appeals, Sixth Circuit. *Education:* Miami University (B.A., 2001); University of Cincinnati (J.D., 2004). Order of the Coif. *Member:* Akron, Ohio State and American Bar Associations. ***PRACTICE AREAS:*** Labor and Employment; Litigation.

OF COUNSEL

PHILIP A. LLOYD, born Youngstown, Ohio, February 13, 1947; admitted to bar, 1972, Ohio; 1996, Colorado. *Education:* Ohio Wesleyan University (B.A., 1969); University of Akron (J.D., 1972). ***PRACTICE AREAS:*** Banking; Bankruptcy; Creditors Rights; Business; Corporate. ***Email:*** palloyd@vssp.com

JOHN W. SOLOMON, born New York, New York, May 7, 1944; admitted to bar, 1973, Ohio; U.S. District Court, Northern District of Ohio; 1977, U.S. Court of Appeals, Sixth Circuit; 1978, U.S. Supreme Court. *Education:* Cornell University (A.B., 1966); University of Michigan (J.D., 1973). United States Department of State, 1967-1971. Foreign Service Officer, American Embassy in Quito, Ecuador and in the Bureau of Intelligence and Research in Washington, D.C. ***LANGUAGES:*** Spanish. ***PRACTICE AREAS:*** Litigation. ***Email:*** jwsolomon@vssp.com

JAY P. PORTER, born Canonsburg, Pennsylvania, April 16, 1953; admitted to bar, 1978, Ohio; U.S. District Court, Northern District of Ohio; U.S. Court of Appeals, Sixth Circuit. *Education:* Grove City College (B.A., 1975); College of William & Mary (J.D., 1978). Vice Chair, Summit County Planning Commission. Listed in The Best Lawyers in America, Real Estate Law, 1995—. *Member:* Cleveland, Akron, Ohio State (Member, Real Property Section) and American (Member, Real Property Section) Bar Associations; National Association of Bond Lawyers. ***PRACTICE AREAS:*** Real Estate; Finance; Environmental. ***Email:*** jpporter@vssp.com

J. BRUCE HUNSICKER, born Akron, Ohio, November 9, 1954; admitted to bar, 1980, Ohio; U.S. District Court, Northern District of Ohio; U.S. Court of Appeals, Sixth Circuit; U.S. Supreme Court. *Education:* The Ohio State University (B.A., 1977); University of Akron (J.D., 1980). Formerly with Brouse McDowell LPA. Former Adjunct Professor at The University of Akron School of Law. ***PRACTICE AREAS:*** Banking; Bankruptcy; Creditors Rights; Litigation; Real Estate. ***Email:*** jbhunsicker@vssp.com

J. BRET TREIER, born Columbus, Ohio, March 7, 1960; admitted to bar, 1985, Ohio; U.S. Court of Appeals, Sixth Circuit; U.S. District Court, Northern District of Ohio. *Education:* Bowling Green State University (B.S., magna cum laude, 1982); Case Western Reserve University (J.D., cum laude, 1985). Phi Delta Phi (President, 1984-1985; 1985-1987). Merit Scholar, 1982-1985. First Editor, 1984-1985 and Associate Editor, 1983-1984, Case Western Reserve University Law Review. Federal Judicial Clerk, The Honorable Leroy J. Contie, Jr., U.S. Court of Appeals, Sixth Circuit. Vice President, Leadership Akron, Class XVIII. President, University Park Development Corporation. Summit County Trustee and Former President, Ohio Division Trustee, American Cancer Society. Endowment Foundation Trustee and Canal Square Branch Former Chair, Akron Metro YMCA. Vice President, Kiwanis Club of Akron. *Member:* American Bar Association. ***PRACTICE AREAS:*** Business Organizations; Mergers, Acquisitions and Divestitures; Closely Held Businesses; Directors' and Officers' Liability; Banking and Finance Law; Commercial Banks; Private Placements; Public Offerings; Securities Law; Non-Profit and Tax-Exempt Organizations. ***Email:*** jbtreier@vssp.com

THOMAS RICHARD CROOKES, born Dowagiac, Michigan, September 16, 1960; admitted to bar, 1987, Ohio; U.S. District Court, Northern District of Ohio; U.S. District Court, Eastern District of Michigan; U.S. Court of Appeals, Fourth and Sixth Circuits. *Education:* University of Michigan (A.B., 1984); University of Detroit (J.D., 1987). *Member:* American Bar Association (Section of Labor and Employment Law). ***PRACTICE AREAS:*** Litigation; Labor and Employment. ***Email:*** trcrookes@vssp.com

VINCENT J. TERSIGNI, born Akron, Ohio, January 7, 1963; admitted to bar, 1988, Ohio, U.S. District Court, Northern District of Ohio, U.S. Court of Appeals, Sixth Circuit and U.S. Supreme Court. *Education:* Miami University (A.B., 1985); Case Western Reserve University (J.D., 1988). Recognized by: "Inside Business Magazine" in 2001 and 2002 as a Leading Lawyer in Labor and Employment Law in Northeast Ohio, as voted by his peers; "Cincinnati Magazine" since 2004 as an Ohio Super Lawyer, as voted by his peers. OSBA Certified Specialist in Labor & Employment Law, 2003. *Member:* Akron Bar Association (Member, Board of Trustees, 2000-2003; Chair, Labor and Employment Law Committee, 1994-1996 and 2000-2002); Ohio State Bar Association (Member, Board of Governors; Labor & Employment Law Committee, 2003—). ***PRACTICE AREAS:*** Management Labor Law; Management Employment Law; Employment Litigation; Civil Rights; ERISA Litigation; OSHA; Wage and Hour Law. ***Email:*** vjtersigni@vssp.com

REPRESENTATIVE CLIENTS: Abercrombie & Fitch; Airborne Express, Inc.; American Showa; Bob Evans Farms, Inc.; Cardinal Health; Columbus Blue Jackets; Consolidated Stores Corp.; Dominion Homes; Eaton Corporation; Greif Bros.; Honda of America Mfg., Inc.; Insurance Federation of Ohio; M/I Homes; Martin Marietta Energy Systems; National City Bank; Fraternal Order of Police; Ohio Casualty Corporation; Ohio League of Financial Institutions; R.G. Barry Corp.; Showa Aluminum Corporation; Techneglas; The Children's Hospital; The Limited, Inc.; The Ohio State University; The Scotts Company; Value City Department Stores; Filene's Basement; DSW; Wendy's International, Inc.; Worthington Industries, Inc.; Hamilton County.

LOCAL COUNSEL: Abbott Laboratories; American Telephone & Telegraph Co.; Anheuser-Busch, Inc.; Ashland Oil, Inc.; B.F. Goodrich Co.; BP America; Emerson Electric; General Electric Company; General Motors Corp.; Goodyear Tire & Rubber; Household Finance

(This Listing Continued)

Corp.; Mac Tools, Inc.; Navistar International; The Kroger Co.; United States Playing Card Co.; Waste Management; Western Southern Life Insurance Company.

EDWARD C. WEBER

Established in 1971

159 SOUTH MAIN STREET, SUITE 1002

AKRON, OHIO 44308-1318

Telephone: 330-535-6185

Fax: 330-996-4014

Email: edweazer@aol.com

URL: http://www.edwardcweberlaw.com

Trials and Appeals in all Courts. Criminal, DUI, Traffic Violations, Personal Injury, Defense, Probate and Estates Drug Crimes, Assault, Domestic Violence.

EDWARD C. WEBER, born Akron, Ohio, February 17, 1944; admitted to bar, 1972, Ohio. *Education:* The Ohio State University; Ohio Dominican College (B.S., 1967); University of Akron (J.D., 1971). Assistant Law Director, City of Akron, Ohio. *Member:* Akron and Ohio State Bar Associations; The Association of Trial Lawyers of America; Ohio Association of Criminal Defense Lawyers Association; National Association of Criminal Defense Lawyers; American Civil Liberties Union. ***LANGUAGES:*** Spanish. ***TRANSACTIONS:*** Key Bank. ***PRACTICE AREAS:*** Trials and Appeals in all Courts; Criminal Law; DUI; Traffic Violations; Personal Injury Law; Defense Law; Probate Law; Estates Law; Felonies; Misdemeanors.

KEITH D. WEINER & ASSOCIATES CO., L.P.A.

AKRON, OHIO

(See Cleveland)

Collections, Bankruptcy, Foreclosures, Evictions, Replevins, Mechanic Liens, Commercial Litigation, Post Judgment Collections.

WHALEN & COMPTON

A LEGAL PROFESSIONAL ASSOCIATION

565 WOLF LEDGES PARKWAY

P.O. BOX 2020

AKRON, OHIO 44309-2020

Telephone: 330-376-1112; 1-800-376-1112 in Ohio

Telecopier: 330-376-3200

URL: http://www.whalenandcompton.com

General Civil Trial and Appellate Practice. Educational and School Law, Labor Law, Management, Civil Rights and Equal Employment Law. Real Estate regarding University and School Law.

DENNIS M. WHALEN, born Akron, Ohio, June 25, 1938; admitted to bar, 1966, Ohio; 1968, U.S. District Court, Northern District of Ohio; 1972, U.S. Supreme Court; 1974, Florida; 1975, U.S. Court of Appeals, Sixth Circuit. *Education:* College of Wooster (B.A., 1960); Akron University Law School (J.D., 1966). Phi Alpha Delta. *Member:* Akron, Ohio State and American Bar Associations; The Florida Bar (Board of Governors, 1999-2003); The Association of Trial Lawyers of America; National School Board Attorneys Association. ***PRACTICE AREAS:*** School Law; Labor Management Law; Litigation. ***Email:*** dwhalen@whalenandcompton.com

G. FREDERICK COMPTON, JR., born New Brighton, Pennsylvania, March 25, 1948; admitted to bar, 1973, Ohio; 1974, Florida and U.S. District Court, Northern District of Ohio; 1980, U.S. Court of Appeals, Sixth Circuit. *Education:* Rutgers University (B.A., 1970); Akron University Law School (J.D., 1973). Phi Alpha Delta. Member, American Arbitration Association Labor Advisory Council, 1994-1998. *Member:* Akron, Ohio State and American Bar Associations; The Florida Bar; Ohio Council of School Board Attorneys (Chairman, 1989). ***PRACTICE AREAS:*** Civil Rights Law; Equal Employment Law; School Law. ***Email:*** fcompton@whalenandcompton.com

HELEN S. CARROLL, born Cleveland, Ohio, 1952; admitted to bar, 1992, Ohio. *Education:* University of Akron (B.A., 1989; J.D., 1992). ***PRACTICE AREAS:*** Labor and Employment. ***Email:*** hcarroll@whalenandcompton.com

---

ELIZABETH GROOMS TAYLOR, born Tachikawa AFB, Tokyo, Japan, April 18, 1966; admitted to bar, 1991, Ohio; 1993, U.S. District Court, Northern District of Ohio. *Education:* Ohio University (B.S., with honors, 1988); University of Akron (J.D., 1991). Intern, Staff and Senior Staff, University of Akron Law Review, 1989-1991. Teaching Adjunct, Legal Writing, University of Akron School of Law, 1991—. *Member:* Akron, Ohio State and American Bar Associations. ***LANGUAGES:*** French. ***PRACTICE AREAS:*** School Law; Labor Management Law. ***Email:*** btaylor@whalenandcompton.com

MARI ALICE ZACHARYASZ, born Berea, Ohio, October 18, 1961; admitted to bar, 2000, Ohio; 2002, U.S. District Court, Northern District of Ohio. *Education:* Baldwin-Wallace College (B.A., cum laude, 1995); Cleveland-Marshall College of Law (J.D., 1999). Alumni Senate Officer, Delta Theta Phi., 2000—. *Member:* Ohio State Bar Association; Ohio Council of School Boards Association; Free Clinic of Greater Cleveland (Associate Board Member, 2000—). ***PRACTICE AREAS:*** School Law. ***Email:*** mazacharyasz@whalenandcompton.com

ANDREW F. PECK, born Rochester, New York, June 2, 1960; admitted to bar, 1985, Ohio; 1986, U.S. District Court, Northern District of Ohio. *Education:* University of Akron (B.A., 1981; J.D., 1985; LL.M., Tax, 1992). *Member:* Akron, Ohio State and American Bar Associations. ***PRACTICE AREAS:*** School Law; Labor Relations. ***Email:*** apeck@whalenandcompton.com

(This Listing Continued)

REPRESENTATIVE CLIENTS: Akron City School District; Cuyahoga Falls City School District; Winton Woods City School District; Kent City School District; Munroe Falls City School District; Stow City School District; Centerville City School District.

WILLIAMS, SENNETT & SCULLY CO., L.P.A.

AKRON, OHIO

(See Twinsburg)

General Civil Trial and Appellate Practice in all Courts. Insurance, Casualty and Surety, Life, Accident and Health, Negligence Litigation, Medical-Legal, Products Liability, Labor and Employment Law, Commercial Litigation.

BRUCE H. WILSON

789 WEST MARKET STREET

AKRON, OHIO 44303

Telephone: 330-253-8300

Email: BruceWilsonEsq@aol.com

Antitrust, Deceptive Trade Practices, Commercial Litigation, Intellectual Property Litigation, Unfair Competition.

BRUCE H. WILSON, admitted to bar, 1964, Ohio; U.S. Supreme Court and U.S. Court of Appeals, Sixth, Second and Eighth Circuits; U.S. Court of Appeals for the Federal Circuit, U. S. District Court, Northern and Southern Districts of Ohio, U.S. District Court, Eastern District of Michigan and U.S. Tax Court; registered to practice before U.S. Patent and Trademark Office. *Education:* Case Institute of Technology (B.S., 1959); University of Akron (J.D., 1963). Adjunct Faculty, University of Akron School of Law. Life Member, USCA Sixth Circuit Judicial Conference. *Member:* Akron, Ohio State (Member, Council of Delegates, Federal Courts and Practice Committee, Intellectual Property Law Section), Federal, Federal Circuit and American Bar Associations; Cleveland Intellectual Property Law Association; American Inns of Court. ***PRACTICE AREAS:*** Litigation; Intellectual Property; Environmental; Products Liability; Business; Trial Practice Litigation; Appellate Practice Litigation; Commercial; Antitrust.

OF COUNSEL

TERENCE E. SCANLON, born Akron, Ohio, October 11, 1945; admitted to bar, 1975, Massachusetts; 1976, Ohio. *Education:* Holy Cross College (B.A., 1967); The Ohio State University; Wayne State University (J.D., 1973). Legal Author: The Prairie Pleader (A Newsletter for lawyers). Adjunct Professor, University of Akron, School of Law, 1986. Lecturer: Walsh College, North Canton, Ohio, 1979. Ohio Legal History Seminar, 1995. ***PRACTICE AREAS:*** Legal Research; Appellate Practice.

WITSCHEY WITSCHEY & FIRESTINE CO., L.P.A.

405 ROTHROCK ROAD

SUITE 103

AKRON, OHIO 44321-3125

Telephone: 330-665-5117

Fax: 330-665-7615

Email: witschey@witscheylaw.com

URL: http://www.witscheyandwitschey.com

Corporate and Business Law, Real Estate, Zoning, Condominium and Construction Law, Oil and Gas Law, Probate, Estate and Business Succession Planning, Elder Care, Tax Law, Civil Litigation involving the above practice areas.

FRANK J. WITSCHEY, born Wadsworth, Ohio, December 22, 1966; admitted to bar, 1992, Ohio; 1993, U.S. District Court, Northern District of Ohio and U.S. Court of Appeals, 6th Circuit. *Education:* Bowling Green State University (B.A., 1989); University of Akron (J.D., 1992). Lambda Chi Alpha. Trial Team, University of Akron, School of Law (1990-1992); Most Outstanding Advocate, Gourley Moot Court. *Member:* Akron, Medina County (Member, Estate Planning Committee), Ohio State and American Bar Associations. ***PRACTICE AREAS:*** Real Estate; Corporate; Commercial Litigation; Business Succession; Estate Planning; Probate. ***Email:*** fjw@witscheylaw.com

JEFFREY T. WITSCHEY, born Wadsworth, Ohio, December 22, 1966; admitted to bar, 1992, Ohio; 1993, U.S. District Court, Northern District of Ohio; 1997, U.S. Supreme Court. *Education:* Bowling Green State University (B.A., 1989); University of Akron (J.D., cum laude, 1992). Lambda Chi Alpha. University of Akron School of Law (1990-1992) Trial Team. *Member:* Akron, Medina County, Summit County, Ohio State and American Bar Associations. ***PRACTICE AREAS:*** Business Litigation; Real Estate Litigation; Business Law; Real Estate; Condominium Law; Zoning Law; Employment Law; Oil and Gas Law. ***Email:*** jtw@witsheylaw.com

DAVID L. FIRESTINE, born Elyria, Ohio, July 9, 1974; admitted to bar, 2000, Ohio and U.S. District Court, Northern District of Ohio. *Education:* Baldwin-Wallace College (B.A., cum laude, 1997); University of Akron (J.D., 2000). Board of Directors: The Young Professionals of Akron; Greater Akron Chamber, Small Business Council. *Member:* Akron and Ohio State Bar Associations. ***PRACTICE AREAS:*** Commercial Litigation; Real Estate Litigation; Business Law; Estate Planning; Real Estate; Oil and Gas Law. ***Email:*** dlf@witscheylaw.com

---

KELLY A. MOLNAR, born Anaheim, California, January 18, 1972; admitted to bar, 2000, Ohio; 2002, U.S. District Court, Northern District of Ohio. *Education:* University of Akron (B.S., magna cum laude, 1994; J.D., magna cum laude, 2000). Certified Public Ac-

(This Listing Continued)

WITSCHEY WITSCHEY & FIRESTINE CO., L.P.A., Akron—Continued

countant, 1998—. *Member:* Akron and Ohio State Bar Associations; Ohio Society of Certified Public Accountants. ***PRACTICE AREAS:*** Probate; Tax Law; Estate Planning; Corporate Law. **Email:** kam@witscheylaw.com

CRAIG S. HORBUS, born Oberline, Ohio, August 4, 1978; admitted to bar, 2004, Ohio and U.S. District Court, Northern District of Ohio. *Education:* Baldwin-Wallace College (B.A., cum laude, 2001); Cleveland-Marshall College of Law (J.D., 2004). Lambda Chi Alpha. Executive Editor, Cleveland-Marshall Journal of Law and Health, 2003-2004. *Member:* Akron, Cleveland, Cuyahoga County, Ohio State and American Bar Associations; Young Professionals of Akron. ***PRACTICE AREAS:*** Commercial Law; Business Law; Construction Law; Real Estate Litigation; Corporate Law; Probate; Land Use. **Email:** csh@witscheylaw.com

AMY M. MONTANA, born Lewisburg, Pennsylvania, August 5, 1975; admitted to bar, 2001, Ohio; U.S. District Court, Northern District of Ohio and U.S. Court of Appeals, Sixth Circuit. *Education:* Youngstown State University (B.S.A.S., summa cum laude, 1998); University of Akron School of Law (J.D., magna cum laude, 2001). Phi Alpha Delta. Managing Editor, Akron Law Review. Member, ABA National Appellate Advocacy Competition; National Appellate Advocacy Competition; New York Bar National Moot Court Competition. *Member:* Cleveland and Ohio State Bar Associations; Scanlon Inn of Court. ***PRACTICE AREAS:*** Business Law; Employment Law; Corporate Law; Commercial Litigation; Litigation.

ZAVARELLO AND DAVIS, CO., L.P.A.

Established in 1981

313 SOUTH HIGH STREET, CORNER SOUTH HIGH AND BUCHTEL

AKRON, OHIO 44308-1532

Telephone: 330-762-9700
Fax: 330-762-1680
Email: RhDavis3205@netlink.net
Email: wzavarello@netlink.net

General Civil, Trial and Appellate Practice. Negligence, Medical, Legal Malpractice, Product Liability.

A. WILLIAM ZAVARELLO, born Johnstown, Pennsylvania, September 29, 1937; admitted to bar, 1964, Ohio. *Education:* University of Akron (B.A., 1959; J.D., 1964). Student Bar President, Assistant Prosecutor, City of Akron, 1964-1966. Member, University of Akron Alumni Board, 1967-1970. *Member:* Akron (Member, Executive Committee, 1979-1981), Ohio State (Member, Council of Delegates (1988-1992) Bar Associations; Summit County Trial Lawyers Association (Board of Trustees, 1986—); Ohio Academy of Trial Lawyers (President, 1988-1989); The Association of Trial Lawyers of America (Board of Governors, 1989-1996 and 2000—); American Board of Trial Advocates; Trial Lawyers for Public Justice; National Lawyers Guild; Scanlon Inn of Court (President, 2005-2006). ***PRACTICE AREAS:*** Medical Malpractice; Negligence; Product Liability; Legal Malpractice. **Email:** wzavarello@netlink.net

RHONDA GAIL DAVIS, born Jonesboro, Arkansas, April 17, 1964; admitted to bar, 1991, Tennessee, Arkansas, and U.S. District Court, Middle District of Tennessee; 1994, Ohio. *Education:* Arkansas State University (B.A., cum laude, 1986); MacQuarie University School of Law, Sydney, Australia (1987-1988); University of Mississippi (J.D., 1991). Phi Kappa Phi. Member: National Trial Competition Team, 1991; Jessup International Law Moot Court Team, University of Mississippi, 1989-1990, 1990-1991 and Macquarie University School of Law, 1987-1988. Rotary Foundation Scholar. Member, 1989-1991 and Editor, 1990-1991, Journal of Space Law. *Member:* Akron (Member, Grievance Committee, 2004-2005; Investigation Subcommittee, 2003-2004), Ohio State and Arkansas Bar Associations; The Association of Trial Lawyers of America Women's Caucus (Vice President and Secretary, 2002-2003; Ohio Liaison, 1999—); Summit County Trial Lawyers Association (Treasurer, 2002-2003; Member, Board of Trustees, 2001-2002); Ohio Academy of Trial Lawyers (Vice President; Member, Board of Trustees, 1997—; Chair, Negligence Section, 2000-2001); Arkansas Trial Lawyers Association; The Association of Trial Lawyers of America; Ohio Women's Bar Association (Member, Board of Trustees, 2001-2003); Scanlon Inn of Court (Member, 2001—). ***PRACTICE AREAS:*** Medical Malpractice; Personal Injury; Antitrust; Professional Malpractice. **Email:** RhDavis3205@netlink.net

REFERENCES: First National Bank of Ohio; National City Bank, Akron.

KRUGLIAK, WILKINS, GRIFFITHS & DOUGHERTY CO., L.P.A.

KEYBANK BUILDING
960 WEST STATE STREET

ALLIANCE, OHIO 44601

Telephone: 330-823-9262
Facsimile: 330-821-2447
Email: legal@kwgd.com
URL: http://www.kwgd.com

Canton, Ohio Office: 4775 Munson Street N.W. Telephone: 330-497-0700.
New Philadelphia, Ohio Office: 158 N. Broadway Street. Telephone: 330-364-3472.

Corporate Law, Mergers and Acquisitions, Labor and Employment (Private and Public Sector), Employee Benefits, Real Estate, Taxation, Complex Litigation, Contracts, Insurance Defense, Estates and Trusts, Probate, Elder Law, Commercial Litigation, Oil and Gas, Occupational Safety and Health, Environmental Law, Health Care Law, Hospital Law, Bankruptcy, Banks and Banking, Securities, Construction Law, Family Law, Education Law, Workers Compensation, Personal Injury Litigation, Collections, Debtor and Creditor, Government, Media Law and Electronic Commerce.

(For Complete Biographical Data on all Personnel, see Professional Biographies at Canton, Ohio)

JASON HENNEKES

AMELIA, OHIO

(See Cincinnati)

Criminal Law, Driving While Intoxicated, Felonies, Misdemeanors, Homicide, Theft, Drug crimes, Traffic Violations, Domestic Violence, Assault.

RICHARD S. RAMSEY

238 CHURCH STREET

AMHERST, OHIO 44001

Telephone: 440-988-3300
Fax: 440-988-9521
Email: RichardSRamsey@hotmail.com
URL: http://www.ramseylawfirm.net

Domestic Relations, Family Law, Divorce, Child Custody, Criminal Law, Business Law, Landlord and Tenant Law, Civil Litigation.

RICHARD S. RAMSEY, born Amherst, Ohio, November 12, 1977; admitted to bar, 2003, Ohio. *Education:* Capital University (B.A., 2000); Cleveland-Marshall College of Law, Cleveland State University (J.D., 2002). *Member:* Ohio State Bar Association. ***PRACTICE AREAS:*** Domestic Relations; Family Law; Divorce; Child Custody; Criminal Law; Business Law; Landlord and Tenant Law; Civil Litigation.

PLASSMAN, RUPP, SHORT & HAGANS

Established in 1935

302 NORTH DEFIANCE STREET
P.O. BOX 178

ARCHBOLD, OHIO 43502-0178

Telephone: 419-445-8815
Fax: 419-445-1080
Email: attorneys@prshlaw.com

General Civil Practice in all Courts. Corporation, Probate and Estate Planning, Insurance Law, Personal Injury, Real Estate, Taxation, Municipal Law, Family/Domestic Relations and Trials.

MEMBERS OF FIRM

OWEN RICE (1900-1978)

HAROLD H. PLASSMAN, born Deshler, Ohio, April 5, 1929; admitted to bar, 1957, Michigan; 1959, Ohio. *Education:* Capital University (A.B., 1951); University of Michigan (J.D., 1956). Order of the Coif. Member, Board of Regents, Capital University, 1977-1987. *Member:* Fulton County, Northwestern Ohio, Ohio State and American Bar Associations; State Bar of Michigan. ***PRACTICE AREAS:*** Probate and Estate Planning; Corporation Law; Taxation Law. **Email:** hhp@prshlaw.com

DAVID P. RUPP, JR., born Wauseon, Ohio, July 23, 1941; admitted to bar, 1965, Ohio. *Education:* The Ohio State University (B.S., 1962; J.D., 1965). Phi Delta Phi. *Member:* Fulton County, Northwestern Ohio, Ohio State (Member, Board of Governors, 1989-1992) and American Bar Associations. ***PRACTICE AREAS:*** Negligence Law; Trials; Personal Injury; Insurance; Family Law. **Email:** dpr@prshlaw.com

PETER D. SHORT, born Wauseon, Ohio, June 8, 1953; admitted to bar, 1978, Ohio. *Education:* Ohio Northern University (B.S., 1974); University of Cincinnati (J.D., 1978). Solicitor Village of Archbold, 1989-1999. Mayor, Village of Archbold, 2000-2004. *Member:* Fulton County, Northwestern Ohio, Ohio State and American Bar Associations. ***PRACTICE AREAS:*** Real Estate Law; Municipal Law; Estate Planning; Corporate Law. **Email:** pds@prshlaw.com

MARK D. HAGANS, born Marquette, Michigan, November 12, 1966; admitted to bar, 1994, Ohio; 1995, U.S. District Court, Northern District of Ohio. *Education:* Ohio Wesleyan University (B.A., cum laude, 1989), University of Toledo (J.D., cum laude, 1994). Solicitor, Village of Archhold and Village of Fayette, 2004—. *Member:* Fulton County, Northwest Ohio, Ohio State and American Bar Associations. ***PRACTICE AREAS:*** Probate; Estate Planning; Real Estate; Corporation Law; General Practice. **Email:** hagans@rtecexpress.net

REPRESENTATIVE CLIENTS: Lugbill Bros., Inc.; The Farmers & Merchants State Bank; Pettisville Grain Co.; Miller Bros. Const., Inc.; Sauder Woodworking Co.; Sauder Manufacturing Co.; Archbold Elevator, Inc.; Allied Moulded Products, Inc.; Brookview Farm, Inc.; Kahrs Tractor Sales, Inc.; Wauseon Woodworking Co.; Archbold Medical Group, Inc.; Archbold Refuse Service; Werlor, Inc.; Gardenscape; Rupp Furniture Co.
REFERENCE: The Farmers & Merchants State Bank, Archbold and Wauseon, Ohio.
APPROVED AGENTS: First American Title Insurance Company.

CRITCHFIELD, CRITCHFIELD & JOHNSTON, LTD.

ASHLAND, OHIO

(See Wooster)

General Practice in all Courts. Business, Corporate Law, Insurance, Estate Planning, Wills and Probate, Labor and Employment, ERISA, Health Care, Environmental Law, Workers Compensation, Banking, Taxation, Antitrust and Trade Regulation, Oil and Gas Law, Litigation, Debtor and Creditor, Municipal Law, School Law, Real Estate, Commercial Law, Construction Law.

GEORGE R. KEYSER

ASHLAND, OHIO

(See Mansfield)

Civic and Criminal Litigation in all Courts. Personal Injury, Automobile Accidents, Slip and Fall, Products Liability, Wrongful Death, Family Law, Divorce, Child Custody, Child Support, Visitation Rights, Adoption Law, Juvenile Law, Criminal Defense, Driving While Intoxicated, Drug Crimes, Felonies, Misdemeanors.

RICHARD LAW OFFICE, LLC

ASHLAND, OHIO

(See Wooster)

Corporate, Business Law, Oil and Gas, Personal Injury, Wrongful Death, Estate Planning, Probate, Divorce, Dissolution, Real Estate, Litigation, Probate Avoidance.

DAVID WIRTH

ASHLAND, OHIO

(See Columbus)

Insurance Law, Negligence, Legal Malpractice, Subrogation, Personal Injury, Probate.

ANDREWS & PONTIUS LLC

4817 STATE ROAD
SUITE 100
P.O. BOX 10
ASHTABULA, OHIO 44005-0010
Telephone: 440-998-6835
Fax: 440-992-6336
URL: http://www.andrewspontius.com

General and Trial Practice. Civil Litigation, Corporation and Business Law, Personal Injury, Medical Malpractice, Complex Tort, Commercial Litigation, Municipal Law, Insurance Defense, Labor and Employment, School Law, Domestic Relations and Family Law, Real Estate Probate and Estate Planning.

DAVID E. PONTIUS, born Ashtabula, Ohio, December 10, 1952; admitted to bar, 1979, Ohio. *Education:* The Ohio State University (B.A., 1974); University of Toledo (J.D., 1979). Rock Creek Village Solicitor, 1988—. Orwell Village Solicitor, 1999-2003; City Solicitor, Ashtabula, 1983-1985. Jefferson Village Solicitor, 1989-1992. Member, Ohio Supreme Court Commission on Certification of Attorneys as Specialists, 1993-2000. Member, Board of Directors, Northeast Region, FirstMerit Bank, N.A. *Member:* Ashtabula County (President, 1992-1993), Ohio State and American Bar Associations; The Association of Trial Lawyers of America; Ohio Academy of Trial Lawyers (Former Member, Board of Governors). ***PRACTICE AREAS:*** Negligence Law; Medical Malpractice; Legal Malpractice; Complex Tort; Commercial Litigation; Municipal Law; Estate Planning; Trial Practice. ***Email:*** dpontius@andrewspontius.com

MARK W. ANDREWS, born Ashtabula, Ohio, March 21, 1950; admitted to bar, 1976, Ohio and U.S. District Court, Northern District of Ohio. *Education:* The Ohio State University (B.S., 1972); Cleveland Marshall College of Law (J.D., 1976). Acting Judge, Ashtabula Municipal Court. *Member:* Ashtabula County and Ohio State Bar Associations; Ohio Association of School Board Attorneys; National Association of School Board Attorneys. ***PRACTICE AREAS:*** School Law; Labor and Employment Law; Commercial Litigation; Probate; Insurance Defense; Corporate; Business Law; Real Estate; Trial Practice. ***Email:*** mandrews@andrewspontius.com

JEFFREY A. FORD, born Conneaut, Ohio, April 17, 1956; admitted to bar, 1982, Ohio. *Education:* Harding College; Ohio State University (B.S., 1979); Ohio State University (J.D., 1982). *Member:* Ashtabula County and Ohio State Bar Associations. ***PRACTICE AREAS:*** Negligence Law; Insurance Defense; Domestic Relations; Commercial Litigation; Probate; Trial Practice; Real Estate; Business Law. ***Email:*** jford@andrewspontius.com

PAMELA D. HOUSTON, born Warren, Ohio, July 30, 1970; admitted to bar, 1999, Ohio. *Education:* University of Akron (B.A., 1992); Cleveland Marshall College of Law (J.D., 1999). *Member:* Ashtabula County (Chairperson, Legal Aid Pro Bono Committee, 2003), Ohio State and American Bar Associations; Ohio Women's Bar Association (11th District Trustee, 2000-2002; Executive Board Member, 2003—; Vice President, 2004); Ohio Academy of Trial Lawyers; Association of Trial Lawyers of America. ***PRACTICE AREAS:*** Domestic Relations; Negligence; Medical Malpractice; Trial Practice; Personal Injury. ***Email:*** phouston@andrewspontius.com

---

PHILIP E. CORDOVA, born Clark Air Force Base, Philippines, September 17, 1967; admitted to bar, 2001, Ohio. *Education:* Kent State University (B.B.A., 1990); University of Akron (J.D., 2001). *Member:* Ashtabula County, Lake County and Ohio State Bar Associations. ***PRACTICE AREAS:*** Domestic Relations; Juvenile Law; Criminal Defense. ***Email:*** pcordova@andrewspontius.com

DUANE J. DUBSKY, born Cleveland, Ohio, April 10, 1947; admitted to bar, 1973, Ohio. *Education:* Ohio University (B.A., cum laude, 1969); Cleveland State University (J.D., 1973). *Member:* Ashtabula County (President, 1988-1989) and Ohio State Bar Associations; Ohio Academy of Trial Lawyers; Association of Trial Lawyers of America. ***PRACTICE AREAS:*** Insurance Law; Negligence Law; Trial Practice; Domestic Relations; Probate; Estate Planning; Real Estate. ***Email:*** ddubsky@andrewspontius.com

REPRESENTATIVE CLIENTS: Heritage Insurance Co.; Lightning Rod Mutual Insurance Co.; Motorists Insurance Co.; Ohio Casualty Insurance Co.; Ohio Insurance Guaranty Assn.; Ohio Mutual Insurance Corp.; State Automobile Insurance Co.; The Cincinnati Insurance Co.; United Ohio Insurance Co.; Western Reserve Mutual Insurance Co.; Jenneco Chemicals, Inc.; EPEC Polymers, Inc.; A.E. Steel Erectors, Inc.; Arthur Louis Steel Co.; Dalin Mold & Machine; Lake city Plating Co.; Penco Tool Inc.; Pickens Plastics, Inc.; Premium Air, Inc.; Resinet Products U.S., Inc.; The ESAB Group, Inc.; White Consolidated Industries, Inc.; Ashtabula Area City Schools Board of Education; Conneaut Area City Schools Board of Education; Geneva Area City Schools Board of Education; Saybrook Township Board of Trustees; Village of Rock Creek, Ohio; CIR, Inc.; Delta Railroad Construction, Inc.; Detrick Industrial Piping, Inc.; Girard Nurseries; Halman, Inc.; Hughes Roller Building Co.; James Drilling Co.; Meridan Oil & Gas Enterprises, Inc.; Nelson Sand & Gravel; Perry Construction Co.; Simak Trucking; Union Industrial Contractors, Inc.; Nassief Ford Mercury Toyota Hyundai; Nassief Pontiac Cadillac, Inc.; North Coast Auto Group; Conncaut, Ltd.; Sunset West; Kinnunen Realty, Inc.; Lake Erie Real Estate Co.; Ashtabula Yacht Sales & Services, Inc.; Jack's Marine, Inc.; Ashtabula Broadcasting Corporation, Inc.; Carpet Mart of Ashtabula, Inc.; C. Herron & Associates, Inc.; Kennedy-Billman Funeral Home, Inc.; Premiere Fitness & Health, Inc.; Radio Enterprises of Ohio, Inc.; Ross-Billman Funeral Home, Inc.
REFERENCE: First Merit, N.A.

BASHEIN & BASHEIN CO., L.P.A.

ASHTABULA, OHIO

(See Cleveland)

Product Liability, Automobile Accidents, Insurance Law, Appellate Practice, Personal Injury Defense, Medical Malpractice, Workers Compensation, Commercial Litigation. Labor and Employment, General Practice.

KLEIN & CARNEY CO., L.P.A.

ASHTABULA, OHIO

(See Cleveland)

Personal Injury, Medical Malpractice, Insurance Law, Wrongful Death, Motor Vehicle Accidents, Nursing Home Negligence, Workers Compensation.

DAVID C. SHELDON

4109 LAKE AVENUE
P.O. BOX 1152
ASHTABULA, OHIO 44005-1152
Telephone: 440-998-6923
Fax: 440-998-3442
Email: dcshel@alltel.net
URL: http://www.lawyers.com/davidcsheldon

Personal Injury, Automobile Accidents and Injuries, Wills, Estates, Probate, Criminal, Family Law, Divorce, Domestic Relations, Commercial Transactions.

DAVID C. SHELDON, born Conneaut, Ohio, July 17, 1945; admitted to bar, 1973, Ohio. *Education:* Miami University (B.A., 1967); University of Virginia (J.D., 1973). Assistant County Prosecutor, 1976-1979, 1984-1996. *Member:* Ashtabula County and Ohio State Bar Associations; Ohio Academy of Trial Lawyers. ***PRACTICE AREAS:*** Personal Injury Law; Automobile Accidents and Injuries; Wills; Estates; Probate; Criminal; Family Law; Divorce; Domestic Relations; Commercial Transactions.

DAVID M. SPOTTS

Established in 1991
6847 LAKE ROAD WEST
P.O. BOX 3046
ASHTABULA, OHIO 44005-3046
Telephone: 440-964-6466
Fax: 440-964-6502
Email: admiral@maritimelaw.com
URL: http://www.maritimelaw.com

Admiralty, General Civil Practice in all State and Federal Courts, Personal Injury, Insurance, Products, Environmental, Liability Law, Trials/and Appeals.

DAVID M. SPOTTS, born Cleveland, Ohio, September 28, 1949; admitted to bar, 1975, Ohio; 1986, Illinois. *Education:* United States Merchant Marine Academy (B.S., 1972); Cleveland Marshall College of Law (J.D., cum laude, 1975). *Member:* Cuyahoga County and Ashtabula County Bar Associations; Federal Bar Association; Maritime Law Association of the United States; International Shipmasters Association; American Bureau Yachting Council.

REPRESENTATIVE CLIENTS: AMAX Incorporated; Cyprus Minerals Corporation; Lakes Pilots Association, Inc.; Erie Leasing, Inc.; Western Great Lakes Pilots Association; ACE-Inamar Insurance Company; Marine Officers Protective Syndicate; Goudreau Management Corp.; Pinney Dock & Transport Company; AIG Marine Insurance.

WARREN AND YOUNG PLL

134 WEST 46TH STREET
P.O. BOX 2300
ASHTABULA, OHIO 44005-2300
Telephone: 440-997-6175
Facsimile: 440-992-9114
URL: http://www.warrenyoung.com

General and Trial Practice. Corporation and Business Law, Labor and Employment Law, Insurance Defense, Civil Litigation, Real Estate, Probate and Estate Planning Law.

FIRM PROFILE: Warren and Young PLL has provided high-quality, cost-effective legal services in northeast Ohio since 1921. Our clients range from individuals and families, to locally based manufacturing and service businesses, to Fortune 500 companies with a regional presence. Our attorneys apply their knowledge, experience and judgment in their areas of concentration, and utilize up-to-date technology to deliver timely, professional advice and service in

(This Listing Continued)

WARREN AND YOUNG PLL, Ashtabula—Continued

the areas of business formation and transactions, employment and labor matters, general and defense litigation, real estate, and estate planning and administration. Our objective is to add value to each engagement we undertake.

THEODORE E. WARREN (1897-1969)

MYRON H. YOUNG (1910-1971)

WILLIAM E. RIEDEL, born September 6, 1942; admitted to bar, 1969, Ohio; 1973, U.S. District Court, Northern District of Ohio; 1974, U.S. Tax Court; 1994, U.S. Supreme Court. *Education:* Adelbert College of Case Western Reserve University (B.B.A., cum laude, 1964); Graduate School of Business of Case Western Reserve University (M.B.A., 1966); Case Western University School of Law (J.D., 1969). *Member:* Cleveland and Ohio State (Member, Litigation Section Board of Governors, 1992-1998) Bar Associations; Ohio Association of Civil Trial Attorneys; Defense Research Institute. ***REPORTED CASES:*** U.S. Supreme Court, Reynoldsville Casket Co. vs. Hyde (1995) 514 U.S. 749. ***PRACTICE AREAS:*** Civil Litigation; Insurance Law; Negligence Law. ***Email:*** wriedel@warrenyoung.com

CARL F. MULLER, born September 12, 1947; admitted to bar, 1972, Ohio; 1973, U.S. District Court, Northern District of Ohio and U.S. Supreme Court. *Education:* Grinnell College (B.A., with honors, 1969); Cornell University (J.D., 1972). Author: (OACTA) "The Defense of Sexual Harassment Claims," 1988; (Ohio CLE Institute) "New Issues Affecting Employment," 1989, 1991, 1992, 1993, 1995; "Critical Employment & Environmental Issues in the Transfer of a Small Business," 1993, 1996; "Emerging Issues in the Wake of Ellerth & Faragher," 1999-2001; "Mandatory Arbitration of Ohio Employment Claims," 1997-2004; (Institute of Business Law) "Reductions in Force: Planning and Risk Management Strategies," 1994, 1996; (Business Laws, Inc.) "Critical Employment Law Issues in the Sale of a Small Business: An Overview for the General Practitioner," 1994; "Effective Risk Management of FMLA, ADA, and Related Liabilities," 2004; (FICC) "The Defense of Sexual Harassment Claims," 1994; "Sexual Harassment Claims: A Risk Management Primer for Law Firms and Law Departments," 1995; Employment Law Discrimination Editor, FICC Update, 1995; "Mandatory Arbitration of Employment Claims," Vol. 48, No. 4, FICC Quarterly; "Heading Off Harassment Suits," The Ohio Lawyer, 1998; The Corporate Analyst, Vol. 7, No. 2, Feb. 1995 "The Defense of Sexual Harassment Claims." Lecturer: OACTA Annual Meeting, 1988, "Defense of Sexual Harassment Claims"; Ohio CLE Institute "Effective Risk Management of FMLA, ADA and Related Liabilities," 2003; "Employment Law," 1989, 1991, 1993 and 1994; "Employment Litigation," 1992, 1993, 1995, 1996; "Buying and Selling a Small Business the Right Way," 1993, 1994, 1995, 1996; Trial Demonstration, "Jury Trial Litigation of the Wrongful Discharge Case," 1994; Workshop, "Jury Trial Litigation of the Sexual Harassment Case," 1994; Workshop, "Advising Employers On How to Discipline and Terminate Employees," 1995, 1996; "Corporate Counsel: Strategies for Success: Employment Issues: How to Stay Out of Court and More." Ohio Courts of Appeals Judges Association Summer Seminar, "Top Ten Ohio Employment Law Decisions," 1994; FICC Annual Meeting, "The Defense of Sexual Harassment Claims," 1994; "Enforcing Employment Agreements Requiring Compulsory Arbitration of Employment Claims in the Wake of Gilmer," 1996; Cleveland Bar Association Labor and Employment Law Seminar, "Investigating Sexual Harassment Complaints," 1997; ABA Annual Meeting of General Practice Section, "Sexual Harassment Litigation," with Judge Susan Webber Wright, 1999. Co-Author: "Critical Employment and Environmental Law Issues in the Transfer of a Small Business," Vol. 46, No. 3 (1996) FICC Quarterly. Editor: The Best of Labor and Employment Law (Ohio CLE Institute, 1st, 2nd, 3rd Editions); Employment Law Editor, FICC Update, 1995, 1996. *Member:* Ashtabula County (President, 1983-1984; Chairman Certified Local Grievance Committee, 1992-1993), Cleveland (Labor Section), Lake County (Labor and Employment Committee), Ohio State (Board of Governors, Labor Law and Employment Law Section, 1988-1998; Chairman, Labor and Employment Specialty Certification Board, 1997-2002) and American (Labor and Employment Law Section - Equal Employment Opportunity Committee) Bar Associations; Federation of Insurance & Corporate Counsel (Chairman, Employment and Civil Rights Section, 1996-1998); American Arbitration Association National Panel of Employment Neutrals. ***PRACTICE AREAS:*** Employment Litigation; Labor Law; Civil Litigation. ***Email:*** cmuller@warrenyoung.com

STUART W. CORDELL, born July 26, 1956; admitted to bar, 1981, Ohio and U.S. District Court, Northern District of Ohio. *Education:* Cornell University (A.B., 1978); Case Western Reserve University (J.D., 1981). Lecturer: OSBA CLE Institute, Business Curriculum, 1994-1999; Ohio Grantmakers Forum, 2002-2004; National Conference of Bar Foundations, 2004. Member, 2002—, and Treasurer, 2003—, Ashtabula County Convention Facilities Authority. *Member:* Cleveland Bar Association; Ohio State Bar Association (Member, Council of Delegates, 2001—); Ohio State Bar Foundation (Trustee, 1999—; President Elect, 2003; President, 2004; Immediate Past President, 2005); Civic Development Corporation of Ashtabula County (Trustee, 1993—; President, 2001—); Ohio Grantmakers Forum (Member, Public Policy Committee); Robert S. Morrison Foundation (Trustee, 1990—). ***LANGUAGES:*** French. ***PRACTICE AREAS:*** Business and Corporation Law; Nonprofit Organizations; Real Estate Law; Estate Planning; Probate. ***Email:*** scordell@warrenyoung.com

JEFFREY L. COXON, born November 25, 1966; admitted to bar, 1992, Ohio; 1994, U.S. District Court, Northern District of Ohio. *Education:* Miami University (B.S., magna cum laude, 1989); The Ohio State University (J.D., 1992). Order of the Coif. Ohio State Law Journal. Member, Board of Directors 1997-2002, Chairman 2000, Ashtabula Area Chamber of Commerce. Member, Board of Directors, American Red Cross (Ashtabula Chapter) 1997-1999. Ashtabula County Rotary Foundation, 1997-2000; Ashtabula County Council on Aging, 1994-1997; ACMC Foundation, 2005—. ***PRACTICE AREAS:*** Business and Corporation Law; Real Estate; Estate Planning; Probate. ***Email:*** jcoxon@warrenyoung.com

CRAIG F. SERNIK, born March 8, 1971; admitted to bar, 1997, Ohio and U.S. District Court, Northern District of Ohio; 2003, U.S. District Court, Western District of Pennsylvania. *Education:* Allegheny College (B.A., with honors, 1993); Case Western Reserve University (J.D., 1997). Co-Author with Carl F. Muller (Partner) "Mandatory Arbitration of Employment Claims," Federation of Insurance and Corporate Counsel, Quarterly, Vol. 48, N.4, Summer, 1998. Lecturer: "Documenting the Hiring and the Termination Process," March, 1999; "Sexual Harassment Update in the Wake of *Oncale, Ellerth, Faragher and Kolstad,*" December, 1999; "Top Ten Deadly FMLA Traps for Unwary Employers," July, 2003; "Substance Abuse Programs and Substance Testing by Ohio Employers"; "Human Resources Management in a Violent World: Managing the Risks While Still Managing Your Employees,"; "Legal and Testing Issues for Drug-Free Employers," Ohio Bureau of Workers' Compensation State-Wide Annual Safety Congress and Exposition, 2004, 2005; "The Bermuda Triangle of Employment Law: The Deadly Intersection of ADA, FMLA and Workers' Compensation," September, 2005. Member: Board of Directors, Ashtabula County Workforce Improvement Board, 2002—; Geauga Ashtabula Portage Partnership Workforce Improvement Board, 2004—; Geauga Ashtabula Portage Partnership, Inc., 2004—. ***PRACTICE AREAS:*** Labor and Employment; Civil Litigation; Workers Compensation. ***Email:*** csernik@warrenyoung.com

RANDY A. VERMILYA, born Canton, Pennsylvania, May 13, 1958; admitted to bar, 1999, Ohio; 2000, U.S. District Court, Northern District of Ohio. *Education:* University of Pittsburgh (B.S., 1980); Cleveland State University (M.S., 1989); Case Western Reserve University (J.D., 1998). Member: American Oil Chemist Society, 1989-1996; American Chemical Society, 1996-2004. ***PRACTICE AREAS:*** Intellectual Property; Corporate; Litigation. ***Email:*** rvermilya@warrenyoung.com

KATHERINE S. BERNARDO, born Ashtabula, Ohio, February 14, 1974; admitted to bar, 2000, Ohio. *Education:* Cornell University (B.A., 1996); University of Pittsburgh (J.D., 1999). ***PRACTICE AREAS:*** Insurance Defense; Personal Injury; Criminal Law; Employment Litigation; Real Estate. ***Email:*** kbernardo@warrenyoung.com

RYAN M. ELLIS, born January 1, 1979; admitted to bar, 2004, Ohio; 2005, U.S. District Court, Northern District of Ohio. *Education:* Bowling Green State University (B.S., summa cum laude, 2001); Case Western Reserve University (J.D., cum laude, 2004). Case Western Reserve Law Review. Author: '"Electioneering Communication' Under the Bipartisan Campaign Reform Act of 2002; A Constitutional Reclassification of 'Express Advocacy,"' 54 Case W. Res. Law Rev. 187, 2003; "Absenteeism Due to a Work-Related Injury: A Critique of Ohio's Most Recent Public Policy Exceptions," 54 Case W. Res. Law Rev. 1415, 2004. ***PRACTICE AREAS:*** Litigation; Business Law; Real Estate. ***Email:*** rellis@warrenyoung.com

All attorneys are members of the Ashtabula County, Ohio State and American Bar Associations.

COLLEY SHROYER & ABRAHAM CO., L.P.A.

ATHENS, OHIO

(See Columbus)

Civil Trial Practice. Personal Injury, Medical Malpractice, Automobile Accidents, Wrongful Death, Railroad Accidents, Slip and Fall, Negligence, Product Liability and Toxic Torts.

LAVELLE LAW OFFICES, L.P.A.

Established in 1952

8 NORTH COURT STREET, 2ND FLOOR
P.O. BOX 661
ATHENS, OHIO 45701-0661
Telephone: 740-593-3347
Fax: 740-592-6656
Email: flavelle@eurekanet.com

Meigs County Office: 66717 State Route 124, Reedsville, 45772. Telephone: 740-378-6456. Fax: 740-592-6656.

Personal Injury, Real Estate, Oil and Gas Law, Custody, Divorce, Domestic Relations, Probate, Estate Planning, Public Sector, Administrative Agencies, Juvenile Law, Criminal Defense, Insurance Defense.

FRANCIS (FRANK) A. LAVELLE, born Athens, Ohio, April 15, 1955; admitted to bar, 1982, Ohio; 1984, U.S. District Court, Southern and Eastern Districts of Ohio; 1986, U.S. Court of Appeals, Sixth Circuit; 2001, U.S. Supreme Court. *Education:* Ohio University (B.A., cum laude, 1977); University of Cincinnati; Capital University Law School (J.D., 1982). Phi Gamma Mu. City Law Director, Nelsonville, 1995-1996. Solicitor, Village of Jacksonville, 1984—. Solicitor, Villages of Buchtel and Trimble, 1992—. Solicitor, Villages of Shawnee and Corning, 1999—. Special Counsel, Ohio Attorney General, 1985-1995. Title Insurance Agent, Ohio Bar Title Insurance Company. *Member:* Ohio Municipal Attorneys Association; Ohio Land Title Association. ***LANGUAGES:*** Spanish. ***PRACTICE AREAS:*** Personal Injury; Real Estate; Oil and Gas Law; Child Custody; Divorce; Domestic Relations; Probate; Estate Planning; Public Sector; Administrative Agencies; Juvenile Law; Criminal Defense; Insurance Defense. ***Email:*** flavelle@eurekanet.com

REPRESENTATIVE CLIENTS: Trimble Twp.; Waste Water Dist.; Southern Perry County Water District; Century Energy Management Co.; Biscayne Petroleum Corp.; Wayne Mutual Insurance Co.; Athens Apartments.

OLIVER LAW OFFICE

ATHENS, OHIO

(See Columbus)

Products Liability, Personal Injury, Wrongful Death, Latex Allergy Litigation, Medical Malpractice, Vioxx Litigation, Automobile Accidents, Insurance Law, Employment Discrimination.

(This Listing Continued)

THE PLYMALE PARTNERSHIP LLP

ATHENS, OHIO

(See Columbus)

Personal Injury, Products Liability, Wrongful Death, Medical Malpractice, Professional Negligence, Traumatic Brain Injury, Automobile Accidents, Nursing Home Torts, Civil Litigation.

ROURKE & BLUMENTHAL, LLP

ATHENS, OHIO

(See Columbus)

Personal Injury, Negligence, Products Liability, Medical Malpractice, Nursing Home Litigation, Wrongful Death, Intentional Tort, Insurance Disputes, Automobile Accidents, Civil Trial Practice, Aviation, Professional Liability.

SLOWIK & ROBINSON, LLC

ATHENS, OHIO

(See Columbus)

Labor and Employment Law, Immigration Law, Small Business Law, Alternative Dispute Resolution, Business Formations.

SOWASH, CARSON & FERRIER

Established in 1980

39 NORTH COLLEGE STREET
P.O. BOX 2629
ATHENS, OHIO 45701
Telephone: 740-594-8388
Fax: 740-593-6490
Email: scf@eurekanet.com

Criminal and Traffic Practice. Domestic Relations and Family Law, Labor and Employment Law, General Civil Trial and Appellate Practice, Nonprofit and Charitable Organizations, Business Law, Personal Injury, Wrongful Death, Historic Preservation Law, Employee Benefits, Agricultural Law, Zoning, Probate, Estate Planning, Intellectual Property Licensing, Technology Transfer.

MEMBERS OF FIRM

JONATHAN SOWASH, born Mansfield, Ohio, February 5, 1954; admitted to bar, 1980, Ohio; 1983, U.S. District Court, Southern District of Ohio; 1990, U.S. Court of Appeals, Sixth Circuit. *Education:* Bowling Green State University (B.A., magna cum laude, 1975); Ohio State University (J.D., 1979). Founding Member and Legal Counsel, Rural Action, 1981. Author: "Legal Issues Involving Worker Ownership in Ohio," The Ohio Buyout Handbook, Kent State University, 1987; "Poverty and the Environment: Making the Link," Appalachian Ohio Public Interest Report, Winter 1992. Managing Partner, Sowash, Carson & Ferrier, 1988—. Legal Counsel: Sunpower, Inc., www.sunpower.com; Appalachian Center for Economic Networks. *Member:* Athens County and Ohio State Bar Associations. ***PRACTICE AREAS:*** Business Law; Business Formation; Business Succession Planning; Buying and Selling of Businesses; Emerging Growth Companies; International Joint Ventures; Strategic Alliances; Intellectual Property; International Intellectual Property; International Licensing; Conservation Easements; Land Trusts; Farm and Ranch Law; Forestry Law; Economic Development; Timber and Logging Law; Historic Preservation; Trusts and Estates; Wills.

HERMAN A. CARSON, born Parkersburg, West Virginia, August 4, 1955; admitted to bar, 1980, Ohio; 1981, U.S. District Court, Southern District of Ohio; 1990, U.S. Court of Appeals, Sixth Circuit. *Education:* Ohio Northern University (B.A., 1977); Ohio State University (J.D. with honors, 1980). Rule 65 Certified Lead Counsel for Capital Cases, 1987—. Chairman, Athens County Public Defender Commission, 1981-1991. Solicitor, Village of Glouster, 1987-1993 and 2005. Acting Judge, Athens County Municipal Court, 1986—. *Member:* Athens County (President, 1997-1998) and Ohio State (Member, Criminal Justice Committee, 1986—) Bar Associations; Ohio Academy of Trial Lawyers (Member, Board of Trustees, 1991-1993); Ohio Association of Criminal Defense Lawyers (Founding Member and Board of Directors, 1987—; Treasurer, 1995-1999; President, 2000-2001). ***PRACTICE AREAS:*** Criminal Defense; Driving While Intoxicated; Personal Injury; Wrongful Death; General Civil Litigation; Insurance Litigation; Automobile Insurance Defense; General Liability Defense; Real Estate Litigation; Wills; Probate.

BETH B. FERRIER, born Akron, Ohio, January 19, 1958; admitted to bar, 1985, Ohio; 1987, Georgia; 1995, U.S. District Court, Southern District of Ohio. *Education:* College of Wooster; University of Miami (A.B., 1980); Case Western Reserve University (J.D., 1985). Associate, Roetzel & Andress, Akron, OH, 1985-1987. Member, Board of Directors, Appalachian By Design, A Training and Development Corporation for Appalachian Artisans, 1994—; Member, Athens County Board of MR/DD, 1996-1999. *Member:* Athens County and Ohio State Bar Associations. ***PRACTICE AREAS:*** Business Law; Nonprofit and Charitable Organizations; Intellectual Property Licensing; Trusts and Estates; Wills; Probate; Employee Benefits; Elder Law; Labor and Employment.

MADELINE RAMBO, born Zanesville, Ohio, June 20, 1954; admitted to bar, 1991, Ohio; 1993, U.S. District Court, Southern District of Ohio. *Education:* Ohio University (B.S.Ed., 1976); Ohio State University (J.D., 1991). Athens County Assistant Prosecutor, CSEA, 1991-1992. *Member:* Athens County and Ohio State Bar Associations. ***PRACTICE AREAS:*** Family Law; Adoption Law; Education Law.

ROBERT A. MILLER, born Zanesville, Ohio, March 17, 1964; admitted to bar, 1989, Ohio, U.S. District, Southern District of Ohio. *Education:* Kentucky Christian College (B.S., 1986); Capital University (J.D., 1989). Former Associate: Robert Allen Miller Co. LPA; Graham, McClelland & Ransbottom. *Member:* Ohio State Bar Association; Ohio Association of Criminal Defense Lawyers; National Association of Criminal Defense Lawyers. ***PRACTICE AREAS:*** Criminal Law; Personal Injury; Civil Practice; Family Law. ***Email:*** miller@scflawoffice.com

(This Listing Continued)

REPRESENTATIVE CLIENTS: Rural Action; Ohio Casualty Insurance Co.; Tri-County Mental Health and Counseling Services, Inc.; West American Insurance; Appalachian Center for Economic Networks; Appalachian By Design, Inc.; Sunpower Inc.; ReUse Industries; Ohio Public Defender Commission; Athens AIDS Task Force; Ohio Mutual Insurance; United Ohio Insurance.

WALKER & WALKER CO., L.P.A.

Established in 1982

211 COLUMBUS ROAD
P.O. BOX 2470
ATHENS, OHIO 45701
Telephone: 740-594-8228
Fax: 740-593-5456
Email: walker@walkerlawlpa.com
URL: http://www.walkerlawlpa.com

General Civil and Criminal Practice. Probate and Real Estate Law. School Law, Elder Law. Insurance Defense. Personal Injury. Family and Domestic Law. Corporate and Business Law. Oil and Gas, Coal and Mineral Law.

WM. PARKER WALKER (1917-1985)

WILLIAM R. WALKER, born Athens, Ohio, August 18, 1950; admitted to bar, 1978, Ohio. *Education:* Ohio University (A.B., 1975); University of Toledo (J.D., 1978). Member, Athens City Board of Education, 1979-1982. Board of Directors: Big Brothers/Big Sisters of Athens, 1994—; McClure Foundation, 1994—. *Member:* Athens County (President, 1987-1988), Ohio State and American Bar Associations; Ohio School Boards Association. [Officer, JAGC, USAR]. ***PRACTICE AREAS:*** Civil Trial; Real Estate; Probate Law; Business Organization and Law. ***Email:*** bill@walkerlawlpa.com

BRIAN R. WALKER, born Athens, Ohio, February 29, 1956; admitted to bar, 1985, Ohio; 1986, U.S. District Court, Northern District of Ohio; 1993, U.S. District Court, Southern District of Ohio. *Education:* Ohio University (B.F.A., cum laude, 1978); University of Toledo (J.D., cum laude, 1985). Instructor, Ohio University 1999—. Member, Board of Directors, Athens County Chapter of the American Red Cross, 1998-2001 (Chairman, 1999-2000). Trustee, Athens County Convention and Visitors Bureau, 2005—. Athens County Young Life Committee, 2003—; Chairman, 2005—. *Member:* Athens County and Ohio State Bar Associations; Ohio Academy of Trial Lawyers; The Association of Trial Lawyers of America. ***PRACTICE AREAS:*** Personal Injury; Insurance Defense; General Civil Litigation; Family Law; Domestic Relations; Misdemeanors. ***Email:*** brian@walkerlawlpa.com

REPRESENTATIVE CLIENTS: State Automobile Mutual Insurance Co.; Athens Landmark, Inc.; Stewart MacDonald Manufacturing Co.; National Business Incubation Association; Oak Hill Bank; Century National Bank; Tri-County Joint Vocational School; First National Bank of McConnelsville; Integrated Services Systems, Inc.; SOG-Southeastern Ohio Voluntary Education Cooperative; Wyngate Condominium Association; Athens Metropolitan Housing Authority.
AGENTS FOR: Lawyers Title Insurance Co. References: Century National Bank; Hocking Valley Bank of Athens.

L. E. BELARDO LLC

36368 DETROIT ROAD, SUITE A
P.O. BOX 419
AVON, OHIO 44011-0419
Telephone: 440-934-2199
Fax: 440-934-2289
Email: belardo@centurytel.net
URL: http://www.belardolaw.com

Family Law, Divorce, Child Custody, Child Support, Visitation Rights, Wills and Probate, Criminal Law, Drug Crimes, DUI/DWI, Juvenile Crimes, Parole and Probation, Traffic Violations, Real Estate, General Practice.

MEMBER OF FIRM

LEE E. BELARDO, born Pittsburgh, Pennsylvania, July 24, 1967; admitted to bar, 1995, Ohio; 1996, U.S. District Court, Northern District of Ohio. *Education:* Youngstown State University (B.S., 1988); Cleveland Marshall College of Law (J.D., 1995). *Member:* Lorain County, Ohio State (Member, Board of Governors, 2005-2007) and American Bar Associations; Ohio Association of Criminal Defense Lawyers. ***PRACTICE AREAS:*** Wills; Probate; Domestic Relations; Criminal Defense.

THE SPIKE & MECKLER LAW FIRM, LLP

AVON, OHIO

(See Elyria)

General Civil Trial Practice. Personal Injury, Medical Malpractice, Family and Domestic Relations, Real Estate, Probate.

WICKENS, HERZER, PANZA, COOK & BATISTA

A LEGAL PROFESSIONAL ASSOCIATION

Established in 1932

35765 CHESTER ROAD
AVON, OHIO 44011-1262
Telephone: 440-930-8000
Facsimile: 440-937-4466
Cleveland Direct Line: 216-447-4418
Cleveland Facsimile: 216-447-0998
Email: pdahm@wickenslaw.com
URL: http://www.wickenslaw.com

General Civil Practice. Corporate, Taxation, Professional Corporations, Pension, Profit Sharing, Employee Benefits, ERISA, Partnership, Real Estate, Environmental, Labor and Employment Relations; Health Care and Hospital, Public Law, Municipal Bonds, Libel and Media Law, Probate and Estate Planning Law, Insurance Defense, Trials and Appeals, Banking, Bankruptcy.

D. A. COOK (1883-1968)

DAN K. COOK (1915-1976)

WILLIAM G. WICKENS (1905-2002)

DANIEL P. BATISTA, born Toledo, Ohio, December 3, 1934; admitted to bar, 1959, Ohio. *Education:* Miami University (B.A., 1956); Western Reserve University (LL.B., 1959). Special Agent, Federal Bureau of Investigation, 1959-1962. *Member:* Lorain County and Ohio State Bar Associations. ***PRACTICE AREAS:*** Health Care; Banking; General Civil Practice; Real Estate; Corporate Law. **Email:** dbatista@wickenslaw.com

DANIEL A. COOK, born Lorain, Ohio, February 28, 1943; admitted to bar, 1968, Ohio. *Education:* Bucknell University (B.S.B.A., 1965); University of Michigan (J.D., 1967). *Member:* Lorain County (Past Chairman, Legal Ethics and Grievance Committee) and Ohio State Bar Associations. ***PRACTICE AREAS:*** Litigation. **Email:** dcook@wickenslaw.com

DAVID L. HERZER, born Lorain, Ohio, March 3, 1945; admitted to bar, 1970, Ohio; 1976, U.S. Tax Court; 1982, Florida; 1985, U.S. Supreme Court and Colorado; 1989, New York. *Education:* Yale University (B.A., magna cum laude, Phi Beta Kappa; Omicron Delta Epsilon, 1967); Harvard University (J.D., 1970). Member, Yale Alumni Association of Cleveland. *Member:* Lorain County, Ohio State and New York State Bar Associations; The Florida Bar. ***PRACTICE AREAS:*** Mergers and Acquisitions; Business Successions; Business Planning; Corporate; Hospital Law; Health Care; Business Organization; Business Taxation. **Email:** dherzer@wickenslaw.com

RICHARD D. PANZA, born Troy, New York, June 8, 1947; admitted to bar, 1973, Ohio; 1983, Florida; 1977, U. S. District Court, Northern District of Ohio; 1980, U.S. Tax Court; 1982, U.S. Claims Court; 1985, U.S. Supreme Court and Colorado; 1986, New York. *Education:* Marist College; State University of New York at Albany (B.A., 1970); Cleveland-Marshall College of Law (J.D., 1973). *Member:* Lorain County, Ohio State (Media Law and Environmental Law Sections), New York and American Bar Associations; The Florida Bar; Ohio Association of Civil Trial Attorneys. ***REPORTED CASES:*** Milkovich vs. Lorain Journal, 497 U.S. 1 (1990); Digital & Analog Design Corp. vs. North Supply Co., 63 Ohio St. 3d 657 (1992); Digital & Analog Design Corp. vs. North Supply Co., 44 Ohio St. 3d 36 (1989); Oney vs. Allen, 39 Ohio St. 3d 103 (1988); Scott vs. News Herald, 25 Ohio St. 3d 243 (1986); Masley vs. Lorain, 48 Ohio St. 2d 335 (1976); DeSario vs. I.E.L., 68 Ohio App. 3d 117 (1991). ***PRACTICE AREAS:*** Litigation; Environmental; Libel Defense. **Email:** rpanza@wickenslaw.com

ROBERT P. ELLIS, JR., born Lorain, Ohio, December 2, 1949; admitted to bar, 1975, Ohio; 1976, U.S. Tax Court; 1985, Colorado. *Education:* Massachusetts Institute of Technology (B.S., 1972); The Ohio State University (J.D., cum laude, 1975). Lecturer: Seminars for Lorain County Association of Realtors; Building Industries Association; Lorain County Bar Association. Instructor: Real Estate Law, Lorain County Community College, 1985-1990. *Member:* Lorain County Bar Association (President, 1988-1989). ***PRACTICE AREAS:*** Commercial Real Estate; Residential Real Estate Development; Business Organization; Tax Law. **Email:** rellis@wickenslaw.com

DAVID C. WIERSMA, born Lakewood, Ohio, May 11, 1947; admitted to bar, 1976, Ohio. *Education:* University of Pittsburgh (B.A., 1969); Cleveland-Marshall College of Law (J.D., cum laude, 1976). License, Ohio Title Insurance. Member: North Coast Estate Planning Council; Estate Planning Council of Cleveland; Board of Trustees, Specialty Hospital of Lorain; President, Lorain Foundation; Former Trustee, Lorain County Law Library Association. *Member:* Lorain County (Chairman, Probate and Trust Section) and Ohio State Bar Associations. (Certified Specialist in Estate Planning, Trust and Probate Law, Ohio State Bar Association). ***PRACTICE AREAS:*** Probate; Trust Law; Estate Planning. **Email:** dwiersma@wickenslaw.com

JAMES W. MOENNICH, born Cleveland, Ohio, April 26, 1951; admitted to bar, 1977, Ohio. *Education:* The Ohio State University (B.S., 1973); Case Western Reserve University (J.D., 1977). *Member:* Cleveland, Lorain County and Ohio State Bar Associations; American Health Lawyers Association. ***PRACTICE AREAS:*** Bankruptcy; Debtor and Creditor; International Transactions; Corporate; Commercial Law; Banking Law; Real Estate; Health Care. **Email:** jmoennich@wickenslaw.com

THOMAS PILLARI, born Lorain, Ohio, May 28, 1947; admitted to bar, 1973, Ohio; 1982, Florida; 2003, U.S. Supreme Court. *Education:* United States Air Force Academy (B.S., 1969); University of Chicago (J.D., 1972); University of Miami (LL.M. Estate Planning, 1990). Fellow, American College of Trust and Estates Counsel, 2002. Assistant Professor, Department of Law, United States Air Force Academy, 1976-1978. Lecturer: Estate and Gift Taxation, Cleveland-Marshall College of Law, 1981-1982; Ohio Society of Certified Public Accountants, 1988-1993. Member, Board of Trustees, LCCC Foundation. Trustee, John R. Nichol Foundation. *Member:* Lorain County, Cleveland (Member, Estate Planning Council), Ohio State (Member, Board of Governors, Estate Planning, Trusts and Probate Law Section) and American Bar Associations; The Florida Bar. [Captain, JAG, U.S. Air Force, 1969-1978]. (Certified Specialist in Estate Planning, Trust and Probate Law,

(This Listing Continued)

Ohio State Bar Association). ***PRACTICE AREAS:*** Probate; Estate Planning; Probate Litigation; Wills; Trust Planning; Business Succession Planning. **Email:** tpillari@wickenslaw.com

RICHARD A. NAEGELE, born Sandusky, Ohio, February 25, 1951; admitted to bar, 1979, Ohio; 1980, U.S. District Court, Northern District of Ohio and U.S. Tax Court; 1985, U.S. Supreme Court; 1986, Colorado. *Education:* Ohio University (B.A., cum laude, 1973; M.A., 1975); Case Western Reserve University (J.D., 1979). Author: "Pension Overview and Update for Non-Pension Attorneys," Ohio State Bar Association, 1999, updated annually; "Protect Your Investments: Creditors' Rights Against Tax Qualified Plans and IRAs," Tennessee CPA Journal, January 2003, republished, Journal of Pension Planning and Compliance, Spring 2003; "Creditors' Rights: Tax-Qualified Plans and IRAs," The CPA Journal, New York State Society of CPAs, October 2000, republished, Journal of Pension Planning and Compliance, Winter, 2001; "Individual Retirement Accounts after TRA '97," The CPA Journal, July 1998; "Individual Retirement Accounts: A User's Guide to the New and Varied World of IRAs," Journal of Deferred Compensation, Spring 1998; "Multiemployer Pension Plan Withdrawal Liability," Journal of Pension Planning and Compliance, Winter 1996; "Working through the IRS and DOL Voluntary Compliance Programs," Journal of Pension Planning and Compliance, Spring 1996; "An Overview of Form 5500 Filing Requirements," Journal of Pension Planning and Compliance, Fall 1996. Lecturer: Ohio State Bar Association; Ohio Academy of Trial Lawyers; Ohio, Indiana, Kentucky, New Mexico, Oklahoma, Rhode Island, Tennessee and West Virginia Societies of Certified Public Accountants; Case Western Reserve University School of Law Tax Seminars; University of Montana School of Law Tax Institutes; Ohio State University School of Law Pension and Benefits Seminars. Named Outstanding Seminar Instructor 1988-1989 by AICPA and Ohio Society of CPAs. Appointed Special Master by U.S. District Court to oversee operation of multiemployer pension plan, 1994. Appointed Plan Administrator by U.S. Bankruptcy Court to Oversee distress termination of defined benefit pension plans with PBCG, 1994-1995. Board of Editorial Advisors, Journal of Pension Planning & Compliance, 1996—. *Member:* Lorain County and Ohio State Bar Associations. ***PRACTICE AREAS:*** Pension; Employee Benefits; ERISA; ESOP; Pension Litigation. **Email:** rnaegele@wickenslaw.com

MARSHA L. COLLETT, born Urbana, Ohio, September 15, 1950; admitted to bar, 1980, Ohio; 1987, Colorado. *Education:* The Ohio State University (B.A., summa cum laude, 1972); Case Western Reserve University (J.D., 1980). Member, Order of the Coif. License, Ohio Title Insurance, Ohio Department of Insurance, 1994. Former Board Member, Lorain Palace Civic Center, Inc. Former Chair, Ohio Coastal Resources Advisory Council. *Member:* Lorain County Bar Association (President, 1999-2000; Chair, Real Estate/Environmental Law Section). ***PRACTICE AREAS:*** Real Estate; Environmental; Securities; Administrative Law. **Email:** mcollett@wickenslaw.com

WILLIAM F. KOLIS, JR., born Pittsfield, Massachusetts, November 4, 1955; admitted to bar, 1980, Ohio; 1981, U.S. District Court, Northern District of Ohio; 1985, U.S. Tax Court; 1986, U.S. Supreme Court; 1987, U.S Claims Court; U.S. Court of Appeals, Sixth Circuit. *Education:* Case Western Reserve University (B.A., with honors, cum laude, in History, 1977; J.D., 1980). *Member:* Lorain County and Ohio State (Member, Media Law Committee) Bar Associations. ***PRACTICE AREAS:*** Litigation; Business Law; Environmental; Media Law; Construction Law; Personal Injury; Family Law. **Email:** wkolis@wickenslaw.com

CHARLES J. PAWLUKIEWICZ, born Grand Rapids, Michigan, December 13, 1946; admitted to bar, 1983, Ohio; U.S. District Court, Northern District of Ohio; 1984, U.S. Court of Appeals, Sixth Circuit; 1992, U.S. District Court, Eastern District of Michigan. *Education:* Murray State University (B.S., 1970); Cleveland-Marshall College of Law (J.D., cum laude, 1983). *Member:* Lorain County and American Bar Associations. ***PRACTICE AREAS:*** Insurance; Environmental; General Civil Litigation; Lender Liability; RICO. **Email:** chuckp@wickenslaw.com

MARK P. ALTIERI, born New Rochelle, New York, June 19, 1952; admitted to bar, 1980, Ohio. *Education:* Ohio University (B.S., summa cum laude, 1974); Cleveland-Marshall College of Law (J.D., 1979); New York University (LL.M., in Taxation, 1982). Certified Public Accountant. Certified Management Accountant. Certified Financial Planner. Author: "Providing Life Insurance and Other Incidental Benefits Through Qualified Retirement Plans After TEFRA," The Tax Adviser, 1984; "Functional Disparity Between Section 336 and 337 Liquidations," The Tax Adviser, 1984; "Discriminatory Methods of Compensating Key Employees in Closely Held Corporations," The Tax Adviser, 1984; "Church Maintained Tax-Sheltered Annuity Plans," The Journal of Pension Planning and Compliance, 1989; "Nonqualified Deferred Compensation Arrangements," The Tax Adviser, 1995; "Income Tax Distinctions Between S Corporations and LLC's," Ohio CPA Journal, 1995; "Considerations in Determining Whether to Elect S Corporation and LLC Status," The Tax Adviser, 1996; "Deferred Compensation Agreements and ERISA Pension Plan Compliance," Ohio CPA Journal, 1996; "Attacks on the Substance of S Stock Transfers," The Tax Adviser, 1997; "Nonqualified Deferred Compensation Agreements: Tax and Accounting Implications," The CPA Journal, 1998; "Avoiding the Section 7206(2) Criminal Tax Penalty for False or Fraudulent Return Preparation," The Tax Adviser, 1998; "IRA's After TRA '97," The CPA Journal, 1998; "Creditors Rights and Tax Qualified Plans," The CPA Journal, 2000; "Political Affiliation of Appointing President and the Outcome of Tax Court Cases," Judicature, 2001; "Partnerships LLC's and S Corporations: Selected Tax Issues," The CPA Journal, 2002; "Creditor Rights Against Tax Qualified Plans," The Journal of Pension Planning and Compliance," 2003. Associate Professor of Accounting, Kent State University, 1992—. *Member:* American Institute of CPAs; Ohio Society of CPAs. ***PRACTICE AREAS:*** Business Organization; Tax Law. **Email:** maltieri@wickenslaw.com

LINDA C. ASHAR, born Lorain, Ohio; admitted to bar, 1985, Ohio, U.S. Court of Appeals, Sixth Circuit and U.S. District Court, Northern District of Ohio; 1993, U.S. Tax Court. *Education:* Muskingum College (B.A., 1969); Kent State University (M.A., 1974); Akron University Law School (J.D., 1985). Member, University of Akron Law Review, 1983-1985. Author: "Statute of Limitations-Malpractice" and "Admissibility of Scientific Evidence," 17 Akron Law Review 701 (1984); "Surviving an OSHA Inspection," Stamping Journal, May 1998. Instructor: Legal Writing, University of Akron School of Law, 1985-1988. Member, Board of Trustees, United Way of Greater Lorain. *Member:* Lorain County Bar Association (Member, Executive Committee). ***PRACTICE AREAS:*** Litigation; Em-

(This Listing Continued)

ployment Relations; Fringe Benefits; Labor and Employment; EEOC; OSHA; Immigration Law; Government Agency Practice; Employment Civil Rights; National Labor Relations Act; Equine Law. **Email:** lashar@wickenslaw.com

JOHN D. RYBARCZYK, born Lorain, Ohio, July 1, 1962; admitted to bar, 1987, Ohio. *Education:* John Carroll University (B.S., cum laude, 1984); Cleveland-Marshall College of Law (J.D., cum laude, 1987). Lecturer, Ohio Society of CPA's, Lormon Education. *Member:* Lorain County and Ohio State Bar Associations. ***PRACTICE AREAS:*** Business Organization; Tax Law; Corporate; Mergers, Acquisitions and Divestitures; Debtor and Creditor; Health and Hospital; Non-Profit Corporations; Tax-Exempt Corporations. **Email:** johnr@wickenslaw.com

MATTHEW W. NAKON, born Cleveland, Ohio, November 4, 1963; admitted to bar, 1988, Ohio. *Education:* Baldwin-Wallace College (B.A., 1985); Cleveland-Marshall College of Law (J.D., cum laude, 1988). Member, Editorial Staff, Journal of Law and Health, 1987-1988. Member: Moot Court Board of Governors; National Order of Barristers. Recipient: Hugo Black Award, 1987; Dean's Award for Excellence in Oral Advocacy; West Publishing Award for Greatest Contribution to Scholarship. *Member:* Lorain County and Ohio State Bar Associations. ***PRACTICE AREAS:*** Litigation. **Email:** mnakon@wickenslaw.com

WILLIAM P. PRESCOTT, born Cleveland, Ohio; admitted to bar, 1989, Ohio. *Education:* Cleveland State University (B.B.A., 1972); Baldwin-Wallace College (Executive M.B.A., 1984); Cleveland-Marshall College of Law (J.D., 1988). Author: "Business, Legal, and Tax Planning for the Dental Practice," Second Edition, Penn Well Books, 2001, First Edition, 1994; Quarterly Supplement to Business, Legal and Tax Planning for the Dental Practice; "The Practice Acquisition Handbook," Randall K. Berning and Affiliates, 1997; "The Limited Liability Company and Other Entities for Dentistry," Randall K. Berning and Affiliates, 1996. *Member:* American Bar Association (Member, Taxation Section); Ohio State, Cleveland and Lorain County Bar Associations. ***PRACTICE AREAS:*** Representation of Dental Practices; Business Organization; Mergers and Acquisitions; Business Succession Planning; Corporate; Employee Benefits. **Email:** wprescott@wickenslaw.com

RACHELLE KUZNICKI ZIDAR, born Cleveland, Ohio, January 4, 1971; admitted to bar, 1996, Ohio. *Education:* Bowling Green State University (B.A., magna cum laude, 1993); Cleveland-Marshall College of Law (J.D., cum laude, 1996). National Order of Barrister, Inns of Court. Member, Moot Court Board of Governors. *Member:* Lorain County, Ohio State and American Bar Associations. ***PRACTICE AREAS:*** Litigation.

MICHAEL R. NIEDERBAUMER, born Cincinnati, Ohio, October 30, 1970; admitted to bar, 2000, Ohio. *Education:* Miami University (B.S., 1993); Case Western Reserve University (J.D., cum laude, 2000). *Member:* Lorain County and Ohio State Bar Associations. ***PRACTICE AREAS:*** Litigation. **Email:** michaeln@wickenslaw.com

RENNIE CARYN RUTMAN, born New York, N.Y., October 14, 1972; admitted to bar, 2001, Ohio. *Education:* John Carroll University (B.S., summa cum laude, 1998); Case Western Reserve University (J.D., cum laude, 2001). *Member:* Ohio State and American Bar Associations. ***PRACTICE AREAS:*** Estate Planning; Probate; Business Succession Planning; Elder Law. **Email:** rrutman@wickenslaw.com

SPENCER A. RYAN, born Elyria, Ohio, January 29, 1976; admitted to bar, 2001, Ohio. *Education:* Bloomsburg University (B.A., cum laude, 1998); Ohio Northern University (J.D., with distinction, 2001). Order of the Barristers. Chief Justice, Moot Court, 2000-2001. *Member:* Ohio State Bar Association. ***PRACTICE AREAS:*** Litigation. **Email:** sryan@wickenslaw.com

JAMES EDWARD PETERS, born Sandusky, Ohio, April 10, 1971; admitted to bar, 1997, Ohio. *Education:* Ohio University (B.B.A., cum laude, 1993); University of Akron School of Law (J.D., 1997). Member, Board of the Directors, Goodwill Industries of Lorain County. *Member:* Lorain County and Bar Association. ***PRACTICE AREAS:*** Business Organization; Tax Law; Health Care; Nonprofit Organizations Law; HIPPA Compliance. **Email:** jpeters@wickenslaw.com

TODD A. SCHRADER, born Cleveland, Ohio, April 18, 1965; admitted to bar, 1996, Ohio; 2002, U.S. Tax Court. *Education:* Case Western Reserve University (B.A., philosophy and public policy, magna cum laude, 1993); Cleveland-Marshall College of Law (J.D., 1996). Member: National Order of Barristers; Moot Court, 1994-1996. Chairman, Moot Court Board of Governors, 1995-1996. License, Ohio Title Insurance, Ohio Department of Insurance, 2004. Former Board Member, North Ridgeville Chamber of Commerce; Secretary, Board of Directors and Chair, Ambassadors Committee, Member, Membership Committee and Build PAC, North Coast Builders Industry Association; Member, Board of Directors, Smart Growth Education Foundation. *Member:* Cleveland, Lorain County and Ohio State Bar Associations. ***PRACTICE AREAS:*** Business Organization; Business Taxation; Tax Law. **Email:** tschrader@wickenslaw.com

DANIEL C. URBAN, born Parma, Ohio, October 2, 1970; admitted to bar, 1996, Ohio; 2000, Illinois. *Education:* Yale University (B.A., 1993); Cleveland-Marshall College of Law (J.D., cum laude, 1996). Member, Moot Court Board of Governors, 1995-1996. Editor, Cleveland-Marshall Law Review, 1995-1996. *Member:* Lorain County and Ohio State Bar Associations. ***PRACTICE AREAS:*** Business Organization; Tax Law; Mergers and Acquisitions. **Email:** durban@wickenslaw.com

THOMAS J. STEFANIK, JR., born Cleveland, Ohio, January 8, 1969; admitted to bar, 1996, Ohio; 1997, U.S. District Court, Northern District of Ohio; 1998, U.S. Court of Appeals, Sixth Circuit. *Education:* College of Wooster (B.A., 1991); Cleveland-Marshall College of Law (J.D., 1996). *Member:* Ohio State Bar Association. ***PRACTICE AREAS:*** Workers Compensation; Employment Law; Litigation. **Email:** tstefanik@wickenslaw.com

JASON ROTHMAN, born Oberlin, Ohio, August 28, 1977; admitted to bar, 2003, Ohio. *Education:* The Ohio State University (B.S.B.A., 2000); Cleveland-Marshall College of Law (J.D., cum laude, 2003). Recipient, Suggs I. Garber Award, 2003. *Member:* Lorain County, Ohio State and American Bar Associations. ***PRACTICE AREAS:*** Pension Plans; Employee Benefits; ERISA; Tax Law; Business Organization. **Email:** jrothman@wickenslaw.com

REPRESENTATIVE CLIENTS: Ross Environmental Services, Inc. (hazardous waste treatment facility); North Ohio Heart Center, Inc.; Community Health Partners of Ohio; Stow Dental Group; The Lorain National Bank; Ohio Edison Co.; Drs. Russell, Berkebile and Associates, Radiologists; South Shore Transportation Co.; Industrial Nut Corp.; Liberty Ford Lincoln-Mercury, Inc.; The Morning Journal; Schlessman Seed Co.; Lake County News Herald; Cleveland Glass & Glazing Industry Pension Fund; IBEW Local 972 Pension Fund; Lake Erie Electric Co.; Sandusky Machine & Tool, Inc.; Cabbage, Inc.; Mansfield News Journal; Acacia Mutual Insurance Co.; Sortino Real Estate Management Development Co.; Gross Plumbing, Inc.; Sharpnack Chevrolet; Jack Matia Chevrolet, Inc.; Lorain Glass Co.; Joyce Buick-Pontiac, Inc.; Mike Bass Ford; Mental Health Services of Lorain County (Nord Center); Beaver Park Marina, Inc.; Romp's Water Port, Inc.; Century Telephone Co.; Sprenger Retirement Centers; The Community Foundation of Greater Lorain County; Clark & Post Architects, Inc.; Lorain County Medical Society.

(This Listing Continued)

STOURTON SCOTT SMITH CO., LPA

AVON LAKE, OHIO

(See Cleveland)

Criminal Law, DWI, Bankruptcy, Personal Injury, Divorce, Family Law.

THE SPIKE & MECKLER LAW FIRM, LLP

AVON LAKE, OHIO

(See Elyria)

General Civil Trial Practice. Personal Injury, Medical Malpractice, Family and Domestic Relations, Real Estate, Probate.

JAMES S. ARNOLD & ASSOCIATES

BATAVIA, OHIO

(See Cincinnati)

General Practice, focusing on Driving Under the Influence, Driving while Intoxicated, DUI, DWI, OVI, Personal Injury, Wrongful Death, Medical Malpractice, Real Estate, Domestic Relations, Bankruptcy and Probate.

PHYLLIS G. BOSSIN CO., L.P.A.

BATAVIA, OHIO

(See Cincinnati)

Domestic Relations and Family Law. Child Custody, Support, Divorce, Premarital Agreements.

BUECHNER, HAFFER, O'CONNELL, MEYERS, HEALEY & KOENIG CO., L.P.A.

BATAVIA, OHIO

(See Cincinnati)

General Practice. Estate and Gift Taxation, Probate, Family Law, Corporate, Negligence, Medical Legal Products Liability, Real Estate, Construction, Land Use, Zoning and Eminent Domain Law. Trials and Appeals, Pension and Profit Sharing, Federal Income.

CHALFIE & FARLEY, CO., L.P.A.

BATAVIA, OHIO

(See Cincinnati)

Probate Litigation, Probate Administration, Estate Planning, Trials and Appeals, Estate and Gift Tax, Trusts, Estates, Wills, Family Law, Negligence, Wrongful Death, Will Contests, Living Trusts and Automobile Collisions.

JASON HENNEKES

BATAVIA, OHIO

(See Cincinnati)

Criminal Law, Driving While Intoxicated, Felonies, Misdemeanors, Homicide, Theft, Drug crimes, Traffic Violations, Domestic Violence, Assault.

LOPEZ, HODES, RESTAINO, MILMAN & SKIKOS

A LAW CORPORATION

BATAVIA, OHIO

(See Cincinnati)

Mass Tort Litigation, Medical Malpractice, Products Liability, Employment Law, Personal Injury and Elder Law.

MANLEY BURKE

A LEGAL PROFESSIONAL ASSOCIATION

BATAVIA, OHIO

(See Cincinnati)

Litigation, Local Government Law, Land Use and Zoning Law, Civil Rights, Probate. Fraternal Law. Personal Injury, Labor Law, Workers Compensation, Employee Benefits and Professional Malpractice.

THE LAW FIRM OF TINA R. MILLS, LLC

BATAVIA, OHIO

(See Cincinnati)

Business Law, Buying and Selling of Businesses, Family Business Law, Limited Liability Company Law, Partnership Law, Small Business Law, Consumer Law, Corporate Law, Criminal Law, Debtor and Creditor, Collections, Creditors Rights, Nonprofit and Charitable Organizations, Charitable Giving, Landlord and Tenant Law, Trusts and Estates, Asset Protection, Estate Litigation, Estate Planning, Guardianship and Conservatorship, Wills and Probate.

NICHOLS, SPEIDEL & NICHOLS

Established in 1926
HAMILTON BUILDING
237 MAIN STREET
BATAVIA, OHIO 45103-2979
Telephone: 513-732-1420
FAX: 513-732-0357
Email: nicholslaw@fuse.net
URL: http://www.nsnlaw.com

General Civil Practice. Wrongful Death and Personal Injury, Family, Corporate, Banking, Probate, Real Estate, Taxation, Divorce, Insurance Law. Trials and Appeals in all Courts, Litigation, Business, Trusts and Estates.

MEMBERS OF FIRM

JAMES G. NICHOLS, born Batavia, Ohio, December 9, 1939; admitted to bar, 1968, Ohio. *Education:* Miami University (B.A., 1961); University of Cincinnati (J.D., 1968). Special Assistant Attorney General, 1971-1994. Member, 1984-1997 and President, 1990, Batavia Board of Education. Member, Board of Trustees, 1972-1980 and President, 1976-1977, American Cancer Society. *Member:* Clermont County (President, 1979-1980), Ohio State and American Bar Associations. [Lieut., U.S. Navy, 1962-1965]. ***PRACTICE AREAS:*** Banking Law; Probate Law; Real Estate; Family Law. ***Email:*** JGN.nicholslaw@fuse.net

DONALD W. WHITE, born Cincinnati, Ohio, April 9, 1946; admitted to bar, 1973, Ohio, U.S. District Court, Southern District of Ohio and U.S. Court of Appeals, Sixth Circuit; 1979, U.S. Supreme Court. *Education:* University of Cincinnati (B.B.A., 1969); Salmon P. Chase College of Law (J.D., 1973). County Prosecutor, 1989—. *Member:* Cincinnati, Clermont County (Vice President, 1986-1987; President, 1988), Ohio State and American Bar Associations; The Association of Trial Lawyers of America; Ohio Academy of Trial Lawyers. ***PRACTICE AREAS:*** Personal Injury Law; Insurance Defense Law; Family Law; Wrongful Death; Business Litigation. ***Email:*** DWW.nicholslaw@fuse.net

DAVID J. FREY, born Dayton, Ohio, October 15, 1950; admitted to bar, 1975, Ohio. *Education:* University of Cincinnati (B.A., 1972; J.D., 1975). Member, University of Cincinnati Law Review, 1973-1974. Assistant County Prosecutor, Civil Division, 1989—. Solicitor, Village of Owensville, 1978—. Chairman, Board of Trustees, Mercy Health Partners - Southwest Ohio. *Member:* Clermont County (President, 1992), Ohio State and American Bar Associations. ***PRACTICE AREAS:*** Probate; Real Estate; Corporate; Family; Trusts and Estates. ***Email:*** DJF.nicholslaw@fuse.net

THOMAS H. FLESSA, born Hamilton County, Ohio, May 19, 1955; admitted to bar, 1982, Ohio and U.S. District Court, District of Ohio. *Education:* University of Cincinnati (B.A., 1977; M.A.I.R., 1978; J.D., 1981). Solicitor, Village of Batavia, 1982-1997. Assistant County Prosecutor, 1989—. *Member:* Cincinnati, Clermont County and Ohio State Bar Associations. ***PRACTICE AREAS:*** Family Law; Real Estate; Personal Injury Law; Probate Law. ***Email:*** THF.nicholslaw@fuse.net

TODD S. STOFFEL, born Cincinnati, Ohio, March 21, 1964; admitted to bar, 1989, Ohio; 1990, U.S. District Court, Southern District of Ohio; 1991, U.S. Court of Appeals, Sixth Circuit. *Education:* Northern Kentucky University (B.A., 1986); University of Cincinnati College of Law (J.D., 1989). Assistant County Prosecutor, 1990—. *Member:* Clermont County and Ohio State Bar Associations; Ohio Academy of Trial Lawyers. ***PRACTICE AREAS:*** Personal Injury Law; Insurance Defense Law; Landlord and Tenant Law; Wrongful Death; Consumer Protection. ***Email:*** TSS.nicholslaw@fuse.net

DAVID E. CARTER, born Cincinnati, Ohio, April 23, 1955; admitted to bar, 1991, Ohio. *Education:* University of Cincinnati (B.B.A., 1977); Xavier University (M.B.A., 1986); Salmon P. Chase College of Law (J.D., 1991). Member, Northern Kentucky Law Review, 1990-1991. Assistant County Prosecutor, 1995—. Certified Public Accountant, Ohio, 1982. *Member:* Clermont County and Ohio State Bar Associations. ***PRACTICE AREAS:*** Corporate Law; Individual, Partnership and Corporate Taxation Law; Estate Planning Law; Probate. ***Email:*** DEC.nicholslaw@fuse.net

GENERAL COUNSEL FOR: Locust Corner Land Co.; Kramer-Myers Ins, Co.; Mastercraft Poured Foundations, Inc.; L & I Trucking and Construction, Inc.; Poured Wall Contractors, Inc.; L & I Group, Inc.; L & I Natural Resources, Inc.; Croswell Bus Lines, Inc.; Jeff Wyler Dealer Group, Inc.
LOCAL COUNSEL FOR: National Land Title Ins. Co.; National Bank & Trust Co.; Castrucci Ford and Chevrolet; First Financial Title Agency of Ohio, Inc.; Sportsman's Market Inc.; Auto Owners Insurance Co. *References:* Auto Owners Insurance Co.; Stacey Moving and Storage, Inc.

GEORGE E. PATTISON

Established in 1972
285 EAST MAIN STREET
BATAVIA, OHIO 45103
Telephone: 513-732-3800
Fax: 513-732-6003
Email: gepattison@aol.com
URL: http://www.lawyers.com/pattisonlaw

Probate, Real Estate, Trusts and Estates, Wills, Estate Planning, Social Security, Disability, General Practice, Family Law, Adoptions, Child Custody, Child Support, Divorce, Domestic Violence, Premarital Agreements, Zoning Law, Elder Law, Eminent Domain, Condemnation, Criminal Law, Business Law, Family Business Law, Small Business Law, Contracts, Driving While Intoxicated, Drug Crimes, Felonies, Homicide, Juvenile Law, Misdemeanors, Parole and Probation, Sexual Assault, Traffic Violations.

FIRM PROFILE: Established in 1972, former Prosecuting Attorney of Clermont County now in practice directly across from Clermont County Seat Courthouse downtown Batavia, Ohio.

GEORGE E. PATTISON, admitted to bar, 1972, Ohio; 1980, U.S. Supreme Court. *Education:* The Ohio State University (B.S., Education, 1967); University of Cincinnati (J.D., 1972). Recipient, Special Award for Assistance to Law Enforcement, Clermont Chamber of Commerce, 1984. First Prize State and National Winner, National Environmental Legal Essay Contest, American Trial Lawyers Association, 1972. Licensed Private Pilot, 1967. Author: "Legal Aspects of Air Pollution Law in Ohio," 1971; "Critique and Proposals," 40 U. Cin. L. Rev. 511-533, 1971. Course Director and Lecturer, Environmental Law and U.S. Environmental Protection Agency, University of Cincinnati, Cincinnati, Ohio, 1971-1979, 1977, 1979. Legal Editor, The W.H. Anderson Company, Cincinnati, Ohio, 1972-1975. Assistant Prosecuting Attorney, Clermont County, Ohio, 1975-1981. Prosecuting Attorney, Clermont County, Ohio, 1981-1989. *Member:* American Bar Association.

PURDY & RING

BATAVIA, OHIO

(See Georgetown)

Criminal Law, DUI, Family Law, Divorce, Dissolution of Marriage, Personal Injury, Estates, Wills, Probate, Business Law, Real Estate, Appellate Practice.

WAITE, SCHNEIDER, BAYLESS & CHESLEY CO., L.P.A.

BATAVIA, OHIO

(See Cincinnati)

General Civil Practice. Aviation, Antitrust Litigation, Class Action, Commercial Litigation, Complex Litigation, Corporate Law, Federal Employees Liability, General Civil Trials and Appeals in all Courts, Insurance, Labor, Consolidated and Multi-district Litigation, Products Litigation, Securities Litigation and Wrongful Death.

HUNT & COOK LLC

BAY VILLAGE, OHIO

(See Westlake)

Civil Litigation and Appeals, Business and Commercial Law, Commercial Collections, Criminal Law, Divorce and Family Law, Wills and Estates, Personal Injury.

BERNARD & HAFFEY CO., L.P.A.

BEACHWOOD, OHIO

(See Cleveland)

General Civil and Criminal Practice. Corporate, Probate, Commercial Law, Bankruptcy, Trusts and Estates, Negligence, Family Law, Divorce, Juvenile, and Real Estate. Trial and Appellate Practice, Personal Injury.

KARBERG, KURANT, WACHTER & TURNER CO., L.P.A.

BEACHWOOD, OHIO

(See Cleveland)

Business and Corporate, Mergers and Acquisition, Employment Litigation, Real Estate, Taxation, Probate, Estate Planning, Litigation in all Courts.

LEVY & DUBYAK

25200 CHAGRIN BOULEVARD, SUITE 310
BEACHWOOD, OHIO 44122
Telephone: 216-896-5600
Fax: 216-896-5601
URL: http://www.ldlawfirm.com

Real Estate, Corporate Law, Business Law, Business Litigation, Finance, Employment Law, Commercial Law, Contracts, Mergers and Acquisitions, Real Estate Litigation.

(This Listing Continued)

PARTNERS

GREGG S. LEVY, born Cleveland, Ohio, June 22, 1966; admitted to bar, 1991, Ohio; 1992, U.S District Court, Northern District of Ohio. *Education:* Indiana University (B.S., with distinction, 1988); The Ohio State University (J.D., with honors, 1991). Member: The International Council of Shopping Centers (ICSC); Home Builders Association of Greater Cleveland (Member, Board of Trustees). *Member:* Cleveland and Ohio State Bar Associations. ***PRACTICE AREAS:*** Real Estate; Corporate Law; Business Law; Finance. ***Email:*** glevy@ldlawfirm.com

ROBERT J. DUBYAK, born Cleveland, Ohio, August 26, 1967; admitted to bar, 1992, Ohio; 1997, U.S. District Court, Northern District of Ohio. *Education:* Miami University-Ohio (B.A., 1989); Case Western Reserve University (J.D., 1992). Assistant Cuyahoga County Prosecutor, 1992-1997. *Member:* Cleveland and Ohio State Bar Associations. ***PRACTICE AREAS:*** Business Litigation; Real Estate Litigation; Employment Law; Business Law. ***Email:*** rdubyak@ldlawfirm.com

ASSOCIATES

AILEEN S. SEXTON, born Rochester, New York, January 24, 1972; admitted to bar, 1999, Ohio. *Education:* John Carroll University (B.A., 1994); Case Western Reserve University (J.D., 1999). *Member:* Cuyahoga County, Ohio State and American Bar Associations; Ohio Women's Bar Association; International Council of Shopping Centers. ***PRACTICE AREAS:*** Real Estate Law; Corporate Law. ***Email:*** asexton@ldlawfirm.com

MARK LESKOVEC, born Youngstown, Ohio, April 27, 1961; admitted to bar, 1986, Ohio and U.S. District Court, Northern District of Ohio; 1988, U.S. Court of Appeals, 6th Circuit. *Education:* Youngstown State University (A.B., 1983); Case Western Reserve University (J.D., cum laude, 1986). Member, Case Western Reserve Law Review, 1984-1985. *Member:* Cleveland, Ohio State and American Bar Associations. ***PRACTICE AREAS:*** Real Estate; Commercial Law; Contracts; Corporate Law; Business Law; Finance. ***Email:*** mleskovec@ldlawfirm.com

KEVIN M. BROKAW, born Elizabeth, New Jersey, August 24, 1974; admitted to bar, 2000, Ohio. *Education:* Bowling Green State University (B.A., 1997); Cleveland-Marshall College of Law (J.D., M.B.A., 2000). Carl D. Glickman, Academic Excellence, Cleveland Marshall College of Law. *Member:* Cleveland and Ohio State Bar Associations; The International Council of Shopping Centers. ***PRACTICE AREAS:*** Real Estate; Contracts; Corporate; Business Law. ***Email:*** kbrokaw@ldlawfirm.com

TIMOTHY J. WEYLS, JR., born Lakewood, Ohio, January 7, 1972; admitted to bar, 1998, Ohio; 1999, U.S. District Court, Northern District of Ohio. *Education:* Kent State University (B.A., 1994); Case Western Reserve University (M.B.A., 1998; J.D., 1998). *Member:* Cleveland, Ohio State and American Bar Associations; The International Council of Shopping Centers. ***PRACTICE AREAS:*** Construction Law; Business Law; Real Estate; Commercial Transactions; Finance. ***Email:*** tjweyls@ldlawfirm.com

EDWARD H. CHYUN, born Seoul, Korea, October 6, 1977; admitted to bar, 2003, Ohio. *Education:* University of Southern California (B.A., cum laude, 2000); The Ohio State University (J.D., with honors, 2003). *Member:* Ohio State Bar Association. ***PRACTICE AREAS:*** Business Litigation; Business Law; Employment Law. ***Email:*** echyun@ldlawfirm.com

OF COUNSEL

ROBERT D. SCHWARTZ, born Cleveland, Ohio, May 2, 1970; admitted to bar, 1997, Ohio, U.S. District Court, Northern District of Ohio and U.S. Court of Appeals, Sixth Circuit. *Education:* Emory Univeristy (B.A., 1992); Cleveland-Marshall College of Law (J.D., 1996). Chi Phi. *Member:* Cleveland and Ohio State Bar Associations; Ohio Academy of Trial Lawyers. ***PRACTICE AREAS:*** Litigation; Commercial Litigation; Personal Injury; Employment Law; Creditors Rights. ***Email:*** rschwartz@ldlawfirm.com

PERSKY, SHAPIRO & ARNOFF CO., L.P.A.

Established in 1927

SIGNATURE SQUARE II
25101 CHAGRIN BOULEVARD, SUITE 350
BEACHWOOD, OHIO 44122
Telephone: 216-360-3737
Telecopier: 216-593-0921

General Practice, Corporate Law, Real Estate, Finance, Health Care, Taxation, Professional Corporations, Trusts and Estates, Estate Planning, Probate Law, Employee Benefits, Antitrust, Litigation, Family Law, Bankruptcy and Debtor and Creditor.

EZRA Z. SHAPIRO (1902-1977)

JOSEPH H. PERSKY (1914-1987)

SHERMAN S. HOLLANDER (1920-1987)

EDWARD N. SALIM (Retired)

PAUL Y. SHAPIRO, born August 27, 1938; admitted to bar, 1963, Ohio; U.S. District Court, Northern District of Ohio. *Education:* Case Western Reserve University (B.A., 1960; J.D., 1963). Order of the Coif; Tau Epsilon Rho. Member, Board of Editors, Western Reserve Law Review, 1962-1963. Trial Attorney, Antitrust Division, U.S. Department of Justice, 1963-1968. *Member:* Association of Commercial Finance Attorneys. ***PRACTICE AREAS:*** Antitrust; Corporate Law; Employee Benefits; Estate Planning; Finance; General Practice; Health Care; Professional Corporations; Real Estate. ***Email:*** pshapiro@perskylaw.com

FRED J. ARNOFF, born October 4, 1950; admitted to bar, 1975, Ohio; U.S. District Court, Northern District of Ohio. *Education:* Miami University (B.S., 1972); University of Akron (J.D., 1975). Phi Alpha Delta. ***PRACTICE AREAS:*** Bankruptcy; Commercial Law; Corporate Law; Debtor and Creditor; Employment Law; General Practice. ***Email:*** fjarnoff@perskylaw.com

(This Listing Continued)

JERROLD L. GOLDSTEIN, born October 28, 1941; admitted to bar, 1967, Ohio; 1969, U.S. District Court, Northern District of Ohio; 1972, U.S. Tax Court; 1974, U.S. Supreme Court. *Education:* The Ohio State University (B.S. in B.A., 1963); Case Western Reserve University (J.D., 1967). Tau Epsilon Rho; Order of the Coif. Associate Editor, Western Reserve Law Review, 1966-1967. Law Clerk, Cuyahoga County Probate Court, Cuyahoga County, Ohio, 1967. ***PRACTICE AREAS:*** Estate Planning; Probate; Trusts and Estates; Corporate Law. ***Email:*** jerrygee@perskylaw.com

STEWART D. ROLL, born July 28, 1949; admitted to bar, 1978, Connecticut; 1987, Ohio; 1993, Pennsylvania; U.S. District Court, Northern District of Ohio; U.S. District Court, District of Connecticut; U.S. District Court, Southern and Eastern Districts of New York, and Western District of Pennsylvania; U.S. Court of Appeals, Third and Sixth Circuits; U.S. Supreme Court. *Education:* Ohio University (B.G.S., 1974); Gonzaga University (J.D., cum laude, 1977). Phi Alpha Delta. Recipient, American Jurisprudence Award in Administrative Law. Assistant General Counsel, Combustion Engineering, Inc., 1980-1987. Commercial Arbitrator, American Arbitration Association, 1994—. [With U.S. Air Force, 1969-1973]. ***PRACTICE AREAS:*** Litigation; Corporate Law; Environmental Law. ***Email:*** sdanl@msn.com

MICHAEL J. SHAPIRO, born July 29, 1968; admitted to bar, 1994, Ohio. *Education:* Miami University (B.A., 1990); Case Western Reserve University (J.D., 1994). Certified Specialist, Federal Taxation, Ohio State Bar Association, 2002. ***PRACTICE AREAS:*** Taxation; Corporate Law; Finance; Real Estate. ***Email:*** mshapiro@perskylaw.com

PAUL R. ROSENBERGER, born November 2, 1972; admitted to bar, 1998, Ohio and U.S. District Court, Northern District of Ohio. *Education:* Northwestern University (B.A., 1995); The Ohio State University (J.D., 1998). Managing Editor, The Ohio State University Journal on Dispute Resolution, 1997-1998. ***PRACTICE AREAS:*** Litigation; Bankruptcy. ***Email:*** prosenberger@perskylaw.com

MARY ANN SCHLEIMER, born Cleveland, Ohio, September 8, 1951; admitted to bar, 2002, Ohio; U.S. District Court, Northern District of Ohio. *Education:* Baldwin-Wallace College (B.A., 1980); Lake Erie College (M.B.A., 1983); Cleveland-Marshall College of Law (J.D., 2000). Certified Public Accountant, Ohio, 1997. ***PRACTICE AREAS:*** Probate; Estate Planning. ***Email:*** maschleimer@perskylaw.com

OF COUNSEL

DONALD N. JAFFE, born February 20, 1938; admitted to bar, 1961, Ohio; U.S. District Court, Northern District of Ohio; U.S. District Court, Eastern District of Michigan and Northern District of Illinois; U.S. Court of Appeals, Sixth and Seventh Circuits, U.S. Court of Appeals for the Armed Forces and U.S. Supreme Court. *Education:* Case Western Reserve University (A.B., 1959; J.D., 1961). Delta Sigma Rho; Pi Sigma Alpha; Kappa Kappa Psi; Tau Epsilon Rho. Instructor, American Institute for Paralegal Studies, 1990-1994. Law Clerk, Judge Paul C. Weick, U.S. Court of Appeals, Sixth Circuit, 1962-1964. Assistant Director of Law and Prosecutor, City of Cleveland Heights, Ohio, 1964-1966. Assistant U.S. Attorney and Chief, Civil Division, Northern District of Ohio, 1969-1972. Councilman, City of Cleveland Heights, 1976. Acting Judge: Cleveland Heights Municipal Court, 1972-1975; Shaker Heights Municipal Court, 1982-1994; Mediator/Fact Finder, Ohio State Employment Relation Board, 1986—. Arbitrator, American Arbitration Association (Member, Labor Panel; Commercial Law Panel). Arbitrator, American Registry of Arbitrators. Arbitrator, Better Business Bureau; Hearing Officer, Ohio Department of Education. Fellow, Ohio State Bar Foundation. *Member:* Ohio State Bar Association (Member, Council of Delegates, 1986— Board of Governors, Labor and Employment Law Section). [Capt., JAGC, USAR, 1961-1971; Ohio Military Reserve, Col., JA, 1986—]. ***PRACTICE AREAS:*** Litigation; Labor and Employment; Arbitration; Estate Planning.

PATRICIA M. RITZERT, born September 22, 1952; admitted to bar, 1977, Ohio; 1978, U.S. District Court, Northern District of Ohio; 1982, U.S. Court of Appeals, Sixth Circuit; 1985, U.S. Supreme Court; 1997, U.S. Court of Federal Claims and U.S. Tax Court. *Education:* University of Akron (B.A., magna cum laude, 1974; J.D., 1977; M., Tax, 1983); Case Western Reserve University (LL.M., Taxation, 2001). Case and Comment Editor, Akron Law Review, 1976-1977. Judicial Clerk, Summit County Court of Common Pleas, 1976-1978. Assistant Director of Law, City of Cuyahoga Falls, 1978-1979. Assistant Director of Law, City of Akron, 1984-1987. ***PRACTICE AREAS:*** Employee Benefits; Estate Planning; Taxation; Corporate Law; Commercial Litigation. ***Email:*** pritzert@perskylaw.com

REPRESENTATIVE CLIENTS: American Processing LLC; Baja Fresh Franchisees; Bamcor, LLC; Cleveland Physicians, Inc.; Computer Quest Ltd.; DMI Sports, Inc.; Fallsway Equipment Co., Inc.;.Healthcare Management and Investment Holdings LLC; Huntington National Bank; JPMorgan Chase Bank, N.A.; John G. Johnson Construction Co.; L.C. Properties Ltd.; Middleburg Radiology Associates, Inc.; National City Bank; National Land Title Insurance Corp.; Northcoast Urology, Inc.; Novak Aircraft & Helicopter Maintenance, LLC; Product Development Corp.; Schneider-Dorsey Insurance Agency, Inc.; Security Union Title Insurance Co.; Singer Steel Co.; Stern Advertising, Inc.; Stewart Title Guaranty Co.; Stotter Realty, LLC; Vendome Associates, Inc.; Westside Gastroenterologists, Inc.; Worldwide Steel LLC.

TOEREK CO., LPA

BEACHWOOD, OHIO

(See Cleveland)

Copyrights, Trademarks, Business Law.

ZIPKIN WHITING CO., L.P.A.

Established in 1965

THE ZIPKIN WHITING BUILDING
3637 SOUTH GREEN ROAD
BEACHWOOD, OHIO 44122-5717
Telephone: 216-514-6400
Fax: 216-514-6406
Email: info@zipkinwhiting.com
URL: http://www.zipkinwhiting.com

Age Discrimination, Bankruptcy, Discrimination, Race Discrimination, Sex Discrimination, Criminal Law, Disability Discrimination, Americans With Disabilities Act, Family Law, Divorce, Consumer Violations, Nursing Home Abuse and Neglect, Employment Law, Employment Age Discrimination, Employment Disability Discrimination, Employment Discrimination, Harassment, National Origin Discrimination, Negligent Hiring, Retaliatory Discharge, Sexual Harassment, Title VII Discrimination, Wrongful Termination, Medical Malpractice, Personal Injury, Accidents, Automobile Accidents and Injuries, Wrongful Death.

LEWIS A. ZIPKIN, admitted to bar, 1964, Ohio; 1976, U.S. District Court, Northern District of Ohio. *Education:* Miami University (B.S., Business Administration, 1961); Case Western Reserve University (J.D., 1964). Zeta Beta Theta. Advisor, Shaker Heights City Council. Vice President and Trustee, Coventry Village Special Improvement District. Vice President, Cleveland Chapter; Member, National Board; Member, National Campaign, Central Committee and Finance and Budget Committee, American Organization for Rehabilitation Through Training. Member: Cleveland Clinic Cancer Care Center; United Way; City Club of Cleveland. *Member:* Cuyahoga County, Greater Cleveland and Ohio State Bar Associations; American Trial Lawyers of America; Ohio Trial Lawyers Association; Cleveland Employment Lawyer's Association; Ohio Employment Lawyer's Association; National Employment Lawyer's Association. ***PRACTICE AREAS:*** Employment Law; Discrimination; Sexual Harassment. ***Email:*** laz@zipkinwhiting.com

---

SAMUEL J. MAMICH, born Cleveland, Ohio, July 19, 1938; admitted to bar, 1973, Ohio and U.S. District Court, Northern District of Ohio; 1976, U.S. Supreme Court and U.S. Tax Court; 1980, U.S. District Court, Western District of Pennsylvania and U.S. Court of Appeals, Third Circuit and Sixth Circuit. *Education:* Kent State University (B.A., 1964); Cleveland-Marshall College of Law (J.D., 1973). ***PRACTICE AREAS:*** Personal Injury; Criminal Defense; Small Business Law; Family Law; Bankruptcy; Tax; Probate; Traffic Violations.

JAMES T. SCHUMACHER, admitted to bar, 1990, Ohio and U.S. District Court, Northern District of Ohio; 1991, U.S. Court of Appeals, Sixth Circuit. *Education:* University of Dayton (B.A, 1983); Cleveland-Marshall College of Law (J.D., 1990). With: Nurenburg, Plevin, Heller & McCarthy Co., L.P.A. ***PRACTICE AREAS:*** Employment Discrimination; Sexual Harassment. ***Email:*** jschumacher@zipkinwhiting.com

CHASTITY CHRISTY, born New Castle, Pennsylvania, January 18, 1978; admitted to bar, 2003, Ohio; 2004, U.S. District Court, Northern District of Ohio. *Education:* Clarion University (B.A., 2000); Case Western Reserve University (J.D., 2003). *Member:* Cleveland and Ohio State Bar Associations; National Employment Lawyers Association. ***PRACTICE AREAS:*** Employment Discrimination; Sexual Harassment. ***Email:*** cchristy@zipkinwhiting.com

NEIL S. RUBIN, admitted to bar, 1998, Ohio; 1999, U.S. District Court, Northern District of Ohio; 2001, U.S. Court of Appeals, Sixth Circuit; 2002, U.S. Supreme Court. *Education:* The Ohio State University (B.S.); Cleveland-Marshall College of Law (J.D., 1997); The University of Toledo (M.S.). *Member:* Cuyahoga County, Ohio State and American Bar Associations; National Employment Lawyers Association; Ohio Employment Lawyers Association; Cleveland Employment Lawyers Association. ***PRACTICE AREAS:*** Employment Discrimination; Sexual Harassment. ***Email:*** nsrubin@zipkinwhiting.com

MICHAEL L. FINE, admitted to bar, 1992, California and U.S. District Court, Southern District of California; 2003, Ohio. *Education:* Colorado College (B.A, cum laude, 1987); Southwestern University School of Law (J.D., summa cum laude, 1992). ***PRACTICE AREAS:*** Employment Discrimination; Litigation. ***Email:*** mfine@zipkinwhiting.com

---

ROTH BIERMAN LLP

5196 RICHMOND ROAD
BEDFORD HEIGHTS, OHIO 44146
Telephone: 216-595-0071
Fax: 216-595-0073
URL: http://www.darothlaw.com
Email: dar@rothbierman.com
URL: http://www.rothbierman.com

Health Care Law, Strategic Planning, Financial, Corporate Law, Business Litigation.

FIRM PROFILE: Roth Bierman LLP takes great pride in providing clients with value added services through creative legal, business and strategic solutions and the firm counsels its clients in a broad spectrum of areas, including corporate, real estate, financial transactions, a broad spectrum of health care matters, litigation strategy, and estate planning and probate administration. Our firm's attorneys frequently act as advisors and general counsel to a number of Ohio's premier growing companies and regularly engage in complex matters involving secured financing transactions, mergers and acquisitions, receivership proceedings, debtor/creditor workout transactions, venture capital funding, business and asset leasing transactions, estate planning, business succession planning, business partner disputes, commercial litigation, commercial construction activities and many other related business and legal matters. As a fast-paced and rapidly-expanding practice, our firm's roots originate from a significant in-depth knowledge of and expertise in all aspects of healthcare transactional, financing, reimbursement and regulatory issues.

(This Listing Continued)

DENNIS A. ROTH, born Cleveland, Ohio, April 15, 1941; admitted to bar, 1967, Ohio. *Education:* The Ohio State University (B.S., Accounting, 1963); Cleveland Marshall College of Law (J.D., 1967). Member: Montifiore Home, 1990-1996, 1999—; Ohio State, Medicaid Reimbursement Study Committee, 1991-1994; Assisted Living Task Force, 1994; Certificate of Need Review Board Task Force, 1988; Ohio Department of Health Long-Term Care Task Force, 1984; Ohio Health Care Associate Reimbursement Committee. Trustee and Treasurer, Centers for Dialysis Care, 1973—. Mediator, Cuyahoga County Court of Common Pleas, 1999. Foreman, Cuyahoga County Grand Jury, 2002. *Member:* Ohio Health Care Association; Northeast Ohio Health Care Association; Association of Ohio Philanthropic Homes for the Aged. ***PRACTICE AREAS:*** Health Care Law; Strategic Planning; Financial; Corporate Law; Business Litigation. ***Email:*** dar@rothbierman.com

VICTOR J. BIERMAN, III, born Philadelphia, Pennsylvania, 1967; admitted to bar, 1999, Ohio. *Education:* University of Notre Dame (B.B.A., Finance, Business Economics, 1991); University of Toledo (J.D., cum laude, 1999). *Member:* American Bar Association (Member, Business and Corporate and Health Law Sections); American Health Care Lawyers Association; Ohio Health Care Association; Ohio Academy of Nursing Homes. ***PRACTICE AREAS:*** Health Care; Corporate Law; Commercial Transactions; Finance. ***Email:*** vjb@rothbierman.com

VINCENT E. FISHER, born Rochester, New York, July 29, 1970; admitted to bar, 1999, Ohio; 2000, Pennsylvania; 2001, Florida. *Education:* Canisius College (B.A., 1996); University of Toledo College of Law (J.D., cum laude, 1999). *Member:* American Bar Association (Member, Health Law and Real Property and Probate Sections); American Health Lawyers Association; Ohio State Bar Association (Member, Trust and Estate Section). ***PRACTICE AREAS:*** Health Care Law; Successions; Estate Planning; Commercial Transactions; Estate Administration; Corporate Law. ***Email:*** vef@rothbierman.com

---

BETH STOLLER ROSENBAUM, born Bronx, New York, May 20, 1963; admitted to bar, 1989, Ohio. *Education:* Miami University (B.A., 1985); Cleveland Marshall College of Law (J.D., 1988). *Member:* Ohio State Bar Association. ***Email:*** bsr@rothbierman.com

JACKSON R. WILLIAMS, born Springfield, Ohio, March 29, 1978; admitted to bar, 2003, Ohio. *Education:* Clark State Community College (A.A., 1998); University of Dayton (B.A., 2000); University of Toledo College of Law (J.D., 2003). *Member:* Cleveland, Ohio State and American Bar Associations. ***PRACTICE AREAS:*** Health Care; Commercial Transactions; Litigation. ***Email:*** jrw@rothbierman.com

HAYLEY L. BUTERA, born Pittsburgh, Pennsylvania, July 18, 1979; admitted to bar, 2005, Ohio. *Education:* Vanderbilt University (B.A., 2001); University of Maryland (J.D., 2004). *Member:* Cleveland Bar Association; American Health Lawyers Association. ***PRACTICE AREAS:*** Health Care Law; Commercial Transactions; Corporate Law.

MARY L. L'HOMMEDIEU, born New Castle, Pennsylvania, May 8, 1968; admitted to bar, 1996, Ohio. *Education:* St. Mary's College (B.A., 1989); University of Akron (J.D., cum laude, 1996). *Member:* Akron Bar Association. ***PRACTICE AREAS:*** Business Litigation; Employment Law; Health Care Law; Corporate Law.

REPRESENTATIVE CLIENTS: Multi-Care Management; Royal Manor Nursing Home; GemCare Corporation; Montefiore Home.

LANCIONE & LLOYD LAW OFFICE CO., L.P.A.

Established in 1929

THE PROFESSIONAL COMPLEX
3800 JEFFERSON STREET, SUITE 101
P.O. BOX 560
BELLAIRE, OHIO 43906
Telephone: 740-676-2034
Fax: 740-676-3931
Email: richardlancione@comcast.net
URL: http://www.lancionelloyd.com

Auto Accidents, Trial Practice. Personal Injury, Medical Malpractice, Workers Compensation, Wrongful Death, Corporation Law, Insurance, Real Estate, Probate and Wills.

FIRM PROFILE: Established in 1929, our law firm has been providing personalized legal services to persons who have suffered injuries because of the fault of another or to the families of those who have suffered wrongful death. The firm's lawyers have experience in automobile accidents, personal injury, worker's compensation and social security disability. We handle cases in both Ohio and West Virginia. The senior member of the firm, Richard L. Lancione, is a Board Certified Civil Trial Advocate.

RICHARD L. LANCIONE, born Bellaire, Ohio, April 26, 1941; admitted to bar, 1966, Ohio; 1967, U.S. District Court, Southern District of Ohio; 1971, U.S. Claims Court; 1974, U.S. Supreme Court. *Education:* Wittenberg University; The Ohio State University (B.S., 1963; J.D., 1966). Phi Delta Phi. Member, Regional Council for Ohio University, Eastern, 1975-2005. Member, Panel of Arbitrators, American Arbitration Association. *Member:* Belmont County (President, 1975-1976), Ohio State (Negligence Committee, 1989—) and American Bar Associations; Ohio Academy of Trial Lawyers (Member, Medical Negligence Committee, 1986); The Association of Trial Lawyers of America; The American Board of Trial Advocates; Board Certified Civil Trial Advocate. ***REPORTED CASES:*** Miller v. Bike Athletic Co., 80 Ohio St. 3rd607; Helms v. Skalican, 112 Ohio App 3rd 377. ***PRACTICE AREAS:*** Personal Injury Law; Trials; Auto Accidents; Medical Malpractice; Wrongful Death. ***Email:*** richardlancione@comcast.net

TRACEY J. LLOYD, born Columbus, Ohio, March 27, 1965; admitted to bar, 1990, Ohio; 1991, U.S. District Court, Southern District of Ohio. *Education:* The Ohio State University (B.A., 1987); Capital University (J.D., 1990). Member, National Organization of Social Security Claimants Representatives. *Member:* Belmont County and Ohio State Bar

(This Listing Continued)

Associations; Ohio Academy of Trial Lawyers. ***PRACTICE AREAS:*** General Law; Social Security Disability Law; Estate Planning; Real Estate Law; Auto Accidents; Personal Injury. ***Email:*** traceylloyd@comcast.net

SCOTT ALAN LLOYD, born Joplin, Missouri, September 23, 1963; admitted to bar, 1991, West Virginia, U.S. District Court, Southern and Northern Districts of West Virginia; 1993, Ohio. *Education:* Slippery Rock University (B.S., 1986); University of Notre Dame (1988); Capital University (J.D., 1990). Delta Theta Phi, 1987. Assistant Prosecuting Attorney, Ohio County, West Virginia, April 1991 - January 1993. Assistant Prosecuting Attorney, Belmont County, Ohio, January 2005—. *Member:* Belmont County, Ohio County, Ohio State and West Virginia State Bar Associations; Ohio Academy of Trial Lawyers; The Association of Trial Lawyers of America. ***PRACTICE AREAS:*** General Law; Workers' Compensation; Domestic Relations; Labor and Employment; Auto Accidents; Personal Injury. ***Email:*** badlands923@comcast.net

APPROVED ATTORNEYS FOR: Stewart Title Company.
REFERENCE: Progressive Bank.

GOSLEE & GOSLEE

Established in 1948

114 SOUTH MAIN STREET
P.O. BOX 416
BELLEFONTAINE, OHIO 43311
Telephone: 937-593-8075
Fax: 937-592-4806

General Civil Practice. Corporation, Negligence, Probate, Commercial and Commercial Collections, Insurance, Family and Domestic Relations Law, Construction Law. Trials and Appeals.

MEMBERS OF FIRM

JAMES R. GOSLEE (1911-1997)

WILLIAM THOMAS GOSLEE, born Bellefontaine, Ohio, January 22, 1953; admitted to bar, 1989, Ohio and U.S. District Court, Northern and Southern Districts of Ohio. *Education:* Ohio State University (B.A., Political Science, 1974); Ohio Northern University (J.D., 1989). Recipient, Book Awards: Contract; Criminal Law. Member, Ohio Northern University Law Review, 1988-1989. Chief City Prosecutor, City of Bellefontaine, 1989—. Solicitor to Village of Russels Point, 1990—. Chapter 7 Trustee, 1990-1992. Assistant to Logan County Prosecutor, 1988-1989. *Member:* Ohio State Bar Association. ***REPORTED CASES:*** State v. Harper, (1995), 74 Ohio St. 3d 2; State v. Hamilton, (1994), 97 Ohio App. 3d 648; State v. Williams, (1992), 82 Ohio App. 3d 39; State v. Scott, (1992), 79 Ohio App. 3d 77; State v. Hengstler, (1991), 75 Ohio App. 3d 400. ***PRACTICE AREAS:*** Commercial Collections; Construction; Personal Injury; Domestic Relations; Trials; Appeals.

REPRESENTATIVE CLIENTS: Eaton Well Drilling, Inc.; Culligan Water Conditioning; C. E. Duff & Son, Inc.; Ohio Lumber & Building Supply, Inc.; Ohio Ready-Mix, Inc.; Humble Construction Co.; Wagner Paving, Inc.; Dayton Door Sales, Inc.; Assemblers, Inc.; Mr. Concrete; Star Homes, Inc.
REFERENCES: The Huntington National Bank of Bellefontaine; Citizens Federal Savings and Loan.

OLIVER LAW OFFICE

BELLEFONTAINE, OHIO

(See Columbus)

Products Liability, Personal Injury, Wrongful Death, Latex Allergy Litigation, Medical Malpractice, Vioxx Litigation, Automobile Accidents, Insurance Law, Employment Discrimination.

PAULIG & SINGER

BELLEFONTAINE, OHIO

(See Urbana)

General Civil and Criminal Trial and Appellate Practice in all Courts. Negligence, Personal Injury, Probate and Estate Planning, Family and Domestic Relations and Insurance Law.

LARGENT, BERRY, PRESTON & JAMISON CO., L.P.A.

1 BEREA COMMONS, SUITE 216
BEREA, OHIO 44017
Telephone: 440-816-0600
Toll Free: 888-891-4263
Fax: 440-816-0604;
URL: http://www.lbpj.com
Email: lawyers@lbpj.com
URL: http://www.largentberryprestonandjamison.com

Medina, Ohio Office: 232 North Court Street, 44256. Telephone: 330-723-8828. Fax: 330-723-8898.

JEFFREY W. LARGENT (1946-2004). ***PRACTICE AREAS:*** Personal Injury; Insurance; Litigation; Medical Malpractice; Torts.

RALPH A. BERRY, JR., born Cleveland, Ohio, October 14, 1942; admitted to bar, 1973, Ohio. *Education:* Ohio Northern University (B.A., 1964); Cleveland Marshall College of Law (J.D., 1973). County Auditor, Medina County, Ohio, 1978-1982. Medina County Commissioner, 1982-1994. Judge, Medina County Common Pleas Court, Domestic Relations Division, 1994-1998. Facilitator, Ohio Commission on Dispute Resolution. Mediator, Medina County Domestic Relations Court. [1st Lt., U.S. Army, 1966-1968]. ***PRACTICE AREAS:*** Business Law; Family Law; Probate; Real Estate; Trusts and Estates; Divorce. ***Email:*** ralph.berry@lbpj.com

KEVIN M. PRESTON, born Garfield Heights, Ohio, March 19, 1956; admitted to bar, 1981, Ohio and U.S. District Court, Northern District of Ohio. *Education:* Bucknell University (B.A., cum laude, 1978); Cleveland Marshall College of Law (J.D., cum laude, 1980). Beachwood and Middleburg Heights Mayors Court Magistrate, 2004—. Acting Judge, Berea Municipal Court 1994 - 2004. ***PRACTICE AREAS:*** Family Law; Trusts and Estates; Real Estate; Children; Guardianship and Conservatorship; Business Law; Wills; Divorce; Child Custody. ***Email:*** Kevin.preston@lbpj.com

NEAL M. JAMISON, born Cleveland, Ohio, August 11, 1958; admitted to bar, 1983, Ohio; 1984, U.S. District Court, Northern District of Ohio; 1995, U.S. Court of Appeals, Sixth Circuit and U.S. Supreme Court. *Education:* Cleveland State University (B.A., magna cum laude, 1980); Cleveland Marshall College of Law (J.D., 1983). Assistant Director of Law, City of Brook Park, 1988—. ***PRACTICE AREAS:*** Municipal Law; Criminal Law; Wills; Zoning, Planning and Land Use; Probate; Litigation; Real Estate; Driving While Intoxicated; Traffic Violations. ***Email:*** Neal.jamison@lbpj.com

THOMAS J. KRAUS, born February 3, 1958; admitted to bar, 1984, Ohio; 1986, U.S. District Court, Northern District of Ohio. *Education:* Ashland University (B.A., magna cum laude, 1980); Cleveland-Marshall College of Law (J.D., 1983). ***PRACTICE AREAS:*** Litigation (Civil and Criminal); Personal Injury; Criminal Defense; Insurance Defense; Probate; Estates; Wills; Guardianship; Conservatorship; Automobile Accidents and Injuries; Dog Bites. ***Email:*** Tom.kraus@lbpj.com

DENIO A. LEONE, born Youngstown, Ohio, November 25, 1958; admitted to bar, 1984, Ohio. *Education:* Ohio State University (B.A., Humanities, 1980); Case Western Reserve University (J.D., 1983). ***LANGUAGES:*** Italian. ***PRACTICE AREAS:*** Workers Compensation; Probate; Family Law; Personal Injury. ***Email:*** Denio.leone@lbpj.com

MATTHEW J. SELBY, born Rochester, New York, 1977; admitted to bar, 2003, Ohio. *Education:* John Carroll University (B.A., 2000); Cleveland-Marshall College of Law (J.D., 2003). ***PRACTICE AREAS:*** Civil Litigation; Criminal Law; Personal Injury; Landlord/Tenant; Corporate Law. ***Email:*** Matt.selby@lbpj.com

OF COUNSEL

KENNETH G. PRESTON, born Cleveland, Ohio, December 2, 1933; admitted to bar, 1960, Ohio; 1963, U.S. District Court, Northern District of Ohio; 1976, U.S. Court of Appeals, Sixth Circuit. *Education:* Case Western Reserve University (B.S., 1955); Cleveland State University, Cleveland Marshall College of Law (LL.B., 1959; LL.M., 1961; J.D., 1968). Director of Law, City of Berea, 1983-1987. Acting Judge, Berea Municipal Court, 1976-1983 & 1988-1993. Ohio Water Development Authority, 1990-1996. ***LANGUAGES:*** French and German. ***PRACTICE AREAS:*** Aged and Aging; Family Law; Municipal Law; Probate; Wills. ***Email:*** Ken.preston@lbpj.com

POWERS & GROH-WARGO

BEREA, OHIO

(See Cleveland)

Real Estate Leasing, Land Use and Acquisition, Condominiums, Construction, Estate Planning and Administration, Corporate Law, Domestic Relations, Civil Litigation.

CLEMENTS, MAHIN & COHEN, LPA CO.

BLUE ASH, OHIO

(See Cincinnati)

Civil Litigation, Workers Compensation, Personal Injury, Products Liability, Medical Malpractice, Legal Malpractice, Appellate Practice, Social Security.

CHEETWOOD LAW OFFICES

300 NORTH MAIN STREET
BOWLING GREEN, OHIO 43402
Telephone: 419-352-4659
Fax: 419-354-4550
Email: Cheetwood.law@wcnet.org
URL: http://www.wcnet.org/~jcheet/

General Civil, Personal Injury, Probate, Estate Planning, Real Estate.

JOHN S. CHEETWOOD, born Bryan, Ohio, May 13, 1944; admitted to bar, 1969, Ohio; 1971, U.S. District Court, Northern District of Ohio; 1975, U.S. Court of Appeals, Sixth Circuit and U.S. Supreme Court; 1990, California. *Education:* Duke University (A.B., 1966); Ohio State University (J.D., 1969). Bowling Green City Attorney, 1973-1976. Prosecuting Attorney, Wood County, 1977-1981. *Member:* Ohio State and American Bar Associations; State Bar of California; Ohio Academy of Trial Lawyers; Ohio Land Title Association; American Land Title Association. Fellow, Ohio State Bar Foundation.

APPROVED ATTORNEYS FOR: First American Title Insurance Company (Agent); Chicago Title Insurance Company (Agent).
REFERENCES: Huntington National Bank; Sky Financial Group.

DAVIES & RUCK, PLL

441 FRAZEE AVENUE, SUITE C
BOWLING GREEN, OHIO 43402
Telephone: 419-287-3233
Fax: 419-287-3215
Email: ndaviesruck@aol.com
URL: http://www.lawyers.com/davies&ruck

Pemberville, Ohio Office: 427 W. College Ave., P.O. Box 412. Telephone: 419-287-3233. Fax: 419-287-3215.

Woodville, Ohio Office: 109 W. Main Street, 43469. Telephone: 419-849-2583. Fax: 419-849-3211.

General Civil Trial Litigation in all Local Courts, Estate and Tax Planning, Probate, Trusts, Real Estate Law and Development, Business Law, Corporations and Partnerships, Family Law, Personal Injury, Criminal Law and Traffic Violations.

FIRM PROFILE: We are a general practice, full service firm. Our goal is to provide a full range of legal services to meet the needs of individuals, families, businesses and community organizations in Wood and Sandusky Counties. We strive to provide top quality professional service, and to do so promptly, efficiently, courteously, and at a reasonable cost to our clients.

MEMBERS OF FIRM

R. NIGEL DAVIES, born Swansea, Britain, January 3, 1949; admitted to bar, 1976, Ohio; U.S. District Court, Northern District of Ohio. *Education:* Exeter University (LL.B., cum laude, 1970); University of Cambridge, Cambridge, England (Criminology, 1971); University of Toledo (J.D., 1976). *Member:* Wood County, Northwest Ohio, Ohio State (Member, Estate Planning, Trust and Probate Law Section) and American Bar Associations; Toledo Estate Planning Council. ***PRACTICE AREAS:*** Real Estate; Real Estate Development; Condominium Law; Probate; Estate Planning; Tax Free Exchanges; Family Law; Elder Law. **Email:** ndaviesruckrnd@aol.com

J. DOUGLAS RUCK, born Lima, Ohio, May 28, 1969; admitted to bar, 1997, Ohio; U.S. District Court, Northern District of Ohio. *Education:* Bowling Green State University (B.S., 1992); University of Toledo (J.D., cum laude, 1997). Note & Comment Editor, University of Toledo Law Review, 1996-1997. *Member:* Wood County (Immediate Past President, 2004), Ohio (Member, Family Law Committee) and American Bar Associations; Ohio Academy of Trial Lawyers. ***PRACTICE AREAS:*** Family Law; Divorce; Real Estate; Business Law; Civil Practice; Trial Practice; Litigation; Personal Injury. **Email:** ndaviesruckjdr@aol.com

APPROVED ATTORNEYS FOR: Port Lawrence Title & Trust Co.

EASTMAN & SMITH LTD.

BOWLING GREEN, OHIO

(See Toledo)

General Civil Practice: Corporate, Business, Banking, Taxation, Real Estate, Securities, Antitrust, Environmental, Public, Labor and Employment, Civil Rights, Employee Benefits, Insurance, Hospital and Health Care, Estate Planning, Pension and Estate Planning, Probate, Workers Compensation, Commercial Litigation, Litigation, Immigration and Naturalization.

FECH & FECH, L.L.C.

BOWLING GREEN, OHIO

(See Toledo)

Criminal Law, Juvenile Law, Delinquency, Misdemeanors, Felonies, Driving While Intoxicated, White Collar Crimes, Traffic Violations, Family Law, Divorce, Child Custody, Visitation Rights, Child Support, Dissolution.

HANNA & HANNA

Established in 1892

HANNA LAW BUILDING
700 NORTH MAIN STREET
P.O. BOX 25
BOWLING GREEN, OHIO 43402-0025
Telephone: 419-352-6501
Fax: 419-352-7008
URL: http://www.hannaandhanna.com

General Civil Trial Litigation, Eminent Domain, Condemnation, Personal Injury, Wrongful Death, Automobile Accidents, Corporation, Wills and Probate, Trusts and Estates, Estate Planning, Medical and Legal Malpractice, Insurance, Real Estate Law, Family Law.

MEMBERS OF FIRM

S. W. BOWMAN (1876-1957)

MARTIN L. HANNA (1909-1994)

MARTIN SHAD HANNA (1940-2001)

HAROLD M. HANNA, born Bowling Green, Ohio, June 17, 1946; admitted to bar, 1971, Ohio; 1977, U.S. Court of Appeals, Sixth Circuit and U.S. Supreme Court. *Education:* Culver Military Academy; Northwestern University (B.S., 1967); University of Toledo College of Law (J.D., 1970). Recipient, Ohio Legal Center Award of Merit. Author and Speaker: On Eminent Domain and related subjects, American Bar Association, Ohio Bar Association, Ohio Legal Center Institute and the National Business Institute. *Member:* Wood County (President, 1980), Toledo, Ohio State (President, District 3, 1980) and American Bar Associations. Fellow, Ohio State Bar Foundation. ***REPORTED CASES:*** Ohio Dept of Trans. vs. Wolber (Ohio App. 3 Dist., 2002); Ohio Dept of Trans vs. Stvartak (Ohio App. 6 Dist., 1997); Hardesty vs. Blanchard Valley Hospital Assn. (Ohio Supreme Court, 1982(as cuted in Baldwins Ohio Revised Code and Ohio Jurisprudence, 3d. ***PRACTICE AREAS:*** Wrongful Death; Eminent Domain/Condemnation; Personal Injury; Product Liability; Civil Trial; Family Law.

DREW A. HANNA, born Bowling Green, Ohio, November 29, 1947; admitted to bar, 1972, Ohio and U.S. District Court, Western District of Ohio. *Education:* Culver Military Academy; Northwestern University (B.S., with honors, 1968); The Ohio State University and University of Toledo (J.D., 1971). Member: Order of the Barristers; Moot Court. Member, University of Toledo Law Review, 1971-1972. Recipient, American Jurisprudence Award for Excellence in the Study of Evidence, 1970. *Member:* Toledo, Wood County, Northwestern Ohio, Ohio State (Member, 1973— and Chairman, 1977 and 1985—, Eminent Domain Committee; Member, Council of Delegates, 1988—) and American Bar Associations; Ohio Association of Insurance Defense Attorneys (OACTA); Defense Research Institute. ***PRACTICE AREAS:*** Insurance Defense Law; Personal Injury Law; Malpractice Law; Civil Trial.

REPRESENTATIVE CLIENTS: Welded Construction Co. (pipe line); O.H. Materials Co. (oil and toxic waste cleanup); Northwestern Ohio Volunteer Firemen's Assn.; Dow Jones & Co., Inc. (Wall Street Journal); Tractor Supply Corp.; Norfolk & Southern Railway; Union Oil Co. of California; General Telephone Co. of Ohio; Owens Technical College; Nationwide Insurance Co.; Holiday Inns; Prudential Insurance Co.; Transamerica Insurance Group; Bowling Green State University; Eminent Domain; J.C. Penney Casualty Ins. Co.; Metropolitan Property & Casualty Ins. Co.; American Home Group; Auto-Owners Insurance Co.; State Automobile Mutual Insurance Co.; Mid-American National Bank & Trust Co.; Goodyear Tire & Rubber Co.; Fuqua Industries, Inc.; Bob Schmidt Chevrolet; H. J. Heinz Co.; E. I. DuPont; United Parcel Service; American Group Insurance Co.; Erie Insurance Co.; International Insurance Co.; Crum & Forster Underwriters Group; American International Insurance Group; Celina Group; Central Insurance Cos.; Indiana Insurance Cos.; Universal Underwriters Insurance Co.; National Union Fire Insurance Co.; Faisho Marine & Fire Insurance Co., Ltd.; Wood Cable TV.

MARSH & MARSH

249 SOUTH MAIN STREET
BOWLING GREEN, OHIO 43402-0347
Telephone: 419-352-2518

General Civil Practice. Commercial, Corporation, Banking, Probate and Estate Planning, Real Estate Law. Abstracting.

FIRM PROFILE: Since 1959 the firm has maintained a general practice, serving the Wood County and Northwest Ohio area from two offices. The partners are extremely active in local business, political and civic affairs.

C. RICHARD MARSH, admitted to bar, 1955, Ohio; 1977, Florida. *Education:* Bowling Green State University; University of Cincinnati (J.D., 1955). Assistant Attorney General of Ohio, 1957-1959. City Solicitor, Bowling Green, 1964-1973. Legal Counsel to Bowling Green State University, 1960-1985.

MICHAEL J. MARSH, admitted to bar, 1979, Ohio and Florida. *Education:* Bowling Green State University (B.B.A., 1976); The Ohio State University (J.D., 1978). City Attorney, Bowling Green, 1988—. ***PRACTICE AREAS:*** Real Estate; Corporate; Banking; Estate Planning; Municipal.

REPRESENTATIVE CLIENTS: Sky Bank; Thayer Chevrolet-Toyota, Inc.; Village of Grand Rapids; City of Bowling Green; Great Lakes Ford-Nissan, Inc.; Holley Properties Management; Preferred Properties Co.; Eagle Ridge Development Co.; Village of Pemberville.
AGENT AND APPROVED ATTORNEYS FOR: Port Lawrence Title & Trust Co.; The Guarantee Title and Trust Co.

RITTER, ROBINSON, McCREADY & JAMES

BOWLING GREEN, OHIO

(See Toledo)

General Civil Practice. Insurance, Trials and Appeals, Municipal Law, Corporation, Probate, Estate Planning, Real Estate, Personal Injury, Product Liability, Labor and Employment. Federal Practice.

SPITLER, HUFFMAN, YOON & NEWLOVE, LLP

Established in 1936

131 EAST COURT STREET
BOWLING GREEN, OHIO 43402-2495
Telephone: 419-352-2535
Fax: 419-353-8728
Email: svh@shynlaw.com
URL: http://www.shynlaw.com

Rossford, Ohio Office: 932 Dixie Highway. Telephone: 419-666-7130.

General Civil Practice in all Courts. Corporation, Business, Personal Injury, Wrongful Death, Product Liability, Medical Malpractice, Probate and Estate Planning, Administrative and Real Estate Law, Public Utility, Trials and Appeals, Bankruptcy, Criminal Defense, Family Law, Criminal Law.

EMMETT V. SPITLER (1911-1995)

MEMBERS OF FIRM

DANIEL T. SPITLER, born Toledo, Ohio, September 20, 1939; admitted to bar, 1965, Ohio; 1970, U.S. Supreme Court. *Education:* University of Arizona; The Ohio State University (B.S. in B.A., 1962); Ohio Northern University (J.D., 1965). Prosecuting Attorney, Wood County, 1969-1976. *Member:* Wood County, Northwestern Ohio and Ohio State Bar Associations; Ohio Academy of Trial Lawyers; American Board of Trial Advocates; The Association of Trial Lawyers of America. ***PRACTICE AREAS:*** Civil Litigation; Professional Negligence; Public Utility Law. **Email:** dspitler@shynlaw.com

(This Listing Continued)

ROBERT E. SPITLER, born Perrysburg, Ohio, September 8, 1949; admitted to bar, 1974, Ohio. *Education:* Muskingum College; The Ohio State University (B.A., summa cum laude, 1971); Georgetown University (J.D., 1974). Phi Beta Kappa. *Member:* Wood County, Northwestern Ohio and Ohio State Bar Associations; Ohio Academy of Trial Lawyers; Ohio Land Title Association. ***PRACTICE AREAS:*** Corporate Law; Land Use Law; Business Law; Trusts and Estates; Estate Planning; Probate. ***Email:*** rspitler@shynlaw.com

REX H. HUFFMAN, born Piqua, Ohio, January 1, 1953; admitted to bar, 1979, Ohio; 1980, U.S. District Court, Northern District of Ohio. *Education:* Miami University (B.S., 1975); University of Toledo (J.D., 1978). Member, University of Toledo Law Review, 1977-1978. *Member:* Wood County, Northwestern Ohio and Ohio State Bar Associations; Ohio Academy of Trial Lawyers; Ohio Association of Criminal Defense Attorneys. ***PRACTICE AREAS:*** Insurance Defense Law; Trial Practice; Product Liability. ***Email:*** rhuffman@shynlaw.com

DIANE RAUSCH HUFFMAN, born Napoleon, Ohio, November 25, 1952; admitted to bar, 1982, Ohio and U.S. District Court, Northern District of Ohio. *Education:* Miami University (B.S., 1975); University of Toledo (J.D., 1981). *Member:* Wood County, Northwestern Ohio, Ohio State and American Bar Associations; Ohio Land Title Association. ***PRACTICE AREAS:*** Real Estate Law; Probate Law; Estate Planning. ***Email:*** dhuffman@shynlaw.com

STEVEN L. SPITLER, born Bowling Green, Ohio, March 29, 1967; admitted to bar, 1996, Ohio; 1997, Michigan and U.S. District Courts, Northern District of Ohio and Eastern District of Michigan; 1999, U.S. Court of Appeals, Sixth Circuit. *Education:* Ohio University (B.A., 1989); Ohio Northern University (J.D., 1995). *Member:* Toledo, Wood County and Ohio State Bar Associations; Ohio Academy of Trial Lawyers; Ohio Association of Criminal Defense Attorneys; Maumee Valley Criminal Defense Lawyers Association; Toledo Area Trial Lawyers Association. ***PRACTICE AREAS:*** Criminal Law; Personal Injury; Litigation; Bankruptcy Chapter 7; Driving While Intoxicated. ***Email:*** sspitler@shynlaw.com

MIMI S. YOON, born Houston, Texas, December 28, 1966; admitted to bar, 1992, Ohio; 1997, U.S. District Court, Eastern District of Michigan; 1998, U.S. District Court, Northern District of Ohio; 1999, U.S. Court of Appeals, Sixth Circuit. *Education:* Smith College (B.A., 1989); Ohio State University College of Law (J.D., 1992). *Member:* Ohio State and Wood County Bar Associations; Ohio Academy of Trial Lawyers. ***PRACTICE AREAS:*** Domestic Relations; Civil Litigation; Mediation. ***Email:*** myoon@shynlaw.com

MEGAN E. NEWLOVE, born Defiance, Ohio, September 1, 1970; admitted to bar, 1995, Ohio; 1997, Michigan. *Education:* Miami University (B.S., 1992); University of Toledo (J.D., 1995). Student Articles Editor, University of Toledo Law Review. *Member:* Wood County and Ohio State Bar Associations. ***PRACTICE AREAS:*** Real Estate; Business Law; Estate Planning. ***Email:*** mnewlove@shynlaw.com

REPRESENTATIVE CLIENTS: Wood County Board of Realtors; Arlington Hospitality, Inc.; Northwestern Water & Sewer District; Rossford/Perrysburg Township Joint Economic Development Authority/Port Authority; Sky Bank-Mid Am Region; American Title Agency, Inc.; Westfield Insurance Co.; First Federal Bank of the Midwest; Ottawa Indian Tribe of Oklahoma.
APPROVED ATTORNEYS FOR: Ohio Bar Title Insurance Co.; Port Lawrence Title and Trust Co.; First American Title Insurance Co.
REFERENCE: Sky Bank-Mid Am Region.

STELTENPOHL, JAMES & MENACHER CO. LPA

BOWLING GREEN, OHIO

(See Toledo)

Family Law, Divorce, Dissolution, Child Custody, Child Support, Visitation Rights, Adoption, Bankruptcy, Criminal Law, Juvenile Law, Traffic Violations, DWI, Misdemeanors, Felonies, Trusts and Estates, Wills and Probate, Corporate Law, Business Law, Business Litigation, Business Formation, Personal Injury, Slip and Fall, Automobile Accidents, Truck Accidents, Real Estate Law.

BARAN, PIPER, TARKOWSKY, FITZGERALD & THEIS CO., L.P.A.

8748 BRECKSVILLE ROAD, SUITE 200
BRECKSVILLE, OHIO 44141
Telephone: 440-746-1177
Fax: 440-746-9637
URL: http://www.baranlaw.com

General Civil Practice. Trials in all Courts. Insurance Defense, Corporate, Family Law, Estate Planning, Personal Injury, Products Liability and Construction Law. Commercial Litigation. Suretyship. Environmental and Governmental Liability. Professional Liability, Worker's Compensation.

(For Complete list of all Personnel and Biographical data, see Professional Biographies at Mansfield, Ohio)

THE BERNARD LAW FIRM

BRECKSVILLE, OHIO

(See Cleveland)

Complex Business Litigation, Accountants Malpractice, Stockbroker Malpractice, Banking Litigation, Employment Litigation, Personal Injury, Wrongful Termination, Employment Discrimination, Race Discrimination, Sex Discrimination, Sexual Harassment, Americans with Disabilities, Age Discrimination in Employment, Employment Termination, Family and Medical Leave Act, Breach of Contract, Contract Litigation, Insurance, Class Actions, Securities Litigation, Shareholder Derivative Actions, Lender Liability, Antitrust, Consumer Litigation, Consumer Fraud, Construction Defects, Construction Accidents, Construction Law, Automobile Accidents and Injuries, Wrongful Death, Dog Bites, Slip and Fall, Nursing Home Litigation, Products Liability.

THE LAW OFFICES OF MICHAEL MOTYLINSKI

Established in 2003

1000 WEST WALLINGS ROAD, SUITE A
BROADVIEW HEIGHTS, OHIO 44147
Telephone: 440-746-1000
Fax: 440-746-1003
URL: http://www.motylinskilaw.com
Email: mm@motylinski-law.com
URL: http://www.motylinski.com

Business Law, Real Estate, Estate Planning, Collections, Criminal.

MICHAEL MOTYLINSKI, born February, 1976; admitted to bar, 2001, Ohio. *Education:* University of Akron (B.A., Political Science, magna cum laude); Case Western Reserve University School of Law (J.D.). Executive Notes Editor, Case Western Reserve University Journal of International Law. Member: Craven Moot Court Team; Jean Pictet International Moot Court Team. *Member:* Cleveland, Cuyahoga County, Ohio State and American (Real Property, Probate and Trust Section) Bar Associations. ***PRACTICE AREAS:*** Business Law; Real Estate; Estate Planning; Collections; Criminal Law.

AMANDA R. McGRAW, admitted to bar, 2005, Ohio. *Education:* Indiana University Bloomington (B.A., 1999); Cleveland-Marshall College of Law (J.D., 2004). ***Email:*** mcgrawamanda@yahoo.com

REPRESENTATIVE CLIENTS: S.A. Comunale; R&R Consulting; The Staffing Specialists, LLC; Credex Auto Leasing; Fred-Vincent Volkswagen, Inc.

DAVID S. RIEHL

3695 CENTER ROAD
BRUNSWICK, OHIO 44212
Telephone: 330-273-3450
Telecopier: 330-225-9770
Email: dsr@davidsriehlatty.com
URL: http://www.lawyers.com/davidsriehlatty

Domestic Relations, Family Law, Divorce, Child Custody, Adoption Law, Premarital Agreements, Real Estate, Commercial Real Estate, Residential Real Estate, Small Business Law, Business Organization, Contracts, Probate, Estate Planning, Trust Law, Wills, Elder Care, Personal Injury, Automobile Accidents and Injuries, Negligence, Criminal Law, Driving While Intoxicated, Traffic Violations, Civil Practice.

DAVID S. RIEHL, born Columbus, Ohio, May 16, 1948; admitted to bar, 1974, Ohio; 1975, U.S. District Court, Northern District of Ohio. *Education:* The Ohio State University (B.A., 1971); Cleveland-Marshall College of Law (J.D., 1974). Medina City Prosecutor, 1977-1979. Acting Judge, Medina Municipal Court, 1994-1997. *Member:* Medina County and Ohio State (Member, Probate and Real Estate Committee) Bar Associations. [Captain, U.S. Army, 1971-1981]. ***PRACTICE AREAS:*** Domestic Relations; Family Law; Divorce; Child Custody; Adoption Law; Premarital Agreements; Real Estate; Commercial Real Estate; Residential Real Estate; Small Business Law; Business Organization; Contracts; Probate; Estate Planning; Trust Law; Wills; Elder Care; Personal Injury; Automobile Accidents and Injuries; Negligence; Criminal Law; Driving While Intoxicated; Traffic Violations; Civil Practice.

GALLAGHER, STELZER & YOSICK, LTD.

Established in 1946

216 SOUTH LYNN STREET
BRYAN, OHIO 43506
Telephone: 419-636-3166
Fax: 419-636-5743
URL: http://www.nwohiolaw.com

General Trial Practice. (Personal Injury, Wrongful Death and Commercial), Corporate, Probate and Estate Planning, Real Estate, Criminal Law, Domestic Relations, Trials and Appeals, Mediation.

MEMBERS OF FIRM

FREDERICK R. PARKER (1907-1980)

GIBSON L. FENTON (1904-1994)

RALPH W. GALLAGHER, born Youngstown, Ohio, November 28, 1941; admitted to bar, 1970, Ohio; 1988, Indiana. *Education:* The Ohio State University (B.S., 1966); University of Toledo (J.D., 1969). *Member:* Ohio State Bar Association; Ohio Academy of Trial Lawyers; The Association of Trial Lawyers of America. ***PRACTICE AREAS:*** Civil Trial Practice; Estate Planning; Estate Administration; Corporate; Real Estate. ***Email:*** rgallagher@nwohiolaw.com

J. T. STELZER, born Celina, Ohio, October 13, 1955; admitted to bar, 1981, Ohio. *Education:* The Ohio State University (B.S., 1978); University of Cincinnati (J.D., 1981). *Member:* Williams County, Northwestern Ohio, Ohio State and American Bar Associations. ***PRACTICE AREAS:*** Criminal Law; Domestic Relations; Banking Law; Bankruptcy; Personal Injury; Probate; Civil Practice; Real Estate; Mediation. ***Email:*** jtstelzer@nwohiolaw.com

(This Listing Continued)

GALLAGHER, STELZER & YOSICK, LTD., Bryan—Continued

KAREN K. GALLAGHER, born Saginaw, Michigan, May 9, 1961; admitted to bar, 1986, Ohio. *Education:* Bowling Green State University (B.S., 1983); University of Toledo (J.D., 1986). *Member:* Williams County, Northwestern Ohio, Ohio State and American Bar Associations. ***PRACTICE AREAS:*** Domestic Relations; Juvenile; Criminal Law; Civil Practice; Personal Injury; Probate; Mediation. ***Email:*** kgallagher@nwohiolaw.com

KIRK E. YOSICK, born Mansfield, Ohio, September 17, 1965; admitted to bar, 1998, Ohio; 1999, Indiana. *Education:* University of Toledo (M.B.A., 1993; B.B.A., 1988; J.D., 1998). *Member:* Williams County, Ohio State and American Bar Associations. ***PRACTICE AREAS:*** Criminal; Civil Practice; Personal Injury; Real Estate; Probate. ***Email:*** kyosick@nwohiolaw.com

GENERAL COUNSEL: Northwestern Electric Cooperative, Inc.; Anderson and Vreeland Midwest, Inc.; Quadco Rehabilitation Center; Potter, Inc.; HRH Industries, Inc.; YMCA Inc.; L.E. Smith, Co.; Bridgewater Dairy, LLC; Bryan Chamber of Commerce; C.E. Electronics, Inc.; John Essman Company, Inc.; Miller's Markets - Ohio/Michigan/Indiana; Ney Oil Company; Ohio Gas Company; The Sanctuary of Williams County; Trufast Corporation; Watson Well Drilling, Inc.
LOCAL COUNSEL FOR: Sky Bank; Cincinnati Insurance Co.; Farmers & Merchants State Bank
TITLE INSURANCE AGENTS FOR: Port Lawrence Title & Trust Co.

BROWN, BEMILLER, MURRAY, McINTYRE, VETTER & HECK, L.L.P.

BUCYRUS, OHIO

(See Mansfield)

General Civil Practice, Corporate Law, Banking, Business, Casualty and Life Insurance, Trusts and Estates, Wills and Probate, Estate Planning, Real Estate Law, Labor, Employment, Personal Injury, Medical Malpractice, Legal Malpractice. Trials and Appeals, Arbitration and Mediation.

CULTICE & BROWN

CAMBRIDGE, OHIO

(See Zanesville)

Business, Business Formation, Partnerships, Limited Liability Companies, Banking, Bankruptcy, Creditors Rights, Health Care, Hospital, Elder Law, Estate Planning, Probate, Estate and Trust, Administration, Taxation, Employment and Labor, Real Estate, Title Insurance, Construction Law, Employee Benefits, Discrimination, Wrongful Termination, Natural Resources, Environmental, Oil & Gas, Matrimonial and Family Law, Divorce, Child Custody, Child Support, Personal Injury, Wrongful Death, Automobile Accidents, Insurance Defense and General Civil Litigation.

DENMEAD LAW OFFICE

CAMBRIDGE, OHIO

(See Columbus)

Civil Trial and Appellate Practice and Personal Injury, Traumatic Brain Injury (TBI), Professional Negligence and Complex Litigation including Class Actions, Patents, Civil Rights, Civil Litigation, RICO, Employment and Political Subdivision Liability issues.

KINCAID, TAYLOR & GEYER

CAMBRIDGE, OHIO

(See Zanesville)

Business, Banks and Banking, Health Care, Estate Planning, Estate Administration, Real Estate, Title Insurance, Environmental, Oil and Gas, Civil Litigation, Domestic Relations, Family Law, Construction, General Civil and Criminal Trial and Appellate Practice.

KNOWLTON & BENNETT

Established in 1987

126 NORTH 9TH STREET
CAMBRIDGE, OHIO 43725
Telephone: 740-439-2719
Fax: 740-432-4937
URL: http://www.lawyers.com/knowlton&bennett

Banks and Banking, Aged and Aging, Foreclosures, Juvenile Law, Commercial Real Estate, Criminal Law, Family Law, Probate, Wills, Trusts and Estates, Real Estate, Business Law, Creditors Rights, Collections, Divorce, Driving While Intoxicated, Traffic Violations.

WILLIAM MARK BENNETT, born Zanesville, Ohio, June 12, 1951; admitted to bar, 1977, Ohio. *Education:* Bowling Green State University (B.A., 1973); Ohio Northern University (J.D., 1977). *Member:* Guernsey County (President, 1982) and Ohio State Bar Associations. ***PRACTICE AREAS:*** Probate Law; Corporate Law; Domestic Law; Real Estate Law; Criminal Law. ***Email:*** bbennett@knowltonbennett.com

DAVID B. BENNETT, born Cambridge, Ohio, February 17, 1960; admitted to bar, 1985, Ohio; 1986, U.S. District Court, Southern District of Ohio. *Education:* Bowling Green State University (B.S. cum laude, 1982); Capital University Law School (J.D., 1985). Phi Eta Sigma; Pi Sigma Alpha; Kappa Delta Pi; Phi Alpha Theta; Phi Alpha Delta. *Member:* Guernsey County (President, 1991), Ohio State (Member: Board of Governors, 2000-2003; Board of Governors, Real Property Section, 2004—; Commission on Judicial Candidates, 2004—; Council of Delegates, 2000—; Ohio State Bar Foundation Board of Trustees, 2003—; Member, Solo, Small Firms and General Practice; Real Property Section) and

(This Listing Continued)

American (Member, Sections on: Real Property, Probate and Trust Law) Bar Associations. ***PRACTICE AREAS:*** Real Estate Law; Probate Law; Family Law; Criminal Law; Corporate Law. ***Email:*** dbennett@knowltonbennett.com

DANIEL D. KNOWLTON (1924-2002)

REPRESENTATIVE CLIENTS: Eastern Ohio Mutual Fire & Tornado Insurance Co.; The Guernsey Bank; Cambridge Area Board of Realtors; Guernsey Anesthesia Services, Inc.; Hondros Market Inc.; Degenhart Paperweight and Glass Museum; National City Bank; Guernsey Residential Inc.; Lake Seneca Resorts Inc.; Utility Operators Inc.; General Wholesale Inc.; Buckeye Guard Service Inc.; National City Mortgage Co.; Cambridge Area Regional Airport Authority; Precision Land Title Agency Inc.; American General Finance; Farmers and Merchants Bank; Bruner Land Company Inc.; Peoples Bank; North Maple Buy Here Pay Here Inc.; Bennett Title Agency Inc.; Southeastern Ohio Credit Union; Thorn-Black Funeral Home.
APPROVED ATTORNEYS FOR: Veterans Administration; Farmers Home Administration; Chicago Title Insurance Co.
AGENTS FOR: First American Title Insurance Co.; Lawyers Title Insurance Co.

TRIBBIE, SCOTT, PLUMMER AND PADDEN

Established in 1952

139 COURT HOUSE SQUARE
P.O. BOX 640
CAMBRIDGE, OHIO 43725-0640
Telephone: 740-432-6322
Fax: 740-439-1795
Email: tspp@verizon.net
URL: http://www.tspplaw.com

General Civil Trial Practice. Corporation, Real Estate, Negligence, Insurance Defense, Insurance and Probate Law. Family Law, Divorce, Child Custody, Child Support.

MEMBERS OF FIRM

THOMAS L. TRIBBIE, born Cambridge, Ohio, December 17, 1926; admitted to bar, 1952, Ohio; 1966, U.S. Supreme Court. *Education:* The Ohio State University (B.A., 1950; J.D., 1952). Delta Theta Phi. Prosecuting Attorney, Guernsey County, 1960-1968. Member, 1965-1979 and President, 1973-1975, Board of Trustees, Guernsey Memorial Hospital. *Member:* Guernsey County (President, 1960) and Ohio State Bar Associations. ***PRACTICE AREAS:*** Civil Practice; Probate; Estate Planning; Corporate Law; Insurance Defense; Insurance. ***Email:*** tspp@cambridgeoh.com

JAMES R. SCOTT, born Cambridge, Ohio, August 29, 1932; admitted to bar, 1962, Ohio. *Education:* Miami University (B.S., 1954); The Ohio State University (J.D., summa cum laude, 1962). Phi Delta Phi. Assistant Prosecuting Attorney, 1963-1968 and Prosecuting Attorney, 1969-1984, Guernsey County. *Member:* Guernsey County (President, 1967) and Ohio State Bar Associations. ***PRACTICE AREAS:*** Civil Practice; Probate; Estate Planning; Corporate Law; Insurance Defense; Insurance. ***Email:*** tspp@cambridgeoh.com

C. KEITH PLUMMER, born Dayton, Ohio, June 6, 1955; admitted to bar, 1981, Ohio; U.S. District Court, Southern District of Ohio; U.S. Court of Appeals, Sixth Circuit; U.S. Supreme Court. *Education:* The Ohio State University (B.A., 1976); Capital University (J.D., 1981). Assistant Prosecuting Attorney, 1981-1984 and Prosecuting Attorney, 1985-2005, Guernsey County. *Member:* Guernsey County, Ohio State and American Bar Associations; National District Attorneys Association; Ohio Prosecuting Attorneys Association. ***PRACTICE AREAS:*** Civil Practice; Probate; Estate Planning; Corporate Law; Insurance; Insurance Defense; Commercial Litigation. ***Email:*** tspp@cambridgeoh.com

DANIEL G. PADDEN, born Steubenville, Ohio, November 14, 1961; admitted to bar, 1987, Ohio; 1988, West Virginia. *Education:* Ohio Northern University (B.S.B.A., Accounting, 1984; J.D., 1987). Delta Theta Phi. Assistant Prosecuting Attorney, 1989-2005 and Prosecuting Attorney, 2005—, Guernsey County. *Member:* Guernsey County and Ohio State Bar Associations; West Virginia State Bar; National District Attorneys Association; Ohio Prosecuting Attorneys Association; Ohio Society of Certified Public Accountants. ***PRACTICE AREAS:*** Family Law; Taxation; Civil Practice; Probate; Estate Planning; Corporate Law; Insurance; Insurance Defense. ***Email:*** tspp@cambridgeoh.com

---

KENT D. BIEGLER, born Berea, Ohio, November 14, 1956; admitted to bar, 1982, Ohio. *Education:* Muskingum College (B.A., 1979); Capital University (J.D., 1982). Assistant Prosecuting Attorney, Guernsey County, 1998—. *Member:* Guernsey County and Ohio State Bar Associations. ***PRACTICE AREAS:*** Family Law; Juvenile Law; Civil Practice; Probate; Estate Planning; Corporate Law. ***Email:*** tspp@cambridgeoh.com

STEPHANIE L. MITCHELL, born Zanesville, June 12, 1973; admitted to bar, 2001, Ohio. *Education:* Muskingum College (B.A., 1997); Capital University (J.D., magna cum laude, 2001). Assistant Prosecuting Attorney, 2001—. *Member:* Guernsey County, Ohio State and American Bar Associations. ***PRACTICE AREAS:*** Criminal Law; Domestic Relations; Civil Practice; Bankruptcy. ***Email:*** tspp@cambridgeoh.com

REPRESENTATIVE CLIENTS: Metropolitan Insurance Co.; State Farm Insurance Co.; The Westfield Cos.; Grange Insurance Co.; The Dailey Jeffersonian Co. (Newspaper); Slabe Tool Co.; Holiday Inn (Cambridge); Hinchcliff Products Co.; Southeast Ohio Physicians, Inc.; Southeastern Equipment Co.; Southeastern Ohio Regional Medical Center; Cambridge Tool and Die Co.; The Hartley Co.; Fehrman Tool & Dye Inc.; Champion Spark Plug Co.-Cambridge; Columbus National Bank.

DAVID WIRTH

CAMBRIDGE, OHIO

(See Columbus)

Insurance Law, Negligence, Legal Malpractice, Subrogation, Personal Injury, Probate.

DOUGLAS M. TOOT

Established in 1973

106 SOUTH BROAD STREET
CANFIELD, OHIO 44406
Telephone: 330-533-9810
Fax: 330-533-2124
Email: dougtoot@zoominternet.net
URL: http://www.dougtootlawoffices.com

Wills and Trusts, Estate Planning, Probate, Elder Law, Business Planning, Corporate and Business Law, Real Estate.

FIRM PROFILE: We have served the Northwestern Ohio area in wills, trusts, estate planning, probate, elder, real estate, taxation and business law since 1973.

DOUGLAS M. TOOT, born Youngstown, Ohio, November 17, 1947; admitted to bar, 1973, Ohio. *Education:* Duke University (A.B., 1969); University of Wisconsin; The Ohio State University (J.D., cum laude, 1973). Phi Eta Sigma; Phi Delta Phi. Lecturer, Estate Planning and Probate topics, National Business Institute, Kent State University, Youngstown State University Tax Institute. *Member:* Mahoning County (Chair, Estate Planning and Taxation Committee, 1996—; Member, Grievance Committee, 1999—), Cleveland, American (Member, Sections of: Real Property, Probate and Trust Law; Taxation) and Ohio State Bar Associations. (Certified Specialist in Estate Planning, Trust and Probate Law, Ohio State Bar Association). ***LANGUAGES:*** English.

LAW OFFICES OF GERALD L. BAKER

3711 WHIPPLE AVENUE, N.W.
CANTON, OHIO 44718-2933
Telephone: 330-492-1001
Fax: 330-492-4577
Email: jbaker3094@aol.com

Corporate Law, Commercial Litigation, Environmental Law, Secured Transactions, Probate Law.

GERALD L. BAKER, born Lorain, Ohio, 1943; admitted to bar, 1968, Ohio; 1970, U.S. District Court, Northern District of Ohio; 1981, U.S. Court of Appeals, Sixth Circuit. *Education:* Heidelberg College; Bowling Green State University (B.A., 1965); The Ohio State University (J.D., 1968). Formerly with Amerman Burt & Jones Co. LPA, 1968-1981. *Member:* Stark County (Member, Judicial Candidates Committee and Bar Journal Committee), Ohio State (Member, Sections on: Corporate Counsel; Litigation; Labor and Employment Law) and American (Member, Sections on: Labor and Employment Law; Business Law) Bar Associations. ***LANGUAGES:*** German. ***REPORTED CASES:*** Openings Inc. v. Sedon Construction Co., 1 Ohio Misc.2d.5, 1982. ***TRANSACTIONS:*** American Disposal Services Inc Acquisition of R.E. Miller Enterprises Inc.; Represented AT&T as Real Estate Counsel when fiber optic line laid across Ohio. ***PRACTICE AREAS:*** Corporate Law; Commercial Litigation; Environmental Law; Secured Transactions; Probate Law.

REPRESENTATIVE CLIENTS: The Stark Development Board Finance Corporation; Stark Metal Sales; C.N.D. Machine Inc.; Cross Truck Equipment Co.
TITLE AGENT FOR: Guardian National Title Insurance Company.

BAKER, DUBLIKAR, BECK, WILEY & MATHEWS

CANTON, OHIO

(See North Canton)

General Civil Trial and Appellate Practice in all Courts. Insurance, Products Liability, Environmental, Malpractice, Political Subdivision, Real Estate, Corporate, Commercial and Family Law.

BLACK McCUSKEY SOUERS & ARBAUGH

A LEGAL PROFESSIONAL ASSOCIATION

Established in 1922

220 MARKET AVENUE SOUTH, SUITE 1000
CANTON, OHIO 44702
Telephone: 330-456-8341; 877-656-8341
Fax: 330-456-5756; 877-456-5746
Email: info@bmsa.com
URL: http://www.bmsa.com

Dover, Ohio Office: Black McCuskey Hanhart Deeds & Bauer, A Legal Professional Association, 130 W. Third Street, 44622. Telephone: 330-364-6553. Fax: 330-364-2739.

General Civil Practice in all State and Federal Courts. Administrative, Acquisitions, Antitrust, Banking, Bankruptcy, Commercial, Construction, Corporate, Divorce, Environmental, Estate Planning and Trusts, Estate Administration, Family Law, Government, Health Care Law, Insurance, Labor, Litigation, Oil and Gas, Personal Injury, Real Estate, Securities, Taxation Law, Workers' Compensation and Wrongful Death and Zoning.

FIRM PROFILE: Since 1922, the lawyers of Black, McCuskey have provided innovative approaches to problem solutions for our diverse clients from Fortune 100 companies to start-up businesses in the full spectrum of legal services.

(This Listing Continued)

ANTHONY E. EFREMOFF, born Battle Creek, Michigan, 1938; admitted to bar, 1963, Ohio. *Education:* University of Michigan (A.B., 1959; J.D., 1963). Order of the Coif. ***PRACTICE AREAS:*** Corporate Law; Securities Regulation Law; Mergers and Acquisitions Law; Taxation Law. ***Email:*** tefremoff@bmsa.com

ROBERT I. FRIEDMAN, born Columbus, Ohio, 1939; admitted to bar, 1964, Ohio. *Education:* Indiana University (B.A., 1961); The Ohio State University (J.D., 1964). Fellow, Ohio State Bar Foundation. ***PRACTICE AREAS:*** Corporate Law; Estate Planning Law; Probate Law; Health Care. ***Email:*** bfriedman@bmsa.com

ARNOLD R. SHIFMAN, born Canton, Ohio, 1940; admitted to bar, 1964, Ohio. *Education:* The Ohio State University (B.A., 1961; J.D., 1964). ***PRACTICE AREAS:*** Real Property Law; Probate Law. ***Email:*** ashifman@amtitle.com

VICTOR R. MARSH, born New Philadelphia, Ohio, 1940; admitted to bar, 1966, Ohio. *Education:* Ohio Wesleyan University; University of Colorado (B.A., 1963); The Ohio State University (J.D., 1966). ***PRACTICE AREAS:*** Environmental Law; Estate Planning Law; Real Property Law. ***Email:*** vmarsh@bmsa.com

DANIEL M. JONAS, born Montclair, New Jersey, 1941; admitted to bar, 1968, Ohio. *Education:* Case Western Reserve University (A.B., 1964; J.D., 1968). ***PRACTICE AREAS:*** Employment and Labor Management Law; Employment Discrimination. ***Email:*** djonas@bmsa.com

RANDOLPH L. SNOW, born Bucyrus, Ohio, 1946; admitted to bar, 1971, Ohio. *Education:* College of Wooster (B.A., 1968); The Ohio State University (J.D., cum laude, 1971). (Managing Director). ***PRACTICE AREAS:*** Litigation Practice; Construction Law; Education Law; Malpractice Defense; Oil and Gas Law. ***Email:*** rsnow@bmsa.com

TERRENCE P. KESSLER, born Canton, Ohio, 1950; admitted to bar, 1975, Ohio. *Education:* Yale University (B.A., 1972); The Ohio State University (J.D., cum laude, 1975). ***PRACTICE AREAS:*** General Practice; Corporate Law; Oil and Gas Law; Taxation Law. ***Email:*** tkessler@bmsa.com

JAMES R. STRAWN, born Canton, Ohio, 1951; admitted to bar, 1976, Ohio. *Education:* Wittenberg University (A.B., 1973); Case Western Reserve University (J.D., 1976). ***PRACTICE AREAS:*** Corporate Law; Labor Law; Employment Litigation. ***Email:*** jstrawn@bmsa.com

JOEL K. DAYTON, born Fontainebleau, France, 1952; admitted to bar, 1977, Ohio. *Education:* Weber State University (B.S., Business Administration, magna cum laude, 1974); The Ohio State University (J.D., cum laude, 1977). ***PRACTICE AREAS:*** Commercial Law; Bankruptcy Law; Banking Law; Finance; Creditors Rights; Workouts. ***Email:*** jdayton@bmsa.com

GUST CALLAS, born Canton, Ohio, 1953; admitted to bar, 1978, Ohio. *Education:* University of Akron (B.S., summa cum laude, 1975; J.D., 1978). (Certified Specialist in Ohio Workers' Compensation Law and Labor and Employment Law, Ohio State Bar Association). ***PRACTICE AREAS:*** Labor Litigation; Employment Litigation; Products Liability Law; Workers' Compensation Law; Education Law; Civil Litigation. ***Email:*** gcallas@bmsa.com

BRUCE M. SOARES, born Fall River, Massachusetts, 1955; admitted to bar, 1980, Ohio. *Education:* Providence College (B.A., summa cum laude, 1977); Case Western Reserve University (J.D., 1980). Order of the Coif. ***PRACTICE AREAS:*** Banking Law; Finance; Real Estate Law; Commercial Law; Condominium Law; Oil and Gas Law. ***Email:*** bsoares@bmsa.com

JAMES P. KAMERER, born Canton, Ohio, 1949; admitted to bar, 1974, Ohio. *Education:* Kent State University (B.A., 1971); University of Akron (J.D., 1974). (Certified Specialist in Estate Planning, Trust and Probate Law, Ohio State Bar Association). ***PRACTICE AREAS:*** Estate Planning; Probate Administration; Trust Law; Corporate Law. ***Email:*** jkamerer@bmsa.com

RICHARD D. DODEZ, born St. Louis, Missouri, 1942; admitted to bar, 1969, Ohio. *Education:* University of California; The Ohio State University (B.S., 1964; J.D., 1969). ***PRACTICE AREAS:*** Employee Benefits Law; Corporation Law; Probate Administration. ***Email:*** ddodez@bmsa.com

MARY E. REYNOLDS, born Canton, Ohio, 1953; admitted to bar, 1983, Ohio. *Education:* Kent State University (B.A., summa cum laude, 1980); University of Akron (J.D., 1983). (Certified Specialist in Ohio Workers' Compensation Law, Ohio State Bar Association). ***PRACTICE AREAS:*** Workers' Compensation; Litigation; Labor and Employment Law; Medical Malpractice Defense. ***Email:*** mreynolds@bmsa.com

JOHN J. RAMBACHER, born Akron, Ohio, 1960; admitted to bar, 1986, Ohio. *Education:* University of Akron (B.S., summa cum laude, 1982; J.D., cum laude, 1986). Phi Sigma Alpha. ***PRACTICE AREAS:*** Business Law; Real Property; Banking Law; Finance; Estate Planning. ***Email:*** jrambacher@bmsa.com

THOMAS W. CONNORS, born Norfolk, Virginia, 1952; admitted to bar, 1978, Ohio. *Education:* Miami University; John Carroll University (B.A., 1974); Case Western Reserve University; Cleveland State University (J.D., 1978). ***PRACTICE AREAS:*** Litigation; Appellate Law; Commercial Law. ***Email:*** tconnors@bmsa.com

DAVID M. HANHART, born Dover, Ohio, 1955; admitted to bar, 1980, Ohio. *Education:* Denison University (B.A., 1977); Case Western Reserve University (J.D., 1980). (Dover Office). ***PRACTICE AREAS:*** Corporate Law; Real Estate; Mortgage Lending; Trusts and Estates. ***Email:*** dhanhart@bmsa.com

C. JASON DEEDS, born Dover, Ohio, 1962; admitted to bar, 1989, Ohio; 1997, U.S. Supreme Court. *Education:* Denison University (B.A., 1985); Ohio Northern University (J.D., 1988). (Dover Office). ***PRACTICE AREAS:*** Corporate Law; Labor and Employment; Real Estate; Trusts and Estates. ***Email:*** jdeeds@bmsa.com

ERICK L. BAUER, born Columbus, Ohio, 1964; admitted to bar, 1991, Ohio. *Education:* Ohio State University (B.A., 1987); Ohio Northern University (J.D., 1991). (Dover Office). ***PRACTICE AREAS:*** Commercial Law; Creditors Rights; Business Law; Corporate Law; Litigation; Divorce; Family Law. ***Email:*** ebauer@bmsa.com

FRANCIS G. CENTRONE, born Brooklyn, New York, 1943; admitted to bar, 1968, Ohio. *Education:* Duquesne University (B.A., 1965); Ohio Northern University (J.D., 1968). ***PRACTICE AREAS:*** Family Law; Divorce. ***Email:*** fcentrone@bmsa.com

(This Listing Continued)

BLACK McCUSKEY SOUERS & ARBAUGH , A LEGAL PROFESSIONAL ASSOCIATION, Canton—Continued

TODD S. BUNDY, born Pittsburgh, Pennsylvania, 1954; admitted to bar, 1980, Ohio. *Education:* Southern Connecticut State College; University of Connecticut (B.A., cum laude, 1976); Capital University (J.D., cum laude, 1980). Order of the Curia. ***PRACTICE AREAS:*** Corporate Law; Business Law; Commercial Litigation; Banking Law; Finance. ***Email:*** tbundy@bmsa.com

GORDON D. WOOLBERT, II, born Lafayette, Indiana, 1970; admitted to bar, 1997, Ohio. *Education:* Stanford University (B.A., 1994); Vanderbilt School of Law (J.D., 1997). ***PRACTICE AREAS:*** Corporate Law; Commercial Litigation. ***Email:*** gwoolbert@bmsa.com

BRIAN R. MERTES, born Canton, Ohio, 1970; admitted to bar, 1995, Ohio. *Education:* University of Dayton (B.S., 1992); University of Akron (J.D., 1995). ***PRACTICE AREAS:*** Workers' Compensation; Labor and Employment; Litigation; Construction Law. ***Email:*** bmertes@bmsa.com

---

JOHN L. JUERGENSEN, born Youngstown, Ohio, 1970; admitted to bar, 1999, Ohio. *Education:* Wittenberg University (B.B.A., cum laude, 1993); University of Akron (J.D., 1999). ***PRACTICE AREAS:*** General Litigation; Business Law; Construction Law; Divorce; Family Law. ***Email:*** jjuergensen@bmsa.com

CHRYSANTHE E. VASSILES, born Kew Gardens, New York, 1971; admitted to bar, 1996, Ohio; 1997, U.S. District Court, Northern District of Ohio. *Education:* Kent State University (B.A., 1993); The Ohio State University (J.D., 1996). ***PRACTICE AREAS:*** Corporate Law; Bankruptcy; Commercial Law; Creditors Rights; Workouts.

KRISTIN R. ZEMIS, born Worcester, Massachusetts, 1967; admitted to bar, 1993, Ohio; 1996, Alabama; 2000, Georgia. *Education:* Emory University (B.A., 1989); University of Dayton School of Law (J.D., 1993). (Dover Office). ***PRACTICE AREAS:*** Health Care; Divorce; Family Law; Business Law; Corporate Law; Environmental Law.

FAITH R. DYLEWSKI, born Canton, Ohio, 1972; admitted to bar, 2002, Ohio. *Education:* Kent State University (B.A., magna cum laude,1995); University of Akron (J.D., summa cum laude, 2002). ***PRACTICE AREAS:*** Labor and Employment; Business Law; Environmental Law; Copyrights. ***Email:*** fdylewski@bmsa.com

DANIEL R. GRIFFITH, born Canton, Ohio, 1977; admitted to bar, 2002, Ohio. *Education:* Mount Union College (B.A., cum laude, 1999); The Ohio State University (J.D., 2002). ***PRACTICE AREAS:*** Trusts and Estates; Corporate Law; Estate Planning; Medicaid Planning. ***Email:*** dgriffith@bmsa.com

ROBERT B. PRESTON, III, born Cleveland, Ohio, 1970; admitted to bar, 2004, Ohio. *Education:* Cleveland State University (B.A., 1999); Akron University Law School (J.D., 2003). ***PRACTICE AREAS:*** Labor and Employment; Workers Compensation; Collections.

ROBERT J. MURPHY, born Canton, Ohio, 1979; admitted to bar, 2004, Ohio. *Education:* Kenyon College (B.A., 2001); Case Western Reserve University (J.D., magna cum laude, 2004). Order of the Coif. *Member:* Stark County Bar Association. ***PRACTICE AREAS:*** Real Estate; Construction Law; Commercial Transactions; Business Law; Corporate Law.

OF COUNSEL

CHARLES J. TYBURSKI, born New Kensington, Pennsylvania, 1934; admitted to bar, 1964, Ohio. *Education:* Ohio Wesleyan University (B.A., 1956); The Ohio State University (J.D., 1964). (Certified Specialist in Estate Planning, Trust and Probate Law, Ohio State Bar Association). ***PRACTICE AREAS:*** Corporate Law; Estate Planning Law; Taxation Law; Education Law. ***Email:*** ctyburski@bmsa.com

GENE BARNHART, born Pineville, West Virginia, 1928; admitted to bar, 1953, Ohio. *Education:* West Virginia University; College of Steubenville; University of Cincinnati (J.D., 1953). Order of the Coif. ***PRACTICE AREAS:*** Real Property Law; Zoning Law; Subdivision Law. ***Email:*** gbarnhart@bmsa.com

RICHARD M. HANHART, born Dover, Ohio, December 23, 1926; admitted to bar, 1951, Ohio and U.S. District Court, Northern District of Ohio; 1981, U.S. Supreme Court. *Education:* Bowling Green State University, University of Notre Dame; Denison University (B.A., 1948); Case Western Reserve University (LL.B., 1951). ***PRACTICE AREAS:*** Litigation; Business Law; Corporate Law; Trusts and Estates.

REPRESENTATIVE CLIENTS: *Financial:* Unizan Bank National Association; Key Bank; Firsmerit Bank; Morgan Bank; GE Commercial Finance. *Manufacturing:* Diebold, Incorporated; The Hoover Mortgage Company; Union Metal Corporation; Alpha Security Products; Gradall Company; N Expak Corporation. *Energy:* Belden & Blake Corp.; First Energy. *Medical:* Mercy Medical Center; North Canton Medical Foundation; Spectrum Orthopaedics, Inc.; Aultman Health Foundation. *Clay Products:* Belden Brick Co.; Stark Ceramics, Inc.; Whitacre Greer; Fireproofing Co.; Stonecreek Brick Co.; Hall China Co. *Insurance:* CIGNA; Guardian Title Insurance Co.; Aetna Insurance Co.; U.S. Aetna Health Care, Inc.; SAFECO. *Other:* Hilscher-Clarke Electric Co.; Canton Regional Transit Authority; Park Poultry, Inc.; Malone College; Standards Testing Labs, Inc.; Graphic Enterprises, Inc.; Developers Diversified, Inc.; Walsh University; Stark Tuscarawas-Wayne; Wayne Joint Solid Waste Management District; Brewster Dairy, Inc.

BUCKINGHAM, DOOLITTLE & BURROUGHS, LLP

4518 FULTON DRIVE, NORTHWEST
P.O. BOX 35548
CANTON, OHIO 44735-5548
Telephone: 330-492-8717; Toll Free: 888-811-2825
Fax: 330-492-9625
Email: bdb@bdblaw.com
URL: http://www.bdblaw.com

Akron, Ohio Office: 50 South Main Street, P.O. Box 1500, 44309-1500. Telephone: 330-376-5300. Toll Free: 800-686-2825. Fax: 330-258-6559.

(This Listing Continued)

Cleveland, Ohio Office: 1375 East Ninth Street, Suite 1700, 44114. Telephone: 216-621-5300. Toll Free: 888-843-2825. Fax: 216-621-5440.
Columbus, Ohio Office: 191 West Nationwide Boulevard, 43215-3506. Telephone: 614-221-8448. Toll Free: 888-686-2825. Fax: 614-221-8590.
Boca Raton, Florida Office: 2500 North Military Trail, Suite 480, 33431. Telephone: 561-241-0414. Toll Free: 800-682-2825. Fax: 561-241-9766.

Appellate, Closely Held Companies, Commercial Law and Litigation, Computer and Technology, Construction Law, Copyrights, Corporate and Business, Creditors Rights/Bankruptcy, Criminal Law, Employment Law, Environmental, Estate Planning, Family Law, Finance and Public Law, Franchise, Health Care, Immigration Law, Insurance Defense, Intellectual Property, Labor and Employment, Land Use and Zoning, Medical Malpractice Defense, Mergers and Acquisitions, Patents, Probate, Publicly Held Companies, Real Estate, School Law, Securities, Succession Planning, Taxation and Employee Benefits, Toxic Tort/Complex Litigation, Trademarks/Service Marks, Trade Secrets, Trial, Trusts and Estates, Venture Capital/Emerging Companies, Workers' Compensation.

FIRM PROFILE: Established in 1913, Buckingham, Doolittle & Burroughs, LLP is a full-service law firm with offices in Akron, Cleveland, Canton and Columbus, Ohio and Boca Raton, Florida. Its attorneys represent clients from the sole proprietor to multinational corporations, tax-exempt organizations, governmental bodies, charities, foundations and public organizations.

The focus of the Firm's corporate practice is on legal issues affecting closely held businesses including start-up joint ventures, agreements among shareholders, corporate reorganization and business contracts. Buckingham attorneys have expertise in mergers and acquisitions, intellectual property, succession planning and related areas of significance to rapidly expanding business organizations and also provide trusts and estates and probate services to individual clients.

The Litigation Practice of Buckingham, Doolittle & Burroughs, LLP has steadily grown to meet the increasingly complex legal demands of the Firm's clients. Areas of focus include appellate, commercial law and litigation, construction, domestic relations, employment, school law, medical malpractice and workers' compensation. The Firm is committed to finding innovative solutions to clients' legal problems. The breadth of its practice in all forums often enables the Firm to avoid disputes by providing legal guidance before problems arise.

Buckingham's clients are representative of virtually every industry and trade, including transportation, food production, chemical manufacturing and distribution, rubber and tire manufacturing, technology, automotive, steel, agriculture and horticulture, financial and banking, insurance and medical, accounting and other professional practices.

MANAGING PARTNER

JEFFREY A. HALM, born Sandusky, Ohio, October 1, 1947; admitted to bar, 1973, Ohio; U.S. District Court, Northern District of Ohio; U.S. Court of Appeals, Sixth Circuit; U.S. Tax Court; U.S. Supreme Court. *Education:* Denison University (B.A., 1969); The Ohio State University (J.D., 1972). Stark State College of Technology Board of Trustees and Planned Giving Committee; American Heart Association President-Elect of Board of Directors; Jackson-Belden Chamber of Commerce, Board of Directors; Canton Symphony Orchestra, Board of Trustees; Jackson Township Rotary, Board of Directors; Stark Community Foundation, Trust and Estates Committee;Buckeye Council, Boy Scouts, Endowment Fund Committee and Advisory Board. Author: "Integrated Planning: Your Wills and Trusts ard Done- Are You Finished?" M.D. News/Northeast Ohio, April, 2005. *Member:* Stark County (Member, Real Property, Probate and Trust Law Section), Ohio State and American Bar Associations. ***PRACTICE AREAS:*** Estate Planning; Asset Protection; Corporate Law. ***Email:*** JHalm@bdblaw.com

SHAREHOLDERS

RALPH D. AMIET, born Apple Creek, Ohio, January 2, 1941; admitted to bar, 1967, Ohio. *Education:* College of Wooster; The Ohio State University (B.S.B.A., cum laude, 1964; J.D., 1967). Phi Delta Phi. Judge, Wayne County Municipal Court, Wayne County, Ohio, 1976-1982. Member: Shisler Conference Center Board, Ohio State University; Community Advisory Board, First Merit Bank,N.A. *Member:* Ohio State and American Bar Associations. ***PRACTICE AREAS:*** Corporate Law; Business Law; Estate Planning. ***Email:*** RAmiet@bdblaw.com

STEVEN A. ARMATAS, born Canton, Ohio, 1959; admitted to bar, 1984, Ohio; U.S. District Court, Northern District of Ohio. *Education:* Harvard University (B.A., cum laude, 1981; J.D., cum laude, 1984). John Harvard Scholar; Felix Frankfurter Scholar. Article, "State Educational Institutions Granted Immunity for Patent and Trademark Infringement," ITPE Journal, 1999. *Member:* Stark County, Ohio State and American Bar Associations. ***LANGUAGES:*** Greek. ***PRACTICE AREAS:*** Corporate Law; Mergers and Acquisitions; Securities Regulation; Copyrights. ***Email:*** SArmatas@bdblaw.com

LEE J. BELL, born Little Falls, New York, December 22, 1947; admitted to bar, 1973, Ohio; 1974, U.S. District Court, Northern District of Ohio. *Education:* State University of New York (B.S., 1969); Indiana University School of Law - Bloomington (J.D., 1973). *Member:* Stark County (Past-Member, Executive Committee), Ohio State and American Bar Associations; Ohio Academy of Trial Lawyers. [With U.S. Army Reserves, 1970-1976]. ***PRACTICE AREAS:*** Plaintiffs Personal Injury Litigation; Business Litigation; Plaintiffs Insurance Coverage Litigation. ***Email:*** LBell@bdblaw.com

DAVID PATRICK DURESKA, born Canton, Ohio, March 17, 1958; admitted to bar, 1987, Ohio; 1988, U.S. Court of Appeals, Sixth Circuit; 2004, U.S. Court of Appeals for the Federal Circuit; registered to practice before U.S. Patent and Trademark Office. *Education:* Ohio State University (B.S., 1980; J.D., 1986). *Member:* Stark County and Ohio State Bar Associations; American and Cleveland Intellectual Property Law Associations. ***PRACTICE AREAS:*** Intellectual Property; Patents; Trademarks; Copyrights. ***Email:*** DDureska@bdblaw.com

WILLIAM W. EMLEY, SR., born Berea, Ohio, 1945; admitted to bar, 1971, Ohio; 1984, U.S. Court of Appeals, Sixth Circuit. *Education:* Berea High School (Valedictorian,

(This Listing Continued)

1963); Princeton University (A.B., 1967); University of California, Boalt Hall School of Law, Berkeley (J.D., 1971). *Member:* Tuscarawas County, Stark County (President, 2006-2007; Chairman, Notary Committee; Member: Disputed Fee Committee; Unauthorized Practice Committee; Municipal Court Committee), Ohio State and American Bar Associations; Ohio Creditors Attorney's Association (Treasurer). [U.S. Army Reserves; Ohio National Guard]. ***PRACTICE AREAS:*** Financial Institutions; Collections; Commercial Litigation; Banks and Banking; Bankruptcy; Family Law. ***Email:*** WEmley@bdblaw.com

JOSEPH J. FELTES, born Cleveland, Ohio, August 2, 1948; admitted to bar, 1978, Ohio. *Education:* John Carroll University (A.B., magna cum laude, 1970); University of Pittsburgh (M.A., with distinction, 1972) Mellon Fellow; Georgetown University Law Center (J.D., cum laude, 1978). Topics Editor, American Criminal Law Review, 1977-1978. Author: "Going Bare?" Ophthalmology Management, September 2005; "Disruptive Physicians: An Alternative to Formal Corrective Action," The Cleveland Bar Journal, March 2004; "'I'm Sorry' A Prescription for Preventing Suits," M.D. News, September-October 2004. *Member:* Ohio State (Member, Health Law Committee) and American (Memver, Sections on: Health Law; Antitrust) Bar Associations; American Academy of Hospital Attorneys; Society of Ohio Hospital Attorneys. ***PRACTICE AREAS:*** Health Law; Health Litigation; Products Liability Defense. ***Email:*** JFeltes@bdblaw.com

MARK D. FRASURE, born Dayton, Ohio, July 12, 1947; admitted to bar, 1974, Ohio. *Education:* Georgetown College (B.A., summa cum laude, 1969); The Ohio State University (J.D., summa cum laude, 1974). *Member:* American Board of Trial Advocates. [Officer, U.S. Navy, 1969-1971]. ***PRACTICE AREAS:*** Insurance Defense; Medical Malpractice. ***Email:*** MFrasure@bdblaw.com

STEPHEN P. GRIFFIN, born Pennsylvania, February 11, 1960; admitted to bar, 1988, Ohio; 1998, Pennsylvania; U.S. District Court, Northern District of Ohio; U.S. Court of Appeals, Sixth Circuit. *Education:* Grove City College (B.A., 1982); University of Pittsburgh (M.P.A., 1983); Akron University Law School (J.D., 1987). Author: "For Love or Money," Stark County Medical Society News, May/June 2005; MD News, May/June 2005; "The Other Oath," Stark County Medical Society News, March 2005; MD News, November/December 2004; "Election of Consent," BDB Health and Medicine Reporter; MD News, November/December 2004; Martindale Hubbell Counsel to Counsel Health Care Alert, May 5, 2005. Member, Board of Directors and Coach: Jackson Youth Football; Jackson Youth Basketball. Legal Advisor, Jackson High School Mock Trial Team. Member, St. Michael's Parish. *Member:* Stark County, Ohio State, Pennsylvania and American Bar Associations; International Association of Defense Counsel; Defense Research Institute; Ohio Association of Civil Trial Attorneys (District Director); Pennsylvania Association of Defense Attorneys. ***PRACTICE AREAS:*** Medical Malpractice; Drug and Medical Device Defense; Products Liability Defense. ***Email:*** SGriffin@bdblaw.com

CHRISTOPHER S. HUMPHREY, admitted to bar, 1993, Ohio. *Education:* Bob Jones University (B.A., 1988); Grand Rapids Baptist Seminary (M.T.S., cum laude, 1990); The University of Akron School of Law (J.D., cum laude, 1993). Akron Law Review, Case and Comment Editor, 1992-1993. Recognized as one of Ohio's Super Lawyers - Rising Stars, in the 2005 Cincinnati Magazine, as voted by his peers. *Member:* Akron, Canton, Ohio State and American Bar Associations. ***PRACTICE AREAS:*** Trial Practice; Medical Malpractice Defense; Long Term Care; Legal Malpractice. ***Email:*** CHumphrey@bdblaw.com

RICHARD J. LOLLI, born Alliance, Ohio, February 11, 1951; admitted to bar, 1976, Ohio; 1977, U.S. District Court, Northern District of Ohio. *Education:* Georgetown University, Washington, D.C. (B.S.F.S., 1973); Case Western Reserve University (J.D., 1976). Member, Ohio Land Title Association. President, Certified Title Agency, Inc. Secretary, Saint Joseph Care Center. Executive Committee, Stark County Unique Club. Member, Georgetown University Alumni Admission Committee. *Member:* Ohio State Bar Association; Stark County Bar Association. ***LANGUAGES:*** Italian. ***PRACTICE AREAS:*** Real Estate; Title Insurance; Estate Planning; Probate; General Practice; Business. ***Email:*** rlolli@bdblaw.com

ROBERT C. MEYER, born Lorain, Ohio, July 30, 1953; admitted to bar, 1978, Ohio; U.S. Court of Military Appeals; 1983, U.S. District Court, Northern District of Ohio. *Education:* Wittenberg University (B.A., 1975); University of Toledo (J.D., 1978). *Member:* Stark County, Ohio State and American Bar Associations. [Capt., JAGC, U.S. Army, 1979-1981]. ***PRACTICE AREAS:*** Workers Compensation; Insurance Defense; Family Law. ***Email:*** BMeyer@bdblaw.com

RICHARD S. MILLIGAN, born Canton, Ohio, August 26, 1954; admitted to bar, 1980, Ohio; U.S. District Court, Northern and Southern Districts of Ohio; U.S. Court of Appeals, Sixth Circuit; U.S. Supreme Court. *Education:* Kenyon College (A.B., 1976); Akron University Law School (J.D., 1980). Articles Editor, Akron Law Review, 1978-1979. Author: Comment, "The Use of Prior Inconsistent Statements of Opinion to Impeach: Ohio's Position," 13 Akron L. Rev. 86, 1979; Note, 11 Akron L. Rev. 333, 1977. Commissioner, Board of Commissioners of Grievance and Discipline of the Supreme Court of Ohio, 1994-1996. Member, Board of Education, Canton City Schools, 2002—. Speaker: "Ethics and the Elder Law Practice," Stark County Bar Association; "Ohio Ethics Law 2004," Stark County Bar Association; "Ethics and Deposition Practice," National Association of Railroad Trial Counsel, Winter Meeting; "Ethics for the Legal Aid Practitioner," Community Legal Aid Services; "Documentation and Legal Liability for the Coronary Care Nurse," Guidant Corporation; "Risk Management in Obstetrics," OB/GYN Residents. *Member:* Stark County and Ohio State Bar Associations; Ohio Association of Civil Trial Attorneys; The Defense Research Institute; International Association of Defense Counsel; Ohio State Bar Foundation. ***PRACTICE AREAS:*** Health Care; Hospital Law; Legal Ethics and Professional Responsibility; Litigation; Medical Malpractice; Professional Liability. ***Email:*** rmilligan@bdblaw.com

TOD T. MORROW, born Canton, Ohio, 1961; admitted to bar, 1989, Ohio. *Education:* Mount Union College (B.A., magna cum laude, 1983); Kent State University (M.A., 1986); Ohio State University (J.D., 1989). Speaker: "Workplace Accidents: How to Minimize Your Company's Liability Exposure," Ohio Safety Congress & Expo, 2005; "Effective Claims Management," H.J. Heinz Annual Safety Conference, Bonita Springs, FL, 2004; "Employment Law for Medical Office Managers," Stark County Medical Office Managers Association, 2004; "OSHA Compliance for Nursing Homes," Ohio Health Care Association Annual Convention, Columbus, OH, 2002; "Avoiding Liability for Employment Discrimination," Tusc. County SHRM, 2002; "Effective Use of Employee Separation Agreements," Buckingham Employment Law Seminar, 2002; "OSHA Compliance Update in Ohio," National Business Institute Seminar, 2001; "Selecting and Terminating Employees," Lorman Education Services, 2001; "Navigating Your Way Through the Disability Minefield: The Interrelationship Between the FMLA, ADA and Workers' Compensation," Lorman Education Services, 2001; "Advanced Workers' Compensation in Ohio," National Business Institute, 2000; "Avoiding OSHA Citations and Liabilities in Ohio," Lorman Education Services, 2000; "OSHA Legislative and Legal Update," NEOUCOM Occupational Safety & Health Conference, 1998-2004. Assistant Law Director, City of North Canton. Graduate, Thirteenth Class of Leadership Stark County. Chairman, Board of Directors, American Cancer Society, Stark County Branch. Member: Board of Trustees, Canton Montessori School; Canton Regional Chamber of Commerce, Economic Development Committee and Labor and Employment and Workers' Compensation Subcommittees; North Canton Board of Zoning Appeals, 1999-2002. President, Stark County Safety Council, 1997-1999. Treasurer, The Arthritis Foundation of Northeastern Ohio, Stark County Branch, 1993-1999. (Certified Specialist in Workers' Compensation Law, Ohio State Bar Association). ***PRACTICE AREAS:*** Employment Law; OSHA; Workers Compensation; Construction Law. ***Email:*** tmorrow@bdblaw.com

PAUL J. PUSATERI, born Cleveland, Ohio, January 4, 1964; admitted to bar, 1991, New Mexico; 1993, U.S. District Court, District of New Mexico; 1997, Ohio and U.S. District Court, Northern District of Ohio. *Education:* Walsh College (B.A., summa cum laude, 1987); Case Western Reserve University (M.A., 1988; J.D., 1991). Adjunct Professor, Walsh University. Member, Walsh University Alumni Board. Board Member, Canton Players. City Attorney, City of Hobbs, New Mexico, 1993-1997. *Member:* Stark County, Ohio State and American Bar Associations; State Bar of New Mexico; Ohio Association of Civil Trial Attorneys; Ohio Municipal League; Municipal Attorneys. ***PRACTICE AREAS:*** Employment Law; Litigation; Public Law. ***Email:*** ppusateri@bdblaw.com

JOHN C. ROSS, born Conneaut, Ohio, February 24, 1957; admitted to bar, 1982, Ohio; U.S. District Court, Northern District of Ohio; U.S. Court of Appeals, Sixth Circuit. *Education:* Ohio University (A.B., summa cum laude, 1979); Ohio State University (J.D., 1982). Former Member, Board of Directors, Stark Metropolitan Housing Authority; SARTA. Former Member, Board of Directors, Canton Urban League. Member, Board of Trustees, Builder's Exchange of East Central Ohio. *Member:* Stark County, Ohio State and American Bar Associations. ***PRACTICE AREAS:*** Construction; Labor and Employment Law; Business Law. ***Email:*** jross@bdblaw.com

JOHN P. VAN ABEL, born Quincy, Illinois, February 12, 1932; admitted to bar, 1959, Ohio. *Education:* Miami University; Mount Union College (B.A., 1956); The Ohio State University (J.D., 1958). Phi Delta Phi. Member, American Academy of Hospital Attorneys, Board Member 1984-1990. President, Ohio Society of Hospital Attorneys, 1982-1983. Inducted into the Ohio Bar Title Insurance Company's "Distinguished Agent," program in 2003. Member, Panel of Arbitrators, American Arbitration Association. *Member:* Stark County, Ohio State and American Bar Associations. [U.S. Army, 1952-1954]. ***PRACTICE AREAS:*** Business Law; Real Estate Law; Health Law; Corporate Law. ***Email:*** JVanAbel@bdblaw.com

PARTNERS

DIANNE BLOCKER BRAUN, born Canton, Ohio, January 10, 1951; admitted to bar, 1976, Ohio; 1977, U.S. District Court, Southern District of Ohio; 1984, U.S. District Court, Northern District of Ohio; 1987, U.S. Court of Appeals, Sixth Circuit. *Education:* Indiana University (B.A., with honors, 1972); Indiana University School of Law (J.D., 1976). Trustee, Canton Museum of Art. Member, Trust & Estates Committee, Stark Community Foundation. Member, Women's Initiative Network. Member, Hadassah - JNF Committee Chair. Trustee, Market Hills Association. *Member:* Cleveland, Stark County and Ohio State Bar Associations. ***PRACTICE AREAS:*** Estate Planning; Trust Administration; Estate Administration; Probate; Closely Held Business Law. ***Email:*** DBraun@bdblaw.com

THOMAS R. HIMMELSPACH, born Salem, Ohio, August 29, 1951; admitted to bar, 1987, Ohio. *Education:* Ohio University (B.G.S., 1976); Akron University Law School (J.D., 1987). Member, Akron Law Review, 1986-1987. Author: Casenote, "Commodity Futures Trading Commission v. Weintraub," Vol. 19, No. 1, Akron Law Review, Summer, 1985; "Limits on Expert Testimony under Daubert v. Merrell Dow Pharmaceuticals, Inc.," National Research Council, Transportation Research Board, 36th Annual Workshop on Transportation Law, Chicago, Illinois, July 21, 1997; "A Broad Overview of EMTALA, The Federal 'Patient Anti-Dumping Act'," Buckingham, Doolittle, & Burroughs, LLP Health & Medicine Reporter; Martindale Hubbell, Counsel to Counsel Health Care Alert, May 5, 2005. *Member:* Stark County, Ohio State and American (Member, Sixth Circuit Editor: Tort and Insurance Practice Section, Appellate Advocacy Committee Newsletter) Bar Associations. ***PRACTICE AREAS:*** Medical Malpractice; Health Law; Insurance Defense; Appellate Practice; Railroad Litigation. ***Email:*** thimmelspach@bdblaw.com

PHILIP E. HOWES, born Canton, Ohio, October 9, 1935; admitted to bar, 1960, Ohio; 1965, U.S. District Court, Northern District of Ohio; 1968, U.S. District Court, Southern District of Ohio; 1975, U.S. Court of Appeals, Sixth Circuit; 1986, U.S. Supreme Court. *Education:* Pennsylvania State University (B.S., 1957); Case Western Reserve University (LL.B., 1960). *Member:* Stark County (President, 1980-1981) and Ohio State Bar Associations; National Association of Railroad Trial Counsel; Ohio Association of Civil Trial Attorneys; The Defense Research Institute, Inc.; International Association of Defense Counsel. Fellow: American College of Trial Lawyers; Ohio State Bar Foundation. ***PRACTICE AREAS:*** Medical Malpractice; Health Law; Litigation; Railroad Law. ***Email:*** phowes@bdblaw.com

BARBARA A. KNAPIC, born Akron, Ohio; admitted to bar, 1986, Ohio. *Education:* Kent State University (B.S., in Journalism, cum laude, 1979); University of Akron (J.D., 1986). Recipient, Patrick O'Neill Award. Member, University of Akron Law Review, 1984. Recipient, Scripps-Howard Scholarship. Member, Ohio Industrial Commission, 1994-1999 and (Chairperson,1994-1995). Chair, Ohio Self Insured Employer Board 1994-1999. Member, Board of Directors, Women Executives in State Government. Member, National Association of Female Executives. Certified Workers' Compensation Specialist, Ohio State Bar Association, Jan. 2001. Member, Workers' Compensation Committee and Chair, Industrial Commission Liaison Subcommittee, OSBA. Participant, Leadership Knox. Mem-

(This Listing Continued)

BUCKINGHAM, DOOLITTLE & BURROUGHS, LLP, Canton—Continued

ber, Ohio Bar Association Mock Trial Committee, 2003—.; Ohio Super Lawyer 2004-2006. Ohio Manufacturers' Association Workers' Compensation Committee. Former Co-chair, Dispute Resolution Committee, International Association of Injury and Accident Boards and Commission. Former Vice-President and Trustee, Self Insured Group of Ohio.Member, Board of Wayne Center for the Arts (Wooster, Ohio). Board Member, Friends & Neighbors of Every Women's House. *Member:* Stark County, Columbus, Ohio State and American Bar Associations. Ohio Bar Foundation. (Certified Specialist in Workers' Compensation Law, Ohio State Bar Association). ***LANGUAGES:*** Spanish. ***PRACTICE AREAS:*** Workers Compensation; Employment Law. ***Email:*** bknapic@bdblaw.com

OF COUNSEL

ARTHUR S. LEB, born Cleveland, Ohio, June 26, 1930; admitted to bar, 1955, Ohio; 1976, U.S. Supreme Court. *Education:* Columbia University (A.B., 1952); Case Western Reserve University (LL.B., 1955). Phi Delta Phi. Executive Committee, 1974-1984 and President, 1983-1984, Ohio Council of School Board Attorneys. *Member:* Stark County Bar Association (President, 1984-1985). ***PRACTICE AREAS:*** Business Law. ***Email:*** ALeb@bdblaw.com

ASSOCIATES

KAREN D. BUTERA, born Cleveland, Ohio; admitted to bar, 1999, Ohio, U.S. District Court, Northern District of Ohio and U.S. Court of Appeals, Sixth Circuit. *Education:* Kent State University (A.S., 1981); Malone College (B.A., 1986); University of Akron (J.D., cum laude, 1999). Member, Trial Competition Team, University of Akron School of Law. Member, University of Akron Law Review, 1997-1999. Recipient: Outstanding Woman Student Award; Stark County Legal Association Scholarship. Alumnus, Leadership Stark County, 14th Class. Member: Executive Women's Golf Association; Grand Parade Committee, Pro Football Hall of Fame; Advancement Committee Plan, Canton Museum of Art. Business Manager and School Treasurer, Ohio School. Speaker: "E-Contracting: E-Business When and Where You Want To" (E-Commerce Seminar); "Trade Secret Law" (Akron Bar Association Seminar); "Legal Aspects of E-Commerce" (Kent State University - Stark Campus); "E-Gossip: Defamation and Disparagement on the Internet"; "Identity Theft" (North Canton Kiwanis). ***PRACTICE AREAS:*** Litigation; Intellectual Property. ***Email:*** KButera@bdblaw.com

G. BRENDA COEY, born Lewisburg, Pennsylvania; admitted to bar, 2003, Ohio. *Education:* Pennsylvania State University (B.S., Health Planning and Administration, 1986); University of Akron (J.D., 2002). Licensed Nursing Home Administrator. Speaker: "How To Survive the Nursing Home Survey Process" (Autumn Enterprises); "Conducting Abuse/Neglect Investigations" (AOPHA). *Member:* Stark County, Ohio State and American Bar Associations. ***PRACTICE AREAS:*** Health and Medicine; Litigation; Employment Law; Workers Compensation; Administrative Law. ***Email:*** bcoey@bdblaw.com

DENISE A. GARY, born Ashtabula, Ohio, December 3, 1972; admitted to bar, 1998, Ohio. *Education:* University of Akron (B.A., magna cum laude, 1995); Case Western Reserve University School of Law (J.D., 1998). Health Matrix: The Journal of Law-Medicine, Editor (1995-1997). Member: Psi Chi, The National Honor Society in Psychology; Golden Key National Honor Society. Phi Sigma Alpha, Buchtel College of Arts and Science Honorary. *Member:* Stark County, Ohio State and American Bar Associations. ***PRACTICE AREAS:*** Workers Compensation. ***Email:*** dgary@bdblaw.com

JUSTIN S. GREENFELDER, born Canton, Ohio, September 22, 1978; admitted to bar, 2004, Ohio. *Education:* Dension University (B.A., Chemistry, 2001); University of Akron School of Law (J.D., IP Certificate Program, 2004). Member, University of Akron Intellectual Property and Trademark Law Association, 2001-2004. Legal Advisor, Jackson High School Mock Trial Team, 2004—. Co-Legal Advisor, Jackson Youth Basketball Association. Recipient: CALI Award for Excellence in Civil Procedure, International Law, Taxation of Intellectual Property, Current Policy Issues Affecting Intellectual Property (award signifies highest grade received in course), 2003. Member, Denison Univeristy, Varsity D Alumni Association, 2001—. Assistant Varsity Baseball Coach, Jackson High School, 2002-2004. Basketball Coach, Jackson Friends Church, 1995—. *Member:* Stark County Bar Association; Summit County Bar Association; Ohio State Bar Association; American Bar Association. ***PRACTICE AREAS:*** Health; Medicine; Intellectual Property; Litigation; Medical Malpractice Defense. ***Email:*** jgreenfelder@bdblaw.com

KRISTINA M. HARLESS, born Belleville, Illinois, October 17, 1967; admitted to bar, 1999, Ohio. *Education:* Mary Washington College (B.A., History, 1991); University of Akron School of Law (J.D., 1999). Member, Stark County Safety Council Steering Committee. Member, Board of Directors, Stark County Law Library Association. *Member:* Ohio State and American Bar Associations; Northeast Ohio Corporate Counsel Association; Promotion Marketing Association. ***PRACTICE AREAS:*** Employment Law; Workers Compensation. ***Email:*** kharless@bdblaw.com

EDWARD T. KENNEDY, born Youngstown, Ohio, August 6, 1967; admitted to bar, 2000, Ohio and U.S. District Court, Northern District of Ohio; registered to practice before U.S. Patent and Trademark Office. *Education:* Youngstown State University (B.E., 1990; M.S., 1992); University of Dayton (J.D., cum laude, 2000). Speaker: "The Intersection of Financial Methods and Patents: Business Method Patents," Society of Financial Service Professionals and the Columbus Bar Association, Columbus, Ohio, April 21, 2005; "Intellectual Property for Employers," Buckingham, Doolittle & Burroughs' 16th Annual Employment Law Seminar, Akron, Cleveland and Canton, October 2004; "Protecting Your Intellectual Property," SCORE Small Business and Law Seminar, Canton, Ohio, October 16, 2004; "Business Methods Patents," Columbus Estate Planning Group, Columbus, Ohio, September 8, 2004; "Intellectual Property in Business," Seminar on Innovative Strategies for Growing and Protecting Your Business in a Challenging Economy, Massillon, Ohio, March 18, 2004. Member, Society of Plastics Engineers. *Member:* Stark County, Ohio State and American Bar Associations; Cleveland Intellectual Property Law Association (Chair of Admissions and Membership Committee); American Intellectual Property Law Association. ***PRACTICE AREAS:*** Intellectual Property; Patents; Trademarks; Copyrights; Trade Secrets; Litigation. ***Email:*** ekennedy@bdblaw.com

(This Listing Continued)

SHILA J. NALAWADI, born Barberton, Ohio; admitted to bar, 2001, Ohio; 2003, U.S. District Court, Northern District of Ohio. *Education:* Mount Union College (B.S., 1989); University of Illinois (M.P.H., 1991); Case Western Reserve University (J.D., cum laude, 2001). Editor-in-Chief, Health Matrix: Journal of Law-Medicine, 2000-2001. *Member:* Stark County, Ohio State and American Bar Associations; American Health Lawyers Association. ***PRACTICE AREAS:*** Health Care; Medical Malpractice Defense. ***Email:*** snalawadi@bdblaw.com

SUSAN CHAE RANK, admitted to bar, 1998, California; 1999, Ohio. *Education:* University of Pennsylvania (B.A., 1992); Stanford University (M.A., 1994); Santa Clara University School of Law (J.D., 1998). Member: Angel Auction Committee, Aultman Women's Board; Selection Committee, Leadership Stark County. Author: "Ohio Encourages 'Good Samaritans' with New Law," (M.D. News) May/June 2005; Speaker: "Labor Arbitrations," BDB Public Law Seminar. *Member:* Ohio State Bar Association; Stark County Bar Association; American Bar Association. ***PRACTICE AREAS:*** Employment and Workers; Health Law. ***Email:*** srank@bdblaw.com

REPRESENTATIVE CLIENTS: Akron General Medical Center; American Physicians Capital Inc.; Aultman Hospital; Crystal Clinic; Extendicare Health Services, Inc.; First Physicians Insurance Company; Fred Olivieri Construction Company; The Ford Motor Company; GE Medical Protective Insurance Company; Haines & Company, Inc.; HCR Manor Care; Hendrickson USA, L.L.C.; The J.M. Smucker Company; Medical Justice; Medina General Hospital; Ohio Bar Liability Insurance Co.; Ohio Hospital Insurance Company; Ohio Insurance Guarantee Association; OMNOVA Solutions, Inc.; Suarez Corp.; The Wooster Brush Company; TREK Bicycle, Inc.; U.S. Technology, Inc.

DAY KETTERER LTD.

Established in 1872

MILLENNIUM CENTRE, SUITE 300
200 MARKET AVENUE NORTH
P.O. BOX 24213
CANTON, OHIO 44701-4213
Telephone: 330-455-0173
Telecopier: 330-455-2633
URL: http://www.dayketterer.com
URL: http://www.day-ketterer.com

General Civil Practice in all the Courts. General Business, Corporation, Insurance, Antitrust, Banking, Labor Law, Commercial Transactions, Bankruptcy, Environmental, Occupational Safety and Health, Workers Compensation, Estate Planning, Real Estate, Taxation, Family Law and Probate Law. Trials and Appeals in all Courts. Administrative Law.

MEMBERS OF FIRM

JOHN R. WERREN, born Canton, Ohio, March 26, 1937; admitted to bar, 1961, Ohio and U.S. District Court, Northern District of Ohio. *Education:* Grove City College (A.B., cum laude, 1958); Case-Western Reserve University (LL.B., 1961). Omicron Delta Kappa; Delta Theta Phi. *Member:* Stark County, Ohio State and American Bar Associations. [Capt., U.S. Air Force, 1963-1966]. ***PRACTICE AREAS:*** Estate Planning; Estate Administration; Civil Litigation; Corporate; Family Law. ***Email:*** jrwerren@day-ketterer.com

WILLIAM B. BADGER, born Millersburg, Ohio, May 20, 1937; admitted to bar, 1961, Ohio and U.S. District Court, Northern District of Ohio. *Education:* Denison University; The Ohio State University (J.D., 1961). Phi Delta Phi. *Member:* Stark County, Ohio State and American Bar Associations. [Capt., US Army, 1963-1965]. ***PRACTICE AREAS:*** Estate Planning; Estate Administration; Real Estate. ***Email:*** wbbadger@day-ketterer.com

JAMES K. BROOKER, born Longstreth, Ohio, March 27, 1938; admitted to bar, 1962, Ohio and U.S. District Court, Northern District of Ohio; 1966, Illinois. *Education:* Kent State University; The Ohio State University (LL.B., 1962). Order of the Coif; Phi Delta Phi. Case Note Editor, The Ohio State Law Journal, 1961. *Member:* Stark County, Ohio State and American Bar Associations. [Capt., U.S. Army, 1963-1965]. ***PRACTICE AREAS:*** Business Organizations; Employment Law; Real Estate; Litigation; Insurance Law. ***Email:*** jkbrooker@day-ketterer.com

J. SEAN KEENAN, born Akron, Ohio, November 14, 1942; admitted to bar, 1967, Ohio and U.S. District Court, Northern District of Ohio; 1984, U.S. Court of Appeals, 6th Circuit. *Education:* Walsh College (B.A., summa cum laude, 1964); University of Notre Dame (LL.B., 1967). *Member:* Stark County, Ohio State and American Bar Associations. [Lt., USNR, 1968-1971]. ***PRACTICE AREAS:*** Civil Rights Defense; Commercial Litigation; Corporate. ***Email:*** jskeenan@day-ketterer.com

WAYNE C. KYHOS, born Washington, D.C., January 23, 1944; admitted to bar, 1969, Ohio; 1970, U.S. Court of Military Appeals; 1973, Georgia and U.S. District Court, Northern District of Ohio. *Education:* DePauw University (B.A., 1966); University of Akron (J.D., 1969). Phi Alpha Delta. *Member:* Stark County, Ohio State and American Bar Associations; State Bar of Georgia; Defense Research Institute; Ohio Association of Civil Trial Attorneys. Fellow: Ohio State Bar Foundation. [Capt., JAGC, U.S. Army, 1970-1973]. ***PRACTICE AREAS:*** Litigation; Insurance Defense. ***Email:*** wckyhos@day-ketterer.com

SHEILA MARKLEY BLACK, born Canton, Ohio, October 7, 1947; admitted to bar, 1972, Ohio; 1977, U.S. District Court, Northern District of Ohio; 1981, U.S. Court of Appeals, 6th Circuit; 1985, U.S. Court of Appeals, 3rd Circuit; 1994, U.S. Supreme Court. *Education:* Mount Holyoke College (B.A., 1969); Duke University (J.D., 1972). *Member:* Stark County, Ohio State and American Bar Associations. ***PRACTICE AREAS:*** Employee Benefits; Labor Relations; Antitrust. ***Email:*** smblack@day-ketterer.com

JAMES R. BLAKE, born Pittsburgh, Pennsylvania, April 18, 1948; admitted to bar, 1973, Ohio and U.S. District Court, Northern District of Ohio; 1984, U.S. Court of Appeals, 6th Circuit; 2003, U.S. District Court, Southern District of Ohio. *Education:* Duke University (B.A., 1970); The Ohio State University (J.D., cum laude, 1973). Instructor, Labor Relations, Malone College, 1975. *Member:* Stark County, Ohio State and American (Member, Sections of: Labor and Employment Law; Litigation) Bar Associations; Ohio Association

(This Listing Continued)

of Civil Trial Attorneys; Federation of Insurance and Corporate Counsel; Defense Research Institute, Inc. (Managing Member). ***PRACTICE AREAS:*** Employment Law; General Litigation; Electrical Injury Litigation. ***Email:*** jrblake@day-ketterer.com

JOHN H. BRANNEN, born Dover, Ohio, July 22, 1949; admitted to bar, 1975, Ohio and U.S. District Court, Northern District of Ohio; 1984, Florida and U.S. Court of Appeals, 6th Circuit. *Education:* Ohio University (B.A., summa cum laude, 1972); University of Michigan (J.D., cum laude, 1975). Phi Beta Kappa. *Member:* Stark County, Ohio State and American Bar Associations; The Florida Bar. ***PRACTICE AREAS:*** Business Organizations and Transactions; Securities; Aircraft Finance and Leasing. ***Email:*** jhbrannen@day-ketterer.com

RICHARD A. PRINCIC, born Cleveland, Ohio, December 13, 1950; admitted to bar, 1976, Ohio and U.S. District Court, Northern District of Ohio; 1980, U.S. Court of Appeals, 6th Circuit. *Education:* Allegheny College (B.A., cum laude, 1973); The Ohio State University (J.D., cum laude, 1976). *Member:* Stark County (Bankruptcy Law Committee Chairman, 1981-1982), Ohio State (Member, Banking, Bankruptcy and Commercial Law Committee) and American Bar Associations; American Bankruptcy Institute. ***PRACTICE AREAS:*** Creditors' Rights; Bankruptcy Law; Secured Transactions; Commercial Litigation. ***Email:*** raprincic@day-ketterer.com

TIM A. POWELL, born North Canton, Ohio, September 2, 1942; admitted to bar, 1976, Ohio and U.S. District Court, Northern District of Ohio. *Education:* Northwestern University (B.A., 1964); Capital University (J.D., 1976). Member, Order of the Curia. *Member:* Stark County, Ohio State and American Bar Associations. ***PRACTICE AREAS:*** Employment Law; Labor Relations; Estate Planning; Estate Administration; Real Estate; Corporate. ***Email:*** tapowell@day-ketterer.com

ALICIA M. WYLER, born Akron, Ohio, July 19, 1946; admitted to bar, 1978, Ohio and U.S. District Court, Northern District of Ohio; U.S. Court of Appeals, 6th Circuit. *Education:* University of Akron (B.A., 1969; J.D., 1977). Phi Alpha Theta. *Member:* Stark County, Ohio State (Member: Young Lawyers Committee, 1981-1983; Criminal Law Committee, 1983—) and American Bar Associations; Ohio Association of Civil Trial Lawyers; Defense Research Institute. ***PRACTICE AREAS:*** Litigation; Medical Malpractice Defense; Hospital Law; Drug and Medical Device Defense; Products Liability Defense; Commercial Litigation; Real Estate Litigation. ***Email:*** amwyler@day-ketterer.com

WILLIAM S. CLINE, born Athens, Ohio, December 11, 1949; admitted to bar, 1978, Ohio and U.S. District Court, Northern District of Ohio; U.S. Court of Appeals, 6th Circuit. *Education:* Kenyon College (A.B., with High Honors, 1972); Case Western Reserve University (J.D., 1978). *Member:* Stark County and Ohio State Bar Associations; Ohio Association of Civil Trial Lawyers; Defense Research Institute, Inc. ***PRACTICE AREAS:*** Commercial Litigation; Products Liability; Litigation; Commercial Law; Internet Law; Electronic Commerce; OSHA; Litigation Management. ***Email:*** wscline@day-ketterer.com

DANIEL A. MINKLER, born Youngstown, Ohio, January 25, 1952; admitted to bar, 1979, Ohio, U.S. District Court, Northern District of Ohio and U.S. Tax Court. *Education:* College of Wooster; University of Idaho (B.S., 1974); Colgate University (M.A.T., 1978); Cleveland State University (J.D., summa cum laude, 1979). Member of Staff, 1977-1978 and Research Editor, 1978-1979, Cleveland State Law Review. *Member:* Stark County, Ohio State and American Bar Associations. ***PRACTICE AREAS:*** Business Organizations; Mergers and Acquisitions; Commercial Law; Commercial Litigation; Real Estate. ***Email:*** daminkler@day-ketterer.com

MATTHEW YACKSHAW, born Clinton, Iowa, September 29, 1953; admitted to bar, 1979, Ohio and U.S. Claims Court; 1981, U.S. District Court, Northern District of Ohio; 1984, U.S. Tax Court; 1986, U.S. Court of Appeals, 6th Circuit; 1993, U.S. Supreme Court and U.S. Court of International Trade; 1995, U.S. Court of Appeals, Federal Circuit. *Education:* John Carroll University (B.A., magna cum laude, 1976); Ohio State University (J.D., with honors, 1979). Law Clerk to Trial Judge Kenneth R. Harkins, U.S. Court of Claims, 1979-1980. Trial Attorney, U.S. Department of Justice, Tax Division, 1980-1984. Recipient: Outstanding Attorney, U.S. Department of Justice, Tax Division, 1983; Special Commendation, 1984. *Member:* Stark County (Member: Executive, Finance and Grievance Committees); Ohio State (Member, Environmental Law Committee) and American (Member, Sections on: Taxation, Environment, Energy and Resources) Bar Associations. ***PRACTICE AREAS:*** Tax; Environmental Law; Toxic Torts Litigation; Construction Litigation; Commercial Litigation; Insurance Litigation. ***Email:*** myackshaw@day-ketterer.com

RAYMOND T. BULES, born Akron, Ohio, October 21, 1956; admitted to bar, 1981, Ohio and U.S. District Court, Northern District of Ohio. *Education:* College of Wooster (B.A., 1978); College of William & Mary (J.D., 1981). Phi Alpha Delta. *Member:* Stark County, Ohio State and American Bar Associations. ***PRACTICE AREAS:*** Family Law. ***Email:*** rtbules@day-ketterer.com

JOHN A. MURPHY, JR., born Tiffin, Ohio, March 29, 1956; admitted to bar, 1981, Ohio and U.S. District Court, Northern District of Ohio. *Education:* University of Toledo (B.B.A., 1978); Tulane University of Louisiana (J.D., 1981). Phi Alpha Delta. *Member:* Stark County, Ohio State and American Bar Associations; Ohio Association of Civil Trial Attorneys; Defense Research Institute. ***PRACTICE AREAS:*** Insurance Defense Litigation; Real Estate Errors and Omissions; Construction; Commercial Litigation; Products Liability. ***Email:*** jamurphy@day-ketterer.com

MERLE D. EVANS III, born Washington, D.C., September 21, 1957; admitted to bar, 1983, Ohio and U.S. District Court, Northern District of Ohio. *Education:* Duke University (B.A., cum laude, 1980); Case Western Reserve University (J.D., 1983). Member, Case Western Reserve Law Review, 1981-1982. *Member:* Stark County, Ohio State and American Bar Associations; Ohio Association of Civil Trial Attorneys; Defense Research Institute, Inc. ***PRACTICE AREAS:*** Insurance Defense; Insurance Coverage Litigation; Commercial Litigation; General Litigation; Electrical Injury Litigation. ***Email:*** mdevans@day-ketterer.com

ROBERT E. ROLAND, born Youngstown, Ohio, December 19, 1959; admitted to bar, 1985, Ohio. *Education:* Miami University (B.A., cum laude, Honors Program, 1982); The Ohio State University (J.D., 1985). Psi Chi; Phi Alpha Delta. *Member:* Stark County, Ohio State and American Bar Associations. ***PRACTICE AREAS:*** Business Law; Business Organization; Buying and Selling of Businesses; Shopping Center Law; Residential Real Estate Development; Banking Law; Family Business Law; Business Succession Planning; Commercial Real Estate Development; Construction Contracts; Mechanics Liens. ***Email:*** reroland@day-ketterer.com

JILL C. McQUEEN, born Alliance, Ohio, February 6, 1961; admitted to bar, 1986, Ohio and U.S. District Court, Northern District of Ohio. *Education:* Case Western Reserve University (B.A., magna cum laude, 1983); The Ohio State University College of Law (J.D., 1986). Phi Beta Kappa. Member, 1984-1985 and Articles Editor, 1985-1986, Ohio State Journal of Dispute Resolution. *Member:* Stark County, Ohio State and American Bar Associations. ***PRACTICE AREAS:*** Employment Law; Labor Relations; Corporate. ***Email:*** jcmqueen@day-ketterer.com

J. CURTIS WERREN, born Canton, Ohio, December 24, 1967; admitted to bar, 1992, Ohio. *Education:* Grove City College (B.A., 1989); The Ohio State University (J.D., 1992). *Member:* Stark County, Ohio State and American Bar Associations. ***PRACTICE AREAS:*** Family Law; General Practice; Corporate; General Litigation; Adoptions. ***Email:*** jcwerren@day-ketterer.com

THOMAS E. HARTNETT, born Suffern, New York, June 30, 1966; admitted to bar, 1993, Ohio. *Education:* University of Vermont (B.A., 1988); State University of New York at Buffalo; University of Cincinnati (J.D., 1993). *Member:* Stark County, Ohio State and American Bar Associations. ***PRACTICE AREAS:*** Real Estate; Litigation; Title Insurance; Estate Planning. ***Email:*** tehartnett@day-ketterer.com

RICHARD W. ARNOLD, born Canton, Ohio, February 17, 1963; admitted to bar, 1994, Ohio; 1996, District of Columbia, U.S. District Court, Northern District of Ohio and U.S. Tax Court. *Education:* Bowling Green State University (B.S.B.A., 1985); University of Akron (J.D., 1993). *Member:* Ohio State and American Bar Associations; American Institute of Certified Public Accountants; Ohio Society of Certified Public Accountants. ***PRACTICE AREAS:*** Tax Law; Estate Planning. ***Email:*** rwarnold@day-ketterer.com

JACK B. COOPER, born Akron, Ohio, December 3, 1962; admitted to bar, 1992, Florida; 1993, U.S. District Court, Middle District of Florida; 1998, Ohio and U.S. District Court, Northern District of Ohio. *Education:* University of Akron (B.A., summa cum laude, 1986); Ohio State University (J.D., with honors, 1992). Recipient, American Jurisprudence Awards for Remedies and Conflicts of Law. Articles Editor, Ohio State Law Journal. *Member:* Stark County, Ohio State and American (Member, Sections on: Tort and Insurance Practice; Litigation) Bar Associations; Defense Research Institute, Inc. ***PRACTICE AREAS:*** Insurance Litigation; General Litigation. ***Email:*** jbcooper@day-ketterer.com

ROBERT J. McBRIDE, born Youngstown, Ohio, June 24, 1966; admitted to bar, 1995, Ohio; 1996, U.S. District Court, Northern District of Ohio; 1997, U.S. Court of Appeals, Sixth Circuit; 2000, U.S. District Court, Southern District of Ohio. *Education:* University of Dayton (B.A., magna cum laude, 1988); University of Akron (M.P.A., 1991); University of Notre Dame (J.D., cum laude, 1995). *Member:* Stark County, Ohio State and American Bar Associations. ***PRACTICE AREAS:*** Labor Relations; Employment Law; Civil Rights Defense; Civil Litigation; Construction Law. ***Email:*** rjmcbride@day-ketterer.com

STEPHEN E. MATASICH, born Euclid, Ohio, September 22, 1969; admitted to bar, 1996, Ohio; 1997, U.S. District Court, Northern District of Ohio. *Education:* University of Akron (B.A., 1991); Cleveland-Marshall College of Law (J.D., 1995). *Member:* Stark County, Ohio State and American Bar Associations. ***PRACTICE AREAS:*** Workers Compensation; Occupational Safety and Health; Insurance Defense; Civil Litigation. ***Email:*** sematasich@day-ketterer.com

ASSOCIATES

JOHN P. ARCHER, born Pittsburgh, Pennsylvania, August 14, 1975; admitted to bar, 2001, Ohio. *Education:* Denison University (B.A., 1998); The Ohio State University (J.D., 2001). *Member:* Stark County, Ohio State and American Bar Associations. ***PRACTICE AREAS:*** Litigation; Insurance Defense; Commercial Law; Corporate Law. ***Email:*** jparcher@day-ketterer.com

JOANNE G. PAULINO, born Cleveland, Ohio, July 18, 1970; admitted to bar, 1996, Ohio. *Education:* University of Akron (B.S., magna cum laude, 1993; J.D., 1996; M.A., 1997). *Member:* Stark County, Ohio State and American Bar Associations. ***PRACTICE AREAS:*** Bankruptcy; Commercial Law. ***Email:*** jgpaulino@day-ketterer.com

JOHN M. PRELAC, born Warren, Ohio, August 16, 1959; admitted to bar, 1984, Ohio; 1989, U.S District Court, Northern District of Ohio; 1990, U.S. Court of Appeals, Sixth Circuit. *Education:* Mount Union College (B.A., 1981); University of Akron (M.T., 1984; J.D., 1984). Omicron Delta Epsilon. University of Akron Law Review, 1983-1984. Professor, American Institute for Paralegal Studies, Inc., 1990-1991. Assistant Prosecuting Attorney, Summit County, 1987-1992. *Member:* Stark County and Ohio State Bar Associations. ***PRACTICE AREAS:*** Corporate Law; Litigation; Estate Planning; Probate; Wills; Trust Law.

R. CLINT ZOLLINGER, born Canton, Ohio, November 20, 1970; admitted to bar, 1999, Ohio and U.S. District Court, Northern District of Ohio; 2002, U.S. Court of Appeals, Sixth Circuit. *Education:* Washington & Jefferson College (B.A., 1993); University of Akron School of Law (J.D., 1999). Instructor, Malone College Legal Environment of Business Course; ETI Technical College (Paralegal Program). *Member:* Stark County, Ohio State and American Bar Associations. ***PRACTICE AREAS:*** Business Litigation; Commercial Litigation; Workers Compensation; Construction Law.

JOHN S. KAMINSKI, born Canton, Ohio, October 12, 1977; admitted to bar, 2003, Ohio and U.S. District Court, Northern District of Ohio. *Education:* Northwestern University (B.A., Economics, 2000); Indiana University School of Law-Bloomington (J.D., cum laude, 2003). *Member:* Stark County and Ohio State Bar Associations. ***PRACTICE AREAS:*** Civil Litigation; Commercial Litigation; Insurance Defense.

DAVID DAVIS, born Fairmont, West Virginia, May 5, 1978; admitted to bar, 2003, Ohio; 2004, U.S. District Court, Northern District of Ohio. *Education:* Case Western Reserve University (B.A., magna cum laude, 2000); The Ohio State University Moritz College of Law (J.D., cum laude, 2003). *Member:* Stark County and Ohio State Bar Associations. ***PRACTICE AREAS:*** Business Law; Corporate Law.

STEVEN D. SHANDOR, born Youngstown, Ohio, September 13, 1973; admitted to bar, 2004, Ohio. *Education:* Youngstown State University (B.A., 1997; M.A., with honors,

(This Listing Continued)

DAY KETTERER LTD., Canton—Continued

2001); The Ohio State University (J.D., 2004). Phi Kappa Phi. *Member:* Stark County, Ohio and American Bar Associations. ***PRACTICE AREAS:*** Health Care; Litigation; Business Law. ***Email:*** sdshandor@day-ketterer.com

OF COUNSEL

LARRY R. BROWN, born Newark, Ohio, 1935; admitted to bar, 1960, Ohio. *Education:* The Ohio State University (B.S.B.A., 1957); The Ohio State University College of Law (J.D., summa cum laude, 1960). Beta Gamma Sigma; Phi Delta Phi. Managing Partner, Day, Ketterer, Raley, Wright & Rybolt, 1985-1990. *Member:* Stark County, Ohio State and American (Member, Section of Labor and Employment Law) Bar Associations; American Law Institute.

LOUIS A. BOETTLER, born North Canton, Ohio, June 24, 1931; admitted to bar, 1955, Ohio and U.S. District Court, Northern District of Ohio. *Education:* Kent State University (A.B., 1953); The Ohio State University College of Law (J.D., summa cum laude, 1955). Delta Theta Phi. *Member:* Stark County, Ohio State and American Bar Associations; Ohio Association of Civil Trial Attorneys; International Association of Defense Counsel. ***PRACTICE AREAS:*** Litigation; Medical Malpractice Defense; Legal Malpractice Defense; Product Liability Litigation. ***Email:*** laboettler@day-ketterer.com

ROBERT J. NEWBOLD, born Buffalo, New York, January 13, 1963; admitted to bar, 1989, Ohio. *Education:* Mount Union College (B.A., 1985); The University of Akron School of Law (J.D., 1988). Listed in The Best Lawyers in America, 2003-2004. Recognized by "Inside Business Magazine" in 2001 and 2002 as a Leading Lawyer in Tax Law in Northeast Ohio, as voted by his peers. Member: North Canton Rotary, Canton Chamber of Commerce, International Franchise Association, Council of Franchise Suppliers. Former Member, Buckingham, Doolittle & Burroughs, Co. LPA. *Member:* Stark County, Ohio State and American Bar Associations; International Franchise Association. ***PRACTICE AREAS:*** Franchise Law; Business Law; Corporate Law. ***Email:*** rjnewbold@day-ketterer.com

REPRESENTATIVE CLIENTS: American Electric Power; Detroit Diesel Corp.; Everhard Products, Inc.; General Motors Acceptance Corp.; General Motors Corp.; Latrobe Steel Co.; Lauren International; Ohio Power Co.; Press of Ohio, Inc.; The Stark Community Foundation; The Timken Co.; United Foundries, Inc.; Walsh University; Wayne-Dalton Corp.; Whitacre-Greer; Chubb Group; CGU Insurance Co.; Government Employees Insurance Co.; GRE America; Great West Casualty Co.; Motorists Insurance Cos.; St. Paul Insurance Co.; Bank One, Akron; KeyBank; National City Bank; Aultman Hospital; Mercy Medical Center.

DENMEAD LAW OFFICE

CANTON, OHIO

(See Columbus)

Civil Trial and Appellate Practice and Personal Injury, Traumatic Brain Injury (TBI), Professional Negligence and Complex Litigation including Class Actions, Patents, Civil Rights, Civil Litigation, RICO, Employment and Political Subdivision Liability issues.

ELK & ELK CO., L.P.A.

CANTON, OHIO

(See Cleveland)

Automobile Accidents, Product Defects, Nursing Home Neglect, Medical Malpractice, Personal Injury.

FISCHER, EVANS & ROBBINS, LTD.

4505 STEPHEN CIRCLE NW SUITE 100
CANTON, OHIO 44718
Telephone: 330-244-0997
Fax: 330-244-8966
URL: http://www.fer-law.com

Civil Trial and Appellate Practice in all State and Federal Courts, Litigation, Insurance Defense, Insurance Coverage, Products Liability Defense, Political Subdivisions, Premises Liability.

MEMBERS OF FIRM

MARK F. FISCHER, born Massillon, Ohio, September 28, 1960; admitted to bar, 1988, Florida; 1989, U.S. District Court, Middle District of Florida; 1991, Ohio; 1992, U.S. District Court, Northern District of Ohio; 2005, U.S. District Court, Southern District of Ohio. *Education:* University of Notre Dame (B.B.A., in Accounting, 1983); Ohio State University (J.D., 1988). *Member:* Stark County, Ohio State and American Bar Associations; The Florida Bar; Ohio Association of Civil Trial Attorneys; Defense Research Institute. ***PRACTICE AREAS:*** Litigation; Insurance Defense; Products Liability Defense; Insurance Coverage; Political Subdivision Liability; Premises Liability; Construction Litigation. ***Email:*** mff@fer-law.com

CARI FUSCO EVANS, born Kansas City, Missouri, June 6, 1969; admitted to bar, 1993, Ohio; U.S. District Court, Northern District of Ohio; 2000, U.S. Court of Appeals, Sixth Circuit; 2005, U.S. District Court, Southern District of Ohio. *Education:* Muskingum College (B.S., summa cum laude, 1990); Case Western Reserve University (J.D., magna cum laude, 1993). Order of the Coif. *Member:* Stark County, Ohio State and American Bar Associations. ***PRACTICE AREAS:*** Litigation; Insurance Defense; Products Liability Defense; Insurance Coverage; Construction Litigation; Premises Liability; Political Subdivision Liability. ***Email:*** cfevans@fer-law.com

DONALD L. ROBBINS, JR., born Bradford, Pennsylvania, November 23, 1966; admitted to bar, 2002, Ohio; 2005, U.S. District Court, Northern District of Ohio. *Education:* University of Akron (B.S., Accounting, 1991; J.D., cum laude, 2002). Certified Public Accountant, Ohio, 1998. *Member:* Stark County, Ohio State and American Bar Associations.

(This Listing Continued)

PRACTICE AREAS: Litigation; Insurance Defense; Insurance Coverage; Construction Litigation; Premises Liability; Political Subdivision Liability. ***Email:*** dlrobbins@fer-law.com

GRISI & RIEGLER

CANTON, OHIO

(See Akron)

Personal Injury, Medical Malpractice, Divorce, Probate and Estates, Municipal Zoning, Corporate.

GUY, LAMMERT & TOWNE

Established in 1973

P.O. BOX 6426
CANTON, OHIO 44706-0426
Telephone: 330-452-1818
Fax: 330-535-9048
Email: guylaw2210@aol.com

Akron, Ohio Office: 2210 First National Tower. Telephone: 330-535-2151. Fax: 330-535-9048

Bankruptcy, Banking, Business Torts, Corporation, Commercial Litigation, Creditors Rights and Reorganization Law. Domestic Relations, Employment Law, Probate, Personal Injury, Taxation, Trial Practice, Malpractice and Products Liability Law. General Litigation.

RESIDENT MEMBER

THOMAS E. LAMMERT, born Pittsburgh, Pennsylvania, March 26, 1947; admitted to bar, 1976, Ohio and U.S. District Court, Northern District of Ohio; 1982, U.S. Supreme Court; 1983, Florida and U.S. Court of Appeals, Sixth Circuit. *Education:* College of Wooster; University of Pittsburgh (B.S., 1969); University of Akron (J.D., 1976). *Member:* Akron (Vice-Chairman, 1990-1991 and Chairman, 1991-1993, Law Office Management Committee), Stark County, Ohio State and American Bar Associations; The Florida Bar. [With U.S. Navy, 1971-1973]. ***PRACTICE AREAS:*** Bankruptcy Law; Commercial Litigation; Creditors Rights Law; Personal Injury Law. ***Email:*** Telammert@aol.com

(For complete personnel and biographical data, See Professional Biographies at Akron, Ohio).

HENNING & YOST, L.P.A.

5022 YUKON STREET, SUITE D
CANTON, OHIO 44708
Telephone: 330-479-9825
Fax: 330-479-9827
Email: henninglaw@neo.rr.com
URL: http://www.henninglaw.com

Employment Law, Human Resource Management, Civil Litigation.

RICHARD L. HENNING, born Canton, Ohio, November 2, 1949; admitted to bar, 1976, Ohio; 1978, U.S. District Court, Northern District of Ohio. *Education:* Ohio State University (B.S., 1972); University of Akron (J.D., 1976). Delta Theta Phi. Tuscarawas Valley Public Defender's Office, 1976-1979. Assistant Prosecuting Attorney, Stark County, 1979-1984. ***PRACTICE AREAS:*** Employment Law; Civil Litigation. ***Email:*** henninglaw@neo.rr.com

SALLY D. HENNING, born Washington, D.C., December 10, 1950; admitted to bar, 1978, Ohio. *Education:* Ohio State University; University of Maryland (B.A., Philosophy, 1970); University of Akron (J.D., 1978). Speaker: Ohio CLE Institute, "Using Computer Scanned Documents," 1995; "Writing to Persuade," Akron Bar Association and University of Akron Law School, 1994; "Sexual Harassment Update," Rubber Manufacturers Association, 1991; "A.D.A." American Corporation Counsel Association, 1991; "Managing Litigation," National Employment Foundation, 1990. Chairman: *Legal Writing,* 1993; *Aids in the Work Place,* 1992. *Previous Employment*: Formerly with, Henning & Henning; Roetzel and Andress; Brouse & McDowell. Founder, EEO Forum. ***PRACTICE AREAS:*** Employment Law; Civil Litigation. ***Email:*** henninglaw@neo.rr.com

HERBERT & BENSON

4571 STEPHEN CIRCLE, N.W.
CANTON, OHIO 44718
Telephone: 330-499-1016
Fax: 330-499-0790
Email: herblegal@aol.com
URL: http://www.lawyers.com/herblegal

Insurance, Malpractice and Products Liability Defense, Commercial and Corporate Law, Business Law, Buying and Selling of Businesses, Family Business Law, Limited Liability Company Law, Partnership Law, Professional Practices, Small Business Law, Family Law, Franchises and Franchising, General Practice, Health Care, Real Estate, Wills and Probate, Contested Wills, Trusts and Estates. Trial and Appellate Practice.

MEMBERS OF FIRM

DAVID L. HERBERT, born Cleveland, Ohio, October 1, 1948; admitted to bar, 1974, Ohio; 1975, U.S. District Court, Northern District of Ohio; 1984, U.S. Court of Appeals, Sixth Circuit. *Education:* Kent State University (B.B.A., 1971); University of Akron (J.D., 1974). ***PRACTICE AREAS:*** Corporate; Business; Commercial; Insurance; Products Liability; Malpractice; Government. ***Email:*** herblegal@aol.com

DON M. BENSON

(This Listing Continued)

JOSEPH L. PICCIN, born Wheeling, West Virginia, October 11, 1974; admitted to bar, 2000, Ohio; 2001, U.S.District Court, Southern District of Ohio. *Education:* Miami University (B.S., 1997); University of Akron (J.D., 2000). Assistant Attorney General, Antitrust Section, Ohio, 2000-2002; Constitutional Offices Section, Tobacco Unit, 2002-2003. *Member:* Columbus and Ohio State Bar Associations. ***PRACTICE AREAS:*** Civil Litigation; Family Law. **Email:** jlp760@sbcglobal.net

OF COUNSEL

JAMES J. COLLUM (Also practicing individually)

WARREN R. PRICE

LYNN A. ZONDORAK

TIMOTHY J. JEFFRIES

437 MARKET NORTH
CANTON, OHIO 44702
Telephone: 330-456-0061
Fax: 330-456-1344
Email: tjeffries@sbcglobal.net

Business Litigation, Real Estate, Commercial Real Estate, Landlord and Tenant Law, Residential Real Estate, Zoning Law, Land Use, Business Law, Business Acquisitions, Business Sales, Bankruptcy, Business Formation, Business Planning, Business Taxation, Collections, Contracts, Corporate, Partnership Law, Family Business Law, Franchise Law, Estate Planning.

FIRM PROFILE: Experienced in handling collections and real estate matters on behalf of out of state clients.

TIMOTHY J. JEFFRIES, born Canton, Ohio, April 21, 1974; admitted to bar, 2000, Ohio; 2001, U.S. District Court, Northern District of Ohio. *Education:* The Ohio State University (B.A., 1996; J.D., 2000). Licensed Title Agent. *Member:* Stark County and Ohio State Bar Associations. ***PRACTICE AREAS:*** Real Estate; Business Law; Collections; Creditors Rights; Contracts; Litigation.

JOHNSON LAW GROUP

CANTON, OHIO 44718
Telephone: 877-333-2889
Fax: 309-827-3991
Email: johnson.law@verizon.net

Okemos, Michigan Office: 3474 Alaiedon Parkway, 47764. Telephone: 877-333-2889.
Bloomington, Illinois Office: 115 W. Front Street, 61701. Telephone: 309-827-3670.
South Bend, Indiana Office: 218 W. Washington Street, 46601. Telephone: 877-333-2889.

Felonies, Murder, White Collar Crime, Drugs, Domestic Violence, DWI.

FIRM PROFILE: Johnson Law Group provides aggressive criminal defense representation throughout the entire States of Illinois, Indiana, Michigan and Ohio. Our Criminal Defense Attorneys are recognized in Illinois, Indiana, Michigan and Ohio for providing premier criminal defense services. The attorneys at Johnson Law Group place cutting edge aggressive defensive strategies at the top of their priority list. Johnson Law Group has developed a process that allows a client 24 hours a day, 7 days a week access to a client service representative who will work closely with the client and our experienced criminal defense lawyers to make sure that every possible angle in a case is covered. To learn more about our process, visit our website at johnsoncriminaldefenselawgroup.com.

Languages: Japanese and Greek.

(For complete biographical data on all personnel, see Professional Biographies at Bloomington, Illinois)

DOUGLAS D. JONES CO., LPA

Established in 1998
2867 SHARONWOOD AVENUE NW
CANTON, OHIO 44708
Telephone: 330-477-5570
Fax: 330-477-4744
Email: djones@neo.rr.com
URL: http://www.dougdjones.com

Wills, Probate, Trusts and Estates, Family Law, Bankruptcy, Real Estate, Property Law, Personal Injury, Torts, Automobile Accidents, Adoptions, Divorce, Child Custody, Child Support, Debtor and Creditor, Estate Planning, Medical Malpractice and Products Liabilities.

FIRM PROFILE: The firm was established in July 1998 by its founder and owner, Douglas D. Jones, who has had over 24 years of experience in northeastern Ohio in a major law firm and private practice. The firm's mission is to provide affordable quality legal services with a personal caring approach to clients needs.

DOUGLAS D. JONES, born Youngstown, Ohio, 1955; admitted to bar, 1980, Ohio; 1981, U.S. District Court, Northern District of Ohio. *Education:* Oral Roberts University (B.A., Ancient Literature, summa cum laude, 1977); University of Akron School of Law (J.D., 1980). *Member:* Akron and Stark County Bar Associations; Christian Legal Society. ***LANGUAGES:*** German and Hebrew. ***SPECIAL AGENCIES:*** 6th Circuit Bankruptcy Appellate Panel. ***PRACTICE AREAS:*** Probate; Wills; Trust Law; Family Law; Bankruptcy; Real Estate; Property Law; Personal Injury; Torts; Automobile Accidents and Injuries; Adoption Law; Divorce; Child Custody; Child Support; Debtor and Creditor; Medical Malpractice; Products Liability. **Email:** djones@neo.rr.com

Languages: German, Hebrew, Greek.

REPRESENTATIVE CLIENTS: Provided upon request.

KRUGLIAK, WILKINS, GRIFFITHS & DOUGHERTY CO., L.P.A.

Established in 1958
4775 MUNSON STREET, N.W.
P.O. BOX 36963
CANTON, OHIO 44735-6963
Telephone: 330-497-0700
Fax: 330-497-4020
Email: legal@kwgd.com
URL: http://www.kwgd.com

Alliance, Ohio Office: KeyBank Building, 960 West State Street. Telephone: 330-823-9262.
New Philadelphia, Ohio Office: 158 N. Broadway Street. Telephone: 330-364-3472.
Sugarcreek, Ohio Office: 233 Factory Street, Suite 4. Telephone: 330-852-3355.

Corporate Law, Mergers and Acquisitions, Labor and Employment (Private and Public Sector), Employee Benefits, Real Estate, Taxation, Complex Litigation, Contracts, Insurance Defense, Estates and Trusts, Probate, Elder Law, Commercial Litigation, Oil and Gas, Occupational Safety and Health, Environmental Law, Health Care Law, Hospital Law, Bankruptcy, Banks and Banking, Securities, Construction Law, Family Law, Education Law, Workers Compensation, Personal Injury Litigation, Collections, Debtor and Creditor, Government, Media Law and Electronic Commerce.

F. STUART WILKINS (Retired)

RAYMOND E. GRIFFITHS, born 1932; admitted to bar, 1957, Ohio. *Education:* Bethany College (B.A., with honors, 1954); Western Reserve University (LL.B., 1957). Order of the Coif. ***PRACTICE AREAS:*** Labor/Employment Law (Public and Private Sectors); Alternative Dispute Resolution; Trusts and Estates; Wills; Probate; Corporate Law. **Email:** rgriffiths@kwgd.com

RONALD W. DOUGHERTY, born 1932; admitted to bar, 1960, Ohio. *Education:* Dartmouth College (A.B., 1954); University of Virginia (LL.B., 1960). *Member:* Ohio State (Distinguished Life Fellow) and American Bar Associations. ***PRACTICE AREAS:*** Litigation; Estate Planning; Corporate Law; Media Law; Family Law; Trusts and Estates; Wills. **Email:** rdougherty@kwgd.com

DAVID L. SIMIELE, born 1936; admitted to bar, 1963, Ohio, U.S. District Court, Northern District of Ohio and U.S. Court of Appeals, Sixth Circuit. *Education:* The Ohio State University (B.S., 1960); Western Reserve University (LL.B., 1963). ***PRACTICE AREAS:*** Banking Law; Complex Litigation; Commercial Law; Real Estate; Corporate Reorganization. **Email:** dsimiele@kwgd.com

FRED J. HAUPT, born 1941; admitted to bar, 1967, Ohio. *Education:* Mount Union College (B.A., 1963); Western Reserve University (J.D., 1967). Order of the Coif. *Member:* National Health Lawyers Association. ***PRACTICE AREAS:*** Professional Corporation Law; Corporate Law; Health Care; Trusts and Estates; Real Estate. **Email:** fjhaupt@kwgd.com

JOHN BOGNIARD, born 1947; admitted to bar, 1972, Ohio. *Education:* Allegheny College (B.A., 1969); The Ohio State University (J.D., cum laude, 1972). ***PRACTICE AREAS:*** Labor and Employment; Mergers and Acquisitions; Business Law. **Email:** jbogniard@kwgd.com

MICHAEL A. THOMPSON, born 1948; admitted to bar, 1974, Ohio and U.S. District Court, Northern District of Ohio. *Education:* Union College (B.A., 1970); Case Western Reserve University (J.D., with honors, 1974). Order of the Coif. ***PRACTICE AREAS:*** Litigation. **Email:** mthompson@kwgd.com

WILLIAM G. WILLIAMS, born 1950; admitted to bar, 1975, Ohio. *Education:* University of Steubenville (B.A., 1972); Cleveland Marshall College of Law (J.D., 1975). Special Counsel, Ohio Attorney General. Legal Counsel, Better Business Bureau Canton Regional, 1994—. Director, Stark State College Foundation, 1994-2005. ***PRACTICE AREAS:*** Commercial Litigation; Business Law; Real Estate; Natural Resources. **Email:** bwilliams@kwgd.com

RICHARD E. DAVIS, born 1950; admitted to bar, 1976, Ohio; 1999, Florida. *Education:* College of Wooster (B.A., with honors, 1972); University of Southern California (M.A., 1973; J.D., 1976). Member, Editorial Board, Probate Law Journal of Ohio. Certified Elder Law Attorney by the National Elder Law Association. Listed in The Best Lawyers in America. (Certified Specialist in Estate Planning, Trust and Probate Law, Ohio State Bar Association). ***PRACTICE AREAS:*** Elder Law; Trusts and Estates; Asset Protection Planning; Probate. **Email:** rdavis@kwgd.com

RANDALL C. HUNT, born 1953; admitted to bar, 1978, Ohio. *Education:* Mount Union College (B.A., magna cum laude, 1975); Case Western Reserve University (J.D., 1978). *Member:* American Health Lawyers Association; American Academy of Healthcare Attorneys; Society of Ohio Hospital Attorneys. ***PRACTICE AREAS:*** Health Care; Corporate Law; Mergers and Acquisitions. **Email:** rchunt@kwgd.com

SAM O. SIMMERMAN, born 1953; admitted to bar, 1979, Ohio. *Education:* Kent State University (B.A., magna cum laude, 1976); The Ohio State University (J.D., with honors, 1979). ***PRACTICE AREAS:*** Commercial Law; Bankruptcy; Securities; Business Law; Commercial Real Estate; Corporate Law; Contracts; Debtor and Creditor; Finance; Mortgages; Public Finance; Real Estate. **Email:** sosimmerman@kwgd.com

TERRY A. MOORE, born 1955; admitted to bar, 1980, Ohio. *Education:* Youngstown State University (B.A., cum laude, 1977); University of Cincinnati (J.D., 1980). ***PRACTICE AREAS:*** Corporate Law; Mergers and Acquisitions; Professional Corporations; Physician Practices; Accountants Liability; Banking Law; Real Property. **Email:** tmoore@kwgd.com

PAUL H. MALESICK II, born 1955; admitted to bar, 1981, Ohio, U.S. District Court, Northern District of Ohio, U.S. Court of Appeals, Third, Fourth and Sixth Circuits and U.S. Supreme Court. *Education:* Kent State University (B.A., magna cum laude, 1978); University of Akron (J.D., 1981). ***PRACTICE AREAS:*** Employee Benefits; Labor and Employment Law; Corporate Law. **Email:** pmalesick@kwgd.com

(This Listing Continued)

KRUGLIAK, WILKINS, GRIFFITHS & DOUGHERTY CO., L.P.A., Canton—Continued

KAREN SOEHNLEN McQUEEN, born 1959; admitted to bar, 1984, Ohio. *Education:* Ohio Northern University (B.S.B.A., 1981); Ohio State University (J.D., summa cum laude, 1984). Order of the Coif. ***PRACTICE AREAS:*** Labor and Employment; Litigation; Employment and Civil Rights Litigation. ***Email:*** kmcqueen@kwgd.com

JACQUELINE BOLLAS CALDWELL, born 1959; admitted to bar, 1985, Ohio. *Education:* University of Notre Dame (B.A., 1982) Valedictorian; Phi Beta Kappa; Ohio State University (J.D., summa cum laude, 1985). Order of the Coif. Member and Author, Ohio State University Law Journal. ***PRACTICE AREAS:*** Business Law; Corporate Law; Environmental Law; Occupational Safety and Health. ***Email:*** jcaldwell@kwgd.com

DAVID E. BUTZ, born 1961; admitted to bar, 1987, Ohio, U.S. District Court, Northern District of Ohio and U.S. Court of Appeals, Sixth Circuit. *Education:* Bethany College (B.A., 1984); Case Western Reserve (J.D., 1987). ***PRACTICE AREAS:*** Litigation; Personal Injury; Family Law; Business Law. ***Email:*** dbutz@kwgd.com

LESLIE IAMS KUNTZ, born 1961; admitted to bar, 1986, Ohio. *Education:* Miami University (B.A., 1983); University of Akron (J.D., 1986). ***SPECIAL AGENCIES:*** State Employment Relations Board; SERB. ***PRACTICE AREAS:*** Public Sector Employment Law; Employment Discrimination Litigation; Education Law; Labor and Employment. ***Email:*** likuntz@kwgd.com

CHARLES E. RINGER, born 1962; admitted to bar, 1989, Ohio, U.S. District Court, Northern and Southern Districts of Ohio and U.S. Court of Appeals, Sixth Circuit. *Education:* University of Akron (B.A., with honors, 1986); Ohio State University (J.D., 1989). ***PRACTICE AREAS:*** Corporate Transactions; Commercial Litigation; Construction Litigation; Estate Planning; Probate; Taxation; Eminent Domain. ***Email:*** cringer@kwgd.com

EDWARD D. MURRAY, born 1965; admitted to bar, 1991, Ohio; 1992, U.S. District Court, Northern District of Ohio and U.S. Court of Appeals, Sixth Circuit. *Education:* Ohio State University (B.A., 1987; J.D., with honors, 1991). (Certified Specialist in Workers' Compensation Law, Ohio State Bar Association). ***PRACTICE AREAS:*** Workers Compensation; Debtor and Creditor; Corporate and Employment Law. ***Email:*** emurray@kwgd.com

JAMES F. CONTINI II, born 1967; admitted to bar, 1992, Ohio. *Education:* University of Akron (B.S., magna cum laude, 1989); Case Western Reserve University (J.D., cum laude, 1992). *Member:* National Association of Elder Law Attorneys. (Certified Specialist in Estate Planning, Trust and Probate Law, Ohio State Bar Association). ***PRACTICE AREAS:*** Trusts and Estates; Probate; Elder Law; Business Law; Real Estate. ***Email:*** jcontini@kwgd.com

JOHN M. TUCKER, born 1971; admitted to bar, 1996, Ohio. *Education:* Miami University, Oxford (B.S., summa cum laude, 1993); Case Western Reserve University (J.D., cum laude, 1996). ***PRACTICE AREAS:*** Corporate Law; Real Estate; Health Care; Trusts and Estates. ***Email:*** jtucker@kwgd.com

JOHN D. CLARK, born 1971; admitted to bar, 1997, Ohio. *Education:* Kenyon College (B.A., 1993); Emory University (J.D., 1997). (Certified Specialist in Estate Planning, Trust and Probate Law, Ohio State Bar Association). ***PRACTICE AREAS:*** Trusts and Estates; Probate; Elder Law; Asset Protection; Business Succession Planning. ***Email:*** jclark@kwgd.com

MICHAEL A. WARKALL, born 1968; admitted to bar, 1994, Ohio. *Education:* Kent State University (B.A., 1990); University of Toledo (J.D., 1994). ***PRACTICE AREAS:*** Estate Planning; Corporate Law; Real Estate. ***Email:*** mwarkall@kwgd.com

MATTHEW P. MULLEN, born 1969; admitted to bar, 1994, Ohio; 1997, U.S. District Court, Northern District of Ohio; 2004, U.S. District Court, Southern District of Ohio. *Education:* University of Akron (B.A., cum laude, 1991); University of Akron School of Law (J.D., magna cum laude, 1994). ***PRACTICE AREAS:*** Civil Litigation; Insurance Law. ***Email:*** mmullen@kwgd.com

SCOTT R. MILLER, born 1970; admitted to bar, 1997, Ohio. *Education:* Kent State University (B.A., summa cum laude, 1993); University of Akron (J.D., magna cum laude, 1997). ***PRACTICE AREAS:*** Real Estate; Zoning, Planning and Land Use; Corporate Law; Estate Planning. ***Email:*** srmiller@kwgd.com

---

GREGORY D. SWOPE, born 1963; admitted to bar, 1995, Ohio; 1996, U.S. District Court, Northern District of Ohio; 1999, U.S. Tax Court. *Education:* Kent State University (B.A., 1986); Akron University Law School (J.D., cum laude, 1995). ***PRACTICE AREAS:*** Civil Litigation; Commercial Law; Debtor and Creditor; Construction Law. ***Email:*** gswope@kwgd.com

SCOTT M. ZURAKOWSKI, born 1972; admitted to bar, 1998, Ohio; 1999, U.S. District Court, Northern District of Ohio. *Education:* Mount Union College (B.A., 1994); Ohio Northern University (J.D., 1997). ***PRACTICE AREAS:*** Labor and Employment; Litigation; Corporate Law. ***Email:*** szurakowski@kwgd.com

JASON M. BAASTEN, born 1974; admitted to bar, 1999, Ohio. *Education:* University of Notre Dame (B.A., 1996); University of Cincinnati (J.D., 1999). ***PRACTICE AREAS:*** Workers Compensation; Labor and Employment. ***Email:*** jbaasten@kwgd.com

JEFFREY A. FICKES, born 1967; admitted to bar, 2001, Ohio. *Education:* The University of Akron (B.S., 1990); The Ohio State University (M.B.A., Finance, 2000; J.D., 2001). ***PRACTICE AREAS:*** Corporate Law; Business Law; Mergers and Acquisitions; Business Taxation; Commercial Lending and Finance; Real Estate. ***Email:*** jfickes@kwgd.com

JASON F. HAUPT, born 1976; admitted to bar, 2002, Ohio. *Education:* Miami University (B.S., 1999); Case Western Reserve University School of Law (J.D., cum laude, 2002). ***PRACTICE AREAS:*** Corporate Law; Health Care; Real Estate. ***Email:*** jhaupt@kwgd.com

(This Listing Continued)

OWEN J. RARRIC, born 1976; admitted to bar, 2002, Ohio. *Education:* Hiram College (B.A., magna cum laude, 1999); University of Akron School of Law (J.D., summa cum laude, 2002). ***PRACTICE AREAS:*** Civil Litigation; Environmental Law. ***Email:*** orarric@kwgd.com

MICHAEL J. BOGDAN, born 1979; admitted to bar, 2004, Ohio. *Education:* John Carroll University (B.A., magna cum laude, 2000); The Ohio State University (M.A., 2004; J.D., 2004). ***PRACTICE AREAS:*** Corporate Law; Employee Benefits; Labor and Employment. ***Email:*** mbogdan@kwgd.com

NATHAN D. VAUGHAN, born 1979; admitted to bar, 2004, Ohio. *Education:* The Ohio State University (B.S., with honors and distinction, 2001); University of Akron (J.D., summa cum laude, 2004). ***PRACTICE AREAS:*** General Corporate Law; Estate Planning; Business; Labor and Employment; Health Care. ***Email:*** nvaughan@kwgd.com

JESSICA A. MORRISON, born 1979; admitted to bar, 2004, Ohio. *Education:* University of Cincinnati (B.B.A., 2001); University of Akron (J.D., 2004). ***PRACTICE AREAS:*** Litigation. ***Email:*** jmorrison@kwgd.com

SCOTT G. HASTINGS, born 1975; admitted to bar, 2005, Ohio. *Education:* Malone College (B.A., 1998); University of Akron School of Law (J.D., magna cum laude, 2005). ***PRACTICE AREAS:*** Corporate Law; Real Estate Law. ***Email:*** shastings@kwgd.com

JENNIFER L. LILE, born 1968; admitted to bar, 2000, Ohio. *Education:* Kent State University (B.S., summa cum laude, 1990); University of Akron (J.D., cum laude, 2000). ***Email:*** jlile@kwgd.com

OF COUNSEL

BENJAMIN B. DE FOREST, born 1957; admitted to bar, 1984, Ohio. *Education:* State University of New York at Buffalo (B.A., 1980); Ohio Northern University (J.D., 1983). ***PRACTICE AREAS:*** Trusts and Estates; Elder Law; Asset Protection Planning; Probate. ***Email:*** bdeforest@kwgd.com

REPRESENTATIVE CLIENTS: *Financial:* Bank One, Akron, N.A.; FirstMerit Citizens National Bank; KeyBank. *Manufacturing:* H-P Products, Inc.; Portage Electric Products, Inc.; Gregory Industries; National Feedscrew and Machining Industries, Inc.; Stark Truss Co., Inc.; Earnest Machine Products Co. *Health Care:* Alliance Community Hospital. *Real Estate:* Prudential DeHoff Real Estate Agency; Monogram Development Company. *Food and Food Processing:* Nickles Bakery, Inc; Superior Dairy; Fresh Mark, Inc. *Printing & Graphics:* Graphic Enterprises. *News Media:* WHBC, The Repository; The Independent; The Times Reporter. *Transportation:* Peoples Services Inc.; Wheeling & Lake Erie Railway. *Construction:* Standard Plumbing; Hammond Construction Co.; Henry A. Selinski, Inc.; Schumacher Homes. *Insurance:* Chubb Group of Insurance Companies; Cincinnati Insurance. *Education:* Mount Union College; Stark State College; Academy of Court Reporting, Inc.; Jackson Local Schools; Perry Schools. *Government:* Stark County Board of Mental Retardation and Developmental Disabilities; Stark County Sheriff's Office; City of Massillon. *Environmental:* Environmental Restoration Corporation; Bjaam Environmental Co. *Oil and Gas:* Great Lakes Energy, LLC. *Uniform and Rental Companies:* Rentwear, Inc.; Fallsway Equipment Co.
COUNSEL FOR: National Pro Football Hall of Fame; Better Business Bureau/Canton Regional.
APPROVED ATTORNEYS FOR: Lawyers Title Insurance Company; Stewart Title Guaranty; American Title.

THOMAS WILLIAM LALLY

BELPAR LAW CENTER
4571 STEPHEN CIRCLE, N.W.
CANTON, OHIO 44718-3629
Telephone: 330-499-5474
Fax: 330-433-1313
Email: TLally4571@sbcglobal.net
URL: http://www.lawyers.com/tlally4571

General Civil Trial Practice in State and Federal Courts.

THOMAS WILLIAM LALLY, born Canton, Ohio, September 6, 1939; admitted to bar, 1973, Ohio; 1974, U.S. District Court, Northern District of Ohio. *Education:* Kent State University (B.A., 1966); University of Akron (J.D., 1972). ***PRACTICE AREAS:*** Bankruptcy; Real Estate; Personal Injury; Medical Malpractice; Wrongful Death; Social Security; Workers Compensation; Sports Law; Product Liability; Corporate Law; Business Law; Divorce; Family Law; Probate; Trusts and Estates; Criminal Law.

AGENT FOR: Ohio Bar Title Insurance Co.

MILLISOR & NOBIL

A LEGAL PROFESSIONAL ASSOCIATION

Established in 1975

4117 WHIPPLE AVENUE NW
CANTON, OHIO 44718
Telephone: 330-493-8525; 888-867-6869
Telefax: 330-493-8606
Email: laborlaw@millisor.com
URL: http://www.millisor.com

Cleveland, Ohio Office: 9150 South Hills Boulevard, Suite 300, 44147-3599. Telephone: 440-838-8800. Telefax: 440-838-8805.

Columbus, Ohio Office: 300 East Broad Street, Suite 190, 43215. Telephone: 614-221-2234. Telefax: 614-221-1278.

Employment Law including Labor Relations, Equal Employment Opportunity, Public Sector, OSHA, Arbitration Law, Litigation, Workers Compensation Law, Human Resources Consulting and Employee Benefit Law.

All Personnel are Members of Ohio State and American Bar Associations.

(For complete biographical data on all personnel, see Professional Biographies at Cleveland, Ohio)

PELINI & ASSOCIATES LLC

BRETTON COMMONS, SUITE 400
8040 CLEVELAND AVENUE, N.W. (NORTH CANTON)
CANTON, OHIO 44720
Telephone: 330-305-6400
Fax: 330-305-0042
URL: http://www.lawyers.com/pelini&associates

Litigation, Insurance Defense, Medical Malpractice Defense, Products Liability Defense, Political Subdivision Representation, Tort and Business Litigation, Construction Litigation, Insurance Coverage Litigation, Labor and Employment Law.

FIRM PROFILE: Pelini & Associates LLC is comprised of five attorneys, three paralegals, and a full support staff. Ours is a litigation-centered insurance defense practice, devoted to providing aggressive, cost-effective, and skilled legal representation to our clients and their insureds throughout Northeastern Ohio. Our attorneys regularly practice in courts at all levels in the Fifth, Seventh, Eighth, Ninth, and Eleventh Appellate Districts of Ohio, and our attorneys have enjoyed substantive litigation experience in the counties of Ashland, Ashtabula, Belmont, Carroll, Columbiana, Coshocton, Cuyahoga, Guernsey, Holmes, Jefferson, Lake, Mahoning, Medina, Muskingum, Portage, Richland, Stark, Summit, Trumbull, Tuscarawas, and Wayne. We strive to maintain the highest levels on integrity, preparedness, and zealous legal representation in all of our dealings with our clients, our colleagues, and the judiciary, as we believe that we are best able to offer high quality legal representation to our clients when we also have the respect of our peers, the judges before whom we practice, and even our adversaries. This philosophy is exemplified in the firm's legal highest ability rating that has been maintained by Craig Pelini for thirteen consecutive years.

As litigation attorneys, our experience has taught us that we can be most effective in representing our clients' interests by fostering and maintaining reputations in the legal community as attorneys who will, and who do, regularly try cases in the courtroom. Among the five attorneys who comprise the firm, our collective trial experience encompasses well over 150 jury trials, including more than 50 jury trials in the past seven years. We have tried cases before judges and juries throughout Northeastern Ohio, including Ashland, Ashtabula, Belmont, Carroll, Columbiana, Coshocton, Cuyahoga, Guernsey, Holmes, Jefferson, Lake, Mahoning, Medina, Muskingum, Portage, Richland, Stark, Summit, Trumbull, Tuscarawas, and Wayne counties. Our emphasis on preparation, skill, and experience, has enabled us to produce generally very favorable results for our clients in the trial arena.

Our firm also utilizes technology to deliver the highest level of quality services as efficiently as possible. We have implemented up-to-date technologies with respect to legal research, document preparation, file management and storage, communications, scheduling, billing, and security, so that we can provide high quality work in an efficient and reliable manner while also protecting our work product and the confidentiality of our clients. We regularly use all available computerized and on-line court systems in order to maintain current and dependable access to court dockets, filings, forms, and rules, in common pleas and federal district courts throughout Ohio.

CRAIG G. PELINI, born Latrobe, Pennsylvania, October 17, 1958; admitted to bar, 1984, Ohio and U.S. District Court, Northern District of Ohio. *Education:* Washington and Jefferson College (B.A., cum laude, 1981); University of Pittsburgh (J.D., 1984). *Member:* Stark County, Ohio State and American Bar Associations; Ohio Association of Civil Trial Attorneys; Defense Research Institute. ***PRACTICE AREAS:*** Litigation; Insurance Defense; Insurance Coverage; Business Litigation; Medical Malpractice Defense; Products Liability Defense. ***Email:*** cgp@pelini-law.com

---

JULIE A. GEISER, born Alliance, Ohio, August 19, 1968; admitted to bar, 1994, Ohio; 1995, U.S. District Court, Northern District of Ohio; 2000, U.S. Court of Appeals, Sixth Circuit. *Education:* Yale University (B.A., cum laude, 1989); University of Arizona (J.D., 1994). Phi Alpha Delta. Member, Arizona Law Review, University of Arizona. *Member:* Stark County, Ohio State and American Bar Associations. ***LANGUAGES:*** Russian, German and Spanish. ***PRACTICE AREAS:*** Commercial Litigation; Insurance Defense; Real Estate; Construction Litigation; Employment Law; Insurance Coverage Litigation. ***Email:*** jageiser@pelini-law.com

KRISTEN E. CAMPBELL, born Canton, Ohio, February 12, 1971; admitted to bar, 1996, Ohio; 2003, U.S. District Court, Northern District of Ohio. *Education:* Duquesne University (B.A., magna cum laude, 1993); The Ohio State University (J.D., 1996). ***PRACTICE AREAS:*** Litigation; Insurance Defense; Employment Litigation. ***Email:*** kec@pelini-law.com

ERIC J. WILLIAMS, born Marion, Indiana, June 19, 1973; admitted to bar, 2000, Ohio. *Education:* Kent State University (B.A., cum laude, 1995); University of Akron, School of Law (J.D., cum laude, 2000). Member, University of Akron Law Review, 1998-1999. *Member:* Stark County, Ohio State and American Bar Associations. ***PRACTICE AREAS:*** Litigation; Insurance Defense; Medical Malpractice Defense; Real Estate; Construction Litigation; Political Subdivision Liability; Torts; Business Litigation; Commercial Litigation. ***Email:*** ejwilliams@pelini-law.com

RANDALL M. TRAUB, born Ft. Monmouth, New Jersey, December 1, 1967; admitted to bar, 1999, Ohio; 2002, U.S. District Court, Northern District of Ohio. *Education:* University of South Florida (B.A., 1994); University of Akron School of Law (J.D., magna cum laude, 1999). *Member:* Stark County and Ohio State Bar Associations. ***PRACTICE AREAS:*** Torts; Business Litigation; Medical Malpractice Defense; Commercial Litigation; Creditors Rights; Health Care Litigation; Insurance Defense. ***Email:*** rmtraub@pelini-law.com

REPRESENTATIVE CLIENTS: Auto-Owners Insurance Company; Castle Insurance Company; Cincinnati Equitable Ins. Co.; Citizens Insurance Company; ESIS; GoAmerica Auto Insurance (formerly Globe American Casualty Company); Indiana Insurance (formerly GRE Insurance Group); Liberty Mutual Group; Plain Township; Tuscarawas Township; Ohio Mutual Insurance Company; Founders Insurance Company; Federated Mutual Insurance Company; Campbell Oil Company; Preferred Physicians Risk Retention Group; State Farm Insurance Company; The St. Paul Companies (formerly USF&G); Westfield Insurance Companies; Zurich Insurance Company.

RENNER, KENNER, GREIVE, BOBAK, TAYLOR & WEBER

A LEGAL PROFESSIONAL ASSOCIATION
CANTON, OHIO
(See Akron)

U.S. and Foreign Patent, Trademark and Copyright Law and Licensing. Antitrust and Unfair Competition Law. Litigation.

STANLEY R. RUBIN

Established in 1976
437 MARKET AVENUE, NORTH
CANTON, OHIO 44702-1423
Telephone: 330-455-5206
Fax: 330-455-5200
Email: srrubin22@aol.com

Personal Injury Law, Medical Negligence Law, Insurance Bad Faith Litigation, Domestic Relations Law, Business Litigation, Commercial Litigation.

STANLEY R. RUBIN, born Canton, Ohio, September 4, 1951; admitted to bar, 1976, Ohio, Pennsylvania and U.S. District Court, Northern District of Ohio. *Education:* Case Western Reserve University (B.A., 1973; J.D., 1976). Assistant Prosecuting Attorney, Stark County, 1976-1980. Referee, Stark County Domestic Relations Court, 1980-1985. *Member:* Stark County (Past Secretary; Vice President, 1998; President, 2000) and Ohio State Bar Associations; Stark County Academy of Trial Lawyers (Secretary, 1990; Treasurer, 1993; Vice-President, 1995; President, 1998); Association of Trial Lawyers of America. ***LANGUAGES:*** German. ***REPORTED CASES:*** Staff Builders v. Aetna. ***PRACTICE AREAS:*** Personal Injury Law; Medical Negligence Law; Insurance Bad Faith Litigation; Domestic Relations Law; Business Litigation; Commercial Litigation.

THE RUFO LAW FIRM

Established in 1983
BANK ONE TOWER
101 CENTRAL PLAZA SOUTH, SUITE 900
CANTON, OHIO 44702
Telephone: 330-456-8389
Fax: 330-456-5328
URL: http://www.divorcesource.com/OH/pages/kenandrea.html
Email: grufolaw@yahoo.com
URL: http://www.grufolaw.com
Mailing Address: P.O. Box 36793, Canton, OH 44735

Criminal Law, Domestic Relations, Business Law, Family Law, Divorce, Marriage Dissolution, Child Support, Child Custody, Visitation Rights, Alimony, Spousal Support, Criminal Defense, Misdemeanors, Felonies, DUI, Traffic Violations, Drug Crimes, Incorporation, Partnerships, Dissolution of Business, Business Contracts, Business Litigation, Collections.

GREGORY J. RUFO, born Canton, Ohio, April 17, 1954; admitted to bar, 1983, Ohio and U.S. District Court, Northern District of Ohio. *Education:* John Carroll University (B.A., 1976); Akron University Law School (J.D., 1983). Listed: Who's Who in America; Who's Who in American Law. *Member:* Stark County, Ohio State and American Bar Associations. ***Email:*** grufolaw@yahoo.com

REPRESENTATIVE CLIENTS: J&J Motors, Inc.; Advanced Industrial Roofing; Tel-Com Systems of Ohio; Preferred Temporary Services, Inc.; Alset Power Guard, Inc.; Brownlee Engineering & Manufacturing, Inc.; Thermo Devices, Inc.; Clary Construction Co., Inc.; Saibene & Son Masonry, Inc.; S&L Properties, Inc.; Marzilli Construction; Hill & Associates, Inc.; B&B Holdings, Inc.; Christian Fabricators, Inc.; Commercial Press, Inc.; Easterdays, Inc.

TIPPING CO., L.P.A.

A LEGAL PROFESSIONAL ASSOCIATION
CANTON, OHIO
(See Akron)

General Civil Trial and Appellate Practice, Negligence, Personal Injury, Business, Commercial, Corporate, Probate, Workers Compensation, Administrative, Insurance, Real Estate, Bankruptcy, Estate Planning, Labor/Employment, Zoning, Municipal Law and Social Security Disability Law.

ZINK, ZINK & ZINK CO., L.P.A.

Established in 1976
3711 WHIPPLE AVENUE, N.W.
CANTON, OHIO 44718
Telephone: 330-492-2225
Fax: 330-492-3956
Email: lazohio@aol.com

Hillsboro Beach, Florida Office: 1198 Hillsboro Mile, Suite 244, 33062. Telephone: 945-428-3672.

(This Listing Continued)

ZINK, ZINK & ZINK CO., L.P.A., Canton—Continued

General Civil Practice. Corporation and Business Law. Real Estate, Probate, Contract, Environmental, Commercial and Construction Litigation. Federal and State Trial Practice.

EDWARD J. ZINK (1921-1996)

LARRY A. ZINK, born Canton, Ohio, June 16, 1951; admitted to bar, 1975, Ohio and U.S. Tax Court; 1976, U.S. District Court, Northern and Southern Districts of Ohio; 1980, U.S. Court of Appeals, Third and Sixth Circuits, and U.S. Supreme Court; 1989, Pennsylvania and U.S. District Court, Western District of Pennsylvania; 1997, Florida. *Education:* Kent State University (B.A., 1972); Case Western Reserve University (J.D., 1975). Assistant U.S. Attorney, U.S. Department of Justice, Northern District of Ohio, 1979-1980. *Member:* Stark County, Ohio State and American Bar Associations; The Association of Trial Lawyers of America; Ohio Academy of Trial Lawyers. ***REPORTED CASES:*** Palm Beach Polo, Inc. v. Columbia Propane Corp., 782 So.2d 938, (Fla 4th DCA 2001); Spring Industries v. Ohio Dept. of Transportation, 51 Ohio Misc. 2nd 6 555 NE 2nd 339, 1989; Spring Industries v. Ohio Dept. of Transportation, 61 Ohio Misc 2nd 105 575 NE 2nd 226, 1990; Garcia v. Siffrin, 63 Ohio St. 2nd 259 (1980); GBJ v. Eastern Ohio Paving Co., 950 F. Supp. 816 (1996); GBJ v. Eastern Ohio Paving Co., 139 F.3rd 1080 (1998). ***PRACTICE AREAS:*** Construction Litigation; Commercial Litigation; Business Litigation; Environmental Litigation; Estate Planning and Estates; Real Estate; Wills; Trust Law.

ARBITRATION OFFICES OF JACQUELIN DRUCKER, ESQ.

806 HARBOR POINT DRIVE
CELINA, OHIO 45822
Telephone: 800-810-4174
Email: jdrucker@aol.com
URL: http://www.druckerarbitration.com

New York, N.Y. Office: 432 East 58th Street, Suite 2. Telephone: 212-688-3919. Fax: 212-935-1870.

Arbitration, Labor and Employment Law and Commercial Disputes.

FIRM PROFILE: Jacquelin F. Drucker maintains a nationwide and international practice in which she arbitrates the full range of employment, labor, and commercial issues.

JACQUELIN F. DRUCKER, ESQ., born Celina, Ohio, October 15, 1954; admitted to bar, 1981, Ohio and New York. *Education:* The Ohio State University (B.A., 1977; J.D., 1981). Faculty Member: Cornell University School of Industrial and Labor Relations; Cornell Institute on Conflict Resolution.*Member:* New York State (Chair, Labor and Employment Section, 2003-2004; Chair-Elect, Labor Section, 2002-2003; Neutral-Chair, ADR in Employment Committee, 1998-2000; CLE Chair, 2000-2002) and American (Neutral-Chair, ADR in Labor and Employment Law Committee, Labor and Employment Law Section, 2001—) Bar Associations; New York County Lawyers Association (Chair, Labor Relations and Employment Law Committee, 1996-1998); National Academy of Arbitrators (Chair, 2006 Program Committee; Task Force on Employment Arbitration; Liaison to the National Academy of Arbitrators, 2004—; Neutral Chair, Regional CLE Programs, 2005—). Fellow: American Bar Foundation; College of Labor and Employment Lawyers. ***PRACTICE AREAS:*** Arbitration; Labor & Employment; Commercial.

THOM L. COOPER CO., LPA

36 WEST MAIN STREET
P.O. BOX 747
CENTERBURG, OHIO 43011
Telephone: 740-625-5215
Toll-Free: 1-800-798-5297
Fax: 740-625-6881
Email: tlc@cooperelderlaw.com
URL: http://www.cooperelderlaw.com

Estate Planning, Estate Administration, Elder Law, Nursing Home Planning, Medicaid and Medicare, Disability Planning, Long Term Care, Guardianships, Conservatorships, Estate and Gift Tax Planning, Fiduciary Administration, Inter Vivos, Decedent's Estate Administration, Fiduciary Tax Administration, Trusts and Estates, Charitable Remainder Trusts, Insurance Trusts, Supplemental Care Trusts, Living Wills, Living Trusts.

THOM L. COOPER, born Miami, Florida, February 15, 1945; admitted to bar, 1983, Ohio. *Education:* Allegheny College (B.A., 1967); Ohio State University (M.S., Ph.D, 1975); Capital University (J.D., 1983). Certified Elder Law Specialist as certified by the National Elder Law Foundation. *Member:* National Academy of Elder Law Attorneys. ***PRACTICE AREAS:*** Estate Planning; Elder Law; Disabilities; Medicare and Medicaid; Long Term Care; Guardianships; Conservatorship; Trusts and Estates; Estate and Gift Taxation; Fiduciary Taxation; Decedents Estates; Living Trusts; Advanced Medical Directives; Probate; Estate Administration; Trust Administration. ***Email:*** Tcooper@TLCElderLaw.com

---

CHRISTOPHER LAVIN, born New York, N.Y., July 22, 1968; admitted to bar, 1998, Ohio. *Education:* Xavier University (B.S.B.A., 1991); University of Dayton (J.D., 1998). *Member:* Cincinnati and Ohio State Bar Associations; National Academy of Elder Law Attorneys. ***PRACTICE AREAS:*** Estate Planning; Elder Law; Disabilities; Medicare and Medicaid; Long Term Care; Guardianships; Conservatorship; Trusts and Estates; Estate and Gift Taxation; Fiduciary Taxation; Decedents Estates; Living Trusts; Advanced Medical Directives; Probate; Estate Administration; Trust Administration. ***Email:*** Clavin@TLCElderLaw.com

DAVID WIRTH

CENTERBURG, OHIO

(See Columbus)

Insurance Law, Negligence, Legal Malpractice, Subrogation, Personal Injury, Probate.

ALTICK & CORWIN CO., L.P.A.

CENTERVILLE, OHIO

(See Dayton)

General Practice. Administrative, Bankruptcy, Business, Collections, Condominium, Creditors' Rights, Criminal, Commercial Law, Decedent's Estates, Employee Benefits, Elder Law, Employment, Estate Planning, Family Law, Immigration and Naturalization, Insurance Defense, Labor Relations, Local Government, Military Law, Municipal, Personal Injury, Probate, Products Liability, Real Estate, Social Security, Taxation, Workers' Compensation, Zoning.

BRAD A. CHALKER

848-C EAST FRANKLIN ST.
CENTERVILLE, OHIO 45459
Telephone: 937-436-1893
Fax: 937-436-1894
Email: BAC@chalkerlaw.com
URL: http://www.chalkerlaw.com
Mailing Address: P.O. Box 750726, Dayton, OH 45475-0726

General Civil Practice, Employment Law, Workers' Compensation Defense, OSHA, Product Liability and Civil Litigation.

BRAD A. CHALKER, born Warren, Ohio, 1950; admitted to bar, 1981, Ohio; 1982, Florida; 1986, Texas; U.S. District Court, Southern District of Ohio and U.S. Court of Appeals, Sixth Circuit. *Education:* United States Naval Academy (B.S., 1973); University of Miami (J.D., with honors, 1981). Member, University of Miami Law Review, 1980-1981. Instructor of Business Law at Sinclair Community College. *Member:* Dayton, Ohio State, and American Bar Associations; The Florida Bar; State Bar of Texas.

REPRESENTATIVE CLIENTS: Corning Incorporated; Hartzell Propeller Inc.; Honeywell International, Inc.; Palm Harbor Homes.

DAVID M. DEUTSCH CO., L.P.A.

CENTERVILLE, OHIO

(See Dayton)

Personal Injury, Product Liability, Wrongful Death, Medical Malpractice.

GREGORY C. GIBSON CO., L.P.A.

CENTERVILLE, OHIO

(See Dayton)

Medical Malpractice, Serious Personal Injury, Wrongful Death.

MAURER LAW OFFICES, LLC

Established in 2004

800 EAST FRANKLIN STREET
CENTERVILLE, OHIO 45459
Telephone: 937-291-3400
Fax: 937-291-0757
URL: http://www.maurerlaw.com
Email: rmaurer@maurerlaw.com
URL: http://www.maurerlawoffices.com

Criminal Law, Driving While Intoxicated, Drug Crimes, Traffic Violations, White Collar Crime, Insurance, Personal Injury, Automobile Accidents and Injuries, Dog Bites, Sexual Abuse, Slip and Fall, Wrongful Death, Family Law, Divorce, Child Custody, Child Support, Domestic Violence, Visitation Rights, Employment Law, Disabled Access, Discrimination, Sexual Harassment, General Practice.

FIRM PROFILE: Civil and criminal litigation in all state and federal courts, Insurance, Domestic Relations, Criminal and Personal Injury, General Practice.

MEMBER OF FIRM

RONALD J. MAURER, born Findlay, Ohio, March 6, 1969; admitted to bar, 1994, Ohio and U.S. District Court, Southern District of Ohio; 2001, Kentucky. *Education:* Otterbein College (B.A., 1991); University of Dayton School of Law (J.D., 1994). Mock Trial Regional Champion. Author: "Ohio Psychotherapist Liability for Sexual Relations with Former Patients," University of Toledo Law Review, Vol. 26, No. 3, 1995; The Federal Sentencing Guidelines for Organizations: How Do They Work and What Are They Supposed to Do?" 18 Univ. of Dayton Law Review 799 (1993). *Member:* Dayton, Ohio State, Kentucky and American Bar Associations; The Ohio Association of Trial Lawyers; The Kentucky Association of Trial Attorneys; Ohio Association of Criminal Defense Lawyers. ***REPORTED CASES:*** Santos v. Ohio Bur. of Workers' Comp., 101 Ohio St. 3d 74 (2004); Ross v. Farmers Ins. Group of Cos., 82 Ohio St. 3d 281 (1998); Hollon v. Clary, 155 Ohio App. 3d 195 (2003); Bass v. Lucas, 131 Ohio App. 3d 627 (1999). ***PRACTICE AREAS:*** Criminal Law; Driving While Intoxicated; Drug Crimes; Traffic Violations; White Collar Crime; Insurance; Personal Injury; Automobile Accidents and Injuries; Dog Bites; Sexual Abuse; Slip and Fall; Wrongful Death; Family Law; Divorce; Child Custody; Child Support; Domestic

(This Listing Continued)

Violence; Visitation Rights; Employment Law; Disabled Access; Discrimination; Sexual Harassment; General Practice. ***Email:*** rmaurer@maurerlaw.com

SHERRETS LAW OFFICES, LLC

CENTERVILLE, OHIO

(See Kettering)

DON P. BROWN, RICHARD H. BROWN

10 CENTER STREET
CHAGRIN FALLS, OHIO 44022
Telephone: 440-247-9100
Fax: 440-247-9109
URL: http://www.immigrationohio.com
Email: rhbrown@ameritech.net
Email: dpbrown@ameritech.net
URL: http://www.dpbrownlaw.com

Probate Law, Estate Law, Estate Planning, Estate and Gift Taxation, Successions, Trusts, Wills, Probate Administration, Elder Care, Corporate Law, Immigration, Real Estate, Business Law.

DON P. BROWN, born Cleveland, Ohio, November 9, 1936; admitted to bar, 1961, Ohio. *Education:* Denison University (B.A., 1958); Western Reserve University (LL.B., 1961). Blue Key; Omicron Delta Kappa. Member, Board of Editors, Western Reserve Law Review, 1960-1961. Arbitrator, American Arbitration Association, 1974-1998. Councilman: City of Warrensville Heights, 1964-1969; Village of Orange, 1972-1974. Member, Estate Planning Council, Cleveland, Ohio, 1968—. *Member:* Cleveland and Ohio State Bar Associations. ***PRACTICE AREAS:*** Probate Law; Estate Law; Estate Planning; Estate and Gift Taxation; Successions; Trusts; Wills; Probate Administration; Elder Care; Corporate Law; Immigration Law; Real Estate; Business Law. ***Email:*** dpbrown@ameritech.net

RICHARD H. BROWN, born Cleveland, Ohio, August 8, 1943; admitted to bar, 1968, Ohio. *Education:* Ohio University (B.B.A., 1965); Case Western Reserve University (J.D., 1968). Phi Delta Phi. *Member:* Cleveland, Cuyahoga County, Geauga County, Ohio State and Federal Bar Associations; American Immigration Lawyers Association (Past Chair, Ohio Chapter and Member, Board of Governors, 1993-1995). ***PRACTICE AREAS:*** Immigration; Corporate; Real Estate; Business Law. ***Email:*** rhbrown@ameritech.net

JAMES P. GRUBER

CHAGRIN FALLS, OHIO

(See Cleveland)

Probate, Wills, Trusts, Estate Planning, Business, Corporations, Partnerships, LLC's, Business Succession Planning, Tax and Real Estate.

MARY A. LENTZ CO., L.P.A.

100 NORTH MAIN STREET, SUITE 210
CHAGRIN FALLS, OHIO 44022-2766
Telephone: 440-247-8701
Fax: 440-247-8741
URL: http://www.lawyers.com/lentz

Public School Law, Private Education Law, Personal Policies, Appeals, Administrative Hearings, Child Abuse and Neglect, Child Sexual Abuse.

FIRM PROFILE: The firm carries the highest legal ability rating in Martindale-Hubbell.

MARY A. LENTZ, admitted to bar, 1973, Ohio; 1974, U.S. District Court, Northern District of Ohio; 1975, U.S. Court of Appeals, Sixth Circuit; 1977, U.S. Supreme Court; 1984, Pennsylvania; 1986, District of Columbia. *Education:* Ursuline College (B.A., 1964); Georgetown University (M.A., 1968); Cleveland Marshall College of Law of Cleveland State University (J.D., 1973). Editor: Ohio School Law Journal, West Group, West Publishing, 1975—. Author: "Lentz School Security," Thomson-West Publishers, 2004, 2005, 2006; "Preventing Child Sexual Abuse-A Parent's Guide," Stellar Resources, Inc. (Spanish/English editions), 2003; "Child Sexual Abuse Prevention Curriculum: Kindergarten-Grade 12," Stellar Resources, Inc., 2003.

MARY K. BENDER CO. L.P.A.

Established in 1986
VILLAGE STATION BLDG. 4A
401 SOUTH STREET
CHARDON, OHIO 44024
Telephone: 440-285-4332
Fax: 440-285-9562
URL: http://www.lawyers.com/marybender

General Civil Trial Practice, Trials and Appeals in all Courts, Family, Custody and Support, Domestic Relations, Divorce, Juvenile, Real Estate.

MARY K. BENDER, born Cleveland, Ohio, September 21, 1947; admitted to bar, 1981, Ohio; 1983, U.S. District Court, Northern District of Ohio. *Education:* Bowling Green State University (B.A., 1968); John Carroll University; Case Western Reserve University (J.D., 1981). Member, Board of Trustees of Western Reserve Area Agency on Aging, 1990-1992. *Member:* Geauga County (Treasurer, 1985-1989; Secretary, 1989-1992; Vice-President, 1992-1993; President, 1993), Ohio State and American Bar Associations. ***PRACTICE AREAS:*** Family Law.

COOPER & FORBES

CHARDON, OHIO

(See Painesville)

Commercial and Retail Collections, Commercial Law, Bankruptcy, Domestic Relations, Chapter 11, Debtors Rights, General Civil Trial Practice, Creditors Rights. Trials and Appeals in all Courts.

DRIGGS, HOGG & FRY CO., LPA

CHARDON, OHIO

(See Willoughby Hills)

Corporate Law, Trusts and Estate, Business Law, Real Estate, Intellectual Property, Patents, Copyrights, Trademarks, Trade Secrets, Unfair Competition.

WILLIAM C. HOFSTETTER

155 MAIN STREET
CHARDON, OHIO 44024
Telephone: 440-285-2247
Fax: 440-285-4140
Email: wchofstetter@aol.com
URL: http://www.lawyers.com/hofstetter

Civil Practice, Real Estate, Estate Planning, Wills, Trusts and Estates, Estate Administration, Probate, Banking Law.

WILLIAM C. HOFSTETTER, born Cleveland, Ohio, April 28, 1950; admitted to bar, 1975, Ohio and U.S. District Court, Northern District of Ohio; 1997, U.S. Court of Appeals, Fourth Circuit. *Education:* Ohio State University (B.A., 1972); Cleveland Marshall College of Law (J.D., 1975). *Member:* Cleveland, Geauga County and Ohio State Bar Associations; Ohio Academy of Trial Lawyers; The Association of Trial Lawyers of America.

PETERSEN & IBOLD

Established in 1980
401 SOUTH STREET
CHARDON, OHIO 44024-1495
Telephone: 440-285-3511
Telecopier: 440-285-3363
Email: p&i@peteribold.com
URL: http://www.lawyers.com/peteribold

Personal Injury, Real Estate and Zoning, Family Law, Criminal, Wills, Probate, Estate Planning and Elder Law, Corporate, Business and Labor Law, Bankruptcy, School Law and Workers Compensation.

JERRY A. PETERSEN, born Chesterland, Ohio, July 30, 1938; admitted to bar, 1966, Ohio. *Education:* Kent State University (B.S., 1961); The Ohio State University (J.D., 1965). *Member:* Geauga and Ohio State Bar Associations; Ohio Council of School Board Attorneys. ***PRACTICE AREAS:*** Real Estate; Zoning; School Law; Labor Law; Personal Injury; Litigation; Domestic Relations. ***Email:*** jp@peteribold.com

DENNIS J. IBOLD, born Cleveland Ohio, June 2, 1948; admitted to bar, 1973, Ohio. *Education:* Marquette University (B.A., 1970); Cleveland Marshall College of Law (J.D., 1973). *Member:* Geauga County, Ohio State and American Bar Associations; American Academy of Matrimonial Lawyers. ***PRACTICE AREAS:*** Family Law; Real Estate; Personal Injury; Business Law. ***Email:*** dji@peteribold.com

MICHAEL G. IBOLD, born Cleveland, Ohio, June 25, 1955; admitted to bar, 1980, Ohio. *Education:* Wittenberg University (B.A., 1977); Cleveland Marshall College of Law (J.D., 1980). *Member:* Geauga County, Ohio State and American Bar Associations; The Association of Trial Lawyers of America. ***PRACTICE AREAS:*** Workers Compensation; Bankruptcy; Personal Injury; Domestic Relations. ***Email:*** mgi@peteribold.com

C. LYNNE DAY, born Cleveland, Ohio, July 6, 1968; admitted to bar, 1993, Ohio. *Education:* Wittenberg University (B.A., cum laude, 1990); The Ohio State University (J.D., 1993). *Member:* Geauga County (Past President), Ohio State and American Bar Associations. ***PRACTICE AREAS:*** Litigation; Domestic Relations; Collections. ***Email:*** lday@peteribold.com

TODD E. PETERSEN, born Chesterland, Ohio, October 2, 1970; admitted to bar, 1996, Ohio. *Education:* Carnegie Mellon University (B.S., 1993); Ohio State University College of Law (J.D., with honors, 1996). *Member:* Geauga, Ohio State and American Bar Associations. ***PRACTICE AREAS:*** Litigation; Real Estate; Zoning Law; School Law; Personal Injury; Business Law. ***Email:*** tp@peteribold.com

CASEY P. O'BRIEN, born Ashtabula, Ohio, August 4, 1975; admitted to bar, 2000, Ohio. *Education:* Walsh University (B.A., 1997); Cleveland-Marshall College of Law (J.D., 2000). *Member:* Geauga, Ashtabula, Ohio State and American Bar Associations. ***PRACTICE AREAS:*** Litigation; Criminal Law; Juvenile Law; Family Law; Personal Injury; Business Law; Estate Planning; Collections. ***Email:*** casey@peteribold.com

ASSOCIATE

Robin Stanley

OF COUNSEL

Keith K. Brooks ***Susan E. Peterson***

STERNBERG & ZEID CO., L.P.A.

CHARDON, OHIO

(See Mentor)

Personal Injury, Automobile Accidents, Wrongful Death, Workers Compensation, Municipal Law, Zoning Law, Bankruptcy, Domestic Relations, Family Law, Divorce, Child Custody, Guardianship, Real Estate, Probate, Estate Planning, Trusts and Wills, Business, Corporate, Contract Law, General Civil Trial Practice in State and Federal Courts.

SVETE, McGEE & CARRABINE CO., L.P.A.

100 PARKER COURT
CHARDON, OHIO 44024-1141
Telephone: 440-286-9571
Fax: 440-286-7504

Insurance Defense, Personal Injury, Products Liability, Professional Malpractice, Commercial, Governmental Construction and General Negligence Litigation, Automobile Accidents, Wrongful Death, Medical Negligence, Real Estate and Zoning, Contracts, Deeds, Easements, Leases, Family Law, Divorce, Dissolution, Child Custody and Support, Paternity, Adoption, Child Abuse and Neglect, Criminal Defense, Felonies, Misdemeanors, Juvenile and Traffic Offenses, D.U.I., Wills, Probate, Estate Planning, Elder Law, Trusts, Powers of Attorney, Living Wills, Guardianships, Asset Preservation, Medicare/Medicaid Planning, Litigation, Corporate and Business Law, Partnerships, Limited Liability Companies, Buying and Selling of a Business.

JOSEPH T. SVETE, born 1937; admitted to bar, 1964, Ohio; 1965, U.S. District Court, Northern District of Ohio; 1992, U.S. Supreme Court. *Education:* Case Western Reserve University (B.S., 1960); Cleveland Marshall College of Law (J.D., 1964). President: Geauga County Law Library Association, 1972-1974. *Member:* Lake County, Geauga County (President, 1974-1976), Ohio State (President, 1988-1989) and American (Member, House of Delegates, 1989-1991) Bar Associations; Geauga County Bar Foundation (President, 1987); Fellow: Ohio State Bar Foundation, American Bar Foundation. ***PRACTICE AREAS:*** Real Estate; Estate Planning; Family Law; Personal Injury; Business Organization; Trial Practice.

DAVID A. McGEE, born Yonkers, N.Y., November 10, 1952; admitted to bar, 1982, Ohio; 1983, U.S. District Court, Northern District of Ohio; 1992, U.S. Supreme Court. *Education:* Fordham University (A.B., 1976); Cleveland Marshall College of Law (J.D., 1981). President, Geauga County Bar Association, 1993. Chairman, Lake County Board of Alcohol, Drug Addiction and Mental Health Services, 1993. Treasurer, Geauga County Law Library Association, 1993. Panel Attorney, Aircraft Owners and Pilot Association. *Member:* Geauga County, Lake County and Ohio State Bar Associations. ***PRACTICE AREAS:*** Civil Litigation; Commercial Law; Construction Law; Consumer Law; Aviation Law; Personal Injury; Criminal Law; Appellate Practice; General Practice.

JAMES P. CARRABINE, born Cleveland, Ohio, December 7, 1955; admitted to bar, 1984, Ohio; 1985, U.S. District Court, Northern District of Ohio; 1992, U.S. Supreme Court. *Education:* John Carroll University (B.S., magna cum laude, 1978); Cleveland-Marshall College of Law (J.D., magna cum laude, 1984). *Member:* Lake County, Geauga County, Ohio State and American Bar Associations; The Association of Trial Lawyers of America. ***PRACTICE AREAS:*** Personal Injury; Trial Practice; Insurance Defense.

JAMES W. REARDON, born Cleveland, Ohio, December 6, 1966; admitted to bar, 1992, Ohio; 1995, U.S. District Court, Northern District of Ohio. *Education:* Miami University (A.B., 1989); Case Western Reserve University (J.D., 1992). *Member:* Geauga County (President, 2004), Lake County and Ohio State Bar Associations. ***REPORTED CASES:*** Stoops v. Miller 97 Ohio App 3d 265 (1994). ***PRACTICE AREAS:*** Family Law (50%); Criminal Law (25%); Personal Injury (10%); Collections (10%). ***Email:*** reardon@smc-law.com

---

LISA J. CAREY, born Glen Dale, West Virginia, December 19, 1967; admitted to bar, 1993, Ohio. *Education:* Bethany College (B.A., summa cum laude, 1990); University of Cincinnati College of Law (J.D., 1993). Order of the Barristers. Moot Court. *Member:* Geauga County, Lake County and Ohio State (Member: Health Care Committee; Negligence Committee) Bar Associations; Ohio Women's Bar Association. ***PRACTICE AREAS:*** Personal Injury; Family Law; Civil Litigation.

JAMES R. FLAIZ, admitted to bar, 2002, Ohio. *Education:* Ohio State University (B.A., 1999); Cleveland-Marshall College of Law (J.D., 2002). ***PRACTICE AREAS:*** Civil Law; Personal Injury; Domestic. ***Email:*** flaiz@smc-law.com

REPRESENTATIVE CLIENTS: Cincinnati Insurance Co.; State Farm Insurance Co.; Thwing-Mills Development Co.; Burton Maple Leaf Co.; Hopkins Properties, Inc.; Newbury Industrial Park; Country Heritage Homes, Inc.; Derus Construction, Inc.; Huntington Banks.

THRASHER, DINSMORE & DOLAN

A LEGAL PROFESSIONAL ASSOCIATION

Established in 1931

100 7TH AVENUE, SUITE 150
CHARDON, OHIO 44024-1079
Telephone: 440-285-2242
Cleveland Line: 440-942-1034
Facsimile: 440-285-9423

General Civil and Criminal Practice. Corporation, Probate, Municipal, Communication Law, Real Estate, Taxation, Zoning, Banking and Insurance Law. Estate Planning. Trials and Appeals. Labor Law. Domestic and Creditors Rights.

RAY K. THRASHER (1906-1973)
JAMES W. DINSMORE (1916-1975)

(This Listing Continued)

LAWRENCE J. DOLAN (Retired)

DAVID E. LOWE, born Goose Creek, Texas, April 7, 1937; admitted to bar, 1970, Ohio. *Education:* John Carroll University (A.B., 1959); Cleveland State University (J.D., 1970). Assistant Attorney General, State of Ohio, 1971-1983. *Member:* Greater Cleveland, Geauga County and Ohio State Bar Associations; Defense Research Institute; Ohio Association of Civil Trial Attorneys; American Academy of Matrimonial Lawyers. (Certified Specialist in Family Relations Law, Ohio State Bar Association). ***PRACTICE AREAS:*** Trials; Domestic Law; Insurance Defense. ***Email:*** DLowe@dolan.law.pro

DALE H. MARKOWITZ, born Cleveland, Ohio, July 4, 1950; admitted to bar, 1975, Ohio and U.S. District Court, Northern District of Ohio; 1981, U.S. Supreme Court and U.S. Court of Appeals, Sixth Circuit. *Education:* The Ohio State University (B.S., 1972); Cleveland Marshall College of Law (J.D., magna cum laude, 1975). *Member:* Geauga County, Ohio State and American Bar Associations. ***PRACTICE AREAS:*** Banking Law; Municipal Law; Real Estate Law; Zoning; Litigation; Corporate Law. ***Email:*** DMarkowitz@dolan.law.pro

JOSEPH R. ZNIDARSIC, born Cleveland, Ohio, August 22, 1951; admitted to bar, 1976, Ohio. *Education:* Bowling Green State University (B.S., 1973); Case Western Reserve University (J.D., 1976). Vice-President and General Counsel, Cleveland Indians Professional Baseball Team. ***PRACTICE AREAS:*** Corporate Law; Tax Planning; Estate Planning; Real Estate Law; Professional Sports Law. ***Email:*** JZnidarsic@dolan.law.pro

DAVID M. ONDREY, born Cleveland, Ohio, October 12, 1951; admitted to bar, 1980, Ohio; 1995, U.S. Court of Appeals, Sixth Circuit. *Education:* Miami University (B.A., 1973); Cleveland Marshall College of Law (J.D., 1980). Solicitor, Burton Village, South Russell Village, 1986—. Trustee, Geauga Regional Hospital, 1998—. *Member:* Geauga County (President, 1998) and Ohio State Bar Associations. ***PRACTICE AREAS:*** Litigation; Municipal Law; Zoning Law; Personal Injury; Employment and Labor Law. ***Email:*** DOndrey@dolan.law.pro

HEIDI M. CISAN, born Cleveland, Ohio, March 17, 1959; admitted to bar, 1989, Ohio. *Education:* Bucknell University; Ohio State University (B.A., 1980); Case Western Reserve University (J.D., summa cum laude, 1989). *Member:* Geauga County, Ohio State Bar Associations. ***PRACTICE AREAS:*** Family Law; Probate Law; Condominium Law. ***Email:*** HCisan@dolan.law.pro

TODD C. HICKS, born Cleveland, Ohio, June 11, 1969; admitted to bar, 1994, Ohio; 1995, U.S. District Court, Northern District of Ohio; 1995, New York; 1997, U.S. Court of Appeals, Sixth Circuit. *Education:* University of Cincinnati (B.A., magna cum laude, 1991); Ohio State University (J.D., honors, 1994). *Member:* Cleveland, Geauga County and Ohio State Bar Associations. ***PRACTICE AREAS:*** Civil Litigation; Labor and Employment; Real Estate. ***Email:*** THicks@dolan.law.pro

MATTHEW J. DOLAN, born Painesville, Ohio, January 12, 1965; admitted to bar, 1990, Ohio. *Education:* Boston College (A.B., 1987); Case Western Reserve University (J.D., 1990). *Member:* Geauga and Ohio State Bar Associations. ***PRACTICE AREAS:*** Municipal Law; Real Estate; Criminal Law. ***Email:*** MDolan@dolan.law.pro

---

J. JAREDD FLYNN, born October 16, 1976; admitted to bar, 2003, Ohio and U.S. District Court, Northern District of Ohio. *Education:* Miami University (B.S., 1999); Case Western Reserve University (J.D., 2003). *Member:* Geauga County, Portage County and Ohio State Bar Associations. ***PRACTICE AREAS:*** Civil Litigation; Real Estate; Trademarks. ***Email:*** JFlynn@dolan.law.pro

KELLY A. SLATTERY, born Cleveland, Ohio, 1977; admitted to bar, 2002, Ohio. *Education:* University of Notre Dame (B.A., magna cum laude, 1999); Case Western Reserve University (J.D., 2002). Order of the Coif. *Member:* Geauga County, Cleveland and American Bar Associations. ***PRACTICE AREAS:*** Corporate Law; Trusts and Estates; Wills & Probate; Mergers and Acquisitions; Real Estate. ***Email:*** KSlattery@dolan.law.pro

REPRESENTATIVE CLIENTS: Ameri-Con Homes; Cablevision Systems Corporation; Carlisle Engineered Products, Division of Carlisle Corporation; Cleveland Indians Baseball Company Ltd. Partnership; FedEx Ground Package Systems, Inc.; Gold Key Processing, Ltd.; Huntington National Bank; Manor Care, Inc.; McGill Property Group; Motorists Mutual Insurance Co.; Eltech Systems Corp.

MARY K. BENDER CO. L.P.A.

CHESTERLAND, OHIO

(See Chardon)

General Civil Trial Practice, Trials and Appeals in all Courts, Family, Custody and Support, Domestic Relations, Divorce, Juvenile, Real Estate.

WILLIAM C. BOULGER

45 WEST FOURTH STREET
P.O. BOX 204
CHILLICOTHE, OHIO 45601
Telephone: 740-774-1625
Fax: 740-774-1625

General Practice. Probate and Tax Law. Trials.

WILLIAM C. BOULGER, born Columbus, Ohio, April 2, 1924; admitted to bar, 1951, Ohio; 1952, U.S. District Court, Southern District of Ohio; 1957, U.S. Supreme Court. *Education:* Harvard University (A.B., 1948); University of Cincinnati (LL.B., 1951). Phi Alpha Delta. *Member:* Ross County, Ohio State (Member: Probate and Trust Law Section; Federal District Court Committee, 1971) and American (Member, Real Property, Probate and Trust Law Section) Bar Associations. ***PRACTICE AREAS:*** Probate; Estate and Tax Planning; Trust Law; Civil Trials.

CALIG & HANDELMAN, LPA

CHILLICOTHE, OHIO

(See Columbus)

Bankruptcy, Personal Injury, Probate, Real Estate, Social Security, Social Security Disability, Medical Malpractice, Wrongful Death, Civil Litigation, Domestic Relations Law.

COLLEY SHROYER & ABRAHAM CO., L.P.A.

CHILLICOTHE, OHIO

(See Columbus)

Civil Trial Practice. Personal Injury, Medical Malpractice, Automobile Accidents, Wrongful Death, Railroad Accidents, Slip and Fall, Negligence, Product Liability and Toxic Torts.

ROBERT C. HESS

ROOM 2 - FOULKE BLOCK
14 SOUTH PAINT STREET
CHILLICOTHE, OHIO 45601
Telephone: 740-774-6152
Fax: 740-774-6153

Wills and Probate, Estates, Trusts, Elder Law, Real Estate, Personal Injury and Civil Litigation.

ROBERT C. HESS, born Columbus, Ohio, September 19, 1948; admitted to bar, 1974, Ohio; 1979, U.S. District Court, Southern District of Ohio; 1990, U.S. Supreme Court. *Education:* Xavier University (A.B., 1970); St. Louis University (J.D., 1974). Phi Delta Phi. Member, Ohio Supreme Court Commission on Character and Fitness of Bar Applicants, 1979-1983. Assistant Law Director, Chillicothe, Ohio, 1988—. Seminar: Program of Instruction for Lawyers, Harvard Law School, 1981. *Member:* Ross County, Ohio State and American Bar Associations.

LIVORNO & ARNETT CO., LPA

CHILLICOTHE, OHIO

(See Columbus)

Workers Compensation, Labor and Employment, Discrimination, Americans with Disabilities Act, Sexual Harassment, Employment Contracts, Wrongful Termination, Civil Service, Government Agency Practice, Union Labor Law, Bankruptcy.

MALEK & MALEK

CHILLICOTHE, OHIO

(See Columbus)

Workers Compensation, Personal Injury, Railroad Accidents and Injuries, Automobile Accidents and Injuries, Wrongful Death, Dog Bites.

OLIVER LAW OFFICE

CHILLICOTHE, OHIO

(See Columbus)

Products Liability, Personal Injury, Wrongful Death, Latex Allergy Litigation, Medical Malpractice, Vioxx Litigation, Automobile Accidents, Insurance Law, Employment Discrimination.

THE PLYMALE PARTNERSHIP LLP

CHILLICOTHE, OHIO

(See Columbus)

Personal Injury, Products Liability, Wrongful Death, Medical Malpractice, Professional Negligence, Traumatic Brain Injury, Automobile Accidents, Nursing Home Torts, Civil Litigation.

TWYFORD & DONAHEY, P.L.L.

CHILLICOTHE, OHIO

(See Columbus)

Personal Injury Litigation, Wrongful Death, Medical Malpractice, Products Liability, Automobile Accidents, Trucking Accidents, Head and Spinal Injuries, Motorcycle Accidents and Injuries, Uninsured Motorists, Insurance Law, Airplane Crash Litigation, Railroad Accidents, Slip and Fall, Dog Bites, Work Related Injuries, Birth Injuries, Nursing Home Abuse and Neglect.

ADAMS, STEPNER, WOLTERMANN & DUSING, P.L.L.C.

CINCINNATI, OHIO

(See Covington, Kentucky)

General Practice. Corporation, Taxation, Insurance and Commercial Law, Real Estate and Construction Law, Torts, Products Liability, Probate, Workers Compensation, Administrative Law, Banking Law, Personal Injury, Employment Law, Bankruptcy, Trials and Appeals.

D. DAVID ALTMAN CO.

A LEGAL PROFESSIONAL ASSOCIATION

15 EAST EIGHTH STREET, SUITE 200W
CINCINNATI, OHIO 45202
Telephone: 513-721-2180
Fax: 513-721-2299
URL: http://www.environlaw.com
Email: daltman@one.net
URL: http://www.lawyers.com/environlaw

Environmental Law, Toxic Torts. Local Governmental and Municipality, Environmental Representation, Class Actions. General Litigation. Art Agency.

D. DAVID ALTMAN, born Waycross, Georgia, March 1, 1946; admitted to bar, 1974, Ohio; U.S. District Court, Southern District of Ohio. *Education:* University of Cincinnati (B.A., 1968; J.D., 1974). Member, 1975-1987 and Chairman, 1977-1978; 1982-1985, Environmental Advisory Council, City of Cincinnati. Ohio Governors Environmental Task Force, 1970-1972. Adjunct Professor, Environmental Law, University of Cincinnati, 1981—. Lecturer in Environmental Law: ATLA/NJTL Seminar, 1987-1988; USEPA Seminar, 1993; Ohio Academy of Trial Academy of Trial Lawyers Environmental Law Workshops, 1987-1993; Executive Enterprises Environmental Regulation Course, 1992-1994; Ohio State Bar Association Environmental Law Seminar, 1989, 1991. Misc. Seminars on Environmental Law, U.C. College of Law, Christ Church, Cincinnati Bar Association, 1996-1998; Testimony on Audit Privilege before U.S. House of Representatives Committee on Oversight, 1998. *Publications*: Local Health Agencies: The Silent Partners in the Environmental Enforcement Network, 18 Northern Kentucky Law Review 213 (Ohio Trial Magazine, Spring 1992). *Member:* Cincinnati, Ohio State and American (Member, Litigation Section) Bar Associations; Ohio Academy of Trial Lawyers (Chairman, Environmental Law Section, 1989-1995); The Association of Trial Lawyers of America; Hamilton County Trial Lawyers Association. ***PRACTICE AREAS:*** Environmental Law; Superfund Litigation; Toxic Torts; Local Government; Art Agency. ***Email:*** daltman@one.net

AMY J. LEONARD, born Kokomo, Indiana, August 6, 1963; admitted to bar, 1988, Ohio; U.S. District Court, Northern and Southern Districts of Ohio. *Education:* University of Tennessee (B.A., with highest honors, 1985); Phi Beta Kappa; Tulane University (J. D., cum laude, 1988). Editor-in-Chief, Tulane Environmental Law Journal, 1987-1988. Member, Moot Court Honor Board. Environmental Advisory Committee, City of Cincinnati, 1993-1997. *Member:* Cincinnati and Ohio State Bar Associations; Ohio Academy of Trial Lawyers (Chair, Environmental Law Committee, 1998-2000); The Association of Trial Lawyers of America. ***PRACTICE AREAS:*** Environmental Law; Superfund Litigation; Toxic Torts; Local Government. ***Email:*** aleonard@environlaw.com

AMY M. BEIERSDORFER, born Cincinnati, Ohio, January 10, 1972; admitted to bar, 2002, Ohio. *Education:* Northland College (B.S., 1995); Vermont Law School (J.D., M.S., 2001). ***PRACTICE AREAS:*** Environmental Law; Superfund; Toxic Torts. ***Email:*** abeiersdorfer@environlaw.com

JAMES S. ARNOLD & ASSOCIATES

Established in 1993

9737 LOVELAND MADEIRA ROAD
CINCINNATI, OHIO 45140
Telephone: 513-984-8313
Fax: 513-984-8480
URL: http://www.jarnoldlaw.com
Email: jarnold@rLtagency.com
URL: http://www.jalawfirm.com

General Practice, focusing on Driving Under the Influence, Driving while Intoxicated, DUI, DWI, OVI, Personal Injury, Wrongful Death, Medical Malpractice, Real Estate, Domestic Relations, Bankruptcy and Probate.

FIRM PROFILE: Aggressive firm practicing in Kentucky and Ohio.

JAMES S. ARNOLD, born Fort Thomas, Kentucky, May 26, 1965; admitted to bar, 1993, Ohio; 1994, Kentucky and U.S. District Court, Southern District of Ohio. *Education:* William Carey College (B.A., 1987); Salmon P. Chase College of Law (J.D., cum laude, 1993). Dean's List. Listed: Who's Who Among Students in American Universities and Colleges, 1985, 1986; Who's Who Among American Law Students, 1992. Member, Better Business Bureau. *Member:* Cincinnati, Ohio and Kentucky Bar Associations; Graduate National Institute for Trial Lawyers; National Association of Criminal Defense Lawyers; Ohio Association of Criminal Defense Lawyers; The Association of Trial Lawyers of America; Ohio Trial Lawyers Association; American Land Title Association; Southwest Ohio Land Title Association; National Association of Mortgage Brokers; Ohio Association of Mortgage Brokers; Professional Mortgage Brokers Association; Kentucky Academy of Trial Attorneys. ***REPORTED CASES:*** Hamilton v. Callon, 119 Ohio App.3d 759 (1997).

ASSOCIATE

GREGORY E. SMITH, born Cincinnati, Ohio, January 26, 1979; admitted to bar, 2004, Ohio; 2005, U.S. District Court, Southern District of Ohio. *Education:* Miami University (B.A., 2000); University of Dayton (J.D., 2004). *Member:* Cincinnati and Ohio State Bar Associations. ***PRACTICE AREAS:*** General Practice; Bankruptcy; Probate.

ARNZEN, WENTZ, MOLLOY, LABER & STORM, P.S.C.

CINCINNATI, OHIO

(See Covington, Kentucky)

General Civil Trial and Appellate Practice in all Courts. Personal Injury, Products Liability, Aviation, Admiralty, Insurance, Medical Malpractice, Consumer Actions, ERISA, Probate, Real Estate, Bankruptcy and Workers' Compensation Law. Corporate, Taxation, Pension and Profit Sharing and Labor Law.

ARONOFF, ROSEN & HUNT

A LEGAL PROFESSIONAL ASSOCIATION

Established in 1928

2200 U.S. BANK TOWER

425 WALNUT STREET

CINCINNATI, OHIO 45202

Telephone: 513-241-0400

Telecopier: 513-241-2877

Real Estate, Construction, Mechanic's Lien, Corporate, Estate Planning, Probate, Trusts, Administrative and Zoning, Taxation and Civil Litigation.

IRWIN I. ARONOFF (1905-1987)

STANLEY J. ARONOFF, born Cincinnati, Ohio, June 8, 1932; admitted to bar, 1957, Ohio. *Education:* Harvard University (A.B., 1954; LL.B., 1957). Member: Ohio House of Representatives, 1960-1966; Ohio State Senate, 1967-1997 (President, 1989-1997); Ohio Arts Council, 1979-1996; Board of Trustees, Children's Protective Service, 1986-1996; Executive Committee, National Conference of State Legislatures, 1982-1996; Board of Governors and Executive Committee, 1986-1996 and Chair, 1996, Council of State Governments. *Member:* Cincinnati, Ohio State and American Bar Associations. ***PRACTICE AREAS:*** Federal Agency Practice; Litigation; Tort Law; Corporate Counseling; Strategic Planning.

STEPHEN R. HUNT, born Dayton, Ohio, May 5, 1955; admitted to bar, 1980, Ohio, U.S. District Court, Southern District of Ohio and U.S. Tax Court; 1987, Kentucky. *Education:* University of Cincinnati (B.B.A., cum laude, 1977; J.D., 1980). *Member:* Cincinnati and Ohio State Bar Associations. ***PRACTICE AREAS:*** Real Estate Law; Condominium Law; Corporate Law.

MARK W. REIS, born Cincinnati, Ohio, July 7, 1952; admitted to bar, 1983, Ohio, U.S. District Court, Southern District of Ohio and U.S. Tax Court; 1984, Kentucky; 1989, U.S. Supreme Court. *Education:* Rollins College; Marietta College (B.S., 1974); University of Cincinnati (J.D., 1983). Beta Beta Beta; Order of the Coif. *Member:* Cincinnati, Ohio State, Kentucky and American Bar Associations. ***PRACTICE AREAS:*** Business Law; Municipal Bond Law; General Corporate; Tax Law.

RICHARD A. PAOLO, born Cincinnati, Ohio, May 21, 1956; admitted to bar, 1982, Ohio. *Education:* University of Cincinnati (B.A., cum laude with honors, 1979; J.D., 1982). ***PRACTICE AREAS:*** Real Estate Law; Real Estate Financing; Construction Law; Corporate Law.

PATRICK M. O'NEILL, born Chicago, Illinois, June 27, 1961; admitted to bar, 1993, Ohio and U.S. District Court, Southern District of Ohio; 1995, U.S. Court of Appeals, Sixth Circuit; 1997, U.S. Supreme Court. *Education:* Ohio University (B.A. in History, 1987); University of Dayton (J.D., 1993). Order of the Barristers. Member, National Moot Court Team, 1993. Winner, Best Brief and Best Oralist, Walter H. Rice Moot Court Competition. Member, American Subcontractors Association, 1995—. *Member:* Cincinnati, Columbus, Ohio State and American (Member, Forum on the Construction Industry) Bar Associations. ***PRACTICE AREAS:*** Construction Law; Construction Arbitration; Construction Mediation; Mechanics Liens; Trial and Appellate Practice.

EDMONDE P. DEGREGORIO, born Yonkers, New York, October 16, 1952; admitted to bar, 1977, Ohio; 1984, Kentucky. *Education:* Columbia University (B.A., 1974); Boston University (J.D., 1977). *Member:* Cincinnati, Ohio State, Northern Kentucky and Kentucky Bar Associations. ***PRACTICE AREAS:*** Commercial Real Estate; Title Insurance; Construction; Commercial Leasing.

VALERIE L. VAN VALKENBURG, born Columbus, Ohio, August 15, 1960; admitted to bar, 1986, Ohio; 1987, U.S. District Court, Southern District of Ohio; 1994, Kentucky; 1997, U.S. Court of Appeals, Sixth Circuit; 2001, U.S. District Court, Eastern District of Kentucky. *Education:* College of Mt. St. Joseph (B.A., magna cum laude, 1983); University of Cincinnati (J.D., 1986). Phi Alpha Delta. *Member:* Cincinnati, Kentucky, and Ohio State Bar Associations. ***PRACTICE AREAS:*** Litigation; Municipal Defense.

TINA M. DONNELLY, born Cincinnati, Ohio, January 11, 1971; admitted to bar, 2000, Ohio. *Education:* University of Cincinnati (B.A., 1993); Salmon P. Chase College of Law (J.D., 1998). Licensed Title Agent, State of Ohio. *Member:* Cincinnati and Ohio State Bar Associations. ***PRACTICE AREAS:*** Real Estate; Probate.

EDWARD P. AKIN, born Houston, Texas, June 23, 1963; admitted to bar, 2001, Ohio; 2002, U.S. District Court, Southern District of Ohio. *Education:* Southwestern University (B.A., 1985); University of Notre Dame Law School (J.D., 2001). *Member:* Cincinnati and Ohio State Bar Associations. ***PRACTICE AREAS:*** Civil Litigation.

OF COUNSEL

IRVING H. ROSEN, born Cincinnati, Ohio, April 16, 1928; admitted to bar, 1957, Ohio; 1958, U.S. Court of Appeals, Sixth Circuit and U.S. District Court, Southern District of Ohio; 1959, U.S. District Court, Southern District of Indiana; 1971, U.S. Supreme Court; 1975, U.S. Tax Court; 1985, Kentucky and U.S. Claims Court. *Education:* University of Cincinnati (B.A., 1949; J.D., 1957). Phi Beta Kappa; Phi Eta Sigma; Phi Delta Phi. *Member:* Cincinnati, Ohio State, Kentucky and American Bar Associations; American Judicature Society; Lawyers Club. ***PRACTICE AREAS:*** Business Law; Tax Law; Real Estate Law.

(This Listing Continued)

REPRESENTATIVE CLIENTS: The Drees Co.; Fifth Third Bank; First Equity Mortgage, Inc.; D. E. Foxx & Associates, Inc.; Cintech Construction, Inc.; Tri-State Land Title Agency, Inc.; Benenson Capital Co.; Home Builders Assn. of Greater Cincinnati; Cobblestone Development Co.; Casco, Inc.; Towne Properties, Inc.; KZF Design, Inc.; Robert C. Rhein Interests, Inc.; John Henry Homes; Classic Properties, Inc.; Robt. Lucke Homes, Inc.
REFERENCE: U.S. Bank.

BAKER & HOSTETLER LLP

Established in 1916

312 WALNUT STREET

SUITE 3200

CINCINNATI, OHIO 45202-4074

Telephone: 513-929-3400

Telecopier: 513-929-0303

To contact an attorney on the Internet use first initial and surname followed by @bakerlaw.com

URL: http://www.bakerlaw.com

In Cleveland, Ohio: 3200 National City Center, 1900 East Ninth Street. Telephone: 216-621-0200.
In Columbus, Ohio: Capitol Square, Suite 2100, 65 East State Street. Telephone: 614-228-1541.
In Costa Mesa, California: 600 Anton Boulevard, Suite 900. Telephone: 714-754-6600.
In Denver, Colorado: 303 East 17th Avenue, Suite 1100. Telephone: 303-861-0600.
In Houston, Texas: 1000 Louisiana, Suite 2000. Telephone: 713-751-1600.
In Los Angeles, California: 333 South Grand Avenue, Suite 1800. Telephone: 213-975-1600.
In Orlando, Florida: SunTrust Center, Suite 2300, 200 South Orange Avenue. Telephone: 407-649-4000.
In Washington, D. C.: Washington Square, Suite 1100, 1050 Connecticut Avenue, N.W. Telephone: 202-861-1500.
In New York, N.Y.: 666 Fifth Avenue. Telephone: 212-589-4200.

General Practice.

OFFICE MANAGING PARTNER

WILLIAM APPLETON, born Pittsburgh, Pennsylvania, February 15, 1949; admitted to bar, 1978, Ohio. *Education:* University of Pittsburgh (B.A., 1971); New York University (J.D., 1978). Phi Beta Kappa. *Member:* Cincinnati (Member, Securities Law Section) and American Bar Associations. ***PRACTICE AREAS:*** Business; Mergers and Acquisitions; Securities Law. ***Email:*** wappleton@bakerlaw.com

PARTNERS

MICHAEL F. BIGLER, born Chillicothe, Ohio, 1957; admitted to bar, 1983, District of Columbia (inactive); 1984, Ohio and U.S. Court of Appeals, Seventh Circuit. *Education:* University of Cincinnati (B.A., 1979); University of Notre Dame (J.D., 1983). *Member:* Cincinnati and Ohio State Bar Associations. ***PRACTICE AREAS:*** Corporate Finance; Equipment Leasing; Bankruptcy and Reorganization; Mergers and Acquisitions. ***Email:*** mbigler@bakerlaw.com

MARTINÉ R. DUNN, born July 24, 1959; admitted to bar, 1985, Ohio; 1986, U.S. District Court, Southern District of Ohio. *Education:* Northwestern University (B.S., 1981); University of Michigan Law School (J.D., 1984). *Member:* Cincinnati, Ohio State, American and National Bar Associations; Black Lawyers Association of Cincinnati; National Association of Industrial and Office Properties. ***PRACTICE AREAS:*** Real Estate; Financing Transactions; Business Law. ***Email:*** mdunn@bakerlaw.com

ERIC J. GEPPERT, born Glens Falls, New York, May 7, 1963; admitted to bar, 1988, Maryland (inactive); 1989, District of Columbia; 1998, Ohio. *Education:* Ithaca College (B.S., cum laude, 1985); George Washington University (J.D., 1988). *Member:* The District of Columbia Bar; Cincinnati, Maryland State, Ohio State and American (Section of Business Law) Bar Associations; Greater Cincinnati Venture Capital Association. ***PRACTICE AREAS:*** Real Estate; Mergers and Acquisitions; Finance; Technology Transactions. ***Email:*** egeppert@bakerlaw.com

ROBIN E. HARVEY, born Los Angeles, California, June 26, 1952; admitted to bar, 1978, Maryland; 1983, Ohio. *Education:* Pitzer College (B.A., 1974); Antioch School of Law (J.D., 1977). ***PRACTICE AREAS:*** Litigation; Labor and Employment; Telecommunications; Appellate Practice. ***Email:*** rharvey@bakerlaw.com

DAVID G. HOLCOMBE, born Newark, Ohio, September 26, 1955; admitted to bar, 1981, Ohio. *Education:* Denison University (B.A., 1978) Class Valedictorian; Case Western Reserve University (J.D., 1981). Phi Beta Kappa; Order of the Coif. *Member:* Cincinnati, Ohio State and American Bar Associations. ***PRACTICE AREAS:*** Employment Law; Litigation. ***Email:*** dholcombe@bakerlaw.com

THOMAS W. KAHLE, born Toledo, Ohio, June 27, 1950; admitted to bar, 1975, Ohio. *Education:* University of Dayton (B.A., summa cum laude, 1972); The Ohio State University (J.D., summa cum laude, 1975). Order of the Coif. *Member:* Cincinnati, Ohio State and American Bar Associations; National Healthcare Lawyers Association. ***PRACTICE AREAS:*** Health Care Law; Hospital Law; Corporate Law; Mergers, Acquisitions and Divestitures. ***Email:*** tkahle@bakerlaw.com

TED T. MARTIN, born Cincinnati, Ohio, October 2, 1956; admitted to bar, 1982, Ohio and U.S. District Court, Southern District of Ohio; 1987, U.S. Court of Appeals, Sixth Circuit; 1999, Kentucky; 2004, U.S. District Court, Western District of Kentucky. *Education:* College of the Holy Cross (A.B., 1979); University of Cincinnati (J.D., 1982). *Member:* Cincinnati and American Bar Associations; American Health Lawyers Association; Defense Research Institute. ***PRACTICE AREAS:*** Civil Litigation; Technology. ***Email:*** tmartin@bakerlaw.com

(This Listing Continued)

ASSOCIATES

BENJAMIN G. DUSING, born Covington, Kentucky, October 17, 1975; admitted to bar, 2002, Kentucky; 2003, U.S. Court of Appeals, Sixth Circuit and U.S. District Court, Eastern and Western Districts of Kentucky; 2004, Ohio and U.S. District Court, Southern District of Ohio. *Education:* Georgetown University (B.S., Foreign Service, 1997); University of Kentucky College of Law (J.D., 2001). *Member:* Cincinnati, Northern Kentucky, Kentucky, Ohio State, Federal and American Bar Associations. ***LANGUAGES:*** Russian. ***PRACTICE AREAS:*** Litigation; Appellate Practice; Products Liability; Toxic Torts; Labor and Employment. ***Email:*** bdusing@bakerlaw.com

ROBERT F. MORWOOD, admitted to bar, 2004, Ohio. *Education:* The Ohio State University (B.A., summa cum laude, 1998; J.D., with honors, 2003). ***Email:*** rmorwood@bakerlaw.com

ELENI V. STRATIGEAS, born Salt Lake City, Utah, 1971; admitted to bar, 1998, Mississippi; 2001, Ohio. *Education:* University of Utah (B.A., cum laude, 1995); Vanderbilt University (J.D., 1998). Member of the Young Professionals of the World Affairs Council, Legacy. *Member:* Ohio State and American Bar Associations; The Mississippi Bar. ***PRACTICE AREAS:*** Mergers and Acquisitions; Corporate Finance; Securities Law; Media Law. ***Email:*** estratigeas@bakerlaw.com

STAFF ATTORNEY

ANGELA HAYDEN, born Cincinnati, Ohio, September 7, 1972; admitted to bar, 1999, Ohio. *Education:* College of Mount St. Joseph (B.A., 1995); University of Akron (J.D., 1998). ***PRACTICE AREAS:*** Products Liability.

BARRETT & WEBER

A LEGAL PROFESSIONAL ASSOCIATION

Established in 1990

500 FOURTH & WALNUT CENTRE
105 EAST FOURTH STREET
CINCINNATI, OHIO 45202
Telephone: 513-721-2120
Facsimile: 513-721-2139
URL: http://www.barrettweber.com

General Civil Practice including Commercial, Condominium, Construction, Corporate, Eminent Domain, Estate and Gift Taxation, Estate Planning, Federal and State Income Tax, Land Use and Planning, Local Government, Negligence, Probate, Real Estate, Tax Valuation of Real Estate, Title Insurance and Zoning. Administrative, Trial and Appellate Practice.

C. FRANCIS BARRETT, born Cincinnati, Ohio, January 24, 1946; admitted to bar, 1971, Ohio; 1972, U.S. District Court, Southern District of Ohio; 1977, U.S. District Court, Northern District of Ohio; 1978, U.S. Court of Appeals, Sixth Circuit. *Education:* Xavier University (B.S., 1968); University of Cincinnati (J.D., 1971). Board Member, Ohio Building Authority, 1996—. Board Member, Ohio Building Authority, 1996—. *Member:* Cincinnati, Ohio State and American Bar Associations; The Association of Trial Lawyers of America; Ohio Academy of Trial Lawyers. ***PRACTICE AREAS:*** Litigation; Zoning, Planning and Land Use; Appellate Practice; Trial Practice; Administrative Law. ***Email:*** CFBARRETT@BARRETTWEBER.com

H. PATRICK WEBER, born Cincinnati, Ohio, January 25, 1949; admitted to bar, 1974, Ohio, U.S. District Court, Southern District of Ohio and U.S. Tax Court; 1990, Kentucky; 1991, U.S. Claims Court. *Education:* University of Notre Dame (B.B.A., 1971; J.D., 1974). *Member:* Cincinnati (Chairman: Estate Planning and Probate Committee, 1995-1996; Estate Planning Institute, 1992-1993), Ohio State, Kentucky and American Bar Associations; Cincinnati Estate Planning Council. (Certified Specialist in Estate Planning, Trust and Probate Law, Ohio State Bar Association). ***PRACTICE AREAS:*** Estate Planning; Probate; Taxation; Corporate Law; Business Law; Partnership Law; Trusts and Estates; Wills. ***Email:*** HPWEBER@BARRETTWEBER.com

MICHAEL R. BARRETT, born Cincinnati, Ohio, January 14, 1951; admitted to bar, 1977, Ohio; 1981, U.S. District Court, Southern District of Ohio; U.S. Court of Appeals, Sixth Circuit. *Education:* University of Cincinnati (B.A., 1974; J.D., 1977). Assistant Prosecutor, 1978-1983 and Chief Assistant Prosecutor, 1983-1984, Hamilton County. Member, Hamilton County Board of Elections. Chairman, Hamilton County Republican Party. Trustee: Citizen Advisory Board of River City Correctional Center; Charles P. Taft Memorial Fund; Boys Hope/Girls Hope. Member, Supreme Court of Ohio Board of Commissioners on Grievances and Discipline. *Member:* Cincinnati Bar Association; National Association of Criminal Defense Attorneys. ***PRACTICE AREAS:*** Litigation; Criminal Law; Domestic Relations; Environmental Law; Driving While Intoxicated; White Collar Crime. ***Email:*** MRBARRETT@BARRETTWEBER.com

M. MICHELE FLEMING, born Cincinnati, Ohio, December 25, 1953; admitted to bar, 1979, Ohio, U.S. District Court, Southern District of Ohio and U.S. Court of Appeals, Sixth Circuit; 1981, Indiana. *Education:* Purdue University (B.S., 1975); University of Cincinnati (J.D., 1979). Student Articles Editor, University of Cincinnati Law Review, 1978-1979. Barrister, Potter Stewart American Inn of Court, 1985-1987. *Member:* Cincinnati, Ohio State and American Bar Associations. ***LANGUAGES:*** Spanish. ***PRACTICE AREAS:*** Civil Appeals; Wireless Communications; Civil Litigation; Probate Litigation; Land Use Litigation; Eminent Domain; Zoning Law. ***Email:*** MMFLEMING@BARRETTWEBER.com

JANET L. BELL, born Cleveland, Ohio, October 23, 1948; admitted to bar, 1984, Ohio; 1985, U.S. District Court, Southern District of Ohio. *Education:* American University (B.A., 1970); University of Cincinnati (M.P.A., 1980); Salmon P. Chase College of Law (J.D., 1984). Member, Order of the Curia. Member, Chase Law Review, 1983-1984. Member, Commercial Real Estate Women (CREW). *Member:* Cincinnati, Ohio State and American Bar Associations. ***PRACTICE AREAS:*** Real Estate Law; Estate Planning; Corporate Law. ***Email:*** JLBELL@BARRETTWEBER.com

(This Listing Continued)

KENNETH J. ELING, born Cincinnati, Ohio, February 5, 1964; admitted to bar, 1993, Ohio and U.S. District Court, Southern District of Ohio; 2000, Kentucky. *Education:* Xavier University (B.S., 1987); Salmon P. Chase College of Law (J.D., 1992). *Member:* Cincinnati, Ohio State, Kentucky, Northern Kentucky and American Bar Associations. ***PRACTICE AREAS:*** Corporate Law; Real Estate Law; Estate Planning; Probate Law; Aviation Law; Criminal Defense. ***Email:*** KJELING@BARRETTWEBER.com

KARRI K. HAFFNER, born Cincinnati, Ohio, January 24, 1970; admitted to bar, 1994, Ohio. *Education:* Rollins College (B.A., 1991); University of Cincinnati (J.D., 1994); University of Cincinnati (Master of Community Planning, 1996). *Member:* Cincinnati, Ohio State and American Bar Associations; American Planning Association (1995—); Ohio Planning Conference (1995—). ***PRACTICE AREAS:*** Land Use Litigation; Zoning, Planning and Land Use; Eminent Domain; Inverse Condemnation; Land Annexation; Property Law. ***Email:*** KKHAFFNER@BARRETTWEBER.com

STEPHANIE K. BOWMAN, born Kankakee, Illinois, December 16, 1974; admitted to bar, 2000, Ohio; 2002, U.S District Court, Southern District of Ohio; 2003, U.S. Court of Appeals, Sixth Circuit; 2004, U.S. District Court, Northern District of Ohio. *Education:* University of Illinois, Urbana-Champaign (B.A., 1997); DePaul University (J.D., 2000). *Member:* Cincinnati, Ohio State and American Bar Associations. ***PRACTICE AREAS:*** Estate Planning; Real Estate; Corporate Law. ***Email:*** skbowman@barrettweber.com

THOMAS W. BREIDENSTEIN, born Cincinnati, Ohio, February 13, 1962; admitted to bar, 1993, Kentucky; 1994, Ohio and U.S. District Court, Eastern District of Kentucky; 1995, U.S. District Court, Southern District of Ohio. *Education:* Miami University (B.A., 1984); Salmon P. Chase College of Law, Northern Kentucky University (J.D., 1993). Formerly with: Cors & Bassett; Deters, Benzinger & Lavelle. Member, American Institute of Certified Planners. Glendale Planning & Historic Preservation Commission, 2000—. *Member:* Cincinnati, Northern Kentucky, Kentucky and Ohio State Bar Associations. ***PRACTICE AREAS:*** Zoning, Planning and Land Use; Litigation. ***Email:*** twbreidenstein@barrettweber.com

REPRESENTATIVE CLIENTS: Allied Waste Industries, Inc.; American Self Storage; Ashland Oil, Inc.; AT&T; Bridgestone/Firestone Inc.; The Cincinnati Reds; Cintas Corporation; The Coca Cola Company; E.S.I., Inc.; Great Traditions Development Group; Holiday Homes, Inc.; Jewish Hospital; Kimco Development Corporation; The Kroger Co.; LaSalle Partners, Inc.; Marathon Oil Company; McDonald's Corporation; Meijer, Inc.; The Monsanto Company; North American Properties, Inc.; Sherwin-Williams Company; State Teachers Retirement Board of Ohio; Streetside Records, Inc. SuperAmerica Group, Inc.; United Dairy Farmers; Valvoline Instant Oil Change Inc.; Western and Southern Life Insurance Co.; E. A. Zicka Company.

BARTLETT & WEIGLE CO., L.P.A.

Established in 1981

SUITE 1100 TRI-STATE BUILDING
432 WALNUT STREET
CINCINNATI, OHIO 45202
Telephone: 513-241-3992
Fax: 513-241-1816
Email: bartlettlaw@fuse.net
URL: http://www.bartlettlaw.com

Covington, Kentucky Office: 211 East Fourth Street. Telephone: 859-491-1122.

General Civil and Criminal Law. Estate Planning, Real Estate and Corporate Franchise Law. Immigration and Naturalization Law. Business Bankruptcy. Trials and Appeals in all Courts.

FIRM PROFILE: William T. Bartlett and Douglas S. Weigle are both graduates of Salmon P. Chase College of Law. What drew these partners together was a single principle —to provide excellent legal counsel in the personal setting of a small general practice firm. While today the Firm has expanded, adding attorneys and support staff, with offices in both Covington, Kentucky and Cincinnati, Ohio, this principle is still paramount.

The Firm remains committed to serving the client -- this means taking the time to listen and understand each client's concerns, providing timely, practical, result-oriented responses to legal matters.

WILLIAM T. BARTLETT, born Erie, Pennsylvania, February 2, 1945; admitted to bar, 1974, Ohio; 1982, U.S. District Court, Southern District of Ohio. *Education:* Pennsylvania State University (B.S.I.E., 1967); Salmon P. Chase School of Law (J.D., 1974). *Member:* Cincinnati (Member, Sections on: Corporate and Securities; Trusts, Wills and Estate Planning) and American (Member, Franchising Section) Bar Associations; American Immigration Lawyers Association. ***PRACTICE AREAS:*** Immigration Law; Corporate Law; Franchise Law; Estate Planning Law. ***Email:*** wbartlett@bartlettlaw.com

DOUGLAS S. WEIGLE, born Cincinnati, Ohio, August 15, 1950; admitted to bar, 1976, Ohio and U.S. District Court, Southern District of Ohio; 1977, Kentucky, U.S. Tax Court and U.S. Court of Appeals, Sixth Circuit; 1979, U.S. District Court, Eastern District of Kentucky; 1980, U.S. Supreme Court. *Education:* Bowling Green State University (B.S., 1972); Northern Kentucky University (J.D., 1976). Omicron Delta Kappa. Co-editor: Process & Procedures - A Guide To Visa Processing At U.S. Consultants And Embassies, Ninth Edition, AILA, 2004, ISBN, 1-57370-122-X. *Member:* Cincinnati (Chairman, Lawyer Referral Service, 1981-1984; Chairman, Criminal Law Committee, 1985-1987), Kentucky, Northern Kentucky (Member, Lawyer Referral Service Committee) and Federal (President, Cincinnati Chapter, 1997-1998; Chair, Immigration Law Section, 2003-2005);) Bar Associations; American Immigration Lawyers Association (Chair, Ohio Chapter, 1985-1989; Director, 1991-1994). ***REPORTED CASES:*** Leonid Petkiewytsch v. INS 945F2nd 871 USCA 6th Circuit, 1991 (Limited Application of the Holtzman Amendment). ***PRACTICE AREAS:*** Immigration Law; Federal Law; Civil and Criminal Trials. ***Email:*** dweigle@bartlettlaw.com

DARRELL S. WRIGHT, born Covington, Kentucky, June 18, 1956; admitted to bar, 1985, Kentucky; 1986, Ohio. *Education:* Northern Kentucky University (B.S., 1978);

(This Listing Continued)

BARTLETT & WEIGLE CO., L.P.A., Cincinnati—Continued

Salmon P. Chase College of Law (J.D., 1984). *Member:* Kentucky and Northern Kentucky (Member, Probate Committee) Bar Associations; American Immigration Lawyers Association. ***PRACTICE AREAS:*** Estate Planning Law; Bankruptcy Law; Immigration Law. ***Email:*** dwright@bartlettlaw.com

MATTHEW L. BENSON, born Covington, Kentucky, January 26, 1977; admitted to bar, 2003, Ohio; 2004, Kentucky; U.S. District Court, Southern District of Ohio and U.S. Court of Appeals, Sixth Circuit. *Education:* University of Kentucky (B.S., Biology, 1999); Salmon P. Chase College of Law (J.D., magna cum laude, 2003). Member: Moot Court Board; Law Review. Author: "Casenote: United States v. Smithers," 30 N. Ky. L. Rev. 605. *Member:* Cincinnati, Kentucky and Federal Bar Associations. ***PRACTICE AREAS:*** Immigration Law; Civil Litigation; Collections; Criminal Law. ***Email:*** mbenson@bartlettlaw.com

IMMIGRATION COUNSEL: Northern Kentucky University; Central State University, Ohio.

KAREN H. BAUERNSCHMIDT CO., LPA

CINCINNATI, OHIO

(See Cleveland)

Real Estate Tax, Litigation, Appellate Practices and Procedure.

E. HANLIN BAVELY

850 TRI STATE BUILDING
432 WALNUT STREET
CINCINNATI, OHIO 45202-3914
Telephone: 513-621-6621
Fax: 513-721-4129

Bankruptcy, Debtor/Creditor, Commercial Collections, Civil Litigation, Probate.

E. HANLIN BAVELY, born Cincinnati, Ohio, August 9, 1938; admitted to bar, 1964, Ohio; 1965, U.S. District Court, Southern District of Ohio; 1970, U.S. Court of Appeals, Sixth Circuit; 1973, U.S. Supreme Court; 1977, U.S. District Court, Eastern District of Kentucky. *Education:* University of Cincinnati (B.A., 1961; J.D., 1964). Panel Trustee, U.S. Bankruptcy Court, 1963—. *Member:* Cincinnati Bar Association (Member and Chairman, 1984-1985, Bankruptcy Committee; Chairman, Certified Grievance Committee, 1990-1993); Member, Board of Trustees, 1995-1999); National Association of Bankruptcy Trustees. ***PRACTICE AREAS:*** Bankruptcy Law; Probate Law; Civil Litigation.

BECKMAN WEIL SHEPARDSON LLC

1200 MERCANTILE CENTER
120 EAST 4TH STREET
CINCINNATI, OHIO 45202-4010
Telephone: 513-621-2100
Telecopier: 513-621-0106
URL: http://www.beckman-weil.com

General Practice. Civil Litigation, Corporation, Domestic Relations, Employment, Tax, Labor, Trademark, Real Estate, Insurance, Medical Malpractice, Hospital, Health Care, Probate, Estate Planning, Elder Law, Medicaid and University Law. Trials and Appeals.

VINCENT H. BECKMAN (Retired)

MEMBERS OF FIRM

SIDNEY WEIL, born Cincinnati, Ohio, 1926; admitted to bar, 1950, Ohio; 1971, U.S. Supreme Court. *Education:* University of Cincinnati (LL.B., 1950). Order of the Coif; Phi Delta Phi. Editor, University of Cincinnati Law Review, 1950. Lecturer on Law, University of Cincinnati, 1951-1967. Member, Hamilton County Board of Elections, 1966-1982. Member, Board of Directors, University of Cincinnati, 1973-1975. *Member:* Cincinnati and American Bar Associations; National Association of College and University Attorneys. ***PRACTICE AREAS:*** Administrative Law; Public Law; Alternative Dispute Resolution; Mediation; Communications Law; Cable Franchising; Construction Law; Public Construction Law; Education Law; College and University Law; Hospital Law; Labor and Employment; Public Sector Employment Law; Municipal Law; Municipal Corporation Law. ***Email:*** sweil@beckman-weil.com

W. PHILIP SHEPARDSON, JR., born Lowell, Massachusetts, June 11, 1945; admitted to bar, 1971, Ohio. *Education:* University of Cincinnati (B.A., 1968; J.D., 1971). *Member:* Cincinnati and American (Member, Section on Business Law) Bar Associations; National Association of College and University Attorneys. ***PRACTICE AREAS:*** Business Law; Business Associations Law; Business Formation; Business Regulation; Buying and Selling of Businesses; Limited Liability Company Law; Corporate Law; Nonprofit and Charitable Organizations; Partnership Law; Probate; Trusts and Estates; Estate Planning; Living Trusts. ***Email:*** pshepardson@beckman-weil.com

DAVID E. HATHAWAY, born Flushing Meadows, New York, January 22, 1944; admitted to bar, 1972, Florida; 1980, Ohio, U. S. Tax Court and U.S. Claims Court. *Education:* Miami University (B.S., 1966); Ohio State University (J.D., cum laude, 1972). ***PRACTICE AREAS:*** Federal Income, Estate and Gift Taxation Law; Corporate Law; Estate Planning; Probate Law. ***Email:*** dhathaway@beckman-weil.com

RICHARD M. HOPPLE, born Cincinnati, Ohio, January 25, 1948; admitted to bar, 1973, Ohio; U.S. District Court, Northern and Southern Districts of Ohio; U.S. District Court, Eastern District of Kentucky; U.S. Court of Appeals, Sixth Circuit; U.S. Court of Federal Claims. *Education:* University of Cincinnati (B.A., with high honors in Economics, 1970; J.D., 1973). *Member:* Cincinnati (Member, 1974—; Member-at-Large, Executive Committee, 1985-1987; Arbitration Committee, Chair, 1986-1989, 1992-1995, Vice-Chair, 1983-1986, Secretary, 1981-1983; Finance Committee Member, 1978-1984, Vice-Chair,

(This Listing Continued)

1982-1984, Secretary, 1981-1982) and Ohio State (Member, 1974—; Council of Delegates, 1988-1992) Bar Associations. ***PRACTICE AREAS:*** Litigation; Negligence; Wrongful Death; Medical Malpractice; Medical Injury; Negligence Defense; Fiduciary Law; Trusts and Estates; Wills; Elder Law; Medicaid; Education Law; Fraternity Law and Liability. ***Email:*** rhopple@beckman-weil.com

PETER L. CASSADY, born Cincinnati, Ohio, November 11, 1947; admitted to bar, 1974, Indiana; 1980, U.S. Supreme Court; 1983, Ohio. *Education:* College of the Holy Cross (B.A., 1970); Boston University (J.D., 1974). *Member:* Cincinnati, Indiana State and American Bar Associations. ***PRACTICE AREAS:*** Alternative Dispute Resolution; Mediation; Civil Practice; Federal Civil Practice; Civil Rights; Civil Rights Defense; Education Law; College and University Law; School Law; Family Law; Collaborative Family Law; Divorce; Matrimonial Law; Premarital Agreements; Labor and Employment; Employment Discrimination; Employment Law; Federal Employment Law; Litigation; Civil Litigation; Personnel Policies; Business Litigation; Insurance Agents and Brokers Defense; Harassment; Wrongful Death. ***Email:*** petercassady@beckman-weil.com

JOSEPH H. FELDHAUS, born Cincinnati, Ohio, December 30, 1951; admitted to bar, 1979, California; 1982, Ohio; 1990, Kentucky. *Education:* Xavier University; University of Cincinnati (B.S., 1974); Southwestern University School of Law (J.D., 1979). *Member:* Cincinnati (Member: Real Estate Committee; Construction Law Committee) and Ohio State (Member, Real Estate Law Committee) Bar Associations. ***PRACTICE AREAS:*** Commercial Real Estate; Construction Law; Eminent Domain; Housing Law; Real Estate; Taxation; Ad Valorem Tax; Low Income Housing Tax Credits; Low Income Tax Credits; Property Tax; Property Tax Abatement; Property Tax Appeals; Property Tax Assessments; Zoning, Planning and Land Use. ***Email:*** jfeldhaus@beckman-weil.com

MARGARET A. HILVERT, born Cincinnati, Ohio, August 8, 1942; admitted to bar, 1989, Ohio. *Education:* College of Mount St. Joseph (B.A., 1964); Miami University (M.A., 1974); University of Cincinnati (J.D., 1989). Editor-in-Chief, University of Cincinnati Law Review, 1988-1989. *Member:* Cincinnati and American Bar Associations. ***PRACTICE AREAS:*** Real Estate; Condominium Law; Business Law; Employment Law. ***Email:*** mhilvert@beckman-weil.com

JANET EILEEN PECQUET, born Akron, Ohio, November 21, 1955; admitted to bar, 1981, California, Ohio and Arkansas. *Education:* California State University Long Beach (B.A., 1978); Southwestern University School of Law (J.D., 1980). Member, Southwestern University Law Review. *Member:* Cincinnati (Member, Past Chair, Past Secretary, Elder Law Committee) and Ohio State (Member, Elder Law Committee) Bar Associations; National Academy of Elder Law Attorneys. ***PRACTICE AREAS:*** Elder Law; Guardianship and Conservatorship; Elder Guardianship; Medicare and Medicaid; Medicaid Planning; Medicaid Hearings; Probate; Probate Administration; Probate Litigation; Trusts and Estates; Estate Litigation; Estate Planning for Parents of Handicapped Children; Estate Planning for the Disabled; Estate Planning for the Elderly; Special Needs Trusts. ***Email:*** jpecquet@beckman-weil.com

BRIAN G. DERSHAW, born Columbus, Ohio, September 30, 1975; admitted to bar, 2000, Ohio; 2001, U.S. District Court, Southern District of Ohio; 2001, Kentucky. *Education:* Capital University (B.A., cum laude, 1997); University of Cincinnati College of Law (J.D., 2000). Justice, Phi Alpha Delta. Member, Moot Court Board. Listed in Madison Who's Who Among American Law Students. Board Member, Peaslee Neighborhood Center, 2004—. *Member:* Cincinnati, Ohio State, Kentucky and American Bar Associations. ***PRACTICE AREAS:*** Labor and Employment; Employment Litigation; Employment Discrimination; Harassment; Personnel Policies; Civil Litigation; Business Litigation; Construction Litigation; Commercial Real Estate Litigation; College and University Law; Insurance Agents and Brokers Defense; Government Contracts; Banking Law; Personal Injury.

ASSOCIATES

BRIAN R. REDDEN, born Cincinnati, Ohio, October 27, 1972; admitted to bar, 1999, Ohio and U.S. District Court, Southern District of Ohio. *Education:* Xavier University (B.A. with honors, magna cum laude, 1994); Salmon P. Chase College of Law, Northern Kentucky University (J.D., cum laude, 1999). Who's Who in American Colleges and Universities. Constable, Judge Steven E. Martin, Hamilton County Court of Common Pleas, 1997-1999. Precinct Executive, Precinct 25-U, Hamilton County, Ohio, 1998—. NFLPA Contract Advisor, 2001—. CFLPA Contact Advisor, 1999—. Trustee: Greater Cincinnati Sports Corp.; Teen Response, Inc. *Member:* Cincinnati (Member, Practical Law Institute and Young Lawyers Section) and Ohio State Bar Associations; Sports Lawyers Association. ***PRACTICE AREAS:*** Labor and Employment; Employment Litigation; Employment Discrimination; Harassment; Personnel Policies; Civil Litigation; Business Litigation; Construction Litigation; Commercial Real Estate Litigation; College and University Law; Sports Law; Misdemeanors Criminal; Traffic Violations; Driving While Intoxicated. ***Email:*** bredden@beckman-weil.com

JENNIFER GRIFFIN ANSTAETT, born Sikeston, Missouri, December 14, 1975; admitted to bar, 2001, Ohio. *Education:* Centre College of Kentucky (B.A., History and English, 1998); Washington & Lee University School of Law (J.D., 2001). *Member:* Cincinnati and Ohio State Bar Associations; American Health Lawyers Association. ***PRACTICE AREAS:*** Elder Law; Limited Liability Company Law; Closely Held Corporations; Corporate Contracts; Corporate Dissolutions; Corporate Governance; Health Care Compliance; Health Care Contracts; Health Insurance Portability and Accountability Act (HIPAA); Health Law; Physician Practices; Medicaid Planning. ***Email:*** janstaett@beckman-weil.com

LAURIE A. LAMB, born Fort Thomas, Kentucky, June 18, 1978; admitted to bar, 2003, Ohio and U.S. District Court, Southern District of Ohio; 2004, Kentucky. *Education:* Northern Kentucky University (B.S., summa cum laude, 2000); Salmon P. Chase College of Law (J.D., magna cum laude, 2003). Editor, Northern Kentucky Law Review, 2001. Author: "The Establishment Clause: A Survey of Recent Religion Cases Decided Within the Sixth Circuit," 29 N. Ky. L. Rev. 73 (2002). *Member:* Cincinnati, Ohio State and American Bar Associations. ***PRACTICE AREAS:*** Business Litigation; Contract Litigation; Domestic Relations; Civil Litigation; Defense Litigation; Construction Litigation; Divorce; Landlord and Tenant Law. ***Email:*** llamb@beckman-weil.com

(This Listing Continued)

KRISTEN M. MYERS, born Cincinnati, Ohio; admitted to bar, 2004, Ohio. *Education:* Hiram College (B.A., 2001); University of Cincinnati (J.D., 2004). Phi Beta Kappa. Order of the Barristers. Best Petitioner's Brief at Pepperdine University National Entertainment Law Moot Court Competition. Recipient, Jorge Carro Consummate Advocate Award; Provident Bank Prize for Wills, Trusts & Future Interests. Member, Association of Professional in Aging, 2004-2005. Book Review: Daniel J. Tichenor, "Diving Lines: The Politics of Immigration Control in America," Published in Immigration and Nationality Law Review, Volume 23 (2002). Executive Director, University of Cincinnati Moot Court Honors Board, 2003-2004. *Member:* Cincinnati, Ohio State and American Bar Associations. ***PRACTICE AREAS:*** Elder Law (25%); Institutional Law (25%); Litigation (20%); Finance (10%); Tax Law (10%); Estate Planning (5%); Probate Administration (5%). ***Email:*** kmyers@beckman-weil.com

MR. FELDHAUS IS A LICENSED AGENT FOR: The Ohio Bar Title Insurance Company; Old Republic National Title Insurance Company.
REPRESENTATIVE CLIENTS: Cincinnati Financial Corp.; University of Cincinnati; Xavier University; Cincinnati Insurance Co.; Cincinnati Life Insurance Co.; Cincinnati Equitable Insurance Co.; Continental Mineral Processing Corp.; Time Warner Entertainment Co., L.P.; USI Midwest, Inc.; Cincinnati Metropolitan Housing Authority; Central Clinic; U.S. Bank.

BENJAMIN, YOCUM & HEATHER, LLC

Established in 1962

312 ELM STREET
SUITE 1850
CINCINNATI, OHIO 45202-2740
Telephone: 513-721-5672
Fax: 513-562-4388
Email: info@byhlaw.com
URL: http://www.byhlaw.com

General Civil Practice. Insurance, Construction Law, Personal Injury, Employment Relations and Labor Law, Estate Planning, Probate, Litigation, Business, Corporate, Bankruptcy Law, and Creditors' Rights.

MEMBERS OF FIRM

JOHN A. BENJAMIN, born September 21, 1914; admitted to bar, 1940, Ohio. *Education:* The Ohio State University (B.A., 1936); Yale Law School (J.D., 1939). Phi Beta Kappa. Recipient, Cincinnati Bar Association Trustees' Award, 2001. Author: "Selling Real Estate in Bankruptcy," Federal Bar Association Seminars, February, 1965. President, Hamilton County Good Government League, 1953-1955. President, Mercantile Library, 1970-1973. President, Isaac M. Wise Temple, 1971-1973. President, United Jewish Cemeteries, 1987-1988. *Member:* Cincinnati (Chairman: Bankruptcy Committee, 1971-1973), Ohio State and American Bar Associations. ***PRACTICE AREAS:*** Probate Law; Bankruptcy Law; Corporate Law; Real Estate Law; Estate Planning.

THOMAS R. YOCUM, born Steubenville, Ohio, November 17, 1953; admitted to bar, 1979, Ohio and U.S District Court, Southern District of Ohio; 1980, Kentucky and Florida; 1981, U.S. District Court, Eastern District of Kentucky; 1982, U.S. Court of Appeals, Sixth Circuit; 1986, U.S. Supreme Court. *Education:* The Ohio State University (B.A., summa cum laude, 1975); California Western University; University of Cincinnati (J.D., 1979); New College, Oxford University, England. Recipient, American Jurisprudence Award for Excellence in Agency-Partnership Course. Arbitrator and Member of Construction Advisory Council, American Arbitration Association. Chapter Attorney and Chair, Legal Committee, Construction Specifications Institute, Cincinnati Chapter. Member, American Subcontractors Association of Cincinnati. Chair, Constructor Magazine Committee, Allied Construction Industries, Cincinnati. *Member:* Cincinnati, Northern Kentucky, Kentucky and Ohio State Bar Associations; The Florida Bar. ***PRACTICE AREAS:*** Construction Law; Insurance Law; Commercial Litigation; Corporate Law; Business Law; Creditors Rights Law. ***Email:*** tryocum@byhlaw.com

TIMOTHY P. HEATHER, born Cincinnati, Ohio, April 10, 1955; admitted to bar, 1980, Ohio; 1981, U.S. District Court, Northern and Southern Districts of Ohio. *Education:* University of Cincinnati (B.F.A., 1977; J.D., 1980). Phi Alpha Delta. Member, National Moot Court Team. Recipient, Best Orator Award and Best Brief Award, Ohio Tri-School Moot Court Competition. *Member:* Cincinnati (Member, Sections on: Negligence Law; Common Pleas Court) and Ohio State (Member: Torts and Insurance Practice Section) Bar Associations; Cincinnati Claims Association; Ohio Association of Civil Trial Attorneys; Defense Research Institute. ***REPORTED CASES:*** Littrell v. Wigglesworth (2001), 91 Ohio St. 3d 425; Noonan v. Rogers (1994), 97 Ohio App. 3d 621; Davis v. Mutual Life Ins. Co. of New York (6th Cir. 1993) 6 F.3d 367; Kueber v. Haas (1988), 47 Ohio App. 3d 62; McMillan v. Bruine-Harpenau-Torbeck Builder's Inc. (1983), 8 Ohio St. 3d 3; Lord v. Daugherty (1981), 66 Ohio St. 2d 441. ***PRACTICE AREAS:*** Personal Injury Law; Civil Trials; General Insurance Defense; Insurance Coverage; Litigation. ***Email:*** tpheather@byhlaw.com

ANTHONY J. IACIOFANO, born Cincinnati, Ohio, June 24, 1960; admitted to bar, 1985, Ohio; 1986, U.S. District Court, Southern District of Ohio; 1999, Kentucky. *Education:* Thomas More College (B.A., cum laude, Accounting and History, 1982); University of Dayton (J.D., 1985). Phi Alpha Theta. Member, Board of Trustees, Chairman, Cincinnati Local # 387 Glazier's Union Pension Fund; National Society of Professional Insurance Investigators; Southwest Ohio Investigators. *Member:* Cincinnati, Ohio State and Kentucky Bar Associations; Cincinnati Claims Association (Vice President). ***REPORTED CASES:*** Friedrich v. Friedrich, 983 F.2d 1396 (6th Cir. C.A. 1993); Paul, et al. v. Moore, et al. (1995) 102 Ohio App. 3d 748. ***PRACTICE AREAS:*** Insurance Defense Law; Construction Law; Personal Injury Law; Fraud Investigations; Insurance Bad Faith Defense. ***Email:*** ajiaciofano@byhlaw.com

LISA MARIE BITTER, born Columbus, Ohio, August 14, 1961; admitted to bar, 1991, Ohio and U.S. District Court, Southern District of Ohio. *Education:* Ohio University (B.S., summa cum laude, 1983); University of Cincinnati (M.A., 1985; J.D., 1990); Ohio State University. *Member:* Cincinnati (Member, Estate Planning, Trusts and Probate Law Committee; Elder Law Committee) and Ohio State Bar Associations; Pro Seniors of Cincinnati; ARAG Group. ***PRACTICE AREAS:*** Estate Planning and Probate; Guardianship; Insurance Defense Law; Personal Injury Law; Employment Law; Sexual Harassment; Real Estate; OSHA Defense. ***Email:*** lmbitter@byhlaw.com

ASSOCIATES

CHRISTOPHER J. MULVANEY, born Dayton, Ohio, June 13, 1963; admitted to bar, 1997, Ohio; 1998, Kentucky and U.S. District Court, Southern District of Ohio and Eastern District of Kentucky. *Education:* The Ohio State University (B.A., 1985); Salmon P. Chase College of Law (J.D., cum laude, 1997). Moot Court Board, 1995-1997 and Executive Board, 1996-1997. *Member:* Cincinnati, Northern Kentucky, Kentucky and Ohio State Bar Associations. ***REPORTED CASES:*** Parker v. I&F Insulation Co. (89 Ohio St. 3D 261, 2000). ***PRACTICE AREAS:*** Civil Litigation; Insurance Defense; Personal Injury; Employment Law; Construction Law. ***Email:*** cjmulvaney@byhlaw.com

BRADFORD C. WEBER, born Lawrenceburg, Indiana, March 23, 1970; admitted to bar, 1997, Ohio and U.S. District Court, Southern District of Indiana; 1998, Kentucky, Indiana, U.S. District Court, Eastern and Western Districts of Kentucky and U.S. Court of Appeals, Sixth Circuit; 1999, U.S. District Court, Southern District of Ohio. *Education:* Miami University (B.A., 1992); University of Kentucky (J.D., 1997). *Member:* Cincinnati, Ohio State and Kentucky Bar Associations. ***PRACTICE AREAS:*** Civil Litigation; Insurance Defense; Insurance Law; Personal Injury; Business Law; Corporate Law; Intellectual Property; Construction Law; Contracts; Estate Planning; Probate. ***Email:*** bcweber@byhlaw.com

RICHARD O. HAMILTON, JR., born Cincinnati, Ohio, June 23, 1968; admitted to bar, 2000, Ohio; 2002, U.S. District Court, Southern District of Ohio. *Education:* Cincinnati State Technical & Community College (A.A.S., cum laude, 1992); The Union Institute (B.S., 1996); Salmon P. Chase College of Law (J.D., 2000). *Member:* Cincinnati, Ohio State and American Bar Associations. [Specialist Fourth Class, U.S. Army, 1986-1988]. ***PRACTICE AREAS:*** Construction Law; Business Law; Debtor and Creditor Rights; Civil Litigation; Real Estate. ***Email:*** rohamilton@byhlaw.com

BRIAN A. LEE, born Cincinnati, Ohio, July 24, 1970; admitted to bar, 2000, Ohio; 2002, U.S. District Court, Southern District of Ohio. *Education:* Northern Kentucky University (B.A., cum laude, 1994); Fordham University (M.A., 1995); Salmon P. Chase College of Law (J.D., cum laude, 2000). *Member:* Cincinnati and Ohio State Bar Associations. ***PRACTICE AREAS:*** Insurance Defense; Insurance; Civil Litigation; Labor and Employment. ***Email:*** balee@byhlaw.com

CHARLES F. HOLLIS, III, born Covington, Kentucky, August 25, 1971; admitted to bar, 1997, Ohio; 1998, Kentucky; 1999, Indiana. *Education:* Northern Kentucky University (B.A., summa cum laude, 1993); University of Cincinnati (J.D., 1997); University of Helsinki (LL.M., International Law, 2002). Dean's Scholar (full tuition), 1992-1993. Phi Alpha Theta. Pi Sigma Alpha. Alpha Chi. Recipient, W. Frank Steely Award for the Outstanding Senior History/Social Studies Major, 1993. Author: "Perpetual Mistrial: The Impropriety of Transnational Human Rights Litigation in United States Courts," Santa Clara Journal of International Law, Spring 2003. *Member:* Cincinnati (Member, International Law Committee, 2003), Ohio State, Kentucky and Indiana State Bar Associations. ***LANGUAGES:*** German, French. ***PRACTICE AREAS:*** Civil Litigation; International Law; Immigration Law. ***Email:*** cfhollis@byhlaw.com

REPRESENTATIVE CLIENTS: *Insurance:* Allstate Insurance Co.; Royal Insurance Co.; Reliance Insurance Co.; Frankenmuth Insurance Co.; Globe American Insurance Co.; Cincinnati Equitable Insurance Co.; Capitol Indemnity Insurance Co.; American Ambassador Casualty Company; Certified Insurance Adjusters, Inc.; Farm Family Insurance Co.; Trans World Assurance Co.; Century Surety Co.; Crawford and Co.; Great American Insurance Co.; Cincinnati Insurance Co.; Walton Risk Services, Inc.; Grange Guardian Insurance Co. *Construction:* Allied Construction Industries; American Subcontractors Association of Cincinnati; Cincinnati Floor Co.; Harrison Concrete, Inc.; Performance Site Management Co.; U.S. Trackworks, Inc.; Bray Trucking, Inc.; West Side Paving, Inc.; Riemeier Lumber Co.; Kelley Bros. Roofing; Bobcat Enterprises, Inc.; Central Acoustical Supply House; Tri-State Plastering Institute, Inc.; Walls and Ceiling Contractors of Greater Cincinnati; Hansco Home Remodelers, Inc.; Security Fence Co.; Best Home Improvement, Inc.; Denier Electric Co.; Hoge-Warren-Zimmerman Co. *Other:* Answering Exchange, Inc.; ESC Administrators, Inc.; Display Specialties, Inc.; Brown Architects; Healthcare Recoveries, Inc.; Messaging, Inc; In Touch Communication, Inc; Rumpke Waste Collection; Tricon Distributors, Inc.

BLANK ROME LLP

PNC CENTER
201 EAST FIFTH STREET, SUITE 1700
CINCINNATI, OHIO 45202
Telephone: 513-362-8700
Fax: 513-362-8787
Email: webmaster@BlankRome.com
URL: http://www.BlankRome.com

Philadelphia, Pennsylvania Office: One Logan Square, 18th & Cherry Streets, 19103-6998. Telephone: 215-569-5500. FAX: 215-569-5555.

Media, Pennsylvania Office: Rose Tree Corporate Center, 1400 N. Providence Road, Building 1, Suite 301, 19063. Telephone: 610-891-7800. FAX: 610-891-7804.

Cherry Hill, New Jersey Office: 210 Lake Drive East, Woodland Falls Corporate Park, Suite 200, 08002-1164. Telephone: 856-779-3600. FAX: 856-779-7647.

Boca Raton, Florida Office: 1200 North Federal Highway, Suite 417, 33432. Telephone: 561-417-8100. FAX: 561-417-8101.

Allentown, Pennsylvania Office: 1620 Pond Road, Suite 200, 18104-2255. Telephone: 610-706-4300. FAX: 610-706-4343.

Wilmington, Delaware Office: Chase Manhattan Centre, 1201 Market Street, Suite 800, 19801. Telephone: 302-425-6400. FAX: 302-425-6464.

Washington, D.C. Office: Watergate, Eleventh Floor, 600 New Hampshire Avenue N.W., 20037. Telephone: 202-772-5800. Fax: 202-772-5858.

Trenton, New Jersey Office: 200 West State Street, 08608. Telephone: 609-278-2320. FAX: 609-278-2323.

Baltimore, Maryland Office: 1 North Charles Street, Suite 1905, 21201. Telephone: 410-659-3939. FAX: 410-659-3969.

(This Listing Continued)

BLANK ROME LLP, Cincinnati—Continued

New York, New York Office: The Chrysler Building, 405 Lexington Avenue, 10174. Telephone: 212-885-5000. FAX: 212-885-5001.

Administrative Law, Administrative Adjudications; Administrative Agency Practice, Administrative Hearings and Appeals, Administrative Litigation, Federal Administrative Law, Professional Licensing, Professional Licensing Regulation, Public Law, Admiralty and Maritime Law, Marine Law, Maritime Contracts, Maritime Finance, Maritime Law, Maritime Liens, Ship Sales and Mortgages, Aged and Aging, Age Discrimination, Elder Care, Elder Law, Agency and Distributorships, Distribution Agreements, International Distribution, Alcoholic Beverages, Liquor Licensing, Alternative Dispute Resolution, Arbitration, International Arbitration, International Dispute Resolution, Mediation, Antitrust and Trade Regulation, Antitrust, Business Combinations, Competition, Covenants Not To Compete, Deceptive Trade Practices, Noncompetition and Non-Solicitation Agreements, Price-Fixing, Restrictive Covenants, Trade Regulation, Unfair Trade, Appellate Practice, Civil Appeals, Art Law, Artists Rights, Museum Law, Asset Protection, International Asset Protection, Aviation and Aerospace, Aircraft Finance and Leasing, Aircraft Sales, Airline Labor Law, Aviation Law, Aviation Defense, Aviation Insurance, Aviation Litigation, Aviation Products Liability, Aviation Regulation, Bankruptcy, Bankruptcy Arbitration, Bankruptcy Chapter 7, Bankruptcy Chapter 11, Bankruptcy Chapter 12, Bankruptcy Chapter 13, Bankruptcy Collections, Bankruptcy Litigation, Bankruptcy Mediation, Bankruptcy Reorganization, Bankruptcy Taxation, Bankruptcy Trustees Rights, Commercial Bankruptcy, Commercial Foreclosure, Commercial Insolvency, Commercial Recovery, Commercial Workouts, Foreclosures, Fraudulent Conveyance, Insolvency, International Bankruptcy, International Insolvency, Liquidations, Out of Court Debt Restructuring, Pre-Bankruptcy Workouts, Receiverships, Repossessions, Workouts, Workouts Taxation, Banks and Banking, ATM Networks, Bank Collections, Bank Directors and Officers Liability, Bank Foreclosures, Bank Mergers and Acquisitions, Banking Antitrust, Banking Law, Banking Litigation, Commercial Banking, Commercial Credit, Commercial Loans, Consumer Banking, Credit Card Law, Credit Finance, Credit Law, Electronic Banking, Fair Lending, Financial Law, Interest and Usury, International Banking Law, International Loans, Lender Law, Lender Liability, Lender Regulation, Lenders Rights, Letters of Credit, Loan Restructuring, Loan Workouts, Loans, Savings and Loan Law, Secured Lending, Truth in Lending, Biotechnology, Biomedical Technology, Biotechnology Licensing, Business Law, Business Arbitration, Business Associations Law, Business Crimes, Business Development, Business Dissolutions, Business Estate Planning, Business Formation, Business Fraud, Business Litigation, Business Mediation, Business Organization, Business Planning, Business Regulation, Business Reorganization, Business Sales, Business Succession Planning, Business Successions, Business Syndication, Business Taxation, Business Torts, Business Transactions, Business Transfers, Business Trusts, Business Valuation, Buying and Selling of Businesses, Capital Formation, Closely Held Business Estate Planning, Closely Held Business Law, Closely Held Business Taxation, Complex Business Litigation, Emerging Business Law, Emerging Growth Companies, Entrepreneurial Business Law, Family Business Law, Family Business Mediation, Family Business Successions, International Business Law, International Joint Ventures, Joint Ventures, Limited Liability Company Law, Privatization, Professional Practices, Small Business Law, Sole Proprietorships, Strategic Alliances, Chancery and Equity, Chancery Practice, Children, Child Custody, Child Support, Civil Practice, Federal Civil Practice, Sex Discrimination, Commercial Collections, Post Judgment Collections, Commercial Law, Commercial Litigation, Complex Commercial Litigation, Secured Transactions, Uniform Commercial Code, Commercial Real Estate, Commercial Real Estate Acquisitions, Commercial Real Estate Development, Commercial Real Estate Finance, Commercial Real Estate Foreclosure, Commercial Real Estate Sales, Commercial Real Estate Syndication, Commercial Real Estate Workouts, Industrial Real Estate Law, Shopping Center Acquisitions, Shopping Center Development, Shopping Center Law, Complex and Multi-District Litigation, Computers and Software, Computer Contracts, Computer Law, Computer Security, Computer Software Law, Computer Technology, Electronic Commerce, Information Technology, Information Technology Contracts, Information Technology Licensing, International Computer Law, Internet Law, Software Copyright, Software Licensing, Software Protection, Year 2000 Computer Conversion, Constitutional Law, First Amendment Law, Construction Law, Construction Finance, Construction Litigation, Construction Workouts, Environmental Construction Law, International Construction Law, Public Construction Law, Consumer Law, Consumer Arbitration, Consumer Class Actions, Consumer Credit, Consumer Credit Compliance, Consumer Finance, Consumer Fraud, Consumer Litigation, Consumer Protection, Consumer Rights, Fair Credit Reporting Act, Contracts, Breach of Contract, Commercial Contracts, Contract Fraud, Contract Litigation, International Commercial Contracts, International Contracts, Copyrights, Copyright Infringement, Copyright Litigation, Copyright Prosecution, Copyright Protection, Copyright Registration, International Copyright Law, Corporate Law, Closely Held Corporations, Corporate Banking Law, Corporate Commercial Law, Corporate Contracts, Corporate Control Contests, Corporate Criminal Law, Corporate Dissolutions, Corporate Ethics, Corporate Fiduciary Law, Corporate Finance, Corporate Formation, Corporate Governance, Corporate Income Tax, Corporate Insurance, Corporate Insurance Defense, Corporate Investigations, Corporate Litigation, Corporate Organization, Corporate Partnerships, Corporate Planning, Corporate Real Estate, Corporate Reorganization, Corporate Successions, Corporate Tax Controversies, Corporate Tax Planning, Corporate Taxation, Corporate Trusts, Corporate Workouts, Family Corporations, Foreign Sales Corporations, Hostile Takeovers, Incorporation, International Corporate Finance, International Corporate Law, International Corporate Taxation, Nonprofit Corporations, Offshore Corporations, Professional Corporations; Proxy Contests, Public Corporations, S Corporations, Securitization, Small Business Corporations, Takeovers, Tender Offers, Transfer Pricing, Criminal Law, Debtor and Creditor, Creditor Bankruptcy, Creditors Rights, Creditors Rights in Bankruptcy, Debtor and Creditor Bankruptcy, Debtor and Creditor Collections, Debtor and Creditor Remedies, Debtor and Creditor Reorganization, Debtor and Creditor Rights, Debtor and Creditor Workouts, Debtor Bankruptcy, International Creditors Rights, Secured Creditors Rights, Unsecured Creditors Rights, Disabilities, Americans with Disabilities Act, Academic Employment, College and University Law, Administrative Lobbying, Executive Lobbying, Legislative Lobbying, Lobbying, Eminent Domain, Employee Benefits, COBRA, Deferred Compensation, Employee Benefit Taxation, Employee Benefit Trusts, Employee Compensation, Employee Stock Ownership Plans, ERISA, Executive Compensation, Executive Compensation Taxation, Flexible Benefit Plans, Multi-Employer Benefits, Multi-Employer Pensions, Non-Qualified Benefits, Pension and Profit Sharing Plans, Pension Plans, Pension Taxation, Profit Sharing, Public Pension Plans, Qualified Retirement Plans, Retirement Benefit Plans, Taft-Hartley Plans, Unemployment Compensation, Music Copyright, Environmental Law, Environmental Compliance, Environmental Liability, Environmental Litigation, Environmental Mediation, International Environmental Law, Equipment Finance and Leasing, Equipment Finance, Equipment Leasing, Vehicle Leasing, Family Law, Divorce, Matrimonial Law, Finance, Asset Based Finance, Financial Institution Reorganization, Financial Institutions Law, Financial Institutions Taxation, Financial Restructuring, International Commercial Finance, International Finance, Franchises and Franchising, Franchise Law, Franchise Licensing, Franchise Litigation, Franchise Taxation, International Franchising, General Practice, Federal Practice, Government, County Government Law, Federal Government Law, Government Affairs, Government Agency Practice, Government Relations, Legislative Practice, Local Government Law, Public Policy, Qui Tam Litigation, State Government Law, State Legislative Practice, Township Law, Government Contracts, Government Construction Contracts, Government Contract Arbitration, Government Contract Fraud, Government Procurement, International Government Contracts, Local Government Contracts, Public Bidding, Public Contract Law, Public Works Contracts, Guardianship and Conservatorship, Health Care, Alternative Health Care Delivery System, Certificates of Need, Health Care Administration, Health Care Contracts, Health Care Corporate Law, Health Care Facility Licensing, Health Care Facility Regulation, Health Care Finance, Health Care Fraud, Health Care Legislation, Health Care Licensing, Health Care Mergers and Acquisitions, Health Care Regulation, Health Care Reimbursement, Health Care Taxation, Health Insurance, Health Insurance Coverage, Health Insurance Defense, Health Insurance Trusts, Health Law, Health Maintenance Organizations, Integrated Health Care Delivery Systems, Long Term Care, Managed Care, Managed Care Contracts, Medical Antitrust, Mental Health Law, Nursing Home Regulation, Pharmacy Law, Physicians Contracts, Hospital Law, Hospital Administration, Medical Staff Contracts, Medical Staff Credentialing, Housing Law, Affordable Housing, Apartment Projects, Housing Finance, Insurance, Commercial Insurance, Insurance Company Taxation, Insurance Litigation, Insurance Defense, Intellectual Property, Artistic Property, Chemical Intellectual Property, Electrical Intellectual Property, Intellectual Property Infringement, Intellectual Property Licensing, Intellectual Property Litigation, International Intellectual Property, International Licensing, Mechanical Intellectual Property, Medical Intellectual Property, Pharmaceutical Intellectual Property, Piracy, Proprietary Rights, Taxation of Intellectual Property, International Law, International Trade, Antidumping, Countervailing Duties, Customs Law, Export Regulation, Import and Export Law, International Trade Regulation, Latin America Trade, Russia Trade, Investments, Financial Services Law, Financial Services Regulation, Foreign Investment, Foreign Investment in the United States, International Investment, Investment Banking Law, Investment Company Law, Investment Partnerships, Investment Regulation, Labor and Employment, Affirmative Action, Collective Bargaining, Employee Drug Testing, Employer Liability, Employment at Will, Employment Contracts, Employment Discrimination, Employment Litigation, Employment Mediation, Executive Employment Law, Executive Severance Contracts, Fair Labor Standards, Family and Medical Leave Act, Federal Employment Law, Harassment, International Employment Contracts, International Labor Law, Labor Arbitration, Management Labor Law, National Labor Relations Act, Personnel Policies, Public Sector Collective Bargaining, Public Sector Labor Relations, Sexual Harassment, Unfair Labor Practices, Union Contract Negotiations, Union Elections, Union Organization, Wage and Hour Law, WARN Act, Workplace Violence, Wrongful Termination Defense, Leases and Leasing, Commercial Leasing, International Leasing, Landlord and Tenant Law, Lease Finance, Leasing, Leveraged Leasing, Office Leasing, Retail Leasing, Shopping Center Leasing, Legal Ethics and Professional Responsibility, Legal Ethics, Litigation, Civil Litigation, Complex Litigation, Defense Litigation, Federal Civil Litigation, Federal Litigation, International Litigation, Long-Arm Litigation, Trial Practice, U.S. Supreme Court Litigation, Newspaper Contracts, Publishing Contracts, Medical Malpractice, Medicare and Medicaid, Medicaid Planning, Medicare and Medicaid Reimbursement, Medicare Fraud and Abuse, Mergers, Acquisitions and Divestitures, Business Acquisitions, Business Divestitures, International Mergers and Acquisitions, Leveraged Acquisitions, Leveraged Buyouts, Merger Reorganization, Mergers and Acquisitions, Mergers and Acquisitions Finance, Mortgages, Commercial Mortgages, Mortgage Banking Law, Mortgage Bankruptcy, Mortgage Finance, Mortgage Foreclosure, Mortgage Insurance, Mortgage Lien Foreclosure, Mortgage Refinancing, Mortgage Securitization, Mortgage Tax, Mortgage Workouts, Secondary Mortgage Market, Municipal Bonds, Municipal Bonds Taxation, Municipal Contracts, Municipal Corporation Law, Municipal Derivative Products, Municipal Finance, Municipal Labor Law, Municipal Leasing, Municipal Pension Law, Municipal Redevelopment, Municipal Securities, Municipal Taxation, Tax Increment Finance, Natural Resources, Nonprofit and Charitable Organizations, Charitable Limited Partnerships, Charitable Organizations Law, Charitable Trusts and Foundations, Nonprofit Organizations Law, Nonprofit Tax Law, Private Foundations, Tax Exempt Organizations, Occupational Safety and Health, OSHA, Partnership Law, Family Limited Partnerships, Family Partnerships, Limited Liability Partnerships, Limited Partnerships, Partnership Dissolution, Partnership Formation, Partnership Organization, Partnership Syndication, Partnership Taxation, Patents, Biochemical Patents, Biotechnology Patent Prosecution, Biotechnology Patents, Chemical Patent Prosecution, Chemical Patents, Computer and Software Patents, Design Patents, Electrical Patent Prosecution, Electrical Patents, Electronic Patents, International Patents, Mechanical Patent Prosecution, Mechanical Patents, Medical Patents, Metallurgical Patents, Molecular Biology Patents, Patent Applications, Patent Infringement, Patent Interference Practice, Patent Licensing, Patent Litigation, Patent Prosecution, Patent Protection, Pharmaceutical Patents, Personal Injury, Premises Security, Probate, Ancillary Probate, International Probate, Probate Administration, Probate Litigation, Probate Taxation, Products Liability, Drug and Medical Device Defense, Firearms Products Liability, Professional Liability, Public Finance, Bond Finance, Economic Development, Housing and Urban Development, Industrial Development, International Economic Development, International Project Finance, Project Finance, Public Authority Finance, Public Finance Taxation, Public-Private Development, Tax Exempt Bonds, Tax Exempt Finance, Railway Labor Law, Real Estate, Condominium Association Law, Condominium Conversions, Condominium Development, Condominium Law, Conveyancing, Cooperative Association Law, Cooperative Conversions, Cooperative Housing Law, Easements, International Real Estate, Land Acquisitions, Land Sales, Land Trusts, Planned Unit Development Law, Real Estate Acquisitions, Real Estate Arbitration, Real Estate Banking Law, Real Estate Bankruptcy, Real Estate Brokers Licensing, Real Estate Contracts, Real Estate Development, Real Estate Finance, Real Estate Foreclosure, Real Estate Investment, Real Estate Investment Taxation, Real Estate Investment Trusts, Real Estate Joint Ventures, Real Estate Leasing, Real Estate Litigation, Real Estate Mediation, Real Estate Partnerships, Real Estate Restructuring, Real Estate Sales, Real Estate Secured Lending, Real Estate Securities, Real Estate Settlements, Real Estate Syndication, Real Estate Tax Appeals, Real Estate Tax Assess-

(This Listing Continued)

(This Listing Continued)

ment, Real Estate Taxation, Real Estate Title, Real Estate Transfers, Real Estate Valuation, Real Estate Workouts, Real Property, Real Property Acquisitions, Real Property Development, Real Property Finance, Residential Real Estate, Residential Real Estate Development, Waterfront Development, Regulatory Law, Drug and Medical Device Regulation, Federal Regulatory Law, Regulated Industries, Regulatory Agency Practice, Regulatory Investigations, Religious Nonprofit Corporation Law, RICO, Securities, Bank Securities, Broker-Dealer Arbitration, Broker-Dealer Regulation, Initial Public Offerings, Private Placement, Private Placement Syndication, Public Offerings, SEC Enforcement, Securities Arbitration, Securities Litigation, Securities Offerings, Securities Registration, Securities Regulation, Shareholder Agreements, Shareholder Disputes, Tax Exempt Securities, Sports Contracts, Sports Licensing, Taxation, Employment Tax, Estate and Gift Taxation, Federal Income Tax, Federal Tax Controversies, Federal Taxation, Fiduciary Income Tax, Income Tax, Individual Taxation, International Tax Controversies, International Taxation, Like Kind Exchanges, Local Taxation, Low Income Housing Tax Credits, Property Tax Abatement, Property Tax Appeals, Sales and Use Tax, State Taxation, Tax Appeals, Tax Audits, Tax Collection, Tax Deferred Exchanges, Tax Planning, Tax Shelters, Trusts and Estates Taxation, Electronics, High Technology Contracts, Semiconductor Technology, Technology Contracts, Technology Licensing, Technology Protection, Technology Transfers, Torts, Trade Association Law, Toxic Torts, Trade Secrets, Theft of Trade Secrets, Trademarks, International Trademarks, Trade Dress, Trade Names, Trademark Arbitration, Trademark Infringement, Trademark Licensing, Trademark Litigation, Trademark Prosecution, Trademark Protection, Trademark Registration, Transportation, Common Carrier Law, Mass Transit Law, Public Transportation Law, Transit Labor, Trusts and Estates, Decedents Estates, Estate Administration, Estate Litigation, Estate Planning, Family Trusts, Family Wealth Transfer, Fiduciary Law, Fiduciary Liability, Fiduciary Litigation, Financial Planning, International Estate Planning, International Trusts, Living Trusts, Offshore Trusts, Personal Planning, Retirement Planning, Trust Administration, Trust Law, Trust Litigation, Trust Planning, Wealth Preservation, Unfair Competition, Utility Law, Utility Acquisitions, Utility Contracts, Utility Taxation, White Collar Crime, Embezzlement, White Collar Criminal Defense, White Collar Fraud, Wills, Contested Wills, Inheritance, Living Wills, Successions, Zoning, Planning and Land Use, Building and Public Safety Codes, Cemetery Law, Environmental Land Use, Fire Districts, Improvement Districts, Land Conservation, Land Development, Land Entitlement, Land Use, Land Use Litigation, Land Use Permitting, Land Use Regulation, Rezoning, Special Districts, Subdivisions, Water Districts, Zoning Law, Zoning Variances, Retail Industry Development.

FIRM PROFILE: Blank Rome LLP is a full-service law firm representing domestic and international publicly-traded and private companies, governmental and other non-profit entities, as well as individuals. With nearly 500 attorneys, in offices in New York, Washington, DC, Pennsylvania, Delaware, Maryland, New Jersey, Ohio and Florida, Blank Rome advises clients in a wide range of industries including: real estate; financial services; health care; gaming; hospitality; life sciences; manufacturing; maritime; energy; telecommunications; technology, and transportation. In addition, Blank Rome clients benefit from the services of the Firm's affiliate, Blank Rome Government Relations LLC, which is staffed by attorneys and lobbyists who guide companies through the complex processes of federal, state and local government.

Blank Rome's New York office represents some of the area's leading real estate, financial services and technology companies. Blank Rome counsels businesses and organizations ranging in size from multi-billion dollar international companies to startups in areas such as: capital formation; mergers and acquisitions; insolvency and restructuring; taxation; intellectual property; labor; and all aspects of litigation. The Firm has had many high-profile representations in the areas of white collar defense, and has prosecuted significant class actions in the environmental, securities and insurance areas. The New York office also has one of the largest and most visible matrimonial and estates & trusts practices in the United States. Blank Rome represents high net worth clients in all aspects of matrimonial law including divorce, mediation, equitable distribution of property, support, paternity, custody and visitation rights, as well as trusts and estates.

PARTNERS

MICHAEL L. CIOFFI, born Cincinnati, Ohio, February 2, 1953; admitted to bar, 1979, Ohio. *Education:* University of Notre Dame (B.A., 1975); University of Cincinnati (J.D., 1979). Co-Author: Sixth Circuit Federal Practice Manual, 1993, 1999. Author: Ohio Pretrial Litigation, 1991, 1998. *Member:* Cincinnati, Ohio State, Federal (President, Cincinnati Chapter, 1993-1994) and American (Member, Sections on: Litigation; International Law, 1980—) Bar Associations. ***PRACTICE AREAS:*** Litigation; Environmental Law. ***Email:*** cioffi@BlankRome.com

MATTHEW J. SIEMBIEDA, born Buffalo, New York, September 4, 1945; admitted to bar, 1970, Pennsylvania (Not admitted in Ohio). *Education:* Canisius College (B.A., 1967); University of Pennsylvania (J.D., 1970). Law Clerk, Honorable William H. Hastie, U.S. Court of Appeals, Third Circuit, 1971-1972. *Member:* Philadelphia, Pennsylvania and American Bar Associations. (Also at Philadelphia, Pennsylvania Office). ***PRACTICE AREAS:*** Environmental Litigation; Complex Business Litigation; Commercial Law; Complex Commercial Litigation; Corporate Criminal Law; Corporate Litigation; Intellectual Property; Securities. ***Email:*** siembieda@BlankRome.com

SHARON J. ZEALEY, born St. Paul, Minnesota, August 30, 1959; admitted to bar, 1984, Ohio; 1985, U.S. District Court, Southern District of Ohio; 1986, U.S. Court of Appeals, Sixth Circuit; 1990, U.S. Supreme Court. *Education:* Xavier University of Louisiana (B.S., cum laude, 1981); University of Cincinnati (J.D., 1984). Adjunct Instructor of Law, University of Cincinnati College of Law, 1997—. Administrator, U.S. Bank (formerly First National Bank of Cincinnati), Corporate Trust Department, 1984-1986. Staff Attorney, United Autoworkers Legal Services, 1986-1988. Associate, Manley Burke LPA, 1988-1991. Deputy Attorney General, Ohio Attorney General's Office, 1991-1995. Assistant U.S. Attorney, U.S. Department of Justice, 1995-1997. U.S. Attorney, Southern District of Ohio, U.S. Department of Justice, 1997-2001. Partner, Blank Rome LLP, 2001—. *Member:* Cincinnati, Federal, American and National Bar Associations; Black Lawyers Association of Cincinnati; Potter Stewart Inn of Court. ***PRACTICE AREAS:*** Civil Litigation; Employment Litigation; White Collar Criminal Defense; Government Compliance. ***Email:*** zealey@BlankRome.com

(This Listing Continued)

SENIOR COUNSEL

NATHANIEL R. JONES, born Youngstown, Ohio, May 13, 1926; admitted to bar, 1957, Ohio. *Education:* Youngstown State University (A.B., 1951; LL.B. 1956). Alpha Delta Boule; Sigma Pi Phi; Kappa Alpha Psi. Listed in: "Who's Who In America"; "Who's Who In Black America". U.S. Circuit Judge, United States Court of Appeals for the Sixth Circuit, 1979-2002. General Counsel, National Association for the Advancement of Colored People (NAACP), 1969-1979. Assistant General Counsel, National Advisory Commission on Civil Disorders (Kerner Commission), 1967-1968. Assistant United States Attorney, Northern District of Ohio at Cleveland, 1960-1967. Executive Director, Fair Employment Practices Commission, City of Youngstown, Ohio, 1956-1959. Co-Chair, Board of Directors, National Underground Railroad Freedom Center. Member, Toyota Motor Manufacturing, North America, Inc. Diversity Advisory Board. Member, Knowledge-Works Foundation Board of Trustees. Member, Executive Committee, Cincinnati Youth Collaborative. Member, Legal Aid Society of Greater Cincinnati Board of Trustees. Co-Chairman, Cincinnati Black-Jewish Coalition. Member, Advisory Committee of the Urban Morgan International Human Rights Institute. Master, Potter Stewart American Inns of Court. Trustee: Interrights USA; National Conference on Community and Justice. Chair, National Conference on Racial and Ethnic Justice. Member: Buckeye Lodge I.B.P.O.E.; Gothic Lodge #22 King Solomon Consistory No. 20; 33rd Degree - United Supreme Council, Mason. Member: United Way and Community Chest Board of Trustees; Metropolitan Club. Charter Member, Youngstown Area Development Corporation. Member: Houston Law Club; University of Cincinnati College of Law Board of Visitors. Former Member, Case Western Reserve University, School of Law In Cleveland, Board of Visitors. Member: Back Bencher Society; Indiana University Board of Visitors; Nova University Law Center, Ft. Lauderdale, Florida, Board of Visitors; The American Bar Association Law School Accreditation Committee Commission on Opportunities for Minorities in the Profession. *Member:* Mahoning County, Cinncinnati, Ohio State, National, American and Federal Bar Associations; Black Lawyers Association of Cincinnati; American Arbitration Association. [U.S. Army Air Corps]. ***PRACTICE AREAS:*** Litigation; Dispute Resolution. ***Email:*** jones-n@BlankRome.com

ASSOCIATE

WILLIAM M. HUSE, admitted to bar, 2003, Ohio and U.S. District Court, Southern District of Ohio. *Education:* Purdue University (B.S., 1999); University of Cincinnati (J.D., 2003). Delta Theta Phi. Master of Scrolls (Re-Chartering Member, 2000-2001). Member: American Institute of Chemical Engineers, 1997—; American Morgan Horse Association, 1990—. ***PRACTICE AREAS:*** Commercial Litigation. ***Email:*** huse@BlankRome.com

A list of Representative Clients will be furnished upon request.

BOEHM, KURTZ & LOWRY

Established in 1990

SUITE 1510, URS CENTER
36 EAST SEVENTH STREET
CINCINNATI, OHIO 45202
Telephone: 513-421-2255
Telecopier: 513-421-2764
Email: KIUC@AOL.COM

Public Utility, Electricity, Natural Gas, Water, Estate Planning and Corporate Law.

FIRM PROFILE: David F. Boehm and Michael L. Kurtz represent large industrial and commercial utility customers in electric, gas and water rate cases, contract negotiations, electric deregulation and restructuring proceedings and other utility matters principally in the states of Ohio, Indiana, Kentucky, Pennsylvania, Michigan and Minnesota. John P. Lowry represents small and mid-size businesses and individuals in contract matters, business planning, and related business litigation, with a focus on health care providers and individuals for estate planning matters.

MEMBERS OF FIRM

DAVID F. BOEHM, born Cincinnati, Ohio, August 21, 1944; admitted to bar, 1972, Ohio; 1993, Kentucky; 1994, Pennsylvania. *Education:* Xavier University (B.S., 1967); University of Cincinnati (J.D., 1972). Member, University of Cincinnati Law Review, 1970-1972. Law Clerk to Judge Timothy S. Hogan, U.S. District Court, Southern District of Ohio, 1972-1974. *Member:* Cincinnati, Ohio State, Kentucky and Pennsylvania Bar Associations; Federal Energy Bar. ***PRACTICE AREAS:*** Public Utility Law; Electricity Law; Water Law; Gas Law. ***Email:*** dboehm@bkllawfirm.com

MICHAEL L. KURTZ, born Cincinnati, Ohio, November 5, 1959; admitted to bar, 1986, Ohio; 1992, Kentucky; 1993, Pennsylvania; 2004, Michigan. *Education:* Princeton University (A.B., Economics, 1982); University of Cincinnati (J.D., 1986). ***PRACTICE AREAS:*** Electricity Law. ***Email:*** mkurtz@bkllawfirm.com

JOHN P. LOWRY, born Youngstown, Ohio, November 12, 1960; admitted to bar, 1986, Ohio. *Education:* Miami University (B.A., Economics, 1983); University of Cincinnati (J.D., 1986). *Member:* Cincinnati, Ohio State and American Bar Associations; National Association of Chiropractic Attorneys. ***PRACTICE AREAS:*** Business and Commercial Transactions; Business Formation; Estate Planning. ***Email:*** jlowry@bkllawfirm.com

ASSOCIATE

KURT J. BOEHM, born Cincinnati, Ohio, June 1, 1977; admitted to bar, 2002, Kentucky; 2003, Ohio. *Education:* University of Colorado at Boulder (B.A., Anthropology, 1999); Washington University (J.D., 2002). *Member:* Kentucky and Ohio State Bar Associations. ***PRACTICE AREAS:*** Public Utility Law; Electric Utilities; Commercial Transactions. ***Email:*** KBOEHM@BKLLAWFIRM.COM

REPRESENTATIVE CLIENTS: ENERGY COUNSEL FOR: Air Products and Chemicals, Inc.; AK Steel Corporation; Alcan Aluminum; Arch Chemicals; BP; Calgon Carbon Corporation; Carbide Industries, LLC; Century Aluminum; Commonwealth Aluminum Corp.; Corning, Inc.; Daimler-Chrysler; Dow Corning; E.I. DuPont de Nemours & Company; Ford Motor Company;

(This Listing Continued)

BOEHM, KURTZ & LOWRY, Cincinnati—Continued

Gallatin Steel; General Electric; ISG Steel; Kimberly-Clark Corporation; Kosmos Cement; Kroger Co.; Lexmark International, Inc.; Marathon-Ashland Petroleum Corp.; MeadWestvaco; 3-M Corporation; North Star Bluescope Steel; OSRAM Sylvania; Owens-Illinois; Protein Technologies; Proctor and Gamble; PPG; RR Donnelley; Rohm & Haas; Square D; Toyota Motor Manufacturing, USA and Weyerhaeuser.
GENERAL COUNSEL FOR: Kentucky Industrial Utility Customers, a state-wide organization of Kentucky's largest industrial consumers of utility services; Ohio Energy Group, a state-wide organization of large industrial utility customers.
COUNSEL FOR: Kramer Graphics, Inc.; CSI Waste Services; Fly Ash Direct Ltd.; Mt. Lookout Chiropractic Center, Inc.; Motion Palpation Institute.

PHYLLIS G. BOSSIN CO., L.P.A.

Established in 1977

SUITE 1210, 36 EAST FOURTH STREET
CINCINNATI, OHIO 45202
Telephone: 513-421-4420
Fax: 513-421-0691
URL: http://www.bossinlaw.com
Email: PBossin@bossinlaw.com
URL: http://www.lawyers.com/phyllisbossin

Domestic Relations and Family Law. Child Custody, Support, Divorce, Premarital Agreements.

FIRM PROFILE: The Phyllis G. Bossin Co., L.P.A., is a legal professional association practicing mostly in the field of matrimonial and family law. Additionally, the firm has well-established relationships with specialists in related fields such as tax counsel, C.P.A.'s, business and real estate appraisers. In addition to handling complex divorce litigation, the firm is well known for its work involving contested custody cases. The firm has wide experience in both negotiating settlements in complex cases as well as litigating these cases when necessary. The firm works closely with clients to meet both their financial and personal needs during the termination of their marriages.

PHYLLIS G. BOSSIN, born Cleveland, Ohio, August 6, 1950; admitted to bar, 1977, Ohio and U.S. District Court, Southern District of Ohio; 2002, District of Columbia. *Education:* University of Cincinnati (B.A., 1972; M.P.A., 1973); Salmon P. Chase College of Law (J.D., 1977). Author and frequent lecturer, Family Law; "Same-Sex Unions, The New Civil Rights Struggle or An Assault on Traditional Marriage?", published in University of Tulsa Law School Law Review, Spring 2005. Faculty, American Bar Association Family Law Section, Trial Advocacy Institute, University of Houston Law School, 1999-2001. Listed in Best Lawyers in America in Family Law, 1995—. Diplomate, American College of Family Trial Lawyers. *Member:* Cincinnati (Member, Domestic Relations Committee; Chairperson, 1990-1992), Ohio State (Member: Family Law Committee; Women in the Profession Section) and American (Chair, Family Law Section, 2003-2004; Vice-Chair, 2001-2002; Secretary, 2000-2001; Council Member 1992-1998; Parliamentarian, 1998-1999; Liaison, Commission on Women in the Profession, 1998—; Member, Board of Editors, *Family Advocate* , 1997-2000) Bar Associations; The District of Columbia Bar; Ohio Women's Bar Association. Fellow: American Academy of Matrimonial Lawyers; International Academy of Matrimonial Lawyers; American Bar Foundation. (Certified Specialist in Family Relations Law, Ohio State Bar Association). ***LANGUAGES:*** French. ***PRACTICE AREAS:*** Domestic Relations; Family Law; Custody; Juvenile. ***Email:*** PBossin@bossinlaw.com

---

SHANNON F. ECKNER, admitted to bar, 2003, Ohio. *Education:* University of Cincinnati (B.A., magna cum laude, 2000; J.D., 2003). Phi Beta Kappa; Order of the Coif. Articles Editor, University of Cincinnati Law Review. *Member:* Cincinnati, Ohio State and American Bar Associations. ***PRACTICE AREAS:*** Family Law. ***Email:*** seckner@bossinlaw.com

SARA BRADFORD

407 VINE STREET, SUITE 146
CINCINNATI, OHIO 45202
Telephone: 513-381-5094
Fax: 513-861-2932

Estate Planning, Wills, Trust, Elder Law, Real Estate.

SARA BRADFORD, admitted to bar, 1996, Kentucky; 2004, Ohio. *Education:* University of Kentucky (B.S., 1992; J.D., 1996). ***PRACTICE AREAS:*** Estate Planning; Wills; Trust Law; Elder Law; Real Estate.

BROOKING, MOEVES & HALLORAN

CINCINNATI, OHIO

(See Fort Wright, Kentucky)

Probate, Wills, Trusts, Family Law, Bankruptcy, Employment Law, Real Estate, Corporate Law, Business Law, Environmental Law, Personal Injury, Domestic Relations, General/Civil Litigation, Criminal Litigation.

LAW OFFICES OF PHYLLIS E. BROWN

119 EAST COURT STREET
CINCINNATI, OHIO 45202
Telephone: 513-412-7681
Fax: 513-412-7683
Email: pebrown@fuse.net

False Claims Act, Complex Litigation, Representation of Charter Schools, Education of Individuals with Disabilities, Disciplinary Issues.

(This Listing Continued)

PHYLLIS E. BROWN, born Newark, New Jersey, November 30, 1939; admitted to bar, 1986, Ohio and U.S. District Court, Southern District of Ohio; 1987, U.S. Court of Appeals, Sixth Circuit; 1994, Kentucky. *Education:* Smith College (B.A., magna cum laude, 1961); Harvard University-Kennedy School of Government (M.P.A., with honors, 1963); University of Cincinnati (J.D., 1986). Editor, The Federal Lawyer, 1992-2002. *Member:* Cincinnati, Ohio State, American and Federal (President, Cincinnati Chapter) Bar Associations; American Health Lawyers Association; Master, Inns of Court.

BUCKLEY KING

A LEGAL PROFESSIONAL ASSOCIATION

1420 PNC CENTER
201 EAST FIFTH STREET
CINCINNATI, OHIO 45202-4182
Telephone: 513-412-5400
National Watts Line: 800-255-2825
Telecopier: 513-412-5401
Email: bkb-cincinnati.com
URL: http://www.buckleyking.com

Cleveland, Ohio Office: 1400 Fifth Third Center. Telephone: 216-363-1400. Telecopier: 216-579-1020.
Columbus, Ohio Office: One Columbus, 10 West Broad Street, Suite 1300. Telephone: 614-461-5600. Telecopier: 614-461-5630.
Atlanta, Georgia Office: Suite 1220 Lennox Building, 3399 Peachtree Road. Telephone: 404-816-7791. Telecopier: 404-816-9786.

Corporate, Litigation, Commercial, Estate Planning, Banking and Finance, Real Estate, Merger and Acquisition, Appellate, Bankruptcy, Professional and Executive (Directors and Officers) Liability, Insurance Law, Products Liability, Health Care, Hospital Law, Medical Malpractice Defense, Immigration and Naturalization, Toxic and Hazardous Materials, ERISA, Taxation, Environmental, Labor and Litigation for Management, Public Employment Relations, Employee Benefits and NLRB Matters.

FIRM PROFILE: Founded in 1983, Buckley King has established itself as a leading full service business and commercial law firm with offices in Cleveland, Columbus, Cincinnati and Atlanta. The attorneys at Buckley King are dedicated to delivering creative, efficient and precise legal solutions for businesses and individuals.

The Firm's clients include individuals, closely-held businesses, Fortune companies, financial institutions, insurance companies, and governmental entities. Each client is highly-valued, and the preservation of long-standing client relationships is every bit as important to us as fostering new relationships.

Client service is the single most important goal of Buckley King. As a mid-sized firm, Buckley King delivers legal services with the depth, agility and resources necessary for timely and practical legal advice. Individualized attention and interactive communication with our clients is vital to our client relationships.

Because the Firm carefully chooses each of its attorneys, our clients receive the highest quality legal product from a skilled, innovative legal team. Although our attorneys may have different resident offices, Buckley King's success is providing solutions, analysis and advice from a range of complementary practice areas through its practice groups.

We take great pride in our ability to respond immediately to any situation, whether to an emergency court hearing, a critical incident, a client crisis, or to a complex and volatile legal situation requiring thoughtful and effective solutions. Even when our counsel is sought due to urgent, complex, or unique circumstances, we react with clear, focused and strategic advice and options.

When your legal or business needs require insight, clarity, focus and strategic direction, contact us.

We intend to exceed your expectations.

DALE A. STALF, born Cincinnati, Ohio, September 6; admitted to bar, 1983, Ohio. *Education:* Xavier University (B.S.B.A., summa cum laude, 1978); University of Cincinnati (J.D., 1983). ***PRACTICE AREAS:*** Commercial Litigation; Employment Practices Litigation; Professional Liability; Personal Injury; Insurance Law. ***Email:*** stalf@bucklaw.com

STEPHEN J. BREWER, born Covington, Kentucky, March 10; admitted to bar, 1977, Ohio; 1984, Kentucky. *Education:* Thomas More College (B.A., 1971); Salmon P. Chase College of Law (J.D., 1975). (Also at Hamilton, Ohio Office). ***PRACTICE AREAS:*** Insurance Defense; Insurance Coverage; Personal Injury Law; Commercial Litigation; Mediation. ***Email:*** sbrewer@bucklaw.com

---

JACK S. HEALY, born Cincinnati, Ohio, June 12; admitted to bar, 1973, Ohio. *Education:* Washington & Jefferson College (B.A., 1970); University of Cincinnati College of Law (J.D., 1973). ***PRACTICE AREAS:*** Insurance Defense; Personal Injury. ***Email:*** healy@bucklaw.com

WM. ERIC MINAMYER, born Salem, Ohio, June 26; admitted to bar, 1979, Ohio; 1995, Kentucky. *Education:* University of Akron (B.A., 1975); The American University (J.D. 1978); Georgetown University (LL.M., Labor, 1982). ***PRACTICE AREAS:*** Labor and Employment; Medical Malpractice; Personal Injury; Sarbanes-Oxley. ***Email:*** minamyer@bucklaw.com

TIMOTHY E. ROGUS, born Dayton, Ohio, April 29; admitted to bar, 1994, Ohio; 1996, Kentucky. *Education:* University of Dayton (B.S., summa cum laude, 1991); University of Cincinnati (J.D., 1994). ***PRACTICE AREAS:*** Litigation; Insurance Defense. ***Email:*** rogus@bucklaw.com

(This Listing Continued)

MELISSA CAMPBELL SUBIT, born Wheeling, West Virginia, September 21; admitted to bar, 1999, Ohio; 2002, Kentucky. *Education:* Wheeling Jesuit College (B.A., summa cum laude, 1996); The Ohio State University (J.D., 1999). ***PRACTICE AREAS:*** Insurance Defense. ***Email:*** subit@bucklaw.com

(For complete biographical data on all personnel, see Professional Biographies at Cleveland, Ohio)

BUECHEL & CONLEY

CINCINNATI, OHIO

(See Covington, Kentucky)

Business Law, Commercial Litigation, Employment Litigation, Construction Litigation, Products Liability, Wills, Probate, Trusts and Estates, and Estate Planning.

BUECHNER, HAFFER, O'CONNELL, MEYERS, HEALEY & KOENIG CO., L.P.A.

105 EAST FOURTH STREET
SUITE 300
CINCINNATI, OHIO 45202
Telephone: 513-579-1500
Fax: 513-977-4361
URL: http://www.bhomhlaw.com

General Practice. Estate and Gift Taxation, Probate, Family Law, Corporate, Negligence, Medical Legal Products Liability, Real Estate, Construction, Land Use, Zoning and Eminent Domain Law. Trials and Appeals, Pension and Profit Sharing, Federal Income.

FIRM PROFILE: We have chosen to remain a small firm in order to provide the highest quality legal service to our clients in a personal and timely manner. A client is best served, in our opinion, when the client receives timely, cost-efficient, personal service and is kept current on the status of the pending matter. In our firm, we strive to meet these objectives by providing expert advice through the attorney or attorneys most qualified to handle the matter.

ROBERT W. BUECHNER, born Syracuse, New York, October 29, 1947; admitted to bar, 1974, Ohio and Florida; 1976, U.S. Tax Court; 1992, Kentucky. *Education:* Princeton University (B.S.E., cum laude, 1969); University of Michigan (J.D., 1974). Author: *Prosper Through Tax Planning,* published by Coward, McCahn and Geoghagan, 1982; *Living Gangbusters,* published by Jason Publishing, Inc., 1986; *The 8 Pathways to Financial Success,* published by Jason Publishing, Inc., 1987, 1993 and 1998. Co-author: *Accumulating Wealth with Before Tax Dollars,* published by The National Underwriter Company, 1979; *Why Universal Life,* published by the National Underwriter Company, 1982. Assistant Adjunct Professor, Taxation, Salmon P. Chase College of Law, 1975-1982. Chairman, Southwestern Ohio Tax Institute, 1981. *Member:* Cincinnati (Member: Taxation Section; Estate Planning and Probate Section; Co-Chairman, Joint Committee of Bar and Life Underwriters, 1978-1981), Ohio State (Member, Taxation Section) and American (Member: Employee Benefit Plans Subcommittee, 1978-1982; 1985-1991; Taxation Section) Bar Associations. ***PRACTICE AREAS:*** Estate Planning Law; Tax Planning Law; General Corporate Law. ***Email:*** rbuechner@bhomhk.com

GLORIA S. HAFFER, born Cincinnati, Ohio, January 28, 1941; admitted to bar, 1977, Ohio and U.S. Court of Appeals, Sixth Circuit; 1982, Kentucky; 1984, U.S. Supreme Court. *Education:* H. Sophie Newcomb College; University of Cincinnati (B.A., 1962); Salmon P. Chase College of Law (J.D., 1977). Recipient, Lawyers Co-Operative Publishing Company Award. Council Member, Amberley Village, Ohio, 1975-1991; Vice Mayor, 1983-1987; Mayor, 1987-1991. Member: Best Lawyers in America, Who's Who in America, Family Law Section; Jewish Hospital of Cincinnati, Chairman, Board of Trustees; Health Alliance of Cincinnati, Board of Trustees, 1996—. Ohio Judicial College Domestic Relations Panelist, Dec., 1994. *Member:* Cincinnati (Member: Estate Planning and Probate Section; Domestic Relations Section), Ohio State (Member, Probate and Trust Section), Kentucky and American (Member, Real Property, Probate and Trust Law and Family Law Sections) Bar Associations. ***PRACTICE AREAS:*** Family Law; Probate Law; General Civil Practice. ***Email:*** ghaffer@bhomhk.com

EDWARD M. O'CONNELL, JR., born Washington, D.C., September 15, 1947; admitted to bar, 1973, Ohio and U.S. District Court, Southern District of Ohio; 1977, U.S. Tax Court; 1982, Kentucky; 1983, U.S. District Court, Eastern District of Kentucky. *Education:* Wheeling Jesuit College (B.S., 1969); University of Cincinnati (J.D., 1973). Phi Alpha Delta. Member, Panel of Arbitrators, American Arbitration Association. *Member:* Cincinnati (Member: Negligence Law Committee; Tort and Insurance Committee; Member, Conferences with Academy of Medicine), Kentucky and Ohio State Bar Associations; Ohio Academy of Trial Lawyers; Cincinnati Lawyers Club. ***PRACTICE AREAS:*** Civil Trial Practice; Products Liability Law; Personal Injury Law; Family Law. ***Email:*** eoconnell@bhomhk.com

ROBERT J. MEYERS, born Philadelphia, Pennsylvania, November 16, 1950; admitted to bar, 1975, Ohio and U.S. District Court, Southern District of Ohio; 1976, U.S. Court of Appeals, Sixth Circuit. *Education:* University of Notre Dame (B.A., magna cum laude, 1972); Georgetown University Law Center, (J.D., 1975). Editor, Georgetown University Law and Policy in International Business Journal, 1974-1975. Author: Note Article, "Administrative Survey, 1974, Bureau of International Commerce," Georgetown Law and Policy in International Business Journal, 1975. Board Member, Cincinnati Board of Health, 1986-1990; Chairman, Operations and Planning Committee, 1986-1990. *Member:* Cincinnati (Member: Common Pleas Court and Domestic Relations Court; Conferences with the Academy of Medicine Committees) and Ohio State (Member, Sections on: Litigation; General Practice) Bar Associations; National Lawyers Bar Association; Cincinnati Lawyers Club. ***PRACTICE AREAS:*** Trial Practice; Business Law; Family Law. ***Email:*** rmeyers@bhomhk.com

ROGER W. HEALEY, born Lynn, Massachusetts, June 7, 1949; admitted to bar, 1976, Ohio and U.S. District Court, Southern District of Ohio; 1985, U.S. Court of Appeals, Sixth Circuit; 1992, U.S. Tax Court; 1993, U.S. Court of Federal Claims. *Education:* Ohio University (B.A., cum laude, 1971); Institute of Touraine, France; University of Tours Law School, France (1971); University of Cincinnati (J.D., 1976). Member, World Trade Association; Board of Trustees, Kenwood Country Club, 1992-1998. *Member:* Cincinnati (Member, International Law Committee) and Ohio State (Member, Litigation Section) Bar Associations. ***LANGUAGES:*** French. ***PRACTICE AREAS:*** Commercial Law; Product Liability Litigation; Business Law; Estate Planning; Construction Litigation. ***Email:*** rhealey@bhomhk.com

FRANCIS X. MARNELL, born New York, N.Y., July 24, 1955; admitted to bar, 1982, Ohio; 1992, Kentucky; 1994, Indiana. *Education:* Stanford University (A.B., 1976); University of Cincinnati (M.A., 1980); College of William & Mary (J.D., 1982). Phi Delta Phi. Fellow, John Marshall Society, 1981-1982. *Member:* Cincinnati (Member, Sections on: Taxation; Estate Planning and Probate; Corporate and Securities Law), Northern Kentucky, Ohio State, Kentucky and Indiana State Bar Associations. ***PRACTICE AREAS:*** Estate Planning Law; Tax Planning Law; General Corporate Law. ***Email:*** fmarnell@bhomhk.com

PETER E. KOENIG, born Cincinnati, Ohio, July 19, 1956; admitted to bar, 1981, Ohio and U.S. District Court, Southern District of Ohio; 1983, U.S. Court of Appeals, Sixth Circuit and U.S. District Court, Eastern District of Kentucky; 1986, U.S. Supreme Court; 1998, Kentucky. *Education:* Ohio University (B.A., summa cum laude, 1978); Case Western Reserve University (J.D., 1981). Phi Beta Kappa; Order of the Barristers. Law Clerk to the Honorable Gilbert Bettman, Court of Common Pleas, Hamilton County, Ohio, 1981-1982. Barrister, Potter Stewart American Inn of Court, 1985-1987. *Member:* Cincinnati (Judicial Candidate Rating Committee, 1987-1995), Ohio State, Kentucky and American Bar Associations. ***PRACTICE AREAS:*** Litigation; Land Use; Real Estate Law; Personal Injury; Probate Litigation. ***Email:*** pkoenig@bhomhk.com

STEPHEN B. HOFFSIS, born Columbus, Ohio, March 28, 1961; admitted to bar, 1986, Ohio; 1989, U.S. Court of Appeals, Sixth Circuit; 1993, U.S. Court of Federal Claims. *Education:* Miami University (B.A., 1983); University of Cincinnati (J.D., 1986). *Member:* Cincinnati, Ohio and American Bar Associations; Cincinnati Lawyers Club. ***PRACTICE AREAS:*** Probate Law; Litigation; Real Estate Law. ***Email:*** shoffsis@bhomhk.com

DAVID RANDOLPH VALZ, born Cincinnati, Ohio, September 18, 1968; admitted to bar, 1994, Ohio; 1995, Kentucky; 1995, U.S. District Court, Southern District of Ohio. *Education:* Vanderbilt University (B.S., 1991); Salmon P. Chase College of Law (J.D., 1994). *Member:* Cincinnati, Ohio State and Kentucky Bar Associations. ***PRACTICE AREAS:*** Estate Planning; Taxation; Corporate Law. ***Email:*** dvalz@bhomhk.com

MICHAEL E. NEIHEISEL, born Cincinnati, Ohio, December 30, 1944; admitted to bar, 1969, Ohio. *Education:* Xavier University (H.A.B., 1966); University of Michigan (J.D., 1969). Certified Public Accountant, Ohio, 1972. *Member:* Cincinnati and Ohio State Bar Associations. ***PRACTICE AREAS:*** Taxation Law; Estate Planning Law; Probate Law. ***Email:*** mneiheisel@bhomhk.com

LAURIE M. HARMON, born Cleveland, Ohio, January 28, 1967; admitted to bar, 1992, Ohio; 1994, U.S. District Court, Southern District of Ohio; 1997, U.S. District Court, Western District of Michigan and U.S. Court of Appeals, Sixth Circuit. *Education:* Miami University (B.S., 1989); Capital University (J.D., cum laude, 1992). Pi Sigma Alpha National Political Science Honorary; Order of the Curia. Recipient, American Jurisprudence Award for Corporations. Member, 1990-1991 and Notes Editor, 1991-1992, Capital University Law Review, Staff Attorney for the Honorable Richard S. Sheward, Franklin County, Ohio, Court of Common Pleas, 1993-1995. *Member:* Cincinnati and Ohio State Bar Associations. ***PRACTICE AREAS:*** Civil Trial Practice. ***Email:*** lharmon@bhomhk.com

REPRESENTATIVE CLIENTS: Kentucky Motor Service, Inc.; Monarch Construction Co.; KOI Warehouse, Inc.; Dennis Ott Builders, Inc.; Image House, Inc.; Loveland Oil Co.; Midwest Ear Foundation; Qualified Emergency Specialists, Inc.; Spencer & Spencer Systems, Inc.; Ohio High School Athletic Association; Dynamis, Inc.; Anchor Associates, Inc.; Danis LaSalle Americas, Inc.; Mid-American Development Co.; Northgate Mall; Pep Boys-Manny, Moe & Jack, Inc.; RE/Max of Southern Ohio, Inc.; Brennan Electric, Inc.

THE LAW OFFICES OF LYNN A. BUECKMAN

THE BUECKMAN LAW BUILDING
7124 VINE STREET
CINCINNATI, OHIO 45216
Telephone: 513-821-4844
Email: bueckmanlaw@cinci.rr.com
URL: http://www.bueckmanlawfirm.com

Bankruptcy, Immigration, DUI, Business Law, Corporate Law, Contracts, Consumer Law.

LYNN A. BUECKMAN, born Belleville, Illinois, May 27, 1958; admitted to bar, 2000, Ohio; 2004, U.S. District Court, Southern District of Ohio and U.S. Court of Appeals, Sixth Circuit. *Education:* University of Redlands (B.S., Business Administration, 1994); Capital University Law School (J.D., 1999; MBA, 1999). *Member:* Cincinnati and Ohio State Bar Associations. ***PRACTICE AREAS:*** Bankruptcy; Immigration Law; Driving While Intoxicated; Business Law; Corporate Law.

CASPER AND CASPER

Established in 1936

119 EAST COURT STREET, FOURTH FLOOR, SUITE 410
CINCINNATI, OHIO 45202
Telephone: 513-381-7096

Middletown, Ohio Office: Gas and Electric Building, One North Main Street, P.O. Box: 510, 45042. Telephone: 513-424-2401.

(This Listing Continued)

CASPER AND CASPER, Cincinnati—Continued

Dayton, Ohio Office: First National Plaza Building, 130 West Second Street, Suite 1950, 45402. Telephone: 937-224-1122.
Hamilton Office: 2 South 3rd Street, Suite 360, 45011. Telephone: 513-892-2560.

Personal Injury, Workers Compensation and Social Security Disability Law. Products Liability Litigation. Trials.

REFERENCES: First National Bank of S.W. Ohio; Bank One of Middletown, Ohio.

(For complete biographical data on all personnel, see Professional Biographies at Middletown, Ohio)

ANTHONY D. CASTELLI

11085 MONTGOMERY ROAD, SUITE 200
CINCINNATI, OHIO 45249
Telephone: 513-621-2345
Fax: 513-621-2519
URL: http://www.castellilaw.com
Email: tony@castellilaw.com
URL: http://www.lawyers.com/castellilaw

Automobile Accidents, Workers Compensation, Personal Injury, Social Security Disability, Wrongful Death, Product Liability, Dog Bites.

FIRM PROFILE: I have been in practice for over twenty-three years fighting for the rights of accident and injury victims. My practice extends throughout the greater Cincinnati region, including Hamilton, Butler, Clermont and Warren Counties.

ANTHONY D. CASTELLI, born Cincinnati, Ohio, April 28, 1951; admitted to bar, 1981, Ohio. *Education:* University of Cincinnati (B.S., 1973); Salmon P. Chase College of Law, Northern Kentucky University (J.D., 1981). *Member:* Cincinnati Bar Association; Ohio State Bar Association; Ohio Academy of Trial Lawyers; The Association of Trial Lawyers of America. (Certified Specialist in Workers' Compensation Law, Ohio State Bar Association). ***LANGUAGES:*** English. ***REPORTED CASES:*** Bowling v. Heil, 31 St 3d. 277.

CHALFIE & FARLEY, CO., L.P.A.

36 EAST SEVENTH STREET, SUITE 1600
CINCINNATI, OHIO 45202
Telephone: 513-381-8616
Fax: 513-381-8619
Email: jimc@one.net
URL: http://www.chalfielaw.com

Probate Litigation, Probate Administration, Estate Planning, Trials and Appeals, Estate and Gift Tax, Trusts, Estates, Wills, Family Law, Negligence, Wrongful Death, Will Contests, Living Trusts and Automobile Collisions.

FIRM PROFILE: Serving and Visiting Clients in Northern Kentucky, Boone, Kenton, Campbell and in Warren, Butler, Clermont and Hamilton County.

JAMES J. CHALFIE, born Cincinnati, Ohio, July 24, 1941; admitted to bar, 1966, Ohio. *Education:* Brandeis University (A.B., 1963); University of Cincinnati (J.D., 1966). Member, Editorial Board, University of Cincinnati Law Review, 1965-1966. Author: "How to Avoid Post-Death Litigation," Estate Planning, June/July, 1999. Lecturer, Cincinnati Estate Planning Institute, 1986, 1989. Assistant County Prosecutor, 1966-1971. Member, Cincinnati Estate Planning Council. *Member:* Cincinnati (Member, Sections on: Probate and Estate Planning (Chairman, 1984-1987), Ohio State (Member: Probate and Trust Law Section) and American Bar Associations; Hamilton County Trial Lawyers Association; Potter Stewart Inns of Court. ***PRACTICE AREAS:*** Probate Litigation; Estate and Gift Taxation; Trust Law; Wills; Trial Practice; Appellate Practice; Estate Planning. ***Email:*** jimc@one.net

KATRINA Z. FARLEY, born Indianapolis, Indiana, August 7, 1963; admitted to bar, 1992, Ohio; 1993, Kentucky. *Education:* Ball State University (B.S., magna cum laude, 1985); Salmon P. Chase College of Law (J.D., magna cum laude, 1992). Author: "How to Avoid Post-Death Litigation," Estate Planning, June/July, 1999. *Member:* Cincinnati (Committees: Elder Law; Family Law; Torts; Insurance), Ohio State, Northern Kentucky, and Kentucky Bar Associations; Ohio Trial Lawyers Academy; Hamilton County Trial Lawyers Association. Member, Potter Stewart Inns of Court; Kentucky Academy of Trial Attorneys; Estate Planning Council of Northern Kentucky. ***PRACTICE AREAS:*** Estate Planning; Probate Litigation; Negligence; Trials & Appeals; Family Law. ***Email:*** katrinaf@one.net

CLEMENTS, MAHIN & COHEN, LPA CO.

Established in 1988
THE EXECUTIVE BUILDING
35 EAST SEVENTH STREET, SUITE 710
CINCINNATI, OHIO 45202-4009
Telephone: 513-721-6500
Facsimile: 513-763-6415
URL: http://www.cmclawyers.com
Email: info@cmclawyers.com
URL: http://www.lawyers.com/cmclawyers

Civil Litigation, Workers Compensation, Personal Injury, Products Liability, Medical Malpractice, Legal Malpractice, Appellate Practice, Social Security.

FIRM PROFILE: Civil Litigation and Appellate Practice, emphasizing Ohio Workers' Compensation Law, Social Security Disability, Personal Injury Law and Professional Malpractice.

(This Listing Continued)

MEMBERS OF FIRM

WILLIAM E. CLEMENTS, born Cincinnati, Ohio, December 17, 1953; admitted to bar, 1979, Ohio and U.S. District Court, Southern District of Ohio; 1981, U.S. Court of Appeals, Sixth Circuit. *Education:* Miami University (B.A., cum laude, 1976); University of Cincinnati (J.D., 1979). Phi Beta Kappa; Phi Alpha Delta; Moot Court. Lecturer: Cincinnati Bar Association Practical Law Institute, 1982-1983; Cincinnati Bar Association Workers Compensation Seminar, 1989, National Business Institute, Inc., Workers Compensation, 1988-1993; Lorman Education Services, 1993. *Member:* Cincinnati (Member, Workers Compensation Committee; Negligence Law Committee; Grievance Committee), Ohio State (Member, Workers Compensation Committee) and American Bar Associations; Ohio Academy of Trial Lawyers; Association of Trial Lawyers of America. (Certified Specialist in Workers' Compensation Law, Ohio State Bar Association). ***REPORTED CASES:*** Blankenship v Cincinnati Milacron Chemicals, Inc., 69 Ohio St.2d 608 (1982); State ex rel. Noll v. I.C., 57 Ohio St.3d 203 (1991). ***PRACTICE AREAS:*** Workers Compensation Law; Negligence Law; Torts; Litigation; Appellate Practice. ***Email:*** wec@cmclawyers.com

JOHN E. MAHIN, born Cincinnati, Ohio, May 19, 1952; admitted to bar, 1977, Ohio, U.S. District Court, Southern District of Ohio and U.S. Court of Appeals, Sixth Circuit. *Education:* Marquette University (B.A., 1974); University of Dayton (J.D., 1977). Member, University of Dayton Law Review, 1976-1977. *Member:* Cincinnati (Member, Lawyer Referral Board Advisory Committee; Negligence Law Committee; Workers Compensation Committee; Chairman, Lawyer Referral Service, 1984-1987), Ohio State and American Bar Associations; Ohio Academy of Trial Lawyers; The Association of Trial Lawyers of America. ***PRACTICE AREAS:*** Civil Litigation; Personal Injury Law; Medical Malpractice. ***Email:*** jem@cmclawyers.com

EDWARD COHEN, born Hamilton, Ohio, December 20, 1954; admitted to bar, 1982, Ohio, U.S. District Court, Southern District of Ohio and U.S. Court of Appeals, Sixth Circuit. *Education:* University of Cincinnati (B.A., 1976; J.D., 1982); Indiana University (M.A., 1982). Moot Court Board (Director, 1981-1982); Order of Barristers. Winner, Midwest Regional, Giles Sutherland Rich Patent Law Competition. Recipient: Research and Teaching Scholarship; Interdisciplinary Doctoral Fellowship; College of Law Scholarship; Rawson Collins School Scholarship. Visiting Instructor, Legal Research and Writing and Appellate Advocacy, University of Cincinnati College of Law, 1982-1983. Lecturer: Cincinnati Bar Association; National Business Institute, Inc. Member, American Society for Composers, Artists and Producers, 1975—. Member, American Speech and Hearing Association, 1976-1978. *Member:* Cincinnati (Member, Workers Compensation Committee, Chairman, 1992-1993; Tort/Insurance Law Committee), Ohio State (Member: Workers Compensation Committee; Negligence Law Committee) and American Bar Associations; Cincinnati Academy of Medicine (Member, Joint Committee). ***REPORTED CASES:*** State ex rel Adams v. Aluchan, of al (2003) 101 Ohio St. 3d 1452; Walters v. Commercial Union Ins. Co. (1999 - 1st Dist. Ct. Appeals); Flora v. Cincinnati Milacrom 88 Ohio App 3d 306 (1993); State Farm Mutual Ins Co. v. Mahin, 92 Ohio App 3d 291 (1993); State ex rel Adams v. Aluchom et al, 78 Ohio App 3d 261 (1992); Lanhart v. Southern Ohio Fabricators 61 Ohio App 31 432 (1991); Johnson v. University of Cincinnati 68 Ohio App 3d M1 (1991); State ex rel Amenniti Dunn Service v. Industrial Commission (1989); Steely v. Boweil et al, 65 Ohio App 3d 161 (1989). ***PRACTICE AREAS:*** Workers Compensation Law; Negligence Law; Torts; Litigation; Social Security; Appellate Practice. ***Email:*** ecohen@cmclawyers.com

CATHARIN R. TAYLOR, born Cleveland, Ohio, March 10, 1966; admitted to bar, 1992, Ohio. *Education:* University of Cincinnati (B.B.A., 1989; J.D., 1992). Member, Moot Court Board. *Member:* Cincinnati Bar and Ohio State Bar Associations; Ohio Academy of Trial Lawyers. (Certified Specialist in Workers' Compensation Law, Ohio State Bar Association). ***REPORTED CASES:*** Cole v. Complete Auto Transit. ***PRACTICE AREAS:*** Worker's Compensation; Personal Injury; Medical Malpractice; Social Security. ***Email:*** ctaylor@cmclawyers.com

ASSOCIATE

LANE N. COHEN, born Hamilton, Ohio, January 2, 1951; admitted to bar, 1988, Ohio and U.S. District Court, Southern District of Ohio and U.S. Court of Appeals, Sixth Circuit. *Education:* University of Cincinnati (B.A., 1973); University of Dayton (J.D., 1988). Order of Barristers. Winner, Mock Trial Team Regional Competition. *Member:* Cincinnati (Member, Workers' Compensation Committee), Ohio State and American Bar Associations. (Certified Specialist in Workers' Compensation Law, Ohio State Bar Association). ***REPORTED CASES:*** State ex rel. Gay v. Mihm 68 Ohio St.3d 315 (1994). ***PRACTICE AREAS:*** Workers Compensation Law; Negligence Law; Torts; Litigation; Social Security; Appellate Practice.

LEGAL SUPPORT PERSONNEL

Peggy Collier ***Beth Otto***
Jackie Powell

COHEN, TODD, KITE & STANFORD, LLC

Established in 1894
250 EAST FIFTH STREET.
SUITE 1200
CINCINNATI, OHIO 45202-4139
Telephone: 513-421-4020
Fax: 513-241-4490
URL: http://www.ctks.com

Banking, Bankruptcy and Reorganization, Corporate and Business, Employee Benefits, Estate Planning and Probate, Litigation, Real Estate and Taxation, General and White Collar Criminal Defense, and Juvenile Delinquency Defense.

FIRM PROFILE: Cohen, Todd, Kite & Stanford, LLC was originally established in 1894 by Alfred M. Cohen and Alfred Mack. The evolution of the original partnership of Cohen & Mack over the last century has developed into what is today known as Cohen, Todd, Kite & Stanford LLC, a firm comprised of 30 members engaging in the general practice of law.

(This Listing Continued)

MEMBERS OF FIRM

STANLEY L. STANFORD, born Cincinnati, OH, 1930; admitted to bar, 1958, OH. *Education:* Eastern Kentucky State College (B.S., 1953); University of Cincinnati (J.D., 1958). ***PRACTICE AREAS:*** Real Estate; Banks and Banking; Estate Planning; Probate.

JOHN G. COBEY, born Cleveland, OH, 1943; admitted to bar, 1969, OH; 1979, KY. *Education:* Cornell University (B.S., 1966); Universidad de Deusto, Bilbao, Spain; University of Cincinnati (J.D., 1969); University of Exeter, Exeter, England. ***PRACTICE AREAS:*** Business Law; Corporate Law. ***Email:*** jcobey@ctks.com

TERRENCE A. MIRE, born Cincinnati, OH, 1947; admitted to bar, 1972, OH. *Education:* Florida State University (B.A., 1969); University of Cincinnati (J.D., 1972). ***PRACTICE AREAS:*** Corporate Law; Business Law; Real Estate Banking Law; Trusts and Estates; Probate. ***Email:*** tmire@ctks.com

MARC W. RUBIN, born Cincinnati, OH, 1949; admitted to bar, 1974, OH. *Education:* University of Cincinnati (B.A., 1971; J.D., 1974); New York University (LL.M., 1975). ***PRACTICE AREAS:*** Corporate Law; Business Law; Estate Planning; Probate; Taxation. ***Email:*** mrubin@ctks.com

MICHAEL J. BOYLAN, born Detroit, MI, 1946; admitted to bar, 1976, OH. *Education:* Xavier University (B.S., 1968); Catholic University of America (J.D., 1976). ***PRACTICE AREAS:*** Civil Litigation; Personal Injury; Probate Litigation; Zoning, Planning and Land Use. ***Email:*** mboylan@ctks.com

RICHARD D. NELSON, born Columbus, OH, 1949; admitted to bar, 1974, OH. *Education:* Miami University (B.A., 1971); University of Cincinnati (J.D., 1974). ***PRACTICE AREAS:*** Bankruptcy; Business Reorganization; Corporate Law; Business Law; Banks and Banking; Litigation. ***Email:*** rnelson@ctks.com

ROBERT S. RUBIN, born Cincinnati, OH, 1954; admitted to bar, 1979, OH. *Education:* University of Wales, Aberystwyth (LL.B., 1976); University of Cincinnati (J.D., 1979). ***PRACTICE AREAS:*** Banks and Banking; Lender Liability; Real Estate Law; Commercial Law; Commercial Litigation. ***Email:*** rrubin@ctks.com

STANTON H. VOLLMAN, born Cincinnati, OH, 1940; admitted to bar, 1966, OH. *Education:* Xavier University (B.S.B.A., 1962); Salmon P. Chase College of Law (J.D., 1966). Certified Public Accountant, Ohio, 1969. (Certified Specialist in Estate Planning, Trust and Probate Law, Ohio State Bar Association). ***PRACTICE AREAS:*** Taxation; Estate Planning; Probate; Corporate Law; Business Law; Elder Law. ***Email:*** svollman@ctks.com

MICHAEL R. SCHMIDT, born Cincinnati, OH, 1951; admitted to bar, 1981, OH; 1982, KY. *Education:* Xavier University (B.A., summa cum laude, 1974); Salmon P. Chase College of Law (J.D., 1981). ***PRACTICE AREAS:*** Litigation. ***Email:*** mschmidt@ctks.com

KEVIN C. McDONOUGH, born Cincinnati, Ohio, July 5, 1955; admitted to bar, 1989, Ohio. *Education:* Xavier University (B.S.B.A., 1983); University of Cincinnati (J.D., 1988). ***PRACTICE AREAS:*** Civil Litigation; Municipal Law; White Collar Criminal Defense. ***Email:*** kmcdonough@ctks.com

DONALD J. RAFFERTY, born Vicksburg, MI, 1962; admitted to bar, 1989, OH. *Education:* Kalamazoo College (B.A., 1984); University of Cincinnati (J.D., 1989). ***PRACTICE AREAS:*** Bankruptcy; Business Reorganization; Litigation; Corporate Law; Business Law; White Collar Criminal Defense. ***Email:*** drafferty@ctks.com

JOHN L. O'SHEA, born Toledo, OH, 1960; admitted to bar, 1989, OH. *Education:* University of Toledo (B.S., 1984); University of Cincinnati (J.D., 1989). ***PRACTICE AREAS:*** White Collar Criminal Defense; Municipal Law; Property Tax Appeals; Personal Injury; Wrongful Death. ***Email:*** joshea@ctks.com

RICHARD M. STONE, born Easton, PA, 1946; admitted to bar, 1971, PA; 1977, OH; 1985, DC. *Education:* Lafayette College (B.S., 1967); University of Pennsylvania (J.D., 1970). ***PRACTICE AREAS:*** Commercial Real Estate; Commercial Transactions. ***Email:*** rstone@ctks.com

MATTHEW McD. KITE, born Cincinnati, OH, 1964; admitted to bar, 1995, OH. *Education:* The Colorado College (B.A., 1987); Capital University (J.D., 1995). ***PRACTICE AREAS:*** Business Law; Corporate Law; Real Estate Banking Law; Construction Law; Probate; Trusts and Estates. ***Email:*** mkite@ctks.com

CURTIS E. KISSINGER, born Cincinnati, Ohio, April 23, 1965; admitted to bar, 1990, Ohio; 1995, U.S. District Court, Southern District of Ohio. *Education:* University of Cincinnati (B.A., 1987); University of Dayton (J.D., 1990). ***PRACTICE AREAS:*** Litigation; Criminal Defense; Corporate Law; Business Law. ***Email:*** ckissinger@ctks.com

SENIOR ATTORNEY

JANET B. CAMPBELL, born Mountain Home, ID, 1952; admitted to bar, 1979, OH. *Education:* Duke University (B.A., cum laude, 1974); University of Cincinnati (J.D., 1979). ***PRACTICE AREAS:*** Labor and Employment; Litigation. ***Email:*** jcampbell@ctks.com

ASSOCIATES

HEIDI A. SELDEN, born Queens, New York, July 8, 1970; admitted to bar, 1996, Ohio; 2003, Pennsylvania. *Education:* University of Dayton (B.A., 1992); University of Arkansas at Little Rock (J.D., 1995). ***PRACTICE AREAS:*** Litigation; Criminal Defense; Estate Planning; Probate. ***Email:*** hselden@ctks.com

JEFFREY S. VOLLMAN, born Cincinnati, Ohio, 1971; admitted to bar, 1997, OH. *Education:* Xavier University (B.S., 1993); Salmon P. Chase Law School (J.D., 1997). ***PRACTICE AREAS:*** Corporate Law; Business Law; Estate Planning; Probate; Taxation. ***Email:*** jvollman@ctks.com

JOSEPH M. HUTSON, born Zanesville, Ohio, October 26, 1972; admitted to bar, 1998, Ohio. *Education:* Ohio University (B.A., 1995); University of Cincinnati (J.D., 1998). ***PRACTICE AREAS:*** Civil Litigation; Criminal Defense; Municipal Law; White Collar Criminal Defense. ***Email:*** jhutson@ctks.com

(This Listing Continued)

MONICA V. KINDT, born San Juan, PR, November 21, 1974; admitted to bar, 1999, Ohio. *Education:* St. Olaf College (B.A., 1996); Florida Coastal School of Law (J.D., 1999). ***LANGUAGES:*** French, Spanish and Portuguese. ***PRACTICE AREAS:*** Bankruptcy; Business Reorganization; Corporate Law; Business Law; Litigation. ***Email:*** mkindt@ctks.com

ANGELA M. HUGHES, born Fort Wayne, Indiana, September 11, 1972; admitted to bar, 2004, Ohio; registered to practice before U.S. Patent and Trademark Office 2005, Indiana. *Education:* Indiana University (B.S., 1999); University of Dayton School of Law (J.D., 2004). ***PRACTICE AREAS:*** Criminal Defense; Civil Litigation; General Practice. ***Email:*** ahughes@ctks.com

OF COUNSEL

ALFRED M. COHEN, born Cincinnati, OH, 1929; admitted to bar, 1953, OH. *Education:* Miami University (A.B., 1950); University of Cincinnati (LL.B., 1953). ***PRACTICE AREAS:*** Probate; Corporate Law.

JOHN W. KILCOYNE, born Huntington, WV, 1908; admitted to bar, 1934, OH. *Education:* Xavier University (A.B., 1931); University of Cincinnati (J.D., 1934). ***PRACTICE AREAS:*** Trusts and Estates; Corporate Law; Taxation; Real Estate.

THOMAS C. KILCOYNE, born Cincinnati, OH, 1958; admitted to bar, 1984, OH; 1985, KY. *Education:* Dartmouth College (A.B., 1981); University of Cincinnati (J.D., 1984). ***PRACTICE AREAS:*** Business Reorganization; Litigation; Trusts and Estates. ***Email:*** tkilcoyne@ctks.com

REPRESENTATIVE CLIENTS: Bank One, N.A.; R.G. Properties, Inc.; CamVic Corporation; Hoeweler Group, Inc.; City of St. Bernard; City of Deer Park; Cincinnati Sub-Zero Products, Inc.; Frisch's Restaurants, Inc.; MAE Holding Company; Casual Restaurant Concepts, Inc.; Elegant Fare, Inc.; TP Mechanical Contractors, Inc.; Dorian Development Company; National Bank & Trust Company.

CATHY R. COOK

114 EAST EIGHTH STREET
CINCINNATI, OHIO 45202-1103
Telephone: 513-241-4029
Fax: 513-723-8634
Email: cathy.cook@cathycooklaw.com
URL: http://www.cathycooklaw.com

Criminal Law, Criminal Appeals, Criminal Defense, Drivers License Suspension, Felonies, Homicide, Manslaughter, Misdemeanors, Murder, Sex Crimes, Sexual Assault, Theft, Traffic Violations. Family Law-Alimony, Cohabitation Agreements, Divorce, Domestic Relations, Domestic Violence, Equitable Distribution, Marital Property Distribution, Marital Property Law, Marital Property Settlements, Matrimonial Law, Non-Traditional Family Law, Paternity, Post-Divorce, Premarital Agreements, Separation Agreements, Spousal Support.

CATHY R. COOK, born July 16, 1957; admitted to bar, 1982, Ohio. *Education:* Miami University (B.A., 1979); University of Cincinnati (J.D., 1982). The Order of Barristers. Recipient, John W. Peck Trial Practice Award. Seminar Speaker: Sophisticated Pretrial Preparation, Ohio Association of Criminal Defense Lawyers, 1994; Domestic Relations Institute, 1996; Competence & NGRI, Greater Cincinnati Criminal Defense Lawyers Association, 1997; Equitable Distribution in Divorce, National Business Institute, 1997 and 2002; Direct Examination, Greater Cincinnati Criminal Defense Lawyers Association, 1998; Plea Negotiation, Ohio Association of Criminal Defense Lawyers, 1998; Superstar Seminar-Drug Cases, Ohio Association of Criminal Defense Lawyers, 2000; Nuts and Bolts of Divorce, Lorman Education Services, 2000; Gay and Lesbian Issues in the Law, Cincinnati Bar Association, 2000; Juvenile Law Symposium, Ohio Association of Criminal Defense Lawyers, 2001; Support Issues in Ohio Divorce Proceedings, National Business Institute, 2003; Lecturer: National Institute for Trial Advocacy, 2003, 2004; Handling Ohio Divorce Cases from Start to Finish, National Business Institute, 2004. *Member:* Cincinnati (Chairperson, Criminal Law Committee, 1987-1990); Ohio State and American Bar Associations; Greater Cincinnati Criminal Defense Lawyers Association (President, 1995-1996; Chair, Board of Trustees, 1996-1997); Ohio Association of Criminal Defense Lawyers (Member: Board of Directors, 1990—; President, 1998-1999; Chair, Board of Directors, 1999-2000); National Association of Criminal Defense Lawyers; Cincinnati Law Library (Member, Board of Trustees, 1997—; Vice President, 1998-2002; President, 2002—).

LEGAL SUPPORT PERSONNEL

SCOTT BROOKS. *Education:* American Institute For Paralegal Studies (Certificate, 1987). (Paralegal). ***Email:*** scott.brooks@cathycooklaw.com

---

DAVID M. COOK LLC

Established in 1999
22 W. NINTH STREET
CINCINNATI, OHIO 45202
Telephone: 513-721-7500
Fax: 513-721-1178
Email: dcook@dmcllc.com
URL: http://www.davidmcookllc.com

COBRA, Employee Benefit Trusts, Litigation, Employee Stock Ownership Plans, ERISA, Class Actions, Litigation Health Benefits, Multi Employer Benefits, Multi Employer Pensions, Pension Plans, Profit Sharing, Taft-Hartley, 401k Plans, Unemployment Compensation, Wrongful Termination, Family Medical Leave Act, Labor Law, Arbitration, Union Organization, Union Contracts, Sexual Harassment, Labor and Employment, Employee Benefits, Toxic Torts, representing Labor Organizations and Labor Unions.

FIRM PROFILE: Representation of Labor Organizations, Benefit/Pension Funds, Employees and Fiduciaries, Labor and Employment Law, Employee Benefits (ERISA), Toxic Torts, Executive Severance.

(This Listing Continued)

DAVID M. COOK LLC, Cincinnati—Continued

DAVID M. COOK, born Vineland, New Jersey, November 22, 1953; admitted to bar, 1978, Ohio and U.S. District Court, Southern District of Ohio; 1983, U.S. Court of Appeals, Sixth Circuit; 1991, U.S. Court of Appeals, Eighth Circuit; 1995, U.S. Court of Appeals, Ninth Circuit. *Education:* Indiana University (A.B., 1975); University of Cincinnati (J.D., 1978). *Member:* Cincinnati, Ohio State and American Bar Associations. ***REPORTED CASES:*** Horn et al v. McQueen et al 215 F.Supp.2d 862 (W.D.Ky 2002); Hamilton v. Carell, 243 F.3d 992 (6th Cir. 2001); Best v. Cyrus, 310 F.3d 932 (6th Cir. 2002); Horn v. McQueen, 215 F. Supp.2d 867 (W.D. Ky 2002); Grindstaff v. Green, 133 F.3d 416 (6th Cir. 1998); Armco Employees' Independent Federation, Inc. v. Armco Steel Co., LP, 65 F.3d 492 (6th Cir. 1995); USW Local 4839 v. New Idea Farm Equipment Corp., 917 F.2d 964 (6th Cir. 1990); National Post Office Mailhandlers v. United States Postal Service, 751 F.2d 834 (6th Cir. 1985); United Paperworkers International Union v. Jefferson Smurfit Corporation, 961 F.2d 1384 (8th Cir. 1992); Steen v. John Hancock Mutual Life Insurance Company, 106 F.3d 904 (9th Cir. 1997); Dennis v. Sawbrook Steel Castings Co., 792 F. Supp. 552 (S.D. OH 1991); Grimes, et al. v. Dayton-Walther Corporation, 680 F. Supp. 1110 (W.D. OH 1987); In re: Valley Kitchens, Inc., 65 B.R. 113 (Bankruptcy Court, S.D. OH 1986); In re: Smith Jones, Inc., 17 B.R. 126 (Bankruptcy Court, D. Minn. 1981); Chamberlain v. AK Steel, 82 Ohio St. 3d 389 (1998); Laborers' International Pension Fund v. DOD Contracts, Inc., 1996 Ohio App. LEXIS 4280 (4th District 1996); Cincinnati Bell Inc. v. Douglas, 1982 Ohio App. LEXIS 12815 (1st District 1982); Craft v. Giles, 1981 Ohio App. LEXIS 12600 (3rd District 1981). ***PRACTICE AREAS:*** Labor and Employment; Employee Benefits; Toxic Torts. ***Email:*** dcook@dmcllc.com

ASSOCIATES

STEPHEN A. SIMON, born Waltham, Massachusetts, September 7, 1968; admitted to bar, 1997, Ohio; 1998, Kentucky, U.S. District Court, Southern District of Ohio and U.S. District Court, Eastern and Western Districts of Kentucky. *Education:* University of Michigan (B.A., 1990); University of Cincinnati (J.D., 1997). *Member:* Cincinnati, Ohio State and American Bar Associations. ***PRACTICE AREAS:*** Labor Relations; ERISA; Mass Torts; Employment Discrimination. ***Email:*** ssimon@dmcllc.com

ROBERT E. RICKEY, born Cincinnati, Ohio; admitted to bar, 2002, Ohio; 2003, U.S. District, Southern District of Ohio. *Education:* Wittenberg University (B.A., summa cum laude, 1999); University of Cincinnati College of Law (J.D., 2002). *Member:* Cincinnati, Ohio State and American Bar Associations. ***PRACTICE AREAS:*** Labor and Employment; Pension Plans; Employee Benefits; Toxic Torts; Discrimination; Executive Compensation; Executive Severance Contracts. ***Email:*** brickey@dmcllc.com

LEGAL SUPPORT PERSONNEL

TRICIA E. ROTH (Legal Assistant)

REPRESENTATIVE CLIENTS: GMP International Union; International Association of Machinists Eastern Region and District 34; Central States Pension Fund; Kentucky State AFL-CIO, Consulting Engineers & Land Surveyors of California Health Insurance Trust; Air Line Pilots Association; UFCW Local 7A; UFCW Local 342; CWA and Local 4400; UAW.

CORS & BASSETT, LLC

Established in 1929

537 EAST PETE ROSE WAY, SUITE 400

CINCINNATI, OHIO 45202-3502

Telephone: 513-852-8200

Fax: 513-852-8222

URL: http://www.corsbassett.com

Ft. Wright, Kentucky Office: 1881 Dixie Highway, Suite 350, 41011. Telephone: 859-331-6440.

General Practice. Corporation, Securities, Labor Relations and Employment Law, Transportation, Environmental, Energy, Land Use Planning and Zoning, International Law, Taxation, Bankruptcy, Estate Planning, Probate, Domestic Relations, Products Liability, Negligence, Franchising, Real Estate Law, Construction Contract and Claims Litigation, and E-Commerce. Trial and Appellate Practice in State and Federal Courts.

FIRM PROFILE: Proud of our seventy-five year history serving Cincinnati and Northern Kentucky, the attorneys at Cors & Bassett have built on the traditional practice areas of a law firm to offer a comprehensive range of legal expertise to serve the needs of individuals and businesses in today's legal environment.

The firm's principal office is located in downtown Cincinnati and one additional office is located in northern Kentucky. The attorneys of Cors & Bassett are admitted to practice in the state of Ohio and many are also admitted in Kentucky. Our attorneys are all members of national, state and local bar associations as well as numerous community and charitable organizations.

Our attorneys emphasize the provision of the highest quality service and guidance to our clients consistent with our clients' individual needs. The attorneys and staff at Cors & Bassett who will work on any particular matter are selected based on the preferences of the client, the experience and skill required, the complexity of the matter and the urgency of prompt action, all with the objective of achieving the best possible representation with maximum effectiveness, efficiency and client satisfaction.

At Cors & Bassett we continuously strive to improve our technology and update our informational sources as our clients' needs for in-depth research and increased productivity grow. In these ways, we continue to build on our tradition of providing high-quality advice to our clients resulting in innovative, proficient and effective legal representation.

MEMBERS OF FIRM

L. BARRY CORS, born Cincinnati, Ohio, June 12, 1932; admitted to bar, 1961, Ohio. *Education:* University of Cincinnati (B.A., 1954; LL.B., 1961). Phi Delta Phi. *Member:* Cincinnati and Ohio State Bar Associations. [Captain, USAF, 1954-1957]. ***PRACTICE AREAS:*** Estate Planning Law; Trust Administration Law. ***Email:*** lbc@corsbassett.com

PAUL R. MORAN, born Cincinnati, Ohio, September 4, 1933; admitted to bar, 1959, Ohio. *Education:* University of Cincinnati (B.A., 1957); University of Virginia (LL.B., 1959). Phi Alpha Delta. *Member:* Cincinnati, Ohio State and American Bar Associations. [Captain, USAF, 1960-1963]. ***PRACTICE AREAS:*** Litigation Law; Labor Law. ***Email:*** prm@corsbassett.com

WILLIAM G. KOHLHEPP, born Cincinnati, Ohio, July 3, 1941; admitted to bar, 1965, Kentucky; 1969, Ohio. *Education:* Thomas More College (A.B., 1961); University of Kentucky (LL.B., 1965). Order of the Coif. Member, 1962-1965 and Comment Editor, 1965, Kentucky Law Journal. With Securities and Exchange Commission, 1965-1968. *Member:* Cincinnati, Ohio State, Kentucky and American Bar Associations. ***PRACTICE AREAS:*** Corporate Law; Securities Law. ***Email:*** wgk@corsbassett.com

RICHARD J. VALLEAU, born Chicago, Illinois, June 19, 1936; admitted to bar, 1962, Ohio and U.S. District Court, Southern District of Ohio; 1963, U.S. District Court, Eastern District of Kentucky; 1964, U.S. Court of Appeals, 6th Circuit. *Education:* Xavier University (B.S., 1959); University of Cincinnati (J.D., 1962). *Member:* Cincinnati and Ohio State Bar Associations. ***PRACTICE AREAS:*** Corporate Law; Probate Law; Trust Administration Law. ***Email:*** rjv@corsbassett.com

JOSEPH H. VAHLSING, born Covington, Kentucky, March 29, 1947; admitted to bar, 1972, Ohio; 1978, Kentucky. *Education:* University of Cincinnati (B.A., 1969); University of Kentucky (J.D., 1972). Order of the Coif; Delta Theta Phi. Member: Kentucky Law Journal, 1971-1972; Campbell County, Kentucky, Board of Education, 1990-2003. *Member:* Cincinnati, Kentucky, Ohio State and Northern Kentucky Bar Associations. ***PRACTICE AREAS:*** Litigation; Labor Law. ***Email:*** jhv@corsbassett.com

ROBERT J. HOLLINGSWORTH, born Dayton, Ohio, September 29, 1948; admitted to bar, 1973, Ohio. *Education:* Xavier University (A.B., summa cum laude, 1970); University of Cincinnati (J.D., 1973). Order of the Coif. Member, University of Cincinnati Law Review, 1971-1973. Law Clerk to Judge Timothy S. Hogan, U.S. District Court, Southern District of Ohio, 1973-1975. *Member:* Cincinnati, Ohio State and American Bar Associations. ***PRACTICE AREAS:*** Litigation; Labor and Employment Law. ***Email:*** rjh@corsbassett.com

DAVID L. BARTH, born Covington, Kentucky, January 25, 1954; admitted to bar, 1978, Ohio; 1984, Kentucky. *Education:* Xavier University (H.A.B., 1974); Salmon P. Chase College of Law (J.D., 1978). Alpha Sigma Nu; Phi Alpha Delta. Member: Moot Court Board; Order of the Curia. Technical Editor, Northern Kentucky Law Review, 1977-1978. *Member:* Ohio State, Cincinnati, Kentucky, Northern Kentucky and American Bar Associations. (Also at Fort Wright, Kentucky Office). ***PRACTICE AREAS:*** Litigation; Labor and Employment; Construction Law. ***Email:*** dlb@corsbassett.com

MICHAEL L. GAY, born Cincinnati, Ohio, June 22, 1952; admitted to bar, 1977, Ohio; 1978, U.S. Court of Appeals, Sixth Circuit. *Education:* The Ohio State University (B.A., 1974); University of Cincinnati (J.D., 1977). *Member:* Cincinnati and Ohio State Bar Associations; Ohio Academy of Trial Lawyers; The Association of Trial Lawyers of America. ***PRACTICE AREAS:*** Litigation; Personal Injury Law; Domestic Relations Law. ***Email:*** mlg@corsbassett.com

ELIZABETH A. HORWITZ, born Cincinnati, Ohio, March 19, 1951; admitted to bar, 1983, Illinois; 1984, Kentucky; 1985, Ohio. *Education:* University of Cincinnati (B.U.P., magna cum laude, 1975); Salmon P. Chase College of Law; Northern Kentucky University (J.D., 1983). Order of the Curia. Member, Northern Kentucky University Law Review, 1982-1983. *Member:* Cincinnati, Ohio State, Kentucky, Illinois State and American Bar Associations. ***PRACTICE AREAS:*** Corporate Law; Securities Law; Land Use Law. ***Email:*** eah@corsbassett.com

JEFFREY J. HARMON, born Covington, Kentucky, March 20, 1958; admitted to bar, 1981, Ohio; 1982, Kentucky, U.S. District Court, Eastern District of Kentucky and U.S. District Court, Southern District of Ohio; 1983, U.S. Court of Appeals, Sixth Circuit; 1985, U.S. Supreme Court. *Education:* Xavier University (A.B., summa cum laude, 1978); George Washington University (J.D., with honors, 1981). *Member:* Cincinnati, Ohio State, Kentucky and American Bar Associations. ***PRACTICE AREAS:*** Environmental Law. ***Email:*** jjh@corsbassett.com

STEPHEN S. HOLMES, born Cincinnati, Ohio, August 27, 1957; admitted to bar, 1982, Ohio and U.S. District Court, Southern District of Ohio. *Education:* Transylvania University (B.A., 1979); University of Kentucky (J.D., 1982). *Member:* Cincinnati and Ohio State Bar Associations; Transportation Lawyers Association. ***PRACTICE AREAS:*** Business Law; Transportation Law. ***Email:*** ssh@corsbassett.com

KATHARINE C. WEBER, born Ashland, Kentucky, February 22, 1965; admitted to bar, 1989, Ohio; 1990, Kentucky. *Education:* University of Kentucky (B.B.A., 1986); Salmon P. Chase College of Law (J.D., 1989). Moot Court Board. Frequently provides on-site seminars for employers on how to formulate and enforce effective personnel policies to avoid and minimize employee lawsuits. Presented seminars and mock trials involving labor and employment law at a host of local, state, and national conferences. Guest faculty lecturer, Denver University Sturm College of Law lecturing on labor and employment law in the transportation industry. Guest, nationally syndicated radio talk show "The Bill Cunningham Show" taking live calls and answering questions on various employment law issues. Monthly columnist for the Kentucky Motor Transport Newspaper regarding labor and employment issues. Co-Author: Kentucky Bench & Bar Magazine article on the Americans With Disabilities Act. Named, "Ohio's Super Lawyers", 2004-2005 by Cincinnati Magazine. *Member:* Cincinnati, Northern Kentucky, Ohio State, Kentucky and American Bar Associations; Transportation Lawyers Association (Executive Committee); National Association of Transportation Employers Resources Association (Board of Directors, 2005, Vice Chairman; 2006, Chairman); Society for Human Resource Management. ***PRACTICE AREAS:*** Labor and Employment Law; Commercial Litigation. ***Email:*** kcw@corsbassett.com

HANS M. ZIMMER, born Cincinnati, Ohio, March 20, 1962; admitted to bar, 1984, Ohio; 1985, U.S. District Court, Southern District of Ohio and U.S. Tax Court. *Education:*

(This Listing Continued)

University of Cincinnati (B.A., cum laude, 1981; J.D., 1984). Order of the Coif. *Member:* Cincinnati and Ohio State Bar Associations. ***LANGUAGES:*** German. ***PRACTICE AREAS:*** Employee Benefits Law; Estate Planning. ***Email:*** hmz@corsbassett.com

JANET L. HOUSTON, born Cincinnati, Ohio, January 19, 1964; admitted to bar, 1989, Ohio; 1991, U.S. Tax Court. *Education:* University of Oklahoma (B.B.A., Accounting, 1985); University of Cincinnati (J.D., 1989); New York University (LL.M., Taxation, 1990). Order of the Coif, Lead Articles Editor, University of Cincinnati. Graduate Editor, New York University Tax Law Review. *Member:* Cincinnati Bar Association. ***PRACTICE AREAS:*** Estate Planning; Taxation; Business Law. ***Email:*** jlh@corsbassett.com

DAVID J. SCHMITT, born Cincinnati, Ohio, March 24, 1962; admitted to bar, 1991, Ohio; 1992, U.S. District Court, Southern District of Ohio. *Education:* Marietta College (B.S., 1983); University of Maine (M.S., Forestry, 1987); University of Cincinnati (J.D., 1991). Phi Alpha Delta (Vice-Justice, 1989-1991). *Member:* Cincinnati (Member, Section on Environmental Law), Ohio State and American Bar Associations. ***LANGUAGES:*** German. ***PRACTICE AREAS:*** Environmental Law; Litigation. ***Email:*** djs@corsbassett.com

KEVIN R. FEAZELL, born Cincinnati, Ohio, December 26, 1960; admitted to bar, 1992, Ohio; 1993, Kentucky. *Education:* University of Cincinnati (B.A., 1988; J.D., 1992). Member, Moot Court. *Member:* Cincinnati, Ohio State, Kentucky, Northern Kentucky and American Bar Associations. ***PRACTICE AREAS:*** Business Law; Commercial Litigation; Construction Litigation; General Litigation; Consumer Law. ***Email:*** krf@corsbassett.com

CURTIS L. CORNETT, born Alamogordo, New Mexico, November 24, 1962; admitted to bar, 1993, Ohio; 1994, U.S. District Court, Southern District of Ohio. *Education:* University of Alabama (B.M., 1984); University of Cincinnati (M.M., 1987; J.D., 1993). Alpha Lambda Delta; Phi Eta Sigma. Editor, University of Cincinnati Law Review. Author: "Ohio Disciplinary Rule 2-107: A Practical Solution to the Referral Fee Dilemma," 61 U. Cin. L. Rev. 239. *Member:* Cincinnati, Ohio State and American Bar Associations; American Inns of Court. ***PRACTICE AREAS:*** Labor and Employment Law; Commercial Litigation; General Litigation. ***Email:*** clc@corsbassett.com

TRACY BYRD JAMISON, born Cincinnati, Ohio, April 14, 1967; admitted to bar, 1993, Kentucky; 1996, Ohio. *Education:* Heidelberg College (B.S., magna cum laude, 1989); University of Cincinnati (J.D., 1993; M.B.A., 1993). ***PRACTICE AREAS:*** Securities; Corporate. ***Email:*** tbj@corsbassett.com

SARA STRAIGHT WOLF, born Huntington, West Virginia, June 17, 1947; admitted to bar, 1976, Ohio and U.S. District Court, Southern District of Ohio. *Education:* Miami University (B.S. Ed., 1969); University of Cincinnati (J.D., cum laude, 1976). Articles Editor, University of Cincinnati Law Review. Author: comment, "Copyright and Misappropriation," 176 Dayton Law Review 951 (1992); "Limitations on Joinder of Defendants in the Ohio Court of Claims," 45 University of Cincinnati Law Review 460 (1976). Certified Mediator, Butler County Common Pleas Court. Board Member: Legal Aid Society of Greater Cincinnati; Fort Hamilton Healthcare Corporation; The Health Alliance. *Member:* Butler County, Cincinnati, Ohio State and American Bar Associations. ***LANGUAGES:*** French. ***PRACTICE AREAS:*** Business Law; Trademark and Copyright Law; Technology Law. ***Email:*** ssw@corsbassett.com

VICTOR C. HALPIN, born Lawrenceburg, Indiana, September 26, 1969; admitted to bar, 1997, Ohio. *Education:* University of Cincinnati (B.B.A., 1994; J.D., 1997). *Member:* Cincinnati and Ohio State Bar Associations. ***PRACTICE AREAS:*** Corporate; Securities; Real Estate. ***Email:*** vch@corsbassett.com

SUSAN R. BELL, born Findlay, Ohio, November 10, 1957; admitted to bar, 1998, Ohio; 1999, U.S. District Court, Southern District of Ohio. *Education:* University of Cincinnati (B.Mus., magna cum laude, 1980; M.Mus., 1984; M.Ed., 1988; J.D., 1998). Publications Editor, Cincinnati Law Review. Author: "Ohio Gets Tough on Juvenile Crime: An Analysis of Ohio 1996 Amendments Concerning the Bindover of Violent Juvenile Offenders to the Adult System and Related Legislation," 66 U. Cin. L. Rev. 207, reprinted in Ohio Crime, Ohio Justice, by Keith Haley and James Todd, p.246, McGraw Hill Co., Inc., 1998. *Member:* Cincinnati, Ohio State and American Bar Associations. ***PRACTICE AREAS:*** Labor and Employment; Litigation. ***Email:*** srb@corsbassett.com

ANDREW C. EMMERT, born Cincinnati, Ohio, January 13, 1959; admitted to bar, 1988, Ohio. *Education:* University of Cincinnati (B.B.A., Accounting and Finance, cum laude, 1982; J.D., 1988). Phi Alpha Delta (President). *Member:* Cincinnati and Ohio State Bar Associations. ***PRACTICE AREAS:*** Real Estate; Business Law; Mergers and Acquisitions; Trusts and Estates. ***Email:*** ace@corsbassett.com

ASSOCIATES

KENNETH H. KINDER II, born Brigham City, Utah, September 4, 1969; admitted to bar, 2000, Ohio and U.S. Tax Court; 2001, Kentucky. *Education:* Transylvania University (B.A., 1991); Salmon P. Chase College of Law (J.D., magna cum laude, 2000). Order of the Curia. Executive Editor, Northern Kentucky Law Review, 1999-2000. Certified Public Accountant, Kentucky, 1994. *Member:* Cincinnati, Ohio State, Kentucky and Northern Kentucky Bar Associations; Cincinnati Estate Planning Council; Kentucky Society of Certified Public Accountants; American Institute of Certified Public Accountants. ***PRACTICE AREAS:*** Tax Law; Corporate Law; Estate Planning. ***Email:*** khk@corsbassett.com

JOSEPH S. BURNS, born Hillsboro, Ohio, January 9, 1975; admitted to bar, 2002, Ohio. *Education:* Northern Kentucky University (B.A., summa cum laude, 1999); Salmon P. Chase College of Law (J.D., summa cum laude, 2002). *Member:* Cincinnati and Ohio State Bar Associations. ***PRACTICE AREAS:*** Litigation; Labor and Employment. ***Email:*** jsb@corsbassett.com

R. SCOTT HUGHES, born Covington, Kentucky, January 6, 1974; admitted to bar, 1999, Ohio; 2000, Kentucky and U.S. District Court, Southern District of Ohio; 2001, U.S. District Court, Eastern District of Kentucky. *Education:* Thomas More College (B.A., English, summa cum laude, 1996; A.A., Pre-Law, summa cum laude, 1996); University of Cincinnati (J.D., 1999). *Member:* Ohio State, Kentucky, Northern Kentucky and American Bar Associations. ***PRACTICE AREAS:*** Litigation; Labor and Employment Law; Personal Injury; Products Liability; Insurance. ***Email:*** rsh@corsbassett.com

(This Listing Continued)

OF COUNSEL

KENNETH B. BASSETT, born Cincinnati, Ohio, January 20, 1931; admitted to bar, 1956, Ohio. *Education:* Denison University (B.A., 1953); University of Cincinnati (LL.B., 1956). Member, University of Cincinnati Law Review, 1954-1956. *Member:* Cincinnati, Ohio State and American Bar Associations. [Lieut., JAG, USNR, 1956-1959]. ***PRACTICE AREAS:*** Corporate Law; Estate Planning Law; Real Estate Law. ***Email:*** kbb@corsbassett.com

JAMES W. HALLORAN, born Louisville, Kentucky, February 20, 1934; admitted to bar, 1960, Ohio. *Education:* Princeton University (A.B., 1956); University of Virginia (LL.B., 1959). Phi Alpha Delta. *Member:* Cincinnati Bar Association. ***PRACTICE AREAS:*** Construction Law; Estate Planning Law. ***Email:*** jwh@corsbassett.com

D. LYNN SPRAETZ, born Virginia Beach, Virginia, July 11, 1963; admitted to bar, 1988, Ohio. *Education:* Miami University (B.S., 1985); Ohio State University (J.D., 1988). *Member:* Cincinnati, Ohio State and American Bar Associations. ***PRACTICE AREAS:*** Corporate Law; Tax Law. ***Email:*** dls@corsbassett.com

MICHELLE A. MULLEE, born Cincinnati, Ohio, January 19, 1960; admitted to bar, 1985, Ohio and U.S. District Court, Southern District of Ohio. *Education:* University of Notre Dame (B.A., cum laude, 1982); Boston College (J.D., 1985). *Member:* Cincinnati, Ohio State and American (Member: Forum on Franchising; Section on Intellectual Property Law) Bar Associations. ***PRACTICE AREAS:*** Corporate Law; Intellectual Property Law; Franchise Law. ***Email:*** mam@corsbassett.com

JAMES J. CARROLL, born Cincinnati, Ohio, August 1, 1946; admitted to bar, 1978, Ohio. *Education:* University of Cincinnati (B.B.A., 1969); Salmon P. Chase College of Law, Northern Kentucky University (J.D., 1978). Phi Alpha Delta. *Member:* Cincinnati and Ohio State Bar Associations. ***PRACTICE AREAS:*** Corporate Law; Real Estate Law. ***Email:*** jjc@corsbassett.com

HAL F. FRANKE, born Cincinnati, Ohio, September 29, 1928; admitted to bar, 1953, Ohio; 1954, West Virginia. *Education:* Xavier University (1948-1950); University of Cincinnati (LL.B., 1953). ***PRACTICE AREAS:*** Labor Law; Contract Law; Administrative Law.

DAVID P. HEIDRICH, born Covington, Kentucky, March 29, 1959; admitted to bar, 1983, Kentucky (Not admitted in Ohio). *Education:* Xavier University (B.S.B.A.; 1971); Salmon P. Chase College of Law (J.D.; 1983). ***Email:*** dph@corsbassett.com

ROBERT GRAY EDMISTON, born Louisville, Kentucky, 1954; admitted to bar, 1981, Kentucky; 1982, Ohio. *Education:* University of Kentucky (B.A., with high distinction, 1977; J.D., 1981). Phi Beta Kappa. *Member:* Cincinnati, Ohio State, Northern Kentucky, Kentucky and American Bar Associations. ***PRACTICE AREAS:*** Estate Planning; Trusts and Estates; Real Estate; Corporate; Charitable Corporations; General Practice. ***Email:*** rge@corsbassett.com

DAVID H. TODD, born Cincinnati, Ohio, 1938; admitted to bar, 1963, Ohio. *Education:* Denison University (B.A., 1960); University of Cincinnati (J.D., 1963). Title Agent, First American Title Insurance Company. Founder, Clermont County Bar Association Fund. Former treasurer and member of the appraisal, executive, and loan committees of a large savings and loan association. *Member:* Clermont County and Ohio State Bar Associations; Ohio Land Title Association. ***PRACTICE AREAS:*** Real Estate; Real Estate Title Insurance. ***Email:*** dht@corsbassett.com

REPRESENTATIVE CLIENTS: Roadway Express, Inc.; The Hillman Group, Inc.; Pomeroy Computer Resources, Inc.; Kenwood Dealer Group; The Midland Company; Citizens Bank of Northern Kentucky; PC on Call, Inc.; Paycor, Inc.; Valley Interior Systems, Inc.; R & L Carriers; Hyatt Hotels; The Dapper Co.; Beechmont Automile: YMCA of Greater Cincinnati; Dugan & Meyers Construction Co.; The Bistro Group, Inc.

CRABBE, BROWN & JAMES LLP

30 GARFIELD PLACE
SUITE 740
CINCINNATI, OHIO 45202
Telephone: 513-784-1525
Fax: 513-784-1250
Email: info@cbjLawyers.com
URL: http://www.cbjLawyers.com

Columbus, Ohio Office: 500 South Front Street, Suite 1200. Telephone: 614-228-5511. Fax: 614-229-4559.
Cleveland, Ohio Office: 1280 W. Third Street. Telephone: 216-574-9312.
Lancaster, Ohio Office: 111 South Broad Street, Suite 209, 43130. Telephone: 740-689-1743. Fax: 740-689-1746.
Urbana, Ohio Office: 118 Scioto Street. Telephone: 937-652-4000.

General Insurance Defense, Product Liability, Professional Malpractice, Premises Liability, Environmental and Toxic Tort Claims, Employment and Labor Law, Tax Matters, General Business and Corporate Law and Litigation, Banking and Securities, Real Estate, Probate and Estate Planning, Criminal Law, Administrative, Regulatory and Governmental Law, Workers Compensation, Intellectual Property, Fire, Arson and Fraud, Fidelity and Surety Life, Accident and Health, Insurance Coverage Law, Construction Claims, Health and Hospital Law, Oil, Gas and Energy Law, Transportation Law, Automobile Dealer Law, Zoning, International Practice and Domestic Law, Land Use Planning, and Eminent Domain.

BRIAN E. HURLEY, born Cleveland, Ohio, December 15, 1953; admitted to bar, 1979, Ohio and U.S. District Court, Southern District of Ohio; 1983, U.S. Court of Appeals, Sixth Circuit. *Education:* John Carroll University (B.A., summa cum laude, 1976); The Ohio State University (J.D., cum laude, 1979); Xavier University (M.S., summa cum laude, 1989). Adjunct Professor: University of Cincinnati College of Law, 1987—; Northern Kentucky University, 1989—. Assistant County Prosecutor, Hamilton County, Ohio, 1982-1988. *Member:* Cincinnati and Ohio State Bar Associations; Ohio Association of Civil Trial Attorneys. ***PRACTICE AREAS:*** Commercial Litigation; Insurance Litigation; Governmental Law; Legal Malpractice; Medical Malpractice Defense; Civil Rights Defense; Law Enforcement; Products Liability; Personal Injury. ***Email:*** BHurley@cbjLawyers.com

(This Listing Continued)

CRABBE, BROWN & JAMES LLP, Cincinnati—Continued

ROBERT J. GEHRING, born Cincinnati, Ohio, February 11, 1954; admitted to bar, 1980, Ohio and U.S. District Court, Southern District of Ohio; 1981, Kentucky; 1988, U.S. Court of Appeals, Sixth Circuit; 1992, U.S. Supreme Court. *Education:* Miami University (B.A., 1976); Salmon P. Chase College of Law, Northern Kentucky University (J.D., 1980). Phi Alpha Delta. Author: "Ohio Personal Injury Practice Forms," Banks Baldwin Publishing Co., 1994; "Products Liability After Tort Reform," Ohio Lawyer, August, 1988; "Overview of Section 1983 Actions," Ohio Municipal Service, December, 1989. Village Solicitor, Newtown, Ohio, 1982-1988. Potter Stewart American Inn of Court, 1986-1988. *Member:* Cincinnati Bar Association (President, 2004; Chairman, Torts and Insurance Practice Committee, 1988-1990; Chairman, Professionalism Committee, 1998-2000; Member, Board of Trustees, Grievance Committee). ***Email:*** RGehring@cbjLawyers.com

ASSOCIATE

BETH WAYNE, born Louisville, Kentucky, May 11, 1954; admitted to bar, 1989, Ohio; 1991, U.S. District Court, Southern District of Ohio. *Education:* Vanderbilt University (B.S.N., 1976); University of Cincinnati (J.D., 1989). *Member:* Cincinnati, Ohio State and American Bar Associations; Ohio Womens Bar Association. ***Email:*** BWayne@cbjLawyers.com

(For biographical data on other personnel, see Professional Biographies at Columbus, Ohio)

CROSKERY LAW OFFICES

Established in 1999

7746 BEECHMONT AVENUE
CINCINNATI, OHIO 45255
Telephone: 513-232-LAWS (5297)
Fax: 513-701-5528
Email: rcroskery@croskerylaw.com
URL: http://www.croskerylaw.com

Sexual Harassment, Wrongful Death, Serious Personal Injury, Auto Accidents, Small Business Representation.

FIRM PROFILE: General Civil Litigation. Represent victims of sexual harassment, wrongful death, serious personal injury.

Small business representation.

ROBERT F. CROSKERY, born Connecticut, July 13, 1956; admitted to bar, 1995, Ohio; 1996, Kentucky; 2005, Florida. *Education:* University of Cincinnati (B.G.S., 1983; J.D., 1995). [Lt. Col., U.S. Army Reserves, serving Special Operations Command]. ***PRACTICE AREAS:*** Sexual Harassment; Wrongful Death; Personal Injury. ***Email:*** rcroskery@croskerylaw.com

MELINDA E. KNISLEY, born Atlanta, Georgia, August 11, 1955; admitted to bar, 1984, Ohio and Federal Bar; 2005, Florida. *Education:* Miami University of Ohio (B.A., 1977); University of Cincinnati (J.D., 1984). ***PRACTICE AREAS:*** Sexual Harassment; Wrongful Death; Personal Injury. ***Email:*** mknisley@croskerylaw.com

REPRESENTATIVE CLIENTS: Terry Lee Chevrolet; The Hair Club for Men and Women of Cincinnati.

CUNI, FERGUSON & LEVAY CO., L.P.A.

Established in 1988

10655 SPRINGFIELD PIKE
CINCINNATI, OHIO 45215-1120
Telephone: 513-771-6768
Fax: 513-771-6781

Real Estate, Corporate, Community and Condominium Association (including Foreclosure), Estate Planning and Probate, and Civil Litigation.

THOMAS L. CUNI, born Logan, West Virginia, October 4, 1947; admitted to bar, 1975, Ohio and U.S. District Court, Southern District of Ohio. *Education:* University of Cincinnati (B.A., 1969; J.D., 1975). *Member:* Cincinnati (Member of the Board of Trustees; Secretary); Ohio State (Member, Continuing Legal Education Committee; Member, Sections on: Real Estate; Corporate Law) and American (Member, Litigation Section) Bar Associations. [1st Lt. U.S. Army, Field Art., 1969-1972]. ***PRACTICE AREAS:*** Corporation Law; Probate Law; Estate Planning Law; Real Estate Law. ***Email:*** TCuni@cfl-law.com

AMY SCHOTT FERGUSON, born Neubrucke, West Germany, February 19, 1968; admitted to bar, 1992, Ohio; 1994, Kentucky. *Education:* University of Cincinnati (B.S., cum laude, 1989); Case Western Reserve University (J.D., cum laude, 1992). Ault Mock Trial Team, 1991-1992. Agent For: Ohio Bar Title Insurance Company. CLE presenter on Community Association Law. *Member:* Butler County, Kentucky, Cincinnati, and Ohio State Bar Associations. ***PRACTICE AREAS:*** Real Estate Law; Community Association Law; Condominium Association Law; Foreclosures. ***Email:*** AFerguson@cfl-law.com

HELEN FANZ LEVAY, born Dayton, Ohio, August 30, 1960; admitted to bar, 1985, Ohio; 1986, U.S. District Court, Southern District of Ohio. *Education:* Ohio State University (B.A., 1982; J.D., 1985). Recipient: Alberta Scott Fellowship for Sociology Award. Instructor, Estate Planning, Midwest Trust School, Cincinnati, Ohio. *Member:* Cincinnati (Member, Estate Planning and Taxations Sections), Ohio State (Member: Taxation Committee; Trust and Probate and Real Property Sections) and American Bar Associations. ***PRACTICE AREAS:*** Estate Planning; Tax Planning; Probate Law. ***Email:*** HLeVay@cfl-law.com

(This Listing Continued)

ASSOCIATES

MARK A. WILDER, born Cincinnati, Ohio; admitted to bar, 1999, Ohio 2004, U.S. District Court, Southern District of Ohio 2005, Kentucky. *Education:* University of Cincinnati (B.A., 1987; J.D., 1999). Agent For: Ohio Bar Title Insurance Company. *Member:* Cincinnati Bar Association. ***PRACTICE AREAS:*** Real Estate; Foreclosures; Community Association Law. ***Email:*** MWilder@cfl-law.com

JOSEPH V. PITSTICK, born Fort Wayne, Indiana, February 19, 1968; admitted to bar, 1993, Ohio. *Education:* Kent State University (B.A., 1990); University of Cincinnati (J.D., 1993). ***PRACTICE AREAS:*** Criminal Law; Real Estate Law; Corporate Law; Commercial Law; Litigation. ***Email:*** JPitstick@cfl-law.com

AGENT FOR: Ohio Bar Title Insurance Co.

DENICOLA & CO., L.P.A.

Established in 1981

36 EAST SEVENTH STREET, SUITE 2020
CINCINNATI, OHIO 45202
Telephone: 513-621-9660
Fax: 513-345-3900
Email: rdenicola@fuse.net
URL: http://www.denicolalaw.com

Corporation and Business Law, Civil Litigation, Commercial Litigation and Collections, Subrogation, Probate, Real Estate, Transportation, Motor Carrier Law, Personal Injury, Automobile Accidents.

FIRM PROFILE: Serving Southwest Ohio and Northern Kentucky area in Commercial Litigation and Small Business Practice, over 37 years experience.

RONALD J. DENICOLA, born Cincinnati, Ohio, November 2, 1941; admitted to bar, 1967, Ohio; 1968, U.S. District Court, Southern District of Ohio; 1970, U.S. Court of Appeals, Sixth Circuit; 1971, U.S. Supreme Court; 1974, U.S. District Court, Eastern District of Kentucky; 1988, Kentucky; 1991, U.S. Tax Court; 2004, U.S. District Court, Northern District of Ohio. *Education:* Xavier University (A.B., 1964); University of Cincinnati College of Law (J. D., 1967). Adjunct Professor, Business Law, Xavier University, 1994-2002. *Member:* Cincinnati (Member: Corporate and Securities Law Committee, 1982—; Trust, Wills and Estates Committee, 1982—), Ohio State, Kentucky and American Bar Associations. ***PRACTICE AREAS:*** Corporate Law; Business Law; Commercial Litigation; Probate; Transportation; Personal Injury; Collections; Subrogation; Bankruptcy; Creditors Rights. ***Email:*** rdenicola@fuse.net

DENLINGER, ROSENTHAL & GREENBERG

A LEGAL PROFESSIONAL ASSOCIATION

425 WALNUT STREET, SUITE 2310
CINCINNATI, OHIO 45202-3918
Telephone: 513-621-3440
Fax: 513-621-4449
URL: http://www.drgfirm.com

Labor and Employment Law.

FIRM PROFILE: Denlinger, Rosenthal & Greenberg's practice is limited to the field of labor and employment law, representing management. The firm's lawyers have substantial experience representing employers in union organizing campaigns, labor negotiations, administrative agency matters (including NLRB, EEOC, OSHA and OFCCP), arbitrations, and litigation (including discrimination, wrongful discharge, wage and hour, benefits, workplace tort, breach of contract and noncompete cases).

The firm's clients range from small to very large companies in a wide variety of businesses, including manufacturing, hotels and restaurants, construction, retail sales, health care and professional firms. Denlinger, Rosenthal & Greenberg also represents municipalities and other governmental entities.

All of the firm's lawyers who have been partners (technically shareholders) for five years or more have equal compensation and equity. Compensation criteria used by other firms that tend to be divisive or to result in excessive client charges - like the amount of bills a lawyer sends or the number of hours he records - are not considered.

Partly as a consequence of this compensation approach, there is much collegiality, trust and consultation among our lawyers. All lawyers help each other take care of our clients' needs. No one is proprietary about a client, nor is there any incentive to be.

DEAN E. DENLINGER (1929-2000)

DANIEL G. ROSENTHAL, born Springfield, Ohio, January 14, 1953; admitted to bar, 1977, Ohio. *Education:* Wittenberg University (B.A., magna cum laude, 1974); Duke University (J.D., with distinction, 1977). *Member:* Cincinnati and Ohio State (Member, Labor-Employment Law Section) Bar Associations. (Certified Specialist in Labor and Employment Law, Ohio State Bar Association). ***PRACTICE AREAS:*** Labor and Employment. ***Email:*** rosenthal@drgfirm.com

GARY L. GREENBERG, born Cincinnati, Ohio, July 8, 1953; admitted to bar, 1978, Ohio. *Education:* University of Pennsylvania (B.A, cum laude, 1974); University of Michigan (J.D., magna cum laude, 1978). *Member:* Cincinnati, Dayton and Ohio State (Member, Labor-Employment Law Section) Bar Associations; The Federalist Society (Member, Labor & Employment Practice Group). ***PRACTICE AREAS:*** Labor and Employment. ***Email:*** garygreenberg@drgfirm.com

JOHN W. FISCHER, II, born Dayton, Ohio, August 28, 1956; admitted to bar, 1981, Ohio. *Education:* University of Cincinnati (B.B.A., cum laude, 1978); Case Western Reserve University (J.D., 1981). *Member:* Cincinnati, Ohio State (Member, Labor-Employ-

(This Listing Continued)

ment Law Section) and American (Member: Labor and Employment Law Section; Occupational Safety and Health Law Committee) Bar Associations. ***PRACTICE AREAS:*** Labor and Employment. ***Email:*** johnfischer@drgfirm.com

MARK E. LUTZ, born Heidelberg, West Germany, November 16, 1956; admitted to bar, 1981, Ohio; 1988, Kentucky. *Education:* Kent State University (B.A., magna cum laude, 1978); University of Chicago (J.D., 1981). Phi Beta Kappa. Member, University of Chicago Law Review, 1979-1981. Law Clerk to Judge Nathaniel R. Jones, Sixth Circuit Court of Appeals, 1981-1982. *Member:* Cincinnati, Ohio State (Member, Labor-Employment Law Section) and Kentucky (Member, Labor and Employment Law Section) Bar Associations. ***PRACTICE AREAS:*** Labor and Employment. ***Email:*** lutz@drgfirm.com

JAMES A. MILLS, born Springfield, Massachusetts, August 5, 1955; admitted to bar, 1980, Ohio. *Education:* Purdue University (B.A., with distinction, 1977); University of Cincinnati (J.D., 1980). Phi Kappa Phi. Editor, University of Cincinnati Law Review, 1979-1980. Law Clerk to Judge Timothy S. Hogan, U.S. District Court, 1982. NLRB Field Attorney, 1983-1986. *Member:* Cincinnati and Ohio State (Member, Labor-Employment Law Section) Bar Associations; The Federalist Society (Member, Labor & Employment Practice Group). ***PRACTICE AREAS:*** Labor and Employment. ***Email:*** jimmills@drgfirm.com

---

JILL STANFORTH TAUBER, born Cincinnati, Ohio, July 30, 1974; admitted to bar, 2001, Ohio. *Education:* Xavier University (B.S., magna cum laude, 1996); The Ohio State University (M.A., 1997); University of Cincinnati (J.D., 2001). *Member:* Cincinnati and Ohio State (Member, Labor-Employment Law Section) Bar Associations; The Federalist Society (Member, Labor & Employment Practice Group). ***PRACTICE AREAS:*** Labor and Employment. ***Email:*** jst@drgfirm.com

EMILY J. GELHAUS, born Cincinnati, Ohio, March 24, 1978; admitted to bar, 2003, Ohio. *Education:* University of Cincinnati (B.A., summa cum laude, 2000) Phi Beta Kappa; University of Cincinnati (J.D., 2003). Order of the Coif. Member, University of Cincinnati Law Review, 2002-2003. *Member:* Cincinnati and Ohio State (Member, Labor-Employment Law Section) Bar Associations. ***PRACTICE AREAS:*** Labor and Employment. ***Email:*** ejg@drgfirm.com

MICHAEL P. MAJBA, born Parma, Ohio, July 21, 1978; admitted to bar, 2003, Ohio. *Education:* University of Notre Dame (B.A., cum laude, 2000); University of Cincinnati (J.D., 2003). University of Cincinnati Immigration and Nationality Law Review, 2001-2003. Law Clerk to the Honorable Mark P Painter, Ohio First District Court of Appeals, 2003-2005. *Member:* Cincinnati and Ohio State Bar Associations. ***PRACTICE AREAS:*** Labor and Employment. ***Email:*** mpm@drgfirm.com

REPRESENTATIVE CLIENTS: Angell-Demmel North America, Inc.; Arkay Industries; Caraustar Industrial & Consumer Products Group; Cedar Village; CCL Container; Columbia Sussex Corp.; CompuNet Clinical Laboratories; Duro Bag Manufacturing Co.; Ernst Enterprises; Ferno Washington, Inc.; Fluor Fernald, Inc.; Georgia-Pacific Corp.; Hubert Distributing Co.; The City of Kettering; The Kroger Co.; Lake Tahoe Horizon Casino Resort; LaRosa's, Inc.; Lighthouse Point Casino; Lion Apparel, Inc.; Lutheran Social Services of Mid America; Lykins Cos.; Moraine Materials Co.; NuTone, Inc.; The Ohio Masonic Home; Overhead Door Corp.; Phototype Engraving Co.; The City of Piqua; Rippe & Kingston Co. PSC; Seligman Distributing Co.; The Standard Textile Co.; Standard Publishing; Trimble Navigation Ltd.; The City of Troy; Twin Towers Nursing Home; Varland Metal Service, Inc.; Winston Heat Treating, Inc.; Zenith Logistics, Inc.

DENMEAD LAW OFFICE

CINCINNATI, OHIO

(See Columbus)

Civil Trial and Appellate Practice and Personal Injury, Traumatic Brain Injury (TBI), Professional Negligence and Complex Litigation including Class Actions, Patents, Civil Rights, Civil Litigation, RICO, Employment and Political Subdivision Liability issues.

DETERS, BENZINGER & LaVELLE, P.S.C.

3500 CAREW TOWER
441 VINE STREET
CINCINNATI, OHIO 45202-3007
Telephone: 513-241-4110
Telecopier: 513-241-4551
URL: http://www.dbllaw.com

Covington, Kentucky Office: Thomas More Park, 207 Thomas More Parkway. Telephone: 859-341-1881. Telecopier: 859-341-1469.

General Practice. Trials and Appeals. Banking, Health Care, Corporate, Personal Injury, Real Estate, Insurance, Labor and Employee Relations, Media, Antitrust, Employee Benefits, Family, Adoption, Collections, Internet, Computer, Information Technology, International, Equine, Probate, Estate Planning, Administrative, Workers' Compensation, Taxation, Zoning, Commercial, Agricultural, Bankruptcy, Construction, Eminent Domain and Criminal Law.

JOSEPH A. CLEVES, JR., born Covington, Kentucky, November 26, 1955; admitted to bar, 1978, Kentucky; 1980, Ohio. *Education:* Thomas More College (B.A., cum laude, 1975); St. Louis University (J.D., 1978). Member, Northern Kentucky Homebuilders Land Development Council. *Member:* Cincinnati, Northern Kentucky, Ohio State, Kentucky and American Bar Associations; Construction Law Forum. ***PRACTICE AREAS:*** Construction Law; Real Estate Law; Banking Law; Commercial Law. ***Email:*** jcleves@dbllaw.com

ALAN J. HARTMAN, born Covington, Kentucky, April 28, 1952; admitted to bar, 1978, Kentucky; 1984, Ohio. *Education:* Duns Scotus College (B.A., with honors, 1974); Northern Kentucky University, Salmon P. Chase College of Law (J.D., 1978). Private Practitioner: Newport, KY., 1978-1983; Cincinnati, Ohio, 1998-2000. Assistant County Attorney, Campbell County, Newport, Kentucky, 1979-1983. Counsel, 1983-1996 and General Counsel, 1993-1996, Cincom Systems, Inc., Cincinnati, Ohio. Vice-President and General Counsel, LanVision Systems, Inc., Cincinnati, Ohio, 1996-1998. *Member:* Cincinnati (Member, Internet/eCommerce and Computer Law Committee, 1983—, Chair, 1992-1994; International Law Committee, 1983—; Corporate Counsel Committee, 1983—), Ohio

(This Listing Continued)

State (Member, Computer Law Committee, 1984—), Kentucky and Northern Kentucky Bar Associations; Christian Legal Society; Computer Law Association. [USAF, 1971-1973]. ***PRACTICE AREAS:*** Computer Law; International Law; Information Technology Law; Corporate Law; Commercial Law. ***Email:*** ahartman@dbllaw.com

WILLIAM J. MORAN, JR., born Indianapolis, Indiana July 3, 1965; admitted to bar, 1992, Ohio; 1993, U.S. District Court, Southern District of Ohio; 1994, U.S. Court of Appeals, Sixth Circuit; 2001, Kentucky and U.S. District Court, Eastern District of Kentucky. *Education:* Xavier University (B.S.B.A., 1987); Capital University (J.D., 1992). Order of the Curia. Recipient, American Jurisprudence Award for Creditors and Debtors Rights. *Member:* Cincinnati, Kentucky, Northern Kentucky and Ohio State Bar Associations; Ohio Association of Civil Trial Attorneys. (Also at Covington, Kentucky Office). ***PRACTICE AREAS:*** Insurance; Commercial Litigation; Construction Law. ***Email:*** bmoran@dbllaw.com

DAVID W. BURLEIGH, born Evansville, Indiana, April 17, 1968; admitted to bar, 1995, Ohio; 1996, Kentucky, U.S. District Court, Eastern District of Kentucky and U.S. Court of Appeals, Sixth Circuit; 1997, U.S. District Court, Western District of Kentucky; 2003, U.S. District Court, Southern District of Ohio and U.S. Court of Appeals, Third Circuit. *Education:* DePauw University (B.A. Honor Scholar, cum laude, 1990); University of Dallas (M.A., 1992); University of Cincinnati (J.D., 1995). Co-Author: Vols. 6 & 7, Kentucky Practice, "Rules of Civil Procedure Annotated," 6th edition 2005 (West Publishing Co.). *Member:* Cincinnati, Northern Kentucky, Ohio State and Kentucky Bar Associations. (Also at Covington, Kentucky Office). ***PRACTICE AREAS:*** Business Litigation; Computer Law; Information Technology; Construction Law; Collections. ***Email:*** dburleigh@dbllaw.com

ASSOCIATES

CARLA M. VENHOFF, born Somerset, Kentucky, May 17, 1974; admitted to bar, 1999, Kentucky (Not admitted in Ohio). *Education:* Thomas More College (B.A., summa cum laude, 1996); Louis D. Brandeis School of Law, University of Louisville (J.D., cum laude, 1999). *Member:* Northern Kentucky and Kentucky Bar Associations. ***PRACTICE AREAS:*** Real Estate Law; Commercial Law; Banking Law; Construction Law. ***Email:*** cvenhoff@dbllaw.com

PETER A. SCHMID, born Cincinnati, Ohio, October 7, 1973; admitted to bar, 2004, Ohio; 2005, Kentucky and U.S. District Court, Southern District of Ohio. *Education:* College of William & Mary (B.S., 1995); Ohio State University (M.A., 1998); Salmon P. Chase College of Law, Northern Kentucky University (J.D., 2003). *Member:* Ohio, Cincinnati, Kentucky and American Bar Associations. ***PRACTICE AREAS:*** Commercial Litigation. ***Email:*** pschmid@dbllaw.com

OF COUNSEL

PIERCE E. CUNNINGHAM, born Cincinnati, Ohio, August 18, 1934; admitted to bar, 1960, Ohio; U.S. District Court, Southern District of Ohio; U.S. Court of Appeals, Sixth Circuit. *Education:* College of the Holy Cross (A.B., 1956); Georgetown University (LL.B., 1959). Trial Counsel for Ohio Attorney General, Columbus Ohio. Chairman: Cincinnati City Planning Commission; Cincinnati Zoning Board of Appeals; Cincinnati Riverfront Development. Advocate, American Board of Trial Attorneys. (Also Member, The Law Offices of Pierce E. Cunningham Co., LPA). ***PRACTICE AREAS:*** Litigation; Dispute Resolution; Real Estate. ***Email:*** pcunningham@dbllaw.com

REPRESENTATIVE CLIENTS: Ace U.S.A.; American Financial Corp.; American General Financial Services; August Groh & Sons Inc.; Chelsea Moore, Inc.; Cincinnati Country Day School; Engineering Excellence, Inc.; Ford Motor Co.; General Cable Corp.; Hunt Development; The Huntington National Bank; LanVision Systems, Inc.; Little Sisters of the Poor, Inc.; MAC Productions, Inc.; Mercy Health Partners; The Mortgage Source, Inc.; New Plan Realty, Inc.; Penn Central Corp.; Projetech, Inc.; Queen City Physicians, Ltd.; Schottenstein Stores, Inc.; Securities Investor Protection Corporation; Standard Life Insurance Co. of Indiana; U.S. Digital Partners, LLC; Vertical Solutions Inc.; Yavneh Day School.

(For complete biographical data on all personnel, see Professional Biographies at Covington, Kentucky)

DeVITA & HOWE, LLP

117 EAST COURT STREET
CINCINNATI, OHIO 45202-1203
Telephone: 513-632-5332
Fax: 513-241-7434

General Business, Real Estate, Tax, Estate Planning and Probate.

MEMBERS OF FIRM

DAVID DeVITA, born Lima, Ohio, January 19, 1952; admitted to bar, 1978, Ohio and Kentucky. *Education:* University of Notre Dame (B.A., 1974); The Ohio State University (J.D., 1978). Order of the Coif. *Member:* Cincinnati and Ohio State Bar Associations. ***PRACTICE AREAS:*** Business; Commercial Practice; Business Acquisitions; Estate Planning. ***Email:*** devita@devhowe.com

WILLIAM D. HOWE, born Cincinnati, Ohio, May 11, 1952; admitted to bar, 1977, Ohio. *Education:* Xavier University (B.A., 1974); University of Cincinnati (J.D., 1977); New York University (LL.M. in Taxation, 1978). Order of the Coif. Member, University of Cincinnati Law Review, 1975-1977. *Member:* Cincinnati and American Bar Associations. ***PRACTICE AREAS:*** Taxation; Estate Planning; Business Law. ***Email:*** howe@devhowe.com

DINSMORE & SHOHL LLP

255 EAST FIFTH STREET, SUITE 1900
CINCINNATI, OHIO 45202-4700
Telephone: 513-977-8200
FAX: 513-977-8141
Email: info@dinslaw.com
URL: http://www.dinslaw.com

Dayton, Ohio Office: One Dayton Centre, One South Main Street, Suite 1300, 45402. Telephone: 937-449-6400. FAX: 937-449-6405.
Columbus, Ohio Office: 10th Floor, 175 South Third Street, 43215-5134. Telephone: 614-628-6880. FAX: 614-628-6890.
Lexington, Kentucky Office: Lexington Financial Center, 250 West Main Street, Suite 1400, 40507. Telephone: 859-425-1000. FAX: 859-425-1099.
Louisville, Kentucky Office: 1400 PNC Plaza, 500 West Jefferson Street, 40202. Telephone: 502-540-2300. FAX: 502-585-2207.
Pittsburgh, Pennsylvania Office: The Grant Building, 330 Grant Street, Suite 2415, 15219. Telephone: 412-281-5000. FAX: 412-281-5055.
Charleston, West Virginia Office: 900 Lee Street, Huntington Square, Suite 600, 25301. Mailing Address: P.O. Box 11887, 25339. Telephone: 304-357-0900. FAX: 304-357-0919.

General Practice: Antitrust, Aviation Law, Banking, Bankruptcy, Business Crimes Law, Computers, Construction, Corporations, Creditors' Rights, Drug and Medical Device, Employee Benefits, Environmental, ERISA, Estate Planning, Franchising, Healthcare, Hospitals, Intellectual Property, International, Immigration, Insurance Law, Labor and Employment Law, Litigation, Medical Malpractice Defense, Mergers and Acquisitions, OSHA, Probate, Products Liability, Real Estate, Securities, State and Local Government Law, Taxation, Transportation Law, Trial and Appellate Practice in State and Federal Courts, Trusts, Workers' Compensation, Zoning.

FIRM PROFILE: Our Foundation

For over 95 years, Dinsmore & Shohl LLP has been providing quality legal counsel to our clients. In recent years, our practice has grown to include seven offices and taken on national and international clients. Today's full-service practice with more than 260 attorneys continues to live up to the ideals set in 1908 by Frank F. Dinsmore and Walter M. Shohl: efficient, cost-effective and comprehensive solutions for every client.

Our Service

At Dinsmore & Shohl LLP, we put our clients first in every element of our full-service practice. The Firm's commitment to quality service extends from our highly-skilled attorneys to our experienced professional staff. By establishing client relationships based on trust, communication and responsiveness, we listen to our clients' concerns and expectations while refining our service to ensure that these needs are met. We recognize that service begins with accessibility and ends with fulfilled expectations.

Our Clients

With over 35 practice areas, Dinsmore & Shohl LLP has the experience and variety to meet your legal needs. Our clients range from public and private corporations to charitable organizations and encompass healthcare providers, local and state governments, financial institutions, real estate developers, franchisors and distributors and pharmaceutical companies.

Our Technology

By embracing and utilizing the latest technology, our efficiencies are passed on to clients. We continuously assess and update our case management systems, intranet, extranets, billing systems, document management systems, and other practice-specific software to ensure our work product can be leveraged and measured. In addition, our legal library uses technology to keep important, up-to-date information close at hand. These combined resources help us strategize, plan, develop and integrate our practice to meet your business needs.

Our Innovation

Our commitment to client service extends to our growing subsidiaries: DinsNet Technologies LLC, Great Water Capital Partners, LLC, and Mercantile Title Agency, Inc. which provide various portals for client collaboration. These unique services help optimize e-business, business intelligence and knowledge management solutions for clients.

Our Future

Utilizing the latest technology and resources, we embrace the future today while maintaining our historical values. With attorneys and staff skilled in a broad range of legal and ancillary subjects, we will continue to offer the knowledge and experience needed to maintain our strict standard of excellence. This commitment has continued to drive our growth and will sustain our foundation into the future.

FRANK F. DINSMORE (1891-1962)

WALTER M. SHOHL (1908-1970)

MEMBERS OF FIRM

JEROME H. KEARNS, born Cincinnati, Ohio, February 17, 1941; admitted to bar, 1966, Ohio. *Education:* Xavier University (B.S., 1963); University of Cincinnati (M.B.A., 1970); University of Michigan (J.D., 1965). *Member:* of the National Association of Estate Planning. ***PRACTICE AREAS:*** Personal Taxation Law; Corporate Law; Business Law; Estate Planning Law. ***Email:*** kearns@dinslaw.com

CLIFFORD A. ROE, JR., born Elyria, Ohio, November 5, 1942; admitted to bar, 1967, Ohio. *Education:* Xavier University (B.S., 1964); University of Notre Dame (J.D., 1967). Note Editor, Notre Dame Law Review, 1966-1967. ***PRACTICE AREAS:*** Corporate and Securities Law; Mergers and Acquisitions Law; Health Care Law; Financial Institutions Law. ***Email:*** roe@dinslaw.com

LAWRENCE R. ELLEMAN, born Hamilton, Ohio, November 21, 1940; admitted to bar, 1966, Ohio. *Education:* The Ohio State University (B.S., 1963; J.D., 1966). Order of the Coif. Associate Editor, Ohio State Law Journal, 1965-1966. Law Clerk to Judge Don J. Young, U.S. District Court, Northern District of Ohio, 1966-1968. Master of the Bench, Potter Stewart Inn of Court. *Member:* Cincinnati, Ohio State and American (Member, Dispute Resolution Section) Bar Associations; Ohio Supreme Court (Member: Board of Bar Examiners; Rules Advisory Committee; Commission on Certification of Lawyers as Specialists). Fellow, Ohio State Bar Foundation. ***PRACTICE AREAS:*** General Litigation; Alternative Dispute Resolution. ***Email:*** larry.elleman@dinslaw.com

JOHN M. KUNST, JR., born Dayton, Ohio, October 10, 1941; admitted to bar, 1966, Ohio; U.S. Supreme Court; U.S. Court of Appeals, Sixth Circuit; U.S. District Court, Southern District of Ohio. *Education:* Wittenberg University (A.B., 1963); University of Cincinnati (J.D., 1966). Law Clerk to Judge David S. Porter, U.S. District Court, Southern District of Ohio, 1966-1968. Member, Product Liability Advisory Council, 1991—. ***PRACTICE AREAS:*** General Litigation; Product Liability; Labor and Employment Law; Commercial Litigation; Mediation Neutral. ***Email:*** kunst@dinslaw.com

THOMAS J. SHERMAN, born Cincinnati, Ohio, January 16, 1944; admitted to bar, 1969, Ohio; U.S. District Court, Southern District of Ohio. *Education:* University of Cincinnati (B.A., 1966; J.D., 1969). Order of the Coif. Editorial Note Editor, University of Cincinnati Law Review, 1968-1969. *Member:* Cincinnati and Ohio State Bar Associations. ***PRACTICE AREAS:*** Real Estate; Corporate Law; Mortgages; Property Law; Leases and Leasing. ***Email:*** tom.sherman@dinslaw.com

VINCENT B. STAMP, born Louisville, Kentucky, May 24, 1944; admitted to bar, 1969, Ohio; U.S. District Court, Southern and Northern District of Ohio; U.S. Court of Appeals, Sixth Circuit. *Education:* Bellarmine College (A.B., 1966); University of Notre Dame (J.D., 1969). *Member:* Cincinnati Bar Association (Former Chair, Environmental Law Committee); Ohio Association of Civil Trial Attorneys (Former Chair, Environmental Law Committee). ***PRACTICE AREAS:*** General Litigation; Environmental Law; Administrative Law; Commercial Law. ***Email:*** stamp@dinslaw.com

FRANK C. WOODSIDE, III, born Glen Ridge, New Jersey, April 18, 1944; admitted to bar, 1969, Ohio; 1991, Kentucky; 1993, Tennessee, Missouri, U.S. District Court, Southern and Northern Districts of Ohio, Eastern and Western Districts of Kentucky, Eastern District of Michigan, Eastern District of Wisconsin, Northern District of California, Western District of Texas, U.S. Court of Appeals, First, Third, Fifth, Sixth, Eighth, Eleventh and District of Columbia and U. S. Supreme Court. *Education:* Lehigh University; Ohio State University (B.S., 1966; J.D., cum laude, 1969); University of Cincinnati (M.D., 1973). Editor, Drug Product Liability, Matthew Bender, 1985—. Adjunct Professor of Law, University of Cincinnati College of Law, 1973-1993. Member, Product Liability Advisory Council, 1991—. Diplomate: American Board of Professional Liability Attorneys; American College of Legal Medicine; American Society of Hospital Attorneys; Society of Ohio Hospital Attorneys. *Member:* International Association of Defense Counsel; Defense Research Institute. ***PRACTICE AREAS:*** Drug & Medical Device, Products Liability Defense Law; Medical Malpractice Defense Law; Health Care Law. ***Email:*** frank.woodside@dinslaw.com

MARK L. SILBERSACK, born Cincinnati, Ohio, December 27, 1946; admitted to bar, 1971, Ohio; U.S. Supreme Court; U.S. Court of Appeals, Third and Sixth Circuits; U.S. District Court, Southern District of Ohio. *Education:* Boston College (A.B., 1968); University of Chicago (J.D., 1971). *Member:* Cincinnati, Ohio State, American and Federal Bar Associations. [USAR (Retired)]. ***PRACTICE AREAS:*** Antitrust Law; General Litigation; Products Liability; Professional Liability. ***Email:*** silbersa@dinslaw.com

GERALD V. WEIGLE, JR., born Cincinnati, Ohio, June 15, 1947; admitted to bar, 1971, Ohio; U.S. District Court, Southern District of Ohio; U.S. Supreme Court; U.S. Court of Appeals, Second, Third, Fifth, Sixth, District of Columbia and Federal Circuits. *Education:* Northwestern University (B.S., 1968); University of Michigan (J.D., 1971). *Member:* Defense Research Institute. ***PRACTICE AREAS:*** General Litigation; Insurance Law. ***Email:*** weigle@dinslaw.com

MICHAEL W. HAWKINS, born Detroit, Michigan, May 10, 1947; admitted to bar, 1972, Ohio; 1989, Kentucky; U.S. Court of Appeals, Sixth Circuit; U.S. District Court, Southern District of Ohio; U.S. District Court, Eastern and Western Districts of Kentucky; U.S. Supreme Court. *Education:* University of Kentucky (B.B.A., 1969; J.D., 1972). Order of the Coif. Lead Articles and Book Reviews Editor, Kentucky Law Journal, 1971-1972. Master, Potter Stewart Inn of Court; Master of the Bench, Samuel P. Chase Inn of Court. ***PRACTICE AREAS:*** Labor and Employment Law and Litigation; Construction Labor Law; Arbitration; Mediation. ***Email:*** hawkins@dinslaw.com

MARK A. VANDER LAAN, born Akron, Ohio, September 14, 1948; admitted to bar, 1973, Ohio; 1973, U.S. District Court, Southern District of Ohio; 1978, U.S. Court of Appeals, Sixth Circuit; 1979, U.S. Supreme Court; U.S. Tax Court; U.S. District Court, Northern District of Ohio. *Education:* Hope College (A.B., 1970); University of Michigan (J.D., 1972). Special Counsel for the Ohio Attorney General, 1983—. Assistant Special Prosecutor, State of Ohio, 1985-1997. Member, Rules of Practice Committee, Ohio Supreme Court, 1991-1992. City Solicitor, Blue Ash, Ohio, 1987—. City Solicitor, Silverton, Ohio, 1999—. President, Cincinnati Railway, 2001—. Master of the Bench, Potter Stewart Inn of Court. Life Member, Sixth Circuit Judicial Conference. *Member:* Cincinnati, Ohio State and American Bar Associations. ***PRACTICE AREAS:*** General Litigation; Commercial Law; State and Local Government Law; Business Crimes Law. ***Email:*** mark.vanderlaan@dinslaw.com

WILLIAM M. FREEDMAN, born Washington, D.C., December 8, 1946; admitted to bar, 1973, Ohio; U.S. District Court, Southern District of Ohio; U.S. Tax Court. *Education:* Carleton College (B.A., 1968); Harvard Law School (J.D., 1973). Adjunct Professor, Health Law & Policy, Department of Health Services Administration, Xavier University, Cincinnati Ohio. *Member:* Cincinnati, Ohio State (Member, Estate Planning and Probate Section) and American (Member, Employee Benefits Committee, Section of Taxation; Health Law Section) Bar Associations; American Health Lawyers Association; Ohio Society of Hospi-

(This Listing Continued)

tal Attorneys. [U.S. Army, 1968-1970]. ***PRACTICE AREAS:*** Business Law; Corporate Law; Employee Benefits; Health Care; Taxation. ***Email:*** bill.freedman@dinslaw.com

PAUL R. MATTINGLY, born Cincinnati, Ohio, February 1, 1950; admitted to bar, 1975, Ohio; 1976, Indiana; U.S. District Court, Southern District of Ohio. *Education:* University of Dayton (B.A., 1972); University of Notre Dame (J.D., 1975). Notes Editor, Notre Dame Law Review, 1974-1975. *Member:* Cincinnati and Ohio State Bar Associations. ***PRACTICE AREAS:*** Corporate Law; Mergers, Acquisitions and Divestitures; Franchises and Franchising; Business Law. ***Email:*** paul.mattingly@dinslaw.com

J. MICHAEL COONEY, born Maysville, Kentucky, May 6, 1950; admitted to bar, 1975, Ohio; 1978, U.S. Tax Court. *Education:* Xavier University (A.B., magna cum laude, 1972); University of Michigan (J.D., magna cum laude, 1975). *Member:* Cincinnati, Ohio State (Council Member, 2003— and Member, Estate Planning, Trust & Probate Law Section; Member, Specialization Committee 2005—) and American Bar Associations; Cincinnati Estate Planning Council (Trustee, 1987-1993; President, 1991-1992). American College of Trust and Estate Counsel. (Certified Specialist in Estate Planning, Trust and Probate Law, Ohio State Bar Association). ***PRACTICE AREAS:*** Estate Planning Law; Personal Taxation Law; Business Law. ***Email:*** mike.cooney@dinslaw.com

MICHAEL S. GLASSMAN, born Toledo, Ohio, December 4, 1951; admitted to bar, 1976, Ohio; U.S. Supreme Court; U.S. Court of Appeals, Fifth, Sixth and Eighth Circuits; U.S. District Court, Southern District of Ohio. *Education:* University of Cincinnati (B.A., summa cum laude, 1973; J.D., 1976). Phi Beta Kappa; Order of the Coif. Production Editor, University of Cincinnati Law Review, 1975-1976. *Member:* Cincinnati (Member, Labor and Employment Section), Ohio State (Member, Labor and Employment Section) and American (Member, Sections on: Labor and Employment; Litigation) Bar Associations; Employment Law Alliance. ***PRACTICE AREAS:*** Labor and Employment; Occupational Safety and Health; Litigation; Class Actions; Alternative Dispute Resolution. ***Email:*** michael.glassman@dinslaw.com

NANCY A. LAWSON, born Plainfield, New Jersey; admitted to bar, 1975, Ohio and U.S. District Court, Northern District of Ohio; 1977, U.S. District Court, Southern District of Ohio; 1978, U.S. Court of Appeals, Sixth Circuit; 1979, U.S. Supreme Court; 1991, U.S. District Court, Northern District of California; 1997, Kentucky. *Education:* Skidmore College (B.A., 1970); Boston University (M.Ed., 1971); University of Toledo (J.D., 1975). Co-author: *The Law of Medical Practice in Ohio,* Lawyers Cooperative Publishing, 1989. *Member:* Defense Research Institute; International Association of Defense Counsel. ***PRACTICE AREAS:*** Business Litigation; Products Liability; General Civil Litigation. ***Email:*** nancy.lawson@dinslaw.com

MICHAEL D. EAGEN, born Cincinnati, Ohio, August 24, 1946; admitted to bar, 1974, Ohio; 2005, Kentucky; U.S. District Court, Southern and Northern Districts of Ohio; U.S. District Court, Eastern District of Kentucky; U.S. Court of Appeals, Sixth Circuit; U.S. Supreme Court. *Education:* College of the Holy Cross (A.B., 1968); University of Michigan (J.D., 1974). *Member:* Cincinnati, Ohio State, Kentucky, Federal (Member, Cincinnati Chapter, Executive Committee) and American Bar Associations; Defense Research Institute; Sixth Circuit Judicial Conference (Life Member); Ohio Association of Civil Trial Attorneys; Potter Stewart Inn of Court (Master of the Bench); American Board of Trial Advocates. Fellow, American College of Trial Lawyers. ***PRACTICE AREAS:*** Litigation; Products Liability; Toxic Torts; Insurance Coverage Defense; Commercial Litigation. ***Email:*** michael.eagen@dinslaw.com

PAUL A. OSE, born Champaign, Illinois, December 19, 1951; admitted to bar, 1977, Ohio; U.S. District Court, Southern District of Ohio. *Education:* Indiana University (A.B., with highest distinction, 1974), Phi Beta Kappa; University of Michigan (J.D., cum laude, 1977). ***PRACTICE AREAS:*** Corporate Law; Mergers and Acquisitions; Securities; Public Company Compliance; International Law. ***Email:*** ose@dinslaw.com

CHARLES F. HERTLEIN, JR., born Cincinnati, Ohio, July 17, 1955; admitted to bar, 1980, Ohio; U.S. District Court, Southern District of Ohio. *Education:* University of Cincinnati (B.A., summa cum laude, 1977); University of Michigan (J.D., cum laude, 1980). Co-author, "Corporate Secretary's Answer Book", Aspen Publishing (2002). *Member:* Cincinnati and Ohio State Bar Associations. ***PRACTICE AREAS:*** Corporate Law; Securities Law; Acquisitions and Mergers; Commercial Transactions. ***Email:*** hertlein@dinslaw.com

JOANNE M. SCHREINER, born Akron, Ohio, October 26, 1954; admitted to bar, 1979, Arizona; 1980, Ohio. *Education:* University of Akron (B.A., summa cum laude, 1976); University of Chicago (J.D., 1979). ***PRACTICE AREAS:*** Business Law; Real Estate Law; Commercial Law. ***Email:*** Joanne.Schreiner@dinslaw.com

JOHN D. LUKEN, born Dayton, Ohio, October 18, 1956; admitted to bar, 1981, Ohio; U.S. Supreme Court; U.S. Court of Appeals, Fifth and Sixth Circuits; U.S. District Court, Southern District of Ohio. *Education:* Northwestern University (B.A., 1978); Stanford University (J.D., 1981). *Member:* Cincinnati and Ohio State Bar Associations. ***PRACTICE AREAS:*** Commercial Litigation; Intellectual Property Litigation; Civil Litigation. ***Email:*** john.luken@dinslaw.com

DEBORAH R. LYDON, born Cincinnati, Ohio, June 7, 1955; admitted to bar, 1981, Ohio; 1991, Kentucky; U.S. Supreme Court; U.S. District Court, Southern and Northern Districts of Ohio; U.S. District Court, Eastern and Western Districts of Kentucky; U.S. Court of Appeals, Sixth and Eighth Circuits. *Education:* University of Cincinnati (B.G.S., 1977; J.D., 1981). Member, Order of the Barristers. Adjunct Professor, University of Cincinnati College of Law, 1986-1999. Co-author: *The Law of Medical Practice in Ohio,* Lawyers Cooperative Publishing, 1989 (Supplements, 1991-1995). Editor, *Emergency Legal Briefings,* 1990-1995. *Member:* Defense Research Institute; Ohio Association of Civil Trial Attorneys; Society of Ohio Hospital Attorneys. ***PRACTICE AREAS:*** General Litigation; Health Care Law; Product Liability Litigation. ***Email:*** lydon@dinslaw.com

GEORGE H. VINCENT, born Ann Arbor, Michigan, May 11, 1957; admitted to bar, 1982, Ohio. *Education:* University of Michigan (B.A., 1979; J.D., 1982). Member, Barristers. Member, 1995-2004 and Chairman, 1998-2004, Hamilton County Tax Levy Review Committee. Member, 1991-1997 and Chairman, 1992-1994, Cincinnati Metropolitan Housing Authority. Member, Hamilton County Public Defender Commission, 2001-2005. Chairman, Hamilton County Republican Party, 2005—. Member, 1997— and Chairman, 2005—, Cincinnati Museum Center. *Member:* Cincinnati Bar Association (Chairman, Corporate and Securities Law Committee, 1991-1993). ***PRACTICE AREAS:*** Corporate Law; Contracts; Mergers and Acquisitions; Securities Law. ***Email:*** george.vincent@dinslaw.com

LYNDA E. ROESCH, born Dayton, Ohio, August 27, 1953; admitted to bar, 1979, Ohio; U.S. District Court, Northern and Southern Districts of Ohio; U.S. Court of Appeals, First and Sixth Circuits; registered to practice before U.S. Patent and Trademark Office. *Education:* University of Notre Dame (B.S., 1975); University of Michigan (M.S., 1976); University of Toledo (J.D., 1979). Member, State of Ohio Board of Commissioners on Character and Fitness, 1997-2000. *Member:* State of Ohio Board of Commissioners, Character and Fitness, 1997-2000; International Trademark Association (Board of Directors, 1995-1997; Chair, Legislation Analysis Committee, 1997-1998; Vice Chair, Internet Committee, 1999-2001); Chair, Internet Committee, 2001-2003; Trademark Offices Practices Group (Past Chair). ***PRACTICE AREAS:*** Trademark and Unfair Competition Law; Copyright Law; Intellectual Property Law; General Litigation. ***Email:*** lroesch@dinslaw.com

GEORGE B. WILKINSON, born Lima, Ohio, December 11, 1951; admitted to bar, 1982, Ohio; U.S. District Court, Southern District of Ohio. *Education:* University of Virginia (B.A., 1974); Georgetown University (J.D., 1981). Third Year Editor, Law and Policy in International Business, 1980-1981. Law Clerk to Judge K. K. Hall, U.S. Court of Appeals, Fourth Circuit, 1981. Co-Author: *Ohio Workers' Compensation Act, 1993 House Bill 107.* . ***PRACTICE AREAS:*** General Litigation; Workers' Compensation Law. ***Email:*** wilkinso@dinslaw.com

JOHN E. JEVICKY, born Indiana, Pennsylvania, August 2, 1954; admitted to bar, 1980, Pennsylvania; 1981, Ohio; U.S. District Court, Southern District of Ohio; U.S. Court of Appeals, Sixth Circuit; U.S. District Court, Northern District of Texas. *Education:* Indiana University of Pennsylvania (B.A., 1976); University of Dayton (J.D., 1980). Associate Editor, University of Dayton Law Review, 1979-1980. Law Clerk to the Hon. Carl B. Rubin, Chief Judge, U.S. District Court for the Southern District of Ohio, 1980-1982. *Member:* Food and Drug Law Institute. ***PRACTICE AREAS:*** General Litigation; Commercial Litigation; Product Liability Defense Litigation; Health Care Law; Drug and Medical Device Regulation; Premarket Clearance Notifications; Consumer Product Safety Law; FDA Enforcement Actions. ***Email:*** jevicky@dinslaw.com

JERRY S. SALLEE, born Columbus, Ohio, November 13, 1954; admitted to bar, 1980, Ohio; U.S. District Court, Southern District of Ohio; U.S. District Court, Northern District of Ohio; U.S. Court of Appeals, Sixth Circuit. *Education:* University of Cincinnati (B.B.A., magna cum laude, 1976); Capital University (J.D., cum laude, 1980). Order of the Curia. ***PRACTICE AREAS:*** Labor and Employment Law; Litigation. ***Email:*** sallee@dinslaw.com

MARK C. BISSINGER, born Steubenville, Ohio, June 4, 1957; admitted to bar, 1983, Ohio; 1993, Kentucky; U.S. Court of Appeals, Sixth Circuit; U.S. District Court, Southern District of Ohio. *Education:* Purdue University (B.S.C.E., 1979); University of Cincinnati (J.D., 1983). Order of the Coif. ***PRACTICE AREAS:*** Commercial Transactions; General Litigation; Construction Law. ***Email:*** bissinge@dinslaw.com

GARY E. BECKER, born Hamilton, Ohio, December 1, 1958; admitted to bar, 1984, Ohio; U.S. District Court, Southern and Northern Districts of Ohio; U.S. Court of Appeals, Sixth Circuit. *Education:* Valparaiso University (B.A., 1980); University of Cincinnati (J.D., 1984). Order of the Coif. Business Manager, University of Cincinnati Law Review, 1983-1984. *Member:* Butler County, Hamilton County and Ohio State Bar Associations; Defense Research Institute. ***PRACTICE AREAS:*** Civil Rights; Litigation; Products Liability; Toxic Torts; Workers' Compensation. ***Email:*** gary.becker@dinslaw.com

NEAL D. BAKER, born Bronx, New York, August 25, 1957; admitted to bar, 1984, Ohio; 1989, New Jersey; U.S. District Court, Southern District of Ohio; U.S. Court of Appeals, Sixth Circuit; U.S. District Court, District of New Jersey. *Education:* State University of New York at Binghamton Harpur College (B.A., 1979); Rutgers University (J.D., 1984). ***PRACTICE AREAS:*** Commercial Litigation; Securities Litigation; Religious Institutions. ***Email:*** nbaker@dinslaw.com

CHARLES M. ROESCH, born Hamilton, Ohio, October 10, 1958; admitted to bar, 1984, Ohio; 1994, Kentucky; U.S. District Court, Southern and Northern Districts of Ohio, Eastern District of Kentucky, Eastern District of Wisconsin, Southern and Northern Districts of Indiana, Southern District of Illinois and Eastern District of Arkansas; U.S. Court of Appeals, Sixth, Seventh and Eleventh Circuits. *Education:* University of Notre Dame (B.B.A., 1981); University of Cincinnati College of Law (J.D., 1984). Note Editor Chairperson, University of Cincinnati Law Review, 1983-1984. *Member:* Cincinnati, Ohio State and Kentucky Bar Associations. ***PRACTICE AREAS:*** Labor and Employment Law and Litigation; Public Employment Relations Law. ***Email:*** croesch@dinslaw.com

K. C. GREEN, born Columbus, Ohio, July 31, 1958; admitted to bar, 1984, Ohio; U.S. Supreme Court; U.S. Court of Appeals, Third, Fifth and Sixth Circuits; U.S. District Court, Southern and Northern Districts of Ohio. *Education:* Case Western Reserve University (B.A., 1980); University of Virginia (J.D., 1984). *Member:* Cincinnati, Ohio State and American Bar Associations; Defense Research Institute. ***PRACTICE AREAS:*** General Litigation; Health Care Law; Product Liability Law. ***Email:*** kc.green@dinslaw.com

M. GABRIELLE HILS, born Covington, Kentucky, November 18, 1959; admitted to bar, 1984, Ohio; 1985, Kentucky, U.S. Supreme Court, United States Court of Appeals, Fifth and Sixth Circuits, U.S. District Court, Southern District of Ohio, Eastern District of Kentucky, Western District of Kentucky, Northern District of California. *Education:* Thomas More College (B.A., 1981); University of Kentucky (J.D., 1984). Order of the Coif. Managing Editor, Kentucky Law Journal, 1983-1984. ***PRACTICE AREAS:*** General Litigation; Products Liability Law. ***Email:*** gabrielle.hils@dinslaw.com

STEPHEN G. SCHWELLER, born Dayton, Ohio, February 5, 1959; admitted to bar, 1984, Ohio; U.S. District Court, Southern and Northern Districts of Ohio; U.S. Court of Appeals, Third and Sixth Circuits. *Education:* Denison University (B.A., with honors, 1981); Washington and Lee University (J.D., magna cum laude, 1984). Order of the Coif. *Member:* Ohio Association of Civil Trial Attorneys; International Association of Insurance Receivers. ***PRACTICE AREAS:*** General Litigation; Insurance Coverage; Insurance Insolvency. ***Email:*** stephen.schweller@dinslaw.com

STEVEN H. SCHREIBER, born Cincinnati, Ohio, August 25, 1948; admitted to bar, 1981, Ohio; 1999, Kentucky and U.S. District Court, Southern District of Ohio. *Education:*

(This Listing Continued)

DINSMORE & SHOHL LLP, Cincinnati—Continued

The Ohio State University (B.A., 1970; M.A., 1972; J.D., 1980). Member, 1979-1980 and Articles Editor, 1980, Ohio State Law Journal. Member, Ohio Board of Bar Examiners, 1985-1990. ***PRACTICE AREAS:*** Real Estate Law; Commercial Transactions; Title Insurance. ***Email:*** steve.schreiber@dinslaw.com

CALVIN D. BUFORD, born Cincinnati, Ohio, April 21, 1959; admitted to bar, 1985, Ohio. *Education:* Northwestern University (B.A., 1981); Harvard University, John F. Kennedy School of Government (M.P.P., 1985); Harvard Law School (J.D., 1985). ***PRACTICE AREAS:*** Corporate Law; Mergers and Acquisitions; Financings. ***Email:*** calvin.buford@dinslaw.com

GREGORY A. HARRISON, born Lima, Ohio, February 1, 1961; admitted to bar, 1985, Ohio; U.S. Supreme Court; U.S. Court of Appeals, Fourth and Sixth Circuits; U.S. Court of Federal Claims; U.S. District Court, Southern and Northern Districts of Ohio. *Education:* Bowling Green State University (B.S. in B.A., 1982); University of Dayton (J.D., magna cum laude, 1985). Editor-in-Chief, University of Dayton Law Review, 1984-1985. Trial Attorney, U.S. Department of Justice, Civil Division, 1985-1989. ***PRACTICE AREAS:*** Commercial Litigation; Product Liability; Insurance. ***Email:*** greg.harrison@dinslaw.com

BEN F. WELLS, born Cincinnati, Ohio, September 28, 1958; admitted to bar, 1983, Ohio; U.S. District Court, Southern District of Ohio. *Education:* University of Cincinnati (B.B.A., 1980); University of Cincinnati College of Law (J.D., 1983). *Member:* Cincinnati and American (Member, Employee Benefits Committee, Taxation Section) Bar Associations. ***PRACTICE AREAS:*** Employee Benefits; Tax Law; Business Law; Executive Compensation. ***Email:*** ben.wells@dinslaw.com

HOLLY D. KOZLOWSKI, born Pittsburgh, Pennsylvania, May 27, 1958; admitted to bar, 1984, Virginia; 1996, Ohio; U.S. District Court, Eastern District of Virginia; U.S. Court of Appeals, Fourth and Federal Circuits; U.S. Supreme Court; registered to practice before U.S. Patent and Trademark Office. *Education:* Bucknell University (B.S., Ch.E., 1980); George Mason University School of Law (J.D., 1984). *Member:* American Intellectual Property Law Association. ***PRACTICE AREAS:*** Intellectual Property. ***Email:*** kozlowsk@dinslaw.com

FREDERICK M. ERNY, born Pittsburgh, Pennsylvania, August 30, 1961; admitted to bar, 1987, Ohio; 1988, Pennsylvania; 2004, Kentucky; U.S. District Court, Southern and Northern Districts of Ohio; U.S. District Court, Eastern and Western Districts of Pennsylvania; U.S. District Court Eastern and Western Districts of Kentucky; U.S. Court of Appeals, Third and Sixth Circuits and U.S. Supreme Court. *Education:* University of Pittsburgh (B.A., 1983); Duquesne University (J.D., 1987). Duquesne University Law Review. *Member:* Cincinnati, Ohio State, Kentucky and American Bar Associations; Defense Research Institute. ***PRACTICE AREAS:*** Drug and Medical Device Defense; Products Liability; General Litigation. ***Email:*** fred.erny@dinslaw.com

TIMOTHY A. TEPE, born Cincinnati, Ohio, May 31, 1960; admitted to bar, 1987, Ohio; U.S. District Court, Southern District of Ohio. *Education:* University of Cincinnati (B.A., 1984; J.D., 1987). ***PRACTICE AREAS:*** Trusts Law; Estates Law; Family Law. ***Email:*** tepe@dinslaw.com

HARVEY JAY COHEN, born Hamilton, Ohio, July 19, 1960; admitted to bar, 1987, Ohio. *Education:* Georgetown University (A.B., cum laude, 1982); Columbia University (Masters in International Affairs, 1986); University of Cincinnati (J.D., 1987). Order of the Coif. University of Cincinnati Law Review. Rotary International Fellowship to University of Yaounde, Cameroon (1983-1984). School of African and Asian Studies, University of Sussex, Brighton, England (1980-1981). Professor, International Business Transactions, University of Cincinnati College of Law. *Member:* Cincinnati (Past Chair/International Law Committee) and Ohio State (Past Chair/International Law Committee) Bar Associations; Greater Cincinnati Chamber of Commerce Foreign Investment Attraction Team (Chair); International Trade Council (Board Member); Southern Ohio Export Council; Kentucky District Export Council; Northern Kentucky International Trade Association (Board Member); French-American Chamber of Commerce (Secretary; Board Member); International Family Resource Center (Past President); Art Academy (Counsel); United Way Neighborhood Services (Co-Chair); ALFA International (Co-Chair, International Law Practice Group). ***LANGUAGES:*** French. ***TRANSACTIONS:*** Several recent $10 - $100M domestic and transnational acquisitions and sales, foreign joint ventures, computer alliance agreements and complex executive employment compensation arrangements. ***PRACTICE AREAS:*** Domestic and International Business Transactions; Computer Law; Foreign Owned Companies; Mergers and Acquisitions; Executive Compensation Agreements; Securities. ***Email:*** harvey.cohen@dinslaw.com

JAMES A. COMODECA, born Cleveland, Ohio, January 6, 1962; admitted to bar, 1987, Ohio; 1996, Kentucky; U.S. District Court, Southern and Northern Districts of Ohio, Eastern District of Michigan and Eastern and Western Districts of Kentucky; U.S. Court of Appeals, Sixth Circuit; U.S. Tax Court. *Education:* Miami University (A.B., 1984); University of Akron School of Law (J.D., 1987). Member, Akron Law Review, 1985-1986. Adjunct Faculty, Sports Management Master Program, Xavier University. *Member:* Cincinnati, Warren County, Northern Kentucky, Ohio State and Kentucky Bar Associations; Defense Research Institute; International Association of Defense Counsel. ***PRACTICE AREAS:*** Products Liability Defense; Medical Malpractice Defense; General Litigation; Sports and Entertainment Law. ***Email:*** jim.comodeca@dinslaw.com

JOSEPH (JAY) L. SALLEE, JR., born Lexington, Kentucky, April 4, 1955; admitted to bar, 1985, Ohio; 1986, Kentucky; U.S. District Court, Eastern and Western Districts of Kentucky; U.S. District Court, Southern District of Ohio; U.S. Court of Appeals, Sixth Circuit. *Education:* University of Kentucky (B.S., 1977); Auburn University (1984); Salmon P. Chase College of Law (J.D., 1985). Order of the Curia. Executive Editor, Northern Kentucky Law Review, 1985. Law Clerk to Hon. William O. Bertelsman, U.S. District Court, Eastern District of Kentucky. *Member:* Cincinnati, Northern Kentucky, Ohio State and Kentucky Bar Associations. (Certified Specialist in Workers Compensation Law, Ohio State Bar Association). ***PRACTICE AREAS:*** Litigation; Workers' Compensation; OSHA; Products Liability. ***Email:*** jay.sallee@dinslaw.com

(This Listing Continued)

JOAN M. VERCHOT, born Paterson, New Jersey, May 2, 1961; admitted to bar, 1986, Ohio; U.S. District Court, Southern District of Ohio; U.S. Supreme Court. *Education:* University of Maryland (B.A., 1983); Capital University (J.D., 1986). Student Notes Editor, Capital University Law Review, 1985-1986. Assistant Attorney General, State of Ohio, 1986-1989. Chairperson, Workers' Compensation Law Committee; Member, Commission on Judicial Candidates, Ohio State Bar Association. Past Chairperson, Workers Compensation Committee and Member, Grievance Committee, Cincinnati Bar Association. *Member:* Ohio State Bar Association (Chairperson, Workers' Compensation Law Committee). (Certified Specialist in Workers Compensation Law, Ohio State Bar Association). ***PRACTICE AREAS:*** General Litigation; Workers' Compensation Law. ***Email:*** joan.verchot@dinslaw.com

KIM MARTIN LEWIS, born Lancaster, Pennsylvania, May 23, 1962; admitted to bar, 1987, California; 1989, Ohio; U.S. District Court, Southern District of Ohio; U.S. District Court, Central District of California. *Education:* Ball State University (B.S., cum laude, 1984); Southwestern University (J.D., cum laude, 1987). Deans Scholar. Research Editor, Southwestern University School of Law Review. ***PRACTICE AREAS:*** Business Bankruptcy. ***Email:*** klewis@dinslaw.com

JOHN E. BARNES, born Cincinnati, Ohio, August 9, 1956; admitted to bar, 1981, Kentucky; 1983, Ohio. *Education:* St. Louis University (B.A., 1978); University of Cincinnati (J.D., 1981). ***PRACTICE AREAS:*** Corporate and Securities Law. ***Email:*** barnes@dinslaw.com

CHARLES H. BROWN, III, born Cincinnati, Ohio, August 19, 1957; admitted to bar, 1987, Ohio; U.S. District Court, Southern and Northern Districts of Ohio; U.S. Court of Appeals, Fourth, Sixth and Federal Circuits; U.S. Supreme Court; registered to practice before the U.S. Patent and Trademark Office. *Education:* University of Virginia, School of Engineering and Applied Science (B.S.M.E., 1979); Marshall-Wythe School of Law, College of William and Mary (J.D., 1987). *Member:* Cincinnati, Ohio State and Federal Bar Associations; American Intellectual Property Law Association. ***PRACTICE AREAS:*** Commercial Litigation; Intellectual Property; Products Liability; Trade Secrets; Unfair Competition; Litigation. ***Email:*** chip.brown@dinslaw.com

BRIAN S. SULLIVAN, born Cincinnati, Ohio, July 16, 1964; admitted to bar, 1988, Ohio; U.S. District Court, Northern and Southern Districts of Ohio. *Education:* University of Cincinnati (B.A., 1985; J.D., 1988). ***PRACTICE AREAS:*** Aviation; Employment; General Litigation. ***Email:*** bsulliva@dinslaw.com

COLLEEN P. LEWIS, born Cincinnati, Ohio, April 2, 1959; admitted to bar, 1989, Ohio; 1999, Kentucky; U.S. District Court, Southern District of Ohio, U.S. District Court, Eastern District of Kentucky and U.S. Court of Appeals, Sixth Circuit. *Education:* Northern Kentucky University (B.S., summa cum laude, 1985; A.A.S., 1985); Northern Kentucky University, Salmon P. Chase College of Law (J.D., cum laude, 1989). Articles Editor, Salmon P. Chase Law Review, 1988-1989. *Member:* Cincinnati, Ohio State, Kentucky and Federal Bar Associations. ***PRACTICE AREAS:*** Labor and Employment Law and Litigation; Public Employment Law. ***Email:*** clewis@dinslaw.com

SUSAN B. ZAUNBRECHER, born Bangor, Maine, July 28, 1959; admitted to bar, 1990, Ohio; U.S. District Court, Southern District of Ohio. *Education:* Tulane University (B.A., 1981); University of Cincinnati (J.D., 1990). Student Articles Editor, University of Cincinnati Law Review, 1989-1990. *Member:* Cincinnati and Ohio State Bar Associations. (Chair, Banking and Financial Institutions Practice Group). ***PRACTICE AREAS:*** Banks and Banking; Corporate Law; Business Law; Securities; Mergers, Acquisitions and Divestitures. ***Email:*** susan.zaunbrecher@dinslaw.com

CHRISTOPHER A. BENINTENDI, born Rockville Centre, New York, June 9, 1965; admitted to bar, 1990, Ohio. *Education:* Wittenberg University (B.A., 1987); University of Dayton School of Law (J.D., cum laude, 1990). ***PRACTICE AREAS:*** Workers Compensation Law; Litigation. ***Email:*** beninten@dinslaw.com

WILLIAM A. SHERMAN, II, born Hamilton, Ohio, November 18, 1960; admitted to bar, 1987, Ohio; 1990, Maryland. *Education:* Morgan State University (B.A., 1983); University of Maryland (J.D., 1986). ***PRACTICE AREAS:*** Product Liability Defense; Business Litigation; Commercial Litigation. ***Email:*** wsherman@dinslaw.com

JEFFREY P. HINEBAUGH, born Fairfax, Virginia, July 17, 1967; admitted to bar, 1992, Ohio. *Education:* Grove City College (B.A., summa cum laude, 1989); University of Michigan (J.D., cum laude, 1992). ***PRACTICE AREAS:*** Product Liability Law. ***Email:*** hinebaug@dinslaw.com

CLYDE BENNETT, II, born Cincinnati, Ohio, February 21, 1965; admitted to bar, 1992, Ohio. *Education:* University of Cincinnati (B.S., 1987); University of Dayton School of Law (J.D., 1992). Recipient, American Jurisprudence Award for Constitutional Law and Federal Income Taxation. ***PRACTICE AREAS:*** Criminal Defense; White Collar Crime; Civil Litigation. ***Email:*** cbennett@dinslaw.com

MARTIN J. MILLER, born Toledo, Ohio, August 29, 1963; admitted to bar, 1991, Ohio, U.S. Supreme Court, U.S. Court of Appeals, Federal Cicuit, U.S. District Court, Southern District of Ohio; registered to practice before U.S. Patent and Trademark Office. *Education:* Purdue University (B.S., Chemical Engineering, B.S., Chemistry, 1986); University of Toledo (J.D., magna cum laude, 1991). Order of the Coif. Editor, The University of Toledo Law Review. *Member:* Cincinnati and American Bar Associations; American Intellectual Property Law Association. ***PRACTICE AREAS:*** Intellectual Property. ***Email:*** mmiller@dinslaw.com

MARY-JO MIDDELHOFF, born Bellevue, Kentucky, August 15, 1959; admitted to bar, 1991, Ohio; 1997, Kentucky. *Education:* Xavier University (B.S.N., 1984); University of Cincinnati College of Law (J.D., 1991). Registered Nurse, Ohio, 1980. ***PRACTICE AREAS:*** Medical Malpractice; Products Liability. ***Email:*** maryjo.middelhoff@dinslaw.com

BONNIE G. CAMDEN, born Hanover, Pennsylvania, November 5, 1950; admitted to bar, 1989, Ohio. *Education:* Western Maryland College (B.A., cum laude, Mathematics, 1972); University of Kansas (M.B.A., 1974); University of Cincinnati College of Law (J.D., 1989). Order of the Coif. Lead Articles Chair, University of Cincinnati Law Review, 1987-1989. Member, YWCA of Cincinnati (Planned Giving Committee). *Member:* Cincinnati and Ohio State Bar Associations. (Certified Specialist in Estate Planning, Trust and Probate

(This Listing Continued)

Law, Ohio State Bar Association). ***PRACTICE AREAS:*** Estate Planning Law (60%); Personal Taxation Law (5%); Estate Administration (20%); Probate Law (15%). ***Email:*** bonnie.camden@dinslaw.com

DEBORAH DeLONG, born Louisville, Kentucky, September 5, 1950; admitted to bar, 1975, Ohio; 1982, U.S. Supreme Court; 1999, Kentucky. *Education:* Vanderbilt University (B.A., 1972); University of Cincinnati (J.D., 1975). Recipient, Leading Women of Cincinnati Award, 2000. Member: Defense Research Institute; Arbitration Tribunal, United States District Court, Southern District of Ohio. Member, Common Pleas Court Arbitration Panel, 1975—. Solicitation Committee, American Heart Association. Member, Junior League of Cincinnati. Board of Directors, Family Education Center. *Member:* Cincinnati (Member, Grievance and Domestic Relations Pleas Court Committee), Ohio State (Member, Labor and Employment Law Committee), Kentucky, Federal (Member, Executive Committee) and American (Litigation Committee on Pretrial Practice Discovery; Labor and Litigation Section) Bar Associations. ***LANGUAGES:*** French. ***PRACTICE AREAS:*** Litigation; Labor Law; Employment Law; Health Care; Business Litigation; Mediation Services. ***Email:*** ddelong@dinslaw.com

ALAN H. ABES, born Akron, Ohio, January 1, 1968; admitted to bar, 1993, Ohio. *Education:* The Ohio State University (B.A., Political Science, summa cum laude, with distinction and with honors, 1990); Northwestern University School of Law (J.D., cum laude, 1993). ***PRACTICE AREAS:*** Litigation. ***Email:*** alan.abes@dinslaw.com

MICHAEL A. MANZLER, born Cincinnati, Ohio, May 17, 1966; admitted to bar, 1992, Ohio and U.S. District Court, Southern District of Ohio; 1995, U.S. Court of Appeals, Sixth Circuit; 2001, U.S. Supreme Court. *Education:* Yale University (B.A., magna cum laude, 1988); University of Chicago (J.D., 1992). Member, Human Resources Committee, 1997— and Chair, 2004—, United Way of Greater Cincinnati. *Member:* Cincinnati (Community Service Committee Board, 1996-2003; Member, Labor and Employment Section, 1992—; Vice Chair, 2004—) and Ohio State (Member, Labor and Employment Section) Bar Associations. ***REPORTED CASES:*** Appalachian Regional Healthcare, Inc. v. United Steelworkers of America, 245 F.3d 601 (6thcir. 2001); Piette v. CSX Transportation, Inc., 1999 U.S. App. LEXIS 15164 (6th Cir. 1999). ***PRACTICE AREAS:*** Labor and Employment; Litigation. ***Email:*** michael.manzler@dinslaw.com

BARBARA SCHWARTZ BROMBERG, born Newark, New Jersey, March 1, 1941; admitted to bar, 1965, New York; 1969, U.S. Tax Court; 1973, Ohio. *Education:* University of Buffalo (B.A., 1962); Columbia University (LL.B., 1965). Phi Beta Kappa. Recipient: Cincinnati Bar Association's Trustees' Award, 1996. Author: Regular Tax Column "Fraternal Law" and Numerous other articles and frequent lecturer. *Member:* Cincinnati Bar Association(Past Chairman); Past Internal Revenue Service Commissioner's Advisory Group (Exempt Organizations) Cincinnati Estate Planning Council; National Health Lawyers Association; Cincinnati Bar Foundation (Past President and Trustee). ***PRACTICE AREAS:*** Foundations and Other Tax Exempt Organizations; Corporations; Taxation; Estate Planning and Probate. ***Email:*** bbromberg@dinslaw.com

MARY J. HEALY, born Covington, Kentucky, November 8, 1952; admitted to bar, 1978, Ohio; 1988, Kentucky. *Education:* University of Cincinnati (B.A., 1974); Northern Kentucky University (J.D., 1978). Listed in: Best Lawyers in America, 1999-2004. Past President, Cincinnati Bar Foundation. Fellow, American College of Trust and Estate Counsel. *Member:* Cincinnati (Estate Planning and Probate Section; Past Chair, Taxation Section) and Kentucky Bar Associations. Fellow, American College of Trust and Estate Counsel. (Certified Specialist in Estate Planning, Trust and Probate Law, Ohio State Bar Association). ***PRACTICE AREAS:*** Estate Planning and Probate. ***Email:*** mhealy@dinslaw.com

RICHARD B. TRANTER, born Cincinnati, Ohio, August 23, 1958; admitted to bar, 1985, Ohio. *Education:* Georgetown University (B.A., 1980); University of Dayton (J.D., 1985). Author: "Real Estate," Chapter to Doing Business in the U.S. 1st & 2nd Eds.; "Zoning and Planning Boards," Ohio CLE Institute, 1997; "Current Zoning Issues," Cincinnati Bar Association, 1996; "Commercial Real Estate Development Issues," Professional Education Systems, 1995; "Regulatory Takings: The Public Need Versus Private Property Rights," Ohio CLE Institute, 1992. Leadership Cincinnati Class XXIII, 1999-2000. Public Defender's Commission for Hamilton County, Ohio, 1994-2000. Member, Hamilton County Zoning Update Advisory Group (ZUAG), 1989-1996. Member, Hamilton County Subdivision Update Advisory Group (SUAG), 1990-1992. Legal Action Network for Development Strategies (LANDS), 1990—. *Member:* Ohio State Bar Association. ***PRACTICE AREAS:*** Commercial Real Estate Law; Zoning, Planning and Land Use; Commercial Finance. ***Email:*** richard.tranter@dinslaw.com

JOHN J. SCHMIDT, born Cincinnati, Ohio, November 25, 1960; admitted to bar, 1992, Ohio and U.S. District Court, Southern District of Ohio; 1993, U.S. Court of International Trade; 1994, U.S. Court of Appeals, Sixth Circuit; 2005, U.S. Court of Appeals, Third Circuit. *Education:* Xavier University (B.A., English, 1982); University of Cincinnati (J.D., 1992). Order of the Coif. Member, University of Cincinnati Law Review, 1990-1991. Student Articles Editor, U.S., Law Review, 1991-1992. Author: "Preemption of Failure to Warn and Misrepresentation Claims Under the Cigarette Act: Dewey v. R.J. Reynolds Tobacco Co.," 577 A.2d 1239 (N.J. 1990), 60 U. Cinn. L. Rev. 251, 1991; "The Fraud Created the Market Theory: The Presumption of Reliance in the Primary Issue Context," 60 U. Cinn. L. Rev. 439, 1991. *Member:* Cincinnati and Ohio State Bar Associations. ***PRACTICE AREAS:*** Corporate; Business Reorganization; Bankruptcy; General Business Representation. ***Email:*** john.schmidt@dinslaw.com

SEAN P. CALLAN, born Fairfax, Virginia, March 27, 1968; admitted to bar, 1993, Ohio; 1994, Kentucky. *Education:* Dartmouth College (A.B., 1990); University of Cincinnati (J.D., 1993). Order of the Coif. *Member:* Cincinnati, Northern Kentucky, Kentucky, Ohio State and American Bar Associations. ***PRACTICE AREAS:*** Real Estate; Litigation; Zoning and Land Use. ***Email:*** scallan@dinslaw.com

BRIAN J. O'CONNELL, born Cincinnati, Ohio, April 2, 1962; admitted to bar, 1992, Ohio. *Education:* University of Dayton (B.A., 1984; J.D., magna cum laude, 1992). Editor, University of Dayton Law Review. ***PRACTICE AREAS:*** Litigation. ***Email:*** oconnell@dinslaw.com

BRIAN P. PERRY, born Cincinnati, Ohio, July 24, 1968; admitted to bar, 1993, Ohio. *Education:* University of Cincinnati (B.A., 1990); University of Cincinnati College of Law

(This Listing Continued)

(J.D., 1993). *Member:* Cincinnati and Ohio State Bar Associations. (Certified Specialist in Workers Compensation Law, Ohio State Bar Association). ***PRACTICE AREAS:*** General Litigation; Workers' Compensation. ***Email:*** brian.perry@dinslaw.com

STEVEN H. RAY, born Lindsborg, Kansas, December 24, 1961; admitted to bar, 1988, Ohio; 1989, U.S. District Court, Southern District of Ohio and U.S. Court of Appeals, Sixth Circuit; 1999, U.S. Court of Appeals, Eighth Circuit. *Education:* University of Nebraska (B.A., 1984); Rutgers University (J.D., with honors, International Law, 1988). *Member:* Cincinnati, Ohio State and American Bar Associations. ***PRACTICE AREAS:*** General Litigation; Product Liability; Railroad Law; Transportation Law. ***Email:*** steve.ray@dinslaw.com

ROBERT J. REID, born Cincinnati, Ohio, December 28, 1967; admitted to bar, 1993, Ohio; 2000, Kentucky. *Education:* Xavier University (B.A., Political Science, 1990); University of Cincinnati College of Law (J.D., 1993). Member, University of Cincinnati Law Review. *Member:* Cincinnati and Ohio State Bar Associations. (Certified Specialist in Labor and Employment Law, Ohio State Bar Association). ***PRACTICE AREAS:*** Labor and Employment Law. ***Email:*** rob.reid@dinslaw.com

LINDA A. ASH, born Sarnia, Ontario, May 7, 1955; admitted to bar, 1991, Ohio and U.S. District Court, Southern District of Ohio; 1994, U.S. District Court, Northern District of Ohio; 1999, U.S. Supreme Court. *Education:* University of Arizona (B.A., 1976); Salmon P. Chase College of Law, Northern Kentucky University (J.D., 1991). Member, Supreme Court Historical Society. *Member:* Cincinnati and Ohio State Bar Associations; American Immigration Lawyers Association. ***PRACTICE AREAS:*** Butter Flavoring/Popcorn Plant Litigation; Immigration; Mold Litigation. ***Email:*** linda.ash@dinslaw.com

DAVID D. BLACK, born Hopkinsville, Kentucky, December 20, 1968; admitted to bar, 1994, Ohio; 1995, Kentucky. *Education:* Murray State University (B.A., 1990); Salmon P. Chase College of Law, Northern Kentucky University (J.D., 1994). ***PRACTICE AREAS:*** Litigation. ***Email:*** david.black@dinslaw.com

J. DAVID BRITTINGHAM, born Birmingham, Alabama, March 3, 1965; admitted to bar, 1993, Ohio; 1994, Kentucky and U.S. District Court, Eastern District of Kentucky; 1995, U.S. District Court, Western District of Kentucky; 1997, U.S. District Court, Southern and Northern Districts of Ohio, U.S. Court of Appeals, Sixth Circuit and U.S. Supreme Court. *Education:* University of Mississippi (B.F.A., 1988); Salmon P. Chase College of Law, Northern Kentucky University (J.D., cum laude, 1993). Member, Moot Court Board. Editor, Northern Kentucky Law Review, 1992-1993. ***PRACTICE AREAS:*** General Litigation; Products Liability; Commercial Litigation; Complex Litigation. ***Email:*** david.brittingham@dinslaw.com

JOHN E. CHRISTOPHER, born Charlottesville, Virginia, May 18, 1967; admitted to bar, 1994, Kentucky and U.S. Tax Court; 1995, Ohio. *Education:* University of Kentucky (B.A., 1990); Salmon P. Chase College of Law (J.D., cum laude, 1993); University of Florida (LL.M., Taxation, 1994). ***PRACTICE AREAS:*** Estate Planning; Business Organizations and Transactions; Taxation; Foundations and other Tax Exempt Organizations. ***Email:*** john.christopher@dinslaw.com

STERLING W. COLVIN, born Lexington, Kentucky, December 28, 1969; admitted to bar, 1995, Kentucky; 1998, Ohio; U.S. District Court, Eastern District of Kentucky. *Education:* University of Kentucky (B.A., with distinction, 1992); Salmon P. Chase College of Law (J.D., cum laude, 1995). Phi Alpha Delta; Order of Curia. *Member:* Cincinnati, Ohio State and Kentucky Bar Associations. ***PRACTICE AREAS:*** Real Property Law; Corporate. ***Email:*** sterling.colvin@dinslaw.com

JASON B. SIMS, born Cincinnati, Ohio, October 8, 1965; admitted to bar, 1994, Ohio; 1997, U.S. Court of International Trade and U.S. Court of Federal Claims. *Education:* Wright State University (B.S., 1988); University of Cincinnati (J.D., with distinction, 1993). *Member:* Cincinnati, Ohio State, Kentucky and American Bar Associations. ***PRACTICE AREAS:*** General Corporate; Franchise Law; Securities; Commercial Law. ***Email:*** jason.sims@dinslaw.com

LEE M. STAUTBERG, born St. Paul, Minnesota; admitted to bar, 1993, Ohio. *Education:* Ohio State University (B.S.B.A., cum laude, 1990; J.D., 1993). Certified Public Accountant, Ohio (inactive). *Member:* Cincinnati and Ohio State Bar Associations. ***PRACTICE AREAS:*** Corporate; Tax. ***Email:*** stautber@dinslaw.com

A. SCOTT FRUECHTEMEYER, born Cincinnati, Ohio, May 25, 1969; admitted to bar, 1995, Ohio; 1998, Georgia. *Education:* University of Michigan (B.A., 1991); University of Minnesota (J.D., cum laude, 1995). *Member:* Ohio State and American Bar Associations. ***PRACTICE AREAS:*** Corporate Law; Mergers and Acquisitions; Securities. ***Email:*** scott.fruechtemeyer@dinslaw.com

LOUISE SADOWSKY BROCK, born Chicago, Illinois, May 27, 1971; admitted to bar, 1996, Ohio; 1997, U.S. District Court, Southern District of Ohio; 1998, U.S. Court of Appeals, Sixth Circuit; 2000, U.S. Supreme Court; 2005, U.S. District Court, Western District of Michigan. *Education:* University of Illinois (B.A., summa cum laude, 1993); University of Michigan (J.D., cum laude, 1996). Listed in: 2005 Forty Under 40, Cincinnati Business Courier; Ohio Super Lawyers Rising Stars in 2005; Rising Star, YWCA of Greater Cincinnati, 2002; Cincinnati Academy of Leadership for Lawyers, 2005. *Member:* Cincinnati, Ohio State and American Bar Associations. ***REPORTED CASES:*** N.L.R.B. v. Kentucky River Community Care, Inc., 532 U.S. 706 (2001); Paquette v. City of Mason, 250 F.Supp.2d 840 (S.D. Ohio 2002); Brown v. EG&G Mound Applied Technologies, Inc., 117 F.Supp.2d 671 (S.D. Ohio 2000). ***PRACTICE AREAS:*** Employment Law (90%); Labor Law (10%). ***Email:*** louise.brock@dinslaw.com

ROBERT A. CARPENTER, born Columbus, Ohio, January 4, 1970; admitted to bar, 1995, Ohio; 1998, Kentucky; 1999, Indiana; U.S. Supreme Court; U.S. Court of Appeals, Sixth Circuit; U.S. District Court, Southern and Northern Districts of Ohio; U.S. District Court, Eastern and Western Districts of Kentucky; U.S. District Court, Northern and Southern Districts of Indiana. *Education:* Hanover College (B.A., magna cum laude, 1992); University of Cincinnati (J.D., 1995). Recipient: American Jurisprudence Award in Civil Procedure; James Helmer Award, 1994-1995 for Most Valuable Contribution to University of Cincinnati Law Review. Member, 1993-1994 and Citations Editor, 1994-1995, University of Cincinnati Law Review. Eagle Scout. *Member:* Cincinnati, Ohio State, Kentucky and

(This Listing Continued)

DINSMORE & SHOHL LLP, Cincinnati—Continued

Indiana State Bar Associations; Defense Research Institute. ***PRACTICE AREAS:*** Complex and Multi-District Litigation; Medical Malpractice; Products Liability. ***Email:*** bob.carpenter@dinslaw.com

JOHN V. HARMEYER, born Cincinnati, Ohio, October 12, 1969; admitted to bar, 1996, Ohio; U.S. District Court, Southern District of Ohio; registered to practice before U.S. Patent and Trademark Office. *Education:* University of Dayton (B.S. in Electrical Engineering, magna cum laude, 1992); University of Cincinnati (J.D., 1996). Order of Coif. Named Ohio Super Lawyer Rising Star, 2005. *Member:* Cincinnati and American Bar Associations; American Intellectual Property Law Association; Cincinnati Intellectual Property Law Association. ***PRACTICE AREAS:*** Intellectual Property; Patents; Computers and Software; Copyrights; Trademarks; Intellectual Property Licensing. ***Email:*** john.harmeyer@dinslaw.com

GREGORY P. ADAMS, born Montreal, Canada, September 5, 1954; admitted to bar, 1979, Massachusetts; 1991, Ohio. *Education:* Middlebury College (A.B., 1976); University of Exeter, England; Suffolk University (J.D., 1979). Senior Editor, Immigration and Nationality Law. Listed in: "The Best Lawyers in America" since 1991; "An International Who's Who of Corporate Immigration Lawyers" since 1997. Named "Ohio Super Lawyer," 2004—. *Member:* Cincinnati Bar Association; American Immigration Lawyers Association. ***PRACTICE AREAS:*** Immigration; Naturalization Law. ***Email:*** gregory.adams@dinslaw.com

DOUGLAS HALPERT, born Brooklyn, New York, November 9, 1962; admitted to bar, 1989, New York; 1994, Ohio. *Education:* University of Chicago (B.A., 1984); Fordham University (J.D., 1988). Author, "Transferring Foreign Employees to Work in the United States: The L Visa," Northern Kentucky Business Journal, April 2001. *Member:* Cincinnati Bar Association; American Immigration Lawyers Association. ***PRACTICE AREAS:*** Immigration (100%); Nationality Law. ***Email:*** douglas.halpert@dinslaw.com

ASSOCIATES

G. FRANKLIN MILLER, born Mansfield, Ohio, March 24, 1938; admitted to bar, 1963, Ohio. *Education:* Columbia University (B.A., 1960); University of Michigan (J.D., 1963). Order of the Coif. Assistant Editor, Michigan Law Review, 1962-1963. ***PRACTICE AREAS:*** Real Estate Law.

CHRISTINE L. McBROOM, born Indianapolis, Indiana, October 23, 1953; admitted to bar, 1981, Ohio; U.S. Supreme Court; U.S. District Court, Southern District of Ohio. *Education:* The Ohio State University (B.S., 1975); University of Dayton (J.D., 1981). Law Clerk to the Hon. Robert A. Steinberg, Magistrate, U.S. District Court, Southern District of Ohio, 1981-1982. *Member:* Cincinnati, Ohio State and American Bar Associations; Better Housing League (Member, Board of Trustees, 1988-1997); Central Committee of the Milford Exempted Village School District. ***PRACTICE AREAS:*** Real Estate; Finance; Leases and Leasing. ***Email:*** chris.mcbroom@dinslaw.com

RICHARD D. POROTSKY, JR., born Cincinnati, Ohio, October 10, 1970; admitted to bar, 1996, Ohio and U.S. District Court, Southern District of Ohio; 2000, U.S. Court of Appeals, Sixth Circuit; 2004, Kentucky. *Education:* Vanderbilt University (B.S., summa cum laude, 1993; J.D., 1996). Editorial Board Member, Vanderbilt Journal of Transitional Law. ***PRACTICE AREAS:*** Litigation; Insurance Coverage. ***Email:*** porotsky@dinslaw.com

STEVE N. SIEGEL, born Newark, Ohio, January 19, 1950; admitted to bar, 1997, Ohio; 1999, U.S. District Court, Southern District of Ohio. *Education:* Denison University (B.A., 1972); Capital University Law School (J.D., cum laude, 1997). *Member:* Cincinnati, Ohio State, American and Federal Bar Associations. ***PRACTICE AREAS:*** Business Litigation; Environmental Litigation; Environmental Compliance; Environmental Compliance Audits. ***Email:*** steve.siegel@dinslaw.com

ROBERT H. HOSKINS, born Hamilton, Ohio, April 28, 1964; admitted to bar, 1997, Ohio and U.S. District Court, Southern and Northern Districts of Ohio; 1998, Kentucky; 1999, U.S. District Court, Western District of Kentucky. *Education:* Earlham College (B.A., 1986); University of Dayton (J.D., 1997). *Member:* Cincinnati, Ohio State and Kentucky State Bar Associations. ***PRACTICE AREAS:*** Litigation; Domestic Relations. ***Email:*** robert.hoskins@dinslaw.com

BRYAN E. PACHECO, born Akron, Ohio, March 21, 1969; admitted to bar, 1997, Ohio; 1998, U.S. District Court, Southern District of Ohio; 2001, U.S. Court of Appeals, Sixth Circuit. *Education:* University of Akron (B.A., 1992); University of Cincinnati (J.D., 1997). Order of the Coif. Member, Cincinnati Law Review. ***PRACTICE AREAS:*** General Litigation. ***Email:*** bryan.pacheco@dinslaw.com

CHRISTOPHER L. MUZZO, born Cincinnati, Ohio, May 13, 1972; admitted to bar, 1997, Ohio; 1998, Kentucky; U.S. District Court, Southern District of Ohio. *Education:* Northwestern University (B.A., 1994; J.D., cum laude, 1997). ***PRACTICE AREAS:*** Litigation. ***Email:*** muzzo@dinslaw.com

MATTHEW D. SHULER, born Lexington, Ohio, July 24, 1972; admitted to bar, 1998, Ohio; 2000, Kentucky and U.S. District Court, Southern District of Ohio. *Education:* The Ohio State University (B.S.B.A., 1995); Cleveland-Marshall College of Law (J.D., summa cum laude, 1998). *Member:* Cincinnati, Ohio State and Kentucky Bar Associations. ***PRACTICE AREAS:*** Litigation; Products Liability; Medical Malpractice Defense. ***Email:*** matthew.shuler@dinslaw.com

HELANA A. DARROW, born Ashland, Kentucky, May 1, 1972; admitted to bar, 1998, Ohio. *Education:* Morehead State University (B.A., 1994); University of Cincinnati (J.D., 1998). *Member:* Cincinnati and Ohio State Bar Associations. ***PRACTICE AREAS:*** Employee Benefits; Taxation. ***Email:*** helana.darrow@dinslaw.com

NEAL A. FRINK, born Bloomington, Indiana, February 18, 1963; admitted to bar, 1999, Ohio; registered to practice before U.S. Patent and Trademark Office. *Education:* Carnegie Mellon University (B.S., Chemical Engineering, 1985); Northern Kentucky University (J.D., cum laude, 1998). Member, Institute of Hazardous Materials Management, 1994-2000. Certified Hazardous Materials Manager, 1994-2000. *Member:* Cincinnati and Ohio State Bar Associations. ***PRACTICE AREAS:*** Environmental Law; Litigation. ***Email:*** nfrink@dinslaw.com

DANIEL L. JONES, JR., born Fort Thomas, Kentucky, May 18, 1967; admitted to bar, 1999, Ohio and U.S. District Court, Southern District of Ohio; 2000, Kentucky. *Education:* Northern Kentucky University (B.O.S., 1994; J.D., cum laude, 1999). *Member:* Cincinnati, Kentucky and Ohio State Bar Associations. ***PRACTICE AREAS:*** Insurance Defense; Products Liability. ***Email:*** daniel.jones@dinslaw.com

DAVID P. FORNSHELL, born Lebanon, Ohio, March 23, 1973; admitted to bar, 1999, Ohio; 2000, U.S. District Court, Southern District of Ohio; 2004, U.S. District Court, Northern District of Ohio and U.S. Supreme Court. *Education:* Ohio University (B.B.A., summa cum laude, 1995); Pepperdine School of Law (J.D., cum laude, 1999). Order of the Barristers. Prosecuting Attorney, City of Blue Ash, Ohio. Board Member, Executive Committee, Warren County Republican Party. *Member:* Cincinnati, Warren County and American Bar Associations. ***PRACTICE AREAS:*** Commercial Litigation; Criminal Law; Municipal Law. ***Email:*** dfornshe@dinslaw.com

MICHAEL G. DAILEY, born Cincinnati, Ohio, September 22, 1966; admitted to bar, 1999, Ohio. *Education:* Miami University (B.S., 1988); University of Cincinnati (J.D., 1999). Author: "Preemption of State Court Class Action Claims for Securities Fraud: Should Federal Law Trump?" 67 University Cincinnati Law Review, 1999. *Member:* Cincinnati and Ohio State Bar Associations. ***PRACTICE AREAS:*** Corporate; Mergers and Acquisitions; Commercial Transactions; Banking. ***Email:*** mdailey@dinslaw.com

NOAH J. STERN, born Albany, New York, April 26, 1971; admitted to bar, 1999, Ohio. *Education:* University of California, Berkeley (B.A., 1993); Indiana University at Bloomington (M.A., 1996); New York University School of Law (J.D., 1999). *Member:* Cincinnati and Ohio State Bar Associations. ***PRACTICE AREAS:*** Tax; Corporate. ***Email:*** noah.stern@dinslaw.com

H. TOBY SCHISLER, born Washington, D.C., January 19, 1972; admitted to bar, 1997, Ohio, U.S. District Court, Southern District of Ohio; 1998, U.S. Court of Appeals, Sixth Circuit. *Education:* Miami University (B.A., cum laude, 1994); University of Cincinnati College of Law (J.D., 1997). Member: Moot Court Board; Order of the Barristers. Recipient: College Moot Court Award; American Jurisprudence Award for Constitutional Law. *Member:* Cincinnati, Ohio State, Federal and American Bar Associations. ***PRACTICE AREAS:*** Litigation; Product Liability; Commercial Litigation; Employment Litigation. ***Email:*** tschisle@dinslaw.com

JENNIFER O. MITCHELL, born Warren, Ohio, November 16, 1973; admitted to bar, 1998, Ohio; 1999, U.S. District Court, Northern District of Ohio; 2000, U.S. District Court, Southern District of Ohio; 2001, Kentucky and U.S. Court of Appeals, Sixth Circuit; 2004, U.S. District Court, Eastern District of Kentucky. *Education:* Miami University (B.A., 1995); University of Akron (J.D., cum laude, 1998). Phi Delta Phi. Adjunct Professor, University of Akron School of Law, Legal Writing, 1998-1999. Colerain High School, Legal Advisor, Mock Trial (1999-2001). Mother of Mercy High School, Legal Advisor, Mock Trial (2001-2005). *Member:* Cincinnati (Member, Committees on: Health Care Law, Mentoring, and Membership), Ohio State, Kentucky and American Bar Associations; Defense Research Institute; American Health Lawyers Association; Ohio Association of Civil Trial Attorneys; United Way (Healthy People Vision Council and HPVC Program Review Committee). ***PRACTICE AREAS:*** Litigation; Health Care Law; Products Liability; Medical Malpractice; Medicare and Medicaid; Privacy Law; Regulatory Law; Antitrust and Trade Regulation; Torts. ***Email:*** jennifer.mitchell@dinslaw.com

CHRISTOPHER R. McDOWELL, born Huntington, West Virginia, February 5, 1969; admitted to bar, 1994, West Virginia; 2000, Ohio; 2002, Kentucky; U.S. Supreme Court; U.S. Court of Appeals, Sixth and Eleventh Circuits; U.S. District Court, Southern Districts of Ohio and U.S. District Court, Southern District of West Virginia; U.S. District Court, Eastern District of Kentucky. *Education:* Marshall University (B.A., 1991); West Virginia University (J.D., 1994). [U.S. Army Judge Advocate General's Corps.]. ***PRACTICE AREAS:*** Civil Litigation; Criminal Litigation. ***Email:*** christopher.mcdowell@dinslaw.com

BECKY BARLOW FITZSIMMONS, born Princeton, New Jersey, April 2, 1968; admitted to bar, 2000, Ohio. *Education:* Western Maryland College (B.A., 1990); University of Maryland at Baltimore (J.D., 2000). Phi Beta Kappa. ***PRACTICE AREAS:*** Commercial Real Estate; Corporate Law. ***Email:*** becky.fitzsimmons@dinslaw.com

MELISSA L. KORFHAGE, born Louisville, Kentucky, June 16, 1975; admitted to bar, 2000, Ohio and U.S. District Court, Southern District of Ohio; 2001, Kentucky. *Education:* Bellarmine College (B.A., 1997); University of Louisville, Louis D. Brandeis School of Law (J.D., 2000). *Member:* Cincinnati, Ohio State and Kentucky Bar Associations. ***PRACTICE AREAS:*** Products Liability; Litigation. ***Email:*** mkorfhag@dinslaw.com

SUZANNE CAHILL McNABB, born Cincinnati, Ohio, January 20, 1972; admitted to bar, 2000, Ohio. *Education:* Trinity College (B.A., 1994); Vanderbilt University (J.D., 2000). *Member:* Cincinnati and Ohio State Bar Associations. ***PRACTICE AREAS:*** Business Law; Corporate Law; Mergers, Acquisitions and Divestitures. ***Email:*** smcnabb@dinslaw.com

AMANDA P. LENHART, born Cincinnati, Ohio, May 1, 1975; admitted to bar, 2000, Ohio; 2001, U.S. District Court, Southern District of Ohio and U.S. Court of Appeals, Sixth Circuit. *Education:* Miami University (B.Phil., 1997); University of Cincinnati (J.D., 2000). Author: "Corporate Confines to Parent Liability Under CERCLA: United States v. Bestfoods," 67 U. Cin. L. Rev. 1357, 1999; "Manipulated by Miranda: A Critical Analysis of Bright Lines and Voluntary Confines Under United States v. Dickinson," 68 U. Cin. L. Rev. 555, 2000. *Member:* Cincinnati and Ohio State Bar Associations. ***PRACTICE AREAS:*** General Litigation; Securities Litigation. ***Email:*** aprebble@dinslaw.com

DAVID S. SULLIVAN, born Pikeville, Kentucky, November 18, 1975; admitted to bar, 2000, Ohio and U.S. District Court, Southern District of Ohio; 2001, Kentucky. *Education:* Grove City College (B.A., magna cum laude, 1997); University of Kentucky (J.D., magna cum laude, 2000). Phi Delta Phi. Order of the Coif. Author: "Disappointed Bidder Standing to Challenge a Government Contract Award: A Proposal for Change in Kentucky Procure-

(This Listing Continued)

ment Law," Kentucky Law Journal, Volume 88, No. 1, 1999-2000. *Member:* Cincinnati, Ohio State and Kentucky Bar Associations. ***PRACTICE AREAS:*** Complex Commercial Litigation. ***Email:*** david.sullivan@dinslaw.com

JAMES A. MARX, born Dayton, Ohio, May 20, 1964; admitted to bar, 1997, Ohio. *Education:* University of Cincinnati (B.A., 1986; M.B.A., 1989); Ohio State University (J.D., 1997). *Member:* Cincinnati and Ohio State Bar Associations. ***PRACTICE AREAS:*** Corporate; Corporate Finance; Commercial; Real Estate. ***Email:*** jmarx@dinslaw.com

SCOTT A. CRISLER, born Columbia, South Carolina, June 16, 1965; admitted to bar, 1995, Georgia; 1996, District of Columbia; 2001, Ohio; 2003 Kentucky. *Education:* University of Georgia (B.B.A., 1990); University of Oklahoma (J.D., 1995). Member, American Indian Law Review. *Member:* Cincinnati, Ohio State, Kentucky and American Bar Associations; State Bar of Georgia; The District of Columbia Bar. ***PRACTICE AREAS:*** Products Liability Litigation and Mass Tort (50%); Business Litigation (25%); General Practice (15%); Criminal (10%). ***Email:*** scrisler@dinslaw.com

JON B. ALLISON, born Dayton, Ohio, October 25, 1970; admitted to bar, 2001, Ohio; U.S. Court of Appeals, Sixth Circuit and U.S. District Court, Southern District of Ohio. *Education:* University of Michigan (B.A., 1994); University of Cincinnati (J.D., 2001). ***PRACTICE AREAS:*** Labor and Employment; Employment Litigation; National Labor Relations Act. ***Email:*** jon.allison@dinslaw.com

CLAYTON L. KUHNELL, born Cincinnati, Ohio, December 18, 1975; admitted to bar, 2001, Ohio, U.S. District Court, Southern District of Ohio and registered to practice before U.S. Patent and Trademark Office. *Education:* University of Cincinnati (B.S.Ch.E., magna cum laude, 1998; J.D., 2001). Dean's List. *Member:* Cincinnati, Ohio State and American Bar Associations. ***PRACTICE AREAS:*** Intellectual Property; Patent Prosecution and Litigation. ***Email:*** ckuhnell@dinslaw.com

JOSHUA A. LORENTZ, born Orlando, Florida, February 12, 1975; admitted to bar, 2001, Ohio, U.S. District Court, Southern District of Ohio, U.S. Court of Appeals, Sixth and Federal Circuits and registered to practice before the U.S. Patent and Trademark Office. *Education:* Ohio University (B.S., Biology; B.A., Political Science, 1998); University of Dayton School of Law (J.D., 2001). Member, American Intellectual Property Law Association, 1999. ***LANGUAGES:*** Spanish. ***PRACTICE AREAS:*** Litigation; Intellectual Property. ***Email:*** jlorentz@dinslaw.com

M. DAVE O'GUINN, III, born December 29, 1969; admitted to bar, 2001, Ohio; 2002, U.S. District Court, Southern District of Ohio. *Education:* DePauw University (B.S., 1992); Political Science Indiana University (M.S., 1994); Notre Dame Law School (J.D., magna cum laude, 2001). *Member:* Cincinnati, Ohio State and American Bar Associations. ***PRACTICE AREAS:*** Labor and Employment. ***Email:*** goguinn@dinslaw.com

ERIC M. ROBBINS, born Cincinnati, Ohio, June 10, 1974; admitted to bar, 2001, Ohio; U.S. Court of Appeals, Sixth and Federal Circuits; U.S. District Court, Southern District of Ohio; registered to practice before the United States Patent and Trademark Office. *Education:* University of Notre Dame (B.S.E.E., 1996); University of Cincinnati (J.D., 2001). Dean's List; Order of the Coif. *Member:* Cincinnati and Ohio State Bar Associations. ***PRACTICE AREAS:*** Patents; Intellectual Property; Litigation; Trademarks. ***Email:*** eric.robbins@dinslaw.com

LORI S. DRASNIN, born Cincinnati, Ohio, February 19, 1976; admitted to bar, 2001, Ohio; U.S. District Court, Southern District of Ohio. *Education:* University of Michigan (B.A., English; B.A., Psychology, 1998); Emory University School of Law (J.D., 2001). *Member:* Cincinnati and Ohio State Bar Associations. ***PRACTICE AREAS:*** Litigation; Products Liability; Toxic Torts. ***Email:*** lori.drasnin@dinslaw.com

ALICIA L. WILHELMY, born Fayetteville, Arkansas, 1975; admitted to bar, 2001, Ohio. *Education:* Xavier University (H.B.A., cum laude, 1997); University of Cincinnati (J.D., 2001). *Member:* Cincinnati (Member, Employee Benefits Committee) and Ohio State Bar Associations. ***PRACTICE AREAS:*** Employee Benefits; Benefits and Compensation. ***Email:*** alicia.wilhelmy@dinslaw.com

DONALD W. MALLORY, born Hamilton, Ohio, May 21, 1966; admitted to bar, 1999, Ohio; 2001, Kentucky, U.S. Supreme Court, U.S. Court of Appeals, Sixth Circuit, U.S. District Court, Southern District of Ohio, U.S. District Court, Eastern District of Kentucky, U.S. District Court, Western District of Kentucky and U.S. Tax Court. *Education:* University of Cincinnati (B.B.A., 1995); Northern Kentucky University, Salmon P. Chase College of Law (J.D., magna cum laude, 1999). Adjunct Professor, Salmon P. Chase College of Law. Certified Public Accountant (Ohio). *Member:* Cincinnati, Ohio State, Kentucky and American Bar Associations. ***LANGUAGES:*** German. ***PRACTICE AREAS:*** Bankruptcy And Workout; Federal Tax; Corporate Transactions. ***Email:*** donald.mallory@dinslaw.com

TRACY ROTTNER YU, born Cincinnati, Ohio, September 17, 1974; admitted to bar, 1999, Ohio. *Education:* University of Notre Dame (B.A., cum laude, 1996); University of Cincinnati (J.D., 1999). Order of the Coif. Member, 1998 and Editorial Board Member, 1999, University of Cincinnati Law Review. Author: "'Standing' in a Quagmire, Raines v. Byrd, 117 SCT 2312 (1997)," University of Cincinnati Law Review, Volume 67, P. 639. *Member:* Cincinnati, Ohio State and American Bar Associations; International Council of Shopping Centers; Notre Dame Club of Cincinnati. ***PRACTICE AREAS:*** Leases and Leasing; Commercial Real Estate; Zoning, Planning and Land Use. ***Email:*** tracy.yu@dinslaw.com

GEOFFREY L. OBERHAUS, born Bowling Green, Ohio, December 15, 1969; admitted to bar, 1998, Ohio; 1999, U.S. District Court, Southern District of Ohio; registered to practice before U.S. Patent and Trademark Office. *Education:* University of Detroit (B.Chem.Eng., cum laude, 1992); Rutgers University, Camden (J.D., 1998). Author: "The Dormant Commerce Clause Dumps New Jersey's Solid Waste Flow Control Regulations," Vol. 29, No. 2. Rutgers Law Journal. *Member:* Cincinnati and American Bar Associations; American Intellectual Property Law Association; Cincinnati Intellectual Property Law Association; Intellectual Property Owners Association. ***PRACTICE AREAS:*** Litigation; Intellectual Property; Patents. ***Email:*** geof.oberhaus@dinslaw.com

ALLYSON B. HANDLER, born Brooklyn, New York, May 18, 1971; admitted to bar, 1996, Maryland; 1998, District of Columbia; 2003, Ohio. *Education:* University of Pennsylvania (B.A., 1993); Georgetown University Law Center (J.D., magna cum laude, 1996). Order of the Coif. ***PRACTICE AREAS:*** Labor and Employment. ***Email:*** allyson.handler@dinslaw.com

(This Listing Continued)

JAMES M. WHERLEY, JR., born Dover, Ohio, July 15, 1974; admitted to bar, 2001, Ohio; U.S. District Court, Southern District of Ohio. *Education:* Grove City College (B.S., 1997); University of Cincinnati (J.D., 2001). Order of the Coif. Member, University of Cincinnati Law Review, 2000-2001.*Member:* Ohio Bar Association. ***PRACTICE AREAS:*** Litigation; Health Care. ***Email:*** james.wherley@dinslaw.com

DOUGLAS J. FEICHTNER, born Cincinnati, Ohio, July 15, 1977; admitted to bar, 2002, Ohio; U.S. District Court, Southern District of Ohio. *Education:* Miami University (B.A., 1999); University of Cincinnati College of Law (J.D., 2002). Evans Scholars, Par Club Member. *Member:* Cincinnati and Ohio State Bar Associations. ***PRACTICE AREAS:*** Litigation. ***Email:*** douglas.feichtner@dinslaw.com

PETER J. GEORGITON, born Columbus, Ohio, December 19, 1976; admitted to bar, 2002, Ohio. *Education:* Wittenberg University (B.A., summa cum laude, 1999); The Ohio State University, Moritz College of Law (J.D., with honors, 2002). Phi Beta Kappa. Editor-in-Chief, Ohio State Law Journal. *Member:* Cincinnati and Ohio State Bar Associations. ***PRACTICE AREAS:*** Litigation; Insurance Coverage; Commercial Litigation; Workers' Compensation. ***Email:*** peter.georgiton@dinslaw.com

ANDREW R. KWIATKOWSKI, born Milwaukee, Wisconsin, October 20, 1976; admitted to bar, 2002, Ohio; U.S. District Court, Southern District of Ohio. *Education:* Duquesne University (B.A., English/Psychology, 1999; J.D., 2002). *Member:* Cincinnati and Ohio State Bar Associations. ***PRACTICE AREAS:*** Litigation; Health Care; Medicare and Medicaid; Consumer Law. ***Email:*** andrew.kwiatkowski@dinslaw.com

SUSAN M. LUKEN, born Cincinnati, Ohio, December 5, 1969; admitted to bar, 2002, Ohio; U.S. District Court, Southern District of Ohio. *Education:* University of Cincinnati (B.A., 1993); University of Cincinnati College of Law (J.D., 2002). *Member:* Cincinnati and Ohio State Bar Associations. ***PRACTICE AREAS:*** Insurance Coverage; Litigation. ***Email:*** susan.luken@dinslaw.com

MARGARET M. MAGGIO, born Covington, Kentucky, March 26, 1954; admitted to bar, 2002, Ohio; 2003, Florida and Kentucky. *Education:* Loyola University of Chicago (B.S.N., summa cum laude, 1976); University of Illinois (M.S., 1982); Salmon P. Chase College of Law, Northern Kentucky University (J.D., summa cum laude, 2002). *Member:* Cincinnati, Ohio, Florida, Kentucky, Northern Kentucky and American Bar Associations; The American Association of Nurse Attorneys, The Defense Research Institute, Ohio Association of Civil Trial Attorneys. ***PRACTICE AREAS:*** Litigation. ***Email:*** margaret.maggio@dinslaw.com

EMERSON C. MOSER, born Muncie, Indiana, June 1, 1976; admitted to bar, 2002, Ohio. *Education:* Purdue University (B.A., 1999; B.S., 1999); Wake Forest University School of Law (J.D., magna cum laude, 2002). *Member:* Cincinnati, Ohio State (Member, Labor & Employment Section) and American (Member, Labor & Employment Section) Bar Associations. ***PRACTICE AREAS:*** Labor and Employment; Employment Litigation; Equal Employment Opportunity Law; Employment Discrimination and Harassment; WARN Act; Disability Discrimination; Noncompete Litigation; National Labor Relations Act. ***Email:*** emerson.moser@dinslaw.com

MICHAEL J. NEWMAN, born Somerville, New Jersey, July 15, 1960; admitted to bar, 1989, Ohio; 1990, U.S. District Court, Southern District of Ohio; 1993, U.S. Court of Appeals, Sixth Circuit; 2003, U.S. District Court, Northern District of Ohio. *Education:* New York University (B.F.A., 1982); American University (J.D., with honors, 1989); Harvard Law School (Advanced Mediator Training Certificate, 2004). Recipient: Certificate of Appreciation, Chase Law School Dean, 1993; U.S. District Court Special Service Award, 1999. Law Clerk to: U.S. Magistrate Judge Jack Sherman, Jr., Southern District of Ohio, 1989-1998, 1999-2003; Judge Nathaniel R. Jones, Sixth U.S. Circuit Court of Appeals, 1998-1999. Adjunct Professor of Law: Pretrial Litigation, University of Cincinnati College of Law, 1996, 1998; Salmon P. Chase College of Law, Northern Kentucky University, 1991-2002; Appellate Advocacy, University of Dayton School of Law, 1997. Author: "United States Magistrate Judges: Suggestions to Increase the Efficiency of their Civil Role," 19 Northern Kentucky Law Review 99, 1991; "Judicial Profile: Honorable Jack Sherman, Jr.," 47 Federal Lawyer 16, January 2000; "Reflections on the Bench-Bar Handbook," 47 Federal Lawyer 4, March/April 2000; "Working as a Career Law Clerk," Cincinnati Bar Association Report, April 2000; "In-House Court Mediation in the U.S. District Courts," 48 Federal Lawyer 4, October 2001; "Current Reflections on Two ADR Efforts in the Federal Courts," 51 Federal Lawyer 4, January 2004. Co-Author, "The Bench-Bar Handbook for the Southern District of Ohio," 1999. Member, National Editorial Board, 1997— and Judicial Profiles Editor, 2003—, "The Federal Lawyer" Magazine. Frequent Lecturer, Employment Law. Volunteer Mediator: United States District Court for the Southern District of Ohio, 2003—; "Advanced Mediation Workshop," Harvard Law School, 2004. Member, Board of Trustees. Collaborative Law Center of Cincinnati, Inc., 1997-2003. Former Member, Board of Trustees, Big Brothers/Big Sisters Association of Cincinnati. Volunteer Big Brother. *Member:* Cincinnati (Member, 1993-1995 and Co-Chair, 1995-1997, Young Lawyers Community Service Committee; Member: Community Service Board of Trustees Committee, 1997-1999; Oral History Committee, 1994-1995) and Federal (Member: Executive Committee, Cincinnati-Northern Kentucky Chapter, 1995—; National Council, 2001—; Membership Chair, 1996-2000; Treasurer, 2000-2001; Secretary, 2001-2002; Vice President, 2003-2004; Chapter President, 2004-2005) Bar Associations; Potter Stewart Inns of Court (Barrister). ***PRACTICE AREAS:*** Labor and Employment; Alternative Dispute Resolution; Litigation. ***Email:*** michael.newman@dinslaw.com

JENNIFER K. SWARTZ, born Marion, Ohio, July 19, 1975; admitted to bar, 2000, Ohio; 2001, Iowa; 2002, U.S. Court of Appeals, Fourth Circuit; 2003, U.S. District Court, Southern District of Ohio; 2004, U.S. District Court, Northern District of Ohio and U.S. Court of Appeals, Sixth Circuit. *Education:* Bowling Green State University (B.A., magna cum laude, 1997); Drake University (J.D., with high honors, 2000). Order of the Coif. *Member:* Cincinnati, Ohio State and Federal Bar Associations. ***PRACTICE AREAS:*** Labor and Employment. ***Email:*** jennifer.swartz@dinslaw.com

KATRINA R. ATKINS, born Cincinnati, Ohio, February 27, 1975; admitted to bar, 2003, Ohio and U.S. District Court, Southern District of Ohio. *Education:* University of Cincinnati (B.S.W., cum laude, 2003); Salmon P. Chase College of Law (J.D., summa cum laude, 2003). ***PRACTICE AREAS:*** Complex Litigation; Litigation; Products Liability; Medical Malpractice. ***Email:*** katrina.atkins@dinslaw.com

(This Listing Continued)

DINSMORE & SHOHL LLP, Cincinnati—Continued

JESSICA S. HYLANDER, admitted to bar, 2003, Ohio. *Education:* Miami University (B.A., 1999); University of Michigan (J.D., 2003). *Member:* Cincinnati and Ohio State Bar Associations. ***PRACTICE AREAS:*** Litigation; Municipal Law; Government; Products Liability; Workers Compensation. ***Email:*** jessica.hylander@dinslaw.com

SARAH V. LEWIS, admitted to bar, 2003, Ohio. *Education:* DePauw University (B.A., cum laude, 1995); College of William & Mary (J.D., 2003). Order of the Coif. *Member:* Cincinnati and Ohio State Bar Associations. ***PRACTICE AREAS:*** Litigation; Commercial Litigation; Banking Litigation; Products Liability. ***Email:*** sarah.lewis@dinslaw.com

PETE S. SINGER, born Cincinnati, Ohio, July 3, 1977; admitted to bar, 2003, Ohio; 2004, U.S. District Court, Southern District of Ohio; 2005, U.S. District Court, Northern District of Ohio. *Education:* Miami University (B.A., cum laude, 1999); University of Dayton (J.D., magna cum laude, 2003). Member, Mock Trial Team, University of Dayton School of Law. Executive Editor, University of Dayton Law Review. Author: "The Three Stooges' Latest Act: Attempting to Define the Scope of Protection the First Amendment Provides to Works of Art Depicting Celebrities," 27 U. Dayton L. Rev. 313 (2002); "Mounting a Fair Use Defense to the Anti-Circumvention Provisions of the Digital Millenium Copyright Act," 28 U. Dayton L. Rev. 111 (2002); "Requests for Admission," Drug Product Liability, Vol. 3, Ch. 26. (Matthew Bender & Co. Inc.). *Member:* Cincinnati Bar Association. ***PRACTICE AREAS:*** Construction Law; Health Care; Products Liability Defense; Medical Malpractice Defense. ***Email:*** peter.singer@dinslaw.com

DAVID A. WHALEY, born Indianapolis, Indiana, June 20, 1978; admitted to bar, 2003, Ohio. *Education:* University of Dayton (B.S., 2000; J.D., magna cum laude, 2003). University of Cincinnati College of Law Rendigs Fry Products Liability Moot Court Competition, 2002. Recipient, Computer Assisted Learning Institute Award, Commercial Paper, 2002, Secured Transactions, 2003, Conflicts of Law, 2002 and Evidence for Civil Litigators, 2002. Research Editor, University of Dayton Law Review, 2002-2003. Law Clerk to Hon. A.J. Wagner, Court of Common Pleas for Montgomery County, 2001-2002. *Member:* Cincinnati, Ohio State and American Bar Associations. ***PRACTICE AREAS:*** Employee Benefits. ***Email:*** david.whaley@dinslaw.com

BRIAN K. GROEMMINGER, admitted to bar, 2003, Indiana; 2004, Ohio. *Education:* Indiana State University (B.S., summa cum laude, 1992; M.B.A., summa cum laude, 1994; J.D., summa cum laude, 2003). *Member:* Cincinnati and Indiana State Bar Associations. ***PRACTICE AREAS:*** Real Estate; Corporate. ***Email:*** brian.groemminger@dinslaw.com

MARY E. WIDDOWSON, born Cincinnati, Ohio, December 30, 1968; admitted to bar, 1998, Arizona; 2000, Navajo Nation Bar and Hopi Bar; 2004, Ohio. *Education:* Indiana State University (B.A., 1991); University of Cincinnati (M.A., 1994); University of Toledo (J.D., 1998). *Member:* Cincinnati, Coconino County and Ohio State Bar Associations; State Bar of Arizona; Navajo Nation Bar Association. ***PRACTICE AREAS:*** Products Liability. ***Email:*** mary.widdowson@dinslaw.com

CHARLES A. BRUCH, born Schenectady, New York, August 16, 1960; admitted to bar, 2003, Ohio and U.S. District Court, Southern District of Ohio. *Education:* Ohio University (B.B.A., summa cum laude, 1984); University of Cincinnati (J.D., 2002). Articles Editor, University of Cincinnati Law Review, 2001-2002. Author: "Taking the Pay Out of Payday Loans: Putting An End to the Usurious and Unconscionable Interest Rates Charged by Payday Lenders," 69 University of Cincinnati Law Review 1257, 2001. Member, University of Cincinnati Alumni Association. *Member:* Cincinnati, Ohio State and American Bar Associations. ***PRACTICE AREAS:*** Litigation. ***Email:*** charles.bruch@dinslaw.com

POLLY RICKARD PATEL, born Middletown, Ohio, November 19, 1976; admitted to bar, 2002, Ohio; U.S. District Court, Southern District of Ohio. *Education:* Miami University (B.A., 1998); Capital University (J.D., summa cum laude, 2002). *Member:* Cincinnati, Columbus and Ohio State Bar Associations. ***PRACTICE AREAS:*** Commercial Real Estate; Leases and Leasing; Real Estate. ***Email:*** polly.patel@dinslaw.com

ALISON N. SACKENHEIM, born Hamilton, Ohio, January 14, 1978; admitted to bar, 2003, Ohio and U.S. District Court, Southern Distict of Ohio. *Education:* Miami University (B.S., 2000); University of Cincinnati (J.D., 2003). *Member:* Cincinnati, Dayton and Ohio State Bar Associations; Association of Civil Trial Attorneys. ***PRACTICE AREAS:*** Workers Compensation; Litigation. ***Email:*** alison.sackenheim@dinslaw.com

STEVEN A. ABREU, born Lowell, Massachusetts, June 26, 1979; admitted to bar, 2004, Ohio. *Education:* University of Illinois at Urbana-Champaign (B.A., Political Science, 2001); The Ohio State University, Moritz College of Law (J.D., 2004). Order of the Coif. *Member:* Cincinnati, Ohio State and American Bar Associations. ***PRACTICE AREAS:*** Intellectual Property; Trademarks; Copyrights; Civil Litigation. ***Email:*** steven.abreu@dinslaw.com

SHAWN P. BURTON, born Cincinnati, Ohio, February 4, 1977; admitted to bar, 2004, Ohio. *Education:* Wittenberg University (B.A., 1999); Miami University (M.A., 2000); Toledo University College of Law (J.D., magna cum laude, 2004). Order of the Coif. ***PRACTICE AREAS:*** Employment Law; Appellate Practice; Employment Litigation; National Labor Relations Act. ***Email:*** shawn.burton@dinslaw.com

CHARLES SHANE CRASE, born Dayton, Ohio, September 2, 1972; admitted to bar, 2004, Ohio and U.S. District Court, Southern District of Ohio. *Education:* United States Naval Academy (B.S., 1994); Salmon P. Chase College of Law (J.D., magna cum laude, 2004). *Member:* Cincinnati and Federal Bar Associations. [Captain, U.S. Marine Corps, 1994-1999]. ***PRACTICE AREAS:*** Labor and Employment. ***Email:*** shane.crase@dinslaw.com

SHANA N. EATON, born Peoria, Illinois, March 9, 1977; admitted to bar, 2004, Ohio. *Education:* Indiana University, Bloomington (B.A., 1998); Georgetown University Law Center (J.D., 2004). ***LANGUAGES:*** French. ***PRACTICE AREAS:*** Litigation. ***Email:*** shana.eaton@dinslaw.com

BEN GERLACH, born Louisville, Kentucky, July 14, 1974; admitted to bar, 2004, Ohio. *Education:* University of Louisville (B.A., 1998); Salmon P. Chase College of Law (J.D., 2004). *Member:* Ohio State Bar Association. ***PRACTICE AREAS:*** Products Liability. ***Email:*** ben.gerlach@dinslaw.com

(This Listing Continued)

NICHOLAS J. KEMPHAUS, born Covington, Kentucky, August 6, 1978; admitted to bar, 2004, Ohio and U.S. District Court, Southern District of Ohio; 2005, Kentucky and U.S. District Court, Eastern District of Kentucky. *Education:* Thomas More College (B.S., Chemistry, summa cum laude, 2001); Salmon P. Chase College of Law (J.D., summa cum laude, 2004). Order of the Curia. *Member:* Cincinnati, Ohio State and Kentucky Bar Associations. ***PRACTICE AREAS:*** Litigation; Products Liability; Torts. ***Email:*** nicholas.kemphaus@dinslaw.com

ANGELINA N. JACKSON, born Dayton, Ohio, October 30, 1975; admitted to bar, 2004, Ohio and U.S. District Court, Southern District of Ohio; 2005, Kentucky. *Education:* Florida A & M University (B.A., 1998); University of Cincinnati College of Law (J.D., 2004). *Member:* Cincinnati, Ohio State (Member, Health Law Committee) and Kentucky Bar Associations. ***PRACTICE AREAS:*** Medical Malpractice; Products Liability; Torts. ***Email:*** angelina.jackson@dinslaw.com

TOBY D. MERCHANT, born Kettering, Ohio, August 29, 1978; admitted to bar, 2004, Ohio. *Education:* Cornell University (B.S., Industrial and Labor Relations, 2001); Case Western Reserve University School of Law (J.D., cum laude, 2004). ***PRACTICE AREAS:*** Corporate; Mergers and Acquisitions; Securities. ***Email:*** toby.merchant@dinslaw.com

DAVID J. MYERS, born Cincinnati, Ohio, February 26, 1978; admitted to bar, 2004, Ohio and U.S. Tax Court. *Education:* University of Cincinnati (B.B.A., cum laude, 2001); University of Notre Dame (J.D., magna cum laude, 2004). *Member:* Cincinnati, Ohio State and American Bar Associations. ***PRACTICE AREAS:*** Corporate Law; Taxation; Trusts and Estates. ***Email:*** david.myers@dinslaw.com

JAMES T. SUTTON, born Henderson, Kentucky, September 12, 1979; admitted to bar, 2004, Ohio. *Education:* Xavier University (B.S.B.A., magna cum laude, 2001); University of Kentucky College of Law (J.D., summa cum laude, 2004). Order of the Coif. *Member:* Cincinnati and Ohio State Bar Associations. ***PRACTICE AREAS:*** Corporate Law; Securities; Mergers, Acquisitions and Divestitures; Banks and Banking. ***Email:*** jay.sutton@dinslaw.com

ANDREW J. WAMSLEY, born Columbus, Ohio, February 15, 1979; admitted to bar, 2004, Ohio. *Education:* Boston University (B.A., cum laude, 2001); Georgetown University Law Center (J.D. 2004). Dean's List, 2003-2004. *Member:* Cincinnati, Ohio State and American Bar Associations. ***PRACTICE AREAS:*** Corporate; Real Estate. ***Email:*** andrew.wamsley@dinslaw.com

JODY H. ARMSTRONG, admitted to bar, 1992, Ohio. *Education:* University of Iowa (B.A., English and Political Science, 1988); DePaul University (J.D., 1992). *Member:* Dayton and Ohio State Bar Associations; International Trademark Association. ***PRACTICE AREAS:*** Intellectual Property; Trademark Licensing; Trademarks; Copyrights. ***Email:*** jody.armstrong@dinslaw.com

CLARE M. IERY, admitted to bar, 2001, Ohio; registered to practice before the U.S. Patent and Trademark Office. *Education:* University of Cincinnati (B.A., high honors, 1997; B.S., 1997); University of Cincinnati (J.D., 2001). ***PRACTICE AREAS:*** Intellectual Property; Patents; Trademarks; Copyrights. ***Email:*** clare.iery@dinslaw.com

JEFFREY A. WILLIS, born Dover, Ohio, February 21, 1975; admitted to bar, 2002, Ohio; 2004, Kentucky; 2005, U.S. District Court, Southern District of Ohio. *Education:* Bowling Green State University (B.S., Criminal Justice, 1998); University of Cincinnati (J.D., 2002). *Member:* Cincinnati, Ohio State and Kentucky Bar Associations. ***PRACTICE AREAS:*** Litigation. ***Email:*** jeffrey.willis@dinslaw.com

GWENDOLYN M. ODMARK, born South Bend, Indiana, April 29, 1973; admitted to bar, 2000, Ohio. *Education:* University of Notre Dame (B.A. and M.A., cum laude, 1995); Emory University (J.D., 1999). Author: "Q-T-M-T-: Denial of Humanitarian Relief for Aggravated Felows," Emory International Law Review, Spring 1999. ***PRACTICE AREAS:*** Immigration Law. ***Email:*** gwen.odmark@dinslaw.com

JAMES A. BROWNING, born Dayton, Ohio, May 1, 1978; admitted to bar, 2003, Kentucky; U.S. District Court, Western and Eastern Districts of Kentucky (Not admitted in Ohio). *Education:* Centre College of Kentucky (B.S., Economics, 2000); Northern Kentucky University (J.D., 2003). Member, Moot Court. Member, Northern Kentucky University Law Review. Law Clerk, Honorable John William Graves, Kentucky Supreme Court. Assistant Commonwealth Attorney, 52nd Judicial District, 2003-2004. Associate Attorney, Hargrove & Foster, Paducah, Kentucky, 2003-2004. Member, Supreme Court Historical Society. *Member:* Cincinnati, Kentucky and American Bar Associations. ***PRACTICE AREAS:*** Litigation; Products Liability; Health Care. ***Email:*** james.adam.browning@dinslaw.com

DAWNE McKENNA PARRISH, born Mansfield, Ohio, July 03, 1969; admitted to bar, 1996, Ohio; 1997, U.S. District Court, Southern District of Ohio. *Education:* Kent State University (B.B.A., magna cum laude, 1991); University of Cincinnati (M.B.A., 1995; J.D., 1996). Contract Attorney, The Kroger Co., 2000-2005. Assistant Counsel, The Western & Southern Life Insurance, 1996-2000. *Member:* Cincinnati and Ohio State Bar Associations. ***PRACTICE AREAS:*** Employee Benefits; Labor and Employment. ***Email:*** dawne.parrish@dinslaw.com

JEREMY A. KLOTZ, born Cincinnati, Ohio, October 3, 1973; admitted to bar, 2002, Indiana, U.S. District Court, Northern and Southern Districts of Indiana and U.S. Court of Appeals, Seventh Circuit (Not admitted in Ohio). *Education:* Indiana University (B.A., Psychology, 1996); DePaul University (J.D., cum laude, 2002). Recipient, CALI Awards in: Excellence in Torts, 1999; Advanced Trial Advocacy, 2002. *Member:* Indiana State and American Bar Associations; National Institute for Trail Advocacy; Defense Research Institute. ***REPORTED CASES:*** Golub v. Giles, 814 N.E.2d 1034 (Ind.App. 2004), trans. denied; In re Strahle, 294 F.Supp.2d 998 (N.D. Ind. 2003) (summary judgment granted); In re Strahle, 250 F.Supp.2d 997 (N.D. Ind. 2003) (motion to dismiss defeated). ***PRACTICE AREAS:*** Litigation; Products Liability; Commercial Litigation; Torts. ***Email:*** jeremy.klotz@dinslaw.com

MAX V. LANGENKAMP, born Cincinnati, Ohio, March 18, 1974; admitted to bar, 2002, Ohio; U.S. District Court, Southern District of Ohio and U.S. Court of Appeals, Sixth Circuit. *Education:* The Ohio State University (B.A., English, with honors, 1998); Univer-

(This Listing Continued)

sity of North Carolina at Chapel Hill (J.D., 2002). ***PRACTICE AREAS:*** Litigation; Labor and Employment; Sports Law; Workers Compensation. ***Email:*** max.langenkamp@dinslaw.com

MATTHEW A. WHITLOW, born Louisville, Kentucky, January 11, 1977; admitted to bar, 2003, Ohio; 2004, Kentucky. *Education:* University of Kentucky (B.S., Accounting and Finance, 1999); University of Dayton School of Law (J.D., 2003). Editor-in-Chief, University of Dayton Law Review. Author: "The Electronic Communications Privacy Act Protects Individual Privacy But Not at the Expense of the Media's Free Press Right: Bartnicki v. Vopper," 532 U.S. 514 (2001), 27 U. Dayton L. Rev. 339 (2002). *Member:* Cincinnati, Ohio State and Kentucky Bar Associations. ***PRACTICE AREAS:*** Corporate Law; Real Estate. ***Email:*** matthew.whitlow@dinslaw.com

JOHN P. SELLERS, III, born 1955; admitted to bar, 1982, Ohio; 2005, California. *Education:* Auburn University (B.A., 1978); University of Cincinnati (J.D., 1982); New York University (LL.M., 1987). ***PRACTICE AREAS:*** Immigration Law. ***Email:*** john.sellers@dinslaw.com

PETER A. DRAUGELIS, born Dayton, Ohio, July 2, 1973; admitted to bar, 2000, Ohio. *Education:* The Ohio State University (B.A., 1996); University of Dayton (J.D., 2000). *Member:* Cincinnati and Ohio State Bar Associations. ***PRACTICE AREAS:*** Corporate Law. ***Email:*** peter.draugelis@dinslaw.com

CARRIE W. RYAN, born Park Hills, Kentucky, February 4, 1971; admitted to bar, 1997, Illinois and U.S. District Court, Northern District of Illinois; 2000, Ohio. *Education:* University of Kentucky (B.A., 1993); Loyola University (J.D., 1997). *Member:* Cincinnati and Ohio State Bar Associations. ***PRACTICE AREAS:*** Business Law; Corporate Law; Mergers, Acquisitions and Divestitures. ***Email:*** carrie.ryan@dinslaw.com

STEPHANIE B. DANIEL, born 1976; admitted to bar, 2004, Tennessee and Georgia (Not admitted in Ohio). *Education:* East Tennessee State University (B.S., magna cum laude, 1999); University of Tennessee at Knoxville (J.D., magna cum laude, 2003). Research Editor, Tennessee Law Review, 2002-2003. *Member:* State Bar of Georgia. ***PRACTICE AREAS:*** Labor and Employment. ***Email:*** stephanie.daniel@dinslaw.com

JESSICA A. DIPRE, born Granville, Ohio, June 27, 1980; (admission pending). *Education:* Ohio University (B.S., Journalism, cum laude, 2002); University of Dayton (J.D., 2005). Member, Moot Court. Recipient, Presidential Merit Scholarship. Member, University of Dayton Law Review. ***PRACTICE AREAS:*** Insurance; Litigation. ***Email:*** jessica.dipre@dinslaw.com

JOHN T. DIPRE, born Erie, Pennsylvania, January 4, 1980; (admission pending). *Education:* University of Rochester (B.S., with high distinction, 2002); University of Dayton (J.D., cum laude, 2005). ***PRACTICE AREAS:*** Intellectual Property; Patents. ***Email:*** todd.dipre@dinslaw.com

CARRIE FISCHESSER, born Covington, Kentucky, August 20, 1969; (admission pending). *Education:* Northern Kentucky University (B.S., Finance/Marketing, 1993); Indiana University (M.B.A., 2000); Salmon P. Chase College of Law (J.D., magna cum laude, 2005). Phi Kappa Phi. Member, Inn of Court. Member, Moot Court. Recipient, Wall Street Journal Award for Excellence. Member, Salmon P. Chase Law Review. *Member:* Kentucky, Ohio State and American Bar Associations. ***PRACTICE AREAS:*** Labor and Employment; Litigation. ***Email:*** carrie.fischesser@dinslaw.com

DANIEL J. GREENBERG, born Fort Lauderdale, Florida, February 9, 1980; (admission pending). *Education:* University of Florida (B.A., with honors, 2002); The Ohio State University (J.D., 2005). *Member:* Cincinnati, Ohio State and American Bar Associations. ***PRACTICE AREAS:*** Alternative Dispute Resolution; Labor and Employment; Occupational Safety and Health. ***Email:*** daniel.greenberg@dinslaw.com

CARRIE A. MORGAN, born Middletown, Ohio, May 28, 1976; (admission pending). *Education:* University of Rochester (B.S., Cell & Developmental Biology, 1999); University of Dayton (J.D., summa cum laude, 2005). Author, "After the Fire and Rain, Lilly Still Stands," University of Dayton Law Review, Fall 2005. Member: Community Tutoring Program; Special Olympics; American Cancer Society. *Member:* Ohio State and American Bar Associations. ***Email:*** carrie.morgan@dinslaw.com

R. WARNER OFF, born Cincinnati, Ohio, January 20, 1980; (admission pending). *Education:* Yale University (B.A., 2002); Emory University School of Law (J.D., 2005). Managing Editor, Emory Bankruptcy Developments Journal, 2004-2005. *Member:* Cincinnati and Ohio State Bar Associations. ***PRACTICE AREAS:*** Corporate Law; Mergers, Acquisitions and Divestitures; Securities. ***Email:*** warner.off@dinslaw.com

ROBERT E. RICHARDSON, born Cincinnati, Ohio, November 25, 1978; (admission pending). *Education:* University of Cincinnati (B.S.E., 2002; J.D., 2005). Recipient, Presidential Leadership Medal of Excellence, University of Cincinnati, 2002. *Member:* Cincinnati and Ohio State Bar Associations. ***LANGUAGES:*** Spanish. ***PRACTICE AREAS:*** Contracts; Medicare and Medicaid.

JULIE E. SHERMAN, born Cleveland, Ohio, September 27, 1977; (admission pending). *Education:* Smith College (B.A., magna cum laude, 2000); University of Virginia (J.D., 2005). Phi Beta Kappa. ***PRACTICE AREAS:*** Corporate Law. ***Email:*** julie.sherman@dinslaw.com

LAURA M. STEWART, born Lancaster, California, May 21, 1975; (admission pending). *Education:* University of Florida (B.S., Telecommunication - News, 1997); University of Dayton (J.D., magna cum laude, 2005). Author, "Take Flight by Cyber-Sight: The Failure of Courts to Require the Americans with Disability Act Title III Public Accommodations Provision to Govern Public Places Such as an Airline's Website," 30 U. Dayton L. Rev. 275 (2004). *Member:* American Bar Association. ***PRACTICE AREAS:*** Litigation; Workers Compensation. ***Email:*** laura.stewart@dinslaw.com

PHILIP J. TRUAX, born Chicago, Illinois, April 1, 1979; (admission pending). *Education:* Ohio University (B.S., 2001); Case Western Reserve University (J.D., cum laude, 2005). *Member:* Ohio State and American Bar Associations. ***PRACTICE AREAS:*** Construction Law; Litigation; Medical Malpractice. ***Email:*** philip.truax@dinslaw.com

ROBERT ZIMMERMAN, born Dallas, Texas, October 29, 1979; (admission pending). *Education:* Vanderbilt University (B.A., 2002); University of Cincinnati (J.D., 2005). ***PRACTICE AREAS:*** Commercial Law; Litigation. ***Email:*** robert.zimmerman@dinslaw.com

(This Listing Continued)

OF COUNSEL

CAROLYN A. BETTS, born Cambridge, Massachusetts; admitted to bar, 1984, Ohio; 1985, U.S. District Court, Southern District of Ohio; 1988, District of Columbia. *Education:* Bryn Mawr College (A.B., 1975); University of Cincinnati (M.B.A., Finance, 1978); Salmon P. Chase College of Law (J.D., 1984). Recipient: American Jurisprudence Book Award in Agency and Partnership; Coy Holstein Award in Coal Law, 1984. Author, "Foregone But Not Forgotten: Interest-Free Loans," Vol. 11, No. 2, Northern Kentucky Law Review, 1984. *Member:* Cincinnati and American Bar Associations; The District of Columbia Bar. ***PRACTICE AREAS:*** Health Care; Litigation; Corporate Finance; Securities; Real Estate. ***Email:*** carolyn.betts@dinslaw.com

HARRIS K. WESTON, born Cincinnati, Ohio, March 12, 1918; admitted to bar, 1946, Ohio. *Education:* Harvard College (A.B., 1940); Harvard Law School (LL.B., 1946). Editor, Harvard Law Review, 1941-1942; 1945-1946. Law Clerk to Justice Harold H. Burton, 1946-1947. *Member:* Cincinnati, Ohio State and American Bar Associations; American Law Institute. ***PRACTICE AREAS:*** Estate Planning Law; Probate Law; Business Law. ***Email:*** weston@dinslaw.com

POWELL McHENRY, born Cincinnati, Ohio, May 14, 1926; admitted to bar, 1951, Ohio. *Education:* University of Cincinnati (A.B., 1949); Harvard Law School (LL.B., 1951). Editor, Harvard Law Review, 1949-1951. General Counsel, Federated Department Stores, 1971-1975. General Counsel, The Procter & Gamble Company, 1976-1991. *Member:* American Law Institute; The Association of General Counsel; Hamilton County Public Defender Commission. ***PRACTICE AREAS:*** General Corporate Law and Litigation. ***Email:*** mchenry@dinslaw.com

JOHN E. McDOWELL, born Toledo, Ohio, November 22, 1927; admitted to bar, 1952, Ohio. *Education:* Miami University (A.B., 1949); University of Michigan (J.D., 1952). Order of the Coif. *Member:* Cincinnati, Ohio State and American Bar Associations. ***PRACTICE AREAS:*** Corporate Law; Business Law; International Law. ***Email:*** mcdowell@dinslaw.com

HARRY L. RIGGS, JR., born Covington, Kentucky, July 18, 1930; admitted to bar, 1957, Ohio and Kentucky; U.S. District Court, Eastern and Western Districts of Kentucky; U.S. District Court, Northern and Southern Districts of Ohio; U.S. Court of Appeals, Sixth Circuit; U.S. Court of Appeals for the District of Columbia Circuit; U.S. Supreme Court. *Education:* Centre College of Kentucky (A.B., 1952); University of Cincinnati (J.D., 1957). Associate Editor, University of Cincinnati Law Review, 1956-1957. City Prosecutor, City of Erlanger, Kentucky, 1958-1964. City Attorney, Erlanger, Kentucky, 1964-1974. *Member:* EAA Legal Advisory Council (Chairman); National Transportation and Safety Board Bar Association (Past President); NBAA (Tax Committee). [LT U.S. Navy, Active Duty 1952-1954, Executive Officer USS PCS 1384]. ***PRACTICE AREAS:*** Products Liability Law; Aviation Law; General Litigation. ***Email:*** riggs@dinslaw.com

THOMAS S. CALDER, born Worcester, Massachusetts, June 10, 1932; admitted to bar, 1957, Ohio; U.S. Court of Appeals, Sixth Circuit. *Education:* University of Notre Dame (A.B., 1954; LL.B., 1957). Associate Editor, Notre Dame Lawyer, 1956-1957. Law Clerk to Judge Potter Stewart, Sixth Circuit Court of Appeals, 1957-1958. Master, Potter Stewart Inn of Court. Member, Product Liability Advisory Council, 1991—. Fellow: American College of Trial Lawyers; American Law Firm Association (Director/Secretary, 1994-1998). ***PRACTICE AREAS:*** General Litigation; Product Liability; Commercial Litigation. ***Email:*** tcalder@dinslaw.com

HAROLD S. FREEMAN, born Chattanooga, Tennessee, March 13, 1933; admitted to bar, 1960, Ohio; U.S. District Court, Southern District of Ohio; U.S. District Court, Eastern District of Kentucky; U.S. Court of Appeals, Fourth, Fifth, Sixth and Eighth Circuits; U.S. Supreme Court. *Education:* University of Chattanooga (B.S., 1955); University of Cincinnati (LL.B., 1960). Order of the Coif. Associate Editor, University of Cincinnati Law Review, 1959-1960. ***PRACTICE AREAS:*** Labor and Employment Law and Litigation; Public Employment Relations Law. ***Email:*** freeman@dinslaw.com

JOHN W. BEATTY, born Paris, France, February 27, 1936; admitted to bar, 1965, Ohio; U.S. District Court, Southern and Northern Districts of Ohio; U.S. District Court, Eastern District of Kentucky; U.S. Court of Appeals, Third and Sixth Circuits; U.S. Supreme Court. *Education:* Villanova University (B.Ch.E., 1957); University of Notre Dame (J.D., 1965). Research Editor, Notre Dame Law Review, 1964-1965. *Member:* The National Center for State Courts (1985-1993). ***PRACTICE AREAS:*** General Commercial Litigation; Antitrust Law. ***Email:*** beatty@dinslaw.com

KATHRYN K. PRZYWARA, born Cincinnati, Ohio, October 22, 1957; admitted to bar, 1982, Illinois (inactive) and U.S. District Court, Northern District of Illinois; 1986, Michigan (inactive) and U.S. District Court, Western District of Michigan; 1990, Ohio and U.S. District Court, Southern District of Ohio; 1992, U.S. Court of Appeals, Sixth Circuit; 1995, U.S. Supreme Court. *Education:* University of Notre Dame (B.A., English, 1979); Indiana University (J.D., magna cum laude, 1982). Order of the Coif; Order of the Barristers. Recipient, Indiana Bar Foundation Scholarship. *Member:* Cincinnati (Member, Grievance Committee, 2001—), Ohio State and American Bar Associations. ***REPORTED CASES:*** Rahn v. Drake Center, Inc., 31 F.3d 407, (6th Cir. 1994) cert. denied, 515 U.S. 1142 (1995); Eboigbe v. Zoological Society of Cinti, 96 Ohio App. 3d 102, 644 N.E. 2d 693 (1994); Belinky v. Drake Center, Inc., 117 Ohio App. 3d 497, 690 N.E. 2d 1302 (1996); In re Swallen's Inc., 205 Bankr. 879 (Bankr. S.D. Ohio 1997). ***PRACTICE AREAS:*** Commercial Law; Litigation. ***Email:*** kathryn.przywara@dinslaw.com

THOMAS J. WESTERFIELD, born Cincinnati, Ohio, April 19, 1955; admitted to bar, 1981, Ohio. *Education:* University of Notre Dame (B.A., Government and International Relations, 1977); Xavier University (M.B.A., Finance, 1978); University of Cincinnati College of Law (J.D., 1981). Participant in the 2005 Investment Company Institute Mutual Fund Compliance Programs Conference Panel entitled "The CCO's Interaction with the Fund Board". Participant in the 2005 Greater Cincinnati Mutual Funds Association Directors' Workshop Panel entitled "Board Effectiveness". *Member:* Cincinnati and American Bar Associations; Investment Company Institute; National Association of Corporate Directors; Society of Corporate Secretaries and Governance Professionals. ***PRACTICE AREAS:*** Business Law; Corporate Law; Finance; Investments. ***Email:*** thomas.westerfield@dinslaw.com

(This Listing Continued)

DINSMORE & SHOHL LLP, Cincinnati—Continued

JOHN B. PERSIANI, born Ohio; admitted to bar, 1989, Pennsylvania and U.S. District Court, Western District of Pennsylvania; 2003, Ohio. *Education:* Wheeling Jesuit College (B.A., 1983); Duke University (J.D., 1989). *Member:* Pennsylvania Bar Association. ***PRACTICE AREAS:*** Bankruptcy; Corporate Reorganization; Corporate Law; Lending. ***Email:*** jpersian@dinslaw.com

REPRESENTATIVE CLIENTS: Archdiocese of Cincinnati; Aventis Pharmaceuticals Inc.; Bally's; Beverly Enterprises, Inc.; Burke, Inc.; Castellini Company; CECO Environmental, Inc.; Chemed Corporation; Cincinnati Children's Hospital Medical Center; Cincinnati Incorporated; City of Blue Ash; Clopay Corporation; Deaconess Hospital; Dover Resources Division/OPW Fueling Components; Enerfab, Inc.; Formica Corporation; Franciscan Health Partnership; General Electric; General Electric Capital Corp.; General Motors Corp.; Halma PLC; Hamilton County Hospital Commission; Hennegan Company; Huffy Corporation; IDS Financial Corporation; International Flavors and Fragrances, Inc.; Jeffrey R. Anderson Real Estate, Inc.; Lenscrafters; Liberty Mutual Insurance Co.; Lucent Technologies, Inc.; Milacron, Inc.; Plastic Moldings Corp.; R. J. Tobacco Company; Roto-Rooter, Inc.; Sawbrook Steel Castings Co.; Sears, Roebuck and Co.; SENCORP; Sherwin Williams; SST Corporation; Sun Financial Group; The Kroger Co.; The Procter & Gamble Co.; The U. S. Playing Card Co.; United Dairy Farmers; United Medical Resources; US Bank; Valeo Thermal Systems.

LAW OFFICES OF JACK A. DONENFELD

A LEGAL PROFESSIONAL ASSOCIATION

119 EAST COURT STREET
CINCINNATI, OHIO 45202
Telephone: 513-632-5311
Fax: 513-721-1213
URL: http://www.donenfeldlawoffice.com
URL: http://www.donenfeldlawfirm.com
Email: JAD@DonenfeldLaw.com
URL: http://www.donenfeldlawoffices.com

Securities, Closely Held Corporations, Limited Liability Companies, Partnerships, Business Planning, Mergers and Acquisitions, Corporate Finance, Franchising and Real Estate, Asset Protection, International Asset Protection, Business Law, Business Formation, Business Succession Planning, Joint Ventures, Profession Practices, Small Business Law, Strategic Alliances, Corporate Law, Corporate Formation, Corporate Governance, Incorporation, Offshore Corporations, Private Finance, Investments, International Investments, Partnerships, Private Equity, Syndication, Venture Capital, Leverage Buyouts, Partnership Law, Real Estate Investments, Private Residence Clubs, Blue Sky Law, Private Placement, Securities Offerings, Securities Registration, Trusts and Estates, Estate Planning.

JACK A. DONENFELD, born Dayton, Ohio, October 9, 1951; admitted to bar, 1976, Ohio; 1977, District of Columbia; 1983, U.S. Supreme Court; 1987, U.S. District Court, Southern District of Ohio. *Education:* Northwestern University (B.A., with honors, Economics, 1973); Boston College Law School (J.D., 1976). Harvard Law School Program of Instruction for Lawyers, 1981, 1988. Legal Intern, Office of the Attorney General of the State of Massachusetts, 1976. Member, Registration and Exemption Advisory Committee, Ohio Division of Securities, 1988—. Member, 1983— and Director, 1985-1986, University of Cincinnati Real Estate Roundtable. Adjunct Associate Professor of Real Estate Law, University of Cincinnati College of Business Administration, 1983—. Member, 1985— and President, 1993-1994, Real Estate Investment Association (formerly known as the Real Estate Securities and Syndication Institute). Arbitrator, Securities and Exchange Commission vs. Prudential Securities Incorporated, C.A. No. 93-2164 (HHG), D.D.C. *Member:* Cincinnati (Member, Committees on: Real Property; Business Law), Ohio State and American (Member, Asset Protection Planning Committee, Real Property, Probate and Trust Law Section) Bar Associations; The District of Columbia Bar. (Also Of Counsel to Thiedmann & Edler, Chicago, Illinois). ***LANGUAGES:*** French. ***SPECIAL AGENCIES:*** Securities and Exchange Commission. ***PRACTICE AREAS:*** Real Estate; Investments; Business Law; Closely Held Business Law; Securities; Asset Protection.

OF COUNSEL

ROBERT W. EDLER, born June 25, 1936; admitted to bar, 1962, Illinois and U.S. District Court, Northern District of Illinois (Not admitted in Ohio). *Education:* Durham University (England) and DePauw University (B.A., with highest distinction, 1958); University of Chicago (M.A., 1959); Stanford University (LL.B., 1962). Phi Beta Kappa. (Also Member of Thiedmann & Edler, Chicago, Illinois). ***SPECIAL AGENCIES:*** Securities and Exchange Commission.

BRUCE S. FENTON, born Port Chester, New York, April 19, 1946; admitted to bar, 1970, District of Columbia and New York; 1971, U.S. District Court, District of Columbia and U.S. Court of Appeals for the District of Columbia Circuit (Not admitted in Ohio). *Education:* Yale University (B.A., 1967); Harvard University (J.D., 1970). *Member:* The Association of the Bar of the City of New York; American Bar Association.

DONNELLON, DONNELLON AND MILLER

A LEGAL PROFESSIONAL ASSOCIATION

9079 MONTGOMERY ROAD
CINCINNATI, OHIO 45242
Telephone: 513-891-7087
Fax: 513-891-7125

Negligence, Insurance, Family, Probate, Criminal, Real Estate Corporations, Taxation and Municipal Law. Trials.

FIRM PROFILE: Founded in 1951 by Judge Edward J. Donnellon, Donnellon, Donnellon and Miller has grown into one of the most respected law firms in Cincinnati. A tradition of service and commitment continues today with Tom & Terry Donnellon. The firm is very knowledgeable *(This Listing Continued)* *in all respects of personal and corporate law. The attorneys not only contribute to the communities with their legal expertise, but are involved in many civic, charitable and local business associations.*

THOMAS E. DONNELLON, born Cincinnati, Ohio, January 1, 1950; admitted to bar, 1976, Ohio; 2002, Kentucky. *Education:* University of Cincinnati (B.A., 1972); Salmon P. Chase College of Law of Northern Kentucky University (J.D., 1976). Assistant Solicitor, City of Cincinnati, 1976-1983. Solicitor, City of Silverton, Ohio, 1984-1997. Registered Land Title Examiner, Common Pleas Court, 1986—. *Member:* Cincinnati, Ohio State, Kentucky and American Bar Associations. ***PRACTICE AREAS:*** Probate Law; Real Estate Law; Municipal Law; Business Law; Automotive Franchises and Dealerships. ***Email:*** ted@donnellonlaw.com

TERRENCE M. DONNELLON, born Cincinnati, Ohio, April 9, 1954; admitted to bar, 1979, Ohio. *Education:* University of Cincinnati (B.A., 1976; J.D., 1979). Solicitor, Golf Manor, 1981—; Past President, Cincinnati Bar Association, 1996; Law Director, City of Montgomery, 1997—. *Member:* Cincinnati, Ohio State and American Bar Associations; Ohio Academy of Trial Lawyers; Ohio Association of Civil Trial Attorneys. ***PRACTICE AREAS:*** Negligence Law; Insurance Law; Municipal Law; Trials; Business Law; Automotive Franchises and Dealerships. ***Email:*** tmd@donnellonlaw.com

R. DOUGLAS MILLER, born Cincinnati, Ohio, June 18, 1955; admitted to bar, 1981, Ohio. *Education:* Vanderbilt University; University of Cincinnati (B.B.A., magna cum laude, 1977); Salmon P. Chase College of Law, Northern Kentucky University (J.D., 1981). Member, Hamilton County, Ohio Board of Zoning Appeals, 1986-1991. Solicitor, Village of Newtown, Ohio, 1988—. Law Director, Deerfield Township, 1996—; Law Director, Sycamore Township, 1991—. Certified Public Accountant, Ohio, 1978. *Member:* Cincinnati, Ohio State and American Bar Association. ***PRACTICE AREAS:*** Probate Law; Real Estate Law; Corporation Law; Municipal Law; Taxation Law. ***Email:*** miller@donnellonlaw.com

---

ROBERT T. BUTLER, born Hamilton, Ohio, July 29, 1962; admitted to bar, 1990, Ohio. *Education:* Metropolitan State College (B.A., in English, 1984); University of Wyoming (J.D., 1990). *Member:* Cincinnati, Ohio State and American Bar Associations. [U.S. Army, 1984-1986; 1990-1991]. ***PRACTICE AREAS:*** Negligence Law; Insurance Law; Criminal Law; DUI Law. ***Email:*** butler@donnellonlaw.com

OF COUNSEL

EDWARD J. DONNELLON, born Cincinnati, Ohio, March 22, 1924; admitted to bar, 1951, Ohio. *Education:* University of Cincinnati; Salmon P. Chase College of Law (J.D., 1951). Solicitor: Golf Manor, 1969-1981; Elmwood Place, 1982-1983. Assistant Attorney General, 1971-1983. President, Hamilton County Municipal Attorneys, 1977-1979. Judge, Hamilton County Municipal Court, 1981-1993. Ohio State Bar Examiner, 1978-1983. *Member:* Cincinnati, Ohio State and American Bar Associations. ***PRACTICE AREAS:*** Negligence Law; Insurance Law; Municipal Law.

REPRESENTATIVE CLIENTS: John Nolan Ford, Inc.; 32 Ford, Inc.; Ridgeview Lincoln-Mercury, Sidney Ford, Inc.; Automobile Club Insurance Co.; Village of Golf Manor; City of Montgomery, Deerfield Twp.; Village of Newtown; Sycamore Township; Pella Windows of Cincinnati and Kentucky; Harley Davidson of Cincinnati; Center for Local Government; Advantage Ford Lincoln Mercury.
REFERENCE: PNC Bank.

DONOVAN LAW

910 RACE STREET
CINCINNATI, OHIO 45202
Telephone: 513-362-2190
Fax: 513-651-4937
Email: mjdonovan@irowco.com
URL: http://www.donovan-law.com

Criminal Defense, Driving While Intoxicated, Family Law, Divorce, Civil Litigation, Juvenile Law, Real Estate, Personal Injury, Auto Accidents.

MARY JILL H. DONOVAN, born Park Hills, Kentucky, March 22, 1962; admitted to bar, 2001, Ohio; 2002, Florida. *Education:* College of Mt. St. Joseph (B.A., 1998); University of Cincinnati (J.D., 2001). Florida Institute of Police Technology, 1990-1991. Ohio State Patrol Academy, DUI Prosecution, 1990. Member, City of Cincinnati, Department of Safety, Police Division: Police Officer, 1987-1992; Vehicular Homicide Investigator, 1990-1992. Law Clerk, General Electric Aircraft Engines, Legal Department, Litigation Division, 2000. President, Indiana Right of Way Company, 2001—. Speaker and Panel Member, Continuing Legal Education Seminar, Client Development, Cincinnati Bar Association. *Member:* Cincinnati Bar Association (Secretary and Vice-Chair, Women Lawyers Committee); The Florida Bar; National Association Criminal Defense Lawyers.

MICHAEL P. McCAFFERTY, born Cincinnati, Ohio; admitted to bar, 2004, Ohio. *Education:* Miami University (Finance); Vanderbilt University (J.D., 2004). ***PRACTICE AREAS:*** Real Estate; Small Business.

RENE B. HEINRICH, born Rosenheim, Germany, 1973; admitted to bar, 2000, Kentucky (Not admitted in Ohio). *Education:* Eastern Kentucky University (B.A., with honors, 1995); Salmon P. Chase College of Law (J.D., 2000). ***LANGUAGES:*** German. ***PRACTICE AREAS:*** DUI; Driving While Intoxicated; Divorce; Probate; Estate Administration; Criminal Law; Felonies; Misdemeanors; Contract Representation; Contract Negotiation; Real Estate.

DREW & WARD

A LEGAL PROFESSIONAL ASSOCIATION

Established in 1958

24TH FLOOR, FOURTH & VINE TOWER
ONE WEST FOURTH STREET
CINCINNATI, OHIO 45202
Telephone: 513-621-8210
Telecopier: 513-621-5444
Email: info@drewlaw.com
URL: http://www.drewlaw.com

General Practice. Civil Trial Litigation. Corporation, Employee Benefits, Family Law, Estate Planning, Franchise Law, Negligence, Probate, Real Estate, Tax, Zoning and Planning Law.

FIRM PROFILE: Drew & Ward is a legal professional association located in Cincinnati, Ohio, and dedicated to providing a range of quality legal services.

The knowledge and experience of Drew & Ward's attorneys are valued by the firm's clients, who range from individuals to families and small businesses to large corporations. Each attorney at Drew & Ward is committed to providing the highest level of service and expertise in the course of representing the firm's clients. Our attorneys adhere to the highest standards of professionalism and stay abreast of the most current legal developments in their respective fields. The goal of this philosophy is to achieve the best available results for clients.

Founded in 1958, Drew & Ward has the expertise to serve its clients in the areas of Tax and Estate Planning, Probate, Business and Corporate Law, Civil Litigation, Domestic Relations, and more.

RICHARD H. WARD, born Cincinnati, Ohio, June 8, 1923; admitted to bar, 1949, Ohio. *Education:* Denison University; University of Cincinnati (LL.B., 1948). Phi Delta Phi. Assistant Prosecuting Attorney, Hamilton County, 1953-1956. Member, Village Council, Mariemont, Ohio, 1954-1958. Member, 1965-1973 and President, 1968-1970, Mariemont City School Board. *Member:* Cincinnati (Member, Grievance Committee, 1956-1975; President, 1976-1977), Ohio State and American (Member: House of Delegates, 1978-1984; Board of Elections, 1985-1989) Bar Associations. Fellow: Ohio State Bar Foundation; American Bar Foundation. [Air Force, 1942-1945; 1951-1953; Lt. Col., 1962]. ***PRACTICE AREAS:*** Civil Litigation; Estate Planning; Probate. ***Email:*** rward@drewlaw.com

JAMES H. COOGAN, born Cincinnati, Ohio, August 23, 1937; admitted to bar, 1961, Ohio and U.S. District Court, Southern District of Ohio. *Education:* University of Cincinnati (B.A., 1959; J.D., 1961). Phi Delta Phi. Master of the Bench, Potter Stewart American Inn of Court, 1993—. Editor, "The Restatement," University of Cincinnati College of Law, 1960-1961. Lecturer on Law, University of Cincinnati, College of Business, 1971-1980. *Member:* Cincinnati (Vice-Chairman Ethics Committee, 1982-1985, Chairman, 1985-1987; Probate Committee, 1977—; Trusts, Wills and Estate Planning Committee, 1977—; Lawyers Assistance Committee, 1981—, Chairman, 1983-1985; Recipient, Trustees Award, 2004) and Ohio State (Member, Joint Property Committee, Probate Section, 1982—; Lawyers Assistance Committee, 1984— and Chairman, 1985-1987) Bar Associations. ***PRACTICE AREAS:*** Civil Litigation; Corporate Law; Estate Planning; Probate; Probate Litigation; Life Insurance; Closely Held Business Law. ***Email:*** jcoogan@drewlaw.com

FREDERIC L. GOEDDEL, born Cincinnati, Ohio, September 18, 1948; admitted to bar, 1973, Ohio; U.S. District Court, Southern District of Ohio; 1985, U.S. Supreme Court. *Education:* Denison University (B.A., 1970); University of Cincinnati (J.D., 1973). Omicron Delta Kappa. Member, National Moot Court Team. Councilman, City of Wyoming, 1979-1981. Mayor, City of Wyoming, 1981-1985. *Member:* Cincinnati (Member, Committees on: Domestic Relations; Trusts, Wills and Estate Planning; Ethics; Judicial Rating, Chairman, 1986-1987) and Ohio State Bar Associations. ***PRACTICE AREAS:*** Family Law; Estate Planning; Corporate Law; Civil Litigation. ***Email:*** fgoeddel@drewlaw.com

ANTHONY G. COVATTA, JR., born Louisville, Kentucky, July 11, 1944; admitted to bar, 1979, Ohio; 1980, U.S. District Court, Southern District of Ohio; 1997, Kentucky. *Education:* Bellarmine College (B.A., 1966); Columbia University (M.A., 1967; Ph.D., 1971); University of Cincinnati (J.D., 1979). Order of the Coif. Editor, University of Cincinnati Law Review. ***LANGUAGES:*** Spanish. ***PRACTICE AREAS:*** Civil Litigation; Corporate Law; Securities; Health Care; Franchises and Franchising; Zoning, Planning and Land Use. ***Email:*** acovatta@drewlaw.com

RUTH I. ROUNDING, born Ottawa, Canada, September 26, 1952; admitted to bar, 1976, Illinois and U.S. District Court, Northern District of Illinois; 1979, Ohio and U.S. District Court, Southern District of Ohio; 1982, U.S. Court of Federal Claims. *Education:* University of Western Ontario (B.A., with honors, 1973); Harvard Law School (J.D., cum laude, 1976). Fellow, American College of Trust and Estate Counsel. Author: "Financial and Health Care Planning for the Elderly in Ohio," (Anderson Publishing 3ed., 1998). *Member:* Cincinnati (Chairman, Taxation Section, 1988-1989; Chairman, Estate Planning Section, 1986-1987) and Ohio State (Member, Board of Governors, Estate Planning, Trust & Probate Law Section, 2000—) Bar Associations. (Certified Specialist, Estate Planning, Trust and Probate Law, Ohio State Bar Association). ***LANGUAGES:*** French. ***PRACTICE AREAS:*** Probate; Trusts and Estates; Taxation; Elder Law; Nonprofit and Charitable Organizations. ***Email:*** rounding@drewlaw.com

RICHARD J. RUEBEL, born Cincinnati, Ohio, March 9, 1948; admitted to bar, 1973, Ohio. *Education:* Cornell University (B.A., 1970); University of Cincinnati (J.D., 1973). Order of the Coif. *Member:* Cincinnati, Ohio State and American Bar Associations; Cincinnati Estate Planning Council. Fellow, American College of Trusts and Estates Counsel. ***PRACTICE AREAS:*** Estate Planning; Estate and Gift Taxation; Corporate Law; Real Estate; Probate; Wills; Trusts and Estates; Fiduciary Law; Closely Held Corporations; Taxation; Nonprofit and Charitable Organizations. ***Email:*** rruebel@drewlaw.com

MICHAEL D. McNEIL, born Redondo Beach, California, August 30, 1964; admitted to bar, 1991, Ohio; 1992, U.S. District Court, Southern District of Ohio. *Education:* Wake Forest University (B.A., 1986); University of Cincinnati (J.D., 1991). *Member:* Cincinnati and Ohio State Bar Associations. ***PRACTICE AREAS:*** Family Law; Civil Litigation; Probate Litigation. ***Email:*** mmcneil@drewlaw.com

(This Listing Continued)

ROBERT M. SMYTH, born Pittsburgh, Pennsylvania, April 2, 1969; admitted to bar, 1994, Ohio; 1995, U.S. District Court, Southern District of Ohio. *Education:* Miami University (B.A., 1991); University of Cincinnati (J.D., 1994). Member, Moot Court Board. Clerk, 1st District of Ohio, Court of Appeals, 1996-1997. *Member:* Cincinnati (Secretary, Court of Appeals Committee, 2004—; Co-Chair, Young Lawyers Membership Committee, 2003—), Ohio State and American Bar Associations. ***PRACTICE AREAS:*** Employment Law; Civil Litigation; Corporate Law; Probate Litigation. ***Email:*** bsmyth@drewlaw.com

RICHARD G. WARD, born Cincinnati, Ohio, February 7, 1955; admitted to bar, 1986, Ohio; 1987, U.S. District Court, Southern District of Ohio and U.S. Court of Appeals, Sixth Circuit. *Education:* Denison University (B.A., 1978); University of Cincinnati College of Law (J.D., 1986). *Member:* Cincinnati, Ohio State and American Bar Associations. ***LANGUAGES:*** French. ***REPORTED CASES:*** Brookbank v. Gray (1996), 74 Ohio St. 3d 279 658 N.E. 2d 724. ***PRACTICE AREAS:*** Civil Litigation; Real Estate; Corporate Law; Estate Planning; Probate; Family Law; Personal Injury. ***Email:*** rward@drewlaw.com

WILLIAM C. SULAU, born Cincinnati, Ohio, September 9, 1950; admitted to bar, 1981, Ohio. *Education:* Denison University (B.A., 1972); Xavier University (M.A., 1976); Thomas M. Cooley Law School (J.D., 1980). *Member:* Cincinnati and Ohio State Bar Associations. ***PRACTICE AREAS:*** Real Estate; Probate; Estate Planning; Contracts.

MARK W. JORDAN, born August 5, 1955; admitted to bar, 1980, Ohio; 1995, Kentucky. *Education:* The American College (C.L.U., 1983; C.h.F.C., 1984); Life Office Management Association (F.L.M.I. 1986); Georgetown University (B.S.F.S., 1977); University of Cincinnati (J.D., 1980). Phi Beta Kappa; Pi Sigma Alpha; Phi Alpha Theta. National Winner of Giles Sutherland Rich Moot Court Competition. Life Member, National Registry of Who's Who. *Member:* Cincinnati and Kentucky Bar Associations; Greater Cincinnati Estate Planning Council. ***PRACTICE AREAS:*** Estate Planning Law; Probate Law; Insurance Law; Business Law. ***Email:*** mward@drewlaw.com

SYBIL B. MULLIN, born Saratoga Springs, New York, October 21, 1965; admitted to bar, 1995, Ohio; 1996, Kentucky. *Education:* Denison University (B.A., cum laude, 1987); Salmon P. Chase College of Law of Northern Kentucky University (J.D., 1995). *Member:* Cincinnati, Kentucky, Ohio State and American Bar Associations. ***LANGUAGES:*** Spanish. ***PRACTICE AREAS:*** Real Estate; Estate Planning; Estate Administration; Corporate Law; Probate Administration. ***Email:*** smullin@drewlaw.com

JAMES R. SCHAEFER, born Zanesville, Ohio, August 11, 1962; admitted to bar, 1992, Ohio; 1993, Colorado; 1994, U.S. District Court, Southern District of Ohio. *Education:* Ohio State University (B.A., 1989); Capital University Law School (J.D., 1992). Licensed Title Insurance Agent: Ohio Bar Title Ins. Co.; Old Republic Nat'l Title Ins. Co. *Member:* Cincinnati (Member, Real Estate Committee) and Ohio State (Member, Real Estate Committee) Bar Associations; Southwest Ohio Land Title Association. (Certified Specialist in Residential Real Estate Law, Ohio State Bar Association). ***LANGUAGES:*** Spanish. ***REPORTED CASES:*** McDonalds Co. Sec. Inc., Gradison Div. v. Alzheimer's Disease & Related Disorders Assn., 140 Ohio App. 3d. ***PRACTICE AREAS:*** Real Estate; Business Law; Civil Litigation; Domestic Relations. ***Email:*** jschaefer@drewlaw.com

OF COUNSEL

GEORGE RAYMOND DREW, born Cambridge, Massachusetts, May 4, 1918; admitted to bar, 1940, Massachusetts; 1950, Ohio. *Education:* Columbia University; Suffolk University (LL.B., with honors, 1939). *Member:* Cincinnati, Ohio State and American Bar Associations. [Lt. Col., Air Force, 1941-1945]. ***PRACTICE AREAS:*** Corporation Law; Probate Law; Hospital Law. ***Email:*** esqdrew1@aol.com

FLACH DOUGLAS, born Cincinnati, Ohio, May 17, 1931; admitted to bar, 1957, Ohio; U.S. District Court, Southern District of Ohio and U.S. Court of Appeals, Sixth Circuit; 1975, U.S. Tax Court; 1978, U.S. Supreme Court. *Education:* University of Cincinnati (A.B., 1953; LL.B., 1957). Omicron Delta Kappa. Member, University of Cincinnati Law Review, 1954-1957. Registered Land Examiner, Ohio, 1986. Instructor, Real Estate Law, Clermont College Branch, University of Cincinnati, 1978—. *Member:* Cincinnati, Clermont County (Chairman: Notary Public Committee, 1979—; Arbitration Committee, 1980) and Ohio State Bar Associations. [1st Lt., U.S. Army Artillery, 1954-1956]. (Also practicing individually, Milford, Ohio). ***PRACTICE AREAS:*** Real Estate; General Civil Litigation.

REPRESENTATIVE CLIENTS: AAA Allied Group, Inc.; American National Life Insurance Co.; Baxter Precast, Inc.; Cardiology Associates of Cincinnati, Inc.; Cheviot Savings Bank; Cincinnatus Savings & Loan, Co.; Cinfield Federal Credit Union; Fraternity Printing Co.; Gardner Publications, Inc.; G. C. Fuller Mfg. Co., Inc.; Greater Cincinnati Associated Physicians, Inc.; Greater Cincinnati Foundation, Inc.; John Finn Company; Late for the Sky Production Company, Inc.; Lightborne Publishing, Inc.; Macke Bros. Book Bindery, Inc.; Medical Recovery Systems, Inc.; PNC Bank; Stevenson, The Color Company; University Radiology Associates; U.S. Financial Life Insurance Co.; Watkins Machinery, Inc.; WesBanco Savings & Loan, Co.
REFERENCES: PNC Bank; Fifth-Third Bank.

M. FREEMAN DURHAM

2725 JOHNSTONE PLACE
CINCINNATI, OHIO 45206-1822
Telephone: 513-651-4900
Email: freeman.durham@usa.net

Trusts and Estates, Employee Benefits, Taxation.

M. FREEMAN DURHAM, born Cincinnati, Ohio, August 11, 1958; admitted to bar, 1983, Ohio. *Education:* Vanderbilt University (B.A., magna cum laude, 1980); Northwestern University (J.D., cum laude, 1983). Phi Beta Kappa. Order of the Coif. Senior Corporate Counsel, Great American Financial Resources, Inc. ***PRACTICE AREAS:*** Trusts and Estates Law; Employee Benefits Law; Taxation Law.

EBNER & RIKER, L.L.P.

Established in 1979

1900 KROGER BUILDING
1014 VINE STREET
CINCINNATI, OHIO 45202-1141
Telephone: 513-621-2888; 800-699-6446
Fax: 513-345-4449
URL: http://www.erlaw.org
URL: http://www.lawyers.com/ebner&riker

Civil Litigation, Personal Injury, Small Business and Corporate Law, Insurance Defense, Probate, Trusts and Estates, Domestic Relations.

J. TIMOTHY RIKER, born Lima, Ohio, July 25, 1948; admitted to bar, 1977, Ohio; 1979, U.S. District Court, Southern District of Ohio. *Education:* Baldwin-Wallace College (B.A., 1970); The Capital University (J.D., cum laude, 1977). *Member:* Cincinnati, Ohio State and American Bar Associations. [Rear Admiral, U.S. Coast Guard and Reserve, 1970-2000]. **Email:** jtriker@erlaw.org

SHARON M. J. SHARTZER, born Bryan, Ohio, June 22, 1974; admitted to bar, 2004, Ohio. *Education:* East Tennessee State University (B.A., cum laude, 2000); Northern Kentucky University (J.D., 2004). Phi Kappa Phi. *Member:* Cincinnati, Ohio State and American Bar Associations.

EICHEL & KRONE CO., L.P.A.

Established in 1971

302 GWYNNE BUILDING
602 MAIN STREET
CINCINNATI, OHIO 45202
Telephone: 513-241-1234
Fax: 513-241-2731
Email: bak@baklaw.com

Trusts and Estates, Wills, Probate, Real Estate, Taxation, Business Law, Charitable Trusts and Foundations, Private Foundations and Tax-Exempt Organizations.

LAWRENCE E. EICHEL (1908-1981)

PAUL W. KRONE (1925-1995)

BRUCE A. KRONE, born Cincinnati, Ohio, June 29, 1954; admitted to bar, 1982, Ohio; 1989, Kentucky. *Education:* The Ohio State University (B.S., 1977); Xavier University (M.B.A., 1979); University of Dayton (J.D., 1982). *Member:* Cincinnati (Member, Estate Planning and Taxation Committees, 1982—), Ohio State, Kentucky (Member: Probate and Trust Law Committee; Taxation Committee, 1989—) and American (Member, Taxation Law Section) Bar Associations. **PRACTICE AREAS:** Estate Planning; Taxation; Corporate; Real Estate; Business Law; Wills; Trust Law; Probate. **Email:** Bruce@BAKLAW.com

REPRESENTATIVE CLIENTS: Furnished Upon Request.

ANNE EINSPANIER

CINCINNATI, OHIO

(See Anne Einspanier Krehbiel, Lebanon, Ohio)

ELK & ELK CO., L.P.A.

CINCINNATI, OHIO

(See Cleveland)

Automobile Accidents, Product Defects, Nursing Home Neglect, Medical Malpractice, Personal Injury.

JOHN H. ENGLE
ATTORNEY AND COUNSELOR AT LAW

FEDERATED BUILDING
SUITE 1800
7 WEST 7TH STREET
CINCINNATI, OHIO 45202
Telephone: 513-241-7332; 513-241-0572
Fax: 513-621-5410
URL: http://www.jenglelaw.com

Insurance Defense, Arson, Insurance Fraud, Personal Injury, Subrogation, Construction, Casualty Insurance and Commercial Litigation.

JOHN H. ENGLE, born Detroit, Michigan, June 8, 1943; admitted to bar, 1968, Ohio; 1970, U.S. District Court, Southern District of Ohio; 1978, U.S. Supreme Court. *Education:* Cornell University (A.B., 1965; J.D., 1968). Seminar Writer and Speaker: American Insurance Fraud Seminar, 1990. Member, Defense Research Institute Litigation Research Group. *Member:* Cincinnati, Ohio and Federal Bar Associations; Ohio Association of Civil Trial Attorneys; National Society of Professional Insurance Investigators. **PRACTICE AREAS:** Insurance Defense Law; Arson Law; Insurance Fraud Defense Law; Subrogation; Litigation; Fraud; Construction Law; Commercial Law; Casualty Insurance; Personal Injury.

RAYMOND T. FALLER

Established in 1976

THE KROGER BUILDING
1014 VINE STREET, SUITE 1450
CINCINNATI, OHIO 45202-1116
Telephone: 513-579-1266
Email: rfall@aol.com
URL: http://www.rtfaller.com

Criminal Law, DUI, Felonies, Misdemeanors, Homicide, Theft, Drug Crimes, Driving Suspensions, Domestic Violence, Assault, Drug Offenses.

FIRM PROFILE: Mr. Faller is a criminal defense lawyer and also a former prosecutor. Since 1982 Mr. Faller has tried over 200 jury trials including four capital cases and has over 60 cases reported in LEXIS.

RAYMOND T. FALLER, born Cincinnati, Ohio, December 23, 1950; admitted to bar, 1976, Ohio; 1977, U.S. District Court, Southern District of Ohio; 1980, U.S. Court of Appeals, Sixth Circuit; 1982, U.S. Supreme Court. *Education:* Xavier University (A.B., cum laude, 1973); University of Cincinnati (J.D., 1976). Lecturer, "Drug Treatment in Lieu of Conviction," Cincinnati Bar Association CLE Seminar, 1989. Assistant Hamilton County Prosecutor, 1978-1982. *Member:* Cincinnati, Ohio State and American Bar Associations; Greater Cincinnati Criminal Defense Lawyers Association (Member, Board of Directors, 1989); Ohio Association of Criminal Defense Lawyers; National Association of Criminal Defense Lawyers. **REPORTED CASES:** State vs. Gover (1989), 61 Ohio App. 3d 330; State vs. Whiting (1987), 41 Ohio App 3d 107; State vs. Sowell, (1988) 39 Ohio St. 3d 322; State vs. Jackson et al, 92 Ohio App 3rd 467 636 N.E. 2nd 332 (1993).

FAULKNER & TEPE, LLP

2200 FOURTH AND VINE TOWER
1 WEST FOURTH STREET
CINCINNATI, OHIO 45202-3606
Telephone: 513-421-7500
Fax: 513-421-7502
URL: http://www.faulknertepe.com

Insurance Defense, General Practice, Bankruptcy, Insolvency, Negligence, Probate, Litigation, Complex Litigation, Construction and Surety Law and Criminal Defense.

MEMBERS OF FIRM

DAVID P. FAULKNER (1929-1999)

R. EDWARD TEPE (1939-2003)

JOHN C. SCOTT, born Cincinnati, Ohio, May 25, 1960; admitted to bar, 1985, Ohio and U.S. District Court, Southern District of Ohio; U.S. Court of Appeals, 6th Circuit. *Education:* Xavier University (A.B., magna cum laude, 1982); University of Cincinnati (J.D., 1985). Recipient, American Jurisprudence Award for Criminal Procedure. *Member:* Cincinnati, Ohio State and American Bar Associations; Ohio Association of Civil Trial Attorneys; Defense Research Institute. **PRACTICE AREAS:** Insurance Defense; Civil Litigation; Bankruptcy; Corporate; Probate; Construction. **Email:** jscott@faulkner-tepe.com

A. NORMAN AUBIN, born Joliet, Illinois, March 25, 1954; admitted to bar, 1983, Ohio and U.S. District Court, Southern District of Ohio, U.S. Court of Appeals, 6th Circuit; U.S. Supreme Court. *Education:* Northeastern University (B.S., 1976); University of Dayton (J.D., 1983). Staff Attorney, Court of Claims, State of Ohio, 1984-1987; Deputy Clerk, Court of Claims, State of Ohio, 1985-1987. *Member:* Cincinnati, Ohio State and American Bar Association; Ohio Association of Criminal Defense Lawyers, Hamilton County Association of Criminal Defense Lawyers; National Association of Criminal Defense Lawyers. **PRACTICE AREAS:** Criminal; Probate; Insurance Defense; General Civil Litigation; Civil Rights Litigation; Mental Health Law. **Email:** naubin@faulkner-tepe.com

JOSEPH T. MORDINO, born Buffalo, New York, February 27, 1971; admitted to bar, 1995, Ohio and U.S. District Court, Southern District of Ohio; 2002, Kentucky. *Education:* St. Lawrence University (B.A., magna cum laude, 1992); University of Cincinnati (J.D., 1995). Phi Beta Kappa. *Member:* Cincinnati and Ohio State Bar Associations. **PRACTICE AREAS:** Insurance Defense; Civil Litigation. **Email:** jmordino@faulkner-tepe.com

ASSOCIATE

ANN E. WALTER, born Cincinnati, Ohio, March 13, 1973; admitted to bar, 1999, Ohio and U.S. District Court, Southern District of Ohio. *Education:* University of Arizona (B.A., 1995); Capital University (J.D., 1998). *Member:* Cincinnati (Member, Young Lawyers Section) and American Bar Associations. **PRACTICE AREAS:** Insurance Defense; Criminal Defense; Civil Litigation. **Email:** annwalter@faulkner-tepe.com

REPRESENTATIVE CLIENTS: The St. Paul Companies, Inc.; Hoosier Insurance Company; General Casualty Insurance Co.; Chubb Group of Insurance Companies; Meridian Insurance Companies; State Auto Insurance Co.; Adjusting Services Unlimited, Inc.; Gallagher Bassett Services, Inc.; Davis Baldwin/Wachovia Insurance Services, Inc.; Western Heritage Insurance Co.; JWF Specialty Co., Inc.; Fulcrum Insurance Company; John R. Jurgensen Company; Valley Asphalt Corporation; Morrow Gravel Co.; Eaton Asphalt Paving Co., Inc.; Southern Ohio Aggregates; Northern Kentucky Aggregates; Fourth Street Financial Group, Inc.; Hamilton County Community Mental Health Board.
REFERENCE: Fifth-Third Bank

STEPHEN R. FELSON

617 VINE STREET, SUITE 1401
CINCINNATI, OHIO 45202
Telephone: 513-721-4900
Fax: 513-639-7011
Email: steveF8953@aol.com
URL: http://www.cincylawyer.com

Consumer Class Actions, Appellate Practice, Civil Litigation, Employment Law, Credit Fraud, Auto Fraud, Consumer Fraud, Civil Rights, Lemon Law, Landlord Tenant Law, Medical Malpractice, Personal Injury.

STEPHEN R. FELSON, born Tulsa, Oklahoma, October 1, 1941; admitted to bar, 1966, Ohio; 1993, U.S. Supreme Court. *Education:* Harvard University (B.A., 1963); University of Cincinnati (J.D., 1966). Order of the Coif. Recipient, American Jurisprudence Prizes for Agency, Civil Procedure II (Pleading), and Administrative Law; Frederick Closs Memorial Prize for Contracts I and Robert S. Marx Foundation Prize for Scholarship in the Law of Torts, University of Cincinnati, 1963-1964; Ohio State Bar Association Foundation Prizes for highest scholastic standing at end of first, second and third year. Editor-in-Chief, University of Cincinnati Law Review, 1965-1966. *Member:* Cincinnati, Ohio State and Federal Bar Associations. ***LANGUAGES:*** Hebrew. ***PRACTICE AREAS:*** Consumer Class Actions; Appellate Practice; Civil Litigation; Employment Law; Credit Fraud; Auto Fraud; Consumer Fraud; Civil Rights; Lemon Law; Landlord Tenant Law; Medical Malpractice; Personal Injury.

FINKELMEIER & FARRELL

36 EAST SEVENTH STREET, SUITE 1660
CINCINNATI, OHIO 45202-4461
Telephone: 513-621-9921
Fax: 513-621-9923
Email: finkelmeier@fuse.net

Workers Compensation, Sports Injury and Social Security Disability.

LOUIS J. FINKELMEIER, born Fort Bragg, North Carolina, March 13, 1943; admitted to bar, 1968, Ohio; 1969, U.S. District Court, Southern District of Ohio; 1974, U.S. Court of Appeals, Sixth Circuit. *Education:* University of Cincinnati (B.A., 1965; J.D., 1968). Phi Delta Phi. Listed in *The Best Lawyers of America,* Woodward/White, Inc., (Workers' Compensation). Member, National Football League Players Association Workers' Compensation Panel. *Member:* Cincinnati (Member, 1968— and Chairman, 1974-1977, Workmen's Compensation Committee), Ohio State and American Bar Associations; The Association of Trial Lawyers of America; Ohio Academy of Trial Lawyers (Member, Board of Governing Trustees, 1974-1978). [Commissioned Officer, U.S. Army Reserve, 1968-1974]. (Board Certified Specialist, Ohio Workers' Compensation Law, Ohio State Bar Association). ***PRACTICE AREAS:*** Workers Compensation; Sports Injury; Probate. ***Email:*** finkelmeier@fuse.net

WILLIAM I. FARRELL, born Charleston, South Carolina, December 23, 1963; admitted to bar, 1989, Ohio; 1990, U.S. District Court, Southern District of Ohio. *Education:* Miami University (B.A., 1986), University of Cincinnati (J.D., 1989). Delta Theta Phi. Member, National Football League Players Association Workers' Compensation Panel; Member, Professional Hockey Players Association Workers' Compensation Panel. *Member:* Cincinnati (CLE Chair, 1995-1996, Secretary, 1997-1998, Vice-Chairman, 1999-2001, Chairman, 2001-2003, Workers' Compensation Committee; Secretary, 1996—, Social Security Committee) and Ohio State Bar Associations; Cincinnati Academy of Leadership for Lawyers; The Ohio Academy of Trial Lawyers (Member, Workers' Compensation Executive Committee, 1999-2002). (Board Certified Specialist, Ohio Workers' Compensation Law, Ohio State Bar Association). ***PRACTICE AREAS:*** Workers Compensation; Sports Injury; Social Security Disability; Personal Injury. ***Email:*** billfarrell@fuse.net

REFERENCE: The Fifth Third Bank.

RICHARD I. FLEISCHER & ASSOCIATES

Established in 1973

917 MAIN STREET
CINCINNATI, OHIO 45202
Telephone: 513-977-4209
Fax: 513-977-4238
Email: fleischer@immigrate2usa.com
URL: http://www.immigrate2usa.com

Practice Limited to Immigration Law.

FIRM PROFILE: Richard I. Fleischer & Associates, founded in 1973, exclusively practices U.S. immigration law throughout the United States and around the world representing individuals, companies, and organizations.

Attorneys Richard I. Fleischer and Neil I. Fleischer hope to be your source for U.S. immigration law.

RICHARD I. FLEISCHER, born Cincinnati, Ohio, February 25, 1944; admitted to bar, 1971, Ohio, U.S. District Court, Southern District of Ohio and U.S. Court Appeals, Sixth Circuit; 1973, The District of Columbia and U.S. District Court, Eastern District of Kentucky; 1974, U.S. Supreme Court; 1977, Kentucky. *Education:* University of Cincinnati (B.B.S., 1967); University of Kentucky (J.D., 1970). Member, Board of Trustees, World Affairs Institute, 1980-1985. President, 1979-1980 and Member, Board of Directors, 1977-1980, International Visitors Center, Inc. Named, Ohio Super Lawyer, 2006. *Member:* American Immigration Lawyers Association. ***PRACTICE AREAS:*** Immigration and Nationality (99%).

(This Listing Continued)

ASSOCIATE

NEIL IAN FLEISCHER, born Cincinnati, Ohio, January 16, 1975; admitted to bar, 2000, Ohio. *Education:* Hobart (A.B., 1997); Capital University (J.D., 2000). Order of the Curia. ***PRACTICE AREAS:*** Immigration Law. ***Email:*** nfleischer@immigrate2usa.com

FREUND, FREEZE & ARNOLD

A LEGAL PROFESSIONAL ASSOCIATION

FOURTH AND WALNUT CENTRE
105 EAST FOURTH STREET
SUITE 1400
CINCINNATI, OHIO 45202-4006
Telephone: 513-665-3500
Telecopier: 513-665-3503
Email: ffalawci@ffalaw.com
URL: http://www.ffalaw.com

Dayton, Ohio Office: One Dayton Centre, One South Main Street, Suite 1800, 45402-2017. Telephone: 937-222-2424. Telecopier: 937-222-5369. Email: ffalawda@ffalaw.com.

Columbus, Ohio Office: Capitol Square Office Building, 65 East State Street, Suite 800, 43215. Telephone: 614-827-7300. Telecopier: 614-827-7303. Email: ffalawco@ffalaw.com.

Covington, Kentucky Office Suite: RiverCenter, 50 East RiverCenter Boulevard, Suite 408, 41011. Telephone: 859-292-2088. Telecopier: 859-292-2514. Email: ffalawky@ffalaw.

Civil Litigation including Commercial Litigation, Employment Defense, Professional Malpractice Defense, Employer Intentional Torts, Construction Litigation, Civil Rights Defense, Local Government Defense, Nursing Home Defense, Environmental Litigation and Insurance Defense.

FIRM PROFILE: Freund, Freeze & Arnold is a full service litigation firm, with offices in Dayton, Cincinnati, Columbus and Covington, Kentucky. The firm's practice emphasizes civil litigation including commercial litigation, employment litigation, municipal government defense, malpractice defense of doctors, lawyers, realtors, insurance agents and other professionals; civil rights defense; employer intentional torts defense; nursing home defense; environment litigation and insurance defense. The firm holds the highest rating given by Martindale-Hubbell and is listed in the Bar Register of Preeminent Lawyers. The firm is an equal opportunities employer. The attorneys in the firm are active in community and professional groups, including local, state and national bar associations. They also have enjoyed strong academic backgrounds.

Geographic area of practice: The firm represents clients in Ohio, southeastern Indiana, and Kentucky, handling an extensive amount of cases in the cities of Dayton, Cincinnati, and Columbus, in the surrounding Ohio counties of Darke, Shelby, Miami, Clark, Champaign, Logan, Madison, Greene, Preble, Butler, Warren, Clermont, Clinton and Franklin, the Kentucky counties of Boone, Kenton and Campbell, and the Indiana counties of Clark, Dearborn, Decatur, Delaware, Franklin, Henry, Jennings, Ohio, Randolph, Ripley, Rush, Scott, Switzerland, Union and Wayne. The firm practices in the local, state and federal courts of northern Kentucky, southeastern Indiana and southern and central Ohio, including Columbus and Franklin County. The firm has offices in Dayton, Cincinnati, Columbus and Covington, Kentucky. The firm's central location in southwestern Ohio allows it to efficiently and economically serve its clients in all of southwestern Ohio and surrounding areas. Dayton, Springfield, Columbus and Indianapolis are closely linked by Interstate 70. Dayton, Cincinnati and Covington are closely linked by Interstate 75. All four offices are at the junction of the area's major highways.

THOMAS B. BRUNS, born Chicago, Illinois, November 22, 1965; admitted to bar, 1990, Ohio; 1993, Kentucky. *Education:* Miami University (B.A., 1987); University of Cincinnati (J.D., 1990). *Member:* Cincinnati, Northern Kentucky, Ohio State and Kentucky Bar Associations; Ohio Association of Civil Trial Attorneys; Defense Research Institute. ***PRACTICE AREAS:*** Insurance Defense; Construction Law; Appellate Practice; Civil Trial; Commercial Litigation. ***Email:*** tbruns@ffalaw.com

MARK A. MACDONALD, born Boston, Massachusetts, November 29, 1953; admitted to bar, 1980, Ohio; 1983, U.S. District Court, Southern District of Ohio; 1984, U.S. Court of Appeals, Sixth Circuit; 1994, U.S. District Court, Eastern District of Kentucky; 1995, Kentucky. *Education:* University of Cincinnati (B.A., with high honors, 1975; J.D., 1980). Member, Board of Editors, University of Cincinnati Law Review, 1979-1980. *Member:* Cincinnati, Northern Kentucky, Ohio State and Kentucky Bar Associations; Ohio Association of Civil Trial Attorneys. ***PRACTICE AREAS:*** Personal Injury; Medical Malpractice. ***Email:*** mmacdona@ffalaw.com

DEE SHERIFF-MACDONALD, born Covington, Kentucky, November 30, 1943; admitted to bar, 1984, Ohio; 1985, U.S. District Court, Southern District of Ohio; 1990, Kentucky and U.S. District Court, Eastern District of Kentucky. *Education:* Northern Kentucky University (A.A.S., 1974; B.A., 1980); Salmon P. Chase College of Law (J.D., 1984). Order of the Curia. Associate Editor, Northern Kentucky Law Review, 1983-1984. Judicial Law Clerk to the Honorable William O. Bertelsman, U.S. District Court, Eastern District of Kentucky, 1984-1985. Adjunct Professor, Salmon P. Chase College of Law, Northern Kentucky University, 1995. Registered Nurse: Ohio, 1974; Kentucky, 1983. *Member:* Cincinnati, Northern Kentucky, Ohio State and Kentucky Bar Associations; Ohio Association of Civil Trial Attorneys; Defense Research Institute. ***PRACTICE AREAS:*** Medical Malpractice Defense; Professional Malpractice Defense; Insurance Defense. ***Email:*** dsheriff@ffalaw.com

TIMOTHY B. SCHENKEL, born Cincinnati, Ohio, August 24, 1966; admitted to bar, 1992, Kentucky and U.S. District Court, Eastern District of Kentucky; 1993, Ohio; 1996, U.S. District Court, Southern District of Ohio. *Education:* University of Dayton (B.S., cum laude, 1988); Salmon P. Chase College of Law (J.D., 1992). Member, Salmon P. Chase Law Review. *Member:* Cincinnati, Northern Kentucky, Ohio State and Kentucky Bar Associa-

(This Listing Continued)

FREUND, FREEZE & ARNOLD, A LEGAL PROFESSIONAL ASSOCIATION, Cincinnati—Continued

tions; Ohio Association of Civil Trial Attorneys. ***PRACTICE AREAS:*** Commercial Litigation; Construction Litigation; Workers Compensation; Insurance Defense. ***Email:*** tschenke@ffalaw.com

JENNIFER K. NORDSTROM, born Steubenville, Ohio, August 13, 1971; admitted to bar, 1996, Ohio; 1997, U.S. District Court, Southern and Northern Districts of Ohio; 1999, Indiana, Kentucky and U.S. District Court, Northern and Southern Districts of Indiana; 2002, U.S. Court of Appeals, Sixth Circuit; U.S. District Court, Eastern and Western Districts of Kentucky. *Education:* Ohio Northern University (B.A., 1993); University of Cincinnati (J.D., 1996). Member, University of Cincinnati Law Review. Treasurer, Student Bar Association, 1994-1995. *Member:* Cincinnati, Northern Kentucky, Kentucky, Indiana State and Ohio State Bar Associations; Ohio Association of Civil Trial Attorneys; Defense Trial Counsel of Indiana; Defense Research Institute. ***PRACTICE AREAS:*** Civil Trial; Professional Malpractice Defense; Insurance Coverage. ***Email:*** jnordstro@ffalaw.com

JOHN J. GARVEY, III, born Columbus, Ohio, May 21, 1966; admitted to bar, 1991, Kentucky; 1992, Ohio, U.S. District Court, Eastern and Western Districts of Kentucky and U.S. Court of Appeals, Sixth Circuit; 1993, U.S. District Court, Southern District of Ohio; 1999, Indiana, U.S. District Court, Southern and Northern Districts of Indiana. *Education:* Xavier University (H.A.B., Honors, Bachelor of Arts (Classics); A.B., History, 1988); Salmon P. Chase College of Law, Northern Kentucky University (J.D., 1991). Member, Kentucky House of Delegates. President, Student Bar Association, 1990-1991. Northern Kentucky Kenton Law Library Trustee, 1995—. *Member:* Cincinnati (Member, Character and Fitness Committee, 1995—), Northern Kentucky (Kenton County Law Library Trustee, 1995-1999; Secretary, 2000, Treasurer, 2001-2002), Kentucky (House of Delegates, 1998-2004), and Ohio State Bar Associations; Ohio Association of Civil Trial Attorneys; Salmon P. Chase, American Inns of Court (Barrister). ***PRACTICE AREAS:*** Civil Litigation; Commercial Litigation; Construction Litigation. ***Email:*** jgarvey@ffalaw.com

DAVID A. SHEARER, JR., born Lexington, Kentucky, April 20, 1968; admitted to bar, 1993, Kentucky, U.S. District Court, Eastern District of Kentucky and U.S. Court of Appeals, Sixth Circuit; 1999, Ohio. *Education:* Vanderbilt University (B.A., 1990); University of Kentucky (J.D., 1993). *Member:* Cincinnati, Northern Kentucky, Kentucky, Ohio State and American Bar Associations; Ohio Association of Civil Trial Attorneys. ***Email:*** dshearer@ffalaw.com

---

JUDD R. UHL, born September 18, 1973; admitted to bar, 1999, Ohio and U.S. District Court, Northern and Southern Districts of Ohio; 2003, Kentucky. *Education:* Miami University (B.A., 1995); University of Akron (J.D., 1999). *Member:* Cincinnati, Northern Kentucky, Ohio State and Kentucky Bar Associations; Ohio Association of Civil Trial Attorneys. ***PRACTICE AREAS:*** Automobile Products Liability; Trucking; Medical Malpractice; Products Liability. ***Email:*** juhl@ffalaw.com

DAVID W. ZAHNISER, born Lexington, Kentucky, February 5, 1965; admitted to bar, 1996, Kentucky; 1997, U.S. District Court, Eastern and Western Districts of Kentucky, U.S. Court of Appeals, Sixth Circuit; 2004, Ohio. *Education:* Greenville College (B.S., 1987); University of Kentucky College of Law (J.D., 1996). *Member:* Cincinnati, Kentucky, Ohio State and Northern Kentucky Bar Associations; Ohio Association of Civil Trial Attorneys. ***REPORTED CASES:*** Stone v. Glass, 35 S.W.3d 827 (Ky. App. 2000). ***PRACTICE AREAS:*** Insurance; Civil Practice. ***Email:*** dzahnise@ffalaw.com

JAMES M. CAWOOD, III, born Ft. Thomas, Kentucky, April 28, 1972; admitted to bar, 1999, Kentucky; 2000, U.S. District Court, Eastern District of Kentucky; 2001, U.S. District Court, Western District of Kentucky; 2004, Ohio. *Education:* University of Kentucky (B.A., 1995); Salmon P. Chase College of Law (J.D., 1999). *Member:* Cincinnati, Northern Kentucky, Kentucky, Ohio State and American Bar Associations; Kentucky Academy of Trial Attorneys; Ohio Association of Civil Trial Attorneys; Defense Research Institute; American Inns of Court (Salmon P. Chase Inn of Court). ***PRACTICE AREAS:*** Insurance Defense; Personal Injury Defense; Medical Malpractice Defense. ***Email:*** jcawood@ffalaw.com

MICHELLE L. DONOGHUE, born Cincinnati, Ohio, June 22, 1976; admitted to bar, 2001, Ohio; 2003, Indiana; 2004, Kentucky and U.S. District Court, Southern District of Ohio and Northern and Southern Districts of Indiana; 2005, U.S. District Court, Eastern and Western Districts of Kentucky. *Education:* University of Kentucky (B.S., cum laude, Biotechnology, 1998; J.D., 2001). *Member:* Cincinnati, Ohio State, Kentucky, Indiana State and Northern Kentucky Bar Associations; Ohio Association of Civil Trial Attorneys (OACTA). ***Email:*** mdonoghue@ffalaw.com

KELLY A. ARMSTRONG, born September 4, 1977; admitted to bar, 2002, Wisconsin; 2003, Ohio; 2004, Indiana and Kentucky; 2005, Illinois. *Education:* University of Kentucky (B.A., English and Sociology, 2000); University of Wisconsin (J.D., 2002). *Member:* Cincinnnati, Illinois State, Ohio State and Indiana State Bar Associations; State Bar of Wisconsin; Ohio Association of Civil Trial Attorneys; Potter Stewart Inn of Court. ***PRACTICE AREAS:*** Insurance Coverage Analysis; Insurance Defense; Litigation; Libel, Slander and Defamation; Federal Civil Practice; Products Liability; Premises Liability; Toxic Torts; Mold Defense. ***Email:*** karmstro@ffalaw.com

ILONA I. KATRUS, born Cincinnati, Ohio, April 2, 1977; admitted to bar, 2003, Ohio; 2004, Kentucky, U.S. District Court, Southern District of Ohio and U.S. District Court, Eastern and Western Districts of Kentucky. *Education:* Xavier University (B.S., Natural Sciences/Pre-Med, 1999); University of Cincinnati College of Law (J.D., 2003). *Member:* Cincinnati, Northern Kentucky, Ohio State, Kentucky and American Bar Associations; Ohio Association of Civil Trial Attorneys. ***PRACTICE AREAS:*** Personal Injury Litigation; Construction Law; Premises Liability. ***Email:*** ikatrus@ffalaw.com

POUL H. LEMASTERS, born Bellaire, Ohio, December 5, 1970; admitted to bar, 2004, Ohio and U.S. District Court, Southern District of Ohio; 2005, Kentucky. *Education:* Cincinnati College of Mortuary Science (B.S., Mortuary Science, cum laude, 1997); Salmon P. Chase College of Law (J.D., magna cum laude, 2003). *Member:* Cincinnati, Northern Kentucky and Ohio State Bar Associations; Ohio Association of Civil Trial Attorneys. ***PRACTICE AREAS:*** Insurance Defense; Litigation; Workers Compensation; Construction Law. ***Email:*** plemaste@ffalaw.com

JASON A. MOSBAUGH, born Cincinnati, Ohio; admitted to bar, 2003, Ohio, Kentucky, Indiana and U.S. District Court, Southern District of Ohio. *Education:* Miami University (B.A.); Salmon P. Chase College of Law; Georgetown Law Center (J.D.). *Member:* Cincinnati, Clermont County, Northern Kentucky, Ohio State, Indiana State and American Bar Associations; Ohio Association of Civil Trial Attorneys. ***PRACTICE AREAS:*** Construction Law; Insurance Defense; Civil Litigation; Appellate Practice. ***Email:*** jmosbaug@ffalaw.com

RUTH T. KELLY, born Cincinnati, Ohio, May 9, 1978; admitted to bar, 2005, Ohio and U.S. District Court, Southern District of Ohio. *Education:* Ohio Wesleyan University (B.A., 2000, cum laude); Chase College of Law (J.D., 2004). Staff, 2002-2003 and Editor, 2003-2004, Northern Kentucky Law Review. Co-Author: "Of Innocents and Offenders: A Survey of Kentucky Juvenile Law," Northern Kentucky Law Review; Symposium Issue: "Campaign "Finance Reform". *Member:* Cincinnati and Ohio State Bar Associations; Northern Kentucky Bar Association; Ohio Association of Civil Trial Attorneys. ***LANGUAGES:*** Spanish. ***PRACTICE AREAS:*** General Insurance Defense; MVA; Premises Liability; Medical Malpractice Defense. ***Email:*** rkelly@ffalaw.com

LOCAL COUNSEL FOR: Special Trial Counsel: City of Dayton; Miami Valley Hospital; Children's Medical Center; Dayton Power & Light Company; Commercial Clients: Bottlers Services, Inc.; Lutheran Social Services. Insurance Company Clients: Auto-Owners Insurance Company; Cincinnati Ins. Co.; CNA Insurance Company; Erie Insurance Group; Farmers Insurance Group; Government Employees Ins. Co.; GRE Insurance Group; Great American Insurance Company; Kemper Group; Media/Professional Insurance, Inc.; Motorists Insurance Company; OHIC Insurance Co.; St. Paul Fire & Marine Insurance Co.; State Auto Insurance Co.; State Farm Mutual Automobile Insurance Company; Liberty Mutual Ins. Co.; Indiana Ins. Co.; Met Life; GE Medical Protective Ins. Co.; American Empire Group.

(For Complete Biographical Data on Dayton and Columbus, Ohio Personnel, See Professional Biographies at Dayton and Columbus, Ohio)

FROST BROWN TODD LLC

Established in 1919
2200 PNC CENTER
201 EAST FIFTH STREET
CINCINNATI, OHIO 45202-4182
Telephone: 513-651-6800
Telecopier: 513-651-6981
Email: info@fbtlaw.com
URL: http://www.frostbrowntodd.com

Columbus, Ohio Office: One Columbus, 10 West Broad Street, 43215-3467. Telephone: 614-464-1211. Telecopier: 614-464-1737.
Middletown, Ohio Office: 300 North Main Street, Suite 200, 45042-1919. Telephone: 513-422-2001. Telecopier: 513-422-3010.
Lexington, Kentucky Office: 250 West Main Street, Suite 2700, 40507-1742. Telephone: 859-231-0000. Telecopier: 859-231-0011.
Louisville, Kentucky Office: 400 West Market Street, 32nd Floor, 40202-3363. Telephone: 502-589-5400. Telecopier: 502-581-1087.
Nashville, Tennessee Office: 424 Church Street, Suite 1600, 37219-2308. Telephone: 615-251-5550. Telecopier: 615-251-5551.
New Albany, Indiana Office: 120 West Spring Street, Suite 400, 47150-3655. Telephone: 812-948-2800. Telecopier: 812-948-7994.

Alternative Dispute Resolution, Bankruptcy and Reorganization, Business Acquisitions, Business and Corporate, Commercial Finance, Commercial Litigation, Commercial/Real Estate, Construction, Copyright, Corporate Responsibility and Defense, Employee Benefits, Energy and Natural Resources, Entrepreneurial, Environmental, Equine, Estate Planning and Administration, Financial Institutions, Fire and Explosion, Health Care, Immigration, International, Intellectual Property, International Business, Internet and Electronic Commerce, Labor and Employment Law, Litigation, Media, Mold and Water Intrusion, Multi-District Litigation, Patent Litigation, Personal Planning and Family Business, Privacy and Information Security, Product Liability, Public Finance, Securities, Tax, Tort & Insurance Law, Trademark, Venture Capital, General Trial Practice in all State and Federal Courts.

FIRM PROFILE: Frost Brown Todd LLC is the result of the November 1, 2000 merger of Frost & Jacobs LLP and Brown, Todd & Heyburn PLLC. This super-regional law firm of approximately 370 attorneys has seven offices in Cincinnati, Columbus and Middletown, Ohio; Louisville and Lexington, Kentucky; Nashville, Tennessee; and New Albany, Indiana. The increased breadth of practice experience, combined with the depth of service and expanded geographic scope, allows the combined firm to effectively serve the growing and changing needs of its institutional, commercial and individual clients at the local, regional, national and international level.

48 Frost Brown Todd LLC attorneys were recognized by their peers in the new 10th Edition of The Best Lawyers in America (2003 - 2004).

Frost Brown Todd LLC was ranked in the Top Ten U.S. Patent Litigation firms by Managing Intellectual Proerty (2002).

MEMBERS

EDWIN R. ACHESON, JR., born Joplin, Missouri, September 14, 1955; admitted to bar, 1982, Indiana; 1989, Ohio; registered to practice before U.S. Patent and Trademark Office. *Education:* University of Missouri (B.S., Mechanical and Aerospace Engineering, 1977); Duke University (J.D., 1980). Adjunct Faculty, Univesity of Cincinnati Law School, 1997—. ***PRACTICE AREAS:*** Patents; Copyrights; Computer Law; Licensing; Intellectual Property Litigation. ***Email:*** eacheson@fbtlaw.com

DEBORAH S. ADAMS, born Cincinnati, Ohio, May 17, 1955; admitted to bar, 1982, Ohio; 1983, Kentucky. *Education:* University of Cincinnati (B.A., 1977); Harvard Univer-

(This Listing Continued)

sity (M.A., 1979); Harvard Law School (J.D., 1982). *Member:* Cincinnati and Ohio State Bar Associations. ***PRACTICE AREAS:*** Employment Discrimination; Wrongful Discharge. ***Email:*** dadams@fbtlaw.com

STEPHEN R. ALBAINY-JENEI, born Massillon, Ohio, November 7, 1964; admitted to bar, 1995, Ohio and U.S. District Court, Southern District of Ohio; registered to practice before U.S. Patent and Trademark Office. *Education:* University of Dayton (B.S., 1986; M.S., 1988); University of Cincinnati (J.D., 1995; Ph.D. Candidate, A.B.D., 1990). Designated one of Chambers & Partners' "America's Leading Business Lawyers," 2003-2006. Author: "Building and Managing University Patent Portfolios," IP Value 2005, Globe White Pages; "Early-Stage Companies Face New Challenges," National Law Journal, December 8, 2003. Speaker: "Commercialization 101, Intellectual Property," Life Sciences Without Boundaries: Bridges to Collaboration Conference, 2003; "Software Licensing Agreements," Multilaw Americas Regional Conference, San Jose, Costa Rica, 2003; "Emerging Legal Issues in Intellectual Property," Attorney General's Annual Conference of Public College and University Attorneys, 2000. Assistant General Counsel and Assistant Director, Intellectual Property for the University of Cincinnati, 1995-2000. Acting Director, Intellectual Property and University Patent Officer, 2000. Member, Leadership Council, CincyTechUSA, 2003—. Presenter's Committee, Greater Cincinnati Venture Association, 2004—. Life Member, University of Cincinnati College of Law Alumni Association. *Member:* Cincinnati and American (Member, Intellectual Property Section) Bar Associations; American Intellectual Property Law Association (Member, Biotechnology Committee); Cincinnati Intellectual Property Law Association; Licensing Executive Society. ***PRACTICE AREAS:*** Intellectual Property Law; Patents; Patent Prosecution; Biotechnology; Licensing; Copyrights; Computer Technology. ***Email:*** salbainyjenei@fbtlaw.com

THOMAS D. ANTHONY, born Cleveland, Ohio, July 23, 1952; admitted to bar, 1977, Ohio. *Education:* Miami University (B.S., 1974); Case Western Reserve University (J.D., 1977). ***PRACTICE AREAS:*** Health Care; Corporate Law. ***Email:*** tanthony@fbtlaw.com

JOHN H. APPEL, born Cincinnati, Ohio, June 1, 1949; admitted to bar, 1974, Ohio. *Education:* University of Cincinnati (B.A., 1971); Harvard Law School (J.D., 1974). ***PRACTICE AREAS:*** Employee Benefits. ***Email:*** jappel@fbtlaw.com

G. RANDALL AYERS, born New Castle, Indiana, August 9, 1962; admitted to bar, 1988, Ohio; 1996, Kentucky. *Education:* Earlham College (A.B., cum laude, 1984); The Ohio State University School of Law (J.D., 1988). Order of the Barristers. Listed in Best Lawyers in America. Member, NLRB DOL State Labor Agencies. *Member:* Ohio State (Member, Labor and Employment Section) and American (Member, Labor and Employment Section) Bar Associations. ***SPECIAL AGENCIES:*** NLRB DOL State Labor Agencies. ***PRACTICE AREAS:*** Labor and Employment. ***Email:*** rayers@fbtlaw.com

GERALD L. BALDWIN, born Dayton, Kentucky, July 10, 1946; admitted to bar, 1969, Ohio; 1971, Kentucky. *Education:* Thomas More College (A.B., 1966); University of Cincinnati (J.D., 1969). *Member:* Cincinnati, Ohio State, Kentucky and American Bar Associations; Federal Bar Association; American Bankruptcy Institution. [U.S. Army Reserve, 1969-1975]. ***PRACTICE AREAS:*** Bankruptcy; Creditors Rights; Commercial Litigation. ***Email:*** gbaldwin@fbtlaw.com

DAVID S. BENCE, born Cincinnati, Ohio, April 19, 1965; admitted to bar, 1990, Ohio. *Education:* University of Michigan (A.B., with distinction, 1987); The Ohio State University College of Law (J.D., 1990). ***PRACTICE AREAS:*** Secured Transactions; Commercial and Construction Lending; Sale of Goods. ***Email:*** dbence@fbtlaw.com

MATTHEW C. BLICKENSDERFER, born Tuscola, Illinois, July 16, 1970; admitted to bar, 1995, Illinois and U.S. District Court, Northern District of Illinois; 1996, U.S. Court of Appeals, Sixth Circuit; 1999, U.S. Court of Appeals, Seventh Circuit; 2000, Ohio; 2001, U.S. District Court, Southern District of Ohio; 2002, U.S. District Court, Eastern District of Michigan; 2003, U.S. Supreme Court. *Education:* Northwestern University (B.A., with highest distinction, 1992); Harvard University (J.D., cum laude, 1995). Law Clerk, Honorable David A. Nelson, U.S. Court of Appeals, Sixth Circuit, 1996-1997. Editor-in-Chief, Sixth Circuit Practice Manual (Third Edition) (forthcoming). Adjunct Professor, University of Cincinnati College of Law, 2002—. Author: "Federal Trade Commission Rediscovers the Robinson-Patman Act," Corporate Counsel, May 2000; "Unleashing RICO," 17 Harvard Journal of Law & Public Policy 867, 1994. ***PRACTICE AREAS:*** Appellate Practice; Antitrust; Trade Regulation; Commercial Litigation. ***Email:*** mblickensderfer@fbtlaw.com

SCOTT R. BROWN, born Cincinnati, Ohio, July 28, 1956; admitted to bar, 1995, Ohio; 1997, U.S. District Court, Southern and Western Districts of Ohio. *Education:* University of Cincinnati (B.A., 1978); Salmon P. Chase College of Law (J.D., magna cum laude, 1995). Order of the Curia. First Place, Kentucky Bar Association Student Writing Competition, 1994. Publications: Kentucky Bench and Bar, Vol. 58, No. 4, 1994; Northern Kentucky Law Review, Vol. 22, No. 2, 1995. *Member:* Cincinnati, Ohio State and American Bar Associations. ***REPORTED CASES:*** Jennings v. Univ. Bar Nose & Throat Specialists,1999 Ohio App. LEXIS 6329 (Ohio Ct. App. Dec. 30, 1999); Bargo v. R&L Transfer, 2000 Ohio App. LEXIS 3869 (Ohio Ct. App. Aug. 28, 2000); Houser v. Motorists Mutual, 2002 Ohio App. LEXIS 2913 (June 4, 2002); Kentucky Medical Ins. Co. v. Jones, No. 02AP-817 (Ohio Ct. App., June 24, 2003). ***PRACTICE AREAS:*** Litigation; Insurance; Real Estate; Business Litigation; Construction. ***Email:*** srbrown@fbtlaw.com

PAUL W. CASPER, JR., born Greensburg, Pennsylvania, November 14, 1946; admitted to bar, 1981, Ohio; U.S. Federal District Court and U.S. Ditrict Court, Southern District of Ohio; U.S. Court of Appeals, Sixth Circuit. *Education:* St. Vincent College (B.A., 1968); University of Dayton (M.S., 1975; J.D., 1981). Member: Greater Cincinnati Rotary Club; Greater Cincinnati Area Chamber of Commerce. Past Chair, Dayton Area Chamber of Commerce Environmental Law Committee. Past Member: Steering Committee of Dayton Area; Chamber of Commerce Legislative & Governmental Affairs Committee. Professional Experience: U.S. Steel-Chemical Engineer; Instructor, University of Dayton. *Member:* Cincinnati and Ohio State Bar Associations. [U.S. Army, 18th Airborne Corps, 1969-1972]. ***PRACTICE AREAS:*** Environmental Law. ***Email:*** pcasper@fbtlaw.com

KEVIN L. COONEY, born 1969; admitted to bar, 1997, Indiana and U.S. District Court, Southern and Northern Districts of Indiana; 1998, Ohio. *Education:* Purdue University (B.S., Che.E., 1992); Washington University (J.D., 1997). Editor-in-chief, Washington University Law Quarterly. *Member:* Cincinnati, Indiana State, Ohio State and American Bar Associations. ***PRACTICE AREAS:*** Mergers and Acquisitions; Corporate Law; Securities; Investment Company Law. ***Email:*** kcooney@fbtlaw.com

GRANT S. COWAN, born Cincinnati, Ohio, July 22, 1959; admitted to bar, 1985, Ohio; 1987, Florida. *Education:* University of Virginia (B.A., 1981); University of Cincinnati (J.D., 1985). Recipient, Distinguished Service Award, Ohio Association of Civil Trial Attorneys, 1996. Leadership Cincinnati, Class XXII. President, BMF Pediatric Clinics, 1996-1999. Member, Board of Trustees: Cincinnati Parks Foundation; Cincinnati Nature Center. *Member:* The Florida Bar. ***PRACTICE AREAS:*** Business Litigation; Unfair Competition; Securities Litigation. ***Email:*** gcowan@fbtlaw.com

MYRON L. DALE, born Cincinnati, Ohio, May 19, 1949; admitted to bar, 1975, Ohio. *Education:* Yale University (B.A., cum laude, 1971); Georgetown University (J.D., 1975). ***PRACTICE AREAS:*** Antitrust and Trade Regulation; Commercial Litigation; Accountant Liability. ***Email:*** mdale@fbtlaw.com

JOSEPH J. DEHNER, born Cincinnati, Ohio, November 28, 1948; admitted to bar, 1973, Ohio; 1986, Florida; U.S. Court of Appeals, Sixth Circuit, U.S. Court of International Trade, U.S. District Court, Southern and Northern Districts of Ohio and U.S. District Court, Eastern District of Kentucky. *Education:* Princeton University (A.B., cum laude, 1970); Harvard Law School (J.D., cum laude, 1973). Recipient, Governor's E-Award, Excellence in Exporting, 2003. Chairman, Southern Ohio District Export Council, 2002—. Ohio Commodore, 2003—. Chair, firm's International Services Group, 1988—. Trustee, Princeton University, 1970-1974. Member, Ohio Historical Society, 1974-1978. Member, Heimlich Institute Foundation, 1980—; Chairman, Foreign Policy Leadership Council Cincinnati Chapter, 2005—. President, French-American Chamber of Commerce of Greater Cincinnati, 2004—. *Member:* Cincinnati, Ohio State and American (Vice-Chair, International Litigation Committee, 2002-2004) Bar Associations; Public Investors Arbitration Bar Association. ***LANGUAGES:*** Russian. ***REPORTED CASES:*** Cohen v. J.B. Oxford, No. C-1-02-571, S.D. Ohio 2002) (confirming punitive damage award against clearing broker); Wiepking v. Prudential Securities, (6th Cir. 1988) (ordering trial rather than arbitration of investor claims); Counterpart International, Inc. v. Freedom Farm International, Inc., International Arbitration (1998 decision by now Chief Justice John Roberts). ***TRANSACTIONS:*** International transactions and counseling, including cross-border acquisitions; representation of claimants in over 150 securities arbitrations; class-action victories for defrauded investors. ***PRACTICE AREAS:*** International Business (50%); Securities Disputes (50%). ***Email:*** jdehner@fbtlaw.com

ROBERT A. DIMLING, born Fort Worth, Texas, August 14, 1941; admitted to bar, 1966, Ohio. *Education:* Bowling Green State University (B.A., 1963); University of Michigan (J.D., 1966). ***PRACTICE AREAS:*** Labor and Employment; Occupational Safety and Health; Workers' Compensation. ***Email:*** bdimling@fbtlaw.com

RICHARD J. ERICKSON, born Pontiac, Michigan, July 16, 1946; admitted to bar, 1971, Ohio. *Education:* Denison University (B.A., 1968); Vanderbilt University (J.D., 1971). ***PRACTICE AREAS:*** Commercial Law; Creditors Rights. ***Email:*** derickson@fbtlaw.com

SUSAN GROGAN FALLER, born Cincinnati, Ohio, March 1, 1950; admitted to bar, 1975, Ohio and U.S. District Court, Southern District of Ohio; 1982, U.S. Supreme Court, U.S. Court of Appeals, Sixth Circuit and U.S. Claims Court; 1984, U.S. Tax Court; 1989, Kentucky; 1990, U.S. District Court, Eastern District of Kentucky; 1996, U.S. District Court, Western District of Kentucky; 2003, U.S. District Court, Northern District of Ohio. *Education:* University of Cincinnati (B.A., magna cum laude, 1972) University of Michigan (J.D., cum laude, 1975). Phi Beta Kappa. Note Editor, Michigan Law Review. Author: "Media Law Resource Center Annual 50-State Survey of Current Developments in Media Libel Law"; "Annual 50-State Survey of Employment Libel adn Privacy Law - Ohio Preparer". Member, Class XVII of Leadership Cincinnati. Member, YWCA Academy of Achieving Career Women. Listed in "Best Lawyers in America" and "Who's Who" publications. *Member:* Cincinnati, Ohio State (Member and Former Chair, Media Law Committee), Kentucky and American (Member: Forum Committee on Communications; First Amendment & Media Litigation Committee; Sections on: Litigation; Tort, Trial & Insurance Practice) Bar Associations; Media Law Resource Center (Chair, Membership Committee and Former President, Executive Committee, Defense Counsel Section); Potter Stewart American Inn of Court. ***PRACTICE AREAS:*** Media Law; First Amendment Law; Libel Litigation; Commercial Litigation; Business Litigation; Tax Litigation. ***Email:*** sfaller@fbtlaw.com

HENRY G. FROST (1875-1951)

NEIL GANULIN, born New York, N.Y., July 20, 1948; admitted to bar, 1973, Ohio. *Education:* University of Cincinnati (B.A., magna cum laude, 1970); University of Michigan (J.D., 1973). ***PRACTICE AREAS:*** Securities; Mergers and Acquisitions; Corporate. ***Email:*** nganulin@fbtlaw.com

JOANNE WISSMAN GLASS, born Covington, Kentucky, November 6, 1969; admitted to bar, 1994, Ohio; 1995, Kentucky and U.S. District Court, Eastern and Western Districts of Kentucky; U.S. District Court, Southern District of Ohio. *Education:* Xavier University (B.A., 1991); Salmon P. Chase College of Law (J.D., 1994). Listed in Who's Who. *Member:* Cincinnati (Member: Workers' Compensation Committee and Executive Committee; CLE Chair, Young Lawyers Section), Northern Kentucky (Member, Young Lawyers Section; Workers' Compensation Committee) Kentucky, Ohio State and American Bar Associations. (Certified Specialist in Workers Compensation Law, Ohio State Bar Association). ***PRACTICE AREAS:*** Workers' Compensation. ***Email:*** jglass@fbtlaw.com

RICHARD M. GOEHLER, born Massillon, Ohio, November 29, 1956; admitted to bar, 1982, Ohio; U.S. Supreme Court; U.S. Court of Appeals, Sixth, Seventh and Ninth Circuits; U.S. District Court, Southern and Northern Districts of Ohio. *Education:* Miami University (A.B., magna cum laude, 1979); University of Notre Dame (J.D., magna cum laude, 1982). Recipient, International Academy of Trial Lawyers Award, 1982. Editor, Frost Brown Todd Media Law Advisory. Author: "The Media Law Handbook for Radio Broadcasters," Editor, National Association of Broadcasters; "Expansion of Tort Law at the Expense of the First Amendment: Has the Jones Court Gone Too Far?" Northern Kentucky Law Review, Symposium Issue 2000; MLRC 50-State Survey of Media Libel Law; MLRC 50-State Survey of Employment Libel & Privacy Law. Co-Author, "Business and Commercial Litigation in Federal Courts," Chapter on Sales Litigation, The West Group, 1999,

(This Listing Continued)

FROST BROWN TODD LLC, Cincinnati—Continued

2005. Member, Boards / Civic Association. Member, Board of Directors, The Ruth Lyons Foundation. Member, Media Law Resource Center, Defense Counsel Section, Advertising and Commercial Speech Committee. Member, Cincinnati Academy of Leadership for Lawyers Steering Committee. Member, Communications Advisory Committee. *Member:* Cincinnati, Ohio State (Member, Media Law Committee) American (Governing Board Member, Forum Committee on Communications; Member, Litigation Section; First Amendment and Media Litigation Committee) Bar Associations; National Institute for Trial Advocacy. ***PRACTICE AREAS:*** Media Law; First Amendment; Libel, Slander and Defamation; Privacy Law; Advertising and Marketing; Litigation; Trademark; Copyright; Business Litigation. ***Email:*** rgoehler@fbtlaw.com

RONALD E. GOLD, born Erie, Pennsylvania, October 18, 1964; admitted to bar, 1989, Illinois; 1993, Ohio; U.S. Court of Appeals, Sixth Circuit; U.S. District Court, Northern District of Illinois; U.S. District Court, Eastern District of Wisconsin; U.S. District Court, Western District of Kentucky; U.S. District Court, Southern District of Indiana. *Education:* University of Michigan (B.A., 1986); University of Pittsburgh (J.D., magna cum laude, 1989). Order of the Coif. ***PRACTICE AREAS:*** Bankruptcy; Creditors' Rights; Workouts. ***Email:*** rgold@fbtlaw.com

STEVEN J. GOLDSTEIN, born New York, N.Y., September 1, 1951; admitted to bar, 1975, Ohio; registered to practice before U.S. Patent and Trademark Office. *Education:* Massachusetts Institute of Technology (B.S., 1972); Boston University (J.D., 1975). Trustee, BioStart, Southern Ohio Biomed Incubator. Member, Research and Education Committee, Cincinnati Children's Research Foundation. Member, MIT Educational Council. Listed, Best Lawyers in America, Intellectual Property. Selected Leading IP Lawyers in Ohio, Chambers USA, 2005. *Member:* Cincinnati Bar Association; American Intellectual Property Law Association. ***PRACTICE AREAS:*** Intellectual Property Law; Patents; Trade Secret; International. ***Email:*** sgoldstein@fbtlaw.com

D. SCOTT GURNEY, born Cincinnati, Ohio, April 28, 1961; admitted to bar, 1986, Ohio; 1987, U.S. District Court, Southern District of Ohio. *Education:* Indiana University (B.A., high distinction, 1983), Phi Beta Kappa; Indiana University School of Law (J.D., 1986). Chair, Construction Law Group. Ranked Top Construction Lawyer in Cincinnati by Chambers USA Client's Guides 2003, 2004, 2005. Listed in Ohio Super Lawyers 2005 and CincyBusiness Leading Lawyers 2005 for construction. Member, Legislative Committee, Associated General Contractors of Ohio; Education Committee and Membership Committee, Allied Construction Industries. *Member:* Cincinnati (Past Chairman, Construction Law Committee) and American (Member: Forum on the Construction Industry; Committee on Construction Litigation) Bar Associations. ***TRANSACTIONS:*** Represents national CM/constructor in multi-million dollar claims relating to building collapse during construction project. Represented national CM/constructor in successfully defeating a project owner's $5 Million delay and cost-overrun claim in a two-week arbitration hearing. Represented national CM/constructor in multi-party claims by hospital alleging defective design and construction of exterior insulated finish system ("EIFS"). Represented masonry contractor in multi-party litigation against public school owner and architect for equitable adjustment to contract resulting from schedule delays and acceleration. Represented national home builder in successful arbitration against panel manufacturer relating to breach of contract and defective workmanship. Represented electrical contractor and steel erector in acceleration and disruption claims against public owner relating to construction of new baseball park. ***PRACTICE AREAS:*** Construction Law; Construction Claims; Construction Litigation; Construction Arbitration and Mediation; Construction Liens; Construction Contracts; Construction Defects; Construction Insurance. ***Email:*** sgurney@fbtlaw.com

CHRISTOPHER S. HABEL, born Cincinnati, Ohio, October 14, 1969; admitted to bar, 1995, Ohio; 1999, U.S. District Court, Northern and Southern Districts of Ohio; U.S. Court of Appeals, Sixth Circuit. *Education:* University of Cincinnati College of Engineering (B.S. Civil & Environmental Engineering, 1992); The Ohio State University College of Law (J.D., 1995). Chi Epsilon Civil Engineering Honor Society. Engineer in Training, Ohio. Articles Editor, Ohio State Law Journal. Author, "Satsky v. Paramount Communications, Inc.: Mining The Ore From Consent Decrees In Environmental Cases," 55 Ohio St. L.J. 983. Listed in: Ohio Super Lawyers Rising Star, 2005; Best Lawyers in America, 2006. Member, Metropolitan Sewer District of Greater Cincinnati, Combined Sewer Overflow Long Term Control Plan Steering Committee. Member, Hamilton County Earthworks Appeals Board. President, Valley View Foundation. *Member:* Cincinnati (Chair, Environmental Law Committee, 2004-2005) and Ohio State (Member, Environmental Law Committee) Bar Associations. ***PRACTICE AREAS:*** Environmental Law; Construction Law. ***Email:*** chabel@fbtlaw.com

WALTER E. HAGGERTY, born Nashville, Tennessee, December 23, 1951; admitted to bar, 1978, Ohio; 1979, Kentucky. *Education:* Xavier University (B.S.B.A., 1973); Salmon P. Chase College of Law (J.D., 1978). *Member:* Northern Kentucky Bar Association; National Association of Railroad Trial Counsel. *Member:* Cincinnati, Ohio State and Kentucky Bar Association. ***PRACTICE AREAS:*** Medical Malpractice Defense; Personal Injury Law; FELA Defense. ***Email:*** whaggerty@fbtlaw.com

ADAM P. HALL, born Glendale, West Virginia, August 21, 1964; admitted to bar, 1989, Ohio. *Education:* The Ohio State University (B.A., 1986); Case Western Reserve University (J.D., 1989). ***PRACTICE AREAS:*** Commercial Litigation; Securities Litigation. ***Email:*** ahall@fbtlaw.com

JACK B. HARRISON, born Chattanooga, Tennessee December 7, 1955; admitted to bar, 1993, Ohio; 1994, U.S. District Court, Southern District of Ohio; 1995, U.S. District Court, Northern District of Ohio; 1996, U.S. Court of Appeals, Sixth Circuit; 1997, U.S. Court of Appeals, District of Columbia Circuit and U.S. Supreme Court; 2000, U.S. District Court, Eastern and Western Districts of Kentucky; 2002, U.S. Court of Appeals, Seventh Circuit. *Education:* University of Tennessee at Chattanooga (B.A., 1978); St. Mary's Seminary (M.A., 1985); University of Cincinnati (J.D., 1993). *Member:* Cincinnati, Ohio State and American Bar Associations. ***REPORTED CASES:*** Iowa Utilities Board v. FCC, 120 F.3d 753 (8th Cir. 1997); Southwestern Bell Tele. Co. v. FCC, 116 F.3d 593 (D.C. Cir. 1997); Kurczi v. Eli Lilly & Co., et al., 113 F.3d 1426 (6th Cir. 1997); Bouchard v. American Home Products Corp., 213 F. Supp. 2d 802 (N.D. Ohio 2002); Philpot v. Haviland, 880 S.W.2d 550 (Ky. 1994); Sutowski v. Eli Lilly & Co, et al., 696 N.E.2d 187 (Ohio 1998); Hicks v. Westinghouse Materials Co., 676 N.E.2d 872 (Ohio 1997). ***PRACTICE AREAS:*** General Litigation (10%); Product Liability Defense (60%); Employment Litigation (25%); Telecommunications Regulatory (5%). ***Email:*** jharrison@fbtlaw.com

DOUGLAS E. HART, born Richmond, Indiana, September 10, 1958; admitted to bar, 1982, Ohio and U.S. Tax Court; U.S. Supreme Court; U.S. Court of Appeals, Fifth, Sixth and Tenth and District of Columbia Circuits. *Education:* Indiana University (B.A., 1979); University of Michigan (J.D., magna cum laude, 1982). *Member:* Cincinnati, Ohio, American Bar Associations; National Association of Railroad Trial Counsel. ***REPORTED CASES:*** Texas Office of Public Utility Counsel v. FCC, 183 F.3d 393 (5th Cir. 1999), cert. denied sub nom. AT&T Corp. v. Cincinnati Bell Tel. Co., 530 U.S. 1223 (2000); National Association of Professional Baseball Leagues, Inc. v. Very Minor Leagues, Inc., 223 F.3d 1143 (10th Cir. 2000); Cincinnati Bell Tel. Co. v. FCC, 69 F.3d 752 (6th Cir. 1995); State, ex rel. Cincinnati Bell Tel. Co. v. Public Utilities Commission of Ohio, 105 Ohio St.3d 177, 2005-Ohio-1150. ***PRACTICE AREAS:*** Litigation; Telecommunications; Transportation. ***Email:*** dhart@fbtlaw.com

STEPHEN N. HAUGHEY, born Dayton, Ohio, April 7, 1955; admitted to bar, 1984, Ohio; U.S. District Court, Southern and Northern Districts of Ohio and U.S. Court of Appelas, Sixth Circuit. *Education:* Wright State University (B.S., 1978); University of Dayton (J.D., 1984). ***PRACTICE AREAS:*** Environmental; Occupational Safety and Health. ***Email:*** shaughey@fbtlaw.com

CARL M. JACOBS (1886-1967)

FREDERICK W. KINDEL, born Akron, Ohio, February 10, 1952; admitted to bar, 1980, Ohio; 1987, Tennessee. *Education:* University of Kentucky (B.A., 1974); University of Tennessee (J.D., 1979). *Member:* Ohio State, Tennessee and American Bar Associations. ***PRACTICE AREAS:*** Real Estate Development and Leasing; Real Estate and Off Balance Sheet Financing; Loan Restructuring; Loan Workouts; Tax Incentives Leasing and Development; Tax Credits. ***Email:*** fkindel@fbtlaw.com

JOHN C. KRUG, born Columbus, Ohio, January 15, 1964; admitted to bar, 1989, Ohio. *Education:* University of Pennsylvania (B.A., cum laude, 1986); George Washington University Law School (J.D., 1989). ***PRACTICE AREAS:*** Business Law; Commercial Law; Commercial Real Estate Transactions; Commercial Real Estate Finance. ***Email:*** jkrug@fbtlaw.com

LORI A. LANDRUM, born Cincinnati, Ohio, August 15, 1968; admitted to bar, 1993, Ohio; 1996, U.S. District Court, Southern District of Ohio; 1998, U.S. Court of Appeals, Sixth Circuit; 2002, U.S. District Court, Eastern District of Michigan. *Education:* Wittenberg University (B.A., cum laude, 1990); University of Cincinnati (J.D., 1993). ***PRACTICE AREAS:*** Litigation. ***Email:*** llandrum@fbtlaw.com

PATRICIA D. LAUB, born Louisville, Kentucky, November 6, 1958; admitted to bar, 1983, Ohio. *Education:* University of Dayton (B.A., summa cum laude, 1979); University of Cincinnati (J.D., 1983). Member, Executive Committee. Order of the Coif. Note Editor, University of Cincinnati Law Review. Author: "Uniform Trust Code Article 5 Creditors' Claims; Spendthrift and Discretionary Trusts" March/April 2001 Probate Law Journal of Ohio. Chair Personal Planning and Family Business Department. Member, Board of Trustees, and Chiar of Development Committee, Cincinnati Association for the Blind. Member, Planned Giving Committee, Cincinnati Art Museum. Past Chair, Cincinnati Bar Association Estate Planning and Probate Section. Certified Estate Planning, Trust and Probate Law Specialist, Ohio State Bar Association. *Member:* Cincinnati and Ohio State (Member: Emeritus Board of Governors Estate Planning; Probate and Trust Law Section) Bar Associations; Cincinnati Estate Planning Council. ***PRACTICE AREAS:*** Trusts and Estates; Probate; Probate Litigation; Taxation; Business Succession Planning; Retirement Benefit Planning; Charitable Gift Planning. ***Email:*** plaub@fbtlaw.com

JAMES K. L. LAWRENCE, born New Rochelle, New York, October 8, 1940; admitted to bar, 1965, Ohio; 1971, U.S. Court of Appeals, Sixth Circuit; 1978, U.S. Court of Appeals, Fourth Circuit. *Education:* The Ohio State University (A.B., 1962; J.D., 1965). (Certified Specialist in Labor and Employment Law, Ohio State Bar Association). ***PRACTICE AREAS:*** Labor and Employment Law; Alternative Dispute Resolution. ***Email:*** jlawrence@fbtlaw.com

P. REID LEMASTERS, born Shelbyville, Indiana, July 28, 1946; admitted to bar, 1971, Indiana; 1972, Ohio; 1990, Kentucky. *Education:* Indiana University (B.A., 1968; J.D., 1971). ***PRACTICE AREAS:*** Commercial Loan; Real Estate Law; Title Insurance Law. ***Email:*** rlemasters@fbtlaw.com

DOUGLAS L. LUTZ, born Cincinnati, Ohio, August 1, 1965; admitted to bar, 1991, Michigan; 1995, Ohio. *Education:* Miami University (B.S., 1987); University of Toledo (J.D., 1991). ***PRACTICE AREAS:*** Bankruptcy; Creditors Rights; Commercial Real Estate. ***Email:*** dlutz@fbtlaw.com

FREDERICK J. McGAVRAN, born Columbus, Ohio, April 24, 1943; admitted to bar, 1972, Ohio; 1992, Kentucky; U.S. District Courts, Northern and Southern Districts of Ohio; U.S. District Court for Kentucky; U.S. Court of Appeals, Sixth Circuit; U.S. Supreme Court. *Education:* Kenyon College (B.A., summa cum laude, 1965); Harvard Law School (J.D., 1972). *Member:* Cincinnati, Northern Kentucky (Chapter), Kentucky, Ohio State and Federal Bar Associations. [Lt., U.S. Navy, 1965-1969]. ***PRACTICE AREAS:*** Complex Litigation; Federal Civil Litigation; Psychiatric Malpractice. ***Email:*** fmcgavran@fbtlaw.com

BERNARD L. McKAY, born Maysville, Kentucky, July 3, 1969; admitted to bar, 1994, Ohio; 1995, Kentucky. *Education:* Morehead State University (B.B.A., 1991); Salmon P. Chase College of Law (J.D., 1994). Certified Specialist in Estate Planning, Probate and Trust Law by the Ohio State Bar Association. Former Chair, Estate Planning and Probate Section, Cincinnati Bar Association. Member, Cincinnati Estate Planning Council. Member, Advanced Estate Planning and Probate Institute Committee of the Cincinnati Bar Association. Chairman, Board of Governors of Salmon P. Chase College of Law. Member, Cincinnati Academy of Leadership for Lawyers. President, Leadership Northern Kentucky Class of 2004. Member, Women's Crisis Center Board of Directors. *Member:* Cincinnati, Ohio State, Kentucky, Northern Kentucky and American Bar Associations. ***PRACTICE AREAS:*** Estate Planning; Probate; Trust Administration; Taxation; Charitable Giving; Family Business Succession. ***Email:*** bmckay@fbtlaw.com

(This Listing Continued)

KEVIN N. McMURRAY, born Columbus, Ohio, January 7, 1963; admitted to bar, 1989, Ohio. *Education:* University of Cincinnati (B.S.ChE., 1986); University of Cincinnati (J.D., 1989). Order of the Coif. Member, Executive Committee, Frost Brown Todd LLC, 1998-2003. Chair, Client Relations Committee, 2000—. Listed in The Best Lawyers in America, 2003-2006. Selected as an "Ohio Super Lawyer" by Ohio Law & Politics, 2003-2005. Selected for recognition as a "Forty Under 40" by Cincinnati Business Courier, 2000. Member, Port of Greater Cincinnati Development Authority, Brownfields Advisory Committee, 2001—. Member, Hamilton County Integrating Committee Brownfields Workgroup, 2003—. *Member:* Cincinnati (Member and Past Chair of Environmental Law Committee), Ohio (Member, Environmental Law Committee) and American (Member, Section of Environment, Energy and Resources) Bar Associations; American Institute of Chemical Engineers. ***PRACTICE AREAS:*** Environmental Law (100%). ***Email:*** kmcmurray@fbtlaw.com

MARTIN E. MOONEY, born Cincinnati, Ohio, October 24, 1952; admitted to bar, 1978, Ohio. *Education:* Princeton University (A.B., cum laude, 1974); University of Notre Dame (M.B.A., cum laude, J.D., cum laude, 1978); New York University (LL.M., 1982). ***PRACTICE AREAS:*** General Tax with primary focus on Corporate and Partnership Transactions. ***Email:*** mmooney@fbtlaw.com

KATHERINE COOK MORGAN, born Concord, North Carolina, December 26, 1969; admitted to bar, 1997, Ohio and U.S. Court of Appeals, Sixth Circuit. *Education:* Swarthmore College (B.A., with honors, 1992); University of Cincinnati College of Law (J.D., 1997). Order of the Coif. Recipient: John W. Peck Trial Practice Award; American Jurisprudence Book Award. Editor-in-Chief, University of Cincinnati Law Review, 1996-1997. *Member:* Cincinnati, Ohio State and American Bar Associations. ***PRACTICE AREAS:*** Labor and Employment Law. ***Email:*** kmorgan@fbtlaw.com

BETH SCHNEIDER NAYLOR, born Cincinnati, Ohio, June 7, 1961; admitted to bar, 1986, Wisconsin; 1989, Ohio. *Education:* Miami University (B.A., 1982); University of Notre Dame Law School (J.D., cum laude, 1986). Author, "An Ounce of Prevention is Worth a Pound of Cure," Cincinnati Business Courier, May 2002. DRI Products Liability Conference, "National Litigation Counsel Perspective," February 2001. Listed in: Outstanding Lawyers of America, 2003; International Who's Who of Product Liability Defense Lawyers, 2003. ***PRACTICE AREAS:*** Preventive Product Safety Counseling; National Products Liability Management; Toxic Tort/Chemical Exposure Litigation; Commercial Litigation. ***Email:*** bnaylor@fbtlaw.com

RAYMOND D. NEUSCH, born Pittsburgh, Pennsylvania, February 21, 1947; admitted to bar, 1978, Ohio. *Education:* Duquesne University (B.A., 1969); Salmon P. Chase College of Law (J.D., 1978). ***PRACTICE AREAS:*** Labor Law. ***Email:*** rneusch@fbtlaw.com

SANDRA L. NUNN, born Decatur, Indiana; admitted to bar, 1995, Ohio. *Education:* University of Cincinnati (B.S., 1987; J.D., 1995). Order of the Coif. Law Review Editor. University of Cincinnati Law Review, Vol. 63, No. 2 and Vol. 63, No. 3. *Member:* Cincinnati, Ohio State and American Bar Associations; Commercial Real Estate Women (CREW); CREW of Greater Cincinnati. ***PRACTICE AREAS:*** Commercial Real Estate Law; Real Estate Transactions. ***Email:*** snunn@fbtlaw.com

E. RICHARD OBERSCHMIDT, born Cincinnati, Ohio, April 28, 1953; admitted to bar, 1978, Ohio. *Education:* Miami University (B.A., 1975), Phi Beta Kappa; University of Virginia (J.D., 1978). Chair, Commercial Transactions and Real Estate Department. Member, Ohio Land Title Association. Member, Board of Zoning Appeals, Anderson Township, Ohio. *Member:* Cincinnati, Ohio State and American Bar Associations. ***PRACTICE AREAS:*** Real Estate Law and Mortgage Financing. ***Email:*** roberschmidt@fbtlaw.com

MICHAEL J. O'GRADY, born Cincinnati, Ohio, 1970; admitted to bar, 1995, Ohio; 1996, U.S. District Court, Southern District of Ohio; 2002, U.S. Court of Appeals, Sixth Circuit. *Education:* University of Michigan (B.A., 1992); University of Cincinnati (J.D., 1995; M.B.A., 1996). *Member:* Cincinnati, Ohio State and American Bar Associations; American Bankruptcy Institute. ***PRACTICE AREAS:*** Bankruptcy; Real Estate; Commercial. ***Email:*** mjogrady@fbtlaw.com

DAVID C. OLSON, born Ashtabula, Ohio, June 27, 1949; admitted to bar, 1978, Ohio; U.S. District Court, Southern District of Ohio; U.S. Court of Appeals, Sixth Circuit; U.S. Supreme Court. *Education:* Williams College (B.A., cum laude, 1971); The Ohio State University (J.D., 1978). Vice-Chair, ABA's Fidelity and Surety Committee. ***PRACTICE AREAS:*** Complex Litigation; Construction; Fidelity and Surety. ***Email:*** dolson@fbtlaw.com

SCOTT D. PHILLIPS, born Dayton, Ohio, October 14, 1962; admitted to bar, 1989, Ohio. *Education:* Southern Methodist University (B.A. and B.B.A., 1984); The Washington College of Law, The American University (J.D., cum laude, 1989). ***PRACTICE AREAS:*** Litigation; Real Estate Litigation; Land Use Litigation; Commercial Litigation. ***Email:*** sphillips@fbtlaw.com

T. STEPHEN PHILLIPS, born Tennyson, Indiana, October 1, 1941; admitted to bar, 1966, Ohio; 1967, Indiana. *Education:* DePauw University (A.B., 1963); Duke University (LL.B., 1966). ***PRACTICE AREAS:*** Estate Planning and Probate; Individual Income Tax Planning; Closely Held Business Representation. ***Email:*** tsphillips@fbtlaw.com

ANN GALLAGHER ROBINSON, born Fort Leonard Wood, Missouri, July 4, 1962; admitted to bar, 1994, Ohio; 1995, U.S. Court of Appeals, Federal Circuit; registered to practice before U.S. Patent and Trademark Office. *Education:* University of Notre Dame (B.S.Ch.E., 1984); Salmon P. Chase College of Law (J.D., 1994). ***PRACTICE AREAS:*** Intellectual Property Litigation; Patent Prosecution. ***Email:*** arobinson@fbtlaw.com

JEFFREY S. ROSENSTIEL, born Florence, Kentucky, September 13, 1966; admitted to bar, 1996, Ohio; 1997, Kentucky, U.S. District Court, Southern District of Ohio and U.S. District Court, Eastern District of Kentucky. *Education:* Kentucky State University (B.A., magna cum laude, 1989); Northern Kentucky University, Salmon P. Chase College of Law (J.D., cum laude, 1996). Adjunct Professor, Chase College of Law (since 1996). City of Ft. Thomas Planning Commission (since1998). Director: Girl Scout Council of Licking Valley (since 1999); Board of Advisor, Northern Kentucky Chamber of Commerce (since 2003).*Member:* Cincinnati, Northern Kentucky, Ohio State, Kentucky and American Bar Associations; American Bankruptcy Institute. ***PRACTICE AREAS:*** Financial Institution Litigation (50%); Bankruptcy Litigation (50%). ***Email:*** jrosenstiel@fbtlaw.com

(This Listing Continued)

JEFFERY R. RUSH, born Montgomery, Alabama, September 18, 1950; admitted to bar, 1975, Ohio. *Education:* Wharton School, University of Pennsylvania (B.S., 1972); Vanderbilt University (J.D., 1975). Listed in Woodward & White's The Best Lawyers in America and Chambers USA. ***PRACTICE AREAS:*** Banks and Banking; Real Estate; Corporate; Workouts. ***Email:*** jrush@fbtlaw.com

DAVID E. SCHMIT, born Charleston, West Virginia, February 18, 1947; admitted to bar, 1975, Ohio; U.S. Court of Appeals, Federal, Fourth and Sixth Circuits; U.S. Court of Federal Claims; registered to practice before U.S. Patent and Trademark Office. *Education:* University of Cincinnati (B.S.E.E., 1969; M.S.E.E., 1976); Salmon P. Chase College of Law (J.D., 1975). *Member:* Cincinnati and Ohio Bar Associations; Cincinnati Intellectual Property Law Association. ***REPORTED CASES:*** Warner-Jenkinson v. Hilton Davis (United States Supreme Court); Ethicon v. Quigg; Mas-Hamilton Group v. La Gard; Senmed v. Richard-Allan Medical(Court of Appeals for the Federal Circuit); Valco v. N&D Machining Service (Ohio Supreme Court). ***PRACTICE AREAS:*** Intellectual Property Litigation (90%, 12); Intellectual Property Counseling (10%, 75); Patent, Trademark, and Copyright Law; Trade Secrets; Unfair Competition. ***Email:*** dschmit@fbtlaw.com

CHARLES E. SCHROER, born Covington, Kentucky, August 11, 1954; admitted to bar, 1979, Ohio and U.S. District Court, Southern District of Ohio; 1980, Kentucky. *Education:* Georgetown University (A.B., 1976); St. Louis University (J.D., 1979). Phi Alpha Delta. Member, International Council of Shopping Centers. *Member:* Cincinnati, Ohio State and Kentucky Bar Associations. ***PRACTICE AREAS:*** Commercial Real Estate; Shopping Center Law; Public Incentives; Historic Preservation; Transportation Law. ***Email:*** cschroer@fbtlaw.com

SAMUEL M. SCOGGINS, born Shreveport, Louisiana, May 8, 1950; admitted to bar, 1975, Ohio. *Education:* Denison University (B.A., with honors, 1972); University of Virginia (J.D., 1975). *Member:* Counselors of Real Estate. ***REPORTED CASES:*** Princeton City School Dist. Bd. of Educ. v. Zaino (2002), 94 Ohio St.3d 66 (upheld township's tax increment financing of public improvements). ***PRACTICE AREAS:*** Corporate; State and Local Taxation; Property Tax Appeals; Real Estate; Real Estate Brokerage Law. ***Email:*** sscoggins@fbtlaw.com

ROBERT D. SHANK, born Cincinnati, Ohio, April 8, 1971; admitted to bar, 1996, Indiana; 1998, Ohio. *Education:* Xavier University (B.A., summa cum laude, 1992); Vanderbilt University (J.D., 1996). Vanderbilt Journal of Transnational Law, 1994-1996. Vanderbilt Moot Court Board. *Member:* Defense Research Insitute. ***PRACTICE AREAS:*** Litigation; Products Liability; Complex and Multi-District Litigation; Labor and Employment; Unfair Competition; Trade Secrets. ***Email:*** rshank@fbtlaw.com

DAVID A. SKIDMORE, JR., born Cincinnati, Ohio, May 9, 1965; admitted to bar, 1991, Ohio and U.S. District Court, Southern District of Ohio; 1992, U.S. Court of Appeals, Sixth Circuit; 2003, U.S. District Court, Northern District of Ohio, U.S. District Court, Central District of Illinois and U.S. Court of Appeals, Ninth Circuit; 2005, U.S. Supreme Court. *Education:* Duke University (B.A., magna cum laude, with distinction, 1987); University of Kent at Canterbury (M.A., 1988); Northwestern University (J.D., cum laude, 1991). Recipient, Cincinnati Business Courier 40 under 40 Award. Associate Editor, Northwestern Law Review. Law Clerk to Honorable S. Arthur Spiegel, U.S. District Court, Southern District of Ohio, 1991-1993. Harry S. Truman Scholar. Named: Best Lawyers in America; Rising Legal Star. Rotary Scholar. Cincinnati Academy for Leadership for Lawyers. Member: Board of Trustees, Stepping Stones Center; Board of Trustees, Bethany House; Law Committee Cincinnati Works. Published in The Labor Law Journal, The National Law Journal, The Federal Lawyer, The Ohio Labor Letter, Personnel Law Update, The Cincinnati Business Courier, and The Ohio State Bar Association Labor and Employment Law News. *Member:* Cincinnati (Member: Labor and Employment Law Committee; Common Pleas Committee) and Ohio State (Member, Board of Governors, Labor and Employment Law Committee) Bar Associations. ***REPORTED CASES:*** Duggins v. Steak 'n Shake, Inc., 195 F.3d 828 (6th Cir. 1999); Dalton v. Jefferson Smurfit Corp., 979 F. Supp. 1187 (S.D. Ohio 1997); Wiltz v. M/G Transport Servs., 925 F. Supp. 500 (S.D. Ohio 1996); Knecht v. Collins, 903 F. Supp. 1193 (S.D. Ohio 1995); National Equity Title Agency, Inc. v. Rivera, 770 N.E.2d 76 (Hamilton Cty. 2001). ***PRACTICE AREAS:*** Employment Litigation; Wrongful Termination; Unfair Competition. ***Email:*** dskidmore@fbtlaw.com

KEVIN S. SPRECHER, born Willingboro, New Jersey, February 24, 1968; admitted to bar, 1995, Ohio and U.S. Court of Appeals for the Federal Circuit; registered to practice before U.S. Patent and Trademark Office. *Education:* Purdue University (B.S.I.E., 1992); Valparaiso University (J.D., 1995). Delta Theta Phi. Notes Editor, Valparaiso University Law Review. *Member:* American Bar Association (Member, Intellectual Property Law Section); Institute of Industrial Engineers; American Intellectual Property Law Association; Cincinnati Intellectual Property Law Association; Cincinnati and Ohio State Bar Associations. ***PRACTICE AREAS:*** Intellectual Property; Patent Prosecution and Litigation. ***Email:*** ksprecher@fbtlaw.com

WILLIAM C. STRANGFELD, born Paterson, New Jersey, September 23, 1945; admitted to bar, 1984, Ohio. *Education:* Kansas Wesleyan University (B.A., 1979); Ohio State University (M.A., 1980; J.D., summa cum laude, 1983). ***PRACTICE AREAS:*** Employee Benefits Law; ERISA; Executive Compensation. ***Email:*** wstrangfeld@fbtlaw.com

JEFFREY R. TEETERS, born Jackson Center, Ohio, July 18, 1968; admitted to bar, 1993, Ohio and U.S. District Court, Southern District of Ohio; 1998, U.S. Court of Appeals, Sixth Circuit; 2005, U.S. Supreme Court. *Education:* University of Dayton (B.A., magna cum laude, 1990); University of Cincinnati (J.D., 1993). Member, 1991-1993, Executive Editor, 1992-1993, University of Cincinnati Law Review. Author: Casenote, "Internal Consistency of Ohio Jury Interrogatories," 61 U. Cinn. L. Rev. 365. Co-Editor of ABA Litigation Section's "Business Torts Journal" 2004-present. *Member:* Cincinnati, Ohio State and American Bar Associations (Member, Sections on: Antitrust; Litigation; Business Torts Litigation Committee). ***REPORTED CASES:*** Nilavar v. Mercy Health System- Western Ohio, 2005 U.S. Dist. LEXIS 13417 (S.D. Ohio 2005). ***PRACTICE AREAS:*** Covenants Not to Compete; Trade Secrets; Antitrust; Civil Litigation; Accountants Liability. ***Email:*** jteeters@fbtlaw.com

DOUGLAS D. THOMSON, born Quantico, Virginia, June 4, 1960; admitted to bar, 1986, Ohio. *Education:* DePauw University (B.A., 1983); Wake Forest University (J.D., 1986); New York University (LL.M., 1987). ***PRACTICE AREAS:*** Nonprofit Corporations and Associations; Corporate Law; Taxation. ***Email:*** dthomson@fbtlaw.com

(This Listing Continued)

FROST BROWN TODD LLC, Cincinnati—Continued

JILL MEYER VOLLMAN, born Cincinnati, Ohio, October 11, 1971; admitted to bar, 1996, Ohio; 1997, Kentucky, U.S. Court of Appeals, Sixth Circuit, U.S. District Court, Northern and Southern Districts of Ohio and U.S. District Court, Eastern District of Kentucky. *Education:* College of Mount St. Joseph (B.A., magna cum laude, 1993); Salmon P. Chase College of Law (J.D., magna cum laude, 1996). Order of the Curia. Lead Articles Editor, Northern Kentucky Law Review, 1995-1996. Author: "In Search of a Right to Escape from a Pornographic Society," 23 Northern Kentucky Law Review 553 (1996). *Member:* Cincinnati, Ohio State, Kentucky and American (Co-Chair, Forum on Communications Law Training & Development Committee, 2003-2004) Bar Associations. ***PRACTICE AREAS:*** Media Law; Advertising Law; Business Litigation. ***Email:*** jvollman@fbtlaw.com

JAMES S. WACHS, born Cincinnati, Ohio, July 18, 1933; admitted to bar, 1958, Ohio. *Education:* University of Cincinnati (B.A., 1955); Harvard Law School (LL.B., 1958). ***PRACTICE AREAS:*** Estate Planning, Probate and Trust Administration; Counseling Privately Held Business. ***Email:*** jwachs@fbtlaw.com

H. LAWSON WALKER, II, born Cincinnati, Ohio, February 10, 1949; admitted to bar, 1975, Ohio, U.S. Court of Appeals, Sixth Circuit and U.S. District Court, Southern District of Ohio; 1976, Kentucky and U.S. District Court, Eastern District of Kentucky. *Education:* University of Cincinnati (B.B.A., 1972; J.D., 1975). Member, Board of Directors, Northern Kentucky/Cincinnati International Airport, 2001—. Member and Vice Chairman, Executive Committee, Northern Kentucky Chamber of Commerce, 1999—. Member, Board of Directors, University of Cincinnati Law School Alumni Association, 1999—. Director, Kentucky Historical Society 2003—. Member, Kentucky House of Representatives, 1987-1993. Vice Chair, Banking and Insurance Committee, 1989-1993. Director, University of Cincinnati Alumni Association, 1986-1994. Candidate for Lt. Governor of Kentucky, 1991. Chairman, Republican Party of the Fourth Congressional District, 1992-1997. Director and Member Emeritus, Northern Kentucky Easter Seal Society, 1982-1990. Director, Sanitation District, 1992-2001. President 1981, and Legislative Chair, Northern Kentucky. *Member:* Cincinnati, Kentucky (Life Fellow) and Ohio State Bar Associations. ***PRACTICE AREAS:*** Government Relations; Planning and Zoning; Civil Litigation; Products Liability Litigation; Municipal Law; Civil Rights Litigation. ***Email:*** lwalker@fbtlaw.com

W. RUSSELL WILSON, born Cincinnati, Ohio, January 23, 1957; admitted to bar, 1983, Ohio. *Education:* Princeton University (A.B., 1980); University of Cincinnati (J.D., 1983). ***PRACTICE AREAS:*** Commercial Real Estate; Shopping Center Law. ***Email:*** rwilson@fbtlaw.com

GEORGE E. YUND, born Chicago, Illinois, April 15, 1952; admitted to bar, 1977, Ohio; U.S. District Court, Southern and Northern Districts of Ohio; U.S. Supreme Court; U.S. Court of Appeals for the Fourth, Sixth, Ninth, Eleventh Circuits and U.S. Court of Appeals, District of Columbia Circuit. *Education:* The Ohio State University (B.A., summa cum laude, 1974), Phi Beta Kappa; University of Michigan (J.D., cum laude, 1977). ***PRACTICE AREAS:*** Labor Law; Employment Law. ***Email:*** gyund@fbtlaw.com

HILLA M. ZERBST, born Florence, South Carolina, December 1, 1949; admitted to bar, 1978, Ohio. *Education:* The Ohio State University (B.A., 1970); Capital University (J.D., 1978). *Member:* Cincinnati and Ohio State Bar Associations. (Certified Specialist in Workers' Compensation Law, Ohio State Bar Association). ***PRACTICE AREAS:*** Workers Law. ***Email:*** hzerbst@fbtlaw.com

SENIOR ASSOCIATES

KIMBERLY S. AMRINE, born Lansing, Michigan, May 25, 1971; admitted to bar, 2000, Ohio. *Education:* Northwestern University (B.A., 1993); George Washington University (J.D., cum laude, 1999). Member, Moot Court Board. Editor, Public Contracts Law Journal. Chair, Cincinnati Bar Association Women Lawyer's Committee. *Member:* Cincinnati, Ohio and American Bar Associations. ***PRACTICE AREAS:*** Advertising Law (40%); Commercial Litigation (60%). ***Email:*** kamrine@fbtlaw.com

STACY CHRISTMAN BLOMEKE, born Cincinnati, Ohio; admitted to bar, 2000, Ohio. *Education:* Xavier University (B.S., cum laude, 1995); University of Cincinnati (M.S., 1996); University of Dayton (J.D., magna cum laude, 2000). Member: Mortar Board; Psi Chi Society, Xavier University. Recipient: Criminal Justice Department Honor Award, Xavier University; American Jurisprudence Award in Estate Planning, Alternative Dispute Resolution, Criminal Trial Practice; Walter H. Rice Moot Court Competition, Best Brief, University of Dayton. Associate Editor, University of Dayton Law Review, 1999-2000. Author: "A Surrogacy Agreement That Could Have and Should Have Been Enforced: R.R. v. M.H., 689 N.E.2d 790 (Mass. 1998)," University of Dayton Law Review, Vol. 24, issue 3, Spring 1999. *Member:* Cincinnati (Member, Committees on: Estate Planning; Probate; Taxation), Ohio State (Member, Sections on: Estate Planning; Trust and Probate Law) State and American (Member: Real Property; Probate and Trust; Young Lawyers Division; Family Law Sections) Bar Associations. ***PRACTICE AREAS:*** Tax; Estate Planning; Probate Administration; Family Law. ***Email:*** sblomeke@fbtlaw.com

KASEY BOND, born Fort Thomas, Kentucky, January 1, 1973; admitted to bar, 1998, Georgia; 1999, Texas; 2004, Ohio. *Education:* University of Kentucky (B.A., summa cum laude, 1995); Vanderbilt University School of Law (J.D., 1998). ***PRACTICE AREAS:*** Labor and Employment. ***Email:*** kbond@fbtlaw.com

JULIE M. TOMLINSON BRUNS, born Dayton, Ohio, May 14, 1974; admitted to bar, 1999, Ohio; 2000, U.S. District Court, Southern District of Ohio. *Education:* Miami University (B.A., summa cum laude, 1996); University of Cincinnati (J.D., 1999). Phi Beta Kappa. *Member:* Cincinnati and Ohio State Bar Associations. ***PRACTICE AREAS:*** Labor and Employment; Workers Compensation. ***Email:*** jbruns@fbtlaw.com

CRAIG M. BRYSON, born Toledo, Ohio, May 3, 1974; admitted to bar, 2001, New York; 2003, Ohio. *Education:* Université de Pau et des Pays de L'Adour, Diplôme D'Université (Certificat Pratique de Langue Francaise, 1994); Miami University (B.A., cum laude, 1996); The Ohio State University College of Law (J.D., with honors, 2000). Recipient, OSU Certificate in International Trade and Development Law. Associate Editor, ABA/OSU Journal on Dispute Resolution. *Member:* Cincinnati, Ohio State and American

(This Listing Continued)

Bar Associations. ***LANGUAGES:*** French. ***PRACTICE AREAS:*** Mergers, Acquisitions and Divestitures; Securities; International Transactions. ***Email:*** cbryson@fbtlaw.com

STEVEN W. CALDWELL, born 1968; admitted to bar, 2002, New York; registered to practice before U .S. Patent and Trademark Office (Not admitted in Ohio). *Education:* University of Kentucky (B.S., 1997); Syracuse University (J.D., 2001).

DIANA R. CHRISTY, born Cincinnati, Ohio, September 21, 1974; admitted to bar, 2001, Ohio. *Education:* University of North Carolina at Wilmington (B.A., Environmental Chemistry, 1997); Salmon P. Chase College of Law (J.D., magna cum laude, 2001). Order of the Curia. Member, Northern Kentucky Law Review, 1999-2001. Editor, Northern Kentucky Law Review, Symposium Issue, 2000-2001. *Member:* Cincinnati, Ohio State and American Bar Associations. ***PRACTICE AREAS:*** Environmental Law. ***Email:*** dchristy@fbtlaw.com

DEANNE E. CLARKE, born Key West, Florida, September 19, 1973; admitted to bar, 1998, Illinois; 2000, Ohio. *Education:* University of Cincinnati (B.A., with high honors, 1995); Loyola University of Chicago (J.D., cum laude, 1998). ***PRACTICE AREAS:*** Commercial Real Estate. ***Email:*** dclarke@fbtlaw.com

DOUGLAS R. DENNIS, born Cleveland, Ohio, March 28, 1963; admitted to bar, 1995, Ohio; 2000, U.S. District Court, Southern and Northern Districts of Ohio and U.S. Court of Appeals, Sixth Circuit; 2003, U.S. Supreme Court. *Education:* United States Military Academy (B.S., 1985); University of Cincinnati (J.D., 1995). Recipient: Mulligan-Moeller Negotiations Award; American Jurisprudence Prizes in Appellate Practice and Corporations. Member, University of Cincinnati Law Review, 1994-1995. Law Clerk to the Honorable Mark P. Painter, Ohio Court of Appeals, First Appellate District, 1995-1997. Co-Author, Ohio Appellate Practice Handbook with Judge Mark P. Painter for West Publishing, 2004—. Author: "Framing the Assignment of Error on Civil Appeals," appearing in the September 2000 issue of the Cincinnati Bar Association report; "Participation on Social Events Breeds Civility," appearing in the November 2000 issue of the Cincinnati Bar Association report; "Delivering a Knockout Punch-Oral Argument in Civil Appeals," appearing in the February 2001 issue of the Cincinnati Bar Association report; "No Just Reason for Delay-Ohio Civil Rule 54(B)," appearing in the May 2001 issue of the Cincinnati Bar Association report; "Effective Appellate Argument Construction," appearing in the July 2001 issue of the Cincinnati Bar Association report; "Preserving Error for Civil Appeals in Ohio," appearing in the December 2001 issue of the Cincinnati Bar Association report; "Avoid the Kitchen Sink Approach," (with Judge Mark P. Painter) appearing in the March 25, 2002 Ohio Lawyers Weekly at 5 O.L.W. 191; "Some Basics for Getting Cases Before the Supreme Court of Ohio," appearing in the May 2002 issue of the Cincinnati Bar Association report; "New Citation Rules in Ohio" appearing in the August 2002 issue of the Cincinnati Bar Association report; "What Impact Will Health Care Reform Have on Vaccine and Drug Makers?" Defense Counsel Journal, Vol. 62, No. 2, pp. 165-176, April 1995. *Member:* Cincinnati Bar Association (Former Chair, Court of Appeals Committee; Member, Professionalism Committee), Ohio State Bar Association (Co-Chair, Court of Appeals Subcommittee to the Litigation Section; Member, Litigation Section Board of Governors) and American Bar Association. [Captain, Armored Cavalry, U.S. Army, 1985-1990.]. ***PRACTICE AREAS:*** Appellate Practice; Products Liability. ***Email:*** ddennis@fbtlaw.com

DAVID E. FRANKLIN, born Topeka, Kansas, January 2, 1962; admitted to bar, 1995, Ohio, U.S. Court of Appeals, Sixth Circuit and U.S. District Court, Northern District of Ohio; 1996, U.S. District Court, Northern District of Ohio, U.S. Court of Appeals for Armed Forces and U.S. Court of Appeals for the Federal Circuit; 1997, Missouri (inactive); registered to practice before U.S. Patent and Trademark Office, 1995. *Education:* University of Kansas (B.S.E.E., 1985); University of Dayton (M.S.E.E., 1990); St. Louis University (J.D., 1995). Professional Engineer, Missouri, 1992 (inactive). *Member:* American Intellectual Property Law Association; Cincinnati Intellectual Property Law Association. [Air Force, 1985-1989, ANG, 1992-1996; Lt. Col., JAG, Air Force Reserves, 1996—.]. ***PRACTICE AREAS:*** Patent Prosecution; Intellectual Property; Government Contracts; Intellectual Property Infringement; Intellectual Property Licensing. ***Email:*** dfranklin@fbtlaw.com

MARY M. GODAR, born Cedar Rapids, Iowa, June 29, 1970; admitted to bar, 1995, California; 1996, Virginia; 2002, Ohio. *Education:* Purdue University (B.A., 1992); McGeorge School of Law, University of the Pacific (J.D., 1995). Phi Beta Kappa. Traynor Honor Society. CLE Coordinator Women Lawyers Committee, 2002-2004. *Member:* Cincinnati (Chair, Women Lawyers Committee) and American Bar Associations; American Immigration Lawyers Association. ***PRACTICE AREAS:*** Immigration and Naturalization. ***Email:*** mgodar@fbtlaw.com

KYLE R. GRUBBS, born Cincinnati, Ohio, April 1, 1976; admitted to bar, 2001, Ohio and U.S. District Court, Southern District of Ohio; 2004, U.S. District Court, Southern District of Indiana. *Education:* Thomas More College (B.A., 1998); University of Cincinnati (J.D., 2001). Order of the Coif. *Member:* Cincinnati, Ohio State, Federal and American Bar Associations. ***REPORTED CASES:*** Menninger v. First Franklin Financial Corp. (In re Fryman), 314 B.R. 137 (Bankr. S.D. Ohio 2004). ***PRACTICE AREAS:*** Commercial Transactions; Real Estate; Financial Restructuring; Banking Law. ***Email:*** kgrubbs@fbtlaw.com

COLLEEN M. HAAS, born Lompoc, California, February 5, 1970; admitted to bar, 1997, Ohio. *Education:* University of Notre Dame (B.B.A., 1992; J.D., 1997). *Member:* Cincinnati, Ohio State and American Bar Associations. ***PRACTICE AREAS:*** Commercial Lending; Real Estate. ***Email:*** chaas@fbtlaw.com

MAUREEN P. HANEY, born Cleveland, Ohio, September 14, 1973; admitted to bar, 1999, Ohio and U.S. District Court, Southern and Norhtern Districts of Ohio. *Education:* Miami University (B.A., 1996); Ohio State University College of Law (J.D., with honors, 1999). Order of the Coif. Author: "The Buckley Conspiracy and how Congress Authorized the Cover-up of Campus Crime," Ohio State Law Journal, Spring 1999. Chair, First Amendment Subcommittee of the ABA's Consumer and Personal Rights Committee. *Member:* Cincinnati, Ohio State and American (Vice-Chair, Young Lawyer's Division Law and Media Committee) Bar Associations. ***PRACTICE AREAS:*** Media Law; First Amendment Law; Advertising Law; Business Litigation. ***Email:*** mhaney@fbtlaw.com

JOHN S. HIGGINS, born Cincinnati, Ohio, January 11, 1966; admitted to bar, 1997, Ohio; 1998, U.S. District Court, Northern District of Ohio; 1998, U.S. Court of Appeals,

(This Listing Continued)

Fourth and Sixth Circuits; 2001, U.S. District Court, Southern District of Ohio; 2003, U.S. District Court, Eastern District of Kentucky; 2004, U.S. Supreme Court; 2005 U.S. District Court, Southern District of Indiana. *Education:* University of Cincinnati (B.S., cum laude, 1993); Cleveland Marshall College of Law (J.D., cum laude, 1997). Recipient: Spangenberg Trial Practice Award; CALI, Excellence for the Future Award, Capital Punishment Law; Corpus Juris Secundum Award for Scholastic Excellence in Contracts; Dean's Award for Outstanding Academic Achievement. Past Law Clerk, Cleveland Municipal Court. Member, Board of Directors, Architecture, Construction and Engineering (ACE). *Member:* Cincinnati, Ohio State, Federal and American (Member, Forum of the Construction Industry) Bar Associations. ***PRACTICE AREAS:*** Commercial Litigation; Business Litigation; Construction Litigation. ***Email:*** jhiggins@fbtlaw.com

KEVIN K. MALOF, born Cincinnati, Ohio, November 27, 1967; admitted to bar, 2000, Ohio. *Education:* Miami University (B.S., 1990); Salmon P. Chase College of Law (J.D., 2000). Member, National Moot Court Board, 1998-2000. Speaker, "Commercial Real Estate Finance," Lorman Continuing Education Seminar, 2004, 2005. *Member:* Cincinnati and Ohio State Bar Associations. ***PRACTICE AREAS:*** Commercial Real Estate; Commercial Loans; Construction Law. ***Email:*** kmalof@fbtlaw.com

CHRISTINA M. SPRECHER, born Wabash, Indiana, March 1, 1970; admitted to bar, 1996, Ohio. *Education:* Indiana University at Bloomington (B.A., 1992); Valparaiso University School of Law (J.D., 1995). Moot Court Society, National Team - Valparaiso University School of Law. Member, International Council of Shopping Centers. Trustee, Executive Committee Member, Cincinnati Ballet Board. *Member:* Cincinnati, Ohio State and American (Member: ABA Real Property; Probate and Trust Law Section) Bar Associations. ***PRACTICE AREAS:*** Commercial Real Estate Transactions; Shopping Center Law; Residential Real Estate Transactions. ***Email:*** csprecher@fbtlaw.com

STEVEN M. WESLOH, born St. Louis, Missouri, March 22, 1971; admitted to bar, 1996, Ohio. *Education:* Indiana University (B.A., 1993); University of Cincinnati College of Law (J.D., 1996). Member, University of Cincinnati Law Review, 1994-1996. Co-author: "Short-Changing Short-Term Risk: A Study In Superfund Remedy Selection," 15 Yale J. Reg. 198 (1998). *Member:* Cincinnati (Member, Environmental Law Committee), Ohio State (Member, Environmental Law Committee) and American (Member, Section on: Environment; Energy and Resources) Bar Associations. ***PRACTICE AREAS:*** Environmental Law. ***Email:*** deswesloh@fbtlaw.com

ASSOCIATES

R. MARISSA ALBERT, born St. Louis, Missouri, 1976; (admission pending). *Education:* Washington University (B.A., 1999); University of Missouri (J.D., 2005). ***PRACTICE AREAS:*** Commercial Transactions; Commercial Real Estate. ***Email:*** malbert@fbtlaw.com

PAMELA BROWN BOSLEY, born Chesapeake, Virginia, 1977; (admission pending). *Education:* University of Virginia (B.A., Economics, French, 1999); University of North Carolina at Chapel Hill (J.D., 2005). ***PRACTICE AREAS:*** Labor and Employment. ***Email:*** pbosley@fbtlaw.com

DANIELLE M. BRIM, born Dayton, Ohio, July 25, 1979; (admission pending); admitted to bar, 2005, Ohio. *Education:* College of William and Mary (B.S., cum laude, 2002); Vanderbilt University (J.D., 2005). Member, Vanderbilt Journal of Transnational Law, 2003-2005. Author: "The Roles of Precaution and Political Accountability in the Regulation of Polybrominated Diphenyl Ethers," 38 Vand. J. Trans. L. 791, 2005. ***PRACTICE AREAS:*** Environmental Law. ***Email:*** dbrim@fbtlaw.com

BETH A. BUCHANAN, born Medina, Ohio, April 21, 1964; admitted to bar, 1997, Ohio and U.S. District Court, Southern District of Ohio. *Education:* Ohio State University (B.S.B.A., 1986); University of Dayton (J.D., summa cum laude, 1997). Phi Delta Phi. Executive Editor, University of Dayton Law Review. Author: "Liens Pass Through Bankruptcy Unaffected" - Or Do They? In re Penrod - Challenging on Adage, University of Dayton Law Review, Vol. 21, Winter 1996; "Use of Restraints in the Hospital Setting: Is the Law a Help or Hindrance to the Advancement of Changing Medical Ideology?" University of Dayton Law Review, Vol. 22, Fall 1996. *Member:* American Bankruptcy Institute; American Bankruptcy Law Forum; American Immigration Lawyers Association. ***PRACTICE AREAS:*** Bankruptcy; Creditor's Rights; Workouts. ***Email:*** bbuchanan@fbtlaw.com

JANDÁ M. CARTER, born Yoakum, Texas, June 11; admitted to bar, 2002, Ohio. *Education:* Purdue University (B.S.E.); University of Dayton (J.D.); University of Illinois (M.S.E.). Editor, UD Journal of Law & Technology, Student Writing, 1999-2000. Recipient: 2004 "Rising Star" Award; NSBE Freshman of the Year Award (4 year Kodak scholarship); Highest Grade-Products Liability, 2000. President, Intellectual Property Law Association, 1999-2000. Engineer, Mechanical Engineering, General Motors Corporation. Food Process Engineering, The Quaker Oats Company. Publications and Presentations: "The Art of Interviewing," National BLSA Conference, October 2005; "The Challenge of Keeping Things Secret: Trade Secrets, Covenants Not-to-Compete, and Confidentiality Agreements," Greater Cincinnati Minority Council Program, November 2004; "What Else Can I Do With My Engineering Degree?" University of Akron Engineering Class, November 2004; "Lexicographical Issues in Patent Prosecution," Franklin Pierce Law Center (IP Symposium), November 2002; "Understanding The Electoral Process," (Mock Election Seminar), April 2003; "The Three B's of Success," Optimist International, Flint Chapter, Annual Scholarship Breakfast, 1998. Affiliations: Trustee, Alumni Board, University of Dayton School of Law, 2004—. Board Member, YWCA of Cincinnati Annual Fund Drive and Heart to Heart Racial Justice Divisions, 2002—. Tutor and Mentor, Cincinnati Youth Collaborative (Cin Public Schools), 2002—. Board Member, Urban Minority Alcohol and Drug Abuse Outreach Program (UMADAOP), 2002—. Board Member, Give Others Will Live, Inc. (focus: organ/tissue donation), 2001—. Member, Purdue Black Alumni Organization, Cincinnati Chapter, 1995—. Mentor, Purdue Women in Engineering Program, 1991—. Member, NAACP. *Member:* Cincinnati (Member, Intellectual Property Law Section; Corresponding Secretary, Black Lawyers Association of Cincinnati), Ohio State and American (Member, Intellectual Property Law Section) Bar Associations; American Intellectual Property Law Association; American Society of Mechanical Engineers; Interdisciplinary Engineering Alumni Association; American Association of Automotive Engineers

(This Listing Continued)

(inactive). ***LANGUAGES:*** Sign Language. ***PRACTICE AREAS:*** Intellectual Property; Patent Prosecution; Patentability and Freedom to Practice Opinions; Patent; Counseling; FDA Consumer Labeling and Packaging Law Issues. ***Email:*** jcarter@fbtlaw.com

NEIL DESAI, born 1980; (admission pending). *Education:* Miami University (B.S., magna cum laude, 2002); University of Cincinnati (J.D., 2005). ***PRACTICE AREAS:*** Litigation. ***Email:*** ndesai@fbtlaw.com

MONICA L. DIAS, born Paducah, Kentucky, 1962; admitted to bar, 2001, Ohio; 2002, Kentucky, U.S. District Court, Eastern District of Kentucky and U.S. Court of Appeals, Sixth Circuit; 2003, U.S. District Court, Southern District of Ohio. *Education:* Western Kentucky University (B.A., 1984); Salmon P. Chase College of Law (J.D., 2001). Legal Fellow, Reporters Committee for Freedom of the Press, Arlington, VA, 2001-2002. *Member:* Cincinnati, Ohio State, Northern Kentucky and Kentucky Bar Associations. ***PRACTICE AREAS:*** Media Law; Libel, Slander and Defamation; Commercial Law. ***Email:*** mdias@fbtlaw.com

EUGENE J. DRODER, III, born 1978; admitted to bar, 2004, Ohio and U.S. District Court, Southern District of Ohio. *Education:* Miami University (B.A., cum laude); University of Dayton (J.D., magna cum laude, 2004). Order of the Coif. *Member:* Cincinnati, Ohio State and American Bar Associations. ***PRACTICE AREAS:*** Labor and Employment; Wage and Hour Law; Fair Labor Standards; Civil Litigation; Complex Litigation. ***Email:*** edroder@fbtlaw.com

CLAIRE SELTZ EICHNER, born Cincinnati, Ohio, April 21, 1965; admitted to bar, 1990, Illinois; 1999, Ohio. *Education:* Washington University (B.A., 1987); Northwestern University (J.D., cum laude, 1990). Phi Beta Kappa; Psi Chi. Executive Editor, 1989-1990 and Staff Member, 1988-1989, The Journal of Criminal Law and Criminology. Author: "Sixth Amendment-The Confrontation Clause, Witness Memory Loss and Hearsay Exceptions: What are the Defendant's Constitutional and Evidentiary Guarantees-Procedure or Substance?" The Journal of Criminal Law and Criminology, Vol. 79, 1988. *Member:* Chicago, Illinois State and American Bar Associations. ***PRACTICE AREAS:*** Litigation. ***Email:*** ceichner@fbtlaw.com

JENNIFER FULLER, admitted to bar, 2004, Ohio. *Education:* Missouri State University (B.S., magna cum laude, 2000). The Ohio State University, Moritz College of Law (J.D., with honors in Law, 2004). Recipient: ABA Award for Excellence in the Study of Labor and Employment Law, 2004; First Place Winner, Herman Moot Court Competition, 2003. First Place Winner, Colley Mock Trial Competition, 2003; Lett Memorial Award for Service to the Moritz College of Law, 2002. Member, Middfest International Executive Committee, 2005. Member, Ohio Public Employer Labor Relations Association (OHPELRA), 2004. Member, National Moot Court Team, 2003-2004. Member, Moritz College of Law Moot Court Governing Board, 2003-2004. *Member:* Butler County, Ohio State and American Bar Associations (Member, Labor & Employment Section). ***PRACTICE AREAS:*** Labor and Employment (70%); Education Law (15%); Township and Municipal Law (15%). ***Email:*** jfuller@fbtlaw.com

STEPHEN M. GRACEY, born Covington, Kentucky, December 31, 1976; admitted to bar, 2003, Ohio; 2004, Kentucky. *Education:* Columbia University (B.A., 1999); University of Cincinnati (J.D., 2003). ***PRACTICE AREAS:*** Litigation. ***Email:*** sgracey@fbtlaw.com

ELIZABETH A. GRAY, born Kirksville, Missouri, 1979; (admission pending). *Education:* John Carroll University (B.A., summa cum laude, 2002); University of Notre Dame (J.D., 2005). Judicial Extern to Honorable William H. Baughman, Jr., U.S. Magistrate Judge, U.S. District Court, Northern District of Ohio, 2003. ***PRACTICE AREAS:*** Bankruptcy. ***Email:*** egray@fbtlaw.com

CHELSEA C. GREEN, born Columbus, Ohio, November 12, 1968; admitted to bar, 2000, Ohio. *Education:* Miami University (B.S., in Accounting, 1991); University of Cincinnati (J.D., 2000); Illinois Institute of Technology (M.S., in Financial Markets, 2000). Certified Public Accountant, 1992. *Member:* Cincinnati, Ohio State and American Bar Associations. ***PRACTICE AREAS:*** Securities; Corporate Law; Investment Company Law; Investment Adviser Law; Broker-Dealer Regulation. ***Email:*** cgreen@fbtlaw.com

MELISSA GREEN, born East Lansing, Michigan; admitted to bar, 2004, Ohio. *Education:* Michigan State University (B.A., 2001); University of Michigan Law School (J.D., 2004). Member: Executive Board: Black Law Students Association; Michigan Journal of Race and Law. *Member:* Cincinnati, Ohio State and American Bar Associations; American Health Lawyers Association. ***PRACTICE AREAS:*** Health Law (50%); Corporate Responsibility and Defense (30%); Mergers and Acquisitions (20%). ***Email:*** mgreen@fbtlaw.com

MURRAY W. GRIESS, born Cincinnati, Ohio September 14, 1965; admitted to bar, 1995, Ohio; 1998, Kentucky. *Education:* Oberlin College (B.A., 1987); University of Michigan Law School (J.D., 1995). *Member:* Cincinnati and Ohio State Bar Associations. ***LANGUAGES:*** Spanish. ***PRACTICE AREAS:*** Labor and Employment. ***Email:*** mgriess@fbtlaw.com

ERIN N. HALENKAMP, born Covington, Kentucky, March 26, 1977; admitted to bar, 2002, Ohio; 2003, Kentucky and U.S. District Court, Southern District of Ohio; 2004, U.S. District Court, Eastern District of Kentucky. *Education:* Transylvania University (B.A., 1999); Salmon P. Chase College of Law (J.D., 2002). Salmon P. Chase Law Review, 2001-2002. Member, Student Bar Association, 2001-2002. *Member:* Cincinnati, Ohio State, Kentucky, Northern Kentucky, and American Bar Associations. ***PRACTICE AREAS:*** Litigation. ***Email:*** erieger@fbtlaw.com

CATHERINE ANN HEITCHUE REED, born Mt. Clemens, Michigan, June 8, 1978; admitted to bar, 2003, Ohio. *Education:* University of Michigan (A.B., 2000; J.D., 2003). *Member:* Cincinnati, Ohio State and American Bar Associations. ***PRACTICE AREAS:*** Labor and Employment (100%). ***Email:*** creed@fbtlaw.com

NICOLETTE R. HUDSON, born Springfield, Ohio, March 8, 1972; admitted to bar, 1999, Ohio and U.S. District Court, Southern District of Ohio. *Education:* Miami University (B.A., 1994); University of Cincinnati College of Law (J.D., 1999). *Member:* Ohio State Bar Association (Member, IP Board of Governors, 2003); International Trademark Association. ***PRACTICE AREAS:*** Trademark; Copyright; Unfair Competition; Trade Secrets; Intellectual Property Litigation. ***Email:*** nhudson@fbtlaw.com

(This Listing Continued)

FROST BROWN TODD LLC, Cincinnati—Continued

ANDREW R. KAAKE, born New York, New York, March 13, 1975; admitted to bar, 2000, Ohio; 2001, U.S. District Court, Southern District of Ohio. *Education:* Northern Kentucky University (B.S., 1997); University of Cincinnati (J.D., 2000) Order of the Coif. Phi Alpha Delta. Author: "Sexual Harrassment: The Supreme Court Couldn't Have Meant 'And'," Labor Law Journal, Summer, 2001. *Member:* Cincinnati and Ohio State Bar Associations. ***Email:*** akaake@fbtlaw.com

ALLISON HILTZ KROPP, born Covington, Kentucky, July 3; admitted to bar, 2003, Ohio. *Education:* Georgetown University (B.S.F.S., 1997; J.D., 2003). *Member:* Cincinnati, Ohio State and American Bar Associations. ***PRACTICE AREAS:*** Personal Planning and Family Business. ***Email:*** akropp@fbtlaw.com

SCOTT A. MARTZ, born 1979; (admission pending). *Education:* Xavier University (B.A., magna cum laude, 2002); Vanderbilt University (J.D., 2005). ***PRACTICE AREAS:*** Tax Law; Corporate Law. ***Email:*** smartz@fbtlaw.com

BRIDGET GANNON McGRAW, born Cincinnati, Ohio, July 21, 1978; admitted to bar, 2003, Ohio. *Education:* Miami University (B.A., Phi Beta Kappa, 1999); University of Cincinnati (J.D., 2003). *Member:* Cincinnati, Ohio State and American Bar Associations. ***PRACTICE AREAS:*** Litigation; Real Estate Litigation; Land Use Litigation; Condemnation; Zoning Law; Commercial Litigation; Business Litigation. ***Email:*** bmcgraw@fbtlaw.com

JOEL F. McGUIRE, born Hamilton, Ohio, August 25, 1971; admitted to bar, 2001, Ohio. *Education:* Ohio University (B.A., cum laude, 1993); Northwestern University (J.D., 2001). Member: City Council, Harrison, Ohio; Veterans of Foreign Wars; American Legion; US Army Ranger Association. *Member:* Cincinnati, Ohio State and American Bar Associations. [U.S. Army, 1993-1997, Captain]. ***PRACTICE AREAS:*** Commercial Litigation; International Litigation; Consumer Litigation; Real Estate Litigation. ***Email:*** jmcguire@fbtlaw.com

KELLY P. MOORE, born Seattle, Washington, June 11, 1977; admitted to bar, 2002, Ohio; 2003, Florida. *Education:* Valparaiso University (B.S., 1999); Franklin Pierce College (J.D., 2002). *Member:* Cincinnati, Ohio State and American Bar Associations; The Florida Bar; American Intellectual Property Law Association. ***PRACTICE AREAS:*** Intellectual Property; Litigation; Patent Prosecution. ***Email:*** kmoore@fbtlaw.com

RODGER W. MOORE, born Topeka, Kansas, March 27, 1968; admitted to bar, 2001, Ohio. *Education:* University of Arkansas (B.S., 1991); Tulane University (M.B.A., 1994); Emory University School of Law (J.D., 2001). Sutherland Award for Academic Excellence in Corporate and Tax Law, 2001. Second Best Oralist, Jessup Moot Court Competition - Southeast Region, 2001. Recipient, First Place, Best Brief, Jessup Moot Court Competition - National Competition, 2001; First Place, Best Brief, Jessup Moot Court Competition - World Competition, 2001. Law Clerk to Honorable Stephanie B. Manis, Fulton County Superior Court, Georgia, 2000. Member, Master of Business Administration, Tulane University, 1994. Dean's List, Emory Law School, Multiple Semesters. Author: "Ten Tips for Effective Electronic Discovery," CBA Report, September 2004; "An Attorney's Duty to Conduct an Informed Electronic Discovery Project," Media Law Resource Center: Media Law Center - Ethics Corner, October 2004; "Wading Into the Swamp of Electronic Discovery," Fidelity & Surety Law Committee Newsletter, January 2005; "Ten Tips for an Effective Electronic Discovery Project," Defense Research Institute, April 2005. Speaker: "Spoliation & Document Retention Policies," Continuing Legal Education Seminar, August 2004. "Electronic Discovery" Continuing Legal Education Seminar, September 2004; "Electronic Discovery Issues," Continuing Legal Education Seminar, February 2005; "Ethics in the Electronic Era," Cincinnati Bar Association Continuing Legal Education Conference, March 2005; "Effectively Conducting Electronic Discovery in Ohio," Continuing Legal Education Seminar, June 2005; "Understanding Electronic Discovery," Ohio State Bar Association Continuing Legal Education Conference, September 2005; "Current Issues in Electronic Discovery," Continuing Legal Education Seminar, September 2005. Chairman of the Board, Cincinnati Film Commission. Member, Cincinnati Bar Association E-Commerce Committee. *Member:* Cincinnati, Ohio State and American Bar Associations. ***PRACTICE AREAS:*** Litigation. ***Email:*** rmoore@fbtlaw.com

SHANNAH J. MORRIS, born 1977; (admission pending). *Education:* Ball State University (B.S.W., 1999); University of Dayton (J.D., cum laude, 2005). ***PRACTICE AREAS:*** Litigation; Insurance Defense; Construction Law; Commercial Law. ***Email:*** smorris@fbtlaw.com

WILLIAM S. MORRISS, admitted to bar, 2005, Ohio. *Education:* University of Southern California (B.S., magna cum laude, 2002); Georgetown University (J.D., magna cum laude, 2005). Order of the Coif. Recipient, ABA/BNA Award For Excellence as a Student of Intellectual Property, 2005. Author: "Use of the Accused Device in Patent Claim Construction," 23 Intell. Prop. L. Newsl. 18, 2004. ***Email:*** wmorriss@fbtlaw.com

MICHAEL E. NITARDY, born Huntington, West Virginia, 1974; (admission pending). *Education:* Marshall University (B.B.A., summa cum laude, 1996); Salmon P. Chase College of Law (J.D., summa cum laude, 2005). ***PRACTICE AREAS:*** Corporate Law; Business Law. ***Email:*** mnitardy@fbtlaw.com

MONICA H. NORRIS, born Hamilton, Ohio, April 30, 1974; admitted to bar, 1999, Ohio. *Education:* Miami University (B.S., 1996); University of Cincinnati (J.D., 1999). *Member:* Cincinnati and Ohio State Bar Associations. ***PRACTICE AREAS:*** Medical Malpractice Litigation; Product Liability Litigation; Employment Intentional Tort Litigation. ***Email:*** mnorris@fbtlaw.com

JENNIFER A. O'GUINN, admitted to bar, 2003, Massachusetts, Ohio and U.S. District Court, Southern District of Ohio. *Education:* Kalamazoo College (B.A., 1999); University of Notre Dame (J.D., 2002). ***PRACTICE AREAS:*** Bankruptcy; Commercial Transactions. ***Email:*** joguinn@fbtlaw.com

BILL J. PALIOBEIS, born Cleveland, Ohio, October 2, 1969; admitted to bar, 1996, Ohio; 1997, Kentucky and U.S. District Court, Eastern District of Kentucky; 1998, U.S. District Court, Southern District of Ohio. *Education:* University of Toledo (B.A., 1992); Case Western Reserve University (J.D., 1996). *Member:* Cleveland, Kentucky and American Bar Associations; Northern Kentucky Bar Association; Defense Research Institute. ***PRACTICE AREAS:*** Medical Malpractice Defense; Personal Injury Defense. ***Email:*** bpaliobeis@fbtlaw.com

SCOTT RICHARDSON, born Pontiac, Michigan, June 5, 1975; admitted to bar, 2002, Ohio. *Education:* Kettering University (B.S.M.E., 1998); University of Dayton (J.D., cum laude, 2002). Pi Tau Sigma; Tau Beta Pi. *Member:* Ohio State Bar Association. ***PRACTICE AREAS:*** Intellectual Property; Intellectual Property Prosecution; Mechanical Intellectual Property. ***Email:*** srichardson@fbtlaw.com

RIA FARRELL SCHALNAT, born Canton, Ohio, September 3, 1971; admitted to bar, 1999, Ohio. *Education:* Northern Kentucky University (B.S., 1995); University of Dayton School of Law (J.D., magna cum laude, 1999). ***PRACTICE AREAS:*** Patent Prosecution; Patent Litigation; Software Copyright; Software Licensing; Trademark. ***Email:*** rschalnat@fbtlaw.com

KARLYN A. SCHNAPP, PH.D, born Toledo, Ohio, August 14, 1962; admitted to bar, 2000, Ohio. *Education:* University of Cincinnati (B.S., with honors in Chemistry, 1984; Ph.D., in Organic Chemistry, 1989); Salmon P. Chase College of Law (J.D., 2000). *Member:* Cincinnati, Ohio State and American (Member, Intellectual Property Law Section) Bar Associations; American Chemical Society; American Intellectual Property Law Association; Cincinnati Intellectual Property Law Association. ***PRACTICE AREAS:*** Patent Prosecution; Licensing. ***Email:*** kschnapp@fbtlaw.com

JAMES D. SCHOENY, born Cincinnati, Ohio, September 17, 1977; admitted to bar, 2003, Ohio. *Education:* Loyola University, Chicago (B.A., magna cum laude, 2000); University of Cincinnati (J.D., 2003). Member, University of Cincinnati Law Review, 2001-2002. *Member:* Cincinnati, Ohio State and American Bar Associations. ***PRACTICE AREAS:*** Litigation. ***Email:*** jschoeny@fbtlaw.com

YVETTE R. SIMPSON, born Cincinnati, Ohio, August 2, 1978; admitted to bar, 2004, Ohio; 2005, U.S. District Court, Southern District of Ohio. *Education:* Miami University (B.A., Political Science; B.S., Mass Communications, 2000); University of Cincinnati College of Law (J.D., 2004). *Member:* Cincinnati (Member, Sections on: Labor and Employment; Alternative Dispute Resolution; Young Lawyers; CBA/BLAC Roundatable), Ohio State (Member, Sections on: Labor and Employment; Media Law), American and National Bar Associations; Black Lawyers' Association of Cincinnati; American Inns of Court; Association of Trial Lawyers of America. ***PRACTICE AREAS:*** Labor and Employment; Communications and Media; Workers Compensation. ***Email:*** ysimpson@fbtlaw.com

JUD B. SIMS, born Danville, Illinois, November 18, 1971; admitted to bar, 1999, Ohio; 2001, U.S. Tax Court. *Education:* Miami University (B.S., 1994); Case Western Reserve University (J.D., 1997). *Member:* Cincinnati Bar Association. ***PRACTICE AREAS:*** Federal Taxation; State Taxation; Local Taxation; Corporate Law; Business Law; Entrepreneurial Business Law. ***Email:*** jsims@fbtlaw.com

RITA M. STOLPER, born New York, New York, September 4, 1954; admitted to bar, 1979, Maryland; 1985, New York; 1991, Ohio. *Education:* Emory University (B.A., 1976); University of Maryland (J.D., 1979). ***PRACTICE AREAS:*** Real Estate. ***Email:*** rstolper@fbtlaw.com

NICOLE M. TEPE, (admission pending). *Education:* Thomas More College (B.A., Biology, 1994); University of Cincinnati (Ph.D., Pharmacology and Cell Biophysics, 2000); University of Cincinnati (J.D., 2005). ***PRACTICE AREAS:*** Intellectual Property. ***Email:*** ntepe@fbtlaw.com

JOSEPH A. TOMAIN, born Long Branch, New Jersey, January 21, 1976; admitted to bar, 2001, Illinois; 2003, Ohio. *Education:* University of Notre Dame (B.A., 1998; J.D., cum laude, 2001). *Member:* Cincinnati, Chicago, Illinois State, Ohio State and American Bar Associations; American Constitution Society (Member, Cincinnati Lawyer Chapter); Defense Research Institute. ***PRACTICE AREAS:*** Civil Litigation; Products Liability; Complex Business Litigation; Media Law Litigation; Appellate. ***Email:*** jtomain@fbtlaw.com

ANDREW B. ULMER, born Columbus, Ohio, January 14, 1977; admitted to bar, 2003, Ohio; registered to practice before the U.S. Patent and Trademark office. *Education:* Ohio State University (B.A., 1999); University of Cincinnati (J.D., 2003). Order of the Coif. Associate Member, University of Cincinnati Law Review, 2001-2002. Author, "To Pee or Not to Pee? That Should Not Be the Question for the Academic Team," 70 U. Cin. L. Rev. 1443 (2002). *Member:* Cincinnati, Ohio State, and American (Member, Intellectual Property Section) Bar Associations; Cincinnati Intellectual Property Law Association; American Intellectual Property Law Association. ***PRACTICE AREAS:*** Intellectual Property. ***Email:*** aulmer@fbtlaw.com

VANCE V. VANDRAKE, III, admitted to bar, 2005, Ohio; registered to practice before the U.S. Patent and Trademark Office. *Education:* Butler University (B.A.); University of Cincinnati (J.D.). ***PRACTICE AREAS:*** Intellectual Property; Electrical Intellectual Property; Intellectual Property Procurement; Intellectual Property Rights; Internet Intellectual Property; Mechanical Intellectual Property; Medical Intellectual Property. ***Email:*** vvandrake@fbtlaw.com

JOSHUA L. VINEYARD, born Cincinnati, Ohio, February 3, 1977; admitted to bar, 2004, Ohio and U.S. District Court, Southern District of Ohio. *Education:* University of Cincinnati (B.S., cum laude, 2000; M.S., magna cum laude, 2001; J.D., magna cum laude, 2004). Order of the Coif. *Member:* Cincinnati and Ohio State and American Bar Associations. ***Email:*** jvineyard@fbtlaw.com

JOSEPH W. WALKER, born 1978; (admission pending). *Education:* Ohio University (B.B.A., cum laude, 2001); University of Dayton School of Law (J.D., summa cum laude, 2005). ***PRACTICE AREAS:*** Litigation. ***Email:*** jwalker@fbtlaw.com

DAVID W. WALULIK, born Steubenville, Ohio, June 23, 1971; admitted to bar, 1999, Pennsylvania; 2003, Ohio. *Education:* The Ohio State University (B.S.B.A., 1994; J.D., 1999). Order of the Coif. Ohio State Moot Court. Member, The Ohio Stae Law Journal. ***PRACTICE AREAS:*** Complex Commercial Litigation; Insurance Coverage.

CLINT C. WATSON, born 1979; admitted to bar, 2005, Ohio. *Education:* Wake Forest University (B.A.); University of Michigan (J.D.). ***PRACTICE AREAS:*** Litigation; Civil Litigation; Complex Litigation; Defense Litigation; Trial Practice. ***Email:*** cwatson@fbtlaw.com

(This Listing Continued)

KRISTIN K. WHITAKER, born Pittsburgh, Pennsylvania, September 7, 1975; admitted to bar, 2002, Ohio. *Education:* University of Richmond (B.A., 1997); Salmon P. Chase College of Law (J.D., magna cum laude, 2002) Order of the Curia. Editor in Chief, Northern Kentucky Law Review. ***PRACTICE AREAS:*** Immigration. ***Email:*** kwhitaker@fbtlaw.com

JANICE BAKER WHITLOW, born Erie, Pennsylvania, February 15, 1977; admitted to bar, 2003, Ohio. *Education:* University of Dayton (B.S.E.E., 1999; J.D., 2003). Member, Moot Court, 2002-2003. Member, Law Review, 2001-2003. *Member:* Cincinnati and Ohio State Bar Associations; American Intellectual Property Law Association. ***PRACTICE AREAS:*** Intellectual Property; Litigation; Patents. ***Email:*** jwhitlow@fbtlaw.com

JEFFREY L. ZACKERMAN, born Cincinnati, Ohio, July 1, 1963; admitted to bar, 1997, Ohio; 1999, U.S. District Court, Southern District of Ohio. *Education:* University of Cincinnati (B.A., 1986); University of Cincinnati College of Law (J.D., 1997). Phi Beta Kappa. Order of the Coif. Student Articles Editor, University of Cincinnati Law Review, 1996-1997. Judicial Clerk to the Hon. Burton Perlman, U.S. Bankruptcy Court for the Southern District of Ohio, 1997-1999. ***PRACTICE AREAS:*** Bankruptcy; Commercial Loans; Real Estate. ***Email:*** jzackerman@fbtlaw.com

COUNSEL

EDMUND J. ADAMS, born Lansing, Michigan, June 6, 1938; admitted to bar, 1963, Ohio. *Education:* Xavier University (A.B., 1960); University of Notre Dame (LL.B., 1963). Fellow, American College of Bankruptcy. Chairman, Ohio Board of Regents. ***SPECIAL AGENCIES:*** Chairman, Ohio Board of Regents. ***PRACTICE AREAS:*** Corporate and Commercial Law, including Business Bankruptcy. ***Email:*** eadams@fbtlaw.com

JAMES R. ADAMS, born Coffeyville, Kansas, August 11, 1938; admitted to bar, 1963, Ohio. *Education:* Denison University (A.B., 1960); Northwestern University (J.D., 1963). ***PRACTICE AREAS:*** Complex Commercial Litigation; Class Actions; Securities and RICO Matters; Accounting and Attorney Malpractice. ***Email:*** jadams@fbtlaw.com

BARBARA F. APPLEGARTH, born Portland, Connecticut, January 7, 1952; admitted to bar, 1979, Ohio; 1982, New Mexico. *Education:* Connecticut College (A.B., 1973); Case Western Reserve University (J.D., 1979); New York University (LL.M., Taxation, 1982). ***PRACTICE AREAS:*** Trusts and Estates; Taxation. ***Email:*** bapplegarth@fbtlaw.com

WILLIAM D. BASKETT, born Evanston, Illinois, July 29, 1939; admitted to bar, 1964, Ohio. *Education:* Harvard College (B.A., 1961); Harvard Law School (LL.B., 1964). ***PRACTICE AREAS:*** Corporate Law.

LISA WEEKLEY COULTER, born Charleston, West Virginia, January 31, 1961; admitted to bar, 1988, Ohio; 1989, U.S. District Court, Southern District of Ohio; 1991, U.S. District Court, Northern District of Ohio; 1994, U.S. Court of Appeals, Sixth Circuit. *Education:* Marietta College (B.A., cum laude, 1983); The Ohio State University (J.D., 1988). Delta Theta Phi. Associate Editor, Fidelity and Surety Digest for the Fidelity and Surety Law Committee. Author and Speaker, ABA Tips, Fidelity and Surety Law Committee and The Surety Claims Institute. Former Partner, McNamara and McNamara, Columbus, Ohio. Volunteer Mediator and Arbitrator, Franklin County Pleas Court. Member, Board of Examiners, 2002—. *Member:* Columbus, Ohio State and American (Member, Fidelity and Surety Committee and Litigation Section) Bar Associations. ***PRACTICE AREAS:*** Extra Contractual Insurance Claims; Litigation; Insurance Defense; Fidelity and Surety; Negligence. ***Email:*** lcoulter@fbtlaw.com

WILLIAM E. GALLAGHER, born Pittsburgh, Pennsylvania, February 5, 1962; admitted to bar, 1992, Pennsylvania; 2001, Ohio. *Education:* Pennsylvania State University (B.S.M.E., 1984); University of Pittsburgh (J.D., 1992). ***PRACTICE AREAS:*** Intellectual Property Litigation. ***Email:*** wgallagher@fbtlaw.com

ALBERT E. HEEKIN, III, born Cincinnati, Ohio, March 25, 1940; admitted to bar, 1965, Ohio. *Education:* University of Notre Dame (B.B.A., 1962); Xavier University (M.B.A., 1968); University of Cincinnati (J.D., 1965). ***PRACTICE AREAS:*** Closely-Held Corporations and Small Businesses. ***Email:*** theekin@fbtlaw.com

JAMES A. KATSANIS, born 1931; admitted to bar, 1957, Ohio and Texas. *Education:* University of Cincinnati (A.B. and LL.B.). Director, Anderson Bank Company of Cincinnati, Ohio. [Staff Judge Advocate, U.S. Air Force, 1955-1959; U.S. Air Force Reserve (24 years)]. ***PRACTICE AREAS:*** Probate (50%); Real Estate (20%); Business Law (5%); Estate Planning (25%). ***Email:*** jkatsanis@fbtlaw.com

LINDA M. KECK, born 1969; admitted to bar, 1996, Ohio; U.S. District Court, Northern and Southern Districts of Ohio and U.S. Court of Appeals, Sixth Circuit. *Education:* Georgetown University (B.S.L.A., Japanese Studies, 1991); University of Illinois (M.A., Japanese Studies, 1995; J.D., 1996). ***LANGUAGES:*** Japanese and German. ***Email:*** lkeck@fbtlaw.com

JAMES M. KIPLING, born Cincinnati, Ohio; admitted to bar, 1972, Ohio. *Education:* University of Cincinnati (B.S.M.E., 1968); Georgetown University (J.D., 1972). *Member:* Cincinnati, Ohio State and American Bar Associations; American Patent Law Association; Cincinnati Patent Law Association. ***TRANSACTIONS:*** Entertainment, sports, celebrity, patent, trademark, copyright, technology and inventorship licenses for merchandising and consumer goods manufacturers. Examples of properties include: "Star Wars", "Batman", "Jurassic Park", "Pokemon", "Care Bears", etc.; NFL, NBA, MLB, NHL, NASCAR. Various Intellectual Propertiy transactions, protections, policing and enforcements. ***PRACTICE AREAS:*** Intellectual Property; Transactions; Licensing; Intellectual Property Protection; Policing Actions; Enforcement; Children's Advertising; General Transactional Matters; Entertiainment and Sports Practice. ***Email:*** jkipling@fbtlaw.com

KAREN ECKER KRATZ, born Cincinnati, Ohio, February 17, 1966; admitted to bar, 1992, Ohio. *Education:* University of Dayton (B.A., summa cum laude, 1988); University of Notre Dame (J.D., magna cum laude, 1992). Senior Editor, Notre Dame Law Review, 1991-1992. Co-Author: "Simon & Schuster, Inc. v. Fischetti: Can New York's Son of Sam Law Survive First Amendment Challenge?" 66 Notre Dame Law Review 1075, 1991. Member, Greater Cincinnati Planned Giving Council. *Member:* Cincinnati (Member, Sections on: Estate Planning; Probate), Ohio State and American Bar Associations. ***PRACTICE AREAS:*** Trusts and Estates; Nonprofit and Charitable Organizations. ***Email:*** kkratz@fbtlaw.com

(This Listing Continued)

LAWRENCE H. KYTE, JR., born Cincinnati, Ohio, February 6, 1938; admitted to bar, 1966, Ohio. *Education:* University of Notre Dame (A.B., 1960); University of Virginia (LL.B., 1963). *Member:* Cincinnati and Ohio State Bar Associations. ***PRACTICE AREAS:*** Real Estate Development Law; Closely Held Corporations; Small Business; Corporate Law. ***Email:*** lkyte@fbtlaw.com

KIMBERLY K. MAUER, born Pella, Iowa, June 28, 1959; admitted to bar, 1984, Iowa; 1987, Ohio. *Education:* Morningside College (B.A., 1981); Drake University (J.D., 1984). ***PRACTICE AREAS:*** Commercial Loans; Bank Regulation; Loan Workouts. ***Email:*** kmauer@fbtlaw.com

VINCENT E. MAUER, born Sioux City, Iowa, October 18, 1958; admitted to bar, 1985, Iowa; 1987, Ohio. *Education:* Morningside College (B.S., summa cum laude, 1981); Drake University (M.B.A., 1984; J.D., 1984). ***PRACTICE AREAS:*** Litigation of Bankruptcy, Commercial and Real Estate Issues; Litigation of Insurance Coverage; International Insurance Litigation. ***Email:*** vmauer@fbtlaw.com

KAREN M. McLAUGHLIN, born St. Louis, Missouri, March 30, 1951; admitted to bar, 1981, Ohio. *Education:* Thomas More College (A.B., magna cum laude, 1973); Salmon P. Chase College of Law of Northern Kentucky University (J.D., 1981). ***PRACTICE AREAS:*** Securities; Investment Management. ***Email:*** kmclaughlin@fbtlaw.com

DAVID J. McPHERSON, born Norwalk, Ohio, April 7, 1954; admitted to bar, 1986, Ohio. *Education:* Bowling Green State University (B.S., 1976; M.A., 1977); University of Cincinnati (J.D., 1986). ***PRACTICE AREAS:*** Employment Law. ***Email:*** dmcpherson@fbtlaw.com

VICTOR C. MORENO, born Peoria, Illinois, July 14, 1966; admitted to bar, 1995, Ohio; registered to practice before U.S. Patent and Trademark Office. *Education:* The Ohio State University (B.S.M.E., 1989); University of Cincinnati College of Law (J.D., 1995). ***PRACTICE AREAS:*** Intellectual Property Litigation; Technology and Science. ***Email:*** vmoreno@fbtlaw.com

LJUBOMIR NACEV, born Skopje, Macedonia, April 3, 1952; admitted to bar, 1976, Illinois (Not admitted in Ohio). *Education:* Johns Hopkins University (B.A., 1973); John Marshall Law School (J.D., 1976); New York University School of Law (LL.M., 1978). ***PRACTICE AREAS:*** Federal Taxation; Tax Litigation. ***Email:*** lnacev@fbtlaw.com

JOHN K. ROSE, born Cincinnati, Ohio, December 11, 1929; admitted to bar, 1960, Ohio. *Education:* University of Cincinnati (A.B., 1951; A.M., 1953); Harvard Law School (LL.B., 1960). ***PRACTICE AREAS:*** Antitrust Law; Telecommunications Law. ***Email:*** jrose@fbtlaw.com

CARLA HAUNZ RUSCONI, born Louisville, Kentucky, October 26, 1963; admitted to bar, 1988, Ohio. *Education:* University of Notre Dame (B.A., 1985); University of Virginia (J.D., 1988). ***PRACTICE AREAS:*** Mergers and Acquisitions; Healthcare; General Corporate. ***Email:*** crusconi@fbtlaw.com

MARY ANN SCHENK, born Cincinnati, Ohio, January 12, 1951; admitted to bar, 1976, Ohio. *Education:* Edgecliff College (B.A., cum laude, 1972); Salmon P. Chase College of Law of Northern Kentucky University (J.D., 1976). Order of the Curia. Trustee, Southwestern Ohio Land Title Association. Former Lecturer, Real Estate Law at University of Cincinnati Evening College. Former Law Director, Treasurer and Council Member, City of Mt. Healthy, Ohio. Former Trustee, Ohio Land Title Association. *Member:* Cincinnati, Ohio and American Bar Associations; Ohio Land Title Association. ***PRACTICE AREAS:*** Real Estate Law. ***Email:*** mschenk@fbtlaw.com

JANE HILS SHEA, born Covington, Kentucky, July 13, 1953; admitted to bar, 1979, Ohio; U.S. District Court, Federal District; U.S. District Court, Southern District of Ohio. *Education:* St. Joseph's College (B.A., 1975); University of Cincinnati College of Law (J.D., 1979). *Member:* Cincinnati and Ohio State Bar Associations. ***PRACTICE AREAS:*** Commercial Transactions; Banking Regulatory Law; Privacy Law; Electronic Commerce. ***Email:*** jshea@fbtlaw.com

All Partners are members of the Cincinnati, Columbus, Butler County, or Fayette County, Kentucky or Ohio State and American Bar Associations.

REPRESENTATIVE CLIENTS: AAF-McQuay Inc.; AEGON USA Realty Advisors, Inc.; AIG Insurance Group; AK Steel Corporation; Anthem Health Plans; Ashland, Inc.; BB&T Corporation; Bank One, NA; Bass Hotels & Resorts, Inc.; Bridgestone/Firestone, Inc.; Brown & Williamson Tobacco Corporation; Catholic Healthcare Partners; Central Bank & Trust Company; Chapelthorp plc; Chiquita Brands International; Cincinnati Bell Inc.; ClubLink Corporation; Convergys Corporation; Coolmore Castlehyde and Associated Stud Farms; Federated Department Stores, Inc.; FieldTurf, Inc.; Taco Bell Franchise Management Advisory Council (FRANMAC); General Electric Company; Hilliard Lyons Government Fund, Inc.; Hilliard Lyons Growth Fund, Inc.; ICI Paints World Group; Jewish Hospital HealthCare Services, Inc.; LensCrafters, Inc.; Lexis-Nexis; LG&E Energy Corp./E.On; Liberty Mutual Insurance Group; New Horizon Resources, Inc.; NTS Development Company; OneBeacon Insurance Group; Progressive Insurance Company; PNC Bank Corp. and PNC Bank; Res-Care, Inc.; The Rouse Companies, LLC; Services Net Incorporated; Smithkline Beecham Clinical Lab; Sud-Chemie Inc.; Terex Corporation; Touchstone Family of Funds; Turner Construction Company; Unified Foodservice Purchasing Co-op, LLC; United Parcel Service; U.S. Bank National Association; Vincor International Inc.; The WWW Funds; Waste Management of North America; Western Southern Life Insurance Company; Wyeth.

FROST & JACOBS LLP

CINCINNATI, OHIO

(See Frost Brown Todd LLC)

MICHAEL F. GEHRIG

1140 BARTLETT BUILDING
36 EAST FOURTH STREET
CINCINNATI, OHIO 45202-3811
Telephone: 513-421-9010
Fax: 513-421-4464
Email: gehriglaw@zoomtown.com
URL: http://www.lawyers.com/gehriglaw

Negligence, Trial Practice, Personal Injury, Professional Liability and Product Liability.

MICHAEL F. GEHRIG, born Cincinnati, Ohio, January 25, 1947; admitted to bar, 1974, Ohio, U.S. District Court, Northern and Southern Districts of Ohio and Eastern District of Kentucky and U.S. Supreme Court. *Education:* The Ohio State University (B.A., 1970); Salmon P. Chase College of Law (J.D., 1974). Co-Author: "Products Liability in Ohio," Negligence Law Committee Newsletter, Ohio State Bar Association, 1979. Author: "Evaluation, Investigation and Case Development Prior to Suit," Ohio Legal Center Institute, 1981; "Evaluation, Investigation and Development of the Product Liability Case Prior to Trial," Trial Litigation Journal, 1983; "Cross-examination and Impeachment, Personal Injury Litigation in Ohio," The Ohio Legal Institute, 1984; "Ohio Uninsured & Underinsured Motorist Coverage Issues," Professional Education Systems, Inc., 1986, 1988, 1990. Lecturer: Practical Law Institute, Cincinnati Bar Association, 1978-1981; Regional Education Seminar, Ohio Academy of Trial Lawyers, 1979; Product Liability Seminar, Ohio Legal Center Institute, 1981; Annual Meeting, Ohio Academy of Trial Lawyers, 1983; Regional Seminar Program, Ohio Academy of Trial Lawyers, l983-1984: Medical Negligence Seminar, Chase College of Law, 1984; Personal Injury Litigation in Ohio, Cross-Examination, Ohio Legal Center Institute, 1984; Regional Seminar Program Ohio Academy of Trial Lawyers, 1986; Ohio Uninsured and Underinsured Motorist Coverage Issues, Professional Education Systems, Inc., 1986, 1988, 1990, Annual Convention, Ohio Academy of Trial Lawyers, 1987; Ohio's New Tort Law, Ohio Academy of Trial Lawyers, 1987, 1988; Prejudgment Interest, Annual Convention, Ohio Academy of Trial Lawyers, 1989, 1990. Cincinnati Bar Association, Arbitration and Product Liability, 1989; Chase College of Law, Damages, Apportionment and Insurance Coverages, 1990; Chase College of Law, Personal Injuries/Medical Malpractice, 1991; Professional Education Systems, Medicine Made Easy for Lawyers, 1992; Cincinnati Bar Association, National Institute of Trial Advocacy, 1992. Cincinnati Bar Association, Arbitration, 1993; Ohio Academy of Trial Lawyers, Cross Examination of the Defense Examiner, 1997, Chase College of Law, ADR, 1997; Ohio Academy of Trial Lawyers, Cross Examination of the Defense Examiner, 1998. Cincinnati Bar Association, Presuit Discovery, 2001; Lorman Education Services, Conducting an Effective Cross-Examination, 2002, 2003, 2004 and 2005; Ohio Academy of Trial Lawyers, Regional Seminar, Summation, 2005; Cincinnati Bar Association, How Much Should I Ask For, 2004. Ohio Academy of Trial Lawyers, Justice Through Communication, 2003. Moderator: Regional Seminar Program, Ohio Academy of Trial Lawyers, 1987; Ohio's New Tort Law, Kentucky Academy of Trial Lawyers, Seminar Series, 1988. *Member:* Cincinnati (Member, Committees on: Conferences with the Academy of Medicine, 1975-1977; Fee Arbitration, 1978-1979; Negligence Law, 1975—; Secretary, 1979), Ohio State (Member, Negligence Law Committee, 1977-1979; Member, Arbitration and Product Liability, 1989) and American Bar Associations; The Association of Trial Lawyers of America (Sustaining Member); Ohio Academy of Trial Lawyers (Member, Negligence Law Standing Committee, 1980-1981; Sustaining Member); American Board of Trial Advocates. ***REPORTED CASES:*** Huffman v. Hair Surgeon (1985) 19 Ohio St. 3rd 83, 482 NE2 1248; Stanton v. Nationwide Insurance Co. (1994) 99 Ohio St. 34d, L. ***PRACTICE AREAS:*** Trial Practice; Negligence; Personal Injury; Products Liability; Professional Liability.

ALBERT R. FINGERMAN (Retired)

REFERENCE: U.S. Bank.

RICHARD H. GLAZER CO., L.P.A.

8180 CORPORATE PARK DRIVE
SUITE 300
CINCINNATI, OHIO 45242
Telephone: 513-489-7200
Fax: 513-489-4044
Email: glazerlaw@fuse.net
URL: http://www.lawyers.com/glazerlaw

Personal Injury, Wrongful Death, Medical Malpractice, Civil Litigation and Eminent Domain, Taking of Property by Appropriation & Condemnation Proceedings.

FIRM PROFILE: The firm's business is devoted principally to matters involving plaintiff's bodily injury, medical malpractice, wrongful death, eminent domain, and other civil litigation. Richard H. Glazer has over 30 years of experience in eminent domain litigation in state and federal courts, representing both condemnors and condemnees.

RICHARD H. GLAZER, born Cleveland, Ohio, September 21, 1944; admitted to bar, 1970, Ohio and U.S. District Court, Southern District of Ohio. *Education:* University of Cincinnati (B.B.A., Econ., 1966); The Ohio State University (J.D., 1969). Special Counsel-Assistant Attorney General, 1971-1993. Lecturer: Business Law, University of Cincinnati College of Business Administration, 1971-1978. *Member:* Cincinnati, Ohio State and American Bar Associations; Ohio Academy of Trial Lawyers; The Association of Trial Lawyers of America; Hamilton County Trial Lawyers Association.

BRIAN M. GOLDBERG

4300 CAREW TOWER
441 VINE STREET
CINCINNATI, OHIO 45202
Telephone: 513-721-3111
Fax: 513-721-3077
Email: rgoldbri@aol.com
URL: http://www.riverfrontsportsmanagement.com

Sports Law. Athlete Representation and Contract Negotiation.

BRIAN M. GOLDBERG, born Cincinnati, Ohio, May 4, 1960; admitted to bar, 1985, Ohio, U.S. District Court, Southern District of Ohio, and U.S. Court of Appeals, Sixth Circuit. *Education:* University of Cincinnati (B.A., econ., 1982); University of Toledo (J.D., 1985). Member, Moot Court Team. Lecturer: "Sports Law/Athlete Representation," Cincinnati Bar Association, Chase College of Law and University of Cincinnati College of Education, 1988—. *Member:* Cincinnati, Ohio State and American (Member, Sports and Entertainment Section) Bar Associations. ***LANGUAGES:*** Spanish. ***PRACTICE AREAS:*** Sports Law; Athlete Representation; Contract Negotiation.

GONZALEZ, SAGGIO & HARLAN, L.L.P.

Established in 1989

CAREW TOWER
441 VINE STREET, SUITE 3615
CINCINNATI, OHIO 45202
Telephone: 513-651-3456
Fax: 513-651-3446
Email: main@gshllp.com
URL: http://www.gshllp.com

Indianapolis, Indiana Office: 201 North Illinois Street, Suite 1900, 46204. Telephone: 317-686-9800. Fax: 317-686-9821.
West Des Moines, Iowa Office: 1501 42nd Street, Suite 465, 50266. Telephone: 515-453-8509. Fax: 515-267-1408.
Milwaukee, Wisconsin Office: 225 East Michigan, 4th Floor, 53202-4900. Telephone: 414-277-8500. Fax: 414-277-8521.
Chicago, Illinois Office: 208 LaSalle Street, Suite 1460, 60604. Telephone: 312-236-0475. Facsimile: 312-236-1750.

Business and Corporate Law, Civil Litigation, Insurance Defense Law, Equal Opportunities and Employment, School Law, Municipal Finance, Business and Commercial Litigation, Patents, Trademarks, Copyrights, Intellectual Property Licensing, Real Estate, Construction, Condemnation Law, Environmental, Taxation, Utilities Law, Trials and Appeals, Government Relations.

FIRM PROFILE: Gonzalez, Saggio & Harlan, L.L.P. is one of the fastest growing law firms in the Midwest. This growth is a reflection of the firm's devotion to quality, efficiency and frank communication in servicing client needs. Furthermore, as a minority-owned law firm, we believe that our diverse backgrounds add value to those clients wanting to better serve a changing and dynamic environment.

JOHN J. WILLIAMS, born Southhampton, New York, April 29, 1963; admitted to bar, 1989, New York and Ohio; 1990, U.S. District Court, Sixth Circuit and U.S. District Court, Southern District of Ohio; 1997, U.S. Court of Federal Claims; 2001, Kentucky; 2003, U.S. District Court, Northern District of Ohio; U.S. Court of Appeals for the Federal Circuit. *Education:* State University of New York College at Purchase (B.A., 1985); State University of New York at Buffalo (J.D., 1988). Board Member, Editorial Board, Ohio Lawyer. Member, Ohio State Bar Foundation Community Service Award for Lawyers age 40 and Under (District 1 and Statewide, 1997) . *Member:* Cincinnati (Member, Executive Committee; Chair, Community Service Committee; Chair, Young Lawyers Section), Ohio State and American Bar Associations. Cincinnati Bar Foundation (Vice-President, Trustee). ***PRACTICE AREAS:*** Defense Litigation; Equal Employment Opportunity Law. ***Email:*** john_williams@gshllp.com

ELIZABETH CONKIN, born Muncie, Indiana, October 8, 1960; admitted to bar, 1986, Illinois and U.S. District Court, Northern District of Illinois; 1995, Ohio and U.S. District Court, Northern and Southern Districts of Ohio. *Education:* DePauw University (B.A., 1983); IIT Chicago-Kent College of Law (J.D., 1986). ***PRACTICE AREAS:*** Litigation; Equal Employment Opportunity Law; Medical Malpractice; Insurance Coverage; Products Liability; Torts.

REPRESENTATIVE CLIENTS: Accenture; Alliant Energy; Bear, Stears & Co.; Chubb Insurance Company; City of Milwaukee; CNH Global N.V.; Darden Restaurants, Inc.; Denny's; Eastman Kodak Company; E.I. du Pont de Nemours and Company; Family Dollar Stores, Inc.; Forest County Potawatomi Community; Harley-Davidson Motor Company; Kohl's Corporation; Luxottica Group; Menard, Inc.; Midwest Airlines; PepsiAmericas, Inc.; Starwood Hotels & Resorts Worldwide, Inc.; State of Wisconsin; Target Corporation; Time Warner Cable; We Energies; Wisconsin Housing and Economic Development Authority (WHEDA); Zale Corporation.

(For complete biographical data on all personnel, see Professional Biographies at Milwaukee, Wisconsin)

GOODSON & COMPANY, LTD.

Established in 1999

110 EAST EIGHTH STREET

SUITE 200

CINCINNATI, OHIO 45202

Telephone: 513-621-5631

Fax: 513-621-3855

URL: http://www.goodsonandcompany.com

Email: brettgoodson@goodsonandcompany.com

URL: http://www.lawyers.com/goodsonandcompany

Personal Injury, Insurance Law, Professional Negligence, Trials and Appeals, Wrongful Death, Products Liability.

FIRM PROFILE: Goodson & Company, Ltd., Attorneys and Counsellors at Law, was established to provide high quality legal representation in a comfortable friendly atmosphere. We strive for a professional yet relaxed relationship with our clients. That means prompt response to telephone calls and letters as well as being available at any time to meet and discuss the case.

Brett Goodson and Stephanie Day are trial attorneys who have worked together for over five years representing clients in civil litigation. They have over 30 years of combined experience as trial attorneys. Goodson & Company vigorously represents mostly plaintiffs who have suffered an injury or death as a result of accidents, medical negligence or faulty products. The firm can handle most civil litigation.

While most of our practice is in Ohio, we are licensed to practice in Kentucky and Indiana and have handled many cases in both states.

The attorneys are supported by an excellent staff including paralegals Bridget Kellner and Cathy Oney, office manager Carolyn Stein and secretary Velma Hollenkamp. If the attorneys are not available, there is usually someone from our staff who can help you.

BRETT C. GOODSON, born Washington, D.C., March 12, 1951; admitted to bar, 1976, Ohio; 1980, U.S. Supreme Court; 1989, Kentucky; 1990, Indiana. *Education:* Ohio University (B.G.S., 1973); University of San Diego (J.D., 1976). Member, 1982— and President, 1987-1989, Volunteer Lawyers for the Poor Foundation. *Member:* Cincinnati (Member: Executive Committee, 1980-1981; Grievance Committee, 1983-1988; Board of Trustees, 1987-1990; Member, 1979— and Chairman, 1993-1995, Tort and Insurance Committee; Member, 1980-1990 and Chairman, 1988-1989, Judicial Candidate Rating Committee; Chairman, Young Lawyers Section, 1980-1981; Trustee, 1990-1992), Ohio State and Kentucky Bar Associations; Ohio Academy of Trial Lawyers; Kentucky Academy of Trial Lawyers; Indiana Trial Lawyers Association; The Association of Trial Lawyers of America; Hamilton County Trial Lawyers Association (President, 1999-2001); American Board of Trial Advocates (Associate Member, 2004—). ***PRACTICE AREAS:*** Civil Practice; Personal Injury; Wrongful Death; Products Liability; Medical Negligence; Professional Negligence. ***Email:*** brettgoodson@goodsonandcompany.com

---

STEPHANIE M. DAY, born Hamilton, Ohio, December 3, 1969; admitted to bar, 2000, Ohio. *Education:* Ball State University (B.S., 1992); Salmon P. Chase College of Law (J.D., cum laude, 2000). *Member:* Cincinnati and Ohio State Bar Associations; Ohio Academy of Trial Lawyers; Hamilton County Trial Lawyers Association; The Association of Trial Lawyers of America. ***PRACTICE AREAS:*** Personal Injury; Wrongful Death; Civil Practice; Medical Negligence; Products Liability; Professional Negligence. ***Email:*** stephanieday@goodsonandmullins.com

LEGAL SUPPORT PERSONNEL

BRIDGET KELLNER

CATHY ONEY

REFERENCE: Fifth Third Bank.

GRAF / STIEBEL / MOYERS

A LEGAL PROFESSIONAL ASSOCIATION

SUITE 2400, U.S. BANK TOWER

425 WALNUT STREET

CINCINNATI, OHIO 45202

Telephone: 513-618-7800

Fax: 513-618-7801

URL: http://www.grafstiebel.com

Closely-Held Business Law, Taxation, Estate Planning, Probate and Trust Administration, Employee Benefits, Retirement Distribution Planning, Litigation of Tax, Probate, and Trust Matters.

FIRM PROFILE: We combine age old values like integrity, hard work, and the pursuit of excellence with modern technology and state of the art legal resources that are updated daily. To better serve our clients, we limit our practice to the specific areas described above. We encourage proactive planning, and we firmly believe that doing things right saves time and money in the long run. While we are available to work on a project basis, most of our client relationships are long term.

WILLIAM R. GRAF, born Cincinnati, Ohio, July 1, 1950; admitted to bar, 1976, Ohio; 1986, U.S. Tax Court. *Education:* Denison University (B.A., 1972); The Ohio State University (J.D., cum laude, 1976). *Member:* Cincinnati, Ohio State and American Bar Associations; Cincinnati Estate Planning Council. (Certified Specialist in Estate Planning, Trust and Probate Law, Ohio State Bar Association). ***PRACTICE AREAS:*** Estate Planning; Estate and Gift Taxation; Fiduciary Income Tax; Probate and Trust Administration; Closely-Held Business Law; Contested Trusts and Estates. ***Email:*** wgraf@grafstiebel.com

MARK A. STIEBEL, born Cincinnati, Ohio, February 24, 1955; admitted to bar, 1980, Ohio; 1984, U.S. Tax Court. *Education:* University of Cincinnati (B.B.A., summa cum laude, 1977; J.D., 1980); University of Florida (LL.M. in Taxation, 1983). Beta Gamma Sigma. Certified Public Accountant, Ohio, 1982. *Member:* Cincinnati, Ohio State and American Bar Associations. ***PRACTICE AREAS:*** Employee Benefits; Taxation; Estate Planning; Closely-Held Business Law. ***Email:*** mstiebel@grafstiebel.com

MICHAEL K. MOYERS, born Los Gatos, California, April 20, 1966; admitted to bar, 1991, Illinois and U.S. District Court, Northern District of Illinois; 1998, Ohio. *Education:* Stanford University (A.B., with distinction, 1988); Stanford Law School (J.D., with distinction, 1991). Phi Beta Kappa; Order of the Coif. Associate Editor, Stanford Law Review. Author: "Survey of Illinois Law Trusts and Estates," 20 Southern Illinois Law Review 959, 1996; "Charitable Remainder Trusts Offer Noncharitable Benefits," 58 Tax'n Acc't 285, 1997. *Member:* Illinois State and Ohio State Bar Associations. ***PRACTICE AREAS:*** Estate Planning; Trust Law; Taxation; Probate; Closely-Held Business Law. ***Email:*** mmoyers@grafstiebel.com

DEBBE A. LEVIN, born Cincinnati, Ohio, March 11, 1954; admitted to bar, 1979, Ohio, U.S. Court of Appeals, 6th Circuit, U.S. District Court, Southern District of Ohio and U.S. Tax Court. *Education:* Washington University (B.A., 1975); University of Cincinnati College of Law (J.D., 1979); New York University (LL.M. in Taxation, 1983). Order of the Coif. Member, Cincinnati Law Review. *Member:* Cincinnati, Ohio State and American Bar Associations; Cincinnati Estate Planning Council; Greater Cincinnati Planned Giving Council; National Academy of Elder Law Attorneys. ***PRACTICE AREAS:*** Employee Benefits; Estate Planning; Probate; Retirement Distribution Planning; Elder Law. ***Email:*** dlevin@grafstiebel.com

MARK S. BEVER, born Zanesville, Ohio, April 27, 1959; admitted to bar, 1984, Ohio. *Education:* University of Notre Dame (B.A., 1981); University of Toledo, College of Law (J.D., 1984); Washington University School of Law (LL.M., Taxation, 1995). Member, The University of Toledo Law Review. Author: "Manville Corporation and the 'Good Faith' Standard for Reorganization Under the Bankruptcy Code," 14 University of Toledo Law Review 1467 (1983). Magistrate, Hamilton County Common Pleas Court, Probate Division, 2000-2003. *Member:* Cincinnati and Ohio State Bar Associations. ***PRACTICE AREAS:*** Trust Administration; Federal Estate and Gift Taxation; Probate Administration; Ancillary Probate; Contested Trusts and Estates; Estate Planning; Income Tax. ***Email:*** mbever@grafstiebel.com

---

NANCY J. BURNS, born Royal Oak, Michigan, February 22, 1958; admitted to bar, 1995, Ohio. *Education:* Northern Kentucky University (B.A., 1992); Salmon P. Chase College of Law of Northern Kentucky University (J.D., 1995). Chartered Property Casualty Underwriter, 1986. *Member:* Cincinnati and Ohio State Bar Associations. ***PRACTICE AREAS:*** Estate Planning for Unmarried Couples; Estate Planning for Parents of Handicapped Children; Estate Planning for the Elderly; Trust Administration; Powers of Attorney; Living Trusts; Estate Planning; Estate Administration; Income Tax; Federal Estate and Gift Taxation; Probate Administration. ***Email:*** nburns@grafstiebel.com

SEAN K. MANGAN, born West Chester, Pennsylvania, March 26, 1973; admitted to bar, 2002, Virginia; 2004, Ohio. *Education:* University of Notre Dame (B.A., 1995); University of Virginia (J.D., 2002). Associate Editor, Virginia Law Review, 2001-2002. Author: "Compensation for 'Certain' Victims of Terrorism Under 2002 of the Victims of Trafficking and Violence Protection Act of 2002," 42 Va. J. Int'l L. 1037 (2002). Member, Ohio Innocence Project. *Member:* Cincinnati, Ohio State and American Bar Associations; Virginia State Bar. [Captain, U.S. Marine Corps, 1995-1999.]. ***PRACTICE AREAS:*** Employee Benefits; Taxation; Closely Held Business Law; Estate Planning. ***Email:*** smangan@grafstiebel.com

REPRESENTATIVE CLIENTS: Charles F. Shiels & Co.; Comstock Valuation Advisors, Inc.; CSP Group, Inc.; Curless Printing Company; GTC Foodservice, Inc.; H. Hafner & Sons, Inc.; Lightborne Publishing, Inc.; MRA Advertising/Production Support Services, Inc.; Varland Metal Service, Inc.; Wil-Cut Co.; Mike Albert Leasing, Inc.; Professional Radiology, Inc.; Feintool U.S. Operations, Inc.; University Radiology Associates of Cincinnati, Inc.; MedicOne, Inc.; Steam Economies Company; Wetherington Family Medicine.

GRAYDON HEAD & RITCHEY LLP

Established in 1871

1900 FIFTH THIRD CENTER

511 WALNUT STREET

P.O. BOX 6464

CINCINNATI, OHIO 45202-3157

Telephone: 513-621-6464

Fax: 513-651-3836

Email: info@graydon.com

URL: http://www.graydon.com

Fort Mitchell, Kentucky Office: 2500 Chamber Center Drive, Suite 300, P.O. Box 17070, 41017. Telephone: 859-282-8800. Fax: 859-525-0214.

Antitrust, Banking, Bankruptcy, Computer, Construction, Corporate, Creditors' Rights, Employee Benefits, Employment, Environmental, Equine, Estate Planning, Finance, Health Care, Human Resources, Intellectual Property, International, Internet Commerce, Labor Relations, Legislative, Litigation, Media Law, Mergers and Acquisitions, Probate, Products Liability, Real Estate, Securities, Succession Planning, Tax, Trial and Appellate Practice in State and Federal Courts, Workers' Compensation.

FIRM PROFILE: Commitment to customer satisfaction is the highest priority for everyone on the Graydon Head & Ritchey team. In focus groups, our clients have described us as "dealmakers, not deal breakers." Comments like this are what fuel our firm, what make us strive to serve our clients even better. We do our homework on our clients' industries and "roll up our sleeves." We also travel to our clients facilities to gain practical knowledge of the business to

(This Listing Continued)

GRAYDON HEAD & RITCHEY LLP, Cincinnati—Continued

inform our advice. Our Downtown Cincinnati and Northern Kentucky offices provide convenient access to clients, but we are not "office bound" lawyers; we get out and see the operations of our clients. Working together with our clients, we have achieved excellent results.

Our motto is "We Represent Success" in recognition that our clients' success is our goal. More than any titles or awards, our clients best reflect the scope and quality of our practice. A diverse group of individuals and entities with local, national and international interests, GH&R clients share a common bond in their quest for business and personal success.

GH&R joined the Center for Quality of Management in 2003, took home the Ohio Governor's Excellence in Exporting Award in 2004 and, according to a survey conducted by "Corporate Board Member" magazine, has been named by corporate directors of publicly traded U.S. corporations as one of Cincinnati's top five law firms for three years in a row.

Our commitment to the Greater Cincinnati community is exemplified in the efforts of our team members to foster volunteerism throughout the entire firm with the attorney and staff driven Community Service Team. Our establishment and continued support of the Women's Professional Development Group is another example of our on-going commitment to diversity and to the service of its clients.

PARTNERS

HENRY G. ALEXANDER, JR., born Cincinnati, Ohio, February 22, 1949; admitted to bar, 1975, Ohio and U.S. Tax Court. *Education:* University of Cincinnati (B.A., 1971; J.D., 1975). Phi Beta Kappa.Member, Midwest Benefits Conference. *Member:* Cincinnati, Ohio State and American Bar Associations. ***PRACTICE AREAS:*** Taxation (Federal, State and Local) Law; Business Planning Law; Employee Benefits and Executive Compensation. ***Email:*** aleh@graydon.com

WILLIAM J. BAECHTOLD, born Cincinnati, Ohio, May 11, 1947; admitted to bar, 1972, Ohio. *Education:* Xavier University (B.S.B.A., magna cum laude, 1969); University of Cincinnati (J.D., 1972). ***PRACTICE AREAS:*** Estate Planning; Trust Law; Estate Law; Business Planning Law. ***Email:*** baew@graydon.com

STEPHEN L. BLACK, born Cincinnati, Ohio, December 3, 1948; admitted to bar, 1974, Ohio; 1975, U.S. Court of Appeals, Sixth Circuit. *Education:* Harvard University (A.B., magna cum laude, 1971; J.D., 1974). Law Clerk to the Hon. George Edwards, U.S. Court of Appeals, Sixth Circuit, 1974-1975. *Member:* Cincinnati and Ohio State Bar Associations. ***PRACTICE AREAS:*** Civil Litigation; Trust Law; Estate Litigation; Environmental Litigation. ***Email:*** sblack@graydon.com

THOMAS A. BREITENBACH, born Cleveland, Ohio, November 27, 1961; admitted to bar, 1990, Ohio; 1991, U.S. District Court, Southern District of Ohio. *Education:* University of Notre Dame (B.B.A., 1984); University of Notre Dame Graduate School of Business (M.B.A., 1985); The Ohio State University College of Law (J.D., 1990). Recipient, Business Courier Forty Under 40 Award, 2000. Chair, Crayons to Computers. Member, Midwest Benefits Conference. Member, National Conference for Community and Justice-.*Member:* Cincinnati Bar Association. ***PRACTICE AREAS:*** Employee Benefits and Executive Compensation. ***Email:*** tbreitenbach@graydon.com

THOMAS A. BRENNAN, born Cleveland, Ohio, April 2, 1938; admitted to bar, 1966, Ohio. *Education:* The Ohio State University (B.A., 1963; J.D., 1966). Instructor, Labor Law, University of Cincinnati, 1979—. Phi Delta Phi. *Member:* Cincinnati and Ohio State Bar Associations. ***PRACTICE AREAS:*** Employment Law; Corporate Law; Health Care Law. ***Email:*** bret@graydon.com

DANIEL E. BURKE, born Cincinnati, Ohio, February 7, 1962; admitted to bar, 1988, Ohio; 1996, Kentucky. *Education:* University of Notre Dame (B.A., cum laude, 1984); University of Cincinnati College of Law (J.D., 1988). Order of the Coif. Member, Southwestern Ohio Self Insurers Association. *Member:* Cincinnati and Ohio State Bar Associations. (Certified Specialist in Workers' Compensation Law, Ohio State Bar Association). ***PRACTICE AREAS:*** Human Resources; Private and Family Businesses. ***Email:*** dburke@graydon.com

CHRISTINE A. BUTTRESS, born Cambridge, Ohio, November 24, 1953; admitted to bar, 1979, Ohio; 1980, U.S. Tax Court; 1985, Kentucky; U.S. District Court, Southern District of Ohio. *Education:* John Carroll University (B.S., magna cum laude, 1976); University of Cincinnati (J.D., 1979). Fellow, American College of Trust and Estate Counsel. *Member:* Cincinnati, Northern Kentucky, Ohio State, Kentucky and American Bar Associations. (Certified Specialist in Estate Planning, Trust and Probate Law, Ohio State Bar Association). ***PRACTICE AREAS:*** Non-Profits and Tax Exempt Organizations; Private Business; Family Business. ***Email:*** butc@graydon.com

HARRY W. CAPPEL, born Salem, Oregon, May 25, 1970; admitted to bar, 1996, Ohio; 2002, Kentucky; 2003, Indiana. *Education:* University of Cincinnati (B.A., 1993); University of Cincinnati College of Law (J.D., 1996). *Member:* Cincinnati, Ohio State, Kentucky, Indiana State Bar Associations. ***PRACTICE AREAS:*** Creditors Rights; Real Estate; Bankruptcy. ***Email:*** hcappel@graydon.com

J. MICHAEL DEBBELER, born Newport, Kentucky, March 10, 1955; admitted to bar, 1980, Ohio and U.S. District Court, Southern District of Ohio; 1981, Kentucky; 1982, U.S. District Court, Eastern District of Kentucky; 1983, U.S. District Court, Northern District of Ohio and Western District of Kentucky; 1988, U.S. Court of Appeals, Federal Circuit and U.S. District Court, Southern and Northern Districts of Indiana; 1992, U.S. Court of Appeals, Sixth Circuit. *Education:* College of Arts and Sciences, University of Kentucky (B.A., History, cum laude, 1976); University of Cincinnati, College of Law (J.D., 1980). Order of the Barristers. Founding Committee Member, Bench Bar Conference, U.S. Bankruptcy Court, Southern District of Ohio. Member: Executive Committee, Midwest Regional Bankruptcy Seminar; Merit Selection Panel for the U.S.Court of Appeals for the Sixth Circuit Judicial Council. *Member:* Cincinnati, Northern Kentucky, Ohio State and Kentucky Bar Associations; American Bankruptcy Institute; American Bankruptcy Law Forum; Tri-State Association for Corporate Renewal. ***PRACTICE AREAS:*** Bankruptcy; Creditors Rights. ***Email:*** mdebbeler@graydon.com

(This Listing Continued)

HARRY J. FINKE IV, born Cincinnati, Ohio, March 21, 1955; admitted to bar, 1982, Ohio; 1984, U.S. District Court, Southern District of Ohio; 1988, U.S. Court of Appeals, Sixth Circuit; 1994, U.S. Supreme Court. *Education:* Brown University (A.B., magna cum laude, 1977); Duke University (J.D., 1982). Law Clerk to the Hon. Carl B. Rubin, U.S. District Court, Southern District of Ohio, 1982-1984. Barrister, Potter Stewart Inn of Court, 1984-1986. Life Member, Sixth Circuit Judicial Conference. *Member:* Cincinnati and Ohio State Bar Associations. ***PRACTICE AREAS:*** Litigation; Employment Law; Banking Litigation. ***Email:*** finh@graydon.com

JOHN A. FLANAGAN, born Sioux City, Iowa, November 29, 1942; admitted to bar, 1968, Iowa; 1971, U.S. Tax Court; 1972, U.S. Supreme Court; 1975, District of Columbia; 1977, Ohio. *Education:* State University of Iowa (B.A., 1964); Georgetown University (J.D., 1968). Order of the Coif. Attorney Advisor to Judge John F. Mulroney, U.S. Tax Court, 1968-1970. Trial Attorney, Tax Division, U.S. Department of Justice, 1970-1974. Associate Professor of Law, Taxation and Trial Practice, 1974-1978; Adjunct Professor, Tax Law and Media Law, University of Cincinnati College of Law, 1978—. *Member:* Cincinnati Bar Associations; The District of Columbia Bar. ***PRACTICE AREAS:*** Taxation (Federal, State and Local) Law; Business Planning Law; Media Law. ***Email:*** jflanagan@graydon.com

WILLIAM G. GEISEN, born Covington, Kentucky, November 27, 1958; admitted to bar, 1983, Kentucky; U.S. District Court, Eastern and Western Districts of Kentucky (Not admitted in Ohio). *Education:* Xavier University (H.A.B., magna cum laude, 1979); University of Kentucky (J.D., 1982). Member, Midwest/Midsouth Construction Law Institute. *Member:* Kentucky and American Bar Associations; American Arbitration Association. ***PRACTICE AREAS:*** Construction Law; Litigation; Dispute Resolution; Commercial Real Estate. ***Email:*** wgeisen@graydon.com

JOHN C. GREINER, born Cincinnati, Ohio, October 23, 1958; admitted to bar, 1983, Ohio. *Education:* Miami University (B.A., cum laude, 1980); University of Notre Dame (J.D., cum laude, 1983). Note Editor, Notre Dame Law Review, 1982-1983. Member: Order of the Barristers; Adjunct Instructor, University of Cincinnati Law School, 2001—. Member, Ohio Coalition of Open Government.*Member:* Cincinnati and Ohio State Bar Associations. ***PRACTICE AREAS:*** Media Law; Commercial Litigation; Banking Law. ***Email:*** grej@graydon.com

JEFFREY M. HENDRICKS, born La Mesa, California, March 27, 1971; admitted to bar, 1996, Ohio; 1997, Kentucky; 1999, U.S. District Court, Southern and Northern Districts of Ohio and U.S. District Court, Eastern and Western Districts of Kentucky. *Education:* Xavier University (B.A., magna cum laude, 1993); University of Cincinnati (J.D., 1996). *Member:* Cincinnati, Ohio State and Kentucky Bar Associations. ***PRACTICE AREAS:*** Creditors Rights; Bankruptcy. ***Email:*** jhendricks@graydon.com

DANIEL C. HEYD, born Cincinnati, Ohio, June 27, 1961; admitted to bar, 1986, Ohio; U.S. District Court, Southern District of Ohio. *Education:* Xavier University (B.S.B.A., summa cum laude, 1983); University of Cincinnati (J.D., 1986). Order of the Coif. Member: Editorial Board, University of Cincinnati Law Review, 1985-1986. *Member:* Cincinnati and Ohio State Bar Associations. ***PRACTICE AREAS:*** Corporate Law; Computer Law; Business Law; Mergers and Acquisitions; Construction Law; Intellectual Property. ***Email:*** heyd@graydon.com

MICHAEL A. HIRSCHFELD, born Sidney, Ohio, June 7, 1951; admitted to bar, 1977, Ohio. *Education:* Kenyon College (A.B., magna cum laude, 1973); University of Virginia (M.B.A., 1977; J.D., 1977). Phi Beta Kappa. *Member:* Cincinnati, Ohio State and American Bar Associations. ***PRACTICE AREAS:*** Closely Held Business Law; Corporate Law; Mergers and Acquisitions; International Law; Computer Law. ***Email:*** mhirschfeld@graydon.com

BRUCE A. HOFFMAN, born Cleveland, Ohio, February 24, 1950; admitted to bar, 1975, Ohio. *Education:* Denison University (B.A., with honors, 1972); Cornell University (J.D., cum laude, 1975). Phi Beta Kappa. *Member:* Cincinnati, Ohio State and American Bar Associations. ***PRACTICE AREAS:*** Employment Law; Corporate Law; Employee Benefits and Executive Compensation Law; Health Care; Litigation. ***Email:*** hofb@graydon.com

MICHAEL S. JONES, born Omaha, Nebraska, March 11, 1965; admitted to bar, 1994, Ohio; 1996, U.S. District Court, Southern District of Ohio. *Education:* University of Cincinnati (B.A., Economics, 1990); Louisiana State University (J.D., 1993). *Member:* Cincinnati Bar Association. ***PRACTICE AREAS:*** Litigation; Creditors; Insurance; Construction Law. ***Email:*** jonm@graydon.com

JOSEPH E. KANE, born Wyandotte, Michigan, April 26, 1945; admitted to bar, 1970, Ohio. *Education:* University of Notre Dame (B.A., cum laude, 1967; J.D., 1970); University of London, London, England (Certificate in English and American Law, 1969). Member, Ohio Land Title Association. Member: National Association of Industrial and Office Parks; National Diocesan Attorneys Association. ***PRACTICE AREAS:*** Real Estate Law; Commercial Leasing Law; Construction Law. ***Email:*** jkane@graydon.com

MONICA DONATH KOHNEN, born Covington, Kentucky, May 24, 1960; admitted to bar, 1985, Ohio; 2001, Kentucky. *Education:* Duke University (B.A., cum laude, 1982); University of Cincinnati (J.D., 1985). Member, The Hamilton County Board of Building Standards. Licensed Ohio Title Agent. *Member:* Cincinnati Bar Association. ***PRACTICE AREAS:*** Commercial Real Estate; Private and Family Businesses; Securities; Financing Transactions. ***Email:*** kohm@graydon.com

ROBERT L. KREIDLER, born Cincinnati, Ohio, January 27, 1937; admitted to bar, 1962, Ohio. *Education:* Yale University (A.B., 1959); University of Cincinnati (J.D., 1962). Phi Alpha Delta. *Member:* Cincinnati Bar Association. ***PRACTICE AREAS:*** Mergers and Acquisitions; Business Financing Law. ***Email:*** krer@graydon.com

JOHN J. KROPP, born Dobbs Ferry, New York, September 25, 1946; admitted to bar, 1972, Ohio. *Education:* University of Cincinnati (B.A., 1969); Georgetown University (J.D., 1972). *Member:* Cincinnati Bar Association. ***PRACTICE AREAS:*** Corporate Law; Securities; Litigation; Equine Law. ***Email:*** jkropp@graydon.com

RICHARD T. LA JEUNESSE, born Dearborn, Michigan, December 7, 1953; admitted to bar, 1980, Ohio. *Education:* Xavier University (B.S., summa cum laude, 1975); Universite de Paris, Sorbonne, France; Katholieke Universiteit de Leuven, Belgium; Universite Libre de Bruxelles, Belgium; University of Michigan (M.A., 1977; J.D., 1980). Alpha Sigma Nu. Ohio State Bar Association Certified Specialist in Business, Commercial and

(This Listing Continued)

Industrial Real Property Law. Member, International Council of Shopping Centers. Member, International Ambassadorial Fellowship. *Member:* Cincinnati and Ohio State Bar Associations;. ***LANGUAGES:*** French. ***PRACTICE AREAS:*** Real Estate Law; Environmental Law; Corporate Law. ***Email:*** lajr@graydon.com

J. JEFFREY LANDEN, born July 13, 1957; admitted to bar, 1982, Ohio; 1983, Kentucky; 1984, U.S. District Court, Eastern District of Kentucky; 1986, U.S. District Court, Western District of Kentucky. *Education:* Centre College of Kentucky (B.A., magna cum laude, 1978); University of Kentucky (J.D., magna cum laude, 1982). Phi Beta Kappa; Order of the Coif. Managing Editor, 70 Kentucky Law Journal, 1981-1982. *Member:* Kentucky and Northern Kentucky Bar Associations; American Bankruptcy Institute. ***PRACTICE AREAS:*** Advertising and Media; Construction Law; Bankruptcy; Creditors Rights; Intellectual Property and Technology; Litigation; Dispute Resolution. ***Email:*** lanj@graydon.com

MICHAEL R. MILLER, born Dayton, Ohio, November 29, 1957; admitted to bar, 1983, Ohio; U.S. District Court, Southern District of Ohio. *Education:* Bowling Green State University (B.S., 1980); University of Dayton School of Law (J.D., 1983). Member: University of Dayton Law Review, 1981-1982; National Mock Trial Team; Order of The Barristers. Recipient, Lewis Powell Award. Certified Financial Planner (TM); Vice President, ProSeniors Inc. Board of Trustees. *Member:* Cincinnati and Ohio State Bar Associations. ***PRACTICE AREAS:*** Trusts and Estates. ***Email:*** mmiller@graydon.com

GERALD F. O'CONNELL, JR., born Dayton, Ohio, August 17, 1959; admitted to bar, 1984, Ohio. *Education:* The Ohio State University (B.S., 1981); University of Cincinnati (J.D., 1984). Phi Alpha Delta; Order of the Coif. Editorial Board, University of Cincinnati Law Review, 1983-1984. Member: International Council of Shopping Centers. ***PRACTICE AREAS:*** Corporate Law; Commercial Law; Real Estate Law. ***Email:*** goconnell@graydon.com

ERIC C. OKERSON, born Ventura, California, August 31, 1949; admitted to bar, 1980, New York and Ohio. *Education:* Boston University (B.A., 1971); Tulane University (J.D., summa cum laude, 1979). Ohio Board of Education, Member, 2005—. Order of the Coif. Editor in Chief, Tulane Law Review, 1978-1979. Law Clerk to the Honorable George Edwards, Chief Judge, U.S. Court of Appeals for the Sixth Circuit, 1979-1980. *Member:* Cincinnati Bar Association. ***PRACTICE AREAS:*** Corporate Law; Secured Transactions Law; Creditors; Intellectual Property. ***Email:*** eokerson@graydon.com

BRUCE I. PETRIE, JR., born Cincinnati, Ohio, January 25, 1954; admitted to bar, 1980, Ohio; U.S. District Court, Southern District of Ohio; U.S. District Court, Northern District of Kentucky; U.S. Court of Appeals, Sixth Circuit; U.S. Supreme Court. *Education:* Brown University (B.A., magna cum laude, 1976); Northwestern University (J.D., 1979). Phi Beta Kappa. Order of the Barristers. Articles Editor, Northwestern University Law Review, 1978-1979. Law Clerk to the Honorable John F. Grady, U.S. District Court, Northern District of Illinois, 1979-1980. President: Legal Aid Society of Cincinnati, 1992-1994; Cincinnati Parks Foundation, 2002—. Leadership Cincinnati, 1992-1993. *Member:* Cincinnati and Ohio State Bar Associations; National Association of School Attorneys; Ohio Association of School Board Attorneys; Ohio River Way Board. ***PRACTICE AREAS:*** Labor Law; Health Care; Employment Law; Education Law; Advertising Law; Media Law. ***Email:*** bpetriejr@graydon.com

JOHN B. PINNEY, born Clinton, Iowa, August 5, 1947; admitted to bar, 1972, Michigan; 1974, Ohio; 1991, Kentucky; U.S. Supreme Court; U.S. Court of Appeals, Sixth Circuit; U.S. District Court, Southern District of Ohio, Eastern and Western Districts of Kentucky, Eastern District of Michigan, District of Colorado, Southern District of Indiana and Eastern District of Wisconsin. *Education:* University of Pennsylvania (B.S. in Economics, Wharton School, 1969); University of Michigan (J.D., cum laude, 1972). Law Clerk to the Honorable Philip Pratt, U.S. District Court, Eastern District of Michigan, 1972-1974. Master of the Bench, Potter Stewart Inn of Court, 1990—. Chairman, Local Rules Committee U.S. Court of Appeals for the Sixth Circuit, 2004—. Member, U.S. Court of Appeals, Sixth Circuit Judicial Conference, 2004—. Speaker: Barriers to Free Movement of Civil Justice, Salzburg, Austria, Nov., 2001; International Colloquium on Commercial Arbitration, Salzburg, Austria, June 2004; International Arbitration Committee of CPR Institute; Center for Resolution of Disputes; Supreme Court Historical Society. *Member:* Cincinnati, Ohio State, Northern Kentucky, Michigan, Kentucky, Federal and American Bar Associations; London International Court of Arbitration; International Bar Associaton; American Arbitration Association. ***PRACTICE AREAS:*** Litigation; Dispute Resolution; International Litigation and Arbitrations. ***Email:*** jpinney@graydon.com

THOMAS A. PREWITT, born Lexington, Kentucky, August 26, 1963; admitted to bar, 1988, Kentucky; 1993, Ohio; U.S. District Court, Eastern and Western District of Kentucky; U.S. Court of Appeals, Sixth Circuit. *Education:* Ohio University (B.S., 1985); University of Kentucky (J.D., 1988). Leadership Northern Kentucky, 1999, President, Madison E-Zone. Family Nurturing Center. Covington Business Council. Northern Kentucky Chamber of Commerce, Board of Advisors. Recipient, 2002 Forty Under 40 Award. Member, CPR Institute for Dispute Resolution. *Member:* Northern Kentucky and Kentucky Bar Associations. ***PRACTICE AREAS:*** Commercial Litigation; Business Litigation. ***Email:*** pret@graydon.com

KAREN J. RENZ, born Chicago, Illinois, March 2, 1964; admitted to bar, 1996, Florida; 1997, Ohio. *Education:* East Carolina University (B.S.B.A., cum laude, 1986); University of Miami School of Law (J.D., cum laude, 1996). Phi Delta Phi. *Member:* Cincinnati, Florida, Ohio State and American Bar Associations; American Institute of Certified Public Accountants; Ohio Society of Certified Public Accountants. ***PRACTICE AREAS:*** Corporate Law; Mergers and Acquisitions. ***Email:*** renk@graydon.com

MICHAEL A. ROBERTS, born St. Louis, Missouri, October 13, 1963; admitted to bar, 1990, Ohio; U.S. District Court, Northern and Southern Districts of Ohio; U.S. Court of Appeals, Sixth Circuit; U.S. Supreme Court. *Education:* University of Notre Dame (B.S., 1986; J.D., 1990). ***PRACTICE AREAS:*** Commercial Litigation; ERISA Litigation; Employment Law; Health Care Litigation. ***Email:*** mroberts@graydon.com

RICHARD L. ROBINSON, born Ft. Lauderdale, Florida, March 5, 1958; admitted to bar, 1983, Kentucky; 1984; U.S. District Court, Eastern District of Kentucky; 1994, U.S. Court of Appeals, Sixth Circuit (Not admitted in Ohio). *Education:* Eastern Kentucky University (B.A., Political Science, 1980); Salmon P. Chase College of Law, Northern Kentucky University (J.D., 1983). Legislative Director/General Counsel, U.S. Rep. Jim Bunning, 1987-1993. *Member:* Kentucky Bar Association. ***PRACTICE AREAS:*** Real Estate Law; Corporate Law; Litigation. ***Email:*** robr@graydon.com

JEFFREY L. ROHR, born Canton, Ohio, April 3, 1960; admitted to bar, 1985, Ohio. *Education:* Miami University (B.S., magna cum laude, 1982); Georgetown University (J.D., cum laude, 1985). ***PRACTICE AREAS:*** Corporate Law; Business Planning Law; Commercial Law. ***Email:*** rohj@graydon.com

ROBERT R. SAELINGER, born Melbourne, Kentucky, January 23, 1957; admitted to bar, 1980, Kentucky and U.S. District Court, Western District of Kentucky; 1984, U.S. Tax Court; 1988, Ohio. *Education:* Xavier University (B.A., 1977); University of Kentucky (J.D., 1980); Boston University (LL.M., in Taxation, 1984). Member, Midwest Benefits Conference. *Member:* Cincinnati, Northern Kentucky and Kentucky Bar Associations. ***PRACTICE AREAS:*** Employee Benefits; Executive Compensation; Taxation. ***Email:*** saer@graydon.com

RICHARD G. SCHMALZL, born Pittsburgh, Pennsylvania, October 20, 1956; admitted to bar, 1982, Pennsylvania and U.S. District Court, Western District of Pennsylvania; 1984, District of Columbia; 1987, Ohio. *Education:* University of Pittsburgh (B.S., summa cum laude, 1978); University of Virginia (J.D., 1982); Georgetown University (LL.M. in Taxation, 1989). *Member:* Cincinnati Bar Association. ***PRACTICE AREAS:*** Securities Law; Corporate Law; Corporate Governance; Mergers and Acquisitions. ***Email:*** rschmalzl@graydon.com

JAMIE D. SCOTT, born Dayton, Ohio, February 29, 1956; admitted to bar, 1983, Texas; 1987, Ohio. *Education:* University of Cincinnati (B.B.A., summa cum laude, 1978); Brigham Young University (J.D., cum laude, 1983). Note and Comment Editor, Brigham Young University Law Review, 1982-1983. Member, Midwest Benefits Conference. *Member:* Cincinnati and Warren County Bar Associations. ***PRACTICE AREAS:*** Employee Benefits; Estate Planning. ***Email:*** jscott@graydon.com

MARK E. SIMS, born Dayton, Ohio, April 15, 1955; admitted to bar, 1980, Ohio; 1981, Florida; 1983, U.S. Tax Court and U.S. Claims Court. *Education:* University of Cincinnati (B.B.A., 1977; J.D., 1980); University of Florida (LL.M., Taxation, 1981). Adjunct Professor, University of Cincinnati College of Law. *Member:* Cincinnati, Ohio State and American Bar Associations; The Florida Bar. ***PRACTICE AREAS:*** Federal Taxation; Corporate Law; Partnership Law; Health Care. ***Email:*** msims@graydon.com

PETER M. SLATER, born Evanston, Illinois; admitted to bar, 1992, New York; 1993, Ohio. *Education:* Skidmore College (B.S., 1987); Case Western Reserve University (J.D., 1992); Georgetown University (LL.M., 1993). Certified Financial Planner. ***PRACTICE AREAS:*** Estate Planning; Trusts and Estates. ***Email:*** pslater@graydon.com

DAVID S. WARREN, born Lima, Ohio, August 27, 1963; admitted to bar, 1989, Ohio. *Education:* Bowling Green State University (B.A., summa cum laude, 1985); Georgetown University School of Foreign Service (M.S.F.S., 1989); Georgetown University (J.D., cum laude, 1989). Phi Beta Kappa; Omicron Delta Kappa; Phi Kappa Phi. *Member:* Cincinnati and Ohio State Bar Associations; American Health Lawyers Association. ***PRACTICE AREAS:*** Business Law; Health Care Law; International Law. ***Email:*** dwarren@graydon.com

KENT WELLINGTON, born Circleville, Ohio, December 29, 1965; admitted to bar, 1991, Ohio; U.S. District Court, Southern District of Ohio; U.S. Court of Appeals, Sixth Circuit. *Education:* Kenyon College (B.A., magna cum laude, English and Economics, 1988, Phi Beta Kappa); The Ohio State University College of Law (J.D., 1991). Member: Ohio State Law Journal; National Moot Court Team. *Member:* Cincinnati Bar Association. ***PRACTICE AREAS:*** Litigation; Employment Law; Media Law. ***Email:*** welk@graydon.com

A. CHRISTIAN WORRELL III, born Ashland, Kentucky, October 24, 1951; admitted to bar, 1985, Ohio; 1986, Kentucky. *Education:* University of Cincinnati (B.A., cum laude, 1975; M.S., Environmental Studies, 1977); Salmon P. Chase College of Law, Northern Kentucky University (J.D., magna cum laude, 1985). Member: Order of Curia. Memeber, American Institute of Architects. *Member:* Cincinnati and Kentucky Bar Associations. ***PRACTICE AREAS:*** Real Estate Law; Commercial Real Estate Law; Construction Law. ***Email:*** cworrell@graydon.com

ASSOCIATES

PAUL ALLEY, born Middletown, Ohio, February 4, 1969; admitted to bar, 1994, Kentucky; 1997, U.S. District Court, Eastern and Western Districts of Kentucky; 1998, U.S. Court of Appeals, Sixth Circuit; 2002, Ohio. *Education:* Miami University (B.A. in History and Political Science, cum laude, 1991); University of Kentucky (J.D., 1994). *Member:* Northern Kentucky and Kentucky Bar Associations; Leadership Northern Kentucky. [With U.S. Navy, JAGC, 1993-1997]. (Resident, Fort Mitchell, Kentucky Office). ***PRACTICE AREAS:*** Commercial Litigation; Dispute Resolution; Construction Law; Advertising and Media Law. ***Email:*** palley@graydon.com

AINE M. BALDWIN, born Cincinnati, Ohio, September 20, 1975; admitted to bar, 2002, Ohio; 2003, U.S. District Court, Eastern District of Tennessee. *Education:* Davidson College (B.A., in history 1998); University of Cincinnati (J.D., 2002). Member, Editorial Board, University of Cincinnati Law Review, 2001-2002. Clerkship, U.S. District Court, Eastern District of Tennessee. *Member:* Cincinnati, Ohio State and Federal Bar Association. ***PRACTICE AREAS:*** Real Estate. ***Email:*** abaldwin@graydon.com

LYNDSEY R. CATER, born Toledo, Ohio, August 1, 1979; admitted to bar, 2004, Ohio. *Education:* Miami University (B.S. Accountancy, 2000); University of Cincinnati College of Law (J.D., 2004); Northwestern University School of Law (LL.M. Taxation, 2005). Associate Member, Law Review. President, Volunteer Income Tax Assistance Group. Winner: Eugene M. Corbin Memorial Award; Reeta Brendamour Prize in Tax Law Studies. *Member:* Cincinnati Bar Association. ***PRACTICE AREAS:*** Employee Benefits; Executive Compensation; Human Resources. ***Email:*** lcater@graydon.com

ALLYSON TRUE COOK, born Carrollton, Kentucky, September 20, 1964; admitted to bar, 1989, Kentucky (Not admitted in Ohio). *Education:* University of Kentucky (B.A.,

(This Listing Continued)

GRAYDON HEAD & RITCHEY LLP, Cincinnati—Continued

Finance, departmental honors, 1986; Minor, Economics, 1986; J.D., 1989). *Member:* Northern Kentucky and Kentucky Bar Associations. ***PRACTICE AREAS:*** Litigation; Construction Law; Dispute Resolution. ***Email:*** acook@graydon.com

KARA A. CZANIK, admitted to bar, 2002, Ohio; U.S. District Court, Southern District of Ohio; 2005, U.S. District Court, Northern District of Ohio. *Education:* Wittenberg University (B.A., 1999); University of Cincinnati College of Law (J.D., 2002). *Member:* Cincinnati, Dayton, Ohio State and American Bar Associations; Potter Stewart Inn of Court. ***PRACTICE AREAS:*** Litigation. ***Email:*** kczanik@graydon.com

NEIL FAIRWEATHER, born Dundee, Scotland, January 11, 1968; admitted to bar, 1995, Kentucky and U.S. District Court, Western and Eastern Districts of Kentucky; 2000, Ohio; 2003, Indiana; U.S. District Court, Southern District of Ohio and U.S. District Court, Northern and Southern Districts of Indiana. *Education:* Hanover College (B.A., 1989); University of Kentucky College of Law (J.D., 1995). Member, International Council of Shopping Centers. *Member:* Cincinnati, Ohio State, Kentucky and Indiana State Bar Associations. ***PRACTICE AREAS:*** Bankruptcy; Creditors Rights; Commercial Real Estate; Litigation; Dispute Resolution. ***Email:*** nfairweather@graydon.com

LEE P. GEIGER, born Cincinnati, Ohio, May 12, 1975; admitted to bar, 2000, Ohio; 2001, U.S. District Court, Southern District of Ohio. *Education:* Miami University (B.A. in Political Science, 1997); University of Toledo (J.D., magna cum laude, 2000). Order of the Coif. Member, 1998-1999 and Assistant Managing Editor, 1999-2000, University of Toledo Law Review. Author: "Cheering for the Home Team, An Analysis of Public Funding of Professional Sports Stadia in Cincinnati, Ohio," The University of Toledo Law Review, Vol. 30, No.3, Spring, 1999. *Member:* Cincinnati Bar Association. ***PRACTICE AREAS:*** Education Law; School Law; Health Care; Labor and Employment; Commercial Litigation. ***Email:*** lgeiger@graydon.com

EVERETT L. GREENE, born Cincinnati, Ohio, December 13, 1947; admitted to bar, 2004, Ohio; 2005, U.S. District Court, Southern District of Ohio. *Education:* United States Naval Academy (B.S., Naval Science,1970); Naval Postgraduate School (M.S., Systems Technology, 1981); Howard University (J.D., 2003). *Member:* Cincinnati and Ohio State Bar Associations. [Capt., U.S. Navy, 1970-2000, retired]. ***PRACTICE AREAS:*** Labor and Employment. ***Email:*** egreene@graydon.com

CHRISTOPHER ALLEN GRIFFIN, born Columbus, Indiana, March 29, 1976; admitted to bar, 2003, Ohio. *Education:* University of Kentucky (B.B.A., cum laude, 1999); Stetson College of Law (J.D., 2003; M.B.A., with honors, 2003). ***PRACTICE AREAS:*** Commercial Real Estate; Construction Law; Litigation; Alternative Dispute Resolution. ***Email:*** cgriffin@graydon.com

MATTHEW B. LAKE, born East Chicago, Indiana, January 7, 1972; admitted to bar, 1999, Ohio. *Education:* Indiana University (B.S. in Finance, with distinction, 1994); University of Cincinnati (J.D., 1999). Order of the Coif. Corporate Law Fellow. Member, Cincinnati Law Review, 1998-1999. Certified Public Accountant, Illinois, 1997. Member, Academy of Medicine Foundation. Member, Southwest Ohio Tax Institute Planning Committee. *Member:* Cincinnati and Ohio State Bar Associations. ***PRACTICE AREAS:*** Business Taxation. ***Email:*** mlake@graydon.com

KATHERINE M. LASHER, born Cincinnati, Ohio, April 11, 1972; admitted to bar, 1999, Ohio; U.S. District Court, Southern District of Ohio; 2005, U.S. Court of Appeals, Sixth Circuit. *Education:* University of Cincinnati (B.A., magna cum laude, 1994; J.D., 1998). Phi Beta Kappa. *Member:* Cincinnati and American Bar Associations; American Immigration Lawyers Association. ***PRACTICE AREAS:*** Labor and Employment; Immigration; Appellate Practice. ***Email:*** klasher@graydon.com

AMY E. LIPPERT, born Cincinnati, Ohio, January 8, 1976; admitted to bar, 2001, Ohio; 2002, U.S. District Court, Northern District of Ohio. *Education:* University of Michigan (B.A., 1998); University of Cincinnati (J.D., 2001). Member, Order of the Coif. Member and Student Articles Editor, University of Cincinnati Law Review, 2000-2001. Law Clerk to the Honorable Nancy A. Vecchiarelli, U.S. Magistrate Judge, Northern District of Ohio, 2001-2003. Co-Author: "Deregulating Voluntary Dismissals," University of Michigan Journal of Law Reform, 2003. *Member:* Cincinnati and Ohio State Bar Associations. ***PRACTICE AREAS:*** Workers Compensation; Labor and Employment. ***Email:*** alippert@gradon.com

SHARON S. PARSLEY, born Cincinnati, Ohio, November 14, 1961; admitted to bar, 2004, Ohio; 2005, Kentucky. *Education:* Xavier University (B.S.B.A., cum laude, Accounting, 1986; M.B.A., summa cum laude, concentration in Finance, 1990); Salmon P. Chase College of Law (J.D., cum laude, 2004). Recipient: Commonwealth Scholarship; "Best Petitioner's Brief" Award, Grosse Moot Court Competition. *Member:* Cincinnati, Kentucky and Ohio State Bar Associations. ***PRACTICE AREAS:*** Health Care; Commercial Real Estate. ***Email:*** sparsley@graydon.com

JENNIFER S. PEARSON, born Austin, Texas, December 9, 1977; admitted to bar, 2003, Ohio. *Education:* University of Cincinnati (B.B.A., 2000); University of Cincinnati College of Law (J.D., 2003). Corporate Law Fellow, 2001-2003. Student Articles Editor, University of Cincinnati Law Review, 2002-2003. *Member:* Cincinnati, Ohio State and American Bar Associations. ***PRACTICE AREAS:*** Corporate Law; Commercial Law; Commercial Real Estate. ***Email:*** jpearson@graydon.com

DANIEL E. REITZ, born Islamabad, Pakistan, February 23, 1977; admitted to bar, 2001, Ohio. *Education:* John Dolibois European Center, Luxembourg; Miami University (B.A., cum laude, 1998); University of Cincinnati (J.D., Order of the Coif, 2001). Member and Student Articles Editor, University of Cincinnati Law Review, 2000-2001. Author: "Raising a Paper Tiger: Public Law No. 105-277 § 117(D) and the Gutting of the State-Sponsored Terrorism Exception to the Foreign Sovereign Immunities Act," 69 University of Cincinnati Law Review 357, 2000; "An Unbearable Burden: United States v. Kaluna and U.S.C. § 3559 (c)(3)(a)," 69 University of Cincinnati Law Review 717, 2001. Cincinnati Youth Collaborative Outstanding Mentor and Tutor, 2005. *Member:* Cincinnati Bar Association. ***PRACTICE AREAS:*** Corporate Law; Real Estate; Mergers and Acquisitions. ***Email:*** dreitz@graydon.com

ANN K. SCHOOLEY, born New York, N.Y., June 15, 1971; admitted to bar, 1999, Ohio. *Education:* University of Cincinnati (B.B.A., 1993); Indiana University, Bloomington (J.D., 1998). Phi Delta Phi (Treasurer, 1997-1998). Author: "FDA Regulation of Telemedicine: A Fatal Misdiagnosis," Federal Communications Law Journal. *Member:* Cincinnati Bar Association. ***PRACTICE AREAS:*** Commercial Litigation; Real Estate Litigation; Construction. ***Email:*** aschooley@graydon.com

(This Listing Continued)

MICHAEL C. SURREY, admitted to bar, 1998, Ohio; 1999, Kentucky, U.S. District Court, Southern District of Ohio and U.S. Court of Appeals, Sixth Circuit. *Education:* Centre College of Kentucky (B.S., cum laude, 1995); University of Kentucky (J.D., cum laude, 1998). Order of the Coif. Leadership Northern Kentucky, Class of 2001. *Member:* Ohio State, Northern Kentucky and Kentucky Bar Associations. ***PRACTICE AREAS:*** Construction; Litigation; Dispute Resolution. ***Email:*** msurrey@graydon.com

BRIAN C. THOMAS, born Akron, Ohio, September 30, 1976; admitted to bar, 2001, Ohio; 2002, U.S. District Court, Southern District of Ohio. *Education:* Georgia Institute of Technology (B.S., with honors, 1998); University of Dayton School of Law (J.D., cum laude, 2001). Author: "Examining a Beggar's First Amendment Right to Beg in an Era of Anti-Begging Ordinances: The Presence and Persistence Test," 26 U. Dayton L. Rev. 155 (2000). *Member:* Cincinnati and Ohio State Bar Associations; Potter Stewart Inn of Court. ***PRACTICE AREAS:*** Employment Litigation; Creditors Rights; Litigation. ***Email:*** bthomas@graydon.com

HANS M. TINKLER, born May 1, 1968; admitted to bar, 2002, Ohio; 2003, Kentucky. *Education:* United States Air Force Academy (B.S., Behavioral Science, 1990); Chaminade University of Honolulu (M.B.A., 1994); University of Cincinnati (J.D., 2002). [Captain, Signals Intelligence, U.S. Air Force, 1990-1995]. ***PRACTICE AREAS:*** Personal Tax Planning; Private Business; Family Business; Business Law; Transactions; Estate Administration. ***Email:*** htinkler@graydon.com

OF COUNSEL

SUSAN M. ARGO, born Davenport, Iowa, January 3, 1971; admitted to bar, 1996, Ohio; 1997, Kentucky, U.S. District Court, Northern, Southern and Federal District of Ohio and U.S. District Court, Eastern, Western and Federal District of Kentucky. *Education:* St. Ambrose University (B.A., summa cum laude, 1993); Drake University Law School (J.D. with honors, 1996). *Member:* Cincinnati, Ohio State, Kentucky and Northern Kentucky Bar Associations. ***LANGUAGES:*** Spanish. ***PRACTICE AREAS:*** Bankruptcy; Commercial Workouts; Real Estate; Civil Litigation. ***Email:*** sargo@graydon.com

REPRESENTATIVE CLIENTS: A summary of major clients include the following: Ackermann Group, AK Steel Corporation, Alliance Primary Care, Aluchem, Inc., Ameriquest Mortgage Company, Archdiocese of Cincinnati, Bascon, Inc., Battelle Memorial Institute, Bio/Start, Inc., Bob Sumerel Tire Co. Inc., Butler Technology and Career Development Schools, Cast-Fab Technologies, Inc., CET (Greater Cincinnati Television Educational Foundation), Christ Hospital, Cincinnati Bell, Cincinnati Enquirer, Cincinnati Eye Institute, Cincinnati Mills, Cincinnati Zoo, Clear Channel Communications, Inc., Consolidated Metal Products, Council on Aging of Southwestern Ohio, Deerfield Construction Company, E.W. Scripps, E-BEAM Services, Inc., Ellis & Watts, Intl., Episcopal Retirement Homes, Inc., Fifth Third Bancorp & Fifth Third Bank, First Watch Restaurants, Fort Hamilton Hospital, Gannett Co., Inc., Girindus America, Inc., Grote Industries, Inc., Health Alliance of Greater Cincinnati, Hilltop Basic Resources, Inc., Hixson Architects & Engineers, Home City Ice Company, Hummel Industries, Indian Hill Board of Education, International Technegroup, Inc., Jewish Hospital, John Morrell & Company, KAO Brands, LanVision Systems, Inc., LaRosa Corporation, LifeSphere, Madison E-Zone, Mazak Corporation, Merrill Lynch, Motz Group, MVD Communications, LLC, National City Bank, OfficeWare, Inc., OKI Systems Limited, Otterbein Homes, Paramount Parks Inc., Portman Equipment Company, Ralph J. Stolle Company, Reading Rock Inc., Regent Communications, Inc., Reliable Castings Corporation, River Cities Capital Fund, Robbins, Inc., Rotex, Inc., Rubin Pachulski Properties (f.k.a. Sycamore Plaza LLC), SENCORP, St. Luke Hospitals, Superior Linen & Apparel Services, Inc., Union Institute and University, Union Savings Bank, University Hospital, Viox Services, Wesley Services Organization, and the West Chester Chamber Alliance.

F. HARRISON GREEN CO., L.P.A.

4015 EXECUTIVE PARK DRIVE, SUITE 130
CINCINNATI, OHIO 45241-4017
Telephone: 513-769-0840
Fax: 513-563-2953
Email: fhgreen@ix.netcom.com
URL: http://www.lawyers.com/f_harrison_green_co-lpa

Litigation, Family Law, Personal Injury, Medical Malpractice, Workers Compensation, Employment Law, Civil Rights, Wills and Trust Law.

F. HARRISON GREEN, born East Orange, New Jersey, August 26, 1946; admitted to bar, 1972, Ohio and U.S. District Court, Southern District of Ohio; 1990, U.S. Court of Appeals, Sixth Circuit; 2000, Indiana and U.S. District Court, Southern District of Indiana. *Education:* Indiana University; University of Mississippi (B.A., 1968); University of Louisville (J.D., 1972). Delta Theta Phi. Recipient, Silver Key Award, ABA-LSD. Judge, Butler County Court, 1978-1981. Solicitor, College Corner, Ohio, 1989—. *Member:* Cincinnati, Indiana State and Ohio State Bar Associations; Federalist Society. (Also Of Counsel, Smith Law Offices, Muncie, Indiana). ***PRACTICE AREAS:*** Civil Litigation; Civil Rights; Corporate Law; Personal Injury; General Practice; Medical Malpractice. ***Email:*** fhgreen@fuse.net

---

DOUGLAS A. MACKINNON, born Hamilton, Ohio, January 24, 1971; admitted to bar, 2001, Ohio; 2003, Tennessee; 2004, U.S. District Court, Southern District of Ohio. *Education:* Miami University, Ohio (B.S., 1993); Salmon P. Chase College of Law (J.D., 2001). Alpha Mu Alpha. Member, National Honor Society. *Member:* Dayton, Ohio State and American Bar Associations. ***PRACTICE AREAS:*** Civil Litigation; Civil Rights; Medical Malpractice; Personal Injury; Family Law. ***Email:*** dmackinnon@fuse.net

REPRESENTATIVE CLIENTS: Thomas Products Co.; King International, Inc.; Access Benefits Corp.; Aluxier Trucking & Excavating; Peoples Trust Company.

GREENEBAUM DOLL & McDONALD PLLC

Established in 1952
2800 CHEMED CENTER
255 EAST FIFTH STREET
CINCINNATI, OHIO 45202-4728
Telephone: 513-455-7600
Fax: 513-455-8500
Email: lrv@gdm.com
URL: http://www.greenebaum.com

Louisville, Kentucky Office: 3300 National City Tower, 101 S. Fifth Street. Telephone: 502-589-4200. Fax: 502-587-3695.
Lexington, Kentucky Office: Suite 1100, 300 West Vine Street. Telephone: 859-231-8500. Fax: 859-255-2742.
Covington, Kentucky Office: 50 East RiverCenter Boulevard. Telephone: 859-655-4200. Fax: 859-655-4239.
Frankfort, Kentucky Office: Suite 101, 229 West Main Street. Telephone: 502-875-0050. Fax: 502-875-0850.
Nashville, Tennessee Office: 700 Two American Center, 3102 West End Avenue. Telephone: 615-760-7100. Fax: 615-760-7300.
Atlanta, Georgia Office: 1175 Peachtree Street, N.E., 100 Colony Square, Suite 780. Telephone: 404-879-2170. Fax: 404-879-2180.
Washington, D.C. Office: 1146 19th Street, N.W., Suite 250. Telephone: 202-293-7000. Fax: 202-293-9700.

General Civil Trial and Appellate Practice in all Courts, Litigation, Corporate Law, Business Law, Commercial Law, Securities, Mergers and Acquisitions, Finance, Electronic Commerce, Economic Development, Banks and Banking, Commercial Credit, Bankruptcy, Health Care, Insurance, Environmental Law, Natural Resources, Mining Law, Oil and Gas Law, Labor and Employment, Employee Benefits, Taxation, Probate, Trusts and Estates, Real Estate, Zoning, Planning and Land Use, Intellectual Property Law, Trademark Law, Patent Law, International Trade, Immigration and Naturalization, Antitrust and Trade Regulation, Franchises and Franchising, Equine, Products Liability Defense, Professional Liability Defense, Alternative Dispute Resolution, Administrative Law, Workers Compensation.

FIRM PROFILE: Greenebaum Doll & McDonald PLLC is a full service business law firm with offices in Louisville, Lexington, Covington, and Frankfort, Kentucky; Cincinnati, Ohio; Nashville, Tennessee; and Atlanta, Georgia, all of which are connected through state of the art information systems. Firm-wide practice groups allow concentration in specific areas of law or specialized industries. The Firm has been recognized in several studies for excellence in client service. Newsletters on a variety of legal issues are published at various times during the year. The Firm is a member of TerraLex, an association of independent law firms providing legal resources throughout the world. Our attorneys are also members of 22 state bar associations, several international bar associations and their respective local bar associations, plus many hold leadership positions with the American Bar Association.

MEMBERS OF FIRM

S. L. GREENEBAUM (1902-1973)

EDWARD L. McDONALD (1870-1961)

ANGUS W. McDONALD (1912-1980)

W. VANMETER ALFORD (1916-1981)

LARAMIE L. LEATHERMAN (1932-1994)

WM. T. (BILL) ROBINSON III, born Covington, Kentucky, 1945; admitted to bar, 1971, Ohio; 1972, Kentucky; 1999, Tennessee. *Education:* University of Kentucky (J.D., 1971). 1989 Outstanding Lawyer in Kentucky, Kentucky Bar Association. Listed in Best Lawyers in America, 1999—. ***PRACTICE AREAS:*** Litigation; Business Litigation; Products Liability; Medical Malpractice. ***Email:*** wtr@gdm.com

JOHN A. WEST, born Cincinnati, Ohio, May 19, 1940; admitted to bar, 1967, Ohio; 1968, Kentucky. *Education:* University of Kentucky (B.A., 1963); University of Cincinnati (J.D., 1967). Assistant U.S. Attorney, Eastern District of Kentucky, 1976-1979. ***PRACTICE AREAS:*** Litigation; Alternative Dispute Resolution; Federal Criminal Law. ***Email:*** jaw@gdm.com

MARK H. LONGENECKER, born Akron, Ohio, February 16, 1951; admitted to bar, 1975, Illinois; 1979, Ohio. *Education:* Denison University (B.A., summa cum laude, 1973) Phi Beta Kappa; Harvard University (J.D., cum laude, 1976). Formerly with Lord Bissell & Brook, Frost & Jacobs, and Frost Brown Todd. *Member:* Cincinnatio Bar Association; United States Bar Association. ***PRACTICE AREAS:*** Corporate Mergers and Acquisitions; Commercial Mergers and Acquisitions; Corporate Venture Capital; Commercial Venture Capital; Corporate Securities; Commercial Securities. ***Email:*** mhl@gdm.com

RICHARD BOYDSTON, admitted to bar, 1977, Ohio; 1992, Kentucky; U.S. District Court, Southern District of Indiana; U.S. District Court, Eastern and Western Districts of Kentucky; U.S. District Court, Northern District of Ohio; U.S. District Court, Southern District of Ohio; U.S. Court of Appeals, Sixth Circuit; U.S. Supreme Court. *Education:* Harvard University (A.B., 1974); University of Pennsylvania (J.D., 1977). *Member:* American, Kentucky, Ohio State and Cincinnati Bar Associations; American Bankruptcy Institute; Tri-State Association for Corporate Renewal. (Certified in Business Bankruptcy Law by the American Board of Certification). ***PRACTICE AREAS:*** Bankruptcy Reorganization; Bankruptcy Litigation; Lender Litigation; Commercial Transactions; Equipment Leasing. ***Email:*** rb2@gdm.com

P. RICHARD ANDERSON, JR., born Jacksonville, Florida, 1947; admitted to bar, 1973, Ohio; 1980, Kentucky. *Education:* University of Maryland (B.A., 1969); College of William & Mary (J.D., 1973). ***PRACTICE AREAS:*** Corporate Law; Mergers and Acquisitions; International Law. ***Email:*** pra@gdm.com

C. CHRISTOPHER MUTH, born Hinsdale, Illinois, June 13, 1955; admitted to bar, 1980, Ohio; 1982, U.S. Tax Court; U.S. District Court, Southern District of Ohio. *Education:* University of Cincinnati (B.B.A., 1977); Chicago-Kent College of Law (J.D., 1980). ***PRACTICE AREAS:*** Mergers, Acquisitions and Divestitures; Taxation; State Taxation; Local Taxation. ***Email:*** ccm@gdm.com

WILLIAM L. MONTAGUE, born Cincinnati, Ohio, 1957; admitted to bar, 1982, Kentucky and U.S. Tax Court; 1986, Ohio. *Education:* Wittenberg University (B.A., magna cum laude, 1979); University of Cincinnati (J.D., 1982). ***PRACTICE AREAS:*** Trusts and Estates; Taxation; Closely Held Corporations; Charitable Giving. ***Email:*** wlm@gdm.com

MARK T. HAYDEN, born Louisville, Kentucky, March 3, 1961; admitted to bar, 1986, Kentucky; 1996, Ohio. *Education:* Indiana University (B.A., 1983; J.D., cum laude, 1986). Member, Kentucky Defense Counsel and Defense Research Institute. ***PRACTICE AREAS:*** Products Liability; Insurance Defense; Professional Liability; Commercial Law; Business Torts; Professional Malpractice.

LOUIS K. EBLING, born Grand Rapids, Michigan, December 8, 1961; admitted to bar, 1987, Illinois; 1994, Ohio. *Education:* Albion College (A.B., English, with honors, 1984); University of Michigan (J.D., 1987). Phi Beta Kappa; Sigma Tau Delta (President); Phi Eta Sigma. Albion College Fellow. Formerly employed by Gardner Carton & Douglas and Frost Brown Todd. *Member:* International Trademark Association (Member, Meetings Committee). ***PRACTICE AREAS:*** Intellectual Property; Trademark; International Trademark. ***Email:*** lke@gdm.com

MICHAEL H. BROWN, born Cincinnati, Ohio, September 7, 1958; admitted to bar, 1981, Kentucky; 1982, Ohio. *Education:* Xavier University (B.S.B.A., 1978); University of Notre Dame (J.D., 1981). Lecturer, University of Cincinnati School of Law, 1983-1987. ***PRACTICE AREAS:*** Taxation Law; Tax Controversies; Corporate Law; Finance Law. ***Email:*** mhb@gdm.com

PHILIP J. SCHWORER, born Covington, Kentucky, June 24, 1955; admitted to bar, 1986, Ohio; 1987, Kentucky. *Education:* University of Cincinnati (B.S., 1977; M.S., 1980); Northern Kentucky University (J.D., 1986). Order of the Curia. Author: Overview of Brownfield Redevelopment Initiatives, No. R. Ky. Law Review, Salmon P. Chase College of Law, Vol. 25, No. 1, 1997. ***PRACTICE AREAS:*** Environmental Law; OSHA Defense; Environmental Health and Safety. ***Email:*** pjs@gdm.com

ROBERT D. HUDSON, born Owensboro, Kentucky, May 24, 1962; admitted to bar, 1987, Ohio; 1988, Kentucky and U.S. District Court, Southern District of Ohio; 1991, U.S. District Court, Eastern District of Kentucky. *Education:* University of Kentucky (B.S., with high distinction, 1984; J.D., 1987). ***PRACTICE AREAS:*** Labor and Employment. ***Email:*** rdh@gdm.com

SUZANNE P. LAND, born Youngstown, Ohio, October 26, 1964; admitted to bar, 1990, Ohio. *Education:* Case Western Reserve (J.D., summa cum laude, Order of the Coif, 1990). Editor, Law Review. Adjunct Professor, University of Cincinnati, 1996—; Noted in Best Lawyers of America, 2002-2003, Trusts and Estates. Formerly with Katz Teller Brant & Hild. ***PRACTICE AREAS:*** Trusts and Estates. ***Email:*** spl@gdm.com

STEVEN R. SMITH, admitted to bar, 1984, Ohio and U.S. District Court, Southern District of Ohio. *Education:* University of Cincinnati (B.A., Political Science, with honors, 1981); University of Dayton (J.D., summa cum laude, 1984). ***PRACTICE AREAS:*** Real Estate; Finance; Banking Law; Commercial and Consumer Lending; Bankruptcy; Lender Litigation. ***Email:*** srs2@gdm.com

STEPHEN E. GILLEN, born Gallipolis, Ohio, July 24, 1953; admitted to bar, 1980, Ohio and U.S. District Court, Southern District of Ohio and U.S. Court of Appeals, Sixth Circuit. *Education:* Miami University (B.S.B.A., 1975); Salmon P. Chase College of Law (J.D., 1980). ***PRACTICE AREAS:*** Intellectual Property. ***Email:*** seg@gdm.com

MIKIO NISHIZU, born November 15, 1944; admitted to bar, 1994, Indiana; 2000, Ohio. *Education:* Jochi University (B.A., 1968); University of Chicago (Ph.D., 1982); Indiana University School of Law (J.D., 1993). Indiana Supreme Court Licensed Mediator. *Member:* Cincinnati, Ohio State, Indiana State and American Bar Associations; American Immigration Lawyers Association; Japan American Society of Greater Cincinnati (Secretary, 2003—; Board Trustee, 2002—); Japan America Society of Indiana (Board of Directors, 1999—). ***LANGUAGES:*** Japanese. ***PRACTICE AREAS:*** Immigration Law; Labor and Employment; Corporate Law; Securities. ***Email:*** mn@gdm.com

OF COUNSEL

GLENN D. BELLAMY, born Lebanon, Ohio, March 10, 1962; admitted to bar, 1988, Washington, U.S. District Court, Western District of Washington and U.S. Court of Appeals, Ninth and Federal Circuits; 1991, U.S. Supreme Court; 1998, U.S. Court of Appeals, Sixth Circuit; 1999, Ohio, U.S District Court, Southern District of Ohio and U.S. Court of International Trade; registered to practice before U.S. Patent and Trademark Office. *Education:* University of Cincinnati (B.S., Nuc. Med., 1984; J.D., 1987). *Member:* Cincinnati, Washington State and Federal Bar Associations; Washington State Patent Law Association (Officer, 1994-1998); International Intellectual Property Law Association; American Intellectual Property Law Association; Cincinnati Intellectual Property Law Association; International Trademark Association. ***PRACTICE AREAS:*** Intellectual Property Law. ***Email:*** gdb@gdm.com

ASSOCIATES

NANCY J. BRIDE, born October 7, 1970; admitted to bar, 1997, Ohio. *Education:* Bowdoin College (B.A., magna cum laude, 1992); Notre Dame University Law School (J.D., 1997). Author: "Supreme Court's Botched Surgery of the Indian Gaming Regulatory Act," 124 Notre Dame J. Leg 149, 1998. *Member:* Ohio State Bar Association. ***PRACTICE AREAS:*** Litigation. ***Email:*** njb@gdm.com

KEVIN R. GHASSOMIAN, born Ashland, Kentucky, June 18, 1973; admitted to bar, 1999, Kentucky and Nevada; 2002, Ohio. *Education:* University of Kentucky (B.A., 1995); Vanderbilt University School of Law (J.D., 1998). Phi Beta Kappa; Omicron Delta Kappa. ***PRACTICE AREAS:*** Business Planning; Estate Planning; Charitable Giving; Tax Planning. ***Email:*** krg@gdm.com

W. ASHLEY HESS, born May 25, 1973; admitted to bar, 1998, Kentucky; 2003, Ohio. *Education:* University of Virginia (B.A., 1995), Echols Scholars Program; Washington &

(This Listing Continued)

GREENEBAUM DOLL & McDONALD PLLC, Cincinnati—Continued

Lee University (J.D., 1998). Staff Writer, Environmental Law Digest. ***PRACTICE AREAS:*** Mergers, Acquisitions and Divestitures; Corporate Law; Computer Software Law. ***Email:*** wah@gdm.com

LORI E. KRAFTE, born Newark, New Jersey, May 16, 1955; admitted to bar, 1998, Ohio. *Education:* Indiana University (B.A., 1976); Claremont University Graduate School (Ph.D., 1989); University of Cincinnati College of Law (J.D., 1998). ***PRACTICE AREAS:*** Intellectual Property; Trademark Prosecution; Trademark Licensing; Trademark and Copyright Enforcement; Software Licensing; Media Law; Publishing Transactions; Domain Name Disputes; Internet Law; E-Commerce; Due Diligence. ***Email:*** lek@gdm.com

REPRESENTATIVE CLIENTS: A.M. Kinney, Inc.; American Life; Ashland Inc.; Atria Communities; Bethlehem Steel Corp.; Columbia Natural Resources, Inc.; Commonwealth Industries, Inc.; Continental General Tire, Inc.; Curtis Maruyasu America; Fifth Third Bank; Gainsborough Farm; HCA-The Healthcare Co.; Hillerich & Bradsby Co.; Huffy Corporation; Humana Inc.; Jewish Hospital Healthcare Services, Inc.; Joseph-Beth Booksellers, LLC; Kroger Co. (The); LG&E Energy Corp.; Lodestar Energy, Inc.; Louisville Bedding Co.; Louisville Forge & Gear Works, LLC; Mitsui & Co., Ltd.; Multi-Color Corporation; National City Bank, Kentucky; Papa John's International, Inc.; Peabody Holding Co., Inc.; Phillips Electronics North Am. Corp.; Shoney's Inc.; Spectracare, Inc.; Toyota Motor Manufacturing North America, Inc.; Toyotomi America Corp.; University of Louisville; Westmoreland Coal Co.; Zeon Chemicals U.S.A., Inc.

(For additional biographical data, see Professional Biographies at Louisville, Lexington, Covington and Frankfort, Kentucky; Nashville, Tennessee; Atlanta, Georgia)

GRIFFIN - FLETCHER, LLP

Established in 1936

3500 RED BANK ROAD

CINCINNATI, OHIO 45227

Telephone: 513-421-1313

Fax: 513-421-1118

Email: ltcincy.com

Email: griffin-fletcher.com

General Practice, General Business, Real Estate, Probate, Estate Planning, Real Estate Litigation.

FIRM PROFILE: Griffin - Fletcher, LLP practices in the fields of Real Estate, Estate Planning, Probate, General Business, and litigation involving Real Estate. The firm handles virtually every type of matter involving real estate, probate, estate planning and real estate litigation. The firm for a number of years has represented savings & loans, banks and lending institutions in the Greater Cincinnati area. The firm is one of the oldest and most respected law firms practicing in the area of real estate matters in the southwestern Ohio area.

EARL W. GRIFFIN (1890-1970)

EDWARD P. HACKETT (1922-1989)

JOHN R. FLETCHER (1920-2004)

MEMBERS OF FIRM

MICHAEL C. FLETCHER, born Erie, Pennsylvania, June 12, 1944; admitted to bar, 1969, Ohio. *Education:* Miami University (B.A., 1966); University of Cincinnati (J.D., 1969). *Member:* Cincinnati, Ohio State and American Bar Associations. ***PRACTICE AREAS:*** Real Estate Law (50%); Title Insurance Law (25%); Litigation (25%). ***Email:*** mfletcher@griffin-fletcher.com

KAREN L. MASTRUSERIO, L.P.A., born Ashland, Ohio, May 5, 1953; admitted to bar, 1986, Ohio and U.S. District Court, Southern District of Ohio. *Education:* University of Cincinnati (B.A., 1978; J.D., 1986). *Member:* Cincinnati and Ohio State Bar Associations. ***PRACTICE AREAS:*** Real Estate (75%); Probate (15%); Litigation (10%). ***Email:*** kmastruserio@griffin-fletcher.com

RICHARD D. HERNDON, born Cincinnati, Ohio, March 16, 1961; admitted to bar, 1986, Ohio. *Education:* University of Cincinnati (B.A., 1983; J.D., 1986). *Member:* Cincinnati, Ohio and American Bar Associations; National Association of Industrial and Office Properties; International Council of Shopping Centers. ***PRACTICE AREAS:*** Real Estate; Business Law. ***Email:*** rherndon@griffin-fletcher.com

KEVIN R. FLYNN, born Cincinnati, Ohio, December 17, 1960; admitted to bar, 1987, Ohio; 1988, U.S. District Court, Southern District of Ohio. *Education:* University of Cincinnati (B.A., Philosophy, 1983; J.D., 1987). Order of the Coif; Delta Theta Phi. *Member:* Cincinnati and Ohio State Bar Associations. ***PRACTICE AREAS:*** Business Law; Real Estate Development; Real Estate Finance. ***Email:*** kflynn@griffin-fletcher.com

HAROLD L. ANNESS, born Cincinnati, Ohio, January 8, 1953; admitted to bar, 1978, Ohio. *Education:* Miami University (B.S., 1975); Ohio Northern University (J.D., 1978). Formerly with: Lindhorst & Dreidame; Thompson-Hine. *Member:* Cincinnati and Ohio State Bar Associations; Hamilton County Regional Planning Commission. ***PRACTICE AREAS:*** Real Estate. ***Email:*** hanness@griffin-fletcher.com

ASSOCIATES

JAMES C. BODLEY, born Loveland, Ohio, April 12, 1947; admitted to bar, 1978, Ohio. *Education:* University of Cincinnati (B.B.A., 1964); Xavier University (M.B.A., 1971); Case Western Reserve University (J.D., 1978). *Member:* Cincinnati, Ohio State and American Bar Associations. ***PRACTICE AREAS:*** Real Estate Law (100%). ***Email:*** jbodley@griffin-fletcher.com

ANDREW D. GRAF, born Cincinnati, Ohio, April 22, 1972; admitted to bar, 1997, Ohio. *Education:* University of Dayton (B.A., 1994); Vanderbilt University (J.D., 1997). *Member:* Cincinnati and Ohio State Bar Associations; National Association of Industrial and Office Properties. ***PRACTICE AREAS:*** Real Estate; Business Law. ***Email:*** agraf@griffin-fletcher.com

(This Listing Continued)

DAVID L. HUPRICH, born Dover, Ohio, August 2, 1933; admitted to bar, 1958, Ohio; 1977, California. *Education:* Miami University; Muskingum College (B.A., 1955); Ohio State University (J.D., 1958). Phi Delta Phi. Member, Editorial Board, Shopping Center Legal Update, International Council for Shopping Centers Law Symposium. Regular Speaker, ICSC Law Conference Panels, Planning Committee Presentations, Ohio, Kentucky and Indiana. Former In-House Counsel, Federated Department Stores. Former General Counsel, Coldwell Banker Commercial Brokerage Company, Los Angeles, CA. *Member:* Ohio State, Illinois State and American Bar Associations; State Bar of California. ***PRACTICE AREAS:*** Real Estate; Commercial Real Estate. ***Email:*** dhuprich@griffin-fletcher.com

BRUCE G. HOPKINS, born Fort Worth, Texas, October 13, 1957; admitted to bar, 1990, Ohio; 1991, Kentucky. *Education:* Yale University (B.A., 1981); Salmon P. Chase College o f Law (J.D., cum laude, 1989). ***PRACTICE AREAS:*** Real Property (50%); Leasing (50%). ***Email:*** bhopkins@griffin-fletcher.com

REPRESENTATIVE CLIENTS: Lawyers Title Insurance Corp.; Fifth Third Bank; Tipton Interests, Inc.; Neyer Properties, Inc.; Anchor Associates; Miami Savings & Loan; Winton Savings & Loan; Eagle Savings Bank; General Electric Employees Federal Credit Union; Regency Realty Group, Inc.; Cottage Savings Bank; Foundation Savings Bank.
REFERENCES: Fifth Third Bank; FirStar Bank, N.A.; Park National Bank.

HAMMOND LAW GROUP, LLC

Established in 1991

3311 CAREW TOWER

441 VINE STREET

CINCINNATI, OHIO 45202

Telephone: 513-381-2011

Fax: 513-381-2227

URL: http://www.hammondlawfirm.com

Immigration and Nationality Law.

FIRM PROFILE: The firm serves the global immigration needs of business, Hammond Law Group has offices in Cincinnati, San Francisco, Washington, D.C. and Toronto.

MICHAEL F. HAMMOND, born April 16, 1964; admitted to bar, 1989, Ohio and U.S. District Court, Southern District of Ohio; 1990, Kentucky and U.S. District Court, Northern District of Kentucky; 1993, U.S. Court of Appeals, Sixth Circuit. *Education:* Cedarville College (B.A., 1986); University Of Cincinnati (J.D., 1989). *Member:* American Immigration Lawyers Association. ***PRACTICE AREAS:*** Immigration and Naturalization. ***Email:*** mfh@hammondlawfirm.com

SHERRY L. NEAL, born July 5, 1969; admitted to bar, 1994, Ohio; 1995, Kentucky; 1996, U.S. District Court, Southern District of Ohio. *Education:* Cedarville College (B.A., 1991); The University of Dayton School of Law (J.D., 1994). *Member:* American Immigration Lawyers Association. ***PRACTICE AREAS:*** Immigration and Naturalization. ***Email:*** sln@hammondlawfirm.com

CHRISTOPHER T. MUSILLO, born May 8, 1970; admitted to bar, 1998, Ohio; 1999, U.S. District Court, Southern District of Ohio. *Education:* Villanova University (B.S.B.A., Finance, 1992); University of Cincinnati (J.D., 1998). *Member:* American Immigration Lawyers Association. ***PRACTICE AREAS:*** Immigration and Naturalization. ***Email:*** cmusillo@hammondlawfirm.com

HARLAN SIMON, born February 17, 1957; admitted to bar, 1986, California (Not admitted in Ohio). *Education:* Colorado College (B.A., 1980); New York University (J.D., M.B.A., 1985). Member, 1982-1983 and Executive Editor, 1983-1984, Annual Survey of American Law. Adjunct Professor, Southwestern University School of Law, 1989-1990. Deputy Public Defender, Los Angeles County, 1986-1990. ***PRACTICE AREAS:*** Business Litigation. ***Email:*** hgs@hammondlawfirm.com

---

CRAIG S. CLARK, born September 19, 1933; admitted to bar, 1963, Ohio; 1964, U.S. District Court, Southern District of Ohio; 2002, U.S. Supreme Court. *Education:* Salmon P. Chase School of Commerce (B.S.C., 1961); Salmon P. Chase College of Law (J.D., 1963). *Member:* Ohio Bar Association; American Immigration Lawyers Association. ***PRACTICE AREAS:*** Immigration and Naturalization; Business Law. ***Email:*** csc@hammondlawfirm.com

PETER LONG LE, born November 7, 1973; admitted to bar, 2003, Ohio. *Education:* University of Cincinnati (B.A., 1998); University of Dayton (J.D., 2002). *Member:* American Immigration Lawyers Association; Greater Cincinnati Criminal Defense Association; Ohio State and American Bar Associations. ***PRACTICE AREAS:*** Immigration and Nationality Law; Criminal Defense. ***Email:*** pll@hammondlawfirm.com

CINDY J. UNKENHOLT, born Cincinnati, Ohio, March 13, 1971; admitted to bar, 1998, Connecticut (Not admitted in Ohio). *Education:* University of Cincinnati (B.S., Criminal Justice, 1994); University of Connecticut (J.D., 1997). *Member:* American Immigration Lawyers Association. ***PRACTICE AREAS:*** Immigration and Nationality Law. ***Email:*** cju@hammondlawfirm.com

AMY R. DALAL, born July 14, 1978; admitted to bar, 2004, Ohio; 2005, U.S. District Court, Southern District of Ohio. *Education:* Emory University (B.A., 1999); University of Cincinnati (M.B.A., 2002; J.D., 2004). *Member:* American Immigration Lawyers Association. ***PRACTICE AREAS:*** Immigration and Naturalization. ***Email:*** ard@hammondlawfirm.com

JUDITH M. PENDERGAST, born December 15, 1948; admitted to bar, 1992, Wisconsin (Not admitted in Ohio). *Education:* Mercy Medical Center School of Nursing (nursing diploma, 1970); Marian College School of Nursing (B.S.N., 1989); Marquette University School of Law (J.D., 1992). *Member:* Cincinnati Bar Association; The American Association of Nurse Attorneys; American Immigration Lawyers Association. ***PRACTICE AREAS:*** Health Care; Immigration Law. ***Email:*** jmp@hammondlawfirm.com

ANNE CATHERINE HARVEY

Established in 1991

TRI-STATE BUILDING
432 WALNUT STREET, SUITE 1001
CINCINNATI, OHIO 45202
Telephone: 513-721-2960
Fax: 513-621-3017
Email: lawyeranneharvey@yahoo.com
URL: http://www.lawfirmanneharvey.com

Dayton Office: 5335 Far Hills Avenue, Suite 313, 45429. Telephone: 937-439-5708. Fax: 937-439-5710.

Trials, Appeals, Federal, State and Municipal Criminal Defense, Divorce, Dissolution, Child Custody, Military Domestic Relations Law.

FIRM PROFILE: One attorney and staff; Independent Association of 2 attorneys.

ANNE CATHERINE HARVEY, born Dayton, Ohio, January 26, 1961; admitted to bar, 1985, Texas; 1991, Ohio; Federal Circuit Court of Appeals, Sixth Circuit; U.S. District Court, Southern District of Ohio; U.S. District Court, Northern District of Texas. *Education:* University of Dayton (B.S., 1981; J.D., 1985). Psi Chi. Member, University of Dayton Law Review, 1984-1985. Author: "Negligent Infliction of Emotional Distress," University of Dayton Law Review, Fall Ed., 1983. Teaching Assistant, Legal Research and Writing, University of Dayton, 1984-1985. Montgomery County Assistant Public Defender, 2001-2003. Acting Judge, Miamisburg Municipal Court, 1997-2003. Member, Greene County Ethics Committee, 2000-2002. Dayton Volunteer Lawyer's Project, 1991-2000. Civilian Trial Attorney, Wright Patterson Air Force Base, 1989-1991. *Member:* Greene County, Dayton, Ohio State, American and Federal Bar Associations; Family Law Forum, Dayton, Ohio. ***LANGUAGES:*** American Sign Language. ***PRACTICE AREAS:*** Criminal Defense; Divorce; Child Custody.

Languages: Sign Language.

HEEKIN & HEEKIN

817 MAIN STREET, SUITE 200
CINCINNATI, OHIO 45202
Telephone: 513-345-5560
Fax: 513-345-5565
Fax: 1-800-300-3210
Email: attorneys@heekinattorneys.com
URL: http://www.heekinattorneys.com

Civil Litigation, Financial Institutions, Commercial Law, Real Estate Law, Personal Injury, Wrongful Death, Landlord and Tenant Law, Mortgages, Criminal Law, DUI, Driving While Intoxicated, Drug Crimes, Felonies, Homicide, Juvenile Law, Misdemeanors, Parole and Probation, Sexual Assault, Traffic Violations.

MEMBERS OF THE FIRM

THOMAS DONALD HEEKIN, JR., born 1960; admitted to bar, 1988, Ohio. *Education:* Colorado College (B.A., Environmental Conservation, 1983); University of Cincinnati (J.D., 1988). *Member:* Cincinnati and Ohio State Bar Associations. ***PRACTICE AREAS:*** Criminal Law; DUI; Driving While Intoxicated; Drug Crimes; Felonies; Homicide; Juvenile Law; Misdemeanors; Parole and Probation; Sexual Assault; Traffic Violations; Juvenile Criminal Law; Business Crimes; Business Fraud; Theft; Sex Crimes; Search and Seizure; Murder; Manslaughter; Forgery; Federal Criminal Law; Drivers License Suspension; Criminal Defense; Burglary; Assault and Battery; Capital Offenses; Drug Trafficking; School Law. ***Email:*** heekin.thomas@heekinattorneys.com

CHRISTOPHER R. HEEKIN, born Cincinnati, Ohio, November 2, 1962; admitted to bar, 1989, Ohio. *Education:* Trinity College (B.A., English and Religion, 1985); Boston University (J.D., 1989). *Member:* Cincinnati and Ohio State Bar Associations. ***PRACTICE AREAS:*** Civil Litigation; Financial Institutions; Personal Injury; Commercial Law; Real Estate; Condominium Law; Landlord and Tenant Law; Wrongful Death; Medical Malpractice; Collections; Small Business Law; Nursing Home Negligence. ***Email:*** heekin.chris@heekinattorneys.com

JOHN L. HEILBRUN

Established in 1984

3536 EDWARDS ROAD, SUITE 100
CINCINNATI, OHIO 45208-1368
Telephone: 513-321-3940
Fax: 513-321-3929
URL: http://www.johnheilbrun.com
Email: heilbrun@one.net.
URL: http://www.heilbrunlaw.com

Plaintiffs' Personal Injury, Automobile/Motor Vehicle Accidents and Injuries, Automobile Insurance, Catastrophic Injuries, Head Injuries, uninsured and Underinsured Motorists, Wrongful Death, Collaborative Family Law, Child Custody, Divorce, Domestic Relations, Criminal Defense, Driving While Intoxicated, Domestic Violence, Search and Seizure, Felonies and Misdemeanors.

FIRM PROFILE: Concentrates on Plaintiffs' Personal Injury, Family Law and Criminal Defense.

JOHN L. HEILBRUN, born Cincinnati, Ohio, February 9, 1951; admitted to bar, 1977, Ohio and U.S. District Court, Southern District of Ohio. *Education:* State University of New York at Stony Brook (B.A., cum laude, 1973); University of Cincinnati (J.D., 1977). *Member:* Cincinnati, Ohio State and American Bar Associations; Ohio Academy of Trial Lawyers (Former Board Member of Trustees and Former Chairman, Criminal Law Section); Hamilton County Trial Lawyers Association; The Association of Trial Lawyers of America; Greater Cincinnati Criminal Defense Lawyers Association; Ohio Academy of Criminal Defense Lawyers; Collaborative Family Lawyers of Cincinnati.

(This Listing Continued)

HELMER, MARTINS, RICE & POPHAM CO., L.P.A.

Established in 1983

1900 FOURTH AND WALNUT CENTRE
105 EAST FOURTH STREET
CINCINNATI, OHIO 45202-4009
Telephone: 513-421-2400
513-421-7902
Email: support@fcalawfirm.com
URL: http://www.fcalawfirm.com

Civil Trial and Appellate Practice; False Claims Act Litigation.

FIRM PROFILE: Helmer, Martins, Rice & Popham Co., L.P.A. has prosecuted qui tam cases longer than any law firm in America. Our complex litigation practice concentrates on representation of whistleblowers in cases under the False Claims Act. Our book, False Claims Act: Whistleblower Litigation, is the first and only book written specifically to help whistleblowers and their attorneys successfully leap the many procedural hurdles of the False Claims Act. We frequently are consulted by attorneys throughout the country regarding False Claims Act cases, and sometimes join with them to help present their clients' cases.

Since 1984, we have lectured, authored treatises and articles, litigated, and lobbied for the rights of whistleblowers who come forward to protect the public treasury. We have represented whistleblowers in dozens of qui tam False Claims Act cases. In some of our cases the United States Government has not intervened, but we have nonetheless pursued the defendants on behalf of our clients and the United States, settling many and seeing others through to jury verdict. False Claims Act cases in which we have represented whistleblowers have led to the return of more than $700,000,000 to the United States Treasury, with proportional amounts to our clients.

We filed a case on behalf of Brett Roby, a quality assurance engineer, against The Boeing Company concerning defective Chinook CH-47d helicopter transmission gears. That case was settled for $65,000,000 in 1999, and in September 2002, the federal court of appeals in Cincinnati affirmed the principle, never before established in a False Claims Act case, that a manufacturer can be liable for the entire value of an aircraft which crashes as the result of a defective part. Mr. Roby was awarded $10,000,000 as a result of the settlement.

Also in September 2002, we and the United States settled for $6,200,000 a case brought in 1997 on behalf of Rudy Anderson, also a quality assurance engineer, against General Electric and Lockheed Martin for placing defective flight computer components in F/A 18 "Hornet" aircraft. The F/A 18 is the Navy's workhorse jet fighter, and the defective components posed a risk that the aircraft would turn sharply on takeoff, causing a loss of pilot control.

Later, in 2002, we resolved another qui tam action against Lockheed Martin concerning mischarging on a F 15E "Strike Eagle" computer simulator program for $1.4 million.

In 2003 one of our False Claims Act cases was partially resolved in a $680 million settlement reached with the Columbia HCA Corporation.

In addition to our False Claims Act work, we represent clients in other kinds of complex litigation, including in the areas of franchise rights, employment rights, civil rights, and environmental law. Highlights for 2002 include completing a $22,000,000 environmental class action settlement against Georgia Pacific Corporation on behalf of a disadvantaged Columbus, Ohio neighborhood for damages resulting from a 1998 chemical factory explosion. We were also successful in preventing a major independent Pepsi Cola bottler from being terminated as a franchisee by the PepsiCo Corporation, as well as convincing a Cincinnati federal judge to award in excess of $3.5 million to a worker injured on an Ohio River towboat.

In 2004, in a rare summary judgment in a civil rights case, a federal court found the City of Cincinnati, the Village of Golf Manor, both of their Chiefs of Police, and against five of their individual police officers liable for violating constitutional rights leading to the death of a Cincinnati citizen.

JAMES B. HELMER, JR., born Piqua, Ohio, May 20, 1950; admitted to bar, 1975, Ohio; 1979, U.S. Supreme Court; 1983, District of Columbia. *Education:* Denison University (B.A., with honors, 1972); University of Cincinnati (J.D., 1975). Member: Order of the Coif; Scribes; Emeritus Master, 1984—, Treasurer, 1990-1991, Potter Stewart American Inn of Court. Member, 1973-1975 and Editor-in-Chief, 1974-1975, University of Cincinnati Law Review. Author: "False Claims Act: Whistleblower Litigation," 3d. Ed., 2002, Supp. 2003, Lexis Nexis; "How Great is Thy Bounty: Relator's Share Calculations Pursuant to the False Claims Act," 68 U.Cin.L.Rev. 737 (2000). Co-Author: Attorney Fees in Employment Cases, Litigating Wrongful Discharge Claims §8.22, Clark Boardman Callaghan, 1987. Co-Author: "Representing the Terminated Employee In Ohio: Evaluating, Settling and Litigating State and Federal Claims," Anderson Publishing, 1990, 2d. Ed. 1997. Law Clerk to Hon. Timothy S. Hogan, Chief Judge of the U.S. District Court, Southern District of Ohio, 1975-1977. Charter Member, Arbitration Council, U.S. District Court, Southern District of Ohio, 1984—. Best Lawyers in America, Woodward-White, 1987—. *Member:* The District of Columbia Bar; Cincinnati and Federal (Member, Constitutional Law Section) Bar Associations; The American Society of Writers on Legal Subjects. ***PRACTICE AREAS:*** Complex Litigation. ***Email:*** jhelmer@fcalawfirm.com

PAUL B. MARTINS, born Honolulu, Hawaii, January 5, 1954; admitted to bar, 1979, Ohio; 1985, U.S. Supreme Court; 1986, U.S. Court of Appeals, Sixth Circuit. *Education:* University of Notre Dame (A.B., magna cum laude, 1976); University of San Diego (J.D., 1979). Order of the Barristers. Member, Moot Court Board. Member, San Diego Law Review, 1978-1979. Author: "Title 4.5, California Liquidated Damages," 16 San Diego Law

(This Listing Continued)

HELMER, MARTINS, RICE & POPHAM CO., L.P.A., Cincinnati—Continued

Review, 967, 1979. Master, Potter Stewart Inn of Court. U.S. Army Judge Advocate, General's Corps, 1980-1986. *Member:* Cincinnati, Ohio State and American Bar Associations. ***PRACTICE AREAS:*** Complex Litigation. ***Email:*** pmartins@fcalawfirm.com

ROBERT M. RICE, born Centerville, Ohio, February 7, 1968; admitted to bar, 1993, Ohio. *Education:* University of Dayton (B.A., summa cum laude, 1990); University of Cincinnati (J.D., 1993). Member, Moot Court Board. Co-Author: "The False Claims Act and Implied Certification: An Overview," 34 False Claims Act and Qui Tam Quarterly Review 51 (2004). *Member:* Cincinnati Bar Association. ***PRACTICE AREAS:*** Complex Litigation. ***Email:*** rrice@fcalawfirm.com

JULIE WEBSTER POPHAM, born Covington, Kentucky, July 17, 1967; admitted to bar, 1992, Ohio; 1993, Kentucky; 1997, U.S. Supreme Court and U.S. Court of Appeals, Sixth and Tenth Circuits. *Education:* Thomas More College (B.A., magna cum laude, 1989); University of Cincinnati (J.D., 1992). Sigma Tau Delta. Co-Author, "Materiality and the False Claims Act," 71 U.Cin.L. Rev. 839 (2003); "The Last Privateers Encounter Sloppy Seas: Inconsistent Original Source Jurisprudence Under the Federal False Claims Act," 24 Ohio N.U.L. Rev. 163 (1998). Staff Attorney, Second District Court of Appeals of Ohio, 1992-1994. *Member:* Cincinnati and Kentucky Bar Associations. ***PRACTICE AREAS:*** Complex Litigation. ***Email:*** jpopham@fcalawfirm.com

---

DONALD G. STIENS, JR., born Springboro, Ohio, March 20, 1966; admitted to bar, 2003, Ohio. *Education:* Miami University (B.A., 1988); University of Cincinnati (J.D., 2002). *Member:* Ohio Bar Association. [Active Duty, U.S.N., 1988-1992; Reserve Duty, U.S.N., 1992-1999, 2004]. ***LANGUAGES:*** Spanish. ***PRACTICE AREAS:*** Complex Litigation. ***Email:*** dstiens@fcalawfirm.com

JENNIFER L. LAMBERT, born Philadelphia, Pennsylvania, December 30, 1970; admitted to bar, 2002, Ohio. *Education:* University of Cincinnati (B.A., with high honors, 1996); Northern Kentucky University (J.D., 2000). *Member:* American Bar Association. ***Email:*** jlambert@fcalawfirm.com

OF COUNSEL

ROBERT CLARK NEFF, JR., born Bucyrus, Ohio, December 18, 1956; admitted to bar, 1983, Ohio; 1985, U.S. Court of Appeals, Sixth Circuit. *Education:* College of Wooster; Kent State University (B.A., cum laude, 1980); University of Toledo (J.D., magna cum laude, 1983). Order of the Coif. Technical Editor, University of Toledo Law Review, 1982-1983. Law Clerk to Hon. S. Arthur Spiegel, U.S. District Court, Southern District of Ohio, 1983-1985. Co-Author, "False Claims Act: Whistleblower Litigation," 1st Ed., Michie Co. (1994); "War Stories: A History of the Qui Tam Provisions of the False Claims Act, the 1986 Amendments to the False Claims Act, and their Application in the United States ex rel. Gravitt v. General Electric Litigation," 18 Ohio Northern University Law Review 35 (1991). (Also practicing with The Neff Law Firm, Ltd., Bucyrus, Ohio). ***Email:*** support@fcalawfirm.com

REFERENCE: Huntington National Bank.

JASON HENNEKES

830 MAIN STREET
CINCINNATI, OHIO 45202
Telephone: 513-721-2850
Fax: 513-241-0584
Email: jayhennekes@hotmail.com
URL: http://www.jasonhennekes.com

Criminal Law, Driving While Intoxicated, Felonies, Misdemeanors, Homicide, Theft, Drug crimes, Traffic Violations, Domestic Violence, Assault.

JASON HENNEKES, born November 4, 1977; admitted to bar, 2002, Ohio. *Education:* University of Cincinnati (B.S., 1977); Northern Kentucky University (J.D., 2002).

DEAN EDWARD HINES

CINCINNATI, OHIO

(See Dayton)

Taxation, Business Taxation, Estate and Gift Taxation, Property Tax Appeals, IRS Audits, Domestic Relations, Family Law, Divorce, Child Custody, Domestic Violence, Child Custody, Visitation Rights, Adoption Law, Alimony.

JON HOFFHEIMER

1200 MERCANTILE LIBRARY BUILDING
414 WALNUT STREET
CINCINNATI, OHIO 45202-3906
Telephone: 513-421-7666
Fax: 513-421-7693
Email: Jon@jonhoffheimer.com

Estate Planning, Probate Law, Wills, Trusts, General Practice.

JON HOFFHEIMER, born Indianapolis, Indiana, February 2, 1941; admitted to bar, 1965, Ohio. *Education:* Colgate University (B.A., 1962); Northwestern University (J.D., 1965). Contributing Editor, "Addams & Hosford, Ohio Probate Practice," 6th edition, 1972, 1978 and 1980. *Member:* Cincinnati (Trusts, Wills and Estate Planning Committee), Ohio State (Probate and Trust Law Section) and American (Real Property, Probate and Trust Law Section) Bar Associations. Fellow: American College of Trust and Estate Counsel; American Bar Foundation; Ohio State Bar Foundation. (Certified Specialist in Estate Planning, Trust and Probate Law, Ohio State Bar Association). ***PRACTICE AREAS:*** Wills; Trusts and Estates; Federal Estate and Gift Taxation; Fiduciary Income Tax.

(This Listing Continued)

THE HORWITZ LAW FIRM, P.S.C.

CINCINNATI, OHIO

(See Crescent Springs, Kentucky)

Federal and State Civil and Criminal Tax Defense, Estate, Taxation, Business Law, Corporate Law, Tax Planning, IRS Audits.

BARBARA J. HOWARD CO., L.P.A.

960 MERCANTILE CENTER
120 EAST FOURTH STREET
CINCINNATI, OHIO 45202
Telephone: 513-421-7300
Fax: 513-562-3532
Email: bjhowardco@aol.com

Family Law, Divorce, Collaborative Law, Litigation.

BARBARA J. HOWARD, born Toledo, Ohio, August 23, 1954; admitted to bar, 1979, Ohio and U.S. District Court, Southern District of Ohio. *Education:* Xavier University (B.A., magna cum laude, 1976); University of Cincinnati (J.D., 1979). Alpha Sigma Nu; Order of Barristers. Author, "1993 Domestic Relations Practice in Ohio," LexisNexis, 1993. Trustee: Xavier University, 1995— Volunteer Lawyers for the Poor Foundation, 1997— Certified in Collaborative Family Law. *Member:* Cincinnati (President, 2001-2002; Board Member, 1983-1990, 1994-1997, 1998-2003; Domestic Relations Committee), Ohio State (Member: Board of Governors, 2005-2008; Council of Delegates, 1985—; Family Law Committee; Past Chair, Women in the Profession Section) and American (Member: House of Delegates, 1986—; Chair, House Select Committee; Standing Committee on Substance Abuse; Board of Directors, ABA Journal; Sections of: Litigation; Family Law) Bar Associations; American Judicature Society; American Council Association (Immediate Past President). (Certified Specialist in Family Relations Law, Ohio State Bar Association). ***PRACTICE AREAS:*** Family Law; Domestic Relations; Divorce; Litigation. ***Email:*** barbhoward@aol.com

---

APRIL MARIE PAYNE, born Germany, May 3, 1971; admitted to bar, 1998, Ohio. *Education:* University of Cincinnati (B.A., 1994); University of Akron (J.D., 1998). Cincinnati Academy of Leadership for Lawyers, Class of 2005. *Member:* Cincinnati (Member, Domestic Relations Committee), Ohio State and American Bar Associations. ***PRACTICE AREAS:*** Family Law; Domestic Relations; Divorce; Litigation. ***Email:*** apayne@howardbodnar.com

LEGAL SUPPORT PERSONNEL

PATRICIA MAYNARD

JAGTIANI + GUTTAG

Established in 1995
5332 KINDLEWOOD DRIVE, WEST CHESTER
CINCINNATI, OHIO 45069
Telephone: 513-856-7272

Fairfax, Virginia Office: 10363-A Democracy Lane, 22030. Telephone: 703-591-2664. Fax: 703-591-5907.

Charlottesville, Virginia Office: 300 Preston Avenue, Suite 300, 22902. Telephone: 703-591-2664.

Patents, Trademarks, Copyrights, Trade Secrets, International Trade, Litigation, Technology Transfer, Mergers and Acquisitions, Intellectual Property.

(For complete biographical data on all personnel, see Professional Biographies at Fairfax, Virginia)

GARY L. JONES CO., L.P.A.

CINCINNATI, OHIO

(See Columbus)

General Civil Practice. Administrative, Alcoholic Beverages, Liquor and Licensing Law, Real Estate Taxation and Appeals.

KATZ, GREENBERGER & NORTON

Established in 1942
105 EAST FOURTH STREET
4TH FLOOR
CINCINNATI, OHIO 45202-4011
Telephone: 513-721-5151
Fax: 513-621-9285
Email: kgnlaw.com
URL: http://www.kgnlaw.com

General Practice. Corporate, Negligence, Labor, Tax, Probate and Immigration Law, Trials and Bankruptcy.

(This Listing Continued)

FIRM PROFILE: Katz, Greenberger & Norton's history began when Leonard Freiberg opened his practice of law in 1911. In the years that followed, the name changed from time to time until 1986 when the name became Katz, Greenberger & Norton.

Katz, Greenberger & Norton first established its reputation as a business law firm. The firm has continued to experience dynamic growth, particularly in the areas of personal injury litigation, corporate, probate and business law. Katz, Greenberger & Norton is a full-service law firm with the experience, expertise and commitment needed to satisfy the most complex and sophisticated legal problems.

Katz, Greenberger & Norton prides itself on a philosophy and tradition that emphasizes providing clients with legal services of the highest quality in a timely and cost-effective manner. Put into practice, this philosophy means anticipating clients' needs and finding solutions, often innovative ones, for legal problems of business and private life. It means organizing the firm's practice to respond with the right people to act responsibly, effectively, quickly and thoroughly. It means delivering legal services that have value and that produce results. And this philosophy means dedicating our resources to excellence through extensive continuing legal education, skill development and current awareness programs.

MARK ALAN GREENBERGER, born Sharon, Pennsylvania, October 26, 1940; admitted to bar, 1966, Ohio; 1967, U.S. District Court, Southern District of Ohio; 1970, U.S. Court of Appeals, 6th Circuit; 1978, U.S. Supreme Court. *Education:* Marietta College; University of Cincinnati (B.A., 1962; J.D., 1965). Tau Kappa Alpha; Delta Sigma Rho; Phi Alpha Delta. Member, Young Leadership Cabinet of the United Jewish Appeal, 1971—. City of Cincinnati Chairman, Israel Bond Committee, 1981-1984. Chairman: Midwest Regional Bankruptcy Seminar. Bankruptcy Trustee, 1964—. *Member:* Cincinnati, Ohio State and American Bar Associations; National Association of Bankruptcy Trustees. ***PRACTICE AREAS:*** Debtor Creditor Law; Labor (Management or Employees) Law; Mergers and Acquisitions; Corporate Law; Business Acquisitions Law. ***Email:*** MAG@kgnlaw.com

LOUIS H. KATZ, born Cincinnati, Ohio, January 30, 1949; admitted to bar, 1973, Ohio. *Education:* University of Wisconsin (B.A., 1970); University of Cincinnati (J.D., 1973). Recipient, Corpus Juris Secundum Award. *Member:* Ohio State Bar Association. ***PRACTICE AREAS:*** Alcohol Beverage Law; Construction Law; Domestic Relations Law; Estate Planning; Real Estate. ***Email:*** LHK@kgnlaw.com

RICHARD L. NORTON, born Warren, Ohio, October 11, 1939; admitted to bar, 1964, Ohio; 1965, U.S. District Court, Northern District of Ohio; 1970, U.S. Supreme Court; 1983, Kentucky. *Education:* The Ohio State University (B.A., 1961); The Ohio State University College of Law (J.D., 1964). Phi Delta Phi. Co-authored: "Ohio Personal Injury Practice Forms," (Banks-Baldwin Law Publishing Co., 1994). President, B'nai B'rith, Lodge # 4, 1970-1971. Special Counsel For Attorney General, Ohio, 1972—. *Member:* Cincinnati (Chairman, Tort and Insurance Practice Committee), Ohio State and Kentucky Bar Associations; Ohio Academy of Trial Lawyers; The Association of Trial Lawyers of America; Hamilton County Trial Lawyers Association. ***PRACTICE AREAS:*** Medical Malpractice Law; Personal Injury Law; Products Liability Law. ***Email:*** RLN@kgnlaw.com

STEVEN M. ROTHSTEIN, born Dayton, Ohio, December 9, 1953; admitted to bar, 1977, Ohio and U.S. District Court, Southern District of Ohio. *Education:* Miami University (A.B., 1974); University of Cincinnati (J.D., 1977). Member, Cincinnati Public Schools Superintendents Advisory Committee. *Member:* Cincinnati Bar Association; American Immigration Lawyers Association; Hamilton County Trial Lawyers Association. ***PRACTICE AREAS:*** Immigration Law; Litigation Law; Real Estate (Property) Law; Medical Malpractice Law; Products Liability Law. ***Email:*** SMR@kgnlaw.com

ELLEN ESSIG, born Cincinnati, Ohio, February 7, 1950; admitted to bar, 1986, Ohio. *Education:* University of Miami; The Ohio State University (B.S., in Education, 1972); Salmon P. Chase College of Law, Northern Kentucky University (J.D., 1986). Recipient, The Lawyers Cooperative Publishing Company & Northern Kentucky University Scholarship Fund Award, 1986. *Member:* Cincinnati and Ohio State Bar Associations; American Academy of Adoption Attorneys. (Certified Specialist in Family Relations Law, Ohio State Bar Association). ***PRACTICE AREAS:*** Domestic Relations Law; Family Law; Divorce; Adoption Law; Surrogacy Law; Egg Donation. ***Email:*** EE@kgnlaw.com

ROSS M. EVANS, born New York, New York, July 30, 1960; admitted to bar, 1986, Ohio; 1987, U. S. District Court, Southern District of Ohio. *Education:* University of Cincinnati (B.A., 1983; J.D., 1986). Omicron Delta Kappa; Mortar Board; Psi Chi; Assistant County Prosecutor 1986-1988; Magistrate Hamilton County Juvenile Court 1988-1996; Ohio Association of Court Referees and Magistrates 1988-1996; Faculty, Ohio Judicial College, 1992-1996; Founding Member, Collaborative Family Lawyers of Cincinnati, 1997 . *Member:* Cincinnati Bar Association (Member: Domestic Relations Committee; Juvenile Court Committee); Ohio State Bar Association; International Academy of Collaborative Professionals; Collaborative Family Lawyers of Cincinnati. ***PRACTICE AREAS:*** Family Law; Domestic Relations; Juvenile Court Matters; Collaborative Practice; Probate; Adoptions.

JEFFREY J. GREENBERGER, born Cincinnati, Ohio, December 17, 1966; admitted to bar, 1992, Ohio; 1993, Kentucky. *Education:* Miami University (B.S., 1989); University of Dayton (J.D., 1992). Phi Alpha Delta. Author: "Legal Perspectives," Inside Self-Storage Magazine. Featured Speaker, Inside Self Storage Trade Show and Exposition, Las Vegas, Nevada, 2000 and 2001, Nashville, Tennessee, 2000 and 2001. Legal Counsel to: The Greater Cincinnati Northern Kentucky Apartment Association; The Ohio Storage Owners Society, Inc. (self-storage); The Kentucky Self-Storage Association; The Clermont County Humane Society. *Member:* Cincinnati, Ohio State, Northern Kentucky, Kentucky and American Bar Association. ***PRACTICE AREAS:*** Real Estate; Property Law; Landlord and Tenant Law; Corporate Law; Bankruptcy. ***Email:*** jjg@kgnlaw.com

STEPHEN E. IMM, born Cincinnati, Ohio July 23, 1962; admitted to bar, 1987, Ohio; 1988, U.S. Court of Appeals, Sixth Circuit. *Education:* University of Cincinnati (B.A., summa cum laude, 1984); Georgetown University (J.D., 1987). Phi Beta Kappa. *Member:* Ohio State Bar Association. ***PRACTICE AREAS:*** Employment Law; Civil Rights; Personal Injury; Litigation.

ASSOCIATES

KEVIN R. BREWER, born Cincinnati, Ohio, July 10, 1972; admitted to bar, 1997, Ohio; 1998, U.S. District Court, Southern District of Ohio. *Education:* University of Dayton (B.S., 1994); University of Cincinnati (J.D., 1997). *Member:* Cincinnati, Ohio State and American Bar Associations.

CHRISTINA S. YAGER, born Marion, Ohio, June 27, 1953; admitted to bar, 1999, Ohio; 2000, Kentucky. *Education:* The Ohio State University (B.S.S.W., 1977); Salmon P. Chase College of Law (J.D., magna cum laude, 1999). Author, Northern Kentucky Law Review, Vol. 26, Summer 1999. Formerly with: Lawrence Firm; McKinney & Namei. *Member:* Cincinnati, Ohio State and Kentucky Bar Associations. ***PRACTICE AREAS:*** Family Law; Immigration Law. ***Email:*** csy@kgnlaw.com

CHERYL L. BORLAND, born Louisville, Kentucky, March 21, 1962; admitted to bar, 1994, Kentucky; 1995, Ohio. *Education:* Northern Kentucky University (B.S., 1991); Salmon P. Chase College of Law (J.D., 1994). Formerly with: Kepley Gilligan & Eyrich; Thompson Hine LLP. *Member:* Ohio State, Kentucky and American Bar Associations. ***PRACTICE AREAS:*** Real Estate; Corporate. ***Email:*** clb@kgnlaw.com

LISA M. ELLIS, born Charleston, South Carolina, September 20, 1966; admitted to bar, 1991, Ohio; 1994, Kentucky; 2001, U.S. District Court, SOuthern District of Ohio. *Education:* Miami University (B.A., cum laude, Phi Beta Kappa, 1988); University of Cincinnati College of Law (J.D., 1991). ***PRACTICE AREAS:*** Real Estate; Bankruptcy. ***Email:*** lme@kgnlaw.com

TAWANDA J. EDWARDS, born Cincinnati, Ohio, October 12, 1972; admitted to bar, 2000, Ohio; 2002, U.S. District Court, Southern District of Ohio. *Education:* University of Cincinnati (B.A., 1995; J.D., 2000). Formerly with Legal Aid Society of Greater Cincinnati. *Member:* Cincinnati and Ohio State Bar Associations; Black Lawyers Association of Cincinnati. ***PRACTICE AREAS:*** Domestic Relations; Juvenile Law. ***Email:*** TJE@kgnlaw.com

OF COUNSEL

Alfred B. Katz (Retired)

REPRESENTATIVE CLIENTS: Gateway Distribution, Inc.; Cordes Lumber, Inc.; Johnson-Nash Metal Products, Inc.; Radio Theatre Group, Inc.; E.A. Zicka Company; Chubb Group of Insurance Companies; CVS International; McSwain Floor Company; Bluford Jackson & Son, Inc.; Hunting Industrial Coodings; Van Orsdel, Inc. (Wood Brokerage Firm); Allied Glass; Diversity Management Systems; Gateway Transport; Computer Graphics Group; J-V Security Systems; Redbank Transport; Relay Express; Clermont County Humane Society; Community Management Corporation; First Industrial Realty Trust; RCC Property Advisors.

KATZ, TELLER, BRANT & HILD

A LEGAL PROFESSIONAL ASSOCIATION

Established in 1980

255 EAST FIFTH STREET, SUITE 2400
CINCINNATI, OHIO 45202-4787
Telephone: 513-721-4532
Telecopier: 513-721-7120
Email: ktbh@katzteller.com
URL: http://www.katzteller.com

General Civil Practice. Banking, Bankruptcy, Business Acquisitions, Business, Civil Litigation, Corporation, ERISA, Estate Planning, Family, Health Care and Hospital, Municipal Law and Zoning Law, Environmental Law, Labor and Employment Law, Pension and Profit Sharing, Probate, Real Estate, Securities, Sports and Entertainment, Tax and Tax Litigation.

REUVEN J. KATZ, born Cincinnati, Ohio, 1924; admitted to bar, 1950, Ohio. *Education:* University of Cincinnati (B.A., 1988); Harvard Law School (J.D., 1950). *Member:* Sports Lawyers Association (Board Member). ***PRACTICE AREAS:*** Health Care; Estate Planning; Sports Law. ***Email:*** rkatz@katzteller.com

JEROME S. TELLER, born Toledo, Ohio, 1930; admitted to bar, 1953, Ohio. *Education:* University of Cincinnati (B.A., 1951; J.D., 1953). Order of the Coif. Associate Editor, University of Cincinnati Law Review, 1952-1953. President, University of Cincinnati College of Law Alumni Association, 1980-1981. Fellow, American Academy of Matrimonial Lawyers. ***PRACTICE AREAS:*** Family Law; Health Care; Real Estate. ***Email:*** jteller@katzteller.com

GUY M. HILD, born Cincinnati, Ohio, 1937; admitted to bar, 1962, Ohio; 1968, U.S. Supreme Court. *Education:* University of Cincinnati (B.A., 1959; J.D., 1962). Fellow, American Academy of Matrimonial Lawyers. ***PRACTICE AREAS:*** Family Law; Business Law; Trusts and Estates. ***Email:*** ghild@katzteller.com

ROBERT A. PITCAIRN, JR., born Pittsburgh, Pennsylvania, 1948; admitted to bar, 1973, Ohio. *Education:* College of Wooster (B.A., 1970); University of Cincinnati (J.D., 1973). Order of the Coif. Executive Editor, University of Cincinnati Law Review, 1972-1973. Fellow, American College of Trial Lawyers. ***PRACTICE AREAS:*** Litigation. ***Email:*** rpitcairn@katzteller.com

ROBERT E. BRANT, born Cincinnati, Ohio, 1949; admitted to bar, 1974, Ohio. *Education:* Vanderbilt University; University of Cincinnati (B.A., magna cum laude, 1971); Stanford University (J.D., 1974); New York University (LL.M. in Taxation, 1975). Phi Beta Kappa. ***PRACTICE AREAS:*** Taxation; Employee Benefits; Trusts and Estates; Closely Held Corporations. ***Email:*** rbrant@katzteller.com

RONALD J. GORET, born Detroit, Michigan, 1937; admitted to bar, 1964, Ohio. *Education:* University of Cincinnati (B.B.A., 1960); Salmon P. Chase College of Law (J.D., 1964). Phi Alpha Delta. Member, Order of the Curia. Referee, Court of Domestic Relations, 1969-1971. Member, National Panel of Arbitrators, American Arbitration Association, 1971-2000. ***PRACTICE AREAS:*** Real Estate. ***Email:*** rgoret@katzteller.com

STEPHEN C. KISLING, born Dayton, Ohio, 1951; admitted to bar, 1976, Ohio; 1978, District of Columbia; 1979, Florida; 1987, U.S. Tax Court. *Education:* Ohio Wesleyan Uni-

(This Listing Continued)

KATZ, TELLER, BRANT & HILD, A LEGAL PROFESSIONAL ASSOCIATION, Cincinnati—Continued

versity (B.A., 1973); Franklin Pierce Law Center (J.D., 1976). *Member:* District of Columbia Bar; The Florida Bar. ***PRACTICE AREAS:*** Employee Benefits; Taxation; Tax Exempt Organizations. ***Email:*** skisling@katzteller.com

JAMES F. McCARTHY, III, born Cincinnati, Ohio, 1952; admitted to bar, 1977, Ohio; 1978, U.S. District Court, Southern District of Ohio; 1981, U.S. Court of Appeals, Sixth Circuit; 1989, U.S. Supreme Court and U.S. Court of Military Appeals. *Education:* Xavier University (B.A., summa cum laude, 1974); The Ohio State University (J.D., 1977). [Cmdr., Judge Advocate General, U.S. Naval Reserve, 1974-1978]. (Also of Counsel, Sand & Sebolt, Canton, Ohio). ***PRACTICE AREAS:*** Litigation; Eminent Domain; Business Torts; Intellectual Property. ***Email:*** jmccarthy@katzteller.com

ANDREW R. BERGER, born Norfolk, Virginia, 1955; admitted to bar, 1978, Ohio; 1990, Kentucky. *Education:* University of Nebraska (B.A., 1975); Cornell University (J.D., cum laude, 1978). Phi Beta Kappa. *Member:* American Health Lawyers Association. ***PRACTICE AREAS:*** Corporate Law; Health Care; Mergers Acquisitions and Divestitures; Real Estate. ***Email:*** aberger@katzteller.com

MARK J. JAHNKE, born Cincinnati, Ohio, 1954; admitted to bar, 1979, Ohio. *Education:* The Ohio State University (B.A., summa cum laude, 1976; M.A., 1976); Northwestern University (J.D., 1979). ***PRACTICE AREAS:*** Mergers, Acquisitions and Divestitures; Health Care; Corporate Law. ***Email:*** mjahnke@katzteller.com

WILLIAM F. RUSSO, born Cincinnati, Ohio, 1955; admitted to bar, 1979, Ohio; 1980, U.S. Tax Court and U.S. Court of Appeals, Sixth Circuit. *Education:* University of Cincinnati (B.A., 1976; J.D., 1979). Order of the Coif; Phi Beta Kappa. Editorial Board, University of Cincinnati Law Review, 1978-1979. ***PRACTICE AREAS:*** Business Taxation; Family Business Successions; Family Trusts; Estate Planning. ***Email:*** wrusso@katzteller.com

WILLIAM T. HAYDEN, born Cincinnati, Ohio, 1954; admitted to bar, 1979, Ohio. *Education:* Denison University (B.A., 1976); University of Cincinnati (J.D., 1979). Special Master, In re Fernald Litigation, 1990—. ***PRACTICE AREAS:*** Corporate Governance; Business Planning; Bankruptcy; Insurance; Debtor and Creditor Relations. ***Email:*** whayden@katzteller.com

JOHN R. GIERL, born Pittsburgh, Pennsylvania, 1958; admitted to bar, 1983, Ohio. *Education:* Miami University (B.A., 1980); The Ohio State University (J.D., with honors, 1983). ***PRACTICE AREAS:*** Corporate Law; Franchises and Franchising; Securities. ***Email:*** jgierl@katzteller.com

BRUCE A. HUNTER, born St. Louis, Missouri; admitted to bar, 1984, Ohio; 1992, Kentucky. *Education:* University of Cincinnati (B.A., 1977; J.D., 1984). Order of the Coif. Note Editor, University of Cincinnati Law Review, 1983-1984. ***PRACTICE AREAS:*** Family Law. ***Email:*** bhunter@katzteller.com

BRADLEY G. HAAS, born Cincinnati, Ohio; admitted to bar, 1986, Ohio. *Education:* University of Cincinnati (B.B.A., magna cum laude, 1982; J.D., 1986). Order of the Coif. Articles Editor, University of Cincinnati Law Review, 1985-1986. ***PRACTICE AREAS:*** Corporate Law; Real Estate Law; Mergers, Acquisitions and Divestitures. ***Email:*** bhaas@katzteller.com

DANIEL P. UTT, born Toledo, Ohio; admitted to bar, 1986, Ohio. *Education:* Bowling Green State University (B.S., 1983); University of Dayton (J.D., summa cum laude, 1986). Executive Editor, University of Dayton Law Review, 1985-1986. ***PRACTICE AREAS:*** Real Estate; Construction Law; Environmental Law; Corporate Law. ***Email:*** dutt@katzteller.com

CYNTHIA L. GIBSON, born Sylva, North Carolina, 1964; admitted to bar, 1989, Ohio; 1999, Kentucky. *Education:* Wake Forest University (B.A. magna cum laude, 1986; Phi Beta Kappa; Phi Alpha Theta; Mortar Board); University of Virginia (J.D., 1989; Dillard Fellow). Notes Editor, Journal of Law & Politics, 1988-1989. ***PRACTICE AREAS:*** Employment Law; Probate Litigation; Privacy Law; Insurance Law. ***Email:*** cgibson@katzteller.com

TEDD H. FRIEDMAN, born Cincinnati, Ohio, 1967; admitted to bar, 1992, Ohio. *Education:* University of Wisconsin-Madison (B.S., 1989); University of Cincinnati (J.D., 1992). Order of the Coif. University of Cincinnati Law Review. ***PRACTICE AREAS:*** Business Law; Health Care; Corporate Law; Computer Law. ***Email:*** tfriedman@katzteller.com

WIJDAN JREISAT, born Amman, Jordan, 1970; admitted to bar, 1994, Ohio. *Education:* Centre College (B.A., 1991); University of Virginia (J.D., 1994). Phi Beta Kappa. ***PRACTICE AREAS:*** Litigation; General Practice; Employment Law. ***Email:*** wjreisat@katzteller.com

LAURA A. HINEGARDNER, born Detroit, Michigan, 1971; admitted to bar, 1996, Kentucky; 1997, Ohio. *Education:* University of Kentucky (B.A., 1993); University of Cincinnati (J.D., 1996). ***PRACTICE AREAS:*** Litigation; Employment Law. ***Email:*** lhinegardner@katzteller.com

---

JOEL S. BRANT, born Cincinnati, Ohio, 1968; admitted to bar, 1997, Ohio. *Education:* Dartmouth College (B.A., 1991); Georgetown University (J.D., 1997); New York University (LL.M., Taxation, 1998). ***PRACTICE AREAS:*** Estate Planning; Taxation; Corporate Law; Health Care. ***Email:*** jsbrant@katzteller.com

TARA A. KLEE, born Cincinnati, Ohio, 1972; admitted to bar, 1998, Ohio; 1999, Kentucky. *Education:* Miami University (B.S., magna cum laude, 1995, Phi Beta Kappa); University of Cincinnati (J.D., 1998, Order of the Coif). Member, Moot Court Board, 1996-1998. Member, University of Cincinnati Law Review, 1997-1998. ***PRACTICE AREAS:*** Corporate Law; Real Estate Law. ***Email:*** tgrause@katzteller.com

(This Listing Continued)

SHERI E. AUTTONBERRY, born Pensacola, Florida, 1974; admitted to bar, 1999, Ohio. *Education:* Louisiana Tech University (B.A., summa cum laude, 1996); Vanderbilt University (J.D., 1999). ***PRACTICE AREAS:*** Litigation. ***Email:*** sauttonberry@katzteller.com

JEROME C. BISHOP, born 1969; admitted to bar, 2002, Ohio. *Education:* Georgetown University (B.A., 1994; J.D., 2001). ***PRACTICE AREAS:*** Insurance; Litigation.

ADAM D. COLVIN, born 1977; admitted to bar, 2003, Ohio. *Education:* Harvard University (A.B., 2000); University of California at Los Angeles (J.D., 2003). ***PRACTICE AREAS:*** Corporate Law; Real Estate; Environmental Law.

OF COUNSEL

JOSEPH A. BRANT, born Cincinnati, Ohio, 1937; admitted to bar, 1961, Ohio. *Education:* University of Cincinnati (B.A., 1959; J.D., 1961); New York University (LL.M. in Taxation, 1962). Adjunct Professor, Estate Planning, 1977—, University of Cincinnati Law School. Fellow, American College of Trust and Estate Counsel. ***PRACTICE AREAS:*** Estate Planning; Federal Taxation; Probate. ***Email:*** jabrant@katzteller.com

REPRESENTATIVE CLIENTS: Acordia; American Modern Home Insurance Group; Ampac Packaging, LLC; Assurant; Bank One; Chemed Corp.; Cincinnati Eye Institute; Columbia Sussex Corp.; Comisar La Normandie Maisonette, Inc.; Duke Energy; Fortis Health; GE Aircraft Engine; Greater Cincinnati Associated Physicians, Inc.; Hebrew Union College-Jewish Institute of Religion; Jeff Ruby Culinary Entertainment; Jeff Wyler Automotive Family; Johnny Bench; Johnson & Johnson; Key Bank; Lion Apparel, Inc.; Loveland Pet Products, Inc.; The Midland Company; Mini-Mix, Inc.; Montgomery Inn, Inc.; The Ohio Heart Health Center, Inc.; The Provident Bank; Roto-Rooter, Inc.; Scanner Applications, Inc.; US Bank; University of Cincinnati Medical Physicians, Inc.

KEATING MUETHING & KLEKAMP PLL

Established in 1954

ONE EAST FOURTH STREET, SUITE 1400
CINCINNATI, OHIO 45202
Telephone: 513-579-6400
Facsimile: 513-579-6457
URL: http://www.kmklaw.com

General Practice: Administrative, Banking, Bankruptcy, Corporations, Criminal, Employee Benefits Law, Environmental, ERISA, Estate Planning, Health Care, Immigration, Intellectual Property, Labor, Mergers and Acquisitions, Probate, Real Estate, Securities, Taxation, Trials and Appeals.

FIRM PROFILE: Keating Muething & Klekamp PLL, founded in 1954, is a service-oriented law firm with approximately 100 lawyers and a support staff of more than 150 people based in Cincinnati, Ohio. We are committed to providing efficient, valuable and cost-conscious counseling.

Our lawyers offer practical advice and time-tested business solutions. We focus on business representation and transactions, commercial finance, labor and employment, employee benefits, private client services, litigation, real estate development and bankruptcy related legal services. For more than 50 years, we have contributed to the success of many businesses from small start-up companies and international corporations to non-profit organizations and government entities.

MEMBERS OF FIRM

JOHN L. MUETHING, born Covington, Kentucky, August 7, 1921; admitted to bar, 1948, Ohio; 1952, U.S. Court of Appeals, Sixth Circuit; 1954, U.S. District Court, Eastern District of Kentucky; 1955, U.S. District Court, Southern District of Ohio; 1964, U.S. Supreme Court. *Education:* Xavier University (B.A., 1943); University of Cincinnati College of Law (J.D., 1948). ***PRACTICE AREAS:*** Commercial and Securities Litigation; Business Planning and Formation.

DONALD P. KLEKAMP, born Cincinnati, Ohio, June 9, 1932; admitted to bar, 1957, Ohio; 1959, U.S. District Court, Southern District of Ohio and U.S. Court of Appeals, Sixth Circuit; 1970, U.S. Tax Court; 1971, U.S. Supreme Court. *Education:* Xavier University (A.B., 1954); University of Cincinnati College of Law (J.D., 1957). ***PRACTICE AREAS:*** Mergers and Acquisitions; Private Offerings; Business Planning and Formation. ***Email:*** DKlekamp@KMKlaw.com

TIMOTHY A. GARRY, born Detroit, Michigan, January 30, 1936; admitted to bar, 1961, Ohio; 1962, U.S. District Court, Southern District of Ohio; 1971, U.S. Supreme Court; 1979, U.S. District Court, Eastern District of Kentucky. *Education:* Xavier University (A.B., 1957); Case Western Reserve University Law School (J.D., 1961). ***PRACTICE AREAS:*** Mergers and Acquisitions; Construction and Development; Private Offerings; Employment Litigation; Trust Administration; Executive Compensation; Estate Planning; Business Planning and Formation. ***Email:*** TGarry@KMKlaw.com

GARY P. KREIDER, born Newark, Ohio, June 7, 1938; admitted to bar, 1964, Ohio; 1966, U.S. District Court, Southern District of Ohio; 1971, U.S. Supreme Court. *Education:* University of Cincinnati (B.A., 1960; M.A., 1961); University of Cincinnati College of Law (J.D., 1964). ***PRACTICE AREAS:*** Corporate Law; Securities Regulation and Compliance; Public Offerings; Private Offerings; Mergers and Acquisitions; Business Planning and Formation. ***Email:*** GKreider@KMKlaw.com

DON R. GARDNER, born Cincinnati, Ohio, March 26, 1935; admitted to bar, 1960, Ohio; 1961, U.S. District Court, Southern District of Ohio; 1964, U.S. Court of Appeals, Sixth Circuit; 1971, U.S. Supreme Court. *Education:* University of Cincinnati (B.A., 1957); University of Notre Dame Law School (J.D., 1960). ***PRACTICE AREAS:*** Zoning, Planning and Land Use; Construction and Development; Bankruptcy and Reorganizations; Creditors Rights Litigation; Real Estate Law; Title Insurance Law. ***Email:*** DGardner@KMKlaw.com

LOUIS F. GILLIGAN, born Darby, Pennsylvania, September 4, 1943; admitted to bar, 1968, Ohio; 1970, U.S. District Court, Southern District of Ohio; 1971, U.S. Supreme Court; 1974, U.S. Court of Appeals, Sixth Circuit. *Education:* University of Scranton (B.S.,

(This Listing Continued)

1965); University of Cincinnati College of Law (J.D., 1968). ***PRACTICE AREAS:*** Class Actions; Professional Liability; Civil Appeals; Personal Injury/Wrongful Death; Antitrust; Intellectual Property Litigation; False Claims Act and Qui Tam Litigation; Commercial and Securities Litigation; Complex and Multi-District Litigation; Mass Torts; Insurance Coverage; Arbitration and Mediation. ***Email:*** LGilligan@KMKlaw.com

HERBERT B. WEISS, born Hamilton, Ohio, January 1, 1940; admitted to bar, 1965, Ohio and U.S. District Court, Southern District of Ohio. *Education:* University of Cincinnati (B.A., 1962); University of Cincinnati College of Law (J.D., 1965). ***PRACTICE AREAS:*** Real Estate Law; Business Law; Government Relations; Government Affairs; Economic Development; Real Estate Finance; Construction and Development; Zoning, Planning and Land Use; Real Estate Taxation; Title Insurance. ***Email:*** HWeiss@KMKlaw.com

JOSEPH P. ROUSE, born Cincinnati, Ohio, November 10, 1944; admitted to bar, 1970, Ohio and U.S. District Court, Southern District of Ohio; 1971, U.S. Tax Court; U.S. Supreme Court. *Education:* University of Notre Dame (B.A., 1966); University of Cincinnati College of Law (J.D., 1970). ***PRACTICE AREAS:*** Personal Tax Services; Trust Administration; Trusts and Estates; Business Taxation; Mergers and Acquisitions; Business Planning and Formation. ***Email:*** JRouse@KMKlaw.com

RICHARD D. SIEGEL, born Moline, Illinois, September 26, 1944; admitted to bar, 1971, Ohio; 1974, U.S. Court of Appeals, 6th Circuit. *Education:* University of Kentucky (B.S., 1966); University of Kentucky College of Law (J.D., 1971). ***PRACTICE AREAS:*** General Corporate Law; Equipment Leasing and Aircraft Finance; Venture Capital Financing; Commercial and Finance Transactions; Mergers and Acquisitions; Commercial Loans; Business Planning and Formation. ***Email:*** RSiegel@KMKlaw.com

JOSEPH L. TRAUTH, JR., born Cincinnati, Ohio, April 22, 1945; admitted to bar, 1973, Ohio and U.S. District Court, Southern District of Ohio; 1976, U.S. District Court, Northern District of Ohio; 1988, U.S. Supreme Court; 2000, Kentucky and U.S. District Court, Eastern District of Kentucky. *Education:* Xavier University (B.S., 1967); University of Cincinnati College of Law (J.D., 1973). ***PRACTICE AREAS:*** Real Estate Law; Real Estate Litigation; Real Estate Taxation; Title Insurance; Zoning Planning and Land Use; Governmental Affairs and Economic Development; Construction and Development. ***Email:*** JTrauth@KMKlaw.com

JAMES R. WHITAKER, born Wauseon, Ohio, March 19, 1946; admitted to bar, 1973, Ohio and U.S. District Court, Southern District of Ohio; 1976, U.S. Court of Appeals, Sixth Circuit. *Education:* Ohio University (B.B.A., 1968); University of Arizona College of Law (J.D., 1973). [With U.S. Army, 1968-1970]. ***PRACTICE AREAS:*** Capital Financing; Mergers and Acquisitions; Banking Regulation. ***Email:*** JWhitaker@KMKlaw.com

J. DAVID ROSENBERG, born Lexington, Kentucky, April 30, 1949; admitted to bar, 1974, Ohio, Kentucky and U.S. District Court, Southern District of Ohio; 1983, U.S. District Court, Eastern District of Kentucky. *Education:* Wharton School, University of Pennsylvania (B.S., 1971); University of Kentucky College of Law (J.D., 1973). ***PRACTICE AREAS:*** Venture Capital Financing; Mergers and Acquisitions; Financial Institutions Law; Business Planning and Formation. ***Email:*** JDRosenberg@KMKlaw.com

ROBERT W. MAXWELL II, born Waynesburg, Pennsylvania, September 6, 1943; admitted to bar, 1968, Ohio; 1969, U.S. Court of Appeals, Sixth Circuit; 1970, U.S. District Court, Southern District of Ohio; 1993, U.S. Supreme Court. *Education:* Hampden-Sydney College (B.S., 1965); Duke University School of Law (J.D., 1968). ***PRACTICE AREAS:*** Labor Law Compliance; Labor Management Relations; Employment Practices and Procedures; Employment Litigation. ***Email:*** RMaxwell@KMKlaw.com

RICHARD D. SPOOR, born Cincinnati, Ohio, October 31, 1944; admitted to bar, 1972, Ohio; 1980, Kentucky. *Education:* University of Cincinnati (A.B., 1966); Harvard Law School (J.D., 1972). ***PRACTICE AREAS:*** Economic Development; Government Affairs; Commercial Loan Documentation; Real Estate Taxation; Real Estate Financing; Bond Finance; Municipal Finance. ***Email:*** RSpoor@KMKlaw.com

J. NEAL GARDNER, born Cincinnati, Ohio, July 12, 1944; admitted to bar, 1969, Ohio; 1972, U.S. Tax Court; 1974, U.S. Court of Appeals, Sixth Circuit; 1975, U.S. District Court, Southern District of Ohio. *Education:* University of Notre Dame (B.S.M.E., 1966); Georgetown University Law Center (J.D., 1969). ***PRACTICE AREAS:*** Corporate Law; Business Planning and Formation; Business Taxation; Private Offerings; Estate Planning Law; Taxation Law. ***Email:*** JGardner@KMKlaw.com

RICHARD L. CREIGHTON, JR., born Wheeling, West Virginia, March 13, 1948; admitted to bar, 1973, Ohio and U.S. District Court, Southern District of Ohio; 1974, U.S. Court of Appeals, Sixth Circuit; 1981, U.S. District Court, Eastern District of Kentucky; 1989, U.S. Supreme Court. *Education:* Xavier University (B.A., 1970); St. Louis University School of Law (J.D., 1973). ***PRACTICE AREAS:*** Complex and Multi-District Litigation; Antitrust Law; Aviation Law; Arbitration and Mediation; Commercial and Securities; Products Liability. ***Email:*** RCreighton@KMKlaw.com

PAUL V. MUETHING, born Cincinnati, Ohio, July 28, 1952; admitted to bar, 1977, Ohio and U.S. District Court, Southern District of Ohio. *Education:* Xavier University (B.A., 1974); University of Cincinnati College of Law (J.D., 1977). ***PRACTICE AREAS:*** Securities Regulation; Mergers and Acquisitions; Public Offerings; Business Planning and Formation. ***Email:*** PMuething@KMKlaw.com

JAMES E. BURKE, born Cincinnati, Ohio, January 24, 1953; admitted to bar, 1978, Ohio and U.S. District Court, Southern District of Ohio; 1983, U.S. Court of Appeals, Sixth Circuit; 1988, U.S. Supreme Court; 1993, U.S. Court of Appeals, Seventh Circuit; 1996, U.S. Court of Appeals, Ninth Circuit; 2002, U.S. Court of Appeals, Eleventh Circuit. *Education:* Yale University (B.A., 1975); University of Cincinnati College of Law (J.D., 1978). ***PRACTICE AREAS:*** Corporate and Securities Litigation; Complex and Multi-District Litigation; Arbitration and Mediation; Appellate Practice. ***Email:*** JBurke@KMKlaw.com

KEVIN E. IRWIN, born Lorain, Ohio, April 18, 1951; admitted to bar, 1977, Ohio and U.S. District Court, Northern District of Ohio; 1979, U.S. District Court, Southern District of Ohio; 1984, U.S. Court of Appeals, Sixth Circuit, 1989, U.S. Supreme Court; 1996, U.S. District Court, Eastern District of Michigan; 2001, U.S. District Court, Northern District of Illinois. *Education:* Miami University (B.A., 1973); Cleveland-Marshall College of Law (J.D., 1977). ***PRACTICE AREAS:*** Bankruptcy Reorganization; Mass Tort Settlement Trusts; Mass Tort Bankruptcy. ***Email:*** KIrwin@KMKlaw.com

(This Listing Continued)

TIMOTHY B. MATTHEWS, born Middlesboro, Kentucky, July 14, 1956; admitted to bar, 1981, Kentucky and U.S. District Court, Eastern District of Kentucky; 1982, Ohio, U.S. District Court, Southern District of Ohio, U.S. Tax Court and U.S. Court of Appeals, Sixth Circuit. *Education:* Harvard University (A.B., 1978); Harvard Law School (J.D., 1981). ***PRACTICE AREAS:*** Commercial Finance; Business Taxation; Mergers and Acquisitions; Private Offerings; Trust Administration; Capital Financing; Estate Planning; Project Finance; Leveraged Leasing; Commercial Loans; Personal Tax Services; Public Finance; Business Planning and Formation. ***Email:*** TMatthews@KMKlaw.com

WILLIAM J. KEATING, JR., born Cincinnati, Ohio, December 19, 1953; admitted to bar, 1979, Ohio, U.S. Supreme Court, U.S. District Court, Southern District of Ohio and U.S. Tax Court. *Education:* University of Cincinnati (B.B.A., 1976; M.B.A., 1976); University of Cincinnati College of Law (J.D., 1979). ***PRACTICE AREAS:*** Mergers and Acquisitions; Estate Planning; Executive Compensation; Business Planning and Formation. ***Email:*** WKeating@KMKlaw.com

WILLIAM A. POSEY, born Cincinnati, Ohio, June 15, 1954; admitted to bar, 1979, Ohio and U.S. District Court, Southern District of Ohio; 1986, U.S. District Court, Eastern District of Kentucky; 1988, U.S. Supreme Court; 1989, U.S. Court of Appeals, Sixth Circuit; 1995, U.S. Court of Appeals, Eleventh Circuit; 2002, U.S. District Court, Eastern District of Michigan. *Education:* University of Cincinnati (B.A., 1976); University of Cincinnati College of Law (J.D., 1979). ***PRACTICE AREAS:*** Mass Torts; Products Liability; Insurance Coverage; Professional Liability; Aviation Litigation; Personal Injury/Wrongful Death; Appellate Practice; Arbitration and Mediation. ***Email:*** WPosey@KMKlaw.com

JOSEPH P. MELLEN, born Sandusky, Ohio, September 7, 1949; admitted to bar, 1977, Ohio; 1979, U.S. District Court, Southern District of Ohio, U.S. Court of Appeals, Sixth Circuit and U.S. Tax Court. *Education:* Xavier University (B.S., 1971); University of Toledo College of Law (J.D., 1977). ***PRACTICE AREAS:*** Business Taxation; Estate Planning; Business Planning and Formation. ***Email:*** JMellen@KMKlaw.com

MARK J. WEBER, born Pittsfield, Massachusetts, September 23, 1954; admitted to bar, 1980, Ohio and U.S. District Court, Southern District of Ohio. *Education:* Duke University (A.B., 1977); University of Cincinnati College of Law (J.D., 1980). ***PRACTICE AREAS:*** Municipal Bonds; Construction and Development; Zoning, Planning and Land Use; Real Estate Finance and Leasing; Title Insurance; Real Estate Taxation. ***Email:*** MWeber@KMKlaw.com

GREGORY M. UTTER, born Cincinnati, Ohio, May 20, 1956; admitted to bar, 1981, Ohio; 1982, U.S. District Court, Southern District of Ohio; 1986, U.S. Court of Appeals, Sixth Circuit; 1996, U.S. Supreme Court. *Education:* University of Cincinnati (B.B.A., 1978); University of Cincinnati College of Law (J.D., 1981). ***PRACTICE AREAS:*** Personal Injury/Wrongful Death; Commercial and Securities Litigation; False Claims Act; Qui Tam Litigation; Class Actions; Mass Torts; Products Liability; Insurance Coverage; Professional Liability; Appellate Practice; Arbitration and Mediation. ***Email:*** GMUtter@KMKlaw.com

ROBERT E. COLETTI, born New York, N.Y., May 2, 1957; admitted to bar, 1982, Ohio and U.S. District Court, Southern District of Ohio. *Education:* Miami University (B.S., 1979); University of Cincinnati College of Law (J.D., 1982). ***PRACTICE AREAS:*** Business Planning and Formation; Acquisitions and Mergers; Securities Regulation Compliance; Public and Private Offerings. ***Email:*** RColetti@KMKlaw.com

JAMES M. JANSING, born Cincinnati, Ohio, August 23, 1956; admitted to bar, 1982, Ohio and U.S. District Court, Southern District of Ohio. *Education:* University of Cincinnati (B.S., 1978; M.A.I.R., 1979); University of Cincinnati College of Law (J.D., 1982). ***PRACTICE AREAS:*** Business Planning and Formation; Project Finance; Mergers and Acquisitions; Private Offerings; Commercial Loans; Public Finance. ***Email:*** JJansing@KMKlaw.com

PATRICK F. FISCHER, born Covington, Kentucky, December 30, 1957; admitted to bar, 1983, Texas; 1984, U.S. District Court, Northern District of Texas; 1988, Ohio and U.S. District Court, Southern District of Ohio. *Education:* Harvard University (A.B., 1980); Harvard Law School (J.D., 1983). ***PRACTICE AREAS:*** Commercial and Securities Litigation; Class Actions; Professional Liability; Appellate Practice; Arbitration and Mediation. ***Email:*** PFischer@KMKlaw.com

DAVID K. MONTGOMERY, born Cincinnati, Ohio, June 14, 1958; admitted to bar, 1984, Georgia; 1985, U.S. District Court, Northern District of Georgia and U.S. Court of Appeals, Eleventh Circuit; 1986, California, U.S. District Court, Central District of California and U.S. Court of Appeals, Ninth Circuit; 1988, Ohio; 1989, U.S. District Court, Southern District of Ohio; 1997, U.S. Supreme Court. *Education:* Miami University (B.A., 1980); Vanderbilt University Law School (J.D., 1984). ***PRACTICE AREAS:*** Labor Law Compliance; Management Labor Law; Employment Practices and Procedures; Employment Litigation. ***Email:*** DMontgomery@KMKlaw.com

JAMES R. MATTHEWS, born Cincinnati, Ohio, February 17, 1960; admitted to bar, 1985, Arizona; U.S. District Court, District of Arizona; U.S. Court of Appeals, Ninth Circuit; 1990, Ohio, U.S. District Court, Southern District of Ohio; U.S. Court of Appeals, Sixth Circuit; U.S. Supreme Court. *Education:* University of Cincinnati (B.A., 1982); University of Cincinnati College of Law (J.D., 1985). ***PRACTICE AREAS:*** Commercial and Securities Litigation; Insurance Coverage; Professional Liability; Appellate Law; Arbitration and Mediation; Personal Injury/Wrongful Death; Products Liability; Mass Torts. ***Email:*** JMatthews@KMKlaw.com

EDWARD E. STEINER, born Cleveland, Ohio, May 1, 1955; admitted to bar, 1983, Ohio. *Education:* University of Virginia (B.A., 1977); Johns Hopkins University (M.A., 1980); Yale University College of Law (J.D., 1983). ***PRACTICE AREAS:*** Mergers and Acquisitions; Corporate Law; Franchise Law; Business Planning and Formation; Securities Regulation and Compliance; Private Offerings; Public Offerings. ***Email:*** ESteiner@KMKlaw.com

STEPHEN M. GOODSON, born Minneapolis, Minnesota, October 2, 1955; admitted to bar, 1980, Ohio; 1981, U.S. Tax Court. *Education:* University of Cincinnati (B.B.A., 1977); Georgetown University Law Center (J.D., 1980). ***PRACTICE AREAS:*** Employee Compensation; Regulatory Compliance; Executive Compensation; Plan Administration; Employee Benefit and Compensation Programs; Mergers, Acquisitions and Divestitures. ***Email:*** SGoodson@KMKlaw.com

(This Listing Continued)

KEATING MUETHING & KLEKAMP PLL, Cincinnati—Continued

ROBERT G. SANKER, born Cincinnati, Ohio, February 15, 1962; admitted to bar, 1987, Ohio and U.S. District Court, Southern District of Ohio; 1990, U.S. Court of Appeals, Sixth Circuit; 2000, U.S. District Court, District of Colorado; 2002, U.S. Court of Appeals, Fourth Circuit. *Education:* Xavier University (B.A., 1984); Georgetown University Law Center (J.D., 1987). ***PRACTICE AREAS:*** Bankruptcy; Business Reorganizations; Bankruptcy Reorganizations; Creditors; Commercial Transactions. ***Email:*** RSanker@KMKlaw.com

LISA WINTERSHEIMER MICHEL, born Covington, Kentucky, October 28, 1963; admitted to bar, 1988, Ohio and U.S. District Court, Southern District of Ohio; 1989, Kentucky. *Education:* Xavier University (B.A., 1985); University of Cincinnati College of Law (J.D., 1988). ***PRACTICE AREAS:*** Executive Compensation; Plan Administration; Employee Benefits and Compensation; Employee Compensation; Mergers, Acquisitions and Divestitures; Business Divestitures. ***Email:*** LMichel@KMKlaw.com

W. KEITH NOEL, born Covington, Kentucky, August 27, 1962; admitted to bar, 1988, Ohio and U.S. District Court, Southern District of Ohio; 1989, Kentucky; 1991, U.S. Court of Appeals, Sixth Circuit; 1993, U.S. District Court, Eastern District of Kentucky. *Education:* University of Kentucky (B.A., 1984); University of Cincinnati College of Law (J.D., 1988). ***PRACTICE AREAS:*** Construction Law; Personal Injury; Wrongful Death; Environmental and Mold Claims. ***Email:*** WNoel@KMKlaw.com

DANIEL J. DONNELLON, born Cincinnati, Ohio, July 15, 1961; admitted to bar, 1986, Ohio; U.S. District Court, Southern District of Ohio; 1994, U.S. Court of Appeals, Sixth Circuit; 1998, U.S. Supreme Court; 2003, U.S. District Court, Eastern District of Michigan. *Education:* Bowling Green State University (B.A., 1983); University of Cincinnati College of Law (J.D., 1986). ***PRACTICE AREAS:*** Securities Litigation; Insurance Coverage; Appellate Practice; Mass Tort Litigation; Business Injunctions; Contract Litigation; General Liability Litigation; Intellectual Property Litigation. ***Email:*** DDonnellon@KMKlaw.com

BRIAN M. BABB, born Cleveland, Ohio, December 19, 1956; admitted to bar, 1986, Ohio; 1989, U.S. District Court, Northern District of Ohio; 1993, U.S. Court of Appeals, Sixth Circuit and U.S. Supreme Court. *Education:* The Ohio State University (B.S., 1980); Capital University School of Law (J.D., 1985). ***PRACTICE AREAS:*** Environmental and Mold Claims; Environmental; Construction and Development. ***Email:*** BBabb@KMKlaw.com

DANIEL E. IZENSON, born Dayton, Ohio, February 20, 1964; admitted to bar, 1990, Ohio; U.S. District Court, Southern District of Ohio; U.S. Court of Appeals, Sixth Circuit. *Education:* Indiana University (B.S., 1986); The Ohio State University Moritz College of Law (J.D., 1990). ***PRACTICE AREAS:*** Arbitration and Mediation; Commercial and Securities Litigation; Appellate Law; Professional Liability. ***Email:*** DIzenson@KMKlaw.com

GAIL T. KING, born Cleveland, Ohio, September 20, 1964; admitted to bar, 1990, Ohio; 1991, U.S. District Court, Southern District of Ohio. *Education:* University of Cincinnati (B.A., 1986); University of Cincinnati College of Law (J.D., 1990). ***PRACTICE AREAS:*** Finance; Business Acquisitions Formation; Public Finance; Business Planning and Formation; Project Finance; Securities Regulation and Compliance; Mergers and Acquisitions; Public Offerings; Commercial Loan Documentation; Real Estate Finance and Leasing. ***Email:*** GKing@KMKlaw.com

KENNETH P. KREIDER, born Cincinnati, Ohio, June 5, 1964; admitted to bar, 1989, Ohio and U.S. District Court, Southern District of Ohio. *Education:* Kenyon College (A.B., 1986); University of Cincinnati College of Law (J.D., 1989). ***PRACTICE AREAS:*** Construction and Development; Real Estate Finance and Leasing; Real Estate Taxation; Title Insurance; Zoning, Planning and Land Use; Environmental Real Estate. ***Email:*** KPKreider@KMKlaw.com

GAIL GLASSMEYER PRYSE, born Cincinnati, Ohio, February 11, 1963; admitted to bar, 1988, Ohio. *Education:* Miami University (B.S., 1985); University of Notre Dame Law School (J.D., 1988). ***PRACTICE AREAS:*** Construction and Development; Real Estate Finance and Leasing; Zoning, Planning and Land Use; Title Insurance. ***Email:*** GPryse@KMKlaw.com

MARY ELLEN MALAS, born Cincinnati, Ohio, March 20, 1962; admitted to bar, 1991, Ohio and U.S. District Court, Southern District of Ohio. *Education:* University of Cincinnati (B.A., 1984); Salmon P. Chase College of Law, Northern Kentucky University (J.D., 1991). ***PRACTICE AREAS:*** Family Law; Collaborative Family Law; Divorce; Premarital Agreements; Marital Property Settlements; Post-Divorce Modification; Separation Agreements; Spousal Supprot. ***Email:*** mmalas@kmklaw.com

MICHAEL L. SCHEIER, born Brooklyn, New York, July 8, 1960; admitted to bar, 1991, Ohio and U.S. District Court, Southern District of Ohio; 1994, U.S. Court of Appeals, Sixth Circuit; 1995, U.S. District Court, Eastern District of Michigan; 1998, U.S. Court of Appeals, Eleventh Circuit; 2001, U.S. District Court, Northern District of Illinois; 2002, U.S. Court of Appeals, Second Circuit. *Education:* Hobart College (B.A., 1983); University of Cincinnati College of Law (J.D., 1991). ***LANGUAGES:*** Hebrew. ***PRACTICE AREAS:*** Creditors; Banking Litigation; Bankruptcy Litigation; Commercial Insolvency; Mass Tort Bankruptcy Practice; Mass Tort Settlements Trusts; Commercial Litigation; Alternative Dispute Resolution. ***Email:*** MScheier@KMKlaw.com

JODY T. KLEKAMP, born Cincinnati, Ohio, November 10, 1965; admitted to bar, 1992, Ohio. *Education:* Miami University (B.A., 1988); University of Cincinnati College of Law (J.D., 1991). ***PRACTICE AREAS:*** Zoning, Planning and Land Use; Real Estate Finance and Leasing; Construction and Development; Title Insurance. ***Email:*** JKlekamp@KMKlaw.com

PAMELA MORGAN HODGE, born Cincinnati, Ohio, December 7, 1962; admitted to bar, 1989, Ohio and U.S. District Court, Southern District of Ohio; 1990, Kentucky and U.S. District Court, Eastern District of Kentucky; 1994, U.S. Supreme Court. *Education:* University of Cincinnati (A.S., 1983; B.S., 1986); Georgetown University Law Center (J.D., 1989). ***PRACTICE AREAS:*** Insurance Coverage; Construction Law; Arbitration and Mediation; Environmental and Mold Claims; Commercial Litigation; Securities Litigation. ***Email:*** PHodge@KMKlaw.com

(This Listing Continued)

PAUL D. DORGER, born Cincinnati, Ohio, July 27, 1965; admitted to bar, 1992, Ohio, U.S. Court of Appeals, Sixth Circuit and U.S. District Court, Southern District of Ohio. *Education:* University of Notre Dame (B.A., 1987); University of Cincinnati College of Law (J.D., 1992). ***PRACTICE AREAS:*** Labor Law Compliance; Labor Management Relations; Employment Practices and Procedures; Employment Litigation. ***Email:*** PDorger@KMKlaw.com

MARK A. WEISS, born Cincinnati, Ohio, November 5, 1966; admitted to bar, 1992, Ohio. *Education:* University of Michigan (A.B., 1989); University of Cincinnati College of Law (J.D., 1992). ***PRACTICE AREAS:*** Private Placement; Public Offerings; Private Offerings; Securities Regulation Compliance; Business Planning and Formation; Mergers and Acquisitions; Venture Capital Financing. ***Email:*** MWeiss@KMKlaw.com

JAMES H. BRUN, born Dayton, Ohio, September 26, 1951; admitted to bar, 1976, Ohio. *Education:* St. Joseph's College (B.A., 1973); University of Cincinnati College of Law (J.D., 1976). ***PRACTICE AREAS:*** Estate and Gift Taxation; Estate Planning; Estate Trust Administration. ***Email:*** JBrun@KMKlaw.com

JOSEPH M. CALLOW JR., born Cleveland, Ohio, May 24, 1968; admitted to bar, 1993, Ohio and U.S. District Court, Southern District of Ohio; 1997, U.S. Court of Appeals, Sixth Circuit. *Education:* Miami University (B.A., 1990); University of Cincinnati College of Law (J.D., 1993). ***PRACTICE AREAS:*** Tort Law; Antitrust; Commercial and Securities Litigation; Complex and Multi-District Litigation; Product Liability; Appellate Practice; Mass Torts. ***Email:*** JCallow@KMKlaw.com

ALAN S. FERSHTMAN, born Cincinnati, Ohio, April 25, 1966; admitted to bar, 1994, Ohio and U.S. District Court, Southern District of Ohio. *Education:* Miami University (B.S., 1988); University of Cincinnati College of Law (J.D., 1994). ***PRACTICE AREAS:*** Business Planning and Formation; Mergers and Acquisitions; Business Taxation; Private Offerings; Trusts and Estates. ***Email:*** AFershtman@KMKlaw.com

JAMES J. McGRAW, JR., born Cincinnati, Ohio, September 4, 1949; admitted to bar, 1974, Ohio and U.S. District Court, Southern District of Ohio; 1975, U.S. Court of Military Appeals; 1980, U.S. Supreme Court; 1983, Kentucky. *Education:* University of Notre Dame (B.B.A., 1971); University of Akron School of Law (J.D., 1974). ***PRACTICE AREAS:*** Nonprofit Organizations; Business Planning and Formation; Government Affairs; Economic Development; Mergers and Acquisitions. ***Email:*** JMcGraw@KMKlaw.com

STEVEN C. COFFARO, born Cincinnati, Ohio, July 31, 1970; admitted to bar, 1995, Ohio and U.S. District Court, Southern District of Ohio; 1996, Kentucky; 1997, Indiana and U.S. District Court, Northern and Southern Districts of Indiana; 1998, U.S. District Court, Western and Eastern Districts of Kentucky; 2002, U.S. Court of Appeals, Sixth Circuit; 2005, U.S. District Court, Northern District of Ohio. *Education:* Miami University (B.A., 1992); University of Cincinnati College of Law (J.D., 1995). ***PRACTICE AREAS:*** Commercial and Securities Litigation; Products Liability; Insurance Coverage; Appellate Practice; Arbitration and Mediation. ***Email:*** SCoffaro@KMKlaw.com

JOHN F. MEISENHELDER, born Indianapolis, Indiana, July 11, 1963; admitted to bar, 1991, Ohio. *Education:* The Ohio State University (B.S., M.I.S., 1986); University of Cincinnati College of Law (J.D., 1991). ***PRACTICE AREAS:*** Employee Benefits; Qualified Retirement Plans; Retirement Benefit Plans; Employee Stock Ownership Plans; Executive Compensation; HIPAA; ERISA Litigation; Mergers and Acquisitions. ***Email:*** JMeisenhelder@KMKlaw.com

MARK J. CHUMLEY, born Ann Arbor, Michigan, December 7, 1966; admitted to bar, 1996, Ohio; 1998, U.S. District Court, Southern District of Ohio. *Education:* University of Michigan (B.A., 1989); University of Cincinnati College of Law (J.D., 1996). ***PRACTICE AREAS:*** Labor Law Compliance; Management Labor Law; Employment Practices and Procedures; Employment Litigation. ***Email:*** MChumley@KMKlaw.com

SUE A. ERHART, born Cincinnati, Ohio, October 6, 1971; admitted to bar, 1996, Ohio; 1999, Indiana. *Education:* Xavier University (B.S., 1993); University of Cincinnati College of Law (J.D., 1996). ***PRACTICE AREAS:*** Intellectual Property Litigation; Commercial and Securities Litigation; Insurance Coverage; Appellate Practice; Arbitration and Mediation; Environmental and Mold Claims; Professional Liability. ***Email:*** SErhart@KMKlaw.com

F. MARK REUTER, born South Bend, Indiana, September 13, 1971; admitted to bar, 1996, Ohio. *Education:* University of Notre Dame (B.A., 1992); University of Notre Dame Law School (J.D., 1996). ***PRACTICE AREAS:*** Securities Regulation; Mergers and Acquisitions; Private Offerings; Public Offerings; Business Planning and Formation. ***Email:*** FReuter@KMKlaw.com

ADRIENNE J. ROACH, born London, Ohio, November 30, 1971; admitted to bar, 1996, Ohio; 1998, Kentucky. *Education:* University of Richmond (B.A., 1993); University of Cincinnati College of Law (J.D., 1996). ***LANGUAGES:*** Spanish. ***PRACTICE AREAS:*** Custody; Family Law; Adoption; Juvenile Law. ***Email:*** ARoach@KMKlaw.com

RACHAEL A. ROWE, born Cincinnati, Ohio, July 5, 1971; admitted to bar, 1996, Ohio; 1997, Kentucky; U.S. District Court, Southern District of Ohio and Eastern and Western Districts of Kentucky; U.S. Court of Appeals, Sixth Circuit. *Education:* Miami University (B.A., 1993); University of Cincinnati College of Law (J.D., 1996). ***PRACTICE AREAS:*** Professional Liability; Appellate Practice; Arbitration and Mediation; Employment Litigation; Class Actions; Commercial and Securities Litigation. ***Email:*** RRowe@KMKlaw.com

JILL A. WELLER, born Warren, Ohio, June 27, 1956; admitted to bar, 1981, District of Columbia; 1985, Ohio. *Education:* Georgetown University (A.B., 1978); Columbus School of Law of the Catholic University of America (J.D., 1981). ***PRACTICE AREAS:*** Environmental Law. ***Email:*** JWeller@KMKlaw.com

JOHN S. FRONDUTI, born Pittsburgh, Pennsylvania, August 18, 1972; admitted to bar, 1998, New York; 2003, Ohio. *Education:* University of Notre Dame (B.B.A., 1994); University of Cincinnati College of Law (J.D., 1997). ***PRACTICE AREAS:*** Aviation and Aerospace; Mergers, Acquisitions and Divestitures; Equipment Finance and Leasing; Banks and Banking. ***Email:*** JFronduti@KMKlaw.com

KAREN KREIDER GAUNT, born Cincinnati, Ohio, August 14, 1971; admitted to bar, 1997, Ohio; 1999, U.S. Court of International Trade and U.S. District Court, Southern

(This Listing Continued)

District of Ohio. *Education:* Denison University (B.A., 1993); University of Cincinnati College of Law (J.D., 1997). ***PRACTICE AREAS:*** Business Planning and Formation; Intellectual Property Litigation; Intellectual Property. ***Email:*** KGaunt@KMKlaw.com

MATTHEW K. BUCK, born Columbus, Ohio, May 27, 1968; admitted to bar, 1996, Ohio; 2003, Kentucky, U.S. District Court, Eastern District of Kentucky and U.S. District Court, Southern District of Ohio. *Education:* The Citadel (B.A., 1990); Temple University James E. Beasley School of Law (J.D., 1996). ***PRACTICE AREAS:*** Commercial and Securities Litigation; Professional Liability; Personal Injury; Class Actions; Insurance Coverage; Arbitration and Mediation; Products Liability. ***Email:*** MBuck@KMKlaw.com

PATRIÇIA B. HOGAN, born Cincinnati, Ohio, July 6, 1948; admitted to bar, 1989, Ohio and U.S. District Court, Southern District of Ohio. *Education:* University of Cincinnati (B.A., 1971); University of Cincinnati College of Law (J.D., 1989). ***PRACTICE AREAS:*** Trademarks; Copyrights; False Advertising; Intellectual Property Litigation; Intellectual Property. ***Email:*** PHogan@KMKlaw.com

E. TODD WILKOWSKI, born Clark Air Force Base, Philippines, June 2, 1967; admitted to bar, 1998, Ohio; 1999, U.S. District Court, Southern District of Ohio. *Education:* United States Air Force Academy (B.S., 1989); Regent University School of Public Policy (M.A., 1998); Regent University School of Law (J.D., 1998). ***PRACTICE AREAS:*** Construction Litigation; Arbitration and Mediation; Estate Litigation; Probate Litigation; Commercial Litigation; ERISA Litigation; Environmental and Mold Claims. ***Email:*** EWilkowski@KMKlaw.com

ASSOCIATES

JOHN N. WINSTEAD, born Madisonville, Kentucky, October 14, 1967; admitted to bar, 1998, Ohio; 1999, Kentucky. *Education:* University of Kentucky (B.A., 1989; B.S., 1991); University of Kentucky College of Law (J.D., 1998). ***PRACTICE AREAS:*** Business Planning and Formation; Commercial Loans; Mergers and Acquisitions; Structured Finance; Private Offerings; Venture Capital Financing. ***Email:*** JWinstead@KMKlaw.com

BENJAMIN A. SCHNEIDER, born Cincinnati, Ohio, April 6, 1971; admitted to bar, 2000, Ohio. *Education:* Miami University (B.A., 1994); Salmon P. Chase College of Law, Northern Kentucky University (J.D., 2000). ***PRACTICE AREAS:*** Construction and Development; Real Estate Finance and Leasing. ***Email:*** BSchneider@KMKlaw.com

CAROLINE M. DIMAURO, born Cincinnati, Ohio, May 13, 1969; admitted to bar, 1999, Ohio and U.S. District Court, Southern District of Ohio. *Education:* Indiana University (B.A., 1991); University of Cincinnati College of Law (J.D., 1999). ***PRACTICE AREAS:*** Employment Litigation; Employment Law; Labor Law Compliance; Management Labor Law. ***Email:*** CDimauro@KMKlaw.com

JAMIE M. RAMSEY, born Ft. Thomas, Kentucky, March 14, 1974; admitted to bar, 1999, Ohio and U.S. District Court, Southern District of Ohio; 2000, Kentucky and U.S. District Court, Eastern District of Kentucky; 2001, U.S. Court of Appeals, Sixth Circuit; 2003, U.S. District Court, Western District of Kentucky; 2004, U.S. Tax Court. *Education:* Northern Kentucky University (B.S., 1996); Salmon P. Chase College of Law, Northern Kentucky University (J.D., 1999). ***PRACTICE AREAS:*** Commercial Litigation; Securities Litigation; Insurance Coverage; Appellate Practice; Mass Torts; Class Actions; Professional Liability. ***Email:*** JRamsey@KMKlaw.com

D. BROCK DENTON, born Bowling Green, Kentucky, December 14, 1974; admitted to bar, 2000, Ohio; 2001, Kentucky. *Education:* University of Kentucky (B.S., 1997); Salmon P. Chase College of Law, Northern Kentucky University (J.D., 2000). ***PRACTICE AREAS:*** Business Planning and Formation; Mergers and Acquisitions; Private Offerings; Public Offerings; Securities Regulation Compliance; Franchise Law; Banking Law; Bank Mergers and Acquisitions; Banking Regulation. ***Email:*** DDenton@KMKlaw.com

THOMAS M. TEPE, JR., born Cincinnati, Ohio, June 16, 1972; admitted to bar, 1999, Ohio and U.S. District Court, Southern District of Ohio; 2001, U.S. Court of Appeals, Sixth Circuit. *Education:* Ohio State University (B.A., 1995); Michigan State University, Detroit College of Law (J.D., 1999). ***PRACTICE AREAS:*** Real Estate Tax Litigation; Zoning, Planning and Land Use; Real Estate Taxation; Governmental Affairs; Economic Development; Construction and Development. ***Email:*** TTepe@KMKlaw.com

MICHAEL J. MOEDDEL, born Cincinnati, Ohio, April 6, 1978; admitted to bar, 2002, Ohio. *Education:* The Ohio State University (B.A., 1999); University of Cincinnati College of Law (J.D., 2002). ***PRACTICE AREAS:*** Business Transactions; Business Taxation; Mergers and Acquisitions; Estate Planning; Private Offerings; Capital Financing. ***Email:*** MMoeddel@kmklaw.com

JASON M. COHEN, born Cincinnati, Ohio, November 21, 1973; admitted to bar, 1999, California and U.S. District Court, Northern District of California; 2003, Ohio, U.S. Court of Appeals, Fifth and Sixth Circuits and U.S. District Court, Southern District of Ohio; 2004, U.S. Court of Appeals, Ninth Circuit. *Education:* Harvard University (A.B., 1995); Stanford University Law School (J.D., 1999). ***PRACTICE AREAS:*** Commercial and Securities Litigation; Antitrust; Appellate Practice; Professional Liability; Insurance Coverage. ***Email:*** JCohen@KMKlaw.com

DANIELLE M. D'ADDESA, born Staten Island, New York, August 9, 1977; admitted to bar, 2003, Ohio. *Education:* Rollins College (B.A., 1999); University of Cincinnati College of Law (J.D., 2003). ***Email:*** ddaddesa@kmklaw.com

DREW M. HICKS, born Dayton, Ohio, September 11, 1976; admitted to bar, 2003, Ohio. *Education:* Duke University (B.A., 1999); University of Cincinnati College of Law (J.D., 2003). ***Email:*** dhicks@kmklaw.com

BRIAN P. MUETHING, born Cincinnati, Ohio, August 7, 1978; admitted to bar, 2003, Ohio. *Education:* Miami University (B.A., 2000); University of Cincinnati College of Law (J.D., 2003). ***Email:*** bmuething@kmklaw.com

ARI B. REDBORD, born December 26, 1974; admitted to bar, 2000, New Jersey; 2001, New York; 2000, District of Columbia (Not admitted in Ohio). *Education:* Duke University (B.A., 1997); Georgetown University Law Center (J.D., 2000). ***PRACTICE AREAS:*** Commercial and Securities Litigation; False Claims Act; Qui Tam Litigation. ***Email:*** aredbord@kmklaw.com

(This Listing Continued)

COLE D. BOND, born Lawrence, Kansas, April 29, 1973; admitted to bar, 1999, Texas; U.S. District Court, Northern and Eastern Districts of Texas; 2004, Ohio. *Education:* University of Kansas (B.A., 1996); Vanderbilt University Law School (J.D., 1999). ***PRACTICE AREAS:*** Labor Law; Employment Law. ***Email:*** cbond@kmklaw.com

JASON V. STITT, born Cleveland, Ohio, June 21, 1975; admitted to bar, 2002, Kentucky, Ohio and U.S. District Court, Eastern District of Kentucky. *Education:* University of Kentucky (B.A., 1997); University of Kentucky College of Law (J.D., 2002). ***PRACTICE AREAS:*** Bankruptcy; Commercial Finance. ***Email:*** JStitt@KMKlaw.com

JOSEPH C. ALTER, born Cincinnati, Ohio, May 28, 1977; admitted to bar, 2002, California and U.S. District Court, Southern District of California; 2003, U.S. Court of Federal Claims; 2005, Ohio. *Education:* Miami University (B.A., 1999); University of San Diego School of Law (J.D., 2002). ***PRACTICE AREAS:*** Securities Regulation and Compliance; Mergers and Acquisitions; Private Placements; Public Offerings; Business Planning; Business Formation. ***Email:*** JAlter@KMKlaw.com

CHRISTY M. NAGELEISEN, born Fort Thomas, Kentucky, April 28, 1978; admitted to bar, 2003, Ohio; 2004, Kentucky. *Education:* Thomas More College (B.A., 1999); University of Cincinnati College of Law (J.D., 2003). ***Email:*** CNageleisen@KMKlaw.com

WILLIAM D. SPOOR, born Cincinnati, Ohio, June 29, 1979; admitted to bar, 2002, Kentucky (Not admitted in Ohio). *Education:* Xavier University (B.A., 1999); University of Cincinnati College of Law (J.D., 2002). ***PRACTICE AREAS:*** Government Affairs; Economic Development; Real Estate Taxation; Real Estate Finance; Bond Finance; Municipal Finance. ***Email:*** WSpoor@KMKlaw.com

M. SCOTT McINTYRE, born Lexington, Kentucky, May 22, 1975; admitted to bar, 2002, Ohio and U.S. Court of Appeals, Sixth Circuit; 2003, Kentucky and U.S. Disrict Court, Southern District of Ohio and Eastern District of Kentucky; 2004, U.S. Court of Appeals, Seventh Circuit. *Education:* Thomas More College (B.A., 1997); University of Kentucky College of Law (J.D., 2001). ***PRACTICE AREAS:*** Labor and Employment; Management Labor Law; Employment Litigation; Labor Law; Labor Relations. ***Email:*** MMcintyre@kmklaw.com

ALISON J. BOUFFARD, born Cleveland, Ohio, June 15, 1979; admitted to bar, 2004, Ohio; 2005, U.S. District Court, Southern District of Ohio. *Education:* Indiana University (B.A., 2001); University of Cincinnati College of Law (J.D., 2004). ***Email:*** abouffard@kmklaw.com

BRIAN A. RIDDELL, born Covington, Kentucky, June 3, 1977; admitted to bar, 2004, Ohio; 2005, Kentucky. *Education:* University of Kentucky (B.A., 1999); Salmon P. Chase College of Law, Northern Kentucky University (J.D., 2004). ***Email:*** BRiddell@kmklaw.com

STEVEN W. SEBASTIAN, born Lexington, Kentucky, October 12, 1969; admitted to bar, 2000, Ohio; 2002, North Carolina. *Education:* University of Kentucky (B.S., 1997); University of Michigan Law School (J.D., 2000). ***PRACTICE AREAS:*** Employee Benefits; Employee Compensation; Executive Compensation; Regulatory Compliance; Plan Administration. ***Email:*** SSebastian@kmklaw.com

SEAN S. SUDER, born Cincinnati, Ohio, February 17, 1978; admitted to bar, 2004, Ohio. *Education:* University of Virginia (B.S., 2000); University of Virginia School of Law (J.D., 2004). ***Email:*** SSuder@kmklaw.com

JENNIFER K. WALWYN, born Springfield, Oregon, July 28, 1978; admitted to bar, 2003, California; 2004, Ohio. *Education:* Cornell University (B.S., 2000); University of California, School of Law, Los Angeles (J.D., 2003). ***Email:*** JWalwyn@kmklaw.com

DAVID A. MEYER, born Fort Thomas, Kentucky, March 13, 1969; admitted to bar, 1996, Ohio; 1997, Kentucky; 2003, U.S. District Court, Southern District of Ohio. *Education:* Thomas More College (B.S., 1991); Salmon P. Chase College of Law, Northern Kentucky University (J.D., 1996). ***PRACTICE AREAS:*** Environmental Law; Insurance Coverage; Environmental and Mold Claims; Construction and Development. ***Email:*** DMeyer@kmklaw.com

PAULA YASUYO BOGGS, born Ft. Knox, Kentucky, June 19, 1974; admitted to bar, 2003, Kentucky; 2004, U.S. District Court, Eastern and Western Districts of Kentucky; 2005, U.S. Court of Appeals, Sixth Circuit (Not admitted in Ohio). *Education:* University of Kentucky (B.S., B.A., 1998); University of Cincinnati College of Law (J.D., 2003). ***Email:*** PBoggs@kmklaw.com

DANIEL G. DUTRO JR., born Yokosuka, Japan, February 17, 1966; admitted to bar, 1994, Ohio; 1995, U.S. District Court, Southern District of Ohio. *Education:* Yale University (B.A., 1988); University of Cincinnati College of Law (J.D., 1994). ***PRACTICE AREAS:*** Real Estate Finance; Construction and Development. ***Email:*** ddutro@kmklaw.com

DONYETTA D. BAILEY, born Newark, New Jersey, January 25, 1975; admitted to bar, 2000, Ohio; 2000, U.S. District Court, Southern District of Ohio; 2004, U.S. Court of Appeals, Sixth Circuit. *Education:* University of Illinois at Springfield (B.A., 1997); Capital University Law School (J.D., 2000). ***PRACTICE AREAS:*** Workers Compensation; Management Labor Law; Employment Litigation; Labor Law; Antitrust; Labor and Employment; Labor Relations. ***Email:*** DBailey@kmklaw.com

ANDREW D. BOWERS, born Lima, Ohio, July 31, 1973; admitted to bar, 1999, Ohio; 2000, U.S. District Court, Southern District of Ohio. *Education:* Wittenberg University (B.A., 1996); The Ohio State University Moritz College of Law (J.D., 1999). ***PRACTICE AREAS:*** Government Affairs; Municipal Bonds; Economic Development. ***Email:*** abowers@kmklaw.com

JENNIFER J. MORALES, born Bryn Mawr, Pennsylvania, April 7, 1978; admitted to bar, 2003, Ohio; 2004, U.S. District Court, Southern District of Ohio and U.S. Tax Court; 2005, District of Columbia. *Education:* Harvard University (A.B., 1999); New York University School of Law (J.D., 2002). ***Email:*** JMorales@kmklaw.com

W. JEFFREY SEFTON, born Columbus, Ohio, March 18, 1970; admitted to bar, 2002, Ohio, U.S. District Court, Southern District of Ohio and U.S. Court of Appeals, Sixth Circuit; 2003, U.S. Tax Court. *Education:* The Ohio State University (B.A., 1999); Capital

(This Listing Continued)

KEATING MUETHING & KLEKAMP PLL, Cincinnati—Continued

University Law School (J.D., 2000); Capital University (LL.M., 2003). ***PRACTICE AREAS:*** Antitrust; Appellate Practice; Class Actions; Securities; Commercial Law; Intellectual Property Litigation. ***Email:*** JSefton@kmklaw.com

OF COUNSEL

WILLIAM J. KEATING, born Cincinnati, Ohio, March 30, 1927; admitted to bar, 1950, Ohio; 1952, U.S. Court of Appeals, Sixth Circuit and U.S. District Court, Southern District of Ohio; 1971, U.S. Supreme Court. *Education:* University of Cincinnati (B.B.A., 1950); University of Cincinnati College of Law (J.D., 1950).

GEHL P. BABINEC, born Indianapolis, Indiana, September 27, 1942; admitted to bar, 1967, Ohio; 1969, U.S. District Court, Southern District of Ohio. *Education:* Xavier University (B.S.B.A., 1964); University of Cincinnati College of Law (J.D., 1967). ***PRACTICE AREAS:*** Mergers and Acquisitions Finance; Finance; Commercial Loan Documentation; Bankruptcy Reorganizations; Creditors. ***Email:*** GBabinec@KMKlaw.com

THOMAS A. HAYES, born Milwaukee, Wisconsin, January 5, 1943; admitted to bar, 1968, Ohio; 1973, U.S. Supreme Court. *Education:* Xavier University (B.S., 1965); University of Michigan Law School (J.D., 1968). ***PRACTICE AREAS:*** Corporate Planning; Business Divestitures; Executive Compensation. ***Email:*** THayes@KMKlaw.com

CHARLES H. GERHARDT, III, born Cincinnati, Ohio, October 31, 1959; admitted to bar, 1986, Ohio. *Education:* University of Notre Dame (B.B.A., 1982); St. Louis University School of Law (J.D., 1986). ***Email:*** cgerhardt@kmkconsulting.com

R. PATRICK DeWINE, born Hamilton, Ohio, February 22, 1968; admitted to bar, 1995, Ohio; 1996, U.S. District Court, Southern District of Ohio and U.S. Court of Appeals, Sixth Circuit. *Education:* Miami University (B.A., B.S., 1990); University of Michigan Law School (J.D., 1994). ***PRACTICE AREAS:*** Appellate Practice; Professional Liability; Commercial Securities Litigation. ***Email:*** RDewine@KMKlaw.com

REPRESENTATIVE CLIENTS: A.K. Steel Corp.; Al Neyer, Inc.; American Financial Group; Ameritek Custom Homes; Argosy Casino & Hotel; The Bank of Kentucky, Inc.; Belcan Corporation.; BP America Inc.; Charter One Bank, N.A.; Chiquita Brands International, Inc.; Cincinnati Equitable Insurance Company.; The Cincinnati Equity Fund Ltd.; Cincinnati New Markets Fund, LLC; The Cincinnati Reds; Cincom Systems, Inc.; Cintas Corporation; Comair, Inc.; The Community Builders; Corporex Companies, Inc.; Delphi Corporation; Delta AirElite Business Jets, Inc.; Duke Realty Limited Partnership; Fenton Rigging and Contracting, Inc.; Ferno Washington, Inc.; Fifth Third Bank; The Fischer Group; F&M Mafco, Inc.; Force Control Industries, Inc.; The Frederic H. Mayerson Group; General Tool Company; George E. Fern Co.; Goettsch International, Inc.; Gorilla Glue Company; Great American Insurance Co.; Hal Homes, Inc.; Hemagen Diagnostics; Hills Communities; The Hillstreet Fund, LP; Holiday Homes, Inc.; Infinity Property & Casualty Corporation; Jaguar of Cincinnati, Inc.; Joseph Automotive Group; Kendle International; Land Rover of Cincinnati, Inc.; Leisure Systems, Inc.; Lone Star Industries, Inc.; LSI Industries Inc.; The Mayerson Co.; Mercedes Benz of Cincinnati, LLC; Meridian Bioscience, Inc.; Meritage Hospitality Group, Inc.; The Midland Co.; Modern Ice Equipment and Supply Co.; Modern Office Methods; Multi-Color Corporation; National City Bank; National City Corporation; New Energy Corp.; Ohio Fresh Eggs; Planet Products Company; Rumpke Consolidated Companies, Inc.; Schumacher-Dugan Construction Co.; Seneca Insurance Company; Stewart Filmscreen Corporation; Sundance Property Management, Inc.; Superior Label Systems, Inc.; Tab Products Co., LLC; Techsolve, Inc.; Towne Properties; Trans-Ash Inc.; United Dairy Farmers Inc.; Uptown Consortium, Inc.; Wallingford Coffee Mills, Inc.; Walnut Investment Partners, L.P.; Walnut Private Equity Fund, L.P.; Williamsburg Properties, Inc.; Worldwide Equipment, Inc.
APPROVED ATTORNEYS FOR: Chicago Title Insurance Co.; Commonwealth Land Title Insurance Co.; First American Title Co.; Guarantee Title and Trust Co.; Midland Title; Ohio Bar Title Insurance Co.; Old Republic National Title Insurance Company; Ticor Title Insurance Co.

KILLWORTH, GOTTMAN, HAGAN & SCHAEFF, L.L.P.

CINCINNATI, OHIO

(See Dinsmore & Shohl LLP)

ROBERT A. KLINGLER CO., L.P.A.

525 VINE STREET, SUITE 2320
CINCINNATI, OHIO 45202-3124
Telephone: 513-665-9500
Fax: 513-621-3240
Email: rak@klinglerlaw.com
URL: http://www.klinglerlaw.com

Commercial and Business Litigation, Labor and Employment, Personal Injury, Medical Malpractice, Sexual Harassment.

ROBERT A. KLINGLER, born Indianapolis, Indiana, July 20, 1952; admitted to bar, 1985, Ohio; 1986, U.S. District Court, Southern District of Ohio; 1988, U.S. Court of Appeals, 6th Circuit; 1998, Kentucky. *Education:* Phillips University, Marburg, Germany; Manchester College (B.A., with distinction, 1976); University of Cincinnati (J.D., 1985). Order of the Coif. Lead Articles Editor, University of Cincinnati Law Review, 1984-1985. *Member:* Cincinnati, Ohio State and American (Member, Litigation Section) Bar Associations. (Board Certified Civil Trial Advocacy Specialist by the National Board of Trial Advocacy). ***PRACTICE AREAS:*** Commercial and Business Litigation; Labor and Employment; Personal Injury; Medical Malpractice; Sexual Harassment. ***Email:*** rak@klinglerlaw.com

---

ROBERT M. LAMB, born Cincinnati, Ohio, May 29, 1952; admitted to bar, 1982, Michigan; 1989, Ohio. *Education:* University of Cincinnati (B.A., magna cum laude, 1975); University of Michigan (J.D., cum laude, 1982); Judge Advocate General's School (LL.M., 1988). *Member:* Cincinnati, Clermont County, Ohio State (Member, Labor-Employment Law Section) and American (Member, Labor and Employment Law Section) Bar Associations; State Bar of Michigan (Member, Labor and Employment Law Section). [Lieutenant Colonel, U.S. Army Reserve, Retired]

SUSAN MARIE SAUTER, born Ann Arbor, Michigan, March 29, 1966; admitted to bar, 1991, Ohio; 1993, U.S. District Court, Southern District of Ohio and U.S. Court of Appeals, Sixth Circuit. *Education:* The Ohio State University (B.A., summa cum laude, 1988); University of Cincinnati College of Law (J.D., 1991). Phi Beta Kappa. Order of the Coif. Lecturer, University of Cincinnati, 1993-1995. Authorship: Tobias & Sauter, Job Rights and Survival Strategies: A Handbook for Terminated Employees (National Employee Rights Institute 1997). Contributing Author/Editor, Litigating Wrongful Discharge Cases (West). Contributing Author, Ohio Jurisprudence 3d (West): Contracts, Constitutional Law, Public Utilities. The 1989 Whistleblower Protection Act: The Possibility of Federal Enforcement of the Public Policy Exception to Employment At Will, 59 U. Cin. L.Rev. 513-57. *Member:* Ohio State Bar Association. ***REPORTED CASES:*** Atkinson v. Internatl Technegroup, Inc., 106 Ohio App.3d 349, 666 NE2d 257. ***PRACTICE AREAS:*** Employment Litigation; Commercial Litigation. ***Email:*** sms@klinglerlaw.com

---

RONALD J. KOCH

CINCINNATI, OHIO

(See Columbus)

Litigation, Copyrights, Trademarks, Patents, Intellectual Property, Contracts, Forensic Science, Engineering, Juvenile, Criminal, Patent Law.

KOHNEN & PATTON LLP

Established in 1974

PNC CENTER, SUITE 800
201 EAST FIFTH STREET
CINCINNATI, OHIO 45202
Telephone: 513-381-0656
FAX: 513-381-5823
Email: info@kohnenpatton.com
URL: http://www.kohnenpatton.com

Ft. Mitchell, Kentucky Office: 211 Grandview Drive, Suite 236 41017. Telephone: 859-341-0009. Facsimile: 859-341-0034.

Litigation, Insurance Law, Probate, Securities, Real Estate Law, Banking Law, Technology, Medical Malpractice Defense, Mediation, Corporate Law, Business Law, Estate Planning.

MEMBERS OF FIRM

RALPH B. KOHNEN (Retired)

W. ANDREW PATTON, born Cincinnati, Ohio, December 18, 1942; admitted to bar, 1968, Ohio; 1970, U.S. District Court, Southern District of Ohio; 1972, U.S. Court of Appeals, Sixth Circuit; 1976, U.S. Supreme Court; 1992, U.S. District Court, Northern District of Texas. *Education:* Miami University (A.B., 1965); University of Cincinnati (J.D., 1968). ***PRACTICE AREAS:*** Litigation; Business Law; Corporate Law; Insurance Law; Medical Malpractice Defense; Mediation. ***Email:*** apatton@kohnenpatton.com

MARK J. ZUMMO, born Dayton, Ohio, August 17, 1955; admitted to bar, 1980, Ohio; 1981, U.S. District Court, Southern District of Ohio. *Education:* University of Virginia (B.A., with high distinction, 1977); University of Cincinnati (J.D., 1980). Phi Beta Kappa. ***PRACTICE AREAS:*** Business Law; Corporate Law; Securities; Mergers and Acquisitions; Real Estate Law. ***Email:*** mzummo@kohnenpatton.com

JOSEPH BEECH, III, born Cincinnati, Ohio, August 16, 1945; admitted to bar, 1973, Ohio. *Education:* Amherst College (B.A., 1967); Stanford University; University of Cincinnati (J.D., 1973). ***PRACTICE AREAS:*** Corporate Law; Mergers and Acquisitions; Banking Law. ***Email:*** jbeech@kohnenpatton.com

JOSEPH L. DILTS, born Zanesville, Ohio, January 8, 1956; admitted to bar, 1981, Ohio; 1982, U.S. District Court, Southern District of Ohio; 1983, Florida; 1985, U.S. Court of Appeals, Sixth Circuit. *Education:* University of Cincinnati (B.A., summa cum laude, with honors, 1978; J.D., 1981). ***PRACTICE AREAS:*** Trial Practice; Insurance Law. ***Email:*** jdilts@kohnenpatton.com

JOHN J. KELLEY, JR., born Cleveland, Ohio, June 17, 1936; admitted to bar, 1960, Ohio; 1963, U.S. District Court, Northern District of Ohio; 1968, U.S. Court of Appeals, Sixth Circuit. *Education:* Ohio University (B.S.C., cum laude, 1958); Case Western Reserve University (LL.B., 1960). ***PRACTICE AREAS:*** Corporate Law; Real Estate Development; Business Law. ***Email:*** jkelley@kohnenpatton.com

KEITH D. MEYER, born Cincinnati, Ohio, February 14, 1955; admitted to bar, 1980, Ohio; 1981, Illinois; 1985, U.S. Tax Court; 1986, U.S. District Court, Northern District of Illinois; 1990, U.S. District Court, Southern District of Ohio. *Education:* University of Cincinnati (B.B.A., magna cum laude, 1977; J.D., 1980). Certified Public Accountant, Illinois, 1982. ***PRACTICE AREAS:*** Estate Planning; Business Law; Mediation. ***Email:*** kmeyer@kohnenpatton.com

K. ROGER SCHOENI, born Alliance, Ohio, July 17, 1955; admitted to bar, 1982, Minnesota, U.S. District Court, District of Minnesota and U.S. Court of Appeals, Eighth Circuit; 1983, Ohio; 1985, U.S. District Court, Southern District of Ohio and U.S. Court of Appeals, Sixth Circuit; 1989, Kentucky and U.S. District Court, Eastern District of Kentucky. *Education:* Heidelberg College; Bowling Green State University (B.S., 1977); University of Minnesota (J.D., 1982). ***PRACTICE AREAS:*** Trial Practice; Products Liability Law; Insurance Law. ***Email:*** rschoeni@kohnenpatton.com

RICHARD M. HAINES, born Cincinnati, Ohio, February 9, 1950; admitted to bar, 1976, Ohio and U.S. District Court, Southern District of Ohio; 1988, Kentucky. *Education:* Denison University (B.A., cum laude, 1972); University of Cincinnati (J.D., 1976). Mem-

(This Listing Continued)

ber, Board of Trustees Southern Ohio Regional Transit Authority, 1991. ***PRACTICE AREAS:*** Banking Law; Creditors Rights Law; Corporate Law; Business Law. ***Email:*** rhaines@kohnenpatton.com

JOHN L. CAMPBELL, born Minneapolis, Minnesota, February 6, 1948; admitted to bar, 1977, Ohio; 1978, U.S. District Court, Southern District of Ohio; 1987, U.S. Court of Appeals, Sixth Circuit; 1990, New Zealand. *Education:* Colorado College (B.A., 1970); University of Cincinnati (J.D., 1977). ***PRACTICE AREAS:*** Estate and Gift Taxation; Estate Planning; Estate Administration; International Estate Planning; International Trust. ***Email:*** jcampbell@kohnenpatton.com

JEFFREY C. SHIPP, born Louisville, Kentucky, January 20, 1959; admitted to bar, 1985, Kentucky and U.S. District Court, Eastern District of Kentucky; 1987, Ohio and U.S. District Court, Southern District of Ohio. *Education:* Northern Kentucky University (B.A., 1982); Salmon P. Chase College of Law (J.D., 1985). ***PRACTICE AREAS:*** Insurance Law; Personal Injury; Municipal Law; Workers' Compensation; Mediation. ***Email:*** jshipp@kohnenpatton.com

ANTHONY J. CARUSO, born Cincinnati, Ohio, March 16, 1962; admitted to bar, 1988, Ohio; U.S. District Court, Southern District of Ohio; 1992, U.S. Court of Appeals, Sixth Circuit; 1994, Kentucky; U.S. District Court, Eastern District of Kentucky. *Education:* University of Cincinnati (B.A., 1984); Ohio State University (J.D., 1988). ***PRACTICE AREAS:*** Medical Malpractice Defense; Employment Law; Litigation; Trial Practice. ***Email:*** tcaruso@kohnenpatton.com

ANN RULEY COMBS, born Cincinnati, Ohio, August 24, 1952; admitted to bar, 1977, Ohio and U.S. District Court, Southern District of Ohio; U.S. Court of Appeals, Sixth Circuit. *Education:* University of Michigan (B.S.N., 1974); Southern Methodist University (J.D., 1977). Sigma Theta Tau. Contract Mediator, Center for Resolution of Disputes. Registered Nurse, USA, 1974. Adjunct Professor, College of Mount St. Joseph, 1999—. Formerly with: Porter, Wright, Morris & Arthur; Roetzel & Andress. *Member:* Cincinnati (Member, Professionalism Committee, 2000—), Ohio State and American Bar Associations. ***PRACTICE AREAS:*** Medical Malpractice Defense; Health Care Law; Insurance Law; Mediation. ***Email:*** acombs@kohnenpatton.com

ANDREW R. LEEPER, born Wooster, Ohio, March 7, 1956; admitted to bar, 1983, New York; 1985, Ohio. *Education:* The College of Wooster (B.A., 1978); The Ohio State University (J.D., with honors, 1982). Phi Beta Kappa; Order of the Coif. ***PRACTICE AREAS:*** Securities; Banking Law; Mergers and Acquisitions. ***Email:*** aleeper@kohnenpatton.com

TERRY E. MOORE, born Dayton, Ohio, November 8, 1960; admitted to bar, 1986, Ohio; 1987, U.S. District Court, Southern District of Ohio. *Education:* University of Cincinnati (B.B.A., cum laude, 1983; J.D., 1986). ***PRACTICE AREAS:*** Business Law; Health Care; Franchise Law; Real Estate; Corporate Law. ***Email:*** tmoore@kohnenpatton.com

ANDREW J. HOGAN, born Burlington, Vermont, February 26, 1962; admitted to bar, 1987, Ohio; U.S. District Court, Southern District of Ohio. *Education:* Bucknell University (B.A., 1984); Case Western Reserve University (J.D., 1987). ***PRACTICE AREAS:*** Contract Law; Corporate Law; Real Estate Law; Business Law. ***Email:*** ahogan@kohnenpatton.com

KAREN A. CARROLL, born Jacksonville, North Carolina, June 29, 1954; admitted to bar, 1987, Ohio; 1988, U.S. District Court, Southern District of Ohio; 1994, Kentucky; U.S. Court of Appeals, Sixth Circuit. *Education:* College of Mount St. Joseph-on the Ohio (B.S.N., 1979); University of Cincinnati (J.D., 1987). Order of the Coif. Recipient, Trial Advocacy Award. Member, Cincinnati Law Review. Formerly with: Roetzel & Andress; Porter, Wright, Morris & Arthur. Member, Board of Trustees, University of Cincinnati Law Alumni. *Member:* Cincinnati and Kentucky Bar Associations; Joint Committee of Bar & Academy (Secretary, 1994-1996). ***PRACTICE AREAS:*** Medical Malpractice Defense. ***Email:*** kcarroll@kohnenpatton.com

COLLEEN M. BLANDFORD, born Cincinnati, Ohio, April 15, 1969; admitted to bar, 1993, Ohio; 1994; U.S. District Court, Southern District of Ohio. *Education:* University of Cincinnati (B.A., 1990; J.D., 1993). ***PRACTICE AREAS:*** Banking Law; Insurance Law; Trial Practice. ***Email:*** cblandford@kohnenpatton.com

PEGGY MURPHY BARKER, born Covington, Kentucky, November 11, 1966; admitted to bar, 1993, Kentucky; 1995, Ohio; U.S. District Court, Eastern and Western Districts of Kentucky; 2000, U.S. District Court, Southern District of Ohio. *Education:* Eastern Kentucky University (B.A., 1988); Salmon P. Chase College of Law (J.D., 1993). Delta Theta Phi. Premises Liability Editor, The Advocate, 1995—. Author: "Recreational Use Statutes: No Fun for the Injured," The Advocate, Journal of the Kentucky Academy of Trial Attorneys, Volume 22, No. 5, September/October, 1995, pages 10-11, 26; "Keep a Step Up on Snow and Ice or Don't Slip and Fall at the Courthouse Doors," The Advocate Journal of the Kentucky Academy of Trial Attorneys, Volume 22, No. 1, January/February 1997, pages 4-10, 12-13. Co-Author: "Independent Medical Examinations-What Every Attorney Should Know About Protecting His or Her Client's Rights," The Advocate Journal of the Kentucky Academy of Trial Attorneys, Volume 24, No. 2, March/April 1997, pages 12-13, 15-16, 21-26. Member, Barrister and Treasurer, 1999—, Salmon P. Chase American Inn of Court. *Member:* Cincinnati, Kentucky and Northern Kentucky Bar Associations; Kentucky Academy of Trial Attorneys,. ***PRACTICE AREAS:*** Corporate Law; Employment Law; Business Litigation; Products Liability; Insurance. ***Email:*** pbarker@kohnenpatton.com

KIMBERLY A. MAYER, born Cincinnati, Ohio, May 15, 1966; admitted to bar, 1996, Ohio; 1997, Kentucky and U.S. District Court, Southern District of Ohio; 1998, Indiana. *Education:* Miami University (B.A., 1988); Xavier College (M.Ed., 1990); Salmon P. Chase College of Law (J.D., cum laude, 1996). ***PRACTICE AREAS:*** Litigation; Banking Law. ***Email:*** kmayer@konenpatton.com

MICHAEL J. STEGMAN, born Fort Thomas, Kentucky, April 17, 1958; admitted to bar, 1983, Ohio; 1984, Kentucky. *Education:* University of Notre Dame (A.B., magna cum laude, 1980); New York University (J.D., 1983). Phi Beta Kappa. ***PRACTICE AREAS:*** Real Estate; Estate Planning; Administration; Business Law. ***Email:*** mstegman@kohnenpatton.com

(This Listing Continued)

ASSOCIATES

MALINDA L. LANGSTON, born Lexington, Kentucky, May 10, 1971; admitted to bar, 1997, Ohio; 1999, Kentucky. *Education:* Georgia Southern University (B.S., 1993); University of Dayton (J.D., 1997). *Member:* Cincinnati, Ohio State, Kentucky and Northern Kentucky Bar Associations. ***PRACTICE AREAS:*** Litigation. ***Email:*** mlangston@kohnenpatton.com

KIMBERLY KYLE ZAMARY, born Lexington, Kentucky, June 27, 1975; admitted to bar, 2000, Ohio; 2001, Kentucky. *Education:* The Ohio State University (B.A., cum laude, with honors, Liberal Arts, 1997); University of Cincinnati (J.D., cum laude, 2000). Student Articles Editor, University of Cincinnati Law Review, 1999-2000. Author: "License, Registration and Your Constitutional Rights, Please: Merrett v. Moore," University of Cincinnati Law Review, 68-Z. *Member:* Cincinnati and Ohio State Bar Associations. ***LANGUAGES:*** Spanish. ***PRACTICE AREAS:*** Litigation. ***Email:*** kzamary@kohnenpaatton.com

H. DREWRY GORES, born Cincinnati, Ohio, April 6, 1954; admitted to bar, 2001, Ohio. *Education:* Cornell University (B.A., 1977); Salmon P. Chase College of Law (J.D., 2001). ***PRACTICE AREAS:*** Estate Planning; Business Law. ***Email:*** dgores@kohnenpatton.com

JEFFREY M. HINES, born Parma, Ohio, June 5, 1970; admitted to bar, 1999, Ohio. *Education:* Ohio University (B.A., 1992); Northern Kentucky University (J.D., 1998). Editor, Northern Kentucky Law Review. Formerly with Roetzel & Andress. *Member:* Cincinnati, Ohio State and American Bar Associations. ***PRACTICE AREAS:*** Medical Malpractice Defense; Litigation. ***Email:*** jhines@kohnenpatton.com

DAVID GRAHAM KERN, born Cincinnati, Ohio, August 28, 1973; admitted to bar, 2000, Ohio; 2001, U.S. District Court, Southern District of Ohio. *Education:* University of South (B.A., 1996); The Ohio State University (J.D., 2000). Assistant Attorney General, Ohio, 2000-2002. ***PRACTICE AREAS:*** Litigation. ***Email:*** dkern@kohnenpatton.com

LOUIS C. SCHNEIDER, born Mariemont, Ohio, October 1, 1976; admitted to bar, 2003, Ohio. *Education:* Miami University (B.S., Business-Economics, B.A., Spanish, 1998); University of Cincinnati (J.D., 2003). Member, Executive Board, University of Cincinnati College of Law Moot Court, 2002-2003. Recipient: Miami University Philip R. Shrine Scholarship for Academic Achievement; Corbin Prize, University of Cincinnati College of Law. *Member:* Cincinnati Bar Association (Member, Young Lawyers' Community Service; Co-Chair). ***PRACTICE AREAS:*** Litigation; Estate Planning. ***Email:*** lschneider@kohnenpatton.com

DAVID JOSEPH BROSS, born Cincinnati, Ohio, August 22, 1978; admitted to bar, 2004, Ohio. *Education:* University of Kentucky (Bachelor of Business Administration, 2001); Salmon P. Chase College of Law (J.D., 2004). Author: "The Use of Pattern-and-Practice by Individuals in Non-Class Claims," 28 Nova Law Review 795 (2004). ***PRACTICE AREAS:*** Insurance Defense; Employment Law; Personal Injury. ***Email:*** dbross@kohnenpatton.com

LESLIE E. GHIZ, born Norfolk, Virginia, June 7, 1969; admitted to bar, 1994, Ohio; 1995, West Virginia. *Education:* West Virginia University (B.A., 1991); Capital University (J.D., 1994). ***PRACTICE AREAS:*** Labor and Employment; Municipal Law. ***Email:*** lghiz@kohnenpatton.com

OF COUNSEL

JOHN P. TAFARO, born East Orange, New Jersey, March 17, 1955; admitted to bar, 1982, Kentucky; 1983, Ohio. *Education:* Wittenberg university (B.A., 1976); Salmon P. Chase College of Law (J.D., 1982). ***PRACTICE AREAS:*** Commercial; Real Estate; Litigation. ***Email:*** jtafaro@kohnenpatton.com

REPRESENTATIVE CLIENTS: Allianz Life Insurance Company of North America; Brown & Williamson Tobacco Co.; Brown Publishing Company; Burlington Insurance Group; Cannon Express Corp.; Catholic Healthcare Partners; The Christ Hospital; The Cincinnati Insurance Companies; City of Williamstown, Kentucky; Colorado Western Insurance Co.; CRST, Inc.; Deep South Insurance; DPI Electronic Imaging, Inc.; Drake Center, Inc.; Faison Associates, Inc.; FRCH Design Worldwide; Geoff Coy Management Group dba Bernard Haldane Associates; Gilkey Window Co., Inc.; Grant County Deposit Bank; Guilford Specialty Group; Huntington National Bank; Intrieve Incorporated; The Jewish Hospital; J.B. Hunt Transport, Inc.; Lykins Oil, Inc.; Maxim Crane Works; A/K/A/ Carlisle Equipment Group; Carlisle Construction Co.; Mercy Hospital (Anderson, Clermont, Fairfield, Western Hills and Mt. Airy); Minnesota Life; KONE, Inc.; National Bank & Trust Company; North East Insurance Company; The Provident Bank; Restaurant Management, Inc.; Reynolds Dewitt & Co.; St. Louis Cardinals, L.P.; St. Paul Fire & Marine Insurance Co.; Sena Weller Rohs Williams, Inc.; Skyline Chili, Inc.; Structural Analysis Engineering Corp.; Thoma & Sutton Eye-Care Professionals, LLC; Tradewinds Beverage Company; Tyson Foods, Inc.; Union Institute & University; The Visiting Nurse Association; Woodman Accident & Life Company.

THE LAWRENCE FIRM, L.P.A.

Established in 1971

8804 MONTGOMERY ROAD, SUITE 700
CINCINNATI, OHIO 45236
Telephone: 513-651-4130
Fax: 513-651-0525
Email: lawrence@lawrencefirm.com
URL: http://www.lawrencefirm.com

Northern Kentucky Office: The Lawrence Firm, PSC, 606 Philadelphia Street, Covington, Kentucky, 41011. Telephone: 859-578-9130. Facsimile: 859-578-1032.

Civil Litigation, Personal Injury, Medical Malpractice, Trucking Accidents, Automobile Accidents, Head and Spinal Injuries, Drug and Medical Device Litigation. Plaintiffs and Defense.

FIRM PROFILE: The Lawrence Firm, L.P.A., is a well established firm located in Cincinnati, Ohio and Northern Kentucky. We concentrate our practice on wrongful death, personal injury, and severe injuries from medical malpractice. The firm is owned by Richard D. Lawrence, employs 7 lawyers, RNs and has quick access to medical consultants.

(This Listing Continued)

THE LAWRENCE FIRM, L.P.A., Cincinnati—Continued

RICHARD D. LAWRENCE, born Jefferson City, Missouri, September 20, 1944; admitted to bar, 1971, Ohio and U.S. District Court, Southern District of Ohio; 1989, Kentucky. *Education:* University of Cincinnati (B.A., 1967); Salmon P. Chase College of Law (J.D., with honors, 1971). Phi Alpha Delta. Recipient: Kentucky Trial Lawyer of the Year Award, 1996; Most Distinguished Lawyer Award, Northern Kentucky Bar Association, 1996; Listed in: Best Lawyers in America; Who's Who in American Law. Contributing Author: "Wrongful Death and Survival Actions," Chapter 26 of "Litigating Tort Cases," The Association of Trial Lawyers of America; "Birth Injuries," Chapter 21 of "Operative Obstetrics"; "Missing the Beat, Failure to Diagnose Heart Attack Cases," Trial Magazine. *Member:* Kentucky Bar Association; The Association of Trial Lawyers of America (Chair: Professional Negligence Section, 1995-1996; Birth Trauma Litigation Section, 1997-1998; Trustee: ATLA; PAC; Co-Chair, Stalwart Committee, International Section, 1998-1999); Inner Circle of Advocates; International Society of Barristers; Salmon P. Chase American Inns of Court (Designated Master and Past President); Kentucky Academy of Trial Attorneys (Present Board Member, 1995—; Sixth District Vice President, 1997-1998; Treasurer, 1998-1999); Ohio Academy of Trial Lawyers (Board Member, 1995-1998). ***PRACTICE AREAS:*** Medical Malpractice; Personal Injury; Wrongful Death.

THOMAS C. KORBEE, born Cincinnati, Ohio, March 21, 1948; admitted to bar, 1977, Ohio; 1978, U.S. District Court, Southern District of Ohio; 1980, U.S. Court of Appeals, 6th Circuit; 1984, U.S. District Court, Eastern District of Kentucky; 1994, Kentucky; 1999, U.S. Supreme Court. *Education:* Xavier University (B.S., cum laude, 1970); University of Cincinnati (J.D., 1977). Alpha Sigma Nu. *Member:* Cincinnati (Chair, Labor and Employment Law Section, 1991-1992), Ohio State and Kentucky Bar Associations; Hamilton County Trial Lawyers Association; The Association of Trial Lawyers of America (Member, Sections on: Professional Negligence; Product Liability; Motor Vehicle Collision); Ohio Academy of Trial Lawyers; Kentucky Academy of Trial Lawyers. ***PRACTICE AREAS:*** Medical Malpractice; Negligence Law; Labor Law; Employment Law. **Email:** tckorbee@lawrencefirm.com

JENNIFER L. LAWRENCE, born Cincinnati, Ohio, May 30, 1971; admitted to bar, 1996, Ohio; 1997, Kentucky; U.S. District Court, Southern District of Ohio. *Education:* Ohio State University (B.A., 1993); Salmon P. Chase College of Law (J.D., 1996). Co-Author, "Medical Malpractice: Understanding the Evolution, Rebuking the Revolution," Northern Kentucky Law Review. Adjunct Professor, Advocacy Skills, Salmon P. Chase College of Law. Member: Birth Trauma Litigation Board. Past Member, Alumni Board, Salmon P. Chase College of Law. *Member:* Cincinnati and Northern Kentucky Bar Associations; Kentucky Academy of Trial Lawyers (Board Member); Ohio Academy of Trial Lawyers; The Association of Trial Lawyers of America (Member, Professional Negligence and Birth Trauma Litigation Group). ***PRACTICE AREAS:*** Medical Malpractice; Nursing Home Negligence; Personal Injury. **Email:** jllawrence@lawrencefirm.com

JILL GUSTAFSON, born Youngstown, Ohio, August 29, 1958; admitted to bar, 1990, Ohio; 2004, Kentucky and U.S. District Court, Southern District of Ohio. *Education:* Ohio State University (B.S.N., 1980); University of Akron (J.D., 1990). Author: "Missing the Beat: Failure to Diagnose Heart Attack," Case Trial Sept. 96. *Member:* Cincinnati and Ohio State Bar Associations; The Association of Trial Lawyers of America (Member, Professional Negligence and Birth Trauma Litigation Group); Ohio Academy of Trial Lawyers (Trustee); Kentucky Bar Association; Kentucky Academy of Trial Attorneys. ***PRACTICE AREAS:*** Plaintiffs Personal Injury; Plaintiffs Medical Malpractice. **Email:** jgustafson@lawrencefirm.com

PATRICK J. BEIRNE, born Cincinnati, Ohio, February 3, 1971; admitted to bar, 1996, Ohio; 1997, U.S. District Court, Southern District of Ohio; 2004, Kentucky. *Education:* Miami University (B.A., 1993); Northern Kentucky University (J.D., 1996). Author, "The Supreme Court Places the Endangered Species Act in 'Harm's' Way," Northern Kentucky Law Review. Instructor, Legal Writing, Salmon P. Chase College of Law, 1998-1999. Court Sponsored Arbitrator, Hamilton County. *Member:* Ohio State, Cincinnati and Kentucky Bar Associations; Kentucky Academy of Trial Lawyers; The Association of Trial Lawyers of America; American Trial Attorneys. ***PRACTICE AREAS:*** Medical Negligence (80%); Products Liability. **Email:** pjbeirne@lawrencefirm.com

ROBERT DONNELLY LEWIS JR., born Cincinnati, Ohio, June 20, 1967; admitted to bar, 1997, Ohio; 1998, U.S. District Court, Southern District of Ohio; 2004, Kentucky. *Education:* Miami University (B.A., 1989); University of Cincinnati (J.D., 1997). Member and Editor, University of Cincinnati Law Review, 1995-1997. Clerk, Hon. William O. Bertelsman, Chief Judge, Eastern District of Kentucky. Speaker: Cincinnati Bar Association New Lawyers Seminar on Litigation; Kentucky Academy of Trial Attorneys on Medical Device and Product Liability. Member, The University of Cincinnati, College of Law Alumni Association Board of Trustees. *Member:* Ohio State, Kentucky, Cincinnati and Northern Kentucky Bar Associations; Association of Trial Lawyers of America; Kentucky Academy of Trial Attorneys. [Lt., U.S. Navy, 1989-1993]. ***PRACTICE AREAS:*** Commercial Litigation; Personal Injury; Medical Malpractice; Products Liability. **Email:** rdlewis@lawrencefirm.com

ANNE L. GILDAY, born Cincinnati, Ohio, June 16, 1978; admitted to bar, 2003, Ohio; 2004, Kentucky. *Education:* College of Charleston (B.A., 2000); Salmon P. Chase College of Law (J.D., 2003). *Member:* Cincinnati, Ohio State, Kentucky and Northern Kentucky Bar Associations; Kentucky Academy of Trial Attorneys; Ohio Academy of Trial Attorneys; The Association of Trial Lawyers of America. ***PRACTICE AREAS:*** Medical Malpractice; Personal Injury; Products Liability. **Email:** algilday@lawrencefirm.com

---

DAVID LAZARUS

Established in 1990

7 WEST SEVENTH STREET, SUITE 1850
CINCINNATI, OHIO 45202
Telephone: 513-241-7460
Fax: 513-684-7777

Real Estate Tax Appeals, Governmental Law, Lobbying and General Civil Practice.

(This Listing Continued)

DAVID LAZARUS, born Cincinnati, Ohio, December 23, 1932; admitted to bar, 1982, Ohio and U.S. District Court, Southern District of Ohio; 1983, Florida, U.S. Court of Appeals, Sixth Circuit and U.S. Tax Court. *Education:* Harvard University (A.B., cum laude, 1954; M.B.A., 1958); University of Cincinnati (J.D., 1982). Member: Commercial Dispute Panel; American Arbitration Association. Member, 1991-1997, and Chairman, 1993-1995, City of Cincinnati, Human Relations Commission. *Member:* Cincinnati, Ohio State and American Bar Associations; The Florida Bar.

RICHARD F. LESSER

36 EAST SEVENTH STREET, SUITE 2020
CINCINNATI, OHIO 45202
Telephone: 513-621-9660
FAX: 513-345-3900
Email: rflesser@fuse.net
URL: http://www.lesserlaw.com

Probate, Elder Law, Real Estate, Bankruptcy, Estate Planning, Trusts, Wills, Guardianship, Personal Injury, Auto Accidents, Collection.

FIRM PROFILE: General Civil and Criminal Trial Practice in all Courts and agencies in Hamilton, Butler, Warren and Clermont Counties.

RICHARD F. LESSER, born Dayton, Ohio, July 29, 1949; admitted to bar, 1982, Ohio and U.S. District Court, Southern District of Ohio; 1987, U.S. Supreme Court. *Education:* University of Cincinnati (B.S., magna cum laude, 1978); Salmon P. Chase College of Law, Northern Kentucky University (J.D., 1982). *Member:* Cincinnati, Ohio State and American Bar Associations. ***PRACTICE AREAS:*** Probate; Elder Law; Real Estate; Bankruptcy.

LINDHORST & DREIDAME CO., L.P.A.

Established in 1949

312 WALNUT STREET, SUITE 2300
CINCINNATI, OHIO 45202-4091
Telephone: 513-421-6630
Telecopier: 513-421-0212
Email: info@lindhorstlaw.com
URL: http://www.lindhorstlaw.com

General Civil Practice, including Insurance, Tort, Medical Legal, Admiralty, Corporate, Commercial, Real Estate, Labor, Taxation, Probate and Estate Planning. General Trial Practice in all State and Federal Courts.

FIRM PROFILE: Lindhorst & Dreidame provides the full range of business and personal legal services at competitive rates. By attracting knowledgeable attorneys with expertise and experience in virtually every specific area of law, we make it our practice to pair each client with the attorney whose particular qualifications best suit that client's needs. Our clients receive the personal attention they deserve, without paying for more than they need. This approach has enabled Lindhorst & Dreidame to successfully serve the law and our clients for over sixty years.

AMBROSE H. LINDHORST (1913-1997)
ROBERT F. DREIDAME (1914-1978)
WILLIAM J. WALSH (1919-1996)
LEO J. BRESLIN (1928-2000)

MEMBERS OF FIRM

JAMES L. O'CONNELL, born Cincinnati, Ohio, July 6, 1931; admitted to bar, 1958, Ohio. *Education:* Xavier University (A.B., 1953); University of Cincinnati (J.D., 1958). Order of the Coif. Master of the Bench, Potter Stewart Inn of Court. *Member:* Cincinnati, Ohio State and Federal Bar Associations; National Association of Railroad Trial Counsel (Vice President, 1986-1988); Ohio Association of Civil Trial Attorneys. Fellow, American College of Trial Lawyers; Advocate, American Board of Trial Advocates. ***PRACTICE AREAS:*** General Civil Litigation; Railroad Law; Negligence Law; Insurance Law. **Email:** joconnell@lindhorstlaw.com

CHARLES J. KELLY, born Cincinnati, Ohio, December 11, 1940; admitted to bar, 1965, Ohio; 1973, U.S. Tax Court. *Education:* Xavier University (B.S., 1962); University of Cincinnati (J.D., 1965). Phi Delta Phi. *Member:* Cincinnati and Ohio State Bar Associations. ***PRACTICE AREAS:*** Corporate Law; Taxation; Estate Planning; Real Estate. **Email:** ckelly@lindhorstlaw.com

JOHN A. GOLDBERG, born Cincinnati, Ohio, July 15, 1941; admitted to bar, 1973, Ohio. *Education:* Loyola University (B.A., 1964); Xavier University (M.Ed., 1965); Salmon P. Chase College of Law of Northern Kentucky University (J.D., 1973). *Member:* Cincinnati and Ohio State Bar Associations. ***PRACTICE AREAS:*** General Civil Litigation; Medical Malpractice Defense; Negligence Law; Insurance Law. **Email:** jgoldberg@lindhorstlaw.com

JAMES M. MOORE, born Cedar Rapids, Iowa, September 19, 1947; admitted to bar, 1972, Ohio. *Education:* Creighton University (A.B., magna cum laude, 1969); University of Cincinnati (J.D., 1972). *Member:* Cincinnati and Ohio State Bar Associations. ***PRACTICE AREAS:*** Civil Litigation; Commercial Law; Negligence Law; Insurance Law; Employment Law. **Email:** jmoore@linhorstlaw.com

JAY R. LANGENBAHN, born Covington, Kentucky, April 25, 1950; admitted to bar, 1976, Ohio; 1983, Kentucky. *Education:* Xavier University; University of Kentucky (B.S., 1972); Salmon P. Chase College of Law (J.D., 1976). *Member:* Cincinnati and Ohio State Bar Associations; Ohio Association of Civil Trial Attorneys. ***PRACTICE AREAS:*** Civil Litigation; Negligence; Business Law; Insurance Law; Domestic Relations Law. **Email:** jlangenbahn@lindhorstlaw.com

(This Listing Continued)

JAMES H. SMITH, III, born Cleveland, Ohio, May 24, 1950; admitted to bar, 1975, Ohio. *Education:* Kenyon College (A.B., 1972); University of Toledo (J.D., cum laude, 1975); New York University (LL.M. in Taxation, 1976). *Member:* Cincinnati and Ohio State Bar Associations. ***PRACTICE AREAS:*** Taxation; Estate Planning; Corporate Law. ***Email:*** jsmith@lindhorstlaw.com

MICHAEL F. LYON, born Chicago, Illinois, March 15, 1947; admitted to bar, 1975, Ohio and U.S. District Court, Southern District of Ohio. *Education:* Xavier University (B.A., 1969); Salmon P. Chase College of Law (J.D., 1975). Author: "Informed Consent," Cincinnati Bar Association Reports, April 1987; "An Ohio Trial Lawyer's Experience in Medical Malpractice," Litigation Journal Commentary Section, American Bar Association, August 13, 1991. Frequent Lecturer in seminars and professional presentations in medical malpractice since 1983. Lecturer: "Chest Pain and the Emergency Room Physician," The Inside Edge Publications, March 1, 1991; National Business Institute Seminars; Seminar for Professional Education Systems; Masters in Trial Demonstrations, American Board of Trial Advocates, 1995—; Medical Malpractice Seminars, Kentucky Medical Physicians; Member, National Business Association of Education Foundation. *Member:* Cincinnati (Chairman, Negligence Law Committee, 1986-1988) and American (Chairman, National Task Force of Tort and Insurance Practice Section relative to proposed National Medical Malpractice Legislation, 1992) Bar Associations; American Board of Trial Advocates (Advocate); Ohio Academy of Trial Lawyers (Chairman, Amicus Curiae, 1982-1988). Fellow, International Society of Barristers (1996). ***PRACTICE AREAS:*** Medical Malpractice. ***Email:*** mlyon@lindhorstlaw.com

THOMAS E. MARTIN, born Cincinnati, Ohio, October 15, 1954; admitted to bar, 1979, Ohio; 1981, U.S. Tax Court. *Education:* Wittenberg University (B.A., cum laude, 1976); University of Cincinnati (J.D., 1979). Member, Order of the Coif. *Member:* Cincinnati and Ohio State Bar Associations. ***PRACTICE AREAS:*** Corporate Law; Estate Planning; Tax Law. ***Email:*** tmartin@lindhorstlaw.com

JAMES F. BROCKMAN, born Houston, Texas, December 9, 1952; admitted to bar, 1981, Ohio. *Education:* University of Cincinnati (B.S., 1975; J.D., 1981); Rutgers University (M.A., 1977). Member, Order of the Barristers. Member, National Moot Court Team. *Member:* Cincinnati and Ohio State Bar Associations; National Association of Railroad Trial Counsel; Ohio Association of Civil Trial Attorneys; American Board of Trial Advocates. ***PRACTICE AREAS:*** Civil Litigation; Negligence Law; Insurance Law. ***Email:*** jbrockman@lindhorstlaw.com

EDWARD S. DORSEY, born Chicago, Illinois, June 29, 1952; admitted to bar, 1987, Ohio. *Education:* Georgetown University (A.B., 1974); Catholic University (J.D., 1977). Attorney, Appellate Court Branch, National Labor Relations Board, Washington, D.C., 1977-1983. Trial Attorney, Contempt Litigation Branch, National Labor Relations Board, Washington, D.C., 1983-1984. *Member:* Cincinnati and Ohio State Bar Associations. ***PRACTICE AREAS:*** Labor Law; Employment Law; Civil Litigation. ***Email:*** edorsey@lindhorstlaw.com

BARRY F. FAGEL, born Cincinnati, Ohio, October 6, 1965; admitted to bar, 1991, Kentucky; 1992, Ohio. *Education:* Xavier University (B.S., 1987); University of Cincinnati (J.D., 1991). *Member:* Cincinnati, Ohio State, Kentucky and Northern Kentucky Bar Associations. ***PRACTICE AREAS:*** Civil Litigation; Insurance; Negligence; Business; Commercial; Construction; Domestic Relations; Workers Compensation; Criminal Law. ***Email:*** bfagel@lindhorstlaw.com

---

CHARLES G. SKIDMORE, born Cincinnati, Ohio, December 3, 1966; admitted to bar, 1992, Ohio; 1993, U.S. Tax Court. *Education:* DePauw University (B.A., 1989); University of Cincinnati (J.D., 1992); Capital University (L.L.M., 1993). *Member:* Cincinnati and Ohio State Bar Associations. ***PRACTICE AREAS:*** Taxation; Corporate Matters; Estate Planning and Administration; Employee Benefits. ***Email:*** cskidmore@lindhorstlaw.com

MARGARET G. KUBICKI, born Regina, Canada, June 13, 1968; admitted to bar, 1993, Ohio. *Education:* University of Ohio (B.S., magna cum laude, 1990); Salmon P. Chase College of Law (J.D., summa cum laude, 1993); University of Florida College of Law (LL.M., Taxation, 1994). Member: Northern Kentucky Law Review, 1991-1993; Florida Tax Review, 1993-1994. *Member:* Cincinnati and Ohio State Bar Associations. ***PRACTICE AREAS:*** Taxation; Estate Planning; Corporate Law. ***Email:*** mkubicki@lindhorstlaw.com

MICHELLE L. CLEMONS, born Toledo, Ohio, January 28, 1970; admitted to bar, 1997, Ohio; 1998, U.S. Tax Court; 2000, U.S. District Court, Southern District of Ohio. *Education:* University of South Florida (B.S., 1992); Capital University (J.D., 1997; LL.M., Taxation, 1997). *Member:* Cincinnati and Ohio State Bar Associations. ***PRACTICE AREAS:*** Taxation; Estate Planning; Corporate Law. ***Email:*** mclemons@lindhorstlaw.com

BRADLEY McPEEK, born Cincinnati, Ohio, February 5, 1973; admitted to bar, 1999, Ohio. *Education:* University of Notre Dame (B.A., 1995); University of Cincinnati (J.D., 1999). *Member:* Cincinnati and Ohio State Bar Associations. ***PRACTICE AREAS:*** Civil Litigation; Corporate Litigation; Commercial Litigation. ***Email:*** bmcpeek@lindhorstlaw.com

DAVID WILLIAMSON, born Cincinnati, Ohio, May 12, 1973; admitted to bar, 1999, Ohio. *Education:* Hanover College (B.A., 1995); Salmon P. Chase College of Law (J.D., 1999). *Member:* Cincinnati and Ohio State Bar Associations. ***PRACTICE AREAS:*** General Civil Litigation; Insurance; Commercial Law; Real Estate Law. ***Email:*** dwilliamson@lindhorstlaw.com

EDWARD ROBERTS, born Cincinnati, Ohio, August 12, 1964; admitted to bar, 1995, Ohio; 1996, Kentucky; 1999, U.S. District Court, Southern District of Ohio. *Education:* University of Cincinnati (B.A., 1988); Salmon P. Chase College of Law (J.D., magna cum laude, 1995). Member, Order of the Curia. ***PRACTICE AREAS:*** Civil Litigation. ***Email:*** eroberts@lindhorstlaw.com

LAURIE A. McCLUSKEY, born Cincinnati, Ohio, October 16, 1973; admitted to bar, 2002, Ohio. *Education:* University of Cincinnati (B.S.N., 1996); Salmon P. Chase College of Law (J.D., 2002). *Member:* Cincinnati, Ohio State and American Bar Associations. ***PRACTICE AREAS:*** Medical Malpractice; Litigation. ***Email:*** lmccluskey@lindhorstlaw.com

CHRISTOPHER H. HURLBURT, born Cincinnati, Ohio, February 27, 1975; admitted to bar, 2000, Ohio; 2001, Kentucky. *Education:* Xavier University (B.A., with honors, 1997); University of Cincinnati (J.D., 2000). Recipient: Thomas J. Walker Founders Scholarship; American Bankruptcy Institute Award of Excellence. Member, American Land Title Association, 2000-2003). *Member:* Ohio State, Kentucky State and Cincinnati Bar Associations; Ohio Land Title Association (Publication Committee Appointee, 2002-2005). ***LANGUAGES:*** English. ***PRACTICE AREAS:*** Commercial Real Estate; Title Insurance; Creditors Rights Litigation. ***Email:*** churlburt@lindhorstlaw.com

JOSHUA J. NOLAN, born Trenton, Michigan, November 7, 1974; admitted to bar, 2004, Ohio. *Education:* University of Toledo (B.A., International Relations, 2001); University of Cincinnati College of Law (J.D., 2004). University of Cincinnati Moot Court; Order of the Barristers. *Member Ohio State Bar Association.* ***PRACTICE AREAS:*** Transportation; Real Estate; Collections; Plaintiffs Personal Injury. ***Email:*** jnolan@lindhorstlaw.com

JOHN D. MOSCHANDREAS, born Washington, D.C., November 28, 1975; admitted to bar, 2003, Ohio and U.S. District Court, Southern District of Ohio. *Education:* Carleton College (B.A., 1997); College of William & Mary (J.D., 2003). *Member:* Cincinnati, Ohio State and American Bar Associations. ***PRACTICE AREAS:*** Civil Litigation; Commercial Litigation; Medical Malpractice. ***Email:*** jmoschandreas@lindhorstlaw.com

REPRESENTATIVE CLIENTS: American Physicians Assurance; Autotemp, Inc.; Baldwin & Lyons; Brotherhood Mutual Insurance Co.; CSX Corp.; Cambridge Integrated Services Group; Canal Insurance Co.; Central Mutual Insurance Co.; Church Mutual Insurance Co.; Cincinnati Insurance Cos.; Conway Clutch Co.; Crum & Forster Group; Fireman's Fund-American Group; Frontier Insurance Group; Gainsco Insurance Co.; Gallenstein Bros.; Hertz Claims Management; Kemper Insurance; Martin Management Group; Medical Protective Co.; Middletown Regional Hospital; Norfolk Corp.; North Side Bank and Trust Company; Ohio Insurance Guaranty Association; Pepsi Americas; Prudential Insurance Co.; St. Paul/Travelers; Sentry Claims Service; UNITRIN; Universal Underwriters Group; Westport Insurance Company.
GENERAL COUNSEL FOR: Alliance Knife, Inc.; Downing Displays, Inc.; Lindsey Motor Express, Inc.; P.L. Marketing, Inc.; Pomeroy IT Solutions, Inc.; Pyramid Controls, Inc.; Ram Universal, Inc.; Sibcy Cline, Inc.; Southside River-Rail Terminal, Inc.; Volunteer of America; Walter P. Dolle Insurance Agency, Inc.

LOPEZ, HODES, RESTAINO, MILMAN & SKIKOS

A LAW CORPORATION

312 WALNUT STREET, SUITE 2090
CINCINNATI, OHIO 45202
Telephone: 513-852-5600
Fax: 513-852-5611
Email: info@lopez-hodes.com
URL: http://www.lopezhodes.com

Newport Beach, California Office: 450 Newport Center Drive, 92660. Telephone: 949-640-8222. Fax: 949-640-8294.
San Francisco, California Office: 625 Market Street, 11th Floor, 94105. Telephone: 415-956-5257. Fax: 415-956-4416.
Shorewood, Minnesota Office: 27995 Boulder Circle, 55331. Telephone: 952-401-4377. Fax: 425-963-3467.
Boston, Massachusetts Office: 95 Commercial Wharf, 02110. Telephone: 617-973-9777. Fax: 617-589-0789.

Mass Tort Litigation, Medical Malpractice, Products Liability, Employment Law, Personal Injury and Elder Law.

FIRM PROFILE: Lopez, Hodes, Restaino, Milman & Skikos is a dynamic, growing and nationally-known firm representing seriously injured plaintiffs throughout the United States, with offices in Newport Beach and San Francisco, California, Minneapolis, Minnesota and Cincinnati, Ohio. The Firm is considered a pioneer in the fields of Mass Torts, Medical Malpractice/HMO Litigation, Pharmaceutical/Medical Device Litigation and Employment Law. Members of the Firm have sat on state and national steering committees in a variety of mass torts, including breast implant, Albuterol, Norplant, L-Tryptophan and Diet Pill (Fen-Phen) and currently sit on such committees in Rezulin, Propulsid, PPA, Sulzer Hip, Ford-Firestone and Baycol. The Firm is listed in the Bar Register of Preeminent Lawyers.

JANET G. ABARAY, born Cincinnati, Ohio, August 19, 1957; admitted to bar, 1982, Ohio. *Education:* University of Cincinnati (B.A., 1979; J.D., 1982). Phi Beta Kappa; Order of the Coif. Business Manager, University of Cincinnati Law Review, 1981-1982. Member, Plaintiffs' Coordinating Committee and Plaintiffs' Liaison Counsel, Ephreda MDL Litigation. *Member:* Cincinnati, Ohio and American Bar Associations; Association of Trial Lawyers of America. Barrister, American Inns of Court. ***REPORTED CASES:*** Trial Counsel for Defendant Merrell-Dow Pharmaceuticals, Inc. in "In Re Bendectin Products Liability Litigation No. 486"; Trial Counsel for Plaintiffs, Class Action of 2,500 Physicians in "Thompson vs. Midwest Foundations Independent Physician Association, D.B.A. Choice-Care"; Trial Counsel for Plaintiffs, Class Action of 8,000 Farmers in "Lutmer vs. Chubb Insurance Co.". ***PRACTICE AREAS:*** Complex Litigation; Civil Litigation; Products Liability; Mass Torts; Personal Injury; Breach of Contract; Insurance Litigation. ***Email:*** jabaray@lopez-hodes.com

---

JANE E. JOSEPH, born Cleveland, Ohio, December 28, 1957; admitted to bar, 1985, Minnesota; U.S. District Court, District of Minnesota; U.S. Court of Appeals, Eighth Circuit; 2002, Ohio. *Education:* Edinburgh University, Edinburgh, Scotland; Oberlin College (B.A., 1980); William Mitchell College of Law (J.D., cum laude, 1985). Member, William Mitchell Law Review. *Member:* Hennepin County and Minnesota State Bar Associations;

(This Listing Continued)

LOPEZ, HODES, RESTAINO, MILMAN & SKIKOS, A LAW CORPORATION, Cincinnati—Continued

Minnesota Trial Lawyers Association; Minnesota Women Lawyers; Association of Trial Lawyers of America. (Resident, Cincinnati, Ohio Office). ***PRACTICE AREAS:*** Personal Injury; Products Liability; Mass Torts. ***Email:*** jjoseph@lopez-hodes.com

BEVERLY H. PACE, born Cincinnati, Ohio, August 7, 1947; admitted to bar, 1986, Ohio; 1988 U.S. District Court, Southern District of Ohio and U.S. Court of Appeals, Sixth Circuit. *Education:* University of Cincinnati (B.A., 1969; J.D., 1986). Member, 1984-1985 and Lead Articles Editor, 1985-1986, University of Cincinnati Law Review. Law Clerk to Hon. John W. Peck, Senior Judge, Sixth Circuit Court of Appeals. *Member:* Cincinnati and Ohio Bar Associations. ***PRACTICE AREAS:*** Mass Torts; Litigation; Employment Law. ***Email:*** bpace@lopez-hodes.com

CALVIN S. TREGRE, JR., born New Orleans, Louisiana. April 9, 1974; admitted to bar, 2001, Ohio. *Education:* Xavier University of Louisiana (B.S., 1996); University of Cincinnati, College of Law (J.D., 2000). Member: Order of Barristers; Moot Court Honors Board. *Member:* Cincinnati and Ohio State Bar Associations; Black Lawyers Association of Cincinnati. ***PRACTICE AREAS:*** Mass Torts; Pharmaceutical Litigation; Products Liability; Class Actions; Personal Injury. ***Email:*** ctregre@lopez-hodes.com

MELANIE S. BAILEY, born Covington, Kentucky, May 17, 1971; admitted to bar, 1997, Kentucky; 1998, U.S. District Court, Eastern District of Kentucky; 2003, Ohio. *Education:* Northern Kentucky University (B.A., 1993); Salmon P. Chase College of Law (J.D., 1996). ***PRACTICE AREAS:*** Class Actions; Commercial Litigation. ***Email:*** mbailey@lopez-hodes.com

JOSEPH M. LYON, born Cincinnati, Ohio; admitted to bar, 2003, Ohio; 2005, U.S. District Court, Southern District of Ohio. *Education:* Loyola College in Maryland (B.A., 1999); Chicago-Kent College of Law, Illinois Institute of Technology (J.D., 2002). *Member:* Cincinnati, Ohio State and Federal Bar Associations; American Constitutional Society, Association of Trial Lawyers of America (Member, New Lawyers Board of Governors); Ohio Academy of Trial Lawyers. ***PRACTICE AREAS:*** Products Liability; Medical Malpractice; Personal Injury. ***Email:*** jlyon@lopez-hodes.com

(For Complete Biographical Data on All Personnel, See Professional Biographies at Newport Beach, California)

STEPHAN D. MADDEN CO., LPA

Established in 1993

601 MAIN STREET, 3RD FLOOR
CINCINNATI, OHIO 45202
Telephone: 513-621-8700
Fax: 513-241-1572
Email: madlaw@fuse.net
URL: http://www.stevemaddenlaw.com

Criminal Law, Family Law, Personal Injury, Driving While Intoxicated.

FIRM PROFILE: General Practice Focuses primarily on Criminal and Misdemeanors, DUI, Traffic, and Appellate Cases. Practice also include Real Estate, Domestic Relations and Family Law, and Personal Injury.

STEPHAN D. MADDEN, born Oakland, California, June 12, 1954; admitted to bar, 1980, Ohio and U.S. District Court, Southern District of Ohio; 2004, U.S. Court of Appeals, 6th Circuit. *Education:* Miami University (A.B., 1976); Salmon P. Chase College of Law (J.D., 1980). *Member:* Cincinnati, Warren County and Ohio State Bar Associations. ***PRACTICE AREAS:*** Criminal Law (90%); Family Law (5%); Personal Injury (5%). ***Email:*** madlaw@fuse.net

Language: English.

REPRESENTATIVE CLIENT: ReMax.

JAMES V. MAGEE, JR.

Established in 1974

36 EAST 7TH STREET, SUITE 2020
CINCINNATI, OHIO 45202
Telephone: 513-621-9660
Fax: 513-345-3900
URL: http://www.jamesvmageelaw.com
Email: jvmageejr@mageelaw.com
URL: http://www.mageelaw.com

Real Estate Law, Litigation, Title Insurance Law, Commercial Litigation, Bankruptcy.

FIRM PROFILE: Serving clients for over 30 years in Cincinnati and Northern Kentucky.

JAMES V. MAGEE, JR., born Philadelphia, Pennsylvania, September 12, 1946; admitted to bar, 1974, Ohio and U.S. District Court, Southern District of Ohio; 1981, U.S. District Court, Northern District of Ohio; 1984, Kentucky and U.S. Court of Appeals, Sixth Circuit; 1986, U.S. District Court, Western District of Kentucky; 1990, U.S. District Court, Eastern District of Kentucky. *Education:* Allentown College (A.B., 1969); Eastern Kentucky University (M.A., 1971); Northern Kentucky University (J.D., 1974). Registered Land Examiner. General Counsel, Cambridge Savings and Loan Association, Cambridge, Ohio, 1978-1984; Associate General Counsel- Litigation, Farm Credit Bank of Louisville, Kentucky, 1984-1986. Co-Editor: Ohio Real Property Law and Practice (Michie. Co. 4th ed); Land Patents: "A Misconception," 58 Ohio State Bar Association Report 34, 1985; "Ohio's New Estate: Tenancy by Entireties," 2 Northern Kentucky State Law Forum 69, 1974. Adjunct Professor of Law, Northern Kentucky University, 1976-1978, 1990. Faculty Member, North Central Bankruptcy Law Institute of Capital University Law Center, 1985-1989. Lecturer: Cincinnati, Louisville, Ohio and Kentucky Bar Associations. *Member:* Cincinnati, Ohio State and Kentucky Bar Associations. ***REPORTED CASES:*** Farmers

(This Listing Continued)

Production Credit Asso. v. Johnson, Nos. 84-1915, 85-860, Supreme Court of Ohio, 24 Ohio St. 3d 69; 493 N.E.2d 946; 1986 Ohio Lexis 650; 24 Ohio B. Rep. 217, June 11, 1986, Decided; Kenney v. Henry Fischer Builder, Inc., APPEAL No. C-970658, COURT Of APPEALS OF OHIO, FIRST APPELLATE DISTRICT, HAMILTON COUNTY, 129 Ohio App. 3d 27 ; 716 N.E.2d 1189; 1998 Ohio App. LEXIS 2999, July 2, 1998, Date of Judgment Entry on Appeal; Cincinnati Cent. Credit Union v. Benson, APPEAL No. C-971030, COURT OF APPEALS OF OHIO, FIRST APPELLATE DISTRICT, HAMILTON COUNTY, 130 Ohio App. 3d 755; 721 N.E.2d 410; 1998 Ohio App. LEXIS 6058, December 18, 1998, Date of Judgment Entry on Appeal; Wiley v. Federal Land Bank, IP No. 85-1441-C UNITED STATES DISTRICT COURT FOR THE SOUTHERN DISTRICT OF INDIANA, INDIANAPOLIS DIVISION, 657 F. Supp. 964; 1987 U.S. Dist. LEXIS 5094, March 31, 1987, Decided.

REPRESENTATIVE CLIENTS: Downtown Property Management, Inc.; Group 2000, LLC; Somerset Refinery; Eden Park Realtors; Landco, Inc.; Jets Title Agency, LLC; Somerset Oil; Nations Title Agency; Licensed Insurance Title Agent for First American Title Insurance Co.; Ohio Bar Title Insurance Company; Stewart Title Guaranty Company.

MANLEY BURKE

A LEGAL PROFESSIONAL ASSOCIATION

Established in 1979

225 WEST COURT STREET
CINCINNATI, OHIO 45202
Telephone: 513-721-5525
Fax: 513-721-4268
Email: info@manleyburke.com
URL: http://www.manleyburke.com

Litigation, Local Government Law, Land Use and Zoning Law, Civil Rights, Probate. Fraternal Law. Personal Injury, Labor Law, Workers Compensation, Employee Benefits and Professional Malpractice.

FIRM PROFILE: Manley Burke's attorneys practice in a variety of areas including complex litigation, land use, zoning and eminent domain law, employment law, municipal law, personal injury, class actions, representation of labor unions and their members, employee benefits law, workers' compensation, social security disability, international energy law, fraternity law, non-profit corporation law, and administrative law.

The firm's attorneys practice throughout Ohio and often in other states across the nation in association with local counsel. The firm publishes a nationally circulated newsletter entitled Fraternal Law, the result of the firm's representation of fraternal organizations nationwide, both as general and special counsel. Several members of the firm teach at area universities; all actively participate in professional associations and civic organizations.

ROBERT E. MANLEY, born Cincinnati, Ohio, November 24, 1935; admitted to bar, 1960, Ohio; 1970, U.S. Supreme Court. *Education:* Xavier University (Sc.B., 1956); University of Cincinnati (A.M., 1957); Harvard University (J.D., 1960). Taft Teaching Fellow of Economics, University of Cincinnati, 1956-1957. Lecturer on Law: Salmon P. Chase College of Law, 1965-1971; University of Cincinnati, 1977-1980. Adjunct Professor of Law, 1980—. Author: "The Effect of Aesthetic Considerations on the Validity of Zoning Ordinances," Monograph with Timothy A. Fischer, 1974; "A Cincinnati Strategy for Environmental Quality Overlay Zones," 7 The Urban Lawyer 96, 1975; "School Desegregation in the North: A Post-Milliken Strategy for Obtaining Metropolitan Relief," 20 St. Louis U.L.J. 585, 1976; "The Next Thirty Years of Civil Rights Litigation," 13 The Urban Lawyer 541, 1981; "Federalism and Management of the Environment," 19 The Urban Lawyer 661, 1987. Chairman, Cincinnati Environmental Advisory Council, 1975-1976. *Member:* Cincinnati (Chairman: Committee on Antitrust Law, 1968; Committee on Housing, Urban Development and Land Planning Law, 1973-1976), Ohio State and American (Chairman, Committee on Government Liability, 1972-1978; Member of Council, Urban, State and Local Government Law Section, 1976-1980, 1982-1986, 1988-1993; Chairman, Editorial Advisory Committee, The Urban Lawyer, 1986-1996) Bar Associations; American Judicature Society; American College of Real Estate Lawyers. Owners Counsel of America. Fellow, American Bar Foundation. ***LANGUAGES:*** Spanish and Portuguese. ***REPORTED CASES:*** Haddon View Investments vs. Coopers & Lybrand, 70 Ohio St. 2d 154 (1982); Pembaur vs. City of Cincinnati, 475 U.S. 469 (1986). ***PRACTICE AREAS:*** Complex Litigation; Land Use Development Law; Environmental Law; Government Law; Probate Law; Civil Rights Law. ***Email:*** rmanley@manleyburke.com

TIMOTHY M. BURKE, born Cleveland, Ohio, February 10, 1948; admitted to bar, 1973, Ohio; 1979, U.S. Supreme Court. *Education:* Xavier University (A.B., 1970); University of Cincinnati (J.D., 1973). Alpha Sigma Nu. Adjunct Associate Professor, Criminal Justice, University of Cincinnati, 1977-1979. Adjunct Associate Professor, Constitutional Law, Xavier University, 1975-1995. Lecturer, Health and the Legislative Process, Xavier University 1982-1995. Special Counsel to Attorney General of Ohio, 1978-1995. Law Director, Village of Lockland, 1981—. Trustee and Chairman of Law Committee, Cincinnati Zoological Society, Inc., 1981-1991, Secretary, 1989-1991. Commissioner, Cincinnati Park Board, 1991-1994. Chair, Hamilton County Board of Elections, 1993—. Chair, 1993-1999, Co-Chair, 1999-2004, Chair, 2004—, Hamilton County Democratic Party. Chair Cincinnati Democratic Party, 1982-1992, 1995-1998. Member: Chamber of Commerce Local Government Committee, 1992—; Chamber of Commerce Ballot Issues Committee, 1992—, Chair, 1993-1994. Ohio Democratic Party Executive Committee, 1994—. Ohio Democrat of the Year, 1995. Justice Team Leader, Cincinnati Community Action Now (Mayor's Commission Appointed in response to civil unrest), 2001-2003. Legislative Assistant to City Councilman, 1971-1974. Special Assistant to U.S. Congressman, 1974-1975 and 1977. U.S. Congressional Candidate, 1978. *Member:* Cincinnati, Ohio State and American Bar Associations. ***REPORTED CASES:*** Nat'l Trust for Historic Pres. v. United States Army Corps of Eng'rs (1983), 570 F. Supp. 465 (S.D. Ohio); Nat'l Trust v. United States Army Corps of Eng'rs (1982), 552 F. Supp. 784 (S.D. Ohio); Gerijo, Inc. vs. Fairfield, 70 Ohio St. 3d 223 (1994); Little Miami, Inc. v. Kinney (1981), 68 Ohio St. 2d 102, 428 N.E. 2d 859; State ex rel. Bryco Co. v. City of Milford, 2001 Ohio App. LEXIS 2773 (12th Dist); Bryco Co. v. City of Milford, 1999 Ohio App. LEXIS 4750 (12th Dist.); Ober v. City

(This Listing Continued)

of Deer Park, 1998 Ohio App. LEXIS 2998 (1st Dist); Asher Invs. v. City of Cincinnati (1997), 122 Ohio App. 3d 126, 701 N.E. 2d 4000 (1st Dist); Newsom v. Kunnen Bros. Serv., 1996 Ohio App. LEXIS 5032 (1st Dist); Cincinnati City Sch. Dist. v. State Bd. of Educ. (1996), 113 Ohio App. 3d 305, 680 N.E. 2d 1061 (10th Dist); Camp Wash. Community Bd. v. Rece (1995), 104 Ohio App. 3d 750, 663 N.E. 2d 373 (1st Dist); Balke v. Pierce Township, 1994 Ohio App. LEXIS 5692 (10th Dist); Gleason V. Council of Cincinnati, 1993 Ohio App. LEXIS 2884 (1st Dist); Thompson v. 5060 Bar, 1989 Ohio App. LEXIS 369 (1st Dist); Cincinnati ex rel. Cincinnati Private Police Asso. v. Cincinnati (1987), 40 Ohio App. 3d 1888, 532 N.E. 2d 175 (1st Dist); State, ex rel. McVey v. Banks, 1983 Ohio App. LEXIS 11947 (12th Dist); Hamilton County v. Paul, 1980 Ohio App. LEXIS 10676 (1st Dist); Mirlisena v. Fellerhoff (1984), 11 Ohio Misc. 2d 7, 463 N.E. 2d 115. ***PRACTICE AREAS:*** Litigation; Local Government Law; Employment Law; Land Use and Zoning Law; Civil Rights. ***Email:*** tburke@manleyburke.com

GARY E. POWELL, born Lima, Ohio, September 24, 1958; admitted to bar, 1984, Ohio; 1985, U.S. District Court, Southern District of Ohio; 1985, U.S. Court of Appeals, Sixth Circuit; 1987, U.S. District Court, Eastern District of Kentucky; 1988, U.S. Supreme Court. *Education:* University of Cincinnati (B.A., magna cum laude, 1981; J.D., 1984). Omicron Delta Kappa. Associate Editor, Fraternal Law, 1987—. Adjunct Assistant Professor, Business Law, University of Cincinnati, 1986—. *Member:* Cincinnati (Board of Trustees, 1993-1995; Chair, Young Lawyers Section, 1994-1995), Ohio State and American Bar Associations; Cincinnati Bar Foundation (Trustee, 1993-2000; Treasurer, 1996-1998; President, 1998-2000). Fellow, American Bar Foundation. ***REPORTED CASES:*** Gerijo, Inc. vs. Fairfield, 70 Ohio St.3d 223 (1994); Oberer Dev. Co. v. City of Fairborn, 1999 Ohio App. LEXIS 1812 (2nd Dist. 1999); Hunsche v. City of Loveland, 1999 Ohio App. LEXIS 1665 (1st Dist. 1999); Riddle v. City of Loveland, 1998 Ohio App. LEXIS 1281 (12th Dist. 1998); State ex rel. Moeller v. Bd. of Trustees of Colerain Twp., 1997 Ohio App. LEXIS 4538 (1st Dist. 1997); Health Mgmt. v. Union Twp. Bd. of Zoning Appeals, 118 Ohio App.3d 281 (12th Dist. 1997); Loreto Dev. Co. v. Village of Chardon, 119 Ohio App.3d 524 (11th Dist. 1996); Singer v. City of Fairborn, 73 Ohio App.3d 809 (2nd Dist. 1991). ***PRACTICE AREAS:*** Litigation; Land Use and Zoning Law; Municipal Law; Eminent Domain; Appellate Practice. ***Email:*** gpowell@manleyburke.com

ROBERT H. MITCHELL, born Cincinnati, Ohio, February 15, 1960; admitted to bar, 1986, Ohio. *Education:* Wabash College (B.A., 1982); University of Cincinnati (J.D., 1986). Order of the Barristers. *Member:* Cincinnati and Ohio State Bar Associations; Ohio Employment Lawyers Association. ***PRACTICE AREAS:*** Litigation; ERISA; Labor and Employment Law. ***Email:*** rhm@manleyburke.com

MATTHEW W. FELLERHOFF, born Cincinnati, Ohio, December 1, 1966; admitted to bar, 1994, Ohio; 1995, U.S. District Court, Southern District of Ohio; 1997, U.S. Court of Appeals, 6th Circuit. *Education:* Miami University (B.A., 1989); Salmon P. Chase College of Law, Northern Kentucky University (J.D., 1994). *Member:* Cincinnati, Ohio State and American Bar Associations; National Employment Lawyers Association. ***REPORTED CASES:*** City of Cincinnati v. Banks (2001) 143 Ohio App. 3d 272, 757 N.E., 2d 1205; Thompson v. Sydnor, 2000 Ohio App. LEXIS 2040 (4th Dist., 2000); Wright v. Goshen Twp., 1997 Ohio App. LEXIS 2452 (12th Dist., 1997). ***PRACTICE AREAS:*** Litigation; Eminent Domain; Employment Law; Local Government Law; Land Use; Zoning Law. ***Email:*** mwf@manleyburke.com

---

EMILY T. SUPINGER, born Cincinnati, Ohio, December 13, 1975; admitted to bar, 2001, Ohio; 2002, U.S. District Court, Southern District of Ohio; 2004, U.S. Court of Appeals, 6th Circuit. *Education:* Ohio University (B.S., 1998); University of Akron (J.D., 2001). *Member:* Cincinnati, Ohio State and American Bar Associations; Ohio Academy of Trial Lawyers; Association of Trial Lawyers of America. ***PRACTICE AREAS:*** Litigation; Eminent Domain; Employment Law; Local Government Law; Land Use; Zoning Law. ***Email:*** egehlert@manleyburke.com

DANIEL J. McCARTHY, born Peoria, Illinois, June 1, 1977; admitted to bar, 2002, Missouri; 2003, Illinois; 2004, Ohio. *Education:* University of Missouri, Columbia (B.A., 1999); St. Louis University (J.D., 2002). *Member:* Cincinnati, Ohio State, Illinois State and American Bar Associations; The Missouri Bar. ***PRACTICE AREAS:*** Litigation; Eminent Domain; Municipal Law. ***Email:*** dmccarthy@manleyburke.com

NATHAN W. SPRONG, born Syracuse, New York, July 15, 1972; admitted to bar, 2004, Ohio. *Education:* Georgetown University (B.A., 1994); University of Dayton (J.D., 2004). *Member:* Cincinnati, Ohio State and American Bar Associations. ***PRACTICE AREAS:*** Eminent Domain; Municipal Law; Land Use; Zoning Law; Litigation; Real Estate. ***Email:*** nsprong@manleyburke.com

RETIRED

WILLIAM A. McCLAIN, born Sanford, North Carolina, 1913; admitted to bar, 1938, Ohio. *Education:* Wittenberg College (A.B., 1934); University of Michigan (J.D., 1937). Awarded: LL.D., Wilberforce University, 1963; LL.D., University of Cincinnati, 1971; LH.D., Wittenberg University, 1972; LL.D., University of Michigan, 2002. Visiting Lecturer on Law: University of Cincinnati, 1963-1972; Salmon P. Chase College of Law, 1965-1972. Author: "Loitering Ordinances," NIMLO Municipal Law Review, Vol. 34B, 1970; "Environment of Fear," Report No. 155, 1970 on Urban Violence Problems, National Institute Municipal Law Officers; "Modern Concepts of Police Power and Eminent Domain," Ninth Institute on Eminent Domain, The Southwestern Legal Foundation, 1969; "An Age of Dramatic Dimensions," Ohio Cities and Villages, Ohio Municipal League, June and July, 1968, Vol. 16. Editor, Fraternal Law, 1982—. City Solicitor, City of Cincinnati, 1963-1972. Judge, Court of Common Pleas, Hamilton County, Ohio, 1975-1976. *Member:* Cincinnati (Chairman, Committee on Housing, Urban Development and Land Planning Law, 1971-1973), Ohio State and American (Member, Civil Rights and Responsibilities Section, 1968-1973) Bar Associations; American Judicature Society; National Bar Association; Black Lawyers Association of Cincinnati. Fellow, American Bar Foundation. ***PRACTICE AREAS:*** Government Law; Civil Litigation; Administrative Law; Civil Rights Law; Constitutional Law.

(This Listing Continued)

OF COUNSEL

GEORGE FABE, born Gary, Indiana, November 14, 1921; admitted to bar, 1981, Ohio. *Education:* University of Cincinnati (B.A., econ, 1943; J.D., 1981). Business: Construction and Real Estate Development, 1946-1976; Commissioner of Insurance, Ohio 1983-1991; Member, Panel of Arbitrators, American Arbitration Association. Chairman, Ohio Health Care Board, 1993-1994, 1995. *Member:* Columbus Bar Association. ***PRACTICE AREAS:*** Insurance Regulation; Insurance Litigation; Construction Litigation; Arbitration; Mediation.

GEORGE F. MOELLER, born Cincinnati, Ohio, October 27, 1954; admitted to bar, 1985, Ohio; 1987, Florida. *Education:* Miami University, Oxford, Ohio; University of Cincinnati (B.B.A., 1981; J.D., 1984). *Member:* Cincinnati Bar Association; Ohio Academy of Trial Lawyers; National Organization of Social Security Claimants' Representatives. ***PRACTICE AREAS:*** Workers' Compensation Law; Social Security Disability Law; Labor Law. ***Email:*** gmoeller@manleyburke.com

GARY MOORE EBY, born Cincinnati, Ohio, March 30, 1951; admitted to bar, 1976, Ohio and U.S. District Court, Southern District of Ohio; 1977, U.S. Court of Appeals, Sixth Circuit; 1982, U.S. District Court, Eastern District of Kentucky; 1984, U.S. Court of Appeals, Fourth Circuit; 1990, District of Columbia Court of Appeals; 1992, Kentucky. *Education:* University of Cincinnati (B.A., 1973; M.A.I.R., 1984; J.D., 1976). Phi Alpha Delta. Member: Ohio State Bar Association Labor and Employment Specialty Board, 1997—; AFL-CIO Lawyers Coordinating Committee, 1982—. Contributing Editor, "The Developing Labor Law," 2nd Ed. (BNA Books), 1983). *Member:* Cincinnati (Member, Labor and Employment Law Committee, 1980—; District of Columbia, Ohio State (Member, Labor and Employment Law Section, 1977—) and American (Member, Labor and Employment Law Section, 1977—; Committee on Development of the Law Under the National Labor Relations Act, 1977—; Sub-committee Co-Chair, 1990—) Bar Associations. ***LANGUAGES:*** German. ***REPORTED CASES:*** Hopkins v. Giles, 7 Ohio App 3d. 79 (1982); D'Andrea v. American Postal Workers Union, 700 F.2d. 335 (6th Cir 1983); Virginia Holding Company, d/b/a Hotel Roanoke, 293 NLRB No. 16 (1989); U.S. Abatement Inc. 303 N.R.B. No. 73 (1991); CHAVIS, et al. vs. Sycamore Community School District Board of Education. 71 Ohio St. 30 26 (1994); I&F Corporation, 322 NLRB No. 191 (1996). ***Email:*** garyeby@manleyburke.com

GERALD DAVID PRAGER, born Norfolk, Virginia, October 25, 1940; admitted to bar, 1993, Texas; 2000, Ohio. *Education:* University of Kansas (B.S., 1962); University of Cincinnati (Ph.D., 1971); Northeastern University (C.A.G.S., 1978); University of Houston (J.D., 1993). Order of the Coif; Order of the Barons. Certified Petroleum Geologist, 1982. Author: "Pemex at the Crossroads: National Oil Industry in Crisis," Houston Journal of International Law, 1992. Member, American Association of Petroleum Geologists, 1981—. Member, Association of International Petroleum Negotiators, 1994—. *Member:* Houston, Cincinnati, Ohio State and American Bar Associations; State Bar of Texas. [Lt., U.S. Navy, 1962-1966]. ***LANGUAGES:*** Spanish. ***PRACTICE AREAS:*** International Law; Energy; Oil and Gas Law; Commercial Law; Corporate Law; Immigration Law. ***Email:*** gprager@manleyburke.com

W. KELLY LUNDRIGAN, born Covington, Kentucky, February 8, 1966; admitted to bar, 1992, Ohio; 1993, U.S. District Court, Southern District of Ohio and U.S. Court of Appeals, Sixth Circuit. *Education:* University of Cincinnati (B.A., 1988; J.D., 1992). *Member:* Cincinnati, Ohio State and American Bar Associations; Ohio Academy of Trial Lawyers; Association of Trial Lawyers of America. ***PRACTICE AREAS:*** Commercial Litigation; Construction Law; Wrongful Death; Civil Rights; Local Government Law; Land Use; Zoning Law. ***Email:*** wkl@manleyburke.com

MARTIN & BAILEY

Established in 1994

SUITE 420, 120 EAST FOURTH STREET
CINCINNATI, OHIO 45202
Telephone: 513-333-0990
Facsimile: 513-333-0066
Email: mblaw@one.net
URL: http://www.martinbaileylaw.com

Insurance Defense, Auto Accidents, Personal Injury, Product Liability, Uninsured, Underinsured Motorists, Malpractice Prevention Consulting, Arson and Property Damage, Insurance Coverage, Construction and Contractor Liability, Corporate Litigation, Contract Disputes, Litigation, Accidents, Worker's Compensation, Theft, False Arrest, Malicious Prosecution, Defamation, Probate, Tax Law.

FIRM PROFILE: Welcome to Martin & Bailey. With more than 90 years of combined experience, a shared work ethic and a common interest in providing quality, cost-effective legal services, the partners of Martin & Bailey formed this firm. Our concentrated areas of practice - individual and corporate litigation and law - and our proven expertise in these areas set us apart in the industry.

In addition, as a smaller firm, we see distinct opportunities to better serve our clients through more personalized attention, greater cost efficiencies and quicker results.

We invite you to take a closer look at the law firm of Martin & Bailey.

MEMBERS OF FIRM

J. ROGER BLUST (1938-1995)

ROBERT C. MARTIN, born Georgetown, Ohio, May 6, 1926; admitted to bar, 1953, Ohio. *Education:* University of Cincinnati (B.B.A., 1949); Salmon P. Chase College of Law (LL.B., 1953). Beta Gamma Sigma. Recipient, Rebecca Bloom Award. *Member:* Cincinnati Bar Association (Member: Taxation Committee; Estate Planning Committee, 1978-1995). ***PRACTICE AREAS:*** Corporate Law; Business Law; Tax Planning; Estate Planning.

STEPHEN A. BAILEY, born Hobbs, New Mexico, August 10, 1945; admitted to bar, 1971, Ohio. *Education:* Xavier University (B.S., 1968); University of Cincinnati (J.D.,

(This Listing Continued)

MARTIN & BAILEY, Cincinnati—Continued

1971). *Member:* Cincinnati, Ohio State and American Bar Associations; Ohio Association of Civil Trial Attorneys; Defense Research Institute. ***PRACTICE AREAS:*** Insurance Defense; Civil Litigation; Personal Injury.

C. CURTIS WALDEN, born Cincinnati, April 5, 1959; admitted to bar, 1984, Ohio. *Education:* University of Cincinnati (B.A., magna cum laude, 1981; J.D., 1984). Recipient, Anderson Award for Appellate Advocacy, U.S. Department of Labor, 1986-1987. *Member:* Cincinnati, Ohio State and American Bar Associations. ***PRACTICE AREAS:*** Insurance Defense; Civil Litigation.

J. STEPHEN COX, born Cincinnati, Ohio, January 31, 1957; admitted to bar, 1991, Ohio. *Education:* University of Cincinnati (B.F.A., 1979); Salmon P. Chase College of Law (J.D., 1991). *Member:* Cincinnati and Ohio State Bar Associations. ***PRACTICE AREAS:*** Insurance Defense; Workers Compensation; Domestic Relations; Entertainment Law.

DOUGLAS J. MAY, born Cincinnati, Ohio, April 10, 1963; admitted to bar, 1989, Ohio; 1991, Kentucky; U.S. District Court, Eastern District of Kentucky; 1994, U.S. District Court, Southern District of Ohio. *Education:* Ohio State University (B.A., 1986); University of Cincinnati (J.D., 1989). *Member:* Cincinnati, Ohio State and Kentucky Bar Associations; Defense Research Institute. ***PRACTICE AREAS:*** Insurance Defense; Civil Litigation; Real Estate Litigation. ***Email:*** dmay@martinandbailey.com

GENERAL COUNSEL FOR: LaRosa's; Schottco Corp.; Schweitzer Construction Co.
REPRESENTATIVE CLIENTS: American Family Insurance; CNI Claims Service, Inc.; Chubb & Son, Inc.; EMC/Hamilton Mutual Insurance Cos.; Encompass Insurance; Erie Insurance Group; Grocers Insurance Group; Hartford Insurance; Indiana Insurance; Lancer Insurance Co.; La Rosa's; Northland Insurance Co.; Specialty Risk Services; Western World Insurance Co.; Wullenweber Jeep-Eagle.

MASON, SCHILLING & MASON CO., L.P.A.

Established in 1973

11340 MONTGOMERY ROAD, SUITE 210
CINCINNATI, OHIO 45249-2313
Telephone: 513-489-0829
800-840-3514
Fax: 513-489-0834
Email: msm@mason-law.com
URL: http://www.mason-law.com

Covington, Kentucky Office: Heritage International, Suite 203, P.O. Box 2158. Telephone: 513-489-0829. Fax: 513-489-0834.
Columbus Office: 460 E. Main Street. Telephone: 513-489-0829. Fax: 513-489-0834.
Dayton Office: 319 Liberty Tower. Telephone: 513-489-0829. Fax: 513-489-0834.
Lima Office: P.O. Box 937. Telephone: 513-489-0829. Fax: 513-489-0834.
Madison, Indiana Office: 201 East Main Street. Telephone: 513-489-0829. Fax: 513-489-0834.

Commercial, Creditors Rights, Bankruptcy, Collection, Banking and Financial Institution Law, Civil Litigation, Federal Consumer Law Litigation, Foreclosures, Automobile Deficiencies, Credit Cards, Medical Debts, Bad Checks, Business Loans/Commercial Debt, Vehicle and Property Repossessions, Landlord Representation/Evictions/Lease Litigation, Equipment Leasing.

FIRM PROFILE: Mason, Schilling & Mason Co., L.P.A., since its founding over 30 years ago, exclusively concentrates in the areas of creditor representation, in all aspects of commercial litigation, banking law, leasing law, bankruptcy law, and creditors' rights law.

We have developed a full service staff of attorneys in all aspects of representation to the credit granting community. Our legal services concentrate exclusively on representing creditors in all facets of legal representation concerning credit management and credit granting, commercial law, and bankruptcy law on behalf of the credit management community.

Further, of particular attention, is the providing of legal services to the banking and credit management community throughout the entire States of Ohio and Kentucky. Our attorneys appear in all State and federal courts in both states.

The value of our law firm rests with the dependable level of service that we provide to all creditor-clients. We pride ourselves in the personalized service and the conscientious follow through that has been a trade mark throughout over three decades of providing legal services to our creditor and banking clients.

JONATHAN A. MASON, born Cleveland, Ohio, January 6, 1947; admitted to bar, 1973, Kentucky and U.S. District Court, Eastern District of Kentucky; 1977, U.S. Supreme Court; 1979, Ohio; 1992, U.S. Court of Appeals, Sixth Circuit. *Education:* University of Cincinnati (B.A., with high honors, 1969; M.A., 1970; J.D., 1973). General Motors Scholar, 1968-1969. Taft Graduate Fellow, 1969-1970. National Moot Court Counsel, 1972. Listed in Who's Who in American Law, 1994—. Author: "Documentary Evidence in Collection Cases," Business Credit, Vol. 95, No. 6, June, 1993; Collection Law in Ohio, Lorman Educational Services, 1995. Co-Author, "In Re Strumpf, Bankruptcy Rights," Business Credit, Vol. 98, No. 9, Oct. 1996. Lecturer: National Business Institute, Bankruptcy and Commercial Law Seminar, 1988, 1990, 1992; Loman Business Institute, 1993—; Bankers Collection Conference, 1993. Faculty Member, Ohio Continuing Legal Education Institute, 1994—. Regional Counsel, Resolution Trust Corp. (RTC), 1992—. City Attorney: City of Crescent Park, Kentucky, 1973-1983; Crescent Springs, Kentucky, 1975-1985. Member: Dean's Council, College of Law, University of Cincinnati, 1987—; Credit Professional, Inc. *Member:* Cincinnati (Member, Bankruptcy Committee), Kenton County (Treasurer, 1977-1980; Member, Executive Committee, 1977-1980), Northern Kentucky, Kentucky, Ohio State (Member: Bankruptcy Committee; Banking Committee) and American Bar Associations; Kenton County Public Defender, Inc.; The Association of Trial Lawyers of America; Commercial Law League of America (Member: Creditors' Rights Section; Bankruptcy Committee); American Bankruptcy Institute; Corporation Collection Attorneys Association of America; Southeastern Bankruptcy Institute; Uniform Commercial Code Institute; American Association of Creditors Attorneys; National Institute of Credit Management; International Credit Conference Institute; Ohio Creditors' Association (Founding Member); Credit Management Leadership Institute; Credit Research Foundation; The Banking Law Institute; INSOL; The Institute of Credit; American Bank Attorneys Association; National Association of Retail Collection Recovery Attorneys; National Mortgage Bank Attorneys Association. ***PRACTICE AREAS:*** Commercial Law; Creditors Rights Law; Bankruptcy Law; Collections; Financial Institution Law; Banking Law. ***Email:*** jon@mason-law.com

RICHARD D. SCHILLING, born Cincinnati, Ohio, April 13, 1952; admitted to bar, 1977, Ohio and U.S. District Court, Southern District of Ohio; 1997, Kentucky, U.S. District Court, Eastern District of Kentucky and U.S. Court of Appeals, 6th Circuit. *Education:* Principia College (B.A., 1974); University of Cincinnati (J.D., 1977). Lecturer: National Business Institute, 1993; Ohio; Ohio State Bar Association Annual Convention, 1997. Member: Equipment Leasing Association of America, 1996—; Commercial Law League of America. *Member:* Cincinnati, Clermont County, Ohio State and American Bar Associations. ***PRACTICE AREAS:*** Equipment Leasing; Creditors Rights; Collections; Commercial Law; Litigation; Banking Law; Bankruptcy. ***Email:*** rick@mason-law.com

JEREMY R. MASON, born Cincinnati, Ohio, August 1, 1974; admitted to bar, 2000, Ohio; 2001, U.S. District Court, Southern District of Ohio. *Education:* Cornell University (B.S., with honors, 1997); The Ohio State University (J.D., with honors, 2000). Recipient: Delta Kappa Epsilon Scholar Award; CALI Award, Business Association, 1998; American Bankruptcy Institute Medal of Excellence, May 2000. Cornell University National Scholar, 1996-1997. Co-Author: Case Analysis, "First Circuit Bap Denies Chapter 13 Debtors a 'Hardship Discharge' in its Clarification of 11 U.S.C. § 1328 (b)," CLLA Bankruptcy Section, Vol. 19, Issue 5, CLLA Bulletin, November 1999. *Member:* Cincinnati and Ohio State Bar Associations; Commercial Law League; American Bankruptcy Institute. ***PRACTICE AREAS:*** Creditors Rights; Bankruptcy; Banking Law; Collections. ***Email:*** jeremy@mason-law.com

---

JOSEPH M. RUWE, born Fort Thomas, Kentucky, December 13, 1965; admitted to bar, 1998, Kentucky and Ohio; 1999, U.S. District Court, Eastern District of Kentucky; 2000, U.S. District Court, Southern District of Ohio. *Education:* Northern Kentucky University (B.A., 1990; J.D., cum laude, 1998). *Member:* Cincinnati, Northern Kentucky, Kentucky and Ohio State Bar Associations. ***PRACTICE AREAS:*** Commercial Law; Leasing; Banking Law; Bankruptcy. ***Email:*** joe@mason-law.com

RACHEL J. MASON, born Cincinnati, Ohio, December 8, 1977; admitted to bar, 2003, Ohio. *Education:* Lehigh University (B.A., high honors, 2000); Dickinson School of Law of the Pennsylvania State University (J.D., 2003). Recipient, Award of Excellence, Commercial Law. ***PRACTICE AREAS:*** Commercial Law; Bankruptcy; Creditors Rights; Collections. ***Email:*** rachel@mason-law.com

KATHRYN H. HOGAN, born Berwyn, Illinois, June 19, 1962; admitted to bar, 1988, Illinois; 1989, Kentucky and U.S. District Court, Western and Eastern Districts of Kentucky and Southern District of Indiana; U.S. Court of Appeals, Sixth Circuit (Not admitted in Ohio). *Education:* University of Dayton (B.A., 1984); University of Louisville School of Law (J.D., 1988). Delta Theta Phi. *Member:* Louisville, Kentucky and American Bar Associations; Women Lawyers Association. ***PRACTICE AREAS:*** Commercial Litigation; Bankruptcy; Creditors Rights; Creditor Collections. ***Email:*** kathy@mason-law.com

OF COUNSEL

FRED H. SUMME, born Covington, Kentucky, April 11, 1949; admitted to bar, 1976, Kentucky and U.S. District Court of Kentucky (Not admitted in Ohio). *Education:* Thomas More College (B.A., 1973); Salmon P. Chase College of Law, Northern Kentucky University (J.D., 1976). *Member:* Kentucky and Northern Kentucky Bar Associations. (Resident, Covington, KY Office). ***PRACTICE AREAS:*** Collections. ***Email:*** msm@mason-law.coom

RICHARD L. LEVINE, born Columbus, Ohio, February 12, 1958; admitted to bar, 1984, Georgia, Ohio, U.S. District Court, Northern District of Georgia and U.S. Court of Appeals, 11th Circuit; 1987, Minnesota; 1988, U.S. District Court, Southern District of Ohio. *Education:* Indiana University (B.A., 1980); Emory University (J.D., 1984). *Member:* Columbus, Ohio State and American Bar Associations; State Bar of Georgia. (Resident, Columbus Office). ***LANGUAGES:*** Hebrew. ***PRACTICE AREAS:*** Real Estate; Civil Litigation; Commercial Law. ***Email:*** msm@mason-law.com

KRISTEN D. VANDEWATER, born Carrolton, Kentucky, October 24, 1976; admitted to bar, 2002, Indiana (Not admitted in Ohio). *Education:* Indiana University, New Albany (D.Psych., 1999); University of Louisville (J.D., 2002). Member, Indiana Pro Bono Council, 2002—. *Member:* Jefferson County and Indiana State Bar Associations; Indiana Trial Lawyers Association; The Association of Trial Lawyers of America. (Also Associate, Barlow Law Office, Madison, Indiana). ***PRACTICE AREAS:*** Banking Law; Commercial Law; Collections; Real Estate; Family Law; Criminal Law; Personal Injury. ***Email:*** msm@mason-law.com

SENIOR LEGAL SUPPORT PERSONNEL

BRENDA L. NORTON (Law Firm Manager and Executive Legal Secretary)

LISA K. SPENCER (Sr. Case Manager; Accounting Manager)

MARILYN E. MASON. *Education:* State University of New York; University of Cincinnati (B.S.; M.Ed.). (Sr. Legal Assistant-Accounting)

SARAH HOSKINS (Senior Legal Assistant-Recovery)

ANNA DOOLEY (Legal Assistant-Recovery)

CONNIE SHUTT. *Education:* University of Cincinnati (A.A.). (Paralegal-Litigation)

LORI HENSLEY. *Education:* Northern Kentucky University (B.A., Criminal Justice). (Paralegal-Litigation and Bankruptcy)

YELENA SHUSTER (Legal Assistant)

(This Listing Continued)

LINDA TYE, (Legal Assistant)

TRACY KINCAID, (Legal Assistant-Recovery)

REPRESENTATIVE CLIENTS: First Interstate Bank; Global Leasing Corp.; Barnett Banks; Share Fax Credit Union; Republic Bank; Mohawk Industries; The Fifth Third Bancorp; The Fifth Third Bank; Citicorp and Citibank, N.A.; Contel Credit Corp.; Borg-Warner Acceptance Corporation; Caterpillar Financial Corp.; Commercial Union Insurance Co.; First Financial Savings Bank; General Ionics, Inc., Subsidiary of Ionics, Inc.; Health and Education Credit Union; Superior Savings Bank; Hobart Corporation; Central Transport, Inc.; Dunlop Tire Co.; General Electric Credit Corporation; GTE Leasing Corp.; Hallmark Cards Inc.; Globe Furniture Rentals, Inc.; 84 Lumber Company; Transamerica Commercial Finance, Inc.; Transit Credit Union; Toyota Motor Credit Corp.; Mercedes-Benz Credit Corp.; Mason-Dixon Lines, Inc.; Novus Financial Services (formerly Sears); GCM Group of Pittsburgh and Cleveland, Inc.; Connecticut Mutual Life Insurance Co.; Jewish Hospital Credit Union; Union Federal Savings Bank; ITT Hartford Insurance Co.; ORIX Leasing Services; Parisian Credit Services; Xerox Credit Services; Key Corp Bank; Autofinance Group; Nationsbank; Cincinnati Bell, Inc.; Nike, Inc.; Arcadia Health Services; Volvo Financial Services; Mellon Bank; Colonial Pacific Corp.; U.S. Bank; Provident Bank Information Leasing Corp.; Park National Bank; Morgan Stanley Dean Witter; Fairfield National Bank; Century National Bank; Richland Bank; Unity National Bank; Second National Bank.
SPECIAL COUNSEL FOR: State of Wisconsin; State of Minnesota; State of Arizona; State of New York; Allstate Insurance Co.; Nationwide Insurance Co.; Liberty Mutual Insurance Co.; Midwest Payment Systems; Bank of Louisiana; Associates Financial; ITT Credit Corp.; Fifth-Third Leasing Co.
REFERENCES: Fifth-Third Bank of Cincinnati; Fifth-Third Bank of Northern Kentucky.

MASUDA, FUNAI, EIFERT & MITCHELL, LTD.

CINCINNATI, OHIO

(See Chicago, Illinois)

International Business, Corporations, Corporate Financing and Reorganizations, Mergers and Acquisitions, Joint Ventures, Real Estate, Environmental Law, Banking, Finance and Lending, Antitrust and Trade Regulations, Unfair Competition, Commercial Transactions, Employment and Labor Relations, Immigration, Technology Licensing, Intellectual Property, Multi-state and Local Taxation, Probate, Insurance Defense, Product and Professional Liability, Arbitration, Corporate and Commercial Litigation and Trials in all Courts, and General Civil Practice.

McCASLIN, IMBUS & McCASLIN

A LEGAL PROFESSIONAL ASSOCIATION

Established in 1947

THE PROVIDENT BUILDING
632 VINE STREET
SUITE 900
CINCINNATI, OHIO 45202-2442
Telephone: 513-421-4646
Fax: 513-421-7929
URL: http://www.mimlaw.com

West Chester, Ohio Office: 7969 Cincinnati-Dayton Road, 45069. Telephone: 513-759-9123. Fax: 513-759-7688.

Alternative Dispute Resolution, Bonds, Business Law, Civil Rights, Civil Litigation, Contracts, Domestic Relations, Environmental Law, Guardianship and Conservatorship, Insurance, Labor and Employment, Legal Malpractice, Medical Malpractice, Personal Injury, Probate, Products Liability, Professional Liability, School Law, Trade Secrets; Trust and Estates, Workers' Compensation, Wills.

PHILIP J. MARSICK, born Cleveland, Ohio, October 14, 1941; admitted to bar, 1972, Ohio; 1988, Kentucky. *Education:* Xavier University (B.S., 1963; M.B.A., 1967); Salmon P. Chase College of Law (J.D., 1972). Member, Defense Research Institute. *Member:* Cincinnati, Northern Kentucky, Ohio State and Kentucky Bar Associations. ***Email:*** pjmarsick@mimlaw.com

JOHN K. HURD, born Warren, Ohio, December 27, 1943; admitted to bar, 1974, Ohio. *Education:* Miami University (B.S., B.A., 1970); Salmon P. Chase College of Law (J.D., 1974). Member, Order of the Curia. *Member:* Cincinnati, Ohio State and American Bar Associations; Ohio Association of Civil Trial Attorneys. ***Email:*** jkhurd@mimlaw.com

R. GARY WINTERS, born East Liverpool, Ohio, March 4, 1948; admitted to bar, 1976, Ohio; 1995, Kentucky. *Education:* University of Cincinnati (B.A., 1970; M.A., 1972; J.D., with honors, 1976). Law Clerk, Hon. Carl B. Rubin, U.S. District Court, Southern District of Ohio, 1976-1978. *Member:* Cincinnati, Ohio State and Kentucky Bar Associations; Defense Research Institute; Ohio Association of Civil Trial Attorneys. American Board of Trial Advocates. Fellow, American College of Trial Lawyers. ***Email:*** rgwinters@mimlaw.com

THOMAS J. GRUBER, born Cincinnati, Ohio, May 3, 1954; admitted to bar, 1979, Ohio; 2000, Kentucky. *Education:* Xavier University (B.A., 1976); University of Cincinnati (J.D., 1979). *Member:* Cincinnati, Kentucky and Ohio State Bar Associations; American Board of Trial Advocates; Ohio Association of Civil Trial Attorneys. ***Email:*** tjgruber@mimlaw.com

JOSEPH C. GRUBER, born Cincinnati, Ohio, July 2, 1961; admitted to bar, 1986, Ohio. *Education:* University of Notre Dame (B.A., 1983); University of Cincinnati (J.D., 1986). *Member:* Cincinnati, Ohio State and American Bar Associations. ***Email:*** jcgruber@mimlaw.com

BERNARD W. WHARTON, born San Diego, California, November 26, 1967; admitted to bar, 1994, Ohio. *Education:* Pomona College (B.A., 1989); University of Cincinnati (J.D., 1994). Recipient, American Jurisprudence Award-Civil Procedure. Member, University of Cincinnati, Law Review, 1992-1993. *Member:* Cincinnati and Ohio State Bar Associations; Defense Research Institute; Ohio Council of School Board Attorneys; Ohio Association of Civil Trial Attorneys. ***Email:*** bwwharton@mimlaw.com

(This Listing Continued)

MICHAEL P. CUSSEN, born Cincinnati, Ohio, September 15, 1969; admitted to bar, 1995, Ohio; 1998, U.S. District Court, Southern District of Ohio; 2002, Kentucky. *Education:* Xavier University (B.A., 1991); Salmon P. Chase College of Law (J.D., 1995). *Member:* Cincinnati and Ohio State Bar Associations. ***Email:*** mpcussen@mimlaw.com

IAN R. SMITH, born Cincinnati, Ohio, December 1, 1971; admitted to bar, 1997, Ohio; 1998, U.S. District Court, Southern District of Ohio. *Education:* Kenyon College (B.A., 1994); University of Cincinnati (J.D., 1997). *Member:* Cincinnati and Ohio State Bar Associations; Ohio Association of Civil Trial Attorneys. ***Email:*** irsmith@mimlaw.com

STEPHEN M. BERNAT, born Cincinnati, Ohio, February 16, 1971; admitted to bar, 1998, Ohio; 1999, U.S. District Court, Southern District of Ohio; 2003, Indiana. *Education:* Ohio University (B.B.A., 1993); Chase College of Law at Northern Kentucky University (J.D., 1998). Member, Student Bar Association, 1996-1998. *Member:* Cincinnati and Ohio State Bar Associations. ***Email:*** smbernat@mimlaw.com

WILLIAM M. CUSSEN, born Boston, Massachusetts, November 26, 1943; admitted to bar, 1969, Ohio. *Education:* Wheeling College; Xavier University (B.S., 1965); Salmon P. Chase College of Law (J.D., 1969). Member, Board of Visitors, Salmon P. Chase College of Law, 1994—. *Member:* Cincinnati and Ohio State Bar Associations; Ohio Association of Civil Trial Attorneys; Defense Research Institute; American Board of Trial Advocates. ***PRACTICE AREAS:*** General Civil Litigation; Negligence Law; Insurance Law.

OF COUNSEL

JOHN P. CONCANNON, born Chicago, Illinois, May 19, 1949; admitted to bar, 1976, Ohio. *Education:* Xavier University (B.S., 1971; M.S., 1976); Salmon P. Chase College of Law (J.D., 1976). *Member:* Cincinnati Bar Association. ***Email:*** jpcwon@aol.com

REPRESENTATIVE CLIENTS: Acuity Insurance Co.; American Bankers Insurance Co.; Armor Elevator Co.; Becor-Western, Inc.; Broadspire; Champion Home Builders Co.; Cincinnati Public Schools; C.L Zimmerman Co.; Coca Cola Enterprises, Inc.; Colony Management Co.; Continental Plastic Containers, Inc.; Crown Cork & Seal Co.; Inc.; Fluor Corp.; General Reinsurance Co.; Genesis Insurance Co.; Great American Insurance Co.; Harsco Corp.; Hylant Claims Service; Indiana Insurance Co.; Liberty Mutual Insurance Co.; 3M; Nationwide Mutual Insurance Co.; The North Side Bank and Trust Company; Orbis Manufacturing Co.; Queen City Metro; Rock-Tenn Co.; Schering-Plough Corp.; Seven Hills Financial, LLC; Smith & Nephew, Inc.; Southwest Ohio Regional Transit Authority; Sun Microsystems; St. Paul Fire & Marine Insurance Co.; Textron; TIG Insurance Co.; Time Warner Cable, Inc.; Travelers Property Casualty; TRW Inc.; U.S. Financial, LLC; Wallgreen Co.; Watkins Motor Lines; Westfield Group.

McKINNEY & NAMEI CO., L.P.A.

Established in 1983

15 EAST EIGHTH STREET
CINCINNATI, OHIO 45202
Telephone: 513-721-0200
Fax: 513-632-5898
Email: firooz@zoomtown.com

Covington, Kentucky Office: 700 Scott Street, P.O. Box 120008, 41012-0008. Telephone: 513-721-0200. Fax: 513-632-5898.

General Civil and Criminal, Trial and Appellate Practice in all Courts. Business, Corporate, Personal Injury, Immigration, ERISA, Real Estate, Insurance, Family Law and Divorce. Alternative Dispute Resolution, Estate Planning, Probate, Employee Benefits, Pension and Profit Sharing and Federal and State Taxation.

DANIEL H. McKINNEY, born Cincinnati, Ohio, December 1, 1929; admitted to bar, 1955, District of Columbia; 1959, Ohio. *Education:* The Ohio State University (A.B., 1951); Harvard University (J.D., 1954). Certified in Estate Planning, Trust and Taxation. *Member:* Ohio State (Member, Trust and Probate Sections) and American (Member, Committees on: Employee Benefits, 1976-1982; Personal Service Corporations, 1982—; Section of Taxation) Bar Associations. [Capt., USMCR, 1954-1963]. ***LANGUAGES:*** Spanish and Russian. ***PRACTICE AREAS:*** ERISA Litigation; Commercial Litigation; Employee Benefit Law; Estate and Probate; Taxation; Corporate; Estate Planning; Immigration Law. ***Email:*** dhmc@msn.com

FIROOZ T. NAMEI, born Tehran, Iran, November 10, 1941; admitted to bar, 1982, Ohio, U.S. District Court, Northern District of Ohio and U.S. Court of Appeals, Fourth, Sixth and Seventh Circuits; 1983, U.S. District Court, Southern District of Ohio; 1995, Kentucky. *Education:* University of Cincinnati (B.S., 1971; J.D., 1982). Member, Board of Editors, University of Cincinnati Law Review, 1981-1982. *Member:* Cincinnati Bar Association; American Immigration Lawyers Association; American Association of Criminal Defense Lawyers. ***LANGUAGES:*** Farsi. ***PRACTICE AREAS:*** Civil Litigation; Criminal Litigation; Personal Injury; Immigration; Family Law. ***Email:*** firooz@zoomtown.com

ASSOCIATES

JOHN ROBERT NATKEVICIUS, born Garfield, Ohio, June 10, 1969; admitted to bar, 2002, Ohio; U.S. Supreme Court; Kentucky Supreme Court. *Education:* John Carroll University (B.A., 1992); University of Ohio (M.A., 1996); University of Toledo School of Law (J.D., 2001). ***PRACTICE AREAS:*** Immigration (50%); Criminal Defense (50%). ***Email:*** johnnynatk@juno.com

BLAKE P. SOMERS, born Nashville, Tennessee, September 2, 1979; admitted to bar, 2004, Ohio; 2005, U.S. District Court, Southern District of Ohio. *Education:* Xavier University (B.A., History, 2001); University of Cincinnati (J.D., 2004). *Member:* Ohio State Bar Association. ***PRACTICE AREAS:*** Criminal Defense (40%); Immigration (40%); Domestic Relations (10%); Probate (10%). ***Email:*** blakesomers@hotmail.com

REPRESENTATIVE CLIENTS: Apollo Glass, Mirror, Window & Screen Co.; Aria's Oriental Rugs, Inc.; Business Information Solutions, Inc.; Westvaco Corporation; Center For Economic Initiatives, Inc.; Crowne Travel and Tours; H.A.G. Steel Contractors, Inc.; Huntington National Bank; Samaritan Counseling Center of Cincinnati, Inc.; Water Quality Insurance Syndicate; Village of Woodlawn, Ohio.

MEZIBOV & JENKINS, LLP

401 EAST COURT STREET, SUITE 600
CINCINNATI, OHIO 45202
Telephone: 513-723-1600
Fax: 513-723-1620
Email: esteelman@mezibovjenkins.com
URL: http://www.mezibovjenkins.com

Employment Discrimination, Title VII Discrimination, Sexual Harassment, Civil Rights, Constitutional Law, Litigation, Employment Law, Class Actions.

MARC D. MEZIBOV, born Newark, New Jersey, September 23, 1945; admitted to bar, 1970, New Jersey; 1974, Ohio. *Education:* American University (B.A., 1967); Boston University (J.D., 1970). Phi Alpha Theta. Member, 1981— and General Counsel and Member, Board of Directors, 1982—, Cincinnati Chapter, American Civil Liberties Union. *Member:* Cincinnati (Member, Committee on Criminal Law, 1974—; Chairman, Civil Rights Committee, 1984-1986) and Ohio State Bar Associations. ***REPORTED CASES:*** City of Cincinnati v. Discovery Network, Inc. 507 U.S. 410 (1993); State ex. Rel. The Miami Student v. Miami University, 79 Ohio St. 3d 168 (1997), 680 N.F.2d 956 (1997); Johnson v. University of Cincinnati, 215 F.3d 561 (2000); Chabad of Southern Ohio, et al. v. City of Cincinnati, 363 F.3d 427 (6th Cir. 2004); S.J. v. Hillcrest Training School, et al., 374 F.3d 416 (6th Cir. 2004). ***PRACTICE AREAS:*** Employment Discrimination; Title VII Discrimination; Sexual Harassment; Civil Rights; Constitutional Law; Litigation.

CHRISTIAN A. JENKINS, born Sharon, Connecticut, January 29, 1969; admitted to bar, 1995, Wisconsin and U.S. District Court, Western and Eastern Districts of Wisconsin and Northern District of Illinois; 1999, Ohio and U.S. District Court, Southern District of Ohio and U.S. Court of Appeals, Sixth Circuit. *Education:* Pennsylvania State University (B.A., with distinction, 1991); Georgetown University Law Center; University of Wisconsin Law School (J.D., cum laude, 1995). Recipient, ABA/BNA Labor and Employment Award, 1995. Author: "Effective Agreements to Arbitrate Statutory Employment Claims," Wisconsin Lawyer, April 1998; Reviser, "Wisconsin Employment Law," Vol. III, State Bar of Wisconsin, 1998. *Member:* Ohio State and American Bar Associations; State Bar of Wisconsin. ***REPORTED CASES:*** Frantz v. Village of Bradford, 245 F.3d 869 (6th Cir. 2001); Pollitt v. Roadway Express, 228 F.Supp.2d 854 (S.D. Ohio 2002); Cervantes v. Sugar Creek Packing, 210 F.R.D. 611 (S.D. Ohio 2002); Seifer v. Adam and Eve, 196 F.Supp.2d 622 (S.D. Ohio 2002). ***PRACTICE AREAS:*** Employment Law; Civil Rights; Class Actions; Litigation.

STACY HINNERS, born Huron, Ohio, August 25, 1978; admitted to bar, 2003, Ohio and U.S. District Court, Southern District of Ohio. *Education:* Ohio Wesleyan University (B.A., with distinction, 2000); University of Dayton (J.D., 2003). Omicron Delta Kappa. Member: Moot Court Team; Mock Trial Team. Staff Attorney for Judge John W. Kessler, Dayton, Ohio, 2003-2004. *Member:* Cincinnati and Ohio State Bar Associations. ***PRACTICE AREAS:*** Employment Law; Civil Rights; Litigation.

OF COUNSEL

WENDY R. CALAWAY, born Houston, Texas, December 2, 1973; admitted to bar, 1998, Ohio; 1999, U.S. District Court, Southern District of Ohio and U.S. Court of Appeals, Sixth Circuit. *Education:* University of Cincinnati (B.A., with honors, 1995; J.D., 1998). *Member:* Cincinnati and Ohio State Bar Associations; Cincinnati Criminal Defense Lawyers Association. ***PRACTICE AREAS:*** Criminal Defense; Business Law; Business Litigation; Estate Planning.

SUSAN E. BRABENEC, born Jacksonville, Florida, March 20, 1975; admitted to bar, 2002, Ohio. *Education:* Florida State University (B.A., 1997); University of Cincinnati (J.D., 2002). Author: "The Art of Determining 'Stolen Property:' U.S. v. Portrait of Wally, A Painting by Egon Schiele, 105 F.Supp.2d 288 (S.D.N.Y. 2000)," 69 U. Cin. L.Rev. 1369 (2001). ***PRACTICE AREAS:*** Employment Discrimination; Title VII Discrimination; Sexual Harassment; Civil Rights; Class Actions; Litigation.

THE LAW FIRM OF TINA R. MILLS, LLC

Established in 2000

4351 GLENESTE WITHAMSVILLE ROAD
CINCINNATI, OHIO 45245
Telephone: 513-732-9999
Fax: 513-735-2455
Email: mills@millslegal.com
URL: http://www.millslegal.com

Business Law, Buying and Selling of Businesses, Family Business Law, Limited Liability Company Law, Partnership Law, Small Business Law, Consumer Law, Corporate Law, Criminal Law, Debtor and Creditor, Collections, Creditors Rights, Nonprofit and Charitable Organizations, Charitable Giving, Landlord and Tenant Law, Trusts and Estates, Asset Protection, Estate Litigation, Estate Planning, Guardianship and Conservatorship, Wills and Probate.

TINA RENEE MILLS, born Cincinnati, Ohio, January 22, 1972; admitted to bar, 1999, Ohio; 2001, U.S. District Court, Southern District of Ohio. *Education:* College of Mount St. Joseph-on the Ohio (B.A., cum laude, 1994); Dayton Law School (J.D., 1997). Phi Delta Phi. Member: Recipient, C.A.L.I. Awards: Business Planning, Criminal Procedure-Police, Commercial and Business Drafting. Clermont Chamber of Commerce, 2000— Cincinnati Chamber of Commerce, 2002— Clermont Leadership Institute, 2001—. Adjunct Professor, Taxation for Paralegals and Introduction to Business, University of Cincinnati, 2001. Lecturer: Small Business Administration and Small Business Seminars; Clermont County League of Women Voters-"Now You're 18" Program. *Member:* Cincinnati, Clermont, Ohio State, Federal and American Bar Associations; Association of Trial Lawyers of America; Ohio Academy of Trial Lawyers. ***PRACTICE AREAS:*** Business Planning; Estate Planning; Probate; Personal Injury; Criminal Law; Civil Litigation. ***Email:*** mills@millslegal.com

(This Listing Continued)

MONTGOMERY, RENNIE & JONSON

Established in 1989

36 EAST SEVENTH STREET, SUITE 2100
CINCINNATI, OHIO 45202-4413
Telephone: 513-241-4722
Fax: 513-241-8775
Email: mrjlaw@mrj.cc

Civil Trial and Appellate Practice in: Automotive, Aviation, Civil Rights, Commercial Construction, Consumer, Employment, Environmental, Motor Carrier Liability, Personal Injury, Premises Liability, Products Liability, Professional Malpractice.

FIRM PROFILE: As regional or national counsel for several clients, the firm is involved in litigation throughout the United States. The firm members and associates are admitted to the state and federal courts of Ohio, Kentucky, Pennsylvania, Indiana, Texas, Florida, New York, and Michigan and have tried lawsuits in California, Illinois, Iowa, Louisiana, Nevada, New York, North Carolina, North Dakota, Oklahoma, South Carolina, Texas, Washington and West Virginia, as well as Ohio and Kentucky. The firm represents Ohio state court judges in civil damages litigation.

MEMBERS OF FIRM

JAMES J. MONTGOMERY, born Cincinnati, Ohio, August 1, 1948; admitted to bar, 1976, Ohio; 1991, Kentucky. *Education:* Miami University at Oxford (B.S.Ed., 1970); Salmon P. Chase College of Law of Northern Kentucky University (J.D., 1976). Member, Order of the Curiae. *Member:* Cincinnati, Ohio State, Kentucky and American Bar Associations. ***PRACTICE AREAS:*** Commercial Litigation; Construction Law; Machinery, Tools and Equipment. ***Email:*** jmontgomery@mrj.cc

DOUGLAS W. RENNIE, born Minneapolis, Minnesota, June 27, 1952; admitted to bar, 1978, Ohio; 1979, Kentucky. *Education:* Miami University at Oxford (B.A., 1974); Salmon P. Chase College of Law (J.D., 1978). *Member:* Cincinnati, Ohio State, Kentucky and American Bar Associations; Trucking Industry Defense Association. ***PRACTICE AREAS:*** Products Liability; Transportation; Motor Carrier Liability. ***Email:*** drennie@mrj.cc

GEORGE D. JONSON, born Columbus, Ohio, July 4, 1957; admitted to bar, 1983, Ohio; 1991, Kentucky. *Education:* Miami University at Oxford, Ohio (B.A., 1979); University of Cincinnati (J.D., 1983). *Member:* Cincinnati, Ohio State, Kentucky and American Bar Associations. ***PRACTICE AREAS:*** Professional Malpractice; Commercial Litigation; Personal Injury. ***Email:*** gjonson@mrj.cc

KELLY CARBETTA SCANDY, born Mansfield, Ohio, June 14, 1960; admitted to bar, 1986, Ohio; 1992, Kentucky. *Education:* Bowling Green State University (B.A., cum laude, 1982); University of Cincinnati (J.D., 1986). Member, University of Cincinnati Law Review, 1984-1986. *Member:* Cincinnati, Ohio State, Kentucky and American Bar Associations. ***PRACTICE AREAS:*** Vehicle Products Liability; Motor Carrier Liability; Consumer Litigation; Commercial Arbitration. ***Email:*** kscandy@mrj.cc

LINDA L. WOEBER, born Pittsburgh, Pennsylvania, November 6, 1962; admitted to bar, 1987, Ohio; 1993, Kentucky and Pennsylvania. *Education:* Miami University (B.S., 1984); University of Cincinnati (J.D., 1987). *Member:* Cincinnati (Past Chair, Labor and Employment Law Committee) Ohio State, Kentucky and Pennsylvania Bar Associations. (Certified Specialist in Labor and Employment Law, Ohio State Bar Association). ***PRACTICE AREAS:*** Employment Law. ***Email:*** lwoeber@mrj.cc

ELIZABETH P. SHERWOOD, born Manchester, Tennessee, March 24, 1958; admitted to bar, 1987, Ohio. *Education:* University of Tennessee at Chattanooga (B.S., 1980; M.S., 1984); University of Cincinnati (J.D., 1987). *Member:* Cincinnati (Vice-Chair, Alternative Dispute Resolution Committee), Ohio State and American Bar Associations; Ohio Academy of Trial Lawyers; Kentucky Academy of Trial Lawyers. ***PRACTICE AREAS:*** Asbestos Litigation; Personal Injury; Commercial Litigation; Insurance; Mediation; Collaborative Law. ***Email:*** esherwood@mrj.cc

JANET A. SELF, born Clovis, New Mexico, May 11, 1954; admitted to bar, 1988, Ohio and U.S. Court of Appeals, Sixth Circuit. *Education:* University of Cincinnati (B.A., 1980; M.P.A., 1982; J.D., 1988). *Member:* Cincinnati, Ohio State and American Bar Associations; Defense Research Institute. ***PRACTICE AREAS:*** Motor Carrier Liability; Premises Liability for Violent Crimes; Neuropsychological and Psychological Injury Claims; Personal Injury. ***Email:*** jself@mrj.cc

RALPH E. BURNHAM, born Palo Alto, California, September 19, 1964; admitted to bar, 1991, Texas; 1997, Ohio; 1998, Kentucky. *Education:* University of Texas at Austin (B.A., 1987); University of Houston (J.D., 1991). Phi Delta Phi. *Member:* Ohio State and Kentucky Bar Associations; State Bar of Texas. ***LANGUAGES:*** Spanish. ***PRACTICE AREAS:*** Professional Malpractice; Products Liability; Commercial Litigation; Employment Litigation; Personal Injury; Insurance. ***Email:*** rburnham@mrj.cc

G. TODD HOFFPAUIR, born Lafayette, Louisiana, July 18, 1966; admitted to bar, 1995, Ohio; 1998, U.S. Court of Appeal, Sixth Circuit; 1999, U.S. Court of Appeals, Fifth Circuit. *Education:* University of Southwestern Louisiana (B.S., 1988); Loyola University (J.D., 1994). *Member:* Cincinnati, Ohio State and American Bar Associations. ***PRACTICE AREAS:*** Products Liability; Motor Carrier Liability; Commercial Litigation; Personal Injury. ***Email:*** thoffpauir@mrj.cc

MATTHEW E. STUBBS, born Kettering, Ohio, February 12, 1970; admitted to bar, 1996, Ohio; 1999, Indiana. *Education:* Ohio State University (B.A., 1992); University of Cincinnati (J.D., 1996). Member, Moot Court, 1994-1996. *Member:* Cincinnati, Ohio State, Indiana State and American Bar Associations. ***PRACTICE AREAS:*** Products Liability; Commercial Litigation; Consumer Litigation; Insurance Law; Personal Injury. ***Email:*** mstubbs@mrj.cc

(This Listing Continued)

KIMBERLY VANOVER RILEY, born Huntington, West Virginia, May 7, 1973; admitted to bar, 1997, Ohio and U.S. District Court, Southern District of Ohio; 1998, U.S. District Court, Northern District of Ohio; U.S. Court of Appeals, Sixth Circuit; 2004, Kentucky. *Education:* University of Cincinnati (B.A., 1994; J.D., 1997). Member, Moot Court, 1995-1997. *Member:* Cincinnati (Member: Labor and Employment Law Committee, 1997—; Civil Rights Committee, 2001—), Ohio, Federal and American Bar Associations. (Certified Specialist in Labor and Employment Law, Ohio State Bar Association). ***PRACTICE AREAS:*** Employment Law; Civil Rights Litigation. ***Email:*** kriley@mrj.cc

TIMOTHY C. AMMER, born Stoneham, Massachusetts, July 18, 1971; admitted to bar, 1998, Ohio; 1999, Indiana. *Education:* University of North Carolina (B.S.B.A., Minor: History, 1993); University of Cincinnati (J.D., 1998). *Member:* Cincinnati, Ohio State, Indiana State and American Bar Associations. ***PRACTICE AREAS:*** Mass Torts; Asbestos Litigation; Products Liability; Premises Liability; Commercial Litigation; Personal Injury; Consumer Litigation; Insurance Law. ***Email:*** tammer@mrj.cc

JASON A. GOLDEN, born Knoxville, Tennessee, February 24, 1970; admitted to bar, 1995, New York; 1998, Florida; 2003, Ohio. *Education:* Indiana University (B.S., 1991); Tulane University Law School (J.D., cum laude, 1994). Co-Author: "Passenger Claims (Cruise Ships, Gambling Ships and Small Boats)," Southeastern Admiralty Law Seminar, Savannah, Georgia, 1998. *Member:* Cincinnati and Ohio State Bar Associations. [Lt. Cmdr., JAGC, U.S. Naval Reserve, 1993—]. ***PRACTICE AREAS:*** Transportation; Motor Carrier Liability; Consumer Litigation; Admiralty and Maritime Law. ***Email:*** jgolden@mrj.cc

HOPE A. SMITH, born Philadelphia, Pennsylvania, May 22, 1976; admitted to bar, 2001, Kentucky; 2002, Ohio and U.S. District Court, Southern District of Ohio; 2003, U.S. District Court, Northern, District of Ohio, U.S. District Court, Eastern District of Kentucky, U.S. Court of Appeals, Sixth and Eleventh Circuits. *Education:* University of Pennsylvania (B.A., 1998); University of Cincinnati College of Law (J.D., 2001). Member, University of Cincinnati Law Review, 1999-2000. President, Student Bar Association, 2000-2001. *Member:* Cincinnati, Kentucky, Ohio State and American Bar Associations. ***PRACTICE AREAS:*** Professional Malpractice; Employment Law; Commercial Litigation; Personal Injury; Insurance. ***Email:*** hsmith@mrj.cc

JENNIFER D. DINE, born Findlay, Ohio, March 30, 1977; admitted to bar, 2003, Ohio; 2004, Michigan and U.S. District Court, Southern District of Ohio. *Education:* University of Michigan, Ann Arbor (B.A., 1998); University of Cincinnati College of Law (J.D., 2003). Member, Moot Court Honor Board, University of Cincinnati, 2001-2003. ***LANGUAGES:*** Spanish. ***PRACTICE AREAS:*** Consumer Litigation; Products Liability; Motor Carrier Liability. ***Email:*** jdine@mrj.cc

PAMELA MARSHALL, born Hamilton, Ontario, Canada, April 24, 1965; admitted to bar, 2004, Ohio. *Education:* Northern Kentucky University (B.S., 2000); Salmon P. Chase College of Law (J.D., 2004). *Member:* Cincinnati, Ohio State and American (Member, Construction Law Section) Bar Associations. ***PRACTICE AREAS:*** Construction Law; Construction Litigation; Products Liability; Motor Carrier Liability; Employment Law. ***Email:*** pmarshall@mrj.cc

OF COUNSEL

KEVIN J. HOPPER, born Cincinnati, Ohio, December 10, 1950; admitted to bar, 1978, Ohio. *Education:* University of Cincinnati (B.S.M.E., 1973); Salmon P. Chase College of Law (J.D., 1978). *Member:* Cincinnati (Member, Wills and Probate Committee, 1980; Chairman, Environmental Law Subcommittee, 1984-1986), Clermont County, Ohio State and American (Member, Sections of: Natural Resources Law; Real Property, Probate and Trust Law) Bar Associations. (Also practicing individually at 7434 Jager Court, Cincinnati, Ohio, 45230)

ELIZABETH A. McCORD, born Gassaway, West Virginia, January 16, 1952; admitted to bar, 1982, Ohio; 1994, U.S. Court of Appeals, Sixth Circuit; 1996, U.S. Supreme Court; 2001, Kentucky. *Education:* Alderson-Broaddus College; Berea College (B.A., 1973); Eastern Kentucky University (M.A., 1975); University of Kentucky (J.D., 1981). Law Review. Moot Court, National Team. *Member:* Ohio State and Kentucky Bar Associations. ***LANGUAGES:*** French. ***PRACTICE AREAS:*** Employment; Civil Rights Defense; Commercial Litigation; Appellate Practice. ***Email:*** emccord@mrj.cc

REPRESENTATIVE CLIENTS: Admiral Insurance Company; American Honda Motor Co., Inc.; ATC Leasing; Averitt Express, Inc.; The Braun Corporation; Cambridge Integrated Services Group, Inc.; The Coleman Company, Inc.; Commercial Truck Claims Management; Commonwealth Insurance Co.; Countrywide Services Corporation; C.R. England, Inc.; Dart Transit; Delta Airlines, Inc.; DHL Worldwide Express; Ford New Holland, Inc.; Freightliner LLC; Gainey Corporation; Great American Insurance; Great West Casualty Company; Infinity / Leader National Insurance; International Truck & Engine Corporation; Komatsu America International Company; Lancer Insurance Company; Landair Transport, Inc.; Mattei Companies; Mazda Motors of America; Millis Transfer, Inc.; National Claims Management; National Interstate Insurance Company; Network Adjusters; Nissan Motor Corporation in U.S.A., Inc.; NTA, Inc.; PACCAR Inc.; Permanent General Assurance Corp.; Ralston Purina Company; Roadway Express; Sigmatek Corp.; St. Paul Fire & Marine Insurance; Swift Transportation Co.; Tecumseh Products Company; The Terminix International Company, L.P.; TIG Insurance; Toyota Motor Sales, U.S.A., Inc.; The Tokio Marine and Fire Insurance Co., Ltd.; Transportation Claims, Inc.; Transport Service Co.; United States Aviation Underwriters, Inc.; U.S. Xpress Enterprises, Inc.; W.E. Love & Associates; Yellow Cab (Claims Service).

MOSKOWITZ & MOSKOWITZ

4300 CAREW TOWER
441 VINE STREET
CINCINNATI, OHIO 45202
Telephone: 513-721-3111
Fax: 513-721-3077
URL: http://www.lawyers.com/mm-law

Domestic Relations, Civil Litigation, Appeals and Probate Law, Automobile Accidents and Injuries, Divorce, Post Divorce Modifications, Child Custody, Child Support, Visitation Rights, Business Litigation, Breach of Contract.

(This Listing Continued)

MEMBERS OF FIRM

JOEL S. MOSKOWITZ, born Cincinnati, Ohio, May 17, 1940; admitted to bar, 1965, Ohio; 1970, U.S. Supreme Court. *Education:* University of Cincinnati (B.A., 1962; J.D., 1965). Phi Alpha Delta. Referee, Court of Domestic Relations, Hamilton County, 1969-1973. *Member:* Cincinnati (Member, 1968-1988 and Chairman, 1984-1985, Bankruptcy Committee; Member, 1969— and Chairman, 1986-1988, Domestic Relations Committee; Member: Grievance Committee, 1992-1995; Ethics Committee, 1987—), Ohio State (Member, Family Law Committee, 1979—; Chairman, 1987-1991; Secretary, 1986) and American Bar Associations. ***PRACTICE AREAS:*** Domestic Relations Law; Corporate Law; Probate Law; Civil Litigation; Business Law. ***Email:*** joel@cincyattorneys.com

MICHAEL A. MOSKOWITZ, born Cincinnati, Ohio, November 20, 1964; admitted to bar, 1989, Ohio; 1995, Kentucky. *Education:* University of Michigan (B.A., 1986); Ohio State University (J.D., 1989). *Member:* Cincinnati Bar Association (Member, Unauthorized Practice of Law Committee, 1991-2004; Chair, 2000-2002); Ohio State Bar Association; Kentucky Bar Association; American Bar Association. ***PRACTICE AREAS:*** Civil Litigation; Corporate; Personal Injury; Appellate Practice. ***Email:*** mam@cincyattorneys.com

JAMES H. MOSKOWITZ, born Cincinnati, Ohio, April 26, 1969; admitted to bar, 1994, Ohio. *Education:* Ohio State University (B.A., 1991); Salmon P. Chase College of Law (J.D., 1994). *Member:* Cincinnati (Member, Domestic Relations Committee), Ohio State and American Bar Associations. ***PRACTICE AREAS:*** Domestic Relations; Estate Law; Civil Practice; Probate. ***Email:*** jhm@cincyattorneys.com

REPRESENTATIVE CLIENTS: ACE Exterminating Co.; Lighting EFX; Three Rivers Nursing and Rehabilitation Center, LLC.
REFERENCES: U.S. Bank; Fifth Third Bank.

MURDOCK GOLDENBERG SCHNEIDER & GROH, L.P.A.

35 EAST SEVENTH STREET, SUITE 600
CINCINNATI, OHIO 45202-2446
Telephone: 513-345-8291
Facsimile: 513-345-8294
Email: info@mgsglaw.com
URL: http://www.mgsglaw.com

Complex Civil Litigation, Class Actions, Consumer Law, Products Liability, Personal Injury, Wrongful Death, Commercial Litigation, Environmental Law, Toxic Torts, Corporate Law.

JOHN C. MURDOCK, born Cincinnati, Ohio, November 24, 1964; admitted to bar, 1994, Ohio; U.S. District Court, Southern and Northern Districts of Ohio; U.S. Court of Appeals, Sixth Circuit; U.S. Court of Federal Claims; U.S. Supreme Court. *Education:* Miami University (B.S., 1987); University of Notre Dame (J.D., 1994). Special Counsel to State and Political Subdivisions. *Member:* Cincinnati, Ohio State and American Bar Associations. [USMC Officer, Active Duty, 1987-1991]. ***PRACTICE AREAS:*** Complex Civil Litigation; Class Actions; ERISA; Fair Labor Standards Act; Consumer Law; Warranty Law; Products Liability; Antitrust; Toxic Torts. ***Email:*** jmurdock@mgsglaw.com

JEFFREY S. GOLDENBERG, born Cincinnati, Ohio, November 8, 1965; admitted to bar, 1994, Ohio; U.S. District Court, Southern and Northern Districts of Ohio. *Education:* Indiana University (B.A., 1988; M.S.E.S., 1994; J.D., 1994). ***PRACTICE AREAS:*** Complex Civil Litigation; Environmental Compliance; Environmental Litigation; Toxic Torts; Products Liability; Commercial Litigation; Consumer Class Actions. ***Email:*** jgoldenberg@mgsglaw.com

THEODORE J. SCHNEIDER, born Ft. Thomas, Kentucky, December 11, 1957; admitted to bar, 1992, Ohio; 1993, Kentucky. *Education:* Thomas More College (B.A., 1980); Purdue University (M.S., 1983); Salmon P. Chase College of Law (J.D., 1992). *Member:* Ohio, Kentucky and Cincinnati Bar Associations; National Lawyers Association. ***PRACTICE AREAS:*** Environmental Law; Environmental Auditing; Environmental Compliance; Utility Regulation; Corporate Law; Estate Planning; Probate; Administrative Agency Practice. ***Email:*** tschneider@mgsglaw.com

THERESA L. GROH, born Cincinnati, Ohio, February 13, 1960; admitted to bar, 1985, Ohio; 1998, U.S. Supreme Court, U.S. Court of Appeals, Sixth Circuit, U.S. District Court, Southern District of Ohio, U.S. Claims Court. *Education:* Miami University (B.A., 1982); University of Cincinnati (J.D., 1985). Member, Order of the Barristers. Law Clerk to Hon. Herman J. Weber, U.S. District Court, Southern District of Ohio. *Member:* Cincinnati, Ohio State and American Bar Associations. ***PRACTICE AREAS:*** Complex Civil Litigation; Consumer Class Actions; Employment Class Actions; ERISA; Antitrust; Personal Injury; Wrongful Death; Product Liability; Toxic Torts. ***Email:*** tgroh@mgsglaw.com

TODD B. NAYLOR, born Plainfield, New Jersey, September 16, 1972; admitted to bar, 1997, Ohio; 2000, U.S. District Court, Southern District of Ohio; 2004, U.S. Court of Appeals, Sixth Circuit, U.S. District Court, Northern District of Ohio and U.S. Supreme Court. *Education:* Bradley University (B.A., 1994); University of Colorado at Boulder (J.D., 1997). Omicron Delta Kappa. Recipient: Legal Aid Award; Trial Advocacy Scholarship. *Member:* Cincinnati and Ohio State Bar Associations; Ohio Academy of Trial Lawyers (Board of Trustees; Chair, Sections on: Toxic; Environmental; Pharmaceutical Torts, 1999-2004); The Association of Trial Lawyers of America. ***PRACTICE AREAS:*** Complex Litigation; Civil Litigation; Toxic Tort Litigation; Products Liability; Medical Malpractice; Personal Injury. ***Email:*** tnaylor@mgsglaw.com

OF COUNSEL

NORMAN A. MURDOCK, born Cincinnati, Ohio, November 6, 1931; admitted to bar, 1968, Ohio; U.S. District Court, Southern District of Ohio, U.S. Court of Federal Claims and U.S. Tax Court. *Education:* Xavier University (B.S., Political Science, Economics, 1955); University of Cincinnati (J.D., 1968). Judge, Court of Common Pleas. Hamilton County Commissioner. State Representative, Ohio House Representative; Delhi Township Clerk/Treasurer. [Honorable Discharge Army Officer.]. ***PRACTICE AREAS:*** Business

(This Listing Continued)

MURDOCK GOLDENBERG SCHNEIDER & GROH, L.P.A., Cincinnati—Continued

Law; Employment Law; Litigation; Personal Injury; Government; Arbitration; Mediation. ***Email:*** higmur@aol.com

NIELSON & SHERRY, PSC

CINCINNATI, OHIO

(See Newport, Kentucky)

Creditors Rights, Foreclosure, Replevin, Bankruptcy, Real Estate, Estate Planning, Corporate Law, Banks and Banking, Business Law, Commercial Law, Debtor/Creditors Rights, Probate, and Tax Practice.

LINDA S. NOVAKOV & ASSOCIATES, PLLC

CINCINNATI, OHIO

(See Erlanger)

Real Estate, Residential, Commercial, Landlord and Tenant, Leases, Foreclosures, Land Contracts and Acquisitions, Condominium Development and Conversion, Conveyancing, Real Estate Acquisitions and Development, Joint Ventures, Title Insurance.

AMY L. OWENS

THE KROGER BUILDING
1014 VINE STREET, SUITE 1525
CINCINNATI, OHIO 45202
Telephone: 513-381-5094
Fax: 513-396-6477

Commercial Law, Corporate Law.

AMY L. OWENS, admitted to bar, 1994, Ohio. *Education:* Campbellsville University (B.A., 1991); University of Cincinnati (J.D., 1994). *Member:* Cincinnati Bar Association. ***PRACTICE AREAS:*** Commercial Law; Corporate Law.

PECK, SHAFFER & WILLIAMS LLP

201 E. 5TH STREET, SUITE 900
CINCINNATI, OHIO 45202
Telephone: 513-621-3394; 800-927-2663
Telecopier: 513-621-3813
Email: lawinfo@peck-shaffer.com
URL: http://www.peck-shaffer.com

Atlanta, Georgia Office: Peck, Shaffer & Williams LLP, Atlanta Financial Center, Suite M20, 3353 Peachtree Road, N.E. Telephone: 404-995-3850. Fax: 404-995-3851.
Chicago, Illinois Office: Peck, Shaffer & Williams LLP, 11 South LaSalle Street, Suite 2100. Telephones: 312-372-6060; 877-372-6060. Fax: 312-372-6085.
Columbus, Ohio Office: Peck, Shaffer & Williams LLP, 175 South Third Street, Suite 600, 43215. Telephone: 614-224-5205; 888-900-5205. Telecopier: 614-224-0069.
Covington, Kentucky Office: Peck, Shaffer & Williams LLP, 118 West 5th Street, 41011. Telephones: 859-431-7000; 888-431-7511. Telecopier: 859-431-0673.
Denver, Colorado Office: Peck, Shaffer & Williams LLP, 555 17th Street, Suite 845 South, 80202. Telephone: 303-296-3996; 877-296-0333. Fax: 303-296-0344.
Louisville, Kentucky Office: Peck, Shaffer & Williams LLP, 239 S. Fifth Street, Suite 1603, 40202. Telephone: 502-561-0054. Telecopier: 502-561-0058.

Public Finance, Municipal Bonds, Municipal Bond Taxation, Municipal Securities, Tax Exempt Bonds, Housing and Urban Development, Health Care Finance, Tax Increment Finance, Municipal Leasing, Public Finance Taxation, Securities Finance, Blue Sky Law, Low Income Housing, Industrial Development Bonds, Municipal Bankruptcy, Public Construction Law.

FIRM PROFILE: Peck, Shaffer & Williams LLP (PS&W) is a law firm with the experience, knowledge and creativity to guide its clients (hundreds of municipalities, counties, school districts, townships, special districts and underwriters) in issuing bonds and other debt instruments. The capital improvements financed with the proceeds of this debt include traditional governmental projects, such as roads, sewers, water systems, all types of public buildings, public infrastructure facilities, such as stadiums, convention centers and single-, multifamily and public housing; facilities for 501(c)(3) organizations, such as hospitals, university and long term care facilities and "exempt facilities" for industrial and commercial users, such as factories, waste recovery plants and port facilities. PS&W's expertise also extends to lease transactions and public construction counsel matters and has helped finance thousands of low-income housing projects in virtually every state.

MEMBERS OF FIRM

HIRAM D. PECK (1844-1914)
FRANK HOLMES SHAFFER (1857-1936)
FLOYD C. WILLIAMS (1884-1963)

BRUCE D. AGIN, born Cleveland, Ohio, September 13, 1961; admitted to bar, 1986, Illinois (Not admitted in Ohio). *Education:* University of Michigan (B.A., Economics/Accounting, 1983) ; University of California School of Law, Los Angeles (J.D., 1986). (Resident Member, Chicago, Illinois Office). ***PRACTICE AREAS:*** Municipal Bonds; Tax Exempt Bonds; Public Finance Taxation. ***Email:*** bagin@peck-shaffer.com

DIRK M. BEDARFF, born Dusseldorf, Germany, March 10, 1960; admitted to bar, 1989, Kentucky. *Education:* University of Denver (B.S.B.A., 1981); University of Kentucky (J.D., 1984). (Resident Member, Covington and Louisville, Kentucky Offices). ***PRACTICE AREAS:*** Municipal Bonds; Tax Exempt Bonds; Public Finance. ***Email:*** dbedarff@peck-shaffer.com

ROBERT T. BRUNS, born Philadelphia, Pennsylvania, April 26, 1950; admitted to bar, 1975, Ohio; 1976, U.S. District Court, Southern District of Ohio; 1988, Pennsylvania. *Education:* Drexel University; University of Cincinnati (B.B.A., summa cum laude, 1972; J.D., 1975). ***PRACTICE AREAS:*** Municipal Bonds; Tax Exempt Bonds; Housing and Urban Development. ***Email:*** bbruns@peck-shaffer.com

GEORGE D. BUZARD III, born Evanston, Illinois, January 31, 1953; admitted to bar, 1978, Illinois. *Education:* University of Illinois (B.S., 1975; J.D., 1978). (Resident Member, Chicago, Illinois Office). ***PRACTICE AREAS:*** Municipal Bonds; Tax Exempt Bonds; Public Finance. ***Email:*** gbuzard@peck-shaffer.com

RICHARD A. CARDWELL, born Ironton, Ohio, August 30, 1963; admitted to bar, 1991, Ohio. *Education:* The Ohio State University (B.A., 1986); Capital University Law School (J.D., 1990). (Resident Member, Columbus, Ohio Office). ***PRACTICE AREAS:*** Municipal Contracts; Construction Contracts; Public Construction Law. ***Email:*** rcardwell@peck-shaffer.com

EDWARD CAVEZZA, born Scranton, Pennsylvania, March 28, 1957; admitted to bar, 1982, Ohio; 1983, U.S. District Court, Southern District of Ohio. *Education:* University of Scranton (B.S., summa cum laude, 1979); University of Notre Dame (J.D., cum laude, 1982). (Resident Member, Columbus, Ohio Office). ***PRACTICE AREAS:*** Municipal Bonds; Tax Exempt Bonds; Public Finance. ***Email:*** ecavezza@peck-shaffer.com

TODD L. COOPER, born Philadelphia, Pennsylvania, July 9, 1955; admitted to bar, 1981, Ohio; 1982, U.S. District Court, Southern District of Ohio. *Education:* Amherst College (A.B., 1977); University of Notre Dame (M.B.A., with honors, 1981; J.D., 1981). ***PRACTICE AREAS:*** Municipal Bonds; Tax Exempt Bonds; Public Finance Taxation. ***Email:*** tcooper@peck-shaffer.com

MARY S. DUFFEY, born Columbus, Ohio, July 4, 1957; admitted to bar, 1987, Ohio; 1988, U.S. District Court, Southern District of Ohio and U.S. Court of Appeals, Sixth Circuit. *Education:* University of Michigan (B.A., 1983); The Ohio State University (J.D., with honors, 1987). (Resident Member, Columbus, Ohio Office). ***PRACTICE AREAS:*** Municipal Bonds; Tax Exempt Bonds; Public Finance. ***Email:*** mduffey@peck-shaffer.com

JOHN W. FISCHER III, born Cincinnati, Ohio, August 1, 1943; admitted to bar, 1968, Ohio. *Education:* University of Michigan (A.B., with honors in Journalism, 1965; J.D., 1968). ***PRACTICE AREAS:*** Municipal Bonds; Tax Exempt Bonds; Health Care Finance. ***Email:*** jfischer@peck-shaffer.com

STEPHEN P. GRASSBAUGH, born Mount Vernon, Ohio, December 2, 1951; admitted to bar, 1984, Ohio. *Education:* The Ohio State University (B.S.B.A., 1973); Case Western Reserve University (J.D., 1984). (Resident Member, Columbus, Ohio Office). ***PRACTICE AREAS:*** Municipal Bonds; Tax Exempt Bonds; Tax Exempt Finance. ***Email:*** sgrassbaugh@peck-shaffer.com

MARY L. GROVES, born New York, New York, April 29, 1952; admitted to bar, 1978, Colorado and U.S. Court of Appeals, Tenth Circuit; 1984, Texas. *Education:* University of Northern Colorado; University of Colorado at Denver (B.A., 1974); University of Denver College of Law (J.D., 1978); Regis University (M.A., 1999). (Resident Member, Denver, Colorado Office). ***PRACTICE AREAS:*** Tax Exempt Finance; Securities and Disclosure; Structured Finance; Housing; Health Care; Non Profit Corporations.

SUSAN PEASE LANGFORD, born Chicago, Illinois, October 17, 1953; admitted to bar, 1977, Georgia (Not admitted in Ohio). *Education:* Mount Holyoke College (B.A. in Math and Political Science, 1974); Emory University School of Law (J.D., 1976). (Resident Member, Atlanta, Georgia Office). ***PRACTICE AREAS:*** Municipal Bonds; Tax Exempt Bonds; Public Finance. ***Email:*** slangford@peck-shaffer.com

DOLORIS F. LEARMONTH, born Charlotte, North Carolina, October 2, 1943; admitted to bar, 1978, Ohio. *Education:* Duke University (A.B., 1965); University of Cincinnati (M.A., 1970; J.D., 1978). ***PRACTICE AREAS:*** Municipal Bonds; Tax Exempt Bonds; Public Finance. ***Email:*** dlearmonth@peck-shaffer.com

THOMAS A. LUEBBERS, born Cincinnati, Ohio, January 22, 1942; admitted to bar, 1966, Ohio; 1967, U.S. District Court, Southern District of Ohio; 1968, U.S. Court of Appeals, Sixth Circuit; 1970, U.S. Supreme Court. *Education:* University of Notre Dame (A.B., 1963); Yale University (LL.B., 1966). ***PRACTICE AREAS:*** Municipal Bonds; Tax Exempt Bonds; Tax Increment Finance. ***Email:*** tluebbers@peck-shaffer.com

MICHAEL J. MELLIERE, born St. Paul, Minnesota, 1967; admitted to bar, 1991, Indiana; 1997, Ohio. *Education:* Purdue University (B.S., 1988); University of Michigan - Ann Arbor (J.D., 1991). (Resident Member, Columbus, Ohio Office). ***PRACTICE AREAS:*** Structured Finance; Health Care Finance; Municipal Securities; Public Finance Taxation; Asset Based Finance. ***Email:*** mmelliere@peck-shaffer.com

JOHN C. MERCHANT, born Lexington, Kentucky, April 1, 1957; admitted to bar, 1982, Kentucky; 1983, U.S. District Courts, Eastern and Western Districts of Kentucky; 1992, Ohio. *Education:* Morehead State University (B.A., cum laude, 1979); University of Kentucky (J.D., 1982). (Resident Member, Louisville, Kentucky Office). ***PRACTICE AREAS:*** Municipal Bonds; Tax Exempt Bonds; Municipal Leasing. ***Email:*** jmerchant@peck-shaffer.com

CAROL DUANE OLSON, born Cambridge, Massachusetts, December 3, 1946; admitted to bar, 1972, New York; 1990, Ohio. *Education:* Newton College (B.A., 1968); University of Virginia (LL.B., 1971); New York University (LL.M., Taxation, 1975). ***PRACTICE AREAS:*** Municipal Bonds; Tax Exempt Bonds; Public Finance Taxation. ***Email:*** colson@peck-shaffer.com

SUJYOT S. PATEL, born Toledo, Ohio, December 5, 1964; admitted to bar, 1991, Ohio; 2001, Kentucky. *Education:* Ohio State University; University of Toledo (B.B.A., 1988); Ohio Northern University (J.D., 1991). (Resident Member, Louisville, Kentucky Office). ***PRACTICE AREAS:*** Municipal Bonds; Tax Exempt Bonds; Housing and Urban Development. ***Email:*** spatel@peck-shaffer.com

JOHN WELD PECK, born Cincinnati, Ohio, January 29, 1944; admitted to bar, 1969, Ohio; 1970, U.S. District Court, Southern District of Ohio; 1971, U.S. Court of Appeals,

(This Listing Continued)

Sixth Circuit; 1977, U.S. Supreme Court. *Education:* Miami University (B.S., 1966; J.D., Hon., 1992); University of Cincinnati (J.D., 1969). ***PRACTICE AREAS:*** Municipal Bonds; Tax Exempt Bonds; Housing and Urban Development. ***Email:*** jpeck@peck-shaffer.com

ROGER L. PETERMAN, born Ypsilanti, Michigan, October 26, 1953; admitted to bar, 1979, Kentucky. *Education:* University of Kentucky (B.A., 1975; J.D., 1979). (Resident Member, Covington and Louisville, Kentucky Offices). ***PRACTICE AREAS:*** Municipal Bonds; Tax Exempt Bonds; Public Finance. ***Email:*** rpeterman@peck-shaffer.com

JERRY G. PETERSON, born St. Paul, Minnesota, July 31, 1942; admitted to bar, 1969, Georgia (Not admitted in Ohio). *Education:* Wheaton College (A.B., 1964); Vanderbilt University (J.D., 1968). (Resident Member, Atlanta, Georgia Office). ***PRACTICE AREAS:*** Municipal Bonds; Tax Exempt Bonds; Public Finance. ***Email:*** jpeterson@peck-shaffer.com

GLENDON B. PRATT, born Cincinnati, Ohio, September 11, 1957; admitted to bar, 1982, Ohio. *Education:* Miami University (B.A., magna cum laude, 1978); University of Michigan (J.D., 1982). (Resident Member, Columbus, Ohio Office). ***PRACTICE AREAS:*** Municipal Bonds; Tax Exempt Bonds; Industrial Development Bonds. ***Email:*** gpratt@peck-shaffer.com

BRADLEY N. RUWE, born Fort Lee, Virginia, September 18, 1970; admitted to bar, 1997, Ohio. *Education:* Xavier University (B.S.B.A., 1992); Salmon P. Chase College of Law (J.D., 1996). ***PRACTICE AREAS:*** Municipal Bonds; Tax Exempt Bonds; Public Finance. ***Email:*** bruwe@peck-shaffer.com

DENNIS G. SCHWALLIE, born Cincinnati, Ohio, April 27, 1953; admitted to bar, 1978, Ohio; 1980, U.S. District Court, Southern District of Ohio. *Education:* University of Cincinnati (B.B.A., with honors, 1975); The Ohio State University (J.D., 1978). (Resident Member, Columbus, Ohio Office). ***PRACTICE AREAS:*** Municipal Bonds; Tax Exempt Bonds; Public Finance. ***Email:*** dschwallie@peck-shaffer.com

ABBOT A. THAYER, born Cincinnati, Ohio, April 30, 1953; admitted to bar, 1980, Ohio. *Education:* Harvard College (A.B., cum laude, 1975); University of Cincinnati (J.D., 1980). ***PRACTICE AREAS:*** Municipal Bonds; Tax Exempt Bonds; Public Finance. ***Email:*** athayer@peck-shaffer.com

BRENDA K. WEHMER, born Anderson, Indiana, July 7, 1964; admitted to bar, 1991, Ohio; 1992, U.S. District Court, Southern District of Ohio. *Education:* University of Cincinnati (B.A., 1987; M.B.A., 1988; J.D., 1991). ***PRACTICE AREAS:*** Municipal Bonds; Tax Exempt Bonds; Public Finance. ***Email:*** bwehmer@peck-shaffer.com

THOMAS A. WILSON, born Port Huron, Michigan, January 13, 1960; admitted to bar, 1985, Michigan; 1990, Ohio. *Education:* Albion College (A.B., magna cum laude, with honors in Philosophy, 1982); Georgetown University (J.D., 1985). (Resident Member, Columbus, Ohio Office). ***PRACTICE AREAS:*** Municipal Bonds; Tax Exempt Bonds; Public Finance. ***Email:*** twilson@peck-shaffer.com

OF COUNSEL

H. C. BUCK NIEHOFF, born Cincinnati, Ohio, May 7, 1947; admitted to bar, 1973, Ohio. *Education:* Denison University (B.A., 1969); University of Exeter, Exeter, England; University of Cincinnati (J.D., 1972); Indiana University. ***Email:*** bniehoff@peck-shaffer.com

MARY W. SULLIVAN, born Cincinnati, Ohio, October 23, 1956; admitted to bar, 1980, Ohio; 1982, U.S. District Court, Southern District of Ohio. *Education:* University of Vienna, Vienna, Austria; Xavier University (B.A., summa cum laude, 1977); University of Cincinnati (J.D., 1980). ***Email:*** msullivan@peck-shaffer.com

ASSOCIATES

JENNIFER R. BLASER, born Akron, Ohio, December 1, 1973; admitted to bar, 1999, Ohio. *Education:* Ohio University (B.A., Finance, 1996); The Ohio State University (J.D., 1999). (Resident Associate, Columbus, Ohio Office). ***PRACTICE AREAS:*** Municipal Bonds; Tax Exempt Bonds; Public Finance. ***Email:*** jblaser@peck-shaffer.com

JASON L. GEORGE, born Waukegan, Illinois, December 8, 1972; admitted to bar, 1998, Ohio. *Education:* DePauw University (B.A., 1995); Indiana School of Law-Bloomington (J.D., 1998). (Resident Associate, Columbus, Ohio Office). ***PRACTICE AREAS:*** Municipal Bonds; Tax Exempt Bonds; Municipal Bankruptcy. ***Email:*** jgeorge@peck-shaffer.com

MELISSA N. HAWKINS, born Columbus, Georgia, January 1, 1978; admitted to bar, 2003, Ohio. *Education:* Bowling Green State University (B.A., Political Science, cum laude, 1999); Emory University School of Law (J.D., 2003). ***PRACTICE AREAS:*** Municipal Bonds; Tax Exempt Bonds; Public Finance. ***Email:*** mhawkins@peck-shaffer.com

ALYSSE E. HOLLIS, born Honolulu, Hawaii, August 30, 1972; admitted to bar, 2000, Colorado (Not admitted in Ohio). *Education:* Colorado State Univeristy (B.A., Technical Journalism, 1994); University of California Hastings College of Law (J.D., 2000). ***PRACTICE AREAS:*** Municipal Bonds; Tax Exempt Bonds; Housing and Urban Development. ***Email:*** ahollis@peck-shaffer.com

MARC KAMER, born Columbus, Ohio, November 28, 1972; admitted to bar, 1998, Ohio. *Education:* The Ohio State University (B.A., Liberal Arts, summa cum laude, with honors, 1995; J.D., with honors in Law, 1998). (Resident Associate, Columbus, Ohio Office). ***PRACTICE AREAS:*** Public Construction Law; Municipal Bonds; Tax Exempt Bonds; Tax Exempt Finance. ***Email:*** mkamer@peck-shaffer.com

IAN F. KOFFLER, born Washington, D.C., July 23, 1977; admitted to bar, 2004, Kentucky (Not admitted in Ohio). *Education:* University of Richmond (B.A., 1999); University of Kentucky, Martin School (M.P.A., 2001); University of Kentucky (J.D., 2004). *Member:* Cincinnati Bar Association. ***PRACTICE AREAS:*** Municipal Bonds; Tax Exempt Bonds; Public Finance. ***Email:*** ikoffler@peck-shaffer.com

NICOLLE STALLWORTH, born 1974; admitted to bar, 2004, New York and New Jersey (Not admitted in Ohio). *Education:* Hampton University (B.S., Marketing, 1996); Fordham Law School (J.D., 2003). *Member:* Ohio State and New York State Bar Associations. (Resident Associate, Columbus, Ohio Office). ***PRACTICE AREAS:*** Tax Exempt Bonds; Municipal Bonds; Public Finance. ***Email:*** nstallworth@peck-shaffer.com

(This Listing Continued)

LONA J. VALENTINE, born Ashland, Kentucky, November 17, 1972; admitted to bar, 2000, Ohio. *Education:* Bellarmine University (B.S. in Mathematics/Actuarial Science, magna cum laude, 1994); University of Kentucky (M.B.A., 1995; J.D. 2000). ***PRACTICE AREAS:*** Municipal Bonds; Tax Exempt Bonds; Public Finance Taxation. ***Email:*** lvalentine@peck-shaffer.com

CHARLES H. WATERMAN, IV, born Columbus, Ohio, March 4, 1974; admitted to bar, 2001, Ohio. *Education:* University of Arizona (B.A., 1996); The Ohio State University College of Law (J.D., with honors, 2001). (Resident Associate, Columbus, Ohio Office). ***PRACTICE AREAS:*** Municipal Bonds; Tax Exempt Bonds; Public Finance; Economic Development. ***Email:*** cwaterman@peck-shaffer.com

DAVID H. WILLIAMS, JR., born Columbus, Ohio, January 7, 1974; admitted to bar, 2000, Georgia. *Education:* University of Georgia (A.B. in Political Science, 1996); Mercer University (J.D., 2000). (Resident Associate, Atlanta, Georgia Office). ***PRACTICE AREAS:*** Municipal Bonds; Tax Exempt Bonds; Public Finance. ***Email:*** dwilliams@peck-shaffer.com

PATRICK WOODSIDE, born Cincinnati, Ohio, 1976; admitted to bar, 2005, Ohio. *Education:* Columbia University School of Engineering and Applied Sciences (B.S. 1999); The Ohio State University, Fisher College of Business (M.B.A. 2002); The Ohio State University, Mortiz College of Law (J.D. 2005). ***PRACTICE AREAS:*** Municipal Bonds; Tax Exempt Bonds; Public Finance Taxation. ***Email:*** pwoodside@peck-shaffer.com

(For Additional Biographical Data on all Personnel, see Professional Biographies at http.www.peck-shaffer.com)

THE PEREZ LAW FIRM CO.

A LEGAL PROFESSIONAL ASSOCIATION

Established in 1983

7672 MONTGOMERY ROAD, SUITE 378
CINCINNATI, OHIO 45236-4204
Telephone: 513-891-8777
Fax: 513-891-0317
Email: rperez@perezfirm.com
URL: http://www.perezfirm.com

Civil Litigation, Class Actions, Employee Benefit Litigation of Pension, Health and Disability, and Insurance Bad Faith.

ROBERT ARMAND PEREZ SR., born Cincinnati, Ohio, September 2, 1951; admitted to bar, 1983, Ohio, U.S. District Court, Southern District of Ohio, U.S. Court of Appeals, Sixth Circuit; 1991, U.S. Supreme Court. *Education:* University of Cincinnati (B.A., 1972; M.S., 1975); Indiana University (J.D., 1982). *Member:* Cincinnati, Ohio State and American Bar Associations; Ohio Academy of Trial Lawyers; Hamilton County Association of Trial Lawyers; The Association of Trial Lawyers of America. ***Email:*** rperez@perezfirm.com

PORTER & PORTER

Established in 1929

2100 FOURTH & VINE TOWER
ONE WEST FOURTH STREET
CINCINNATI, OHIO 45202
Telephone: 513-621-3993
Fax: 513-621-1746

General Civil Practice in all Courts. Estate Planning, Probate, Corporate, Federal and State Taxation, Bankruptcy, Negligence, Real Estate and Family Law. Trials and Appeals. Employee/Fringe Benefits, Charitable Foundations, Insurance Law.

MEMBERS OF FIRM

ROBERT C. PORTER (1890-1954)

ROBERT C. PORTER, JR., born Cincinnati, Ohio, September 21, 1927; admitted to bar, 1952, Ohio; 1956, U.S. Supreme Court and U.S. Court of Military Appeals; 1981, U.S. Tax Court. *Education:* University of Michigan (B.A., 1949); Harvard University (J.D., 1952). Phi Beta Kappa. *Member:* Cincinnati, Ohio State (Member: Public Relations Committee, 1960-1972; Special Probate Committee, 1967-1969) and American Bar Associations. [Capt., USAFR, 1952-1961]. ***PRACTICE AREAS:*** Estate Planning Law; Probate Law; Corporate Law; Trials and Appeals; Federal and State Taxation Law.

ROBERT C. PORTER, III, born Cincinnati, Ohio, December 3, 1954; admitted to bar, 1979, Ohio and U.S. District Court, Southern District of Ohio. *Education:* University of Michigan (A.B., 1976); University of Cincinnati (J.D., 1979). *Member:* Cincinnati, Ohio State and American Bar Associations. ***PRACTICE AREAS:*** Family Law; Real Estate Law; Estate Planning Law; Probate Law; Corporate Law; Trials and Appeals. ***Email:*** RCP3NKP@FUSE.NET

BANK REFERENCES: P.N.C. Bank; Fifth Third Bank; U.S. Bank; The Provident Bank.

PORTER WRIGHT MORRIS & ARTHUR LLP

Established in 1846

250 E. FIFTH STREET, SUITE 2200
CINCINNATI, OHIO 45202-5117
Telephone: 513-381-4700; (800-582-5813)
Fax: 513-421-0991
Email: cincinnati@porterwright.com
URL: http://www.porterwright.com

Columbus, Ohio Office: 41 South High Street, 43215-6194. Telephones: 614-227-2000; (800-533-2794). Fax: 614-227-2100. Internet: columbus@porterwright.com.
Dayton, Ohio Office: One Dayton Centre, One South Main Street, Suite 1600, 45402-2028. Telephones: 937-449-6810; (800-533-4434). Fax: 937-449-6820. Internet: dayton@porterwright.com.
Cleveland, Ohio Office: 925 Euclid Avenue, Suite 1700, 44115-1483. Telephones: 216-443-9000; (800-824-1980). Fax: 216-443-9011. Internet: cleveland@porterwright.com.
Washington, D.C. Office: 1919 Pennsylvania Avenue, N.W., Suite 500, 20006-3434. Telephones: 202-778-3000; (800-456-7962). Fax: 202-778-3063. Internet: washington@porterwright.com.
Naples, Florida Office: 5801 Pelican Bay Boulevard, Suite 300, 34108-2709. Telephones: 239-593-2900; (800-876-7962). Fax: 239-593-2990. Internet: naples@porterwright.com.

Alternative Dispute Resolution, Agricultural Law, Antitrust and Trade Regulation, Business and Corporate, Complex Litigation, Construction, Employee Benefits, Energy and Utilities, Environment, Federal Administrative Law, Federal Contracting and Procurement, Financial Institutions, General Practice, Governmental Affairs, Health Care, Insurance, Intellectual Property, International Business, Labor and Employment, Litigation, Public Law, Public Finance, Real Estate, Securities, Taxation, Technology, Trusts and Estates.

FIRM PROFILE: Porter Wright Morris & Arthur LLP is a nationally known business law firm delivering creative solutions for large, mid-size and entrepreneurial businesses. Porter Wright's Cincinnati presence traces to 1982. Attorneys in Cincinnati emphasize litigation, corporate law, financial transactions, transportation law, trade associations, intellectual property, real estate, bankruptcy and debt workout, and estate planning and probate. The Firm, which traces its origins to 1846, has over 280 lawyers practicing in Cincinnati, Cleveland, Columbus, and Dayton, Ohio; Washington, D.C.; and Naples, Florida.

RESIDENT PARTNERS

DAVID T. CROALL, born Plainfield, New Jersey, June 27, 1955; admitted to bar, 1981, Ohio, Virginia (inactive), U.S. District Court, Southern District of Ohio and U.S. Court of Appeals, Sixth Circuit; 1992, U.S. Supreme Court; 2003, Kentucky. *Education:* College of William & Mary (A.B., 1977); Harvard Law School (J.D., 1980). Phi Beta Kappa. *Member:* Virginia State Bar; Kentucky State, Ohio State, Cincinnati (Grievance Committee, 1990- 2001) and American Bar Associations. ***REPORTED CASES:*** Jacobson v. Bd. of Ed., 961 F. 2d 100 (6th Cir. 1992); Holthaus v. Bd. of Ed., 986 F. 2d 1044 (6th Cir. 1993); Warmack v. Delta Airlines 827 F. Supp. 1345 (S.D. Ohio 1993); Chapman v. Adia, 116 Ohio App. 3d 455 (2000); Cincinnati Bar Ass'n v. Stidham, 87 Ohio St. 3d 455 (2000); Cincinnati Bar Ass'n v. Bertsche, 84 Ohio St. 3d 170 (1998). ***PRACTICE AREAS:*** Employment Law; Employment Defense; Employment Litigation; Employment Litigation Defense; Employment Discrimination; Employment Discrimination Defense; Wage and Hour Case Law. ***Email:*** dcroall@porterwright.com

MARK E. ELSENER, born Fort Thomas, Kentucky, September 29, 1954; admitted to bar, 1980, Ohio and U.S. District Court, Southern District of Ohio; 1983, U.S. Court of Appeals, Sixth Circuit. *Education:* University of Cincinnati (B.A., 1976; M.A., 1977; J.D., 1980). Research Editor, University of Cincinnati Law Review, 1979-1980. ***PRACTICE AREAS:*** Civil Trial and Appellate Practice; Insurance Law; Commercial Litigation. ***Email:*** melsener@porterwright.com

THEODORE D. GROSSER, born Cincinnati, Ohio, October 24, 1952; admitted to bar, 1977, Ohio; 1978, Kentucky. *Education:* University of Cincinnati (B.A., summa cum laude, with honors, 1974); Washington and Lee University (J.D., cum laude, 1977). ***PRACTICE AREAS:*** Commercial Law; Mergers, Acquisitions and Divestitures; Corporate Law. ***Email:*** tgrosser@porterwright.com

JEROME J. METZ, JR., born Cincinnati, Ohio, December 25, 1950; admitted to bar, 1980, Ohio. *Education:* Xavier University (B.S., summa cum laude, 1976); University of Cincinnati (J.D., 1980). Alpha Sigma Nu. Order of the Coif. Editorial Board, University of Cincinnati Law Review, 1979-1980. Presentation: "Fundamentals of Commercial Bankruptcy," Lorman Education Services, 2003. *Member:* Cincinnati (Member, Bankruptcy Committee), Ohio State, Federal and American (Member, Sections of Litigation and Business Law) Bar Associations. ***PRACTICE AREAS:*** Bankruptcy; Business Torts; Civil Litigation; Finance; Commerce. ***Email:*** jmetz@porterwright.com

MICHAEL G. REED, born Columbus, Ohio, August 8, 1956; admitted to bar, 1981, Ohio, U.S. District Court, Southern District of Ohio and U.S. Court of Appeals, Sixth Circuit; 1985, U.S. District Court, Eastern District of Kentucky. *Education:* Miami University (B.S.B.A., 1978); University of Cincinnati (J.D., 1981). *Member:* Cincinnati and Ohio State Bar Associations; Ohio Land Title Association. ***PRACTICE AREAS:*** Business; Financial Institutions; Real Estate; Trade Association Law. ***Email:*** mreed@porterwright.com

DAVID REICHERT, born Cincinnati, Ohio, November 23, 1929; admitted to bar, 1954, Ohio. *Education:* Bowling Green State University (B.A., 1951); University of Cincinnati (LL.B., 1954). *Member:* Cincinnati and Ohio State Bar Associations. ***PRACTICE AREAS:*** Estate Planning and Probate; Corporate Law; Trade Associations; Business. ***Email:*** dreichert@porterwright.com

R. JEFFREY SCHLOSSER, born Fort Thomas, Kentucky, November 6, 1957; admitted to bar, 1983, Kentucky; 1984, Ohio. *Education:* Centre College of Kentucky (B.A., 1980); Salmon P. Chase College of Law (J.D., 1983). [U.S. Marine Corps, 1984-1987]. ***PRACTICE AREAS:*** Commercial Transactions; Business Law; Employment Law; Finance; Commerce; Real Estate. ***Email:*** jschlosser@porterwright.com

JOHN S. STITH, born Cincinnati, Ohio, April 15, 1939; admitted to bar, 1964, Ohio. *Education:* Princeton University (A.B., cum laude, 1961); University of Cincinnati (J.D., summa cum laude, 1964). *Member:* Ohio State Bar Association (President-Elect, 2005—). ***PRACTICE AREAS:*** Corporate Law; Securities Regulation; Mergers, Acquisitions and Divestitures; Business; Securities. ***Email:*** jstith@porterwright.com

CHRISTINE S. WHEATLEY, born Pittsburgh, Pennsylvania, February 27, 1971; admitted to bar, 1996, Ohio. *Education:* University of Notre Dame (B.A., 1993); The Ohio State University (J.D., 1996). Author: "A Survey of the Rules of Evidence in Russian Criminal Procedure," The Parker School Journal of East European Law, Vo. 2, No. 3. ***PRACTICE AREAS:*** Corporate; Mergers and Acquisitions; Business; Securities. ***Email:*** cwheatley@porterwright.com

RESIDENT OF COUNSEL

DANIEL W. SCHARFF, born Cincinnati, Ohio, December 15, 1959; admitted to bar, 1990, Kentucky; 1991, Ohio. *Education:* Northern Kentucky University (B.S., cum laude, 1982); Salmon P. Chase College of Law (J.D., magna cum laude, 1990). ***PRACTICE AREAS:*** Health Care Corporate Law; Closely Held Corporations; Income Tax; Business; Securities; Finance; Commerce. ***Email:*** dscharff@porterwright.com

RESIDENT ASSOCIATE

RACHEL E. BURKE, born Newcastle Upon Tyne, England, August 31, 1971; admitted to bar, 1996, Ohio; 1997, U.S. District Court, Southern District of Ohio. *Education:* Miami University (B.S., 1993); College of William & Mary (J.D., 1996). Order of the Coif. *Member:* Cincinnati and Ohio State Bar Associations. ***PRACTICE AREAS:*** Employment Law; Employment Litigation Defense. ***Email:*** rburke@porterwright.com

(See Listings at Dayton, Cleveland and Columbus, Ohio, Washington, D.C. and Naples, Florida for professional biographies on attorneys resident in those offices)

LAW OFFICE OF WILLIAM CATES RAMBO

414 WALNUT STREET, SUITE 508
CINCINNATI, OHIO 45202-3913
Telephone: 513-768-8901
Fax: 513-768-8909
Email: bill@iplawrambo.com
URL: http://www.iplawrambo.com

Preparation and Prosecution of Domestic and Foreign Patents, Trademark and Copyright Registrations, Litigation and Licensing of Intellectual Property, Patent and Trademark Searches and Infringement Studies.

WILLIAM CATES RAMBO, born Columbus, Ohio, June 17, 1948; admitted to bar, 1982, Ohio and U.S. District Court, Southern District of Ohio; 1985, U.S. Court of Appeals for the Federal Circuit; 1991, U.S. District Court, Northern District of Ohio; registered to practice before U.S. Patent and Trademark Office. *Education:* The Ohio State University (B.S., 1976); Capital University (J.D., cum laude, 1982). ***PRACTICE AREAS:*** Copyrights; Intellectual Property; Patents; Trademarks; Trade Secrets.

DEBORAH PRICE RAMBO, born Charleston, West Virginia, December 28, 1956; admitted to bar, 1987, Ohio. *Education:* University of Cincinnati (B.A., summa cum laude, 1984); Harvard University (J.D., 1987). ***Email:*** deborah@iplawrambo.com

RENDIGS, FRY, KIELY & DENNIS, L.L.P.

Established in 1946

1 WEST FOURTH STREET, SUITE 900
CINCINNATI, OHIO 45202
Telephone: 513-381-9200
FAX: 513-381-9206
Email: info@rendigs.com
URL: http://www.rendigs.com

Trial and General Practice, Appellate Practice, Products Liability, Insurance Litigation, Personal Injury, Medical Liability, Medical Malpractice, Nursing Home Litigation, Health Law, Hospital Law, Professional Liability, Construction Law, Mold Claims, Corporate Law, Business Law, Maritime Law, Aviation Law, Commercial Law, Taxation, Real Estate, Probate, Trusts and Estates, Wills, Bankruptcy, Family Law, Environmental Law, Transportation, Medical Devices, Civil Rights, Premises Liability, Premises Security, Labor Law, Employment Law, Employee Benefits, Criminal Law, Class Actions, Complex and Multi-District Litigation, Alternative Dispute Resolution, Legal Professional Liability, Workers' Compensation Defense, Zoning, Planning and Land Use.

FIRM PROFILE: For over half of a century Rendigs, Fry, Kiely & Dennis L.L.P has developed lasting working relationships with institutional and individual clients of all types, stressing innovation and service. Our goal is to serve the needs of our clients in a quality manner, striving to obtain outstanding results while upholding the principles of value and efficiency.

The firm's practice has spread throughout Ohio, Kentucky and Indiana with lawyers practicing in both state and federal courts of those states. The firm is located at the Fourth and Vine Tower in downtown Cincinnati.

PARTNERS OF THE FIRM

AUGUST A. RENDIGS, JR. (1895-1988)
ROBERT M. DENNIS (1917-1973)
WILLIAM H. FRY (1905-1975)
JOHN A. KIELY (1899-1986)

(This Listing Continued)

W. ROGER FRY, born Cincinnati, Ohio, March 10, 1940; admitted to bar, 1966, Ohio; 1986, District of Columbia; 1990, Kentucky. *Education:* University of Cincinnati (B.A., 1962); Salmon P. Chase College of Law (J.D., 1966). Phi Alpha Delta; Order of the Curia. Co-Author: "Interpreting the Pollution Exclusion Clause and the Comprehensive General Liability Policy - Ohio's Next Step," 23 Akron Law Review 507, 1990; "The Ohio Supreme Court's Interpretation of the Pollution Exclusion Clause —A Step Not Yet Taken," 16 University of Dayton Law Review 679, 1991. *Member:* Cincinnati, Ohio (Member: Environmental Law Committee, Natural Resources Law Committee and Negligence Law Committee), Kentucky and American (Member, Sections on: Tort and Insurance Practice; Litigation) Bar Associations; Ohio Association of Civil Trial Attorneys; Defense Research Institute; Federation of Insurance and Corporate Counsel; American Board of Trial Advocates (Advocate). Fellow, American College of Trial Lawyers. ***PRACTICE AREAS:*** Environmental Law; Products Liability; Commercial Litigation; Construction Litigation; Art Law; Indian Law; Class Actions. ***Email:*** wfry@rendigs.com

DAVID WINCHESTER PECK, born Cincinnati, Ohio, June 1, 1939; admitted to bar, 1966, Ohio; 1970, U.S. District Court, Southern District of Ohio; 1974, U.S Court of Appeals, Sixth Circuit; 1976, U.S. Supreme Court; 1989, Kentucky. *Education:* Miami University (B.S. in Bus. Admin., 1962); Salmon P. Chase College of Law (J.D., 1966). Phi Alpha Delta. Assistant Solicitor, Criminal Division, City of Cincinnati, 1966-1969. City of Wyoming School Board, 1981-1989. Adjunct Professor of Law, Trial Practice, Salmon P. Chase College of Law, Northern Kentucky University, 1993—. *Member:* Cincinnati, Ohio State (Chairman, Litigation Section, Board of Governors 1990, 1991; Co-Chair, Medical Malpractice Committee, Legal Malpractice and Other Professional Liability, 1997) and American Bar Associations; Ohio Association of Civil Trial Attorneys; International Association of Defense Counsel; Defense Research Institute. Advocate, American Board of Trial Advocates. Fellow, American College of Trial Lawyers. ***PRACTICE AREAS:*** Medical Malpractice Defense; Hospital Law; Medical Device Products Liability; Employment Litigation. ***Email:*** dpeck@rendigs.com

PAUL F. WENKER, born Cincinnati, Ohio, May 15, 1942; admitted to bar, 1967, Ohio; 1968, U.S. Claims Court; 1969, U.S. Tax Court. *Education:* Xavier University (B.S., cum laude, 1964); Georgetown University (J.D., 1967); George Washington University (LL.M. in Taxation, 1970). Delta Theta Phi. *Member:* Cincinnati, Ohio State and American Bar Associations. ***PRACTICE AREAS:*** Estate Planning; Probate; Taxation. ***Email:*** pwenker@rendigs.com

EDWARD R. GOLDMAN, born Cincinnati, Ohio, February 28, 1943; admitted to bar, 1973, Ohio and U.S. District Court, Southern District of Ohio; 1977, U.S. Supreme Court; 1982, U.S. Court of Appeals, Sixth Circuit. *Education:* University of Cincinnati (B.S., Eng. 1969); Salmon P. Chase College of Law (J.D., 1973). Phi Alpha Delta. Member, Order of the Curia. Author: "The Case of Anderson v. United Realty Co. and The Doctrine of Implied Gifts to Issue in Ohio," 1 N. Ky. St. L.F. 67, 1973. Part Time Instructor, Municipal Court Practice, Chase College of Law, 1975-1981. *Member:* Cincinnati (Member, Committee on Ethics and Professional Responsibility, 1989-1990), Ohio State and American Bar Associations. ***PRACTICE AREAS:*** Products Liability; Insurance; Professional Liability; Civil Rights. ***Email:*** egoldman@rendigs.com

JOSEPH W. GELWICKS, born Baltimore, Maryland, January 13, 1949; admitted to bar, 1976, Ohio; 1977, Kentucky; 1981, U.S. Supreme Court; 1982, Indiana; 1992, Minnesota. *Education:* Northern Kentucky University (A.B., 1973); Salmon P. Chase College of Law of Northern Kentucky University (J.D., 1976). *Member:* Cincinnati, Ohio State, Kentucky, Northern Kentucky and Indiana State Bar Associations; Defense Research Institute; Ohio Association of Civil Trial Attorneys; Trucking Industry Defense Association. ***PRACTICE AREAS:*** Insurance; Personal Injury. ***Email:*** jgelwicks@rendigs.com

LEONARD A. WEAKLEY, JR., born Cincinnati, Ohio, August 29, 1946; admitted to bar, 1977, Ohio; 1978, Kentucky and U.S. Court of Appeals, Sixth Circuit; 1979, U.S. District Court, Southern District of Ohio; 1982, U.S. District Court, Eastern District of Kentucky; 1985, U.S. Supreme Court. *Education:* University of Cincinnati (B.B.A., 1970; M.B.A., 1973); Salmon P. Chase College of Law (J.D., 1977). *Member:* Cincinnati (Member, Committees on: Construction Law, First District Court of Appeals), Ohio State (Member, Litigation Section, Bar Foundation), Kentucky (Member, Construction and Public Contract Law Section), Northern Kentucky (Member, Construction Law Committee), Federal (Member, Litigation Section) and American (Member, Forum on the Construction Industry, Litigation Section, Construction Law Committee and Architects and Engineers Liability Subcommittee) Bar Associations; Defense Research Institute (Member, Construction Law Committee); Ohio Association of Civil Trial Lawyers; American Arbitration Association (Construction Arbitrator; Member, Cincinnati Construction Advisory Committee); Center for Resolution of Disputes (Construction Law Arbitrator). [U.S. Army Combat Engineers, 1970-1972]. ***PRACTICE AREAS:*** Construction Law; Architects and Engineers Liability. ***Email:*** lweakley@rendigs.com

CAROLYN A. TAGGART, born Xenia, Ohio, October 6, 1951; admitted to bar, 1978, Ohio and U.S. District Court, Southern District of Ohio; 1984, U.S. Court of Appeals, Sixth Circuit; 1994, Kentucky, U.S. District Court, Eastern District of Kentucky and U.S. Supreme Court. *Education:* Miami University (B.S.Ed., cum laude, 1973); University of Cincinnati (J.D., 1978). Order of the Barristers. Member, National Moot Court Team. Faculty Member, National Institute of Trial Advocacy, 1993—. Mediator, U.S. District Court, Southern District of Ohio, Settlement Week, 1994—. *Member:* Cincinnati (Chair, Grievance Committee, 1995-1997), Ohio State, Kentucky, Northern Kentucky and American Bar Associations; American College of Trial Lawyers; Ohio Association of Civil Trial Attorneys (Vice President); Defense Research Institute; International Association of Defense Counsel; American Board of Trial Advocates. ***PRACTICE AREAS:*** Products Liability; Legal Malpractice; Premises Security; Nursing Home Liability; Employer Intentional Torts. ***Email:*** ctaggart@rendigs.com

DONALD C. ADAMS, JR., born Cincinnati, Ohio, March 18, 1957; admitted to bar, 1982, Ohio and U.S. District Court, Southern District of Ohio; 1987, U.S. Court of Appeals; 1991, Kentucky. *Education:* Miami University (B.A., magna cum laude, 1979); University of Cincinnati (J.D., 1982). *Member:* Cincinnati, Ohio State, Northern Kentucky, Kentucky, Federal and American Bar Associations; Maritime Law Association of the United States; Ohio Association of Civil Trial Attorneys; Trucking Industry Defense Association. ***PRACTICE AREAS:*** Admiralty and Maritime Law; Labor Law; Insurance Coverage. ***Email:*** dadams@rendigs.com

(This Listing Continued)

WILSON G. WEISENFELDER, JR., born Cheyenne, Wyoming, March 8, 1953; admitted to bar, 1985, Ohio. *Education:* University of Cincinnati (B.B.A., 1975; M.B.A., 1977); Salmon P. Chase Law School (J.D., 1985). *Member:* Cincinnati, Warren County and Ohio State Bar Associations. ***PRACTICE AREAS:*** Civil Rights; Professional Liability; General Litigation. ***Email:*** wweisenfelder@rendigs.com

STEVEN D. HENGEHOLD, born Cincinnati, Ohio, November 21, 1959; admitted to bar, 1985, Ohio; 1986, U.S. District Court, Southern District of Ohio. *Education:* Xavier University (B.S.B.A., 1982); University of Cincinnati (J.D., 1985). *Member:* Cincinnati and Ohio State Bar Associations; Ohio Association of Civil Trial Attorneys. ***PRACTICE AREAS:*** Architects and Engineers Liability; Civil Litigation. ***Email:*** shengehold@rendigs.com

THOMAS M. EVANS, born Dayton, Ohio, March 9, 1960; admitted to bar, 1986, Ohio and U.S. District Court, Southern District of Ohio. *Education:* Colorado State University; University of Colorado (B.A., cum laude, 1982); University of Cincinnati (J.D., 1985). *Member:* Cincinnati, Ohio State and American Bar Associations. ***PRACTICE AREAS:*** Medical Malpractice; Hospital Law. ***Email:*** tevans@rendigs.com

FELIX J. GORA, born Joliet, Illinois, May 23, 1955; admitted to bar, 1980, Ohio; 1983, U.S. District Court, Southern District of Ohio; 1991, Kentucky. *Education:* Miami University (A.B., 1977); University of Cincinnati (J.D., 1980). Phi Beta Kappa. *Member:* Cincinnati, Ohio State, Kentucky and American Bar Associations. ***PRACTICE AREAS:*** Employment Law; Products Liability; Civil Rights; Aviation Law. ***Email:*** fgora@rendigs.com

JOHN F. McLAUGHLIN, born Salem, Massachusetts, September 21, 1961; admitted to bar, 1987, Virginia; 1988, Massachusetts, District of Columbia and U.S. District Court, Eastern District of Virginia, U.S. District Court for the District of Columbia; 1989, Kentucky; 1991, Ohio and Florida. *Education:* Assumption College (B.A., 1983) Valedictorian; Georgetown University Law Center (J.D., 1987). *Member:* Cincinnati, Northern Kentucky and American Bar Associations. ***PRACTICE AREAS:*** Litigation; Personal Injury Defense; Products Liability Defense; Insurance Coverage; Aviation Law. ***Email:*** jmclaughlin@rendigs.com

PETER L. NEY, born Cincinnati, Ohio, September 2, 1961; admitted to bar, 1987, Ohio and U.S. District Court, Southern District of Ohio; 1993, Kentucky; 1994, U.S. Court of Appeals, Sixth Circuit. *Education:* University of Notre Dame (B.S., 1983); University of Cincinnati College of Law (J.D., 1987). Dean's List. Recipient: University Scholarship; Lawrence Maxwell Memorial Prize for Excellence in Oral Advocacy; American Jurisprudence Awards for Excellence in Constitutional Law and Products Liability. Regional Counsel, Related Elevator Companies. Past President, Mercy Montessori Parents Association. Member, Alumni Board of University of Cincinnati College of Law. Active in Down Syndrome Association of Greater Cincinnati. Past Board Member, Down Syndrome Association of Greater Cincinnati, Parks and Recreation Board, City of Madeira, Ohio. Past Member: Hamilton County Association of Retarded Citizens; Local Interagency Consortium. Arbitrator, Hamilton County Court of Common Pleas. *Member:* Cincinnati (Member, Tort and Insurance Law Committee), Ohio State, Kentucky, Northern Kentucky and Federal Bar Associations; Ohio Association of Civil Trial Attorneys; Defense Research Institute. ***PRACTICE AREAS:*** Commercial Law; Insurance; Products Liability; Premise Liability; Professional Liability. ***Email:*** pney@rendigs.com

ROBERT F. BROWN, born Sandusky, Ohio, May 2, 1963; admitted to bar, 1988, Ohio; 1989, U.S. District Court, Southern District of Ohio and U.S. Court of Appeals, Sixth Circuit; 1995, Kentucky. *Education:* Miami University (B.S., 1985); Ohio State University (J.D., 1988). Pi Mu Epsilon. Executive Editor, The Ohio State Journal on Dispute Resolution, 1987-1988. Recipient, Judge Joseph M. Harter Memorial Award for Achievement in Trial Practice. *Member:* Cincinnati (Vice Chairman, Admissions Committee), Ohio State, Kentucky and American Bar Associations; Ohio Association of Civil Trial Attorneys (Chairman, Commercial Litigation Committee); Defense Research Institute. ***PRACTICE AREAS:*** Corporate Law; Commercial Litigation; Bankruptcy; Real Estate; Professional Malpractice Defense. ***Email:*** rbrown@rendigs.com

KENNETH B. FLACKS, born New York, N.Y., October 17, 1948; admitted to bar, 1973, Ohio and U.S. District Court, Southern District of Ohio; 1997, Kentucky; U.S. District Court, Eastern District of Kentucky. *Education:* Miami University (B.S., 1970); University of Cincinnati (J.D., 1973). *Member:* Cincinnati, Dayton, Ohio State and American Bar Association; Ohio Association of Civil Trial Attorneys; Defense Research Institute. ***PRACTICE AREAS:*** Products Liability; Premises Liability; Civil Litigation; Insurance Coverage; Construction Law. ***Email:*** kflacks@rendigs.com

PAUL W. McCARTNEY, born Pittsburgh, Pennsylvania, July 3, 1962; admitted to bar, 1988, Ohio; 1989, U.S. District Court, Southern District of Ohio and U.S. Court of Appeals, Sixth Circuit. *Education:* Kenyon College (B.A., 1984); Ohio State University (J.D., 1988). Order of the Coif. *Member:* Cincinnati and Ohio State Bar Associations. ***PRACTICE AREAS:*** Medical Malpractice. ***Email:*** pmccartney@rendigs.com

JONATHAN P. SAXTON, born New Haven, Connecticut, April 30, 1964; admitted to bar, 1989, Ohio and U.S. District Court, Southern District of Ohio; 1996, Kentucky. *Education:* Miami University (B.S., 1986); University of Cincinnati (J.D., 1989). Order of the Coif; Order of the Barristers. Co-Author: "Interpreting the Pollution Exclusion Clause in the Comprehensive General Liability Policy - Ohio's Next Step," 23 Akron L. Rev. 1990; "The Ohio Supreme Court's Interpretation of the Pollution Exclusion Clause —A Step Not Yet Taken," 16 University of Dayton Law Review 679, 1991. *Member:* Cincinnati (Member, Environmental Law Committee and Legal Education and Admission Committee) and Ohio State (Member, Environmental Law Committee) Bar Associations; Defense Research Institute; Ohio Association of Civil Trial Attorneys. ***PRACTICE AREAS:*** Toxic Torts; Mold Claims; Products Liability; Insurance Coverage; Class Actions; Fire Loss. ***Email:*** jsaxton@rendigs.com

ARTHUR E. PHELPS, JR., born Cleveland, Ohio, July 21, 1960; admitted to bar, 1985, Ohio; 1986, U.S. District Court, Northern District of Ohio; 1987, U.S. District Court, Southern District of Ohio; 1992, U.S. Court of Appeals, Sixth Circuit; 1995, Kentucky and U.S. District Court, Eastern District of Kentucky. *Education:* Denison University (B.A., 1982); Case Western Reserve University (J.D., 1985). Law Clerk, Hon. Thomas D. Lambros, U.S. District Court, Northern District of Ohio, 1985-1986. Adjunct Professor, Paralegal Studies, Mount St. Joseph College, 1993-1994. *Member:* Cincinnati (Chair, Common

(This Listing Continued)

RENDIGS, FRY, KIELY & DENNIS, L.L.P., Cincinnati—Continued

Pleas Court Committee, 1993-1995), Ohio State and Kentucky Bar Associations. (Certified Specialist in Workers' Compensation Law, Ohio State Bar Association). ***PRACTICE AREAS:*** Workers Compensation; Medical Malpractice; Personal Injury. ***Email:*** aphelps@rendigs.com

JAMES J. ENGLERT, born Cincinnati, Ohio, January 8, 1953; admitted to bar, 1990, Ohio; 1992, Kentucky, U.S. District Court, Eastern and Western Districts of Kentucky, U.S. District Court, Southern District of Ohio and U.S. Court of Appeals, Sixth Circuit. *Education:* Boston College (B.A., 1975); University of Cincinnati (J.D., 1990). Editor in Chief, University of Cincinnati Law Review, 1989-1990. Law Clerk to U.S. District Court Judge Wm. O. Bertlesman, Eastern District of Kentucky, 1990-1991. *Member:* Cincinnati, Ohio State, Kentucky, Northern Kentucky and American Bar Associations. ***LANGUAGES:*** French. ***PRACTICE AREAS:*** Construction Law; Litigation. ***Email:*** jenglert@rendigs.com

JAMES E. McLEAN, JR., born Cleveland, Ohio, January 6, 1965; admitted to bar, 1990, Ohio; 1994, U.S. District Court, Southern District of Ohio. *Education:* Wittenberg University (B.A., 1987); University of Cincinnati (J.D., 1990). *Member:* Cincinnati and Ohio State (Member: Tort and Insurance Committee; Domestic Relations Committee) Bar Associations. ***PRACTICE AREAS:*** Insurance Defense; Family Law; Employment Law. ***Email:*** jmclean@rendigs.com

MICHAEL P. FOLEY, born Grand Forks, North Dakota, April 24, 1966; admitted to bar, 1993, Ohio; 1994, U.S. District Court, Southern District of Ohio and U.S. Court of Appeals, Sixth Circuit; 1995, Kentucky and U.S. District Court, Eastern and Western Districts of Kentucky. *Education:* Xavier University (B.A., 1988); Ohio Northern University (J.D., 1992). Phi Alpha Delta. *Member:* Ohio State, Kentucky, Northern Kentucky and American Bar Associations; Ohio Association of Civil Trial Attorneys; Defense Research Institute. ***PRACTICE AREAS:*** Construction Law; Professional Liability; Products Liability; Personal Injury; Municipal Liability; Fire Loss; Insurance Coverage. ***Email:*** mfoley@rendigs.com

CHRISTOPHER R. CARVILLE, born Rochester, New York, October 5, 1972; admitted to bar, 1997, Ohio. *Education:* Xavier University (B.S.B.A., magna cum laude, 1994); University of Cincinnati (J.D., 1997). *Member:* Cincinnati and Ohio State Bar Associations; Ohio Association of Trial Attorneys. ***PRACTICE AREAS:*** Construction Law; Civil Litigation; Insurance Defense; Personal Injury; Criminal Law. ***Email:*** ccarville@rendigs.com

CHRISTOPHER J. ALUOTTO, born Riverdale, Maryland, May 16, 1967; admitted to bar, 1992, Ohio; 1993, U.S. District Court, Southern District of Ohio and U.S. Court of the Armed Forces; 1999, U.S. Court of Federal Claims; 2002, Kentucky. *Education:* American University (B.A., 1989); University of Dayton (J.D., 1992); George Washington University (LL.M., 1999). *Member:* Cincinnati, Ohio State and Kentucky Bar Associations; Ohio Association of Civil Trial Attorneys; Defense Research Institute. ***PRACTICE AREAS:*** Products Liability; Toxic Torts; Government Contracts; Environmental Law. ***Email:*** caluotto@rendigs.com

RETIRED PARTNER

WILLIAM H. HUTCHERSON, JR., born Washington, D.C., May 2, 1925; admitted to bar, 1954, Ohio. *Education:* Denison University (A.B., 1950); University of Virginia (LL.B., 1953). ***PRACTICE AREAS:*** Automobile Liability; Premises Liability; Insurance. ***Email:*** whutcherson@rendigs.com

OF COUNSEL

J. KENNETH MEAGHER, born Cincinnati, Ohio, July 11, 1933; admitted to bar, 1960, Ohio; 1975, Kentucky; 1978, U.S. District Court, Southern District of Ohio; U.S. District Court, Eastern District of Kentucky and U.S. Court of Appeals, Sixth Circuit. *Education:* University of Cincinnati (B.A., 1957; J.D., 1960). *Member:* Cincinnati, Kenton County, Kentucky, Ohio State and American Bar Associations; International Association of Defense Counsel; Defense Research Institute. ***PRACTICE AREAS:*** Personal Injury; Medical Malpractice; Workers' Compensation. ***Email:*** jmeagher@rendigs.com

GORDON C. GREENE, born Cincinnati, Ohio, August 2, 1935; admitted to bar, 1960, Ohio; 1961, U.S. District Court, Southern District of Ohio; 1963, U.S. Court of Appeals, Sixth Circuit; 1965, U.S. District Court, Northern District of Kentucky. *Education:* University of Cincinnati (B.A., 1957; J.D., 1960). *Member:* Cincinnati (Chairman: Admiralty Law Committee, 1964-1967; Common Pleas Court, Civil Law and Procedure Committee, 1965-1978; Applicants and Admissions to bar Committee, 1971-1974; Member, Grievance Committee, 1972-1994; Chairman, Conferences with the Academy of Medicine Committee), Ohio State and American Bar Associations; Ohio Civil Trial Lawyers Association; American Board of Trial Advocates; American College of Trial Lawyers; International Association of Insurance Counsel; American Arbitration Association. ***PRACTICE AREAS:*** Litigation; Medical Malpractice; Hospital Liability; Products Liability; Admiralty and Maritime. ***Email:*** ggreene@rendigs.com

C. THOMAS DUPUIS, born Pittsburgh, Pennsylvania, November 15, 1938; admitted to bar, 1968, Ohio; 1969, U.S. Court of Military Appeals and U.S. District Court, Southern District of Ohio; 1972, U.S. District Court, Eastern District of Kentucky and U.S. Court of Appeals, Sixth Circuit; 1974, U.S. Supreme Court. *Education:* Lafayette College (B.S., 1960); University of Cincinnati (J.D., 1968). Phi Delta Phi. *Member:* Cincinnati, Ohio State (Board of Governors, General Practice Section, 1988-1994) and American Bar Associations; American Arbitration Association. [Capt. JAGC, U.S.N.R.-Ret., 1960-1992]. ***PRACTICE AREAS:*** Business Law; Commercial Law; Construction Law; Family Law; Alternative Dispute Resolution; Estate Planning. ***Email:*** tdupuis@rendigs.com

PAUL J. KELLOGG, born Avon Lake, Ohio, June 13, 1967; admitted to bar, 1993, Ohio; 1994, U.S. District Court, Southern District of Ohio; 1998, U.S. Tax Court. *Education:* Ohio University (B.S., 1989); University of Dayton (J.D., 1993). *Member:* Cincinnati and American Bar Associations. ***PRACTICE AREAS:*** Estate Planning; Corporate Law; Tax Law. ***Email:*** pkellogg@rendigs.com

(This Listing Continued)

ASSOCIATES

KAREN A. ROLCIK, born Elizabeth, New Jersey, July 7, 1961; admitted to bar, 1986, Ohio; 1992, Texas; U.S. District Court, Southern District of Ohio, U.S. Court of Appeals, Federal Circuit, U.S. Court of Federal Claims and U.S. Tax Court. *Education:* Butler University (B.S., cum laude, 1983); Indiana University School of Law - Bloomington (J.D., magna cum laude, 1986). Order of the Coif. Managing Editor, Indiana University Law Journal, 1985-1986. Certified Mediator and Neutral, Texas. *Member:* Dallas (Member, Sections on: Probate, Trusts and Estates; Tax), Ohio State (Member: Elder Law Committee; Estate Planning, Trust & Probate Law Section) and American (Member, Sections on: Real Property, Probate and Trust Law; Taxation) Bar Associations; State Bar of Texas (Member, Sections on: Real Property, Probate, Trust Law; Taxation); College of the State Bar of Texas; Dallas Estate Planning Council; Cincinnati Estate Planning Council. ***PRACTICE AREAS:*** Business Continuation Planning; Business Services; Domestic Relations; Estate Planning; Probate; Tax Law. ***Email:*** krolcik@rendigs.com

CYNTHIA M. CHIARO, born Youngstown, Ohio, December 1, 1961; admitted to bar, 1996, Ohio; 1998, U.S. District Court, Southern District of Ohio. *Education:* University of Oklahoma (B.B.A., 1988); University of Cincinnati (J.D., 1996). *Member:* Cincinnati, Ohio State and American Bar Associations; Ohio Association of Civil Trial Attorneys. ***PRACTICE AREAS:*** Insurance Defense; Insurance Coverage. ***Email:*** cchiaro@rendigs.com

PETER B. JURS, born Toledo, Ohio, August 8, 1972; admitted to bar, 1997, Ohio; 1998, U.S. Court of Appeals, Sixth Circuit; 1999, U.S. District Court, Southern District of Ohio; 2000, Kentucky. *Education:* Miami University (B.A., 1994); University of Cincinnati (J.D., 1997). Law Clerk to the Honorable James G. Carr, U.S. District Judge, Western Divisions, Northern District of Ohio, 1997-1998. *Member:* Cincinnati, Ohio State, Kentucky and American Bar Associations; Northern Kentucky Bar Association; Defense Research Institute; Ohio Association of Civil Trial Attorneys. ***PRACTICE AREAS:*** Products Liability; Construction; Litigation; Admiralty. ***Email:*** pjurs@rendigs.com

CHAD E. WILLITS, born Columbus, Ohio, October 28, 1969; admitted to bar, 1996, Ohio; 1997, U.S. District Court, Southern District of Ohio; 1999, Indiana and U.S. District Court, Northern and Southern Districts of Indiana; 2001, U.S. Court of Appeals, Sixth Circuit. *Education:* University of Dayton (B.A., 1992); University of Cincinnati (J.D., 1996). Phi Alpha Delta. *Member:* Cincinnati and Ohio State Bar Associations. ***PRACTICE AREAS:*** General Litigation; Labor and Employment Law. ***Email:*** cwillits@rendigs.com

LYNNE M. LONGTIN, born Cincinnati, Ohio, May 18, 1971; admitted to bar, 1999, Ohio. *Education:* Indiana University, Bloomington (B.A., 1993); University of Cincinnati (J.D., 1999). Order of the Coif. Associate Member, University of Cincinnati Law Review, 1997-1998. Author: The EEOC'S Position on Mandatory Arbitration, University of Cincinnati, Ohio - Winter 1999. *Member:* Cincinnati and Ohio State Bar Associations. ***PRACTICE AREAS:*** General Litigation; Professional Malpractice; Insurance Defense; Corporate; Commercial Litigation. ***Email:*** llongtin@rendigs.com

GEORGE J. ZAMARY, born Youngstown, Ohio, December 16, 1972; admitted to bar, 1999, Ohio; 2000, U.S. District Court, Southern District of Ohio. *Education:* Ohio University (B.S., summa cum laude, 1995); Capital University (J.D., 1998). Law Clerk to the Honorable Arthur M. Ney, Jr., 1999-2001. *Member:* Cincinnati and Ohio State Bar Associations. ***PRACTICE AREAS:*** Litigation; Product Liability; Construction Defects; Class Actions; Personal Injury. ***Email:*** gzamary@rendigs.com

ROBERT J. THUMANN, born Cincinnati, Ohio, November 5, 1972; admitted to bar, 2002, Ohio; 2004, U.S. Court of Federal Claims. *Education:* University of Cincinnati (B.A., Criminal Justice, 1995); Salmon P. Chase College of Law (J.D., 2002). ***PRACTICE AREAS:*** Personal Injury; Premises Liability; Products Liability. ***Email:*** rthumann@rendigs.com

LAURA I. HILLERICH, born Lancaster, Pennsylvania, April 28, 1977; admitted to bar, 2002, Ohio. *Education:* Wittenberg University (B.A., Psychology, 1999); University of Cincinnati (J.D., 2002). ***PRACTICE AREAS:*** Personal Injury; Premises Liability; Commercial Litigation. ***Email:*** lhillerich@rendigs.com

REPRESENTATIVE CLIENTS: Academy of Model Aeronautics Inc.; AIG; Alex Fries & Bros., Inc.; American Outdoor Advertising Co.; American National Red Cross; Applied Data Management; A-T Controls, Inc.; AT&T; Bar Investment Group; Barrett Paving Materials, Inc.; Bix Box Company; Boy Scouts of America; Business Software Alliance, Inc.; Carestar, Inc.; Catalina Lighting, Inc.; City of Cincinnati; Cincinnati Insurance Company; CNA; Colas, Inc.; Consolidated Stores Corp.; Crum & Forster Insurance Group; CUMIS/CUNA Mutual Insurance Co.; Delta Airlines, Inc.; Dillard's, Inc.; Engineering Methods, Inc.; Federated Mutual Insurance Co.; Games, Inc.; General Motors Acceptance Corp.; General Star Indemnity Company; Good Samaritan Hospital; Grange Mutual Insurance Company; The Harleysville Insurance Group; HNTB Design/Build, Inc.; IBM; Indiana Insurance Company; Ingram Barge Company; Jefferson Insurance Company; Liberty Mutual Insurance Company; Mach III Clutch, Inc.; Marriott International, Inc.; MDM iNet, LLC; Medical Protective Company; Motorists Mutual Insurance Company; Ohio Insurance Guaranty Association; Park-Ohio Holdings Corp.; Park Ohio Industries; PERJAM; The PMA Insurance Group Inc.; Princeton Employees Credit Union; Pro-Copy, Ltd.; Scott Technologies, Inc.; St. Paul Insurance Company; Stand Energy Corporation; State Farm Fire & Casualty; The Taylor Company; ThyssenKrupp Elevator Corporation; ThyssenKrupp Elevator Manufacturing, Inc.; Vertical Systems Elevator Company; W.I.B.-Cincinnati, Inc.; Zurich Insurance Group.

RICE AND DIEDRICHS, LLP

Established in 1974

3530 EDWARDS ROAD

CINCINNATI, OHIO 45208-1358

Telephone: 513-871-1545

Fax: 513-871-1545

URL: http://www.lawyers.com/rice&diedrichs

Federal, State and Local Taxation (Compliance and Planning), Estate Planning, Probate, Business and Real Estate.

JAMES K. RICE, born Charleston, West Virginia, September 30, 1942; admitted to bar, 1967, Ohio and West Virginia; 1977, U.S. Tax Court; 2003, Kentucky. *Education:* University of Cincinnati (B.B.A., 1964; J.D., 1967). *Member:* Cincinnati Bar Association (Member: Grievance Committee, 1993—. ***PRACTICE AREAS:*** Taxation Law; Business Law; Probate Law; Estate Planning; Real Estate. ***Email:*** jkrice@cinci.rr.com

(This Listing Continued)

FRANK M. DIEDRICHS, born Cincinnati, Ohio, February 10, 1943; admitted to bar, 1976, Ohio; 1997, Kentucky. *Education:* University of Cincinnati (A.B., 1965); University of Michigan (M.B.A., 1967); Salmon P. Chase College of Law (J.D., 1976). *Member:* Cincinnati Bar Association (President, 1999-2000; Member, Estate Planning and Probate Committee) and Ohio State Bar Association. ***PRACTICE AREAS:*** Probate Law; Estate Planning Law; Real Estate; Business Law. ***Email:*** fmdiedrichs@cinci.rr.com

ROBBINS, KELLY, PATTERSON & TUCKER

A LEGAL PROFESSIONAL ASSOCIATION

Established in 1965

THE FEDERATED BUILDING, SUITE 1400
7 WEST SEVENTH STREET
CINCINNATI, OHIO 45202-2417
Telephone: 513-721-3330
Telecopier: 513-721-5001
URL: http://www.rkpt.com

Mason, Ohio Office: 315 West Main Street, 45040. Telephone: 513-336-7550. Fax: 513-336-7750.

FIRM PROFILE: Robbins, Kelly, Patterson & Tucker is a Cincinnati legal association practicing in the areas of Business and Employment Law, Real Estate, Litigation, Estate Planning and Probate, Taxation and Family Law. The firm's practice focuses in Ohio, Kentucky, Indiana and Florida.

FREDRIC J. ROBBINS, born Brooklyn, New York, October 5, 1949; admitted to bar, 1974, Ohio; 1984, Florida. *Education:* Miami University (B.S., 1971); University of Cincinnati (J.D., 1974). ***PRACTICE AREAS:*** Corporate Law; Estate Planning; Probate Law; Real Estate. ***Email:*** frobbins@rkpt.com

JAMES M. KELLY, born Lawton, Oklahoma, January 4, 1952; admitted to bar, 1976, Ohio and U.S. District Court, Southern District of Ohio; 1984, U.S. Tax Court; U.S. Court of Appeals, Sixth Circuit; 1993, U.S. Supreme Court. *Education:* Xavier University (A.B., summa cum laude, 1973); University of Cincinnati (J.D., cum laude, 1976). ***PRACTICE AREAS:*** Commercial Litigation; Employment Law; Personal Injury; Business Law; Management Labor Law. ***Email:*** jkelly@rkpt.com

MARK C. PATTERSON, born Cincinnati, Ohio, April 19, 1949; admitted to bar, 1979, Ohio; 2002, Kentucky. *Education:* Xavier University (B.A., 1971); Salmon P. Chase College of Law (J.D., 1979). ***PRACTICE AREAS:*** Estate Planning; Business Law; Probate Law. ***Email:*** mpatterson@rkpt.com

JACK L. TUCKER, born Cincinnati, Ohio, December 12, 1957; admitted to bar, 1983, Ohio; 1985 Kentucky. *Education:* Wittenberg University; Georgetown College (B.S., cum laude, 1980); University of Cincinnati (J.D., 1983). Licensed Title Insurance Agent, 1986. ***PRACTICE AREAS:*** Real Property; Corporate; Secured Lending; Partnership; Estate Planning. ***Email:*** jtucker@rkpt.com

THOMAS M. GAIER, born Cincinnati, Ohio, August 12, 1949; admitted to bar, 1975, Ohio, U.S. District Court, Southern District of Ohio and U.S. Tax Court. *Education:* University of Cincinnati (B.A., cum laude, 1971; J.D., 1975). ***PRACTICE AREAS:*** Estate Planning; Probate Law; Taxation; Real Estate; Business Law; Adoptions. ***Email:*** tgaier@rkpt.com

DANIEL J. TEMMING, born Cincinnati, Ohio, June 25, 1951; admitted to bar, 1979, Ohio and U.S. District Court, Southern District of Ohio; 1980, Indiana and U.S. District Court, Southern District of Indiana. *Education:* Xavier University; University of Cincinnati (B.S., 1974); Salmon P. Chase College of Law (J.D., 1979). ***PRACTICE AREAS:*** Negligence; Torts; Insurance Law; Family Law; Business Law; Probate Law. ***Email:*** dtemming@rkpt.com

RANDY J. BLANKENSHIP, born Covington, Kentucky, August 7, 1961; admitted to bar, 1986, Ohio; 1987, Kentucky and U.S. District Court, Southern District of Ohio; 1988, U.S. District Court, Eastern District of Kentucky; 1989, U.S. Court of Appeals, Sixth Circuit; 1993, U.S. Supreme Court; 1999, U.S. Court of Appeals, Seventh Circuit and U.S. District Court, Western District of Kentucky. *Education:* Northern Kentucky University (B.A., magna cum laude, 1983); Salmon P. Chase College of Law (J.D., magna cum laude, 1986). ***PRACTICE AREAS:*** Personal Injury; Consumer Protection; Commercial Litigation; Domestic Relations; Business Law; Employment Law. ***Email:*** rblankenship@rkpt.com

WILLIAM D. SHERMAN, born Cincinnati, Ohio, June 12, 1968; admitted to bar, 1994, Ohio and U.S. District Court, Southern District of Ohio. *Education:* University of Notre Dame (B.A., 1990); University of Cincinnati (J.D., 1994). ***PRACTICE AREAS:*** Estate Planning and Probate; Taxation; Corporate Law. ***Email:*** bsherman@rkpt.com

BARRY A. SPAETH, born Cincinnati, Ohio, August 20, 1953; admitted to bar, 1994, Ohio and U.S. District Court, Southern District of Ohio. *Education:* Westminster College (B.A., cum laude, 1975); University of Cincinnati (J.D., 1994). ***PRACTICE AREAS:*** Domestic Relations; Litigation; Business Law; Estate Planning; Probate; Real Estate. ***Email:*** bspaeth@rkpt.com

---

RICHARD T. LAUER
ELIZABETH SLONE DeHAAN
ESTHER MARIA NORTON
MICHAEL A. GALASSO
STEPHEN M. SAGER
JARROD M. MOHLER
JASON R. HINNERS

(This Listing Continued)

OF COUNSEL

RICHARD L. NURRE

STEPHEN L. ROBISON

4500 COOPER ROAD, SUITE 305
CINCINNATI, OHIO 45242
Telephone: 513-412-3483
Fax: 513-412-3482
URL: http://www.robinsontaxlaw.com
Email: steve@robisiontaxlaw.com
URL: http://www.stephenlrobison.com

Taxation, Estate Planning and Corporate Law, Like Kind Exchanges, Tax Planning, Tax Controversies.

FIRM PROFILE: Stephen L. Robison, Esq. has focused on providing sophisticated and creative tax and business counsel to successful business and individual clients since 1986. He practices before the U.S. Tax Court and at all levels with the federal and state taxing authorities. His objective for each of his clients is to reduce their rate of tax and to increase their net personal wealth.

STEPHEN L. ROBISON, born Cleveland, Ohio, May 21, 1960; admitted to bar, 1986, Ohio. *Education:* University of Cincinnati (B.A., 1982; J.D., 1985); University of Bridgeport (LL.M., 1986). Phi Alpha Delta (President, 1984-1985). Member, Cleveland Bar Association, 1986-1989. *Member:* Cincinnati, Ohio (Member, Tax Section; Tax Committee) and American (Member, Tax Section) Bar Associations. (Certified Specialist in Federal Tax Law, Ohio State Bar Association). ***PRACTICE AREAS:*** Taxation Law; Estate Planning Law; Corporate Law.

ROETZEL & ANDRESS

A LEGAL PROFESSIONAL ASSOCIATION

Established in 1876

310 CHIQUITA CENTER
250 EAST FIFTH STREET
CINCINNATI, OHIO 45202
Telephone: 513-361-0200
Telecopier: 513-361-0335
Email: inquiries@ralaw.com
URL: http://www.ralaw.com

Akron, Ohio Office: 222 South Main Street. Telephone: 330-376-2700. Telecopier: 330-376-4577.
Columbus, Ohio Office: National City Center, 155 E. Broad Street, 12th Floor. Telephone: 614-463-9770. Telecopier: 614-463-9792.
Naples, Florida Office: 850 Park Shore Drive, Trianon Centre, 3rd Floor. Telephones: 239-649-6200; 800-535-7239. Telecopier: 239-261-3659.
Cleveland, Ohio Office: One Cleveland Center, 1375 East Ninth Street, 9th Floor. Telephone: 216-623-0150. Telecopier: 216-623-0134.
Fort Myers, Florida Office: 2320 First Street, Suite 1000. Telephone: 239-337-3850. Telecopier: 239-337-0970.
Toledo, Ohio Office: One SeaGate, 9th Floor. Telephone: 419-242-7985. Facsimile: 419-242-0316.
Tallahassee, Florida Office: 225 South Adams Street, Suite 250, P.O. Box 10369. Telephone: 850-222-7718. Telecopier: 850-222-8222.
Washington, D.C. Office: 1025 Connecticut Avenue, NW, Suite 220. Telephone: 202-625-0600. Telecopier: 202-338-6340.

General Corporate and Business Law, Banking and Finance, Mergers, Acquisitions and Divestitures, Securities Law, Real Estate Law, Real Estate Development/Syndication/Condominium Law, Tax Law, Intellectual Property Law, Computer Law, Hospital and Health Care Law, Public Law and Finance, Governmental Relations, School Law, Commercial/Bankruptcy Law, Employment Law, Pension, Employee Benefits, Workers' Compensation, OSHA, Business and Commercial Litigation, Complex and Multidistrict Litigation, Antitrust Law, RICO, Federal Court Practice, Product Liability, Environmental Law/Toxic Torts, Insurance Law, Information Technology Law, Medical Malpractice Defense, Asbestos Litigation, Construction Law, 1st Amendment/Media Law, White Collar Criminal Defense, Railroad and FELA, Trucking and Transportation Law, Probate and Estate Planning, Utility Law, International Law, Trial and Appellate Practice.

FIRM PROFILE: Founded in 1876, Roetzel & Andress is one of the largest and fastest growing full-service, corporate law firms with nine offices throughout Ohio, Florida, and Washington, D.C. Roetzel & Andress represents a wide range of clients from individuals and closely-held businesses to multi-national corporations, financial institutions, and government entities. Our lawyers serve as general counsel to many clients, and many of those relationships have existed for much of our history. Our lawyers provide a broad range of legal services to clients on a local, national, and international basis.

PARTNERS

ERIC G. BRUESTLE, born Cincinnati, Ohio, April 23, 1953; admitted to bar, 1977, Ohio. *Education:* University of Cincinnati (B. Mus., 1974; J.D., 1977). *Member:* Cincinnati (Past Chair, Workers' Compensation Committee) and Ohio State (Member, Workers' Compensation Committee) Bar Associations. (Managing Partner) (Certified Specialist in Workers' Compensation Law, Ohio State Bar Association). ***PRACTICE AREAS:*** Workers' Compensation; Labor and Employment; Probate; Estate Planning. ***Email:*** ebruestle@ralaw.com

PETER K. NEWMAN, admitted to bar, 1980, Ohio and U.S. District Court, Southern District of Ohio; 1984, Illinois; 1988, U.S. Court of Appeals, Sixth Circuit; 1990, U.S. Dis-

(This Listing Continued)

ROETZEL & ANDRESS, A LEGAL PROFESSIONAL ASSOCIATION, Cincinnati—Continued

trict Court, Northern District of Ohio and U.S. Court of Appeals, Ninth Circuit; 1998, U.S. District Court, Western District of Kentucky; 1999, Kentucky. *Education:* Miami University (B.A., Economics and Political Science, cum laude, 1977); Georgetown University Law Center (J.D., 1980). *Member:* Cincinnati, Kentucky, Ohio State and American Bar Associations. ***PRACTICE AREAS:*** Employment Litigation; Intellectual Property; Labor and Employment; Regulatory Compliance; Union Labor Law. ***Email:*** pnewman@ralaw.com

JEFFREY S. SHOSKIN, born Pittsburgh, Pennsylvania, July 7, 1958; admitted to bar, 1983, Ohio and U.S. District Court, Southern District of Ohio; 1990, U.S. Court of Appeals, Sixth Circuit. *Education:* Grove City College (B.A., magna cum laude, 1980); Temple University (J.D., cum laude, 1983). Named an Ohio Super Lawyer. Co-Author, Chapter, "Defenses to Wrongful Termination Claims," Litigating Wrongful Discharge Claims, Clark Boardman Callaghan. Member, Inaugural Class, Cincinnati Academy of Leadership for Lawyers. *Member:* Cincinnati (Chair, Labor and Employment Committee, 2000-2004; Vice President, Board of Trustees; Former Secretary and Treasurer; Former Chair, Young Lawyers Section), Ohio State (Member, Labor & Employment Law Committee) and American (Member, Labor & Employment Law Committee) Bar Associations; Potter Stewart American Inn of Court (Member, Executive Committee). ***PRACTICE AREAS:*** Labor and Employment (95%); Alternative Dispute Resolution (5%). ***Email:*** jshoskin@ralaw.com

---

GREGORY S. KESSLER, born Cincinnati, Ohio, January 26, 1966; admitted to bar, 1996, Ohio; Kentucky; U.S. District Court, Northern District of Ohio; U.S. District Court, Southern District of Ohio; U.S. Court of Appeals, Sixth Circuit. *Education:* University of Cincinnati (B.S.A.E., 1988; J.D., 1996). Member: Law Review, 1994-1996; Moot Court, 1994-1996. *Member:* Cincinnati and Ohio State Bar Associations. ***PRACTICE AREAS:*** Civil Litigation; Commercial Law; Consumer Law; Insurance Defense; Personal Injury; Products Liability; Breach of Contract. ***Email:*** gkessler@ralaw.com

ELIZABETH SHAFFER, born 1978; admitted to bar, 2003, Ohio; 2004, Kentucky. *Education:* Centre College (B.A., 2000); University of Cincinnati College of Law (J.D., 2003). Order of the Coif. *Member:* Cincinnati, Ohio State and Kentucky Bar Associations. ***PRACTICE AREAS:*** Bankruptcy; Employment Litigation; Labor and Employment; Litigation; Products Liability; Regulatory Compliance; Union Labor Law. ***Email:*** lshaffer@ralaw.com

REPRESENTATIVE CLIENTS: General Motors Corporation; Ford Motor Company; Rite Aid Corporation; PMC Chemicals, Inc.; Mercy Hospital/Anderson; Mutual Assurance Company; AAMOS.

(For complete biographical data on all personnel, see Professional Biographies at Akron, Ohio)

JAY A. ROSENBERG, LPA

ONE FINANCIAL WAY, SUITE 312
CINCINNATI, OHIO 45242
Telephone: 513-792-6729
Fax: 513-745-0747
Email: jrosenberg@fandtlaw.com
URL: http://www.dodeeds.com

Real Estate, Title Insurance, Corporate.

JAY A. ROSENBERG, born Philadelphia, Pennsylvania, October 23, 1939; admitted to bar, 1966, Ohio; 1986, Kentucky. *Education:* Wharton School of the University of Pennsylvania (B.S., Economics, 1961); University of Michigan (J.D., with distinction, 1965). Title Insurance Agent, Ohio, 1968—. Member, Banker's Club, Cincinnati, Ohio. *Member:* Cincinnati (Real Estate, Bankruptcy and Continuing Education Law Sections), Kentucky (Real Estate Law Section) and Ohio State (Board of Governors, Real Estate Law Section) Bar Associations; Ohio Land Title Association (Trustee, 1979-1984; President, 1983-1984; Secretary-Treasurer Trustee, 1992-1993; Chairman Lender's Council, 1996-1998; Political Action Committee, Trustee, 1997-2001); Southwestern Ohio Land Title Association (Trustee, 1993-2004). (Also Of Counsel to Furnier & Thomas, LLP). ***PRACTICE AREAS:*** Real Estate; Title Insurance Claims; Corporate.

SANDERS & ASSOCIATES, LPA

9122 MONTGOMERY ROAD, SUITE 201
CINCINNATI, OHIO 45242
Telephone: 513-891-8900
Fax: 513-891-8937
Email: lawfirm@sandersassociates.net
URL: http://www.sandersassociates.net

General Civil and Trial Practice in all Courts. National Litigation Practice, Commercial Disputes, Insurance Coverage, Crop Insurance and Personal Injury.

M. BRADFORD SANDERS, born Cincinnati, Ohio, 1954; admitted to bar, 1985, Missouri; 1986, Illinois; 1988, Ohio; U.S. District Court, Southern District of Ohio; U.S. District Court, Eastern District of Missouri and U.S. Court of Appeals, Sixth Circuit. *Education:* Kenyon College (B.A., 1976); Washington University (J.D., 1985). *Member:* Cincinnati, Ohio State and American Bar Associations. ***PRACTICE AREAS:*** Insurance Coverage Litigation; Crop Insurance; Civil Litigation; Commercial Disputes. ***Email:*** bsanders@sandersassociates.net

---

THOMAS C. JAMES, JR., born Savannah, Georgia, 1966; admitted to bar, 1992, Georgia; 2001, Ohio; U.S. District Court, Southern District of Ohio. *Education:* Oglethorpe University (B.A., 1988); Emory University School of Law (J.D., 1992). *Member:* Cincinnati and Ohio State Bar Associations; State Bar of Georgia. ***PRACTICE AREAS:*** Insurance Coverage Litigation; Crop Insurance; Civil Litigation; Commercial Disputes; Customs Law. ***Email:*** tjames@sanderassociates.net

KATHERINE S. CARMODY

THE SANDERS LAW FIRM

CINCINNATI, OHIO

(See Covington, Kentucky)

Personal Injury and Wrongful Death, including: Automobile, Products Liability, Medical Malpractice, Premises Liability, F.E.L.A., General Negligence, Insurance Law, Legal Malpractice, Civil and Commercial Litigation, including Business Disputes, Land-use Planning, Zoning, and Contracts, Probate, Criminal Law, Environmental, including Regulatory and Toxic Tort.

SANTEN & HUGHES

A LEGAL PROFESSIONAL ASSOCIATION
SUITE 3100
312 WALNUT STREET
CINCINNATI, OHIO 45202
Telephone: 513-721-4450
Fax: 513-721-0109
URL: http://www.santen-hughes.com

FIRM PROFILE: For more than forty years, Santen and Hughes has enjoyed an excellent reputation, and is well connected with businesses and other professionals in the greater Cincinnati/Northern Kentucky area. The firm specializes in litigation and the representation of privately-held businesses, their owners and executives. With respect to litigation, we routinely appear in all courts located in Hamilton, Clermont, Warren, Butler, and Montgomery Counties in Ohio, and Kenton, Campbell, and Boone Counties in Kentucky, the Federal District Courts, and the Sixth Circuit Court of Appeals. We handle plaintiff's medical malpractice and personal injury cases, family law matters including collaborative law and mediation, and the whole spectrum of commercial, corporate, collection, bankruptcy, employment, and probate litigation. As part of our general business representation, we also specialize in handling transactions, real estate development, securities, financing, employment matters, estate planning, probate and trust administration, tax planning and tax controversies.

WILLIAM E. SANTEN, born Cincinnati, Ohio, June 14, 1928; admitted to bar, 1955, Ohio. *Education:* Georgetown University (B.S.S., 1950); University of Cincinnati (LL.B., 1955). Assistant Attorney General, State of Ohio, 1957-1958. Assistant City Solicitor, Cincinnati, Ohio, 1960. *Member:* Cincinnati, Ohio State and American (Member, Litigation Section) Bar Associations; The Association of Trial Lawyers of America; Ohio Academy of Trial Lawyers; Hamilton County Trial Lawyers Association (Past Trustee). ***PRACTICE AREAS:*** Eminent Domain Law; Negligence Law; Medical Malpractice Law. ***Email:*** wes@santen-hughes.com

CHARLES M. MEYER, born Cincinnati, Ohio, December 31, 1951; admitted to bar, 1977, Massachusetts; 1978, Ohio and Florida; 1993, Kentucky, U.S. Supreme Court, U.S. Court of Appeals, Sixth Circuit, U.S. District Court, Southern Disrict of Ohio and U.S. District Court, Eastern District of Kentucky. *Education:* Boston College (A.B., 1974; J.D., 1977). ***PRACTICE AREAS:*** Business Litigation; Commercial Litigation; Chapter 11 Bankruptcy; Collections; Business Transactions.

CHARLES E. REYNOLDS, born Chattanooga, Tennessee, April 4, 1954; admitted to bar, 1981, Ohio. *Education:* University of North Carolina (B.S., 1976); University of Tennessee (J.D., 1980). *Member:* Cincinnati and American (Member, Section on Business Law) Bar Associations. ***PRACTICE AREAS:*** Corporate Law; Mergers and Acquisitions; Commercial Litigation; Contract Litigation. ***Email:*** cer@santen-hughes.com

JOHN D. HOLSCHUH, JR., born Columbus, Ohio, December 21, 1955; admitted to bar, 1980, Ohio and U.S. District Court, Southern District of Ohio; 1986, U.S. Court of Appeals, Sixth Circuit and U.S. Supreme Court; 1987, U.S. District Court, Eastern District of Kentucky; 1991, Kentucky. *Education:* Miami University (B.S., 1977); University of Cincinnati (J.D., 1980). National Institute of Trial Advocacy Faculty, 1990, 1996, 2004, 2005. Prosecuting Attorney, City of Loveland, 1988-1992; Magistrate, 1992—; Magistrate, Village of Fairfax, 1999—. Recognized in The Best Lawyers in America 1996—; Ohio Super Lawyers 2004. *Member:* Cincinnati (Board of Trustees, 1995-2004; President, 2002-2003), Ohio State and Kentucky Bar Associations; Hamilton County Trial Lawyers Association (President, 1990-1992; Member, Board of Trustees, 1992-1994); Ohio Academy of Trial Lawyers (Member, Board of Trustees, 1991-1995, 1998-2000); The Association of Trial Lawyers of America; American Board of Trial Advocates. Sixth Circuit Judicial Conference (Life Member); The Potter Stewart Inn of Court (Emeritus Member). ***REPORTED CASES:*** Hester v. Dwivedi, et.al, 89 O.S.3d 575 (2000); Lawyer's Cooperative Publishing Co. v. Muething, 65 O.S. 3d 273, 603 N.E.2d 969 (1992); King v. Lekamp, 50 O.App.3d 4, 553 N.E.2d 701 (Ham.Co. 1988); Ryne v. Garvey, 87 O.App.3d 145, 621 N.E.2d 1320 (Montg.Co. 1993); McKinney v. Schlatter, 118 O.App.3d 328 (Butler Co. 1997). ***PRACTICE AREAS:*** General Negligence Trial Law; Appeals; Medical Malpractice Law; Personal Injury Law. ***Email:*** jdh@santen-hughes.com

JAMES P. WERSCHING, born Columbus, Ohio, March 14, 1955; admitted to bar, 1980, Ohio. *Education:* University of Notre Dame (B.B.A., 1977); University of Cincinnati (J.D., 1980); New York University (LL.M., taxation, 1984). Certified Public Accountant, Ohio, 1983. *Member:* Cincinnati (Former Chair, Taxation Section), Ohio State Bar Associations; American Institute of Certified Public Accountants (Section of Taxation). ***PRACTICE AREAS:*** Business Law; Federal Income Tax Law; Estate Planning and Probate Law; Real Estate Law.

C. GREGORY SCHMIDT, born Cincinnati, Ohio, May 14, 1955; admitted to bar, 1980, Ohio and U.S. District Court, Southern District of Ohio; 1981, U.S. Court of Appeals, Sixth Circuit; 1992, Kentucky and U.S. District Court, Eastern District of Kentucky. *Edu-*

(This Listing Continued)

cation: University of Cincinnati (B.B.A., 1977); University of Dayton (J.D., 1980). Member, Board of Trustees, Madeira and Indian Hill Fire Company, 1992—; Secretary, 1995-1999; Vice President, 1999—, Madiera and Indian Hill Joint Fire District. *Member:* Cincinnati, Ohio State and Kentucky Bar Associations. ***PRACTICE AREAS:*** Corporate Law; Business Law; Construction Law; Probate Law; Estate Planning Law; Real Estate Law; Mergers and Acquisitions. ***Email:*** cgs@santen-hughes.com

WILLIAM E. SANTEN, JR., born Cincinnati, Ohio, August 16, 1955; admitted to bar, 1984, Ohio. *Education:* University of Cincinnati (B.A., 1977); Thomas M. Cooley Law School (J.D., 1983). *Member:* Cincinnati, Ohio State and American Bar Associations; The Association of Trial Lawyers of America; Ohio Academy of Trial Lawyers; Hamilton County Trial Lawyers Association. ***PRACTICE AREAS:*** General Negligence Law; Product Liability Law; Personal Injury Law; Medical Malpractice Law; Land Use Law; Appropriation.

WILLIAM A. DECENSO, born Cincinnati, Ohio, November 12, 1953; admitted to bar, 1979, Ohio; 1986, U.S. Court of Appeals, Sixth Circuit. *Education:* Boston College (A.B., 1975); University of Cincinnati (J.D., 1978). *Member:* Cincinnati Bar Association (Member, Domestic Relations Committee); Ohio State Bar Association; Collaborative Family Lawyers of Cincinnati. ***PRACTICE AREAS:*** Domestic Relations; Business. ***Email:*** wad@santen-hughes.com

SARAH TANKERSLEY, born Radford, Virginia, February 5, 1969; admitted to bar, 1997, Ohio; 1998, Kentucky. *Education:* Northern Kentucky University (B.A., 1993); University of Kentucky (J.D., 1997). *Member:* Cincinnati, Northern Kentucky, Ohio and Kentucky State Bar associations; Ohio Association of Trial Lawyers. ***PRACTICE AREAS:*** Medical Malpractice; Personal Injury. ***Email:*** sbt@santen-hughes.com

---

FANON A. RUCKER, born Gary, Indiana, October 19, 1971; admitted to bar, 1996, Ohio; 2000, U.S. District Court, Southern District of Ohio; U.S. Court of Appeals, Sixth Circuit. *Education:* Hampton University (B.A., 1993); University of Cincinnati (J.D., 1996). *Member:* Cincinnati (Trustee, 2002—), Ohio State, American and National Bar Associations; Black Lawyers Association of Cincinnati (President, 2001-2003). ***PRACTICE AREAS:*** Litigation; Civil Rights; Employment Law; Municipal Law. ***Email:*** far@santen-hughes.com

DEEPAK K. DESAI, born Cincinnati, Ohio, December 19, 1968; admitted to bar, 1993, Ohio; 2005, U.S. District Curt, Southern District of Ohio. *Education:* Northern Kentucky University (B.A., summa cum laude, University Honors Scholar, 1988); Salmon P. Chase College of Law (J.D., summa cum laude, 1991). *Member:* Cincinnati and Ohio State Bar Associations. ***PRACTICE AREAS:*** Business Law; Bankruptcy; Real Estate; Estate Planning; Litigation. ***Email:*** dkd@santen-hughes.com

WILLIAM J. LISS, born Los Angeles, California, January 26, 1971; admitted to bar, 1997, Ohio; 1998, Nevada and U.S. District Court, Southern District of Ohio; 1999, Florida; U.S. Tax Court. *Education:* The Ohio University (B.A., 1993); University of Cincinnati (J.D., 1997); University of Florida (LL.M., Taxation, 1999). Phi Beta Kappa. *Member:* Cincinnati and Ohio State Bar Associations. ***PRACTICE AREAS:*** Business Taxation; Estate Planning. ***Email:*** wjl@santen-hughes.com

J. ROBERT LINNEMAN, born Cincinnati, Ohio; admitted to bar, 2001, Ohio. *Education:* Miami University (B.A., 1991); Salmon P. Chase College of Law (J.D., 2001). ***PRACTICE AREAS:*** Litigation; Business Law; Real Estate; Construction Law. ***Email:*** jrl@santen-hughes.com

ANDREW WEISENBERGER, born Cincinnati, Ohio, September 12, 1977; admitted to bar, 2002, Ohio; 2003, U.S. District Court, Southern District of Ohio; 2004, Kentucky. *Education:* Miami University (B.S., 1999); Louis D. Brandeis School of Law, University of Louisville (J.D., 2002); Georgetown University (LL.M., with distinction, 2003). *Member:* Kentucky Bar Association. ***PRACTICE AREAS:*** Taxation; Business Law; Probate; Estate Planning. ***Email:*** aww@santen-hughes.com

SCHOTTENSTEIN ZOX & DUNN CO., LPA

BANK ONE TOWERS
8044 MONTGOMERY ROAD, SUITE 630
CINCINNATI, OHIO 45236-2926
Telephone: 513-792-0792
Fax: 513-792-0803
Email: info@szd.com
URL: http://www.szd.com

Columbus, Ohio Office: 250 West Street, 43215-2538. Telephone: 614-462-2700. Telecopier: 614-462-5135. Telex: 650 24 444 365.
Cleveland, Ohio Office: USBank Centre, 1350 Euclid Avenue, Suite 1400, 44115. Telephone: 216-621-6501. Fax: 216-621-6502.

Business (Corporate, Banking and Lending, Real Estate/Land Use, General Tax, State and Local Tax, Employee Benefits, Estate Planning, White Collar Crime, E-Commerce, Intellectual Property/Technology Protection, International); Labor and Employment Law, Litigation, Health Law, Construction Law, Bankruptcy Law, Environmental Law, Debtor/Creditor Rights, Workers' Compensation, Municipal Law, Government Affairs.

FIRM PROFILE: Since its founding in 1966, Schottenstein Zox & Dunn has grown from four lawyers to over 100. The firm is dedicated to viewing the law from varied perspectives for the variety of local, regional and national clients it represents as either general counsel or in one or more of the above practice areas. Schottenstein Zox & Dunn is a complete law firm offering comprehensive services to businesses, governmental entities and individuals. Our position in the marketplace combined with the experience of our lawyers enables us to provide our clients with the responsive answers they need to succeed.

(This Listing Continued)

MARCIA J. MYERS, born Salem, Ohio, 1959; admitted to bar, 1985, Ohio. *Education:* Bowling Green State University (B.A., magna cum laude, 1982); The Ohio State University (J.D., 1985). ***PRACTICE AREAS:*** Health Law; Corporate Law; Hospital Law. ***Email:*** mmyers@szd.com

All of the firm's attorneys are members of the Cincinnati, Ohio State and American Bar Associations.

(For biographical data on all personnel, see Professional Biographies at Columbus, Ohio)

SCHROEDER, MAUNDRELL, BARBIERE & POWERS

11935 MASON ROAD, SUITE 110
CINCINNATI, OHIO 45249
Telephone: 513-583-4200
Fax: 513-583-4203
Email: tpowers@smbplaw.com
URL: http://www.smbplaw.com

Litigation.

MEMBERS OF FIRM

JOHN W. HUST, born Cincinnati, Ohio, May 3, 1949; admitted to bar, 1975, Ohio; 1993, Kentucky. *Education:* The Ohio State University (B.S., 1971); University of Cincinnati (J.D., 1975). Member, University of Cincinnati Law Review, 1973-1975. *Member:* Cincinnati and Ohio State Bar Associations; Northern Kentucky Bar Association. ***PRACTICE AREAS:*** Professional Liability Law; Products Liability; School Law; Employment Law; Commercial Litigation. ***Email:*** jhust@smbplaw.com

ROBERT S. HILLER, born Memphis, Tennessee, December 19, 1951; admitted to bar, 1977, Ohio and U.S. District Court, Southern District of Ohio; 1982, U.S. Court of Appeals, Sixth Circuit; 1993, Kentucky; 2000, U.S. District Court, Eastern District of Kentucky. *Education:* Indiana University (A.B., 1973); University of Tennessee (J.D., 1976). *Member:* Cincinnati, Warren County and Ohio State Bar Associations; Northern Kentucky Bar Association. ***PRACTICE AREAS:*** Premises Liability Law; Automobile Liability Law; Personal Injury Law; Wrongful Death Litigation; Insurance Law; General Litigation. ***Email:*** rhiller@smbplaw.com

LAWRENCE E. BARBIERE, born Dayton, Ohio, March 6, 1951; admitted to bar, 1977, Ohio and U.S. District Court, Southern District of Ohio; 1980, U.S. Court of Appeals, Sixth Circuit; 1993, Kentucky; 2002, U.S. Supreme Court. *Education:* Indiana University (A.B., 1973); University of Cincinnati (J.D., 1977). Member, University of Cincinnati Law Review, 1976-1977. Author: "The Seizure of a Tenant's Property by His Landlord Pursuant to State Statute Does Not Involve State Action for Purposes of the Fourteenth Amendment," 45 U. Cinn. L. Rev. 301, 1976. *Member:* Cincinnati, Ohio State Bar Associations; Ohio Association of Civil Trial Attorneys; Cincinnati Bar Association Ethics Committee; Northern Kentucky Bar Association. ***PRACTICE AREAS:*** Civil Rights Law; Intentional Torts; Products Liability Law; Property Law; Insurance Law; Zoning Law. ***Email:*** lbarbiere@smbplaw.com

TODD M. POWERS, born Cincinnati, Ohio, December 7, 1958; admitted to bar, 1984, Ohio, U.S. District Court, Southern District of Ohio and U.S. District Court, Eastern District of Kentucky; 1985, U.S. Court of Appeals, Sixth Circuit; 1991, Kentucky; 1994, West Virginia, U.S. District Court, Southern District of West Virginia, U.S Court of Appeals, Fourth Circuit and U.S. Supreme Court. *Education:* Ohio State University (B.A., 1981); University of Cincinnati (J.D., 1984). *Member:* Cincinnati, Ohio State, West Virginia, Kentucky and American (Member, Litigation Section, Tort and Insurance Practice Section) Bar Associations; Ohio Association of Civil Trial Attorneys; Defense Research Institute; Maritime Law Association of United States. ***PRACTICE AREAS:*** Admiralty Law; Personal Injury Law; General Litigation. ***Email:*** tpowers@smbplaw.com

CHRISTOPHER L. MOORE, born Cincinnati, Ohio, October 24, 1967; admitted to bar, 1993, Ohio and U.S. District Court, Southern District of Ohio; 1999 U.S. District Court, Eastern District of Kentucky. *Education:* Xavier University (B.S./B.A., 1989); University of Toledo (J.D., 1993). *Member:* Cincinnati, Ohio State and American Bar Associations; Northern Kentucky Bar Association; Ohio Association of Civil Trial Attorneys; Defense Research Institute. ***PRACTICE AREAS:*** Insurance Defense; Premises Liability; Products Liability; Employment Litigation; Personal Injury; General Litigation. ***Email:*** cmoore@smbplaw.com

ASSOCIATES

JAY D. PATTON, born Wilmington, Ohio, January 30, 1970; admitted to bar, 1997, Ohio; 1998, U.S. District Court, Southern District of Ohio; 1999, Indiana and U.S. District Court, Northern and Southern Districts of Indiana; 2000, Kentucky and U.S. District Court, Eastern District of Kentucky. *Education:* Ball State University (B.S., 1994); University of Cincinnati (J.D., 1997). *Member:* Cincinnati, Indiana, Kentucky and Ohio State Bar Associations. ***PRACTICE AREAS:*** Admiralty Law; Personal Injury; Insurance Coverage. ***Email:*** jpatton@smbplaw.com

DEREK W. SCRANTON, born South Weymouth, Massachusetts, March 23, 1970; admitted to bar, 2002, Ohio. *Education:* Ohio University (B.A., 1992); University of Cincinnati (J.D., 2002). ***PRACTICE AREAS:*** Admiralty and Maritime Law; Premises Liability; Slip and Fall; Insurance Defense; Insurance Coverage; Uninsured and Underinsured Motorists; Municipal Law; Employment Law. ***Email:*** dscranton@smbplaw.com

MEGAN C. AHRENS, born Cincinnati, Ohio, November 27, 1977; admitted to bar, 2003, Ohio; 2004, U.S. District Court, Southern District of Ohio and U.S. District Court, Southern District of Indiana. *Education:* Indiana University, Bloomington (B.A., 2000); University of Cincinnati (J.D., 2003). *Member:* Cincinnati, Ohio State and American Bar Associations. ***PRACTICE AREAS:*** Admiralty and Maritime Law; Personal Injury; Premises Liability; Litigation. ***Email:*** mahrens@smbplaw.com

(This Listing Continued)

SCHROEDER, MAUNDRELL, BARBIERE & POWERS, Cincinnati—Continued

OF COUNSEL

WILLIAM P. SCHROEDER, born Cincinnati, Ohio, November 1, 1942; admitted to bar, 1968, Ohio; 1990, Kentucky. *Education:* University of Cincinnati (B.S., 1964); Salmon P. Chase College of Law (J.D., 1968). Phi Alpha Delta; Omicron Delta Kappa. Member, Order of the Curia. Adjunct Professor of Law, Salmon P. Chase College of Law, Northern Kentucky University, 1970. Adjunct Professor of Law, University of Cincinnati College of Law, 1987. *Member:* Cincinnati, Ohio State and American Bar Associations; Maritime Law Association of the United States; International Association of Defense Counsel. ***PRACTICE AREAS:*** Admiralty Law; Commercial Litigation; Mining Law; Zoning Law; Environmental Law; Personal Injury Law; Estate Planning; Business Planning. ***Email:*** bschroeder@smbplaw.com

MICHAEL E. MAUNDRELL, born Cincinnati, Ohio, December 11, 1946; admitted to bar, 1974, Ohio. *Education:* University of Michigan (B.A., 1969); University of Cincinnati (J.D., 1974). *Member:* Cincinnati, Ohio State and American Bar Associations; Maritime Law Association of the United States. ***PRACTICE AREAS:*** Legal Malpractice Law; Employment Law; Civil Rights Law.

REPRESENTATIVE CLIENTS: Ashland Oil, Inc.; Arosy Gaming Co.; The Ohio River Co.; Midland Enterprises Inc.; Madison Coal & Supply Co.; McGinnis, Inc.; American Electric Power; Indiana Insurance Co.; B & B Riverboats; CNA; Kroger Co.; K & K Insurance Co.; Princeton City School District; Kentucky Fried Chicken; Ohio Bar Liability Insurance Co.; Restaurant Management, Inc.; Neare, Gibbs & Co.; St. Paul Fire & Marine Insurance Co.; Ohio Government Risk Management Plan; Midwest Claims Service; Roadway Express.

SCHWARTZ, MANES & RUBY

A LEGAL PROFESSIONAL ASSOCIATION

Established in 1976

2900 CAREW TOWER
441 VINE STREET
CINCINNATI, OHIO 45202-3090
Telephone: 513-579-1414
Telecopier: 513-579-1418
URL: http://www.smrfirm.com

Administrative Law, Business Planning, Civil Trial Practice, Taxation, Estate Planning, Employee Benefits, Real Estate, Intellectual Property, Mergers and Acquisitions, Probate, Securities, Personal Injury, Retirement Planning, Labor, Employment, Family Law, Information Technology, Copyright, Trademark, Corporate Partnerships, Trusts, Government Contracts, Health Care Law.

FIRM PROFILE: Since 1976, Schwartz, Manes & Ruby has provided sophisticated legal counsel and expertise with an added dimension- a determination to see problems and opportunities from a client's perspective. Our creative, independent-thinking lawyers recognize the importance of detail in fulfilling the needs of a diverse group of individual and business clients.

RICHARD M. SCHWARTZ, born Brooklyn, New York, September 19, 1936; admitted to bar, 1962, New York and U.S. Tax Court; 1968, Ohio. *Education:* Queens College (B.S., 1957); Boston University (LL.B., 1961; LL.M. in Taxation, 1962). Lecturer: Federal Income Tax and Estate Planning, American College of Chartered Life Underwriters, 1976—; Southwestern Ohio Tax Institute, 1976—. Tax Attorney, Office of Chief Counsel, Internal Revenue Service, 1962-1967. *Member:* Cincinnati, Ohio State, New York State, Federal and American (Member, Taxation Section) Bar Associations. ***PRACTICE AREAS:*** Taxation; Estate Planning; Corporate Law; Real Estate. ***Email:*** rschwartz@smrfirm.com

STANLEY L. RUBY, born Louisville, Kentucky, February 23, 1937; admitted to bar, 1963, Kentucky; 1965, U.S. Tax Court; 1966, District of Columbia; 1970, Ohio. *Education:* Vanderbilt University (B.A., 1959; LL.B., 1961); New York University (LL.M. in Taxation, 1964). Member, Editorial Board, Vanderbilt Law Review, 1960-1961. Lecturer: Income Taxation, Legal Environment of Business and Financial and Estate Planning Applications, The American College, 1978—; Basic Estate and Gift Taxation and Planning, ABA, 1978—; New York University Institute on Federal Taxation, 1985. Attorney-Advisor, U.S. Tax Court, 1964-1966. Attorney, Tax Division, Department of Justice, 1968-1970. *Member:* Cincinnati, Ohio State, Kentucky and American (Member, Sections on: Business Law; Taxation) Bar Associations. ***PRACTICE AREAS:*** Real Estate; Taxation; Securities. ***Email:*** sruby@smrfirm.com

SCOTT M. SLOVIN, born Cincinnati, Ohio, April 29, 1952; admitted to bar, 1977, Ohio; 1979, U.S. District Court, Southern District of Ohio; 1981, U.S. Tax Court; 1989, U.S. Court of Appeals, Sixth Circuit; 1990, U.S. Supreme Court. *Education:* Indiana University (B.S., with honors, 1974); University of Cincinnati (J.D., 1977); New York University (LL.M. in Taxation, 1978). Phi Eta Sigma; Beta Gamma Sigma. Adjunct Professor, University of Cincinnati Graduate School of Business, 1984. Recipient: American Jurisprudence Award in Torts; Michael R. Lowengart Memorial Prize for Trade Regulations. Member, Board of Directors, Indiana Memorial Union, Indiana University, 1973-1974. *Member:* Cincinnati, Ohio State and American (Member, Sections on: Business Law; Taxation) Bar Associations. ***REPORTED CASES:*** Cottage Savings v. Commissioner, 499 U.S. 554 (1991). ***PRACTICE AREAS:*** Taxation; Corporate Law; Franchise Law; Estate Planning; Retirement Planning. ***Email:*** sslovin@smrfirm.com

DONALD B. HORDES, born Newport News, Virginia, September 25, 1944; admitted to bar, 1969, District of Columbia; 1972, U.S. Court of Appeals for the District of Columbia Circuit; 1982, Ohio. *Education:* University of Maryland (B.A., 1966); George Washington University (J.D., 1969; LL.M., 1976). Phi Beta Kappa; Phi Delta Phi; Phi Kappa Phi. Member, George Washington University Law Review, 1968-1969. Editor, Employment Law Section, Ohio State Bar Association Newsletter, 1984-1987. Adjunct Professor, The Master of Arts, Labor and Employment Relations, University of Cincinnati, 1980-1991. National Labor Relations Board Staff Counsel to Member John H. Fanning, 1972-1976. Trial Attorney, Region 9, Cincinnati, Ohio, 1976-1981. *Member:* Cincinnati (Chairman, Labor and Employment Committee, 1992-1994), Ohio State and American Bar Associations; The District of Columbia Bar. [Capt., USAF, JAG, 1969-1972]. ***PRACTICE AREAS:*** Labor Law; Employment Relations; Administrative Law; Civil Trial Practice. ***Email:*** dhordes@smrfirm.com

WILLIAM S. WYLER, born Cincinnati, Ohio, March 28, 1946; admitted to bar, 1972, Ohio, U.S. District Court, Southern District of Ohio and U.S. Court of Appeals, District of Columbia Circuit; 1973, U.S. Court of Appeals, Sixth Circuit; 1975, U.S. Supreme Court; 1989, U.S. Court of Appeals, Federal Circuit. *Education:* American University (B.A., 1969); University of Cincinnati (J.D., 1972). Member, Supreme Court Advisory Committee on Court Technology, 1987-1998. Adjunct Professor of Law, University of Cincinnati and Salmon P. Chase School of Law. Registered Canadian Trademarks Agent. *Member:* Cincinnati (Chairman, Computer Law Committee, 1985-1987), Ohio State (Chairman, Computer Law Committee, 1987-1990; Board of Governors, Intellectual Property Section, 1992-1994; Board of Governors, Patent, Trademark and Copyright Section) and American (Member, Committee on Science and Technology) Bar Associations; Computer Law Association; American Intellectual Property Law Association. ***PRACTICE AREAS:*** Information Technology; Copyrights; Trademarks. ***Email:*** wwyler@smrfirm.com

JAMES K. KELLER, born Fort Wayne, Indiana, January 3, 1956; admitted to bar, 1994, Ohio and U.S. District Court, Southern District of Ohio. *Education:* St. Francis College (B.A., 1978); Indiana University (M.B.A., 1985); University of Cincinnati (J.D., 1994). Certified Public Accountant. *Member:* Cincinnati and Ohio State Bar Associations. ***PRACTICE AREAS:*** Corporate Law; Civil Trial Practice; Real Estate; Mergers and Acquisitions; Business Planning; Taxation. ***Email:*** jkeller@smrfirm.com

ASSOCIATES

RALPH J. CONRAD, born Canton, Ohio, September 22, 1962; admitted to bar, 1987, Ohio. *Education:* Ohio Northern University (B.S.B.A., with distinction, 1984); University of Akron (M.A. Taxation, 1987; J.D., magna cum laude, 1987). Moot Court Team. Tax Editor, The Akron Law Review, 1986-1987. Law Clerk to the Hon. Nicholas J. Walinkski, U.S. District Court for the Northern District of Ohio, 1987-1989. *Member:* American Bar Association; Ohio State Bar Association College. (Certified Specialist in Estate Planning, Trust and Probate Law, Ohio State Bar Association). ***PRACTICE AREAS:*** Estate Planning; Probate; Taxation; Business Planning. ***Email:*** rconrad@smrfirm.com

HALLIE L. SCHNEIDER, born Akron, Ohio August 29, 1978; admitted to bar, 2003, Ohio; U.S. District Court, Southern District of Ohio. *Education:* Xavier University (H.A.B., magna cum laude, 2000); University of Cincinnati College of Law (J.D., 2003). *Member:* Cincinnati, Ohio State and American Bar Associations. ***PRACTICE AREAS:*** Corporate Law; Civil Practice. ***Email:*** hschneider@smrfirm.com

OF COUNSEL

DENNIS L. MANES, born Akron, Ohio, October 19, 1948; admitted to bar, 1973, Ohio; 1976, U.S. Tax Court; 1989, U.S. Court of Appeals, Sixth Circuit; 1990, U.S. Supreme Court. *Education:* Kent State University (B.B.A., 1970); University of Toledo (J.D., 1973); New York University (LL.M. in Taxation, 1974). Delta Theta Phi. *Member:* Cincinnati, Ohio State and American (Member, Taxation Section) Bar Associations. ***PRACTICE AREAS:*** Taxation; Estate Planning; Corporate Law. ***Email:*** dmanes@smrfirm.com

HERBERT BASS, born Cincinnati, Ohio, December 22, 1923; admitted to bar, 1949, Ohio; 1956, U.S. Supreme Court. *Education:* University of Cincinnati (LL.B., 1948). Instructor, Contract Law, Air Force Institute of Technology, 1963-1970. Member, Board of Commissioners on the Unauthorized Practice of Law, 1980-1985. *Member:* Cincinnati, Ohio State and Federal Bar Associations. ***PRACTICE AREAS:*** Government Contracts. ***Email:*** hbass@smrfirm.com

ORLY R. RUMBERG, born Cleveland, Ohio, August 28, 1968; admitted to bar, 1993, Ohio. *Education:* Case Western Reserve University (B.A., cum laude, 1990); Case Western Reserve School of Law (J.D., 1993). Managing Editor, Health Matrix, Journal of Law-Medicine, 1992-1993. Author: "Increasing the Supply of Cadaver Organs for Transplantation: Recognizing That The Real Problem if Psychological Not Legal," 3 Health Matrix, Journal of Law-Medicine 219, 1993. *Member:* Cincinnati Bar Association; American Health Lawyers Association. ***LANGUAGES:*** Hebrew. ***PRACTICE AREAS:*** Corporate Law; Mergers and Acquisitions; Health Care Law. ***Email:*** orumberg@smrfirm.com

REPRESENTATIVE CLIENTS: *FINANCIAL:* Emery Federal Credit Union; Miami University Employees Federal Credit Union. *COMMERCIAL:* Baker Concrete Construction, Inc.; Bankhardts, Inc.; Batesville Products, Inc.; La-Z-Boy Recliner Shops, Inc.; Champion Window Manufacturing & Supply Co.; King Wrecking Co., Inc.; JP Flooring Systems, Inc.
APPROVED ATTORNEYS FOR: Stewart Title Insurance Company.

SHEA & ASSOCIATES

Established in 1979

444 CHIQUITA CENTER
250 E. FIFTH STREET
CINCINNATI, OHIO 45202-4119
Telephone: 513-621-8333
Telecopier: 513-651-3272
Email: jshea@shea-associates.com
Email: scoffey@shea-associates.com
Email: jscheper@shea-associates.com
URL: http://www.shea-associates.com

Civil Litigation, Catastrophic Personal Injury, Negligence Law, Medical Malpractice and Products Liability.

FIRM PROFILE: Shea & Associates limits its practice to civil litigation. The firm is available for the presentation or defense of general negligence, professional liability, product liability, and business litigation.

(This Listing Continued)

JOSEPH W. SHEA III, born Cincinnati, Ohio, January 3, 1947; admitted to bar, 1974, Ohio. *Education:* University of Cincinnati (B.A., 1969); Northern Kentucky University (J.D., 1974). Editor, The Verdict Reporter, pub., Ohio Academy of Trial Lawyers, 1976—. Author: *Ohio Forms for Civil Trial Practice,* Harrison Publishing Company, 1984; Contributing Author: *Wrongful Death in Ohio,* Anderson Publishing Co., 1983; *Personal Injury Litigation in Ohio,* Ohio Legal Center Institute of the State Bar Association, 1990; *Civil Litigation in Ohio,* Ohio Legal Center Institute of the State Bar Association, 1991, 1993, 1995 and 1998-2000. Member, 1984-1990 and Chairman, 1988-1989, Board of Bar Examiners, Supreme Court of Ohio. Listed in: Best Lawyers in America, Woodward/White, 1995—(Personal Injury; Products & Malpractice); Ohio Super Lawyer, 2004.*Member:* Ohio Academy of Trial Lawyers (President, 1981-1982); American Board of Trial Advocates (Advocate, 1989—, National Board of Directors, 1989—); National Board of Trial Advocacy (State Representative, 1990—; National Bar Examiner, 1984-1987, 1989, 1991, 1994 and 2001); International Society of Barristers. Fellow, American College of Trial Lawyers. American Inns of Court (Emeritus Master, 1985—). Certified Civil Trial Advocate by the National Board of Trial Advocacy. ***PRACTICE AREAS:*** Civil Litigation; Personal Injury; Negligence Law; Medical Malpractice; Products Liability. ***Email:*** jshea@shea-associates.com

ASSOCIATES

SHIRLEY A. COFFEY, born Tallahassee, Florida, August 15, 1959; admitted to bar, 1992, Ohio; 1999, Kentucky. *Education:* University of Cincinnati, College Conservatory of Music (B.Mus., summa cum laude, 1980); University of Cincinnati College of Law (J.D., 1992). Order of the Coif. Member, University of Cincinnati Law Review. Author: "One Bankruptcy is Enough, 78,000 is Too Many. . . Protection of Retirement Benefits Under the Retiree Benefits Bankruptcy Protection Act of 1988," 61 U. Cinn. L. Rev. 715, 1992. Listed in: Who's Who in American Law and International Who's Who. *Member:* Cincinnati, Ohio State, Kentucky and American Bar Associations; The Association of Trial Lawyers of America; Ohio Academy of Trial Attorneys; Trial Lawyers for Public Justice. ***PRACTICE AREAS:*** Products Liability; Medical Malpractice; General Civil Litigation; Personal Injury. ***Email:*** scoffey@shea-associates.com

JAMES H. SCHEPER, born Bellevue, Kentucky, March 7, 1942; admitted to bar, 1968, Ohio; 1980, California. *Education:* Xavier University (B.S.B.A., 1964); Salmon P. Chase College of Law (J.D., 1968). Listed in: Best Lawyers in America, 2004; Ohio Super Lawyer, 2004. *Member:* Butler County and Ohio State Bar Associations; State Bar of California; International Association of Defense Counsel; American Board of Trial Advocates; Butler County Trial Lawyers; Ohio Association of Civil Trial Lawyers; American College of Trial Lawyers. ***PRACTICE AREAS:*** Malpractice Law; Personal Injury Law. ***Email:*** jscheper@shea-associates.com

LEGAL SUPPORT PERSONNEL

CONNIE DEFILLIPPO, born Lancaster, Ohio, August 23, 1953. *Education:* Capital University (B.S.N., 1977). Registered Nurse, 1977. Certified Legal Nurse Consultant, 2000. ***Email:*** cdefillippo@shea-associates.com

BETH SILVERMAN

Established in 1984

SUITE 920, 30 GARFIELD PLACE
CINCINNATI, OHIO 45202
Telephone: 513-241-9844
FAX: 513-241-9908
Email: attybeth@aol.com
URL: http://www.bethsilverman.com

Domestic Relations, Divorce, Custody, and Juvenile Law.

BETH SILVERMAN, born Toledo, Ohio, January 19, 1957; admitted to bar, 1984, Ohio. *Education:* Miami University (B.S., cum laude, 1978); Xavier University (M.S., magna cum laude, 1981); University of Cincinnati (J.D., 1984). Listed in Best Lawyers in America, 2001-2004.

JANE FINK SILVERS CO., LTD.

SUITE 400-A
1080 NIMITZVIEW
CINCINNATI, OHIO 45230
Telephone: 513-624-6720
Fax: 513-624-6720
Email: jsilvers@silvers-law.com
URL: http://www.lawyers.com/janefinksilvers

Business Estate Planning, Estate Planning, Business Transactions, Probate, Business Successions, Professional Practices, Limited Liability Company Law, Small Business Law, Family Limited Partnerships, Tax Law, Estate Administration, Trust Administration.

JANE FINK SILVERS, born Columbus, Ohio, March 7, 1961; admitted to bar, 1986, Ohio, U.S. District Court, Southern District of Ohio and U.S. Tax Court. *Education:* The Ohio State University (B.S.B.A., 1983); University of Cincinnati (J.D., 1986). Certified Public Accountant, Ohio, 1990. Author: "Adequate Disclosure of the Value of Gifts," Ohio CPA Journal, October-December, 1999. *Member:* Cincinnati (Member, Sections on: Taxation; Trusts; Wills and Estate Planning) and Ohio State (Member, Sections on: Estate Planning; Taxation) Bar Associations; Ohio and Cincinnati Society of CPA's; Cincinnati Estate Planning Council. ***PRACTICE AREAS:*** Estate Planning; Business Transactions; Probate; Professional Practices; Limited Liability Company Law; Small Business Law; Family Limited Partnerships; Tax Law; Estate Administration; Trust Administration. ***Email:*** jsilvers@silvers-law.com

SIRKIN PINALES & SCHWARTZ LLP

Established in 1977

920 FOURTH & RACE TOWER
105 WEST FOURTH STREET
CINCINNATI, OHIO 45202-2726
Telephone: 513-721-4876
Telecopier: 513-721-0876
Email: hschwartz@sirkinpinales.com
URL: http://www.sirkinpinales.com

Criminal Law, First Amendment Law, Constitutional Law, Wills and Probate, Trusts and Estates, Township Law, Municipal Law, Appellate Practice, White Collar Criminal Defense, Trials and Appeals in all State and Federal Courts, Corporate Law, Business Law, Personal Injury, Civil Rights.

MEMBERS OF FIRM

H. LOUIS SIRKIN, born Cincinnati, Ohio, April 19, 1940; admitted to bar, 1965, Ohio; 2001, U.S. Supreme Court; U.S. Court of Appeals, Third, Fourth, Fifth, Sixth, Eighth, Ninth and Eleventh Circuits. *Education:* University of Cincinnati (A.B., 1962; J.D., 1965). Recipient, Distinguished Alumni Award. Adjunct Faculty, University of Cincinnati Law School. *Member:* Cincinnati and Ohio State Bar Associations; First Amendment Lawyers Association (National Chairman, 1994-1995); National Association of Criminal Defense Lawyers. Fellow: American College of Trial Lawyers. ***REPORTED CASES:*** Aschcroft v. Free Speech Coalition, 535 U.S. 234, 2002. ***PRACTICE AREAS:*** First Amendment Law; Criminal Law; Constitutional Law. ***Email:*** lsirkin@sirkinpinales.com

MARTIN S. PINALES, born Cincinnati, Ohio, August 8, 1942; admitted to bar, 1968, Ohio; U.S. Court of Appeals; U.S. Supreme Court. *Education:* University of Cincinnati (B.B.A., 1964); Salmon P. Chase College of Law (J.D., 1968). Author: "Representing A Witness Before the Grand Jury," Criminal Defense Techniques, Matthew Bender & Co., Inc. Lecturer, White Collar Crime, University of Cincinnati, 1974—. Faculty, National College for Criminal Defense, Mercer University Law School, 1985—. Adjunct Faculty: Trial Advocacy, Chase College of Law, 1993—; Cardozo School of Law. *Member:* Cincinnati, Ohio State and American Bar Associations; National Association of Criminal Defense Lawyers (President Elect). Fellow, American Board of Criminal Defense Lawyers. ***PRACTICE AREAS:*** White Collar Criminal Defense; Criminal Law; Federal Criminal Law; Grand Jury Practice. ***Email:*** mpinales@sirkinpinales.com

HOWARD M. SCHWARTZ, born Cincinnati, Ohio, February 7, 1948; admitted to bar, 1975, Ohio. *Education:* University of Cincinnati (B.S.E.E., 1971); Salmon P. Chase College of Law (J.D., 1975). *Member:* Cincinnati and Ohio State Bar Associations. ***PRACTICE AREAS:*** Wills; Probate; Trusts and Estates; Corporate Law; Business Law; Personal Injury. ***Email:*** hschwartz@sirkinpinales.com

LAURA A. ABRAMS, born Cincinnati, Ohio, October 24, 1965; admitted to bar, 1991, Ohio; 1992, U.S. District Court, Southern District of Ohio; 1994, U.S. Court of Appeals, Sixth Circuit; 2001, U.S. Supreme Court. *Education:* University of Dayton (B.A., Economics, magna cum laude, 1988); University of Cincinnati College of Law (J.D., 1991). Phi Alpha Theta; Alpha Sigma Tau; Omicron Delta Epsilon. Recipient: Gustavis Henry Wald Memorial Prize. Editor, University of Cincinnati College of Law, Law Review. Judicial Law Clerk to the Honorable William H. Wolff, Jr., Second District Court of Appeals, State of Ohio, 1991-1994. *Member:* Cincinnati and Ohio State Bar Associations. ***PRACTICE AREAS:*** Administrative Law; Municipal Law; Public Law; Township Law. ***Email:*** labrams@sirkinpinales.com

ASSOCIATES

JOHN P. FELDMEIER, born Columbus, Ohio, March 16, 1966; admitted to bar, 1991, Ohio; 1997, U.S. District Court, Southern District of Ohio and U.S. Court of Appeals, 6th Circuit. *Education:* Ohio Dominican College (B.A., magna cum laude, Political Science, 1988); Capital University (J.D., 1991); Miami University (M.A., Political Science, 1993; Ph.D., Political Science, 1996). Delta Theta Phi. Order of the Curia, 1991. Member, Capital University Law Review, 1990-1991. *Member:* Cincinnati and Ohio State Bar Associations. ***PRACTICE AREAS:*** Criminal Law; First Amendment Law. ***Email:*** jfeldmeier@sirkinpinales.com

JENNIFER M. KINSLEY, born Charleston, South Carolina, June 12, 1975; admitted to bar, 1999, Ohio; U.S. District Court, Southern District of Ohio; U.S. Court of Appeals, Third, Sixth and Eleventh Circuits. *Education:* University of Florida (B.A., 1996); Duke University (J.D., 1999). Phi Beta Kappa. Adjunct Faculty, University of Cincinnati Law School. *Member:* Cincinnati and Ohio State Bar Associations; First Amendment Lawyers Association; Association of Trial Lawyers of America; Greater Cincinnati Criminal Defense Lawyers Association. ***PRACTICE AREAS:*** Criminal Law; Juvenile Law; First Amendment Law; Civil Rights. ***Email:*** jkinsley@sirkinpinales.com

CANDACE C. CROUSE, born Texarkana, Texas, February 17, 1975; admitted to bar, 2000, Ohio; 2002, U.S. District Court, Southern District of Ohio and U.S. Court of Appeals, Sixth Circuit. *Education:* West Virginia University (B.A., 1997); Ohio State University (J.D., 2000). Phi Kappa Phi; Phi Beta Kappa; Golden Key. Law Clerk to Honorable Frederick, P. Stamp, U.S. District Court, Northern District of West Virginia. *Member:* Ohio State and American Bar Associations; First Amendment Lawyers Association; National Association of Criminal Defense Lawyers. ***PRACTICE AREAS:*** Criminal Defense; Constitutional Law; First Amendment Law. ***Email:*** ccrouse@sirkinpinales.com

REFERENCE: The Huntington National Bank.

SLOVIN & CUMMINS CO., LPA

9435 WATERSTONE BOULEVARD, SUITE 270
CINCINNATI, OHIO 45249
Telephone: 513-683-9000
Fax: 513-683-9073
Email: sclpa@sclpa.com
URL: http://www.attorneysonline.us/sclaw.htm

Crescent Springs, Kentucky Office: 2335 Buttermilk Crossing, Suite 330, 41017. Telephone: 513-683-900. Fax: 513-683-9073.

Commercial Litigation, Collections, Bankruptcy, Landlord and Tenant Law, Federal Consumer Law, Compliance and Defense, Commercial Litigation, Consumer Litigation.

FIRM PROFILE: The attorneys at Slovin & Cummins Co., LPA have over 40 years of combined experience in representation of creditors. The firm handles matters for banks, insurance companies, hospitals, leasing companies, credit card providers, debt buyers, landlords, trade creditors, and asset-based lenders. Their practice includes representing creditors in a multitude of related areas such as collections, bankruptcy proceedings, commercial litigation, consultation and defense of litigation under federal and state consumer laws, including the Fair Debt Collection Practice Act and the Fair Credit Reporting Act, repossessions, foreclosures, and evictions.

RANDY T. SLOVIN, born Cincinnati, Ohio, September 23, 1958; admitted to bar, 1983, Ohio; 1984, Kentucky and U.S. District Court, Southern District of Ohio and Eastern District of Kentucky. *Education:* Indiana University (B.A., 1980); University of Cincinnati (J.D., 1983). Chair, Fair Debt Collection Practices Act Committee. Member, Commercial Law League of America, 2000-2005. Creditor's Right Section, Executive Council, Commercial Law League of America, 2004—. Chair, Midwest Region, Commercial Law League of America, 2004-2005. *Member:* Cincinnati, Ohio State and Kentucky Bar Associations; National Association of Retail Collection Attorneys; American Collectors Association International; National Association of Credit Management. ***PRACTICE AREAS:*** Commercial Litigation; Collections; Landlord and Tenant Law; Federal Consumer Litigation. ***Email:*** rtslovin@sclpa.com

JOHN R. CUMMINS, born Cincinnati, Ohio, January 7, 1960; admitted to bar, 1986, Ohio; 1987, Indiana; 1993, Kentucky. *Education:* Northwestern University (B.A., 1982); Ohio State University (J.D., 1986). *Member:* Cincinnati, Kentucky and Ohio State Bar Associations. ***LANGUAGES:*** French. ***PRACTICE AREAS:*** Collections; Commercial Litigation; Consumer Litigation. ***Email:*** jrcumming@sclpa.com

REPRESENTATIVE CLIENTS: American Express; Wells Fargo Bank; Equilease,; International Paper Company; Ameritech Publishing, Inc.; Arrow Financial Services; CNA Insurance; Merchant Bank; Hewlett Packard Financial Services; Autovest; Boulder Credit Services; hh Gregg; Triad Financial; Jewish Hospital of Louisville; Norton Hospital; Citifinancial; Bellsouth; Sagmore Insurance; Check-N-Go; Grady Memorial Hospital; Guardian National Acceptance Corp.

SHERRI GOREN SLOVIN CO., L.P.A.

30 GARFIELD PLACE, SUITE 920
CINCINNATI, OHIO 45202-4322
Telephone: 513-241-9844
Fax: 513-241-9908
Email: sgslovin@slovinlaw.com
URL: http://www.slovinlaw.com

Other Cincinnati Office (Field-Ertel): 9435 Waterstone Boulevard, Suite 270, 45249. Telephone: 513-241-9844.

Domestic Relations, Collaborative Family Law, Mediation, Parenting and Child Related Issues, Child Support, Spousal Support, Family Law, Divorce, Dissolution, Visitation, Post-Divorce Matters, Collaborative Divorce.

SHERRI GOREN SLOVIN, born Cleveland, Ohio, February 26, 1954; admitted to bar, 1979, Ohio. *Education:* University of Cincinnati (B.A., magna cum laude, 1974; J.D., 1979). Phi Beta Kappa. Listed in: *Best Lawyers in America*; *Ohio Superlawyers*. Author and Lecturer, Trainer, Collaborative Law Workshops. Past Chairperson, Collaborative Family Lawyers of Cincinnati. Board Member, International Academy of Collaborative Professionals. *Member:* Cincinnati, Ohio State and American Bar Associations. ***PRACTICE AREAS:*** Family Law; Mediation; Collaborative Family Law; Spousal Support; Visitation Rights; Divorce; Child Support. ***Email:*** sgslovin@slovinlaw.com

SLOWIK & ROBINSON, LLC

CINCINNATI, OHIO

(See Columbus)

Labor and Employment Law, Immigration Law, Small Business Law, Alternative Dispute Resolution, Business Formations.

SQUIRE, SANDERS & DEMPSEY L.L.P.

312 WALNUT STREET, SUITE 3500
CINCINNATI, OHIO 45202-4036
Telephone: 513-361-1200
Fax: 513-361-1201
URL: http://www.ssd.com

REVISOR OF THE OHIO AND TEXAS LAW DIGESTS FOR THIS DIRECTORY

The Americas Offices: Cleveland, Columbus, Houston, Los Angeles, Miami, New York, Palo Alto, Phoenix, San Francisco, Tallahassee, Tampa, Tysons Corner, Washington DC, West Palm Beach, Caracas, Santo Domingo, Rio de Janeiro.

(This Listing Continued)

European Offices: Bratislava, Brussels, Budapest, London, Madrid, Milan, Moscow, Prague, Warsaw.
Asia Offices: Beijing, Hong Kong, Shanghai, Tokyo.
Associated Offices: Bucharest, Dublin, Kyiv, Buenos Aires, Santiago.

Bankruptcy and Reorganization, Chemicals, Communications, Construction and Engineering, Corporate Transactions and Securities Regulation, E-Commerce, Economic Regulation, Education, Energy, Environmental, Health and Safety, Financial Institutions and Services, Financial Services, Gaming and Casinos, Government and Administrative Agencies, Health Care and Hospitals, Health Sciences, Hospitality and Recreation, Insurance, Intellectual Property, International Dispute Resolution, Labor and Employment, Life Sciences, Litigation, Manufacturing, Media and Entertainment, Private Equity, Project Finance, Public Finance, Real Estate, Real Estate and Hospitality, Sports, Steel, Taxation, Technology, Transportation and Utilities.

FIRM PROFILE: The Cincinnati office of Squire, Sanders & Dempsey L.L.P. affords clients from southern Ohio, the United States and the global community the resources of a major worldwide firm with local business and cultural ties. The office is home to lawyers with concentrations in corporate and business law, commercial and appellate litigation, business reorganizations and bankruptcy, financial services, mergers and acquisitions, corporate financing, intellectual property and international matters. Carrying on more than 100 years of Squire Sanders' appellate work, the Cincinnati office is ideally positioned and uniquely qualified to serve the needs of clients seeking representation in the U.S. Court of Appeals for the Sixth Circuit. Several of our Cincinnati lawyers have held prominent clerking positions in the Sixth Circuit, and many have briefed and argued cases before various state and federal appellate tribunals, combining their significant appellate experience with skilled and creative advocacy techniques.

PARTNERS - CINCINNATI OFFICE

JAMES J. BARRESI, born Detroit, Michigan, 1966; admitted to bar, 1991, Ohio; U.S. District Court, Southern District of Ohio. *Education:* Alma College (B.A., 1988); Wake Forest University (J.D., 1991). *Member:* American Bar Association (Member, Banking Law Committee, Business Financing Committee and Negotiated Acquisitions Committee, Business Law Section). ***PRACTICE AREAS:*** Corporate; Finance; Securities; Financial Services. ***Email:*** jbarresi@ssd.com

RONALD A. BELL, born Jamaica, West Indies, 1967; admitted to bar, 1994, Ohio; U.S. District Court, Southern District of Ohio; U.S. Tax Court. *Education:* Polytechnic University (B.S.A.E., 1988); University of Cincinnati (M.S.A.E., 1991); The Ohio State University (J.D., 1994). Member, CFA Institute. ***PRACTICE AREAS:*** Employee Benefits; ERISA; Taxation; Executive Compensation; Corporate Law; Securities; Finance; Financial Services; Venture Capital. ***Email:*** rbell@ssd.com

SCOTT A. KANE, born Carson City, Michigan, 1969; admitted to bar, 1997, Ohio; U.S. District Court, Southern District of Ohio; U.S. Court of Appeals, Sixth Circuit. *Education:* Western Michigan University (B.S., summa cum laude, 1994); University of Cincinnati (J.D., 1997). Order of the Coif. ***PRACTICE AREAS:*** Litigation. ***Email:*** skane@ssd.com

STEPHEN D. LERNER, born New York, N.Y., 1960; admitted to bar, 1986, New York; 1991, Ohio; U.S. Court of Appeals, Sixth Circuit; U.S. District Court, Eastern and Southern Districts of New York and Southern District of Ohio. *Education:* University of Pennsylvania (B.A., 1982; M.A., 1982; J.D., 1985). Founding and Current Board Member, Tri-State Association for Corporate Renewal. Member, Executive Committee, Midwest Regional Bankruptcy Seminar, Inc. *Member:* Cincinnati, Ohio State, New York State and American Bar Associations; American Bankruptcy Institute. Fellow, American College of Bankruptcy. ***PRACTICE AREAS:*** Bankruptcy; Workouts; Business Reorganization; Commercial Transactions; Commercial Loans. ***Email:*** slerner@ssd.com

STEPHEN C. MAHON, born New Rochelle, New York, 1964; admitted to bar, 1989, New York; 1992, District of Columbia; 1993, Ohio; U.S. Court of Appeals, District of Columbia Circuit. *Education:* Vanderbilt University (B.A., 1986; J.D., 1989). *Member:* Cincinnati Bar Association; The Entrepreneurship Institute (Member, Board of Directors). ***PRACTICE AREAS:*** Corporate Law; Finance; Securities. ***Email:*** smahon@ssd.com

MARK J. RUEHLMANN, born Cincinnati, Ohio, 1961; admitted to bar, 1987, Ohio; U.S. District Court, Southern District of Ohio; U.S. Court of Appeals, Sixth Circuit. *Education:* University of Notre Dame (B.A., 1984); Vanderbilt University (J.D., 1987). Member and Chairman of the Board, Sisters of Charity Senior Care Corporation; Chair of Board, Zoological Society of Cincinnati. *Member:* Cincinnati and Ohio State Bar Associations. ***PRACTICE AREAS:*** Litigation; Class Actions. ***Email:*** mruehlmann@ssd.com

BRYAN J. VENESY, born Evanston, Illinois, 1963; admitted to bar, 1988, Ohio. *Education:* Ohio Wesleyan University (B.A., 1985); University of Cincinnati (J.D., 1988). *Member:* Columbus, Ohio State and American Bar Associations. ***PRACTICE AREAS:*** Real Estate; Finance; Corporate. ***Email:*** bvenesy@ssd.com

OF COUNSEL - CINCINNATI OFFICE

TIMOTHY L. COYLE, born Covington, Kentucky, 1957; admitted to bar, 1987, Ohio; 1990, Kentucky. *Education:* University of Kentucky (B.S., 1981; M.S., 1982); Northern Kentucky University (J.D., 1986). Certified Public Accountant, Ohio, 1984. International Tax Counsel: AT&T, 1988-1990; Procter & Gamble, 1986-1988. *Member:* Kentucky Bar Association. ***PRACTICE AREAS:*** Corporate Law. ***Email:*** tcoyle@ssd.com

JEFFREY A. MARKS, born Cleveland, Ohio, 1955; admitted to bar, 1981, Ohio; U.S. District Court, Southern District of Ohio; U.S. Court of Appeals, Sixth Circuit; U.S. District Court, Eastern District of Kentucky; U.S. District Court, Eastern District of Michigan. *Education:* The Ohio State University (B.A., 1977); University of Cincinnati (J.D., 1980). Member, 1978-1980 and Student Articles Editor, 1979-1980, University of Cincinnati Law Review. Law Clerk to Hon. Burton Perlman, U.S. Bankruptcy Court, Southern District of Ohio, 1980-1982. Member, Advisory Committee on Local Rules of the U.S. Bankruptcy Court, Southern District of Ohio, 1990-2001. *Member:* Cincinnati (Member and Past Chair, Bankruptcy Law Committee) and American (Member, Business Law Section) Bar Asso-

(This Listing Continued)

ciations; American Bankruptcy Institute; Tri-State Association for Corporate Renewal. ***PRACTICE AREAS:*** Bankruptcy; Business Reorganizations; Debtor/Creditor Rights. ***Email:*** jemarks@ssd.com

GEORGE N. OTI, born New York, New York, 1961; admitted to bar, 1992, New York (Not admitted in Ohio). *Education:* Michigan State University (B.A., with high honors, 1983); Columbia University (J.D., 1986); Cambridge University (LL.M., 1988). Phi Beta Kappa. ***PRACTICE AREAS:*** Corporate Law; Project Finance. ***Email:*** goti@ssd.com

GREGORY A. RUEHLMANN, born Cincinnati, Ohio, 1955; admitted to bar, 1981, Ohio; U.S. District Court, Southern District of Ohio; U.S. Court of Appeals, Sixth Circuit. *Education:* Northwestern University (B.A., 1978); Vanderbilt University (J.D., 1981). *Member:* Cincinnati, Ohio State and American Bar Associations. ***PRACTICE AREAS:*** Trials and Appeals; Construction Law; Personal Injury Litigation; Commercial Litigation. ***Email:*** gruehlmann@ssd.com

ASSOCIATES - CINCINNATI OFFICE

PIERRE H. BERGERON, born Knoxville, Tennessee, 1974; admitted to bar, 1999, Ohio; 2005, Kentucky; U.S. District Court, Southern District of Ohio and U.S. Court of Appeals, Sixth Circuit; U.S. District Court, Eastern District of Michigan and U.S. Court of Appeals, Ninth Circuit; U.S. Court of Appeals, Fifth Circuit; U.S. Supreme Court; U.S. Court of Appeals, Second Circuit. *Education:* Centre College (B.A., cum laude, 1996); University of Virginia (J.D., 1999). ***PRACTICE AREAS:*** Litigation. ***Email:*** pbergeron@ssd.com

P. CASEY COSTON, born Muskegon, Michigan, 1964; admitted to bar, 1993, Michigan; U.S. District Court, Eastern and Western Districts of Michigan (Not admitted in Ohio). *Education:* Kalamazoo College (B.A., with honors, 1987); George Washington University (J.D., 1990); Georgetown University (LL.M., Securities Regulation, 1991). ***PRACTICE AREAS:*** Bankruptcy. ***Email:*** ccoston@ssd.com

KENNETH R. CRAYCRAFT, JR., born Georgetown, Ohio, 1962; admitted to bar, 2001, Ohio; U.S. District Court, Southern District of Ohio. *Education:* Malone College (B.A., 1985); University of Cincinnati (M.A., 1988); Cincinnati Christian University (M.A., M.Div., 1988); Boston College (Ph.D., 1993); Duke University (J.D., 2001). ***PRACTICE AREAS:*** Litigation. ***Email:*** kcraycraft@ssd.com

CHRISTOPHER A. DEABLER, born Media, Pennsylvania, 1974; admitted to bar, 2002, Massachusetts; 2004, Ohio. *Education:* University of Tampa (B.A., magna cum laude, 1996); Texas A&M University (M.A., 1998); Northwestern University (J.D., 2001). ***PRACTICE AREAS:*** Corporate Law. ***Email:*** cdeabler@ssd.com

JILL S. KIRILA, born Sharon, Pennsylvania, 1972; admitted to bar, 1997, Ohio; U.S. Court of Appeals, Sixth Circuit; U.S. District Court, Northern District of Ohio; U.S. District Court, Southern District of Ohio. *Education:* The Ohio State University (B.A., summa cum laude, 1994); Georgetown University (J.D., 1997). ***LANGUAGES:*** Spanish. ***PRACTICE AREAS:*** Labor and Employment. ***Email:*** jkirila@ssd.com

DAVID A. PEPPER, born Cincinnati, Ohio, 1971; admitted to bar, 1999, Ohio. *Education:* Yale University (B.A., magna cum laude, 1993; J.D., 1999). ***PRACTICE AREAS:*** Litigation. ***Email:*** dpepper@ssd.com

KIM D. SEATON, born Findlay, Ohio, 1964; admitted to bar, 1997, Ohio; U.S. District Court, Southern District of Ohio. *Education:* Bowling Green State University (B.S., 1985; M.S., 1987); Northwestern University (J.D., 1997). ***PRACTICE AREAS:*** Bankruptcy. ***Email:*** kseaton@ssd.com

JEFFREY D. SIEHL, born Dayton, Ohio, 1972; admitted to bar, 1998, Ohio; U.S. District Court, Southern District of Ohio. *Education:* Miami University (B.A., 1995); The Ohio State University (J.D., 1998). Order of the Coif. ***PRACTICE AREAS:*** Litigation. ***Email:*** jsiehl@ssd.com

ELLIOT M. SMITH, born Lakewood, New Jersey, 1979; admitted to bar, 2004, Ohio; U.S. District Court, Southern District of Ohio. *Education:* Ner Israel Rabbinical College (B.T.L., 2001); University of Maryland (J.D., 2004). ***PRACTICE AREAS:*** Bankruptcy.

RYAN D. WALTERS, born Oregon, Ohio, 1976; admitted to bar, 2003, Ohio; U.S. Court of Appeals, First, Second, Third, Fourth, Fifth, Sixth, Seventh, Eighth, Ninth, Tenth and Eleventh Circuits; U.S. District Court, Northern and Southern Districts of Ohio. *Education:* The Ohio State University (B.A., summa cum laude, 2000); University of Michigan (J.D., cum laude, 2003). Associate Editor, University of Michigan Journal of Law Reform. ***PRACTICE AREAS:*** Litigation. ***Email:*** rwalters@ssd.com

DAVID L. WHEELER, born Augsburg, Germany, 1967; admitted to bar, 1996, Ohio and U.S. Tax Court. *Education:* University of Vermont (B.S.B.A., 1990); University of Cincinnati (J.D., 1996). ***PRACTICE AREAS:*** Corporate Law. ***Email:*** dwheeler@ssd.com

REVISOR OF THE OHIO AND TEXAS LAW DIGESTS FOR THIS DIRECTORY

(For Biographical Data on Cleveland and Columbus, Ohio, Miami and Tampa, Florida, Houston, Texas, New York, New York, Phoenix, Arizona, Washington, D.C., Los Angeles, Palo Alto and San Francisco, California, Tysons Corner, Virginia, Rio de Janeiro, Brazil, Bratislava, Slovak Republic, Brussels, Belgium, Budapest, Hungary, London, England, Madrid, Spain, Milan, Italy, Moscow, Russian Federation, Prague, Czech Republic, Warsaw, Poland, Beijing and Hong Kong, China and Tokyo, Japan Personnel, see Professional Biographies at those Points Respectively).

STATMAN, HARRIS, SIEGEL & EYRICH, LLC

2900 CHEMED CENTER
255 EAST FIFTH STREET
CINCINNATI, OHIO 45202-2912
Telephone: 513-621-2666
Facsimile: 513-587-4477

Dayton, Ohio Office: Fifth Third Center, 110 North Main Street, Suite 1520, 45402. Telephone: 937-222-1090. Fax: 937-222-1046.

Chicago, Illinois Office: 333 West Wacker Drive, Suite 1710, 60606. Telephone: 312-263-1070. Fax: 312-263-1201.

(This Listing Continued)

General Civil Trial and Appellate Practice in Federal and State Courts. Commercial Litigation, Bankruptcy, Banking, Personal Injury and Family Law. Corporate Acquisitions, Dispositions, Spin-Offs, Corporate Formation, Financings, Real Estate, Banking and Commercial Law, Reorganizations, Restructurings, Bankruptcy, Civil Litigation, General Business, Intellectual Property, Taxation, Estate Planning.

ALAN J. STATMAN, born Cincinnati, Ohio, February 11, 1958; admitted to bar, 1983, Ohio, U.S. District Court, Southern District of Ohio and U.S. Court of Appeals, Sixth Circuit; 1993, Kentucky and U.S. Court of International Trade; 1994, U.S. District Court, Eastern District of Kentucky. *Education:* University of Cincinnati (B.A., 1979); University of Dayton (J.D., 1983). Phi Alpha Delta. Member, International Law Moot Court Team. *Member:* Cincinnati, Ohio State, Kentucky, Federal and American Bar Associations. ***REPORTED CASES:*** In Re: Hurst Lincoln Mercury, Inc., AD B.R. 894 (Bankr. S.D. Oh. 1987); In Re: LCL Income Properties, L.P. VI, 177 B.R. (Bankr. S.D. Oh. 1995). ***PRACTICE AREAS:*** Bankruptcy; Workouts; Corporate Restructuring; Debtor and Creditor Rights; Commercial Litigation; Real Property; Personal Injury. ***Email:*** ajstatman@shselegal.com

JEFFREY P. HARRIS, born Cincinnati, Ohio, April 6, 1951; admitted to bar, 1976, Ohio and U.S. District Court, Southern District of Ohio. *Education:* Trinity College (B.A., 1973); Boston University (J.D., 1976). Panel of Trustees, Bankruptcy Court, 1979—. *Member:* Cincinnati, Ohio State, Federal and American Bar Associations. ***TRANSACTIONS:*** Store Closing Agreements with B. Altman, Bonwit Teller, Alexanders Department Stores et al. Purchase inventory Yugo North America, DeLorean Motor Car Co. Real Estate-Acquisition and capitalization of shopping centers. ***PRACTICE AREAS:*** Commercial Transactions; Real Estate; Bankruptcy Law; Corporate Restructuring; Creditor Rights; Mergers and Acquisitions. ***Email:*** jharris@shselegal.com

ROBERT H. SIEGEL, born Cincinnati, Ohio, November 16, 1945; admitted to bar, 1975, Ohio. *Education:* University of Cincinnati (B.A., 1968); Salmon P. Chase College of Law, Northern Kentucky University (J.D., 1975). Omicron Delta Epsilon. Assistant City Solicitor, (Real Estate Division), Cincinnati, 1975-1979. Lenders Counsel, American Land Title Association. *Member:* American College of Mortgage Attorneys. ***PRACTICE AREAS:*** Real Estate Law; Corporate Law; Mergers and Acquisitions; Title Insurance Law; Banking Law. ***Email:*** rsiegel@shselegal.com

DAVID J. EYRICH, born Cincinnati, Ohio, December 24, 1946; admitted to bar, 1973, Ohio; U.S. District Court, Southern District of Ohio. *Education:* Ohio Wesleyan University (B.A., cum laude, 1969); University of Cincinnati (J.D., 1973). Omicron Delta Kappa. *Member:* Cincinnati Bar Association; Ohio Land Title Association. ***PRACTICE AREAS:*** Corporate Law; Financial Institutions Law; Real Estate Law; Probate; Estate Planning Law. ***Email:*** deyrich@shselegal.com

ROBERT A. BARDACH, born Cincinnati, Ohio, May 5, 1963; admitted to bar, 1989, Ohio. *Education:* University of Michigan (B.A., 1985); University of Toledo (J.D., 1988). Approved Attorney for Stewart Title Guaranty Company. *Member:* Cincinnati, Ohio State and American Bar Associations. ***PRACTICE AREAS:*** Real Estate Law; Shopping Center Acquisitions; Shopping Center Leasing; Title Insurance Law; Business Planning; Landlord and Tenant Law; Probate; Estate Administration. ***Email:*** bbardach@shselegal.com

HOWARD L. RICHSHAFER, born Denver, Colorado, June 27, 1945; admitted to bar, 1975, Ohio. *Education:* University of Cincinnati (B.A., 1968); Salmon P. Chase College of Law, Northern Kentucky University (J.D., 1975). Adjunct Professor of Tax Law, University of Cincinnati Graduate School of Business, 1982—. Internal Revenue Agent, 1968-1978. Tax Manager, Alexander Grant & Company, 1978-1979. Certified Public Accountant, Ohio, 1978. *Member:* Cincinnati (Chairman, Tax Committee, 2001) and Ohio State (Chairman, Federal Taxation Specialty Board, 1998-2002) Bar Associations. ***PRACTICE AREAS:*** Taxation Law; Corporate Law; Estate Planning; Mergers and Acquisitions. ***Email:*** hrichshafer@shselegal.com

THOMAS S. SAPINSLEY, born Dayton, Ohio, December 14, 1955; admitted to bar, 1982, Ohio; 1992, Kentucky. *Education:* Indiana University (B.A., 1978); University of Cincinnati (J.D., 1981). ***PRACTICE AREAS:*** Litigation; Domestic Relations; Personal Injury; Family Law. ***Email:*** tsapinsley@shselegal.com

---

WILLIAM B. FECHER, born Wilmington, Delaware, March 9, 1962; admitted to bar, 1987, Ohio, U.S. District Court, Southern District of Ohio and U.S. Court of Appeals, Sixth Circuit; 1989, U.S. Supreme Court. *Education:* Butler University (B.A., 1984); University of Dayton (J.D., 1987). Member, University of Dayton Law Review, 1985-1987. Lecturer on Creditor Rights, Foreclosures, Consumer Law and Fair Debt Collection Practices Act. *Member:* Dayton and Ohio State Bar Associations; American Bankruptcy Law Forum. ***PRACTICE AREAS:*** Bankruptcy Law; Collection; Foreclosures; Creditors Rights; Banking Law; Corporate Law; Credit Union Law. ***Email:*** wbfecher@shselegal.com

FERN E. GOLDMAN, born Brooklyn, New York, October 30, 1957; admitted to bar, 1981, Ohio; 1997, Kentucky; U.S. District Court, Southern District of Ohio. *Education:* Brandeis University (B.A., cum laude, 1978); New York University (J.D., 1981). Law Clerk to Honorable Randall J. Newsome, U.S. Bankruptcy Court, Southern District of Ohio, 1984-1986. *Member:* Cincinnati and Ohio State Bar Associations. ***PRACTICE AREAS:*** Complex Commercial Litigation; Finance; Corporate Law. ***Email:*** fgoldman@shselegal.com

THOMAS A. WIETHOLTER, born Covington, Kentucky, March 28, 1951; admitted to bar, 1986, Kentucky; 1987, Ohio and U.S. District Court, Eastern District of Kentucky. *Education:* Northern Kentucky University (A.A.S., Fire Science, 1980; B.S., Public Administration, 1981); Salmon P. Chase College of Law (J.D., 1986). *Member:* Cincinnati, Kentucky, Ohio State and American Bar Associations; Northern Kentucky Bar Association. ***PRACTICE AREAS:*** Family Law; Labor Law; Municipal Law; Local Government Law; Litigation; Fire Loss. ***Email:*** tawietholter@shselegal.com

TRACY L. HAWKINS, born Cincinnati, OH, September 23, 1971; admitted to bar, 2000, Ohio; 2001, U.S. District Court, Southern District of Ohio. *Education:* University of Evansville (B.S., 1993); Salmon P. Chase College of Law (J.D., 1999). *Member:* Cincinnati,

(This Listing Continued)

STATMAN, HARRIS, SIEGEL & EYRICH, LLC, Cincinnati—Continued

Ohio State and American Bar Associations; Ohio Land Title Association. ***PRACTICE AREAS:*** Commercial Real Estate; Residential Real Estate; Corporate Law. ***Email:*** thawkins@shselegal.com

BRIAN T. GILES, born Louisville, Kentucky, December 30, 1974; admitted to bar, 2000, Ohio. *Education:* Miami University (B.A., 1996); University of Kentucky (J.D., 2000). ***PRACTICE AREAS:*** Corporate Law; Tax Law. ***Email:*** bgiles@shselegal.com

KIMBERLY A. SCHMALTZ, born Cincinnati, Ohio, October 4, 1960; admitted to bar, 1999, Ohio and Indiana. *Education:* College of Mount St. Joseph (B.A., 1983); Salmon P. Chase College of Law (J.D., 1999). Member, Indiana School Bar Association. *Member:* Cincinnati, Dearborn, Ohio County, Ohio State and Indiana State Bar Associations. ***PRACTICE AREAS:*** Business Law; Corporate Law; Litigation; Criminal Defense; Probate; Estate Planning.

CHRISSY M. DUNN, (admission pending). *Education:* Western Kentucky University (B.A., 2001); Salmon P. Chase College (J.D, 2005). *Member:* Association of Trial Lawyers of America. ***PRACTICE AREAS:*** Banking Litigation; Insurance Defense.

OF COUNSEL

LAWRENCE A. FLEMER, born Summit, New Jersey, August 17, 1951; admitted to bar, 1980, Ohio and U.S. District Court, Southern District of Ohio; 1981, U.S. District Court, Eastern District of Kentucky; U.S. Court of Appeals, Sixth Circuit. *Education:* University of Cincinnati (B.A., 1974); Salmon P. Chase College of Law of Northern Kentucky University (J.D., 1980). Member: Order of the Curia. Master, Potter Stewart Inn of Court. ***PRACTICE AREAS:*** Commercial Litigation; Franchise Law; Insurance Defense; Employment Law; Personal Injury. ***Email:*** lflemer@shselegal.com

COLLEEN M. HEGGE, born Covington, Kentucky, June 23, 1962; admitted to bar, 1987, Ohio and U.S. District Court, Southern District of Ohio; 1988, Kentucky and U.S. District Court, Eastern District of Kentucky; 1989, U.S. District Court, Western District of Kentucky; 1991, U.S. Claims Court. *Education:* Northern Kentucky University; Morehead State University (B.S., 1984); Salmon P. Chase College of Law (J.D., 1987). Phi Kappa Phi. Dean's List. Recipient, Trial Advocacy Award. Vice-President, Environmental Science Club. *Member:* Cincinnati, Ohio State, Kentucky and American Bar Associations; The Association of Trial Lawyers of America; Cincinnati Women Lawyers Association; Kentucky Women Lawyers Association; Kentucky Academy of Trial Attorneys. ***PRACTICE AREAS:*** Complex Litigation; Torts; Insurance Law; Personal Injury; Wrongful Death; Medical Malpractice; Product Liability; Class Actions; Drug and Medical Device Litigation. ***Email:*** chegge@shselegal.com

REPRESENTATIVE CLIENTS: Bank One, N.A.; Schottenstein Stores Corporation; Value City Department Stores, Inc.; Crown Shoe Stores; American Eagle Outfitter Stores; Valley Fair Corporation; Gentry Clothiers, Inc.; Totes Incorporated; Tudor Properties, Inc.; Colerain Hills Shopping Center; St. Bernard Square Shopping Center; Skyway Luggage Company; Tampa Electric Company (TECO); Higher Education Assistance Foundation (HEAF); Roslyn Realty Company; Seneca Environmental Products, Inc.; Pipe Products, Inc.; Samex Trading Company, Inc.; Pella Window; AHF Industries; Peoples Bank Corporation (Indianapolis); HRC Limited Partnership (Hyatt Regency Cincinnati); The Fifth Third Bank; Rohr Corporation; H.R. Chally; Brennan Builders; K&L Investment Corp.
REFERENCES: The Fifth Third Bank; Bank One, N.A.

JOHN E. STILLPASS

Established in 2001

9545 KENWOOD ROAD, SUITE 103
CINCINNATI, OHIO 45242-6100
Telephone: 513-936-0800
Fax: 513-794-8800
Email: jstillpass@stillpass.com
URL: http://www.stillpass.com

General Practice. Marine, Automobile Franchises and Dealerships, Admiralty and Maritime, Probate Law, Real Estate, Business and Commercial Law.

JOHN E. STILLPASS, born Cincinnati, Ohio, May 13, 1956; admitted to bar, 1981, Ohio, U.S. District Court, Southern District of Ohio and U.S. Court of Appeals, Sixth Circuit; 1982, Florida; 1988, U.S. District Court, Southern District of Florida; 1991, U.S. Tax Court. *Education:* University of Pennsylvania, Wharton School (B.S.E., 1978); Case Western Reserve University (J.D., 1981). Senior Associate Editor: Case Western Reserve Journal of Intl. Law, 1980-1981; Canada-U.S. Law Journal, 1980-1981. Assistant Zone Manager, AB Volvo, Car Marketing Division, Gothenburg, Sweden. (1973-1978). Panel Chairman, Arbitration Program, Clermont Court of Common Pleas. *Member:* Cincinnati, Palm Beach and Ohio State Bar Associations; The Florida Bar. ***PRACTICE AREAS:*** Commercial Law; Business Law; Real Estate; Probate; Admiralty and Maritime Law; Marine Law; General Practice; Automotive Franchises and Dealerships; Dealership Law.

STRAUSS & TROY

A LEGAL PROFESSIONAL ASSOCIATION

Established in 1953

THE FEDERAL RESERVE BUILDING
150 EAST FOURTH STREET
CINCINNATI, OHIO 45202-4018
Telephone: 513-621-2120
Fax: 513-241-8259
Email: info@strausstroy.com
URL: http://www.strausstroy.com

Northern Kentucky Office: 50 East RiverCenter Boulevard, Covington, Kentucky, 41011. Telephone: 513-621-8900. Fax: 513-629-9444.

(This Listing Continued)

General Civil Practice, Litigation, Alternative Dispute Resolution, Corporate, Probate, Tax, Estate Planning, Real Estate, Securities, Employment Law, Trade Regulation, Antitrust, Patent and Trademark Litigation, Real Estate and Development Law, Housing and Urban Development, Syndication Law, Land Use and Zoning, Trials and Appeals, Pension and Profit Sharing Law, ERISA, Franchise Law, Hospitality and Lodging.

FIRM PROFILE: Strauss & Troy, founded in 1953, is a full-service law firm that is well-established in Cincinnati, Northern Kentucky and throughout the tri-state area. The firm's main office is in the heart of the Cincinnati central business district; the second office is located in the RiverCenter office complex in Covington, Kentucky.

Strauss & Troy's broad legal practice can be divided into five primary areas:

1. Litigation including Arbitration, Mediation and other forms of Alternative Dispute Resolution of business and commercial matters and involving class actions, securities, shareholder rights, Patents and Trademarks, insurance, banking, bankruptcy, real estate, construction, employment, manufacturer's representation issues, tax, products liability, medical malpractice, personal injury, and domestic relations.

2. Corporate, including general business and commercial, banking, securities, hospitality industry, franchise, insurance, and mergers and acquisitions.

3. Tax, including individual and corporate tax planning, pension and profit sharing, and tax shelters.

4. Real Estate, including development, acquisitions, financing, title insurance, workouts, housing and urban development, limited liability companies, partnerships and syndications, construction, landlord/tenant, leasing and environmental law.

5. Estate Planning and Probate, including wills, trusts, estates, and international estate planning.

All attorneys in the firm are licensed to practice in Ohio and a number of attorneys are also licensed to practice in Kentucky and other jurisdictions.

LUCIEN G. STRAUSS (1900-1982)
ORVILLE A. TROY (1896-1967)
KENNETH D. TROY (1918-1993)
ALAN C. ROSSER (1946-2001)

MARK H. BERLIANT, born Chicago, Illinois, April 1, 1932; admitted to bar, 1956, Virginia; 1957, Ohio. *Education:* University of Virginia (B.A., Accounting, 1953; LL.B., 1956). Member, Editorial Board, Virginia Law Review. Adjunct Professor, Partnerships and Tax Shelter, University of Cincinnati Law School, 1981-1986. Tax Trial Attorney, Cincinnati Region, Office of Chief Counsel, Internal Revenue Service, 1956-1961. Listed in "The Best Lawyers in America," 1983-2003 Editions. *Member:* Cincinnati (Chairman, Tax Committee, 1976) and American (National Chairman, Committee on Real Estate Tax Problems, 1983-1985; Vice Chairman, 1981-1983; Subcommittee Chairman, "Syndications," 1979-1981; Member, 1978-2001; Member: Committee on Tax Shelter, 1980-1987; Committee on Tax Structure and Simplification, 1985-1988) Bar Associations. ***PRACTICE AREAS:*** Taxation Law; Tax and Succession Planning; Estate Planning; Real Estate Development; Gaming Law. ***Email:*** mhberliant@strausstroy.com

WILLIAM V. STRAUSS, born Cincinnati, Ohio, July 5, 1942; admitted to bar, 1967, Ohio. *Education:* Harvard University (A.B., cum laude, 1964); University of Pennsylvania (J.D., 1967). *Member:* Cincinnati, Ohio State and American (Real Property, Probate and Trust Law Sections) Bar Associations; Security Title and Guaranty Agency, Inc. (President). ***PRACTICE AREAS:*** Housing and Urban Development Law; Real Estate Law; Title Insurance Law; Commercial Law; Estate Planning. ***Email:*** wvstrauss@strausstroy.com

LARRY A. NEUMAN, born Lexington, Kentucky, March 20, 1942; admitted to bar, 1967, Kentucky; 1970, Ohio. *Education:* Tulane University of Louisiana (B.A., 1964); University of Kentucky (J.D., 1967). Order of the Coif. Staff Member, Kentucky Law Journal, 1966-1967. *Member:* Cincinnati, Ohio State, Kentucky and American Bar Associations. [Captain, U.S. Army, 1967-1969]. ***PRACTICE AREAS:*** ERISA; Pension and Profit Sharing Law; Real Estate Law; Estate Planning. ***Email:*** laneuman@strausstroy.com

WILLIAM S. ABERNETHY, JR., born Philadelphia, Pennsylvania, February 21, 1942; admitted to bar, 1967, Ohio; 1968, U.S. Tax Court and U.S. District Court, Southern District of Ohio. *Education:* University of Cincinnati (B.A., 1964; J.D., 1967). Phi Delta Phi; Omicron Delta Kappa. *Member:* Cincinnati, Ohio State and American Bar Associations. ***PRACTICE AREAS:*** Litigation; Family Law; Corporate Law; Probate Law. ***Email:*** wsabernethy@strausstroy.com

THOMAS C. RINK, born Rock Island, Illinois, May 26, 1945; admitted to bar, 1970, Ohio. *Education:* University of Notre Dame (B.B.A., 1967; J.D., 1970); George Washington University (LL.M. in Taxation, 1974). Chairman, Southwest Ohio Tax Institute, 1980. Listed in "Best Lawyers in America." *Member:* Cincinnati (Chairman, Taxation Section, 1982-1983), Ohio and American (Member, Taxation Section) Bar Associations. [U.S. Marines, 1970-1974]. ***PRACTICE AREAS:*** Estate Planning; Probate Law; Real Estate Development and Syndication; Lease Law; Taxation; Tax Controversies. ***Email:*** tcrink@strausstroy.com

FRANKLIN A. KLAINE, JR., born Covington, Kentucky, November 20, 1941; admitted to bar, 1967, Ohio; 1991, Kentucky. *Education:* College of the Holy Cross (B.S., 1963); University of Cincinnati (J.D., 1967). Phi Delta Phi. City Solicitor: Wyoming, Ohio, 1980—; Loveland, Ohio, 2001—. *Member:* Cincinnati, Ohio State, Kentucky and American Bar Associations. ***PRACTICE AREAS:*** Corporate; Employment; Municipal; School; Real Estate; Estate Planning. ***Email:*** faklaine@strausstroy.com

WILLIAM R. JACOBS, born Cincinnati, Ohio, June 14, 1948; admitted to bar, 1973, Ohio. *Education:* Washington University (A.B., 1970); University of Cincinnati (J.D., 1973). Order of the Coif. Casenote Editor, University of Cincinnati Law Review, 1972-1973. Assistant Professor of Law, Corporations, Business Planning and Legal Drafting, University of Cincinnati College of Law, 1976-1978. Adjunct Professor, Corporate Law,

(This Listing Continued)

Securities Regulation and Trial Practice, University of Cincinnati College of Law, 1979-1980, 1984-1992. *Member:* Cincinnati, Ohio State and American Bar Associations. ***PRACTICE AREAS:*** Trial Practice; Construction Law; Corporate Law. ***Email:*** wrjacobs@strausstroy.com

DANIEL H. DEMMERLE, II, born Cincinnati, Ohio, October 20, 1948; admitted to bar, 1973, Ohio and U.S. District Court, Southern District of Ohio; 1981, Kentucky. *Education:* Denison University (B.A., with honors, 1970); Vanderbilt University (J.D., 1973). Member, Order of the Coif. Case Editor, Vanderbilt Law Review, 1972-1973. *Member:* Cincinnati, Ohio State, Northern Kentucky and Kentucky Bar Associations. ***PRACTICE AREAS:*** Real Estate Finance; Real Estate-Commercial; Hospitality Law; Closely Held Businesses; Medical Professional Associations; Commercial Lendings and Closings. ***Email:*** dhdemmerle@strausstroy.com

JAMES G. HELDMAN, born Cincinnati, Ohio, March 7, 1949; admitted to bar, 1975, District of Columbia, U.S. District Court for the District of Columbia and U.S. Court of Appeals for the District of Columbia Circuit; 1980, U.S. Supreme Court; 1981, Ohio. *Education:* Harvard University (A.B., cum laude, 1971); George Washington University (J.D., with honors, 1974). *Member:* The District of Columbia Bar; Cincinnati, Ohio State and American Bar Associations. ***PRACTICE AREAS:*** Real Estate Finance; Real Estate-Commercial; Closely Held Business; Buying and Selling of Businesses; Corporate Financing Law; Franchise Law; Multi-Unit Residential Real Estate. ***Email:*** jgheldman@strausstroy.com

CHARLES JAY POSTOW, born Washington, D.C., November 10, 1950; admitted to bar, 1975, Maryland and Florida; 1976, District of Columbia; 1977, Ohio. *Education:* University of Maryland (B.S., 1972); American University (J.D., 1975); Georgetown University (LL.M. in Taxation, 1979). *Member:* Maryland, Ohio State and American Bar Associations; The Florida Bar; The District of Columbia Bar. ***PRACTICE AREAS:*** Finance Law; Acquisitions, Divestitures and Mergers Law; Real Estate Development Law. ***Email:*** cjpostow@strausstroy.com

STUART C. BRINN, born Cincinnati, Ohio, February 2, 1951; admitted to bar, 1976, Ohio and U.S. District Court, Southern District of Ohio; 1985, Kentucky. *Education:* Wharton School of Finance; University of Pennsylvania (B.S., cum laude, 1973); University of Cincinnati (J.D., 1976). Arbitrator, Hamilton County, Ohio Court of Common Pleas, 1978—; Arbitrator, American Arbitration Association.. *Member:* Cincinnati (Former Chairman, Fee Arbitration Committee), Ohio State and Northern Kentucky Bar Associations; American Arbitration Association. ***PRACTICE AREAS:*** Business Law and Litigation; Loan Workouts; Banking; Bankruptcy; Collection. ***Email:*** scbrinn@strausstroy.com

MARTIN C. BUTLER, born Covington, Kentucky, October 5, 1951; admitted to bar, 1977, Ohio; 1978, Kentucky. *Education:* Thomas More College (B.A., 1973); Salmon P. Chase College of Law of Northern Kentucky University (J.D., 1977). *Member:* Cincinnati, Ohio State and Kentucky Bar Associations. (Resident, Covington, Kentucky Office). ***PRACTICE AREAS:*** Real Estate Development Law; Probate Law; Business Law. ***Email:*** mcbutler@strausstroy.com

R. GUY TAFT, born Cincinnati, Ohio, November 30, 1949; admitted to bar, 1976, Ohio. *Education:* University of Cincinnati (B.A., with high honors, 1972; J.D., 1976). Order of the Coif. Member, Editorial Board, University of Cincinnati Law Review, 1974-1976. *Member:* Cincinnati, Ohio State, American and Federal Bar Associations. ***PRACTICE AREAS:*** Federal and State Court Litigation; Arbitrations and Mediations; Patent and Trademark Litigation; Employment Law; Contract Fraud Litigation; Appeals; Administrative Law; Health Care Law; Partnership and Corporate Litigation. ***Email:*** rgtaft@strausstroy.com

ANN W. GERWIN, born St. Louis, Missouri, September 14, 1949; admitted to bar, 1979, Ohio and U.S. District Court, Southern District of Ohio. *Education:* Ohio Wesleyan University (B.A., 1971); Salmon P. Chase College of Law of Northern Kentucky University (J.D., 1979). Member, Order of the Curia. Manuscript Editor, Northern Kentucky Law Review, 1978-1979. *Member:* Cincinnati (Chairman, Corporate and Securities Law Section, 1986-1987), Ohio State and American Bar Associations. ***PRACTICE AREAS:*** Business Law; Securities Regulation; Mergers and Acquisitions. ***Email:*** awgerwin@strausstroy.com

RICHARD S. WAYNE, born Cincinnati, Ohio, June 5, 1952; admitted to bar, 1979, Ohio and U.S. District Court, Southern District of Ohio; 1983, U.S. Court of Appeals, Sixth Circuit; 1984, U.S. Court of Appeals, Fourth, Fifth and Ninth Circuits and U.S. District Court, Eastern District of Michigan. *Education:* University of Cincinnati (B.A., 1974); University of Dayton (J.D., 1978). Member, 1976-1977 and Associate Editor, 1977-1978, University of Dayton Law Review. *Member:* Cincinnati, Ohio State, Federal and American Bar Associations. ***PRACTICE AREAS:*** Complex Litigation; Corporate Planning; Class Actions; Shareholder Derivative Actions; Arbitrations and Mediations. ***Email:*** rswayne@strausstroy.com

PAUL B. CALICO, born Berea, Kentucky, August 24, 1954; admitted to bar, 1980, Ohio and U.S. District Court, Southern District of Ohio; 1981, Kentucky; 1982, U.S. District Court, Eastern District of Kentucky; 1989, U.S. Court of Appeals, Sixth Circuit; 1995, U.S. Tax Court. *Education:* Western Kentucky University (B.S., magna cum laude, 1976); University of Kentucky (J.D., with distinction, 1980). Omicron Delta Kappa; Order of the Coif. Member, Kentucky Law Journal, 1978-1980. *Member:* Cincinnati, Ohio State, Kentucky, Northern Kentucky and American Bar Associations; The Ohio Association of Civil Trial Attorneys; The Collaborative Law Institute (Member, Board of Trustees). ***REPORTED CASES:*** Estate of Swallen v. Commissioner, 98 F.3d 919 (6th Cir. 1996); Rheinecker v. Forest Lab., 826 F. Supp. 256 (S.D. Ohio 1993); Rheinecker v. Forest Lab., 813 F. Supp. 1307 (S.D. Ohio 1993); Bray v. Forest Pharmaceuticals, Inc., 812 F. Supp. 115 (S.D. Ohio 1993); In re Alpco, Inc., 62 B.R. 184 (Bankr. S.D. Ohio 1986); Schreiner v. Ohio Dep't of Educ., 88 Ohio St. 3d 1432; 724 N.E.2d 809 (Ohio 2000); Crowinshield/Old Town Community Urban Redevelopment Corp. v. Campeon Roofing & Waterproofing, 129 Ohio App. 3d 819; 719 N.E.2d 89 (1st Dist. 1998); S. Paul Matthews & Robert A. Davis v. Swallen, 1995 Ohio App. LEXIS 4669 (1st Dist. 1998); Sears, Roebuck & Co. v. Boone County Bd. of Assessment Appeals, 715 S.W.2d 888 (Ky. App. 1986). ***PRACTICE AREAS:*** Litigation; Mediation and Arbitration; Employment Law; Contract Law; Construction Law. ***Email:*** pbcalico@strausstroy.com

(This Listing Continued)

ANDREW M. SHOTT, born Cincinnati, Ohio, March 7, 1955; admitted to bar, 1981, Ohio and U.S. District Court, Southern District of Ohio. *Education:* University of Virginia (B.A., with high distinction, 1977; J.D., 1981). Phi Beta Kappa. *Member:* Cincinnati and American Bar Associations. ***PRACTICE AREAS:*** Real Estate Development and Syndication; Housing and Urban Development Law; Real Estate-Commercial Law; Financial Restructuring; Landlord and Tenant Law. ***Email:*** amshott@strausstroy.com

CLAUDIA G. ALLEN, born Rockville Center, New York, October 23, 1948; admitted to bar, 1979, Illinois; 1980, U.S. District Court, Northern District of Illinois; 1981, U.S. Court of Appeals, Seventh Circuit; 1982, U.S. Tax Court; 1988, Ohio. *Education:* State University of New York at Buffalo (B.F.A., 1970; M.A., 1975; J.D., 1979). Senior Editor, Buffalo Law Review, 1978-1979. Coordinator of Business Law and Lecturer, North Carolina State University, 1983-1987. Bigelow Fellow and Lecturer in Law, University of Chicago Law School, 1979-1980. Affiliated Scholar, American Bar Foundation, 1980. Clerk to Judge Harlington Wood, Jr., U.S. Court of Appeals, Seventh Circuit, 1980-1981. Adjunct Professor, Corporate Tax, University of Cincinnati Law School. Member, Southwestern Ohio Tax Institute Committee. *Member:* Cincinnati Bar Association (Member, Sections on: Employee Benefits Committee; Labor and Employment Committee; Admissions Committee). ***PRACTICE AREAS:*** Employee Benefits; ERISA Litigation; Pension and Profit Sharing; Qualified Retirement Plans; Deferred Compensation; Employment Law. ***Email:*** cgallen@strausstroy.com

TIMOTHY B. THEISSEN, born Covington, Kentucky, October 3, 1957; admitted to bar, 1980, Kentucky; 1983, U.S. District Court, Eastern District of Kentucky; 1985, U.S. Court of Appeals, Sixth Circuit; 1987, Ohio. *Education:* Xavier University; Northern Kentucky University (B.A., 1977); Salmon P. Chase (J.D., 1980). Assistant Professor, Adjunct, University of Cincinnati, 1986-1989. Member, American Planning Association. Commissioner, 1989— and Chairman, 1995—, Kenton County Planning Commission. *Member:* Northern Kentucky, Kentucky, Ohio State and American Bar Associations. (Resident, Covington, Kentucky Office). ***PRACTICE AREAS:*** Domestic Relations Law; Real Estate; Zoning; Civil Litigation. ***Email:*** tbtheissen@strausstroy.com

WILLIAM K. FLYNN, born Cincinnati, Ohio, January 23, 1960; admitted to bar, 1985, Ohio, U.S. District Court, Southern District of Ohio, Eastern District of Kentucky and U.S. Court of Appeals, Sixth Circuit; 1986, Kentucky. *Education:* Miami University (B.A., 1982); University of Cincinnati (J.D., 1985). Pi Sigma Alpha. Member, National Moot Court Team. Recipient: First Place and Best Brief Awards, National Administrative Law Moot Court Competition. *Member:* Cincinnati, Ohio State, Kentucky and American Bar Associations; Public Investor Arbitration Bar Association. ***PRACTICE AREAS:*** Complex Litigation; Securities Arbitration and Investment Fraud Litigation; Corporate Law. ***Email:*** wkflynn@strausstroy.com

CHARLES C. ASHDOWN, born New York, N.Y., 1961; admitted to bar, 1986, Ohio; 1987, U.S. District Court, Southern District of Ohio; 1994, U.S. Court of Appeals, Sixth Circuit. *Education:* Fordham University (B.A., magna cum laude, in cursu honorum, 1983); University of Notre Dame (J.D., 1986). *Member:* Cincinnati, Ohio State and American Bar Associations. ***PRACTICE AREAS:*** Commercial Transactions; Real Estate Law; Business Litigation; Construction Law; Mechanics Liens; Liquor Licensing. ***Email:*** ccashdown@strausstroy.com

MARILYN J. MAAG, born Cincinnati, Ohio, October 10, 1956; admitted to bar, 1986, Ohio. *Education:* University of Cincinnati (B.S., magna cum laude, 1979; J.D., 1986). Articles Editor, University of Cincinnati Law Review, 1985-1986. Co-Author: *Anderson's Ohio Probate Practice and Procedure,* 7th ed. Anderson Publishing Co., 1990 (and annual updates from 1991—). Author: *The Simple Will in Ohio,* Anderson Publishing Co., 1992 (and annual updates from 1993—). *Member:* Cincinnati, Ohio State (Member, Board of Governors, Estate Planning, Trust & Probate Law Section, 1997—) and American Bar Associations. ***PRACTICE AREAS:*** Estate Planning Law; Probate Law. ***Email:*** mjmaag@strausstroy.com

THOMAS L. STACHLER, born Cincinnati, Ohio, July 14, 1960; admitted to bar, 1989, Ohio and U.S. District Court, Southern District of Ohio. *Education:* Centre College (B.S., 1982); University of Cincinnati (J.D., 1989). Recipient: American Jurisprudence Award in Trial Practice; Henry A. Morrill Prize For Excellence in Constitutional Law. Author: Case Note, "Repose v. Right-to-a-Remedy: Physician vs. Patient Under the Ohio Constitution," 57 University of Cincinnati Law Review 423, 1988. Student Articles Editor, University of Cincinnati Law Review, 1988-1989. Adjunct Professor University of Cincinnati College of Law Trial Practice and Practical Litigation. Barrister, Potter Stewart Inn of Court, 1990-1992, 2002. *Member:* Cincinnati, Ohio State and American Bar Associations. ***PRACTICE AREAS:*** Civil (General Civil) Practice; Complex and Multi-District Litigation; Commercial Law; Negligence Law; Malpractice Law. ***Email:*** tlstachler@strausstroy.com

ANTHONY M. BARLOW, born Pembroke, Ontario, Canada, April 13, 1959; admitted to bar, 1990, Ohio. *Education:* Selkirk College, University of British Columbia; University of Cincinnati (B.A., magna cum laude, 1987; J.D., 1990). Member, Order of the Coif. Law Review Junior Member, 1988-1989. Author: Comment, "Restricting Election Day Exit Polling," U. Cinn. L. Rev., Vol. 58, 1990; Casenote, "City of Lakewood v. Plain Dealer Pub. Co. (1988)," U. Cinn. L. Rev., Vol. 58, 1990. Co-Author: Anderson's Ohio Probate Practice and Procedure, 7th ed. Anderson Publishing Co., 1990 and updates. ***PRACTICE AREAS:*** Real Estate (Property) Law; Real Estate; Asset Based Finance; Commercial Leasing; Construction Law; Small Business Counseling; Condominium Development; Multi/Single Family Housing Development; Commercial Foreclosure; Loan Workouts; Zoning Law; Like Kind Exchanges. ***Email:*** ambarlow@strausstroy.com

MARSHALL K. DOSKER, born Louisville, Kentucky, December 21, 1963; admitted to bar, 1991, Ohio; 1992, Kentucky. *Education:* University of Louisville (B.S.B.A., 1985); Salmon P. Chase College of Law (J.D., 1991). (Resident, Covington, Kentucky Office). ***PRACTICE AREAS:*** Tax Law; Estate Planning; Business Law; Litigation. ***Email:*** mkdosker@strausstroy.com

SHAWN M. YOUNG, born Cincinnati, Ohio, January 29, 1955; admitted to bar, 1987, Ohio. *Education:* Northern Kentucky University (B.S., cum laude, 1977); Salmon P. Chase College of Law (J.D., magna cum laude, 1987). Order of the Curia. Articles Editor, Northern Kentucky Law Review, 1986-1987. Author: "Lemon Reconstituted: Aguilar vs. Felton and Public Aid to Parochial Schools," Northern Kentucky Law Review, Vol. 13, No. 2,

(This Listing Continued)

STRAUSS & TROY, A LEGAL PROFESSIONAL ASSOCIATION, Cincinnati—Continued

1986. *Member:* Cincinnati, Ohio State and American Bar Associations. ***PRACTICE AREAS:*** General Business and Corporate Law; Mergers and Acquisitions; Securities Regulation Law; Trademark Law. ***Email:*** smyoung@strausstroy.com

AUGUST T. JANSZEN, born Cincinnati, Ohio, November 17, 1966; admitted to bar, 1993, Ohio and U.S. District Court, Southern District of Ohio; 1995, Kentucky and U.S. Court of Appeals, Sixth Circuit. *Education:* St. Louis University (B.A., 1989); Villanova University; University of Dayton (J.D., cum laude, 1993). Member, 1991-1993; Executive Editor, 1992-1993, University of Dayton Law Review. *Member:* Cincinnati, Northern Kentucky, Kentucky and Ohio State Bar Associations; The Ohio Association of Civil Trial Attorneys. ***REPORTED CASES:*** Burgess v. Doe, 116 Ohio App.3d 61, 686 N.E.2d 1141 (1996); Heard v. Meijer, Inc., 113 Ohio App.3d 224, 680 N.E.2d 719 (1996); Hobler v. Motorists Mutual Ins. Co., 105 Ohio App.3d 629, 664 N.E.2d 999 (1995); Progressive Specialty Ins. Co. v. Edwards, 126 Ohio App.3d 171, 709 N.E.2d 1231 (1998). ***PRACTICE AREAS:*** Commercial Litigation; Non-Competition Agreements; Computer Law; Internet Law; Intellectual Property Law; Trademark, Copyright and Unfair Competition. ***Email:*** atjanszen@strausstroy.com

PETE A. SMITH, born St. Marys, Ohio, March 29, 1969; admitted to bar, 1994, Ohio; 1995, Kentucky. *Education:* University of Cincinnati (B.A., magna cum laude, 1991); University of Notre Dame (J.D., cum laude, 1994). Phi Beta Kappa, Omicron Delta Kappa, Mortar Board. Author: "Potential Liability of University Owned and Operated Medical and Dental Clinics," Journal of College and University Law, Fall, 1994. *Member:* Cincinnati, Ohio State, Kentucky and American Bar Associations. (Resident, Covington, Kentucky Office). ***PRACTICE AREAS:*** Real Estate; Corporate Law; Estate Planning; Domestic Relations. ***Email:*** pasmith@strausstroy.com

THOMAS P. GLASS, born Xenia, Ohio, May 3, 1964; admitted to bar, 1993, Ohio and U.S. District Court, Southern District of Ohio; 1997, Kentucky, U.S. District Court, Eastern District of Kentucky and U.S. Court of Appeals, Sixth Circuit. *Education:* Wright State University (B.A., 1989); University of Dayton (J.D., 1993). Member, 1991-1993; Associate Editor, 1992-1993, University of Dayton Law Review. *Member:* Ohio State and Kentucky Bar Associations. ***PRACTICE AREAS:*** Corporate Litigation; Insurance Litigation. ***Email:*** tpglass@strausstroy.com

MICHAEL A. RUH, JR., born Fort Mitchell, Kentucky, May 27, 1968; admitted to bar, 1996, Ohio; 1997, Kentucky. *Education:* University of Kentucky (B.B.A., with high distinction, 1990; M.B.A., 1991); University of Cincinnati (J.D., 1996). Beta Gamma Sigma. Recipient, Corpus Juris Secundum Award in Torts. President, Student Bar Association, 1996. *Member:* Cincinnati, Ohio State, Kentucky and American Bar Associations. ***PRACTICE AREAS:*** Real Estate; Corporate; Business Law; Commercial Real Estate Acquisitions; Commercial Transactions; Commercial Loans; Construction Contracts; Commercial Real Estate Development; Property Rights; Condominium Conversions; Condominium Development; Conveyancing; Easements; Land Acquisitions; Property Management; Real Estate Acquisitions; Real Estate Contracts; Real Estate Development; Real Estate Finance; Real Estate Leasing; Real Estate Sales; Real Property; Residential Real Estate; Residential Real Estate Development; Residential Real Estate Sales; Commercial Real Estate Finance; Commercial Real Estate Sales; Business Dissolutions; Business Formation; Business Litigation; Business Organization; Business Planning; Business Sales; Business Transactions; Business Transfers; Buying and Selling of Businesses; Joint Ventures; Limited Liability Company Law; Small Business Corporations; Closely Held Corporations; Corporate Contracts; Corporate Dissolutions; Corporate Finance; Corporate Formation; Corporate Organization; Corporate Planning; Incorporation. ***Email:*** maruh@strausstroy.com

---

MICHAEL B. STONER, born Los Angeles, California, June 26, 1963; admitted to bar, 1997, Ohio. *Education:* University of Dayton (B.A., magna cum laude, 1994; J.D., cum laude, 1997). Phi Theta Kappa. Phi Alpha Theta. Member, Golden Key National Honor Society. University of Dayton Mentor Program. *Member:* Cincinnati and Ohio State Bar Associations; Ohio Land Title Association. ***PRACTICE AREAS:*** Real Estate; Real Estate Finance. ***Email:*** mbstoner@strausstroy.com

JOSEPH J. BRAUN, born Cincinnati, Ohio, August 6, 1973; admitted to bar, 1998, Ohio; 2000, U.S. District Court, Southern District of Ohio. *Education:* University of Kentucky (B.A., 1994); University of Toledo (J.D., 1998). Member: Clermont County Mental Health Board, 1998-1999; Clermont County Public Library Board of Trustees, 1999—. Mayor's Court Prosecutor, City of Wyoming, Ohio. *Member:* Cincinnati, Ohio State and American Bar Associations; Ohio Trial Lawyers Association; The Association of Trial Lawyers of America. ***PRACTICE AREAS:*** General Litigation; Complex Litigation; Employment Law; Negligence; Contracts. ***Email:*** jjbraun@strausstroy.com

STEPHANIE A. DILL, born Cincinnati, Ohio, January 20, 1972; admitted to bar, 1999, Ohio. *Education:* Miami University (B.S., cum laude, 1994); University of Cincinnati (M.B.A./J.D., 1999). *Member:* Cincinnati, Ohio State and American Bar Associations. ***PRACTICE AREAS:*** Real Estate; Business Law; Corporate Law. ***Email:*** sadill@strausstroy.com

LORI A. ROSS, born Cincinnati, Ohio, April 14, 1975; admitted to bar, 2000, Ohio and U.S. District Court, Southern District of Ohio; 2001, Kentucky. *Education:* Miami University (B.A. in Psychology and Sociology, magna cum laude, 1997); University of Cincinnati (J.D., 2000). Order of the Coif; Phi Kappa Phi; Phi Beta Kappa. *Member:* Cincinnati, Kentucky and Ohio State Bar Associations. ***PRACTICE AREAS:*** Civil Litigation; Employment Law; Constitutional Law; Complex and Multi-District Litigation. ***Email:*** laross@strausstroy.com

JEREMY A. HAYDEN, born Henderson, Kentucky, April 17, 1974; admitted to bar, 2000, Kentucky; 2002, Ohio. *Education:* Western Kentucky University (B.A., 1996); University of Kentucky (J.D., 2000); University of Cincinnati (M.S.B.A., Taxation, 2002). Phi Delta Phi. Order of Omega. Articles Editor, Journal of Natural Resources and Environmental Law. Trial Advocacy Board. *Member:* Cincinnati (Section on Taxation), Ohio State, Kentucky, Northern Kentucky (Business and Tax Sections) and American (Section on Taxation) Bar Associations. (Resident, Covington, Kentucky Office). ***PRACTICE AREAS:*** Federal, State and Local Taxation; Business Organization and Planning; Estate Planning and Probate. ***Email:*** jahayden@strausstroy.com

MATTHEW R. CHASAR, born Buffalo, New York, June 8, 1976; admitted to bar, 2002, Ohio. *Education:* Miami University (B.S., 1998); University of Cincinnati (J.D., 2002). *Member:* Cincinnati and Ohio State Bar Associations. ***PRACTICE AREAS:*** Litigation. ***Email:*** mrchasar@strausstroy.com

NICOLE M. LUNDRIGAN, born Piqua, Ohio, 1977; admitted to bar, 2002, Ohio and U.S. District Court, Southern District of Ohio; 2003, U.S. Court of Appeals, Sixth Circuit. *Education:* University of Dayton (B.A., 1998); Ohio Northern University (J.D., 2002). *Member:* Dayton, Cincinnati and Ohio State Bar Associations. ***PRACTICE AREAS:*** Commercial Litigation; Complex Litigation. ***Email:*** nmlundrigan@strausstroy.com

JASON D. TONNE, born Cincinnati, Ohio, November 18, 1977; admitted to bar, 2003, Ohio; 2005, Kentucky. *Education:* University of Cincinnati (B.B.A. in Accounting and Real Estate, 2000; J.D., 2003). Order of Omega. Coach, St. Xavier Mock Trial Team. Member: Sigma Chi Alumni Association; Business Network International; Cincinnati Real Estate Club. *Member:* Cincinnati (Member, Continuing Legal Education Committee, Young Lawyers Section), Ohio State and American Bar Associations. ***PRACTICE AREAS:*** Corporate Law; Real Estate Law; Litigation. ***Email:*** jdtonne@strausstroy.com

WILLIAM O. WILLIAMSON, born Cincinnati, Ohio, June 22, 1977; admitted to bar, 2004, Ohio. *Education:* The University of Akron (B.S.B.A., Finance, magna cum laude, 1999); The University of Cincinnati Graduate School of Business (M.B.A., 2002); The University of Cincinnati College of Law (J.D., 2004). Corporate Law Fellow for the University of Cincinnati College of Law Center for Corporate Law. *Member:* Cincinnati, Ohio State, and American Bar Associations. ***PRACTICE AREAS:*** Real Estate; Business. ***Email:*** wowilliamson@strausstroy.com

JOHN M. LEVY, born La Jolla, California, April 19, 1978; admitted to bar, 2004, Ohio and U.S. District Court, Southern District of Ohio. *Education:* University of Vermont (B.A., 2000); University of Cincinnati (J.D., 2004). Associate Member, University of Cincinnati Law Review, 2002-2003. *Member:* Cincinnati, Ohio State and American Bar Associations; The Association of Trial Lawyers of America. ***Email:*** jmlevy@strausstroy.com

STEPHEN G. NESBITT, born Cincinnati, Ohio, October 21, 1978; admitted to bar, 2004, Ohio; 2005, Kentucky. *Education:* Miami University (B.S., Business Administration, 2001); Salmon P. Chase College of Law (J.D., 2004). Order of the Curia. Executive Editor, Northern Kentucky Law Review, 2002-2003. *Member:* Cincinnati, Ohio State and Kentucky Bar Associations. (Resident, Covington, Kentucky Office). ***PRACTICE AREAS:*** Commercial and Residential Real Estate; Corporate and Business Law. ***Email:*** sgnesbitt@strausstroy.com

OF COUNSEL

SAMUEL M. ALLEN, born Glendale, Ohio, August 24, 1929; admitted to bar, 1957, Ohio; 1958, U.S. District Court, Southern District of Ohio; 1962, U.S. Court of Appeals, Sixth Circuit; 1982, U.S. Supreme Court; 1989, Kentucky. *Education:* Harvard University (A.B., 1951); University of Cincinnati (J.D., 1957). Member, Editorial Board, University of Cincinnati Law Review, 1955-1957. Chancellor, Episcopal Diocese of Southern Ohio, 1975-1997. *Member:* Cincinnati and Ohio State Bar Associations. (Resident, Covington, Kentucky Office). ***PRACTICE AREAS:*** Charitable Trusts and Foundations; Corporate Planning; Employment Law; Labor (Management) Law; General Practice. ***Email:*** smallen@strausstroy.com

GORDON H. HOOD, born Cincinnati, Ohio, May 2, 1928; admitted to bar, 1953, Ohio; 1954, Kentucky; 1965, U.S. District Court, Southern District of Ohio; 1980, U.S. District Court, Eastern District of Kentucky. *Education:* Dartmouth College (A.B., 1950); University of Cincinnati (LL.B., 1953). Phi Delta Phi. Chairman, Kentucky Council on Higher Education, 1970-1975. *Member:* Cincinnati, Northern Kentucky and American Bar Associations. (Resident, Covington, Kentucky Office). ***PRACTICE AREAS:*** Corporate Law; Real Estate Law; Banking Law; Probate Law. ***Email:*** ghhood@strausstroy.com

CHARLES G. ATKINS, born Covington, Kentucky, August 19, 1935; admitted to bar, 1962, Ohio and Kentucky; 1988, U.S. District Court, Southern District of Ohio, U.S. District Court, Eastern District of Kentucky, U.S. Court of Appeals, Sixth Circuit, U.S. Tax Court and U.S. Supreme Court. *Education:* University of Cincinnati (B.A., 1959; J.D., 1962). Adjunct Professor of Law, University of Cincinnati College of Law, 1985—. Lecturer on Evidence to Ohio Judicial College, 1986. Master of the Bench, Potter Stewart Inn of Court. *Member:* Cincinnati, Ohio State, Commonwealth of Kentucky and American Bar Associations; The Association of Trial Lawyers of America. ***PRACTICE AREAS:*** Commercial Litigation; Litigation Defense; Malpractice Law; False Claims Act Litigation. ***Email:*** cgatkins@strausstroy.com

MITCHELL B. GOLDBERG, born Cincinnati, Ohio, January 24, 1944; admitted to bar, 1968, Ohio. *Education:* University of Cincinnati (B.A., 1965; J.D., 1968). Order of the Coif. Member, Board of Editors, University of Cincinnati Law Review, 1967-1968. Adjunct Professor, University of Cincinnati College of Law, 1988-1992. Member, American Arbitration Association, Federal Mediation and Conciliation Service, and The Center for Resolution of Disputes. *Member:* Cincinnati, Ohio State and American Bar Associations; National Academy of Arbitrators. (Certified Specialist in Labor and Employment Law, Ohio State Bar Association). ***PRACTICE AREAS:*** Litigation; Alternative Dispute Resolution; Employment Law; Civil Rights Law; Business Law. ***Email:*** mgoldlaw@alltel.net

LEON L. WOLF, born Cincinnati, Ohio, November 14, 1926; admitted to bar, 1950, Ohio; 1951, U.S. District Court, Southern District of Ohio and U.S. Court of Appeals, Sixth Circuit; 1978, U.S. District Court, Eastern District of Kentucky; 1998, U.S. Supreme Court. *Education:* Ohio University and University of Cincinnati (LL.B., 1950). Order of the Coif; Phi Alpha Delta. Editor, Cincinnati Law Review, 1950. *Member:* Cincinnati, Ohio State and American Bar Associations. ***PRACTICE AREAS:*** Manufacturer's Representation Law; Contract Law; Litigation; Business Torts; Litigation of Restrictive Covenants; Land Use Law. ***Email:*** llwolf@strausstroy.com

PAUL J. THEISSEN, born Covington, Kentucky, September 12, 1929; admitted to bar, 1953, Ohio; 1954, Kentucky and U.S. District Court, Eastern District of Kentucky. *Education:* Xavier University (B.S., 1950); University of Cincinnati (J.D., 1953). *Member:* North-

(This Listing Continued)

ern Kentucky (President, 1960-1961), Kentucky and Ohio State Bar Associations. (Resident, Covington, Kentucky Office). **PRACTICE AREAS:** Estate Planning; Foreclosure Law; Mortgage Law; Real Estate Law; Wills. **Email:** pjtheissen@strausstroy.com

DIANE SCHNEIDERMAN, born New York, N.Y., September 9, 1947; admitted to bar, 1972 Connecticut; 1989, Ohio. *Education:* Cornell University (B.A., with distinction, 1968); Yale University (J.D., 1972). Phi Beta Kappa. *Member:* Cincinnati, Ohio State and American Bar Associations. **PRACTICE AREAS:** Commercial Real Estate; Affordable Housing (Low Income Housing Tax Credits and HOPE VI); Shopping Center Law; Shopping Center Development; Retail Leasing; Corporate Contracts. **Email:** dtschneiderman@strausstroy.com

CHARLES H. MELVILLE, born Cincinnati, Ohio, January 18, 1937; admitted to bar, 1962, Ohio; 1963, U.S. District Court, Southern District of Ohio; 1964, U.S. Court of Appeals, Sixth Circuit; 1967, U.S. Court of Appeals, First Circuit; 1971, U.S. Court of Customs and Patent Appeals; 1994, U.S. Supreme Court. *Education:* Princeton University (A.B., with honors in Economics, 1959); University of Cincinnati (J.D., 1962). Order of the Coif. Editor-in-Chief, Cincinnati Law Review. **PRACTICE AREAS:** Intellectual Property; Manufacturers' Representative Law; Contracts and Restrictive Covenants; Business Torts; Litigation. **Email:** chmelville@strausstroy.com

PHILOMENA SALDANHA ASHDOWN, born Madras, India, May 29, 1958; admitted to bar, 1986, Ohio; 1987, Madras, India; 1990, District of Columbia. *Education:* University of Madras; Stella Maris College (B.S., 1978); University of Madras, Madras Law School (LL.B., 1984); University of Notre Dame (J.D., 1986). **PRACTICE AREAS:** Creditors' Rights; Commercial and Bankruptcy Law. **Email:** psashdown@strausstroy.com

REPRESENTATIVE CLIENTS: AIMCO (Apartment Investment and Management Co.); BP Oil Co.; The City of Loveland, Ohio; The City of Wyoming, Ohio; Coldwell Banker Residential Real Estate; Cole + Russell Architects, Inc.; Corporex Companies, Inc.; Forest Laboratories; Greenfield Research, Inc.; Hauck Holdings, Ltd.; ING Investment Management; JP Morgan Chase (Bank One); LaSalle Bank National Association; Lion Apparel; Mamar, Inc.; Meijer, Inc.; NexGen Enterprises, Inc.; P&G, Inc.; PNC Bank, N.A. (Ohio and Kentucky); PNC Business Credit; Republic Financial Corporation; The Richard E. Jacobs Co., Inc.; Standard Textile Co., Inc.; Stern-Hendy Properties, Inc.; Storopak, Inc.; Sycamore School District; United Magazine Co.; US Bank National Association; Vandercar Holdings, Inc.; The Verdin Co.; Victory Wholesale Grocers.
APPROVED ATTORNEYS FOR: Chicago Title Insurance Co.; Commonwealth Land Title Insurance Co.; First American Title Insurance Co.; Old Republic National Title Insurance Co.

WILLIAM B. STRUBBE

1525 KROGER BUILDING
CINCINNATI, OHIO 45202
Telephone: 513-621-4775
Fax: 513- 621-4789
Email: wstrubbe@one.net
URL: http://www.strubbelaw.net

Insurance Coverage and Defense Litigation, Product Liability, Commercial Litigation, Personal Injury, Copyright, Legal Malpractice.

WILLIAM B. STRUBBE, born Cincinnati, Ohio, August 30, 1952; admitted to bar, 1979, Ohio; 1980, U.S. District Court, Southern District of Ohio; 1985, U.S. Court, of Appeals, Sixth Circuit; 1990, Kentucky; 1991, U.S District Court, Eastern District of Kentucky. *Education:* University of Oregon (B.A., 1975); University of Cincinnati (J.D., 1979). Student Articles Editor, University of Cincinnati Law Review, 1978-1979. Assistant Adjunct Professor, University of Cincinnati, 2001—. *Member:* Cincinnati (Vice Chair, Ethics Committee; Member, Common Pleas Court Committee), Northern Kentucky, Clermont County, Ohio State (Vice Chair, Insurance Law Committee, 1999-2000; Chair, 2000—; Vice-Chair, 2002— and Secretary, 2000-2002, Negligence Law Committee; Member, Jury Instructions Committee, 2001—), Kentucky and American Bar Associations; Association of Trial Lawyers of America; Ohio Academy of Trial Lawyers. **REPORTED CASES:** In re Kkemko, Inc. 181 B.R. 47 Bkrtcy, S.D.Ohio, 1995; Beil v. Lakewood Engineering and Mfg. Co., 15 F.3d 546 C.A.6 (Ky.), 1994; State Auto. Mut. Ins. Co. v. Newman 65 Oh. Misc. 2d 23, 640 N.E.2d 627 Ohio Mun., 1994; Heile v. Herrmann, 136 Ohio App.3d 351, 736 N.E.2d 566 Ohio App. 1 Dist. Dec 17, 1999; Carlson v. Rabkin, 152 Ohio App. 3d 672, 789 N.E. 2nd 1122 (2003).

LAW OFFICES OF
SURDYK, DOWD & TURNER, CO., L.P.A.

CINCINNATI, OHIO

(See Dayton)

TAFT, STETTINIUS & HOLLISTER LLP

Established in 1885
425 WALNUT STREET, SUITE 1800
CINCINNATI, OHIO 45202-3957
Telephone: 513-381-2838
Facsimile: 513-381-0205
URL: http://www.taftlaw.com

Columbus, Ohio Office: Twelfth Floor, 21 East State Street. Telephone: 614-221-2838.
Covington, Kentucky Office: 1717 Dixie Highway, Suite 340. Telephone: 859-331-2838; 513-381-2838.
Cleveland, Ohio Office: 3500 BP Tower, 200 Public Square. Telephone: 216-241-2838.
Dayton, Ohio Office: 110 North Main Street, Suite 900. Telephone: 937-228-2838.

Antitrust, Bankruptcy and Debtor/Creditor Rights, Business and Finance, E-Business (Internet and E-Commerce), Employee Benefits/ERISA and Tax-Planning, Environmental Law, Family Law, Family Business Planning, Franchise, General Litigation, Health Care, Immigration, Institutional Finance, Intellectual Property and Technology Group, International, Japanese

(This Listing Continued)

Practice, Labor and Employment, Mergers and Acquisitions, Nonprofit and Tax-Exempt Organizations, Product Liability and Personal Injury, Public Finance, Real Property, Securities, Tax, Probate and Estate Planning, Workers' Compensation.

MEMBERS OF FIRM

ROBERT A. TAFT (1889-1953)

JOHN L. STETTINIUS (1882-1924)

JOHN B. HOLLISTER (1890-1979)

L. CLIFFORD CRAIG, born Cincinnati Ohio, August 1, 1938; admitted to bar, 1964, Ohio. *Education:* Duke University (A.B., 1961; LL.B., 1964). Fellow, American College of Trial Lawyers.

ROBERT J. TOWNSEND, born Charlotte, Michigan, November 11, 1938; admitted to bar, 1964, Ohio. *Education:* Michigan State University (B.A., 1960); Harvard Law School (LL.B., 1963).

JEROLD A. FINK, born Dayton, Ohio, July 16, 1941; admitted to bar, 1966, Ohio. *Education:* Duke University (A.B., 1963; LL.B., 1966).

THOMAS D. HEEKIN, born Cincinnati, Ohio, August 15, 1937; admitted to bar, 1962, Ohio. *Education:* Williams College (A.B., 1959); University of Michigan (J.D., 1962).

MELVIN S. SHOTTEN, born Detroit, Michigan, March 22, 1943; admitted to bar, 1968, Ohio. *Education:* University of Michigan (B.S., 1965; J.D., 1968).

GERALD J. RAPIEN, born Cincinnati, Ohio, February 11, 1943; admitted to bar, 1968, Ohio; 2000, Kentucky. *Education:* Xavier University (A.B., 1965); University of Notre Dame (LL.B., 1968). Fellow, American College of Trial Lawyers.

STEPHEN M. NECHEMIAS, born St. Louis, Missouri, July 27, 1944; admitted to bar, 1969, Ohio. *Education:* The Ohio State University (B.S., 1966); University of Cincinnati (J.D., 1969).

†††STEPHEN M. O'BRYAN, born Dayton, Ohio, December 9, 1944; admitted to bar, 1969, Ohio. *Education:* Bowling Green State University (B.A., 1966); Case Western Reserve University (J.D., 1969).

ROBERT E. RICH, born Corbin, Kentucky, February 4, 1944; admitted to bar, 1970, Ohio; 1999, Michigan; 2003, Kentucky. *Education:* University of Kentucky (A.B., 1966); Harvard Law School (J.D., 1969).

R. JOSEPH PARKER, born St. Louis, Missouri, June 29, 1944; admitted to bar, 1969, Ohio. *Education:* Georgetown University (A.B., 1966); Boston College Law School (J.D., 1969). Fellow, American College of Trial Lawyers.

TIMOTHY E. HOBERG, born Cincinnati, Ohio, August 14, 1944; admitted to bar, 1970, Ohio. *Education:* The Ohio State University (B.E.E., 1967); University of Virginia (J.D., 1970).

G. JACK DONSON JR., born Dayton, Ohio, August 25, 1946; admitted to bar, 1971, Ohio. *Education:* The Ohio State University (B.A., 1968); University of Cincinnati (J.D., 1971).

†DAVID L. JOHNSON, born Lima, Ohio, September 23, 1946; admitted to bar, 1971, Ohio; 1973, Hawaii. *Education:* Ohio Wesleyan University (B.A., 1968); Harvard Law School (J.D., 1971).

THOMAS C. HILL, born Prestonsburg, Kentucky, July 17, 1946; admitted to bar, 1973, Ohio. *Education:* Case Western Reserve University (A.B., 1968); University of Chicago (J.D., 1973).

LAWRENCE J. BARTY, born Detroit, Michigan, June 17, 1942; admitted to bar, 1973, Ohio. *Education:* Florida State University (B.A., 1969); Duke University (J.D., 1973).

†††MARGARET ANNE CANNON, born Highland, Illinois, January 19, 1948; admitted to bar, 1973, Ohio. *Education:* Oberlin College (A.B., 1970); Case Western Reserve University (J.D., 1973).

THOMAS T. TERP, born Fountain Hill, Pennsylvania, August 12, 1947; admitted to bar, 1973, Ohio. *Education:* Albion College (B.A., 1969); College of William and Mary (J.D., 1973).

†LAWRENCE D. WALKER, born Syracuse, New York, July 10, 1948; admitted to bar, 1973, Ohio. *Education:* Fordham University (B.A., 1970); Northwestern University (J.D., 1973).

ROGER A. WEBER, born Wauseon, Ohio, February 12, 1949; admitted to bar, 1973, Ohio. *Education:* The Ohio State University (B.A., 1970); Harvard Law School (J.D., 1973).

ROSS E. WALES, born Youngstown, Ohio, October 17, 1947; admitted to bar, 1974, Ohio. *Education:* Princeton University (A.B., 1969); University of Virginia (J.D., 1974).

†TIMOTHY P. NAGY, born Elyria, Ohio, April 18, 1949; admitted to bar, 1974, Ohio. *Education:* Wake Forest College; The Ohio State University (B.A., 1971); Capital University (J.D., 1974).

WILLIAM STUART DORNETTE, born Washington, D.C., March 2, 1951; admitted to bar, 1975, Ohio. *Education:* Williams College (B.A., 1972); University of Virginia (J.D., 1975).

TIMOTHY J. QUINN, born Cincinnati, Ohio, March 9, 1947; admitted to bar, 1975, Ohio. *Education:* Yale University (B.A., 1969); Trinity College, Dublin, Ireland; The Ohio State University (J.D., 1975).

EDWARD D. DILLER, born Bluffton, Ohio, August 7, 1947; admitted to bar, 1976, Ohio. *Education:* Bluffton College (B.A., 1969); University of Oregon; Harvard Law School (J.D., 1976).

DANIEL J. HOFFHEIMER, born Cincinnati, Ohio, December 28, 1950; admitted to bar, 1976, Ohio. *Education:* Harvard University (A.B., 1973); University of Virginia (J.D., 1976). Fellow, American College of Trust and Estate Counsel.

(This Listing Continued)

TAFT, STETTINIUS & HOLLISTER LLP, Cincinnati—Continued

TIMOTHY J. HURLEY, born Cleveland, Ohio, November 6, 1951; admitted to bar, 1976, Ohio. *Education:* Xavier University (A.B., 1973); St. Louis University (J.D., 1976).

JOHN J. McCOY, born Cincinnati, Ohio, March 15, 1952; admitted to bar, 1977, Ohio. *Education:* Xavier University (B.S., 1974); University of Chicago (J.D., 1977).

STEVEN W. WEEKS, born Topeka, Kansas, March 7, 1950; admitted to bar, 1977, Ohio. *Education:* Washburn University of Topeka (B.S., 1972); Harvard Law School (J.D., 1977).

TIMOTHY P. REILLY, born Cincinnati, Ohio, June 23, 1953; admitted to bar, 1978, Ohio. *Education:* University of Notre Dame (B.A., 1975); University of Cincinnati (J.D., 1978).

WILLIAM J. SEITZ III, born Cincinnati, Ohio, October 29, 1954; admitted to bar, 1978, Ohio. *Education:* Wake Forest University; University of Cincinnati (B.A., 1975; J.D., 1978).

THOMAS R. SCHUCK, born Findlay, Ohio, February 7, 1950; admitted to bar, 1976, Ohio. *Education:* DePauw University (B.A., 1972); University of Kent, Canterbury, England (M.A., 1974); Harvard Law School (J.D., 1976).

MICHAEL J. ZAVATSKY, born Wheeling, West Virginia, December 15, 1948; admitted to bar, 1980, Ohio. *Education:* The Ohio State University (B.A., 1970); University of Hawaii (M.A., 1972); University of Cincinnati (J.D., 1980).

KIM K. BURKE, born Pittsburgh, Pennsylvania, September 13, 1955; admitted to bar, 1980, Pennsylvania; 1981, Ohio. *Education:* Indiana University of Pennsylvania (B.S., 1977); University of Pittsburgh (J.D., 1980).

MARK J. STEPANIAK, born Cincinnati, Ohio, July 21, 1955; admitted to bar, 1980, Ohio. *Education:* Thomas More College (B.A., 1977); University of Cincinnati (J.D., 1980).

†††JOHN D. BROWN, born Cleveland, Ohio, November 1, 1942; admitted to bar, 1969, Ohio. *Education:* University of Colorado (B.A., 1966); Case Western Reserve University (J.D., 1969).

†††JOEL A. MAKEE, born Cleveland, Ohio, May 27, 1944; admitted to bar, 1969, Ohio. *Education:* Wittenberg University (B.A., 1966); Case Western Reserve University (J.D., 1969).

†††THOMAS J. LEE, born Cleveland, Ohio, March 27, 1952; admitted to bar, 1977, Ohio. *Education:* Wittenberg University (B.A., 1974); Case Western Reserve University (J.D., 1977).

†††CARL A. MURWAY, born Lakewood, Ohio, May 6, 1958; admitted to bar, 1983, Ohio. *Education:* Oberlin College (B.A., 1980); University of Wisconsin (J.D., 1983). Fellow, American Academy of Matrimonial Lawyers.

CHARLES MICHAEL STEPHAN, born Cincinnati, Ohio, March 23, 1949; admitted to bar, 1979, Ohio. *Education:* Xavier University (B.A., 1970); University of Cincinnati (J.D., 1979).

GERALD S. GREENBERG, born Philadelphia, Pennsylvania, July 27, 1951; admitted to bar, 1977, New York; 1988, Ohio. *Education:* Dickinson College (B.A., 1973); Harvard Law School (J.D., 1976).

MARGARET AVRIL LAWSON, born Cincinnati, Ohio, May 12, 1957; admitted to bar, 1982, Ohio. *Education:* Dartmouth College (B.A., 1979); Harvard University (J.D., 1982).

TOSHIO NAKAO, born Wakayama, Japan, June 10, 1952; admitted to bar, 1984, District of Columbia; 1992, Ohio. *Education:* International Christian University, Japan (B.A., 1977); Duke University (J.D., 1983).

††ROBERT B. CRAIG, born Cincinnati, Ohio, September 13, 1955; admitted to bar, 1981, Ohio; 1984, Kentucky. *Education:* Duke University (A.B., 1977); University of Chicago (J.D., 1981).

STEPHEN M. GRIFFITH JR., born Chicago, Illinois, October 26, 1953; admitted to bar, 1981, Ohio. *Education:* Northwestern University (B.A., 1975); Marshall-Wythe School of Law, College of William & Mary (J.D., 1981).

THOMAS E. GROSSMANN, born Cincinnati, Ohio, October 20, 1956; admitted to bar, 1982, Ohio. *Education:* Miami University (B.A., 1979); University of Cincinnati (J.D., 1982).

†††MARK J. VALPONI, born Cleveland, Ohio, March 23, 1952; admitted to bar, 1977, Ohio. *Education:* Purdue University (B.S., 1974); Cleveland State University (J.D., 1977; M.B.A., 1981).

JEFFREY S. SCHLOEMER, born Cincinnati, Ohio, December 3, 1958; admitted to bar, 1983, Ohio. *Education:* University of Notre Dame (A.B., 1980); Duke University (J.D., 1983).

†††STEVEN A. MARRER, born Cincinnati, Ohio, March 25, 1958; admitted to bar, 1983, Ohio. *Education:* Northwestern University (B.A., 1980); Case Western Reserve University (J.D., 1983).

TIMOTHY C. SULLIVAN, born Cincinnati, Ohio, February 19, 1961; admitted to bar, 1985, Ohio. *Education:* Cornell University (A.B., 1982); University of Cincinnati (J.D., 1985).

PATRICK J. MITCHELL, born Columbus, Ohio, November 25, 1951; admitted to bar, 1986, Ohio. *Education:* University of Cincinnati (B.B.A., 1975; M.S., 1983); Washington College of Law, American University (J.D., 1986).

†MICHAEL A. BYERS, born Columbus, Ohio, October 20, 1953; admitted to bar, 1978, Ohio. *Education:* The Ohio State University (B.A., 1975); University of Akron (J.D., 1978).

SAMUEL M. DURAN, born Columbus, Ohio, August 9, 1956; admitted to bar, 1984, Ohio. *Education:* University of Michigan (A.B., 1978); University of Denver (M.A., 1980); The Ohio State University (J.D., 1984).

(This Listing Continued)

SUSAN E. WHEATLEY, born Cincinnati, Ohio, November 26, 1960; admitted to bar, 1986, Ohio. *Education:* Yale University (B.A., 1982); Northwestern University (J.D, 1986).

†††BRUCE L. WATERHOUSE, JR., born Pittsburgh, Pennsylvania, May 17, 1955; admitted to bar, 1982, Colorado; 1988, Ohio. *Education:* University of Michigan (B.S., 1977); American University (J.D., 1982).

DOREEN CANTON, born Wilkes Barre, Pennsylvania, October 3, 1948; admitted to bar, 1988, Ohio. *Education:* Canisius College (B.A., 1970); University of Cincinnati (J.D., 1988).

GREGORY PARKER ROGERS, born Chicago, Illinois, October 30, 1964; admitted to bar, 1989, Ohio. *Education:* Miami University (B.S., 1986); Emory University (J.D., 1989).

MARK A. KOBASUK, born Cleveland, Ohio, November 21, 1957; admitted to bar, 1990, Ohio. *Education:* Hiram College (B.A., 1980); Georgetown University (M.A., 1988; J.D., 1988).

RONALD C. CHRISTIAN, born Paducah, Kentucky, June 22, 1962; admitted to bar, 1987, Ohio. *Education:* Murray State University (B.S., 1984); Salmon P. Chase College of Law (J.D., 1987).

MARCIA VOORHIS ANDREW, born Pelham, New York, September 30, 1962; admitted to bar, 1988, Ohio. *Education:* Williams College (B.A., 1984); University of Virginia (J.D., 1988).

ROBERT A. BILOTT, born Albany, New York, August 2, 1965; admitted to bar, 1990, Ohio. *Education:* New College of the University of South Florida (B.A., 1987); Cambridge University, Cambridge, England; The Ohio State University College of Law (J.D., 1990).

RUSSELL S. SAYRE, born Alexandria, Virginia, July 13, 1964; admitted to bar, 1990, Ohio. *Education:* Mary Washington College (B.A., 1986); University of Virginia (J.D., 1990).

PATRICIA O. LOWRY, born Baltimore, Maryland, January 13, 1947; admitted to bar, 1985, Ohio. *Education:* Mount Holyoke College (A.B., 1969); University of Virginia (J.D., 1972).

EARL K. MESSER, born Patterson, New Jersey, February 11, 1954; admitted to bar, 1991, Ohio. *Education:* United Wesleyan College (B.S., 1977); University of Cincinnati (M.A., 1984); Salmon P. Chase College of Law (J.D., 1991).

†††ROBERT P. McMANUS, born New York, N.Y., October 15, 1953; admitted to bar, 1978, Ohio. *Education:* University of Notre Dame (B.B.A., 1975); The Ohio State University (J.D., 1978).

†ROBERT W. McADAMS, JR., born Bradford, Pennsylvania, November 9, 1954; admitted to bar, 1987, Ohio. *Education:* University of Dayton (B.S., 1976); University of Virginia (M.B.A., 1980); University of California, Hastings College of the Law (J.D., 1986).

†TIMOTHY B. MITCHELL, born Dallas, Texas, January 5, 1956; admitted to bar, 1982, Ohio. *Education:* The Ohio State University (B.A., 1979); Capital University Law School (J.D., 1982).

†††DAVID H. WALLACE, born Cleveland, Ohio, February 28, 1961; admitted to bar, 1986, Ohio. *Education:* Middlebury College (B.A., 1983); Case Western Reserve University (J.D., 1986).

†††PETER M. POULOS, born Roslyn, New York, September 3, 1965; admitted to bar, 1990, Ohio. *Education:* Washington University (B.S.E.E., 1987); Case Western Reserve University (J.D., 1990).

W. TIMOTHY MILLER, born Indianapolis, Indiana, May 13, 1967; admitted to bar, 1992, Ohio. *Education:* DePauw University (B.Mus., 1989); Cornell University (J.D., 1992).

DAVID HAMILTON PECK, born Dearborn, Michigan, August 25, 1959; admitted to bar, 1992, Ohio. *Education:* Eastern Michigan University (B.S., 1988); University of Michigan (J.D., 1992).

DANIEL E. FAUSZ, born Fort Thomas, Kentucky, September 13, 1961; admitted to bar, 1993, Kentucky; 1994, Ohio. *Education:* Northwestern University (B.A., 1983); Vanderbilt University (M.A., 1985); New York University (J.D., 1989).

GEORGE D. MOLINSKY, born Cincinnati, Ohio, November 16, 1966; admitted to bar, 1994, Ohio. *Education:* University of Notre Dame (B.B.A., 1989); Notre Dame Law School (J.D., 1994).

†††DONNA M. FLAMMANG, born Cleveland, Ohio, January 15, 1951; admitted to bar, 1975, Ohio. *Education:* Albion College (B.A., 1971); Cleveland State University (J.D., 1975).

†††MARY GRACE BALAZS, born Cleveland, Ohio, December 19, 1953; admitted to bar, 1980, Ohio. *Education:* John Carroll University (B.A., 1976); Cleveland Marshall College of Law (J.D., 1979).

†††GREGORY J. O'BRIEN, born Cleveland, Ohio, May 27, 1966; admitted to bar, 1994, Ohio. *Education:* University of Toledo (B.B.A., 1989); Cleveland State University (J.D., 1994).

†††JILL FRIEDMAN HELFMAN, born Akron, Ohio, February 20, 1962; admitted to bar, 1987, Ohio. *Education:* University of Michigan (A.B., 1984); Case Western Reserve University (J.D., 1987). Fellow, American Academy of Matrimonial Lawyers.

DAVID A. MANCINO, born Youngstown, Ohio, December 25, 1965; admitted to bar, 1994, Ohio; registered to practice before U.S. Patent and Trademark Office. *Education:* University of Michigan (B.S.E.E., 1988); University of Cincinnati (J.D., 1994).

DANIEL R. WARNCKE, born Wauseon, Ohio, March 3, 1959; admitted to bar, 1993, Ohio. *Education:* University of Maryland (B.A., 1987); Webster University (M.A., 1990); University of Cincinnati (J.D., 1993).

(This Listing Continued)

TRACEY CHRISKE PUTHOFF, born St. Louis, Missouri, January 11, 1966; admitted to bar, 1995, Ohio; registered to practice before U.S. Patent and Trademark Office. *Education:* University of Missouri-Rolla (B.S.A.E., 1989); Salmon P. Chase College of Law (J.D., 1995).

††††J. STEVEN JUSTICE, born Dayton, Ohio, December 2, 1958; admitted to bar, 1994, Ohio. *Education:* Anderson University (B.A., 1981); Southern Baptist Theological Seminary (M.Div., 1987); University of Cincinnati (J.D., 1994).

MICHAEL A. LAING, born Orlando, Florida, February 23, 1961; admitted to bar, 1986, Florida; 2004, Ohio. *Education:* Auburn University (B.S., 1983); University of Alabama (J.D., 1986); University of Florida (LL.M. in Taxation, 1987).

††††HUGH E. WALL, III, born Dayton, Ohio, November 5, 1946; admitted to bar, 1972, Ohio. *Education:* College of St. Thomas (B.A., 1968); University of Cincinnati (J.D., 1972).

†††WILLIAM J. STAVOLE, born Parma, Ohio, March 23, 1963; admitted to bar, 1988, Ohio. *Education:* Kenyon College (B.A., 1985); The Ohio State University (J.D., 1988).

†††DANIEL K. WRIGHT, II, born Cleveland, Ohio, April 21, 1954; admitted to bar, 1979, Ohio. *Education:* Hillsdale College (B.L.S., 1976); Case Western Reserve University (J.D., 1979).

†††BRUCE J. L. LOWE, born Brighton, Sussex, England, 1949; admitted to bar, 1976, England and Wales; 1979, Ohio. *Education:* St. Edmunds Hall, Oxford University (B.A., 1972; M.A., 1976); Inns of Court School of Law, London, England (Barrister at Law, 1976).

†JOHN P. CURP, born Dayton, Ohio, February 17, 1970; admitted to bar, 1995, Ohio. *Education:* Miami University (B.S., 1992); Indiana University (J.D., 1995).

†††DAVID V. ALLEN, born Fort Meade, Maryland, June 20, 1961; admitted to bar, 1987, Ohio. *Education:* Baldwin-Wallace College (B.A., 1983); Akron University Law School (J.D., 1987).

AIMEE L. KELLER, born Wilmington, Delaware, February 13, 1966; admitted to bar, 1993, Ohio. *Education:* Cornell University (B.S., 1988; J.D., 1993).

JOHN B. NALBANDIAN, born Fort Ord, California, March 15, 1969; admitted to bar, 1997, District of Columbia; 2001, Ohio. *Education:* University of Pennsylvania (B.S., Econ., 1991); University of Virginia (J.D., 1994).

†††TIMOTHY L. ZIX, born Cincinnati, Ohio, July 20, 1965; admitted to bar, 1991, Ohio. *Education:* University of Dayton (B.S., 1987); Cleveland Marshall College of Law (J.D., 1991).

†JAMES B. FARMER, born Corpus Christi, Texas, May 5, 1949; admitted to bar, 1976, Ohio. *Education:* Cornell University (B.A., 1971); The Ohio State University (M.C.R.P., 1976; J.D., 1976).

†††STEPHEN H. JETT, born Augusta, Georgia, July 2, 1962; admitted to bar, 1990, Ohio. *Education:* University of Kentucky (B.A., 1984; J.D., 1990).

JULIA B. MEISTER, born Fort Thomas, Kentucky, November 16, 1969; admitted to bar, 1995, Ohio. *Education:* Xavier University (B.A., 1991); Notre Dame Law School (J.D., 1995).

ERIC K. COMBS, born West Union, Ohio, August 10, 1971; admitted to bar, 1996, Ohio. *Education:* Miami University (B.A., 1993); University of Wisconsin-Madison (J.D., 1996).

KERRY P. HASTINGS, born Cincinnati, Ohio, October 27, 1971; admitted to bar, 1996, Ohio. *Education:* University of Michigan (B.A., 1993); Harvard University (J.D., 1996).

†††CHARLES A. BOWERS, born Haverhill, Massachusetts, March 15, 1967; admitted to bar, 1994, Ohio. *Education:* Lafayette College (B.A., 1989); Case Western Reserve University (J.D., 1994).

OF COUNSEL

J. MACK SWIGERT, born Carthage, Illinois, September 25, 1907; admitted to bar, 1935, Illinois; 1937, Ohio. *Education:* Grinnell College, 1925-1927; Harvard College (S.B., 1930); Harvard Law School (LL.B., 1935).

CHARLES D. LINDBERG, born Moline, Illinois, September 11, 1928; admitted to bar, 1954, Ohio. *Education:* Augustana College (A.B., 1950); Yale Law School (LL.B., 1953).

ROBERT G. STACHLER, born St. Marys, Ohio, December 16, 1929; admitted to bar, 1957, Ohio. *Education:* University of Dayton (B.S., 1951); University of Cincinnati (LL.B., 1957).

†††FRED J. LIVINGSTONE, born Cleveland, Ohio, February 20, 1926; admitted to bar, 1950, Ohio. *Education:* Western Reserve University; Harvard University (LL.B., 1950).

JAMES J. RYAN, born Cincinnati, Ohio, June 17, 1929; admitted to bar, 1954, Ohio. *Education:* Xavier University (A.B., 1951); University of Cincinnati (LL.B., 1954).

CYNTHIA F. BLANK, born New York, N.Y., March 5, 1925; admitted to bar, 1956, Ohio. *Education:* Western Reserve University (B.A., 1944); Salmon P. Chase College of Law (J.D., 1956); New York University (LL.M., 1973).

†††DAVID E. BURKE, born Chicago, Illinois, November 3, 1937; admitted to bar, 1964, Ohio. *Education:* University of Dayton (B.A., 1959); Case Western Reserve University (J.D., 1963).

JAMES J. MAYER, born Cincinnati, Ohio, November 27, 1938; admitted to bar, 1969, Ohio; 1975, Kentucky. *Education:* University of Cincinnati (B.S.E.E., 1961); Salmon P. Chase College of Law (J.D., 1969).

LAURA A. RINGENBACH, born Cincinnati, Ohio, September 2, 1953; admitted to bar, 1983, Ohio. *Education:* Xavier University (B.S., 1975); University of Cincinnati (M.S., 1978; J.D., 1983).

(This Listing Continued)

†††GEORGE J. DUNN, born Cleveland, Ohio, April 29, 1935; admitted to bar, 1960, Ohio. *Education:* Yale University (B.S., 1957); Harvard University (LL.B., 1960).

†FRANK A. TITUS, born Gallipolis, Ohio, June 28, 1946; admitted to bar, 1979, Ohio. *Education:* The Ohio State University (B.A., 1970; M.A., 1973); Capital University Law School (J.D., 1979).

†††RICHARD D. TOMSICK, born Euclid, Ohio, August 3, 1959; admitted to bar, 1984, Ohio. *Education:* Case Western Reserve University (B.A., 1981; J.D., 1984).

J. ALAN LIPS, born Louisville, Kentucky, May 7, 1938; admitted to bar, 1968, Ohio. *Education:* University of Kentucky (B.S., 1960; J.D., 1967).

†DIANE D. REYNOLDS, born Akron, Ohio, 1959; admitted to bar, 1985, Ohio. *Education:* The Ohio State University (B.A., 1982); Capital University (J.D., 1985); University of Chicago (M.B.A., 1999).

RETIRED PARTNERS

JAMES R. BRIDGELAND JR., born Cleveland, Ohio, February 16, 1929; admitted to bar, 1957, Ohio. *Education:* University of Akron (A.B., 1951); Harvard University (A.M., 1955); Harvard Law School (LL.B., 1957).

FRANK H. STEWART, born Mexico City, Mexico, May 19, 1931; admitted to bar, 1957, District of Columbia; 1959, Ohio. *Education:* Harvard University (B.A., 1952); University of Virginia (LL.B., 1957).

WILBUR L. COLLINS, born Columbus, Ohio, May 18, 1930; admitted to bar, 1954, Ohio. *Education:* The Ohio State University (B.S., 1954; LL.B., 1954); New York University (LL.M., 1960).

WILLIAM K. ENGEMAN, born Baltimore, Maryland, August 19, 1939; admitted to bar, 1965, Ohio. *Education:* Brown University (B.A., 1961); University of Virginia (LL.B., 1964).

ASSOCIATES

RAYMOND W. LEMBKE, born Mariemont, Ohio, July 25, 1959; admitted to bar, 1983, Washington (inactive); 1984, Ohio; 1986, Kentucky. *Education:* Northwestern University (B.A., 1980); Vanderbilt University (J.D., 1983).

PATRICIA D. BRAXTON, born Amery, Wisconsin, February 21, 1961; admitted to bar, 1990, Ohio. *Education:* City University of New York (B.B.A., 1983); Brooklyn Law School; University of Dayton (J.D., 1989).

CYNTHIA C. FELSON, born Boston, Massachusetts, August 23, 1955; admitted to bar, 1993, Ohio. *Education:* University of Cincinnati (B.A., 1989); Salmon P. Chase College of Law (J.D., 1993).

MARY L. RUST, born Cincinnati, Ohio, June 16, 1962; admitted to bar, 1987, Ohio; 1999, Kentucky. *Education:* Miami University (B.S., 1984); University of Cincinnati (J.D., 1987).

†††CHRISTINE LEWANSKI, born Cleveland, Ohio, August 11, 1970; admitted to bar, 1996, Ohio. *Education:* Hollins College (B.A., 1992); Case Western Reserve University (J.D., 1995).

LORI E. JEFFRIES, born Cincinnati, Ohio, July 24, 1972; admitted to bar, 1997, Ohio. *Education:* Miami University (B.S., 1994); Salmon P. Chase College of Law (J.D., 1997).

BRENDA M. BREITKREUTZ, born West Point, Nebraska, November 3, 1971; admitted to bar, 1998, Ohio. *Education:* Wayne State University (B.S., 1992); University of Michigan (J.D., 1997).

††THOMAS P. VERGAMINI, born Seneca Falls, New York, December 31, 1950; admitted to bar, 1980, Ohio; 1982, Kentucky. *Education:* The Ohio State University (B.A., 1973); University of Kentucky (M.S.L.S., 1975); Salmon P. Chase College of Law (J.D., 1980).

ANTONIA MITROUSSIA, born Athens, Greece, November 29, 1961; admitted to bar, 1991, Ohio. *Education:* University of Cincinnati (B.A., 1983; M.A., 1986; J.D., 1990).

PATRICIA ANDERSON PRYOR, born Nürnberg, Germany, February 27, 1973; admitted to bar, 1998, Ohio. *Education:* Ohio University (B.A., 1994); University of Cincinnati (J.D., 1998).

JEANNE MARIE BRUNS, born Bowling Green, Ohio, January 7, 1968; admitted to bar, 1999, Ohio. *Education:* Marquette University (B.A., 1989); Georgetown University (J.D., 1999).

PAIGE L. ELLERMAN, born Covington, Kentucky, May 11, 1974; admitted to bar, 1999, Ohio; 2000, Kentucky; 2001, Indiana. *Education:* University of Kentucky (B.A., 1995); Salmon P. Chase College of Law (J.D., 1999).

JUSTIN D. FLAMM, born Dayton, Ohio, June 10, 1974; admitted to bar, 1999, Ohio. *Education:* Miami University (B.A., 1996); Washington and Lee University (J.D., 1999).

ALLISON S. RUSSELL, born Dayton, Ohio, August 19, 1974; admitted to bar, 1999, Ohio. *Education:* DePauw University (B.A., 1996); Case Western Reserve University (J.D., 1999).

TRACY T. WARD, born Dayton, Ohio, April 1, 1969; admitted to bar, 1999, Ohio; 2000, Indiana. *Education:* University of Cincinnati (B.A., 1995; J.D., 1999).

JAMES M. ZIMMERMAN, born Cincinnati, Ohio, April 7, 1974; admitted to bar, 1999, Ohio. *Education:* Vanderbilt University (B.A., 1996; J.D., 1999).

SARA SIMRALL RORER, born Cincinnati, Ohio, December 6, 1953; admitted to bar, 1988, Ohio. *Education:* Miami University (B.A., 1976); University of Tennessee (M.S.S.W., 1979); University of Cincinnati (J.D., 1988).

JOSHUA A. SHAPIRO, born Cincimati, Ohio, January 21, 1972; admitted to bar, 1999, Ohio. *Education:* University of Cincinnati (B.A., 1994); Indiana University School of Law (J.D., 1999).

††††LISA L. PATTERSON, born Niagara Falls, New York, 1968; admitted to bar, 1996, Ohio. *Education:* University of Toronto (B.A., 1990); Capital University (J.D., 1995).

(This Listing Continued)

TAFT, STETTINIUS & HOLLISTER LLP, Cincinnati—Continued

J. DONALD MOTTLEY, born Alamogordo, New Mexico, August 29, 1954; admitted to bar, 1991, Ohio. *Education:* Wright State University (B.A., 1975; M.S., 1976); Salmon P. Chase College of Law (J.D., 1991).

†††ROBERT B. OWEN, born Willoughby, Ohio, October 31, 1967; admitted to bar, 2000, Ohio. *Education:* Hiram College (B.A., in Business Administration, 1995); Cleveland-Marshall College of Law (J.D., 2000).

†††PATRICK J. KREBS, born Euclid, Ohio, June 8, 1975; admitted to bar, 2000, Ohio. *Education:* Villanova University (B.A., 1997); Case Western Reserve University (J.D., 2000).

AMY C. ASHTON, born Lubbock, Texas, July 22, 1971; admitted to bar, 2000, Ohio. *Education:* Miami University (B.A., 1993); University of Virginia (J.D., 2000).

†SHELLI TURNER CLARK, born Westerville, Ohio, December 3, 1974; admitted to bar, 2000, Ohio. *Education:* Wittenberg University (B.A., 1997); The Ohio State University (J.D., 2000).

MELISSA KURZHALS COVER, born Cincinnati, Ohio, September 22, 1973; admitted to bar, 2000, Ohio. *Education:* University of Cincinnati (B.S., 1995; B.A., 1996; J.D., 2000).

DAWN R. LANDERS, born Troy, Ohio, April 26, 1973; admitted to bar, 2000, Ohio. *Education:* The Ohio State University (B.S.N., 1996; J.D., 2000).

DANIEL F. OBERKLEIN, born Cincinnati, Ohio, January 26, 1975; admitted to bar, 2000, Ohio. *Education:* Xavier University (B.S., 1997); University of Chicago (J.D., 2000).

SHARON I. SHANLEY, born Thomson, Georgia, December 1, 1961; admitted to bar, 1999, Ohio. *Education:* University of Georgia (B.A., 1982; J.D., 1985).

††J. STEPHEN SMITH, born Cincinnati, Ohio, June 17, 1966; admitted to bar, 1995, Ohio; 1996, Kentucky; 2003, Indiana. *Education:* Denison University (B.A., 1988); Patterson School of Diplomacy and International Commerce, University of Kentucky (M.A., 1990); University of Cincinnati (J.D., 1995).

RICHARD L. FERRELL, III, born Washington, D.C., October 2, 1969; admitted to bar, 1994, Ohio; 2004, Kentucky. *Education:* High Point College (B.A., 1991); University of Akron (J.D., 1994).

TAMARA A. MIANO, born Lexington, Kentucky, 1965; admitted to bar, 2001, Ohio. *Education:* Cornell University (B.S., 1998); Salmon P. Chase College of Law (J.D., 2001).

RYAN L. WILLIS, born Dayton, Ohio, January 27, 1976; admitted to bar, 2001, Ohio; registered to practice before U.S. Patent and Trademark Office. *Education:* Rose-Hulman Institute of Technology (B.S.ChE., 1998); University of Dayton (J.D., 2001).

THERESA H. VELLA, born St. Louis, Missouri, 1973; admitted to bar, 1999, Missouri; 2000, Illinois; 2001, Ohio. *Education:* Boston State College (B.A., 1995); St. Louis University School of Law (J.D., 1999).

MONICA L. GEARDING, born Dallas, Texas, April 5, 1967; admitted to bar, 1998, Ohio. *Education:* The Ohio State University (B.A., 1995); Case Western Reserve University (J.D., 1998).

†††MATTHEW T. VIOLA, born Cleveland, Ohio, November 11, 1973; admitted to bar, 2000, Ohio. *Education:* Miami University (B.S.B.A., 1996); Cleveland-Marshall College of Law (J.D., 2000).

GREGORY W. BEE, born Akron, Ohio, June 17, 1973; admitted to bar, 2002, Ohio. *Education:* Ohio University (A.B., 1995; M.A., 1997); University of Michigan (J.D., 2002).

NATASHA M. CAVANAUGH, born Cincinnati, Ohio, April 10, 1977; admitted to bar, 2002, Ohio; 2005, Florida. *Education:* Stanford University (B.A., 1999; M.A., 1999); University of Virginia (J.D., 2002).

RYAN C. EDWARDS, born Ashland, Kentucky, September 3, 1977; admitted to bar, 2002, Ohio; 2003, Kentucky. *Education:* University of Kentucky (B.A., 1999; J.D., 2002).

BRIDGET C. HOFFMAN, born Cincinnati, Ohio, February 22, 1977; admitted to bar, 2002, Ohio. *Education:* Xavier University (B.A., 1998); University of Cincinnati (J.D., 2002).

MATTHEW C. LOFTUS, born Cincinnati, Ohio, January 1, 1976; admitted to bar, 2002, Ohio. *Education:* Miami University (B.S., 1998); The Ohio State University (M.B.A., 2002; J.D., 2002).

PATRICK E. NOSER, born Mansfield, Ohio, March 12, 1976; admitted to bar, 2002, Ohio. *Education:* University of Cincinnati (B.A., 1998; J.D., 2002).

BRIE S. ROGERS, born Cincinnati, Ohio, May 26, 1978; admitted to bar, 2002, Ohio. *Education:* Auburn University (B.A., 1998); University of Cincinnati (J.D., 2002).

KATHERINE A. RUWE, born Cincinnati, Ohio, March 9, 1977; admitted to bar, 2002, Ohio. *Education:* University of Dayton (B.A., 1999); University of Cincinnati (J.D., 2002).

JILLIAN M. SUWANSKI, born Owensboro, Kentucky, September 7, 1977; admitted to bar, 2002, Ohio. *Education:* Kentucky Wesleyan College (B.A., 1999); University of Kentucky (J.D., 2002).

JULIA E. TARVIN, born Cincinnati, Ohio, October, 22, 1974; admitted to bar, 2002, Ohio. *Education:* Northern Kentucky University (B.A., 1997); Salmon P. Chase College of Law (J.D., 2002).

RACHEL S. ZAHNISER, born Campbellsville, Kentucky, December 12, 1972; admitted to bar, 1999, Kentucky; 2003, Ohio. *Education:* Centre College of Kentucky (B.A., 1994); University of Kentucky (M.S.L.S., 1995; J.D., 1999).

†††HEATHER L. TONSING, born Cleveland, Ohio, July 29, 1972; admitted to bar, 1998, Ohio. *Education:* University of Akron (B.S., 1994); Cleveland-Marshall College of Law (J.D., 1998).

(This Listing Continued)

JOHN M. MUELLER, born New York, N.Y., February 11, 1970; admitted to bar, 1997, Ohio; registered to practice before U.S. Patent and Trademark Office. *Education:* Purdue University (B.S.ChE., 1993); Indiana University (J.D., 1997).

†††ROBERT H. FISCHER, JR., born Akron, Ohio, November 19, 1973; admitted to bar, 1999, Ohio. *Education:* Ohio University (B.A., 1996); Vanderbilt University (J.D., 1999).

†††MAJEED G. MAKHLOUF, born Jerusalem, West Bank, Palestine, January 2, 1977; admitted to bar, 2001, Ohio; 2003, District of Columbia. *Education:* Hiram College (B.A., 1998); The Ohio State University (J.D., 2001).

†††KIMBERLIE L. HUFF, born Park Ridge, Illinois, April 21, 1975; admitted to bar, 2000, Ohio; 2001, Illinois. *Education:* Valparaiso University (B.A., 1996); University of Illinois (J.D., 2000).

†††LAWRENCE C. DAVISON, born Alliance, Ohio, March 29, 1966; admitted to bar, 1991, Ohio. *Education:* University of Dayton (B.S.B.A., 1988); Case Western Reserve University (J.D., 1991).

PAULA J. DEHAN, born Cincinnati, Ohio, July 9, 1963; admitted to bar, 2003, Ohio. *Education:* Xavier University (B.A., 1985); University of Cincinnati (M.B.A., 1987); Salmon P. Chase College of Law (J.D., 2003).

CATHERINE E. HOWARD, born Louisville, Kentucky, September 26, 1978; admitted to bar, 2003, Ohio. *Education:* University of Louisville (B.A., 2000); Salmon P. Chase College of Law (J.D. 2003).

BRIAN R. HYLANDER, born Waltham, Massachusetts, August 8, 1973; admitted to bar, 2003, Ohio. *Education:* Providence College (B.A., 1995); University of Michigan (J.D., 2003).

LORA N. McINTURF, born Cincinnati, Ohio, December 3, 1977; admitted to bar, 2003, Ohio. *Education:* Ohio University (B.B.A., 1999); Indiana University (M.P.A., 2000); The Ohio State University (J.D., 2003).

†BENJAMIN J. PARSONS, born Columbus, Ohio, February 16, 1978; admitted to bar, 2003, Ohio. *Education:* Miami University (B.A., 1999); The Ohio State University (J.D., 2003).

LAQUITA S. WILSON, born Louisville, Kentucky, August 30, 1978; admitted to bar, 2003, Ohio. *Education:* University of Kentucky (B.A., 2000); University of Cincinnati (J.D., 2003).

BRYAN E. WISE, born Morristown, New Jersey, March 10, 1978; admitted to bar, 2003, Ohio. *Education:* University of Notre Dame (B.A., 2000; J.D., 2003).

PATRICK G. JOHNSON, born Spokane, Washington, February 7, 1974; admitted to bar, 2003, Ohio. *Education:* University of Washington (B.A., 1996); University of Virginia (J.D., 2003).

†††PATRICIA FLEMING KREWSON, born Warren, Ohio, July 4, 1979; admitted to bar, 2003, Ohio. *Education:* Bowling Green State University (B.A., 2000); Case Western Reserve University (J.D., 2003).

KRISTEN L. SAFIER, born Ridgefield Park, New Jersey, September 9, 1977; admitted to bar, 2001, Ohio. *Education:* Miami University (B.A., 1997); University of Cincinnati (J.D., 2001).

†††ADAM D. CORNETT, born Mayfield Heights, Ohio, December 11, 1975; admitted to bar, 2004, Ohio. *Education:* College of Wooster (B.A., 1998); Cleveland-Marshall College of Law (J.D., 2004).

†††KRISTIN R. ERENBURG, born Springfield, Illinois, July 1, 1974; admitted to bar, 2004, Ohio. *Education:* University of Michigan (B.A., 1996); Cleveland-Marshall College of Law (J.D., 2004).

JOHN R. POTTER, born Ashland, Kentucky, February 25, 1978; admitted to bar, 2003, Ohio; 2005, Kentucky. *Education:* Davidson College (B.A., 2000); University of Virginia (J.D., 2003).

††††GREGORY TURNER, born Harlan, Kentucky, May 15, 1964; admitted to bar, 2001, Ohio. *Education:* University of Dayton (B.S., 1986; J.D., 2001).

BRIAN S. SETTLES, born Frankfort, Kentucky, May 17, 1979; admitted to bar, 2004, Ohio; 2005, Kentucky. *Education:* Miami University, Ohio (B.S., 2001); University of Kentucky (J.D., 2004).

MARCELLA KAY SMITH, born St. Louis, Missouri, November 19, 1978; admitted to bar, 2004, Ohio. *Education:* Miami University, Ohio (B.A., 2001); Boston University (J.D., 2004).

††††MATTHEW J. WILES, born Akron, Ohio, March 26, 1977; admitted to bar, 2002, Ohio. *Education:* Bowling Green State University (B.S., 1999); Dayton Law School (J.D., 2002).

VANESSA A. WERNICKE, born New York, N.Y., July 22, 1976; admitted to bar, 2004, Ohio. *Education:* Cornell University (B.S., 1998); University of Cincinnati (J.D., 2004).

†††KRISTI J. KMETZ, born Youngstown, Ohio, February 6, 1977; admitted to bar, 2003, Ohio. *Education:* Youngstown State University (B.A., 1999); Ohio Northern University (J.D., 2002).

†††RONN J. GEHRING, born Hubbard, Ohio, November 5, 1977; admitted to bar, 2003, Ohio. *Education:* Bowling Green State University (B.A., 2000) University of Akron (J.D., 2002).

†BARBARA A. McNEIL, born Buffalo, New York, July 19, 1948; admitted to bar, 1980, Ohio. *Education:* The Ohio State University (B.S.S.W., 1970); Capital University (J.D., 1979).

† Columbus Office
†† Covington, Kentucky Office
††† Cleveland Office
†††† Dayton Office

(This Listing Continued)

COUNSEL FOR: AK Steel Corporation; Arena Management Holdings, Inc.; Avon Products, Inc.; BASF Corporation; Belvedere Corp.; Bethesda Hospital; Blue Chip Venture Company, Ltd.; Brenntag North America, Inc.; Chiquita Brands International Inc.; Cincinnati Bengals, Inc.; Cincinnati Children's Hospital Medical Center; Cintas Corporation; CINergy Corp.; Cleveland Municipal School District; Cornerstone Brands, Inc.; David J. Joseph Company; Diebold Incorporated; Dura-Med Pharmaceuticals; Evenflo Company, Inc.; Federal Home Loan Bank of Cincinnati; Ford Motor Co.; Frisch's; Globalstar LLC; Good Samaritan Hospital; Goodyear Tire & Rubber Company; Harsco Corporation; Helena Chemical Company; Kimball International; LCA-Vision Inc./LasikPlus; Leggett & Platt, Incorporated; Messer Construction Co.; National Stock Exchange; Nissan Motor Acceptance; Riverside Radiology Associates, Inc.; Sandusky International, Inc.; State Teachers Retirement System of Ohio; Thermo Development, Inc.; The Ohio Casualty Insurance Company; University of Cincinnati; U.S. Bancorp; U.S. Bank National Association; Volocys, Inc.; Xspedius Communications LLC; Zaremba Group, LLC.

(For biographical data on all other personnel, see Covington, Kentucky, Columbus, Cleveland and Dayton, Ohio professional biographies)

TALIAFERRO, MEHLING, SHIROONI, CARRAN & KEYS, PLLC

CINCINNATI, OHIO

(See Covington, Kentucky)

Accident and Personal Injury, Automobile Negligence, Workers' Compensation, Trial Practice, Products Liability Law, FELA, Labor (Management or Employees) Law, Insurance Defense Law, Condemnation Law, Administrative Hearings and Appeals, Civil (General Civil) Practice, Uninsured Motorist, Domestic Relations Law, Criminal Law, Social Security Disability Law and Estate Planning.

THOMPSON & COMPANY, L.P.A.

Established in 1975

SOUTHAMPTON SQUARE
7434 JAGER COURT
CINCINNATI, OHIO 45230-4344
Telephone: 513-232-7576
Fax: 513-232-7654
Email: thompson@colpa.com
URL: http://www.lawyers.com/thompson

General Civil Practice including Taxation, Business Organization, Real Estate, Business Acquisitions and Sales, Estate Planning and Probate Law and Commercial Litigation.

JAMES W. THOMPSON, born Cincinnati, Ohio, March 31, 1941; admitted to bar, 1968, Ohio and U.S. District Court, Southern District of Ohio. *Education:* Kent State University (B.A., 1963); Salmon P. Chase College of Law of Northern Kentucky State College (J.D., 1968). Phi Alpha Delta. *Member:* Cincinnati and Ohio State Bar Associations. ***PRACTICE AREAS:*** Taxation; Business Organization; Business Acquisitions; Business Sales; Real Estate; Estate Planning; Probate; Commercial Litigation.

REFERENCE: Huntington National Bank, Cincinnati.

THOMPSON HINE LLP

312 WALNUT STREET, 14TH FLOOR
CINCINNATI, OHIO 45202-4089
Telephone: 513-352-6700
Fax: 513-241-4771
Email: info@ThompsonHine.com
URL: http://www.ThompsonHine.com

Cleveland, Ohio Office: 3900 Key Center, 127 Public Square, 44114-1291. Telephone: 216-566-5500. Fax: 216-566-5800. Email: info@ThompsonHine.com.
Columbus, Ohio Office: 10 West Broad Street, Suite 700, 43215-3435. Telephone: 614-469-3200. Fax: 614-469-3361. Email: info@ThompsonHine.com.
Dayton, Ohio Office: 2000 Courthouse Plaza, N.E., P.O. Box 8801, 45401-8801. Telephone: 937-443-6600. Fax: 937-443-6635. Email: info@ThompsonHine.com.
Washington, D.C. Office: 1920 N Street, N.W., Suite 800, 20036-1600. Telephone: 202-331-8800. Fax: 202-331-8330. Email: info@ThompsonHine.com.
New York, N.Y. Office: One Chase Manhattan Plaza, 58th Floor, 10005-1401. Telephone: 212-344-5680. Fax: 212-809-6890. Email: info@ThompsonHine.com.
Brussels, Belgium Office: Avenue Louise 375 - b8, 1050 Brussels, Belgium, Telephone: 011 (32-2) 626-3280. Fax: 011 (32-2) 626-3299. Email: info@ThompsonHine.com.
Atlanta, Georgia Office: Proscenium Center, Suite 1200, 1170 Peachtree Street, 30309-7673. Telephone: 404-541-2900. Fax: 404-541-2905. Email: info@ThompsonHine.com.

Administrative Law, Admiralty and Maritime Law, Agency and Distributorships, Antitrust and Trade Regulation, Aviation and Aerospace, Bankruptcy, Banks and Banking, Biotechnology, Business Law, Business Litigation, Business Regulation, Business Transactions, Closely Held Business Law, Joint Ventures, Class Actions, Commercial Law, Commercial Real Estate, Communications and Media, FCC Regulation, Computers and Software, Construction Law, Contracts, Copyrights, Corporate Law, Corporate Finance, Corporate Litigation, Corporate Tax Controversies, Debtor and Creditor, Employee Benefits, ERISA, Energy, Energy Regulation, Environmental Law, Finance, Commercial Finance, Franchises and Franchising, General Practice, Government, False Claims Act, Qui Tam Litigation, Government Contracts, Health Care, Insurance Coverage, Insurance Regulation, Intellectual Property, International Law, International Trade, Internet Law, Labor and Employment, Life Sciences, Litigation, Complex Litigation, Medicare Fraud and Abuse, Mergers, Acquisitions and Divestitures, Natural Resources, Nonprofit and Charitable Organizations, Occupational Safety and Health, OSHA, Partnership Law, Patents, Probate, Products Liability, Product Safety, Professional Liability, Public Finance, Railroad Law, Real Estate, Regulatory Law, Drug and Medical Device Regulation, Food and Drug Regulation, International Regulatory Law, Regulated Industries, Securities, Initial Public Offerings, Public Offerings, Taxation, Tax Controversies, Toxic Torts, Trade Secrets, Trademarks, Transportation, Trusts and Estates, Unfair Competition, Utility Law, White Collar Crime, Zoning, Planning and Land Use.

(This Listing Continued)

FIRM PROFILE: Established in 1911, Thompson Hine today is among the nation's largest corporate law firms and was recently selected as one of the Best Corporate Law Firms in America (in a survey of 32,000 corporate directors conducted by Corporate Board Member magazine). Thompson Hine attorneys serve some of the premier businesses in the world, including:

Alltel, Anthem Blue Cross/Blue Shield, Avery Dennison, BIC Corporation, Chiquita Brands International, Eaton Corporation, Eveready (Energizer), Ford Motor Company, Ford Motor Credit, Formica Corp., Goodrich Corporation, Goodyear Tire and Rubber Co., Hartford Insurance, Intimate Brands, Inc. (Victoria's Secret, Bath & Body Works), Jo-Ann Stores, Inc., Kelly Services, Inc., KeyCorp/KeyBank, Lexis-Nexis, The Mead Corporation, Medical Mutual of Ohio, Milacron Inc., Newell Rubbermaid, Nordson Corporation, Oglebay Norton Company, Ohio Bankers Association, Omnicare, Inc., Parker Hannifin, Polyone Corporation, Procter & Gamble, S.C. Johnson & Son, Inc., Sherwin-Williams, Smythe Cramer Co., SuperValu, Time Warner Cable, Toro Company, Verizon Wireless, and Whirlpool Corporation.

Thompson Hine attorneys provide a wide range of corporate legal services, represented by the following practice groups:

BANKRUPTCY - We represent major secured and unsecured lenders, creditors" committees, credit enhancement providers, debtors and various other parties of interest in finance transactions, workouts and bankruptcy matters.

BUSINESS LITIGATION - We represent corporate clients in a wide variety of business litigation - from corporate control contests and insurance disputes, to class actions, securities fraud, and tax controversies.

BANKING & INSURANCE - Our lawyers provide recognized experience in virtually all areas of financial institutions matters. We provide regulatory, transactional, government relations and litigation services to clients on matters related to insurance. Our clients include all types of insurance companies and other financial services organizations including large, publicly held, multinational financial holding companies; banks and thrifts; investment banking organizations; securities broker-dealers; registered investment advisor organizations; mutual funds; and mortgage banking and broker organizations.

COMMERCIAL & PUBLIC FINANCE - We handle complex commercial finance transactions (including senior debt, subordinated debt and mezzanine financing transactions and private debt placements), public finance, asset securitizations and general bank regulatory law.

COMPETITION, ANTITRUST & WHITE-COLLAR CRIME - We represent clients in antitrust and competition matters, trade restraint and price discrimination issues, franchising and distribution, misappropriation of trade secrets, false advertising, enforcement of noncompetition covenants and interference with business relationships.

CONSTRUCTION - We represent owners, design professionals, construction managers, contractors and sureties in connection with all facets of the building industry and have served in the role of Project Counsel for billions of dollars of construction at sites across the United States.

CORPORATE, M&A AND SECURITIES - We represent both emerging and established businesses in their most important business transactions, from start-up through IPOs, joint ventures, mergers, acquisitions and beyond.

eBUSINESS & EMERGING TECHNOLOGIES - This group unites experienced counsel from various disciplines around one central goal: helping business realize the opportunities and manage the risks of electronic and technological commerce.

EMPLOYEE BENEFITS - We advise clients regarding qualified, non-qualified and welfare benefit plans; resolution of controversies with the IRS, DOL, PBGC and other agencies; incentive and equity-based compensation arrangements; statutory and regulatory compliance; ERISA fiduciary duties; ESOPs; multi-employer plans; and ERISA litigation.

ENERGY - We provide a broad range of services to our clients in the energy industry, including those that: Generate and sell electric energy into the nation's wholesale and retail energy markets. Transport and sell natural gas and oil. Transmit and distribute electricity and natural gas in retail markets. Purchase natural gas, electric energy and coal. Conduct energy trading operations. Manufacture, construct and/or buy and sell facilities and assets associated with the energy industry. Undertake energy-related projects, such as distributed generation, conservation or energy management projects. Manage information used by the energy industry.

ENVIRONMENTAL - We help clients understand the environmental aspects of their business transactions, craft methods of allocating risk and counsel them on their compliance obligations under local, state and federal laws.

HEALTH CARE - We represent physician groups, hospitals, clinical laboratories, diagnostic service providers, pharmaceutical manufacturers, medical device manufacturers and health insurance providers.

INTELLECTUAL PROPERTY - We assist clients with patents, trademarks, copyrights, trade secrets, computer software, internet related issues, employment relationships and intellectual property litigation.

INTERNATIONAL - We advise clients on trade regulation issues, customs and duty matters, foreign investment and joint ventures, NAFTA matters, importing and exporting issues, intellectual property protection, and immigration matters.

(This Listing Continued)

THOMPSON HINE LLP, Cincinnati—Continued

LABOR & EMPLOYMENT - We represent clients in employment litigation, workers" compensation proceedings, immigration matters, collective bargaining, administrative proceedings before the Department of Labor, OSHA, EEOC, NLRB and various state agencies.

LIFE SCIENCES - We provide legal and regulatory management services to established and emerging companies in the food, pharmaceuticals, biotech, and medical device industries.

PERSONAL & SUCCESSION PLANNING - We assist clients in the management and transmission of wealth, the succession to the control of businesses and other personal and family concerns.

PRODUCT LIABILITY - We have handled thousands of product liability matters involving mechanical, chemical, electrical, medical, aerospace, automotive and other products.

REAL ESTATE - We represent clients in Real Estate Development; Corporate Real Estate; Zoning and Land Use; Real Estate Investment and Financing; and Real Estate Investment Trusts.

TAXATION - We counsel clients in business transactions and financings, tax controversy, litigation, legislative and regulatory activities, executive compensation and tax planning, international taxation, state and local taxation and foundation and exempt organization matters.

TELECOMMUNICATIONS - Our Telecommunications group provides clients with wide-ranging guidance on the regulations and laws affecting telecommunications, broadcasting and other electronic communications companies. Our representation includes transactional matters, regulatory compliance, telecommunications services contracting, licensing and legislative/regulatory advocacy. We also have experience in issues involving communications land use and environmental matters, including human exposure to electromagnetic energy.

TRANSPORTATION - One of the largest transportation practices in the United States, our team has more than 100 years of collective experience representing transportation interests. We are involved in matters relating to commercial relationships and arrangements as well as the extensive and complex structure of rights, remedies and regulatory requirements involved in the domestic and international transportation of goods by rail, motor, ship, barge, air and pipeline.

WORKERS COMPENSATION - We represent employers in workers" compensation matters before state courts and industrial commissions. We have extensive experience representing and counseling clients in the area of workers' compensation.

AMOS BURT THOMPSON (1871-1965)
CHARLES P. HINE (1877-1942)
WALTER L. FLORY (1880-1951)
MICHAEL L. HARDY (Partner-in-Charge, Cleveland)
PATRICIA MANN SMITSON (Partner-in-Charge, Cincinnati)
ANTHONY C. WHITE (Partner-in-Charge, Columbus)
ROBERT M. CURRY (Partner-in Charge, Dayton)
NICHOLAS J. DiMICHAEL (Partner-in-Charge, Washington, DC)
GEORGE J. WALSH III (Partner-in-Charge, New York City)
LUDO DEKLERCK (Partner-in-Charge, Brussels)
WALT A. LINSCOTT (Partner-in-Charge, Atlanta)

PARTNERS

PAUL ALLAER, born Brussels, Belgium, August 1, 1960; admitted to bar, 1986, Ohio; 1998, Brussels (Associated Member). *Education:* University of Antwerp, Belgium (B.A., 1980); University of Leuven, Belgium (J.D., 1983); Washington College of Law of American University (LL.M., in International Law, 1984); George Washington University National Law Center (M.C.L., 1986). Lecturer: "Doing Business in China", Miami Valley International Trade Association, Dayton, May 2004; "Why Invest in the US Midwest", ABN-AMRO, Amsterdam, May 2004; "Purchasing Law: International Aspects", Lorman Education Series, Cincinnati, March 2003; "Growing Your Business in China: Legal Aspects," Cincinnati, February 2003; "Global Technology Symposium," Greater Cincinnati Chamber of Commerce, August 2002; "EU Law and Business after the Euro: Perspectives from Brussels," Chicago Bar Association, Chicago, March 2002; "Data Privacy Regulations: The EU and Beyond," Cincinnati Bar Association, March 2002; "Privacy and Data Protection Law: The Emerging Frontier," Association of Corporate Counsel (SW Ohio Chapter), October 2001; "Doing Business in the European Union," Kentucky World Trade Conference, November 2000; "The Global Market Is Right Around The Corner," ABA Teleconference, April 2000; "International Contract Negotiation Essentials," Miami Valley International Trade Association, September 1999; "Legal Aspects of International Business," International Management Association, Akron-Canton Chapter, March 1999; "Preparing Your Business for the Euro," Fifth Third International Seminar Series, November 1998; "Recent Developments in EU Competition Law," ABA Section of Business Law, St. Louis, April 1998; "Legal Aspects of Selling into Mexico," Cinergy Department of Regional Development, January 1998; "Doing Business in Chile," Kentucky World Trade Conference, November 1997; "Acquisitions of European Businesses: Employment and Quasi-Employment Related Pitfalls," ABA Section of Business Law, Boston, April 1997; "International Strategic Alliances," Ohio Global Trade Conference, Columbus, December 1996. "Legal Aspects of Doing Business in Belgium," Flanders Foreign Investment Office, San Diego and Chicago, May 1996. Author: "Avoiding Global Conflicts," ABA Journal, April 2000; "Welcome to Euroland: What U.S. Lawyers Should Know About the Euro," ABA Journal, March 1999; "Cincinnati-Brussels Flight Means Export Growth," Cincinnati Business Courier, January 27, 1997; "EU Member State Liability for Non-Implementation of Directives Clarified," EuroWatch, May 3, 1996; "Sweeping Change Heralded by EU Contract Terms Directive," Corporate Counsel's International Advisor, April 1994. Honorary Consul of Belgium, 1997—. Cincinnati Academy of Leadership for Lawyers, Class of 2000. Chair, Greater Cincinnati Chamber of Commerce's International Trade Council, 2000-. Member, Greater Cincinnati Chamber of Commerce's Foreign Investment Attraction Team; Cincinnati Business Courier's "Forty Under Forty," Class of 1999. Immediate Past President, International Visitors Council of Greater Cincinnati. Secretary and Treasurer, Consular Corps of Cincinnati. Board of Advisors, EuroWatch (bi-weekly publication). *Member:* Cincinnati (Chair, International Business Law Committee, 1994-1995) and American (Chair, European Law Subcommittee of the Business Section's International Business Law Committee, 1991-2001) Bar Associations; Miami Valley International Trade Association (Board of Trustees, 2002—); Cincinnati Bar Foundation (Board of Trustees, 2003—); Northern Kentucky International Trade Association. (Also at Brussels, Belgium). ***LANGUAGES:*** Dutch, French. ***TRANSACTIONS:*** Represented a variety of public and privately-held companies relative to establishing manufacturing and distribution operations in China, some of which were structured as wholly foreign-owned enterprises (WFOEs), others as equity or coopoerative joint ventures. Represented public company in acquisition of its distributor in Mexico. Represented privately-held manufacturer in acquiring majority equity interest in its distributor in England. Assisted privately-held manufacturer in restructuring of EU-wide distributor network. Assisted public company with corporate restructuring of its foreign subsidiaries in 17 countries on four continents. Represented large privately-held manufacturer in share acquisition of company located in France. Assisted privately-held industrial manufacturer in acquisitions of substantially all of the assets of its distributor in the Netherlands. Represented public company in the establishment of a 50-50 joint venture in Mexico. Representated manufacturer in share acquisition of competitor in Belgium. Assisted privately-held company in the sale to a US public company of substantially all of its assets, including the stock of its wholly-owned subsidiaries in Germany, Mexico, Czech Republic and Sweden. Represented a variety of US companies, both public and privately-held, in the establishment of manufacturing, distribution and/or administrative headquarter operations in the European Union. Represented a variety of foreign companies, in particular from Europe, establishing manufacturing, distribution and/or administrative headquarter operations in the US, including negotiations of and assistance relative to investment incentives on local and state basis. Provide trouble-shooting analysis to numerous companies relative to the structure and operations of their international agency and distribution network. Worked with numerous client to craft tailor-made forms of international contracts that respond to the need of the business people. In addition to providing counsel relative to matters in virtually all countries located in the biggest trading areas around the world (Western Europe, Central and South American and the Far East), also have provided counsel to less traditional places of business such as Algeria, Antigua, Barbados, Bulgaria, Cayman Islands, Dominican Republic, Granada, India, Israel, Lebanon, New Zealand, Oman, Pakistan, Philippines, Poland, Romania, Russia, Saudi Arabia, St. Kitts Nevis, St. Lucia, South Africa and former Yugoslavia. ***PRACTICE AREAS:*** Corporate Law; International Law; European Union Law; Belgian Law. ***Email:*** Paul.Allaer@ThompsonHine.com

BRUCE M. ALLMAN, born McKeesport, Pennsylvania, January 11, 1943; admitted to bar, 1974, Ohio; 1999, Kentucky; U.S. District Court, Northern and Southern Districts of Ohio, U.S. District Court, Eastern and Western Districts of Kentucky and U.S. Supreme Court. *Education:* University of Cincinnati (B.S., 1971; J.D., 1974). Fellow, American College of Trial Lawyers. Listed in: *Who's Who in American Law*. Member, Center for Public Resources (N.Y. Alternate Dispute Resolution Organization). *Member:* Cincinnati, Ohio State, Kentucky and American Bar Associations; Defense Research Institute. [USNR, 1962-1964]. ***PRACTICE AREAS:*** Litigation; Mass Torts; Class Actions; Commercial; Product Liability; Personal Injury; Construction; Insurance Coverage and Insurance Bad Faith Litigation. ***Email:*** Bruce.Allman@ThompsonHine.com

CHRISTOPHER M. BECHHOLD, born New York, N.Y., January 19, 1954; admitted to bar, 1980, Ohio. *Education:* Yale University (B.A., 1977); Case Western Reserve University (J.D., 1980). *Member:* Cincinnati (Member, Litigation and Insurance Sections); Ohio State Bar Associations; Defense Research Institute; Federation of Defense and Corporate Counsel. ***PRACTICE AREAS:*** Litigation; Catastrophic Loss Law; Insurance Law; Construction Law; Products Liability. ***Email:*** Chris.Bechhold@ThompsonHine.com

DANIEL O. BERGER, born Cincinnati, Ohio, January 1, 1945; admitted to bar, 1973, Ohio. *Education:* Denison University (B.A., cum laude, 1967); University of Michigan (J.D., 1972). Phi Beta Kappa. Lecturer, Ohio Continuing Legal Education Institute. Peace Corps. Volunteer: Colombia and St. Lucia. Executive Committee, The Hill & Griffith Company. Trustee, Secretary, The Glendale Cemetery Association. Chairman, Board of Trustees, Spring Grove Cemetery and Arboretum. *Member:* Cincinnati and Ohio State Bar Associations. ***LANGUAGES:*** French and Spanish. ***PRACTICE AREAS:*** Real Estate Law; General Business. ***Email:*** Dan.Berger@ThompsonHine.com

DEBORAH S. BRENNEMAN, born Marietta, Ohio, August 8, 1962; admitted to bar, 1993, Ohio; 1994, U.S. District Court, Southern District of Ohio. *Education:* Ohio University (B.S., summa cum laude, 1983; M.A., 1984); University of Cincinnati (J.D., 1993). Order of the Coif. Editor, University of Cincinnati Law Review, 1992-1993. Author: "Sexual Harassment Claims and Ohio's Workers' Compensation Statute," University of Cincinnati Law Review, 1993; "From a Woman's Point of View: The Use of the Reasonable Woman Standard in Sexual Harassment Cases," University of Cincinnati Law Review, 1992. Presentations: "Electronic Monitoring: Big Brother or Smart Business," Thompson Hine LLP, May 2002; "So What is a Disability?: The Ever-Changing Scope of the ADA and What it Means for Employers," Thompson Hine LLP, May 2002. Board of Trustees: Cincinnati Ballet; Dominican Community Services. Member, Cincinnati Academy of Leadership for Lawyers, Class VI. *Member:* Cincinnati (Member, Women Lawyers Committee) and Ohio State Bar Associations. ***PRACTICE AREAS:*** Labor and Employment; Business Litigation. ***Email:*** Debbie.Brenneman@ThompsonHine.com

TIMOTHY R. BROWN, born Hamilton, Ohio, July 21, 1962; admitted to bar, 1987, Georgia and Ohio. *Education:* Xavier University (B.S.B.A., magna cum laude, 1984); Emory University (J.D., 1987). Recipient, Georgia Bankers' Association, Award in Estate Planning, 1987. Listed in: Ohio Super Lawyers, 2003, 2004, 2005; Best Lawyers in America, 1995—. Author: "Firms Not Providing Proper Retirement Training," Cincinnati Business Courier, 1996; "Changes in Benefits Part of Trade Treaty," Cincinnati Business Courier, 1995. Contributing Author: Welfare Benefits Guide 1990-91; Issue I; Pensions in Perspective; 3rd Edition. Lecturer: "Pension Crisis," WXVU Simply Money, 2004; "Mutual Fund Investigations & Effect on 401(K) Plans," WVXU Simply Money, 2003; "New Millenium Employment Strategies - Managing Changing Obligations and Expectations,"

(This Listing Continued)

Thompson Hine LLP, May 2002; "Post-Enron Retirement Legislation," WVXU Simply Money, 2002; "Insurance Company Demutualization and Effect on Benefit Plans," Certified Employee Benefits Specialists, March 2002; "EGTRRA" Seminar, Thompson Hine LLP, October 2001; "Basics of Client Development and Client Relations," Cincinnati Bar Association, 1996, 1997, 1998, 2000; "Employee Benefits Update," Cincinnati Chapter of OSCPA, 1998; "Participant Education," WVXU, Simply Money, 1997, 1998; "Current Retirement Plan Trends," WVXU, Simply Money, 1997; "Tax Issues in Separation Agreements & Post-Employment Health Insurance & Other Benefits," Ohio CLE Institute, 1997; "Conflicts in Employee Benefits Work," 10th Annual Cincinnati Employee Benefits Conference, 1997; "Pension Simplification," Cincinnati Chamber of Commerce Tax Legislation Update Seminar, 1997; "Pension Simplification & Health Care Legislation," Thompson Hine Seminar, 1996; "Employee Benefits Update '96 - Recent Developments and Future Trends," Cincinnati Chapter of OSCPA, 1996; "Participant Education and Plan Investments", WVXU, Simply Money, 1995; "Retirement Plan Update," Thompson Hine and Society National Bank Seminar, 1995; "401(k) Plans - The Next Generation," Thompson Hine, WVXU and Financial Group, Ltd. Seminar, 1995; "Introduction to Qualified Retirement Plans and Overview of ERISA" Cincinnati/Dayton Chapter of International CEBS Society; 1994, 1996; "Overview of Qualified and Non-Qualified Retirement Plans," Cincinnati Chapter of OSCPA, 1994, 1995; "Maximizing Owner Benefits Through Qualified and Non-Qualified Retirement and Health Care Plans," Ohio CLE Institute, Summer Tax Institute, 1994; "1994 Employment Law and Employee Benefit Issues: A Checklist Approach to Compliance," Thompson Hine Seminar, 1994; "What You Need to Know About Current Compliance Issues When Working With Qualified Plans and How to Design Alternate Plans to Maximize Your Client's Wealth," Cincinnati Chapter of IAFP, 1994; PNC Bank "Money Matters" Seminar Series; "Retirement Planning," 1993; PNC Bank "For Your Financial Health" Seminar Series; "Retirement Plans for Professional Businesses," 1993; "Qualification Requirements for Retirement Plans," Dayton Bar Association, 1993. Member, Personnel Committee, 1988-2002; Chairman, 1997-2000, Cincinnati Area Chapter of the American Red Cross. Volunteer, Member, 1996 Abracadabra Fundraiser Committee, Cincinnati Playhouse in the Park. Member, Sparkle Fundraiser Committee, Cystic Fibrosis Foundation, 2002, 2003, 2004. *Member:* Cincinnati (Chair, Employee Benefits Committee, 1995-1997; Member, Continuing Legal Education Advisory Committee, 1997-1998; Member, BLAC-CBA RoundTable, 1990-1994; Co-Chair, 9th Annual Cincinnati Employee Benefits Conference, 1996) and American (Member, Tax Section and Employee Benefits Committee) Bar Associations; State Bar of Georgia. (Practice Group Leader, Employee Benefits & Executive Compensation). ***PRACTICE AREAS:*** Taxation Law; Employee Benefits Law. ***Email:*** Tim.Brown@ThompsonHine.com

STEPHEN J. BUTLER, born Cincinnati, Ohio, January 5, 1952; admitted to bar, 1977, Ohio; 1978, U.S. District Court, Southern District of Ohio and U.S. Court Appeals, Sixth Circuit; 1979, U.S. Tax Court. *Education:* St. Joseph's College (B.A., magna cum laude, 1974); University of Cincinnati (J.D., 1977). Order of the Coif. Editor-in-Chief, University of Cincinnati Law Review, 1976-1977. *Member:* Cincinnati (Member, Judicial Candidate Rating Committee), Ohio State and American (Member, Litigation and Antitrust Section) Bar Associations. ***PRACTICE AREAS:*** Commercial Litigation; Antitrust Law; Competition; Business Litigation. ***Email:*** Steve.Butler@ThompsonHine.com

FRANK D. CHAIKEN, born Cincinnati, Ohio, July 18, 1960; admitted to bar, 1987, Pennsylvania and New Jersey; 1994, Ohio; 1998, Kentucky. *Education:* Harvard College (A.B., 1983); Boston College (J.D., magna cum laude, 1987). Member, Boston College Law Review. Member, Cincinnati Academy of Leadership for Lawyers (CALL), Class of 1998. "Choice of Business Entities in Ohio", Lorman Education Services, Fall 2003; Moderator, Midwest International Law Conference, Cincinnati, Ohio, Spring 2002. Author: "Mergers & Acquisitions", Doing Business in and with the United States, Thompson Hine LLP, 1999; "Terms of Trade" Newsletter, Huntington Bank, 1998; Revised Contracts Chapter, Couse's Ohio Form Book, 1997; "Going Global" Article Series, Cincinnati Business Courier, 1995-1998. Lecturer: "Buying and Selling a Business in Ohio," Lorman Education Services, July 2000; "Enforcement of Judgments Across Borders," Cincinnati Bar Association, International Law Committee, April 2000; Cincinnati Bar Association, Corporate Counsel Committee, Mergers and Acquisitions, 1998; Client Briefing on Foreign Corrupt Practices, Thompson Hine LLP, 1997. Founding Member: Kentucky German Business Council; Japan America Society of Greater Cincinnati; Board of Advisors, University of Cincinnati College of Business Administration, Center for Global Competitiveness; Schools Committee, Harvard Club of Cincinnati; Former Trustee, Cincinnati Chapter, American Jewish Committee. Trustee: Vocal Arts Ensemble of Cincinnati; World Affairs Council of Greater Cincinnati; Isaac M. Wise Temple. *Member:* Cincinnati (Past Chair, International Law Committee, 2000-2002), Ohio State, Kentucky and American (Member, Business and International Law Sections) Bar Associations. ***LANGUAGES:*** German. ***TRANSACTIONS:*** Acquisition of stock of consumer products distribution company by US subsidiary of European public company; advised Asia-Pacific company in proposed auction of business; purchase of manufacturing business in Europe by US public company; purchase of US packaging machinery manufacturer by UK public company; acquisition of industrial and consumer products businesses by NYSE corporation; acquisition of plastics manufacturing businesses in Germany; purchase and sale of numerous industrial knife and saw manufacturing and servicing businesses; purchase of US software development and licensing business by UK public company; sale of industrial products divisions by NYSE company; acquisition of institutional pharmacies by NYSE company; joint ventures in Asia, Latin American and Europe; production and technology licensing agreements; software license, development and servicing agreements; employment and consulting agreements; business organizations and financing; private placements; product distribution and sales representation agreements. ***PRACTICE AREAS:*** International Joint Ventures; Commercial Contracts; Agency and Distributorships; Business Formation; Business Organization; Business Transactions; Buying and Selling of Businesses; Closely Held Corporations; Contracts; Corporate Law; International Business Law; Joint Ventures; Limited Liability Company Law; Mergers, Acquisitions and Divestitures; Strategic Alliances; International Commercial Contracts. ***Email:*** Frank.Chaiken@ThompsonHine.com

WILLIAM H. CORDES, born Cincinnati, Ohio, December 13, 1945; admitted to bar, 1973, Ohio. *Education:* University of Michigan (B.B.A., magna cum laude, 1968; J.D., magna cum laude, 1973). Order of the Coif. Member, University of Michigan Law Review. Lecturer: "How to Choose the Right Business Structure," Ohio CLE Institute seminar, 1993, 1994; New Business Seminar Series, Greater Cincinnati Chamber of Commerce,

(This Listing Continued)

1990. Former Vice Chairman and Trustee, Cincinnati Ballet Company. Trustee, Greater Cincinnati Arts and Education Center. Former Trustee, Cincinnati Nature Center. Education Committee, Former Trustee, Greater Cincinnati Chamber of Commerce. Member, Leadership Cincinnati, 1985-1986. *Member:* Cincinnati (Securities Law Committee); Ohio State (Member, Corporate Law Section) and American (Member, Corporation, Banking and Business Law Section) Bar Associations. ***LANGUAGES:*** French. ***PRACTICE AREAS:*** Corporate Law; Securities Law. ***Email:*** William.Cordes@ThompsonHine.com

SCOTT B. CROOKS, born Cincinnati, Ohio, March 9, 1943; admitted to bar, 1968, Ohio; 1969, U.S. Tax Court. *Education:* University of Michigan (B.A., cum laude, 1965; J.D., 1968). Listed in: *Best Lawyers in America,* 1999-2000, 2001-2002. Author: "Productivity Correlates Highly with Employee Ownership", The Business Record, 1995. Contributing Author, Seaver; Ohio Corporation Law. Lecturer: "Compensation and Benefits Provisions of the Taxpayer Relief Act of 1997," Ohio Society of Certified Public Accountants, 1998; "Corporate Governance in ESOP Companies," National Center for Employee Ownership, 1994; "How ESOP's Work," National Center for Employee Ownership, 1993, 1995, 1998. Chairman, City of Wyoming Economic Development Commission. Trustee, President and Secretary, Wyoming School Foundation. Member, Past Chairman, Midwest Benefits Conference. Member, National Center for Employee Ownership. *Member:* Cincinnati (Member: Taxation Committee; Employee Benefits Committee); Ohio State and American (Member, Employee Benefits Committee; Taxation Section; Real Property, Probate and Trust Law Section; Litigation Committee on Pretrial Practice Discovery Section; Labor and Litigation Section) Bar Associations; The ESOP Association. ***PRACTICE AREAS:*** Employee Benefits; Employee Stock Ownership Plans; Executive Compensation. ***Email:*** Scott.Crooks@ThompsonHine.com

RENEE S. FILIATRAUT, born Dearborn, Michigan, July 21, 1963; admitted to bar, 1988, Ohio; 1999, Kentucky. *Education:* University of Michigan (A.B., with distinction, 1985); State University of New York at Buffalo (J.D., 1988). *Member:* Cincinnati Bar Association, Board Of Directors;(Member, Women Lawyers Committee); Cincinnati Bar Foundation, Board of Directors: Ohio State and Kentucky Bar Associations; Black Lawyers Association of Cincinnati Roundtable (Member and Co-Chair, Retention Committee). ***PRACTICE AREAS:*** Business Litigation; Insurance Law; Health Care; Environmental Litigation. ***Email:*** Renee.Filiatraut@ThompsonHine.com

JACK F. FUCHS, born Cincinnati, Ohio, August 21, 1952; admitted to bar, 1982, Ohio; 1992, Kentucky. *Education:* University of Chicago (B.A., 1974); University of Cincinnati (M.A., 1976; J.D., 1982). Order of the Coif. Lead Articles Editor, University of Cincinnati Law Review, 1981-1982. Author: "The Cash Balance Controversy: Fitting Square Pegs Into Round Holes" Federal Tax Mgmt. Mem. (Dec. 1, 2003); "Federalizing State Law Tort and Contract Claims," 39 Fed B. News & J. 582 (Nov. 1992). Comment, "Exhaustion of State Administrative Remedies in Section 1983 Actions," Cincinnati Law Review, 1982. Note, "Rhode Island v. Inglis," Cincinnati Law Review, 1981. Lecturer, "ERISA Litigation in Ohio," NBI, Nov. 2000; "ERISA Subrogation," KATA, May 2002; "ERISA Ethics," IRS-CBA, May 2003. *Member:* Cincinnati, Ohio State, Federal and American (Joint Committee on Employee Benefits; Professional Liability Committee) Bar Associations. ***REPORTED CASES:*** Ramsey v. Formica Corp., 398 F.3d 421 (6th Cir. 2005); Tolton v. Ohio Biodyne, Inc., 48 F.3d 937 (6th Cir. 1994); Washburn v. UNUM Life Ins. Co., 43 F. Supp. 2d 848 (S.D. Ohio 1998); Ratliff Enterprises, Inc. v. American Employers Ins. Co., 334 Ark. 547, 975 S.W.2d 837 (1998); Aetna Cas. & Surety Co. v. Ply Gem Indus., Inc., 343 N.J. Super. 430, 778 A.2d 1132 (N.J. App. 2001); Countrymark Cooperative, Inc. v. Smith, 124 Ohio App. 3d 159, 705 N.E.2d 738 (1997), cert. denied, 81 Ohio St. 3d 1496, 691 N.E.2d 1058 (1998). ***PRACTICE AREAS:*** ERISA Litigation (65%, 20); Professional Liability (20%, 3); Litigation (5%, 3); Labor and Employment (5%, 3); Employee Benefits (5%). ***Email:*** Jack.Fuchs@ThompsonHine.com

JANE E. GARFINKEL, born New York, N.Y., December 2, 1952; admitted to bar, 1980, Ohio; 1997, Kentucky. *Education:* Dartmouth College (Rufus Choate Scholar, 1972-1973); Wheaton College, Massachusetts (B.A., summa cum laude, 1974, Phi Beta Kappa); University of Michigan (M.A., 1975; J.D., cum laude, 1979). Lecturer: "The Emergency Medical Treatment and Active Labor Act (EMTALA)," Academy of Medicine of Cincinnati and Cincinnati Bar Association, September 16, 1999; "The Limitations of Pap Smears and the Significance of Clinical Findings in the Diagnosis of Cervical Dysplasia—A Legal Perspective," Health Alliance of Cincinnati, October 18, 2000; "Risk Management for Health and Fitness Professionals—Avoiding Liability for Personal Injuries," Alliance of Cincinnati Hospitals, March 16, 2000; "Healthcare Law Update," Healthcare Financial Management Association of Ohio; "Transmittal of Diagnostic Information—Is it the Unauthorized Practice of Medicine?" Client Seminar; "Alternative Dispute Resolution in Lease Disputes - Panacea or Pandora's Box?" International Council of Shopping Centers; "Tax Appeals in Ohio—A Fistful of Dollars," Institute of Real Estate Management. Presenter: "HIPAA Update," Labor and Employment Seminar, May 2002; "Doctor-Pharmacy Rep Guidelines Not Panacea," Cincinnati Business Courier, June 24, 2002; "After Lease Breach, Landlord Required to Find New Tenant," Cincinnati Business Courier, August 8, 2003. *Member:* Cincinnati, Ohio State and Kentucky Bar Associations; American Health Lawyers Association. ***LANGUAGES:*** French. ***PRACTICE AREAS:*** Litigation; Commercial Law; Malpractice Law; Real Estate; Health Care Law; Trade Secret Litigation; Products Liability Litigation. ***Email:*** Jane.Garfinkel@ThompsonHine.com

KENNETH B. GERMAIN, born New York, N.Y., September 16, 1945; admitted to bar, 1970, California; 1988, District of Columbia; 1989, Ohio. *Education:* Rutgers College (A.B., magna cum laude, 1966); New York University School of Law (J.D., 1969). Recipient, American Jurisprudence Prizes for Excellence. Listed in: The Best Lawyers in America, 1991-1992 and all later editions; Listed in: Marquis' Who's Who in America Law; Marquis' Who's Who in the World; Guide to the World's Leading Experts in Trade Mark Law, 1996—; Who's Who Legal, An International Who's Who of Trademark Lawyers; Chambers USA America's Leading Lawyers for Business, 2004—. Associate Editor, New York University Law Review. Over 20 Legal Publications and over 190 Professional Lectures. Adjunct Professor, University of Cincinnati College of Law, 1988—. Member, Board of Advisors: Restatement (Third) of Unfair Competititon, 1987-1992; Patent, Trademark and Copyright Journal (BNA), 1987—. Founder and Chair, All Ohio Annual Institute on Intellectual Property, 1990—. Member: Board of Directors, United States Trademark Association, 1990-1992; Cincinnati Intellectual Property Law Association, 1988—; CPR/INTA Panel of Neutrals, 2000—; Advisory Council, J. Thomas McCarthy Center for Intel-

(This Listing Continued)

THOMPSON HINE LLP, Cincinnati—Continued

lectual Property and Technology Law, 2001—*Member:* Cincinnati and Ohio State Bar Associations; State Bar of California; District of Columbia Bar; Cincinnati Intellectual Property Law Association; International Trademark Association. ***PRACTICE AREAS:*** Trademarks (90%); Unfair Competition (10%). ***Email:*** Ken.Germain@ThompsonHine.com

GARY M. GLASS, born Perth Amboy, New Jersey, June 25, 1964; admitted to bar, 1989, Ohio; 1995, Kentucky. *Education:* Colgate University (B.A., cum laude, 1986); University of Notre Dame (J.D., 1989). Member: Colgate University Alumni Fund Raising Committee; United Way Volunteer Leadership Development Program. Board of Trustees: Enjoy the Arts; At. Aloysius Orphanage. *Member:* Cincinnati (Member, Admissions Committee), Ohio State and Kentucky Bar Associations; Defense Research Institute. ***TRANSACTIONS:*** Representation of manufacturers of automobiles, asbestos-containing products, construction and industrial machinery, and food preparation equipment in product liability cases; Representation of numerous insurers in coverage, policy construction, and bad faith litigation; Representation of various manufacturers in all types of business litigation, including U.C.C., warranty, consumer sales practices and contract disputes; Representation of health, life and disability insurers in cases stemming from claims determinations; Representation of employers in intentional tort cases involving product injuries; Representation of employers in OSHA cases involving machine guarding issues. ***PRACTICE AREAS:*** Products Liability; Business Litigation. ***Email:*** Gary.Glass@ThompsonHine.com

ROBERT P. JOHNSON, born Blacksburg, Virginia, September 5, 1963; admitted to bar, 1988, Ohio; 1996, Kentucky, U.S. District Court, Southern District of Ohio and U.S. Court of Appeals, Sixth Circuit; U.S. District Court, Eastern and Western Districts of Kentucky. *Education:* College of William and Mary (B.A., 1985); Vanderbilt University (J.D., 1988). Author: "Rethinking 'Narrowing the ERISA Preemption': A Defense Perspective," Mealey's Managed Care Liability Report, October 8, 1999; "Liability issues confront insurers, employers," Cincinnati Business Courier, January 20, 2000. Lecturer: "Premises and Workplace Liability: Legal Issues," Thompson Hine LLP, AON Risk Services and the Payne Firm, Inc., Risk Management for Business: Issues and Strategies, 1996. *Member:* Cincinnati, Kentucky, Ohio State and American Bar Associations. ***REPORTED CASES:*** Lenning v. Commercial Union Ins. Co., 260 F.3d 574 (6th Cir 2001); GTE Wireless of the Midwest Inc. v. Anderson Township, 134 Ohio App 3d 352, 731 NE2d 201 (1999); Sammarco v. Anthem Ins. Cos., 131 Ohio App 3d 544, 723 NE2d 128 (1998). ***PRACTICE AREAS:*** Business Litigation; Commercial Litigation; Insurance Coverage and Defense; ERISA; Health Care Litigation; Products Liability. ***Email:*** Rob.Johnson@ThompsonHine.com

STEPHEN M. KING, born Christchurch, New Zealand, October 18, 1960; admitted to bar, 1985, Ohio. *Education:* Washington and Lee University (B.A., 1982); Ohio State University (J.D., 1985). Approved Speaker, Practicing Law Institute. President, Board of Directors, Ensemble Theatre. Member, Steering Committee, Cincinnati District Council for Urban Land Institute. *Member:* Cincinnati (Past Chairman, Real Property Law Section), Ohio State and American Bar Associations. ***PRACTICE AREAS:*** Commercial Real Estate; Banks and Banking; Energy. ***Email:*** Steve.King@ThompsonHine.com

THOMAS J. KIRKWOOD, born Buffalo, New York April, 27, 1949; admitted to bar, 1974, Ohio, U.S. District Court, Southern District of Ohio and U.S. Tax Court; 1990, Kentucky and U.S. District Court, Eastern District of Wisconsin. *Education:* Michigan State University; University of Cincinnati (B.A., 1971); University of Cincinnati College of Law (J.D., 1974). Editor, University of Cincinnati Law Review, 1973-1974. Author: "The Cost Effective Solution of Dispute Resolution," Allied Construction Industries 'Cincinnati Constructor', Seminar, 1999; "Private Mediation Can Save Time and Money," Cincinnati Business Courier, 1997; "Records Retention & The Ten Year Statute," The Cincinnati Constructor, 1994; "Waters and Watercourses - Public Trust Doctrine," New Jersey Law Journal, 1973. Lecturer: "Ohio Builds 2002: Project Close Out"; "Designer-Led Design Build," Cincinnati Large A-E Firms, Seminar; 1999; "Risk Management," Home Builders Association of Greater Cincinnati, Seminar, 1998. Presenter: "Construction Law," Cincinnati Bar Association, 2000; "Can this Project be Saved? Delay Damages and Differing Site Conditions," Cleveland Construction Contracting Community, Seminar; 1998, 1999, 2001. "Construction Partnering," 9th Biennial Midwest/Midwouth Construction Law Institute, January 2003. Member: Board of Trustees, Cincinnati Nature Center; Board of Trustees, Center for Resolution of Disputes; Construction Partnering Facilitation. Certified Mediator, CPR Institute for Dispute Resolution, 1996. *Member:* Northern Kentucky, Cincinnati, Kentucky, Ohio State and American (Member, Forum on the Construction Industry) Bar Associations. ***PRACTICE AREAS:*** Construction Law (30%); Construction Litigation (40%); Construction Mediation and Facilitation (30%). ***Email:*** Tom.Kirkwood@ThompsonHine.com

BRENDA M. KLOOS, born Lansing, Michigan, March 3, 1956; admitted to bar, 1982, Ohio; 1983, U.S. Tax Court. *Education:* Alma College (B.A., magna cum laude, 1978); University of Dayton School of Law (J.D., summa cum laude, 1982). *Member:* Cincinnati (Former Chair, Estates and Trusts Section; Former Chair, Estate Planning Institute Committee), Ohio State and American Bar Associations. ***PRACTICE AREAS:*** Trusts and Estates; Charitable Planning; Retirement Planning. ***Email:*** brenda.kloos@thompsonhine.com

ANDREW L. KOLESAR, born Cincinnati, Ohio, August 31, 1958; admitted to bar, 1990, Pennsylvania; 1991, District of Columbia; 1994, U.S. District Court, District of Columbia; 1996, Ohio; 2000, Kentucky. *Education:* Virginia Military Institute (B.S., Distinguished Graduate, 1981); Ohio State University (M.S., 1983); Georgetown University (J.D., cum laude, 1990). Practice Group Leader. Phi Kappa Phi; Tau Beta Phi. Associate Editor, Georgetown Law Journal. Author: "Get a Grip on Liabilities for Contaminated Sites - Cleanup Costs Can Haunt Failed Businesses," Cincinnati Business Courier, July 13, 2001; "Buying and Selling Brownfield Properties: A Practical Guide for Successful Transactions," Northern Kentucky Law Review, 2000; "Implementing an EMS Could Be Best Defense," Cincinnati Business Courier, May 5, 2000; "Superfund Liability Net Expands," Butler-Warren Business Journal, Feb. 1999; "Internal Investigations of Potential Criminal Misconduct Under Environmental Laws," Environment Reporter, February 3, 1995; "Proposed Rule Regarding Post-Closure Care at RCRA Interim Status Facilities: A Step in the Right Direction," EPA Administrative Law Reporter, January 1995; "Criminal Procedures Project - Right to Counsel," Georgetown Law Journal, 1988-1989. Board of Trustees, Montessori Center Room, Cincinnati Ohio. Advisory Board, Talbert House, Cincinnati, Ohio. Lecturer: Environmental Issues in Property Development - National Business Institute, August 21, 2002; Managing the Risks of Toxic Mold in Buildings - Lorman Seminar, August 6, 2002; Mold Litigation and Risk Management Issues - Cincinnati Exchange Club, June 19, 2002; Voluntary Reporting of Non-Compliance: Strategies to Minimize Liabilities - Annual Business & Industry's Environmental Symposium, March 21, 2002; Brownfields, Voluntary Action Program and Issue 1 - Ohio Municipal League Annual Conference, October 10, 2001; Voluntary Action Program and Brownfields Development - The Mayors Association of Ohio Annual Conference, May 24, 2001; Avoiding OSHA Citations and Liabilities in Ohio - Lorman Education Services, February 8, 2001; Ohio Land Use: Current Issues in Subdivision Annexation and Zoning Law, Environmental Concerns for Developers - National Business Institute, October 19, 2000; Buying and Selling Brownfield Properties: Cleaning Up After the Closing - Annual Business & Industry's Environmental Symposium, March 23, 2000; Superfund Current Developments - OSBA Environmental Seminar, March 11, 1999; Proactively Managing Compliance - Annual Business & Industry's Environmental Symposium, April 1998. *Member:* Cincinnati and Ohio State Bar Associations; District of Columbia Bar. ***PRACTICE AREAS:*** Environmental; OSHA. ***Email:*** Andrew.Kolesar@ThompsonHine.com

EARLE JAY MAIMAN, born Scranton, Pennsylvania, October 21, 1948; admitted to bar, 1981, Ohio; 2000, Kentucky. *Education:* Ohio University (B.S., 1970); University of Wisconsin-Milwaukee (M.A., 1973); University of Cincinnati (J.D., 1981). Order of the Coif. Member, University of Cincinnati Law Review. Civil Service Commission, Maderia, Ohio. *Member:* Cincinnati, Kentucky, Ohio State and American Bar Associations. ***PRACTICE AREAS:*** Business Litigation; Product Liability; Health Care; Insurance. ***Email:*** Earle.Maiman@ThompsonHine.com

MELVIN E. MARMER, born Salisbury, Maryland, May 8, 1933; admitted to bar, 1962, Maryland; 1966, Ohio. *Education:* University of Maryland (B.S., 1955; M.B.A., 1957); George Washington University (LL.B., 1962). Certified Public Accountant, Maryland, 1960. *Member:* Cincinnati, Ohio State and American Bar Associations. ***PRACTICE AREAS:*** Personal Planning; Successions; Closely Held Businesses; Employee Benefit Law; Estate Planning; Professional Corporations Law; Taxation. ***Email:*** Mel.Marmer@ThompsonHine.com

WILLIAM L. MARTIN, JR., born Cincinnati, Ohio, November 4, 1946; admitted to bar, 1971, Ohio. *Education:* College of the Holy Cross (B.A., 1968); University of Cincinnati (J.D., 1971). Speaker, Continuing Education Issues, Professional Development Seminars. Member, Collaborative Law Group. President and Board Member, Children, Inc. *Member:* Cincinnati and Ohio State Bar Associations. ***PRACTICE AREAS:*** Real Estate Law; Corporate Law; Domestic Relations Law; Estate Planning. ***Email:*** William.Martin@ThompsonHine.com

DONALD S. MENDELSOHN, born Cincinnati, Ohio, October 24, 1949; admitted to bar, 1975, Ohio and U.S. District Court, Southern District of Ohio. *Education:* Yale University (B.A., magna cum laude, 1971); Stanford University (J.D., 1975). Phi Beta Kappa (1970). Student Marshall (1971). *Member:* Cincinnati and American (Member: Committee on Federal Regulation of Securities; Subcommittee on Investment Companies and Investment Advisers) Bar Associations. ***PRACTICE AREAS:*** Investment Company Law; Investment Adviser Law; Securities Law; Corporate Law; Business Law; Mergers and Acquisitions. ***Email:*** Don.Mendelsohn@ThompsonHine.com

MICHAEL J. NIEBERDING, born Cincinnati, Ohio, May 13, 1968; admitted to bar, 1994, Ohio; registered to practice before U.S. Patent and Trademark Office. *Education:* University of Dayton (B.S.E.E., cum laude, 1990); University of Cincinnati (J.D., 1994). Tau Beta Pi; Eta Kappa Nu. Recipient, American Jurisprudence Award in Real Estate Transactions. Member, Board of Directors, mscenter, 2004—. *Member:* Cincinnati Bar Association; American Intellectual Property Law Association; Cincinnati Intellectual Property Law Association; Dayton Intellectual Property Law Association. ***PRACTICE AREAS:*** Intellectual Property (100%). ***Email:*** Mike.Nieberding@ThompsonHine.com

MICHAEL R. OESTREICHER, born Cincinnati, Ohio, June 20, 1950; admitted to bar, 1976, New York; 1978, Ohio;. *Education:* Miami University (B.A., 1972); Boston University (J.D., 1975). Author: "Drafting International Technology License Agreements," *Negotiating and Structuring International Commercial Transaction,* ABA (1991, 1999, 2003); "International Technology License Agreements," in Counseling Emerging Companies in Going International, ABA (1994). Board of Advisers, *International Quarterly;* "Politics may be new but it's business as usual in Japan," Cincinnati Business Courier, Sep 27 - Oct 3, 1999; "Twilight Zone cases on agents, distributors," Cincinnati Business Courier, November 14-20, 1994; "Joint ventures can work with focus on long term," Cincinnati Business Courier, March 6-12, 1995; "Don" Cincinnati Business Courier, July 4-10, 1994; "Italy" Cincinnati Business Courier, January 23-29, 1995; "Winning the 'race' of global economy not an easy task," Cincinnati Business Courier, February 16-22, 1987; "Vietnam: Door is now open, but going through it isn't," Cincinnati Business Courier, Feb 28 - Mar 6, 1994. "Legal Due Diligence Checklist - International Acquisitions," Corporate Counsel's International Advisor, Business Laws, Inc., December 1, 1995; "Foreign investments needed for area's future economic health," Cincinnati Business Courier, April 6-12, 1987. Lecturer: "Legal: Tax and Policy Consideration," International Software and Hardware Marketing Seminar, International Computer/Software Executives Association, Inc., November 9, 1988; "Negotiating and Drafting Technology Transfer and Design and Development Agreements," ABA National Institute on Negotiating and Drafting International Commercial Transactions: A Case Study with Sample Documents, November 8-9, 1990; "Marketing Through Agents and Distributors," World Trade Association and the Cincinnati Bar Association, Introduction to Legal Aspects of International Trade and Investment, May 24, 1988; "Technology Transfer - Who's Doing What to Whom?" Joint Meeting of the Dayton Council on World Affairs and the Miami Valley International Trade Association, May 20, 1987; "Letters of Credit - Legal Issues" Bank One, Dayton, NA Standby Letter of Credit Seminar, September 28, 1988, March 16, 1989; "Doing Business in the U.K.," sponsored by Clark, Schaeffer, Hackett & Co., June 27, 1995; "Transactions Involving the Japanese," Current International Issues for Corporate Counsel with Emphasis on Joint Ventures and Other Strategic Alliances, Continuing Legal Education Satellite Network Program, June 27, 1990; "International Technology Transfers and Intellectual Property Law Regimes," Counseling Emerging Companies in Going International, ABA Section of Business Law,

(This Listing Continued)

Section of International Law and Practice, May 9, 1991, June 20, 1991; "Intellectual Property Licensing and Transfers," ABA National Institute on Negotiating and Structuring International Commercial Transactions, June 10-11, 1999; "Formalizing the Agent/Distributor Relationship," International Marketing through Agents and Distributors, International Management Training Institute, World Trade Association/Greater Cincinnati Chamber of Commerce, February 18, 1988; "Expanding Internationally Through Foreign Acquisitions," Midwest Conference on International Law, 1995; "International Joint Ventures and Strategic Alliances," Miami Valley International Trade Association, 1994; "How Do Clients View Global Expansion With Limited Resources and How Does the Service Professional Position Himself to Fulfill These Needs?" The Continental Association of CPA Firms/Intercontinental Accounting Associates Convention, 1992; "Expanding Internationally - Strategies for the Company With Limited Resources," World Trade Association, 1991; "U.S. and Foreign Legal Considerations - A Case Study," World Trade Association's International Strategic Planning Seminar, 1989; "Patterns of Success and Failures of Doing Business in China," International Management Training Institute, China Trade Seminar & Workshop, 1988; "Economic Development and Export Promotion: A Private Sector Perspective," National Conference of State Legislatures, International Trade Committee Annual Meeting, 1987; "Distributorship Agreements," United States Department of Commerce International Trade Administration Midwestern Conference on Legal Aspects of International Business, 1985. Board of Trustees, Past President, Isaac M. Wise Temple. Emeritus, Cincinnati Board of Overseers, Hebrew Union College - Jewish Institute of Religion. Past Chairman, International Law Committee of the Cincinnati Bar Association, 1987-1990. Member, Board of Trustees: Cincinnati State Technical and Community College; Jewish Cemeteries of Greater Cincinnati. *Member:* Ohio State and American Bar Associations. (Member, Executive Committee). ***PRACTICE AREAS:*** International Law; Corporate Law; Intellectual Property. ***Email:*** Michael.Oestreicher@ThompsonHine.com

KIMBERLY E. RAMUNDO, born Covington, Kentucky, December 23, 1971; admitted to bar, 1996, Ohio; 1998, U.S. District Court, Southern District of Ohio; 2001, U.S. Court of Appeals, Sixth Circuit; 2002, Kentucky and U.S. District Court, Eastern District of Kentucky. *Education:* Miami University (B.A., cum laude, 1993); University of Cincinnati (J.D., cum laude, 1996). Member: Board of Directors and Officer (Secretary), Tallstacks Music Arts & Heritage Festival; Cincinnati Academy of Leadership for Lawyers, 2003; YWCA Rising Star, 2003. *Member:* Cincinnati, Ohio State and American Bar Associations. ***PRACTICE AREAS:*** Construction Law; Business Litigation; Copyright Infringement Litigation. ***Email:*** Kim.Ramundo@ThompsonHine.com

STEPHEN L. RICHEY, born Cincinnati, Ohio, August 12, 1946; admitted to bar, 1993, Ohio, U.S. District Court, Northern and Southern Districts of Ohio and U.S. Court of Appeals, Sixth Circuit; 2000, Kentucky; U.S. District Court, Eastern District of Kentucky. *Education:* Xavier University (B.A., cum laude, 1969; M.Ed., summa cum laude, 1979); Chase College of Law (J.D., summa cum laude, 1993). Law Clerk, Honorable S. Arthur Spiegel, U.S.D.C., S.D.Ohio. Author: "Episcopal Retirement Homes, Inc. v. Ohio Dept. Of Industrial Relations; Judicial Rehearing in the Ohio Supreme Court," Northern Kentucky Law Review; 1992; "Employers' Responsibilities and Duties to Today's Citizen Soldier," Employee Relations Law Journal, Vol. 29, No. 4, Spring 2004; "Employers' Responsibilities and Duties to Today's Citizen Soldiers," Month's Feature Article, Cincinnati Bar Assn. Report, Jan. 2005; "Drafting Effective Non-Compete Agreements," Cincinnati Business Courier, Sept. 9, 2005. Lecturer: "How to Avoid Liability When Hiring and Firing," March 2000; "ADA, FMLA and Workers' Compensation Seminar," June 2000; "Buying and Selling a Business in Ohio," July 2000; "Wage and Hour Law Update," February 2001; "Treating Employees with Dignity and Respect," February 2001; "Family and Medical Leave Act in Ohio," April 2001; "Disability Discrimination," March 2002; "Ohio Public Employment Law Conference," April 2002; "New Millennium Employment Strategies," May 2002; "Managing Employee Relationships in Ohio," September 2002; "Best Practice in FMLA Administration," January 2003; "Proposed Changes to FLSA," June 2003; "Avoiding Liability in Hiring and Firing," September 2003; "ADA, FMLA and Workers' Compensation," Feb. 2004; "Non-Compete Agreements and Injunctive Relief," April 2004; "Changes to 'White Collar' Regulations," Sept. 2004; "Workplace Violence," Sept. 2004; "Exempt or Non-Exempt, Applying the New Wage and Hour Regulations to Your Workplace," May 2005. Mediator, U.S.D.C. S.D.Ohio; Adjunct Faculty, Chase College of Law; Member, Local Rules Committee, U.S.D.C., S.D.Ohio; General Counsel, Children's Meeting House Montessori School. *Member:* Cincinnati (Member, Employment Law Group), Ohio State and Federal (Member, Executive Committee) Bar Associations; Greater Cincinnati Human Resources Association; Potter Stewart Inns of Court. ***LANGUAGES:*** French and Latin. ***REPORTED CASES:*** Ramsey v. Formica Corporation, U.S. Dist. LEXIS 9558, 33 Emp. Ben. Cases (BNA) 1095 (S.D. Ohio 2004); D.E.I., Inc. v. Ohio & Vicinity Reg'l Council of Carpenters, 2004 U.S. Dist. LEXIS 886 (N.D. Ohio 2004); Cervantes v. Sugar Creek Packing Co., 210 F.R.D. 611 (S.D. Ohio 2000); Shepherd v. Babcock & Wilcox of Ohio, 2000 U.S. Dist LEXIS 6349 (S.D. Ohio 1998). ***PRACTICE AREAS:*** Labor and Employment Law; Litigation. ***Email:*** Stephen.Richey@ThompsonHine.com

DOUGLAS D. ROBERTS, born Hamilton, Ohio, May 5, 1963; admitted to bar, 1989, California; 1993, Ohio; 1994, U.S. District Court, Southern District of Ohio; U.S. District Court, Central, Northern, Southern and Eastern Districts of California and U.S. Court of Appeals, Sixth and Ninth Circuits. *Education:* John E. Dolibois European Center, Luxembourg City, Luxembourg (1983-1984); Miami University (A.B., magna cum laude, 1985); University of California, Los Angeles (J.D., 1988). Phi Beta Kappa; Phi Kappa Phi; Pi Sigma Alpha; Phi Eta Sigma; Alpha Lambda Delta. Member, Moot Court Honors Program, 1986. Recipient, University of California, Los Angeles Chancellor's Marshal Award, 1988. Member and Executive Editor, Pacific Basin Law Journal, 1985-1988. Intern: European Community Secretariat of the European Parliament, Trade Division, Luxembourg, 1983-1984; and U.S. Securities and Exchange Commission, Division of Enforcement, Washington, D.C., 1987. *Member:* Cincinnati Bar Association; State Bar of California. ***LANGUAGES:*** French. ***Email:*** Doug.Roberts@ThompsonHine.com

ROBERT A. SELAK, born Wheeling, West Virginia, September 5, 1954; admitted to bar, 1979, Ohio. *Education:* Wheeling Jesuit College (B.S., 1976); Harvard University (J.D., 1979). *Member:* Cincinnati (Member, Admissions Committee), Ohio State and American (Member: Business Law Section, Urban, State and Local Government Law Section) Bar Associations; National Association of Bond Lawyers. ***PRACTICE AREAS:*** Public Finance; Structured Finance. ***Email:*** Bob.Selak@ThompsonHine.com

(This Listing Continued)

GERALD W. SIMMONS, born Oak Park, Illinois, January 11, 1943; admitted to bar, 1967, Ohio; 1974, U.S. Supreme Court; 1986, U.S. Tax Court. *Education:* Georgetown University (A.B., 1964); Yale University (LL.B., 1967). *Member:* Cincinnati and Ohio State Bar Associations. [U.S. Army, 1967-1969; resigned as a Captain in Military Intelligence; served one year in Vietnam]. ***TRANSACTIONS:*** Complex securities litigation for client Gulf & Western; statewide multiple accounting malpractice claims for client Grant Thornton. ***PRACTICE AREAS:*** Complex Litigation; Civil Litigation; NASD Arbitration; Securities Fraud Arbitration; Antitrust; Business Combinations; Covenants Not To Compete; Labor and Employment. ***Email:*** Jerry.Simmons@ThompsonHine.com

PATRICIA MANN SMITSON, born Glasgow, Kentucky; admitted to bar, 1977, Ohio. *Education:* University of Cincinnati (B.A., 1967; J.D., 1977). Partner-in-Charge, Cincinnati Office. Phi Beta Kappa. Recipient: Leading Women of Cincinnati Award, 1997; YWCA Career Women of Achievement Award, 1999. Presenter: University of Cincinnati College of Law Fourteenth Annual Corporate Law Symposium, *Corporate Law Firms in the 21st Century,* March 9, 2001; "Choice of Law and the Corporate Law Firm"; Education Finance Council/NCHELP Student Loan Finance Legal Issues Conferences: 2001 Meeting, "Understanding the Unique Legal and Financing Characteristics of Private Student Loans"; 2002 Meeting, "Current Topics Relating to Corporate Governance and Board Liability Issues". Member: Board of Trustees, United Way of Greater Cincinnati, 2002—; Board of Directors, Downtown Cincinnati Inc., 2001—; Public Affairs Council, Greater Cincinnati Chamber of Commerce, 2002—; Leadership Cincinnati, Class XVII; Board of Visitors, University of Cincinnati College of Law, 1992—; Board of Directors, National Speaking of Women's Health, 1999—. Board of Trustees, Ohio Legal Assistance Foundation, 2000—; May Festival Board of Trustees,1997—; Member, Board of Directors, 1989-1997 and President, 1995-1997, YWCA of Cincinnati. Member, YWCA Academy of Career Women of Achievement, 1999—. *Member:* Cincinnati, Ohio and American (Member, Business Law Section) Bar Associations; National Association of Bond Lawyers. (Partner-in-Charge). ***LANGUAGES:*** French. ***TRANSACTIONS:*** Representation of student loan originators and secondary markets on matters relating to federally guaranteed student loan program and private consumer loans; Representation of student loan authorities in connection with conversions from tax-exempt status to for profit status, including making an election under Section 150(d) of the Internal Revenue Code; Representation of issuers of tax-exempt and taxable student loan obligations; Representation of underwriters in connection with issuance of student loan asset-backed securities; Representation of clients in connection with conduit warehousing facilities, lines of credit, letters of credit and interest rate protection products. ***PRACTICE AREAS:*** Corporate; Securities; Commercial Finance; Public Finance. ***Email:*** Trish.Smitson@ThompsonHine.com

LOUIS F. SOLIMINE, born New York, N.Y., August 30, 1952; admitted to bar, 1976, Ohio. *Education:* Wright State University (B.A., summa cum laude, 1973); University of Cincinnati (J.D., 1976). Listed in Best Lawyers in America, 1994-2003. Executive Editor, University of Cincinnati Law Review. Tri-State Chapter, Turnaround Management Association. Arbitration Panel, Chairman, National Association of Securities Dealers (NASD). Arbitration Panel, Chairman, Hamilton County Court of Common Pleas. Past Vice Chairman and Secretary, St. Ursula Villa School. *Member:* Cincinnati (Member, Corporate and Securities Law Committee; Bankruptcy Committee) and Ohio State Bar Associations. ***PRACTICE AREAS:*** Corporate Law; Commercial Law; Bankruptcy Law; Creditors Rights. ***Email:*** Louis.Solimine@ThompsonHine.com

KEITH P. SPILLER, born Georgetown, Ohio; admitted to bar, 1989, Ohio; 2000, Kentucky. *Education:* Miami University (B.A., 1986); Wake Forest University (J.D., 1989). Lecturer: "Labor and Employment Law Update," Thompson Hine LLP, May 25, 2005; "Labor and Employment Law Update," Thompson Hine LLP, May 27, 2004; "Labor and Employment Law Update," Thompson Hine LLP, June 19, 2003; "Managing Employee Relationships in Ohio," September 13, 2002; "Labor Law Update," Thompson Hine LLP, May 23, 2002; "The Family and Medical Leave Act," ADP Users Group Meeting, March 21, 2002; "How to Write and Implement Effective Employee Handbooks and Human Resources Policies," May 23, 2000; "Defending Against the "New" Labor Movement," July 27, 1999; "Employee Discharge and Documentation in Ohio," June 2, 1999; "The Family and Medical Leave Act and The Americans With Disabilities Act: An Overview of Recent Developments," Employment and Labor Law Seminar, Washington, D.C., January 29, 1999; Various client seminars on the Family and Medical Leave Act, Sexual Harassment, Union Avoidance, Role of Documentation in the Employment Process. *Member:* Cincinnati, Kentucky and Ohio State Bar Associations; Defense Research Institute. ***TRANSACTIONS:*** First-chair jury trial experience in various discrimination and wrongful discharge litigation in both federal and state courts; Substantial experience in counseling employers on defeating unionization attempts; Defending charges of discrimination filed with the Equal Employment Opportunity Commission and other state organizations such as the Ohio Civil Rights Commission; Handling grievances and arbitrations for unionized employers, as well as the defense of unfair labor practice charges before the National Labor Relations Board; Serving as Management's Chief Spokesperson during union negotiations for initial and subsequent collective bargaining agreements; Designing and assisting in the implementation of various workplace policies, including drug and alcohol testing, medical exams, hiring protocol, severance and reduction-in-force plans; Advising employers on compliance with affirmative action obligations, including the design and drafting of affirmative action plans and the defense of OFCCP compliance and glass-ceiling audits; General counseling of human resource professionals concerning all aspects of employment, such as wage and hour compliance, trade secrets and competition, and disciplinary issues. ***PRACTICE AREAS:*** Employment Discrimination (30%); Union Labor Law (30%); Affirmative Action (20%); Competition (10%); Wage and Hour Law (5%); Wrongful Termination (5%). ***Email:*** Keith.Spiller@ThompsonHine.com

J. SHANE STARKEY, born East Liverpool, Ohio, November 28, 1969; admitted to bar, 1995, Florida; 1996, Ohio. *Education:* Wittenberg University (B.A., magna cum laude, 1992); University of Cincinnati (J.D., 1995); University of Florida (LL.M., Taxation, 1997). Author: "Tax Treatment of Employee Stock Options in Mergers and Acquisitions," 90 Tax Notes 1231, February 26, 2001. Committee Member, Southwestern Ohio Tax Institute. *Member:* Cincinnati, Ohio State and American Bar Associations; The Florida Bar. ***PRACTICE AREAS:*** Taxation; Executive Compensation. ***Email:*** Shane.Starkey@ThompsonHine.com

JOANN M. STRASSER, born Cincinnati, Ohio, June 12, 1959; admitted to bar, 1994, Ohio. *Education:* University of Cincinnati (B.U.P., magna cum laude, 1982; J.D., 1994).

(This Listing Continued)

THOMPSON HINE LLP, Cincinnati—Continued

Board of Trustees, Greater Cincinnati Mutual Association, 2002—. *Member:* Cincinnati and Ohio State Bar Associations. ***PRACTICE AREAS:*** Investment Company Law; Investment Management; Investment Partnerships; Investment Regulation; Mutual Funds; Securities; Corporate Law; Business Law. ***Email:*** JoAnn.Strasser@ThompsonHine.com

JOHN H. WENDELN, born Dayton, Ohio, May 6, 1959; admitted to bar, 1984, Ohio. *Education:* University of Dayton (B.S., Accounting, 1981; J.D., 1984); Law Review, University of Dayton School of Law; Author: Interest-Free Loans: The Court of Claims Attempts to Correct Dean - Hardee v. United States, 8 U. Dayton L. Rev. 377 (1983). Recipient, Burton Award for Legal Achievement, 2002. Member, University of Dayton Law Review, 1982-1983. Certified Public Accountant, Ohio (inactive). Author, "Interest-Free Loans: The Court of Claims Attempts to Correct Dean - Hardee v. United States," 8 U. Dayton L. Rev. 377 (1983). Co-Author: "IRS Issues New Proposed Regulations Simplifying Minimum Distribution Rules," The Banking Law Journal (March 2001); "The Cash Balance Controversy: Fitting Square Pegs Into Round Holes," BNA Tax Management Memorandum (2003). National Panelist, "A Second Look at the Cash Balance Proposed Regulations: What Do They Really Mean?" ABA Joint Committee on Employee Benefits (JCEB) Teleconference Program, 2003. Adjunct Instructor, CEBS Employee Benefit Courses, 2004-2005. Former Chair, Member, Benefits Committee, Ohio Society of CPAs, 1994-2002. *Member:* Cincinnati (Former Chairman, Employee Benefits Committee), Ohio State and American (Member, Tax Section; Employee Benefits Committee) Bar Associations. ***TRANSACTIONS:*** Co-Author: IRS Issues New Proposed Regulations Simplifying Minimum Distribution Rules, The Banking Law Journal (2001); Burton Award for Legal Achievement (2002); National Panelist: A Second Look at the Cash Balance Proposed Regulations: What Do They Really Mean?, ABA Joint Committee on Employee Benefits (JCEB) Teleconference Program (2003); Co-Author: The Cash Balance Controversy: Fitting Square Pegs Into Round Holes, BNA Tax Management Memorandum (2003). ***PRACTICE AREAS:*** Employee Benefits Law. ***Email:*** John.Wendeln@ThompsonHine.com

RODNEY M. YOUNG, born Tokyo, Japan, August 26, 1960; admitted to bar, 1994, Indiana; 1995, Ohio; U.S. Court of Appeals, Federal Circuit; registered to practice before U.S. Patent and Trademark Office. *Education:* University of Alabama (B.S.M.E., 1982); Salmon P. Chase College of Law (J.D., 1994). Member, Leadership Cincinnati. *Member:* Ohio State, National and American Bar Associations; American Intellectual Property Law Association; Cincinnati Intellectual Property Law Association; Black Lawyers Association of Cincinnati; Cincinnati Academy of Leadership for Lawyers. ***PRACTICE AREAS:*** Intellectual Property. ***Email:*** Rodney.Young@ThompsonHine.com

DEBORAH A. YOUTSEY, admitted to bar, 1985, Connecticut; 1988, Ohio. *Education:* Kenyon College (A.B., 1978); Western New England College, School of Law (J.D., 1985). *Member:* American Immigration Lawyers Association; National Association of Foreign Student Advisors. ***PRACTICE AREAS:*** Immigration Law. ***Email:*** Debbie.Youtsey@ThompsonHine.com

ASSOCIATES

GARY D. BLACHMAN, born Glenridge, New Jersey, December 25, 1965; admitted to bar, 1994, Illinois; 1995 Ohio and New Jersey. *Education:* Rutgers University (B.A., 1987); City of University of New York, Bernard Baruch College (M.B.A., 1991);John Marshall Law School (J.D., 1994). Phi Alpha Delta (Marshall). Vice President, Moot Court Board. Secretary, International Law Society. Lecturer: QDROs and Other Pension Law Issues," Toledo Bar Association, 2000. Member: ASPA Benefits Council of Greater Cincinnati; Great Lakes TE/GE Council; Midwest Benefits Conference. Ohio State Leader and Secretary, Board of Directors, Juvenile Diabetes Research Foundation. *Member:* Cincinnati (Chair, Employee Benefits Committee) and Ohio Bar Associations. ***PRACTICE AREAS:*** Employee Benefits; ERISA; Tax Law. ***Email:*** Gary.Blachman@ThompsonHine.com

BRET F. BUSACKER, born 1970; admitted to bar, 2000, Ohio. *Education:* Brigham Young University (B.A., 1995); Washington State University (M.B.A., 1997); The Ohio State University (J.D., 2000). *Member:* Cincinnati, Ohio State and American Bar Associations. ***LANGUAGES:*** Italian. ***Email:*** Bret.Busacker@ThompsonHine.com

ERIN C. CHILDS, born Chicago, Illinois, 1977; admitted to bar, 2002, Ohio and U.S. District Court, Southern District of Ohio 2004, U.S. Court of Appeals, Sixth Circuit. *Education:* Saint Louis University (B.A., 1998); University of Cincinnati (J.D., 2002). Court Appointed Special Advocate, ProKids. *Member:* Cincinnati (Secretary, Young Lawyers Division), Ohio State and American Bar Associations. ***PRACTICE AREAS:*** Business Law. ***Email:*** Erin.Childs@ThompsonHine.com

ERIC S. CLARK, born 1974; admitted to bar, 1999, Ohio; 2001, Massachusetts. *Education:* John Carroll University (B.S., 1996; B.A., 1996); University of Cincinnati College of Law (J.D., 1999). Presentations: "Using Alternative Dispute Resolution in Employment Matters," sponsored by AAA; "Drafting an Alternative Dispute Resolution Program," sponsored by Nixon Peabody; "Reductions in Force: The Selection Process," sponsored by Thompson Hine LLP; "Drafting Employee Relations Documents," sponsored by Sterling Group. *Member:* Cincinnati, Ohio State and Massachusetts Bar Associations. ***PRACTICE AREAS:*** Alternative Dispute Resolution; Civil Practice; Class Actions; General Practice; Labor and Employment; Litigation; Unfair Competition. ***Email:*** Eric.Clark@ThompsonHine.com

JEFFREY M. CLARKE, born May 22, 1969; admitted to bar, 1999, Ohio and U.S. District Court, Northern District of Ohio; 2000, U.S. Court of Appeals, Sixth Circuit. *Education:* University of Cincinnati (B.A., 1992); Case Western Reserve University (J.D., cum laude, 1999). *Member:* Ohio State and American Bar Associations. ***PRACTICE AREAS:*** Corporate Transactions; Securities; Commercial Finance; Public Finance. ***Email:*** Jeffrey.Clarke@ThompsonHine.com

JOHN P. COLBERT, born Euclid, Ohio, June 19, 1971; admitted to bar, 1996, Ohio; 1999, U.S. District Court, Southern District of Ohio; registered to practice before U.S. Patent and Trademark Office. *Education:* Ohio University (B.S., Chemistry, summa cum laude, 1993); University of Dayton (J.D., 1996). Phi Beta Kappa. *Member:* Cincinnati Bar Association; Cincinnati Intellectual Property Association. ***PRACTICE AREAS:*** Intellectual Property; Chemical Patents; Chemical Patent Prosecution; Trademarks; Trademark Licensing; Domain Names. ***Email:*** John.Colbert@ThompsonHine.com

(This Listing Continued)

JOHN COTTINGHAM, admitted to bar, 2002, New York; 2005, Ohio. *Education:* University of Michigan (B.S.E., cum laude, 1991); New York University (J.D., 2001). [Lieutenant, U.S. Navy, 1990-1998]. ***TRANSACTIONS:*** EMC's $1.9 billion 2004 acquisition of Documentation; Sprint's $35 billion 2004 tracking stock recombination; PricewaterhouseCoopers Consulting's $3.5 billion 2002 sale to IBM; Cherokee International's $110 million 2004 initial public offering; Research in Motion's $1.0 billion 2004 secondary common stock offering. ***PRACTICE AREAS:*** Mergers and Acquisitions; Private Equity; Public Company Finance; Public Finance; Investment Company Representation; Corporate. ***Email:*** John.Cottingham@ThompsonHine.com

MATTHEW CURRAN, born Cincinnati, Ohio, February 10, 1975; (admission pending). *Education:* Indiana University (B.A., 1997); Boston College Law School (J.D., 2003). *Member:* Cincinnati and Ohio State Bar Associations. ***PRACTICE AREAS:*** Commercial Litigation; Commercial Torts. ***Email:*** Matt.Curran@ThompsonHine.com

CHRISTOPHER ELSWICK, admitted to bar, 2002, Massachusetts; 2005, Ohio; registered to practice before U.S. Patent and Trademark Office. *Education:* University of Kentucky (B.S., Mechanical Engineering, 1998); The Ohio State University (J.D., 2002). *Member:* American Intellectual Property Law Association. ***PRACTICE AREAS:*** Patents. ***Email:*** Christopher.Elswick@ThompsonHine.com

BETH FREEMAL, born Cincinnati, Ohio, July 6, 1968; admitted to bar, 1997, Illinois; 2005, Ohio. *Education:* Northwestern University (B.S., 1990); Chicago-Kent University College of Law (J.D., with high honors, 1997). Order of the Coif. Editor-in-Chief, Chicago-Kent Law Review, 1996-1997. *Member:* Illinois State Bar Association. ***PRACTICE AREAS:*** Finance; Corporate. ***Email:*** Beth.Freemal@ThompsonHine.com

DIANE M. GODERRE, born Kettering, Ohio, September 21, 1971; admitted to bar, 1998, Ohio and U.S. District Court, Southern District of Ohio. *Education:* University of Cincinnati (B.A., 1993; J.D., 1998). Member, Moot Court Board, 1997-1998. Student Articles Editor, University of Cincinnati Law Review, 1997-1998. Author, "International Negotiations Gone Sour: Precontractual Liability Under the United Nations Sales Convention," University of Cincinnati Law Review, Vol. 66:1. *Member:* Cincinnati Bar Association Federal Bar Association. ***PRACTICE AREAS:*** Business Litigation. ***Email:*** Diane.Goderre@ThompsonHine.com

JAMES HOUSTON, born Cincinnati, Ohio, October 30, 1971; admitted to bar, 2000, Ohio and U.S. District Court, Southern District of Ohio. *Education:* Miami University (B.A., History, 1994); University of Dayton (J.D., cum laude, 2000). Executive Editor, University of Dayton Law Review, 1999-2000. Member, BEAM Committee, Lighthouse Youth Services. *Member:* Cincinnati (Member: Ethics Committee; Young Lawyers Section; Secretary, Construction Law Committee; Co-Chair, Mock Trial Competition), Ohio State and American Bar Associations. ***PRACTICE AREAS:*** Commercial Litigation; Construction Litigation. ***Email:*** James.Houston@ThompsonHine.com

JENNIFER KINNEN, born Middleburg Heights, Ohio; admitted to bar, 2002, Ohio and U.S. District Court, Southern District of Ohio. *Education:* The Ohio State University (B.A., magna cum laude, 1999); University of Cincinnati (J.D., 2002). Order of the Coif. Associate Member, 2000-2001 and Student Articles Editor, 2001-2002, University of Cincinnati Law Review. Member, Editorial Staff, Human Rights Quarterly, 1999. *Member:* Cincinnati, Ohio State and American Bar Associations. ***PRACTICE AREAS:*** Commercial Real Estate; Commercial Law; Finance; Construction Law. ***Email:*** Jennifer.Kinnen@ThompsonHine.com

BRYCE A. LENOX, born Cincinnati, Ohio, September 23, 1971; admitted to bar, 1998, Ohio and U.S. District Court, Southern District of Ohio. *Education:* University of Notre Dame (B.B.A., 1993); University of Dayton (J.D., cum laude, 1998). Executive Editor, University of Dayton Law Review, 1997-1998. Author: Casenote, "Personal Jurisdiction in Cyberspace: Teaching the Stream of Commerce Dog New Internet Tricks," 22 University of Dayton Law Review 331. Author, Comment, "Genetic Discrimination in Insurance and Employment: Spoiled Fruits of the Human Genome Project," 23 University of Dayton Law Review 189. *Member:* Dayton, Cincinnati, Ohio State and Federal Bar Associations. ***PRACTICE AREAS:*** Litigation. ***Email:*** Bryce.Lenox@ThompsonHine.com

ERIN M. MANAHAN ALKIRE, born Sacramento, California, April 14, 1976; admitted to bar, 2001, Ohio; 2002, Kentucky; U.S. Court of Appeals, Sixth Circuit; U.S. District Court, Northern and Southern Districts of Ohio; U.S. District Court, Eastern and Western Districts of Kentucky. *Education:* Clemson University (B.A., 1998); College of William & Mary (J.D., 2001). ***PRACTICE AREAS:*** Litigation. ***Email:*** Erin.Alkire@ThompsonHine.com

KELLY L. REBLIN, born Berea, Ohio, March 29, 1971; admitted to bar, 1997, Ohio; 2002, Virginia. *Education:* Baldwin-Wallace College (B.A., cum laude, 1993); St. Mary's University of San Antonio (J.D., 1997). Phi Delta Phi. Staff Writer, 1995-1996 and Symposium Editor, 1996-1997, St. Mary's Law Journal. Author: "Inadequate Fiduciary Guidance on Adequate Consideration," Newsletter, Mid-Atlantic Chapter of the ESOP Association, Spring 2002; "Mandatory Coverage for Prescription Contraceptives," News & Notes, Hampton Roads Society for Human Resource Management, March 2002; "NAFTA and the Environment: Dealing with Abnormally High Birth Defect Rates in Texas-Mexico Border Towns," 27 St. Mary's L.J. 4 (1996). *Member:* Cincinnati Bar Association. ***PRACTICE AREAS:*** Employee Benefits (100%). ***Email:*** Kelly.Reblin@ThompsonHine.com

DAVID A. RINES, born 1966; admitted to bar, 1995, Connecticut; 1998, Massachusetts; 2004, Ohio. *Education:* University of Notre Dame (B.S., with high honors, 1989); University of Virginia (J.D., 1995). American Bar Association Ohio State Bar Association Cincinnati Bar Association. ***PRACTICE AREAS:*** Corporate Transactions; Securities; Business Formation; Business Organization; Business Start-Ups; Business Transactions; Limited Liability Company Law; Emerging Growth Companies; Joint Ventures; Pass-Through Entities; Commercial Transactions; Sale of Goods; Commercial Contracts; Closely Held Corporations; Corporate Contracts; Corporate Finance; Corporate Formation; Corporate Governance; Corporate Organization; Corporate Partnerships; Incorporation; Public Corporations; Equity Finance; Private Finance; Limited Partnerships; Partnership Formation; Partnership Organization; Blue Sky Law; Initial Public Offerings; Private Placement; Securities Disclosure; Securities Offerings; Securities Registration; Securities Regulation; Shareholder Agreements; Mergers and Acquisitions; Business Acquisitions; Business Divestitures; Private Equity; Venture Capital. ***Email:*** David.Rines@ThompsonHine.com

(This Listing Continued)

JEFFREY L. STAINTON, born Dixon, Illinois, February 25, 1965; admitted to bar, 1997, Ohio. *Education:* Northwestern University (B.A., 1987); Xavier University (M.B.A., 1993); University of Cincinnati (J.D., 1997). ***PRACTICE AREAS:*** Mergers, Acquisitions and Divestitures (40%); Commercial Finance (40%); Corporate Law (20%). ***Email:*** Jeff.Stainton@ThompsonHine.com

KIMBERLY D. WILCOXON, born Newport News, Virginia, November 16, 1976; admitted to bar, 2001, Ohio. *Education:* Miami University (B.A., 1998); University of Cincinnati College of Law (J.D., 2001). *Member:* Cincinnati and Ohio State Bar Associations. ***PRACTICE AREAS:*** Employee Benefits. ***Email:*** Kim.Wilcoxon@ThompsonHine.com

DAVID WILLBRAND, born Cambridge, Massachusetts, May 11, 1970; admitted to bar, 1996, Ohio; 1998, Colorado. *Education:* Harvard College (A.B., 1992); University of Cincinnati College of Law (J.D., 1996). ***PRACTICE AREAS:*** Corporate Law; Business Law; Computers and Software; Contracts; Intellectual Property. ***Email:*** David.Willbrand@ThompsonHine.com

M. SCOTT YOUNG, born San Jose, Costa Rica, February 22, 1967; admitted to bar, 1993, Ohio; 1994, U.S. District Court, Northern District of Ohio; 1995, U.S. Court of Appeals, Sixth Circuit; 1997, U.S. District Court, Northern District of New York; 2004, U.S. Court of Appeals, Federal Circuit and U.S. District Court, Southern District of Ohio. *Education:* St. John's College (B.A., 1989); Case Western Reserve University (J.D., 1993). *Member:* Cincinnati, Ohio State and American Bar Associations; Ohio Self-Insuring Association. ***REPORTED CASES:*** State ex rel. Sysco Food Service of Cleveland, Inc. v. Industrial Commission of Ohio (2000), 89 Ohio St. 3d 612; State ex rel. LTV Steel Co. v. Industrial Commission of Ohio, et al. (1999), 85 Ohio St. 3d 75; State ex rel. Hillside Dairy Co. v. Conrad (1999), 84 Ohio St. 3d 314; State, ex rel. Eaton Corporation v. Industrial Commission of Ohio, et al. (1998), 83 Ohio St. 3d. 330; State, ex rel. Eaton Corporation v. Industrial Commission of Ohio, et al. (1997), 80 Ohio St. 3d 352; F. Buddie Contracting Ltd., et al. v. Cuyahoga Community College District, et al. (N.D. Ohio 1998), 31 F. Supp. 2d 584; F. Buddie Contracting Ltd., et al. v. Cuyahoga Community College District, et al. (N.D. Ohio 1998), 31 F. Supp. 2d 571. ***PRACTICE AREAS:*** Workers Compensation; Labor and Employment; Litigation; Insurance Defense; Transportation. ***Email:*** Scott.Young@ThompsonHine.com

OF COUNSEL

JAMES J. CROWE, born New Castle, Pennsylvania, June 9, 1935; admitted to bar, 1963, Virginia; 1966, Ohio. *Education:* Youngstown State University (B.A., 1958); Georgetown University (J.D., 1963). Counsel, Kepley, Gilligan & Eyrich, 1996-2000. Vice President, Secretary and General Counsel, U.S. Shoe Corporation, 1972-1995. Senior Attorney, Eaton Corporation, 1968-1972. Corporate Attorney, General Tire & Rubber Co., 1965-1968. Attorney, U.S. Securities and Exchange Commission, 1963-1965. *Member:* Cincinnati Bar Association; American Society of Corporate Secretaries. [Lt. U.S. Army, 1958-1959]. ***PRACTICE AREAS:*** General Corporate; Mergers and Acquisitions; Securities; Arbitration. ***Email:*** James.Crowe@ThompsonHine.com

LISA MAY EVANS, born Birmingham, Alabama, August 11, 1963; admitted to bar, 1994, Ohio; 1999, U.S. District Court, Southern District of Ohio. *Education:* Howard University; University of Cincinnati (B.A., Communications, 1985); Salmon P. Chase College of Law (J.D., cum laude, 1994). Member, Ohio Inns of Court, 1992-1993. Chase College of Law Representative, Student Bar Association, 1992-1993. Member, Class of 2000, Cincinnati Bar Association Academy of Leadership for Lawyers. Named YWCA Rising Star, 2002. Nominee, Cincinnati Business Courier 40 Over 40, 2002. Listed in Who's Who Among Black Cincinnatians, 2005. Recipient: Marcus Darby Award for Dedication to Advocacy, 1994; Academic Scholarships Award, 1991-1994. Student Articles Editor, 1993-1994 and Member, Salmon P. Chase Law Review. Member, Board of Directors: Volunteer Lawyers Project, 1999-2002; Millcreek Valley Restoration Project, 2002. Employment Counsel, 2002-2004 and Human Resources Director, 2004-2005, Sara Lee Corporation. Member, Board of Trustees, 2003-2005, Member, Board of Directors, Central Clinic, 2003-2005 and Chair, Domestic Violence in the Workplace Committee, 2004-2005, Cincinnati YWCA. Formerly with: Dinsmore & Shohl; Santen & Hughes. *Member:* Cincinnati, Ohio State and American Bar Associations. ***LANGUAGES:*** Spanish. ***REPORTED CASES:*** Wade v. General Electric, 1997 U.S. Dist. LEXIS 23752 (S.D. Ohio 1997); Bector v. Harte Hanks Marketing, 1998 U.S. App. LEXIS 23727 (4th Cir. 1998); Talbott v. Anthem Blue Cross and Blue Shield of Ohio, 147 F.Supp 2d 860 (S.D. Ohio 2001). ***PRACTICE AREAS:*** Civil Practice; Civil Rights Defense; Discrimination; Labor and Employment; Employment Defense; Class Action Defense; Mediation; Arbitration; Alternative Dispute Resolution. ***Email:*** LisaMay.Evans@ThompsonHine.com

LEONARD S. MERANUS, born Newark, New Jersey, January 7, 1928; admitted to bar, 1954, Ohio; 1955, U.S. District Court, Southern District of Ohio; U.S. Court of Appeals, Sixth Circuit. *Education:* Rutgers University (Litt.B., magna cum laude, 1948); Harvard Law School (LL.B., cum laude, 1954). Co-Editor, Law and the Writer, Writers Digest Books,1978, 1981 and 1985. Trustee, Secretary/Treasurer, The Andrew Jergens Foundations, 1962-1996. Past Chairman, Past Trustee, The Jewish Hospital Of Cincinnati. *Member:* Cincinnati, Ohio State and American (Member, Business Law) Bar Associations; American Arbitration Association (Member, Regional Advisory Council; Chairman, Commercial Arbitration Committee of the Regional Advisory Council; Member, Ohio Advisory Committee for Large, Complex Cases; Member, Large, Complex Case Arbitration Panel). ***LANGUAGES:*** French. ***PRACTICE AREAS:*** Business Law; Corporate Law; Securities; Mergers and Acquisitions. ***Email:*** Leonard.Meranus@ThompsonHine.com

SENIOR ATTORNEY

LISA M. WHARTON, born Ames, Iowa, October 10, 1956; admitted to bar, 1988, California; 1992, Ohio; 1999, Kentucky. *Education:* Wheaton College (B.A., 1977); Fuller Theological Seminary; Santa Clara University (J.D., 1987). *Member:* Cincinnati and Kentucky Bar Associations; State Bar of California. ***PRACTICE AREAS:*** Real Estate. ***Email:*** Lisa.Wharton@ThompsonHine.com

(For complete biographical data on Lawyers in Offices other than Cincinnati, see Professional Biographies at the Respective Office Location)

MARK T. TILLAR

105 EAST MAIN STREET, SUITE 202
CINCINNATI, OHIO 45040
Telephone: 513-770-0264
Fax: 513-770-0267
Email: info@marktillar.com
URL: http://www.marktillar.com

Criminal Law, DUI/DWI, Entertainment, Sports and Leisure Law, White Collar Crimes, Domestic Violence.

MARK T. TILLAR, born Cincinnati, Ohio, September 15, 1955; admitted to bar, 1985, Ohio; 1986, U.S. District Court, Southern District of Ohio; 2004, U.S. Court of Appeals, 6th Circuit. *Education:* University of California, at Berkeley (B.A., Political Science, 1981); University of Puget Sound (J.D., 1985). *Member:* Cincinnati and Ohio State Bar Associations; Washington State Bar Associations. ***PRACTICE AREAS:*** Criminal Law.

TRIONA CALDERHEAD & LOCKEMEYER

2909 VERNON PLACE
CINCINNATI, OHIO 45219
Telephone: 513-569-9999
Fax: 513-569-9998

Milford, Ohio Office: 200 Techne Center Drive, Suite 100, 45150. Telephone: 513-576-1060.

Medical Malpractice Defense, Professional Liability, Appellate Practice, Civil Litigation, Insurance Defense, Health Care, Consumer Law Defense, Negligence Defense, Family Law, Criminal Law, Entertainment Law.

DAVID C. CALDERHEAD, born Mansfield, Ohio, July 30, 1961; admitted to bar, 1987, Ohio; 1990, U.S. District Court, Southern District of Ohio; 1995, Kentucky. *Education:* Taylor University (B.A., 1983); Cleveland-Marshall College of Law (J.D., cum laude, 1987). *Member:* Cincinnati, Clermont County, Kentucky and Ohio State Bar Associations. (Also Member, Calderhead Law Office, LLC). ***PRACTICE AREAS:*** Medical Malpractice Defense; Professional Liability; Appellate Practice; Civil Litigation; Insurance Defense; Health Care; Consumer Law Defense.

MEMBERS OF FIRM

JAMES P. TRIONA, born Mount Clemens, Michigan, February 3, 1953; admitted to bar, 1978, Ohio; 1991, Kentucky. *Education:* Georgetown College (B.A., summa cum laude, 1975); The Ohio State University College of Law (J.D., 1978). Former Member, Tiona & Lockemeyer, Ltd.; Jacobson, Maynard & Tuschman, LPA; Spenger Nathanson PLL. *Member:* Toledo, Ohio State, Kentucky and American Bar Associations; American Board of Trial Advocates.

DAVID S. LOCKEMEYER, born Clifton Springs, New York, December 24, 1955; admitted to bar, 1992, Ohio; U.S. District Court, Northern and Southern Districts of Ohio and U.S. Court of Appeals, Sixth Circuit; 1998, Kentucky; U.S. Supreme Court. *Education:* Heidelberg College (B.M., 1978); Central Michigan University (M.S.A., 1988); Cleveland-Marshall College of Law (J.D., 1992). Managing Editor, Cleveland State Law Review. Author: "At What Cost Will the Court Impose a Duty to Save the Life of a Child," Cleveland State Law Review. Recipient: American Jurisprudence Award for Family Law; Reminger & Reminger Award, Meritorious Writing in the Field of Law and Medicine. Former Member: Tiona Lockemeyer, Ltd.; Roetzel & Andress; Jacobson, Maynard & Tuschman. Department Director, Assistant Director, Miami Valley Hospital, 1983-1987. Zone Manager, Henco Co., 1982. *Member:* Cincinnati, Ohio State and Kentucky Bar Associations; Defense Research Institute. (Resident). ***PRACTICE AREAS:*** Medical Malpractice; General Litigation Defense. ***Email:*** lockemeyer@trionalaw.com

ASSOCIATES

STEPHANIE P. FRANCKEWITZ, born Wheeling, West Virginia, November 28, 1965; admitted to bar, 2001, Ohio. *Education:* West Virginia University (B.S., B.A., 1989); University of Pittsburgh (M.B.A., 1991); Northern Kentucky University (J.D., 2000). *Member:* Ohio State Bar Association. ***PRACTICE AREAS:*** Medical Malpractice Defense; Appellate Practice; Civil Litigation; Professional Liability.

JOEL L. PESCHKE, born West Allis, Wisconsin, September 10, 1972; admitted to bar, 2000, Ohio. *Education:* University of Memphis (B.A., cum laude, 1995); University of Cincinnati College of Law (J.D., 2000). *Member:* Ohio State Bar Association. ***PRACTICE AREAS:*** Negligence Defense; Family Law; Criminal Law; Entertainment Law.

RUTH M. TOROK, born Pittsburgh, Pennsylvania, November 30, 1959; admitted to bar, 1985, Ohio; U.S. District Court, Southern District of Ohio; U.S. Court of Appeals, Sixth Circuit. *Education:* Kent State University (B.A., Political Science, cum laude, 1980); University of Cincinnati (J.D., 1983). Recipient: United States Law Week Prize; 1983 West Publishing Company Corpus Juris Secundum Student Award. Former Associate: Roetzel & Andress, 1997-2000; TriHealth, 1995-1996. (Resident). ***PRACTICE AREAS:*** Medical Malpractice Defense.

LEGAL SUPPORT PERSONNEL

JESSICA A. VONTSOLOS, (Paralegal)

REPRESENTATIVE CLIENTS: Pro Assurance, Inc.

ULMER & BERNE LLP

Established in 1908

600 VINE STREET, SUITE 2800
CINCINNATI, OHIO 45202
Telephone: 513-698-5000
FAX: 513-698-5001
Email: infocincinnati@ulmer.com
URL: http://www.ulmer.com

Cleveland, Ohio Office: Skylight Office Tower, 1660 West 2nd Street, Suite 1100. Telephone: 216-583-7000. FAX: 216-583-7001.

Columbus, Ohio Office: 88 East Broad Street, Suite 1600. Telephone: 614-229-0000. FAX: 614-229-0001.

Chicago, Illinois Office: One North Franklin Street, Suite 1825. Telephone: 312-324-8000. FAX: 312-324-8001.

Antitrust; Banking and Commercial Lending; Broker/Dealer and Securities Litigation; Business Law; Business Litigation; Business Restructuring; Class Action Defense; Construction Law; Corporate Finance; Corporate Restructuring and Creditors' Rights; Corporate Succession Planning; Emerging Businesses; Employee Benefits; Employment and Labor; Environmental; Fair Housing; Financial Institution Compliance; General Counsel Services; Health Care; Income Tax; Insurance Coverage; Intellectual Property and Technology; Joint Ventures; Liability Defense; Mass Torts; Mergers, Acquisitions and Divestitures; Nonprofit; OSHA; Pharmaceutical; Product Liability; Public Law; Real Estate; Securities; Securities Regulatory Compliance; Subrogation; Tax; Technology Transactions; Toxic Tort Defense; Trade Secrets/ Unfair Competition; Trusts and Estates; Venture Capital; Workers' Compensation; Trial and Appellate Practice in All Courts.

FIRM PROFILE: Ulmer & Berne LLP, established in 1908, is one of Ohio's largest law firms, as well as one of its fastest growing. The firm has doubled in size in the last five years and tripled in size in the last 10. In the last 18 months alone, the firm has added 47 new lawyers. A full-service firm with over 185 attorneys in Cleveland, Columbus, Cincinnati and Chicago, Ulmer & Berne represents publicly traded and privately held companies, financial institutions, pharmaceutical companies, family businesses, international joint ventures and affiliations, investor groups, start-ups and emerging businesses, public bodies and nonprofit organizations. For more information, visit www.ulmer.com.

LAW FIRM ALLIANCES/ASSOCIATIONS: **LAWYERS ASSOCIATED WORLDWIDE (L.A.W.)**

BUSINESS COUNSEL, INC.

PARTNERS

B. SCOTT BOSTER, born September 18, 1959; admitted to bar, 1985, Ohio; 1993, Kentucky. *Education:* Miami University (B.S., cum laude, 1981); University of Cincinnati (J.D., 1985). ***PRACTICE AREAS:*** Business Law; Corporate Law; Trusts and Estates; Probate; Taxation. ***Email:*** sboster@ulmer.com

MATTHEW V. BRAMMER, born March 18, 1959; admitted to bar, 1993, Ohio; 2000, Kentucky. *Education:* The Ohio State University (B.S., 1984); University of Cincinnati College of Law (J.D., 1993). ***PRACTICE AREAS:*** Complex Litigation; Drug and Medical Device Defense; Products Liability Defense; Civil Litigation; Business Litigation. ***Email:*** mbrammer@ulmer.com

ANDREW R. GIANNELLA, born April 1, 1970; admitted to bar, 1996, Ohio; 2003, Kentucky. *Education:* Colgate University (B.A., 1992); University of Cincinnati (J.D., 1996). Member, Ohio State Bar Association Real Property Law Specialty Certification Board, 2002-2004. ***PRACTICE AREAS:*** Real Estate; Real Estate Finance; Corporate Counseling; Corporate Finance; Corporate Planning. ***Email:*** agiannella@ulmer.com

JENNIFER BOUCHARD HAGEMAN, born January 7, 1970; admitted to bar, 1996, Ohio; 1997, Kentucky. *Education:* Xavier University (B.A., 1992); University of Cincinnati (J.D., 1996). Order of the Coif. *Member:* Defense Research Institute; Ohio Womens' Bar Association (First District Trustee). ***PRACTICE AREAS:*** Products Liability Defense; Drug and Medical Device Litigation; Mass Tort Defense; Business Litigation. ***Email:*** jhageman@ulmer.com

JOHN M. HANDS, born May 9, 1961; admitted to bar, 1988, Ohio; 1995, Kentucky. *Education:* Miami University (B.A., 1983); University of Cincinnati (J.D., 1988). Delta Theta Phi. *Member:* Ohio Association of Civil Trial Attorneys (Member, Board of Trustees); Cincinnati Academy of Leadership for Lawyers; Defense Research Institute. ***PRACTICE AREAS:*** Products Liability; Business Litigation; Construction Law. ***Email:*** jhands@ulmer.com

JOHN R. IPSARO, born December 8, 1966; admitted to bar, 1993, Ohio; 1994, Kentucky. *Education:* State University of New York at Buffalo (B.S., Criminal Justice, magna cum laude, 1989); University of Dayton (J.D., summa cum laude, 1993). ***PRACTICE AREAS:*** Products Liability; Drug and Medical Device Litigation; Business Litigation; Liability Defense. ***Email:*** jipsaro@ulmer.com

SCOTT P. KADISH, born May 19, 1960; admitted to bar, 1985, Ohio. *Education:* Boston University (B.S., in Business Administration, cum laude, 1982); American University (J.D., 1985). (Partner-in-Charge, Cincinnati Office; Member, Management Committee). ***PRACTICE AREAS:*** Corporate; Real Estate; Real Estate Leasing. ***Email:*** skadish@ulmer.com

BRADLEY D. KAPLAN, born 1961; admitted to bar, 1987, Illinois; 1988, Ohio; 1998, Kentucky. *Education:* Indiana University (B.A., Economics, 1983); Capital University (J.D., 1986). *Member:* Chicago, Cincinnati, Illinois State, Ohio State, Kentucky and American Bar Associations. ***PRACTICE AREAS:*** Corporate Transactions; Real Estate Development; Conveyancing; Finance; Leasing. ***Email:*** bkaplan@ulmer.com

LINDA E. MAICHL, born September 1, 1958; admitted to bar, 1989, Ohio. *Education:* University of Cincinnati (B.B.A., 1984; M.B.A., 1988; J.D., 1989). Order of the Coif. ***PRACTICE AREAS:*** Drug and Medical Device Litigation; Products Liability Litigation; Class Action Defense; Mass Torts; Business Litigation; Civil Appeals; Federal Administrative Law; Drug and Medical Device Regulation. ***Email:*** lmaichl@ulmer.com

MICHAEL A. MARRERO, born July 8, 1953; admitted to bar, 1977, Ohio. *Education:* Xavier University (A.B., magna cum laude, 1974); University of Paris, Sorbonne, Paris, France (Diplôme Annuel); University of Michigan (J.D., 1977). Alpha Sigma Nu. Law Clerk to Hon. Timothy S. Hogan, U.S. District Judge, Southern District of Ohio, 1977-1979. ***PRACTICE AREAS:*** Trademarks; Intellectual Property; Corporate; Mergers, Acquisitions and Divestitures; Advertising; Licensing; Promotion Law. ***Email:*** mmarrero@ulmer.com

DONALD J. MOONEY, JR., born November 14, 1950; admitted to bar, 1975, Ohio; 2004, New Mexico and Florida. *Education:* University of Notre Dame (B.A., cum laude, 1972); University of Cincinnati (J.D., with honors, 1975). Order of the Coif. Member, 1985—, and Chairman, 1998-2004, Cincinnati Planning Commission. ***PRACTICE AREAS:*** Litigation; Antitrust and Trade Regulation; Labor and Employment; Zoning, Planning and Land Use; Intellectual Property. ***Email:*** dmooney@ulmer.com

JEFFREY F. PECK, born August 1, 1957; admitted to bar, 1982, Ohio. *Education:* Miami University (B.A., 1979); University of Cincinnati College of Law (J.D., 1982). Order of the Barristers. (Chair, Product Liability Group). *Member:* Cincinnati Bar Association (Chairman, Judicial Candidate Rating Committee; Member, Tort and Insurance Practice Committee; Member, Risk Management Committee, Tall Stacks, 1999); Cincinnati Academy of Leadership for Lawyers (Member, Steering Committee); Cincinnati Bar Association/Black Lawyers Association of Cincinnati Roundtable Retention Committee. ***PRACTICE AREAS:*** Liability Defense; Complex Litigation; Risk Management; Labor and Employment Law; Products Liability Defense; Drug and Medical Device Defense; Litigation; Occupational Safety and Health; Toxic Torts. ***Email:*** jpeck@ulmer.com

STUART A. SCHLOSS, JR., born July 12, 1947; admitted to bar, 1972, Ohio. *Education:* University of Colorado (B.A., 1969); University of Michigan (J.D., 1972). ***PRACTICE AREAS:*** Business Law; Fine Arts; Nonprofit Organizations Law; Closely Held Business Law; Family Business Law; Divorce Taxation; Physicians Practices; Estate Planning. ***Email:*** sschloss@ulmer.com

FREDERIC X. SHADLEY, born November 17, 1955; admitted to bar, 1981, Ohio; 1982, Illinois; 1990, Kentucky; 1994, Indiana. *Education:* University of Notre Dame (B.S.E.E., 1978; J.D., 1981). Eta Kappa Nu. ***PRACTICE AREAS:*** Products Liability; Construction Litigation; Commercial Litigation; Intellectual Property Litigation; Class Actions. ***Email:*** fshadley@ulmer.com

MICHAEL J. SUFFERN, born January 1, 1962; admitted to bar, 1990, Illinois; 1993, Ohio; 2001, Kentucky. *Education:* University of Notre Dame (B.A., 1984); Loyola University of Chicago (J.D., magna cum laude, 1990). ***PRACTICE AREAS:*** Product Liability Defense; Mass Torts; Insurance Coverage Litigation; Commercial Litigation. ***Email:*** msuffern@ulmer.com

STUART R. SUSSKIND, born October 10, 1944; admitted to bar, 1969, Ohio. *Education:* University of Cincinnati (B.B.A., 1966; J.D., 1969). Phi Delta Phi. Lecturer: University of Cincinnati, 1973-1992; Salmon P. Chase College of Law of Northern Kentucky University, 1974-1977. ***PRACTICE AREAS:*** Trust and Estates; Tax Planning; Corporate Law; Business Law. ***Email:*** ssusskind@ulmer.com

JOSEPH P. THOMAS, born March 15, 1956; admitted to bar, 1988, Ohio; 1989, New Jersey; 1999, Kentucky; registered to practice before U.S. Patent and Trademark Office. *Education:* Washington State University (Bachelor of Pharmacy, 1980); University of Cincinnati (Doctor of Pharmacy, 1982); Northern Kentucky University (J.D., cum laude, 1988). Rho Chi Pharmaceutical Honor Society. Licensed Pharmacist, Washington, 1980. (Co-Chair, Litigation Department; Chair, Pharmaceutical Industry Practice). ***PRACTICE AREAS:*** Drug and Medical Device Litigation; Toxic Tort Defense; Products Liability Defense; Commercial Litigation. ***Email:*** jthomas@ulmer.com

OF COUNSEL

GINA M. SAELINGER, born May 29, 1969; admitted to bar, 1993, Ohio; 2001, Kentucky. *Education:* Xavier University (B.S., summa cum laude, 1990); University of Cincinnati (J.D., 1993). Order of the Coif; Order of the Barristers. ***PRACTICE AREAS:*** Class Action Defense; Complex and Multi-District Litigation; Drug and Medical Device Defense; Products Liability Defense; Business Litigation; Civil Litigation. ***Email:*** gsaelinger@ulmer.com

SENIOR ATTORNEY

REUEL D. ASH, born May 1, 1957; admitted to bar, 1991, Ohio. *Education:* Stanford University (A.B., Music, 1979); Eastman School of Music (M.M., Performance and Literature, 1981); University of Cincinnati (J.D., 1991). ***PRACTICE AREAS:*** Bankruptcy; Insolvency; Business Law; Commercial Litigation. ***Email:*** rdash@ulmer.com

ASSOCIATES

JENNIFER PASCHEN BERGERON, born March 13, 1973; admitted to bar, 2002, Ohio. *Education:* Centre College of Kentucky (B.A., summa cum laude, 1995) Phi Beta Kappa; University of Virginia (M.A., Foreign Affairs, 1998); University of Cincinnati (J.D., 2002). Associate Member, Law Review. Senior Articles Editor, Human Rights Quarterly. *Member:* Cincinnati Bar Association (CLE Coordinator, Women Lawyers Committee). ***PRACTICE AREAS:*** Labor and Employment; Civil Rights Litigation. ***Email:*** jbergeron@ulmer.com

CHRISTOPHER D. CATHEY, born November 2, 1973; admitted to bar, 1999, Ohio; 2003, Florida and Kentucky. *Education:* University of Florida (B.A., 1994); University of Cincinnati (J.D., 1999). Fellow, Cincinnati Academy of Leadership for Lawyers. ***PRACTICE AREAS:*** Business Litigation; Employment Litigation; Lender Liability; Tort and Insurance Litigation. ***Email:*** ccathey@ulmer.com

(This Listing Continued)

TIFFANY REECE CLARK, born October 15, 1973; admitted to bar, 1999, Pennsylvania; 2001, Massachusetts; 2002, Ohio. *Education:* Wake Forest University (B.A., 1996); University of Cincinnati College of Law (J.D., 1999). ***PRACTICE AREAS:*** Liability Defense; Business Litigation. ***Email:*** tclark@ulmer.com

JASON P. CONTE, born November 7, 1973; admitted to bar, 1999, Ohio. *Education:* University of Notre Dame (B.A., magna cum laude, 1996); Vanderbilt University (J.D., 1999). ***PRACTICE AREAS:*** Civil Litigation; Defense Litigation; Federal Litigation; Construction Litigation; Tort Liability; Mold Litigation; Automobile Negligence; Product Defects. ***Email:*** jconte@ulmer.com

PAUL J. (P.J.) COSGROVE, born January 7, 1973; admitted to bar, 1999, New Jersey; 1999, Pennsylvania; 2001, Ohio. *Education:* The Ohio State University (B.A., 1995); Rutgers University Law School, Camden (J.D., 1999); Temple University Beasley School of Law (LL.M., Trial Advocacy, 2003). Certified by State of New Jersey Judiciary as Small Claims Mediator. ***PRACTICE AREAS:*** Drug and Medical Device Litigation; Complex Litigation; Liability Defense; Alternative Dispute Resolution. ***Email:*** pcosgrove@ulmer.com

JEFFREY GEOPPINGER, born September 11, 1975; admitted to bar, 2001, Ohio. *Education:* Boston College (B.A., 1998); University of Cincinnati College of Law (J.D., 2001). ***PRACTICE AREAS:*** Products Liability Defense; Insurance Defense; Pharmaceutical Litigation. ***Email:*** jgeoppinger@ulmer.com

PAMELA GINSBURG, born April 18, 1955; admitted to bar, 1990, Tennessee; 2000, Ohio. *Education:* Belmont College (B.A., cum laude, 1976); Vanderbilt University (J.D., 1990). ***PRACTICE AREAS:*** Civil Litigation; Securities Litigation; Construction Litigation; Business Litigation. ***Email:*** pginsburg@ulmer.com

SHARON E. GRONOTTE, born January 28, 1975; admitted to bar, 1999, Ohio; 2000, Kentucky. *Education:* Thomas More College (B.A., History, summa cum laude, 1996); University of Kentucky (J.D., magna cum laude, 1999). Order of the Coif. Managing Editor, Kentucky Law Journal, 1998-1999. *Member:* Cincinnati, Ohio State and Kentucky Bar Associations. ***PRACTICE AREAS:*** Products Liability; General Liability Defense; Drug and Medical Device Defense. ***Email:*** sgronotte@ulmer.com

PRENTISS W. HALLENBECK, JR., born April 25, 1955; admitted to bar, 1998, Ohio; 2000, Kentucky. *Education:* University of Virginia (B.A., 1978; J.D., 1998). ***PRACTICE AREAS:*** Products Liability; Personal Injury; Litigation; Trademark; Insurance. ***Email:*** phallenbeck@ulmer.com

JEANETTE HARGREAVES, born January 4, 1966; admitted to bar, 1995, Ohio. *Education:* University of Kentucky (B.B.A., with distinction, 1988); University of Cincinnati (J.D., 1995). Order of the Coif. ***PRACTICE AREAS:*** Products Liability; Drug and Medical Device Litigation. ***Email:*** jhargreaves@ulmer.com

JENNIFER SNYDER HEIS, born March 17, 1976; admitted to bar, 2001, Georgia; 2003, Ohio. *Education:* Kenyon College (B.A., 1998); Emory University School of Law (J.D., 2001). ***PRACTICE AREAS:*** Litigation; Medical Malpractice; Products Liability. ***Email:*** jheis@ulmer.com

KAREN L. IMBUS, born November 8, 1962; admitted to bar, 1996, Ohio. *Education:* University of Notre Dame (B.A., 1984); The London School of Economics (M.Sc., 1985); University of Cincinnati College of Law (J.D., 1995). ***PRACTICE AREAS:*** Litigation; Drug and Medical Device Defense. ***Email:*** kimbus@ulmer.com

KAREN E. JONES, born July 27, 1966; admitted to bar, 2004, Ohio. *Education:* University of Kentucky (B.A., 1988); University of Cincinnati (J.D., 2004). ***PRACTICE AREAS:*** Business Litigation; Complex Litigation. ***Email:*** kjones@ulmer.com

JOSEPH C. KLEIN, born December 9, 1968; admitted to bar, 1997, Washington and Ohio. *Education:* University of Michigan (B.A., Economics, 1991; B.A., Philosophy, 1991; J.D., summa cum laude, 1995). Phi Delta Phi; Order of the Coif. Judicial Clerkship, Judge Thomas P. Griesa, U.S. District Court, Southern District of New York, 1996-1997. ***PRACTICE AREAS:*** Litigation; Tort Defense. ***Email:*** jklein@ulmer.com

THOMAS G. McINTOSH, born September 5, 1976; admitted to bar, 2003, Ohio; 2004, Kentucky. *Education:* University of Kentucky (B.S., magna cum laude, 1998; J.D., 2003). ***PRACTICE AREAS:*** Products Liability Defense; Drug and Medical Device Defense; Defense Litigation. ***Email:*** tmcintosh@ulmer.com

JAMES L. SALMON, born May 22, 1967; admitted to bar, 1994, Wyoming; 2000, Ohio and Kentucky. *Education:* Texas Tech University (B.A., 1991); University of Cincinnati (J.D., 1994). Law Clerk to the Honorable William A. Taylor, Wyoming Supreme Court, 1994-1996. ***PRACTICE AREAS:*** Civil Litigation; Business Litigation; Insurance Bad Faith. ***Email:*** jsalmon@ulmer.com

JEFFREY R. SCHAEFER, born May 3, 1955; admitted to bar, 1993 Ohio. *Education:* Colgate University (A.B., Chemistry, 1977); Salmon P. Chase College of Law, Northern Kentucky University (J.D., magna cum laude, 1992). ***PRACTICE AREAS:*** Appellate Practice; Class Action Defense; Intellectual Property Litigation; Complex Litigation; Patent Litigation; Drug and Medical Device Defense; Products Liability Defense; Mass Torts. ***Email:*** jschaefer@ulmer.com

MICHAEL C. SCHMIDT, born November 2, 1972; admitted to bar, 2001, Ohio. *Education:* University of Kentucky (B.A., 1995); Salmon P. Chase College of Law (J.D., 2001). ***PRACTICE AREAS:*** Real Estate; Business Law. ***Email:*** mschmidt@ulmer.com

JACQUELINE R. SHERIDAN, born December 16, 1977; admitted to bar, 2003, Indiana; 2005, Ohio. *Education:* Purdue University (B.A., 2000); University of Notre Dame (J.D., 2003). ***PRACTICE AREAS:*** Products Liability; Drug and Medical Device Litigation; Mass Torts; Tort Defense. ***Email:*** jsheridan@ulmer.com

DENISE M. SMITH, born October 17, 1971; admitted to bar, 1996, Kentucky; 1997, Ohio. *Education:* University of Louisville (B.A., 1993); Salmon P. Chase College of Law (J.D., magna cum laude, 1996). Order of the Curia. *Member:* Defense Research Institute. ***PRACTICE AREAS:*** Drug and Medical Device Litigation; Products Liability Defense; Toxic Torts; Civil Litigation. ***Email:*** dsmith@ulmer.com

JULIE C. SMITH, born May 26, 1969; admitted to bar, 1998, New Jersey; 1999, New York; 2001, Georgia (Not admitted in Ohio). *Education:* College of William & Mary (B.A., 1991); Seton Hall University School of Law (J.D., 1998). ***PRACTICE AREAS:*** Products Liability Defense; Mass Tort Defense; Drug and Medical Device Litigation; Class Action Defense. ***Email:*** jsmith@ulmer.com

RONALD G. SMITH, born October 14, 1968; admitted to bar, 1998, Ohio. *Education:* Miami University (B.S., 1991); University of Cincinnati (J.D., 1998). ***PRACTICE AREAS:*** Corporate; Real Estate; Mergers and Acquisitions. ***Email:*** rsmith@ulmer.com

MARY LYNN TATE, born October 17, 1961; admitted to bar, 1999, Kentucky; 2002, Ohio. *Education:* College of William & Mary (B.S., 1983); University of Kentucky (J.D., 1999). ***PRACTICE AREAS:*** Drug and Medical Device Litigation; Products Liability Defense. ***Email:*** mtate@ulmer.com

TRACI L. WALLACE, born January 20, 1968; admitted to bar, 2000, Ohio. *Education:* Miami University (B.A., summa cum laude, 1992); Salmon P. Chase College of Law (J.D., magna cum laude, 1998). ***PRACTICE AREAS:*** Liability Defense. ***Email:*** twallace@ulmer.com

VOLKEMA, THOMAS, MILLER, BURKETT, SCOTT & MERRY

A LEGAL PROFESSIONAL ASSOCIATION

Established in 1988

700 WALNUT STREET, SUITE 400
CINCINNATI, OHIO 45202-2015
Telephone: 513-651-4400
Fax: 513-651-4405
Email: attorneys@vt-law.com

Columbus, Ohio Office: 140 East Town Street, Suite 1100. 43215-5183. Telephone: 614-221-4400. Fax: 614-221-6010.

Qui Tam (Whistleblower), False Claims Act, Civil State and Federal Trial and Appellate Practice. Personal Injury. Malpractice, Nursing Home Negligence, HMO Liability, Class Actions, Wrongful Death, Automobile Accidents, Product Liability, Employee Benefits, Insurance Bad Faith, Aviation and Tort Law, ERISA.

FIRM PROFILE: A Plaintiff Tort Litigation Firm.

FREDERICK M. MORGAN, JR., born Wheeling, West Virginia, September 19, 1956; admitted to bar, 1983, Ohio; 1997, U.S. Court of Appeals, Fifth, Sixth, Tenth and Eleventh Circuits and U.S. Supreme Court. *Education:* Denison University (B.A., 1978); University of Cincinnati (J.D., 1983). Co-Author, "The Last Privateers Encounter Sloppy Seas: Inconsistent Original Source Jurisprudence Under the Federal False Claims Act," 24 Ohio N.U.L. Rev. 163 (1998). Law Clerk to the Honorable David S. Porter, U.S. Senior District Judge, Southern District of Ohio, 1983-1985. Trial Attorney, Federal Programs Branch, Civil Division, U.S. Department of Justice, Washington, D.C., 1985-1989. *Member:* Cincinnati and American Bar Associations; The Association of Trial Lawyers of America. Member Emeritus: The Charles Fahy American Inn of Court; Potter Stewart Inn of Court. ***Email:*** rmorgan@vt-law.com

JENNIFER M. VERKAMP, born Cincinnati, Ohio, August 9, 1970; admitted to bar, 1996, Ohio and U.S. Court of Appeals, Sixth and Eleventh Circuits. *Education:* Xavier University (B.S., 1992); Georgetown University (J.D., 1996). Recipient, BNA Legal Scholar Award. Co-Author, "Notes From the Field: Practicalities of the Qui Tam 'Working Partnership' Under the 1986 False Claims Act Amendments," 29 False Claims Act and Qui Tam Quarterly Review 31 (2003). *Member:* Cincinnati Bar Association; Cincinnati Academy of Leadership for Lawyers. ***Email:*** jverkamp@vt-law.com

REFERENCE: Huntington National Bank.

(For complete biographical data on all personnel, see Professional Biographies, Columbus, Ohio)

VORYS, SATER, SEYMOUR AND PEASE LLP

Established in 1909

ATRIUM TWO, SUITE 2000
221 EAST FOURTH STREET
P.O. BOX 0236
CINCINNATI, OHIO 45201-0236
Telephone: 513-723-4000
Facsimile: 513-723-4056
URL: http://www.vssp.com

Columbus, Ohio Office: 52 East Gay Street, P.O. Box 1008, 43216-1008. Telephone: 614-464-6400. Facsimile: 614-464-6350.

Cleveland, Ohio Office: 2100 One Cleveland Center, 1375 East Ninth Street, 44114-1724. Telephone: 216-479-6100. Facsimile: 216-479-6060.

Washington, D.C. Office: 1828 L Street, N.W., Suite 1111, 20036-5104. Telephone: 202-467-8800. Facsimile: 202-467-8900.

Alexandria, Virginia Office: 277 South Washington Street, Suite 310, 22314. Telephone: 703-837-6999. Facsimile: 703-549-4492.

Akron, Ohio Office: First National Tower, 106 South Main Street, Suite 1100, 44308. Telephone: 330-208-1000. Facsimile: 330-208-1001.

Banking, Civil/Commercial Litigation, Commercial Transactions/Bankruptcy, Environmental, Estate Planning/Probate, Health Care, Savings and Loan/Thrifts.

PARTNERS

GLENN V. WHITAKER, born Cincinnati, Ohio, July 23, 1947; admitted to bar, 1972, Maryland; 1973, District of Columbia; 1980, Ohio. *Education:* Denison University (B.A., magna cum laude, 1969); George Washington University (J.D., cum laude, 1972). Phi Beta Kappa; Order of the Coif; Master of the Bench, Potter Stewart Inn of Court. Fellow, American College of Trial Lawyers. Associate, American Board of Trial Advocates. Trial Attorney

(This Listing Continued)

VORYS, SATER, SEYMOUR AND PEASE LLP, Cincinnati—Continued

and Special Litigation Counsel, Civil Division, U.S. Department of Justice, 1976-1980. *Member:* Ohio State and American Bar Associations. ***PRACTICE AREAS:*** Litigation; Criminal Defense; Commercial Litigation. ***Email:*** gvwhitaker@vssp.com

STEPHEN S. EBERLY, born Toledo, Ohio, December 7, 1945; admitted to bar, 1973, Ohio; 1992, Kentucky. *Education:* University of Wisconsin (B.B.A., with honors, 1967); University of Michigan (J.D., cum laude, 1972). Board Member, Former President and Counsel, Cincinnati Association for the Blind. Member, Society for American Baseball Research. *Member:* Cincinnati, Ohio State, Kentucky and American Bar Associations. ***PRACTICE AREAS:*** Labor and Employment; Litigation; Public Employment Relations Law. ***Email:*** sseberly@vssp.com

DANIEL J. BUCKLEY, born Ann Arbor, Michigan, January 20, 1949; admitted to bar, 1974, Ohio; 1982, U.S. Supreme Court. *Education:* University of Aberdeen, Aberdeen Scotland; Ohio Wesleyan University (B.A., 1971); University of Exeter, Exeter, England; University of Cincinnati (J.D., 1974). Case Note Editor, University of Cincinnati Law Review, 1973-1974. Law Clerk to U.S. District Judge Julius J. Hoffman, Northern District of Illinois, 1974-1976. Adjunct Professor, University of Cincinnati College of Law. Listed in Best Lawyers in America, Commercial and Personal Injury Litigation. Best Lawyers: Business Litigator Corporate Counsel Magazine. Master of the Bench, Potter Stewart Inn of Court. *Member:* Cincinnati, Ohio State and American (Member, Sections on: Corporation, Banking and Business Law; Litigation) Bar Associations; Ohio Bar Foundation; American College of Trial Lawyers. ***PRACTICE AREAS:*** General Civil Trial Practice; State and Federal Courts Law; Hospital Law. ***Email:*** djbuckley@vssp.com

DONALD J. SHULLER, born Cincinnati, Ohio, March 18, 1951; admitted to bar, 1976, Ohio. *Education:* University of Virginia (B.S., 1973; J.D., 1976). Beta Gamma Sigma. *Member:* Cincinnati, Ohio State and American (Member, Real Estate Finance Committee, Loan Practices and Lender Liability Subcommittee) Bar Associations. ***PRACTICE AREAS:*** Commercial Transactions; Real Estate Law; Real Estate Finance Law; Secured Transactions. ***Email:*** djshuller@vssp.com

CHARLES C. BISSINGER, JR., born Columbus, Ohio, January 4, 1955; admitted to bar, 1979, Ohio and U.S. District Court, Southern District of Ohio; 1990, Kentucky; 1996, Massachusetts. *Education:* University of Michigan (B.B.A., 1976); Harvard University (J.D., cum laude, 1979). Phi Beta Kappa; Beta Gamma Sigma. *Member:* Cincinnati and Kentucky Bar Associations. ***PRACTICE AREAS:*** Housing Development; Real Estate; Real Estate Development; Real Estate Syndication; Commercial Real Estate. ***Email:*** ccbissinger@vssp.com

ROGER E. LAUTZENHISER, born Portland, Indiana, February 24, 1954; admitted to bar, 1979, Ohio. *Education:* Stanford University (A.B., with distinction, 1976); University of California at Los Angeles (J.D., 1979). Phi Beta Kappa. ***PRACTICE AREAS:*** Corporate Law; Securities Regulation; Business Law. ***Email:*** relautzenhiser@vssp.com

DAVID A. GROENKE, born Cincinnati, Ohio, February 13, 1956; admitted to bar, 1981, Ohio and U.S. District Court, Southern District of Ohio. *Education:* University of Michigan (A.B., 1978); Vanderbilt University (J.D., 1981). *Member:* Cincinnati (Past Chair, Estate Planning and Probate Committee) and American Bar Associations. ***PRACTICE AREAS:*** Trusts and Estates; Wills; Estate Planning; Taxation; Real Estate; Like Kind Exchanges; Closely Held Business Law. ***Email:*** dagroenke@vssp.com

TERRI REYERING ABARE, born Cincinnati, Ohio, June 2, 1954; admitted to bar, 1983, Ohio; 1985, U.S. District Court, Southern District of Ohio. *Education:* Miami University (B.A., 1975); Georgetown University Law Center (J.D., cum laude, 1983). *Member:* Cincinnati (Member, Corporate and Securities Law Committee) and Ohio State Bar Associations. ***PRACTICE AREAS:*** Corporate Law; Securities; Banking Law. ***Email:*** trabare@vssp.com

ANDREW M. KAPLAN, born Cincinnati, Ohio, January 6, 1957; admitted to bar, 1983, Ohio and U.S. District Court, Southern District of Ohio; U.S. Court of Appeals, Sixth Circuit. *Education:* Amherst College (B.A., 1979) Phi Beta Kappa; Georgetown University Law Center (J.D., magna cum laude, 1983). Editor, Georgetown Law Journal, 1983. *Member:* Cincinnati, Ohio State and American Bar Associations. ***PRACTICE AREAS:*** Litigation; Workers Compensation Law. ***Email:*** amkaplan@vssp.com

MARK A. NORMAN, born South Bend, Indiana, June 5, 1956; admitted to bar, 1983, Ohio and U.S. District Court, Northern and Southern Districts of Ohio; U.S. Court of Appeals, Sixth Circuit. *Education:* George Washington University (B.A., honors, 1977); Georgetown University Law Center (J.D., cum laude, 1983). Phi Beta Kappa. Trustee's Scholar. Co-Author: "RCRA and Superfund," Shepard's McGraw-Hill. Administrative Assistant and Press Secretary to U.S. Representative John J. LaFalce (NY-32), 1978-1983. Chairman, Hamilton County Environmental Action Commission. Chairman, Cincinnati Chamber of Commerce Environmental, Occupational Safety and Health Committee. *Member:* Cincinnati and Ohio State Bar Associations. ***PRACTICE AREAS:*** Environmental Law; Administrative Law; Occupational Safety and Health. ***Email:*** manorman@vssp.com

MELVIN A. BEDREE, born Fort Wayne, Indiana, August 12, 1959; admitted to bar, 1984, Ohio and U.S. District Court, Southern District of Ohio. *Education:* Depauw University (B.A., magna cum laude, 1981); University of Cincinnati (J.D., 1984). Phi Beta Kappa; Order of the Coif. Research Editor, University of Cincinnati, College of Law, Law Review, 1983-1984. *Member:* Ohio State and American Bar Associations. ***PRACTICE AREAS:*** Commercial Law; Franchising; Business. ***Email:*** mabedree@vssp.com

THOMAS L. GABELMAN, born Cincinnati, Ohio, May 12, 1958; admitted to bar, 1984, Ohio; 1990, Kentucky; U.S. District Court, Southern District of Ohio and U.S. Court of Appeals, Sixth Circuit. *Education:* University of Cincinnati (B.A., summa cum laude, 1980; J.D., 1984). Phi Beta Kappa, Omicron Delta Kappa. District Representative for the Honorable Willis D. Gradison, Jr., U.S. Representative, 2nd District, Ohio, 1980-1981. *Member:* Cincinnati (Chair, Construction Law Committee, 1990-1993) and Northern Kentucky Bar Associations; American Arbitration Association (Chair, Regional Construction Law Committee, 1990—). ***PRACTICE AREAS:*** Construction Law; Litigation; Real Estate. ***Email:*** tlgabelman@vssp.com

(This Listing Continued)

W. BRECK WEIGEL, born Bronxville, New York, November 1, 1960; admitted to bar, 1985, Ohio and U.S. District Court, Southern District of Ohio; 1987, U.S. Court of Appeals, Sixth Circuit; 1988, U.S. District Court, Eastern District of Kentucky; 1993, Colorado. *Education:* University of Colorado (B.A., 1982); University of Cincinnati School of Law (J.D., with honors, 1985). Faculty Member, National Institute of Trial Advocacy. *Member:* Cincinnati (Member: Grievance Committee; Admissions Committee; Board of Trustee), Ohio State (Member, Litigation Committee) and American (Member, Litigation Section) Bar Associations. Master of the Bench, Potter Stewart Inn of Court. ***PRACTICE AREAS:*** Commercial Litigation; Construction Litigation; Intellectual Property Litigation; Civil Practice; Federal Civil Practice; Business Law; Intellectual Property; Banking Law. ***Email:*** wbweigel@vssp.com

WILLIAM D. HAYES, born Geneva, New York, May 14, 1961; admitted to bar, 1986, Ohio and U.S. District Court, Southern District of Ohio. *Education:* Denison University (B.A., 1983); Capital University (J.D., 1986). Staff Attorney, 1986-1990 and Managing Attorney, 1990-1991, Ohio Environmental Protection Agency. Listed in Best Lawyers in America 2003-2004. *Member:* Cincinnati (Chair, Environmental Committee) and Ohio State (Member, Environmental Committee) Bar Associations; Air and Waste Management Association; Cincinnati Chamber of Commerce (Member, Air Quality Committee); Ohio Small Business Clean Air Act Stationary Source Advisory Panel (Appointed Member; Chair). ***PRACTICE AREAS:*** Environmental Law; Air Quality. ***Email:*** wdhayes@vssp.com

NATHANIEL LAMPLEY, JR., born Hamilton, Ohio, May 31, 1963; admitted to bar, 1989, Ohio. *Education:* University of Dayton (B.A., with honors, 1985); University of Cincinnati (J.D., 1988). ***PRACTICE AREAS:*** Litigation; Sports Law; Employment Law. ***Email:*** nlampley@vssp.com

ELIOT N. MEYERS, born Cincinnati, Ohio, May 6, 1965; admitted to bar, 1991, New York and District of Columbia; 1994, Ohio. *Education:* Harvard College (A.B., summa cum laude, 1987); Harvard University (J.D., cum laude, 1990). Phi Beta Kappa. Author: Tax Management Memorandum, (12/14/92) Vol. 33, No. 25; Journal of Real Estate Taxation, Vol. 12, No. 1, Fall, 1993; Journal of Taxation of Investments, Vol. 11 No. 1, Autumn, 1993; Journal of S Corporation Taxation, Vol. 6, No. 3, Winter, 1995. ***PRACTICE AREAS:*** Taxation; Small Business Law; Estate Planning. ***Email:*** enmeyers@vssp.com

VICTOR A. WALTON, JR., born Cincinnati, Ohio, December 15, 1964; admitted to bar, 1991, Ohio and U.S. District Court, District of Ohio; 1996, U.S. Court of Appeals, Sixth Circuit; 1998, U.S. District Court, Northern District of Ohio. *Education:* Georgetown University (B.S.F.S., 1987; J.D., 1991). Member, Journal of Law and Technology. ***PRACTICE AREAS:*** Commercial Litigation; Construction Litigation; False Claims Act; Whistleblower Litigation; Environmental Law; Environmental Litigation; Toxic Torts; Mold Litigation; Health Care Litigation; Health Care Fraud; Health Care Compliance; Bankruptcy Workouts. ***Email:*** vawalton@vssp.com

SCOTT A. CARROLL, born Cincinnati, Ohio, April 1, 1967; admitted to bar, 1993, Ohio; 1995, U.S. District Court, Southern District of Ohio. *Education:* University of Cincinnati (B.S., 1990; J.D., 1993). Phi Alpha Delta. Member, Cincinnati Law Review, 1990-1993. Emergency Medical Technician, 1992. Law Clerk for the Hon. Sandra S. Belkwith, Judge, U.S. District Court, Southern District of Ohio. *Member:* Ohio State Bar Association. ***PRACTICE AREAS:*** Employment Law; Litigation. ***Email:*** sacarroll@vssp.com

RICHARD L. MOORE, born Cincinnati, Ohio, May 17, 1965; admitted to bar, 1993, Ohio; 1994, U.S. District Court, Southern District of Ohio; 1995, U.S. Court of Appeals, Sixth Circuit. *Education:* Bowling Green State University (B.S., 1987); University of Cincinnati (J.D., 1993). Member, University of Cincinnati Law Review, 1992-1993. Chairman, 1997— and Board Chair, Board of Trustees, Urban League of Greater Cincinnati. *Member:* Black Lawyers Association of Cincinnati (Former Vice President). ***PRACTICE AREAS:*** Litigation; Criminal Defense; Workers Compensation. ***Email:*** rlmoore@vssp.com

HANI R. KALLAS, born Kettering, Ohio, December 30, 1968; admitted to bar, 1994, Ohio. *Education:* Miami University (B.S., 1991); University of Cincinnati College of Law (J.D., 1994). Order of the Coif. Articles Editor, University of Cincinnati Law Review. Author: "The Undercharge Dilemma: How the Interstate Commerce Commission has Aided Shippers Defending Against Bankrupt Carriers," 62 U. Cinn. L.Rev. 173 (1993). ***PRACTICE AREAS:*** Commercial; Real Estate. ***Email:*** hrkallas@vssp.com

PHILLIP J. SMITH, born Fargo, North Dakota, October 29, 1968; admitted to bar, 1994, Ohio and U.S. District Court, Southern District of Ohio; 1996, U.S. Court of Appeals, Sixth Circuit. *Education:* Miami University (B.A., summa cum laude, 1991); University of Michigan (J.D., cum laude, 1993). Phi Beta Kappa. Member, University of Michigan Journal of Law Reform. *Member:* Cincinnati and Ohio State Bar Associations. ***PRACTICE AREAS:*** Litigation. ***Email:*** pjsmith@vssp.com

ERIC W. RICHARDSON, born Fort Thomas, Kentucky, 1973; admitted to bar, 1996, Ohio; 1997, Kentucky; U.S. Supreme Court; U.S. Court of Appeals, Sixth and Federal Circuits; U.S. District Court, Southern District of Ohio; U.S. District Court, Eastern and Western Districts of Kentucky. *Education:* Thomas More College (B.A., 1993); University of Cincinnati (J.D., 1996). Delta Epsilon Sigma. Order of the Coif. Author: "Who Is a Qualified Individual with a Disability Under the ADA," Vol. 64, Univ. of Cincinnati Law Review; "Due Process Requirements of Jury Charges in Capital Cases," Vol. 64, Univ. of Cincinnati Law Review. Law Clerk to the Hon. R. Guy Cole, Jr., U.S. Court of Appeals, Sixth Circuit, 1996-1997. *Member:* Cincinnati and Kentucky Bar Associations. ***PRACTICE AREAS:*** Litigation; Bankruptcy Workouts. ***Email:*** ewrichardson@vssp.com

WILLIAM D.G. BALDWIN, born Rockford, Illinois, April 1, 1967; admitted to bar, 1997, Ohio. *Education:* University of Wisconsin-Madison (B.A., 1989); Northern Kentucky University (J.D., magna cum laude, 1997). Student Articles Editor, Northern Kentucky Law Review, 1996-1997; Member, 1995-1996. Board Member and Treasurer, Hamilton County Alcohol and Drug Addiction. *Member:* Cincinnati and American Bar Associations. ***PRACTICE AREAS:*** Commercial; Finance; Real Estate; Housing and Development. ***Email:*** wdbaldwin@vssp.com

(This Listing Continued)

ASSOCIATES

ROBERT M.M. SHAFFER, born Cincinnati, Ohio, June 6, 1968; admitted to bar, 1996, Ohio. *Education:* Yale University (B.A., 1990); University of Cincinnati (J.D., 1996). *Member:* Cincinnati and Ohio State Bar Associations. ***LANGUAGES:*** Spanish. ***Email:*** rshaffer@vssp.com

KENT A. BRITT, born Indianapolis, Indiana, November 27, 1970; admitted to bar, 1997, Ohio and U.S. District Court, Southern District of Ohio. *Education:* Indiana University (B.S., 1994); University of Cincinnati (J.D., 1997). Phi Alpha Delta. *Member:* Cincinnati, Ohio State and American (Member, Litigation Section, 1997—) Bar Associations. ***PRACTICE AREAS:*** Litigation. ***Email:*** kabritt@vssp.com

KIMBERLY J. SCHAEFER, born Pittsburgh, Pennsylvania; admitted to bar, 1998, Ohio and U.S. District Court, Southern District of Ohio. *Education:* Miami University (B.S., summa cum laude, 1995); Duke University School of Law (J.D., magna cum laude, 1998). *Member:* Cincinnati Bar Association. ***PRACTICE AREAS:*** Corporate Law; Securities; Banking Law. ***Email:*** kjschaefer@vssp.com

ANTHONY L. OSTERLUND, born Denison, Iowa, April 19, 1967; admitted to bar, 1999, Ohio; 2000, U.S. District Court, Southern District of Ohio; 2001, U.S. Court of Appeals, Sixth Circuit. *Education:* Iowa State University (B.A., 1989); University of Cincinnati (J.D., 1999). Editor-in-Chief, University of Cincinnati Law Review, 1998-1999. Author: "Showdown at the Constitutional Corral: Self-Incrimination v. Potential Foreign Prosecution, 67 U. CIN. L. Rev. 615 (1999); "The Unequal Balancing Act Between HIV-Positive Patients and Physicians, 25 OHIO N.U. 149 (1999). *Member:* Columbus, Cincinnati and Ohio State Bar Associations. [Captain, U.S. Marine Corp]. ***PRACTICE AREAS:*** Litigation; General Civil Trial Practice; Federal Practice; Employment Discrimination; Commercial Litigation; Toxic Tort Litigation; Alternative Dispute Resolution. ***Email:*** alosterlund@vssp.com

TARA K. BURKE, born Cincinnati, Ohio; admitted to bar, 2000, Ohio. *Education:* Xavier University (B.A., 1997); University of Cincinnati College of Law (J.D., 2000). *Member:* Cincinnati and Ohio State Bar Associations. ***Email:*** tkburke@vssp.com

JASON L. HODGES, born Williamsburg, Kentucky, January 21, 1975; admitted to bar, 2000, Ohio and U.S. District Court, Southern District of Ohio; 2001, Kentucky. *Education:* Centre College of Kentucky (B.A., 1997); University of Kentucky College of Law (J.D., cum laude, 2000). *Member:* Cincinnati, Ohio State, Kentucky and American Bar Associations. ***PRACTICE AREAS:*** Corporate Law; Financial Institutions Law; Banking Law; Securities; Business Law. ***Email:*** jlhodges@vssp.com

MR. KORY A. JACKSON, born Oxford, Ohio; admitted to bar, 2000, Ohio; 2001, U.S. District Court, Southern District of Ohio; 2005, U.S. District Court, Southern District of Indiana and U.S. Court of Appeals, Sixth Circuit. *Education:* University of Cincinnati (B.A., English Literature, 1997; J.D., 2000). Member, Conference Committee, Greater Cincinnati Minority Counsel Program. Volunteer Legal Consultant, School of Creative and Performing Arts. *Member:* Cincinnati, Ohio State and American Bar Associations. ***PRACTICE AREAS:*** Litigation (100%); Criminal Law; Personal Injury Defense; Products Liability; Insurance Law; Toxic Torts.

MICHAEL J. BRONSON, born Cincinnati, Ohio, May 14, 1976; admitted to bar, 2001, Ohio. *Education:* Denison University (B.A., magna cum laude, 1998); Vanderbilt University School of Law (J.D., 2001). Phi Beta Kappa. Managing Editor, Vanderbilt Law Review. ***PRACTICE AREAS:*** Litigation. ***Email:*** mjbronson@vssp.com

COREY A. DONOVAN, born Toledo, Ohio, May 17, 1977; admitted to bar, 2002, Ohio; 2003, U.S. District Court, Northern District of Ohio. *Education:* University of Cincinnati (B.A., magna cum laude,1999; J.D., 2002). Phi Beta Kappa; Distinguished Honors Scholar; Executive Member, Moot Court Board; Director of University of Cincinnati College of Law National Moot Court Competition. *Member:* Ohio State and American Bar Associations. ***PRACTICE AREAS:*** General Civil Litigation. ***Email:*** cadonovan@vssp.com

SARAH B. FAIRWEATHER, admitted to bar, 2002, Ohio; 2003, Kentucky and U.S. District Court, Southern District of Ohio. *Education:* Xavier University (B.A., 1995); University of Cincinnati College of Law (J.D., 2002). Member, Public Policy Committee, Greater Cincinnati Alzheimer's Association. *Member:* Cincinnati, Kentucky and American Bar Associations. ***PRACTICE AREAS:*** Litigation. ***Email:*** sbfairweather@vssp.com

ADAM C. SHERMAN, born Dayton, Ohio; admitted to bar, 2002, New York; 2003, California and Ohio; 2004, U.S. Court of Appeals, Sixth Circuit. *Education:* University of Michigan (B.A., Philosophy, with high honors, 1997); Ohio State University/Oxford, United Kingdom (Pre-law program, 1997); New York University School of Law (J.D., 2001). ***PRACTICE AREAS:*** Litigation. ***Email:*** acsherman@vssp.com

MICHAEL L. RICH, born Toronto, Canada, November 11, 1978; admitted to bar, 2003, New York and U.S. Court of Appeals, Sixth Circuit; 2004, Ohio; U.S. District Court, Southern District of Ohio. *Education:* University of Delaware (B.A., Physics, English, magna cum laude, 1997); Stanford University Law School (J.D, 2000). Phi Beta Kappa. Law Clerk to the Honorable Susan J. Dlott, Southern District of Ohio. ***PRACTICE AREAS:*** Litigation; Appellate Practice. ***Email:*** mlrich@vssp.com

WARD B. WASHINGTON, born Dawson Creek, British Columbia, Canada, July 18, 1969; admitted to bar, 2003, Ohio. *Education:* University of Victoria, British Columbia, Canada (B.A., with honors, 1999); Duke University School of Law (J.D., 2003). ***PRACTICE AREAS:*** Litigation. ***Email:*** wbwashington@vssp.com

GEOFFREY M. WHITE, born Miami, Florida, March 26, 1978; admitted to bar, 2003, Ohio. *Education:* Mary Washington College (B.A., 2000); University of Michigan (J.D., 2003). *Member:* Cincinnati Bar Association. ***PRACTICE AREAS:*** Commercial; Real Estate. ***Email:*** gmwhite@vssp.com

ERICA D. GANN, born Lexington, Kentucky; admitted to bar, 2004, Ohio and U.S. District Court, Southern District of Ohio. *Education:* University of Cincinnati (B.A., cum laude, 1995; J.D., 2004); Austin Peay State University (M.M., Vocal Performance, with honors, 1997). Order of the Coif. Managing Editor, University of Cincinnati Law Review, 2003-2004. Author, "Judicial Action in Retrograde: The Case for Applying Section 804 of the Sarbanes-Oxley Act to All Fraud Actions Under the Securities Laws," 72 U.Cin. L. Rev. 1043 (2004). *Member:* Ohio State Bar Association. ***Email:*** edgann@vssp.com

MR. WHITNEY C. GIBSON, born Dayton, Ohio; admitted to bar, 2004, Ohio. *Education:* Pennsylvania State University (B.S., 2000); University of Cincinnati (J.D., 2004). Member, Student Court. Author, "Rethinking The Sixth Circuit's Erosion of First Amendment Rights in Rose v. Stephens," Cincinnati Law Review. ***PRACTICE AREAS:*** Litigation. ***Email:*** wcgibson@vssp.com

JACKIE R. KRUGER, admitted to bar, 2004, Ohio and California. *Education:* University of California, Berkeley (B.A., 2001); University of Michigan (J.D., 2003). *Member:* Cincinnati and American Bar Associations; State Bar of California. ***LANGUAGES:*** Russian. ***Email:*** jrkruger@vssp.com

OF COUNSEL

EUGENE P. RUEHLMANN, born Cincinnati, Ohio, February 23, 1925; admitted to bar, 1950, Ohio. *Education:* University of Cincinnati (A.B., 1948); Harvard University (LL.B., 1950). Phi Beta Kappa. Councilman, 1959-1971 and Mayor, 1967-1971, City of Cincinnati. ***PRACTICE AREAS:*** Corporate Law; Estate Planning; Probate and Trust Law. ***Email:*** epruehlmann@vssp.com

ROGER A. YURCHUCK, born Amityville, New York, June 9, 1938; admitted to bar, 1962, Ohio. *Education:* Northwestern University (A.B., cum laude, 1959); Harvard University (J.D., 1962). Phi Beta Kappa. Vice President and General Counsel, Federal Home Loan Mortgage Corporation, 1971-1973. Vice Chairman and Director, Securities Investor Protection Corporation, 1982-1988. ***PRACTICE AREAS:*** Savings and Loan Law; Real Estate; Financial Institutions Law. ***Email:*** rayurchuck@vssp.com

BARBARA BISON JACOBSON, born Washington, D.C., August 17, 1948; admitted to bar, 1975, Ohio; 1976, District of Columbia; 1979, U.S. Supreme Court; 1980, Proctor in Admiralty. *Education:* Miami University (B.A., 1970); The Ohio State University (J.D., summa cum laude, 1975); National Institute for Trial Advocacy (Diploma, Advanced Trial Advocacy, 1983). Order of the Coif. Recipient, American Jurisprudence Award for Federal Practice and Procedure. Member, 1973-1975 and Issue Planning Editor, 1974-1975, Ohio State Law Journal. Law Clerk to the Honorable William K. Thomas, U.S. District Judge, Northern District of Ohio, 1975-1976. Master of the Bench of the Potter Stewart Inn of Court, 1984-1996/2002-2004. Faculty, Trial Advocacy Institute, National Institute for Trial Advocacy and University of Cincinnati College of Law, 1993-1999. Board of Editors, 1993-1996 and Editor, 1994-1996, Ohio Trial Magazine. Recognized in the Best Lawyers in America, 1993—. Recognized in the Ohio Super Lawyer, 2003. *Member:* Cincinnati (Chair: Intellectual Property Litigation Committee, 2000-2002; Tort and Insurance Committee, 1995-1996; Vice-Chair, 1991-1995), Ohio State and American Bar Associations; The Association of Trial Lawyers of America; Ohio Academy of Trial Lawyers (Member, Board of Trustees, 1993-1997); Hamilton County Trial Lawyers Association (Member, Board of Trustees, 1990-2000; Vice President, 1992-1996; President, 1996-1999); Ohio Women's Bar Association (Co-Chair, Membership committee, 2002—). ***PRACTICE AREAS:*** Litigation; Intellectual Property; Plaintiffs Personal Injury. ***Email:*** bbisonjacobson@vssp.com

DONALD B. LEWIS, born Pittsburgh, Pennsylvania, February 18, 1950; admitted to bar, 1976, Pennsylvania; 1977, Ohio. *Education:* Yale University (B.A., 1972); University of Michigan (J.D., 1976). Formerly with: City of Cincinnati Law Department, 1977-2000; Vorys, Sater, Seymour and Pease LLP, 2000—. *Member:* Cincinnati Bar Association (Member, Local Government Law Committee). ***PRACTICE AREAS:*** Commercial Real Estate; Economic Development; Municipal Law. ***Email:*** dblewis@vssp.com

MARY C. HENKEL, born Cincinnati, Ohio, November 21, 1954; admitted to bar, 1979, Mississippi; 1983, Texas; 1988, Ohio. *Education:* Xavier University (A.B., summa cum laude, 1976); Harvard Law School (J.D., 1979). *Member:* Cincinnati and Ohio State Bar Associations. ***PRACTICE AREAS:*** Litigation; Health Care. ***Email:*** mchenkel@vssp.com

DOUGLAS S. TRIPP, born Ann Arbor, Michigan, August 17, 1957; admitted to bar, 1985, Oklahoma, U.S. District Court, Northern District of Oklahoma and U.S. Court of Appeals, Federal Circuit; 1986, U.S. Court of Appeals, 10th Circuit; 1987, U.S. District Court, Eastern District of Oklahoma; 1992, Ohio and U.S. District Court, Southern District of Ohio; 2005, U.S. District Court, Eastern District of Michigan. *Education:* Eastern Michigan University (B.S., 1980); University of Tulsa (J.D., 1985). ***PRACTICE AREAS:*** Bankruptcy; Workouts; Outsourcing.

CYNTHIA A. SHAFER, born Park Ridge, Illinois, August 19, 1960; admitted to bar, 1986, Ohio; 1987, U.S. Court of Appeals, Sixth Circuit. *Education:* Bowling Green State University (B.S., magna cum laude, 1981); University of Cincinnati (J.D., 1986). Order of the Coif. Clerk for Judge David Nelson, U.S. Court of Appeals, Sixth Circuit, 1985-1987. *Member:* Cincinnati and Ohio State Bar Associations. ***PRACTICE AREAS:*** Financial Institutions Law; Mergers and Acquisitions Law; Securities Law. ***Email:*** cashafer@vssp.com

MICHAEL G. SCHWARTZ, born Cincinnati, Ohio, April 8, 1966; admitted to bar, 1992, Ohio. *Education:* University of Pennsylvania (B.S., Economics, 1988); University of Cincinnati (J.D., 1991); University of Florida (LL.M., Taxation, 1992). Member, Cincinnati Estate Planning Council. Member, Financial Planning Association of Cincinnati. Member, Wharton Club of Cincinnati. *Member:* Cincinnati Bar Association (Member, Board of Trustees and Membership Services Committee). (Certified Specialist in Federal Taxation Laws and Estate Planning, Trust and Probate Law, Ohio State Bar Association). ***PRACTICE AREAS:*** Estate Planning (50%); Closely Held Business (50%). ***Email:*** mgschwartz@vssp.com

ROSEMARY D. WELSH, born Thief River Falls, Minnesota; admitted to bar, 1995, Ohio, Kentucky and U.S. District Court, Southern District of Ohio; U.S. District Court, Eastern and Western Districts of Kentucky. *Education:* Gustavus Adolphus College (B.A., magna cum laude); University of Minnesota (M.A.); University of Cincinnati (J.D., 1995). Lead Articles Editor, University of Cincinnati Law Review, 1994-1995. Author: "Negligent Credentialing: Ohio Expands Hospital Liability in the Wake of Surgery of Love," 73 U.

(This Listing Continued)

VORYS, SATER, SEYMOUR AND PEASE LLP, Cincinnati—Continued

Cinn. L.R. 607, Fall 1994. ***PRACTICE AREAS:*** Litigation; Health Care Law; Workers' Compensation; Retaliatory Discharge; Products Liability; Premises Liability. ***Email:*** rdwelsh@vssp.com

STAFF ATTORNEY

STEVEN R. MILLER, born Marquette, Michigan, March 18, 1969; admitted to bar, 1994, Ohio; 1995, Michigan. *Education:* Albion College (A.B., 1991); Michigan State University - Detroit College of Law (J.D., summa cum laude, 1994). Staff Member, Michigan State University - Detroit College of Law Review, 1992-1994. *Member:* State Bar of Michigan; Ohio State Bar Association; Society for Human Resource Management. ***PRACTICE AREAS:*** Labor and Employment. ***Email:*** srmiller@vssp.com

REPRESENTATIVE CLIENTS: Abercrombie & Fitch; Airborne Express, Inc.; American Showa; Bob Evans Farms, Inc.; Cardinal Health; Columbus Blue Jackets; Consolidated Stores Corp.; Dominion Homes; Eaton Corporation; Greif Bros.; Honda of America Mfg., Inc.; Insurance Federation of Ohio; M/I Homes; Martin Marietta Energy Systems; National City Bank; Fraternal Order of Police; Ohio Casualty Corporation; Ohio League of Financial Institutions; R.G. Barry Corp.; Showa Aluminum Corporation; Techneglas; The Children's Hospital; The Limited, Inc.; The Ohio State University; The Scotts Company; Value City Department Stores; Filene's Basement; DSW; Wendy's International, Inc.; Worthington Industries, Inc.; Hamilton County.
LOCAL COUNSEL: Abbott Laboratories; American Telephone & Telegraph Co.; Anheuser-Busch, Inc.; Ashland Oil, Inc.; B.F. Goodrich Co.; BP America; Emerson Electric; General Electric Company; General Motors Corp.; Goodyear Tire & Rubber; Household Finance Corp.; Mac Tools, Inc.; Navistar International; The Kroger Co.; United States Playing Card Co.; Waste Management; Western Southern Life Insurance Company.

(For Complete Biographical Data on all Personnel, see Professional Biographies at Columbus, Ohio)

WAITE, SCHNEIDER, BAYLESS & CHESLEY CO., L.P.A.

Established in 1860

1513 FOURTH AND VINE TOWER
FOURTH AND VINE STREETS
CINCINNATI, OHIO 45202
Telephone: 513-621-0267
Fax: 513-381-2375; 621-0262
Email: wsbclaw@aol.com
URL: http://www.wsbclaw.com

General Civil Practice. Aviation, Antitrust Litigation, Class Action, Commercial Litigation, Complex Litigation, Corporate Law, Federal Employees Liability, General Civil Trials and Appeals in all Courts, Insurance, Labor, Consolidated and Multi-district Litigation, Products Litigation, Securities Litigation and Wrongful Death.

FIRM PROFILE: Waite, Schneider, Bayless & Chesley Co., L.P.A. one of the oldest law firms in Cincinnati, Ohio, was founded in 1860 as the law firm of Bowler & Cleveland. From its inception until the early 1960's, the law firm maintained primarily a defense practice, representing a multitude of railroads, manufacturing entities and insurance companies. Thereafter, Waite, Schneider, Bayless & Chesley established a plaintiffs' civil practice and today the law firm offers a wide range of legal services with concentration in the areas of complex, class action, consolidated and multidistrict, tort, commercial, antitrust and securities litigation. Continuing professional legal education is a requirement of all attorneys and members of the firm are actively involved in professional associations and civic affairs.

STANLEY M. CHESLEY, born Cincinnati, Ohio, March 26, 1936; admitted to bar, 1960, Ohio; 1978, Kentucky. *Education:* Walnut Hills High School, Cincinnati; University of Cincinnati (B.A., 1958); University of Cincinnati Law School (LL.B., 1960). Omicron Delta Kappa. Member, Lead Counsel Committee, Beverly Hills Fire Litigation, 1978. Member, Lead Counsel Committee, MGM Grand Hotel Fire Litigation, 1980. Co-Chairman, Plaintiffs' Legal Committee, MGM Grand Hotel Fire Litigation, 1981. Member, Lead Counsel Committee, "Bendectin" Litigation, 1982. Member, Plaintiffs' Steering Committee Pan Am Air Disaster, 1982. Lead Counsel, Zimmer Nuclear Power Plant, Cincinnati Gas & Electric, 1982. Member, Agent Orange Plaintiff Committee, 1982. Co-Chairman, Executive Committee, Union Carbide Gas Plant Disaster, Bhopal, India, 1985. Plaintiffs' Lead Counsel Committee, Arrow Air Aircrash, 1986. Lead Counsel, Plaintiffs' Steering Committee, Northwest Air Crash Litigation, 1987. Co-Lead Counsel, ChoiceCare Insurance Litigation, 1987. Plaintiffs' Lead Counsel Committee, Chubb Insurance Co., 1988. Member Plaintiffs' Lead Counsel Committee Fernald Nuclear Power Plant. Member Plaintiffs' Lead Counsel Committee Miamisburg Train Derailment Litigation. Member Plaintiffs' Lead Counsel Committee Pan Am Flight #103, Lockerbie Scotland. Worldwide Class Counsel Bjork Shiley "C/C" Heart Valve Litigation. Co-Chair Plaintiffs' Steering Committee In Re: Breast Implant Litigation, Fen Phen Litigation. Listed in Best Lawyers in America and the Martindale-Hubbell Bar Register of Preeminent Lawyers *Member:* Cincinnati, Ohio State, Kentucky, West Virginia, Federal and American Bar Associations; State Bar of Texas; State Bar of Nevada; The Association of Trial Lawyers of America (Ohio State Committeeman, 1969-1972; Sustaining Member, 1970—; Ohio Chairman, Environmental Law Section, 1970—; Chairman, Tort Section, 1973-1974; National Program Chairman, 1973-1974); Maritime Law Association of the United States; Melvin M. Belli Society; Board of Commissioners on Grievances and Discipline of the Ohio Supreme Court. ***PRACTICE AREAS:*** General Civil Practice; Aviation; Antitrust Litigation; Class Action; Complex Litigation; Consolidated and Multi-District Litigation; Products Liability; Commercial Litigation.

JAMES R. CUMMINS, born Findlay, Ohio, May 13, 1942; admitted to bar, 1967, Ohio; 1970, U.S. District Court, Southern District of Ohio; 1991, U.S. District Court, Northern District of Ohio; 1995, U.S. Court of Appeals, Sixth Circuit; 1999, Kentucky; 2004, U.S. District Court, District of Columbia; 2005, U.S. District Court, Northern District of Illinois. *Education:* Princeton University (A.B., 1964); University of Cincinnati (J.D., 1967); New York University (LL.M. in Foreign and Comparative Law, 1968). Phi Delta Phi. Case Note Editor, University of Cincinnati Law Review, 1966-1967. Listed, International Who's Who of Corporate Governance Lawyers, 2004. Editor, New York International Law Review, 1967-1968. Lecturer: "Attorney Responses to Accountant Opinion Request Letters," Cincinnati Bar Association, 1987; "Civil RICO," Ohio Northern University, 1988; "The Year 2000 Time Bomb: Legal & Corporate Governance Implications for Board of Directors, Trustees and Officers," Cincinnati and Columbus Bar Associations, 1999; "Corporate Ethics: Can Trust Be Rebuilt - Pro-Active Steps Toward Effective Corporate Governance," Cincinnati Bar Association, 2002. Listed in, International Who's Who of Corporate Governance Lawyer, 2004. Member, Board of Commissioners on Grievances and Discipline of Supreme Court of Ohio, 1989-1994. Member, Advisory Committee on Local Rules, U.S. District Court for the Southern District of Ohio. *Member:* Cincinnati (Member, Long Range Planning Subcommittee, 1989), Ohio State, Kentucky and American (Member, Committee on Federal Regulation of Securities, 1981—; Member, Subcommittee on Investment Companies and Investment Advisers, 1981—) Bar Associations. ***PRACTICE AREAS:*** Securities Law; Corporate Law; Commercial Litigation; Health Care; Antitrust. ***Email:*** jcummins@wsbclaw.com

FAY E. STILZ, born Pittsburgh, Pennsylvania, December 24, 1951; admitted to bar, 1978, Ohio. *Education:* Miami University; Xavier University (B.S., 1974); University of Cincinnati (J.D., 1978). *Member:* Cincinnati, Ohio State and American Bar Associations; The Association of Trial Lawyers of America; Ohio Trial Lawyers Association. ***PRACTICE AREAS:*** General Civil Practice; Class Action; Complex Litigation; Consolidated and Multi-District Litigation; Products Liability; Commercial Litigation.

ROBERT A. STEINBERG, born Baltimore, Maryland, December 25, 1942; admitted to bar, 1967, Ohio; 1968, U.S. District Court, Southern District of Ohio; U.S. Court of Appeals, Sixth Circuit. *Education:* Ohio State University (B.A., 1964; J.D., 1966). Teaching Positions: University of Dayton School of Law, 1977-1995, Trial Practice' Evidence, Professional Responsibility, Criminal Law; University of Cincinnati Law School, 1984-1990, Trial Practice; Salmon P. Chase Law School, 1969-1972, Criminal Constitutional Law. Assistant U.S. Attorney, 1968-1977; U.S. Magistrate Judge, 1978-1996. *Member:* Ohio State Bar Association; Federal Bar Association, Cincinnati Chapter (President, 1996), Dayton Chapter (President); Federal Bar Association (National Vice-President); National Council of Magistrate Judges, 1984-1995; Member, Southern District of Ohio Civil Justice Reform Committee and Ohio Local Rules Committee, 1993-1996. Potter Stewart Inn of Court; Master of the Bench. ***PRACTICE AREAS:*** Complex and Multi-District Litigation; Class Action Litigation; Major Tort Litigation; Antitrust Litigation; Shareholders Litigation; Employment Discrimination; Private Mediation Services. ***Email:*** bobsteinberg@wsbclaw.cc

LOUISE M. ROSELLE, born Cleveland, Ohio, November 30, 1948; admitted to bar, 1972, Ohio. *Education:* The Ohio State University (B.S., 1969; J.D., cum laude, 1971); University of Cincinnati (M.B.A., 1977). Author: Article 19 - "Clean Air Act Amendments of 1970," published in the 1974 issue of the Boston College Commercial Business and Law Review. *Member:* Cincinnati, Ohio State and American Bar Associations; The Association of Trial Lawyers of America. ***PRACTICE AREAS:*** Environmental; Toxic Torts; Class Actions. ***Email:*** louiseroselle@wsbclaw.com

THOMAS F. REHME, born Cincinnati, Ohio, April 1, 1929; admitted to bar, 1954, Ohio. *Education:* Georgetown University (B.S.S., 1951); Yale University (LL.B., 1954). Phi Alpha Delta. House Counsel, Diamond Shamrock Chemical Corp., Cleveland, Ohio, 1964-1969. Assistant City Solicitor, Cincinnati, Ohio, 1969-1993. *Member:* Cincinnati and Federal Bar Associations. ***PRACTICE AREAS:*** Municipal Law; Contractual Law; Real Estate; Probate; Taxation.

D. ARTHUR RABOURN, born Ashland, Kentucky, January 22, 1953; admitted to bar, 1979, Ohio. *Education:* Morehead State University (A.B., 1975); Salmon P. Chase College of Law of Northern Kentucky University (J.D., 1978). *Member:* Cincinnati, Ohio State and American Bar Associations; Ohio Academy of Trial Lawyers; The Association of Trial Lawyers of America. ***PRACTICE AREAS:*** Complex Litigation; Trial Practice; General Tort; Employer Intentional Torts; Product Liability; FELA Litigation.

TROY W. SKEENS, JR., born Cincinnati, Ohio, August 6, 1954; admitted to bar, 1981, Ohio; 1982, U.S. District Court, Southern District of Ohio and U.S. Court of Appeals, Sixth Circuit; 1983, U.S. District Court, Eastern District of Kentucky; 1987, Kentucky; 2004, U.S. District Court, Northern District of Ohio. *Education:* University of Cincinnati (B.A., 1977); Pettit College of Law, Ohio Northern University (J.D., 1981). Delta Theta Phi; Order of Barristers. Author: "The Role of Trial Counsel," Kentucky Civil Practice at Trial, Civil Practice Handbook Series, Vol. II, 1990. *Member:* Cincinnati, Northern Kentucky, Kentucky and Ohio State Bar Associations. ***PRACTICE AREAS:*** Litigation; Personal Injury; Maritime Law; Class Actions; Complex Litigation. ***Email:*** tws@wsbclaw.com

PAUL M. DE MARCO, born Youngstown, Ohio, August 13, 1959; admitted to bar, 1984, California; 1989, Ohio; U.S. Supreme Court; U.S. Court of Appeals, 1st Circuit; U.S. Court of Appeals, 5th Circuit; U.S. Court of Appeals, 6th Circuit; U.S. Court of Appeals, 7th Circuit; U.S. Court of Appeals, 9th Circuit; U.S. Court of Appeals, 10th Circuit; U.S. District Court, Southern District of Ohio; U.S. District Court, Northern District of Ohio; U.S. District Court, Eastern District of California; U.S. District Court, Central District of California; U.S. District Court, Southern District of California. *Education:* College of Wooster (B.A., 1981); McGeorge School of Law, University of the Pacific (J.D., with distinction, 1983); University of Cambridge (1985). Phi Beta Kappa; Order of the Coif. Recipient: American Jurisprudence Award, Civil Procedure. Traynor Moot Court Competition Team. Traynor Honor Society. Research Attorney to Presiding Justice Robert K. Puglia, California Court of Appeals, Third Appellate District, 1984-1985; to Associate Justice Frances N. Carr, California Court of Appeals, Third Appellate District, 1986. Secretary, Collaborative Law Center. Member: Grievance Committee; Prison Reform Advocacy Center; Cincinnati Citizens Police Review Panel, 1999-2002. *Member:* Federal Bar Association, Ohio State Bar Association; Cincinnati Bar Association; American Bar Association. ***REPORTED CASES:*** Procter & Gamble Co. v. Amway Corp., 242 F.3d 539 (5th Cir. 2001); Baker v. LaBoeuf, Lamb, Leiby & MacRae, 105 F.3d 1102 (6th Cir. 1997); In re NLO, Inc., 5 F.3d 154 (6th Cir. 1993); In re Allied-Signal, Inc., 891 F.2d 974 (1st Cir. 1989); In re Allied Signal, Inc., 891 F.2d 967 (1st Cir. 1989); City of Cincinnati v. Beretta U.S.A. Corp., 768

(This Listing Continued)

N.E.2d 1136 (Ohio 2002); Norgard v. Brush Wellman, Inc., 766 N.E.2d 977 (Ohio 2002); Wallace v. Ohio Dep't of Commerce, 773 N.E.2d 1018 (Ohio 2002); Chamberlain v. AK Steel Corp., 696 N.E.2d (Ohio 1998); State of Ohio ex rel. A & D Ltd. P'ship v. Keefe, 671 N.E.2d 13 (Ohio 1996); Tulloh v. Goodyear Atomic Corp., 584 N.E.2d 729 (Ohio 1992); Begala v. PNC Bank, Ohio, N.A., 756 N.E.2d 215 (Ohio App. 2001). ***PRACTICE AREAS:*** Appellate Practice; Complex Litigation; Class Actions; Commercial Litigation; Multi-District Litigation.

TERRENCE L. GOODMAN, born Detroit, Michigan, March 30, 1958; admitted to bar, 1984, Ohio; U.S. District Court, Southern District of Ohio. *Education:* Albion College (B.A., summa cum laude, 1981); Washington & Lee University (J.D., 1984). Phi Beta Kappa. Recipient, American Jurisprudence Award in Contracts, 1984. Author: "Minimum Contacts and Contracts, The Breached Relationship," 40 Washington & Lee University Review. *Member:* Cincinnati, Ohio State and American Bar Associations. ***PRACTICE AREAS:*** Complex Litigation; Multi-District Litigation; Class Action Litigation.

ROBERT HEUCK II, born Cincinnati, Ohio, December 5, 1956; admitted to bar, 1985, Oregon; 1987, U.S. District Court, District of Oregon and U.S. Court of Appeals, Ninth Circuit; 1988, California and U.S. District Court, Northern District of California; 1989, U.S. District Court, Eastern District of California; 1990, U.S. District Court, Southern District of California and U.S. Supreme Court; 1991, Ohio and U.S. District Court, Southern District of Ohio; 1999, U.S. Court of Appeals, Tenth Circuit. *Education:* Reed College (B.A., 1981); University of Oregon (J.D., 1985). Order of the Coif. Law Clerk, U.S. Court of Appeals, Ninth Circuit, 1985-1987. *Member:* Cincinnati and Ohio State Bar Associations; Oregon State Bar; State Bar of California. ***PRACTICE AREAS:*** Complex Litigation; Products Liability; Personal Injury; Commercial Litigation. ***Email:*** Heuck@wsbclaw.cc

JANE HANNA WALKER, born Cincinnati, Ohio, July 18, 1957; admitted to bar, 1984, Ohio; 1988, U.S. District Court, Southern District of Ohio. *Education:* University of Cincinnati (B.A., 1980); Ohio Northern University College of Law (J.D., 1983). Member, National Moot Court. *Member:* Cincinnati, Ohio State and American Bar Associations; Ohio Academy of Trial Lawyers. ***PRACTICE AREAS:*** Civil Litigation; Personal Injury Litigation; Class Action Litigation; Multi-District Litigation. ***Email:*** Janehwalker@wsbclaw.com

JEAN M. GEOPPINGER, born Cincinnati, Ohio, June 1, 1965; admitted to bar, 1990, Ohio; 1991, U.S. District Court, Southern District of Ohio; 1992, U.S. Court of Appeals, Sixth Circuit; 2004, U.S. Court of Appeals, Eleventh Circuit; 2005, U.S. Court of Appeals, Second Circuit. *Education:* Miami University European Center (1986); Miami University (B.A., cum laude, University Honors, 1987); University of Cincinnati College of Law (J.D., 1990). Phi Beta Kappa; Phi Alpha Delta. Recipient, American Jurisprudence Award in Advocacy. University of Cincinnati Law Review, Member, 1988-1989, Business Manager, 1989-1990. Counselor/Executive Director, Member, Potter Stewart American Inn of Court. *Member:* Cincinnati, Ohio State and American Bar Associations. ***LANGUAGES:*** German. ***PRACTICE AREAS:*** Litigation; Complex Litigation; Class Action; Aviation Litigation. ***Email:*** jeangeoppinger@wsbclaw.com

MELANIE S. CORWIN, born Cincinnati, Ohio, July 9, 1962; admitted to bar, 1990, Ohio; 1991, U.S. District Court, Southern District of Ohio; 1992, U.S. Court of Appeals, Sixth Circuit; 1999, Kentucky. *Education:* Eastern Kentucky University (B.A., 1984); Salmon P. Chase College of Law, Northern Kentucky University (J.D., 1990). *Member:* Cincinnati, Ohio State, Kentucky and American Bar Associations. ***PRACTICE AREAS:*** Employment Law; Corporate Law; Corporate Governance Law; Business Law; Securities Law; Litigation; Employment Litigation; Commercial Litigation. ***Email:*** mcorwin@wsbclaw.com

RENÉE A. INFANTE, born Youngstown, Ohio, March 9, 1965; admitted to bar, 1991, Ohio and U.S. District Court, Southern District of Ohio; 1992, U.S. Court of Appeals, Sixth Circuit; 1997, Kentucky; 2001, U.S. District Court, Eastern District of Kentucky. *Education:* Miami University (B.A., 1987); Oxford University, Oxford, England; Ohio State University (J.D., 1990). *Member:* Cincinnati, Northern Kentucky, Kentucky, Ohio State and American Bar Associations; Association of Trial Lawyers of America; Ohio Association of Trial Lawyers (Member, Board of Trustees); Kentucky Association of Trial Lawyers. ***PRACTICE AREAS:*** Civil Litigation; Personal Injury Litigation; Class Action Litigation.

RODGER N. WALK

THE NATHANIEL ROPES BUILDING
917 MAIN STREET, SUITE 400
CINCINNATI, OHIO 45202
Telephone: 513-977-4220
Fax: 513-977-4218
Email: rnwalklaw@fuse.net
URL: http://www.lawyers.com/rnwalklaw

Catastrophic Injury and Loss, Wrongful Death, Medical Malpractice, Personal Injury, Complex Commercial Litigation, Collaborative Divorce, Business and Commercial Law, Family Law, Litigation and Appeals, Alternative Dispute Resolution, Employee Employment Law, Products Liability.

RODGER N. WALK, born Chicago, Illinois, August 19, 1948; admitted to bar, 1974, Ohio, U.S. District Court, Southern District of Ohio, Eastern District of Kentucky and Northern District of California, and U.S. Court of Appeals, Sixth Circuit. *Education:* University of Cincinnati (B.A., 1970; M.A., 1972; J.D., 1974). Omicron Delta Epsilon. *Member:* Cincinnati, Ohio State and American Bar Associations; The Association of Trial Lawyers of America. ***PRACTICE AREAS:*** Catastrophic Injury; Wrongful Death; Medical Malpractice; Personal Injury; Commercial Litigation; Complex Litigation; Divorce; Business Law; Commercial Law; Family Law; Appellate Practice; Alternative Dispute Resolution; Bankruptcy; Employment Law; Products Liability.

WELTMAN, WEINBERG & REIS CO., L.P.A.

525 VINE STREET, SUITE 800
CINCINNATI, OHIO 45202
Telephone: 513-723-2200
Fax: 513-723-2239
Email: wwr@weltman.com
URL: http://www.weltman.com

Burlington, New Jersey Office: Telephone: 609-914-0437.
Deerfield, Illinois Office: Telephone: 847-940-9812.
Chicago, Illinois Office: Telephone: 312-786-9676.
Cleveland, Ohio Office: Telephone: 216-685-1000.
Columbus, Ohio Office: Telephone: 614-228-7272.
Philadelphia, Pennsylvania Office: Telephone: 215-599-1500.
Pittsburgh, Pennsylvania Office: Telephone: 412-434-7955.
Troy, Michigan Office: Telephone: 248-362-6100.

See Firm Profile and Statement of Practice under Cleveland, Ohio Listing.

FRANK J. VENEZIANO, born Fremont, Ohio, December 3, 1959; admitted to bar, 1985, Ohio; 1991, U.S. District Court, Southern District of Ohio. *Education:* Ohio Wesleyan University (B.A., with departmental honors, 1982); University of Cincinnati College of Law (J.D., 1985). *Member:* Cincinnati and Ohio State Bar Associations. ***PRACTICE AREAS:*** Creditors Rights; Commercial and Consumer Litigation; Foreclosure/Evictions; Banking; Collection Law; Litigation and Defense. ***Email:*** fveneziano@weltman.com

GLENN E. ALGIE, born Fort Thomas, Kentucky, June 6, 1963; admitted to bar, 1988, Kentucky; 1989, Ohio; 1990, U.S. District Court, Eastern District of Kentucky; 2001, U.S. District Court, Southern District of Ohio. *Education:* University of Kentucky (B.A., with distinction, 1985); University of Kentucky School of Law (J.D., 1988). *Member:* Cincinnati, Ohio State, Kentucky and Northern Kentucky Bar Associations. ***PRACTICE AREAS:*** Creditors Rights; Legal Action Recovery; Litigation and Defense; Civil Litigation; Bankruptcy. ***Email:*** galgie@weltman.com

BRIAN E. CHAPMAN, born Ashland, Kentucky, January 26, 1962; admitted to bar, 1987, Kentucky; 1988, Ohio; 1989, U.S. District Court, Eastern and Western Districts of Kentucky; 1990, U.S. District Court, Southern District of Ohio; 1996, U.S. Court of Appeals, Sixth Circuit. *Education:* University of Kentucky (B.B.A., 1984); Salmon P. Chase College of Law (J.D., 1987). Counselor, Kentucky Lawyers Assistance Program (Kentucky Bar Association). *Member:* Cincinnati, Ohio State, Northern Kentucky and Kentucky Bar Associations. ***PRACTICE AREAS:*** Creditors Rights; Commercial Law; Collections; Legal Action Recovery. ***Email:*** bchapman@weltman.com

DAVID W. CLIFFE, born Fostoria, Ohio, December 6, 1966; admitted to bar, 1992, Ohio; 1993, U.S. District Court, Southern District of Ohio; 1995, U.S. District Court, Northern District of Ohio. *Education:* Yale University (B.A., 1989); University of Cincinnati College of Law (J.D., 1992). Merit Scholar, University of Cincinnati College of Law. *Member:* Hancock County and Ohio State Bar Associations. ***PRACTICE AREAS:*** Foreclosure/Evictions; Creditor. ***Email:*** dcliffe@weltman.com

JEANNETTE M. CONRAD, born Oak Park, Illinois, August 14, 1972; admitted to bar, 2003, Kentucky, U.S. District Court, Eastern and Western Districts of Kentucky and U.S. District Court, Northern and Southern Districts of Indiana; 2004, Indiana (Not admitted in Ohio). *Education:* Sullivan University (BS., cum laude, Business, 1998); University of Louisville, Louis D. Brandeis School of Law (J.D., 2003). *Member:* Louisville (Member, Sections on: Bankruptcy; Business Law; Litigation; Young Lawyers), Indianapolis, Kentucky (Member, Sections on: Bankruptcy; Young Lawyers), Indiana State and American Bar Associations. ***PRACTICE AREAS:*** Creditors Rights; Bankruptcy. ***Email:*** jconrad@weltman.com

JOHN L. DAY, JR., born Covington, Kentucky, January 9, 1949; admitted to bar, 1981, Kentucky and Ohio; 1982, U.S. District Court, Southern District of Ohio; 1983, U.S. Court of Appeals, Sixth Circuit; 1996, U.S. District Court, Western District of Kentucky; 1998, U.S. District Court, Southern District of Indiana; 2001, U.S. District Court, Northern District of Ohio; 2002, U.S. District Court, Eastern District of Kentucky. *Education:* University of Kentucky (B.A., 1973); Salmon P. Chase College of Law (J.D., 1981). Associate Editor, Northern Kentucky Law Review, 1980-1981. *Member:* Kentucky and Ohio State Bar Associations. ***PRACTICE AREAS:*** Bankruptcy Law; Banking Law; Creditors Rights; Commercial Litigation. ***Email:*** jday@weltman.com

LAURA R. FAULKNER, born Columbus, Ohio, August 18, 1974; admitted to bar, 1999, Ohio; 2000, U.S. District Court, Southern District of Ohio; 2001, U.S. District Court, Northern District of Ohio. *Education:* Miami University (B.A. in Political Science and English Literature, 1996); University of Dayton (J.D., 1999). *Member:* Cincinnati and Ohio State Bar Associations; American Bankruptcy Law Forum. ***PRACTICE AREAS:*** Bankruptcy; Creditors Rights. ***Email:*** lfaulkner@weltman.com

GAIL C. HERSH, JR., born Fort Lauderdale, Florida, December 7, 1964; admitted to bar, 1992, Ohio; 1994, Kentucky; 1995, U.S. District Court, Eastern District of Kentucky and U.S. District Court, Southern District of Ohio. *Education:* Kenyon College (B.A., 1987); University of Cincinnati (J.D., 1991). *Member:* Cincinnati and Kentucky Bar Associations. ***PRACTICE AREAS:*** Creditors Rights; Foreclosure/Evictions; Real Estate. ***Email:*** ghersh@weltman.com

SUSAN B. KLINEMAN, born Indianapolis, Indiana, August 9, 1965; admitted to bar, 1993, Indiana, U.S. Court of Appeals, Seventh Circuit and U.S. District Court, Northern and Southern Districts of Indiana; 2001, Ohio. *Education:* Purdue University (B.A., 1987); Indiana University School of Law- Indianapolis (J.D., 1993). *Member:* Indiana State Bar Association; Cincinnati Bar Association; Indianapolis Bar Association. ***PRACTICE AREAS:*** Real Estate; Creditors Rights; Bankruptcy; Foreclosure/Evictions. ***Email:*** sklineman@weltman.com

AMY TRIPLETT MORGAN, born Ashland, Kentucky, December 19, 1971; admitted to bar, 1999, Ohio and Kentucky; 2000, U.S. District Court, Southern District of Ohio; 2001, U.S. District Court, Eastern District of Kentucky; 2003, U.S. District Court, Western

(This Listing Continued)

WELTMAN, WEINBERG & REIS CO., L.P.A., Cincinnati—Continued

District of Kentucky and U.S. District Court, Northern District of Ohio. *Education:* Marshall University (B.A., 1995); The University of Toledo College of Law (J.D., 1998). *Member:* Cincinnati Bar Association; Northern Kentucky Bar Association. **Email:** amorgan@weltman.com

THOMAS R. MYERS, born Louisville, Kentucky, August 27, 1963; admitted to bar, 1988, Ohio; 2001, Kentucky. *Education:* University of Cincinnati (B.A., cum laude, 1985); University of Cincinnati College of Law (J.D., 1988). *Member:* Cincinnati and Kentucky Bar Associations. ***PRACTICE AREAS:*** Creditors Rights; Commercial Law; Collections; Legal Action Recovery. ***Email:*** tmyers@weltman.com

KAROLINA F. PERR, born Columbus, Indiana, December 5, 1964; admitted to bar, 1989, Pennsylvania and U.S. District Court, Eastern District of Pennsylvania; 1996, Indiana, Ohio, U.S. District Court, Southern and Northern Districts of Indiana and U.S. District Court, Southern District of Ohio; 2004, U.S. District Court, Eastern and Western Districts of Michigan. *Education:* Indiana University (B.A., in Psychology, 1986); University of Dayton School of Law (J.D., 1989). *Member:* Indiana State and Cincinnati Bar Associations. ***LANGUAGES:*** Hungarian, French. ***PRACTICE AREAS:*** Creditors Representation; Bankruptcy. ***Email:*** kperr@weltman.com

PHILIP Q. RATLIFF, born South Williamson, Kentucky, November 19, 1960; admitted to bar, 1992, Kentucky, U.S. District Court, Eastern District of Kentucky and U.S. Court of Appeals, Sixth Circuit; 1995, U.S. District Court, Western District of Kentucky; 1999, West Virginia and U.S. District Court, Southern District of West Virginia (Not admitted in Ohio). *Education:* Eastern Kentucky University (B.B.A., 1982); University of Louisville (J.D., 1991); Morehead State University (M.B.A., 1994). *Member:* Kentucky and West Virginia Bar Associations. ***PRACTICE AREAS:*** Creditors Rights; Real Estate; Foreclosure/Evictions. ***Email:*** pratliff@weltman.com

NICHOLAS K. ROHNER, born Cincinnati, Ohio, September 14, 1974; admitted to bar, 2001, Ohio and U.S. District Court, Southern District of Ohio; 2002, Indiana and U.S. District Court, Northern and Southern Districts of Indiana. *Education:* Miami University (B.A., 1997); University of Cincinnati College of Law (J.D., 2001). *Member:* Indiana State, Ohio State and Cincinnati Bar Associations. ***PRACTICE AREAS:*** Creditors Rights; Collections; Civil Litigation; Legal Action Recovery; Litigation and Defense. ***Email:*** nrohner@weltman.com

ANNE M. SMITH, born Memphis, Tennessee, July 26, 1963; admitted to bar, 1989, Ohio; 1993, Kentucky; 1995, U.S. District Court, Western District of Kentucky. *Education:* Murray State University (B.S., 1985); Salmon P. Chase College of Law (J.D., 1989). Vice-President, Salmon P. Chase Student Bar Association, 1988-1989. Recipient, Commonwealth Scholarship for Legal Studies, 1985. Assistant County Attorney, Livingston County, 1999-2004. Solo Practitioner, 1999-2004. *Member:* Kentucky, Ohio State and Marshall County Bar Associations. ***PRACTICE AREAS:*** Foreclosure/Evictions (80%); Creditors Rights (10%); Real Estate Title Insurance (10%). ***Email:*** ansmith@weltman.com

CHARLES L. TATE, born Cincinnati, Ohio, November 20, 1962; admitted to bar, 2000, Ohio. *Education:* University of Cincinnati (B.A., 1995); University of Cincinnati College of Law (J.D., 1999). *Member:* Cincinnati and Ohio State Bar Associations. ***PRACTICE AREAS:*** Creditors Rights; Legal Action Recovery; Litigation. ***Email:*** ctate@weltman.com

R. MATTHEW VAN SICKLE, born Rome, New York, December 6, 1978; admitted to bar, 2003, Indiana and U.S. District Court, Southern District of Indiana; 2004, U.S. District Court, Northern District of Indiana; 2005, North Carolina (Not admitted in Ohio). *Education:* Wake Forest University (B.A., 2000); Indiana University School of Law - Bloomington (J.D., 2003). *Member:* Indiana State Bar Association; Indianapolis Bar Association. ***PRACTICE AREAS:*** Creditors Rights; Legal Action Recovery. ***Email:*** mvansickle@weltman.com

(For complete biographical data, see Professional Biographies at other locations)

WHITE, GETGEY & MEYER CO., L.P.A.

1700 FOURTH & VINE TOWER
1 WEST FOURTH STREET
CINCINNATI, OHIO 45202-3621
Telephone: 513-241-3685
Fax: 513-241-2399

Civil Litigation, Personal Injury Law, Medical Malpractice Law, Workers Compensation Law, Appellate Practice.

RONALD A. MEYER, born New York, New York, May 14, 1944; admitted to bar, 1969, Ohio, U.S. District Court, Southern District of Ohio and U.S. Claims Court. *Education:* The Ohio State University (B.A., 1966); University of Cincinnati (J.D., 1969). *Member:* Cincinnati and Ohio State Bar Associations; The Association of Trial Lawyers of America; Hamilton County Trial Lawyers Association; Ohio Academy of Trial Lawyers. ***PRACTICE AREAS:*** Medical Malpractice Law; Personal Injury Law; Product Liability Law; Insurance Law; Civil Litigation.

NICHOLAS E. BUNCH, born Indianapolis, Indiana, October 23, 1953; admitted to bar, 1980, Ohio and U.S. District Court, Southern District of Ohio; 1982, U.S. Tax Court; 1990, U.S. Claims Court. *Education:* The Ohio State University (B.S., 1975); University of Dayton (J.D., 1980). *Member:* Butler County, Cincinnati and Ohio State Bar Associations; Ohio Academy of Trial Lawyers. ***PRACTICE AREAS:*** Medical Malpractice Law; Legal Malpractice Law; Personal Injury Law; Insurance Law; Product Liability Law. ***Email:*** nbunch@wgmlpa.com

DAVID P. KAMP, born Cincinnati, Ohio, August 10, 1952; admitted to bar, 1981, Ohio, U.S. District Court, Northern and Southern Districts of Ohio, District of Tennessee, District of Kansas and District of New Jersey, and U.S. Court of Appeals, Sixth Circuit. *Education:* Thomas More College (B.A., 1978); University of Cincinnati (J.D., 1981). Barrister, Potter Stewart Inn of Court. Member, Editorial Board, University of Cincinnati Law Review, 1980. Past Chairman, Board of Trustees, Ohio Client Security Fund. Member: National Association of Securities Dealers; American Stock Exchange; Center for Mediation of Disputes. *Member:* Cincinnati, Ohio State and American Bar Associations; The Association of Trial Lawyers of America; Ohio Academy of Trial Lawyers; Past President, Hamilton County Trial Lawyers Association. ***PRACTICE AREAS:*** Civil Litigation; Commercial Litigation; Personal Injury; Medical Malpractice; Family Law; Securities Litigation; ERISA; Product Liability.

GLENDA MORGAN HERTZMAN, born Middletown, Ohio, August 31, 1946; admitted to bar, 1979, Ohio and U.S. District Court, Southern District of Ohio. *Education:* Muskingum College (B.A., 1970); Capital University Law School (J.D., magna cum laude, 1979). Order of the Curia. Editor-in-Chief, Capital University Law Review, 1978-1979. *Member:* Cincinnati (Chairperson, Unauthorized Practice of Law Committee) and Ohio State Bar Associations; Ohio Academy of Trial Lawyers; Association of Trial Lawyers of America; Hamilton County Trial Lawyers Association. (Certified Specialist in Workers' Compensation Law, Ohio State Bar Association). ***PRACTICE AREAS:*** Civil Litigation; Workers Compensation Law; Social Security Disability Law. ***Email:*** GHertzman@wgmlpa.com

CARL J. STICH, JR., born Louisville, Kentucky, April 18, 1953; admitted to bar, 1980, Ohio; 1981, Kentucky; U.S. District Court, Southern and Northern Districts of Ohio; U.S. District Court, Eastern and Western Districts of Kentucky; U.S. District Court, Eastern and Western District of Arkansas; U.S. Court of Appeals, Sixth Circuit; U.S. Supreme Court. *Education:* University of Kentucky (B.S., 1976; J.D., 1980). Member, Kentucky Law Journal, 1978-1980. Moot Court Board, National Team. Assistant Special Prosecutor, State of Ohio, 1985-1994. Special Prosecutor, Commonwealth of Kentucky, 1991-1994. Assistant Independent Counsel (Whitewater Investigation) 1994. *Member:* Ohio State, Kentucky and American Bar Association. ***PRACTICE AREAS:*** Civil Litigation. ***Email:*** cstich@wgmlpa.com

---

LEONA BETH ZAHNEIS, born Louisville, Kentucky, October 22, 1971; admitted to bar, 2001, Ohio. *Education:* Eastern Kentucky University (B.S., Nursing, 1993); Salmon P. Chase College of Law (J.D., 2001). Order of the Curia. Recipient, Judge West Award, Northern Kentucky Bar Association. Nursing License, Kentucky, 1993. *Member:* Cincinnati, Ohio State and Northern Kentucky Bar Associations. ***PRACTICE AREAS:*** Medical Malpractice; Litigation. ***Email:*** bzahneis@wgmlpa.com

C. JOSEPH MCCULLOUGH, born October 25, 1973; admitted to bar, 1998, Ohio, U.S. District Court, Southern District of Ohio and U.S. Court of Appeals, Sixth Circuit. *Education:* Butler University (B.S., 1995); University of Dayton (J.D., 1998). ***PRACTICE AREAS:*** Civil Litigation. ***Email:*** jmccullough@wgmlpa.com

OF COUNSEL

REETA H. BRENDAMOUR, born Chicago, Illinois, October 3, 1958; admitted to bar, 1996, Ohio; 1997, Illinois. *Education:* Hanover College (B.A., 1981); University of Cincinnati (J.D., 1996). Instructor, Family Law, University of Cincinnati College of Law, 2000—. *Member:* Cincinnati and Ohio State Bar Associations. ***PRACTICE AREAS:*** Domestic Relations. ***Email:*** rbrendmour@wgmlpa.com

TODD H. BAILEY, born Middletown, Ohio, April 24, 1951; admitted to bar, 1976, Ohio and U.S. District Court, Southern District of Ohio; 1978, U.S. District Court, Eastern District of Kentucky; 1980, U.S. Court of Appeals, Sixth Circuit; registered to practice before U.S. Patent and Trademark Office. *Education:* Miami University, Ohio (B.A., magna cum laude, 1973; honorary Doctor of Laws, 1992); Duke University (J.D., with distinction, 1976). Phi Beta Kappa. Formerly with: Frost Brown Todd, Cincinnati, Ohio; Greenebaum, Doll & McDonald LLP, Cincinnati, Ohio. Affiliate Member, Industrial Designers Association of America. Adjunct Professor, 2002-2005 and Markley Visiting Professor, 2005, Miami University; Adjunct Professor, Xavier M.B.A. Program, 2004-2005. Mediator, Center for Resolution of Disputes, Cincinnati, Ohio. *Member:* Cincinnati (Chair, Intellectual Property Litigation Committee), Ohio State (Member: Litigation Committee; Intellectual Property Law Section), Federal (Member, Sections on: Intellectual Property; Litigation; Alternative Dispute Resolution) and American (Member, Sections on: Intellectual Property; Litigation; Litigation & Alternative Dispute Resolution) Bar Associations; Defense Research Institute; Ohio Association of Trial Attorneys; Industrial Designer Society of America (Member, Litigation Committee). ***SPECIAL AGENCIES:*** Collaberative Law Center, Trained Mediator. ***PRACTICE AREAS:*** Civil Litigation. ***Email:*** tbailey@wgmlpa.com

BRUCE B. WHITMAN

Established in 1982

3536 EDWARDS ROAD, SUITE 100
CINCINNATI, OHIO 45208
Telephone: 513-321-3940
Fax: 513-321-3929
Email: bbwhits123@aol.com
URL: http://www.whitmanlawoffice.com

Civil Litigation, Product Liability, Employment Law, Medical Malpractice, Wrongful Death, Criminal Defense and Personal Injury, Divorce/Dissolution, Business Litigation.

FIRM PROFILE: We handle complex civil litigation and criminal defense. This includes medical malpractice, plaintiff and defense.

BRUCE B. WHITMAN, born Chicago, Illinois, December 15, 1951; admitted to bar, 1980, Ohio and U.S. District Court, Southern District of Ohio; 1981, U.S. Court of Appeals, 6th Circuit; 1983, U.S. District Court, Eastern District of Kentucky; 1984, U.S. Supreme Court. *Education:* University of Cincinnati (B.A., with honors in History, 1975; J.D., 1980). Phi Alpha Theta. Author: "The Use of Rule 17C in Preparing a Defense," The Vindicator, Winter 1989. Judicial Candidate, 2002. Member, Board of Cincinnati Human Relations Commission, 1991-1997, Treasurer, 1993-1995. *Member:* Cincinnati, Ohio State and

(This Listing Continued)

American Bar Associations; Cincinnati Criminal Defense Lawyers Association; Ohio Criminal Defense Lawyers Association; The Association of Trial Lawyers of America; Ohio Academy of Trial Lawyers; Hamilton County Trial Lawyers Association (Trustee, 1993-1997).

VIRGINIA CONLAN WHITMAN

Established in 1993

ONE WEST FOURTH STREET, SUITE 1700
CINCINNATI, OHIO 45202-3621
Telephone: 513-352-0401
FAX: 513-241-2399
Email: vwhitman@wgmlpa.com

General Civil Litigation in State and Federal Courts. Employment Discrimination, Employee Counseling, Business Litigation.

VIRGINIA CONLAN WHITMAN, born Cincinnati, Ohio, May 26, 1949; admitted to bar, 1981, Ohio; 1982, U.S. District Court, Southern District of Ohio and U.S. Court of Appeals, Sixth Circuit. *Education:* University of Cincinnati (B.A., high honors in Political Science, 1978); Marquette University; University of Cincinnati (J.D., 1981). Barrister, Counselor, Potter Stewart American Inn of Court, 1984-1986. Student Articles Editor, University of Cincinnati Law Review, 1980-1981. Recipient: Best Editorial Note, 1980-1981; Best Casenote, 1979-1980. Law Clerk to Hon. S. Arthur Spiegel, Judge, U.S. District Court, Southern District of Ohio. Special Master: Teletronics/Accufix Class Action Settlement, S.D. Ohio, 1998—; Miller v. CCC Class Action Settlement, S.D. Ohio, 2003-2004. Member: Local Federal Rules Committee, S.D. Ohio, 2004—; Federal Magistrate Selection Committee, 2005. Life Member, Sixth Circuit Judicial Conference of the United States. *Member:* Cincinnati and Ohio State Bar Associations; Cincinnati Employment Lawyers Association; National Employment Lawyers Association; Hamilton County Trial Lawyers Association; American Arbitration Association (Arbitrator, Employment Law Panel).

MICHAEL J. WIETHE

SUITE 1800 FEDERATED BUILDING
7 WEST SEVENTH STREET
CINCINNATI, OHIO 45202
Telephone: 513-241-7332
Fax: 513-621-5410
Email: mjwiethe@fuse.net
URL: http://www.mjwiethe.com

General Practice.

MICHAEL J. WIETHE, born Cincinnati, Ohio, 1947; admitted to bar, 1972, Ohio. *Education:* St. Louis University (B.A., 1969); University of Cincinnati (J.D., 1972). *Member:* Cincinnati, Ohio State and Federal (Member, Board of Directors) Bar Associations. ***PRACTICE AREAS:*** Domestic Relations (25%, 40); Bankruptcy (25%, 50); Small Business Corporations (25%, 40); Personal Injury (25%, 15).

THE WOLFE PRACTICE, LPA

Established in 2000

4445 LAKE FOREST DRIVE, SUITE 420
CINCINNATI, OHIO 45242
Telephone: 513-618-8700
Fax: 513-618-8740
Email: jwolfe@twplaw.com
URL: http://www.twplaw.com

Banks and Banking, Business Law, Business Litigation, Business Transactions, Closely Held Business Law, Joint Ventures, Commercial Law, Commercial Real Estate, Communications and Media, Construction Law, Contracts, Copyrights, Corporate Law, Corporate Finance, Corporate Litigation, Environmental Law, Finance, Commercial Finance, Franchises and Franchising, General Practice, Health Care, Intellectual Property, Internet Law, Labor and Employment, Litigation, Mergers, Acquisitions and Divestitures, Nonprofit and Charitable Organizations, Partnership Law, Probate, Real Estate, Taxation, Trade Secrets, Trademarks, Trusts and Estates, Unfair Competition, Zoning, Planning and Land Use. Adoption, Cohabitation Agreements; Divorce Law; Domestic Relations Law; Marital Property Law; Matrimonial Law; Non-Traditional Family Law; Paternity Law; Post-Divorce Law; Premarital Agreements; Separation Agreements; Spousal Support Law.

FIRM PROFILE: The largest woman-owned law firm in Ohio, The Wolfe Practice provides the highest quality in long-term, multidimensional legal services. Client service is at the heart of everything we do. Our highly-skilled attorneys, who have broad range of experience across business, law, and government, work in teams to develop a full understanding of the circumstances and issues that affect clients' lives and businesses and anticipate and help them to resolve problems efficiently and cost-effectively.

Our motto is "Serving Clients For Life". Our attorney's practice law with passion for building long term trusted relationships with our clients through a team approach where our clients' goals become our goals. We strive to minimize conflict through strategic negotiation and communication, and cost effectively resolve legal disputes preserving important business relationships to our clients.

JENNIFER C. WOLFE, born Kansas City, Missouri, November 16, 1971; admitted to bar, 1999, Ohio; 2005, U.S. Supreme Court. *Education:* Ball State University (B.S., Journalism, 1993); University of Cincinnati (M.A., 1999; J.D., 1999). ***PRACTICE AREAS:*** Corporate; Franchise; Licensing; Intellectual Property; Real Estate. ***Email:*** jwolfe@twplaw.com

(This Listing Continued)

TINA J. BARRETT, born Hamilton, Ohio, December 7, 1962; admitted to bar, 2004, Ohio; 2005, U.S. District Court, Southern District of Ohio. *Education:* Miami University (B.A., Philosophy, 1997; M.A., Philosophy, 1999); University of Cincinnati (J.D., 2003). *Member:* Cincinnati, Ohio State and American Bar Associations. ***PRACTICE AREAS:*** Labor and Employment; Business Litigation; Domestic Relations; Employment Law; Construction Litigation. ***Email:*** tbarrett@twplaw.com

DANIELLE M. WILSON, born Cleveland, Ohio, May 13, 1979; admitted to bar, 2004, Ohio. *Education:* Ohio University (B.S., Legal Communications, 2001); Cleveland State University, Cleveland-Marshall College of Law (J.D., 2004). *Member:* Ohio State and American Bar Associations. ***PRACTICE AREAS:*** Real Estate; Probate; Wills; Trusts; Estate Planning. ***Email:*** dwilson@twplaw.com

JANET ELLEN BEERS, born Cape Girardeau, Missouri, August 10, 1976; admitted to bar, 2004, Ohio; 2005, U.S. District Court, Southern District of Ohio. *Education:* Miami University of Ohio (B.A., English Literature, 1999); University of Cincinnati (J.D., 2003). Member, Women's Wealth Network. *Member:* Cincinnati, Ohio State and American Bar Associations. ***PRACTICE AREAS:*** Estate Planning; Asset Protection; Taxation; Business Law. ***Email:*** ebeers@twplaw.com

APPROVED ATTORNEYS FOR: First American Title Co.; WealthCounsel; Midwest Mediation Group; Wolfe Title & Trust Co.

THE LAW OFFICE OF REX A. WOLFGANG

CINCINNATI, OHIO

(See Hamilton)

Civil Practice, Environmental Law, Product Liability, Personal Injury, Real Estate, Construction Law, Community Association Law.

WOLNITZEK & ROWEKAMP, P.S.C.

CINCINNATI, OHIO

(See Covington, Kentucky)

General Civil Trial and Appellate Practice in all Courts. Personal Injury, Wrongful Death, Immigration and Naturalization, Criminal Law, School Law, Product Liability, Insurance, Estate Planning and Probate, Corporation, Real Estate and Family Law.

WOOD, HERRON & EVANS, L.L.P.

Established in 1868

2700 CAREW TOWER
CINCINNATI, OHIO 45202
Telephone: 513-241-2324
Fax: 513-421-7269
Email: info@whepatent.com
URL: http://www.whepatent.com

Intellectual Property and Related Litigation; Computer Law, Patents, Trademarks and Copyrights.

FIRM PROFILE: The firm was founded over 130 years ago, making us one of the most experienced firms in the Midwest. We engage exclusively in the practice of intellectual property law, including patent, trademark, trade secret, copyright and unfair competition matters.

Wood, Herron & Evans is a steadily growing law firm located in Cincinnati, Ohio. We are proud that six members of our firm are listed among the Best Lawyers in America, and that we are one of only a few firms in the country to have that many listed.

About one-third of our practice involves litigation, with the balance in United States and foreign patent and trademark prosecution, evaluation of inventions, licensing and counseling work. Our practice has a broad and stable client base extending from coast to coast. We also serve a growing number of foreign clients.

MEMBERS OF FIRM

EDMUND E. WOOD (1868-1916)
WILLIAM R. WOOD (1893-1935)
EDMUND P. WOOD (1923-1968)
TRUMAN A. HERRON (1935-1976)
EDWARD B. EVANS (1937-1971)

BRUCE TITTEL, born Carbondale, Illinois, October 24, 1938; admitted to bar, 1963, Tennessee; 1964, Ohio; registered to practice before U.S. Patent and Trademark Office. *Education:* Vanderbilt University (B.A., 1960; LL.B., 1963). Phi Delta Phi. Associate Editor, Vanderbilt Law Review, 1962-1963. Co-author, "The Law of Trade Secrets in Ohio," Ohio Bar Journal, 1974. Author, "Protecting a Client's Trademark," Report, 1986. Co-Author, "What Every Engineer Should Know About Patents," Marcel Dekker, Inc., 1979, 1988. Listed in all issues of Best Lawyers in America. *Member:* Cincinnati, Ohio State and American Bar Associations; Cincinnati Intellectual Property Law Association (President, 1977); American Intellectual Property Law Association; The Association of Trial Lawyers of America. ***PRACTICE AREAS:*** Intellectual Property; Intellectual Property Litigation; Patent, Trademark and Copyright.

DONALD F. FREI, born New York, N.Y., June 2, 1938; admitted to bar, 1965, Ohio; 1972, District of Columbia; registered to practice before U.S. Patent and Trademark Office. *Education:* Cornell University (B.M.E., 1961); Georgetown University (J.D., 1965). Delta Theta Phi. Lecturing Law, University of Cincinnati, 1967-1978. Adjunct Professor of Intellectual Property Law, Northern Kentucky University Law School, 1988—. Member, Advisory Board of IP Litigator, 1995—. Co-Author, "What Every Engineer Should Know

(This Listing Continued)

WOOD, HERRON & EVANS, L.L.P., Cincinnati—Continued

About Patents," Marcel Dekker, Inc., 1979, 1988. Author: "Trademark Concerns of the Corporate General Counsel," Cincinnati Bar Association Corporate and Securities Law Institute, 1987; listed in Best Lawyers in America, 1991-2002; "International Protection of Trademarks," Ohio State Bar Association Institute on International Law, 1994; "Intellectual Property Law Developments of Interest to Corporate Counsel," Cincinnati Bar Association Corporate and Securities Law Institute, 1995; "Trademark Law as it Affects Fraternal Organizations," Fraternal Law Conference, 1986; "Trademarks and Copyrights from a Fraternity's Viewpoint," Fraternal Law Conference, 1987; Copyright Liability," Fraternal Law Conference, 1988; "Generating Income From Fraternity/Sorority Marks," Fraternal Law Conference, 1995; "Overview of Patent Law," Cincinnati Bar Association Seminar on Intellectual Property, 1995; Trademark Implications for Corporate Counsel, 1987; Northern Kentucky University College of Law Seminar on Intellectual Property, 1992, 1993. Panelist, Northern Kentucky University Law School, "Overview of Recent Patent Legislation," 1999; Commentator, Northern Kentucky University Law School Symposium on "Cyberlaw", 2001. Member, Regional Advisory Council and Panel of Arbitrators, American Arbitration Association. Member, University of Cincinnati Department of Physics Corporate Advisory Board, 1991-1993. Member: Cincinnati, Ohio State (Chairman, Executive Committee, Patent Trademark and Copyright Section, 1972-1975) and American Bar Associations; American Intellectual Property Law Association; Cincinnati Intellectual Property Law Association. ***PRACTICE AREAS:*** Intellectual Property; Patent, Trademark and Copyright. ***Email:*** dfrei@whepatent.com

DAVID J. JOSEPHIC, born Trafford, Pennsylvania, June 3, 1935; admitted to bar, 1966, Ohio; registered to practice before U.S. Patent and Trademark Office. *Education:* Xavier University (B.S., in Chemistry, magna cum laude, 1957; M.S., in Chemistry, 1959); Georgetown University (J.D., 1965). Delta Theta Phi. *Member:* Cincinnati, Ohio State and American Bar Associations; Cincinnati Intellectual Property Law Association; American Intellectual Property Law Association. ***PRACTICE AREAS:*** Intellectual Property; Patent, Trademark and Copyright.

DAVID S. STALLARD, born Lexington, Kentucky, February 23, 1944; admitted to bar, 1968, Kentucky; 1970, Ohio; registered to practice before U.S. Patent and Trademark Office. *Education:* Georgetown College (B.S., in Physics, 1966); University of Louisville (J.D., 1968). Phi Alpha Delta (Justice, 1967-1968). Co-Author, "What Every Engineer Should Know About Patents," Marcel Dekker, Inc., 1979, 1988. *Member:* Kentucky and Ohio State (Chairman, Patent Section, 1983 and 1984) Bar Associations; Cincinnati Intellectual Property Law Association (Vice President, 1978; President, 1979); American Intellectual Property Law Association. ***PRACTICE AREAS:*** Intellectual Property; Patent, Trademark and Copyright. ***Email:*** dstallard@whepatent.com

J. ROBERT CHAMBERS, born Bloomsburg, Pennsylvania, August 29, 1945; admitted to bar, 1972, Michigan; 1974, Ohio; registered to practice before U.S. Patent and Trademark Office. *Education:* The Ohio State University (B.Met.E.; M.Sc., 1968); Wayne State University (J.D., magna cum laude, 1972). Author: "Jury Trials in Patent Cases: The Uncertain Course of the Federal Circuit," 13 AIPLA Quarterly Journal, 361, 1985; "Jury Trials in Patent Cases," 1988 Indiana Continuing Legal Education Forum; "Jury Trials in Patent Cases: The First Six Years of the Federal Circuit," 29 IDEA 275, 1989; "Doctrine of Equivalents," 1995 Winter Meeting, Association of Corporate Patent Counsel, "Doctrine of Equivalents after Hilton Davis Chemical Co. v. Warner-Jenkinson," ALI-ABA Current Developments in Patent Law, 1995. *Member:* Cincinnati, Ohio State and American (Member, Sections on: Litigation; Patent, Trademark and Copyright Law) Bar Associations; Cincinnati Intellectual Property Law Association; American Intellectual Property Law Association. ***PRACTICE AREAS:*** Intellectual Property Litigation; Patent, Trademark and Copyright. ***Email:*** bchambers@whepatent.com

GREGORY J. LUNN, born Covington, Kentucky, November 14, 1955; admitted to bar, 1978, Kentucky; 1979, Ohio; registered to practice before U.S. Patent and Trademark Office. *Education:* Thomas More College (B.A., Chemistry, 1975); University of Kentucky (J.D., 1978). *Member:* Cincinnati, Ohio State, Kentucky (Chairman, Patent, Trademark and Copyright Committee, 1985-1988) and American Bar Associations; Cincinnati Intellectual Property Law Association (President, 1987); American Intellectual Property Law Association. ***PRACTICE AREAS:*** Intellectual Property; Patent, Trademark and Copyright. ***Email:*** glunn@whepatent.com

KURT L. GROSSMAN, born Youngstown, Ohio, February 12, 1955; admitted to bar, 1981, District of Columbia; 1983, Ohio; registered to practice before U.S. Patent and Trademark Office. *Education:* University of Cincinnati (B.S.E.E., cum laude, 1978); George Washington University (J.D., with honors, 1981). Eta Kappa Nu; Omicron Delta Kappa; Phi Delta Phi. Law Clerk/Technical Advisor to Hon. Helen W. Nies, U.S. Court of Appeals for the Federal Circuit, 1981-1983. Arbitrator, Hamilton County Courts. Listed in Best Lawyers in America, 2001-2002. *Member:* Cincinnati, Ohio State and American Bar Associations; Cincinnati Intellectual Property Law Association; American Intellectual Property Law Association; Institute of Electrical and Electronic Engineers. ***PRACTICE AREAS:*** Intellectual Property; Patent, Trademark and Copyright. ***Email:*** kgrossman@whepatent.com

CLEMENT H. LUKEN, JR., born Cincinnati, Ohio, July 11, 1956; admitted to bar, 1986, Ohio; registered to practice before U.S. Patent and Trademark Office. *Education:* Xavier University (B.S., in Chemistry, magna cum laude, 1978; M.S., in Chemistry, 1981); Salmon P. Chase College of Law, Northern Kentucky University (J.D., 1986). Arbitrator, Hamilton County Courts. *Member:* Cincinnati, Ohio State and American Bar Associations; Cincinnati Intellectual Property Law Association (President, 1996); American Intellectual Property Law Association; American Chemical Society (Member, Executive Committee). ***PRACTICE AREAS:*** Intellectual Property; Patent, Trademark and Copyright. ***Email:*** cluken@whepatent.com

THOMAS J. BURGER, born Cincinnati, Ohio, April 4, 1960; admitted to bar, 1986, Ohio; registered to practice before U.S. Patent and Trademark Office. *Education:* University of Notre Dame (B.S.E.E., 1982; J.D., 1986). *Member:* Cincinnati and Ohio State Bar Associations; National Lawyers Association; American Intellectual Property Law Association; Cincinnati Intellectual Property Law Association; German Association for Industrial Property and Copyrights (GRUR). ***PRACTICE AREAS:*** Intellectual Property; Patent, Trademark and Copyright. ***Email:*** tburger@whepatent.com

GREGORY F. AHRENS, born Cleveland, Ohio, November 18, 1961; admitted to bar, 1987, Wisconsin and Ohio; registered to practice before U.S. Patent and Trademark Office. *Education:* University of Texas at Austin (B.S.Ch.E., 1983); Hamline University; University of Wisconsin at Madison (J.D., 1987). Phi Alpha Delta. Member: National Moot Court Team; Hamline Law Review. Managing Editor, Wisconsin International Law Journal. *Member:* Cincinnati, Ohio State and American Bar Associations; State Bar of Wisconsin; Cincinnati Intellectual Property Law Association; American Intellectual Property Law Association. ***PRACTICE AREAS:*** Intellectual Property; Intellectual Property Litigation; Patent, Trademark and Copyright. ***Email:*** gahrens@whepatent.com

WAYNE L. JACOBS, born Madison, Wisconsin, August 23, 1960; admitted to bar, 1990, Ohio; registered to practice before U.S. Patent and Trademark Office. *Education:* Texas A & M University (B.S.M.E., cum laude, 1981); Southern Methodist University (M.S.E.M., 1985); University of Louisville (J.D., 1990). *Member:* Cincinnati and Ohio State Bar Associations; National Lawyers Association; Cincinnati and American Intellectual Property Law Associations. ***PRACTICE AREAS:*** Intellectual Property; Patent, Trademark and Copyright. ***Email:*** wjacobs@whepatent.com

KURT ANDREW SUMME, born Fort Mitchell, Kentucky, April 4, 1965; admitted to bar, 1991, Ohio; 1992, U.S. District Court, Southern District of Ohio; U.S. District Court, Central District of Illinois; registered to practice before U.S. Patent and Trademark Office. *Education:* University of Cincinnati (B.S., Electrical Engineering, 1988; J.D., 1991). Recipient: Honors Scholarship, University of Cincinnati; Honors Scholarship, University of Cincinnati School of Law. Member, University of Cincinnati Law Review. *Member:* Cincinnati, Ohio State, Federal and American Bar Associations; American Intellectual Property Law Association; Cincinnati Intellectual Property Law Association. ***PRACTICE AREAS:*** Intellectual Property; Patent, Trademark and Copyright. ***Email:*** ksumme@whepatent.com

KEVIN G. ROONEY, born Fremont, Ohio, May 10, 1964; admitted to bar, 1992, Ohio; registered to practice before U.S. Patent and Trademark Office. *Education:* University of Cincinnati (B.S.M.E., 1987); George Washington University (J.D., with honors, 1992). Patent Examiner, U.S. Patent & Trademark Office, 1987-1992. *Member:* American Bar Association; Cincinnati Intellectual Property Law Association; American Intellectual Property Law Association. ***PRACTICE AREAS:*** Intellectual Property; Patent, Trademark and Copyright. ***Email:*** krooney@whepatent.com

KEITH R. HAUPT, born Cincinnati, Ohio, January 19, 1963; admitted to bar, 1992, Ohio; 1993, U.S. District Court, Southern District of Ohio; registered to practice before U.S. Patent and Trademark Office. *Education:* Vanderbilt University (B.E., 1985); The Ohio State University (J.D., with honors, 1992). Pi Tau Sigma. Recipient, John E. Hallen Memorial Award. Member, American Society of Mechanical Engineers, 1983-1988. Listed in, Who's Who Among American Law School Students. *Member:* Cincinnati, Ohio State and American Bar Associations; American Intellectual Property Law Association. ***PRACTICE AREAS:*** Intellectual Property; Patent, Trademark and Copyright. ***Email:*** khaupt@whepatent.com

THEODORE R. REMAKLUS, born Coldwater, Ohio, July 24, 1962; admitted to bar, 1993, Ohio, U.S. District Court, Southern District of Ohio, U.S. District Court, Eastern District of Michigan and U.S. Court of Appeals, Federal Circuit; registered to practice before U.S. Patent and Trademark Office. *Education:* University of Cincinnati (B.S.M.E., 1985; J.D., 1993); Polytechnic University (M.S.M.E., 1990). Member: Moot Court; Order of the Barristers; Order of the Coif. *Member:* Ohio State (Member, Board of Governors, Intellectual Property Group) and American Bar Associations; Cincinnati Intellectual Property Law Association. ***PRACTICE AREAS:*** Intellectual Property; Intellectual Property Litigation; Patent, Trademark and Copyright. ***Email:*** tremaklus@whepatent.com

THOMAS W. HUMPHREY, born St. Charles, Illinois, March 26, 1966; admitted to bar, 1993, Ohio; 1994, U.S. District Court, Southern District of Ohio; registered to practice before U.S. Patent and Trademark Office. *Education:* Massachusetts Institute of Technology (B.S.E.E.; M.S.E.E., 1989); Harvard University (J.D., cum laude, 1993). Tau Beta Pi; Eta Kappa Nu. Author: "Copyright for Non-literal Aspects of Functional Software," Harvard Thesis; Lecturer, "Software Patents," "Discovery Issues Relating to Electronic Mail," "Establishing and Defending Trademarks on the Internet," "Connecting Your Law Practice to the WWW", "The Digital Millenium Copyright Act," "Software and Internet Patents," and "Business Model Patents," Cincinnati Bar Association Continuous Legal Education Seminars, Xavier University College of Management and Entrepreneurship, Northern Kentucky University, Salmon P. Chase College of Law. *Member:* Cincinnati Bar Association (Chair, Internet, E-Commerce and Computer Law Committee, 1997-1999); Cincinnati Intellectual Property Law Association. ***PRACTICE AREAS:*** Intellectual Property; Patent, Trademark and Copyright. ***Email:*** thumphrey@whepatent.com

SCOTT A. STINEBRUNER, born Louisville, Kentucky, December 19, 1968; admitted to bar, 1993, Minnesota; 1998, Ohio; registered to practice before U.S. Patent and Trademark Office. *Education:* Washington University (B.S.E.E., cum laude, 1989); University of Minnesota (J.D., cum laude, 1993). *Member:* Cincinnati, Ohio State and American Bar Associations; Cincinnati Intellectual Property Law Association; American Intellectual Property Law Association. ***PRACTICE AREAS:*** Intellectual Property; Patent, Trademark and Copyright. ***Email:*** sstinebruner@whepatent.com

DAVID H. BRINKMAN, born Cincinnati, Ohio, February 12, 1961; admitted to bar, 1994, Ohio; 1995, U.S. District Court, Southern District of Ohio; registered to practice before U.S. Patent and Trademark Office. *Education:* Tufts University (B.S.E.E., 1983); University of Dayton (J.D., 1994). Phi Alpha Delta. *Member:* Cincinnati, Ohio State and American Bar Associations; American Intellectual Property Law Association; Cincinnati Intellectual Property Law Association. ***PRACTICE AREAS:*** Intellectual Property; Patent, Trademark and Copyright. ***Email:*** dbrinkman@whepatent.com

BEVERLY A. LYMAN, born Philadelphia, Pennsylvania, August 22, 1956; admitted to bar, 1996, Ohio; registered to practice before U.S. Patent and Trademark Office. *Education:* Thomas Jefferson University (B.S., Medical Technology, 1978); University of Pennsylvania (M.S., Science Education, 1982); Hahnemann Medical College (Ph.D., M.S., Biochemistry, 1986, 1984); University of Memphis (J.D., cum laude, 1996). Moot Court. *Member:* Cincinnati, Ohio State and American Bar Associations; Cincinnati and American Intellectual Property Law Associations; American Association for the Advancement of Sci-

(This Listing Continued)

ence; American Society of Biochemistry and Molecular Biology; Society of Toxicology; Sigma-Xi. ***PRACTICE AREAS:*** Intellectual Property; Patent, Trademark and Copyright. ***Email:*** blyman@whepatent.com

SENIOR ASSOCIATES

JOSEPH R. JORDAN, born Warren, Ohio, January 23, 1942; admitted to bar, 1968, Ohio and Virginia; 1972, U.S. District Court, Southern District of Ohio; 1973, District of Columbia, U.S. Court of Appeals, Sixth Circuit and U.S. Supreme Court; 1983, U.S. District Court, Eastern District of Kentucky; 1996, Colorado; registered to practice before U.S. Patent and Trademark Office. *Education:* University of Notre Dame (B.S. in Eng. Sci., 1964); Georgetown University (J.D., 1968). *Member:* Cincinnati, Ohio State and American Bar Associations; Virginia State Bar; District of Columbia Bar; Cincinnati Intellectual Property Law Association. ***PRACTICE AREAS:*** Intellectual Property; Patent, Trademark and Copyright. ***Email:*** jjordan@whepatent.com

C. RICHARD EBY, born Cincinnati, Ohio, October 28, 1941; admitted to bar, 1968, Ohio; registered to practice before U.S. Patent and Trademark Office. *Education:* University of Cincinnati (B.S.E.E., 1964); Xavier University (M.B.A., 1987); Chase College of Law (J.D., 1968). ***PRACTICE AREAS:*** Intellectual Property; Patent, Trademark and Copyright. ***Email:*** reby@whepatent.com

ASSOCIATES

J. DWIGHT POFFENBERGER, JR., born Cincinnati, Ohio, June 22, 1964; admitted to bar, 1994, Ohio; registered to practice before U.S. Patent and Trademark Office. *Education:* University of Michigan (B.S.M.E., 1987); George Mason University (J.D., 1993). ***SPECIAL AGENCIES:*** U.S. Patent and Trademark Office; U.S. Environmental Protection Agency. ***PRACTICE AREAS:*** Intellectual Property; Patent, Trademark and Copyright. ***Email:*** dpoffenberger@whepatent.com

KATHRYN E. SMITH, born Cincinnati, Ohio, June 17, 1970; admitted to bar, 1996, Ohio. *Education:* Kenyon College (B.A., magna cum laude, History, 1992); University of Toledo (J.D., 1996). Phi Beta Kappa. *Member:* Cincinnati, Ohio State and American Bar Associations; American Intellectual Property Law Association; International Trademark Association. ***PRACTICE AREAS:*** International Trademarks; Domestic Trademarks; Unfair Competition; Patent, Trademark and Copyright. ***Email:*** ksmith@whepatent.com

KRISTI L. DAVIDSON, born Willoughby, Ohio, October 12, 1971; admitted to bar, 1997, Ohio; registered to practice before U.S. Patent and Trademark Office. *Education:* Case Western Reserve University (B.S., 1994); University of Dayton (J.D., cum laude, 1997). Phi Alpha Delta. Secretary, Intellectual Property Law Society, 1995-1996. Author: "Supreme Court Says Yes to Color: Qualitex v. Jacobson Products," 21 Dayton L. Rev. 855 (1996). *Member:* Cincinnati and Ohio State Bar Associations; American Intellectual Property Law Association; Cincinnati Intellectual Property Law Association. ***PRACTICE AREAS:*** Intellectual Property; Patent, Trademark and Copyright. ***Email:*** kdavidson@whepatent.com

P. ANDREW BLATT, born Huntington, West Virginia, January 19, 1966; admitted to bar, 1998, Ohio; 1999, U.S. District Court, Southern District of Ohio; registered to practice before U.S. Patent and Trademark Office. *Education:* Embry-Riddle Aeronautical University (B.S., Aeronautical Engineering, cum laude, 1988); Purdue University (M.S., Aeronautical and Astronautics, 1990; Ph.D., Aeronautical and Astronautics, 1993); University of Cincinnati (J.D., 1998). Student Articles Editor, University of Cincinnati Law Review, 1997-1998; Associate Member, 1996-1997. *Member:* Cincinnati, Ohio State and American Bar Associations; American Intellectual Property Law Association; Cincinnati Intellectual Property Law Association. ***PRACTICE AREAS:*** Intellectual Property; Patent, Trademark and Copyright. ***Email:*** dblatt@whepatent.com

DAVID E. JEFFERIES, born St. Louis, Missouri, September 28, 1970; admitted to bar, 1998, Ohio; 1999, U.S. District Court, Southern District of Ohio; registered to practice before U.S. Patent and Trademark Office. *Education:* Earlham College (B.A., Biology, 1992); Northwestern University (M.S., Biotechnology, 1993); Indiana University School of Law (J.D., 1998). Delta Theta Phi. Associate Member, 1996-1997 and Articles Editor, 1997-1998, Indiana Journal of Global Legal Studies. Author, "The Body as Commodity: The Use of Markets to Cure the Organ Deficit," 5 Ind. J. Global Legal Studies 621, Spring 1998. *Member:* Cincinnati, Ohio State and American Bar Associations; Cincinnati and American Intellectual Property Law Associations; American Association for the Advancement of Science. ***PRACTICE AREAS:*** Intellectual Property; Patent, Trademark and Copyright. ***Email:*** djefferies@whepatent.com

WILLIAM R. ALLEN, born Abingdon, Virginia, October 18, 1957; admitted to bar, 2000, Ohio. *Education:* Emory and Henry College (B.S., Physics/Mathematics, 1980); University of North Carolina at Chapel Hill (Ph.D., Physics, 1986); University of Tennessee at Knoxville (J.D., 1999). Member, Tennessee Law Review. *Member:* Cincinnati, Ohio State and American Bar Associations; Cincinnati and American Intellectual Property Law Association. ***PRACTICE AREAS:*** Intellectual Property; Patent, Trademark and Copyright. ***Email:*** wallen@whepatent.com

JOHN P. DAVIS, born Madison, Wisconsin, December 29, 1964; admitted to bar, 1995, Illinois; 1998, District of Columbia and Minnesota; 2001, Ohio. *Education:* Purdue University (B.S.E.E., 1987); Regent University (J.D., 1995). Member, Regent University Law Review, 1993-1995. *Member:* Cincinnati, Illinois, Minnesota, Federal and American Bar Associations; The District of Columbia Bar; Cincinnati and American Intellectual Property Law Associations; Christian Legal Society; Computer Law Association; Institute of Electrical and Electronic Engineers. [U.S. Air Force, 1988-1992; U.S. Air Force Reserve, 1992—]. ***PRACTICE AREAS:*** Intellectual Property; Patent, Trademark and Copyright. ***Email:*** jdavis@whepatent.com

DOUGLAS A. SCHOLER, born Goshen, Indiana, May 13, 1971; admitted to bar, 2000, Ohio. *Education:* University of Notre Dame (B.S.E.E., 1994); Northern Kentucky University (J.D., 2000). *Member:* Cincinnati, Ohio State and American Bar Associations; Institute of Electrical and Electronic Engineers. [Capt. USAF, 1994-2000]. ***PRACTICE AREAS:*** Intellectual Property; Patent, Trademark and Copyright. ***Email:*** dscholer@whepatent.com

(This Listing Continued)

BRETT A. SCHATZ, born Cincinnati, Ohio, August 9, 1972; admitted to bar, 2000, Ohio, Kentucky and Indiana; U.S. District Court, Southern District of Ohio and U.S. District Court, Eastern and Western Districts of Kentucky. *Education:* University of Cincinnati (B.S.M.E., 1995); Salmon P. Chase College of Law (J.D., cum laude, 2000). Adjunct Professor, Salmon P. Chase College of Law, 2000—. *Member:* Cincinnati and Ohio State Bar Associations; American Intellectual Property Law Association. ***PRACTICE AREAS:*** Intellectual Property; Patent, Trademark and Copyright. ***Email:*** bschatz@whepatent.com

DAVID WESLEY DORTON, born Alexandria, Virginia, January 9, 1967; admitted to bar, 2001, Ohio. *Education:* Virginia Polytechnic Institute and State University (M.S.M.E., 1991); University of Dayton School of Law (J.D., 2001). Member, University of Dayton Law Review. *Member:* Ohio State and American Bar Associations; American Intellectual Property Law Association. ***PRACTICE AREAS:*** Intellectual Property; Patent, Trademark and Copyright. ***Email:*** ddorton@whepatent.com

SARAH OTTE GRABER, born Indianapolis, Indiana, May 4, 1972; admitted to bar, 1997, Ohio. *Education:* Indiana University College of Arts & Sciences (B.A., 1994); University of Dayton School of Law (J.D., 1997). *Member:* Cincinnati, Ohio State and American Bar Associations; International Trademark Association; American Intellectual Property Law Association; Lawyers Club of Cincinnati. ***PRACTICE AREAS:*** Trademarks; Copyrights; Intellectual Property; Unfair Competition. ***Email:*** sgraber@whepatent.com

STEVEN W. BENINTENDI, born Georgetown, Ohio, March 22, 1969; (admission pending). *Education:* University of Dayton (B.S., Mechanical Engineering; M.S., Mechanical Engineering, 1992); Georgia Institute of Technology (Ph.D., Mechanical Engineering, 1992); University of Dayton School of Law (J.D., 2003). *Member:* Cincinnati Bar Association; American Intellectual Property Law Association. ***PRACTICE AREAS:*** Patents; Trademarks; Copyrights; Intellectual Property. ***Email:*** sbenintendi@whepatent.com

RANDALL S. JACKSON, JR., born Cincinnati, Ohio, April 25, 1972; admitted to bar, 1998, Ohio; 1999, Kentucky; U.S. District Court, Southern District of Ohio and U.S. Court of Appeals, Sixth and Federal Circuits; registered to practice before U.S. Patent and Trademark Office. *Education:* St. Louis University (B.A., Chemistry, cum laude, 1994; J.D., 1998; Certificate in Health Law, 1998); University of Cincinnati (M.S., Chemistry, cum laude, 2003). Author: "Plan of Care Requirements for Kentucky Home Health Agencies," *Kentucky Medical News,* Volume 6, Number 5, p. 22, October 1999; "The Year 2000 Bug," *Communique,* The Official Newsletter of the Indiana Association for Home and Hospice Care, Inc., April 1999; "The Year 2000 Bug, *The Executive Edge,* A News Brief of the Kentucky Home Health Association, Vol. 3 Legal Issues Edition, April 1999. *Member:* Dayton (Vice-Chairman, Judges Committee on Notaries Public, 2002-2003), Cincinnati, Kentucky, Ohio State and American Bar Associations; American Intellectual Property Law Association. ***PRACTICE AREAS:*** Patents; Biochemical Patents; Chemical Patents; Biotechnology Patents; Pharmaceutical Patents.

OF COUNSEL

JOHN D. POFFENBERGER, born Adrian, Michigan, May 24, 1934; admitted to bar, 1961, Virginia, District of Columbia and Ohio; registered to practice before U.S. Patent and Trademark Office. *Education:* The Ohio State University (B.S., in I.E., 1957); George Washington University (LL.B., 1961). *Member:* Cincinnati and American Bar Associations; Cincinnati Intellectual Property Law Association; American Intellectual Property Law Association. ***PRACTICE AREAS:*** Intellectual Property; Patent, Trademark and Copyright. ***Email:*** jpoffenberger@whepatent.com

THOMAS W. FLYNN, born Amsterdam, New York, April 7, 1933; admitted to bar, 1963, Virginia; 1969, Ohio. *Education:* University of South Carolina (B.S. in C.E., 1956); The George Washington University Law School (J.D., 1963). Delta Theta Phi. Patent Examiner, U.S. Patent Office, 1959-1963. Listed in "The Best Lawyers in America." *Member:* Ohio State Bar Association (Chairman, Patent, Trademark and Copyright Section, 1975-1978). [Capt., U.S. Air Force, 1956-1959]. ***REPORTED CASES:*** Dorr-Oliver, Incorporate v. Fluid-Quip, Inc., 94 F. 3d 376 (7th Cir. 1996); DAP Products, Inc. v. Color Tile Manufacturing, Inc., 821 F.Supp. 488 (S.D. Ohio, 1993); Chemlawn Services Corporation v. GNC Pumps, Inc. 690 F.Supp. 560 (S.D. Tex., 1988). ***PRACTICE AREAS:*** Intellectual Property; Patent, Trademark and Copyright. ***Email:*** tflynn@whepatent.com

BRADLEY D. BECK, born Cincinnati, Ohio; admitted to bar, 1988, Ohio; registered to practice before U.S. Patent and Trademark Office. *Education:* University of Cincinnati (B.S.A.E., 1970); University of Central Florida (M.S.E., Mechanical Engineering, 1979); Salmon P. Chase College of Law (J.D., 1987). Registered Professional Engineer, Ohio. Engineer: Mechanical Design and Lead Systems, General Electric Aircraft Engines, Evendale, Ohio, 1978-1989; Test Operations, Pratt & Whitney Aircraft, West Palm Beach, Florida, 1972-1978. Formerly with: Butler, Snow, O'Mara, Stevens & Caldwell; Garrison, Morrison, Haight & Morrow; Baker, Donelson, Bearman & Caldwell. *Member:* Cincinnati, Ohio State and American Bar Associations; American Intellectual Property Law Association. ***PRACTICE AREAS:*** Patents; Mechanical Patents.

LEGAL SUPPORT PERSONNEL

JAMES CROSSET, born Cincinnati, Ohio, June 13, 1958. *Education:* Indiana University (B.S., 1980); University of Cincinnati (M.B.A., 1982). Certified Public Accountant, Illinois, 1984. Certified Legal Manager. Member, Audit Committee, Cincinnati Public Schools, 2002-2003. ***Email:*** jcrosset@whepatent.com

---

WOOD & LAMPING, L.L.P.

Established in 1927

600 VINE STREET, SUITE 2500
CINCINNATI, OHIO 45202-2491
Telephone: 513-852-6000
Fax: 513-852-6087

Lawrenceburg, Indiana Office: Wood, Lamping & Lehner, 208 Walnut Street, 47025. Telephone: 812-537-2375. Fax: 812-537-2368.

(This Listing Continued)

WOOD & LAMPING, L.L.P., Cincinnati—Continued

Civil and Commercial Litigation, Corporate and Business, including Mergers and Acquisitions, Tax, Labor and Employment, Workers Compensation, Real Estate, Municipal and Administrative, Admiralty, Products Liability Defense, Insurance Defense, Securities, Bankruptcy, Estate Planning, Probate, Family Law, Land Use and Zoning, Employee Benefits, Health and Hospital Law.

FIRM PROFILE: Wood & Lamping's proud tradition of serving greater Cincinnati began in 1927, making it one of the most experienced firms in the area. Our attorneys serve the constantly changing needs of clients ranging from multinational corporations, governments, health care and financial institutions to nonprofit organizations, as well as medium and small business organizations, individuals and sole proprietorships.

LAW FIRM ALLIANCES/ASSOCIATIONS: **LEGAL NETLINK ALLIANCE**

MEMBERS OF FIRM

KENNETH J. SCHNEIDER, born Cincinnati, Ohio, April 10, 1937; admitted to bar, 1966, Ohio; 1970, U.S. Supreme Court; U.S. District Court, Southern District of Ohio. *Education:* Xavier University (B.S., magna cum laude, 1959; M.B.A., 1960); Salmon P. Chase College of Law (J.D., 1966). General Counsel, Springdale and Mason, Ohio. Formerly, Bank Board of Directors, Chairman and General Counsel, Procter & Gamble Brand Management. Board of Governor's Chairman, (Emeritus), Cincinnati Banker's Club. *Member:* Cincinnati, Ohio State and American Bar Associations. ***PRACTICE AREAS:*** Corporate Law; Governmental and Municipal Law; Estate/Probate Law; Real Estate Law. ***Email:*** kjschneider@woodlamping.com

WILLIAM R. ELLIS, born Pittsburgh, Pennsylvania, August 14, 1949; admitted to bar, 1975, Pennsylvania; U.S. District Court, Western District of Pennsylvania; 1976, U.S. Court of Appeals, Third Circuit; 1980, U.S. District Court, Eastern District of Kentucky; 1981, U.S. Court of Appeals, Fourth Circuit; 1983, U.S. District Court, Eastern District of Texas; 1985, Ohio, U.S. Court of Appeals, Sixth Circuit; U.S. District Court, Southern District of Ohio; 1987, U.S. Supreme Court. *Education:* University of Dayton (B.A., 1970); Duquesne University (J.D., 1975). Crier-Clerk of the Honorable Rabe F. March, Chief Justice of the U.S. District Court, Western District of Pennsylvania, 1972-1975. Speaker, New Developments in Longshoreman and Harborworkers Compensation Act Cases, Ohio Valley Improvement Association National Convention, 1983; "Prosecution of the Defense of Jones Act Cases," National Waterways Conference, 1992. *Member:* Cincinnati (Member, Marine Law Panel, 1985—), Allegheny County, Pennsylvania and American Bar Associations; Master of the Bench, Potter Stewart Inns of Court. ***PRACTICE AREAS:*** Civil Litigation; Maritime Law; Products Liability Law; Insurance Defense Law. ***Email:*** wrellis@woodlamping.com

HAROLD G. KORBEE, born Cincinnati, Ohio, September 29, 1939; admitted to bar, 1965, Ohio; 1966, U.S. District Court, Southern District of Ohio; 1967, U.S. Court of Appeals, Sixth Circuit; 1969, U.S. Tax Court; 1979, U.S. Supreme Court. *Education:* Xavier University (B.S., 1961); Salmon P. Chase College of Law (J.D., 1965). Member, National Panel of Arbitrators, American Arbitration Association, 1967—. President, The Lawyers Club of Cincinnati, 1978. *Member:* Cincinnati (Member, 1966— and Chairman, 1979—, Negligence Law Committee; Member, Labor Law Committee, 1977—), Ohio State and American Bar Associations; Ohio Academy of Trial Lawyers; American Board of Trial Advocates; The Association of Trial Lawyers of America. ***LANGUAGES:*** English. ***REPORTED CASES:*** Chapman v. Audia Services 116 Ohio App 3d 534 (1997); Rosser v. Pipe Fitters Union Local No. 392, Case No. 92-3016 US Court of Appeals 6th Cir. (1993); Seale v. Citizens Savings & Loan 806 F2d 99 (6th Cir. 1986); Pipefitters Union Local No. 392 v. NLRB 712 F.2d 225 (1983). ***PRACTICE AREAS:*** Civil Litigation; Labor Law; Employee Benefits Law. ***Email:*** hgkorbee@woodlamping.com

ERIC C. HOLZAPFEL, born Sandusky, Ohio, May 22, 1946; admitted to bar, 1972, Ohio; U.S. District Court, Southern District of Ohio; 1975, U.S. Court of Appeals, Sixth Circuit; U.S. District Court, Eastern District of Kentucky. *Education:* Denison University (B.A., 1968); Emory University (J.D., 1971). Editor, Emory Law Review, 1970-1971. *Member:* Cincinnati, Ohio State and American (Member, Litigation, Business Committee; Construction Law) Bar Associations. ***PRACTICE AREAS:*** Civil Litigation; Construction Law; Commercial Law; Employment Law; Real Estate Law. ***Email:*** echolzapfel@woodlamping.com

PAUL R. BERNINGER, born Cincinnati, Ohio, December 25, 1943; admitted to bar, 1971, Ohio. *Education:* Xavier University (B.S., 1965); Salmon P. Chase College of Law (J.D., 1971). *Member:* Cincinnati and Ohio State Bar Associations. ***PRACTICE AREAS:*** Labor and Employment Law; Public School Law. ***Email:*** prberninger@woodlamping.com

ROBERT P. MALLOY, born Pittsburgh, Pennsylvania, August 25, 1943; admitted to bar, 1974, Ohio. *Education:* University of Cincinnati (B.A., high honors, 1967; J.D., 1974). Member, Editorial Board, University of Cincinnati Law Review, 1973-1974. President, Hamilton County Municipal Attorney Association, 1985-1988. Solicitor: Village of Terrace Park; Law Director, City of Madeira. Law Director, Symmes Township, Ohio, 1994—. *Member:* Cincinnati, Ohio State and American Bar Associations. [With USAF, 1967-1972]. ***PRACTICE AREAS:*** Land Use Litigation; Public Sector Law; Zoning Law; Administrative Law. ***Email:*** rpmalloy@woodlamping.com

JEFFREY M. ROLLMAN, born Covington, Kentucky, October 15, 1945; admitted to bar, 1974, Ohio. *Education:* Ohio University (B.A., 1967); Salmon P. Chase College of Law (J.D., 1974). Order of the Curia. *Member:* Cincinnati, Ohio State and American (Past Chair, Domestic Relations Committee) Bar Associations; Domestic Relations Collaborative Law of Cincinnati. ***PRACTICE AREAS:*** Domestic Relations Law; Business Law. ***Email:*** jmrollman@woodlamping.com

MARK S. RECKMAN, born Cincinnati, Ohio, October 2, 1953; admitted to bar, 1979, Ohio. *Education:* University of Vermont (B.A., 1975); University of Cincinnati (J.D., 1979). Board Chairman, Columbia Savings Bank, 1985—. Board of Directors, Hyde Park Lumber Co, 1986—. *Member:* Cincinnati Bar Association (Chairman, Legal Problems of the Elderly Committee, 1993-1994). ***PRACTICE AREAS:*** Probate Law; Real Estate Law; Business Law. ***Email:*** msreckman@woodlamping.com

(This Listing Continued)

JAN M. FRANKEL, born Cincinnati, Ohio, January 5, 1951; admitted to bar, 1978, Ohio; U.S. District Court, Southern District of Ohio. *Education:* Stephens College (B.A., 1972); Salmon P. Chase College of Law (J.D., 1978). *Member:* Cincinnati (Member, Law for the Elderly and Probate and Estate Planning Committees; Wills, Trusts and Estate Planning Committee) and Ohio State (Member, Estate Planning, Trust and Probate Law Section Board of Governors, 1993—) Bar Associations. ***PRACTICE AREAS:*** Probate Law; Estate Planning; Elder Law; Family Law; Domestic Relations. ***Email:*** jmfrankel@woodlamping.com

GARY J. DAVIS, born Cincinnati, Ohio, June 30, 1954; admitted to bar, 1979, Ohio; U.S. Tax Court; U.S. District Court, Eastern District of Kentucky; U.S. District Court, Southern District of Ohio; U.S. Court of Appeals, Sixth Circuit; 1988, Kentucky. *Education:* Northern Kentucky University (B.S., cum laude, 1976); Salmon P. Chase College of Law (J.D., 1979). Member, Order of the Curia. Member and Notes Editor, N. Kentucky Law Review, 1977-1979. Certified Public Accountant, Ohio, 1981. *Member:* Cincinnati, Kentucky and Northern Kentucky Bar Associations. ***PRACTICE AREAS:*** Corporate Law; Taxation Law; Business Law; Real Estate. ***Email:*** gjdavis@woodlamping.com

JAMES B. HARRISON, born Covington, Kentucky, May 14, 1957; admitted to bar, 1983, Ohio; 1984, Kentucky. *Education:* University of Kentucky (B.A., 1979); Salmon P. Chase College of Law (J.D., 1983). Member, Northern Kentucky Law Review, 1982-1983. *Member:* Ohio State and Kentucky Bar Associations. ***PRACTICE AREAS:*** Business Law; Computer Law; Corporate Law; Estate Planning. ***Email:*** jbharrison@woodlamping.com

HENRY E. MENNINGER, JR., born Cincinnati, Ohio, May 16, 1950; admitted to bar, 1977, Ohio; 1979, U.S. Tax Court; 1981, U.S. Supreme Court; U.S. District Court, Southern District of Ohio; U.S. Court of Appeals, Sixth Circuit; U.S. Court of Customs and Patent Appeals; U.S. Court of International Trade. *Education:* University of Cincinnati (B.A., 1972); Salmon P. Chase College of Law (J.D., 1977). Phi Alpha Delta (Vice Justice, 1975-1976; Justice, 1976-1977). Member, Order of the Curia. Adjunct Professor, Salmon P. Chase College of Law (Bankruptcy Law, Modern Real Estate Transactions), 1989—. Member: Panel of Bankruptcy Trustees, United States Bankruptcy Court, Southern District of Ohio, 1988—. Special Counsel to the Attorney General for the State of Ohio, 1983-1995. Juvenile Referee, City of Harrison, 1987-1993. Board of Zoning Appeals, City of Harrison, Ohio, 2000—. *Member:* Cincinnati (Chairman, Continuing Legal Education Committee, 1980; Lecturer, 1979-1981; Chairman, 1981, Practical Law Institute; Chairman, Real Property Committee, 1985-1988) Ohio State and Federal Bar Associations; Lawyers Club of Cincinnati; National Association of Bankruptcy Trustees; American Bankruptcy Law Institute. ***PRACTICE AREAS:*** Bankruptcy Law; Real Estate Law; Probate Law. ***Email:*** hemenninger@woodlamping.com

C. J. SCHMIDT, III, born Cincinnati, Ohio, May 14, 1957; admitted to bar, 1983, Ohio; U.S. District Court, Southern District of Ohio; U.S. Court of Appeals, Sixth Circuit. *Education:* University of Cincinnati (B.S., 1979; J.D., 1983); Georgetown University (LL.M., 1987). *Member:* Cincinnati and Ohio State Bar Associations. ***PRACTICE AREAS:*** Labor and Employment Law; Employee Benefits Law; Civil Litigation. ***Email:*** cjschmidt@woodlamping.com

THOMAS M. WOEBKENBERG, born Cincinnati, Ohio, October 6, 1960; admitted to bar, 1986, Ohio; U.S. District Court, Southern District of Ohio. *Education:* University of Virginia (B.A., 1982); Ohio Northern University (J.D., 1986). Associate Editor, Ohio Northern University Law Review. Certified United States Small Business Administration 504 Closing Attorney. *Member:* Cincinnati and Ohio State Bar Associations; Cincinnati Academy of Leadership for Lawyers. ***PRACTICE AREAS:*** Real Estate Law. ***Email:*** tmwoebkenberg@woodlamping.com

ARTHUR D. WEBER, JR., born Jersey City, New Jersey, September 7, 1947; admitted to bar, 1973, Ohio; U.S. District Court, Southern District of Ohio; U.S. Court of Appeals, Sixth Circuit; U.S. Supreme Court; 2000, Kentucky. *Education:* University of Dayton (B.A., 1969); Salmon P. Chase College of Law (J.D., 1973). *Member:* Cincinnati, Ohio State (Member, Real Estate Law Section Board of Governors), Kentucky and American Bar Associations. ***PRACTICE AREAS:*** Real Estate Law; Business Law; Estate Planning; Mediation. ***Email:*** adweber@woodlamping.com

THOMAS J. BREED, born Hammond, Indiana, July 26, 1949; admitted to bar, 1974, Ohio; U.S. District Court, Southern District of Ohio. *Education:* Indiana University (B.A., 1971; J.D., 1974). Certified Specialist, Estate Planning, Trust and Probate Law. *Member:* Ohio State and American Bar Associations (Member, Estate Planning Council). ***PRACTICE AREAS:*** Estate Planning; Probate; Real Estate; Business Law. ***Email:*** tjbreed@woodlamping.com

JOHN W. EILERS, JR., born Cincinnati, Ohio, November 21, 1939; admitted to bar, 1967, Ohio; U.S. District Court, Southern District of Ohio; U.S. Court of Appeals, Sixth Circuit; U.S. Supreme Court. *Education:* Marietta College (B.A., 1961); Salmon P. Chase College of Law (J.D., 1967). Certified Specialist, Estate Planning, Trust and Probate Law. Author: Effective Postmortem Reformation of a Client's Estate Plan, Estate Planning, May 1996. Lecturer: Ohio Legal Institute, 1972—; Cincinnati Estate Planning Institute. *Member:* Cincinnati, Ohio State (Board of Governors of Probate and Trust Law Section, 1983-1992) and American Bar Associations. Fellow, The American College of Trust and Estate Counsel. ***PRACTICE AREAS:*** Probate Law; Taxation Law; Estate Planning; Tax Exempt Organizations. ***Email:*** jweilers@woodlamping.com

LISA DEHART LEHNER, born Lawrenceburg, Indiana, March 31, 1966; admitted to bar, 1993, Arizona; 1996, Indiana; 2001, Ohio. *Education:* Miami University (B.A., 1988); American University (J.D., 1992). Member, American University Journal of International Law and Policy. *Member:* Cincinnati, Dearborn County, Ohio State and Indiana State Bar Associations. (Also at Lawrenceburg, Indiana Office). ***LANGUAGES:*** German. ***PRACTICE AREAS:*** Business Law; Estate Planning; Real Estate; Governmental Law. ***Email:*** ldlehner@woodlamping.com

PETER M. BURRELL, born Pittsburgh, Pennsylvania, May 8, 1959; admitted to bar, 1984, Oregon; 1990, Ohio; 1994, U.S. District Court, Southern District of Ohio. *Education:* Ohio Wesleyan University (B.A., 1981); University of Notre Dame (J.D., 1984). *Member:* Cincinnati, Ohio State, Oregon and American Bar Associations. ***PRACTICE AREAS:*** Bad Faith Insurance Law; Employment Litigation; Business Litigation; Noncompete Litigation. ***Email:*** pmburrell@woodlamping.com

(This Listing Continued)

JEFFREY P. McSHERRY, born Davenport, Iowa, October 17, 1965; admitted to bar, 1991, Ohio; 1992, Kentucky; 1996, Indiana; U.S. District Court, Northern and Southern Districts of Ohio; U.S. District Court, Northern and Southern Districts of Indiana; U.S. District Court, Eastern and Western Districts of Kentucky; U.S. Court of Appeals, Sixth Circuit; U.S. Bankruptcy Court, Northern and Southern Districts of Ohio and Indiana; U.S. Bankruptcy Court, Eastern and Western Districts of Kentucky. *Education:* Bowling Green State University (B.S., cum laude, 1988); University of Dayton (J.D., 1991). *Member:* Cincinnati, Ohio State, Indiana State and Kentucky Bar Associations. ***PRACTICE AREAS:*** Civil Litigation; Insurance Defense; Construction; Business Litigation; Creditors Rights; Fraud; Bad Faith Insurance Law. ***Email:*** jpmcsherry@woodlamping.com

LISA M. RAMMES, born Dayton, Ohio, March 4, 1969; admitted to bar, 1996, Ohio; 1997, U.S. District Court, Southern District of Ohio. *Education:* Miami University (B.A., 1991); University of Cincinnati (J.D., 1996). *Member:* Cincinnati and Ohio State Bar Associations. ***PRACTICE AREAS:*** Corporate; Business Law; Municipal; Real Estate. ***Email:*** lmrammes@woodlamping.com

OF COUNSEL

ROBERT F. RECKMAN, born Cincinnati, Ohio, April 7, 1922; admitted to bar, 1948, Ohio. *Education:* DePauw University (A.B., 1943); University of Cincinnati (LL.B., 1948). *Member:* Cincinnati Bar Association. ***PRACTICE AREAS:*** Estate Planning; Probate; Real Estate Law.

WILLIAM H. EDER, JR., born Cincinnati, Ohio, August 9, 1938; admitted to bar, 1963, Ohio; U.S. District Court, Eastern District of Kentucky; U.S. District Court, Southern District of Ohio; U.S. Court of Appeals, Sixth Circuit. *Education:* University of Cincinnati (B.A., 1959; J.D., 1963). *Member:* Cincinnati Bar Association (Chairman, Bankruptcy Law Committee, 1982-1984). ***PRACTICE AREAS:*** Corporate Law; Bankruptcy; Business; Business Acquisitions; Automobile Dealerships Law. ***Email:*** wheder@woodlamping.com

AMY GASSER CALLOW, born Rochester, New York, February 12, 1969; admitted to bar, 1994, Ohio; 1995, U.S. District Court, Southern District of Ohio. *Education:* Miami University (B.S., 1991); University of Cincinnati (J.D., 1994). Order of the Barristers. Recipient, Best Brief Award in National Sports Law Competition, 1994. Member, Moot Court Team. *Member:* Cincinnati, Ohio State and American Bar Associations. ***PRACTICE AREAS:*** Insurance Defense; General Litigation. ***Email:*** agcallow@woodlamping.com

ASSOCIATES

DOUGLAS L. WESTENDORF, born Cincinnati, Ohio, January 12, 1947; admitted to bar, 1974, Ohio; U.S. District Court, Southern District of Ohio. *Education:* Fordham University (B.A., magna cum laude, 1969); Columbia University (J.D., 1974). Phi Beta Kappa. *Member:* Cincinnati (Chairman, Corporate and Securities Law Committee, 1984-1985) and Ohio State Bar Associations. ***PRACTICE AREAS:*** Business; Securities; Mergers and Acquisitions; Corporate; Contracts. ***Email:*** dlwestendorf@woodlamping.com

RAYMOND J. PIKNA, JR., born Akron, Ohio, September 19, 1954; admitted to bar, 1979, Ohio; 1981, U.S. District Court, Southern District of Ohio; 1984, U.S. District Court, Northern District of Ohio; 1985, U.S. Court of Appeals, Sixth Circuit; 1986, U.S. Supreme Court; 1987, U.S. District Court, Northern District of Texas; 1989, Texas; 1991, U.S. Court of Appeals, Fifth Circuit and U.S. District Court, Western District of Texas; 2005, U.S. District Court, Southern District of Indiana. *Education:* University of Notre Dame (B.B.A., 1976); Case Western Reserve University (J.D., 1979). Member: American Bankruptcy Law Forum. Member; Tri-State Association for Corporate Renewal; Notre Dame Monogram Club. *Member:* Cincinnati and Ohio State Bar Associations. ***LANGUAGES:*** French. ***REPORTED CASES:*** United States v. Noland, 517 U.S. 535, 134 L.Ed.2d 748, 116 S. Ct. 1524 (1996); In re Jenny Lynn Mining Co., 780 F.2d 585 (6th Cir. 1986), cert. denied 477 U.S. 905. ***PRACTICE AREAS:*** Commercial; Bankruptcy; Business. ***Email:*** rjpikna@woodlamping.com

ROCCINA S. NIEHAUS, born Cincinnati, Ohio, February 27, 1956; admitted to bar, 1981, Ohio; 1982, U.S. District Court, Southern District of Ohio. *Education:* Xavier University (B.A., 1978); University of Cincinnati (J.D., 1981). Alpha Sigma Nu. Title Insurance License: Ohio, 1985; Indiana, 2001. *Member:* Cincinnati Bar Association (Member, Real Property Committee, 1985—). ***PRACTICE AREAS:*** Real Estate. ***Email:*** rsniehaus@woodlamping.com

TIMOTHY A. GARRY, JR., born Cleveland, Ohio, June 25, 1960; admitted to bar, 1986, Ohio; U.S. District Court, Southern District of Ohio. *Education:* Georgetown University (B.A., 1982); University of Cincinnati (J.D., 1985). Assistant Prosecutor, Hamilton County, 1988-1994. Law Director, City of Norwood, 1996-1999. *Member:* Cincinnati (Member, Tort and Insurance Practice Committee, Estate Planning and Probate Committee; Chair, Local Government Law Committee, 1998—) and Ohio State Bar Associations; Cincinnati Academy of Leadership for Lawyers; Potter Stewart Inn of Courts (Barrister, 1989-1991). ***PRACTICE AREAS:*** Governmental Law; Municipal Law; Litigation. ***Email:*** tagarry@woodlamping.com

EDWARD D. BENDER, born Cincinnati, Ohio, October 16, 1968; admitted to bar, 1995, Ohio. *Education:* University of Cincinnati (B.A., 1992); Salmon P. Chase College of Law (J.D., 1995). *Member:* Cincinnati and Ohio State Bar Associations. ***PRACTICE AREAS:*** Probate; Estate Planning; Corporate Law. ***Email:*** edbender@woodlamping.com

MARK A. DENNEY, born Cincinnati, Ohio, December 16, 1964; admitted to bar, 1995, Ohio. *Education:* Xavier University (B.A., 1987; M.B.A., 1989); University of Dayton (J.D., 1994). *Member:* Cincinnati Bar Association (Vice Chair, Corporate Counsel Committee, 1999-2005; University of Dayton School of Law Alumni (Board of Trustees, 2001-2005). ***PRACTICE AREAS:*** Business; Taxation; Employment; Non-Profits. ***Email:*** madenney@woodlamping.com

JANET Y. CASTAÑEDA, born Lorain, Ohio, March 15, 1959; admitted to bar, 1996, Ohio. *Education:* Baldwin-Wallace College (B.S., 1985); University of Toledo (J.D., 1996). *Member:* Cincinnati and Ohio State Bar Associations; Trial Lawyers of America; Defense Research Institute (Member, Workers' Compensation Committee; Women Lawyers Committee; Insurance Committee; Labor and Employment Law Committee). ***PRACTICE AREAS:*** Litigation; Employment Law; Workers' Compensation; Personal Injury; Medical Negligence. ***Email:*** jycastaneda@woodlamping.com

(This Listing Continued)

KEVIN K. FRANK, born San Francisco, California, June 9, 1970; admitted to bar, 1997, California; 2004, Ohio. *Education:* University of California at Davis (B.A., 1992); University of San Francisco (J.D., 1997). ***PRACTICE AREAS:*** Civil Litigation; Construction Law; Commercial Law; Eminent Domain. ***Email:*** kkfrank@woodlamping.com

KAREN A. NICEWANDER, born Norman, Oklahoma, March 10, 1973; admitted to bar, 1998, Ohio; 1999, U.S. District Court, Southern District of Ohio. *Education:* Miami University (B.A., 1994); University of Dayton (J.D., 1998). Phi Alpha Delta (Member, Domestic Relations Committee). *Member:* Cincinnati and Ohio State Bar Associations. ***PRACTICE AREAS:*** Domestic Relations; Labor and Employment. ***Email:*** kanicewander@woodlamping.com

JEFFREY D. FORBES, born Rochester, Pennsylvania, October 6, 1972; admitted to bar, 2001, Ohio; U.S. District Court, Southern District of Ohio. *Education:* Ohio University (B.S.Ed., 1996); University of Cincinnati (J.D., 2001). Order of the Barristers. *Member:* Cincinnati and Ohio State Bar Associations. ***PRACTICE AREAS:*** Municipal Law; Government; Land Use; Zoning Law; Public Sector Labor Relations; Employment Law. ***Email:*** jdforbes@woodlamping.com

V. BRANDON McGRATH, born Burlington, North Carolina, May 11, 1972; admitted to bar, 2000, Ohio and Kentucky; U.S. District Court, Southern District of Ohio; U.S. Court of Appeals, Sixth Circuit; 2003, U.S. District Court, Eastern District of Kentucky; 2004, U.S. District Court, Western District of Kentucky and U.S. District Court, Northern District of Ohio. *Education:* University of Kentucky (B.S., 1994); University of Cincinnati (J.D., 1999). *Member:* Cincinnati, Ohio State and Kentucky Bar Associations. ***PRACTICE AREAS:*** Civil Litigation; Maritime Law; Insurance Defense Law; Products Liability Law. ***Email:*** vbmcgrath@woodlamping.com

NATHAN H. BLASKE, born Louisville, Kentucky, July 1, 1978; admitted to bar, 2003, Ohio; U.S. District Court, Southern District of Ohio; 2004, Kentucky and Indiana; U.S. District Court, Northern and Southern Districts of Indiana; U.S. Court of Appeals, Sixth Circuit. *Education:* University of Kentucky (B.B.A., 2000); Salmon P. Chase College of Law (J.D., cum laude, 2003). *Member:* Cincinnati, Ohio State, Indiana State, Kentucky and American Bar Associations. ***Email:*** nhblaske@woodlamping.com

SARAH B. ELLINGTON, born Lexington, Kentucky, October 29, 1977; admitted to bar, 2003, Ohio; U.S. District Court, Southern District of Ohio. *Education:* University of Miami (B.A., 2000); University of Cincinnati (J.D., 2003). *Member:* Cincinnati and Ohio State Bar Associations; International Foundation of Employee Benefits. ***Email:*** sbellington@woodlamping.com

WEDNESDAY OSTER, born Stratesville, North Carolina, April 16, 1979; admitted to bar, 2004, Ohio. *Education:* Transylvania University (B.A., 2000); University of Cincinnati (J.D., 2004). Order of the Barristers. ***PRACTICE AREAS:*** Business; Municipal; Education. ***Email:*** enoster@woodlamping.com

REPRESENTATIVE CLIENTS: American Bank & Trust; American Electric Power System; Ashland Inc.; Atlantic-Richfield Co.; Bardes Corporation; Beechmont Ford, Inc.; Bridge Technologies LLC; Center Bank; Chase Manhattan; Cincinnati Barge Company, Inc.; CIT Small Business Lending, Corp.; Columbia Savings and Loan; Disability Management Services, Inc.; Exxon Company, U.S.A.; Fifth Third Bank; Fuller Ford, Inc.; Granite Banc, Inc.; Hamilton County Development Co., Inc.; Hartford Insurance Co.; Houston Casualty Co.; IBEW Union Local 212 Employee Benefit Funds, Plumber and Pipefitters Local 392 Benefits Fund, Cincinnati Symphony Orchestra Musicians Fund; Libby, Perszyk, Kathman, Inc.; Paul Revere Insurance Co.; Manufacturer's Agent's National Association; Marine Equipment Management Co.; Marsh & McLennan; Metropolitan Life Insurance Co.; Mon River Towing Co.; Midland Enterprises; Neare Gibbs & Company; PNC Bank; Reichold Chemicals, Inc.; St. Paul Fire & Marine Insurance Co.; Society Bank; Sun Refining & Minerals Co.; Sun Trust Mortgage Inc.; Tencon, Inc.; Traveler's Insurance Co.; UBE Automotive North America, LLC; US Bank; United Southern Assurance Co.; Volvo North American; Washington Mutual Homeloans; UNUM/Provident Corp.; United Community Bank. *Municipal Corporations:* Dayton; Forest Park; Greenhills; Madeira; Mason; New Richmond; Reading; St. Bernard; Springdale; Symmes Township; Terrace Park. Counties: Clermont; Hamilton; Warren. School District: Norwood City; Princeton Local, Cincinnati Public.
TITLE AGENTS FOR: Chicago Title Insurance Co.

ZEGARSKI & ICE CO., L.P.A.

700 WALNUT STREET, SUITE 220
CINCINNATI, OHIO 45202
Telephone: 513-651-4226
Fax: 513-651-0224
Email: dzegarski@fuse.net

Bankruptcy, Consumer Bankruptcy, Foreclosures, Family Law, Adoptions, Child Custody, Child Support, Divorce, Domestic Violence, Premarital Agreements, Spousal Support, Visitation Rights, Dissolution, Modifications, Garnishments, Harassment, Lawsuits, Alimony, Paternity, Personal Injury.

DANIEL S. ZEGARSKI, born 1970; admitted to bar, 1995, Ohio and U.S. District Court, Southern District of Ohio; 1996, U.S. Court of Appeals, 6th Circuit. *Education:* University of Dayton (B.A., 1995); Dayton Law School (J.D., 1995). ***PRACTICE AREAS:*** Bankruptcy; Business Law; Commercial Law; Litigation; Appellate Practice; Personal Injury; Plaintiffs Personal Injury; Consumer Bankruptcy; Debtors Rights.

ANDREW G. ICE, born 1968; admitted to bar, 1996, Ohio; 1997, U.S. Court of Appeals, 6th Circuit. *Education:* University of Cincinnati (B.A., Political Science); University of Toledo College of Law (J.D.). ***PRACTICE AREAS:*** Family Law; Personal Injury; Plaintiffs Personal Injury; Divorce; Child Support; Adoption Law.

ZIEGLER & SCHNEIDER, P.S.C.

CINCINNATI, OHIO

(See Covington)

Business, Condominium, Construction Law, Corporate, Creditor's Rights, Eminent Domain, Bankruptcy, Employment, Environmental, Estate Planning, Admiralty, Family Law, Foreclosures, Insurance Defense, Lending, Municipal, Products Liability, Personal Injury, Probate, Real Estate Acquisitions and Development and Zoning Law.

MICHAEL E. BENSON

CIRCLEVILLE, OHIO

(See Columbus)

Bankruptcy Law, Foreclosures, Debtor and Creditor, Real Estate, Landlord and Tenant, Buying and Selling, Wills, Living Wills, Healthcare, Powers of Attorney.

CALIG & HANDELMAN, LPA

CIRCLEVILLE, OHIO

(See Columbus)

Bankruptcy, Personal Injury, Probate, Real Estate, Social Security, Social Security Disability, Medical Malpractice, Wrongful Death, Civil Litigation, Domestic Relations Law.

COLLEY SHROYER & ABRAHAM CO., L.P.A.

CIRCLEVILLE, OHIO

(See Columbus)

Civil Trial Practice. Personal Injury, Medical Malpractice, Automobile Accidents, Wrongful Death, Railroad Accidents, Slip and Fall, Negligence, Product Liability and Toxic Torts.

WILLIAM L. GEARY

CIRCLEVILLE, OHIO

(See Columbus)

Family Law, Divorce, Separation Agreements, Child Custody, Child Support, Visitation Rights, Alimony.

GOLDMAN & ROSENTHAL

CIRCLEVILLE, OHIO

(See Columbus)

Personal Injury, Family Law, Real Estate, Commercial Leasing, Construction and Mechanics Lien Law, Collections, Estate Planning and Probate, Corporate, Juvenile Law, Criminal. Civil and Criminal Trials in all Courts.

SUSAN KENNEY-PFALZER

CIRCLEVILLE, OHIO

(See Columbus)

Family Law, Divorce, Dissolution, Child Custody, Spousal and Child Support, Visitation Rights, Adoptions, Paternity, Juvenile Law, Collaborative Law, Restraining Orders.

LAMKIN, VAN EMAN, TRIMBLE, BEALS & DOUGHERTY, LLC

CIRCLEVILLE, OHIO

(See Columbus)

Personal Injury, Medical Malpractice, Products Liability, Negligence, Insurance Coverage, Stockbroker Malpractice & Fraud. Litigation and Trial Practice.

OLIVER LAW OFFICE

CIRCLEVILLE, OHIO

(See Columbus)

Products Liability, Personal Injury, Wrongful Death, Latex Allergy Litigation, Medical Malpractice, Vioxx Litigation, Automobile Accidents, Insurance Law, Employment Discrimination.

THE PLYMALE PARTNERSHIP LLP

CIRCLEVILLE, OHIO

(See Columbus)

Personal Injury, Products Liability, Wrongful Death, Medical Malpractice, Professional Negligence, Traumatic Brain Injury, Automobile Accidents, Nursing Home Torts, Civil Litigation.

ROURKE & BLUMENTHAL, LLP

CIRCLEVILLE, OHIO

(See Columbus)

Personal Injury, Negligence, Products Liability, Medical Malpractice, Nursing Home Litigation, Wrongful Death, Intentional Tort, Insurance Disputes, Automobile Accidents, Civil Trial Practice, Aviation, Professional Liability.

REBECCA J. STUMLER

CIRCLEVILLE, OHIO

(See Columbus)

Family Law, Divorce, Child Custody, Child Support, Visitation Rights, Adoption Law, Paternity, Domestic Violence, Bankruptcy Law, Civil Litigation.

TWYFORD & DONAHEY, P.L.L.

Established in 1968

214 SOUTH COURT STREET
CIRCLEVILLE, OHIO 43113
Telephone: Toll Free: 1-800-686-1699
Fax: 614-849-0475
Email: help@twyforddonahey.com
URL: http://www.twyforddonahey.com

Columbus, Ohio Office: 495 South High Street, 43215-5058. Telephone: Toll Free: 1-800-686-1699. Email: help@twyforddonahey.com.
Delaware, Ohio Office: 163 N. Sandusky Street, Suite 103, 43015. Telephone: Toll Free: 1-800-686-1699. Email: help@twyforddonahey.com.
Lancaster, Ohio Office: 3794 Old Columbus, N.W., 43130. Telephone: Toll Free: 1-800-686-1699. Email: help@twyforddonahey.com.
Newark, Ohio Office: 137 West Main Street, Suite C., 43025. Telephone: Toll Free: 1-800-686-1699. Email: help@twyforddonahey.com.
London, Ohio Office: 25 West Fifth Street, 43140. Telephone: Toll Free: 1-800-686-1699. Email: help@twyforddonahey.com.

Personal Injury Litigation, Wrongful Death, Medical Malpractice, Products Liability, Automobile Accidents, Trucking Accidents, Head and Spinal Injuries, Motorcycle Accidents and Injuries, Uninsured Motorists, Insurance Law, Airplane Crash Litigation, Railroad Accidents, Slip and Fall, Dog Bites, Work Related Injuries, Birth Injuries, Nursing Home Abuse and Neglect.

FIRM PROFILE: Tom Twyford and Dick Donahey have been partners since 1968 and have practiced exclusively in the areas of personal injury, medical malpractice and products liability law. We have never represented insurance companies! In recent years, we have obtained some of the largest verdicts in Franklin County. We have purposely remained small in order to concentrate on a limited number of cases. We have six offices and will handle cases in any part of the state of Ohio.

(For complete biographical data on all personnel, see Professional Biographies at Columbus, Ohio.)

ABEL & ZOCOLO, LPA

Established in 1974

THE SUPERIOR BUILDING - SUITE 1915
815 SUPERIOR AVENUE
CLEVELAND, OHIO 44114
Telephone: 216-621-6138
Fax: 216-241-5620
Email: lorizocolo@aol.com
URL: http://www.lawyers.com/jackabellaw

Family Law, Divorce, Custody, Interstate Custody, International Custody, Domestic Violence, Personal Injury, Divorce Taxation, Probate, Guardianship Law, Sports Law representing professional athletes in Family Law matters.

JACK W. ABEL, born Cleveland, Ohio, June 1, 1948; admitted to bar, 1974, Ohio and U.S. District Court, Northern District of Ohio; 1984, U.S. Supreme Court. *Education:* The Ohio State University (B.A., 1970); University of North Carolina at Chapel Hill (J.D., 1974). Court Appointed Arbitrator. Court Appointed Guardian Ad Litem. *Member:* Cleveland Bar Association (Member and Former Chairman, Family Law Section). ***REPORTED CASES:*** Pasqualone v. Pasqualone, 63 Ohio St 2d 96, 406 N.E. 22 1121 (Ohio 1980); Strother v. Hutchinson, 67 Ohio St 2d 282, 423 N.E. 2d 467 (Ohio 1981); Mayor v. Mayor, 71 Ohio App 3d 789, 595 N.E. 2d 436 (Ohio App. 8 Dist, 1991). ***PRACTICE AREAS:*** Family Law; Divorce; Child Custody; Interstate Child Custody; International Child Custody; Domestic Violence; Personal Injury Law; Divorce Taxation; Probate; Guardianship; Sports Law. ***Email:*** jwabel@sbcglobal.net

LORI A. ZOCOLO, born Salem, Ohio, December 19, 1959; admitted to bar, 1998, Ohio and U.S. District Court, Northern District of Ohio. *Education:* Ohio University (B.A., 1982); Case Western Reserve University (J.D., 1998). Former Adjunct Professor, Case Western Reserve University School of Law. *Member:* Cleveland Bar Association. ***PRACTICE AREAS:*** Family Law; Domestic Violence; Personal Injury; Criminal Law; Driving While Intoxicated; Divorce; Child Custody. ***Email:*** lorizocolo@sbcglobal.net

ASSOCIATE

SHARON R. DITKO-BEVIONE, born Cleveland, Ohio, April 30, 1975; admitted to bar, 2004, Ohio. *Education:* Cleveland State University (B.A., summa cum laude, 1998); Case Western Reserve University (J.D., cum laude, 2004). Recipient, William E. Davis Prize. Treasurer, Jonathan Ault Mock Trial Team, 2003-2004. ***PRACTICE AREAS:*** Family Law; Divorce; Child Custody; Juvenile Law; Domestic Violence. ***Email:*** ditkobevione@sbcglobal.net

AGGERS, JOSEPH & CHEVERINE CO., L.P.A.

Established in 1994

EXECUTIVE COMMONS EAST
29525 CHAGRIN BOULEVARD, SUITE 306
CLEVELAND, OHIO 44122-4601
Telephone: 216-765-8520
Fax: 216-765-8817
Email: ajc@ajclawfirm.com
URL: http://www.ajclawfirm.com

Business Law, Commercial, Admiralty and Maritime, Environmental, Contracts, Corporate, Employment Law, Construction Law, Wills, Probate, Real Estate, State and Federal Litigation.

(This Listing Continued)

FIRM PROFILE: Since its formation in 1994, Aggers, Joseph & Cheverine Co., L.P.A. has provided a broad range of litigation services to its clients in matters of admiralty, business and contract law, real estate, probate and estate administration matters, employment law, telecommunications law, computer law, construction litigation and creditor representation in bankruptcy proceedings, with particular emphasis on trial work. The principals of Aggers, Joseph & Cheverine Co., L.P.A. have dedicated themselves to providing the highest quality legal services at the most reasonable cost to their clients. Focusing primarily on litigation matters, Aggers, Joseph & Cheverine Co., L.P.A. services both individual clients and business entities. The firm has earned the recognition and respect of its clients, the bar and the bench in its many areas of practice.

DAVID F. AGGERS, born Youngstown, Ohio, December 1, 1947; admitted to bar, 1983, Ohio and U.S. District Court, Northern District of Ohio; U.S. Court of Appeals, Sixth Circuit; U.S. District Court, Eastern District of Michigan. *Education:* John Carroll University (B.A., 1970); Cleveland State University, Cleveland Marshall College of Law (J.D., 1982). *Member:* Ohio State Bar Association. ***PRACTICE AREAS:*** Admiralty and Maritime Law; Environmental Law; Real Estate Law; Civil Litigation; Commercial Law; Federal Litigation; Debtor and Creditor Law. ***Email:*** dfa@ajclawfirm.com

KATHRYN THERESA JOSEPH, born Cleveland, Ohio, August 9, 1960; admitted to bar, 1986, Ohio and U.S. District Court, Northern District of Ohio; U.S. Court of Appeals, Sixth Circuit; U.S. District Court, Eastern District of Wisconsin; U.S. District Court, Eastern District of Michigan. *Education:* University of Rochester (B.A., cum laude, 1982); Case Western Reserve University (J.D., 1986). Adjunct Professor, Case Western Reserve University, Trial Tactics. *Member:* Ohio State Bar Association. ***PRACTICE AREAS:*** Real Estate Law; Probate Law; Civil Litigation; Commercial Law; Business Litigation; Contract Law; Federal Litigation. ***Email:*** ktj@ajclawfirm.com

VINCENT L. CHEVERINE, born Parma, Ohio, October 21, 1963; admitted to bar, 1990, Washington and U.S. District Court, Western District of Washington; 1993, U.S. Court of Appeals, Ninth Circuit; 1995, Ohio and U.S. District Court, Northern District of Ohio; 2001, U.S. Court of Appeals, Sixth Circuit. *Education:* University of Virginia (B.A., cum laude, 1985; J.D., 1990). Executive Editor, Journal of Law and Politics, 1989-1990. *Member:* Ohio State and Washington State Bar Associations. ***PRACTICE AREAS:*** Employment Discrimination; Sexual Harassment; Employment Law; Wrongful Termination; Labor Law; Covenants Not To Compete; Civil Litigation; Federal Litigation; Construction Litigation; Mechanics Liens; Commercial Litigation. ***Email:*** vlc@ajclawfirm.com

OF COUNSEL

JOHN V. SCHARON, JR., born Massillon, Ohio, April 2, 1953; admitted to bar, 1978, Ohio. *Education:* Walsh College; University of Akron (B.A., cum laude, 1975); Case Western Reserve University (J.D., 1978). Member, National Mock Trial Team, 1978. Listed in Marquis' Who's Who in American Law, 1992. Coordinator, People's Law School, 1990. *Member:* Cleveland and Ohio State Bar Associations; The Association of Trial Lawyers of America; Ohio Academy of Trial Lawyers; Cleveland Academy of Trial Attorneys (Trustee, 1985-1987; Newsletter Editor, 1986-1987; Secretary, 1987-1988; CLE Coordinator, 1987-1988; Treasurer, 1988-1989; President, 1989-1990); 8th District Judicial Conference (Life Member). ***PRACTICE AREAS:*** Personal Injury; Medical Malpractice; Products Liability; Litigation. ***Email:*** jvs@ajclawfirm.com

AGIN AND AGIN CO. L.P.A.

Established in 1986

5910 LANDERBROOK DRIVE
SUITE 200
CLEVELAND, OHIO 44124
Telephone: 440-460-1415
Fax: 440-446-1240
Email: bernieagin@aol.com
URL: http://www.lawyers.com/agin&agin

Business, Family and Probate Law, Personal Injury, Elder Care Law, General Civil Trials.

FIRM PROFILE: The firm presents a unique ability to bring both sophisticated financial analysis and legal problem solving to cases undertaken by the office. In addition to their backgrounds as attorneys at law, both Sandra Agin and Bernard I. Agin are certified public accountants. Bernard I. Agin also has his masters degree in Economic and Statistical Analysis. The firm is available to the general public and to other law firms wishing to avail themselves of the firm's resources for litigation support.

BERNARD I. AGIN, born Cleveland, Ohio, November 21, 1946; admitted to bar, 1975, Ohio; 1977, U.S. District Court, Northern District of Ohio. *Education:* The Ohio State University (B.S. in B.A., cum laude, 1969; M.A. in Economic Theory and Econometrics, 1969); Cleveland Marshall College of Law, Cleveland State University (J.D., 1975). Beta Gamma Sigma. Certified Public Accountant, Ohio, 1977. Certified Valuation Analyst, 1998. Publications: "When Experts Disagree," Domestic Relations Journal of Ohio, July/August 1992; "Spousal Support - Guidelines or Methodology?" Domestic Relations Journal of Ohio, March/April 1993; "Marital vs. Non-Marital Interests - Value in Closely Held Corporations," Domestic Relations Journal of Ohio, July/August 1996. Co-Author of Computerized "Spousal Support Analysis Program," DomRel Support Services, Inc., 1994; "Tracing Assets in the Martial Estate," Domestic Relations Journal of Ohio, 1998. Lecturer in the areas of valuation of closely held businesses, divorce taxation and spousal support analysis for Ohio Family Law Institute, Professional Education Seminars, Inc., Cleveland Bar Association, Cuyahoga County Bar Association, Lake County Bar Association and the National Business Institute. Selected for inclusion in The Best Lawyers in America: Directory of Expert Witnesses (Woodward/White, Inc., 1992). *Member:* Cleveland, Ohio State and Cuyahoga Bar Associations; Ohio Society of Certified Public Accountants; The Institute of Business Appraisers; National Association of Certified Valuation Analysts. ***PRACTICE AREAS:*** Domestic Relations; Litigation; Probate; Business Law. ***Email:*** bernieagin@aol.com

(This Listing Continued)

SANDRA K. AGIN, born Germany, October 11, 1948; admitted to bar, 1978, Ohio and U.S. District Court, Northern District of Ohio. *Education:* Cleveland State University (B.B.A., 1970); Cleveland Marshall College of Law (J.D., 1977). Beta Alpha Psi. Certified Public Accountant, Ohio, 1972. *Member:* Cleveland and Ohio State Bar Associations. ***PRACTICE AREAS:*** Personal Injury; Elder Care; Probate; Business Law. ***Email:*** skagin@aol.com

REFERENCE: National City Bank.

THOMAS F. ALLEN

1801 EAST NINTH STREET, SUITE 1300
CLEVELAND, OHIO 44114
Telephone: 216-771-4000
Fax: 216-771-0422

Tax and Business Law.

THOMAS F. ALLEN, born Norwalk, Ohio, 1942; admitted to bar, 1968, Ohio. *Education:* Yale University (B.A., 1965; LL.B., 1968).

AMIN & TUROCY, LLP

24TH FLOOR, NATIONAL CITY CENTER
1900 EAST 9TH STREET
CLEVELAND, OHIO 44114
Telephone: 216-696-8730
Fax: 216-696-8731
URL: http://www.thepatentattorneys.com

Patents, Patent Prosecution, Trademarks, Trademark Prosecution, Copyrights, Litigation, Intellectual Property.

PARTNERS

HIMANSHU S. AMIN, born Mumbai, India, January, 1965; admitted to bar, 1995, Ohio; 1996, U.S. District Court, Northern District of Ohio; 1997, U.S. Court of Appeals for the Federal Circuit; registered to practice before U.S. Patent and Trademark Office. *Education:* The Ohio State University (B.S.E.E., 1988); Weatherhead School of Management, Case Western Reserve University (M.B.A., 1993); Case Western Reserve University (J.D., 1995). Recipient: Nathan Burkan Award, Copyright Law, Case Western Reserve University, 1994; Second Place, Boalt Law School National High Technology Writing Competition, 1995. Author, "The Lack of Protection Afforded Software Under the Current Intellectual Property Laws," 43 Clev.St.L.Rev. 1, 19 (1995). *Member:* Ohio State Bar Association; American Bar Association; American Intellectual Property Law Association; Cleveland Intellectual Property Association. ***Email:*** hamin@thepatentattorneys.com

GREGORY TUROCY, born Cleveland, Ohio, 1963; admitted to bar, 1991, Ohio; U.S. District Court, Northern District of Ohio and U.S. Court of Appeals, Federal Circuit; registered to practice before U.S. Patent and Trademark Office. *Education:* The Ohio State University (B.A., in Chem., 1986); University of Georgia (M.S., Organic Chemistry, 1988); Mercer University (J.D., 1991). Co-Author, "The Synthesis of Racemic E and Z 2,3-Methantyrosine: New Cyclopropyl Analogs of Tyrosine," Journal of Organic Chemistry, 1989, 54, 145. *Member:* American Bar Association (Member, Patent, Trademark and Copyright Section); Cleveland Intellectual Property Law Association (Chairperson, Chemical/Biotech Practice Committee); American Intellectual Property Law Association; American Chemical Society. ***Email:*** gturocy@thepatentattorneys.com

JEFFREY R. SADLOWSKI, born June 1, 1963; admitted to bar, 1990, Ohio; U.S. District Court, Northern District of Ohio and the U.S. Court of Appeals, Sixth Circuit; 2001, U.S. Federal District Court of Appeals and U.S. Supreme Court. *Education:* Case Western Reserve University (B.S., Engineering, 1985); Cleveland State University (J.D., magna cum laude, 1989).

DEBORAH CORPUS, admitted to bar, 2000, Ohio; registered to practice before U.S. Patent and Trademark Office. *Education:* University of California at Davis (B.S., 1996); Case Western Reserve University (J.D., 2000). Research Assistant, Department of Neurology, University of California Davis School of Medicine and Department of Anatomy/Physiology/Cell Biology, University of California Davis School of Veterinary Medicine. ***Email:*** dliu@thepatentattorneys.com

JEFFREY D. HALE, born January 26, 1965; admitted to bar, 1997, New York; 1998, Minnesota and District of Columbia; registered to practice before U.S. Patent and Trademark Office (Not admitted in Ohio). *Education:* University of Missouri, Columbia (B.S.E.E., cum laude, with honors, 1987); Franklin Pierce Law Center (J.D., 1996).

ERIC D. JORGENSON, born Montevideo, Minnesota, May 20, 1951; admitted to bar, 2002, Ohio and U.S. District Court, Northern District of Ohio; registered to practice before U.S. Patent and Trademark Office. *Education:* Moorhead State University (B.A., Math, 1980); North Dakota State University (B.S.E.E., 1980); Texas Wesleyan University School of Law (J.D., 1997). ***Email:*** ejorgenson@thepatentattorneys.com

ASSOCIATES

DANIEL B. BORTNICK, born Meadville, Pennsylvania, September 17, 1960; admitted to bar, 2000, Ohio. *Education:* Cleveland State University (B.S.E.E., 1994); Cleveland-Marshall College of Law, Cleveland State University (J.D., 1998). ***Email:*** dbortnick@thepatentattorneys.com

CARLOS GARRITANO, admitted to bar, 2004, Ohio. *Education:* Case Western Reserve University (B.S., Electrical Engineering with Signal and Systems, cum laude, 2001); The Ohio State University Moritz College of Law. ***Email:*** cgarritano@thepatentattorneys.com

(This Listing Continued)

AMIN & TUROCY, LLP, Cleveland—Continued

DAVID W. GRILLO, admitted to bar, 2003, Ohio; registered to practice before U.S. Patent and Trademark Office. *Education:* The Ohio State University (B.A., Computer Science and Engineering, 2000); Cleveland-Marshall College of Law (J.D., 2003). ***Email:*** dgrillo@thepatentattorneys.com

JOHN M. LING, born Atlanta, Georgia, December 1, 1973; admitted to bar, 2000, Arizona and Ohio; registered to practice before U.S. Patent and Trademark Office. *Education:* University of Michigan (B.A., Biology and English Literature, 1996); University of Arizona (Medicinal and Chemical Pharmacology; J.D., 2000). ***Email:*** jling@thepatentattorneys.com

MICHAEL J. MEDLEY, admitted to bar, 2004, Ohio; registered to practice before U.S. Patent and Trademark Office. *Education:* Ohio University (B.S., Electrical Engineering, cum laude, with Microprocessors, 2001); The Ohio State University Moritz College of Law. ***Email:*** mmedley@thepatentattorneys.com

JAMES J. PINGOR, born 1966; admitted to bar, 1998, Ohio; U.S. District Court, Northern District of Ohio; registered to practice before U.S. Patent and Trademark Office. *Education:* University of Pittsburgh (B.S., 1988); Capital University (J.D., 1998). ***Email:*** JPingor@thepatentattorneys.com

JEFFREY N. PRULHIERE, born Akron, Ohio, June 10, 1957; admitted to bar, 1984, Ohio; registered to practice before U.S. Patent and Trademark Office. *Education:* University of Akron (B.S.E.E., summa cum laude, 1980; J.D., cum laude, 1984; M.A., 1986). ***Email:*** jprulhiere@thepatentattorneys.com

VAHID SHARIFI, born Tehran, Iran, May 16, 1967; admitted to bar, 2000, Illinois and California; registered to practice before U.S. Patent and Trademark Office (Not admitted in Ohio). *Education:* Tehran University (B.S., 1990); Northwestern University (M.S., 1993); Loyola University of Chicago (J.D., 2000). ***Email:*** vsharifi@thepatentattorneys.com

LEGAL SUPPORT PERSONNEL

TODD BEHRENS, (admission pending). *Education:* Duke University (B.S., Biomedical Engineering, cum laude, 2000); Case Western Reserve University School of Law. ***Email:*** tbehrens@thepatentattorneys.com

---

APICELLA AND TRAPP

Established in 1965
1200 PENTON MEDIA BUILDING
1300 EAST NINTH STREET
CLEVELAND, OHIO 44114-1503
Telephone: 216-696-3550
Fax: 216-696-3830
Email: aptrapp@msn.com

General Trial and Appellate Practice. Negligence, Federal Employers Liability, Railroad, Family, Professional Liability, Products Liability, Probate Litigation, Nursing Home Litigation.

FIRM PROFILE: Mr. F.M. Apicella and Mrs. Mary Jane Trapp are a husband-and-wife team that has been in practice together for over 19 years. They practice throughout the state of Ohio in legal matters of Personal Injury, Professional Liability, Products Liability, Family Law, Railroad Law and Nursing Home Litigation.

MEMBERS OF FIRM

F. M. APICELLA, born Cleveland, Ohio, August 10, 1930; admitted to bar, 1954, Ohio; 1964, U.S. Supreme Court. *Education:* The Ohio State University (B.A., 1952); The Ohio State University College of Law (J.D., 1954). Acting Judge, South Euclid, Ohio Municipal Court, 1965-1968. Chairman, Arbitration Panel, Cuyahoga County Common Pleas Court, 1970—. *Member:* Cleveland, Cuyahoga County (Trustee, 1971—; President, 1980-1981), Geauga County, Eighth Judicial District of Ohio (Life Member, Judicial Conference), Ohio State (Member, Council of Delegates, 1979—; Member, Litigation Section Council; Chairman, Unauthorized Practice of Law Committee, 2001-2003) and American (Member, House of Delegates, 1983—) Bar Associations; Cleveland Academy of Trial Attorneys (Member, Board of Directors, 1971-1981; President, 1975-1976). Fellow: Cuyahoga County Bar Foundation (President, 1986-1988); Ohio State Bar Foundation. [1st Lt., U.S. Army, 1954-1956]. ***PRACTICE AREAS:*** Personal Injury Law; Federal Employers Liability Law; Railroad Law; Products Liability Law; Nursing Home Litigation; Professional Liability. ***Email:*** aptrapp@msn.com

MARY JANE TRAPP, born Columbus, Ohio, July 6, 1956; admitted to bar, 1981, Ohio; 1987, U.S. Supreme Court. *Education:* Mount Holyoke College (A.B., cum laude, 1978); Case Western Reserve University (J.D., 1981). Commissioner, Supreme Court of Ohio CLE Commission, 2005—. Commissioner, Supreme Court of Ohio Board of Commissioners on the Unauthorized Practice of Law, 1986-1989. Member: Supreme Court Task Force on the Unauthorized Practice of Law, 1990-1994; Supreme Court Records Management Task Force, 1995-1997; Supreme Court Rules Advisory Committee, 1997-2002. Attorney Representative, Ohio Judicial Conference, Civil Law and Procedure Committee, 1995-1997. Member, Privacy and Public Access Subcommittee, Supreme Court of Ohio Advisory Committee on Technology and the Courts. *Member:* Cleveland (Trustee, 1995-1998), Cuyahoga County (Trustee, 1986-1993, 1999—; Treasurer, 1993-1994), Geauga County, Ohio State (President, 2001-2002; Member: District 12 Board of Governors Representative, 1995-1998; Council of Delegates, 1986—; Women in the Profession Section Council; Chairman, Judicial Administration and Legal Reform Committee, 1993-1995; Trustee, 1995-1999, and Treasurer, 1997-1998, Chair, 1999, Ohio Continuing Legal Education Institute; Eighth Judicial District Life Member Judicial Conference; Membership Committee, National Conference of Bar Presidents, 2001-2003) and American (Member, House of Delegates, 2002—) Bar Associations; Ohio Academy of Trial Lawyers. Fellow: American Bar Foundation; Ohio State Bar Foundation. ***PRACTICE AREAS:*** Personal Injury Law; Family Law; Child Custody; Products Liability Law; Probate Litigation; Nursing Home Litigation; Professional Liability. ***Email:*** aptrapp@msn.com

(This Listing Continued)

REFERENCE: Key Bank.

ARMSTRONG, MITCHELL, DAMIANI & ZACCAGNINI

Established in 1981
1725 MIDLAND BUILDING
101 PROSPECT AVENUE WEST
CLEVELAND, OHIO 44115-1091
Telephone: 216-566-0064
Fax: 216-566-0224

Personal Injury, Product Liability, Medical Malpractice, Wrongful Death, School Law, State and Federal Litigation and Appellate Practice, Federal, State and Local Taxation, Real Estate, Commercial Law, Administrative Law, Probate and Estate Planning, Labor Law, Attorney Disciplinary Law, Government Law and Criminal Law.

MEMBERS OF FIRM

TIMOTHY J. ARMSTRONG, born Cleveland, Ohio, June 6, 1944; admitted to bar, 1972, Ohio; 1973, U.S. District Court, Northern District of Ohio; 1978, U.S. Supreme Court. *Education:* John Carroll University (B.A., 1967); Case Western Reserve University (J.D., 1972). Assistant Prosecuting Attorney, Cuyahoga County, 1975-1979. Prosecutor, City of Brook Park, Ohio, 1984-1987. Special Counsel, Office of the Ohio Attorney General, 1983-1991. *Member:* American Bar Association. ***SPECIAL AGENCIES:*** Boards of Revision; Ohio Board of Tax Appeals. ***PRACTICE AREAS:*** School Law; Real Estate; Commercial Law; Administrative Law. ***Email:*** tim@law-amdz.com

WILLIAM MITCHELL, born Martins Ferry, Ohio, February 5, 1949; admitted to bar, 1978, Ohio; 1979, U.S. District Court, Northern District of Ohio; 1989, U.S. Court of Appeals, Sixth Circuit; 1995, U.S. Court of Appeals, Third Circuit; 1996, U.S. Supreme Court. *Education:* Ohio University (B.S., 1971; M.S., 1972); Cleveland-Marshall College of Law (J.D., 1978). Assistant Prosecuting Attorney, Cuyahoga County, 1979-1980. Commissioner, Victims of Crime Division, Court of Claims of Ohio, 1982-1987. *Member:* The Association of Trial Lawyers of America; Ohio Academy of Trial Lawyers. ***PRACTICE AREAS:*** Personal Injury; Product Liability; Medical Malpractice; Wrongful Death; Administrative Law; School Law. ***Email:*** bill@law-amdz.com

LOUIS C. DAMIANI, born Bellaire, Ohio, May 23, 1953; admitted to bar, 1979, Ohio and U.S. District Court, Northern District of Ohio; 1980, U.S. Court of Appeals, Sixth Circuit; 1985, U.S. Supreme Court. *Education:* The Ohio State University (B.A., 1975); Cleveland-Marshall College of Law (J.D., 1979). Director, Supreme Court of Ohio, 1983-1986. Foreman, Cuyahoga County Grand Jury, September 1993 Term. Special Counsel, Cuyahoga County Treasurer, 1987-1994. Special Counsel, Clerk of Courts, Cleveland Municipal Court, 1994—. Life Member, Judicial Conference of the Eighth Judicial District of Ohio. *Member:* American Bar Association; Ohio Council of School Board Attorneys; National School Board Association's Council of School Attorneys. ***PRACTICE AREAS:*** School Law; Governmental Law; Administrative Law; Labor Law. ***Email:*** lou@law-amdz.com

BRUCE A. ZACCAGNINI, born Bellaire, Ohio, October 7, 1960; admitted to bar, 1986, Ohio; 1987, U.S. District Court, Northern District of Ohio; 1990, West Virginia, U.S. District Court, Southern District of West Virginia and U.S. Court of Appeals, Sixth Circuit. *Education:* Ohio State University (B.S.B.A., 1983); Cleveland-Marshall College of Law (J.D., 1986). Deputy Clerk, Supreme Court of Ohio, 1984-1986. Staff Attorney, Office of the Director of the Supreme Court, Ohio, 1986. Assistant Prosecuting Attorney, Cuyahoga County, 1986-1989. *Member:* West Virginia State and American Bar Associations. ***PRACTICE AREAS:*** School Law; Commercial Law; Administrative Law; Criminal Law; Domestic Relations. ***Email:*** bruce@law-amdz.com

ASSOCIATES

VICTOR V. ANSELMO, born Cleveland, Ohio, April 8, 1963; admitted to bar, 1988, Ohio; 1995, U.S. District Court, Northern District of Ohio. *Education:* University of Dayton (B.S., 1985); Cleveland-Marshall College of Law (J.D., 1988). Referee, Cuyahoga County Court of Common Pleas, Division of Domestic Relations, 1990-1991. ***PRACTICE AREAS:*** Workers Compensation; Personal Injury; Medical Malpractice; Real Estate Tax Litigation; Probate; Criminal Law; Domestic Relations; School Law; Special Education; Collective Bargaining; Labor Relations; Arbitration. ***Email:*** victor@law-amdz.com

MAURA NORTON, born Cleveland, Ohio, April 12, 1965; admitted to bar, 1991, Ohio; 1995, U.S. District Court, Northern District of Ohio. *Education:* John Carroll University (B.A., 1987); Case Western Reserve University (J.D., 1991). Delta Theta Phi. ***PRACTICE AREAS:*** Real Estate Tax Litigation; Criminal Law; Small Business Law; Probate. ***Email:*** maura@law-amdz.com

REFERENCE: National City Bank of Cleveland.

JASON T. BAKER

55 PUBLIC SQUARE, SUITE 1330
CLEVELAND, OHIO 44113
Telephone: 216-771-3966
Fax: 216-771-4124
URL: http://www.jbakerlaw.com

Bankruptcy, Criminal Law, DUI, Drug Crimes, Traffic Violations, Divorce, Probate, Wills, Child Custody, Child Support.

JASON T. BAKER, born 1974; admitted to bar, 1999, Ohio. *Education:* The Ohio State University (B.S.B.A., 1996; J.D., 1999). ***PRACTICE AREAS:*** Bankruptcy; Criminal Law; Divorce; Probate; Wills; Child Support; Child Custody.

BAKER & HOSTETLER LLP

Established in 1916

3200 NATIONAL CITY CENTER
1900 EAST NINTH STREET
CLEVELAND, OHIO 44114-3485
Telephone: 216-621-0200
Telecopier: 216-696-0740
To contact an attorney on the Internet use first initial and surname followed by @bakerlaw.com
URL: http://www.bakerlaw.com

In Cincinnati, Ohio: 312 Walnut Street, Suite 3200. Telephone: 513-929-3400.
In Columbus, Ohio: Capitol Square, Suite 2100, 65 East State Street. Telephone: 614-228-1541.
In Costa Mesa, California: 600 Anton Boulevard, Suite 900. Telephone: 714-754-6600.
In Denver, Colorado: 303 East 17th Avenue, Suite 1100. Telephone: 303-861-0600.
In Houston, Texas: 1000 Louisiana, Suite 2000. Telephone: 713-751-1600.
In Los Angeles, California: 333 South Grand Avenue, Suite 1800. Telephone: 213-975-1600.
In Orlando, Florida: SunTrust Center, Suite 2300, 200 South Orange Avenue. Telephone: 407-649-4000.
In Washington, D.C.: Washington Square, Suite 1100, 1050 Connecticut Avenue, N.W. Telephone: 202-861-1500.
In New York, N.Y.: 666 Fifth Avenue. Telephone: 212-589-4200.

General Practice.

NEWTON D. BAKER (1871-1937)
JOSEPH C. HOSTETLER (1885-1958)
THOMAS L. SIDLO (1888-1955)

EXECUTIVE PARTNERS

R. STEVEN KESTNER, born August 6, 1954; admitted to bar, 1979, Ohio. *Education:* Ohio Wesleyan University (B.A., cum laude, 1976); The Ohio State University (J.D., 1979). Pi Mu Epsilon (Mathematics); Omicron Delta Epsilon (Economics); Omicron Delta Kappa (Leadership). Member, 1977-1979, Issue Planning Editor, 1978-1979, Ohio State Law Journal. Member, Firm's Policy Committee. Firmwide Group Chair, Business Group Practice Area. *Member:* Cleveland (Member, Sections of: Securities Law; Corporations, Banking and Business Law), Ohio State and American Bar Associations (Member, Business Law Section). ***PRACTICE AREAS:*** Mergers and Acquisitions; Private Equity; Venture Capital; Securities Law. ***Email:*** skestner@bakerlaw.com

ALEC WIGHTMAN, born Cleveland, Ohio, January 23, 1951; admitted to bar, 1975, Ohio; 1982, U.S. Tax Court. *Education:* Duke University (A.B., cum laude, 1972); The Ohio State University (J.D., cum laude, 1975). (Resident, at Columbus Office). ***PRACTICE AREAS:*** Business Law; Bankruptcy Law. ***Email:*** awightman@bakerlaw.com

OFFICE MANAGING PARTNER

HEWITT B. SHAW, JR., born Altoona, Pennsylvania, February 6, 1955; admitted to bar, 1980, Ohio and U.S. District Court, Northern District of Ohio; 1982, U.S. Tax Court. *Education:* Grove City College (A.B., 1977); Case Western Reserve University (J.D., 1980). Delta Mu Delta; Order of the Coif. Member, Case Western Reserve Law Review, 1979-1980. *Member:* Ohio State and American (Member: Taxation Section; Committee on S Corporations) Bar Associations. ***PRACTICE AREAS:*** Tax Law; Business/Corporate Law. ***Email:*** hshaw@bakerlaw.com

PARTNERS

ALBERT T. ADAMS, born Cleveland, Ohio, December 20, 1950; admitted to bar, 1977, Ohio. *Education:* Harvard University (B.A., 1973; M.B.A., 1977; J.D., 1977). ***PRACTICE AREAS:*** Business. ***Email:*** aadams@bakerlaw.com

FRANK H. ANDORKA, born Lorain, Ohio, July 25, 1946; admitted to bar, 1975, Ohio. *Education:* Ohio University (A.B., summa cum laude with high honors in History, 1968) Phi Beta Kappa; Cornell University (J.D., magna cum laude, 1975). Order of the Coif. Note and Comment Editor, Cornell Law Review. Author: *A Practical Guide to Copyrights and Trademarks*. *Member:* Cleveland and American (Member, ABA Intellectual Property Section; Chairman, 1984-1986, Committee 302; International Copyright Laws and Treaties; Chairman, 1986-1988, Committee 308, Government Relations to Copyright; Chairman, 1988-1990, Committee 306, Broadcasting, Sound Recording & Performing Artists; Chairman, 1990-1992, Division III, Copyrights) Bar Associations. ***PRACTICE AREAS:*** Intellectual Property; Copyrights/Trademarks and Licensing; Television. ***Email:*** fandorka@bakerlaw.com

DANA ROUNTREE ANDRASSY, born Charlotte, North Carolina, February 27, 1964; admitted to bar, 1993, South Carolina; 1994, Ohio. *Education:* University of South Carolina (B.S., 1986; J.D., 1993); New York University School of Law (LL.M., 1994). ***PRACTICE AREAS:*** Tax; Business. ***Email:*** dandrassy@bakerlaw.com

BARRY W. ANDREWS, born Cleveland, Ohio, September 25, 1968; admitted to bar, 1995, Ohio. *Education:* Yale University (B.A., 1990); University of Notre Dame (J.D., 1995). ***PRACTICE AREAS:*** Business; Corporate; Mergers and Acquisitions; Securities. ***Email:*** bandrews@bakerlaw.com

OAKLEY V. ANDREWS, born Cleveland, Ohio, April 15, 1940; admitted to bar, 1965, Ohio; 1968, U.S. Tax Court; U.S. District Court, Northern District of Ohio; U.S. Court of Appeals, Sixth Circuit. *Education:* Yale University (B.A., 1962); Western Reserve University (J.D., 1965). Phi Delta Phi. *Member:* Cleveland (Member, Estate Planning, Probate and Trust Law Section; Chairman, 1984-1985) and Ohio State Bar Associations; Estate Planning Council of Cleveland (President, 1982-1983). Fellow, The American College of Trust and Estate Counsel. ***PRACTICE AREAS:*** Trusts and Estates. ***Email:*** oandrews@bakerlaw.com

(This Listing Continued)

ELLIOT S. AZOFF, born Cleveland, Ohio, September 20, 1946; admitted to bar, 1972, Massachusetts; 1973, Ohio; 1988, U.S. Supreme Court. *Education:* Yale University (B.A., magna cum laude, 1968) Phi Beta Kappa; Harvard Law School (J.D., magna cum laude, 1972). Member, Harvard Law Review, 1970-1972. Law Clerk to Simon E. Sobeloff, Fourth Circuit Court of Appeals, 1972-1973. Author: "The Drug-Free Workplace Act - It's Contractor's Friend, Not An Enemy," Construction Digest, October, 1989. Co-Author: "Practice and Procedure Before the National Labor Relations Board," BNA, 1984, 1989, 1992; "Guide to Wage and Hour Regulation," BNA, 1987, 1998. *Member:* Cleveland, Ohio State and American Bar Associations. ***PRACTICE AREAS:*** Negotiations; Arbitrations; Employment Relations; Supervisory Training; Wage-Hour; National Labor Relations Matters; Public Law; Litigation of Discrimination and Wrongful Discharge Claims. ***Email:*** eazoff@bakerlaw.com

JEFFREY BADDELEY, born Batavia, New York, July 6, 1955; admitted to bar, 1983, Ohio. *Education:* University of Chicago (A.B., 1977); Case Western Reserve University (J.D., 1983). Editor, Case Western University Law Review, 1982-1983. Adjunct Professor, Case Western Reserve University School of Law, 1992—. *Member:* Cleveland, Ohio State and American Bar Associations. ***PRACTICE AREAS:*** Bankruptcy; Commercial Law. ***Email:*** jbaddeley@bakerlaw.com

RICHARD H. BAMBERGER, born Cleveland, Ohio, September 18, 1945; admitted to bar, 1972, Ohio. *Education:* Bowdoin College (B.A., 1967); Case Western Reserve University (J.D., 1972). Order of the Coif. Law Clerk Federal Judge William K. Thomas, N.D., Ohio, 1972-1974. Adjunct Professor in Employee Benefits in Masters Tax Program at Case Western Reserve University Law School. *Member:* Cleveland, Ohio State and American (Member, Employee Benefits Committee) Bar Associations; Midwest Pension and Benefits Conference. ***PRACTICE AREAS:*** Employment Law and Benefits, Litigation; Tax Law. ***Email:*** rbamberger@bakerlaw.com

BRIAN A. BASH, born Columbus, Ohio, September 21, 1949; admitted to bar, 1975, Ohio; 1976, U.S. District Court, Northern District of Ohio; 1987, U.S. Court of Appeals, 6th Circuit; 2003, U.S. District Court, Southern District of Ohio. *Education:* Tulane University (B.A., 1971; J.D., 1975). Author: Banking Law, Vols. 7, 8 and 8A, (Matthew Bender Co.), Ohio Collection Law (Professional Education Systems), Ohio Real Estate Update (Professional Education Systems), Ohio Mortgage Foreclosures (Professional Education Systems), Lender Liability in Ohio (National Business Institute, Inc.). Adjunct Professor, Commercial Law, Cleveland Marshall School of Law, 1979-1982. Member, Federal Court Panel, 1992—. *Member:* Cleveland, Cuyahoga County, Ohio State and American Bar Associations; Commercial Law League of America; American Bankruptcy Institute; National Association of Bankruptcy Trustees (Panel Trustee, 1986—); Euromoney's List of Leading U.S. Insolvency Attorneys. ***PRACTICE AREAS:*** Debtor Creditor Law; Bankruptcy; Banking Law. ***Email:*** bbash@bakerlaw.com

BRUCE O. BAUMGARTNER, born St. Louis, Missouri, August 21, 1942; admitted to bar, 1967, Ohio; U.S. District Court, Northern District of Ohio; U.S. Court of Appeals, First, Sixth, Eleventh and Federal Circuits; U.S. Court of Claims. *Education:* Northwestern University (B.A., 1964; J.D., cum laude, 1967). Editor, Northwestern Law Review. Author: Counterfeiting and Piracy in the U.S.--A General Overview of the Law and Practice to Combat Counterfeiting and Piracy, Common Law Institute of Intellectual Property Limited in London, England (1983); "The Gray Market--The *Copiat* Supreme Court Appeal, the Effective Copyright Alternative, and Possible Legislation," Practicing Law Institute (1988); "Enforcement of Intellectual Property Rights Through the Courts," Taipei, Taiwan, U.S. Department of Commerce Presentation to the Taiwan Judiciary (1989); "Developments in Worldwide Intellectual Property Rights in a Global Marketplace," Taiwan Intellectual Property Institute, Taipei, Taiwan (1991); "Developments in United States Intellectual Property Law in the Global Economy," University of Philippines, Manila, Philippines, (1991)' "Copyright Enforcement Worldwide," ABA-Section of Patent, Trademark & Copyright Law, 1992 Annual Meeting: "How to Police Your Trade Mark From Competing Applications and Registrations on Global Registers," International Trademark Association's 118th Annual Meeting (1996). Adjunct Professor of Law on Intellectual Property, Case Western Reserve University School of Law (1993-1994). *Member:* Cleveland, Ohio State and American (Member: Litigation, International and Patent, Trademark and Copyright Law Sections) Bar Associations; International Trademark Association; American Intellectual Property Law Association; Association of College Licensing Administrators; Asian-Pacific Lawyers Association. [Lieut., JAGC, USNR, Active Duty, 1968-1971; Legal Officer, NATO Base, Siganello, Sicily, 1969-1971]. ***PRACTICE AREAS:*** Intellectual Property; Intellectual Property Litigation; Business and Commercial Litigation; International Intellectual Property. ***Email:*** bbaumgartner@bakerlaw.com

MARY M. BITTENCE, born Houghton, Michigan, January 10, 1952; admitted to bar, 1982, Ohio. *Education:* Cleveland State University (B.A., summa cum laude, 1976; J.D., summa cum laude, 1982). Business Editor, Cleveland State Law Review, 1981-1982. *Member:* Cleveland, Ohio State and American Bar Associations. ***PRACTICE AREAS:*** Litigation; Environmental Law; Product Liability. ***Email:*** mbittence@bakerlaw.com

MAUREEN A. BRENNAN, born Morristown, New Jersey, August 7, 1949; admitted to bar, 1977, Pennsylvania; 1978, U.S. District Court, Eastern District of Pennsylvania; 1989, Ohio. *Education:* Bryn Mawr College (B.A., magna cum laude with honors in Phil., 1971); Boston College (J.D., cum laude, 1977). Attorney, U.S. Environmental Protection Agency, 1977-1980. Assistant District Attorney, Philadelphia Trial and Appellate Divisions, 1980-1984. Adjunct Professor, Case Western University Law School, Environmental Law, 1990-1992 and 2000. Member: Steering Committee, The Ohio Voluntary Action Program, Brownfields, 1994—; Cuyahoga County Brownfields Working Group, 1993-1995. *Member:* Cleveland, Cuyahoga County, Ohio State, Pennsylvania (Member, Environmental Law Committee, 1997—) and American Bar Associations. ***PRACTICE AREAS:*** Environmental Law; Administrative Law; Litigation; Regulatory Law. ***Email:*** mbrennan@bakerlaw.com

TERRY M. BRENNAN, born Cleveland, Ohio, May 26, 1970; admitted to bar, 1995, Ohio; 1997, New York. *Education:* Miami University (B.A., 1992); Indiana University at Bloomington (J.D., cum laude, 1995). Omicron Delta Kappa; Phi Alpha Delta. Member, 1992-1995 and Managing Editor, 1994-1995, Indiana Law Journal. *Member:* Cleveland, Ohio State and American Bar Associations. ***PRACTICE AREAS:*** Litigation. ***Email:*** tbrennan@bakerlaw.com

(This Listing Continued)

BAKER & HOSTETLER LLP, Cleveland—Continued

GARY L. BRYENTON, born Lodi, Ohio, October 21, 1939; admitted to bar, 1965, Ohio; 1967, U.S. Court of Appeals, Sixth Circuit; 1972, U.S. Supreme Court. *Education:* Heidelberg College (A.B., 1961); Western Reserve University (J.D., 1965). Order of the Coif. *Member:* Cleveland, Ohio State and American Bar Associations. ***PRACTICE AREAS:*** Business; Real Estate; Partnerships; Reorganizations; Mergers and Acquisitions. ***Email:*** gbryenton@bakerlaw.com

PHILLIP M. CALLESEN, born Manistee, Michigan, February 24, 1962; admitted to bar, 1987, Ohio. *Education:* Bowling Green State University (B.A., magna cum laude, 1984); Case Western Reserve University (J.D., magna cum laude, 1987). Phi Beta Kappa; Order of the Coif. *Member:* Cleveland, Ohio State and American Bar Associations. ***PRACTICE AREAS:*** Debt Finance; Business Law; Real Estate Law. ***Email:*** pcallesen@bakerlaw.com

DIANE P. CHAPMAN, born Lowell, Massachusetts; admitted to bar, 1978, Ohio. *Education:* Duquesne University (B.A., 1974); Cleveland State University (J.D., 1978). ***PRACTICE AREAS:*** General Litigation; Products Liability; Construction Law. ***Email:*** dchapman@bakerlaw.com

ELAINE A. CHOTLOS, born Granville, Ohio, February 5, 1958; admitted to bar, 1983, Ohio. *Education:* University of Cincinnati (B.A., 1980); The Ohio State University (J.D., with honors, 1983). Phi Beta Kappa. ***PRACTICE AREAS:*** Corporate and Real Estate Law; Solid Waste Industry; Environmental Law. ***Email:*** echotlos@bakerlaw.com

AVERY S. COHEN, born Youngstown, Ohio, November 29, 1936; admitted to bar, 1961, Ohio; 1982, Florida. *Education:* Case Western Reserve University (A.B., 1958); Harvard Law School (J.D., 1961). Author: "The Outside Director-Selection, Responsibilities and Contribution to the Public Corporation," XXXIV Washington & Lee Law Review 837, 1977. Instructor, Teaching Damages and Business Planning, Cleveland State University Law School, 1965-1976. Co-Chairman: "Corporate Governance," 1979; NYLJ Institute, "Compensating the Corporate Executive," 1978, "The New Disclosure Rules," 1980 and "Going Public in the 80s," 1982; "Retooling Your Firm," American Bar Association, Dec., 1991; "Administrative Strategic Planning in the 90's," Update, Dec., 1991. Lecturer: Effective Law Firm Planning, ICLE and ILFM Institutes, 1983-1995; Corporate Disclosure After the Securities Litigation Reform Act, Fulcrum, 1996. ***Email:*** acohen@bakerlaw.com

LOUIS A. COLOMBO, born Cleveland, Ohio, November 29, 1947; admitted to bar, 1973, Ohio; 1974, U.S. District Court, Northern District of Ohio; 1982, U.S. Court of Appeals, Ninth Circuit; 1984, U.S. Court of Appeals, Sixth Circuit; 1988, U.S. Supreme Court; 1990, U.S. Court of Appeals, Fourth Circuit; 1992, U.S. Court of Appeals, Fifth and Second Circuits; 1995, U.S. Court of Appeals, Third Circuit; 1999, U.S. Court of Appeals, Eleventh Circuit. *Education:* Michigan State University (B.A., magna cum laude, 1969); University of Michigan (J.D., magna cum laude, 1973). Phi Beta Kappa; Order of the Coif. Associate Editor, Michigan Law Review, 1972-1973. ***PRACTICE AREAS:*** Litigation; Defamation; Media; Intellectual Property. ***Email:*** lcolombo@bakerlaw.com

WAYNE C. DABB, JR., born Ogden, Utah, September 20, 1946; admitted to bar, 1971, Ohio; 1972, U.S. District Court, Northern District of Ohio and U.S. Court of Appeals, Sixth Circuit; 1974, U.S. Court of Appeals, Tenth Circuit; 1977, U.S. Court of Appeals, Seventh Circuit; 1981, U.S. Supreme Court; 1982, U.S. Court of Appeals, Eleventh Circuit; 1995, U.S. Court of Appeals, Second Circuit; 1996, U.S. Court of Appeals, Third and Eighth Circuits. *Education:* University of Utah (B.S., Economics, magna cum laude, 1968); University of Michigan (J.D., cum laude, 1971). Phi Beta Kappa; Phi Alpha Delta. Assistant Director of Law, City of Cleveland, 1972. Fellow, The Ohio State Bar Foundation. *Member:* Cleveland, (Member, Appellate Committee), Ohio State (Member, Council of Delegates, 1983-1987), Federal and American Bar Associations; Defense Research Institute. ***PRACTICE AREAS:*** Antitrust; Appeals; Litigation. ***Email:*** wdabb@bakerlaw.com

ELIZABETH A. DELLINGER, born Cleveland, Ohio, November 1, 1961; admitted to bar, 1987, Ohio. *Education:* Kenyon College (A.B., summa cum laude, 1984); Case Western Reserve University (J.D., cum laude, 1987). Phi Beta Kappa. Member, Case Western Reserve Law Review, 1986-1987. ***PRACTICE AREAS:*** Mergers and Acquisitions; Corporate Law; Commercial Law; Corporate Finance. ***Email:*** edellinger@bakerlaw.com

JOHN D. DRINKO, born St. Marys, West Virginia, June 17, 1921; admitted to bar, 1945, Ohio. *Education:* Marshall College (B.A., 1942; honorary LL.B., 1980); University of Texas; The Ohio State University (J.D., 1944; Honorary LL.D., 1986); John Carroll University (Honorary LL.D., 1987); Capital University (Honorary LL.D., 1988); Cleveland State University (Honorary LL.D., 1990); Dyke College (Honorary DH.L., 1990); Cleveland Clinic Foundation (Distinguished Fellow - 1991); University of New Hampshire (Honorary LL.D., 1992); Baldwin-Wallace College (Honorary DH.L., 1993); Ursuline College (Honorary DH.L., 1994); Notre Dame College of Ohio (Honorary DH.L., 1997); Marietta College Honorary (DH.L., 2001). Order of the Coif. ***PRACTICE AREAS:*** Business. ***Email:*** jdrinko@bakerlaw.com

DENNIS E. ECKART, born Euclid, Ohio, April 6, 1950; admitted to bar, 1974, Ohio. *Education:* Xavier University (B.A., cum laude, 1971); Cleveland-Marshall College of Law (J.D., 1974). *Member:* Ohio State and American Bar Associations. ***PRACTICE AREAS:*** Public Policy; Legislative.

STEVEN A. EISENBERG, born Cleveland, Ohio, April 21, 1970; admitted to bar, 1995, Ohio. *Education:* Miami University (B.S., 1992); Cleveland-Marshall College of Law (J.D., cum laude, 1995); DePaul University College of Law (LL.M., Health Law, 1997). *Member:* Cleveland and Ohio State Bar Associations; American Health Lawyers Association. ***PRACTICE AREAS:*** Corporate Law; Health Law. ***Email:*** seisenberg@bakerlaw.com

PAUL P. EYRE, born Dublin, Ireland, March 13, 1947; admitted to bar, 1975, Wisconsin; 1982, Ohio and U.S. District Court, Northern District of Ohio; 1991, U.S. Court of Appeals, Sixth Circuit; 1994, U.S. Court of Appeals, Second Circuit. *Education:* University of Wisconsin-Madison (B.A., 1971; J.D., 1975). Assistant Regional Director, 1977-1979 and Regional Director, 1979-1982, Federal Trade Commission. *Member:* Ohio State Bar Association. [With U.S. Navy, 1967-1969]. (Managing Partner, New York Office). ***PRACTICE AREAS:*** Litigation; Trade Regulation. ***Email:*** peyre@bakerlaw.com

(This Listing Continued)

MICHAEL K. FARRELL, born Berea, Ohio, January 31, 1962; admitted to bar, 1988, Ohio and U.S. District Court, Northern District of Ohio; 1997, U.S. Court of Appeals, Fourth Circuit; 2000, U.S. Court of Appeals, Sixth Circuit. *Education:* Miami University (B.A., 1984); Case Western Reserve School of Law (J.D., 1988). Order of the Coif. Editor, Case Western Law Review, 1988. ***PRACTICE AREAS:*** First Amendment; Libel; Media Litigation; Litigation; Copyright and Trademark Litigation. ***Email:*** mfarrell@bakerlaw.com

PAUL H. FEINBERG, born Yonkers, New York, November 24, 1938; admitted to bar, 1965, New York; 1979, Ohio. *Education:* University of Pennsylvania (A.B., 1960); Harvard Law School (LL.B., cum laude, 1963); New York University (LL.M. in Taxation, 1970). Speaker: Federal Deposit Insurance Corporation Community Development Conference, Dallas, 1999; Ohio CLE Institute Non-Profit Conference, 1998; PESI The Law of Tax Exempt Organizations (Ohio), 1998. Assistant General Counsel, The Ford Foundation, 1971-1977. *Member:* Cleveland (Treasurer, 1996-1999), Ohio State, New York State and American (Member, Section of Taxation, Committee on Exempt Organizations; Co Chair, Private Foundations Subcommittee, 1995—) Bar Associations. ***PRACTICE AREAS:*** Tax. ***Email:*** pfeinberg@bakerlaw.com

JOSÉ C. FELICIANO, born Yauco, Puerto Rico, March 7, 1950; admitted to bar, 1975, Ohio and U.S. District Court, Northern District of Ohio; 1978, U.S. Supreme Court; 1981, U.S. Court of Appeals, Sixth Circuit; 1992, U.S. Court of Appeals, Third Circuit and U.S. District Court, Western District of Pennsylvania; 1996, U.S. District Court, Eastern District of Michigan. *Education:* John Carroll University (B.A., cum laude, 1972); Cleveland State University (J.D., 1975; M.B.A., 1984). Delta Theta Phi. Chief Prosecuting Attorney, City of Cleveland, 1980-1984. White House Fellow, 1984-1985. Member, American College of Trial Lawyers, 1995. Life Member, Judicial Conference, Eighth Judicial District, Cuyahoga County, Ohio. *Member:* Cleveland (President, 2000-2001), Ohio State and American (Member: Board of Governors, 2001; House of Delegates, 1999-2002) Bar Associations; Ohio Hispanic Bar Association (Vice President, 1982-1984). ***LANGUAGES:*** Spanish. ***PRACTICE AREAS:*** Commercial Litigation; Employment Litigation. ***Email:*** jfeliciano@bakerlaw.com

CHARLES J. FRENCH, III, born Chicago, Illinois, March 30, 1951; admitted to bar, 1978, Ohio; 1982, U.S. District Court, Northern District of Ohio; 1989, U.S. Court of Appeals, Sixth Circuit; 1991, U.S. Supreme Court. *Education:* Cleveland State University (B.A., 1973); Cleveland Marshall College of Law (J.D., 1977). Assistant County Prosecutor, Cuyahoga County, 1978-1982. Trial Attorney, Criminal Division, Cleveland Strike Force, U.S. Department of Justice, 1982-1985. *Member:* Cleveland and Ohio State (Member, Litigation and Labor Law Sections) Bar Associations; Defense Research Institute (Member, Employment Law Section). ***PRACTICE AREAS:*** Employment; Insurance; General Litigation. ***Email:*** cfrench@bakerlaw.com

ROBERT R. GALLOWAY, born Indianapolis, Indiana, April 28, 1963; admitted to bar, 1988, Ohio and U.S. District Court, Northern District of Ohio. *Education:* Hamilton College (B.A., 1985); Case Western Reserve University (J.D., 1988). Order of the Coif. *Member:* Cleveland and Ohio State Bar Associations. ***PRACTICE AREAS:*** Tax; Estate Planning; Conservation Easements. ***Email:*** rgalloway@bakerlaw.com

JOHN M. GHERLEIN, born Cleveland, Ohio, April 24, 1955; admitted to bar, 1980, Ohio; 1982, U.S. Court of Appeals, Ninth Circuit; 1983, U.S. Court of Appeals, Sixth Circuit. *Education:* Bucknell University (B.A., 1977); Case Western Reserve University (J.D., 1980). Editor, Case Western Reserve Law Review, 1979-1980. *Member:* American, Ohio State and Cleveland Bar Associations. ***PRACTICE AREAS:*** Business; Corporate and Securities Law; Mergers and Acquisitions. ***Email:*** jgherlein@bakerlaw.com

WENDY J. GIBSON, born Englewood, New Jersey, November 13, 1953; admitted to bar, 1979, Ohio; 1980, U.S. District Court, Northern District of Ohio and U.S. Court of Appeals, Sixth Circuit; 1995, U.S. District Court, Eastern District of Michigan; 2001, U.S. Court of Appeals, Fourth Circuit. *Education:* Principia College (B.A., 1975); New York University (J.D., 1979). *Member:* Cleveland, Ohio State and American Bar Associations; American Bankruptcy Institute. ***PRACTICE AREAS:*** Bankruptcy and Commercial Law. ***Email:*** wgibson@bakerlaw.com

EDWARD S. GINSBURG, born Bronx, New York, April 24, 1948; admitted to bar, 1975, Ohio. *Education:* State University of New York at Binghamton, New York (B.A., 1969); The Ohio State University College of Law(J.D., 1975). Order of the Coif. ***PRACTICE AREAS:*** Business. ***Email:*** eginsburg@bakerlaw.com

MATTHEW R. GOLDMAN, born New York, N.Y., May 27, 1952; admitted to bar, 1979, New York; 1980, U.S. District Court, Southern and Eastern Districts of New York; 1982, U.S. District Court, Northern District of Ohio; 1982, Ohio; 1997, U.S. District Court, District of Maryland. *Education:* State University of New York at Buffalo (B.A., History, magna cum laude, 1974; B.A., American Studies, magna cum laude, 1975); University of Pennsylvania (J.D., 1978). Phi Beta Kappa. Author: William J. O'Neill Seminar, "Post-Confirmation Issues" 1998; and "Guarantor Rights Under Ohio Law," 1995. Co-Author: Clark-Boardman, *Federal Rules of Bankruptcy,* 1988-1991. *Member:* Cleveland, Ohio State and American Bar Associations; American Bankruptcy Institute. ***PRACTICE AREAS:*** Bankruptcy and Commercial Law. ***Email:*** mgoldman@bakerlaw.com

MATTHEW D. GRABAN, born Youngstown, Ohio, December 1, 1971; admitted to bar, 1997, Ohio. *Education:* University of Akron (B.S., summa cum laude, 1994); Case Western Reserve University (J.D., magna cum laude, 1997). Order of the Coif. *Member:* Cleveland, Ohio State and American Bar Associations. ***PRACTICE AREAS:*** Corporate Law; Mergers and Acquisitions; Securities; Venture Capital Financing. ***Email:*** mgraban@bakerlaw.com

JAMES B. GRISWOLD, born Cleveland, Ohio, June 20, 1946; admitted to bar, 1974, Ohio. *Education:* Harvard University (A.B., 1968); University of Michigan (J.D., 1974). Lecturer: "Creative Approaches to Acquisitions: Negotiating the Deal: Strategies, Danger Signals and Pitfalls"; "Growing Your Company and Protecting its Value". Instructor, Continuing Legal Education Program presentation: "Venture Capital Financing". *Member:* American Bar Association (Member, Subcommittee on Negotiated Acquisitions). ***PRACTICE AREAS:*** Business. ***Email:*** jgriswold@bakerlaw.com

J. RICHARD HAMILTON, born Wadsworth, Ohio, June 21, 1929; admitted to bar, 1956, Ohio. *Education:* Ohio University (B.S.C., 1951); The Ohio State University (J.D.,

(This Listing Continued)

1956). Phi Alpha Delta; Order of the Coif. Editor-in-Chief, Ohio State Law Journal. *Member:* Cleveland, Ohio State and American (Member, Sections of Business Law and International Law) Bar Associations. ***PRACTICE AREAS:*** Business. ***Email:*** rhamilton@bakerlaw.com

SUZANNE K. HANSELMAN, born Cleveland, Ohio, March 5, 1963; admitted to bar, 1991, Ohio. *Education:* Miami University (B.A., 1985); The Ohio State University (J.D., 1991). Order of the Coif. Business Manager, Ohio State Law Journal. ***Email:*** shanselman@bakerlaw.com

JANE T. HAYLOR, born Cincinnati, Ohio, December 30, 1946; admitted to bar, 1986, Ohio. *Education:* Case Western Reserve University (B.S., 1968; J.D., 1986). Member, 1984-1985 and Articles Editor, 1985-1986, Case Western Reserve University Law Review. *Member:* Ohio State and American Bar Associations. ***PRACTICE AREAS:*** Trusts and Estates. ***Email:*** jhaylor@bakerlaw.com

L. DENNIS HOFFMAN JR., born Lexington, Kentucky, July 8, 1968; admitted to bar, 1997, Ohio. *Education:* University of Michigan (B.G.S., 1990); Cleveland-Marshall College of Law (J.D., summa cum laude, 1997). Articles Editor, Cleveland State Law Review. *Member:* Cleveland, Ohio State and American Bar Associations. ***PRACTICE AREAS:*** Corporate; Real Estate; Commercial Finance; Mergers and Acquisitions. ***Email:*** dhoffman@bakerlaw.com

RICHARD R. HOLLINGTON, JR., born Findlay, Ohio, November 12, 1932; admitted to bar, 1957, Ohio; 1960, U.S. Customs Court and U.S. Tax Court; 1962, U.S. District Court, Northern District of Ohio; 1964, U.S. Supreme Court; 1966, U.S. Court of Appeals, Sixth Circuit. *Education:* Williams College (B.A., 1954); Harvard University (LL.B., 1957). Special Counsel to Attorney General of Ohio, 1963-1966. Member, Ohio Legislature, 1967-1970. Law Director, City of Cleveland, 1971-1972. Life Member, 6th Circuit Judicial Conference and 8th Appellate District Conference. Member, Board of Commissioners on Grievance and Discipline, 1993-1995. Lead Director, Sky Financial Group, Inc. ***PRACTICE AREAS:*** Business; Litigation; Banking. ***Email:*** rhollington@bakerlaw.com

JOSEPH F. HUTCHINSON, JR., born Akron, Ohio, May 13, 1949; admitted to bar, 1974, Ohio; U.S. District Court, Northern District of Ohio; U.S. Court of Appeals, Sixth Circuit; U.S. Supreme Court. *Education:* The University of Michigan (B.A., with honors, 1971); The Ohio State University Moritz College of Law (J.D., 1973). *Member:* Akron, Cleveland, Ohio State and American Bar Associations. ***PRACTICE AREAS:*** Business; Bankruptcy; Workouts; Commercial Litigation. ***Email:*** jhutchinson@bakerlaw.com

SCOTT D. IRWIN, admitted to bar, 1992, Ohio; 1995, Florida. *Education:* Kent State University (B.A., summa cum laude, 1989); The Ohio State University (J.D., summa cum laude, 1992). Phi Beta Kappa; Order of the Coif. Editor, The Ohio State Law Journal, 1990-1992. Associate, Foley & Lardner, 1995-1997. Counsel, General Electric Company, 1997-1999. *Member:* American Bar Association (Member, Negotiated Acquisitions Committee, Task Force on Public Company Acquisitions, 1995—). ***PRACTICE AREAS:*** Mergers and Acquisitions; Venture Capital; Private Equity; Corporate Finance; E-Business; International Law; International Commerce; Technology Law; Business Law. ***Email:*** sirwin@bakerlaw.com

SUZANNE M. JAMBE, born New Bedford, Massachusetts, October 13, 1960; admitted to bar, 1993, Ohio. *Education:* University of Virginia (B.A., 1984); University of Toledo (J.D., magna cum laude, 1993). Order of the Coif. *Member:* Cleveland, Ohio State and American Bar Associations. ***PRACTICE AREAS:*** Litigation; Domestic Relations; Division of Employee Benefits in Domestic Relations matters. ***Email:*** sjambe@bakerlaw.com

AMY ELIZABETH KELLOGG, born Lorain, Ohio, March 28, 1962; admitted to bar, 1986, Indiana and Ohio. *Education:* University of Toledo (B.B.A., summa cum laude, 1983); The Ohio State University (J.D., 1986). Order of the Coif. Articles Editor, Ohio State Law Journal, 1985-1986. Author: "Hawaii Housing Authority v. Midkiff: The Continued Validity of the Public Use Doctrine," Ohio State Law Journal, Vol. 47 No. 2, 1986. *Member:* Cleveland, Ohio State and American Bar Associations. ***PRACTICE AREAS:*** Real Estate Law. ***Email:*** akellogg@bakerlaw.com

TOM A. KING, born Pittsburgh, Pennsylvania, August 23, 1954; admitted to bar, 1990, Ohio; 1993, U.S. District Court, Northern District of Ohio; 1994, U.S. Court of Appeals, Sixth Circuit. *Education:* Allegheny College (B.A., 1976); Cleveland Marshall College of Law (J.D., magna cum laude, 1990). Inns of Court. Managing Editor, Cleveland Marshall Law Review, 1989-1990. Trustee, Council for Economic Opportunities of Greater Cleveland, 1990—. Trustee, Inner City Renewal Society, 1990—. *Member:* American, Ohio State and Cleveland Bar Associations. ***PRACTICE AREAS:*** Employment Law. ***Email:*** tking@bakerlaw.com

CALVIN B. KIRCHICK, born New York, N.Y., April 6, 1946; admitted to bar, 1972, Ohio. *Education:* University of Michigan (A.B., 1968; J.D., 1972). Phi Beta Kappa; Order of the Coif. ***PRACTICE AREAS:*** Trusts and Estates. ***Email:*** ckirchick@bakerlaw.com

ROBERT K. LEASE, born Cleveland, Ohio, 1948; admitted to bar, 1976, Ohio and U.S. District Court, Northern District of Ohio. *Education:* Dartmouth College (A.B., magna cum laude, 1970, Phi Beta Kappa); University of Connecticut (J.D., cum laude, 1976). Member, University of Connecticut Law Review. ***PRACTICE AREAS:*** Trusts and Estates. ***Email:*** rlease@bakerlaw.com

TODD H. LEBOWITZ, born Baltimore, Maryland, May 2, 1972; admitted to bar, 1997, Ohio; 1998, U.S. District Court, Northern District of Ohio and U.S. Court of Appeals, Sixth Circuit; 2002, U.S. District Court, Eastern District of Wisconsin; 2005, U.S. District Court, Northern District of Illinois. *Education:* University of Michigan (B.A., 1993; J.D., cum laude, 1997). Author: Evaluating Purely Reproductive Disorders Under The Americans with Disabilities Act, Michigan Law Review, Dec., 1997. *Member:* Greater Cleveland Bar Association; Ohio State and American Bar Associations. ***PRACTICE AREAS:*** Employment Litigation. ***Email:*** tlebowitz@bakerlaw.com

EARL M. LEIKEN, born Cleveland, Ohio, January 19, 1942; admitted to bar, 1967, Ohio. *Education:* Harvard University (B.A., magna cum laude, 1964; LL.B., cum laude, 1967). Author: "Pref. Treatment in the Skilled Building Trades," 56 Cornell Law Review 84, 1970; *Unionization and Collective Bargaining,* with H. Sherman and W. Murphy, published by Bureau of National Affairs, Inc., 1971. Associate Professor of Law and Assistant Dean, Case Western Reserve School of Law, 1967-1971. *Member:* Cleveland, Ohio State and American Bar Associations. ***PRACTICE AREAS:*** Employment Law. ***Email:*** eleiken@bakerlaw.com

MELISSA A. LEONARD, born Akron, Ohio, October 6, 1969; admitted to bar, 1995, Ohio. *Education:* Miami University (B.S., 1992); University of Michigan (J.D., 1994). *Member:* Greater Cleveland, Ohio State and American Bar Associations. ***PRACTICE AREAS:*** Business; Mergers and Acquisitions; Venture Capital and Private Equity; Capital Formation; Commercial Finance; Mezzanine Finance. ***Email:*** mleonard@bakerlaw.com

RICHARD H. LEUKART, II, born Detroit, Michigan, March 15, 1942; admitted to bar, 1967, Ohio. *Education:* Amos Tuck Graduate School of Business Administration; Dartmouth College (A.B., 1964); University of Michigan (J.D., 1967). Group Chair of Employment Law; Employee Benefits. ***PRACTICE AREAS:*** Employment Law; Employee Benefits; Health Care; Closely Held Corporations. ***Email:*** dleukart@bakerlaw.com

JOHN B. LEWIS, born Poplar Bluff, Missouri, 1947; admitted to bar, 1972, Missouri; 1973, U.S. Court of Appeals, Eighth Circuit and U.S. District Court, Eastern District of Missouri; 1979, U.S. District Court, Northern District of Ohio; 1980, Ohio; 1982, U.S. Court of Appeals, Sixth Circuit; 1983, U.S. District Court, Eastern District of Michigan; 1987, U.S. Court of Appeals, Third Circuit and U.S. Supreme Court; 1989, U.S. District Court, Northern District of California; 1990, U.S. Court of Appeals, Seventh Circuit; 2003, U.S. District Court, Southern District of Ohio. *Education:* University of Missouri (B.A., 1969; J.D., 1972); Columbia University (LL.M., 1978). Articles: Author or Co-author: "Title VII and Friendship, Commerce and Navigation Treaties: Prognostications Based Upon Sumitomo Shoji," 44 Ohio State Law Journal 45, 1983; "New York Times v. Sullivan: A Retrospective Examination," 33 DePaul L. Rev. 741, 1984; "Drug Screening in the Public Sector, Municipalities and Government Workers," 2 J. Law and Health 39, 1987-1988; "Defamation and the Workplace: A Survey of the Law and Proposals for Reform," 54 Mo. L. Rev. 797, 1989; "Defamation Actions Arising From Arbitration and Related Dispute Resolution Procedures Preemption, Collateral Estoppel and Privilege: Why the Absolute Privilege Must Be Expanded," 45 DePaul L. Rev. 677, 1996; "I Know What You E-Mailed Last Summer," Security Management Magazine, January 2002 at 93. Listed in the Best Lawyers in America. *Member:* Cleveland (Member, Labor Law Section), Ohio State (Member, Labor and Employment Law Section) and American (Member: Labor and Employment Law Section, Committee on Equal Employment Opportunity Law; Forum Committee on Communications Law) Bar Associations; The American Law Institute. ***PRACTICE AREAS:*** Labor and Employment Litigation; Civil Rights Defense; Libel and Slander; Class Action. ***Email:*** jlewis@bakerlaw.com

LAWRENCE V. LINDBERG, born Youngstown, Ohio, December 21, 1947; admitted to bar, 1973, Ohio. *Education:* College of Wooster (B.A., 1970); New York University (J.D., 1973). ***PRACTICE AREAS:*** Real Estate Law; Real Estate Tax; Business Law. ***Email:*** llindberg@bakerlaw.com

JAMES A. LOEB, born Shaker Heights, Ohio, May 3, 1963; admitted to bar, 1988, Ohio and U.S. District Court, Northern District of Ohio. *Education:* The Ohio State University (B.A. Political Science, 1985; J.D., with honors in Law, 1988). Pi Sigma Alpha; Delta Theta Phi. Extern U.S. District Court, Northern District of Ohio for Judge George W. White, 1987. Instructor, Legal Writing Program, The Ohio State University, 1987. *Member:* Cleveland, Ohio State and American Bar Associations. ***PRACTICE AREAS:*** Litigation; Family Law. ***Email:*** jloeb@bakerlaw.com

ROBERT M. LOESCH, born Lakewood, Ohio, January 24, 1964; admitted to bar, 1992, Ohio. *Education:* Fairfield University (B.A., American Studies, 1986); Case Western University (J.D., 1991). Staff Attorney, Division of Enforcement, Securities and Exchange Commission, 1991-1995. ***PRACTICE AREAS:*** Corporate Law; Mergers and Acquisitions; Securities; Venture Capital. ***Email:*** rloesch@bakerlaw.com

THOMAS R. LUCCHESI, born Ann Arbor, Michigan, October 18, 1959; admitted to bar, 1984, Ohio and U.S. District Court, Northern District of Ohio; 1987, U.S. Court of Appeals, Sixth Circuit; 1995, U.S. Supreme Court. *Education:* University of Michigan (B.A., 1981; J.D., 1984). Member, Journal of Law Reform, 1982-1983. ***PRACTICE AREAS:*** Litigation. ***Email:*** tlucchesi@bakerlaw.com

ARTHUR H. LUNDBERG, born Riverhead, New York, April 7, 1966; admitted to bar, 1994, Ohio. *Education:* Boston College (B.S., 1988); Case Western Reserve University (J.D., 1994). Order of the Coif. Member, Case Western Reserve University Law Review. *Member:* Ohio State and American Bar Associations. ***PRACTICE AREAS:*** Mergers and Acquisitions; Securities. ***Email:*** alundberg@bakerlaw.com

RAYMOND M. MALONE, born Cleveland, Ohio, April 18, 1957; admitted to bar, 1982, Ohio; 1986, Colorado; U.S. District Court, Northern District of Ohio, U.S. District Court, District of Colorado and U.S. Tax Court. *Education:* Miami University (B.S., cum laude, 1979); Case Western Reserve University (J.D., 1982). Beta Gamma Sigma; Order of the Coif. Editor, Case Western Reserve Law Review, 1981-1982. Certified Public Accountant, Ohio, 1984 (nonpracticing). ***PRACTICE AREAS:*** Employee Benefit; Business; Employment Law; Tax Law. ***Email:*** rmalone@bakerlaw.com

RUTH ANN MALONEY, born Columbus, Ohio, December 10, 1958; admitted to bar, 1990, Ohio. *Education:* The Ohio State University (B.S., summa cum laude, 1982); University of Toledo (J.D., magna cum laude, 1990). Order of the Coif. ***PRACTICE AREAS:*** Employment Law and Benefits. ***Email:*** rmaloney@bakerlaw.com

DAVID L. MARBURGER, born New Castle, Pennsylvania, September 27, 1954; admitted to bar, 1983, Ohio; 1984, Pennsylvania. *Education:* Syracuse University (B.S. 1976); University of Pittsburgh (J.D., 1983). Member, University of Pittsburgh Law Review, 1981-1983. Author: "More Protection For the Press: The Third Circuit Expands the Fair Report Privilege," 43 U. Pitt. L. Rev. 1143, 1982; "In Defense Of Broadcaster Access To Evidentiary Video and Audio Tapes," U. Pitt. L. Rev. 647, 1983. ***PRACTICE AREAS:*** Litigation; First Amendment Law; Libel Law. ***Email:*** dmarburger@bakerlaw.com

ROBERT G. MARKEY, born Cleveland, Ohio, February 25, 1939; admitted to bar, 1964, Ohio. *Education:* Brown University (A.B., 1961); Case Western Reserve University (J.D., 1964). ***PRACTICE AREAS:*** Corporate. ***Email:*** rmarkey@bakerlaw.com

MARK R. MAZANEC, born Cleveland, Ohio, October 8, 1961; admitted to bar, 1988, Ohio; 1989, Florida. *Education:* University of Notre Dame (B.S., cum laude, 1983); University of Michigan (J.D., 1988). Tau Beta Pi. Counsel, Environmental Affairs, Manager,

(This Listing Continued)

BAKER & HOSTETLER LLP, Cleveland—Continued

EAS Europe, 6-sigma Quality Leader and Supply Chain Manager, General Electric. *Member:* Cleveland, Ohio State and American Bar Associations; American Institute of Chemical Engineers. ***PRACTICE AREAS:*** Environmental Law; Health and Safety. ***Email:*** mmazanec@bakerlaw.com

JOHN J. McGOWAN, JR., born Toledo, Ohio, August 2, 1956; admitted to bar, 1984, Ohio and U.S. District Court, Northern District of Ohio; 1986, U.S. Court of Appeals, Sixth Circuit and U.S. Tax Court; 1994, U.S. Court of Appeals, Fourth and District of Columbia Circuits, U.S. District Court, District of Arizona; 1996, U.S. Court of Appeals, Eleventh Circuit; 1999, U.S. Supreme Court. *Education:* University of Toledo (B.B.A., 1978; J.D., 1983). Author: "Title Holding Companies Provide Tax-Exempt Real Estate Financing," 1 Ohio Law 4 (April, 1988). ERISA Counsel, Owens-Corning Fiberglas Corporation, 1984-1985. Publications: "Borrowing Employee Contributions for Other Purposes is A High Stakes Game Not Worth the Risk, *Tax Employee Benefits,* (July 1997); "Fall Out From the Tax Court's Decision in *Lozon v. Comm'r:* New Questions for Independent Contractors And the Plans in which they Participate," *Pension & Benefits Week (RIA)* (July 28, 1997); "Assessing the Impact of Workers Misclassification After *Vizcaino v. Microsoft*" *Pension & Benefits Week (RIA)* (Sept 15 & 22, 1997). *Member:* Cleveland, Ohio State (Member, Labor Law Section) and American (Member, Sections of: Taxation; Labor and Employment Law, Employee Benefits Committee and Tort and Insurance, Employee Benefits Committee) Bar Associations. ***PRACTICE AREAS:*** Tax Law; ERISA Litigation; Employee Benefits; Executive Compensation; Class Action. ***Email:*** jmcgowan@bakerlaw.com

MICHAEL P. McNAMARA, JR., born Cleveland, Ohio, February 6, 1971; admitted to bar, 1996, Ohio. *Education:* The Catholic University of America (B.A., magna cum laude, 1993); Case Western Reserve University (J.D., magna cum laude, 1996). *Member:* Ohio State and American Bar Associations. ***PRACTICE AREAS:*** Business; Mergers and Acquisitions; Real Estate; Securities; Commercial Financing. ***Email:*** mmcnamara@bakerlaw.com

GREGORY V. MERSOL, born Euclid, Ohio, August 9, 1960; admitted to bar, 1985, Ohio and Ohio Supreme Court; 1986, U.S. District Court, Northern District of Ohio and U.S. Court of Appeals, Sixth and Eighth Circuits; 1987, U.S. Court of Appeals, Third Circuit; 1988, U.S. District Court, Southern District of Ohio; 1992, U.S. Supreme Court; 1999, U.S. District Court, District of North Dakota; 2003, U.S. District Court, Northern District of Indiana. *Education:* Case Western Reserve University (B.A., 1982; J.D., magna cum laude, 1985). Order of the Coif. Research Editor, Case Western University Law Review, 1984-1985. Co-Author: "Defamation in the Workplace: A Survey of the Law and Proposals for Reform," 54 Missouri L.Rev. 797, 1989. *Member:* American, Ohio State (Member, Labor and Employment Law Section) and Cleveland Bar Associations. ***PRACTICE AREAS:*** Employment Litigation; Class Action. ***Email:*** gmersol@bakerlaw.com

WADE A. MITCHELL, born Cleveland, Ohio, November 11, 1954; admitted to bar, 1985, Ohio; 1986, U.S. Court of Military Appeals; 1987, U.S. District Court, Northern District of Ohio; 1992, U.S. Court of Appeals, Sixth Circuit; U.S. District Court, Eastern District of Michigan; 1993, U.S. Supreme Court; 1996, U.S. Court of Appeals, Federal Circuit. *Education:* United States Coast Guard Academy (B.S. with high honors, 1977); George Washington University (J.D. with high honors, 1985). *Member:* Cleveland, Ohio State and American Bar Associations. [With U.S. Coast Guard, 1977-1987]. ***PRACTICE AREAS:*** Products Defense; Toxic Tort; Patent and Commercial Litigation. ***Email:*** wmitchell@bakerlaw.com

KAREN B. NEWBORN, born Cleveland, Ohio, October 30, 1944; admitted to bar, 1976, Ohio and U.S. District Court, Northern District of Ohio; 1978, U.S. Court of Appeals, Sixth Circuit; 1984, U.S. District Court, Eastern District of Michigan; 1988, U.S. Supreme Court; 2002, U.S. District Court, Eastern District of Wisconsin. *Education:* Goucher College (B.A. 1966); Cleveland State University (J.D., summa cum laude, 1976). Assistant Law Director, City of Cleveland, 1976-1979. Adjunct Instructor Teaching Trial Advocacy, Cleveland State University, 1987. Faculty, ICLE 42nd Annual Advocacy Institute, 1991. *Member:* Cleveland (Board of Trustees, 1989-1992; Commission on Women in the Law; Member and Chair, 1987-1989, Judicial Selection Committee, 1993 and 1994; Nominating Committee, 1994, 2001, Chair, 2002), Ohio State (Council of Delegates, 1990-1993; Presentation, Defense Strategy in Superfund Cases, 1982) and American Bar Associations; Anthony J. Celebrezze Inn of Court (Master Bencher); State of Ohio Eighth Judicial District Conference (Life Member). ***PRACTICE AREAS:*** Litigation; Employment; Environmental Law. ***Email:*** knewborn@bakerlaw.com

PATRICIA J. O'DONNELL, born Cleveland, Ohio, December 17, 1948; admitted to bar, 1982, Ohio. *Education:* Cleveland State University (B.A., summa cum laude, 1979); Cleveland Marshall College of Law (J.D., summa cum laude, 1982). Editor, Cleveland Marshall Law Review, 1981-1982. Author: Note, "The Antitrust Improvements Act of 1976, Parens Patriae Act; Paper Tiger or Sleeping Giant," Cleveland State Law Review, Vol. 31, No. 1, Pages, 107-144, 1982. Listed in The Best Lawyers in America, published by Woodward & White. Trustee, Member, Executive Committee and Chair, Legal Affairs, Cleveland Zoological Society. Member, Visiting Committee to the Cleveland State University Maxine Goodman Levin College of Urban Affairs and Recipient of The Dean's Distinguished Alumni Award for 2002. *Member:* Cleveland, Ohio State and American Bar Associations. ***PRACTICE AREAS:*** Real Estate Law; Business. ***Email:*** podonnell@bakerlaw.com

RONALD S. OKADA, born Cleveland, Ohio, June 11, 1960; admitted to bar, 1985, Ohio and U.S. District Court, Northern District of Ohio; 1988, U.S. Court of Appeals, Sixth and Eleventh Circuits; 1999, U.S. Supreme Court. *Education:* Carleton College (B.A., magna cum laude, 1982); University of Michigan Law School (J.D., magna cum laude, 1985). Phi Beta Kappa. Order of the Coif. *Member:* Cleveland, Ohio State and American Bar Associations. ***PRACTICE AREAS:*** Litigation; Class Action. ***Email:*** rokada@bakerlaw.com

W. JAMES OLLINGER, born Kittanning, Pennsylvania, April 5, 1943; admitted to bar, 1968, Ohio. *Education:* Capital University (B.A., 1965); Western Reserve University (J.D., 1968). Order of the Coif; Phi Delta Phi. ***PRACTICE AREAS:*** Employee Benefits; Employee Compensation; Tax; Labor; Business. ***Email:*** jollinger@bakerlaw.com

JEFFREY H. PARAVANO, born Westlake, Ohio, February 7, 1966; admitted to bar, 1991, Ohio; 1992, District of Columbia and Colorado, U.S. Tax Court, U.S. Court of Appeals for the District of Columbia, Federal, Fourth, Fifth, Sixth and Ninth Circuits; 1993, New York, Maryland and Connecticut, U.S. Court of Federal Claims, U.S. Court of Appeals, Third, Seventh and Eleventh Circuits; 1994, U.S. District Court for the District of Columbia, U.S. Court of Appeals, Tenth Circuit; 1995, U.S. District Court, Northern District of Ohio and U.S. Supreme Court. *Education:* John Carroll University (B.S.B.A., Accounting, cum laude, 1988); Georgetown University Law Center (J.D., magna cum laude, 1991; LL.M. in Taxation, with distinction, 1993). *Member:* American Bar Association (Member, Business and Taxation Sections). (Also at Washington DC Office). ***PRACTICE AREAS:*** Mergers, Acquisitions and Dispositions; Tax Controversies; Tax Litigation; Venture Capital; Start-Ups; Private Equity Transactions; Partnership Taxation; Joint Ventures; LLC Agreements; Consolidated Returns Issues; Taxation of Real Estate Investment Trusts; Inbound and Outbound Investment Planning and Tax Treaty Issues; Spin-Offs, Split-Offs and Split-Ups; Taxation of S Corporations; State and Local Taxation; Tax Legislation; Tax Policy. ***Email:*** jparavano@bakerlaw.com

JOHN D. PARKER, born Cleveland, Ohio, February 11, 1958; admitted to bar, 1983, Ohio; U.S. Court of Appeals, Sixth, Seventh and Ninth Circuits; U.S. Tax Court; U.S. Supreme Court. *Education:* Wheaton College; Bowling Green State University (B.A.C., summa cum laude, 1979); Case Western Reserve University (J.D., 1983). ***PRACTICE AREAS:*** Commercial Litigation; Antitrust; Class Action. ***Email:*** jparker@bakerlaw.com

PATRICK J. PAUKEN, born Perrysburg, Ohio, 1952; admitted to bar, 1978, Ohio. *Education:* Ohio University (B.G.S., 1975); Case Western Reserve University (J.D., 1978). *Member:* Cleveland, Ohio State (Real Property Section) and American (Real Property, Probate and Trust Law Section) Bar Associations. ***PRACTICE AREAS:*** Real Estate. ***Email:*** ppauken@bakerlaw.com

STEPHEN J. PETRAS, JR., born Lakewood, Ohio, February 28, 1954; admitted to bar, 1979, Ohio and U.S. District Court, Northern District of Ohio. *Education:* Wittenberg University (B.A. Physics, 1976); Case Western Reserve University (J.D., 1979). Omicron Delta Kappa; Phi Alpha Delta. *Member:* Cleveland (Member, Ethics Committee, 1982-1989), Ohio State and American (Member, International Law Section) Bar Associations; Cleveland World Trade Association (President, 1996-1998; Greater Cleveland International Lawyers Group (President, 1994-2001); Greater Cleveland International Trade Alliance (Director, 1996-1998); World Trade Center Cleveland (Advisory Board); Cleveland Committee on Foreign Relations; Metrowest Kiwanis Charitable Foundation (Chairman); Cleveland Council on World Affairs (Trustee); Case Western Reserve University School of Law (International LL.M. Advisory Board, 1996—); Northern Ohio District Export Council. Head, International Practice, Baker & Hostetler. ***PRACTICE AREAS:*** International Business Law; Corporate; Commercial. ***Email:*** spetras@bakerlaw.com

ROBERT C. PETRULIS, born Parma, Ohio, October 15, 1961; admitted to bar, 1988, Ohio and U.S. District Court, Northern District of Ohio; 1994, U.S. Supreme Court; 1995, U.S. Court of Appeals, Sixth Circuit. *Education:* Case Western Reserve University (B.A., magna cum laude, with honors in American Studies, 1983); The Ohio State University (M.P.A., 1985); University of Michigan (J.D., 1988). Phi Alpha Theta; Phi Kappa Phi; Phi Beta Kappa. Author: "Commissions Use Negotiated Settlements to Expedite Regulatory Process," The National Regulatory Research Institute Quarterly Bulletin, October, 1985. *Member:* Cleveland, Ohio State and American Bar Associations. (Certified Specialist in Labor & Employment Law, Ohio State Bar Association). ***PRACTICE AREAS:*** Employment Law; Public Law; Administrative and Regulatory Law. ***Email:*** rpetrulis@bakerlaw.com

THOMAS J. PIATAK, admitted to bar, 1989, Ohio. *Education:* Case Western Reserve University (B.A., summa cum laude, 1986); University of Michigan (J.D., cum laude, 1989). *Member:* Ohio State Bar Association. ***PRACTICE AREAS:*** Employment Litigation; Occupational Safety and Health Law; Client Counseling. ***Email:*** tpiatak@bakerlaw.com

PATRICIA A. POOLE, born Cleveland, Ohio, December 10, 1954; admitted to bar, 1991, Ohio. *Education:* Huron Road Hospital School of Nursing; Bowling Green State University (B.S.N., summa cum laude, 1987); Cleveland-Marshall College of Law (J.D., 1991). Sigma Theta Tau; Golden Key; Order of Barristers. Registered Nurse, Ohio, 1976. *Member:* Cleveland, Ohio State and American Bar Associations; National League of Nursing; American Association of Nurse Attorneys. ***PRACTICE AREAS:*** Toxic Tort; Product Liability; Litigation; Occupational Safety; Health Care; Environmental; Workers Compensation. ***Email:*** ppoole@bakerlaw.com

DAVID A. POSNER, born Cleveland, Ohio, April 13, 1964; admitted to bar, 1989, Ohio; 1990, U.S. Court of Appeals, Sixth Circuit and U.S. District Court, Northern District of Ohio; 1992, U.S. Court of Appeals, Fifth Circuit; 1994, U.S. District Court, Eastern District of Michigan; 2002, U.S. Supreme Court; 2003, U.S. District Court, Southern District of Ohio. *Education:* Indiana University (B.S., 1986); Case Western Reserve University (J.D., 1989). *Member:* Cleveland, Cuyahoga County, Ohio State, Federal and American Bar Associations. ***SPECIAL AGENCIES:*** EEOC; OCRC; NLRB; SERB. ***REPORTED CASES:*** Brock v. Morton, 2002 Ohio App. LEXIS 1691 (2002); Morenz v. Progressive Casualty Ins. Co., 2002 Ohio App. LEXIS 2474 (2002); Cole v. UFCW-Employer Health & Welfare Fund, 238 F3d 420 (6th Cir. 2000); Clark vs. Central Cartage Co., 1995 U.S. App. LEXIS 38820, 73 F.3d 361 (6th Cir. 1995); Alexander vs. Electronic Data Systems Corp.; 13 F.3d 940 (6th Cir. 1994); Electronic Data Systems Corp. vs. NLRB, 985 F.2d 801 (5th Cir. 1993); Tanks vs. Greater Cleveland Regional Transit Authority, 930 F.2d 475 (6th Cir. 1991) Hopkins vs. Electronic Data Systems Corp., 1997 U.S. Dist. LEXIS 19422 (E.D. Mich. 1997) aff'd, 196 F3d 655 (6th Cir. 1999); Van Waters & Rogers, Inc. vs. Truck Drivers Union, Local 407, 897 F. Supp. 1017 (N.D. Ohio 1995); Slappey vs. Forest City, Inc., 1995 U.S. Dist. LEXIS 5625 (E.D. Mich. 1995); Emser vs. Curtis Industries, 744 F.Supp. 1076 (N.D. Ohio 1991). ***PRACTICE AREAS:*** Employment Litigation; Employment Law.

EDWARD G. PTASZEK, JR., born Cleveland, Ohio, September 29, 1950; admitted to bar, 1978, Ohio. *Education:* Bowling Green State University (B.S., 1972); Case Western Reserve University (J.D., 1978). Order of the Coif; Beta Gamma Sigma. ***PRACTICE AREAS:*** Tax. ***Email:*** eptaszek@bakerlaw.com

KEVIN G. ROBERTSON, born Detroit, Michigan, January 11, 1960; admitted to bar, 1984, Ohio. *Education:* Case Western Reserve University (B.S., with highest honors, 1981;

(This Listing Continued)

J.D., 1984). Order of the Coif. ***PRACTICE AREAS:*** Trusts and Estates; Income, Gift and Estate Taxation; Retirement Plans; Employee Benefits. ***Email:*** krobertson@bakerlaw.com

McKINLEY HOBART SAUER III, born Massillon, Ohio, September 25, 1960; admitted to bar, 1987, Ohio; 1988, Arizona, U.S. District Court, Northern District of Ohio and U.S. Tax Court; 2001, U.S. District Court, District of Arizona. *Education:* The University of Akron (B.S.A., cum laude, 1984); The Ohio State University (J.D., with honors, 1987). Phi Alpha Delta. *Member:* Cleveland, Ohio State and American Bar Associations; State Bar of Arizona. ***PRACTICE AREAS:*** Corporate; Securities; Finance. ***Email:*** BSauer@bakerlaw.com

PAULA F. SEGER, born Cleveland, Ohio, October 10, 1954; admitted to bar, 1979, Ohio; 1987, U.S. Court of Appeals, Sixth Circuit. *Education:* Indiana University (B.A., summa cum laude, 1976); The Ohio State University (J.D., honors, 1979). ***PRACTICE AREAS:*** Employment Law; NLRB Practice. ***Email:*** pseger@bakerlaw.com

THOMAS M. SEGER, born Cleveland, Ohio, October 11, 1946; admitted to bar, 1972, Ohio and U.S. Court of Appeals, First Circuit; 1976, U.S. Court of Appeals, Sixth Circuit; 1987, U.S. Court of Appeals, Seventh Circuit. *Education:* Miami University (B.A., magna cum laude, 1968); Harvard Law School (J.D., 1972). Law Clerk, Hon. Ed. McEntee, U.S. First Circuit Court of Appeals, 1972-1973. Phi Beta Kappa. Author: "The Majority Status of Incumbent Bargaining Representatives," 47 Tulane Law Review, 961, 1973. *Member:* Cuyahoga County, Ohio State and American Bar Associations. ***PRACTICE AREAS:*** Employment Law; NLRB, EEOC, Employment-at-Will; Affirmative Action Programs; Employee Relations; Bargaining Agreements; School Law. ***Email:*** tseger@bakerlaw.com

THOMAS H. SHUNK, born Elmira, New York, December 27, 1954; admitted to bar, 1979, Ohio. *Education:* Yale University (B.A., cum laude, 1976); Columbia University (J.D., 1979). Harlan Fiske Stone Scholar. Moot Court Student Editor, 1977-1978. Co-author: "The Summary Jury Trial," 29 Cleveland State Law Review 43, 1980. Law Clerk to Hon. Thomas D. Lambros, U.S. District Court, Northern District of Ohio, 1980. *Member:* Cleveland, Ohio State and American Bar Associations. ***PRACTICE AREAS:*** Litigation. ***Email:*** tshunk@bakerlaw.com

RANDALL L. SOLOMON, born Dayton, Ohio, June 8, 1948; admitted to bar, 1973, Ohio, U.S. District Court, Northern District of Ohio and U.S. Court of Appeals, Sixth Circuit; U.S. Court of Appeals for the Federal Circuit. *Education:* Wright State University (B.A., summa cum laude, 1970); Case Western Reserve University (J.D., 1973). Order of the Barristers. Fellow, American College of Trial Lawyers. *Member:* Cleveland (Chairman, Litigation Section, 1991-1992), Ohio State and American (Member, Litigation and Torts and Insurance Practice Sections) Bar Associations; Defense Research Institute; Eighth District, Ohio, Judicial Conference (Life Member); Master of the Bench, Judge Anthony J. Celebrezze Inn of Court. ***PRACTICE AREAS:*** Toxic Tort Litigation; Commercial Litigation; Construction Litigation. ***Email:*** rsolomon@bakerlaw.com

JAMES SPALLINO, JR., born Charleroi, Pennsylvania, 1959; admitted to bar, 1993, Ohio. *Education:* Duquesne University (B.S., 1991); University of Akron (J.D., summa cum laude, 1993). Editor-in-Chief, Akron Law Review, Akron Tax Journal. Author: "The Search for the Fourth Amendment Seizure: It Won't Be Found on a Bus-Florida v. Bostick," 25 Akron L. Rev. 457, Fall 1991. *Member:* Cleveland, Ohio State and American Bar Associations. ***PRACTICE AREAS:*** Estate Planning; Estate and Trust Administration; Asset Protection Planning; Family Business Succession Planning; Charitable Planning and Exempt Organizations; Estate Planning for Resident Alien and Noncitizen Individuals; College Planning. ***Email:*** jspallino@bakerlaw.com

RONALD A. STEPANOVIC, born Cleveland, Ohio, October 14, 1963; admitted to bar, 1988, Ohio. *Education:* Case Western Reserve University (B.S., 1985; J.D., magna cum laude, 1988). Order of the Coif. Member, Case Western Reserve Law Review, 1987-1988. ***PRACTICE AREAS:*** Business; Venture Capital Financing. ***Email:*** rstepanovic@bakerlaw.com

DAVID J. STRAUSS, born Chicago, Illinois, January 26, 1943; admitted to bar, 1967, Iowa and Ohio. *Education:* University of Iowa (B.B.A., 1964; J.D., 1967). Phi Delta Phi; Order of the Coif. ***PRACTICE AREAS:*** Tax; Real Estate; Partnership Law. ***Email:*** dstrauss@bakerlaw.com

VICTOR STRIMBU, JR., born New Philadelphia, Ohio, November 25, 1932; admitted to bar, 1960, Ohio; 1967, U.S. Court of Claims; 1988, U.S. Court of Appeals, Sixth Circuit; 1972, U.S. Supreme Court. *Education:* Heidelberg College (B.A., 1954); Columbia University (J.D., 1960). Pi Sigma Alpha. ***PRACTICE AREAS:*** Employment Relations; Media Law. ***Email:*** vstrimbu@bakerlaw.com

MICHELLE PIERCE STRONCZER, born September 21, 1958; admitted to bar, 1996, Ohio; 1997, U.S. District Court, Northern District of Ohio and U.S. Court of Appeals, Sixth Circuit; 2003, U.S. District Court, Southern District of Ohio; 2004, U.S. District Court, Eastern District of Michigan. *Education:* University of Akron (B.A., magna cum laude, 1993); University of Akron School of Law (J.D., summa cum laude, 1996). *Member:* Ohio State (Member, Labor and Employment Law Section) and American (Member, Labor and Employment Law Section) Bar Associations. ***PRACTICE AREAS:*** Employment Litigation; Civil Rights Defense; ERISA Litigation. ***Email:*** mstronczer@bakerlaw.com

JOHN E. SULLIVAN, born Cleveland, Ohio, December 9, 1958; admitted to bar, 1984, Ohio; 1985, U.S. District Court, Northern District of Ohio; 1999, U.S. Court of Appeals, Sixth Circuit. *Education:* Denison University (B.A., cum laude, 1981), Phi Beta Kappa; Omicron Delta Kappa; Pi Sigma Alpha; Mortar Board; Vanderbilt University (J.D., 1984). Senior Student Writing Editor, Vanderbilt Law Review 1983-1984. Author: Note, "First Amendment Protection of Artistic Entertainment: Toward Reasonable Municipal Regulation of Video Games," 36 Vand. L. Rev. 1223, 1983; "Implied Private Causes of Action and the Recoverability of Damages Under the RCRA Citizen Suit Provision," 25 ELR News & Analysis 10408, 1995. ***PRACTICE AREAS:*** Litigation; Environmental Law. ***Email:*** jsullivan@bakerlaw.com

STEPHEN C. SUTTON, born Rochester, New York, February 18, 1966; admitted to bar, 1991, Ohio; 1992, U.S. District Court, Northern District of Ohio; 1994, U.S. Circuit Court, Sixth Circuit and U.S. District Court, District of Arizona; 2000, U.S. District Court, Northern District of New York; 2002, U.S. District Court, Western District of New York; 2004, U.S. District Court, Eastern District of Michigan; 2005, U.S. Court of Appeals, Second Circuit. *Education:* State University of New York at Albany (B.A., magna cum laude, 1988); Cleveland-Marshall College of Law (J.D., magna cum laude, 1991). *Member:* Cleveland and Ohio State (Member, Labor and Employment Section) Bar Associations. ***SPECIAL AGENCIES:*** Equal Employment Opportunity Commission; Ohio Civil Rights Commission; National Labor Relations Board; State Employment Relations Board. ***PRACTICE AREAS:*** Labor and Employment; Employment Litigation. ***Email:*** ssutton@bakerlaw.com

CHRISTOPHER J. SWIFT, born Piqua, Ohio, March 6, 1955; admitted to bar, 1980, Ohio and U.S. District Court, Northern District of Ohio; 1983, U.S. Tax Court; 1987, U.S. Court of Appeals, Sixth Circuit. *Education:* Ohio Wesleyan University (B.A., summa cum laude, 1977); The Ohio State University (J.D., summa cum laude, 1980). Phi Beta Kappa; Omicron Delta Kappa; Order of the Coif. Member, Board of Trustees, Ohio Wesleyan University, 1977-1980. Author: "Corporate Liquidations under I.R.C. Section 336 and the Tax Benefit Rule: Tennessee-Carolina Transportation, Inc. v. Commissioner," 40 Ohio St. L.J. 517, 1979. Speaker: 1986, 1994, 1995, 1996 and 2001 Cleveland Tax Institute; 1987, 1995, 1997 and 1998 (Chair) Cleveland Health Care Law Institute; 1988, 1990, 1992 (Chair), 1994, 1996, 1998, 2000 and 2002 Cleveland State and Local Tax Institute. *Member:* Cleveland, Ohio State and American Bar Associations. ***PRACTICE AREAS:*** Tax and Personal Planning; State and Local Taxes; Health Law. ***Email:*** cswift@bakerlaw.com

ALEXANDER J. SZILVAS, born Parma, Ohio, April 22, 1962; admitted to bar, 1987, Ohio. *Education:* University of Notre Dame (B.B.A., with high honors, 1984); Georgetown University Law Center (J.D., cum laude, 1987). Beta Gamma Sigma; Beta Alpha Psi. ***PRACTICE AREAS:*** Tax. ***Email:*** aszilvas@bakerlaw.com

HALLE FINE TERRION, born Cleveland, Ohio, May 15, 1968; admitted to bar, 1993, Ohio. *Education:* University of Michigan (A.B., with distinction; with highest honors, 1990); Case Western Reserve University (J.D., magna cum laude, 1993). Order of the Coif. Contributing Editor, Case Western Reserve University Law Review. *Member:* Cleveland (Member, Securities and Corporate, Banking and Business Sections) and American (Member, Business Section) Bar Associations. ***PRACTICE AREAS:*** Mergers and Acquisitions; Private Capital; Debt Finance; Joint Ventures; Business. ***Email:*** hterrion@bakerlaw.com

WILLIAM M. TOOMAJIAN, born Troy, New York, September 26, 1943; admitted to bar, 1968, New York and U.S. District Court, Northern District of New York; 1972, U.S. District Court, Southern District of New York; 1975, U.S. Court of Appeals, Second Circuit; 1976, U.S. Supreme Court, U.S. Tax Court and U.S. Claims Court; 1978, Ohio. *Education:* Hamilton College (B.A., 1965); University of Michigan (J.D., 1968); New York University (LL.M. in Taxation, 1975). Chairman, Cleveland Tax Institute, 1985. *Member:* Cleveland (Chairman, Tax Committee, 1985-1986), Ohio State and American (Tax Section Advisor to Conference of Commissioners of Uniform State Law Personal Property Leasing Committee) Bar Associations; Tax Club of Cleveland (President, 1986-1987; Member, Board of Editorial Advisors to the Tax Adviser). ***PRACTICE AREAS:*** Taxation; Equipment Leasing; International Law. ***Email:*** wtoomajian@bakerlaw.com

ERNEST E. VARGO, JR., born St. Clairsville, Ohio, September 2, 1960; admitted to bar, 1985, Ohio; 1986, U.S. District Court, Northern District of Ohio; 1994, U.S. Court of Appeals, Sixth Circuit; 2002, U.S. Court of Appeals, District of Columbia Circuit. *Education:* The Ohio State University (B.A., summa cum laude, 1982); University of Michigan (J.D., cum laude, 1985). *Member:* Cleveland, Ohio State and American (Member, Antitrust Section) Bar Associations. ***PRACTICE AREAS:*** Litigation; Antitrust; Trade Regulation; Class Action. ***Email:*** evargo@bakerlaw.com

R. BYRON WALLACE, born Seattle, Washington, December 19, 1945; admitted to bar, 1974, Ohio. *Education:* Harvard University (A.B., 1968); Case Western Reserve University (J.D., 1974). Order of the Coif. ***PRACTICE AREAS:*** Employment Law and Benefits. ***Email:*** bwallace@bakerlaw.com

DANIEL R. WARREN, born Cleveland, Ohio, October 11, 1956; admitted to bar, 1982, Illinois; 1990, U.S. Supreme Court; 1991, Ohio. *Education:* Brown University (B.A., magna cum laude, 1978); University of California at Berkeley (J.D., 1982). Member, Harold M. Burton Inns of Court. Co-Author: "Representing Corporate Clients Suspected of Crime," The Champion, January 1984. Faculty Member, NITA and ABA Litigation Section Trial Justice Clinics. *Member:* Cleveland Bar Association. (Group Leader, Business Litigation). ***PRACTICE AREAS:*** Complex Commercial Litigation; Civil Litigation; Business Litigation. ***Email:*** dwarren@bakerlaw.com

THOMAS D. WARREN, born Cleveland, Ohio, June 22, 1966; admitted to bar, 1992, California; 1994, U.S. District Court, Central District of California amd U.S. Court of Appeals, Ninth Circuit; 2003, U.S. District Court, Northern District of Ohio and U.S. Courts of Appeals, Sixth Circuit; 2004, Ohio, U.S. Supreme Court and U.S. Courts of Appeals, Fifth Circuit. *Education:* Harvard College (A.B., Government, 1988); Stanford Law School (J.D., with distinction, 1992). Phi Beta Kappa. Finalist, Marion Rice Kirkwood Moot Competition. Recipient, Elliot and Mary Perkins Prize for Superior Academic and Extracurricular Achievement. Senior Note Editor, Stanford Law Review, 1991-1992. ***PRACTICE AREAS:*** Appellate Practice; Civil Litigation; Business Crimes; Corporate Investigations. ***Email:*** twarren@bakerlaw.com

ROBERT A. WEIBLE, born Dover, Ohio, June 25, 1953; admitted to bar, 1978, Ohio. *Education:* Wittenberg University (B.A., summa cum laude, 1975); The Ohio State University (J.D., summa cum laude, 1978). Order of the Coif. Note and Comment Editor, Ohio State Law Journal, 1977-1978. ***PRACTICE AREAS:*** Securities Law; Mergers and Acquisitions; Corporate Governance. ***Email:*** rweible@bakerlaw.com

DEBORAH A. SCHAFF WILCOX, born Wausau, Wisconsin, March 2, 1963; admitted to bar, 1987, Wisconsin and Ohio; 1991, U.S. Court of Appeals, Fourth Circuit. *Education:* University of Wisconsin (B.A., with distinction, 1984; J.D., with honors, 1987). Author: Monthly Article on, "Character Licensing," Licensing Journal, 2001-2002; "Legal Issues and Search Engines," (2001-2002); "Understanding Basic Copyright Law in Ohio," CLE Program (2000-2002); "Protecting Intellectual Property in Cyberspace," Ohio Lawyers Weekly, 1999; "Policing Trademarks," INTA Forum (1999). Adjunct Professor, Trademarks, Case Western Reserve University School of Law, 2002. *Member:* Cleveland, Ohio State and American Bar Associations; International Trademark Association; International Anti-Counterfeiting Coalition. ***LANGUAGES:*** French. ***PRACTICE AREAS:*** Intellectual Property. ***Email:*** dwilcox@bakerlaw.com

(This Listing Continued)

BAKER & HOSTETLER LLP, Cleveland—Continued

JAMES R. WOOLEY, born Cleveland, Ohio, April 11, 1957; admitted to bar, 1983, New York; 1986, Ohio, U.S. District Court, Northern District of Ohio and U.S. Court of Appeals, Sixth Circuit. *Education:* University of Cincinnati (B.F.A, magna cum laude, 1979); Case Western Reserve University (J.D., 1982, Order of the Coif). Member, Case Western Reserve Law Review, 1982. Author: "Handling a DNA Case: Practice Pointers," U.S. Department of Justice Handbook, 1992; "A Response to Lander: The Courtroom Perspective," American Journal of Human Genetics, 49:892, 1991; "The Ethnicity Issue in DNA Litigation: Leave the Lawyering to the Lawyers," Promega Proceedings Publication, 1992; "DNA Testing: A Legal Practice of its Very Own," Promega Proceedings Publication, 1993; "A Response to the NY Times," In Brief, Case Western Reserve Law School, 1991; "Using DNA Analysis to Fight Crime in Ohio," Ohio DNA Advisory Council Report, Introduction and Admissibility Chapters, 1994; "Why We Will Never All Agree About DNA Testing in Criminal Cases," Promega Proceedings Publication, 1994; "DNA Evidence," U.S. Department of Justice Violent Crime Book Chapter, 1996; "Presenting DNA Evidence at Trial: the K.I.S.S. Principle," Profiles in DNA, 1:3, May, 1997; "STR Litigation Strategies," International Symposium on Human Identification, Promega Proceedings Publication, 1998. Co-Author: "The Forensic DNA Brouhaha: Science or Debate?" with Rocke Harmon, American Journal of Human Genetics, 51:1164, 1992; "Reliability of Statistical Estimates in Forensic DNA Typing," with Bruce Budowle, DNA on Trial: Genetic Identification and Criminal Justice, Cold Spring Harbor Press, 1992. Adjunct Professor, Case Western Reserve University, 1995—. Assistant District Attorney, Manhattan District Attorney's Office, 1982-1986. United States Attorney's Office, Organized Crime Strike Force, 1990-2000. *Member:* Cleveland, Ohio State and New York State Bar Associations. ***REPORTED CASES:*** United States v. Yee, 134 F.R.D. 161 (N.D. Ohio, 1991); United States v. Yee, 129 F.R.D. 629 (N.D. Ohio, 1990); United States v. Bonds, 18 F. 3d 1327 (6th Cir. App., 1994); United States v. Liberatore, 856 F. Supp. 358 (N.D. Ohio, 1994); United States v. Liberatore, 846 F. Supp. 569 (N.D. Ohio, 1994); United States v. Kraig, 99 F. 3d 1361 (6th Cir. App., 1996); United States v. Dusenbery, 114 F. 3d 1189 (6th Cir. App., 1997); United States v. Dusenbery, 80 F. Supp. 2d 744 (N.D. Ohio, 1998); United States v. Cencer, 90 F. 3d 1103 (6th Cir. App., 1996). ***PRACTICE AREAS:*** White Collar Crime; Corporate Criminal Investigations; Complex Commercial Litigation. ***Email:*** jwooley@bakerlaw.com

MARTIN T. WYMER, born Ravenna, Ohio, November 12, 1957; admitted to bar, 1984, Ohio and U.S. District Court, Northern District of Ohio; 1985, U.S. Court of Appeals, Sixth Circuit; 1990, Michigan, U.S. District Court, Eastern District of Michigan and U.S. Court of Appeals, Fifth Circuit; 1993, U.S. Supreme Court; 2000, U.S. District Court, District of Colorado; 2001, U.S. District Court, Western District of Michigan; 2002, U.S. Court of Appeals, Eleventh Circuit; 2003, U.S. Court of Appeals, Third Circuit. *Education:* University of Cincinnati (B.S., summa cum laude, 1980); Ohio State University (J.D., honors graduate, 1984). Phi Beta Kappa. *Member:* American, Ohio State and Cleveland Bar Associations; State Bar of Michigan. ***REPORTED CASES:*** Monette vs. Electronic Data System, 90 F.3d 1173 (6th Cir. 1996); Richard Brothers vs. AT&T, 885 F.Supp. 1043 (N.D. Ohio, 1995); Electronic Data Systems vs. National Labor Relations Board, 985 F.2d 801 (5th Cir. 1993); Janis Cox vs. Electronic Data Systems, 751 F. Supp. 680 (E.D. Mich. 1990); Anthony Holloman vs. Greater Cleveland Regional Transit Authority, 741 F. Supp. 677 (N.D. Ohio 1990); The State, ex rel. Clark et al. vs. Greater Cleveland Regional Transit Authority, 48 Ohio St. 3d 19 (1990). ***PRACTICE AREAS:*** Employment and Labor Litigation; Equal Employment Opportunity Law; Executive Termination Litigation; Complex Business Litigation; Collective Bargaining. ***Email:*** mwymer@bakerlaw.com

OF COUNSEL

WILLIAM L. ARNOLD, born Cleveland, Ohio, October 7, 1952; admitted to bar, 1977, Ohio. *Education:* Bowling Green State University (B.A., 1974); Cleveland State University (J.D., 1977). Omicron Delta Kappa. *Member:* Cleveland, Ohio State and American Bar Associations. ***PRACTICE AREAS:*** Real Estate; Real Estate Taxation. ***Email:*** warnold@bakerlaw.com

CHRIS BATOR, born Cleveland, Ohio, March 31, 1962; admitted to bar, 1987, Ohio, U.S. District Court, Northern District of Ohio and U.S. Court of Appeals, Sixth Circuit; 1988, U.S. District Court, Southern District of Ohio; 1989, District of Columbia. *Education:* John Carroll University (B.A., magna cum laude, 1984); Case Western Reserve University (J.D., cum laude, 1987). *Member:* Cleveland Bar Association; Ohio State Bar Association; American Bar Association. ***PRACTICE AREAS:*** Civil Litigation; Insurance Defense; Insurance Law. ***Email:*** cbator@bakerlaw.com

THOMAS S. CAMPANELLA, born Cleveland, Ohio, January 13, 1950; admitted to bar, 1977, Ohio. *Education:* Ohio University (B.A., 1972; M.A., 1973); Cleveland-Marshall College of Law (J.D., 1977). Certified Public Accountant, 1984 (inactive status). Cleveland City Council, 1979-1980. Auditor/Consultant Arthur Young & Company, 1982-1985. Vice President, Managed Care for Medical Mutual of Ohio, 1985-1997. Associate Dean, Ohio University College of Medicine, 1997-2000. ***PRACTICE AREAS:*** Health Care; Employee Benefits. ***Email:*** TCampanella@bakerlaw.com

VICTORIA JOHNSON, admitted to bar, 1990, Ohio. *Education:* Baldwin Wallace College (B.A., 1983); Case Western Reserve University (J.D., 1990). ***PRACTICE AREAS:*** Real Estate; Construction; Business. ***Email:*** vjohnson@bakerlaw.com

MELINDA L. REYNOLDS, born Cleveland, Ohio, October 10, 1962; admitted to bar, 1997, Ohio. *Education:* Cleveland State University (B.B.A., 1987); Case Western Reserve University (J.D., 1997). Order of the Coif. Certified Public Accountant, Ohio, 1991. ***PRACTICE AREAS:*** Domestic and International Tax Planning; Tax Controversies. ***Email:*** mreynolds@bakerlaw.com

MARY A. WILSON, born 1955; admitted to bar, 1981, New York and U.S. District Court, Western District of Texas; 1983, Ohio and U.S. District Court, Northern District of Ohio. *Education:* State University of New York at Albany (B.A., Russian and Political Science, 1977); State University of New York at Buffalo (J.D., 1980); Case Western Reserve University (LL.M., 1996). ***PRACTICE AREAS:*** International Taxation. ***Email:*** mwilson@bakerlaw.com

(This Listing Continued)

ASSOCIATES

JOHN J. ALLOTTA, born Toledo, Ohio, October 7, 1975; admitted to bar, 2001, Ohio. *Education:* Ohio Wesleyan University (B.A., cum laude, 1998); Case Western Reserve University (J.D., magna cum laude, 2001). *Member:* Ohio State and American Bar Associations. ***PRACTICE AREAS:*** Mergers and Acquisitions; Commercial Financing. ***Email:*** jallotta@bakerlaw.com

MICHELLE B. ANSELMO, admitted to bar, 1989, Illinois and U.S. District Court, Northern District of Illinois; 1992, U.S. Court of Appeals, Sixth Circuit; 1995, U.S. Court of Appeals, Seventh Circuit, U.S. District Court, Eastern District of Wisconsin and U.S. District Court, Southern District of Florida; 2004, Ohio. *Education:* Marquette University (B.A., with honors, 1985); Case Western Reserve University (J.D., with honors, 1989). *Member:* American Bar Association (Member, Sections on: Litigation; Employment and Labor Law). ***PRACTICE AREAS:*** Employment Litigation. ***Email:*** mbarrett@bakerlaw.com

MATHEW B. BEREDO, born Cleveland, Ohio, August 17, 1972; admitted to bar, 1998, Ohio; 1999, U.S. District Court, Northern District of Ohio. *Education:* Yale College (B.A., cum laude, 1994); University of Michigan (J.D., cum laude, Order of the Coif, 1998). *Member:* Cleveland and Ohio State Bar Associations. ***LANGUAGES:*** Spanish. ***PRACTICE AREAS:*** Commercial Litigation; Labor and Employment Law. ***Email:*** mberedo@bakerlaw.com

BRIDGET MEEHAN BRENNAN, born Camp Hill, Pennsylvania, November 28, 1974; admitted to bar, 2000, Ohio; 2001, U.S. District Court, Northern District of Ohio; 2002, U.S. Court of Appeals, Sixth Circuit. *Education:* John Carroll University (B.A., 1997); Case Western Reserve University (J.D., 2000). *Member:* Cleveland, Ohio State and American Bar Associations. ***PRACTICE AREAS:*** Commercial Litigation; First Amendment. ***Email:*** bbrennan@bakerlaw.com

KIMBERLY C. BRUNNER, born Kettering, Ohio; admitted to bar, 2002, Ohio. *Education:* Vanderbilt University (B.A., cum laude, 1995); The Ohio State University College of Law (M.B.A. 1999; J.D., with honors, 2002);. Order of the Coif. ***PRACTICE AREAS:*** Business. ***Email:*** kbrunner@bakerlaw.com

KELLY S. BURGAN, admitted to bar, 2001, Ohio. *Education:* The Ohio State University (B.A., 1993); Cleveland-Marshall College of Law (J.D., summa cum laude, 2001). *Member:* Ohio State and American Bar Associations; International Women's Insolvency and Restructuring Confederation. ***PRACTICE AREAS:*** Bankruptcy; Creditors' Rights; Commercial Law. ***Email:*** kburgan@bakerlaw.com

WAN COLLIER, born Taipei, Taiwan, June 18, 1971; admitted to bar, 1998, New York; 2002, Ohio. *Education:* Cornell University (B.A., 1994; J.D., 1997). *Member:* New York State Bar Association. ***PRACTICE AREAS:*** Business Law; Finance; Venture Capital. ***Email:*** wcollier@bakerlaw.com

DEANNA M. CONRAD, born Cleveland, Ohio, May 2, 1976; admitted to bar, 2004, Ohio. *Education:* Barnard College, Columbia University (B.A., cum laude, 1998); Case Western Reserve University School of Law (J.D., magna cum laude, 2004). Order of the Coif. ***PRACTICE AREAS:*** General Practice. ***Email:*** dconrad@bakerlaw.com

EMANUEL J. COTRONAKIS, admitted to bar, 1998, Ohio; 1999, U.S. Court of Appeals, Sixth Circuit and U.S. District Court, Northern District of Ohio. *Education:* Case Western Reserve University (B.A., 1992); Georgetown University (J.D., 1998). *Member:* Ohio State and American Bar Associations. ***PRACTICE AREAS:*** Business; Securities; Debt Finance; Mergers and Acquisitions. ***Email:*** ecotronakis@bakerlaw.com

ANDREA L. CSOMOS, admitted to bar, 2001, Ohio. *Education:* University of Toledo (B.A., summa cum laude, 1998; J.D., summa cum laude, Valedictorian, 2001) Order of the Coif. *Member:* Cleveland, Ohio State and American Bar Associations. ***PRACTICE AREAS:*** Business; Real Estate. ***Email:*** acsomos@bakerlaw.com

WILLIAM J. CULBERTSON, born Washington, D.C., 1966; admitted to bar, 1995, Ohio. *Education:* Bates College (B.A., cum laude, 1989); Case Western Reserve University (J.D., 1995). Member, National Committee on Planned Giving, 1995—. ***PRACTICE AREAS:*** Trusts and Estates; Nonprofit Organizations Law. ***Email:*** wculbertson@bakerlaw.com

ANNE M. DAVET, born Cleveland, Ohio; admitted to bar, 2004, Ohio. *Education:* John Carroll University (B.A., History, cum laude, 2001); University of Notre Dame (J.D., cum laude, 2004). ***PRACTICE AREAS:*** General Practice. ***Email:*** adavet@bakerlaw.com

TODD DAWSON, born Warren, Ohio, September 30, 1973; admitted to bar, 1998, Ohio and U.S. District Court, Northern District of Ohio. *Education:* Youngstown State University (B.A., 1994); Duke University (J.D., 1998). *Member:* Ohio State and American Bar Associations. ***PRACTICE AREAS:*** Labor Relations; Employment Discrimination. ***Email:*** tdawson@bakerlaw.com

MICHAEL P. DeMINICO, born Cleveland, Ohio, April 20, 1975; admitted to bar, 2003, Ohio. *Education:* The College of William & Mary (B.A., Economics, 1997); The George Washington University Law School (J.D., high honors, 2003) Order of the Coif.

PATRICK J. EGAN, admitted to bar, 2001, Ohio. *Education:* Moravian College & Theological Seminary (B.A., 1997); Duquesne University (J.D., 2001). *Member:* Ohio State and American Bar Associations. ***PRACTICE AREAS:*** Employee Benefits; ERISA Litigation. ***Email:*** pegan@bakerlaw.com

BETHANY L. FABIAN, born Syracuse, New York; admitted to bar, 2002, Ohio; 2003, U.S. District Court, Northern District of Ohio; 2005, U.S. Court of Appeals, Sixth Circuit. *Education:* State University of New York at Geneseo (B.A., 1996); Georgetown University Law Center (J.D., 2002). *Member:* Ohio State and American Bar Associations. ***PRACTICE AREAS:*** Employment and Labor. ***Email:*** bfabian@bakerlaw.com

(GUENTHER) KARL FANTER, born Cleveland, Ohio; admitted to bar, 2002, Ohio. *Education:* Bowling Green State University (B.A., 1999); Harvard Law School (J.D., 2002). ***PRACTICE AREAS:*** Litigation. ***Email:*** kfanter@bakerlaw.com

MEGAN P. FRIENT, born St. Louis, Missouri, August 8, 1973; admitted to bar, 1998, Ohio. *Education:* University of Dayton (B.A., magna cum laude, 1995); Case Western Reserve University (J.D., cum laude, 1998). Member, 1996-1998 and Managing Editor, 1997-

(This Listing Continued)

1998, Case Western Reserve University Law Review. ***PRACTICE AREAS:*** White Collar Crime; Antitrust; Complex Civil Litigation; Intellectual Property; Franchise Distribution Law. ***Email:*** mfrient@bakerlaw.com

RUTH E. HARTMAN, admitted to bar, 2005, Ohio. *Education:* University of Wisconsin (B.A., English and History) Phi Beta Kappa; University of Michigan (M.A., United States History, 1999; J.D., 2004). ***PRACTICE AREAS:*** General Practice. ***Email:*** rhartman@bakerlaw.com

MICHELLE M. HERVEY, born Copley, Ohio, September 8, 1972; admitted to bar, 2000, Ohio; 2001, U.S. District Court, Northern District of Ohio; 2003, U.S. Tax Court. *Education:* Case Western Reserve University (B.S., magna cum laude, 1994; J.D., summa cum laude, 2000). Certified Public Accountant, Ohio, 1996. *Member:* Ohio State and American Bar Associations; Ohio Society of CPAs. ***PRACTICE AREAS:*** Mergers and Acquisitions; Limited Liability Companies; Partnerships; Real Estate Investment Trusts; Business and Tax Planning for Closely Held Businesses; Tax Controversies. ***Email:*** mhervey@bakerlaw.com

SCOTT C. HOLBROOK, born Cleveland, Ohio, August 28, 1975; admitted to bar, 2000, Ohio; 2001, U.S. Court of Appeals, Sixth Circuit; 2004, U.S. Court of Appeals, Fifth Circuit. *Education:* Ohio Wesleyan University (B.A., 1997); University of Virginia (J.D., 2000). Order of the Coif. Member, Virginia Law Review. Law clerk to the Honorable Karen Nelson Moore, U.S. Court of Appeals for the Sixth Circuit. Member: Ohio State Bar Association, 2000-2001; William K. Thomas Inn of Court, 2001-2002. *Member:* Cleveland, Ohio State and American Bar Associations. ***PRACTICE AREAS:*** Commercial Litigation. ***Email:*** sholbrook@bakerlaw.com

F. ARTHUR JONES, II, born January 29, 1977; admitted to bar, 2003, Virginia, U.S. District Court, Eastern and Western Districts of Virginia and U.S. Courts of Appeals, Fourth Circuit; 2004, District of Columbia; 2005, Ohio and U.S. District Court, Northern District of Ohio and Northern District of Texas. *Education:* Harvard University (A.B., cum laude, 1999); Georgetown University Law Center (J.D., 2003). *Member:* Virginia and American Bar Associations; Virginia State Bar; The District of Columbia Bar. ***PRACTICE AREAS:*** Litigation; Employment Litigation. ***Email:*** fajones@bakerlaw.com

SEAN M. KAMMER, born Rittman, Ohio, 1980; admitted to bar, 2004, Ohio. *Education:* University of Wyoming (B.A., magna cum laude); Duke University (J.D., cum laude, 2004). ***PRACTICE AREAS:*** General Practice. ***Email:*** skammer@bakerlaw.com

BRANDON E. KEPPLE, born March 3, 1978; admitted to bar, 2003, Ohio. *Education:* Miami University (B.S., 2000); The Ohio State University College of Law (J.D., with honors, 2003). Order of the Coif.

KELLY M. KING, admitted to bar, 2003, Ohio; 2004, U.S. District Court, Northern District of Ohio and U.S. Court of Appeals, Sixth Circuit. *Education:* Miami University (B.A., cum laude, 2000); Case Western Reserve University School of Law (J.D., magna cum laude, 2003). Order of the Coif. ***Email:*** kking@bakerlaw.com

ANDREW W. KIRKPATRICK, born July 13, 1975; admitted to bar, 2003, Ohio; 2004, U.S. District Court, Northern District of Ohio. *Education:* University of Colorado at Boulder (B.A., 1998); Washington College of Law, American University (J.D., 2003); Kogod School of Business, American University (M.B.A., 2003). *Member:* Ohio State and American Bar Associations.

DAVID E. KITCHEN, born Provo, Utah, April 25, 1977; admitted to bar, 2004, Ohio. *Education:* Brigham Young University (B.S., Manufacturing Engineering and Technology, 2001); University of Chicago Law School (J.D., 2004). Tau Alpha Pi. ***Email:*** dkitchen@bakerlaw.com

MELINDA M. KLINE, born Syracuse, New York; admitted to bar, 2004, Ohio. *Education:* University of Rochester (B.A., cum laude, 2001); Case Western Reserve University School of Law (J.D., magna cum laude, 2004). Order of the Coif. ***Email:*** mkline@bakerlaw.com

DEBORAH L. KOERWITZ, born Willoughby, Ohio, February 11, 1971; admitted to bar, 1999, Ohio. *Education:* Miami University (B.S., 1993); Washington University (J.D., 1999). Member, 1997-1998 and Articles Editor, 1998-1999, Washington University Law Quarterly. *Member:* Ohio State and American Bar Associations. ***PRACTICE AREAS:*** Employee Benefits; Business. ***Email:*** dkoerwitz@bakerlaw.com

LAURIE G. KOSANOVICH, born Lexington, Virginia, May 4, 1972; admitted to bar, 1997, Ohio; 1998, U.S. District Court, Northern District of Ohio. *Education:* College of Wooster (B.A., 1994); Case Western Reserve University (J.D., 1997). *Member:* Cleveland, Cuyahoga County and Ohio State Bar Associations. ***PRACTICE AREAS:*** Business Law. ***Email:*** lkosanovich@bakerlaw.com

REBECCA C. LUTZKO, born Parma, Ohio, July 8, 1971; admitted to bar, 1998, Ohio. *Education:* Boston University (B.A., magna cum laude, 1993); Georgetown University Law Center (J.D., cum laude, 1997). Law Clerk to The Honorable Alice M. Batchelder, United States Court of Appeals for the Sixth Circuit, 1997-1998. Co-author: with Judge Alice M. Batchelder and J. Clegg Ivey, "Sixth Circuit Year in Review," University of Tennessee Law Review. *Member:* Cleveland, Ohio State and American Bar Associations. ***PRACTICE AREAS:*** General Civil Litigation; First Amendment Litigation; Intellectual Property Litigation; Securities Litigation. ***Email:*** rlutzko@bakerlaw.com

MICHAEL D. MIERAU, JR., born Cuyahoga Falls, Ohio; admitted to bar, 1998, Ohio; 1999, U.S. Court of Appeals, District of Columbia Circuit and U.S. District Court, Northern District of Ohio. *Education:* University of Akron (B.A., 1989); Cleveland-Marshall College of Law (J.D., magna cum laude, 1998). *Member:* Cleveland (Member, Labor and Employment Law Section), Ohio State (Member, Labor and Employment Law Section) and American (Member, Labor and Employment Law Section) Bar Associations. ***PRACTICE AREAS:*** Employment Litigation. ***Email:*** mmierau@bakerlaw.com

TANYA F. MILLER, born Seattle, Washington, October 3, 1973; admitted to bar, 1999, Ohio; 2002, U.S. District Court, Southern District of New York. *Education:* Case Western Reserve University (B.A., Sociology and Philosophy, cum laude, 1996); Case Western Reserve University School of Law (J.D., cum laude, 1999). ***PRACTICE AREAS:*** Litigation; Business Crimes; Corporate Investigations. ***Email:*** tmiller@bakerlaw.com

JENNIFER A. MILLS, born Cincinnati, Ohio, 1968; admitted to bar, 1996, Ohio. *Education:* University of Cincinnati (B.S., 1991); Case Western Reserve University (M.S. in Physics, 1993; LL.M. in Taxation, 1997); The Ohio State University (J.D., 1996). *Member:* Cleveland, Ohio State and American Bar Associations. ***PRACTICE AREAS:*** Taxation; Employee Benefits. ***Email:*** jamills@bakerlaw.com

CHRISTINA J. MOSER, born Pittsburgh, Pennsylvania, August 30, 1973; admitted to bar, 1998, California; 2001, Ohio. *Education:* Ohio University Honors Tutorial College (B.S., Interpersonal Communications, with highest honor, 1995); Pepperdine University School of Law (J.D., magna cum laude, 1998); London School of Economics and Political Science (LL.M., Intellectual Property, with merit, 2001). ***PRACTICE AREAS:*** Intellectual Property; Litigation. ***Email:*** cmoser@bakerlaw.com

MICHAEL E. MUMFORD, admitted to bar, 2001, Ohio; 2002, U.S. District Court, Central District of Illinois and U.S. District Court, Northern District of Ohio. *Education:* Case Western Reserve University (B.A., cum laude, 1998; M.A., 1998; J.D. cum laude, 2001). *Member:* Cleveland, Ohio State and American Bar Associations. ***PRACTICE AREAS:*** Commercial Litigation; Class Action Defense. ***Email:*** mmumford@bakerlaw.com

ANDREW J. MURRAY, born Bryan, Ohio, September 24, 1972; admitted to bar, 1998, Kentucky; 2004, Ohio. *Education:* The Ohio State University (B.S., Accounting, magna cum laude, 1995; J.D., 1998). *Member:* Kentucky and American Bar Associations; American Health Lawyers Association. ***PRACTICE AREAS:*** Health Care; Corporate Transactions. ***Email:*** amurray@bakerlaw.com

EDWARD D. PAPP, born Cleveland, Ohio, December 28, 1971; admitted to bar, 1997, Ohio. *Education:* John Carroll University (B.A., 1994); Ohio State University College of Law (J.D., 1997). *Member:* Cleveland, Ohio State and American Bar Associations. ***PRACTICE AREAS:*** Civil Litigation; Products Liability; Toxic Torts Litigation. ***Email:*** epapp@bakerlaw.com

CHRISTOPHER D. PELLICCIONI, born Chicago, Illinois, October 1, 1976; admitted to bar, 2003, Ohio and U.S. District Court, Northern District of Ohio. *Education:* University of Southern California (B.A., 1999); Case Western Reserve University School of Law (J.D., magna cum laude, 2003);. Order of the Coif.

JASON P. PERDION, born Cleveland, Ohio, February 28, 1970; admitted to bar, 1998, Ohio; 1999, U.S. District Court, Northern District of Ohio. *Education:* The Ohio State University (B.S.N.R., 1993); University of Toledo (J.D., cum laude, 1998). Author: Protecting Wetlands Through the Clean Water Act and the 1985 and 1990 Farm Bills: A Winning Trio, 28 U. Tol. L. Rev. 867. ***PRACTICE AREAS:*** Environmental; Litigation. ***Email:*** jperdion@bakerlaw.com

DAVID F. PROAÑO, born Quito, Ecuador, May 15, 1976; admitted to bar, 2005, Ohio. *Education:* Calvin College (B.S., 1998); Harvard Law School (J.D., 2004). ***PRACTICE AREAS:*** General Practice. ***Email:*** dproano@bakerlaw.com

LORA M. REECE, admitted to bar, 2002, Ohio. *Education:* North Carolina State University (B.A., summa cum laude, Phi Kappa Phi, 1992); University of Michigan Law School (J.D. 2002). ***PRACTICE AREAS:*** Litigation. ***Email:*** lreece@bakerlaw.com

TIMOTHY J. RICHARDS, born Cleveland, Ohio, October 2, 1976; admitted to bar, 2004, Ohio. *Education:* Wesleyan University (B.A., Philosophy and Classical Civilization, 1999); The Ohio State University, Moritz College of Law (J.D., with honors, 2004). ***Email:*** trichards@bakerlaw.com

JAMES H. ROLLINSON, born Morristown, New Jersey, October 29, 1969; admitted to bar, 1998, New York; 2001, Massachusetts; 2002, U.S. District Court, District of Massachusetts; 2003, U.S. Court of Appeals, First Circuit; 2005, U.S. District Court, Northern District of Ohio (Not admitted in Ohio). *Education:* University of Richmond (B.S., magna cum laude, 1992); Cornell Law School (J.D., 1997). Phi Beta Kappa. ***PRACTICE AREAS:*** Commercial Litigation; Criminal Defense. ***Email:*** jrollinson@bakerlaw.com

AARON J. RUPERT, born Cleveland, Ohio, 1976; admitted to bar, 2002, Ohio. *Education:* College of Wooster (B.A., cum laude, 1998); University of Michigan (J.D., cum laude, 2002). ***LANGUAGES:*** Mandarin and Chinese. ***PRACTICE AREAS:*** Litigation. ***Email:*** arupert@bakerlaw.com

STEPHAN J. SCHLEGELMILCH, born Cleveland, Ohio, April 11, 1974; admitted to bar, 2000, Ohio; 2001, U.S. District Court, Northern District of Ohio and U.S. Court of Appeals, Sixth Circuit. *Education:* Case Western Reserve University (B.A., 1997; J.D., 2000). ***PRACTICE AREAS:*** White Collar Crime; Commercial Litigation. ***Email:*** SSchlegelmilch@bakerlaw.com

KARIN M. SCHOLZ, admitted to bar, 2003, Ohio. *Education:* Miami University (B.A.); Cleveland Marshall School of Law (J.D., cum laude). ***PRACTICE AREAS:*** First Amendment.

DOUGLAS R. SERGENT, born Cleveland, Ohio, July 20, 1966; admitted to bar, 1999, Ohio; 2000, U.S. District Court, Northern District of Ohio. *Education:* Case Western Reserve University (B.A., cum laude, 1996); Cleveland-Marshall College of Law (J.D., magna cum laude, 1999). *Member:* Cleveland, Ohio State and American Bar Associations. ***PRACTICE AREAS:*** Employment and Labor; Labor Relations. ***Email:*** dsergent@bakerlaw.com

JEREMY J. SHARP, admitted to bar, 1999, Ohio; 2003, U.S. District Court, Northern District of Ohio. *Education:* College of William and Mary (B.A., 1995); The Ohio State University, Michael E. Moritz College of Law (J.D., 1999). *Member:* Cleveland, Ohio State and American (Member, Sections on: Labor and Employment Law; Tax Law) Bar Associations. ***PRACTICE AREAS:*** Taxation; Employee Benefits. ***Email:*** jjsharp@bakerlaw.com

JAMES A. SLATER, admitted to bar, 2002, Ohio, U.S. Court of Appeals, Sixth Circuit and U.S. District Court, Northern District of Ohio. *Education:* Muskingum College (B.S., 1998); Ohio State University College of Law (J.D., 2001). *Member:* American and Ohio State Bar Associations. ***PRACTICE AREAS:*** Litigation. ***Email:*** jslater@bakerlaw.com

JANET A. SPREEN, admitted to bar, 1999, Massachusetts; 2005, Ohio. *Education:* The Ohio State University (B.A., summa cum laude, 1995); Georgetown University Law Center (J.D., magna cum laude, 1999). ***PRACTICE AREAS:*** Securities; Mergers and Acquisitions; Business. ***Email:*** jspreen@bakerlaw.com

(This Listing Continued)

BAKER & HOSTETLER LLP, Cleveland—Continued

KEVIN R. TALBOT, born Buffalo, New York; admitted to bar, 2001, Ohio. *Education:* Canisius College (B.A., 1998); University of Notre Dame (J.D., 2001). *Member:* Ohio State and American Bar Associations. ***PRACTICE AREAS:*** Mergers and Acquisitions; Commercial Financing. ***Email:*** ktalbot@bakerlaw.com

MATTHEW A. TENEROWICZ, born Cleveland, Ohio, April 6, 1973; admitted to bar, 1998, Ohio. *Education:* Ohio Wesleyan University (B.A., summa cum laude, 1995); The Ohio State University (J.D., with honors, 1998). *Member:* Ohio State and American Bar Associations. ***Email:*** mtenerowicz@bakerlaw.com

ROGER G. TRIM, born Royal Oak, Michigan, September 21, 1976; admitted to bar, 2003, Ohio; 2004, U.S. District Court, Northern District of Ohio. *Education:* University of Michigan (B.B.A., cum laude, 1998); Case Western Reserve University School of Law (J.D., magna cum laude, 2003). Order of the Coif.

CORINNE M. TYLER, admitted to bar, 1998, Ohio. *Education:* Case Western Reserve University (B.A., Political Science, with honors, 1995); Cleveland-Marshall College of Law (J.D., cum laude, 1998). *Member:* Ohio State and American Bar Associations. ***PRACTICE AREAS:*** Employee Benefits. ***Email:*** ctyler@bakerlaw.com

MARGARET M. VANDEHEY, born Marshfield, Wisconsin; admitted to bar, 1999, Ohio and U.S. District Court, Northern District of Ohio; 2000, Wisconsin. *Education:* University of Wisconsin, Madison (B.A., 1990; J.D., cum laude, 1999). Managing Editor, Wisconsin Law Review, 1998-1999. Registered Nurse, Wisconsin, 1996. *Member:* Cleveland, Ohio State and American Bar Associations; State Bar of Wisconsin. ***PRACTICE AREAS:*** Real Estate. ***Email:*** mvandehey@bakerlaw.com

AARON M. VANDERKAAY, born Akron, Ohio, October 22, 1975; admitted to bar, 2001, Ohio. *Education:* Cornell University (B.S., 1998); The Ohio State University College of Law (J.D. with honors, 2001). Delta Theta Phi. *Member:* Cleveland, Ohio State and American Bar Associations. ***PRACTICE AREAS:*** Business Law; Commercial Real Estate; Securities. ***Email:*** avanderkaay@bakerlaw.com

PETER W. VAN EUWEN, III, born Grand Rapids, Michigan, January 9, 1973; admitted to bar, 1998, Ohio. *Education:* Ohio University (B.B.A., summa cum laude, 1995); The Ohio State University College of Law (J.D., summa cum laude, 1998). Order of the Coif. *Member:* Ohio State and American Bar Associations. ***PRACTICE AREAS:*** Business Law; Mergers and Acquisitions; Securities; Debt Finance. ***Email:*** pvaneuwen@bakerlaw.com

MICHAEL A. VANNIEL, admitted to bar, 2001, Ohio; 2003, U.S. District Court, Northern District of Ohio. *Education:* The Ohio State University (B.A., 1995); University of Toledo (J.D., magna cum laude, 2001). Order of the Coif. *Member:* Ohio State and American Bar Associations. ***PRACTICE AREAS:*** Bankruptcy; Commercial Law. ***Email:*** mvanniel@bakerlaw.com

MONICA S. VERMA, admitted to bar, 1993, U.P., India; 2000, Ohio. *Education:* University of Lucknow, India (B.A., with honors, 1990; LL.B., summa cum laude, 1993); Case Western Reserve University (LL.M., with honors, 1999). *Member:* Ohio Asian American Bar Association; Women in International Trade in North East Ohio; Asian Indian Americans for Better Government. ***PRACTICE AREAS:*** Intellectual Property; Internet; Software; Technology; International Transactions; Outsourcing/Offshoring. ***Email:*** mverma@bakerlaw.com

BRETT A. WALL, born Laramie, Wyoming, February 19, 1971; admitted to bar, 1998, Ohio and U.S. District Court, Northern District of Ohio. *Education:* Ohio State University (B.A., 1995; J.D., 1998). ***PRACTICE AREAS:*** Commercial Litigation; Class Action Defense; Antitrust. ***Email:*** bwall@bakerlaw.com

NATHAN F. WARE, born Cleveland, Ohio, April 3, 1974; admitted to bar, 2000, Ohio. *Education:* The Ohio State University (B.S., summa cum laude, 1996; M.B.A., with honors, 1999; J.D., with honors in Law, 1999); Case Western Reserve University (LL.M., Taxation, 2004). ***PRACTICE AREAS:*** Business; Mergers and Acquisitions; Securities; Partnership and Corporate Tax. ***Email:*** nware@bakerlaw.com

THOMAS M. WEARSCH, born August 4, 1975; admitted to bar, 2002, New York (Not admitted in Ohio). *Education:* Harvard University (A.B., magna cum laude, 1998); University of Virginia (J.D., 2001). ***PRACTICE AREAS:*** Bankruptcy; Creditors Rights.

STAFF ATTORNEYS

GINA A. BEREDO, born Louisville, Kentucky, June 21, 1974; admitted to bar, 1999, Ohio; 2000, U.S. District Court, Northern District of Ohio; 2004, U.S. Court of Appeals, Sixth Circuit. *Education:* St. Louis University (B.A., cum laude, 1996); Indiana University (J.D., 1999). Phi Alpha Delta. *Member:* Cleveland, Ohio State and American (Member, Individual Rights and Responsibilities) Bar Associations. ***PRACTICE AREAS:*** Litigation; Intellectual Property. ***Email:*** gberedo@bakerlaw.com

GERALDINE J. BUTLER, admitted to bar, 2000, Ohio. *Education:* John Carroll University (B.A., 1993); Cleveland-Marshall College of Law (J.D., 1998). ***PRACTICE AREAS:*** Litigation. ***Email:*** gbutler@bakerlaw.com

LIDIA V. CARR, born Moscow, Russia; admitted to bar, 2001, Ohio. *Education:* Moscow State Institute of International Relations (M.S., Economics, high honors, 1994); Ohio Wesleyan University (B.A., summa cum laude, 1995) Phi Beta Kappa; University of Akron (J.D., magna cum laude, 2000). *Member:* Cleveland, Ohio and American Bar Associations. ***PRACTICE AREAS:*** Trusts and Estates. ***Email:*** lcarr@bakerlaw.com

MELANIE S. CORCORAN, born Cleveland, Ohio, November 27, 1955; admitted to bar, 1991, Ohio. *Education:* Otterbein College; Kent State University (B.A., 1977); Cleveland-Marshall School of Law (J.D., 1991). *Member:* Cleveland, Ohio State and American Bar Associations. ***Email:*** mcorcoran@bakerlaw.com

JOSEPH E. DIBAGGIO, admitted to bar, 2002, Ohio. *Education:* University of Dayton (B.A., Criminal Justice Studies, 1996); Cleveland Marshall College of Law (J.D., 2001). *Member:* Ohio State Bar Association. ***PRACTICE AREAS:*** Litigation; Asbestos. ***Email:*** jdibaggio@bakerlaw.com

(This Listing Continued)

JENNIFER L. ESCHEDOR, born Sandusky, Ohio, October 20, 1967; admitted to bar, 1993, Ohio. *Education:* Bowling Green State University (B.A., 1989); The Ohio State University (J.D., 1993). ***Email:*** jeschedor@bakerlaw.com

DIANE L. FEIGI, born December 24, 1972; admitted to bar, 1998, Ohio; 1999, U.S. District Court, Northern District of Ohio. *Education:* University of Akron (B.A., summa cum laude, 1995); Cleveland-Marshall College of Law (J.D., 1998). *Member:* American, Ohio State and Cleveland Bar Associations. ***PRACTICE AREAS:*** Products Liability; Toxic Tort. ***Email:*** dfeigi@bakerlaw.com

JULIE E. FIRESTONE, born San Pedro, California, December 29, 1970; admitted to bar, 1996, Ohio. *Education:* Miami University (B.S./B.A., 1993); Case Western Reserve University (J.D., 1996). Certified Public Accountant, Ohio, 1999. ***Email:*** jfirestone@bakerlaw.com

KRISTIN J. JAKIEL, born Buffalo, New York, January 27, 1973; admitted to bar, 1998, Ohio. *Education:* Ohio State University (B.A., magna cum laude, 1995); American University Washington College of Law (J.D., summa cum laude, 1998). Member, American University Law Review. *Member:* Cleveland, Ohio State and American Bar Associations. ***PRACTICE AREAS:*** Employment Litigation. ***Email:*** kjakiel@bakerlaw.com

LANCE T. MASON, admitted to bar, 1992, Pennsylvania (inactive); 1996, Ohio; 2004, U.S. District Court, Northern District of Ohio. *Education:* College of Wooster (B.A., 1989); University of Michigan Law School (J.D., 1992). ***PRACTICE AREAS:*** Litigation; Employment Litigation; White Collar Crime; Legislative Practice. ***Email:*** lmason@bakerlaw.com

NICHOL M. SCHOENFIELD, born Willoughby, Ohio, October 8, 1970; admitted to bar, 1996, Ohio and U.S. District Court, Northern District of Ohio. *Education:* University of Notre Dame (B.A., cum laude, 1993); The Ohio State University (J.D., cum laude, 1996). Member, The Ohio State Journal of Dispute Resolution. *Member:* Cleveland, Ohio State and American Bar Associations. ***PRACTICE AREAS:*** Commercial Litigation; Civil Litigation. ***Email:*** nschoenfield@bakerlaw.com

DIANE D. WILCOX, born Dayton, Ohio, November 6, 1957; admitted to bar, 1988, Ohio. *Education:* Ohio University (B.S.J., with honors, 1979); University of Akron (J.D., cum laude, 1988). Member, Akron Law Review, 1986-1988. Editor, Akron Tax Journal, 1987-1988. ***PRACTICE AREAS:*** Employee Benefits Law. ***Email:*** ddwilcox@bakerlaw.com

LEGAL SUPPORT PERSONNEL

BOB CRAIG (Chief Information Officer)

ALVIN M. PODBOY, JR., born Cleveland, Ohio, February 10, 1947; admitted to bar, 1972, Ohio; 1973, U.S. District Court, Northern District of Ohio; 1992, U.S. Supreme Court. *Education:* Ohio University (A.B., cum laude, 1969); Case Western Reserve University (J.D., 1972; M.L.S., 1977). Phi Gamma Mu; Phi Alpha Theta. President, Case Western Reserve University Library School Alumni Association, 1981. *Member:* Cleveland (Chair, Technology Committee, 2001—), Ohio State (Chairman, Law Libraries Committee, 1987-1991) and American Bar Associations; American Association of Law Libraries (Chair, Committee on Relations with Information Vendors, 1990-1991; Chair, National Legal Resources Committee, 1992-1993; Chair, Private Law Libraries Special Interest Section, 1994-1995; Chair, Mentoring Committee, 2000-2001; Member, Executive Board, 2001—); Ohio Regional Association of Law Libraries (President, 1984-1985). [Capt., U.S.A.F., 1972]. (Firmwide Director of Libraries). ***Email:*** apodboy@bakerlaw.com

CHARLES B. THOMAS, born Aurora, Illinois, March 6, 1945. *Education:* Colgate University (A.B., 1967); Northeastern University (M.S., M.B.A., 1968). Certified Public Accountant, Illinois, 1971. *Member:* American Bar Association; American Institute of Certified Public Accountants. (Firmwide Director of Finance). ***Email:*** cthomas@bakerlaw.com

MICHAEL E. BANTA

75 PUBLIC SQUARE
SUITE 525
CLEVELAND, OHIO 44113
Telephone: 216-566-0770

General Civil and Criminal Trial Practice. DUI, Driving While Intoxicated; Traffic Violations, Personal Injury, Automobile Accidents, Domestic Relations Law, Family Law, Divorce. Wills and Probate.

MICHAEL E. BANTA, born Dayton, Ohio, February 26, 1947; admitted to bar, 1973, Ohio and U.S. District Court, Northern District of Ohio; 1983, U.S. Court of Appeals, Sixth Circuit and U.S. Supreme Court. *Education:* Ohio State University (B.A., 1969); Case Western Reserve University (J.D., 1972). Phi Alpha Delta. Instructor, Criminal Law, Case Western Reserve University Law School's Center for Criminal Justice, 1973-1993. Member, U.S. Department of Transportation's YOUTHS Safety Advisory Committee, 1970-1972. *Member:* Cleveland (Member, Criminal Law Committee) and Ohio State Bar Associations. [Captain, U.S. Army Reserve, Infantry, 1969-1977]

BASHEIN & BASHEIN CO., L.P.A.

35TH FLOOR
TERMINAL TOWER
50 PUBLIC SQUARE
CLEVELAND, OHIO 44113
Telephone: 216-771-3239; 800-771-4457
Fax: 216-781-5876
URL: http://www.basheinlaw.com
URL: http://www.lawyers.com/basheinlaw

Product Liability, Automobile Accidents, Insurance Law, Appellate Practice, Personal Injury Defense, Medical Malpractice, Workers Compensation, Commercial Litigation. Labor and Employment, General Practice.

(This Listing Continued)

W. CRAIG BASHEIN, born Cleveland, Ohio, October 5, 1960; admitted to bar, 1986, Ohio and U.S. District Court, Northern District of Ohio; 1998, U.S. Court of Appeals, Sixth Circuit; 1999, U.S. Supreme Court. *Education:* The Ohio State University (B.A., 1983; J.D., 1986). Delta Theta Phi. Member, Order of the Coif. Recipient, The American Jurisprudence Award for Excellence in the Study of Law. Named: "Top 10 Lawyers in Ohio;" One of Ohio's Super Lawyers for 2004. *Ohio Lawyer's Weekly,* 2001. Arbitrator and Mediator: Commercial Disputes; Personal Injury; Labor Disputes. *Member:* Cleveland and Ohio State Bar Associations; Ohio Academy of Trial Lawyers; The Association of Trial Lawyers of America. ***REPORTED CASES:*** Westfield Ins. Co. v. Galatis, 100 Ohio St.3d 216 (2003); Santos v. BWC, 101 Ohio St.3d 74 (2004); Rolf v. Tri State Motor Transit Co., 91 Ohio St.3d 380 (2001); Clark v. Chubb Group of Ins. Cos., 337 F.3d 687 (6th Cir. 2003); Golem v. Village of Put-In-Bay, 222 F.Supp.2d 924 (N.D. Ohio 2002). ***PRACTICE AREAS:*** Personal Injury Litigation; Medical Negligence Litigation; Commercial Litigation; FELA; Products Liability; Automobile Accidents and Injuries; Employment; Civil Rights; Insurance Law; Appellate Practice. ***Email:*** cbashein@basheinlaw.com

RICHARD W. BASHEIN, born Cleveland, Ohio, May 1, 1964; admitted to bar, 1989, Ohio and U.S. District Court, Northern District of Ohio. *Education:* The Ohio State University (B.A., 1986); Cleveland-Marshall College of Law (J.D., 1989). Phi Alpha Delta. *Member:* Cleveland and Ohio State Bar Associations; The Association of Trial Lawyers of America; Ohio Academy of Trial Lawyers; Cleveland Workers Compensation Attorneys. ***PRACTICE AREAS:*** Workers Compensation; Litigation. ***Email:*** rbashein@basheinlaw.com

KAREN H. BAUERNSCHMIDT CO., LPA

700 WEST ST. CLAIR AVENUE, SUITE 214
CLEVELAND, OHIO 44113
Telephone: 216-566-8500
Fax: 216-566-0942
URL: http://www.khbtaxlaw.com
Email: kbauerns@mindspring.com
URL: http://www.ohiorealestatetax.com

Real Estate Tax, Litigation, Appellate Practices and Procedure.

KAREN H. BAUERNSCHMIDT, born Cleveland, Ohio, April 14, 1951; admitted to bar, 1976, Ohio; 1980, U.S. District Court, Northern District of Ohio. *Education:* Wittenberg University (B.A., 1973); Case Western Reserve University (J.D., 1976). Co-author: "Cash Equivalency in Ohio Real Property Taxation," Ohio Tax Review, Capital University Law Review. *Member:* Cleveland and Ohio State (Member, Taxation Committee) Bar Associations; Ohio Women's Bar Association. ***REPORTED CASES:*** Oberlin Manor vs. Lorain County (1989) 45 Ohio St 3d 56; Alliance Towers vs. Bd. of Revision (1988) 37 Ohio St 3d 16; James Ratner vs. Stark County Bd. of Revision (1986); Wynwood Apts. vs. Bd. of Revision (1979) 59 Ohio St 2d 34; Ratner vs. Stark Co. Bd. of Revision (1988) 35 Ohio St 3d 26 Bd. of Ed. of Mentor Exemp. Vill School Dist vs. Bd. of Revision (1988) 37 Ohio St 3d 318; Sears Roebuck & Co. vs. Franklin Co BOR (1991) Sup Ct Case No. 90-2373; Gates Mills Club vs. Cuy. City BOR (1992 64 Ohio St 3d 198). ***PRACTICE AREAS:*** Real Estate Tax; Litigation; Appellate Practice. ***Email:*** kbauerns@mindspring.com

BAUGHMAN & JOYCE, LLC

2500 BROOK PARK ROAD
SUITE E
CLEVELAND, OHIO 44134
Telephone: 216-687-1244
Fax: 216-621-4066

Civil Litigation and Appeals, Employment Law, Personal Injury, Products Liability, Construction Law, Workers' Compensation, Toxic Torts, Railroad (FELA) Law, Maritime Law, Administrative Law.

EILEEN M. JOYCE, born Parma, Ohio, January 17, 1969; admitted to bar, 1998, Ohio; 2000, U.S. District Court, Northern District of Ohio and Eastern District of Michigan; 2002, U.S. Court of Appeals, Eighth Circuit. *Education:* Cleveland State University (B.B.A. Finance, summa cum laude, 1993); Case Western Reserve University School of Law (J.D., 1997). Member, Niagara Moot Court Team. Staff Editor, Health-Matrix Journal of Law Medicine. *Member:* Cleveland and Ohio State Bar Associations. ***REPORTED CASES:*** Franklin v. USX Corporation, 87 Cal. App. 4th 615 (2001); Cleveland Bar Assn. v. Dixon, 95 Ohio St. 3d 490 (2002); Britton v. USS Great Lakes Fleet, Inc., 302 F.3d 812 (8th Cir. 2002); State ex rel. Pittsburgh & Conneaut Dock Co. v. Industrial Commission of Ohio, 160 Ohio App. 3d (2005). ***PRACTICE AREAS:*** Civil Litigation; Toxic Torts; Product Liability; Maritime Law. ***Email:*** eileen@baughmanlaw.com

OF COUNSEL

R. PATRICK BAUGHMAN, born Zanesville, Ohio, November 18, 1938; admitted to bar, 1963, Ohio; U.S. District Court, Northern District of Ohio; U.S. District Court, Eastern District of Michigan; U.S. Court of Appeals, Sixth Circuit; U.S. Supreme Court. *Education:* The Ohio State University (B.S., 1960; J.D., 1962). Chief, Workmen's Compensation Section, Ohio Attorney General's Office, 1971. Member, Labor Advisory Committee, Ohio Chamber of Commerce, 1981—. *Member:* Cuyahoga County (Member, Committees on: Workers' Compensation, 1973—; Unauthorized Practice, 1975-1980), Ohio State (Member, Workers' Compensation Committee, 1973—) and American (Member, Tort and Insurance Practice Section) Bar Associations; Defense Research and Trial Lawyers Association; Maritime Law Association. ***PRACTICE AREAS:*** Workers Compensation Law; Maritime Law; Products Liability; Toxic Torts; Trial Practice; Appellate Practice. ***Email:*** pat@baughmanlaw.com

REPRESENTATIVE CLIENTS: U.S. Steel Corporation; LTV Steel; Ameritech; USS Great Lakes Fleet; Marathon Oil; Litton Great Lakes Fleet; Ingalls Shipbuilding; Copperweld Steel Company; USS/Kobe Steel Company; Associated Materials, Inc.; Lake Terminal Railroad; Litton Industries; Michigan Tankers; Selby, Battersby & Co.; Transtar Inc.

BENESCH, FRIEDLANDER, COPLAN & ARONOFF LLP

Established in 1938
2300 BP TOWER
200 PUBLIC SQUARE
CLEVELAND, OHIO 44114-2378
Telephone: 216-363-4500
Facsimile: 216-363-4588
URL: http://www.bfca.com

Columbus, Ohio Office: 88 East Broad Street, Suite 900, 43215-3506. Telephone: 614-223-9300. Facsimile: 614-223-9330.

Bankruptcy, Bankruptcy Reorganization, Banks and Banking, Business Law, Casino and Gambling, Class Actions, Collections, Commercial Law, Commercial Real Estate, Complex and Multi-District Litigation, Construction Law, Consumer Law, Contracts, Copyrights, Corporate Law, Debtor and Creditor, Election Campaign and Political Law, Electronic Commerce, Employee Benefits, Environmental Law, Finance, Health Care, Immigration Law, Intellectual Property, Internet and Technology, Labor and Employment, Leases and Leasing, Mergers, Acquisitions, Divestitures, Mortgages, Patent, Probate, Product Liability, Real Estate, Resort and Leisure, Securities, Taxation, Trademarks, Transportation, Trusts and Estates, Wills, Workers Compensation, Zoning, Planning and Land Use.

FIRM PROFILE: We counsel clients in a number of industries, including broadcasting, computer software, consumer finance, distribution, energy, financial institutions, gaming, health care, investment banking, leisure and entertainment, manufacturing, medical devices, professional services, real estate development and leasing, and retail. Our clients include publicly-held, mid-market, and emerging companies as well as public entities, entrepreneurs, non-profit organizations, trusts and estates. We advise clients on the full spectrum of issues related to owning and operating a business in addition to regulatory compliance, strategic alliances, joint ventures and brownfields. Our lawyers appear regularly before state and federal courts, alternative dispute resolution panels and administrative and legislative bodies to protect and advance the interests of our clients. We are a member of TerraLex, an international network of law firms which enables us to extend assistance to our clients in over 90 countries.

LAW FIRM ALLIANCES/ASSOCIATIONS: ***TERRALEX, THE WORLDWIDE NETWORK OF INDEPENDENT LAW FIRMS***

MEMBERS OF FIRM

GEORGE N. ARONOFF, born Cleveland, Ohio, 1933; admitted to bar, 1958, Ohio. *Education:* Case Western Reserve University (A.B., 1956; LL.B., 1958). Order of the Coif. Recipient, 1994 Centennial Medal, highest award granted by Case Western Reserve University Law School to a graduate. Editor, Case Western Reserve Law Review. Member: U.S. Senate Judiciary Committee Shareholder Rights Subcommittee Advisory Board; Case Western Reserve University Society of Benchers. Trustee: Case Western Reserve University, Development and Alumni Affairs Committee; Cleveland Orchestra. ***PRACTICE AREAS:*** Corporate Law; Mergers, Acquisitions and Divestitures; Securities. ***Email:*** garonoff@bfca.com

STEVEN M. AUVIL, born Canton, Ohio, 1964; admitted to bar, 1994, Ohio; registered to practice before U.S. Patent and Trademark Office. *Education:* The Ohio State University (B.S.M.E., 1988); Cleveland State University (J.D., summa cum laude, 1993); New York University (LL.M., Trade Regulation, 1994). Editor, Cleveland State Law Review. Author: "Staying Patent Validity," 41 Cleve. St. L. Rev. 315 (1993); "Gray Market Goods...," 28 Akron L. Rev. 437 (1995). Adjunct Professor of Law, Patent Law and Practices, Cleveland State University, 2000—. *Member:* Cleveland Bar Association (Chair, Intellectual Property Committee, 1997-1998); Cleveland Intellectual Property Association (Chair, Antitrust Law Committee, 1996-1998). ***PRACTICE AREAS:*** Patent; Trademark; Copyright; Trade Secrets; Litigation. ***Email:*** sauvil@bfca.com

LAWRENCE M. BELL, born Cleveland, Ohio, 1935; admitted to bar, 1961, Ohio. *Education:* Miami University (B.S., 1957); Case Western Reserve University (LL.B., 1961). Order of the Coif. Member, Board of Editors, Case Western Reserve Law Review. Former Chair, Corporation, Business and Banking Law Section, Cleveland Bar Association. Former Co-Chair, Cleveland Bar Association Securities Law Institute. Former Adjunct Professor: Contracts Law, Case Western Reserve University School of Law, Cleveland State University School of Law. Member, Case Western Reserve University Society of Benchers. Former Member: Steering Committee of Leadership Cleveland. Chairman of the Board of Governors, Laura and Alvin Siegal College of Judaic Studies. ***PRACTICE AREAS:*** Business Law; Mergers and Acquisitions; Securities; Contracts; Corporate Law. ***Email:*** lbell@bfca.com

GARY B. BILCHIK, born Cleveland, Ohio, 1945; admitted to bar, 1971, Ohio; 1981, Florida. *Education:* Ohio University (B.B.A., 1967); The Ohio State University (J.D., cum laude, 1971). Trustee: Jewish Family Service Association, Parents Volunteer Association. *Member:* Cleveland Bar Association (Member, Estate Planning Section). ***PRACTICE AREAS:*** Estate Planning; Probate; Fiduciary Income Tax; Federal Estate and Gift Taxation Law. ***Email:*** gbilchik@bfca.com

GREGORY G. BINFORD, born Canton, Ohio, 1948; admitted to bar, 1973, Ohio. *Education:* Case Western Reserve University (A.B., 1970; J.D., 1973). Associate Editor, Case Western Reserve University Law Review. Credentialed: American Medical Association Doctor Advisory Network. Certified Mediator: American Health Lawyers Association Alternative Dispute Resolution Service; American Arbitration Association; National Arbitration Forum. Former Chair: Cleveland Bar Association, Health Law Section; Health Law Institute. ***PRACTICE AREAS:*** Health Care; Hospital Law; Alternative Health Care Delivery Systems; Integrated Health Care Delivery Systems. ***Email:*** gbinford@bfca.com

HARRY M. BROWN, born Oradea, Romania, 1947; admitted to bar, 1972, Ohio. *Education:* Yeshiva University (B.A., magna cum laude, 1969); New York University (J.D., 1972). Former Member: Rules Revisions Committee, Ohio Certificate of Need Review Board; American Bar Association Task Force on Housing for the Elderly. Member: Advi-

(This Listing Continued)

BENESCH, FRIEDLANDER, COPLAN & ARONOFF LLP, Cleveland—Continued

sory Board for the Case Western Reserve University Law/Medicine Center. Former Chair: Ohio Department of Health Certificate of Need Task Force; Ethics Committee, Cuyahoga County Bar Association. ***PRACTICE AREAS:*** Health Care; Medicare and Medicaid; Long Term Care; Health Care Facility Licensing; Certificates of Need. ***Email:*** hbrown@bfca.com

THOMAS R. BRULE, born Rochester, New York, 1954; admitted to bar, 1980, Kentucky; 1982, U.S. District Court, Western District of Kentucky; 1983, U.S. Court of Appeals, 6th Circuit; 1993, Ohio; 1994, U.S. District Court, Northern District of Ohio. *Education:* Indiana University of Pennsylvania (B.S., 1976); University of Kentucky (M.B.A., 1977); University of Louisville (J.D., 1980). Member: International Franchise Association, Cleveland State University School of Business Visiting Committee. Former adjunct professor: University of Akron School of Law. *Member:* Cleveland, Ohio State, Kentucky, Federal and American (Member, Forum on Franchising) Bar Associations. ***PRACTICE AREAS:*** Franchise Law; Business Law; Distribution. ***Email:*** tbrule@bfca.com

MAYNARD A. BUCK, III, born Wheeling, West Virginia, 1958; admitted to bar, 1983, Ohio. *Education:* Wright State University (B.A., 1980); Georgetown University; University of Toledo (J.D., 1983). Student Articles Editor, University of Toledo Law Review. Judicial Clerk, U.S. District Court, Southern District of Ohio, 1984-1985. ***PRACTICE AREAS:*** Employment Law; Employment Discrimination; Unfair Labor Practices; Management Labor Law. ***Email:*** mbuck@bfca.com

THOMAS O. CRIST, born Euclid, Ohio, 1970; admitted to bar, 1995, Ohio and U.S. District Court, Southern District of Ohio; 1997, U.S. District Court, Northern District of Ohio and U.S. Court of Appeals, Sixth Circuit. *Education:* The Ohio State University (B.A., cum laude, 1992); Capital University (J.D., 1994) Order of the Curia. *Member:* Cleveland Bar Association; Ohio State Bar Association (Construction Law Committee); Columbus Bar Association (Litigation Section); American Bar Association (Forum on the Construction Industry). ***PRACTICE AREAS:*** Construction Arbitration; Construction Claims; Construction Defects; Construction Litigation; Contractors Liability. ***Email:*** tcrist@bfca.com

LESLIE A. DROCKTON, born Akron, Ohio, 1960; admitted to bar, 1986, Ohio. *Education:* Connecticut College (B.A., 1982); Case Western Reserve University (J.D., magna cum laude, 1986) Order of the Coif. *Member:* Cleveland Bar Association; Ohio State Bar Association; National Association of Stock Plan Professionals. ***PRACTICE AREAS:*** Mergers and Acquisitions; Public Finance; Private Finance. ***Email:*** ldrockton@bfca.com

GREGG A. EISENBERG, born Cleveland, Ohio, 1971; admitted to bar, 1997, Ohio. *Education:* University of Rochester (B.A., magna cum laude, 1994) Phi Beta Kappa; The Ohio State University (J.D., 1997). Member: Anti Defamation League, Civil Rights Division; Cystic Fibrosis Foundation, Rainbow Chapter. Alumni and Admissions Representative, The University of Rochester. *Member:* Cleveland Bar Association; Ohio State Bar Association. ***PRACTICE AREAS:*** Mergers and Acquisitions; Mergers and Acquisitions Finance; Public Corporations. ***Email:*** geisenberg@bfca.com

PETE C. ELLIOTT, born Danville, Pennsylvania, 1959; admitted to bar, 1984, Ohio; 1988, U.S. Supreme Court. *Education:* Dickinson College (B.A., 1981); Case Western Reserve University (J.D., 1984). Associate, Case Western Reserve Law Review. Law Clerk to John M. Manos, United States District Court, Northern District of Ohio, 1984-1986. Assistant General Counsel, Ernst & Young LLP, 1991-1994. Member, Defense Research Institute. ***PRACTICE AREAS:*** Trial Practice; Defense Litigation; Federal Litigation; Complex Business Litigation; Directors and Officers Liability; Accountants Malpractice; Securities Litigation; Labor Litigation. ***Email:*** pelliott@bfca.com

IRWIN M. FELDMAN, born Milwaukee, Wisconsin, 1939; admitted to bar, 1964, Wisconsin and Ohio. *Education:* University of Wisconsin-Madison (B.B.A., 1961; J.D., 1964). Order of the Coif. Note Editor, University of Wisconsin Law Review. *Member:* Cleveland Bar Association (Member, Health Care Section); American Health Lawyers Association; Society of Ohio Hospital Attorneys. ***PRACTICE AREAS:*** Health Care; Nonprofit and Tax-Exempt Organizations; Employee Benefits. ***Email:*** ifeldman@bfca.com

JAMES M. FRIEDMAN, born Cleveland, Ohio, 1941; admitted to bar, 1966, Ohio. *Education:* Dartmouth College (A.B., summa cum laude, 1963); Harvard University (J.D., cum laude, 1966). Phi Beta Kappa. Law Clerk to Chief Judge Paul C. Weick, U.S. of Appeals, Sixth Circuit, 1966-1967. Co-Author: "Balkanization of Interstate Energy Markets: New Variations of Sovereign Self-Interest," 30 Case Western Reserve Law Review 291, 1980; "The Silent Alliance," Regnery Gateway, 1984. Author: "Clean Air Act Proceedings Affecting National Coal Markets: An Examination of the Authority of the President to Allocate Markets," 82 West Virginia Law Review 867, 1980. Executive Counsel to Governor of Ohio, 1971-1972. Chairman, Ohio Civil Rights Commission, 1972-1974. Director, Overseas Private Investment Corporation, 1978-1981. Special Counsel to the Attorney General of Ohio, 1983-1995. President, Federation for Community Planning, 1989-1992. ***PRACTICE AREAS:*** Environmental Law; Election Campaign and Political Law; Legislative Practice. ***Email:*** jfriedman@bfca.com

GREGORY K. GALE, born LaJolla, California, 1970; admitted to bar, 1994, Georgia; 1995, Maryland; 2003, Ohio. *Education:* Michigan State University (B.A. 1991); College of William & Mary (J.D., 1994). Recipient, Marshall-Wythe Professionalism Award. ***Email:*** ggale@bfca.com

JEREMY GILMAN, born Brooklyn, New York, 1955; admitted to bar, 1983, Ohio; 1985, Florida. *Education:* Columbia College (A.B., 1979); Case Western Reserve University (J.D., 1983). Editor, Case Western Reserve University Law Review, 1982-1983. Author: "Game Day," 25 Legal Studies Forum 281, 2001; "Light Banter: The Faculty at Lunch," 24 Legal Studies Forum 343, 2000; "Catskills on Court Street," 24 Legal Studies Forum 463, 2000; "Personal Jurisdiction and the Internet: Traditional Jurisprudence for a New Medium," 56 The Business Lawyer 395, 2000; "The Real World School of Law," New England Review, Vol. 20 (2), Spring 1999 (Nominated for a Pushcart Prize); "Rethinking the Role of Caveat Emptor in Execution Sales," 32 Case Western Reserve Law Review 735, 1992; "When Brands Collide: Adventures in Advertising Litigation," Cleveland Bar Journal, Vol. 76, No. 2, 2004. Member, Ohio Interagency Early Intervention Council, 1992-1995. Vice Chairman, Board of Trustees, Cleveland Better Business Bureau. Chairman, Membership Committee, Cleveland Better Business Bureau. Legal Advisor, Cleveland Advertising Association. Member, Executive Council, Litigation Section, Cleveland Bar Association. *Member:* American Bar Association (Member, Sections on: Business Law; Litigation). ***PRACTICE AREAS:*** Complex Litigation; Business Litigation; Commercial Litigation; Securities Litigation; Class Actions; Bankruptcy Litigation; Administrative Litigation; Health Care Litigation; Advertising and Marketing; Unfair Competition; Environmental Litigation; Employment Litigation. ***Email:*** jgilman@bfca.com

ALLAN GOLDNER, born Czechoslovakia, 1947; admitted to bar, 1973, Ohio. *Education:* Ohio University (A.B., cum laude, 1969); Cleveland State University (J.D., cum laude, 1973). Editor-in-Chief, Cleveland State Law Review, 1972-1973. *Member:* Cleveland (Member, Securities Law Section), Ohio State (Member, Corporation Law Committee), American (Member, Sections on: Corporations and Banking Law) and Federal Bar Associations. ***PRACTICE AREAS:*** Mergers and Acquisitions; Joint Ventures; Strategic Alliances; Public Finance; Private Finance; Corporate Law; Business Law. ***Email:*** agoldner@bfca.com

BERNARD D. GOODMAN, born Cleveland, Ohio, 1935; admitted to bar, 1960, Ohio. *Education:* University of Michigan (A.B., 1957); Case Western Reserve University (LL.B., 1960). Order of the Coif. Member, Board of Editors, Case Western Reserve Law Review, 1959-1960. *Member:* American College of Real Estate Lawyers (Chairman, Insurance Committee). ***PRACTICE AREAS:*** Commercial Real Estate Development; Syndication; Finance; Workouts; Real Estate Leasing. ***Email:*** bgoodman@bfca.com

JOSEPH N. GROSS, born Kansas City, Missouri, 1951; admitted to bar, 1991, Ohio; 1992, U.S. Court of Appeals, Sixth Circuit and U.S. District Court, Northern District of Ohio. *Education:* University of Missouri (B.S.I.E., with honors, 1976); Southern Illinois University (M.B.A., 1980); St. Louis University; Cleveland State University (J.D., summa cum laude, 1991). *Member:* Cleveland Bar Association (Chair, 1999-2000, Professional Ethics Committee). ***PRACTICE AREAS:*** Employment Litigation; Management Employment Law; Management Labor Law; Workers Compensation Defense; Attorney Discipline. ***Email:*** jgross@bfca.com

NORMAN W. GUTMACHER, born Cleveland, Ohio, 1946; admitted to bar, 1971, Ohio. *Education:* The Ohio State University (B.S., 1968); University of Cincinnati (J.D., 1971). Order of the Coif. Note Editor, University of Cincinnati Law Review, 1970-1971. Listed in: "Ohio Super Lawyers;" "Best Lawyers in America;" "Strathmore's Who's Who;" "Who's Who in American Law." Author: "Leases: A Landlord's Environmental Concerns," NAIOP News, November, 1989; "Obtaining A Real Estate Loan in Today's Market: How to Minimize Your Risks," Development Magazine, July/August, 1989; "Better Safe than Sued: Security Measures to Limit Liability," Skylines Magazine, May 1989; "Negotiating Real Estate Loans - A Frontal Approach," NMM Weekly Legal Review, July, 1984; "Revoke Security Deposit Concession if Tenant Defaults," Commercial Lease Law Institute, March, 1992; "Liability for Third Party Criminal Acts on Property," The Alert, December 1997. Member, Ohio Division of Securities Real Estate Syndications Committee, 1981-1984. *Member:* American College of Real Estate Lawyers; International Council of Shopping Centers. ***PRACTICE AREAS:*** Commercial Lending; Commercial Leasing; Construction Law; Workouts; Commercial Real Estate. ***Email:*** ngutmacher@bfca.com

DOUGLAS E. HAAS, born Cleveland, Ohio, 1950; admitted to bar, 1977, Ohio; 1980, District of Columbia. *Education:* Tufts University (B.A., magna cum laude, 1973); Washington University (M.B.A., 1977; J.D., 1977). *Member:* Cleveland Bar Association (Securities Law Planning Committee). ***PRACTICE AREAS:*** Business Law; Securities; Mergers, Acquisitions and Divestitures; Private Finance; Debt and Equity Finance; Corporate Law; Securities Offerings. ***Email:*** dhaas@bfca.com

JAMES M. HILL, born Sioux City, Iowa, 1953; admitted to bar, 1979, Illinois; 1988, Ohio. *Education:* University of Iowa (B.A., with highest honors, 1975); Yale University (J.D., 1978). Phi Beta Kappa. Author: "Subordinated Lenders Troubled Companies: A Volatile Mix," Venture Capital Journal, Feb., 1992. ***PRACTICE AREAS:*** Entrepreneurial Business Law; Venture Capital; Securities; Mergers, Acquisitions and Divestitures; Corporate Law. ***Email:*** jhill@bfca.com

EDWARD KANCLER, born Cleveland, Ohio, 1939; admitted to bar, 1964, Ohio. *Education:* Lewis & Clark College; Ohio University (A.B., 1961); Case Western Reserve University (J.D., 1964). Phi Beta Kappa; Phi Kappa Phi. Managing Editor, Case Western Reserve Law Review, 1963-1964. Author: "Litigating the Zoning Case in Ohio: Suggestions to Fill the Text Book Void," Cleveland State Law Review, 1975. Lecturer, National Institute of Trial Advocacy. Member, Federal Court Panel of Alternative Dispute Resolution Neutrals for Northern District of Ohio. Member, National Panel, American Arbitrators Association. ***PRACTICE AREAS:*** Alternative Dispute Resolution; Zoning, Planning and Land Use; Litigation. ***Email:*** ekancler@bfca.com

IRA C. KAPLAN, born Cleveland, Ohio, 1954; admitted to bar, 1979, Ohio. *Education:* University of Rochester (B.A., cum laude, 1976); George Washington University (J.D., 1979). ***PRACTICE AREAS:*** Securities; Entrepreneurial Business; Corporate Finance; Mergers, Acquisitions and Divestitures; Equity Finance; Public Equity; Private Equity; Electronic Commerce. ***Email:*** ikaplan@bfca.com

PETER N. KIRSANOW, born Cleveland, Ohio, 1953; admitted to bar, 1979, Ohio; 1984, U.S. District Court, Northern District of Ohio. *Education:* Cornell University (A.B., 1976); Cleveland State University (J.D., cum laude, 1979). Article Editor, Cleveland State Law Review, 1992-1993. Lecturer, Cleveland Marshall College of Law, 1992-1993. (Labor Counsel). ***PRACTICE AREAS:*** Employment Litigation; National Labor Relations Act; Equal Employment Opportunity Law; Labor Arbitration; Management Labor Law; Sports Law. ***Email:*** pkirsanow@bfca.com

ANN E. KNUTH, born Euclid, Ohio, 1963; admitted to bar, 1993, Ohio. *Education:* State University of New York College of Environmental Science and Forestry (B.S., magna cum laude, 1985); Grand Valley State University (M.B.A., with distinction, 1989); Case Western Reserve University (J.D., cum laude, 1993). ***PRACTICE AREAS:*** Employment Discrimination; Management Employment Law; Management Labor Law; Immigration Law. ***Email:*** aknuth@bfca.com

HOWARD A. LEVY, born Winfield, Kansas, 1944; admitted to bar, 1973, Ohio. *Education:* Kenyon College (B.A., magna cum laude, 1967); John Carroll University (M.A.T.,

(This Listing Continued)

1969); Case Western Reserve University (J.D., 1972). Phi Beta Kappa. Member, Editorial Board, Case Western Reserve Law Review, 1971-1972. Author: "Bankruptcy and the Land Sale Contract," 23 Case Western Reserve Law Review 393, 1972. Chairman, 1989-1990, Labor Law Section, Cleveland Bar Association. (Certified Specialist in Labor and Employment Law, Ohio State Bar Association). ***PRACTICE AREAS:*** Employment Litigation; Employment Discrimination; Management Labor Law. ***Email:*** hlevy@bfca.com

RICHARD G. LILLIE, born Cleveland, Ohio, 1950; admitted to bar, 1979, Ohio; 1980, U.S. District Court, Northern District of Ohio; 1983, U.S. Court of Appeals, Sixth Circuit; 1990, District of Columbia and U.S. Supreme Court; 1991, U.S. Court of Appeals for the District of Columbia Circuit and U.S. Court of Claims; 1992, U.S. Court of Appeals, Seventh Circuit; 2000, New York. *Education:* Baldwin-Wallace College; Cleveland State University (B.A., 1975); Cleveland-Marshall College of Law (J.D., 1979); Case Western Reserve University (Ph.D., 1990). Delta Theta Phi. Recipient: U.S. Attorney General's Special Achievement Award, 1986. Judge, Cuyahoga County Court of Common Pleas, 1998. Assistant U. S. Attorney, 1982-1987. Instructor, U.S. Attorney General's Advocacy Institute, 1987. Congressional Staff Aide to Congressman William E. Minshall, 1973-1975. Assistant Law Director, 1993-1994 and Law Director, 1994-1995, City of Westlake, Ohio. Law Director, Village of Grafton, Ohio, 1994-1998, 1999—. Counsel to the Board of Public Affairs, Village of LaGrange, Ohio, 1994-1996. Assistant Law Director/Assistant Prosecutor, City of Lakewood, Ohio, 1991-1992. Adjunct Professor of Law: Case Western Reserve University, School of Law, 2002—; Cleveland-Marshall College of Law, 1991-2000. Legal Commentator: NBC; ABC; CNN. *Member:* Cleveland (Member: Criminal Law Section, 1979—, Chairman, 1984-1985; Federal Court Committee, 1982—), Cuyahoga County, New York State, Ohio State and American Bar Associations; The District of Columbia Bar; National Association of Criminal Defense Lawyers. (Board Certified Trial Advocate, (Criminal Law), National Board of Trial Advocacy). ***REPORTED CASES:*** United States v. Chichy, 1 F.3d 1501 (6th Cir. 1993); Village of Grafton v. Ohio Edison Company, et al. 77 Ohio St. 3d 102, 671 N.E. 2d 241 (1996); United States v. Dedhia 134 F.3d 802 (6th Cir. 1998); Village of Grafton v. Ohio Edison Company, et al. 100 Ohio App. 3d 327, 653 N.E. 2d 1254 (9th Dist. 1995); State of Ohio v. Walker 66 Ohio App.3d 518, 585 N.E.2d 848 (8th Dist. 1990). ***PRACTICE AREAS:*** Litigation; Criminal Law; Professional Malpractice; Commercial Litigation; Catastrophic Injury. ***Email:*** rlillie@bfca.com

EZIO A. LISTATI, born Cleveland, Ohio, 1965; admitted to bar, 1990, Ohio. *Education:* John Carroll University (B.S., 1987); Case Western Reserve University (J.D., 1990). ***PRACTICE AREAS:*** Contracts; Commercial; Business; Real Estate; Insurance. ***Email:*** elistati@bfca.com

KEVIN D. MARGOLIS, born Cleveland, Ohio, 1963; admitted to bar, 1989, Ohio. *Education:* Northwestern University (B.A., 1986); Case Western Reserve University (J.D., 1989). Co-Author: "Brownfields - A Comprehensive Guide To Redeveloping Contaminated Property," ABA, 1997. ***PRACTICE AREAS:*** Environmental Law; Environmental Business Law; Environmental Real Estate; Environmental Corporate Law; Property Remediation. ***Email:*** kmargolis@bfca.com

DAVID R. MAYO, born Cleveland, Ohio, 1951; admitted to bar, 1976, Ohio. *Education:* Miami University (B.S., 1973); Cleveland State University (J.D., 1976). ***PRACTICE AREAS:*** Commercial Law; Litigation; Foreclosures; Commercial Litigation; Creditors Rights. ***Email:*** dmayo@bfca.com

MEGAN LUM MEHALKO, born Ann Arbor, Michigan, 1965; admitted to bar, 1990, Ohio. *Education:* Bucknell University (B.A., 1987); Case Western Reserve University (J.D., 1990). ***PRACTICE AREAS:*** Corporate Law; Mergers, Acquisitions and Divestitures; Business Law; Contracts. ***Email:*** mmehalko@bfca.com

DAVID W. MELLOTT, born Springfield, Ohio, 1953; admitted to bar, 1978, Ohio; 1980, U.S. District Court, Northern District of Ohio; 1989, U.S. Court of Appeals, Sixth Circuit. *Education:* Miami University (B.A., magna cum laude, 1975); The Ohio State University (J.D., 1978). Phi Beta Kappa. *Member:* International Association of Defense Counsel; Ohio Association of Civil Trial Attorneys. Arbitration Chairman, Cuyahoga County Court of Common Pleas. ***PRACTICE AREAS:*** Litigation; Products Liability; Contracts; Insurance. ***Email:*** dmellott@bfca.com

BARRY J. MILLER, born Rochester, New York, 1954; admitted to bar, 1983, Ohio; 1985, District of Columbia. *Education:* Miami University (B.S., 1977); Kent State University (M. Architecture, 1979); Case Western Reserve University (J.D., 1983). Associate Editor, 1981-1982, Notes Editor, Case Western Reserve University Law Review, 1982-1983. Author: Note, "The Architect in the Design-Build Model: Designing and Building the Case for Strict Liability in Tort," 33 Case Western Reserve University Law Review 116, 1982. Contributing Author: Ohio Public Contract Law and Construction Claims (3rd Ed., 1994); State-by-State Guide to Construction and Design Law (ABA, 1998). Professional Registered Architect, 1981, Ohio. *Member:* Cleveland, Ohio State, American and Federal Bar Associations; American Arbitration Association (Regional Advisory Committee; Large Complex Case Arbitrator; Mediator). ***PRACTICE AREAS:*** Construction Law; Public Construction Law; Real Estate. ***Email:*** bmiller@bfca.com

MARK A. PHILLIPS, born Berea, Ohio, 1952; admitted to bar, 1990, Ohio. *Education:* Ohio University (B.A., summa cum laude, 1974); Cleveland State University (J.D., summa cum laude, 1990). *Member:* Cleveland and American Bar Associations; American Arbitration Association (Regional Advisory Committee). ***PRACTICE AREAS:*** Complex Business Litigation; Corporate Litigation; Bankruptcy Litigation; Intellectual Property; Securities Litigation; Trade Secrets Litigation. ***Email:*** markphillips@bfca.com

MICHAEL A. PRIMROSE, born Whitinsville, Massachusetts, 1960; admitted to bar, 1989, Ohio. *Education:* University of Texas at Houston (B.A., with honors, 1986); University of Michigan (J.D., cum laude, 1989). ***PRACTICE AREAS:*** Entrepreneurial Business Law; Corporate Finance; Venture Capital; Securities; Mergers, Acquisitions and Divestitures; Corporate Law; Equity Finance; Public Equity; Private Equity. ***Email:*** mprimrose@bfca.com

ANNA K. RASKE, born Toledo, Ohio, 1971; admitted to bar, 1996, Ohio; 1997, U.S. District Court, Northern District of Ohio; 1998, U.S. Court of Appeals, Sixth Circuit. *Education:* Miami University (B.A., 1993); University of Dayton (J.D., cum laude, 1996). Member, 1994-1995 and Associate Editor, 1995-1996, University of Dayton Law Review. ***Email:*** araske@bfca.com

(This Listing Continued)

ALAN E. SCHABES, born Cleveland, Ohio, 1957; admitted to bar, 1981, Ohio. *Education:* Duquesne University (B.S., magna cum laude, 1978); Hofstra University (J.D., 1981). Associate Editor, Hofstra Law Review, 1979-1981. Member, Health Law Section, 1986— and Licensure Subcommittee of Health Law Section, 1987, Ohio State Bar Association, 1991. Member, Board of Editors, Nursing Home Regulations Survey, Certification and Enforcement Manual, Thompson Publishing Co., 1993—. Recipient, Ohio Chapter of American College of Health Care Administrators Journalism Award, 1992. Member, Publications Committee, National Health Lawyers Association. Author: "The Omnibus Budget Reconciliation Act of 1987: A Major Change in Long Term Care Law," Ohio Law, 1989; "Medicine's Big Brother," 93 Chicago Medicine 18, 1990; "Long-Term Care Surveys," The Long-Term Care Handbook, National Health Lawyers Association, 1991; "Negotiation of Managed Care Contracts for Long Term Care Facilities," *The Long Term Care Handbook—Update,* 1999. Co-Chair and Author: *The Long Term Care Handbook— Update*, American Health Lawyers Association, 1999. Co-General Editor and Author: *The Long Term Care Handbook: Regulatory, Operational and Financial Guideposts* (second edition), 2000. *Member:* American Health Lawyers Association. ***PRACTICE AREAS:*** Health Care; Long Term Care; Medicare and Medicaid Reimbursement; Integrated Health Care Delivery Systems; Hospitals. ***Email:*** aschabes@bfca.com

WILLIAM E. SCHONBERG, born Cleveland, Ohio, 1954; admitted to bar, 1979, Ohio. *Education:* Ohio University (B.G.S., cum laude, 1976); Cleveland State University (J.D., 1979). Author: Bankruptcy Law Sections of "Ohio Collection Law," 1987 and "Ohio Postjudgment Collection Law," 1988 published by Professional Education Systems, Inc. Co-Author: "Basic Bankruptcy in Ohio, 1988 published by National Business Institute, Inc. Member of Board of Directors of American Board of Certification; Chair, ABC Standards Committee, 1995-1997. Member, Board of Directors, Northern Ohio Chapter of Turnaround Management Association, 1994-1998. *Member:* Cleveland (Member, Section of Commercial and Bankruptcy Law), Ohio and American Bar Associations; American Bankruptcy Institute. ***PRACTICE AREAS:*** Bankruptcy Chapter 11; Corporate Reorganization; Corporate Workouts; Commercial Law; Secured Transactions Law. ***Email:*** wschonberg@bfca.com

H. JEFFREY SCHWARTZ, born Cleveland, Ohio, 1954; admitted to bar, 1980, Ohio. *Education:* Cleveland State University (B.A., 1976; J.D., 1979). Judicial Clerk, United States Bankruptcy Court, Northern District of Ohio, 1980-1983. Author: "Treatment of Postpetition Real Property Taxes in Bankruptcy," Prentice Hall Law & Business, Nov., 1991; "The Alternatives: Workout or Bankruptcy," The Bankers Magazine, (WG&L 1992); "Break Up Fees, Topping Fees, and Overbid Procedures for the Chapter 11 Purchaser," (Prentice Hall Law & Business, 1993); "The Bankruptcy Reform Act of 1994," (Cleveland Bar Journal, 1994). Faculty Member, Fifteenth Annual Bankruptcy Litigation Institute, Prentice Hall Law & Business. *Member:* Cleveland (Chairman, 1994-1995, Bankruptcy and Commercial Law Section) and American (Member, Section on Business Law; Subcommittees on: Tax and Chapter 11; American Bankruptcy Institute. ***PRACTICE AREAS:*** Bankruptcy Reorganization; Commercial Workouts; International Bankruptcy; International Insolvency; Out of Court Debt Restructuring. ***Email:*** jschwartz@bfca.com

PETER K. SHELTON, born Dallas, Texas, 1961; admitted to bar, 1993, Ohio. *Education:* University of Colorado (B.A., 1984); Cleveland State University (J.D., 1993). ***PRACTICE AREAS:*** Corporate Law; Mergers and Acquisitions; Corporate Finance. ***Email:*** pshelton@bfca.com

HOWARD A. STEINDLER, born Cleveland, Ohio, 1942; admitted to bar, 1967, Ohio. *Education:* Miami University (B.S., 1964); The Ohio State University (J.D., cum laude, 1967). Adjunct Professor of Law, Cleveland State University Law School, 1981-1985. *Member:* Lenders' Counsel Group of the American Land Title Association; Cleveland Bar Real Estate Institute (Lecturer, 1978; 1983; 1985; 1990; 1996; 1999; 2000); American College of Real Estate Lawyers; National CLE Conference (Lecturer, 2000). ***PRACTICE AREAS:*** Business Law; Real Estate Law; Shopping Center Law. ***Email:*** hsteindler@bfca.com

MICHAEL K. SWEARENGEN, born Toledo, Ohio, 1960; admitted to bar, 1989, Ohio. *Education:* University of Toledo (B.A., cum laude, 1982); Georgetown University (J.D., cum laude, 1989). Articles Editor, American Criminal Law Review. ***PRACTICE AREAS:*** Real Estate. ***Email:*** mswearengen@bfca.com

JOSEPH G. TEGREENE, born Lakewood, Ohio, 1953; admitted to bar, 1984, Ohio. *Education:* Kenyon College (B.A., cum laude, 1974); Cleveland State University (J.D., 1983). ***PRACTICE AREAS:*** Corporate Law; Securities; Business Law; Contracts. ***Email:*** jtegreene@bfca.com

RONALD J. TEPLITZKY, born Cleveland, Ohio, 1961; admitted to bar, 1987, Ohio. *Education:* Ohio University (A.B., summa cum laude, 1984); Case Western Reserve University (J.D., magna cum laude, 1987). Phi Beta Kappa; Order of the Coif. Member, Case Western Reserve University Law Review. ***PRACTICE AREAS:*** Bank Law; Lender Law; Mergers, Acquisitions and Divestitures; Business Law; Investments; Health Care. ***Email:*** rteplitzky@bfca.com

RICHARD F. TRACANNA, born Washington, Pennsylvania, 1959; admitted to bar, 1984, Pennsylvania; 1987, Ohio. *Education:* University of Notre Dame (B.B.A., with highest honors, 1981); University of North Carolina at Chapel Hill (J.D., with honors, 1984). Beta Gamma Sigma; Beta Alpha Psi. Staff Member, North Carolina Law Review, 1982-1983. Author: Contributor, "A Survey of Developments in North Carolina Law," North Carolina Law Review LXI-61, 1983. ***PRACTICE AREAS:*** Taxation; Corporate Tax Planning; Partnership Taxation; Workouts Taxation; Executive Compensation. ***Email:*** rtracanna@bfca.com

JEFFRY L. WEILER, born New York, N.Y., 1942; admitted to bar, 1970, Ohio; 1981, Florida. *Education:* Miami University (B.S., 1964); Cleveland State University (J.D., cum laude, 1970). Internal Revenue Agent, Internal Revenue Service, Field Audit Division, Cleveland, Ohio, 1965-1970. Certified Public Accountant, Ohio, 1968. Adjunct Associate Professor of Law, Cleveland State University Law School, 1980-1987. Chairman: Cleveland Tax Institute, 1983; Cleveland Estate Planning Institute, 1979. President, Tax Club of Cleveland, 1999-2000.*Member:* Ohio State Bar Association (Member: Board of Governors; Estate Planning, Trust and Probate Law Section, 1999—). Fellow, American College

(This Listing Continued)

BENESCH, FRIEDLANDER, COPLAN & ARONOFF LLP, Cleveland—Continued

of Trust and Estate Counsel, 1990—. (Board Certified Tax Lawyer, Florida Bar Board of Legal Specialization and Education). ***PRACTICE AREAS:*** Estate Planning; Taxation; Tax Controversies. ***Email:*** jweiler@bfca.com

JEFFREY J. WILD, born New York, New York, 1972; admitted to bar, 1997, Ohio. *Education:* Yeshiva University (B.A., cum laude, 1994); Benjamin N. Cardozo School of Law (J.D., 1997). ***Email:*** jwild@bfca.com

ERIC L. ZALUD, born Cleveland, Ohio, 1960; admitted to bar, 1985, Indiana; 1987, Ohio. *Education:* Miami University (A.B., 1981); Vanderbilt University (J.D., 1985). Associate Editor, Vanderbilt Journal of Transnational Law, 1984-1985. International Court of Justice, Public International Law, The Hague, The Netherlands, 1983. Member: Executive Committee, Transportation Lawyers of America; Association for Transportation Law Logistics and Policy; Ohio Foreign Commerce Association; Transportation Consumer Protection Council; Conference of Freight Counsel; Cleveland Traffic Club; Defense Research Institute, Trucking Law Committee; Cleveland Trucking Association. ***LANGUAGES:*** Spanish, Portuguese. ***PRACTICE AREAS:*** Transportation; Commercial Litigation; Product Liability Defense; Insurance Coverage; Construction Law. ***Email:*** ezalud@bfca.com

JEFFREY D. ZIMON, born Boston, Massachusetts, 1963; admitted to bar, 1992, Ohio. *Education:* Brandeis University (A.B., 1985); Case Western Reserve University (J.D., 1992). Winner, Dunn Moore Moot Court Competition, 1991. Member, Niagra International Law Moot Court Team, 1992. ***PRACTICE AREAS:*** Employee Benefits; Employee Compensation; Employee Benefits Litigation; Business Law. ***Email:*** jzimon@bfca.com

SENIOR ATTORNEY

SHEILA M. NINNEMAN, born Toledo, Ohio, 1959; admitted to bar, 1989, Ohio. *Education:* University of Dayton (B.A., cum laude, 1982); Cleveland State University (J.D., magna cum laude, 1989). ***Email:*** sninneman@bfca.com

ASSOCIATES

JESSICA N. ANGNEY, born Lorain, Ohio, 1975; admitted to bar, 2001, Ohio. *Education:* Baldwin-Wallace College (B.A., cum laude, 1997); Cleveland State University (J.D., 2000). Moot Court, 1998-1999. Editor, Cleveland State Law Review, 1999-2000. Author: "It's New But is it Improved: The New 'Innocent Spouse' Provision," Cleveland State Law Review, Vol. 47, No. 4, 2000. Certified Public Accountant, 2001. ***Email:*** jangney@bfca.com

MARK E. AVSEC, born Cleveland, Ohio, 1954; admitted to bar, 1995, Ohio. *Education:* Cleveland State University (B.A., summa cum laude, 1992; J.D., magna cum laude, 1994). ***Email:*** mavsec@bfca.com

LINDSAY C. BABBITT, born Cleveland, Ohio, 1976; admitted to bar, 2004, Ohio; 2005, Wisconsin. *Education:* University of Michigan (B.A., 1999); University of Wisconsin (J.D., 2004). ***Email:*** lbabbitt@bfca.com

SUSAN E. CLADY, born Parma, Ohio, 1971; admitted to bar, 1996, Ohio. *Education:* The Ohio State University (B.A., summa cum laude, 1993; J.D., with honors, 1996). ***Email:*** sclady@bfca.com

JEFFREY A. CROSSMAN, born Wickliffe, Ohio, 1972; admitted to bar, 2001, Ohio and U.S. District Court, Northern District of Ohio. *Education:* Mount Union College (B.A., 1994); University of Akron (M.A., 1996); Cleveland-Marshall College of Law (J.D., 2000). ***Email:*** jcrossman@bfca.com

JACOB DERENTHAL, born Ann Arbor, Michigan, 1977; admitted to bar, 2005, Ohio. *Education:* University of Michigan (B.A., 1999); St. John's University (J.D., 2004). ***Email:*** jderenthal@bfca.com

JOHN S. GAMBACCINI, born Akron, Ohio, 1975; admitted to bar, 2000, Ohio. *Education:* University of Akron (B.A., summa cum laude, 1997); George Washington University (J.D., 2000). ***Email:*** jgambaccini@bfca.com

W. SCOTT HARDERS, born Takoma Park, Maryland, 1964; admitted to bar, 1997, California; 1999, Ohio; registered to practice before U.S. Patent and Trademark Office. *Education:* University of Notre Dame (B.S.E.E., 1986); University of San Diego (J.D., 1997). Author: "Recent Developments in Patent Law," The Key, Intellectual Property Newsletter, January 2001; "Highlights of the Last 100 Years - Intellectual Property Law," Cleveland Bar Journal, January 2000. *Member:* Cleveland Bar Association (Chair, Intellectual Property Law Section, 2000-2001); State Bar of California; Institute of Electrical and Electronics Engineers; American Intellectual Property Association. [Lt., U.S. Navy, 1986-1994]. ***Email:*** sharders@bfca.com

RYAN P. HOOPER, born Beverly, Massachusetts, 1976; admitted to bar, 2001, Ohio. *Education:* University of Dayton (B.A., magna cum laude, 1998); Georgetown University (J.D., 2001). ***Email:*** rhooper@bfca.com

BRYAN JAKETIC, born Cleveland, Ohio, 1976; admitted to bar, 2004, Ohio. *Education:* Cornell University (B.S., 1998); George Washington University (J.D., with honors, 2004). ***Email:*** bjaketic@bfca.com

JEFFREY P. JONES, born San Diego, California, 1964; admitted to bar, 1993, California; 2001, Ohio. *Education:* University of California, Berkeley (B.A., 1986); Georgetown University (M.A., 1989); McGeorge School of Law (J.D., with great distinction, 1993). Order of the Coif. Assistant Comment Editor, Pacific Law Journal. ***Email:*** jjones@bfcacom

TAMARA L. KAREL, born Cincinnati, Ohio, 1970; admitted to bar, 2005, Ohio. *Education:* Bowling Green State University (B.S., 1994); Cleveland State University (J.D., 2004). ***Email:*** tkarel@bfca.com

ROSS J. KIRCHICK, born Cleveland, Ohio, 1974; admitted to bar, 2000, Ohio. *Education:* University of Michigan (B.A., with distinction, 1996); The Ohio State University (J.D., with honors, 2000). ***Email:*** rkirchick@bfca.com

(This Listing Continued)

RITA KLINE, born Cleveland, Ohio, 1974; admitted to bar, 2000, Ohio. *Education:* John Carroll University (B.S., 1996); Cleveland State University (J.D., 2000). *Member:* Cleveland Intellectual Property Law Association. ***LANGUAGES:*** Hungarian. ***PRACTICE AREAS:*** Patents. ***Email:*** rkline@bfca.com

GREGORY S. KOLOCOURIS, (admission pending). *Education:* Bucknell University (B.S., 1994); University of Pittsburgh (J.D., 1997). ***Email:*** gkolocouris@bfca.com

LEE KORLAND, (admission pending). *Education:* Brandeis University (B.A., cum laude, 1999); Case Western Reserve University, Weatherhead School of Management (M.B.A., 2003); Case Western University School of Law (J.D., magna cum laude, 2003). ***Email:*** lkorland@bfca.com

JEAN KERR KORMAN, born Mentor, Ohio, 1958; admitted to bar, 1990, Ohio. *Education:* The Ohio State University (B.S., 1981); Cleveland State University (J.D., cum laude, 1989). *Member:* Cleveland, Lake, Ohio State and American Bar Associations. ***Email:*** jkorman@bfca.com

M. CASEY KUCHARSON, born Cleveland, Ohio, 1979; admitted to bar, 2004, Ohio. *Education:* Miami University (B.S., 2001); University of Akron (J.D., 2004).

STUART A. LAVEN, JR., born Cleveland, Ohio, 1972; admitted to bar, 1999, Ohio. *Education:* George Washington University (B.S., 1995); The Ohio State University (J.D., 1999). Associate Editor, Ohio State Law Journal. *Member:* American Bar Association (Member, Business Bankruptcy Section). ***Email:*** slaven@bfca.com

NATHAN L. LUTZ, born Warren, Ohio, 1973; admitted to bar, 2002, Ohio. *Education:* The Ohio State University (B.S., summa cum laude, 1997); University of Chicago (J.D., 2002). ***Email:*** nlutz@bfca.com

ROBERT A. MARCHANT, born Boston, Massachusetts, 1972; admitted to bar, 2001, Ohio. *Education:* Brigham Young University (B.S., 1997); Willamette University (J.D., 2001). ***Email:*** rmarchant@bfca.com

CRAIG L. MOORE, born Cleveland, Ohio, 1966; admitted to bar, 1994, Ohio; 1999, U.S. Supreme Court; 2001, U.S. District Court, Southern District Ohio. *Education:* University of Cincinnati (B.A., 1988); Cleveland State University (J.D., 1994). ***PRACTICE AREAS:*** Antitrust and Trade Regulation; Litigation. ***Email:*** cmoore@bfca.com

DAVID M. NEUMANN, born Boston, Massachusetts, 1967; admitted to bar, 1997, Ohio; 1998, Massachusetts. Member: Turnaround Management Association; Cleveland Counsel of World Affairs. ***LANGUAGES:*** Russian. ***Email:*** dneumann@bfca.com

JULIE M. PRICE, born Cleveland, Ohio, 1974; admitted to bar, 1999, Ohio. *Education:* Bowling Green State University (B.S., 1996); Cleveland State University (J.D., cum laude, 1999). ***Email:*** jprice@bfca.com

ROBERT C. PSAROPOULOS, born Elyria, Ohio, 1970; admitted to bar, 1996, Ohio and U.S. District Court, Northern District of Ohio; 1999, U.S. Court of Appeals, Sixth Circuit. *Education:* The Ohio State University (B.S.B.A., 1993); Cleveland State University (J.D., 1996); John Carroll University (M.B.A., 1999). Associate, Cleveland-Marshall Journal of Law & Health, 1994-1995. ***Email:*** rpsaropoulos@bfca.com

CHRISTOPHER P. REUSCHER, born Massillon, Ohio, 1975; admitted to bar, 2002, Ohio. *Education:* Malone College (B.A., 1998); University of Akron (J.D., cum laude, 2002). Member, Akron Law Review. ***Email:*** creuscher@bfca.com

WILLIAM J. SHIN, born Chicago, Illinois, 1977; admitted to bar, 2002, Ohio. *Education:* Duke University (A.B., cum laude, 1999); University of Notre Dame (J.D., 2002). Executive Editor, Notre Dame Journal of Law. ***Email:*** wshin@bfca.com

NICK D. SHOFAR, born Cleveland, Ohio, 1953; admitted to bar, 1987, Ohio. *Education:* Boston University (B.A., 1975); Dyke College (Paralegal Cert., 1981); Cleveland State University (J.D., 1986). ***Email:*** nshofar@bfca.com

TODD L. SLADEK, born Merrill, Wisconsin, 1956; admitted to bar, 2004, Ohio. *Education:* University of Notre Dame (B.S., 1979); University of Rochester (M.S., 1983; Ph.D., 1984); University of Akron (J.D., 2004). ***Email:*** tsladek@bfca.com

EDWARD J. STOLL, JR., born Lakewood, Ohio, 1966; admitted to bar, 1994, Ohio; 1995, U.S. District Court, Northern District of Ohio; 2003, U.S. Supreme Court. *Education:* Denison University (B.A., 1989); Cleveland State University (J.D., 1994). ***Email:*** estoll@bfca.com

CLARE R. TAFT, born Cleveland, Ohio, 1978; admitted to bar, 2003, Ohio. *Education:* John Carroll University (B.A., 2000); Cleveland State University (J.D., cum laude, 2003). ***Email:*** ctaft@bfca.com

MARK D. TRAINER, born McKeesport, Pennsylvania, 1977; admitted to bar, 2002, Ohio. *Education:* Harding University (B.A., summa cum laude, 1999); Indiana University, Indianapolis (J.D., summa cum laude, 2002). ***Email:*** mtrainer@bfca.com

THEOLOGOS VERGINIS, born Manchester, New Hampshire, 1974; admitted to bar, 2002, Ohio. *Education:* University of Akron (B.S., magna cum laude, 1996; J.D., magna cum laude, 2002); The Ohio State University (M.S.W., magna cum laude, 1997). ***Email:*** tverginis@bfca.com

YANPING WANG, born Yushe, Shanxi Province, P.R. China, 1969; admitted to bar, 1992, China; 2000, Ohio. *Education:* Political Science & Law University of China (LL.B., with honors, 1991); Renmin University of China (LL.M., 1994); University of Kansas (J.D., 2000). ***LANGUAGES:*** Chinese. ***Email:*** ywang@bfca.com

OF COUNSEL

MARIANN E. BUTCH, born Bay City, Michigan, 1958; admitted to bar, 1996, Ohio and U.S. District Court, Northern District of Ohio. *Education:* University of Michigan (B.A., 1980); Case Western Reserve University (J.D., cum laude, 1996). Articles Editor, Case Western Reserve Law Review. ***Email:*** mbutch@bfca.com

ROBERT C. CROSS, born East Cleveland, Ohio, 1956; admitted to bar, 1987, Ohio. *Education:* Case Western Reserve University (B.A., 1982; M.B.A., 1991); University of Illinois (J.D., 1986). ***PRACTICE AREAS:*** Commercial Loans; Secured Lending; Asset Based Finance; Workouts. ***Email:*** rcross@bfca.com

(This Listing Continued)

GRETCHEN A. HOLDERMAN, born Cleveland, Ohio, 1964; admitted to bar, 1992, Ohio and U.S. District Court, Northern District of Ohio; 1993, U.S. Court of Appeals, Sixth Circuit; 1998, U.S. Supreme Court; 2001, U.S. Court of Appeals, Seventh Circuit. *Education:* Ohio University (B.A., 1987; M.A., summa cum laude, 1988); Cleveland Marshall College of Law (J.D., 1991). ***PRACTICE AREAS:*** Litigation; Criminal Law; Habeas Corpus; Corporate Law; Partnership Law; Professional Malpractice; Contracts; Catastrophic Injury. ***Email:*** gholderman@bfca.com

MARGARET A. KENNEDY, born Minneapolis, Minnesota, 1946; admitted to bar, 1976, Ohio. *Education:* Creighton University (B.S., 1968); University of Denver (M.A., 1971); Case Western Reserve University (J.D., 1976). Lecturer in Law, Lawyering Process, Case Western Reserve University, 1981-1995. ***PRACTICE AREAS:*** Employment Law; Employment Discrimination; Management Labor Law. ***Email:*** pkennedy@bfca.com

LISA C. KIMMEL, born Cleveland, Ohio, 1960; admitted to bar, 1986, Ohio. *Education:* Bucknell University (B.A., 1982); Case Western Reserve University (J.D., 1986). ***PRACTICE AREAS:*** Employee Benefits; Deferred Compensation; ERISA; Pension and Profit Sharing Plans. ***Email:*** lkimmel@bfca.com

ALLAN D. KLEINMAN, born Cleveland, Ohio, 1926; admitted to bar, 1952, Ohio. *Education:* Case Western Reserve University (B.B.A., 1949; LL.B., 1952). ***PRACTICE AREAS:*** Trusts and Estates. ***Email:*** akleinman@bfca.com

DEANNA COE KURSH, born Cleveland, Ohio, 1942; admitted to bar, 1974, Ohio. *Education:* The Ohio State University (B.S., 1963); Case Western Reserve University (J.D., 1974). Order of the Coif. ***PRACTICE AREAS:*** Business Law; Corporate Law. ***Email:*** dkursh@bfca.com

RICHARD D. MARGOLIS, born Cleveland, Ohio, 1938; admitted to bar, 1963, Ohio. *Education:* University of Pennsylvania (B.S., Economics, 1960); Yale University (J.D., 1963). ***PRACTICE AREAS:*** Business Law; Mergers, Acquisitions and Divestitures; Securities. ***Email:*** rmargolis@bfca.com

GINGER FULLER MLAKAR, born Chillicothe, Ohio, 1963; admitted to bar, 1992, Ohio; 2000, Florida. *Education:* The Ohio State University (B.S.B.A., summa cum laude, 1985; J.D., 1992). Managing Editor, The Ohio State Journal on Dispute Resolution, 1991-1992. Certified Public Accountant, Ohio, 1994. *Member:* Cleveland (Treasurer, Estate Planning, Probate and Trust Law Section, 2002—) and Ohio State (Member, Estate Planning, Trust and Probate Law Section, 1998—) Bar Associations; Estate Planning Council of Cleveland (Executive Committee, 2001—). (Certified Specialist in Estate Planning, Trust and Probate Law, Ohio State Bar Association). ***PRACTICE AREAS:*** Trusts and Estates. ***Email:*** gmlakar@bfca.com

ROBERT M. SPIRA, born Cleveland, Ohio, 1947; admitted to bar, 1972, Ohio. *Education:* Miami University (B.A., 1969); Case Western Reserve University (J.D., 1972). Order of the Coif. Articles Editor, Case Western Reserve Law Review. Author: Trends in Contract Logistics Agreements, 65 J.Transp.Logist. & Pol'y 243-259 (Spring 1998). Member: Counsel of Logistics Management; Transportation Intermediaries Association; Ohio Trucking Association; Regional Logistics Committee; Northeast Ohio Logistics; Growth Association of Greater Cleveland. *Member:* Transportation Lawyers Association. ***PRACTICE AREAS:*** Transportation and Logistics. ***Email:*** rspira@bfca.com

MICHAEL D. ZAVERTON, born Binghamton, New York, 1953; admitted to bar, 1987, Ohio, U.S. District Court, Northern District of Ohio, U.S. Court of Appeals, Sixth Circuit and U.S. Supreme Court. *Education:* Colgate University (A.B., 1975); Case Western Reserve University (J.D., 1987). ***Email:*** mzaverton@bfca.com

RETIRED COUNSEL

ALFRED A. BENESCH (1879-1973)

ROBERT C. COPLAN (1918-2003)

JEROME M. FRIEDLANDER (1900-1993)

RICHARD L. PHILLIPS, born Cleveland, Ohio, 1926; admitted to bar, 1955, Ohio. *Education:* The Ohio State University (B.S., 1949); Cleveland State University (J.D., summa cum laude, 1955).

(For complete Biographical data on Personnel at Columbus, Ohio see Professional Biographies at that location)

BERGER & ZAVESKY CO., L.P.A.

Established in 1950

ROCKEFELLER BUILDING, SUITE 1425
614 W. SUPERIOR AVENUE
CLEVELAND, OHIO 44113
Telephone: 216-830-9000
Toll Free in Ohio: 1-877-515-5677
Fax: 216-830-4200
Email: bergzav@earthlink.net
URL: http://www.bergzal.com

Personal Injury, Medical Malpractice, Pharmaceutical Drug and Medical Device Litigation, Automobile Accidents, Products Liability, Wrongful Death, Nursing Home Abuse and Neglect, Worker's Compensation, Employment Law, Sexual Harassment, Real Estate, Family Law, Child Abuse, Intentional Torts. Trial Practice in State and Federal Court.

FIRM PROFILE: Our staff of highly rated attorneys bring experience and solutions to a variety of legal matters. The law must be stable, but ever changing, and with our firm you will find qualified attorneys to help you with your legal problems. In addition, former Chief U.S. District Court Judge George White, who is Of Counsel, brings a wealth of knowledge and experience to the firm which he has been able to utilize as a mediator and arbitrator.

I. JOSEPH BERGER, born Cleveland, Ohio, October 4, 1925; admitted to bar, 1950, Ohio; 1965, U.S. Supreme Court. *Education:* Case Western Reserve University (B.B.A., 1947; J.D., 1950). Life Member: Sixth Circuit Federal Judicial Conference. Special Counsel to Ohio Attorney General's Office, 1970.

(This Listing Continued)

ROBERT J. ZAVESKY, born Cleveland, Ohio, July 9, 1953; admitted to bar, 1983, Ohio and U.S. District Court, Northern District of Ohio; 1984, U.S. Court of Appeals, Sixth Circuit; 1986, Illinois; 2002, U.S. Supreme Court. *Education:* Cuyahoga Community College (A.A., 1977); Baldwin-Wallace College (B.A., 1980); Cleveland State University (J.D., cum laude, 1983).

JEFFREY D. LOJEWSKI, born Cleveland, Ohio, September 29, 1957; admitted to bar, 1982, Ohio and U.S. District Court, Northern District of Ohio; 1983, U.S. Court of Appeals, Sixth Circuit. *Education:* Miami University (A.B., cum laude, 1979); Cleveland Marshall College of Law, Cleveland State University (J.D., 1982).

DOUGLAS L. WINSTON, born Cleveland, Ohio, February 11, 1960; admitted to bar, 1986, Ohio; 1989, U.S. District Court, Northern District of Ohio; 1990, U.S. District Court, Southern District of Ohio; 1991, U.S. Court of Appeals, Sixth Circuit. *Education:* Case Western Reserve University (B.A., 1983); The Ohio State University College of Law (J.D., 1986).

OF COUNSEL

GEORGE W. WHITE, born Duquesne, Pennsylvania, May 6, 1931; admitted to bar, 1956, Ohio. *Education:* Baldwin-Wallace College; Cleveland Marshall College of Law (J.D., 1955). Common Pleas Court Judge, Cuyahoga County, Ohio, 1968-1980. U.S. District Court Judge, 1980-1999 and Chief Judge, 1995-1999, Northern District of Ohio. ***Email:*** bergzav@earthlink.net

SAM THOMAS, III, born Montgomery, Alabama, November 15, 1947; admitted to bar, 1997, Ohio. *Education:* Cleveland State University (B.A., 1973); Indiana University, Bloomington (M.S., 1975); Cleveland-Marshall College of Law (J.D., 1996).

BERKMAN, GORDON, MURRAY & DEVAN

Established in 1964

2121 THE ILLUMINATING BUILDING
55 PUBLIC SQUARE
CLEVELAND, OHIO 44113-1949
Telephone: 216-781-5245
Fax: 216-781-8207
Email: bgmdclvld@aol.com
URL: http://www.lawyers.com/berkmangordonmurray&devanlaw

Trial and Appellate Practice in Civil, Criminal and Constitutional Law. Labor, Civil Rights and Employment Law, Corporate, Personal Injury, Administrative, Family Law and General Practice.

FIRM PROFILE: Berkman, Gordon, Murray & DeVan was established in 1964. The firm practices in the fields of Civil, Criminal, Constitutional, First Amendment, Personal Injury, Medical Malpractice and Family Law. Serving clients throughout Ohio and elsewhere, the firm devotes a considerable amount of its time to Criminal and Civil Trial work. We serve as advisors to a full spectrum of clients ranging from individuals to large corporations.

MEMBERS OF FIRM

BERNARD A. BERKMAN (1929-1985)

J. MICHAEL MURRAY, born Cleveland, Ohio, June 15, 1950; admitted to bar, 1976, Ohio and U.S. District Court, Northern District of Ohio; 1978, U.S. Court of Appeals, Sixth Circuit; 1982, U.S. Supreme Court; 1990, U.S. Court of Appeals, Ninth Circuit; 1993, U.S. Court of Appeals, Second and Fifth Circuits; 1998, U.S. Court of Appeals, Eighth Circuit; 2001, U.S. District Court, Northern District of New York, U.S. District Court, Southern District of Ohio and U.S. Court of Appeals, Third and Fourth Circuits; 2003, U.S. District Court, Western District of Michigan; 2004, U.S. District Court, Northern District of Indiana, U.S. District Court, Northern District of Texas and U.S. Court of Appeals, Seventh Circuit; 2005, U.S. Court of Appeals, Eleventh Circuit. *Education:* University of Notre Dame (B.A., 1972); Cleveland Marshall College of Law, Cleveland State University (J.D., summa cum laude, 1976). Listed in: The Best Lawyers in America, 1993—; Ohio Super Lawyers; Leading Lawyers Inside Business; Top Lawyers Northern Ohio Live. *Member:* Ohio State Bar Association; First Amendment Lawyers Association (President, 1997-1998; National Chairman, 1998-1999); The Association of Trial Lawyers of America; National Association of Criminal Defense Lawyers; Cuyahoga Criminal Defense Lawyers Association. Fellow, American College of Trial Lawyers. ***PRACTICE AREAS:*** Civil Litigation; Criminal Litigation; First Amendment Law; Constitutional Law; Civil Rights; Medical Malpractice; Wrongful Death; Personal Injury. ***Email:*** jmmurray@bgmdlaw.com

MARK R. DEVAN, born Cleveland, Ohio, May 30, 1948; admitted to bar, 1974, Ohio and U.S. District Court, Northern District of Ohio; 1975, U.S. Court of Appeals, Sixth Circuit; 1982, U.S. Supreme Court. *Education:* Ashland College (B.A., 1971); Cleveland State University (J.D., 1974). Phi Alpha Delta. Listed in: The Best Lawyers in America; Who's Who in American Law; Ohio's Super Lawyers. Author: "Conducting a Defense Jury Voir Dire Through the Judge in Federal District Court," The Champion, Vol. XI, No. 2; "Whose Grand Jury Is It, Anyway? An Account of the Reform of the Cuyahoga County Grand Jury," The Vindicator, Summer, 1988; "Other Acts Evidence: A New Approach," Criminal Law Journal of Ohio, Vol. 2, No. 3, May/June 1990. *Member:* Ohio State Bar Association; Cuyahoga Criminal Defense Lawyers Association (President, 1988-1989; Chairman, Grand Jury Committee, 1986-1988; Amicus Committee, 1985-1986); Ohio Association of Criminal Defense Lawyers (Treasurer, 1992; Chairman, Grand Jury Committee, 1987-1989, Vice President of Publications, 1989-1991; President, 1993-1994); National Association of Criminal Defense Lawyers (Vice-Chairman, Hotline Panel of Experts, 1986-1987); Eighth Judicial District Conference, Life Member. Fellow: American College of Trial Lawyers, 1995 —; American Board of Criminal Defense Lawyers, 1999 —. ***PRACTICE AREAS:*** Criminal Law; Appellate Practice. ***Email:*** mdevan@bgmdlaw.com

LORRAINE R. BAUMGARDNER, born Lakewood, Ohio, April 1, 1955; admitted to bar, 1980, Ohio; 1982, U.S. Court of Appeals, Sixth Circuit. *Education:* College of Wooster

(This Listing Continued)

BERKMAN, GORDON, MURRAY & DeVAN, Cleveland—Continued

(B.A., 1977); Case Western Reserve University (J.D., 1980). Phi Beta Kappa. *Member:* Ohio State Bar Association; First Amendment Lawyers Association. ***PRACTICE AREAS:*** Constitutional Law; Employment Law; Civil Rights; Nursing Home Negligence; Wrongful Death; Products Liability. ***Email:*** lbaumgardner@bgmdlaw.com

JEREMY A. ROSENBAUM, born Lorain, Ohio, June 12, 1958; admitted to bar, 1985, Ohio and U.S. District Court, Northern District of Ohio; 1986, U.S. Court of Appeals, Sixth Circuit. *Education:* University of Cincinnati (B.A., 1980); Cleveland Marshall College of Law, Cleveland State University (J.D., 1985). *Member:* Cuyahoga County, Ohio State and Federal Bar Associations; First Amendment Lawyers Association. ***PRACTICE AREAS:*** Civil Litigation; Criminal Litigation; First Amendment Law; Constitutional Law; Civil Rights; Employment Law; Appellate Practice. ***Email:*** jrosenbaum@bgmdlaw.com

STEVEN D. SHAFRON, born Cleveland, Ohio, July 15, 1962; admitted to bar, 1987, Ohio; 1988, U.S. District Court, Northern District of Ohio; 1989, U.S. Court of Appeals, Sixth Circuit; 2001, U.S. Court of Appeals, Third and Fourth Circuits; 2003, U.S. District Court, Eastern and Western Districts of Michigan; 2004, U.S. District Court, Northern District of Indiana and U.S. Court of Appeals, Seventh Circuits. *Education:* University of Michigan (B.A., 1984); Case Western Reserve University (J.D., 1987). Member: Jessup International Law Moot Court Team; Order of Barristers. *Member:* Cleveland and Ohio State Bar Associations; First Amendment Lawyers Association. ***PRACTICE AREAS:*** Litigation; Constitutional Law; Appellate Practice. ***Email:*** sshafron@bgmdlaw.com

BROOKE F. KOCAB, born Cleveland, Ohio, October 10, 1960; admitted to bar, 1985, Ohio and U.S. District Court, Northern District of Ohio; 1989, U.S. Court of Appeals, Sixth Circuit. *Education:* Lakeland Community College (A.A.S., 1980); Garfield Senior College (B.S., 1982); Cleveland Marshall College of Law, Cleveland State University (J.D., 1985). Member, Moot Court Board of Governors, 1985. Order of the Barristers. Secretary/Treasurer, Lake County Law Library Association, 1988—. *Member:* Lake County (Trustee, 2000-2003) and Ohio State Bar Association; First Amendment Lawyers Association. ***PRACTICE AREAS:*** Civil Litigation; Medical Malpractice; Family Law. ***Email:*** bkocab@bgmdlaw.com

ASSOCIATES

ERIN L. REIFFER, born Grand Rapids, Michigan, January 14, 1978; admitted to bar, 2004, Ohio; 2005, U.S. District Court, Northern District of Ohio. *Education:* Calvin College (B.A., 1999); Case Western Reserve University (J.D., magna cum laude, 2004). *Member:* Cleveland Bar Association; First Amendment Lawyers Association. ***PRACTICE AREAS:*** Constitutional Law; First Amendment Law; Civil Litigation. ***Email:*** ereiffer@bgmdlaw.com

RAYMOND VASVARI, born Youngstown, Ohio, April 3, 1965; admitted to bar, 1991, Ohio and U.S. District Court, Northern District of Ohio; 1993, U.S. Court of Appeals, Sixth Circuit; 1995, U.S. Supreme Court; 2001, U.S. District Court, Southern District of Ohio; 2004, U.S. District Court, Northern District of Texas. *Education:* Harvard University (A.B., cum laude, 1987); Case Western Reserve University (J.D., 1991). Co-Author: "Counter-Demonstration as Protected Speech," 23 Hastings Const. L.Q. Dec. 1995. Adjunct Professor, Case Western Reserve University School of Law, 1994-2003. *Member:* Cleveland Bar Association; First Amendment Lawyers Association. ***PRACTICE AREAS:*** Civil Litigation; First Amendment Law; Constitutional Law; Criminal Law; Civil Rights. ***Email:*** rvasvari@bgmdlaw.com

OF COUNSEL

LARRY S. GORDON, born Cleveland, Ohio, April 4, 1931; admitted to bar, 1956, Ohio; 1959, U.S. District Court, Northern District of Ohio; 1966, U.S. Supreme Court; 1973, U.S. Court of Appeals, Sixth Circuit; 1981, U.S. Tax Court. *Education:* Adelbert College, Western Reserve University (B.A., 1953); Western Reserve University (LL.B., 1956). *Member:* Ohio State Bar Association. ***Email:*** lgordon@bgmdlaw.com

REFERENCE: First National Bank of Ohio.

BERNARD & HAFFEY CO., L.P.A.

Established in 1971

JEFFERSON CENTRE
5001 MAYFIELD ROAD #301
P.O. BOX 24005
CLEVELAND, OHIO 44124-0005
Telephone: 216-291-3600
FAX: 216-291-0159
Email: bernardhaffey@sbcglobal.net
URL: http://www.lawyers.com/bernard&haffey

General Civil and Criminal Practice. Corporate, Probate, Commercial Law, Bankruptcy, Trusts and Estates, Negligence, Family Law, Divorce, Juvenile, and Real Estate. Trial and Appellate Practice, Personal Injury.

CLIFFORD H. BERNARD (1907-1985)

J. ROSS HAFFEY, JR., born Cleveland, Ohio, August 26, 1938; admitted to bar, 1964, Ohio. *Education:* John Carroll University (B.S., 1960); Cleveland Marshall College of Law (J.D., 1964). Delta Theta Phi. Foreman, Cuyahoga County Grand Jury 1974. Member, Board of Commissioners on Grievances and Discipline of the Supreme Court of Ohio, 1983-1987. President, Cuyahoga Criminal Defense Lawyers Association. 1989-1990. *Member:* Ohio State Bar Association; Cuyahoga Criminal Defense Lawyers; Cleveland Academy of Trial Attorneys. ***PRACTICE AREAS:*** Criminal Law; Business Law; Family Law; Divorce; Probate; Litigation. ***Email:*** gfratianne@sbcglobal.net

TIMOTHY P. HAFFEY, born Cleveland, Ohio, December 3, 1959; admitted to bar, 1989, Ohio; 1995, U.S. Federal District Court and U.S. District Court, Northern District of Ohio. *Education:* John Carroll University (B.A., 1984); Cleveland-Marshall College of Law (J.D., 1988). Counsel, Criminal Justice Act. *Member:* Cleveland, Lake County, Geauga County Bar Associations; Cuyahoga Criminal Defense Lawyers Association. ***PRACTICE AREAS:*** Criminal Law; Juvenile Trial Practice; Personal Injury; Business Law; Appellate Practice. ***Email:*** tphaffey@sbcglobal.net

KIRK W. LIEDERBACH, born Cleveland, Ohio, September 8, 1960; admitted to bar, 1992, Ohio and U.S. Federal District Court. *Education:* Cleveland-Marshall College of Law (J.D., 1992). *Member:* Ohio State Bar Association. ***PRACTICE AREAS:*** Real Estate; Construction Law; Insurance Law; Trusts and Estates; Personal Injury; Creditors Rights; Litigation. ***Email:*** kliederbach@sbcglobal.net

REPRESENTATIVE CLIENTS: McStay Engineered Products, Co.; Republic Bank; Brooks & Stafford Co., Ins.; The Kennedy Group; Ocwen Federal Bank; Domino Logistics Co.; Custom Warehousing Inc.
REFERENCE: National City Bank (Cleveland).

THE BERNARD LAW FIRM

CROWN CENTRE BUILDING, SUITE 600
5005 ROCKSIDE ROAD
CLEVELAND, OHIO 44131-6808
Telephone: 440-546-7500
Fax: 440-546-7501
URL: http://www.bernardlaw.com
Email: bernardlaw@aol.com
URL: http://www.lawyers.com/bernardlaw

Complex Business Litigation, Accountants Malpractice, Stockbroker Malpractice, Banking Litigation, Employment Litigation, Personal Injury, Wrongful Termination, Employment Discrimination, Race Discrimination, Sex Discrimination, Sexual Harassment, Americans with Disabilities, Age Discrimination in Employment, Employment Termination, Family and Medical Leave Act, Breach of Contract, Contract Litigation, Insurance, Class Actions, Securities Litigation, Shareholder Derivative Actions, Lender Liability, Antitrust, Consumer Litigation, Consumer Fraud, Construction Defects, Construction Accidents, Construction Law, Automobile Accidents and Injuries, Wrongful Death, Dog Bites, Slip and Fall, Nursing Home Litigation, Products Liability.

DALE A. BERNARD, born Cleveland, Ohio, March 8, 1959; admitted to bar, 1984, Ohio, U.S. District Court, Northern District of Ohio and U.S. Court of Appeals, Sixth Circuit; 2003, U.S. District Court, Southern District of Ohio. *Education:* Ohio State University (B.A., 1981); Cleveland State University (J.D., 1984). *Ohio State Bar Association; The Association of Trial Lawyers of America; National Association of Consumer Advocates.* ***REPORTED CASES:*** Michaels Building Company, et al. v. Ameritrust Co., N.A., et al., 848 F.2d 674 (6th Cir. 1988) (Tetralogy of Class Action and RICO/Antitrust Appeals); Zackaroff v. Koch Transfer Co., 862 F.2d 1263 (6th Cir. 1988); Bowman v. Koch Transfer Co., 862 F.2d 1257 (6th Cir. 1988); Michaels Bldg. Co. v. Cardinal Fed. S & L, 54 Ohio App. 3d 180 (Cuy. Cty. 1988).

BERNS, OCKNER & GREENBERGER, LLC

3733 PARK EAST DRIVE
SUITE 200
CLEVELAND, OHIO 44122
Telephone: 216-831-8838
Fax: 216-464-4489

Zoning, Land Use, Real Estate, Construction, Business Litigation, Insurance and Unfair Competition Law.

MEMBERS

SHELDON BERNS, born Cleveland, Ohio, December 13, 1932; admitted to bar, 1960, Ohio; 1961, U.S. Court of Appeals, 6th Circuit; 1970, U.S. Court of Appeals, 2nd Circuit and U.S. Supreme Court; 1981, U.S. Claims Court. *Education:* The Ohio State University (B.S., summa cum laude, 1958); Case Western Reserve University (LL.B., 1960). Beta Gamma Sigma; Order of the Coif. Editor, Case Western Reserve Law Review, 1959-1960. Member, Beachwood City Council, 1971-1977. Life Member, Eighth Judicial Conference. Listed in Best Lawyers in America, 1995—. *Member:* Cleveland, Ohio State and American (Member, Sections of: Litigation; Urban, State and Local Government Law) Bar Associations. ***PRACTICE AREAS:*** Zoning Law; Land Use; Real Estate; Construction Law; Litigation. ***Email:*** sberns@bernsockner.com

JORDAN BERNS, born Cleveland, Ohio, October 9, 1965; admitted to bar, 1990, Ohio; 1991, U.S. District Court, Northern District of Ohio; 1994, U.S. Court of Appeals, 6th Circuit. *Education:* University of Michigan (A.B., with distinction, 1987); The Ohio State University (J.D., summa cum laude, 1990). Order of the Coif. Author: "Is There Something Suspicious About the Constitutionality of Loitering Laws?" 50 Ohio St. L.J., 717, 1989. *Member:* Cleveland, Ohio State and American Bar Associations. ***PRACTICE AREAS:*** Commercial Litigation; Real Estate; Construction Law; Unfair Competition; Insurance. ***Email:*** jberns@bernsockner.com

BENJAMIN J. OCKNER, born Columbus, Ohio, December 20, 1960; admitted to bar, 1986, Ohio; 1987, U.S. District Court, Northern District of Ohio; 1994, U.S. Tax Court; 1997, U.S. Court of Appeals, 6th Circuit. *Education:* Miami University (A.B., 1982); Georgetown University Law Center (J.D., 1986). Judicial Clerkship, Thomas D. Lambros, U.S. District Court, Northern District of Ohio, 1987-1988. *Member:* Cleveland (Member, Business Litigation Committee), Ohio State and American Bar Associations. ***PRACTICE AREAS:*** Business Litigation; Unfair Competition; Real Estate; Zoning, Planning and Land Use. ***Email:*** bockner@bernsockner.com

PAUL M. GREENBERGER, born Cleveland, Ohio, November 5, 1949; admitted to bar, 1975, Ohio. *Education:* Purdue University; Ohio State University (B.S. Chem., Eng., 1971); George Washington University (J.D., 1975). Lecturer: Continuing Legal Education for Lawyers, Ohio Bar Association; Real Property Law Institute of the Columbus Ohio Bar Association. Former Trial Attorney, U.S. Department of Justice, Criminal Division (Member, Organized Crime and Racketeering Section). Member, Cleveland Ohio Strike Force.

(This Listing Continued)

Former Asst. Dir. of Law and City Prosecutor, Cleveland Heights, Ohio. Commissioner, Commission On The Unauthorized Practice of Law, Ohio Supreme Court. ***PRACTICE AREAS:*** Commercial Litigation; Real Estate; Insurance; Civil Rights. ***Email:*** pgreenberger@bernsockner.com

GARY F. WERNER, born Cleveland, Ohio, February 22, 1962; admitted to bar, 1994, California and U.S. District Court, Central District of California; 1998, U.S. District Court, Northern District of Ohio; 1999, Ohio and U.S. Court of Appeals, Sixth Circuit; 2000, U.S. District Court, Southern District of Ohio. *Education:* University of California at Los Angeles (B.A., Economics, summa cum laude, 1991); Loyola Law School, Los Angeles (J.D., 1994). Phi Beta Kappa; Phi Delta Phi. Certified Arbitrator, Better Business Bureau. Councilman, City Council, Brunswick, Ohio. Chairman, Planning and Zoning Committee, Brunswick City Council. Past Member, Board of Zoning Appeals, Brunswick, Ohio. Member, Medina County Home Builders Association. *Member:* Medina County and American Bar Associations. ***PRACTICE AREAS:*** Zoning and Land Use; Business Litigation; Mechanics Liens; Construction Litigation. ***Email:*** gwerner@bernsockner.com

TIMOTHY J. DUFF, born Patchogue, New York, May 12, 1964; admitted to bar, 1990, Ohio; 1996, U.S. District Court, Northern District of Ohio; 1997, U.S. Court of Appeals, Sixth Circuit. *Education:* Denison University (B.A., 1986); Case Western Reserve University (J.D., 1990). *Member:* Cleveland, Ohio State and Federal (Board of Directors, Northern Ohio Chapter, 2004-2005) Bar Associations. ***PRACTICE AREAS:*** Business Litigation; Zoning, Planning and Land Use; Construction Law. ***Email:*** tduff@bernsockner.com

STEPHEN E. BLOOM CO, L.P.A.

526 SUPERIOR LEADER BUILDING
CLEVELAND, OHIO 44114
Telephone: 216-575-9100
Email: seb216@sebloomlaw.com
URL: http://www.lawyers.com/sebloomlaw

Personal Injury, Workers Compensation, Contracts, Auto Accidents, Nursing Home Abuse, Head and Spinal Cord Injuries, Wrongful Death, Medical Malpractice, Motorcycle Accidents, Slip and Fall, Dog Bites, Trucking Accidents.

STEPHEN E. BLOOM, born Canton, Ohio, July 17, 1953; admitted to bar, 1985, Ohio; 1987, Florida. *Education:* University of Cincinnati (B.A., 1975); Cleveland-Marshall College of Law (J.D., 1985). *Member:* Cleveland, Ohio State and American Bar Associations; The Association of Trial Lawyers of America; Ohio Academy of Trial Lawyers. ***PRACTICE AREAS:*** Personal Injury; Workers Compensation; Contracts; Automobile Accidents and Injuries; Nursing Home Abuse and Neglect; Spinal Injury; Head Injury; Wrongful Death; Medical Malpractice; Motorcycle Accidents; Slip and Fall; Dog Bites; Truck Accidents. ***Email:*** seb216@sebloomlaw.com

JOSEPH E. BOLEK, JR.

3659 GREEN ROAD, SUITE 200
CLEVELAND, OHIO 44122
Telephone: 216-831-0004
Fax: 216-831-5051
URL: http://www.josephbolekjr.com
Email: bolekslaw@adelphia.net
URL: http://www.bolekslaw.com

Family Law, Divorce, Child Custody, Child Support, Alimony, Personal Injury.

FIRM PROFILE: I have 38 years experience with emphasis on Divorce and Family Law. There is no charge for the first 1/2 hour consultation.

JOSEPH E. BOLEK, JR., born Ravenna, Ohio, July 30, 1941; admitted to bar, 1967, Ohio; 1971, U.S. District Court, Northen District of Ohio; 1977, U.S. Tax Court. *Education:* John Carroll University (A.B., 1964); Case Western Reserve University (J.D., 1967). *Member:* Cleveland and American Bar Associations; The Association of Trial Lawyers of America.

BONEZZI SWITZER MURPHY & POLITO CO. L.P.A.

Established in 1998
526 SUPERIOR AVENUE, SUITE 1400
CLEVELAND, OHIO 44114-1491
Telephone: 216-875-2767
Fax: 216-875-1570
Email: bsmp@bsmplaw.com
URL: http://www.bsmplaw.com

Asbestos Litigation, Consumer Protection Law, Contract Law, Employment Law, General Insurance Defense, including Construction Litigation, Motor Vehicle Accidents, Premises Liability, Product Liability and Personal Injury, Hospital Defense, Hospital Risk Management, Medical Malpractice, Nursing Home Litigation, Pharmaceutical, Professional Negligence, Toxic Tort, Uninsured Motorist Law, UCC Law and Appellate Practice.

FIRM PROFILE: Bonezzi Switzer Murphy & Polito Co., L.P.A. is located in suite 1400 of the historic Lender Building located on the southwest corner of East 6th Street and Superior Avenue in Cleveland, Ohio.

BSMP is a relatively new law firm, having opened its doors in January of 1998. However, many of its attorneys have devoted twenty years or more of their professional practice to the defense of physicians and hospitals in medical malpractice litigation. Several of our attorneys specialize in additional areas of civil litigation.

(This Listing Continued)

BSMP commenced operations with eight attorneys. The firm now employs seventeen attorneys, two nurse consultants, four paralegals and a highly effective, hard working support staff of over twenty.

BSMP is a civil defense trial firm. While several shareholders remain focused on defending medical malpractice lawsuits, the firm has attracted attorneys to its staff with expertise in asbestos defense litigation, employment discrimination, nursing home defense and general insurance defense matters.

The asbestos litigation group represents clients with a very diverse range of products. We currently represent many local suppliers of asbestos containing products, several asbestos-containing product manufacturers, equipment manufacturers, premise defendants, a maritime manufacturer and a ship builder. Our joint defense agreement among our current clients provide us an opportunity to save significant litigation expense by contributing only a pro rata share of the cost in every case. BSMP has experienced trial attorneys and a support staff capable of handling any type of asbestos case. We also specialized in the medical aspects of the litigation and have nurse paralegals available to assist in providing the best medical defense available in our jurisdiction.

BSMP has several attorneys at both the shareholder and associate level who devote a substantial amount of their practice to employment law litigation. Attorneys in the firm have represented clients in both state and federal courts, state and federal administrative agencies (EEOC, OCRC, NLRB) and in arbitrations/mediation with respect to a multitude of employment issues, including alleged wrongful terminations, breach of contracts, hiring/promotion practices and discrimination (sex, gender, racial/ethnicity, age, religious and handicap). Jury verdict results, as well as punished opinions in this area of law, are available upon request.

BSMP prides itself on its ability to obtain excellent results for its clients, whether by motion practice, settlements or trial. On average, the attorneys at BSMP try between twenty and thirty jury trials per year. We are proud of our trial record. BSMP also has an in-house department of hundreds of exhibits that can be used in trial without our clients incurring additional expense. We Also maintain a library with many thousands of depositions, reports and trial testimony from expert witnesses whom we encounter on a regulars basis.

BSMP has developed many close friends in the legal and medical profession. Many of these friends are also our clients.

WILLIAM D. BONEZZI, born Cambridge, England, November 25, 1945; admitted to bar, 1973, Ohio. *Education:* Bowling Green State University (B.S., 1970); Cleveland State University (J.D., 1973). Member of Panel, American Arbitration Association. *Member:* Cleveland and Ohio State Bar Associations; Defense Research Institute; American Society of Law and Medicine. ***PRACTICE AREAS:*** Medical Malpractice; Insurance Defense; Toxic Tort; Product Liability; Professional Negligence; Premises Liability. ***Email:*** wbonezzi@bsmplaw.com

STEVEN J. HUPP, born Youngstown, Ohio, August 19, 1963; admitted to bar, 1988, Ohio; 1990, U.S. District Court, Northern District of Ohio; 1992, U.S. Court of Appeals, Sixth Circuit; 2001, U.S. Supreme Court. *Education:* John Carroll University (B.A., 1985); Cleveland-Marshall College of Law (J.D., 1988). Associate Member, 1986-1987 and Managing Editor, 1987-1988, Cleveland-Marshall Law Review. Author: Note, "Ford v. Wainwright, Statutory Changes and a New Test for Sanity: You Can't Execute Me, I'm Crazy!" Cleveland State Law Review, (1987) Vol. 35, Number 4, p. 515. *Member:* Ohio State Bar Association. ***PRACTICE AREAS:*** Medical Malpractice; Hospital Defense; Nursing Home Litigation. ***Email:*** shupp@bsmplaw.com

KEVIN O. KADLEC, born Cleveland, Ohio, October 18, 1956; admitted to bar, 1987, Ohio; 1988, U.S. District Court, Northern District of Ohio; 1991, U.S. Court of Appeals, Sixth Circuit. *Education:* Cleveland State University (B.A., cum laude, 1978); Cleveland-Marshall College of Law (J.D., cum laude, 1986). Editor, Cleveland State Law Review, 1986. Author: "The National Minimum Drinking Age Act of 1984," Cleveland State Law Review, 34, No. 4, 1985-1986. *Member:* Ohio State Bar Association; Cleveland Association of Civil Trial Attorneys; Joint Medical-Legal Committee, Cleveland Academy of Medicine/Cleveland Bar Association. ***PRACTICE AREAS:*** Asbestos Litigation; Toxic Tort; Superfund; Medical Malpractice; Product Liability; Insurance Defense; Premises Liability; Motor Vehicle Accidents and Injuries. ***Email:*** kkadlec@bsmplaw.com

PATRICK J. MURPHY, born Cleveland, Ohio, February 13, 1949; admitted to bar, 1974, Ohio; 1990, U.S. District Court, Northern and Southern Districts of Ohio. *Education:* Villanova University (A.B., 1971); Case Western Reserve University (J.D., 1974). *Member:* Cleveland and Ohio State Bar Associations; Professional Liability Underwriter's Society. ***PRACTICE AREAS:*** Medical Malpractice Defense; Insurance Defense; Motor Vehicle Accidents and Injuries; Premises Liability; Construction Accident; Product Liability; Commercial Litigation. ***Email:*** pmurphy@bsmplaw.com

JOHN S. POLITO, born Cleveland, Ohio, June 17, 1952; admitted to bar, 1977, Ohio; 1978, U.S. District Court, Northern District of Ohio; 1980, U.S. Court of Appeals, Sixth Circuit. *Education:* Xavier University (B.A., summa cum laude, 1974); Cleveland-Marshall College of Law (J.D., cum laude, 1977). *Member:* Cuyahoga County Board of Arbitrators; Ohio State and American Bar Associations; Cleveland Association of Civil Trial Attorneys; Defense Research Association. ***PRACTICE AREAS:*** Insurance Defense; Motor Vehicle Accidents and Injuries; Premises Liability; Product Liability; Medical Malpractice; Asbestos Litigation; Toxic Tort. ***Email:*** jpolito@bsmplaw.com

BETH A. SEBAUGH, born Zanesville, Ohio, July 20, 1954; admitted to bar, 1980, Ohio; 1981, U.S. District Court, Northern District of Ohio; 1982, U.S. Court of Appeals, Sixth Circuit; 1993, U.S. Supreme Court. *Education:* Ohio University (B.S.E., 1976); Cleveland-Marshall College of Law (J.D., 1980). *Member:* Cleveland Bar Association (Fee Dispute Committee, 1985 (Vice-Chairman, 1996); Council, Litigation Section, 1992-1995; Judicial Selection Committee, 1996); Ohio State Bar Association; Defense Research Institute. ***PRACTICE AREAS:*** Medical Malpractice; Product Liability; Employment Law; Equal Employment Opportunity Law; Personal Injury; Toxic Tort; Professional Negligence. ***Email:*** bsebaugh@bsmplaw.com

(This Listing Continued)

BONEZZI SWITZER MURPHY & POLITO CO. L.P.A., Cleveland—Continued

DONALD H. SWITZER, born Atlanta, Georgia, May 31, 1950; admitted to bar, 1978, Ohio; 1979, U.S. District Court, Northern District of Ohio. *Education:* Texas A & M University (B.A., 1972); University of Virginia (J.D., 1978). Quarterly Case Editor, 1984-1995. *Member:* Cleveland and Ohio State Bar Associations; Ohio Association of Civil Trial Attorneys (Member of the Year 1990). [Captain, United States Army, 1972-1975]. ***PRACTICE AREAS:*** Medical Malpractice; Toxic Tort; Hospital Risk Management; Personal Injury; Premises Liability; Product Liability; Construction Litigation; Contracts; Insurance Coverage; Uniform Commercial Code. ***Email:*** dswitzer@bsmplaw.com

---

PETER A. HOLDSWORTH, born Cleveland, Ohio, February 14, 1975; admitted to bar, 2002, Ohio. *Education:* University of Cincinnati (B.S., 1997); Cleveland-Marshall College of Law (J.D., 2002). *Member:* Ohio State Bar Association. ***PRACTICE AREAS:*** Medical Malpractice; Employment Law; Nursing Home Litigation; Insurance Defense. ***Email:*** pholdsworth@bsmplaw.com

LYNETTE E. KISS, born Walbridge, Ohio, September 3, 1974; admitted to bar, 2000, Ohio. *Education:* University of Dayton (B.A., cum laude, 1996); Case Western Reserve University (J.D., 1999). *Member:* Ohio State and American Bar Associations. ***PRACTICE AREAS:*** Asbestos Litigation; Toxic Tort; Medical Malpractice. ***Email:*** lkiss@bsmplaw.com

BRETT A. MILLER, born Columbus, Ohio, October 5, 1974; admitted to bar, 2001, Ohio and U.S. District Court, Northern District of Ohio; 2002, Illinois. *Education:* Bowling Green State University (B.A., cum laude, 1997); Cleveland-Marshall College of Law (J.D., cum laude, 2001). Delta Theta Phi Law Fraternity, International: State Chancellor for Ohio. *Member:* Cleveland and Ohio State Bar Associations. ***PRACTICE AREAS:*** Medical Malpractice; Hospital Law; Nursing Home Litigation; Insurance Defense. ***Email:*** bmiller@bsmplaw.com

BRET C. PERRY, born Offutt Air Force Base, Nebraska, September 4, 1972; admitted to bar, 2001, Ohio; 2002, U.S. District Court, Northern District of Ohio. *Education:* Bowling Green State University (B.S., 1997); Cleveland-Marshall College of Law (J.D., 2000). Clerk to the Honorable Michael J. Corrigan, Eighth District Court of Appeals, 1999-2000; Clerk to the Honorable Nancy R. McDonnell, Cuyahoga County Court of Common Pleas, 2000-2002; Clerk to the Honorable Frank D. Celebrezze, Jr., Eighth District Court of Appeals, 2002-2003. *Member:* Cleveland and Ohio State Bar Associations. [Third Class Petty Officer (E-4), United States Navy, 1991-1993]. ***PRACTICE AREAS:*** Medical Malpractice; Insurance Defense; Appellate Practice. ***Email:*** bperry@bsmplaw.com

PATRICK J. QUALLICH, born Cleveland, Ohio, September 1, 1971; admitted to bar, 1999, Ohio; 2002, U.S. District Court, Northern District of Ohio and U.S. Court of Appeals, Sixth Circuit. *Education:* University of Cincinnati (B.S., 1994); Cleveland-Marshall College of Law (J.D., cum laude, 1999). Associate Member, 1997-1998 and Managing Editor, 1998-1999, Cleveland State Law Review. Member: National Moot Court Team, 1997-1998; Moot Court Board of Governors, 1998-1999. Order of the Barristers. *Member:* Harold D. Burton Chapter of the American Inns of Court; Cleveland Bar Association; Ohio State Bar Association (Health Care Law Committee Appointee). ***PRACTICE AREAS:*** Medical Malpractice; Asbestos Litigation; Toxic Tort; Employment Law; Premises Liability; Nursing Home Litigation; Appellate Practice. ***Email:*** pquallich@bsmplaw.com

SUSAN M. REINKER, born Cleveland, Ohio; admitted to bar, 1979, Ohio; 1980, U.S. District Court, Northern District of Ohio. *Education:* Lutheran Hospital School of Nursing (R.N., 1967); Cleveland State University (B.A., 1970); Kent State University (M.A., 1975); Case Western Reserve University (J.D., 1979). *Member:* Cleveland and Ohio State Bar Associations. ***PRACTICE AREAS:*** Medical Malpractice; Professional Negligence; Pharmacy Law; Nursing Home Litigation. ***Email:*** sreinker@bsmplaw.com

TIMOTHY G. SWEENEY, born Lorain, Ohio, December 20, 1957; admitted to bar, 1984, Ohio; 1985, U.S. District Court, Northern District of Ohio; 1990, U.S. Court of Appeals, Sixth Circuit. *Education:* Ohio State University (B.A., 1981); Cleveland-Marshall College of Law (J.D., 1984). Winner, Hugo Black Award and Dean's Award in Oral Advocacy. Order of the Barristers. Member: Moot Court National Team, 1983-1984; Moot Court Board of Governors, 1983-1984. *Member:* Cleveland and Ohio State Bar Associations. ***PRACTICE AREAS:*** Insurance Defense; Premises Liability; Product Liability; Employment Law; Equal Employment Opportunity Law; Contracts; Consumer Protection; Professional Liability; Medical Malpractice; Nursing Home Litigation; Uninsured and Underinsured Motorists. ***Email:*** tsweeney@bsmplaw.com

KIMBERLY A. THOMAS, born Cleveland, Ohio, August 31, 1965; admitted to bar, 2004, Ohio; registered to practice before U.S. Patent and Trademark Office. *Education:* Ursuline College (B.S.N., 1987); Case Western Reserve University (M.S., Nursing, 1991); Kent State University (Adult Nurse Practitioner Certificate, 1998); Cleveland-Marshall College of Law (J.D., 2003). Sigma Theta Tau. *Member:* Cuyahoga County, Medina County and Ohio State Bar Associations; American Heart Association; Society of Critical Care Medicine; American Association of Critical Care Nurses. ***PRACTICE AREAS:*** Medical Malpractice; Hospital Defense; Nursing Home Litigation. ***Email:*** kthomas@bsmplaw.com

REPRESENTATIVE CLIENTS: Affiliated FM Insurance; AO Smith; AP Capital; ASE USA; Ashtabula General Medical Center; Baltimore Ennis Land Company; Brandon Drying Fabrics; California Insurance Guarantee Assoc.; Catholic Cemetaries; Catholic Charities Services Corporation; Chase Brass and Copper, Inc.; Chubb Group of Insurance Companies; CNA; Congoleum Corporation; Crown Cork & Seal; Donald McKay Smith; Elliott Company; Elyria Memorial Hospital; Empire Abrasives Equipment; FB Wright of Cincinnati; Flexo; Hersh Packing; Hollow Center Packing; Industrial Holdings Corporation; Interstate Insurance Company; Kaiser Permanente; Ken Randall America, Inc.; Mahoning Valley Supply Company; Metro Health Medical Center; MF Murdock; Moldex-Metric, Inc.; Nationwide Insurance; Nordan Smith; Industrial Welding Supplies of Hattiesburg, Inc.; Pangborn Corporation; Physicians Insurance Company of Ohio; Pro Assurance; Royal & Sun Alliance; Sly, Inc.; Soehnlen Piping Company; Southwest General Health Center; Sprinkman & Sons; St. Paul Fire & Marine; St. Paul Insurance; Standard Oil Company; The Cleveland Catholic Diocese; The Cleveland Clinic Foundation; The Doctors Company; The Hartford; The Ohio Hospital Insurance Company; Todd Shipyards Corporation; Travelers; Unifrax Corporation; University Hospitals of Cleveland; Westfield Group; Yohe Supply Company; Zurich-American.

BRICKER & ECKLER LLP

Established in 1944

1375 EAST NINTH STREET, SUITE 1500
CLEVELAND, OHIO 44114-1718
Telephone: 216-523-5405
Fax: 216-523-7071
Email: info@bricker.com
URL: http://www.bricker.com

Columbus, Ohio Office: 100 South Third Street, 43215-4291. Telephone: 614-227-2300. Fax: 614-227-2390.

Antitrust and Competitive Business Practices, Banking, Bankruptcy, Commercial, Construction, Corporate Governance, Corporation and Partnership, Cyberlaw, Creditor-Debtor, Education, Emerging Business, Employment Relations, Energy, Entertainment/Sports, Environmental, Federal Taxation, Governmental Agencies and Legislative Law, Health Care, Insurance, Intellectual Property, International Transactions, Litigation, Mental Retardation and Developmental Disabilities, Mergers and Acquisitions; Mortgage Lending, Oil and Gas, Pension and Employee Benefits, Public Finance, Public Utilities, OSHA, Real Estate, Securities, State and Local Taxation, Trusts and Estates, Workers' Compensation.

FIRM PROFILE: Bricker & Eckler LLP is one of Ohio's leading law firms. Located in Columbus and Cleveland, the firm represents individuals as well as corporations, nonprofit organizations, government agencies, health care facilities, school districts, and municipalities. Dedicated to comprehensive client service, Bricker & Eckler offers services focused on both industry sectors and traditional practice areas. Bricker & Eckler LLP was founded in 1944 by John W. Bricker, a three-term Ohio governor, two-term Ohio senator, and a former candidate for vice president of the United States. Today, we continue our founder's tradition of public service by placing our clients and our communities first.

LAW FIRM ALLIANCES/ASSOCIATIONS: **LEGALINK**

PARTNERS

ALAN J. ROSS, born Cleveland, Ohio, June 8, 1947; admitted to bar, 1975, Ohio and U.S. District Court, Northern District of Ohio; 1983, U.S. Court of Appeals, Sixth Circuit; 1986, U.S. Court of Appeals for the Federal Circuit; 2004, New York; registered to practice before the U.S. Patent and Trademark Office. *Education:* Cleveland State University (B.C.E., 1970); Cleveland-Marshall College of Law (J.D., 1975). ***PRACTICE AREAS:*** Intellectual Property; Business Litigation; Antitrust; Computer Law. ***Email:*** aross@bricker.com

GLENN S. KRASSEN, born Santa Monica, California, June 29, 1955; admitted to bar, 1980, Ohio; 1981, District of Columbia, U.S. District Court, Northern District of Ohio, U.S. Court of Appeals for the District of Columbia and U.S. Court of Appeals, Sixth Circuit. *Education:* George Washington University (B.A., with distinction, 1977); The Ohio State University College of Law (J.D., 1980). ***PRACTICE AREAS:*** Energy; Public Utility; Corporate Law; Public Finance. ***Email:*** gkrassen@bricker.com

RICHARD M. KNOTH, born Indianapolis, Indiana, October 8, 1958; admitted to bar, 1983, Indiana and Illinois; 1985, U.S. Court of Appeals, Seventh Circuit; 1989, Ohio, Ohio Supreme Court and U.S. Court of Appeals, Sixth Circuit; 1993, Court of Federal Claims; 1994, U.S. Court of Appeals, Eighth Circuit; 1996, U.S. Supreme Court; 1998, U.S. Court of Appeals, Fifth and Eleventh Circuits; 2004, Texas. *Education:* Boston College (A.B., cum laude, 1980) De Paul University (J.D., 1983). ***REPORTED CASES:*** *Circuit City Stores v. Artz Group*; 165 F3d 1047 (6th Cir. 1999) (Trademark injunction, Internet infringement); Coles v. Cleveland Bd. of Educ., 950 F.Supp. 1337, 115 Ed. Law Rep. 926 (N.D. Ohio 1996) (defense of constitutional challenges to board practices); City of Cleveland v. Cleveland Elec. Illuminating Co., 115 Ohio App. 3d 1 (Ohio App. 8 Dist. 1996) (injunction action in anti-competition utility energy wheeling case); Berg v. Health and Hosp. Corp. of Marion County, Ind., 865 F.2d 797 (7th Cir. 1989) (defense of governmental entity's health ordinance against constitutional claims). ***PRACTICE AREAS:*** Business Litigation; Intellectual Property. ***Email:*** rknoth@bricker.com

SUZANNE KLENSMITH SAGANICH, born Detroit, Michigan, May 20, 1961; admitted to bar, 1987, Texas; 1998, Ohio. *Education:* Kalamazoo College (B.A., 1983); Case Western Reserve University (J.D, 1986). ***PRACTICE AREAS:*** Real Estate; Commercial Law; Mortgage Financing; Banking. ***Email:*** ssaganich@bricker.com

JAYNE L. JAKUBAITIS, born Cleveland, Ohio; admitted to bar, 1992, Ohio; 1993, U.S. District Court, Northern District of Ohio; 1997, U.S. Court of Appeals, Sixth Circuit; 1998, U.S. District Court, Northern and Southern Districts of Texas and U.S. Court of Appeals, Fifth and Eleventh Circuits; 2002, U.S. District Court, Eastern District of Michigan; 2004, Texas. *Education:* University of Notre Dame (B.A., 1979); Cleveland-Marshall College of Law (J.D., 1992). ***PRACTICE AREAS:*** Business Litigation; Intellectual Property. ***Email:*** jjakubaitis@bricker.com

OF COUNSEL

BREADEN M. DOUTHETT, born Oak Hill, Ohio, July 31, 1966; admitted to bar, 1991, Ohio; U.S. District Court, Northern District of Ohio; U.S. Court of Appeals, Sixth Circuit; U.S. Supreme Court. *Education:* Denison University (B.A., 1988); Ohio State University (J.D., 1991). ***PRACTICE AREAS:*** Intellectual Property; Business Litigation. ***Email:*** bdouthett@bricker.com

JOEL S. HEISER, born Cleveland, Ohio, December 14, 1966; admitted to bar, 1994, Ohio; 1995, U.S. District Court, Northern District of Ohio; 1996, U.S. Court of Appeals, Sixth Circuit; 2002, U.S. Supreme Court. *Education:* American University (B.S.B.A., 1989); Thomas M. Cooley Law School (J.D., 1994). ***PRACTICE AREAS:*** Corporate Law; Energy; Public Finance; Secured Lending. ***Email:*** jheiser@bricker.com

---

MAURA L. BROZOVIC, born Canton, Ohio, March 11, 1973; admitted to bar, 2000, Ohio. *Education:* Case Western Reserve University (B.A., cum laude, 1995; J.D., 1998). ***PRACTICE AREAS:*** Business Litigation. ***Email:*** mbrozovic@bricker.com

(This Listing Continued)

JOSHUA M. MARKS, born Cleveland, Ohio, June 15, 1970; admitted to bar, 1996, Ohio; 1998, U.S. District Court, Northern District of Ohio and U.S. Court of Appeals, Sixth Circuit. *Education:* Ohio University (B.A., Management Information Systems; Business Law, cum laude, 1992); Cleveland-Marshall College of Law (J.D., 1996). ***PRACTICE AREAS:*** Intellectual Property; Business Litigation; Computer Law. ***Email:*** jmarks@bricker.com

MICHAEL J. MONTGOMERY, born Youngstown, Ohio, July 26, 1974; admitted to bar, 1999, Ohio. *Education:* The Ohio State University (B.A., magna cum laude, 1996; J.D., summa cum laude, 1999). ***PRACTICE AREAS:*** Litigation. ***Email:*** mmontgomery@bricker.com

REPRESENTATIVE CLIENTS: American Insurance Association; Association of Ohio Life Insurance Companies; Bank One Corp.; CEMEX, Inc.; City of Columbus; County of Franklin; Dayton City School District; Dublin City School District; Duke Energy Corporation; Fairfield Medical Center; Fifth Third Bank; General Motors Corporation; Kenyon College; The McGraw-Hill Companies, Inc.; MetLife Auto & Home; Morgan Stanley Dean Witter/Discover Financial Services, Inc.; Nationwide Insurance Enterprise; New Par/Verizon Wireless; Ohio Hospital Association; OhioHealth Corp.; Ohio Manufacturers' Association; PhRMA; The Ohio State University; Turner Construction Company; U.S. Bridge; Von Roll America, Inc.; Westfield Insurance Group; Whirlpool Corporation.

BRITTON, SMITH, PETERS & KALAIL CO., L.P.A.

SUMMIT ONE, SUITE 540
4700 ROCKSIDE ROAD
CLEVELAND, OHIO 44131-6814
Telephone: 216-642-0323
Facsimile: 216-642-0747
URL: http://www.ohioedlaw.com

Limited to the representation of boards of education in all aspects of Education Law, including School Law, Management Employment Law, Management Labor Law, Collective Bargaining, Employment Arbitration, School Board Defense, Defense Litigation, Special Education, Civil Rights Defense, General Liability Defense, Public Finance, Public Construction Law, Real Estate Valuation, Real Estate Tax Appeals, Workers' Compensation Defense.

MEMBERS OF THE FIRM

JOHN E. BRITTON, born Charleston, West Virginia, December 15, 1955; admitted to bar, 1981, Ohio, U.S. District Court, Northern District of Ohio and U.S. Court of Appeals, Sixth Circuit. *Education:* Valparaiso University (B.A., 1978); University of Toledo (J.D., 1981). Assistant Attorney General, State of Ohio, 1983-1984. *Member:* Akron and Ohio State Bar Associations; National School Boards Association Council of School Attorneys; Ohio Council of School Board Attorneys (Member, Executive Committee); Education Law Association. ***PRACTICE AREAS:*** Education Law; Special Education; Management Labor Law; Management Employment Law; Collective Bargaining. ***Email:*** jbritton@ohioedlaw.com

DAVID KANE SMITH, born Cleveland, Ohio, January 2, 1947; admitted to bar, 1984, Ohio, U.S. District Court, Northern and Southern Districts of Ohio and U.S. Court of Appeals, Sixth Circuit. *Education:* Case Western Reserve University (B.A., 1969); Cleveland State University (M.Ed., 1979); Cleveland-Marshall College of Law (J.D., magna cum laude, 1984). *Member:* Cleveland, Ohio State and American Bar Associations; Ohio Council of School Board Attorneys; Education Law Association; National School Board Association Council of School Attorneys; Defense Research Institute; Ohio Association of Civil Trial Attorneys. ***PRACTICE AREAS:*** Education Law; Management Employment Law; School Board Defense; Defense Litigation; Civil Rights Defense. ***Email:*** dsmith@ohioedlaw.com

SCOTT C. PETERS, born Cleveland, Ohio, January 16, 1967; admitted to bar, 1992, Ohio, U.S. District Court, Northern District of Ohio and U.S. Court of Appeals, Sixth Circuit. *Education:* Kenyon College (A.B., cum laude, 1989); Case Western Reserve University (J.D., 1992). Executive Editor, Case Western Reserve Journal of International Law, 1991-1992. *Member:* Cleveland, Ohio State and American Bar Associations; Ohio Council of School Board Attorneys; National School Boards Association Council of School Attorneys; Education Law Association. ***PRACTICE AREAS:*** Education Law; Management Employment Law; Management Labor Law; School Board Defense; Collective Bargaining; Special Education. ***Email:*** speters@ohioedlaw.com

KARRIE M. KALAIL, born Akron, Ohio, January 22, 1963; admitted to bar, 1988, Ohio and U.S. District Court, Northern District of Ohio. *Education:* Ohio University (B.A., cum laude, 1985); University of Akron (J.D., 1988). Member, 1986-1987; Case and Comment Editor, Akron Law Review. *Member:* Akron and Ohio State Bar Associations; Ohio Council of School Board Attorneys; National Association of Educational Negotiators. ***PRACTICE AREAS:*** Education Law; Management Labor Law; Public Construction Law; Real Estate Valuation; Real Estate Tax Appeals. ***Email:*** kkalail@ohioedlaw.com

KRISTA K. KEIM, born Youngstown, Ohio, July 7, 1971; admitted to bar, 1996, Ohio, U.S. District Court, Northern and Southern Districts of Ohio and U.S. Court of Appeals, Sixth Circuit. *Education:* Miami University (B.A., 1993); Case Western Reserve University (J.D., 1996). *Member:* Cleveland and Ohio State Bar Associations; Ohio Council of School Board Attorneys. ***PRACTICE AREAS:*** Education Law; Management Employment Law; School Board Defense; Civil Rights Defense; Workers Compensation. ***Email:*** kkeim@ohioedlaw.com

DAVID H. SEED, born Cleveland, Ohio, May 19, 1968; admitted to bar, 1996, Ohio. *Education:* Kenyon College (A.B., 1990); Case Western Reserve University (M.B.A., 1992); Cleveland State University (J.D., 1995). Beta Gamma Sigma (Case Western Reserve University). *Member:* Cleveland (Member, Taxation and Probate Sections), Ohio State (Member, Taxation, Probate and Estate Planning Sections) Bar Associations; Ohio Council of School Board Attorneys. ***PRACTICE AREAS:*** Education Law; Real Estate Valuation; Real Estate Tax Appeals; Public Finance. ***Email:*** dseed@ohioedlaw.com

ASSOCIATES

JOSEPH W. BOATWRIGHT, IV, born Richmond, Virginia, April 14, 1980; admitted to bar, 2004, Ohio and U.S. District Court, Northern District of Ohio; 2005, U.S. District Court, Southern District of Ohio. *Education:* George Mason University (B.A., 2001); William & Mary School of Law (J.D., 2004). Member, William and Mary Environmental Law and Policy Review. *Member:* Cleveland and Ohio State Bar Associations. ***PRACTICE AREAS:*** Education Law; Labor and Employment; Litigation. ***Email:*** jboatwright@ohioedlaw.com

SHERRIE D. CLAYBORNE, born Cleveland, Ohio, November 25, 1969; admitted to bar, 1996, Ohio; 1999, District of Columbia, U.S. District Court, Northern District of Ohio and U.S. Court of Appeals, Sixth Circuit. *Education:* College of Wooster (B.A., 1992); The Ohio State University (J.D., 1995). *Member:* Cleveland and Ohio State Bar Associations; District of Columbia; Ohio Council of School Board Attorneys. ***PRACTICE AREAS:*** Education Law; Management Employment Law; Management Labor Law; Special Education; Workers Compensation Defense. ***Email:*** sclayborne@ohioedlaw.com

LORI A. KOSAKOWSKI, born Parma, Ohio, September 4, 1978; admitted to bar, 2003, Ohio. *Education:* Baldwin-Wallace College (B.A., 2000); Valparaiso University School of Law (J.D., 2003). Associate Editor, Valparaiso University Law Review. *Member:* Cuyahoga County, Ohio State and American Bar Associations. ***PRACTICE AREAS:*** Education Law; Management Employment Law; Management Labor Law; School Board Defense; Collective Bargaining. ***Email:*** lkosakowski@ohioedlaw.com

DAVID A. ROSE, born Bridgeport, Connecticut, August 14, 1975; admitted to bar, 2001, Ohio; U.s. District Court, Northern District of Ohio; U.S. Court of Appeals, Sixth Circuit. *Education:* Providence College (B.A., 1997); University of Toledo (J.D., 2000). *Member:* Cleveland, Ohio State and American Bar Associations; Ohio Council of School Board Attorneys. ***PRACTICE AREAS:*** Education Law; Real Estate Valuation; Management Employment Law. ***Email:*** drose@ohioedlaw.com

MICHAEL E. STINN, born Ft. Smith, Arkansas, October 12, 1958; admitted to bar, 1984, Ohio; 1985, U.S. District Court, Northern District of Ohio. *Education:* Georgetown University (B.S., 1980); Cleveland-Marshall College of Law (J.D., 1984). Member, Ohio Council of School Board Attorneys. Treasurer, Georgetown University Alumni Club of Cleveland. Member, Advisory Board, Cleveland Schools Special Olympic Program. *Member:* Cleveland Bar Association (Member, Litigation Council). ***PRACTICE AREAS:*** Personal Injury Defense; Employment Discrimination Defense; Insurance Defense; Worker's Compensation Defense; Probate Defense. ***Email:*** mstinn@ohioedlaw.com

BROUSE McDOWELL

A LEGAL PROFESSIONAL ASSOCIATION
Established in 1919
1001 LAKESIDE AVENUE, SUITE 1600
CLEVELAND, OHIO 44114
Telephone: 216-830-6830
Toll Free: 877-837-5711
Telex: 216-830-6807
Email: brouse@brouse.com
URL: http://www.brouse.com

Akron, Ohio Office: 388 S. Main Street, Suite 500. Telephone: 330-535-5711. Toll Free: 800-837-5711. Facsimile: 330-253-8601. URL: http://www.brouse.com.

Administrative, Bankruptcy, Business, Business Litigation, Commercial, Corporation, Creative Technologies, Creditors' Rights, E-Commerce, Environmental, Estate Planning, Federal Securities, General Civil, Health Care, Immigration, Insurance, Intellectual Property, Labor and Employment, Litigation, Mediation, Mergers and Acquisitions, Municipal and Bond, OSHA Compliance, Probate, Real Estate, Succession Planning, Tax, Trademarks, Trial and Appellate Practice, Venture Capital.

FIRM PROFILE: Brouse McDowell is particularly noted for its experience in the areas of business, commercial law, insurance recovery litigation, and environmental compliance and litigation. The firm has a strong business practice, assisting clients with public and private debt, equity offerings, securities law compliance, venture capital arrangements, joint ventures and mergers, acquisitions and divestitures. The firm has an equally strong commercial law practice, including creditors' rights and debtors' protection issues, loan workouts, restructuring strategies, and the implications of creditors' rights issues in leveraged buy-outs. In addition, the firm has a national health care practice, representing hospitals, physician practice groups, and other health care providers.

SHAREHOLDERS

LINDA L. BLUSO, born Cleveland, Ohio, September 25, 1954; admitted to bar, 1982, Ohio and U.S. District Court, Northern District of Ohio; 1986, U.S. Supreme Court. *Education:* Cleveland State University (B.A., magna cum laude, 1979; J.D., 1982). (Resident). ***PRACTICE AREAS:*** Business; Corporate; Real Estate; Commercial. ***Email:*** lbluso@brouse.com

CHRISTOPHER J. CARNEY, born Cleveland, Ohio, June 1, 1961; admitted to bar, 1986, Ohio; U.S. District Court, Northern and Southern Districts of Ohio; U.S. Court of Appeals, 6th Circuit. *Education:* John Carroll University (B.A., 1983); Case Western Reserve University (J.D., 1986). (Resident). ***PRACTICE AREAS:*** Litigation; Labor and Employment; OSHA. ***Email:*** ccarney@brouse.com

JOSEPH T. DATTILO, born Italy, 1948; admitted to bar, 1973, Ohio; U.S. District Court, Northern District of Ohio; U.S. District Court, Western District of Pennsylvania; U.S. District Court, Central District of Illinois; U.S. Court of Appeals, Third, Fourth, Sixth and Seventh Circuits; U.S. Supreme Court. *Education:* Kent State University (B.A., 1970); The Ohio State University (J.D., 1973). (Resident). ***PRACTICE AREAS:*** Litigation; Environmental. ***Email:*** jdattilo@brouse.com

MS. KEVEN DRUMMOND EIBER, born Elyria, Ohio, July 26, 1958; admitted to bar, 1983, District of Columbia; 1985, Maryland; 1990, Ohio; U.S. District Court, Northern District of Ohio; U.S. District Court for the District of Columbia; U.S. Court of Appeals,

(This Listing Continued)

BROUSE McDOWELL, A LEGAL PROFESSIONAL ASSOCIATION, Cleveland—Continued

Fourth and Sixth Circuits. *Education:* Michigan State University; University of Illinois (B.A., 1980); American University (J.D., 1983). (Resident). ***PRACTICE AREAS:*** Environmental; Litigation. ***Email:*** keiber@brouse.com

CATHRYN R. ENSIGN, born Uniontown, Pennsylvania, November 12, 1954; admitted to bar, 1986, Ohio; U.S. District Court, Northern District of Ohio; U.S. Supreme Court. *Education:* Cleveland State University (B.A., 1981); Cleveland-Marshall College of Law (J.D., 1986). (Resident). ***PRACTICE AREAS:*** Labor and Employment; Banking; Bankruptcy; Creditors Rights. ***Email:*** censign@brouse.com

PATRICIA A. GAJDA, born Cleveland, Ohio, January 18, 1965; admitted to bar, 1990, Ohio. *Education:* John Carroll University (B.S.B.A., Economics, magna cum laude, 1987); Case Western Reserve University (J.D., magna cum laude, 1990). (Resident). ***PRACTICE AREAS:*** Business; Corporate. ***Email:*** pgajda@brouse.com

THOMAS A. GATTOZZI, born Cleveland, Ohio, December 14, 1968; admitted to bar, 1994, Ohio; U.S. District Court, Nothern District of Ohio. *Education:* University of Pennsylvania (B.A., English, 1991); Case Western Reserve University (J.D., 1994). (Resident). ***PRACTICE AREAS:*** Real Estate; Business; Corporate. ***Email:*** tgattozzi@brouse.com

ALAN M. KOSCHIK, born Detroit, Michigan, October 2, 1961; admitted to bar, 1989, California; 1996, Ohio; U.S. District Court, Nothern District of Ohio; U.S. District Court, Northern, Eastern, Central and Southern Districts of California; U.S. District Court, District of Arizona. *Education:* University of Michigan (B.A., with high distinction, 1983; M.P.P., 1987; J.D., cum laude, 1987). (Resident). ***PRACTICE AREAS:*** Banking; Bankruptcy; Creditors Rights; Commercial. ***Email:*** akoschik@brouse.com

DAVID A. LUM, born Cleveland, Ohio, May 21, 1969; admitted to bar, 1994, Ohio; U.S. District Court, Northern District of Ohio. *Education:* Tufts University of Massachusetts (B.A., English, 1991); Case Western Reserve University (J.D., cum laude, 1994). (Resident). ***PRACTICE AREAS:*** Real Estate; Business; Corporate. ***Email:*** dlum@brouse.com

CHARLES D. PRICE, born Cleveland, Ohio, October 14, 1969; admitted to bar, 1995, Ohio; U.S. District Court, Northern District of Ohio. *Education:* University of Dayton (B.S., magna cum laude, 1992); Case Western Reserve University (J.D., 1995). (Resident). ***PRACTICE AREAS:*** Environmental; Litigation. ***Email:*** cprice@brouse.com

JESSICA E. PRICE, born Cleveland, Ohio, July 13, 1972; admitted to bar, 1997, Ohio; U.S. District Court, Northern District of Ohio. *Education:* Miami University (B.A., 1994); Ohio Northern University (J.D., with distinction, 1997). (Resident). ***PRACTICE AREAS:*** Commercial. ***Email:*** jprice@brouse.com

THOMAS J. UBBING, born Columbus, Ohio, November 1, 1957; admitted to bar, 1985, Ohio; U.S. District Court, Nothern District of Ohio. *Education:* Ohio State University (B.S., 1980); University of Toledo College of Law (J.D., cum laude, 1984). (Resident). ***PRACTICE AREAS:*** Tax; Business; Corporate. ***Email:*** tubbing@brouse.com

ROBERT M. WALTER, born Somerset, Pennsylvania, August 5, 1947; admitted to bar, 1972, Pennsylvania; 1981, Ohio. *Education:* Pennsylvania State University (B.A., magna cum laude, 1969); University of Pennsylvania (J.D., cum laude, 1972). ***PRACTICE AREAS:*** Environmental. ***Email:*** rwalter@brouse.com

TIMOTHY D. WOOD, born Cleveland, Ohio, June 12, 1942; admitted to bar, 1972, Ohio, U.S. District Court, Northern District of Ohio; and U.S. Court of Appeals, Second and Sixth Circuits. *Education:* Muskingum College (B.A., 1964); Cleveland Marshall College of Law (J.D., 1972). (Resident). ***PRACTICE AREAS:*** Labor and Employment; Employment Law; Employment Litigation; Labor Negotiaions; Union Elections; Personal Policies; Best Practices; Public Sector. ***Email:*** twood@brouse.com

---

MICHAEL C. BRINK, born Toledo, Ohio, September 12, 1976; admitted to bar, 2003, Ohio. (Resident)

MICHAEL P. O'DONNELL, admitted to bar, 2004, Ohio. *Education:* John Carroll University (B.S.B.A., Finance, 2001); Cleveland-Marshall College of Law (J.D., summa cum laude, 2004). ***PRACTICE AREAS:*** Commercial Law; Litigation. ***Email:*** modonnell@brouse.com

OF COUNSEL

THEODORE A. WARD, born Cleveland, Ohio, March 21, 1946; admitted to bar, 1971, Ohio. *Education:* Denison University (B.A., 1968); Case Western Reserve University School of Law (J.D., 1971). ***PRACTICE AREAS:*** Health Care. ***Email:*** tward@brouse.com

COUNSEL FOR: A. Schulman, Inc.; Americhem, Inc.; Bekaert Corporation; Goodrich Company; BP Amoco Corporation; Centers for Dialysis Care; Children's Hospital Medical Center of Akron; Electrolux; FirstEnergy Corp.; The Goodyear Tire & Rubber Co.; The Lubrizol Corp.; Myers Industries, Inc.; Sterling Jewelers, Inc.

(For complete biographical data on other personnel, see Professional Biographies at Akron, Ohio)

BROWN & SZALLER CO., L.P.A.

Established in 1979

14222 MADISON AVENUE
CLEVELAND, OHIO 44107-4510
Telephone: 216-228-7200
Fax: 216-228-7207
URL: http://www.lawandhelp.com
Email: atty@lawandhelp.com
URL: http://www.lawyers.com/brownszaller

General Civil Trial and Appellate Practice. Personal Injury, Accidents, Products Liability and Medical Malpractice Law.

(This Listing Continued)

JAMES F. SZALLER, born Cleveland, Ohio, January 22, 1945; admitted to bar, 1975, Ohio and U.S. District Court, Northern District of Ohio; 1982, U.S. Supreme Court; 1983, U.S. Court of Appeals, Sixth Circuit; 1986, U.S. Court of Appeals, Fourth Circuit. *Education:* Cleveland State University (B.A., 1970; J.D., cum laude, 1975). Honorary Member, Who's Who In Practicing Attorney's, 1990; Who's Who in American Law, 7th Edition (1992-1993); Who's Who in American Law, 8th Edition (1994-1995); Who's Who in American Law, 9th Edition (1996-1997); Who's Who in American Law, 10th Edition (1998-1999); Who's Who in American Law, 11th Edition (2000-2001); Who's Who in American Law, 12th Edition (2002-2003). Who's Who in the World, 11th Edition (1993-1994); Who's Who in the World, 12th Edition (1995-1996); Who's Who in the World, 17th Edition (2000); Who's Who in the World, 18th Edition (2002-2003). Recipient: Corpus Juris Secundum Award, Graduating Senior Contributing Most to Legal Scholarship, 1974; W.H. Anderson Co. Award for Most Meritorious Law Review Article, 1974-1975; Ohio Title Corporation Award, 1973; Sindell Tort Competition Award, 1974-1975; Law Review Outstanding Achievement Award (First Recipient of this Award), 1974-1975; Ohio Academy of Trial Lawyers Distinguished Service Award, 1996. Member, Editorial Board, The Cleveland State Law Review, 1973-1975. Editor and originator of Exegesis, Cuyahoga Bar Journal, 1973-1975. Advocate, National College of Advocacy, 1993. Lecturer on Law, Cleveland State University College of Law, 1977-1983. Amicus Curiae for ATLA and OATL in U.S. Supreme Court in *Reynoldsville Casket Co. v. Hyde,* 514 U.S. 749 (1995). *Member:* Cleveland and Ohio State Bar Associations; Cleveland Academy of Trial Lawyers; Ohio Academy of Trial Attorneys; The Association of Trial Lawyers of America (Treasurer, Propulsid Litigation Group, 2001—;Co-Chair, Baycol Litigation Group, 2002—). ***Email:*** szaller@lawandhelp.com

KENNETH J. KNABE, born Bay Village, Ohio, January 21, 1954; admitted to bar, 1979, Ohio and U.S. District Court, Northern District of Ohio; 1981, Florida. *Education:* University of Cincinnati (B.A., summa cum laude, 1976); Cleveland-Marshall College of Law (J.D., cum laude, 1979). Recipient, Charles Auerbach Memorial Award for Outstanding Student in the Law of Evidence, Cleveland-Marshall College of Law, 1977. *Member:* Cleveland, Ohio State and American Bar Associations; The Florida Bar; Cleveland Academy of Trial Lawyers (Treasurer, 2000-2001; Vice President, 2001-2002; President, 2002-2003); Ohio Academy of Trial Attorneys (Lecturer). ***Email:*** knabe@lawandhelp.com

REFERENCE: Fifth Third Bank.

BROWNER AND HENDERSON LLC

THE LEADER BUILDING
526 SUPERIOR AVENUE EAST, SUITE 545
CLEVELAND, OHIO 44114
Telephone: 216-774-0000
Fax: 216-774-0493
URL: http://www.lawyers.com/brownerandhenderson

Consumer Bankruptcy, Civil Litigation, Collections, Business Formation, Criminal Law, Real Estate.

MEMBERS OF FIRM

JEREMY TODD BROWNER, born Albany, New York, June 10, 1975; admitted to bar, 2002, New York and U.S. District Court, Northern District of Ohio; 2003, Ohio. *Education:* Embry-Riddle Aeronautical University (B.S., 1997); Hofstra University (J.D., 2001). Member, Certified Grievance Committee, 2003—. *Member:* Cuyahoga County, Cleveland and Ohio State Bar Associations. ***PRACTICE AREAS:*** Consumer Bankruptcy; Plaintiff Civil Litigation; Civil Litigation Defense; Collections; Business Formation. ***Email:*** brownerhenderson@sbcglobal.net

BRANDON HENDERSON, born Cleveland, Ohio, July 21, 1976; admitted to bar, 2002, Ohio; 2004, U.S. District Court, Northern District of Ohio. *Education:* Ohio University (B.A., 1998); Case Western Reserve University (J.D., 2001). *Member:* Cuyahoga County and Ohio State Bar Associations; Cuyahoga Criminal Defense Lawyers Association. ***PRACTICE AREAS:*** Criminal Law (70%); Civil Litigation (15%); Real Estate (15%). ***Email:*** brownerhenderson@sbcglobal.net

THE BRUNN LAW FIRM CO., LPA

700 WEST ST. CLAIR AVENUE, SUITE 208
CLEVELAND, OHIO 44113-1230
Telephone: 216-623-7300
Fax: 216-623-7330
Email: brunn@core.com

Medical Malpractice, Product Liability, Litigation.

THOMAS L. BRUNN, SR., born Ionia, Michigan, March 14, 1937; admitted to bar, 1967, Ohio. *Education:* John Carroll University (B.S., 1959); Cleveland-Marshall Law School (J.D., 1967). Author: "Manufacturers Duty to Warn," Federation of Insurance and Corporate Counsel Quarterly, vol. 44, No. 4. *Member:* Cuyahoga County and American Bar Associations; Eighth Judicial Conference (Life Delegate); Federation of Defense and Corporate Counsel (Vice Chair, Products Liability Section); Cleveland Association of Civil Trial Attorneys (President, 1982-1983); Ohio Association of Civil Trial Attorneys; Defense Research Institute; Trial Lawyers Association. ***PRACTICE AREAS:*** Civil Litigation; Product Liability; Medical Malpractice. ***Email:*** brunn@core.com

THOMAS L. BRUNN, JR., born Cleveland, Ohio, July 1, 1964; admitted to bar, 1989, Ohio; 1992, U.S. District Court, Northern District of Ohio. *Education:* John Carroll University (B.A., 1986); Cleveland Marshall College of Law (J.D., 1989). Life Delegate, Eighth Judicial Conference. *Member:* Cleveland and Ohio State Bar Associations' Ohio Academy of Trial Lawyers; The Association of Trial Lawyers of America. ***PRACTICE AREAS:*** Civil Litigation; Medical Malpractice; Product Liability. ***Email:*** brunn@core.com

(This Listing Continued)

ALISON D. RAMSEY, born Cleveland, Ohio, November 11, 1976; admitted to bar, 2004, Ohio. *Education:* University of Michigan, Ann Arbor (B.A., 1998); Case Western Reserve University (J.D., cum laude, 2004). Phi Beta Kappa. *Member:* Cleveland and Ohio State Bar Associations. ***LANGUAGES:*** Spanish. ***PRACTICE AREAS:*** Civil Litigation; Products Liability; Medical Malpractice. ***Email:*** brunn@core.com

BRZYTWA, QUICK & McCRYSTAL, LLC

900 SKYLIGHT OFFICE TOWER
1660 WEST SECOND STREET
CLEVELAND, OHIO 44113-1411
Telephone: 216-664-6900
Fax: 216-664-6901
Email: METZLER@BQMLAW.COM
URL: http://www.bqmlaw.com

Litigation, Alternative Dispute Resolution, Appellate Practice, Torts, Toxic Tort Defense, Products Liability, Aviation Litigation, Medical Malpractice, Professional Malpractice, Legal Ethics, Personal Injury, Commercial Litigation, Trade Regulation, Banking Litigation, Business Law, Construction Law, Contracts, Intellectual Property Litigation, Insurance Litigation, Insurance Coverage and Constitutional Law.

FIRM PROFILE: Brzytwa, Quick & McCrystal, LLC is a firm respected for its expertise in the trial of lawsuits throughout the United States. The firm was established in 1994 and specializes in litigation and dispute resolution with emphasis on products liability defense, aviation litigation, construction litigation, professional liability defense, business litigation, and intellectual property litigation.

MEMBERS OF FIRM

E. JOHN BRZYTWA, born Cleveland, Ohio, January 19, 1943; admitted to bar, 1968, Ohio. *Education:* Baldwin-Wallace College (B.A., 1965); Georgetown University (J.D., 1968). ***PRACTICE AREAS:*** Aviation Litigation; Intellectual Property Litigation; Commercial Litigation; Products Liability. ***Email:*** BRZYTWA@BQMLAW.COM

HARRY T. QUICK, born Cleveland, Ohio, August 27, 1939; admitted to bar, 1965, Ohio. *Education:* John Carroll University (B.S. in S.S., 1962); Case Western Reserve University (J.D., 1965). ***PRACTICE AREAS:*** Litigation; Products Liability; Medical Malpractice; Toxic Tort Defense; Commercial Litigation. ***Email:*** QUICK@BQMLAW.COM

JAMES L. McCRYSTAL, JR., born Sandusky, Ohio, November 6, 1948; admitted to bar, 1973, Ohio. *Education:* John Carroll University (A.B., 1970); University of Notre Dame (J.D., 1973). ***PRACTICE AREAS:*** Alternative Dispute Resolution; Products Liability; Medical Malpractice; Professional Liability; Commercial Litigation; Business Torts; Insurance Coverage; Toxic Tort Defense. ***Email:*** MCCRYSTAL@BQMLAW.COM

DANIEL F. PETTICORD, born Amherst, Ohio, January 6, 1968; admitted to bar, 1992, Ohio. *Education:* Bucknell University (B.A., 1989); Cleveland Marshall College of Law (J.D., cum laude, 1992). ***PRACTICE AREAS:*** Litigation; Medical Malpractice; Intellectual Property Litigation; Toxic Tort Defense; Products Liability. ***Email:*** PETTICORD@BQMLAW.COM

ASSOCIATES

ROBERT E. CAHILL, born Cleveland, Ohio, March 4, 1974; admitted to bar, 2000, Ohio. *Education:* University of Notre Dame (B.A., cum laude, 1997); Case Western Reserve University (J.D., 2000). ***PRACTICE AREAS:*** Litigation; Products Liability; Personal Injury Defense; Aviation Litigation; Commercial Litigation; Professional Liability. ***Email:*** CAHILL@BQMLAW.COM

BETH M. ADAMS, born Cleveland, Ohio, May 8, 1976; admitted to bar, 2002, Ohio. *Education:* Baldwin-Wallace College (B.A., 1998); Cleveland-Marshall College of Law (J.D.; M.B.A., 2001). Member, Ohio State Bar Association, 2002. *Member:* Cleveland Bar Association. ***PRACTICE AREAS:*** Litigation; Products Liability; Toxic Tort Defense. ***Email:*** adams@bqmlaw.com

BUCKINGHAM, DOOLITTLE & BURROUGHS, LLP

Established in 1990

1375 EAST NINTH STREET, SUITE 1700
CLEVELAND, OHIO 44114
Telephone: 216-621-5300; Toll Free: 1-888-843-2825
Fax: 216-621-5440
Email: bdb@bdblaw.com
URL: http://www.bdblaw.com

Akron, Ohio Office: 50 South Main Street, P.O. Box 1500, 44309-1500. Telephone: 330-376-5300. Toll Free: 800-686-2825. Fax: 330-258-6559.
Canton, Ohio Office: 4518 Fulton Drive Northwest, P.O. Box 35548, 44735-5548. Telephone: 330-492-8717. Toll Free: 888-811-2825. Fax: 330-492-9625.
Columbus, Ohio Office: 191 West Nationwide Boulevard, 43215-3506. Telephone: 614-221-8448. Toll Free: 888-686-2825. Fax: 614-221-8590.
Boca Raton, Florida Office: 2500 North Military Trail, Suite 480, 33431. Telephone: 561-241-0414. Toll Free: 800-682-2825. Fax: 561-241-9766.

Appellate, Closely Held Companies, Commercial Law and Litigation, Computer and Technology, Construction Law, Copyrights, Corporate and Business, Creditors Rights/Bankruptcy, Criminal Law, Employment Law, Environmental, Estate Planning, Family Law, Finance and Public Law, Franchise, Health Care, Immigration Law, Insurance Defense, Intellectual Property, Labor and Employment, Land Use and Zoning, Medical Malpractice Defense, Mergers and Acquisitions, Patents, Probate, Publicly Held Companies, Real Estate, School Law, Securities, Succession Planning, Taxation and Employee Benefits, Toxic Tort/Complex Litigation, Trademarks/Service Marks, Trade Secrets, Trial, Trusts and Estates, Venture Capital/Emerging Companies, Workers' Compensation.

FIRM PROFILE: Established in 1913, Buckingham, Doolittle & Burroughs, LLP is a full-service law firm with offices in Akron, Cleveland, Canton and Columbus, Ohio and Boca Raton, Florida. Its attorneys represent clients from the sole proprietor to multinational corporations, tax-exempt organizations, governmental bodies, charities, foundations and public organizations.

The focus of the Firm's corporate practice is on legal issues affecting closely held businesses including start-up joint ventures, agreements among shareholders, corporate reorganization and business contracts. Buckingham attorneys have expertise in mergers and acquisitions, intellectual property, succession planning and related areas of significance to rapidly expanding business organizations and also provide trusts and estates and probate services to individual clients.

The Litigation Practice of Buckingham, Doolittle & Burroughs, LLP has steadily grown to meet the increasingly complex legal demands of the Firm's clients. Areas of focus include appellate, commercial law and litigation, construction, domestic relations, employment, school law, medical malpractice and workers' compensation. The Firm is committed to finding innovative solutions to clients' legal problems. The breadth of its practice in all forums often enables the Firm to avoid disputes by providing legal guidance before problems arise.

Buckingham's clients are representative of virtually every industry and trade, including transportation, food production, chemical manufacturing and distribution, rubber and tire manufacturing, technology, automotive, steel, agriculture and horticulture, financial and banking, insurance and medical, accounting and other professional practices.

MANAGING PARTNER

RONALD M. WILT, born Bluffton, Ohio, December 30, 1965; admitted to bar, 1992, Ohio; 1994, Kentucky. *Education:* Earlham College (B.A., with honors, 1988); University of Cincinnati (J.D., 1992). Scholastic Distinctions: University of Cincinnati, Moot Court Board; John W. Peck Trial Practice Award. *Member:* Cleveland, Ohio State and Kentucky Bar Associations. ***PRACTICE AREAS:*** Medical Malpractice Defense; Litigation. ***Email:*** RWilt@bdblaw.com

SHAREHOLDERS

GERALD B. CHATTMAN, born Cleveland, Ohio, September 15, 1942; admitted to bar, 1967, Ohio. *Education:* University of Michigan (B.A., cum laude, 1964); Case Western Reserve University (J.D., 1967). Listed in Best Lawyers in America, 2001-2002; 2003-2004, 2005-2006 and given special Award for being recognized for 20 Years or more. Recognized as one of Ohio Super Lawyers in 2004 and 2005 Cincinnati Magazine, as voted by his peers. Member, Cleveland State University, Cleveland Marshall College of Law Visiting Committee. Member, Labor Arbitration Panel, American Arbitration Association; Federal Mediation and Conciliation Service (Member, Labor Arbitration Panel, 1973—); Institute for the Elimination of Workplace Violence. Visiting Associate Professor, Evidence, and Instructor, Research and Writing, Administrative Law and Trial Practice, Case Western Reserve School of Law. Adjunct Professor, Trial Advocacy and Labor Arbitration, Cleveland State University Cleveland-Marshall College of Law. *Member:* Cleveland, Ohio State and American Bar Associations. ***PRACTICE AREAS:*** Labor Law; Corporate Law; Nonprofit Organizations Law. ***Email:*** gchattman@bdblaw.com

ALAN P. DIGIROLAMO, born Akron, Ohio, November 17, 1963; admitted to bar, 1989, Ohio. *Education:* Arizona State University (B.S., cum laude, 1985); Case Western Reserve University (J.D., 1989). *Member:* Akron, Cleveland, Ohio State and American Bar Associations. ***PRACTICE AREAS:*** Commercial Litigation; Bankruptcy; Collections. ***Email:*** adigirolamo@bdblaw.com

DAVID L. DRECHSLER, born Beachwood, Ohio, September 2, 1963; admitted to bar, 1989, Ohio. *Education:* Ohio State University (B.S., 1986); Case Western Reserve University (J.D., cum laude, 1989). *Member:* Cleveland, Akron, Ohio State and American Bar Associations. ***PRACTICE AREAS:*** Commercial Litigation; Probate Litigation; Intellectual Property Litigation; Federal Litigation; Complex Litigation; Employment Litigation. ***Email:*** DDrechsler@bdblaw.com

ROBERT A. HAGER, born September 21, 1962; admitted to bar, 1988, Ohio and U.S. District Court, Northern District of Ohio; 1991, U.S. Court of Appeals, Sixth Circuit; 1997, U.S. Supreme Court. *Education:* John Carroll University (B.A., 1985); Cleveland-Marshall College of Law (J.D., cum laude, 1988). Listed in: The Best Lawyers in America, 2003-2006; Recognized as one of Ohio's Super Lawyers, 2004-2005, as voted by his peers. Vice-Chair, Board of Regents, John Carroll University. President's Council, Board of Trustees, Walsh Jesuit High School. Member, Executive Committee and Past President, Lawyers' Guild for the Catholic Diocese of Cleveland. Frequent lecturer and author relating to construction law issues. Expert witness in various construction litigation matters. Member: Associated General Contractors of Ohio; Associated Builders and Contractors; American Institute of Constructors. *Member:* Cleveland, Ohio State (Chair, Construction Law Committee) and American (Member: Forum on the Construction Industry; Litigation Section; Construction Litigation Committee) Bar Associations. ***PRACTICE AREAS:*** Commercial Litigation (50%); Construction Law; Construction Litigation (50%). ***Email:*** BHager@bdblaw.com

WILLIAM B. LEAHY, born Detroit, Michigan, November 2, 1943; admitted to bar, 1968, Ohio; U.S. District Court, Northern District of Ohio; U.S. Supreme Court; U.S. Court of Appeals, Third, Fourth and Sixth Circuits. *Education:* The Ohio State University (B.A., 1965; J.D., 1968). National Moot Court Team, The Ohio State University College of Law, 1967-1968. Listed: Best Lawyers in America, 1997-2006; Ohio Super Lawyer in the 2004 and 2005 Law & Politics, Inc., as recognized by his peers. U.S. Army Judge Advocate General's Corps, 1969-1973 (principally prosecuted felony cases). Adjunct Professor of Law, teaching pre-trial practice to third year law students, Case Western Reserve University School of Law. Author, articles in National Law Journal; CPR Institute publication, *Alter-*

(This Listing Continued)

BUCKINGHAM, DOOLITTLE & BURROUGHS, LLP, Cleveland—Continued

natives; Defense Research Institute publication, *For the Defense;* Crain's Cleveland Business. Presenter at U.S. District Court, Northern District of Ohio, beginner and advanced courses for ADR neutrals and instructor on the subject of alternative dispute resolution for Ohio CLE Institute. Judge, CPR Institute Awards for Excellence in ADR; former President and Executive Vice-President, present Lifetime Trustee, Retired and Senior Volunteer Program of Greater Cleveland, Inc.; Past President, Western Reserve Area Agency on Aging. Member, Product Liability Committee, CPR Institute for Dispute Resolution. Panel Member, Distiguished Neutrals, CPR Institute. Mediator: Federal Court Panel of Alternate Dispute Resolution Neutrals; Court of Common Pleas, Cuyahoga County. Past Clerk of Session, Fairmount Presbyterian Church; Past Chair, Board of Trustees, Fairmount Presbyterian Church. *Member:* Ohio State Bar Association; Cleveland Bar Association; Defense Research Institute. ***LANGUAGES:*** Spanish. ***TRANSACTIONS:*** Besides appearing as trial and appellate counsel in numerous Ohio state and federal courts, has been admitted pro hac vice as trial or appellate counsel in 24 states and numerous out-of-state federal courts; has represented numerous product manufacturers in numerous jurisdictions; has appeared as counsel in arbitrations, mediations and other alternative dispute resolution proceedings in nine states. ***PRACTICE AREAS:*** Litigation; Insurance Coverage; Products Liability; Torts; Commercial Litigation; Construction Litigation; Alternative Dispute Resolution; Mediation. ***Email:*** wleahy@bdblaw.com

DOUGLAS J. PAUL, born Newark, New Jersey, October 16, 1949; admitted to bar, 1974, Ohio and U.S. District Court, Northern District of Ohio; 1979, U.S. Court of Appeals, Sixth Circuit; U.S. Supreme Court; U.S. Tax Court. *Education:* Johns Hopkins University (B.A., 1971); Case Western Reserve University (J.D., 1974). Member, National Moot Court Team, 1972-1973. Associate Editor, Case Western Reserve Law Review, 1972-1973. Adjunct Faculty Member, Trial Advocacy, Cleveland-Marshall College of Law. *Member:* Cleveland (Member, Certified Grievance Committee), Cuyahoga County and Ohio State Bar Associations. ***PRACTICE AREAS:*** Business Litigation; Employment Law; Restrictive Covenants; Mediation; Construction Litigation; Computer Law. ***Email:*** dpaul@bdblaw.com

DIRK E. RIEMENSCHNEIDER, born Lakewood, Ohio, May 29, 1966; admitted to bar, 1991, Ohio; 1992, U.S. District Court, Northern District of Ohio. *Education:* Baldwin Wallace College (B.A., 1988); Cleveland Marshall College of Law (J.D., 1991). *Member:* Cleveland and Ohio State Bar Associations. ***PRACTICE AREAS:*** Trial Practice; Medical Malpractice. ***Email:*** DRiemenschneider@bdblaw.com

DEBORAH SESEK, born Cleveland, Ohio, November 19, 1950; admitted to bar, 1976, Ohio; 1987, California. *Education:* University of Dayton (B.A., 1972); University of Innsbruck, Austria; Cleveland State University (J.D., cum laude, 1976). Cleveland State Law Review. Listed in Best Lawyers in America, 1997-2006. Recognized as one of Ohio's Super Lawyers in the 2004 and 2005 Cincinnati Magazine, as voted by her peers. Member, Board of Advisors, Villa Angela-St. Joseph High School. Chairperson, 2002— and Member, Board of Trustees, Villa Angela-St. Joseph High School Education Endowment Fund. Chairperson, 1996— and Member, Board of Trustees, Our Lady of the Elms. *Member:* Cleveland, Akron, Ohio State (Past Chair: Worker's Compensation Law Committee; Seminar Subcommittee) and American Bar Associations; Ohio Self-Insurers Group. ***PRACTICE AREAS:*** Workers Compensation. ***Email:*** DSesek@bdblaw.com

JOHN P. SLAGTER, born Erie, Pennsylvania, March 31, 1966; admitted to bar, 1991, Ohio, U.S. District Court, Northern District of Ohio and U.S. Court of Appeals, 6th Circuit. *Education:* John Carroll University (B.A., 1988); Case Western Reserve University (J.D., 1991). Recognized as one of Ohio's Super Lawyers, Cincinnati Magazine, 2004, 2005 and 2006. Author, Articles on Real Estate & Construction Matters, Properties Magazine. Member: International Council of Shopping Centers; Home Builders Association of Summit and Portage Counties; Home Builders Association of Cleveland Suburban Counties; Land Use Council; Associated Builders and Contractors; American Institute of Contractors. Author: "U.S. Supreme Court Extends Reach of Eminent Domain"; Cleveland Bar Association Journal "U.S. Supreme Court Decides Landmark Eminent Domain Case"; "Mutual Mistake in the Calculation of the Square Footage of a Commercial Lease"; "The Power of Eminent Domain in Economic Revitalization Projects"; "Acceleration of Rent"; "Ohio's New Condominium Law: An Overview of the Changes"; "Yes, You Can Fight City Hall - When Zoning is a 'Regulatory Taking' "; "Can the Government Stop Development Without Compensating You?"; "Real Property Tax: Assessment and Appeals"; "Don't Forget About CAUV When Purchasing Real Estate"; "You Pick the Time and Place - I Will Be There! - Forum Selection Clauses in Commercial Leases"; "Rain, Rain, Go Away: Understanding Legal Issues Surrounding Control of Surface Water Runoff". Speaker: "House Bill 175: Changes to Current Practice," (Cleveland Bar Association); "Advanced Zoning and Land Use," (Lorman Education Seminar); "HBA Forms Seminar," (Home Builders Association of Summit and Portage Counties); "Construction Lien Law," (Lorman Education Seminar); "Land Use Law," (CLE International); "Mechanics' Lien Law and Fairness in Contracting Law" (American Society of Professional Estimators - Northeast Ohio Chapter); "The Legality of Impact Fees" (CLE International); "Zoning and Land Use" (Cleveland Bar Association); "Recent Judicial Decisions & Legislation" (Buckingham Real Estate & Construction Law Seminar); "Legal Aspects of Construction Law" (Associated Builders and Contractors); "Legal Issue Involving Ohio Local Governments" (National Business Institute); "Eminent Domain Update and Impact Fees" (Lorman Education Seminar); "Update on Township Zoning Law" (Lorman Education Seminar). *Member:* Cleveland (Member: Legal Fee Dispute Committee; Real Estate Section; Litigation Section), Ohio State (Member, Sections on: Real Estate; Litigation) and American (Member, Section on: Litigation; Real Property; Construction Law) Bar Associations. ***PRACTICE AREAS:*** Commercial Litigation; Real Estate; Construction Law; Zoning Law; Land Use. ***Email:*** JSlagter@bdblaw.com

TERRY W. VINCENT, born Akron, Ohio, 1955; admitted to bar, 1987, Ohio and U.S. Tax Court; U.S. District Court, Northern District of Ohio. *Education:* The University of Akron (B.S., summa cum laude, 1983); The University of Akron College of Business (M.A. in Taxation, 1986); The University of Akron School of Law (J.D., 1986). Former Adjunct Professor, LL.M. Tax Program, Case Western Reserve School of Law. Board Member: Harvest for Hunger - Allocations Committee; Executive Committee of the Lawyer's Guild, Catholic Diocese of Cleveland. Member: Lakewood Chamber of Commerce. Trustee, Partnership for a Safer Cleveland. *Member:* Ohio State Bar Association; Cleveland Bar Association. [United States Air Force]. (Former Managing Partner, Cleveland). ***PRACTICE AREAS:*** Taxation; Business Law; Public Finance; Litigation. ***Email:*** TVincent@bdblaw.com

RONALD F. WAYNE, born Cleveland, Ohio, July 9, 1953; admitted to bar, 1978, Ohio; 1979, U.S. District Court, Northern District of Ohio; 1990, U.S. Tax Court; 1994, New Jersey; 1995, Florida; 1998, U.S. Supreme Court. *Education:* Cleveland State University (B.A., magna cum laude, 1974); Cleveland Marshall College of Law, Cleveland State University (J.D., cum laude, 1978). Author, "Getting Back to Basics: What Estate Planning Clients Really Care About," Cleveland Bar Journal, June, 2003. Delegate, Estate Planning Council of Cleveland. *Member:* Cleveland and Ohio State Bar Associations; The Florida Bar. (Certified Specialist in Estate Planning, Trusts and Probate Law, Ohio State Bar Association). ***PRACTICE AREAS:*** Estate Planning; Trust Law; Probate. ***Email:*** rwayne@bdblaw.com

GRANT M. YOAKUM, born Delaware, Ohio, August 21, 1969; admitted to bar, 1994, Ohio; 1996, Florida. *Education:* University of Dayton (B.A., 1991); Cleveland-Marshall College of Law (J.D., cum laude, 1994). Member, Board of Trustees, Rebuilding Together, Summit County. Recognized as one of Ohio's Super Lawyers - Rising Stars, in the 2005 Cincinnati Magazine, as voted by his peers. ***PRACTICE AREAS:*** Real Estate; Business Law; Workers Compensation Defense. ***Email:*** GYoakum@bdblaw.com

PARTNERS

JOHN F. BALLARD, born Boston, Massachusetts, July 1, 1947; admitted to bar, 1978, Ohio; U.S. District Court, Northern District of Ohio; 1983, U.S. Tax Court. *Education:* Harvard University (B.A., magna cum laude, 1969); Case Western Reserve University (J.D., 1978). *Member:* Cleveland, Ohio State and American Bar Associations; National Association of Stock Plan Professionals. ***PRACTICE AREAS:*** Securities; Corporate Law; Mergers and Acquisitions; Closely Held Businesses. ***Email:*** JBallard@bdblaw.com

EDWARD C. COAXUM, JR., born Cleveland, Ohio; admitted to bar, 1971, Ohio; U.S. District Court, Northern District of Ohio; U.S. Court of Appeals, 6th Circuit. *Education:* Williams College (B.A., 1966); Boston University (J.D., 1969). Member: Board of Directors, American Automobile Association; Board of Elections, Cuyahoga County. Member, Board of Trustees, Past Chairman and Member, Corporate Board, AAA Ohio Motorists Association. Member, Governing Board, AAA East Central. Member, Commission on Racial Fairness, appointed by Chief Justice Thomas J. Moyer, Ohio Supreme Court. Past President, Society of Alumni, Williams College; Past Trustee, Greater Cleveland Roundtable. Member, Ohio Municipal Attorneys Association. Member, Investment and Growth Task Force, Greater Cleveland Partnership. Director of Law, City of Warrensville Heights. *Member:* Cleveland (Former Trustee and Former Vice Chair, Corporation, Banking and Business Law Committee, Securities Law Section; Vice Chair, Minority Outreach Committee), Ohio State and American (Member, Section on Corporate, Banking and Business Law) Bar Associations; National Association of Bond Lawyers. Life Member, Judicial Conference of the Eighth Judicial District of Ohio. ***PRACTICE AREAS:*** Business Law; Public Finance; Commercial Transactions; Municipal Law; Real Estate. ***Email:*** ecoaxum@bdblaw.com

LISA M. DEFILIPPIS, born Alexandria, Virginia, August 15, 1955; admitted to bar, 1986, Ohio. *Education:* University of Virginia (B.A., 1977); Suffolk University (J.D., cum laude, 1986). Member: Worldwide Employee Benefits Network, Cleveland Chapter; PTA Board, Roxboro Middle School. Member, Pension Committee and Insurance Committee, Buckingham, Doolittle & Burroughs. ***PRACTICE AREAS:*** ERISA; Employee Benefits. ***Email:*** LdeFilippis@bdblaw.com

PAUL A. DZENITIS, born Louisville, Kentucky, July 6, 1967; admitted to bar, 1994, Kentucky; 2003, Ohio. *Education:* Princeton University (B.A., 1989); University of Kentucky School of Law (J.D., 1994). Author, "Advice for the Doctor Defendant," Louisville Medicine, Volume 49, No. 6, November 2001. Recognized as one of Ohio's Super Lawyers - Rising Stars, in the 2005 Cincinnati Magazine, as voted by peers. *Member:* Ohio State Bar Association; Kentucky Bar Association. ***PRACTICE AREAS:*** Medical Malpractice. ***Email:*** pdzenitis@bdblaw.com

LAWRENCE FRIEDLANDER, born Cleveland, Ohio, October 6, 1940; admitted to bar, 1965, Ohio; 1966, U.S. District Court, Northern District of Ohio; 1973, U.S. Supreme Court; 1981, U.S. Court of Appeals, 6th Circuit. *Education:* Brandeis University (A.B., 1962); Boston College; Case Western Reserve University (J.D., 1965). *Member:* Greater Cleveland, Cuyahoga County and Ohio State Bar Associations. ***PRACTICE AREAS:*** Civil Litigation; Personal Injury; Negligence; Workers Compensation; Social Security; Elder Law; Administrative Hearings and Appeals; General Practice; Arbitration. ***Email:*** lfriedlander@bdblaw.com

DALE A. NOWAK, born Cleveland, Ohio, June 7, 1953; admitted to bar, 1980, Ohio; 1981, U.S. District Court, Northern District of Ohio. *Education:* Cleveland State University (B.A., cum laude, 1976); Cleveland Marshall College of Law, Cleveland State University (J.D., magna cum laude, 1980). Member, Law Review. Co-Author, "Multiple Convictions Statute in Ohio: Has it Achieved its Intended Result?" Cleveland State Law Review, Vol. 31, No. 2, 1982. Part Time Instructor, Cleveland Marshall College of Law, 1982. *Member:* Cleveland, Cuyahoga County and Ohio State Bar Associations. ***PRACTICE AREAS:*** Civil Litigation; Commercial Litigation; Appellate Litigation; Personal Injury; Workers Compensation. ***Email:*** dnowak@bdblaw.com

HENRY I. REDER, born Akron, Ohio, October 7, 1950; admitted to bar, 1979, Ohio; 1983, U.S. District Court, Northern District of Ohio; 2003, U.S. Court of Appeals, 6th Circuit. *Education:* International University of the Arts, Florence, Italy; Kent State University (B.Arch., cum laude, 1973); Cleveland-Marshall College of Law (J.D., 1979). Delta Theta Phi (Vice Dean for Evening Students); Tau Sigma Delta, 1978-1979. Recipient: Presidential Citation, American Institute of Architects, Ohio Chapter, 2003; Presidents Award for Outstanding Service, Cleveland Chapter, American Institute of Architects, 2001. Registered Architect, Ohio, 1976. Member, Editorial Advisory Staff, Code News. Member, Construction Specification Institute. Former Member, Construction Industry Affairs Council of Cleveland, Ohio. Commercial Panelist, Arbitrator, Large Complex Case Panel, 1979-2005 and Member, Advisory Committee, Construction Industry, 1993-2004, American Arbitra-

(This Listing Continued)

tion Association. *Member:* Geauga County, Ohio State (Member, Construction Law Subcommittee) and American (Member: Construction Law Forum; Construction Law Committee, Litigation Section) Bar Associations; American Institute of Architects (Member); AIA Ohio (Secretary, 2003-2004; President Elect, 2005; President, 2006; Member: Seal Law Task Force, 1995; Board of Directors, 1998-2002; Design Build Task Force, 1999-2004; Financial Oversight Committee, 2000-2003); AIA Cleveland (President, 1994 and Member, Board of Directors, 1998-2003, Cleveland Chapter). ***Email:*** hreder@bdblaw.com

ASSOCIATES

MARK F. CRAIG, born Akron, Ohio; admitted to bar, 2002, Ohio; 2003, U.S. District Court, Northern District of Ohio; 2004, U.S. Court of Appeals, Sixth and Federal Circuits. *Education:* Charleston Southern (B.A., magna cum laude, 1994); University of Akron School of Law (J.D., magna cum laude, 2001). Recognized as one of Ohio's Super Lawyers - Rising Stars in the 2005 Cincinnati Magazine, as voted by his peers. Member, University of Akron Law Review, 2000-2001. Board of Directors, Transitional Housing, Inc. *Member:* Cleveland, Ohio State and American Bar Associations. [U.S. Navy, 1990-1998]. ***PRACTICE AREAS:*** Construction Law; Litigation. ***Email:*** mcraig@bdblaw.com

CHRISTINE M. FARANDA, admitted to bar, 1996, Ohio. *Education:* Cleveland State University (B.B.A., 1992); Cleveland-Marshall College of Law (J.D., 1996). *Member:* Cleveland and Ohio State Bar Associations. ***PRACTICE AREAS:*** Workers' Compensation; Employment Law. ***Email:*** cfaranda@bdblaw.com

DAVID J. LINDNER, born Cleveland, Ohio, September 19, 1973; admitted to bar, 2001, Ohio. *Education:* The Ohio State University (B.A., magna cum laude, 1995; J.D., 2001). Member, Managing Board, 2000-2001 and Staff Member, 1999-2000, The Ohio State Law Journal. Recipient, CALI Excellence for the Future Award in Real Estate Finance, 2000. *Member:* Cleveland, Ohio State and American Bar Associations. ***PRACTICE AREAS:*** Real Estate Law; Condominium Law; Community Association Law; Construction Law; Zoning Law. ***Email:*** dlindner@bdblaw.com

WALTER A. (SCOTT) LUCAS, born Parma, Ohio, February 27, 1971; admitted to bar, 1997, Ohio; 1998, U.S. District Court, Northern District of Ohio; 2002, U.S. Court of Appeals, Sixth Circuit. *Education:* Baldwin Wallace College (B.A., cum laude, 1994); Cleveland State University, Cleveland-Marshall College of Law (J.D., cum laude, 1997). ***PRACTICE AREAS:*** State and Federal Criminal Defense; White Collar Crime; Civil Litigation; Government Investigations; Business Litigation; Juvenile Law. ***Email:*** SLucas@bdblaw.com

RYAN J. MORLEY, born Cleveland, Ohio, February 22, 1976; admitted to bar, 2001, Connecticut; 2002, U.S. District Court, District of Connecticut; 2004, Ohio; 2005, U.S. District Court, Northern District of Ohio. *Education:* Miami University (B.A., International Studies, 1998; B.A., Political Science, 1998); Quinnipiac University (J.D, cum laude, 2001). Editor-In-Chief, Quinnipiac Probate Law Journal, 2000-2001. *Member:* Connecticut, Cleveland, Ohio State and American Bar Associations. ***LANGUAGES:*** Spanish. ***PRACTICE AREAS:*** Litigation; Commercial Litigation; Employment Litigation; Labor Law. ***Email:*** rmorley@bdblaw.com

BETH A. NAGEL, born Lorain, Ohio; admitted to bar, 1997, Ohio. *Education:* University of Akron (B.S.N., 1985); Cleveland Marshall College of Law (J.D., cum laude, 1996). Editor, Cleveland Marshall College of Law Law Review, 1995-1996. Registered Nurse, Ohio, 1986. *Member:* Ohio State Bar Association. ***PRACTICE AREAS:*** Medical Malpractice Defense. ***Email:*** bnagel@bdblaw.com

BRIAN K. NAM, born Wheaton, Maryland, July 14, 1975; admitted to bar, 2004, Ohio; 2005, U.S. District Court, Northern District of Ohio. *Education:* American University (B.A., 1998); The Ohio State University (J.D., 2004). *Member:* Cleveland Bar Association; Cuyahoga County Bar Association; Ohio State Bar Association; American Bar Association. ***PRACTICE AREAS:*** Real Estate; Construction Litigation. ***Email:*** bnam@bdblaw.com

TIMOTHY A. SPIRKO, born Cleveland, Ohio, September 26, 1971; admitted to bar, 1999, Ohio; U.S. District Court, Northern District of Ohio. *Education:* Pennsylvania State University (B.A., 1994); Cleveland-Marshall College of Law (J.D., 1998). *Member:* Ohio State and American Bar Associations. ***PRACTICE AREAS:*** Medical Malpractice; Litigation. ***Email:*** tspirko@bdblaw.com

REPRESENTATIVE CLIENTS: Deloitte & Touche, LLP; GAR Foundation; J.M. Smucker Company; Yellow Roadway Corporation; R.W. Sidley, Inc.; WACO Scaffolding & Equipment; HCR-Manor Care.

BUCKLEY KING

A LEGAL PROFESSIONAL ASSOCIATION

1400 FIFTH THIRD CENTER
CLEVELAND, OHIO 44114
Telephone: 216-363-1400
National Watts Line: 800-255-2825
Telecopier: 216-579-1020
Email: bkb@bucklaw.com
URL: http://www.buckleyking.com

Columbus, Ohio Office: One Columbus, 10 West Broad Street, Suite 1300. Telephone: 614-461-5600. Telecopier: 614-461-5630.

Cincinnati, Ohio Office: 1420 PNC Center, 201 East Fifth Street. Telephone: 513-412-5400. Telecopier: 513-412-5401.

Atlanta, Georgia Office: Suite 1220 Lennox Building, 3399 Peachtree Road. Telephone: 404-816-7791. Telecopier: 404-816-9786.

Corporate, Litigation, Commercial, Estate Planning, Banking and Finance, Real Estate, Merger and Acquisition, Appellate, Bankruptcy, Professional and Executive (Directors and Officers) Liability, Insurance Law, Products Liability, Health Care, Hospital Law, Medical Malpractice Defense, Immigration and Naturalization, Toxic and Hazardous Materials, ERISA, Taxation, Environmental, Labor and Litigation for Management, Public Employment Relations, Employee Benefits and NLRB Matters.

(This Listing Continued)

FIRM PROFILE: Founded in 1983, Buckley King has established itself as a leading full service business and commercial law firm with offices in Cleveland, Columbus, Cincinnati and Atlanta. The attorneys at Buckley King are dedicated to delivering creative, efficient and precise legal solutions for businesses and individuals.

The Firm's clients include individuals, closely-held businesses, Fortune companies, financial institutions, insurance companies, and governmental entities. Each client is highly-valued, and the preservation of long-standing client relationships is every bit as important to us as fostering new relationships.

Client service is the single most important goal of Buckley King. As a mid-sized firm, Buckley King delivers legal services with the depth, agility and resources necessary for timely and practical legal advice. Individualized attention and interactive communication with our clients is vital to our client relationships.

Because the Firm carefully chooses each of its attorneys, our clients receive the highest quality legal product from a skilled, innovative legal team. Although our attorneys may have different resident offices, Buckley King's success is providing solutions, analysis and advice from a range of complementary practice areas through its practice groups.

We take great pride in our ability to respond immediately to any situation, whether to an emergency court hearing, a critical incident, a client crisis, or to a complex and volatile legal situation requiring thoughtful and effective solutions. Even when our counsel is sought due to urgent, complex, or unique circumstances, we react with clear, focused and strategic advice and options.

When your legal or business needs require insight, clarity, focus and strategic direction, contact us.

We intend to exceed your expectations.

BRENT M. BUCKLEY, born Cleveland Heights, Ohio, November 25; admitted to bar, 1982, Ohio. *Education:* Case Western Reserve University (B.A., 1977); Cleveland State University (J.D., 1982). ***PRACTICE AREAS:*** Corporate Law; Finance; Corporate Litigation; Professional and Executive Liability Law. ***Email:*** buckley@bucklaw.com

WOODS KING III, born Mount Clemens, Michigan, June 25; admitted to bar, 1983, Ohio. *Education:* Washington & Lee University (B.A., 1979); Cleveland State University (J.D., 1982). ***PRACTICE AREAS:*** Corporate Finance; Trusts and Estates. ***Email:*** king@bucklaw.com

RICHARD J. DISANTIS, born Cleveland, Ohio, July 11; admitted to bar, 1966, Ohio. *Education:* Kenyon College (A.B., 1963); University of Michigan (J.D., 1966). ***PRACTICE AREAS:*** Products Liability; Toxic Substances; Hazardous Materials. ***Email:*** disantis@bucklaw.com

HARRY W. GREENFIELD, born Cleveland, Ohio, May 15; admitted to bar, 1970, Ohio. *Education:* Ohio University (B.B.A., 1967); Cleveland State University (J.D., cum laude, 1970). ***PRACTICE AREAS:*** Debt Reorganization; Bankruptcy Law; Commercial Law; Creditors Rights; General Corporate. ***Email:*** greenfield@bucklaw.com

DAVID C. ENGLE, born Mount Vernon, Ohio, April 13; admitted to bar, 1981, Ohio. *Education:* Asbury College; The Ohio State University (B.S., 1976); University of Akron (J.D., 1981). ***PRACTICE AREAS:*** Insurance Defense; Accident and Personal Injury Law; Product Liability; Workers Compensation. ***Email:*** engle@bucklaw.com

ROSEMARY SWEENEY, born Cleveland, Ohio, December 14; admitted to bar, 1987, Ohio. *Education:* John Carroll University (B.S., cum laude, 1976); Kent State University (M.Ed, 1977); Case Western Reserve University (J.D., 1987). ***PRACTICE AREAS:*** Corporate and Business Law; Banking Law; Commercial Law. ***Email:*** sweeney@bucklaw.com

DANIEL P. CARTER, born Massillon, Ohio, March 22; admitted to bar, 1974, Pennsylvania; 2002, Ohio. *Education:* St. Joseph's University (B.S., 1971); Villanova University (J.D., 1974). ***PRACTICE AREAS:*** Environmental Litigation; Insurance Defense; Municipal; Complex Federal Litigation. ***Email:*** carter@bucklaw.com

BARBARA LEE ARMSTRONG, born Lakewood, Ohio, January 16; admitted to bar, 1987, Ohio. *Education:* College of Wooster (B.A., 1984); Case Western Reserve University (J.D., 1987). ***PRACTICE AREAS:*** Banking Litigation; Equine Law; Appellate Practice. ***Email:*** bl_armstrong@bucklaw.com

JEFFREY C. TOOLE, born Ithaca, New York, October 12; admitted to bar, 1985, Indiana; 1995, Ohio. *Education:* Kenyon College (B.A., summa cum laude, 1982); Cornell University (J.D., cum laude, 1985). ***PRACTICE AREAS:*** Reorganization and Bankruptcy; Commercial Transactions; Creditors. ***Email:*** toole@bucklaw.com

RICHARD M. BAIN, born Cleveland, Ohio, April 15; admitted to bar, 1979, Ohio. *Education:* Miami University (B.A., 1976); Case Western Reserve University (J.D., cum laude, 1979). ***PRACTICE AREAS:*** Commercial Litigation; Business Law; Personal Injury Litigation. ***Email:*** bain@bucklaw.com

THEODORE M. DUNN, JR., born Lexington, Kentucky, November 24; admitted to bar, 1982, Ohio. *Education:* Miami University (B.A., 1976); Cleveland State University (J.D., cum laude, 1982). ***PRACTICE AREAS:*** Insurance Defense; Products Liability; Casualty; Professional Liability; Labor and Employment; Commercial Litigation. ***Email:*** dunn@bucklaw.com

PAUL PSOTA, born Cleveland, Ohio, August 18; admitted to bar, 1989, Ohio. *Education:* Baldwin-Wallace College (B.A., Bus. Adm., 1983); Cleveland State University (J.D., 1989); University of Akron (LL.M., Taxation, 1993). ***LANGUAGES:*** German. ***PRACTICE AREAS:*** Tax Law; Business Law; Corporate Law; Health Care Law. ***Email:*** psota@bucklaw.com

HAROLD R. RAUZI, born Litchfield, Illinois, October 1; admitted to bar, 1989, Ohio. *Education:* Lewis & Clark Community College (A.S., 1973); Ottawa University (B.A., 1984); Case Western Reserve University (J.D., cum laude, 1989). ***PRACTICE AREAS:*** Appellate; General Litigation; Health and Hospital Law. ***Email:*** rauzi@bucklaw.com

(This Listing Continued)

BUCKLEY KING, A LEGAL PROFESSIONAL ASSOCIATION, Cleveland—Continued

DOUGLAS N. BARR, born Cleveland, Ohio, January 14; admitted to bar, 1972, Ohio. *Education:* Middlebury College (B.A., 1969); Case Western Reserve University (J.D., 1972). ***PRACTICE AREAS:*** Litigation; Products Liability; Toxic Torts; Mediation Services. ***Email:*** barr@bucklaw.com

KEVIN R. KEOGH, born Cleveland, Ohio, July 2; admitted to bar, 1983, Ohio; 1989, Florida. *Education:* Baldwin Wallace College (B.A., 1979); Cleveland State University (J.D., 1982). ***PRACTICE AREAS:*** Business Law; Estate Planning; Taxation (Local, State and Federal); Probate Law; Real Estate. ***Email:*** keogh@bucklaw.com

REGINA M. MASSETTI, born Anniston, Alabama, September 12; admitted to bar, 1981, Ohio; 1982, Alabama. *Education:* Baldwin-Wallace College (B.A., 1976); Cleveland-Marshall College of Law (J.D., 1981). ***PRACTICE AREAS:*** Environmental Law; Insurance Defense. ***Email:*** massetti@bucklaw.com

MICHAEL J. SPISAK, born Lakewood, Ohio, February 10; admitted to bar, 1994, Ohio. *Education:* Case Western Reserve University (B.A. cum laude, 1991); Cleveland State University (J.D., 1994). ***PRACTICE AREAS:*** Labor and Employment; Workers Compensation. ***Email:*** spisak@bucklaw.com

---

LORRAINE DEBOSE, born Cleveland, Ohio, May 14; admitted to bar, 2003, Ohio. *Education:* Emory University (B.A., 1997); Case Western Reserve University (J.D., 2001). ***PRACTICE AREAS:*** Toxic Torts; Insurance Defense; Medical Malpractice. ***Email:*** debose@bucklaw.com

DOV Y. FRANKEL, admitted to bar, 1994, Maryland; 2004, Ohio; U.S. Court of Appeals, Fourth Circuit; U.S. District Court, Northern District of Ohio; U.S. District Court, District of Maryland. *Education:* Ner Israel Rabbinical College (B.A., 1991); University of Maryland School of Law (J.D., 1994). ***PRACTICE AREAS:*** Bankruptcy; Reorganization; Creditors Rights; Commercial Litigation; Commercial Transactions; Real Estate. ***Email:*** frankel@bucklaw.com

NATHAN HASKELL, (admission pending). *Education:* Baldwin-Wallace College (B.A., 1998); Case Western Reserve University (J.D., 2005). ***Email:*** haskell@bucklaw.com

ERIC D. KRAJEWSKI, born Cleveland, Ohio, January 10; admitted to bar, 2004, Ohio. *Education:* Bowling Green State University (B.S., 2000); Cleveland Marshall College of Law (J.D., cum laude, 2004). ***PRACTICE AREAS:*** Litigation; Insurance Defense; Personal Injury. ***Email:*** krajewski@bucklaw.com

LINDSAY MAXWELL, born Milwaukee, Wisconsin, October 23; admitted to bar, 1993, Ohio. *Education:* Denison University (B.A.,1978), Phi Beta Kappa; University of Toledo (J.D.,cum laude, 1990). ***PRACTICE AREAS:*** Corporate Law; Banks and Banking; Real Estate. ***Email:*** maxwell@bucklaw.com

HEIDI J. MILICIC, born Cleveland, Ohio, January 25; admitted to bar, 1996, Ohio. *Education:* Michigan State University (B.A., 1993); Case Western Reserve University (J.D., 1996). ***PRACTICE AREAS:*** Commercial Litigation; Business Litigation; Complex Litigation. ***Email:*** milicic@bucklaw.com

JAMES L. MILLER, born Lorain, Ohio, May 9; admitted to bar, 1996, Ohio. *Education:* Ohio State University (B.S., 1989); Cleveland State University (J.D., magna cum laude, 1996). ***PRACTICE AREAS:*** Corporate; Commercial Law; Banking Transactions. ***Email:*** miller@bucklaw.com

JEFFREY W. RUPLE, born Cleveland, Ohio, July 19; admitted to bar, 1997, Ohio; 1999, Kentucky. *Education:* Denison University (B.A., 1994); University of Dayton (J.D., 1997). ***PRACTICE AREAS:*** Toxic Torts; Insurance Coverage; Environment; Insurance Defense; Litigation. ***Email:*** ruple@bucklaw.com

DEBORAH D. ZIELINSKI, born Cleveland, Ohio, September 13; admitted to bar, 2000, Ohio. *Education:* Bowling Green State University (B.S.B.A., 1987; M.B.A. and Masters of Organization Development, 1989); Cleveland State University (J.D., magna cum laude, 1999). ***PRACTICE AREAS:*** Commercial Real Estate; Real Estate; Corporate Law; Business Law; Leases and Leasing; Banks and Banking. ***Email:*** zielinski@bucklaw.com

OF COUNSEL

JOHN A. HALLBAUER, born Camden, New Jersey, October 23; admitted to bar, 1966, Ohio. *Education:* Albion College (B.A., 1963); Case Western Reserve University (J.D., 1966). ***PRACTICE AREAS:*** Litigation; Business Law; Fiduciary Law; Creditors; Foreclosures. ***Email:*** hallbauer@bucklaw.com

ELLIOT M. KAUFMAN, born Cleveland, Ohio, March 8; admitted to bar, 1964, Ohio. *Education:* Ohio State University (B.S.C. in B.A., 1961; J.D., 1964). ***PRACTICE AREAS:*** Real Estate; Corporate Law; Commercial Law; Litigation. ***Email:*** kaufman@bucklaw.com

---

ROGER M. BUNDY

4766 BROADVIEW ROAD
CLEVELAND, OHIO 44109
Telephone: 216-781-1720
Fax: 216-622-2714
Email: rbundy@rogerbundylaw.com
URL: http://www.rogerbundylaw.com

Personal Injury Litigation, Automobile Accidents, Slip and Fall, Trucking Accidents, Consumer Bankruptcy, Litigation, Estate Planning, Probate, Wills, Trusts, Nursing Home Abuse, Sexual Abuse, Real Estate, Commercial Leasing, Consumer Law, Truth-in-Lending, Lemon Law, Consumer Fraud.

(This Listing Continued)

ROGER M. BUNDY, born Port Huron, Michigan, April 12, 1971; admitted to bar, 2002, Ohio. *Education:* Michigan State University (B.A., 1995); Cleveland-Marshall College of Law (J.D., 2001). Formerly with: Garson & Associates Co., LPA; Dennis Seaman & Associates Co., LPA. *Member:* Cleveland and Ohio State Bar Associations.

DAVID A. BURGE CO., L.P.A.

Established in 1975

2901 SOUTH PARK BOULEVARD
CLEVELAND, OHIO 44120-1842
Telephone: 216-921-8900
Fax: 216-921-0209

Patent and Trademark Practice.

DAVID A. BURGE, born Anderson, Indiana, July 22, 1943; admitted to bar, 1970, Kentucky; 1971, Ohio; 1972, U.S. District Court, Northern District of Ohio; 1974, U.S. Court of Customs and Patent Appeals; 1978, U.S. Supreme Court; 1982, U.S. Court of Appeals, Federal Circuit; registered to practice before U.S. Patent and Trademark Office. *Education:* University of Illinois (B.S., with highest honors, 1966); Georgetown University; University of Louisville (J.D., 1970). Phi Kappa Phi; Phi Eta Sigma; Sigma Tau; Gamma Epsilon; Sigma Delta Kappa. Author: *Patent and Trademark Tactics and Practice,* John Wiley & Sons, 1980, 1984, 1999; "Patents" Chapter in Mechanical Engineers' Handbook, John Wiley & Sons, 1986, 1998, 2005. *Member:* Greater Cleveland (Member, Board of Trustees, 1979-1980; Member, Executive Council, 1977-1980, Vice-Chairman, 1978-1979 and Chairman, 1979-1980, Young Lawyers Section; Member, 1997-2000, Small Practices) and American Bar Associations; Cleveland Patent Law Association; American Intellectual Property Law Association; Associated Locksmiths of America; Penn-Ohio Locksmiths Association.

CHARLES S. BUTLER

35 SEVERANCE CIRCLE, SUITE 809
CLEVELAND, OHIO 44118-1519
Telephone: 216-691-9404; 216-691-9959
Fax: 216-297-1972
URL: http://www.cbutlerjusticeforvictims.com
Email: cbutlerjustice@ameritech.net
URL: http://www.lawyers.com/justiceforvictims

Sexual Harassment, Fired Unjustly, Discrimination, Labor and Employment, Malpractice, Personal Injury, Wrongful Death, Probate, Criminal.

CHARLES S. BUTLER, born 1942; admitted to bar, 1967, Ohio. *Education:* University of Pennsylvania, the Wharton School (B.S., 1964); University of Michigan (J.D., 1967). ***PRACTICE AREAS:*** Sexual Harassment; Discrimination; Harassment; Sex Discrimination; Race Discrimination; Employment Discrimination; Wrongful Termination; Wrongful Death; Wills; Labor Law; Employment Law; Disabilities; Accidents; Personal Injury; Medical Malpractice; Workers Compensation; Inheritance; Guardianship; Estate Planning; Social Security; Living Wills; Whistleblower Litigation; Social Security Disability; Birth Trauma; Retaliatory Discharge; Probate; Civil Rights; Legal Malpractice; Nursing Home Abuse and Neglect; Police Brutality; Judicial Discipline.

CALFEE, HALTER & GRISWOLD LLP

1400 MCDONALD INVESTMENT CENTER
800 SUPERIOR AVENUE
CLEVELAND, OHIO 44114-2688
Telephone: 216-622-8200
Telecopier: 216-241-0816
Telex: 980499
URL: http://www.calfee.com

Columbus, Ohio Office: 1100 Fifth Third Center, 21 East State Street. Telephone: 614-621-1500. Fax: 614-621-0010.

Antitrust and Trade Regulation, Banking and Bank Regulation, Bankruptcy and Creditors' Rights, Commercial Business and Finance, General Corporate, Corporate Succession Planning, Employee Benefits, Labor and Employment Relations, Environmental, Estate Planning and Administration, Executive Compensation, Federal Government Contracts and Agency Regulation, Franchise Law, Government Relations and Legislation, Healthcare, Information Technology, Intellectual Property and Technology, International, Litigation, Oil and Gas, Partnerships and Joint Ventures, Public Finance, Public Law, Real Estate, Securities, Tax.

LAW FIRM ALLIANCES/ASSOCIATIONS: **LEX MUNDI**

PARTNERS

HAROLD W. BABBIT, born Ottawa, Kansas, 1941; admitted to bar, 1967, Ohio. *Education:* University of Iowa (B.A., 1963); Yale University (LL.B., 1967). Author: "Ohio Municipal Law." Adjunct Professor, Municipal Law, Cleveland State Law School, 1980—. ***PRACTICE AREAS:*** Public Law; Public Finance. ***Email:*** hbabbit@calfee.com

BRENT D. BALLARD, born Columbus, Ohio, 1955; admitted to bar, 1985, Ohio. *Education:* Bates College (B.A., 1978); Cornell University (M.P.S., 1980); Case Western Reserve University (J.D., 1985). Associate Member, Case Western Reserve Law Review, 1983-1984. *Member:* Cleveland, Ohio State and American Bar Associations; Lawyer-Pilot Bar Association. ***PRACTICE AREAS:*** Corporate Law; Real Estate. ***Email:*** bballard@calfee.com

MURAD A. BEG, born Toledo, Ohio, 1969; admitted to bar, 1995, New York and New Jersey; 2000, Ohio. *Education:* Kenyon College (B.A., 1991); Pace University School of

(This Listing Continued)

Law (J.D., cum laude, 1995). Member, Environmental Law Review, 1993-1995. *Member:* Ohio State and American Bar Associations. ***PRACTICE AREAS:*** Corporate Law; Mergers and Acquisitions; Securities. ***Email:*** mbeg@calfee.com

VIRGINIA D. BENJAMIN, born Orange, New Jersey, 1951; admitted to bar, 1976, Ohio. *Education:* Smith College (A.B., 1973); Boston University (J.D., cum laude, 1976). Member, Board of Directors, National Association of Bond Lawyers, 1996-1997; 1999-2002. *Member:* Cleveland and Ohio State Bar Associations; National Association of Bond Lawyers. ***PRACTICE AREAS:*** Public Finance; Public Law; Government Relations; Legislative Practice; Health Care; Long Term Care. ***Email:*** vbenjami@calfee.com

KARL S. BEUS, born Idaho Falls, Idaho, 1964; admitted to bar, 1992, Ohio. *Education:* Brigham Young University; University of Utah (B.A., 1989); University of Idaho (J.D., magna cum laude, 1992). Member, Idaho Law Review, 1991-1992. ***LANGUAGES:*** German. ***PRACTICE AREAS:*** Commercial Finance; Information Technology. ***Email:*** kbeus@calfee.com

MITCHELL G. BLAIR, born Bellefonte, Pennsylvania, 1957; admitted to bar, 1982, Ohio. *Education:* Union University (B.A., magna cum laude, 1979); College of William & Mary (J.D., 1982). ***PRACTICE AREAS:*** Litigation. ***Email:*** mblair@calfee.com

MICHAEL E. BRITTAIN, born Cleveland, Ohio, 1954; admitted to bar, 1979, Ohio and U.S. District Court, Northern District of Ohio; 1984, U.S. Court of Appeals, Sixth Circuit; 1986, U.S. Supreme Court. *Education:* Ohio University (A.B., summa cum laude, 1976); Case Western Reserve University (J.D., 1979). Phi Beta Kappa; Order of the Coif. ***PRACTICE AREAS:*** Litigation; Insurance Coverage; Toxic Torts. ***Email:*** mbrittain@calfee.com

JOHN R. CERNELICH, born Cleveland, Ohio, 1959; admitted to bar, 1986, Ohio. *Education:* Harvard University (A.B., cum laude, 1982); University of Virginia (J.D., 1986). ***PRACTICE AREAS:*** Labor and Employment. ***Email:*** jcernelich@calfee.com

THOMAS A. CICARELLA, born Gary, Indiana, 1949; admitted to bar, 1974, Ohio. *Education:* Indiana University (A.B., 1971; J.D., magna cum laude, 1974). Associate Editor, Indiana Law Review, 1973-1974. Adjunct Associate Professor of Law, Cleveland Marshall College of Law, 1981—. ***PRACTICE AREAS:*** Commercial Finance; Bankruptcy; Creditors Rights. ***Email:*** tcicarella@calfee.com

JOHN S. CIPOLLA, born Cleveland, Ohio, 1963; admitted to bar, 1989, Ohio; registered to practice before U.S. Patent and Trademark Office. *Education:* Bowling Green University (B.S., cum laude, 1985); Cleveland-Marshall College of Law (J.D., magna cum laude, 1989). ***PRACTICE AREAS:*** Intellectual Property. ***Email:*** jcipolla@calfee.com

PETER J. COMODECA, born Cleveland, Ohio, 1954; admitted to bar, 1984, Massachusetts; 1990, Ohio. *Education:* United States Military Academy (B.S., 1977); Harvard University (J.D., 1984); The Judge Advocate General's School (LL.M., 1988). [Major, U.S. Army, 1977-1990]. ***PRACTICE AREAS:*** Construction Law; Arbitration/Mediation; Government Contracts; Government Agency Practice; International Law; Litigation; Probate Litigation. ***Email:*** pcomodeca@calfee.com

TIMOTHY J. CONNORS, born Chicago, Illinois, 1964; admitted to bar, 1989, Ohio. *Education:* Michigan State University (B.A., with honors, 1986); University of Michigan (J.D. 1989). ***PRACTICE AREAS:*** Information Technology; Intellectual Property. ***Email:*** tconnors@calfee.com

WILLIAM E. COUGHLIN, born Cleveland, Ohio, 1956; admitted to bar, 1983, Ohio; 1984, U.S. District Court, Northern District of Ohio and U.S. Court of Appeals, District of Columbia Circuit; 1987, U.S. Court of Appeals, Sixth Circuit; 2002, U.S. Court of Appeals, First Circuit. *Education:* Georgetown University (A.B., magna cum laude, 1978; M.S.F.S., 1983; J.D., magna cum laude, 1983). Fulbright Scholar, University of Geneva, 1978-1979. Phi Beta Kappa. Topics Editor, Law and Policy in International Business, 1981-1982. Law Clerk, U.S. Court of Appeals for the District of Columbia Circuit, 1983-1984. ***LANGUAGES:*** French. ***PRACTICE AREAS:*** Litigation; Environmental Law. ***Email:*** wcoughlin@calfee.com

DAVID J. CRANDALL, born Cleveland, Ohio, 1966; admitted to bar, 1991, Ohio. *Education:* Allegheny College (B.S., magna cum laude, 1989); Syracuse University (J.D., cum laude, 1991). Phi Beta Kappa. *Member:* Cleveland, Ohio State and American Bar Associations. ***PRACTICE AREAS:*** Corporate Law; Mergers and Acquisitions; Partnership Law; Limited Liability Company Law; Joint Ventures; Tax Law. ***Email:*** dcrandall@calfee.com

MARA E. CUSHWA, born Youngstown, Ohio, 1965; admitted to bar, 1990, Ohio. *Education:* University of Notre Dame (B.A., 1987); Case Western Reserve University (J.D., 1990). *Member:* Cleveland, Ohio State and American (Member, Real Property & Probate Section) Bar Associations. ***PRACTICE AREAS:*** Commercial Real Estate; Finance; Land Development; Joint Ventures; Zoning, Planning and Land Use; Environmental Law; Partnership Law; Limited Liability Company Law. ***Email:*** mcushwa@calfee.com

CHERYL A. D'AMICO, born Cleveland, Ohio; admitted to bar, 1996, Ohio; 2005, Florida. *Education:* Baldwin-Wallace College (B.A., 1992); Cleveland State University (J.D., 1995). *Member:* Cleveland (Member, Estate Planning, Probate and Trust Law Section), Ohio State and American Bar Associations; The Florida Bar. (Certified Specialist in Estate Planning, Trust and Probate Law, Ohio State Bar Association). ***PRACTICE AREAS:*** Estate Planning; Trust Planning; Estate Administration; Trust Administration. ***Email:*** cdamico@calfee.com

ANTHEA R. DANIELS, born Cleveland, Ohio, 1964; admitted to bar, 1989, Ohio. *Education:* Denison University (B.A., 1986); Case Western Reserve University (J.D., 1989). Jessup International Moot Court. Co-Author: "The Discovery of Medical Records Maintained by Health Care Facilities: Inconsistent Law in Need of Legislative Correction," Journal of Law and Health, 1990-1991. ***LANGUAGES:*** Spanish. ***PRACTICE AREAS:*** Corporate Law; Health Care; Long Term Care; Information Technology. ***Email:*** adaniels@calfee.com

PHILIP M. DAWSON, born Jamestown, New York, 1945; admitted to bar, 1972, Ohio. *Education:* Miami University (B.A., 1967); Emory University (J.D., 1972). ***PRACTICE AREAS:*** Corporate Succession; Corporate Law; Mergers and Acquisitions; Estate Planning. ***Email:*** pdawson@calfee.com

(This Listing Continued)

SHELLY G. DEDMON, born Iowa City, Iowa, 1961; admitted to bar, 1988, Ohio. *Education:* Stephens College (B.A., 1983); University of Iowa (J.D., with high distinction, 1988). Co-Chair, Joint Subcommittee, International Business and Domestic Business Documentation, Business Law Section, American Bar Association. ***PRACTICE AREAS:*** Commercial Finance; Information Technology; International Law. ***Email:*** sdedmon@calfee.com

JOHN J. EKLUND, born New York, N.Y., 1955; admitted to bar, 1980, Ohio; 1981, U.S. District Court, Northern District of Ohio; 1986, U.S. Court of Appeals, Sixth Circuit; 1994, U.S. Court of Appeals, Seventh Circuit; 1997, U.S. District Court, Western District of Wisconsin; 1999, U.S. Supreme Court. *Education:* Union University (B.A., cum laude, 1977); Washington & Lee University (J.D., cum laude, 1980). Lead Articles Editor, Washington and Lee Law Review, 1979-1980. *Member:* Cleveland, Ohio State (Chair, Board of Governors, Antitrust Section, 2001-2003) and American (Member, Sections on: Antitrust; Litigation) Bar Associations. ***PRACTICE AREAS:*** Antitrust and Trade Regulation; Litigation. ***Email:*** jeklund@calfee.com

LYNN M. GATTOZZI, born Cleveland, Ohio, 1962; admitted to bar, 1987, Ohio. *Education:* University of Notre Dame (B.A., 1984); Case Western Reserve University School of Law (J.D., cum laude, 1987). Associate Member, 1985-1986 and Contributing Editor, 1986-1987, Case Western Reserve Law Review. ***PRACTICE AREAS:*** Real Estate. ***Email:*** lgattozz@calfee.com

RICHARD P. GODDARD, born South Bend, Indiana, 1952; admitted to bar, 1979, Ohio and U.S. District Court, Northern District of Ohio; 1981, U.S. Court of Appeals, Sixth Circuit; 1983, U.S. Supreme Court; 1999, U.S. District Court, Southern District of Ohio. *Education:* Oberlin College (B.A., 1974); Washington & Lee University (J.D., magna cum laude, 1979). Order of the Coif. Research Editor, Washington & Lee Law Review, 1978-1979. *Member:* Cleveland, Ohio State and American Bar Associations. ***PRACTICE AREAS:*** Litigation; Labor and Employment; Civil Rights Section 1983; Discrimination; Construction Law; Construction Arbitration; Construction Claims; Construction Contracts; Construction and Design Law; Construction and Surety Law; Construction Defects; Construction Labor Law; Construction Liens; Construction Litigation; Construction Mediation. ***Email:*** rgoddard@calfee.com

GUY F. GUINN, born New York, N.Y., 1949; admitted to bar, 1975, Wisconsin; 1976, U.S. Tax Court; 1981, Ohio. *Education:* Duke University (B.A., summa cum laude, 1971); University of Michigan (J.D., cum laude, 1975). Phi Beta Kappa. Listed in: The Best Lawyers in America, 1995-2005; Chambers USA , America's Leading Lawyers for Business, 2004, 2005. *Member:* Cleveland, Ohio State and American (Past Chair, Joint Subcommittee, International and Domestic Business Transactions, Business Law Section) Bar Associations. ***PRACTICE AREAS:*** Commercial Finance; Creditor Rights; International Law. ***Email:*** gguinn@calfee.com

ARTHUR C. HALL III, born West Chester, Pennsylvania, 1962; admitted to bar, 1993, Texas; 1995, Ohio. *Education:* Franklin and Marshall College (B.A., 1984); Duke University (M.B.A., 1986); University of Notre Dame (J.D., magna cum laude, 1993). Research and Projects Editor, Notre Dame Law Review. ***PRACTICE AREAS:*** Securities; Corporate Law; Mergers and Acquisitions. ***Email:*** ahall@calfee.com

WALTER G. HARPER, born Los Angeles, California, 1944; admitted to bar, 1974, Ohio. *Education:* United States Military Academy (B.S., 1966); Vanderbilt University (J.D., 1974). Associate Editor, Vanderbilt Law Review, 1973-1974. ***PRACTICE AREAS:*** Public Law; Public Finance; Real Estate. ***Email:*** wharper@calfee.com

JULIE A. HARRIS, born Akron, Ohio, 1970; admitted to bar, 1995, Ohio. *Education:* Bowling Green State University (B.L.S., magna cum laude, 1990); Georgetown University Law Center (J.D., 1995). Senior Articles Editor, Georgetown Journal of Legal Ethics. ***PRACTICE AREAS:*** Litigation. ***Email:*** jharris@calfee.com

RICHARD J. HAUER, JR., born Cleveland, Ohio, 1950; admitted to bar, 1975, Ohio. *Education:* Boston College (B.A., magna cum laude, 1972); Case Western Reserve University (J.D., 1975). Editor, Case Western Reserve Law Review, 1974-1975. ***PRACTICE AREAS:*** Employee Benefits; Executive Compensation; Tax Law. ***Email:*** rhauer@calfee.com

MAURA L. HUGHES, born Cleveland, Ohio, 1967; admitted to bar, 1993, Ohio; 1994, U.S. District Court, Northern District of Ohio; 1995, U.S. Court of Appeals, Tenth Circuit; 1996, U.S. Court of Appeals, Sixth Circuit; 2001, U.S. District Court, Southern District of Ohio. *Education:* Brown University (A.B., magna cum laude, 1990); Harvard University (J.D., cum laude, 1993). Phi Beta Kappa. Senior Editor, Harvard Environmental Law Review, 1992-1993. Law Clerk to Judge Ann Aldrich, U.S. District Court, Northern District of Ohio, 1993-1994. 1999 Pegasus Scholar, Inner Temple, London. ***PRACTICE AREAS:*** Antitrust and Trade Regulation; Litigation; Civil Rights Section 1983. ***Email:*** mhughes@calfee.com

JOHN J. JENKINS, born Trenton, New Jersey, 1962; admitted to bar, 1986, Ohio. *Education:* Canisius College (B.A., 1983); University of Virginia (J.D., 1986). ***PRACTICE AREAS:*** Corporate Law; Information Technology; Mergers and Acquisitions; Private Finance; Securities. ***Email:*** jjenkins@calfee.com

TRACY SCOTT JOHNSON, born McCook, Nebraska, 1963; admitted to bar, 1995, Ohio; U.S. District Court, Northern District of Ohio, U.S. District Court, Eastern District of Michigan, U.S. Court of Appeals, Sixth Circuit and U.S. Supreme Court; registered to practice before U.S. Patent and Trademark Office. *Education:* United States Naval Academy (B.S., with distinction, 1985); Widener University School of Law (J.D., magna cum laude, 1994). Recipient, Donald E. Pease Best Student Article Award. Staff, Delaware Journal of Corporate Law, 1993-1994. Author, "Pay for Performance: Corporate Executive Compensation in the 1990's," 20 Del. J. Corp. L. 183, 1995. *Member:* Cleveland, Ohio State and American Bar Associations. ***PRACTICE AREAS:*** Litigation; Intellectual Property; Intellectual Property Litigation; Intellectual Property Enforcement; Intellectual Property Infringement; Civil Litigation; Complex Litigation; U.S. Supreme Court Litigation; Federal Civil Litigation. ***Email:*** tjohnson@calfee.com

THOMAS A. JORGENSEN, born Washington, D.C., 1943; admitted to bar, 1968, District of Columbia and Ohio. *Education:* Columbia College (A.B., 1964); Duke University (LL.B., 1967). Order of the Coif. Member, Editorial Board, Duke Law Journal, 1966-1967. Author: "ESOPS as Corporate Planning Tools," The Corporate Analyst, August

(This Listing Continued)

CALFEE, HALTER & GRISWOLD LLP, Cleveland—Continued

1993; "Handling Employee Benefits in Mergers and Acquisitions," The Corporate Analyst, May 1993; "The Ultimate Decision—Lump Sum, Installments Or IRA Rollover," Property and Probate, March/April 1991; "Takeover Benefits—Corporate Acquisitions Can Make Employee Benefit Programs into Hidden Assets—or Legal Landmines," Ohio Law, January 1989; "Terminating Defined Benefit Pension Plans," 46 NYU Institute on Federal Taxation, Conference on Employee Benefits and Executive Compensation, Chapter 4, 1988; "Handling Terminations after COBRA," 45 NYU Institute on Federal Taxation, 10-1, 1987. Member, Advisory Group, Commissioner of Internal Revenue Service, 1985-1986. Vice Chair and Chair, Employee Benefits Committee, Section on Taxation, 1993-1998; Chairman: Plan Terminations, Mergers, Asset Transfers and Termination Insurance Committee of the Real Property, Probate and Trust Law Section, 1986-1989; Chair of Joint Committee on Employee Benefits of the American Bar Association, 1993-1994; Chairman, Midwest Pension Conference, Northeast Ohio, 1987. Chairman, U.S. Chamber of Commerce Task Force on Nondiscrimination Regulations, 1990-1993; Council Member, Section of Taxation of the American Bar Association, 2003—; Member of Steering Committee, International Pension and Employee Benefits Lawyers Association, 2003—; Chair, Employee Benefits Practice Group, Lex Mundi, 2003—. ***PRACTICE AREAS:*** Employee Benefits; Executive Compensation. ***Email:*** tjorgens@calfee.com

JOSEPH K. JUSTER, born Quincy, Massachusetts, 1957; admitted to bar, 1984, Massachusetts; 1989, Ohio. *Education:* Williams College (B.A., cum laude, 1979) Phi Beta Kappa; Boston University (J.D., 1984). Associate Editor, 1983 and Editor, 1984, Annual Review of Banking Law. ***PRACTICE AREAS:*** Corporate Law; Mergers and Acquisitions. ***Email:*** jjuster@calfee.com

TARA A. KASTELIC, born Chester, Pennsylvania, 1965; admitted to bar, 1991, Ohio; registered to practice before U.S. Patent and Trademark Office. *Education:* University of Toledo (B.S.C.S.E., 1988; J.D., 1991). Order of the Coif. Member, 1989-1990 and Student Articles Editor, 1990-1991, University of Toledo Law Review. ***PRACTICE AREAS:*** Information Technology; Intellectual Property. ***Email:*** tkastelic@calfee.com

MATTHEW J. KLABEN, born Syracuse, New York, 1969; admitted to bar, 1995, Ohio. *Education:* Canisius College (B.A., summa cum laude, 1991); University of Bonn, Germany (Fulbright Certificate, 1992); Cornell University (J.D., magna cum laude, 1995). Order of the Coif. Note Editor, Cornell Law Review, 1994-1995. *Member:* Cleveland, Ohio State and American Bar Associations. ***LANGUAGES:*** German. ***PRACTICE AREAS:*** Corporate Law; Securities; Executive Compensation; Information Technology; Mergers and Acquisitions. ***Email:*** mklaben@calfee.com

BRIAN E. KONDAS, born Cleveland, Ohio, 1965; admitted to bar, 1995, Ohio; registered to practice before U.S. Patent and Trademark Office. *Education:* University of Michigan (B.S.E.E., 1987); Cleveland-Marshall College of Law (J.D., 1995). *Member:* American Intellectual Property Law Association. ***PRACTICE AREAS:*** Intellectual Property. ***Email:*** bkondas@calfee.com

STEPHEN P. KRESNYE, born Cleveland, Ohio, 1949; admitted to bar, 1977, Ohio. *Education:* John Carroll University (B.S.B.A., magna cum laude, 1971); The University of Michigan (M.B.A., with distinction, 1974; J.D., magna cum laude, 1976). Order of the Coif. ***PRACTICE AREAS:*** Corporate Law; Mergers and Acquisitions; Partnership Law; Limited Liability Company Law; Joint Ventures; Tax Law. ***Email:*** skresnye@calfee.com

ANTHONY J. LaCERVA, born Youngstown, Ohio, 1959; admitted to bar, 1986, Ohio. *Education:* Kent State University (B.A., 1982); University of Toledo College of Law (J.D., magna cum laude, 1985). Order of the Coif. Member, University of Toledo Law Review, 1984-1985. Law Clerk to Hon. Robert E. DeMascio, U.S. District Court, Eastern District of Michigan, 1985-1987. ***PRACTICE AREAS:*** Complex Commercial Litigation; Corporate and Securities Litigation; Intellectual Property Litigation; Products Liability Litigation. ***Email:*** alacerva@calfee.com

JAMES F. LANG, born Cleveland, Ohio, 1963; admitted to bar, 1992, Ohio and U.S. District Court, Northern District of Ohio; 1993, U.S. Court of Appeals, Sixth Circuit. *Education:* Wake Forest University (B.A., cum laude, 1986); University of Virginia (J.D., 1992). Co-Author, Gotherman, Babbit & Lang, Local Government Law - Municipal, 1st ed., 2004. Author: "Are you Ready for the Internet?" 12 Babbit's Ohio Municipal Service 73, Sept./Oct. 2000; "Tort Reform Could Benefit Municipalities," 9 Babbit's Ohio Municipal Service 1, Jan./Feb. 1997; "Federal Preemption of Local Pesticide Use Regulation: The Past, Present and Future of Wisconsin Public Intervenor v. Mortier," 11 Va. Envtl. L.J. 241, 1991-1992. *Member:* Cleveland, Ohio State and American Bar Associations. ***PRACTICE AREAS:*** Litigation; Public Utility Law; Telecommunications Law; Local Government Law; Information Technology. ***Email:*** jlang@calfee.com

JAMES M. LAWNICZAK, born Toledo, Ohio, 1951; admitted to bar, 1977, Michigan; 1979, Illinois; 1989, Ohio. *Education:* University of Michigan (B.A., 1974; J.D., magna cum laude, 1977). Order of the Coif. Associate Editor, Michigan Law Review, 1975-1977. Author: "A Comparison of the American Sherman Antitrust Act and the British Restrictive Trade Practices Act: The Trade Association Experience," with Martin H. Malin, 59 U. Det. J. Urban L. 147, 1982; "Did Congress Always Say What It Meant in the Bankruptcy Reform Act of 1994?" 101 Comm. L.J. 372, 1996. Law Clerk, Hon. Robert E. DeMascio, United States District Court, Eastern District of Michigan, 1977-1979. Contributing Author: revised 15th edition of Collier on Bankruptcy; Bankruptcy Chapter, Lexis's Asset Based Financing Treatise. *Member:* Cleveland Bar Association (Trustee, 2005—; Chair, 2003-2004 and Member, Bankruptcy and Commercial Law Section). ***PRACTICE AREAS:*** Bankruptcy; Creditors Rights; Commercial Finance. ***Email:*** jlawniczak@calfee.com

LEONARD L. LEWIS, born Lancaster, Pennsylvania, 1954; admitted to bar, 1984, Ohio; registered to practice before U.S. Patent and Trademark Office. *Education:* University of Notre Dame (B.S.E.E., magna cum laude, 1976); Cleveland State University (J.D., cum laude, 1983). ***PRACTICE AREAS:*** Intellectual Property. ***Email:*** llewis@calfee.com

CHARLES B. LYON, born Kansas City, Missouri, 1944; admitted to bar, 1971, Ohio; registered to practice before U.S. Patent and Trademark Office. *Education:* University of Oklahoma (B.S.M.E., 1967); George Washington University (J.D., with honors, 1970). Examiner, United States Patent and Trademark Office, 1967-1969. *Member:* Cleveland Patent Law Association (Director, 1983-1984). ***PRACTICE AREAS:*** Intellectual Property. ***Email:*** clyon@calfee.com

MICHAEL F. MARHOFER, born Akron, Ohio, 1965; admitted to bar, 1991, Ohio. *Education:* Miami University (B.S., 1987); The University of Akron (J.D., magna cum laude, 1991; M.B.A., 1991). Managing Editor, The University of Akron Law Review, 1990-1991. Member of The University of Akron, College of Business Administration, Advancement Council, 2003—. *Member:* Cleveland, Ohio State and American Bar Associations. ***PRACTICE AREAS:*** Corporate Law; Mergers and Acquisitions. ***Email:*** mmarhofe@calfee.com

DARLENE EVANS McCOY, born Cleveland, Ohio, 1953; admitted to bar, 1979, Ohio. *Education:* Kent State University (B.G.S., 1975); University of Akron (J.D., 1979). Chief of Staff, Mayor Michael White, Cleveland, Ohio, 1991-1993. Director, Ohio Civil Right Commission, 1988-1990. Executive Secretary, Ohio Industrial Commission, 1983-1988. *Member:* Cleveland, Ohio State and American Bar Associations. ***PRACTICE AREAS:*** Government Relations; Legislative Practice; Public Law; Public Finance; Workers Compensation. ***Email:*** dmccoy@calfee.com

THOMAS F. McKEE, born Cleveland, Ohio, 1948; admitted to bar, 1975, Ohio and U.S. Supreme Court. *Education:* University of Michigan (A.B., with high distinction, 1970); Case Western Reserve University (J.D., 1975). Order of the Coif. Associate Editor, Case Western Reserve Law Review, 1973-1974. *Member:* Cleveland (Member, Securities Law Section), Ohio State (Member, Securities Law Section) and American (Member, Federal Regulation of Securities Committee) Bar Associations. ***PRACTICE AREAS:*** Corporate Law; Mergers and Acquisitions; Public and Private Offerings; Securities. ***Email:*** tmckee@calfee.com

BRIAN A. McMAHON, born Lorain, Ohio, 1967; admitted to bar, 1994, Ohio. *Education:* The Ohio State University (B.S.B.A., 1989; J.D., 1994). Order of the Coif. Articles Editor, 1992-1993 and Managing Editor, 1993-1994, Ohio State Law Journal. Law Clerk, Hon. James H. Williams, U.S. Bankruptcy Court, Northern District of Ohio, 1994-1996. ***PRACTICE AREAS:*** Commercial Finance. ***Email:*** bmcmahon@calfee.com

DANIEL J. McMULLEN, born Youngstown, Ohio, 1956; admitted to bar, 1983, Ohio; 1988, District of Columbia; 1990, U.S. Supreme Court. *Education:* Harvard University (B.A., magna cum laude, 1978; J.D., cum laude, 1982). Law Clerk to Chief Judge Frank J. Battisti, U.S. District Court, Northern District of Ohio, 1982-1983. Author: "Stubborn Facts of History,"; "Likelihood of Confusion? Trademark and Jurisdiction Issues on the Internet," University of Akron Annual Symposium on Intellectual Property Law and Policy, March 2002; "On Heroes and Idealists," 42 Cleveland State Law Review 373, 1994; 44 Case Western Reserve Law Review 75, 1993. ***PRACTICE AREAS:*** Information Technology; Intellectual Property. ***Email:*** dmcmullen@calfee.com

THOMAS I. MICHALS, born Cleveland, Ohio, 1956; admitted to bar, 1988, Ohio. *Education:* Coffeyville Kansas Junior College; Central Missouri State University (B.S., 1977); Case Western Reserve University (J.D., magna cum laude, 1988). Order of the Coif. *Member:* Lake County Bar Association. ***PRACTICE AREAS:*** Litigation. ***Email:*** tmichals@calfee.com

ROBERT A. MILLER, born Columbus, Ohio; admitted to bar, 1982, Ohio. *Education:* College of Wooster (B.A., 1979); Case Western Reserve University (J.D., 1982). *Member:* Cleveland, Ohio State and American (Member, Sections on: Taxation; Real Property, Probate and Trust) Bar Associations. ***PRACTICE AREAS:*** Employee Benefits; Executive Compensation. ***Email:*** rmiller@calfee.com

JoELLEN M. MINCHAK, born Cleveland, Ohio, 1960; admitted to bar, 1985, Ohio. *Education:* Hiram College (B.A., magna cum laude, 1982); Harvard University (J.D., 1985). Phi Beta Kappa. ***PRACTICE AREAS:*** Commercial Finance; Bankruptcy; Creditors Rights. ***Email:*** jminchak@calfee.com

JOHN M. MINO, born Cleveland, Ohio, 1959; admitted to bar, 1984, Ohio. *Education:* Georgetown University (B.S.F.S., cum laude, 1981); Georgetown University Law Center (J.D., 1984). Editor, Law and Policy in International Business, 1983-1984. ***PRACTICE AREAS:*** Corporate Law; Government Relations; Legislative Practice; Partnership Law; Limited Liability Company Law; Joint Ventures; Private Finance; Public Law; Public Finance; Public Utility Law; Telecommunications Law. ***Email:*** jmino@calfee.com

GERALD A. MONROE, born Cleveland, Ohio, 1964; admitted to bar, 1992, Ohio. *Education:* Northwestern University (B.S.J., 1986); Cleveland-Marshall College of Law (J.D., summa cum laude, 1992). ***PRACTICE AREAS:*** Investment Funds; Venture Capital Transactions; Corporate Law; Mergers and Acquisitions; Securities. ***Email:*** gmonroe@calfee.com

EDWARD W. MOORE, born Warren, Ohio, 1957; admitted to bar, 1982, Ohio. *Education:* Miami University (B.A., 1978); Case Western Reserve University (J.D., 1982). Order of the Coif. Notes Editor, Case Western Reserve Law Review, 1981-1982. *Member:* Cleveland, Ohio State and American Bar Associations. ***PRACTICE AREAS:*** Corporate Law; Mergers and Acquisitions; Securities. ***Email:*** emoore@calfee.com

SEAN T. MOORHEAD, born Columbus, Ohio, 1964; admitted to bar, 1993, Ohio; 1994, U.S. District Court, Northern District of Ohio; registered to practice before U.S. Patent and Trademark Office. *Education:* University of Michigan (B.S.E., E.E., cum laude, 1986); The Ohio State University College of Law (J.D., with honors, 1993). Order of the Coif. Articles Editor, Ohio State Law Journal, 1991-1993. Author: "The Doctrine of Equivalents: The Second Prong of Patent Infringement Charges," 53 Ohio St. L.J. 1421, 1992. *Member:* American Intellectual Property Law Association; Cleveland Intellectual Property Law Association. ***PRACTICE AREAS:*** Intellectual Property; Patent Prosecution; Patent Litigation; Trademark; Copyright; Trade Secret; Unfair Competition; Licensing; Agreements; Technology Transfer; Information Technology. ***Email:*** smoorhead@calfee.com

KIMBERLY MOSES, born Cleveland, Ohio, 1958; admitted to bar, 1985, Ohio. *Education:* Trinity College (B.A., 1981); Cleveland Marshall College of Law (J.D., magna cum laude, 1985). Author: "Developing an Early Strategic Defense Paramount in Class Actions"; "Litigation Tactics and Strategy in the Defense of Class Actions." Speaker, Defense of Class Actions and The Class Action Fairness Act of 2005. *Member:* Cleveland (Member, Sections on: Litigation; Women in the Law), Ohio State (Member, Litigation Section) and

(This Listing Continued)

American (Member: Committee on Class and Derivative Litigation, Business Law Section; Litigation Section) Bar Associations. ***PRACTICE AREAS:*** Litigation. ***Email:*** kmoses@calfee.com

DOUGLAS A. NEARY, born Detroit, Michigan, 1960; admitted to bar, 1985, Ohio. *Education:* University of Michigan (B.A., 1982); Boston University (J.D., 1985). James B. Angell Scholar. Vice Chairman, Firm's Corporate Group. Chair, Firm's Client Services Committee. Member, Firm's Executive Committee. *Member:* Ohio State and American Bar Associations. ***PRACTICE AREAS:*** Corporate Law; Venture Capital; Private Equity; Mergers and Acquisitions; Securities. ***Email:*** dneary@calfee.com

RONALD H. NEILL, born Akron, Ohio, 1944; admitted to bar, 1969, Ohio. *Education:* College of Wooster (B.A., 1966); Duke University (J.D., 1969). Member, Board of Editors, Duke Law Journal, 1968-1969. Assistant Professor of Law in Federal Income Taxation and Federal Estate and Gift Taxation, University of Akron, 1969-1970. ***PRACTICE AREAS:*** Corporate Law; Mergers and Acquisitions; Partnership Law; Limited Liability Company Law; Joint Ventures; Private Finance; Tax Law. ***Email:*** rneill@calfee.com

TODD F. PALMER, born Berea, Ohio, 1965; admitted to bar, 1990, Ohio. *Education:* Miami University (B.A., 1987); Ohio State University (J.D., 1990). (Certified Specialist in Labor & Employment Law, Ohio State Bar Association). ***PRACTICE AREAS:*** Labor and Employment. ***Email:*** tpalmer@calfee.com

MICHAEL D. PHILLIPS, born Charlottesville, Virginia, 1951; admitted to bar, 1977, Ohio. *Education:* University of Virginia (B.A., 1973); College of William & Mary (J.D., 1977). Articles Editor, William & Mary Law Review, 1976-1977. ***PRACTICE AREAS:*** Health Care; Corporate Law; Partnership; Limited Liability Company; Joint Ventures; Mergers and Acquisitions; Oil and Gas Law; Tax Law. ***Email:*** mphillips@calfee.com

WILLIAM M. PHILLIPS, born Cleveland, Ohio, 1957; admitted to bar, 1983, Ohio; 1986, California. *Education:* Miami University of Ohio (B.S. in Economics, 1979); The Ohio State University College of Law (J.D., with honors, 1983). Editor-in-Chief, The Ohio State Law Journal, 1982-1983. *Member:* State Bar of California. ***PRACTICE AREAS:*** Real Estate. ***Email:*** bphillips@calfee.com

ROBERT N. RAPP, born Erie, Pennsylvania, 1947; admitted to bar, 1972, Ohio; 1973, U.S. District Court, Northern District of Ohio; 1980, U.S. Supreme Court; 1981, U.S. Court of Appeals, Sixth Circuit; 2002, U.S. District Court, Western District of Pennsylvania; 2005, U.S. District Court, Southern District of Ohio. *Education:* Case Western Reserve University (B.A., 1969; J.D., 1972); Cleveland State University (M.B.A., 1989). Articles Editor, Case Western Reserve Law Review, 1971-1972. Contributing Author: *Federal Securities Act of 1933,* (c) Matthew Bender & Co. Author: "*Blue Sky Regulation*" (2003 ed.), (c) Matthew Bender & Co. Practitioner in Residence, Cornell Law School, 1993. Adjunct Professor, Law, Theory and Practice in Financial Markets, Case Western Reserve University School of Law, 1994-1998. Member, Legal Advisory Board, National Association of Securities Dealers, Inc., 1992-1996. Member, Market Operations Review Committee, Nasdaq Stock Market, Inc., 1996—. Member, Enforcement Advisory Comm., Ohio Div. Securities. Arbitrator, Securities, AAA and Futures Industry Forums. Private Mediator. ***PRACTICE AREAS:*** Litigation; Securities; Financial Market Regulation; Alternative Dispute Resolution. ***Email:*** rrapp@calfee.com

MARY M. REIL, born Dover, New Hampshire, 1956; admitted to bar, 1982, Ohio. *Education:* University of Miami (B.A., magna cum laude, 1977); Georgetown University (J.D., 1982). Associate Editor, The Tax Lawyer, 1981-1982. ***PRACTICE AREAS:*** Employee Benefits; Executive Compensation. ***Email:*** mreil@calfee.com

SANDRA G. ROLITSKY, born Cleveland, Ohio, 1954; admitted to bar, 1980, Michigan; 1982, Ohio. *Education:* University of Michigan (B.A., 1976); University of Detroit (J.D., 1980). Articles Editor, Detroit Law Review, 1979-1980. ***PRACTICE AREAS:*** Employee Benefits; Executive Compensation. ***Email:*** srolitsky@calfee.com

ROBERT A. ROSS, born Detroit, Michigan, 1960; admitted to bar, 1985, Ohio. *Education:* Miami University (B.S., magna cum laude, 1982); Georgetown University Law Center (J.D., magna cum laude, 1985). Associate Editor, The Tax Lawyer, 1984-1985. ***PRACTICE AREAS:*** Corporate Law; International Transactions; Mergers and Acquisitions; Partnership Law; Limited Liability Company Law; Joint Ventures; Private Finance; Tax Law. ***Email:*** rross@calfee.com

WILLIAM L. S. ROSS, born Jakarta, Indonesia, 1956; admitted to bar, 1982, Ohio; 1983, U.S. District Court, Northern District of Ohio; 1986, U.S. Court of Appeals, Sixth Circuit. *Education:* University of Virginia, Woodrow Wilson School of Government and Foreign Affairs (B.A., cum laude, 1979); College of William & Mary (J.D., 1982). Member, William & Mary Law Review, 1981-1982. Chair, Workers' Compensation Specialization Board of Examiners. Secretary, National Workers' Compensation Defense Network. *Member:* Cleveland, Ohio State (Past Chair, Workers' Compensation Law Committee) and American Bar Associations. ***PRACTICE AREAS:*** Workers Compensation Defense; OSHA; Employment Law; Litigation. ***Email:*** wross@calfee.com

RAYMOND RUNDELLI, born Cleveland, Ohio, January 31, 1960; admitted to bar, 1985, Ohio. *Education:* Miami University (A.B., summa cum laude, 1982); University of Michigan Law School (J.D., magna cum laude, 1985). *Member:* Cleveland, Ohio State and Federal Bar Associations; International Trademark Association; Cleveland Intellectual Property Law Association. ***PRACTICE AREAS:*** Intellectual Property; Intellectual Property Litigation. ***Email:*** rrundelli@calfee.com

LAWRENCE N. SCHULTZ, born Elyria, Ohio, 1948; admitted to bar, 1979, Ohio. *Education:* Ohio Northern University (B.A., 1970); Cleveland Marshall College of Law (J.D., magna cum laude, 1978). ***PRACTICE AREAS:*** Bankruptcy; Creditors Rights; Commercial Finance; Corporate Law; Information Technology; International Law; Mergers and Acquisitions; Partnership Law; Limited Liability Company Law; Joint Ventures; Private Finance. ***Email:*** lschultz@calfee.com

RONALD C. STANSBURY, born Port Clinton, Ohio, 1948; admitted to bar, 1974, Ohio. *Education:* The Ohio State University (B.A., 1970; J.D., summa cum laude, 1974). Adjunct Professor, Case Western Reserve University School of Law, 1990-1992. Chair, Northeast Ohio Chapter of the Midwest Pension and Employee Benefits Conference, 1995-1996. ***PRACTICE AREAS:*** Employee Benefits; Executive Compensation. ***Email:*** rstansbu@calfee.com

(This Listing Continued)

JAMES F. STREICHER, born Ashtabula, Ohio, 1940; admitted to bar, 1966, Ohio. *Education:* The Ohio State University (B.A., 1962); Case Western Reserve University (J.D., 1966). ***PRACTICE AREAS:*** Corporate Law; Partnership Law; Limited Liability Company Law; Joint Ventures; Private Finance. ***Email:*** jstreicher@calfee.com

JAMES C. VANDERWIST, born Cleveland, Ohio, 1958; admitted to bar, 1983, Ohio. *Education:* Duke University (B.A., magna cum laude, 1980); Georgetown University (J.D., 1983). Member, American Criminal Law Review. *Member:* American Bar Association (Member, Forum on Franchising). ***PRACTICE AREAS:*** Corporate Law; Mergers and Acquisitions; Franchising and Distribution Law. ***Email:*** jvanderwist@calfee.com

THOMAS E. WAGNER, born Erie, Pennsylvania, 1944; admitted to bar, 1973, Ohio. *Education:* United States Military Academy (B.S., 1966); Vanderbilt University (J.D., 1973). Associate Editor, Vanderbilt Law Review, 1972-1973. Law Director, 1979-1981, and Chief Administrative Officer, 1981, City of Cleveland. *Member:* Cleveland, Ohio State and American Bar Associations. ***PRACTICE AREAS:*** Corporate Law; Government Relations; Public Utility Law. ***Email:*** twagner@calfee.com

MARK I. WALLACH, born Cleveland, Ohio, 1949; admitted to bar, 1974, Ohio and U.S. District Court, Northern District of Ohio; 1985, U.S. Court of Appeals, Sixth Circuit and U.S. Supreme Court; 1991, U.S. District Court, Western District of Michigan and U.S. Court of Appeals, Eighth Circuit; 2001, U.S. District Court, Southern District of Ohio; 2004, U.S. District Court, Eastern District of Michigan. *Education:* Wesleyan University (B.A., magna cum laude, 1971); Harvard University (J.D., cum laude, 1974). Co-Chair, Firm's Litigation Group. Law Clerk to Chief Judge Frank J. Battisti, U.S. District Court, Northern District of Ohio, 1974-1975. Associate, Baker & Hostetler, 1975-1979. Chief Trial Counsel, City of Cleveland, 1979-1981. *Member:* Greater Cleveland, Ohio State, Federal and American Bar Associations; Cuyahoga County Law Directors Association. ***PRACTICE AREAS:*** Litigation; Municipal Law. ***Email:*** mwallach@calfee.com

MARCIA J. WEXBERG, born Cleveland, Ohio, 1953; admitted to bar, 1980, Pennsylvania; 1991, Ohio. *Education:* Miami University (B.A., magna cum laude, 1975); University of Pennsylvania (J.D., 1979); Temple University (LL.M, Taxation, 1984). Phi Beta Kappa. Lecturer and Author: "Federal Income Taxation of Trusts & Estates and Generation Skipping Tax," Pennsylvania Bar Quarterly, 1986; "Estate & Gift Tax Changes Made By the 1987 Omnibus Budget Reconciliation Act," Pennsylvania Bar Quarterly, 1988; "Estate, Gift and Generation-Skipping Transfer Taxes: Changes Made by the Miscellaneous Revenue Act of 1988," Pennsylvania Bar Quarterly, 1989; "The Omnibus Budget Reconciliation Act of 1989—Changes Affecting Estate, Gift and Generation-Skipping Transfer Taxes," Pennsylvania Bar Quarterly, 1990; "Estate Freezes Under the Revenue Reconciliation Act of 1990—Section 2036(c), Its Demise and Disinterment," Pennsylvania Bar Quarterly, 1991. Fellow, American College of Trust and Estate Counsel. ***PRACTICE AREAS:*** Corporate Succession; Estate Planning; Trust Planning; Estate Administration; Trust Administration; Charitable Planning. ***Email:*** mwexberg@calfee.com

CORNELIUS J. WHITFORD, born Parma, Ohio, 1964; admitted to bar, 1989, Ohio. *Education:* Fordham University (B.A., summa cum laude, 1986); Columbia Law School (J.D., 1989). Phi Beta Kappa. *Member:* Cleveland and Ohio State Bar Associations. ***PRACTICE AREAS:*** Corporate Successions; Corporate Law; Mergers, Acquisitions and Divestitures. ***Email:*** nwhitford@calfee.com

JOHN T. WIEDEMANN, born Hammond, Indiana, 1952; admitted to bar, 1977, California; 1996, Ohio; registered to practice before U.S. Patent and Trademark Office. *Education:* United States Air Force Academy; University of Cincinnati (B.S., Chemistry, cum laude, 1974); The Ohio State University (J.D., cum laude, 1977). *Member:* American Intellectual Property Law Association (Chair, Public Information Committee, 1992-1994; Chair, Licensing Committee, 1994-1996; Chair, Patent Law Committee, 2001-2002; Member, Board of Directors, 1997-2000). Fellow, American Intellectual Property Law Association, 2003. ***PRACTICE AREAS:*** Intellectual Property; Patents; Patent Litigation. ***Email:*** jwiedemann@calfee.com

CHRISTOPHER S. WILLIAMS, born Sandusky, Ohio, 1964; admitted to bar, 1990, Ohio; U.S. District Court, Northern and Southern Districts of Ohio, U.S. Court of Appeals, Fifth, Sixth and Ninth Circuits and U.S. Supreme Court. *Education:* Miami University (B.A., 1986); Georgetown University (J.D., 1989). *Member:* Cleveland, Ohio State, Federal and American Bar Associations. ***PRACTICE AREAS:*** Civil Litigation; ERISA Litigation; Trial Practice. ***Email:*** cwilliams@calfee.com

SCOTT R. WILSON, born Cleveland, Ohio, 1951; admitted to bar, 1977, Ohio. *Education:* University of Michigan (A.B., with high distinction, 1974); Case Western Reserve University (J.D., 1977). Phi Beta Kappa; Order of the Coif. Associate Editor, 1975-1976 and Editor, 1976-1977, Case Western Reserve Law Review. *Member:* Cleveland, Ohio State and American Bar Associations. ***PRACTICE AREAS:*** Corporate Law; Closely Held Corporations; Corporate Contracts; Corporate Formation; Corporate Governance; Corporate Reorganization; Corporate Successions; Corporate Taxation; Mergers, Acquisitions and Divestitures; Leveraged Buyouts; Finance; Partnership Law; Limited Liability Company Law. ***Email:*** swilson@calfee.com

RETIRED PARTNERS

FREDERICK W. ASSINI, born Koppel, Pennsylvania, 1943; admitted to bar, 1968, Ohio. *Education:* College of the Holy Cross (B.S., 1965); Duke University (J.D., 1968). ***PRACTICE AREAS:*** Corporate Succession Planning; Corporate Law; International Law; Mergers and Acquisitions. ***Email:*** rassini@calfee.com

WILLIAM A. BOYD, born Hillsboro, Ohio, 1946; admitted to bar, 1974, Ohio. *Education:* The Ohio State University (B.A.A.E., 1970; J.D., summa cum laude, 1974). Member, Editorial Staff, Ohio State Law Journal, 1973. (Retired). ***Email:*** wboyd@calfee.com

RICHARD CUSICK, born Northampton, Massachusetts, 1931; admitted to bar, 1955, Ohio. *Education:* John Carroll University (B.S., 1952); Case Western Reserve University (LL.B., 1955). Editor, Western Reserve Law Review, 1954-1955. Member, Sixth Circuit Judicial Conference, 1977—. ***PRACTICE AREAS:*** Litigation.

BRIAN M. EISENBERG, born Chicago, Illinois, 1942; admitted to bar, 1967, Ohio; 1979, Florida. *Education:* University of Pennsylvania (B.S., in Econ., cum laude, 1964); University of Michigan (J.D., 1967). Law Clerk, Chief Justice Kingsley A. Taft, Ohio Su-

(This Listing Continued)

CALFEE, HALTER & GRISWOLD LLP, Cleveland—Continued

preme Court, 1967-1968. Attorney, Office of General Counsel, Securities and Exchange Commission, 1968-1970. ***PRACTICE AREAS:*** Litigation. ***Email:*** beisenbe@calfee. com

DANIEL L. EKELMAN, born Cleveland, Ohio, 1926; admitted to bar, 1952, Ohio. *Education:* Ohio Wesleyan University (A.B., 1950); Case Western Reserve University (LL.B., 1952). Order of the Coif. Editor, Western Reserve Law Review, 1951-1952.

CHARLES R. EMRICK, JR., born Lakewood, Ohio, 1929; admitted to bar, 1958, Ohio. *Education:* Ohio University (B.S.C., 1951; M.S.J., 1952); The Cleveland-Marshall Law School (J.D., 1958). (Retired)

DALE C. LaPORTE, born Cleveland, Ohio, 1942; admitted to bar, 1966, Ohio. *Education:* University of Notre Dame (B.S., 1963); Case Western Reserve University (J.D., 1966). Order of the Coif. Managing Editor, Case Western Reserve Law Review, 1965-1966. ***PRACTICE AREAS:*** Corporate Law; Mergers and Acquisitions; Corporate Finance; Securities. ***Email:*** dlaporte@calfee.com

F. RUSH McKNIGHT, born Toledo, Ohio, 1929; admitted to bar, 1955, Ohio. *Education:* University of Pennsylvania; Case Western Reserve University (A.B., 1952; LL.B., 1955). Attorney Advisor to the Chairman, National Labor Relations Board, 1955-1956. Attorney, Cincinnati Regional Office, 1957. ***PRACTICE AREAS:*** Information Technology; Intellectual Property; International Law.

MICHAEL L. MILLER, born Miamisburg, Ohio, 1941; admitted to bar, 1966, Ohio. *Education:* Ohio University (A.B., 1963); Duke University (LL.B., 1966). Consul of Sweden (Ohio). ***PRACTICE AREAS:*** General Business; International Business Law; Transactions; Securities. ***Email:*** mmiller@calfee.com

JOHN L. NAYLOR, JR., born Springfield, Illinois, 1927; admitted to bar, 1951, Ohio and Michigan. *Education:* Wabash College (A.B., 1948); University of Michigan (J.D., 1951). Phi Beta Kappa. ***PRACTICE AREAS:*** Corporate; Employee Benefits.

TIMOTHY J. NOLAN, born Cleveland, Ohio; admitted to bar, 1967, Ohio. *Education:* Ohio University (B.B.A., 1964); The Ohio State University (J.D., 1966). ***Email:*** tnolan@calfee.com

RICHARD N. OGLE, born Springfield, Ohio, 1936; admitted to bar, 1961, Ohio. *Education:* Wittenberg College (A.B., 1958); University of Chicago (J.D., 1961). Law Clerk to Justice Henry L. Burman, Illinois Appellate Court, 1961-1962. ***Email:*** rogle@calfee.com

WILLIAM A. PAPENBROCK, born Cleveland, Ohio, 1938; admitted to bar, 1963, Ohio. *Education:* Miami University (B.S., 1960); Case Western Reserve University (LL.B., 1963). Editor, Western Reserve Law Review, 1962-1963. Law Clerk, Chief Justice Kingsley A. Taft, Ohio Supreme Court, 1963-1964.

KENNETH R. SCHMEICHEL, born Chicago, Illinois, 1947; admitted to bar, 1973, Ohio. *Education:* Elmhurst College (B.A., magna cum laude, 1969); University of Chicago (J.D., 1973). Certified Public Accountant, Illinois, 1970. ***PRACTICE AREAS:*** Taxation; Retirement Planning; Business Planning. ***Email:*** kschmeic@calfee.com

JOSEPH D. SULLIVAN, born Toledo, Ohio, 1931; admitted to bar, 1958, Ohio and District of Columbia. *Education:* Cornell University; John Carroll University (B.S., 1953); University of Michigan (LL.B., 1958). (Retired)

KEVIN M. SULLIVAN, born Worcester, Massachusetts, 1944; admitted to bar, 1974, Ohio. *Education:* College of the Holy Cross (B.S., 1966); University of Notre Dame (M.B.A., 1969); Case Western Reserve University (J.D., 1974). Order of the Coif. ***PRACTICE AREAS:*** Public Utility Law; Telecommunications Law. ***Email:*** ksullivan@calfee. com

JOHN D. WHEELER, born Conneaut, Ohio, 1940; admitted to bar, 1964, Ohio. *Education:* Allegheny College (B.S., 1961); Case Western Reserve University (J.D., 1964). ***PRACTICE AREAS:*** Corporate Law; Government Relations; Legislative Practice; Health Care; Long Term Care; College and University Law; Information Technology; Partnership Law; Limited Liability Company Law; Joint Ventures; Private Finance; Real Estate. ***Email:*** jwheeler@calfee.com

ASSOCIATES

W. ERIC BAISDEN, born Wadsworth, Ohio; admitted to bar, 1991, Ohio. *Education:* Ashland College (B.S., 1986); Case Western Reserve University (J.D., 1991). ***PRACTICE AREAS:*** Labor and Employment. ***Email:*** ebaisden@calfee.com

ALYSSA J. BELL, born Park Ridge, Illinois, 1971; admitted to bar, 2002, Ohio. *Education:* Miami University (B.S., 1993); Ohio State University (M.S., 1995); Case Western Reserve University (J.D., magna cum laude, 2002). Order of the Coif. *Member:* Cleveland, Ohio State and American Bar Associations. ***PRACTICE AREAS:*** Environmental; Real Estate. ***Email:*** abell@calfee.com

STACY R.C. BERLINER, born Lorain, Ohio, 1978; admitted to bar, 2003, Ohio. *Education:* University of Aberdeen, Scotland, 1998; College of Wooster (B.A., cum laude, 2000); Cleveland-Marshall College of Law (J.D., summa cum laude, 2003). Editor-in-Chief, Cleveland-Marshall Law Review. *Member:* Cleveland Bar Association. ***PRACTICE AREAS:*** Litigation; Business; Commercial; Insurance Coverage; ERISA; Contract Litigation. ***Email:*** sberliner@calfee.com

CHET J. BONNER, born Geneva, Ohio, 1966; admitted to bar, 2002, Ohio and U.S. District Court, Northern District of Ohio; 2005, U.S. District Court, Western District of Michigan; registered to practice before U.S. Patent and Trademark Office. *Education:* Ohio University (B.S., 1989); Cleveland State University (M.B.A., summa cum laude, 1998); Cleveland-Marshall College of Law (J.D., summa cum laude, 2002). *Member:* Cleveland, Ohio State and American Bar Associations; Cleveland Intellectual Property Law Association. ***PRACTICE AREAS:*** Intellectual Property. ***Email:*** cbonner@calfee.com

ALAN C. BRANDT, born Cleveland, Ohio; admitted to bar, 2001, Ohio; 2002, U.S. District Court, Northern District of Ohio; registered to practice before U.S. Patent and Trademark Office. *Education:* Ohio (DeVry) Institute of Technology (B.S. in Electronics Engineering Technology, with honors, 1982); Johns Hopkins University (M.A.S., 1988); Case Western Reserve University (J.D., 2000). *Member:* Cleveland, Ohio State and American Bar Associations; Cleveland Intellectual Property Law Association; American Intellectual Property Law Association. ***PRACTICE AREAS:*** Intellectual Property; Information Technology; Intellectual Property Licensing. ***Email:*** abrandt@calfee.com

JARON R. BROWN, born Columbus, Ohio, 1976; admitted to bar, 2002, Ohio. *Education:* University of Hartford (B.S., magna cum laude, 1999); Case Western Reserve University (J.D., 2002). *Member:* Ohio and Cleveland Bar Associations. ***PRACTICE AREAS:*** Securities; Corporate; Mergers, Acquisitions and Divestitures. ***Email:*** jbrown@calfee.com

MATTHEW E. BURKE, born Cleveland, Ohio, 1968; admitted to bar, 1995, Ohio. *Education:* University of Michigan (B.A., 1991); Case Western Reserve University School of Law (J.D., 1995). *Member:* Ohio State and American Bar Associations. ***PRACTICE AREAS:*** Corporate Law; Mergers and Acquisitions; Closely Held Corporations; Corporate Formation; Leveraged Buyouts; Spin-Offs; Leveraged Acquisitions. ***Email:*** mburke@calfee.com

MASSIMO CAPRETTA, born Castel di Sangro, Italy, 1974; admitted to bar, 2000, Illinois (Not admitted in Ohio). *Education:* University of Chicago (A.B., with honors, 1997); University of Michigan (J.D., magna cum laude, 2000). *Member:* American Bar Association. ***PRACTICE AREAS:*** Commercial Business; Finance. ***Email:*** mcapretta@calfee.com

ZOE K. CARLISLE, born Erie, Pennsylvania, 1979; admitted to bar, 2004, Ohio. *Education:* Case Western Reserve University (B.A., summa cum laude, 2001); Emory University (J.D., with honors, 2004). ***PRACTICE AREAS:*** Litigation. ***Email:*** zcarlisle@calfee.com

S. PAIGE CHRISTOPHER, born Ridgewood, New Jersey, 1968; admitted to bar, 1995, Illinois; 1996, Ohio; registered to practice before U.S. Patent and Trademark Office. *Education:* Duke University (B.A., 1990); The John Marshall Law School (J.D., 1995). Regional Champion, 1995 National Mock Trial Competition, ABA, Young Lawyers Division. Executive Editor, The Journal of Computer and Information Law, 1994-1995. *Member:* American Intellectual Property Law Association; Cleveland Intellectual Property Law Association. ***PRACTICE AREAS:*** Intellectual Property. ***Email:*** pchristopher@calfee.com

SUZANNE M. CONROY, born Columbus, Ohio, 1969; admitted to bar, 1995, Ohio. *Education:* Ohio University (B.S., 1991); Cleveland-Marshall College of Law (J.D., 1995). ***PRACTICE AREAS:*** Real Estate. ***Email:*** sconroy@calfee.com

HEATHER C. CORRIGAN, born Shaker Heights, Ohio, 1973; admitted to bar, 2001, Ohio. *Education:* Kent State University (B.A., magna cum laude, 1995); Cleveland-Marshall College of Law (J.D., magna cum laude, 2001). *Member:* Cleveland and Ohio State (Member, Legal Education Committee) Bar Associations. ***PRACTICE AREAS:*** Real Estate. ***Email:*** hcorrigan@calfee.com

TRACY D. CRANDALL, born Brooklyn, New York, 1972; admitted to bar, 1997, Ohio. *Education:* Bucknell University (B.A., cum laude, 1994); Cleveland-Marshall College of Law (J.D., summa cum laude, 1997). ***PRACTICE AREAS:*** Corporate; Information Technology; Mergers and Acquisitions; International; Partnerships, LLCs and Joint Ventures. ***Email:*** tcrandall@calfee.com

DIANE HUGHES DOBREA, born Taipei, Taiwan, 1964; admitted to bar, 1994, Ohio; registered to practice before U.S. Patent and Trademark Office. *Education:* Case Western Reserve University (B.A., 1986; M.S., with honors, 1990; J.D., cum laude, 1994). *Member:* Cleveland and Ohio State Bar Associations; American Intellectual Property Law Association; Cleveland Intellectual Property Law Association; Association of University Technology Managers. ***PRACTICE AREAS:*** Intellectual Property; Technology Transfer; Biotechnology Licensing; Biotechnology; Biotechnology Patent Prosecution; International Patents; Mechanical Patent Prosecution; Medical Patents; Patent Licensing; Trademarks; Trademark Licensing; Contracts. ***Email:*** ddobrea@calfee.com

RYAN W. FALK, born Pittsburgh, Pennsylvania, 1977; admitted to bar, 2003, Ohio; registerd to practice before U.S. Patent and Trademark Office. *Education:* University of Akron (B.S., 2000); Case Western Reserve University College of Law (J.D., magna cum laude, 2003). Order of the Coif. *Member:* Cleveland, Ohio State and American Bar Associations; American Intellectual Property Law Association; Cleveland Intellectual Property Law Association. ***PRACTICE AREAS:*** Intellectual Property; Information Technology. ***Email:*** rfalk@calfee.com

KRISTIN J. FROST, born St. Louis, Missouri, 1972; admitted to bar, 2001, Ohio; registered to practice before U.S. Patent and Trademark Office. *Education:* University of Missouri at St. Louis (B.S., 1995); The Ohio State University (M.S., 1998); Ohio State University College of Law (J.D., with honors, 2001). *Member:* Cleveland, Ohio State and American Bar Associations; Cleveland Intellectual Property Law Association; American Intellectual Property Law Association. ***PRACTICE AREAS:*** Intellectual Property. ***Email:*** kfrost@calfee.com

ALEXANDER E. GERTSBURG, born Moldavia, U.S.S.R., 1975; admitted to bar, 2001, Ohio and U.S. District Court, Northern and Southern Districts of Ohio. *Education:* Miami University (B.A., 1997); Cleveland-Marshall College of Law (J.D., magna cum laude, 2000); U.S. Army Transportation Officer School (2000). Order of Barristers. *Member:* Cleveland, Cuyahoga County, Ohio State and Federal Bar Associations. [With U.S.A.R., Transportation Corps, 1993-2004; Served in Iraq in support of Operation Iraqi Freedom, 2003]. ***LANGUAGES:*** Russian. ***PRACTICE AREAS:*** Litigation; Business Law; Commercial Law; First Amendment; Unfair Competition; Defamation; Securities; Broker-Dealer Arbitration. ***Email:*** agertsburg@calfee.com

MELISSA M. GLEESPEN, born Wheaton, Illinois, 1968; admitted to bar, 2000, Massachusetts; 2003, Ohio. *Education:* Harvard University (A.B.A., cum laude, 1997); Northeastern University (J.D., 2000). *Member:* Boston, Cleveland and American Bar Associations. ***PRACTICE AREAS:*** Securities; Capital Markets; Corporate; Mergers and Acquisitions. ***Email:*** mgleespen@calfee.com

JAMES D. GRAHAM, born Cleveland, Ohio, 1965; admitted to bar, 1995, Ohio. *Education:* Hiram College (B.A., cum laude, 1988); University of Michigan (M.A., French Literature, 1990); Case Western Reserve University (J.D., cum laude, 1995). Phi Beta Kappa. Articles Editor, Case Western Reserve Journal of International Law, 1994-1995. Author: "Re-evaluation of the Dispute Resolution Mechanism in the Canada-U.S. Free Trade

(This Listing Continued)

Agreement: The Softwood Lumber Dispute," 28 Case W. Res. J. of Int'l L 473, 1996. Co-Author: "Development of International Arbitration in 18th and 19th Century United States-Great Britain Relations and its Relevancy Today," Dispute Resolution J., Jan.-Mar., 1996. ***LANGUAGES:*** French. ***PRACTICE AREAS:*** Commercial Finance; Information Technology; International Law. ***Email:*** jgraham@calfee.com

GINA K. HAGEDORN, born Cincinnati, Ohio, 1977; admitted to bar, 2004, Ohio. *Education:* Miami University (B.S., magna cum laude, 2000); Case Western Reserve University (M.B.A., 2000); Case Western Reserve University School of Law (J.D., magna cum laude, 2004). ***PRACTICE AREAS:*** Corporate. ***Email:*** ghagedorn@calfee.com

WARREN M. HAINES II, born Topeka, Kansas; admitted to bar, 1995, North Carolina; 1998, Missouri and Kansas; 2000, Ohio; 2002, U.S. Supreme Court; registered to practice before U.S. Patent and Trademark Office. *Education:* University of Kansas (B.S., Chem.E., 1984); Duquesne University Law School (J.D., magna cum laude, 1995). *Member:* Ohio State (Member, Intellectual Property Section) and American (Member, Intellectual Property Section) Bar Associations; American Intellectual Property Law Association. ***PRACTICE AREAS:*** Intellectual Property. ***Email:*** whaines@calfee.com

SHELLY K. HILLYER, born Ashtabula, Ohio; admitted to bar, 1994, Pennsylvania; 2000, U.S. District Court, Eastern District of Pennsylvania; 2001, U.S. District Court, Northern District of Ohio; 2002, Ohio. *Education:* Ohio State University (B.A., 1988); Temple University School of Law (J.D., cum laude, 1994). Member, Temple Law Review. Law Clerk to the Hon. Edward G. Biester, Jr., Bucks County, Pennsylvania, 1994-1995. Author, "The Attorney-Client Privilege, Ethical Rules of Confidentiality and Other Arguments Bearing on Disclosure of a Fugitive Client's Whereabouts," Temple Law Review, 1995. Co-Author: with Michael Brittain, "General Counsel: Think You're Fully Covered by Your Company's D&O Policy? Think Again," Insights, Summer 2005; with Michael Brittain, "The Keys to Directors' and Officers' Coverage," Directorship, January 2005; with Michael Brittain, "Maximizing Insurance Coverage in the Wake of Ohio's Asbestos Tort Reform," Mealey's Litigation Report: Insurance, Dec. 7, 2004. Assistant District Attorney, Philadelphia District Attorney's Office, 1995-2000. Litigation Associate, Drinker, Biddle & Reath LLP, Philadelphia, Pennsylvania, 2000-2001. *Member:* Cleveland, Ohio State and Pennsylvania Bar Associations. ***PRACTICE AREAS:*** Insurance Coverage; Business Litigation; Commercial Litigation. ***Email:*** shillyer@calfee.com

GEORGE HOSKINS, born Columbus, Ohio, 1972; admitted to bar, 1998, Ohio. *Education:* University of Chicago (B.A., 1995); Ohio State University College of Law (J.D., 1998). ***PRACTICE AREAS:*** Information Technology; Intellectual Property. ***Email:*** ghoskins@calfee.com

MARK R. HULL, born Rochester, New York, 1968; admitted to bar, 2004, Ohio and U.S. District Court, Northern District of Ohio; registered to practice before U.S. Patent and Trademark Office. *Education:* The Pennsylvania State University (B.S., cum laude, 1990); Case Western Reserve University Weatherhead School of Management (M.B.A., 1998); University of Akron School of Law (J.D., summa cum laude, 2004). *Member:* Cleveland and Ohio State Bar Associations. ***PRACTICE AREAS:*** Intellectual Property. ***Email:*** mhull@calfee.com

WILLIAM A. JOHNSTON, born Lima, Ohio, 1966; admitted to bar, 1999, Ohio; registered to practice before U.S. Patent and Trademark Office. *Education:* The Pennsylvania State University (B.S., 1988); Cleveland-Marshall College of Law (J.D., cum laude, 1999). ***PRACTICE AREAS:*** Intellectual Property; Patents; Trademark Prosecution. ***Email:*** wjohnston@calfee.com

LAURA K. KENDALL, born Youngstown, Ohio, 1977; admitted to bar, 2004, Ohio. *Education:* University of Akron (B.A. summa cum laude, 1999); Case Western Reserve University (J.D., magna cum laude, 2004). *Member:* Ohio State and American Bar Associations. ***PRACTICE AREAS:*** Labor and Employment. ***Email:*** lkendall@calfee.com

DENEEN LAMONICA, born Euclid, Ohio; admitted to bar, 2001, Ohio; 2005, Illinois. *Education:* Cleveland State University (B.A., summa cum laude, 1997); Cleveland-Marshall College of Law (J.D., 2000). Dean's Merit Scholar. Recipient: Outstanding Achievement in Psychology, Cleveland State University. *Member:* Chicago, Cleveland, Cuyahoga County (Co-Chair, Leadership Academy, 2002-2003) and Ohio State Bar Associations; Justinian Forum. ***PRACTICE AREAS:*** Toxic Torts; Products Liability. ***Email:*** dlamonica@calfee.com

JEFFREY J. LAUDERDALE, born Allentown, Pennsylvania, 1975; admitted to bar, 2002, Ohio; 2003, U.S. District Court, Northern District of Ohio, U.S. District Court, Western District of Michigan, U.S. Court of Appeals, Sixth and Federal Circuits and U.S. Tax Court. *Education:* Ohio University (A.B., 1998); The Ohio State University (J.D., with honors, 2001); New York University (LL.M., Taxation, 2002). Member, The Ohio State Law Journal, 2000-2001. Law Clerk to the Hon. Richard F. Suhrheinrich, U.S. Court of Appeals, Sixth Circuit, 2002-2003. Author, "A New Trend in the Law of Privilege: The Federal Settlement Privilege and the Proper Use of Federal Rule of Evidence 501 for the Recognition of New Privileges," 35 U. Mem. L. Rev. 255 (2005). *Member:* Cleveland, Ohio State, Federal and American Bar Associations. ***PRACTICE AREAS:*** Litigation. ***Email:*** jlauderdale@calfee.com

SHARON A. LUARDE, born Decatur, Indiana, 1964; admitted to bar, 1995, Indiana and U.S. District Court, Northern and Southern Districts of Indiana; 1999, Ohio and U.S. District Court, Northern District of Ohio. *Education:* Indiana University (B.A., 1991; J.D., cum laude, 1994). *Member:* Cleveland, Ohio State and American Bar Associations. ***PRACTICE AREAS:*** Litigation. ***Email:*** sluarde@calfee.com

SCOTT C. MATASAR, born Philadelphia, Pennsylvania, 1970; admitted to bar, 1996, New York and U.S. District Court, Southern and Eastern Districts of New York; 1997, Maryland; 1998, New Jersey; 2000, Ohio and U.S District Court, Northern District of Ohio. *Education:* Columbia College, Columbia University (B.A., 1992); Boston University (J.D., with honors in Health Law concentration, 1995); University College of Wales, Aberystwyth, United Kingdom (1st Class, Welsh and Celtic Studies). Managing Editor, Boston University International Law Journal, 1994-1995. Author, "False Memory Syndrome and Sex Abuse Cases," 22 J. of L., Med. & Ethics 286, 1994. *Member:* American Bar Association (Member, Tort Trial and Insurance Practice Section). ***LANGUAGES:*** Welsh. ***REPORTED CASES:*** Estate of Lola Brewer v. Dowell & Jones, et al., (8th Dist. Ct. App. 2002), 2002 Ohio 3440. ***PRACTICE AREAS:*** Insurance Coverage; Securities Litigation; Commercial Litigation. ***Email:*** smatasar@calfee.com

LAURA C. McBRIDE, born Augusta, Georgia, 1974; admitted to bar, 2003, California (Not admitted in Ohio). *Education:* College of Wooster (B.A., 1996); Dartmouth College (M.S., 1997); George Washington University (J.D., 2003). *Member:* State Bar of California; American Bar Association. ***PRACTICE AREAS:*** Litigation. ***Email:*** lmcbride@calfee.com

STEPHEN L. McCAULEY, born Ravenna, Ohio, 1960; admitted to bar, 1993, Ohio. *Education:* Kent State University (B.S., with honors, 1982); The Ohio State University (J.D., cum laude, 1992); John Marshall Law School (LL.M., with honors, 1993). ***PRACTICE AREAS:*** Intellectual Property. ***Email:*** smccaule@calfee.com

AMY B. McGANN, born Warren, Ohio, 1976; admitted to bar, 2001, Ohio. *Education:* Boston College, Carroll School of Management (B.S., cum laude, 1998); Case Western Reserve University, Weatherhead School of Management (M.B.A., 2001); Case Western Reserve University School of Law (J.D., cum laude, 2001). *Member:* Cleveland, Ohio State and American Bar Associations. ***PRACTICE AREAS:*** Corporate; Mergers and Acquisitions; Securities; Capital Markets. ***Email:*** amcgann@calfee.com

JOHN J. McGUIRE, born Cleveland, Ohio, 1973; admitted to bar, 1998, Ohio. *Education:* University of Pennsylvania (B.A., B.S., in Economics, 1995); Case Western Reserve University (J.D., magna cum laude, 1998). Order of the Coif. ***PRACTICE AREAS:*** Corporate Law; Mergers and Acquisitions; Commercial Business; Finance. ***Email:*** jmcguire@calfee.com

RONALD M. McMILLAN, born Cleveland, Ohio, 1968; admitted to bar, 2000, Ohio; 2001, U.S. District Court, Northern District of Ohio; 2003, U.S. Court of Appeals, Sixth Circuit. *Education:* Cleveland State University (B.A., 1996; J.D., summa cum laude, 2000). *Member:* Cleveland, Ohio State and American Bar Associations. ***PRACTICE AREAS:*** Commercial Litigation; Construction Litigation; Civil Litigation; Tort Defense. ***Email:*** rmcmillan@calfee.com

WESLEY C. MEINERDING, born Canton, Ohio, 1974; admitted to bar, 2002, Ohio. *Education:* University of Notre Dame (B.S.M.E., 1998); University of Toledo (J.D., 2002). ***PRACTICE AREAS:*** Intellectual Property. ***Email:*** wmeinerding@calfee.com

MATTHEW M. MENDOZA, born Cincinnati, Ohio, 1970; admitted to bar, 1997, Ohio. *Education:* Kent State University (B.A., summa cum laude, 1994); Ohio State University (J.D., with honors in law, 1997). ***PRACTICE AREAS:*** Business Litigation; Commercial Litigation; Insurance Coverage Litigation; Tort Litigation; Accident Litigation; Products Liability Litigation; Civil Litigation. ***Email:*** mmendoza@calfee.com

BRIAN M. MURRAY, born Bayonne, New Jersey, 1974; admitted to bar, 1999, Ohio. *Education:* Case Western Reserve University (B.A., 1996; J.D., 1999). *Member:* Cleveland, Ohio State and American Bar Associations. ***PRACTICE AREAS:*** Employee Benefits. ***Email:*** bmurray@calfee.com

THOMAS R. O'DONNELL, born Cleveland, Ohio; admitted to bar, 1996, Ohio. *Education:* John Carroll University (B.A., 1991); Cleveland Marshall College of Law (J.D., 1996). ***PRACTICE AREAS:*** Environmental Law. ***Email:*** todonnell@calfee.com

COLLEEN MORAN O'NEIL, born Cleveland, Ohio, 1970; admitted to bar, 1996, Ohio. *Education:* John Carroll University (B.A., 1992); Cleveland-Marshall College of Law (J.D., magna cum laude, 1996). ***PRACTICE AREAS:*** Litigation. ***Email:*** coneil@calfee.com

NENAD PEJIC, born Cleveland, Ohio, 1967; admitted to bar, 1996, Ohio; U.S. District Court, Northern District of Ohio; registered to practice before U.S. Patent and Trademark Office;. *Education:* The Ohio State University (B.S., Electrical Engineering, 1991); Cleveland State University (J.D., cum laude, 1996). *Member:* Ohio State and American Bar Associations; Cleveland Intellectual Property Law Association. ***PRACTICE AREAS:*** Intellectual Property; Electrical Intellectual Property; Electronic Intellectual Property; Intellectual Property Litigation; Intellectual Property Procurement; Intellectual Property Prosecution; Intellectual Property Rights; Mechanical Intellectual Property; Intellectual Property Portfolio Management. ***Email:*** npejic@calfee.com

DANIEL P. PETROV, born Cleveland, Ohio, 1976; admitted to bar, 2001, Ohio; 2002, U.S. District Court, Northern District of Ohio and U.S. Court of Appeals, Sixth Circuit; 2005, U.S. Court of Appeals, Fifth Circuit. *Education:* Columbia University (B.A., 1998); Case Western Reserve University (J.D., 2001). Appointed Member: Columbia University Alumni Representation Committee, 2002; Case Western Reserve University Law Alumni Board, 2004; Leadership Board, Cleveland Playhouse Square Partners, 2005. *Member:* Cleveland, Ohio State and American Bar Associations. ***PRACTICE AREAS:*** Labor and Employment. ***Email:*** dpetrov@calfee.com

GREGORY J. PHILLIPS, born Washington, D.C., 1970; admitted to bar, 1998, Virginia; 1999, District of Columbia; 2004, Ohio; U.S. District Court, Northern District of Ohio, U.S. District Court, Eastern District of Virginia, U.S. Court of Appeals, Sixth and Eleventh Circuits and U.S. Court of Federal Claims. *Education:* Princeton University (A.B., magna cum laude, 1993); University of Virginia School of Law (J.D., 1998). ***PRACTICE AREAS:*** Litigation; Antitrust Litigation; Business Litigation; Commercial Litigation; Corporate Litigation; Securities Litigation. ***Email:*** gphillips@calfee.com

BRENT M. PIETRAFESE, born Mayfield Heights, Ohio, 1978; admitted to bar, 2003, Ohio. *Education:* Miami University (B.S., cum laude, 2000); Case Western Reserve University (J.D., 2003; M.B.A., 2003). *Member:* Cleveland, Cuyahoga County, Ohio State and American Bar Associations. ***PRACTICE AREAS:*** Mergers and Acquisitions; Corporate Restructuring; Succession Planning; Corporate. ***Email:*** bpietrafese@calfee.com

BILLY CARTER RAULERSON, born Fort Myers, Florida, 1970; admitted to bar, 2001, Ohio; 2002, District of Columbia; registered to practice before U.S. Patent and Trademark Office. *Education:* University of South Florida (B.S.C.S., summa cum laude, 1998; B.S.C.I.S., summa cum laude, 1998); University of Dayton (J.D., cum laude, 2001). *Member:* Ohio State Bar Association; The District of Columbia Bar; American Intellectual Property Law Association. ***PRACTICE AREAS:*** Intellectual Property; Information Technology. ***Email:*** braulerson@calfee.com

(This Listing Continued)

CALFEE, HALTER & GRISWOLD LLP, Cleveland—Continued

KARLA M. ROGERS, born Minerva, Ohio, 1970; admitted to bar, 1997, Ohio. *Education:* University of Akron (B.S., cum laude, 1992); Cleveland Marshall College of Law (J.D., cum laude, 1996). *Member:* Cleveland and Ohio State Bar Associations. ***PRACTICE AREAS:*** Telecommunications Law; Real Estate; Private and Public Finance. ***Email:*** krogers@calfee.com

JENNIFER L. ROTH, born Ravenna, Ohio, 1974; admitted to bar, 2002, Ohio. *Education:* Ohio State University (B.S., 1996); Case Western Reserve University (J.D., cum laude, 2002). *Member:* American Bar Association. ***PRACTICE AREAS:*** Public Law; Finance. ***Email:*** jroth@calfee.com

DAVID A. RUIZ, born Toledo, Ohio, 1973; admitted to bar, 2000, Pennsylvania and U.S. District Court, Western District of Pennsylvania; 2002, Ohio; 2003, U.S. District Court, Northern District of Ohio. *Education:* The Ohio State University (B.A., 1997); The Ohio State University, Moritz College of Law (J.D., 2000). *Member:* Pennsylvania, Ohio State and American Bar Associations. ***PRACTICE AREAS:*** Corporate Litigation; Commercial Litigation; Antitrust Compliance Litigation. ***Email:*** druiz@calfee.com

KENNETH J. SMITH, born Elyria, Ohio, 1972; admitted to bar, 2000, Ohio; registered to practice before U.S. Patent and Trademark Office. *Education:* University of Toledo (B.S., 1995); Cleveland-Marshall College of Law (J.D., magna cum laude, 2000). *Member:* Cleveland Bar Association. ***PRACTICE AREAS:*** Intellectual Property. ***Email:*** ksmith@calfee.com

KRISTOFER K. SPREEN, born Indianapolis, Indiana, 1974; admitted to bar, 1999, Massachusetts; 2005, Ohio. *Education:* University of Washington (B.A., 1996); Georgetown University (J.D., 1999). *Member:* Cleveland, Ohio State and American Bar Associations. ***PRACTICE AREAS:*** Securities and Capital Markets; General Corporate. ***Email:*** kspreen@calfee.com

VARNESH SRITHARAN, born Colombo, Sri Lanka, 1975; admitted to bar, 2001, Minnesota; 2005, Ohio. *Education:* University of Massachusetts (B.A., 1998); University of Illinois College of Law (J.D., 2001). *Member:* Cleveland and American Bar Associations. ***PRACTICE AREAS:*** Securities; Capital Markets; Corporate. ***Email:*** vsritharan@calfee.com

ANTHONY F. STRINGER, born Melbourne, Florida, 1973; admitted to bar, 1999, Ohio. *Education:* Fordham University (B.A., 1995); The Ohio State University College of Law (J.D., 1999). ***PRACTICE AREAS:*** Litigation. ***Email:*** astringer@calfee.com

K. JAMES SULLIVAN, born Manassas, Virginia, 1976; admitted to bar, 2001, Ohio; 2002, U.S. District Court, Northern District of Ohio. *Education:* John Carroll University (B.A., magna cum laude, 1998); University of Virginia Law School (J.D., 2001). *Member:* Cleveland, Ohio State and Federal Bar Associations. ***PRACTICE AREAS:*** Banks and Banking; Class Action Defense; Class Actions; Civil Litigation; Federal Civil Litigation; Insurance Litigation. ***Email:*** kjsullivan@calfee.com

ALEXANDER N. TEETER, born Albany, New York, 1975; admitted to bar, 2002, Massachusetts; 2003, U.S. District Court, District of Massachusetts; 2005, Ohio. *Education:* Colgate University (B.A., cum laude, with high honors in Philosophy, 1998); Boston College (J.D., cum laude, 2002). Senior Editor, Law Review. *Member:* Boston, Cleveland, Massachusetts, Ohio State and American Bar Associations. ***PRACTICE AREAS:*** Commercial Business; Finance. ***Email:*** ateeter@calfee.com

JENNIFER L. VERGILII, born Manhasset, New York, 1972; admitted to bar, 1997, Illinois; 1999, Iowa; 2001, Ohio. *Education:* College of the Holy Cross (B.A., 1994); Case Western Reserve University (J.D., 1997). ***PRACTICE AREAS:*** Corporate Law; Information Technology; Mergers and Acquisitions. ***Email:*** jvergilii@calfee.com

KAREN A. VISOCAN, born Cleveland, Ohio; admitted to bar, 1993, Ohio. *Education:* Ohio University (B.S., magna cum laude, 1990); Case Western Reserve University (J.D., 1993). Order of the Barristers. Author: "Prescription Drug Importation and Reimportation: But Everybody's Doing It," Cleveland Bar Association Journal, April 2005; "What Every Lawyer Should Know About Health Law," Cleveland Bar Association Journal, April 2004; "Recent Changes in Medicare Managed Care: A Step Backwards?" 6 (1) The Elder Law Journal, 1998; "Managed Care Organizations and Appeals," J. of the National Academy of Elder Law Attorneys, 1997; "Managed Care: What Are The Costs," The Ohio Lawyer, 1997; "Medicare Appeals," Elder Law Desk Reference, 1997; "Medicare and Medicaid Are They Just Health Care Systems," University of Houston Law Review, 1992. Adjunct Professor: Case Western Reserve University School of Law; Cleveland-Marshall College of Law; Ursuline College. Committee Chair, Health Care Financial Management Association. *Member:* Cleveland (Vice President, Health Law Section) and Ohio State (Former Chair, Managed Care Subcommittee) Bar Associations; National Health Lawyers Association. ***PRACTICE AREAS:*** Health Care; Bankruptcy; Corporate Law; Long Term Care; Creditors Rights. ***Email:*** kvisocan@calfee.com

THOMAS M. WELSH, born Akron, Ohio, 1977; admitted to bar, 2003, Ohio. *Education:* Miami University (B.A., 1999); Case Western Reserve University School of Law (J.D., 2003). *Member:* Ohio State and American Bar Associations; American Health Lawyers Association. ***PRACTICE AREAS:*** Corporate; Healthcare. ***Email:*** twelsh@calfee.com

NATHAN A. WHEATLEY, born Conneaut, Ohio, 1969; admitted to bar, 2000, Ohio and U.S. District Court, Northern District of Ohio. *Education:* Kent State University (B.A., 1993); University of Akron School of Law (J.D., summa cum laude, 1999). Member, American Mensa. *Member:* Ohio State and American Bar Associations; American Trial Lawyers Association. ***PRACTICE AREAS:*** Commercial Litigation; Bankruptcy Litigation; Bankruptcy; Utility Law. ***Email:*** nwheatley@calfee.com

JENNIFER L. WICK, born Boston, Massachusets, 1976; admitted to bar, 2001, Ohio. *Education:* Washington & Lee University (B.S., magna cum laude, 1998; J.D., magna cum laude, 2001). Order of the Coif. ***PRACTICE AREAS:*** Intellectual Property. ***Email:*** jbuckey@calfee.com

(This Listing Continued)

GEORGIA E. YANCHAR, born Morgantown, West Virginia, October 4, 1974; admitted to bar, 1999, Ohio; 2004, New York. *Education:* University of Pittsburgh (B.S., 1996); Pepperdine University (J.D., 1999). ***PRACTICE AREAS:*** Intellectual Property. ***Email:*** gyanchar@calfee.com

LISA M. YERRACE, born Youngstown, Ohio, 1977; admitted to bar, 2002, Ohio; 2003, U.S. District Court, Northern District of Ohio. *Education:* Case Western Reserve University (B.A., 1999); The Ohio State University (J.D., 2002). Law Clerk to U.S. Bankruptcy Judge Russ Kendig, Canton, Ohio. *Member:* American Bankruptcy Institute; International Women's Insolvency and Restructuring Confederation, Northeast Ohio Network. ***PRACTICE AREAS:*** Bankruptcy; Creditors Rights; Commercial Transactions. ***Email:*** lyerrace@calfee.com

SENIOR ATTORNEYS

SEAN C. BECKSTROM, born Cleveland, Ohio, 1967; admitted to bar, 1995, Ohio. *Education:* Ohio University (A.B., 1990); Cleveland-Marshall College of Law (J.D., 1995). Phi Beta Kappa. *Member:* Cleveland and Ohio State Bar Associations. ***PRACTICE AREAS:*** Partnership Law; Limited Liability Company Law; Joint Ventures; Private Finance; Real Estate; Construction Law; Real Estate Exchanges. ***Email:*** sbeckstrom@calfee.com

PETER A. CARFAGNA, born Shaker Heights, Ohio, 1953; admitted to bar, 1979, Ohio; U.S. Court of Appeals, Sixth Circuit. *Education:* Harvard University (A.B., summa cum laude, 1975; B.A., 1977); Oxford University, Oxford, England (M.A., with honours, 1977); Harvard Law School (J.D., magna cum laude, 1979). Phi Beta Kappa; Rhodes Scholar. Member: Case Western Reserve University School of Law's first Distinguished Visiting Practitioner; Diocese of Cleveland Finance Council Member; United Way of Lake County Board Member; Chairman of the Board, Secretary/Treasurer, Lake County Captains; Greater Cleveland Sports Commission Board Member. Elected Director: Worldwide Harvard Alumni Association; Association of American Rhodes Scholars. ***PRACTICE AREAS:*** Litigation; Government Relations and Legislation; General Corporate. ***Email:*** pcarfagna@calfee.com

WADE DOUGLASS CLARK, born Canton, Ohio, 1954; admitted to bar, 1980, Ohio; 1981, Florida. *Education:* Youngstown State University (B.A., cum laude, 1976); University of Akron School of Law (J.D., 1980). Articles Editor, Akron Law Review, 1979-1980. *Member:* Cleveland and American Bar Associations. ***PRACTICE AREAS:*** Employee Benefits; Executive Compensation. ***Email:*** wclark@calfee.com

CORINE R. CORPORA, born Cleveland, Ohio, 1963; admitted to bar, 1992, Ohio. *Education:* Cleveland State University (B.B.A., 1988); Case Western Reserve University (J.D., 1992). *Member:* Cleveland, Ohio State and American Bar Associations. ***PRACTICE AREAS:*** Employee Benefits; Executive Compensation. ***Email:*** ccorpora@calfee.com

PAMELA A. DOCHERTY, born Youngstown, Ohio, 1944; admitted to bar, 1994, Ohio; registered to practice before U.S. Patent and Trademark Office. *Education:* Washington College (B.S., Biology, summa cum laude, 1965); Pennsylvania State University (Ph.D., Physiology, 1979); University of Akron (J.D., summa cum laude, 1994). Case and Comment Editor, Akron Law Review, 1993-1994. Author: "The Human Genome, A Patenting Dilemma," 26 Akron Law Review 525, 1993. ***PRACTICE AREAS:*** Intellectual Property. ***Email:*** pdochert@calfee.com

MARY E. GOLRICK, born Cleveland, Ohio, 1957; admitted to bar, 1985, Ohio; registered to practice before U.S. Patent and Trademark Office. *Education:* Cleveland State University (B.S., cum laude, 1979); Cleveland Marshall College of Law, Cleveland State University (J.D., magna cum laude, 1985). Member, Board of Editors, Cleveland State Law Review, 1984-1985. ***PRACTICE AREAS:*** Intellectual Property. ***Email:*** mgolrick@calfee.com

JEAN M. HILLMAN, born Cleveland, Ohio, 1960; admitted to bar, 1994, Ohio. *Education:* Baldwin-Wallace College (B.A., 1989); Cleveland Marshall College of Law (J.D., 1994). *Member:* Cleveland, Ohio State and American Bar Associations; Estate Planning Council of Cleveland. ***PRACTICE AREAS:*** Estate Planning; Trust Planning; Estate Administration; Trust Administration. ***Email:*** jhillman@calfee.com

SHERYL K. KELLY, born Knob Knoster, Missouri, 1956; admitted to bar, 1980, Ohio. *Education:* St. Bonaventure University; University of Akron (B.A., 1977); C. Blake McDowell School of Law, University of Akron (J.D., 1980). Delta Theta Phi. Author: "Commercial Speech and Advertising," Akron Law Review, Fall, 1978. *Member:* Cleveland and American Bar Associations; Commercial Law League of America. ***PRACTICE AREAS:*** Commercial Finance. ***Email:*** skelly@calfee.com

DONALD E. LAMPERT, born Philadelphia, Pennsylvania, 1948; admitted to bar, 1986, Ohio. *Education:* University of Pittsburgh (B.A., 1969); University of Pennsylvania (M.A., 1971); Rutgers University (Ph.D., 1975); Case Western Reserve University (J.D., 1986). Adjunct Professor, Case Western Reserve University School of Law. Academic Advisor, Ohio State Bar Association Workers' Compensation Specialty Board. *Member:* Cleveland, Ohio State and American Bar Associations. ***PRACTICE AREAS:*** Workers Compensation; OSHA. ***Email:*** dlampert@calfee.com

KENNETH L. LOHISER, born Painesville, Ohio, 1963; admitted to bar, 1988, Ohio. *Education:* The Ohio State University (B.A., cum laude, 1985); University of Cincinnati (J.D., 1988). Member, Moot Court Board. ***PRACTICE AREAS:*** Real Estate. ***Email:*** klohiser@calfee.com

RUTH L. LOVETT, born Schenectady, New York, 1950; admitted to bar, 1985, Ohio. *Education:* Lycoming College (A.B., 1972); Case Western Reserve University (J.D., magna cum laude, 1985). Order of the Coif. ***PRACTICE AREAS:*** Employee Benefits; Executive Compensation. ***Email:*** rlovett@calfee.com

JOHN E. MILLER, JR., born Berwyn, Illinois, 1944; admitted to bar, 1970, District of Columbia; 1997, Ohio; registered to practice before U.S. Patent and Trademark Office. *Education:* Purdue University (B.S.Chem.E., 1966); Georgetown University (J.D., 1970). *Member:* Licensing Executives Society. ***PRACTICE AREAS:*** Intellectual Property. ***Email:*** jmiller@calfee.com

(This Listing Continued)

MICHAEL T. MULCAHY, born 1951; admitted to bar, 1976, Ohio; 1985, Michigan; 1989, Illinois. *Education:* Bowling Green State University (B.S., 1973); Cleveland-Marshall College of Law (J.D., 1976). ***PRACTICE AREAS:*** Public Utility Law; Telecommunications Law. ***Email:*** mmulcahy@calfee.com

CYNTHIA KRIPS PORT, born Washington, D.C., 1969; admitted to bar, 1998, Maryland; 2001, Virginia; 2002, Ohio. *Education:* University of Maryland (B.A., 1991); American University, Washington College of Law (J.D., magna cum laude, 1997). *Member:* Cleveland, Cuyahoga County, Ohio State and Maryland State Bar Associations. ***PRACTICE AREAS:*** Estate Planning; Estate Administration. ***Email:*** cport@calfee.com

GRETCHEN ROGGE, born Toledo, Ohio, 1969; admitted to bar, 1997, Ohio. *Education:* Northwestern University (B.A., 1992); Boston University (J.D., 1997). ***PRACTICE AREAS:*** Employee Benefits; Executive Compensation. ***Email:*** grogge@calfee.com

CRISTIN ROSE SNODGRASS, born Ft. Riley, Kansas, May 17, 1977; admitted to bar, 2003, Ohio; 2004, Florida. *Education:* The Ohio State University (B.A., Humanities, Major in History, 1999); Case Western Reserve University (J.D., 2003). *Member:* Cleveland, Ohio State and American Bar Associations; The Florida Bar. ***PRACTICE AREAS:*** Estate and Succession Planning; Estate Administration; Estate Planning. ***Email:*** csnodgrass@calfee.com

JACK R. STARKOFF, born Cleveland, Ohio, 1969; admitted to bar, 1994, Ohio; 1995, Florida and U.S. District Court, Southern District of Ohio; 2002, U.S. District Court, Northern District of Ohio. *Education:* University of Wisconsin-Madison (B.S., 1991); Emory University School of Law (J.D., 1994). *Member:* Cleveland, Ohio State and American Bar Associations. (Certified Specialist in Workers' Compensation Law, Ohio State Bar Association). ***PRACTICE AREAS:*** Workers Compensation; Labor and Employment. ***Email:*** jstarkoff@calfee.com

CHRISTOPHER M. STEVENS, born Providence, Rhode Island, 1965; admitted to bar, 1991, California; U.S. District Court, Southern, Central, Eastern, and Northern Districts of California; U.S. Court of Appeals, Ninth Circuit (Not admitted in Ohio). *Education:* Boston University (B.A., 1987); Syracuse University (J.D., 1990). *Member:* State Bar of California. ***PRACTICE AREAS:*** Litigation. ***Email:*** cstevens@calfee.com

SUSAN R. STROM, born Toronto, Ontario, Canada, 1951; admitted to bar, 1978, New York; 1983, New Jersey; 1990, Ohio. *Education:* University of Cincinnati (B.A., 1973); University of Cincinnati College of Law (J.D., 1977). Law Clerk to Honorable Paul G. Levy, Superior Court, State of New Jersey, 1983-1984. Assistant Counsel to Honorable Thomas H. Kean, Governor of New Jersey, 1986-1988. ***PRACTICE AREAS:*** Environmental Law; Real Estate. ***Email:*** sstrom@calfee.com

MAGDA B. SZABO, born Cleveland, Ohio, 1953; admitted to bar, 1977, Ohio, U.S. District Court, Northern District of Ohio and U.S. Tax Court. *Education:* Cleveland-Marshall College of Law (J.D., 1977); Cleveland State University (M.A.F.I.S., 1984); Case Western Reserve University School of Law (LL.M., Taxation, 2003). Certified Public Accountant, Ohio. Author: "Estate Tax Planning in a Climate of Change," Tax Notes Today, August 23, 2004; "Asset Protection Trusts: A Planning Opportunity in Some States," Journal of Taxation of Investments, Autumn 2004; "Asset Protection," Cleveland Bar Association Journal, October 2004; "Tax Practitioner Responsibilities Expand Under Circular 230," Catalyst Magazine (OSCPA), September/October 2004. Speaker, "Asset Protection" & "Estate Planning Updates," OSCPA Ohio State Tax Institute, December 2004; "Asset Protection," National Business Institute, March 2005; "Nonprofits in Ohio," National Business Institute, June 2005. *Member:* Cleveland and American (Member: Tax Club, Estate Planning Council) Bar Associations; American Institute of Certified Public Accountants; Ohio State Certified Public Accountants (Editorial Advisory Board, Catalyst Magazine); International Lawyers' Group; Northern Ohio Planned Giving Council. ***PRACTICE AREAS:*** Taxation; Estate Planning; Probate Litigation; Asset Protection; International. ***Email:*** mszabo@calfee.com

PAUL E. SZABO, born Cleveland, Ohio, 1953; admitted to bar, 1979, Ohio; 1981, U.S. District Court, Northern District of Ohio; 1989, U.S. Court of Appeals for the Federal Circuit; registered to practice before U.S. Patent and Trademark Office. *Education:* St. John's College (B.A., 1974); Cleveland Marshall College of Law (J.D., 1978). Law Clerk to Judge Thomas O. Matia and Judge Daniel O. Corrigan, Common Pleas Court of Cuyahoga County, Ohio, 1979-1981. *Member:* Cleveland, Ohio State and American Bar Associations; Cleveland Intellectual Property Law Association. ***PRACTICE AREAS:*** Patent; Trademark. ***Email:*** pszabo@calfee.com

CHRISTINA TAIT, born Frankfurt, Indiana, 1964; admitted to bar, 1995, Ohio. *Education:* Boston University (B.A., 1986); Case Western Reserve University (J.D., cum laude, 1995). Member, International City and County Managers Association. *Member:* Ohio State Bar Association. [Officer, U.S. Navy, 1986-1992]. ***PRACTICE AREAS:*** Public Law; Finance; Public Partnerships; Private Partnerships. ***Email:*** ctait@calfee.com

INNA VYSMAN, born Krasnoyarsh, Russia, 1967; admitted to bar, 1994, Connecticut; 1995, New York (Not admitted in Ohio). *Education:* Siberian Technological Institute (B.S., summa cum laude, 1989); Fordham University School of Law (J.D., 1994). ***PRACTICE AREAS:*** Investments; Partnership Law; Limited Liability Company Law; Securities. ***Email:*** ivysman@calfee.com

WILLIAM E. ZITELLI, born Pittsburgh, Pennsylvania, 1941; admitted to bar, 1986, Pennsylvania (Not admitted in Ohio). *Education:* University of California at Los Angeles (B.S.E., 1969); Duquesne University (J.D., 1986). *Member:* Cleveland Intellectual Property Law Association. ***PRACTICE AREAS:*** Intellectual Property. ***Email:*** wzitelli@calfee.com

STAFF ATTORNEYS

ROBERT J. BONKO, born Cleveland, Ohio, 1955; admitted to bar, 1993, Ohio. *Education:* University of Akron (B.A., 1977); Cleveland State University (M.P.A., 1984; J.D., 1992). *Member:* Cleveland and Ohio State Bar Associations; Defense Research Institute. ***PRACTICE AREAS:*** Antitrust and Trade Regulation; Environmental Law; Litigation. ***Email:*** rbonko@calfee.com

(This Listing Continued)

LINDA U. ELLIOTT, born Cleveland, Ohio; admitted to bar, 1991, Ohio. *Education:* Cleveland State University (B.A., 1987); Cleveland Marshall College of Law (J.D., cum laude, 1990). *Member:* Cleveland, Ohio State and American Bar Associations. ***PRACTICE AREAS:*** Workers Compensation; Workers Compensation Defense. ***Email:*** lelliott@calfee.com

DAVID E. GRAY, II, born Martinsburg, West Virginia, 1970; admitted to bar, 1999, Ohio. *Education:* Marshall University (B.A., cum laude, 1996); Cleveland-Marshall College of Law (J.D., 1999). *Member:* Cleveland, Ohio State and American Bar Associations. [U.S. Army Paratrooper, 1989-1992; Veteran of the Persian Gulf War]. ***PRACTICE AREAS:*** Workers Compensation; OSHA; Products Liability Litigation; Labor and Employment Litigation. ***Email:*** dgray@calfee.com

SENIOR COUNSEL

MARC L. OBERDORFF, born Lakewood, Ohio, 1953; admitted to bar, 1980, Ohio; 2000, Kentucky. *Education:* Princeton University (A.B., 1980); Georgetown University (J.D., 1980). Editor, Georgetown Law Journal, 1979-1980. Lecturer in Law, Cleveland-Marshall College of Law, 1991—. *Member:* Kentucky Bar Association. ***LANGUAGES:*** French and Italian. ***PRACTICE AREAS:*** College and University Law; Information Technology; Public Law; Public Finance; Tax Law. ***Email:*** moberdor@calfee.com

OF COUNSEL

JOHN PAUL BATT, born Buffalo, New York, 1952; admitted to bar, 1978, Ohio. *Education:* Williams College (B.A., 1974); Case Western Reserve University (J.D., 1978). Phi Beta Kappa; Order of the Coif. Case Western Reserve Law Review, 1976-1978. ***PRACTICE AREAS:*** Partnership Law; Limited Liability Company Law; Joint Ventures; Private Finance; Real Estate; Securities; Tax Law. ***Email:*** jbatt@calfee.com

All Attorneys are Members of the Greater Cleveland, Ohio State and American Bar Associations.

CARLISLE, McNELLIE, RINI, KRAMER & ULRICH CO., L.P.A.

24755 CHAGRIN BOULEVARD, SUITE 200
CLEVELAND, OHIO 44122-5690
Telephone: 216-360-7200
FAX: 216-360-7210
URL: http://www.carlisle-law.com

Columbus, Ohio Office: Suite 200, 155 West Main Street. Telephone: 614-464-2704.

General Civil Practice. Real Estate, Mortgage, Corporation, Probate, Bankruptcy and Family Law. Trials.

GERALD K. CARLISLE, born Akron, Ohio, December 2, 1934; admitted to bar, 1960, Ohio. *Education:* College of Wooster (B.A., 1956); The Cleveland-Marshall Law School (LL.B., 1960). Delta Theta Phi. *Member:* Cleveland, Ohio State and American Bar Associations. (Retired) (Also of Counsel to Carlisle-Kesling, Morgan, Conlan, LLC). ***PRACTICE AREAS:*** Housing and Urban Development; Partnerships; Limited Liability Companies; Commercial Litigation; Construction Contracts; Mortgage Finance.

RICHARD L. McNELLIE, born Oil City, Pennsylvania, September 8, 1948; admitted to bar, 1975, Ohio. *Education:* Case Western Reserve University (B.A., 1970); Cleveland Marshall College of Law (J.D., 1975). *Member:* Cuyahoga County, Ohio State and American Bar Associations. ***PRACTICE AREAS:*** Real Estate Bankruptcy; Real Estate Finance; Real Estate Foreclosure; Real Estate Title; Real Estate Workouts.

WILLIAM T. RINI, born Cleveland, Ohio, October 6, 1949; admitted to bar, 1975, Ohio. *Education:* Baldwin-Wallace College (B.A., 1971); Cleveland Marshall College of Law (J.D., 1975). Phi Alpha Delta. Assistant Prosecutor, City of Cleveland, 1978. *Member:* Ohio State and American Bar Associations; Ohio Academy of Trial Lawyers; The Association of Trial Lawyers of America. ***PRACTICE AREAS:*** Civil Litigation; Divorce; Criminal Defense; Estate Probate; Real Estate.

HERBERT J. KRAMER, born Cleveland, Ohio, October 24, 1958; admitted to bar, 1984, Ohio; 1986, U.S. District Court, Northern District of Ohio; 1996, U.S. Court of Appeals, Sixth Circuit and U.S. Supreme Court. *Education:* John Carroll University (B.S.B.A., 1980); Cleveland-Marshall College of Law (J.D., 1984). *Member:* Cleveland, Ohio State and American Bar Associations. ***PRACTICE AREAS:*** Real Estate Finance; Commercial Real Estate; Closely Held Business; Commercial Law; Estate Administration; Estate Planning; Foreclosures.

PHYLLIS A. ULRICH, born Columbus, Ohio, May 18, 1966; admitted to bar, 1991, Ohio and U.S. District Court, Northern District of Ohio; 1993, U.S. Court of Appeals, Sixth Circuit; 1995, U.S. District Court, Southern District of Ohio; 1996, U.S. Supreme Court. *Education:* The University of Akron (B.A., magna cum laude 1988; J.D. 1991). *Member:* Akron (Member and Past Chair, Bankruptcy and Commercial Law Section), Cleveland (Member, Bankruptcy and Commercial Law Sections) and Ohio State (Member, Litigation Section) Bar Associations; American Bankruptcy Institute. ***REPORTED CASES:*** In Re Price, (Bkrtcy. N.D. Ohio 2004), 304 B.R. 769; In Re Crawford, (Bkrtcy. N.D. Ohio 1999), 232 B.R. 92; In Re Andersson, (6th Cir. BAP, Ohio, 1997), 209 B.R. 76. ***PRACTICE AREAS:*** Bankruptcy; Foreclosures; Banking Law; Creditors Rights; Commercial Litigation.

RICHARD A. UTZ, born Bucyrus, Ohio, November 26, 1952; admitted to bar, 1977, Ohio. *Education:* Ohio State University (B.A., 1974; J.D., 1977). Phi Alpha Sigma; Phi Delta Phi. *Member:* Columbus, Crawford County, Ohio State and American (Member, Real Property, Probate and Trust Law Section) Bar Associations. (Resident at Columbus Office). ***PRACTICE AREAS:*** Real Estate Title; Real Estate Title Insurance; Quiet Title; Real Estate Finance; Real Estate Workouts.

(This Listing Continued)

CARLISLE, McNELLIE, RINI, KRAMER & ULRICH CO., L.P.A., Cleveland—Continued

JAMES L. SASSANO, born Cleveland, Ohio, November 3, 1964; admitted to bar, 1993, Ohio; 1998, U.S. District Court, Northern District of Ohio. *Education:* Bowling Green State University (B.S.B.A., 1988); Cleveland Marshall College of Law (J.D., 1993). *Member:* Cleveland and Ohio State (Member, Real Estate Section, 1995—) Bar Associations. ***PRACTICE AREAS:*** Real Estate; Foreclosures. ***Email:*** jsassano@carlisle-law.com

ERIC T. DEIGHTON, born Cleveland, Ohio, February 28, 1973; admitted to bar, 1999, Ohio. *Education:* Wheeling Jesuit College (B.A., 1996); Case Western Reserve School of Law (J.D., 1999). ***PRACTICE AREAS:*** Foreclosures; Evictions; Creditors Representation. ***Email:*** edeighton@carlisle-law.com

AMY M. BLYTHE-GLAZE, born Akron, Ohio, December 26, 1972; admitted to bar, 1999, Ohio and U.S. District Court, Northern District of Ohio. *Education:* Ohio Northern University (B.A., 1995); Akron University Law School (J.D., 1999). Order of Omega. Member, Mortar Board. *Member:* Cleveland and Ohio State Bar Associations. ***PRACTICE AREAS:*** Bankruptcy; Creditors Rights; Probate. ***Email:*** aglaze@carlisle-law.com

MARK A. POLAND, born Cincinnati, Ohio, May 9, 1970; admitted to bar, 2000, Ohio. *Education:* University of Cincinnati (B.B.A., 1993); Cleveland-Marshall College of Law (J.D., 1999). *Member:* Ohio State and American Bar Associations. ***PRACTICE AREAS:*** Real Estate; Foreclosures; Collections; Bankruptcy. ***Email:*** mpoland@carlisle-law.com

RICHARD J. FEUERMAN, born Cleveland, Ohio, October 6, 1972; admitted to bar, 1999, Ohio and U.S. District Court, Northern District of Ohio. *Education:* The Ohio State University (B.A., 1994); Cleveland-Marshall College of Law (J.D., 1998). *Member:* Cleveland, Cuyahoga County and Ohio State Bar Associations. ***LANGUAGES:*** Spanish and Hungarian. ***PRACTICE AREAS:*** Foreclosures; Real Estate; Civil Litigation. ***Email:*** rfeuerman@carlisle-law.com

GEORGE J. ANNOS, born Warren, Ohio, June 3, 1958; admitted to bar, 1992, Ohio. *Education:* Mount Union College (B.A., 1980); University of Akron (J.D., 1992). *Member:* Trumbull County Bar Association. ***PRACTICE AREAS:*** Real Estate Foreclosure; Probate Administration; Domestic Relations. ***Email:*** gannos@carlisle-law.com

OSCAR E. ALBORES, born Cleveland, Ohio, May 14, 1977; admitted to bar, 2002, Ohio. *Education:* John Carroll University (B.S., 1999); The Ohio State University (J.D., 2002). Delta Theta Phi. *Member:* Ohio State Bar Association. ***LANGUAGES:*** Spanish. ***PRACTICE AREAS:*** Real Estate Foreclosure; Real Estate. ***Email:*** oalbores@carlisle-law.com

SANDOR W. STERNBERG, born Budapest, Hungary, August 2, 1954; admitted to bar, 1984, Ohio and U.S. District Court, Northern District of Ohio. *Education:* Case Western Reserve; Cleveland State University (B.A., 1982); Ohio Northern University (J.D., 1984). Member, National Moot Court Team. *Member:* Cleveland, Cuyahoga County and Ohio State Bar Associations. ***LANGUAGES:*** Hungarian. ***PRACTICE AREAS:*** Litigation; Real Estate; Business Law. ***Email:*** ssternberg@carlisle-law.com

REPRESENTATIVE CLIENTS: Federal National Mortgage Assn.; Dollar Bank, FSB; First Merit Bank N.A.; Security Savings Mortgage Corp.; Shamrock Graphics Inc.; Principal Residential Mortgage Corp.; Ohio Title Corp.; T.A. Title Insurance Company.
REFERENCE: First Merit Bank N.A.

JOSEPH D. CARNEY & ASSOCIATES, L.L.C.

Established in 1994

2001 CROCKER ROAD, SUITE 440
CLEVELAND, OHIO 44145
Telephone: 440-899-1551
Fax: 440-892-4147
Email: info@jdcarney.com
URL: http://www.jdcarneylaw.com

Small, Medium and Large Business Counseling, Corporate Law, Litigation, Commercial and Residential Real Estate, Estate Planning, Employment Law Compliance, Securities Law, Capital Formation, Commercial Contracts, Mergers and Acquisitions, Financing Related Law, Employment Law, Construction, Regulatory, Liquor Law, Broker-Dealers, Insurance Law.

JOSEPH D. CARNEY, born Berea, Ohio, 1952; admitted to bar, 1977, Ohio; 1980, District of Columbia. *Education:* Boston University (B.A., 1974; M.S., 1977); Case Western Reserve University (J.D., 1977); Georgetown University (LL.M., Securities Regulation, 1983). Phi Alpha Delta. Staff, Securities and Exchange Commission, 1977-1983. Attorney: Division of Investment Management, 1977-1980; Division of Enforcement, 1980-1982. Special Counsel, Office of General Counsel, 1982-1983. Arbitrator: New York Stock Exchange, Inc.; National Association of Securities Dealers, Inc.; American Arbitration Association. Ohio Division of Securities Advisory Committees: Member, Licensing Advisory Committee, 1988—; Member, 1989— and Co-Chairperson, 1990-1992, Enforcement Advisory Committee. Calfee, Halter & Griswold, Associate, 1984-1986; Partner, 1987-1993. *Member:* Cleveland (Chair, 1993-1994; Chair-Elect, 1992-1993; Secretary, 1991-1992; Treasurer, 1990-1991; Securities Law Section), Ohio State, Federal (Chairperson, 1988-1989; Deputy Chairperson, 1987-1988; Secretary, 1986-1987; Director, 1985-1986, Young Lawyer Division; President, 1993-1994; President-Elect, 1992-1993; Vice President, 1991-1992; Treasurer, 1990-1991; Director, 1989-1990, Cleveland Chapter) and American Bar Associations; Ohio Venture Association; Urban Land Institute. ***Email:*** jdc@jdcarney.com

ASSOCIATE

BRYAN S. MOLLOHAN, admitted to bar, 1998, Ohio and U.S. District Court, Northern District of Ohio. *Education:* Baldwin-Wallace College (B.A., Business Finance, History, 1995); Cleveland State University (J.D., 1998).: Member: Cleveland, Ohio State and American (Member, Sections of: Corporations, Banking and Business Law; Real Property; Taxation; Litigation; Administrative Law; Estate Planning) Bar Associations. ***PRACTICE AREAS:*** Corporate Finance; Employment Law; Real Estate; Estate Planning; Wills; Litigation. ***Email:*** bsm@jdcarney.com

(This Listing Continued)

CAVITCH, FAMILO, DURKIN & FRUTKIN CO., L.P.A.

Established in 1886

1717 EAST NINTH STREET, FOURTEENTH FLOOR
CLEVELAND, OHIO 44114-2876
Telephone: 216-621-7860
Telecopier: 216-621-3415
Email: law@cfdf.com
URL: http://www.cfdf.com

Business Law, Taxation, Estate Planning, Probate, Pension and Profit Sharing, Real Estate, Trial and Appellate Practice.

FIRM PROFILE: Cavitch, Familo, Durkin & Frutkin, is engaged in the general civil and business practice of law. Our practice embraces all civil specialties as they relate to the problems and planning concerns of business entities and their owners. Our firm traces its history to the late 1800's and enjoys an enviable reputation as one of the top firms in the Cleveland area.

The firm's clients include manufacturers, service and retail businesses, hospitals, real estate developers, brokerage firms and builders. In addition, the firm represents professional practices, such as physicians, attorneys, accountants, and professional athletes, as well as financial enterprises such as brokerages, venture capitalists, banks and insurance companies. In addition, the firm serves as an editor for the Matthew Bender publications, Rabkin & Johnson Current Legal Forms, and the Ohio Transaction Guide.

HARVEY L. FRUTKIN, born San Antonio, Texas, April 22, 1945; admitted to bar, 1972, Ohio. *Education:* Ohio University (A.B., cum laude, 1967); University of Michigan (J.D., magna cum laude, 1971). Order of the Coif; Phi Beta Kappa. Member of Faculty, Ohio Corporation Law with Federal Tax Analysis, Case Western Reserve University Law School, 1977-1981. University of Akron Law School Symposium, 1983. Author: *Taxation of Executive Compensation:* Planning and Practice, Matthew Bender & Co., 1983; *Pension and Profit-Sharing Plans:* Forms and Practice, Matthew Bender & Co., 1989. General Chairman, Cleveland Tax Institute, 1987. ***PRACTICE AREAS:*** Business Planning; Corporate Succession; Taxation; Estate Planning; Health Care. ***Email:*** hfrutkin@cfdf.com

THOMAS G. BELDEN, born Cincinnati, Ohio, June 15, 1944; admitted to bar, 1971, Ohio. *Education:* University of Notre Dame (B.B.A., 1966); University of Michigan (M.B.A., 1967); Case Western Reserve University (J.D., 1971). Order of the Coif. Member, National Moot Court Team. Note Editor, Case Western Reserve Law Review, 1970-1971. Member, Adjunct Faculty, Real Estate Planning, Case Western Reserve Law School, 1985-1986. ***PRACTICE AREAS:*** Business Law; Taxation; Real Estate. ***Email:*** tbelden@cfdf.com

ROBERT M. NELSON, born Youngstown, Ohio, November 21, 1946; admitted to bar, 1971, Ohio. *Education:* John Carroll University (B.S., 1968); University of Notre Dame; Case Western Reserve University (J.D., 1971). Order of the Coif. Note Editor, Case Western Reserve Law Review, 1970-1971. ***PRACTICE AREAS:*** Estate Planning; Business Law; Probate. ***Email:*** rnelson@cfdf.com

JAMES DICKINSON, born Cleveland, Ohio, 1948; admitted to bar, 1973, Ohio; 1991, Florida. *Education:* Washington & Lee University (B.A., 1970); University of Virginia (J.D., 1973). Phi Beta Kappa. Fellow, American College of Trust and Estate Counsel. ***PRACTICE AREAS:*** Estate Planning; Trust Planning; Estate Administration; Trust Administration; Corporate Law.

MICHAEL C. COHAN, born Boston, Massachusetts, November 7, 1952; admitted to bar, 1977, Ohio. *Education:* Boston College (A.B., magna cum laude, 1974); Loyola University (J.D., 1977). Phi Alpha Delta; Alpha Sigma Nu. Case and Index Editor, Loyola Law Review, 1976-1977. ***PRACTICE AREAS:*** Employment Law; Commercial Litigation; Civil Litigation; Real Estate Litigation. ***Email:*** mcohan@cfdf.com

STEPHEN E. PIGOTT, born Cleveland, Ohio, December 26, 1954; admitted to bar, 1980, Ohio; 1981, U.S. District Court, Northern District of Ohio; 1985, U.S. Tax Court. *Education:* Pennsylvania State University (B.S., 1977); The Ohio State University (J.D., 1980). ***PRACTICE AREAS:*** Business Law; Partnerships and Limited Liability Companies; Taxation; Nonprofit Corporations. ***Email:*** spigott@cfdf.com

DOUGLAS A. DIPALMA, born Euclid, Ohio, May 17, 1955; admitted to bar, 1980, Illinois; 1985, Ohio, U.S. District Court, Northern Districts of Illinois and Ohio. *Education:* University of Notre Dame (B.A., cum laude, 1977); Case Western Reserve University (J.D., 1980). Order of the Coif. ***PRACTICE AREAS:*** Commercial Litigation; Employment Law; Civil Litigation. ***Email:*** ddipalma@cfdf.com

THOMAS M. CAWLEY, born Cleveland, Ohio, June 23, 1956; admitted to bar, 1982, Ohio; 1983, Florida. *Education:* Grove City College (B.A., 1978); Case Western Reserve University (J.D., 1982). Order of the Coif. Member: Order of the Barristers; National Moot Court Team, 1981-1982. *Member:* The Florida Bar. ***PRACTICE AREAS:*** Business Law; Taxation; ERISA. ***Email:*** tcawley@cfdf.com

MOHAMMED J. BIDAR, born Cleveland, Ohio, November 26, 1958; admitted to bar, 1984, Ohio. *Education:* Case Western Reserve University (B.S., cum laude, 1981; J.D., 1984). Beta Alpha Psi. ***PRACTICE AREAS:*** Estate Planning; Elder Law; Tax Law; Probate; Tax Exempt Organizations. ***Email:*** mbidar@cfdf.com

HAROLD O. MAXFIELD, JR., born Cleveland, Ohio, July 7, 1961; admitted to bar, 1986, Ohio. *Education:* Baldwin-Wallace College (B.A., 1983); Cleveland Marshall College of Law (J.D., cum laude, 1986). Staff Member, Cleveland Marshall College Law Review, 1984-1985. *Member:* Cleveland Bar Association (Co-Chairperson, Real Estate Institute, 1999-2001; Vice Chairman, Real Estate Section, 2002-2003). ***PRACTICE AREAS:*** Business Law; Real Estate. ***Email:*** hmaxfield@cfdf.com

(This Listing Continued)

RONALD D. HOLMAN, II, born Cleveland, Ohio, 1959; admitted to bar, 1986, Ohio. *Education:* Dartmouth College (B.A., 1982); Columbia University (J.D., 1986). ***PRACTICE AREAS:*** Civil Litigation; Employment Law; Commercial Litigation. ***Email:*** rholman@cfdf.com

MARK A. TRUBIANO, born Cleveland, Ohio, July 31, 1963; admitted to bar, 1988, Ohio. *Education:* Case Western Reserve University (B.S., 1985; J.D., cum laude, 1988). Beta Alpha Psi. ***PRACTICE AREAS:*** Business Law; Estate Planning; Probate; Successions; Elder Law. ***Email:*** mtrubiano@cfdf.com

ALEXANDER E. GOETSCH, born Chicago, Illinois, February 28, 1969; admitted to bar, 1995, Ohio; 1996, Florida. *Education:* Heidelberg College (B.A., 1991); Cleveland Marshall College of Law (J.D., 1995). Editor, Cleveland State Law Review, 1993-1995. *Member:* The Florida Bar. ***PRACTICE AREAS:*** Civil Litigation. ***Email:*** agoetsch@cfdf.com

RETIRED PARTNERS

ZOLMAN CAVITCH, born Traverse City, Michigan, November 17, 1925; admitted to bar, 1951, Ohio. *Education:* University of Michigan (A.B., 1948; J.D., 1950). Order of the Coif. Associate Editor, Michigan Law Review, 1949-1950. Author: *Ohio Corporation Law with Federal Tax Analysis,* Matthew Bender & Co., 1961; *Business Organizations with Tax Planning,* Matthew Bender & Co., 1965; *Tax Planning For Corporations and Shareholders,* Matthew Bender & Co., 1974. Co-Author: *Michigan Corporation Law with Federal Tax Analysis,* Matthew Bender & Co., 1963; *Massachusetts Corporation Law with Federal Tax Analysis,* Matthew Bender & Co., 1963. Member of Faculty, Law School, Western Reserve University, 1954-1973.

EDWARD D. FAMILO, born Detroit, Michigan, July 15, 1921; admitted to bar, 1948, Ohio. *Education:* Western Reserve University (A.B., 1943; J.D., 1948). Phi Delta Phi. Lecturer on Federal Practice and Bankruptcy, Cleveland-Marshall Law School. ***PRACTICE AREAS:*** Business Law. ***Email:*** efamilo@cfdf.com

OF COUNSEL

GEORGE J. DURKIN, born Cleveland, Ohio, December 12, 1934; admitted to bar, 1962, Ohio. *Education:* University of Notre Dame (B.B.S., 1956); Western Reserve University (LL.B., 1962). Order of the Coif. Member of Faculty, Federal Income Tax Law and Ohio Corporations Law with Federal Tax Analysis, Case Western Reserve University, 1971-1977. ***PRACTICE AREAS:*** Taxation Law; Business Law. ***Email:*** gdurkin@cfdf.com

HOWARD P. KASDAN, born Cleveland, Ohio, February 7, 1945; admitted to bar, 1969, Ohio; U.S. Supreme Court. *Education:* Ohio University (A.B., 1966); Case-Western Reserve University (J.D., 1969). *Member:* Ohio State Bar Association. ***PRACTICE AREAS:*** Domestic Relations; Family Law; Business Planning.

ROBERT C. HEINTEL, born Cleveland, Ohio, August 17, 1971; admitted to bar, 1996, Ohio; 1997, U.S. District Court, Northern District of Ohio. *Education:* John Carroll University (B.S.B.A., cum laude, 1993); Case Western Reserve University School of Law (J.D., cum laude, 1996). Managing Editor, Case Western Reserve University Law Review, 1995-1996. Co-Editor: Ohio Transaction Guide, Matthew Bender & Co., 2000-2001; Current Legal Forms, Matthew Bender & Co., 2000-2001. Author, "The Need for an Alternative to Antitrust Regulation of the National Football League," Note 46 C.W.R.U. Law Review 1033 (1996). Associate Attorney, Cavitch, Familo, Durkin & Frutkin, Cleveland, Ohio, 1996-2001. *Member:* Cleveland Bar Association. (Corporate Counsel)

SHANNON L. McEANENEY, born Columbus, Ohio, May 22, 1972; admitted to bar, 1998, Ohio. *Education:* John Carroll University (B.A., 1994); Cleveland-Marshall College of Law, Cleveland State University (J.D., cum laude, 1998). ***PRACTICE AREAS:*** Estate Planning; Probate. ***Email:*** smceaneney@cfdf.com

MATTHEW E. SENRA, born Rocky River, Ohio, February 21, 1971; admitted to bar, 2000, Ohio. *Education:* University of Rochester (B.M., 1993); Cleveland-Marshall College of Law (J.D., 2000). Order of the Barristers. Member: National Moot Court Team, 1998-2000. ***LANGUAGES:*** Spanish. ***PRACTICE AREAS:*** Business Transactions; ERISA. ***Email:*** msenra@cfdf.com

SARA E. DeCARO, born Garfield Heights, Ohio, November 20, 1974; admitted to bar, 2000, Ohio; 2001, U.S. District Court, Northern District of Ohio. *Education:* Baldwin Wallace College (B.A., 1997); Cleveland-Marshall College of Law (J.D., 2000). *Member:* Cleveland and Ohio State Bar Associations; William K. Thomas Inn of Court. ***PRACTICE AREAS:*** Commercial Litigation; Business Litigation; Employment Law. ***Email:*** sdecaro@cfdf.com

REBECCA S. MOLYNEAUX, born Cleveland, Ohio, August 12, 1976; admitted to bar, 2002, Ohio. *Education:* Syracuse University (B.S., 1998); Syracuse University College of Law (J.D., 2002).

JEFFREY W. GALLUP, born Bradford, Pennsylvania, September, 1972; admitted to bar, 2003, Ohio. *Education:* Boston University (B.S., 1994); Case Western Reserve University (J.D., cum laude, 2003). ***Email:*** jgallup@cfdf.com

---

JAMES CHIN

745 LEADER BUILDING
526 SUPERIOR AVENUE, EAST
CLEVELAND, OHIO 44114-1402
Telephone: 216-241-0646; 800-653-7161
Telefax: 216-241-4246
Email: JimmyChin@aol.com
URL: http://www.lawyers.com/oh-immigration

Business, Immigration, Labor Certifications, Real Estate, Civil Litigation, International Laws Corporation.

(This Listing Continued)

JAMES CHIN, born Cleveland, Ohio, May 17, 1950; admitted to bar, 1976, Ohio. *Education:* Northwestern University (B.A., 1973); Case Western Reserve University (J.D., 1976). *Member:* Cleveland, Ohio State, American and The Federal Bar Associations. ***LANGUAGES:*** Chinese.

MARY L. CIBELLA

614 WEST SUPERIOR AVENUE
SUITE 1300
CLEVELAND, OHIO 44113
Telephone: 216-344-9220
Facsimile: 216-664-6999

Disciplinary Defense, Legal Malpractice Defense, Pre-Admission Licensure, Ethics Advisory Opinions, The Grievance Process.

MARY L. CIBELLA, born Warren, Ohio, January 11, 1956; admitted to bar, 1984, Ohio; 1999, U.S. District Court, Northern District of Ohio. *Education:* Kent State University (B.S., 1980); Cleveland Marshall College of Law (J.D., 1983). *Member:* Cleveland, Cuyahoga County and Ohio State Bar Associations; National Organization of Bar Counsel; Association of Professional Responsibility Counsel. (Of Counsel to McGinty Hilow & Spellacy Co., L.P.A.)

R. JACK CLAPP & ASSOC. CO., L.P.A.

ONE CLEVELAND CENTER
SUITE 2420
1375 EAST NINTH
CLEVELAND, OHIO 44114
Telephone: 800-334-8500
Fax: 216-861-1401
Email: info@rjackclapp.com
URL: http://www.rjackclapp.com

Washington, D.C. Office: 444 North Capital Street, N.W. Hall of States Building, Suite 828. 20001. Telephone: 888-334-8500.
Mentor, Ohio Office: 7784 Reynolds Road. Telephone: 216-946-1100. Fax: 216-946-1756.

Wrongful Death, Personal Injury, Medical Malpractice, Professional Malpractice, Defective Products, Automobile Accidents, Aviation Law, Nursing Home Negligence, Commercial Vehicle Liability, Tourist Injuries, Farm Equipment Liability.

(For complete biographical data on all personnel, see Professional Biographies at Washington, D.C.)

CLIMACO, LEFKOWITZ, PECA, WILCOX & GAROFOLI CO., L.P.A.

Established in 1969
1220 HURON ROAD, SUITE 1000
CLEVELAND, OHIO 44115-1711
Telephone: 216-621-8484
Telecopier: 216-771-1632
Email: japeca@climacolaw.com
URL: http://www.climacolaw.com

Washington, D.C. Office: 818 Connecticut Avenue, N.W., Suite 857, 20006. Telephone: 202-887-4777. Fax: 202-887-4778.

General Civil, Corporate, Environmental, Government and Labor Law. E.R.I.S.A., Litigation. Bankruptcy, Real Estate, Criminal, Securities, Public Utility, Municipal, Class Actions, Mass Torts, Securities Litigation, Personal Injury, Workers Compensation, Family, Public Employment Relations, Commercial and Public Financing, Entertainment, Television (CATV), School and Intellectual Property.

FIRM PROFILE: General Practice mid-sized law firm located in Cleveland, Ohio, specializing in litigation, commercial law, municipal law, employment law, class actions and mass torts.

JOHN R. CLIMACO, born Cleveland, Ohio, September 24, 1941; admitted to bar, 1967, Ohio and U.S. Court of Appeals, Sixth Circuit; 1968, U.S. District Court, Northern District of Ohio; 1973, U.S. Supreme Court; 1980, U.S. Court of Appeals, Sixth Circuit; 1984, U.S. Tax Court; 1990, U.S. Court of Appeals, Second Circuit; 2002, U.S. District Court, Eastern District of Texas; 2004, U.S. District Court, Southern District of Ohio. *Education:* The Ohio State University (B.S., 1964); Western Reserve University (J.D., 1967). Recipient, Ellis Island Medal of Honor, 2000. Special Counsel to Ohio Attorney General, 1975-1994. Board Member: Alzheimer's Association, Cleveland Chapter, 1989—; Leadership, Cleveland, 1993. Life Member: Judicial Conference of the Sixth Circuit, Judicial Conference of the Eighth Judicial District of Ohio. Member, Northern District of Ohio Advisory Group. *Member:* Cleveland, Ohio State, Federal and American Bar Associations; The Association of Trial Lawyers of America. ***REPORTED CASES:*** Inland Refuse Transfer Co. v. Browning-Ferris Industries of Ohio, Inc., 15 Ohio St.3d 321, 474 N.E.2d 271, 15 O.B.R. 448 (Ohio Dec. 31, 1984) (NO. 83-1826); O'Shea v. Fayard, 2003 WL 21956534 (2003); Millstein v. Millstein, 2002 WL 31031676 (2002); White v. Smith & Wesson, 97 F. supp. 2d 816, N.D. Ohio, 2000. ***PRACTICE AREAS:*** Complex Litigation; Securities Litigation; Mass Torts; Labor Law; White Collar Crime. ***Email:*** jrclim@climacolaw.com

JOHN A. PECA, born Cleveland, Ohio, August 9, 1952; admitted to bar, 1977, Ohio; 1978, U.S. Tax Court; 1980, U.S. District Court, Northern District of Ohio; 1986, District of Columbia and U.S. Court of Appeals, 6th, 7th and District of Columbia Circuits; 1987, U.S. Supreme Court. *Education:* John Carroll University (B.S., 1974); Case Western Reserve University (J.D., 1977). Certified Public Accountant, Ohio, 1978. Member, Board of Trustees: Gilmour Academy; Cleveland Central Catholic High School, NOIA Foundation; Neighborhood Centers Association. *Member:* Cleveland, Ohio State and American Bar As-

(This Listing Continued)

CLIMACO, LEFKOWITZ, PECA, WILCOX & GAROFOLI CO., L.P.A., Cleveland—Continued

sociations; American Association of Attorney-Certified Public Accountants; Ohio Society of Certified Public Accountants; American Institute of Certified Public Accountants. ***SPECIAL AGENCIES:*** U.S. Tax Court. ***PRACTICE AREAS:*** Business Law; Business Planning. ***Email:*** japeca@climacolaw.com

DENNIS R. WILCOX, born Norwalk, Ohio, November 9, 1951; admitted to bar, 1977, Ohio; 1980, U.S. District Court, Northern District of Ohio; 1986, U.S. District Court, Eastern District of Michigan; 1987, District of Columbia, U.S. Tax Court and U.S. Court of Appeals, Third Circuit; 1991, U.S. Court of Appeals, Sixth Circuit; 2004, U.S. District Court, Southern District Ohio. *Education:* The Ohio State University (B.A., cum laude, 1974); Case Western Reserve University (J.D., 1977). Order of the Coif. Member, Cleveland Heights Fair Housing Board, 1998-1999; Cleveland Heights Board of Zoning Appeals, 1999-2000; Cleveland Heights City Council, 2000—. *Member:* Cleveland, Cuyahoga County, and Ohio State Bar Associations; National Association of Bond Lawyers. ***PRACTICE AREAS:*** Municipal Law; Public Finance; Business Law. ***Email:*** drwilc@climacolaw.com

THOMAS J. TARANTINO, born Cleveland, Ohio, March 16, 1963; admitted to bar, 1990, Ohio; U.S. District Court, Northern District of Ohio; U.S. Court of Appeals, Sixth Circuit. *Education:* Cleveland State University (B.A., 1987); Cleveland Marshall College of Law (J.D., 1990). Pi Sigma Alpha. *Member:* Lake County, Cuyahoga County and Ohio State Bar Associations; National Association of Bond Lawyers. ***REPORTED CASES:*** Miele vs. Ribovich, 90 Ohio St. 3d. 439 (2000). ***PRACTICE AREAS:*** Corporate; Real Estate; Municipal Law; Public Finance. ***Email:*** tjtara@climacolaw.com

DAVID M. CUPPAGE, born Cleveland, Ohio, September 16, 1964; admitted to bar, 1990, Ohio; 1995, U.S. District Court, Northern and Southern Districts of Ohio; U.S. Court of Appeals, Sixth Circuit. *Education:* Kent State University (B.A., 1986); Cleveland-Marshall College of Law (J.D., 1990). Senior Editor, Cleveland State Law Review. Law Clerk to: Hon. Francis E. Sweeney, Eight District Court of Appeals, Ohio, 1991-1992; Hon. Donald C. Nugent, Eighth District Court of Appeals, Ohio, 1993-1994. *Member:* Cleveland (Member: Intellectual Property Committee; Environmental Law Section) and Ohio State (Member, Intellectual Property Law Section) Bar Associations. ***REPORTED CASES:*** Resource Title Agency, Inc. v. Morreale Real Estate Services, Inc., 314 F.Supp.2d 763 (N.D. Ohio 2004); State ex rel. White v. Koch, 96 Ohio St.3d 395, (2002); Cleveland ex rel. O'Malley v. White, 148 Ohio App.3d 564, (2002); City of Berea ex rel. Ward v. Trupo, 141 Ohio App.3d 772, (2001); Hauser v. Cleveland Cuyahoga County Port Authority, 2000 WL 709017 (2000); Olmsted Twp. Bd. of Trustees v. City of Berea, 134 Ohio App. 3d 688; Liberty Steel Products, Inc. v. Francosteel Corp., 57 F.Supp. 2d 459, (1999); Automated Tracking Systems, Inc. v. Great American Ins. Co., 130 Ohio App.3d 238, (1998). ***PRACTICE AREAS:*** Business Litigation; Municipal Law; Commercial Litigation; Employment Law; Intellectual Property. ***Email:*** dmcupp@climacolaw.com

KEITH T. VERNON, born Montgomery County, Pennsylvania, July 11, 1969; admitted to bar, 1996, Ohio; 1997, U.S. District Court, Northern District of Ohio; 2003, District of Columbia. *Education:* St. Josephs University (B.S., 1991); Loyola University (J.D., 1996). International Moot Court. Loyola National Trial Team. (Also at Washington, D.C. Office). ***PRACTICE AREAS:*** Products Liability; Class Actions; Tobacco Litigation; Employment Law. ***Email:*** ktvern@climacolaw.com

DAVID W. NEEL, born Cleveland, Ohio, May 2, 1958; admitted to bar, 1986, Ohio, U.S. District Court, Northern District of Ohio and U.S. Court of Appeals, Sixth Circuit; 1992, U.S. Supreme Court. *Education:* Kenyon College (B.A., cum laude, 1980); Cleveland-Marshall College of Law (J.D., cum laude, 1984); Columbia University Law School (LL.M., 1985). Editor, Cleveland State Law Review, 1983-1984. Law Clerk to the Hon. Ann Aldrich, U.S. District Court, Northern District of Ohio, 1985-1986. Adjunct Professor, Evidence, Cleveland-Marshall College of Law. Volunteer, Free Clinic of Greater Cleveland Legal Services Program. General Counsel, New House Communications, Inc. *Member:* Cleveland (Secretary, Litigation Section, 2004-2005), Ohio State and American Bar Associations. ***REPORTED CASES:*** Treadway v. Local 911, UFCW, 2000 U.S. App. LEXIS 14494 (6th Cir., June 20, 2000); Blue Cross & Blue Shield v. Klein, U.S. App. LEXIS 17753 (6th Cir., July 11, 1997); Budish v. Gordon, 784 F.Supp. 1320 (N.D. Ohio, 1992); In re Mansfield Tire & Rubber Co., LEXIS 13656 (N.D. Ohio, 1990); State ex rel. Geauga County Bd. of Comm'rs v. Milligan, 100 Ohio St. 3d 366 (2003); American Seaway Foods v. Belden S. Assocs. Ltd. Partnership, 72 Ohio St. 3d 514 (1995); Universal Oil Co. v. Limbach, 63 Ohio St. 3d 476 (1992); Geauga County Bd. of Comm'rs v. Geauga County Sheriff, 2003 Ohio 7201 (11th Dist., 2003); Cuyahoga County Bd. of Comm'rs v. Richard L. Bowen & Assocs., Inc., 2003 Ohio App. LEXIS 2125 (8th Dist., July 10, 2003); Waters v. Allied Mach. & Eng'g Corp., 2003 Ohio App. LEXIS 2125 (5th Dist., April 30, 2003); Swiggum v. Ameritech Corp., 1999 Ohio App. LEXIS 4634 (10th Dist., September 30, 1999); Tepper v. Heck, 1992 Ohio App. LEXIS 6291 (8th Dist., December 10, 1992); Fenn v. Triton Transport, Inc., 1991 Ohio App. LEXIS 557 (9th Dist., February 6, 1991); Tepper v. Heck, 1990 Ohio App. LEXIS 2760 (8th Dist., July 5, 1990). ***PRACTICE AREAS:*** Employment Litigation; Commercial Litigation. ***Email:*** dwneel@climacolaw.com

PAUL S. LEFKOWITZ (Retired)

ANTHONY J. GAROFOLI (1936-2003)

JACK D. MAISTROS (1956-2001)

JOHN F. CORRIGAN, born Cleveland, Ohio, August 1, 1961; admitted to bar, 1986, Ohio. *Education:* John Carroll University (B.A., cum laude, 1983); Cleveland-Marshall College of Law (J.D., 1986). Formerly with Cuyahoga County Prosecutors Office, 1986-1997. *Member:* Cleveland and Ohio State Bar Associations. ***PRACTICE AREAS:*** Litigation; Criminal Law; Personal Injury. ***Email:*** jfcorr@climacolaw.com

MARGARET M. METZINGER, born Erie, Pennsylvania, January 15, 1965; admitted to bar, 1995, Ohio. *Education:* Hiram College (B.A., 1987); Cleveland-Marshall College of Law (J.D., 1995). *Member:* Cleveland and Ohio State Bar Associations; Ohio Women's Bar Association. ***PRACTICE AREAS:*** Probate; Domestic Relations; Business Litigation; Employment Litigation. ***Email:*** mmmetz@climacolaw.com

SCOTT D. SIMPKINS, born Delaware, Ohio, August 23, 1970; admitted to bar, 1996, Ohio; 1997, U.S. District Court, Northern District of Ohio; 2003, U.S. District Court, Southern District of Ohio. *Education:* Ohio Wesleyan University (B.A., 1992); Capital University (J.D., cum laude, 1996). Order of the Curia. Associate Editor, Capital University Law Review, 1994-1996. Member, Federalist Society. *Member:* Ohio State and American Bar Associations. ***PRACTICE AREAS:*** Litigation; Class Actions. ***Email:*** sdsimp@climacolaw.com

JENNIFER L. STUEBER, born Cleveland, Ohio, 1969; admitted to bar, 1996, Ohio; 2003, U.S. District Court, Northern District of Ohio. *Education:* Ohio State University (B.A., 1991); Cleveland Marshall College of Law (J.D., 1996). *Member:* Ohio State and American Bar Associations. ***PRACTICE AREAS:*** Business Law; Real Estate Law; Public Finance; Private Finance. ***Email:*** jlstue@climacolaw.com

JOSEPH P. FEGEN, born Cleveland, Ohio, March 23, 1969; admitted to bar, 1995, Ohio; 1996, Colorado (inactive); U.S. District Court, Northern District of Ohio; U.S. District Court, District of Colorado. *Education:* University of Dayton (B.A., with honors, 1991); Capital University School of Law (J.D., cum laude, 1995); Case Western Reserve University School of Law (LL.M., Taxation, 2002). Listed in Who's Who of American Law Students, 14th Ed., 1994, 15th Ed., 1995. *Member:* Cleveland and Ohio State Bar Associations. ***PRACTICE AREAS:*** Business Law; Real Estate; Municipal Law; Public Finance. ***Email:*** jpfege@climacolaw.com

P. WESLEY LAMBERT, born Chillicothe, Ohio, February 24, 1978; admitted to bar, 2003, Ohio; 2004, U.S. District Court, Northern District of Ohio. *Education:* The Ohio State University (B.S., 2000); Case Western Reserve University (J.D., magna cum laude, 2003). Contributing Editor, Case Western Reserve University Law Review, 2001-2003. Author: "Worlds are Colliding: A Critique of the Need for the Additional Criminal Securities Fraud Section in Sarbanes-Oxley," 53 Case W. Res. Law Rev. 839 (Spring 2003). ***PRACTICE AREAS:*** Commercial Litigation; Business Litigation; Employment Litigation; Municipal Law. ***Email:*** pwlamb@climacolaw.com

LISA ANN GORSHE, born St. Cloud, Minnesota, March 9, 1969; admitted to bar, 1997, Florida; 1999, Minnesota (Not admitted in Ohio). *Education:* Augsburg College (B.A., 1991); St. Thomas University School of Law (J.D., 1997). *Member:* Minnesota State Bar Association; The Florida Bar; Richfield Human Rights Commission. ***PRACTICE AREAS:*** Class Actions; Mass Torts. ***Email:*** lagors@climacolaw.com

DAWN M. CHMIELEWSKI, born Euclid, Ohio, October 14, 1973; admitted to bar, 2004, Ohio. *Education:* University of Akron (B.S.N., 1996); Cleveland-Marshall College of Law (J.D., magna cum laude, 2004). ***PRACTICE AREAS:*** Class Actions; Product Liability; Mass Torts. ***Email:*** dmchmi@climacolaw.com

TERRI A. LIGHTNER, born Cleveland, Ohio; admitted to bar, 2004, Ohio. *Education:* Ursuline College (B.S.N., 1992); Cleveland-Marshall College of Law (J.D., 2004). *Member:* Cleveland and Ohio State Bar Associations. ***PRACTICE AREAS:*** Class Actions; Products Liability; Mass Torts; Medical Malpractice. ***Email:*** taligh@climacolaw.com

REFERENCES: National City Bank; Security Federal Savings & Loan.

COHEN ROSENTHAL & KRAMER LLP

THE WESTERN RESERVE BUILDING - SUITE 705
1468 WEST NINTH STREET
CLEVELAND, OHIO 44113
Telephone: 216-781-7956
Fax: 216-781-8061
URL: http://www.crklaw.com

Trial Practice, Appellate Practice, Complex Litigation, Complex Civil Litigation, Class Action, Securities Litigation, Antitrust, Corporate Law, Shareholders Rights, Contract Law, Commercial Litigation, Fraud, Bankruptcy.

JOSHUA R. COHEN, born Knob Noster, Missouri, June 7, 1959; admitted to bar, 1984, Ohio. *Education:* University of Texas (B.A., with high honors, 1981; J.D., with honors, 1984). Phi Beta Kappa. *Member:* Cleveland, Ohio State, Federal and American Bar Associations. ***REPORTED CASES:*** Coles v. Board ofEduc., 171 F.3d 369 (6th Cir. 1999); Cole v. Mileti, 133 F3d 433 (6th Cir. 1998); Merrill Lynch v. Jaros, 70 F. 3d 418 (6th Cir, 1995); Thompson v. Karr, 4 F. Supp. 2d 731 (ND Ohio 1998); In re Revco Sec. Litig., (1993 Transfer Binder) Fed. Sec. L. Rep. ¶97,809 (N.D. Ohio Sep. 14, 1993); Baker v. BP AM., Inc. 749 F. Supp. 840 (N.D. Ohio 1990); Merrill Lynch v. Stark (1994), 65 Ohio St. 3d 312; Mentor Lagoons Inc. v. Rubin (1987), 31 Ohio St. 3d 256; Lesser v. Burry (1999), 132 Ohio App. 3d 319; Beder v. Cleveland Browns, Inc. (1998), 129 Ohio App. 3d 188; Cooper v. Metal Sales Mftg. Corp. (1995), 104 Ohio App 3d 34; Firt Nat. Supermarkets v. Merrill Lynch (1994), 104 Ohio App. 3d 289; State ex rel. Sun Newspapers, Inc. v. Board of Educ. (1991), 76 Ohio App. 3d 170; Obenauf v. CIDCO Inv. Serv. (1990), 54 Ohio App. 3d 131; Fine v. America Online, Inc. (2000) 139 Ohio App. 3d 133. ***PRACTICE AREAS:*** Complex Civil Litigation; Class Action; Securities Litigation; Commercial Litigation. ***Email:*** jrc@crklaw.com

JAMES B. ROSENTHAL, born Cleveland, Ohio, 1962; admitted to bar, 1990, Virginia; 1991, District of Columbia; 1994, Ohio, U.S. Court of Appeals, District of Columbia Circuit; U.S. Court of International Trade; U.S. District Court, Northern District of Ohio. *Education:* Yale University (B.A., magna cum laude, 1984); Georgetown University (J.D., cum laude, 1990). *Member:* Cleveland, Ohio State and Federal Bar Associations; Virginia State Bar; Judge Anthony J. Celebrezze American Inn of Court. ***REPORTED CASES:*** BP Chem v. Jiangsu Sopo Corp., 285 F.3d 677 (8th Cir. 2002); Edmondson & Gallagher v. Alban Towers Tenants Ass'n, 48 F.3d 1260 (D.C. Cir. 1995); Ductmate Indus. v. Famous Sup. Corp., 55 F.Supp 2d 777 (N.D. Ohio 1999); State v. Hill (2001), 92 Ohio St.3d 191 (amicus curiae); T.W. Grogan Co. v. Grogan (2001), 143 Ohio App.3d 1235. ***PRACTICE AREAS:*** Complex Litigation; Antitrust; Corporate Law; Shareholder Rights; Contract Litigation; Fraud. ***Email:*** jbr@crklaw.com

(This Listing Continued)

ELLEN MAGLICIC KRAMER, born Cleveland, Ohio, March 10, 1966; admitted to bar, 1991, Ohio and U.S. District Court, Northern and Southern District of Ohio; U.S. Court of Appeals, Sixth Circuit. *Education:* John Carroll University (B.A., magna cum laude, 1988); Ohio State University College of Law (J.D., 1991). *Member:* Ohio State Bar Association. ***REPORTED CASES:*** In re Koenig Sporting Goods, 203 F.3d 986 (6th Cir. 2000); In re Economy Lodging Sys., 234 B.R. 691 (6th Cir. BAP 1999); Thomson v. Karr, 4 F. Supp. 2d 731 (N.D. Ohio 1998); First Nat. Bank v. From Forge Mach. (1996), 113 Ohio App.3d 722. ***PRACTICE AREAS:*** Litigation; Bankruptcy. ***Email:*** emk@crklaw.com

JASON R. BRISTOL, born Amherst, New York, October 10, 1975; admitted to bar, 2000, Ohio; 2001, U.S. District Court, Northern District of Ohio; 2002, U.S. District Court, Southern District of Ohio; 2003, U.S. Court of Appeals, Sixth Circuit; 2004, U.S. Supreme Court. *Education:* Bowling Green State University (B.A., with honors, 1997); Cleveland-Marshall College of Law (J.D., 2000). Order of Barristers. Moot Court Board of Governors, 1999-2000. Advocate, Fiftieth Annual National Moot Court Competition, 1999. Recipient: Cleveland-Marshall College of Law Moot Court Alumni of the Year, 2003-2004. Adjunct Faculty Member, Cleveland-Marshall College of Law, 2001—. Member, Board of Trustees, Bowling Green State University, 1995-1997. *Member:* Lorain County, Cleveland and Ohio State Bar Associations. ***PRACTICE AREAS:*** Complex Civil Litigation; Class Action Litigation; Securities Litigation; Pension Litigation; Civil Rights. ***Email:*** jbristol@crklaw.com

CATHLEEN M. BOLEK, born Cleveland, Ohio, December 16, 1966; admitted to bar, 1992, Ohio; 1993, U.S. District Court, Northern District of Ohio; 1995, U.S. Court of Appeals, Sixth Circuit; 2001, U.S. District Court, Central District of Illinois. *Education:* Syracuse University (B.A., cum laude, 1988) Eta Pi Upsilon; Case Western Reserve University (J.D., 1992). *Member:* Cleveland and Cuyahoga County Bar Associations; The Association of Trial Lawyers of America; Ohio Academy of Trial Lawyers; Cleveland Academy of Trial Lawyers; Cleveland Employment Lawyers Association; Ohio Employment Lawyers Association; National Employment Lawyers Association; Cleveland Employment Inns of Court. ***REPORTED CASES:*** Cehrs v. Northeast Ohio Alzheimer's Research Ctr, 155 F 3d 775 (6th Cir. 1998); Gliner v. Saint-Gobain Norton Indus. Ceramics Corp., 89 Ohio St.3d 414 (2000) (amicus); Cleveland Bar Assn. v. Feneh, 86 Ohio St.3d 102 (1999) (amicus); Cleveland Bar Assn v. Allanson, 83 Ohio St.3d 304 (1998) (amicus); Phillips v. Burt, 77 Ohio St.3d 1229 (1997) (amicus); Hyde v. Reynoldsville Casket Co., 68 Ohio St. 3d 240 (1994) (amicus); Hardwick v. Sherwin Williams Co., 91 Fair Empl. Prac.Cas.(BNA) 142 (2003); Johnson v. Univ. Hosp. of Cleveland, 150 Ohio App.3d 256 (2002); Blanton v. Cayahoga Cty. Bd.of Elections, 150 Ohio App.3d 61 (2002); Shalkauser v. Medina, 148 Ohio App.3d 41 (2002); Hood v. Diamond Prod., Inc., 137 Ohio App.3d 9 (2000); Takach v. Am Med Tech., 128 Ohio App.3d 457 (1998); Harmon v. Philip Morris, 120 Ohio App.3d 187 (1997); Reese v. Euclid Cleaning Contrs., 103 Ohio App.3d 141 (1995); Mathis v. St. Alexis Hosp. Assoc., 99 Ohio App.3d 159 (1994); Steele v. Auburn Vocational School Dist., 104 Ohio App.3d 204 (1994). ***PRACTICE AREAS:*** Litigation; Employment Discrimination and Retaliation; Whistleblower Retaliation; Sexual Harassment; Medical Malpractice; Personal Injury; Appellate Advocacy.

HOWARD M. COHN
PATENT ATTORNEY, LLC

21625 CHAGRIN BOULEVARD, SUITE 220
CLEVELAND, OHIO 44122-5335
Telephone: 216-752-0955
Fax: 216-752-0957
URL: http://www.cohnpatents.com
Email: howard.cohn@cohnpatents.com
URL: http://www.lawyers.com/howardmcohn

Patents, Trademarks, Copyrights, Licensing, Intellectual Property.

HOWARD M. COHN, born Baltimore, Maryland, February 14, 1943; admitted to bar, 1969, Virginia; 1972, Maryland; 1980, New York; 1988, Connecticut; 1992, Ohio; registered to practice before U.S. Patent and Trademark Office. *Education:* University of Maryland (B.S.M.E., 1965); American University (J.D., 1969). *Member:* Virginia State Bar; Ohio State Bar Association; New York State Bar Association; Cleveland Intellectual Property Law Association. ***PRACTICE AREAS:*** Patents; Trademarks; Copyrights; Licensing; Intellectual Property. ***Email:*** howard.cohn@cohnpatents.com

COLLINS & SCANLON LLP

Formerly Donahue & Scanlon

3300 TERMINAL TOWER
50 PUBLIC SQUARE
CLEVELAND, OHIO 44113-2294
Telephone: 216-696-0022
Telecopier: 216-696-1166
Email: lawyers@collins-scanlon.com
URL: http://www.collins-scanlon.com

General Civil Practice. Corporate, Business, Securities, Real Estate, Condominium, Taxation, Secured Transactions, Commercial, Probate, Trust and Estate Planning Law. Trials.

MEMBERS OF FIRM

TIM L. COLLINS, born Northampton, Massachusetts, October 2, 1957; admitted to bar, 1986, Ohio and U.S. District Court, Northern District of Ohio; 1987, U.S. Court of Appeals, Sixth Circuit; 1990, U.S. Supreme Court; 1994, Pennsylvania and U.S. District Court, Eastern and Western Districts of Michigan; 1995, U.S. District Court, Southern District of Ohio; 1998, U.S. Court of Appeals, Eighth Circuit. *Education:* University of Massachusetts; Baldwin-Wallace College (B.A., 1981); Cleveland Marshall College of Law (J.D., 1985). Member, Moot Court Board of Governors, 1983-1984. Chair, Cleveland Heights Cable Television Commission. Vice Chair, Cleveland Heights Recreation Advisory Board. Member, Ohio Supreme Court Advisory Committee on Technology and the Courts, 2000—. Life Member, Eighth Appellate District Judicial Conference. *Member:* Cleveland (Member, Litigation Section) and Ohio State (Member, Litigation Section; Board of Governors, 1999—; Chair, Computer Law Committee, 1997-1999; Member, Counsel of Delegates, 1999—) Bar Associations. ***PRACTICE AREAS:*** Corporate Law; Business Law; Litigation; Computer Law; Franchise Law; Class Actions. ***Email:*** tcollins@collins-scanlon.com

RUSSELL DAVID KORNBLUT, born Cleveland, Ohio, September 17, 1960; admitted to bar, 1985, Florida; 1986, Ohio; 1988, U.S. District Court, Northern District of Ohio. *Education:* Indiana University (B.A., 1982); Cleveland-Marshall College of Law (J.D., 1985). Phi Eta Sigma; Tau Epsilon Rho. Member, Indiana University Honor Society. Member: Mortgage Bankers Association; Ohio Mortgage Bankers Association; Greater Cleveland Mortgage Bankers Association. *Member:* Cleveland, Cuyahoga County and Ohio State Bar Associations. ***PRACTICE AREAS:*** Creditors Rights; Mortgage Banking Law; Corporate Law; Real Estate; Litigation; Workers Compensation; Bankruptcy; Business Law. ***Email:*** rkornblut@collins-scanlon.com

HARVEY LABOVITZ, born Cleveland, Ohio, December 25, 1944; admitted to bar, 1969, Ohio; 1971, U.S. District Court, Northern District of Ohio; 1977, U.S. Supreme Court; 1987, U.S. Court of Appeals, Sixth Circuit; 1994, U.S. District Court, Eastern District of Michigan. *Education:* Miami University (A.B., 1966); Boalt Hall School of Law, University of California at Berkeley (J.D., 1969). Member, American Arbitration Association. Chairman, Cuyahoga County Court of Common Pleas Arbitration Panels. Chairman, Ohio Division of Securities Ad Hoc Committee on Promoters' Compensation on Oil and Gas Programs, 1986. ***PRACTICE AREAS:*** Corporate Law; Real Estate Law; Secured Transactions Law; Trial and Appeals Law; Construction Law; Condominium Law. ***Email:*** hlab@collins-scanlon.com

THOMAS J. SCANLON, born Cleveland, Ohio, March 25, 1938; admitted to bar, 1963, Ohio; 1964, U.S. District Court, Northern District of Ohio; 1975, U.S. Tax Court; 1976, U.S. Court of Appeals, Sixth Circuit; 1978, U.S. Claims Court; 1987, U.S. Supreme Court. *Education:* John Carroll University (B.S., 1959); Cleveland Marshall College of Law (J.D., cum laude, 1963). Special Assistant to Ohio Attorney General, 1991-1995. Member, Board of Bar Examiners State of Ohio. Alternative Dispute Resolution and Professional Ethics Committee. Member, U.S. District Court Mediation Panel. Member, College, Ohio State Bar Association. Life Member, Judicial Conference, Eighth Judicial District. Delegate, Judicial Conference, Sixth Judicial District, United States District Court, 2002-2003. Member, Merit Selection Panel, U.S. District Court, Northern District of Ohio. *Member:* Cleveland (Member, Estate Planning, Probate and Trust Law, Real Estate Law Sections), Ohio (Member, Real Property and Probate and Trust Law Section) and American (Member, Real Property and Probate and Trust Law and Taxation Section) Bar Associations; American Arbitration Association (Member, National Panel on Commercial and Construction Law); National Association of Industrial and Office Properties, Northern Ohio Chapter (Member and Trustee). ***PRACTICE AREAS:*** Business Law; Real Estate Law; Condominium Law; Taxation; Probate Law; Estate Planning Law; Trials and Appeals Law. ***Email:*** tscanlon@collins-scanlon.com

M. SCOTT WILSON, born Salem, Ohio, March 18, 1952; admitted to bar, 1984, Ohio. *Education:* Eastman School of Music (B.M., cum laude, 1974); University of Notre Dame (M.M., 1976); University of Michigan (J.D., 1984). ***PRACTICE AREAS:*** Mergers and Acquisitions; Corporate Law; Succession Planning; Trust; Estates; Health Care Law. ***Email:*** swilson@collins-scanlon.com

ASSOCIATE

KRISTIE MARIE WEIBLING, born Youngstown, Ohio, September 24, 1975; admitted to bar, 2001, Ohio. *Education:* Youngstown State University (B.S., 1997); Cleveland-Marshall College of Law (J.D., 2001). Delta Theta Phi. Executive Editor, Journal of Law and Health. Author: "Genetic Research: Are More Limitations Needed in the Field?" Journal of Law and Health, Cleveland-Marshall College of Law, Vol. 15, Issue 1; "Beware of the Tortious Requests for Medical Records," August 2000 Newsletter to the Litigation Section of the Ohio State Bar Association. *Member:* Ohio State and American Bar Associations. ***Email:*** ksosnowski@collins-scanlon.com

REPRESENTATIVE CLIENTS: Activities Press, Inc.; Aero Mark, Inc.; Automotive Acceptance Corp.; Avondale Shopping Center; B & B Oval Track Products, Inc.; Campus Medical Arts Building Ltd; China Merchandise Exhibit, Inc.; CCollar Bank; Core-Tech, Inc.; Ehle Morrison Group Ltd.; Fluid Line Products, Inc.; Foundry Support Operations, Inc.; Foundry Support Services, Inc.; GE Capital Corp.; GE Healthcare; Gulf States Manufactures; Heartland Developers, Inc.; Hunters Pointe Townhouses; The Huntington National Bank; Kelly Genealogical Service; King James Group Development Cos.; Lake Hospitality; Lake Hospitality; Lawyers Title Insurance Corp.; Tele-com, Inc.; Marbelle Industries, Inc.; Metropolitan Windows and Glass Block; Mr. Brisket, Inc.; National Association of Industrial and Office Parks, Northern Ohio Chapter; ORG Holdings; Records Deposition Service of Ohio; Records Imaging Service, Inc.; Saxon Mortgage, Inc.; Sentro-Tech, Inc.; Squires Roofing and Construction Co.; Summit Office Park LLC; Sun America Management Corp.; Tink Hall Food Market; Vantage Financial Group, Inc.; Wachovia Mortgage Corporation.

COWDEN, HUMPHREY, NAGORNEY
& LOVETT CO., L.P.A.

1414 TERMINAL TOWER
50 PUBLIC SQUARE
CLEVELAND, OHIO 44113-2204
Telephone: 216-241-2880
Telecopier: 216-241-2881
URL: http://www.cowdenlaw.com

Outsourced general counsel, Corporate and international, Corporate formation and structure, Finance and capital formation, Securities, mergers and acquisitions, Lender and borrower representation, Real estate and Urban Development, Business succession counseling, Bankruptcy and creditors rights.

(This Listing Continued)

COWDEN, HUMPHREY, NAGORNEY & LOVETT CO., L.P.A., Cleveland—Continued

FIRM PROFILE: CHNL was founded in 1991 as a law firm committed to providing legal guidance and counsel to the owners and managers of entrepreneurial and closely held businesses. Our firm blends experience, knowledge, wisdom, faith and perseverance to provide solutions for the unique business, legal and life decisions that our clients' success requires.

Our focus is to guide our clients from formation to growth to financing to success to succession and beyond.

We are proud to say that we are a law firm of entrepreneurs advising entrepreneurs.

GERALD W. COWDEN, born Monongahela, Pennsylvania, September 2, 1949; admitted to bar, 1975, Ohio. *Education:* Washington & Jefferson College (B.A., 1971); University of Akron (J.D., 1975). Member: Board of Editors, Akron Law Review, 1974-1975. *Member:* Akron (Member: Young Lawyers School Program 1975-1980, Corporate Section), Ohio State (Member: Corporation Section; Taxation Committee; Partnership Subcommittee) and American (Member: Corporation Law Committee; Taxation Committee) Bar Associations. ***PRACTICE AREAS:*** Corporate; Corporate Finance; Banking Law; Securities. ***Email:*** gcowden@cowdenlaw.com

ROBERT M. HUMPHREY, born Cleveland, Ohio, November 26, 1954; admitted to bar, 1982, Ohio; 1984, U.S. District Court, Northern District of Ohio; 1985, U.S. Tax Court; 1989, Illinois. *Education:* University of Cincinnati; Bridgewater State College (B.A., 1978); Suffolk University (J.D., 1982); Georgetown University (LL.M., in Taxation, 1988). Author: Case Comment, "Indigents' Right to Appointed Counsel in Parental Rights Termination Proceedings - Lassiter v. Department of Social Services of Durham County, North Carolina, 101 S. Ct. 2153 (1981)," Suffolk University Law Review, Vol. XVI, Number 1; "Stumbling Over the Dog: Treatment of Withdrawing Employers Under the Multiemployer Pension Plan Amendments Act of 1980," 359-2nd Tax Management Portfolio, Multiemployer Plans Special Rules, B-401. *Member:* Cleveland, Ohio State and American Bar Associations. ***PRACTICE AREAS:*** Corporate; Corporate Finance; Federal Taxation; International Transactions; Intellectual Property. ***Email:*** rhumphrey@cowdenlaw.com

MARY FORBES LOVETT, born Lynn, Massachusetts, May 31, 1953; admitted to bar, 1985, Ohio. *Education:* The Ohio State University (B.S., cum laude, 1974); Cleveland-Marshall College of Law (J.D., magna cum laude, 1985). Editor, Cleveland State University Law Review; Managing Editor Journal of Law & Health. Frequent Lecturer: Cleveland Bar Association Real Estate Institute; Urban Land Institute; CREW; Maxine Goodman Levin College of Urban Affairs. Past President and Board Member, Commercial Real Estate Women, Inc.; Past President, Greater Cleveland Real Estate Organizations. *Member:* Cleveland (Past, Real Estate Section Chair), Ohio State and American Bar Associations; Urban Land Institute. (Certified Specialist in Business, Commercial and Industrial Real Property Law, Ohio State Bar Association). ***PRACTICE AREAS:*** Real Estate; Land Use; Corporate Finance; Environmental; Corporate Law. ***Email:*** mlovett@cowdenlaw.com

FRANK P. NAGORNEY, born Cleveland, Ohio, 1950; admitted to bar, 1975, Ohio. *Education:* Case Western Reserve University (B.S., 1972); New York University (J.D., 1975). Member: Council of Smaller Enterprises, National Association of Metal Finishers, 1991-1995; Institute of Packaging Professionals, 1993-1995. Member, Ohio Organization for Recycling & Reuse; United States Fencing Association (USOC). *Member:* Cleveland, Ohio State and American Bar Associations. ***PRACTICE AREAS:*** Corporate; Finance; Taxation; Bankruptcy; Environmental; Estate Planning; Intellectual Property; International Taxation; Real Estate. ***Email:*** fnagorney@cowdenlaw.com

JAMES S. HOGG, born August 5, 1952; admitted to bar, 1978, New York; 1985, Ohio. *Education:* Kalamazoo College (B.A., cum laude, 1974); University of Michigan (J.D., cum laude, 1977). *Member:* Cleveland, Ohio State and American Bar Association. ***PRACTICE AREAS:*** Securities; Mergers and Acquisitions; Corporate Law. ***Email:*** jhogg@cowdenlaw.com

TERRENCE J. STEEL, born Akron, Ohio, March 3, 1946; admitted to bar, 1971, Ohio; 1973, U.S. District Court, Northern District of Ohio; 1975, U.S. Court of Appeals, Sixth Circuit. *Education:* The Ohio State University (B.A., 1968; J.D., 1970). *Member:* Akron (Member, Executive Committee, 1981-1983; Treasurer, 1984-1985; President, 1992-1993; Member, Bankruptcy Section, 1989—; Vice-President, 1996-1997), Ohio State (Member: House of Delegates, 1989-1990; 1994-1996; Real Property & Litigation Sections) and American (Member, National Conference of Bar Presidents, 1991-1993.) Bar Associations. [With JAGC, USAF, 1972]. ***PRACTICE AREAS:*** Bankruptcy; Real Property; Probate; Estate Planning. ***Email:*** tsteel@cowdenlaw.com

DEBORA S. LASCH, born Cape May Court House, New Jersey, October 28, 1958; admitted to bar, 1988, Ohio and U.S. District Court, Northern District of Ohio; 1991, U.S. Court of Appeals, Sixth Circuit; U.S. District Court, Central District of Illinois; U.S. District Court, Eastern District of Wisconsin. *Education:* Miami University (B.A., 1981); Cleveland State University (J.D., cum laude, 1988). Delta Theta Phi. Editor, Cleveland State University Law Review. Recipient, American Jurisprudence Awards in: Civil Procedure; Property; Contracts; Criminal Law; Corporations. Author, "How to Spot a Bad Phase I Environmental Assessment," Cleveland Bar Association, April 1, 2003. Lecturer: "Reciprocal Easement Agreements," CREW Fall, Professional Development Seminar, 2003; "The Small Business Liability Relief & Brownfield Revitalization Act," Cleveland Bar Association's Environmental Law Symposium, November 15, 2002; "Introduction to Cleanup Liability Laws: Superfund and RCRA," Cleveland Bar Association's Spring Environmental Law Symposium, 2001; "Environmental Issues Facing Real Estate Developers," Cleveland Bar Association's Fall Seminar, 1998; "Lead Paint and Asbestos Update," Cleveland Bar Association's Environmental Law Institute, 1997; "A Practical Approach to Acquiring and Disposing of Contaminated Properties," Cleveland Bar Association's Real Estate Institute, 1996; "The Petroleum Underground Storage Tank Release Compensation Board," Ohio State Bar Association's Environmental Law Conference, 1995; "Consultant Liability," Cleveland Bar Association's Environmental Law Institute, 1995. Board Member, Commercial Real Estate Women, Inc., Cleveland. *Member:* Cleveland, Ohio State and American (Member, Environmental Sections) Bar Associations; Urban Land Institute. (Certified Specialist in Business, Commercial and Industrial Real Property Law, Ohio State Bar Association). ***PRACTICE AREAS:*** Real Estate; Brownfields Redevelopment; Environmental Compliance; Corporate Law; Mergers and Acquisitions; Finance. ***Email:*** dlasch@cowdenlaw.com

KARL E. MAY, born 1949; admitted to bar, 1974, Ohio. *Education:* Ohio Northern University (B.A., with high distinction, 1971); The Ohio State University (J.D., summa cum laude, 1974). ***PRACTICE AREAS:*** Securities; Corporate Law; Business Law.

FREDERIC P. SCHWIEG, born Boston, Massachusetts; admitted to bar, 1985, Ohio; U.S. District Court, Northern District of Ohio and U.S. Court of Appeals, Sixth Circuit. *Education:* Case Western Reserve University (B.A., 1981; J.D., cum laude, 1985). Moot Court. Member, Niagra International Moot Court Team. Journal of International Law. Member, Turnaround Management Association. *Member:* Cleveland and Ohio State Bar Associations. ***REPORTED CASES:*** Suhar v. Burns, —F.3d— 6th Cir. 2001. ***PRACTICE AREAS:*** Bankruptcy Law; Commercial Litigation. ***Email:*** fschwieg@cowdenlaw.com

---

MATTHEW J. LENHARD, born Fairview Park, Ohio, May 23, 1974; admitted to bar, 1999, Ohio. *Education:* University of Notre Dame (B.A., magna cum laude, 1996); Vanderbilt University School of Law (J.D., 1999). ***PRACTICE AREAS:*** Corporate Law; Mergers and Acquisitions; Real Estate; Securities; Estate Planning. ***Email:*** mlenhard@cowdenlaw.com

JOHN STOREY, admitted to bar, 2005, Ohio. *Education:* College of Wooster (B.A., 2001); Cleveland-Marshall College of Law (J.D., 2005). *Member:* Ohio State Bar Association. ***PRACTICE AREAS:*** Real Estate; Corporate Law; Urban Planning; Banking Law.

PHILLIP A. HELON, born Akron, Ohio, February 11, 1978; admitted to bar, 2004, Ohio. *Education:* The Ohio State University (B.S.B.A., 2000); Case Western Reserve University (J.D./M.B.A., 2004). Recipient: Certificate of Concentration in Business Organizations, with honors; CALI Excellence for the Future Award; highest grade in Venture Capital and Entrepreneurial Financing Law. *Member:* Cleveland, Ohio State and American Bar Associations. ***PRACTICE AREAS:*** Corporate Law; Securities; Mergers and Acquisitions; Real Estate; Banking Law; Finance. ***Email:*** phelon@cowdenlaw.com

---

CRABBE, BROWN & JAMES LLP

1280 W. THIRD STREET
CLEVELAND, OHIO 44113
Telephone: 216-574-9312
Email: info@cbjLawyers.com
URL: http://www.cbjLawyers.com

Columbus, Ohio Office: 500 South Front Street, Suite 1200. Telephone: 614-228-5511. Fax: 614-229-4559.

Cincinnati, Ohio Office: 30 Garfield Place, Suite 740, 45202. Telephone: 513-784-1525. Fax: 513-784-1250.

Lancaster, Ohio Office: 111 South Broad Street, Suite 209, 43130. Telephone: 740-689-1743. Fax: 740-689-1746.

Urbana, Ohio Office: 118 Scioto Street. Telephone: 937-652-4000.

General Insurance Defense, Product Liability, Professional Malpractice, Premises Liability, Environmental and Toxic Tort Claims, Employment and Labor Law, Tax Matters, General Business and Corporate Law and Litigation, Banking and Securities, Real Estate, Probate and Estate Planning, Criminal Law, Administrative, Regulatory and Governmental Law, Workers Compensation, Intellectual Property, Fire, Arson and Fraud, Fidelity and Surety Life, Accident and Health, Insurance Coverage Law, Construction Claims, Health and Hospital Law, Oil, Gas and Energy Law, Transportation Law, Automobile Dealer Law, Zoning, International Practice and Domestic Law, Land Use Planning, and Eminent Domain.

(For biographical data on other personnel, see Professional Biographies at Columbus, Ohio)

CULLEN CO. LPA

THE SUPERIOR BUILDING
815 SUPERIOR AVENUE, SUITE 1210
CLEVELAND, OHIO 44114
Telephone: 216-621-2090
Fax: 216-621-2062
URL: http://www.ohioelaw.com

Civil Litigation, Employment Law, Wrongful Termination, For Labor Standards Act, Age Discrimination, Sexual Harassment, Racial Discrimination, Personal Injury, Medical Malpractice, Nursing Home Malpractice, Class and Collective Actions, Municipal Laws.

JOHN L. CULLEN, born Cleveland, Ohio, June 25, 1965; admitted to bar, 1993, Ohio; 1994, U.S. District Court, Northern District of Ohio and U.S. Court of Appeals, Sixth Circuit. *Education:* Bradford College (B.A., 1988); Cleveland Marshall College of Law (J.D., 1993). Assistant Law Director, Civil Division, City of Cleveland, Ohio, 1996-1997. *Member:* Ohio State and American Bar Associations.

CURATOLO SIDOTI
A LEGAL PROFESSIONAL ASSOCIATION

24500 CENTER RIDGE ROAD
SUITE 280
CLEVELAND, OHIO 44145
Telephone: 440-808-0011
Fax: 440-808-0657
Email: cleveland@patentandtm.com
URL: http://www.patentandtm.com

Intellectual Property Law.

(This Listing Continued)

JOSEPH G. CURATOLO, born Cleveland, Ohio, May 2, 1952; admitted to bar, 1977, Ohio and U.S. District Court, Northern District of Ohio; 1978, U.S. Court of Customs and Patent Appeals; 1980, U.S. Court of Appeals, Federal Circuit; registered to practice before U.S. Patent and Trademark Office. *Education:* John Carroll University (B.S., cum laude, 1974); Cleveland Marshall College of Law (J.D., 1977). Member, International Union of Pure and Applied Chemistry. *Member:* Federal Circuit, Ohio State and American Bar Associations; American Intellectual Property Law Association; Cleveland Intellectual Property Law Association; American Chemical Society; American Institute of Chemical Engineering; American Association for the Advancement of Science. ***PRACTICE AREAS:*** Intellectual Property Law; Patents; Trademarks.

SALVATORE A. SIDOTI, born Cleveland, Ohio, November 11, 1970; admitted to bar, 1999, Ohio, U.S. District Court, Northern District of Ohio and U.S. Court of Appeals, Sixth and Federal Circuits; registered to practice before U.S. Patent and Trademark Office. *Education:* Hiram College (B.A., Biology, 1993); Cleveland Marshall College of Law (J.D., 1999). Secretary, Intellectual Property Section of the Ohio State Bar Association. Vice-Chair, PCT Issues Committee, American Intellectual Property Association. *Member:* Cleveland, Federal Circuit, Ohio State and American (Member, Intellectual Property Law Section) Bar Associations; American Intellectual Property Law Association; Cleveland Intellectual Property Law Association. ***PRACTICE AREAS:*** Intellectual Property Law; Patents; Trademarks.

ASSOCIATE

JAMES E. OEHLENSCHLAGER, born Cleveland, Ohio, July 12, 1968; admitted to bar, 2001, Ohio; registered to practice before U.S. Patent and Trademark Office. *Education:* University of Akron (B.S., 1991; J.D., 2000); University of Cincinnati College of Medicine (M.S., 1997). *Member:* American Intellectual Property Law Association; Cleveland Intellectual Property Law Association. [U.S. Army, 1985-1991]. ***LANGUAGES:*** German. ***PRACTICE AREAS:*** Intellectual Property Law; Patents; Trademarks.

STEVEN S. DAVIS CO., L.P.A.

450 STANDARD BUILDING
1370 ONTARIO STREET
CLEVELAND, OHIO 44113
Telephone: 216-781-3311
Fax: 216-781-3312
Email: sdavis@epitrustee.com
URL: http://www.rabbanddavis.com

Bankruptcy, Bankruptcy Chapter ll, Bankruptcy Chapter 13, Bankruptcy Chapter 7, Debtor and Creditor, Commercial.

STEVEN S. DAVIS, born 1950; admitted to bar, 1975, Ohio and U.S. District Court, Northern District of Ohio. *Education:* University of Rochester (B.A., 1972); Cleveland State University (J.D., 1975). *Member:* Cleveland, Cuyahoga County and Ohio State Bar Associations. ***PRACTICE AREAS:*** Bankruptcy; Commercial Law; Debtor and Creditor; Bankruptcy Chapter 11; Bankruptcy Chapter 13; Bankruptcy Chapter 7. ***Email:*** sdavis@epitrustee.com

---

DAVIS & YOUNG

A Legal Professional Association
1700 MIDLAND BUILDING
CLEVELAND, OHIO 44115
Telephone: 216-348-1700
Fax: 216-621-0602
Email: atty@davisyoung.com
URL: http://www.davisyoung.com

Akron, Ohio Office: National City Center, One Cascade Plaza, Suite 800, 44308. Telephone: 330-376-1717. Fax: 330-376-1797.
Youngstown, Ohio Office: The Commerce Building, 201 East Commerce Street, Suite 100, 44503. Telephone: 330-743-1717.
Warren, Ohio Office: 108 Main Street, SW, Suite 1000, 44481. Telephone: 330-373-1717. Fax: 330-395-0610.

General Trial and Appellate Practice, Products Liability, General Tort, Insurance Coverage, Personal Injury, Toxic Torts, Complex Mass Tort Claims, Legal and Medical Malpractice, Municipal Liability, Civil Rights, Employment Practices Liability, and Environmental and Commercial Liability.

FIRM PROFILE: Many of Davis & Young's attorneys are members of the following organizations: Cleveland, Cuyahoga and Ohio State Bar Associations, Defense Research Institute (DRI), Ohio Association of Civil Trial Attorneys (OACTA), and Cleveland Association of Civil Trial Attorneys (CACTA).

REES H. DAVIS, SR. (1892-1965)

FRED J. YOUNG (1889-1946)

GEORGE W. LUTJEN, admitted to bar, 1964, Ohio. *Education:* John Carroll University (B.S., 1959); University of Detroit; Cleveland-Marshall Law School (J.D., 1964). ***Email:*** jmelton@davisyoung.com

C. RICHARD McDONALD, admitted to bar, 1973, Ohio. *Education:* DePauw University (B.A., 1970); Case Western Reserve University (J.D., 1973). ***Email:*** cmcdonal@davisyoung.com

PAUL D. EKLUND, admitted to bar, 1978, Ohio. *Education:* Miami University (A.B., 1975); Case Western Reserve University (J.D., 1978). Assistant Attorney General of Ohio, 1978-1979. "Leading Lawyer" for Insurance Law in Northeast Ohio, 2001, 2002; "The Best Lawyers in America" 2003. *Member:* Cleveland Association of Civil Trial Attorneys (President, 1994-1995). ***Email:*** peklund@davisyoung.com

(This Listing Continued)

JAN L. ROLLER, admitted to bar, 1980, Massachusetts; 1983, Ohio. *Education:* Denison University (B.A., cum laude, 1976); Case Western Reserve University School of Law (J.D., 1979). Assistant District Attorney, Suffolk and Plymouth Counties, 1980-1982. Life Delegate, Eighth District Judicial Conference. *Member:* Barrister-Cleveland Inns of Court; Cleveland Bar Foundation (Trustee); International Association Defense Counsel. ***Email:*** jroller@davisyoung.com

THOMAS W. WRIGHT, admitted to bar, 1984, Ohio. *Education:* Ohio University (A.B., summa cum laude, 1981); Case Western Reserve University (J.D., 1984). Phi Beta Kappa. ***Email:*** twright@davisyoung.com

DAVID J. FAGNILLI, admitted to bar, 1986, Ohio; 2002, U.S. Supreme Court. *Education:* Southern California College (B.A., 1980); Cleveland Marshall College of Law (J.D., 1986). Life Delegate, Eighth District Judicial Conference. *Member:* Federal Bar Association; Justinian Forum; Midwest Environmental Claims Association; National Forum for Environmental and Toxic Tort Issues. ***Email:*** dfagnill@davisyoung.com

WILLIAM VANCE, admitted to bar, 1981, Ohio. *Education:* Bowling Green State University (B.S., 1976); Cleveland-Marshall College of Law (J.D., 1981). Omicron Delta Epsilon. Law Clerk to the Honorable John T. Patton, Court of Appeals of Ohio, Eighth Appellate District, 1981-1983. Assistant Prosecuting Attorney, Cuyahoga County, 1983-1987. ***Email:*** wvance@davisyoung.com

PATRICK F. ROCHE, admitted to bar, 1976, Ohio. *Education:* Hofstra University (B.B.A., 1972); Cleveland Marshall Law School (J.D., 1976). Assistant Cuyahoga County Prosecutor, 1976-1980. Chief Trial Counsel, City of Cleveland Prosecutor, 1980-1984. Chief Police Prosecutor, City of Cleveland, 1984-1986. Law Director, Fairview Park, Ohio, 1991-2001. Prosecutor, City of Westlake, 2000-2001. ***Email:*** proche@davisyoung.com

DENNIS R. FOGARTY, admitted to bar, 1991, Ohio. *Education:* John Carroll University (B.A., 1987); Cleveland-Marshall Law School (J.D., 1991). Business Editor, Cleveland State University Law Review, 1990-1991. ***Email:*** dfogarty@davisyoung.com

RICHARD M. GARNER, admitted to bar, 1993, Ohio; 1994, U.S. District Court, Southern District of Ohio; 1995, U.S. Court of Appeals, Sixth Circuit; 1999, U.S. District Court, Northern District of Ohio. *Education:* Ohio State University (B.A., 1990; J.D., 1993). Author/Lecturer: "The Implication of Scott-Pontzer and its Progeny on Ohio UM/UIM cases", National Business Institute, March 2003; "Annual UM/UIM Seminar", Cuyahoga County Bar Association/Akron Bar Association, December 2002; "Insurance Settlements In Ohio", National Business Institute, Sept. 2002; "Annual UM/UIM Seminar", Cuyahoga County Bar Association/Akron Bar Association, December 2001; "UM/UIM Update 2000-2001", Cleveland Marasahll College of Law, December 2001. Former Prosecutor, 1993-1997; Former Magistrate, 1997-1999.*Member:* Federalist Society. ***Email:*** rgarner@davisyoung.com

ASSOCIATES

THOMAS J. CONNICK, admitted to bar, 1999, Ohio, U.S. Court of Appeals, Sixth Circuit and U.S. District Court, Northern District of Ohio. *Education:* John Carroll University (B.A., 1992); Cleveland-Marshall College of Law (J.D., 1999). ***Email:*** tconnick@davisyoung.com

SHAWN A. CORMIER, admitted to bar, 1998, Ohio. *Education:* Ohio Northern University (B.A., with honors, 1990); Cleveland State University (M.A., with honors, 1991); Cleveland Marshall College of Law (J.D., 1998). ***Email:*** scormier@davisyoung.com

KRISTI L. HAUDE, admitted to bar, 2002, Ohio. *Education:* Kent State University (B.A., 1999); Cleveland-Marshall College of Law (J.D., 2002). ***Email:*** khilbish@davisyoung.com

SHANNON M. PIETRAFESE, admitted to bar, 2004, Ohio. *Education:* Bowling Green State University (B.A., 2001); Case Western Reserve University (J.D., 2004). ***Email:*** spietraf@davisyoung.com

PATRICK M. ROCHE, admitted to bar, 1999, Ohio. *Education:* University of Dayton (B.S., 1995); Cleveland-Marshall College of Law, Cleveland State University (J.D., 1999). ***Email:*** pmroche@davisyoung.com

JENNIFER SARDINA, born Buffalo, New York, May 21, 1973; admitted to bar, 2000, Ohio; 2002, Florida. *Education:* Canisius College (B.A., 1995); Cleveland-Marshall College of Law (J.D., 2000). Delta Theta Phi. Arbitrator: Cuyahoga County Court of Common Pleas Alternative Dispute Resolution Department. *Member:* Cuyahoga County Bar Association (Member, Board of Trustees; Chair, New Lawyer Section; Member, Committee on Bar Admissions; Participant, Leadership Academy, 2001-2002); The Florida Bar; Cleveland-Marshall College of Law Alumni Association; Justinian Forum. ***Email:*** jsardina@davisyoung.com

RONALD J. ZIEHM, admitted to bar, 1991, Ohio. *Education:* Bowling Green State University (B.S., 1988); Cleveland-Marshall College of Law (J.D., 1991). ***Email:*** rziehm@davisyoung.com

OF COUNSEL

MARTIN J. MURPHY, admitted to bar, 1963, Ohio. *Education:* John Carroll University (B.S.S., 1960); Western Reserve University (LL.B., 1963). Life Delegate, Judicial Conference of the Eighth Judicial District. Member, Board of Directors, Westfield Companies. *Member:* Cleveland (Chairman, 1997-1998 and Member, Litigation Section) and American (Member, Sections of Tort and Insurance Practice and Litigation) Bar Associations; Cleveland Association of Civil Trial Attorneys (President, 1983-1984). Fellow: American College of Trial Lawyers; International Academy of Trial Lawyers; International Society of Barristers. ***Email:*** mmurphy@davisyoung.com

HENRY A. HENTEMANN, admitted to bar, 1963, Ohio. *Education:* John Carroll University (A.B., 1957); The Cleveland-Marshall Law School (J.D., 1963). Delta Theta Phi. Author: "Damages For Potential Residuals of Brain Injuries," 11 Cleveland-Marshall Law Review 554, September, 1962; "Uninsured Motorist Coverage," 12 Cleveland-Marshall Law Review 66, January, 1963 (reprinted in *Personal Injury Commentator,* Vol. VI, No. 3, page 18, May, 1963); "Uninsured Motorist Defined," 16 Cleveland Marshall Law Review 504, 1967; "Expected or Intended: What Does It Mean," XLVI Insurance Counsel Journal, July, 1979; "Underinsured Motorist Coverage; A New Coverage with New Problems," 56

(This Listing Continued)

DAVIS & YOUNG, Cleveland—Continued

Ohio State Bar Report 5, 1983; "The Hentemann Handbook for Civil Jury Trials," Cuyahoga County Bar Association, 1984; "Uninsured Motorist Coverage Claims and The Bad Faith Issue," Defense Counsel Journal, April, 1988. Member, Judicial Conference, Eighth Judicial District, Ohio. Faculty, Defense Counsel Trial Academy, 1989. *Member:* International Association of Defense Counsel (President, 1992-1993; Board Member, 1988-1994); Defense Research Institute (Board Member, 1991-1994); Cleveland Association of Civil Trial Attorneys (President, 1988-1989); Lawyers For Civil Justice (Board Member, 1991-1994). Fellow, American College of Trial Lawyers. ***Email:*** pcooper@davisyoung.com

J. MICHAEL CREAGAN, admitted to bar, 1985, Ohio. *Education:* University of Notre Dame (A.B., 1967); Cleveland Marshall College of Law (J.D., cum laude, 1985). [1st. Lt., U.S. Army, 1967-1969]. ***Email:*** mcreagan@davisyoung.com

R. EMMETT MORAN, admitted to bar, 1977, Ohio; 1984, U.S. Court of Military Appeals; 1987, U.S. District Court, Northern District of Ohio. *Education:* University of Detroit (B.A., 1969); Cleveland Marshall College of Law, Cleveland State University (J.D., 1976). Assistant Cuyahoga County Prosecutor, 1977-1987. [MAJ, JAGC, Ohio Army National Guard, 1979—]. ***Email:*** dreddy@davisyoung.com

PAMELA BARKER, admitted to bar, 1982, Ohio. *Education:* Kenyon College (B.A., magna cum laude, 1979); Ohio State University College of Law (J.D., 1982). Magistrate for the City of Brecksville. ***Email:*** pbarker@davisyoung.com

COUNSEL FOR: Amerisure Companies; Avis Rent-A-Car System, Inc.; The Cafaro Co.; Central Mutual Insurance Co.; Cincinnati Insurance Co.; CNA Insurance Co.; Dana Corporation; Erie Insurance Group; GMAC Insurance; Grange Mutual Casualty Co.; Greenwich Insurance Company; The Hartford; Heritage Cos.; Investors Insurance Group; KAISER Foundation Health Plan of Ohio; Merit Plan Insurance Co.; MIC General Insurance Corp.; Motorists Mutual Insurance Cos.; Ohio Casualty Insurance Co.; Ohio Insurance Guaranty Association; Progressive Cos.; St. Paul Insurance Cos.; Security Insurance Company of Hartford; State Automobile Mutual Insurance Co.; State Farm Mutual Automobile Insurance Co.; State Farm Fire and Casualty Insurance Co.; SYSCO Food Services of Cleveland, Inc.; T.J. Maxx Stores; Travelers Insurance Co.; Unigard Insurance Group; United of Ohio Insurance Co.; University Hospitals of Cleveland; Westfield Companies; Wolverine Mutual Insurance Co.

RICHARD L. DEMSEY CO., L.P.A.

1350 EUCLID AVENUE
CLEVELAND, OHIO 44115
Telephone: 216-263-7900
Fax: 216-263-7901
Email: rdemseylaw.com
URL: http://www.demseylawoffice.com

Construction Accidents, Nursing Home Negligence, Obstetric Malpractice, Wrongful Death, Automobile Accidents, Brain Injury, Catastrophic Injury, Motorcycle Accidents and Injuries, Plaintiff's Personal Injury, Severe Burns, Spinal Injury, Railroad Accidents and Injuries, Railroad Crossing Accidents, Aviation Law, Trucking Accidents, Medical Malpractice, Sexual Harassment, Premise Liability, Product Liability.

FIRM PROFILE: Richard Demsey was one of the Senior Partners with the law firm Nurenberg, Plevin, Heller & McCarthy who after 23 years has opened his own firm and continues to handle all injury matters.

RICHARD L. DEMSEY, born Cleveland, Ohio, November 27, 1953; admitted to bar, 1982, Ohio; U.S. District Court, Northern District of Ohio; U.S. Court of Appeals, Sixth Circuit. *Education:* Ohio University (B.F.A., 1976); Cleveland State University (B.A., 1979); Case Western Reserve University (J.D., 1982). Adjunct Professor, Law, Case Western Reserve University, 1996—. Adjunct Faculty, Trial Advocacy, Cleveland-Marshall College of Law, Cleveland State University, 1996—. *Member:* Ohio Academy of Trial Lawyers; The Association of Trial Lawyers of America. ***PRACTICE AREAS:*** Construction Accidents; Nursing Home Negligence; Obstetric Malpractice; Wrongful Death; Automobile Accidents; Brain Injury; Catastrophic Injury; Motorcycle Accidents; Plaintiff's Personal Injury; Severe Burns; Spinal Injury; Railroad Accidents and Injuries; Railroad Crossing Accidents; Aviation Law; Truck Accidents; Medical Malpractice; Sexual Harassment; Premises Liability; Products Liability.

DENMEAD LAW OFFICE

CLEVELAND, OHIO

(See Columbus)

Civil Trial and Appellate Practice and Personal Injury, Traumatic Brain Injury (TBI), Professional Negligence and Complex Litigation including Class Actions, Patents, Civil Rights, Civil Litigation, RICO, Employment and Political Subdivision Liability issues.

DETTELBACH, SICHERMAN & BAUMGART

A LEGAL PROFESSIONAL ASSOCIATION
Established in 1960
1100 OHIO SAVINGS PLAZA
1801 EAST 9TH STREET
CLEVELAND, OHIO 44114-3169
Telephone: 216-696-6000
Telecopier: 216-696-3338
Email: dsb@dsb-law.com

Bankruptcy, Chapter 11 Reorganization, Commercial Bankruptcy and Transactions, Corporate, Insolvency, Uniform Commercial Code, Real Estate, Commercial. General Civil Trial and Appellate Practice.

(This Listing Continued)

FIRM PROFILE: Dettelbach, Sicherman & Baumgart, a Legal Professional Association, and its predecessors have been actively engaged in the practice of law in Cleveland, Ohio, since 1960. The firm is a boutique with a practice concentrated in bankruptcy, debtor-creditor and commercial law. The firm's primary client base consists of multiple major corporate clients, for whom legal matters are handled both locally and throughout the United States.

ARTHUR H. DETTELBACH (1904-1972)

MARVIN A. SICHERMAN, born Cleveland, Ohio, December 27, 1934; admitted to bar, 1960, Ohio; 1961, U.S. District Court, Northern District of Ohio; 1969, U.S. Court of Appeals, 6th Circuit; 1975, U.S. Supreme Court. *Education:* Case Western Reserve University (B.A., 1957; J.D., 1960). Tau Epsilon Rho. Author: "Sales-Express & Implied Warranties," 9 Western Reserve Law Review 511, 1958; "Debtor-Creditor Outlines," Cleveland Bar Practice & Procedure Clinic, 1961-1980 and 1982-1987; "Truth in Lending Outline," Ohio State Bar Program, 1969; "Preferences Under the Bankruptcy Act," Outline, Ohio Legal Center Institute, Debtor-Creditor Conference, 1972. Co-Author: Outline, "Chapter 13-Adjustment of Debts of an Individual with Regular Income," with David O. Simon, Ohio Legal Center Institute Conference, 1981; "Acquisition of Troubled Companies," The Lawyer's Brief, March, 1996; "Asset Purchase Agreement (For Use in Acquisition of a Company That is in Chapter 11)," Model Agreements for Corporate Counsel, 1996; "Bankruptcy Foreclosure & Related Title Problems," Outline, Ohio Legal Center Institute; "Basic Titles to Real Estate, Bankruptcy, Foreclosure and Related Title Problems," Ohio Legal Center Institute. Member, Board of Editors, Case Western Reserve Law Review, 1959-1960. Member, 1977-1985, President, 1981 and 1985, Vice President, 1983-1984, Beachwood Board of Education. *Member:* Cleveland (Chairman, Bankruptcy Court Committee, 1971-1973; Member, Bankruptcy Section), Cuyahoga County (Chairman, Bankruptcy Court Committee, 1981-1982), and Ohio State Bar Associations; National Association of Bankruptcy Trustees. ***REPORTED CASES:*** U.S. V. Nordic Village Inc., 503 U.S. 30 112 S. Ct. 1011, 1992, (Sovereign Immunity); Sicherman V. Ohio Public Employees Deferred Comp. Prog., 946 F.2d 895, 6th Cir., 1991, cert. gr., Jdmt. Vac., 505 U.S. 1202 112 S. St. 2987, 1992; P.B.G.C. v. Sunar Hauserman (In re Sunar Hauserman, Inc.) 126 F.3d 811, 6th Cir., 1997. ***PRACTICE AREAS:*** Commercial Bankruptcy; Bankruptcy Chapter 11; Commercial Transactions; Insolvency; Real Estate Law; Uniform Commercial Code. ***Email:*** msicherman@dsb-law.com

RICHARD A. BAUMGART, born Cleveland, Ohio, December 30, 1953; admitted to bar, 1978, Ohio and U.S. District Court, Northern District of Ohio; 1986, U.S. Court of Appeals, Sixth Circuit; 1992, U.S. Supreme Court. *Education:* University of Rochester (B.A., with distinction, 1975); The Ohio State University (J.D., 1978). Author: "Receiverships and Acquiring Assets from a Troubled Company," Ohio CLE Institute Outlines, 1998; "Effect of Changes in Bankruptcy Law on Family Law Practice," Ohio Academy of Trial Layers Outline, 1995 and Ohio CLE Institute, 1998; "Preferences from a Plaintiff's Perspective," William J. O'Neill Institute, 1994; "Practical Problems Confronting Real Estate Practitioners in Bankruptcy Proceedings Outline," Bar Association of Greater Cleveland, 1986; "Fraudulent Conveyances & Effects of Selected Title Problems Relating to Bankruptcy Matters," Ohio CLE Institute 1990, Cleveland Bar Association 1989, Cleveland Bar Association Real Estate Institute. Co-Chairman, William J. O'Neill Institute, 1996. *Member:* Cleveland (Member, Bankruptcy Section) and Ohio State Bar Associations; National Association of Bankruptcy Trustees. ***PRACTICE AREAS:*** Bankruptcy Chapter 11; Commercial Bankruptcy; Commercial Transactions; Insolvency; Civil Trials; Real Estate Law; Uniform Commercial Code. ***Email:*** rbaumgart@dsb-law.com

ROBERT D. BARR, born Hudson, Michigan, August 12, 1971; admitted to bar, 1996, Ohio and U.S. District Court, Northern District of Ohio; 1998, U.S. Court of Appeals, Sixth Circuit. *Education:* Albion College (B.A., summa cum laude, 1993); Case Western Reserve University (J.D., 1996). Phi Beta Kappa; Delta Theta Phi. Author: "Exemptions, Objections to Exemptions and Exemption Planning," The Bankruptcy Pro-Bono Project, 2003; "Avoidance of Single Witness Mortgages by Chapter 7 Trustees," The Cleveland-Marshall Law Alumni Association, 2000. *Member:* Cleveland (Co-Chair, Basic Bankruptcy Seminar, 2000; Co-Chair, William J. O'Neill Bankruptcy Institute, 2001; Co-Editor, The Northcoast e-Pipeline, the Newsletter of the Bankruptcy and Commercial Law Section, 2003) and Ohio State Bar Associations. ***PRACTICE AREAS:*** Bankruptcy Chapter 11; Commercial Bankruptcy; Commercial Transactions; Insolvency; Civil Trials; Real Estate Law; Uniform Commercial Code. ***Email:*** rbarr@dsb-law.com

LISA A. VARDZEL, born Pittsburgh, Pennsylvania, July 6, 1978; admitted to bar, 2003, Ohio and U.S. District Court, Northern District of Ohio; 2004, U.S. Court of Appeals, Sixth Circuit. *Education:* Ohio Wesleyan University (B.A., magna cum laude, 2000); Case Western Reserve University (J.D., cum laude, 2003). *Member:* Cleveland and Ohio State Bar Associations. ***PRACTICE AREAS:*** Bankruptcy Chapter 11; Commercial Bankruptcy; Commercial Transactions; Insolvency; Civil Practice. ***Email:*** lvardzel@dsb-law.com

REPRESENTATIVE CLIENTS: A.M. Castle & Co.; Alcan Aluminum Corp.; The Commercial Finance Group; (Commercial Factors); Federal Home Loan Mortgage Corp.; Imperial Tobacco Company, Limited; National City Bank; Novelis, Inc.; Ohio Savings Bank; Patio Enclosures, Inc.; Pubco Corp.; Kroy LLC; Total Plastics, Inc.
REFERENCE: National City Bank.

DINN, HOCHMAN & POTTER, LLC

5910 LANDERBROOK DRIVE, SUITE 200 (MAYFIELD HEIGHTS)
CLEVELAND, OHIO 44124
Telephone: 440-446-1100
Fax: 440-446-1240
Email: dhp@dhplaw.com
URL: http://www.dhplaw.com

General Civil Practice. Corporate Law, Business Law, Civil Litigation, Commercial, Real Estate, Telecommunications, Probate, Estate Planning, Family Law, Workers Compensation and Administrative Agencies.

(This Listing Continued)

MEMBERS OF FIRM

IRWIN J. DINN, born Lorain, Ohio, October 29, 1939; admitted to bar, 1964, Ohio. *Education:* University of Michigan (A.B., 1961; LL.B., 1964). Delta Theta Phi. Law Clerk to Honorable Lester L. Cecil, U.S. Court of Appeals, Sixth Circuit, 1964-1965. Chapter Author: "I Think I Need A Lawyer, Now What?!" Silver Lining Books, 2002. Author: "You Don't Do Estate Planning? Practical Advice for Your Clients," Probate and Property, July/August, 2002. *Member:* Cleveland and Ohio State Bar Associations. ***PRACTICE AREAS:*** Estate Planning; Probate Law; Business Law; Administrative Agency Practice. ***Email:*** idinn@dhplaw.com

DAVID B. HOCHMAN, born Indianapolis, Indiana, October 11, 1949; admitted to bar, 1974, Ohio. *Education:* The Ohio State University (B.S., 1971); Cleveland State University (J.D., 1974). *Member:* Cleveland, Cuyahoga County and Ohio State Bar Associations; Ohio Land Title Association. ***PRACTICE AREAS:*** Real Estate; Litigation; Business Litigation; Corporate Law; Business Law. ***Email:*** dhochman@dhplaw.com

STEVEN B. POTTER, born Cleveland, Ohio, September 28, 1956; admitted to bar, 1981, Ohio and U.S. District Court, Northern District of Ohio; 1988, U.S. District Court, Eastern District of Michigan; 1990, U.S. Court of Appeals, Sixth Circuit; 2003, U.S. Supreme Court. *Education:* Cornell University (A.B., 1978); Case Western Reserve University (J.D., 1981). Member: Moot Court, Executive Board, 1980-1981; Wagner Moot Court Team. Recipient, Heiss Labor Law Award, 1981. Author: "Using Settlement 'Videos' for Creative, Cost Effective Litigation," American Law Journal, September, 2001; "Befriending Payday and Small Loan Businesses - A Smart Move for the Banking Industry?" Banking Law Journal, July/August, 2002. *Member:* Cleveland, Ohio State and American (Member, Section of: Litigation) Bar Associations. ***PRACTICE AREAS:*** Litigation; Employment; Medical Malpractice. ***Email:*** spotter@dhplaw.com

THOMAS A. BARNI, born Cleveland, Ohio, June 5, 1967; admitted to bar, 1995, Ohio and U.S. District Court, Northern District of Ohio. *Education:* Cleveland State University (B.A., 1990); Cleveland-Marshall Ohio College of Law (J.D., 1994). *Member:* Cleveland, Ohio and American Bar Associations. ***PRACTICE AREAS:*** Civil Litigation; Business Law; Commercial Law; Real Estate; Family Law. ***Email:*** tbarni@dhplaw.com

ASSOCIATES

RENEE S. PIENTA, born Parma, Ohio, October 1, 1975; admitted to bar, 2001, Ohio; 2004, U.S. District Court, Northern District of Ohio. *Education:* Miami University (B.S., 1998); Case Western Reserve University (J.D., cum laude, 2001). *Member:* Ohio State and Cleveland Bar Associations. ***PRACTICE AREAS:*** Business Litigation; Civil Litigation. ***Email:*** spicnta@dhplaw.com

RYAN L. RIVCHUN, admitted to bar, 2002, Ohio. *Education:* State University of New York at Albany (B.S., cum laude, 1998); Case Western Reserve University (J.D., magna cum laude, 2002). Order of the Coif. *Member:* Ohio State, American and Cleveland Bar Associations. ***PRACTICE AREAS:*** Real Estate; Business Law; Estate Planning. ***Email:*** rrivchun@dhplaw.com

OF COUNSEL

MICHAEL C. HENNENBERG, born Weiden, West Germany, September 23, 1948; admitted to bar, 1974, Ohio and U.S. District Court, Northern District of Ohio; 1977, U.S. Court of Appeals, Sixth Circuit; 1978, U.S. Supreme Court. *Education:* The Ohio State University (B.S., Business Administration, 1970); Case Western Reserve University; Cleveland State University (J.D., 1974). Certified by the Ohio Supreme Court Committee on the Appointment of Counsel for Indigent Defendant's in Capital Cases. Author: "An Analysis of R.C. 2951.041 - Drug Treatment In Lieu of Conviction," Vol. 1, Issue 5 Criminal Law Journal of Ohio; "Conducting a Defense Jury Voir Dire Through the Judge in Federal District Court". Co-Authored, with Mark R. deVan: "The Champion," Official Publication of National Association of Criminal Defense Lawyers, Vol. II, No. 2, March 1987. Lecturer: "A Practitioner's Guide to Professionalism, Ethics and Substance Abuse," Lorman Education Services, 2000-2004, "Plea Negotiations, "The Ohio State Bar Association CLE Institute, 2000; "Litigation Essentials: Talking to the Jury," Cleveland Marshall Law Alumni Association, 1996; "Pleading and Practice in White Collar Cases," Ohio Association of Criminal Defense Lawyer's Defense of White Collar Criminal Cases, 1992. *Member:* Cleveland Bar Association (Member: Board of Trustees, 1985-1988; Criminal Law Committee; Past Chairman, 1981-1982; Criminal Law Committee, 1974—; Legislative Liaison, 1983-1986; Steering Committee of Task Force on Violent Crime; Co-Chairman, Robbery Sub Task Force, 1982); National Association of Criminal Defense Lawyers; Ohio Association of Criminal Defense Attorneys (Charter Member, Board of Directors, 1986—); Ohio State and American Bar Associations. Fellow, American Board of Criminal Lawyers. ***REPORTED CASES:*** State of Ohio v. Pearson, 62 Ohio St. 2d 291; Pepper Pike v. Doe, 66 Ohio St. 2d 374; Sims v. Engle, 619 F.2d 598, cert. denied 67 L.Ed. 2d 374; State v. Cornell 72 O Op. 2d 428; Lake County Bar Ass'n v. Donald Ezzone, 102 Ohio St. 3d 79. ***PRACTICE AREAS:*** Criminal Defense; Appellate Practice; White Collar Criminal Defense; Health Care Fraud; Antitrust; Regulatory Investigations; Tax Fraud; Civil Fraud; Attorney Discipline; Legal Malpractice Defense.

IRWIN M. FRANK, admitted to bar, 1972, Ohio. *Education:* Miami University (B.S., 1969); Cleveland-Marshall College of Law (J.D., 1972). ***PRACTICE AREAS:*** Real Estate Law (70%, 200); Business Law (30%, 70).

DANIEL K. DISMUKE

CLEVELAND, OHIO

(See Akron)

Real Estate, Business Law, Litigation, Trusts and Estates, Family Law.

DRIGGS, HOGG & FRY CO., LPA

CLEVELAND, OHIO

(See Willoughby Hills)

Corporate Law, Trusts and Estate, Business Law, Real Estate, Intellectual Property, Patents, Copyrights, Trademarks, Trade Secrets, Unfair Competition.

DUVIN, CAHN & HUTTON

A LEGAL PROFESSIONAL ASSOCIATION

Established in 1972

ERIEVIEW TOWER, 20TH FLOOR
1301 EAST NINTH STREET
CLEVELAND, OHIO 44114
Telephone: 216-696-7600
Facsimile: 216-696-2038
Email: attorneys@duvin.com
URL: http://www.duvinlaw.com

Labor Relations Law and Litigation. Public Employment Relations, Civil Trial and Appellate Practice in all State and Federal Courts, Employee Benefit and Equal Opportunity Law, OSHA, Workers' Compensation Law and Commercial Litigation.

FIRM PROFILE: Duvin, Cahn & Hutton is a growing forty-seven member law firm located in Cleveland, Ohio, which represents employers nationally in all areas of labor relations and employment law. In addition, the firm represents corporations in complex commercial litigation.

We have a national comprehensive 'labor relations' practice that includes the direct negotiation of many major collective bargaining agreements for significant employers in both the public and private sector. We also are continuously consulted on the administration of collective bargaining agreements and handle contract arbitrations for our clients. Our labor relations practice also involves extensive union related litigation before both federal and state courts as well as federal and state administrative agencies. Furthermore, we engage in extensive union resistance counseling and all related litigation. Also, we have continuously represented numerous corporate and multi-employer benefit plans, providing counsel on fund administration and compliance issues.

Although collective bargaining and labor relations have been the historic foundation of our firm, we have developed a very sizeable and rapidly expanding 'employment law practice' representing significant corporations throughout the country and large public sector employers within northeast Ohio. Our employment law practice includes full-service counseling and a very active litigation practice in such areas as employment discrimination, employee privacy issues, wrongful discharge, employment related torts, employee benefits, OSHA and workers' compensation. In addition, we provide the full range of day-to-day counseling to our clients on the development and maintenance of sound employee relations practices and policies in light of the increasing number and complexity of state and federal statutes regulating the workplace.

Our intensive litigation experience in the employment area has also led directly to an expansion of our areas of practice outside of our historic roots. Many of our clients liked our approach and results so much in handling labor and employment litigation that they urged us to handle their 'commercial litigation' as well. We initially handled such matters strictly to accommodate these special requests. Now, the scope of this litigation has expanded dramatically. We recently have handled and/or are currently handling complex contract disputes, both in private industry and government, anti-trust actions and unfair competition cases.

ROBERT P. DUVIN, born Evansville, Indiana, May 18, 1937; admitted to bar, 1961, Indiana; 1963, Ohio. *Education:* Indiana University (B.A., 1958; J.D., 1961); Columbia University (LL.M., 1963). Author: "The Duty to Bargain: Law in Search of Policy," 64 Columbia Law Review 248, 1964; "Collective Bargaining," Industrial Relations Law Digest, July, 1964; "The Bargaining Lockout: An Impatient Warrior," 40 Notre Dame Lawyer 137, 1965; "Personnel Management and Training", pp. 291-318, Chain Store Publishing Corp., 1969; "Prepaid Group Practice and Collective Bargaining," Perspective, 2nd Quarter, p. 26, 1970; "Drug Testing in the Workplace: The Employer's Perspective", Business Laws, Inc., p. 149-160, 1987. *Member:* Cleveland and Ohio State Bar Associations. ***SPECIAL AGENCIES:*** NLRB; DOL; EEOC; OCRC; SERB. ***PRACTICE AREAS:*** Management Labor Law; Employment Litigation; General Litigation. ***Email:*** rduvin@duvin.com

STEPHEN J. CAHN, born Syracuse, New York, December 11, 1931; admitted to bar, 1961, Ohio. *Education:* University of Florida (B.S., 1953); Cleveland-Marshall Law School of Cleveland State University (J.D., summa cum laude, 1961). Mediation, Cuyahoga County Common Pleas Court, ADR. *Member:* Cleveland and American Bar Associations. [Major, U.S. Army Reserve, 1953-1965]. ***SPECIAL AGENCIES:*** PBGC; DOL; IRS. ***PRACTICE AREAS:*** Employee Benefit Law; Multi-Employer Benefits; Multi-Employer Pensions. ***Email:*** scahn@duvin.com

LEE J. HUTTON, born Cleveland, Ohio, December 9, 1950; admitted to bar, 1975, Ohio. *Education:* Ohio University (A.B., summa cum laude, 1972); University of Michigan (J.D., magna cum laude, 1975). Phi Beta Kappa; Phi Delta Phi. Director of Clinical Program and Lecturer in Law, Case Western Reserve University, 1976-1981. *Member:* Ohio State (Member, Labor Law Section) and American (Member: Labor and Employment Law Section; Litigation Section) Bar Associations. ***SPECIAL AGENCIES:*** EEOC; NLRB; DOL; OFCCP. ***REPORTED CASES:*** Peters v. The Lincoln Electric Co., 285 F.3d 456 (6th Cir. 2002); Alexander vs. Electronic Data Systems, 13 F.3d 940 (6th Cir. 1994); Tanks vs. Greater Cleveland Regional Transit Authority, 930 F.2d 475 (6th Cir. 1991); Testerman vs. Electronic Data Systems, 98 F3d 297 (7th Cir. 1996); Stinson vs. Ironworkers District Council of Southern Ohio Benefit Trust, 869 F.2d 1014 (7th Cir. 1990); Guinn vs. Electronic Data Systems Corp., 57 F.E.P. Cases 360 (4th Cir. 1991); Mailwell Envelope vs. Int'l Assoc. of Machinists, District 54, 916 F.2d 344 (6th Cir. 1990); Bokunewicz vs. Purolator Products, Inc., 907 F.2d 1396 (3d Cir. 1990); Southern Moldings, Inc. vs NLRB, 728 F.2d 805 (6th Cir. 1984); Midland Steel Products Co. vs. Int'l Union, UAW, 61 Ohio St. 3d 121

(This Listing Continued)

DUVIN, CAHN & HUTTON, A LEGAL PROFESSIONAL ASSOCIATION, Cleveland—Continued

(1991); City of Lakewood vs. State Employment Relations Board, 66 Ohio App. 3d 387 (1990). ***PRACTICE AREAS:*** Management Labor Law; Equal Employment Opportunity Law; Employment Litigation; Employee Benefit Law; Family and Medical Leave Act. ***Email:*** lhutton@duvin.com

MARC J. BLOCH, born Cleveland, Ohio, February 14, 1943; admitted to bar, 1969, Ohio. *Education:* Miami University (B.A., 1965); Cleveland State University (J.D., 1969). Phi Alpha Delta. Member, Editorial Board, Cleveland State Law Review, 1968-1969. Author: "Working to Rule and Other Alternate Job Actions," 9 The Labor Lawyer, No. 2, Spring 1993; "Mechanical Copying, Copyright Law and The Teacher," 17 Cleveland-Marshall Law Review 299, 1968; "The Right to Strike for Public Employees in Ohio," 18 Cleveland-Marshall Law Review 392, 1969. Attorney, National Labor Relations Board, 1969-1972. Vice President, Cleveland Public Sector Labor Relations Association, 1986-1987. President, Cleveland Public Sector Labor Relations Association, 1987-1988. *Member:* Cleveland and American (Member, Section of Labor and Employment Law) Bar Associations. ***SPECIAL AGENCIES:*** NLRB; SERB. ***PRACTICE AREAS:*** Management Labor Law; Public Sector Labor Relations; Collective Bargaining. ***Email:*** mbloch@duvin.com

ANDREW C. MEYER, born New York, N.Y., February 15, 1952; admitted to bar, 1976, Ohio. *Education:* Ohio University (A.B., 1973; M.A., 1973); Case Western Reserve University (J.D., 1976). Phi Beta Kappa; Pi Gamma Mu; Omicron Delta Epsilon. Member, National Championship Team, Robert F. Wagner Memorial National Labor Moot Court Competition. ***SPECIAL AGENCIES:*** NLRB; SERB. ***PRACTICE AREAS:*** Management Labor Law; Equal Employment Opportunity Law; Litigation; Unfair Labor Practices. ***Email:*** ameyer@duvin.com

MARTIN S. LIST, born New York, N.Y., November 26, 1950; admitted to bar, 1975, New Jersey; 1981, Ohio. *Education:* Cornell University (B.S., 1972); Rutgers University (J.D., 1975). Member, Moot Court Board. Instructor, Rutgers University, Labor Law, 1977-1980. Adjunct Faculty, Cleveland Marshall College of Law, Cleveland State University, 2002—; Adjunct, James J. Nance College of Business Administration, Cleveland State University, 2004—; Co-Author: "Defense Perspective on Individual Employment Rights," 67 Nebraska Law Review 193, 1988. ***SPECIAL AGENCIES:*** EEOC; OCRC; SERB; NLRB. ***REPORTED CASES:*** NLRB vs. Medina County Publications, 735 F.2d 199 (6th Cir. 1984); NLRB vs. Apex Paper Box, 976 F2d 733 (6th Cir. 1992); Local No. 1 vs. D.O. Summers Cleaners, 154 LRRM 2574 (N.D. Ohio, 1997); Brickers v. CBOE, 145 F3d 846 (1998). ***PRACTICE AREAS:*** Union Organizing; Collective Bargaining; Management Employment Law; Equal Employment Opportunity Law; Litigation; Public Sector Labor Law. ***Email:*** mlist@duvin.com

CRAIG M. BROWN, born Paterson, New Jersey, August 2, 1954; admitted to bar, 1979, Ohio. *Education:* University of Michigan (B.A., with distinction, 1976); Georgetown University Law Center (J.D., 1979). Administrative Editor, Law & Policy in International Business, Georgetown University Law Center, 1978-1979. Author: "Bounty or Grant: A Call for Redefinition in Light of the Zenith Decision," 9 Law and Policy in International Business 1229, 1978. *Member:* Cleveland, Ohio State and American Bar Associations. ***SPECIAL AGENCIES:*** NLRB; EEOC; SERB; DOL. ***PRACTICE AREAS:*** Management Labor Law; Public Sector Labor Law; Litigation; Equal Employment Opportunity Law; Collective Bargaining. ***Email:*** cbrown@duvin.com

FRANK W. BUCK, born Tuscaloosa, Alabama, April 17, 1954; admitted to bar, 1980, Ohio. *Education:* University of Michigan (B.A., with distinction, 1976; J.D., 1979). *Member:* Cleveland and American Bar Associations. ***SPECIAL AGENCIES:*** NLRB; SERB. ***REPORTED CASES:*** TruServ Corp. v. NLRB, 254 F.3d 1105 (D.C. Cir. 2001), cert.denied, 534 U.S. 1130 (2002); Electronic Data Systems Corp. v. NLRB, 985 F.2d 801 (5th Cir. 1993); Shapiro v. Cook United, Inc., 762 F.2d 49 (6th Cir. 1985); NLRB v. Forest City Enterprises, Inc., 663 F.2d 34 (6th Cir. 1981); USW v. LTV Steel Mining Co., 168 L.R.R.M. 2818 (Mn. 2001); Midland Steel Prods. Co. v. Int'l Union, United Auto., Aero. & Agric. Implement Workers, 61 Ohio St.3d 121 (1991); FOP Lodge No.8 v. City of Cleveland, 1998 Ohio App. LEXIS 1508 (1998); Cleveland Police Patrolmen's Ass'n v. City of Cleveland, 107 Ohio App. 3d 248 (1995). ***PRACTICE AREAS:*** Management Labor Law; Public Sector Labor Law; Equal Employment Opportunity Law; Litigation; Collective Bargaining. ***Email:*** fbuck@duvin.com

NEAL B. WAINBLAT, born Rochester, New York, December 30, 1954; admitted to bar, 1981, New York; 1981, Ohio. *Education:* University of Rochester (B.A., 1977); Case Western Reserve University (J.D., 1980). Order of the Coif. *Member:* Cleveland and American Bar Associations. ***SPECIAL AGENCIES:*** PBGC; DOL; IRS. ***PRACTICE AREAS:*** Employee Benefit Law; Litigation; Multi-Employer Benefits; Multi-Employer Pensions; ERISA Compliance. ***Email:*** nwainblat@duvin.com

JOHN T. BILLICK, admitted to bar, 1973, Ohio; 1974, U.S. District Court, Northern District of Ohio; 1980, U.S Court of Appeals, Sixth Circuit; 1983, U.S. Supreme Court; 1993, U.S. Court of Appeals, Fifth Circuit. *Education:* John Carroll University (B.A., summa cum laude, 1970); Georgetown University (J.D., 1974). Instructor, Business Law, Kent State University; Former Member, Board of Education, Hudson, Ohio City School District, 1995-2000. *Member:* Cleveland, Akron, Ohio State and American (Labor and Employment Law Section; Occupational Safety and Health Committee) Bar Associations. ***PRACTICE AREAS:*** Labor Relations; Employment Litigation. ***Email:*** jbillick@duvin.com

KENNETH B. STARK, born Cleveland, Ohio, April 14, 1948; admitted to bar, 1979, Ohio; 1985, Arizona. *Education:* University of Wisconsin (B.S.Ch.E., 1971); Case Western Reserve University (J.D., 1979). Order of the Coif. Recipient, Labor Law Award. Contributor: Occupational Safety and Health Law, Second Supplement, BNA Books, 1994; Baldwin's Ohio School Law, Banks Baldwin, 1986; Ohio Collective Bargaining Law, Banks Baldwin, 1984. *Member:* Cleveland, Ohio State and American (Member, OSHA Committee) Bar Associations; State Bar of Arizona. ***SPECIAL AGENCIES:*** NLRB; SERB; OSHRC; OCRC; EEOC. ***REPORTED CASES:*** Sec'y of Labor v. B.F. Goodrich Hilton Davis Inc., 19 BNA OSHC 1795 (OSHRCJ 2001); Sec'y of Labor v. S.K. Wellman Friction Co., 18 BNA OSHC 1878 (OSHRCJ 1999); Mack v. BF Goodrich 120 Ohio App 3d 99 (1997); CBOE v. International Bd. of Firemen & Oilers, Local 701 120 Ohio App 3d 63 (1997); Martin v. American Cyanamid 8 F.3d 140 (6th Cir. 1993); State ex rel Brenders v. Hall 71 Ohio St 3d 632 (1995); State ex rel Martines v. Cleveland City Bd Ed 70 Ohio St 3d 416 (1994). Secretary of Labor vs. American Cyanamid 15 BNA OSHC 1497; 1992 CCH OSHD P2 9598 (OSHRC, 1992); Cleveland Electric Illuminating Co. vs. OSHRC 910 F.2d 1333 (6th Cir. 1990). ***PRACTICE AREAS:*** Occupational Safety and Health Law; Environmental Litigation; Public Sector Labor Law; Equal Employment Opportunity Law; Litigation. ***Email:*** kstark@duvin.com

ROBERT M. WOLFF, born Cincinnati, Ohio, February 8, 1955; admitted to bar, 1980, Ohio. *Education:* Oberlin College (B.A., 1977); University of Illinois (J.D., cum laude, 1980). Harno Scholar. Editor, University of Illinois Law Review, 1979-1980. Author: Note "Pacifica's Seven Dirty Words, A Sliding Scale of First Amendment," 1979 University of Illinois Law Forum 696. Chief Assistant Director of Law, City of Cleveland, 1987-1989. Advisory Committee, Cleveland State University Industrial Relations Center, 1988-1989. Illinois Governor's Fellow, 1977. Trustee and Vice Chair, National Multiple Sclerosis Society, Buckeye Chapter, Visiting Committee, Cleveland State University Marshall College of Law. Board of Trustees, Program Chair, National Conference for Community and Justice, Northern Ohio Chapter; Member, Managing Partners Forum, Cleveland Bar Association. ***REPORTED CASES:*** Wright v. Metro Health 58 F.3d 1130, (6th Cir. 1995); Molton vs. City of Cleveland, 839 F.2d 240 (6th Cir. 1988); Hawley vs. City of Cleveland, 773 F.2d 736 (6th Cir. 1985), cert. denied 106 S.Ct. 1266; Jones vs. Shankland, 800 F.2d 77 (6th Cir. 1986) cert. denied 107 S.Ct. 2177 (1987); Baab vs. Amr Services, 811 F.Supp. 1246 (N.D. Ohio 1993); State ex rel Geauga County Board of Commissioners v. Milligan, 100 Ohio St. ed 366 (2003); Oker v. Ameritech Corp., 89 Ohio St. 3d 223 (2000); Ricchetti v. Cleveland City School District, 72 Ohio St. 3d 1214 (1995); Lake County Board of Mental Retardations Developmental Disability v. Professional Association for the Teaching of the Mentally Retarded, 71 Ohio St. 3d 15 (1994); State ex rel Martines v. Cleveland City School District, 70 Ohio St. 3d 416 (1994); City of East Cleveland v. East Cleveland Fire Fighters, 70 Ohio St. 3d 125 (1994); Schwartz vs. ComCorp, 69 Ohio St. 3d (1994); State, ex rel, Gaeta vs. City of Cleveland, 39 Ohio St.3d 338 (1988); State Personnel Board of Review vs. Bay Village Civil Service Commission 28 Ohio St.3d 214 (1986); FOP v. City of Cleveland, 141 Ohio App 3d 63 (2001); Hunter vs. City of Cleveland, 56 Ohio App.3d 22 (App. Cuy. 1988); Hudak vs. Cleveland Civil Service Commission 44 Ohio App.3d 17 (App. Cuy. 1988); Gannon vs. City of Cleveland, 13 Ohio App.3d (App. Cuy, 1984). ***PRACTICE AREAS:*** Civil Litigation; Employment Litigation; Management Labor Relations. ***Email:*** rwolff@duvin.com

SUE MARIE DOUGLAS, admitted to bar, 1981, Ohio. *Education:* Georgetown University (B.A., cum laude, 1976); American University, Washington College of Law (J.D., 1981). *Member:* Akron, Cleveland, Ohio State and American Bar Associations; The District of Columbia Bar. (Certified Specialist in Labor & Employment Law, Ohio State Bar Association). ***PRACTICE AREAS:*** Employment Law; Employment Litigation; Alternative Dispute Resolution. ***Email:*** sdouglas@duvin.com

STEPHEN J. SFERRA, born Youngstown, Ohio, June 12, 1961; admitted to bar, 1986, Ohio. *Education:* Bowling Green State University (B.S., summa cum laude, 1983); Case Western Reserve University (J.D., cum laude, 1986). Omicron Delta Kappa. Member, Mortar Board. Member, Case Western Reserve Law Review, 1985-1986. ***SPECIAL AGENCIES:*** NLRB; SERB; EEOC; OCRC. ***PRACTICE AREAS:*** Management Labor Law; Collective Bargaining; Equal Employment Opportunity Law; Litigation. ***Email:*** ssferra@duvin.com

CHRISTINE C. COVEY, born Cleveland, Ohio, 1955; admitted to bar, 1980, Ohio and U.S. District Court, Northern District of Ohio. *Education:* Bowling Green State University (B.S.B.A., 1976); Cleveland-Marshall College of Law (J.D., 1979). Order of the Barristers. Listed in: The Best Lawyer in America, 1995-2004. *Member:* Cleveland and Ohio State Bar Associations. ***PRACTICE AREAS:*** Workers' Compensation Defense. ***Email:*** ccovey@duvin.com

JON M. DILENO, born Cleveland, Ohio, January 14, 1962; admitted to bar, 1988, Ohio. *Education:* John Carroll University; Baldwin Wallace College (B.A., cum laude, 1984); Tulane University (J.D., cum laude, 1988). Recipient, Outstanding Labor Law Student Honor. Instructor, Public Sector Labor Law, Cleveland State University, Certificate Program, 2000—; Contributing Editor, Elkouri and Elkouri, "How Arbitration Works," 6th Edition. ***SPECIAL AGENCIES:*** NLRB; SERB; EEOC; OCRC. ***PRACTICE AREAS:*** Management Labor Law; Equal Employment Opportunity Law; Litigation. ***Email:*** jdileno@duvin.com

SUELLEN OSWALD, born January 4, 1959; admitted to bar, 1990, Ohio, Pennsylvania, U.S. District Court, Northern and Southern Districts of Ohio, U.S. District Court, Western District of Pennsylvania and U.S. Court of Appeals, Sixth and Third Circuits. *Education:* Edinboro University (B.A., honors convocation, 1979); Case Western Reserve (J.D., 1990). *Member:* Cleveland, Ohio State and American (Member, Section on Labor and Employment Law) Bar Associations. ***SPECIAL AGENCIES:*** NLRB; OFCCP; EEOC; SERB and OCRC. ***REPORTED CASES:*** Smith v. The Cleveland Clinic Foundation, 151 Ohio App. 3d 373 (Cuyahoga Cty. 2003); Ferro Corp. v. Garrison Industries, 142 F.3d 926 (6th Cir. 1998); In re Glass, Molders, Pottery, Plastics and Allied Workers International Union, Local No. 173, 983 F.2d 725 (6th Cir. 1993); Bruno v. United Steelworkers of America, 784 F.Supp. 1286 (N.D. Ohio 1992), aff'd. 983 F 2d 1065 (6th Cir. 1993). ***PRACTICE AREAS:*** Management Labor Law; Collective Bargaining; Public Sector Labor Law; Union Organizing; Unfair Labor Practices; Litigation; Equal Employment Opportunity Law. ***Email:*** soswald@duvin.com

JANETTE McCARTHY LOUARD, born Kingston, Jamaica, April 3, 1961; admitted to bar, 1986, New York; 1996, Ohio. *Education:* Wellesley College (B.A., cum laude, 1983); Columbia University (J.D., 1986). Law Clerk to Honorable John Hargrove, Sr., 1986-1988. Former Assistant U.S. Attorney, U.S. District Court, Eastern District of New York, 1991-1995. ***PRACTICE AREAS:*** Equal Employment Opportunity Law; Employment Litigation. ***Email:*** jlouard@duvin.com

KATHLEEN M. KORDELESKI, born Amherst, Ohio, January 19, 1960; admitted to bar, 1986, Ohio and U.S. District Court, Northern District of Ohio; 1988, U.S. Court of Appeals, Sixth Circuit; 1999, U.S. Court of Appeals, Eighth Circuit. *Education:* Lorain Community College (A.A., cum laude, 1981); University of Toledo (B.B.A., cum laude, 1983); Cleveland Marshall College of Law (J.D., 1986). Member, National Moot Court

(This Listing Continued)

Team. Member, Moot Court Board of Governors. Order of Barristers. *Member:* Cleveland, Cuyahoga County, Lorain County, Ohio State, Federal and American Bar Associations. ***SPECIAL AGENCIES:*** NLRB; EEOC; OCRC; SERB; DOL. ***PRACTICE AREAS:*** Management Labor Law; Collective Bargaining; Unfair Labor Practices; Employment Discrimination; Wrongful Termination. ***Email:*** kkordeleski@duvin.com

KENNETH D. SCHWARTZ, born Bloomington, Indiana; admitted to bar, 1991, Illinois; 1998, Ohio. *Education:* Kent State University (B.A., 1987); University of Illinois (J.D., 1991; M.A., Labor and Industrial Practice, 1991). Phi Beta Kappa; Omicron Delta Kappa. Rickert Scholar. Author: "*Gilman v. Interstate/Johnson Lane Corporation:* The Supreme Court Endorses Arbitration of Age Discrimination Claims," 17 Employee Rel. Law J., Vol. 17, No. 2 (Autumn 1991, Burstein, J. and Schwartz, K.). *Member:* Chicago, Illinois State and American Bar Associations. ***PRACTICE AREAS:*** Management Labor Law; Employment Litigation; Wrongful Termination. ***Email:*** kschwartz@duvin.com

BRADLEY A. SHERMAN, born Cleveland, Ohio, October 23, 1968; admitted to bar, 1994, Ohio. *Education:* Northwestern University (B.A., 1991); Case Western Reserve University (J.D., cum laude, 1994). Notes Editor, Case Western Reserve University Law Review, 1993-1994. *Member:* Cleveland, Ohio State and American Bar Associations. ***SPECIAL AGENCIES:*** NLRB; EEOC; SERB; OCRC; PHRC; MCAD. ***REPORTED CASES:*** Mark Watson v. Electronic Data Sys., 2003-LCA-30 (Kennington, ALJ Nov. 12, 2003); Derungs v. Wal-Mart Stores, Inc., 374 F.3d 428 (6th Cir. 2004); Testerman v. EDS Tech. Prods. Corp., 98 F.3d 297 (6th Cir. 1996); McDaniel v. Wal-Mart Stores, Inc., 94 F.Supp. 2d 878 (N.D. Ohio 2000); State ExRel. Cleveland Police Patrolmen's Ass'n v. City of Cleveland, 702 N.E.2d 926 (Cuyahoga App. 1997); Cleveland Board of Educ. v. Int'l Bhd. of Firemen & Oilers Lo. 701, 696 N.2d 658 (Cuyahoga App. 1997). ***PRACTICE AREAS:*** Management Labor Law; Employment Litigation; Equal Employment Opportunity Law; Union Organization; Computer Law. ***Email:*** bsherman@duvin.com

BARRY Y. FREEMAN, born New York, N.Y., October 13, 1967; admitted to bar, 1993, Ohio and U.S. District Court, Northern District of Ohio; 1994, Michigan; 1997, U.S. District Court, Eastern District of Michigan and U.S. Court of Appeals, Sixth Circuit; 2002, U.S. Supreme Court; 2003, U.S. District Court, Southern District of Ohio and U.S. District Court, District of Colorado. *Education:* University of Chicago (A.B., with honors, 1990); University of Michigan (J.D., 1993). *Member:* Cleveland (Member, Labor and Employment Law Section), Ohio State (Member, Labor and Employment Law Section) and American (Member, Labor and Employment Law Section) Bar Associations; State Bar of Michigan. ***SPECIAL AGENCIES:*** EEOC; OCRC; NLRB; SERB. ***REPORTED CASES:*** Mack v. Strategic Materials, Inc. 270 F.Supp.2d 934 (2003), aff'd. 2004 U.S. App. LEXIS 18960 (2004); Gonzalez v. Moffitt, 1997 U.S. App. LEXIS 6400 (1997); Brown v. Renter's Choice, Inc. 55 F.Supp.2d 788 (1999); Felden v. First Nat'l. Supermarkets, Inc. 1999 Ohio App. LEXIS 2430 (1999); Stallworth v. Greater Cleveland Regional Transit Auth., 1998 Ohio App. LEXIS 5312 (1998); Ragone v. Sentry Ins., 121 Ohio App.3d 362, 700 N.E.2d 48 (1997). ***PRACTICE AREAS:*** Employment Law; Employment Litigation; Management Labor Law; Commercial Litigation; Insurance Law. ***Email:*** bfreeman@duvin.com

LESSIE MILTON JONES, admitted to bar, 1984, Michigan (inactive); 1985, Ohio. *Education:* Kent State University (B.A., 1979); Cleveland-Marshall College of Law (J.D., 1983).

LISA FROIMSON MANN, born Philadelphia, Pennsylvania, June 14, 1956; admitted to bar, 1980, Ohio. *Education:* Indiana University (B.A., 1977); Case Western Reserve University (J.D., 1980). ***SPECIAL AGENCIES:*** EEOC; OCRC; Penn. HRC; NY Div. of HR. ***REPORTED CASES:*** Fisher Foods and United Food and Commercial Workers Local 880, 80 L.A. 133 (Abrams, 1983); Michael S. Becka vs. American Seaway Foods, Inc., et al., Slip Opinion No. 9-009, Court of Appeals, 11th Appellate District; Lake County, Ohio (June 25, 1982); Bethel Robertson vs. James Mayfield, Administrator, Bureau of Worker's Compensation, Slip Opinion No. 50754, Court of Appeals, 8th Appellate District, Cuyahoga County, Ohio (June 19, 1986). ***PRACTICE AREAS:*** Equal Employment Opportunity Law; Employment Law; Litigation. ***Email:*** lmann@duvin.com

M. TERENCE CAWLEY, admitted to bar, 1990, Ohio; 1991, North Carolina; 1995, California. *Education:* Kenyon College (B.A., cum laude, 1983); University of North Carolina School of Law (J.D., 1990). ***PRACTICE AREAS:*** Litigation; Complex Commercial Litigation.

JONATHAN S. FORMAN, admitted to bar, 1994, Ohio; 1997, Oregon. *Education:* University of Michigan (B.A., 1990); University of Cincinnati (J.D., 1994). ***PRACTICE AREAS:*** Management Labor Law; Employment Discrimination; Employment Litigation. ***Email:*** jforman@duvin.com

TERESA R. POFOK, admitted to bar, 1994, Ohio. *Education:* Kent State University (B.A., cum laude, 1991); Rutgers University Law School (J.D., 1994).

PATRICIA S. CONTI, admitted to bar, 1995, Ohio. *Education:* John Carroll University (B.A., magna cum laude, 1989); Cleveland Marshall College of Law (J.D., cum laude, 1995). Adjunct Faculty, Lakeland Community College, 1989-2001; Judicial Staff Attorney, Cuyahoga County Common Pleas Court 1996-1998; Magistrate, Cuyahoga County Court of Common Pleas, 1998-2001. ***SPECIAL AGENCIES:*** EEOC, OCRC, State Unemployment Board. ***PRACTICE AREAS:*** Labor Relations; Employment Law; Litigation; Criminal Law; Commercial LItigation. ***Email:*** pconti@duvin.com

FREDRICK W. ENGLEHART, admitted to bar, 1997, Ohio. *Education:* San Francisco State University (B.A., summa cum laude, 1994); Case Western Reserve University (J.D., cum laude, 1997). ***PRACTICE AREAS:*** Management Labor; Union Organization; Union Elections; Collective Bargaining Litigation. ***Email:*** fenglehart@duvin.com

HEIDI ALTEN, admitted to bar, 1997, Ohio; 1999, U.S. District Court, Northern District of Ohio; 2000, Washington, D.C. *Education:* Columbia University (B.A., 1993; J.D., 1997). *Member:* Ohio State and American Bar Associations. ***PRACTICE AREAS:*** Labor and Employment. ***Email:*** halten@duvin.com

SHANNON K. PATTON, born December 9, 1972; admitted to bar, 1998, Ohio. *Education:* Miami University (B.A., cum laude, 1995); Ohio State University (J.D., 1998). *Member:* Cleveland and Ohio State Bar Associations. ***SPECIAL AGENCIES:*** EEOC; OCRC. ***PRACTICE AREAS:*** Management Labor Law; Employment Litigation. ***Email:*** spatton@duvin.com

TIMOTHY S. ANDERSON, admitted to bar, 1999, Ohio. *Education:* University of Miami (B.A., magna cum laude, 1996); University of Michigan (J.D., cum laude, 1999). ***PRACTICE AREAS:*** Management Labor Law; Employment Litigation. ***Email:*** tanderson@duvin.com

BONNIE L. KRISTAN, born Lakewood, Ohio, December 12, 1970; admitted to bar, 1998, North Carolina; 2001, Ohio. *Education:* Miami University (B.S., B.A., 1993); University of Pittsburgh (J.D., 1998). *Member:* Cleveland, Ohio State and North Carolina Bar Associations. ***PRACTICE AREAS:*** Workers Compensation; Labor and Employment. ***Email:*** bkristan@duvin.com

LISA A. COTTLE, born Hartford, Connecticut, July 11, 1975; admitted to bar, 2000, Ohio; 2002, U.S. District Court, Northern District of Ohio. *Education:* University of Michigan (B.A., high honors in Spanish, 1997); Case Western Reserve University (J.D., 2000). Articles Editor, Case Western Reserve Journal of International Law. Attorney Advisor, Judicial Law Clerk, U.S. Department of Justice Attorney General's Honor Program, Executive Office for Immigration Review, Los Angeles Immigration Court, 2000-2001. *Member:* Cleveland and Ohio State Bar Associations; American Immigration Lawyers Association. ***LANGUAGES:*** Spanish. ***PRACTICE AREAS:*** Labor Relations; Litigation; Immigration Law. ***Email:*** lcottle@duvin.com

JAMES P. SMITH, born January 20, 1976; admitted to bar, 2001, Ohio. *Education:* Yale University (B.A., 1998); University of Cincinnati (J.D., 2001). ***PRACTICE AREAS:*** Labor Relations; Litigation. ***Email:*** jsmith@duvin.com

PATRICK H. LEWIS, admitted to bar, 1985, Ohio. *Education:* Case Western Reserve University (B.A., 1978); Cleveland-Marshall College of Law (J.D., 1984). *Member:* Cuyahoga County (Workers' Compensation, Labor Section), Ohio State (Workers' Compensation) and American (Labor and Employment Law Section) Bar Associations. ***PRACTICE AREAS:*** Workers Compensation; OSHA; Unemployment Compensation; Labor. ***Email:*** plewis@duvin.com

STEPHANIE SEELEY, born July 9, 1976; admitted to bar, 2001, Ohio. *Education:* Allegheny College (B.A., 1998); Syracuse University (J.D., summa cum laude, 2001). Judicial Law Clerk, Northern District of Pennsylvania, 2001-2002. *Member:* Cleveland, Ohio, American Bar Associations. ***PRACTICE AREAS:*** Labor Relations; Litigation. ***Email:*** sseeley@duvin.com

SHERRIE M. MIKHAIL, admitted to bar, 2001, Ohio. *Education:* John Carroll University (B.A., 1998); Case Western Reserve University (J.D., 2001). ***PRACTICE AREAS:*** Labor Relations; Litigation. ***Email:*** smikhail@duvin.com

LISA ORLANDO, admitted to bar, 2002, Ohio; 2003, U.S. District Court, Northern District of Ohio; 2004, U.S. Court of Appeals, Sixth Circuit. *Education:* Boston College (B.S., 1996); Case Western Reserve University (J.D., magna cum laude, 2002). Order of the Coif. *Member:* Ohio State and American Bar Associations. ***SPECIAL AGENCIES:*** EEOC; OCRC. ***PRACTICE AREAS:*** Labor Relations; Employment Litigation. ***Email:*** lorlando@duvin.com

RICHARD D. PORTER, admitted to bar, 2002, Ohio. *Education:* Mount Union College (B.A., 1993); Ohio State University (J.D., 2002). ***PRACTICE AREAS:*** Labor Relations; Litigation. ***Email:*** rporter@duvin.com

MEREDITH A. LOBRITZ, admitted to bar, 2003, Ohio. *Education:* The Ohio State University (B.S., cum laude, 1997; J.D., 2003). *Member:* Cleveland, Ohio State and American Bar Associations. ***PRACTICE AREAS:*** Labor Relations; Litigation. ***Email:*** mlobritz@duvin.com

KATHY SCADDEN, admitted to bar, 2003, Ohio. *Education:* University of Montana (B.S., 1983); Cleveland Marshall College of Law (J.D., summa cum laude, 2003). Recipient: Robert P. Duvin Award for Excellence in Labor and Employment Law; ABA/BNA Award for Excellence in the Study of Labor and Employment Law. *Member:* Cleveland, Ohio State and American Bar Associations. ***PRACTICE AREAS:*** Labor Relations; Litigation. ***Email:*** kscadden@duvin.com

DANIEL CONNELL, admitted to bar, 2004, Ohio. *Education:* Georgetown University (B.A., 2000); Case Western Reserve University (J.D., 2004; M.B.A., 2004).

EMILY FIFTAL, admitted to bar, 2004, Ohio. *Education:* Truman State University (B.A., summa cum laude, 2001); Case Western Reserve University (J.D., magna cum laude, 2004). Class Valedictorian; Order of the Coif. Managing Editor, Law Review, 2003-2004.

JULIA G. WAINBLAT, admitted to bar, 1992, Ohio. *Education:* Miami University (B.A., 1979); Cleveland State University (M.A.; J.D., cum laude, 1992).

OF COUNSEL

JEFFREY A. BELKIN, admitted to bar, 1964, Michigan; 1965, Ohio; 1971, U.S. Supreme Court. *Education:* Brown University (A.B., 1961); University of Michigan (J.D., 1964). Listed in Best Lawyers in America, 1987—. Member, Advisory Committee of the Industrial Relations Center, Cleveland State University, 1987—; Chair, 1990-1991. Attorney, National Labor Relations Board, 1964-1966. Member, National Panel of Arbitrators, American Arbitration Association. President, Cleveland Psychoanalytic Foundation, 1998-2000. *Member:* Cleveland, Ohio State and American Bar Associations. ***Email:*** jbelkin@duvin.com

MARK V. WEBBER, born Cleveland, Ohio, August 8, 1947; admitted to bar, 1974, Ohio. *Education:* Columbia College of Columbia University (B.A., 1969); Boston College (J.D., 1974). *Member:* Cleveland and Ohio State Bar Associations. ***REPORTED CASES:*** DelCostello v. Local 57 IBT, 762 F2d 1219 (4th Cir. 1985); Robinson v. Central Brass Manufacturing Company, 987 F2d 1235 (6th Cir. 1993), cert. denied 510 U.S. 827 (1993); Truserv Corp. v. NLRB 254 F3d 1105 (D.C. Cir. 2001), cert. denied 122 S. Ct.1070 (2002).. ***PRACTICE AREAS:*** Litigation; Labor Law; Employment Law. ***Email:*** mwebber@duvin.com

LINDA HAUSERMAN HARROLD, admitted to bar, 1979, Ohio and U.S. District Court, Northern District of Ohio; 1987, U.S. Court of Appeals, Sixth Circuit; 2003, U.S.

(This Listing Continued)

DUVIN, CAHN & HUTTON, A LEGAL PROFESSIONAL ASSOCIATION, Cleveland—Continued

District Court, Southern District of Ohio. *Education:* Grinnell College (A.B., 1969); Oberlin College (M.A.T., 1970); Case Western Reserve University (J.D., 1979). Phi Beta Kappa. Order of the Coif; Associate Editor, Case Western Reserve Law Review, 1977-1978. Member, Village Council, Kirtland Hills, Ohio, 1994—. *Member:* Cleveland, Lake County, Ohio State and American Bar Associations. ***SPECIAL AGENCIES:*** EEOC; OCRC; DOL; OFCCP. ***PRACTICE AREAS:*** Employment Law; Labor Law; Litigation; Alternative Dispute Resolution. ***Email:*** lharrold@duvin.com

REPRESENTATIVE CLIENTS: Avery Dennison; Bally; City of Cleveland; Cleveland-Akron-Canton Supermarket Industry; Cleveland Browns; Cleveland Clinic Foundation; Cleveland Orchestra; Continental Airlines; Delaware North Sportservice Corp.; Dominion East Ohio Gas Company; Electronic Data Systems; Electrolux; Ford Motor Company; Forest City Enterprises; Goodyear Tire & Rubber Company; House of LaRose; International Steel Group; Richard Jacobs Group; Lamson & Sessions, Inc.; Lincoln Electric; MBNA; McDonald's Corp.; The Metro Health System; Nordstrom; Northeast Ohio Regional Sewer District; Ohio Turnpike Commission; Progressive Insurance Companies; Regional Transit Authority; The Scott Fetzer Co.; Steris; Target Corporation; Wal-Mart.

ROBERT EDELSTEIN

Established in 1997

23825 COMMERCE PARK
SUITE A
CLEVELAND, OHIO 44122-5834
Telephone: 216-514-4981
Fax: 216-514-4987
Email: RECUBE@AOL.com
URL: http://www.edelsteincollectionlaw.com

General Business Practice, Commercial Collections, Debtor and Creditor, Bankruptcy, Landlord and Tenant Law, Litigation.

ROBERT EDELSTEIN, born Havana, Cuba, March 21, 1958; admitted to bar, 1983, Ohio; 1985, U.S. District Court, Northern District of Ohio and U.S. Court of Federal Claims. *Education:* Tulane University (B.A., 1980); Case Western Reserve University (J.D., 1983). Phi Eta Sigma. Assistant Attorney General, Ohio, 1984-1986. Special Counsel, Ohio Attorney General, 1987-1993. *Member:* Cleveland Bar Association. ***LANGUAGES:*** Spanish. ***PRACTICE AREAS:*** Bankruptcy; Collections; Repossessions; Business Law; Commercial Law; Debtor and Creditor; Landlord and Tenant Law.

Language: Spanish

REPRESENTATIVE CLIENTS: Orlean Enterprises, Inc.; ABG Management Inc.; Media Pro, Inc.; Berkowitz, Kumin, Bookatz, Inc.; Famous Enterprises, Inc.; The Window Factory of America, Inc.; Weiss, Inc.; ATM Distributing, Inc.; APT Management, Inc.; IOS Capital, Inc.; Bass Security Services, Inc.; Swift Cleaners, Inc.; Swiger Coil Systems, Inc.; Thompson Aluminum Casting Co.

ELK & ELK CO., L.P.A.

LANDERHAVEN CORPORATE CENTER
6100 PARKLAND BOULEVARD
CLEVELAND, OHIO 44124-4187
Telephone: 888-355-6446
Email: kthompson@elkandelk.com
URL: http://www.elkandelklaw.com

Columbus, Ohio Office: Fifth Third Center, Capital Square, 21 East State Street, Suite 320, 43215. Telephone: 1-888-ELK-OHIO.

Automobile Accidents, Product Defects, Nursing Home Neglect, Medical Malpractice, Personal Injury.

DAVID J. ELK, admitted to bar, 1965, Ohio. *Education:* Case Western Reserve University (B.B.A.; J.D.).

ARTHUR M. ELK, admitted to bar, 1973, Ohio and Florida. *Education:* Case Western Reserve University (B.B.A.); Cleveland State University (J.D.).

FAY, SHARPE, FAGAN, MINNICH & McKEE, LLP

Established in 1884

1100 SUPERIOR AVENUE, SEVENTH FLOOR
CLEVELAND, OHIO 44114
Telephone: 216-861-5582
FAX: 216-241-1666
Email: fs@faysharpe.com
URL: http://www.faysharpe.com

Providing a complete range of Domestic and International Intellectual Property Law services including Patents, Trademarks, Copyrights, Trade Secrets, Licensing Matters, Unfair Competition Law and Litigation.

FIRM PROFILE: Fay Sharpe has focused on supporting the technology advancements of its clients and safeguarding intellectual property rights since 1884. The firm is one of the largest intellectual property speciality firms in the Midwest with IP attorneys, technical consultants, and a worldwide network of intellectual property resources covering biotechnology, chemistry, engineering, physics, computer science and virtually every technology in between.

MEMBERS OF FIRM

MARK E. BANDY, born Flint, Michigan, December 25, 1962; admitted to bar, 1991, Ohio and Michigan; registered to practice before U.S. Patent and Trademark Office. *Education:* Michigan Technological University (B.S.Ch.E., with honors, 1985); Cleveland-Marshall College of Law (J.D., 1990); University of Michigan (M.B.A., 1997). *Member:* Cleveland and Ohio State Bar Associations; American Intellectual Property Law Association. ***PRACTICE AREAS:*** Patent; Trademark; Copyright; Unfair Competition; Licensing; Chemical and Mechanical Arts. ***Email:*** mbandy@faysharpe.com

†JOHN P. CORNELY, born Rome, New York, October 18, 1968; admitted to bar, 1995, Ohio; registered to practice before U.S. Patent and Trademark Office. *Education:* John Carroll University (B.S., cum laude, 1991); The Ohio State University College of Law (J.D., 1994). Patent Examiner, U.S. Patent and Trademark Office, 1996-1997. Registered Patent Attorney, 1998. ***PRACTICE AREAS:*** Patent Prosecution; Trademark; Copyright; Mechanical, Optical, Electrical and Software Arts. ***Email:*** jcornely@faysharpe.com

†JOSEPH D. DREHER, born Cleveland, Ohio, November 1, 1965; admitted to bar, 1991, Ohio, U.S. District Court, Northern District of Ohio, U.S. Court of Appeals, Federal and 6th Circuits; registered to practice before U.S. Patent and Trademark Office. *Education:* University of Dayton (B.E.E., cum laude, 1988); Case Western Reserve University (J.D., cum laude, 1991). Adjunct Professor of Law, Case Western Reserve University. ***PRACTICE AREAS:*** Patent; Trademark; Copyright; Domain Names; Internet Law; Procurement, Counseling and Litigation. ***Email:*** jdreher@faysharpe.com

†JUDE A. FRY, born Youngstown, Ohio, April 8, 1961; admitted to bar, 1991, Ohio and U.S. District Court, Northern District of Ohio; 1992, U.S. Court of Appeals, 6th Circuit; 1996, U.S. Court of Appeals, Federal Circuit; registered to practice before U.S. Patent and Trademark Office. *Education:* Youngstown State University (B.E., 1985); Cleveland-Marshall School of Law (J.D., 1991). Tau Beta Pi; Omega Chi Epsilon. ***PRACTICE AREAS:*** Patent; Trademark; Copyright; Litigation; Chemical Arts. ***Email:*** jfry@faysharpe.com

†STEVEN M. HAAS, born Waterbury, Connecticut, May 8, 1969; admitted to bar, 1994, Ohio; 1996, District of Columbia; registered to practice before U.S. Patent and Trademark Office. *Education:* University of Cincinnati (B.S., 1991); University of Akron (J.D., cum laude, 1994). Law Clerk, Hon. Elinore Marsh Stormer, Akron Municipal Court, 1992-1994. ***PRACTICE AREAS:*** Patent and Trademark Prosecution; Litigation; Mechanical and Computer Arts; Fluid Dispensing Systems; Automotive Engine and Drivetrain Systems; Computer-Implemented Business Methods; Digital Image Processing. ***Email:*** shaas@faysharpe.com

MICHAEL E. HUDZINSKI, born Cleveland, Ohio, May 7, 1961; admitted to bar, 1989, Ohio; U.S. District Court, Northern District of Ohio; registered to practice before the U.S. Patent and Trademark Office. *Education:* Cleveland State University, Fenn College of Engineering (B.E.E., 1983); Cleveland State University, Cleveland-Marshall College of Law (J.D., 1989). *Member:* Cleveland Intellectual Property Association; American Intellectual Property Law Association. ***PRACTICE AREAS:*** Patent; Trademark; Copyright; Electrical and Mechanical Arts. ***Email:*** mhudzinski@faysharpe.com

†RICHARD M. KLEIN, born New York, N.Y., November 30, 1958; admitted to bar, 1985, Ohio and U.S. District Court, Northern District of Ohio; 1987, U.S. Court of Appeals for the Federal and 6th Circuits; 1999, U.S. Supreme Court; registered to practice before the U.S. Patent and Trademark Office. *Education:* Ohio State University (B.S., Biochem-Micro, 1980; M.B.A., Finance, 1982); Case Western Reserve University (J.D., 1985). Author: "State Trademark and Unfair Competition Law, (Clark Boardman), Compiled by the International Trademark Association (INTA), Ohio Section and Update; "Establishing Infringement under the Doctrine of Equivalents after Malta," Journal of Patent and Trademark Office Society, Vol. 75, No. 1, PP 5-19, January 1993; "Helpful Insights to the New Standards Required for Patent Applications Containing Nucleotide and/or Amino Acid Sequence Data," Journal of the Patent and Trademark Office Society, Vol. 73, No. 1, pp. 29-36, January, 1991; "Rule Changes Concerning DNA or Amino Acid Sequence Data," The Journal of Proprietary Rights, Vol. 2, No. 10, pp. 19-20, October, 1990; "A Recent Revision to the General Venue Statute Greatly Expands Plaintiffs' Venue Choices," Journal of the Patent and Trademark Office Society, Vol. 71, No. 11, pp. 886-888, November 1989; "Changes in the Federal Venue Statute Expands Venue Choices for Trademark Infringement or Unfair Competition," The Journal of Proprietary Rights, Vol. 1, No. 9, pp. 25-26, September 1989; "A General Venue Statute Revision Expands a Plaintiff's Choices Against a Corporate Defendant for Trademark Infringement or Unfair Competition," Cleveland Bar Journal, Vol. 60, No. 10, pp. 342-343, September, 1989. *Member:* Cleveland Intellectual Property Law Association (Director); Federal Circuit Bar Association; Patent and Trademark Office Society; The American Institute of Chemists; American Chemical Society. ***REPORTED CASES:*** Antonious v. Spalding & Evenflo Cos., Inc., 281 F.3d 1258, 62 USPQ2d 1060 (Fed. Cir. 2002); Antonious v. Spalding & Evenflo Cos., Inc., 275 F.3d 1066, 61 USPQ2d 1245 (Fed. Cir. 2002); Microsoft Corp. v. Action Software, 136 F.Supp. 2d 735; 58 USPQ2d 1305 (N.D. Ohio 2001); Antonious v. Spalding & Evenflo Companies, Inc., 44 F.Supp. 2d 732 (D.Md. 1998), 217 F.3d 849, 1999 U.S. App. LEXIS 22984 (Fed. Cir. 1999); Dolly, Inc. v. Spalding & Evenflo Cos., 16 F.3d 394, 29 USPQ2d 1767 (Fed. Cir. 1994); Darling v. Spalding & Evenflo Cos., Inc., 30 USPQ2d 1047 (N.D. Ind. 1993), aff'd, 26 F.3d 140 (Fed. Cir. 1994); R.E.F. Golf Co. v. Roberts Metals, Inc., 24 USPQ2d 1070 (M.D. Fla. 1992); Dolly, Inc. v. Spalding & Evenflo Cos., 954 F.2d 734, 23 USPQ2d 1555 (Fed. Cir. 1992); Spalding & Evenflo Companies v. Graco Metal Products Inc., 19 USPQ2d 1479 (N.D. Ohio 1991); and, Spalding & Evenflo Cos., Inc. v. Graco, 18 USPQ2d 2029 (N.D. Ohio 1991). ***PRACTICE AREAS:*** Patent Litigation; Patent, Trademark and Copyright Prosecution; Chemical Arts; Biotechnology; Mechanical Arts. ***Email:*** rklein@faysharpe.com

†THOMAS E. KOCOVSKY, JR., born Newark, New Jersey, March 2, 1947; admitted to bar, 1975, Virginia; 1976, U.S. Court of Federal Claims; 1978, Ohio; 1979, U.S. District Court, Northern District of Ohio; 1981, U.S. Court of Appeals, 6th Circuit; 1983, U.S. Court of Appeals for the Federal Circuit; registered to practice before U.S. Patent and Trademark Office. *Education:* Cornell University (B.S., 1969; M.E., Engr. Phys., 1970); George Washington University (J.D., with honors, 1975). Examiner, United States Patent Office, 1970-1975. Law Clerk: U.S. Court of Customs and Patent Appeals, 1975-1976; U.S. Claims Court, 1976-1977. Adjunct Professor of Patent Law, Capital University American Law Studies Program, Tokyo, 1987. *Member:* Cornell Society of Engineers. ***PRACTICE AREAS:*** Patent; Trademark; Copyright; Electrical Arts. ***Email:*** tkocovsky@faysharpe.com

SANDRA M. KOENIG, born East Cleveland, Ohio, May 2, 1960; admitted to bar, 1987, Ohio; 1988, U.S. District Court, Northern District of Ohio; 2000, U.S. Court of Appeals, Federal Circuit; registered to practice before the U.S. Patent and Trademark Office.

(This Listing Continued)

Education: Cleveland State University (B.Ch.E., 1983); Cleveland-Marshall College of Law (J.D., 1987). CLE Presentations: "Understanding Basic Trademark Law In Ohio," 2001; "Basic Copyright Law," 2001, 2003; "Madrid Protocol Overview," 2004. *Member:* International Trademark Association; Cleveland Intellectual Property Association (Member, Information Resources Committee); American Intellectual Property Association. ***PRACTICE AREAS:*** Patent; Trademark; Copyright; Litigation. ***Email:*** skoenig@faysharpe.com

†***SCOTT ANDREW McCOLLISTER,*** born Garfield Heights, Ohio, May 6, 1964; admitted to bar, 1989, Ohio; registered to practice before U.S. Patent and Trademark Office. *Education:* Purdue University (B.S., 1986); Case Western Reserve University (J.D., 1989). ***PRACTICE AREAS:*** Patent; Trademark; Copyright; Trade Secrets; Chemical Arts. ***Email:*** smccollister@faysharpe.com

†***JAY F. MOLDOVANYI,*** born Budapest, Hungary, August 24, 1948; admitted to bar, 1979, Virginia; 1982, U.S. Court of Appeals for the Federal Circuit; 1983, U.S. Supreme Court; 1984, Ohio; 1985, U.S. District Court, Northern District of Ohio; registered to practice before U.S. Patent and Trademark Office. *Education:* Case Western Reserve University (B.S.M.E., 1972); The Ohio State University (J.D., 1979); George Washington University (LL.M., 1983). Phi Delta Phi. Member: Order of the Barristers; National Moot Court Team. *Author:* "Reduction to Practice by Computer Simulation-Is It Ever Possible?" JPOS, Vol. 65, No. 9, pp. 492-521, September 1983; "Employed Inventors in Ohio: Who owns the Invention?" Ohio Lawyer, Vol. 1, No. 4., pp, 25-27, July/August, 1987; "False Advertising Is Actionable Under the Trademark Laws," Cleveland Bar Journal, Vol. 60, No. 9, pp. 296-297, July-August, 1989. *Member:* Federal Circuit Bar Association; Virginia State Bar; Patent and Trademark Office Society. ***PRACTICE AREAS:*** Patent; Trademark; Copyright; Litigation. ***Email:*** jmoldovanyi@faysharpe.com

†***PHILIP J. MOY, JR.,*** born New York, N.Y., August 6, 1954; admitted to bar, 1984, District of Columbia; 1986, U.S. Court of Appeals for the Federal Circuit; 1989, Ohio, U.S. District Court, Northern District of Ohio and U.S. Court of Appeals, 6th Circuit; registered to practice before U.S. Patent and Trademark Office. *Education:* Dartmouth College (A.B., 1976; B.E., 1977); George Washington University (J.D., 1984). Executive Managing Editor, George Washington Journal of International Law and Economics, 1983-1984. *Author:* "Arbitration of United States Patent Validity and Infringement Under 35 U.S.C. §294," 17 Geo. Wash. J. Int'l L. & Econ. 637 (1983). *Member:* Federal Circuit Bar Association; Association of Patent Law Firms (Board Member, 1998-2002; Secretary, 1999-2000; President, 2000-2001); Dartmouth Society of Engineers; Dartmouth Lawyers Association; Licensing Executives Society. ***PRACTICE AREAS:*** Patent; Trademark; Copyright; Licensing; Litigation. ***Email:*** pmoy@faysharpe.com

†***TIMOTHY E. NAUMAN,*** born Dayton, Ohio, September 26, 1958; admitted to bar, 1983, Ohio; 1985, U.S. District Court, Northern District of Ohio; 1987, U.S. Court of Appeals for the Federal Circuit; registered to practice before U.S. Patent and Trademark Office. *Education:* University of Notre Dame (B.S.C.E., 1980); University of Dayton (J.D., 1983). Examiner, United States Patent Office, 1983-1984. *Member:* Federal Circuit Bar Association; Patent and Trademark Office Society. ***PRACTICE AREAS:*** Patent; Trademark; Copyright; Mechanical and Electro-Mechanical Arts; Preparation and Prosecution; Infringement/Validity Assessment. ***Email:*** tnauman@faysharpe.com

†***PATRICK R. ROCHE,*** born Cleveland, Ohio, March 24, 1952; admitted to bar, 1978, Ohio; 1979, U.S. District Court, Northern District of Ohio; 1981, U.S. Court of Appeals, 6th Circuit; 1983, U.S. Court of Appeals for the Federal Circuit; 1985, U.S. Supreme Court; registered to practice before U.S. Patent and Trademark Office. *Education:* University of Notre Dame (B.S.E.E., 1974); Cleveland Marshall College of Law (J.D., 1978). *Member:* Institute of Electrical and Electronics Engineers. ***PRACTICE AREAS:*** Patent; Trademark; Copyright; Electrical Arts. ***Email:*** proche@faysharpe.com

†***JAMES E. SCARBROUGH,*** born Pittsburgh, Pennsylvania, July 20, 1964; admitted to bar, 1997, Ohio; registered to practice before the U.S. Patent and Trademark Office. *Education:* Pennsylvania State University (B.S.M.E., 1986); Carnegie Mellon University (M.S.I.A., 1991); Case Western Reserve University (J.D., 1997). ***PRACTICE AREAS:*** Patent Prosecution; Patent Opinions; Mechanical Arts; Trademark; Copyright. ***Email:*** jscarbrough@faysharpe.com

ANN M. SKERRY, born Leeds, England, May 16, 1956; admitted to bar, 1997, Ohio; registered to practice before the U.S. Patent and Trademark Office. *Education:* University of Manchester, England (B.Sc., 1977; Ph.D., 1981); Case Western Reserve University (J.D., magna cum laude, 1997). Order of the Coif. *Member:* Cleveland Intellectual Property Law association; Case Western Reserve Law Review. ***PRACTICE AREAS:*** Patent Prosecution; Trademarks; Opinions; Sterilization; Carbon Chemistry; Electrochemistry; Adhesives; Biochemistry; Ceramics; Petroleum and Rubber Chemistry; Lighting Devices; Paper Chemistry. ***Email:*** askerry@faysharpe.com

MARK S. SVAT, born Lorain, Ohio, June 22, 1959; admitted to bar, 1989, Ohio; registered to practice before the U.S. Patent and Trademark Office. *Education:* Cleveland State University (B.S.E.T., 1985); Cleveland-Marshall College of Law (J.D., 1988). *Member:* Institute of Electrical and Electronic Engineers; Cleveland Intellectual Property Law Association. ***PRACTICE AREAS:*** Patent; Trademark; Copyright; Computer Hardware and Software; Internet; E-Commerce. ***Email:*** msvat@faysharpe.com

BRIAN E. TURUNG, born Houston, Texas, June 6, 1963; admitted to bar, 1991, Ohio; registered to practice before the U.S. Patent and Trademark Office. *Education:* University of Houston (B.Ch.E., 1987); St. Louis University (J.D., 1990). *Member:* Cleveland and American Bar Associations; Cleveland Intellectual Property Law Association. ***PRACTICE AREAS:*** Patent, Trademark and Copyright Prosecution, Licensing and Litigation; Chemical Arts; Electrical and Mechanical Arts. ***Email:*** bturung@faysharpe.com

GREGORY S. VICKERS, born Cleveland, Ohio, October 16, 1963; admitted to bar, 1997, Ohio; registered to practice before U.S. Patent and Trademark Office. *Education:* West Virginia University (B.S., Industrial Engineering, 1987); Cleveland-Marshall Law School (J.D., 1997). President, Industrial Engineering Honor Society. ***PRACTICE AREAS:*** Patent; Trademark; Copyright; Unfair Competition; Mechanical Arts. ***Email:*** gvickers@faysharpe.com

ROBERT V. VICKERS, born Anderson, Indiana, May 9, 1934; admitted to bar, 1961, District of Columbia and Ohio; 1967, U.S. District Court, Northern District of Ohio; 1982, U.S. Court of Appeals for the Federal Circuit and U.S. Court of Appeals, Sixth Circuit; 1983, U.S. District Court, Eastern District of Michigan; registered to practice before U.S. Patent and Trademark Office. *Education:* General Motors Institute (B.M.E., 1957); George Washington University (J.D., with honors, 1960). Phi Alpha Delta. *Member:* Cleveland, American and Federal Bar Associations; American Intellectual Property Law Association. ***PRACTICE AREAS:*** Trademark; Unfair Competition; Patent and Trademark Prosecution and Litigation. ***Email:*** rvickers@faysharpe.com

ASSOCIATES

†***MATTHEW P. DUGAN,*** born New Castle, Pennsylvania, August 22, 1967; admitted to bar, 2000, Ohio; registered to practice before the U.S. Patent and Trademark Office. *Education:* Youngstown State University (B.E.M.E., 1992); Cleveland-Marshall College of Law (J.D., 2000). *Member:* American Society of Mechanical Engineers. ***PRACTICE AREAS:*** Patent and Trademark Prosecution; Mechanical and Electro-Mechanical Arts. ***Email:*** mdugan@faysharpe.com

PATRICK D. FLOYD, born Toledo, Ohio, November 28, 1963; admitted to bar, 1993, Ohio; registered to practice before U.S. Patent and Trademark Office. *Education:* University of Cincinnati (B.S.E.E., 1990); University of Toledo (J.D., 1993). *Member:* Cleveland International Property Law Association; American Intellectual Property Law Association. ***PRACTICE AREAS:*** Patents; Trademarks; Copyrights; Electrical and Mechanical Arts. ***Email:*** pfloyd@faysharpe.com

†***COLLEEN FLYNN GOSS,*** born Youngstown, Ohio, March 26, 1955; admitted to bar, 1980, Ohio. *Education:* Tufts University (B.A., 1977); Case Western Reserve University (J.D., 1980). *Member:* International Trademark Assocation. ***PRACTICE AREAS:*** Trademark (U.S. and International); Copyright. ***Email:*** cfgoss@faysharpe.com

KARL WILLIAM HAUBER, born Erie, Pennsylvania, July 30, 1963; admitted to bar, 2001, Ohio; registered to practice before the U.S. Patent and Trademark Office. *Education:* Cleveland State University (B.I.E., 1987); Cleveland-Marshall College of Law (J.D., 2001). *Member:* Lake County, Ohio State and American Bar Associations; Cleveland Intellectual Property Law Association; Cleveland-Marshall Law Alumni Association. ***PRACTICE AREAS:*** Patent and Trademark Prosecution; Copyright; Mechanical Arts. ***Email:*** khauber@faysharpe.com

ERIC M. HIGHMAN, born East Cleveland, Ohio, January 22, 1962; admitted to bar, 1997, Ohio; 1999, U.S. District Court, Northern District of Ohio; registered to practice before U.S. Patent and Trademark Office. *Education:* Cleveland State University (B.S., Electrical Engineering, 1986; M.S., Electrical Engineering, 1991); Cleveland-Marshall College of Law (J.D., cum laude, 1997). *Member:* Cleveland Intellectual Property Law Association. ***PRACTICE AREAS:*** Patent Preparation and Prosecution; Validity Opinions; Microprocessor Electrical Systems; Firmware and Software; Power Systems; Communication Systems; Semiconductor Fabrication Technology; Control Systems; Trademark. ***Email:*** ehighman@faysharpe.com

†***ERIK J. OVERBERGER,*** born Cleveland, Ohio, February 25, 1973; admitted to bar, 2000, Ohio; registered to practice before U.S. Patent and Trademark Office. *Education:* Ohio University (B.S.M.E., 1996); Capital University (J.D., 2000). ***PRACTICE AREAS:*** Patent; Trademark; Copyright; Mechanical Arts. ***Email:*** eoverberger@faysharpe.com

†***SUE ELLEN PHILLIPS,*** born Middleburg Heights, Ohio, December 3, 1958; admitted to bar, 1985, Ohio and U.S. District Court, Northern District of Ohio; registered to practice before U.S. Patent and Trademark Office. *Education:* Ohio University (B.S., 1982); Cleveland Marshall College of Law (J.D., 1985). *Member:* Cuyahoga County Bar Association. ***PRACTICE AREAS:*** Patent; Trademark; Copyright; Chemical Arts. ***Email:*** sphillips@faysharpe.com

ROBERT A. SIDOTI, born Madison, Ohio, July 28, 1971; admitted to bar, 1998, Ohio; registered to practice before U.S. Patent and Trademark Office. *Education:* University of Arizona (B.S.M.E., 1993); Cleveland-Marshall College of Law (J.D., 1998). *Member:* Cleveland Bar Association; Cleveland Intellectual Property Law Association; American Intellectual Property Law Association. ***PRACTICE AREAS:*** Patent; Trademark; Copyright; Litigation; Mechanical Arts. ***Email:*** rsidoti@faysharpe.com

ROBERT M. SIEG, born Berea, Ohio, April 10, 1969; admitted to bar, 2005, Ohio; registered to practice before U.S. Patent and Trademark Office. *Education:* Cleveland State University (B.S., Electrical Engineering, 1992); The Ohio State University (M.S., Electrical Engineering, 1994; Ph.D., Electrical Engineering, 1998); Cleveland-Marshall College of Law (J.D., 2004). Sigma Xi. *Member:* Cleveland Bar Association; Cleveland Intellectual Property Law Association; Institute of Electrical and Electronic Engineers; American Vacuum Society. ***PRACTICE AREAS:*** General Electrical and Mechanical Arts; Medical Imaging; Optoelectronics and Optical Systems; Computer Software; Computer Data Processing; Computer Modeling. ***Email:*** rsieg@faysharpe.com

†***SCOTT M. SLABY,*** born Parma, Ohio, June 11, 1973; admitted to bar, 2003, Ohio and U.S. District Court, Northern District of Ohio; registered to practice before U.S. Patent and Trademark Office. *Education:* John Carroll University (B.S., 1995; M.S., 1997); Cleveland-Marshall College of Law (J.D., 2003). *Member:* American Chemical Society. ***PRACTICE AREAS:*** Patent; Trademark; Copyright; Trade Secrets; Biochemistry; Chemical Arts. ***Email:*** sslaby@faysharpe.com

†***JOSEPH E. WATERS,*** born Cleveland, Ohio, August 14, 1973; admitted to bar, 2000, Ohio; 2001, U.S. District Court, Northern District of Ohio; registered to practice before U.S. Patent and Trademark Office. *Education:* John Carroll University (B.S., Chemistry, 1995); Case Western Reserve University (J.D., cum laude, 2000). ***PRACTICE AREAS:*** Patents; Trademarks; Copyrights; Organic Chemistry; Polymers. ***Email:*** jwaters@faysharpe.com

JONATHAN A. WITHROW, born Ravenna, Ohio, May 11, 1973; admitted to bar, 2002, Ohio; registered to practice before U.S. Patent and Trademark Office. *Education:* The Ohio State University (B.S., 1996); Cleveland State University (J.D., summa cum laude, 2001). *Member:* Cleveland and Ohio State Bar Associations; Cleveland Intellectual Property Law Association; American Intellectual Property Law Association. ***PRACTICE AREAS:*** Patent; Trademark; Mechanical Arts. ***Email:*** jwithrow@faysharpe.com

(This Listing Continued)

FAY, SHARPE, FAGAN, MINNICH & McKEE, LLP, Cleveland—Continued

JEFFREY N. ZAHN, born Euclid, Ohio, March 10, 1962; admitted to bar, 2004, Ohio; registered to practice before U.S. Patent and Trademark Office. *Education:* Cleveland State University (B.S., Electrical Engineering, 1986); Cleveland-Marshall College of Law (J.D., 2000). Patent Examiner, United States Patent and Trademark Office, 2000-2003. *Member:* Cleveland and Ohio State Bar Associations; American Intellectual Property Law Association. ***PRACTICE AREAS:*** Patent Preparation, Prosecution and Counseling; General Electrical Arts; Electronic Controls; Robotics; Systems Navigation Guidance Communications; Systems Hardware and Software. ***Email:*** jzahn@faysharpe.com

*†**MARINA V. ZALEVSKY,*** born Kiev, Ukraine, January 19, 1961; admitted to bar, 2004, Ohio; registered to practice before U.S. Patent and Trademark Office. *Education:* St. Petersburg State University of Water Communications (B.S., Electrical Engineering, 1986); Rensselaer Polytechnic Institute (M.S., Electrical Engineering, 1992); Cleveland-Marshall College of Law (J.D., cum laude, 2004). ***LANGUAGES:*** Russian. ***PRACTICE AREAS:*** Patent Prosecution and Preparation; Medical Imaging Technology; Machine Vision; Optics and Lighting; Power Systems; Robotics; Servo Systems; Electronics; LEDs. ***Email:*** mzalevsky@faysharpe.com

JOHN S. ZANGHI, born Cleveland, Ohio, June 13, 1965; admitted to bar, 1995, Ohio; 1998, U.S. District Court, Northern District of Ohio; registered to practice before U.S. Patent and Trademark Office. *Education:* Cleveland State University (B.E.E., 1988); University of Akron (J.D., cum laude, 1995). Editor-in-Chief, Akron Law Review. *Member:* Cleveland and American Bar Associations; Cleveland Intellectual Property Law Association; American Intellectual Property Law Association. ***PRACTICE AREAS:*** Patent; Trademark; Copyright; Licensing; Electrical and Mechanical Arts. ***Email:*** jzanghi@faysharpe.com

OF COUNSEL

E. KENT DANIELS, JR., born Cleveland, Ohio, July 24, 1932; admitted to bar, 1959, Virginia; 1971, Ohio; 1972, U.S. District Court, Northern District of Ohio; registered to practice before U.S. Patent and Trademark Office. *Education:* West Virginia University (B.S.M.E., 1955); George Washington University (LL.B., 1959). Phi Alpha Delta. Member, Scabbard and Blade. ***PRACTICE AREAS:*** Patent; Trademark; Unfair Competition; Mechanical and Electrical Arts. ***Email:*** ekdaniels@faysharpe.com

CHRISTOPHER B. FAGAN, born South Bend, Indiana, September 1, 1937; admitted to bar, 1965, Ohio; 1967, U.S. District Court, Northern District of Ohio; 1981, U.S. Court of Appeals, 6th Circuit; 1982, U.S. Court of Appeals, 7th Circuit; 1983, U.S. Court of Appeals for the Federal and 1st Circuits; 1985, U.S. Supreme Court; registered to practice before U.S. Patent and Trademark Office. *Education:* University of Notre Dame (B.S.M.E., cum laude, 1959); Georgetown University (J.D., 1965). *Author:* "Proprietary Aspects of Names and Titles," Cleveland Bar Journal, Vol. 47, No. 4. Examiner, United States Patent Office, 1963-1965. Adjunct Professor of Law, Cleveland State University, Cleveland-Marshall College of Law. Listed in The Best Lawyers in America. *Member:* Cleveland and Ohio State Bar Associations; Cleveland Intellectual Property Law Association; American Intellectual Property Law Association. [Lt., U.S. Navy, 1959-1963]. ***PRACTICE AREAS:*** Patent; Trademark; Copyright; Litigation. ***Email:*** cfagan@faysharpe.com

*†**JAMES W. McKEE,*** born Mansfield, Ohio, April 16, 1942; admitted to bar, 1969, Ohio and U.S. District Court, Northern District of Ohio; 1971, U.S. Court of Appeals, 1st Circuit; 1983, U.S. Court of Appeals for the Federal Circuit; registered to practice before U.S. Patent and Trademark Office. *Education:* General Motors Institute (B.M.E., 1966); Case Western Reserve University (J.D., 1969). Phi Delta Phi. ***PRACTICE AREAS:*** Patent; Trademark; Copyright; Mechanical Arts. ***Email:*** jmckee@faysharpe.com

RICHARD J. MINNICH, born Cleveland, Ohio, June 2, 1933; admitted to bar, 1965, Ohio, U.S. District Court, Northern District of Ohio and U.S. Court of Appeals, 6th Circuit; 1983, U.S. Court of Appeals for the Federal Circuit; 1985, U.S. Supreme Court; registered to practice before U.S. Patent and Trademark Office. *Education:* Kent State University (B.S., Chemistry, 1956); Cleveland Marshall College of Law (J.D., 1965). *Member:* Cleveland and Ohio State Bar Associations; Cleveland Intellectual Property Association; American Intellectual Property Law Association; Licensing Executive Society. ***PRACTICE AREAS:*** Patent; Trademark; Copyright; Licensing and Litigation; International Licensing. ***Email:*** rminnich@faysharpe.com

THOMAS E. YOUNG, born Pittsburgh, Pennsylvania, May 18, 1948; admitted to bar, 1975, Ohio; 1976, U.S. District Court, Northern District of Ohio; 1982, U.S. Court of Appeals for the Federal Circuit and U.S. Court of Appeals, Sixth Circuit; registered to practice before U.S. Patent and Trademark Office. *Education:* The Ohio State University (B.S.E.E., 1971); Case Western Reserve University (J.D., 1975). *Member:* Cleveland and Ohio State Bar Associations; Cleveland Intellectual Property Law Association. ***PRACTICE AREAS:*** Patent; Trademark; Unfair Competition; Electrical and Mechanical Arts. ***Email:*** tyoung@faysharpe.com

† Member: Cleveland, Ohio State and American Bar Associations; Cleveland Intellectual Property Law Association; American Intellectual Property Law Association.

MARK B. FELBER

1525 LEADER BUILDING
526 SUPERIOR AVENUE N.E.
CLEVELAND, OHIO 44114
Telephone: 216-363-3900
Fax: 216-241-2286
Email: m.felber.esq@att.net
URL: http://www.lawyers.com/felberlaw

General Civil and Criminal Practice, Drug Crimes, Juvenile Crimes, Parole and Probation, Litigation, Family Law, Divorce, Child Custody, Spousal and Child Support, Domestic Violence, Visitation Rights, Personal Injury, Head and Spinal Injuries, Sexual Abuse, Slip and Fall, Trucking Accidents, Automobile Negligence, Wrongful Death, Nursing Home Litigation, Social

(This Listing Continued)

Security Disability, Dog Bites, Workers' Compensation, Trusts and Estates, Estate Planning, Guardianship, Wills and Probate, DWI, Bankruptcy, Admiralty, Maritime Injuries, Aviation, Airplane Crashes, Consumer Law, Consumer Fraud, Lemon Law, Unsafe Products, Warranties, Education, Employment Law, Sexual Harassment, Wrongful Termination, Medical Malpractice, Products Liability, Drugs and Medical Devices, Real Estate, Buying or Selling a Home, Business Law, Debt and Credit, Collections, Creditor's Rights, Contracts, Lawsuits, Starting a Business.

MARK B. FELBER, born Hartford, Connecticut, March 25, 1958; admitted to bar, 1984, Ohio; 1985, U.S. District Court, Northern District of Ohio. *Education:* Brandeis University (B.A., Philosophy, 1980); Case Western Reserve University (J.D., 1984). Member: Guardian Ad Litem Project, Cuyahoga County Domestic Relations Court, 1998—. Trustee, Broadway School of Music and the Arts (President, 1998-2003). Prosecutor, Village of Bentleyville, Ohio, 1989-1990, 1992-1993. *Member:* The Ohio Academy of Trial Lawyers; Cuyahoga Criminal Defense Lawyers Association. ***PRACTICE AREAS:*** General Practice; Litigation; Administrative Hearings and Appeals; Divorce; Child Custody; Personal Injury; Workers; Consumer Bankruptcy; Trusts and Estates; Driving While Intoxicated; Criminal Law; Social Security Disability.

HENRY B. FISCHER CO., L.P.A.

Established in 1993
26111 BRUSH AVENUE, SUITE 400
P.O. BOX 32644
CLEVELAND, OHIO 44132-0644
Telephone: 216-731-3535
Fax: 216-261-5252
Email: HBFCoLPA@cs.com
URL: http://www.lawyers.com/henryfischerlaw

Civil Litigation and Appeals, Construction, Business, General Practice, Municipal, Real Estate Law, Probate, Trusts and Wills.

FIRM PROFILE: The firm serves individuals, small businesses and corporations, municipalities, school boards, counties and a variety of public officials. The firm strives to provide assured quality service utilizing state of the art computer equipment and trained staff engaged in ongoing continuing legal education.

HENRY B. FISCHER, born Cleveland, Ohio, October 4, 1936; admitted to bar, 1964, Ohio; U.S. District Court, Northern District of Ohio; U.S. Court of Appeals, 6th Circuit; U.S. Supreme Court; registered to practice before U.S. Patent and Trademark Office. *Education:* Northwestern University (B.S.Ch.E., 1960); Cleveland State University School of Law (J.D., cum laude, 1964). Sole Practitioner, 1965—. Partner, Walter & Haverfield, 1985-1993. Principal, Henry B. Fischer Co., L.P.A., 1993—. Special Counsel, 1979-1986, Law Director, 1972-1979, Prosecutor and Assistant Law Director, 1965-1971, City of East Cleveland. Special Counsel, 1978—, Assistant Law Director, 1974-1997 and Special Counsel to Euclid Board of Education, 1980—, City of Euclid. Ohio Attorney General, Assistant and Special Counsel, 1966-1970. With, Lubrizol Corporation Research and Development and Patent Departments, 1960-1964. ***REPORTED CASES:*** Lakewood Ohio Congregation of Jehovah's Witnesses, Inc. v. Lakewood, 20 Ohio App. 3d 338 (Cuy. Cty. 1985), Cert. den.; Lakewood Congregation of Jehovah Witnesses v. Lakewood, 699 F.2d 303 (6th Cir. 1977), Cert. den.; Northern Ohio Sign Contractors Association, et al. v. City of Lakewood & DeLorean Cadillac, Inc., et al. v. City of Lakewood, 32 Ohio St.3d 316 (1987); Lakewood v. Plain Dealer Publishing Co., 486 U.S. 750 (1987). ***PRACTICE AREAS:*** Civil Litigation; Appellate Practice; Real Estate; Business Law; Contracts; Construction Law; Trade Secrets; General Practice; Municipal Law; Estate Planning; Trusts and Estates; Wills; Probate. ***Email:*** HBFCoLPA@cs.com

REPRESENTATIVE CLIENTS: Euclid Board of Education; City of Euclid; City of Mentor.

LAW OFFICES OF MARK S. FISHMAN

THE LEADER BUILDING
526 SUPERIOR AVENUE, SUITE 853
CLEVELAND, OHIO 44114
Telephone: 216-781-4800
Fax: 216-621-4121
Email: msf1400@aol.com
URL: http://www.markfishman.com

Personal Injury, Automobile Accidents, Worker's Compensation, Dog Bites, Insurance Law.

MARK S. FISHMAN, born Cleveland, Ohio, August 30, 1956; admitted to bar, 1981, Ohio; 1982, U.S. District Court, Northern District of Ohio; 1989, U.S. Court of Appeals, 6th Circuit. *Education:* The Ohio State University (B.A., 1978; J.D., 1981). Acting Judge, South Euclid Municipal Court, 1991-2000. *Member:* Cuyahoga County and Ohio State Bar Associations; The Association of Trial Lawyers of America; Ohio Academy of Trial Lawyers; Cleveland Association of Compensation Attorneys; Cleveland Academy of Trial Lawyers; Million Dollar Advocates Forum. ***PRACTICE AREAS:*** Personal Injury Law (50%, 40); Workers Compensation Law (50%, 100).

PAUL W. FLOWERS CO., L.P.A.

Established in 1998

TERMINAL TOWER, 35TH FLOOR
50 PUBLIC SQUARE
CLEVELAND, OHIO 44113-2216
Telephone: 216-344-9393
Fax: 216-344-9395
Email: pwf@pwfco.com
URL: http://www.pwfco.com

Civil Litigation, Civil Appeals, Administrative Hearings and Appeals, Business Litigation, Insurance Litigation, Civil Liability, Corporate Law, Real Estate, Estate Planning and Probate Administration.

FIRM PROFILE: The firm is devoted primarily to appellate representation but also furnishes clients in Ohio and California with general civil, business, real property and probate services.

PAUL WILLIAM FLOWERS, born Grand Rapids, Michigan, October 2, 1964; admitted to bar, 1990, Ohio; 1992, U.S. District Court, Northern District of Ohio; 1993, U.S. Court of Appeals, Sixth Circuit; 1999, U.S. Supreme Court; 2001, California and U.S. District Court, Central District of California. *Education:* University of Kentucky (B.A., with honors, 1987); The Ohio State University (J.D., with honors, 1990). Law Clerk to Hon. John W. Reece, 1990-1992. Lawyer of the Year, Ohio Lawyers Weekly, 2001. Highest Jury Verdict, Ohio Lawyers Weekly, 2002. Author: "Targeting Federal RICO's Pattern Requirement to Long-Term Organized Criminal Activity," 51 Ohio St. L.J. 713 (1990); "H.B. 58: Amendments of the Declaratory Judgment Act," 11 Ohio Trial Magazine 21 (Summer/Fall 2000); "Pontzer Roadblocks - Notice and Consent," 12 Ohio Trial Magazine 25 (Summer 2002). *Member:* Akron, Cleveland and Ohio State Bar Associations; State Bar of California; Ohio Academy of Trial Lawyers (Trustee; Chair, Amicus Committee). (Certified Specialist in Civil Trial Law, Ohio State Bar Association). ***REPORTED CASES:*** Santos v. Ohio Bur. of Worker's Comp., 101 Ohio St. 3d 74, 2004 - Ohio - 28, 801 N.E.2d 441(2004); Rolf v. Tri State Motor Transit Co., 91 Ohio St.3d 380, 2001-Ohio-44, 745 N.E.2d 424 (2001); Clark v. Chubb Group of Ins. Cos., 337 F.3d 687 (6th Cir. 2003); St. Vincent Med. Cntr. v. Sader, 100 Ohio App. 3d 379, 654 N.E.2d 144 (1995). ***Email:*** pwf@pwfco.com

MARK S. FRANK

Established in 1984

323 WEST LAKESIDE AVENUE, SUITE 450
CLEVELAND, OHIO 44113
Telephone: 216-621-5661
Fax: 216-241-5670
Email: markfrank@lawyers.com
URL: http://www.lawyers.com/markfranklaw

Personal Injury, Medical Malpractice, Trial Litigation, Municipal, Collections, Probate Law, Bankruptcy and Criminal Defense Law. General Practice, Driving While Intoxicated, Traffic Violations, Automobile Accidents, Wrongful Death, Premises Liability, Premises Security, Dog Bites, Animal Bites, Torts, Negligence and Insurance Law.

MARK S. FRANK, born Cleveland, Ohio, February 21, 1956; admitted to bar, 1981, Ohio; 1983, U.S. Court of Appeals, Sixth Circuit. *Education:* University of Cincinnati (B.A., 1978); Cleveland State University (J.D., 1981). Member, Board of Governors, Moot Court, 1981. Speaker: "Trying the Automobile Injury Case," Seminar, 1992. *Member:* Greater Cleveland, Cuyahoga County and Ohio State Bar Associations.

REFERENCE: National City Bank.

FRANTZ WARD LLP

2500 KEY CENTER
127 PUBLIC SQUARE
CLEVELAND, OHIO 44114-1230
Telephone: 216-515-1660
Fax: 216-515-1650
Email: attorneys@frantzward.com
URL: http://www.frantzward.com

Corporate Law, Business Law, Litigation, Labor and Employment, Construction Law, College and University Law, Banking Law, Health Care, Worker's Compensation, Antitrust Law, Telecommunications Law, Estate Planning, Probate, Products Liability, Real Estate, Civil Rights, OSHA, Trade Regulation, ERISA, Creditors' Rights, Bankruptcy, Alternative Dispute Resolution Services, Insurance, Taxation.

MEMBERS OF FIRM

BARBARA J. ARISON, born Akron, Ohio, October 10, 1952; admitted to bar, 1975, Ohio; 1980, U.S. Supreme Court; 1991, California. *Education:* University of Akron (B.A., 1972); University of Virginia (J.D., 1975). ***PRACTICE AREAS:*** Litigation; Complex and Multi-District Litigation; Drug and Medical Device Litigation; Products Liability Law; Commercial Litigation. ***Email:*** barison@frantzward.com

KEITH A. ASHMUS, born Cleveland, Ohio, August 19, 1949; admitted to bar, 1974, Ohio; 1980, U.S. Supreme Court; 1991, California. *Education:* Michigan State University (B.A., 1971; M.A., 1972, Phi Beta Kappa); Yale University (J.D., 1974). *Member:* Ohio State Bar Association. ***PRACTICE AREAS:*** Disability; OSHA Law; Litigation/Litigation Defense; Employment Discrimination Law; Employer-Employee Relations; Alternative Dispute Resolution; Wage Hour; Wrongful Termination; Employment at Will; Mediation Services. ***Email:*** kashmus@frantzward.com

BRETT K. BACON, born Perry, Iowa, August 8, 1947; admitted to bar, 1972, Ohio. *Education:* University of Dubuque (B.A., 1969); Northwestern University (J.D., 1972). ***PRACTICE AREAS:*** Business Torts; Civil Trial; Insurance Defense Law; Lender Liability; Products Liability Law; Mediation Services; Alternative Dispute Resolution; Creditors Rights; Commercial Law; Banking Law; Consumer Law; Health Law. ***Email:*** bbacon@frantzward.com

T. MERRITT BUMPASS, JR., born Roxboro, North Carolina, September 10, 1943; admitted to bar, 1969, North Carolina; 1972, Ohio. *Education:* United States Military Academy (B.S., 1965); Wake Forest University (J.D., 1969); Columbia University (LL.M., in Labor, 1971). ***PRACTICE AREAS:*** Employment Law and Litigation; Labor Law; ERISA; OSHA. ***Email:*** mbumpass@frantzward.com

MICHAEL N. CHESNEY, born Ravenna, Ohio, June 16, 1966; admitted to bar, 1992, Ohio. *Education:* Duke University (A.B., 1988); Notre Dame Law School (J.D., summa cum laude, 1992). Lead Note Editor, Notre Dame Law Review, 1992. ***PRACTICE AREAS:*** Labor and Employment Law; Litigation. ***Email:*** mchesney@frantzward.com

IAN H. FRANK, born Chardon, Ohio, July 2, 1971; admitted to bar, 1996, Ohio. *Education:* Baldwin-Wallace College (B.A., magna cum laude, 1993); Cleveland Marshall College of Law (J.D., magna cum laude, 1996). Editor, Cleveland State Law Review, 1994-1996. *Member:* Ohio Contractors Association; American Arbitration Association; Surety Association of Ohio. ***PRACTICE AREAS:*** Construction Law; Litigation; Products Liability Law. ***Email:*** ifrank@frantzward.com

MICHAEL J. FRANTZ, born Piqua, Ohio, May 7, 1951; admitted to bar, 1976, Ohio. *Education:* University of Notre Dame (B.A., magna, cum laude, 1973); Georgetown University (J.D., 1976). Adjunct Lecturer, Labor Relations, Cleveland State University and Oberlin College. *Member:* American Arbitration Association (Member, Labor Advisory Council). ***PRACTICE AREAS:*** Labor Law; Litigation and Employment Law; College and University Law; Construction Law; Health Care; ERISA. ***Email:*** mfrantz@frantzward.com

STEPHEN F. GLADSTONE, born Chicago, Illinois, December 6, 1950; admitted to bar, 1981, Ohio; 1985, U.S. Supreme Court. *Education:* Xavier University (A.B., 1972; M.Ed., 1976); Case Western Reserve University (J.D., 1981). Order of the Coif. ***PRACTICE AREAS:*** Litigation; Health Care; Business Arbitration; Commercial Law; Fraud; Insurance. ***Email:*** sgladstone@frantzward.com

CARL H. GLUEK, born Kalamazoo, Michigan, August 2, 1959; admitted to bar, 1985, Ohio. *Education:* Colby College (B.A., 1982); Case Western Reserve University (J.D., 1985). ***PRACTICE AREAS:*** Labor Law; Employment Law; ERISA; College and University Law. ***Email:*** cgluek@frantzward.com

PATRICK F. HAGGERTY, born Cleveland, Ohio, August 16, 1955; admitted to bar, 1985, Ohio. *Education:* McGill University (B.A., 1978); Cleveland-Marshall College of Law (J.D., 1984). ***PRACTICE AREAS:*** Litigation; Product Liability Law; Construction Law; Insurance. ***Email:*** haggerty@frantzward.com

RALPH P. HIGGINS, JR., born Cleveland, Ohio, May 20, 1955; admitted to bar, 1980, Ohio. *Education:* University of Notre Dame (B.B.A., 1977; J.D., 1980). ***PRACTICE AREAS:*** Estate Planning; Federal Estate and Gift Taxation Law; Probate Law; Trust Administration; Trust Law; Wills. ***Email:*** rhiggins@frantzward.com

JOEL R. HLAVATY, born Cleveland, Ohio, September 10, 1955; admitted to bar, 1983, Ohio. *Education:* John Carroll University (B.A., 1977); University of Akron (J.D., 1983). ***PRACTICE AREAS:*** Labor Law; Employment Law; ERISA; Health Care; OSHA. ***Email:*** jhlavaty@frantzward.com

BRIAN J. KELLY, born Stamford, Connecticut, November 5, 1969; admitted to bar, 1994, Ohio; 1995, U.S. District Court, Northern District of Ohio and U.S. Court of Appeals for the Sixth Circuit; 2003, U.S. District Court, Southern District of Ohio; 2004, U.S. Supreme Court. *Education:* University of Michigan (B.A., with high distinction, 1991; J.D., cum laude, 1994). ***PRACTICE AREAS:*** Labor and Employment Law; Litigation. ***Email:*** bkelly@frantzward.com

CHRISTOPHER C. KOEHLER, born Cleveland, Ohio, March 21, 1967; admitted to bar, 1992, Ohio. *Education:* College of the Holy Cross (B.A., 1989); Case Western Reserve University (J.D., 1992). ***PRACTICE AREAS:*** Civil Litigation; Commercial Litigation; Products Liability; Business Litigation. ***Email:*** ckoehler@frantzward.com

JOHN F. KOSTELNIK, III, born Euclid, Ohio, August 22, 1956; admitted to bar, 1981, Ohio. *Education:* Miami University (B.S., 1978); Ohio State University (J.D., 1981). Former Law Clerk to U.S. Bankruptcy Judge Robert J. Sidman. ***PRACTICE AREAS:*** Bankruptcy; Creditors Rights; Banking Law; Commercial Law; Transactional Law. ***Email:*** jkostelnik@frantzward.com

MARIS J. McNAMARA, born Buffalo, New York, July 3, 1967; admitted to bar, 1993, Ohio. *Education:* Canisius College (B.A., 1989); University of Akron (J.D., 1992). Hearing Officer, The Industrial Commission of Ohio. ***PRACTICE AREAS:*** Labor and Employment Law; Workers' Compensation. ***Email:*** mmcnamara@frantzward.com

COLLEEN C. MURNANE, born Lakewood, Ohio, December 30, 1967; admitted to bar, 1995, Ohio. *Education:* Boston College (B.A., in Political Science, magna cum laude, 1990); The Ohio State University College of Law (J.D., summa cum laude, 1995); Order of the Coif. ***PRACTICE AREAS:*** Litigation; Consumer Finance; Business Litigation; ERISA Litigation; Products Liability Law. ***Email:*** cmurnane@frantzward.com

ANDREW J. NATALE, born Cleveland, Ohio, March 19, 1964; admitted to bar, 1989, Ohio. *Education:* University of Dayton (B.A., 1986); University of Cincinnati (J.D., 1989). *Member:* American (Member, Forum on the Construction Industry) Bar Association; American Arbitration Association (Member, Construction Advisory Counsel; Panel of Construction Arbitrators and Mediators); Associated General Contractors; Ohio Contractors Association; Construction Employers Association. ***PRACTICE AREAS:*** Construction Law and Litigation; Mechanics Lien Law; Bond and Security Law; Insurance Coverage Litigation; General Litigation; Arbitration and Mediation; Alternative Dispute Resolution; Commercial Law; Architects and Engineers Liability Law; Construction Contracts; Construction Claims. ***Email:*** anatale@frantzward.com

BERNARD H. NIEHAUS, born Cleveland, Ohio, January 21, 1930; admitted to bar, 1955, Ohio. *Education:* John Carroll University (B.S.S., 1952); Western Reserve University (LL.B., 1955). Law Director, Westlake, Ohio, 1978-1986. ***PRACTICE AREAS:*** Commercial Law; Probate; Real Estate; Taxation; Municipal Law; Corporate Law; Business Law; Estate Planning. ***Email:*** bniehaus@frantzward.com

(This Listing Continued)

FRANTZ WARD LLP, Cleveland—Continued

JAMES B. NIEHAUS, born Lakewood, Ohio, June 24, 1958; admitted to bar, 1983, Ohio. *Education:* University of Notre Dame (B.A., 1980; J.D., 1983). Contributing Author, Ohio Business Competition Law (Lawyers Coop Publishing 1994). ***PRACTICE AREAS:*** Antitrust; Trade Regulation; Litigation; Commercial Law; College and University Law; Telecommunications. ***Email:*** jniehaus@frantzward.com

M. NEAL RAINS, born Burlington, Iowa, July 26, 1943; admitted to bar, 1968, Ohio. *Education:* University of Iowa (B.A., 1965); Northwestern University (J.D., 1968). Phi Beta Kappa; Omicron Delta Kappa. Fellow, American Bar Foundation. *Member:* American Inns of Court (Master Bencher and former President, William K. Thomas Chapter). ***PRACTICE AREAS:*** Antitrust; Litigation; Products Liability; Alternative Dispute Resolution. ***Email:*** mrains@frantzward.com

MARK L. RODIO, born Cleveland, Ohio, November 23, 1969; admitted to bar, 1995, Ohio. *Education:* Case Western Reserve University (B.S., summa cum laude, 1992); University of Pennsylvania Law School (J.D., cum laude, 1995). *Member:* Ohio State and American Bar Associations. ***PRACTICE AREAS:*** Commercial Litigation; Construction Litigation; Real Estate Litigation. ***Email:*** mrodio@frantzward.com

MARC A. SANCHEZ, born Cleveland, Ohio, May 8, 1966; admitted to bar, 1991, New Hampshire; 1994, Ohio. *Education:* Duke University (A.B., 1988); Stanford University (J.D., 1991). Board Chair, El Barrio, Inc. *Member:* Lillian K. Thomas Inn; American Inns of Court; Eighth Judicial Conference (Life Member); Hispanic National Bar Association; National Association of Securities Dealers (Member, Arbitration Panel). ***PRACTICE AREAS:*** Litigation; Construction Law; Insurance Coverage and Defense. ***Email:*** msanchez@frantzward.com

MICHAEL E. SMITH, born Mantua, Ohio, August 8, 1964; admitted to bar, 1989, Ohio. *Education:* University of Notre Dame (B.A., magna cum laude, 1986); Case Western Reserve University (J.D., summa cum laude, 1989). Order of the Coif. ***PRACTICE AREAS:*** Litigation; Commercial Law; Construction; ERISA; Health Care; Products Liability; Telecommunications. ***Email:*** msmith@frantzward.com

DANIEL A. WARD, born Philadelphia, Pennsylvania, June 17, 1952; admitted to bar, 1982, Pennsylvania and Ohio. *Education:* LaSalle College (B.S., 1978); University of Tulsa (J.D., 1981); New York University (LL.M., in Labor, 1982). ***PRACTICE AREAS:*** Employment Litigation; OSHA Law; Labor Relations Law; Health and Hospital Care Law. ***Email:*** dward@frantzward.com

OF COUNSEL

MICHAEL M. HUGHES, born Cleveland, Ohio, June 21, 1937; admitted to bar, 1962, Ohio; 1964, U.S. District Court, Northern District of Ohio; 1969, U.S. Court of Appeals, Sixth Circuit; 1970, U.S. Supreme Court; 1991, U.S. District Court, Eastern District of Michigan; 1982, U.S. Court of Appeals, Third Circuit; 1994, U.S. Court of Appeals, Fifth Circuit;. *Education:* Georgetown University (B.S., 1959); University of Michigan (J.D., 1962). Order of the Coif. Managing Editor, Michigan Law Review, 1961-1962. *Member:* International Association of Defense Counsel; Cleveland Association of Civil Trial Attorneys (President, 1968-1969). [Capt., U.S. Army (Artillery), 1962-1964]. ***PRACTICE AREAS:*** Products Liability Defense; Commercial Litigation; Tort Defense; Insurance Coverage; Professional Liability. ***Email:*** mhughes@frantzward.com

ASSOCIATES

REBECCA J. BENNETT, born Cleveland, Ohio, January 11, 1973; admitted to bar, 1998, Ohio; 1999, U.S. District Court, Northern and Southern Districts of Ohio, U.S. District Court, Eastern District of Michigan and U.S. Court of Appeals, Sixth Circuit. *Education:* The Ohio State University (B.A., summa cum laude, 1995); Cleveland Marshall College of Law (J.D., magna cum laude, 1998). Member, Moot Court Board of Governors, 1997-1998. Business Editor, Cleveland State Law Review, 1997-1998. ***PRACTICE AREAS:*** Labor Law; Employment Law; OSHA; Litigation; Affirmative Action; Prevailing Wage Litigation; Wage and Hour Law; Alternative Dispute Resolution. ***Email:*** rbennett@frantzward.com

LINDSEY A. CARR, born Cleveland, Ohio, February 14, 1975; admitted to bar, 2001, Ohio. *Education:* Northwestern University (B.S., Journalism, 1997); Case Western Reserve University (J.D., magna cum laude, 2001); New York University (LL.M., General Studies and Constitutional Law, 2003). Order of the Coif. ***PRACTICE AREAS:*** Litigation. ***Email:*** lcarr@frantzward.com

JAY R. CARSON, born Youngstown, Ohio, December 4, 1969; admitted to bar, 1997, Ohio; 2000, U.S. Court of Appeals, Sixth Circuit; 2001, U.S. District Court, Northern District of Ohio; 2002, U.S. District Court, Southern District of Ohio. *Education:* Baldwin-Wallace College (B.A., 1992); The Ohio State University (J.D., 1997). Magistrate, Medina County Common Pleas Court, 1999-2000. Law Clerk to The Honorable Alice M. Batchelder, 6th Circuit Court of Appeals. ***PRACTICE AREAS:*** Business Litigation. ***Email:*** jcarson@frantzward.com

LARRY W. CONNER, born Painesville, Ohio, November 8, 1971; admitted to bar, 1997, Ohio; 1998, U.S. District Court, Central District of Ohio; 2001, U.S. District Court, Northern District of Ohio; 2002, U.S. Court of Appeals, 6th Circuit; 2003, U.S. Distrct Court, Southern District of Ohio; registered to practice before U.S. Patent and Trademark Office. *Education:* Indiana University (B.S., Biochemistry, 1994); Case Western Reserve University School of Law (J.D., 1997). ***PRACTICE AREAS:*** Litigation; Competition. ***Email:*** lconner@frantzward.com

JENNIFER L. CUTHBERTSON, born Jamestown, New York, June 6, 1979; admitted to bar, 2004, Ohio. *Education:* Duke University (B.A., Public Policy, 2001); Case Western Reserve University (J.D., 2004). *Member:* Cleveland and Ohio State Bar Associations. ***PRACTICE AREAS:*** Litigation; Construction Law. ***Email:*** jcuthbertson@frantzward.com

JAMES T. DIXON, born Toledo, Ohio, December 14, 1968; admitted to bar, 1997, California and U.S. District Court, Northern District of California; 1999, U.S. District Court, Central District of California; 2002, U.S. District Court, Eastern District of California; 2004, Ohio and U.S. District Court, Northern District of Ohio. *Education:* Denison University (B.A., English Literature, 1991); Case Western Reserve University (J.D., 1997). Editor in Chief, Case Western Reserve Law Review, 1996-1997. Author, "On Lemon Squeezers and Locking Devices: Consumer Product Safety and Firearms, A Modest Proposal," Case Western Reserve Law Review, Spring 1997. ***PRACTICE AREAS:*** Construction Litigation; Commercial Litigation. ***Email:*** tdixon@frantzward.com

WILLIAM P. DUNN, born Erie, Pennsylvania, January 11, 1972; admitted to bar, 1999, Louisiana (inactive), U.S. District Court, Eastern, Middle and Western Districts of Louisiana and U.S. Court of Appeals, 5th Circuit; 2003, Ohio and U.S. District Court, Northern District of Ohio. *Education:* Rollins College (A.B., 1994); Tulane University (J.D., magna cum laude, Admiralty Certificate, 1999). Articles Editor, Tulane Maritime Law Journal. *Member:* Ohio State Bar Association. ***PRACTICE AREAS:*** Commercial Litigation; Labor and Employment; Insurance Defense. ***Email:*** wdunn@frantzward.com

GREGORY R. FARKAS, born Cincinnati, Ohio, December 27, 1972; admitted to bar, 1998, Ohio. *Education:* Michigan State University (B.A., with high honors, 1994); University of Michigan (J.D., cum laude, 1997). Phi Beta Kappa. ***PRACTICE AREAS:*** Litigation; Bankruptcy; Products Liability. ***Email:*** gfarkas@frantzward.com

TRAVIS F. JACKSON, born Tulsa, Oklahoma, March 26, 1974; admitted to bar, 1999, Ohio. *Education:* Northwestern Oklahoma State University (B.A., History, summa cum laude, 1996); Notre Dame Law School (J.D., summa cum laude, 1999). ***PRACTICE AREAS:*** Litigation; Health Care; Tax Law. ***Email:*** tjackson@frantzward.com

MELISSA A. JONES, born Youngstown, Ohio, January 19, 1974; admitted to bar, 2002, Ohio. *Education:* The Ohio State University (B.A., 1996); Cleveland-Marshall College of Law (J.D., 2002). ***PRACTICE AREAS:*** Litigation. ***Email:*** mjones@frantzward.com

CHRISTOPHER G. KEIM, born Cleveland, Ohio, May 19, 1971; admitted to bar, 1996, Ohio; 2002, U.S. District Court, Northern District of Ohio; 2003, U.S. District Court, Southern District of Ohio. *Education:* The Ohio State University (B.S., 1993); Case Western Reserve University (J.D., 1996). ***PRACTICE AREAS:*** Litigation; Products Liability; Automotive Warranty Law; Consumer Litigation. ***Email:*** ckeim@frantzward.com

HANS L. LARSEN, born Casper, Wyoming, December 11, 1959; admitted to bar, 1992, Ohio. *Education:* United States Naval Academy (B.S., 1982); University of Virginia (J.D., 1992). ***PRACTICE AREAS:*** Corporate Law; Municipal Law; Financial Transactions; College and University Law; Banking Law; Real Estate. ***Email:*** hlarsen@frantzward.com

KELLY SUMMERS LAWRENCE, born Cleveland, Ohio, June 14, 1975; admitted to bar, 2002, Ohio; 2004, New York. *Education:* Miami University (B.A., 1997); Cleveland-Marshall College of Law (J.D., 2002). ***PRACTICE AREAS:*** Labor and Employment (100%). ***Email:*** klawrence@frantzward.com

ANTHONY J. LAZZARO, born Toledo, Ohio, April 28, 1979; admitted to bar, 2004, Ohio. *Education:* Vanderbilt University (B.A., Economics, 2001); Cleveland-Marshall College of Law (J.D., 2004). *Member:* Cleveland and Ohio State Bar Associations. ***PRACTICE AREAS:*** Labor and Employment; Litigation. ***Email:*** alazzaro@frantzward.com

EDWARD J. LEADER, born Gouverneur, New York, March 23, 1972; admitted to bar, 1997, Michigan; 1998, Florida and U.S. District Court, Western District of Michigan; 1999, Ohio. *Education:* University of Notre Dame (B.A., History, magna cum laude, 1994; J.D., cum laude, 1997). ***PRACTICE AREAS:*** Real Estate; Commercial Leasing; Construction Law. ***Email:*** eleader@frantzward.com

BRIAN A. MACIAK, born Cleveland, Ohio, August 29, 1975; admitted to bar, 2000, Ohio; 2001, U.S. District Court, Northern District of Ohio; 2003, U.S. District Court, Southern District of Ohio. *Education:* Kent State University (B.A., magna cum laude, 1997); Syracuse University (J.D., magna cum laude, 2000). Order of the Coif. Member, Moot Court. Lead Articles Editor, Syracuse Law Review, 1999-2000. ***PRACTICE AREAS:*** Labor and Employment. ***Email:*** bmaciak@frantzward.com

MATTHEW H. MATHENEY, born Zanesville, Ohio, March 23, 1971; admitted to bar, 1998, Ohio. *Education:* College of Wooster (B.A., 1995); Cleveland-Marshall College of Law (J.D., cum laude, 1998). Law Clerk to the Honorable Marilyn Shea-Stonum, United States Bankruptcy Court, Northern District of Ohio. ***PRACTICE AREAS:*** Bankruptcy; Creditors Rights; Commercial Law; Commercial Lending Transactions; Banking Law. ***Email:*** mmatheney@frantzward.com

JENIFER E. NOVAK, born Ashtabula, Ohio, June 27, 1970; admitted to bar, 1999, Ohio. *Education:* Kent State University (B.A., 1992); Cleveland-Marshall College of Law (J.D., 1999). ***PRACTICE AREAS:*** Litigation; Products Liability Law; Insurance Coverage; Insurance Defense. ***Email:*** jnovak@frantzward.com

JULIE L. PIETRZEN, born Southfield, Michigan, March 13, 1974; admitted to bar, 2004, Ohio. *Education:* Albion College (B.A., 1996); Case Western Reserve University (J.D., 2004). *Member:* Ohio State Bar Association. ***PRACTICE AREAS:*** Litigation. ***Email:*** jpietrzen@frantzward.com

BRIAN E. ROOF, born Cleveland, Ohio, August 24, 1971; admitted to bar, 1999, Ohio; 2000, U.S. District Court, Northern District of Ohio. *Education:* University of Notre Dame (B.A., cum laude, 1994); University of Notre Dame Law School (J.D., cum laude, 1999). Board Member and Treasurer, Ohio Boys Town, 2000—. ***PRACTICE AREAS:*** Commercial Law; Business Law; Products Liability. ***Email:*** broof@frantzward.com

JENNIFER L. WHITNEY, born Cleveland, Ohio, September 8, 1973; admitted to bar, 1999, Ohio and U.S. District Court, Northern District of Ohio; 2005, U.S. District Court, Southern District of Ohio. *Education:* Ohio Wesleyan University (B.A., 1995); Cleveland Marshall Law School (J.D., cum laude, 1999). *Member:* American Bar Association; The Association of Trial Lawyers of America; Woman's Bar Association; Harold Burton Inn of Court. ***PRACTICE AREAS:*** Labor and Employment (100%). ***Email:*** jwhitney@frantzward.com

STEVEN R. YOO, born Cleveland, Ohio, February 10, 1963; admitted to bar, 1990, Ohio. *Education:* The Ohio State University (B.A., 1985); Cleveland-Marshall College of Law (J.D., 1988). Delta Theta Phi. Moot Court Board of Governors; Benton National Moot Court Team. Recipient, The Jeffrey A. Stein Award. The Order of Barristers; Treasurer, Stu-

(This Listing Continued)

dent Bar Association, 1988. *Member:* Cleveland and Ohio State Bar Associations. ***PRACTICE AREAS:*** Workers Compensation. ***Email:*** syoo@frantzward.com

FRENCH & FRENCH

Established in 1952

820 WEST SUPERIOR AVENUE, SUITE 510
CLEVELAND, OHIO 44113
Telephone: 216-621-4260
Fax: 216-621-4262
Email: frenchandfrench@msw.com

General Civil Trial Practice, Workers Compensation, Probate Law, Social Security Disability and Personal Injury Law.

MEMBERS OF FIRM

JAMES H. FRENCH, born Cleveland, Ohio, March 25, 1945; admitted to bar, 1974, Ohio; 1975, U.S. District Court, District of Ohio; 1981, U.S. Supreme Court; 1983, U.S. Court of Appeals, Sixth Circuit. *Education:* Borromeo College (B.A., 1967); Cleveland Marshall College of Law (J.D., 1974). Secretary, Cuyahoga County Notary Commission, 1988—. Member, Board of Trustees, Cuyahoga County Public Library, 1984-1988. *Member:* Cuyahoga County (Member, Workers Compensation Committee, 1975—), Cleveland (Member: Judicial Selection Committee, 1990-1996; Workers Compensation Committee, 1975—) and Ohio State (Member, Workers Compensation Committee, 1989—) Bar Associations; Ohio Trial Lawyers Association; National Organization of Social Security Claimants' Representatives.

RALPH F. FRENCH (1908-2001)

FRIEDMAN, DOMIANO & SMITH CO., L.P.A.

SIXTH FLOOR, STANDARD BUILDING
1370 ONTARIO STREET
CLEVELAND, OHIO 44113-1701
Telephone: 216-621-0070; 1-800-280-0070
Fax: 216-621-4008
Email: fds@fdslaw.com
URL: http://www.fdslaw.com

Marco Island, Florida Office: 1141 Swallow Building 4, 34145. Telephone: 941-642-0252.

Products Liability, Negligence, Wrongful Death, Medical Malpractice, General Civil Practice. Trials, Personal Injury, Insurance Law, Automobile Accidents.

JEFFREY H. FRIEDMAN, born Cleveland, Ohio, July 8, 1947; admitted to bar, 1973, Ohio, U.S. District Court, Northern District of Ohio and U.S. Court of Appeals, Sixth Circuit; 1976, U.S. Supreme Court; 1987, Florida and U.S. District Court, Southern District of Florida; 1988, District of Columbia Court of Appeals. *Education:* John Carroll University (B.A., 1969); Case Western Reserve University (J.D., 1972). Assistant Attorney General, State of Ohio, 1973-1997. Special Counsel for State of Ohio, 1983—. Founding Sponsor, Civil Justice Foundation, 1986. Advocate, National College of Advocacy. *Member:* Cleveland, Cuyahoga County (Board of Trustees, 1985—), Collier County and Ohio State Bar Associations; The Florida Bar; District of Columbia Bar; Cleveland Academy of Trial Lawyers; Ohio Academy of Trial Lawyers; The Association of Trial Lawyers of America. (Board Certified Civil Trial Advocate by the National Board of Trial Advocacy). ***PRACTICE AREAS:*** Products Liability Law; Negligence Law; Employment Discrimination Law; Insurance Law; Wrongful Death; Railroad Law; Medical Malpractice; FELA. ***Email:*** JeffFriedman@fdslaw.com

JOSEPH C. DOMIANO, born Cleveland, Ohio, October 21, 1928; admitted to bar, 1957, Ohio; 1959, U.S. District Court, Northern District of Ohio; 1981, U.S. Supreme Court; 1983, U.S. Court of Appeals, Sixth Circuit. *Education:* Adelbert College (B.B.A., 1951); Case Western Reserve University; Cleveland State University (J.D., 1956). Special Counsel, Ohio Attorney General, 1960-1962. Prosecutor, City of Maple Heights, 1964-1965. Solicitor, Village of Bentleyville, 1974-1994. Counsel: Maple Heights Board of Education, 1976-1985; Twinsburg City Schools, 1987-1988. Instructor, Law Enforcement, Cuyahoga Community College, 1968. Law Director, City of Olmsted Falls, 1990-1992. *Member:* Cleveland, Cuyahoga County (Trustee, 1980—; President, 1994) and Ohio State Bar Associations; Cleveland Academy of Trial Attorneys; The Association of Trial Attorneys of America; Ohio Academy of Trial Lawyers. ***PRACTICE AREAS:*** Medical Malpractice; Negligence Law; Trial Practice; Torts. ***Email:*** JoeDomiano@fdslaw.com

M. DAVID SMITH, born Cleveland, Ohio, April 8, 1944; admitted to bar, 1970, Ohio; 1987, Florida; U.S. District Court, Northern and Southern Districts of Ohio; U.S. District Court, Southern District of Florida. *Education:* Ohio State University (B.S., 1966); Cleveland Marshall (J.D., 1970). Internal Revenue Service. Former Prosecutor, Village of Bentleyville. *Member:* Cleveland, Cuyahoga County and American Bar Associations. ***PRACTICE AREAS:*** Real Estate Law; Business Law; Trial Practice; Wrongful Death. ***Email:*** DavidSmith@fdslaw.com

---

STEPHEN S. VANEK, born Elyria, Ohio, March 25, 1967; admitted to bar, 1992, Ohio; 1993, U.S. District Court, Northern District of Ohio. *Education:* Lorain City Community College (A.A., highest honors, 1987); Baldwin-Wallace College (B.A., magna cum laude, 1989); Cleveland Marshal College of Law (J.D., 1992). Editor, The Gavel Cleveland Marshall College of Law. *Member:* Cuyahoga County Bar Association. ***PRACTICE AREAS:*** Personal Injury-Negligence; Products Liability; Torts. ***Email:*** StephenVanek@fdslaw.com

MICHAEL L. EISNER, born Cleveland, Ohio, September 30, 1968; admitted to bar, 1995, Ohio and U.S. District Court, Northern District of Ohio. *Education:* Hobart College (B.A., 1990); Cleveland Marshall College of Law (J.D., summa cum laude, 1995). Executive Editor, Cleveland State Law Review, 1994-1995. *Member:* Cleveland, Cuyahoga County and Ohio State Bar Associations; Ohio Academy of Trial Lawyers. ***PRACTICE AREAS:*** Litigation; Personal Injury. ***Email:*** MichaelEisner@fdslaw.com

(This Listing Continued)

KEVIN L. LENSON, born Cleveland, Ohio, April 23, 1970; admitted to bar, 1996, Ohio. *Education:* University of Wisconsin, Madison (B.A., 1992); University of Toledo College of Law (J.D., 1996). *Member:* Cleveland and Ohio State Bar Associations. ***PRACTICE AREAS:*** Personal Injury; Litigation. ***Email:*** KevinLenson@fdslaw.com

DONNA TAYLOR KOLIS, born Richwood, West Virginia, June 12, 1954; admitted to bar, 1984, Ohio; 1985, U.S. District Court, Northern District of Ohio; 1987, U.S. District Court, Southern District of Ohio. *Education:* Virginia Intermont College (B.A., 1976); Cleveland State University (J.D., 1983). Lecturer, The Ohio Academy of Trial Lawyers, 1990-1995. *Member:* Cuyahoga County Bar Association; The Association of Trial Lawyers of America; The Ohio Academy of Trial Lawyers (Trustee, 1990-1992); The Cleveland Academy of Trial Lawyers (Trustee, 1992-1995). ***REPORTED CASES:*** Moskovitz v. MT Sinai, 69 Ost. 3d 638 (1994). ***PRACTICE AREAS:*** Plaintiff Medical Malpractice. ***Email:*** donnakolis@fdslaw.com

DAINA B. VAN DERVORT, born Wilmington, Delaware, August 14, 1955; admitted to bar, 1980, Ohio; 1982, Illinois; 1989, Colorado. *Education:* Case Western Reserve University (B.A., magna cum laude, 1977); University of Notre Dame (J.D., 1980). Phi Beta Kappa. Formerly with: Climaco, Lefkowitz, et. al.; Peterson, Ross; Anderson, Sommermeyer, et. al. *Member:* Chicago, Illinois State, Ohio State, Colorado State and American Bar Associations. ***LANGUAGES:*** Russian. ***PRACTICE AREAS:*** Personal Injury. ***Email:*** dvandervort@fdslaw.com

CHRISTINE M. LaSALVIA, born Cleveland, Ohio, February 3, 1976; admitted to bar, 2003, Ohio. *Education:* Ohio State University (B.S., 1998); Cleveland Marshall College of Law (J.D., 2003). ***PRACTICE AREAS:*** Personal Injury; Intentional Torts; Railroad Law. ***Email:*** christinelasalvia@fdslaw.com

FRIEDMAN & GILBERT

Established in 1980

1700 STANDARD BUILDING
1370 ONTARIO STREET
CLEVELAND, OHIO 44113
Telephone: 216-241-1430
Fax: 216-621-0427
URL: http://www.friedmanandgilbert.com

State and Federal Criminal and Civil Trial and Appellate Practice. Negligence, Civil Rights Law.

FIRM PROFILE: Friedman & Gilbert's emphasis on criminal justice advocacy has lead to specializations in both high profile criminal defense and civil rights litigation. Both Gordon Friedman and Terry Gilbert are as equally skilled in handling Section 1983 police misconduct actions as they are in representing homicide, drug, white collar and environmental law defendants in both state and federal trial and appellate levels.

MEMBERS OF FIRM

GORDON S. FRIEDMAN, born Cleveland, Ohio, January 4, 1942; admitted to bar, 1968, Ohio and U.S. Court of Appeals, Sixth Circuit; 1969, U.S. District Court, Northern District of Ohio. *Education:* Miami University (B.A., 1964); George Washington University (J.D., 1967). Assistant Cuyahoga County Public Defender, 1967-1970. Director, Free Medical Clinic of Greater Cleveland, 1970-1972. Associate Professor of Law, 1972-1976 and Adjunct Professor of Law, 1976—, Cleveland State University, Cleveland-Marshall College of Law. CLE Speaker: "Mitigation and Jury Selection in Capital Cases," Louisiana Criminal Defense Seminar, Spring, 1994; "The U.S. Supreme Court and the Law of Arrest," Cleveland Bar Association Criminal Seminar, 1997; "Police Misconduct Litigation: U.S.C. 42 1983," Ohio Academy of Trial Lawyers; "We the Jury," Ohio Association of Criminal Defense Lawyers; "Psychological Defenses," Ohio Capital Litigation, 2001. Speaker: "Prosecuting Defending Police Liability Cases," Professional Education Systems Institute, 2004. Member, Legal Committee, National Organization for the Reform of Marijuana Laws (NORML). Cuyahoga County Public Defender Commission. *Member:* National Association of Criminal Defense Lawyers; American Civil Liberties Union. ***REPORTED CASES:*** Ohio v. Lawrence 44 Ohio St. 3d 24 1989 (death sentence reversed); Jones v. Jago 575 F.2d 1164 (6th Cir. 1978); Smith, et al. v. City of Lorain, et al., 857 F. Supp. 1203 (N.D. OH, 1994); Bhola v. State of Ohio, 143 Ohio App. 3d 644 (2001). ***Email:*** gorlaw@f-glaw.com

TERRY H. GILBERT, born Cleveland, Ohio, April 29, 1948; admitted to bar, 1973, Ohio; 1974, U.S. District Court, Northern District of Ohio; 1977, U.S. Court of Appeals, 5th, 6th and 8th Circuits. *Education:* Miami University (B.A., 1970); Cleveland State University (J.D., 1973). Recipient, John Minor Wisdom Award, American Bar Association Litigation Section, 2002. Faculty Lecturer, Trial Advocacy, Cleveland State University School of Law. CLE Speaker: "The DNA Revolution," Ohio Death Penalty Seminar, May 1997; "Supreme Court Review," Federal Defender's Criminal Trial and Sentencing Seminar, August 1996; "Deposing Police Officers and Supervisors," Ohio Academy of Trial Lawyers Police Misconduct Seminar, February 1997; "Post-Conviction Relief in Ohio," Cuyahoga County Bar Association Immigration Law Seminar, May 1998; "Criminal Law and the Media," Cuyahoga County Bar Association, November 2001. Speaker, "Section 1983 Law," Ohio Federal-State Bar Conference, Oct. 2003. Cooperating Attorney, Center for Constitutional Rights. *Member:* National Association of Criminal Defense Lawyers; National Lawyers Guild; American Civil Liberties Union; American Academy of Forensic Scientists. ***REPORTED CASES:*** U.S.A. v. Yee, et al, 12 F.3d 540 (6th Cir. 1993) (DNA test); Ohio v. Lessin, 67 Ohio St. 3d 487 (1993) (free speech flag burning); State ex rel. Jones v. Suster, 84 Ohio St.3d 70 (1998) (re-opening Sheppard murder case); Yates v. Cleveland, 941 F.2d 444 (6th Cir. 1991) (no immunity for police shooting); Austin v. Wilkinson, 372 F.3d 346 (6th Cir. 2004) (challenge to Supermax prison). ***Email:*** tgilbert@f-glaw.com

REFERENCE: National City Bank.

GALLAGHER SHARP

Established in 1912

(Formerly Hauxhurst, Sharp, Mollison & Gallagher)

BULKLEY BUILDING, SIXTH FLOOR
1501 EUCLID AVENUE
CLEVELAND, OHIO 44115
Telephone: 216-241-5310
Telecopier: 216-241-1608
URL: http://www.gallaghersharp.com

Toledo, Ohio Office: 420 Madison Avenue, Suite 1250, 43604. Telephone: 419-241-4860. Telecopier: 419-241-4866.

General Civil Practice. Insurance, Product Liability, Aviation, Railroad, Professional Negligence, Mass Tort, Drugs and Devices, Construction, Environmental, Corporation, Securities, Probate Law, Workers' Compensation, Appellate.

FIRM PROFILE: Gallagher Sharp, in the continuous practice of law since 1912, is a trial and business practice firm serving clients throughout Ohio and the United States.

Lawyers in the Firm are active members in many professional organizations, including the Federation of Insurance and Corporate Counsel (FICC), the International Association of Defense Counsel (IADC), the Defense Research Institute (DRI), the Lawyer-Pilots Bar Association, the Ohio State Bar Association and local bar associations.

The firm has long-standing relationships with leading companies in the casualty insurance business, major airframe and engine manufacturers, pharmaceutical companies, and other product manufacturers, major health care providers, architectural, engineering and construction firms, and other large and small companies.

MEMBERS OF FIRM AND SENIOR ATTORNEYS

KEVIN C. ALEXANDERSEN, born Brooklyn, New York; admitted to bar, 1986, Ohio. *Education:* Rochester Institute of Technology (B.S. with high honors, 1981); Ohio Northern University College of Law (J.D., with honors, 1986). Phi Delta Phi. Lead Articles Editor, Ohio Northern Law Review, 1985-1986. *Member:* National Association of Railroad Trial Counsel. ***PRACTICE AREAS:*** Products Liability; Transportation; Asbestos Law.

ERNEST W. AUCIELLO, JR., born Welch, West Virginia; admitted to bar, 1985, Ohio. *Education:* Bowling Green State University (B.S., cum laude, 1982); University of Toledo (J.D., cum laude, 1985). Order of the Coif. Member, Toledo Law Review. Law Clerk to the Honorable James F. Churchill, United States District Judge for the Eastern District of Michigan, Northern Division, 1985-1987. ***PRACTICE AREAS:*** Medical Malpractice; Professional Liability.

TIMOTHY T. BRICK, born Cleveland, Ohio; admitted to bar, 1988, Ohio. *Education:* Wittenberg University (B.A., 1985); Case Western Reserve University (J.D., 1988). ***PRACTICE AREAS:*** Professional Liability; Business.

THOMAS J. CABRAL, born Fall River, Massachusetts. admitted to bar, 1986, Ohio. *Education:* Walsh College (B.A., magna cum laude, 1982); University of Akron (J.D., 1985). [Lt., JAGC, USN, 1986-1989]. ***PRACTICE AREAS:*** General Liability; Insurance Law.

THOMAS E. DOVER, born Waterloo, Iowa; admitted to bar, 1980, Ohio. *Education:* University of Dayton (B.S., summa cum laude, 1977; J.D., magna cum laude, 1980). Phi Alpha Delta. Managing Editor, University of Dayton Law Review, 1979-1980. Listed, Best Lawyers in America. *Member:* National Association of Railroad Trial Counsel (Member, Executive Committee). (Also at Toledo Office). ***PRACTICE AREAS:*** Transportation; Mass Torts.

STANLEY M. DUB, born Montreal, Canada; admitted to bar, 1975, Ohio; 1986, New York. *Education:* The Ohio State University (B.S., 1972); Case Western Reserve University (J.D., 1975). ***PRACTICE AREAS:*** Corporate Law; Franchise Law; Mergers and Acquisitions; Estate Planning; Education Law.

ROBERT H. EDDY, born Toledo, Ohio; admitted to bar, 1979, Ohio. *Education:* University of Notre Dame (B.A., 1976); University of Toledo (J.D., cum laude, 1979). Phi Kappa Phi. Law Clerk to Hon. William K. Thomas, U.S. District Court, Northern District of Ohio, 1979-1981. ***PRACTICE AREAS:*** Insurance Law; Professional Liability.

TIMOTHY J. FITZGERALD, born Lakewood, Ohio; admitted to bar, 1989, Ohio. *Education:* Marquette University (B.S., 1986); Cleveland Marshall College of Law (J.D., 1989). Phi Alpha Theta. (Also at Toledo Office). ***PRACTICE AREAS:*** Business Law; Professional Liability; Appellate Practice.

WILLIAM F. GIBSON, born Johnstown, Pennsylvania; admitted to bar, 1973, Ohio. *Education:* Elizabethtown College (B.A., 1970); Cleveland Marshall College of Law (J.D., 1973). Assistant Prosecuting Attorney, Major Trial Division, Cuyahoga County, Ohio, 1976-1983. *Member:* National Association of Railroad Trial Counsel. ***PRACTICE AREAS:*** Railroad Law; Trucking Law; Transportation Law.

LARRY C. GREATHOUSE, born Columbus, Ohio; admitted to bar, 1983, Ohio. *Education:* The Ohio State University (B.A., History, 1980); The Cleveland Marshall College of Law (J.D., 1983). ***PRACTICE AREAS:*** Insurance Law; General Liability.

MARK A. GREER, born Minot, North Dakota; admitted to bar, 1986, Ohio. *Education:* University of Cincinnati (B.A., 1983); Case Western Reserve University (J.D., 1986). ***PRACTICE AREAS:*** General Liability; Insurance Law.

TODD M. HAEMMERLE, born Dayton, Ohio; admitted to bar, 1993, Ohio. *Education:* Miami University (B.S., 1990); University of Toledo (J.D., magna cum laude, 1993). Order of the Coif. Student Articles Editor, University of Toledo Law Review, 1992-1993. ***PRACTICE AREAS:*** General Liability; Transportation.

JULIE L. JUERGENS, born Lakewood, Ohio; admitted to bar, 1996, Ohio. *Education:* St. Bonaventure University (B.A., 1993); Case Western Reserve University (J.D., 1996). ***PRACTICE AREAS:*** Business Law; Professional Liability.

(This Listing Continued)

JAMES F. KOEHLER, born Cleveland, Ohio; admitted to bar, 1973, Ohio. *Education:* College of Wooster (B.A., 1970); Case Western Reserve University (J.D., 1973). Order of the Coif. Editor, Case Western Reserve University Journal of International Law, 1972-1973. ***PRACTICE AREAS:*** Class Actions; Commercial Law; Corporate Law; Securities Litigation.

ERIC H. MANN, born Painesville, Ohio; admitted to bar, 1980, Ohio. *Education:* Kent State University (B.A., 1976); Case Western Reserve University (J.D., 1980). ***PRACTICE AREAS:*** Mass Torts; Asbestos Litigation.

SHEILA A. McKEON, born Brooklyn, New York; admitted to bar, 1984, Ohio. *Education:* Boston College (B.A., cum laude, 1981); Case Western Reserve University (J.D., 1984). *Member:* National Association of Railroad Trial Counsel. ***PRACTICE AREAS:*** Railroad Law; General Liability; Transportation.

MARGARET MARY MEKO, born Cleveland, Ohio; admitted to bar, 1984, Ohio. *Education:* George Washington University (B.A., 1979); Cleveland State University (J.D., magna cum laude, 1984). Phi Beta Kappa. Editor, Cleveland State University Law Review, 1982-1984. Licensed Private Pilot. ***PRACTICE AREAS:*** Insurance; Transportation.

DANIEL J. MICHALEC, born Akron, Ohio; admitted to bar, 1989, Ohio. *Education:* Kent State University (B.S., cum laude, 1968); University of Akron (M.S., 1980; J.D., 1989). ***PRACTICE AREAS:*** Products Liability; Asbestos Law.

LYNN L. MOORE, born Dayton, Ohio; admitted to bar, 1984, Ohio. *Education:* Ohio University (B.S., cum laude, 1974); Cleveland-Marshall (J.D., 1984). ***PRACTICE AREAS:*** General Liability; Professional Liability.

JOHN T. MURPHY, born Cleveland, Ohio; admitted to bar, 1990, Ohio. *Education:* Miami University, Oxford, Ohio (B.S., 1978); Cleveland Marshall College of Law (J.D., 1990). Chartered Property Casualty Underwriter (C.P.C.U.), 1985. Editor, Cleveland Marshall Law Review, 1989-1990. ***PRACTICE AREAS:*** Litigation; Professional Liability.

GARY L. NICHOLSON, born Fort Thomas, Kentucky; admitted to bar, 1984, Ohio. *Education:* The Ohio State University (B.A., 1980); The University of Toledo College of Law (J.D., 1983). Phi Kappa Phi. ***PRACTICE AREAS:*** Insurance Law.

FORREST A. NORMAN III, born Cleveland, Ohio; admitted to bar, 1992, Ohio. *Education:* Case Western Reserve University (B.A., cum laude, 1986; J.D., 1992). Delta Theta Phi. Editor-in-Chief, CWRU Journal of International Law, 1991-1992. [Capt., USMC, 1986-1989]. ***PRACTICE AREAS:*** Medical Law; Litigation.

JOSEPH W. PAPPALARDO, born Cleveland, Ohio; admitted to bar, 1980, Ohio. *Education:* Case Western Reserve University (B.A., summa cum laude, 1977); The Ohio State University (J.D., 1980). Phi Beta Kappa. *Member:* Trucking Industry Defense Association (TIDA); Transportation Lawyers Association; Anthony J. Celebrezze Inn for Court (Master Bencher); Defense Research Institute; Cleveland Association of Civil Trial Attorneys (President, 1996-1997). ***PRACTICE AREAS:*** Products Liability Law; General Liability; Transportation.

ALAN M. PETROV, born Cleveland, Ohio; admitted to bar, 1974, Ohio. *Education:* Rutgers University (A.B., with honors, 1971); Case Western Reserve University (J.D., 1974). Order of the Coif. Executive Editor, Case Western Reserve International Journal of Law, 1973-1974. ***PRACTICE AREAS:*** Professional Liability Law; Insurance.

JAY CLINTON RICE, born Cleveland, Ohio; admitted to bar, 1979, Ohio. *Education:* Case Western Reserve University (B.A., summa cum laude, 1976; M.A., 1976; J.D., 1979). Phi Beta Kappa; Order of the Coif; Editor, Case Western Reserve University Law Review, 1978-1979. ***PRACTICE AREAS:*** Insurance Law; Appellate Practice.

TIMOTHY PATRICK ROTH, born Columbus, Ohio; admitted to bar, 1994, Ohio. *Education:* Fordham University (B.A., 1991); Case Western Reserve University (J.D., 1994). *Member:* Transportation Lawyers Association. ***PRACTICE AREAS:*** General Liability; Transportation.

MONICA A. SANSALONE, born Cincinnati, Ohio; admitted to bar, 1995, Ohio. *Education:* Loyola University of Chicago (B.A., 1992); Cleveland Marshall College of Law (J.D., cum laude, 1995). Law Clerk to the Hon. Terrence O'Donnell, U.S. Court of Appeals, Eighth Circuit, 1996-1997. Member, Commission on Professionalism, Supreme Court of Ohio, 2004-2007. ***PRACTICE AREAS:*** Professional Liability; Appellate Practice.

JOSEPH J. SANTORO, born Toledo, Ohio; admitted to bar, 1997, Ohio. *Education:* John Carroll University (B.S., 1994); University of Toledo (J.D., cum laude, 1997). Order of the Coif. *Member:* National Association of Railroad Trial Counsel. ***PRACTICE AREAS:*** Litigation; Transportation.

PAUL J. SCHUMACHER, JR., born Cleveland, Ohio; admitted to bar, 1983, Ohio. *Education:* University of Dayton (B.A., 1980); Cleveland-Marshall College of Law (J.D., cum laude, 1983). Editor, Cleveland State Law Review, 1982-1983. *Member:* Federation of Defense and Corporate Counsel (FDCC). ***PRACTICE AREAS:*** Products Liability Law; General Liability.

JOHN A. SIMON, born Cleveland, Ohio; admitted to bar, 1990, Ohio. *Education:* John Carroll University (B.S., 1987); Cleveland Marshall College of Law (J.D., cum laude, 1990). Delta Theta Phi. Law Clerk to the Hon. John T. Patton, Eighth District Court of Appeals, 1990-1993. ***PRACTICE AREAS:*** Medical Law.

ALTON L. STEPHENS, JR., born Beaumont, Texas; admitted to bar, 1975, Ohio. *Education:* Texas A & M University (B.S., 1966; M.S., 1968; Ph.D., Aerospace Engineering, 1970); Northern Kentucky University (J.D., 1975). Sigma Gamma Tau; Tau Beta Pi; Order of Curia. [Capt., U.S. Air Force, 1970-1974]. ***PRACTICE AREAS:*** Professional Liability; Business.

D. JOHN TRAVIS, born Cleveland, Ohio; admitted to bar, 1976, Ohio. *Education:* Ohio State University (B.S., 1973); Ohio State University College of Law (J.D., 1976). Assistant Prosecuting Attorney, Assistant Director of Law, Chief Assistant Director of Law, City of Cleveland, 1977-1982. Member, 1990-1992, 1994— and Chair, 1995-1997, Board of Commissioners on the Unauthorized Practice of Law, Supreme Court of Ohio. *Member:* Federation of Defense and Corporate Counsel (FDCC). ***PRACTICE AREAS:*** General Liability; Insurance Law.

(This Listing Continued)

JAMES T. TYMINSKI, JR., born Cleveland, Ohio; admitted to bar, 1999, Ohio. *Education:* John Carroll University (B.A., 1991); Cleveland Marshall College of Law (J.D., 1998). ***PRACTICE AREAS:*** General Liability; Transportation Law.

JOHN A. VALENTI, born Cleveland, Ohio; admitted to bar, 1980, Ohio. *Education:* Loyola University; Cleveland State University (B.A., 1976); Cleveland-Marshall College of Law (J.D., cum laude, 1980). Member, 1978-1979 and Associate Editor, 1979-1980, Cleveland State Law Review. ***PRACTICE AREAS:*** Mass Torts; Asbestos Litigation.

STEPHEN M. BEAUDRY, born Cleveland, Ohio; admitted to bar, 2003, Ohio. *Education:* John Carroll University (B.A., magna cum laude, 1999); The Ohio State University College of Law (J.D., with honors, 2003). Intern, The Honorable Richard A. Gephardt, Office of the House Democratic Leader, 1997. ***PRACTICE AREAS:*** Medical Malpractice; Mass Torts.

GREGORY K. BOOP, born Cleveland, Ohio; admitted to bar, 1997, Ohio. *Education:* Cleveland State University (B.A., 1993); Cleveland-Marshall College of Law (J.D., 1997). Editor, 1996-1997, Cleveland State Law Review. ***PRACTICE AREAS:*** General Liability; Professional Liability.

LORI E. BROWN, born Cleveland, Ohio; admitted to bar, 1999, Ohio. *Education:* University of Michigan (B.A., with distinction, 1996); Ohio State University College of Law (J.D., with honors, 1999). ***PRACTICE AREAS:*** Business Law; Professional Liability.

GEORGE H. CARR, born Columbus, Ohio; admitted to bar, 1998, Ohio. *Education:* The Ohio State University (B.Music, cum laude, 1994); Cleveland-Marshall College of Law (J.D., 1998). Delta Theta Phi. Assistant Director of Law, City of North Olmsted, 1999-2000. ***PRACTICE AREAS:*** Business; Appellate Practice.

JEREMY G. CHEUNG, born Jefferson City, Missouri; admitted to bar, 2004, Ohio. *Education:* University of Memphis (B.A. 1999); University of Dayton (J.D. 2004). Executive Editor, 2003-2004 and Staff Writer, 2002-2003, University of Dayton Law Review. Law Clerk, The Honorable Michael L. Tucker, Montgomery County Court of Common Pleas, Dayton, Ohio, 2003-2004. Legal Intern, The Honorable Walter H. Rice, Chief Judge, U.S. District Court, Southern District of Ohio, 2002. ***PRACTICE AREAS:*** Professional Liability; Transportation.

COLLEEN R. DEL BALSO, born Cleveland, Ohio; admitted to bar, 2002, Ohio. *Education:* Ohio Wesleyan University (B.A., 1998); Cleveland-Marshall College of Law (J.D., 2002). ***PRACTICE AREAS:*** General Liability; Business.

DONALD G. DRINKO, born Cleveland, Ohio; admitted to bar, 1993, Ohio. *Education:* Cleveland State University (B.A., 1990); Cleveland-Marshall College of Law (J.D., 1993). ***PRACTICE AREAS:*** Litigation; Insurance.

CATHERINE FAZIO, born Cleveland, Ohio; admitted to bar, 2004, Ohio. *Education:* Georgetown University (B.A., 2000); Case Western Reserve University (J.D., cum laude, 2004). Intern, The Honorable Steve C. LaTourette, U.S. Congress, 14th District, Ohio, 1998-1999. ***PRACTICE AREAS:*** Business; Professional Liability.

ANNA S. FISTER, born Cleveland, Ohio; admitted to bar, 2003, Ohio; 2005, Michigan. *Education:* Hiram College (B.A., cum laude, 2000); University of Dayton School of Law (J.D., 2003). Staff Writer, University of Dayton Law Review, 2002-2003. Intern, The Honorable Sherrod Brown, U.S. Congress, 13th District, Ohio, 1999. (Also at Toledo Office). ***PRACTICE AREAS:*** Transportation; Appellate Practice.

ABBY GARDNER, born Cleveland, Ohio; admitted to bar, 1998, Ohio. *Education:* Ohio Wesleyan University (B.A., 1994); Cleveland-Marshall College of Law (J.D., 1998); Cleveland State University (M.A., 1998). Pi Sigma Alpha. Senator, 1995-1997 and Speaker of the Senate, 1996-1997, Cleveland-Marshall College of Law Student Bar Association. ***PRACTICE AREAS:*** Professional Liability; Medical Law.

LEAH M. HOHENBERGER, born Akron, Ohio; admitted to bar, 2002, Ohio. *Education:* John Carroll University (B.A., 1999); Cleveland-Marshall College of Law (J.D., magna cum laude, 2002). Associate Editor, 2000-2001 and Executive Editor, 2001-2002, The Journal of Law and Health. ***PRACTICE AREAS:*** General Liability; Medical Malpractice.

J. COLIN KNISELY, born Williamsport, Pennsylvania; admitted to bar, 1997, Ohio. *Education:* Allegheny College (B.A., magna cum laude, 1993); Case Western Reserve University (J.D., 1997). ***PRACTICE AREAS:*** Transportation Law; Professional Liability.

ELENA N. LOUGOVSKAIA, born Siberia, Russia; admitted to bar, 2000, Ohio. *Education:* Denison University (B.S., 1997); Case Western Reserve University (J.D., 2000). ***LANGUAGES:*** Russian. ***PRACTICE AREAS:*** Products Liability; Litigation.

JENNIFER L. McKEEGAN, born Pittsburgh, Pennsylvania; admitted to bar, 1997, Ohio. *Education:* University of Maryland (B.A., 1994); Cleveland Marshall College of Law, Cleveland State University (J.D., 1997). Layout Editor, 1996-1997, Cleveland State University Law Review. Judicial Staff Attorney, Cuyahoga County Court of Common Pleas, 1997-2000. ***PRACTICE AREAS:*** Products Liability; Professional Liability.

COLLEEN A. MOUNTCASTLE, born Cleveland, Ohio; admitted to bar, 1998, Ohio. *Education:* University of Dayton (B.A., cum laude, 1995); Case Western Reserve University (J.D., 1998). Member, Case Western Reserve University Journal of International Law. Judicial Clerk to the Hon. Colleen Conway Cooney, Eighth District Court of Appeals, 2001-2002. ***PRACTICE AREAS:*** Mass Torts; Appellate Practice.

THOMAS F. NAUGHTON, born Bronx, New York; admitted to bar, 1994, Michigan; 2000, Ohio. *Education:* Ohio State University (B.A., 1989); Michigan State University College of Law (J.D., cum laude, 1994). (Also at Toledo Office). ***PRACTICE AREAS:*** Litigation; Products Liability.

JOHN N. NEAL, born Mexico, Missouri; admitted to bar, 2002, Ohio. *Education:* Miami University (B.A., magna cum laude, 1999); Case Western Reserve University (J.D., cum laude, 2002). Phi Beta Kappa; Phi Delta Phi. Editor-in-Chief, Health Matrix: The Journal of Law Medicine, 2001-2002. Associate Editor, The Internet Law Journal, 2001-2002. ***PRACTICE AREAS:*** Corporate Law; Insurance.

(This Listing Continued)

HOLLY OLARCZUK-SMITH, born Springfield, New Jersey; admitted to bar, 2000, Ohio. *Education:* Pennsylvania State University, The Behrend College (B.A., magna cum laude, 1996); Cleveland-Marshall College of Law (J.D., magna cum laude, 2000). Research Editor, The Journal of Law and Health, 1999-2000. Staff Attorney, Honorable Judith A. Christley, Eleventh District Court of Appeals, 2000-2003. ***PRACTICE AREAS:*** Mass Torts; Appellate.

MARTIN J. PANGRACE, born Cleveland, Ohio; admitted to bar, 2001, Ohio. *Education:* Carnegie Mellon University (B.A., with honors, 1997); Case Western Reserve University (J.D., 2001). ***PRACTICE AREAS:*** Professional Liability; Litigation.

STEPHEN T. PERSIA, born Rochester, New York; admitted to bar, 2004, Ohio. *Education:* Clemson University (B.A. 2000); University of Toledo (J.D., magna cum laude, 2004). Lead Articles Editor, 2003-2004 and Associate, 2002-2003, University of Toledo Law Review. ***PRACTICE AREAS:*** Product Liability; Litigation.

MICHAEL J. PIKE, born Cleveland, Ohio; admitted to bar, 2001, Ohio. *Education:* Fairfield University (B.S., 1997); Case Western Reserve University (J.D., 2001). ***PRACTICE AREAS:*** Products Liability; Mass Torts.

RICHARD C.O. REZIE, admitted to bar, 1999, Ohio. *Education:* Colorado School of Mines (1992); New York College at Oneonta (B.A., magna cum laude, 1996); Case Western University (J.D., magna cum laude, 1999). Order of the Coif. Judicial Staff Attorney to Honorable William G. Batchelder, Ohio Court of Appeals, Ninth Appellate District, 1999-2001. ***PRACTICE AREAS:*** Appellate Practice; Insurance Defense.

THERESA A. RICHTHAMMER, born Buffalo, New York; admitted to bar, 1997, Ohio. *Education:* Michigan State University (B.A., 1994); Cleveland-Marshall College of Law (J.D., magna cum laude, 1997). Member, Cleveland State Law Review, 1995-1997. Staff Attorney, Honorable Janet R. Burnside, Cuyahoga County Court of Common Pleas, 1999-2000. ***PRACTICE AREAS:*** Medical Law; Appellate.

PAUL KOHL SCHNEIDER, born Lakewood, Ohio; admitted to bar, 1992, Ohio. *Education:* University of Notre Dame (B.S., 1989); Cleveland-Marshall College of Law (J.D., 1992). ***PRACTICE AREAS:*** Products Liability; Litigation.

PAMELA S. SCHREMP, born Lorain, Ohio; admitted to bar, 1998, Ohio. *Education:* Bowling Green State University (B.S.N., 1983); University of Cincinnati (M.S.N., 1984); Cleveland Marshall College of Law (J.D., cum laude, 1998). Registered Nurse, Ohio, 1979. ***PRACTICE AREAS:*** Medical Malpractice; Professional Liability.

MARK M. TURNER, born Buffalo, New York; admitted to bar, 2002, Ohio. *Education:* Case Western Reserve University (B.A., 1990); Canisius College (M.B.A., 1995); The Ohio State University (J.D., 2002). ***PRACTICE AREAS:*** Products Liability; Business Law.

KRISTIN L. WEDELL, born Fairview, Ohio; admitted to bar, 2000, Ohio. *Education:* University of Toledo (B.A., magna cum laude, 1997); Case Western Reserve University (J.D., 2000). *Member:* Anthony J. Celebrezze Inn of Court (Associate Member). ***PRACTICE AREAS:*** Business Law; Products Liability.

DARLENE E. WHITE, born Cleveland, Ohio; admitted to bar, 2000, Ohio. *Education:* John Carroll University (B.A., 1992); Cleveland-Marshall College of Law (J.D., 2000). ***PRACTICE AREAS:*** Medical Malpractice; Litigation.

DEBORAH W. YUE, born Pittsburgh, Pennsylvania; admitted to bar, 1994, Ohio. *Education:* Carnegie Mellon University (B.S., 1989); Cleveland-Marshall College of Law (J.D., 1994). ***LANGUAGES:*** Chinese. ***PRACTICE AREAS:*** Insurance Law; Litigation.

STAFF ATTORNEY

JAMIE L. MANNING, born Cleveland, Ohio; admitted to bar, 1980, Ohio. *Education:* University of Wisconsin, Madison; University of Southern California (B.A., 1973); University of San Francisco Law School (J.D., 1976). ***LANGUAGES:*** Spanish. ***PRACTICE AREAS:*** Product Liability; Asbestos Litigation.

OF COUNSEL

WILLIAM H. FULTON, born Wuchang, China; admitted to bar, 1972, Ohio; U.S. District Court, Northern District of Ohio; U.S. Court of Appeals, Sixth Circuit. *Education:* College of Wooster (B.A., 1969); Case Western Reserve University School of Law (J.D., 1972). *Member:* Ohio State Bar Association. ***PRACTICE AREAS:*** Wills; Corporate Law; Probate; Taxation; Estate and Gift Taxation; Trusts and Estates.

Representative Clients Available Upon Request.

MARK GARDNER
ATTORNEY AND COUNSELOR AT LAW

526 SUPERIOR AVENUE, SUITE 1130
CLEVELAND, OHIO 44114
Telephone: 216-696-9800
Fax: 216-696-2200

Criminal Law, Driving While Intoxicated, Traffic Violations, Personal Injury, Wrongful Death, Negligence, Slip and Fall, Small Business Law, Litigation.

MARK GARDNER, born Detroit, Michigan, March 14, 1964; admitted to bar, 1993, Ohio; 1996, U.S. District Court, Northern District of Ohio; U.S. Court of Appeals, Sixth Circuit and U.S. Supreme Court. *Education:* Community College of the U.S. Air Force (A.A., 1986); State University of New York, Manhattan (B.S., 1990); Case Western Reserve University (J.D., 1992). Assistant Public Defender, Lake County Public Defender's Office, 1993-1997. Numerous alcohol related certifications and training. Frequent lecturer/speaker, subject of alcohol and field sobriety testing. [U.S.A.F., Kentucky Air National Guard, Intelligence Operations Analyst, 1981-1986; U.S.C.G., Weapons Controller/Electronic Technician, Drug-Interdiction Team, 1986-1990]. ***REPORTED CASES:*** State v. Hominsky, 107 Ohio App.3d 787, 669 N.E.2d 523 (1995); State v. Martin, 112 Ohio App.3d

(This Listing Continued)

MARK GARDNER ATTORNEY AND COUNSELOR AT LAW, Cleveland—Continued

225, 678 N.E.2d 297 (1996); State v. Miller, 117 Ohio App.3d 750, 691 N.E.2d 703 (1997). ***PRACTICE AREAS:*** Traffic Violations; Criminal Defense; General Practice.

WILLIAM P. GIBBONS

Established in 1973

1525 LEADER BUILDING

CLEVELAND, OHIO 44114

Telephone: 216-623-8000; 241-2500

Facsimile: 216-241-2286

Email: wpgibbonsesq@aol.com

Business and Corporate Law, Business Acquisitions, Development and Organizations, Closely Held Businesses, Federal Income Taxation Law, Estate Planning and Litigation Related to All of the Foregoing.

FIRM PROFILE: Provides a broad array of legal assistance to business owners and entrepreneurs in the acquisition, development and organization of business opportunities, the operation of businesses, the financing of such opportunities, the sale of businesses and litigation involving financial, business and tax matters. See Martindale-Hubbell Bar Register of Preeminent Lawyers - Business Law.

WILLIAM P. GIBBONS, born Cleveland, Ohio, January 1, 1942; admitted to bar, 1973, Ohio. *Education:* John Carroll University (B.S.B.A., 1964); Cleveland-Marshall College of Law (J.D., 1972). Certified Public Accountant, Ohio, 1968 (Ret.). Member, numerous boards of Directors of For-Profit and Not-For-Profit Organizations. *Member:* Greater Cleveland, Cuyahoga County, Ohio State and American (Member, Income Tax, Probate and Property Law Section) Bar Associations; Eighth District Judicial Conference (Life Member). [1st Lt. U.S. Army, Ret.]

GIFFEN & KAMINSKI, LLC

1717 EAST NINTH STREET, SUITE 2100

CLEVELAND, OHIO 44114-2876

Telephone: 216-621-5161

Telecopier: 216-621-2399

URL: http://www.thinkgk.com

Commercial Litigation, Employment Litigation, Real Estate Litigation, Securities Litigation and Arbitration, Creditors Rights, Probate and Trust Litigation, Banking Litigation, Management Labor Relations, Products Liability.

MEMBERS OF THE FIRM

KAREN L. GIFFEN, born Ellwood City, Pennsylvania, March 25, 1958; admitted to bar, 1989, Ohio. *Education:* Cleveland State University (B.A., 1980); Cleveland-Marshall College of Law (J.D., summa cum laude, 1989). Editor, Ohio Transaction Guide. Recipient: Spangenberg Trial Practice Award; Federal Bar Association Award for Excellence in Constitutional Law. *Member:* Cleveland and Ohio State and American Bar Associations; Ohio Women's Bar Association; National Association of Minority and Female Owned Law Firms. ***PRACTICE AREAS:*** Commercial Litigation; Real Estate Litigation; Health Care; Management Labor Relations; Trust Litigation; Probate Litigation; Banking Litigation. ***Email:*** kgiffen@thinkgk.com

KERIN LYN KAMINSKI, born Cleveland, Ohio, March 4, 1958; admitted to bar, 1985, Ohio. *Education:* Ashland College (B.A., cum laude, 1980); Cleveland-Marshall Law School (J.D., magna cum laude, 1984). Listed, Ohio Super Lawyer, 2003 and 2004. Recipient, Federal Bar Association Award for Excellence in Evidence. Editor, Ohio Transaction Guide. *Member:* Cleveland Bar Association (Trustee, 1997-2000; Past Chair Commission on Women in the Law); Ohio State Bar Association; Ohio Women's Bar Association; National Association of Minority and Female Owned Law Firms. ***PRACTICE AREAS:*** Commercial Litigation; Employment Litigation; Real Estate Litigation; Creditors Rights; Probate Litigation; Trust Litigation; Banking Litigation. ***Email:*** kkaminski@thinkgk.com

ASSOCIATES

STEVEN R. MALYNN, born Oakland, California, June 30, 1959; admitted to bar, 1996, Ohio; 1999, U.S. District Court, Northern District of Ohio. *Education:* University of California at Riverside (B.A., 1981); University of Notre Dame Law School (J.D., 1996). Author, "Municipal Liability for Jailhouse Suicide in Ohio, Ohio Municipal Service, Jan.-Feb. 2000. *Member:* Cleveland, Ohio State and American Bar Associations. [Lieutenant Colonel, U.S. Marine Corps Reserve]. ***REPORTED CASES:*** Ward v. Hengle, 124 Ohio App. 3d 396; Martin v. Budd, 128 Ohio App. 3d 115. ***PRACTICE AREAS:*** Commercial Litigation; Securities Litigation; Securities Arbitration; Products Liability; Employment Litigation; Municipal Liability; Constitutional Law.

TRACY A. TUROFF, admitted to bar, 2002, Ohio. *Education:* Case Western Reserve University (B.A., magna cum laude, 1997) Dean's High Honors; Cleveland-Marshall College of Law (J.D., 2002). Pi Sigma Alpha, Case Western Reserve University. Recipient, Pancoast Research and Fellowship Award, Case Western Reserve University. *Member:* Cleveland (Member, Sections on: Women in the Law; Real Estate; Litigation) and Ohio State Bar Associations; William K.Thomas Inn of Court. ***PRACTICE AREAS:*** Commercial Litigation; Employment Litigation; Real Estate Litigation; Business Torts Litigation; Probate Litigation. ***Email:*** tturoff@thinkgk.com

EMILY ALLEGRETTI VLASICH, born Hammond, Indiana; admitted to bar, 2002, Ohio; 2003, U.S. District Court, Northern District of Ohio and U.S. Court of Appeals, Sixth Circuit. *Education:* Case Western Reserve University (B.A., cum laude, 1999; J.D., cum laude, 2002). *Member:* Cleveland (Member, Sections on: Women in Law; Litigation) and

(This Listing Continued)

Ohio State Bar Associations. ***PRACTICE AREAS:*** Commercial Litigation; Employment Litigation; Bankruptcy; Creditors Rights; Trust Litigation; Uniform Commercial Code Litigation. ***Email:*** evlasich@thinkgk.com

KATHLEEN NITSCHKE, born Olney, Maryland; admitted to bar, 2001, Ohio; U.S. District Court, Northern and Southern Districts of Ohio. *Education:* John Carroll University (B.S., cum laude, 1997); Detroit College of Law at Michigan State University (J.D., cum laude, 2000). Psi Chi, Psychology Honors Society; Sigma Delta Phi, Spanish Honor Society; Delta Theta Phi, Law Fraternity. *Member:* Cleveland (Member: Ethics and Grievance Committee; Litigation Section) and Ohio State Bar Associations. ***PRACTICE AREAS:*** Commercial Litigation; Employment Litigation; Uniform Commercial Code Litigation; Real Estate Litigation. ***Email:*** knitschke@thinkgk.com

JEFFREY T. PETERS, born Garfield Heights, Ohio; admitted to bar, 1999, Ohio; 2002, U.S. District Court, Northern District of Ohio; 2004, U.S. District Court, Southern District of Ohio; 2005, U.S. Court of Appeals, Sixth Circuit. *Education:* Bowling Green State University (B.S.B.A., 1996); Cleveland-Marshall College of Law (J.D., 1999). *Member:* Cleveland Bar Association (Member, Labor and Employment Section). ***REPORTED CASES:*** Roberts v. State Farm Mutual Auto Insurance Co., 155 Ohio App.3d 98, 2003 Ohio 5398. ***PRACTICE AREAS:*** Commercial Litigation; Employment Litigation; Litigation; Real Estate Litigation. ***Email:*** jpeters@thinkgk.com

GOLD AND PYLE, LPA

526 SUPERIOR AVENUE E, SUITE 1140

CLEVELAND, OHIO 44114

Telephone: 216-696-6122

Fax: 216-696-3214

General, Criminal and Civil Trial and Appellate Practice in all State and Federal Courts. Business Litigation, Labor and Employment, Employment Discrimination, Real Estate and Construction Law, Professional Liability and Malpractice, Professional Discipline, Education Law, Arbitration and Mediation.

GERALD S. GOLD, born Cleveland, Ohio, February 2, 1931; admitted to bar, 1954, Ohio; 1973, U.S. Supreme Court. *Education:* Western Reserve University (A.B., 1951; J.D., 1954). Order of the Coif. Editor-in-Chief, Western Reserve Law Review, 1953-1954. Author: "Annual Survey, Criminal Law," Western Reserve Law Review, 1960-1963; "Federal Habeas Corpus: A New Outlook for the State Prisoner," 25 Ohio State Law Journal 60, 1964; "Split Loyalty: An Ethical Problem for the Criminal Defense Lawyer," 14 Cleveland Marshall Law Review 65, 1965. Co-author: "Suppression of Illegally Obtained Evidence," Vol. 5, Am. Jur. *Trials.* Lecturer: Western Reserve Law Medicine Center, 1963—; Western Reserve Law School, 1964. Instructor, Cleveland Marshall Law School, 1967-1971. Public Defender, Cuyahoga County, 1961-1965. Secretary, 1963-1965 and Member, 1962-1965, Defender Committee, National Legal Aid and Defender Association. President, Cleveland Association of Trial Lawyers in Criminal Cases, 1964-1965. President, Case Western Reserve Law Alumni Association, 1974-1975. Member, Society of Benchers, Regent, National College of Criminal Defense Lawyers, 1981. Board Member, Greater Cleveland Growth Association, 1982—. *Member:* Fellow, International Society of Barristers. Ohio Academy of Trial Lawyers (Chairman, Criminal Law Section, 1971—); National Association of Criminal Defense Lawyers (Member, Board of Directors, 1973—; Secretary, 1976; Vice President, 1977; President, 1978); National Board of Trial Advocacy. Fellow, American College of Trial Lawyers. Ohio State Bar Foundation. Fellow, American Board of Criminal Lawyers. Greater Cleveland (Chairman: Press-Bar Relations Committee, 1971-1973; Federal Court Committee, 1973-1974; Criminal Law Committee, 1976-1977; Trustee, 1978—; President, 1982-1983), Cuyahoga County, Ohio State (Member, 1962 and Chairman, 1972-1976, Criminal Law Committee) and American (Member: Legal Aid and Indigent Defendants Committee, 1967-1970; Criminal Justice Section; Chairman, Exclusionary Rule Committee, 1976-1977; Member, Council of Criminal Justice, 1981) Bar Associations; Cuyahoga County Criminal Courts Bar Association (President, 1972-1976). ***PRACTICE AREAS:*** Criminal; Civil Trials; Appeals; Administrative Agencies. ***Email:*** ggold@gp-lpa.com

JOHN S. PYLE, born Newark, Ohio, December 8, 1948; admitted to bar, 1974, Ohio; 1978, U.S. District Court, Northern District of Ohio; 1979, U.S. Supreme Court; 1981, U.S. Court of Appeals, Sixth Circuit. *Education:* Hiram College (B.A., 1969); Case Western Reserve University (J.D., 1974). Assistant County Prosecutor, Cuyahoga County, Ohio, 1974-1978. Assistant U.S. Attorney, Northern District of Ohio, 1978-1981. Adjunct Faculty Member, Case Western Reserve University School of Law, 1993-1996. Co-Author: "Volume 4 of Katz and Giannelli, Criminal Law," West Publishing, 1997. President, Board of Governor's, Case Western Reserve University, Law Alumni Association, 1988-1990. *Member:* Greater Cleveland (Chairman, Criminal Law Committee, 1983-1984; Member, Board of Trustees, 1984-1987), Ohio State and Federal Bar Associations; Ohio Academy of Trial Lawyers (Chairman, Criminal Law Section, 1986-1988). [With U.S. Army, 1969-1970]. ***REPORTED CASES:*** Mustafa v. State Medical Bd. of Ohio, 1991 WL 224202 (Ohio App. 10 Dist., Franklin County, Oct 17, 1991); State v. Jenks, 61 Ohio St.3d 259, 574 N.E.2d 492 (1991); Office of Disciplinary Counsel v. Badalian, 51 Ohio St.3d 42, 553 N.E.2d 1080 (1990); State v. Thompson, 33 Ohio St.3d 1, 514 N.E.2d 407 (1987); State v. Shimits, 10 Ohio St.3d 83, 461 N.E.2d 1278 (1984). ***PRACTICE AREAS:*** Appellate Practice; Criminal Trial Practice; Legal Ethics and Discipline Law. ***Email:*** jpyle@gp-lpa.com

DAVID W. GOLDENSE

Established in 1981

TERMINAL TOWER, SUITE 920
50 PUBLIC SQUARE
CLEVELAND, OHIO 44113
Telephone: 216-241-0300
Fax: 216-241-2731
Email: DWGoldense@aol.com
URL: http://www.davidwgoldenselaw.com

Automobile Accidents, Medical Malpractice, Employment Discrimination, Personal Injury, Dog Bites, Employment Law.

DAVID W. GOLDENSE, born Chicago, Illinois, August 2, 1951; admitted to bar, 1977, Ohio. *Education:* Denison University (B.A., 1973); University of Toledo (J.D., 1977). Chairman, Moot Court Board, 1976-1977. Order of the Barristers. Regional Finalist in Oral Argument, Jessup International Moot Court Competition. Lecturer: Hon. Bernard Friedman Litigation Institute; Ohio Academy of Trial Lawyers, 1993—. Member, Eighth District Judicial Conference, 1989—. Cleveland Academy of Trial Attorneys (Trustee, 1987-1991, Treasurer, 1992, Secretary, 1993-1994, Vice-President, 1994-1995, President, 1995-1996). *Member:* Cuyahoga Bar Association; The Association of Trial Lawyers of America. ***PRACTICE AREAS:*** Personal Injury; Medical Malpractice; Employment Law; Workers Compensation; Litigation.

GARY M. GOLDFARB

Established in 1975

2000 STANDARD BUILDING
1370 ONTARIO STREET
CLEVELAND, OHIO 44113
Telephone: 216-579-1117; 216-363-6066
Fax: 216-363-6013; 216-363-6010
Email: gar4law@aol.com
URL: http://www.lawyers.com/garygoldfarb

General, Civil Trial, Personal Injury, Workers Compensation, Domestic Relations, Corporate Law, Automobile Accidents, Divorce, Child Custody, Child Support, Wrongful Death, Medical Malpractice.

GARY M. GOLDFARB, born Cleveland, Ohio, March 13, 1947; admitted to bar, 1972, Ohio. *Education:* Ohio University (B.B.A., 1969); Case Western Reserve University (J.D., 1972). Member, Case Western Reserve Law Review, 1971. American Jurisprudence Award Winner, Administrative Law. *Member:* Cleveland and Ohio State Bar Associations; Ohio Academy of Trial Lawyers.

GOODMAN WEISS MILLER LLP

Established in 1986

100 ERIEVIEW PLAZA, 27TH FLOOR
CLEVELAND, OHIO 44114-1882
Telephone: 216-696-3366
Telecopier: 216-363-5835
Email: gwm@goodmanweissmiller.com
URL: http://www.goodmanweissmiller.com

Business and Complex Litigation. Corporation, Securities, Taxation, Real Estate, Banking, Commercial Finance, Antitrust, International, Computer and Employment Law. Trials and Appeals in Federal and State Courts. Litigation of Restrictive Covenants, Emergency Injunction and Equity Practice, Securities, Business Torts, Warranty, and Franchise Litigation, Creditors Rights; Health Care Law; Intellectual Property Rights.

MEMBERS OF FIRM

STEVEN J. MILLER, born Cleveland, Ohio, June 7, 1956; admitted to bar, 1981, Ohio and, U.S. District Court, Northern District of Ohio; 1987, U.S. Court of Appeals, Sixth Circuit; 1992, U.S. Court of Appeals, Fifth Circuit. *Education:* Brown University (A.B., with honors, 1978); Vanderbilt University; Case Western Reserve University (J.D., 1981). Member: Wagner Moot Court Team, 1980-1981; The Order of Barristers, 1980-1981. Associate Editor, American Bar Association *Litigation* Journal, 1984—. Chair, Cleveland Bar Association Business Litigation Committee, 1998—. Special Counsel, Attorney General of Ohio, 1991-1995. Life Member, Judicial Conference for the Eighth Judicial District, Cuyahoga County, Ohio. Founding Barrister, Harold Burton Inn of Court. *Member:* Cleveland (Member, Litigation Section), Ohio State (Member, Litigation Section) and American (Member, Litigation and Business Law Sections) Bar Associations. ***PRACTICE AREAS:*** Business Litigation; Corporate Litigation; Complex Litigation; Trial Practice; Federal Practice; Emergency Injunction Litigation. **Email:** Miller@goodmanweissmiller.com

JAY R. FAEGES, born Cleveland, Ohio, February 17, 1960; admitted to bar, 1991, Ohio; U.S. District Court, Northern District of Ohio. *Education:* Cleveland State University (B.S., cum laude, 1988); Cleveland Marshall College of Law (J.D., magna cum laude, 1991). Alpha Kappa Nu. Member, Cleveland State Law Review, 1990-1991. *Member:* Cleveland, Ohio State and American Bar Associations; Cleveland Legal Aid Society (Board of Trustees, 1998-2000). ***PRACTICE AREAS:*** Business Transactions; Creditors Rights; Health Care; Securities Offerings; Corporate Law. **Email:** Faeges@goodmanweissmiller.com

MICHAEL D. GOLER, born Shaker Heights, Ohio, June 29, 1952; admitted to bar, 1977, Ohio and U.S. District Court, Northern District of Ohio; 1982, U.S. Court of Appeals, Sixth Circuit. *Education:* Union College, New York (B.A. Classics, with honors, 1974); Case Western Reserve University (J.D., 1977). *Member:* Cleveland (Founder and Chairman, Environmental Law Section, 1991-1995; Chairman, Foreclosure Committee, 1981-1985; Chairman, Real Estate Section, 1989-1990), Ohio State and American (Member: Thrift Subcommittee, Corporation, Banking and Business Law Section; Real Estate Financing Committee; Technology Standing Committee, 1998—; CLE Standing Committee, 1999—; Planning Committee 2004—; Managing Editor of E-Dirt Electronic Real Estate Newsletter, 1999—; Chairman, Committee on Enforcement of Creditor's Rights and Bankruptcy, 1991-1995; Committee on Economics, Technology and Practice Methods, Vice Chair, 1995-1997, Chairman, 1997-2001; Council Member, 2001—; Chair, Practice Management Group 2004 —; Real Property, Probate and Trust Law Section; Vice-Chair Membership and Marketing Committee, 2004 —; SOC Membership Committee 2004 —; Nominating Committee 2005—; Law Practice Management Sections) Bar Associations. American College of Mortgage Attorneys. ***PRACTICE AREAS:*** Real Estate Law; Commercial Lending Law; Banking Law; Workouts; Financial Institution Law; Business Transactions; Corporate Law. **Email:** Goler@goodmanweissmiller.com

DREW A. CARSON, born Cleveland, Ohio, July 10, 1957; admitted to bar, 1986, Ohio; 1988, U.S. Court of Appeals, Sixth Circuit; 1990, U.S. District Court, Northern District of Ohio. *Education:* Oberlin College (B.A., 1979); Case Western Reserve University (J.D., 1986). Assistant Director of Law for the City of Cleveland, Ohio, 1990-1993. Assistant Director of Law for the City of Cleveland Heights, Ohio, 1993-1995. *Member:* Cleveland, Ohio State and American (Member, Business Law Section) Bar Associations. ***LANGUAGES:*** French. ***PRACTICE AREAS:*** Public Sector Law; Employment Law; Business Litigation. **Email:** Carson@goodmanweissmiller.com

ASSOCIATES

DEBORAH J. MICHELSON, born Brooklyn, New York, January 5, 1963; admitted to bar, 1988, New York; 1993, Ohio; U.S. District Court, Northern and Southern Districts of Ohio, and U.S. Court of Appeals, Sixth Circuit. *Education:* Northwestern University (B.A., 1984); Case Western Reserve University (J.D., cum laude, 1987). Recipient, International Academy of Trial Lawyers Advocacy Award. Member, Case Western Reserve Law Review. Assistant District Attorney, New York County (Manhattan), 1987-1992. *Member:* Cleveland (Past Chair, Litigation Section; Current Member, Litigation Section Council), Ohio State and American (Member, Business Law, Litigation and Torts and Insurance Practice Sections) Bar Associations. ***PRACTICE AREAS:*** Business Litigation; Securities Litigation; Complex Litigation; Trial Practice; Appellate Practice; Employment Litigation. **Email:** Michelson@goodmanweissmiller.com

DAVID A. KUNSELMAN, born Elmhurst, Illinois, February 23, 1976; admitted to bar, 2001, Ohio and U.S. District Court, Northern District of Ohio. *Education:* Union College (B.A., cum laude, 1998); Case Western Reserve University (J.D., cum laude, 2001). Omicron Delta Epsilon. Recipient: Jack Cronquist Award; CALI-Excellence for the Future Award. *Member:* Cleveland, Ohio State and American Bar Associations. ***PRACTICE AREAS:*** Business Transactions; Securities Offerings; Corporate Law; Corporate Litigation; Complex and Multi-District Litigation. **Email:** Kunselman@goodmanweissmiller.com

SARAH H. KOSTURA, born Cleveland, Ohio; admitted to bar, 2004, Ohio and U.S. District Court, Northern District of Ohio. *Education:* John Carroll University (B.A., magna cum laude, 2001); Case Western Reserve University (J.D., cum laude, 2004). *Member:* Cleveland, Ohio and American Bar Associations. ***PRACTICE AREAS:*** Business Litigation; Business Transactions. **Email:** boots@goodmanweissmiller.com

OF COUNSEL

ROBERT A. GOODMAN, born Cleveland, Ohio, May 16, 1935; admitted to bar, 1960, Ohio; 1965, Missouri. *Education:* Dartmouth College (B.A., 1957); Case Western Reserve University (LL.B., 1960). Editor, Case Western Reserve Law Review, 1959-1960. Trial Attorney, Bureau of Restraint of Trade, F.T.C., 1962-1964. Chairman, Land Clearance Redevelopment Authority of Kansas City, 1971-1974. Special Counsel, Attorney General of Ohio, 1991-1995. *Member:* Cleveland, Ohio State and American (Member, Sections on: Antitrust Law; Litigation; Business Law) Bar Associations. ***PRACTICE AREAS:*** Complex Litigation; Corporate Governance; Antitrust Law. **Email:** Goodman@goodmanweissmiller.com

RONALD I. WEISS, admitted to bar, 1965, Ohio. *Education:* University of Pennsylvania (B.S., 1962); Case Western Reserve University (J.D., 1965); New York University (LL.M. in Taxation, 1966). ***PRACTICE AREAS:*** Corporate Law; Securities Law; Taxation Law. **Email:** weiss@goodmanweissmiller.com

REPRESENTATIVE CLIENTS: Accrisoft Corporation; Advance Stores Company Incorporated; Aironet Wireless Communications Inc; AMPCO System Parking; Arch Communications, Inc.; Automated Solutions Corporation; Burgess & Niple; Charter One Bank; Chase/JPMorgan; ChemMasters, Inc.; Citi; Citizens Academy; Commonwealth Equity Services, Inc.; Convenient Food Mart, Inc.; Digital Library Resources, Inc.; Edward W. Daniel, LLC; Eton Financial Services; The Equitable Life Assurance Society of the United States; First Place Bank; The Gateway Companies, Inc.; The Glidden Company; Groeneveld Groep B.V.; The Huntington National Bank; Hyva Groep B.V.; International Seaway Trading Corp.; Invesco Funds Group, Inc.; J.G. Wentworth SSC, L.P.; JTM Products, Inc.; LaSalle National Bank; McDonald's Corporation; National Bank of Canada; National City Bank; NationsBank; Nationwide Life Insurance Company; OverDrive, Inc.; Porphyron, Inc.; The Provident Bank; RPM Inc.; Republic Bank; Sonagage, Inc.; Strategic Vista Corp.; US Bank; Vacation Auctions, Inc.; Visual Marking Systems, Inc.

R. BENTON GRAY & COMPANY

Established in 1999

55 PUBLIC SQUARE, SUITE 900
CLEVELAND, OHIO 44113
Telephone: 216-579-0800
Facsimile: 216-781-3066
Email: bengray@bengraylaw.com
Email: rbgraylaw@sbcglobal.net
URL: http://www.bengraylaw.com

Litigation, Employment Law, Equal Employment Opportunity Law, Sexual Harassment, Wrongful Termination, Executive Employment Law, Non-Compete Agreements, Employment Retention and Severance Agreements, Civil Practice, Civil Appeals.

(This Listing Continued)

R. BENTON GRAY & COMPANY, Cleveland—Continued

R. BENTON GRAY, born Cleveland, Ohio, July 5, 1951; admitted to bar, 1983, Ohio. *Education:* Kenyon College (A.B., 1973); Duke University (J.D., 1983). *Member:* Cleveland (Past Chair, Employment and Labor Law Section; Member, Board of Trustees and Committees on: Certified Grievance; Judicial Selection) and Ohio State Bar Associations; The Association of Trial Lawyers of America; Cleveland Employment American Inn of Court (Master of the Bench). ***PRACTICE AREAS:*** Employment Law Claims (80%); Litigation (10%); Appellate Practice (5%); Alternative Dispute Resolution (5%).

SUSAN M. GRAY

21330 CENTER RIDGE RD.
CLEVELAND, OHIO 44116
Telephone: 440-331-3949
Fax: 440-331-8160
Email: smgray@smgraylaw.com
URL: http://www.lawyers.com/susangraylaw

Bankruptcy, Consumer Law, Consumer Fraud, Foreclosures, Debtor and Creditor, Fair Credit Reporting Act, Fair Debt Collection Practices Act.

SUSAN M. GRAY, born Greenville, South Carolina, November 25, 1949; admitted to bar, 1982, Washington; 1993, Ohio and U.S. District Court, Northern District of Ohio. *Education:* University of Chicago (B.A., cum laude, 1972); Seattle University School of Law (J.D., magna cum laude, 1982). *Member:* Cuyahoga County, Cleveland (Member, Bankruptcy and Commercial Law Sections), Ohio State Bar Associations. ***LANGUAGES:*** Spanish. ***PRACTICE AREAS:*** Bankruptcy; Consumer Law; Fraud; Foreclosures; Debtor and Creditor Law; Fair Credit Reporting Act; Fair Debt Collection Practices Act.

JAMES P. GRUBER

50 EAST WASHINGTON STREET
CLEVELAND, OHIO 44022
Telephone: 440-893-9686
Fax: 440-247-1031
URL: http://www.jpglawfirm.com

Probate, Wills, Trusts, Estate Planning, Business, Corporations, Partnerships, LLC's, Business Succession Planning, Tax and Real Estate.

JAMES P. GRUBER, born Cleveland, Ohio, January 3, 1958; admitted to bar, 1989, Ohio. *Education:* University of Colorado at Boulder (B.A., 1982); Case Western Reserve University (J.D., 1988). *Member:* Ohio State Bar Association (Member, Estate Planning, Trust and Probate Section); Estate Planning Council of Cleveland. ***PRACTICE AREAS:*** Probate; Wills; Trusts; Estate Planning; Tax; Business; Business Succession Planning; Real Estate; Corporate Law; Partnership Law; Limited Liability Company Law. ***Email:*** jpglaw@email.com

RUBIN GUTTMAN & ASSOCIATES, L.P.A.

Established in 1981
55 PUBLIC SQUARE
SUITE 1860
CLEVELAND, OHIO 44113-1998
Telephone: 216-696-4006
Fax: 216-696-2778
Email: GUTTLAW@AOL.COM
URL: http://www.guttlaw.com

Plaintiffs Personal Injury, Medical Malpractice, Negligence, Business, Corporate and Real Estate Litigation, Employment Defense, Cable Television and Communication Litigation and Commercial Litigation, Appellate Practice.

FIRM PROFILE: Firm focuses on serious personal injury and medical malpractice, with substantial experience in cases of serious neurological and head injury, disfigurement, wrongful death, and cancer.

RUBIN GUTTMAN, born Brooklyn, New York, June 22, 1952; admitted to bar, 1977, Ohio and U.S. District Court, Northern District of Ohio. *Education:* Brooklyn College (B.A., cum laude, 1974); Cleveland State University (J.D., 1977). Member, Cleveland State Law Review, 1976-1977. Adjunct Professor, Business Law, Cleveland State University, 1980-1982. *Member:* Greater Cleveland and Ohio State Bar Associations; The Association of Trial Lawyers of America; Ohio Academy of Trial Lawyers. ***LANGUAGES:*** Hebrew. ***REPORTED CASES:*** Appellants' Counsel, Gross v. Cablevision of the Midwest, Inc. ***PRACTICE AREAS:*** Personal Injury Law; Medical Malpractice Law; Business Litigation; Appellate Practice. ***Email:*** GUTTLAW@AOL.COM

ANN MARIE STOCKMASTER, born Cleveland, Ohio, April 26, 1958; admitted to bar, 1996, Ohio; 1997, U.S. District Court, Northern District of Ohio. *Education:* Cleveland State University (B.A., magna cum laude, 1990); Cleveland Marshall College of Law (J.D., cum laude, 1996). Associate, 1993-1994, Editor, 1994-1995, Cleveland Marshall Law Review. Member, 1993-1994 and Vice Chairman of Operations, 1994-1995, Moot Court Board of Governors. *Member:* Cleveland and Ohio State Bar Association; Association of Trial Lawyers of America; Ohio Academy of Trial Lawyers. ***PRACTICE AREAS:*** Personal Injury; Medical Malpractice; Business Litigation; Real Estate.

Language: Hebrew.

REPRESENTATIVE CLIENTS: Gross Brothers Development Co.; Gross Builders; Diamond Engineered Space Inc.; Gottlieb & Sons, Inc.; ML Building Corp.; Pinnacle Financial Group, Inc.; Robert L. Stark Enterprise, Inc.; Global Interactive Entertainment Corp.

HAHN LOESER & PARKS LLP

Established in 1920
3300 BP TOWER
200 PUBLIC SQUARE
CLEVELAND, OHIO 44114-2301
Telephone: 216-621-0150
FAX: 216-241-2824/1-877-HAHNLAW
Email: inquiry@hahnlaw.com
URL: http://www.hahnlaw.com

Columbus, Ohio Office: 65 East State Street, Suite 1400, 43215. Telephone: 614-221-0240. Fax: 614-221-5909.
Akron, Ohio Office: One Gojo Plaza, Suite 300, 44311-1076. Telephone: 330-864-5550. Fax: 330-864-7986.
Naples, Florida Office: 3301 Bonita Beach Road, Suite 308, Bonita Springs, 34134. Telephone: 239-949-6989. Fax: 239-949-6687.

Business, Corporate and Securities, Litigation, Taxation and Employee Benefits, Estate Planning, Probate, Real Estate, Labor, Creditors Rights, Reorganization and Bankruptcy, Intellectual Property and Technology, Environmental, Patent, Trademark and Copyright Law, Telecommunications Law, Government Relations, Public Utility and Regulatory Law, Health Care, Construction Law.

FIRM PROFILE: Hahn Loeser & Parks LLP . . . Dedicated, diverse legal counsel serving businesses, industries, institutions and individuals since 1920. We deliver sophisticated and innovative counseling to a wide spectrum of clients from our offices in Cleveland, Columbus and Akron, Ohio, and Bonita Springs and Naples, Florida.

MEMBERS OF FIRM

JEFFREY A. BRAUER, born Boston, Massachusetts, 1968; admitted to bar, 1994, Illinois; 1998, Ohio. *Education:* Northwestern University (B.S., Communications, 1990); Vanderbilt University (J.D., 1994). *Member:* Ohio State (Council of Delegates, 2005-2007; New Lawyer Section, Chair, 2003-2004) and American (Litigation Section; TIPS; Young Lawyers Division: Committee Director, 2004-2005, Litigation Committee Chair, 2002-2004 and Co-Chair) Bar Associations. ***PRACTICE AREAS:*** Litigation; Construction Law. ***Email:*** jabrauer@hahnlaw.com

ERICA L. CALDERAS, born Caracas, Venezuela, November 30, 1968; admitted to bar, 1994, Ohio. *Education:* Cornell University (A.B., with distinction in all subjects, 1991); Northwestern University School of Law (J.D., 1994). ***PRACTICE AREAS:*** Litigation. ***Email:*** elcalderas@hahnlaw.com

DOUGLAS C. CARLSON, born Chicago, Illinois, March 14, 1950; admitted to bar, 1975, Ohio; 1979, U.S. Tax Court; 1982, Florida. *Education:* Kent State University (B.B.A., magna cum laude, 1971; M.P.A., 1972); Case Western Reserve University (J.D., 1975). Beta Gamma Sigma; Beta Alpha Psi. Associate Editor, Case Western Reserve Law Review, 1973-1974. Certified Public Accountant, Ohio, 1978. ***PRACTICE AREAS:*** Tax Law; Business Taxation; Business Law; Nonprofit and Charitable Organizations; Corporate Law; Estate Planning; Probate. ***Email:*** dccarlson@hahnlaw.com

ARTHUR L. COBB, born Rockville Centre, New York, September 15, 1949; admitted to bar, 1975, New York; 1977, Ohio. *Education:* Cornell University (A.B., 1971; J.D., 1974). Listed in the Best Lawyers in America - Health Care and Real Estate Law, 2001-2005. ***PRACTICE AREAS:*** Health Care; Real Estate; Creditors Rights. ***Email:*** alcobb@hahnlaw.com

DEBORAH A. COLEMAN, born Chicago, Illinois, July 19, 1951; admitted to bar, 1976, Ohio. *Education:* Radcliffe College (A.B., magna cum laude, 1973); Harvard University (J.D., 1976). Phi Beta Kappa. Author: "Antitrust Issues in the Litigation and Settlement of Infringement Claims," Akron Law Review, 2004. *Member:* Cleveland (Member and Past Chair, Professional Ethics Committee) and American (Past Member and Chair, Standing Committee on Ethics and Professional Responsibility) Bar Associations; Cleveland Intellectual Property Law Association (Chair, Antitrust Committee). ***PRACTICE AREAS:*** Litigation; Mediation; Arbitration; Antitrust; Intellectual Property; Professional Conduct; Legal Ethics. ***Email:*** dacoleman@hahnlaw.com

DANIEL A. DeMARCO, born Cleveland, Ohio, March 24, 1958; admitted to bar, 1983, Texas; 1987, Ohio. *Education:* University of Chicago (B.A., 1980); University of Michigan (J.D., 1983). Phi Beta Kappa. *Member:* American Bar Association; American Bankruptcy Institute; Turnaround Management Association. (Board Certified in Business Bankruptcy Law by the American Board of Certification). ***PRACTICE AREAS:*** Creditors Rights; Bankruptcy; Bankruptcy Chapter 11; Insolvency; Debtors and Creditors Reorganization; Litigation. ***Email:*** dademarco@hahnlaw.com

JAMES M. DROZDOWSKI, born Cleveland, Ohio, March 10, 1970; admitted to bar, 1995, Ohio. *Education:* University of Cincinnati (B.A., summa cum laude, 1992); Case Western Reserve University (J.D., magna cum laude, 1995). ***PRACTICE AREAS:*** Labor Law; Employment Law; Employer Liability; Employment Litigation; Litigation. ***Email:*** jmdrozdowski@hahnlaw.com

CHRISTINA D'ERAMO EVANS, admitted to bar, 1991, Ohio. *Education:* Miami University (B.A., cum laude, 1988); Case Western Reserve University School of Law (J.D., cum laude, 1991). *Member:* Cleveland (Secretary, Estate Planning, Probate and Trust Law Section) and Ohio State (Council Member, Estate Planning, Probate and Trust Law Section) Bar Associations. (Certified Specialist in Estate Planning, Trust and Probate Law, Ohio State Bar Association). ***PRACTICE AREAS:*** Estate Planning; Trust Law; Estate Settlements. ***Email:*** cdevans@hahnlaw.com

ROSE MARIE L. FIORE, born Cleveland, Ohio, January 24, 1970; admitted to bar, 1995, Ohio. *Education:* Case Western Reserve University (B.A., magna cum laude, 1992; J.D., 1995). ***PRACTICE AREAS:*** Litigation; Franchise Law. ***Email:*** rmfiore@hahnlaw.com

ROBERT J. FOGARTY, born Paterson, New Jersey, January 5, 1952; admitted to bar, 1977, Ohio; 1979, Florida. *Education:* University of Cincinnati (B.A., magna cum laude,

(This Listing Continued)

1974; J.D., 1977). Phi Beta Kappa. Assistant U.S. Attorney for the Southern District of Ohio, 1979-1982. ***PRACTICE AREAS:*** Litigation. ***Email:*** rjfogarty@hahnlaw.com

STEPHEN H. GARIEPY, born Salamanca, New York, December 12, 1952; admitted to bar, 1977, Ohio; 1988, U.S. Tax Court. *Education:* Case Western Reserve University (B.A., magna cum laude, 1974); The Ohio State University (J.D., cum laude, 1977). Co-Author: "Tax Planning Strategies for Credit Shelter Trusts," CCH, 1983; "Taxation of Executive Compensation: Planning and Practice," Matthew Bender & Co., 1983; "Ohio Transaction Guide," Matthew Bender & Co., 1978-1995; "Rabkin and Johnson Current Legal Forms with Tax Analysis," Matthew Bender & Co., 1978-1995; "Ohio State Taxation," Matthew Bender & Co., 1986. Consultant, BNA Estate Tax Spread Sheet, The Bureau of National Affairs, Washington, D.C., 1989—. Member: Cleveland Society of Estate Analysts, 1996—; Estate Planning Council of Cleveland (President, 1997-1998; Trustee, 1993-1999); Estate Planning Advisory Council, Case Western Reserve University, 2002—. Member, 1995— and Chair, 2004—, Planned Giving Council, Cleveland Museum of Art. Trustee and Chair of Planned Giving, Great Lakes Theater Festival, 2004—. *Member:* Cleveland (Chair, Estate Planning Institute, 1990-1991; Member, Continuing Legal Education Committee, 1994-1998), Ohio State (Member, Probate and Trust Law Section, 1982—) and American (Member, Committee on Estate and Gift Taxes, 1988—) Bar Associations; American College of Trust and Estate Counsel. ***PRACTICE AREAS:*** Estate Planning; Business Planning; Probate; Business Law; Family Business Successions. ***Email:*** sgariepy@hahnlaw.com

MICHAEL J. GARVIN, born Cleveland, Ohio, December 30, 1958; admitted to bar, 1984, Ohio. *Education:* Miami University (B.S., 1981); College of William & Mary (J.D., 1984). Co-Author: "A Modest Expansion of the Attorney-Client Privilege Relating to Patent Opinions," Intellectual Property and Technology Law Journal, May, 2002. *Member:* American Bar Association (Member, Section of Litigation; Co-Chair: Programming Subcommittee; Intellectual Property Litigation Committee). ***PRACTICE AREAS:*** Litigation; Intellectual Property; Computer Law. ***Email:*** mjgarvin@hahnlaw.com

WARREN GOLDENBERG, born Brooklyn, New York, August 11, 1957; admitted to bar, 1981, Ohio. *Education:* State University of New York at Albany (B.A., summa cum laude, 1978); University of Michigan (J.D., cum laude, 1981). ***PRACTICE AREAS:*** Intellectual Property; Mergers and Acquisitions; Technology Transfers; Technology Business Startups; Closely Held Business. ***Email:*** wgoldenberg@hahnlaw.com

STEVEN A. GOLDFARB, born Cleveland, Ohio, July 30, 1960; admitted to bar, 1985, Ohio. *Education:* Indiana University (B.A., 1982); Ohio State University College of Law (J.D., 1985). *Member:* Cleveland, Ohio and American (Franchise Forum) Bar Associations; International Franchise Association. ***PRACTICE AREAS:*** Business Litigation; Torts; Franchise Litigation; Employment Litigation. ***Email:*** sagoldfarb@hahnlaw.com

STANLEY R. GOROM III, born Bryan, Ohio, October 18, 1963; admitted to bar, 1993, Ohio. *Education:* Indiana University (B.S., 1987); DePaul University College of Law (J.D., 1993). Member, DePaul Moot Court Society. Member, DePaul Business Law Journal. ***PRACTICE AREAS:*** Corporate Law; Real Estate; Corporate Finance; Banking; Gaming Regulation; Gaming Development. ***Email:*** srgorom@hahnlaw.com

KATHLEEN B. HAVENER, born Pensacola, Florida, June 27, 1954; admitted to bar, 1991, Virginia; 1992, District of Columbia and Maryland; 1998, Ohio. *Education:* Spring Hill College (B.A., summa cum laude, 1976); Trinity College, Dublin, Ireland; Harvard University (J.D., cum laude, 1991). Judicial Law Clerk for the Honorable John M. Ferren, District of Columbia Court of Appeals. Associate Editor, Harvard International Law Journal. ***PRACTICE AREAS:*** Commercial Litigation. ***Email:*** kbhavener@hahnlaw.com

CANDACE M. JONES, born Bucyrus, Ohio; admitted to bar, 1992, Ohio. *Education:* American University (B.A., magna cum laude, 1987); Case Western Reserve University Law School (J.D., summa cum laude, 1992). Order of the Coif. Board of Directors, Cleveland/Cuyahoga County Port Authority, 2002—. *Member:* American Bar Association (Chair, Cyberspace Law Committee). ***PRACTICE AREAS:*** Business Law; Commercial Law; Software Licensing; Technology Licensing. ***Email:*** cmjones@hahnlaw.com

ARTHUR M. KAUFMAN, born Cleveland, Ohio, May 25, 1950; admitted to bar, 1983, Ohio; 1986, U.S. Court of Appeals, Sixth Circuit; 2002, U.S. Supreme Court. *Education:* Ohio State University (B.S., Education, 1973); Cleveland-Marshall College of Law (J.D., cum laude, 1983). Law Clerk to Honorable R.B. Krupansky, U.S. Court of Appeals, Sixth Circuit, 1984-1986. Co-Author, "The Mutuality Doctrine in the Arbitration Agreements: The Elephant in the Road," Franchise Law Journal, Vol. 22, No. 2, Fall 2002. President-Elect: Federal Bar Association, N.D. Chapter; Cleveland Marshall College of Law Visiting Committee. *Member:* Federal and American Bar Associations; International Franchise Association;. ***PRACTICE AREAS:*** Litigation; Franchise Law; Insurance Coverage. ***Email:*** amkaufman@hahnlaw.com

STEPHEN J. KNERLY, JR., born Lakewood, Ohio, December 15, 1949; admitted to bar, 1976, Ohio. *Education:* Ecole Pratique des Hautes Etudes; Bowdoin College (A.B., summa cum laude, magna cum laude, in historium, 1972); Fletcher School of Law and Diplomacy (A.M., 1973); Case Western Reserve University (J.D., 1976). Phi Beta Kappa. Honorary French Consul, Northern Ohio. ***LANGUAGES:*** French. ***PRACTICE AREAS:*** Business Law; Corporate Law; Art Law; Museum Law; International Law. ***Email:*** sjknerly@hahnlaw.com

ALAN S. KOPIT, born Cleveland, Ohio, August 26, 1952; admitted to bar, 1977, Ohio; 1988, U.S. Supreme Court. *Education:* Tufts University (B.A., summa cum laude, 1974); University of Chicago (J.D., 1977). Phi Beta Kappa; Phi Delta Phi. White House Fellow, Special Assistant to the Secretary of Defense, 1987-1988. Recipient of Secretary of Defense Medal for Outstanding Public Service. Consumer Law Contributor, The Today Show, NBC, 2000—. National Legal Commentary (CNN, MSNBC, CNBC, Bloomberg Financial). Staff Attorney appearing on WKYC-TV (NBC) 1982-1991; WEWS-TV (ABC), 1991-2000. Vice-Chair, Cleveland Bicentennial Commission, 1992-1997. Legal Editor of lawyers.com. *Member:* Cleveland (President, 1996-1997) and American (Director, 1995-2002 and Council, 2002-2005, Litigation Section) Bar Associations; William Thomas Inn of Court (Master of the Bench). American Bar Foundation. ***PRACTICE AREAS:*** Creditors Rights; Bankruptcy; Bankruptcy Chapter 11; Insolvency; Debtor and Creditor Reorganization; Litigation; Business Law; Corporate Law; Construction Law. ***Email:*** askopit@hahnlaw.com

(This Listing Continued)

ROBERT D. MARKUS, born Cleveland, Ohio, April 2, 1940; admitted to bar, 1967, Ohio. *Education:* University of Wisconsin (B.S., 1962); Western Reserve University (J.D., 1967). Order of the Coif. Member, Board of Editors, Western Reserve University Law Review, 1966-1967. Listed in the Best Lawyers in America - Real Estate Law, 1993-1994; 1995-1996; 1997-1998; 1999-2000; 2001-2002, 2003-2004. ***PRACTICE AREAS:*** Real Estate; Business Law; Corporate Law. ***Email:*** rdmarkus@hahnlaw.com

JOHN E. MELLYN, JR., born Lynn, Massachusetts, June 16, 1945; admitted to bar, 1973, Ohio. *Education:* Boston College (A.B., magna cum laude, 1967); University of Virginia (J.D., 1973). Omicron Delta Epsilon. [With U.S. Army, 1968-1971]. ***PRACTICE AREAS:*** Real Estate; Banking Law; Financial Services Law; Business Law. ***Email:*** jemellyn@hahnlaw.com

DAVID J. MICHALSKI, born Madison, Wisconsin, June 22, 1966; admitted to bar, 1994, Ohio. *Education:* University of Wisconsin (B.A., 1987) Phi Beta Kappa; University of Chicago (M.A., 1989); Case Western University School of Law (J.D., magna cum laude, 1994). ***PRACTICE AREAS:*** Litigation. ***Email:*** djmichalski@hahnlaw.com

GREGORY M. NOLFI, born Campbell, Ohio, July 24, 1950; admitted to bar, 1977, Ohio; U.S. Supreme Court. *Education:* Youngstown State University (B.S., 1972); University of Toledo (J.D., 1977). *Member:* National Health Lawyers Association. ***PRACTICE AREAS:*** Business Law; Corporate Law; Health Care; Estate Planning; Trusts and Estates. ***Email:*** gmnolfi@hahnlaw.com

F. RONALD O'KEEFE, born Great Neck, New York, October 7, 1950; admitted to bar, 1977, Ohio; 2002, U.S. Supreme Court. *Education:* Georgetown University (A.B., cum laude, 1972); Cleveland-Marshall College of Law (J.D., cum laude, 1977). Editor, Cleveland State Law Review, 1976-1977. Listed in the Best Lawyers in America - Corporate Law, 2001-2002; Corporate, M&A and Securities Law, 2003-2004, 2005-2006. *Member:* Cleveland, Ohio State and American Bar Associations; American Society of Corporate Secretaries;. ***PRACTICE AREAS:*** Corporate Law; Securities; Mergers and Acquisitions. ***Email:*** frokeefe@hahnlaw.com

LAWRENCE E. OSCAR, born Chicago, Illinois, June 2, 1956; admitted to bar, 1981, Ohio. *Education:* University of Pennsylvania, Wharton School (B.S., cum laude, 1978); New York University (J.D., 1981). Listed in Best Lawyers in America, 2005-06. *Member:* American Bar Association (Member, Commercial Financial Services Committee, Business Law Section); American Bankruptcy Institute. ***PRACTICE AREAS:*** Creditors Rights; Reorganizations; Bankruptcy Chapter 11; Business Law; Corporate Law; Dispute Resolution. ***Email:*** leoscar@hahnlaw.com

STEPHEN P. OWENDOFF, born Morristown, New Jersey, August 1, 1943; admitted to bar, 1969, Ohio. *Education:* Bowdoin College; Kent State University (B.A., 1966); Georgetown University (J.D., 1969). Editor, Georgetown Law Journal, 1968-1969. Listed in the Best Lawyers in America - Corporate, Securities & M&A Law, 2001-2006. ***PRACTICE AREAS:*** Business Law; Corporate Law; Entrepreneurial Business Law; Financial Services Law; Real Estate. ***Email:*** spowendoff@hahnlaw.com

ANDREW S. POLLIS, born Pittsburgh, Pennsylvania, May 26, 1964; admitted to bar, 1990, Ohio; 1991, U.S. Court of Appeals, Sixth Circuit; 1999, U.S. Court of Appeals, Federal and Seventh Circuits; 2000, U.S. Court of Appeals, Third, Tenth and Eleventh Circuits; 2002, U.S. Supreme Court; 2004, U.S. Court of Appeals, Eighth Circuit. *Education:* Brown University (A.B., magna cum laude, 1986); Harvard Law School (J.D. cum laude, 1990). Phi Beta Kappa. *Member:* Cleveland (Former Secretary, Appellate Courts Committee, Litigation Section), Ohio (Chair, Litigation Section; Founder and Former Chair, Appellate Practice Committee) and American (Executive Board Member, Founding Member and Secretary, Council of Appellate Lawyers, Appellate Judges Conference of Judicial Division; Co-Chair, Membership Committee, Former Co-Chair, Amicus Curiae Briefs Committee and Former Co-Chair, Appellate Practice Committee, Litigation Section) Bar Associations. ***LANGUAGES:*** Italian and French. ***PRACTICE AREAS:*** Litigation; Appellate Practice. ***Email:*** aspollis@hahnlaw.com

LEE D. POWAR, born Cleveland, Ohio, October 2, 1938; admitted to bar, 1963, Ohio; 1989, U.S. Supreme Court. *Education:* Cornell University (B.A., 1960); University of Michigan (J.D., with honors, 1963). Tau Epsilon Rho. Member, Board of Editors, Michigan Law Review, 1962-1963. Listed in The Best Lawyers in America - Banking Law and Bankruptcy and Creditor-Debtor Rights Law, 2004-2005. Co-Author, "Deciphering Conflicts of Interest in Bankruptcy Representation: An Update," Commercial Law Journal, Vol. 105, No. 2, Summer 2000. *Member:* American Bar Association (Business Law Section, Business Bankruptcy Committee; Chairman, Task Forces on Alternative Dispute Resolution in Bankruptcy, 1997-2000 and Pension, Welfare and Labor Issues, 1989-1997, Commercial Financial Services Committee, Ad Hoc Committee on Bankruptcy Court Structure and Insolvency Processes, Dispute Resolution Section); American Law Institute; American Bankruptcy Institute; Association of Commercial Finance Attorneys; Turnaround Management Association: American College of Commercial Finance Lawyers (President, 2005—). ***PRACTICE AREAS:*** Financial Institutions Law; Creditors Rights; Insolvency; Debtor and Creditor Reorganization; Bankruptcy; Business Law; Corporate Law; Real Estate. ***Email:*** ldpowar@hahnlaw.com

RICHARD T. PRASSE, born Cleveland, Ohio, July 17, 1953; admitted to bar, 1981, Ohio. *Education:* Duke University (B.A., 1975); Case Western Reserve University (J.D., 1981). ***PRACTICE AREAS:*** Labor Relations; Employment Law; Employer Liability; Education Law. ***Email:*** rtprasse@hahnlaw.com

ROYCE R. REMINGTON, born Bozeman, Montana, August 14, 1961; admitted to bar, 1988, Ohio; 1989, District of Columbia. *Education:* Rochester Institute of Technology (B.S., 1983); Cleveland-Marshall College of Law (J.D., cum laude, 1988). Managing Editor, Cleveland State Law Review, 1988. Author, "Management's Unilateral Implementation of Drug Testing: Are the Unions Left Holding the Jar?" 36 Clev. St. L.Rev. 29, 1988. *Member:* American Bar Association (Chair, Construction Litigation Committee, 2002-2005; Member, Forum on the Construction Industry); American Arbitration Association (Member, Construction Advisory Council). ***PRACTICE AREAS:*** Construction Law; Commercial Litigation. ***Email:*** rrremington@hahnlaw.com

DENNIS R. ROSE, born Cleveland, Ohio, 1956; admitted to bar, 1987, Ohio. *Education:* Cleveland State University (B.S., cum laude, 1978; J.D., magna cum laude, 1987). Managing Editor, Cleveland State Law Review, 1986-1987. Law Clerk to the Honorable

(This Listing Continued)

HAHN LOESER & PARKS LLP, Cleveland—Continued

Leroy J. Contie, Jr., U.S. Court of Appeals, Sixth Circuit, 1987-1989. Chair, Northern District of Ohio Advisory Group, 1999-2005. Chair, Northern District of Ohio CJRA Rules Committee, 1995-1999. Life Member, Judicial Conference of the U.S. Court of Appeals, Sixth Circuit. *Member:* Cleveland (Member, Litigation Section), Ohio State (Member: Federal Courts Committee; Litigation and Intellectual Property Sections), Federal (Director, Northern District of Ohio Chapter) and American (Member, Litigation Section; Chair, Federal Rules Subcommittee of Pretrial Practice and Discovery Committee) Bar Associations. ***PRACTICE AREAS:*** Litigation; Intellectual Property; Business Law; Corporate Law. ***Email:*** drrose@hahnlaw.com

MICHAEL P. SHUSTER, born Cleveland, Ohio, May 6, 1967; admitted to bar, 1992, Indiana; 1995, Ohio. *Education:* University of Notre Dame (B.B.A., with honors, 1989); Ohio State University Law School (J.D., with honors, 1992). Co-Author, "Deciphering Conflicts of Interest in Bankruptcy Representation: An Update," Commercial Law Journal, Vol. 105, No. 2, Summer 2000. ***PRACTICE AREAS:*** Creditors Rights; Bankruptcy; Insolvency; Secured Transactions. ***Email:*** mpshuster@hahnlaw.com

STEVEN H. SNEIDERMAN, born Cleveland, Ohio, November 4, 1966; admitted to bar, 1991, Ohio. *Education:* Indiana University (B.S., with high distinction, 1988); The Ohio State University (J.D. with honors, 1991). Phi Delta Phi; Beta Alpha Psi; Beta Gamma Sigma; Golden Key; Phi Eta Sigma; Alpha Lambda Delta; Order of the Coif. *Member:* Cleveland Bar Association (Chair, Corporation, Banking and Business Law Section). ***PRACTICE AREAS:*** Business Law; Corporate Law; Entrepreneurial Business Law. ***Email:*** shsneiderman@hahnlaw.com

MARK E. STAIB, born Tiffin, Ohio, January 31, 1948; admitted to bar, 1973, Ohio. *Education:* John Carroll University (A.B., magna cum laude, honors curriculum, 1970); University of Virginia (J.D., 1973). Alpha Sigma Nu; Delta Sigma Rho-Tau Kappa Alpha; Phi Delta Phi. *Member:* American Bar Association (Litigation News: Managing Editor, 1997-1998; Editor-in-Chief, 1998-2000; Co-Chair, Electronic Publishing Committee, 2000-2004; Council Member, 2004—). ***PRACTICE AREAS:*** Litigation; Environmental Law; Environmental Litigation. ***Email:*** mestaib@hahnlaw.com

MARK F. SWARY, admitted to bar, 1973, Ohio. *Education:* St. Joseph's College (B.A., magna cum laude, 1970) Blue Key, 1970; Case Western Reserve University (J.D., 1973). Listed in Best Lawyers in America, Estate Planning and Probate, 2001-02; Trusts and Estates, 2003-04. Member, Tax Incentive Review Council, City of Cleveland, 1989—. Planned Giving Council, Case Western Reserve University (Chairman, 2002-03). Planned Giving Council, Cleveland Orchestra. Planned Giving Council, Cleveland Museum of Art. *Member:* Attorneys for Family-Held Enterprises (Charter Member, Board of Trustees, President-Elect). Fellow, American College of Trust and Estates Counsel. ***PRACTICE AREAS:*** Estate Planning; Trusts and Estates; Probate; Business Law; Corporate Law; Family Business Successions. ***Email:*** mfswary@hahnlaw.com

EDWARD A. WEINSTEIN, born Cleveland, Ohio, January 8, 1959; admitted to bar, 1986, Ohio. *Education:* Miami University (B.S., 1981); Case Western Reserve University (J.D., 1986). Certified Public Accountant, Ohio, 1984. Co-Author: "Tax Issues Facing Healthcare Internal Auditors," Journal of the Association of Healthcare Internal Auditors, Inc., 2004. Author: "U.S. Tax Treatment of Gains and Losses Realized on Foreign Currency Exchange Rate Hedging," Case Western Reserve Journal of International Law, Summer 1986. ***PRACTICE AREAS:*** Taxation; Corporate Law; Business Law; Mergers, Acquisitions and Divestitures; Health Care Law; Nonprofit Institutions. ***Email:*** eweinstein@hahnlaw.com

CRAIG OWEN WHITE, born Cleveland, Ohio, 1957; admitted to bar, 1983, Ohio. *Education:* Williams College (B.A., 1979); University of Virginia (J.D., 1983). Thomas J. Watson Fellow, 1979. Chairman: Golden Age Centers of Greater Cleveland, Inc.; WECO Fund, Inc.; MWV Pinnacle Capital Fund Board of Advisors; Board of Advisors, Shorebridge Capital, Ltd. *Member:* Ohio State (Member, Corporation Law Committee) and American (Member, Committee on Corporate Laws, Section of Business Law) Bar Associations. ***PRACTICE AREAS:*** Business Law; Corporate Governance. ***Email:*** cowhite@hahnlaw.com

OF COUNSEL

M. PATRICIA CULLER, born Mansfield, Ohio, May 24, 1954; admitted to bar, 1985, Ohio; 2002, U.S. Tax Court. *Education:* University of Notre Dame (B.A., 1976), Phi Beta Kappa; University of Iowa (M.A., 1978); Cleveland State University, Cleveland-Marshall College of Law (J.D., 1984). Listed in Best Lawyers in America - Trusts and Estates, 2005-2006. Adjunct Faculty, Cleveland Marshall College of Law, 1995-1996. *Member:* Cleveland (Member, Council of Delegates, Estate Planning, Probate and Trust Law Section) and Ohio State (Member: Section Council, Estate Planning, Probate and Trust Law Section; Estate Planning, Trust and Probate Specialty Board) Bar Associations; Estate Planning Council of Cleveland. Fellow, American College of Trust and Estate Counsel (State Chair, Ohio). (Certified Specialist in Estate Planning, Trust and Probate Law, Ohio State Bar Association). ***PRACTICE AREAS:*** Estate Planning; Business Succession Planning; Probate; Trusts and Estates; Trust Law. ***Email:*** mpculler@hahnlaw.com

JOAN M. GROSS, born Cleveland, Ohio, January 23, 1950; admitted to bar, 1976, Ohio. *Education:* Boston University (B.S., 1972); Case Western Reserve University (J.D., 1976). Order of the Coif. Associate Editor, Case Western Reserve Law Review, 1974-1975. OSBA Board Certified Specialist in Estate Planning, Trust and Probate Law. Listed in Best Lawyers in America - Trusts and Estates, 2005-2006. ***PRACTICE AREAS:*** Estate Planning; Trusts and Estates. ***Email:*** jmgross@hahnlaw.com

RANDY J. HART, born Cleveland, Ohio, December 18, 1963; admitted to bar, 1990, Ohio. *Education:* Ohio State University (B.S., 1986); Cleveland-Marshall College of Law (J.D., magna cum laude, 1990). ***PRACTICE AREAS:*** Litigation; Public Utility Law; Utility Regulation; Regulatory Law; Telecommunications Law; Telecommunications Regulation; Business Law; Corporate Law. ***Email:*** rjhart@hahnlaw.com

N. HERSCHEL KOBLENZ, born Albany, New York, November 19, 1934; admitted to bar, 1960, New York and Ohio. *Education:* Cornell University (A.B., 1956); Yale University (J.D., 1960). Phi Alpha Delta; Tau Epsilon Rho; Order of the Coif. Editor, Yale Law Journal, 1957-1960. Chairman, Cleveland Tax Institute, 1975. Listed in the Best Lawyers in America - Tax Law, 2001-2002, 2003-2004. ***PRACTICE AREAS:*** Taxation; Business Law; Corporate Law. ***Email:*** nhkoblenz@hahnlaw.com

BARBARA H. LEVINE, born Philadelphia, Pennsylvania, April 4, 1950; admitted to bar, 1977, Maryland; 1978, District of Columbia; 2004, Ohio. *Education:* Douglass College (B.A., in History, 1972); Temple University (J.D., 1977). Recipient, American Jurisprudence Award for excellent achievement in Trusts and Estates. Member, Baltimore Estate Planning Council Board, 1996-1997; Co-Chairman, Programming Committee, Baltimore Association for Financial Planning, Inc., 1996-1997. Member, Cleveland Estate Planning Council. *Member:* The District of Columbia Bar. ***PRACTICE AREAS:*** Estate Planning. ***Email:*** blevine@hahnlaw.com

HARRY D. MERCER, born Coos Bay, Oregon, July 31, 1942; admitted to bar, 1967, Ohio. *Education:* University of Pennsylvania (B.A., 1964; LL.B., cum laude, 1967). Member, Board of Editors, University of Pennsylvania Law Review, 1965-1967. Listed in the Best Lawyers in America - Corporate Law. *Member:* Ohio State (Chair, Committee on Business Courts, 1994-1999) Bar Association and Legal Committee of the Equipment Leasing Association, 1999-2002; American Law Institute. ***PRACTICE AREAS:*** Business Law; Commercial Law; Corporate Law; Equipment Leasing. ***Email:*** hdmercer@hahnlaw.com

COUNSEL

ROBERT A. COOPER, born Schenectady, New York, July 8, 1970; admitted to bar, 1997, Ohio;1998, Georgia. *Education:* University of Hartford (B.A., cum laude, 1992); Cleveland Marshall College of Law (J.D., magna cum laude, 1997). Author, "Blinded by the Hype: Shifting the Burden When Manufacturers Engage in Direct Consumer Advertising of Prescription Drugs," 21 Vermont Law Review 1073 (1997). ***PRACTICE AREAS:*** Business Law; Corporate Law; Corporate Finance; Technology Licensing. ***Email:*** racooper@hahnlaw.com

NEIL K. EVANS, born Harbor Creek, Pennsylvania, November 22, 1936; admitted to bar, 1964, Ohio; U.S. Supreme Court; U.S. Court of Appeals, District of Columbia and Sixth Circuits; U.S. District Court, Northern and Southern Districts of Ohio. *Education:* University of Rochester (B.A., History, with honors, 1958); University of Pennsylvania (LL.B., 1964). *Member:* Cleveland, Ohio State and American Bar Associations; American Arbitration Association (Commercial Panel). ***PRACTICE AREAS:*** Mediation; Arbitration. ***Email:*** nkevans@hahnlaw.com

ASSOCIATES

CATHERINE V. ANDREWS, born May 4, 1973; admitted to bar, 1999, Ohio. *Education:* Tulane University (B.A., 1996); Case Western Reserve University (J.D., 1999). ***PRACTICE AREAS:*** Corporate and Securities. ***Email:*** candrews@hahnlaw.com

SEAN M. ANSBERRY, born Cleveland, Ohio, March 23, 1973; admitted to bar, 1999, Ohio. *Education:* Miami University (B.S., 1995); University of Cincinnati College of Law (J.D., 1999). ***PRACTICE AREAS:*** Business Litigation. ***Email:*** smansberry@hahnlaw.com

CHRISTOPHER S.W. BLAKE, born Cleveland, Ohio, July 25, 1970; admitted to bar, 1999, Ohio. *Education:* University of Missouri-Columbia (B.A., 1992; B.J., 1992; M.A., 1994); Cleveland-Marshall College of Law (J.D., summa cum laude, 1999). ***LANGUAGES:*** Spanish. ***PRACTICE AREAS:*** Business Law; Corporate Law; Mergers and Acquisitions; Commercial Finance; International Law. ***Email:*** cswblake@hahnlaw.com

DOUGLAS E. BLOOM, born Beachwood, Ohio, October 3, 1973; admitted to bar, 2001, Ohio. *Education:* The Ohio State University (B.A., 1996); Cleveland-Marshall College of Law (J.D., cum laude, 2001). Formerly with Charles Kampinski Co. LPA. *Member:* Cleveland Bar Association; Cleveland Academy of Trial Lawyers. ***PRACTICE AREAS:*** Litigation. ***Email:*** dbloom@hahnlaw.com

ROCCO I. DEBITETTO, born August 28, 1976; admitted to bar, 2001, Ohio; U.S. District Court, Northern and Southern Districts of Ohio; U.S. Court of Appeals, Sixth Circuit. *Education:* University of Dayton (B.A., 1998); University of Cincinnati (J.D., 2001). ***PRACTICE AREAS:*** Bankruptcy; Creditors Rights; Commercial Litigation; Restructuring. ***Email:*** ridebitetto@hahnlaw.com

DEREK E. DIAZ, born February 18, 1973; admitted to bar, 1998, Ohio. *Education:* John Carroll University (B.A., magna cum laude, 1995); The Ohio State University (J.D., 1998). ***PRACTICE AREAS:*** Creditors' Rights; Bankruptcy; Litigation. ***Email:*** ddiaz@hahnlaw.com

ROBERT J. DIAZ, born Boston, Massachusetts, 1965; admitted to bar, 1993, Wisconsin; 1994, Illinois; 2004, Ohio; U.S. District Court, Northern and Southern Districts of Ohio; U.S. District Court, Eastern and Western Districts of Wisconsin; registered to practice before U.S. Patent and Trademark Office. *Education:* University of New Hampshire (B.A., 1987); University of Wisconsin-Madison (J.D., 1993). *Member:* Cleveland Intellectual Property Law Association; American Intellectual Property Law Association. ***LANGUAGES:*** Japanese. ***REPORTED CASES:*** State v. Harris, 206 Wis. 2d 243, 557 N.W. 2d 245 (1996). ***PRACTICE AREAS:*** Intellectual Property Litigation; Intellectual Property Prosecution; International Law. ***Email:*** rjdiaz@hahnlaw.com

PASQUALE DIMASSA, JR., born December 19, 1975; admitted to bar, 2001, Ohio. *Education:* Baldwin-Wallace College (B.A., 1998); Case Western Reserve University (J.D., 2001). ***PRACTICE AREAS:*** Litigation. ***Email:*** pdimassa@hahnlaw.com

ARTHUR E. GIBBS, III, born Canton, Ohio, May 1, 1969; admitted to bar, 1996, Ohio. *Education:* Fordham University (B.A., cum laude, 1991); Case Western Reserve University (J.D., cum laude, 1996). ***PRACTICE AREAS:*** Trusts and Estates; Employee Benefits; Probate Administration; Fiduciary Litigation. ***Email:*** aegibbs@hahnlaw.com

DAWN T. HAYNES, born March 1, 1974; admitted to bar, 2001, Ohio. *Education:* Case Western Reserve University (B.S., 1997); Cleveland-Marshall College of Law (J.D., 2001). ***PRACTICE AREAS:*** Litigation; Trademark Litigation; Trademark Prosecution. ***Email:*** dthaynes@hahnlaw.com

(This Listing Continued)

HERBERT HOTCHKISS, born Jamestown, New York, 1970; admitted to bar, 1996, Ohio. *Education:* Bob Jones University (B.A., cum laude, 1992); Cleveland-Marshall College of Law (J.D., cum laude, 1996); Case Western Reserve School of Law (LL.M., in Taxation, 1998). ***Email:*** hhotchkiss@hahnlaw.com

ERIC B. LEVASSEUR, born Rochester, Michigan, October 17, 1976; admitted to bar, 2002, Ohio and U.S. District Court, Northern and Southern Districts of Ohio; U.S. District Court, Eastern District of Michigan; U.S. Court of Appeals, Sixth Circuit. *Education:* Colgate University (B.A., 1999); Case Western Reserve University (J.D., 2002). ***PRACTICE AREAS:*** Litigation. ***Email:*** eblevasseur@hahnlaw.com

YURI R. LINETSKY, admitted to bar, 2000, Ohio and U.S. District Court, Northern District of Ohio; 2001, U.S. District Court, Southern District of Ohio; 2003, U.S. Court of Appeals, Third Circuit; 2004, U.S. Court of Appeals, Sixth Circuit. *Education:* Case Western Reserve University (B.A., 1997; J.D., magna cum laude, 2000). ***LANGUAGES:*** Russian. ***PRACTICE AREAS:*** Litigation. ***Email:*** yrlinetsky@hahnlaw.com

BRADLEY C. LINK, born March 7, 1972; admitted to bar, 2004, Ohio. *Education:* Evangel University (B.A., 1995); Cleveland-Marshall College of Law (J.D., 2004). ***PRACTICE AREAS:*** Real Estate Law; Business Law; Non-Profit Law; Corporate and Securities. ***Email:*** blink@hahnlaw.com

JAMES W. MAY, born December 9, 1976; admitted to bar, 2004, Ohio. *Education:* University of the South (B.A., 1999); University of North Carolina (J.D., 2004). ***PRACTICE AREAS:*** Business; Corporate and Securities. ***Email:*** jmay@hahnlaw.com

CHRISTOPHER W. PEER, admitted to bar, 2003, Ohio. *Education:* Ohio Wesleyan University (B.A., 1994); Cleveland Marshall College of Law (J.D., magna cum laude, 1993). ***PRACTICE AREAS:*** Bankruptcy; Creditors Rights. ***Email:*** cpeer@hahnlaw.com

ROBERT B. PORT, born October 29, 1966; admitted to bar, 2004, Ohio. *Education:* Drexel University (B.S., 1989); The Catholic University of America (M.S., 1994); Case Western Reserve University School of Law (J.D., cum laude, 2004). ***PRACTICE AREAS:*** Litigation. ***Email:*** rport@hahnlaw.com

SONJA C. RICE, born September 21, 1970; admitted to bar, 2001, Ohio. *Education:* Oberlin College (B.A., 1992); Case Western Reserve University (J.D., 2001). Co-Author, "A Modest Expansion of the Attorney-Client Privilege Relating to Patent Opinions," Intellectual Property & Technology Law Journal, May 2002. ***LANGUAGES:*** German and Indonesian. ***PRACTICE AREAS:*** Litigation; Construction Law; Appellate Practice.

STEVEN E. SEASLY, born Willard, Ohio, December 13, 1970; admitted to bar, 1999, Ohio; U.S. District Court, Northern District of Ohio. *Education:* Bowling Green State University (B.S., magna cum laude, 1993); Cleveland-Marshall College of Law (J.D., magna cum laude, 1998). ***PRACTICE AREAS:*** Labor and Employment; Litigation. ***Email:*** sseasly@hahnlaw.com

CATHRYN A. SUSSMAN, born Cleveland, Ohio, January 18, 1970; admitted to bar, 1998, Ohio. *Education:* Ohio University (B.S., summa cum laude, 1992); Cleveland Marshall College of Law (J.D., magna cum laude, 1998). ***PRACTICE AREAS:*** Business Law; Corporate Law; Mergers and Acquisitions; Intellectual Property. ***Email:*** casussman@hahnlaw.com

JONI TODD, born May 11, 1974; admitted to bar, 2005, Ohio. *Education:* Cleveland State University (B.A., summa cum laude, 2001); Cleveland-Marshall College of Law (J.D., summa cum laude, 2005). ***PRACTICE AREAS:*** Litigation. ***Email:*** jtodd@hahnlaw.com

NANCY A. VALENTINE, admitted to bar, 1998, Ohio; U.S. District Court, Northern and Southern Districts of Ohio. *Education:* Vanderbilt University (B.A., cum laude, 1994); The Ohio State University (J.D., 1998). *Member:* Ohio State Bar Association; American Bankruptcy Institute; International Women's Insolvency and Restructuring Confederation. ***PRACTICE AREAS:*** Creditors Rights; Bankruptcy Chapter 11; Business Reorganization; Insolvency; Litigation. ***Email:*** navalentine@hahnlaw.com

CHRISTOPHER B. WICK, born Mayfield Heights, Ohio, May 4, 1975; admitted to bar, 2000, Ohio. *Education:* Washington & Lee University (B.A., Print Journalism and European History, 1997; J.D., 2000). ***PRACTICE AREAS:*** Debtor and Creditor Reorganization; Creditors Rights in Bankruptcy; Litigation. ***Email:*** cwick@hahnlaw.com

ANN C. ZIEGLER, born June 5, 1977; admitted to bar, 2003, Ohio. *Education:* John Carroll University (B.A., 1999); Cleveland-Marshall College of Law (J.D., summa cum laude, 2003). ***PRACTICE AREAS:*** Business Law. ***Email:*** aziegler@hahnlaw.com

COLUMBUS, OHIO
RESIDENT MEMBERS

Stephen E. Chappelear
Marc J. Kessler
Thomas J. Riley
Arland T. Stein
Jeffrey W. Stiltner

RESIDENT ASSOCIATES

Julie E. Brigner
Dawn-Rae Grauel
Anthony J. Miller
Erica K. Williams
Jeffrey A. Yeager

AKRON, OHIO
RESIDENT MEMBERS

R. Eric Gaum
Scott M. Oldham
Mark A. Watkins

RESIDENT OF COUNSEL

Louis F. Kreek, Jr.

RESIDENT ASSOCIATES

Robert J. Clark
W. Edward Crooks
John J. Cunniff
Bret A. Hrivnak
Michael H. Minns
Amanda H. Wilcox

(This Listing Continued)

BONITA SPRINGS, FLORIDA
RESIDENT MEMBERS

Jeffrey M. Folkman
Kim M. Hastings
Andrew J. Krause (Not admitted in OH; Board Certified Wills, Trusts and Estates Lawyer, Florida Bar Board of Legal Specialization and Education)

RESIDENT ASSOCIATE

Starling N. Hendriks

REPRESENTATIVE CLIENTS: Aetna, Inc.; American General Finance, Inc.; Bank of America/Fleet Financial; Bechtel; Biotronik; BMW Financial Services; The CIT Group; Cargill, Inc.; Case Western Reserve University; Cendant; Cleveland-Cliffs Inc; The Cleveland Museum of Art; Corrpro Companies, Inc,; Country Pure Foods; Davel Communications, Inc.; Exxon Mobil Corporation; First Union Real Estate Investments; Great Lakes Cheese; Head USA; Homewood Homes; Hugo Boss USA; Imperial Parking Corporation; Jacobs Entertainment, Inc.; Johnson Controls, Inc.; Liberty Bank, NA; Monsanto; Moosehead Breweries Ltd.; Myers Industries; Notre Dame College of Ohio; The Ohio State University; OM Group, Inc.; Paro Services, Inc.; ProQuest; Standard Parking; Safeco; Textron Financial; TransTechnology Corporation; University of Akron; U.S. Bancorp.

(For complete biographical data on Columbus, Ohio personnel, see Professional Biographies at Columbus, Ohio)
(For complete biographical data on Akron, Ohio personnel, see Professional Biographies at Akron, Ohio)

MICHAEL P. HARVEY CO., L.P.A.

Established in 1994

311 NORTHCLIFF DRIVE
CLEVELAND, OHIO 44116-1344
Telephone: 440-356-9108
Fax: 440-356-9128
Email: mpharveyco@aol.com

Small Business, Employment, Commercial Litigation and Trade Secrets, Labor and Employment, Business Law, Litigation, Unfair Competition, Corporate, Civil Rights, Commercial Law, Computers and Software, Contracts, Disabilities, Franchises and Franchising, Trial and Appellate.

MICHAEL P. HARVEY, born Worcester, Massachusetts, August 7, 1957; admitted to bar, 1987, Ohio; 1988, U.S. Court of Appeals, Sixth Circuit; U.S. District Court, Northern District of Ohio; 2001, U.S. Supreme Court. *Education:* Worcester State College (B.S., 1980); University of Hartford (M.Ed., 1982); Cleveland Marshall College of Law (J.D., 1987). Articles Editor, 1986-1987, Cleveland-Marshall Law Review. Arbitrator, AAA, Commercial/Construction Panel, 1995—. Adjunct Professor, Cleveland-Marshall College of Law, 1988—. Law Clerk to Chief Judge John F. Ray, U.S. Bankruptcy Court, N.D. Ohio, 1987-1988. Extern to Judge Alice Batchelder, U.S. District Court, N.D. Ohio, 1987. Arbitrator, Cuyahoga County, Common Pleas Court, 1993—. Chair, Employment Law Practice and Procedure Seminar, Cleveland Bar Association, 1992-1999. Chair, Cleveland Bar Association, Practice and Procedure Clinic (1992-1995). Co-Chair, Cleveland Bar Labor and Employment Seminar, 2000-2002. Member: COSE Leadership Council (1994-1997); Rocky River Planning Commission, (Chair, 1996—). Trustee, Cleveland-Marshall Law Alumni Association, 2000—. Frequent speaker on labor and business issues. *Member:* Cleveland (Chair, Employment and Labor Law Section, 2001-2002; Chair, Unauthorized Practice of Law Committee) and Ohio State (Member, Business and Litigation Committee) Bar Associations. ***PRACTICE AREAS:*** Antitrust; Trade Regulation; Appellate Practice; Business Law; Civil Practice; Commercial Law; Computers and Software; Corporate Law; Employee Benefits; Franchises and Franchising; Intellectual Property; Labor and Employment; Leases and Leasing; Litigation; Trade Secrets; Trademarks. ***Email:*** mpharveyco@aol.com

HENKIN & SEEWALD

1220 W. 6TH STREET, SUITE 205
CLEVELAND, OHIO 44113
Telephone: 216-781-8288
Fax: 216-781-1273
Email: howardhenkin2@aol.com
URL: http://www.henkinandseewald.com

Estate Planning, Wills and Trusts, Insurance, Medical Malpractice, Probate and Liquor Law.

MEMBERS OF FIRM

HOWARD A. HENKIN, born 1945; admitted to bar, 1971, Ohio. *Education:* Case Western Reserve University (A.B., 1967; J.D., 1970). ***PRACTICE AREAS:*** Real Estate; Probate; Business Law; Estate Planning; Wills; Trust Law; Liquor Liability. ***Email:*** howardhenkin2@aol.com

J. GARY SEEWALD, born 1946; admitted to bar, 1971, Ohio. *Education:* Case Western Reserve University (A.B., 1968; J.D., 1971). ***LANGUAGES:*** German. ***PRACTICE AREAS:*** Personal Injury; Criminal Law; Insurance; Medical Malpractice; Wills; Probate. ***Email:*** PRLodge@mindspring.com

MICHAEL C. HENNENBERG

LANDERBROOK CORPORATE CENTER
5910 LANDERBROOK DRIVE, SUITE 200
CLEVELAND, OHIO 44124-6500
Telephone: 440-544-2000
Fax: 440-544-2002
Email: Hennenberg@aol.com
URL: http://www.hennenberg.com

Criminal Defense, Trial and Appellate Practice, State and Federal Courts, White Collar Defense, Health Care Fraud, Antitrust Defense, Regulatory Investigations, Tax Fraud, Complex Civil Fraud, Attorney Discipline, Legal Malpractice Defense.

MICHAEL C. HENNENBERG, born September 23, 1948; admitted to bar, 1974, Ohio and U.S. District Court, Northern District of Ohio; 1977, U.S. Court of Appeals, Sixth Circuit; 1978, U.S. Supreme Court. *Education:* The Ohio State University (B.S., Business Administration, 1970); Case Western Reserve University; Cleveland State University (J.D., 1974). Certified by the Ohio Supreme Court Committee on the Appointment of Counsel for Indigent Defendant's in Capital Cases. Author: "An Analysis of R.C. 2951.041 - Drug Treatment In Lieu of Conviction," Vol. 1, Issue 5 Criminal Law Journal of Ohio; "Conducting a Defense Jury Voir Dire Through the Judge in Federal District Court". Co-Authored, with Mark R. DeVan: "The Champion," Official Publication of National Association of Criminal Defense Lawyers, Vol. II, No. 2, March 1987. Lecturer: "A Practitioner's Guide to Professionalism, Ethics and Substance Abuse," Lorman Education Services, 2000-2004, "Plea Negotiations, " The Ohio State Bar Association CLE Institute, 2000; "Litigation Essentials: Talking to the Jury," Cleveland Marshall Law Alumni Association, 1996; "Pleading and Practice in White Collar Cases," Ohio Association of Criminal Defense Lawyer's Defense of White Collar Criminal Cases, 1992. *Member:* Cleveland Bar Association (Member: Board of Trustees, 1985-1988; Criminal Law Committee; Past Chairman, 1981-1982; Criminal Law Committee, 1974—; Legislative Liaison, 1983-1986; Steering Committee of Task Force on Violent Crime; Co-Chairman, Robbery Sub Task Force, 1982); National Association of Criminal Defense Lawyers; Ohio Association of Criminal Defense Attorneys (Charter Member, Board of Directors, 1986—); Ohio State and American Bar Associations. American Board of Criminal Lawyers. (Certified as a Criminal Trial Advocacy Specialist by the National Board of Trial Advocacy). ***REPORTED CASES:*** Lake Cty. Bar Assn. v. Donald Ezzone, 102 Ohio St. 3d 79 (Supreme Court of Ohio 2004); James Samuel Sims v. Ted Engle, 619 F.2d 598 (United States Court of Appeals, 6th Circuit, 1980) cert. denied, 67 L.Ed.2d 374 (United States Supreme Court, 1981); Pepper Pike v. Doe, 66 Ohio St. 2d 374 (Supreme Court of Ohio, 1981); State of Ohio v. Thomas Pearson, 62 Ohio St. 2d 291 (Supreme Court of Ohio, 1980); State of Ohio v. Lee, et. al., 48 Ohio St.2d 208 (Supreme Court of Ohio, 1976); State of Ohio v. Robert Cornell, 72 OOp.2d 428 (Cuyahoga County Common Pleas Court, 1975). ***PRACTICE AREAS:*** Criminal Defense; White Collar Criminal Defense; Health Care Fraud; Antitrust; Regulatory Investigations; Tax Fraud; Civil Fraud; Attorney Discipline; Legal Malpractice Defense.

JOHN A. FATICA, born Cleveland, Ohio, August 29, 1963; admitted to bar, 1991, Ohio; 1992, U.S. District Court, Northern District of Ohio and U.S. Court of Appeals, Sixth Circuit; 1999, U.S. Supreme Court. *Education:* Miami University (B.S. accounting, 1985); Cleveland Marshall College of Law (J.D., cum laude, 1991). Assistant Cuyahoga County Public Defender, 1991-1996, Cleveland. ***REPORTED CASES:*** State of Ohio v. Goodlow (1992), 84 App. 3d 529; Akron Bar Association v. Thomas (1999), 84 Ohio St. 3d 395; Lake County Bar Association v. Donald Ezzone, 102 Ohio St. 3d 79. ***Email:*** john@fatica.com

HENRETTA LAW OFFICES

CLEVELAND, OHIO

(See Akron)

Medical Malpractice, Legal Malpractice, Nursing Home Litigation, Insurance Litigation, Automobile Accidents and Injuries and Wrongful Death.

HERMANN, CAHN & SCHNEIDER, LLP

SUITE 500, 1301 EAST NINTH STREET
CLEVELAND, OHIO 44114
Telephone: 216-781-5515
Facsimile: 216-781-1030
Email: hcs@hcsattys.com
Email: hcs@en.com
URL: http://www.hcsattys.com

General Practice, Civil Litigation in all Courts. Complex Litigation, Trial Practice, Asbestos Litigation, Insurance Defense, Products Liability, Environmental, Employment and Trade Practice Litigation, Personal Injury Law, Domestic Relations, Corporate and Business Law, Securities Law, Fidelity and Surety Law, Franchise Law, Taxation, Pension and Profit Sharing Law.

FIRM PROFILE: Hermann, Cahn & Schneider is a law firm specializing in legal representation which requires aggressive advocacy skills and creative approaches to legal problem solving. The firm's litigation clients include Fortune 500 companies, insurance companies, financial institutions, and individuals who have suffered personal injuries or economic loss. In the area of business transactions and representation, the firm's clientele consists of a variety of privately owned enterprises, professional practices and service businesses.

MEMBERS OF FIRM

GARY D. HERMANN, born Cleveland, Ohio, September 20, 1946; admitted to bar, 1971, Ohio; 2005, Montana. *Education:* Hiram College (B.A., 1968); Northwestern University (J.D., 1971). Associate Editor, Northwestern University Journal of Criminal Law, 1970-1971. Author: "The Consumer Expectation Test: Application of a Difficult Standard for Determining Defects," Federation of Insurance and Corporate Counsel Quarterly, Winter, 1991; "Use of Consent Judgment in Insurance Coverage Disputes," Defense Research Institute's For the Defense, 1982. *Member:* Greater Cleveland and Ohio State Bar Associations; Federation of Insurance and Corporate Counsel (Vice Chairman, Products Liability Section); Defense Research Institute (Member, Industrywide Litigation Committee). (Also Member, Axiom Law Group, PLLC, Big Sky, Montana). ***PRACTICE AREAS:*** Products Liability Law; Toxic Torts; Insurance Defense; Environmental Litigation. ***Email:*** ghermann@hcsattys.com

JAMES S. CAHN, born Cleveland, Ohio, April 16, 1946; admitted to bar, 1973, Ohio. *Education:* University of Pennsylvania (B.A., 1968); The Ohio State University (J.D., 1973). *Member:* Greater Cleveland, Cuyahoga (Chairman, Family Law Section, 1990-1991), Ohio State and American (Member, Family Law Section) Bar Associations. Fellow, American Academy of Matrimonial Lawyers (Qualified Divorce Arbitrator through Matrimonial Arbitration Training Program). ***PRACTICE AREAS:*** Domestic Relations Law; Family Law; Custody Law; Civil Litigation. ***Email:*** jcahn@hcsattys.com

KENT B. SCHNEIDER, born Cleveland, Ohio, November 12, 1951; admitted to bar, 1976, Pennsylvania and New Jersey; 1978, Ohio. *Education:* The Ohio State University (B.A., 1973); Rutgers University School of Law (J.D., 1976). *Member:* Celebrezze Inn of Court (Barrister); Cleveland Academy of Trial Attorneys (Director). ***PRACTICE AREAS:*** Plaintiffs Trial Practice; Personal Injury Law; Complex Litigation; Business Litigation. ***Email:*** kschneider@hcsattys.com

ANTHONY J. HARTMAN, born Cleveland, Ohio, January 6, 1943; admitted to bar, 1968, Ohio. *Education:* The Ohio State University (B.S., 1965); Case Western Reserve University (J.D., 1968). Order of the Coif. *Member:* Greater Cleveland (Member, Securities Law Committee) and American Bar Associations. ***PRACTICE AREAS:*** Complex Litigation; Environmental Litigation; Securities Litigation; Business Litigation. ***Email:*** ahartman@hcsattys.com

ROBERT WARREN, JR., born Cleveland, Ohio, August 22, 1949; admitted to bar, 1974, Ohio; 1975, District of Columbia. *Education:* The Ohio State University (B.S., cum laude, 1971; J.D., 1974). Beta Gamma Sigma; Phi Alpha Kappa; Phi Eta Sigma. Attorney, Division of Market Regulation, Securities and Exchange Commission, Washington, D.C., 1974-1978. *Member:* Greater Cleveland (Member, Securities Law Institute Committee, 1992-1993) and American Bar Associations. ***PRACTICE AREAS:*** Corporate Law; Securities Law; Real Estate-Commercial Law. ***Email:*** rwarren@hcsattys.com

KERRY S. VOLSKY, born Tucson, Arizona, January 19, 1954; admitted to bar, 1980, Ohio. *Education:* Kent State University (B.A., magna cum laude, 1976); Case Western Reserve University (J.D., 1980). *Member:* Greater Cleveland and Ohio State Bar Associations. ***PRACTICE AREAS:*** Personal Injury Litigation; Toxic Tort Litigation; Medical Malpractice. ***Email:*** kvolsky@hcsattys.com

PETER J. KREMBS, born Madison, Wisconsin, December 12, 1944; admitted to bar, 1973, Ohio. *Education:* University of Wisconsin (B.S., 1968); Case Western Reserve University (J.D., 1973). *Member:* Greater Cleveland, Ohio State and American Bar Associations; The Association of Trial Lawyers of America; Defense Research Institute. ***PRACTICE AREAS:*** Insurance Defense Litigation; Commercial Litigation; Real Estate; Corporate Law; Business Law. ***Email:*** pkrembs@hcsattys.com

JAY H. SALAMON, born Cleveland, Ohio, May 9, 1954; admitted to bar, 1980, Ohio. *Education:* Kent State University (B.A., magna cum laude, 1977); Case Western Reserve University (J.D., 1980). Pi Sigma Alpha. *Member:* Greater Cleveland and Ohio State Bar Associations. ***PRACTICE AREAS:*** Securities Litigation; Commercial Litigation; Legal Research. ***Email:*** jsalamon@hcsattys.com

HUNTER S. HAVENS, born Cleveland, Ohio, December 6, 1954; admitted to bar, 1984, Ohio and U.S. District Court, Northern District of Ohio. *Education:* Case Western Reserve University (B.A., cum laude, 1980); Cleveland-Marshall College of Law (J.D., 1984). ***PRACTICE AREAS:*** Products Liability; Litigation; Insurance Defense; Construction Law; Employment Litigation; Personal Injury; Appellate Practice. ***Email:*** hhavens@hcsattys.com

HUGH D. BERKSON, born Cleveland, Ohio, September 10, 1968; admitted to bar, 1994, Ohio; 1996, U.S. District Court, Northern District of Ohio. *Education:* University of Texas (B.B.A., 1989); Case Western Reserve University (J.D., 1994). Member, Order of the Barristers. Recipient: American Jurisprudence Award, National Mock Trial, 1993; Jonathan M. Ault Mock Trial Prize, 1993-1994. Adjunct Associate Professor of Law, Mock Trial, Case Western Reserve University School of Law, 1995—. *Member:* Cleveland and Ohio State Bar Associations. ***PRACTICE AREAS:*** Civil Litigation; Commercial Law; Business Law. ***Email:*** hberkson@hcsattys.com

HEIDI P. CHYLLA, born Boston, Massachusetts, January 1, 1969; admitted to bar, 1993, Georgia; 1994, U.S. District Court, Northern District of Georgia and U.S. Court of Appeals, Eleventh Circuit; 1998, U.S. Court of Appeals, Sixth Circuit; 1999, Ohio. *Education:* University of Georgia (B.A., cum laude, 1990); Nova Southeastern University (J.D., 1993). *Member:* Cleveland, Ohio State and American Bar Associations; State Bar of Georgia; Ohio Women's Bar Association; Cuyahoga County Arbitration Panel. ***PRACTICE AREAS:*** Insurance Defense; Commercial Litigation; Products Liability. ***Email:*** hchylla@hcsattys.com

ASSOCIATES

JEFFREY S. MOELLER, born Cincinnati, Ohio, August 22, 1965; admitted to bar, 1989, Alaska; 2002, Ohio. *Education:* Miami University (B.A., magna cum laude, 1986); University of North Carolina at Chapel Hill (J.D., with honors, 1989). Member, Order of the Coif. Appellate Law Clerk, Alaska Supreme Court, Anchorage, Alaska, 1989-1990. Author: "Transnational Movement of People in a Post 9/11 World," World Trade Center (Cleveland) Quarterly Newsletter, Cleveland, OH (2002). Panel Member: "Habeas Corpus and Other Remedies in Federal Court," American Immigration Lawyers' Association National Conference, Chicago, IL (2000); "Update on Removal Defense and Federal Litigation," Northeast Ohio Federal Bar Association Immigration Conference, Cleveland, OH (2001). Speaker: "Alternative Routes to Employment-Based Permanent Residency; Are the Service Centers Adjudicating Petitions According to the Same Philosophy?" Northeast

(This Listing Continued)

Ohio Federal Bar Association Immigration Conference, Cleveland, OH (2001); "2001-02 Changes to Immigration Policies and their Effect of the Flow of International Trade," Ohio Foreign Commerce Association, Cleveland, OH (2002). Book Review: H. Zheng, *Legal Structure of the International Textile Trade* 14 N.C. J.Int'l L. & Com. Reg. 519 (Fall 1989). *Member:* American Immigration Lawyers Association, Ohio State and Cleveland Bar Association. ***LANGUAGES:*** French. ***REPORTED CASES:*** Gallo-Alvarez v. Ashcroft, 266 F.3d 1123 (9th Cir. 2001); Meng Li v. I.N.S., 259 F.3d 1132 (9th Cir. 2001); Andrade v. State of Alaska, Dept. of Revenue, 23 P.3d 58 (Alaska 2001); Said v. Eddy, 87 F.Supp.2d 937 (D. Alaska 2000); Hinojosa-Perez v. Eddy, 55 F.Supp.2d 1001 (D. Alaska 1999); Neal & Company, Inc. v. City of Dillingham, 923 P.2d 89 (Alaska 1996); Katmailand, Inc. v. Lake and Peninsula Borough, 904 P.2d 397 (Alaska 1995); City of Dillingham v. CH2M Hill Northwest, Inc., 873 P.2d 1271 (Alaska 1994). ***PRACTICE AREAS:*** Civil Litigation; Immigration Law. ***Email:*** jmoeller@hcsattys.com

JONETTA J. KAPUSTA-DOROGI, born Cleveland, Ohio, April 1, 1963; admitted to bar, 1992, Ohio. *Education:* Case Western Reserve University (B.A., 1985); Cleveland Marshall College of Law (J.D., 1989). Delta Theta Phi. *Member:* Cleveland, Cuyahoga County and Ohio State Bar Associations. ***PRACTICE AREAS:*** Domestic Relations. ***Email:*** kapusta-dorogi@hcsattys.com

MICHAEL D. BRENNAN, born Erie, Pennsylvania, August 9, 1971; admitted to bar, 1996, Ohio; 1997, U.S. District Court, Northern District of Ohio. *Education:* Bowling Green State University (B.A., 1993); Cleveland-Marshall College of Law (J.D., 1996). Pi Sigma Alpha. Omicron Delta Kappa. Member, Cleveland-Marshall Law Review. *Member:* Cleveland and Ohio State Bar Associations. ***PRACTICE AREAS:*** Litigation; Business Law; Personal Injury; Labor and Employment. ***Email:*** mbrennan@hcsattys.com

JAMES L. LANE, born Akron, Ohio, April 9, 1973; admitted to bar, 1999, Ohio. *Education:* Ohio University (B.B.A., cum laude, 1995); University of Akron (J.D., 1998). *Member:* Akron, Cleveland and Ohio State Bar Associations. ***PRACTICE AREAS:*** Domestic Relations; Family Law; Child Custody. ***Email:*** jlane@hcsattys.com

JANE K. CONRAD, born Cleveland, Ohio; admitted to bar, 2000, Ohio. *Education:* Kent State University (B.A., 1980); Akron University Law School (J.D., cum laude, 2000). Recipient, Honorable Arthur J. Goldberg Prize in Constitutional Law. Member, Akron Law Review. *Member:* Cleveland and Ohio State Bar Associations. ***PRACTICE AREAS:*** Insurance Defense; Personal Injury; Products Liability; Premises Liability; Commercial Litigation; Contract Litigation. ***Email:*** jconrad@hcsattys.com

ALICIA L. MAZZI, born Youngstown, Ohio, April 1, 1977; admitted to bar, 2002, Ohio. *Education:* John Carroll University (B.A., 1999); Case Western Reserve University (J.D., 2002). Phi Delta Phi. Member, Northern Italian American Foundation. *Member:* Ohio State, Cleveland and Cuyahoga County Bar Associations.

OF COUNSEL

CHARLES KAMPINSKI, born Neustadt-Holstein, Germany, April 2, 1947; admitted to bar, 1974, Ohio and U.S. District Court, Northern District of Ohio. *Education:* The Ohio State University (B.A., 1970; J.D., 1974). Member, Ohio State Law Journal, 1973-1974. *Member:* Cuyahoga County and Ohio State Bar Associations; The Association of Trial Lawyers of America (Sustaining Member); Cleveland Association of Civil Trial Attorneys. ***PRACTICE AREAS:*** Negligence; Insurance; Products Liability; Medical Malpractice; Business Law.

HENRY V. KERR, admitted to bar, 1963, Ohio. *Education:* University of Nebraska at Lincoln (B.A.); St. John's University (LL.B.). ***PRACTICE AREAS:*** Securities (90%).

REPRESENTATIVE CLIENTS: Allen-Bradley Co.; Rockwell International; Fleetwood Enterprises, Inc.; Skyline Corporation; The Marmon Group; Novartis Pharmaceuticals, Inc.; Pfizer Inc.; ABM, Inc.; Greyhound Lines, Inc.; Old Dominion Freight Lines; FedEx; Saks Fifth Avenue, Inc.; Van Dorn DeMag Corporation; Ingersoll-Rand Corp.
INSURANCE CLIENTS: Penn National Insurance Co.; Hastings Mutual Insurance Co.; Liberty Mutual Insurance Co.; Western General Management, Inc.; Allstate Insurance Co.; Farmers Insurance Companies; Commercial Union Insurance Co.; Acuity; Crawford & Co.; Royal & SunAlliance.

JOHN V. HEUTSCHE CO., LPA

Established in 1973

310 LAKESIDE AVENUE W., SUITE 500
CLEVELAND, OHIO 44113-1069
Telephone: 216-241-1000
Fax: 216-241-1093
URL: http://www.heutschelaw.com
Email: johnvheutsche@heutschelaw.com
URL: http://www.heutsche.com

Family Law, Domestic Relations, Child Custody, Divorce, Mediation, Separation Agreements, Spousal Support.

JOHN V. HEUTSCHE, born Sharon, Pennsylvania, February 17, 1946; admitted to bar, 1973, Ohio and U.S. District Court, Northern District of Ohio. *Education:* John Carroll University (A.B., 1969); Cleveland State University (J.D., 1973). Delta Theta Phi. Lecturer, Cuyahoga Community College, 1973-1978. Lecturer: Family Law, Cuyahoga County Bar Association (1981-1987; Family Law Institute (1989—); National Business Institute (1991—). Member, Board of Trustees, Divorce Equity, Inc., 1988-1991. Member, Panel of Arbitrators, American Arbitration Association. Certified Mediator: Family, Business and Divorce Conflicts, Mediation and Conflict Management Services, 1992. *Member:* Cuyahoga County (Member, Family Law Section: Chairman, 1987-1988), Medina County and Ohio State (Member, Family Law Section) Bar Associations. ***REPORTED CASES:*** Zigmont vs. Toto 47 Ohio App 3d 181 5 47 NE 2nd 1208 1988 (Modification of Custody Pursuant to Ohio Law in Lieu of Decreeing State Law, Application of Child Support Guidelines When Income Exceeds Charted Amount); The State Ex Rel. Litty vs. Leskovyansky, 77 Ohio St. 97 (1996). ***PRACTICE AREAS:*** Family Law; Domestic Relations; Child Custody; Divorce; Mediation; Separation Agreements; Spousal Support. ***Email:*** johnvheutsche@heutschelaw.com

(This Listing Continued)

GAIL A. HURD, born Fairview Park, Ohio, December 24, 1959; admitted to bar, 1985, Ohio. *Education:* Kenyon College (B.A., 1982); Case Western Reserve University (J.D., 1985). Formerly with U.S. Department of Labor. *Member:* Cleveland and Cuyahoga County Bar Associations. ***PRACTICE AREAS:*** Family Law; Domestic Relations; Child Custody; Separation Agreements; Spousal Support. ***Email:*** ghurd@heutschelaw.com

REFERENCE: First Merit Bank, Cleveland, OH.

HICKMAN & LOWDER CO., L.P.A.

Established in 1979

1370 ONTARIO STREET, SUITE 1620
CLEVELAND, OHIO 44113-1743
Telephone: 216-861-0360
Fax: 216-861-3113
URL: http://www.lawyers.com/h&lcolaw

Administrative Law, Civil Rights, Disability Law, Special Education Law, Elder Law, Estate Planning, Probate, Public Law, Social Security Law, SSI, Special Needs Trusts.

FRANKLIN J. HICKMAN, born Galion, Ohio, July 29, 1946; admitted to bar, 1973, Ohio; 1974, U.S. District Court, Northern District of Ohio; 1982, U.S. Court of Appeals, Sixth Circuit; 1992, U.S. Supreme Court; 2003, U.S. District Court, Southern District of Ohio. *Education:* Catholic University of America (B.A., summa cum laude, 1969; M.A., 1970); University of Pennsylvania (J.D., 1973). Recipient, 1994 John Minor Wisdom Award for Public Service and Professionalism from ABA Litigation Section. Author: "To Stay Home: Analysis of Rights and Recommendations on Procedures for Persons Receiving Mental Health Service in the Community," 7 Journal of Law and Health (Cleveland Marshall) 219, 1993; "Right to Refuse Psychotropic Medication," 6 MDLR 122 (1982); "Civil Commitment of Mentally Ill," Merrick, Rippner, Ohio Probate Law: Practice and Procedure; "Adult Protective Services," Merrick, Rippner, Ohio Probate Law: Practice and Procedure; Adjunct Professor, Psychiatry and Law, School of Medicine, Department of Psychiatry, Case Western Reserve University, 1978—; Adjunct Faculty, School of Law, Case Western Reserve University, 1988—. Lecturer in law, Cleveland-Marshall School of Law, 1978-1986. Attorney, Legal Aid Society of Cleveland, 1973-1982. Member and Officer, Cuyahoga County Board of Mental Retardation and Developmental Disabilities, 1983-1987. ***REPORTED CASES:*** Rone v. Fireman, 473 F. Supp. 92, N.D. Ohio, 1979; Levine v. Torvik, 986 F.2d 1506, 6th Cir., 1993; Knable v. Bexley City School Dist., 238 F.3d 755 (6th Cir. 2001). ***PRACTICE AREAS:*** Public Law; Mental Disability Law; Disabled Rights; Special Education Law; Americans with Disabilities Act; Disability Discrimination; Mental Health Law. ***Email:*** fhickman@hickman-lowder.com

JANET L. LOWDER, born Cleveland, Ohio, October 4, 1952; admitted to bar, 1992, Ohio and U.S. Court of Appeals, Sixth Circuit; 1993, U.S. District Court, Northern District of Ohio. *Education:* Baldwin-Wallace College (B.A., summa cum laude, 1973); Cleveland-Marshall College of Law (J.D., summa cum laude, 1992). Recipient: Banks Baldwin Co. Award; Delta Theta Phi Award. Editor, Cleveland State Law Review, 1991-1992. Author: "The Role of a 'Medicaid Payback Trust' in Personal Injury Awards Granted to Disabled Persons," Ohio Lawyer, March/April 1994; "To Stay at Home: Analysis of Rights and Recommendations on Procedures for Persons Receiving Mental Health Services in The Community," 7 Journal of Law and Health 219, 1993; "New Protections for Persons with Mental Disabilities in the Workplace under the ADA," 40 Clev. St. L. Rev., 1991. Certified in Elder Law, National Elder Law Foundation. *Member:* Lake County, Cleveland (Member: Bar Admissions Committee, 1993—; Estate Planning, Probate and Trust Law Section); Ohio State (Member, Elder Law Committee) and American (Member: Real Property, Probate & Trust Law Section) Bar Associations; National Academy of Elder Law Attorneys. ***PRACTICE AREAS:*** Estate Planning; Estate Planning for the Disabled; Probate Law; Elder Law; Medicaid Planning; Estate Administration; Trust Administration; Guardianship; Guardianship Administration; Tax Planning; Probate Taxation; Mental Disability Law; Disabled Rights; Advance Directives; Medicaid Hearings; Probate Administration; Decedents Estates; Estate Planning for Parents of Handicapped Children; Estate Planning for the Elderly; Special Needs Trusts. ***Email:*** jlowder@hickman-lowder.com

ELENA LIDRBAUCH, born Bratislava, Czechoslovakia, July 4, 1959; admitted to bar, 1999, Ohio. *Education:* Cleveland State University (B.A., 1982); Kent State University (M.Ed., 1983); University of Akron School of Law (J.D., 1999). *Member:* Cleveland, Medina, Ohio State and American Bar Associations. ***PRACTICE AREAS:*** Mediation; Public Law; Mental Disability Law; Disabled Rights; Guardianship Administration; Employment Law. ***Email:*** elidrbauch@hickman-lowder.com

SANDRA J. BUZNEY, born Cleveland, Ohio, September 11, 1951; admitted to bar, 1999, Ohio. *Education:* University of Cincinnati (B.A., Psychology, summa cum laude, 1973) Phi Beta Kappa; University of Michigan (M.S.W., 1975); Case Western Reserve University School of Law (J.D., cum laude, 1999). Recipient, Elaine Osborne Jacobson Award for Women in Health Care Law, 2nd place winner. Licensed Independent Social Worker, State of Ohio, 1985—. *Member:* Cleveland, Cuyahoga County, Ohio State (Member, Elder Law Committee) and American Bar Associations; National Association of Elder Law Attorneys; Greater Cleveland Brain Injury Coalition; Adult Guardianship Services (Member, Advisory Board). ***PRACTICE AREAS:*** Elder Law; Medicaid Planning; Medicaid Hearings; Estate Planning; Probate Administration; Special Needs Trusts; Guardianship Administration. ***Email:*** sbuzney@hickman-lowder.com

JUDITH C. SALTZMAN, born Cleveland, Ohio, July 27, 1949; admitted to bar, 1974, Massachusetts; 1975, U.S. District Court, District of Massachusetts; 1998, Ohio; 2000, U.S. District Court, Northern District of Ohio. *Education:* Wesleyan University (B.A., 1970); Northeastern University (J.D., 1974). Recipient, Greater Boston Legal Services Memorial Service Award for Outstanding Client Advocacy. Member, International Dyslexia Association, Coalition of Parents, Advocates and Attorneys. Former Impartial Hearing Officer, Ohio Department of Education. *Member:* Cleveland and Cuyahoga County Bar Associations. ***REPORTED CASES:*** Avery v. Heckler, 672 F.2d 158 (1st. Cir. 1985) and 797 F. 2d 19 (1st Cir. 1986). ***PRACTICE AREAS:*** Special Education. ***Email:*** jsaltzman@hickman-lowder.com

(This Listing Continued)

HICKMAN & LOWDER CO., L.P.A., Cleveland—Continued

MARY BRESNICKY McKEE, born Cleveland, Ohio, February 3, 1960; admitted to bar, 1985, Pennsylvania; 1986, New Jersey; 1987, Massachusetts; 1993, District of Columbia; 1997, Ohio; 2000, U.S. District Court, Northern District of Ohio. *Education:* Yale University (B.A., magna cum laude, 1982); University of Notre Dame (J.D., 1985). Member, National Organization of Social Security Claimants' Representatives. *Member:* Cleveland and Lorain County Bar Associations. ***PRACTICE AREAS:*** Social Security Disability; Elder Law; Guardianship; Estate Planning; Special Needs Trusts. ***Email:*** mmckee@hickman-lowder.com

D. PETER HOCHBERG CO., L.P.A.

Established in 1984

BAKER BUILDING, SIXTH FLOOR
1940 EAST SIXTH STREET
CLEVELAND, OHIO 44114
Telephone: 216-771-3800
Fax: 216-771-3804
1-800-776-8166
Email: dphochberg@aol.com

Patent, Trademark, Copyright, Unfair Competition and Trade Secrets Law, Trials.

D. PETER HOCHBERG, born Brooklyn, New York; admitted to bar, 1969, Virginia; 1970, New York and U.S. District Court, Northern District of New York; 1971, U.S. Court of Appeals, 2nd Circuit; 1974, U.S. Supreme Court; 1976, Ohio and U.S. District Court, Northern District of Ohio; 1979, U.S. Court of Appeals, 5th Circuit; 1982, U.S. Court of Appeals, Federal Circuit; registered to practice before U.S. Patent and Trademark Office. *Education:* Cornell University (B.M.E., 1964); Georgetown University (J.D., 1969). Phi Delta Phi. Member, Georgetown Law Journal, 1968-1969. Arbitrator, American Arbitration Association. *Member:* Cleveland Intellectual Property Law Association; American Intellectual Property Law Association; Licensing Executive Society; International Trademark Association; International and Intellectual Property Association; Asian Patent Attorneys Association; AIPPI; FICPI. ***LANGUAGES:*** French. ***PRACTICE AREAS:*** Patents; Trademarks; Copyrights; Unfair Competition; Trade Secrets; Trial Practice. ***Email:*** dphochberg@aol.com

KATHERINE R. VIEYRA, born Albany, New York, December 31, 1952; admitted to bar, 1995, Ohio. *Education:* Rice University (B.A., 1974); Case Western Reserve University (J.D., 1995). ***PRACTICE AREAS:*** Intellectual Property; Trademarks. ***Email:*** krvieyra@aol.com

SEAN F. MELLINO, born Cleveland, Ohio, December 8, 1976; admitted to bar, 2001, Ohio. *Education:* Dickinson College (B.S., 1998); Case Western Reserve University (J.D., 2001). Phi Delta Phi. ***LANGUAGES:*** Italian. ***PRACTICE AREAS:*** Patent Law; Trademark Law. ***Email:*** sfmellino@aol.com

OF COUNSEL

PIERO G. RUFFINENGO, born Italy, July 21, 1944; admitted to bar, 1975, Utah; registered to practice before the U.S. Patent and Trademark Office (Not admitted in Ohio). *Education:* University of Arizona (B.S., 1975); University of California/Los Angeles (M.S., Engineering-Operations Research, 1970); University of California/Los Angeles (Ph.D. Engineering, 1972); University of Utah (J.D., 1975). Order of the Coif. Member, University of Utah Law Review, 1974-1975. *Member:* Utah State Bar; American and International Bar Associations. ***LANGUAGES:*** Italian and Spanish. ***Email:*** paralegl@aros.net

JAMES A. RICH, born Stamford, New York, January 24, 1938; admitted to bar, 1971, New York; registered to practice before U.S. Patent and Trademark Office (Not admitted in Ohio). *Education:* Rensselaer Polytechnic Institute (B.S.M.E., 1961); Georgetown University Law Center (J.D., 1970). Tau Beta Pi. Union Carbide Scholar. Former Senior Attorney with Calfee Halter & Griswold, New York. *Member:* Cleveland Intellectual Property Law Association; American Intellectual Property Law Association. ***PRACTICE AREAS:*** Patents; Trademarks; Trade Secrets; Intellectual Property Agreements. ***Email:*** jarich@aol.com

HOFFMAN LEGAL GROUP, LLC

23230 CHAGRIN BOULEVARD, SUITE 232
CLEVELAND, OHIO 44122-5495
Telephone: 216-292-5200
Fax: 216-292-8766
URL: http://www.hoffmanlegalgroup.net

General Practice.

FIRM PROFILE: All members of the Firm have extensive Trial and Appellate experience in both State and Federal Court and administrative agencies. Our Firm specialized in litigation in all areas, including personal injury, malpractice, medical-legal and products liability. The Firm's practice also consists of probate, casualty and surety, commercial and corporate law.

W. ANDREW HOFFMAN, III, born Circleville, Ohio, June 27, 1954; admitted to bar, 1979, Ohio and U.S. District Court, Northern District of Ohio; 1985, U.S. Court of Appeals, Sixth Circuit; 1996, U.S. Supreme Court. *Education:* Purdue University (B.A., 1976); Cleveland Marshall College of Law (J.D., 1979). Delta Theta Phi. Member, Alternative Dispute Resolution Mediator, U.S. District Court, 1992—. Dean, Cleveland Alumni Senate. *Member:* Greater Cleveland (Member, Medical Legal Committee, 1988-1992), Ohio State (Member, Negligence Law Committee, 1989-1991) and American Bar Associations. (Certified as a Civil Trial Advocacy Specialist by the National Board of Trial Advocacy). ***REPORTED CASES:*** Adair v. Koppers Co., 541 F.Supp. 1120, aff'd, 741 F.2d 111 (1984); Mominee v. Scherbarth, 28 Ohio St. 3d 270, 503 N.E.2d 717 (1986); Commonwealth Propane Co. v. Petrosol International, 818 F.2d 522 (1987); Baker v. Hadley 167 F.3d 1014 (6th Cir, 1995). ***PRACTICE AREAS:*** Personal Injury; Products Liability; Probate; Casualty Insurance; Surety Law; Commercial Law; Corporate Law; Slip and Fall; Wrongful Death; Construction Accidents; Automobile Accidents; Insurance Bad Faith; Dog Bites. ***Email:*** hlgllc@aol.com

(This Listing Continued)

DOUGLAS S. HUNTER, born Marion, Ohio, February 25, 1975; admitted to bar, 2000, Ohio; 2002, U.S. District Court, Northern District of Ohio. *Education:* University of Toledo (B.S., 1997); Ohio Northern University (J.D., with distinction, 2000). Associate Editor, Ohio Northern University Law Review. *Member:* Cleveland, Ohio State and American Bar Associations; Ohio Association of Trial Lawyers. ***PRACTICE AREAS:*** Personal Injury; Workers Compensation; Insurance; Consumer Law; Contracts. ***Email:*** dhunterhlg@aol.com

HOHMANN, BOUKIS & CURTIS CO., L.P.A.

Established in 1971

1370 ONTARIO STREET
SUITE 520
CLEVELAND, OHIO 44113-1701
Telephone: 216-696-1076
Fax: 216-696-2317
Email: hbc@clevelandlawyers.cc

General Civil, Trial and Appellate Practice. Corporation, Commercial, Reorganization, Bankruptcy, Probate, Taxation and Real Estate Law. Commercial Collections. Estate Planning. International Transactions.

WILLIAM T. HOHMANN, born Cleveland, Ohio, May 12, 1939; admitted to bar, 1965, Ohio; 1966, U.S. District Court, Northern District of Ohio. *Education:* Kent State University (B.A., 1962); Case Western Reserve University (J.D., 1965). Delta Theta Phi. Author: Mechanic's Liens in Ohio, Business Credit, January 2001. General Counsel, National Association of Credit Management, Greater Cleveland. Trustee, N.A.C.M., Greater Cleveland; Member, Civil Service Commission, North Olmsted, Ohio. *Member:* Cleveland and Ohio State Bar Associations. ***PRACTICE AREAS:*** Corporation Law; Reorganization Law; Bankruptcy Law; International Transactions; Commercial Collections; Litigation. ***Email:*** whohmann@clevelandlawyers.cc

KENNETH BOUKIS, born Cleveland, Ohio, August 28, 1940; admitted to bar, 1966, Ohio; 1970, U.S. District Court, Northern District of Ohio. *Education:* Cleveland State University (B.B.A., 1963; LL.M., 1976); Case Western Reserve University (J.D., 1966). Phi Delta Phi. Member, Case Western Reserve Law Review Board, 1965-1966. Member, Advisory Group, U.S. District Court, Northern District of Ohio. *Member:* Cleveland and Ohio State Bar Associations; National Lawyers Association. ***LANGUAGES:*** Greek. ***PRACTICE AREAS:*** Civil and Criminal Trials; Commercial Law; Real Estate Law; Corporation Law. ***Email:*** kboukis@clevelandlawyers.cc

CHRIST BOUKIS, born Cleveland, Ohio, August 4, 1939; admitted to bar, 1965, Ohio; 1968, U.S. District Court, Northern District of Ohio. *Education:* Cleveland State University (B.B.A., 1962); Case Western Reserve University (J.D., 1965). Phi Delta Phi. *Member:* Cleveland (Chairman, Estate Planning, Probate and Trust Law Section, 1988-1989), 8th Judicial District (Life Member, Judicial Conference) and Ohio State (Member, Estate Planning, Probate and Trust Law Section) Bar Associations; Estate Planning Council of Cleveland. ***LANGUAGES:*** Greek. ***PRACTICE AREAS:*** Corporation Law; Probate Law; Real Estate Law; Estate Planning; Trust Law. ***Email:*** cboukis@clevelandlawyers.cc

JACK CURTIS, born Lorain, Ohio, January 14, 1958; admitted to bar, 1985, Ohio. *Education:* Kent State University (B.A., 1980); Cleveland Marshall College of Law (J.D., 1984). *Member:* Cleveland and Ohio State Bar Associations. ***PRACTICE AREAS:*** Commercial Law; Commercial Collections; Bankruptcy Law; Litigation. ***Email:*** jcurtis@clevelandlawyers.cc

REFERENCE: National City Bank.

HAROLD L. HOM, CO., LPA

1991 CROCKER ROAD
SUITE 600, GEMINI TOWER 1
CLEVELAND, OHIO 44145
Telephone: 440-892-3374
Fax: 440-892-3375
URL: http://www.HomLaw.net
Email: harold@HomLaw.net
URL: http://www.haroldhomlawfirm.com

Estate Planning, Probate, Business Law, Intellectual Property and Immigration Law.

HAROLD L. HOM, born Youngstown, Ohio, April 5, 1962; admitted to bar, 1988, Ohio and U.S. District Court, Northern and Southern Districts of Ohio; registered to practice before U.S. Patent and Trademark Office. *Education:* The Ohio State University (B.S. Chemical Engineering, 1984); Case Western Reserve University (M.B.A., 1988; J.D., 1988). *Member:* Cleveland, Lorain County and Ohio State Bar Associations; American Immigration Lawyers Association. ***PRACTICE AREAS:*** Estate Planning; Probate; Business; Intellectual Property; Immigration.

JAMES A. HUDAK

29425 CHAGRIN BOULEVARD, SUITE 304
CLEVELAND, OHIO 44122-4602
Telephone: 216-292-3900
Fax: 216-292-3930
Email: hudakjames@aol.com

Patent, Trademark, Copyright and Unfair Competition Law.

JAMES A. HUDAK, born Cleveland, Ohio, December 21, 1940; admitted to bar, 1974, Ohio; 1981, U.S. District Court, Northern District of Ohio; registered to practice before U.S. Patent and Trademark Office. *Education:* Case Institute of Technology (B.S., with honors, 1962) Tau Beta Pi; Eta Kappa Nu; Case Western Reserve University (M.B.A., 1967); Cleveland-Marshall College of Law (J.D., 1974). *Member:* Cleveland Intellectual Property Law Association; American Intellectual Property Law Association; Licensing Executives Society.

ILER & ILER

1640 STANDARD BUILDING
CLEVELAND, OHIO 44113
Telephone: 216-696-5700
Email: nancyiler@ameritech.net
URL: http://www.ilerlawoffice.com

General Practice.

DON C. ILER, born 1929; admitted to bar, 1960, Ohio. *Education:* Ohio State University (B.S., 1957); Cleveland Marshall College of Law (LL.B., 1960). Best Lawyers in America, 1987; 1988-1990. Author: "Ohio Personal Injury Practice", Banks-Baldwin Law Publishing Co, 1991. Lecturer, Ohio Negligence and Wrongful Death Law, Ohio Judicial Conference, 1984 and Ohio Academy of Trial Lawyers, 1983. *Member:* Greater Cleveland, Cuyahoga County and Ohio State Bar Associations. Cleveland Trial Lawyers Association. Ohio Academy of Trial Lawyers (President, 1983-1984; Trustee, 1992—); Association of Trial Lawyers of America (Governor, 1992—); Lawyer-Pilots Bar Association. ***PRACTICE AREAS:*** Personal Injury; Medical Malpractice; Products Liability; Libel, Slander and Defamation.

NANCY C. ILER, born Cleveland, Ohio, January 9, 1960; admitted to bar, 1987, Ohio. *Education:* University of Akron (B.S.N., 1982); Cleveland Marshall College of Law (J.D., 1987). Registered Nurse, Ohio, 1982. Formerly with Don C. Iler Co., L.P.A. *Member:* The Association of Trial Lawyers of America; Ohio Academy of Trial Attorneys. ***PRACTICE AREAS:*** Medical Malpractice; Wrongful Death; Nursing Home Negligence. ***Email:*** nancyiler@ameritech.net

KAREN S. IRELAND-PHILLIPS
ATTORNEY AT LAW

ROCKEFELLER BUILDING
614 WEST SUPERIOR AVENUE, SUITE 1448
CLEVELAND, OHIO 44113
Telephone: 216-696-5530
Fax: 216-696-5531
URL: http://www.irelandpnillipslaw.com
Email: ksiplaw@hotmail.com
URL: http://www.ireland-phillips-law.com

Family Law, Workers Compensation, Civil Litigation, Probate, Wills, Social Security, Personal Injury.

KAREN S. IRELAND-PHILLIPS, born Indianapolis, Indiana, October 13, 1958; admitted to bar, 1996, Ohio. *Education:* Cleveland State University (B.A., 1990); Cleveland-Marshall College of Law (J.D., 1993). *Member:* Ohio State Bar Association. ***PRACTICE AREAS:*** Family Law; Workers Compensation; Civil Litigation; Probate; Wills; Social Security; Personal Injury.

JANIK & DORMAN, L.L.P.

9200 SOUTH HILL BOULEVARD, SUITE 300
CLEVELAND, OHIO 44147-3521
Telephone: 440-838-7600
Fax: 440-838-7601
Email: scott.cerny@janiklaw.com
URL: http://www.janiklaw.com

Litigation. Insurance Coverage and Defense, Corporate and Commercial Defense and Labor and Employment. Professional Liability, Casualty, Products Liability, Aviation, Toxic Tort and Environmental Law.

PARTNERS

STEVEN G. JANIK, born Cleveland, Ohio, November 1, 1951; admitted to bar, 1976, Ohio and U.S. District Court, Northern District of Ohio; 1977, U.S. Tax Court; 1978, U.S. Court of Appeals, Sixth Circuit; 1985, U.S. Supreme Court; 1986, U.S. Court of Appeals, Fourth Circuit; 1988, Maryland and District of Columbia; 1989, California; 1990, U.S. District Court, Central and Southern Districts of California. *Education:* Denison University (B.A., 1973); Cleveland State University (J.D., 1975). Delta Theta Phi (National Marshal, 1981-1983). Life Member, Sixth Circuit Judicial Conference. Member, Federal Judicial Center Task Force on Reducing Trial Delay, 1981—. Author: "Accountant Malpractice," Wiley Publications, 1989. *Member:* Cleveland, Orange County, Ohio State and American (Tips/Litigation) Bar Associations; International Association of Defense Counsel; Defense Research Institute; Lawyer-Pilots Bar Association. ***PRACTICE AREAS:*** Litigation; Insurance Coverage and Defense; Professional Liability; Products Liability; Aviation. ***Email:*** sgjanik@compuserve.com

ANDREW J. DORMAN, born Cleveland, Ohio, August 24, 1967; admitted to bar, 1994, Ohio and U.S. District Court, Northern District of Ohio; 1995, Kentucky. *Education:* Bowling Green State University (B.S.B.A., 1989); Cleveland Marshall College of Law (J.D., cum laude, 1994). Editor, Cleveland Marshall Law Review, 1992-1994. *Member:* Cleveland, Cuyahoga County and Ohio State Bar Associations. ***PRACTICE AREAS:*** Professional Liability; Casualty; Insurance Coverage; Complex Litigation.

JONATHAN PHILIPP, born North Olmsted, Ohio, June 6, 1964; admitted to bar, 1989, Ohio; 1999, New Jersey and U.S. District Court, District of New Jersey; 2001, U.S. District Court, Northern District of Ohio. *Education:* Drew University (B.A., Political Science, 1986); George Washington University National Law Center (J.D., with honors, 1989). Formerly with Greenkaum Rowe Smith Ravin Davis & Himmell, LLP, Woodbridge, New Jersey. ***PRACTICE AREAS:*** Health Care; Medical Malpractice; Financial Institutions Litigation; Commercial Litigation. ***Email:*** jonathan.philipp@janiklaw.com

JASON D. WINTER, born Akron, Ohio, May 24, 1974; admitted to bar, 2000, Florida; 2003, Ohio. *Education:* Boston University (B.A., 1996); Georgetown University Law Center (J.D., 2000). ***PRACTICE AREAS:*** Medical Malpractice Defense. ***Email:*** jason.winter@janiklaw.com

ASSOCIATES

BRIAN D. SPITZ, born Cleveland, Ohio, December 23, 1971; admitted to bar, 1997, Ohio. *Education:* American University (B.A., 1993); Case Western Reserve University (J.D., 1997). Order of the Barristers. ***PRACTICE AREAS:*** Insurance Defense; Civil Trial Practice; Product Liability; Environmental Law.

BARRY RONALD MURNER, admitted to bar, 1998, Ohio. *Education:* University of Cincinnati (1993); Cleveland-Marshall College of Law (1997). ***PRACTICE AREAS:*** Criminal Law.

DAVID H. BROWN, born Columbus, Ohio, April 23, 1973; admitted to bar, 2002, Ohio. *Education:* Ohio University (B.A., Philosophy, 1998); Cleveland-Marshall College of Law (J.D., 2002). ***Email:*** david.brown@janiklaw.com

STACY N. LILLY, born Geneva, Ohio, July 29, 1975; admitted to bar, 2000, Ohio; 2001, U.S. District Court, Northern District of Ohio. *Education:* Ohio University (B.A., 1997); University of Toledo College of Law (J.D., 2000). *Member:* Cleveland Bar Association. ***PRACTICE AREAS:*** Insurance Defense; Casualty Insurance. ***Email:*** stacey.lilly@janiklaw.com

LORI ROSS TARK, born Wheeling, West Virginia, October 19, 1969; admitted to bar, 2003, Ohio and U.S. District Court, Northern District of Ohio. *Education:* Cleveland State University (B.S., 1994); Case Western Reserve University (J.D., 2003). ***PRACTICE AREAS:*** Securities Litigation; Business Litigation. ***Email:*** lori.tark@janiklaw.com

CHARLES C. SPAGNOLI, born Syracuse, New York, November 26, 1969; admitted to bar, 1995, New York and U.S. District Court, Northern and Western Districts of New York; 2002, Ohio, U.S. District Court, Northern District of Ohio and U.S. District Court, Northern District of Indiana. *Education:* Yale University (B.A., magna cum laude, 1991); Harvard Law School (J.D., cum laude, 1994). *Member:* American Bar Association. ***PRACTICE AREAS:*** Employment Law; Labor Law. ***Email:*** chris.spagnoli@janiklaw.com

CHRISTOPHER J. VAN BLARGAN, born Euclid, Ohio, November 8, 1967; admitted to bar, 1996, Ohio. *Education:* John Carroll University (B.S., 1990); University of Akron (J.D., 1995). ***PRACTICE AREAS:*** Insurance Defense; Medical Malpractice; Casualty Insurance.

CRYSTAL L. NICOSIA, born Niagara Fall, New York, July 11, 1979; admitted to bar, 2004, Ohio. *Education:* State University of New York at Buffalo (B.A., Sociology, 2001); University of Dayton School of Law (J.D., 2004). Alpha Kappa Delta. *Member:* Ohio State Bar Association and Cleveland Bar Association. ***Email:*** crystal.nicosia@janiklaw.com

ERIC J. WEISS, born Sandusky, Ohio, April 30, 1974; admitted to bar, 2000, Ohio. *Education:* Bowling Green State University (B.A., 1996); Cleveland-Marshall College of Law (J.D., 2000). ***PRACTICE AREAS:*** Insurance Litigation; Insurance Defense.

MATTHEW M. NEE, admitted to bar, 2000, Ohio. *Education:* Union College (B.A., Political Science, 1993); Ohio Northern University, Petit College of Law (J.D., 1999). Law Review Executive Board. ***REPORTED CASES:*** Kansas v. Hendricks 24 Ohio N.U.L. Rev. 619. ***PRACTICE AREAS:*** Insurance. ***Email:*** matthew.nee@janiklaw.com

MARK E. KREMSER, born Cleveland, Ohio, April 10, 1971; admitted to bar, 1996, Ohio. *Education:* Bowling Green State University (B.A., English, 1993); Case Western Reserve University School of Law (J.D., 1996). Phi Beta Kappa; Phi Alpha Delta. Order of Barristers. Member, Niagara Moot Court Team. Recipient, Niagara Moot Court Competition, Best Applicant Brief, 1996. Distinguished Advocate, Dean Dunmore Moot Court Competition. ***PRACTICE AREAS:*** Insurance Litigation.

KELLY H. ROGERS, born Parma, Ohio, November 11, 1979; admitted to bar, 2005, Ohio. *Education:* Albion College (B.A., 2001); University of Michigan (J.D., 2004). ***PRACTICE AREAS:*** Litigation; Insurance Defense. ***Email:*** kelly.rogers@janiklaw.com

MICHAEL J. STANUSZEK, born Owosso, Michigan, January 8, 1979; admitted to bar, 2004, Ohio. *Education:* Central Michigan University (B.S.B.A., cum laude, 2001); University of Tennessee (J.D., 2004). University of Tennessee Law Review. Author: Transactions: The Tennessee Journal of Business Law, Fall 2003. Member, Society of Human Resource Management. *Member:* Akron Bar Association; Ohio State Bar Association. ***PRACTICE AREAS:*** Casualty; Business Litigation. ***Email:*** michael.stanuszek@janiklaw.com

CATHERINE A. DAVIS, born Manhattan, Kansas, March 23, 1970; admitted to bar, 1998, Ohio; 1999, U.S. District Court, Northern District of Ohio; 2004, U.S. District Court, Southern District of Ohio; U.S. Court of Appeals, Sixth Circuit. *Education:* Wright State University (B.A., magna cum laude, 1994); University of Toledo College of Law (J.D., ma-

(This Listing Continued)

JANIK & DORMAN, L.L.P., Cleveland—Continued

gna cum laude, 1998). Order of the Coif. University of Toledo Law Review, Editor, 1997-1998. ***PRACTICE AREAS:*** Insurance Defense Litigation. ***Email:*** catherine.davis@janiklaw.com

W. JOSEPH BAKER, born Benton Harbor, Michigan, May 28, 1974; admitted to bar, 2000, Ohio. *Education:* Northern Michigan University (B.S., Political Science, 1996); Cleveland-Marshall College of Law (J.D., 2000). Associate Member, 1998-1999 and Research Editor, 1999-2000, Law Review. ***PRACTICE AREAS:*** Business Litigation.

OF COUNSEL

THOMAS D. LAMBROS, born Ashtabula, Ohio, February 4, 1930; admitted to bar, 1952, Ohio. *Education:* Fairmont State College; Cleveland Marshall Law School (LL.B., 1952). On April 30, 1996, the United States Congress enacted Public Law 104-136, designating the Thomas D. Lambros Federal Building and United States Courthouse in Youngstown, Ohio. Judge Lambros is the founder and chairman of the board of the Thomas D. Lambros Dispute Management Center, LLC. Recipient: Herbert Harley Award, the highest award given by the American Judicature Society; The Whitney North Seymour, Sr. Arbitration Medal presented by the American Arbitration Association, 1996; National Public Service Award, The Ohio State University School of Public Policy and Management, 1997. Member: National Conference of Federal Trial Judges, 1988-1993; Judicial Conference of the United States, 1993-1995. Author: Summary Jury Trials (Litigation) "The Future of Alternative Dispute Resolution," Founder of Summary Jury Trial Process, 1980, Pepperdine L.Rev., 1990-1995. United States District Judge, Court of Common Pleas of Ashtabula County, Jefferson, Ohio, 1961-1967. Northern District of Ohio, 1967-1995 and Chief Judge, 1990-1995. Panel Member, American Arbitration Association National Mass Torts Panel. Member, National Panel of Distinguished Neutrals, Center for Public Resources. *Member:* Cleveland, Ashtabula County (Past President), Ohio State, Federal (President) and American Bar Associations. Fellow, American Bar Foundation. [With U.S. Army, 1954-1956]. ***REPORTED CASES:*** Special Counsel to the Official Committee of Tort Claimants in Dow Corning Bankruptcy. Managed Pretrial Coordination of Litigation for 1992 Air Crash at New York La Guardia Airport; Managed all Asbestos-Related Personal Injury Cases Pending in the Northern District of Ohio; Formulated $20 Million Settlement of a Consumer Class Action Antitrust Case. ***PRACTICE AREAS:*** Litigation; Alternative Dispute Resolution.

ELLYN B. MEHENDALE, born 1969; admitted to bar, 1994, Ohio. *Education:* Miami University (B.S., 1991); Cleveland Marshall College of Law (J.D., magna cum laude, 1994).

CHRISTOPHER L. PARKER, born Berea, Ohio, 1956; admitted to bar, 1991, Ohio; 1994, U.S. District Court, Northern District of Ohio; 1998, U.S. Court of Appeals, Fourth Circuit. *Education:* Miami University (B.S., 1988); University of Dayton (J.D., 1991). Phi Alpha Delta. Recipient, American Jurisprudence Award in Administrative Law. Fellow, Akron Bar Foundation. ***REPORTED CASES:*** Simmerer v. Dabbas, 89 Ohio St.3d 586, 733 N.E.2d 1169 (Ohio, 2000); Schmidt v. Koval (Ohio App. 7 Dist., 2002); Riley v. Summa Health Systems. ***PRACTICE AREAS:*** Medical Malpractice (80%); Professional Liability Defense (20%).

JAVITCH, BLOCK & RATHBONE L.L.P.

1300 EAST NINTH STREET, 14TH FLOOR
CLEVELAND, OHIO 44114-1503
Telephone: 216-623-0000
Fax: 216-623-0190
Email: bblock@JBandR.com
URL: http://www.JBandR.com

Cincinnati, Ohio Office: 602 Main Street, Suite 500, 45202. Telephone: 513-774-9600. Fax: 513-744-9602

Columbus, Ohio Office: 33 North Third Street, Suite 300, 43215. Telephone: 614-228-9550. Fax: 614-228-2818.

Bankruptcy, Commercial, Corporate, Collection, General Civil Practice, Landlord-Tenant, Real Estate, Trials and Appeals.

VICTOR M. JAVITCH, admitted to bar, 1962, Ohio. *Education:* University of Michigan (B.A., 1959); Western Reserve University (LL.B., 1962). Tau Epsilon Rho. Editor, Western Reserve Law Review, 1961-1962. Lecturer: Topics - Creditor Rights, Landlord/Tenant, Secured Transactions. Court Appointed Receiver, administering complex business liquidations. ***Email:*** vjavitch@JBandR.com

BRUCE A. BLOCK, admitted to bar, 1976, Ohio. *Education:* American University (B.A., 1973); Case Western Reserve University (J.D., 1976). ***Email:*** bblock@JBandR.com

JOEL H. RATHBONE, admitted to bar, 1979, Ohio. *Education:* University of North Carolina (B.A., 1976); Cleveland Marshall College of Law (J.D., 1979). Member, Panel of U.S. Trustees, Bankruptcy Court, Northern District of Ohio, 1979—. ***Email:*** jhr@JBandR.com

MARC A. MELAMED, admitted to bar, 1977, Ohio. *Education:* Case Western Reserve University; Washington University (A.B., 1973); Cleveland Marshall College of Law (J.D., 1977). Member: U.J.A. National Young Leadership Cabinet; Jewish Community Center (Board of Trustees; Vice President, 1991—). ***Email:*** mam@JBandR.com

KENNETH B. BAKER, admitted to bar, 1977, Ohio. *Education:* University of Colorado (B.A., 1972); Cleveland Marshall College of Law (J.D., 1977). ***Email:*** kbaker@JBandR.com

MICHELE POLITO SOUCIE, admitted to bar, 1982, Ohio. *Education:* Baldwin-Wallace College (B.A., summa cum laude, 1979); Cleveland Marshall College of Law (J.D., 1982). Author: "Teamwork Allows Moms to Juggle," The Plain Dealer, Sunday, October 1997; "Facts About the Eviction Process," Properties Magazine, July 1999; "Investment Inquiries Co-Signor of Lease," Properties magazine, May 2000. ***Email:*** msoucie@JBandR.com

MICHAEL D. LINN, admitted to bar, 1986, Ohio. *Education:* Kent State University (B.A., 1983); Cleveland State University (J.D., 1986). Delta Theta Phi. Recipient, Award for Outstanding Student in Civil Procedure, 1985. Staff Member, 1984-1985 and Editor, 1985-1986, Cleveland State Law Review. Author: "Recent Developments in Uninsured/Underinsured Motorist Coverage in Ohio," Law and Fact Vol. 60, No. 3, April/May, 1986. Lecturer: Topics: Creditor Rights; Landlord-Tenant Law. ***Email:*** mlinn@JBandR.com

MICHAEL D. SLODOV, admitted to bar, 1991, Ohio. *Education:* Cleveland State University (B.A., 1985); Case Western Reserve University (J.D., 1990). Articles Editor, Case Western Reserve Law Review. Author: Note, "Criminal Responsibility and the Noncompliant Psychiatric Offender," 40 Western R. L. Rev. 271. ***REPORTED CASES:*** Diebold, Inc. v. Firstcard Financial Services, Inc., 104 F Supp.2d 758 (N.D. Ohio 2000); National Satellite Sports, Inc. v. Eliadis, Inc., 65 F. Supp.2d 662 (N.D. Ohio 1999; aff'd. 253 F.3d 900 (6th Cir. 2001, cert. denied, 122 S. Ct. 1127, 2002); Beecher v. Ohio State Home Services, Inc., 81 Ohio St.3d 599 (1998); Sicheman v. Diamoncut, Inc. (In re Sol Bergman Estate Jewelers, Inc.), 225 B.R. 896 (6th Cir. BAP 1998); Catholic Social Serv. of Cuyahoga Cty. v. Howard (8th Dist. App. 1995), 106 Ohio App.3d 615; State ex rel. Howard v. Ferreri, 70 Ohio St.3d 587 (1994). ***Email:*** mslodov@JBandR.com

JEFFREY E. DUBIN, admitted to bar, 1997, Ohio. *Education:* State University of New York at Buffalo (B.A., 1994); Cleveland-Marshall College of Law (J.D., 1997). *Member:* Ohio State Bar Association; National Association of Subrogation Professionals. ***Email:*** jdubin@JBandR.com

ROBERT N. LURIE, admitted to bar, 1994, Ohio. *Education:* University of Wisconsin (B.A., 1991); Cleveland-Marshall College of Law (J.D., 1994). *Member:* Cuyahoga County and Ohio State Bar Associations; Commercial Law League. ***Email:*** rlurie@JBandR.com

THEODORE A. KONSTANTINOPOULOS, admitted to bar, 1995, Ohio. *Education:* University of Akron (B.A., Marketing, 1991); University of Akron Law School (J.D., 1995). *Member:* Akron and Ohio State Bar Associations. ***Email:*** tkonstantinopoulos@JBandR.com

REPRESENTATIVE CLIENTS: General Motors Acceptance Corp.; Associated Estates Corp.; Dollar Bank; Consolidated Management, Inc.; Chase Manhattan Bank; Bank of America; General Electric Capital Corp.; Household Finance Corporation; Key Bank, National City Corp.; Chrysler Financial Corp.; Bank One; Chrysler Financial Co. L.L.C.; Creditrust; Citibank; State of Ohio; Credit Acceptance Corporation; Toyota Motor Credit.
REFERENCE: Bank One.

(This Listing Continued)

JEFFRIES, KUBE, FORREST & MONTELEONE CO., L.P.A.

Established in 1980
1650 MIDLAND BUILDING
CLEVELAND, OHIO 44115
Telephone: 216-771-4050
Fax: 216-771-0732
Email: attys@jkfmlaw.com
URL: http://www.jkfmlaw.com

Personal Injury, Wrongful Death, Medical Malpractice and Products Liability Law. General Civil, Trial and Appellate Practice.

SALVATORE P. JEFFRIES (1930-1992)

J. MICHAEL MONTELEONE, born Cleveland, Ohio, September 23, 1949; admitted to bar, 1974, Ohio; 1976, U.S. District Court, Northern District of Ohio; 1983, U.S. Court of Appeals, Sixth Circuit. *Education:* John Carroll University (B.A., 1971); Cleveland Marshall College of Law (J.D., cum laude, 1974). Phi Alpha Delta. Author, "Damages Evidence in the Catastrophic Injury Case," 1 Ohio Trial 11 (Summer 1990); "Trial Lawyers and the Health Care Crisis," 8 Ohio Lawyer No. 5, (1994). Assistant Ohio Attorney General, 1974-1975. Selected in "The Best Lawyers in America," 1995-2006. Listed in Ohio Super Lawyers 2004, Top 100 in 2005. *Member:* Cleveland, Cuyahoga County and Ohio State Bar Associations; The Association of Trial Lawyers of America; Ohio Academy of Trial Lawyers (President, 1999-2000; Chairman, Medical Negligence Section, 1991-1994; Member, Board of Trustees, 1987-2005); Cleveland Academy of Trial Lawyers (Member, Board of Trustees, 1986-1989); American Board of Trial Advocacy (Advocate). International Society of Barristers; American College of Trial Lawyers. (Certified as a Civil Trial Advocate by the National Board of Trial Advocacy, 1983; Recertified, 1988, 1993, 1998, 2003). ***REPORTED CASES:*** Morris v. Savoy (1991) 61 O. St. 3rd 684; Jones v. VIP Development Co. (1984) 15 O. St. 3rd 90. ***PRACTICE AREAS:*** Medical Malpractice; Personal Injury Law; Products Liability Law. ***Email:*** jmm923@aol.com

DAVID A. FORREST, born Cleveland, Ohio, May 17, 1954; admitted to bar, 1979, Ohio and U.S. District Court, Northern District of Ohio; 1983, U.S. Court of Appeals, Sixth Circuit. *Education:* Baldwin-Wallace College (B.A., 1976); Cleveland State University (J.D., 1979). Selected as one of Northeast Ohio's Leading Lawyers by Inside Business, 2001-2004. Examiner, National Board of Trial Advocacy, 2002—. Listed, Ohio Super Lawyers, 2004, 2005. *Member:* Bar Association of Greater Cleveland; Ohio State Bar Association; Cleveland Academy of Trial Attorneys (Director, 1993-1996); Ohio Academy of Trial Lawyers (Eighth District Trustee, 1993-1997; Vice-Chairman Products Liability Section, 1995; Chairman, Products Liability Section, 1996); The Association of Trial Lawyers of America. (Certified As A Civil Trial Advocate by the National Board of Trial Advocacy). ***PRACTICE AREAS:*** Personal Injury Law; Products Liability; Medical Malpractice Law; Maritime Law; Jones Act. ***Email:*** dforrest@jkfmlaw.com

M. JANE RUA, born Crestline, Ohio, May 3, 1958; admitted to bar, 1986, Ohio; 1989, U.S. District Court, Northern District of Ohio. *Education:* University of Toledo (B.S.N., cum laude, 1980); Ohio State University College of Law (J.D., 1986). Sigma Theta Tau. Licensed Nurse, Ohio, 1980. *Member:* Lake County and Ohio State Bar Association; Cleveland Academy of Trial Attorneys; Ohio Academy of Trial Lawyers; The Association of Trial Lawyers of America. ***PRACTICE AREAS:*** Medical Malpractice; Personal Injury. ***Email:*** janerua@ix.netcom.com

MARK E. BARBOUR, born Indianapolis, Indiana, April 21, 1959; admitted to bar, 1988, Ohio; 1989, U.S. District Court, Northern District of Ohio. *Education:* Wittenberg

(This Listing Continued)

University (B.A., 1982); Cleveland-Marshall College of Law (J.D., 1988). *Member:* Cleveland and Ohio State Bar Association; Ohio Academy Trial Lawyers (Eighth District Trustee, 1999-2005; Executive Committee, 2003-2005); Cleveland Academy of Trial Attorneys (Member, Board of Directors, 2002—; Treasurer, 2004-2005; Secretary, 2005-2006); The Association of Trial Lawyers of America. ***PRACTICE AREAS:*** Personal Injury; Negligence law; Insurance Law; Motor Vehicle Accidents and Injuries; Torts; Civil Litigation. ***Email:*** mbarbour@jkfmlaw.com

BRADFORD D. ZELASKO, born Cleveland, Ohio, July 19, 1953; admitted to bar, 1978, Ohio and U.S. District Court, Northern District of Ohio. *Education:* University of Notre Dame (B.B.A., 1975); Case Western Reserve University (J.D., 1978). *Member:* Ohio State Bar Association; Cleveland Academy of Trial Lawyers; Ohio Academy of Trial Lawyers (Representative at Large, 1999-2002); The Association of Trial Lawyers of America. ***PRACTICE AREAS:*** Personal Injury Law; Civil Litigation; Insurance Law; Negligence Law; Employment Intentional Torts. ***Email:*** bzelasko@jkfmlaw.com

MICHAEL R. KUBE (Retired)

REFERENCE: First Merit Bank, N.A.

JONES DAY

NORTH POINT
901 LAKESIDE AVENUE
CLEVELAND, OHIO 44114-1190
Telephone: 216-586-3939
Telecopier: 216-579-0212
Email: counsel@jonesday.com
URL: http://www.jonesday.com

In Columbus, Ohio: 325 John H. McConnell Boulevard, Suite 600. Telephone: 614-469-3939. Telecopier: 614-461-4198.
In Atlanta, Georgia: 1420 Peachtree Street, N.E., Suite 800. Telephone: 404-521-3939. Telecopier: 404-581-8330.
In Beijing, China: 3201 China World Tower 1, No. 1 Jianguomenwai Avenue. Telephone: 86-10-5866-1111. Telecopier: 86-10-5866-1122.
In Brussels, Belgium: Boulevard Brand Whitlocklaan 165, 1200 Brussels. Telephone: 32-2-645-14-11. Telecopier: 32-2-645-14-45.
In Chicago, Illinois: 77 West Wacker. Telephone: 312-782-3939. Telecopier: 312-782-8585.
In Dallas, Texas: 2727 North Harwood Street. Telephone: 214-220-3939. Telecopier: 214-969-5100.
In Frankfurt, Germany: Hochhaus am Park, Grüneburgweg 102, 60323 Frankfurt am Main. Telephone: 49-69-9726-3939. Telecopier: 49-69-9726-3993.
In Hong Kong, China: 31st Floor, Edinburgh Tower, The Landmark, 15 Queen's Road, Central. Telephone: 852-2526-6895. Telecopier: 852-2868-5871.
In Houston, Texas: 717 Texas, Suite 3300. Telephone: 832-239-3939. Telecopier: 832-239-3600.
In Irvine, California: 3 Park Plaza, Suite 1100. Telephone: 949-851-3939. Telecopier: 949-553-7539.
In London, England: 21 Tudor Street. Telephone: 44-20-7039-5959. Telecopier: 44-20-7039-5999.
In Los Angeles, California: 555 South Flower Street, Fiftieth Floor. Telephone: 213-489-3939. Telecopier: 213-243-2539.
In Madrid, Spain: Velázquez 51, 4th Floor. Telephone: 34-91-520-39-39. Telecopier: 34-91-520-39-38.
In Menlo Park, California: 2882 Sand Hill Road, Suite 240. Telephone: 650-739-3939. Telecopier: 650-739-3900.
In Milan, Italy: Via Turati, 16/18. Telephone: 39-02-7645-4001. Telecopier: 39-02-7645-4400.
In Moscow, Russia: Smolenskaya Square 3, 9th Floor, 121099 Moscow. Telephone: 7-095-980-6769. Telecopier: 7-095-980-6765.
In Munich, Germany: Prinzregentenstr. 11, 80538 Munich. Telephone: 089-20 60 42-200. Telecopier: 089-20 60 42-293.
In New York, New York: 222 East 41st Street. Telephone: 212-326-3939. Telecopier: 212-755-7306.
In Paris, France: 120, rue du Faubourg Saint-Honoré. Telephone: 33-1-56-59-39-39. Telecopier: 33-1-56-59-39-38.
In Pittsburgh, Pennsylvania: 500 Grant Street, One Mellon Bank Center, 31st Floor. Telephone: 412-391-3939. Telecopier: 412-394-7959.
In San Diego, California: 12750 High Bluff Drive, Suite 300. Telephone: 858-314-1200. Telecopier: 858-314-1150.
In San Francisco, California: 555 California Street, 26th Floor. Telephone: 415-626-3939. Telecopier: 415-875-5700.
In Shanghai, China: 30th Floor, Shanghai Kerry Centre, 1515 Nanjing Road West. Telephone: 86-21-2201-8000. Telecopier: 86-21-5298-6569.
In Singapore, Singapore: 30 Cecil Street, #29-01 Prudential Tower. Telephone: 65 6 538 3939. Telecopier: 65 6 536 3939.
In Sydney, Australia: Australia Square, Level 38, 264-278 George Street. Telephone: 61-2-8272-0500. Telecopier: 61-2-8272-0599.
In Taipei, Taiwan: 6th Floor, 2 Tun Hwa South Road, Section 2. Telephone: (886-2) 2704-6808 or (886-2) 7712-3399. Telecopier: (886-2) 2704-6791.
In Tokyo, Japan: Shiroyama MT Building, 6th Floor, 1-17 Toranomon 4-chome, Minato-ku, Tokyo 105-0001. Telephone: 81-3-3433-3939. Telecopier: 81-3-5401-2725.
In Washington, D.C.: 51 Louisiana Avenue, N.W. Telephone: 202-879-3939. Telecopier: 202-626-1700.

Full-Service Civil Practice, Antitrust and Competition Law, Business Restructuring and Reorganization, Capital Markets, Complex Commercial and Multrijurisdictional Litigation, Corporate Criminal Investigations, Employee Benefits and Executive Compensation, Energy Delivery and Power, Government Regulation, Health Care, Intellectual Property and Technology, International Litigation and Arbitration, Issues and Appeals, Labor and Employment, Lending/Structured Finance and Derivatives, Life Sciences, Mergers and Acquisitions, Oil and Gas, Private Equity, Products Liability, Personal Injury Torts and Health Litigation, Real Estate and Environment, Securities and Shareholder Litigation, Tax.

MEMBERS OF FIRM IN CLEVELAND

STEPHEN J. BROGAN, born Manhattan, New York; admitted to bar, 1977, District of Columbia (Not admitted in Ohio). *Education:* Boston College (A.B., 1974); University of Notre Dame (J.D., 1977). Managing Partner, January 1, 2003. Deputy Assistant Attorney General, Office of Legal Policy, U.S. Department of Justice, 1981-1983. (Also at Washington, D.C. Office). ***PRACTICE AREAS:*** Litigation; Complex Business Litigation; Corporate Investigations; Qui Tam Litigation. ***Email:*** sjbrogan@jonesday.com

KENNETH R. ADAMO, born Staten Island, New York; admitted to bar, 1975, Illinois; 1976, New York; 1984, Ohio; 1988, Texas; registered to practice before U.S. Patent and Trademark Office. *Education:* Rensselaer Polytechnic Institute (B.S., Ch.E., 1972); Albany Law School of Union University (J.D., 1975); John Marshall Law School (LL.M., 1989). ***PRACTICE AREAS:*** Intellectual Property; Patent Litigation; Trademarks; Unfair Competition. ***Email:*** kradamo@jonesday.com

DAVID F. ADLER, born Cleveland, Ohio; admitted to bar, 1986, Ohio. *Education:* University of Michigan (B.A., 1983); Benjamin N. Cardozo School of Law (J.D., 1986). ***PRACTICE AREAS:*** Litigation; Complex Business Litigation; Products Liability; Unfair Competition. ***Email:*** dfadler@jonesday.com

DAVID B. ALDEN, born Syracuse, New York; admitted to bar, 1983, Ohio. *Education:* Oberlin College (B.A., 1980); University of Michigan (J.D., 1983). Phi Beta Kappa; Order of the Coif. ***PRACTICE AREAS:*** Litigation; Products Liability. ***Email:*** dbalden@jonesday.com

RANDAL S. BARINGER, born Youngstown, Ohio; admitted to bar, 1990, Ohio. *Education:* Youngstown State University (B.S., 1981); The Ohio State University (J.D., 1990). Order of the Coif. ***PRACTICE AREAS:*** Litigation; Products Liability. ***Email:*** rsbaringer@jonesday.com

RICHARD J. BEDELL, JR., born Akron, Ohio; admitted to bar, 1987, Ohio. *Education:* University of Akron (B.S.C.E., 1979); University of Colorado (M.S.C.E., 1982); Boston College (J.D., 1987). ***PRACTICE AREAS:*** Litigation; Complex Business Litigation; Products Liability; Insurance Coverage. ***Email:*** rjbedell@jonesday.com

MARK A. BELASIC, born Springfield, Illinois; admitted to bar, 1986, Ohio. *Education:* The College of Wooster (B.A., 1983); Columbia University (J.D., 1986). ***PRACTICE AREAS:*** Litigation; Products Liability. ***Email:*** mabelasic@jonesday.com

THOMAS A. BRIGGS, born Canton, Ohio; admitted to bar, 1994, Ohio; registered to practice before U.S. Patent and Trademark Office. *Education:* University of Akron (B.S.Ch.E., 1987); John Marshall Law School (J.D., 1994). Order of the Coif. ***PRACTICE AREAS:*** Intellectual Property Rights; Intellectual Property Licensing; Strategic Alliances; Joint Ventures; Technology Contracts. ***Email:*** tabriggs@jonesday.com

KATHLEEN B. BURKE, born Brooklyn, New York; admitted to bar, 1973, Ohio. *Education:* St. John's University (B.A., 1969; J.D., 1973). President, Ohio State Bar Association, 1993-1994. ***PRACTICE AREAS:*** Litigation; Complex Business Litigation; Insurance Coverage; Appellate Practice. ***Email:*** kbburke@jonesday.com

ROBERT L. CANALA, born Weirton, West Virginia; admitted to bar, 1986, Ohio. *Education:* West Virginia University (B.S., 1977; M.B.A., 1979); University of Akron (J.D., 1986). Law Clerk to Judge Batchelder, U.S. District Court, Northern District of Ohio, 1986-1988. ***PRACTICE AREAS:*** Intellectual Property; Patent Litigation. ***Email:*** rcanala@jonesday.com

DENISE A. CARKHUFF, born Geneva, Ohio; admitted to bar, 1995, Ohio. *Education:* Miami University (B.A., 1992); University of Toledo (J.D., 1995). Phi Beta Kappa; Order of the Coif. ***Email:*** dcarkhuff@jonesday.com

WILLIAM H. COQUILLETTE, born Boston, Massachusetts; admitted to bar, 1975, Ohio; 1976, Massachusetts. *Education:* Yale University (B.A., 1971); University College, Oxford, England (B.A., 1973); Harvard University (J.D., 1975). Phi Beta Kappa. Marshal Scholar. Law Clerk to Justice Wilkins, Massachusetts Supreme Court, 1975-1976. ***PRACTICE AREAS:*** Mergers and Acquisitions; Leveraged Buyouts; Venture Capital. ***Email:*** whcoquillette@jonesday.com

PAUL G. CRIST, born Denver, Colorado; admitted to bar, 1974, Ohio; 1976, California. *Education:* University of Nebraska (B.A., 1971); New York University (J.D., 1974). Order of the Coif. Fellow, American College of Trial Lawyers. ***PRACTICE AREAS:*** Litigation; Products Liability. ***Email:*** pgcrist@jonesday.com

JOHN D. CURRIVAN, born Paris, France; admitted to bar, 1978, Ohio. *Education:* Cornell University (B.S., 1968; J.D., 1978); University of California, Berkeley (M.S., 1969); University of West Florida (M.S., 1971). Tau Beta Pi; Order of the Coif. Trial Judge, U.S. Navy, 1983-1984. ***PRACTICE AREAS:*** Taxation; Federal Income Tax; Partnership Taxation. ***Email:*** jdcurrivan@jonesday.com

THOMAS C. DANIELS, born Akron, Ohio; admitted to bar, 1986, Ohio. *Education:* Kent State University (B.Mus., 1977; M.Mus., 1982); University of Akron (J.D., 1986). Law Clerk to Judge Potter, U.S. District Court, Northern District of Ohio, 1986-1988. ***PRACTICE AREAS:*** Securities; Initial Public Offerings; Capital Markets. ***Email:*** tcdaniels@jonesday.com

THOMAS DEMITRACK, born Denville, New Jersey; admitted to bar, 1979, Ohio. *Education:* University of Hartford (B.Mus., 1976); The Ohio State University (J.D., 1979). Order of the Coif. ***PRACTICE AREAS:*** Antitrust and Trade Regulation; Price-Fixing. ***Email:*** tdemitrack@jonesday.com

ROBERT P. DUCATMAN, born Cleveland, Ohio; admitted to bar, 1980, Ohio. *Education:* Cleveland State University (B.A., 1977; J.D., 1980). Law Clerk to Judge Manos, U.S. District Court, Northern District of Ohio, 1980-1983. ***PRACTICE AREAS:*** Intellectual Property; Covenants Not To Compete; Patent Infringement; Trademark Infringement. ***Email:*** rducatman@jonesday.com

(This Listing Continued)

JONES DAY, Cleveland—Continued

JOHN P. DUNN, born Tiffin, Ohio; admitted to bar, 1974, Ohio; 1983, New York. *Education:* Marquette University (B.A., 1971); Georgetown University (J.D., 1974). ***PRACTICE AREAS:*** International Commercial Law; Cross Border Investment. ***Email:*** jpdunn@jonesday.com

ROBERT S. FAXON, born La Crosse, Wisconsin; admitted to bar, 1992, Ohio. *Education:* Vanderbilt University (B.A., 1989); Case Western Reserve University (J.D., 1992). ***PRACTICE AREAS:*** Complex Business Litigation; Products Liability; Class Action Defense; Mass Torts; Toxic Tort Defense. ***Email:*** rfaxon@jonesday.com

REGAN J. FAY, born Cleveland, Ohio; admitted to bar, 1974, Ohio; registered to practice before U.S. Patent and Trademark Office. *Education:* Massachusetts Institute of Technology (B.S.Ch.E., 1970); George Washington University (J.D., 1974). Order of the Coif. Law Clerk to Judge Miller, U.S. Court of Customs and Patent Appeals, 1973-1975. Patent Examiner, U.S. Patent and Trademark Office, 1970-1972. ***PRACTICE AREAS:*** Intellectual Property; Patent Litigation; Trademark Litigation. ***Email:*** rjfay@jonesday.com

F. DREXEL FEELING, born Washington, D.C.; admitted to bar, 1995, Ohio; registered to practice before U.S. Patent and Trademark Office. *Education:* University of Pennsylvania (B.S., 1984); Wright State University (M.S., 1992); The Ohio State University (J.D., 1995). ***PRACTICE AREAS:*** Intellectual Property Rights; Patent Prosecution; Patent Litigation; International Patent Prosecution; Electrical Patent Prosecution. ***Email:*** f.dfeeling@jonesday.com

MICHELLE K. FISCHER, born Newark, New Jersey; admitted to bar, 1989, Ohio. *Education:* Yale University (B.A., 1986); University of Chicago (J.D., 1989). ***PRACTICE AREAS:*** Antitrust and Trade Regulation. ***Email:*** mfischer@jonesday.com

TIMOTHY P. FRAELICH, born Ashtabula, Ohio; admitted to bar, 1993, Ohio. *Education:* Youngstown State University (B.A., 1983); Cornell University (J.D., 1993). ***PRACTICE AREAS:*** Intellectual Property; Trademark Prosecution; Trademark Infringement. ***Email:*** tfraelich@jonesday.com

LYLE G. GANSKE, born Toledo, Ohio; admitted to bar, 1984, Ohio. *Education:* Bowling Green State University (B.S., B.A., 1981); The Ohio State University (J.D., 1984). Order of the Coif. Law Clerk to Judge Wright, Ohio Supreme Court, 1985-1986. ***PRACTICE AREAS:*** Mergers and Acquisitions; Takeovers; Corporate Governance. ***Email:*** lgganske@jonesday.com

STEVEN N. GEISE, born Olean, New York; admitted to bar, 1996, Ohio. *Education:* University of Dayton (B.A., 1992); Ohio Northern University (J.D., 1995). Law Clerk to Judge Anderson, U.S. District Court of South Carolina, 1995-1996. ***PRACTICE AREAS:*** Civil Litigation; Complex Litigation; Product Liability Defense; Tobacco Litigation. ***Email:*** sngeise@jonesday.com

STEPHEN Q. GIBLIN, born Baltimore, Maryland; admitted to bar, 1980, Ohio. *Education:* Washington & Lee University (B.A., 1977); Duke University (J.D., 1980). Phi Beta Kappa. ***PRACTICE AREAS:*** Environmental Law; Hazardous Materials and Substances; Toxic Substance Liability. ***Email:*** sqgiblin@jonesday.com

CALVIN P. GRIFFITH, born Warren, Ohio; admitted to bar, 1988, Ohio; registered to practice before U.S. Patent and Trademark Office. *Education:* The Ohio State University (B.S., 1983; J.D., 1987). Order of the Coif. ***LANGUAGES:*** Japanese. ***PRACTICE AREAS:*** Intellectual Property; Patent Infringement; Intellectual Property Licensing. ***Email:*** cpgriffith@jonesday.com

THEODORE M. GROSSMAN, born New York, New York; admitted to bar, 1975, New York; 1987, Ohio. *Education:* Cornell University (A.B., 1971; J.D., 1974). Trial and Appellate Counsel, Civil Division, U.S. Department of Justice, 1980-1984. Fellow, American College of Trial Lawyers. ***PRACTICE AREAS:*** Litigation; Products Liability. ***Email:*** tgrossman@jonesday.com

DANIEL C. HAGEN, born Cleveland, Ohio; admitted to bar, 1980, Ohio. *Education:* Baldwin-Wallace College (B.A., 1977); University of Virginia (J.D., 1980). Order of the Coif. ***PRACTICE AREAS:*** Employee Benefits; ERISA; Executive Compensation; Pension Plans. ***Email:*** dchagen@jonesday.com

THOMAS A. HAMILTON, born Cleveland, Ohio; admitted to bar, 1993, Ohio; 1998, Illinois. *Education:* University of Michigan (B.A., 1990); Case Western Reserve University (J.D., 1993). ***PRACTICE AREAS:*** Environmental Law; Air Pollution; Environmental Risk Management; Brownfields Redevelopment; Environmental Litigation. ***Email:*** tahamilton@jonesday.com

CHARLES W. HARDIN, JR., born Conneaut, Ohio; admitted to bar, 1987, Ohio. *Education:* Ohio Northern University (B.A., 1984); The Ohio State University (J.D., 1987). Order of the Coif. ***PRACTICE AREAS:*** Mergers and Acquisitions; Merchant Banking. ***Email:*** charleswhardin@jonesday.com

DAVID G. HEIMAN, born Cincinnati, Ohio; admitted to bar, 1971, Ohio. *Education:* University of Cincinnati (B.B.A., 1967; J.D., 1970). Order of the Coif. Chairman, Commercial Financial Services Committee, Business Law Section, American Bar Association, 1990-1994. ***PRACTICE AREAS:*** Bankruptcy; Bankruptcy Chapter 11; Lender Liability. ***Email:*** dgheiman@jonesday.com

MARK HERRMANN, born Abington, Pennsylvania; admitted to bar, 1983, California; 1988, Illinois; 1990, Ohio. *Education:* Princeton University (A.B., 1979); University of Michigan (J.D., 1983). Order of the Coif. Law Clerk to Judge Nelson, U.S. Court of Appeals, Ninth Circuit, 1983-1984. ***PRACTICE AREAS:*** Litigation; Class Action Defense; Complex Litigation. ***Email:*** mherrmann@jonesday.com

WILLIAM A. HERZBERGER, born Cleveland, Ohio; admitted to bar, 1987, Ohio. *Education:* Miami University (B.S., 1984); The Ohio State University (J.D., 1987). ***PRACTICE AREAS:*** Real Estate; Real Estate Development; Real Estate Finance. ***Email:*** wherzberger@jonesday.com

CHRISTOPHER J. HEWITT, born Oswego, New York; admitted to bar, 1995, New York; 1998, Ohio. *Education:* University of Toledo (B.B.A., 1990); Georgetown University Law Center (J.D., 1994); Georgetown University (M.B.A., 1994). Order of the Coif. ***PRACTICE AREAS:*** Corporate Law; Business Law; Finance; Mergers, Acquisitions and Divestitures; Securities. ***Email:*** cjhewitt@jonesday.com

KENNETH G. HOCHMAN, born Mt. Vernon, New York; admitted to bar, 1973, Ohio; 1977, Florida; 1981, New York. *Education:* State University of New York at Buffalo (B.A., 1969); Columbia University (J.D., 1972). Phi Beta Kappa. Fellow, American College of Trust and Estate Counsel. ***PRACTICE AREAS:*** Estate Planning; Estate Administration; Family Wealth Transfer. ***Email:*** kghochman@jonesday.com

WALTER S. HOLZER, born Pittsburgh, Pennsylvania; admitted to bar, 1995, Ohio. *Education:* The Ohio State University (B.S., 1991); Capital University (J.D., 1995). ***Email:*** wsholzer@jonesday.com

RONALD R. JANKE, born Milwaukee, Wisconsin; admitted to bar, 1974, Ohio. *Education:* Wittenberg University (B.A., 1969); Duke University (J.D., 1974). Order of the Coif. Chairman, Environmental Controls Committee, Section of Corporation, Banking and Business Law, American Bar Association, 1980-1983. ***PRACTICE AREAS:*** Environmental Law; Environmental Liability; Hazardous Waste. ***Email:*** rrjanke@jonesday.com

CARL M. JENKS, born Cleveland, Ohio; admitted to bar, 1982, Ohio. *Education:* Carleton College (B.A., 1967); Duke University (M.A., 1973; Ph.D., 1979); Harvard University (J.D., 1980). Law Clerk to Judge Mansfield, U.S. Court of Appeals, Second Circuit, 1980-1981. ***LANGUAGES:*** Portuguese. ***PRACTICE AREAS:*** Taxation; Tax Controversies; Federal Income Tax; Bankruptcy Taxation. ***Email:*** cmjenks@jonesday.com

STEPHEN J. KACZYNSKI, born Brooklyn, New York; admitted to bar, 1979, New York; 1986, Ohio. *Education:* St. John's University (B.A., 1976; J.D., 1978); University of Virginia (LL.M., 1984). Trial Attorney, U.S. Army Judge Advocate General Corps, 1979-1985. ***PRACTICE AREAS:*** Litigation; Products Liability. ***Email:*** skaczynski@jonesday.com

ROBERT C. KAHRL, born Mount Vernon, Ohio; admitted to bar, 1975, Ohio. *Education:* Princeton University (A.B., 1968); The Ohio State University (M.B.A., 1975; J.D., 1975). Order of the Coif. Law Clerk to Judge Weick, U.S. Court of Appeals, Sixth Circuit, 1975-1976. ***PRACTICE AREAS:*** Intellectual Property; Intellectual Property Litigation; Electronic Intellectual Property. ***Email:*** rckahrl@jonesday.com

SANJIV K. KAPUR, born Rochester, New York; admitted to bar, 1985, Massachusetts; 1986, New York; 1992, Ohio. *Education:* Harvard University (A.B., 1982; J.D., 1985). Phi Beta Kappa. Fulbright Fellowship, Pontificia Universidad Catolica del Ecuador, 1985-1986. Law Clerk to Judge Nelson, U.S. Court of Appeals, Sixth Circuit, 1987-1988. Deutscher Akademischer Austauschdienst Juristenprogramm, 1988-1989. ***LANGUAGES:*** French, German and Spanish. ***PRACTICE AREAS:*** International Securities; Cross Border Investment; Investment in Latin America. ***Email:*** skapur@jonesday.com

CHRISTOPHER M. KELLY, born Buffalo, New York; admitted to bar, 1988, New York; 2001, Ohio. *Education:* Canisius College (B.A., 1983); Duke University (J.D., 1986). ***PRACTICE AREAS:*** Capital Markets; Corporate Finance; Securities; Technology Finance. ***Email:*** ckelly@jonesday.com

DENNIS M. KELLY, born Cleveland, Ohio; admitted to bar, 1968, Ohio. *Education:* John Carroll University (A.B., 1965); University of Notre Dame (J.D., 1968). Law Clerk to Judge Bright, U.S. Court of Appeals, Eighth Circuit, 1968-1969. ***PRACTICE AREAS:*** Litigation; Complex Business Litigation; Class Action Defense; Environmental Law. ***Email:*** dmkelly@jonesday.com

PAUL D. KOETHE, born Lorain, Ohio; admitted to bar, 1986, Ohio. *Education:* Bucknell University (B.S.B.A., 1981); Case Western Reserve University (J.D., 1986). Order of the Coif. ***PRACTICE AREAS:*** Litigation; Products Liability; Business Litigation. ***Email:*** pdkoethe@jonesday.com

DAVID A. KUTIK, born Paterson, New Jersey; admitted to bar, 1980, Ohio. *Education:* Colgate University (A.B., 1977); Case Western Reserve University (J.D., 1980). Order of the Coif. ***PRACTICE AREAS:*** Litigation; Complex Business Litigation; Complex Commercial Litigation; Energy. ***Email:*** dakutik@jonesday.com

DENNIS W. LABARRE, born Binghamton, New York; admitted to bar, 1968, Ohio. *Education:* Northwestern University (B.A., 1965); University of Virginia (LL.B., 1968). (Also at New York Office). ***PRACTICE AREAS:*** Securities; Corporate Banking Law; Cross Border Investment. ***Email:*** dwlabarre@jonesday.com

RICHARD P. LAYMAN, born Columbus, Ohio; admitted to bar, 1980, Ohio. *Education:* Ohio Northern University (B.A., 1977); University of Michigan (J.D., 1980). Order of the Coif. ***PRACTICE AREAS:*** Estate Planning; International Estate Planning; Personal Planning. ***Email:*** rplayman@jonesday.com

JEFFREY S. LEAVITT, born Cleveland, Ohio; admitted to bar, 1973, Ohio. *Education:* Cornell University (A.B., 1968); Case Western Reserve University (J.D., 1973). Order of the Coif. ***PRACTICE AREAS:*** Employee Benefits; Pension Plans; Tax Exempt Organizations. ***Email:*** jleavitt@jonesday.com

PATRICK J. LEDDY, born Cleveland, Ohio; admitted to bar, 1990, Ohio. *Education:* Cleveland State University (B.B.A., 1987; J.D., 1990). ***PRACTICE AREAS:*** Mergers and Acquisitions; Corporate Finance; Securities. ***Email:*** pjleddy@jonesday.com

HEATHER LENNOX, born Cleveland, Ohio; admitted to bar, 1992, Ohio. *Education:* John Carroll University (B.A., 1989); Georgetown University (J.D., 1992). ***PRACTICE AREAS:*** Bankruptcy; Bankruptcy Chapter 11; Out of Court Debt Restructuring; Commercial Insolvency; Fraudulent Conveyance. ***Email:*** hlennox@jonesday.com

IRVIN A. LEONARD, born Philadelphia, Pennsylvania; admitted to bar, 1967, New York; 1969, Ohio. *Education:* University of Pittsburgh (B.A., 1964); New York University (J.D., 1967). Phi Beta Kappa; Order of the Coif. Law Clerk to Judge Wyatt, U.S. District Court, Southern District of New York, 1967-1969. ***PRACTICE AREAS:*** Real Estate Development; Technology Transfers; Sports Law; Health Care; Corporate Law. ***Email:*** ialeonard@jonesday.com

BARBARA J. LEUKART, born New York, New York; admitted to bar, 1975, Ohio. *Education:* Barnard College (B.A., 1971); Case Western Reserve University (J.D., 1975). Order of the Coif. ***PRACTICE AREAS:*** Labor and Employment; Employment Litigation; Title VII Discrimination. ***Email:*** bjleukart@jonesday.com

(This Listing Continued)

MARY D. MALONEY, born Cleveland, Ohio; admitted to bar, 1987, Ohio. *Education:* University of Akron (B.S., 1984); Cleveland State University (J.D., 1987). ***PRACTICE AREAS:*** Employee Benefits; Deferred Compensation; Retirement Benefit Plans. ***Email:*** mdmaloney@jonesday.com

MICHAEL G. MARTING, born Cleveland, Ohio; admitted to bar, 1974, Ohio. *Education:* Yale University (B.A., 1971; J.D., 1974). Phi Beta Kappa. ***PRACTICE AREAS:*** Mergers and Acquisitions; Public Corporations. ***Email:*** mgmarting@jonesday.com

BERNADETTE MIHALIC MAST, born Lorain, Ohio; admitted to bar, 1988, Ohio. *Education:* The Ohio State University (B.S., 1982); Case Western Reserve University (J.D., 1988). Order of the Coif. Certified Public Accountant, Ohio, 1986. ***PRACTICE AREAS:*** Real Estate; Real Estate Secured Lending; Construction Finance. ***Email:*** bmmast@jonesday.com

STEPHEN C. MIXTER, born Columbus, Ohio; admitted to bar, 1986, Ohio. *Education:* The Ohio State University (B.A., 1983); Duke University (J.D., 1986). Phi Beta Kappa; Order of the Coif. ***PRACTICE AREAS:*** Real Estate; Corporate Real Estate. ***Email:*** smixter@jonesday.com

ANTHONY R. MOORE, born Cleveland, Ohio; admitted to bar, 1975, Ohio. *Education:* Harvard University (A.B., 1972); University of Virginia (J.D., 1975). ***PRACTICE AREAS:*** Mergers and Acquisitions; Venture Capital. ***Email:*** armoore@jonesday.com

DENNIS L. MURPHY, born Philadelphia, Pennsylvania; admitted to bar, 1991, Pennsylvania; 1994, Ohio. *Education:* King's College (B.A., 1988); Case Western Reserve University (J.D., 1991). Order of the Coif. Law Clerk to Judge Kosik, U.S. District Court, Middle District of Pennsylvania, 1991-1993. ***PRACTICE AREAS:*** Litigation; Products Liability. ***Email:*** dlmurphy@jonesday.com

JOHN M. NEWMAN, JR., born Youngstown, Ohio; admitted to bar, 1970, Illinois; 1972, California; 1976, Ohio. *Education:* Georgetown University (B.A., 1966); Harvard University (J.D., 1969). Phi Beta Kappa. Law Clerk to Judge Hill, U.S. District Court, Central District of California, 1969-1970. Assistant U.S. Attorney, Central District of California, U.S. Attorney's Office, 1970-1975. Fellow, American College of Trial Lawyers. ***PRACTICE AREAS:*** Litigation; Complex Business Litigation; Securities Litigation. ***Email:*** jmnewman@jonesday.com

TIMOTHY J. O'HEARN, born Canton, Ohio; admitted to bar, 1984, Ohio; registered to practice before U.S. Patent and Trademark Office. *Education:* University of Cincinnati (B.S.M.E., 1979); University of Akron (J.D., 1983). Tau Beta Pi. ***PRACTICE AREAS:*** Intellectual Property; Intellectual Property Portfolio Management; Trademarks. ***Email:*** tohearn@jonesday.com

ZACHARY T. PARIS, born Cleveland, Ohio; admitted to bar, 1973, Ohio. *Education:* Yale University (B.A., 1970; J.D., 1973). Phi Beta Kappa. Law Clerk to Judge Thomas, U.S. District Court, Northern District of Ohio, 1973-1974. ***PRACTICE AREAS:*** Real Estate; Real Estate Development; Corporate Real Estate. ***Email:*** ztparis@jonesday.com

WILLIAM T. PLESEC, born Cleveland, Ohio; admitted to bar, 1971, Ohio; 1981, District of Columbia. *Education:* John Carroll University (A.B., 1966); Cleveland State University (J.D., 1971). Trial Attorney, Antitrust Division, U.S. Department of Justice, 1971-1975. ***PRACTICE AREAS:*** Complex Business Litigation; Products Liability; Corporate Criminal Law. ***Email:*** wtplesec@jonesday.com

JOSEPH D. POLLACK, born Cleveland, Ohio; admitted to bar, 1984, Ohio. *Education:* Bowling Green State University (B.B.A., 1975); University of Akron (J.D., 1984). ***PRACTICE AREAS:*** Intellectual Property; Patent Litigation; Trade Secrets. ***Email:*** jdpollack@jonesday.com

DAVID P. PORTER, born Hayward, California; admitted to bar, 1981, Ohio. *Education:* University of California, Davis (B.S., 1975); Case Western Reserve University (J.D., 1981). Order of the Coif. ***PRACTICE AREAS:*** Capital Markets; Securities; Corporate Finance. ***Email:*** dporter@jonesday.com

RACHEL L. RAWSON, born Pittsburgh, Pennsylvania; admitted to bar, 1991, New York; 1995, Ohio. *Education:* Kenyon College (B.A., 1987); Columbia University (J.D., 1990). Phi Beta Kappa. ***PRACTICE AREAS:*** Banks and Banking; Secured Lending; Mezzanine Finance; Out of Court Debt Restructuring. ***Email:*** rlrawson@jonesday.com

ROBERT H. RAWSON, JR., born Washington, D.C.; admitted to bar, 1971, Ohio; 1972, District of Columbia. *Education:* Princeton University (A.B., 1966); Oxford University, England (M.A., 1968); Harvard University (J.D., 1971). Phi Beta Kappa; Rhodes Scholar. ***PRACTICE AREAS:*** Antitrust and Trade Regulation; Antitrust Class Actions. ***Email:*** rrawson@jonesday.com

JOHN A. REGO, born Cincinnati, Ohio; admitted to bar, 1988, Ohio. *Education:* Stanford University (B.S., 1982); University of Virginia (J.D., 1986). Tau Beta Pi; Order of the Coif. Law Clerk to Judge Harris, U.S. District Court for the District of Columbia, 1986-1987. ***PRACTICE AREAS:*** Environmental Law; Environmental Risk Management; Brownfields Redevelopment. ***Email:*** jrego@jonesday.com

RICHARD L. REPPERT, born Philadelphia, Pennsylvania; admitted to bar, 1974, Ohio; 1993, Pennsylvania. *Education:* Lehigh University (B.A., 1970); Villanova University (J.D., 1974). Order of the Coif. Member, American College of Real Estate Lawyers. ***PRACTICE AREAS:*** Commercial Real Estate Finance; Mortgages. ***Email:*** rreppert@jonesday.com

JEANNE M. RICKERT, born Cambridge, Massachusetts; admitted to bar, 1980, Ohio. *Education:* Cornell University (B.A., 1975); Case Western Reserve University (J.D., 1978). Order of the Coif. Law Clerk to Judge Contie, U.S. District Court, Northern District of Ohio, 1978-1980. ***LANGUAGES:*** French. ***PRACTICE AREAS:*** Joint Ventures; Limited Liability Company Law. ***Email:*** jmrickert@jonesday.com

GEOFFREY J. RITTS, born Lansing, Michigan; admitted to bar, 1993, Ohio. *Education:* Yale University (B.A., 1989; J.D., 1993). Phi Beta Kappa. Law Clerk to Judge Nelson, U.S. Court of Appeals, Sixth Circuit, 1993-1994. ***PRACTICE AREAS:*** Securities Litigation; Banking Litigation; ERISA Litigation; Multidistrict Litigation. ***Email:*** gjritts@jonesday.com

LISA A. ROBERTS-MAMONE, born Pittsburgh, Pennsylvania; admitted to bar, 1988, Ohio. *Education:* Grove City College (B.A., 1985); Case Western Reserve University

(This Listing Continued)

(J.D., 1988). Order of the Coif. ***PRACTICE AREAS:*** Trusts and Estates; Federal Estate and Gift Taxation; Generation Skipping Taxes. ***Email:*** larobertsmamone@jonesday.com

LOUIS RORIMER, born New York, New York; admitted to bar, 1975, Ohio. *Education:* Harvard University (A.B., 1969); Case Western Reserve University (J.D., 1975). ***PRACTICE AREAS:*** Mergers and Acquisitions; Equity Compensation; Insider Trading. ***Email:*** lrorimer@jonesday.com

JAMES A. RYDZEL, born Worcester, Massachusetts; admitted to bar, 1972, Ohio; 1975, Florida. *Education:* St. Louis University (B.A., 1968); Duke University (J.D., 1971). Phi Beta Kappa. Adjunct Professor of Law, Case Western Reserve University, 1986-1990. ***PRACTICE AREAS:*** Labor and Employment; Employment Litigation; Labor Arbitration. ***Email:*** jarydzel@jonesday.com

JOHN M. SAADA, JR., born Cleveland, Ohio; admitted to bar, 1993, Ohio. *Education:* John Carroll University (B.S., 1988); Case Western Reserve University (J.D., 1993). Order of the Coif. ***PRACTICE AREAS:*** Mergers and Acquisitions; Leveraged Buyouts; Venture Capital. ***Email:*** johnmsaada@jonesday.com

EDWARD J. SEBOLD, born Morgantown, West Virginia; admitted to bar, 1994, Ohio. *Education:* John Carroll University (B.A., 1987); University of Michigan (J.D., 1990). Order of the Coif. Law Clerk to Judge Wilkinson, U.S. Court of Appeals, Fourth Circuit, 1990-1991. ***PRACTICE AREAS:*** Litigation; Complex Commercial Litigation; Class Action Defense; Products Liability. ***Email:*** edwardjsebold@jonesday.com

STEVEN E. SIGALOW, born Akron, Ohio; admitted to bar, 1975, Ohio. *Education:* The Ohio State University (B.A., 1972); Case Western Reserve University (J.D., 1975). Phi Beta Kappa; Order of the Coif. ***PRACTICE AREAS:*** Litigation; Insurance Coverage; Complex Business Litigation. ***Email:*** sesigalow@jonesday.com

DAVID W. SLOAN, born Rahway, New Jersey; admitted to bar, 1974, Ohio. *Education:* Princeton University (A.B., 1963); Stanford University (M.S., 1965); Harvard University (J.D., 1970). Adjunct Professor of Law, Case Western Reserve University, 1975. ***PRACTICE AREAS:*** Technology Contracts; Technology Transfers; Technology Finance. ***Email:*** dwsloan@jonesday.com

STEPHEN G. SOZIO, born Philadelphia, Pennsylvania; admitted to bar, 1983, Ohio. *Education:* Pennsylvania State University (B.A., 1979); Cleveland State University (J.D., 1983). Assistant U.S. Attorney, U.S. Attorney's Office, Northern District of Ohio, 1989-2000. ***PRACTICE AREAS:*** Corporate Criminal Law; Corporate Investigations; Fraud. ***Email:*** sgsozio@jonesday.com

STEPHEN J. SQUERI, born New York, New York; admitted to bar, 1979, Ohio; 2003, Colorado. *Education:* Hofstra University (B.A., 1976); University of Notre Dame (J.D., 1979). Phi Beta Kappa. ***PRACTICE AREAS:*** Antitrust; Complex Litigation; Grand Jury Practice; Franchise Distribution; Trial Practice. ***Email:*** sjsqueri@jonesday.com

JOHN L. STRAUCH, born Pittsburgh, Pennsylvania; admitted to bar, 1963, New York; 1964, Ohio. *Education:* University of Pittsburgh (B.A., 1960); New York University (LL.B., 1963). Phi Beta Kappa; Order of the Coif. Law Clerk to Judge Waterman, U.S. Court of Appeals, Second Circuit, 1963-1964. President, Cleveland Bar Association, 1985-1986. Fellow, American College of Trial Lawyers. ***PRACTICE AREAS:*** Litigation; Complex Business Litigation; Products Liability; Class Action Defense. ***Email:*** jlstrauch@jonesday.com

RICHARD G. STUHAN, born Braddock, Pennsylvania; admitted to bar, 1976, Virginia; 1977, District of Columbia; 1986, Ohio. *Education:* Duquesne University (B.A., 1973); University of Virginia (J.D., 1976). Order of the Coif. ***PRACTICE AREAS:*** Litigation; Products Liability. ***Email:*** rgstuhan@jonesday.com

BRIAN F. TOOHEY, born Niagara Falls, New York; admitted to bar, 1969, New York; 1980, Ohio. *Education:* Niagara University (B.S., 1966); Cornell University (J.D., 1969). ***PRACTICE AREAS:*** Litigation; Insurance Coverage; Professional Liability. ***Email:*** bftoohey@jonesday.com

JEFFERY D. UBERSAX, born Cleveland, Ohio; admitted to bar, 1984, District of Columbia; 1988, Ohio. *Education:* Amherst College (B.A., 1977); Harvard University (M.A., 1978; J.D., 1982). Phi Beta Kappa. Law Clerk to Judge Schwarzer, U.S. District Court, Northern District of California, 1982-1983. ***LANGUAGES:*** German. ***PRACTICE AREAS:*** Litigation; Business Litigation; Class Action Defense; Corporate Criminal Law. ***Email:*** jdubersax@jonesday.com

MICHAEL W. VARY, born Arlington, Virginia; admitted to bar, 1982, Illinois; 1986, Ohio; registered to practice before U.S. Patent and Trademark Office. *Education:* John Carroll University (B.S., 1975); Yale University (M.S., M.Phil., 1978; Ph.D., 1980); Case Western Reserve University (J.D., 1982). ***PRACTICE AREAS:*** Intellectual Property; Intellectual Property Litigation; Chemical Patents. ***Email:*** michaelvary@jonesday.com

ROBERT S. WALKER, born Cleveland, Ohio; admitted to bar, 1982, Ohio. *Education:* Dyke College (B.S., 1979); Cleveland State University (J.D., 1982). ***PRACTICE AREAS:*** Litigation; Products Liability; Insurance Coverage; Class Action Defense. ***Email:*** rswalker@jonesday.com

JAMES L. WAMSLEY, III, born Lakewood, Ohio; admitted to bar, 1975, Ohio; registered to practice before U.S. Patent and Trademark Office. *Education:* University of Virginia (B.S.E.E., 1972); University of Michigan (J.D., 1975). Tau Beta Pi. ***PRACTICE AREAS:*** Intellectual Property; Intellectual Property Litigation; Trade Secrets. ***Email:*** jlwamsleyiii@jonesday.com

ROBERT C. WEBER, born Chester, Pennsylvania; admitted to bar, 1976, Ohio. *Education:* Yale University (B.A., 1972); Duke University (J.D., 1976). Order of the Coif. President, Cleveland Bar Association, 1995-1996. Fellow: American College of Trial Lawyers; International Academy of Trial Lawyers. ***PRACTICE AREAS:*** Litigation; Products Liability; Complex Business Litigation; Class Action Defense. ***Email:*** rcweber@jonesday.com

RICHARD B. WHITNEY, born Corpus Christi, Texas; admitted to bar, 1973, Ohio; 1998, New York. *Education:* Union College, New York (B.A., 1970); Case Western Reserve University (J.D., 1973). Order of the Coif. ***PRACTICE AREAS:*** Litigation; Complex Business Litigation; Insurance Insolvency; Professional Liability. ***Email:*** rbwhitney@jonesday.com

(This Listing Continued)

JONES DAY, Cleveland—Continued

PAULA BATT WILSON, born Buffalo, New York; admitted to bar, 1995, Ohio. *Education:* Brown University (A.B., 1980); Case Western Reserve University (J.D., 1995). Order of the Coif. ***PRACTICE AREAS:*** Civil Litigation. ***Email:*** pbwilson@jonesday.com

JAMES E. YOUNG, born Mentor, Ohio; admitted to bar, 1972, Ohio. *Education:* Ohio University (B.B.A., 1968); The Ohio State University (J.D., 1972). Order of the Coif. Law Clerk to Judge Phillips, U.S. Court of Appeals, Sixth Circuit, 1972-1973. Chief Counsel, 1980-1981 and Law Director, 1981-1982, City of Cleveland, Ohio. ***PRACTICE AREAS:*** Litigation; Complex Litigation; Toxic Tort Defense. ***Email:*** jameseyoung@jonesday.com

SENIOR PARTNER

PATRICK F. McCARTAN, born Cleveland, Ohio; admitted to bar, 1960, Ohio. *Education:* University of Notre Dame (A.B., 1956; LL.B., 1959). Managing Partner, January 1, 1993 - December 31, 2002. Law Clerk to Justice Whittaker, U.S. Supreme Court, 1959-1960. Member, Ohio Board of Bar Examiners, 1970-1975. President, Bar Association of Greater Cleveland, 1977-1978. Member, Standing Committee on Rules of Practice and Procedure for the United States Courts, 1998—. Fellow: American College of Trial Lawyers; International Academy of Trial Lawyers. ***PRACTICE AREAS:*** Litigation; Complex Business Litigation; Class Action Defense; U.S. Supreme Court Litigation. ***Email:*** pmccartan@jonesday.com

SENIOR OF COUNSEL

GEORGE J. MOSCARINO, born Cleveland, Ohio; admitted to bar, 1958, Ohio. *Education:* Ohio University (A.B., 1955); Case Western Reserve University (LL.B., 1958; J.D., 1958). Assistant Attorney General, State of Ohio, 1960. Assistant Prosecuting Attorney, Cuyahoga County, 1961-1970. Member, Grand Jury Committee, 1983-1986, Special Advisor, Grand Jury Committee 1986— and Member, Section Council, 1984-1988, Criminal Justice Section, American Bar Association. Fellow, American College of Trial Lawyers. ***PRACTICE AREAS:*** Litigation; Corporate Criminal Law; Corporate Investigations. ***Email:*** gmoscarino@jonesday.com

OF COUNSEL

DAVID B. COCHRAN, born Cleveland, Ohio; admitted to bar, 1996, Ohio; registered to practice before U.S. Patent and Trademark Office. *Education:* University of Illinois (B.S., 1989); Cleveland State University (J.D., 1996). Order of the Coif. ***Email:*** dcochran@jonesday.com

MICHAEL J. HORVITZ, born Cleveland, Ohio; admitted to bar, 1975, Ohio; 1976, Florida. *Education:* University of Pennsylvania (B.S., 1972); University of Virginia (J.D., 1975); New York University (LL.M., 1980). ***Email:*** mjhorvitz@jonesday.com

RICHARD H. SAYLER, born Rochester, New York; admitted to bar, 1970, New York; 1985, Ohio. *Education:* Dartmouth College (A.B., 1966); University of Michigan (J.D., 1969). Order of the Coif. Law Clerk: to Chief Judge Lumbard, U.S. Court of Appeals, Second Circuit, 1969-1970; to Justice White, U.S. Supreme Court, 1970-1971. Special Assistant to the Assistant Attorney General, Antitrust Division, U.S. Department of Justice, 1972-1974. ***PRACTICE AREAS:*** Litigation; Complex Business Litigation; Appellate Practice; Commercial Arbitration. ***Email:*** richardsayler@jonesday.com

COUNSEL

LEOZINO AGOZZINO, born Cleveland, Ohio; admitted to bar, 1985, Ohio. *Education:* Oberlin College (B.A., 1978); The Ohio State University (J.D., 1981). Phi Beta Kappa. ***Email:*** lagozzino@jonesday.com

RANDALL A. COLE, born Akron, Ohio; admitted to bar, 1973, Ohio. *Education:* Washington & Lee University (B.A., 1967); Case Western Reserve University (J.D., 1973). Attorney, 1973-1979 and Deputy Director, 1980-1986, City of Akron Law Department. ***Email:*** racole@jonesday.com

SANDRA E. GAMMIE, born Elyria, Ohio; admitted to bar, 1986, Ohio. *Education:* University of Maryland (B.S., 1971); George Washington University (M.A., 1977); Georgetown University (J.D., 1986). Order of the Coif. ***Email:*** sgammie@jonesday.com

ELLEN E. HALFON, born Los Angeles, California; admitted to bar, 1988, Ohio. *Education:* Immaculate Heart College (B.A., 1980); Loyola Law School, Los Angeles (J.D., 1987). ***Email:*** eehalfon@jonesday.com

CHARLES D. HASSELL, born New York, New York; admitted to bar, 1973, Ohio; 1974, Vermont. *Education:* New York University (B.E., 1968; M.S., 1970; J.D., 1973). Tau Beta Pi; Order of the Coif. Law Clerk to Judge Waterman, U.S. Court of Appeals, Second Circuit, 1973-1974 and 1976-1978. Assistant Attorney General, Office of the Attorney General, State of Vermont, 1974-1976. ***Email:*** cdhassell@jonesday.com

TED S. HISER, born Tiffin, Ohio; admitted to bar, 1985, Ohio. *Education:* Heidelberg College (B.A., 1969); Cleveland State University (J.D., 1985). ***Email:*** tshiser@jonesday.com

KATHLEEN HOHLER, born Lorain, Ohio; admitted to bar, 1980, Ohio. *Education:* Miami University (B.A., 1972); Georgetown University (J.D., 1980). ***Email:*** khohler@jonesday.com

CHARLES M. KENNEDY, born Pittsburgh, Pennsylvania; admitted to bar, 1980, Ohio. *Education:* Grove City College (B.A., 1977); University of Chicago (J.D., 1980). ***Email:*** cmkennedy@jonesday.com

J. JOSEPH KORPICS, born Palmerton, Pennsylvania; admitted to bar, 1991, Ohio. *Education:* University of Notre Dame (B.S., 1983); Texas A & M University (M.S., 1985); University of Houston (J.D., 1991). Environmental Engineer, U.S. Environmental Protection Agency, 1985-1988. ***Email:*** jkorpics@jonesday.com

KATHY P. LAZAR, born Lorain, Ohio; admitted to bar, 1982, Ohio. *Education:* Kent State University (B.A., 1978); Case Western Reserve University (J.D., 1982). Phi Beta Kappa; Order of the Coif. ***Email:*** kplazar@jonesday.com

(This Listing Continued)

STEPHEN D. SCANLON, born New York, New York; admitted to bar, 1985, Ohio; registered to practice before U.S. Patent and Trademark Office. *Education:* State University of New York at Buffalo (B.S., 1980); University of Cincinnati (J.D., 1985). ***Email:*** sdscanlon@jonesday.com

MARC A. SILVERSTEIN, born Baltimore, Maryland; admitted to bar, 1980, District of Columbia; 1986, Maryland; 1989, Ohio. *Education:* Brown University (Sc.B., 1974); Massachusetts Institute of Technology (M.S.C.E., 1976); Harvard University (J.D., 1980). Tau Beta Pi. ***Email:*** msilverstein@jonesday.com

CHARLES M. STEINES, born Warren, Ohio; admitted to bar, 1977, Ohio. *Education:* Miami University (B.S., 1972); Capital University (J.D., 1977); New York University (LL.M., 1983). Assistant Ohio Attorney General, Taxation Section, 1977-1982. ***Email:*** cmsteines@jonesday.com

H. DUANE SWITZER, born Gladstone, Michigan; admitted to bar, 1964, Ohio; registered to practice before U.S. Patent and Trademark Office. *Education:* Michigan Technological University (B.S., 1960); Georgetown University (LL.B., 1963). Tau Beta Pi. Examiner, U.S. Patent Office, 1960-1963. ***Email:*** hswitzer@jonesday.com

ROSE MARY WENSTRUP, born Jackson, Mississippi; admitted to bar, 1995, Ohio. *Education:* St. Louis University (B.A., 1977); Case Western Reserve University (J.D., 1995). Phi Beta Kappa. ***LANGUAGES:*** French. ***Email:*** rwenstrup@jonesday.com

ASSOCIATES

ATOSSA M. ALAVI, born Mashad, Iran; admitted to bar, 2003, Ohio. *Education:* University College of London (Bachelor of Dental Surgery, 1989; M.Phil, Neuroscience, 2003); Royal College of Surgeons, England (Fellow in Dental Surgery, 1994); Eastman Dental Institute, London (M.Sc., Endodontics, 1995); Case Western Reserve University (J.D., 2003). ***LANGUAGES:*** Farsi. ***Email:*** amalavi@jonesday.com

KATHLEEN M. AMER, born Pittsburgh, Pennsylvania; admitted to bar, 2004, Ohio. *Education:* University of Notre Dame (B.B.A., 1998; J.D., 2004). Certified Public Accountant, Ohio, 2001. ***Email:*** kmamer@jonesday.com

LAURA R. ANDERSON, born New York, New York; admitted to bar, 1990, California; 1997, Ohio. *Education:* Vanderbilt University (B.A., B.A., 1987); Pepperdine University (J.D., 1990). ***Email:*** lranderson@jonesday.com

MARK J. ANDREINI, born Oceanside, California; admitted to bar, 1994, Ohio. *Education:* University of Minnesota (B.M., 1988; M.M., 1990; J.D., 1994). Order of the Coif. ***Email:*** mjandreini@jonesday.com

MICHAEL R. ASAM, born Akron, Ohio; admitted to bar, 2001, Ohio; registered to practice before U.S. Patent and Trademark Office. *Education:* Kenyon College (A.B., 1994); University of North Carolina (Ph.D., 1998); Duke University (J.D., 2001). ***Email:*** mrasam@jonesday.com

BRETT P. BARRAGATE, born Cleveland, Ohio; admitted to bar, 1996, Ohio. *Education:* University of Hartford (B.A., 1992); Cleveland State University (J.D., 1996). ***Email:*** bpbarragate@jonesday.com

GREGORY A. BAUER, born Norwalk, Ohio; admitted to bar, 1997, Ohio. *Education:* John Carroll University (B.A., 1993); The Ohio State University (J.D., 1997). ***Email:*** gabauer@jonesday.com

LAURA BERESH, born Greenwich, Connecticut; admitted to bar, 2000, Ohio. *Education:* Wittenberg University (B.A., 1990); University of Akron (J.D., 2000). ***Email:*** lberesh@jonesday.com

JOHN V. BIERNACKI, born Cleveland, Ohio; admitted to bar, 1995, Michigan; 2001, Ohio; registered to practice before U.S. Patent and Trademark Office. *Education:* University of Detroit (B.Ch.E., 1987; J.D., 1995); John Carroll University (M.A., 1994). Tau Beta Pi. ***Email:*** jvbiernacki@jonesday.com

LAURA A. BIGLER, born Fort Wayne, Indiana; admitted to bar, 2001, Ohio. *Education:* John Carroll University (B.S., 1997); Cleveland State University (J.D., 2001). ***Email:*** labigler@jonesday.com

STEPHEN L. BITTENCE, born Cleveland, Ohio; admitted to bar, 2004, Ohio. *Education:* The Ohio State University (B.S.C.E., 1994); Cleveland State University (Masters; J.D., 2004). ***Email:*** slbittence@jonesday.com

CARL E. BLACK, born Cincinnati, Ohio; admitted to bar, 1998, Ohio. *Education:* Ohio University (B.S., 1989); The Ohio State University (J.D., 1998). Order of the Coif. ***Email:*** ceblack@jonesday.com

PEARSON N. BOWNAS, born Columbus, Ohio; admitted to bar, 1997, Ohio. *Education:* Miami University (B.A., 1994); Loyola University, Chicago (J.D., 1997). ***Email:*** pnbownas@jonesday.com

JENNIFER H. BOYCE, born Orange County, California; admitted to bar, 1996, Ohio. *Education:* Purdue University (B.A., 1991); University of Pittsburgh (J.D., 1996). ***Email:*** jhboyce@jonesday.com

KEVIN D. BOYCE, born Greenwich, Connecticut; admitted to bar, 1996, Ohio. *Education:* Purdue University (B.A., 1993); Boston University (J.D., 1996). ***Email:*** kdboyce@jonesday.com

MARC D. BROWNING, born Cincinnati, Ohio; admitted to bar, 1998, Ohio. *Education:* Miami University (B.S., 1994); University of Virginia (J.D., 1998). ***Email:*** mdbrowning@jonesday.com

JAMES P. BURKE, born Parma, Ohio; admitted to bar, 2001, Ohio. *Education:* University of Chicago (B.A., 1997); University of Notre Dame (M.A., J.D., 2001). ***Email:*** jpburke@jonesday.com

JUSTIN M. CERNANSKY, born Steubenville, Ohio; admitted to bar, 2004, Ohio. *Education:* University of Notre Dame (B.A., 2001); Cornell University (J.D., 2004). ***Email:*** jmcernansky@jonesday.com

ERIC C. CHAFFEE, born Springfield, Ohio; admitted to bar, 2002, Ohio. *Education:* The Ohio State University (B.A., 1999); University of Pennsylvania (J.D., 2002). Phi Beta Kappa. ***Email:*** ecchaffee@jonesday.com

(This Listing Continued)

HOWARD W. CHU, born Xenia, Ohio; admitted to bar, 2004, Ohio. *Education:* Miami University (B.S., 2001); The Ohio State University (J.D., 2004). ***LANGUAGES:*** Chinese (Mandarin). ***Email:*** hwchu@jonesday.com

ROBERT J. COLACARRO, born Cleveland, Ohio; admitted to bar, 2002, Ohio. *Education:* John Carroll University (B.S.B.A., 1998); Boston College (J.D., 2001). ***Email:*** rjcolacarro@jonesday.com

STEPHEN P. COOLBAUGH, born Rochester, New York; admitted to bar, 2001, Ohio; 2003, New York. *Education:* Georgetown University (B.S.F.S., 1997); State University of New York, Buffalo (J.D., 2001). Phi Beta Kappa. ***Email:*** spcoolbaugh@jonesday.com

LORRI W. COOPER, born Allentown, Pennsylvania; admitted to bar, 1995, Connecticut; 1996, New York; 1998, District of Columbia; 2002, Ohio; registered to practice before U.S. Patent and Trademark Office. *Education:* Western New England College (B.S., 1986); Rensselaer Polytechnic Institute (M.S., 1992); University of Connecticut (J.D., 1995). ***Email:*** lwcooper@jonesday.com

STEPHANIE S. COUHIG, born Dayton, Ohio; admitted to bar, 2002, Ohio; registered to practice before U.S. Patent and Trademark Office. *Education:* University of Dayton (B.S.C.E., 1999); University of Notre Dame (J.D., 2002). Tau Beta Pi. ***Email:*** sscouhig@jonesday.com

JOHN D. CURTIN, born Oaklawn, Illinois; admitted to bar, 2003, Ohio. *Education:* University of San Diego (B.A., 2000); Syracuse University (J.D., 2003). Order of the Coif. ***Email:*** jdcurtin@jonesday.com

DAVID L. DeBORD, born Galliapolis, Ohio; admitted to bar, 2003, Ohio. *Education:* Ohio Wesleyan University (B.A., 2000); Vanderbilt University (J.D., 2003). ***Email:*** dldebord@jonesday.com

JAMES P. DOUGHERTY, born Brooklyn, New York; admitted to bar, 1999, New York; 2005, Ohio. *Education:* State University of New York, Geneseo (B.A., 1995); University of California, Los Angeles (J.D., 1998). ***Email:*** jpdougherty@jonesday.com

DAVID W. DULABON, born Erie, Pennsylvania; admitted to bar, 2001, Ohio. *Education:* Pennsylvania State University (B.A., B.A., 1998); Vanderbilt University (J.D., 2001). Phi Beta Kappa. Law Clerk to Judge Buckwalter, U.S. District Court, Eastern District of Pennsylvania, 2002-2003. ***Email:*** dwdulabon@jonesday.com

PATRICIA ESCHBACH-HALL, born Paulding, Ohio; admitted to bar, 1999, Ohio. *Education:* Kenyon College (B.A., 1996); The Ohio State University (J.D., 1999). ***Email:*** peschbachhall@jonesday.com

ADRIENNE M. FERRARO, born Warrensville Heights, Ohio; admitted to bar, 2003, Ohio. *Education:* College of Wooster (B.A., 2000); The Ohio State University (J.D., 2003). Phi Beta Kappa; Order of the Coif. ***Email:*** amferraro@jonesday.com

KEVIN H. FINK, born Cleveland, Ohio; admitted to bar, 2002, New York; 2004, Ohio. *Education:* Miami University (B.S., 1998); Case Western Reserve University (J.D., 2001). ***Email:*** khfink@jonesday.com

ANDREW G. FIORELLA, born Buffalo, New York; admitted to bar, 2003, Ohio. *Education:* State University of New York, Buffalo (B.A., 2000); Cornell University (J.D., 2003). Phi Beta Kappa. ***Email:*** agfiorella@jonesday.com

ANNE OWINGS FORD, born Ann Arbor, Michigan; admitted to bar, 1989, Ohio. *Education:* University of Michigan (B.A., 1985); Vanderbilt University (J.D., 1989). Law Clerk: to Judge Daughtrey, Tennessee Court of Criminal Appeals and Tennessee Supreme Court, 1989-1990; to Magistrate Judge Laurie, U.S. District Court, Northern District of Ohio, 1991-1993; to Judge Aldrich, U.S. District Court, Northern District of Ohio, 1994. ***Email:*** aoford@jonesday.com

PAUL E. FRANZ, born Wright-Patterson AFB, Ohio; admitted to bar, 1999, Indiana; 2002, Ohio; registered to practice before U.S. Patent and Trademark Office. *Education:* North Dakota State University (B.S., 1990); Seattle University (J.D., 1999). ***Email:*** pefranz@jonesday.com

SCOTT F. FRODYMA, born Holyoke, Massachusetts; admitted to bar, 1998, New York and Ohio. *Education:* Middlebury College (B.A., 1988); George Washington University (J.D., 1994); New York University (LL.M., 1997). ***Email:*** sffrodyma@jonesday.com

LISA B. GATES, born Pittsburgh, Pennsylvania; admitted to bar, 1988, Ohio. *Education:* Pennsylvania State University (B.S., 1983); University of Pittsburgh (J.D., 1988). Order of the Coif. ***Email:*** lgates@jonesday.com

SUSAN M. GERBER, born Akron, Ohio; admitted to bar, 1999, Ohio. *Education:* University of Akron (A.A.B., 1987; B.S., 1996; J.D., 1999). Law Clerk to Judge Batchelder, U.S. Court of Appeals, Sixth Circuit, 2000. ***Email:*** smgerber@jonesday.com

AMY E. GERBICK, born Fairview Park, Ohio; admitted to bar, 2002, Ohio. *Education:* Wittenberg University (B.A., 1993); Cleveland State University (J.D., 2002). ***Email:*** aegerbick@jonesday.com

KRISTEN LAU GEST, born Cleveland, Ohio; admitted to bar, 2003, Ohio. *Education:* College of William & Mary (B.A., 1996); Case Western Reserve University (J.D., 2003). Order of the Coif. ***Email:*** klgest@jonesday.com

MICHAEL J. GLEASON, born Lumberton, North Carolina; admitted to bar, 2001, Ohio. *Education:* State University of New York at Buffalo (B.A., 1998); Cornell University (J.D., 2001). Phi Beta Kappa. ***Email:*** mjgleason@jonesday.com

ERIC R. GOODMAN, born Lansing, Michigan; admitted to bar, 2003, Ohio. *Education:* Hope College (B.A., 2000); University of Michigan (J.D., 2002). Phi Beta Kappa. Law Clerk to Chief Judge William T. Bodoh, U.S. Bankruptcy Court, Northern District of Ohio and Bankruptcy Appellate Panel for the Sixth Circuit, 2003-2004. ***Email:*** ergoodman@jonesday.com

THOMAS R. GOOTS, born Cleveland, Ohio; admitted to bar, 1996, Ohio. *Education:* Ohio University (B.S., 1984); University of Akron (J.D., 1995). ***Email:*** trgoots@jonesday.com

(This Listing Continued)

EARNEST B. GREGORY, born Dayton, Ohio; admitted to bar, 2004, Ohio. *Education:* Wright State University (B.S., 1999; M.B.A., 2001); Harvard University (J.D., 2004). ***Email:*** ebgregory@jonesday.com

ELIZABETH A. GROVE, born Canton, Ohio; admitted to bar, 1990, Ohio; 1992, District of Columbia. *Education:* Kent State University (B.A., 1987); Case Western Reserve University (J.D., 1990). Law Clerk to Judge O'Malley, U.S. District Court, Northern District of Ohio, 1994-1996. ***Email:*** eagrove@jonesday.com

BRIAN K. GRUBE, born Lancaster, Ohio; admitted to bar, 1997, Ohio; 1999, District of Columbia. *Education:* Ohio University (B.B.A., 1993); University of Chicago (J.D., 1997). Staff Attorney, Policy Planning, Federal Trade Commission, 1997-1999. ***Email:*** bkgrube@jonesday.com

GINA K. GUNNING, born Akron, Ohio; admitted to bar, 1995, Ohio. *Education:* University of Notre Dame (B.A., 1989; J.D., 1995). ***Email:*** gkgunning@jonesday.com

SCOTT W. HACKWELDER, born Melrose, Massachusetts; admitted to bar, 2004, Ohio; registered to practice before U.S. Patent and Trademark Office. *Education:* Duke University (B.S.E., 1992); Villanova University (M.C.E., 1998); Syracuse University (J.D., 2004). Order of the Coif. ***Email:*** swhackwelder@jonesday.com

JOSEPH D. HATINA, born Cleveland, Ohio; admitted to bar, 1999, Ohio. *Education:* Bowling Green State University (B.S., 1991); University of Alabama (M.S., 1993); Cleveland State University (J.D., 1999). ***Email:*** jdhatina@jonesday.com

TRAVIS M. HEIDORF, born Manitowoc, Wisconsin; admitted to bar, 2003, Ohio. *Education:* University of Wisconsin-Whitewater (B.B.A., 1999); University of Minnesota (J.D., 2003). Order of the Coif. ***LANGUAGES:*** French. ***Email:*** tmheidorf@jonesday.com

PETER G. HILBERT, born Mayfield Heights, Ohio; admitted to bar, 2003, Ohio. *Education:* Syracuse University (B.A., 1999); University of Pennsylvania (J.D., 2003). ***Email:*** pghilbert@jonesday.com

CEDAR R. HOLMGREN, born River Falls, Wisconsin; admitted to bar, 2003, Ohio. *Education:* University of Florida (B.A., 1999); University of Minnesota (J.D., 2003). Order of the Coif. ***Email:*** crholmgren@jonesday.com

MELISSA E. HORN, born Oberlin, Ohio; admitted to bar, 2003, Ohio. *Education:* Taylor University (B.A., 1998); Cleveland State University (J.D., 2003). Law Clerk to Chief Judge Randolph Baxter, U.S. Bankruptcy Court, Northern District of Ohio, 2003-2004. ***Email:*** mehorn@jonesday.com

MARY ELIZABETH HUBER, born Cleveland, Ohio; admitted to bar, 1996, Ohio. *Education:* Saint Mary's College (B.B.A., 1982); University of Notre Dame (J.D., 1996). Certified Public Accountant, Illinois, 1982. Law Clerk to Judge Kelly, U.S. Court of Appeals, Tenth Circuit, 1996-1997. ***Email:*** mhuber@jonesday.com

TIMOTHY M. HUDSON, born Amherst, New York; admitted to bar, 2004, Ohio. *Education:* College of William & Mary (B.A., 2000); Duke University (J.D., 2003). Phi Beta Kappa. Law Clerk to Judge Eldon E. Fallon, U.S. District Court, Eastern District of Louisiana, 2003-2004. ***Email:*** tmhudson@jonesday.com

PETER E. IZANEC, born Philadelphia, Pennsylvania; admitted to bar, 2001, New York; 2005, Ohio. *Education:* Williams College (B.A., 1994); Harvard University (J.D., 1999). Law Clerk to Judge Arnold, U.S. Court of Appeals, Eighth Circuit, 1999-2000. ***Email:*** peizanec@jonesday.com

ANTHONY T. JACONO, born Cleveland, Ohio; admitted to bar, 2000, Ohio. *Education:* Case Western Reserve University (B.S., B.A., 1997); University of Minnesota (J.D., 2000). Phi Beta Kappa; Tau Beta Pi. ***Email:*** atjacono@jonesday.com

LINDSAY C. JENKINS, born Cleveland, Ohio; admitted to bar, 2002, Ohio. *Education:* Miami University (B.S., 1998); Cleveland State University (J.D., 2002). Law Clerk to Judge Solomon Oliver, Jr., U.S. District Court, Northern District of Ohio, 2002-2004. ***Email:*** lcjenkins@jonesday.com

A. GREGORY JUNGE, born Bronxville, New York; admitted to bar, 2004, Ohio. *Education:* Kenyon College (B.A., 1993); Johns Hopkins University (M.S., 1998); George Washington University (J.D., 2004). ***Email:*** agjunge@jonesday.com

SALIM A. KAFITI, born Cleveland, Ohio; admitted to bar, 2001, New York; 2005, Ohio. *Education:* Miami University, Ohio (B.A., 1996); Case Western Reserve University (J.D., 2000). Order of the Coif. ***Email:*** sakafiti@jonesday.com

GUS KALLERGIS, born Akron, Ohio; admitted to bar, 1999, Ohio. *Education:* Yale University (B.A., 1996); University of Notre Dame (J.D., 1999). ***LANGUAGES:*** Greek and Spanish. ***Email:*** gkallergis@jonesday.com

DAINIUS A. KRIVINSKAS, born Cuyahoga Falls, Ohio; admitted to bar, 2003, Ohio. *Education:* Duke University (A.B., 1999); University of Michigan (J.D., 2003). ***LANGUAGES:*** Lithuanian. ***Email:*** dakrivinskas@jonesday.com

LEA J. KRIVINSKAS, born Cuyahoga Falls, Ohio; admitted to bar, 2005, Ohio. *Education:* Duke University (A.B., 2000); Harvard University (J.D., 2004). Phi Beta Kappa. ***LANGUAGES:*** Lithuanian. ***Email:*** ljkrivinskas@jonesday.com

LISA K. KUNKLE, born Toledo, Ohio; admitted to bar, 1994, Ohio. *Education:* Miami University (B.S., 1990); University of Toledo (J.D., 1994). Order of the Coif. Law Clerk to Judge Young, U.S. District Court, Northern District of Ohio, 1994-1995. ***Email:*** lkunkle@jonesday.com

KABIR A. LALCHANDANI, born Santa Barbara, California; admitted to bar, 2004, Ohio. *Education:* Cornell University (B.S., 1999; J.D., 2004). ***LANGUAGES:*** Spanish. ***Email:*** kalalchandani@jonesday.com

LISA S. LATHROP, born Ludington, Michigan; admitted to bar, 2001, Ohio. *Education:* Central Michigan University (B.S., 1998); University of Notre Dame (J.D., 2001). ***Email:*** lslathrop@jonesday.com

JONATHAN B. LEIKEN, born Cleveland, Ohio; admitted to bar, 1997, Ohio; 1998, New York. *Education:* Brandeis University (B.A., 1994); University of Pennsylvania (J.D., 1997). Law Clerk to Judge Sam H. Bell, U.S. District Court, Northern District of Ohio, 1997-1998. Assistant U.S. Attorney, Southern District of New York (Criminal Division), U.S. Department of Justice, 2001-2004. ***Email:*** jleiken@jonesday.com

(This Listing Continued)

JONES DAY, Cleveland—Continued

JENNIFER C. LEWIS, born Chicago, Illinois; admitted to bar, 1995, Ohio. *Education:* John Carroll University (B.A., 1991); Case Western Reserve University (J.D., 1995). Order of the Coif. ***Email:*** jclewis@jonesday.com

JOHN Q. LEWIS, born Big Rapids, Michigan; admitted to bar, 1996, Ohio. *Education:* Kalamazoo College (B.A., 1993); Duquesne University (J.D., 1996). ***Email:*** jqlewis@ jonesday.com

NATHAN T. LEWIS, born Huntington, West Virginia; admitted to bar, 2004, Ohio. *Education:* Marshall University (B.S., 2000); The Ohio State University (J.D., 2004). ***Email:*** ntlewis@jonesday.com

ARTHUR P. LICYGIEWICZ, born Cleveland, Ohio; admitted to bar, 1997, Ohio. *Education:* University of Notre Dame (B.S., 1993); Syracuse University (J.D., 1997). Order of the Coif. ***Email:*** aplicygiewicz@jonesday.com

BURKHART R. LINDAHL, born Bowling Green, Ohio; admitted to bar, 2000, Ohio. *Education:* Nanzan University, Japan (CJS Certification, 1996); Bowling Green State University (B.A., 1997); University of Toledo (J.D., 2000). Phi Beta Kappa. ***Email:*** brlindahl@jonesday.com

SHOSHANA E. LITT, born Cleveland, Ohio; admitted to bar, 2003, Ohio. *Education:* Haverford College (B.A., 1995); Yale University (M.A., 1998); American University, Washington College of Law (J.D., 2003). ***LANGUAGES:*** Japanese. ***Email:*** selitt@ jonesday.com

JULIA ANN LOVE, born Kingston, New York; admitted to bar, 1995, New York and Ohio. *Education:* Boston University (B.A., 1991); Georgetown University (J.D., 1994). ***Email:*** jalove@jonesday.com

SHERYL H. LOVE, born Philadelphia, Pennsylvania; admitted to bar, 1995, Pennsylvania and Ohio. *Education:* Columbia University (B.A., 1988); Villanova University (J.D., 1994). Order of the Coif. Law Clerk to Judge Yohn, U.S. District Court, Eastern District of Pennsylvania, 1994-1995. ***Email:*** shlove@jonesday.com

JOHN PAUL LUCCI, born Parma, Ohio; admitted to bar, 2003, Ohio. *Education:* Case Western Reserve University (B.A., 1997; M.A., 1997; J.D., 2003). Phi Beta Kappa; Order of the Coif. ***Email:*** jplucci@jonesday.com

KARL M. MAERSCH, born Huntington, New York; admitted to bar, 2002, Ohio; registered to practice before U.S. Patent and Trademark Office. *Education:* Purdue University (B.S.M.E., 1995); John Marshall Law School (J.D., 2002). ***Email:*** kmmaersch@jonesday. com

DAVID M. MAIORANA, born Falls Church, Virginia; admitted to bar, 1999, Ohio; registered to practice before U.S. Patent and Trademark Office. *Education:* University of Virginia (B.S., 1992); American University, Washington College of Law (J.D., 1997). Patent Examiner, U.S. Patent and Trademark Office, 1992-1997. ***Email:*** dmaiorana@ jonesday.com

JEFFREY R. A. MANGHILLIS, born Mayfield Heights, Ohio; admitted to bar, 2000, Ohio. *Education:* The Ohio State University (B.A., 1997); Harvard University (J.D., 2000). Phi Beta Kappa. Law Clerk to Judge Gwin, U.S. District Court, Northern District of Ohio, 2002- 2003. ***Email:*** jramanghillis@jonesday.com

SASHA MARKOVIC, born Belgrade, Serbia, Yugoslavia; admitted to bar, 2004, Ohio. *Education:* Cleveland State University (B.S., 1990; J.D., 2004). ***LANGUAGES:*** Serbo-Croation. ***Email:*** smarkovic@jonesday.com

JOHN E. MAZEY, born Cleveland, Ohio; admitted to bar, 1998, Ohio. *Education:* Cleveland State University (B.A., 1995; J.D., 1998). ***Email:*** jemazey@jonesday.com

PHILIP W. McCARTY, born Madison, Wisconsin; admitted to bar, 2003, Ohio. *Education:* Wesleyan University (B.A., 1997); University of Wisconsin (J.D., 2003). ***Email:*** pmccarty@jonesday.com

RYAN B. MCCRUM, born Bangor, Maine; admitted to bar, 1999, Ohio. *Education:* Johns Hopkins University (B.S., 1996); Case Western Reserve University (J.D., 1999). Order of the Coif. ***Email:*** rbmccrum@jonesday.com

DAWN E. McFADDEN, born Abington, Pennsylvania; admitted to bar, 2003, New York; 2005, Ohio. *Education:* Bowling Green State University (B.A., 1992); Case Western Reserve University (J.D., 2002). ***Email:*** demcfadden@jonesday.com

DANIEL A. MESSELOFF, born New York, New York; admitted to bar, 2003, New York; 2005, Ohio. *Education:* Washington University, St. Louis (B.A., 1996); Fordham University (J.D., 2001). ***Email:*** dmesseloff@jonesday.com

HEATHER VARLEY MILLER, born Presque Isle, Maine; admitted to bar, 2003, Ohio. *Education:* Clark University (B.A., 1995); Syracuse University (J.D., 2002). Law Clerk to Judge McAvoy, U.S. District Court, Northern District of New York, 2001-2002. ***Email:*** hvmiller@jonesday.com

NICHOLAS M. MILLER, born Cleveland, Ohio; admitted to bar, 1998, Ohio. *Education:* Cleveland State University (B.A., 1995; J.D., 1998). ***Email:*** nmmiller@jonesday. com

DAVID E. MILLS, born Cleveland, Ohio; admitted to bar, 2002, Ohio. *Education:* Colgate University (B.A., 1999); University of Michigan (J.D., 2002). Phi Beta Kappa. ***Email:*** demills@jonesday.com

KIMBERLEY P.H. MITCHELL, born Lansing, Michigan; admitted to bar, 2002, Massachusetts; 2004, Ohio. *Education:* Michigan State University (B.A., 1994); Case Western Reserve University (M.A., 1996); Cornell University (J.D., 2002). ***Email:*** kpmitchell@jonesday.com

ISAAC A. MOLNAR, born Oxford, Ohio; admitted to bar, 1999, Illinois; 2003, Ohio; registered to practice before U.S. Patent and Trademark Office. *Education:* The Ohio State University (B.Sc., 1996; J.D., 1999). Order of the Coif. ***Email:*** iamolnar@jonesday.com

ANNA L. MOSCIONI, born Ravenna, Ohio; admitted to bar, 2000, Ohio. *Education:* Bowling Green State University (B.A., 1996); Case Western Reserve University (J.D., 2000). Phi Beta Kappa. ***Email:*** almoscioni@jonesday.com

(This Listing Continued)

ERIC H. MOSIER, born Dry Tavern, Pennsylvania; admitted to bar, 1997, Ohio. *Education:* Harvard University (A.B., 1994); Cornell University (J.D., 1997). ***Email:*** ehmosier@jonesday.com

CASSANDRA G. MOTT, born Orrville, Ohio; admitted to bar, 1999, Ohio. *Education:* Ohio Northern University (B.A., 1994); The Ohio State University (J.D., 1999). Order of the Coif. ***Email:*** cgmott@jonesday.com

ADAM D. MUNSON, born Cleveland, Ohio; admitted to bar, 2001, Ohio. *Education:* University of Dayton (B.A., 1998); Duke University (J.D., 2001). Order of the Coif. ***Email:*** admunson@jonesday.com

MELISSA J. NANDI, born Cleveland, Ohio; admitted to bar, 1998, Ohio. *Education:* St. Bonaventure University (B.A., 1995); Albany Law School of Union University (J.D., 1998). ***Email:*** mjnandi@jonesday.com

JOSEPHINE S. NOBLE, born New York, New York; admitted to bar, 2004, Ohio. *Education:* Harvard University (A.B., 2001); State University of New York at Buffalo (J.D., 2004). ***Email:*** jsnoble@jonesday.com

PATRICK J. NORTON, born Cleveland, Ohio; admitted to bar, 1998, Ohio. *Education:* Northwestern University (B.S., 1993); Case Western Reserve University (J.D., 1998). ***Email:*** pjnorton@jonesday.com

AIDANA K. NURGALIYEVA, born Almaty, Kazakhstan; admitted to bar, 2004, Ohio. *Education:* Hartwick College (B.A., 2001); State University of New York at Buffalo (J.D., 2004). ***LANGUAGES:*** Russian. ***Email:*** aknurgaliyeva@jonesday.com

R. JASON OBLANDER, born Liberal, Kansas; admitted to bar, 2000, Ohio. *Education:* Kansas State University (B.A., 1997; B.S., 1997); University of Virginia (M.A., J.D., 2000). Phi Beta Kappa. ***Email:*** rjoblander@jonesday.com

MICHAEL S. OWENDOFF, born Cleveland, Ohio; admitted to bar, 1996, Ohio. *Education:* University of Dayton (B.S., 1992); Cleveland State University (M.B.A., J.D., 1995). ***Email:*** msowendoff@jonesday.com

JOHANNA F. PARKER, born Cleveland, Ohio; admitted to bar, 1999, Ohio. *Education:* University of Notre Dame (B.A., 1996); Case Western Reserve University (J.D., 1999). Phi Beta Kappa; Order of the Coif. ***Email:*** jfparker@jonesday.com

THEODORE C. PARSONS, born Columbus, Ohio; admitted to bar, 1998, Ohio; registered to practice before the U.S. Patent and Trademark Office. *Education:* The Ohio State University (B.S., 1994); Duke University (J.D., 1998). Tau Beta Pi. ***Email:*** tcparsons@ jonesday.com

VIPUL B. PATEL, born Chicago, Illinois; admitted to bar, 2003, Ohio. *Education:* Case Western Reserve University (B.S., 2000); Columbia University (J.D., 2003). ***LANGUAGES:*** Gujarati and Spanish. ***Email:*** vbpatel@jonesday.com

STEPHEN R. PENROD, born Toledo, Ohio; admitted to bar, 2000, Ohio. *Education:* College of Wooster (B.A., 1997); Cleveland State University (J.D., 2000). ***Email:*** srpenrod@jonesday.com

SHANE T. PFLEIDERER, born Galion, Ohio; admitted to bar, 2003, Ohio. *Education:* University of Toledo (B.B.A., 1998; J.D., 2003). Certified Public Accountant, Ohio, 2001. ***Email:*** spfleiderer@jonesday.com

CHRISTINE M. PRZYBYSZ, born Cleveland, Ohio; admitted to bar, 2004, Ohio. *Education:* Ohio Wesleyan University (B.A., 1999); Case Western Reserve University (J.D., 2004). Phi Beta Kappa; Order of the Coif. ***Email:*** cmprzybysz@jonesday.com

CHARLES W. PUGH, born Detroit, Michigan; admitted to bar, 2004, Ohio. *Education:* Kenyon College (B.A., 2001); New York University (J.D., 2004). ***Email:*** cwpugh@ jonesday.com

KIMBERLY J. PUSTULKA, born Buffalo, New York; admitted to bar, 2000, Ohio. *Education:* State University of New York at Buffalo (B.S., 1997); Harvard University (J.D., 2000). ***Email:*** kjpustulka@jonesday.com

MARK B. RADEFELD, born Parma, Ohio; admitted to bar, 2003, Ohio. *Education:* Allegheny College (B.A., 2000); University of Akron (J.D., 2003). ***Email:*** mbradefeld@ jonesday.com

DUSTIN B. RAWLIN, born Parma, Ohio; admitted to bar, 2000, Ohio. *Education:* Boston College (B.A., M.A., 1997); Duke University (J.D., 2000). Phi Beta Kappa. ***Email:*** dbrawlin@jonesday.com

MEGGAN A. RAWLIN, born Morgantown, West Virginia; admitted to bar, 2001, Ohio. *Education:* Princeton University (B.A., 1998); Duke University (J.D., 2001). Law Clerk to Judge John Adams, U.S. District Court, Northern District of Ohio, 2003-2005. ***LANGUAGES:*** Spanish. ***Email:*** mrawlin@jonesday.com

BRIAN E. RAY, born Akron, Ohio; admitted to bar, 2001, Ohio. *Education:* University of Notre Dame (B.A., 1993); Kyoto University (Fulbright Fellow, 1993-1994); University of Pennsylvania (M.A., 1996); The Ohio State University (J.D., 2001). Order of the Coif. Law Clerk to: Judge Alan E. Norris, U.S. Court of Appeals, Sixth Circuit, 2001- 2002; Justice Richard J. Goldstone, Constitutional Court of South Africa, 2003. ***Email:*** beray@ jonesday.com

ROBERT F. RIVERA, born Niles, Ohio; admitted to bar, 2003, Ohio. *Education:* Youngstown State University (B.S., 1994); The Ohio State University (J.D., 2003). Order of the Coif. ***Email:*** rfrivera@jonesday.com

JULIE W. ROGERS, born Winston-Salem, North Carolina; admitted to bar, 2005, Ohio. *Education:* Duke University (A.B., 1997; J.D., 2004). ***Email:*** jwrogers@jonesday. com

RYAN T. ROUTH, born Sandusky, Ohio; admitted to bar, 1999, Ohio. *Education:* Ohio Wesleyan University (B.A., 1994); University of Michigan (J.D., 1998). ***Email:*** rrouth@jonesday.com

JEFFREY SAKS, born Cleveland, Ohio; admitted to bar, 1997, New York; 1999, Ohio. *Education:* Boston University (B.A., B.S., 1988); Fordham University (J.D., 1996). Order of the Coif. ***Email:*** jsaks@jonesday.com

(This Listing Continued)

JOSEPH M. SAUER, born Pittsburgh, Pennsylvania; admitted to bar, 1999, Illinois; 2002, Ohio; registered to practice before U.S. Patent and Trademark Office. *Education:* West Virginia University (B.S.E.E., 1993); Duquesne University (J.D., 1999). ***Email:*** jmsauer@jonesday.com

STEFAN K. SCHNOPP, born Dayton, Ohio; admitted to bar, 1997, Ohio. *Education:* The Ohio State University (B.A., 1993); University of Toledo (J.D., 1997). Order of the Coif. ***Email:*** skschnopp@jonesday.com

ASHA B. SCIELZO, born Baltimore, Maryland; admitted to bar, 1999, Georgia; 2005, Ohio. *Education:* University of Pennsylvania (B.A., 1995); Georgetown University (J.D., 1999). ***LANGUAGES:*** French and Hindi. ***Email:*** abscielzo@jonesday.com

KATHERINE M. SEREVITCH, born Cleveland, Ohio; admitted to bar, 2004, Ohio. *Education:* Villanova University (B.S., 2001); Case Western Reserve University (J.D., 2004). Order of the Coif. ***Email:*** kmserevitch@jonesday.com

PAULA G. SHAKELTON, born Cleveland, Ohio; admitted to bar, 2004, Ohio. *Education:* University of Notre Dame (B.A., 1996); University of Chicago (M.A., 1998); Emory University (J.D., 2003). Order of the Coif. ***Email:*** pgshakelton@jonesday.com

JENNY L. SHEAFFER, born Commerce, Georgia; admitted to bar, 1998, Ohio; registered to practice before U.S. Patent and Trademark Office. *Education:* College of Environmental Science and Forestry, State University of New York at Syracuse (B.S., 1995); Syracuse University (J.D., 1998). Order of the Coif. ***Email:*** jlsheaffer@jonesday.com

MATTHEW P. SILVERSTEN, born Denville, New Jersey; admitted to bar, 2002, Ohio. *Education:* Wake Forest University (B.A., 1998); The Ohio State University (J.D., 2001). Order of the Coif. Law Clerk to Judge Cobb, U.S. District Court, Eastern District of Texas, 2001-2002. ***Email:*** mpsilversten@jonesday.com

JOHN L. SINATRA, JR., born Buffalo, New York; admitted to bar, 1997, New York; 1998, Ohio. *Education:* State University of New York at Buffalo (B.A., 1993; J.D., 1996). Phi Beta Kappa. Law Clerk to the Central Legal Research Staff, New York Court of Appeals, 1996-1998. ***Email:*** jlsinatrajr.@jonesday.com

AMANDA M. SNYDER, born Elkins, West Virginia; admitted to bar, 2003, Ohio. *Education:* Washington & Jefferson College (B.A., 2000); University of Pittsburgh (J.D., 2003). Phi Beta Kappa; Order of the Coif. ***LANGUAGES:*** French. ***Email:*** asnyder@jonesday.com

BRAD A. SOBOLEWSKI, born Cleveland, Ohio; admitted to bar, 2000, Ohio. *Education:* Georgetown University (B.A., 1997); University of Notre Dame (J.D., 2000). ***Email:*** basobolewski@jonesday.com

MICHAEL J. SOLECKI, born Parma, Ohio; admitted to bar, 1998, Georgia; 2001, Ohio. *Education:* Duke University (A.B., 1994); University of Virginia (J.D., 1998). Order of the Coif. ***Email:*** mjsolecki@jonesday.com

NICOLE D. STANGER, born Pittsburgh, Pennsylvania; admitted to bar, 1998, Ohio. *Education:* Pennsylvania State University (B.S., 1991); University of Akron (Masters, J.D., 1998). Certified Public Accountant, Pennsylvania, 1993. ***Email:*** ndstanger@jonesday.com

TRACY K. STRATFORD, born Youngstown, Ohio; admitted to bar, 1998, Ohio. *Education:* The Ohio State University (B.A., 1994; J.D., 1998). ***Email:*** tkstratford@jonesday.com

JESSICA E. TRILLING, born Los Angeles, California; admitted to bar, 2001, Texas; 2003, Ohio. *Education:* University of Michigan (B.A., 1998); University of Pennsylvania (J.D., 2001). Order of the Coif. ***Email:*** jetrilling@jonesday.com

HENRY E. TURNER JR., born Lyndhurst, Ohio; admitted to bar, 2003, Ohio. *Education:* University of Chicago (A.B., 2000); University of Michigan (J.D., 2003). ***Email:*** heturnerjr@jonesday.com

WADE R. WAGATSUMA, born Honolulu, Hawaii; admitted to bar, 1999, Ohio. *Education:* University of Hawaii (B.A., 1994); Case Western Reserve University (J.D., 1997); New York University (LL.M., 1998). Phi Bata Kappa; Order of the Coif. Attorney-Advisor, Judge Nims, III, U.S. Tax Court, 1998-1999. ***Email:*** wrwagatsuma@jonesday.com

CHRISTOPHER J. WAGNER, born Denver, Colorado; admitted to bar, 2003, Ohio. *Education:* University of Denver (B.S., 1999); Case Western Reserve University (J.D., 2003). ***Email:*** cjwagner@jonesday.com

ANDREW M. WALKER, born Youngstown, Ohio; admitted to bar, 2003, Ohio. *Education:* Miami University (B.S.B.A., 1995); The Ohio State University (J.D., 2003). Order of the Coif. ***Email:*** amwalker@jonesday.com

JAMES W. WALWORTH, JR., born Columbus, Ohio; admitted to bar, 2001, Ohio. *Education:* Wabash College (A.B., 1997); Cornell University (J.D., 2001). ***Email:*** jwwalworthjr@jonesday.com

STEPHEN L. WASHINGTON, born Bethesda, Maryland; admitted to bar, 1996, New York; 1998, Ohio. *Education:* University of Wisconsin-Madison (B.A., 1986); Columbia University (M.P.A., 1988); Benjamin N. Cardozo School of Law, Yeshiva University (J.D., 1995). ***LANGUAGES:*** French. ***Email:*** slwashington@jonesday.com

BROOKE D. WERNER, born Salem, Ohio; admitted to bar, 2004, Ohio. *Education:* Catawba College (B.A., 2001); Albany Law School (J.D., 2004). ***Email:*** bdwerner@jonesday.com

MEREDITH M. WILKES, born New York, New York; admitted to bar, 1996, Nebraska; 2000, Ohio. *Education:* Colorado State University (B.A., 1993); Creighton University (J.D., 1996). Legal Writing Instructor, Adjunct Faculty, Creighton University, 1997-1999. ***Email:*** mwilkes@jonesday.com

CAROLINE M. WILLIAMS, born Steubenville, Ohio; admitted to bar, 2004, Ohio. *Education:* Denison University (B.A., 1999); University of Michigan (J.D., 2004). ***Email:*** cmwilliams@jonesday.com

THOMAS A. WILSON, born Chicago, Illinois; admitted to bar, 2003, Ohio. *Education:* Princeton University (A.B., 1993); University of California, Los Angeles (J.D., 2003). ***Email:*** tawilson@jonesday.com

JONATHAN P. WITMER-RICH, born Kimpese, Congo; admitted to bar, 2001, Ohio. *Education:* Goshen College (B.A., 1997); University of Michigan (J.D., 2000). Order of the Coif. Law Clerk to: Judge Michael, U.S. Court of Appeals, Fourth Circuit, 2001-2002; Judge Goodwin, U.S. District Court, Southern District of West Virginia, 2002-2003. ***LANGUAGES:*** Kimpese. ***Email:*** jwitmerrich@jonesday.com

SENIOR STAFF ATTORNEYS

JENNIFER HAY BARINGER, born Ann Arbor, Michigan; admitted to bar, 1995, Michigan; 2002, Ohio. *Education:* University of Michigan (B.A., 1991); Thomas M. Cooley Law School (J.D., 1994). ***Email:*** jhbaringer@jonesday.com

KAREN J. CORRIGAN, born Cleveland, Ohio; admitted to bar, 1993, Ohio. *Education:* John Carroll University (B.A., 1975); Cleveland State University (J.D., 1993). ***Email:*** kjcorrigan@jonesday.com

MARK B. FARRONI, born Willoughby, Ohio; admitted to bar, 1983, Ohio. *Education:* University of Dayton (B.A., 1980); Case Western Reserve University (J.D., 1983). ***Email:*** mbfarroni@jonesday.com

MICHAEL S. MARTIS, born Cleveland, Ohio; admitted to bar, 1985, Ohio. *Education:* The Ohio State University (B.A., 1982); Cleveland State University (J.D., 1985). ***Email:*** msmartis@jonesday.com

STAFF ATTORNEYS

Ronald L. Cappellazzo	***Lynne C. Fischer***
Jennifer J. Chunyo	***Richard S. Geiger***
Noreen DeNuzzo	***Jeffrey D. Roush***

Languages: Chinese (Mandarin), French, German, Greek, Hindi, Japanese, Lithuanian, Portuguese and Spanish.

(For Biographical Data on other Personnel, see respective offices' Professional Biographies)

GARY L. JONES CO., L.P.A.

CLEVELAND, OHIO

(See Columbus)

General Civil Practice. Administrative, Alcoholic Beverages, Liquor and Licensing Law, Real Estate Taxation and Appeals.

JOONDEPH & BITTEL, LLP

CLEVELAND, OHIO

(See Akron)

Civil Trial and Appellate Practice in Federal and State Courts. Taxation, Corporate, Health Care, Administrative, Pension, Real Estate, Construction Litigation, Labor and Employment, Bankruptcy, Estate Planning, Probate Law and Boat Manufacturing Liability.

KADISH, HINKEL & WEIBEL

A LEGAL PROFESSIONAL ASSOCIATION

Established in 1975

1717 EAST NINTH STREET, SUITE 2112
CLEVELAND, OHIO 44114
Telephone: 216-696-3030
Telecopier: 216-696-3492
URL: http://www.khwlaw.com

General Civil Practice. Federal Taxation, Corporation, Business, Real Estate, Trust, Probate, Estate Planning and Pension and Profit Sharing Law. Health Care, State and Local Taxation, Litigation.

FIRM PROFILE: Kadish, Hinkel & Weibel is a progressive law firm with traditional standards of legal excellence. The firm is well-known for its expertise in business and tax law, in its representation of entrepreneurs, small-to-medium-sized businesses, and members of the professional disciplines.

Founded in 1975, the firm has expanded its services and areas of practice to meet the ever-changing needs of today's business and professional clients. The firm's clients benefit from the diverse talents of the firm's attorneys and their team approach toward responding to their clients' needs.

The legal world is constantly changing, and the attorneys at Kadish, Hinkel & Weibel are prepared to address emerging issues, laws and trends. The firm's attorneys and support staff use sophisticated computer systems and extensive libraries of resources to serve clients in a technologically advancing environment.

Kadish, Hinkel & Weibel is a firm broad enough to respond to its clients' varied legal needs, yet small enough to respond to its clients' needs personally, quickly and efficiently.

STEPHEN L. KADISH, admitted to bar, 1965, New York, Ohio and U.S. Tax Court. *Education:* Williams College (B.A., 1960); Columbia University (LL.B., 1963); Georgetown University (LL.M. in Taxation, 1966). Author: "Section 303 Redemptions to Pay Death Taxes and Administrative Expenses: A Relief Provision Liberally Construed," Western Reserve Law Review, Vol. 18, No. 3, March, 1967; "'E' Reorganizations-Recapitalizations and 'F' Reorganizations—Changes in Identity, Form, or Place of Organization," Case Western Reserve Law Review, Vol. 19, No. 4, June, 1968; "Reporting Sales Income by the Installment Method," The Practical Lawyer, May, 1971. Lecturer at Seminars including: ALI-ABA Annual Seminar on Tax and Business Planning, 1975-2001; Case Western Reserve University; Chicago Tax Shelter Institute; Cleveland Bar Real Estate Institute; Cleveland Tax Institute; Colorado Tax Institute; Indiana Tax Institute; NYU Seminar on Partnerships and S Corporations; Ohio CPA Tax Planning Institute; Ohio Accounting Show; South-

(This Listing Continued)

KADISH, HINKEL & WEIBEL, A LEGAL PROFESSIONAL ASSOCIATION, Cleveland—Continued

ern States CPA Tax Institute; West Virginia Tax Institute. Clerk to Judge Russell E. Train, U.S. Tax Court, 1963-1965. *Member:* Greater Cleveland (Chairman, Business Tax Committee, 1975-1977), Cuyahoga County (Chairman, Business Tax Committee, 1975-1977, 1980-1982), Ohio State, Federal and American Bar Associations. Fellow, American College of Tax Counsel. ***PRACTICE AREAS:*** Taxation; Estate Planning; Business Law. ***Email:*** skadish@khwlaw.com

KEVIN M. HINKEL, admitted to bar, 1980, Ohio and U.S. Tax Court. *Education:* John Carroll University (B.S., 1977); Cleveland State University (J.D., magna cum laude, 1980). Research Editor, Cleveland State Law Review, 1979-1980. *Member:* Cleveland and Ohio State Bar Associations. ***REPORTED CASES:*** Sherwin-Williams Company v. Cuyahoga County Board of Revision, et al. (1996), 74 Ohio St. 3d 415, 659, N.E. 2d 1223; Cleveland Board of Education v. Cuyahoga County Board of Revision (1995), 73 Ohio St. 3d 715, 654 N.E. 2d 1224; Kaminsky, Inc. v. Commissioner, 60 TCM 740 (1990). ***PRACTICE AREAS:*** Real Estate; Taxation; Business Law; Health Care; State Taxation; Local Taxation. ***Email:*** khinkel@khwlaw.com

DAVID G. WEIBEL, admitted to bar, 1980, Ohio; 1981, U.S. Tax Court and U.S. District Court, Northern District of Ohio. *Education:* John Carroll University (B.S.B.A., magna cum laude, 1977); Case Western Reserve University (J.D., 1980). Contributing Author: "Business Organizations, Young on Pension and Profit Sharing Plans," Matthew Bender & Co. *Member:* Cleveland and Ohio State Bar Associations. ***PRACTICE AREAS:*** Pension and Profit Sharing; Estate Planning; Probate; Trusts; Corporation; Business Law. ***Email:*** dweibel@khwlaw.com

AARON H. BULLOFF, admitted to bar, 1972, New York; 1981, Ohio. *Education:* Ohio State University (B.A., 1968); University of Michigan (J.D., 1971). Phi Alpha Delta (Chapter Marshall, 1970-1971). *Member:* New York State, Ohio, Federal (National Resolutions Committee Chairman 2002-2003, Northern District of Ohio Chapter President 2001-2002) and American (Member, Antitrust, Litigation and Employment Sections) Bar Associations. ***SPECIAL AGENCIES:*** Federal Trade Commission. ***REPORTED CASES:*** Blank v. Security, Inc., 123 Ohio App. 3d 248 (1997); Valen Mfg. Co. v. U.S., 90 F.3d 1190 (6th Cir., 1996); Babin v. C.I.R., 64 T.C.M. (CCH) 1357, (U.S. Tax Ct., 1992), In the matter of Chrysler Corporation, 96 F.T.C. 134 (1980). ***PRACTICE AREAS:*** Commercial Litigation; Tax Litigation; Administrative Law; Antitrust and Trade Litigation; Consumer Law; Employment Litigation. ***Email:*** abulloff@khwlaw.com

WILLIAM A. DUNCAN, admitted to bar, 1987, Ohio. *Education:* Walsh College (B.A., magna cum laude, 1984); University of Akron School of Law (J.D., 1987). Member: Midwest Pension Conference, 1988—. *Member:* Cleveland and Ohio State (Member, Probate and Trust Law Section) Bar Associations. ***PRACTICE AREAS:*** Pension and Profit Sharing; Estate Planning; Probate; Business Law. ***Email:*** wduncan@khwlaw.com

JAMES H. ROWND, admitted to bar, 1989, Indiana; 1991, U.S. Tax Court; 1993, Ohio. *Education:* Wittenberg University (B.A., cum laude, 1982); Indiana University (M.B.A., 1988; J.D., cum laude, 1988); Case Western Reserve University (LL.M. Tax, 1998). Certified Public Accountant (non-practicing), Ohio, 1984. Certified Financial Planner (non-practicing). Member: American Institute of Certified Public Accountants. *Member:* Cleveland and Ohio State Bar Associations. ***PRACTICE AREAS:*** Corporate; Taxation; Business Law. ***Email:*** jrownd@khwlaw.com

DEAN M. ROONEY, admitted to bar, 1983, Ohio and U.S. District Court, Northern District of Ohio; 1986, U.S. Court of Appeals, Sixth Circuit; 2002, U.S. Supreme Court. *Education:* Cleveland State University (B.A., magna cum laude, 1976); Cleveland Marshall College of Law (J.D., 1983). Recipient: Corpus Juris Secundum Award, 1983; Chief Justice Samuel H. Silbert Award, 1982-1983. Staff Member, 1981-1982 and Managing Editor, 1982-1983, Cleveland State Law Review. Author, "Standard of Proof in Proceedings to Terminate Parental Rights," 31 Cleveland State Law Review 679 (1982). Member, Business Mediation Panel, Cuyahoga County. *Member:* Cleveland, Cuyahoga County, Ohio State and Federal Bar Associations. ***PRACTICE AREAS:*** Business Litigation; Commercial Litigation; Business Law; Corporate Law. ***Email:*** drooney@khwlaw.com

MATTHEW F. KADISH, admitted to bar, 1987, Ohio; 1990, District of Columbia; 1991, Hawaii; 1999, Maryland. *Education:* Williams College (B.A., 1984); Case Western Reserve University (J.D., cum laude, 1987); New York University (LL.M. in Taxation, 1988). Associate, Case Western Reserve Law Review, 1985-1986. Co-Author, "S vs. C - Tax Considerations in Corporate Choice of Entity," Business Entities WGÆ vol. 2 No. 6, November/December, 2000. Attorney-Advisor to Judge Herbert L. Chabot, United States Tax Court, Washington, D.C., 1988-1990. Member, 1997— and Director, 2002—, Small Business Council of America. *Member:* Hawaii State, Ohio State, Federal and American (Member, Tax Sections) Bar Associations; The District of Columbia. ***LANGUAGES:*** French. ***PRACTICE AREAS:*** Taxation; Estate Planning; Business Law. ***Email:*** mkadish@khwlaw.com

---

MARY BETH DUFFY, admitted to bar, 1989, Ohio. *Education:* Miami University (B.S.B.A., cum laude, 1983); Cleveland Marshall College of Law (J.D., 1988). *Member:* Cleveland Bar Association. ***PRACTICE AREAS:*** Real Estate; Estate Planning; Probate; Business Law. ***Email:*** mduffy@khwlaw.com

KENT S. HEDMAN, admitted to bar, 1975, North Carolina; 1997, Ohio. *Education:* University of North Carolina (B.A., 1968; J.D., 1975; M.B.A., 1978). Phi Beta Kappa; Morehead Scholar; Business Foundation Fellow. *Member:* Ohio State Bar Association. [Active U.S. Navy, 1970-1973; Reserve U.S. Navy Commander, 1974-1991]. ***PRACTICE AREAS:*** Estate Planning; Probate. ***Email:*** khedman@khwlaw.com

JEFFREY J. PLATKO, admitted to bar, 1997, Ohio. *Education:* State University of New York at Buffalo (B.S., magna cum laude, 1990); Cleveland-Marshall College of Law (J.D., cum laude, 1997). *Member:* Cleveland and Ohio State Bar Associations. ***PRACTICE AREAS:*** Real Estate; Business Law; Corporate Law. ***Email:*** jplatko@khwlaw.com

RITA M. JARRETT, admitted to bar, 1992, Ohio. *Education:* Cleveland State University (B.B.A., 1984); Cleveland-Marshall College of Law (J.D., 1991). *Member:* Cleveland and Ohio State Bar Associations. ***PRACTICE AREAS:*** Real Estate Taxation. ***Email:*** rjarrett@khwlaw.com

(This Listing Continued)

KAHN & ASSOCIATES, L.L.C.

55 PUBLIC SQUARE, SUITE 650
CLEVELAND, OHIO 44113
Telephone: 216-621-6101; 888-536-6671
Fax: 216-621-6006
Email: help@kahnandassociates.com
URL: http://www.kahnandassociates.com

Lemon Law, Warranty Law, Consumer Bankruptcy, Debt Resolution, Personal Injury, Credit Reporting Violations and Repair.

CRAIG ANTHONY KAHN, admitted to bar, 1994, Ohio. *Education:* Colorado State University (B.A., 1991); Vermont Law School (J.D., 1994; M.S.L., 1994).

KAHN KLEINMAN

Established in 1962

2600 ERIEVIEW TOWER
1301 EAST 9TH STREET
CLEVELAND, OHIO 44114-1824
Telephone: 216-696-3311
Telecopiers: 216-623-4912; 216-696-1009
URL: http://www.kahnkleinman.com

Corporation, Securities, Venture Capital, Real Estate, Bankruptcy, Computer & Technology, Labor and Employment, Litigation, Taxation, Trust and Estate Planning.

FIRM PROFILE: Kahn Kleinman represents entrepreneurs, deal intensive growth companies, public and private, corporate and real estate, as well as the banks, institutions and capital and service providers that support these companies. Kahn Kleinman's practice areas include corporate and securities, real estate and environmental, technology, e-commerce and computer law, litigation, zoning, tax, trust and estate planning, ERISA, labor and employment, creditors' rights, restructuring and bankruptcy law.

LESTER W. ARMSTRONG, born Philadelphia, Pennsylvania, November 15, 1960; admitted to bar, 1986, Ohio and U.S. District Court, Southern District of Ohio; 1987, U.S. District Court, Northern District of Ohio and U.S. Court of Appeals, Sixth Circuit. *Education:* Heidelberg College (B.A., magna cum laude, 1983); University of Toledo College of Law (J.D., cum laude, 1986). Editor-in-Chief, University of Toledo Law Review, 1985-1986. Law Clerk to Judge Walter H. Rice, United States District Court, Southern District of Ohio, 1986-1987. *Member:* Cleveland, Ohio State (Labor and Employment Law Section) and American (Labor and Employment Law Section) Bar Associations. ***PRACTICE AREAS:*** Management Labor Law; Management Employment Law; Employment Litigation. ***Email:*** larmstrong@kahnkleinman.com

KEVIN D. BARNES, born Cleveland, Ohio, January 3, 1954; admitted to bar, 1979, Ohio. *Education:* Harvard College (A.B., 1976); Harvard Law School (J.D., 1979). *Member:* Cleveland and American Bar Associations. ***PRACTICE AREAS:*** Corporate; International; Banking Law; Computer; Technology Law; UCC. ***Email:*** kbarnes@kahnkleinman.com

DOUGLAS V. BARTMAN, born Madison, Wisconsin, May 15, 1967; admitted to bar, 1993, California, U.S. District Court, Northern District of California and U.S. Court of Appeals, Ninth Circuit; 1994, U.S. District Court, District of Arizona; 1996, Illinois and U.S. District Court, Northern District of Illinois; 1997, U.S. District Court, Central District of Illinois; 2000, Ohio and U.S. District Court, Northern District of Ohio. *Education:* University of Michigan (A.B., 1989); University of California, Hastings College of Law (J.D., 1993). ***PRACTICE AREAS:*** Employment Litigation; Construction Litigation; Commercial Litigation. ***Email:*** dbartman@kahnkleinman.com

IRV BERLINER, born Cleveland, Ohio, June 3, 1954; admitted to bar, 1979, Ohio. *Education:* Miami University (B.A., 1976); The Ohio State University (J.D., 1979). ***PRACTICE AREAS:*** Securities; Corporate Law; Casinos and Gambling. ***Email:*** iberliner@kahnkleinman.com

MICHAEL H. DIAMANT, born Cleveland, Ohio, July 30, 1946; admitted to bar, 1971, Ohio; 1973, U.S. District Court, Northern District of Ohio; 1977, U.S. Court of Appeals, 6th Circuit and U.S. Supreme Court; 1981, U.S. Claims Court; 1982, U.S. Court of Appeals, Federal Circuit; 1994, U.S. Court of Appeals, 10th Circuit; 1995, U.S. Court of Appeals, 11th Circuit. *Education:* Case Western Reserve University, Case Institute of Technology (B.S., Engineering, with high honors, 1968); Harvard University (J.D., cum laude, 1971). Special Counsel, Ohio Attorney General, 1974. Chairman, 1993-1999 and Member, 2000—, Visiting Committee, Case School of Engineering, Case Western Reserve University. Member, Visiting Committee, Case Institute of Technology, 1983-1987, Undergraduate Colleges, 1987-1994. Member, Commercial Panel, American Arbitration Association. *Member:* Cleveland (Chairman, Computer Law Institute, 1982-1985; Chairman, Judicial Selection Committee, 1985), Ohio State and American (Member: Computer Programs Committee, Section of Patent, Trademark and Copyright Law, 1980—; Computer Law Committee, 1980— and Information Security Committee, 2002—, Section of Science and Technology; Litigation Section, Trial Practice Committee, 1987—) Bar Associations; Computer Law Association. ***PRACTICE AREAS:*** Business Litigation; Computer Law; Technology Law; Intellectual Property; Unfair Competition. ***Email:*** mdiamant@kahnkleinman.com

DOMINIC A. DIPUCCIO, born Cleveland, Ohio, March 12, 1964; admitted to bar, 1990, Ohio. *Education:* Xavier University (B.S., 1986); Case Western Reserve University (J.D., 1990). ***PRACTICE AREAS:*** Securities; Mergers and Acquisitions; Corporate. ***Email:*** ddipuccio@kahnkleinman.com

ROBERT A. FUERST, born Cleveland, Ohio, April 18, 1953; admitted to bar, 1979, Ohio; 1980, California. *Education:* University of Colorado (B.S., 1975); Case Western Re-

(This Listing Continued)

serve University School of Law (J.D., 1979). *Member:* Cleveland, Ohio State and American Bar Associations. ***PRACTICE AREAS:*** Real Estate; Business Law. ***Email:*** rfuerst@kahnkleinman.com

BRUCE E. GAYNOR, born Cleveland, Ohio, November 27, 1945; admitted to bar, 1972, Ohio. *Education:* Bowling Green State University (B.S., 1968); Cleveland State University (J.D., magna cum laude, 1972); Yale Law School (Graduate Fellow, 1978-1979). Editor-in-Chief, Cleveland State Law Review, 1971-1972. Lecturer, Ohio University, 1973-1975. Assistant Dean and Lecturer, Syracuse University College of Law, 1975-1979. Co-chair, Real Estate and Environmental Law Practice Group, 1997-1998. *Member:* Cleveland and Ohio State Bar Associations. ***PRACTICE AREAS:*** Real Estate Law; Construction Law; Real Estate Development Law. ***Email:*** bgaynor@kahnkleinman.com

NEIL KURIT, born Cleveland, Ohio, August 31, 1940; admitted to bar, 1964, Ohio. *Education:* Miami University (B.S., 1961); Case Western Reserve University (J.D., 1964). Member, Editorial Board, Case Western Reserve Law Review, 1963-1964. *Member:* Cleveland, Ohio State and American Bar Associations. ***PRACTICE AREAS:*** Estate Planning Law; Probate Law. ***Email:*** nkurit@kahnkleinman.com

STUART L. LARSEN, born Cleveland, Ohio, February 24, 1964; admitted to bar, 1993, Ohio; 1997, U.S. District Court, Northern District of Ohio. *Education:* Cleveland State University (B.B.A., 1987); The Ohio State University (J.D., 1993). Law Clerk to The Hon. Walter J. Krasniewski, U.S. Bankruptcy Judge, 1993-1997. ***PRACTICE AREAS:*** Bankruptcy; Creditors Rights; Commercial Litigation. ***Email:*** slarsen@kahnkleinman.com

MARC H. MORGENSTERN, born Cleveland, Ohio, March 29, 1950; admitted to bar, 1975, Ohio; 1979, District of Columbia. *Education:* Yale University (B.A., 1972); Boston University (J.D., 1975). Author: "Meet the Invendor," Venture Capital & Startups, www.Redherring.com, February 2001; "The Definitive Deal Dictionary," www.offroadcapital.com, 1999; "Balancing the Deal - Private Placements - What They Can Mean to Your Client," Business Law Today, Vol. 5, No. 2 (Nov./Dec., 1995); "Private Placement Guidelines--A Lawyer's Letter to a First-Time Issuer," Bus. Law.; "Philosophy of Acquisitions," Corporate Counsel's Quarterly; Lecturer: SEC Forum on Small Business Capital Formation, 1984—; and Member of Forum's Executive Committee, 1994—. Member: Board of Directors, Rock and Roll Hall of Fame and Museum; Dean's Technology Council, Case Western Reserve University Medical School. *Member:* Cleveland (Chairman, Securities Law Section, 1988-1989), Ohio State and American (Co-Chairman, ABA Task Force to Revise Rule 147, 1990—; Member, Task Force on SEC Small Business Initiative Proposal) Bar Associations. ***PRACTICE AREAS:*** Venture Capital Law; Mergers, Acquisitions and Divestitures Law; Securities Law. ***Email:*** morgenstern@kahnkleinman.com

STEVEN M. MOSS, born Cleveland, Ohio, February 20, 1963; admitted to bar, 1991, Ohio; 1992, U.S. District Court, Northern District of Ohio; 1992, U.S. Court of Appeals, Sixth Circuit; 1998, U.S. Court of Appeals, Eighth Circuit; 1999, U.S. Supreme Court; 2000, U.S. Court of Appeals, District of Columbia Circuit. *Education:* Ithaca College (B.S., 1985); Cleveland Marshall College of Law (J.D., 1991). Editor, Cleveland State University Law Review, 1990-1991. *Member:* Cleveland, Ohio State (Member, Labor and Employment Law Section) and American Bar Associations. ***PRACTICE AREAS:*** Management Labor Law; Employment Litigation; Collective Bargaining. ***Email:*** smoss@kahnkleinman.com

RICHARD S. RIVITZ, born Cleveland, Ohio, July 5, 1942; admitted to bar, 1967, Ohio. *Education:* Cornell University (A.B., cum laude, 1964); Harvard University (J.D., 1967). Law Clerk to Honorable Thomas D. Lambros, U.S. District Judge, Northern District of Ohio, 1968. Law Clerk to Honorable Frank J. Battisti, U.S. District Judge, Northern District of Ohio, 1969. Contributing Editor, Ohio Real Property Law, National Law Journal, 1980-1984. Co-Author: "Using Personal Property Lien Priority Insurance (with Form)," The Practical Real Estate Lawyer, March 1995. *Member:* Greater Cleveland (Member, Federal Courts Committee, 1977-1985), Ohio State, Federal (Director, Cleveland Chapter, 1972-1974) and American (Vice-Chairman, 1978-1980 and Chairman, 1981-1982, Committee on Governmentally-Assisted Housing; Chairman, Real Estate Investment Committee of Real Property, Probate and Trust Law Section, 1982-1983; Vice- Chairman, Partnership Subcommittee of Syndication/Securities Commission, 1987-1988; Vice-Chairman, 1992-1993; Co-Chairman, 1993; Chairman, 1994—, Committee on Professional Responsibility; Nominating Committees, 1995; Co-Chair, Goal IX Standing Committee, 1996—; Council Member, Section on Real Property, Probate and Trust Law, 1997—) Bar Associations; American Counsel Association (Trustee, 1977-1986, 1988; Secretary-Treasurer, 1979-1983; President, 1992). ***PRACTICE AREAS:*** Real Estate Law; Corporate Law. ***Email:*** rrivitz@kahnkleinman.com

RICHARD A. ROSNER, born Cleveland, Ohio, September 30, 1939; admitted to bar, 1964, Ohio. *Education:* Case Western Reserve University (B.B.A., 1961; J.D., 1964). Author: "Reducing the Risks of a Failing Common Ownership Community," The Practical Real Estate Lawyer, May, 1995. Co-Chair, Real Property Practice Group. Listed in the Real Estate Law Section of the current edition of "Best Lawyers in America." *Member:* Cleveland (Chairman, Section on Real Property Law, 1990-1991; Co-Chairman, Condominium Committee, 1982; Chairman, Common Ownership Committee, 1993—), Cuyahoga County (Vice Chairman, Real Property Law Section, 1979-1982), Ohio State (Member, Board of Governors, Real Property Law Section, 1981-1984 and 2000—) and American (Chairman, Land Records Improvement Committee, 1993-1995; Vice Chairman, H-1 Committee for Development, Operation and Management of Community Associations, 1998—) Bar Associations; American College of Real Estate Attorneys. ***PRACTICE AREAS:*** Real Estate Law; Real Estate Development Law; Condominium Law; Planned Unit Development Law (including two Jack Nicklaus golf course communities). ***Email:*** rrosner@kahnkleinman.com

DAVID R. TAVOLIER, born Wadsworth, Ohio, June 21, 1961; admitted to bar, 1986, Ohio. *Education:* University of Michigan (B.B.A., with high distinction, 1983); Georgetown University (J.D., cum laude, 1986). Speaker, Cleveland Bar Association Tax Institute, 1996-1997. *Member:* Cleveland (Member, General Tax Committee), Ohio State and American (Member, Tax Section) Bar Associations. ***PRACTICE AREAS:*** Federal Taxation; State Taxation; Local Taxation; Executive Compensation; Employee Benefits; Corporate Law; Partnership Law; Limited Liability Company Law. ***Email:*** dtavolier@kahnkleinman.com

(This Listing Continued)

ROBERT J. VALERIAN, born Cleveland, Ohio, January 13, 1943; admitted to bar, 1976, Ohio; 1977, U.S. Court of Appeals, 6th Circuit; 1982, U.S. Claims Court; 1992, U.S. Court of Appeals, 11th Circuit; 1998, U.S. Court of Appeals, 8th Circuit. *Education:* John Carroll University; Georgetown University, School of Foreign Service (B.S., 1964); Case Western Reserve University (J.D., 1976). Member, Alternative Dispute Resolution Panel, U.S. District Court, Northern District of Ohio. *Member:* Cleveland, Cuyahoga County, Ohio State and American (Member, Section on Litigation) Bar Associations. ***PRACTICE AREAS:*** Complex Business Litigation; Labor and Employment Law; Construction Law. ***Email:*** rvalerian@kahnkleinman.com

MISSIA H. VASELANEY, born Cleveland, Ohio, December 6, 1961; admitted to bar, 1985, Ohio. *Education:* University of Dayton (B.S., 1982); Cleveland-Marshall College of Law (J.D., 1984). Certified Public Accountant, Ohio, 1989. Certified Financial Planner, 1989. *Member:* Cleveland, Cuyahoga County and Ohio State Bar Associations; Estate Planning Council of Cleveland; American Institute of Certified Public Accountants. ***PRACTICE AREAS:*** Tax Planning; Pension Plans; Estate Planning. ***Email:*** mvaselaney@kahnkleinman.com

ROBERT A. ZIMMERMAN, born Cleveland, Ohio, March 4, 1966; admitted to bar, 1991, Ohio; U.S. District Court, Southern and Northern Districts of Ohio and U.S. Court of Appeals, Sixth Circuit. *Education:* The Ohio State University (B.A., cum laude, with honors, 1988; J.D., 1991). Phi Kappa Phi. Assistant Attorney General, Ohio, 1991-1995. Delegate, 2000 Democratic National Convention. Member, Executive Committee, Democratic Party, Cuyahoga County. *Member:* Cleveland, Ohio State and American Bar Associations. ***PRACTICE AREAS:*** Litigation; Employment Law; Public Law. ***Email:*** rzimmerman@kahnkleinman.com

---

PHILIP R. BAUTISTA, born Akron, Ohio, January 4, 1973; admitted to bar, 2001, Ohio; U.S. District Court, Southern District of Ohio and U.S. Court of Appeals, Sixth Circuit. *Education:* Duke University (B.S., Biology, 1995); The Ohio State University (J.D., 2000). Member, Ohio State Law Review, 1998-2000. Managing Editor, The Ohio State Journal of Dispute Resolution, 1999-2000. Former Judicial Extern to Ohio Supreme Court Justice Alice Robie Resnick. Author, "Congress Says, Yooou're Out!!!" The Ohio State Journal on Dispute Resolution, Vol. 15, No. 2, 2000. *Member:* Cleveland, Columbus, Ohio State and American Bar Associations; National Asian and Pacific American Bar Association. ***PRACTICE AREAS:*** Litigation. ***Email:*** pbautista@kahnkleinman.com

HOWARD J. BOBROW, born New York, New York, August 24, 1970; admitted to bar, 1996, Ohio. *Education:* Miami University (B.A., cum laude, 1992); Case Western Reserve University (J.D., cum laude, 1996). *Member:* Cleveland and American Bar Associations; Association for Corporate Growth; Ohio Venture Association. ***PRACTICE AREAS:*** Corporate Finance; Venture Capital; Securities; Mergers and Acquisitions. ***Email:*** hbobrow@kahnkleinman.com

LEIGH A. HELLNER, born Chicago, Illinois, July 11, 1971; admitted to bar, 1996, Illinois; 1999, New York (Not admitted in Ohio). *Education:* Northwestern University (B.A., 1993); University of Pennsylvania (J.D., 1996). ***PRACTICE AREAS:*** Commercial Real Estate. ***Email:*** lhellner@kahnkleinman.com

THEODORE EINHORN, born Washington, D.C., December 26, 1969; admitted to bar, 1997, Ohio. *Education:* Trinity College (B.A., 1991); The Catholic University of America (J.D., magna cum laude, 1997). Author: "Reigning in ERISA Preemption? Any Willing Provides Statues After New York Blue Cross Plans v. Travelers Insurance Co.," 13 Journal of Contemporary Health Law & Policy 265, 1996. *Member:* Cleveland, Ohio State and American Bar Associations. ***PRACTICE AREAS:*** Commercial Real Estate; Environmental Law. ***Email:*** teinhorn@kahnkleinman.com

MARK R. JACOBS, born Cincinnati, Ohio, January 3, 1973; admitted to bar, 1999, Ohio; 2002, U.S. District Court, Northern District of Ohio. *Education:* Washington University (A.B., 1995); The Ohio State University (J.D., 1999). ***PRACTICE AREAS:*** Business Litigation. ***Email:*** mjacobs@kahnkleinman.com

PETER NEALIS, born Pittsburgh, Pennsylvania, April 21, 1975; admitted to bar, 2000, Ohio. *Education:* Colby College (B.A., 1997); The Ohio State University (J.D., 2000). Phi Kappa Phi. Order of the Coif. Member, Jessup Moot Court Team. Managing Editor, Ohio State Law Journal. Author, "Per Se Legality: A New Standard in Antitrust Adjudication Under the Rule of Reason," 61 Ohio State L.J. 347. *Member:* Cleveland, Ohio State and American Bar Associations. ***PRACTICE AREAS:*** Corporate Tax; Business Litigation. ***Email:*** pnealis@kahnkleinman.com

MARK E. OWENS, born Newport News, Virginia, October 3, 1968; admitted to bar, 1997, Ohio. *Education:* Miami University (B.A., 1991); Ohio State University (J.D., 1997). Phi Beta Kappa; Delta Theta Phi. Scholar Leader. Member, Jessup International Moot Court Team. *Member:* Cleveland, Ohio State and American Bar Associations. ***LANGUAGES:*** Spanish. ***PRACTICE AREAS:*** Bankruptcy; Creditors Rights; Commercial Litigation. ***Email:*** mowens@kahnkleinman.com

MARK J. STOCKMAN, born Cleveland, Ohio, August 8, 1961; admitted to bar, 1996, Ohio. *Education:* Kent State University (M.ARCH., 1986); Cleveland State University (J.D., 1996). Registered Architect, Ohio 1988. ***PRACTICE AREAS:*** Real Estate. ***Email:*** mstockman@kahnkleinman.com

MICHAEL R. TUCCI, born Cleveland, Ohio, September 16, 1967; admitted to bar, 1999, Ohio; 2002, U.S. District Court, Northern District of Ohio; 2003, U.S. Court of Appeals, Sixth Circuit. *Education:* Capital University (B.A., summa cum laude, 1995); Case Western Reserve University (J.D., magna cum laude, 1999). Order of the Coif. Adjunct Faculty Member, Case Western Reserve University School of Law. Adjunct Faculty Member, Chair, Scholarship Committee and Member, Advisory Board, Ursuline College Legal Studues Program. Volunteer, Ohio Reads. Co-Coach, Debate Team, Martin Luther King High School. *Member:* Cleveland and Ohio State Bar Associations. ***PRACTICE AREAS:*** Corporate Law; Securities; Intellectual Property. ***Email:*** mtucci@kahnkleinman.com

DEBORAH A. WEISMAN, born Cleveland, Ohio, May 4, 1969; admitted to bar, 1994, Ohio. *Education:* University of Michigan (B.A., with distinction, 1991); George Washington University (J.D., with high honors, 1994). Member, Order of the Coif. *Mem-*

(This Listing Continued)

KAHN KLEINMAN, Cleveland—Continued

ber: Cleveland, Ohio State and American Bar Associations. ***PRACTICE AREAS:*** Mergers, Acquisitions and Divestitures; Corporate Law; Securities; General Practice. ***Email:*** dweisman@kahnkleinman.com

ELIZABETH MARIE ZOLLER, born Cleveland, Ohio, December 12, 1969; admitted to bar, 2001, Ohio. *Education:* Ohio State University (B.A., 1992); Cleveland-Marshall College of Law (J.D., cum laude, 2001). *Member:* Cleveland (Member, Real Estate Section), Ohio State and American Bar Associations. ***PRACTICE AREAS:*** Real Estate; Litigation. ***Email:*** ezoller@kahnkleinman.com

SENIOR COUNSEL

BENNETT YANOWITZ, born Cleveland, Ohio, February 25, 1923; admitted to bar, 1949, Ohio. *Education:* University of Michigan (A.B., 1947) Phi Beta Kappa; Case Western Reserve University (LL.B., summa cum laude, 1949). Order of the Coif. Editor-in-Chief, Case Western Reserve Law Review, 1949. Chairman, National Jewish Community Relations Advisory Council, 1980-1982. President, Jewish Education Service of North America, 1987-1990. President, Jewish Community Federation of Cleveland, 1992-1994. *Member:* Cleveland, Cuyahoga County and Ohio State Bar Associations. ***PRACTICE AREAS:*** Real Estate Law; Real Estate Development; Corporate Law; Estate Planning; Trust Administration. ***Email:*** byanowitz@kahnkleinman.com

OF COUNSEL

ROBERT U. FEIN, born Youngstown, Ohio, October 3, 1963; admitted to bar, 1988, Ohio. *Education:* The Ohio State University (B.S.B.A., 1985; J.D., with honors, 1988). Order of the Coif. *Member:* Cleveland, Ohio State and American Bar Associations. ***PRACTICE AREAS:*** Corporate Law; Partnership Law; Securities Law; Real Estate Law; Commercial Law. ***Email:*** rfein@kahnkleinman.com

PETER A. IGEL, born Columbus Ohio, 1960; admitted to bar, 1986, Ohio. *Education:* Miami University (B.S., 1982); The Ohio State University (J.D., with honors, 1986). Certified Public Accountant, Ohio (inactive), 1987. Chair, Tax Committee, 1998-1999. *Member:* Cleveland Bar Association. ***PRACTICE AREAS:*** Tax Planning; Pension Plans; Estate Planning. ***Email:*** pigel@kahnkleinman.com

REPRESENTATIVE CLIENTS: C & T Access Venture Fund; Austin Powder; Chase Shopping Centers; Cohesant Technologies; Dots Stores; Firstar Bank, N.A.; First Interstate Development; Mazel Stores; National City Bank; Olympic Steel; Orius Central Office Services; Pierre's Ice Cream; Pulte Homes of Ohio Corporation; Rainbow Rentals; Royal Appliance Mfg.; WestCap Partners Equity Fund.

DALE F. KAINSKI

55 PUBLIC SQUARE, SUITE 2020
CLEVELAND, OHIO 44113-1901
Telephone: 216-574-9500
Telefax: 216-241-2920

Federal and State Trial and Appellate Litigation, Business, Commercial, Municipal, Civil Rights, Insurance Defense.

DALE F. KAINSKI, born Cleveland, Ohio, March 26, 1950; admitted to bar, 1975, Ohio and U.S. District Court, Northern District of Ohio; 1977, U.S. Court of Appeals, Sixth Circuit; 1979, U.S. Supreme Court. *Education:* Bowling Green State University (B.S., Accounting, 1972); Notre Dame London Centre for Legal Studies; University of Notre Dame Law School (J.D., 1975). Beta Gamma Sigma; Delta Theta Phi. Law Clerk to U.S. District Judge Robert B. Krupansky, N.D. of Ohio, 1975-1978. Assistant U.S. Attorney, Northern District of Ohio, 1978-1983. Chief Counsel, City of Cleveland, 1983-1986. Special Counsel to Ohio Attorney General, 1997-2000. Instructor, U.S. Attorney General's Advocacy Institute, 1982. *Member:* Cleveland, Ohio State (Member, OSBA College, 1992-1997, 2000), Federal (National Council, 1981-1988; Vice President, Sixth Circuit, 1982-1984, 1986-1987; Chairman, Younger Lawyers Division, 1985-1986; President, Cleveland Chapter, 1981-1982) and American Bar Associations; Cuyahoga County Law Directors Association; Judicial Conference of the U.S. Sixth Circuit (Life Member); Judicial Conference of the Ohio Eighth District (Life Member). ***PRACTICE AREAS:*** Business Law; Commercial Law; Municipal Law; Civil Rights Law; Insurance Defense.

KARBERG, KURANT, WACHTER & TURNER CO., L.P.A.

SUITE 300, PEPPER PIKE PLACE
30195 CHAGRIN BOULEVARD
CLEVELAND, OHIO 44124-5703
Telephone: 216-292-3300
Telecopier: 216-292-3340
Email: lawfirm@lawkkwt.com
URL: http://www.conwaymarken.com

Business and Corporate, Mergers and Acquisition, Employment Litigation, Real Estate, Taxation, Probate, Estate Planning, Litigation in all Courts.

JEFFREY G. WYNER, born Cleveland, Ohio, June 6, 1946; admitted to bar, 1971, Ohio; 1973, U.S. Court of Military Appeals; 2001, U.S. Supreme Court. *Education:* Wharton School of Finance and Commerce, University of Pennsylvania (B.S., cum laude, 1968); University of Michigan (J.D., 1971). Beta Gamma Sigma. Author: "Database Delight: How to Use Tools to Manage that Transaction," Business Law Today, July/Aug. 2001. Member, Civil Service Commission, City of University Heights, Ohio, 1977-1984. *Member:* Cleveland, Ohio State and American (Member, Real Property, Probate and Trust Law Section; Section of Law Practice Management) Bar Associations. [U.S. Navy Judge Advocate General's Corps., 1972-1974]. ***PRACTICE AREAS:*** Real Estate; Business Transactions; Taxation Law; Computer Law; Litigation. ***Email:*** jwyner@lawkkwt.com

(This Listing Continued)

BRUCE K. KARBERG, born Columbus, Ohio, July 15, 1945; admitted to bar, 1975, Ohio and U.S. District Court, Northern District of Ohio. *Education:* Cleveland State University (B.A., cum laude, 1972); Cleveland Marshall College of Law (J.D., 1975). [U.S. Marine Corps., 1964-1968]. ***PRACTICE AREAS:*** Real Estate Development; Finance; Business Formation; Business Transactions; Corporate Financing. ***Email:*** bkarberg@lawkkwt.com

JACK KURANT, born Stuttgart, Germany, June 4, 1946; admitted to bar, 1972, Ohio; 1977, U.S. Supreme Court; U.S. District Court, Northern District of Ohio. *Education:* The Ohio State University (B.A., 1968); Case Western Reserve University (J.D., 1971). Pi Sigma Alpha; Phi Delta Phi. *Member:* Cleveland, Ohio State (Member, Corporation Law Committee; Chairman, Limited Liability Company Subcommittee) and American Bar Associations. ***PRACTICE AREAS:*** Corporate; Real Estate; Business Acquisitions; General Business Law. ***Email:*** jkurant@lawkkwt.com

MARK I. WACHTER, born Cleveland, Ohio, March 1, 1950; admitted to bar, 1977, Ohio and U.S. District Court, Northern District of Ohio; 1979, U.S. Court of Appeals, Sixth Circuit; 1982, Maryland; 1992, U.S. Supreme Court. *Education:* University of Michigan (A.B., 1972; A.M., 1973); American University (J.D., cum laude, 1976). *Member:* Greater Cleveland and Ohio State Bar Associations. ***PRACTICE AREAS:*** Trials and Appeals; Business Litigation; Real Estate Litigation; Foreclosure Law; Mediation; Arbitration. ***Email:*** mwachter@lawkkwt.com

PETER TURNER, born Newark, New Jersey, July 19, 1956; admitted to bar, 1981, Ohio; 1982, U.S. Court of Military Appeals; 1985, District of Columbia; 1986, Maryland, U.S. District Court, Northern and Southern Districts of Ohio, District of Columbia and District of Maryland; U.S. Court of Appeals, Fourth, Sixth and District of Columbia Circuits and U.S. Supreme Court. *Education:* Ohio State University (B.A., 1978); Case Western Reserve University (J.D., 1981). *Member:* Cleveland, Ohio State and American Bar Associations. [Capt., USAF., 1982-1986]. ***PRACTICE AREAS:*** Commercial Law; Construction Law; Products Liability Law; Unfair Competition Law; Litigation. ***Email:*** pturner@lawkkwt.com

---

NEIL S. SARKAR, born Cincinnati, Ohio, June 27, 1971; admitted to bar, 1997, Ohio and U.S. District Court, Northern and Southern Districts of Ohio. *Education:* University of Chicago (B.A., with honors, 1993); Case Western Reserve University (J.D., 1997). *Member:* Cleveland, Ohio State and American Bar Associations. ***LANGUAGES:*** French. ***PRACTICE AREAS:*** Labor and Employment Law; Litigation. ***Email:*** nsarkar@lawkkwt.com

STEPHEN D. DODD, born Rochester, New York, August 22, 1974; admitted to bar, 2000, Ohio, U.S. District Court, Northern District of Ohio and U.S. Court of Appeals, Sixth Circuit. *Education:* Bob Jones University (B.S., cum laude, 1996); Case Western Reserve University (J.D., cum laude, 2000). Member: Mentor Area Chamber of Commerce; Council for Exceptional Children. *Member:* Cleveland, Lake County, Ohio State and American Bar Associations. ***PRACTICE AREAS:*** Business Law; Corporate Law; Real Estate; Estate Planning. ***Email:*** sdodd@lawkkwt.com

LIZA M. FUNKHOUSER, born Denver, Colorado, August 5, 1975; admitted to bar, 2000, Ohio. *Education:* University of Pittsburgh (B.A., cum laude, 1997); Case Western Reserve University (J.D., cum laude, 2000). *Member:* Ohio State Bar Association. ***PRACTICE AREAS:*** Real Estate; Probate; Estate Planning. ***Email:*** lbrady@lawkkwt.com

OF COUNSEL

A. R. (BUD) MAYS, born Cleveland, Ohio, March 9, 1931; admitted to bar, 1956, Ohio; 1959, U.S. District Court, Northern District of Ohio; 1961, U.S. Court of Appeals, Sixth Circuit. *Education:* Kent State University (B.S., 1953); Duke University Law School (LL.B., 1956). Delta Theta Phi. *Member:* Greater Cleveland and Ohio State Bar Associations. [With U.S. Army, 1956-1958]. ***PRACTICE AREAS:*** Real Estate; Business; Contract; Corporate Financing; Partnership. ***Email:*** bmays@lawkkwt.com

JAMES J. CONWAY, born Cleveland, Ohio, October 8, 1928; admitted to bar, 1955, Ohio; 1962, U.S. Supreme Court. *Education:* Kent State University; The Cleveland-Marshall Law School (LL.B., 1955). *Member:* Cleveland, Cuyahoga County (Chairman, Corporate Law Committee, 1978 and 1984), Ohio State and American Bar Associations; Cleveland Academy of Trial Attorneys (President, 1960). ***PRACTICE AREAS:*** Business; Corporate; Estate Planning; Banking Law; Savings Bank Law. ***Email:*** jconway@lawkkwt.com

HOWARD A. MARKEN, born Cleveland, Ohio, February 10, 1924; admitted to bar, 1950, Ohio. *Education:* The Ohio State University (B.Sc., cum laude, 1948); University of Michigan (J.D., 1950). Beta Gamma Sigma; Tau Epsilon Rho. Special Counsel to Attorney General of Ohio, 1979-1988. Member, Shaker Heights City Planning Commission and Board of Zoning Appeals, 1977-1982. *Member:* Cleveland (Member, Real Estate Law Section), Ohio State (Member, Real Property Law Section) and American (Member, Section of Real Property, Probate and Trust Law) Bar Associations; Lawyer-Pilots Bar Association; Urban Land Institute; National Association of Industrial and Office Properties. ***PRACTICE AREAS:*** Real Estate; Business Transactions; Tax Law; Estate Planning; Litigation. ***Email:*** hmarken@lawkkwt.com

KAUFMAN & CUMBERLAND CO., L.P.A.

CLEVELAND, OHIO

(See Thompson Hine LLP)

KEIS / GEORGE LLP

55 PUBLIC SQUARE, SUITE 800
CLEVELAND, OHIO 44113
Telephone: 216-241-4100
Fax: 216-771-3111
Email: info@keisgeorge.com
URL: http://www.keisgeorgellplaw.com

Personal Injury, Insurance Subrogation, Insurance Defense, Construction Law, Products Liability, Insurance, Health Care Subrogation, Automobile Accidents, Medical Malpractice.

MEMBERS OF FIRM

WILLIAM H. KEIS, JR., born Cleveland, Ohio, February 26, 1955; admitted to bar, 1982, Ohio and U.S. District Court, Northern District of Ohio. *Education:* Cleveland State University (B.A., 1977); Cleveland-Marshall College of Law (J.D., 1981). *Member:* Cleveland, Ohio State and American Bar Associations; National Association of Subrogation Professionals. ***PRACTICE AREAS:*** Insurance Subrogation; Products Liability; Insurance Defense; Property Subrogation. ***Email:*** bkeis@keisgeorge.com

WARREN S. GEORGE, born June 19, 1964; admitted to bar, 1989, Ohio and U.S. District Court, Northern District of Ohio. *Education:* Cleveland State University (B.A., 1977); Cleveland-Marshall College of Law (J.D., 1989). *Member:* Cleveland, Ohio State and American Bar Associations; Cleveland Academy of Civil Trial Attorneys; Defense Research Institute. ***PRACTICE AREAS:*** Insurance Defense Litigation; Insurance Coverage; Insurance Subrogation; Products Liability. ***Email:*** wgeorge@keisgeorge.com

HERBERT L. NUSSLE, admitted to bar, 1994, Ohio. *Education:* The Ohio State University (B.A., 1989); Cleveland-Marshall College of Law (J.D., cum laude, 1994). ***PRACTICE AREAS:*** Insurance Subrogation; Lemon Law. ***Email:*** hnussle@keisgeorge.com

ASSOCIATES

PATRICK J. O'MALLEY, born July 3, 1969; admitted to bar, 1995, Ohio; 1996, Illinois; 2000, U.S. District Court, Northern District of Ohio. *Education:* Quincy College (B.S., 1991); Cleveland-Marshall College of Law (J.D., 1995). *Member:* Cleveland, Cuyahoga County, Lorain County, Ohio State and Illinois State Bar Associations. ***PRACTICE AREAS:*** Insurance Subrogation; Automobile Accidents and Injuries; Personal Injury. ***Email:*** pomalley@keisgeorge.com

LISA M. GERLACK, born Lakewood, Ohio, October 4, 1964; admitted to bar, 1989, Ohio, U.S. District Court, Northern District of Ohio and U.S. Court of Appeals, Sixth Circuit. *Education:* Wittenberg University (B.A., 1986); Cleveland-Marshall College of Law (J.D., 1989). Recipient, Moot Court Faculty Advisor's Award. Editor, Law & Fact Cuyahoga County Bar Association Journal. Member: Cleveland Marshall National Moot Court Team; Order of Barrister's Advocacy. Prosecutor, City of Bentleyville, Ohio, 1990. *Member:* Cleveland, Cuyahoga County and Ohio State (Council of, Delegates, 1996-1998) Bar Associations; Ohio Academy of Trial Lawyers; The Association of Trial Lawyers of America; Cleveland Academy of Trial Lawyers (Member, Board of Directors, 1994-1998). ***LANGUAGES:*** Spanish. ***PRACTICE AREAS:*** Insurance; Products Liability; Personal Injury; Employment Law; Appellate Practice. ***Email:*** lgerlack@keisgeorge.com

JEFFREY L. AUSTIN, born Warren, Ohio, January 27, 1972; admitted to bar, 1998, Ohio, U.S. District Court, Northern and Southern Districts of Ohio and U.S. Court of Appeals, Sixth Circuit. *Education:* The Ohio State University (B.A., 1994); John Marshall Law School (J.D., 1997). *Member:* Cleveland, Cuyahoga County and Ohio State Bar Associations. ***PRACTICE AREAS:*** Insurance Defense Litigation; Personal Injury; Products Liability; Contract Disputes; Defamation; Wrongful Death; Bad Faith. ***Email:*** jaustin@keisgeorge.com

TIMOTHY L. SPRAGUE, born Dayton, Ohio, January 27, 1972; admitted to bar, 1999, Ohio and U.S. District Court, Northern District of Ohio. *Education:* The Ohio State University (B.A., 1994); John Marshall College of Law (J.D., 1997). *Member:* Columbus, Ohio State and American Bar Associations. ***PRACTICE AREAS:*** Insurance Defense; Personal Injury; Subrogation; Construction Law; Products Liability. ***Email:*** tsprague@keisgeorge.com

CAROLE A. LOHR, born August 3, 1971; admitted to bar, 2000, Ohio and U.S. District Court, Northern District of Ohio. *Education:* North Carolina State University (B.A., 1995); Cleveland Marshall College of Law (J.D., 1999). *Member:* Ohio State Bar Association. ***PRACTICE AREAS:*** Insurance Subrogation; Creditors Rights; Contract Disputes; Insurance Defense. ***Email:*** clohr@ukglaw.com

SCOTT T. KNOWLES, admitted to bar, 2004, Ohio. *Education:* University of Dayton (B.S., 1999); University of Toledo, College of Law (J.D., 2003). ***PRACTICE AREAS:*** Insurance Subrogation; Insurance. ***Email:*** sknowles@keisgeorge.com

KAREN FOUT, born December 28, 1959; admitted to bar, 2004, Ohio. *Education:* Merrimac College (B.A., 1987); Cleveland-Marshall College of Law (J.D., 2003). ***PRACTICE AREAS:*** Insurance Defense; Casualty Insurance Subrogation; Insurance Coverage; Appellate Practice. ***Email:*** kfout@keisgeorge.com

JASON P. GRABLE, born Conneaut, Ohio, April 7, 1977; admitted to bar, 2003, Ohio. *Education:* The Ohio State University (B.A., 1999); Ohio Northern University College of Law (J.D., with distinction, 2003). Editor-in-Chief, Ohio Northern Law Review, 2002-2003; Staff Editor, 2001-2002. ***PRACTICE AREAS:*** Products Liability; Litigation; Subrogation. ***Email:*** jgrable@gsfn.com

---

ELLEN HOLLAND KELLER

Established in 1997

55 PUBLIC SQUARE, SUITE 1510
CLEVELAND, OHIO 44113
Telephone: 216-771-4830
Fax: 216-771-4615
Email: holland@gwis.com

Consumer Law, Bankruptcy, Business Law, Commercial Law, Mediation.

(This Listing Continued)

ELLEN HOLLAND KELLER, born Chicago, Illinois, March 10, 1940; admitted to bar, 1979, Ohio and U.S. District Court, Northern District of Ohio; 1986, U.S. Court of Appeals, Sixth Circuit. *Education:* Miami University (B.A., 1962); University of Michigan (M.A., 1964); Case Western Reserve University (Ph.D., 1976); Cleveland-Marshall College of Law (J.D., 1979). *Member:* Cleveland (Member: Alternative Dispute Resolution Committee), Ohio State and American (Member, Dispute Resolution Section) Bar Associations; American Bankruptcy Institute. ***PRACTICE AREAS:*** Consumer Law; Bankruptcy; Business Law; Commercial Law; Mediation.

STANLEY S. KELLER & ASSOCIATES CO., LPA

Established in 1977

SUITE 330 THE HANNA BUILDING
1422 EUCLID AVENUE
CLEVELAND, OHIO 44115-1901
Telephone: 216-566-7100
Fax: 216-566-5430
Email: sskeller@en.com

Lorain County, Ohio Office: 5455 Detroit Road, Sheffield Village, 44054. Telephone: 440-930-4039. Fax: 440-934-7205.

General Practice.

FIRM PROFILE: The law firm is engaged in the practice of law with emphasis on insurance defense, insurance coverage and bad faith issues, product liability, automobile negligence, transportation companies, environmental issues, asbestos and hazardous waste litigation. In addition, our firm represents our corporate and business clients with respect to legal concerns which affect their businesses and corporations and includes corporate law, business succession planning, employment law, commercial law, real estate, commercial litigation and internet/online law.

STANLEY S. KELLER, born Cleveland, Ohio, November 25, 1933; admitted to bar, 1958, Ohio; U.S. District Court, Northern District of Ohio. *Education:* Kent State University (A.B., 1956); Western Reserve University (LL.B., 1958). Tau Epsilon Rho. *Member:* Cleveland, Akron, Ohio State and American (Member, Sections on: Tort and Insurance Practice; Litigation) Bar Associations; Defense Research and Trial Lawyers Association; Ohio Association of Civil Trial Attorneys; Defense Research Institute. ***PRACTICE AREAS:*** Insurance Defense Law; Products Liability Law; Negligence Litigation. ***Email:*** sskeller@en.com

WALTER H. KROHNGOLD, born Cleveland, Ohio, October 15, 1956; admitted to bar, 1983, Ohio; U.S. District Court, Northern District of Ohio. *Education:* University of Rochester (B.A., 1979); Case Western Reserve University (J.D., 1983). *Member:* Cleveland, Akron, Cuyahoga County and Ohio State Bar Associations; Defense Research Institute. ***PRACTICE AREAS:*** Insurance Defense Law; Products Liability Law; Negligence Litigation. ***Email:*** wkrohngold@en.com

MARTIN T. POWERS, born Cleveland, Ohio, July 27, 1962; admitted to bar, 1991, Ohio. *Education:* Cleveland State University (B.A., 1985); University of Akron (J.D., 1989). Treasurer, International Law Society. *Member:* Ohio Bar Association. ***PRACTICE AREAS:*** Insurance Defense; Products Liability; Toxic Torts. ***Email:*** mpowers@en.com

MICHAEL L. COLE, born Akron, Ohio, May 16, 1970; admitted to bar, 2000, Ohio and U.S. District Court, Northern District of Ohio. *Education:* Mount Union College (B.A., 1993); University of Akron School of Law (J.D., 1999). Recipient, Communications Proficiency Award, 1988-1992. FCC License, 1988. Formerly with: Cole Co. LPA; Crombie Law Firm. Magistrate, City of Hudson Mayor's Court, 2003—. *Member:* Ohio State and American (Member, Litigation Section) Bar Associations. ***PRACTICE AREAS:*** Insurance Defense; Consumer Bankruptcy; Municipal Law; Domestic Relations; Wills; Trusts and Estates. ***Email:*** mcole@en.com

REPRESENTATIVE CLIENTS: American International Group; Allstate Insurance Company; State Farm Insurance Company; Schneider National Carriers, Inc.; INS Insurance, Inc.; Brotherhood Mutual Insurance Company; Hartford-Omni Insurance Group; Metropolitan Property & Liability Insurance Co.; AFLAC; Infinity Insurance Company; Windsor Group; Atlanta Casualty Company; Sentry Insurance Company; Gallagher Bassett Services, Inc.; Victoria Insurance Group; CNI Claim Service; Superior Insurance Company; Admiral Insurance Company; Covenant Mutual Insurance Co.; Southeastern Fidelity Insurance Co.; O'Brien & Associates; Esis, Inc./CIGNA Cos.; Crum & Forster; Self-Insured Services Co.; C.N.A.; Capital Indemnity Co.; North American Specialty Co.; Hastings Mutual Insurance Company; Brinker International; Fortis Financial Corp.; Yellow Freight Systems; State Auto Insurance Company; Lobo Claims Management, Inc.; Watkins Motor Lines; TIG Insurance Company Environmental Claims; Tops Market, Inc.; Foremost Insurance Company; ACE USA; Continental Western Insurance Company; Roehl Transport; Merastar Insurance Company.
REFERENCE: Bank One, Cleveland.

KELLEY & FERRARO LLP

1300 EAST NINTH STREET, SUITE 1901
CLEVELAND, OHIO 44114
Telephone: 216-575-0777; Toll Free: 1-888-839-8479
Fax: 216-575-0799
Email: k&f@kelley-ferraro.com
URL: http://www.kelley-ferraro.com

Products Liability, Toxic Tort, Wrongful Death, Personal Injury, Medical Malpractice, Asbestos Litigation, Silica Litigation, Welding Road Litigation, Vioxx, Workers Compensation, Sports Law, Entertainment Law, Family Law and Probate Law.

JAMES L. FERRARO, born Greenwich, Connecticut, March 29, 1957; admitted to bar, 1983, Florida; 1984, U.S. District Court, Southern District of Florida; 1985, Massachusetts; 1994, U.S. Court of Appeals, Third Circuit and U.S. Tax Court; 2000, U.S. Court of Appeals, First Circuit; 2002, New York, U.S. Court of Appeals, Fourth Circuit and U.S.

(This Listing Continued)

KELLEY & FERRARO LLP, Cleveland—Continued

District Court, Southern District of New York; 2003, Ohio. *Education:* University of Miami (B.B.A., 1978; M.S., 1979; J.D., 1983). Sigma Alpha Epsilon (1976). Beta Alpha Psi (1977). Certified Public Accountant, Florida, 1980. Contract Advisor: Major League Baseball Players Association, 1994. National Finalist, Trial Lawyer of the Year, 1997. Inducted, Knights of Malta, 1999. Florida State Coordinator, Trial Lawyers for Public Justice, 2000. Awarded, Ellis Island Medal of Honor, 2001. Owner, Las Vegas Gladiators. *Member:* Dade County, Massachusetts, New York State and American Bar Associations; Florida Institute of Certified Public Accountants; American Institute of Certified Public Accountants; Florida Trial Lawyers Association; ATLA; National Italian-American Bar Association; Academy of Florida Trial Lawyers; Million Dollar Advocates Forum. (Also Member, Ferraro & Associates, P.A., Miami, Florida). ***REPORTED CASES:*** Castillo, etc. et al., Petitioners v. E.I. Dupont De Nemours & Co., Inc. et al. Respondents, 854 So.2d 1264 (Fla. 2003). ***PRACTICE AREAS:*** Products Liability; Asbestos Litigation; Toxic Torts; Wrongful Death; Personal Injury; Medical Malpractice; Sports Law; Entertainment Law.

MICHAEL V. KELLEY, born Cleveland, Ohio, September 3, 1951; admitted to bar, 1982, Ohio; 1983, U.S. District Court, Northern District of Ohio; 1984, U.S. Court of Appeals, Sixth Circuit; 1985, U.S. Supreme Court; 1991, District of Columbia; U.S. District Court, Northern District of Illinois; U.S. District Court, Western District of Pennsylvania; 1992, U.S. District Court, Northern District of California; 1996, U.S. Court of Appeals, Fifth Circuit. *Education:* St. Benedict's College; Case Western Reserve University (B.A., 1974); Cleveland Marshall College of Law (J.D., 1981). Member, Board of Trustees, 1984-1986 and President, Board of Trustees, 1987-1990, Cleveland Public Library. Foreman, Appointed by the Court, Cuyahoga County Court of Common Pleas, Grand Jury, May Term, 1981. Life Member, Judicial Conference of the Eighth Judicial District of Ohio. Special Counsel to Ohio Attorney General, 1983—. Member, Million Dollar Advocates Forum. *Member:* Greater Cleveland, Cuyahoga County, Ohio State, Federal and American Bar Associations; The Association of Trial Lawyers of America; American Judicature Society; Ohio Academy of Trial Lawyers. ***PRACTICE AREAS:*** Asbestos Litigation; Products Liability; Toxic Torts; Wrongful Death; Personal Injury; Medical Malpractice; Domestic Relations.

JOHN A. SIVINSKI, born Port Clinton, Ohio, October 21, 1959; admitted to bar, 1986, Ohio and U.S. District Court, Northern District of Ohio; 1987, U.S. Court of Appeals, Seventh and Sixth Circuits. *Education:* John Carroll University (B.S., 1983); Case Western Reserve University (J.D., cum laude, 1986). Member, Million Dollar Advocates Forum. *Member:* Cleveland and Ohio State Bar Associations; The Association of Trial Lawyers of America; Ohio Academy of Trial Lawyers; Trial Lawyers for Public Justice. ***PRACTICE AREAS:*** Asbestos Litigation; Products Liability; Toxic Torts; Personal Injury; Medical Malpractice.

THOMAS M. WILSON, born Cleveland, Ohio, July 12, 1956; admitted to bar, 1987, Ohio; 1988, U.S. Court of Appeals, Sixth Circuit and U.S. District Court, Northern District of Ohio; 1992, U.S. Supreme Court; 1995, U.S. Court of Appeals, Fifth Circuit. *Education:* Cleveland State University (B.A., 1984); Cleveland State University, Cleveland Marshall College of Law (J.D., 1987). Phi Alpha Delta. Recipient, American Jurisprudence Awards in Administrative Law and Jurisprudence. Adjunct Instructor, Cleveland State University, Cleveland Marshall College of Law, 1989-1990. Member, Cleveland Works Legal Advisory Board. *Member:* Cleveland (Bar Admissions Committee, 1993-2001; Certified Grievance Committee, 1996-2002; Professional Ethics Committee, 1996—; Executive Council Member, Young Lawyers Section, 1988-1990; Member, Criminal Law and Environmental Law Sections), Cuyahoga County (Member, Criminal Law Section) and Ohio State Bar Associations; The Association of Trial Lawyers of America; Cuyahoga County Criminal Defense Lawyers Association. ***REPORTED CASES:*** State ex rel. Hubbard v. Industrial Commission (2002), 96 Ohio St. 3d 336; Dombelek v. Ohio Bur. Of Workers' Comp. 154 Ohio App.3d 338; Bedford Hts. v. France 67 Ohio St.3d 55 (1993). ***PRACTICE AREAS:*** Complex Litigation; Toxic Torts; Asbestos Litigation; Products Liability; Medical Malpractice; Wrongful Death; Appellate Practice.

ANTHONY GALLUCCI, born Cleveland, Ohio, December 4, 1969; admitted to bar, 1996, Ohio; 1997, U.S. District Court, Northern District of Ohio; 1998, U.S. Court of Appeals Sixth Circuit; 2002, U.S. Supreme Court. *Education:* Miami University (B.A., 1992); Cleveland Marshall College of Law (J.D., 1996). Managing Editor, Journal of Law and Health. Arbitrator, Council of Better Business Bureaus, Inc. Member, Million Dollar Advocates Forum. *Member:* Cleveland, Ohio State and American Bar Associations; Ohio Academy of Trial Lawyers. ***PRACTICE AREAS:*** Asbestos Litigation; Products Liability; Toxic Torts; Personal Injury; Wrongful Death.

COREY WADE FROST, born Bellefontaine, Ohio, March 15, 1962; admitted to bar, 1987, Ohio. *Education:* Cleveland State University (B.A., magna cum laude, 1984); Case Western Reserve University (J.D., cum laude, 1987). Franklin Thomas Backus Merit Scholar; Homer E. Woodling Scholar. Magistrate, Cuyahoga County Court of Common Pleas, Domestic Relations Division, 1989-1999. ***PRACTICE AREAS:*** Family Law; Workers Compensation; Asbestos Litigation; Products Liability.

JOHN MARTIN MURPHY, born Cleveland, Ohio, October 4, 1970; admitted to bar, 1996, Ohio; 1999, U.S. District Court, Northern District of Ohio; 2000, U.S. Court of Appeals, Sixth Circuit. *Education:* Purdue University (B.A., 1992); Thomas M. Cooley Law School (J.D., 1996). Magistrate: Bratenahl Village; Grand River Village. *Member:* Cleveland and Ohio State Bar Associations. ***PRACTICE AREAS:*** Personal Injury; Asbestos Litigation; Silicosis Litigation; Products Liability; Toxic Torts; Wrongful Death.

SANDRA BECHER SOMMERS, born Steubenville, Ohio, August 30, 1959; admitted to bar, 1985, Ohio and U.S. District Court, Southern District of Ohio; 1999, U.S. District Court, Northern District of Ohio. *Education:* Ohio University (B.A., cum laude, 1981); Capital University (J.D., 1985). Assistant Attorney General, Business and Government Regulations, Workers' Compensation Section, 1987-1990. *Member:* Cleveland and Ohio State Bar Associations. ***REPORTED CASES:*** State ex rel. Vebanek v. Indus. Comm. (1995), 73 Ohio St.3d 562; State, ex rel. LTV Steel Co., v. Indus. Comm. *(1992), 65 Ohio St. 3d 22; State ex rel. Crisp v. Indus. Comm. (1992),* 64 Ohio St.3d 507; State ex rel. Jeffrey Mining Machinery Div., Dresser Industries, Inc. v. Indus. Comm. (1990), 56 Ohio St.3d 91; Fayette Fire & Safety Equip. Co. v. Hennosy (1989), 65 Ohio App.3d 10. ***PRACTICE AREAS:*** Asbestos Litigation; Toxic Torts; Silicosis Litigation; Products Liability.

(This Listing Continued)

SHAWN M. ACTON, born Mayfield Heights, Ohio, March 22, 1975; admitted to bar, 2000, Ohio; 2001, U.S. District Court, Northern District of Ohio; 2003, U.S. Court of Appeals, Sixth Circuit; 2005, U.S. Supreme Court. *Education:* University of Dayton (B.A., 1997); Cleveland-Marshall College of Law (J.D., 2000). *Member:* Cleveland and Ohio State Bar Associations; Trial Lawyers for Public Justice. ***PRACTICE AREAS:*** Workers Compensation; Asbestos Litigation; Personal Injury.

LORI ANN LUKA, born Youngstown, Ohio, December 6, 1973; admitted to bar, 2000, Ohio; 2001, U.S. Court of Appeals, Sixth District and U.S. District Court, Northern District of Ohio. *Education:* Youngstown State University (B.S., Political Science, summa cum laude, 1997); Cleveland-Marshall College of Law (J.D., cum laude, 2000). *Member:* Cuyahoga County, Mahoning County, Cleveland and Ohio State Bar Associations; The Association of American Trial Lawyers; Trial Lawyers for Public Justice. ***PRACTICE AREAS:*** Asbestos Litigation; Personal Injury; Workers Compensation; Toxic Torts; Medical Malpractice.

ROBERT A. MARCIS, II, born Cleveland, Ohio, July 24, 1973; admitted to bar, 1998, Ohio; 2001, U.S. District Court, Northern District of Ohio. *Education:* Duke University (A.B., cum laude, 1995); Wake Forest University (J.D., 1998). Member, Wake Forest Law Review, 1996-1998. Member, Million Dollar Advocates Forum. *Member:* Cleveland and Ohio State Bar Associations. ***PRACTICE AREAS:*** Asbestos Litigation; Workers Compensation; Products Liability.

JAESON L. TAYLOR, born Euclid, Ohio, November 14, 1975; admitted to bar, 2001, Ohio. *Education:* Washington & Jefferson College (B.A., 1997); Case Western Reserve University (J.D., 2000). *Member:* Cleveland and Ohio State Bar Associations. ***PRACTICE AREAS:*** Asbestos Litigation; Workers Compensation; Products Liability; Probate; Personal Injury.

WILLIAM EDWARD UZL, born Cleveland, Ohio, December 17, 1964; admitted to bar, 1990, Ohio; 1991, North Carolina. *Education:* Mount Union College (B.A., magna cum laude, 1987); Case Western Reserve University (J.D., 1990). ***PRACTICE AREAS:*** Workers Compensation; Asbestos Litigation; Probate; Estate Planning; Products Liability.

CATHERINE J. TESTA, born Greensburg, Pennsylvania, December 18, 1976; admitted to bar, 2004, Ohio. *Education:* Washington & Jefferson College (B.A., 1999); Cleveland Marshall College of Law (J.D., 2003). ***PRACTICE AREAS:*** Asbestos Litigation; Workers Compensation; Probate.

JENNIFER L. MANCINO, born Akron, Ohio, January 4, 1976; admitted to bar, 2004, Ohio. *Education:* Kansas Wesleyan University (B.A., 1999); University of Akron (J.D., 2003). ***PRACTICE AREAS:*** Asbestos Litigation; Workers Compensation; Personal Injury.

DAYNA M. DePERRO, born Youngstown, Ohio, August 18, 1979; admitted to bar, 2004, Ohio. *Education:* Miami University (B.A., 2001); Cleveland-Marshall College of Law (J.D., 2004). Member, Cleveland-Marshall Alumni Association. *Member:* Cleveland, Mahoning County, Ohio State and American Bar Associations. ***PRACTICE AREAS:*** Probate Law; Personal Injury. ***Email:*** ddeperro@kelley-ferraro.com

ERIC C. WIEDEMER, born Fairview, Ohio, July 2, 1977; admitted to bar, 2005, Ohio. *Education:* Loyola University (B.B.A., 1999); Cleveland-Marshall College of Law (J.D., 2004). ***PRACTICE AREAS:*** Asbestos Litigation; Toxic Torts; Personal Injury; Workers Compensation. ***Email:*** ewiedemer@kelley-ferraro.com

JENNIFER L. ROZIC, born Maumee, Ohio, March 23, 1977; admitted to bar, 2005, Ohio. *Education:* Ohio University (B.B.A., 1999); Cleveland-Marshall College of Law (J.D., 2004). ***LANGUAGES:*** French. ***PRACTICE AREAS:*** Probate; Asbestos Litigation; Toxic Torts. ***Email:*** jrozic@kelley-ferraro.com

JOHN T. FORRISTAL, born Cleveland, Ohio, February 22, 1973; admitted to bar, 2005, Ohio. *Education:* Fordham University (B.A., 1995); Case Western Reserve University (J.D., 2004). [Sgt., U.S. Army Reserves, 1996-2003.]. ***PRACTICE AREAS:*** Asbestos Litigation; Personal Injury; Workers Compensation; Toxic Torts. ***Email:*** jforristal@kelley-ferraro.com

OF COUNSEL

LYNN ARKO KELLEY, born Cleveland, Ohio, August 25, 1955; admitted to bar, 1985, Ohio. *Education:* Washington & Jefferson College (B.A., 1977); Cleveland Marshall College of Law (J.D., 1983). Member, Board of Trustees, Washington & Jefferson College, 1996-2001. Appointed Judge, Cleveland Heights Municipal Court, September 2002. Acting Judge, Cleveland Heights Municipal Court, 1995-1996. Life Member, Judicial conference of the Eights Judicial District of Ohio. *Member:* Cleveland, Cuyahoga County and American Bar Associations. ***PRACTICE AREAS:*** Children; Family Law.

KELLEY, JASONS, McGUIRE & SPINELLI, L.L.P.

629 EUCLID AVENUE, SUITE 1037
CLEVELAND, OHIO 44114
Telephone: 216-902-4444
Fax: 216-902-4447

Philadelphia, Pennsylvania Office: Centre Square West, Suite 1500, 1500 Market Street, 19102. Telephone: 215-854-0658. Fax: 215-854-8434.
Wilmington, Delaware Office: 800 Delaware Avenue, P.O. Box 194, 19899. Telephone: 302-652-8560. Fax: 302-652-8405.

(For complete biographical data on all personnel, see Biography Listing at Philadelphia, Pennsylvania)

KENNEDY REEVE & KNOLL

75 PUBLIC SQUARE, SUITE 1300
CLEVELAND, OHIO 44113
Telephone: 216-771-5511
Facsimile: 216-771-5511
URL: http://www.krkattorneys.com/

Columbus, Ohio Office: 98 Hamilton Park, 43203. Telephone: 614-228-2050. Facsimile: 614-228-3320.

Sexual Harassment, Americans with Disability Act, Age Discrimination in Employment Act, Title VII Race and Gender Discrimination, Family Medical Leave Act, National Origin Discrimination, Civil Service, State and Federal Civil Rights Litigation, Religion Discrimination, Representation to the Equal Employment Opportunity Commission and Ohio Civil Rights Commission, Administrative Law, Unemployment, Worker's Compensation Retaliation, Whistleblower Statute, Intentional Tort, Equal Protection and Due Process Violations, Employee Benefits, Wrongful Termination, Public Policy, Severance Package Review and Negotiation, Contract Review, Negotiation and Litigation, Small Business Start-Up and Consulting.

ASSOCIATE

PATRICK M. WATTS, admitted to bar, 2002, Ohio. *Education:* The Ohio State University (J.D., 2004).

(For complete biographical data on all personnel, see Professional Biographies at Columbus, Ohio)

KIRSCHENBAUM LAW OFFICES CO., L.P.A.

Established in 1950
1919 EAST 13TH STREET
CLEVELAND, OHIO 44114
Telephone: 216-621-0890
Toll Free in Ohio: 1-877-822-4402
Fax: 216-621-3590
URL: http://www.kirschenbaumlaw.com
Email: kirschenbaumlaw@aol.com
URL: http://www.lawyers.com/kirschenbaumlaw

Personal Injury, Medical Malpractice, Workers' Compensation, Products Liability, Employment Law and Discrimination, Labor Management Relations, Wage and Hour, Real Estate (HUD), Health and Elder Care Law, Family Law, Bankruptcy. Civil Trials and Appeals in all Courts.

DAVID KIRSCHENBAUM, born Cleveland, Ohio, July 26, 1925; admitted to bar, 1950, Ohio; 1965, U.S. Supreme Court. *Education:* The Ohio State University; Ohio Northern University (LL.B., 1950). Life Member, Sixth Circuit Judicial Conference and The Judicial Conference Of The Eighth Judicial District. Member, Northeast Regional Sewer Board of Ohio, 1979-1980. *Member:* Cuyahoga County Bar Association; Judicial Conference of the Eighth Judicial District (Life Member). [With: U.S. Army, 1943-1946; U.S. Merchant Marine, 1946]. ***PRACTICE AREAS:*** Real Estate (HUD); Construction Law; Workers Compensation Law; Health Care Law; Elder Care Law.

DAN G. KIRSCHENBAUM, born Cleveland, Ohio, November 28, 1955; admitted to bar, 1984, Ohio, U.S. Court of Appeals, Sixth Circuit; 1990, Colorado. *Education:* Ohio State University (B.A., 1978); Ohio Northern University (J.D., 1984). Life Member, The Judicial Conference Of The Eighth Judicial District. *Member:* Cleveland Bar Association; Judicial Conference of the Eighth Judicial District (Life Member). ***PRACTICE AREAS:*** Workers Compensation Law; Personal Injury Law; Health Care Law; Elder Care Law.

ROBERT W. TODT, born Cleveland, Ohio, July 5, 1950; admitted to bar, 1986, Ohio and U.S. District Court, Northern District of Ohio. *Education:* Cleveland State University (B.A., 1982); Cleveland-Marshall College of Law (J.D., 1986). ***PRACTICE AREAS:*** Personal Injury Law; Civil Litigation; Criminal Defense Law; Bankruptcy Law.

REPRESENTATIVE CLIENTS: Doan Electric Co.; Good Samaritan Nursing Homes.
REFERENCES: National City Bank; Huntington National Bank.

KLEIN & CARNEY CO., L.P.A.

55 PUBLIC SQUARE, SUITE 1200
CLEVELAND, OHIO 44113
Telephone: 216-861-0111
Toll Free: 1-800-360-2889
Fax: 216-861-8203
Email: kleinandcarney@aol.com
URL: http://www.kleinandcarney.com

Personal Injury, Medical Malpractice, Insurance Law, Wrongful Death, Motor Vehicle Accidents, Nursing Home Negligence, Workers Compensation.

LARRY S. KLEIN, born Cleveland, Ohio, October 12, 1953; admitted to bar, 1980, Ohio, U.S. District Court, Northern District of Ohio and U.S. Tax Court. *Education:* Boston University (B.A. in Psychology and Accounting, cum laude, 1975); Cleveland State University (J.D., 1980). *Member:* Cleveland, Cuyahoga, Ashtabula, Ohio State and American Bar Associations; the Association of Trial Lawyers of America; Ohio Association of Trial Lawyers; Cleveland Academy of Trial Attorneys. ***PRACTICE AREAS:*** Personal Injury; Medical Malpractice; Insurance Law; Motor Vehicle Accidents and Injuries; Nursing Home Negligence. ***Email:*** kleinandcarney@aol.com

CHRISTOPHER J. CARNEY, born Cleveland, Ohio, October 23, 1967; admitted to bar, 1993, Ohio; U.S. District Court, Northern District of Ohio. *Education:* University of Dayton (B.A., 1990); Cleveland Marshall School of Law (J.D., cum laude, 1993). *Member:* Cuyahoga County, Cleveland, Ohio State and American Bar Associations; The Association of Trial Lawyers of America; Ohio Association of Trial Lawyers; Cleveland Academy of Trial Lawyers. ***PRACTICE AREAS:*** Personal Injury; Medical Malpractice; Insurance

(This Listing Continued)

Law; Motor Vehicle Accidents and Injuries; Nursing Home Negligence. ***Email:*** kleinandcarney@aol.com

KNEVEL & ASSOCIATES CO. LPA

629 EUCLID AVENUE, SUITE 519
CLEVELAND, OHIO 44114
Telephone: 216-523-7800
Fax: 216-523-7801
URL: http://www.lawyers.com/knevel&associates

Bankruptcy.

MARK H. KNEVEL, born 1951; admitted to bar, 1977, Ohio. *Education:* University of Notre Dame (B.A., 1974); Case Western Reserve University (J.D., 1977). *Member:* Ohio State Bar Association. ***PRACTICE AREAS:*** Bankruptcy (100%, 1300). ***Email:*** mknevel@knevel.com

KOBLENTZ & KOBLENTZ

Established in 1948
55 PUBLIC SQUARE, SUITE 1170
CLEVELAND, OHIO 44113
Telephone: 216-621-3012
Fax: 216-621-6567

Legal Ethics and Discipline Law. General Practice of Law, including Small Business, Corporate Real Estate, Criminal Defense, Civil Litigation, Domestic Relations, Probate and White Collar Criminal Defense.

RICHARD S. KOBLENTZ, born Cleveland, Ohio, May 19, 1950; admitted to bar, 1975, Ohio and U.S. District Court, Northern District of Ohio; 1988, U.S. Supreme Court. *Education:* The Ohio State University (B.S.Ed., 1972); Cleveland Marshall College of Law, Cleveland State University (J.D., cum laude, 1975). Trustee, 1985-1987, Officer, 1987-1990, President, 1990-1991, Honorary Trustee, 1992—, Alumni of the Year, 1997, Cleveland-Marshall Law Alumni Association. Co-Chairman, Annual Cleveland-Marshall Alumni Luncheon, 1986-1989. Member, 1986-1996 and Chairman, 1988-1991, Cuyahoga County Board of Mental Retardation and Developmental Disabilities. President, 1996— and Member of Executive Committee, Trustee and Counsel, Cleveland Baseball Federation, 1985-1996. Member, Campaign Cabinet of Jewish Community Federation. Co-Chairman, Friends of the Mentally Retarded, 1990. Trustee, American Jewish Congress, 1990, Vice-President, 1991-1995. *Member:* Cleveland, Cuyahoga County (Trustee, 1985-1989, Vice President, 1989-1992; Member, 1980-1995 and Chairman, 1988-1990, Grievance Committee; Member and Secretary, Ethics Committee, 1977-1980), Geauga County and Ohio State Bar Associations; National Association of Criminal Defense Lawyers; Ohio Criminal Defense Lawyers Association (Member, Legislative Committee); Cuyahoga Criminal Defense Lawyers Association (Member, Court Oversight Committee); Judicial Conference, Eighth Judicial District, Charter Life Member. ***PRACTICE AREAS:*** Legal Ethics and Discipline Law; Civil Litigation; Criminal Defense; White Collar Criminal Defense; Real Estate; Domestic Relations; Family Law; Small Business; Corporate Law; Probate. ***Email:*** koblentz@sbcglobal.net

CRAIG J. MORICE, born St. Louis, Missouri, October 25, 1964; admitted to bar, 1995, Ohio; 2000, U.S. Court of Appeals, Sixth Circuit. *Education:* St. Louis University (B.A., cum laude, 1986); Cleveland Marshall College of Law, Cleveland State University (J.D., 1995). *Member:* Ohio State Bar Association. ***PRACTICE AREAS:*** Criminal Defense; Driving While Intoxicated; Civil Litigation; Domestic Relations; Family Law; Legal Ethics.

BRYAN L. PENVOSE, born Gettysburg, Pennsylvania, November 19, 1975; admitted to bar, 2001, Ohio. *Education:* Washington & Jefferson College (B.A., 1998); Cleveland-Marshall College of Law (J.D., 2001). Delta Theta Phi. *Member:* Ohio State and American Bar Associations. ***PRACTICE AREAS:*** Civil Litigation; Business Law; Criminal; Employment Discrimination. ***Email:*** blpenvose@sbcglobal.net

MARVIN A. KOBLENTZ (1922-1995)

RONALD J. KOCH

CLEVELAND, OHIO

(See Columbus)

Litigation, Copyrights, Trademarks, Patents, Intellectual Property, Contracts, Forensic Science, Engineering, Juvenile, Criminal, Patent Law.

KOETH, RICE & LEO CO., L.P.A.

Established in 1919
(Formerly Bertsch, Millican & Winslow Co., L.P.A.)
1280 WEST THIRD STREET
CLEVELAND, OHIO 44113
Telephone: 216-696-1433
Telecopier: 216-696-1439
Email: info@krplpa.com
URL: http://www.krplpa.com

Civil Trial and Appellate Practice. Insurance, Labor and Employment, Environmental Law, Personal Injury, Products Liability, Medical Malpractice.

(This Listing Continued)

KOETH, RICE & LEO CO., L.P.A., Cleveland—Continued

FIRM PROFILE: Koeth, Rice & Leo Co., L.P.A., and its predecessor firms have been practicing law in Cleveland, Ohio since 1919, engaged in general, civil trial and appellate practice, with primary emphasis in insurance, business, tax, real estate development and probate law. Focus on insurance defense litigation began as early as 1925 with a single client and has expanded so that, at present, approximately 70% of its practice involves that specialty, including products, automobile, premises and other personal injury liability, malpractice, libel and slander, environmental, asbestos and contractual coverage issues related to each of these areas.

RICHARD M. BERTSCH (1926-1995)

ROBERT J. KOETH, born Cleveland, Ohio, August 26, 1952; admitted to bar, 1982, Ohio and U.S. District Court, Northern District of Ohio. *Education:* Cleveland State University (B.A., 1974); Cleveland-Marshall College of Law (J.D., 1982). Assistant County Prosecutor, 1983-1986. *Member:* Ohio State and American Bar Associations; Cleveland Defense Attorney's Group; Ohio Association of Civil Trial Attorneys. ***PRACTICE AREAS:*** Insurance Defense Law; Environmental Law; Products Liability; Personal Injury; Intentional Torts. ***Email:*** rkoeth@krplpa.com

CLARK D. RICE, born Cleveland, Ohio, August 19, 1955; admitted to bar, 1980, Ohio. *Education:* Bethany College (B.A., 1977); Cleveland Marshall College of Law (J.D., 1980). Assistant County Prosecutor, 1985-1987. *Member:* Cleveland and Ohio State Bar Associations; Cleveland Defense Attorneys Group; Ohio Association of Civil Trial Attorneys. ***PRACTICE AREAS:*** Insurance Defense Law; Commercial Litigation, Employment Law; Construction Law. ***Email:*** crice@krplpa.com

ANN LEO, born Cleveland, Ohio, June 25, 1953; admitted to bar, 1979, Ohio; 1980, U.S. District Court, Northern District of Ohio; 1982, U.S. Court of Appeals, Sixth Circuit. *Education:* Cleveland State University (B.A., cum laude, 1975); Cleveland Marshall College of Law (J.D., cum laude, 1979). *Member:* Cleveland and Ohio State Bar Associations. ***PRACTICE AREAS:*** Insurance/Contract Law; Appellate Law; Products Liability; Personal Injury; Intentional Torts. ***Email:*** aleo@krplpa.com

---

SHAWN W. SCHLESINGER, born Cleveland, Ohio, August 26, 1973; admitted to bar, 1998, Ohio and U.S. District Court, Northern District of Ohio. *Education:* Ohio University (B.A., cum laude, 1995); Cleveland-Marshall College of Law (J.D., magna cum laude, 1998). *Member:* Cleveland (Member Certified Grievance Committee) and Ohio State Bar Associations. ***PRACTICE AREAS:*** Insurance Defense; Commercial Litigation; Products Liability; Premises Liability; Toxic Tort. ***Email:*** sschlesinger@krplpa.com

OF COUNSEL

JEFFREY H. SPIEGLER, born 1948; admitted to bar, 1974, Ohio. *Education:* Ohio State University (B.S.B.A.); Cleveland Marshall College of Law (J.D.). ***PRACTICE AREAS:*** Personal Injury Law; Medical Malpractice Law; Civil Practice.

REPRESENTATIVE CLIENTS: Farmers Insurance Co.; Greyhound Lines, Inc.; Holiday Inns, Inc.; Euclid Disposal, Inc.; Home Insurance Co.; Surplus Lines Adjusting Co.; Lloyds of London; Inland Mutual Insurance Co.; Transamerica Insurance Group; State Automobile Insurance Co.; Greyhound Corp.; Bituminous Casualty Corp.; Waite Hill Services; Colony Insurance Co.; Figgie International; Excel Insurance Co.; Acceleration Insurance Co.; Ohio Fair Plan; Lumberman's Underwriting Alliance; Meridian Mutual Insurance; State Farm Insurance; Universal Underwriters Insurance Company; Act One, Inc.; Associates in Behavioral Management, Inc.; Claims Management Services, Inc.
REFERENCE: Society Bank.

KOHRMAN JACKSON & KRANTZ P.L.L.

Established in 1984

ONE CLEVELAND CENTER, 20TH FLOOR
1375 EAST NINTH STREET
CLEVELAND, OHIO 44114
Telephone: 216-696-8700
Telecopier: 216-621-6536
URL: http://www.kjk.com

Automotive Franchise and Dealership, Bankruptcy, Banks and Banking, Broker Dealer Arbitration, Business Law, Commercial Litigation, Commercial Real Estate, Computers and Software, Complex Litigation, Corporate Law, E Commerce, Employment Contracts, Employment Termination, Executive Compensation, Family Law, Finance, Health Care, Leveraged Buyouts, Local Government Law, Litigation, Mergers, Acquisitions and Divestitures, Partnership Law, Private Equity, Labor and Employment, Probate, Real Estate, Securities, Securities Class Actions, Software Licensing, Taxation Law, Trusts and Estates, Venture Capital, Wills and Wrongful Termination.

FIRM PROFILE: Kohrman Jackson & Krantz P.L.L. is a Cleveland-based law firm representing individuals and companies throughout Northeast Ohio and the United States. Founded in 1969, we are dedicated to providing our clients with the resources and knowledge needed to solve their legal issues, and have the expertise to handle the most sophisticated business transactions and complex litigation.

MEMBERS OF FIRM

S. LEE KOHRMAN, born Cleveland, Ohio, September 2, 1927; admitted to bar, 1953, Ohio. *Education:* Harvard University (A.B., 1949; LL.B., 1953). *Member:* Cleveland, Cuyahoga and Ohio State Bar Associations. ***PRACTICE AREAS:*** Corporate. ***Email:*** slk@kjk.com

ROBERT H. JACKSON, born Cleveland, Ohio, December 12, 1936; admitted to bar, 1961, Ohio. *Education:* University of Illinois (A.B., 1958); Case Western Reserve University (LL.B., 1961). Author: "Stockbrokers Liability Under Custom Usages and Rules," Cleveland Marshall Law Review, Vol. 12, Issue No. 1, January 1963; "Are Things Awry In Hay-On-Wye?" (with Donna Jackson), Biblio Magazine, April, 1997; "Serial Productions: Essential Parts of the 19th Century Imagination", The Grolier Club, 1996; "The Second Greatest Sport", The Gamut Cleveland State University, 1984; "Public Offerings: A Comparative Study of Disclosure in Western Europe and the United States," Western Reserve Law Review, Vol. 16, No. 1, December, 1964. Financial Attorney, Securities and Exchange Commission, 1961-1966. *Member:* Cleveland, Federal and American (Chairman, Subcommittee on Proxy Solicitations and Tender Offers for Federal Securities Committee, 1969-1972) Bar Associations. ***PRACTICE AREAS:*** Securities Regulation Law; Corporate Law; Corporate Restructures Law; Syndication Law. ***Email:*** rhj@kjk.com

BYRON S. KRANTZ, born Detroit, Michigan, September 26, 1935; admitted to bar, 1962, Ohio. *Education:* Dartmouth College (A.B., 1957); Case Western Reserve University (J.D., 1962). Staff Assistant to U.S. Senator Stephen M. Young, 1965-1970. Co-Author: "The Sixth Circuit and the Securities Law: A Survey of Reasons From 1983 through 1985," 17 University of Toledo Law Review 549, 1986. *Member:* Cleveland (Member: Securities Committee; Executive Committee, Corporation, Banking and Business Law Section, 1989—; Ohio Division of Securities Real Estate Registration Committee), Ohio State and American (Member, Litigation Section) Bar Associations. ***PRACTICE AREAS:*** Securities Regulation Law; Corporate Law; Litigation Law. ***Email:*** bsk@kjk.com

KEVIN T. O'CONNOR, born Cleveland, Ohio, January 24, 1950; admitted to bar, 1977, Ohio; 1982, U.S. Tax Court and U.S. District Court, Northern District of Ohio. *Education:* Georgetown University (B.S., 1972); Cleveland Marshall College of Law (J.D., 1977). Certified Public Accountant, Ohio, 1981. *Member:* Cleveland, Cuyahoga County and Ohio State Bar Associations; American Institute of Certified Public Accountants; Ohio Society of Certified Public Accountants. ***PRACTICE AREAS:*** Federal Income, Estate and Gift Taxation Law. ***Email:*** kto@kjk.com

ALAN M. RAUSS, born Cleveland, Ohio, October 20, 1944; admitted to bar, 1972, Ohio and U.S. District Court, Northern District of Ohio; 1973, U.S. Court of Appeals, Sixth Circuit; 1978, U.S. Supreme Court. *Education:* University of Pennsylvania (B.S., 1967); University of Michigan (J.D., 1972). *Member:* Cleveland (Chairman, Corporate Law Department Section, 1983-1984), Ohio State and American (Co-Chairman, Judicial Developments Subcommittee, Individual Rights and Responsibilities in the Work Place Committee, Labor and Employment Law Section, 1990—) Bar Associations. ***PRACTICE AREAS:*** Corporate Law; Labor Law. ***Email:*** amr@kjk.com

SARAH GABINET, born Salem, Oregon, December 19, 1953; admitted to bar, 1982, Ohio; 1983, U.S. District Court, Northern District of Ohio; 1988, U.S. Court of Appeals, Sixth Circuit. *Education:* Oberlin College (B.A., 1975); Indiana University (M.S., 1977); Case Western Reserve University (J.D., 1982). Member, Center for Principled Family Advocacy. *Member:* Cleveland, Ohio State and Federal (Member, Business Litigation Committee) Bar Associations. ***PRACTICE AREAS:*** Business Litigation; Family Law. ***Email:*** sjg@kjk.com

MARC C. KRANTZ, born Cleveland, Ohio, October 13, 1960; admitted to bar, 1986, Pennsylvania; 1987, District of Columbia; 1993, Ohio. *Education:* Dartmouth College (A.B., cum laude, 1982); University of Pennsylvania (J.D., 1986). *Member:* Cleveland, Washington State and American Bar Associations. ***PRACTICE AREAS:*** Corporate; Securities. ***Email:*** mck@kjk.com

STEVEN C. BERSTICKER, born Cleveland, Ohio, June 6, 1961; admitted to bar, 1986, Ohio. *Education:* The Colorado College (B.A., 1983); Case Western Reserve University (J.D., 1986). Judicial Law Clerk, Ohio Supreme Court, 1986-1987. *Member:* Cleveland, Ohio State and American Bar Associations. ***LANGUAGES:*** Spanish. ***PRACTICE AREAS:*** Corporate; Securities. ***Email:*** scb@kjk.com

CHRISTOPHER J. HUBBERT, born Cleveland, Ohio, March 11, 1966; admitted to bar, 1991, Ohio. *Education:* Boston University; University of Michigan (A.B., summa cum laude, 1988); Case Western Reserve University (J.D., magna cum laude, 1991). Order of the Coif. *Member:* Ohio State Bar Association. ***PRACTICE AREAS:*** Corporate; Securities. ***Email:*** cjh@kjk.com

ARI H. JAFFE, born Cleveland, Ohio, December 11, 1960; admitted to bar, 1987, Ohio and U.S. District Court, Northern District of Ohio; 1989, U.S. Court of Appeals, District of Columbia Circuit. *Education:* Brandeis University (B.A., with honors, 1983); Case Western Reserve University School of Law (J.D., 1986). Editor, Health Matrix, 1985-1986. Intern to Judge William K. Thomas, U.S. District Court, Northern District of Ohio, 1984. Charter Member, Advisory Committee, Law and Medicine Center, Case Western University School of Law. Recipient, Jewish Community Federation of Cleveland, Bennett and Donna Yanowitz Leadership Award, 1999. *Member:* Cleveland, Cuyahoga County (Member: Certified Grievance Committee), Ohio State and American Bar Associations. ***PRACTICE AREAS:*** Litigation; Securities Arbitration; Business Litigation; Health Care Law. ***Email:*** ahj@kjk.com

ROBERT S. GILMORE, born Cleveland, Ohio, June 15, 1961; admitted to bar, 1986, Ohio. *Education:* University of Cincinnati (B.A., 1983); The Ohio State University (J.D., 1986). Phi Beta Kappa. Author: "Attacking The Negligence Rule in Defamation of Private Plaintiffs", 47 Ohio St. L.J. 503 (1986). *Member:* Cleveland, Ohio and American Bar Associations. ***PRACTICE AREAS:*** Employment Law; Labor Law; Litigation. ***Email:*** rsg@kjk.com

VALORIA C. HOOVER, born Tiffin, Ohio, October 1, 1964; admitted to bar, 1992, Ohio; 1996, U.S. District Court, Northern District of Ohio; 1997, U.S. Court of Appeals, Sixth Circuit; 1999, U.S. Supreme Court; 2003, U.S. District Court, Southern District of Ohio. *Education:* Miami University (B.A., magna cum laude, 1989); University of Dayton (J.D., magna cum laude, 1992). Author, "The Rule in Shelley's Case Rears its Ugly Head," 16 U. Dayton L.Rev. 1283 (1991). Special Counsel to the Ohio Attorney General, 2003—. Fellow, Akron Bar Association Foundation, 2000—. Member, Summit County Mediation Advisory Council, 1998—. *Member:* Cleveland, Akron, Ohio State and American Bar Associations. ***PRACTICE AREAS:*** Complex Litigation; Business Litigation. ***Email:*** vch@kjk.com

DAVID R. POSTERARO, born New York, N.Y., November 10, 1952; admitted to bar, 1981, Ohio. *Education:* Fordham University (B.A., summa cum laude, 1974); Case Western Reserve University (J.D., 1981). Cleveland City Records Commission, 2002—. *Mem-*

(This Listing Continued)

ber: Cleveland, Ohio State and American Bar Associations; Licensing Executive Society. ***PRACTICE AREAS:*** Intellectual Property; Licensing; Internet; E-Business; Technology Law. ***Email:*** drp@kjk.com

KAREN L. GRECO, born Cleveland, Ohio, September 29, 1957; admitted to bar, 1982, Ohio. *Education:* John Carroll University (B.A., 1979); Cleveland-Marshall College of Law (J.D., 1982). Editor, Cleveland Marshall Law Review, 1981-1982. *Member:* Cleveland (Member, Estate Planning, Probate and Trust Law and Real Property Sections), Ohio State and American Bar Associations. ***PRACTICE AREAS:*** Estate Planning; Probate Administration. ***Email:*** klg@kjk.com

BRETT S. KRANTZ, born Cleveland, Ohio, July 8, 1963; admitted to bar, 1990, Illinois; 1992, District of Columbia; 1998, Ohio. *Education:* Dartmouth College (A.B., 1985); University of Chicago (J.D., 1990). ***PRACTICE AREAS:*** Commercial Litigation; Securities Litigation. ***Email:*** bk@kjk.com

MARK B. SCHILDHOUSE, born Cleveland, Ohio, March 11, 1952; admitted to bar, 1980, Ohio. *Education:* University of Cincinnati (B.A., 1974); Cleveland Marshall College of Law (J.D., 1979). Member, National Association of Industrial and Office Properties. Member, Greater Cleveland Mortgage Bankers Association. Formerly with Garofoli Kraus Hill & Bartuner. *Member:* Ohio State Bar Association. ***PRACTICE AREAS:*** Real Estate; Contracts; Corporate Law. ***Email:*** mbs@kjk.com

MARY K. WHITMER, born Akron, Ohio, October 29, 1951; admitted to bar, 1975, Ohio; 1980, U.S. District Court, Northern District of Ohio. *Education:* Case Western Reserve University (B.A., 1972; J.D., 1975). Certified Public Accountant, Ohio, 1978. *Member:* Cleveland Bar Association (Treasurer, 1999-2002; Member, Commercial Section); Commercial Law League of America (President, July 2004-July 2005; Member, Bankruptcy Section); Ohio Society of CPA's. ***PRACTICE AREAS:*** Bankruptcy; Commercial Law.

GARY L. JONES, born Cleveland, Ohio, August 3, 1958; admitted to bar, 1997, Ohio. *Education:* Cleveland State University (B.A., 1983); Cleveland Marshall College of Law (J.D., 1996). ***PRACTICE AREAS:*** Real Estate; Intellectual Property; Probate; Corporate Law; Entertainment Law. ***Email:*** glj@kjk.com

CONNIE S. CARR, born Elyria, Ohio, August 22, 1961; admitted to bar, 1991, New York; 1992, District of Columbia; 1994, Ohio. *Education:* Cedarville College (B.A., 1983); Institute on Comparative Political and Economic Systems, Georgetown University (1983); American University (J.D., 1990). Vice Chair, Board of Directors, Lorain Port Authority, 2000—. ***PRACTICE AREAS:*** Corporate; Securities; Real Estate. ***Email:*** csc@kjk.com

MICHELE L. HOZA, born Washington, D.C., September 18, 1971; admitted to bar, 2001, Ohio. *Education:* Kent State University (B.A., 1993); Cleveland-Marshall College of Law (J.D., 2001). Managing Editor, Cleveland State Law Review. ***PRACTICE AREAS:*** Corporate Law; Securities. ***Email:*** mlh@kjk.com

MARK S. O'BRIEN, born Milwaukee, Wisconsin, May 4, 1965; admitted to bar, 2000, Ohio, U.S. District Court, Northern District of Ohio and U.S. Tax Court. *Education:* Ohio State University (B.A., 1994; M.A., 1996); Cleveland-Marshall College of Law (J.D., 2000); New York University (LL.M., Tax, 2003). ***PRACTICE AREAS:*** Tax Law; Corporate Law. ***Email:*** mso@kjk.com

KEVIN L. CHLARSON, born Phoenix, Arizona, November 17, 1971; admitted to bar, 2003, Ohio; 2004, U.S. District Court, Northern District of Ohio. *Education:* Arizona State University (B.A., 1994); University of Iowa (Ph.D., 2000); University of Arizona (J.D., 2003). Author: "Circuit City Stores, Inc. v. Adams and the Unresolved Questions of Mandatory Employment Arbitration Agreements," Employment and Labor Law Section Newsletter, Arizona Bar Association, October 2002. *Member:* Cleveland, Cuyahoga County, Ohio State and American Bar Associations. ***PRACTICE AREAS:*** Business Litigation; Employment Law. ***Email:*** klc@kjk.com

TODD M. BURGER, born Monterey, California, March 4, 1977; admitted to bar, 2002, Ohio. *Education:* Bowling Green State University (B.A., cum laude, 1999); University of Toledo College of Law (J.D., cum laude, 2002). Managing Editor, The University of Toledo Law Review, 2001-2002. Author: "Carrel v. Allied Products Corporation: Is the Ohio Supreme Court Having the Last Word On Product Liability?," 32 U. Tol. L. Rev. 591 (2001). *Member:* Cleveland and Ohio State Bar Associations. ***PRACTICE AREAS:*** Corporate; Securities.

JON J. PINNEY, born Youngstown, Ohio, June 28, 1975; admitted to bar, 2000, Ohio; 2001, U.S. District Court, Northern District of Ohio; U.S. Court of Appeals, Sixth Circuit. *Education:* John Carroll University (B.S., 1997); Cleveland-Marshall College of Law (J.D., 2000). Member and Board of Governors, Cleveland-Marshall Moot Court Team, 1999-2000; Member, 1998-1999 and Advisor, 2000, International Law Society Moot Court Team; Nova Southeastern National Moot Court Competition Runner-Up, 2000. Appointed, National Order of Barristers, 2000. *Member:* Cleveland (Member, Young Lawyers Section, 2001) Ohio State (Member, Young Lawyers Section, 2000—) and American (Member, Business Litigation and Young Lawyers Section, 2000) Bar Associations; International Law Society. ***PRACTICE AREAS:*** Business Litigation; Securities Litigation; Corporate Law.

LAURA L. VOLPINI, born Youngstown, Ohio, October 31, 1977; admitted to bar, 2002, Ohio; 2003, U.S. District Court, Northern District of Ohio. *Education:* John Carroll University (B.S.B.A., 1999); Case Western Reserve University (J.D., 2002). ***PRACTICE AREAS:*** Business Litigation; Employment Law; Construction Law; General Liability. ***Email:*** llv@kjk.com

DAVID S. BLOCKER, born Portland, Oregon, August 18, 1976; admitted to bar, 2002, Ohio; 2003, U.S. District Court, Northern District of Ohio. *Education:* Miami University (B.A., 1998); Case Western Reserve University (J.D., cum laude, 2002). Member, National Moot Court Team. *Member:* Ohio State and American Bar Associations. ***PRACTICE AREAS:*** Litigation; Family Law. ***Email:*** dsb@kjk.com

OF COUNSEL

KENNETH W. KLEINMAN, born New York, N.Y., April 7, 1946; admitted to bar, 1974, Ohio. *Education:* Cornell University (B.S., 1966; M.B.A., 1968); Georgetown University (J.D., 1974). *Member:* Ohio State and American (Member, Health Law Section) Bar Associations. ***PRACTICE AREAS:*** Health. ***Email:*** kwk@kjk.com

(This Listing Continued)

STEPHEN C. WEINGRAD, born Mineola, New York, September 25, 1941; admitted to bar, 1973, Ohio and U.S. District Court, Northern District of Ohio. *Education:* Kenyon College (B.A., 1963); Case Western Reserve University (J.D., 1973). *Member:* Cleveland, Ohio State and American Bar Associations. ***LANGUAGES:*** Spanish. ***PRACTICE AREAS:*** Real Estate Law; Affordable Housing Law. ***Email:*** scw@kjk.com

MARC I. STRAUSS, born Cleveland, Ohio, September 15, 1961; admitted to bar, 1986, Ohio; 1993, Pennsylvania. *Education:* University of Arizona (B.S.B.A., 1983); Cleveland Marshall College of Law (J.D., 1986). ***PRACTICE AREAS:*** Family Law (65%); Criminal Law (20%); Civil Litigation (15%). ***Email:*** mis@kjk.com

STEPHEN D. RICHMAN, born Cleveland, Ohio, July 23, 1957; admitted to bar, 1986, Ohio; U.S. Court of Appeals, Sixth Circuit; U.S. District Court, Northern District of Ohio. *Education:* University of Miami (B.B.A., magna cum laude, 1979; M.B.A., 1980); Cleveland-Marshall College of Law (J.D., 1985). Councilman, Village of Moreland Hills, 2004—. Volunteer Magistrate, Juvenile Division, Village of Moreland Hills, 2000—. *Member:* Cleveland and Ohio State Bar Associations. ***PRACTICE AREAS:*** Real Estate Law; Corporate Law; Commercial Law. ***Email:*** sdr@kjk.com

REPRESENTATIVE CLIENTS: Bridge Ohio Israel Private Equity Fund; Brown Gibbons & Company; Ceres Group; Concord Hotels; Developers Diversified; Famous Enterprises; General Electric Capital; Hawk; Kings Medical; Liberty Self Stor; Merrill, Lynch, Pierce, Fenner & Smith; Ohio Department of Development; Omni Corporate Services; Rostra Technologies; Sky Financial; Paragon Real Estate Investment; Rexam Beverage Can; Starbak Communications; Sunnyside Automotive Group; The Parkland Group; The Rostra Companies; Weinberg & Bell Group.

PHILIP J. KOREY

Established in 1980

SUITE 410, LEADER BUILDING
526 SUPERIOR AVENUE, EAST
CLEVELAND, OHIO 44114
Telephone: 216-771-7030
FAX: 216-771-2421
Email: pjkoreylaw@sbcglobal.net
URL: http://www.lawyers.com/philipjkorey

General Criminal and Personal Injury Trial and Appellate Practice in State and Federal Courts.

PHILIP J. KOREY, born Cleveland, Ohio, June 28, 1952; admitted to bar, 1980, Ohio; 1981, U.S. District Court, Northern District of Ohio; 1982, U.S. Court of Appeals, Sixth Circuit; 1985, U.S. Court of Appeals, Second Circuit and U.S. Supreme Court, 1991. *Education:* John Carroll University (B.S., cum laude, 1974); Cleveland Marshall College of Law (J.D., 1980, Dean's List). National Moot Court Team. Best Brief Award, 1979. Lecturer: Cuyahoga County Common Pleas Court Forensic Clinic, "Insanity Defense," 1988; Academy of Continuing Legal Education, 1991; DUI Trial Seminar Cleveland Marshall College of Law, 1996; Cuyahoga County Criminal Defense Lawyers Association, Discovery 1995; Exculpatory Evidence, 2002. *Member:* Cleveland and Ohio State Bar Associations; The Association of Trial Lawyers of America; Cuyahoga County Criminal Defense Lawyers Association (Chairman, Legislative Committee, Drafter of Organization's Model Rule 16, 1995); National Association of Criminal Defense Lawyers. ***PRACTICE AREAS:*** Criminal Law; Personal Injury; Trial Practice; Appellate Practice.

KOVACH & FARLING CO., LPA

925 LEADER BUILDING
526 SUPERIOR AVENUE EAST
CLEVELAND, OHIO 44114
Telephone: 216-357-3301
Fax: 216-357-3304
Email: tkovach@kflpa.com
URL: http://www.kovachandfarling.com

Commercial Contract Disputes, Business Litigation, Trade Secret Litigation, Business Tort Litigation, Takeover Litigation, Class Action Litigation, Securities Litigation, Restrictive Covenant Litigation, Shareholder Derivative.

FIRM PROFILE: Kovach & Farling Co., LPA was formed in 2003 as a premiere business litigation boutique law firm.

Its principals, Thomas G. Kovach and Harold E. Farling, were partners at two of Cleveland's largest and most prestigious full service law firms. Together, they have a combined twenty-five years of experience in a wide variety of commercial and complex civil litigation matters, including breach of contract cases, class actions, securities and shareholder derivative actions, product liability litigation and trademark and unfair competition actions.

Kovach & Farling Co., LPA is dedicated to providing its clients the highest quality legal representation at reasonable rates. As a business litigation firm, Kovach & Farling Co., LPA represents both plaintiffs and defendants in federal and state trial and appellate courts, as well as in a variety of ADR proceedings, including arbitration and mediation.

THOMAS G. KOVACH, born Cleveland, Ohio, 1964; admitted to bar, 1990, Ohio; U.S. District Court, Northern District of Ohio; U.S. Court of Appeals, Fifth and Sixth Circuits. *Education:* Kenyon College (B.A., 1986); The Ohio State University (J.D., 1990). Order of the Coif. Former Professor, Pretrial Litigation, Case Western Reserve University School of Law. Former Partner, Squire, Sanders & Dempsey L.L.P. *Member:* Ohio State and American (Member, Litigation Section) Bar Associations. ***PRACTICE AREAS:*** Business Litigation; Commercial Contract Disputes; Trade Secret Litigation; Business Tort Litigation; Securities; Takeover Litigation. ***Email:*** tkovach@kflpa.com

HAROLD E. FARLING, born Cleveland, Ohio, March 31, 1966; admitted to bar, 1991, Ohio; 1994, U.S. District Court, Northern District of Ohio; U.S. Court of Appeals, Sixth Circuit. *Education:* Kenyon College (B.A., 1988); Case Western Reserve University

(This Listing Continued)

KOVACH & FARLING CO., LPA, Cleveland—Continued

(J.D., 1991). Formerly with Squire, Sanders & Dempsey L.L.P. Former Partner: Kaufman & Cumberland Co., LPA; Thompson Hine LLP. Member, Anthony J. Celebrezze Inn of Court. ***PRACTICE AREAS:*** Business Litigation; Class Action Litigation; Securities Litigation; Restrictive Covenants; Shareholder Derivative Actions; Class Actions. ***Email:*** hfarling@kflpa.com

LEE R. KRAVITZ

4508 STATE ROAD
CLEVELAND, OHIO 44109
Telephone: 216-749-0808
Fax: 216-749-5389
Email: leekravitz@adelphia.net
URL: http://www.leekravitzlaw.com

Bankruptcy Law, Chapter 7, Chapter 13, Consumer Bankruptcy.

LEE R. KRAVITZ, born Cleveland, Ohio, January 5, 1955; admitted to bar, 1980, Ohio; 1981, Florida and U.S. District Court, Northern District of Ohio; U.S. District Court, Southern District of Florida and U.S. Court of Appeals, Eleventh Circuit. *Education:* Ohio University (B.A., 1977); Cleveland Marshall College of Law (J.D., 1980). Delta Theta Phi. *Member:* Cleveland and Ohio State Bar Associations. ***LANGUAGES:*** French.

ASSOCIATE

DAVID B. BOKOR, born Cleveland, Ohio, November 9, 1961; admitted to bar, 1993, Ohio and U.S. District Court, Northern District of Ohio. *Education:* Ohio University (B.A., 1985); Cleveland-Marshall College of Law (J.D., 1993). *Member:* Ohio State Bar Association. ***PRACTICE AREAS:*** Bankruptcy; Consumer Bankruptcy. ***Email:*** dbbokor@aol.com

KUSHNER & RENDON CO., L.P.A.

2860 BP TOWER
200 PUBLIC SQUARE
CLEVELAND, OHIO 44114
Telephone: 216-696-6700
Fax: 216-696-6772

Civil Litigation, Criminal Litigation, Family Law.

MEMBERS OF THE FIRM

PHILIP S. KUSHNER, born Cleveland, Ohio, February 25, 1959; admitted to bar, 1985, District of Columbia; 1990, Ohio. *Education:* Yale University (B.A., magna cum laude, 1981); University of Chicago (J.D., 1985). Adjunct Faculty, Case Western Reserve University School of Law, 2001-2002. Assistant U.S. Attorney for Northern District of Ohio, 1989-1990. Assistant U.S. Attorney for District of Columbia, 1990-1994. *Member:* Cleveland Bar Association (Member, Judicial Selection Committee, 1997-2000); National Association of Criminal Defense Lawyers; Judicial Conference for the Eighth Judicial District of Ohio (Life Member); William K. Thomas Inn of Court (2000—; Secretary and Treasurer); Ohio Academy of Trial Lawyers. ***PRACTICE AREAS:*** Civil Litigation; Criminal Litigation.

CAROLE SCHWARTZ RENDON, born Cleveland, Ohio, November 8, 1962; admitted to bar, 1989, Illinois, U.S. District Court, District of Massachusetts and U.S. Court of Appeals, First Circuit; 1997, Massachusetts; 1999, Ohio, U.S. District Court, Northern District of Ohio and U.S. Court of Appeals, Sixth Circuit. *Education:* Northwestern University (B.A., summa cum laude, 1984); Northwestern University School of Law (J.D., cum laude, 1987). Phi Beta Kappa; Wigmore Scholar. Editor-in-Chief, Journal of Criminal Law and Criminology. Law Clerk to the Honorable Joel M. Flaum, U.S. Court of Appeals, Seventh Circuit, 1987-1988. Prosecutor, Organized Crime Strike Force Unit, U.S. Attorney's Office, Boston, Massachusetts, 1988-1994. Chief, New England Organized Crime Drug Enforcement Task Force, 1994-1997. *Member:* Cleveland (Trustee; Chair, Criminal Law Section) and American Bar Associations; Anthony J. Celebrezze Inn of Court. ***PRACTICE AREAS:*** Criminal Litigation; Civil Litigation.

MICHAEL R. HAMED, born Cleveland, Ohio, January 21, 1972; admitted to bar, 1998, Ohio. *Education:* Miami University (B.A., summa cum laude, 1994); University of Pennsylvania (J.D., cum laude, 1997). Phi Beta Kappa; Order of the Coif; Moot Court Board. *Member:* Cleveland and American Bar Associations; Harold Burton Inn of Court. ***PRACTICE AREAS:*** Criminal Litigation; Civil Litigation; Family Law.

RACHAEL L. ISRAEL, born Lorain, Ohio, May 18, 1973; admitted to bar, 2000, Ohio; 2002, U.S. District Court, Northern District of Ohio and U.S. Court of Appeals, Sixth Circuit. *Education:* Wittenberg University (B.A., 1995); Case Western Reserve University (J.D., magna cum laude, 2000). Order of the Coif. Member, Case Western Reserve University Law Review. Adjunct Professor, Case Western Reserve University School of Law, 2001—.

LANCIONE & LANCIONE, PLL

200 PUBLIC SQUARE, SUITE 2955
CLEVELAND, OHIO 44114
Telephone: 216-623-4949
Fax: 216-623-3975
Email: jgl@lancionelaw.com
URL: http://www.lancioneandlancione.com

Medical Malpractice, Personal Injury, Automobile Accidents, Hospital Liability, Negligence, Wrongful Death.

(This Listing Continued)

JOHN G. LANCIONE, born Bellaire, Ohio, March 4, 1935; admitted to bar, 1959, Ohio; 1968, U.S. Supreme Court. *Education:* Ohio University (B.S.C., 1957); The Ohio State University (LL.B., 1959). Phi Delta Phi. *Member:* Greater Cleveland (Chairman, Common Pleas Court Committee, 1974), Cuyahoga County (Chairman, Ethics Committee, 1984), Ohio State and American Bar Associations; The Association of Trial Lawyers of America; Cleveland Academy of Trial Lawyers; Ohio Academy of Trial Lawyers; American Board of Trial Advocates (Ohio President, 1993; National Board Representative, 1998-1999); American College of Trial Lawyers; American College of Legal Medicine (Associate in Law, 1973—); Life Delegate to Judicial Conference of the Eighth Judicial District of Ohio. Fellow: International Society of Barristers (President, 1998-1999). ***REPORTED CASES:*** U.S. Supreme Court: Zacchini v. Scripps-Howard Broadcasting Company, 433 U.S. 562, 97 S.Ct. 2849 (1977). United States District Court: Carr v. Armstrong Air Conditioning, Inc., 817 F.Supp. 54 (N.D. Ohio, W.D. 1993); Gamble v. United States, 648 F. Supp. 438 (N.D. Ohio, E.D. 1986); Ohio Public Interest Campaign v. Fisher Foods, Inc., 546 F.Supp. 1 (N.D. Ohio, E.D. 1982). Ohio Supreme Court: Browning v. Burt, 66 Ohio St. 3d 544, 613 N.E.2d 993 (1993); Mominee v. Scherbarth, 28 Ohio St.3d 270, 503 N.E.2d 717 (1986); Vinci v. American Can Company, 9 Ohio St.3d 98, 549 N.E.2d 507 (1984); Zacchini v. Scripps-Howard Broadcasting Co., 54 Ohio St.2d 286, 376 N.E.2d 582 (1978); Zacchini v. Scripps-Howard Broadcasting Co., 47 Ohio St.2d 224, 351 N.E.2d 454 (1976); Moriarty v. Westgate Center, Inc., 172 Ohio St. 402, 176 N.E.2d 410 (1961). Ohio Court of Appeals: Fortman v. Dayton Power & Light Company, 80 Ohio App.3d 525, 609 N.E.2d 1296 (Montgomery Ct. App. 1992); Vinci v. American Can Company, 69 Ohio App.3d 727, 591 N.E.2d 793 (Cuyahoga Ct. App. 1990); Fuedo v. Pavlik, 55 Ohio App.3d 217, 563 N.E.2d 351 (Cuyahoga Ct. App. 1988); Heilprin v. Ohio State University Hospitals of Ohio State University, 31 Ohio App. 3d 35, 508 N.E.2d 178 (Franklin Ct. App. 1986); Shibley v. Time, Inc., 45 Ohio App. 2d 69, 341 N.E.2d 337 (Cuyahoga Ct. App. 1975); Nationwide Mutual Ins. Co. v. Jackson, 10 Ohio App.2d 137, 226 N.E.2d 760 (1967). Roberts v. Ohio Permanente Medical Group, Inc. (1996) 76 Ohio St. 3d 483 (amicus curiae). Ohio Court of Common Pleas: Shibley v. Time, Inc., 40 Ohio Misc. 51, 321 N.E.2d 791 (1974). ***PRACTICE AREAS:*** Medical Malpractice; Hospital Liability Law; Personal Injury Law. ***Email:*** JGL@lancionelaw.com

JOHN A. LANCIONE, born Cleveland Ohio, November 28, 1962; admitted to bar, 1988, Ohio. *Education:* Denison University (B.A., Political Science, 1985); Case Western Reserve University, The Franklin Thomas Backus School of Law (J.D., 1988). *Member:* Cleveland, Cuyahoga County (Member, Negligence Committee, Young Lawyers Committee, Chairman, 1994), Ohio State and American Bar Associations; The Association of Trial Lawyers of America (Member, Membership Oversight Committee, 1993-1996; New Lawyer Division, Ohio Governor, 1994-1995; Leader's Forum, Ohio Chair, 2005); Ohio Academy of Trial Lawyers (Member, New Lawyer Section: Chairman, 1995; Medical Negligence Victims Coalition Committee, 1995; Board of Trustees, 1995-2004; Chairman, Medical Negligence Section, 1998-2000; Treasurer, 2004-2005); Cleveland Academy of Trial Lawyers. ***REPORTED CASES:*** Ohio Supreme Court: Marshall v. Ortega, 87 Ohio St. 3d 522 (2000, Amicus Curiae); Gum v. CEI, 81 Ohio State 3d 1243 (1998). Ohio Court of Appeals: Schlachet v. Cleveland Clinic, 104 Ohio App. 3d 160 (1995); Hallett v. Stow Bd.of Ed., 89 Ohio App. 3d 309 (1993); Fortman v. Dayton Power & Light Co., 80 Ohio App. 3d 525 (1992). ***PRACTICE AREAS:*** Medical Negligence; Personal Injury Law. ***Email:*** JAL@lancionelaw.com

LARGENT, BERRY, PRESTON & JAMISON CO., L.P.A.

CLEVELAND, OHIO

(See Berea)

THE LAWSON FIRM, LLC

Established in 2004

PLAZA WEST EXECUTIVE CENTER
20220 CENTER RIDGE ROAD, SUITE 320
CLEVELAND, OHIO 44116
Telephone: 440-409-0303
Fax: 440-409-0323
Email: slawson@lawsonfirm.net
URL: http://www.lawsonfirm.net

Insurance Law, Insurance Regulation, Internet Law, General Corporate Law, Business Law, Intellectual Property.

FIRM PROFILE: The Lawson Firm, LLC is a Cleveland-based firm focusing on insurance law, insurance regulation, compliance and corporate governance. Further information about the firm may be found at www.lawsonfirm.net.

MEMBER OF FIRM

SCOTT E. LAWSON, born Springville, New York, August 30, 1962; admitted to bar, 1994, Ohio. *Education:* State University of New York at Fredonia (B.A., 1985); Cleveland-Marshall College of Law (J.D., 1994). *Member:* American Bar Association. ***LANGUAGES:*** English. ***PRACTICE AREAS:*** Insurance (70%); Corporate (15%); E-Commerce (5%); Intellectual Property (10%). ***Email:*** slawson@lawsonfirm.net

DANIEL J. LEFFLER
COUNSELOR AT LAW

CLEVELAND, OHIO

(See Akron)

Employment Law, Union Contract Negotiations, Union Labor Law, Civil Litigation.

DAVID WOLFE LEOPOLD & ASSOCIATES CO., LPA

Established in 1994

2000 EAST NINTH STREET, SUITE 300
CLEVELAND, OHIO 44115
Telephone: 216-696-4676
Fax: 216-696-8268
URL: http://www.immvisa.com
Email: info@immvisa.com
URL: http://www.dwllawfirm.com

Immigration, Visa and Citizenship Law.

FIRM PROFILE: We represent corporations, health care institutions, law firms, religious organizations, schools, families and individuals from across the nation and around the world on all matters related to United States immigration, visa and citizenship law. We concentrate on employment-based cases for highly skilled foreign workers, including physicians, scientists, corporate managers and executives, engineers, computer professionals, artists and entertainers, and others; H-1B specialty worker and L-1 international executive visas, alien employment certification from the U.S. Department of Labor as well as national interest waivers of the labor certification requirement; waivers of the two-year foreign residence requirement for physicians; defending corporations from charges of knowingly employing unauthorized workers; and, complex deportation matters, including administrative trials and appeals and federal court litigation.

DAVID W. LEOPOLD, born Detroit, Michigan August 29, 1958; admitted to bar, 1985, Ohio. *Education:* University of Michigan (A.B., 1980); Case Western Reserve University (J.D., 1985). Adjunct Professor of Immigration Law, Case Western Reserve University School of Law, 1997— Adjunct Professor of Immigration Law, Cleveland-Marshall College of Law, Cleveland State University, 2005—. National Secretary, American Immigration Lawyers Association (AILA), 2005-2006. Director, (AILA) National Board of Governors, 2001-2005. Chair: AILA Ohio Chapter, 2001-2002; AILA Department of Homeland Security (DHS). General Counsel Liaison Committee, 2004-2005. Chair, AILA DHS Immigration and Customs Enforcement Liaison Committee, 2003-2004. Faculty, American Immigration Law Foundation Litigation Institute, 2003—. Senior Editor, Immigration and Nationality Law Handbook (AILA 2005-2006). Associate Editor, Litigation Manual (AILA 2002). Contributing Author, Visa Processing Guide (AILA 2005). Associate Commissioner, Beachwood, Ohio Cable Commission, 1999-2004. Trustee, Center for the Prevention of Domestic Violence, 1992-1993. Legislative Assistant, United States Senate, 1993. Legal Aide Society of Cleveland, 1988-1991. *Member:* Cleveland and Ohio State Bar Associations; American Immigration Lawyers Association; National Association of Criminal Defense Lawyers. ***LANGUAGES:*** Hebrew and Russian. ***REPORTED CASES:*** Pak v. Reno, 196 F.3d 666 (6th Cir. 1999); Pulice v. INS, 218 F.3d 505 (6th Cir. 2000); Roman v. Ashcroft, 340 F.3d 314 (6th Cir. 2003); Rosales-Garcia v. Holland, 322 F.3d 386 (6th Cir. 2003)(en banc); Roman v. Ashcroft, 181 F. Supp. 2d 808 (N.D. Ohio 2002); Denko v. Ashcroft, 351 F.3d 717 (6th Cir. 2003); Cline v. Catholic Diocese of Toledo, 206 F.3d 651 (6th Cir. 1999). ***PRACTICE AREAS:*** Immigration; Visa; Citizenship Law. ***Email:*** dleopold@immvisa.com

---

MEHTA KHORZAD ADI, ESQ., born Montreal, Canada, August 7, 1979; admitted to bar, 2004, Ohio. *Education:* Ohio State University (B.A., 2001); Case Western Reserve University School of Law (J.D., 2004). *Member:* Cuyahoga County, Cleveland, Ohio State and American Bar Associations; American Immigration Lawyers Association. ***LANGUAGES:*** Gujarati (Spoken Fluency), Hindi (Intermediate Spoken and Written Fluency) and French (Intermediate Spoken and Written Fluency). ***PRACTICE AREAS:*** Immigration Law; Visas; Citizenship.

MELISSA A. GRECO, born Cleveland, Ohio, May 9, 1979; admitted to bar, 2005, Ohio. *Education:* Hiram College (B.A., 2001); Case Western Reserve University School Of Law (J.D., 2004). Member, American Immigration Lawyers Association (AILA). Ohio Chapter, Executive Office for Immigration Review Liaison Committee, 2005—. *Member:* Cuyahoga County, Cleveland and Ohio State Bar Associations; American Immigration Lawyers Association. ***PRACTICE AREAS:*** Immigration Law; Visas; Citizenship.

LEVIN & ASSOCIATES CO., L.P.A.

TOWER AT ERIEVIEW, SUITE 1100
1301 EAST 9TH STREET
CLEVELAND, OHIO 44114
Telephone: 216-928-0600
Fax: 216-928-0016
URL: http://www.levinandassociates.com
URL: http://www.lawyers.com/levinlaw

Commercial Litigation, Medical Malpractice, Personal Injury, Product Liability.

JOEL LEVIN, born Erie, Pennsylvania, August 22, 1951; admitted to bar, 1977, Massachusetts; 1984, Ohio; 1988, Pennsylvania, U.S. Supreme Court, U.S. Court of Appeals, 5th, 6th and 11th Circuits, U.S. District Court, Northern District of Ohio and U.S. District Court, Northern District of Texas. *Education:* University of Chicago (B.A., 1972; M.A., 1973); University of Oxford, Oxford, England (D. Phil., 1981); Boston University (J.D., 1976). Author: "Balance Theory of Contracts: Seeking Justice in Voluntary Obligations," 19 McGill Law Journal 24 (1983); "Justification and the Law," 32 Emory Law Journal 987 (1983); "The Concept of the Judicial Decision," 33 Case Western Reserve Law Review 208 (1983); "Constitutional Future of Statutes of Repose," Ohio Trial (1988); "Litigating Bad Faith Insurance Claims in Ohio", C.W.R.U. Dept of CLE (1988); "How to Make Sense Out of Uninsured Motorists Law," C.W.R.U., Dept. of C.L.E. (1989); "The Liability Insurer's Duties to Defend and Settle," C.W.R.U. Dept. of C.L.E. (1990); "Striking the Balance in Contract Theory" 39 Cleveland State Law Review (1992); *How Judges Reason: The Logic of Adjudication,* (1992); "The Action in the Transaction: Life Around the Contractual Edges," 58 In Brief 3 (1993); "Charles Dickens and the Uses of History: A Salute to Holdsworth," 14 Vera Lex 1 (1994); "An Uncommon Lawyer," 34 Washburn Law Review 225 (1995); *Revolutions, Institutions, Law,* (1997); "Tort Wars," 39 Tort Trial & Ins. Prac. L.J. 869 (2004); Representing Abused Children: The Changing Law," 76 Clev. B.J. 17 (2004); "Representing Abused Children: Practice and Procedure," 76 Clev. B.J. 20 (2005). Lecturer in Law, Case Western Reserve University, 1982—; Cleveland Marshall College of Law, 1997-1998. Visiting Professor of Law, U.S. Dept. of State Volgorad, Russia, 1996, Novgorad, Russia, 2000. Special Counsel to the Ohio Attorney General, 1994-1997. Trustee, Russian-U.S. Legal Education Foundation. Member, Consortium for the Study of Plaintiff's Lawyering, Harvard Law School. *Member:* Cleveland, Ohio State and American Bar Associations; The Association of Trial Lawyers of America; Cleveland Academy of Trial Attorneys; AMINTAPHIL; American Philosophical Association; The Bentham Society. ***PRACTICE AREAS:*** Commercial Litigation; Medical Malpractice; Personal Injury; Products Liability. ***Email:*** jl@levinandassociates.com

---

APARESH PAUL, born Lexington, Kentucky, May 9, 1972; admitted to bar, 2003, Ohio. *Education:* Vanderbilt University (B.A., 1994); Case Western Reserve University (J.D., 2002). *Member:* Cleveland and Ohio State Bar Associations; Cleveland Academy of Trial Attorneys. ***PRACTICE AREAS:*** Commercial Litigation; Medical Malpractice; Personal Injury; Products Liability. ***Email:*** ap@levinandassociates

CHRISTOPHER M. VLASICH, born Lansing, Michigan, July 2, 1977; admitted to bar, 2002, Ohio; 2005, U.S. District Court, Northern District of Ohio and U.S. Court of Appeals, Sixth Circuit. *Education:* Michigan State University (B.A., 1999); Case Western Reserve University (J.D., 2002). Member, National Mock Trial Team. Recipient, William E. Davis Award. *Member:* Cleveland Bar Association. ***PRACTICE AREAS:*** Commercial Litigation (40%); Medical Malpractice (30%); Personal Injury (20%); Products Liability (10%). ***Email:*** cmv@levinandassociates.com

---

LEVY & DUBYAK

CLEVELAND, OHIO

(See Beachwood)

Real Estate, Corporate Law, Business Law, Business Litigation, Finance, Employment Law, Commercial Law, Contracts, Mergers and Acquisitions, Real Estate Litigation.

LICHKO & SCHECHTER

1600 ILLUMINATING BUILDING
55 PUBLIC SQUARE
CLEVELAND, OHIO 44113
Telephone: 216-928-1503
Fax: 216-619-9846
URL: http://www.lichkoschechter.com

Civil Litigation at the Trial and Appellate Levels in State and Federal Courts, Business Litigation, Construction Litigation, Corporate Law, Real Estate and Securities.

MEMBERS OF FIRM

GREGORY M. LICHKO, born Cleveland, Ohio, April 17, 1947; admitted to bar, 1975, Ohio; U.S. District Court, Northern District of Ohio; U.S. Court of Appeals, 6th Circuit and U.S. Tax Court. *Education:* Ohio University (A.B., Honors College, 1969); Case Western Reserve University (J.D., 1975). Faculty Member, The University of Virginia School of Law, Trial Advocacy Institute. Formerly Litigation Partner and Chief Trial Attorney, Kohrman, Jackson, Krantz, 1981-1993. *Member:* Cleveland, Ohio State and American Bar Associations. ***REPORTED CASES:*** Legros v. Tarr, 44 Ohio St. 3rd 1 (1989); Warren Plaza Company v. Giant Eagle, Inc., 63 Ohio St. 3rd 497 (1992); State, ex. rel. Bd. of Educ. For Fairview Park School Dist. v. Bd. of Educ. For Rocky River School District (1988); Equity Centers Dev. Co. v. S. Coast Centers, Inc., 83 Ohio App. 3rd 643 (Ct. App. Cuyahoga Cty. 1992). ***PRACTICE AREAS:*** Civil Practice; Art Law; Business Law; Business Torts; Construction Law; Architects and Engineers Errors and Omissions; Commercial Law; Professional Liability; Wrongful Termination; Theft of Trade Secrets; Unfair Competition. ***Email:*** glichko@lichkoschechter.com

ROY J. SCHECHTER, born Cleveland, Ohio, September 21, 1958; admitted to bar, 1986, Ohio; 1989, U.S. District Court, Northern District of Ohio and U.S. Court of Appeals, Sixth Circuit. *Education:* Arizona State University (B.S., 1982); Case Western Reserve University (J.D., 1986). Assistant Cuyahoga County Prosecutors Office, 1986-1988. *Member:* Cleveland, Ohio State and Federal Bar Associations. ***REPORTED CASES:*** In re: Tabor, 232 BR 85 (N.D. Ohio 1999); Centimark Corp. v. Brown Sprinkler Service, Inc., 85 Ohio St. 3rd 485 (1993); State v. Levy, 55 Ohio App. 3rd 219 (Ct. App. Cuyahoga Cty. 1988). ***PRACTICE AREAS:*** General Practice; Employment Litigation; Premises Liability; Civil Fraud; Contracts; Personal Injury; Products Liability Law; Torts; Insurance Defense. ***Email:*** rschechter@lichkoschechter.com

OF COUNSEL

GREGORY R. GLICK, born Cleveland, Ohio, September 12, 1948; admitted to bar, 1973, Ohio and U.S. District Court, Northern District of Ohio. *Education:* Case Western Reserve University (B.A., 1970; J.D., 1973). Member, Registration and Exemption Advisory Committee, Ohio Division of Securities. ***PRACTICE AREAS:*** Securities; Real Estate; Banking Law; Corporate Law; Partnership Law.

(This Listing Continued)

WILLIAM S. LIGHTBODY

Established in 1977

32600 FAIRMOUNT BOULEVARD, ATRIUM SUITE, 100
CLEVELAND, OHIO 44124
Telephone: 216-621-7337
Fax: 216-621-7393
URL: http://www.williamlightbodylaw.com

Litigation, Intellectual Property, Patent, Trademark, Copyright, Unfair Competition, Trade Secrets.

WILLIAM S. LIGHTBODY, born Cleveland, Ohio, August 29, 1950; admitted to bar, 1977, Ohio; 1979, U.S. District Court, Northern District of Ohio; 1989, U.S. Court of Appeals for the Federal Circuit; registered to practice before U.S. Patent and Trademark Offices. *Education:* Bethany College (B.S., 1971); Cleveland Marshall School of Law; New York University School of Law (J.D., 1975; LL.M., 1976). *Member:* Ohio State and American Bar Associations.

MICHAEL J. LINDEN CO., LPA

(An Association of Independently Practicing Lawyers)

SUITE 400 PARK PLAZA BUILDING
1111 CHESTER AVENUE
CLEVELAND, OHIO 44114
Telephone: 216-621-0590
Fax: 216-621-5665
Email: michael.linden@lindenlpa.com

Mortgages, Real Estate, Banking, Foreclosures and related Bankruptcy, Financial Institutions, Secured Transactions, Condominium and Real Estate Development Law.

MICHAEL J. LINDEN, born Cleveland, Ohio, October 20, 1950; admitted to bar, 1975, Ohio. *Education:* The Ohio State University (B.S., 1972); Cleveland State University (J.D., 1975). Recipient, American Jurisprudence Award. Special Counsel, Veterans Administration, 1981—. Lecturer, National Business Institute. *Member:* Greater Cleveland, Cuyahoga County and Ohio State Bar Associations. ***PRACTICE AREAS:*** Foreclosure Law; Bankruptcy Law; Condominium Law; Real Estate Law. ***Email:*** michael.linden@lindenlpa.com

REPRESENTATIVE CLIENTS: Third Federal Savings & Loan Assn.; Ohio Savings Bank; U.S. Title Agency, Inc.; Condominium Concepts, Inc.; Flair Corp. (Builders & Developers); The Linden Group; First Nationwide Mortgage Corp.; Homeq Servicing Corporation; Indymac Bank, F.S.B.; Homecoming Financial Services; Saxon Mortgage, Inc.; Fidelity National Foreclosure Solutions; Wendover Financial Services.
REFERENCES: National City Bank; Ohio Savings Bank.

LOWE EKLUND WAKEFIELD & MULVIHILL CO., L.P.A.

TOWER CITY CENTER
610 SKYLIGHT OFFICE TOWER
1660 WEST SECOND STREET
CLEVELAND, OHIO 44113-1454
Telephone: 216-781-2600
Fax: 216-781-2610
Email: lew@lewm.com
URL: http://www.lewm.com

Products Liability, Personal Injury, Medical Malpractice, Commercial Litigation, Wrongful Death, Business Litigation.

FIRM PROFILE: Lowe Eklund Wakefield & Mulvihill Co., L.P.A. was established in 1976. We are a plaintiffs' trial firm and a recognized leader in the areas of products liability, medical malpractice and automobile product safety. The firm carries the highest legal ability rating in Martindale-Hubbell. The partnership includes members who are listed in Best Lawyers in America and who are Board Certified Trial Attorneys.

JAMES A. LOWE, born Cleveland, Ohio, July 15, 1945; admitted to bar, 1972, Ohio; 1973, U.S. Supreme Court; 1979, U.S. District Court, Northern District of Ohio and U.S. Court of Appeals, Sixth Circuit. *Education:* University of Pennsylvania (B.A., 1967); Cleveland State University (J.D., cum laude, 1972). Editor, Cleveland State Law Review, 1971-1972. Author: "Products Liability Litigation Pretrial Practice," Callaghan & Co., 1988; Editor, Products Liability Litigation," Series, Callaghan & Co., 1988; "Product Liability in Ohio After Tort Reform," Professional Education Systems, Inc., 1988. Editor, "Products Liability Case and Comment," Callaghan & Co., 1986-1987. General Editor, Ohio Jur Pleading and Practice Forms, Lawyers Cooperative Publishing, 1994. Instructor: Brief Writing and Oral Advocacy, Remedies, Cleveland State University School of Law, 1974-1976; The Lawyering Process, Case Western Reserve University School of Law, 1981-1986. Member, Faculty National College of Advocacy, Basic Trial College, 1985; Advanced College, 1987, 1988. Lecturer, Products Liability College, ATLA, 1988, 1990. Chairman, "Preparation and Trial of a Products Liability Case," ATLA Seminar, 1988-1989. Listed in Best Lawyers in America, 1993-2002. Director, Attorneys Information Exchange Group. *Member:* Greater Cleveland (Master Bencher, American Inns of Court), Ohio State (Chairman Products Liability Committee, 1985—) and American Bar Associations; Ohio Academy of Trial Lawyers (Chairman, Products Liability Section, 1985-1990); Cleveland Academy of Trial Attorneys (President, 1991-1992; Director, 1987-1992); The Association of Trial Lawyers of America (Chair, Products Liability Section, 1991-1992); American Board of Trial Advocates. Fellow: Roscoe Pound Foundation; American College of Trial Lawyers; International Society of Barristers. (Certified as Civil Trial Advocate by the National Board of Trial Advocacy). ***PRACTICE AREAS:*** Products Liability Law; Personal Injury Law; Civil Trials. ***Email:*** Jlowe@lewm.com

(This Listing Continued)

CLAUDIA RIETH EKLUND, born Cleveland, Ohio, November 9, 1951; admitted to bar, 1979, Ohio; 1982, U.S. District Court, Northern District of Ohio; 1983, U.S. Court of Appeals, Sixth Circuit. *Education:* Cleveland State University (B.A., 1976); Cleveland Marshall College of Law (J.D., 1979). Member, Cleveland Marshall Law Review, 1978-1979. Member, Panel of Arbitrators, American Arbitration Association. Listed in Best Lawyers in America, 2003. *Member:* Cuyahoga County, Ohio State and American Bar Associations; Cleveland Academy of Trial Lawyers; The Association of Trial Lawyers of America; Ohio Academy of Trial Lawyers; American Board of Trial Advocates. (Certified as a Civil Trial Advocate by the National Board of Trial Advocacy). ***PRACTICE AREAS:*** Personal Injury Law; Products Liability Law; Medical Malpractice. ***Email:*** Ceklund@lewm.com

MARK L. WAKEFIELD, born Heidelberg, Germany, May 5, 1956; admitted to bar, 1982, Ohio and U.S. District Court, Northern District of Ohio; 1985, U.S. Court of Appeals, Sixth Circuit. *Education:* St. Lawrence University (B.A./B.S., 1977); Case Western Reserve University (J.D., 1982). Delta Theta Phi. Member, 1982, Alumni Advisor, Case Western Reserve Law School, 1989-1996, Jessup International Moot Court Team. Co-Author: "Products Liability Litigation Pretrial Practice," Callaghan Co., 1997-1998, 2000-2001. *Member:* Greater Cleveland and Ohio State Bar Associations; The Association of Trial Lawyers of America; Ohio Academy of Trial Lawyers; Cleveland Academy of Trial Attorneys; Master, American Inns of Court. ***LANGUAGES:*** Spanish. ***PRACTICE AREAS:*** Personal Injury Law; Products Liability Law; F.E.L.A. Law. ***Email:*** Mwakefield@lewm.com

DENNIS P. MULVIHILL, born Grand Rapids, Michigan, January 11, 1966; admitted to bar, 1994, Ohio; 1995, U.S. District Court, Northern District of Ohio and U.S. Court of Appeals, Sixth Circuit. *Education:* Kenyon College (B.A., 1988); Cleveland-Marshall College of Law (J.D., cum laude, 1994). Author: "The Case Against Electronic Pet Containment Systems, Products Liability & Litigation: Product Studies," The West Group, August 1998; "15-Passenger Vans Slip Through the Safety Gap," Trial Magazine, March 2004. *Member:* Cleveland, Cuyahoga County and Ohio State (Member, Board of Directors) Bar Associations; Cleveland Academy of Trial Attorneys; Ohio Academy of Trial Lawyers (Member, Board of Governing Trustees, 1999—; Chairman, Products Liability Section, 2000-2002, 2003—); The Association of Trial Lawyers of America. ***PRACTICE AREAS:*** Personal Injury; Products Liability; Medical Malpractice; Civil Litigation. ***Email:*** Dmulvihill@lewm.com

---

GREGORY S. SCOTT, born Cleveland, Ohio, June 3, 1969; admitted to bar, 1996, Ohio; 1997, U.S. District Court, Northern District of Ohio. *Education:* Oberlin College (B.A., 1991); Cleveland-Marshall College of Law (J.D., 1996). *Member:* Cleveland, Cuyahoga County and Ohio State Bar Associations; The Association of Trial Lawyers of America; Cleveland Academy of Trial Lawyers; Ohio Academy of Trial Lawyers; Cleveland-Marshall Law Alumni Association. ***PRACTICE AREAS:*** Personal Injury Tort; Products Liability Law; Medical Malpractice. ***Email:*** Gscott@lewm.com

SARA S. RAVAS, born Cleveland, Ohio, July 31, 1978; admitted to bar, 2003, Ohio and U.S. District Court, Northern District of Ohio. *Education:* Wheeling Jesuit College (B.A., Political Science, 2000); Case Western Reserve University (J.D., 2003). Phi Delta Phi. *Member:* Cleveland, Cuyahoga County, Ohio State and American Bar Associations; The Association of Trial Lawyers of America; Ohio Academy of Trial Lawyers. ***PRACTICE AREAS:*** Personal Injury; Medical Malpractice; Products Liability. ***Email:*** sravas@lewm.com

OF COUNSEL

DONALD CYBULSKI, born Cleveland, Ohio, March 18, 1951; admitted to bar, 1975, Ohio and U.S. District Court, Northern District of Ohio; 1983, U.S. Court of Appeals, Sixth Circuit; 1990, U.S. Court of Federal Claims; 1996, Pennsylvania. *Education:* Wharton School, University of Pennsylvania (B.S. in Econ., 1972); Case Western Reserve University School of Law (J.D., 1975). Member, National Moot Court Team, 1973. Assistant Editor, Case Western Reserve Law Review, 1974-1975. *Member:* Cleveland, Ohio State and American Bar Associations; The Association of Trial Lawyers of America; Ohio Academy of Trial Lawyers. ***PRACTICE AREAS:*** Medical Malpractice; Products Liability; Personal Injury. ***Email:*** Dcybulski@lewm.com

MAGUIRE & SCHNEIDER LLP

Established in 1993

1370 ONTARIO STREET, SUITE 1700
CLEVELAND, OHIO 44113
Telephone: 800-600-1222
Fax: 216-274-9808
Email: msandhu@ms-lawfirm.com

Columbus, Ohio Office: 250 Civic Center Drive, Suite 500, 43215. Telephone: 614-224-1222. Fax: 614-224-1236.

Business Litigation, Labor and Employment, Insurance Defense, Directors Liability Errors and Omissions Defense, Real Estate Malpractice Claims, Real Estate, Corporate, Commercial Litigation, Health Care Law, Health Care Fraud and Abuse, Banking Law, Probate and Estate Planning, Family Law, Adoptions, Mediation, White Collar Crime, Criminal Defense, Consumer Law, Administrative Law, Creditor's Rights Law, Financial Institution Law, Intellectual Property, Internet Law, Lemon Law, Product Liability, and Worker's Compensation.

(For complete biographical data on firm personnel, see Professional Biographies at Columbus, Ohio)

MANLEY • DEAS • KOCHALSKI LLC

CLEVELAND, OHIO

(See Columbus)

Real Estate, Mortgages, Foreclosures, Loss Mitigation, Creditors Rights, Bankruptcy, Evictions, Landlord and Tenant Law, Title Service, Mortgage Servicing, Real Estate Development Closings.

THEODORE M. MANN, JR.
LAW FIRM

Established in 1963

644 HUNTINGTON BUILDING
925 EUCLID AVENUE
CLEVELAND, OHIO 44115-1493
Telephone: 216-621-6147
FAX: 216-621-6149
Email: mannlawoffice@ameritech.net
URL: http://www.lawyers.com/tmannlaw

Alternative Dispute Resolution, Mediation, Appellate Practice, Business Law, Business Litigation, Contracts, Corporate Law, Elder Law, Franchises and Franchising, Fraud, General Practice, Labor and Employment, Litigation, Negligence, Personal Injury, Probate, Real Estate, Real Estate Litigation, Residential Real Estate, Torts, Trade Secrets Trusts and Estates, Estate Planning, Trust Administration, Wills.

THEODORE M. MANN, JR., born Cleveland, Ohio, October 12, 1948; admitted to bar, 1976, Ohio and U.S. District Court, Northern District of Ohio; 1978, U.S. Court of Appeals, Sixth Circuit; 1987, U.S. District Court, Eastern District of Michigan; 1988, U.S. Supreme Court; 1991, U.S. District Court, District of Nebraska. *Education:* Allegheny College (B.A., 1970); Case Western Reserve University (J.D., 1976). Member, Moot Court Board, 1975-1976. Recipient, Solo Merit Award, American Bar Association, 1998. Alternate Dispute Resolution Neutral Panel (Member, U.S. District Court, Northern District of Ohio, 1992—). Adjunct Professor, Cleveland State University Law School, 1998—. Life Member, Judicial Conference of the Eighth Appellate District. *Member:* Geauga County, Lake County (Member, Grievance Settlement Week and Probate), Greater Cleveland (Member, Sections on: Labor Law; Litigation; Estate Planning; Fee Mediation Committee), Cuyahoga County (Member, Judicial Selection, Common Pleas Court; Chair, Fee Dispute Committee), Ohio State (Member, Sections on: Labor & Employment Law; Litigation; Board of Governors, Solo, Small Firm and General Practice Section, 1997—; Member Council of Delegates, 1997—; Special Committee on Multidisciplinary Practice and Legal Profession, 1999), American (Member, Sections on: Business Law; Labor & Employment Law; Litigation; Tort and Insurance Practice; General Practice; Law Practice Management; Real Property, Probate and Trust Law) Bar Associations. ***PRACTICE AREAS:*** Alternative Dispute Resolution; Mediation; Appellate Practice; Civil Appeals; Business Law; Business Litigation; Commercial Liability; Commercial Litigation; Contracts; Corporate Law; Corporate Formation; Corporate Litigation; Elder Law; Franchises and Franchising; General Practice; Labor and Employment; Employment Law; Employment Litigation; Leases and Leasing; Landlord and Tenant Law; Litigation; Negligence; Personal Injury; Probate; Real Estate; Residential Real Estate; Torts; Trade Secrets; Trusts and Estates; Estate Planning; Trust Administration; Wills. ***Email:*** mannlawoffice@ameritech.net

OF COUNSEL

THEODORE M. MANN (1921-1999)

REFERENCE: Huntington Bank.

MANNION AND GRAY CO., L.P.A.

Established in 2005

1300 EAST 9TH STREET, SUITE 1625
CLEVELAND, OHIO 44114
Telephone: 216-344-9422
Fax: 216-344-9421
URL: http://www.manniongray.com

Catastrophic Injuries, Medical Malpractice, Products Liability, Medical Device and Class Action, Professional Liability, and Consumer Law.

FIRM PROFILE: We have defended these cases in Ohio, Florida, Illinois, Michigan, Pennsylvania, New York, Missouri, Minnesota, West Virginia, Kentucky, Virginia, and other jurisdictions.

MEMBERS OF FIRM

THOMAS P. MANNION, born Cleveland, Ohio, June 10, 1963; admitted to bar, 1993, Ohio; 1995, West Virginia and U.S. District Court, Northern District of Ohio; 1997, U.S. District Court, Southern District of West Virginia; 2000, U.S. District Court, Northern District of West Virginia. *Education:* Bowling Green State University (B.S., 1986); University of Akron (J.D., summa cum laude, 1993). Author: "Pacific Mutual vs. Cleopatra Haslip—The Constitutionality of Punitive Damages," University of Akron Law Review, Spring 1991; "The Professional Judgment Rule," Insight Matters, Ohio Psychiatric Association, August 1996; "Therapists' Duty to Warn," Ohio Medicine, August 1996. *Member:* Toledo, Lucas County, Stark County and Ohio State, West Virginia and American Bar Associations. ***PRACTICE AREAS:*** Medical Malpractice; Professional Liability; Products Liability; Drug and Medical Device Litigation; Insurance Coverage; Insurance Defense. ***Email:*** tmannion@manniongray.com

TODD A. GRAY, born Ashtabula, Ohio, August 14, 1970; admitted to bar, 1999, Ohio. *Education:* Eastern Michigan University (B.S., 1995); University of Toledo (J.D., cum laude, 1999). *Member:* Ohio State Bar Association. ***PRACTICE AREAS:*** Medical Malpractice; Products Liability; Professional Liability; Insurance Defense; Lemon Law; Transportation. ***Email:*** tgray@manniongray.com

ASSOCIATE

RYAN K. RUBIN, born Chicago, Illinois, August 17, 1978; admitted to bar, 2004, Ohio, Kentucky and U.S. District Court, Northern District of Ohio. *Education:* Miami University (B.A., 2000); Case Western Reserve University (J.D., 2003). *Member:* Cleveland and Ohio State Bar Associations; Defense Research Institute. ***PRACTICE AREAS:*** Medical Malpractice; Products Liability; Drug and Medical Device Litigation; Professional Liability; Insurance Defense; Consumer Law. ***Email:*** rrubin@manniongray.com

(This Listing Continued)

MANSOUR, GAVIN, GERLACK & MANOS CO., L.P.A.

Established in 1954

55 PUBLIC SQUARE, SUITE 2150
CLEVELAND, OHIO 44113-1994
Telephone: 216-523-1500
Telecopier: 216-523-1705
URL: http://www.mggmLPA.com

General Civil Practice. Corporate, Insurance, Real Estate, Labor, Employment, Wrongful Discharge, Discrimination, Municipal, Probate and Condemnation Law, Litigation, Product and Hospital Liability, Environmental Litigation.

FIRM PROFILE: The firm, established in 1954, consists of 19 attorneys plus general support personnel and concentrates in the areas of civil litigation including corporate, employment, insurance, real estate, product and hospital liability, and environmental litigation. Our practice is spread throughout the state of Ohio as well as the United States.

ERNEST P. MANSOUR, born Cleveland, Ohio, January 16, 1931; admitted to bar, 1955, Ohio. *Education:* St. Francis College (B.A., 1952); Western Reserve University (LL.B., 1955). Phi Alpha Delta. *Member:* Greater Cleveland, Ohio State and American Bar Associations; Cleveland Defense Attorneys' Group. ***PRACTICE AREAS:*** Corporate Law; Litigation.

MICHAEL T. GAVIN, born Garfield Heights, Ohio, February 22, 1928; admitted to bar, 1955, Ohio. *Education:* John Carroll University (B.S.S., 1952); Western Reserve University (LL.B., 1955). Phi Alpha Delta. *Member:* Greater Cleveland, Cuyahoga County, Ohio State and American Bar Associations; Cleveland Academy of Trial Lawyers (President, 1964). ***PRACTICE AREAS:*** Real Estate Law; Civil Litigation.

JULIUS R. GERLACK, born Cleveland, Ohio, September 21, 1936; admitted to bar, 1962, Ohio. *Education:* Ohio University (B.S.C., 1959); Western Reserve University (LL.B., 1962). *Member:* Greater Cleveland, Cuyahoga County and Ohio State Bar Associations; Defense Research and Trial Lawyers Association; Cleveland Defense Attorneys' Group; Ohio Association of Civil Trial Attorneys. ***PRACTICE AREAS:*** Insurance Law; Probate Law; Litigation.

ELI MANOS, born Cleveland, Ohio, January 12, 1931; admitted to bar, 1958, Ohio. *Education:* Harvard College (B.A., 1953); Harvard University (LL.B., 1958). *Member:* Greater Cleveland and Cuyahoga County Bar Associations. ***PRACTICE AREAS:*** Real Estate Law; Litigation; Appellate Law.

DALE E. MARKWORTH, born Cleveland, Ohio, February 18, 1948; admitted to bar, 1973, Ohio. *Education:* Denison University (B.A., 1970); Washington University (J.D., 1973). *Member:* Greater Cleveland, Ohio State and American Bar Associations; Defense Research Institute; Cleveland Defense Attorneys' Group; Ohio Association of Civil Trial Attorneys. ***PRACTICE AREAS:*** Litigation; Product Liability; Hospital Liability. ***Email:*** dmarkworth@mggmlpa.com

JEFFREY M. EMBLETON, born Columbus, Ohio, August 23, 1950; admitted to bar, 1975, Ohio. *Education:* Ohio University (B.A., 1972); Case Western Reserve University (J.D., 1975). *Member:* Greater Cleveland, Ohio State and American (Member, Labor and Employment Law Section) Bar Associations; Cleveland Defense Attorneys' Group; Ohio Association of Civil Trial Attorneys. ***PRACTICE AREAS:*** Litigation. ***Email:*** jembleton@mggmlpa.com

ANTHONY J. COYNE, born Cleveland, Ohio, October 2, 1960; admitted to bar, 1988, Ohio. *Education:* John Carroll University (B.A., 1982); Cleveland State University College of Urban Affairs (M.S., 1984); The Cleveland Marshall College of Law (J.D., 1987). Member, Cleveland Planning Commission; Trustee, Ohio Planning Conference, the Ohio Chapter of the American Planning Association. *Member:* Greater Cleveland, Ohio State and American (Member, Urban, State and Local Government Law Section) Bar Associations. ***PRACTICE AREAS:*** Municipal Law; Zoning and Planning; Real Property; Commercial; Litigation. ***Email:*** acoyne@mggmlpa.com

DAVID B. CATHCART, born Cleveland, Ohio, May 23, 1950; admitted to bar, 1975, Ohio. *Education:* Denison University (B.A., 1972); Case Western University (J.D., 1975). Phi Delta Phi. Assistant Instructor, Research and Writing, Case Western Reserve Law School, 1974-1975. *Member:* Greater Cleveland and Ohio State Bar Associations; Defense Research Institute; Cleveland Defense Attorneys' Group; Ohio Association of Civil Trial Attorneys. ***PRACTICE AREAS:*** Corporate Law.

SAMUEL R. MARTILLOTTA, born Albion, New York, October 22, 1951; admitted to bar, 1980, Ohio. *Education:* Ohio Wesleyan University (B.A., 1973); The Cleveland Marshall College of Law (J.D., 1980). *Member:* Greater Cleveland, Ohio State (Member, Environmental Law Section) and American Bar Associations; Defense Research Institute; Cleveland Association of Civil Trial Attorneys. ***PRACTICE AREAS:*** Insurance Defense; Litigation; Mass Tort Litigation; Environmental. ***Email:*** smartillotta@mggmlpa.com

JOHN F. BURKE, III, born South Bend, Indiana, August 2, 1965; admitted to bar, 1992, Ohio; 1994, U.S. District Court, Northern District of Ohio. *Education:* Miami University (B.A., 1988); The Cleveland Marshall College of Law (J.D., cum laude 1992). Recipient, Charles Auerbach Award for Excellence in Evidence. Three times recipients, American Jurisprudence Award. Member, Cleveland Marshall Moot Court Board of Governors. *Member:* Cleveland, Cuyahoga County and Ohio State Bar Associations; Cleveland Association of Civil Trial Attorneys. ***PRACTICE AREAS:*** Labor Law; Worker's Compensation Law; Insurance Defense; General Litigation. ***Email:*** jburke@mggmlpa.com

BRUCE G. RINKER, born Washington, D. C., April 26, 1951; admitted to bar, 1977, Ohio; 1979, U.S. District Court, Northern District of Ohio. *Education:* Hamilton College (B.A., 1973); Case Western Reserve University (J.D., 1976). Executive Editor, Case Western Reserve Journal of International Law, 1975-1976. Author: "The Future of Arbitration in

(This Listing Continued)

MANSOUR, GAVIN, GERLACK & MANOS CO., L.P.A., Cleveland—Continued

Latin America; A Study of Its Regional Development," Case Western Reserve Journal of International Law, 1976. Law Clerk to the Hon. August Pryatel, Eighth District Court of Appeals of Ohio, 1978-1981. Adjunct Instructor of Law, Cleveland-Marshall College of Law, 1980-1985. Assistant County Prosecutor, Criminal Trial Division, Cuyahoga County Prosecutor's Office, 1981-1984. Mayfield Village Council, 1987-1993; Council President, 1991-1993; Mayor, 1993—. CLE Lecturer. *Member:* Cleveland, Ohio State and American Bar Associations; Cleveland and Ohio Association of Civil Trial Attorneys. ***LANGUAGES:*** French. ***PRACTICE AREAS:*** Civil Litigation; Municipal Zoning; General Practice. ***Email:*** brinker@mggmlpa.com

---

EDWARD O. PATTON, born Cleveland, Ohio, May 1, 1964; admitted to bar, 1989, Ohio; 1997, U.S. District Court, Northern District of Ohio. *Education:* Xavier University (B.A., 1986); Cleveland Marshall College of Law (J.D., 1989). *Member:* Cleveland and Ohio State Bar Associations. ***PRACTICE AREAS:*** Insurance Defense; Criminal Defense.

BRADFORD J. PATRICK, born Milwaukee, Wisconsin, June 10, 1968; admitted to bar, 1999, Ohio, U.S. District Court, Eastern District of Ohio and U.S. Court of Appeals, Sixth Circuit. *Education:* University of Dayton (B.S., 1990); Case Western Reserve University (J.D., 1998). Author, "Snuffing Out the First Amendment: The FDA Regulation of Tobacco Company Advertising and Sports Sponsorships Under the Federal Food, Drug and Cosmetic Act," Marquette Sports Law Journal, Vol. 8, No. 1, Fall 1997. *Member:* Cleveland and Ohio State Bar Associations. ***PRACTICE AREAS:*** Civil Litigation; Real Estate; Dealer and Distributor; Computer and Software Law; Trademarks. ***Email:*** bpatrick@mggmlpa.com

LINDA L. JOHNSON, born Brush, Colorado, July 23, 1958; admitted to bar, 1996, Ohio; 1998, U.S. District Court, Northern District of Ohio. *Education:* University of Illinois; University of Colorado (B.S.C.E., 1980); Cleveland State University (J.D., cum laude, 1996). Recipient: American Jurisprudence Award in Legal Writing and Research; Law Fellow Merit Scholarship; CALI Excellence for the Future Award in Remedies. Member, American Water Works Association, 1982-1989. *Member:* Cleveland and Ohio State Bar Associations. ***PRACTICE AREAS:*** Products Liability; Contracts; Environmental Law. ***Email:*** ljohnson@mggmlpa.com

MARY E. DONAHUE, born Charleston, West Virginia, July 26, 1958; admitted to bar, 1994, Ohio and U.S. District Court, Northern District of Ohio. *Education:* University of Dayton (B.S., 1980); Cleveland Marshall College of Law (J.D., 1994). Associate, 1991-1992 and Editor, 1992-1993, Cleveland Marshall Law Review. *Member:* Cleveland and Ohio State Bar Associations. ***PRACTICE AREAS:*** Corporate Law; Finance; Banking Law; Venture Capital; Mergers and Acquisitions. ***Email:*** mdarcy@mggmlpa.com

AMY L. PHILLIPS, born Elyria, Ohio, October 22, 1973; admitted to bar, 1998, Ohio and U.S. District Court, Northern District of Ohio; 1999, U.S. Court of Appeals, Sixth Circuit. *Education:* Kent State University (B.A., summa cum laude, 1995); Cleveland Marshall College of Law (J.D., 1998). Research Editor, Cleveland State Law Review, 1997-1998. *Member:* Cleveland, Ohio State, and American Bar Associations. ***PRACTICE AREAS:*** Labor and Employment Law; Municipal Law; Administrative Law. ***Email:*** aphillips@mggmlpa.com

WILLIAM J. MUNIAK, born Cleveland, Ohio, October 28, 1967; admitted to bar, 1992, Ohio; U.S. District Court, Northern District of Ohio; 1993, U.S. Court of Appeals, Sixth Circuit; 1994, U.S. District Court, Eastern District of Illinois; 1997, U.S. District Court, Southern District of Ohio. *Education:* Bowling Green State University (B.L.S., cum laude, 1989); Cleveland Marshall College of Law (J.D., magna cum laude, 1992). Articles Editor, Law Review. Moot Court Board of Governors. *Member:* Cleveland, Medina County and Ohio State Bar Associations. ***PRACTICE AREAS:*** Insurance Defense; Products Liability; Complex Civil Litigation; Business Litigation; Creditors Rights. ***Email:*** wmuniak@mggmlpa.com

MICHAEL PATRICK QUINLAN, born Willoughby, Ohio; admitted to bar, 1996, Ohio; 2002, U.S. District Court, Northern District of Ohio and U.S. Court of Appeals, Sixth Circuit. *Education:* University of Dayton (B.S., 1993); Cleveland-Marshall College of Law (J.D., 1996). Assistant County Prosecutor, Geauga County, Ohio, 1996-2002. *Member:* Cleveland, Cuyahoga County, Geauga County and Ohio State Bar Associations.

KEITH J. KEARNEY, born Cleveland, Ohio, March 19, 1968; admitted to bar, 1998, Ohio. *Education:* Wheeling Jesuit College (B.A., 1990); Cleveland-Marshall College of Law (J.D., 1998). Psi Chi; Alpha Sigma Nu. Judicial Staff Attorney, Hon. Kenneth R. Callahan, Cuyahoga County Court of Common Pleas. ***PRACTICE AREAS:*** Insurance Defense; Products Liability; Complex Civil Litigation. ***Email:*** kkearney@mggmlpa.com

BRENDON P. FRIESEN, born Pasadena, California, August 29, 1977; admitted to bar, 2003, Ohio; 2004, U.S. District Court, Northern District of Ohio. *Education:* Occidental College (B.A., 1999); The Ohio State University (J.D., 2003). *Member:* Cleveland, Cuyahoga and Ohio State Bar Associations. ***LANGUAGES:*** Spanish. ***PRACTICE AREAS:*** Litigation. ***Email:*** bfriesen@mggmlpa.com

ASHLEY M. ARVIN, born Kokomo, Indiana, September 5, 1971; admitted to bar, 2004, Ohio; 2005, U.S. District Court, District of Ohio and U.S. Court of Appeals, Sixth Circuit. *Education:* Purdue University (B.S., 1997); Cleveland-Marshall College of Law (J.D., 2004). *Member:* Cleveland and Ohio State Bar Associations. ***PRACTICE AREAS:*** Real Estate; Eminent Domain; Land Use; Zoning Law; Probate; Corporate Law; Civil Litigation. ***Email:*** aarvin@mggmlpa.com

REPRESENTATIVE CLIENTS: BP America; Forest City Enterprises; Hartford Insurance Co.; Hilti Inc.; Invacare Corp.; Linderme Tube; McDonald's Systems, Inc.; Michigan Mutual Liability Insurance Co.; Ohio Northern Transit; Pfizer Inc.; Swagelok Co.; Wedge Products, Inc.; Wire Products Co.; Zurich Insurance Co.

SETH B. MARKS

3637 GREEN ROAD
CLEVELAND, OHIO 44122
Telephone: 216-292-2600
Fax: 216-464-7866
Toll Free: 888-514-4600
Email: sethb123@aol.com
URL: http://www.lawyers.com/sethmarkslaw

Residential Real Estate, Wills, Commercial Collections, Trusts, Leases, For Sale By Owner, Deeds, Landlord/Tenant.

SETH B. MARKS, born Cleveland, Ohio, August 24, 1945; admitted to bar, 1971, Ohio; 1974, U.S. District Court, Northern District of Ohio; 1977, U.S. Supreme Court. *Education:* Miami University (B.A., 1967); Case Western Reserve University (J.D., 1970). Acting Judge, Shaker Heights Municipal Court, 1996—. ***PRACTICE AREAS:*** Residential Real Estate; Wills; Trust Law; Commercial Collections; Probate; Leases and Leasing; Small Business Law; Real Estate Sales; Contracts.

MAZANEC, RASKIN & RYDER CO., L.P.A.

Established in 1980
100 FRANKLIN'S ROW
34305 SOLON ROAD
CLEVELAND, OHIO 44139
Telephone: 440-248-7906
Fax: 440-248-8861
Email: mrrlaw.com
URL: http://www.mrrlaw.com

Columbus, Ohio Office: Suite 400, 250 Civic Center Drive. 43215. Telephone: 614-228-5931. Fax: 614-228-5934.

Civil Litigation, Insurance Defense, Construction Law, Negligence, Professional Negligence, Municipal Law, Civil Rights, Real Estate, Business Law, Probate, Estate Planning.

THOMAS S. MAZANEC, born Cleveland, Ohio, November 26, 1949; admitted to bar, 1976, Ohio; 1980, U.S. District Court, Northern District of Ohio; 1981, U.S. Supreme Court; 1986, U.S. Court of Appeals, Sixth Circuit. *Education:* Xavier University (B.S.B.A., 1971); Cleveland Marshall College of Law (J.D., 1976). *Member:* Cleveland, Akron, Ohio State and American Bar Associations; Scanlon Inn of Court, Akron; Ohio Association of Civil Trial Attorneys. ***PRACTICE AREAS:*** Civil Litigation; Business Law; Real Estate Law; Construction Law. ***Email:*** tmazanec@mrrlaw.com

TODD M. RASKIN, born New York, N.Y., June 23, 1950; admitted to bar, 1980, Ohio, U.S. District Court, Northern District of Ohio, 1988, U.S. Court of Appeals, Sixth Circuit; 1985, U.S. Supreme Court. *Education:* Kent State University (B.S., 1972); Cleveland Marshall College of Law (J.D., 1979). *Member:* Cleveland, Cuyahoga County, Ohio State and American Bar Associations; Ohio Association of Civil Trial Attorneys; Defense Research Institute. ***PRACTICE AREAS:*** Litigation; Insurance Defense; Municipal Law. ***Email:*** traskin@mrrlaw.com

EDWARD M. RYDER, born Cleveland, Ohio, May 4, 1948; admitted to bar, 1977, Ohio and U.S. District Court, Northern District of Ohio; U.S. Court of Appeals, Sixth Circuit. *Education:* Cleveland State University (B.A., 1970); Cleveland-Marshall College of Law (J.D., 1977). *Member:* Columbus and Ohio State Bar Associations; Ohio Association of Civil Trial Attorneys. ***PRACTICE AREAS:*** Insurance Defense; Litigation. ***Email:*** eryder@mrrlaw.com

JOHN T. McLANDRICH, born Cleveland, Ohio, July 30, 1957; admitted to bar, 1983, Ohio; 1988, U.S. District Court, Northern District of Ohio and U.S. Supreme Court; 1989, U.S. Court of Appeals, Sixth Circuit. *Education:* John Carroll University (B.S.Ec., 1979); Case Western Reserve University School of Law (J.D., 1983). *Member:* Cleveland, Ohio State and American Bar Associations; Defense Research Institute. ***PRACTICE AREAS:*** Appellate Practice; Insurance Defense; Litigation; Probate Law; Closely Held Corporations Law; Municipal Law; Civil Rights Law. ***Email:*** jmclandrich@mrrlaw.com

JAMES A. CLIMER, born Chillicothe, Ohio, December 17, 1954; admitted to bar, 1980, Ohio; 1981, U.S. District Court, Northern District of Ohio; 1981, U.S. District Court, Southern District of Ohio. *Education:* Miami University, Ohio (B.A., 1977); University of Toledo College of Law (J.D., 1980). *Member:* Parma, Ohio State Bar Associations; Cuyahoga County Law Directors Association. ***PRACTICE AREAS:*** Insurance Defense; Civil Rights; Litigation; Municipal Law. ***Email:*** jclimer@mrrlaw.com

JOSEPH F. NICHOLAS, JR., born Cleveland, Ohio, August 23, 1961; admitted to bar, 1987, Ohio; 1991, U.S. District Court, Northern District of Ohio. *Education:* University of Dayton (B.A., cum laude, 1983); Cleveland Marshall College of Law (J.D., 1986). *Member:* Cleveland and Ohio State Bar Associations. ***PRACTICE AREAS:*** Insurance; Insurance Defense; Litigation; Professional Liability; Torts; Transportation. ***Email:*** jnicholas@mrrlaw.com

PATRICK W. WINSLOW, born Cleveland, Ohio, April 13, 1953; admitted to bar, 1977, Ohio; 1982, U.S. District Court, Northern District of Ohio and U.S. Tax Court; 1984, U.S. Court of Appeals, Sixth Circuit. *Education:* University of Pennsylvania (B.S., 1974); Cleveland State University (J.D., 1977). Certified Public Accountant, Ohio, 1979. *Member:* Greater Cleveland, Cuyahoga County and Ohio State Bar Associations; Ohio Society of Certified Public Accountants. ***PRACTICE AREAS:*** Tax Law; Real Property; Corporate Law; Trusts and Estates; Probate.

PAUL J. CRISTALLO, born Clearwater, Florida, October 19, 1967; admitted to bar, 1993, Ohio; U.S. District Court, Northern District of Ohio; 1999, U.S. Court of Appeals, Sixth Circuit. *Education:* University of Akron (B.A., 1990); Cleveland Marshall College of Law (J.D., 1993). ***PRACTICE AREAS:*** Insurance Defense; Municipal; Civil Litigation. ***Email:*** pcristallo@mrrlaw.com

(This Listing Continued)

TIMOTHY R. OBRINGER, born Alton, Illinois, September 19, 1965; admitted to bar, 1991, Ohio; 1992, U.S. District Court, Northern District of Ohio; 1997, U.S. Court of Appeals, Sixth Circuit. *Education:* The Ohio State University (B.A., 1987); University of Toledo College of Law (J.D., 1991). Formerly with Selker & Assoc., Ltd. ***PRACTICE AREAS:*** Employment Law; Business Litigation; General Practice.

NATASHA A. WELLS-NIKLAS, born Marysville, Ohio, March 24, 1971; admitted to bar, 1996, Ohio; 2002, U.S. District Court, Northern District of Ohio. *Education:* Ohio University (B.A., 1993); University of Toledo College of Law (J.D., 1996). Delta Theta Phi. *Member:* Ohio State Bar Association; Ohio Association of Civil Trial Attorneys. ***PRACTICE AREAS:*** Insurance Defense; Civil Litigation; Personal Injury; General Liability. ***Email:*** nniklas@mrrlaw.com

DAVID R. FENN, born Cleveland, Ohio, May 8, 1958; admitted to bar, 1998, Ohio. *Education:* College of Wooster (B.A., 1980); Cleveland Marshall College of Law (J.D., 1997). *Member:* Ohio State and American Bar Associations. ***LANGUAGES:*** French. ***Email:*** dfenn@mrrlaw.com

EDWARD A. PROCTOR, born Cleveland, Ohio, December 3, 1968; admitted to bar, 1998, Ohio. *Education:* John Carroll University (B.S. in B.A., 1992); Ohio State College of Law (J.D., 1998). Certified Public Accountant, Ohio, 2001. *Member:* Ohio State and American Bar Associations. ***PRACTICE AREAS:*** Taxation; Estate Planning; Probate Administration. ***Email:*** eproctor@mrrlaw.com

JEFFREY T. KAY, born Berea, Ohio, February 2, 1972; admitted to bar, 1998, Ohio; 1999, U.S. District Court, Northern District of Ohio and U.S. Court of Appeals, Sixth Circuit. *Education:* Ashland University (B.S., magna cum laude, 1993); Cleveland Marshall College of Law (J.D., 1997). *Member:* Cleveland, Ohio State and American Bar Associations; National Employment Lawyers Association. ***PRACTICE AREAS:*** Insurance Defense. ***Email:*** jkay@mrrlaw.com

ROBERT F. CATHCART, born San Mateo, California, May 16, 1970; admitted to bar, 1999, Ohio; 2000, U.S. District Court, Northern District of Ohio and U.S. Court of Appeals, Sixth Circuit. *Education:* University of Nevada at Reno (B.A., 1995); Case Western Reserve University (J.D., 1999). ***PRACTICE AREAS:*** Insurance Defense; Municipal Liability; Civil Rights. ***Email:*** rcathcart@mrrlaw.com

GEOFFREY A. BELZER, born New York, N.Y., June 2, 1965; admitted to bar, 2000, Ohio. *Education:* Northwestern University (B.S.J., Journalism, 1987); Akron University Law School (J.D., cum laude, 1990). ***PRACTICE AREAS:*** Professional Liability; General Liability. ***Email:*** gbelzer@mrrlaw.com

CHRISTOPHER P. CONOMY, born Wichita Falls, Texas, February 28, 1970; admitted to bar, 2000, Ohio, U.S. District Court, Northern District of Ohio and U.S. Court of Appeals, Sixth Circuit. *Education:* Ithaca College (B.A., 1992); Cleveland-Marshall College of Law (J.D., magna cum laude, 1998; M.P.A.). ***Email:*** cconomy@mrrlaw.com

DAVID JAMES SIPUSIC, admitted to bar, 2001, Ohio. *Education:* Cleveland-Marshall College of Law (J.D., 2001).

FRANK H. SCIALDONE, born Syracuse, New York, July 22, 1970; admitted to bar, 2002, Ohio and U.S. District Court, Northern District of Ohio. *Education:* Nazareth College of Rochester (B.A., 1994); Cleveland-Marshall College of Law (J.D., magna cum laude, 2002). ***PRACTICE AREAS:*** Municipal Law. ***Email:*** fscialdone@mrrlaw.com

STEVEN J. MOODY, born Cleveland, Ohio, October 9, 1962; admitted to bar, 2002, Ohio. *Education:* Cleveland State University (B.A., 1996); Cleveland-Marshall College of Law (J.D., 2001). Former Associate, Gallagher, Sharp, Fulton & Norman. ***PRACTICE AREAS:*** Insurance Defense.

JULIUS E. TROMBETTO, born Fairview, Ohio, May 19, 1976; admitted to bar, 2002, Ohio. *Education:* Purdue University (B.S., with high distinction, 1998); Case Western Reserve University (J.D., 2002). Phi Beta Kappa; Phi Kappa Phi. ***PRACTICE AREAS:*** Personal Injury; Litigation; Medical Malpractice. ***Email:*** jtrombetto@mrrlaw.com

MARTIN JAMES O'CONNELL, born Mansfield, Ohio, December 28, 1953; admitted to bar, 2003, Ohio and U.S. District Court, Northern District of Ohio; 2004, U.S. Court of Appeals, Sixth Circuit. *Education:* University of Cincinnati (B.A., magna cum laude, 1976; M.S., 1979); Cleveland-Marshall College of Law (J.D., magna cum laude, 2003). Member, Law Review. *Member:* Cleveland, Ohio State and American Bar Associations. (Also practicing individually, Shaker Heights, OH). ***PRACTICE AREAS:*** Litigation; Employment.

REPRESENTATIVE CLIENTS: Acceptance Insurance Co.; American Custom Insurance Services, Inc.; American Indemnity Insurance Co.; American Modern Home Insurance Group; ANPAC General Insurance Company; Best Insurers, Inc.; Carnegie Insurance Services; Century Surety Insurance Co.; Continental Western Insurance Company; Cover X Corporation; Crawford & Co.; First Mercury Syndicate; Frankenmuth Mutual Insurance Co.; German Mutual Insurance Co.; GMAC Insurance Co.; Great American Insurance Co.; Great West Life Assurance and Annuity Co.; Hamilton Mutual Insurance Co.; Indiana Insurance Co.; Jefferson Insurance Group; Kemper National Insurance Company; Lancer Insurance Company; Liberty Mutual Insurance Co.; National Casualty Co.; National Indemnity Co.; National Interstate Co.; Northland Insurance Companies; Ohio Bar Liability Insurance Company; Old Dominion Insurance Co.; Professional Claims Managers, Inc.; Progressive Casualty Insurance Co.; Republic Insurance Co.; Republic Franklin Insurance Co.; Safe Auto Insurance Co.; Scottsdale Insurance Co.; State Farm Fire & Casualty Company; Summit Risk Services, Inc.; Transport Insurance Co.; Tyson Foods, Inc.; Utica Mutual Insurance Co.; Western Heritage Insurance Co.; Windsor Insurance Group.; Zurich American Insurance Co.
REFERENCE: Huntington National Bank.

(For complete biographical data on personnel at Columbus, see that location)

JOHN J. McCARROLL

516 STANDARD BUILDING
1370 ONTARIO STREET
CLEVELAND, OHIO 44113
Telephone: 216-861-6655; 877-861-6655
Fax: 216-861-6653
Email: mccarrol@apk.net
URL: http://www.usavisalaws.com

Victims Rights, Personal Injury, Bankruptcy, Business Law, Probate, Criminal Defense, Immigration Law.

JOHN J. McCARROLL, born Bronx, New York, October 25, 1944; admitted to bar, 1989, Ohio and U.S. District Court, Northern District of Ohio. *Education:* University of Wyoming (B.A., 1969); City University of New York (M.B.A., 1972); Cleveland Marshall College of Law (J.D., 1988). *Member:* Ohio, Cleveland and Cuyohoga County Bar Associations. ***LANGUAGES:*** Spanish.

McCARTHY, LEBIT, CRYSTAL & LIFFMAN CO., L.P.A.

Established in 1959

1800 MIDLAND BUILDING
101 PROSPECT AVENUE, WEST
CLEVELAND, OHIO 44115
Telephone: 216-696-1422
Fax: 216-696-1210
Email: tfa@mccarthylebit.com
URL: http://www.mccarthylebit.com

Corporate and General Business, Real Estate, Taxation, Litigation, Commercial Banking, Estate Planning and Probate, Domestic Relations, Bankruptcy and Creditors Rights, Intellectual Property and Information Technology.

DANIEL R. McCARTHY, born Cleveland, Ohio, August 13, 1924; admitted to bar, 1954, Ohio and U.S. Tax Court; 1973, U.S. Supreme Court; 1981, District of Columbia Bar, U.S. District Court, Northern District of Ohio, U.S. Court of Appeals, Sixth Circuit and U.S. Claims Court,. *Education:* Western Reserve University (B.B.A., 1948); Cleveland Marshall College of Law, Cleveland State University (J.D., cum laude, 1954). Delta Theta Phi. Co-Editor, Cleveland Marshall Law Review, 1953. *Member:* Cleveland, Ohio State, Federal and American Bar Associations; The District of Columbia Bar. [Sgt., U.S. Army, active duty, 1943-1946]. ***PRACTICE AREAS:*** Tax Law; Business Planning Law.

EDWARD A. LEBIT (1936-1988)

LARRY CRYSTAL, born Cleveland, Ohio, December 16, 1938; admitted to bar, 1965, Ohio; 1969, U.S. Tax Court. *Education:* Western Reserve University (B.B.A., 1961); Cleveland Marshall College of Law (J.D., 1965). Certified Public Accountant, Ohio, 1965. *Member:* Cleveland, Cuyahoga County and Ohio State Bar Associations. ***PRACTICE AREAS:*** Mergers and Acquisitions Law; Financing Law; Tax Law; Corporate Law.

IRWIN S. HAIMAN, born Cleveland, Ohio, March 19, 1916; admitted to bar, 1941, Ohio; 1946, U.S. District Court, Northern District of Ohio; 1961, U.S. Supreme Court; 1985, U.S. Court of Appeals, 6th Circuit. *Education:* Adelbert College; Case Western Reserve University (A.B., cum laude, 1938); The Cleveland-Marshall Law School (J.D., cum laude, 1941). *Member:* Cleveland (Chairman, Domestic Relations Committee, 1973-1975) and Ohio State Bar Associations. ***PRACTICE AREAS:*** Federal and State Litigation; Zoning Law; General Municipal Law; Real Estate. ***Email:*** ish@mccarthylebit.com

KENNETH B. LIFFMAN, born Cleveland, Ohio, June 19, 1954; admitted to bar, 1979, Ohio and Florida. *Education:* Miami University (B.S., 1976); Cleveland Marshall College of Law (J.D., magna cum laude, 1979). *Member:* Cleveland, Ohio State and American Bar Associations; The Florida Bar. ***PRACTICE AREAS:*** Real Estate Law; Corporate; Business Law; Commercial Banking Law. ***Email:*** kbl@mccarthylebit.com

MARK B. COHN, born Cleveland, Ohio, December 28, 1947; admitted to bar, 1974, Ohio and U.S. District Court, Northern District of Ohio; 1976, Florida and U.S. District Court, Middle District of Florida; 1980, U.S. Tax Court; 1985, U.S. Claims Court; 1989, U.S. Supreme Court. *Education:* The Ohio State University (B.S., 1969; J.D., summa cum laude, 1973). Order of the Coif. Associate Editor, The Ohio State Law Journal, 1972-1973. Member, National Moot Court Team, 1972. *Member:* Cleveland (Member, 1974 and Chairman, Federal Courts Committee, 1987-1988) and Ohio State Bar Associations; The Florida Bar; The Association of Trial Lawyers of America; American Board of Trial Advocates. Member, Celebrezze Inn of Court. ***PRACTICE AREAS:*** Trials and Appeals; White Collar Crime; Legal Malpractice. ***Email:*** mbc@mccarthylebit.com

JOHN S. SEICH, born Cleveland, Ohio, September 23, 1949; admitted to bar, 1982, Ohio; 1983, Florida, U.S. Tax Court and U.S. Court of Appeals, Sixth Circuit. *Education:* The Ohio State University (B.S., 1971); Case Western Reserve University (J.D., 1982). Certified Public Accountant, Ohio, 1977. *Member:* Cleveland, Ohio State and American Bar Associations; The Florida Bar. (Certified Specialist in Federal Tax Law, Ohio State Bar Association). ***REPORTED CASES:*** O'Neill v. Commissioner of Internal Revenue, 994 F. 2d 302. ***PRACTICE AREAS:*** Taxation Law; Estate Planning Law; Probate Law; Pension and Profit Sharing Plans Law. ***Email:*** jss@mccarthylebit.com

ROBERT S. BALANTZOW, born Cleveland, Ohio, December 7, 1940; admitted to bar, 1965, Ohio; 1966, Michigan, U.S. District Court, Northern District of Ohio, U.S. District Court, Eastern District of Michigan, U.S. Court of Appeals, 6th Circuit; 1976, Florida and U.S. District Court, Southern District of Florida. *Education:* University of Pennsylvania, Wharton School of Finance and Commerce (B.S. in Economics, 1962); Case Western Reserve University (J.D., 1965). *Member:* Cleveland, Cuyahoga (Trustee, 1998-2001) and Ohio State Bar Associations; State Bar of Michigan; The Florida Bar. ***PRACTICE AREAS:*** Debtor Creditor Law; Reorganizations; Bankruptcy; General Commercial Law.

(This Listing Continued)

McCARTHY, LEBIT, CRYSTAL & LIFFMAN CO., L.P.A., Cleveland—Continued

KIMON P. KARAS, born Ashland, Ohio, March 1, 1952; admitted to bar, 1978, Ohio; 1980, U.S. Tax Court. *Education:* Miami University (A.B., 1974); Ohio Northern University (J.D., 1978); University of Florida (LL.M. in Taxation, 1979). Adjunct Professor of Law in Taxation, Case Western Reserve School of Law, 1992—. *Member:* Greater Cleveland (Member: Taxation Committee, 1982—, Chairman, 1991-1992; Member, 1982— and Chairman, 1991-1992, Estate Planning, Probate and Trust Law Section), Ohio State (Member, Taxation Committee; Secretary, Federal Taxation Committee, 1993-1994; Vice-Chairman, 1995, 1996) and American (Member, Sections on: Taxation, 1982—; Real Property, Probate and Trust Law, 1982—) Bar Associations. (Certified Specialist in Federal Tax Law, Ohio State Bar Association). ***PRACTICE AREAS:*** Taxation Law; Corporate Law; Partnership Law; Estate Planning. ***Email:*** kpk@mccarthylebit.com

DAVID A. SCHAEFER, born Cleveland, Ohio, May 3, 1948; admitted to bar, 1974, Ohio. *Education:* Miami University (B.S., cum laude, 1970); Northwestern University (M.A., 1971); Case Western Reserve University (J.D., 1974). National Moot Court Team, 1972-1973. Listed in Best Lawyers in America, 2003-2004. Named to Ohio Super Lawyers, Cleveland Top 50, 2004, Cincinnati. Associate, Case Western Reserve Law Review, 1972-1973. Instructor, National Institute of Trial Advocacy, 1988—. Guest Lecturer, Trial Practice, Case Western Reserve University Law School, 1989-2002. Author: "Effective Voir Dire--Some Tips for the Practitioner," Litigation Basics, Ohio CLE Institute, 1998-2002; "Avoiding Malpractice Claims: Help Yourself Because Juries Won't," Vol. 60, No. 4, Defense Counsel Journal, October 1993; "Business Torts & Antitrust," Ch. 20, Vol. II, Business Torts (J.D. Zamore Editor 1989); "Low-Cost Shadow Juries," 22 Trial 12, 1986. Co-Author: "Exclusive Arrangements in Health Care: Moving Toward Freedom from the Antitrust Threat?" 33 Federal Bar Journal 327, 1986; "Deposition Strategy, Law and Forms," Vols. 3 and 5, Chapter on Contracts and Corporations, Real Property--Unfair Competition, Matthew Bender, 1981; "Unfair Competition and Antitrust: An Uneasy Synthesis," 1 Litigation Journal, The Ohio Academy of Trial Lawyers 19, Autumn, 1979. Author: "Proving the Economic Value of a Destroyed Business," 2 Litigation Journal, The Ohio Academy of Trial Lawyers, No. 2, Winter, 1982; "Plaintiff's Strategy in Trade Secret Litigation," Litigation 48, American Bar Association, Spring, 1980. Instructor: Research, Writing and Advocacy, 1973-1974 and Civil Procedure, 1977, Case Western Reserve University Law School. Founding Member, Anthony J. Celebrezze Inns of Court. Member, International Association of Defense Counsel. President, Federal Bar Association, Cleveland Chapter, 1992-1993. Chairperson, Merit Selection Panel for Replacement of U.S. Magistrate, 1999. ***REPORTED CASES:*** Grover v. Eli Lilly and Co., N.D. Ohio (1995) 896 F.Supp. 725; Cabot Corp. v. King, 790 F. Supp. 153 (N.D. Ohio, 1992); Cleveland Bar Association v. Tolliver, (1996) 75 Ohio St. 3d 178; Boedeker vs. Rogers (2000), 140 O. App. 3211; In re: Cuyahoga Cty. Asbestos Cases (1998), 127 O. App. 3d 358; Ohio Savings Bank v. H.L. Vokes Co. et al (1989), 54 O.App.3d 68; Anderson et al v. A.C.& S., Inc. (1992), 83 O.App.3d 581. ***PRACTICE AREAS:*** Trial; Contract; Professional Liability; Product Liability; Employment Discrimination; Negligence; Construction. ***Email:*** das@mccarthylebit.com

DAVID L. ROSENZWEIG, born Pottsville, Pennsylvania, June 17, 1939; admitted to bar, 1968, Ohio; 1969, U.S. District Court, Northern District of Ohio. *Education:* Youngstown State University (B.S., 1962); Case Western Reserve Law School (J.D., 1968). Order of the Coif. Member, Moot Court Board and National Moot Court Team, 1966-1967. Editor-in-Chief, Case Western Reserve Law Review, 1967-1968. *Member:* Cleveland and Ohio State Bar Associations. ***PRACTICE AREAS:*** Corporate; Banking and Finance; Real Estate; Hotel and Resort Development; Hotel Franchise Law. ***Email:*** dlr@mccarthylebit.com

PAMELA N. HULTIN, born Washington, D.C., November 8, 1945; admitted to bar, 1973, Colorado; 1979, U.S. Supreme Court; 1989, Ohio; 1990, District of Columbia; 1994, U.S. Tax Court. *Education:* Denison University (B.F.A., 1968); University of Colorado (J.D., 1973). Order of the Coif. Recipient, Alice Robie Resnick Lifetime Achievement in Law Award, 1999. Instructor, National Institute of Trial Advocacy, 1979—. Chairperson, Cleveland Courthouse Academy, 1995-1999. Adjunct Professor, Evidence, Cleveland Marshall Law School, 1994-1998. Adjunct Instructor, Trial Tactics, Case Western Reserve Law School, 2001. Visiting Instructor, University of Colorado Law School, 1976. *Member:* Denver (Vice President, 1983-1984), Cuyahoga County (Member, Board of Trustees, 1993-1995) Ohio State (Member, Council of Delegates, 1993-1995) and American Bar Associations; Ohio Womens Bar Association (President, 1991-1993). ***PRACTICE AREAS:*** Trial Practice; Contracts; Products Liability; Commercial Litigation; Employment Discrimination; Negligence. ***Email:*** pnh@mccarthylebit.com

RICHARD A. RABB, born Cleveland, Ohio, April 30, 1963; admitted to bar, 1990, Ohio; 1996, U.S. District Court, Northern District of Ohio. *Education:* Ohio State University (B.A., 1985); Cleveland-Marshall School of Law (J.D., 1989). *Member:* Cuyahoga County and Ohio State (President, Family Law Section, 2001) Bar Associations. ***PRACTICE AREAS:*** Divorce; Child Custody; Juvenile Law; Antenuptial; Commercial Litigation. ***Email:*** rar@mccarthylebit.com

STUART A. MINTZ, born Cleveland, Ohio, September 16, 1953; admitted to bar, 1978, Ohio; 1979, Florida. *Education:* Ohio University (B.A., 1975); Cleveland Marshall College of Law (J.D., 1978). Adjunct Professor, Cleveland Marshall College of Law. *Member:* The Florida Bar. ***PRACTICE AREAS:*** Commercial Law; Uniform Commercial Code; Bank Regulatory Law; Corporate Law. ***Email:*** sam@mccarthylebit.com

CHARLES P. ROYER, born Huntingdon, Pennsylvania, January 17, 1961; admitted to bar, 1986, Ohio; U.S. District Court, Northern District of Ohio; 1989, U.S. Court of Appeals, Sixth Circuit. *Education:* Indiana University of Pennsylvania (B.A., magna cum laude, 1983); University of Pittsburgh School of Law (J.D., 1985). Staff Member, 1985 and Note Editor, 1986, University of Pittsburgh Law Review. *Member:* Cleveland and Ohio State Bar Associations. ***LANGUAGES:*** French. ***REPORTED CASES:*** In re Investigation of National Union Fire Ins. Co. (1993) 66 Ohio St.3d 81; LiCause v. City of Canton (1989) 42 Ohio St.3d 109; Ross v. Belden Park Co., 2001 Ohio App. LEXIS 1862, Court of Appeals for the Fifth Appellate District, April 16, 2001; Willis v. Peoples, 1997 Ohio App. LEXIS 390, Eighth Appellate District, February 6, 1987; Metropolitan Cablevision v. Cox Cable Cleveland Area, (1992) 78 Ohio App.3d 273; American Indoor Soccer Ass'n. v. Capital, 1993 U.S. Dist. LEXIS 20914, N.D. of Ohio, Nov. 15, 1993. ***PRACTICE AREAS:*** General Business Litigation; Creditors Rights; Land Use and Zoning Litigation; Construction Law. ***Email:*** cpr@mccarthylebit.com

(This Listing Continued)

GLENN R. WILSON, born Akron, Ohio, January 10, 1963; admitted to bar, 1990, Ohio; 1991, U.S. Court of Appeals for the Federal Circuit; U.S. Court of Federal Claims; U.S. Tax Court; 1993, U.S. Supreme Court; 1998, U.S. District Court, Northern District of Ohio. *Education:* Bowling Green State University (B.A., 1986); University of Toledo (J.D., 1989). *Member:* Cleveland Bar Association. ***PRACTICE AREAS:*** Intellectual Property; Litigation; Corporate Law. ***Email:*** grw@mccarthylebit.com

ROBERT T. GLICKMAN, born Cleveland, Ohio, June 14, 1966; admitted to bar, 1992, Ohio; 2001, U.S. District Court, Northern District of Ohio. *Education:* University of North Carolina-Greensboro (B.A., 1988); Case Western Reserve University (J.D., 1992). Adjunct Professor of Law, John Marshall College of Law. Judge, Common Pleas Court of Cuyahoga City, 2001-2004. Special City Prosecutor, Mahoning, 1998-2001. Assistant City Prosecutor, Major Trial Unit, Cuyahoga City, 1993-2001. *Member:* Cleveland, Cuyahoga City and Ohio State Bar Associations; William K. Thomas Inn of Court. ***PRACTICE AREAS:*** Commercial Litigation; Business Litigation; Professional Malpractice Litigation; White Collar Crime; Alternative Dispute Resolution. ***Email:*** rtg@mccarthylebit.com

E. ROGER STEWART, born Houston, Texas, October 19, 1951; admitted to bar, 1998, Ohio. *Education:* University of Texas at Austin (B.A., Economics, magna cum laude, 1974); Catholic University of America (M.A., Accounting, 1979); Cleveland-Marshall College of Law (J.D., magna cum laude, 1997). Phi Beta Kappa. Editor, Cleveland-Marshall Law Review, 1996. *Member:* Cleveland and Ohio State Bar Associations. [Capt., Supply Corps, U.S. Naval Reserve, Retired.]. ***PRACTICE AREAS:*** Taxation Law; Corporate Law; Partnerships; Estate Planning Law. ***Email:*** rstewart@mccarthylebit.com

---

ELLEN R. STEIN, born Cleveland, Ohio, September 4, 1964; admitted to bar, 1998, Ohio and U.S. District Court, Northern District of Ohio. *Education:* The Ohio State University (B.S.B.A., 1986); Cleveland State University (M.B.A., 1991); Cleveland Marshall College of Law (J.D., 1998). Guest Lecturer, Sports and Event Marketing, Tulane University and the LPGA (Ladies Professional Golf Association). *Member:* Cleveland, Cuyahoga County Ohio State and American Bar Associations. ***PRACTICE AREAS:*** Corporate Law; Mergers and Acquisitions; Real Estate; Commercial Transactions; Intellectual Property; Information Technology. ***Email:*** ert@mccarthylebit.com

LESLIE ERIN WARGO, born Sandusky, Ohio, June 11, 1975; admitted to bar, 2000, Ohio, U.S. District Court, Northern District of Ohio and U.S. Court of Appeals, Sixth Circuit. *Education:* University of Akron (B.A., cum laude, 1997); Case Western Reserve University (J.D., 2000). Phi Sigma Alpha. Member, Craven Moot Court Team. Senator, Student Bar Association, 1997-1999. Recipient: Scholar-Athlete Award; Distinguished Oral Advocate Award. Co-Author: "Fair Debt Collection Practices Act Update," OSBA, Debt Collection Reference Manual, Volume 00-04, 2000. Co-Author: "How and Why to use a Focus Group as a part of Trial Preparation, Cleveland Bar Journal, October 2003. *Member:* Cleveland, Ohio State, Federal and American (Member, Litigation and Young Lawyers Section) Bar Associations; Anthony Celebreeze Inn of Court. ***PRACTICE AREAS:*** Business Litigation; Personal Injury; Products Liability. ***Email:*** lew@mccarthylebit.com

KIMBERLY A. BRENNAN, born East Cleveland, Ohio, November 4, 1967; admitted to bar, 1993, Ohio and U.S. District Court, Northern District of Ohio. *Education:* Miami University (B.A., 1990); Case Western Reserve University School of Law (J.D., 1993). Interim Coordinator, Legal Service for American Jewish Congress, 1991. *Member:* Cleveland, Ohio State (Member, Board of Governors, Labor and Employment Section) and Federal Bar Associations; Cleveland Association of Civil Trial Attorneys. ***PRACTICE AREAS:*** Commercial Litigation; Employment Law; Professional Liability; Negligence. ***Email:*** kab@mccarthylebit.com

KATHERINE E. WENSINK, born Dearborn, Michigan, November 13, 1974; admitted to bar, 1999, Michigan; 2000, Iowa and U.S. Court of Appeals, 7th Circuit; 2001, Illinois; 2002, Ohio. *Education:* Purdue University (B.A., 1996); University of Michigan (J.D., 1999). *Member:* Cleveland (Member, Sections on: Estate Planning, Probate and Trust Law), Iowa State, Illinois State, Ohio State and American Bar Associations; State Bar of Michigan. ***PRACTICE AREAS:*** Taxation; Estate Planning; Probate; Pension and Profit Sharing Plans. ***Email:*** kew@mccarthylebit.com

MATTHEW B. MURPHY, born Cleveland, Ohio, June 6, 1973; admitted to bar, 2002, Ohio; 2004, U.S. District Court, Northern District of Ohio. *Education:* Cleveland State University (B.A., 1999); Cleveland-Marshall College of Law (J.D., magna cum laude, 2002). Former Associate, Cavitch Familo Durkin & Frutkin. ***PRACTICE AREAS:*** Corporate Law (40%); Commercial Banking (30%); Real Estate (30%). ***Email:*** mbm@mccarthylebit.com

ERIC C. POWELL, born Kalamazoo, Michigan, September 7, 1975; admitted to bar, 2001, Ohio; 2002, U.S. District Court, Southern District of Ohio and U.S. Tax Court. *Education:* The Ohio State University (B.A., 1998); Ohio Northern University (J.D., 2001); Georgetown University (LL.M., Taxation, 2002). Order of the Barristers. Member, Moot Court National Tax Competition. Associate Justice, Moot Court Executive Board. Former Associate, Miller Mast Ltd. *Member:* Holmes County, Ohio State and American Bar Associations. ***PRACTICE AREAS:*** Taxation; Corporate Law; Commercial Banking; Real Estate. ***Email:*** ecp@mccarthylebit.com

OF COUNSEL

WILTON S. SOGG, born Cleveland, Ohio, May 28, 1935; admitted to bar, 1960, Ohio; 1969, U.S. Supreme Court and U.S. Tax Court; 1970, Florida. *Education:* Dartmouth College (A.B., 1956); Harvard Law School (J.D., 1959). Fulbright Fellow, University of London, (1959-1960). Phi Beta Kappa. Recipient, Executive Award, The Graduate School of Credit and Financial Management at the London School of Business Studies, 1976. Editor, Harvard Law Review, 1957-1959. Listed in The Best Lawyers in America-Corporate Law. Adjunct Professor, Cleveland Marshall College of Law, 1960—. Lecturer on Law, Harvard

(This Listing Continued)

Law School, 1978-1979. *Member:* Ohio State Bar Association; The Florida Bar. ***PRACTICE AREAS:*** Estate Planning; Tax Law; Corporate Law; Real Estate. ***Email:*** wss@mccarthylebit.com

JON FITZPATRICK, born Youngstown, Ohio, June 1, 1936; admitted to bar, 1977, Ohio. *Education:* The Ohio State University (B.S.B.A., Economics, 1960); Cleveland Marshall College of Law (J.D., 1977). Certified Public Accountant, Ohio, 1964. Author: "Choosing The Best Retirement Plan For The Closely-Held Company," Taxation For Lawyers, September-October, 1985. *Member:* Ohio State and American Bar Associations; Ohio Society of Certified Public Accountants; American Institute of Certified Public Accountants; The Estate Planning Council of Cleveland. ***PRACTICE AREAS:*** Estate Planning; Trusts; Estate Administration; Business Transactions; Qualified Plans. ***Email:*** jonfitzesq@aol.com

MCCRAY, MUZILLA, SMITH & MEYERS CO., L.P.A.

CLEVELAND, OHIO

(See Elyria)

General Civil Practice, Corporate, Personal Injury, Medical Malpractice, Probate and Estate Planning, Labor and Employment, Government, Real Estate, Insurance Defense, Health, Tax, Civil Litigation, Product Liability, Communications and Copyright Issues and Environment. Trial and Appellate Practice in all Courts.

MCDONALD HOPKINS CO., LPA

Established in 1921

600 SUPERIOR AVENUE, E.
SUITE 2100
CLEVELAND, OHIO 44114-2653
Telephone: 216-348-5400
Telecopier: 216-348-5474
Email: info@mcdonaldhopkins.com
URL: http://www.mcdonaldhopkins.com

West Palm Beach, Florida Office: McDonald Hopkins Co., PA, One Clearlake Centre, 250 Australian Avenue S., Suite 700, 33401-5007. Telephone: 561-472-7510. Fax: 561-472-2975.

Dennis, Massachusetts Office: 956 Main Street, 02638. Telephone: 508-385-5227. Fax: 508-385-4355.

Columbus, Ohio Office: 41 South High Street, Suite 3650, 43215. Telephone: 614-458-0025. Fax: 614-458-0028.

General Civil Trial and Appellate Practice. Corporate, Taxation, Pension and Profit Sharing, Professional Corporations, Insurance, Securities, Estate Planning, Probate, Real Estate, Family Law, Banking, Partnership, Employment and Labor Relations, Equipment Leasing, Bankruptcy, Communications, Computer Law, Health and Hospital Law.

LAW FIRM ALLIANCES/ASSOCIATIONS: ***INTERNATIONAL LAWYERS NETWORK***

SCOTT R. AUSTIN, born Columbus, Ohio, 1956; admitted to bar, 1984, Florida and U.S. District Court, Southern District of Florida; 1986, U.S. District Court, Middle District of Florida; 1994, U.S. Court of Appeals, Eleventh Circuit. *Education:* Ohio University (B.S., summa cum laude, 1979; M.B.A., 1981); Georgetown University Law Center (J.D., 1984). (Resident, West Plam Beach, Florida Office). ***PRACTICE AREAS:*** Intellectual Property; Litigation; Patents. ***Email:*** saustin@mcdonaldhopkins.com

PETER M. BERNHARDT, born New York, N.Y., 1964; admitted to bar, 1993, Florida; U.S. District Court, Southern and Middle Districts of Florida. *Education:* University of Florida (B.A., 1988); Nova Southeastern University (J.D., 1992). (Resident, West Plam Beach, Florida Office). ***LANGUAGES:*** German. ***PRACTICE AREAS:*** Commercial Litigation; Real Estate Litigation; Sports Law. ***Email:*** pbernhardt@mcdonaldhopkins.com

PATRICK J. BERRY, born Cleveland, Ohio, 1964; admitted to bar, 1989, Ohio. *Education:* Bowling Green State University (B.S., 1986); Georgetown University Law Center (J.D., cum laude, 1989). ***PRACTICE AREAS:*** Mergers and Acquisitions; Securities; Corporate Law. ***Email:*** pberry@mcdonaldhopkins.com

JEFFREY P. CONSOLO, born Mansfield, Ohio, 1953; admitted to bar, 1978, Kentucky; 1979, Ohio; 1984, Florida. *Education:* Western Kentucky University (B.S., 1975); University of Louisville (J.D., 1978). ***PRACTICE AREAS:*** Estate Planning Law; Probate Law; Probate Litigation. ***Email:*** jconsolo@mcdonaldhopkins.com

JEROME W. COOK, born Wickliffe, Ohio, 1958; admitted to bar, 1986, Ohio. *Education:* Case Western Reserve University (B.A., History, 1981); Cleveland State University (M.A., 1985); Cleveland-Marshall College of Law (J.D., magna cum laude, 1986). Cleveland-Marshall Law Review. ***PRACTICE AREAS:*** Litigation; Construction Law; Real Estate; Fidelity and Surety. ***Email:*** jcook@mcdonaldhopkins.com

RICHARD S. COOPER, born Whittier, California, 1956; admitted to bar, 1981, Ohio. *Education:* Syracuse University (A.B., cum laude, 1978); Georgetown University (J.D., cum laude, 1981). *Member:* Cleveland (Member, Health Law Section), Ohio State (Chair, Health Care Law Committee, 1994-1996; Member, Payment Issues, Labor and Professional Rights and Licensure Subcommittees) and American (Member, Forum Committee on Health Law) Bar Associations; American Health Lawyers Association. ***PRACTICE AREAS:*** Health and Hospital Law; Professional Corporations Law. ***Email:*** rcooper@mcdonaldhopkins.com

ANNE T. CORRIGAN, born Cleveland, Ohio, 1963; admitted to bar, 1992, Ohio. *Education:* John Carroll University School of Business (B.S., magna cum laude, 1986); Case Western Reserve University (J.D., magna cum laude, 1992). Order of the Coif. Case Western Reserve University Law Review. ***PRACTICE AREAS:*** Commercial Transactions; Real Estate Law; Commercial Banking; Mergers, Acquisitions and Divestitures; Corporate Law. ***Email:*** acorrigan@mcdonaldhopkins.com

(This Listing Continued)

LEONARD M. COSENTINO, born Garfield Heights, Ohio, 1962; admitted to bar, 1987, Ohio. *Education:* Grove City College (B.A., summa cum laude, 1984); Case Western Reserve University, School of Law (J.D., magna cum laude, 1987). ***PRACTICE AREAS:*** Business Law. ***Email:*** lcosentino@mcdonaldhopkins.com

JAMES A. DIMITRIJEVS, born Cleveland, Ohio, 1967; admitted to bar, 1994, Ohio. *Education:* John Carroll University (B.A., 1989); Cleveland-Marshall College of Law (J.D., 1994). ***PRACTICE AREAS:*** Intellectual Property. ***Email:*** jdimitrijevs@mcdonaldhopkins.com

ANTHONY J. DIVENERE, born Bari, Italy, 1941; admitted to bar, 1967, Ohio; 1968, U.S. District Court, Northern District of Ohio; 1977, U.S. Court of Appeals, Sixth Circuit and U.S. Supreme Court. *Education:* John Carroll University (A.B., 1964); The Ohio State University (J.D., 1967). ***PRACTICE AREAS:*** Corporate Litigation; Securities Litigation. ***Email:*** adivenere@mcdonaldhopkins.com

ROBERT H. EARP, III, born Dayton, Ohio, 1970; admitted to bar, 1996, Ohio. *Education:* University of Dayton (B.S., 1993; J.D., 1996). ***PRACTICE AREAS:*** Intellectual Property; Patents; Trademarks; Copyrights. ***Email:*** rearp@mcdonaldhopkins.com

PAUL N. EDWARDS, born Topeka, Kansas, 1953; admitted to bar, 1979, Ohio; 1990, New York. *Education:* The Ohio State University (B.S., cum laude, 1974); Cleveland-Marshall College of Law (J.D., 1979). Cleveland State Law Review. ***PRACTICE AREAS:*** Securities; Corporate; Antitrust. ***Email:*** pedwards@mcdonaldhopkins.com

THEODORE J. ESBORN, born Cleveland, Ohio, 1952; admitted to bar, 1979, Ohio; 1980, U.S. District Court, Northern District of Ohio; 1983, U.S. Court of Appeals, Sixth Circuit. *Education:* Washington & Jefferson College (B.A., 1974); Case Western Reserve University (J.D., 1979). ***PRACTICE AREAS:*** Environmental Law. ***Email:*** tesborn@mcdonaldhopkins.com

BRYAN H. FALK, born Strongsville, Ohio, 1972; admitted to bar, 1997, Ohio. *Education:* Miami University (B.A., Economics, Political Science, 1987); Case Western Reserve University (J.D., cum laude, 1997). ***PRACTICE AREAS:*** Corporate Law; Real Estate; Finance. ***Email:*** bfalk@mcdonaldhopkins.com

RICHARD C. FARRIN, born 1947; admitted to bar, 1972, Ohio; U.S. Supreme Court. *Education:* Miami University (B.A., 1969); The Ohio State University (J.D., cum laude, 1972). (Resident, Columbus, Ohio Office). ***PRACTICE AREAS:*** Local Taxation; State Tax Controversies; State Taxation. ***Email:*** rfarrin@mcdonaldhopkins.com

G. ANDREW GARDNER, born Cleveland, Ohio, 1970; admitted to bar, 1996, Ohio. *Education:* The College of Wooster (B.A., with honors, 1992); The Ohio State University (J.D., with honors, 1996). Phi Beta Kappa. Order of the Coif. ***PRACTICE AREAS:*** Corporate Law; Mergers and Acquisitions; Finance; Leases and Leasing; Real Estate. ***Email:*** agardner@mcdonaldhopkins.com

STEVEN L. GARDNER, born Cleveland, Ohio, 1950; admitted to bar, 1976, Ohio; 1977, U.S. District Court, Northern and Southern Districts of Ohio; 1980, U.S. Supreme Court; 1984, U.S. Court of Appeals, Sixth Circuit; 1985, U.S. Tax Court; 2004, Florida; 2005, U.S. District Court, Southern District of Florida; U.S. Court of Appeals, Eleventh Circuit; Supreme Court of Ohio. *Education:* The Ohio State University (B.S., 1972; J.D., cum laude, 1976); Case Western Reserve University (M.S.M., 1973). ***PRACTICE AREAS:*** Civil Trial Practice; Business Litigation; Unfair Competition; Trade Secrets; Securities Litigation; Contract Litigation; Health Litigation. ***Email:*** sgardner@mcdonaldhopkins.com

VICTOR T. GERACI, born Cleveland, Ohio, 1963; admitted to bar, 1988, Ohio; 1989, U.S. District Court, Northern District of Ohio. *Education:* Case Western Reserve University (B.A., 1985; J.D., 1988). ***PRACTICE AREAS:*** Labor and Employment; Litigation. ***Email:*** vgeraci@mcdonaldhopkins.com

CARL J. GRASSI, born Cleveland, Ohio, 1959; admitted to bar, 1984, Ohio. *Education:* John Carroll University (B.S.B.A., 1981); Cleveland Marshall College of Law (J.D., cum laude, 1984). Certified Public Accountant, Ohio, 1985. ***PRACTICE AREAS:*** Business Law; Mergers and Acquisitions; Taxation; Employee Benefits; Corporate Law; Employee Stock Ownership Plans. ***Email:*** cgrassi@mcdonaldhopkins.com

JAMES A. GRIFFITH, born Cleveland, Ohio, 1933; admitted to bar, 1958, Ohio. *Education:* Case Western Reserve University (B.B.A., 1954; J.D., 1958). ***PRACTICE AREAS:*** Real Estate Law; Corporate Law; Business Law; Mergers and Acquisitions. ***Email:*** jgriffith@mcdonaldhopkins.com

DAVID K. HALES, born Rochester, New York, 1969; admitted to bar, 1996, Ohio. *Education:* State University of New York at Binghamton (B.S., 1991); Boston University School of Law (J.D., magna cum laude, 1996). ***PRACTICE AREAS:*** Real Estate. ***Email:*** dhales@mcdonaldhopkins.com

JEFFREY R. HUNTSBERGER, born Canton, Ohio, 1954; admitted to bar, 1980, Ohio. *Education:* Valparaiso University (B.A., 1977); Case Western Reserve University (J.D., 1980). Order of the Coif. ***PRACTICE AREAS:*** Business Law; Real Estate Law; Secured Transactions; Lender Representation. ***Email:*** jhuntsberger@mcdonaldhopkins.com

BRIAN J. JEREB, born Cleveland, Ohio, 1958; admitted to bar, 1983, Ohio; 1987, U.S. District Court, Northern District of Ohio. *Education:* John Carroll University (B.A., magna cum laude, 1980); University of Toledo College of Law (J.D., cum laude, 1983). Alpha Sigma Nu Honor Society. Order of the Coif. ***PRACTICE AREAS:*** Estate Planning; Probate. ***Email:*** bjereb@mcdonaldhopkins.com

DAVID M. KALL, born Cleveland, Ohio, 1967; admitted to bar, 1993, Ohio. *Education:* Ohio State University (B.A., summa cum laude, honors and distinction in Political Science, 1989; J.D., with honors, 1993). ***PRACTICE AREAS:*** Tax; Business. ***Email:*** dkall@mcdonaldhopkins.com

BERNARD L. KARR, born Conneaut, Ohio, 1947; admitted to bar, 1973, Ohio; 1975, U.S. Tax Court. *Education:* Bowling Green State University (B.S., in Ed., 1969); The Ohio State University (J.D., cum laude, 1973); New York University (LL.M. in Taxation, 1978). Author of numerous tax and estate planning articles. Manager, Estate Planning Department; Chairman, F. Scholl Foundation. Trustee, Bowling Green State University Foundation. Past Chairman, Church of the Savior Foundation. Director, Boys and Girls Clubs of

(This Listing Continued)

McDONALD HOPKINS CO., LPA, Cleveland—Continued

Cleveland. Director, Rock and Roll Hall of Fame and Museum. Trustee, D.E. Mitchell Foundation. *Member:* Cleveland and Ohio State Bar Associations. ***PRACTICE AREAS:*** Estate Planning; Probate; Charitable Organizations Law; Family Business Successions; Taxation. ***Email:*** bkarr@mcdonaldhopkins.com

JEFFREY B. KEIPER, born Cleveland, Ohio, 1964; admitted to bar, 1992, Washington; 1994, Ohio. *Education:* College of Wooster (B.A., honors in English, 1986); Indiana University (M.A., English, 1989); The Ohio State University College of Law (J.D., with honors, 1992). Phi Beta Kappa. The Ohio State University Law Journal. ***PRACTICE AREAS:*** Labor Management Law; Equal Employment Opportunity Law; Arbitration; Employment Litigation; Personnel Policies; Personnel Training. ***Email:*** jkeiper@mcdonaldhopkins.com

ROGER L. KLEINMAN, born Cleveland, Ohio, 1951; admitted to bar, 1984, Ohio; 1985, U.S. District Court, Northern District of Ohio and U.S. Court of Appeals, Sixth Circuit. *Education:* The Ohio State University (B.A., cum laude, 1973); Cleveland Marshall College of Law (J.D., cum laude, 1984). Phi Beta Kappa. Cleveland Marshall Law Review. ***PRACTICE AREAS:*** Litigation; Family Law; Appellate Practice. ***Email:*** rkleinman@mcdonaldhopkins.com

MARK D. KLIMEK, born Columbus, Ohio, 1963; admitted to bar, 1993, Ohio. *Education:* Miami University (B.S., 1987); The Ohio State University (J.D., 1993). Certified Public Accountant, Ohio, 1989. ***PRACTICE AREAS:*** Business Law; Mergers and Acquisitions; Tax Law; Business Transactions. ***Email:*** mklimek@mcdonaldhopkins.com

ANTHONY D. KONKOLY, born Cleveland, Ohio; admitted to bar, 1986, Ohio. *Education:* University of Virginia (B.S., with honors, 1982); Case Western Reserve University (J.D., magna cum laude, 1986). ***PRACTICE AREAS:*** General Business and Commercial Law; Mergers and Acquisitions; Litigation Management; Antitrust. ***Email:*** akonkoly@mcdonaldhopkins.com

PETER KRAGULJAC, born Cleveland, Ohio, 1966; admitted to bar, 1994, Ohio, U.S. District Court, Northern District of Ohio and U.S. Court of Appeals, Federal Circuit; registered to practice before the U.S. Patent and Trademark Office. *Education:* The Ohio State University (B.S., 1989); Cleveland State University, Cleveland-Marshall College of Law (J.D., 1994). ***PRACTICE AREAS:*** Litigation; Intellectual Property; Patents, Trademarks, Copyrights. ***Email:*** pkraguljac@mcdonaldhopkins.com

JOSEPH J. LoPRESTI, JR., born Cleveland, Ohio, 1947; admitted to bar, 1973, Ohio. *Education:* University of Notre Dame (B.B.A., 1969); The Ohio State University (J.D., 1973). (Managing Partner). ***PRACTICE AREAS:*** Corporate Law; Mergers and Acquisitions; Commercial Loans. ***Email:*** jlopresti@mcdonaldhopkins.com

DAN L. MAKEE, born Cleveland, Ohio, 1960; admitted to bar, 1985, Ohio; 1988, U.S. District Court, Northern District of Ohio; 1993, U.S. Court of Appeals, Sixth Circuit; 2001, U.S. District Court, Southern District of Ohio. *Education:* Denison University (A.B., 1982); Case Western Reserve University (J.D., 1985). Law Clerk to Hon. Ralph S. Locher, Supreme Court of Ohio. *Member:* Cleveland and Ohio State Bar Associations; Anthony J. Celebrezze Inn of Court. ***PRACTICE AREAS:*** Litigation; Business Litigation; Employment Litigation; ERISA Litigation. ***Email:*** dmakee@mcdonaldhopkins.com

SEAN D. MALLOY, born Evansville, Illinois, 1968; admitted to bar, 1992, Illinois; 2000, Ohio. *Education:* University of Miami (B.A., cum laude, 1990); University of Virginia School of Law (J.D., 1993). ***PRACTICE AREAS:*** Bankruptcy. ***Email:*** smalloy@mcdonaldhopkins.com

TYLER L. MATHEWS, born Marshall, Michigan, 1968; admitted to bar, 1994, Ohio; 1996, U.S. District Court, Northern and Southern Districts of Ohio and U.S. Court of Appeals, Sixth Circuit; 2002, Michigan. *Education:* Albion College (B.A., magna cum laude, 1991); Cleveland-Marshall College of Law (J.D., magna cum laude, 1994). Judicial Clerk, Hon. John R. Evans, Third District Court of Appeals, 1994-1995. *Member:* Cleveland, Ohio State and American Bar Associations. ***PRACTICE AREAS:*** Litigation. ***Email:*** tmathews@mcdonaldhopkins.com

GEORGE L. McGAUGHEY, JR., born Athens, Georgia, 1945; admitted to bar, 1975, Ohio; 1976, U.S. District Court, Northern District of Ohio. *Education:* Yale University (B.A., 1967); Case Western Reserve University (J.D., 1975). Order of the Coif. Case Western Reserve Law Review. *Member:* Anthony J. Celebrezze Inn of Court (Master Bencher). ***PRACTICE AREAS:*** Commercial Litigation; Securities Arbitration; Noncompete Litigation; Trade Secrets; Litigation; Construction Litigation; Arbitration. ***Email:*** gmcgaughey@mcdonaldhopkins.com

MICHAEL J. MEANEY, born Washington, D.C., 1952; admitted to bar, 1977, Ohio. *Education:* Georgetown University (A.B., cum laude, 1974); The Ohio State University College of Law (J.D., summa cum laude, 1977). ***PRACTICE AREAS:*** Business Law; Corporate Law; Securities; Mergers and Acquisitions. ***Email:*** mmeaney@mcdonaldhopkins.com

JOHN T. METZGER, born Miami, Florida, 1960; admitted to bar, 1986, Florida and U.S. District Court, Middle and Southern Districts of Florida. *Education:* Florida State University (B.A., summa cum laude, 1982); University of Pennsylvania (J.D., 1985). (Board Certified Real Estate Lawyer, Florida Bar Board of Legal Specialization and Education-)(Resident, West Palm Beach, Florida Office). ***PRACTICE AREAS:*** Business Litigation; Real Estate Litigation. ***Email:*** jmetzger@mcdonaldhopkins.com

JOHN T. MULLIGAN, born Cleveland, Ohio, 1946; admitted to bar, 1974, Ohio; 1975, U.S. District Court, Northern District of Ohio; 1982, U.S. Tax Court. *Education:* University of Notre Dame (A.B., cum laude, 1968); Case Western Reserve University (J.D., 1974). Editor, Case Western Reserve Law Review, 1973-1974. ***PRACTICE AREAS:*** Health Law; Corporate Law. ***Email:*** jmulligan@mcdonaldhopkins.com

WILLIAM J. O'NEILL, born Staten Island, New York, 1960; admitted to bar, 1985, Ohio; 1986, U.S. District Court, Northern District of Ohio and U.S. Court of Appeals, Sixth Circuit; 2001, U.S. District Court, Southern District of Ohio. *Education:* Assumption College (B.A., cum laude, 1982); The Ohio State University (J.D., with honors, 1985). *Member:*

(This Listing Continued)

Defense Research Institute; National Health Lawyers Association. ***PRACTICE AREAS:*** Employment Litigation; Health Care Litigation; Commercial Litigation; Class Actions. ***Email:*** woneill@mcdonaldhopkins.com

SCOTT N. OPINCAR, born Parma, Ohio, 1968; admitted to bar, 1994, Ohio; 1995, U.S. District Court, Northern District of Ohio. *Education:* University of Akron (B.A., 1991); Cleveland Marshall College of Law (J.D., 1994). ***PRACTICE AREAS:*** Bankruptcy; Creditors Rights; Business Reorganization. ***Email:*** sopincar@mcdonaldhopkins.com

R. JEFFREY POLLOCK, born San Francisco, California, 1946; admitted to bar, 1976, Ohio and Michigan. *Education:* DePauw University (B.A., 1968); Harvard University (M.T.S., 1971); Northeastern University (J.D., 1976). ***PRACTICE AREAS:*** Litigation; Business Torts; Intellectual Property. ***Email:*** jpollock@mcdonaldhopkins.com

MICHAEL G. RILEY, born Cleveland, Ohio, 1956; admitted to bar, 1987, Ohio and U.S. Tax Court. *Education:* College of the Holy Cross (B.A., 1978); Brown University (M.A.T., 1980); Syracuse University College of Law (J.D., summa cum laude, 1987); Case Western Reserve University (LL.M., Tax, 1996). Justinian Society. Order of the Coif. ***PRACTICE AREAS:*** Employee Benefits Law; Estate Planning Law; Tax Law. ***Email:*** mriley@mcdonaldhopkins.com

SHAWN M. RILEY, born Cleveland, Ohio, 1961; admitted to bar, 1986, Ohio. *Education:* Kent State University (B.A., magna cum laude, 1983); Case Western Reserve University (J.D., magna cum laude, 1986). Order of the Coif. ***PRACTICE AREAS:*** Bankruptcy; Commercial; Corporate. ***Email:*** sriley@mcdonaldhopkins.com

JEAN R. ROBERTSON, born Ashtabula, Ohio, 1965; admitted to bar, 1990, Pennsylvania; 1998, Ohio. *Education:* The Ohio State University (B.A., cum laude, 1986; J.D., 1990). ***PRACTICE AREAS:*** Bankruptcy; Insolvency; Creditors Rights; Commercial Litigation. ***Email:*** jrobertson@mcdonaldhopkins.com

DOUGLAS B. SCHNEE, born Philadelphia, Pennsylvania, 1969; admitted to bar, 1994, Ohio; 1997, U.S. District Court, Northern District of Ohio, 1998, U.S. Court of Appeals, Sixth Circuit; 2000, U.S. District Court, Southern District of Ohio; 2002, U.S. District Court, Northern District of Indiana. *Education:* Tulane University (B.A., 1991); Case Western Reserve University (J.D., cum laude, 1994). Law Clerk, Judge Stephen R. Shaw, Court of Appeals of Ohio, Third Appellate District, 1994-1996. ***PRACTICE AREAS:*** Employment Litigation; Commercial Law; Litigation. ***Email:*** dschnee@mcdonaldhopkins.com

ROGER L. SHUMAKER, born Auburn, Indiana, 1950; admitted to bar, 1976, Indiana and Ohio. *Education:* Manchester College (B.A., 1972); Case Western Reserve University (J.D., 1976). Phi Alpha Delta. ***PRACTICE AREAS:*** Estate Planning Law; Probate Law; Closely Held Business Law. ***Email:*** rshumaker@mcdonaldhopkins.com

MICHELE SMOLIN, born Pittsburgh, Pennsylvania, 1960; admitted to bar, 1992, Ohio; 1993, Pennsylvania; 1994, U.S. District Court, Western District of Pennsylvania; 1996, U.S. District Court, Northern District of Ohio. *Education:* Carlow College (B.A., cum laude, 1982); Case Western Reserve University (J.D., 1992). Order of Barristers. Member, National Moot Court Team. ***PRACTICE AREAS:*** Civil Litigation; Commercial Law; Employment Litigation. ***Email:*** msmolin@mcdonaldhopkins.com

MICHAEL L. SNYDER, born Cuyahoga Falls, Ohio, 1961; admitted to bar, 1988, Ohio. *Education:* Brigham Young University (B.A., 1985); George Washington University (J.D., 1988). ***LANGUAGES:*** Spanish. ***PRACTICE AREAS:*** Commercial Litigation. ***Email:*** msnyder@mcdonaldhopkins.com

GLENN D. SOUTHWORTH, born Poughkeepsie, New York, 1965; admitted to bar, 1991, Maryland; 1993, Ohio; 1994, U.S. District Court, Northern District of Ohio. *Education:* University of Maryland (B.S., 1988); The American University (J.D., 1991). ***PRACTICE AREAS:*** Civil Litigation. ***Email:*** gsouthworth@mcdonaldhopkins.com

JAMES E. STIEF, born Akron, Ohio, 1970; admitted to bar, 1997, Ohio. *Education:* John Carroll University (B.S., cum laude, 1992); University of Notre Dame (J.D., cum laude, 1997). ***PRACTICE AREAS:*** Commercial Finance; Mergers and Acquisitions; Venture Capital. ***Email:*** jstief@mcdonaldhopkins.com

JAMES M. STONE, born Columbus, Ohio, 1952; admitted to bar, 1986, Ohio; 2004, Michigan. *Education:* The Ohio State University (B.A., 1976); Cleveland-Marshall College of Law (J.D., summa cum laude, 1986). Recipient: West Hornbook Award Highest Academic Average in Class; Frew Scholarship for Achievement in Labor Law; William K. Thomas Award; Jaeger Award. Cleveland State Law Review. Contributing Editor, "The Developing Labor Law." *Member:* American Bar Association (Committee on Development of the Law Under the NLRA and Committee on Railway and Airline Labor Law). ***PRACTICE AREAS:*** Labor and Employment Practices Law. ***Email:*** jstone@mcdonaldhopkins.com

DALE R. VLASEK, born Cleveland, Ohio, 1948; admitted to bar, 1982, Wisconsin and Iowa; 1987, Ohio. *Education:* Cleveland State University (B.A., 1970; M.A., 1972); University of Iowa (Ph.D., 1978; J.D., with high distinction, 1982). Order of the Coif. ***PRACTICE AREAS:*** ERISA; Pension and Profit Sharing Law. ***Email:*** dvlasek@mcdonaldhopkins.com

KENNETH J. WALSH, born Cleveland, Ohio, 1945; admitted to bar, 1976, Ohio. *Education:* College of the Holy Cross (A.B., 1967); Case Western Reserve University (J.D., 1973). ***PRACTICE AREAS:*** Civil Litigation; Business Litigation; Civil Appeals. ***Email:*** kwalsh@mcdonaldhopkins.com

DAVID D. WATSON, born Cleveland, Ohio; admitted to bar, 1994, Ohio. *Education:* Harvard University (A.B., 1986); Georgetown University (J.D., 1993). ***PRACTICE AREAS:*** Mergers and Acquisitions; Corporate. ***Email:*** dwatson@mcdonaldhopkins.com

JOHN M. WIRTSHAFTER, born Cleveland, Ohio, 1959; admitted to bar, 1984, Ohio and U.S. Court of Appeals, Sixth Circuit. *Education:* Indiana University (B.S., cum laude, 1981); Case Western Reserve University (J.D., 1984). ***PRACTICE AREAS:*** Employee Benefits; Executive Compensation. ***Email:*** jwirtshafter@mcdonaldhopkins.com

MICHAEL W. WISE, born Cleveland, Ohio, 1962; admitted to bar, 1990, Ohio and District of Columbia. *Education:* Grove City College (B.A., with highest honors, 1984);

(This Listing Continued)

Case Western Reserve University (J.D., cum laude, 1990). *PRACTICE AREAS:* Government Relations; Legislative Practice; Public Law; Public Finance. *Email:* mwise@mcdonaldhopkins.com

JANE MARIE PINE WOOD, born Midland, Texas, 1962; admitted to bar, 1987, Tennessee; 1988, Ohio; 1993, Massachusetts. *Education:* Texas A & M University (B.A., summa cum laude, 1983); Vanderbilt University (J.D., 1987). Phi Kappa Phi. Vanderbilt Journal of Transnational Law. (Resident, Dennis, Massachusetts Office). *PRACTICE AREAS:* Health Care Law. *Email:* jwood@mcdonaldhopkins.com

THOMAS M. ZAINO, born Xenia, Ohio, 1964; admitted to bar, 1989, Ohio. *Education:* University of Cincinnati (B.B.A., 1986); The Ohio State University (J.D., 1989). *PRACTICE AREAS:* State Taxation. *Email:* tzaino@mcdonaldhopkins.com

CHARLES B. ZELLMER, born Cleveland, Ohio, 1947; admitted to bar, 1972, Ohio; 1973, U.S. District Court, Northern District of Ohio; 1980, U.S. Court of Appeals, Sixth Circuit; 1983, U.S. Tax Court. *Education:* Hamilton College (B.A., 1969); Case Western Reserve University (J.D., 1972). *PRACTICE AREAS:* Business Law; Real Estate; Estate Planning; Successions. *Email:* czellmer@mcdonaldhopkins.com

---

GEORGE J. ASIMOU, born Cleveland, Ohio, 1978; (admission pending). *Education:* Johns Hopkins University (B.A., with honors, 2000); Case Western Reserve University School of Law (J.D., Dean's Scholar, 2005). *PRACTICE AREAS:* Labor and Employment; Labor Law; Employment Litigation. *Email:* gasimou@mcdonaldhopkins.com

ROBERT C. BARAONA, born Parma, Ohio; admitted to bar, 1998, Ohio. *Education:* Ohio University (B.S., Chemistry, 1994); The Ohio State University (J.D., 1998). *PRACTICE AREAS:* Intellectual Property; Patent Prosecution; Trademark Prosecution; Patent Licensing. *Email:* Rbaraona@mcdonaldhopkins.com

TODD A. BENNI, born Kearney, Nebraska, 1971; admitted to bar, 1999, Pennsylvania; registered to practice before U.S. Patent and Trademark Office (Not admitted in Ohio). *Education:* Purdue University (B.S.I.E., 1995); University of Pittsburgh (J.D., cum laude, 1998). (Attorney). *PRACTICE AREAS:* Litigation; Intellectual Property; Patent Prosecution; Trademarks; Copyrights. *Email:* tbenni@mcdonaldhopkins.com

M. JOHN BURGESS, born Willoughby, Ohio, 1974; admitted to bar, 2002, Ohio; 2005, Florida. *Education:* University of Cincinnati (B.A., cum laude, 1997); Cleveland-Marshall College of Law (J.D., magna cum laude, 2002); Case Western Reserve University (LL.M., Taxation, 2003). *PRACTICE AREAS:* Tax Law; Business Law; Mergers and Acquisitions. *Email:* jburgess@mcdonaldhopkins.com

RICHARD W. CLINE, born Piscataway, New Jersey, 1969; admitted to bar, 1997, Ohio. *Education:* Rutgers University (B.A., 1992); University of Florida, College of Law (J.D., with honors, 1997). *PRACTICE AREAS:* Commercial Litigation. *Email:* rcline@mcdonaldhopkins.com

DAVID B. CUPAR, born Cleveland, Ohio, 1974; admitted to bar, 1999, Ohio; U.S. District Court, Northern and Southern Districts of Ohio, U.S. District Court, Eastern District of Michigan and U.S. Court of Appeals, Federal Circuit; registered to practice before U.S. Patent and Trademark Office. *Education:* Case Western Reserve University (B.S., cum laude, 1996; J.D., cum laude, 1999). *PRACTICE AREAS:* Intellectual Property; Litigation; Patents; Trademarks; Copyrights; Trade Secrets. *Email:* dcupar@mcdonaldhopkins.com

MAURA S. CURRAN, born Youngstown, Ohio, 1962; admitted to bar, 2000, Ohio; 2002, Florida. *Education:* Kent State University (B.A., 1984); Cleveland-Marshall College of Law (J.D., 2000). (Resident, West Plam Beach, Florida Office). *PRACTICE AREAS:* Real Estate. *Email:* mcurran@mcdonaldhopkins.com

SHERRI L. DAHL, born Columbus, Ohio, 1968; admitted to bar, 2001, Ohio. *Education:* University of Redlands (B.S., 1997); Ohio State University (J.D., 2000). *PRACTICE AREAS:* Bankruptcy; Insolvency; Creditors Rights; Commercial Litigation. *Email:* sdahl@mcdonaldhopkins.com

TARA C. DEVORE, admitted to bar, 2002, Ohio. *Education:* University of Akron (B.S., 1998; M.A., Tax, 2001; J.D., 2001). *PRACTICE AREAS:* Employee Benefits. *Email:* tdevore@mcdonaldhopkins.com

JOHN D. FABIAN, born Columbus, Ohio, 1974; admitted to bar, 2002, Ohio. *Education:* Stanford University (B.A., with honors, 1997); Georgetown University (J.D., 2002). *PRACTICE AREAS:* Litigation. *Email:* jfabian@mcdonaldhopkins.com

JULIE A. FISCHER, born Cleveland, Ohio, May 26, 1971; admitted to bar, 1999, Ohio; U.S. District Court, Northern District of Ohio. *Education:* Kent State University (B.A., 1994); Cleveland-Marshall College of Law (J.D., 1998); Case Western Reserve University (LL.M., 2005). *PRACTICE AREAS:* Estate Planning; Probate. *Email:* jfischer@mcdonaldhopkins.com

SUSAN F. GEORGE, born North Canton, Ohio, 1979; admitted to bar, 2004, Ohio. *Education:* Case Western Reserve University (B.A., cum laude, 2001; J.D., 2004). *LANGUAGES:* French. *PRACTICE AREAS:* Corporate; Securities; Real Estate. *Email:* sgeorge@mcdonaldhopkins.com

MARIA-ALEXA PILAR GUEVARA, born Livingston, New Jersey, 1975; admitted to bar, 2002, Florida; U.S. District Court, Middle District of Florida. *Education:* University of Notre Dame (B.B.A., 1997); University of Florida (J.D., 2002). (Resident, West Plam Beach, Florida Office). *PRACTICE AREAS:* Commercial Real Estate. *Email:* aguevara@mcdonaldhopkins.com

PATRICIA J. HAAS, born Cleveland, Ohio, 1969; admitted to bar, 1999, Ohio; U.S. District Court, Northern and Southern Districts of Ohio and U.S. Court of Appeals, Sixth Circuit. *Education:* Kent State University (B.A., cum laude, 1992); Cleveland-Marshall College of Law (J.D., 1999). *PRACTICE AREAS:* Business Law; Labor and Employment; Labor Law; Employment Litigation. *Email:* phaas@mcdonaldhopkins.com

STEPHEN K. HALL, born Columbus, Ohio, 1971; admitted to bar, 1997, Ohio. *Education:* The Ohio State University (B.A., 1993; J.D., 1997); Capital University (LL.M., Taxation, 2000). *PRACTICE AREAS:* State Taxation. *Email:* shall@mcdonaldhopkins.com

(This Listing Continued)

KRISTIN K. C. HOWARD, born Newark, New Jersey, 1974; admitted to bar, 1999, Ohio. *Education:* Wellesley College (B.A., cum laude, 1996); Harvard Law School (J.D., 1999). *PRACTICE AREAS:* Distressed Mergers and Acquisitions; Mergers and Acquisitions; Creditors' Rights. *Email:* khoward@mcdonaldhopkins.com

MICHAEL J. KACZKA, born Pittsburgh, Pennsylvania, 1978; (admission pending). *Education:* Washington & Lee University (B.A., cum laude, 2000); Case Western Reserve University (J.D., 2003). *PRACTICE AREAS:* Business Reorganization. *Email:* mkaczka@mcdonaldhopkins.com

JOHN "JT" KALNAY, born Belleville, Ontario, 1961; admitted to bar, 1998, Ohio; U.S. District Court, Northern District of Ohio; U.S. Court of Appeals, Federal Circuit; registered to practice before the U.S. Patent and Trademark Office. *Education:* University of Ottawa (B.A., cum laude, 1983); University of Dayton (M.S., magna cum laude, 1985); Case Western Reserve University (J.D., cum laude, 1998). *PRACTICE AREAS:* Litigation; Software Patents; Applications and Prosecution. *Email:* jkalnay@mcdonaldhopkins.com

HEATHER M. KERN, born Cleveland, Ohio, May 5, 1976; admitted to bar, 2004, Ohio; 2005, U.S. District Court, Northern District of Ohio. *Education:* Notre Dame College, Ohio (B.A., 2001); Case Western Reserve University School of Law (J.D., 2004). *PRACTICE AREAS:* Employment Litigation; Business and Commercial Litigation. *Email:* hkern@mcdonaldhopkins.com

KENT C. KIFFNER, born Detroit, Michigan, 1979; admitted to bar, 2004, Ohio. *Education:* Baldwin-Wallace College (B.A., cum laude, 2001); Syracuse University College of Law (J.D., magna cum laude, 2004). *PRACTICE AREAS:* Litigation; Real Estate; Construction. *Email:* kkiffner@mcdonaldhopkins.com

STEPHEN J. LATKOVIC, born Cleveland, Ohio, March 8, 1977; (admission pending). *Education:* George Washington University (Bachelor of Accountancy, 1999); Cleveland-Marshall College of Law (J.D., cum laude, 2005). *PRACTICE AREAS:* Business Law; Tax Law; Accounting Law. *Email:* slatkovic@mcdonaldhopkins.com

PAUL W. LINEHAN, born South Amboy, New Jersey, 1969; admitted to bar, 1998, Ohio. *Education:* University of Notre Dame (B.B.A., 1991); Case Western Reserve University (J.D., cum laude, 1998). Certified Public Accountant, Ohio, 1994. *PRACTICE AREAS:* Bankruptcy; Business Reorganization; Litigation; Creditors Rights. *Email:* plinehan@mcdonaldhopkins.com

MICHAEL MAKOFSKY, born New York, N.Y., 1974; admitted to bar, 1999, Ohio. *Education:* University of Connecticut (B.A., 1996); Case Western Reserve University, School of Law (J.D., 1999). Associate, 1997-1998 and Articles Editor, 1998-1999, Case Western Reserve University Law Review. *PRACTICE AREAS:* Mergers and Acquisitions; Securities; Banking Law; Real Estate. *Email:* mmakofsky@mcdonaldhopkins.com

PATRICK W. MARAIST, born West Palm Beach, Florida, 1967; admitted to bar, 1997, Florida; U.S. Court of Appeals, Eleventh Circuit; U.S. District Court, Southern and Middle Districts of Florida. *Education:* Florida Atlantic University (B.B.A., with high honors, 1993); University of Florida (J.D., with honors, 1996). (Resident, West Plam Beach, Florida Office). *PRACTICE AREAS:* Business and Commercial Litigation; Real Estate and Construction Litigation; Employment Litigation. *Email:* pmaraist@mcdonaldhopkins.com

ADAM D. MARSHALL, born New York, N.Y., 1970; admitted to bar, 1999, Ohio; 2000, U.S. District Court, Northern and Southern Districts of Ohio; 2002, Florida; U.S. District Court, Middle and Southern Districts of Florida. *Education:* Colgate University (B.A., 1993); Case Western Reserve University (J.D., 1999). (Resident, West Plam Beach, Florida Office). *PRACTICE AREAS:* Bankruptcy; Business Restructuring. *Email:* amarshall@mcdonaldhopkins.com

GRANT A. MONACHINO, admitted to bar, 2003, Ohio. *Education:* Mount Union College (B.A., 2000); Cleveland-Marshall College of Law (J.D., 2003). *PRACTICE AREAS:* Litigation; Intellectual Property. *Email:* gmonachino@mcdonaldhopkins.com

NICOLE M. MONACHINO, born Cleveland, Ohio, 1978; admitted to bar, 2003, Ohio. *Education:* Hiram College (B.A., summa cum laude, 2000); University of Notre Dame (J.D., cum laude, 2003). *PRACTICE AREAS:* Labor and Employment. *Email:* nmonachino@mcdonaldhopkins.com

DAVID T. MOVIUS, born Rochester, Minnesota, 1973; admitted to bar, 1998, Ohio. *Education:* University of Puget Sound (B.A., Computer Science, 1995); American University (J.D., magna cum laude, 1998). *PRACTICE AREAS:* Litigation; Intellectual Property. *Email:* dmovius@mcdonaldhopkins.com

VINCENT J. NARDONE, born Mongahela, Pennsylvania, 1970; admitted to bar, 1996, Ohio; U.S. District Court, Southern District of Ohio, U.S. Court of Appeals, Sixth Circuit, U.S. Tax Court and U.S. Supreme Court. *Education:* Duquesne University (B.S., Business Administration, 1993); Capital University (J.D., cum laude, 1996; LL.M., Taxation, 1997). *PRACTICE AREAS:* Tax Controversies; Nonprofit Organizations Law; Corporate Governance; Corporate Investigations. *Email:* vnardone@mcdonaldhopkins.com

LUCY K. O'SHAUGHNESSY, born Cleveland, Ohio, 1964; admitted to bar, 1999, Ohio; 2000, U.S. District Court, Northern District of Ohio. *Education:* Wittenberg University (B.A., cum laude, 1986); Case Western Reserve University (J.D., cum laude, 1999). *PRACTICE AREAS:* Litigation. *Email:* loshaughnessy@mcdonaldhopkins.com

LYNETTE M. PAPUSHAK, born Cleveland, Ohio, 1971; admitted to bar, 1998, Ohio; 2004, Michigan; U.S. District Court, Northern and Southern Districts of Ohio and Eastern and Western Districts of Michigan; U.S. Court of Appeals, Sixth Circuit. *Education:* Baldwin-Wallace College (B.A., summa cum laude, 1995); The Ohio State University, College of Law (J.D., 1998). *PRACTICE AREAS:* Labor and Employment Law. *Email:* lpapushak@mcdonaldhopkins.com

ANDREW S. PERRY, born Lakewood, Ohio, 1968; admitted to bar, 2000, Ohio. *Education:* The Ohio State University (B.S., 1991); Capital University (J.D., magna cum laude, 1999). *PRACTICE AREAS:* Corporate Law; Banking; Real Estate. *Email:* aperry@mcdonaldhopkins.com

MARK E. PORTER, born Sayama-Shi, Japan, 1962; admitted to bar, 2000, Ohio and U.S. Court of Federal Claims. *Education:* U.S. Naval Academy (B.S., 1984); University of

(This Listing Continued)

McDONALD HOPKINS CO., LPA, Cleveland—Continued

Maryland, (M.A., 1986); Rutgers University Law School (J.D.). ***PRACTICE AREAS:*** Commercial Litigation; Construction Litigation; Labor and Employment. ***Email:*** mporter@mcdonaldhopkins.com

MATTHEW R. RECHNER, born Park Ridge, Illinois, 1976; admitted to bar, 2001, Ohio. *Education:* University of Notre Dame (B.A., cum laude, 1998); Case Western Reserve University, School of Law (J.D., 2001). ***PRACTICE AREAS:*** Commercial Litigation; Labor and Employment; Litigation. ***Email:*** mrechner@mcdonaldhopkins.com

KATAYOON SADRE MAY, born Tehran, Iran, December 6, 1978; admitted to bar, 2004, Ohio. *Education:* Northwestern University; University of Virginia (B.A., with distinction, 2000); University of North Carolina at Chapel Hill (J.D., 2004). ***PRACTICE AREAS:*** Business Law; Corporate Law. ***Email:*** kmay@mcdonaldhopkins.com

R. CHRISTOPHER SALATA, born Cleveland, Ohio, 1976; admitted to bar, 2001, Ohio. *Education:* University of Notre Dame (B.S., 1998); Case Western Reserve University (J.D., 2001). ***PRACTICE AREAS:*** Banking; Finance; Corporate Law; Corporate Restructuring; Real Estate Transactions. ***Email:*** csalata@mcdonaldhopkins.com

MATTHEW A. SALERNO, born Cleveland, Ohio, 1974; admitted to bar, 1999, Ohio and U.S. District Court, Northern and Southern Districts of Ohio; 2000, Indiana and U.S. District Court, Northern and Southern Districts of Indiana. *Education:* The Ohio State University (B.A., with distinction in Criminology, 1996); Case Western Reserve University, School of Law (J.D., 1999). ***PRACTICE AREAS:*** Bankruptcy; Creditors Rights. ***Email:*** msalerno@mcdonaldhopkins.com

JASON M. SMITH, born Parma, Ohio, April 9, 1978; (admission pending). *Education:* John Carroll University (B.S.B.A., 2000); Cleveland-Marshall College of Law (J.D., summa cum laude, 2005). ***PRACTICE AREAS:*** Business Law; Business Succession Planning; Banking Law. ***Email:*** jsmith@mcdonaldhopkins.com

RICHARD D. SUMMERS, born Cleveland, Ohio, 1971; admitted to bar, 1998, Ohio. *Education:* Baldwin-Wallace College (B.A., with honors, 1994); University of Akron (J.D., 1998). ***PRACTICE AREAS:*** Litigation. ***Email:*** rsummers@mcdonaldhopkins.com

ANDREW J. VON GUSTEDT, born Tubingen, Germany, 1968; admitted to bar, 1997, Maryland; 1998, Florida. *Education:* West Virginia University (B.A., 1991); Thomas M. Cooley Law School (J.D., 1996); University of Miami School of Law (LL.M., Real Property Development, 1998). (Resident, West Plam Beach, Florida Office). ***PRACTICE AREAS:*** Real Estate. ***Email:*** avongustedt@mcdonaldhopkins.com

DAVID E. WEISBLATT, born New York, N.Y., 1968; admitted to bar, 1994, Ohio. *Education:* Tufts University (B.A., 1991); The Ohio State University, School of Law (J.D., 1994). ***PRACTICE AREAS:*** Labor and Employment Law. ***Email:*** dweisblatt@mcdonaldhopkins.com

JENNIFER A. ZADOR, born Warren, Ohio, 1979; (admission pending). *Education:* John Carroll University (B.A., 2002); Case Western Reserve University Law School (J.D., cum laude, 2005). ***PRACTICE AREAS:*** Intellectual Property Rights; Intellectual Property Litigation; Litigation. ***Email:*** jzador@mcdonaldhopkins.com

---

McFADDEN & ASSOCIATES CO. LPA

Established in 1981

1370 ONTARIO STREET, SUITE 1700
CLEVELAND, OHIO 44113
Telephone: 216-622-0850
Fax: 216-622-0854
Email: mcfadden@mcfaddenlaw.us

Real Estate, Residential Real Estate, Commercial Real Estate, Industrial Real Estate Law, Litigation, Business Enterprises.

FIRM PROFILE: Experienced in all forms of real estate litigation; title insurance claims; foreclosures; creditor rights; creditor bankruptcy; bankruptcy litigation.

DONALD P. McFADDEN, born Cleveland, Ohio; admitted to bar, 1973, Ohio and U.S. District Court, Northern District of Ohio; 1980, U.S. Supreme Court; 1985, U.S. Court of Appeals, Sixth Circuit; 2002, U.S. District Court, Southern District of Ohio. *Education:* St. Louis University (B.A., 1970); Case Western Reserve University (J.D., 1973). *Member:* Cleveland (Member, Sections on: Professional Responsibility, 2003; Judicial, 2003), Cuyahoga County and Ohio State (Chairman; Member: Real Property Specialty Board, 2002—; Board of Governors, Real Property Section) Bar Associations; Ohio Trial Lawyers Association. ***PRACTICE AREAS:*** Real Estate; Residential Real Estate; Commercial Real Estate; Industrial Real Estate Law; Litigation; Business Enterprises. ***Email:*** mcfadden@mcfaddenlaw.us

---

DAVID A. FREEBURG, born Ridgway, Pennsylvania; admitted to bar, 1999, Ohio and U.S. District Court, Northern District of Ohio; 2000, U.S. District Court, Southern District of Ohio; 2002, U.S. Court of Appeals, Sixth Circuit. *Education:* State University of New York at Buffalo (B.A., 1994); Cleveland State University (J.D., 1999). *Member:* Cleveland and Ohio State Bar Associations. ***PRACTICE AREAS:*** Real Estate; Real Estate Litigation; Foreclosures; Bankruptcy. ***Email:*** freeburg@mcfaddenlaw.us

BRADLEY P. TOMAN, born Hubbard, Ohio; admitted to bar, 1989, Ohio; 1990, Michigan. *Education:* College of Wooster (B.A., 1986); Cleveland-Marshall College of Law (J.D., 1989). ***PRACTICE AREAS:*** Real Estate Litigation (120). ***Email:*** toman@mcfaddenlaw.us

Language: Spanish.

McGLINCHEY STAFFORD, PLLC

Established in 1974

25550 CHAGRIN BOULEVARD
SUITE 406
CLEVELAND, OHIO 44122-4640
Telephone: 216-378-9905
Fax: 216-378-9910
URL: http://www.mcglinchey.com

New Orleans, Louisiana Office: 643 Magazine Street, 70130-3477. Telephone: 504-586-1200. Fax: 504-596-2800. TDD: 504-596-2728. Telex: 584327.
Houston, Texas Office: 1001 McKinney, Suite 1500, 77002. Telephone: 713-520-1900. Fax: 713-520-1025.
Dallas, Texas Office: 2711 N. Haskell, Suite 2700 LB25, 75204. Telephone: 214-257-1700. Fax: 214-257-1717.
Baton Rouge, Louisiana Office: One American Place, 14th Floor, 301 Main Street, 70825. Telephone: 504-383-9000. Fax: 504-343-3076.
Jackson, Mississippi Office: Suite 1100 South, City Centre, 200 South Lamar Street, 39201. Telephone: 601-960-8400. Fax: 601-960-8406.
Monroe, Louisiana Office: 1811 Tower Drive, Suite A, 71201. Telephone: 318-651-0807. Fax: 318-651-0809.
Albany, New York Office: 194 Washington Avenue, 6th Floor, 12210. Telephone: 518-432-1200. Fax: 518-432-8711.

General Practice in the State and Federal Courts. Admiralty/Maritime Law, Agricultural, Antitrust and Trade Regulation, Aviation, Banking and Financial Institutions, Bankruptcy/Reorganization/Creditors' Rights, Business Litigation, Collection Law, Commercial Finance/Asset-Based Lending, Construction, Consumer Financial Services Law and Regulation, Corporate and General Business, Employee Benefits/ERISA/Executive Compensation, Gaming Law and Regulation, Energy Law and Regulation, Environmental Law and Regulation, General Litigation and Insurance Defense, Governmental Relations and Legislation, Health Care Law and Regulation, Housing and Housing Finance, Manufactured Housing and Manufactured Housing Finance, Insurance Law and Regulation, Intellectual Property, International Law and Business Transactions, Labor and Employment, Products Liability, Professional Liability/Director and Officer Liability, Project and Structured Finance, Public Finance, Public Law and Finance, Public Utilities Law and Regulation, Real Estate, Securities Law and Regulation, Taxation and Tax Litigation, Trusts/Estate Planning and Administration.

MEMBERS OF FIRM

MARK S. EDELMAN, born Cleveland, Ohio, October 28, 1961; admitted to bar, 1986, Ohio; 1987, Illinois. *Education:* University of Michigan (B.A., 1983); The Ohio State University (J.D., 1986). Articles Editor, Ohio State Law Journal, 1985-1986. Author, "The Walker Case: Is an Assignee Discount a Finance Charge?" The Review of Financial Services, Vol. 14, No. 21. Adjunct Faculty Member, Kent State University, 1990-1991. *Member:* Ohio State and American (Member, Committee on Consumer Financial Services, Business Law Section; Vice Chair, Personal Property Finance Subcommittee) Bar Associations. ***PRACTICE AREAS:*** Consumer Credit Compliance; Banking Regulation; Corporate Law; Business Law; Truth in Lending; E-Commerce. ***Email:*** medelman@mcglinchey.com

DAVID W. THOMPSON, born Lexington, Kentucky, June 24, 1965; admitted to bar, 1990, Tennessee; 1991, Kentucky; 1993, Massachusetts; 1998, Ohio. *Education:* Transylvania University (B.A., magna cum laude, 1987); University of Kentucky (J.D., 1990); Boston University (LL.M., Banking Law, 1994). Author: "The Walker Case: Is an Assignee Discount a Finance Charge?" The Review of Banking and Financial Services, December 1998; "Analysis of Gramm-Leach Privacy Provisions and Related Laws," published in the book "Financial Modernization: Understanding and Implementing the New Requirements," published by AlexInformation, L.P., 1999. *Member:* Ohio State, Kentucky and American (Member, Consumer Financial Services Committee and Banking Law Committee, Business Law Section) Bar Associations. ***PRACTICE AREAS:*** Consumer Finance; Banking Law; E-Commerce; Internet Law; Business Litigation. ***Email:*** dthompson@mcglinchey.com

ARTHUR J. ROTATORI, born Cleveland, Ohio, January 7, 1956; admitted to bar, 1981, Ohio. *Education:* Case Western Reserve University (B.A., summa cum laude, 1978); Northwestern University (J.D., 1981). Phi Beta Kappa. Editor, Journal of Criminal Law and Criminology, 1980-1981. Author: "State Law Developments Affecting Consumer Lenders," 16 The Review of Banking & Financial Services 229A (2000); "New Predatory Lending Initiatives," 18 The Review of Banking & Financial Services 12A (2002). Adjunct Faculty Member, Cuyahoga Community College, 1993. *Member:* Ohio State and American (Member, Consumer Financial Services Committee, Business Law Section) Bar Associations. ***PRACTICE AREAS:*** Consumer Financial Services; Electronic Commerce; Banking Law. ***Email:*** arotatori@mcglinchey.com

BARBARA FRIEDMAN YAKSIC, born Cleveland, Ohio, July 30, 1956; admitted to bar, 1981, Ohio. *Education:* Indiana University (B.S., summa cum laude, 1978); The Ohio State University (J.D., cum laude, 1981). Beta Gamma Sigma. *Member:* Cleveland (Member, Board of Trustees, 1996-1999; Executive Committee, 1998-1999; Chair, Women in the Law, 1991-1992; Chair Justice For All, 2000-2002; Vice Chair, Judicial Selection Committee, 2002—), Ohio State (Member, Council of Delegates, 2001—; Vice Chair, Women in the Profession, 2001—), Federal and American Bar Associations; Ohio Women's Bar Association. ***PRACTICE AREAS:*** Commercial Litigation; Business Litigation. ***Email:*** byaksic@mcglinchey.com

ASSOCIATES

BROOKE TURNER BAUTISTA, born Elyria, Ohio, November 18, 1974; admitted to bar, 2000, Ohio and U.S. District Court, Southern District of Ohio; 2002, U.S. District Court, Northern District of Ohio. *Education:* Ohio University (B.A., 1997); The Ohio State University (J.D., 2000). Phi Alpha Delta. Formerly with, Dagger, Johnston, Miller, Ogilvie

(This Listing Continued)

& Hampson. *Member:* Cleveland, Columbus, Fairfield County and Ohio State Bar Associations. ***PRACTICE AREAS:*** Business Litigation (70%); Consumer Finance (30%). ***Email:*** bbautista@mcglinchey.com

JOY A. DiPALMA, born Cleveland, Ohio; admitted to bar, 2000, Ohio. *Education:* Miami University (B.A., 1997); Cleveland-Marshall College of Law (J.D., 2000). ***PRACTICE AREAS:*** Consumer Finance; Lending; Structured Finance.

KIMBERLY Y. SMITH, born Goshen, Indiana, October 7, 1965; admitted to bar, 1996, Ohio. *Education:* Taylor University (B.A., summa cum laude, 1988); Case Western Reserve University (J.D., cum laude, 1996). Order of Barristers. Recipient, William H. Wallace Award for Excellence in Litigation; International Academy of Trial Lawyers for Outstanding Trial Advocacy. Member, Case Western Reserve University Law Review. President, Case Western Reserve University Mock Trial Team. Arbitrator, Better Business Bureau. *Member:* Cleveland, Ohio State and American Bar Associations. ***PRACTICE AREAS:*** Commercial Litigation. ***Email:*** ksmith@mcglinchey.com

OF COUNSEL

EUGENIA M. SCHMIDLEY, born Denver, Colorado, 1952; admitted to bar, 1978, California; 1985, Ohio. *Education:* Sweet Briar College (B.A., 1974); Fordham University (J.D., 1977). Phi Beta Kappa. Author: "New Judicial Approach to Maintaining Housing Quality in the Cities," Fordham Urban Law Journal, Volume IV, Winter 1976; "FDICA Regulations Heighten Scrutiny of Management," Bank Account and Finance, Winter, 1992-1993. ***PRACTICE AREAS:*** Consumer Credit Compliance; Truth in Lending; Banking Regulation. ***Email:*** eschmidley@mcglinchey.com

MONICA L. LACKS, born Perth Amboy, New Jersey, March 5, 1965; admitted to bar, 1990, Massachusetts; 1995, Louisiana, U.S. District Court, Eastern and Middle Districts of Louisiana and U.S. Court of Appeals, Fifth Circuit; 2005, Ohio. *Education:* Johns Hopkins University (B.A., 1987); Harvard Law School (J.D., cum laude, 1990). Phi Beta Kappa. *Member:* Louisiana State and Massachusetts Bar Associations. ***REPORTED CASES:*** Salard v. Lowe's Home Centers, 904 F.Supp 569 (W.D. La.1995); Harris v. Utica Rental Systems, 1996 WL539954 (E.D. La. 1996); Klaimon v. Cigna Companies 1997 WL79292 (E.D. La. 1997) affd, 138 .F2d 952 (5th Cir. 1998), cert. denied, 525 U.S. 896, 119 S.Ct.221 (1998); Holland v. Hartford Computes Exchange, Inc., 1994 WL326635 (D.Mass. 1994). ***PRACTICE AREAS:*** Labor and Employment; Litigation. ***Email:*** mlacks@mcglinchey.com

JAMES S. WERTHEIM, born Cleveland, Ohio, January 8, 1960; admitted to bar, 1985, Ohio, U.S. District Court, Southern District of Ohio; 1986, U.S. District Court, Northern District of Ohio; 1988, U.S. Court of Appeals, Sixth Circuit; 1998, U.S. Court of Appeals for the Federal Circuit. *Education:* University of Michigan (B.A., 1982); The Ohio State University (J.D., 1985). Author: "Investigating The Insurance Claim," *Insuring Real Property,* Chapter 20, Matthew Bender and Company, Inc., 1989. *Member:* Cleveland, Ohio State and American (Member, Torts, Insurance Practice, Business Law and Litigation Sections) Bar Associations. ***PRACTICE AREAS:*** Business Litigation; Consumer Litigation; Class Action Defense; Corporate Litigation; Product Liability; Trial Practice; Federal Practice; Emergency Injunction Litigation; Insurance Litigation. ***Email:*** jwertheim@mcglinchey.com

REPRESENTATIVE CLIENTS: Advocate Capital, Inc.; AmeriCredit Financial Services; Auto One Acceptance Corp; Automotive Finance Corp.; Bally Total Fitness; Banconsumer Services, Inc.; Bank One Corporation; Bridgestone Firestone, Inc.; Charter One Auto Finance; Chase Manhattan Mortgage; Chrysler Financial; CompliSource LLC; Dell Financial Services; Fleet-Boston Financial Group; FBS Financial; GE Lighting; Grad Partners, Inc.; Household Automotive Finance; Huntington Capital; Hyundi Motor Company; InfiStar Corporation; Iowa Studen Loan Liquidity; J.D. Byrider Systems, Inc.; Key Bank; Magic American Corporation; Monetrics; Nissan Motor Acceptance Corp.; Option One Mortgage Corp.; PNC Bank; Systems & Services Technologies; Toyota Motor Credit Corporation; US Bancorp; Wachovia Corporation; Washington Mutual Bank; Wells Fargo Bank.

(For biographical data on other personnel, see Professional Biographies at New Orleans, Baton Rouge and Monroe, Louisiana, Jackson, Mississippi, Dallas and Houston, Texas and Albany, New York)

McKINZIE AND ASSOCIATES

CLEVELAND, OHIO

(See Akron)

Business Law, Criminal Law, Construction, Personal Injury, Family Law and Civil Practice.

McLAUGHLIN & McCAFFREY, LLP

EATON CENTER, SUITE 1350
1111 SUPERIOR AVENUE
CLEVELAND, OHIO 44114-2500
Telephone: 216-623-0900
Fax: 216-623-0935
Email: law@paladin-law.com
URL: http://www.lawyers.com/paladin-law

Federal and State Trials and Appeals, White Collar Criminal Defense and Complex Civil Litigation.

FIRM PROFILE: McLaughlin & McCaffrey, LLP engages in white collar criminal defense and complex civil litigation throughout the United States. The firm represents individuals and corporations (foreign and domestic) in all phases of complex civil and criminal litigation. The firm's attorneys act as counsel in federal, state and regulatory matters involving individuals and business entities on issues to include: malpractice, personal injury and product liability, insurance defense, corporate, environmental, internal investigations, economic espionage, antitrust, money laundering, RICO, securities fraud, mail fraud, wire fraud, bank fraud, health care fraud, criminal tax matters and immigration and naturalization law. The firm is committed to providing quality legal services for individuals and business entities who desire the personal attention and cost savings of working with a smaller, yet highly sophisticated, litigation firm.

(This Listing Continued)

PATRICK M. McLAUGHLIN, born Monahans, Texas, July 23, 1946; admitted to bar, 1976, Ohio; 1978, U.S. District Court, Northern District of Ohio; 1979, U.S. Court, of Appeals, Sixth Circuit; 1980, U.S. Supreme Court; 1989, U.S. District Court, Southern District of Ohio; 1995, U.S. Court of Appeals, Fifth Circuit. *Education:* Ohio University (B.G.S., cum laude, 1972); Case Western Reserve University (J.D., 1976). Omicron Delta Kappa. Editor-in-Chief, Case Western Reserve Journal of International Law, 1975-1976. Fellow, American College of Trial Lawyers. Independent Special Counsel for Ohio Attorney Generals, 1994-1996. Appointed: U.S. Attorney, Northern District of Ohio by President Ronald Reagan, 1985-1988. U.S. Attorney, Northern District of Ohio by the U.S. District Court, 1984-1985. Chief, Civil Division, Northern District of Ohio, 1982-1984. Assistant U.S. Attorney, Northern District of Ohio, 1978-1982. Inductee: Ohio Veterans Hall of Fame (Class of 2003); Ohio Military Hall of Fame for Valor (Class of 2004). *Member:* Cleveland, Ohio State, Federal (President, Cleveland Chapter, 1987-1988; Delegate to the National Council, 1988-1989) and American Bar Associations; Judge Antony J. Celebrezze Inn of Court (Master Bencher; President). [U.S. Army, 1966-1968; SSG E-6, First Infantry Division, RVN; U.S. Army Reserve, JAG Corps, Major, 1974-1992]. ***PRACTICE AREAS:*** Federal Litigation; State Litigation; Trial Practice; Appellate Practice; Professional Malpractice; White Collar Criminal Defense. ***Email:*** pmm@paladin-law.com

JOHN F. McCAFFREY, born Lakewood, Ohio, June 10, 1961; admitted to bar, 1987, Ohio; 1989, District of Columbia; 1990, New Jersey and U.S. District Court, District of New Jersey; 1991, New York and U.S. District Court, Northern District of Ohio; 1995, U.S. Court of Appeals, Fifth Circuit; 1996, U.S. Court of Appeals, Sixth Circuit; 1999, U.S. Court of Appeals, Eleventh Circuit; 2001, U.S. District Court, Southern District of Ohio; 2002, U.S. Supreme Court. *Education:* John Carroll University (B.A., 1983); Case Western Reserve University (J.D., 1987). Employment: Federal Bureau of Investigation, 1987-1990; Cuyahoga County Prosecutors Office, 1990-1994. Special Assistant, United States Attorney, Northern District of Ohio, 1994. Assistant Independent Special Counsel for Ohio Attorney Generals, 1994-1996. Special Assistant Franklin County Prosecutor, 1995-1996. *Member:* Cleveland, Cuyahoga County (Board of Trustees, 2001-2004), Ohio State, Federal and American Bar Associations. ***SPECIAL AGENCIES:*** Chairman: Society of Former Special Agents of the Federal Bureau of Investigation, Cleveland Chapter; Hon. William K. Thomas Chapter, American Inns of Court, Master Bencher; Advisory Group for the U.S. District Court, Northern District of Ohio, Chairman - Criminal Rules Committee. Acting Judge, Lakewood Municipal Court; St. Edward High School, Legal Eagle Man of the Year, 2004. ***PRACTICE AREAS:*** Federal Litigation; Litigation; Trial Practice; Appellate Practice; Corporate Litigation; Commercial Litigation; White Collar Criminal Defense. ***Email:*** jfm@paladin-law.com

DENNIS P. ZAPKA, born Youngstown, Ohio, June 28, 1949; admitted to bar, 1975, Ohio; 1976, U.S. District Court, Northern District of Ohio; 1980, U.S. Court of Appeals, Sixth Circuit and U.S. Supreme Court; 1987, U.S. District Court, Southern District of Ohio; 2005, U.S. Court of Appeals, Eleventh Circuit. *Education:* Youngstown State University (B.A., magna cum laude, 1972); Georgetown University Law Center (J.D., 1975). Member, Tax Lawyer Journal. Employment: Assistant U.S. Attorney, Northern District of Ohio, 1978-1985; Chief, Civil Division, Northern District of Ohio, 1984-1985; Special Assistant U.S. Attorney, Northern District of Ohio, 1985-1986. 1999 Ohio Lawyer of the Year (Ohio Lawyer Weekly). *Member:* Cleveland, Cuyahoga County, Ohio State (Environmental Law Committee), Federal (Treasurer, 1985-1987; President-Elect, 1988-1989, President, Cleveland Chapter, 1989-1990; Delegate to National Council, 1990-1991; Originator, Elaine R. Boots Fisher Award recognizing community, public and charitable service) and American Bar Associations; Advisory Group for the U.S. District Court, Northern District of Ohio; Association of Trial Lawyers of America. ***PRACTICE AREAS:*** Federal Litigation; Civil Litigation; Trial Practice; Appellate Practice; Personal Injury; Professional Malpractice; Toxic Torts; Environmental Law; Insurance Coverage; Insurance Defense; Corporate Litigation; Commercial Litigation. ***Email:*** dpz@paladin-law.com

ASSOCIATES

ANTHONY R. PETRUZZI, born Cleveland, Ohio, October 1, 1971; admitted to bar, 1998, Ohio, U.S. District Court, Northern District of Ohio and U.S. Court of Appeals, Sixth Circuit; 2004, U.S. District Court, Southern District of Ohio. *Education:* Ohio University (A.B., summa cum laude, 1994); Cleveland Marshall College of Law, Cleveland State University (J.D., 1997). Assistant Independent Special Counsel for Ohio Attorney General, 2000-2001. *Member:* Cleveland, Cuyahoga County, Ohio State, Federal and American Bar Associations. ***PRACTICE AREAS:*** Federal Litigation; Civil Litigation; Appellate Practice; Employment Law; Insurance Coverage; Insurance Defense; White Collar Criminal Defense. ***Email:*** arp@paladin-law.com

DAVID H. BOEHM, born Cleveland Heights, Ohio, January 5, 1974; admitted to bar, 2000, Ohio; 2002, U.S. District Court, Northern District of Ohio; 2004, U.S. District Court, Southern District of Ohio. *Education:* Ohio University (B.A., 1996); Cleveland-Marshall College of Law, Cleveland State University (J.D., 2000). *Member:* Cleveland, Ohio State and American Bar Associations. ***PRACTICE AREAS:*** Federal Litigation; Civil Litigation; Insurance Coverage; Insurance Defense; Corporate Litigation; Commercial Litigation. ***Email:*** dhb@paladin-law.com

ADRIENNE B. KIRSHNER, born Toledo, Ohio, December 29, 1976; admitted to bar, 2002, Ohio; 2003, U.S. District Court, Northern District of Ohio. *Education:* University of Chicago (B.A., with general honors, 1999); Case Western Reserve University (J.D., cum laude, 2002). *Member:* Cleveland and Ohio State Bar Associations. ***PRACTICE AREAS:*** Federal Litigation; Civil Litigation; Appellate Practice; White Collar Criminal Defense. ***Email:*** abk@paladin-law.com

SEAN T. LAVIN, born Cleveland, Ohio, March 21, 1976; admitted to bar, 2001, Ohio; 2003, U.S. District Court, Northern District of Ohio. *Education:* University College Galway, Galway, Ireland (1995); John Carroll University (B.A., 1998); Cleveland-Marshall College of Law (J.D., 2001). Law Clerk to: Judge Anthony O. Calabrese, Jr., Ohio State Court of Appeals, Eighth District, 2003-2005; Judge Ronald Suster, Cuyahoga County Court of Common Pleas, 2001-2003. *Member:* Cleveland, Ohio State and American Bar Associations. ***PRACTICE AREAS:*** Federal Litigation; Civil Litigation; Appellate Practice; White Collar Criminal Defense. ***Email:*** stl@paladin-law.com

McMAHON, DeGULIS, HOFFMANN & LOMBARDI LLP

Established in 1994

THE CAXTON BUILDING - SUITE 650
812 HURON ROAD
CLEVELAND, OHIO 44115-1126
Telephone: 216-621-1312
Telecopier: 216-621-0577
URL: http://www.mdhl.net
Email: envlaw@mdhl.net
URL: http://www.lawyers.com/mdh

Environmental Law and Litigation.

FIRM PROFILE: McMahon, DeGulis, Hoffmann & Lombardi LLP offers a full range of environmental legal services including litigation, compliance, audits, counseling, transactional support, remediation, insurance coverage, Brownfield redevelopment, toxic tort, asbestos defense, and defense of enforcement actions. The firm is a founding member of the Environmental Law Network which is comprised of environmental law firms nationwide.

McMahon, DeGulis, Hoffmann & Lombardi LLP attorneys concentrate their practices in the following major areas of environmental law: Ohio Voluntary Action Program (Brownfields Statute), RCRA, Toxic Tort Litigation, OSHA, Toxic Substances Control Act, CERCLA, Ohio Underground Storage Tank Program, Ohio Solid and Hazardous Waste Program, Safe Drinking Water Act, Wetlands Permitting, Land Use Issues, Clean Water Act and Clean Air Act.

MEMBERS OF FIRM

MICHAEL S. McMAHON, born Crestline, Ohio, October 18, 1955; admitted to bar, 1981, Ohio. *Education:* John Carroll University (B.A., magna cum laude, 1978); Columbia University (J.D., 1981). Recipient, Stone Scholar. Co-Author: "Ohio Adopts a Model Law to Promote Voluntary Cleanup of Contaminated Property," J. Env. Permitting, Spring, 1995; "Does the Sixth Circuit Have a New Standard for Its Review of the EPA's Use of Air Quality Modeling?" 18 Toledo Law Review 569. *Member:* Cleveland (Chair, Environmental Law Section, 1995-1996) and Ohio State (Member, Environmental Law Committee) Bar Associations. ***PRACTICE AREAS:*** Air Pollution; Environmental Auditing; Environmental Compliance; Hazardous Materials Transportation; International Environmental Law. ***Email:*** mcmahon@mdhl.net

GREGORY J. DeGULIS, born Cleveland, Ohio, February 21, 1960; admitted to bar, 1986, Massachusetts and New York; 1990, Ohio and U.S. District Court, Northern District of Ohio; 1995, U.S. District Court, Southern District of Ohio; U.S. Court of Appeals, Sixth Circuit. *Education:* University of Michigan (B.A., 1982); Case Western Reserve University (J.D., 1985). Vice Chair, Toxic and Hazardous Substances and Environmental Law Committee, American Bar Association, 1988-1999. Chair, Environmental Law Committee, Cleveland Bar Association, 1999-2000. Commercial Panel Member, American Arbitration Association. ***PRACTICE AREAS:*** Environmental Cost Recovery; Asbestos Defense; Environmental Insurance Coverage; Superfund; Toxic Tort Defense. ***Email:*** degulis@mdhl.net

MARIA T. LOMBARDI, born Bethpage, New York, 1961; admitted to bar, 1992, Ohio, U.S. District Court, Northern District of Ohio and U.S. Court of Appeals, Sixth Circuit. *Education:* New York State College of Environmental Science & Forestry (B.S., cum laude, 1983); Cleveland-Marshall College of Law (J.D., cum laude, 1992). Secretary, Ohio Chapter of National Brownfields Association; Board Member, Commercial Real Estate Women of Cleveland. *Member:* Cleveland (Member, Environmental Law Committee), Ohio State (Member, Environmental Law Section) and American (Member, Natural Resources Section) Bar Associations. ***REPORTED CASES:*** Centerior Service v. Acme Scrap & Metal Corp., 153 F.3d 344 (6th Cir. 1998). ***PRACTICE AREAS:*** Environmental Real Estate; Property Remediation; Brownfields Redevelopment; Environmental Compliance Auditing; Hazardous Waste; Environmental Insurance. ***Email:*** lombardi@mdhl.net

STEPHEN H. DANIELS, born Cleveland, Ohio, January 25, 1953; admitted to bar, 1978, Ohio and U.S. District Court, Northern District of Ohio; 1988, U.S. Court of Appeals, Sixth Circuit. *Education:* Wittenberg University (B.A., 1975); Georgetown University Law Center (J.D., 1978). Listed in: Who's Who in Practicing Attorneys. Editor, Law and Policy in International Business, Georgetown University. Author: chapter on personal injury law in the United States, International Compensation of Personal Injury, Center for International Studies. Guest Lecturer and Instructor, Environmental Response Systems, Inc., Asbestos Abatement Certification Program. Lecturer, "Economic Loss and Emotional Damages Experts," Lorman Education Services. *Member:* Defense Research Institute. ***PRACTICE AREAS:*** Litigation; Commercial Litigation; Construction Law; Toxic Tort Litigation; Intellectual Property Litigation; Products Liability. ***Email:*** daniels@mdhl.net

ASSOCIATES

SUZANNE WIERY, born Warren, Ohio, 1972; admitted to bar, 1998, Ohio; 1999, U.S. District Court, Northern District of Ohio. *Education:* John Carroll University (B.S., Biology, 1995); Cleveland Marshall College of Law (J.D., cum laude, 1998). *Member:* Cleveland (Member, Environmental Law Executive Committee) and Ohio State (Member, Environmental Law Section; Environmental Law Committee) Bar Associations; Cleveland Commercial Real Estate Women (Committee Chair). ***PRACTICE AREAS:*** Toxic Tort Litigation; Environmental Law; Environmental Real Estate; Underground Storage Tanks; Resource Conservation and Recovery Act. ***Email:*** wiery@mdhl.net

ERICK C. SMITH, born Dunkirk, New York, July 8, 1963; admitted to bar, 1988, Ohio; 1990, Pennsylvania; 1991; U.S. District Court, District of New Jersey; 1999, U.S. Court of Appeals, Third Circuit. *Education:* State University of New York at Geneseo (B.A., cum laude, 1984); Case Western Reserve University (J.D., 1987). ***PRACTICE AREAS:*** Insurance Defense; Environmental Law. ***Email:*** esmith@mdhl.net

EVAN J. PALIK, born East Cleveland, Ohio, April 17, 1960; admitted to bar, 1985, Ohio and U.S. District Court, Northern District of Ohio and U.S. Court of Appeals, Sixth Circuit. *Education:* Miami University (B.S., 1982); University of Akron (J.D., 1985). *Member:* Akron and Ohio State Bar Associations. ***REPORTED CASES:*** Sentinel Sel. Systems v. Medkeff 36 Ohio App 3d 86 (1987); Barbell v. Twinsburg Twp. 69 Ohio App 3d 837 (1990); Torba v. S.M. Smulken Co. 888 F.Supp. 851 (1995). ***PRACTICE AREAS:*** Toxic Tort Class Actions; Insurance Defense. ***Email:*** epalik@mdhl.net

JAMES A. BYRNE, born Cambridge, Massachusetts, January 1, 1962; admitted to bar, 1990, Ohio, U.S. District Court, Northern District of Ohio and U.S. Court of Appeals, Sixth Circuit. *Education:* Suffolk University (B.S., 1984); Cleveland Marshall College of Law (J.D., 1990). Recipient, Spangenberg Trial Practice Award; American Jurisprudence Award for Trial Advocacy. Member, Moot Court Board of Governors, 1989-1990. *Member:* Ohio State Bar Association. ***PRACTICE AREAS:*** Civil Litigation; Insurance Defense; Toxic Tort Class Actions. ***Email:*** byrne@mdhl.net

AMY KLIMEK, born Atlanta, Georgia, July 24, 1967; admitted to bar, 1993, West Virginia; 1995, Ohio. *Education:* Rhodes College (B.A., cum laude, honors in history, 1989); The Ohio State University College of Law (J.D., 1993). Research Editor, Ohio State Law Journal, 1992-1993. Co-Author: "The National Historic Preservation Act and Federally-Delegated State Permitting Programs; A SMCRA-Based Primer," Journal of Environmental Permitting (Autumn, 1994). *Member:* Cleveland, West Virginia and Ohio State (Member, Environmental Law Committee) Bar Associations. ***PRACTICE AREAS:*** Environmental. ***Email:*** klimek@mdhl.net

OF COUNSEL

RICHARD A. GREEN, born Cleveland, Ohio, July 22, 1956; admitted to bar, 1980, Ohio; 1981, U.S. District Court, Southern and Northern Districts of Ohio. *Education:* The Ohio State University (B.A., with honors, 1977); Case Western Reserve University (J.D., 1980). Author, "Hidden Value in a Target's Expired Insurance," Mergers & Acquisitions, 1998. Assistant Ohio Attorney General, 1980-1987. Founder and Member, Board of Trustees, Northeast Ohio Chapter, American Corporate Counsel Association, 1994-2000. ***PRACTICE AREAS:*** Insurance Coverage; Insurance Coverage Litigation; Commercial Litigation; Brownfields Redevelopment. ***Email:*** green@mdhl.net

REPRESENTATIVE CLIENTS: General Electric Company; The Sherwin-Williams Company; BP; Delaware North; RPM, Inc.; Sears, Roebuck & Co.; Norfolk Southern; John Crane, DAP, Inc.; ChevronTexaco; Tops Markets; American Greetings; Rust-Oleum Corp.; Omnova Solutions; YSI, Inc.

McNEAL, SCHICK, ARCHIBALD & BIRO CO., L.P.A.

Established in 1956

VAN SWERINGEN ARCADE
123 WEST PROSPECT AVENUE, SUITE 250
CLEVELAND, OHIO 44115
Telephone: 216-621-9870
Fax: 216-522-1112
Email: msab@apk.net
URL: http://www.msablaw.com

General Civil Trial and Appellate Practice in all State and Federal Courts. Admiralty, Architects and Engineers, Commercial, Corporation, Environmental, Insurance, Malpractice, Products Liability and Toxic Substances Law.

HARLEY J. McNEAL (1911-1996)

THOMAS SCHICK (1923-1997)

ALBERT J. BIRO (1926-1995)

PAUL W. ZIEGLER, born Cleveland, Ohio, March 19, 1946; admitted to bar, 1971, Ohio; 1973, U.S. District Court, Northern District of Ohio; 1982, District of Columbia. *Education:* Georgetown University (A.B., 1968; J.D., 1971). *Member:* Cleveland (Trustee, 1993-1996), Ohio State and American Bar Associations; The District of Columbia Bar; Ohio Association of Civil Trial Attorneys; Association of Defense Trial Attorneys; Defense Research Institute; Cleveland Association of Civil Trial Attorneys; Life Member, Judicial Conference for the Eighth Judicial District. ***PRACTICE AREAS:*** Construction Law; Products Liability; Environmental Law; Toxic Substances Law; Civil Litigation; Insurance Law; Professional Liability Law. ***Email:*** ziggy@msablaw.com

FREDRIC E. KRAMER, born Cleveland, Ohio, June 14, 1937; admitted to bar, 1962, Ohio. *Education:* John Carroll University (B.S.S., 1959); University of Detroit; Case Western Reserve University (LL.B., 1962). Delta Sigma Rho. *Member:* Cleveland (Trustee, 1987-1990) and Ohio State (Council of Delegates, 1997—) Bar Associations; Master Bencher of William K. Thomas Inn of Court; Judicial Conference, Eighth Judicial District (Life Member). ***PRACTICE AREAS:*** Civil Litigation; Insurance Law; Construction Law; Professional Liability Law. ***Email:*** kramer@msablaw.com

JOHN C. CUBAR, born Cleveland, Ohio, April 15, 1952; admitted to bar, 1978, Ohio; 1979, U.S. District Court, Northern District of Ohio; 1980, U.S. Court of Appeals, Sixth Circuit. *Education:* Miami University (A.B., 1974); Cleveland State University (J.D., 1978). *Member:* Ohio State Bar Association; Cleveland Association of Civil Trial Attorneys. ***PRACTICE AREAS:*** Civil Litigation; Insurance Law; Environmental Law; Construction Law; Professional Liability Law; Probate Law. ***Email:*** jcc@msablaw.com

MARILYN J. SINGER, born San Francisco, California, March 7, 1955; admitted to bar, 1979, Ohio; 1980, U.S. District Court, Northern District of Ohio; 1984, U.S. Court of Appeals, Sixth Circuit. *Education:* Bryn Mawr College (A.B., 1976); Case Western Reserve University (J.D., 1979). *Member:* Cleveland and Ohio State Bar Associations; Ohio Association of Civil Trial Attorneys. ***PRACTICE AREAS:*** Civil Litigation; Insurance Law; Products Liability Law; Professional Liability Law. ***Email:*** mjs@msablaw.com

BRIAN T. WINCHESTER, born Cleveland, Ohio, July 19, 1971; admitted to bar, 1998, Ohio; 1999, U.S. District Court, Northern District of Ohio; 2003, U.S. Court of Appeals, Sixth Circuit. *Education:* Xavier University (B.A., 1993); Cleveland Marshall College of Law (J.D., 1997). *Member:* Cleveland and Ohio State Bar Associations; Cleveland

(This Listing Continued)

Association of Civil Trial Attorneys; William K. Thomas American Inn of Court. **PRACTICE AREAS:** Insurance Law; Construction Law; Civil Litigation. **Email:** btw@msablaw.com

ASSOCIATES

KRISTINA M. PACKARD, born Niles, Ohio, December 5, 1973; admitted to bar, 2000, Ohio; 2004, U.S. District Court, Northern District of Ohio. *Education:* John Carroll University (B.A., 1996); Cleveland Marshall College of Law (J.D., 2000). *Member:* Ohio State Bar Association; Ohio Women's Bar Association. ***LANGUAGES:*** French. ***PRACTICE AREAS:*** Construction Law; Professional Liability Law; Civil Litigation; Environmental Law. ***Email:*** kpackard@msablaw.com

DAWN E. SNYDER, born Cleveland, Ohio, July 18, 1978; admitted to bar, 2004, Ohio. *Education:* Allegheny College (B.A., 2000); Cleveland-Marshall College of Law (J.D., 2004). *Member:* Ohio State Bar Association. ***PRACTICE AREAS:*** Insurance Law; Construction Law; Civil Litigation. ***Email:*** dsnyder@msablaw.com

OF COUNSEL

ROBERT D. ARCHIBALD, born Girard, Ohio, January 11, 1931; admitted to bar, 1956, Ohio. *Education:* College of Wooster (A.B., 1953); Youngstown University; Western Reserve University (J.D., 1956). Phi Delta Phi. Author, "Military Jurisdiction Over Discharged Serviceman," 7 Western Reserve Law Review 191, 1955. Member, Editorial Board of Western Reserve Law Review, 1955-1956. *Member:* Cleveland (Trustee, 1979-1982), Ohio State and American Bar Associations; American Academy of Attorney-Mediators. Fellow, American College of Trial Lawyers. ***PRACTICE AREAS:*** Civil Litigation; Insurance Law; Environmental Law; Toxic Substances Law. ***Email:*** arch@msablaw.com

REPRESENTATIVE CLIENTS: Allstate Insurance Company; American International Group; American Safety; Auto-Owners Insurance Company; Burgess & Niple Limited; Cavell America; Church Mutual Insurance Company; Claims Control, Inc.; CNA Insurance Companies; Design Professionals Insurance Company; GEICO; Great West Casualty Company; Home-Owners Insurance Co.; Kemper Insurance Companies; Liberty International Underwriters; Megas Beauty Care, Inc.; ms consultants, inc.; MWH Americas, Inc.; NCMIC; Owners Insurance Company; RiverStone Claims Management, LLC; Safeco Insurance Companies; Unitrin Specialty Lines Insurance; Vesta Companies; Wade-Trim; Walgreen Co.; Ward North America, Inc.

KAREN K. MEADE & ASSOCIATES CO. LPA

Established in 1991

1370 WEST 6TH STREET, SUITE 208
CLEVELAND, OHIO 44113
Telephone: 216-696-3327
Fax: 216-621-8609
Email: immigration_atty@yahoo.com

Immigration and Nationality Law.

KAREN K. MEADE, born Lorain, Ohio, 1956; admitted to bar, 1983, Ohio; 1984, U.S. District Court, Northern District of Ohio; 1990, U.S. Court of Appeals, Sixth Circuit. *Education:* Kent State University (B.A., 1979); Cleveland Marshall College of Law (J.D., 1983). *Member:* American Bar Association; American Immigration Lawyers Association. ***LANGUAGES:*** Spanish. ***PRACTICE AREAS:*** Immigration Law. ***Email:*** immigration_atty@yahoo.com

Languages: Spanish, French, German, Greek, Farsi (Persian).

MELLINO LAW FIRM LLC

55 PUBLIC SQUARE, SUITE 1260
CLEVELAND, OHIO 44113
Telephone: 216-621-8348
Fax: 216-621-8378
Email: cmm@mellinolaw.com
URL: http://www.christophermellino.com

Negligence, Insurance, Products Liability, Medical Malpractice, Nursing Home Negligence.

MEMBER

CHRISTOPHER M. MELLINO, born Cleveland, Ohio, February 5, 1959; admitted to bar, 1984, Ohio and U.S. District Court, Northern District of Ohio. *Education:* Cleveland State University (B.A., 1981); Cleveland Marshall College of Law, Cleveland State University (J.D., cum laude, 1984). Moot Court Board of Governors, 1983-1984. *Member:* Cuyahoga County and Ohio State Bar Associations; Cleveland Academy of Trial Attorneys; Ohio Academy of Trial Lawyers; The Association of Trial Lawyers of America. ***PRACTICE AREAS:*** Negligence; Insurance; Products Liability; Medical Malpractice; Nursing Home Negligence; Birth Trauma; Gynecology Malpractice; Medical Liability; Medical Negligence; Nursing Malpractice; Nursing Negligence; Obstetric Malpractice; Pediatric Malpractice; Pharmacists Liability; Physicians Professional Liability; Surgeons Liability; Head Injury; Plaintiffs Personal Injury; Wrongful Death; Tort Liability. ***Email:*** cmm@mellinolaw.com

ASSOCIATE

PAIGE H. PLATTEN, born Springfield, Illinois, February 2, 1967; admitted to bar, 2004, Ohio. *Education:* Case Western Reserve University (B.S.N., 2000); New England School of Law (J.D., 2003). ***PRACTICE AREAS:*** Medical Malpractice; Personal Injury. ***Email:*** pplatten@mellinolaw.com

LAW OFFICE OF WARNER MENDENHALL

CLEVELAND, OHIO

(See Akron)

False Claims Act, Whistleblower Litigation, Qui Tam Litigation, Employment Law, Government, Municipal Law, Litigation, Bankruptcy.

MEYERS, ROMAN, FRIEDBERG & LEWIS

A LEGAL PROFESSIONAL ASSOCIATION

28601 CHAGRIN BOULEVARD, SUITE 500
CLEVELAND, OHIO 44122
Telephone: 216-831-0042
Fax: 216-831-0542
URL: http://www.meyerslamannarandroman.com
Email: attys@meyersroman.com
URL: http://www.meyersroman.com

Surety and Insurance Defense Law, Business and Corporate Law, Estate Planning, Business Succession, Environmental Law, Commercial Litigation, Construction and General Litigation, Probate, Family Law, Employment Law and Real Estate Law.

MEMBERS OF FIRM

ANNE L. MEYERS, born Brooklyn, New York, March 23, 1951; admitted to bar, 1977, Ohio. *Education:* The Ohio State University (B.A., 1972); Capital University (J.D., 1977). *Member:* Cleveland, Ohio State and American (Member, Fidelity and Surety Committee) Bar Associations. ***PRACTICE AREAS:*** Business Law; Corporate Law; Civil Litigation; Employment Discrimination; Insurance Law; Surety Law. ***Email:*** ameyers@meyersroman.com

BARBARA K. ROMAN, born Cleveland, Ohio, May 22, 1950; admitted to bar, 1977, Ohio; 1982, U.S. District Court, Northern District of Ohio; 1983, U.S. District Court, Southern District of Ohio. *Education:* The Ohio State University (B.A., 1971); Cleveland Marshall College of Law (J.D., 1976). *Member:* Cuyahoga County, Ohio State and American Bar Associations. ***PRACTICE AREAS:*** Civil Litigation; Consumer Law; Domestic Relations; Family Law; Estate Planning; Probate; Real Estate; Surety Law. ***Email:*** broman@meyersroman.com

RONALD P. FRIEDBERG, born Cincinnati, Ohio, January 20, 1965; admitted to bar, 1991, Ohio; 1992, U.S. District Court, Northern District of Ohio and U.S. Court of Appeals, Sixth Circuit. *Education:* University of Michigan (B.B.A., with high distinction, 1987); Case Western Reserve University (J.D., magna cum laude, 1991). *Member:* Cleveland, Ohio State and American Bar Associations. ***PRACTICE AREAS:*** Civil Litigation; Employment Discrimination Law; Insurance Law; Surety Law. ***Email:*** rfriedberg@meyersroman.com

SCOTT M. LEWIS, born Brooklyn, New York, August 19, 1959; admitted to bar, 1984, Ohio. *Education:* University of Michigan (B.A., 1981); University of Chicago (J.D., cum laude, 1984). Phi Beta Kappa. Lecturer, Cleveland Bar Association Practice & Procedures Clinic (Corporate Acquisitions), 1995-1996. Alternate Member, International Hockey League Board of Governors, 1996-2000. *Member:* Cleveland, Cuyahoga County and Ohio State (Member, Corporation and Business Law Sections) Bar Associations. ***PRACTICE AREAS:*** Mergers, Acquisitions and Divestitures Law; Corporate Law; Partnership Law; Securities Law; Commercial Law. ***Email:*** slewis@meyersroman.com

PETER D. BROSSE, born New York, N.Y., April 12, 1959; admitted to bar, 1984, Ohio. *Education:* The Ohio State University (B.S., 1981); University of Toledo (J.D., 1984). Recipient, American Jurisprudence Award in Criminal Procedure. ***PRACTICE AREAS:*** Business Law; Corporate Law; Computer Law; Real Estate Law; Securities Law. ***Email:*** pbrosse@meyersroman.com

ALAN N. HIRTH, born Brooklyn, New York, May 13, 1948; admitted to bar, 1973, Ohio and U.S. District Court, Northern District of Ohio. *Education:* City College of the City University of New York (B.A., 1970); Cleveland Marshall College of Law (J.D., summa cum laude, 1973). *Member:* Cleveland, Ohio State and American Bar Associations. ***PRACTICE AREAS:*** Litigation. ***Email:*** ahirth@meyersroman.com

DEBRA J. HORN, born Plum City, Wisconsin, 1959; admitted to bar, 1986, Ohio; 1988, U.S. District Court, Northern District of Ohio. *Education:* University of Minnesota (B.A., magna cum laude, 1981; J.D., cum laude, 1986). *Member:* Cleveland and Ohio State Bar Associations; Ohio Women's Bar Association. ***LANGUAGES:*** Spanish. ***PRACTICE AREAS:*** Litigation. ***Email:*** dhorn@meyersroman.com

LYNN A. KRIESSLER, born Euclid, Ohio, March 4, 1965; admitted to bar, 1991, Ohio. *Education:* Wellesley College (B.A., 1987); Case Western Reserve University (J.D., 1991). ***PRACTICE AREAS:*** Business Law; Corporate Law; Business Succession; Estate Planning. ***Email:*** lkriessler@meyersroman.com

DEBRA A. PERELMAN, born Cleveland, Ohio, August 29, 1963; admitted to bar, 1989, Texas; 1993, Ohio. *Education:* Miami University (B.S., cum laude, 1985); Case Western Reserve University (J.D., cum laude, 1988). *Member:* Ohio State and American Bar Associations; State Bar of Texas. ***PRACTICE AREAS:*** Mergers, Acquisitions and Divestitures; Corporate Finance; Corporate Law; Business Law; Joint Ventures; Securities. ***Email:*** dperelman@meyersroman.com

ASSOCIATES

F. SCOTT B. GENEVA, born Geneva, Ohio, July 27, 1973; admitted to bar, 2000, Ohio. *Education:* Miami University (B.A., 1995); The Ohio State University (J.D., 1999). *Member:* Cleveland, Cuyahoga County, Ohio State and American Bar Associations. ***PRACTICE AREAS:*** Estate Planning; Probate; Tax Law. ***Email:*** sgeneva@meyersroman.com

MATTHEW E. PARKINS, born Lancaster, Ohio, July 20, 1974; admitted to bar, 2000, Ohio. *Education:* Ohio University (B.A., summa cum laude, 1996); Capital Univer-

(This Listing Continued)

MEYERS, ROMAN, FRIEDBERG & LEWIS, A LEGAL PROFESSIONAL ASSOCIATION, Cleveland—Continued

sity (J.D., magna cum laude, 2000). *Member:* Cleveland, Ohio State and American Bar Associations. ***PRACTICE AREAS:*** Business Law; Corporate Law; Civil Litigation; Employment Law; Insurance; Surety Law. ***Email:*** mparkins@meyersroman.com

KENNEE B. SWITZER, born Montreal, Quebec, December 5, 1953; admitted to bar, 1988, Ohio, U.S. District Court, Northern District of Ohio and U.S. Court of Appeals, Sixth Circuit. *Education:* McGill University (B.A., History, with honors, 1976); London School of Economics and Political Science (Ph.D., History, 1982); Cleveland-Marshall College of Law (J.D., summa cum laude, 1988). *Member:* Ohio State and American Bar Associations; Ohio Women's Bar Association; The Association of Trial Lawyers of America. ***LANGUAGES:*** French. ***PRACTICE AREAS:*** Corporate Litigation; Business Litigation; Employment Law; Civil Litigation. ***Email:*** kswitzer@meyersroman.com

GEOFFREY S. GOSS, born Cleveland, Ohio, August 15, 1969; admitted to bar, 1998, Ohio; 2003, New York. *Education:* Washington & Jefferson College (B.A., 1991); The Ohio State University (J.D., with honors, 1998). *Member:* Ohio State, New York State and American Bar Associations. ***PRACTICE AREAS:*** Corporate Law; Real Estate Law. ***Email:*** ggoss@meyersroman.com

JENIFERE M. REICHARD, born Cleveland, Ohio, March 4, 1978; admitted to bar, 2003, Ohio. *Education:* Villanova University (B.A., Communications); Cleveland-Marshall College of Law (J.D., 2003). *Member:* Cleveland, Cuyahoga County and Ohio State Bar Associations. ***PRACTICE AREAS:*** Domestic Relations; Family Law; Civil Litigation. ***Email:*** jreichard@meyersroman.com

STEPHEN M. NOWAK, born Cleveland, Ohio, August 15, 1977; admitted to bar, 2004, Ohio. *Education:* University of Dayton (B.A., 1999); Cleveland-Marshall College of Law (J.D., cum laude, 2004). *Member:* Cleveland and Ohio State Bar Associations. ***PRACTICE AREAS:*** Business Law; Corporate Law; Civil Litigation; Surety Law. ***Email:*** snowak@meyersroman.com

OF COUNSEL

LOUIS B. GENEVA, born Wilmington, Delaware, February 2, 1947; admitted to bar, 1973, Ohio; 1977, Connecticut. *Education:* Miami University (B.A., 1969); Suffolk University (J.D., 1973); New York University (LL.M., 1974). Cleveland-Marshall College of Law Emeritus Associate Professor. *Member:* Cleveland, Ohio State and American Bar Associations. ***PRACTICE AREAS:*** Estate Planning; Probate Law; Tax Law. ***Email:*** lgeneva@meyersroman.com

MILANO WEISER

ATTORNEYS & COUNSELORS AT LAW
A LEGAL PROFESSIONAL ASSOCIATION

MILANO LAW BUILDING
2639 WOOSTER ROAD
CLEVELAND, OHIO 44116
Telephone: 440-356-2828
Fax: 440-356-2873
Email: inquire@milanolaw.com
URL: http://www.milanolaw.com

Criminal Defense, White Collar Crime, Wrongful Death, Medical Malpractice, Nursing Home Negligence, Internet Law, Consumer Law.

JAY MILANO, born Cleveland, Ohio, June 1, 1951; admitted to bar, 1981, Ohio. *Education:* The Ohio State University (B.A., 1978); Cleveland Marshall College of Law (J.D., 1981). Adjunct Professor, Trial Tactics, Case Western Reserve University College of Law. Trial attorney, Complex Cases, Civil and Criminal, Federal and State Court. Counsel in cases outside of the State of Ohio. Acted as an on air Legal Consultant for both NBC, CBS and WTAM Radio. Featured, as have two of his cases, on "60 Minutes." Appeared on NBC Nightly News, CNN and NPR. *Member:* Cuyahoga County (Founding President and Mensa), Cleveland and Ohio State (Chair, Criminal Law Committee) Bar Associations; Ohio Academy of Trial Lawyers; National Association of Criminal Defense Lawyers; Ohio Association of Criminal Defense Lawyers; Ohio Association of Criminal Defense Lawyers (President); Cuyahoga Criminal Defense Lawyers Association (Member, Council of Delegates). ***PRACTICE AREAS:*** Criminal Defense; White Collar Crime; Wrongful Death; Medical Malpractice; Nursing Home Negligence; Internet Law; Consumer Law; Business Litigation. ***Email:*** jm@milanolaw.com

RACHEL M. WEISER, born Pittsburgh, Pennsylvania, March 17, 1975; admitted to bar, 1998, Ohio. *Education:* University of Pittsburgh (B.A. with honors in English Literature, summa cum laude, 1995); Case Western Reserve University (J.D., 1998). Phi Beta Kappa Honors Society. Awards: Paul J. Hergenroder Award, Top Student in Trial Tactics, Ault Mock Trial Team. Leadership Academy and Co-Chaired, 2001-2002. Alumni, Case Western Reserve University Law Alumni Board. Member: Board of Trustees of the Foundation for Jewish Education; Young Leadership Division Board of the Cleveland Jewish Federation. Instructor, Ursuline College Acclerated Program, Legal Studies Department. Trial Attorney, Medical Malpractice, Personal Injury, Civil Litigation and Criminal Defense. *Member:* Cuyahoga County (Member, Certified Grievance Committee) and American Bar Associations. ***PRACTICE AREAS:*** Personal Injury; Medical Malpractice; Nursing Home Negligence; Wrongful Death; Business Litigation; Internet Law; Consumer Law; Criminal Defense; White Collar Crime. ***Email:*** rmw@milanolaw.com

---

TIKVAH SHACHTER, born Cleveland, Ohio, November 11, 1975; admitted to bar, 2001, New York; 2005, Ohio. *Education:* Yeshiva University (B.A., Political Science, summa cum laude, 1997); Benjamin N. Cardozo School of Law (J.D., 2001). Editor, International and Comparative Law Journal. ***Email:*** ts@milanolaw.com

MILLISOR & NOBIL

A LEGAL PROFESSIONAL ASSOCIATION

Established in 1975

9150 SOUTH HILLS BOULEVARD, SUITE 300
CLEVELAND, OHIO 44147-3599
Telephone: 440-838-8800; 800-800-8806
Telefax: 440-838-8805
Email: laborlaw@millisor.com
URL: http://www.millisor.com

Columbus, Ohio Office: 300 East Broad Street, Suite 190, 43215. Telephone: 614-221-2234. Telefax: 614-221-1278.
Canton, Ohio Office: 4117 Whipple Avenue NW, 44718. Telephone: 330-493-8525; 888-867-6869. Telefax: 330-493-8606.

Employment Law including Labor Relations, Equal Employment Opportunity, Public Sector, OSHA, Arbitration Law, Litigation, Workers Compensation Law, Human Resources Consulting and Employee Benefit Law.

FIRM PROFILE: From its offices in Cleveland, Canton and Columbus, Millisor & Nobil advises and represents management nationally in labor and employment-related matters. Since the formation, in 1975, the firm has continued to grow in size and in client base. Our clients represent a cross-section of business, industry and associations.

The philosophy at Millisor & Nobil is that employers are better served by placing a greater emphasis on the prevention or minimization of problems before they occur. Our practice covers the entire spectrum of employment law - negotiating collective bargaining agreements, defending employers in grievance, arbitration and unfair labor practice hearings, developing union prevention strategies and countering union organizing campaigns and developing strike preparation plans. Millisor & Nobil manages plant relocations, union decertifications and deauthorizations and the often thorny successorship situations so critical to business acquisitions. We regularly appear before the National Labor Relations Board and the State Employment Relations Board.

Our employment law practice includes advice and counseling in such areas as occupational safety and health, prevailing wage, labor cost reduction analysis, workers' compensation, unemployment compensation, affirmative action and employment benefit plans, including health care cost containment.

Consistent success in defending employment-related lawsuits has distinguished Millisor & Nobil's litigation department since the firm's inception. While favorable results are the first priority in any litigation, achieving those results efficiently is essential. Our objective is to resolve all litigation to the client's satisfaction for the lowest total cost. Our lawyers rapidly identify issues and plot case strategy because they do not have to reinvent the wheel in each new lawsuit.

Our philosophy of anticipating and preventing problems before a crisis develops led us to create our human resource management department to assist employers in managing their most critical asset - their employees. This department provides expertise and experience in developing solutions to our clients in the areas of candidate assessment and selection, employee communications as well as practical guidance in the development of policies, procedures and handbooks.

Millisor & Nobil is deeply committed to preventive strategies geared to maintaining positive employee relations and avoiding litigation. The professionals at Millisor & Nobil approach legal issues with special knowledge of client operations and priorities acquired through long-term relationships.

KENNETH R. MILLISOR, born Belle Center, Ohio, 1937; admitted to bar, 1961, Ohio; U.S. Supreme Court; U.S. Court of Appeals, Sixth and District of Columbia Circuits; U.S. District Court, Northern District of Ohio. *Education:* Ohio Wesleyan University (B.A., 1959); The Ohio State University (J.D., 1960). Order of the Coif. Editor-in-Chief, Ohio State Law Journal, 1960. Listed in: "Who's Who in American Law," 1983—; "Best Lawyers in America," Labor and Employment Law Section, 1989—. *Member:* Akron, Ohio State (Member, Board of Governors, 1971— and Chairman, Labor Law Section, 1978-1981) and American (Member, Labor and Employment Law Section) Bar Associations. ***PRACTICE AREAS:*** Labor Management Law; Equal Employment Opportunity Law; Public Sector; Arbitration Law; Employee Benefit Law. ***Email:*** kmillisor@millisor.com

STEVEN M. NOBIL, born Tiffin, Ohio, 1947; admitted to bar, 1972, Ohio; 1975, District of Columbia; U.S. Supreme Court; U.S. Court of Appeals, Sixth Circuit. *Education:* Baldwin-Wallace College (B.A., with distinction, 1969); The Ohio State University (J.D., 1972). Omicron Delta Kappa (President, 1968-1969). Listed in Best Lawyers in America," Labor and Employment Law Section, 1993—. *Member:* Akron, Cleveland, Ohio State (Chairman, Fair Labor Standards Act Subcommittee, Labor Law Section, 1979-1984) and American (Member, Equal Employment Law Committee; Labor and Employment Law and Collective Bargaining and Arbitration Sections) Bar Associations. ***PRACTICE AREAS:*** Labor Management Law; Equal Employment Opportunity Law; Public Sector; OSHA Law; Arbitration Law. ***Email:*** snobil@millisor.com

THOMAS D. ROONEY, born Akron, Ohio, 1947; admitted to bar, 1972, Ohio; U.S. Supreme Court; U.S. Court of Appeals, Sixth Circuit. *Education:* Ohio University (B.B.A., 1969); The Ohio State University (J.D., 1972). Assistant Ohio Attorney General, 1973-1976. *Member:* Cleveland, Ohio State (Member, Labor Law Section) and American (Member, Equal Employment Opportunity Subcommittee, Labor Law Section) Bar Associations. ***PRACTICE AREAS:*** Labor Management Law; Equal Employment Opportunity Law; Public Sector; Arbitration Law; Workers Compensation Law. ***Email:*** trooney@millisor.com

DAVID E. SCHREINER, born Cleveland, Ohio, 1948; admitted to bar, 1973, Ohio; U.S. Court of Appeals, Sixth Circuit. *Education:* Brown University (A.B., 1970); Case Western Reserve University (J.D., 1973). *Member:* Cleveland, Ohio State (Member, Labor

(This Listing Continued)

Section) and American (Member, Labor and Employment Law Section) Bar Associations. ***PRACTICE AREAS:*** Labor Management Law; Equal Employment Opportunity Law; Public Sector; OSHA Law; Arbitration Law. ***Email:*** dschreiner@millisor.com

DAVID P. HILLER, born Canton, Ohio, 1941; admitted to bar, 1969, Ohio; U.S. Court of Appeals, Sixth Circuit; U.S. Supreme Court. *Education:* University of Akron (A.B., with distinction, 1963); University of Michigan (M.A., 1965; J.D., cum laude, 1969). Chief Counsel to the Attorney General of Ohio, 1979-1980. *Member:* Columbus, Ohio State (Member, Labor and Employment Law Section) and American (Member, Labor and Employment Law Section) Bar Associations. (At Columbus Office). ***PRACTICE AREAS:*** Labor Management Law; Collective Bargaining; Defense of Unfair Labor Practices; Equal Employment Opportunity Law; Public Sector Labor Law; College and University Labor Law; Construction Labor Law; Arbitrations; Litigation. ***Email:*** dhiller@millisor.com

MARIBETH GAVIN-WUERTZ, born Cleveland, Ohio, 1955; admitted to bar, 1984, Ohio; U.S. District Court, Northern District of Ohio; U.S. Court of Appeals, Sixth Circuit. *Education:* Bowling Green State University (B.S., magna cum laude, 1978); Cleveland-Marshall College of Law (J.D., 1984). Externship, Hon. John M. Manos, U.S., District Court. Law Clerk to the Hon. Alice M. Batchelder, U.S. District Court, Northern District of Ohio, 1985-1987. *Member:* Cleveland (Member, Labor and Employment Law Section) and American (Member, Labor and Employment Law Section) Bar Associations. ***PRACTICE AREAS:*** Labor Management Law; Equal Employment Opportunity Law; Public Sector; OSHA Law; Arbitration Law; Human Resources Management.

MICHAEL J. REIDY, born Lakewood, Ohio, 1952; admitted to bar, 1978, Ohio. *Education:* University of Akron (B.S., 1974); Case Western Reserve University (J.D., 1978). *Member:* Cleveland and Ohio State Bar Associations. ***PRACTICE AREAS:*** Labor; Workers Compensation. ***Email:*** mreidy@millisor.com

JOHN R. SLATER, born Indianapolis, Indiana, 1946; admitted to bar, 1981, Ohio. *Education:* The Ohio State University (B.A., 1978; J.D., 1980). *Member:* Stark County (Chairman, Workers' Compensation Committee) Ohio State (Member, Workers Compensation Law Committee) and American Bar Associations. (At Canton Office). ***PRACTICE AREAS:*** Workers' Compensation Law; OSHA Law. ***Email:*** jslater@millisor.com

RICHARD A. MILLISOR, born Akron, Ohio, April 3, 1964; admitted to bar, 1990, New Mexico; 1992, Colorado; 1994, Ohio. *Education:* University of St. Andrews, Scotland (M.A. with honors, 1987); University of Colorado (J.D., 1990). Member and Editor, University of Colorado Law Review, 1988-1990. *Member:* Cleveland and Ohio State Bar Associations. (Certified Specialist in Labor and Employment Law, Ohio State Bar Association). ***PRACTICE AREAS:*** Labor Management Law; Arbitration Law; Litigation. ***Email:*** rmillisor@millisor.com

TERRY E. LARDAKIS, born Akron, Ohio, January 23, 1949; admitted to bar, 1977, Ohio. *Education:* University of Akron (B.A., 1972; J.D., 1976). *Member:* Akron and Ohio State Bar Associations. ***PRACTICE AREAS:*** Labor and Employment; Public Sector Labor Relations; Public Sector Employment Law. ***Email:*** tlardakis@millisor.com

PAUL C. MORRISON, born New Castle, Pennsylvania, 1939; admitted to bar, 1964, Ohio. *Education:* Allegheny College (B.A., 1961); Western Reserve University (J.D., 1964). Phi Delta Phi; Order of the Coif. Member, Board of Editors, Western Reserve Law Review, 1962-1964. *Member:* Cleveland, Ohio State and American Bar Associations. ***PRACTICE AREAS:*** Employee Benefits Law. ***Email:*** pmorrison@millisor.com

ROBERT E. DEZORT, born Cleveland, Ohio, December 29, 1966; admitted to bar, 1992, Ohio. *Education:* College of William and Mary (B.A., 1989); Cleveland Marshall College of Law (J.D., magna cum laude, 1992). *Member:* Ashland County, Cleveland, Ohio State and American Bar Associations. ***PRACTICE AREAS:*** Labor Law; Equal Employment Opportunity Law; Litigation. ***Email:*** rdezort@millisor.com

R. SCOT HARVEY, born Akron, Ohio, October 27, 1963; admitted to bar, 1990, Ohio; U.S. District Court, Northern District of Ohio; U.S. Court of Appeals, Fourth and Sixth Circuits; U.S. Supreme Court. *Education:* Syracuse University (B.A., 1986; M.A., 1987); The Ohio State University (J.D., 1990). ***PRACTICE AREAS:*** Labor and Employment; Litigation. ***Email:*** sharvey@millisor.com

DANIEL P. O'BRIEN, born Cleveland, Ohio, January 24, 1959; admitted to bar, 1984, Ohio. *Education:* Albion College (B.A., 1981); Case Western Reserve University (J.D., 1984). *Member:* Ohio State Bar Association. ***PRACTICE AREAS:*** Workers Compensation Law. ***Email:*** dobrien@millisor.com

SCOTT A. LEFELAR, born Cleveland, Ohio, May 19, 1969; admitted to bar, 1994, Illinois and U.S. District Court, Northern, Central and Southern Districts of Illinois; 1999, Ohio. *Education:* American University (B.A., summa cum laude, 1991); Case Western Reserve University (J.D., cum laude, 1994). *Member:* American Bar Association. ***PRACTICE AREAS:*** Employment Litigation. ***Email:*** slefelar@millisor.com

JENNIFER A. WELFLEY, born Akron, Ohio, 1972; admitted to bar, 1997, Ohio; 1998, U.S. District Court, Northern District of Ohio. *Education:* Kent State University (B.S., summa cum laude, 1994); University of Toledo (J.D., cum laude, 1997). Order of the Coif. Member, Board of Editors, University of Toledo Law Review. *Member:* Cleveland, Ohio State and American Bar Associations. ***PRACTICE AREAS:*** Litigation; Labor and Employment Law. ***Email:*** jwelfley@millisor.com

ASSOCIATES

MELANIE L. WEBBER, born Elyria, Ohio, May 12, 1970; admitted to bar, 1999, Ohio. *Education:* Cleveland State University (B.A.A., cum laude, 1995); Cleveland Marshall College of Law (J.D., 1998). *Member:* Cleveland Bar Association. ***PRACTICE AREAS:*** Employment Law; Labor Relations. ***Email:*** mwebber@millisor.com

CAROL D. STRASSMAN, born Cleveland, Ohio, 1955; admitted to bar, 1980, Ohio. *Education:* Miami University (A.B., 1977); Case Western Reserve University School of Law (J.D., 1980). *Member:* Cleveland and Ohio State Bar Associations. (Certified Specialist in Workers' Compensation Law, Ohio State Bar Association). ***PRACTICE AREAS:*** Workers' Compensation Law. ***Email:*** cstrassman@millisor.com

MONICA M. WEBER, born Parma, Ohio, 1979; admitted to bar, 2004, Ohio. *Education:* John Carroll University (B.S.B.A., cum laude, 2001); The Ohio State University (J.D., with honors, 2004). ***PRACTICE AREAS:*** Labor and Employment. ***Email:*** monicaweber@millisor.com

JEFFREY D. SMITH, born Parma, Ohio, 1979; admitted to bar, 2004, Ohio. *Education:* Baldwin-Wallace College (B.S., 2001); Case Western Reserve University (J.D., 2004). ***PRACTICE AREAS:*** Labor and Employment. ***Email:*** jsmith@millisor.com

ROBERT C. PIVONKA, II, born Durango, Colorado, December 16, 1968; admitted to bar, 1996, Ohio. *Education:* Marquette University (B.A., magna cum laude, 1991); Case Western Reserve University (J.D., magna cum laude, 1996). Order of the Coif. ***Email:*** rpivonka@millisor.com

OF COUNSEL

WILLIAM E. BLACKIE, III, born Lakewood, Ohio, October 19, 1954; admitted to bar, 1979, Ohio. *Education:* Ohio Wesleyan University (B.A., 1976); The Ohio State University (J.D., 1979). ***PRACTICE AREAS:*** School Law; Municipal Law; Labor and Employment; Litigation. ***Email:*** wblackie@millisor.com

PARALEGALS

JOAN C. POIRRIER, born Phillipsburg, Pennsylvania, August 22, 1949. *Education:* Business College (1980). ***PRACTICE AREAS:*** Workers Compensation; Litigation. ***Email:*** jpoirrier@millisor.com

MARK E. SNYDER, born Akron, Ohio, October 19, 1971; admitted to bar, 1998, Ohio. *Education:* Bowling Green State University (B.A., magna cum laude, 1994); The University of Akron (J.D., 1997). ***PRACTICE AREAS:*** Labor and Employment Litigation (50%); Workers Compensation (50%). ***Email:*** msnyder@millisor.com

MARGARET M. QUINN, born Parma, Ohio, 1963. ***PRACTICE AREAS:*** Workers Compensation Law. ***Email:*** mquinn@millisor.com

All Personnel are Members of Ohio State and American Bar Associations.

REPRESENTATIVE CLIENTS: Alliance Hospitality Management; Allied Waste Industries, Inc.; Aluminum Precision Products, Inc.; American Steel Foundries; Anderson-Dubose Co.; Blackhawk Automotive Plastics, Inc., BP Amoco Corp.; Case Foods; Cleveland Automobile Dealers Association; Eaton Corp.; Empire Plastics; Ferro Corporation; Goodrich Corp.; Janesville-Sackner Group; Products, Inc., Jo-Ann Stores, Inc.; KeyCorp.; May Department Stores Co. (May Co., Kaufmann's and Payless Shoe Source); McDonald Steel Corporation; Millcraft Paper Co.; National Screw Machine Products Association; Ohio Automobile Dealers Association; Ohio CAT; Ohio Desk Company; Park Ohio Industries; Peco II, Inc.; PolyOne Corp.; Printing Industry of Ohio; Procare Automotive Services, Inc.; Radix Wire Company; RCA Rubber Co.; R. L. Lipton Distributing Co.; Rock & Roll Hall of Fame and Museum, Inc.; Sekely Industries, Inc.; S&G Manufacturing Group; Sourceone Healthcare Technologies; Southwest General Hospital; ThyssenKrupp Gerlach; TJX Companies, Inc.; Vaccar Towers; Worthing Precision Metals; Yokohama Tire Corp.

(This Listing Continued)

MORGANSTERN, MACADAMS & DEVITO CO., L.P.A.

623 WEST ST. CLAIRE AVENUE
CLEVELAND, OHIO 44113
Telephone: 216-621-4244; 216-687-1212
Fax: 216-621-2951
URL: http://www.mmd-law.com

Civil Trial Practice with Emphasis on Family Law, Juvenile Law, Adoption, Custody, Business Litigation and Commercial Litigation.

STANLEY MORGANSTERN, born Cleveland, Ohio, August 27, 1941; admitted to bar, 1967, Ohio. *Education:* The Ohio State University (B.S., 1963); Cleveland-Marshall College of Law (J.D., 1967). *Member:* Cuyahoga County, Ohio State and American Academy of Matrimonial Lawyers. (Certified Specialist in Family Law, Ohio State Bar Association). ***PRACTICE AREAS:*** Family Law; Business Law. ***Email:*** smorgan153@aol.com

PAMELA J. MACADAMS, born Cleveland, Ohio, January 30, 1958; admitted to bar, 1984, Ohio. *Education:* Baldwin-Wallace College (B.A., magna cum laude, 1981); Cleveland-Marshall College of Law (J.D., 1984). *Member:* Ohio State Bar Association; American Academy of Matrimonial Lawyers. (Certified Specialist in Family Relations Law, Ohio State Bar Association). ***PRACTICE AREAS:*** Family Law; Juvenile Law. ***Email:*** pamatty@aol.com

CHRISTOPHER MICHAEL DEVITO, born Washington, D.C., November 27, 1965; admitted to bar, 1990, Ohio. *Education:* University of Notre Dame (B.B.A., in Fin. and Econ., 1987); The Ohio State University (J.D., 1990). *Member:* Cleveland and Ohio State Bar Associations. ***PRACTICE AREAS:*** Corporate Law; Medical Malpractice; Personal Injury; Torts. ***Email:*** devitolaw@yahoo.com

MICHAEL A. PARTLOW, born Scottsburg, Indiana, January 21, 1956; admitted to bar, 1986, Ohio. *Education:* University of Akron (J.D., 1986). ***PRACTICE AREAS:*** Appellate Practice; Family Law; Real Estate; Professional Liability; Torts.

MORIARTY & JAROS, P.L.L.

30000 CHAGRIN BOULEVARD, SUITE 200
CLEVELAND, OHIO 44124
Telephone: 216-360-2124
Telecopier: 216-360-2199
Email: info@moriartyjaros.com
URL: http://www.moriartyjaros.com

General Civil Practice. Corporate, Probate, Real Estate, Administrative, Taxation Law. Estate Planning. Litigation.

(This Listing Continued)

MORIARTY & JAROS, P.L.L., Cleveland—Continued

MEMBERS OF FIRM

RICHARD J. MORIARTY, born Cleveland, Ohio, October 4, 1921; admitted to bar, 1949, Ohio. *Education:* John Carroll University (B.B.A., 1943); The Cleveland-Marshall Law School (J.D., 1949). *Member:* Greater Cleveland and Ohio State (Member, Sections on: Taxation; Real Property, Probate and Trust Law; Corporation, Banking and Business Law) Bar Associations. ***PRACTICE AREAS:*** Corporate Law; Estate Planning; Real Estate. ***Email:*** rjmoriarty@aol.com

STANLEY T. JAROS, born Muskogee, Oklahoma, February 25, 1945; admitted to bar, 1973, Ohio. *Education:* Brown University (A.B., 1967); University of Pennsylvania (M.B.A., 1970); Case Western Reserve University (J.D., 1973). *Member:* Greater Cleveland and Ohio State Bar Associations. ***PRACTICE AREAS:*** Corporate Law; Real Estate. ***Email:*** sjaros@moriartyjaros.com

JEFFREY J. HIGERD, born Columbus, Ohio, October 29, 1948; admitted to bar, 1975, Ohio. *Education:* Ohio Wesleyan University (B.A., 1970); Case Western Reserve University (J.D., 1973). Law Clerk to Ben C. Green, U.S. District Judge, 1976-1979. *Member:* Cleveland and Ohio State Bar Associations. ***PRACTICE AREAS:*** Closely Held Businesses; Contracts; Commercial Litigation; Corporate Banking Law; Trusts; Real Estate; Leases and Leasing. ***Email:*** jhigerd@moriartyjaros.com

HARRY L. ARTHUR, born Cleveland, Ohio, February 12, 1956; admitted to bar, 1982, Ohio. *Education:* Miami University (B.S., 1978); Case Western Reserve University (J.D., 1981). *Member:* Greater Cleveland and Ohio State Bar Associations. ***PRACTICE AREAS:*** Corporate Law; Real Estate. ***Email:*** harthur@moriartyjaros.com

DAVID R. RILEY, born Akron, Ohio, November 2, 1948; admitted to bar, 1980, Ohio. *Education:* Brown University (A.B., 1971); Case Western Reserve University (J.D., 1980). *Member:* Greater Cleveland and Ohio State Bar Associations. [Lt., U.S. Navy, 1972-1977]. ***PRACTICE AREAS:*** Probate; Taxation; Estate Planning Law; Corporate Law; Employee Benefits. ***Email:*** driley@moriartyjaros.com

OF COUNSEL

EDGAR H. BOLES, born Cleveland, Ohio, March 2, 1947; admitted to bar, 1973, Ohio; 1974, U.S. District Court, Northern District of Ohio; 1991, U.S. Court of Appeals, Sixth Circuit; 1995, U.S. District Court, Eastern District of Michigan; 1997, U.S. Supreme Court. *Education:* Ohio Wesleyan University (B.A., 1969); Case Western Reserve University (J.D., 1973). Editor, Case Western Reserve Law Review, 1972-1973. Law Clerk, Eighth District Court of Appeals of Ohio, 1973-1975. Author: Casenote, "General Investment Corp. v. Angelini," 23 Case Wes. Res. L. Rev. 418 (1972). Assistant Prosecuting Attorney, Cuyahoga County, 1975-1976. Member, Court of Nisi Prius, 2001—. Formerly with Buckley King. *Member:* Greater Cleveland, Geauga County, Ohio State and American Bar Associations. ***PRACTICE AREAS:*** Commercial Litigation; Business Law; Labor and Employment; Domestic Relations. ***Email:*** eboles@moriartyjaros.com

---

MOSCARINO & TREU, L.L.P.

THE HANNA BUILDING
1422 EUCLID AVENUE, SUITE 630
CLEVELAND, OHIO 44115
Telephone: 216-621-1000
Fax: 216-622-1556
Email: gmoscarino@mosctreu.com
URL: http://www.lawyers.com/moscarino&treu

General Civil Trial and Appellate Practice. Civil Litigation in all Courts. Complex Litigation, Medical Legal, Product Liability, Business, Banking and Commercial Litigation, Personal Injury and Employment Litigation, White Collar Criminal Defense.

FIRM PROFILE: Moscarino & Treu is a law firm specializing in civil litigation and dispute resolution with a focus on personalized service for clients ranging from large corporations to small businesses and individuals. Founded by two large firm partners with extensive experience in tort and business litigation. The firm provides sophisticated representation in a small firm environment.

GEORGE M. MOSCARINO, born Cleveland, Ohio, September 29, 1958; admitted to bar, 1983, Ohio. *Education:* Denison University (B.A., 1980); Case Western Reserve University (J.D., 1983). Member, National Moot Court Team, 1982-1983. Assistant Prosecuting Attorney, Cuyahoga County, Cleveland, Ohio, 1983-1986. *Member:* Cleveland, Ohio State and American Bar Associations. ***PRACTICE AREAS:*** Litigation; Medical Malpractice. ***Email:*** gmoscarino@mosctreu.com

KRIS H. TREU, born Cleveland, Ohio, October 10, 1957; admitted to bar, 1983, Ohio; 1993, Maine. *Education:* Dartmouth College (A.B., 1980); The Ohio State University (J.D., 1983). Staff Member, 1981-1982, Note and Comment Editor, 1982-1983, The Ohio State University Law Journal. Author: "Loss of Consortium and Engaged Couples: The Frustrating Fate of Faithful Fiancees," 44 Ohio State Law Journal 219. *Member:* Cleveland and Ohio State Bar Associations; Defense Research Institute; Anthony J. Celebrezze Inn of Court. ***PRACTICE AREAS:*** Litigation; Medical Liability; Professional Liability; Commercial Litigation; Product Liability. ***Email:*** ktreu@mosctreu.com

MICHAEL J. BERTSCH, born Canton, Ohio, June 16, 1956; admitted to bar, 1982, Ohio. *Education:* Xavier University (B.S.B.A., magna cum laude, 1978); Cleveland-Marshall College of Law (J.D., 1981). Member, Self Insurers' Group of Ohio. Co-author: "Overview of Ohio Workers' Compensation Law for Employers"; "Martindale-Hubbell Law Digest 2000 Workers' Compensation Law Summary". Lecturer, Employer Intentional Tort Liability, Ohio Workers' Compensation and Related Legislative and Insurance Issues. *Member:* Cleveland and Ohio State Bar Associations; Ohio Association of Civil Trial Attorneys; Cleveland Association of Civil Trial Attorneys; Defense Research Institute. ***PRACTICE AREAS:*** Workers Compensation Defense; Employer Intentional Torts; Employment Law; OSHA; Products Liability; Marketing Law; Consumer Protection. ***Email:*** mbertsch@mosctreu.com

WILLIAM H. FALIN, born Mansfield, Ohio, April 30, 1961; admitted to bar, 1987, Ohio; 1998, Indiana. *Education:* Ohio University (A.B., 1983); Cleveland-Marshall College of Law (J.D., magna cum laude, 1987). Editor, Cleveland State Law Review, 1986-1987. *Member:* Cleveland and Ohio State Bar Associations. ***PRACTICE AREAS:*** Litigation; Commercial Litigation; Securities Litigation; Medical Liability; Professional Liability; Products Liability. ***Email:*** wfalin@mosctreu.com

---

EDWARD S. JERSE, born Cleveland, Ohio, April 8, 1958; admitted to bar, 1983, Ohio. *Education:* Georgetown University (B.A., magna cum laude, 1980); Harvard University (J.D., 1983). Phi Beta Kappa. *Member:* Cleveland and Ohio State Bar Associations. ***PRACTICE AREAS:*** Litigation. ***Email:*** ejerse@mosctreu.com

PATRICIA CASEY CUTHBERTSON, born Cleveland, Ohio, October 27, 1955; admitted to bar, 1990, Ohio. *Education:* Kent State University (B.S.N., cum laude, 1978); Cleveland Marshall College of Law (J.D., summa cum laude, 1990). Sigma Theta Tau. *Member:* Erie and Ohio Bar Associations. ***PRACTICE AREAS:*** Medical Malpractice; Health Care Risk Management. ***Email:*** pcuthbertson@mosctreu.com

JOHN T. BULLOCH, born Cleveland, Ohio, March 20, 1952; admitted to bar, 1991, Ohio. *Education:* University of Toledo (B.S., Pharmacy, cum laude, 1975); Case Western Reserve University (J.D., magna cum laude, 1991). Order of the Coif. Member, Case Western Reserve Law Review, 1989-1990. *Member:* Cleveland and Ohio State Bar Associations; Defense Research Institute. ***PRACTICE AREAS:*** Litigation; Medical Malpractice; Health Care Risk Management. ***Email:*** jbulloch@mosctreu.com

ROBERT L. AUSTRIA, born Milwaukee, Wisconsin, August 1, 1962; admitted to bar, 1998, Ohio. *Education:* Miami University (B.S., in Business, 1985); Baldwin-Wallace College (M.A., Business Administration, 1993); Cleveland-Marshall College of Law (J.D., cum laude, 1998). *Member:* Akron and Ohio State Bar Associations. ***PRACTICE AREAS:*** Real Estate; Business Law. ***Email:*** raustria@mosctreu.com

SEAN M. SWEENEY, born Cincinnati, Ohio, September 1, 1968; admitted to bar, 1999, Ohio. *Education:* University of Cincinnati (B.A., 1995); Cleveland-Marshall College of Law (J.D., 1999). *Member:* Cleveland and Ohio State Bar Associations. ***LANGUAGES:*** German. ***PRACTICE AREAS:*** Medical Liability; Professional Liability; Products Liability; General Liability. ***Email:*** ssweeney@mosctreu.com

MICHAEL W. MATILE, born Toledo, Ohio, December 2, 1972; admitted to bar, 2000, Ohio. *Education:* University of Kentucky (B.B.A., 1995); University of Toledo (J.D., 2000). Law Clerk to Justice Deborah A. Agosti, Nevada Supreme Court, 2001-2002. *Member:* Cleveland and Ohio State Bar Associations. ***PRACTICE AREAS:*** Litigation. ***Email:*** mmatile@mosctreu.com

CAROL J. MOSKOWITZ, born Ann Arbor, Michigan, March 9, 1961; admitted to bar, 2002, Ohio. *Education:* University of Michigan (B.S.N., magna cum laude); Cleveland-Marshall College of Law (J.D., cum laude, 2002). *Member: Ohio State Bar Association.* ***PRACTICE AREAS:*** Medical Malpractice Defense. ***Email:*** cmoskowitz@mosctreu.com

KATHLEEN E. GEE, born Cleveland, Ohio, July 18, 1972; admitted to bar, 2002, Ohio. *Education:* Kent State University (B.B.A., 1994); Cleveland Marshall College of Law (J.D., magna cum laude, 2002). Delta Sigma Pi. Member, Society for Human Resource Management; Student Bar Association; Self-Insured Group of Ohio. *Member:* Cleveland, Ohio State and American Bar Associations. ***PRACTICE AREAS:*** Employment Law; Workers Compensation. ***Email:*** kgee@mosctreu.com

MARY E. WHITE, born Cleveland Ohio, September 21, 1960; admitted to bar, 2003, Ohio. *Education:* St. Vincent Charity Hospital School of Nursing (R.N., 1981); Bowling Green State University (B.S.N., 1990); Cleveland Marshall College of Law (J.D., 2002). Member, American Nurses Association; Ohio Nurses Association. Ohio Northern University Law Review: "Nurses and Hospitals Battling: Hospitals Protect Profits," Nurses Advocate for Quality Patient Care While Turning to Unions, As a Solution, 27 Ohio N.U.L. Rev. 285, 2000. *Member:* Ohio State and American Bar Associations. ***PRACTICE AREAS:*** Medical Malpractice Defense.

SEAMUS J. McMAHON, born Cleveland, Ohio, July 18, 1978; admitted to bar, 2003, Ohio. *Education:* Case Western Reserve University (B.A., 1999); Cleveland-Marshall College of Law (J.D., with honors, 2003). ***PRACTICE AREAS:*** Medical Malpractice Defense. ***Email:*** smcmahon@mosctreu.com

---

MURMAN & ASSOCIATES

CLEVELAND, OHIO

(See Lakewood)

Municipal Law, Probate and Estate, Professional Responsibility Legal Ethics and Criminal Law in regards to Professional Licensing.

A. DALE NATICCHIA

4141 ROCKSIDE ROAD, SUITE 230
CLEVELAND, OHIO 44131
Telephone: 216-520-5297
Fax: 216-642-5355
Email: dale@naticchia.com
URL: http://www.naticchialaw.com

Driving While Intoxicated, Traffic Violations, Juvenile Law, Drivers License Suspension, DUI, Estate Planning, Wills and Probate Law, Contested Wills, Felonies and Collections.

A. DALE NATICCHIA, born Cleveland, Ohio, April 18, 1952; admitted to bar, 1986, Ohio; 1987, U.S. District Court, District of Ohio. *Education:* John Carroll University (B.A.,

(This Listing Continued)

magna cum laude, 1983); Cleveland-Marshall College of Law (J.D., 1986). Special Counsel to Ohio Attorney General. *Member:* Cleveland, Cuyahoga County and Ohio State Bar Associations; The Association of Trial Lawyers of America. ***PRACTICE AREAS:*** DWI; DUI; Juvenile Law; Wills; Probate; Contested Wills; Felonies; Collections; Drivers License Suspension.

NICOLA, GUDBRANSON & COOPER, LLC

Established in 1933

REPUBLIC BUILDING, SUITE 1400
25 W. PROSPECT AVENUE
CLEVELAND, OHIO 44115-1048
Telephone: 216-621-7227
FAX: 216-621-3999
URL: http://www.nicola.com
URL: http://www.nicolalaw.com

Corporations, Transactions, Taxation, Real Estate, Estate Planning, Probate and Trusts, Business and Commercial Litigation and Appeals, Employment Law, Municipal Law, School Law, Products Liability, Health Care Law, Real Estate Ad Valorem Tax Litigation.

FIRM PROFILE: Our Firm was founded in 1933 by Benjamin Nicola.

K. V. NICOLA (1906-1994)

MEMBERS OF FIRM

ROBERT N. GUDBRANSON, born Camden, New Jersey, October 8, 1932; admitted to bar, 1961, Ohio. *Education:* Dartmouth College (A.B., 1955); Case Western Reserve University (LL.B., 1961). ***PRACTICE AREAS:*** Business; Real Estate; Estate Planning; Probate and Trust Law. ***Email:*** gudbranson@nicola.com

RICHARD A. COOPER, born Columbus, Ohio, August 31, 1952; admitted to bar, 1977, Ohio. *Education:* Ohio State University (B.A., magna cum laude, 1974); University of Chicago (J.D., 1977). Phi Beta Kappa. ***PRACTICE AREAS:*** Business; Tax; Estate Planning. ***Email:*** rcooper@nicola.com

JOHN D. SAYRE, born Cleveland, Ohio, May 29, 1950; admitted to bar, 1977, Ohio. *Education:* DePauw University (B.A., cum laude, 1972); Indiana University (M.A., 1974); Case Western Reserve University (J.D., 1977). ***PRACTICE AREAS:*** Business and Commercial Litigation; Real Estate Litigation; Domestic Relations. ***Email:*** sayre@nicola.com

TIMOTHY D. CARNAHAN, born Cleveland, Ohio, April 16, 1954; admitted to bar, 1979, Ohio; 1981, Florida. *Education:* University of Akron (B.S. B.A., magna cum laude, 1976; J.D., 1979); University of Miami (LL.M., taxation, 1980). ***PRACTICE AREAS:*** Business; Tax; Estate Planning; Health Care Law; Real Estate. ***Email:*** carnahan@nicola.com

MATTHEW T. FITZSIMMONS, born Staten Island, New York, October 3, 1953; admitted to bar, 1980, Ohio; 1997, U.S. Supreme Court. *Education:* University of Notre Dame (A.B., with honors, 1975); University of Dayton (J.D., 1980). Law Clerk to Chief Justice Frank D. Celebrezze, Supreme Court of Ohio, 1980-1982. ***PRACTICE AREAS:*** Business and Commercial Litigation; Employment Litigation; Product Liability Litigation; Health Care Law; Ad Valorem Property Tax Litigation. ***Email:*** fitzsimmons@nicola.com

L. JAMES JULIANO, JR., born Cleveland, Ohio, February 20, 1950; admitted to bar, 1977, Ohio; 1986, New York. *Education:* Case Western Reserve University (B.A., 1973; J.D., 1977). ***PRACTICE AREAS:*** Corporate; Real Estate; Municipal; School; Labor; Trials; Italian-American Transactions. ***Email:*** juliano@nicola.com

JAMES H. GROVE, born South Bend, Indiana, January 12, 1962; admitted to bar, 1988, Ohio. *Education:* Michigan State University (B.S., 1984); Case Western Reserve University (J.D., 1988). ***PRACTICE AREAS:*** Business, Commercial and Employment Litigation; Products Liability; Insurance. ***Email:*** grove@nicola.com

RICHARD G. WITKOWSKI, born January 6, 1954; admitted to bar, 1985, Ohio; 1989, California. *Education:* Miami University (B.B.A., cum laude, 1976); Cleveland State University (J.D., 1985). Certified Public Accountant, Ohio, 1978. ***PRACTICE AREAS:*** Complex Litigation; Professional Liability; First and Third Party Insurance Defense. ***Email:*** witkowski@nicola.com

ASSOCIATES

MICHAEL E. CICERO, born Cleveland, Ohio, August 14, 1965; admitted to bar, 1992, Ohio. *Education:* Miami University (B.S., 1987); Cleveland Marshall College of Law (J.D., 1991). ***PRACTICE AREAS:*** Municipal Law; Business; Real Estate; Tax; Commercial Litigation; Trial and Appellate Litigation; Planning and Zoning. ***Email:*** cicero@nicola.com

RONALD C. YINGLING, born Canton, Ohio, June 29, 1968; admitted to bar, 1996, Ohio. *Education:* University of Dayton (B.S., 1990); Cleveland Marshall College of Law (J.D., cum laude, 1996). Editor, Cleveland State Law Review, 1995-1996. ***PRACTICE AREAS:*** Commercial Litigation; Products Liability; Employment Litigation. ***Email:*** yingling@nicola.com

JAMES P. BAUER, born Benton Harbor, Michigan, March 17, 1967; admitted to bar, 1993, Ohio. *Education:* Michigan State University (B.A., with honors, 1989); Ohio State University (J.D., 1993). ***PRACTICE AREAS:*** Business; Real Estate; Commercial Litigation. ***Email:*** bauer@nicola.com

NICHOLAS J. DERTOUZOS, born Rochester, Michigan, December 1, 1973; admitted to bar, 1999, Ohio. *Education:* Michigan State University (B.A., 1996); Case Western Reserve University (J.D., 1999). ***PRACTICE AREAS:*** Litigation; Trial Practice; Appellate Practice; Complex Litigation; Corporate Litigation; Commercial Litigation. ***Email:*** dertouzos@nicola.com

BRENDA L. WOLFF, born Warren, Ohio, July 10, 1965; admitted to bar, 1994, Ohio; 2001, Massachusetts. *Education:* Cleveland State University (B.B.A., cum laude, 1991); Cleveland-Marshall College of Law (J.D., cum laude, 1994). ***PRACTICE AREAS:*** Estate Planning; Estate Administration; Federal Taxation; State Taxation. ***Email:*** wolff@nicola.com

BECKY M. SCHEIMAN, born Brunswick, Ohio, October 23, 1972; admitted to bar, 1998, Wisconsin; 2000, Ohio. *Education:* Washington & Jefferson College (B.A., 1995); Marquette University Law School (J.D., 1998); Case Western Reserve University (LL.M., Taxation, 1999). ***PRACTICE AREAS:*** Corporate Law; Tax Law; Nonprofit Organizations Law; Estate Planning; Estate Administration; School Law. ***Email:*** bscheiman@nicola.com

OF COUNSEL

VINCENT A. FEUDO, born East Cleveland, Ohio, April 28, 1939; admitted to bar, 1965, Ohio. *Education:* Ohio University (B.S.J., 1961); Cleveland-Marshall College of Law (J.D., 1965). Municipal Prosecutor: Mayfield Village, 1973—; Gates Mills, 1976—. Hunting Valley, 1984—. Director of Law and Prosecutor, Mayfield Heights, 1973-1994. Law Director, South Euclid, 1995-2004. ***PRACTICE AREAS:*** Municipal Law; Civil Rights Section 1983 Litigation. ***Email:*** feudo@nicola.com

ANTHONY R. TROIA, born Ravenna, Ohio, March 3, 1938; admitted to bar, 1966, Ohio. *Education:* Kent State University (B.S., 1959); The Ohio State University (J.D., 1966). ***PRACTICE AREAS:*** Corporate Law; Tax Law; Estate Planning; Probate; Real Estate. ***Email:*** troia@nicola.com

JAMES D. ROSEMAN, born Massillon, Ohio, September 9, 1947; admitted to bar, 1972, Ohio. *Education:* Ohio University (A.B., 1969); Case Western Reserve University (J.D., 1972). ***PRACTICE AREAS:*** Estate Planning; Probate; Closely Held Business Law; Taxation. ***Email:*** jroseman@nicola.com

JAMES R. CHRISZT, born Cleveland, Ohio, 1956; admitted to bar, 1987, Ohio. *Education:* University of Notre Dame (B.B.A., 1978); Cleveland-Marshall College of Law, Cleveland State University (J.D., summa cum laude, 1987). Certified Public Accountant, Ohio, 1980 (inactive). ***PRACTICE AREAS:*** Corporate; Corporate Succession Planning; Estate Planning; Finance; Real Estate; Tax. ***Email:*** jchriszt@nicola.com

TIMOTHY L. McGARRY, born Cleveland, Ohio, 1966; admitted to bar, 1991, Ohio. *Education:* Ohio State University (B.S.B.A., summa cum laude, 1988); Northwestern University (J.D., 1991). ***PRACTICE AREAS:*** Commercial Litigation; Corporate Litigation; Civil Litigation; Construction Law. ***Email:*** tmcgarry@nicola.com

ARTHUR L. (TIM) CLEMENTS, III, born Cleveland, Ohio, 1957; admitted to bar, 1985, New York; 1986, Ohio. *Education:* Yale University (B.A., 1979); Ohio State University (J.D., 1984). ***PRACTICE AREAS:*** Estate Planning; Probate; Trust Administration; Elder Law; Trust Litigation; Estate Litigation; Civil Litigation; School Law; Nonprofit Organizations Law; Corporate Law. ***Email:*** tclements@nicola.com

REFERENCES: National City Bank; Key Bank, N.A.

NORCHI, BARRETT & FORBES LLC

Established in 2002

COMMERCE PARK IV
23240 CHAGRIN BOULEVARD, SUITE 600
CLEVELAND, OHIO 44122
Telephone: 216-514-9500
Fax: 216-514-4304
Email: kmn@norchilaw.com

Medical Negligence Defense, Health Care Litigation, Employment Law, Insurance Defense.

FIRM PROFILE: Five attorneys focusing on the defense of medical malpractice and health care organization litigation, employment law, insurance law and general civil litigation. The attorneys are supported by two nurse consultants and two paralegals.

KEVIN M. NORCHI, born Youngstown, Ohio, August 10, 1959; admitted to bar, 1986, Ohio; 1986, U.S. District Court, Northern District of Ohio; 1989, U.S. District Court, Southern District of Ohio; 1992, U.S. Court of Appeals, 6th Circuit. *Education:* Fordham University (A.B., 1983); Case Western Reserve University (J.D., 1986). *Member:* Cleveland and Ohio State Bar Associations; Ohio Association of Civil Trial Attorneys. ***PRACTICE AREAS:*** Litigation; Medical Negligence; Health Care Litigation; Products Liability; Employment Law; Professional Liability. ***Email:*** kmn@norchilaw.com

LISA M. BARRETT, born Lakewood, Ohio, June 4, 1967; admitted to bar, 1992, Ohio; 1995, U.S. Court of Appeals, Sixth Circuit and U.S. District Court, Northern District of Ohio. *Education:* Alma College (B.A., 1989); Case Western Reserve University School of Law (J.D., 1992). Prosecuting Attorney/Assistant Director of Law, Shaker Heights, Ohio, 1992-2000. Moscarino & Treu, LLP, 2000-2002. *Member:* Cuyahoga County, Cleveland and American Bar Associations. ***PRACTICE AREAS:*** Litigation; Medical Malpractice; Labor and Employment; Professional Liability. ***Email:*** lbarrett@norchilaw.com

STEVEN J. FORBES, born Fort Wayne, Indiana, November 10, 1962; admitted to bar, 1989, Ohio; 1994 U.S. District Court, Northern District of Ohio. *Education:* Amherst College (A.B., cum laude, 1986); George Washington University (J.D., with honors, 1989). Member, Felony Division Stark County Public Defenders Office, 1992-1994. *Member:* Cuyahoga County and Ohio State Bar Associations. ***PRACTICE AREAS:*** Litigation; Professional Liability; Employment Law; Insurance. ***Email:*** sforbes@norchilaw.com

MICHAEL L. GOLDING, born Sydney, New South Wales, Australia, September 9, 1968; admitted to bar, 1993, Ohio; U.S. Supreme Court; 1994, U.S. District Court, Northern District of Ohio. *Education:* Bucknell University (B.A., cum laude, 1990); Georgetown University (J.D., 1993). Member, Law and Policy in International Business, 1991-1993. *Member:* Cleveland, Ohio State and American Bar Associations. ***PRACTICE AREAS:*** Litigation; Insurance Defense; Casualty. ***Email:*** mgolding@norchilaw.com

(This Listing Continued)

NORCHI, BARRETT & FORBES LLC, Cleveland—Continued

IVERSON MATTHEW JACKSON, born Cleveland, Ohio; admitted to bar, 2003, Ohio. *Education:* University of Cincinnati (B.A., Urban Planning, 1999); Case Western Reserve University (J.D./M.B.A, 2003). *Member:* Cleveland, Cuyahoga County and Ohio State Bar Associations. ***Email:*** mjackson@norchilaw.com

REPRESENTATIVE CLIENTS: University Hospital Health Systems; Summa Health Systems; St. Paul Insurance Co.; The Doctors Company; ACE USA Insurance Co.; U.S. Liability Insurance Co.; Meridia Health System; National Guardian Risk Retention; Case Western Reserve University; Laurelwood Hospitals & Counseling Centers; Philadelphia Insurance Companies; Markel Insurance Company.

NOVAK, ROBENALT, PAVLIK & SCHARF, LLP

SKYLIGHT OFFICE TOWER, TOWER CITY CENTER
1660 WEST SECOND STREET, SUITE 950
CLEVELAND, OHIO 44113-1498
Telephone: 216-781-8700
Facsimile: 216-781-9227
URL: http://www.ohiomedicalmalpractice.com
Email: nrps@nrpslaw.com
URL: http://www.ohiodebtrelief.com

Medical Malpractice, Birth Trauma, Automobile Accident, Personal Injury, FELA, Products Liability, Debtor-Creditor Law, Personal and Business Bankruptcy and Workouts, Business Law, Real Estate, General and Civil Trial Practice, Litigation.

FIRM PROFILE: Approximately 70 years ago, a firm was established that became known as one of the most prestigious personal injury and litigation law firms in the city of Cleveland. In 1978, a merger diversified that firm's practice into the areas of business, debtor/creditor disputes and bankruptcy.

Today, the firm's primary focus is client satisfaction with a result oriented practice. We specialize in two broad areas: (1) plaintiff's personal injury and medical malpractice litigation, and (2) legal services to small and mid-sized businesses and individuals, including bankruptcy and out-of-court workouts.

We adhere to the belief that results and client satisfaction are the most important tenets upon which our practice is built. Every client should expect this standard of practice.

PARTNERS

WILLIAM J. NOVAK, born Cleveland, Ohio, March 22, 1949; admitted to bar, 1973, Ohio; 1974, U.S. District Court, Northern District of Ohio; 1985, U.S. Court of Appeals, Sixth Circuit and U.S. Supreme Court; 1994, Kentucky. *Education:* Boston University (B.S. in B.A., magna cum laude, 1971; J.D., 1973). Beta Gamma Sigma. Member, Board of Education, City of Maple Heights, 1976-1977. Mediator, Settlement Week, 1989. Lecturer and Member, Panel of Arbitrators, American Arbitration Association. Member, Million Dollar Advocates Forum. Special Counsel to Ohio State Attorney General Betty Montgomery. Special Counsel, Ohio State Attorney General James Petro. Author: "Liability for Inducing A Breach of the Patient-Physician Relationship," CATA News, Spring, 2002; "Malpractice Insurance Disclosure Rule-Are You in Compliance?," Cleveland Bar Journal, January, 2002; "Co-Counsel Fees: Are Referral Fees Permissible?," Cleveland Bar Journal, May, 1999; "Attorney Liens and Retaining Client Files," Cleveland Bar Journal, April, 1998. *Member:* Medina County, Cleveland (Trustee, 1998-2001; Member, Bar Journal Committee, 1998-1999; Member: Medical Legal Committee, 1974-1988; Judicial Selection Committee, 1987-1990, 2000-2004; Bicentennial Constitution Committee; Law Lecturer, 1983 and 1998; Fee Dispute Committee, 1998-2003; Trustee, Litigation Section, 1989-1990; Unauthorized Practice of Law Committee, 1998-2003; Ethics Committee, 1993-2003; Non-Dues Revenue Committee, 1999-2000; Grievance Committee, 2000-2004; Standing Committee on Professionalism, 1999-2001; Chairman, Lawyer Referral Services, 2003-2005; Co-Chairman, First Annual Symposium on Ethics and Professionalism, 2001), Cuyahoga County (Trustee, 1982-1992 and Chairman, 1982-1984, Common Pleas Court Committee; Secretary, 1987; Law Lecturer, 1983-1988; Chairman, Court of Appeals Committee; Chairman, Lawyer Referral Committee, 1989-1993; Chairman Tort Committee, 1988; Chairman, Continuing Legal Education, 1990-1991; Chairman, Greenbriar Seminar, 1991-1994; Chairman, Long Range Planning, 1990), Ohio State and American (Member: Litigation Section; Subcommittee on Malpractice, 1976) Bar Associations; The Association of Trial Lawyers of America; Ohio Academy of Trial Lawyers (Vice Chairman, Specialization Committee, 1977-1978; Lecturer, 1993-1999); Cleveland Academy of Trial Lawyers (Treasurer, 1983; Vice President, 1984; President, 1985); Eighth District Judicial Conference (Life Member; Lecturer, 1986; Member, Litigation Commission, 1992). ***REPORTED CASES:*** Halton v. Great Clips, Inc., 94 F. Supp. 2d 856 (2000); Scarso v. Cuyahoga County Dep't of Human Services, 747 F. Supp. 381 (1989); In re Suburban Motor Freight, 124 B.R. 964 (1990); Butler v. Jordan, 92 Ohio St. 3d 354 (2001); Koch v. Rist, 89 Ohio St. 3d 250 (2000); Petratos v. Markakis, 69 Ohio St. 3d 1219 (1994); Smith v. 10th Inning, Inc., 49 Ohio St. 3d 289 (1989); Cuyahoga County Bar Association v. Gerstenslager, 45 Ohio St. 3d 88 (1989); Oney v. Allen, 39 Ohio St. 3d 103 (1988); Johnson v. New London, 36 Ohio St. 3d 60 (1988); Marrek v. Cleveland Metroparks Bd. Of Commissioners, 9 Ohio St. 3d 194 (1984); Levin v. Hardwig, 60 Ohi St. 2d 81 (1979); Moats v. Metropolitan Bank of Lima, 40 Ohio St. 2d 47 (1974); Mentor Chiropractic Ctr. v. State Farm Fire & Cas. Co., 139 Ohio App. 3d 407 (2000); Braxton-Fountain v. University Hosps., 133 Ohio App. 3d 323 (1999); Brown v. McDonald's Corp., 101 Ohio App. 3d 294 (1995); Fetratos v. Markakis, 92 Ohio App. 3d 626 (1993); Gray v. Jefferson Geriatric & Rehabilitation Center, 75 Ohio App. 3d 499 (1991); Kontos v. Luxmore, 65 Ohio App. 3d 148 (1989); Saultz v. Funk, 64 Ohio App. 2d 29 (1979); Shapiro v. Burkons, 62 Ohio App. 2d 73 (1979). ***PRACTICE AREAS:*** Medical Malpractice; Personal Injury Litigation; FELA. ***Email:*** wnovak@nrpslaw.com

THOMAS D. ROBENALT, born Lima, Ohio, June 26, 1965; admitted to bar, 1991, Ohio; 1992, Florida; U.S. District Court, Northern District of Ohio. *Education:* Miami University (B.A., 1987); Ohio Northern University (J.D., 1991). Judicial Law Clerk, Cuyahoga County, Commons Plea Court, 1991-1993. Associate Attorney, Gallagher Sharp, Fulton & Norman, 1993-1997. Invited Lecturer: Evidence, Ohio State Bar Association, 1999-2000; Ethics and Professionalism, Cleveland Bar Association Tax Institute, 2001; Advanced Trial Advocacy in Ohio, National Business Institute, 2005. *Member:* Cleveland (Chairman, Professionalism and Ethics Committee, 2001-2002) and Ohio State (Member, Section on Litigation) Bar Associations; Association of Trial Lawyers of America; Ohio Association of Trial Lawyers. ***PRACTICE AREAS:*** Professional Malpractice Litigation; Personal Injury Litigation; Business and Franchise Litigation. ***Email:*** trobenalt@nrpslaw.com

THOMAS C. PAVLIK, born Cleveland, Ohio, December 28, 1941; admitted to bar, 1966, Ohio. *Education:* University of Notre Dame (A.B., 1963); Case Western Reserve University (J.D., 1966). Delta Theta Phi. Seminar Speaker, Bankruptcy and Secured Transactions, MCLE for Ohio Lawyers, 1989. *Member:* Cleveland (Member, Bankruptcy Committee, 1974), Cuyahoga County (Chairman, Bankruptcy Section, 1982-1984), Lorain County and Ohio State Bar Associations; War Veterans Bar Association (Vice-President, 1972-1973); Eighth District Judicial Conference. [Capt., U.S. Army, 1966-1969]. ***PRACTICE AREAS:*** Bankruptcy; Debtor-Creditor Law; Financial Workouts; Business Law; Real Estate. ***Email:*** tpavlik@nrpslaw.com

SCOTT H. SCHARF, born Cleveland, Ohio, March 28, 1964; admitted to bar, 1990, Ohio and U.S. District Court, Northern District of Ohio. *Education:* Ohio State University (B.A., with honors, 1986); Case Western Reserve University School of Law (J.D., 1990). Recipient of the Deans' Scholarship and American Jurisprudence Award, 1988. Member, Case Western Reserve University Law Review, 1990. Special Counsel, Ohio State Attorney General. *Member:* Cleveland, Cuyahoga County and American Bar Associations. ***REPORTED CASES:*** Gibson v. Gibson, 219 B.R. 195 (B.A.P. 6th 1998). ***PRACTICE AREAS:*** Debtor-Creditor Law; Financial Workouts; Bankruptcy Law; Business Law; Real Estate. ***Email:*** sscharf@nrpslaw.com

---

COLIN P. SAMMON, born Mayfield Heights, Ohio, November 23, 1976; admitted to bar, 2003, Ohio; 2004, U.S. District Court, Northern District of Ohio. *Education:* Miami University (B.S., Finance, 1999); Ohio Northern University (J.D., with distinction, 2002). Manuscript Editor, Ohio Northern Law Review, 2002. Author: "Insurance Agent and Broker Liability: Crossing the Two Way Street," Ohio N.U.L. Rev. 237, 2002. Law Clerk to the Honorable David T. Evans, Ohio Court of Appeals, Fourth Appellate District, 2002-2004. *Member:* Ohio State Bar Association. ***PRACTICE AREAS:*** Personal Injury; Medical Malpractice; Products Liability. ***Email:*** csammon@nrpslaw.com

SHELLY R. LASALVIA, born Cleveland, Ohio, January 23, 1978; admitted to bar, 2004, Ohio; 2005, U.S. District Court, Northern District of Ohio. *Education:* John Carroll University (B.S., 2000); Cleveland-Marshall College of Law (J.D., 2003). Managing Editor, Cleveland-Marshall College of Law Journal of Law and Health, 2002-2003. ***PRACTICE AREAS:*** Bankruptcy; Debtor and Creditor; Commercial Litigation. ***Email:*** slasalvia@nrpslaw.com

NURENBERG, PLEVIN, HELLER & McCARTHY CO., L.P.A.

1370 ONTARIO STREET
SUITE 100
CLEVELAND, OHIO 44113-1792
Telephone: 216-621-2300; Toll Free: 1-800-562-7438
Fax: 216-771-2242
Email: nphm@nphm.com
URL: http://www.nphm.com

Plaintiff Personal Injury and Wrongful Death Litigation, Airplane Crash Litigation, Aviation Litigation, Civil Litigation, Commercial Litigation, Construction Accidents, Medical and Hospital Negligence, Product Liability, Premises Liability, Railroad Accidents and Injuries, FELA, Class Action Litigation, Appellate Practice, Vehicular Accident Law.

FIRM PROFILE: NURENBERG, PLEVIN, HELLER & MCCARTHY CO., L.P.A. is a trial firm which concentrates its practice in a variety of tort areas, representing plaintiffs who sustain personal injury or death from medical malpractice, product defect, aviation crashes, automobile casualty, construction accidents, railroad injuries among other areas. The firm also represents clients in commercial litigation. In practice for over 75 years, the firm has vast experience in the Trial and Appellate Courts in the state and federal court systems. Members of the firm are additionally licensed to practice in California, District of Columbia, New York and Pennsylvania and with the assistance of local counsel, the firm's members practice and are admitted in courts throughout the United States. The law firm was formed in 1928 by Abraham (Abe) H. Dudnik and Samuel F. Komito. Originally, the focus was railroad law and other cases involving injured workers. The current senior partners have been with the firm for over 30 years. The firm, now known as Nurenberg, Plevin, Heller & McCarthy Co., L.P.A., consists of 15 lawyers and a support staff which includes nurse paralegals, trial paralegals, investigators and additional personnel dedicated to maintaining the highest standards in the personal injury, wrongful death and civil litigation fields of law. In particular, the firm represents clients throughout the United States in complex product liability cases, and in Aviation, Railroad and Vehicular crash cases. The firm also concentrates in the representation of victims and their families in complex physician, surgical and hospital malpractice cases, making use of its ability to team experienced trial lawyers with its in-house nursing support staff. Finally, the firm has long enjoyed a reputation throughout the State and Federal Court Systems in successfully challenging limitations, both statutory and insurance, to claimants' rights to file actions and collect damages. The firm carries the highest legal ability rating in Martindale-Hubbell.

A. H. DUDNIK (1905-1963)

S. F. KOMITO (1902-1984)

MARSHALL I. NURENBERG, born Pittsburgh, Pennsylvania, July 5, 1925; admitted to bar, 1953, Ohio; U.S. District Court, Northern District of Ohio; 1959, U.S. Supreme Court; U.S. Court of Appeals, Sixth Circuit. *Education:* Western Reserve University

(This Listing Continued)

(B.B.A., 1950; LL.B., 1953). Order of the Coif; Tau Epsilon Rho. Recipient: Cleveland Academy of Trial Attorneys, 1991; Cuyahoga County Bar Association, Special Service to the Legal Profession, 1994; Dean Fletcher Reed Andrews Award, Case Western Reserve Law School, 1994. Member, Editorial Board, Western Reserve Law Review, 1952-1953. Member, National Panel of Arbitrators, American Arbitration Association, 1966—. *Member:* Cleveland, Cuyahoga County, Ohio State and American Bar Associations; Cleveland Academy of Trial Attorneys; Ohio Academy of Trial Lawyers; The Association of Trial Lawyers of America (Editor, 1965—); The Cleveland Inns of Court; American Board of Trial Advocacy. Fellow: International Academy of Trial Lawyers; American College of Trial Lawyers. [U.S. Navy, 1943-1946]. (Retired). ***PRACTICE AREAS:*** Airplane Crash Litigation; Construction Accidents; Nursing Home Negligence; Birth Trauma; Obstetric Malpractice; Nursing Malpractice; Wrongful Death; Catastrophic Injury; Motor Vehicle Accidents & Injuries; Plaintiff's Personal Injury; Railroad Accidents and Injuries; Railroad Crossing Accidents. ***Email:*** MNurenberg@nphm.com

MAURICE L. HELLER, born Canton, Ohio, April 9, 1931; admitted to bar, 1956, Ohio; U.S. District Court, Northern District of Ohio; U.S. Court of Appeals, Sixth Circuit; U.S. Supreme Court. *Education:* University of Michigan (B.A., 1953); University of Virginia; Northwestern University (J.D., 1956). Member, National Panel of Arbitrators, American Arbitration Association, 1966. *Member:* Cleveland Academy of Trial Attorneys; Ohio Academy of Trial Lawyers; The Association of Trial Lawyers of America. (Retired). ***PRACTICE AREAS:*** Construction Accidents; Nursing Home Negligence; Insolvency Litigation; Birth Trauma; Obstetric Malpractice; Nursing Malpractice; Wrongful Death; Automobile Accidents; Motor Vehicle Accidents and Injuries; Plaintiff's Personal Injury. ***Email:*** MHeller@nphm.com

JOHN J. McCARTHY, born Cleveland, Ohio, March 7, 1926; admitted to bar, 1955, Ohio; U.S. District Court, Northern District of Ohio; 1987, U.S. Supreme Court; U.S. Court of Appeals, Sixth Circuit. *Education:* Kent State University (B.S.B.A., 1950); The Cleveland-Marshall Law School (LL.B., 1954). (Retired). ***PRACTICE AREAS:*** Construction Accidents; Nursing Home Negligence; Wrongful Death; Catastrophic Injury; Motor Vehicle Accidents and Injuries; Plaintiff's Personal Injury; Railroad Accidents and Injuries; Railroad Crossing Accidents. ***Email:*** JMcCarthy@nphm.com

THOMAS MESTER, born Cleveland, Ohio, January 31, 1944; admitted to bar, 1969, Ohio; U.S. District Court, Northern District of Ohio; U.S. Supreme Court; U.S. Court of Appeals, Sixth Circuit. *Education:* John Carroll University (B.A., cum laude, 1966); Case Western Reserve University (J.D., 1969). Phi Alpha Theta. Member, Case Western Reserve Law Review, 1968-1969. Lecturer in various areas of practice. Delegate and Life Member, Eighth District Court of Appeals Judicial Conference.*Member:* Cuyahoga County Bar Association; Ohio Academy of Trial Lawyers; The Association of Trial Lawyers of America; Million Dollar Advocate Forum. ***PRACTICE AREAS:*** Medical Malpractice; Construction Accidents; Nursing Home Negligence; Birth Trauma; Obstetric Malpractice; Nursing Malpractice; Wrongful Death; Automobile Accidents; Brain Injury; Motor Vehicle Accidents & Injuries; Plaintiff's Personal Injury; Railroad Accidents and Injuries; Railroad Crossing Accidents; Catastrophic Injury; Medical Negligence; Pediatric Malpractice; Surgeons Liability; Toxic Torts. ***Email:*** TMester@nphm.com

HARLAN M. GORDON, born Cleveland, Ohio, January 31, 1943; admitted to bar, 1968, Ohio; U.S. District Court Northern District of Ohio; U.S. Supreme Court; U.S. Court of Appeals, Sixth Circuit. *Education:* Case Western Reserve University (A.B., 1965; J.D., 1968). Tau Epsilon Rho; Order of the Coif. Member, Editorial Board, Case Western Reserve Law Review, 1967-1968. Law Clerk to U. S. District Court Judge Thomas Lambros, 1969-1973. *Member:* Cleveland Academy of Trial Attorneys; Ohio Academy of Trial Lawyers; The Association of Trial Lawyers of America. ***PRACTICE AREAS:*** Airplane Crash Litigation; Construction Accidents; Nursing Home Negligence; Obstetric Malpractice; Wrongful Death; Automobile Accidents; Motor Vehicle Accidents and Injuries; Railroad Accidents and Injuries; Railroad Crossing Accidents; Medical Negligence; Pediatric Malpractice; Surgeons Liability; Toxic Torts. ***Email:*** HGordon@nphm.com

DAVID M. PARIS, born Cleveland Heights, Ohio, October 9, 1952; admitted to bar, 1978, Ohio and California; U.S. District Court, Northern District of Ohio; U.S. District Court, Northern and Central Districts of California; U.S. Supreme Court; U.S. Court of Appeals, Sixth Circuit. *Education:* The Ohio State University (B.A., 1974); The Cleveland-Marshall College of Law (J.D., 1978). Author: "Preparing and Trying The Automobile Accident Case," 1989 and 1994, PESI; "The Supplemental Action," 1990, OATL; "Insurance Litigation in Ohio," 1993, NBI; "The Constitutionality of Ohio's Workers Compensation Subrogation Statute, 2001, CATA;" "The Digital Trial Lawyer: Technology and Trial Practice," 2002. Instructor, Trial Advocacy Institute, Cleveland Marshall College of Law, 1990—. Member, Crane Injury Litigation Group and Electrical Accident Group, 1991-1998. Delegate and Life Member, Eighth District Court of Appeals Judicial Conference. Member, Baycol Litigation Group, 2001-2003. Member, Steering Committee of "City of New Orleans" Amtrak Crash, 1999. *Member:* Ohio State Bar Association; State Bar of California; Cleveland Academy of Trial Attorneys (Member, Board of Directors, 1993-1994; Treasurer, 1998-1999; Secretary, 1999-2000; Vice President, 2000-2001; President, 2001-2002); Ohio Academy of Trial Lawyers; The Association of Trial Lawyers of America; National Board of Trial Advocacy. Fellow, Roscoe Pound Institute. ***REPORTED CASES:*** Lunar v. City of Cleveland, 69 Ohio St.3d 673, 635 N.E.2d 357 (1994); Zelko v. Parsons, 29 Ohio App.3d 302, 505 N.E.2d 271 (1985); Motorists Mutual Ins. Co. v. Handlovic, 23 Ohio St. 3d 179, 492 N.E.2d 417 (1986). Baughman v. State Farm Mutual Insurance Co., 88 Ohio St. 3d 481 (2000); Holeton v. Crouse Cartage Co., 92 Ohio St. 3d 115 (2001). ***PRACTICE AREAS:*** Construction Accidents; Medical Malpractice; Insurance Litigation; Products Liability; Airplane Crash Litigation; Wrongful Death; Automobile Accidents; Plaintiff's Personal Injury; Railroad Crossing Accidents; Employer Intentional Torts; Class Actions; Consumer Law; Consumer Class Actions; Consumer Fraud; Consumer Rights; Toxic Torts. ***Email:*** DParis@nphm.com

JAMES R. LEBOVITZ, born Cleveland, Ohio, September 7, 1956; admitted to bar, 1982, Ohio, U.S. District Court, Northern District of Ohio, U.S. Court of Appeals, Sixth Circuit, U.S. District Court Northern and Central Districts of California, U.S. District Court, Northern District of Illinois, U.S. District Court, Western and Eastern Districts of Pennsylvania, U.S. District Court, Southern District of New York, U.S. District Court, Central District of Utah, U.S. District Court, Northern District of Indiana, U.S. District Court, Southern District of West Virginia, U.S. District Court, District of South Carolina, U.S. District Court, Eastern District of Michigan and U.S. District Court, Third Judicial District of Utah; 2005, District of Columbia. *Education:* Cleveland State University (B.A., cum laude, 1979); Cleveland Marshall College of Law (J.D., 1982). Member, Moot Court, 1981-1982. Featured, "Tragedy's Bottom Line," USA Today, January 5, 2000; "Reaching for the Sky," Scene Magazine, December 20-26, 2001; "Largest Ohio Plane Crash PI Verdict," Ohio Lawyers Weekly, December 22, 1997, Forbes Magazine, Seattle Times, New York Times and numerous other major news publications. Appointed Member, Steering Committee in Mass Disasters including Singapore Airlines Flight 006 crash at Taipei, Taiwan; Alaska Airlines Flight 261 near Los Angeles; Egypt Air Flight 990 Crash near Nantucket, MA; Swissair Flight 111 Crash near Nova Scotia; ValuJet Flight 592 crash near Miami; USAir Flight 427 crash near Pittsburgh; USAir Flight 405 crash near New York; City of New Orleans Amtrak crash near Chicago; USAir Flight 1493 crash at Los Angeles; USAir Flight 4743 crash at Beckley, WV; Comair Flight 3272 crash near Detroit; United Airlines Flight 232 at Sioux City, IA; Delta Flight 810 disaster near Los Angeles; Burlington Northern Train collision near Los Angeles, Ca. Author: "Liability of Homeowners and Private Recreational Operators for Swimming Pool Accidents," Cleveland State University, May 1984; "Physician Liability for Errors/Omissions in Medical Record Documentation," St. Luke's Hospital, Cleveland, OH, 1992. Lecturer: 36th Ohio Academy of Trial Lawyers Award Convention, "An Overview of Commercial Aviation Litigation," May 1993; "Aviation Law and Contracts - Implications of the Warsaw Convention," Columbus, OH, 1994; "Proving Damages in Aviation Cases," Cleveland, Ohio, October 1997. *Member:* Cleveland, Ohio State and American Bar Associations; The District of Columbia Bar; Lawyer-Pilots Bar Associations; Ohio Academy of Trial Lawyers; The Association of Trial Lawyers of America. ***REPORTED CASES:*** Beck v. Alaska Air Group, 2002 U.S. Dist. Lexis 10017 (N.D.Cal. May 24, 2002); In re: Air crash off Point Mugu, 145 Fed.Sup.2d 1156 (N.D.Cal. 2001); Dowe v. Amtrak, 2004 U.S. Dist. Lexis 7233 (N.D. Ill., April 26, 2004); Dowe v. Amtrak, 2003 U.S. Dist. Lexis, 18538 (N.D. Ill., October 21, 2003); Garber v. Provident Life & Accident Ins. Co., 22 Employee Benefits Cas. (BNA) 1090 (6th Cir. 1999). ***PRACTICE AREAS:*** Airplane Crash Litigation; Aviation Accidents; Aviation Litigation; Obstetric Malpractice; Wrongful Death; Automobile Accidents; Catastrophic Injury; Head Injury; Motor Vehicle Accidents and Injuries; Plaintiff's Personal Injury; Railroad Accidents and Injuries; Railroad Crossing Accidents. ***Email:*** JLebovitz@nphm.com

WILLIAM S. JACOBSON, born Cleveland, Ohio, January 27, 1957; admitted to bar, 1984, Ohio and U.S. District Court, Northern District of Ohio; 1993, U.S. Court of Appeals, Sixth Circuit; 1999, U.S. Supreme Court. *Education:* Washington and Jefferson College (B.A., 1979); Case Western Reserve University (J.D., 1983). Author of and Lecturer on: Multiple topics relating to medical malpractice, including obstetrical claims. *Member:* Ohio Academy of Trial Lawyers; The Association of Trial Lawyers of America; Volunteer Legal Aid Society of Cleveland. ***PRACTICE AREAS:*** Nursing Home Negligence; Birth Trauma; Obstetric Malpractice; Nursing Malpractice; Wrongful Death; Automobile Accidents; Brain Injury; Catastrophic Injury; Head Injury; Motor Vehicle Accidents and Injuries; Plaintiff's Personal Injury; Severe Burns; Medical Negligence; Nursing Negligence; Pediatric Malpractice; Surgeons Liability; Spinal Injury; Railroad Accidents and Injuries; Railroad Crossing Accidents. ***Email:*** WJacobson@nphm.com

JEFFREY A. LEIKIN, born Cleveland, Ohio, May 16, 1959; admitted to bar, 1985, Ohio; U.S. District Court, Northern District of Ohio; U.S. Court of Appeals, Sixth Circuit; U.S. Supreme Court. *Education:* University of Colorado (B.A., 1981); Cleveland-Marshall College of Law, Cleveland State University (J.D., 1984). Tau Epsilon Rho. *Member:* Cleveland Bar Association; Cleveland Academy of Trial Attorneys; Ohio Academy of Trial Lawyers; The Association of Trial Lawyers of America. ***PRACTICE AREAS:*** Construction Accidents; Nursing Home Negligence; Birth Trauma; Obstetric Malpractice; Nursing Malpractice; Wrongful Death; Automobile Accidents; Brain Injury; Catastrophic Injury; Head Injury; Motor Vehicle Accidents and Injuries; Plaintiff's Personal Injury; Severe Burns; Spinal Injury; Railroad Accidents and Injuries; Railroad Crossing Accidents. ***Email:*** JLeikin@nphm.com

ELLEN M. McCARTHY, born Cleveland, Ohio, March 14, 1962; admitted to bar, 1990, Ohio and U.S. District Court, Northern District of Ohio; U.S. Court of Appeals, Sixth Circuit. *Education:* St. Leo College (B.A., 1984); Cleveland-Marshall College of Law, Cleveland State University (J.D., 1990). Bar Examiner, Ohio Supreme Court. Member, Board of Bar Examiners. Member: Board of Trustees, Cleveland-Marshall College of Law Alumni Association; Board of Trustees, Women's City Club; Board of Trustees, Cleveland Academy of Trial Attorneys. *Member:* Cleveland and Cuyahoga County Bar Associations; Cleveland Academy of Trial Attorneys; Ohio Academy of Trial Lawyers; Association of Trial Lawyers of America. ***PRACTICE AREAS:*** Construction Accidents; Nursing Home Negligence; Birth Trauma; Obstetric Malpractice; Wrongful Death; Automobile Accidents; Brain Injury; Catastrophic Injury; Motor Vehicle Accidents and Injuries; Plaintiff's Personal Injury; Railroad Accidents and Injuries; Railroad Crossing Accidents. ***Email:*** EMcCarthy@nphm.com

KATHLEEN J. ST. JOHN, born Cleveland, Ohio, November 8, 1956; admitted to bar, 1982, Ohio; U.S. District Court, Northern District of Ohio; U.S. Supreme Court; U.S. Court of Appeals, Sixth and Tenth Circuits. *Education:* Ohio University (B.A., summa cum laude, 1979); Cleveland-Marshall College of Law, Cleveland State University (J.D., cum laude, 1982). Author: "What Lies Beneath: Workers' Compensation Subrogation in the Wake of Holeton v. Crouse Cartage Co.," 12 Ohio Trial, 2001. Lecturer: "Constitutional Challenges in Your Personal Injury Practice," CATA, 2001; "What is the Status of Worker's Compensation Subrogation in Ohio?" 45th Ohio Academy of Trial Lawyers Annual Convention, 2002; "Destroying Subrogation Rights Without the UM/UIM Carrier's Consent," Auto Insurance Seminar, OATL, 2002; "Stare Decisis," Insurance Law Seminar, OATL, 2003. *Member:* Ohio Academy of Trial Lawyers; Cleveland Academy of Trial Attorneys. ***REPORTED CASES:*** Beck v. Alaska Air Group, 2002 U.S. Dist. Lexis 10017 (N.D. Cal. May 24, 2002); In re: Air crash off Point Mugu, 145 Fed.Sup. 2d 1156 (N.D. Cal.2001); Ferrando v. Auto-Owners Mutual, 98 Ohio St. 3d 186 (2002); Holeton v. Crouse Cartage Co., 92 Ohio St. 3d 115 (2001) (amicus curiae); Baughman v. State Farm Mut. Auto. Ins. Co., 88 Ohio St. 3d 480 (2000); Harp v. City of Cleveland Heights, 87 Ohio St. 3d 506 (2000); Minton v. Honda of America Manufacturing, Inc., 80 Ohio St. 3d 62 (1997) (amicus curiae); Gallagher v. Cleveland Browns Football Co., 79 Ohio St. 3d 427 (1996); Moskovitz v. Mt. Sinai Med. Ctr., 69 Ohio St. 3d 638 (1994) (amicus curiae). ***PRACTICE AREAS:*** Airplane Crash Litigation; Appellate Practice; Construction Accidents; Nursing Home Negligence; Wrongful Death; Catastrophic Injury; Plaintiff's Personal Injury; Railroad Accidents and

(This Listing Continued)

NURENBERG, PLEVIN, HELLER & McCARTHY CO., L.P.A., Cleveland—Continued

Injuries; Railroad Crossing Accidents; Aviation Accidents; Consumer Law; Consumer Class Actions; Consumer Fraud; Consumer Rights; Products Liability. ***Email:*** KStJohn@nphm.com

JONATHAN D. MESTER, born Cleveland, Ohio, July 27, 1970; admitted to bar, 1998, Ohio and U.S. District Court, Northern District of Ohio. *Education:* Syracuse University (B.A., cum laude, 1992); The Ohio State University (J.D., 1998). Recipient, First Place Overall and Best Brief Award, 1998 National Civil Rights Moot Court Competition. Chief Managing Editor, The Ohio State Journal on Dispute Resolution, 1997-1998. Author: "The Administrative Dispute Resolution Act of 1996: Will the New Era of ADR in Federal Administrative Agencies Occur at the Expense of Public Accountability?" 13 Ohio St. Journal on Dispute Resolution 167, 1997. *Member:* Cleveland and Ohio State Bar Associations; Ohio Academy of Trial Lawyers; The Association of Trial Lawyers of America. ***PRACTICE AREAS:*** Construction Accidents; Nursing Home Negligence; Obstetric Malpractice; Nursing Malpractice; Wrongful Death; Automobile Accidents; Catastrophic Injury; Motor Vehicle Accidents and Injuries; Plaintiff's Personal Injury; Railroad Accidents and Injuries; Products Liability; Medical Negligence; Toxic Torts. ***Email:*** JMester@nphm.com

---

ROBERT S. ZELLER, born Cleveland, Ohio, March 6, 1952; admitted to bar, 1985, Ohio. *Education:* Cleveland State University (B.A., 1974; J.D., 1984). *Member:* Ohio Academy of Trial Lawyers. ***PRACTICE AREAS:*** Workers Compensation; Wrongful Death; Automobile Accidents; Catastrophic Injury; Motor Vehicle Accidents and Injuries; Plaintiff's Personal Injury. ***Email:*** RZeller@nphm.com

BRENDA M. JOHNSON, born Cleveland, Ohio, September 19, 1962; admitted to bar, 1993, Ohio, U.S. Court of Appeals, Sixth Circuit and U.S. District Court, Northern District of Ohio. *Education:* Kent State University (B.G.S., 1988); Cleveland State University (M.A., 1990); Cleveland Marshall College of Law, Cleveland State University (J.D., cum laude, 1993). Author: "Great-West Life & Annuity Ins. v. Knudson: How to Close the Door on Federal ERISA Subrogation Actions," 17 Ohio Trial, 2003. Articles Editor, Cleveland State University Law Review, 1992-1993. Member, Editorial Board, Ohio Trial, 2004—. *Member:* Ohio Academy of Trial Lawyers; Cleveland Academy of Trial Attorneys. ***REPORTED CASES:*** McMillin v. Davidson Industries, Inc., 2005 Ohio 224 (8th Dist.); Becker v. Metzger, 144 Ohio App 3d 52 (7th Dist. 2001); Vajda v. St. Paul Mercury Ins. Co., 2003 Ohio 160 (8th Dist.); Washington v. Spitzer Mgmt., 2003 Ohio 1735 (8th Dist.); Beck v. Alaska Air Group, 2002 U.S. Dist. Lexis 10017 (N.D.Cal. May 24, 2002); In re: Air crash of Point Mugu, 145 Fed. Sup.2d 1156 (N.D. Cal. 2001); Dowe v. Amtrak, 2004 U.S. Dist. Lexis 7233 (N.D. Ill., April 26, 2004); Dowe v. Amtrak, 2003 U.S. Dist. Lexis, 18538 (N.D. Ill., October 21, 2003). ***PRACTICE AREAS:*** Airplane Crash Litigation; Appellate Practice; Construction Accidents; Nursing Home Negligence; Wrongful Death; Catastrophic Injury; Plaintiff's Personal Injury; Severe Burns; Spinal Injury; Railroad Accidents and Injuries; Railroad Crossing Accidents. ***Email:*** BJohnson@nphm.com

ANDREW R. YOUNG, born Wooster, Ohio, March 14, 1974; admitted to bar, 1999, Ohio; 2000, District of Columbia and U.S. District Court, Northern District of Ohio. *Education:* Ohio Wesleyan University (B.A., magna cum laude, 1996); Case Western Reserve University (J.D., 1999). Member, Order of Barristers. Staff Attorney, U. S. Representative Dennis J. Kucinich, 1999-2000. Member: The Supreme Court of Ohio's Commission on Legal Education Opportunity, 2003; The Planning Commission of North Ridgeville, Ohio, 2003. Councilman, North Ridgeville, Ohio, 2003—. *Member:* Lorain County, Ohio State and American Bar Associations; Cleveland Academy of Trial Attorneys; Ohio Academy of Trial Lawyers (Trustee and Chairperson, Young Lawyers Division, 2002-2004; Recipient, Distinguished Service Award, 2003); The Association of Trial Lawyers of America. ***PRACTICE AREAS:*** Construction Accidents; Explosions; Nursing Home Negligence; Obstetric Malpractice; Medical Malpractice; Wrongful Death; Automobile Accidents and Injuries; Premises Liability; Brain Injury; Catastrophic Injury; Plaintiffs Personal Injury; Railroad Accidents and Injuries; Products Liability; Admiralty and Maritime Law. ***Email:*** ayoung@nphm.com

REFERENCE: Society National Bank of Cleveland.

OBRAL & MAYS & ASSOCIATES

STANDARD BUILDING
1370 ONTARIO STREET
CLEVELAND, OHIO 44113
Telephone: 216-696-4421
Fax: 216-696-3228
Email: tmays@lawmjo.com

Personal Injury, Medical Malpractice, Automobile Accidents, Workers Compensation, Wrongful Death, Truck Accidents, Nursing Home Abuse, Products Liability, Dog Bites, Slip and Fall, Criminal Law.

MARK JOSEPH OBRAL, born 1956; admitted to bar, 1984, Ohio. *Education:* Cleveland State University (B.A., 1980; J.D., 1984). *Member:* Ohio State Bar Association; Ohio Academy of Trial Lawyers. ***PRACTICE AREAS:*** Personal Injury; Medical Malpractice; Automobile Accidents and Injuries; Workers Compensation; Wrongful Death; Truck Accidents; Nursing Home Abuse and Neglect; Products Liability; Dog Bites; Slip and Fall; Criminal Law.

THOMAS CHARLES MAYS, born 1961; admitted to bar, 1986, Ohio. *Education:* Cleveland State University (B.S., 1983); Cleveland-Marshall College of Law (J.D., 1986). ***PRACTICE AREAS:*** Personal Injury; Medical Malpractice; Automobile Accidents and Injuries; Workers Compensation; Wrongful Death; Truck Accidents; Nursing Home Abuse and Neglect; Products Liability; Dog Bites; Slip and Fall; Criminal Law.

OGNE, ALBERTS & STUART, P.C.

CLEVELAND, OHIO

(See Troy, Michigan)

General Civil Litigation Practice in State and Federal Courts. Insurance Defense, General Negligence, Product Liability, Employment and Commercial Litigation, Worker's Compensation, Professional Negligence and Aviation Law. Trials and Appeals, Business Law, Wills, Trusts & Estates, Probate, Criminal Law.

OTT & ASSOCIATES CO., L.P.A.

55 PUBLIC SQUARE, SUITE 1250
CLEVELAND, OHIO 44113
Telephone: 216-771-2600
Fax: 216-830-8939
Email: steven.ott@ottesq.com
URL: http://www.lawyers.com/ottesq

Corporate Law, Real Estate, Condominium Law, Probate, Civil Litigation, Internet Law.

STEVEN M. OTT, born New York, N.Y., September 29, 1955; admitted to bar, 1980, Ohio; 2000, California. *Education:* Ohio Wesleyan University (B.A., 1977); Cleveland Marshall College of Law (J.D., 1980). *Member:* Cuyahoga County, Ohio State and American Bar Associations; State Bar of California. ***PRACTICE AREAS:*** Corporate Law; Real Estate; Condominium Law; Probate; Civil Litigation; Internet Law; Business Law; Construction Law. ***Email:*** steven.ott@ottesq.com

---

PAGANO, WILSON, THOMARIOS, GILLISSIE & LENAHAN LLC

1370 ONTARIO STREET
SUITE 1240
CLEVELAND, OHIO 44113
Telephone: 216-685-9940
Fax: 216-685-9942

Criminal Law, Employment Defense, Personal Injury, Workers Compensation, Social Security Disability, Probate, Estate Planning, Family Law, Business Law, Collections.

JOSEPH V. PAGANO, born May 26, 1970; admitted to bar, 2001, Ohio; 2003, Florida and U.S. District Court, Northern District of Ohio. *Education:* Cleveland-Marshall College of Law (J.D., 1999). ***PRACTICE AREAS:*** Criminal Law; Employment Defense; Personal Injury; Workers Compensation. ***Email:*** joseph@pwtglaw.com

RACHEL C. WILSON, born Columbus, Ohio, October 11, 1971; admitted to bar, 1997, Ohio. *Education:* Ohio University (B.S., Communication, 1994); Cleveland-Marshall College of Law (J.D., 1997). *Member:* Cleveland and Ohio State Bar Associations. ***LANGUAGES:*** Spanish. ***PRACTICE AREAS:*** Social Security Disability; Workers Compensation; Probate. ***Email:*** rachel@pwtglaw.com

ELIZABETH A. THOMARIOS, born Akron, Ohio, December 2, 1973; admitted to bar, 1999, Ohio; 2003, U.S. District Court, Northern District of Ohio. *Education:* Kenyon College (B.A., English, 1996); Cleveland-Marshall College of Law (J.D., 1999). *Member:* Akron Bar Association. ***PRACTICE AREAS:*** Criminal Law; Family Law; Business Law; Personal Injury; Collections. ***Email:*** beth@pwtglaw.com

REBECCA R. GILLISSIE, born Cleveland, Ohio, May 6, 1973; admitted to bar, 2001, Ohio; 2004, U.S. District Court, Northern District of Ohio. *Education:* Miami University (B.A., 1995); Cleveland State University (J.D., 2000). ***PRACTICE AREAS:*** Workers Compensation; Social Security Disabiltiy; Estate Planning; Employment Law. ***Email:*** rebecca@pwtglaw.com

CHRISTOPHER RICHARDS LENAHAN, born Cleveland, Ohio, November 21, 1967; admitted to bar, 2000, Ohio. *Education:* Marquette University (B.A., 1990); Cleveland-Marshall College of Law (J.D., 1999). ***PRACTICE AREAS:*** Criminal Law. ***Email:*** clenahan3@aol.com

---

HERBERT PALKOVITZ

1600 STANDARD BUILDING
CLEVELAND, OHIO 44113
Telephone: 216-771-3777
FAX: 216-771-1950
Email: palkovlaw@aol.com
URL: http://www.lawyers.com/palkovlaw

Divorce, Domestic Relations, Family Law. Trials. Arbitration.

HERBERT PALKOVITZ, born McKeesport, Pennsylvania, December 1, 1942; admitted to bar, 1969, Ohio; 1970, U.S. District Court, Northern District of Ohio; 1972, U.S. Supreme Court; 1982, U.S. Court of Appeals, Sixth Circuit. *Education:* Washington & Jefferson College (B.A., 1964); Cleveland Marshall College of Law (J.D., 1968). Phi Alpha Delta. Listed in: The Best Lawyers in American, Naifeh and Smith, 1991—; Who's Who in American Law, 1992—. Member, Board of Trustees, Cleveland Urban Community School, 1971-1972. Member, Board of Trustees, 1979—, President, 1987-1988, Cleveland Marshall Law School of Cleveland State University Alumni Association. Member, Guardian Ad Litem Panel of Juvenile Court Division of the Court of Common Pleas of Cuyahoga County, 1979-1988. Member, Guardian ad Litem Advisory Committee, Domestic Relations Division of Cuyahoga County Common Pleas Court, 1986-1988. Member, Rules Committee of Division of Domestic Relations, Cuyahoga County Common Pleas Court, 1986-1990. Member, 1984 and Chairman, 1988-1993, Divorce Mediation Advisory Committee of Jewish Family Services Association. Member, National Panel of Arbitrators, American Arbitration Association. Member, Ohio State Supreme Court Committee, Alter-

(This Listing Continued)

nate Dispute Resolution, 1992-2002. Contributing Author, Baldwins Ohio Domestic Relations Law, June, 1987—. Certified Divorce Arbitrator through American Academy of Matrimonial Lawyers, 1989. *Member:* Cleveland (Chairman, Juvenile Court Committee, 1974-1976; Member, 1979-1989 and Chairman, 1985-1986, Family Law Section), Cuyahoga County (Member, 1975-1982 and Chairman, 1979-1980, Committee on Juvenile Court; Member, 1977 and Chairman, 1985-1986, Family Law Section), Ohio State (Member, Family Law Committee; Eighth Judicial Conference (Life Member), 1980—) and American (Member, Family Law Section) Bar Associations; War Veterans Bar Association (President, 1977-1978). Fellow: American Academy of Matrimonial Lawyers (President, Ohio Chapter, 1989; Member, National Board of Governors, 1990-2002; American College of Family Trial Lawyers (Diplomat). Fellow, International Academy of Matrimonial Lawyers.

ASSOCIATE

ADAM J. THURMAN, born Cleveland, Ohio, January 11, 1972; admitted to bar, 1997, Ohio and U.S. District Court, Northern District of Ohio. *Education:* John Carroll University (B.A., cum laude, 1994); Cleveland Marshall College of Law (J.D., summa cum laude, 1997). Alpha Kappa Delta. Executive Editor, Cleveland State Law Review. Regularly Appointed Guardian Gadlitem Cuyhoga County. Recipient, National Collegiate Social Science Award. Listed in: Who's Who in American Colleges and Universities; Who's Who, American Law Students, 1996-1997. *Member:* Cleveland (Member, Young Lawyers Section, 1997), Cuyahoga County, Ohio State (Member, Family Law Committee, 1998) and American Bar Associations. ***PRACTICE AREAS:*** Divorce; Domestic Relations; Family Law; Trials. ***Email:*** ajthurman@aol.com

LEGAL SUPPORT PERSONNEL

SHERRI A. LANZILOTTA (Legal Assistant)

REFERENCES: National City Bank; Society National Bank.

CHARLES J. PALMERI CO., L.P.A.

Established in 1983

SUITE 207, CORPORATE CIRCLE
30100 CHAGRIN BOULEVARD
CLEVELAND, OHIO 44124-5705
Telephone: 216-831-7338
Toll Free: 800-274-7067
Facsimile: 216-504-0240
Email: cjpalmeri@cjpalmeri.com
URL: http://www.cjpalmeri.com

Creditors' Rights, Real Estate Foreclosure, Creditor Bankruptcy, Secured Creditor Rights, Secured Collections and Loan Workouts.

CHARLES J. PALMERI, ESQ., born Cleveland, Ohio, July 17, 1952; admitted to bar, 1977, Ohio; 1978, U.S. District Court, Northern District of Ohio; 2002, U.S. Court of Appeals, Sixth Circuit and 2002, U.S. Supreme Court. *Education:* John Carroll University (B.A., 1974); University of Dayton (J.D., 1977). Adjunct Faculty, School of Business, Instructor of Business Law, John Carroll University, Cleveland since 1989. ***PRACTICE AREAS:*** Real Estate Mortgage Foreclosure; Secured Creditor Rights; Creditor Bankruptcy; Loan Workouts; Real Estate; Collections. ***Email:*** cjpalmeri@cjpalmeri.com

REPRESENTATIVE CLIENTS: National City Bank; National City Mortgage Co.; Charter One Bank F.S.B.; First Place Bank; ShoreBanc; Maxus Leasing Group.

PEARNE & GORDON LLP

1801 EAST 9TH STREET
SUITE 1200
CLEVELAND, OHIO 44114-3108
Telephone: 216-579-1700
Facsimile: 216-579-6073
Email: ip@pearnegordon.com
URL: http://www.pearnegordon.com

Patent, Trademark, Copyright, Trade Secret, Unfair Competition, and Related Intellectual Property Law.

FIRM PROFILE: With roots dating back to the 1910's, Pearne & Gordon is one of the largest and oldest intellectual property law firms in Cleveland. Its attorneys have experience in all areas of technology, including electronics, electrical engineering, chemistry, chemical engineering, mechanical engineering, computers, digital signal processing, software, medical devices, polymers, biotechnology, nuclear science and machine design, and their activities include not only patent, trademark, and copyright prosecution but also licensing and consulting. Members of the firm are experienced in all facets of intellectual property litigation and have handled patent, trademark, copyright, trade secret and unfair competition lawsuits in court and patent interferences and trademark oppositions and cancellations before the Patent and Trademark Office. The firm works closely with patent and trademark law firms in Canada, Mexico, South America, Europe and the Far East to provide full international service to its clients.

MEMBERS OF FIRM

JOHN F. PEARNE (1912-1981)

CHARLES B. GORDON, born Oak Park, Illinois, November 23, 1922; admitted to bar, 1950, District of Columbia; 1952, Ohio; 1970, U.S. Supreme Court and U.S. Court of Appeals, Sixth Circuit; 1982, U.S. Court of Appeals for the Federal Circuit; registered to practice before U.S. Patent and Trademark Office. *Education:* Princeton University (B.S.E., 1943); Harvard Law School (LL.B., 1949). *Member:* Cleveland and American Bar Associations; Cleveland Intellectual Property Law Association; American Intellectual Property Law Association. ***PRACTICE AREAS:*** Patent; Trademark; Copyright; Trade Secret; Unfair Competition. ***Email:*** ip@pearnegordon.com

THOMAS P. SCHILLER, born Cleveland, Ohio, September 25, 1934; admitted to bar, 1960, Ohio; 1970, U.S. Supreme Court; 1982, U.S. Court of Appeals for the Federal Circuit; registered to practice before U.S. Patent and Trademark Office. *Education:* Case Institute of Technology (B.S., 1956); George Washington University; Western Reserve University (J.D., 1960). Phi Delta Phi. *Member:* Cleveland and American Bar Associations; Cleveland Intellectual Property Law Association; American Intellectual Property Law Association; International Trademark Association. ***PRACTICE AREAS:*** Patent; Trademark; Copyright; Trade Secret; Unfair Competition. ***Email:*** ip@pearnegordon.com

DAVID B. DEIOMA, born Dover, Ohio, December 26, 1940; admitted to bar, 1965, Ohio, U.S. Court of Appeals, Sixth Circuit; 1972, U.S. Supreme Court; 1981, U.S. Court of Appeals, Fourth Circuit; 1982, U.S. Court of Appeals for the Federal Circuit; registered to practice before U.S. Patent and Trademark Office. *Education:* Case Western Reserve University (B.S., E.Sc., 1962); Georgetown University (J.D., 1965). Phi Kappa Phi. President, Ohio Venture Association, 1988-1990. Founder, David Deioma Lectureship at Case Western Reserve University. Member, Advisory Committee to Case Western Reserve University, Case School of Engineering Dean. *Member:* Cleveland, Ohio State and American Bar Associations; Cleveland Intellectual Property Law Association; American Intellectual Property Law Association. ***PRACTICE AREAS:*** Patent; Trademark; Copyright; Trade Secret; Unfair Competition. ***Email:*** ddeioma@pearnegordon.com

JOSEPH J. CORSO, born Cleveland, Ohio, March 13, 1942; admitted to bar, 1969, Ohio; registered to practice before U.S. Patent and Trademark Office. *Education:* Ohio University (B.S.Ch.E., 1965); University of Akron (J.D., 1969). *Member:* Cleveland and American Bar Associations; Cleveland Intellectual Property Law Association; American Intellectual Property Law Association. ***PRACTICE AREAS:*** Patent; Trademark; Copyright; Trade Secret; Unfair Competition. ***Email:*** ip@pearnegordon.com

HOWARD G. SHIMOLA, born Cleveland, Ohio, October 14, 1942; admitted to bar, 1970, Ohio; registered to practice before U.S. Patent and Trademark Office. *Education:* Case Institute of Technology (B.S. in M.E., 1965); Cleveland Marshall College of Law (J.D., 1970). *Member:* Cleveland Intellectual Property Law Association; American Intellectual Property Law Association. ***PRACTICE AREAS:*** Patent; Trademark; Copyright; Trade Secret; Unfair Competition. ***Email:*** ip@pearnegordon.com

JEFFREY J. SOPKO, born Cleveland, Ohio, March 10, 1948; admitted to bar, 1975, Ohio; 1978, U.S. Court of Appeals, Sixth Circuit; 1982, U.S. Court of Appeals for the Federal Circuit; registered to practice before U.S. Patent and Trademark Office. *Education:* University of Dayton (B.T., 1970); Cleveland Marshall College of Law (J.D., 1975). Epsilon Delta Tau. *Member:* Cleveland and American Bar Associations; Cleveland Intellectual Property Law Association; American Intellectual Property Law Association; International Federation of Industrial Property Attorneys; Institute of Electrical and Electronic Engineers. ***PRACTICE AREAS:*** Patent; Trademark; Copyright; Trade Secret; Unfair Competition. ***Email:*** jsopko@pearnegordon.com

JOHN P. MURTAUGH, born Orrville, Ohio, February 23, 1952; admitted to bar, 1978, California; 1979, U.S. Court of Appeals, District of Columbia Circuit; 1981, Ohio; 1982, U.S. Court of Appeals, Sixth Circuit; 1989, U.S. Court of Appeals for the Federal Circuit; registered to practice before U.S. Patent and Trademark Office. *Education:* University of Notre Dame (B.A., summa cum laude, 1974); University of Michigan (J.D., magna cum laude, 1978); Case Western Reserve University (B.A., in Chemistry, summa cum laude, 1989). Phi Beta Kappa. Associate Editor, 1976-1977 and Senior Editor, 1977-1978, Michigan Law Review. Co-Author: *Ohio Civil Practice,* Banks-Baldwin Law Pub. Co., 1988. Law Clerk to Hon. John A. Danaher, U.S. Court of Appeals for the District of Columbia Circuit, 1978-1979. *Member:* American Intellectual Property Law Association, Cleveland Intellectual Property Law Association. ***PRACTICE AREAS:*** Patent; Trademark; Copyright; Trade Secrets; Intellectual Property Litigation. ***Email:*** jmurtaugh@pearnegordon.com

JAMES M. MOORE, born Akron, Ohio, February 10, 1948; admitted to bar, 1988, Ohio and U.S. Court of Appeals for the Federal Circuit; 1992, U.S. Supreme Court; registered to practice before U.S. Patent and Trademark Office. *Education:* University of Akron (B.S.E.E., 1971); Southern Methodist University (M.S.E.E., 1972); Cleveland-Marshall School of Law (J.D., cum laude, 1988). Phi Alpha Delta; Eta Kappa Nu. Member: Moot Court Board of Governors; Order of Barristers. *Member:* Cleveland, Ohio State and American Bar Associations; Cleveland Intellectual Property Law Association (President, 1997-1998); American Intellectual Property Law Association; Institute of Electrical and Electronics Engineers. [Major, USAF, 1972-1985]. ***PRACTICE AREAS:*** Patent; Trademark; Copyright; Trade Secret; Unfair Competition. ***Email:*** ip@pearnegordon.com

MICHAEL W. GARVEY, born Oak Park, Illinois, March 18, 1962; admitted to bar, 1991, Ohio and U.S. Court of Appeals for the Federal Circuit; registered to practice before U.S. Patent and Trademark Office. *Education:* University of Notre Dame (B.S.E.E., 1984); College of William and Mary (J.D., 1991). Member, Institute of Electrical and Electronics Engineers. *Member:* Ohio State Bar Association; Cleveland Intellectual Property Law Association (Secretary, 1997-2000; President, 2003-2004); American Intellectual Property Law Association; International Trademark Association; International Federation of Industrial Property Attorneys (FICPI). ***PRACTICE AREAS:*** Patents; Trademarks; Prosecution and Appeals; Intellectual Property. ***Email:*** mgarvey@pearnegordon.com

RICHARD A. SHARPE, born Cleveland, Ohio, March 24, 1965; admitted to bar, 1992, Ohio; 1996, U.S. District Court, Northern District of Ohio; U.S. Court of Appeals, Federal Circuit; registered to practice before U.S. Patent and Trademark Office. *Education:* Otterbein College (B.S., Chem., 1987), Sigma Zeta; Washington College of Law of American University (J.D., 1991). *Member:* Cleveland (Secretary, 1994-1996) and American Intellectual Property Law Associations. ***SPECIAL AGENCIES:*** Patent Examiner, U.S. Patent and Trademark Office, 1989-1990. ***PRACTICE AREAS:*** Intellectual Property; Patents; Trademarks; Copyrights; Litigation. ***Email:*** ip@pearnegordon.com

RONALD M. KACHMARIK, born Cleveland, Ohio, July 31, 1963; admitted to bar, 1994, Ohio; 1995, U.S. District Court, Northern District of Ohio and U.S. Court of Appeals, Federal Circuit; registered to practice before the U.S. Patent and Trademark Office. *Education:* University of Akron (B.S., 1987); Cleveland-Marshall College of Law (J.D., 1994).

(This Listing Continued)

PEARNE & GORDON LLP, Cleveland—Continued

Sigma Pi Sigma. Patent Examiner, U.S. Patent and Trademark Office, 1987-1990. *Member:* American Bar Association; Cleveland Intellectual Property Law Association (Treasurer, 1999-2001); American Intellectual Property Law Association. ***PRACTICE AREAS:*** Intellectual Property; Patent; Trademark. ***Email:*** rkachmarik@pearnegordon.com

PAUL A. SERBINOWSKI, born Buffalo, New York, March 22, 1967; admitted to bar, 1994, Pennsylvania; 1995, Ohio; 1996, U.S. District Court, Northern District of Ohio; registered to practice before U.S. Patent and Trademark Office. *Education:* Alfred University (B.S.C.E., 1989); Widener University (J.D., 1994). Member, American Ceramic Society. *Member:* Cleveland and American Intellectual Property Law Associations. ***PRACTICE AREAS:*** Intellectual Property; Patents; Trademarks; Copyrights; Chemistry; Biotechnology. ***Email:*** ip@pearnegordon.com

BRIAN G. BEMBENICK, born DuBois, Pennsylvania, February 22, 1966; admitted to bar, 1998, Ohio; registered to practice before U.S. Patent and Trademark Office. *Education:* Gannon University (B.S., 1988); Catholic University of America (J.D., 1997). *Member:* American Bar Association; Cleveland Intellectual Property Law Association. ***PRACTICE AREAS:*** Patents; Trademarks; Copyrights. ***Email:*** bbembenick@pearnegordon.com

AARON A. FISHMAN, born Kansas City, Missouri, March 25, 1972; admitted to bar, 1999, Ohio; 2000, U.S. District Court, Northern District of Ohio; registered to practice before U.S. Patent and Trademark Office. *Education:* University of Toledo (B.E.T., 1996; J.D., 1999). Member, Institute of Electrical and Electronics Engineers. *Member:* Cleveland Intellectual Property Law Association; American Intellectual Property Law Association. ***PRACTICE AREAS:*** Patents; Trademarks; Copyrights. ***Email:*** ip@pearnegordon.com

ASSOCIATES

STEPHEN S. WENTSLER, born Akron, Ohio, December 15, 1967; admitted to bar, 1997, Virginia; 2000, Ohio; U.S. Court of Appeals, Federal and Sixth Circuits; U.S. District Court, Southern District of Ohio; registered to practice before U.S. Patent and Trademark Office. *Education:* University of Cincinnati College of Engineering (B.S.M.E., magna cum laude, 1993); Syracuse University College of Law (J.D., 1996). *Member:* Ohio State and American Bar Associations; American Intellectual Property Law Association; Cleveland Intellectual Property Law Association; American Society of Mechanical Engineers (Treasurer, Cincinnati Section). ***PRACTICE AREAS:*** Patents; Intellectual Property.

ROBERT F. BODI, born Cleveland, Ohio, March 8, 1964; admitted to bar, 2000, Ohio; 2001, U.S. District Court, Northern District of Ohio; registered to practice before U.S. Patent and Trademark Office. *Education:* University of Akron (B.S.E.E., B.S., Applied Math, 1988; J.D., summa cum laude, 2000). Pi Mu Epsilon; Eta Kappa Nu. Member, I.E.E.E.; Cleveland Engineering Society; Federalist Society. Online Editor, Akron Law Review, 1999-2000. *Member:* Cleveland and Ohio State Bar Associations; American Intellectual Property Law Association. ***PRACTICE AREAS:*** Patents; Trademarks; Copyrights; Copyright Litigation. ***Email:*** rbodi@pearnegordon.com

SUZANNE B. GAGNON, admitted to bar, 2000, Ohio; 2001, U.S. District Court, Northern District of Ohio; registered to practice before U.S. Patent and Trademark Office. *Education:* University of Dayton (B.E.E., 1991); Capital University (M.B.A., 1998); Ohio State University (J.D., 2000). Eta Kappa Nu; Phi Sigma Rho. *Member:* Ohio State Bar Association; Cleveland Intellectual Property Law Association; American Intellectual Property Law Association; Society of Women Engineers. ***PRACTICE AREAS:*** Patents; Trademarks; Copyrights. ***Email:*** sgagnon@pearnegordon.com

UNA SCHUMACHER, admitted to bar, 2002, Ohio, U.S. District Court, Northern District of Ohio; registered to practice before U.S. Patent and Trademark Office. *Education:* Miami University (B.S., 1996); Cleveland-Marshall College of Law (J.D., 2001). *Member:* Cleveland, Ohio State, American Bar Associations; Cleveland Intellectual Property Law Association. ***PRACTICE AREAS:*** Patents; Trademarks; Copyrights. ***Email:*** uschumacher@pearnegordon.com

STEVEN J. SOLOMON, born Cleveland, Ohio, November 24, 1975; admitted to bar, 2003, Ohio; registered to practice before U.S. Patent and Trademark Office. *Education:* Ohio State University (B.S.Ch.E., 1998); Cleveland State University (J.D., magna cum laude, 2002). Member, American Institute of Chemical Engineers. *Member:* Ohio State Bar Association; Cleveland Intellectual Property Law Association. ***LANGUAGES:*** French. ***PRACTICE AREAS:*** Patents; Trademarks; Copyrights; Intellectual Property Litigation. ***Email:*** ssolomon@pearnegordon.com

GREGORY FERNENGEL, born Danville, Kentucky, June 20, 1975; admitted to bar, 2003, Ohio; registered to practice before U.S. Patent and Trademark Office. *Education:* The Ohio State University (B.S., Pharmacy, 1998); Case Western Reserve University (J.D., 2003). Registered Pharmacist, Ohio, 1999—. Member, American Pharmacist Association. *Member:* Cleveland Bar Association; Cleveland and American Intellectual Property Law Associations. ***PRACTICE AREAS:*** Intellectual Property; Patents; Trademarks; Copyrights; Litigation. ***Email:*** gfernengel@pearnegordon.com

OF COUNSEL

LOWELL L. HEINKE, born Coshocton, Ohio, October 14, 1932; admitted to bar, 1960, Ohio; 1961, U.S. District Court, Northern District of Ohio; 1982, U.S. Court of Appeals, Federal Circuit; registered to practice before U.S. Patent and Trademark Office. *Education:* Case Institute of Technology (B.S. in Eng., with honors, 1954); George Washington University (LL.B., 1959). *Member:* Cleveland, Ohio State and American Bar Associations; Cleveland (President, 1980-1981) and American (Chairman, Antitrust Law Committee, 1978-1980; Member, Board of Managers, 1980-1983) Intellectual Property Law Associations. ***SPECIAL AGENCIES:*** Patent Examiner, U.S. Patent Office, 1955-1958. ***PRACTICE AREAS:*** Intellectual Property; Patents; Trademarks. ***Email:*** ip@pearnegordon.com

THADDEUS A. ZALENSKI, born East Vandergrift, Pennsylvania, December 10, 1936; admitted to bar, 1966, Pennsylvania; 1970, U.S. Court of Appeals, Third Circuit; 1982, U.S. District Court of Appeals for the Federal Circuit; registered to practice before the U.S. Patent and Trademark Office (Not admitted in Ohio). *Education:* Pennsylvania State University (B.S. in P.N.G.E., 1959); Georgetown University Law Center(J.D., 1966). ***SPECIAL AGENCIES:*** Patent Examiner, U.S. Patent and Trademark Office, 1961-1966. ***PRACTICE AREAS:*** Patents; Trademark; Copyright; Trade Secrets; Unfair Competition. ***Email:*** ip@pearnegordon.com

(This Listing Continued)

PERANTINIDES & NOLAN CO., L.P.A.

CLEVELAND, OHIO

(See Akron)

General Civil Trial and Appellate Practice. Negligence, Products Liability, Medical Legal, Malpractice, Construction, Toxic Tort and Commercial Law. Insurance, Environmental, Aviation, Wrongful Death and Civil Rights.

RANDALL M. PERLA

19443 LORAIN ROAD
CLEVELAND, OHIO 44126
Telephone: 440-333-2503
Fax: 440-333-9650
URL: http://www.randallperla.com
Email: theperlas5@aol.com
URL: http://www.perlalaw.com

Domestic Relations, Family Law, Divorce, Personal Injury, Automobile Accidents and Injuries, Probate, Child Custody.

RANDALL M. PERLA, born Cleveland, Ohio, August 19, 1949; admitted to bar, 1974, Ohio. *Education:* Bowling Green State University (B.A., 1971); Cleveland Marshall College of Law (J.D., 1974). Listed in: Martindale-Hubbell's Bar Register of Preeminent Lawyers; Who's Who in American Law. Former Magistrate, Cuyahoga County Domestic Relations Court, 1975-1978. *Member:* Cleveland (Former Officer-Trustee, Family Law Committee), Cuyahoga County, Lorain County and Ohio State Bar Associations; Ohio Academy of Trial Lawyers (Former Chairperson, Family Law Section); The Association of Trial Lawyers of America (Ohio State Chairperson, Family Law Section). ***PRACTICE AREAS:*** Domestic Relations; Family Law; Child Custody; Divorce; Personal Injury Law; Probate Law.

PERSKY, SHAPIRO & ARNOFF CO., L.P.A.

CLEVELAND, OHIO

(See Beachwood)

General Practice, Corporate Law, Real Estate, Finance, Health Care, Taxation, Professional Corporations, Trusts and Estates, Estate Planning, Probate Law, Employee Benefits, Antitrust, Litigation, Family Law, Bankruptcy and Debtor and Creditor.

FRANK PISCITELLI CO., L.P.A.

SUITE 900, THE HALLE BUILDING
1228 EUCLID AVENUE
CLEVELAND, OHIO 44115
Telephone: 216-931-7000
Fax: 216-931-9925
URL: http://www.piscitellilaw.com

Automobile Accidents, Personal Injury, Medical Malpractice and Class Action Litigation.

FIRM PROFILE: Practice limited to plaintiffs personal and financial injuries.

FRANK E. PISCITELLI, JR., born Richmond Heights, Ohio, March 11, 1967; admitted to bar, 1993, Ohio and U.S. District Court, Northern District of Ohio; 1995, U.S. Court of Appeals, Sixth Circuit. *Education:* Cleveland State University (B.A., 1990); Cleveland Marshall College of Law (J.D., 1993). *Member:* Ohio State Bar Association; The Association of Trial Lawyers of America; Ohio Academy of Trial Lawyers. ***PRACTICE AREAS:*** Automobile Accidents and Injuries; Personal Injury; Medical Malpractice; Class Actions. ***Email:*** frank@piscitellilaw.com

DARRYL E. PITTMAN & ASSOCIATES

2940 NOBLE ROAD, SUITE 202
CLEVELAND, OHIO 44121
Telephone: 216-291-1005
Fax: 216-382-8580
Email: dpittman@stratos.net
URL: http://www.pittmanalexanderattorneys.com

Consumer Law, Bankruptcy, Lead Poisoning.

DARRYL E. PITTMAN, born Pittsburgh, Pennsylvania, July 11, 1948; admitted to bar, 1973, Ohio. *Education:* Columbia University (A.B., 1970; J.D., 1973). *Member:* Ohio State Bar Association; The Association of Trial Lawyers of America; Ohio Trial Lawyers Association. ***LANGUAGES:*** Spanish. ***PRACTICE AREAS:*** Consumer Law; Bankruptcy; Lead Poisoning.

PLEVIN & GALLUCCI COMPANY, L.P.A.

Established in 1974

THE ILLUMINATING BUILDING
55 PUBLIC SQUARE, SUITE 2222
CLEVELAND, OHIO 44113
Telephone: 216-861-0804
Fax: 216-861-5322
Email: FGallucci@PGlawyer.com
URL: http://www.plevinandgallucci.com

Personal Injury, Workers' Compensation, Medical Malpractice; Airplane Crash Litigation; Construction Accidents, Nursing Home Negligence; Insurance Litigation, Birth Trauma; Obstetric Malpractice; Nursing Malpractice; Wrongful Death; Automobile Accidents; Brain Injury; Catastrophic Injury; Motor Vehicle Accidents and Injuries; Railroad Accidents and Injuries; Railroad Crossing Accidents.

LEON M. PLEVIN, born Weirton, West Virginia, January 8, 1932; admitted to bar, 1957, Ohio; 1961, U.S. District Court, Northern District of Ohio, U.S. Supreme Court; 1987, Pennsylvania; 1988, New York; U.S. Court of Appeals, Sixth Circuit. *Education:* West Virginia University (A.B., 1953); George Washington University; The Cleveland-Marshall Law School (J.D., 1957). Selected by his peers as one of the 100 outstanding lawyers, from approximately 8,000 lawyers of Northeast Ohio, Inside Business Magazine, December 2001, December 2002 and December 2003. Author: "Setoff under Underinsured Motorist Coverage," 20 Clev. St. L.Rev. 10, 1971. Member: Board of Bar Examiners, Supreme Court of Ohio, 1998-2004; Arts and Sciences Visiting Committee of Cleveland State University, 1998—; Visiting Committee, Cleveland-Marshall Law School, Cleveland State University, 1987-1996. Member, 1965— and Member, Board of Directors, 1970-1982, American Arbitration Association. President, Cleveland Artist Foundation, 1998-2003. President, Cleveland-Marshall Law School Alumni Association of Cleveland State University, 1984-1985 and its outstanding alumnus, 1988. Trustee, Cleveland State University Development Foundation, 1997—. Trustee, Citizens League, 1975-1982. Member and Chairman, Cleveland Regional Advisory Council, American Arbitration Association, 1970-1972. Past Trustee, Cleveland Rape Crisis Center. Founding Life Member, Eighth District Court of Appeals. Trustee, Beck Center for the Performing Arts, 1999-2002. *Member:* Cleveland Bar Association (Chairman: Common Pleas Court Committee, 1969-1970; Joint Medical-Legal Committee, 1970-1971 and Trustee, 1972-1975); Cuyahoga County and American Bar Associations; Cleveland Academy of Trial Attorneys (Trustee); Ohio Academy of Trial Lawyers (Chairperson, Medical Negligence Committee, 1988-1989; Sustaining Member); The Association of Trial Lawyers of America; American Judicature Society. ***PRACTICE AREAS:*** Airplane Crash Litigation; Construction Accidents; Nursing Home Negligence; Insurance Litigation; Birth Trauma; Obstetric Malpractice; Nursing Malpractice; Wrongful Death; Automobile Accidents; Brain Injury; Catastrophic Injury; Motor Vehicle Accidents & Injuries; Plaintiff's Personal Injury; Railroad Accidents and Injuries; Railroad Crossing Accidents. ***Email:*** lplevin@pglawyer.com

FRANK LEWIS GALLUCCI III, born Mayfield, Ohio, September 25, 1975; admitted to bar, 2000, Ohio and U.S District Court, Northern District of Ohio. *Education:* Boston College (B.S., 1997); Cleveland-Marshall College of Law (J.D., 2000). Trustee, Cleveland-Marshall Law School Alumni Association, Cleveland State University, 2004-2005. Vice President, Boston College Alumni Association, Cleveland Chapter. Associate Board Member, Free Medical Clinic of Greater Cleveland. *Member:* Cuyahoga County and Ohio State Bar Associations; Cleveland Academy of Trial Attorneys; Ohio Academy of Trial Lawyers. ***PRACTICE AREAS:*** Workers' Compensation; Airplane Crash Litigation; Construction Accidents; Nursing Home Negligence; Insurance Litigation; Birth Trauma; Obstetric Malpractice; Nursing Malpractice; Wrongful Death; Automobile Accidents; Brain Injury; Catastrophic Injury; Motor Vehicle Accidents and Injuries; Plaintiffs Personal Injury; Railroad Accidents and Injuries; Railroad Crossing Accidents. ***Email:*** fgallucci@pglawyer.com

---

PODOR & ASSOCIATES

CLEVELAND, OHIO

(See Solon)

Family Law, Adoption Law, Child Support, Child Custody, Visitation Rights, Divorce, Business Law, Commercial Law, Civil Rights, Criminal Law, DUI/DWI, Discrimination, Employment Law, Insurance Law, Legal Malpractice, Pediatric Malpractice, Medical Malpractice, Motor Vehicle Accidents, Nursing Home Litigation, Plaintiffs Personal Injury, Products Liability Law, Professional Malpractice Law, Sexual Harassment, Toxic Torts, Traffic Violations, White Collar Crimes, Workers Compensation.

PORTER WRIGHT MORRIS & ARTHUR LLP

Established in 1846

925 EUCLID AVENUE, SUITE 1700
CLEVELAND, OHIO 44115-1483
Telephone: 216-443-9000; (800-824-1980)
Fax: 216-443-9011
Email: cleveland@porterwright.com
URL: http://www.porterwright.com

Columbus, Ohio Office: 41 South High Street, 43215-6194. Telephones: 614-227-2000; (800-533-2794). Fax: 614-227-2100. Internet: columbus@porterwright.com.
Dayton, Ohio Office: One Dayton Centre, One South Main Street, Suite 1600, 45402-2028. Telephones: 937-449-6810; (800-533-4434). Fax: 937-449-6820. Internet: dayton@porterwright.com.
Cincinnati, Ohio Office: 250 E. Fifth Street, Suite 2200, 45202-5117. Telephones: 513-381-4700; (800-582-5813). Fax: 513-421-0991. Internet: cincinnati@porterwright.com.

(This Listing Continued)

Washington, D.C. Office: 1919 Pennsylvania Avenue, N.W., Suite 500 20006-3434. Telephones: 202-778-3000; (800-456-7962). Fax: 202-778-3063. Internet: washington@porterwright.com.
Naples, Florida Office: 5801 Pelican Bay Boulevard, Suite 300, 34108-2709. Telephones: 239-593-2900; (800-876-7962). Fax: 239-593-2990. Internet: naples@porterwright.com.

Alternative Dispute Resolution, Agricultural Law, Antitrust and Trade Regulation, Business and Corporate, Complex Litigation, Construction, Employee Benefits, Energy and Utilities, Environment, Federal Administrative Law, Federal Contracting and Procurement, Financial Institutions, General Practice, Governmental Affairs, Health Care, Insurance, Intellectual Property, International Business, Labor and Employment, Litigation, Public Law, Public Finance, Real Estate, Securities, Taxation, Technology, Trusts and Estates.

FIRM PROFILE: Porter Wright Morris & Arthur LLP is a nationally known business law firm delivering creative solutions for large, mid-size and entrepreneurial businesses. Porter Wright's Cleveland presence traces to 1983 and emphasizes complex litigation issues, employment law, business transactions, commercial and municipal finance, bankruptcy and debt, estate planning and probate. The Firm, which traces its origins to 1846, has over 280 lawyers practicing in Cincinnati, Cleveland, Columbus, and Dayton, Ohio; Washington, D.C.; and Naples Florida.

PARTNERS

ROBERT D. ANDERLE, born Garfield Heights, Ohio, October 27, 1964; admitted to bar, 1990, Pennsylvania; 1995, Ohio. *Education:* Miami University (B.A., cum laude, 1987); Case Western Reserve University (J.D., magna cum laude, 1990). Law Clerk to Honorable Joseph F. Weis, Jr., United States Court of Appeals, Third Circuit. ***PRACTICE AREAS:*** Commercial Litigation; Insurance Coverage; Employee Benefits; Labor and Employment. ***Email:*** randerle@porterwright.com

ANN M. CARESANI, born Cleveland, Ohio, April 27, 1965; admitted to bar, 1994, Ohio. *Education:* Cleveland State University (B.B.A., magna cum laude, 1988; M.B.A., 1993); Cleveland-Marshall College of Law (J.D., magna cum laude, 1994). Certified Public Accountant, Ohio, 1992. *Member:* Cleveland and American Bar Associations. ***PRACTICE AREAS:*** Employee Benefits Law; ERISA. ***Email:*** acaresani@porterwright.com

JAMES W. EHRMAN, born Oberlin, Ohio, September 15, 1948; admitted to bar, 1974, Ohio; 1977, U.S. District Court, Northern District of Ohio; 1989, U.S. Court of Appeals, Sixth Circuit. *Education:* Harvard University (A.B., cum laude, 1971); University of Pennsylvania (J.D., 1974). *Member:* Cleveland, Mahoning County, Ohio State and American Bar Associations; American Bankruptcy Institute. ***REPORTED CASES:*** In re Hunt Energy Co., Inc., 48 B.R. 472 (Bankr. N.D. Ohio, 1985). ***PRACTICE AREAS:*** Bankruptcy Law; Commercial Litigation; Business Law. ***Email:*** jehrman@porterwright.com

MICHAEL A. ELLIS, born Chicago, Illinois, January 19, 1954; admitted to bar, 1977, Ohio. *Education:* University of Pennsylvania (B.A., 1974; M.A., 1974); Duke University (J.D., 1977). Order of the Coif. Instructor, "Mergers and Acqusitions," Cleveland Marshall School of Law, 1999-2000. Lecturer, "PLI, Acquiring or Selling the Privately-Held Company," 1996-2005. *Member:* Cleveland (Chair, Business and Corporation Section, 2005-2006, Chair, Section of Securities, 1991-1992; Section's 1990 Securities Law Institute), Ohio State (Chair, Corporation Law Committee, 1999-2001) and American Bar Associations. ***PRACTICE AREAS:*** Corporate Law; Securities Law; Partnership Law; Technology Law; Finance and Commerce; Labor and Employment. ***Email:*** mellis@porterwright.com

DONALD J. FISHER, born Jamaica, New York, November 15, 1948; admitted to bar, 1976, Ohio; 1978, U.S. District Court, Northern District of Ohio. *Education:* Hiram College (B.A., 1970); Case Western Reserve University (J.D., 1976). *Member:* Ohio State Bar Association. ***PRACTICE AREAS:*** Banking and Commercial Law; Secured Transactions; Real Estate; Finance; Commerce. ***Email:*** dfisher@porterwright.com

DANIEL F. GOURASH, born Wilkinsburg, Pennsylvania, November 18, 1957; admitted to bar, 1983, Ohio; 1984, U.S. District Court, Northern District of Ohio; 1985, U.S. Court of Appeals, Sixth Circuit; 1987, U.S. District Court, Eastern District of Michigan; 1994, U.S. Supreme Court. *Education:* University of New Haven (B.A., summa cum laude, 1980); Duke University School of Law (J.D., 1983). *Member:* American Bar Association (Chairperson, Young Lawyers Division, 1993-1994). ***PRACTICE AREAS:*** Insurance Coverage; Insurance Bad Faith; Bank and Savings and Loan Failures; Fraud; Products Liability; Securities Litigation; Commercial Litigation. ***Email:*** dgourash@porterwright.com

MARGARET M. KOESEL, born Cleveland, Ohio, March 18, 1950; admitted to bar, 1989, Ohio. *Education:* Baldwin-Wallace College (B.A., 1985); Cleveland State University (J.D., magna cum laude, 1988). Editor, Cleveland State University Law Review, 1987-1988. Adjunct Professor, Case Western Reserve University, 1993-1997. Law Clerk: Judge Ann McManamon, Ohio Court of Appeals. Co-author: Spoliation of Evidence: Sanctions and Remedies for Destruction of Evidence in Civil Litigation (ABA, 2000). *Member:* Ohio State and American Bar Associations. ***PRACTICE AREAS:*** Employment Litigation; ERISA Litigation; Commercial Litigation. ***Email:*** mkoesel@porterwright.com

PHILIP E. LANGER, born Dayton, Ohio, 1948; admitted to bar, 1973, Ohio; U.S. District Court, Southern District of Ohio. *Education:* Ohio Wesleyan University; The Ohio State University (B.A., 1970; J.D., 1973). *Member:* Dayton, Ohio State and American Bar Associations. ***PRACTICE AREAS:*** Banking Law; Bankruptcy Law; Commercial Litigation; Finance; Commerce. ***Email:*** planger@porterwright.com

IRENE M. MACDOUGALL, born Northampton, Massachusetts, November 25, 1958; admitted to bar, 1983, Ohio and U.S. District Court, Northern District of Ohio. *Education:* Case Western Reserve University (B.A., magna cum laude, 1980; J.D., 1983). Phi Beta Kappa; Order of the Coif. Member, Mortar Board. Recipient, American Jurisprudence Award, Professional Responsibility. *Member:* Cleveland Bar Association (Member, Real Estate Institute, Planning Committee, 1999-2004). ***PRACTICE AREAS:*** Banking and Finance; Real Estate; Corporate; Health Care; Business; Securities. ***Email:*** imacdougall@porterwright.com

(This Listing Continued)

PORTER WRIGHT MORRIS & ARTHUR LLP, Cleveland— Continued

HUGH E. McKAY, born Cleveland, Ohio, January 18, 1956; admitted to bar, 1982, Ohio and U.S. District Court, Northern District of Ohio and U.S. Court of Appeals, Sixth Circuit; 2002 U.S. Supreme Court. *Education:* Brown University (B.A., 1978); University of Pennsylvania (J.D., 1981). Life Member, Eighth District Judicial Conference. Former President and Master Bencher, William K. Thomas Inn of Court. Vice-Chair, American Red Cross, Board of Directors, Greater Cleveland Chapter, 2005—. Faculty, National Institute for Trial Advocacy Deposition Program. Leadership Cleveland, Class of 1998. *Member:* Cleveland (President-elect, 2005-2006; Vice-President, 2004-2005; Member, Board of Trustees, 1991-1994) and Federal (Vice-President, Northern District of Ohio Chapter, 2005-2006) Bar Associations. ***PRACTICE AREAS:*** Complex Commercial Litigation; Product Liability; Securities Litigation; Business Torts; Financial Institutions. ***Email:*** hmckay@porterwright.com

PAUL R. MATIA, born Cleveland, Ohio, October 2, 1937; admitted to bar, 1962, Ohio; 1969, U.S. District Court, Northern District of Ohio. *Education:* Case Western Reserve University (B.A., cum laude, 1959); Harvard University (J.D., 1962). Member, American Inn of Court, 1991—. Member, Ohio Senate, 1971-1975, 1979-1983. Judge, Cuyahoga County Common Pleas Court, 1985-1991. Judge, 1991-2005, and Chief Judge, 1999-2004, U.S. District Court, Northern District of Ohio, 1991-2005. Life Member, Sixth Circuit Judical Conference, 2005—. Member, U.S. Court of Appeals, Sixth Circuit, 1992-2005. *Member:* Cleveland, Cuyahoga County, Ohio State and Federal Bar Associations. ***PRACTICE AREAS:*** Litigation. ***Email:*** pmatia@porterwright.com

JOHN C. MONICA, JR., born St. Louis, Missouri, November 29, 1964; admitted to bar, 1991, Virginia; 1992, Maryland; 1994, District of Columbia; 2003, Ohio. *Education:* Northwestern University (B.A., 1987); George Washington University (J.D., with honors, 1991). ***PRACTICE AREAS:*** Products Liability Defense; Commercial Litigation. ***Email:*** jmonica@porterwright.com

FRED J. POMPEANI, born Cleveland, Ohio, July 8, 1957; admitted to bar, 1982, Ohio. *Education:* Miami University (B.A., 1979); Case Western Reserve University (J.D., 1982). ***PRACTICE AREAS:*** Workers Compensation; Employment Law; Civil Litigation. ***Email:*** fpompeani@porterwright.com

PATRICIA A. SCREEN, born Naples, Italy, May 31, 1956; admitted to bar, 1985, Ohio. *Education:* Old Dominion University (B.A., magna cum laude, 1978; M.A., 1982); University of Virginia (J.D., 1985). Phi Delta Phi. Member, Virginia Tax Review, 1984. Recipient, National Law Journal's Recognition for the Most Significant Defense Verdict of 2002: Ching Lung Chang v. The Cleveland Clinc Foundation, et. al., Cuyahoga County Ohio Court of Common Pleas, Case No. 403722. ***PRACTICE AREAS:*** Commercial Litigation; Insurance Law; Products Liability; Alternative Dispute Resolution; Intellectual Property; Professional Negligence; Employee Benefits. ***Email:*** pscreen@porterwright.com

LEO M. SPELLACY, JR., born Cleveland, Ohio, September 19, 1969; admitted to bar, 1996, Ohio; U.S. District Court, Northern District of Ohio. *Education:* John Carroll University (B.A., 1992); Cleveland State University (M.P.A., 1996); Cleveland Marshall College of Law (J.D., summa cum laude, 1996). ***PRACTICE AREAS:*** Litigation. ***Email:*** lspellacy@porterwright.com

RALPH STREZA, born Cleveland, Ohio, February 21, 1956; admitted to bar, 1982, Ohio. *Education:* Miami University (B.A., 1978); Cleveland Marshall College of Law (J.D., cum laude, 1982). ***PRACTICE AREAS:*** Negligence; Products Liability; Employer Liability; Litigation. ***Email:*** rstreza@porterwright.com

DAVID C. TRYON, born Cleveland, Ohio, December 20, 1958; admitted to bar, 1985, Ohio. *Education:* Brigham Young University (B.S., magna cum laude, 1981); University of Michigan (J.D., cum laude, 1984). Legal Articles published in Cleveland Bar Journal, various trade publications and Cleveland Plain Dealer; Seminar Speaker on Construction Law and Litigation issues; Visiting Lecturer at Cleve. State Univ. on Trial Advocacy. *Member:* Ohio Bar Association; Federalist Society (President, Cleveland Chapter). ***LANGUAGES:*** Spanish. ***REPORTED CASES:*** RTC v. Fountain Circle Assts., 799 F. Supp. 48 (1992); RTC v. J.B. Centron Dev. Co., 92 Ohio App. 3d 643 (1993); First Natl. Bank v. Bolin (1994 WL 175728). ***PRACTICE AREAS:*** Construction Law; Commercial Litigation; Appellate Litigation; Corporation Law; Business and Securities; Financial Institutions. ***Email:*** dtryon@porterwright.com

TRACEY L. TURNBULL, born Mt. Kisco, New York, June 1, 1969; admitted to bar, 1996, Ohio; 1997, U.S. District Court, Northern District of Ohio. *Education:* Hamilton College (B.A., 1991); Case Western Reserve University (J.D., cum laude, 1996). ***PRACTICE AREAS:*** Litigation. ***Email:*** tturnbull@porterwright.com

JEFFREY J. WEBER, born Cleveland, Ohio, January 21, 1962; admitted to bar, 1993, Ohio. *Education:* United States Naval Academy (B.S., with merit, 1984); University of Virginia (J.D., 1993). Phi Alpha Theta. *Member:* Cleveland and Ohio State Bar Associations. [U.S. Marine Corp., 1984-1991]. ***PRACTICE AREAS:*** Employment Law; Labor Law; Litigation. ***Email:*** jweber@porterwright.com

WILLIAM R. WEIR, born Coshocton, Ohio, January 3, 1959; admitted to bar, 1984, Ohio. *Education:* Northwestern University (B.A., 1981); Case Western Reserve University (J.D., 1984). ***PRACTICE AREAS:*** Banking Law; Secured Transactions; Business and Securities; Finance and Commerce; Real Estate; Lender Law; Commercial Real Estate Finance. ***Email:*** WWEIR@porterwright.com

ALAN D. WRIGHT, born Youngstown, Ohio, October 11, 1929; admitted to bar, 1959, Ohio; 1962, U.S. Supreme Court; 1964, U.S. District Court, Northern District of Ohio and U.S. Court of Appeals, Sixth Circuit. *Education:* Kenyon College (A.B., 1951); Cleveland State University (J.D., 1959). Municipal Law Director, Lake County, Ohio, 1962-1972. Trustee, Ohio Public Expenditure Council, 1975-1990. Vice President and General Counsel, Cleveland Electric Illuminating Co., 1977-1986. Member, National Coal Council, 1991-1997. *Member:* Cleveland (Chairman, Court Management Project, 1971-1972), Lake County and Ohio State Bar Associations. ***PRACTICE AREAS:*** Governmental Affairs; Utility Law; Health Care. ***Email:*** awright@porterwright.com

(This Listing Continued)

RESIDENT ASSOCIATES

AMY L. DELUCA, born Wheeling, West Virginia, January 25, 1976; admitted to bar, 2003, Ohio. *Education:* University of Akron (B.A., magna cum laude, 1998); Cleveland-Marshall College of Law (J.D., summa cum laude, 2002). ***PRACTICE AREAS:*** Litigation. ***Email:*** adeluca@porterwright.com

L. WILLIAM ERB, born Cleveland, Ohio, September 26, 1960; admitted to bar, 2000, Ohio; 2003, U.S. District Court, Northern District of Ohio. *Education:* Kenyon College (B.A., 1982); Thunderbird, The Garvin School of International Management (M.B.A., with distinction, 1985); Cleveland-Marshall College of Law (J.D., summa cum laude, 2000). *Member:* Cleveland and Ohio State Bar Associations. ***PRACTICE AREAS:*** Banking Law; Commercial Lending Transactions; Creditors Rights; Finance and Commerce. ***Email:*** lwerb@porterwright.com

REBECCA KUCERA FISCHER, born Cleveland, Ohio, August 9, 1974; admitted to bar, 1999, Ohio; 2000, U.S. District Court, Northern District of Ohio. *Education:* Baldwin-Wallace College (B.A., magna cum laude, 1996); Case Western Reserve University (J.D., 1999). Dean Dunmore Tournament Award Winner, Niagara Moot Court Team, 1999. ***PRACTICE AREAS:*** Financial Institutions; Bankruptcy; Commercial Litigation; Litigation; Finance and Commerce. ***Email:*** rfischer@porterwright.com

KEVIN KELLEY, born Lorain, Ohio, April 4, 1968; admitted to bar, 2004, Ohio. *Education:* Marquette University (B.S., 1990); Case Western Reserve University (M.S., 1996); Cleveland State University (J.D., 2004). Managing Editor, Cleveland State Law Review, 2004. ***PRACTICE AREAS:*** Litigation. ***Email:*** kkelley@porterwright.com

KENNETH J. KLEPPEL, born Garfield Heights, Ohio, August 15, 1979; admitted to bar, 2005, Ohio. *Education:* University of Notre Dame (B.B.A., magna cum laude, 2001; J.D., 2004). Editor-in-Chief, The Journal of College and University Law, 2003-2004. *Member:* Lake County, Cleveland, Ohio State and American Bar Associations. ***PRACTICE AREAS:*** Litigation. ***Email:*** kkleppel@porterwright.com

SUZANA KRSTEVSKI KOCH, born 1976; admitted to bar, 2001, Ohio; 2002, U.S. Court of Appeals, Sixth Circuit and U.S. District Court, Northern District of Ohio; 2003, U.S. District Court, Western District of Pennsylvania. *Education:* Walsh College (B.A., summa cum laude, 1998); The Ohio State State University (J.D., 2001). National Moot Court Team, 2000-2001. Senior Law Clerk to Honorable William T. Bodoh, U.S. Bankruptcy Court, Northern District of Ohio and Sixth Circuit Bankruptcy Appellate Panel. *Member:* Cleveland, Ohio State and American Bar Associations. ***PRACTICE AREAS:*** Bankruptcy; Insolvency; Workouts; Commercial Litigation; Finance; Commerce; Financial Institutions.

SCOTT LEPENE, born Cleveland, Ohio, March 30, 1975; admitted to bar, 2003, Ohio. *Education:* Ohio University (B.S., summa cum laude, 1997); Vanderbilt University (J.D., 2003). ***PRACTICE AREAS:*** Litigation; Employment Law; Bankruptcy. ***Email:*** slepene@porterwright.com

DAVID M. LEWIS, born Cleveland, Ohio, October 10, 1967; admitted to bar, 2000, Ohio. *Education:* Cleveland State University (B.A., English and Communications, 1991); Case Western Reserve University (J.D., 2000). Order of the Coif. *Member:* Ohio State and American Bar Associations. ***PRACTICE AREAS:*** General Business; Financial Institutions; Commercial Law; Real Estate. ***Email:*** dlewis@porterwright.com

PATRICK T. LEWIS, born Cleveland, Ohio, October 1, 1979; admitted to bar, 2004, Ohio. *Education:* College of William & Mary (A.B., cum laude, 2000); Harvard University (J.D., cum laude, 2004). Phi Beta Kappa. ***PRACTICE AREAS:*** Litigation. ***Email:*** plewis@porterwright.com

MICHELLE POWE MARVINNEY, born Cleveland, Ohio, December 28, 1955; admitted to bar, 1984, Ohio and U.S. District Court, Northern District of Ohio; U.S. Tax Court. *Education:* Miami University (B.S., Accountancy, 1978); Case Western Reserve University (J.D., 1984). Beta Alpha Psi. Member, National Moot Court Team, 1983-1984. Certified Public Accountant, Ohio, 1980. *Member:* Cleveland and Ohio State Bar Associations. ***PRACTICE AREAS:*** Corporate Law; Banking Law; Business; Finance; Commerce; Real Estate. ***Email:*** mmarvinney@porterwright.com

ALLYSON MONDALEK, born Cleveland, Ohio, September 10, 1978; admitted to bar, 2004, Ohio. *Education:* The Ohio State University (B.S., 2001); Case Western Reserve University (J.D., magna cum laude, 2004). Order of the Coif. ***PRACTICE AREAS:*** Corporate Law; Financial Institution Law; Commercial Loans; Real Estate. ***Email:*** amondalek@porterwright.com

JOHN A. MUGNANO, born Cleveland, Ohio, November 12, 1969; admitted to bar, 2001, Ohio. *Education:* Miami University (B.S., Zoology, 1992; B.A., 1992; M.S., Zoology, 1995); Purdue University; Cleveland-Marshall College of Law (J.D., summa cum laude, 2001). Sigma Xi. ***PRACTICE AREAS:*** Litigation. ***Email:*** jmugnano@porterwright.com

JAVIER A. PACHECO, born Lima, Peru, February 17, 1982; (admission pending). *Education:* The Ohio State University (B.A., 2002); Case Western Reserve University (J.D., 2005). ***LANGUAGES:*** Spanish. ***PRACTICE AREAS:*** Litigation. ***Email:*** jpacheco@porterwright.com

NICOLE J. QUATHAMER, born Niles, Ohio, January 24, 1973; admitted to bar, 1999, Ohio; 2000, U.S. District Court, Northern District of Ohio and U.S. Court of Appeals, Sixth Circuit. *Education:* The Ohio State University (B.A., 1995); Cleveland-Marshall College of Law (J.D., magna cum laude, 1999). *Member:* Cleveland, Ohio State and American Bar Associations; Defense Research Institute. ***PRACTICE AREAS:*** Litigation; Employment Law; Workers Compensation. ***Email:*** nquathamer@porterwright.com

NATALIE H. RAUF, born Cincinnati, Ohio, February 24, 1975; admitted to bar, 2001, Ohio. *Education:* Illinois Wesleyan University (B.A., 1997); Case Western Reserve University (J.D., cum laude, 2001). Notes Editor, Case Western Reserve Law Review, 2000-2001. *Member:* Ohio State and American Bar Associations. ***PRACTICE AREAS:*** Banking; Commercial Loans; Real Estate; Finance; Commerce. ***Email:*** nrauf@porterwright.com

HOWARD G. STRAIN, born Pittsburgh, Pennsylvania, January 28, 1964; admitted to bar, 1996, Wisconsin and U.S. District Court, Eastern and Western Districts of Wisconsin;

(This Listing Continued)

1997, U.S. District Court, Northern District of Ohio; 1998, Ohio and U.S. Court of Appeals, Sixth Circuit. *Education:* Antioch University (B.A., Political Science, 1989); The Ohio State University (J.D., 1996). Order of the Coif. Speaker, "Insurance Coverage for Environmental Contamination: What You Need to Know in the Wake of Edgerton, Hills Standard, and WPS," State Bar of Wisconsin, Environmental Law Update, 1997. Speaker, "Securities Litigation and Arbitration," Institute for Paralegal Education, June 1999. *Member:* Ohio State and American Bar Associations. ***REPORTED CASES:*** Lee-Lipstreu v. Chubb Group of Ins. Cos., 329 F.3d 898 (6th Cir. 2003)(Instrumental in this decision, which allowed insurance companies to remove uninsured/underinsured motorist cases to federal court without being improperly remanded to state court). ***PRACTICE AREAS:*** Insurance Coverage Litigation; Complex Commercial Litigation; Bankruptcy; Fraudulent Conveyance. ***Email:*** hstrain@porterwright.com

CHARLES W. ZEPP, born Cleveland, Ohio, June 22, 1972; admitted to bar, 1997, Ohio. *Education:* Xavier University (B.S., 1994); The Ohio State University (J.D., 1997). ***PRACTICE AREAS:*** Litigation. ***Email:*** czepp@porterwrigt.com

OF COUNSEL

LISA A. REID, born Buffalo, New York, December 21, 1961; admitted to bar, 1988, Ohio. *Education:* John Carroll University (B.S., 1983); Cleveland-Marshall College of Law (J.D., 1988). Co-Author: Martindale-Hubbell Law Digest 1994 Workers' Compensation Law Summary; Ohio Workers' Compensation: A Legal Overview for Employers. *Member:* Cleveland (Chair, Workers' Compensation Section) and Ohio State Bar Associations; Ohio Women's Bar Association; Association of Trial Lawyers of America. ***LANGUAGES:*** French. ***PRACTICE AREAS:*** Workers Compensation; Labor and Employment. ***Email:*** lreid@porterwright.com

(See Listings at Dayton, Cincinnati and Columbus, Ohio, Washington, D.C. and Naples, Florida for professional biographies on attorneys resident in those offices)

LAW OFFICES OF LESTER S. POTASH

55 PUBLIC SQUARE, SUITE 1717
CLEVELAND, OHIO 44113
Telephone: 216-771-8400
Fax: 216-771-8404
Email: lsp@potashlaw.com

General Practice, Social Security, Personal Injury, Automobile Accidents, Criminal Law, Drunk Driving, Probate, Litigation, Medical Malpractice, Legal Malpractice.

LESTER S. POTASH, born Cleveland, Ohio, November 12, 1950; admitted to bar, 1975, Ohio; 1978, U.S. Court of Appeals, Sixth Circuit; 1986, U.S. Supreme Court. *Education:* Miami University (B.A., 1971); Case Western Reserve University (J.D., 1975). *Member:* Cuyahoga County (President, 2002-2003), Ohio State and American Bar Associations; The Association of Trial Lawyers of America; Ohio Academy of Trial Lawyers.

POWERS & GROH-WARGO

2 BEREA COMMONS, SUITE 215 (BEREA)
P.O. BOX 1059
CLEVELAND, OHIO 44017
Telephone: 440-243-2955
Facsimile: 440-243-2967
URL: http://www.pgwohio.com

Real Estate Leasing, Land Use and Acquisition, Condominiums, Construction, Estate Planning and Administration, Corporate Law, Domestic Relations, Civil Litigation.

DONALD H. POWERS, born Nicholson, Pennsylvania, July 18, 1930; admitted to bar, 1955, Illinois; 1957, New York; 1958, U.S. Court of Appeals, Second Circuit; 1959, U.S. District Court, Northern District of New York; 1964, Ohio; 1965, U.S. Claims Court and U.S. District Court, Southern District of Ohio; 1972, U.S. District Court, Northern District of Ohio. *Education:* Grove City College (A.B., magna cum laude, 1952); Northwestern University (J.D., 1955). Phi Alpha Delta; Pi Kappa Delta; Pi Gamma Mu; Order of the Coif. Hardy Scholar. Associate Editor, Northwestern University Law Review, 1955. Associate Professor, Teaching Law and Enterprise at New York State University at Binghamton, 1961-1963. Associate Counsel, Middle Eastern Emergency Committee, Suez Crisis, 1956. *Member:* Cleveland, Ohio State and American (Member, Business Law Section; Law Practice Management Section) Bar Associations. ***PRACTICE AREAS:*** Real Estate Leasing; Land Use and Acquisitions; Zoning Law; Condominiums; Construction Law. ***Email:*** don@pgwohio.com

FRANK J. GROH-WARGO, born Cleveland, Ohio, June 7, 1951; admitted to bar, 1980, Ohio and U.S. District Court, Northern District of Ohio; 1983, U.S. Court of Appeals, Sixth Circuit. *Education:* University of Dayton (B.A., 1973; J.D., 1980). Appellate Advocacy: Tri-State Moot Court Competition. Member, City of Berea Planning Commission. Member, Enterprise Zone Tax Review Council, 1990. *Member:* Cuyahoga County and Ohio State Bar Associations. ***PRACTICE AREAS:*** Real Estate Law; Corporate Law; Employment Contracts; Employment Discrimination; Municipal Law. ***Email:*** frank@pgwohio.com

DONNA J. POWERS, born Binghamton, New York, April 17, 1962; admitted to bar, 1988, Ohio. *Education:* Allegheny College (B.A., 1984); University of Puget Sound (J.D., cum laude, 1987). Alden Scholar. Recipient, American Jurisprudence Award for Administrative Law. Member, University of Puget Sound Law Review, 1986 and 1987. *Member:* Cleveland, Ohio State and American Bar Associations. ***PRACTICE AREAS:*** Estate Planning and Administration; Real Estate; Business. ***Email:*** donnap@pgwohio.com

MELINDA L. RUSCHAK, born Sandusky, Ohio, August 18, 1961; admitted to bar, 1986, Ohio; 1993, U.S. District Court, Northern District of Ohio; 1995, U.S. Supreme Court. *Education:* The Ohio State University (B.A., 1983); Capital University (J.D., 1986). Phi Alpha Delta. Order of the Curia. Recipient, American Jurisprudence Award for Civil Procedure and Business Associations. *Member:* Ohio State Bar Association. ***PRACTICE AREAS:*** Domestic Relations. ***Email:*** melinda@pgwohio.com

KATHERINE H. OPSINCS, born Parma, Ohio, February 9, 1979; admitted to bar, 2004, Ohio. *Education:* Wooster College (B.A., 2001); Case Western Reserve University (J.D., 2004). ***PRACTICE AREAS:*** Business Litigation. ***Email:*** kate@pgwohio.com

LEGAL SUPPORT PERSONNEL

MARGARET A. HUSTON, born Lakewood, Ohio, February 22, 1959. *Education:* Bryant & Stratton Business Institute (1986); American Institute for Paralegal Studies (Paralegal Certificate, 1987). (Paralegal). ***PRACTICE AREAS:*** Business Litigation; Real Estate. ***Email:*** marge@pgwohio.com

JENNIFER C. DAMRON, born Cleveland, Ohio, February 13, 1973. *Education:* Wayne County Career Center (Clerical and Business Education Certificate, 1992). ***PRACTICE AREAS:*** Estate Planning; Estate Administration. ***Email:*** jennifer@pgwohio.com

REPRESENTATIVE CLIENTS: Montlack Realty Co.; Nolos, Inc.; Snider Companies; International Physical Fitness Association; Northern Machine Tool Co.; Northern Boiler Co.; Union National Mortgage Co.; Union Escrow Co.

MARLON A. PRIMES

CARL B. STOKES FEDERAL COURTHOUSE, SUITE 400
801 WEST SUPERIOR AVENUE
CLEVELAND, OHIO 44113
Telephone: 216-622-3684
Fax: 216-522-4982
Email: marlon.primes@usdoj.gov

Civil Practice.

MARLON A. PRIMES, born Akron, Ohio, March 8, 1964; admitted to bar, 1990, Ohio; 1991, District of Columbia. *Education:* Ohio University (B.S.J., cum laude, 1986); Georgetown University (J.D., 1989). Law Clerk to Member Wilford W. Johansen, National Labor Relations Board, Washington, D.C., 1987-1989. Assistant U.S. Attorney. *Member:* Cleveland (Member, Board of Trustees, 2001-2004) and National (Vice President, 2001-2003 and 2004—) Bar Associations; The District of Columbia Bar; American Inns of Court (Master); Cleveland Bar Foundation. ***PRACTICE AREAS:*** Civil Practice.

KEVIN PURCELL CO., L.P.A.

19109 OLD DETROIT ROAD
CLEVELAND, OHIO 44116
Telephone: 440-331-5883
Fax: 440-331-9125
Email: kevintrust@stratos.net
URL: http://www.ohioestateplanninglaw.com

Elder Law, Trusts and Estates, Asset Protection, Estate Planning, Guardianship, Wills, Probate, Medicaid Eligibility, Revocable Trusts, Living Trusts, Charitable Giving, Living Will, Health Care Power of Attorney.

KEVIN PURCELL, born Cleveland, Ohio, December 7, 1952; admitted to bar, 1981, Ohio; 1986, District of Columbia. *Education:* John Carroll University (B.A., 1974); Cleveland Marshall College of Law (J.D., 1981). Certified Specialist, Estate Planning, Trust & Probate Law. *Member:* Ohio State Bar Association (Member: Estate Planning and Probate Law Section; Elder Law Section); National Academy of Elder Law Attorneys. ***Email:*** kevintrust@stratos.net

RABIN & RABIN CO., L.P.A.

55 PUBLIC SQUARE, SUITE 1510
CLEVELAND, OHIO 44113
Telephone: 216-771-8084
Fax: 216-771-4615
Email: jrabin@rabinandrabin.com
URL: http://www.lawyers.com/rabin&rabin

Bankruptcy, Real Estate, Probate, Commercial Litigation, Creditors Rights, Debtors Rights, Consumer Bankruptcy, Chapter 7, Chapter 11, Chapter 13.

MARY ANN (MICKEY) RABIN, born St. Louis, Missouri, June 1, 1934; admitted to bar, 1978, Ohio. *Education:* University of Rochester; Washington University (A.B., 1956); Washburn University of Topeka; Case Western Reserve University (J.D., 1978). Member, National Mock Trial Team. Member, Panel of Bankruptcy Trustees, United States Bankruptcy Court for the Northern District of Ohio, 1983—. Life Member, Eighth District Judicial Conference. Member, Women's Professional Cabinet Executive Committee, State of Israel Bonds, 1985-1989. Board Member, Hebrew Free Loan Association, 1981-1990. Board of Governors, Case-Western Reserve University School of Law, 1990-1993. *Member:* Cleveland (Member, Section on: Bankruptcy and Commercial Law, Secretary, 1986; Treasurer, 1987; Vice-Chairman, 1988; Chairman, 1989), Cuyahoga County (Trustee, 1990-1993), Ohio State and American Bar Associations; Ohio Women's Bar Association (Founding Member); National Association of Bankruptcy Trustees; American Bankruptcy Institute. ***PRACTICE AREAS:*** Bankruptcy; Real Estate; Probate; Commercial Litigation. ***Email:*** mrabin@rabinandrabin.com

JULIE E. RABIN, born New Haven, Connecticut, 1956; admitted to bar, 1981, Ohio. *Education:* Hebrew University of Jerusalem; Northwestern University (B.S.J., 1978); New York University (J.D., 1981). Dean's List. Kappa Tau Alpha; Alpha Lambda Delta. Law Clerk, U.S. Bankruptcy Judge John J. Galgay, 1979-1980. Member, Board of Directors, Sidelines, 1993-1996. Founding Member, Ketura Group of Hadassah. Former Cabinet Member, Young Business & Professional Division, Cleveland United Jewish Appeal. *Mem-*

(This Listing Continued)

RABIN & RABIN CO., L.P.A., Cleveland—Continued

ber: Cleveland (Trustee, 1998-2001; Section on: Bankruptcy and Commercial Law, Treasurer, 1997; Secretary, 1998; Vice-Chairman, 1999; Chairman 2000; Chairman Commission, Women in the Law, 1996-1997) and Ohio State Bar Associations. ***PRACTICE AREAS:*** Bankruptcy; Real Estate; Probate; Commercial Litigation. ***Email:*** jrabin@rabinandrabin.com

RADEMAKER, MATTY, McCLELLAND & GREVE

Established in 1974

55 PUBLIC SQUARE, SUITE 1775
CLEVELAND, OHIO 44113
Telephone: 216-621-6570
Fax: 216-621-1127
URL: http://www.rmmglaw.com

General Civil Trial and Appellate Practice before State and Federal Courts and Administrative Agencies, Workers' Compensation Defense, Municipal Law, Personal Injury and Products Liability and Insurance Defense, Banking, Corporation, Partnership, Estate Planning, Probate, Real Estate, Labor and Employment Practices Defense.

FIRM PROFILE: Rademaker, Matty, McClelland & Greve is a general law practice firm with substantial experience in the areas of workers' compensation defense, product liability defense, personal injury defense, employment practices defense and municipal law. Our philosophy is to produce positive results and successful claims management for our clients.

Our emphasis on providing our clients services at reasonable rates has earned us a healthy reputation among diverse industry executives, among automotive and specialty manufacturers, municipalities, hospitals, retail stores, grocery chains and other corporate entities, non-profit organizations and independently owned businesses.

MEMBERS OF FIRM

DENNIS A. RADEMAKER, born Cleveland, Ohio, October 3, 1950; admitted to bar, 1977, Ohio; 1983, Florida. *Education:* Cleveland State University (B.A., 1972); Cleveland-Marshall College of Law (J.D., 1977). Assistant Law Director, City of Cleveland, 1977. Attorney for Administrator, Ohio Bureau of Workers Compensation, 1977-1980. Member, Workers' Compensation, Labor-Management-Government Advisory Committee, 1987-1997. Member, Workers' Compensation Committee, Ohio Manufacturers' Association. Director of Law, City of North Royalton, 1987-1996. *Member:* Cleveland and Ohio State Bar Associations; The Florida Bar; Cleveland Association of Civil Trial Attorneys; Cuyahoga County Law Directors Association. (Certified Specialist in Workers' Compensation Law, Ohio State Bar Association). ***PRACTICE AREAS:*** Workers' Compensation Defense; Municipal Law. ***Email:*** drademaker@rmmglaw.com

DAVID J. MATTY, born Cleveland, Ohio, February 1, 1954; admitted to bar, 1979, Ohio and U.S. Tax Court. *Education:* John Carroll University (B.A., summa cum laude, 1976); Cleveland-Marshall College of Law (J.D., 1979). Law Director: City of Rocky River, 1989—; Law Director: City of Solon, Ohio, 1999—. Prosecutor and Assistant Law Director, City of Rocky River, Ohio, 1980-1988. Assistant Law Director, City of North Royalton, 1987-1988. *Member:* Cleveland and Ohio State Bar Associations; Cuyahoga County Law Directors Association (President, 1989). ***PRACTICE AREAS:*** Municipal Defense; Corporate Law; Business Acquisitions; Estate Planning; Real Estate Law; Banking Law; Probate Law; Workers' Compensation Defense. ***Email:*** dmatty@rmmglaw.com

ROBERT C. McCLELLAND, born Lakewood, Ohio, December 27, 1952; admitted to bar, 1980, Ohio and U.S. Court of Appeals, 6th Circuit. *Education:* Denison University (B.A., 1975); Cleveland-Marshall College of Law (J.D., 1980). Member of Staff, 1978-1979 and Associate, 1979-1980, Cleveland State Law Review. Assistant Law Director, City of Westlake, 1982-1992. *Member:* Cleveland, Cuyahoga County and Ohio State Bar Associations; Cuyahoga County Law Directors Association (Past President, 1993); Ohio Association of Civil Trial Attorneys; Cleveland Association of Civil Trial Attorneys; Defense Research Institute. ***PRACTICE AREAS:*** Personal Injury Defense; Products Liability Defense; Insurance Defense; Workers Compensation Defense; Employment Defense; Banking Law; Municipal Law. ***Email:*** rmcclelland@rmmglaw.com

THOMAS F. GREVE, born Cleveland, Ohio, May 6, 1956; admitted to bar, 1981, Ohio. *Education:* Ohio Wesleyan University (B.A., 1978); Cleveland-Marshall College of Law (J.D., 1981). Omicron Delta Epsilon; Delta Theta Phi. Assistant Law Director and Assistant Prosecutor, City of North Royalton, 1988-1996; Assistant Law Director and City Prosecutor, City of Beachwood, Ohio, 1996—; Assistant County Prosecutor, Cuyahoga County Prosecutor's Office, Cleveland, 1985-1988. *Member:* Cleveland and Ohio State Bar Associations; Cuyahoga County Law Directors Association (Vice President, 1996; President, 1997). ***PRACTICE AREAS:*** Workers' Compensation Defense; Municipal Law; Personal Injury Defense; Probate Law; Criminal Law; Employment Defense; Civil Rights Defense. ***Email:*** tgreve@rmmglaw.com

KIRK R. HENRIKSON, born Painesville, Ohio, April 16, 1965; admitted to bar, 1991, Ohio. *Education:* Miami University (B.A., 1987); Cleveland-Marshall College of Law (J.D., 1990). *Member:* Cleveland and Ohio State Bar Associations; Cuyahoga County Law Directors Association. (Certified Specialist in Workers' Compensation Law, Ohio State Bar Association). ***PRACTICE AREAS:*** Workers' Compensation Defense; Municipal Law; Employment Defense; Civil Rights Defense. ***Email:*** khenrikson@rmmglaw.com

ASSOCIATES

JENNIFER L. WHITT, born Warren, Ohio, October 23, 1974; admitted to bar, 2002, Ohio. *Education:* Mount Union College (B.A., 1997); University of Akron Law School (J.D., 2001). ***Email:*** jwhitt@rmmglaw.com

NICOLE M. HOLT, born Cleveland, Ohio, June 15, 1975; admitted to bar, 2002, Ohio. *Education:* Eastern Michigan University (B.S., 1997); Case Western Reserve University School of Law (J.D., 2001). ***Email:*** nholt@rmmglaw.com

(This Listing Continued)

CHARLES W. KINKOPF, born Cleveland, Ohio, July 17, 1963; admitted to bar, 1994, Ohio. *Education:* Kent State University (B.S., 1988); Ohio Northern University; University of Akron (J.D., 1993). *Member:* Ohio State Bar Association.

REFERENCE: First National Bank of Ohio.

RANKIN, HILL, PORTER & CLARK LLP

925 EUCLID AVENUE, SUITE 700
CLEVELAND, OHIO 44115-1405
Telephone: 216-566-9700
Fax: 216-566-9711
Email: info@rankinhill.com
URL: http://www.rankinhill.com

Lake County, Ohio Office: 4080 Erie Street, 44094-7836. Telephone: 216-566-9700. Fax: 216-566-9711.

Patent, Trademark, Copyright, Unfair Competition Law and Antitrust Law.

MEMBERS OF FIRM

STEPHEN A. HILL, born Ravenna, Ohio, October 1, 1947; admitted to bar, 1974, Ohio and U.S. District Court, Northern District of Ohio; 1976, U.S. Court of Appeals, Sixth Circuit; 1982, U.S. Court of Appeals for the Federal Circuit; 1986, U.S. Court of Appeals, Fourth Circuit; 1994, U.S. Supreme Court; registered to practice before U.S. Patent and Trademark Office. *Education:* Massachusetts Institute of Technology (B.S., 1969); Case Western Reserve University (J.D., 1974). Sigma Gamma Tau. Editor, Case Western Reserve Law Review, 1973-1974. *Member:* Cleveland, Ohio State and American Bar Associations; Cleveland Intellectual Property Law Association; American Intellectual Property Law Association. ***PRACTICE AREAS:*** Patent, Trademark and Copyright. ***Email:*** hill@rankinhill.com

WAYNE D. PORTER, JR., born Brownsville, Pennsylvania, July 27, 1947; admitted to bar, 1975, Virginia; 1976, District of Columbia and U.S. District Court, Northern District of Ohio; 1977, Ohio; 1985, U.S. Court of Appeals for the Federal Circuit; 1980, U.S. Supreme Court; registered to practice before U.S. Patent and Trademark Office. *Education:* West Virginia University (B.S.A.E., 1969); University of Cincinnati; Georgetown University (J.D., 1975). Editor, Georgetown Law Journal, 1974-1975. *Member:* Cleveland (Member, 1979-1986 and Chairman, 1983-1984, Grievance Committee; Member, Ad Hoc Commission to Create the Public Advertising Resource Service, 1986) and Ohio State Bar Associations; Cleveland Intellectual Property Law Association (Member, 1985— and Chairman, 1986-1987, Antitrust Committee). ***PRACTICE AREAS:*** Patent, Trademark and Copyright; Trade Secret and Unfair Competition; Licensing and Litigation. ***Email:*** porter@rankinhill.com

KENNETH A. CLARK, born Cleveland, Ohio, September 15, 1958; admitted to bar, 1986, Ohio; 1986, U.S. District Court, Northern District of Ohio, U.S. Court of Appeals for the Federal Circuit and U.S. Claims Court; registered to practice before U.S. Patent and Trademark Office. *Education:* Cleveland State University (B.Met. E., 1980); Cleveland-Marshall College of Law (J.D., 1985). *Member:* American Intellectual Property Law Association; Cleveland Intellectual Property Law Association; American Society for Metals. (Also Patent Counsel, Ferro Corporation). ***PRACTICE AREAS:*** Patent Prosecution; Licensing Agreements; Trademarks. ***Email:*** clark@rankinhill.com

DAVID E. SPAW, born Cleveland, Ohio, September 7, 1965; admitted to bar, 1991, Ohio; registered to practice before U.S. Patent and Trademark Office. *Education:* Cleveland State University (B.E.E., 1988); Cleveland Marshall College of Law (J.D., cum laude, 1991). *Member:* Cleveland and Lake County Bar Associations; American Intellectual Property Law Association; Cleveland Intellectual Property Law Association. ***PRACTICE AREAS:*** Patent; Trademark; Copyright. ***Email:*** spaw@rankinhill.com

RANDOLPH E. DIGGES, III, born Dallas, Texas, October 16, 1964; admitted to bar, 1992, Ohio; 1993, U.S. District Court, Northern District of Ohio; 1994, U.S., Court of Appeals, Sixth Circuit; 2000, U.S. Supreme Court and Court of Appeals, Federal Circuit; registered to practice before U.S. Patent and Trademark Office. *Education:* The Ohio State University (B.A., Chemistry, 1988); University of Toledo (J.D., 1992). *Member:* Ohio State and Cleveland Bar Associations; Cleveland Intellectual Property Law Association. ***PRACTICE AREAS:*** Patent Prosecution; Patent Litigation; Trademark Prosecution; Trademark Litigation; Copyright Litigation. ***Email:*** digges@rankinhill.com

ASSOCIATES

JAMES A. BALAZS, born Cleveland, Ohio, 1966; admitted to bar, 1999, Ohio; registered to practice before U.S. Patent and Trademark Office. *Education:* Cornell University (B.S.M.E., 1989); Cleveland-Marshall College of law (J.D., 1999). *Member:* Cleveland and American Bar Associations; Cleveland Intellectual Property Law Association. ***PRACTICE AREAS:*** Patent Prosecution; Trademark Prosecution. ***Email:*** balazs@rankinhill.com

CHRISTOPHER KORFF, born Pennsylvania, 1966; admitted to bar, 2003, Ohio, U.S. District Court, Northern District of Ohio; registered to practice before U.S. Patent and Trademark Office. *Education:* Rensselaer Polytechnic Institute, Kent State University, The Ohio State University (B.S., Chemistry, 1996; B.A. Russian, 1996); Case Western Reserve University School of Law (J.D., 2002). Executive Articles Editor, Journal of International Law. *Member:* Cleveland, Ohio State and American Bar Associations; American Intellectual Property Law Association; Cleveland Intellectual Property Law Association. ***LANGUAGES:*** Russian and German. ***PRACTICE AREAS:*** Patent Prosecution; Trademark Prosecution. ***Email:*** korff@rankinhill.com

RAY, ROBINSON, CARLE & DAVIES P.L.L.

1717 EAST 9TH STREET, SUITE 1650
CLEVELAND, OHIO 44114-2878
Telephone: 216-861-4533
Facsimile: 216-861-4568
Email: rayrob@rayrobcle.com
URL: http://www.rayrobcle.com

General Civil Practice in all State and Federal Courts. Trials and Appeals.

FIRM PROFILE: Ray, Robinson, Carle & Davies P.L.L., began as a specialized admiralty law firm in the 1890's. Although it continues to represent domestic and foreign vessel operators and ocean marine insurers in matters of personal injury, cargo damage, collision damages, marine pollution, and vessel-related contracts and documentation, the firm has expanded its expertise into corporate development, estate planning and probate, product liability defense, management representation in employment matters, personal injury, wrongful death, and general litigation.

LAW FIRM ALLIANCES/ASSOCIATIONS: **NETWORK OF LEADING LAW FIRMS**

MEMBERS OF FIRM

DOUGLAS R. DENNY, born Cleveland, Ohio, February 11, 1947; admitted to bar, 1974, Ohio. *Education:* United States Merchant Marine Academy (B.S., with highest honors, 1969); The Ohio State University (J.D., cum laude, 1973). Delta Theta Phi. Licensed as a Second Officer of Unlimited Tonnage by United States Coast Guard. *Member:* Cleveland and American Bar Associations; Maritime Law Association of the United States. [CAPT, U.S. Naval Reserve, Retired]. ***PRACTICE AREAS:*** Admiralty and Maritime Law; Environmental Law; Estate Planning; Probate; Corporate Law; Insurance Defense; Real Estate. ***Email:*** ddenny@rayrobcle.com

GENE B. GEORGE, born Cleveland, Ohio, February 19, 1949; admitted to bar, 1974, Ohio. *Education:* Bowling Green State University (B.A., magna cum laude, 1971); University of Michigan (J.D., 1973). Omicron Delta Kappa. *Member:* Cleveland Bar Association; Maritime Law Association of the United States (Vice Chair, Marine Insurance and General Average Committee, 1997—). ***PRACTICE AREAS:*** Admiralty and Maritime Law; Labor and Employment; Insurance Defense. ***Email:*** ggeorge@rayrobcle.com

JULIA R. BROUHARD, born Indianapolis, Indiana, November 10, 1947; admitted to bar, 1981, Texas and U.S. District Court, Southern District of Texas; 1989, Ohio, U.S. District Court, Northern District of Ohio and U.S. District Court, Eastern District of Michigan; 1992, U.S. District Court, Northern District of Illinois; 1999, U.S. District Court, Western District of Pennsylvania; 2004, U.S. District Court, Southern District of Ohio; 2005, U.S. District Court, Western District of Michigan. *Education:* Ball State University (B.S., 1969); Butler University (M.S., 1972); University of Houston (J.D., 1981). *Member:* Cleveland (Chair, Commission on Women in Law, 1995-1996; Chair Grievance Committee, 2001-2002; Trustee, 2002-2005); Ohio State and American Bar Associations; Maritime Law Association of the United States. ***PRACTICE AREAS:*** Admiralty and Maritime Law; Insurance Defense; Transportation; Litigation; Toxic Torts. ***Email:*** jbrouhard@rayrobcle.com

ROBERT T. CONIAM, born Elyria, Ohio, February 26, 1948; admitted to bar, 1986, Ohio; 1987, U.S. District Court, Northern District of Ohio, Eastern District of Michigan, Northern District of Indiana, and Western District of New York; U.S. Court of Appeals, Sixth, Seventh and Eighth Circuits. *Education:* Ohio Northern University (B.S.M.E., 1971); Cleveland State University (J.D., 1986). *Member:* Cleveland and Ohio State Bar Associations; Maritime Law Association of the United States. ***PRACTICE AREAS:*** Admiralty and Maritime Law; Insurance Defense; Products Liability; Personal Injury. ***Email:*** rconiam@rayrobcle.com

SANDRA MAURER KELLY, born Lakewood, Ohio, July 19, 1960; admitted to bar, 1986, Ohio; 1987, California; 1988, District of Columbia; 1989,U.S. Court of Appeals, Sixth Circuit; 1990, U.S. Court of Appeals, Seventh Circuit. *Education:* Ohio State University (B.S., 1983; M.S., with distinction, 1983); Capital University; Pepperdine University (J.D., 1986). Phi Alpha Delta. Adjunct Professor, Keller Graduate School of Management, 2004. Advisory Board Chair, Network Leading Law Firms. *Member:* Cleveland Bar Association; State Bar of California; District of Columbia Bar; Maritime Law Association of the United States. ***PRACTICE AREAS:*** Admiralty and Maritime Law; Products Liability; Collections; Insurance Defense; Personal Injury; Wrongful Death; Corporate Law. ***Email:*** skelly@rayrobcle.com

THOMAS MORE WYNNE, born Buffalo, New York, January 9, 1968; admitted to bar, 1994, Ohio, U.S. District Court, Northern District of Ohio, U.S. District Court, Eastern and Western Districts of Michigan, U.S. District Court, Northern District of Indiana and U.S. Court of Appeals, Sixth and Seventh Circuits. *Education:* New York State Maritime College (B.S., Marine Transportation, with honors, Third Mate, 1990); University of Toledo (J.D., magna cum laude, 1994). Order of the Coif (Toledo Chapter). University of Toledo Law Review, 1993-1994. Adjunct Instructor, University of Toledo College of Law, 2005. Licensed as a Third Officer of Unlimited Tonnage by United States Coast Guard. *Member:* Cleveland Bar Association; Maritime Law Association of the United States; Ohio Academy of Trial Lawyers. ***PRACTICE AREAS:*** Admiralty and Maritime Law; Insurance Defense; Labor and Employment; Collections; Personal Injury. ***Email:*** twynne@rayrobcle.com

OF COUNSEL

LUCIAN Y. RAY (1903-1987)

THEODORE C. ROBINSON (1916-2002)

WILLIAM D. CARLE, III, born Cleveland, Ohio, May 31, 1929; admitted to bar, 1955, Ohio. *Education:* Miami University (B.S., 1951); The Cleveland-Marshall Law School (J.D., 1955). Delta Theta Phi. Member, Board of Trustees, 1975—and Vice-Chairman, 1992—, Great Lakes Historical Society. *Member:* Cleveland, Ohio State and American Bar Associations; Maritime Law Association of the United States; International Association of Defense Counsel. ***PRACTICE AREAS:*** Admiralty and Maritime Law; Environmental Law; Probate; Insurance Defense; Transportation. ***Email:*** rayrob@rayrobcle.com

DAVID G. DAVIES, born Evanston, Illinois, April 25, 1933; admitted to bar, 1962, Michigan; 1962, Ohio. *Education:* University of Michigan (B.S.E., Naval Architecture and Marine Engineering, 1955; J.D., 1961). Order of the Coif; Tau Beta Pi. Assistant Editor, Michigan Law Review, 1960-1961. Trustee and Chair, 1983-1984, St. John and West Shore Hospital. *Member:* Cleveland (Trustee, 1976-1980), Ohio State and American Bar Associations; Maritime Law Association of the United States (Director, 1997-2000). Fellow, American College of Trial Lawyers. ***PRACTICE AREAS:*** Admiralty and Maritime Law; Products Liability; Insurance Defense; Toxic Torts; Contracts. ***Email:*** ddavies@rayrobcle.com

REPRESENTATIVE CLIENTS: Cleveland-Cliffs, Inc.; Canada Steamship Lines, Ltd.; The M.A. Hanna Co.; Assuranceforeningen Gard; World Shipping, Inc.; Japan Ship Owners' Mutual P & I Assn.; North of England P & I Assn., Ltd.; Standard Steamship Owners' P & I Assn., Ltd.; United Kingdom Mutual Steamship Assn., Ltd.; West of England Ship Owners' P & I Assn., Ltd.; The London Steam-Ship Owners' Mutual Insurance Assn., Ltd.; The Britannia Steam Ship Insurance Assn., Ltd.; The Steamship Mutual Underwriting Assn., Ltd.; The Travelers Cos.; Ispat Inland, Inc.; BP Amoco Corp.; Inland Lakes Management Inc.; ContainerPort Group, Inc.; Canadian Shipowners Assn.; ULS Group; American Steamship Owners P & I Assn.; Great Lakes Protective Association; Viking Corporation; Zimmer, Inc.; Grand River Navigation Company; Lower Lakes Transportation Co.; Key Bank; American Reliable Ins. Co.; HDM Corp.; Rush Trucking; E Trade Consumer Finance Corp.; Lower Lakes Towing Co.; Mittal Steel USA ISG Inc.

RENNER, KENNER, GREIVE, BOBAK, TAYLOR & WEBER

A LEGAL PROFESSIONAL ASSOCIATION

CLEVELAND, OHIO

(See Akron)

U.S. and Foreign Patent, Trademark and Copyright Law and Licensing. Antitrust and Unfair Competition Law. Litigation.

RENNER, OTTO, BOISSELLE & SKLAR, LLP

NINETEENTH FLOOR
1621 EUCLID AVENUE
CLEVELAND, OHIO 44115-2183
Telephone: 216-621-1113
Fax: 216-621-6165
Email: mailroom@rennerotto.com
URL: http://www.rennerotto.com

Patent, Trademark, Copyright, Unfair Competition and Related Antitrust Law.

JOHN F. OBERLIN (1880-1971)

EDWIN E. DONNELLY, JR. (1925-1976)

MEMBERS OF FIRM

DONALD L. OTTO, born Durant, Iowa, June 25, 1936; admitted to bar, 1964, Ohio; 1965, U.S. District Court, Northern District of Ohio and U.S. Court of Appeals, 6th Circuit; 1969, District of Columbia; 1975, U.S. Court of Appeals, District of Columbia Circuit; 1982, U.S. Court of Appeals for the Federal Circuit; registered to practice before U.S. Patent and Trademark Office. *Education:* Iowa State University (B.S.M.E., 1959); George Washington University (LL.B., 1963). Phi Eta Sigma; Pi Tau Sigma. *Member:* American Bar Association; Cleveland Intellectual Property Law Association. ***PRACTICE AREAS:*** Patent; Trademark; Copyright and Intellectual Property.

ARMAND P. BOISSELLE, born Haverhill, Massachusetts, December 16, 1931; admitted to bar, 1965, Ohio; 1967, South Carolina and U.S. District Court, South Carolina; 1971, U.S. Court of Appeals, District of Columbia Circuit and U.S. District Court, Northern District of Ohio; 1976, U.S. Court of Appeals, 7th Circuit; 1982, U.S. Court of Appeals for the Federal Circuit; registered to practice before U.S. Patent and Trademark Office. *Education:* Bridgewater State College (B.S. in Ed., 1953); Boston College (M.S. in Chem., 1957); University of Notre Dame (Ph.D. in Chem., 1961); Western Reserve University (J.D., 1965). Delta Theta Phi. Councilman, Village of Timberlake, Ohio, 1963-1965. *Member:* American Chemical Society; Cleveland Intellectual Property Law Association (Director, 1982-1983; Vice President, 1984-1985; President, 1990-1991); American Intellectual Property Law Association. ***PRACTICE AREAS:*** Patent; Trademark; Copyright and Intellectual Property.

WARREN A. SKLAR, born Cleveland, Ohio, November 6, 1944; admitted to bar, 1971, Virginia; 1973, Ohio and U.S. District Court, Northern District of Ohio; 1982, U.S. Court of Appeals for the Federal Circuit; registered to practice before U.S. Patent and Trademark Office. *Education:* Case Institute of Technology (B.S.E.E., 1966); George Washington University (J.D., 1970). *Member:* Virginia and American Bar Associations; Cleveland Intellectual Property Law Association; American Intellectual Property Law Association. ***PRACTICE AREAS:*** Patent; Trademark; Copyright and Intellectual Property.

NEIL A. DUCHEZ, born Cleveland, Ohio, June 2, 1946; admitted to bar, 1972, Ohio; 1973, U.S. District Court, Northern District of Ohio and U.S. Court of Appeals, 6th Circuit; 1977, U.S. Supreme Court; 1982, U.S. Court of Appeals for the Federal Circuit; registered to practice before U.S. Patent and Trademark Office. *Education:* Cleveland State University (B.Ch.E., 1969; J.D., 1972). Phi Alpha Delta. *Member:* American Bar Association; American Intellectual Property Law Association; Cleveland Intellectual Property Law Association (Treasurer, 1981-1983; Chairman, Chemical Practice Committee, 1985-1986 and 1988-1989; President 1999-2000; Vice President 1996-1997; Chairman, Ethics and Unauthorized Practice Committee 1979-1980). ***PRACTICE AREAS:*** Patent; Trademark; Copyright and Intellectual Property.

(This Listing Continued)

RENNER, OTTO, BOISSELLE & SKLAR, LLP, Cleveland—Continued

DON W. BULSON, born Woonsocket, Rhode Island, June 4, 1951; admitted to bar, 1976, Ohio; 1977, U.S. District Court, Northern District of Ohio; 1982, U.S. Court of Appeals for the Federal Circuit; registered to practice before U.S. Patent and Trademark Office. *Education:* Rensselaer Polytechnic Institute; Ohio University (B.S.M.E., summa cum laude, 1972; M.S.M.E., 1975); The Ohio State University (J.D., cum laude, 1976). Phi Delta Phi. *Member:* American Bar Association; Cleveland Intellectual Property Law Association (President 2001-2002; Treasurer 1991-1993); American Intellectual Property Law Association. ***PRACTICE AREAS:*** Patent; Trademark; Copyright and Intellectual Property.

GORDON D. KINDER, born Cleveland, Ohio, April 25, 1948; admitted to bar, 1977, Ohio; 1980, U.S. District Court, Northern District of Ohio; 1981, U.S. Court of Appeals, Sixth Circuit; 1982, U.S. Court of Appeals for the Federal Circuit; registered to practice before U.S. Patent and Trademark Office. *Education:* Case Western Reserve University (B.S.M.E., with honors, 1974; J.D., 1977). *Member:* Greater Cleveland Bar Association (Member, Ethics Committee, 1980—); Cleveland Intellectual Property Law Association. ***PRACTICE AREAS:*** Patent; Trademark; Copyright and Intellectual Property.

JAY R. CAMPBELL, born Cincinnati, Ohio, November 9, 1962; admitted to bar, 1989, Ohio, U.S. Claims Court, U.S. Court of Appeals for the Federal Circuit, U.S. District Court, Northern District of Ohio; registered to practice before U.S. Patent and Trademark Office. *Education:* Ohio State University (B.S.M.E., 1985); University of Akron (J.D., 1989). Member, University of Akron Law Review, 1988-1989. *Member:* American Bar Association; Cleveland Intellectual Property Law Association. ***PRACTICE AREAS:*** Patent; Trademark; Copyright and Intellectual Property.

MARK D. SARALINO, born Akron, Ohio, March 5, 1961; admitted to bar, 1989, Virginia; 1990, Ohio, U.S. District Court, Northern District of Ohio, U.S. Court of Appeals, Federal Circuit; registered to practice before U.S. Patent and Trademark Office. *Education:* University of Akron (B.S.E.E., 1985; J.D., magna cum laude, 1989). *Member:* Virginia State Bar; American Bar Association; Cleveland Intellectual Property Law Association. ***PRACTICE AREAS:*** Patent; Trademark; Copyright and Intellectual Property.

CYNTHIA S. MURPHY, born St. Louis, Missouri, August 8, 1960; admitted to bar, 1988, Ohio; registered to practice before U.S. Patent and Trademark Office. *Education:* Georgia Institute of Technology (B.M.E., 1982); Cleveland Marshall College of Law (J.D., 1988). Recipient: American Jurisprudence and Charles Auerbach Memorial Award for Outstanding Student in the Law of Evidence; Hugo Black Award; Faculty Advisor's Moot Court Award; Winning Team in Annual Moot Court Competition. Licensed Professional Engineer, Ohio, 1987. *Member:* Cleveland and Ohio State Bar Associations; American Society of Mechanical Engineers; Cleveland Intellectual Property Law Association (Secretary 2002-2004; Chairman, International Committee 2001—). ***PRACTICE AREAS:*** Intellectual Property; Patent; Trademark and Copyright.

CHRISTOPHER B. JACOBS, born Columbus, Ohio, January 18, 1969; admitted to bar, 1995, Ohio; 1996, U.S. District Court, Northern District of Ohio; 1997, U.S. Court of Appeals for the Federal Circuit; registered to practice before U.S. Patent and Trademark Office. *Education:* The Ohio State University (B.S.M.E., 1992; J.D., 1995). *Member:* American Intellectual Property Law Association; Cleveland Intellectual Property Association;. ***PRACTICE AREAS:*** Patents; Trademarks; Copyrights; Intellectual Property. ***Email:*** cjacobs@rennerotto.com

JONATHAN A. PLATT, born Pittsburgh, Pennsylvania, January 10, 1961; admitted to bar, 1997, Ohio; 1998, U.S. District Court, Northern District of Ohio; registered to practice before U.S. Patent and Trademark Office. *Education:* Case Western University (B.S., B.S.M.E., with high honors, 1988; Ph.D., 1991; J.D., summa cum laude, 1997). *Member:* Greater Cleveland Bar Association; American Intellectual Property Law Association; Cleveland Intellectual Property Law Association. ***PRACTICE AREAS:*** Patents; Trademarks; Copyrights; Intellectual Property.

HEIDI A. BOEHLEFELD, born Pittsburgh, Pennsylvania, June 22, 1961; admitted to bar, 1990, Ohio; registered to practice before the U.S. Patent and Trademark Office. *Education:* Case Western Reserve University (B.S., 1983; M.B.A., 1990; J.D., 1990). *Member:* Cleveland Bar Association; Cleveland Intellectual Property Law Association (Treasurer, 1997-1999); American Intellectual Property Law Association. (Corporate Counsel). ***PRACTICE AREAS:*** Patents; Trademarks; Copyrights; Intellectual Property.

THOMAS W. ADAMS, born Tulsa, Oklahoma, April 21, 1949; admitted to bar, 1992, Ohio; 1993, U.S. District Court, Northern District of Ohio and U.S Court of Appeals, Federal Circuit; 1996, Texas and U.S. District Court, Southern District of Texas; registered to practice before U.S. Patent and Trademark Office. *Education:* Austin College (B.A., 1971); Texas Christian University (M.S., 1976); Cleveland State University (J.D., magna cum laude, 1992). *Member:* Cleveland, Houston and American Bar Associations; Cleveland Intellectual Property Law Association; Houston Intellectual Property Law Association; American Chemical Society. ***PRACTICE AREAS:*** Patents; Trademarks; Copyrights; Intellectual Property. ***Email:*** tadams@rennerotto.com

M. DAVID GALIN, born Cambridge, Massachusetts, August 16, 1968; admitted to bar, 1996, Ohio; 1997, U.S. District Court, Northern District of Ohio, U.S. Court of Appeals, Federal Circuit; registered to practice before U.S. Patent and Trademark Office. *Education:* Georgia Institute of Technology (B.E.E., 1990); Case Western Reserve University (J.D., cum laude, 1996). Phi Delta Phi. *Member:* American Bar Association; Cleveland Intellectual Property Law Association; American Intellectual Property Law Association. ***PRACTICE AREAS:*** Patent; Trademark; Copyright; Intellectual Property. ***Email:*** dgalin@rennerotto.com

TODD R. TUCKER, born Urbana, Illinois, November 12, 1969; admitted to bar, 1995, Ohio, U.S. District Court, Northern District of Ohio and U.S. Court of Appeals, Federal and Sixth Circuits; registered to practice before U.S. Patent and Trademark Office. *Education:* The University of Iowa (B.S.E., 1992); The University of Dayton School of Law (J.D., 1995). Phi Delta Phi. Best Orator, Walter Rice Moot Court Competition. Managing Editor, University of Dayton Law Review, 1994-1995. *Member:* Cleveland Intellectual Property Law Association. ***PRACTICE AREAS:*** Patents; Trademarks; Copyrights; Intellectual Property. ***Email:*** ttucker@rennerotto.com

(This Listing Continued)

ASSOCIATES

JOHN J. DEL COL, born Columbus, Ohio, September 15, 1963; admitted to bar, 1998, Ohio; 1999, U.S. District Court, Northern District of Ohio, U.S. Court of Appeals, Federal Circuit; registered to practice before U.S. Patent and Trademark Office. *Education:* Ohio State University (B.S.M.E., 1985); University of Toledo (M.B.A., 1991; J.D., 1997). Member, Society of Automotive Engineers, 1985-1998. *Member:* Ohio State Bar Association; Cleveland Intellectual Property Law Association. ***PRACTICE AREAS:*** Intellectual Property; Patent; Trademark; Copyright. ***Email:*** jdelcol@rennerotto.com

JASON A. WORGULL, born Cleveland, Ohio, July 12,1973; admitted to bar, 1999, Ohio; registered to practice before U.S. Patent and Trademark Office. *Education:* John Carroll University (B.S., in Physics, 1995; M.S., in Physics, 1996); University of Dayton (J.D., 1999). *Member:* Cleveland and Ohio State Bar Associations; Cleveland Intellectual Property Law Association; American Intellectual Property Law Association. ***PRACTICE AREAS:*** Patents; Trademarks; Copyrights; Intellectual Property. ***Email:*** jworgull@rennerotto.com

MARK C. JOHNSON, born Cleveland, Ohio, February 3, 1974; admitted to bar, 2000, Ohio; 2001, U.S. District Court, Northern District of Ohio; registered to practice before U.S. Patent and Trademark Office. *Education:* Marquette University (B.S.E., 1996); Case Western Reserve University (J.D., 2000). ***PRACTICE AREAS:*** Patents; Trademarks; Copyrights; Intellectual Property. ***Email:*** mjohnson@rennerotto.com

KENNETH W. FAFRAK, JR., born Nuremburg, Germany, November 13, 1964; admitted to bar, 2003, Ohio; registered to practice before U.S. Patent and Trademark Office. *Education:* Cleveland State university (B.E.E., cum laude, 1988); Cleveland-Marshall College of Law (J.D., magna cum laude, 2003). Tau Beta Pi. *Member:* Cleveland Intellectual Property Law Association. ***PRACTICE AREAS:*** Patents; Trademarks; Copyrights; Intellectual Property. ***Email:*** kfafrak@rennerotto.com

DANIEL R. LING, born Walnut Creek, California, February 20, 1978; admitted to bar, 2003, Ohio; registered to practice before U.S. Patent and Trademark Office. *Education:* University of Michigan (B.S.C.E., 2000); Case Western Reserve University (J.D., 2003). *Member:* Cleveland Intellectual Property Law Association. ***PRACTICE AREAS:*** Patents; Trademarks; Copyrights; Intellectual Property. ***Email:*** dling@renerotto.com

TIMOTHY E. MANNING, born Cleveland, Ohio, June 12, 1967; admitted to bar, 1998, Ohio; 1999, U.S. District Court, Northern District of Ohio; registered to practice before U.S. Patent and Trademark Office. *Education:* John Carroll University (B.S., 1990); Cleveland- Marshall College of Law (J.D., cum laude, 1998). *Member:* American Intellectual Property Law Association; Cleveland Intellectual Property Law Association. ***PRACTICE AREAS:*** Patents; Trademarks; Copyrights; Intellectual Property. ***Email:*** tmanning@rennerotto.com

MARISA J. ZINK, born Dover, Ohio, March 4, 1975; admitted to bar, 2001, Ohio, U.S. District Court, Northern District of Ohio; 2002, U.S. Court of Appeals, Federal Circuit; registered to practice before U.S. Patent and Trademark Office. *Education:* Case Western Reserve University (B.A., Chemistry, 1997); University of Akron (J.D., 2001). *Member:* Cleveland and Ohio State Bar Associations; American Intellectual Property Law Association; Cleveland Intellectual Property Association. ***PRACTICE AREAS:*** Patents; Trademarks; Copyrights; Intellectual Property. ***Email:*** mzink@rennerotto.com

THOMAS G. FISTEK, born Cleveland, Ohio, November 5, 1976; admitted to bar, 2004, Ohio; registered to practice before U.S. Patent and Trademark Office. *Education:* University of Maryland (B.S.M.E., 2000); Cleveland-Marshall College of Law (J.D., magna cum laude, 2004). Phi Tau Sigma. Member, Cleveland-Marshall Law Review, 2003-2004. *Member:* Cleveland Intellectual Property Law Association. ***PRACTICE AREAS:*** Patents; Trademarks; Copyrights; Intellectual Property. ***Email:*** tfistek@rennerotto.com

MICHELE M. TYRPAK, born Cleveland, Ohio, August 30, 1965; admitted to bar, 1996, Ohio; registered to practice before U.S. Patent and Trademark Office. *Education:* Cleveland State University (B.S., 1987); Cleveland-Marshall College of Law (J.D., 1994). *Member:* American Bar Association; Cleveland Intellectual Property Association; American Intellectual Property Association. ***PRACTICE AREAS:*** Patents; Trademarks; Copyrights; Intellectual Property. ***Email:*** mtyrpak@rennerotto.com

OF COUNSEL

JOHN W. RENNER, born Cleveland, Ohio, September 12, 1929; admitted to bar, 1954, Ohio; 1959, U.S. District Court, Northern District of Ohio; 1965, U.S. Court of Appeals, 6th Circuit; 1982, U.S. Court of Appeals for the Federal Circuit; registered to practice before U.S. Patent and Trademark Office. *Education:* Bethany College (B.S., 1950); Western Reserve University (LL.B., 1953). Phi Delta Phi. Trustee: Hillcrest Hospital, Cleveland, Ohio, 1957—; Bethany College, Bethany, West Virginia, 1980—. *Member:* Greater Cleveland and American Bar Associations; Cleveland Intellectual Property Law Association. ***PRACTICE AREAS:*** Patent; Trademark; Copyright and Intellectual Property.

RIETH & ANTONELLI CO.

BP OFFICE TOWER
200 PUBLIC SQUARE, SUITE 2940
CLEVELAND, OHIO 44114
Telephone: 216-861-2222
Fax: 216-861-2220
Email: dantonelli@riethantonelli.com
URL: http://www.riethantonellilaw.com

Family Law, Divorce, Collaborative Divorce, Child Custody, child Support, Visitation Rights, Premarital Agreements, Collaborative Law, Family Relations Law.

MEMBERS OF FIRM

RICHARD C. RIETH, admitted to bar, 1979, Ohio. *Education:* Cleveland State University (B.A., 1975); Cleveland-Marshall College of Law (J.D., 1979). ***Email:*** rrieth@riethantonelli.com

(This Listing Continued)

DOMINIC M. ANTONELLI, born Cleveland, Ohio, May 19, 1962; admitted to bar, 1987, Ohio. *Education:* Kenyon College (B.A., 1984); Case Western Reserve University (J.D., 1987). ***PRACTICE AREAS:*** Divorce (85%, 80); Matrimonial Law. ***Email:*** dantonelli@riethantonelli.com

CRAIG A. HAIRSTON, born Ironton, Ohio, August 12, 1973; admitted to bar, 1999, Ohio. *Education:* Ohio University (B.S., cum laude, 1966); Capital University Law School (J.D., 1999). Former Law Clerk: Lawrence County Court of Common Pleas, Lawrence County, Ohio; Ohio Rehabilitation Services Commission. *Member:* Columbus, Ohio State and American Bar Associations. ***PRACTICE AREAS:*** Litigation. ***Email:*** chairston@riethantonelli.com

MARIELLEN M. ANTONELLI, admitted to bar, 2002, Ohio. *Education:* Ursuline College (B.A., 1992); Capital University Law School (J.D., 1999). ***Email:*** mantonelli@riethantonelli.com

RIPPNER, SCHWARTZ & CARLIN

CLEVELAND, OHIO

(See Weston Hurd L.L.P.)

GREGORY SCOTT ROBEY

Established in 1991

14402 GRANGER ROAD
CLEVELAND, OHIO 44137
Telephone: 216-581-8200
Fax: 216-581-2822
URL: http://www.gregoryscottrobey.com
Email: robeylaw@aol.com
URL: http://www.robey-law.com

Federal Criminal Cases, Drug Cases, DUI/DWI, Sex Offenses, Homicide, Weapons, White Collar Crime, Arson, Traffic Offenses, Appeals, Juvenile Cases, Defense of Police Officers.

FIRM PROFILE: Gregory S. Robey is an experienced and aggressive trial lawyer who handles defense of criminal matters in Federal, State, Juvenile and Appellate Courts.

GREGORY SCOTT ROBEY, born Cleveland, Ohio, October 2, 1965; admitted to bar, 1991, Ohio; 1992, U.S. District Court, Northern District of Ohio; 1993, U.S. Court of Appeals, Sixth Circuit; 2001, U.S. Supreme Court. *Education:* Wittenberg University (B.A., 1988); University of Richmond (J.D., 1991). Gerry Spence Trial Lawyers College Seminar, Hunt, Texas, 2000. Western Trial Advocacy Institute, University of Wyoming, 2002. Delegate, Ohio Eighth District Judicial Conference. *Member:* Cleveland and Cuyahoga County (Guest Lecturer) Bar Associations; National Association of Criminal Defense Lawyers; Ohio Association of Criminal Defense Lawyers; Cuyahoga County Criminal Defense Lawyers Association; Ohio Academy of Trial Lawyers; Federal Criminal Justice Act Panel Member. (Also Member, Robey & Robey). ***LANGUAGES:*** Spanish. ***REPORTED CASES:*** United States of America v. St. Martin, Sixth Circuit Court of Appeals, Case No. 01-4091. ***PRACTICE AREAS:*** Federal Criminal Law; Drug Crimes; Police Officers Defense; Driving While Intoxicated; Sex Crimes; Homicide; Weapons; White Collar Crime; Arson; Traffic Violations; Appellate Practice; Juvenile Law.

ASSOCIATE

MARGARET A. ROBEY, born Cleveland, Ohio, June 19, 1967; admitted to bar, 1994, Ohio; 1996, U.S. District Court, Northern District of Ohio. *Education:* Case Western Reserve University (B.A., 1991; J.D., 1994). Phi Beta Kappa. *Member:* Cuyahoga County and Ohio State Bar Associations. ***PRACTICE AREAS:*** Criminal Law; Criminal Appeals; Habeas Corpus; Post-Conviction Remedies.

RODGERS AND CO., L.P.A.

1600 GUILDHALL, LANDMARK OFFICE TOWERS
45 PROSPECT AVENUE, WEST
CLEVELAND, OHIO 44115
Telephone: 216-861-6191
Fax: 216-861-4699
Email: attys@rodgersandcolpa.com
URL: http://www.lawyers.com/rodgersandco

General Civil Trial and Appellate Practice in all Courts. Complex Litigation, Professional Liability Defense, Commercial, Construction, Personal Injury, Employment, General Insurance Defense, Toxic Tort, ERISA and Insurance Coverage Litigation, Life and Health Insurance, Environmental Law, Real Estate Law, Alternative Dispute Resolution, Products Liability.

FIRM PROFILE: Rodgers and Co., L.P.A. specializes in a variety of litigation areas. The experience gained by the firm's attorneys working within both small and large law firm structures offers its clients a unique blend of approaches to litigation matters.

The firm's primary goal is client satisfaction in all respects. The high quality of legal services rendered is achieved with cost effective and highly responsive results. Flexibility is offered to fit the legal services to the specific requirements of the firm's clients.

The attorneys in the firm have a combined level of experience with proven results in all practice areas including broad experience in jury trials in both state and federal courts, appellate practice, arbitrations and ADR matters.

WALTER A. RODGERS, born New York, N.Y., 1944; admitted to bar, 1970, Ohio, Florida and U.S. District Court, Northern District of Ohio; 1982, U.S. Supreme Court; 1985, U.S. Court of Appeals, Sixth Circuit. *Education:* Clarion State University (B.S., 1966); Cleveland State University (J.D., 1970). Member, Editorial Board, Cleveland State University Law Review, 1969-1970. Member, Judge Anthony J. Celebrezze Inn of Court.

(This Listing Continued)

Chairman, City of Bay Village Planning Commission, 1993—. *Member:* Cleveland, Cuyahoga County, Ohio State and American (Member, Tort and Insurance Law and Litigation Sections) Bar Associations. Defense Research Institute; Ohio Association of Civil Trial Attorneys: Cleveland Association of Civil Trial Attorneys; Association of Ski Defense Attorneys. ***REPORTED CASES:*** Haag v. Cuyahoga County, 619 F. Supp. 262 (1985); Kolenich v. Limbacher Paint and Color Works, Inc., 62 Ohio St. 3d 1203, 579 N.E. 2d 711, Ohio Lexis 3096 (1991); Zamlen v. City of Cleveland, 686 F. Supp. 631 (1988); Ervinwood Marine, Inc. v. Fireman's Fund Ins. Co., 750 F. Supp. 278 (1990); Bettio v. Village of Northfield, 775 F. Supp. 1545 (1991); Revco D.S., Inc. v. Government Employees Ins. Co., 984 F. 2d 154; U.S. App., Lexis 15960 (1992); Shaheen v. Boston Mills Ski Resort, Inc., 85 Ohio App. 3d 285; 619 N.E.2d. 1037 (1993); Broome v. Ohio Ski Slopes, Inc., 108 Ohio App.3d 86, 670 N.E.2nd 262 (1995); Stone v. Alpine Valley Ski Area (1999) 135 Ohio App.3d 540, 734 N.E.2d 888; Lu-An-Do, Inc. v. Kloots (1999) 131 Ohio App.3d 71, 721 N.E.2d 507; Presrite Corp. v. Commercial Union Ins. Co. (1996) 113 Ohio App.3d 38, 680 N.E.2d 216; Heritage Mutual Ins. Co. v. Stevens (1996) 92 Ohio Misc.2d 9, 699 N.E.2d 1005; MBE Collection, Inc. v. Westfield Companies, Inc., Slip Copy, Ohio App 8. Dist. April 8, 2002; Archer v. ACE, USA (2003) 152 Ohio App. 3d 455, 788 N.E.2d 662. ***PRACTICE AREAS:*** Products Liability; Litigation; Liability Defense; Commercial Construction; Personal Injury; Employment; Insurance Defense; Toxic Tort; Real Estate; ADR. ***Email:*** wrodgers@rodgers-lpa.com

JEFFREY M. ELZEER, born Lorain, Ohio, February 2, 1966; admitted to bar, 1991, Ohio. *Education:* Baldwin-Wallace College (B.A., cum laude, 1988); Case Western Reserve University (J.D., 1991). *Member:* Cleveland and Ohio State Bar Associations; Defense Research Institute; Ohio Association of Civil Trial Attorneys; Cleveland Association of Civil Trial Attorneys; Association of Ski Defense Attorneys. ***PRACTICE AREAS:*** Litigation; Liability Defense; Commercial; Construction; Personal Injury; Insurance Defense; Toxic Tort; Products Liability. ***Email:*** jelzeer@rodgers-lpa.com

KATHRYN A. KERKA, born Cleveland, Ohio, January 24, 1961; admitted to bar, 1985, Ohio; 1987, U.S. District Court, Northern District of Ohio; 1988, U.S. Court of Appeals, Sixth Circuit. *Education:* Cleveland State University (B.A., 1982); Cleveland-Marshall College of Law (J.D., 1985). Staff Member, 1983-1984 and Issue Editor, 1984-1985, Cleveland State Law Review. Law Clerk to the Honorable Thomas J. Parrino, Judge, Court of Appeals of Ohio, Eighth Appellate District, 1985-1986. *Member:* Ohio State Bar Association.

REPRESENTATIVE CLIENTS: Acordia Resort Services; Alpine Valley Ski Resort; American Alternative Insurance Company; American ReInsurance Corporation; Blue Ridge Insurance Co.; Boston Mills Ski Resort, Inc.; Brandywine Ski Resort, Inc.; BTR, Inc.; Clear Fork Ski Resort, Inc.; Coregis Insurance Company; Cotton States Insurance Company; The Eliza Jennings Group; Employers Reinsurance Corporation; Equimeter, Inc.; Fireman's Fund Insurance Companies; First Specialty Insurance Corporation; GAB Robins North America, Inc.; Government Employees Insurance Company; GNB, Inc.; International Administrators, Inc.; K&K Insurance Group; Mad River Valley Hi, Ltd.; Ohio Ski Slopes, Inc.; Pennsylvania Lumbermens Mutual Insurance Company; Pinnacle Insurance Company; Randall America/Seaton Insurance Company; Relmax International, Inc.; Republic Insurance Group; Rexnord Corporation; Richard Oliver Risk Managers, Inc.; United National Insurance Company; URC Risk Managers; Utica Mutual Insurance Company; Ward N.A., Inc.; Westport Insurance Corporation; Willis Corroon Corporation of New Hampshire; Winterthur Swiss Insurance Group.

ROETZEL & ANDRESS

A LEGAL PROFESSIONAL ASSOCIATION

Established in 1876

ONE CLEVELAND CENTER
1375 EAST NINTH STREET, 9TH FLOOR
CLEVELAND, OHIO 44114
Telephone: 216-623-0150
Telecopier: 216-623-0134
Email: inquiries@ralaw.com
URL: http://www.ralaw.com

Akron, Ohio Office: 222 South Main Street. Telephone: 330-376-2700. Telecopier: 330-376-4577.

Columbus, Ohio Office: National City Center, 155 E. Broad Street, 12th Floor. Telephone: 614-463-9770. Telecopier: 614-463-9792.

Naples, Florida Office: 850 Park Shore Drive, Trianon Centre. Telephones: 239-649-6200; 800-535-7239. Telecopier: 239-261-3659.

Cincinnati, Ohio Office: 250 East Fifth Street, 310 Chiquita Center. Telephone: 513-361-0200. Telecopier: 513-361-0335.

Fort Myers, Florida Office: 2320 First Street, Suite 1000. Telephone: 239-337-3850. Telecopier: 239-337-0970.

Toledo, Ohio Office: One SeaGate, 9th Floor. Telephone: 419-242-7985. Facsimile: 419-242-0316.

Tallahassee, Florida Office: 225 South Adams Street, Suite 250, P.O. Box 10369. Telephone: 850-222-7718. Telecopier: 850-222-8222.

Washington, D.C. Office: 1025 Connecticut Avenue, NW, Suite 220. Telephone: 202-625-0600. Telecopier: 202-338-6340.

General Corporate and Business Law, Banking and Finance, Mergers, Acquisitions and Divestitures, Securities Law, Real Estate Law, Real Estate Development/Syndication/Condominium Law, Tax Law, Intellectual Property Law, Computer Law, Hospital and Health Care Law, Public Law and Finance, Governmental Relations, School Law, Commercial/Bankruptcy Law, Employment Law, Pension, Employee Benefits, Workers' Compensation, OSHA, Business and Commercial Litigation, Complex and Multidistrict Litigation, Antitrust Law, RICO, Federal Court Practice, Product Liability, Environmental Law/Toxic Torts, Insurance Law, Information Technology Law, Medical Malpractice Defense, Asbestos Litigation, Construction Law, 1st Amendment/Media Law, White Collar Criminal Defense, Railroad and FELA, Trucking and Transportation Law, Probate and Estate Planning, Risk Management, Utility Law, International Law, Trial and Appellate Practice.

(This Listing Continued)

ROETZEL & ANDRESS, A LEGAL PROFESSIONAL ASSOCIATION, Cleveland—Continued

FIRM PROFILE: Founded in 1876, Roetzel & Andress is one of the largest and fastest growing full-service, corporate law firms with nine offices throughout Ohio, Florida, and Washington, D.C. Roetzel & Andress represents a wide range of clients from individuals and closely-held businesses to multi-national corporations, financial institutions, and government entities. Our lawyers serve as general counsel to many clients, and many of those relationships have existed for much of our history. Our lawyers provide a broad range of legal services to clients on a local, national, and international basis.

PARTNERS

LEWIS W. ADKINS, JR., born Roosevelt, New York, March 8, 1964; admitted to bar, 1993, Ohio. *Education:* City College of the City University of New York (B.S., cum laude, 1988); University of Akron Law School (J.D., 1993). *Member:* Cleveland, Cuyahoga County and Ohio State Bar Associations. (Resident). ***PRACTICE AREAS:*** Labor and Employment Law; Public and School Law. ***Email:*** ladkins@ralaw.com

ROBERT E. BLACKHAM, born Lorain, Ohio, January 14, 1959; admitted to bar, 1987, Ohio and U.S. District Court, Northern District of Ohio; 2001, Pennsylvania and U.S. Supreme Court; 2004, U.S District Court, Southern District of Ohio. *Education:* Ohio State University (B.A., 1984); Cleveland-Marshall College of Law (J.D., 1987). Phi Alpha Delta. Member, Moot Court Board. Member: Cleveland Advanced Manufacturing Program (CAMP); Disability Management Employers Coalition; Ohio Self-Insurers Association. Board Member: Cuyahoga County Public Library Foundation; Cleveland Marshall College of Law Visiting Committee. *Member:* Akron, Greater Cleveland, Cuyahoga County, Ohio State and Federal Bar Associations; Defense Research Institute. (Managing Partner; Also at Akron Office) (Certified Specialist in Workers' Compensation Law, Ohio State Bar Association) (Certified Civil Trial Advocate by the National Board of Trial Advocacy). ***LANGUAGES:*** Spanish. ***PRACTICE AREAS:*** Labor and Employment; Workers; OSHA; Emergency Medical Services Law; Environmental Health and Safety; General Liability Defense; Litigation. ***Email:*** rblackham@ralaw.com

ANNA MOORE CARULAS, born Flint, Michigan, January 12, 1961; admitted to bar, 1986, Ohio; U.S. District Court, Northern District of Ohio. *Education:* Alma College (B.A., cum laude, 1983), Phi Beta Kappa; University of Notre Dame (J.D., 1986). *Member:* Cleveland, Cuyahoga County and Ohio State Bar Associations. (Resident) (Board Certified Civil Trial Advocate by the National Board of Trial Advocacy). ***PRACTICE AREAS:*** Medical Malpractice Defense. ***Email:*** acarulas@ralaw.com

ROBERT B. CASARONA, born Canton, Ohio, November 13, 1960; admitted to bar, 1986, Ohio; 1987, U.S. District Court, Northern and Southern Districts of Ohio; U.S. Court of Appeals, 6th and 8th Circuits. *Education:* Denison University; Arizona State University (B.S., cum laude, 1983); University of Cincinnati (J.D., 1986). Author: "Why Should We Care About Electronic Evidence," Cleveland Bar Journal; "Civil and Criminal Enforcement of Environmental Law in Ohio," Banks Baldwin Law Publishing (1992); "Private Enforcement Actions," Banks Baldwin Law Publishing (1993); "Environmental Criminal Liability," Banks Baldwin Law Publishing (Supplement, 1993); "Special Issues of Civil Liability Under CERCLA," Banks Baldwin Law Publishing (Supplement, 1993); "Environmental Law Compliance: A Business Approach," Cleveland Professional Services Guide, Cleveland Growth Association. Member: The Geauga County Bluecoats; The Justinian Forum; Executive Committee, Geauga County Republican Party. Trustee, The Gathering Place. *Member:* Cleveland, Cuyahoga County, Federal and American (Member, Sections on: Natural Resources; Energy and Environmental Law; Litigation; Intellectual Property Law) Bar Associations; Ohio State Bar Association (Member, Environmental Law Committee; Litigation Section); Northern Ohio Italian American Association. ***PRACTICE AREAS:*** Business Litigation; Environmental; Construction Law. ***Email:*** rcasarona@ralaw.com

CARL J. DYCZEK, born November 22, 1954; admitted to bar, 1980, Ohio; 1980, U.S. District Court, Northern District of Ohio and 1980, U.S. Tax Court. *Education:* State University of New York at Buffalo (B.A.,1976); Cleveland State University (J.D., 1980); Case Western Reserve University (M.B.A., 1986). Member: American Land Title Association; Association for Corporate Growth; Estate Planning Council of Greater Cleveland; Greater Cleveland Mortgage Banker's Association; Growth Capital Corporation; Lawyer's Guild of the Catholic Diocese of Cleveland; Turnaround Management Association; Cleveland World Trade Center, Shoes and Clothes for Kids. *Member:* Ohio State Bar Association; Greater Cleveland Bar Association. ***LANGUAGES:*** German. ***PRACTICE AREAS:*** Financial Transactions; Real Estate; Tax; Creditors Rights; Estate Planning; Banking. ***Email:*** cdyczek@ralaw.com

DAVID H. GUNNING II, born Cleveland, Ohio, June 8, 1967; admitted to bar, 1994, Ohio and U.S. District Court, Northern District of Ohio. *Education:* Lake Forest College (B.A., 1989); Cleveland Marshall School of Law (J.D., 1994). *Member:* Cleveland, Ohio State and American Bar Associations; American Institute of Constructers; Associated Builders and Contractors; Home Builders Association of Greater Cleveland; Association of General Contractors; International Council of Shopping Centers. ***PRACTICE AREAS:*** Commercial Real Estate; Construction Law; Telecommunications Law; Commercial Litigation. ***Email:*** dgunning@ralaw.com

MICHAEL J. HAAS, born Cleveland, Ohio, September 21, 1968; admitted to bar, 1994, Ohio and U.S. District Court, Northern District of Ohio. *Education:* Syracuse University (B.A., 1991); Cleveland Marshall School of Law (J.D., 1994). Sigma Alpha Mu. *Member:* Cleveland, Cuyahoga County, Ohio State and American Bar Associations; International Council of Shopping Centers; National Association of Industrial and Office Properties. (Resident). ***LANGUAGES:*** Hebrew. ***PRACTICE AREAS:*** Real Estate; Finance. ***Email:*** mhaas@ralaw.com

DAVID R. HARBARGER, born Uniontown, Pennsylvania, March 4, 1945; admitted to bar, 1975, Ohio; 1977, U.S. District Court, Northern District of Ohio and U.S. Tax Court; 1980, U.S. Supreme Court; 1985, U.S. Court of Appeals, Sixth Circuit. *Education:* Wichita State University (B.A., 1969); Cleveland State University (J.D., 1975). Law Director: City of Westlake, 1998-2005; City of Lakewood, 1988-1991. Mayor, City of Lakewood, 1991-1995. Practice Group Manager, Public Law Group, 2003—. *Member:* Cleveland, Cuyahoga County, Ohio State and American Bar Associations; American Judicature Society; International Municipal Lawyers Association. [LTC, USAR Retired, 1997]. (Also at Washington, D.C. Office). ***PRACTICE AREAS:*** Public Law (25%); Real Estate Development (25%); Land Use (25%); Governmental Relations (25%). ***Email:*** dharbarger@ralaw.com

JOSEPH E. HERBERT, born Cincinnati, Ohio, May 14, 1965; admitted to bar, 1992, Ohio; 1996, Missouri (inactive). *Education:* Miami University (B.A., 1987); University of Toledo (J.D., cum laude, 1992). Member, National Moot Court Team and Moot Court Board. *Member:* Cleveland, Cuyahoga County and Ohio State Bar Associations; Cleveland Association of Civil Trial Lawyers; Defense Research Institute. (Resident). ***PRACTICE AREAS:*** Medical Malpractice Defense. ***Email:*** jherbert@ralaw.com

TIMOTHY C. IVEY, born Cleveland, Ohio, February 14, 1962; admitted to bar, 1987, Ohio and U.S. District Court, Northern District of Ohio. *Education:* University of Toledo (B.B.A., 1984); Case Western Reserve University (J.D., 1987). Alpha Phi Alpha; Blue Key. Member: Jessup Moot Court Team, 1986-1987; National Mock Trial Team, 1985-1987; American Inns of Court, 1987. Recipient: Dunmore Tournament Moot Court Award, 1986; International Academy of Trial Lawyers Award, 1987; Martin Luther King Award, 1987. *Member:* National Association of Criminal Defense Lawyers; The Ohio Association of Criminal Defense Lawyers. ***Email:*** tivey@ralaw.com

PETER LAWSON JONES, born December 23, 1952; admitted to bar, 1980, Ohio; 1986, U.S. District Court, Northern District of Ohio. *Education:* Harvard University (A.B., magna cum laude, 1975; J.D., 1980). Law Clerk, Supreme Court of Ohio, 1992-1993. Commissioner, Cuyahoga County, Ohio, 2002—. Member, Ohio House of Representatives, 1997-2002. Councilman, Shaker Heights, Ohio, 1984-1991. Former Bar Examiner, Supreme Court of Ohio, Law Director, Woodmere Village, Ohio, and Special Counsel, Office of the Attorney General of Ohio. *Member:* Cleveland, Cuyahoga County and Ohio State Bar Associations; Norman S. Minor Bar Association. (Resident). ***PRACTICE AREAS:*** Public Law (40%); Criminal Defense (20%); Plaintiffs Personal Injury (40%). ***Email:*** pjones@ralaw.com

R. MARK JONES, born Painesville, Ohio, January 13, 1957; admitted to bar, 1983, Ohio and U.S. District Court, Northern District of Ohio. *Education:* University of Colorado at Boulder (B.A., 1979); Case Western Reserve School of Law (J.D., 1983). Member, Ohio Super Lawyers, 2004. *Member:* Cleveland and Ohio State Bar Associations; Defense Research Institute. (Resident)(Certified as a Civil Trial Advocacy Specialist by the National Board of Trial Advocacy). ***PRACTICE AREAS:*** Medical Malpractice Defense; Drug and Medical Device Defense. ***Email:*** mjones@ralaw.com

INGRID A. KINKOPF-ZAJAC, born Cleveland, Ohio, November 12, 1961; admitted to bar, 1996, Ohio; 2003, U.S. District Court, Northern District of Ohio. *Education:* St. Vincent Charity Hospital School of Nursing (R.N. Diploma, 1982); Nazareth College of Rochester (B.A., 1993); Case Western Reserve University School of Law (J.D., 1996). *Member:* Cleveland, Cuyahoga County and Ohio State Bar Associations. (Resident). ***LANGUAGES:*** German. ***PRACTICE AREAS:*** Medical Malpractice Defense. ***Email:*** ikinkopf-zajac@ralaw.com

KENNETH M. LAPINE, born January 30, 1942; admitted to bar, 1967, Ohio and U.S. District Court, Northern District of Ohio; 1994, U.S. Supreme Court. *Education:* Dartmouth College (A.B., 1964); University of Michigan (J.D., 1967). Publications: *Consumer Credit: Law, Transactions and Forms,* (6 vols.), Matthew Bender & Co. (1984—); *Banking Law,* (multiple vols.), Matthew Bender & Co. (1979—); *Rabkin & Johnson, Current Legal Forms,* (Volume 8), Matthew Bender & Co. (1978—). *Member:* Cleveland, Toledo, Cuyahoga County, Ohio State and American Bar Associations. (Resident). ***PRACTICE AREAS:*** Real Estate (35%); Real Estate Finance (15%); Real Estate Syndication (20%); Banking Law (5%); Consumer Credit (15%); Business Law (10%). ***Email:*** klapine@ralaw.com

DOUGLAS G. LEAK, born Buffalo, New York, November 8, 1962; admitted to bar, 1988, New Jersey and Pennsylvania; 1989, Ohio; 1993, U.S. Court of Appeals, Sixth Circuit; 1998, U.S. District Court, Northern District of Ohio. *Education:* Boston University (B.A., cum laude, 1985); Cleveland Marshall College of Law (J.D., 1988). *Member:* Cleveland, Cuyahoga County, Lake County and Ohio State Bar Associations; Defense Research Institute. (Resident). ***REPORTED CASES:*** Heiner v. Moretuzzo (Ohio Supreme Court); Multiple Appellate decisions. ***PRACTICE AREAS:*** Medical Malpractice; Appellate Law. ***Email:*** dleak@ralaw.com

MARK P. McGRIEVY, born March 10, 1963; admitted to bar, 1990, New Jersey; 1993, Ohio. *Education:* Muhlenberg College (B.A., 1985); Cleveland-Marshall College of Law (J.D., 1988). Law Clerk, Hon. Thomas Rumano, Superior Court of New Jersey, 1988-1989. *Member:* American Health Lawyers Association. ***PRACTICE AREAS:*** Health Care; Long Term Care; Business and Corporate Law. ***Email:*** mmcgrievy@ralaw.com

RICHARD S. MITCHELL, born Cleveland, Ohio, June 3, 1959; admitted to bar, 1984, Ohio and U.S. District Court, Northern District of Ohio; 1987, U.S. Court of Appeals, Sixth Circuit; 2002, U.S. Supreme Court. *Education:* Tulane University of Louisiana (B.S., Business Management, 1981); Case Western Reserve University (J.D., 1984). *Member:* Cleveland, Ohio State and American Bar Associations. (Resident). ***REPORTED CASES:*** Telxon Corporation v. Symbol Technologies, 961 F. Supp. 1113 (N.D. Ohio 1996); Stavroff v. Meyo, 987 F.Supp 987 (N.D. Ohio 1995, aff'd, 129 F. 3d 1265 (6th Cir. 1997); Basicomputer v. Scott, 791 F. Supp 1280 (N.D. Ohio 1991), aff'd, 973 F2d 507 (6th Cir. 1992); Stern Enterprises v. Plaza Theatres I and II, Inc., 105 Ohio App 3d 601 (Portage Cty. 1995); Mor-Flo Industries, Inc. v. Board of Review, 817 P.2d 328 (Utah App. 1991). ***PRACTICE AREAS:*** Business and Complex Litigation; Securities Litigation; Class Actions; Emergency Injunctions in Non-Competes; Misappropriation of Trade Secrets; Lanham Act Violations. ***Email:*** rmitchell@ralaw.com

DOUGLAS S. MUSICK, born Cheverly, Maryland, July 11, 1967; admitted to bar, 1992, Ohio. *Education:* University of Michigan (B.A., 1989); Case Western Reserve School of Law (J.D., 1992). *Member:* Cleveland, Cuyahoga County and Ohio State Bar Associations; Self-Insured Employers Association. (Resident). ***PRACTICE AREAS:*** Workers' Compensation; General Civil Litigation; Employment Law. ***Email:*** dmusick@ralaw.com

(This Listing Continued)

BASIL J. MUSNUFF, born Philadelphia, Pennsylvania, January 23, 1964; admitted to bar, 1989, Ohio; 1994, U.S. Court of Appeals, Sixth Circuit; U.S. District Court, Northern and Southern Districts of Ohio. *Education:* Haverford College (B.A., with honors, 1986); Cornell Law School (J.D., magna cum laude, 1989). *Member:* Cleveland, Akron, Ohio State and Federal Bar Associations; Defense Research Institute. ***PRACTICE AREAS:*** Product Liability; General Litigation; Insurance; Civil Litigation; Torts. ***Email:*** bmusnuff@ralaw.com

CHERYL A. O'BRIEN, born Cleveland, Ohio, June 15, 1959; admitted to bar, 1989, Ohio. *Education:* Ursuline College (B.S.N., 1981); Cleveland-Marshall College of Law (J.D., 1988). *Member:* Cleveland and Ohio State Bar Associations. ***PRACTICE AREAS:*** Medical Defense. ***Email:*** cobrien@ralaw.com

RICHARD A. PLEWACKI, born Cleveland, Ohio, November 26, 1948; admitted to bar, 1980, Ohio. *Education:* Bowling Green State University (B.A., 1970); University of Akron School of Law (J.D., 1980). *Member:* Cleveland, Cuyahoga County, Ohio State and American Bar Associations; Transportation Lawyers Association; Canadian Transportation Lawyers Association; Association for Transportation Law, Logistics and Policy; Ohio Trucking Association; Truckload Carriers Association; American Arbitration Association. (Resident). ***PRACTICE AREAS:*** Transportation and Logistics Law; Corporate Law; Commercial Law; Mergers and Acquisitions. ***Email:*** rplewacki@ralaw.com

GEORGE W. ROONEY, JR., born Akron, Ohio, October 23, 1949; admitted to bar, 1974, Ohio and U.S. District Court, Northern District of Ohio; 1977, U.S. Court of Appeals, Sixth Circuit; 1980, U.S. Supreme Court; 1987, U.S. District Court, Southern District of Ohio; 1993, U.S. Tax Court; 1996, U.S. Court of International Trade; 2003, U.S. Court of Appeals, Federal Circuit; registered to practice before U.S. Patent and Trademark Office. *Education:* University of Virginia (B.S.M.E., 1971); The Ohio State University (J.D., cum laude, 1973). Life Member, Sixth Circuit Judicial Conference. Chairman, Federal Court Committee, Akron Bar Association, 1991-1993. Member, Federal Court Panel, Alternative Dispute Resolution, 1992—. Chairman, Technology Committee, Advisory Group of U.S. District Court, Northern District of Ohio, 1999-2002. President, Rotary Club of Akron, 1988-1989. Vice Chairman, Summit County Red Cross, 1988-1991. President, Akron Law Library Association, 1995-1997. President, Great Trail Council, B.S.A., 1996-1997. *Member:* Cleveland, Ohio State (Chairman, Uniform State Law Committee, 1989-1991; Chairman, Law Libraries Committee, 1993-1995) and Federal Bar Associations. (Resident) (Board Certified Civil Trial Advocacy Specialist by the National Board of Trial Advocacy). ***REPORTED CASES:*** Frankl v. Goodyear Tire and Rubber Company, 181 N.J. 1 (2004); Luntz Corp. v. Public Ulilities Comm., 79 Ohio St.3d 509 (1997); Ohio Edison Co. v. Public Utilities Comm., 78 Ohio St.3d 466 (1997); Bank One, Akron, N.A. v. Atwater Enterprises, Inc., 115 Ohio App.3d 461 (1996); R&R Plastics, Inc. v. F.E. Myers Co., 92 Ohio App.3d 789 (1993); Silver Cloud v. National Kitchen Products, 989 F.2d 501 (6th Cir. 1993); Bank One of Cleveland, N.A. v. Abbe, 916 F.2d 1067 (6th Cir. 1990); Van Fossen v. Babcock & Wilcox Company, 36 Ohio St.3d 100 (1988); Michaels Bldg. Co. v. Ameritrust Co., N.A., 848 F.2d 674 (6th Cir. 1988); XXTH Century Heating & Ventilating Co. v. Dept. of Energy, 618 F.2d 1 (6th Cir. 1980). ***PRACTICE AREAS:*** Complex Business Litigation (50%); Alternative Dispute Resolution (10%); Intellectual Property Litigation (40%). ***Email:*** grooney@ralaw.com

ALBERT N. SALVATORE, born Cleveland, Ohio, 1954; admitted to bar, 1982, Ohio. *Education:* John Carroll University (B.S.B.A., cum laude, 1976); Cleveland-Marshall College of Law (J.D., 1982); New York University (LL.M., Taxation, 1983). *Member:* Cleveland, Ohio State and American (Member, Sections on: Corporations; Bank and Business Law; Taxation Law) Bar Associations. ***PRACTICE AREAS:*** Taxation; Corporate Law; Partnership Law; Securities. ***Email:*** asalvatore@ralaw.com

BEVERLY A. SANDACZ, born Euclid, Ohio, August 9, 1960; admitted to bar, 1994, Ohio. *Education:* Ursuline College (B.S.N., magna cum laude, 1982); Cleveland-Marshall College of Law (J.D., summa cum laude, 1994). Law Clerk, Hon. Joseph Mahoney, 11th District Court of Appeals, 1993-1995. *Member:* Cuyahoga County, Lake County and Ohio State Bar Associations. (Resident). ***PRACTICE AREAS:*** Medical Malpractice; Health Care. ***Email:*** bsandacz@ralaw.com

MARK L. SARLSON, born Akron, Ohio, April 20, 1961; admitted to bar, 1986, Ohio and U.S. District Court, Northern District of Ohio. *Education:* University of Virginia (B.A., 1983); Ohio State University (J.D., 1986). Chief Justice, Moot Court Governing Board. Article Editor, The Ohio State Journal on Dispute Resolution, 1985-1986. Member: ABA Appellate Advocacy Team, 1985-1986. *Member:* Cleveland and Ohio State Bar Associations. ***PRACTICE AREAS:*** Corporate Law; Corporate Finance; Commercial Finance; Real Estate. ***Email:*** msarlson@ralaw.com

DONALD S. SCHERZER, born Brooklyn, New York, March 16, 1949; admitted to bar, 1975, Ohio and U.S. District Court, Northern District of Ohio; 1979, U.S. Court of Appeals, Sixth Circuit, U.S. Supreme Court and U.S. Tax Court. *Education:* Bowling Green State University (B.S., 1971); Case Western Reserve University (J.D., 1975). Trial Attorney, U.S. Dept. of Justice, Antitrust Div., 1975-1982. *Member:* Cleveland, Ohio State (Chairman, Antitrust Section, 1997-1998), Federal (President, Cleveland Chapter, 1984-1985; National Chairman Antitrust and Trade Regulation Section, 1985-1986) and American (Member, Antitrust, Litigation and Criminal Law Sections) Bar Associations; Sixth Circuit Judicial Conference (Life Member). (Resident). ***PRACTICE AREAS:*** Antitrust Law; Trade Regulation Law; Civil Litigation; Complex Litigation; Environmental Litigation; Securities Litigation; Criminal Law. ***Email:*** dscherzer@ralaw.com

JAMES C. SCOTT, born Lansing, Michigan, 1961; admitted to bar, 1991, Ohio; registered to practice before U.S. Patent and Trademark Office. *Education:* Hope College (B.S., 1983); Case Western Reserve University (J.D., 1989). *Member:* American Bar Association; Cleveland Intellectual Property Law Association; Lawyer-Pilot Bar Association. ***PRACTICE AREAS:*** Patents; Trademarks; Copyright; Intellectual Property; Litigation and Licensing. ***Email:*** jscott@ralaw.com

DIANA M. THIMMIG, born West Germany, May 5, 1959; admitted to bar, 1983, Ohio, U.S. District Court, Northern District of Ohio and U.S. Court of Appeals, Sixth Circuit; 1993, U.S. Supreme Court; 1996, U.S Court of Appeals, Third Circuit; 1998, U.S. District Court, Western District of Pennsylvania; 2002, U.S. District Court, Western District of Michigan. *Education:* John Carroll University (B.A., cum laude, 1980); Cleveland-Marshall College of Law (J.D., 1982). Bankruptcy Trustee, U.S. Bankruptcy Court, Northern District of Ohio, 1987-1991. Member, Civil Justice Reform Advisory Group, U.S. District Court, Northern District of Ohio, 1995-2003. Honorary Consul, Federal Republic of Germany, 1989—. President, Legal Aid Society of Cleveland, 2003—. Trustee, International Services Center, 1998-2004. *Member:* Cuyahoga County (President, 2005—) and Ohio State Bar Associations; Cuyahoga County Bar Foundation (Trustee, 2002—). (Certified Specialist, Consumer Bankruptcy Law and Business Bankruptcy Law, American Bankruptcy Board of Certification). ***PRACTICE AREAS:*** Bankruptcy; Commercial Litigation; Commercial Transactions. ***Email:*** dthimmig@ralaw.com

OF COUNSEL

JANICE A. ISAKOFF, born Toledo, Ohio, February 22, 1960; admitted to bar, 1986, Ohio. *Education:* Findlay College (B.A., cum laude, 1982); University of Toledo (J.D., 1986). *Member:* Cleveland and Ohio State Bar Associations. ***PRACTICE AREAS:*** Banking; Finance; Closely Held Business; Emerging Business Law; Condominium Association Law; Homeowners Law; Construction Law; Real Estate Law; Land Use Law; Residential Association Litigation; School Law. ***Email:*** jisakoff@ralaw.com

TERESA E. PURTIMAN, admitted to bar, 2001, Ohio. *Education:* The Ohio State University (B.A., Economics, summa cum laude, 1986); The University of Akron School of Law (J.D., magna cum laude, 2001). Phi Beta Kappa. *Member:* Ohio State and American Bar Associations. ***PRACTICE AREAS:*** Intellectual Property; Closely Held Business Law; Emerging Business Law. ***Email:*** tpurtiman@ralaw.com

GARY A. WEISS, born Cleveland, Ohio, November 6, 1963; admitted to bar, 1990, Ohio; 1992, U.S. District Court, Northern District of Ohio; 1995, U.S. District Court, Eastern District of Michigan; 2003, U.S. District Court, Southern District of Ohio and U.S. Court of Appeals, Sixth Circuit. *Education:* University of Akron (B.A., cum laude, 1986); University of Toledo (J.D., 1990). *Member:* Cleveland and Ohio State Bar Associations. (Also at Columbus Office). ***PRACTICE AREAS:*** Insurance Defense; Workers Compensation Defense; Litigation. ***Email:*** gweiss@ralaw.com

---

CHAD ARFONS, born January 9, 1971; admitted to bar, 1997, Ohio; 2004, U.S. Tax Court. *Education:* Unversity of Akron (B.A., 1994); Tulane University Law School (J.D., 1997). Contributing Author, "Consumer Credit Law, Transactions and Forms," Matthews Bender & Co., 1999—. *Member:* Cleveland and Ohio State Bar Associations. ***PRACTICE AREAS:*** Real Estate; Real Estate Finance; Real Estate Syndication; Banking Law; Consumer Credit; Corporate Law; Loan Syndication. ***Email:*** carfons@ralaw.com

RICARDO J. CARDENAS, born Cleveland, Ohio, May 8, 1968; admitted to bar, 1996, Ohio. *Education:* Cleveland State University (B.A., cum laude, 1993); Case Western Reserve (J.D., 1996). ***Email:*** rcardenas@ralaw.com

TAMMI J. CARTER, born Geneva, New York, October 12, 1979; admitted to bar, 2004, Ohio; 2005, U.S. District Court, Northern District of Ohio. *Education:* Le Moyne College (B.A., summa cum laude, 2001); Case Western Reserve University (J.D., cum laude, 2004). Executive Contributing Editor, Case Western Reserve University Law Review, 2003-2004. Author, Note, "The Individual v. The Employer: Who Should Be Held Liable Under Employment Discrimination Law," 54 Case W. Res. L. Rev. 861 (2004). *Member:* Cleveland and Ohio State Bar Associations. ***PRACTICE AREAS:*** Labor and Employment. ***Email:*** tcarter@ralaw.com

STEPHENIE L. CONDE, born Canton, Ohio; admitted to bar, 1994, Ohio. *Education:* Bowling Green State University (B.A., 1991); Cleveland-Marshall College of Law (J.D., 1994). Research Editor, Cleveland-Marshall Law Review. *Member:* Cuyahoga County and Ohio State Bar Associations. ***PRACTICE AREAS:*** Workers; Workers Compensation Defense. ***Email:*** sconde@ralaw.com

LYNN A. GROSS, born Lansing, Michigan, December 3, 1974; admitted to bar, 2000, Ohio and U.S. District Court, Northern District of Ohio; 2001, U.S. Court of Appeals, Sixth Circuit; 2003, U.S. District Court, Southern District of Ohio. *Education:* Michigan State University (B.A., 1997); Case Western Reserve University (J.D., 2000). Recipient, Labor and Employment Law Award, 2000, and Legal Clinic Award, 2000, Case Western Reserve University School of Law. *Member:* Cleveland and Ohio State Bar Associations. (Resident). ***REPORTED CASES:*** Goins v. Cuyahoga Metropolitan Housing Authority, 2004 WL 63966, 20 IER 1449, 2004-Ohio-139, Ohio App. 8th Dist. (Jan. 15, 2004) McGowan v. Cuyahoga Metropolitan Housing Authority, 2004 WL 1752867, 2004-Ohio-4070, Ohio App. 8th Dist. (Aug. 5, 2004). ***PRACTICE AREAS:*** Employment Law; Labor Law; Civil Rights Law; Workers Compensation. ***Email:*** lgross@ralaw.com

CHRISTINE M. KATTOLA, born Flint, Michigan, December 16, 1979; admitted to bar, 2004, Ohio. *Education:* University of Michigan (B.A., Political Science, with distinction, 2001); The Ohio State University (J.D., 2004). ***LANGUAGES:*** Arrabic and Chaldean. ***PRACTICE AREAS:*** Business Litigation; Labor and Employment. ***Email:*** ckattola@ralaw.com

HUGH S. KINAST, born Cleveland, Ohio, August 8, 1977; admitted to bar, 2004, Ohio. *Education:* Indiana University (B.A., 2001); Case Western Reserve University (J.D., cum laude, 2004). *Member:* Cuyahoga County Bar Association; American Health Lawyers Association. ***PRACTICE AREAS:*** Real Estate Leasing; Real Estate Banking Law; Real Estate Sales; Long Term Care; Health Care; Business Law. ***Email:*** hkinast@ralaw.com

LAUREN K. KINKOPF, born Cleveland, Ohio; admitted to bar, 1992, Ohio. *Education:* Medical College of Ohio (B.S. in Nursing, 1986); Cleveland-Marshall College of Law (J.D., 1992). *Member:* Cuyahoga County Bar Association; American Nurses Association; Ohio Nurses Association. ***PRACTICE AREAS:*** Medical Defense. ***Email:*** lkinkopf@ralaw.com

DAVID A. KOTNIK, born 1969; (admission pending); admitted to bar, 2005, Ohio. *Education:* The Ohio State University (B.S., 1992); Cleveland-Marshall College of Law (J.D., 2004). *Member:* Cuyahoga County, Ohio State and American Bar Associations. ***PRACTICE AREAS:*** Business Litigation; Construction Law; Corporate and Business Services; Public Law Litigation; Real Estate, Land Use, and Construction; Real Estate, Land Use, and Construction Litigation. ***Email:*** dkotnik@ralaw.com

(This Listing Continued)

ROETZEL & ANDRESS, A LEGAL PROFESSIONAL ASSOCIATION, Cleveland—Continued

BRIAN H. LINICK, born Cleveland, Ohio; admitted to bar, 2005, Ohio. *Education:* The Ohio State University (B.S., 2002); Cleveland-Marshall College of Law (J.D., 2004). *Member:* Cleveland, Cuyahoga County, Ohio State and American Bar Associations. ***LANGUAGES:*** Spanish. ***PRACTICE AREAS:*** Banking and Finance; Closely-Held and Emerging Businesses; Corporate and Business Services; Real Estate, Land Use, and Construction. ***Email:*** blinick@ralaw.com

RACHEL K. MATHOSLAH, (admission pending); admitted to bar, 2004, Ohio. *Education:* Boston University (B.A., 1999); Case Western Reserve University School of Law (J.D., 2004). *Member:* Cayahoga County and Ohio State Bar Associations. ***PRACTICE AREAS:*** Real Estate; Real Estate Development; Real Estate Finance. ***Email:*** rmathoslah@ralaw.com

ADAM C. MILLER, born Columbus, Ohio, January 27, 1965; admitted to bar, 1994, Ohio. *Education:* The Ohio State University (B.A., English, 1988); Otterbein College (Ohio Teaching Certificate, 1989); Capital University (J.D., 1994). U.S. Army (JAG) Judge Advocate General's School Officer Basic Course (1998), Advanced Course (2002). Author: "OSBA's Sunshine Law Guide," The Ohio School Ethics Guide, Ohio School Records Guide and Managing Employee Leaves. Deputy Director of Legal Services, Ohio School Boards Association, Westerville, Oh., 1995-2000. Local School Superintendent, 2000-2002. Maguire & Schneider, L.L.P., 2002-2005. Ohio Director, Operation Homefront. *Member:* Columbus, Ohio State and American (Member, Legal Assistance to Military Personnel (LAMP) Committee) Bar Associations. [U.S. Army Reserve JAG Corps., 1996—; Commander, HHC, TF Victory, Bagram Air Field, Afghanistan]. ***PRACTICE AREAS:*** Education Law; Special Education; Collective Bargaining; Military Law; Probate; Domestic Relations; Labor and Employment; Administrative Law; International Law; Constitutional Law; Civil Litigation. ***Email:*** amiller@ralaw.com

JAMES P. MYERS, born Cleveland, Ohio, September 28, 1976; admitted to bar, 2002, Ohio; 2003, U.S. District Court, Northern District of Ohio. *Education:* Wake Forest University (B.A., Political Science, 1999); Case Western Reserve University (J.D., 2002). *Member:* Cleveland, Ohio State and American Bar Associations. ***PRACTICE AREAS:*** Civil Litigation; Medical Malpractice Defense. ***Email:*** jmyers@ralaw.com

ERIC M. PIZZUTI, born 1980; (admission pending). *Education:* Miami University, Richard T. Farmer School of Business Administration (B.S., 2002); Catholic University of America, Columbus School of Law (J.D., 2005). ***PRACTICE AREAS:*** Corporate Law. ***Email:*** epizzuti@ralaw.com

BETH ANN SCHENZ, born Barberton, Ohio, November 30, 1970; admitted to bar, 2001, Ohio and U.S. District Court, Northern District of Ohio; 2003, U.S. Court of Appeals, Sixth Circuit. *Education:* Xavier University (B.S., 1992); Cleveland-Marshall College of Law (J.D., 2001). Member, Board of Governors, Moot Court, 2000-2001. *Member:* Cuyahoga County, Cleveland and Ohio State Bar Associations. ***PRACTICE AREAS:*** Bankruptcy; Creditors Rights; Business Litigation. ***Email:*** bschenz@ralaw.com

JOHN J. SCHRINER, JR., born Cleveland, Ohio, December 19, 1973; admitted to bar, 1999, Ohio. *Education:* Northwestern University (B.A., 1996); Ohio State University College of Law (J.D., 1999). Law Clerk, U.S. Magistrate Judge George J. Limbert, Northern District of Ohio, 1999-2001. *Member:* Cleveland, Cuyahoga County and Ohio State Bar Associations. (Resident). ***PRACTICE AREAS:*** Business Litigation. ***Email:*** jschriner@ralaw.com

E. MARK YOUNG, admitted to bar, 2001, Ohio. *Education:* Wake Forest University (B.A., Economics, 1996); University of Toledo (J.D., 2001). *Member:* Cleveland and Ohio State Bar Associations. ***PRACTICE AREAS:*** Creditor Bankruptcy; Business Litigation. ***Email:*** myoung@ralaw.com

REPRESENTATIVE CLIENTS: Advanced Elastomer Systems, Inc.; Akron General Medical Center; Atlantic Tool & Die; Babcock & Wilcox, a McDermott Company; Bank One; Barberton Citizens Hospital; Beacon Journal Publishing Company; BP America; Burger Iron Company; Catholic Healthcare Partners; City of Akron; The Cleveland Clinic Foundation; CSX Transportation; Dart Industries, Inc.; Doctors Hospital; Edward J. Debartolo Corp.; F.E. Myers; FirstEnergy; Ford Motor Company; General Motors Corporation; Grant/Riverside Methodist Hospitals; Honeywell, Inc.; Lloyd's of London; Louisiana Pacific Corporation; Marathon Oil Company; Marriott Corporation; Medtronic, Inc.; MRK Technologies; National City Bank; National Railroad Passenger Corporation (AMTRAK); Norfolk Southern Corporation; Ohio Health Corporation; Ohio Rail Commission; OHM Remediation Services; Pentair, Inc.; PPG Industries, Inc.; Pulte Homes Corporation; Rite-Aid; Seaman Corporation; State of Ohio; Summa Health System; Summit County; The University of Akron; Waste Management, Inc.; Western Parcel Express.

(For complete biographical data on all personnel, see Professional Biographies at Akron, Ohio)

ROLF & GOFFMAN CO., L.P.A.

Established in 1985

350 CORPORATE CIRCLE
30100 CHAGRIN BOULEVARD
CLEVELAND, OHIO 44124-5705
Telephone: 216-514-1100
Telecopier: 216-514-0030
Email: info@rolfgoffman.com
URL: http://www.rolfgoffman.com

Health Care Law, Labor and Employment, General Civil Litigation in all State and Federal Courts, Administrative, Business, Corporate, Banking, Real Estate, Estate Planning and Probate Law.

FIRM PROFILE: For over 20 years, Rolf & Goffman Co., L.P.A., has been representing all forms of business enterprises with concentration in the representation of health care systems, institutions and providers.

CAROL ROLF, born Munich, Germany, March 29, 1952; admitted to bar, 1976, Ohio; U.S. District Court, Northern District of Ohio; U.S. Court of Appeals, Sixth Circuit. *Education:* Case Western Reserve University (B.A., magna cum laude, 1973); Cleveland State University (J.D., 1975). Member: Ohio Department of Health Licensure and Certification Task Force, 1984-1985; Board of Examiners of Nursing Home Administrators, 1992-1994; Special Counsel to Ohio Attorney General, 1993-1997; Board of Trustees: United Church Homes, 1995-1998; Boys and Girls Clubs of Cleveland. *Member:* Cleveland and Ohio State (Member, Health Care Committee) Bar Associations; American Health Lawyers Association; Ohio Women's Bar Association. ***PRACTICE AREAS:*** Health Care Law; Administrative Law. ***Email:*** rolf@rolfgoffman.com

(This Listing Continued)

IRA S. GOFFMAN, born Freeport, New York, August 31, 1956; admitted to bar, 1981, Ohio; 1982, Florida; U.S. District Court, Northern District of Ohio; U.S. Tax Court. *Education:* State University of New York at Binghamton (B.S., Accounting, 1978); University of Toledo (J.D., cum laude, 1981). Phi Kappa Phi. Ohio Certificate of Need Task Force, 1994-1995. Member, Ohio Freestanding Facility Licensure and Inpatient Hospital Service Quality Advisory Committee. *Member:* Cleveland and Ohio State Bar Associations; The Florida Bar; American Health Lawyers Association; Health Care Financial Management Association. (Board Certified Health Law Lawyer, Florida Bar Board of Legal Specialization and Education). ***PRACTICE AREAS:*** Health Care Law; Business Law. ***Email:*** goffman@rolfgoffman.com

RICHARD D. FIKTUS, born Cleveland, Ohio, December 14, 1953; admitted to bar, 1978, Ohio; 1981, U.S. District Court, Northern District of Ohio; 1983, U.S. District Court, Southern District of Ohio; 1985, U.S. Tax Court. *Education:* University of Houston and Ohio University (B.B.A., summa cum laude, 1975); Cleveland State University, Cleveland-Marshall College of Law (J.D., cum laude, 1978). Member: Board of Directors, American Liver Foundation, Northern Ohio Chapter, 1996—. *Member:* Cleveland and Ohio State Bar Associations; American Health Lawyers Association. ***PRACTICE AREAS:*** Real Estate Law; Banking and Financing Law; Corporate Law; Business Law; Estate Planning Law; Probate Law. ***Email:*** fiktus@rolfgoffman.com

ARIC D. MARTIN, born Cincinnati, Ohio, June 15, 1970; admitted to bar, 1995, Ohio; U.S. District Court, Northern District of Ohio; U.S. Court of Appeals, Sixth Circuit. *Education:* Miami University, Oxford, Ohio (B.A., 1992); John E. Dolibois European Center (1990-1991), Luxembourg Ville, Luxembourg; St. Anne's College, Oxford University (1994), Oxford, United Kingdom. The Ohio State University College of Law (J.D., 1995). Associate Editor, The Ohio State Law Review, 1993-1995. *Member:* Cleveland and Ohio State (Member, Health Care Committee) Bar Associations; American Health Lawyers Association. ***PRACTICE AREAS:*** Health Care Law; Administrative Law. ***Email:*** martin@rolfgoffman.com

PAUL A. LANG, born Parma, Ohio, March 7, 1967; admitted to bar, 1992, Ohio. *Education:* Miami University (B.A., 1989); Case Western Reserve University (J.D., cum laude, 1992). *Member:* Ohio State and American Bar Associations; American Health Lawyers Association. ***PRACTICE AREAS:*** Health Care Law; Administrative Law; Business Law. ***Email:*** lang@rolfgoffman.com

SCOTT SALSBURY, born Conneaut, Ohio, September 9, 1962; admitted to bar, 1987, Ohio; 1990, U.S. District Court, Northern District of Ohio; 1997, U.S. Court of Appeals, Sixth Circuit. *Education:* Kent State University (B.A., cum laude, 1984); The Ohio State University (J.D., 1987). *Member:* Akron and Ohio State Bar Associations; American Health Lawyers Association; Ohio Hospital Association. ***REPORTED CASES:*** Sokol v. Akron General Med. Center, 173 F.3d 1026 (6th Cir. 1999). ***PRACTICE AREAS:*** Litigation; Healthcare Law. ***Email:*** salsbury@rolfgoffman.com

---

CHRISTOPHER M. TOST, born Steubenville, Ohio, October 9, 1973; admitted to bar, 1999, Ohio. *Education:* St. Francis College (B.A., magna cum laude, 1996); Case Western Reserve (J.D., cum laude, 1999). Managing Editor, Health Matrix: Journal of Law and Medicine, 1999. *Member:* Ohio State Bar Association. ***PRACTICE AREAS:*** Healthcare Law; Administrative; Employment Law. ***Email:*** tost@rolfgoffman.com

CRAIG HARAN, born Rochester, New York, January 17, 1975; admitted to bar, 2000, Ohio. *Education:* John Carroll University (B.A., 1997); Case Western Reserve University (J.D., 2000). *Member:* Ohio State and American Bar Associations; American Health Lawyers Association. ***PRACTICE AREAS:*** Health Law; Long Term Care; Administrative Law; Medicare and Medicaid Reimbursement. ***Email:*** haran@rolfgoffman.com

REFERENCES: Extendicare Health Services, Inc.; Drs. Hill & Thomas; NEO-PET LLC; The Schroer Group; ProMedica Health System; Marymount Hospital; Ohio Health Care Association; University Hospitals Health System; First Merit Bank; Otterbein Homes, Inc.; United Church Homes, Inc.; Health Care Facilities (HCF); Fifth Third Bank; Dollar Bank.

BARBARA GOLDBERG ROSMAN

LANDMARK CENTRE, SUITE 360
25700 SCIENCE PARK DRIVE
CLEVELAND, OHIO 44122
Telephone: 216-831-7300
Fax: 216-831-7361
Email: BGRLaw@sbcglobal.net
URL: http://www.lawyers.com/barbaragoldbergrosman

Criminal Defense, Civil Practice, Family Law, Divorce, Child Custody, Health Care, Juvenile Law, Medical Collections, Collections, Medical Law, Mediation, Collaborative Law, Debt Collection, Collections, Residential Real Estate, Small Business, Contract Law.

BARBARA GOLDBERG ROSMAN, born Philadelphia, Pennsylvania, June 20, 1951; admitted to bar, 1988, Ohio and U.S. District Court, Northern District of Ohio; 1992, U.S. Supreme Court. *Education:* Temple University (B.A., 1972); Case Western Reserve University (M.S., 1973; J.D., 1988). Assistant Prosecuting Attorney, Trumbull County, 1989-1991. Mediator. Trained Collaborative Lawyer. *Member:* Cleveland, Cuyahoga County, Trumbull County and Ohio State Bar Associations.

ROSS, BRITTAIN & SCHONBERG CO., L.P.A.

Established in 1991

6000 FREEDOM SQUARE DRIVE, SUITE 540
CLEVELAND, OHIO 44131
Telephone: 216-447-1551
Telecopier: 216-447-1554
URL: http://www.rbslaw.com

Practice Limited to the Representation of Management in all aspects of Labor Law, Employment Relations and Workers Compensation Matters.

ALAN G. ROSS, born Cleveland, Ohio, November 4, 1949; admitted to bar, 1975, Ohio; 1977, U.S. District Court, Northern District of Ohio; 1983, U.S. Court of Appeals, Sixth Circuit; 1989, U.S. Supreme Court. *Education:* University of Michigan (B.A., 1971); Cleveland State University, Cleveland-Marshall College of Law (J.D., cum laude, 1975). Co-Editor, Ohio Labor Law Newsletter, 1974-1975. Field Attorney, National Labor Relations Board, 1975-1977. *Member:* Cleveland, Ohio State (Member, Labor Law Section) and American (Member, Labor Relations Law Section) Bar Associations. ***PRACTICE AREAS:*** Labor Law; Employment Relations; Workers Compensation Law; OSHA Law. ***Email:*** aross@rbslaw.com

BRIAN K. BRITTAIN, admitted to bar, 1981, Ohio. *Education:* Mount Union College (B.A., summa cum laude, 1978); Case Western Reserve University (J.D., 1981); Cleveland State University (M.B.A., 1986). Phi Alpha Delta. *Member:* Cleveland, Cuyahoga County, Geauga County, Lorain County and Ohio State Bar Associations. (Certified Specialist, Workers' Compensation Law, Ohio Bar Board of Legal Specialization and Education). ***PRACTICE AREAS:*** Labor Law; Workers Compensation Law; OSHA Law. ***Email:*** bbrittain@rbslaw.com

EVELYN P. SCHONBERG, born Cleveland, Ohio, October 9, 1955; admitted to bar, 1981, Ohio; 1982, U.S. District Court, Northern and Southern Districts of Ohio. *Education:* American University (B.S., 1978); Cleveland State University, Cleveland-Marshall College of Law (J.D., 1981). Lecturer, Oral Advocacy and Brief Writing, Cleveland-Marshall Law School, 1980-1983. Law Clerk to U. S. Magistrate, Northern District of Ohio, 1982-1985. *Member:* Cleveland (Member, Labor Law Section), Ohio State (Member, Labor Law Section) and Federal (Member, Labor Law Section) Bar Associations. (Certified Specialist, Labor and Employment Law, Ohio Bar Board of Legal Specialization and Education). ***PRACTICE AREAS:*** Employment Relations; Labor Law. ***Email:*** lynns@rbslaw.com

DAVID T. ANDREWS, born New Hartford, New York, October 5, 1968; admitted to bar, 1993, Ohio. *Education:* Ohio University (B.A., summa cum laude, 1990); University of Virginia (J.D., 1993). Chairman of the Board, Chamber of Commerce, Solon, Ohio, 2005. Member, Board of Education, Twinsburg City School District. *Member:* Cleveland and Ohio State (Member, Labor and Employment Law Section) Bar Associations. ***PRACTICE AREAS:*** Labor and Employment Law. ***Email:*** dandrews@rbslaw.com

---

ANTHONY A. BAUCCO, born Cleveland, Ohio, February 7, 1978; admitted to bar, 2003, Ohio. *Education:* University of Dayton (B.A., Criminal Justice Studies, 2000); Cleveland-Marshall College of Law (J.D., 2003). Member, Cleveland State Law Review. *Member:* Cleveland and Ohio State Bar Associations. ***PRACTICE AREAS:*** Workers Compensation. ***Email:*** ABaucco@rbslaw.com

JENNIFER A. BENNETT, born Canton, Ohio, July 3, 1968; admitted to bar, 1994, Ohio. *Education:* University of Akron (B.S., magna cum laude, 1991); University of Cincinnati (J.D., 1994). Delta Theta Phi; Omicron Delta Kappa. Member, Moot Court Board. Recipient, American Jurisprudence Award, Pre-trial Practice. *Member:* Cleveland, Stark County, Ohio State and American Bar Associations. ***PRACTICE AREAS:*** Workers Compensation; Employment Law; Litigation. ***Email:*** jbennett@rbslaw.com

JERRY P. CLINE, born Piscataway, New Jersey, December 3, 1969; admitted to bar, 2002, Ohio. *Education:* Rutgers University, New Brunswick (B.A., 1993); Capital University (J.D., 2002). Order of the Curia. *Member:* Cleveland and Ohio State Bar Associations; Lawyers Guild, Catholic Diocese of Cleveland; Federalist Society (Member, Cleveland Lawyers Chapter). ***PRACTICE AREAS:*** Employment Law; Litigation; Workers Compensation. ***Email:*** jcline@rbslaw.com

SCOTT COGHLAN, born Cleveland, Ohio, June 11, 1967; admitted to bar, 1992, Ohio; 1996, U.S. District Court, Northern District of Ohio and U.S. Court of Appeals, Sixth Circuit. *Education:* Bowling Green State University (B.S., 1989); Case Western Reserve University (J.D., 1992). *Member:* Ohio State Bar Association. ***PRACTICE AREAS:*** Workers Compensation. ***Email:*** scoghlan@rbslaw.com

CHRISTOPHER R. DEBSKI, born Pittsburgh, Pennsylvania, October 8, 1971; admitted to bar, 1997, Ohio and U.S. District Court, Northern District of Ohio. *Education:* University of Michigan (B.A., 1993); University of Akron School of Law (J.D., 1996). Formerly with: Brian Law Offices; Law Offices of Debra E. Booher, P.C. *Member:* Cleveland and Ohio State Bar Associations. ***PRACTICE AREAS:*** Workers Compensation Defense. ***Email:*** cdebski@rbslaw.com

DAVID S FARKAS, born Toronto, Ontario, December 25, 1974; admitted to bar, 2003, Ohio. *Education:* Ner Israel Rabbinical College (Bachelor of Talmudic Law, 1996; Master of Talmudic Law, 1998); University of Maryland School of Law (J.D., 2002). Member, Editorial Staff, "The Business Lawyer." *Member:* Cleveland (Member, Labor and Employment Section), Cuyahoga County (Member, Employment Law Section), Ohio State (Member, Labor and Employment Section) and American (Member, Labor and Employment Section) Bar Associations. ***PRACTICE AREAS:*** Labor and Employment. ***Email:*** dfarkas@rbslaw.com

NICK A. NYKULAK, born Parma, Ohio, August 10, 1976; admitted to bar, 2003, Ohio. *Education:* Cleveland State University (B.A, Political Science, 1999); Cleveland Marshall College of Law (J.D., 2002). Executive Editor, Journal of Law and Health, 2002-2003. *Member:* Cleveland and Ohio State Bar Associations. ***PRACTICE AREAS:*** Labor and Employment. ***Email:*** nnykulak@rbslaw.com

(This Listing Continued)

MEREDITH L. ULLMAN, born Toledo, Ohio, January 23, 1977; admitted to bar, 2002, Ohio. *Education:* Ohio University (B.A., cum laude, 1999); Case Western Reserve University (J.D., cum laude, 2002). ***PRACTICE AREAS:*** Workers Compensation; Labor Law; Employment Law. ***Email:*** mullman@rbslaw.com

THOMAS R. WYATT, admitted to bar, 1986, Ohio. *Education:* The Ohio State University (B.A., 1983); University of Akron (J.D., 1986). ***PRACTICE AREAS:*** Workers Compensation; International Tort Defense; OSHA Litigation. ***Email:*** twyatt@rbslaw.com

LEGAL SUPPORT PERSONNEL

PARALEGALS

Kimberly L. Altstadt	***Joyce L. Hale***
Lorraine J. Geiger	***Renee M. Mezera*** (Paralegal Manager)
Megan E. Geist	***Carla E. Reznik***
Arlene M. Golias	

REPRESENTATIVE CLIENTS: Kokosing Construction Co.; Associated Builders and Contractors Inc., Northern Ohio Chapter; O. Ames Co.; AGA Gas, Inc.; Duke-Weeks Construction; A.R.E. Inc.; Dixon Ticonderoga Co.; Northeast Ohio Area Chambers of Commerce, Inc.

ROTATORI, BENDER, GRAGEL, STOPER & ALEXANDER CO. L.P.A.

800 LEADER BUILDING
526 SUPERIOR AVENUE EAST
CLEVELAND, OHIO 44114-1498
Telephone: 216-928-1010
Fax: 216-928-1007
URL: http://www.rotatori.com

Employment Law, Civil Practice, Trial Practice, Appellate Practice, Labor Law, Domestic Relations, Antitrust, Securities Litigation, Trade Secrets, White Collar Criminal Defense, Taxation, Business Law, Civil and Criminal Tax Controversy.

ROBERT J. ROTATORI, born Cleveland, Ohio, March 19, 1937; admitted to bar, 1962, Ohio; 1973, U.S. Supreme Court. *Education:* Case Western Reserve University (B.A., 1959; J.D., 1962). Phi Beta Kappa; Omicron Delta Kappa; Order of the Coif. Editor, Western Reserve Law Review, 1961-1962. Author: "Right to Refuse to Deal," Western Reserve Law Review, 1962. Member, Department of Justice, Anti-Trust Division, 1962-1964. Chief Assistant, U.S. Attorney, Northern District of Ohio, 1964-1969. Member, Supreme Court of Ohio Advisory Committee, Rules of Criminal Procedure, 1970—. Life Member, Sixth Circuit Judicial Conference, 1975—. Member, Board of Trustees, Case Western Reserve Law School, 1975-1976. *Member:* Cleveland (President), Ohio State and American Bar Associations; Greater Cleveland (Chair, Criminal Law Committee, 1971-1972; Member, Board of Trustees, 1973-1976); The Association of Trial Lawyers of America; Sixth Circuit Judicial Conference (Life Member). Fellow, American College of Trial Lawyers. ***Email:*** rjr@rotatori.com

J. TIMOTHY BENDER, born Akron, Ohio, July 26, 1949; admitted to bar, 1978, Ohio and U.S. Tax Court; 1979, U.S. District Court, Northern District of Ohio; 1981, U.S. Court of Appeals, Sixth Circuit; 1994, U.S. Supreme Court. *Education:* University of Akron (B.S., 1973; J.D., 1978). Member, Akron Law Review. Listed in The Best Lawyers in America in Tax Law. *Member:* Cleveland (Member, General Tax Committee, 1980—) and American (Member, Court Procedure Committee, Taxation Section, 1986—) Bar Associations. ***PRACTICE AREAS:*** Taxation; Business Law; Civil and Criminal Tax Controversy. ***Email:*** tbender@rotatori.com

SUSAN L. GRAGEL, born Cleveland, Ohio, September 2, 1955; admitted to bar, 1980, Ohio and U.S. District Court, Northern District of Ohio; 1984, U.S. Supreme Court and U.S. Court of Appeals, Sixth Circuit. *Education:* Cleveland State University (B.A., cum laude, 1977; J.D., cum laude, 1980). Research Editor, Cleveland-Marshall Law Review, 1979-1980. President, Cleveland Marshall Law Alumni, 1985-1986. Author: "Drug Testing--The Labor Union Perspective," J. L. and Health, 1987. Co-Author: "Criminal Justice; Arrest to Trial," Women's Legal Rights Handbook, 1980. *Member:* Greater Cleveland (Past, Trustee; Judicial Selection Committee; Past-Chair, Certified Grievance Committee, Labor Law Section), Ohio State and American Bar Associations; Eighth Judicial Conference (Life Member). ***REPORTED CASES:*** NCS Healthcare, Inc. v. Condleswood Partners LLC., 160 Ohio App.3rd 421, 827 N.E.2d 797 (2005); State ex rel. Kabect v. Shaker Hts. Bd. of Educ., 78 Ohio St. 3d 37, 676 N.E. 2d 101 (1997); Wise v. Ohio Dept. of Education, 863 F.Supp. 570 (N.D. Ohio 1994); United States v Cooperative Theatres of Ohio, Inc., 845 F.2d 1367 (6th Cir. 1988); J.L. Foti Construction Co. v. Laborers International Union of North America, Local No. 310, 742 F.2d 994 (6th Cir. 1984). ***Email:*** sgragel@rotatori.com

RICHARD L. STOPER, JR., born Fairmont, West Virginia, August 20, 1958; admitted to bar, 1984, Ohio; 1986, U.S. District Court, Northern District of Ohio; 1986, U.S. Court of Appeals, Sixth Circuit; 1988, U.S. Court of Appeals, Third Circuit; 1998, U.S. Supreme Court. *Education:* The Ohio State University (B.A., Journalism, 1979); Cleveland-Marshall College of Law (J.D., magna cum laude, 1984). Member, Cleveland State Law Review. Law Clerk to Hon. Leroy J. Contie, Jr., U.S. Court of Appeals, Sixth Circuit, 1984-1986. *Member:* Cleveland, Ohio State Bar Association. ***REPORTED CASES:*** Gettings v. Building Laborers Local 310 Fringe Benefit Fund, 349 F.3d 300 (6th Cir. 2003); Ross v. H.E.R.E. I.U., 266 F. 3d 236 (3d Cir. 2001); United States v. Kassouf, 144 F.3d 952 (6th Cir. 1998); FDIC v. Bates, 42 F.3d 369 (6th Cir. 1994); Nettis Environmental Ltd. v. IWI, Inc, 46 F. Supp. 2d 722 (N.D. Ohio 1999); U.S. v. McCullough, 891 F. Supp. 422 (N.D., Ohio 1995); State ex rel. Jones v. Suster, 84 Ohio St. 3d 70, 701 N.E. 2d 1002 (1998); State v. Ramirez, 135 Ohio App.3d 89, 732 N.E.2d 1065 (1989). ***PRACTICE AREAS:*** Commercial Law; Employee Benefits; Labor and Employment; Litigation; White Collar Crime. ***Email:*** rstoper@rotatori.com

JOSEPH P. ALEXANDER, born Akron, Ohio, April 14, 1956; admitted to bar, 1981, Ohio and U.S. District Court, Northern District of Ohio; 1988, U.S. Tax Court; 1992, U.S. Court of Appeals, Sixth Circuit. *Education:* University of Akron (B.S.B.A., 1977; J.D., 1981); Georgetown University, Law Center (LL.M., Taxation, 1984). Law Clerk to Special

(This Listing Continued)

ROTATORI, BENDER, GRAGEL, STOPER & ALEXANDER CO. L.P.A., Cleveland—Continued

Trial Judge Fred Tansill, U.S. Tax Court, 1985. ***PRACTICE AREAS:*** Tax Controversy; Corporate Law; Business Succession Planning; Taxation; ERISA. ***Email:*** jalexander@rotatori.com

J. SCOTT BROOME, born Chagrin Falls, Ohio, March 19, 1963; admitted to bar, 1989, Ohio and U.S. Tax Court; 1995, U.S. District Court, Northern District of Ohio and U.S. Court of Appeals, Sixth Circuit; 1996, U.S. District Court, Southern District of Ohio. *Education:* The Ohio State University (B.S., Accounting, 1986); Case Western Reserve University (J.D., 1989). Attorney, 1989-1993 and Senior Attorney, 1989-1994, Office of Chief Counsel, Internal Revenue Service. *Member:* Cleveland, Federal and American Bar Associations; Tax Club of Cleveland. ***PRACTICE AREAS:*** Taxation; Civil and Criminal Tax Controversy; White Collar Criminal Defense. ***Email:*** sbroome@rotatori.com

---

CARA L. SANTOSUOSSO, born Cleveland, Ohio, April 25, 1973; admitted to bar, 1998, Ohio; 1999, U.S. District Court, Northern District of Ohio. *Education:* John Carroll University (B.A., magna cum laude, 1995); Cleveland Marshall College of Law (J.D., 1998). Assistant Prosecuting Attorney, Cuyahoga County, 1999-2003. Law Clerk, 8th District Court of Appeals, 2003-2005. *Member:* Cleveland and Ohio State Bar Associations; Justinian Forum. ***Email:*** csantosuosso@rotatori.com

ROTH BIERMAN LLP

CLEVELAND, OHIO

(See Bedford Heights)

Health Care Law, Strategic Planning, Financial, Corporate Law, Business Litigation.

DANIEL J. RYAN LPA

1370 ONTARIO STREET, SUITE 2000
CLEVELAND, OHIO 44113
Telephone: 216-363-6082
Fax: 216-696-1718
Email: offdanryan@msn.com
URL: http://www.lawyers.com/lawyerscomdanieljryan

Personal Injury, Auto Accidents, Civil Litigation, Industrial Injuries, Medical Malpractice, Professional Malpractice, Business Litigation, Employment Law, Wrongful Termination.

DANIEL J. RYAN, born Cleveland, Ohio, March 21, 1945; admitted to bar, 1973, Ohio. *Education:* John Carroll University (B.A., 1968); Cleveland State University College of Law (J.D., 1973). *Member:* Cleveland and Ohio State Bar Associations. ***PRACTICE AREAS:*** Personal Injury; Automobile Accidents and Injuries; Civil Litigation; Industrial Injuries; Medical Malpractice; Professional Malpractice; Business Litigation; Employment Law; Wrongful Termination. ***Email:*** offdanryan@msn.com

SCHNEIDER, SMELTZ, RANNEY & LAFOND P.L.L.

Established in 1895
1111 SUPERIOR AVENUE, SUITE 1000
CLEVELAND, OHIO 44114
Telephone: 216-696-4200
Telecopier: 216-696-7303
URL: http://www.ssrl.com

General Practice, Corporate, Estate Planning and Probate, Real Estate, Taxation, Domestic Relations, Employment Law, Civil Litigation, Health Care.

MEMBERS OF FIRM

JOHN E. SMELTZ, born Salem, Ohio, September 10, 1922; admitted to bar, 1948, Ohio. *Education:* College of Wooster (B.A., 1943); Case Western Reserve University (LL.B., 1948). Phi Delta Phi; Order of the Coif. *Member:* Cleveland, Ohio State and American Bar Associations. Fellow, The American College of Trust and Estate Counsel. (Regent 1985-1992). ***PRACTICE AREAS:*** Estate Planning; Probate Law. ***Email:*** jsmeltz@ssrl.com

PHILLIP ALLYN RANNEY, born Cleveland, Ohio, June 22, 1936; admitted to bar, 1961, Ohio. *Education:* Dartmouth College (B.A., 1958); Case Western Reserve University (LL.B., 1961). Member, Case Western Reserve Law Review, 1960-1961. *Member:* Cleveland, Ohio State and American Bar Associations. ***PRACTICE AREAS:*** Estate Planning; Probate Law. ***Email:*** pranney@ssrl.com

THOMAS J. LAFOND, born Chicago, Illinois, February 25, 1941; admitted to bar, 1966, Ohio. *Education:* John Carroll University (B.S., B.A., 1963); Case Western Reserve University (J.D., 1966). Delta Theta Phi. *Member:* Cleveland (President, 1991-1992), Cuyahoga County, Ohio State and American Bar Associations. ***PRACTICE AREAS:*** Domestic Relations Law. ***Email:*** tlafond@ssrl.com

JAMES D. VAIL, born Cleveland, Ohio, May 26, 1953; admitted to bar, 1979, Ohio. *Education:* Kenyon College; Case Western Reserve University (B.A., 1975; J.D., 1979). *Member:* Cleveland, Ohio State and American Bar Associations. ***REPORTED CASES:*** Spectrum Sports v. McQuillan 506 U.S. 447 (1993). ***PRACTICE AREAS:*** Corporate Law; Employment Law; Health Care Law; Succession Planning; Litigation. ***Email:*** jvail@ssrl.com

JANICE EDGEHOUSE RIETH, born Martins Ferry, Ohio, June 9, 1953; admitted to bar, 1978, Ohio. *Education:* Ohio University (B.A., 1975); Case Western Reserve University (J.D., 1978). Phi Beta Kappa. Cuyahoga County Common Pleas Court Domestic Relations Division, Legal Department and Referee, 1980-1987. *Member:* Cleveland (Member, Family Law Section), Cuyahoga County (Member, Family Law Section) and Ohio State (Member, Family Law Section) Bar Associations; American Bar Association; Ohio Academy of Trial Lawyers; Ohio Women's Bar Association (Member, Judicial Selection Committee). ***PRACTICE AREAS:*** Domestic Relations Law; Divorce; Post Divorce; Separation Agreements; Premarital Agreements. ***Email:*** jrieth@ssrl.com

JAMES P. FARMER, JR., born Cleveland, Ohio, March 24, 1951; admitted to bar, 1981, Ohio. *Education:* Ohio University (B.S., 1975); Cleveland Marshall College of Law (J.D., 1981). *Member:* Cleveland (Member, Real Estate Model Forms Committee), Ohio State and American Bar Associations. ***PRACTICE AREAS:*** Real Estate; Business Law; Estate Planning; Probate. ***Email:*** jfarmer@ssrl.com

CHARLES F. ADLER, born Indianapolis, Indiana, October 4, 1957; admitted to bar, 1983, Ohio and U.S. Tax Court; 1985, Florida. *Education:* Miami University (B.S., 1979); Cleveland-Marshall College of Law, Cleveland State University (J.D., 1983). Certified Public Accountant (inactive), Ohio, 1986. Author, "Creditor Claims Against Non-Private Property," Probate Law Journal of Ohio, Vol. 14, Issue. *Member:* Cleveland (Member, Estate Planning Council of Cleveland), Ohio State and American Bar Associations. Fellow, American College of Trust and Estate Counsel. (Certified Specialist in Estate Planning Trust and Probate Law, Ohio State Bar Association). ***PRACTICE AREAS:*** Estate Planning Law (35%); Probate Law (35%); Taxation Law (30%). ***Email:*** cadler@ssrl.com

JONATHAN L. STARK, born Cleveland, Ohio, June 27, 1967; admitted to bar, 1991, Ohio. *Education:* Boston College (B.A., 1988); Case Western Reserve (J.D., 1991). Phi Delta Phi. Case Western Reserve Law Review, Articles Editor, 1990-1991. *Member:* Cleveland and Ohio State Bar Associations. ***PRACTICE AREAS:*** Litigation; Business; Employment Law. ***Email:*** jstark@ssrl.com

KENNETH J. LAINO, born Amityville, New York, February 6, 1953; admitted to bar, 1979, New York; 1981, Ohio and Florida. *Education:* John Carroll University (A.B., summa cum laude, 1975); University of Michigan (J.D., 1978). Adjunct Faculty (Business Administration), Baldwin-Wallace College, 1985-2002. *Member:* Cleveland, Ohio State and American Bar Associations. ***PRACTICE AREAS:*** Business Law; Nonprofit Corporations; Real Estate; Estate Planning. ***Email:*** klaino@ssrl.com

J. PAUL FIDLER, born Frankfurt, Germany, March 10, 1971; admitted to bar, 1996, Ohio. *Education:* Pennsylvania State University (B.S., 1993); Ohio State University (J.D., 1996). Order of the Coif. *Member:* Cleveland, Ohio State and American Bar Associations. ***PRACTICE AREAS:*** Estate Planning; Probate; Taxation Law; Litigation. ***Email:*** jfidler@ssrl.com

---

SONJA C. RAJKI, born Cleveland, Ohio, 1976; admitted to bar, 2002, Iowa (Not admitted in Ohio). *Education:* Lawrence University (B.A., 1998); Case Western Reserve University (J.D., 2002). ***PRACTICE AREAS:*** Business Law; Health Care; Real Estate; Nonprofit and Charitable Organizations; Trusts and Estates. ***Email:*** srajki@ssrl.com

SANDRA C. LUCAS, born Parma, Ohio, May 4, 1975; admitted to bar, 2000, Ohio. *Education:* John Carroll University (B.A., summa cum laude, 1997); Case Western Reserve University (J.D., magna cum laude, 2000). *Member:* Cleveland, Ohio State and American Bar Associations. ***PRACTICE AREAS:*** Estate Planning; Probate. ***Email:*** slucas@ssrl.com

MICHAEL K. FRENCH, born Cleveland, Ohio, July 11, 1974; admitted to bar, 2001, Ohio. *Education:* Georgetown University (B.S., 1996); Cleveland-Marshall College of Law (J.D., magna cum laude, 2001). *Member:* Cleveland, Ohio State and American Bar Associations. ***PRACTICE AREAS:*** Litigation; Business Law; Real Estate. ***Email:*** mfrench@ssrl.com

ADRIENNE N. CVETKOVIC, born Youngstown, Ohio, July 6, 1979; admitted to bar, 2004, Ohio. *Education:* Hiram College (B.A., magna cum laude, 2001); Case Western Reserve University (J.D., cum laude, 2004). *Member:* Cleveland, Ohio State and American Bar Associations; Ohio Women's Bar Association. ***PRACTICE AREAS:*** Family Law; Litigation; Business Law. ***Email:*** acvetkovic@ssrl.com

OF COUNSEL

JOSEPH P. GIBBONS, born Lakewood, Ohio, July 22, 1954; admitted to bar, 1979, Ohio. *Education:* John Carroll University (B.A., cum laude, 1976); Cleveland-Marshall College of Law (J.D., 1979). Delta Theta Phi. *Member:* Cleveland (Member, Probate and Estate Planning Committee, 1979—), Cuyahoga County, Ohio State and American (Member, Litigation Section) Bar Associations. ***PRACTICE AREAS:*** Corporate Law; Estate Planning; Real Estate. ***Email:*** jgibbons@ssrl.com

REFERENCES: National City Bank; KeyBank.

SCHOTTENSTEIN ZOX & DUNN CO., LPA

USBANK CENTRE
1350 EUCLID AVENUE, SUITE 1400
CLEVELAND, OHIO 44115
Telephone: 216-621-6501
Fax: 216-621-6502
Email: info@szd.com
URL: http://www.szd.com

Columbus, Ohio Office: 250 West Street, 43215-2538. Telephone: 614-462-2700. Telecopier: 614-462-5135. Telex: 650 24 444 365.

Cincinnati, Ohio Office: Bank One Towers, 8044 Montgomery Road, Suite 630, 45236-2926. Telephone: 513-792-0792. Fax: 513-792-0803.

Business (Corporate, Banking and Lending, Real Estate/Land Use, General Tax, State and Local Tax, Employee Benefits, Estate Planning, White Collar Crime, E-Commerce, Intellectual Property/Technology Protection, International); Labor and Employment Law, Litigation, Health Law, Construction Law, Bankruptcy Law, Environmental Law, Debtor/Creditor Rights, Workers' Compensation, Municipal Law, Government Affairs.

(This Listing Continued)

FIRM PROFILE: Since its founding in 1966, Schottenstein Zox & Dunn has grown from four lawyers to over 100. The firm is dedicated to viewing the law from varied perspectives for the variety of local, regional and national clients it represents as either general counsel or in one or more of the above practice areas. Schottenstein Zox & Dunn is a complete law firm offering comprehensive services to businesses, governmental entities and individuals. Our position in the marketplace combined with the experience of our lawyers enables us to provide our clients with the responsive answers they need to succeed.

M. COLETTE GIBBONS, born Cleveland, Ohio, 1951; admitted to bar, 1976, Ohio; 1977, U.S. District Court, Southern District of Ohio. *Education:* John Carroll University (A.B., cum laude, honors program, 1973); Cleveland-Marshall College of Law, Cleveland State University (J.D., 1976). ***PRACTICE AREAS:*** Bankruptcy; Litigation. ***Email:*** cgibbons@szd.com

RAYMOND C. HEADEN, born Cleveland, Ohio, 1960; admitted to bar, 1987, Ohio. *Education:* Williams College (B.A., 1982); University of Pennsylvania Law School (J.D., 1987). *Member:* Norman S. Minor Bar Association. ***PRACTICE AREAS:*** Banking; Finance; Corporate; Public Law. ***Email:*** rheaden@szd.com

H. ALAN ROTHENBUECHER, born Akron, Ohio, 1964; admitted to bar, 1989, Ohio; 1990, Florida; 1991, District of Columbia; U.S. District Court, Northern District of Ohio, U.S. District Court, Middle District of Florida, U.S. District Court, Northern District of Illinois, U.S. Court of Appeals, Sixth Circuit and U.S. Supreme Court. *Education:* University of Michigan (A.B., 1985); Case Western Reserve University (J.D., 1989). *Member:* Akron Bar Association (Fellow); Federal Bar Association. ***LANGUAGES:*** German. ***PRACTICE AREAS:*** Intellectual Property; Litigation; Business Immigration.

ROBERT M. STEFANCIN, born Uniontown, Pennsylvania, 1965; admitted to bar, 1990, Ohio; 1991, U.S. District Court, Northern District of Ohio and U.S. Court of Appeals, Sixth Circuit; 2000, U.S. Tax Court. *Education:* Washington & Jefferson College (B.A., cum laude, 1987); Case Western Reserve University (J.D., cum laude, 1990). *Member:* Akron Bar Association. ***PRACTICE AREAS:*** Bankruptcy; Litigation. ***Email:*** rstefancin@szd.com

MATTHEW J. STOCKSLAGER, born Greenville, Ohio, April 2, 1966; admitted to bar, 1992, Ohio; U.S. District Court, Northern District of Ohio. *Education:* The Ohio State University (B.S., 1989); University of Akron (J.D., cum laude, 1992). *Member:* Akron Bar Association. ***PRACTICE AREAS:*** Corporate Law; Health Care; Real Estate. ***Email:*** mstockslager@szd.com

---

LINDA S. GEMIND, born Detroit, Michigan, April 6, 1958; admitted to bar, 1990, Florida (inactive) and U.S. District Court, Middle District of Florida; 1991, Ohio and U.S. Tax Court; 2003, Pennsylvania. *Education:* Kent State University (B.A., cum laude, 1979); University of Florida College of Law (J.D., with honors, 1989). ***LANGUAGES:*** German. ***PRACTICE AREAS:*** Immigration and Naturalization; Corporate Law; Securities. ***Email:*** lgemind@szd.com

JAY E. KRASOVEC, born Cleveland, Ohio, 1970; admitted to bar, 1998, Ohio and U.S. District Court, Northern District of Ohio; 2003, U.S. District Court, Northern District of Illinois. *Education:* University of Akron (B.A., cum laude, 1995; J.D., cum laude, 1998). ***PRACTICE AREAS:*** Intellectual Property; Litigation. ***Email:*** jkrasovec@szd.com

MEGHAN D. MAJERNIK, born Cleveland, Ohio, 1978; admitted to bar, 2002, Ohio. *Education:* Baldwin-Wallace College (B.A., summa cum laude, 1999); Cleveland-Marshall College of Law (J.D., summa cum laude, 2002). ***PRACTICE AREAS:*** Labor and Employment; Workers Compensation. ***Email:*** mmajernik@szd.com

KATHERINE G. MANGHILLIS, born Cleveland, Ohio, August 14, 1978; admitted to bar, 2004, Ohio and U.S. District Court, Northern District of Ohio; 2005, District of Columbia. *Education:* College of Wooster (B.A., 2000); Akron University Law School (J.D., 2004). ***PRACTICE AREAS:*** Bankruptcy; Litigation. ***Email:*** kmanghillis@szd.com

TAYLOR M. WESLEY, born 1980; (admission pending). *Education:* Dickinson College (B.A., 2002); Case Western Reserve University School of Law (J.D., 2005). ***PRACTICE AREAS:*** Bankruptcy. ***Email:*** twesley@szd.com

OF COUNSEL

JEFFREY A. PERLMUTER, born Cleveland, Ohio, 1949; admitted to bar, 1975, Ohio. *Education:* Tulane University (B.A., 1972); The American University (J.D., 1975); Georgetown University (LL.M., 1979). ***PRACTICE AREAS:*** Estate Planning; Employee Benefits. ***Email:*** jperlmuter@szd.com

All of the firm's attorneys are members of the Cleveland, Ohio State and American Bar Associations.

(For biographical data on all personnel, see Professional Biographies at Columbus, Ohio)

SCHUSTER & SIMMONS CO.

A LEGAL PROFESSIONAL ASSOCIATION

THE BEVELIN HOUSE
2913 CLINTON AVENUE
CLEVELAND, OHIO 44113
Telephone: 216-348-1100
FAX: 216-348-0013
Email: ss@apk.net

Business and Commercial Matters including Federal and State Litigation. White Collar Criminal Defense, Labor and Employment.

NANCY C. SCHUSTER, admitted to bar, 1968, Ohio; U.S. District Court, Northern District of Ohio; U.S. District Court, Eastern and Northern Districts of California; U.S. Court of Appeals, Sixth and Ninth Circuits. *Education:* University of Wisconsin (B.S.); Cleveland State University (J.D., cum laude, 1968). Assistant U.S. Attorney, Northern District of Ohio, 1973-1983, Chief Criminal Division, 1978-1983. Board of Editors, Ohio Lawyer Magazine, Ohio Supreme Court Rules Advisory Committee. District Court ADR Panel. *Member:* Cleveland, Ohio State (Council of Delegates, Judicial Administration and Legal Reform, Former Chair), Federal and American Bar Associations; William K. Thomas Inn of Court. ***PRACTICE AREAS:*** State and Federal Commercial Litigation; White Collar Defense; Business Transactions; Labor and Employment.

KAMI DAVIS ROWLES, born 1973; admitted to bar, 1999, Ohio; U.S. District Court, Northern District of Ohio; U.S. Court of Appeals, Sixth Circuit. *Education:* Miami University (B.A., magna cum laude, 1995); University of Cincinnati College of Law (J.D., 1999). *Member:* Cleveland and Ohio State Bar Associations.

AMI J. PATEL, admitted to bar, 2004, Ohio. *Education:* Ohio University (B.A., magna cum laude, 2001); Case Western Reserve University College of Law (J.D., 2004). *Member:* Cleveland, Ohio State and American Bar Associations.

SCHWARTZ, DOWNEY & CO., L.P.A.

GUILD HALL BUILDING
45 WEST PROSPECT, SUITE 1616
CLEVELAND, OHIO 44115
Telephone: 216-696-7100
Fax: 216-696-7210

Complex Civil and Criminal Litigation in State and Federal Courts. Mediation and Arbitration.

FIRM PROFILE: Schwartz, Downy & Co., L.P.A. represents clients in trial and on appeal in a wide range of litigation, including commercial disputes, criminal defense, professional negligence and discipline, employment disputes, serious personal injury and family law. Members of the firm also serve as arbitrators and mediators and advise clients before litigation regarding resolution of disputes.

MEMBERS OF FIRM

NIKI Z. SCHWARTZ, born Wilkinsburg, Pennsylvania, December 14, 1938; admitted to bar, 1964, Ohio, 1970, U.S. Supreme Court. *Education:* The Ohio State University (B.A., cum laude, 1960; J.D., summa cum laude, 1964). Phi Beta Kappa; Pi Sigma Alpha. Assistant Professor of Law, University of Toledo College of Law, 1965-1968. Listed In: *Best Lawyers in America* for Business Litigation and Criminal Defense; *Ohio Super Lawyers 2004:*Top Ten Super Lawyers, 2nd Highest Point Total; *Chambers USA America's Leading Business Lawyers, 2003-2004; Inside Business,* Leading Lawyers, 2003. Fellow, American College of Trial Lawyers; Master Bencher, American Inn of Court (William K. Thomas Chapter); Member, Supreme Court of Ohio Rules Advisory Committee, 1993-1998; Vice Chair, 1998; Mediator, United States District Court (N.D. Ohio); Distinguished Services Awards From National Association of Criminal Defense Lawyers, Cuyahoga County Bar Association and Ohio House of Representatives for facilitating the settlement of the 1993 Lucasville prison riot. Recipient: William K. Thomas Professionalism Award, Cleveland Bar Association, 2004; Hororee, The Ohio State University Moritz College of Law, 2004. ***REPORTED CASES:*** UNITED STATES SUPREME COURT: Hines v. Anchor Motor Freight, 424 U.S. 554 (1976); Palmer v. City of Euclid, 402 U.S. 544 (1971); Ward v. Monroeville, 409 U.S. 57 (1972); United States v. Calandra, 414 U.S. 338 (1974). ***PRACTICE AREAS:*** Business Litigation; Appellate Practice; Criminal Defense; Labor and Employment; Mediation; Arbitration; Professional Discipline; Professional Malpractice. ***Email:*** nschwartz@sdlpa.com

BRIAN P. DOWNEY, born Cleveland, Ohio, November 7, 1963; admitted to bar, 1989, Ohio, U.S. District Court, Northern District of Ohio; 1990, U.S. Court of Appeals, Sixth Circuit. *Education:* University of Dayton (B.S., cum laude, 1986); Cleveland-Marshall College of Law (J.D., magna cum laude, 1989). *Member:* Cleveland, Ohio State and Federal Bar Associations; Harold J. Burton Inn of Court, 1989-1993, 1996-1999). ***PRACTICE AREAS:*** Commercial Litigation; Real Estate; Construction Law; Labor Law; Criminal Law; Administrative Agencies. ***Email:*** bdowney@sdlpa.com

JENNIFER E. SCHWARTZ, born Toledo, Ohio, June 25, 1966; admitted to bar, 1991, Ohio; 1992, U.S. District Court, Northern District of Ohio. *Education:* The Ohio State University (B.A., 1988); Ohio State College of Law (J.D., 1991). Phi Delta Phi. Articles Editor, Journal on Dispute Resolution, 1990-1991. Law Clerk to the Honorable Thomas D. Lambros, Chief Judge, Northern District of Ohio, 1991-1992. Assistant Public Defender, Cuyahoga County Public Defender Office, 1992-1995. Member, Harold J. Burton Inn of Court, 1993-1999. *Member:* Cleveland and Ohio State Bar Associations. ***PRACTICE AREAS:*** Criminal Defense; Civil Litigation; Labor and Employment Law. ***Email:*** jschwartz@sdlpa.com

---

RALPH J. SCOLA

2628 COURTLAND BOULEVARD
CLEVELAND, OHIO 44118-4738
Telephone: 216-321-3562
Fax: 216-371-2093
Email: Ralphscola@aol.com
URL: http://www.lawyers.com/scola

Business Law, Corporate Law, Commercial Law, Civil Litigation, Health Care, Intellectual Property, International Trade, Non-Profit and Charitable Organizations, Mergers, Acquisitions and Divestitures, Trusts and Estates, Antitrust and Trade Regulation, Entertainment and the Arts.

RALPH J. SCOLA, born Philadelphia, Pennsylvania; admitted to bar, 1969, Ohio and U.S. District Court, Northern District of Ohio; 1981, Kentucky and U.S. Supreme Court; 1991, West Virginia; 1992, Pennsylvania; 1997, New York. *Education:* Drexel University (B.S., 1966); Villanova University (J.D., 1969). Sigma Rho, Blue Key. Staff Member, Vil-

(This Listing Continued)

RALPH J. SCOLA, Cleveland—Continued

lanova University Law Review, 1967-1968. Author: Casenote, "Responsibility for Maintenance and Cure Payments Established Between Co-extensively Liable Shipowners, 1967," Villanova Law Review, 1968; "Licensor Liability in U.S.," Vol. XV No. 3 Les Nouvelles, September, 1980; "Case Study: Dealing with PRC," Vol. XV, No. 3 Les Nouvelles, September, 1980; "Negotiating the Contract: Environmental Concerns," Issue No. 43 The Environmental Counselor, March 15, 1992 and in Model Agreements for Corporate Counsel, Vol. 3, March 1996; "Intellectual Property in Various Types of Business Transactions," and "Perfection of Security Interests in Intellectual Property," Asset Identification, Protection and Valuation in Colorado, National Business Institute, Inc., November 1997; "Introduction to Public Charities," "Public Charities in Ohio," "Protecting Tax-Exempt and Public Charity Status," and "Avoiding Intermediate Sanctions," Ohio Public Charities, Lorman Education Services, June 1999; "Protection and Liabilities of Officers, Directors and Employees of Religious Organizations in Ohio; Ohio Filing Requirements," Religious Corporation Issues, Lorman Education Services, October 2002;. *Member:* Ohio State, New York State and Kentucky Bar Associations; West Virginia State Bar.

REPRESENTATIVE CLIENTS: The Consolidated Core Company; The Consolidated Metals Company, Inc.; The Fasola Family Racing Stables, LLC; The Handel Company; HLR Systems, Inc.; The Internal Medicine Foundation of St. Luke's Medical Center, Inc.; The St. Luke's Surgical Foundation, Inc.; Strike Force Sales & Supply, Inc.; The Surgical Foundation of St. Luke's Medical Center, Inc.

SEELEY, SAVIDGE & EBERT, CO.

A LEGAL PROFESSIONAL ASSOCIATION

Established in 1978

FIFTH THIRD CENTER - SUITE 800
600 SUPERIOR AVENUE, EAST
CLEVELAND, OHIO 44114-2655
Telephone: 216-566-8200
Fax-Telecopier: 216-566-0213
URL: http://www.sse-law.com

Civil Trial /Corporate Commercial Law, Securities, Employment, Labor, Health Care, Real Estate, Environmental, Litigation, Appellate Practice, Insurance Defense, Construction, Municipal, Estate Planning.

FIRM PROFILE: The firm provides specialty representation to Fortune 500 Companies and full service representation to small and mid-market business and institutional clients throughout Ohio. Strongly business-oriented, the firm is structured into basic divisions - business/corporate, litigation, appellate practice, real estate, estate planning. In addition to named partners, the staff consists of: Eric Baker, Pat Frutig, John Norton, David Reed, Glenn Seeley, Matthew Seeley and Matthew Shady.

GREGORY D. SEELEY, born Cleveland, Ohio; admitted to bar, 1972, Ohio; 1986, Wisconsin; 1989, Pennsylvania. *Education:* Kenyon College (B.A., 1969); American University (J.D., 1972). Member, Ohio Division of Securities Enforcement Advisory Board, 1988—. *Member:* Cleveland (Chairman, Corporation, Business and Banking Section, 1985-1987; Member, Certified Grievance Committee, 1989-1990), Ohio State (Member, Committee on: Oil and Gas, 1974-1981; Health Care, 1987-1989; Corporation Law, 1988—), Ohio Greater Cleveland and, American Bar Associations; American Health Lawyers Association; Public Investors Arbitration Bar Association. ***PRACTICE AREAS:*** Business Law; Securities Law; Mergers and Acquisitions Law; Health Care Law. ***Email:*** GDSeeley@sse-law.com

KEITH A. SAVIDGE, born London, England; admitted to bar, 1972, Ohio; 1973, U.S. District Court, Northern District of Ohio; 1985, U.S. Court of Appeals, Sixth Circuit; 1991, U.S. District Court, Eastern District of Michigan; 1990, U.S. Court of Appeals, Fourth Circuit; 1991, U.S. District Court, Eastern District of Michigan. *Education:* Case Western Reserve University (B.A., 1967); Cleveland-Marshall College of Law (J.D., cum laude, 1972). Delta Theta Phi. *Member:* Cleveland, Ohio State and American (Member, Sections on: Litigation; Employment Litigation) Bar Associations; The Defense Research Institute; The Association of Trial Lawyers of America; Cleveland Association of Civil Trial Attorneys. [Col. Ret., JAGC, Ohio Army National Guard]. ***PRACTICE AREAS:*** Appellate Practice; Construction Law; Employment Law; Insurance Defense; Workers Compensation; Litigation; Business Litigation; Occupational Safety & Health; Products Liability; Toxic Torts; Environmental Law. ***Email:*** KASavidge@sse-law.com

GARY A. EBERT, born Sandusky, Ohio; admitted to bar, 1978, Ohio and U.S. District Court, Northern District of Ohio. *Education:* Kent State University; Ashland University (B.S., 1972); Cleveland-Marshall College of Law (J.D., 1975). Phi Delta Theta. Councilman, 1982-1986 and Law Director, 1986—, City of Bay Village. *Member:* Ohio State Bar Association; Ohio Municipal League; Cuyahoga County Law Directors Association; International Municipal Lawyers Association. ***PRACTICE AREAS:*** Corporate; Municipal; Estate Planning; Probate; Business; Construction Law; Education and School Law; Environmental Law; Trusts; Real Estate Law; Zoning and Planning. ***Email:*** GAEbert@sse-law.com

ANDREW D. BEMER, born Cleveland, Ohio; admitted to bar, 1973, Ohio. *Education:* Ohio State University (B.A., 1970); Cleveland-Marshall College of Law (J.D., 1973). ***PRACTICE AREAS:*** Defense Litigation; Employment Law; Municipal Law; Domestic Relations. ***Email:*** adbemer@sse-law.com

MARY DAVIS, born Oak Park, Illinois; admitted to bar, 1988, Ohio. *Education:* Northeastern Illinois University (B.A., cum laude, 1980) Case Western Reserve University (J.D., 1988). ***PRACTICE AREAS:*** Real Estate; Environmental Law. ***Email:*** mdavis@sse-law.com

DOUGLAS P. WHIPPLE, born Sharon, Pennsylvania; admitted to bar, 1980, Ohio; 1986, Pennsylvania. *Education:* Baldwin-Wallace College (B.A., 1974); Cleveland-Marshall College of Law (J.D., cum laude, 1980). ***PRACTICE AREAS:*** Civil Litigation; Torts; Employment Law. ***Email:*** dpwhipple@sse-law.com

(This Listing Continued)

REPRESENTATIVE CLIENTS: Bay Mechanical & Electrical Corporation; Ben Venue Laboratories; City of Bay Village; Community Health Partners; California Concepts; Countywide Petroleum; Diamond Products; Gould Electronics, Inc.; Heinz, U.S.A.; HWC Realty; In-Bay Put Township Port Authority; Kemper Insurance; King James Medical Laboratory; Liberty Mutual Insurance; North American Benefits Network; North American Specialty Insurance Co.; Nylonge Corporation; Sears, Roebuck and Co.; Union Partners.

SELKER & ASSOCIATES LLC

34305 SOLON ROAD, SUITE 100
CLEVELAND, OHIO 44139
Telephone: 440-248-7906
FAX: 440-248-8861
Email: eselker@mrrlaw.com

General Civil Practice in all State and Federal Courts, Real Estate, Civil Litigation, Business Law.

MEMBER OF FIRM

EUGENE I. SELKER, born Cleveland, Ohio, June 16, 1929; admitted to bar, 1953, Ohio. *Education:* Ohio University; Western Reserve University (B.B.A., 1950; LL.B., 1953). Tau Epsilon Rho; Phi Beta Kappa. Member, Board of Editors, Western Reserve Law Review, 1952-1953. Author: "Lottery: Self Executing Constitutional Prohibition," Western Reserve Law Review, 1952; "Rights of Purchaser in Defective House-Warranty," Western Reserve Law Review, 1953. Licensed Real Estate Broker, Ohio, 1954-1980. Member: Cleveland Steering Committee for Governor's Housing and Community Development Advisory Commission, 1972-1973; State of Ohio Board of Examiners, Nursing Home Administrators, 1974-1975. President, Plan Action Tomorrow's Housing Path Association, 1972-1973. Founding Trustee, Cuyahoga Plan (Fair Housing). Law Lecturer, Case Western Reserve University, Legal Aspects of Construction, 1977-1989. Lecturer, Cleveland Bar Association Real Estate Institute, 1983, 1985, 1990, 1991, 1992 and 1997 including subjects of "Negotiating Commercial Occupancy Leases,"; "Real Estate Litigation, Preparation, Trial,"; "Trial of Real Property Actions,"; Co-Chairman, 1986. *Member:* Cleveland (Member, Real Estate Section) and Ohio State Bar Associations. ***LANGUAGES:*** Spanish. ***REPORTED CASES:*** Whitworth Bros. Storage Co. v. Central States, Southeast & Southwest Areas Pension Fund, 982 F.2d 1006; Tilberry v. Body, 24 Ohio St. 3d 117; Abbott v. City of Parma, 112 Ohio App. 3d 570; Hoyt v. Gordon & Assocs., 104 Ohio App. 3d 598. ***PRACTICE AREAS:*** Civil Litigation; Real Estate Litigation; Construction Law; Legal Malpractice; Professional Malpractice; Eminent Domain; Zoning, Planning and Land Use; Business Law. ***Email:*** eselker@mrrlaw.com

REPRESENTATIVE CLIENTS: Amsdell Construction and Amsdell Companies; Ressler Contracting; Gordon & Associates; On The Greens Development Co.

LAW OFFICES OF KENNETH F. SEMINATORE

THE SUPERIOR BUILDING, SUITE 1715
815 SUPERIOR AVENUE, N.E.
CLEVELAND, OHIO 44114
Telephone: 216-344-3838
Fax: 216-344-0515

General Practice, Corporate and Commercial Transactions, Civil Litigation, Health Care and Insurance.

KENNETH F. SEMINATORE, born Cleveland, Ohio, August 17, 1947; admitted to bar, 1971, Ohio; 1976, U.S. District Court, Northern District of Ohio; 1984, U.S. Tax Court; 1985, U.S. Court of Appeals, Sixth Circuit; 1987, District of Columbia; 1988, U.S. Court of Appeals for the District of Columbia Circuit; 1991, West Virginia and U.S. District Court, District of West Virginia; 1992, U.S. Court of Appeals, Fourth Circuit. *Education:* Case Western Reserve University (A.B., magna cum laude, 1968); Harvard University (J.D., cum laude, 1971). Phi Beta Kappa. Woodrow Wilson Fellow. Member, Board of Trustees, Case Western Reserve University, 1972-1974. Member, 1973-1974, Chairman, 1974, Cuyahoga County Board of Mental Retardation. Member, Board of Trustees, Cuyahoga County Hospital Foundation, 1976-1977. Special Counsel to Ohio Attorney General, 1976-1997. Member, Cleveland Board of Education, 1980-1983. Member, Board of Trustees, Citizens League of Greater Cleveland, 1991-1997. *Member:* Cleveland, Cuyahoga County (Chairman, Corporate and Business Law Committee, 1978-1979) and Ohio State Bar Associations; National Association of Bond Lawyers.

SHAPERO & GREEN, LLC

Established in 1971

SIGNATURE SQUARE II, SUITE 220
25101 CHAGRIN BOULEVARD
CLEVELAND, OHIO 44122-5656
Telephone: 216-831-5100
Toll Free 1-877-404-6300
Fax: 216-831-9467

Personal Injury, Medical Malpractice, General Civil, Business Litigation, Corporate Law, Banking, Real Estate, Domestic Relations, Probate.

FIRM PROFILE: Since 1971, the firm has been committed to prompt and effective legal representation with the goal of maintaining long-term relationships with it's clients in the areas of personal injury, medical malpractice, business and commercial litigation, corporate law, banking, real estate, domestic relations and probate.

MEMBERS OF FIRM

MICHAEL I. SHAPERO, admitted to bar, 1971, Ohio; U.S. District Court, Northern District of Ohio and U.S. Supreme Court. *Education:* The Ohio State University (B.S.,

(This Listing Continued)

1966); Cleveland Marshall College of Law (J.D., 1970). Seminar Instructor, Medical Malpractice and Civil Trial Litigation, 1990-1991. Internal Revenue Officer and Special Procedures Advisor, 1966-1971. Member, Homeless Committee, 1999—. *Member:* American Bar Association; Ohio State Bar Association; Cuyahoga County Bar Association; Ohio Academy of Trial Lawyers; Cleveland (Member, Board of Trustees, 1982-1985; Professional Ethics Committee, 1972-1973; Grievance Committee, 1982-1988; Liaison to Committee, 1973-1981, 1987-1991) Bar Association. ***PRACTICE AREAS:*** Personal Injury; Medical Malpractice; General Civil.

BRIAN J. GREEN, born Cleveland, Ohio, June 8, 1969; admitted to bar, 1994, Ohio; 1995, U.S. District Court, Northern and Eastern Districts of Ohio; 1997, U.S. Court of Appeals, Third and Sixth Circuits. *Education:* Indiana University (B.S., Finance, Real Estate, 1991); Washington University (J.D., 1994). Member, Washington University Regional Moot Court Team, Moot Court Finalist. *Member:* Cleveland and Ohio State Bar Associations. ***PRACTICE AREAS:*** Business Litigation; Corporate; Banking; Real Estate. ***Email:*** bgreen@shaperolaw.com

---

DAVID S. MICHEL, admitted to bar, 1984, Ohio and U.S. District Court, Northern District of Ohio. *Education:* University of Michigan (B.A., 1980); Case Western Reserve (J.D., 1983). Phi Delta Phi. *Member:* Cuyahoga County and Cleveland Bar Associations. ***PRACTICE AREAS:*** Personal Injury; Medical Malpractice; Domestic Relations; Probate.

JENNIFER STAKES, born Cleveland, Ohio, July 25, 1975; admitted to bar, 2002, Ohio. *Education:* Ursuline College (B.A., Psychology, cum laude, 1997); Akron University Law School (J.D., 2001). *Member:* Ohio State Bar Association. ***PRACTICE AREAS:*** Business Law; Commercial Law; Litigation. ***Email:*** jstakes@shaperolaw.com

---

SHAPERO & ROLOFF CO., L.P.A.

1350 EUCLID AVENUE, SUITE 1550
CLEVELAND, OHIO 44115-1828
Telephone: 216-781-1700; 800-321-9199
Fax: 216-781-1972
Email: nshapero@shaperoroloff.com
URL: http://www.shaperoroloff.com

Plaintiffs Personal Injury, Wrongful Death, Medical Malpractice, Nursing Home Negligence, Products Liability, FELA, Premises Liability, Class Actions, Employment Law, Employment Discrimination, Wrongful Discharge, Sexual Harassment, Civil Rights, Union Labor Law.

FIRM PROFILE: The law firm of Shapero & Roloff Co., L.P.A., is dedicated to providing services to individuals and labor unions in the areas of personal injury, medical malpractice, nursing home negligence, wrongful death, product liability, labor, employment, civil rights, and railroad employment injuries (FELA). Our highly skilled trial attorneys are well known and respected throughout Ohio and beyond.

NEAL E. SHAPERO, born Lorain, Ohio, December 22, 1958; admitted to bar, 1984, Ohio; 1985, New Jersey; 1986, U.S. District Court, Northern District of Ohio and U.S. Court of Appeals, Sixth Circuit. *Education:* Kent State University (B.S., 1981); University of Akron (J.D., 1984). Assistant City Prosecutor, 1985-1986 and Assistant Director of Law, 1986-1987, City of Akron. CLE Lecturer: Fundamentals of Direct Examination, 1989; Municipal Liability, 1989; FDA and MDA Requirements for Medical Device Litigation, 1990; Premises Liability, 1997-1998; Trying the Soft Tissue Injury Case, 1998; How to Litigate Your First Civil Trial in Ohio, 2000 and 2003; Cross-Examination of the Defense Medical Examiner, 2000, Nursing Home Negligence 2001 & 2003, Orthopedic Issues in Injury Cases 2004 and Taking Your First Deposition 2004. *Member:* Cleveland, Lorain, Cuyahoga County and Ohio State Bar Associations; The Association of Trial Lawyers of America (Member, Sections on: Tort; Railroad Law); Ohio Academy of Trial Lawyers; Cleveland Academy of Trial Lawyers (Director, 1990-1993). ***PRACTICE AREAS:*** Wrongful Death; Medical Malpractice; Nursing Home Liability; Products Liability; Personal Injury; Civil Rights. ***Email:*** nshapero@shaperoroloff.com

---

ABBY K. LILL, born Middleburg Heights, Ohio, July 16, 1979; admitted to bar, 2004, Ohio. *Education:* Case Western Reserve University (B.A., 2001); Cleveland-Marshall College of Law (J.D., cum laude, 2004). Order of Barristers. *Member:* Cuyahoga County, Cleveland and Ohio State Bar Associations; The Association of Trial Lawyers of America; The Ohio Academy of Trial Lawyers. ***PRACTICE AREAS:*** Wrongful Death; Medical Malpractice; Nursing Home Liability; Products Liability; Personal Injury; Civil Rights. ***Email:*** alill@shaperoroloff.com

---

SHAPIRO & FELTY, L.L.P.

1500 WEST THIRD STREET, SUITE 400
CLEVELAND, OHIO 44113-9873
Telephone: 216-621-1530
Fax: 216-621-7646
Email: shapfelt@logs.com

Foreclosure, Bankruptcy, Landlord and Tenant, Real Estate Litigation, Closing and Title Services, Creditor and Collection Services, Probate and Estate Planning, Business and Corporate Law.

FIRM PROFILE: The Law Offices of Shapiro & Felty were founded in 1987 by Gerald M. Shapiro and Kriss D. Felty with the goal of providing clients a broad range of legal services related to real estate and creditor law. Since then, the firm has enjoyed continuous growth to its present status as one of Ohio's premiere real estate firms representing national mortgage lenders and servicers.

(This Listing Continued)

This growth and experience has enabled Shapiro & Felty to expand into the areas of creditor and collection services, probate and estate planning, as well as small business and corporate law while assuring its clients of high quality representation, consistent performance together with comprehensive reporting.

GERALD M. SHAPIRO, born Chicago, Illinois, July 14, 1943; admitted to bar, 1969, Illinois, Florida and U.S. District Court, Northern District of Illinois (Not admitted in Ohio). *Education:* Northwestern University (B.S., 1965); DePaul University (J.D., 1969). Co-founder of LOGS Legal Network. *Member:* Illinois State and American Bar Associations; The Florida Bar; Mortgage Bankers Association; The National Council of Savings Institutions. (Also Member, Shapiro & Burson, Fairfax, Virginia). ***PRACTICE AREAS:*** Foreclosures; Bankruptcy; Real Estate; Real Estate Acquisitions; Real Estate Development; Real Estate Finance.

KRISS D. FELTY, born Cleveland, Ohio, May 5, 1954; admitted to bar, 1983, Ohio; U.S. District Court, Northern District of Ohio; 1984, U.S. Court of Appeals, Sixth Circuit; 1985, Florida; 1986, U.S. Supreme Court; 1988, Texas; 1989, Wisconsin. *Education:* Case Western Reserve University (B.A., Psychology, 1976); University of Akron School of Law (J.D., 1983). Licensed Title Insurance Agent, First American Title Insurance Co. and Guardian Title Insurance Company. Foreclosure Commissioner, Department of Housing and Urban Development. President, First Financial Title Agency of Ohio, Inc. *Member:* Greater Cleveland, Cuyahoga County, Ohio State and American Bar Associations; State Bar of Texas; Mortgage Bankers Association of Greater Cleveland; Mortgage Bankers Association of Ohio. ***PRACTICE AREAS:*** Foreclosures; Bankruptcy; Real Estate Litigation; Probate; Corporate law.

DAVID S. KREISMAN, admitted to bar, 1963, Illinois; U.S. District Court, Northern District of Illinois; 1964, U.S. Court of Appeals (Not admitted in Ohio). *Education:* University of Chicago (B.A., 1960; J.D., 1963). Co-Founder, LOGS Legal Network. Director, National Operations, LOGS Legal Network Offices. *Member:* American Bar Association; Chicago Council of Lawyers; National Association of Chapter 13 Trustees; Illinois Mortgage Bankers Association; Mortgage Bankers Association of America. ***PRACTICE AREAS:*** Real Estate Litigation; Civil Litigation; Foreclosures; Fire Loss Litigation; Condemnation.

MARK R. LEMBRIGHT, born December 11, 1962; admitted to bar, 1989, Ohio and U.S. District Court, Northern and Southern Districts of Ohio; U.S. Court of Appeals, Sixth Circuit. *Education:* Ohio University (B.A., Political Science, 1984); University of Akron School of Law (J.D., 1989). *Member:* Cleveland, Cuyahoga County and Ohio State Bar Associations. ***PRACTICE AREAS:*** Foreclosures; Landlord and Tenant Law; Bankruptcy; Chapter 7; Chapter 11; Chapter 13.

CHRISTOPHER M. KOVACH, born March 23, 1970; admitted to bar, 1995, Ohio; 1996, U.S. District Court, Northern District of Ohio; 2002, U.S. District Court, Southern District of Ohio. *Education:* Ohio University (B.A., Political Science, 1992); Case Western Reserve University (J.D., 1995). *Member:* Ohio State Bar Association. ***PRACTICE AREAS:*** Bankruptcy; Foreclosures; Civil Litigation.

PHILLIP C. BARRAGATE, born Cleveland, Ohio, October 12, 1966; admitted to bar, 1992, Illinois; 1994, Ohio. *Education:* University of Vermont (B.A., 1989); John Marshall Law School (J.D., 1992). ***PRACTICE AREAS:*** Real Estate.

DANIEL SPIRKO, born Lackawanna, New York, March 14, 1972; admitted to bar, 2000, Ohio. *Education:* The Ohio State University (B.S.B.A., 1995); Cleveland-Marshall College of Law (J.D., 2000). ***PRACTICE AREAS:*** Real Estate.

CHRISTIAN ERIC NIKLAS, born Cleveland, Ohio, August 21, 1971; admitted to bar, 1996, Ohio; 1997, U.S. District Court, Northern District of Ohio; 2002, U.S. District Court, Southern District of Ohio. *Education:* Kent State University (B.A., 1993); University of Toledo (J.D., 1996). *Member:* Ohio State Bar Association; American Bankruptcy Institute. ***PRACTICE AREAS:*** Bankruptcy..

ROSS P. MILLER, born August 22, 1976; admitted to bar, 2001, Ohio; 2002, U.S. District Court, Northern District of Ohio. *Education:* Boston University (B.A., 1998); Case Western Reserve University (J.D., 2001). *Member:* Cleveland and Ohio State Bar Associations. ***PRACTICE AREAS:*** Foreclosures.

ROBERT J. LACIVITA, born Youngstown, Ohio, April 29, 1977; admitted to bar, 2002, Ohio. *Education:* Miami University (B.S., Business Administration, 1999); Cleveland-Marshall College of Law (J.D., 2002). *Member:* Cleveland, Cuyahoga County and Ohio State Bar Associations. ***PRACTICE AREAS:*** Real Estate; Foreclosures; Litigation; Creditors Rights.

JOHN A. POLINKO, born Cleveland, Ohio, October 30, 1972; admitted to bar, 2001, Ohio and U.S. District Court, Northern District of Ohio; 2002, U.S. District Court, Northern and Southern Districts of Ohio; 2004, U.S. Court of Appeals, Sixth Circuit. *Education:* The Ohio State University (B.A., 1996); University of Akron School of Law (J.D., 2001). *Member:* Cleveland and Ohio State Bar Associations. ***PRACTICE AREAS:*** Bankruptcy; Foreclosures; Real Estate Litigation.

RICHARD J. LACIVITA, born Youngstown, Ohio, March 29, 1975; admitted to bar, 2000, Ohio; 2003, U.S. District Court, Southern District of Ohio. *Education:* Miami University (B.S., Business, 1997); The Ohio State University (J.D., 2000). ***PRACTICE AREAS:*** Real Estate; Foreclosures; Real Estate Litigation; Business Litigation; Commercial Litigation; Creditors Rights.

ANTONIO J. SCARLATO, born Toledo, Ohio, May 31, 1974; admitted to bar, 2001, Ohio. *Education:* University of Toledo (B.S., 1997; J.D., 2000). *Member:* Ohio State, Cleveland and Toledo Bar Associations. ***PRACTICE AREAS:*** Real Estate; Foreclosures; Real Estate Title; Real Estate Litigation; Creditors Rights.

JENNIFER R. FRANKS, born Youngstown, Ohio, November 18, 1976; admitted to bar, 2002, Ohio. *Education:* St. Mary's College (B.A., History, 1999); University of Akron School of Law (J.D., 2002). ***PRACTICE AREAS:*** Real Estate Title.

LOUIS P. ALEXANDER, JR., born Youngstown, Ohio, April 11, 1977; admitted to bar, 2003, Ohio; U.S. District Court, Northern and Southern Districts of Ohio. *Education:*

(This Listing Continued)

SHAPIRO & FELTY, L.L.P., Cleveland—Continued

Miami University (B.S. Business Administration, 2000); Cleveland State University (M.B.A., 2003); Cleveland-Marshall College of Law (J.D., 2003). *Member:* Cuyahoga County, Cleveland, Columbus, American and Ohio State Bar Associations. ***PRACTICE AREAS:*** Bankruptcy; Real Estate; Creditors Rights.

BRIAN R. GUTKOSKI, born Cleveland, Ohio, July 7, 1978; admitted to bar, 2003, Ohio, U.S. District Court, Northern District of Ohio; 2004, Florida and U.S. District Court, Southern District of Ohio. *Education:* Baldwin-Wallace College (B.A., Business Administration, 2000); Cleveland-Marshall College of Law (J.D., 2003). *Member:* Cuyahoga County, Ohio State and American Bar Associations; The Florida Bar. ***PRACTICE AREAS:*** Bankruptcy; Real Estate; Creditors Rights.

MARTHA R. SPANER, admitted to bar, 2002, Ohio. *Education:* Ohio University (B.S., Telecommunications, 1988); Cleveland-Marshall College of Law (J.D., 2001); University of Findlay (M.S., Environmental Management, 1995).

CHRIS E. MANOLIS, born October 10, 1973; admitted to bar, 2003, Ohio. *Education:* Ohio State University (B.A., 1996); University of Toledo (JD., 2000). ***PRACTICE AREAS:*** Foreclosures.

DAVID O. SIMON

1370 ONTARIO STREET, SUITE 450
CLEVELAND, OHIO 44113-1744
Telephone: 216-621-6201
Telecopier: 216-575-1405
Email: dsimon@epiqtrustee.com

Bankruptcy and Commercial Law.

DAVID O. SIMON, born Youngstown, Ohio, October 2, 1949; admitted to bar, 1975, Ohio, U.S. District Court, Northern District of Ohio, U.S. Court of Appeals, Sixth Circuit and United States Supreme Court. *Education:* Bowling Green State University (B.S.B.A., 1971); Cleveland Marshall College of Law (J.D., 1975). Author: "The Trustee - Rights, Powers and Interactions with Debtors and Creditors," Ohio CLE Institute Basics of Bankruptcy, 1991; "Current Problems and Pitfalls - Preferences and Fraudulent Conveyances," Cuyahoga County Bar Association, 1991; "Clearing the Bankruptcy Cloud on Title; The Automatic Stay and Abandonment," Ohio Land Title Association, Title Topics, 1997; "Receivership Acquisitions," Ohio CLE Institute, 1998; "The Impact of Bankruptcy on Dissolution of Marriage," National Business Institute, 1998. Member, Panel of Trustees, U.S. Bankruptcy Court, 1979—. *Member:* Cleveland (Past Chair, Bankruptcy and Commercial Law Section) and Ohio State Bar Associations. ***PRACTICE AREAS:*** Bankruptcy Law; Commercial Law.

THE SIMON LAW FIRM, LLP

SUITE 1717 PENTON MEDIA BUILDING
1300 EAST NINTH STREET
CLEVELAND, OHIO 44114-1503
Telephone: 216-575-1002
Fax: 216-575-1556
Email: mail@esimonlaw.com

Employment Law, Discrimination, Harassment, Civil Litigation.

STEVEN D. BELL, born Akron, Ohio, February 11, 1953; admitted to bar, 1979, Ohio; 1989, District of Columbia; U.S. Supreme Court; U.S. Court of Appeals, Third, Sixth, District of Columbia and Federal Circuits; U.S. District Court, Northern and Southern Districts of Ohio and U.S. District Court, Eastern District of Michigan. *Education:* University of Notre Dame (B.A., 1975); University of Akron (J.D., 1979). Assistant Director of Law, Akron, 1980-1984. Chief Trial Attorney, 1982-1984. Assistant U.S. Attorney, Cleveland, 1984-1988. Chief, Civil Division, Cleveland, Ohio, 1986-1988. Member, 1986-1988, Ohio Supreme Court Commission, Chair, 1995-1996, Continuing Legal Education. Adjunct Faculty, Cleveland-Marshall College of Law, 1984-2002. *Member:* Ohio State and American Bar Associations; The Ohio Academy of Trial Lawyers. ***PRACTICE AREAS:*** Employee Rights; Discrimination; Class Actions; White Collar Criminal Defense. ***Email:*** sbell@esimonlaw.com

ELLEN S. SIMON, born Cleveland, Ohio, January 10, 1952; admitted to bar, 1979, Massachusetts, U.S. District Court, District of Massachusetts and U.S. Court of Appeals, First Circuit; 1981, Ohio, U.S. District Court, Northern District of Ohio and U.S. Court of Appeals, Sixth Circuit; U.S. Supreme Court. *Education:* Brandeis University (B.A., cum laude, 1974); Suffolk University (J.D., 1979). Law Clerk to Hon. Ann Aldrich, U.S. District Court, Northern District of Ohio, 1984. Professor, Cleveland Marshall College of Law, 1983-1984, 1996-1997. Member, Board of Directors, 1987—, President, 1990-1991, American Civil Liberties Union of Cleveland. Life Delegate to Judicial Conference of the Eighth Judicial District of Ohio. *Member:* Cleveland, Ohio State and American Bar Associations; Ohio Academy of Trial Lawyers; The Association of Trial Lawyers of America (Chair, Employment Rights Section, 1991-1993; Section Leaders Council, 1992-1994); National Employment Lawyers Association. Fellow, International Society of Barristers; American Board of Trial Advocates. ***PRACTICE AREAS:*** Employee Rights; Discrimination; Harassment; Negligence; Medical Malpractice. ***Email:*** mail@esimonlaw.com

---

ANN MARIE AHERN, born Dayton, Ohio, February 16, 1972; admitted to bar, 1998, Ohio and U.S. District Court, Northern District of Ohio. *Education:* University of Dayton (B.A., 1994); Cleveland Marshall College of Law (J.D., cum laude, 1998). Editor, 1997-1998 and Member, 1996-1997, Cleveland State Law Review. *Member:* Cleveland, Ohio State and American Bar Associations; Ohio Employment Lawyers Association; Association

(This Listing Continued)

of Trial Lawyers of America (Treasurer, Employment Rights Section, 2001-2002). ***PRACTICE AREAS:*** Employee Rights; Discrimination; Harassment. ***Email:*** amahern@esimonlaw.com

MATTHEW J. McCRACKEN, born Cleveland, Ohio, March 28, 1977; admitted to bar, 2004, Ohio. *Education:* Vassar College (B.S., 1999); Case Western Reserve University School of Law (J.D., cum laude, 2004). Notes Editor, 2003-2004 and Associate Editor, 2002-2003, Case Western Reserve University Journal of International Law. Author: "Abusing Self-Determination and Democracy: How the TPLF is Looting Ethiopia," 36 Case W. Res. J. Intl. L. 1, 2004. *Member:* Cleveland, Ohio State and American Bar Associations. ***PRACTICE AREAS:*** Employee Rights; Discrimination; Class Actions; White Collar Criminal Defense. ***Email:*** mamccracken@esimonlaw.com

SINDELL, LOWE & GUIDUBALDI

CLEVELAND, OHIO

(See Lowe Eklund Wakefield & Mulvihill Co., L.P.A.)

SINGERMAN, MILLS, DESBERG & KAUNTZ

Established in 2001
3401 ENTERPRISE PARKWAY, SUITE 200
CLEVELAND, OHIO 44122
Telephone: 216-292-5807
Fax: 216-292-5867
URL: http://www.smdklaw.com

Banks and Banking, Secured Lending, Corporate Law, Real Estate, Bankruptcy, Taxation, Limited Liability Company Law, Partnership Law, Estate Planning, Probate, Trusts and Estates, Litigation, Commercial Law, Construction Law.

FIRM PROFILE: Singerman, Mills, Desberg & Kauntz was formed in January, 2001, by Paul J. Singerman, William M. Mills, Gary S. Desberg, and Edmund G. Kauntz. Prior to forming the firm, the principals worked together for nearly 16 years, both at a small Cleveland, Ohio law firm and at a large international law firm headquartered in Cleveland, Ohio. The firm's sophisticated boutique practice concentrates on corporate matters, banking, real estate, taxation, estate planning, estate administration and commercial litigation. The firm has a diverse client base. Clients include: financial institutions; real estate investors and developers; retail and wholesale merchants and distributors; and a broad spectrum of privately-held corporations, entrepreneurial enterprises, professional corporations and individuals.

PAUL J. SINGERMAN, born Cleveland, Ohio, 1958; admitted to bar, 1983, Ohio. *Education:* Miami University; Case Western Reserve University (B.A., 1980); Case Western Reserve University School of Law (J.D., 1983). Order of the Coif. Trustee, Cleveland National Air Show, 1993-2002. Temple Israel Ner Tamid, Trustee, 1990— and President, 2001-2003. Listed in Ohio Super Lawyers, 2004 and 2005. *Member:* Cleveland (Member, Sections on: Corporation, Banking and Business; Bankruptcy and Commercial Law), Ohio State and American (Member, Sections on: Business Law; Real Property, Probate and Trust Law) Bar Associations. ***PRACTICE AREAS:*** Banks and Banking; Secured Lending; Creditors Rights; Commercial Real Estate; Real Estate Law; Business Law. ***Email:*** psingerman@smdklaw.com

WILLIAM M. MILLS, born Cleveland, Ohio, 1950; admitted to bar, 1975, Ohio. *Education:* Dartmouth College (A.B., magna cum laude, 1972); Cornell University (J.D., 1975). Phi Beta Kappa. *Member:* Cleveland (Member, Estate Planning, Probate and Trust Law Section), Ohio State (Member, Probate and Trust Law Section) and American (Member, Sections on: Taxation and Real Property, Probate and Trust Law) Bar Associations; Estate Planning Council of Cleveland. ***PRACTICE AREAS:*** Federal Income Tax; Estate and Gift Taxation; Estate Planning; Probate; Professional Corporations. ***Email:*** wmills@smdklaw.com

GARY S. DESBERG, born Cleveland, Ohio, 1960; admitted to bar, 1985, Ohio; 1986, Florida. *Education:* University of Michigan (A.B., 1982); Case Western Reserve University (J.D., cum laude, 1985). *Member:* Cleveland (Member, Sections on: Corporation, Banking and Business Law; Real Estate Law; Co-Chairman, Real Estate Law Institute, 1996-1997), Ohio State and American (Member, Sections on: Business Law; Real Property, Probate and Trust) Bar Associations. ***PRACTICE AREAS:*** Commercial Real Estate; Leases and Leasing; Corporate Law; Secured Lending; Finance. ***Email:*** GDesberg@smdklaw.com

EDMUND G. KAUNTZ, born Cleveland, Ohio, 1962; admitted to bar, 1987, Ohio. *Education:* Case Western Reserve University (B.S., summa cum laude, 1984; J.D., magna cum laude, 1987). Beta Alpha Psi; Order of the Coif. *Member:* Cleveland (Member, Estate Planning, Probate and Trust Law Section), Ohio State (Member, Probate and Trust Law Section) and American (Member, Sections on: Taxation and Real Property, Probate and Trust) Bar Associations; Estate Planning Council of Cleveland. ***PRACTICE AREAS:*** Partnership Law; Limited Liability Company Law; Taxation; Probate; Trusts and Estates. ***Email:*** EKauntz@smdklaw.com

TROY R. BROWN, born Racine, Wisconsin, October 24, 1944; admitted to bar, 1972, Wisconsin and Ohio. *Education:* University of Wisconsin at Milwaukee (B.S., Senior Honors, 1968); University of Wisconsin at Madison (J.D., magna cum laude, 1972). Listed in: Who's Who in Executives and Professionals, Edition 2003-2004; Best Lawyers in America, Edition 2005-2006. Speaker: Project Development Ground Leases, ICSU US Law Conference; Managing Multi Property, Multi State Property Transactions, ICSC US Law Conference, 1997; Challenges and Issues in Shopping Center Redevelopment and Expansion, ICSC Midwest Symposia, 1995; REITS: Their Use and Formation, Columbus Bar Association Real Estate Institute, 1995. *Member:* Cleveland (Member: Real Estate Law), Ohio State (Member: Real Property Law; Corporate Counsel), Wisconsin and American (Member: Real Property, Probate and Trust Law) Bar Associations; International Council of Shopping Centers; Urban Land Institute; First American Title Insurance Advisory Board. ***PRACTICE AREAS:*** Commercial Real Estate; Secured Lending; Real Estate Law; Leases and Leasing; Construction Law; Financing. ***Email:*** tbrown@smdklaw.com

(This Listing Continued)

JEFFREY A. GORSKI, born Cleveland, Ohio, 1968; admitted to bar, 1994, Ohio. *Education:* Marquette University (B.A., honors, magna cum laude, 1990); Case Western Reserve University (J.D., 1994). *Member:* Cleveland (Member, Sections on: Corporation, Banking and Business Law) and Ohio State Bar Associations. ***PRACTICE AREAS:*** Corporate Law; Mergers and Acquisitions; Real Estate; Secured Lending. ***Email:*** jgorski@smdklaw.com

OF COUNSEL

GARY W. MELSHER, born Cleveland, Ohio, March 8, 1939; admitted to bar, 1964, Ohio. *Education:* The Ohio State University (B.S., 1961); Case Western Reserve University (J.D., 1964). Order of the Coif. Listed: Ohio Super Lawyers, 2004 and 2005; Best Lawyers of America, 2005. Member, Pacesetters. Formerly with Jones Day. ***PRACTICE AREAS:*** Real Estate; Leases and Leasing. ***Email:*** gmelsher@smdklaw.com

ASSOCIATES

MICHAEL R. STAVNICKY, born Cleveland, Ohio, March 24, 1969; admitted to bar, 1994, Ohio. *Education:* Ohio University (B.S., summa cum laude, 1991); Cleveland Marshall College of Law (J.D., cum laude, 1994). Phi Kappa Phi; Phi Eta Sigma; Golden Key. Recipient, American Jurisprudence Award. Member, Cleveland Marshall Law Review, 1994. Member, Board of Directors, Kidney Foundation. *Member:* Cleveland, Ohio and American Bar Associations. ***REPORTED CASES:*** State ex rel. Curtin v. Indus. Comm. (1999) 86 Ohio St.3d 581; Kilrov v. B.H. Lakeshore Co. (1996) 111 Ohio App.3d 357. ***PRACTICE AREAS:*** Litigation; Construction Law; Real Estate; Commercial Law. ***Email:*** mstavnicky@smdklaw.com

JEAN M. CULLEN, born Cleveland, Ohio, January 20, 1954; admitted to bar, 1991, Ohio. *Education:* College of St. Catherine (B.A., 1976); Case Western Reserve University (J.D., 1991). Order of the Coif. *Member:* Cleveland and Ohio State Bar Associations; Estate Planning Council of Cleveland. ***PRACTICE AREAS:*** Estate Planning; Probate Administration. ***Email:*** jcullen@smdklaw.com

JOHN J. BURNS, born Cleveland, Ohio, October 24, 1970; admitted to bar, 1998, Ohio; 1999, U.S. District Court, Northern District of Ohio. *Education:* University of Dayton (B.A., 1993); Cleveland State University (J.D., magna cum laude, 1998). ***PRACTICE AREAS:*** Real Estate; Corporate Law. ***Email:*** jburns@smdklaw.com

JEFFREY A. SAYOC, born Canton, Ohio, January 4, 1972; admitted to bar, 2000, Ohio. *Education:* Bowling Green State University (B.A., 1995); University of Toledo (J.D., 1998). ***PRACTICE AREAS:*** Real Estate; Business Law; Corporate Finance; Secured Lending. ***Email:*** jsayoc@smdklaw.com

SLOWIK & ROBINSON, LLC

CLEVELAND, OHIO

(See Columbus)

Labor and Employment Law, Immigration Law, Small Business Law, Alternative Dispute Resolution, Business Formations.

JIHAD M. SMAILI, ESQ., L.L.C.
ATTORNEYS & COUNSELORS AT LAW

Established in 2000

THE WESTERN RESERVE BUILDING
SOUTH WING
1468 WEST 9TH STREET, SUITE 330
CLEVELAND, OHIO 44113
Telephone: 216-685-9500
Fax: 216-685-9685
URL: http://www.smaililaw.com
Email: jihad@smaililaw.com
URL: http://www.smaililawfirm.com

Criminal Defense, Immigration, Business Formation and Transactions, Civil Litigation, Civil Rights, Contracts, Employment Discrimination, Personal Injury, Medical Malpractice, Workers Compensation, Bankruptcy, Probate, Trusts, Wills and Estates.

JIHAD M. SMAILI, born August 25, 1971; admitted to bar, 1998, Ohio; 1999 U.S. District Court, Northern and Southern Districts of Ohio, U.S. Court of Appeals, Sixth Circuit. *Education:* University of Toledo (B.A., Political Science, 1993); Cleveland-Marshall College of Law (J.D., magna cum laude, 1998). Pi Sigma Alpha. Editor, Cleveland State Law Review, 1996-1998. Staff Editor, The Gavel, 1996-1998. Research Assistant, Law Professors Dena Davis & David Forte. Recipient: James C. Connell Award for Outstanding Student in Criminal Law; CALI Excellence for the Future Award for Outstanding Student in Evidence, Family Law, Trial Advocacy, Real Estate Law & Comparative Law, 1996-1998. Law Clerk, Messerman & Messerman, Cleveland, Ohio, 1996-1998. Treasurer, Criminal Law Society. Assistant County Prosecutor, Felony Division, Cuyahoga County, Ohio, 2000-2002; Citizens' FBI Academy, 2001. Assistant Ohio Attorney General, 1998-2000. Lawyers for Justice Program, Columbus, Ohio, 1999. *Member:* Ohio State and American Bar Associations; American Immigration Lawyers Association (Member, American-Arab Anti-Discrimination Committee). ***LANGUAGES:*** Arabic and Spanish. ***PRACTICE AREAS:*** Criminal Law; Immigration and Naturalization; Civil Rights; Medical Malpractice; Personal Injury. ***Email:*** jihad@smaililaw.com

MATTHEW T. GILMARTIN, born New York, N.Y., 1956; admitted to bar, 1982, Ohio; 1983, U.S. District Court, Northern District of Ohio; 1986, U.S. Court of Appeals, 6th Circuit and U.S. Supreme Court; 1998, U.S. District Court, Northern District of Indiana, U.S. District Court, Northern District of Illinois and U.S. Court of Appeals, 7th Circuit; 1999, U.S. District Court, Southern District of Ohio; 2000, U.S. District Court, Central District of Illinois, U.S. District Court, District of Colorado and U.S. Court of Appeals, 9th and 10th Circuits. *Education:* John Carroll University (B.A., 1979); University of Akron (J.D., 1982). ***PRACTICE AREAS:*** Probate; Taxation; Real Estate; Trusts and Estates; Wills; Civil Litigation; Business Law; Contracts; Bankruptcy.

Languages: English, Spanish and Arabic.

SMITH MARSHALL, LLP

Established in 1953

500 NATIONAL CITY EAST SIXTH BUILDING
1965 EAST SIXTH STREET
CLEVELAND, OHIO 44114
Telephone: 216-781-4994
Telecopier: 216-781-9448
Email: law@smithmarshall.com
URL: http://www.smithmarshall.com

General Civil Practice. Business and Corporate, Commercial, Construction, Environmental, Insurance, Negligence, Probate, Product Liability, Real Estate Law. Trials and Appeals.

FIRM PROFILE: In the 1950's a lawyer at one of Cleveland's largest law firms envisioned providing superior legal services to clients in the personalized setting of a small law firm. This vision became a reality, and for more than fifty years, Smith Marshall, LLP has been a vital member of the Northern Ohio legal community.

From its beginning as a litigation firm, Smith Marshall, LLP has expanded its practice areas to include business, corporate, labor, real estate, probate, tax and estate planning. And as the role of litigation has grown in our society, the firm has broadened its trial and appellate expertise to include disputes involving traditional torts, insurance, commercial and contract claims, fire losses, employer liability, governmental liability, products liability, professional negligence, environmental claims and toxic tort claims.

In the complex legal world of today, the lawyers of Smith Marshall, LLP are committed to offering "big firm" expertise and support in a small firm setting where the representation provided is efficient, result-oriented and personal.

RICHARD C. GREEN (1910-1967)
MELVIN M. ROBERTS (1911-1971)
JOHN M. CRONQUIST (1931-1993)
JACK F. SMITH (1917-1996)

WENTWORTH J. MARSHALL, JR., born Cleveland, Ohio, August 22, 1931; admitted to bar, 1956, Ohio. *Education:* Williams College (B.A., 1953); Western Reserve University (LL.B., 1956). Phi Delta Phi. Board of Editors, Western Reserve Law Review, 1955-1956. *Member:* Cleveland Bar Association. ***PRACTICE AREAS:*** Corporate Law; Estate Planning; Real Estate Law. ***Email:*** wjm@smithmarshall.com

PHILIP J. WEAVER, JR., born Cleveland, Ohio, March 27, 1947; admitted to bar, 1974, Ohio. *Education:* Wittenberg University (A.B., 1969); The Ohio State University (J.D., cum laude, 1974). Member, Panel of Arbitrators, American Arbitration Association. *Member:* Cleveland, Cuyahoga County, Ohio State and American Bar Associations; Ohio and Cleveland Associations of Civil Trial Attorneys; Defense Research Institute. Fellow, Harold F. Burton Inn of Court. ***PRACTICE AREAS:*** Product Liability; Construction Law; Commercial Law; Complex Litigation; Insurance Coverage; Employment Law; Professional Liability; Toxic Torts. ***Email:*** pjw@smithmarshall.com

FREDERICK P. VERGON, JR., born Mesa, Arizona, June 12, 1944; admitted to bar, 1969, Ohio; 1980, U.S. Supreme Court. *Education:* Denison University (B.A., 1966); Case Western Reserve University (J.D., 1969). Phi Delta Phi. Associate Board Member, Case Western Reserve Law Review, 1967-1968. Member, Panel of Arbitrators, American Arbitration Association. *Member:* Cleveland, Ohio State and American Bar Associations; Cleveland and Ohio Associations of Civil Trial Attorneys; The Defense Research Institute; International Association of Defense Counsel. ***PRACTICE AREAS:*** Products Liability; Construction Law; Insurance Coverage; Employment Law; Complex Litigation; Professional Liability; Toxic Torts; Governmental Liability. ***Email:*** fpv@smithmarshall.com

R. ERIC SMEARMAN, born Cleveland, Ohio, February 9, 1968; admitted to bar, 1993, Ohio. *Education:* John Carroll University (B.A., 1990); Case Western Reserve University (J.D., cum laude, 1993). Craven Moot Court Team, Dean Dunmore Award. *Member:* Cleveland, Cuyahoga County, Lake County, Ohio State and American Bar Associations; Ohio Association of Civil Trial Attorneys, Defense Research Institute. ***PRACTICE AREAS:*** General Civil Litigation; Insurance Defense; Insurance Law; Estate Planning; Probate; Corporate Law; Commercial Litigation; Real Estate Law. ***Email:*** res@smithmarshall.com

KARA M. SCHEDLBAUER, born Mineola, New York, April 6, 1978; admitted to bar, 2003, Ohio; 2004, U.S. District Court, Northern District of Ohio. *Education:* Allegheny College (B.A., 2000); Case Western Reserve University (J.D., 2003). *Member:* Cuyahoga County, Cleveland, Ohio State and American Bar Associations; Ohio Association of Civil Trial Attorneys; Defense Research Institute. ***PRACTICE AREAS:*** Civil Litigation; Insurance Defense; Insurance Coverage; Business Law. ***Email:*** kms@smithmarshall.com

REPRESENTATIVE CLIENTS: *Corporations:* Amoco Corp.; A.O. Smith Corp.; Apec Corporation; Avery Engineering Corp.; Conoco, Inc.; Daisy Hill Greenhouses, Inc.; Dynamotors, Inc.; Essex Chemical Corp.; Freightliner Corp.; The Gardner Contracting Co.; International Power Machinery Co.; KKSG & Associates, Inc.; Lutheran Children's Aid & Family Services; Marous & Weiner, Inc.; One Source Facility Services; Orange Crush Soccer, Inc.; Plastic Safety Systems, Inc.; Raymond A. Arnold Masonry & General Contracting Co.; S.E. Mighton Co.; Samsel Rope and Marine Supply Co.; Schindler Elevator Corp.; Snyder General Corp.; State Industries, Inc.; Volvo-GMC Heavy Truck Corp.; Wasacz & Skvoretz, Ltd.; White Castle Systems, Inc.; White Motor Corp.; Wilson Feed Mill, Inc. *Insurance Companies:* Alexsis National; American Family Insurance Co.; The Chubb Group; American Universal Insurance Co.; Auto-Owners Ins. Co.; Capital Indemnity Corp.; DPIC Cos.; Employers Mutual Insurance Co.; FCCI Insurance Group; Federated Mutual Group; Fireman's Fund Insurance Co.; Hartford Insurance Group; The Kemper Group; Leader National Insurance Co.; Lexington Insurance Co.; Liberty Mutual Group; Magna Carta Companies; MetLife Auto & Home Insurance;

(This Listing Continued)

SMITH MARSHALL, LLP, Cleveland—Continued

Pennsylvania National Mutual Insurance Co.; Permanent General Assurance Co.; Prudential Property & Casualty Co.; Risk Administration Management Company; State Automobile Mutual Insurance Co.; State Farm Insurance Cos.; The Travelers Cos.; Victoria Insurance Co.; Westfield Cos.; Zurich-American Insurance Group.

STOURTON SCOTT SMITH CO., LPA

75 PUBLIC SQUARE, SUITE 800
CLEVELAND, OHIO 44113
Telephone: 216-344-9338
Fax: 216-344-9337
Email: stourtonsmith@sbcglobal.net
URL: http://www.aggressivelegalrep.com

Elyria, Ohio Office: 633 West Broad Street, Suite 200, 44035. Telephone 440-284-0101. Fax: 440-322-5509.

Criminal Law, DWI, Bankruptcy, Personal Injury, Divorce, Family Law.

FIRM PROFILE: Criminal Law, DWI, Bankruptcy, Personal Injury, Divorce, Family Law.

STOURTON SCOTT SMITH, born Cleveland, Ohio, March 8, 1969; admitted to bar, 1995, Ohio. *Education:* Ohio University (B.A., 1991); Valparaiso University (J.D., 1994). *Member:* Cuyahoga, Cuyahoga County, Lorain County and Ohio State Bar Associations; Defense Lawyers Association. ***PRACTICE AREAS:*** Driving While Intoxicated; Criminal Law; Juvenile Criminal Law; Bankruptcy; Traffic Violations; Drug Crimes; Parole and Probation; Family Law; Divorce; Child Support; Child Custody; Visitation Rights; Personal Injury; Automobile Accidents and Injuries; Medical Malpractice; Slip and Fall; Wrongful Death.

SPIETH, BELL, McCURDY & NEWELL CO., L.P.A.

Established in 1867
2000 HUNTINGTON BUILDING
925 EUCLID AVENUE
CLEVELAND, OHIO 44115-1496
Telephone: 216-696-4700
Fax: 216-696-2706
Email: law@spiethbell.com
URL: http://www.spiethbell.com

Business Law, Corporate Law, Real Estate Law, Taxation, Trusts and Estates, Wills, Probate, Nonprofit and Charitable Organizations, Litigation, Labor and Employment, Alcoholic Beverage Control.

FIRM PROFILE: Spieth, Bell, McCurdy & Newell Co., L.P.A., is a mid-sized law firm providing quality legal representation and personal service. Established in 1867, Spieth, Bell, McCurdy & Newell is Cleveland's oldest law firm. Within the legal profession and among its clients, the firm has earned a reputation for excellence - based upon the philosophy and performance of its partners and associates.

The attorneys of Spieth, Bell, McCurdy & Newell have served their profession and community, chairing and being members of committees of the American, Ohio and Cleveland Bar Associations, chairing professional symposia such as the Cleveland Tax Institute, Cleveland Corporate Law Institute and Cleveland Estate Planning Institute and serving as elected public officials. All attorneys are members of the American Bar Association, Ohio State Bar Association and Cleveland Bar Association.

The firm provides a full range of legal services to individuals and to closely-held businesses, as well as specialized services to public companies and their legal staffs. The firm also has the specialized knowledge and skills necessary to fulfill the business and personal needs of those who have accumulated substantial amounts of capital, such as entrepreneurs and their families.

The principal practice groups of Spieth, Bell are Corporate and Tax, Employment and Labor, Litigation, Alcoholic Beverage Control and Estate and Trust Planning and Administration.

CLYDE E. WILLIAMS, JR., born Niagara Falls, New York, December 17, 1919; admitted to bar, 1945, Ohio. *Education:* Denison University (A.B., 1942); Harvard University (LL.B., 1945). ***PRACTICE AREAS:*** Corporate Law; Real Estate Law. ***Email:*** cwilliams@spiethbell.com

STERLING NEWELL, JR., born Cleveland, Ohio, September 1, 1921; admitted to bar, 1949, Ohio; 1960, U.S. Customs Court. *Education:* Haverford College (B.S., 1943); New York University (LL.B., 1948). Phi Delta Phi. Special Assistant to U.S. Attorney General, 1953-1955. ***Email:*** snewl22@aol.com

J. DONALD CAIRNS, born Chelsea, Massachusetts, 1931; admitted to bar, 1958, Ohio; 1974, Florida; U.S. Tax Court; U.S. District Court, Northern District of Ohio; U.S. Supreme Court. *Education:* Harvard College (A.B., 1952); The Ohio State University (J.D., 1958). Order of the Coif. Editor-in-Chief, Ohio State Law Journal. (Certified Specialist in Estate Planning, Trust and Probate Law, Ohio State Bar Association) (Board Certified Wills, Trusts and Estates Lawyer, Florida Bar Board of Legal Specialization and Education). ***PRACTICE AREAS:*** Estate and Gift Taxation; Trusts and Estates; Wills; Probate. ***Email:*** dcairns@spiethbell.com

EUGENE STEVENS, born Cleveland, Ohio, December 22, 1934; admitted to bar, 1958, Ohio; 1979, Florida. *Education:* Case Western Reserve University (B.B.A., 1956; LL.B., 1958). ***PRACTICE AREAS:*** Alcoholic Beverage Control. ***Email:*** estevens@spiethbell.com

(This Listing Continued)

RICHARD T. WATSON, born Lakewood, Ohio, August 21, 1933; admitted to bar, 1960, Ohio. *Education:* Harvard College (A.B., 1954); Harvard University (LL.B., 1960). Chairman, Cleveland Tax Institute, 1972. ***Email:*** richardtwatson@worldnet.att.net

HENRY E. SEIBERT, IV, born Columbus, Ohio, December 8, 1942; admitted to bar, 1968, Ohio. *Education:* Princeton University (A.B., 1965); Duke University (J.D., 1968). Phi Delta Phi. Editor-in-Chief, Legal Research Program, Duke Law School, 1967-1968. ***PRACTICE AREAS:*** Business Law; Corporate Law; Real Estate Law. ***Email:*** nseibert@spiethbell.com

FREDERICK I. TAFT, born New Haven, Connecticut, June 26, 1945; admitted to bar, 1972, Ohio. *Education:* Yale University (B.A., 1967; J.D., 1971). Phi Beta Kappa. Adjunct Instructor, Case Western University School of Law, 1973. ***PRACTICE AREAS:*** Business Law; Aircraft Law; Corporate Law; Real Estate Law. ***Email:*** rtaft@spiethbell.com

JAMES M. HAVACH, born Cleveland, Ohio, August 21, 1946; admitted to bar, 1974, Ohio. *Education:* John Carroll University (B.S.B.A., 1968); Washington and Lee University (J.D., cum laude, 1974). Phi Delta Phi; Order of the Coif. Editorial Board, Washington and Lee Law Review, 1974. Certified Public Accountant, Ohio, 1969. ***PRACTICE AREAS:*** Taxation; Real Estate Law; Sports Law; Partnership Law. ***Email:*** jhavach@spiethbell.com

STANLEY DAN PACE, born Dayton, Ohio, December 10, 1947; admitted to bar, 1975, Ohio. *Education:* Denison University (B.A., 1970); University of Toledo (J.D., 1975). ***PRACTICE AREAS:*** Labor and Employment Law; Employment Arbitration; Labor Relations; Employment Discrimination. ***Email:*** dpace@spiethbell.com

BRUCE G. HEAREY, born Philadelphia, Pennsylvania, July 19, 1950; admitted to bar, 1975, New Jersey; 1977, New York and California; 1982, Ohio. *Education:* Wesleyan University (B.A., 1972); Fordham University (J.D., 1975). ***PRACTICE AREAS:*** Litigation; Labor and Employment Law. ***Email:*** bhearey@spiethbell.com

J. TALBOT YOUNG, JR., born San Diego, California, 1948; admitted to bar, 1975, Ohio. *Education:* University of Notre Dame (B.A., 1970; J.D., cum laude, 1975). Assistant Articles Editor, Notre Dame Law Review. *Member:* Cleveland (Member, Estate Planning and Probate and Trust Law Section) and Ohio State (Member, Probate and Trust Law Section) Bar Associations; Estate Planning Council of Cleveland. Fellow, American College of Trust and Estate Counsel. ***PRACTICE AREAS:*** Estate and Gift Taxation; Trusts and Estates; Charitable Trusts and Foundations; International Estate Planning; Estate Planning; Wills; Probate. ***Email:*** tyoung@spiethbell.com

DIANNE FOLEY, born Kearny, New Jersey, June 12, 1947; admitted to bar, 1976, New Jersey and U.S. District Court, District of New Jersey; 1985, Ohio and U.S. District Court, Northern District of Ohio. *Education:* Boston College (B.A., 1969); Seton Hall University (J.D., 1975). Law Clerk, Hon. Lawrence A. Whipple, Chief Judge, U.S. District Court, District of New Jersey, 1975-1976. Board Certified Specialist in Labor and Employment Law, Ohio State Bar Association. ***PRACTICE AREAS:*** Litigation; Labor and Employment Law; Federal Civil Practice. ***Email:*** dhearey@spiethbell.com

JAMES R. BRIGHT, born Lima, Ohio, February 2, 1949; admitted to bar, 1976, Ohio. *Education:* Princeton University (A.B., 1971); Georgetown University (J.D., 1976). Case and Note Editor, Law and Policy in International Business, 1976. ***PRACTICE AREAS:*** Estate and Gift Taxation; Trusts and Estates; Wills; Probate; Charitable Trusts and Foundations. ***Email:*** jbright@spiethbell.com

REBECCA HOLLOWAY DENT, born Dayton, Ohio, November 6, 1947; admitted to bar, 1976, New York; 1991, Ohio. *Education:* Barnard College (B.A., 1970); New York University (M.A., 1972); Columbia University (J.D., 1975). Harlan Fiske Stone Scholar. Senior Research Associate, Columbia University School of Law, 1980-1983. *Member:* New York State Bar Association. ***PRACTICE AREAS:*** Estate and Gift Taxation; Trusts and Estates; Wills; Probate; Charitable Trusts and Foundations. ***Email:*** rdent@spiethbell.com

EUGENE A. KRATUS, born Buffalo, New York, June 26, 1951; admitted to bar, 1976, Ohio; 1979, Florida. *Education:* University of Notre Dame (B.B.A., 1973); Cleveland-Marshall College of Law (J.D., 1976). *Member:* The Florida Bar. ***PRACTICE AREAS:*** Estate and Gift Taxation; Trusts and Estates; Wills; Probate; Business Succession Planning; Corporate Law. ***Email:*** ekratus@spiethbell.com

JOHN M. SLIVKA, born Cleveland, Ohio, January 25, 1953; admitted to bar, 1981, Ohio. *Education:* Cleveland State University (B.B.A., 1975); Cleveland-Marshall College of Law (J.D., cum laude, 1981). ***PRACTICE AREAS:*** Business Law; Corporate Law; Taxation; Business Succession Planning; Partnership Law. ***Email:*** jslivka@spiethbell.com

BENJAMIN CALKINS, born Boston, Massachusetts, 1956; admitted to bar, 1982, District of Columbia; 1983, Ohio; 1990, New York. *Education:* Harvard College (A.B., cum laude, 1978); University of Michigan (J.D., magna cum laude, 1981). Order of the Coif. Editor, Michigan Law Review, 1979-1981. Law Clerk, Honorable Julian Abele Cook, Jr., United States District Court, Eastern District of Michigan, 1981-1983. ***PRACTICE AREAS:*** Business Law; Corporate Law; Real Estate Law; Banks and Banking; Buying and Selling of Businesses; Emerging Growth Companies. ***Email:*** bcalkins@spiethbell.com

M. ELIZABETH MONIHAN, born Cleveland, Ohio, March 22, 1957; admitted to bar, 1984, Ohio. *Education:* John Carroll University (B.S., 1979); Cleveland-Marshall College of Law (J.D., 1984). Member, Cleveland State University Law Review. Member, Estate Planning Council of Cleveland (President, 1994-1995). Fellow, American College of Trust and Estate Counsel. ***PRACTICE AREAS:*** Estate and Gift Taxation; Trusts and Estates; Wills; Probate; Charitable Trusts and Foundations. ***Email:*** emonihan@spiethbell.com

KRISTIN L. UBERSAX, born Cleveland, Ohio, February 8, 1961; admitted to bar, 1987, Ohio. *Education:* Yale University (B.A., summa cum laude, 1983); Harvard University (J.D., cum laude, 1987). Phi Beta Kappa. ***PRACTICE AREAS:*** Business Law; Real Estate Law; Sports Law. ***Email:*** kubersax@spiethbell.com

WADE M. FRICKE, born Cleveland, Ohio, November 7, 1961; admitted to bar, 1989, Ohio. *Education:* Princeton University (A.B., 1984); Washington and Lee University (J.D., 1989). Phi Delta Phi. Benjamin F. Fiery Scholar. Managing Editor, Washington and Lee Law Review, 1988-1989. ***PRACTICE AREAS:*** Labor and Employment Law; Labor Relations. ***Email:*** wfricke@spiethbell.com

TIMOTHY G. WARNER, born Kane, Pennsylvania, March 18, 1964; admitted to bar, 1993, Ohio; 1994, Pennsylvania; U.S. District Court, Northern and Southern Districts of

(This Listing Continued)

Ohio; U.S. Supreme Court. *Education:* Indiana University of Pennsylvania (B.A., with honors, 1986); Syracuse University (J.D., with honors, 1993). Editor, Syracuse University Law Review. Law Clerk, Honorable Alice M. Batchelder, United States Court of Appeals, Sixth Circuit. ***PRACTICE AREAS:*** Corporate Litigation; Commercial Litigation; Products Liability; ERISA; Labor and Employment Litigation. ***Email:*** twarner@spiethbell.com

KEVIN P. GLUNTZ, born Cincinnati, Ohio, December 3, 1959; admitted to bar, 1995, Ohio. *Education:* Kent State University (B.B.A., 1986); University of Akron School of Law (J.D., cum laude, 1995); Case Western Reserve University School of Law (LL.M., Taxation, 1997). *Member:* Cuyahoga County Bar Association. ***PRACTICE AREAS:*** Partnership Law; Investments; Real Estate Law; Business Law; Taxation. ***Email:*** kgluntz@spiethbell.com

---

R. DOUGLAS McCREERY, born Cleveland, Ohio, 1952; admitted to bar, 1986, Ohio. *Education:* Case Western Reserve University (B.S., 1981; M.B.A., 1983; J.D., cum laude, 1986). *Member:* Cleveland and Ohio State Bar Associations. ***PRACTICE AREAS:*** Estate and Gift Taxation; Trusts and Estates; Wills; Probate; Corporate Law; Business Succession Planning; Commercial Transactions. ***Email:*** dmccreery@spiethbell.com

DOUGLAS M. NELSON, II, born Liberty, Maine, April 2, 1967; admitted to bar, 1996, Ohio; 1997, New York. *Education:* Pennsylvania State University (B.S., Economics, 1992); Cleveland-Marshall College of Law (J.D., cum laude, 1996); New York University School of Law (LL.M., Taxation, 1997). ***PRACTICE AREAS:*** Business Law; Corporate Law; Taxation; Estate and Gift Taxation; Trusts and Estates; Wills; Probate. ***Email:*** dnelson@spiethbell.com

ERICA E. McGREGOR, born Ann Arbor, Michigan, June 5, 1973; admitted to bar, 1998, Ohio; 1999, U.S. District Court, Northern District of Ohio. *Education:* University of Michigan (B.A., 1995); Boston University (J.D., 1998). ***PRACTICE AREAS:*** Estate and Gift Taxation; Trusts and Estates; Wills; Probate; Charitable Trusts and Foundations. ***Email:*** emcgregor@spiethbell.com

ALLISON McCALLUM, born Cleveland, Ohio, September 26, 1974; admitted to bar, 1999, Ohio; 2002, U.S. District Court, Northern District of Ohio. *Education:* John Carroll University (B.A., cum laude, 1996); Cleveland-Marshall College of Law (J.D., cum laude, 1999). ***PRACTICE AREAS:*** Litigation; Labor and Employment Law. ***Email:*** amccallum@spiethbell.com

REPRESENTATIVE CLIENTS: Anthem Blue Cross & Blue Shield; The Astrup Co.; Baldwin Wallace; Cavaliers Operating Company, LLC; Cleveland Institute of Art; Command Plastic Corporation; The Cypress Companies; Dougherty-Hanna Resources Co.; Elevation Motorsports LLC; Enpac Corporation; Flow Polymers, Inc.; Neff-Perkins Company; Saint-Gobain; Williams International.

THE SPIKE & MECKLER LAW FIRM, LLP

CLEVELAND, OHIO

(See Elyria)

General Civil Trial Practice. Personal Injury, Medical Malpractice, Family and Domestic Relations, Real Estate, Probate.

DAVID M. SPOTTS

CLEVELAND, OHIO

(See Ashtabula)

Admiralty, General Civil Practice in all State and Federal Courts, Personal Injury, Insurance, Products, Environmental, Liability Law, Trials/and Appeals.

SQUIRE, SANDERS & DEMPSEY L.L.P.

4900 KEY TOWER
127 PUBLIC SQUARE
CLEVELAND, OHIO 44114-1304
Telephone: 216-479-8500
Fax: 216-479-8780
URL: http://www.ssd.com

REVISOR OF THE OHIO AND TEXAS LAW DIGESTS FOR THIS DIRECTORY

The Americas Offices: Cincinnati, Columbus, Houston, Los Angeles, Miami, New York, Palo Alto, Phoenix, San Francisco, Tallahassee, Tampa, Tysons Corner, Washington DC, West Palm Beach, Caracas, Santo Domingo, Rio de Janeiro.
European Offices: Bratislava, Brussels, Budapest, London, Madrid, Milan, Moscow, Prague, Warsaw.
Asia Offices: Beijing, Hong Kong, Shanghai, Tokyo.
Associated Offices: Bucharest, Dublin, Kyiv, Buenos Aires, Santiago

Bankruptcy and Reorganization, Chemicals, Communications, Construction and Engineering, Corporate Transactions and Securities Regulation, E-Commerce, Economic Regulation, Education, Energy, Environmental, Health and Safety, Financial Institutions and Services, Financial Services, Gaming and Casinos, Government and Administrative Agencies, Health Care and Hospitals, Health Sciences, Hospitality and Recreation, Insurance, Intellectual Property, International Dispute Resolution, Labor and Employment, Life Sciences, Litigation, Manufacturing, Media and Entertainment, Private Equity, Project Finance, Public Finance, Real Estate, Real Estate and Hospitality, Sports, Steel, Taxation, Technology, Transportation and Utilities.

FIRM PROFILE: The Cleveland office of Squire, Sanders & Dempsey L.L.P. is the seat of many of the firm's practice areas and much of its leadership. The first and largest office, Cleveland was founded in the late 19th century to accommodate some of the nation's largest companies doing business in Ohio's industrial capital. Clients range from Fortune 100 companies involved in industries and operations worldwide to privately held enterprises, emerging and mature companies and governments of every kind. The office is the hub of several of Squire Sanders' leading national and international practices, including corporate, tax, financial services, health care and nonprofits, public law, litigation, labor and employment and environmental. The Cleveland office is the firm's largest, home to approximately 175 lawyers.

PARTNERS

CLEVELAND OFFICE

ANDREW SQUIRE (1850-1934)

WILLIAM B. SANDERS (1854-1929)

JAMES H. DEMPSEY (1859-1920)

ANDREW AGATI, born Jamestown, New York, 1970; admitted to bar, 1995, Ohio; 1999, Illinois; U.S. District Court, Northern District of Ohio and U.S. Court of Appeals, Sixth Circuit; U.S. District Court, Eastern District of Michigan; U.S. Court of Appeals, Eleventh Circuit. *Education:* Allegheny College (B.A., magna cum laude, 1992); Case Western Reserve University (J.D., magna cum laude, 1995). Phi Beta Kappa; Order of the Coif. ***PRACTICE AREAS:*** Litigation. ***Email:*** aagati@ssd.com

STACY D. BALLIN, born New York, New York, 1958; admitted to bar, 1983, Ohio; U.S. Court of Appeals, Third, Sixth and Tenth Circuits; U.S. District Court, Northern District of Ohio and District of Colorado. *Education:* Bucknell University (B.A., cum laude, 1980); Case Western Reserve University (J.D., 1983). Valedictorian; Order of the Coif. Editor, Case Western Reserve University Law Review. ***PRACTICE AREAS:*** Commercial Litigation; Antitrust Litigation; Construction Litigation; Securities Litigation. ***Email:*** sballin@ssd.com

GEOFFREY K. BARNES, born Cleveland, Ohio, 1945; admitted to bar, 1973, Ohio. *Education:* Denison University (B.A., 1967); Case Western Reserve University (J.D., 1973). Editor-in-Chief, Case Western Law Review. *Member:* Ohio State Bar Association (Member, Environmental Law Committee). ***PRACTICE AREAS:*** Environmental. ***Email:*** gbarnes@ssd.com

DANIEL G. BERICK, born Cleveland, Ohio, 1962; admitted to bar, 1988, New York; 1992, Ohio. *Education:* Columbia University (A.B., 1984); The University of Chicago (J.D., 1987). Author: "It's A Private Matter," Business Law Today, Sept./Oct., 1996; "Engagement Letters For Investment Banking Services," The Practical Lawyer, March, 1997. Co-author: "Confidentiality Agreements for the Sale of a Business," The Practical Lawyer, December 2002. Trustee, Shaker Heights Public Library (1997-2000). Member: Managed Funds Association; The Financial Markets Association; Association for Corporate Growth; American Society of Corporate Secretaries. *Member:* Association of the Bar of the City of New York; Cleveland (Member, Sections on: Securities Law; Corporation, Banking and Financial Services), Ohio State and American (Member, Business Law Section) Bar Associations;. ***PRACTICE AREAS:*** Securities; Corporate Finance; Investment Banking Law; Mergers, Acquisitions and Divestitures; Corporate. ***Email:*** dberick@ssd.com

CAROLYN J. BULLER, born Cleveland, Ohio, 1955; admitted to bar, 1981, Ohio. *Education:* Oberlin College (B.A., 1978); Case Western Reserve University (J.D., 1981). Order of the Coif. Member, Case Western Law Review. *Member:* Cleveland and Ohio State Bar Associations. ***PRACTICE AREAS:*** Corporate; Mergers and Acquisitions; Creditors Rights; Finance. ***Email:*** cbuller@ssd.com

DAVID W. BURCHMORE, born Evanston, Illinois, 1952; admitted to bar, 1986, Ohio; U.S. District Court, Northern District of Ohio; U.S. Court of Appeals, Sixth Circuit; U.S. Court of Appeals, Fourth Circuit; U.S. Court of Appeals, Ninth Circuit; U.S. District Court, Southern District of Ohio; U.S. Court of Appeals, District of Columbia Circuit; U.S. Supreme Court. *Education:* Princeton University (A.B., magna cum laude, 1973); University of Virginia (M.A., 1975; Ph.D., 1979; J.D., 1986). Dillard Fellow. Articles Editor, University of Virginia Law Review. Author: "Wet Weather Consent Decrees: Protecting POTWS in Negotiations," AMSA, 2003. ***PRACTICE AREAS:*** Environmental. ***Email:*** dburchmore@ssd.com

VAN CARSON, born Wheeling, West Virginia, 1938; admitted to bar, 1966, Ohio; U.S. Court of Appeals, Sixth Circuit; U.S. Supreme Court; U.S. Court of Appeals, Seventh Circuit; U.S. District Court, District of Columbia. *Education:* Mount Union College (B.A., 1963); Duke University (LL.B., 1966). Order of the Coif. Editor, Duke University Law Review, 1965-1966. Vice Chairman and Member of the Executive Committee of the Board of Directors, Ohio Chamber of Commerce. *Member:* Cleveland (Member, Environmental Law Committee), Ohio State (Chairman, Environmental Law Committee, 1991-1993) and American (Member, Litigation Section) Bar Associations. (National Coordinator of Environmental Practice). ***PRACTICE AREAS:*** Environmental. ***Email:*** vcarson@ssd.com

CHARLES F. CLARKE, born Hillsboro, Ohio, 1916; admitted to bar, 1940, Michigan; 1946, Ohio; U.S. Court of Appeals, Sixth Circuit and U.S. Supreme Court. *Education:* Washington and Lee University (B.A., summa cum laude, 1938); University of Michigan (LL.B., 1940). Order of the Coif. Awarded LL.D. by Cleveland State University, 1970. President, Amicus Committee, Nominations Committee, Executive Committee, National Association of Railroad Trial Counsel, 1967-1968. President, Trustee, Free Medical Clinic of Greater Cleveland, 1978-1990. *Member:* Cleveland, Ohio State and American Bar Associations; U.S. Sixth Circuit Judicial Conference (Life Member); U.S. Eighth Judicial District (Life Member). Fellow, American College of Trial Lawyers. [U.S. Army, 1941-1945]. ***PRACTICE AREAS:*** Litigation; Trusts and Estates. ***Email:*** cclarke@ssd.com

WILLIAM H. CONNER, born Columbus, Ohio, 1940; admitted to bar, 1967, Ohio; U.S. District Court, Northern District of Ohio; U.S. Tax Court. *Education:* Miami University (A.B., magna cum laude, 1964); University of Michigan (J.D., cum laude, 1967). *Member:* Ohio State (Member and former Chair, Taxation Committee) and American (Member, Tax Section) Bar Associations; National Association of Bond Lawyers (Member, Director, President and former Treasurer); American College of Bond Counsel, Fellow. ***PRACTICE AREAS:*** Tax-Exempt Financing; State and Local Taxation. ***Email:*** wconner@ssd.com

TIMOTHY J. COSGROVE, born Cleveland, Ohio, 1961; admitted to bar, 1987, Ohio. *Education:* Cleveland State University (B.A., 1983; J.D., 1987). Director of Legislation and Policy, Office of the Governor, State of Ohio, 1991-1993. Member and Chair: Board of Trustees, Cleveland State University; Chair, Board of Directors, Northeast Midwest Institute; Public Affairs Committee, Greater Cleveland Partnership; Public Affairs Committee,

(This Listing Continued)

SQUIRE, SANDERS & DEMPSEY L.L.P., Cleveland—Continued

Ohio Chamber of Commerce. *Member:* Ohio State Bar Association; Ohio Lobbying Association. ***PRACTICE AREAS:*** Public Law; Public Finance. ***Email:*** tcosgrove@ssd.com

MARK A. CUSICK, born Pittsburgh, Pennsylvania, 1948; admitted to bar, 1975, Ohio. *Education:* Duquesne University (B.A., 1970); University of Virginia (J.D., 1975). Order of the Coif. Member, University of Virginia Law Review. *Member:* Cleveland, Ohio State and American (Member, Business Law and Law Practice Sections) Bar Associations. (Coordinator, International Practice) (Also at London, England Office). ***PRACTICE AREAS:*** Corporate; International. ***Email:*** mcusick@ssd.com

CAROL F. DAKIN, born Orange, New Jersey, 1943; admitted to bar, 1969, Ohio. *Education:* Mount Holyoke College (A.B., 1964); University of Pennsylvania; Cleveland State University (J.D., 1969). Member, Editorial Board, Cleveland-Marshall Law Review. ***PRACTICE AREAS:*** Employee Benefits; Executive Compensation. ***Email:*** cdakin@ssd.com

ERNIE K. DEMANELIS, born Morgantown, West Virginia, 1956; admitted to bar, 1981, West Virginia (inactive), Ohio; U.S. District, Southern District of West Virginia; U.S. Court of Appeals, Sixth Circuit. *Education:* West Virginia University (B.A., Phi Beta Kappa, 1978; J.D., 1981). Order of the Coif. Editor-in-Chief, West Virginia Law Review. *Member:* Cleveland, Ohio State, West Virginia and American Bar Associations. ***LANGUAGES:*** Greek. ***PRACTICE AREAS:*** Public Finance. ***Email:*** edemanelis@ssd.com

ALAN S. DORIS, born Cleveland, Ohio, 1947; admitted to bar, 1972, Ohio, U.S. District Court, Northern District of Ohio and U.S. Tax Court. *Education:* Miami University (A.B., cum laude; B.S., cum laude, 1969); Harvard University (J.D., cum laude, 1972). Phi Beta Kappa; Beta Gamma Sigma. Chairman, Cleveland Tax Institute, 1992. *Member:* American Bar Association (Member, Section of Taxation, Chairman, 1995-1996, Capital Recovery and Leasing Committee and Principal Author, Section of Taxation Comments on Regulations Under Section 197; Chairman, 1987-1994, Subcommittee, Amortization of Intangibles). ***PRACTICE AREAS:*** Taxation; Corporate Law; Investments; Business Law. ***Email:*** adoris@ssd.com

CARL A. DRAUCKER, born Ravenna, Ohio, 1951; admitted to bar, 1977, Ohio; U.S. Tax Court; U.S. District Court, Northern District of Ohio; U.S. Court of Federal Claims; U.S. Court of Appeals, Ninth Circuit. *Education:* Hiram College (B.A., magna cum laude, 1973); Ohio Northern University (J.D., 1977); Boston University (LL.M., 1978). Phi Beta Kappa. *Member:* Akron and American Bar Associations. ***PRACTICE AREAS:*** Estates and Trusts; Employee Benefits; Executive Compensation; Taxation. ***Email:*** cdraucker@ssd.com

PATRICK J. DUGAN, born Lima, Ohio, 1957; admitted to bar, 1982, Ohio. *Education:* Bowling Green State University (B.S., cum laude, 1979); The Ohio State University (J.D., with honors, 1982). Beta Alpha Psi. Order of the Coif. Included in The Best Lawyers in America, 2006 edition. Member, Board of Directors, Ariel Corporation. Board of Trustees, Raymond E. Mason Foundation. ***PRACTICE AREAS:*** Corporate Law; Financial Services; Capital Markets. ***Email:*** pdugan@ssd.com

ROBERT J. EIDNIER, born Euclid, Ohio, 1957; admitted to bar, 1982, Ohio. *Education:* Miami University (B.S., summa cum laude, 1979); University of Virginia (M.S., 1982; J.D., 1982). Order of the Coif. Editorial Board, University of Virginia Law Review. Certified Public Accountant, Ohio. *Member:* Cleveland and Ohio State Bar Associations; National Association of Bond Lawyers. ***PRACTICE AREAS:*** Corporate and Partnership Taxation; Bankruptcy; Taxation; Tax-Exempt Financing. ***Email:*** reidnier@ssd.com

STEVEN A. FRIEDMAN, born Washington, D.C., 1967; admitted to bar, 1992, Ohio; U.S. District Court, Northern District of Ohio; U.S. Court of Appeals, Sixth Circuit; U.S. District Court, Southern District of Ohio; U.S. Court of Federal Claims. *Education:* Oberlin College (B.A., 1989); University of Chicago (J.D., 1992). Member, Charter Class, Cleveland Bridge Builders Leadership Group. *Member:* Cleveland and Ohio State Bar Associations. Anthony J. Celebrezze Inn of Court. ***PRACTICE AREAS:*** Commercial Litigation; Public Construction Law; Constitutional Law. ***Email:*** sfriedman@ssd.com

D. BRUCE GABRIEL, born Peoria, Illinois, 1954; admitted to bar, 1980, Ohio. *Education:* Coe College (B.A., 1976); Northwestern University (J.D., M.M., 1980). ***PRACTICE AREAS:*** Health Care Finance; Project and Structured Finance; Securities Law; Tax-Exempt Finance. ***Email:*** dbgabriel@ssd.com

DAVID S. GOODMAN, born Cleveland, Ohio, 1952; admitted to bar, 1977, Ohio. *Education:* Oberlin College (B.A., 1974); Harvard University (J.D., 1977). *Member:* Cleveland and Ohio State Bar Associations; National Association of Bond Lawyers. ***PRACTICE AREAS:*** Capital Markets; Public Finance. ***Email:*** dgoodman@ssd.com

RICHARD S. GURBST, born New York, New York, 1946; admitted to bar, 1971, Ohio. *Education:* Brandeis University (B.A., 1968); University of Pennsylvania (J.D., 1971). ***PRACTICE AREAS:*** Litigation; Debtor and Creditor; Bankruptcy Litigation; Personal Injury Defense. ***Email:*** rgurbst@ssd.com

W. MICHAEL HANNA, born Richwood, West Virginia, 1954; admitted to bar, 1980, Ohio. *Education:* Glenville State College (B.A.Ed., 1975); West Virginia University (J.D., 1980). ***PRACTICE AREAS:*** Labor and Employment; Workplace Injury and Environment. ***Email:*** whanna@ssd.com

PAMELA IDDINGS HANOVER, born Troy, Ohio, 1955; admitted to bar, 1980, Ohio. *Education:* Indiana University (B.A., 1977); The Ohio State University (J.D., 1980). Order of the Coif. Member, The Ohio State University Law Journal. *Member:* National Association of Bond Lawyers; Ohio Conference of Community Development (Chairman, Legislative Committee). ***PRACTICE AREAS:*** Public Finance. ***Email:*** phanover@ssd.com

SUSAN C. HASTINGS, born Minneapolis, Minnesota, 1959; admitted to bar, 1985, Ohio. *Education:* Wartburg College; University of Iowa (B.A., 1980; J.D., with distinction, 1985). ***PRACTICE AREAS:*** Labor and Employment; Education Law. ***Email:*** shastings@ssd.com

THOMAS G. HAVENER, born Cleveland, Ohio, 1961; admitted to bar, 1987, Ohio. *Education:* The Ohio State University (B.A., 1983); Case Western Reserve University (J.D., 1987). Case Western Reserve University Law Review. ***PRACTICE AREAS:*** Federal Income Tax; State and Local Tax; Tax-Exempt Obligations; Tax-Exempt Organizations. ***Email:*** thavener@ssd.com

BARBARA L. HAWLEY, born West Liberty, Iowa, 1950; admitted to bar, 1977, Ohio. *Education:* University of Chicago (A.B., general honors, 1972); Case Western Reserve University (J.D., 1977). Order of the Coif. *Member:* Cleveland and Ohio State Bar Associations. ***PRACTICE AREAS:*** Municipal Law; Public Finance; Health Care Finance; University Finance. ***Email:*** bhawley@ssd.com

LAURA KINGSLEY HONG, born Cincinnati, Ohio, 1959; admitted to bar, 1985, Ohio; U.S. District Court, Northern District of Ohio; U.S. Court of Appeals, Sixth Circuit. *Education:* Oberlin College (B.A., 1980); Case Western Reserve University (J.D., 1985). Former Associate Professor, Trial Tactics, Case Western Reserve University School of Law. *Member:* Cleveland, Ohio State and American (Litigation and Tort and Insurance Law Sections) Bar Associations; Ohio Asian Bar Association; Defense Research and Trial Lawyers Association; Ohio Association of Civil Trial Attorneys; Past President, Federal Bar Association, Northern District of Ohio Chapter; Past President, National Asian Pacific American Bar Association. ***PRACTICE AREAS:*** Toxic Tort Defense; Mass Tort; Products Liability; Commercial Litigation. ***Email:*** lhong@ssd.com

BRUCE P. JONES, born Jamestown, New York, 1948; admitted to bar, 1973, Ohio. *Education:* Colgate University (B.A., 1970); Yale University (J.D., 1973). *Member:* Cleveland, Ohio State and American Bar Associations; National Association of Bond Lawyers. ***PRACTICE AREAS:*** Public Law; Public Finance; Governmental Entities; Port Authorities; Bond and Underwriters Counsel; Economic Development; Pollution Control Finance. ***Email:*** bjones@ssd.com

MARY ANN JORGENSON, born Gallipolis, Ohio, 1941; admitted to bar, 1975, Ohio; 1982, New York. *Education:* Agnes Scott College (B.A., 1963); Phi Beta Kappa; Harvard University (M.A., 1964); Case Western Reserve University (J.D., 1975). Order of the Coif. Listed in Best Lawyers in America. *Member:* Ohio State Bar Association (Former Chair, Corporation Law Committee); American Bar Association (Chair, Corporate Law Committee). (National Coordinator of Corporate Practice). ***PRACTICE AREAS:*** Mergers and Acquisitions; Tender Offers; Finance; Executive Compensation; Corporate Governance. ***Email:*** mjorgenson@ssd.com

GORDON S. KAISER, JR., born Lakewood, Ohio, 1948; admitted to bar, 1973, Ohio. *Education:* Baldwin-Wallace College (B.A., 1970); Case Western Reserve University (J.D., 1973). Order of the Coif. Editor, Case Western Reserve University Law Review. *Member:* American Bar Association (Vice Chairman, Corporate Finance Committee, Public Utility, Communications and Transportation Law Section). ***PRACTICE AREAS:*** Corporate. ***Email:*** gkaiser@ssd.com

F. BARRY KEEFE, born Clinton, Iowa, 1942; admitted to bar, 1973, Ohio. *Education:* St. Ambrose University (B.A., 1964); Marquette University (M.S., 1966); Case Western Reserve University (J.D., 1973). Order of the Coif. Editor, Case Western Reserve University Law Review. *Member:* Akron, Ohio State and American (Member, State and Local Government Sections) Bar Associations; Government Finance Officers Association. ***PRACTICE AREAS:*** Public Law; Public Finance. ***Email:*** bkeefe@ssd.com

THOMAS S. KILBANE, born Cleveland, Ohio, 1941; admitted to bar, 1966, Ohio; U.S. District Court, Northern District of Ohio; U.S. Supreme Court; U.S. Claims Court; U.S. District Court, Central District of Illinois; U.S. District Court, Southern District of Texas; U.S. Court of Appeals, First, Second, Third, Fourth, Fifth, Sixth, Seventh, Eighth, Ninth, Tenth and Eleventh Circuits; U.S. District Court, Southern District of Ohio; U.S. Court of Appeals, District of Columbia; U.S. Court of Appeals, Federal Circuit. *Education:* John Carroll University (B.A., magna cum laude, Valedictorian, 1963); Northwestern University (J.D., 1966). Board of Editors, Northwestern University Law Review. Listed in Best Lawyers in America, Guide to the Leading U.S. Litigation Lawyers (2005), International Who's Who of Professionals, Who's Who in the World, Who's Who in American Law and Who's Who in America. Commended as a top-ranked General Commercial Litigator in Ohio in the 2004 and 2005 editions of Chambers USA; America's Leading Business Lawyers; as a Top 100 Super Lawyer in Ohio Super Lawyers magazine; as a top Ohio lawyer by Inside Business magazine and as a highly recommended Dispute Resolution lawyer in Global Counsel 3000. Fellow: American College of Trial Lawyers; American Bar Foundation; International Academy of Trial Lawyers. Master Bencher, Anthony J. Celebrezze Inn of Court. Member: Federal Court Panel of Alternative Dispute Resolution, U.S. District Court, Northern District of Ohio; CPR Institute of Dispute Resolution, Cleveland Panel; American Arbitration Association Complex Litigation Panel of Arbitrator/Mediators. Member, National Committee on Minitrials, National Committee on Construction Disputes. American Arbitration Association, Corporate Counsel Committee, Commercial Panel of Arbitrators, Construction Industry Advisory Counsel. *Member:* Cleveland, Ohio State (Former Chairman, ADR Committee; Corporate/Commercial/Construction Law Subcommittee and Judicial Administration and Legal Reform Committee), Federal and American (Member, Litigation and Antitrust Sections) Bar Associations; Defense Research Institute; American College of Barristers (Member). [Captain, U.S. Army, Vietnam, Bronze Star Recipient]. (National Coordinator of Litigation Practice). ***PRACTICE AREAS:*** Commercial Litigation; Antitrust Litigation; Securities Litigation; Construction Litigation; ADR. ***Email:*** tkilbane@ssd.com

ROBERT D. LABES, born Chicago, Illinois, 1962; admitted to bar, 1988, Ohio; U.S. District Court, Northern District of Ohio and U.S. Court of Appeals, Sixth Circuit. *Education:* University of Michigan (B.A., with high honors and high distinctions, 1985; J.D., cum laude, 1988). Order of the Coif. Editor, University of Michigan Journal of International Law. *Member:* Cleveland and Ohio State Bar Associations. ***PRACTICE AREAS:*** Municipal Finance; Affordable Housing; Health Care Finance; Bond and Underwriter. ***Email:*** rlabes@ssd.com

JOHN S. LARSON, born Akron, Ohio, 1951; admitted to bar, 1977, Ohio. *Education:* Dartmouth College (A.B., summa cum laude, 1974); University of Pennsylvania (J.D., 1977). *Member:* Ohio State and American Bar Associations; National Association of Bond Lawyers. ***PRACTICE AREAS:*** Public Finance; Education Law; Local Government Law. ***Email:*** jlarson@ssd.com

WENDLENE M. LAVEY, born Durham, North Carolina, 1963; admitted to bar, 1989, Ohio, U.S. Court of Appeals, District of Columbia Circuit and U.S. Court of Appeals, Sixth

(This Listing Continued)

Circuit; U.S. District Court, Northern District of Ohio. *Education:* Dickinson College (B.A., 1986); Harvard University (J.D., 1989). ***PRACTICE AREAS:*** Environmental; Civil Litigation. ***Email:*** wlavey@ssd.com

DAMOND R. MACE, born Elizabethtown, Kentucky, 1959; admitted to bar, 1984, Ohio; 1991, California; U.S. District Court, Northern District of Ohio; U.S. Court of Appeals, Third Circuit; U.S. Court of Appeals, Sixth Circuit; U.S. District Court, Eastern District of Wisconsin; U.S. Court of Appeals, Fifth Circuit; U.S. Supreme Court. *Education:* Wittenberg University (B.A., summa cum laude, chemistry, 1981); Harvard University (J.D., cum laude, 1984). Master Bencher, Judge Anthony J. Celebrezze American Inn of Court; American College of Trial Lawyers. ***PRACTICE AREAS:*** Litigation; Contracts; Torts; Products Liability; Civil Practice. ***Email:*** dmace@ssd.com

JAMES J. MAIWURM, born Wooster, Ohio, 1948; admitted to bar, 1974, Ohio and U.S. District Court, Northern District of Ohio; 1975, U.S. Court of Appeals, Sixth Circuit; 1979, U.S. Supreme Court; 1986, District of Columbia and U.S. Court of Appeals for the District of Columbia Circuit; 1987, Maryland and New York. *Education:* College of Wooster (B.A., 1971); University of Michigan, Ann Arbor (J.D., 1974). Phi Beta Kappa. *Member:* The District of Columbia Bar; New York State and American (Member, Communications Law Section) Bar Associations. ***PRACTICE AREAS:*** Business Law; Commercial Law; Joint Ventures; Mergers and Acquisitions; Securities Offerings. ***Email:*** jmaiwurm@ssd.com

RICHARD D. MANOLOFF, born Cleveland, Ohio, 1964; admitted to bar, 1992, Ohio; U.S. Court of Appeals, Sixth Circuit; U.S. District Court, Northern District of Ohio. *Education:* Princeton University (A.B., magna cum laude, 1987) Phi Beta Kappa; Yale University (J.D., 1992). Yale Law Journal. ***PRACTICE AREAS:*** Bond Financing; Education Law; Public Finance; Government Contracts; Municipal Law. ***Email:*** rmanoloff@ssd.com

JEFFREY J. MARGULIES, born Sioux Falls, South Dakota, 1946; admitted to bar, 1973, Ohio. *Education:* University of Iowa (B.A., magna cum laude, 1968; J.D., with high distinction, 1973). Order of the Coif. Executive Editor, University of Iowa Law Review. *Member:* Cleveland, Ohio State and American Bar Associations. ***PRACTICE AREAS:*** Business Law; Securities; Mergers, Acquisitions and Divestitures; Finance; Investment Companies and Investment Advisers; Private Equity; Executive Compensation. ***Email:*** jmargulies@ssd.com

DOUGLAS A. McWILLIAMS, born Cleveland, Ohio, 1960; admitted to bar, 1994, Ohio; U.S. District Court, Northern District of Ohio; U.S. Court of Appeals, Sixth Circuit; U.S. Court of Appeals, Seventh Circuit. *Education:* Oberlin College (B.A., 1984) Phi Beta Kappa; University of California, Berkeley (J.D., 1994). Articles Editor, Ecology Law Quarterly. *Member:* Ohio State and American (Member, Section on Environment, Energy and Resources) Bar Associations. ***PRACTICE AREAS:*** Environmental Law. ***Email:*** dmcwilliams@ssd.com

GEORGE M. von MEHREN, born Boston, Massachusetts, 1950; admitted to bar, 1977, Ohio; U.S. Supreme Court; U.S. Court of Appeals, Sixth Circuit; U.S. District Court, Northern District of Ohio. *Education:* Harvard University (A.B., 1972); Cambridge University, England (B.A., 1974; M.A., 1985); Harvard University (J.D., 1977). Editor, Harvard Law Review. *Member:* Cleveland, Ohio State, Federal and American Bar Associations; Civil Justice Reform Act Advisory Group (Northern District of Ohio). ***PRACTICE AREAS:*** Commercial Litigation; International Dispute Resolution. ***Email:*** gvonmehren@ssd.com

MICHAEL G. MEISSNER, born Panama City, Florida, 1954; admitted to bar, 1979, Ohio; U.S. Court of Federal Claims; U.S. Tax Court. *Education:* University of Notre Dame (B.A., 1976); Harvard University (J.D., cum laude, 1979). Case Editor, Harvard Law Review. *Member:* Cleveland (Former Chairman, General Tax Committee), Ohio State and American (Member, Section on Taxation) Bar Associations; Tax Practitioners of Cleveland; Tax Club. ***PRACTICE AREAS:*** Executive Compensation; Corporate Taxation; Tax Controversy; Exempt Organizations; Financial Instruments; Public Utility Taxation; Workouts. ***Email:*** mmeissner@ssd.com

G. CHRISTOPHER MEYER, born Fremont, Nebraska, 1948; admitted to bar, 1973, Ohio; U.S. District Court, Northern District of Ohio; U.S. Court of Appeals, Sixth Circuit. *Education:* Grinnell College; University of Kansas (B.A., 1970); University of Pennsylvania (J.D., 1973). *Member:* Cleveland (Member, Section of Bankruptcy and Commercial Law) and American (Member: Business Bankruptcy Committee; Commercial and Financial Services Committee) Bar Associations; American College of Bankruptcy; American Bankruptcy Institute; Turnaround Management Association. ***PRACTICE AREAS:*** Bankruptcy Chapter 11; Bankruptcy Reorganization; Insolvency; International Insolvency; Workouts. ***Email:*** cmeyer@ssd.com

OSBORNE MILLS, JR., born Cleveland, Ohio, 1947; admitted to bar, 1975, Ohio. *Education:* Dartmouth College (A.B., 1969); Case Western Reserve University (J.D., 1975). Lecturer in Law, Modern Real Estate Transactions, Case Western Reserve University School of Law, 1976-1982. *Member:* Cleveland (Member, Sections on: Corporation, Banking and Business Law; Bankruptcy and Commercial Law; Real Estate) and Ohio State (Member, Business Law Section) Bar Associations. [Capt., USMC, 1969-1972]. ***PRACTICE AREAS:*** Banks and Banking; Secured Lending; Business Law; Real Estate. ***Email:*** omills@ssd.com

DAVID J. MILLSTONE, born Morgantown, West Virginia, 1946; admitted to bar, 1971, West Virginia and Ohio. *Education:* Johns Hopkins University (A.B., 1968); West Virginia University (J.D., 1971). Articles Editor, West Virginia University Law Review. *Member:* Cleveland and American (Member, Labor and Employment Section, International Labor Law Committee and International Law and Practice Section) Bar Associations. (Member of Labor and Employment Practice). ***PRACTICE AREAS:*** Labor and Employment Law; International Law; Education Law. ***Email:*** dmillstone@ssd.com

KENNETH C. MOORE, born Chicago, Illinois, 1947; admitted to bar, 1973, Ohio; 1975, District of Columbia; U.S. Court of Appeals, Fourth Circuit; U.S. District Court, District of Maryland; U.S. District Court, Northern District of Ohio; U.S. Court of Appeals, Sixth Circuit; U.S. Court of Appeals, District of Columbia Circuit; U.S. Supreme Court. *Education:* Hiram College (B.A., summa cum laude, 1969); Harvard University (J.D., cum laude, 1973). Member, Harvard Law Review. Law Clerk to U.S. Circuit Judge Harrison L. Winter. Speaker, First Circuit Federal Judicial Conference Panel on Managing the Complex Environmental Case. *Member:* Cleveland, Ohio State, Federal and American (Sections: Litigation, Environment, Energy and Resources) Bar Associations. ***PRACTICE AREAS:*** Environmental; Litigation; Ethics and Professional Responsibility. ***Email:*** kmoore@ssd.com

JAMES P. MURPHY, born Jackson, Tennessee, 1944; admitted to bar, 1969, Ohio; 1984, District of Columbia and Maryland; U.S. Court of Appeals, District of Columbia, Federal, Fourth and Sixth Circuits; U.S. Court of Federal Claims; U.S. District Court, Central District of Illinois, District of Columbia, District of Arizona, District of Maryland, Northern District of Ohio; U.S. Supreme Court. *Education:* University of Notre Dame (A.B., 1966); University of Michigan (J.D., cum laude, 1969). Associate Editor, Michigan Law Review. *Member:* The District of Columbia Bar; Ohio State and Maryland State Bar Associations. ***PRACTICE AREAS:*** Litigation. ***Email:*** jmurphy@ssd.com

JAN E. MURRAY, born Barre, Vermont, 1952; admitted to bar, 1978, Ohio. *Education:* University of Vermont (B.A., 1974); Case Western Reserve University (J.D., M.S., 1978). Author, "Disclosure of Corporate Compliance Matters by Healthcare Providers," The Practical Lawyer, Vol. 45, No. 2, March 1999. Adjunct Faculty, Cleveland State University College of Law, 1984-1990. *Member:* Cleveland (Member, 1993-1996, and Chairman, 1995-1996, Health Law Council), Ohio State and American Bar Associations; American Health Lawyers Association; Teaching Hospitals and Academic Medical Centers Commission (Chair). ***PRACTICE AREAS:*** Health Care Regulation; Health Law; Health Care Contracts; Health Care Corporate Law; Physician Contracts. ***Email:*** jmurray@ssd.com

FREDERICK R. NANCE, born Cleveland, Ohio, 1953; admitted to bar, 1978, Ohio; 1987, Florida (inactive); U.S. District Court, Northern District of Ohio; U.S. Court of Appeals, Sixth Circuit. *Education:* Harvard University (B.A., 1975); University of Michigan (J.D., 1978). *Member:* Ohio State, National and American (Member, Litigation Section) Bar Associations; Norman Minor Bar Association; U.S. Court of Appeals, Sixth Circuit Judicial Conference (Life Member). ***PRACTICE AREAS:*** Commercial Litigation; Public Sector Law; Construction Litigation; Sports Law; Alternative Dispute Resolution. ***Email:*** fnance@ssd.com

LAURA D. NEMETH, born Sandusky, Ohio, 1963; admitted to bar, 1989, Ohio. *Education:* Ohio State University (B.S.B.A., 1986; J.D., 1989). *Member:* Cleveland (Member, Sections on: Corporate, Banking and Business Law; Real Estate Law and Securities Law), Ohio State and American (Member, Business Law Section) Bar Associations. ***PRACTICE AREAS:*** Corporate Law; Securities; Commercial Real Estate; Computers and Software; Mergers, Acquisitions and Divestitures; Technology Law. ***Email:*** lnemeth@ssd.com

HOWARD J.C. NICOLS, born Woodhaven, New York, 1956; admitted to bar, 1981, Ohio; 2000, New York; U.S. Court of Appeals, Second Circuit; U.S. Court of Appeals, Sixth, Tenth and Ninth Circuits; U.S. District Court, Northern District of Ohio. *Education:* Fordham University; Albany University (B.A., summa cum laude, 1978); Cornell University (J.D., cum laude, 1981). Chancellor, Cornell Moot Court Board; Board of Editors, International Law Journal. *Member:* Cleveland Bar Association; American Inns of Court. ***PRACTICE AREAS:*** Litigation; Corporate Technology; Securities; Oil and Gas. ***Email:*** hnicols@ssd.com

JAMES P. OLIVER, born Girard, Ohio, 1944; admitted to bar, 1969, Ohio. *Education:* Bowling Green State University (B.S., 1966); University of Cincinnati (J.D., 1969). *Member:* Cleveland and Ohio State Bar Associations. Fellow, The American College of Trust and Estate Counsel. ***PRACTICE AREAS:*** Corporate; Mergers and Acquisitions; Executive Compensation; Estate Planning. ***Email:*** joliver@ssd.com

DANIEL J. O'LOUGHLIN, born Cleveland, Ohio, 1925; admitted to bar, 1951, Ohio. *Education:* John Carroll University (B.S., 1948); University of Michigan (LL.B., 1951). ***PRACTICE AREAS:*** Litigation; Public Law. ***Email:*** doloughlin@ssd.com

DALE E. PAPAJCIK, born Cleveland, Ohio, 1957; admitted to bar, 1986, Ohio; U.S. District Court, Northern District of Ohio. *Education:* University of Akron (B.S., Civil Engineering, 1980; J.D., 1986). *Member:* Ohio State and American Bar Associations. ***PRACTICE AREAS:*** Environmental Law. ***Email:*** dpapajcik.@ssd.com

SAMUEL S. PEARLMAN, born Pittsburgh, Pennsylvania, 1942; admitted to bar, 1967, Ohio; U.S. Court of Appeals, Third Circuit; U.S. District Court, Eastern District of Pennsylvania; U.S. District Court, Northern District of Ohio. *Education:* University of Pennsylvania (A.B., 1963; LL.B., magna cum laude, 1966). Order of the Coif. Editor, University of Pennsylvania Law Review, 1964-1966. Lecturer in Law, Case Western Reserve University School of Law, 1978-1982. Member, Registration Committee, Ohio Division of Securities, 1979-1989. *Member:* Cleveland (Member, Sections on: Securities Law (Chairman, 1985-1986), Real Estate and Corporation and Business Law; Chairman, Securities Law Institute, 1978), Ohio State (Member, Real Estate Section) and American (Member, Business Law Section) Bar Associations. ***PRACTICE AREAS:*** Real Estate; Corporate; Securities; Mergers, Acquisitions and Divestitures; Real Estate Acquisitions. ***Email:*** spearlman@ssd.com

TERRENCE G. PERRIS, born Los Angeles, California, 1947; admitted to bar, 1972, Ohio. *Education:* University of Toledo (B.A., magna cum laude, 1969); University of Michigan (J.D., summa cum laude, 1972). Articles and Book Review Editor, Michigan Law Review. Law Clerk to The Honorable J. Edward Lumbard, U.S. Court of Appeals for the Second Circuit. Law Clerk to Justice Potter Stewart, Supreme Court of the United States. Visiting Professor, University of Michigan Law School, 1996. (National Coordinator of Taxation Practice). ***LANGUAGES:*** Greek. ***PRACTICE AREAS:*** Federal Taxation; Bankruptcy; Constitutional Limitations on Taxing Power. ***Email:*** tperris@ssd.com

HARRIS A. SENTURIA, born Cleveland, Ohio, 1969; admitted to bar, 1993, Ohio and U.S. District Court, Southern District of Ohio; 1996, U.S. District Court, Northern District of Ohio; 2002, U.S. Court of Appeals, Sixth Circuit and U.S. Supreme Court; 2003, U.S. District Court, Eastern District of Wisconsin; 2005, U.S. District Court, Eastern District of Michigan. *Education:* Rice University (B.A., 1990); Columbia University (J.D., 1993). ***Email:*** hsenturia@ssd.com

MICHAEL L. SHARB, born Nelsonville, Ohio, 1966; admitted to bar, 1993, Colorado (inactive); 1997, Ohio. *Education:* Ohio University (B.B.A., 1988); University of Colorado (J.D., 1993). Order of the Coif. Production Editor, The University of Colorado Law Review. ***PRACTICE AREAS:*** Public Finance; Education Law; Local Government Law. ***Email:*** msharb@ssd.com

(This Listing Continued)

SQUIRE, SANDERS & DEMPSEY L.L.P., Cleveland—Continued

TIMOTHY J. SHEERAN, born Cincinnati, Ohio, 1948; admitted to bar, 1975, Ohio, U.S. Court of Appeals, Sixth Circuit; U.S. District Court, Northern District of Ohio. *Education:* The Ohio State University (B.A., 1971); Harvard University (J.D., 1975). Co-Author, Baldwin's *Ohio School Law,* 1991—. *Member:* Cleveland (Labor and Employment Committee), Ohio State (Labor and Employment Law Section) and American (Member, Labor Law Section) Bar Associations; National Council of School Attorneys; Education Law Association; Ohio Council of School Attorneys. ***PRACTICE AREAS:*** Labor and Employment; Education Law. ***Email:*** tsheeran@ssd.com

JOHN F. SHELLEY, born Des Moines, Iowa, 1943; admitted to bar, 1968, Ohio; U.S. District Court, Northern District of Ohio. *Education:* Harvard University (A.B., cum laude, 1965; LL.B., cum laude, 1968). *Member:* Cleveland, Ohio State (Estate Planning and Probate Section) and American (Real Property, Probate and Trust Law Section) Bar Associations. Fellow, American College of Trust and Estate Counsel. ***PRACTICE AREAS:*** Trusts and Estates; Taxation; Nonprofit and Charitable Organizations. ***Email:*** jshelley@ssd.com

CHARNA E. SHERMAN, born Cleveland, Ohio, 1958; admitted to bar, 1985, District of Columbia; 1990, Ohio; U.S. Court of Appeals, District of Columbia, U.S. District Court for the District of Columbia; U.S. District Court, Northern District of Ohio; U.S. Court of Appeals, Sixth Circuit. *Education:* Harvard University (B.A., magna cum laude, 1980); Phi Beta Kappa; Georgetown University (J.D., magna cum laude, 1985). Articles Editor, Law Review: The Georgetown Law Journal. Legislative Assistant, U.S. Senator Daniel Patrick Moynihan, 1980-1982. Judicial Clerk, The Honorable John H. Pratt of the U.S District Court, District of Columbia, 1985-1986. Co-Chair, Corporate Compliance, Investigations and Criminal Defense Practice. *Member:* Cleveland and American (Division Co-Chair, Litigation Section Leadership) Bar Associations. ***PRACTICE AREAS:*** Litigation. ***Email:*** cesherman@ssd.com

R. THOMAS STANTON, born Moline, Illinois, 1943; admitted to bar, 1969, Ohio; 1982, New York. *Education:* Knox College (B.A., 1965); Harvard University; Northwestern University (J.D., 1969). Order of the Coif. Editor, Northwestern University Law Review. (Chairman, Management Committee). ***PRACTICE AREAS:*** Public Finance. ***Email:*** rstanton@ssd.com

DALE E. STEPHENSON, born Ann Arbor, Michigan, 1956; admitted to bar, 1982, Ohio; 1997, Texas; U.S. District Court, Northern District of Ohio; U.S. Court of Appeals, Sixth Circuit; U.S. District Court, Eastern District of Wisconsin; U.S. District Court, Southern and Northern Districts of Texas; U.S. Court of Appeals, Fifth Circuit; U.S. Court of Appeals, Seventh Circuit; U.S. Supreme Court. *Education:* Michigan State University; Spring Arbor University (B.A., summa cum laude, 1979); University of Michigan (J.D., 1982). Author: "European Community Waste Policy: At the Brink of a New Era," *BNA International Environment Reporter,* 403-411 (July 17, 1991); "Environmental Laws Are Stricter In Green - Influenced Europe," *The National Law Journal* (September 30, 1991); "Environmental Regulation in Europe," *Journal of Canada-United States Law Institute* (1992); "Greenhouse Gas Emissions and Emissions Trading in North America: Kyoto Treaty and U.S. Initiatives," Journal of Canada-United States Law Institute (2002). *Member:* State Bar of Texas; Ohio State Bar Association; American Bar Association (Member, Section on Environment, Energy and Resources). ***PRACTICE AREAS:*** Environmental; International. ***Email:*** dstephenson@ssd.com

MARTHA S. SULLIVAN, born Syracuse, New York, 1967; admitted to bar, 1994, Ohio; U.S. District Court, Northern District of Ohio; U.S. Court of Appeals, Seventh Circuit. *Education:* Skidmore College (B.S., 1989); Bryn Mawr College (M.S.S., 1991; M.L.S.P., 1992); Case Western Reserve University (J.D., 1994). ***PRACTICE AREAS:*** Litigation; Bankruptcy; Financial Services. ***Email:*** msullivan@ssd.com

DYNDA A. THOMAS, born Springfield, Illinois, 1959; admitted to bar, 1986, Ohio. *Education:* Miami University (B.A., 1982); University of Nebraska (1982-1983); University of Cincinnati (J.D., 1986). *Member:* Cleveland (Real Property, Probate and Trust Law Section) and American (Public Utility, Communications and Transportation Law, Member, Committee on Global Infrastructure) Bar Associations. ***PRACTICE AREAS:*** Corporate; Project Finance. ***Email:*** dthomas@ssd.com

JAMES D. THOMAS, born Detroit, Michigan, 1961; admitted to bar, 1987, Ohio; U.S. Court of Appeals, Sixth Circuit; U.S. District Court, Northern District of Ohio; U.S. District Court, Southern District of Ohio; U.S. District Court, Western District of Michigan; U.S. District Court, Eastern District of Michigan; U.S. Court of Appeals; Federal Circuit; U.S. Court of Appeals, Fifth Circuit; U.S. Supreme Court. *Education:* Adrian College (B.A., 1984); University of Toledo (J.D., cum laude, 1987). Editor-in-Chief, University of Toledo Law Review. U.S. Magistrate Judge, Northern District of Ohio, 1995-1999. ***PRACTICE AREAS:*** Litigation; Bankruptcy; White Collar Crime; Commercial Law. ***Email:*** jdthomas@ssd.com

JAMES D. TROXELL, born Akron, Ohio, 1946; admitted to bar, 1976, Ohio; U.S. District Court, Northern District of Ohio; U.S. Tax Court; U.S. Court of Federal Claims; U.S. Supreme Court. *Education:* University of Akron (B.A., 1968; J.D., 1975). ***PRACTICE AREAS:*** Information Systems and Technology; Intellectual Property; Technology Licensing. ***Email:*** jtroxell@ssd.com

GREGORY J. VIVIANI, born Euclid, Ohio, 1959; admitted to bar, 1984, Ohio. *Education:* Miami University (B.S., 1981); Case Western Reserve University (J.D., 1984). Order of the Coif. *Member:* American Bar Association (Member, Taxation Section); The WEB Network of Benefit Professionals. ***PRACTICE AREAS:*** Employee Benefits. ***Email:*** gviviani@ssd.com

ROBIN G. WEAVER, born Columbus, Ohio, 1948; admitted to bar, 1974, Ohio; U.S. Supreme Court; U.S. District Court, Southern District of Ohio; The Ohio Supreme Court; U.S. Court of Appeals, Second, Third, Sixth, Seventh and Eleventh Circuits; U.S. District Court, Northern District of Ohio. *Education:* The Ohio State University (B.A., 1970); University of Michigan (J.D., 1973). Publications: "Non-US Firms: How to Enforce Your Foreign Trade Secrets in the US," *International Commercial Litigation* and *United States Litigation Yearbook.* Master Bencher, The Ohio Supreme Court Board of Commissioners on Grievances and Discipline, 1988-1992, 1994—; Chair, 1996-1997; Vice Chair, 1998, 1999. Faculty Member: National Institute for Trial Advocacy, Midwest Regional Trial Program, 1983—; National Institute for Trial Advocacy, Advanced Trial Program, Boulder, Colorado. Judge, Anthony J. Celebrezze Inn of Court. Selected Lawyer of the Year, Ohio Lawyers Weekly, 1998. *Member:* Cleveland (President, 2002; President-Elect, 2001; Vice President, 2000; Chairman, Judicial Selection Committee, 1994; Life Member, Eighth Appellate Judicial Conference), Ohio State and American Bar Associations; Cleveland Association of Civil Trial Attorneys; Defense Research Institute; Life Member, Eighth District Judicial Conference; Ohio Association of Civil Trial Attorneys. Fellow: American College of Trial Lawyers; International Society of Barristers. ***PRACTICE AREAS:*** Commercial; Products Liability; Litigation. ***Email:*** rweaver@ssd.com

JEFFREY J. WEDEL, born McKeesport, Pennsylvania, 1957; admitted to bar, 1983, Michigan (inactive); 1989, Ohio. *Education:* Dickinson College (B.A., 1979); Thomas M. Cooley Law School (J.D., summa cum laude, 1983). ***PRACTICE AREAS:*** Labor and Employment. ***Email:*** jwedel@ssd.com

DAVID C. WEINER, born Cincinnati, Ohio, 1943; admitted to bar, 1968, District of Columbia (inactive); 1969, Ohio; U.S. Supreme Court. *Education:* University of Cincinnati (B.B.A., 1965); Georgetown University (J.D., 1968). Phi Delta Phi; Omicron Delta Kappa. Law Clerk, Senior Circuit Judge E. Barrett Prettyman, U.S. Court of Appeals for the District of Columbia Circuit, 1968-1969. President, Ohio Legal Assistance Foundation, 2003—. *Member:* American Bar Association (Member, Standing Committee on the Federal Judiciary, 1997-2003; Chair, Section of Litigation, 1994-1995; Member, House of Delegates, 1981—); American Judicature Society (Member, Board of Directors, 1978-1986). American Bar Foundation; National Legal Aid and Defender Association (Member, Board of Directors, 1986-1990); International Society of Barristers (1995—). ***PRACTICE AREAS:*** Litigation; Complex Litigation; Alternative Dispute Resolution. ***Email:*** dweiner@ssd.com

JOSEPH C. WEINSTEIN, born Waterbury, Connecticut, 1958; admitted to bar, 1983, Ohio; U.S. Court of Appeals, Sixth Circuit; U.S. District Court, Northern District of Ohio; U.S. Court of Appeals, Fourth Circuit; U.S. Supreme Court; U.S. Court of Appeals, Fifth Circuit; U.S. Court of Appeals, Seventh Circuit; U.S. District Court, Southern District of Texas. *Education:* Case Western Reserve University (B.A., 1980; J.D., 1983). Phi Beta Kappa; Order of the Coif. *Member:* Akron, Ohio State and American (Antitrust and Litigation Sections) Bar Associations. ***PRACTICE AREAS:*** Business Litigation; Securities and Shareholder Litigation; Corporate Compliance and Investigations; Products Liability Litigation. ***Email:*** jweinstein@ssd.com

DAVID A. ZAGORE, born Peru, Indiana, 1963; admitted to bar, 1988, Ohio. *Education:* The Ohio State University (B.A., cum laude, 1985; J.D., 1988). ***PRACTICE AREAS:*** Securities; Mergers and Acquisitions; Tender Offers; Finance; Corporate Governance. ***Email:*** dzagore@ssd.com

SENIOR COUNSEL

CLEVELAND OFFICE

HELEN Z. KRYSHTALOWYCH, born Bad-Verishofen, Germany, 1945; admitted to bar, 1980, Ohio. *Education:* The Ohio State University (B.A., B.S., 1967); Kent State University (M.Ed., magna cum laude, 1971); Cleveland-Marshall (J.D., magna cum laude, 1980). *Member:* Cleveland (International Law Group), Ohio State and American (International Law Practice Committee) Bar Associations; Ukrainian-American Bar Association; Committee of the Ohio — Ukraine Judiciary Program; First World Congress of Ukrainian Lawyers. (Also at Moscow, Russia Office). ***LANGUAGES:*** Ukrainian, Russian and English. ***PRACTICE AREAS:*** International; Corporate; Project Finance. ***Email:*** hkryshtalowych@ssd.com

JOHN F. LEWIS, born Oberlin, Ohio, 1932; admitted to bar, 1958, Ohio; U.S. District Court, Northern District of Ohio; U.S. Supreme Court. *Education:* Eastbourne College (Sussex, England); Amherst College (B.A., 1955); University of Michigan (J.D., 1958). (Managing Partner, Cleveland Office, 1985-2002). ***PRACTICE AREAS:*** Labor and Employment. ***Email:*** jlewis@ssd.com

WALTER J. REKSTIS, III, born San Diego, California, 1945; admitted to bar, 1972, Ohio. *Education:* University of Cincinnati (B.B.A., 1968; J.D., 1972). *Member:* Cleveland and Ohio State Bar Associations; International Association of Defense Counsel. ***PRACTICE AREAS:*** Litigation. ***Email:*** wrekstis@ssd.com

COUNSEL

CLEVELAND OFFICE

JEFFREY A. BOMBERGER, born West Reading, Pennsylvania, 1956; admitted to bar, 1984, Delaware; 1985, Pennsylvania; 1986, Ohio. *Education:* Lebanon Valley College (B.S., magna cum laude, 1978); University of Pennsylvania (J.D., cum laude, 1984). *Member:* National Association of Bond Lawyers. ***PRACTICE AREAS:*** Public Finance. ***Email:*** jbomberger@ssd.com

KATHERINE G. PETREY, born Oak Ridge, Tennessee, 1948; admitted to bar, 1974, Ohio. *Education:* University of Kentucky (B.A., 1970; J.D., 1974). *Member:* Cleveland and Ohio State Bar Associations; National Association of Bond Lawyers; Association for Governmental Leasing & Finance. ***PRACTICE AREAS:*** Public Law; Public Finance. ***Email:*** kpetrey@ssd.com

OF COUNSEL

CLEVELAND OFFICE

GREGORY C. BURKART, born St. Louis, Missouri, 1963; admitted to bar, 1988, Illinois (inactive); 1992, Michigan; U.S. District Court, Eastern District of Michigan (Not admitted in Ohio). *Education:* Spring Hill College (B.S., 1985); St. Louis University (J.D., 1988). *Member:* Detroit, Livingston County and Illinois State Bar Associations; State Bar of Michigan. [Captain, U.S. Army, JAGC, 1988-1992]. ***LANGUAGES:*** Spanish. ***PRACTICE AREAS:*** Public Finance; Public Authority Finance. ***Email:*** gburkart@ssd.com

DAVID B. LAVEY, born Parma, Ohio, 1962; admitted to bar, 1987, Ohio. *Education:* Princeton University (B.A., 1984); University of Georgia (J.D., 1987). ***PRACTICE AREAS:*** Construction Law. ***Email:*** dlavey@ssd.com

(This Listing Continued)

JILL G. OKUN, born Kew Gardens, New York, 1958; admitted to bar, 1983, New York; 1986, Ohio; U.S. District Court, Eastern and Southern Districts of New York; U.S. Court of Appeals, Second Circuit; U.S. District Court, Northern District of Ohio; U.S. Court of Appeals, Sixth Circuit. *Education:* Tufts University (B.A., magna cum laude, 1979); Boston College (J.D., with honors, 1982). *Member:* Cleveland Bar Association (Certified Grievance Committee); Judge Anthony J. Celebrezze American Inn of Court (Barrister). ***PRACTICE AREAS:*** Commercial Litigation; RICO; Antitrust; Class Actions; Contracts. ***Email:*** jokun@ssd.com

SHAWN R. RUSSELL, born Lorain, Ohio, 1958; admitted to bar, 1986, Ohio. *Education:* Indiana University (B.A., 1980); Cleveland State University (J.D., magna cum laude, 1986); Baldwin-Wallace College (M.B.A., 1997). *Member:* Cleveland and American Bar Associations; Credit Card Compliance Association (Past President). ***PRACTICE AREAS:*** Banks and Banking; Corporate Law; Securities. ***Email:*** srussell@ssd.com

LOUIS STOKES, born Cleveland, Ohio, 1925; admitted to bar, 1953, Ohio; 1999, District of Columbia; U.S. Supreme Court. *Education:* Case Western Reserve University (1946-1949); Cleveland State University (J.D., 1953). U.S. Representative, 11th District of Ohio, 1969-1999. [Technician 4th Grade, U.S. Army, 1943-1946]. ***PRACTICE AREAS:*** Transportation. ***Email:*** lstokes@ssd.com

MITCHELL S. THOMPSON, born Erie, Pennsylvania, 1963; admitted to bar, 1994, Ohio; U.S. District Court, Northern District of Ohio. *Education:* Indiana University of Pennsylvania (B.A., 1991); Case Western Reserve University (J.D., summa cum laude, 1994; LL.M., 2001). ***PRACTICE AREAS:*** Taxation. ***Email:*** mthompson@ssd.com

MICHAEL WAGER, born Cleveland, Ohio, 1951; admitted to bar, 1982, New York; 1990, Ohio. *Education:* The American University (B.A., 1973); Columbia University (M.A., 1976); New York University (J.D., 1981). Editor-in-Chief, Journal of International Law, 1981. Fiscal Officer, Cleveland-Cuyahoga County Port Authority. ***PRACTICE AREAS:*** Corporate; Securities; Mergers and Acquisitions. ***Email:*** mwager@ssd.com

CONSULTANT

CLEVELAND OFFICE

HENRY T. KING JR., born Meriden, Connecticut, 1919; admitted to bar, 1943, Connecticut; 1946, New York; 1956, Ohio. *Education:* Yale University (B.A., 1941; J.D., 1943). Advisory Board Member, The Institute for International and Comparative Law of the Center for American and International Law. Senior Adviser, Robert Jackson Center, Jamestown, New York. *Member:* American Bar Association; Canadian Bar Association (Lifetime Member); American Arbitration Association (Corporate Counsel Committee); Greater Cleveland International Lawyers Group; Northern Ohio District Export Council. (Legal Consultant). ***PRACTICE AREAS:*** Corporate. ***Email:*** hking@ssd.com

SENIOR ATTORNEYS

CLEVELAND OFFICE

ROGER M. GOLD, born Cleveland, Ohio, 1965; admitted to bar, 1991, Ohio; U.S. District Court, Northern District of Ohio; U.S. District Court, Southern District of Texas. *Education:* Bowdoin College (B.A., summa cum laude, 1988); New York University (J.D., cum laude, 1991). ***PRACTICE AREAS:*** Litigation. ***Email:*** rgold@ssd.com

MEEGAN LALLY SPICER, born Cleveland, Ohio, 1968; admitted to bar, 1993, Ohio. *Education:* Bowling Green State University (B.S., 1990); Cleveland State University (J.D., 1993). ***PRACTICE AREAS:*** Public Revenue Finance. ***Email:*** mlallyspicer@ssd.com

JAMES W. SATOLA, born Cleveland, Ohio, 1961; admitted to bar, 1989, Ohio; 1991, District of Columbia (inactive); U.S. District Court, Northern District of Ohio; U.S. Court of Appeals, Sixth Circuit; U.S. Supreme Court; U.S. District Court, District of Arizona; U.S. Court of Appeals, Eighth Circuit; U.S. Court of Appeals, Ninth Circuit. *Education:* The Ohio State University (B.S., 1984); Case Western Reserve University (J.D., 1989). ***PRACTICE AREAS:*** Litigation. ***Email:*** jsatola@ssd.com

CHRISTOPHER R. SHEA, born Athens, Ohio, 1966; admitted to bar, 1993, Ohio; U.S. District Court, Northern District of Ohio; U.S. Court of Appeals, Sixth Circuit. *Education:* Kenyon College (A.B., summa cum laude, 1987); University of Virginia (J.D., 1993). ***PRACTICE AREAS:*** Litigation. ***Email:*** cshea@ssd.com

ASSOCIATES

CLEVELAND OFFICE

STEPHEN P. ANWAY, born Akron, Ohio, 1976; admitted to bar, 2002, Ohio; U.S. Court of Appeals, Sixth Circuit; U.S. District Court, Northern District of Ohio. *Education:* Bowling Green State University (B.A., summa cum laude, 1999); The Ohio State University (J.D., with honors in Law, 2002). Managing Editor, Ohio State Law Journal. ***PRACTICE AREAS:*** Litigation. ***Email:*** sanway@ssd.com

CIPRIANO S. BEREDO, III, born Cleveland, Ohio, 1970; admitted to bar, 1999, Ohio. *Education:* Miami University (B.A., 1994); Indiana University (J.D., cum laude, 1999). Co-author: "Confidentiality Agreements for the Sale of a Business," The Practical Lawyer, December 2002. ***PRACTICE AREAS:*** Corporate Law. ***Email:*** cberedo@ssd.com

CHANDRA S. BOWLING, born Elizabethtown, Kentucky, 1964; admitted to bar, 1993, Ohio; 1994, Kentucky; U.S. District Court, Southern District of Ohio, U.S. District Court, Eastern District of Kentucky; U.S. Court of Appeals, Sixth Circuit; U.S. Supreme Court; U.S. Court of Appeals, Seventh Circuit; U.S. District Court, Northern District of Ohio. *Education:* The Ohio State University (B.A., cum laude, 1988); Northern Kentucky University (J.D., cum laude, 1993). ***PRACTICE AREAS:*** Labor and Employment. ***Email:*** cbowling@ssd.com

PATRICK J. BROOKS, born Canton, Ohio, 1971; admitted to bar, 1998, Ohio; U.S. District Court, Northern District of Ohio; U.S. Court of Appeals, Third Circuit. *Education:* The University of Akron (B.A., 1993; J.D., cum laude, 1998). ***LANGUAGES:*** Russian. ***PRACTICE AREAS:*** Corporate Law. ***Email:*** pbrooks@ssd.com

(This Listing Continued)

PATRICK J. BURKE, born Cleveland, Ohio, 1972; admitted to bar, 2003, Ohio. *Education:* The Ohio State University (B.S., cum laude, 1995); Cleveland State University (J.D., summa cum laude, 2003). ***PRACTICE AREAS:*** Corporate Law. ***Email:*** pburke@ssd.com

ALEXANDER G. BURLINGAME, born Cleveland, Ohio, 1971; admitted to bar, 1998, Ohio. *Education:* University of Tulsa (B.A., 1994); Case Western Reserve University (J.D., 1998). ***PRACTICE AREAS:*** Public Revenue Finance. ***Email:*** aburlingame@ssd.com

NAILAH K. BYRD, born New York, N.Y., 1972; admitted to bar, 2000, New York and New Jersey; 2002, Ohio. *Education:* Columbia University (B.A., 1995); Brooklyn Law School (J.D., 1998). ***PRACTICE AREAS:*** Litigation. ***Email:*** nbyrd@ssd.com

AMY L. CADLE, born Charleston, West Virginia, 1975; admitted to bar, 2002, Ohio; U.S. Court of Appeals, Sixth Circuit and U.S. District Court, Northern District of Ohio. *Education:* Hiram College (B.A., cum laude, 1997); Washington and Lee University (J.D., 2002). ***PRACTICE AREAS:*** Litigation. ***Email:*** acadle@ssd.com

J. PHILIP CALABRESE, born Evanston, Illinois, 1971; admitted to bar, 2000, Ohio; U.S. Tax Court; U.S. District Court, Northern District of Ohio; U.S. Court of Federal Claims; U.S. Court of Appeals, Sixth Circuit; U.S. Court of Appeals, Federal Circuit; U.S. Court of Appeals, Seventh Circuit; U.S. Supreme Court and U.S. Court of Appeals, District of Columbia Circuit; U.S. District Court, Southern District of Ohio; U.S. Court of Appeals, Third Circuit; U.S. Court of Appeals, Eighth Circuit; U.S. Court of Appeals, Ninth Circuit. *Education:* College of the Holy Cross (B.A., summa cum laude, 1993); Harvard University (J.D., cum laude, 2000). Phi Beta Kappa. ***PRACTICE AREAS:*** Litigation; Complex Litigation. ***Email:*** pcalabrese@ssd.com

MICHELE L. CONNELL, born Natrona, Pennsylvania, 1972; admitted to bar, 2003, Ohio. *Education:* Georgetown University (B.S., magna cum laude, 1995); Case Western Reserve University (J.D., summa cum laude, 2003). ***LANGUAGES:*** Spanish. ***PRACTICE AREAS:*** Corporate Law. ***Email:*** mconnell@ssd.com

CHRISTINE TOMKO COSSLER, born Warren, Ohio, 1971; admitted to bar, 2002, Ohio; U.S. District Court, Northern District of Ohio. *Education:* Youngstown State University (B.E., 1995); Case Western Reserve University (J.D., summa cum laude, 2002). ***PRACTICE AREAS:*** Labor and Employment. ***Email:*** ccossler@ssd.com

STEPHEN J. CRAWFORD, born Buffalo, New York, 1968; admitted to bar, 1994, New York; 1997, Ohio. *Education:* State University of New York at Buffalo (B.A., summa cum laude, 1990; J.D., 1993). Phi Beta Kappa. ***PRACTICE AREAS:*** Real Estate. ***Email:*** scrawford@ssd.com

MICHAEL A. CULLERS, born Cleveland, Ohio, 1970; admitted to bar, 1995, Ohio; U.S. Tax Court. *Education:* Miami University (B.S., cum laude, 1992); Case Western Reserve University (J.D., magna cum laude, 1995). ***PRACTICE AREAS:*** Taxation. ***Email:*** mcullers@ssd.com

STEVEN A. DELCHIN, born Euclid, Ohio, 1971; admitted to bar, 1997, Ohio; U.S. District Court, Northern District of Ohio; U.S. Court of Appeals, Sixth Circuit. *Education:* John Carroll University (B.A., summa cum laude, 1994); Case Western Reserve University (J.D., summa cum laude, 1997). Order of the Coif. ***PRACTICE AREAS:*** Litigation; Appellate Practice; Complex and Multi-District Litigation; Constitutional Law; Copyrights; Legal Ethics and Professional Responsibility; Products Liability; Securities; Trademarks. ***Email:*** sdelchin@ssd.com

STEPHEN M. FAZIO, born Lawrence, Massachusetts, 1972; admitted to bar, 2003, Ohio; U.S. District Court, Northern District of Ohio. *Education:* University of Massachusetts (B.S., cum laude, 1994); Case Western Reserve University (J.D., magna cum laude, 2003). Order of the Coif. ***PRACTICE AREAS:*** Litigation. ***Email:*** sfazio@ssd.com

L. TODD GIBSON, born 1968; admitted to bar, 1997, New York; 2004, Ohio. *Education:* Denison University (B.A., 1991); Case Western Reserve University (J.D., 1996; M.B.A., 1996). ***PRACTICE AREAS:*** Public Revenue Finance. ***Email:*** tgibson@ssd.com

JILL A. GRINHAM, born Akron, Ohio, 1976; admitted to bar, 2002, Ohio; U.S. District Court, Northern District of Ohio. *Education:* Westminster College (B.S., magna cum laude, 1999); Pace University (J.D., summa cum laude, 2002). ***PRACTICE AREAS:*** Environmental Law. ***Email:*** jgrinham@ssd.com

REBECCA WISTNER HAVERSTICK, born Columbus, Ohio, 1971; admitted to bar, 1996, Ohio; U.S. District Court, Northern District of Ohio; U.S. Court of Appeals, Sixth Circuit. *Education:* Miami University (B.A., magna cum laude, with honors, 1993); Case Western Reserve University (J.D., magna cum laude, 1996). ***PRACTICE AREAS:*** Litigation. ***Email:*** rhaverstick@ssd.com

SARA E. HUTCHINS, born Gallipolis, Ohio, 1978; admitted to bar, 2003, Ohio. *Education:* The Ohio State University (B.A., 2000); Capital University (J.D., cum laude, 2003). Order of the Curia. ***PRACTICE AREAS:*** Litigation. ***Email:*** shutchins@ssd.com

DENISE A. JACKSON, born Palo Alto, California, 1961; admitted to bar, 1994, Ohio. *Education:* Northwestern University (B.M., 1983; M.M., 1987); University of California, Hastings College (J.D., 1994). ***PRACTICE AREAS:*** Employee Benefits. ***Email:*** djackson@ssd.com

DANIEL A. JAFFE, born Cleveland, Ohio, 1960; admitted to bar, 1989, Ohio; U.S. Court of Appeals, Sixth Circuit; U.S. District Court, Northern and Southern Districts of Ohio. *Education:* Columbia University (B.A., 1983; J.D., 1989). ***PRACTICE AREAS:*** Labor and Employment. ***Email:*** djaffe@ssd.com

COLIN R. JENNINGS, born Washington, D.C., 1971; admitted to bar, 1997, Ohio; U.S. District Court, Northern District of Ohio; U.S. Court of Appeals, Sixth Circuit. *Education:* Allegheny College (B.A., 1994); Case Western Reserve University (J.D., 1997). ***PRACTICE AREAS:*** Litigation; Products Liability; White Collar Criminal Defense. ***Email:*** cjennings@ssd.com

ERIC J. JOHNSON, born Cleveland, Ohio, 1975; admitted to bar, 2000, Ohio; U.S. District Court, Northern District of Ohio; U.S. Court of Appeals, Sixth Circuit. *Education:* Denison University (B.A., summa cum laude, 1997); Duke University (J.D., 2000). ***LANGUAGES:*** Spanish and Japanese. ***PRACTICE AREAS:*** Labor and Employment. ***Email:*** ejohnson@ssd.com

(This Listing Continued)

SQUIRE, SANDERS & DEMPSEY L.L.P., Cleveland—Continued

ALLEN A. KACENJAR, born Parma, Ohio, 1974; admitted to bar, 1999, Ohio; U.S. District Court, Northern District of Ohio; U.S. Court of Appeals, Fifth Circuit; U.S. Supreme Court; U.S. District Court, Northern District of Texas; U.S. Court of Appeals for the District of Columbia Circuit. *Education:* Miami University (B.S., 1996); Case Western Reserve University (J.D., magna cum laude, 1999). ***PRACTICE AREAS:*** Environmental Law. ***Email:*** akacenjar@ssd.com

LAURA E. KACENJAR, born Parma, Ohio, 1976; admitted to bar, 2001, Illinois; 2005, Ohio; U.S. District Court, Northern District of Illinois. *Education:* Miami University (B.S., 1998); University of Michigan (J.D., cum laude, 2001). ***PRACTICE AREAS:*** Corporate Law. ***Email:*** lkacenjar@ssd.com

JOAN A. KAVURU, born Akron, Ohio, 1963; admitted to bar, 1992, Ohio. *Education:* Valparaiso University (B.S.N., with distinction, 1985); Case Western Reserve University (J.D., cum laude, 1992). ***PRACTICE AREAS:*** Taxation. ***Email:*** jkavuru@ssd.com

MAUREEN SHERIDAN KENNY, born Lakewood, Ohio, 1971; admitted to bar, 1998, Ohio; U.S. Court of Appeals, Ninth Circuit; U.S. District Court, Northern District of Ohio. *Education:* Bowling Green State University (B.A., 1993); Cleveland State University (J.D., 1998). *Member:* Cleveland and Ohio State Bar Associations. ***PRACTICE AREAS:*** Litigation. ***Email:*** mkenny@ssd.com

SUZANNE K. KETLER, born New Castle, Pennsylvania, 1967; admitted to bar, 2001, Ohio; U.S. District Court, Northern District of Ohio. *Education:* Northwestern University (B.A., 1988; J.D., cum laude, 2001); University of Pittsburgh (Ph.D., 1997). ***LANGUAGES:*** Italian, French. ***PRACTICE AREAS:*** Intellectual Property. ***Email:*** sketler@ssd.com

TODD D. KILPATRICK, born Dennison, Ohio, 1964; admitted to bar, 1990, New York; U.S. Court of Appeals, Second Circuit; U.S. Court of Appeals, Third Circuit; U.S. District Court, Northern District of New York; U.S. District Court, Northern District of Ohio; U.S. District Court, Western District of New York; U.S. Supreme Court (Not admitted in Ohio). *Education:* The College of Wooster (B.A., 1986); Cleveland State University (J.D., 1989). ***PRACTICE AREAS:*** Labor and Employment. ***Email:*** tkilpatrick@ssd.com

CHAUNDRA C. KING, born Cleveland, Ohio, 1977; admitted to bar, 2004, Ohio. *Education:* Harvard University (B.A., cum laude, 1999); Columbia University (J.D., 2004). ***PRACTICE AREAS:*** Litigation. ***Email:*** cking@ssd.com

ANDREW R. KRUPPA, born Bowling Green, Ohio, 1975; admitted to bar, 2000, Ohio; U.S. District Court, Northern District of Ohio. *Education:* Colby College (B.A., magna cum laude, 1997); The Ohio State University (J.D., with honors, 2000). Order of the Coif. ***PRACTICE AREAS:*** Litigation. ***Email:*** akruppa@ssd.com

LIANNE MANTIONE, born Flemington, New Jersey, 1974; admitted to bar, 2003, Ohio; U.S. District Court, Northern District of Ohio. *Education:* Lake Erie College (B.S., 1997); Cleveland State University (M.A., J.D., magna cum laude, 2003). ***PRACTICE AREAS:*** Environmental Law. ***Email:*** lmantione@ssd.com

ERIN ELIZABETH MARKS, born Cleveland, Ohio, 1977; admitted to bar, 2004, Ohio. *Education:* The Ohio State University (B.A., 1999); Case Western Reserve University (M.B.A., 2004; J.D., magna cum laude, 2004). Contributing Editor, Case Western Reserve Law Review. ***LANGUAGES:*** French. ***PRACTICE AREAS:*** Corporate. ***Email:*** emarks@ssd.com

DANIEL C. MAZANEC, born Cleveland, Ohio, 1979; admitted to bar, 2004, Ohio; U.S. District Court, Northern District of Ohio. *Education:* University of Notre Dame (B.A., 2001); University of Virginia (J.D., 2004). ***PRACTICE AREAS:*** Litigation. ***Email:*** dmazanec@ssd.com

JENNIFER JENKINS MEADOWS, born New Orleans, Louisiana, 1976; admitted to bar, 2003, Georgia (Not admitted in Ohio). *Education:* Wake Forest University (B.A., 1998); Georgia State University (M.S., 2000); University of Chicago (J.D., 2003). ***PRACTICE AREAS:*** Litigation.

ELLEN K. MEEHAN, born Columbus, Ohio, 1949; admitted to bar, 1992, Ohio; U.S. District Court, Northern District of Ohio. *Education:* College of Mt. St. Joseph (B.A., 1971); Cleveland State University (J.D., magna cum laude, 1992). ***PRACTICE AREAS:*** Taxation. ***Email:*** emeehan@ssd.com

J. SETH METCALF, born Columbus, Ohio, 1979; admitted to bar, 2004, Ohio. *Education:* Ohio State University (B.A., cum laude, 2001); Cornell University (J.D., 2004). ***PRACTICE AREAS:*** Public Securities. ***Email:*** smetcalf@ssd.com

CYNTHIA C. MOG, born Cleveland, Ohio, 1968; admitted to bar, 1993, Ohio. *Education:* Miami University (B.S., summa cum laude, 1990); Northwestern University (J.D., 1993). ***PRACTICE AREAS:*** Taxation. ***Email:*** cmog@ssd.com

LESLIE A. MORSEK, born Parma, Ohio, 1976; admitted to bar, 2001, Ohio. *Education:* Miami University (B.S., 1998); The University of Akron (J.D., magna cum laude, 2001). ***PRACTICE AREAS:*** Litigation. ***Email:*** lmorsek@ssd.com

STEPHANIE E. NIEHAUS, born Cleveland, Ohio, 1977; admitted to bar, 2002, Ohio; U.S. District Court, Northern District of Ohio; U.S. District Court, Eastern District of Michigan; U.S. District Court, Western District of Michigan. *Education:* Georgetown University (B.A., magna cum laude, 1999); University of Notre Dame (J.D., summa cum laude, 2002). ***PRACTICE AREAS:*** Litigation. ***Email:*** sniehaus@ssd.com

NATALIE E. NORFUS, born Cleveland, Ohio, 1980; admitted to bar, 2004, Ohio. *Education:* American University (B.A., magna cum laude, 2001); George Washington University (J.D., 2004). ***PRACTICE AREAS:*** Labor and Employment. ***Email:*** nnorfus@ssd.com

PHILIP M. OLISS, born Fort Meade, Maryland, 1970; admitted to bar, 1996, Ohio; U.S. District Court, Northern District of Ohio; U.S. District Court, Western District of Pennsylvania; U.S. Court of Appeals, Sixth Circuit. *Education:* The Ohio State University (B.A., 1993); University of Cincinnati (J.D., 1996). ***PRACTICE AREAS:*** Litigation. ***Email:*** poliss@ssd.com

(This Listing Continued)

RAPHAEL J. OMERZA, born Cleveland, Ohio, 1967; admitted to bar, 1994, Massachusetts; 1995, Ohio; U.S. Court of Appeals, Sixth Circuit; U.S. District Court, Northern District of Ohio; U.S. Supreme Court. *Education:* Boston College (B.A., summa cum laude, 1989); Vermont Law School (J.D., magna cum laude, 1993). ***PRACTICE AREAS:*** Corporate Law. ***Email:*** romerza@ssd.com

ELTON L. PARKER, born Ransomville, New York, 1973; admitted to bar, 1999, New York and Ohio. *Education:* State University of New York at Buffalo (B.S., 1995); Case Western Reserve University (J.D., 1998). ***PRACTICE AREAS:*** Environmental Law. ***Email:*** eparker@ssd.com

CHRISTINA HENAGEN PEER, born Kettering, Ohio, 1973; admitted to bar, 1999, Ohio; U.S. District Court, Northern District of Ohio; U.S. Court of Appeals, Sixth Circuit. *Education:* Miami University (B.A., magna cum laude, 1996); Washington University in St. Louis (J.D. 1999). Order of the Coif. ***PRACTICE AREAS:*** Labor and Employment. ***Email:*** cpeer@ssd.com

SEAN T. PEPPARD, born Cleveland, Ohio, 1973; admitted to bar, 2001, Ohio. *Education:* Yale University (B.A., 1995); University of Michigan (J.D., 2001). ***PRACTICE AREAS:*** Corporate Law. ***Email:*** speppard@ssd.com

CHRISTINE MURPHY PIERPONT, born Darwin, Australia, 1958; admitted to bar, 1983, Maine (inactive); 1991, Ohio; U.S. District Court, District of Maine (inactive); U.S. District Court, Northern District of Ohio; U.S. Court of Appeals, Sixth Circuit. *Education:* Kent State University (B.A., cum laude, 1980); University of Southern Maine (J.D., 1983). ***PRACTICE AREAS:*** Bankruptcy. ***Email:*** cpierpont@ssd.com

SARAH K. RATHKE, born Brainerd, Minnesota, 1976; admitted to bar, 2001, Ohio; U.S. District Court, Northern District of Ohio; U.S. District Court, Southern District of Ohio. *Education:* Georgetown University (B.A., cum laude, 1998); University of Michigan (J.D., 2001). ***PRACTICE AREAS:*** Litigation. ***Email:*** srathke@ssd.com

RENEE TRAMBLE RICHARD, born Cleveland, Ohio, 1954; admitted to bar, 1988, Ohio; 2003, District of Columbia. *Education:* Kent State University (B.B.A., 1976); Cleveland State University (M.B.A., 1981; J.D., 1988). ***PRACTICE AREAS:*** Public Revenue Finance. ***Email:*** rtramblerrichard@ssd.com

JOSEPH P. RODGERS, born Lorain, Ohio, 1972; admitted to bar, 1998, Ohio; U.S. District Court, Northern District of Ohio. *Education:* College of Wooster (B.A., 1994); Cleveland State University (J.D., 1998). ***PRACTICE AREAS:*** Litigation. ***Email:*** jrodgers@ssd.com

CATHERINE ZIROLI ROMANCHEK, born Norristown, Pennsylvania, 1978; admitted to bar, 2003, Ohio. *Education:* University of Notre Dame (B.A., magna cum laude, 2000); University of Michigan (J.D., cum laude, 2003). ***PRACTICE AREAS:*** Public Securities. ***Email:*** cromanchek@ssd.com

ELIZABETH M. SANBORN, born Cleveland, Ohio, 1955; admitted to bar, 1981, Ohio. *Education:* University of Northern Colorado (B.A., 1977); Campbell University (J.D., 1981). ***PRACTICE AREAS:*** Labor and Employment. ***Email:*** esanborn@ssd.com

MARK J. SAVAGE, born Cleveland, Ohio, 1973; admitted to bar, 1998, Ohio; U.S. District Court, Northern District of Ohio; U.S. District Court, Southern District of Ohio; U.S. Court of Appeals, Sixth Circuit. *Education:* Baldwin-Wallace College (B.A., 1995); Cleveland State University (J.D., magna cum laude, 1998). ***PRACTICE AREAS:*** Litigation. ***Email:*** mjsavage@ssd.com

WILLIAM V. SHAKLEE, born Lawrence, Kansas, 1976; admitted to bar, 2002, Ohio; U.S. District Court, Eastern District of Michigan; U.S. District Court, Northern District of Ohio; registered to practice before U.S. Patent and Trademark Office. *Education:* University of Rhode Island (B.A., 1998); The Ohio State University (J.D., 2002). Associate Editor, The Ohio State Journal of Alternative Dispute Resolution. ***PRACTICE AREAS:*** Environmental Law. ***Email:*** wshaklee@ssd.com

DHEERAJ K. SINGHAL, born Torrance, California, 1975; admitted to bar, 2001, California; U.S. District Court, Central District of California; U.S. Court of Appeals, Ninth Circuit; U.S. District Court, Northern District of Ohio (Not admitted in Ohio). *Education:* University of California, Los Angeles (B.S., 1997); University of California, Davis (J.D., cum laude, 2001). ***LANGUAGES:*** Hindi. ***PRACTICE AREAS:*** Litigation. ***Email:*** dsinghal@ssd.com

ANTHONY M. SMITS, born Green Bay, Wisconsin, 1972; admitted to bar, 1999, Ohio. *Education:* Marquette University (B.A., honors, 1995); University of Cincinnati (M.B.A., 1997; J.D., 1999). ***PRACTICE AREAS:*** Corporate Law; Securities; Corporate Governance; Technology; E-Commerce. ***Email:*** asmits@ssd.com

CATHERINE M. SWARTZ, born Cleveland, Ohio, 1976; admitted to bar, 2002, Ohio. *Education:* College of Wooster (B.A., magna cum laude, 1998); Ohio State University (J.D., with honors, 2002). ***PRACTICE AREAS:*** Public Finance; Bond Finance; Tax Exempt Bonds; Tax Exempt Finance. ***Email:*** cswartz@ssd.com

TERENCE L. THOMAS, born Cleveland, Ohio, 1962; admitted to bar, 1994, Ohio. *Education:* Cornell University (B.S., 1984); Ohio State University (J.D., 1994). ***PRACTICE AREAS:*** Real Estate. ***Email:*** tthomas@ssd.com

CATHERINE CORRIGAN TOMPKINS, born Cleveland, Ohio, 1968; admitted to bar, 1995, Ohio. *Education:* Georgetown University (A.B., cum laude, 1991); Case Western Reserve University (J.D., 1995). ***PRACTICE AREAS:*** Public Revenue Finance. ***Email:*** ctompkins@ssd.com

JAMES A. VOLLINS, born New York, N.Y., 1968; admitted to bar, 1993, Ohio; U.S. District Court, Northern District of Ohio; U.S. Court of Appeals, Third Circuit; U.S. Court of Appeals, Sixth Circuit; U.S. Court of Appeals for the Federal Circuit; U.S. Supreme Court. *Education:* Wesleyan University (B.A., 1990); Case Western Reserve University (J.D., magna cum laude, 1993). ***PRACTICE AREAS:*** Litigation. ***Email:*** jvollins@ssd.com

DANA B. WEISS, born Livingston, New Jersey, 1975; admitted to bar, 2003, Ohio. *Education:* University of Texas at Austin (B.J., 1997); Cleveland State University (J.D., cum laude, 2003). ***PRACTICE AREAS:*** Public Securities. ***Email:*** dweiss@ssd.com

(This Listing Continued)

KRISTINE M. WELLMAN, born Flint, Michigan, 1970; admitted to bar, 1995, Ohio. *Education:* University of Michigan (A.B., with distinction, 1992); Case Western Reserve University (J.D., 1995). ***PRACTICE AREAS:*** Corporate Law. ***Email:*** kwellman@ssd.com

REVISOR OF THE OHIO AND TEXAS LAW DIGESTS FOR THIS DIRECTORY

(For Biographical Data on Cincinnati and Columbus, Ohio, Miami and Tampa, Florida, Houston, Texas, New York, New York, Phoenix, Arizona, Washington, D.C., Los Angeles, Palo Alto and San Francisco, California, Tysons Corner, Virginia, Rio de Janeiro, Brazil, Bratislava, Slovak Republic, Brussels, Belgium, Budapest, Hungary, London, England, Madrid, Spain, Milan, Italy, Moscow, Russian Federation, Prague, Czech Republic, Warsaw, Poland, Beijing and Hong Kong, China and Tokyo, Japan Personnel, see Professional Biographies at those Points Respectively).

JAMES T. STANCEU

425 WESTERN RESERVE BUILDING
1468 W. NINTH STREET
CLEVELAND, OHIO 44113
Telephone: 216-588-1001; 800-641-7989
Fax: 216-588-1003
Email: jtstanceu@neo.rr.com
URL: http://www.jtstanceulaw.com

Personal Injury, Automobile Accidents and Injuries, Truck Accidents and Injuries, Wrongful Death, Medical Malpractice, Workers Compensation, Workers' Compensation Appeals.

JAMES T. STANCEU, born Canton, Ohio, July 31, 1951; admitted to bar, 1979, Ohio; 2004, U.S. District Court, Northern District of Ohio. *Education:* Ohio State University (B.A., summa cum laude, 1973); Georgetown University (J.D., cum laude, 1979). Phi Beta Kappa. Staff Member, 1977-1978 and Editor, 1978-1979, Law and Policy in International Business. *Member:* Ohio State Bar Association. ***PRACTICE AREAS:*** Personal Injury; Automobile Accidents and Injuries; Truck Accidents; Wrongful Death; Medical Malpractice; Workers Compensation; Workers Compensation Appeals.

STEGE & MICHELSON CO., L.P.A.

32ND FLOOR, BP AMERICA BUILDING
200 PUBLIC SQUARE, SUITE 3220
CLEVELAND, OHIO 44114
Telephone: 216-348-0700
Fax: 216-348-0803
Email: email@stege-law.com
URL: http://www.stege-law.com

Trial Practice in the State and Federal Courts including Personal Injury, Medical Malpractice, Nursing Home Abuse and Neglect, FELA/Railroad Law, Labor and Employment, Insurance Litigation, Commercial Litigation, Business Tort Litigation, Criminal Defense. Elder Law, Estate Planning and Probate Law.

FIRM PROFILE: We are a litigation firm. Personal injury law, in all its dimensions, is our distinctive passion. Our practice also enjoys an excellent track record with employment, commercial, criminal and business tort litigation. Please visit our website.

EDWARD RICHARD STEGE, born Madison, Wisconsin, November 4, 1943; admitted to bar, 1968, Wisconsin and Ohio; 1969, U.S. District Court, Northern District of Ohio; 1970, U.S. Court of Appeals, Sixth Circuit; 1975, U.S. Supreme Court. *Education:* Colgate University (A.B., 1965); University of Wisconsin Law School (J.D., 1968). Member, Order of the Coif, 1968. Member, Board of Editors, University of Wisconsin Law Review, 1966-1968. Adjunct Professor of Law, Case Western Reserve University, 1975-1976, 1996-1999; Cleveland-Marshall College of Law, 1978-1979. Director, Law Reform Section, Legal Aid Society of Cleveland, 1970-1978. Master of the Bench, Harold H. Burton Chapter, American Inns of Court, 1992—. Member, Federal Court Panel of Alternative Dispute Resolution Neutrals, Northern District of Ohio, 1992—. *Member:* Cleveland (Chair, Professional Ethics Committee, 1999; Member, Sections on Litigation and Labor and Employment Law; Division of Fees Mediation and Arbitration Committee), Ohio State (Member, Sections on Litigation and Labor and Employment Law), and American (Member, Sections on: Litigation; Labor and Employment Law; Tort and Insurance Law) Bar Associations; The Association of Trial Lawyers of America; Ohio Academy of Trial Lawyers; Cleveland Academy of Trial Lawyers. ***REPORTED CASES:*** Moore vs. City of East Cleveland, 431 U.S. 494, 1977, argued; Local Union 93 International Association of Firefighters vs. City of Cleveland, 478 U.S. 501, 1986, argued. ***PRACTICE AREAS:*** Trial Practice; Personal Injury; Medical Malpractice; Employment Law; Commercial Litigation; Nursing Home Abuse and Neglect. ***Email:*** rstege@stege-law.com

MICHAEL B. MICHELSON, born Brooklyn, New York, May 4, 1941; admitted to bar, 1971, New York; 1979, Ohio, U.S. District Court, Northern District of Ohio, U.S. District Court, Southern District of New York and U.S. Court of Appeals, Second, Third and Fourth Circuits; U.S. Supreme Court. *Education:* New York University (B.S., 1962); St. John's University (J.D., 1970). Special Attorney, Criminal Division, U.S. Department of Justice, 1974-1979. *Member:* Cleveland, New York State and Ohio State Bar Associations; The Association of Trial Lawyers of America. ***PRACTICE AREAS:*** Personal Injury; Medical Negligence; Railroad Law; Federal Employers Liability Act (FELA); Employment Law; Professional Negligence; Motor Vehicle Accidents and Injuries; Criminal Law. ***Email:*** mmichelson@stege-law.com

---

ANDREW J. THOMPSON, born Hornell, New York, May 28, 1973; admitted to bar, 1999, Ohio. *Education:* Case Western Reserve University (B.A., 1966; J.D., 1999). *Member:* Cleveland (Member, Labor and Employment Section) and Ohio State Bar Associations; The Association of Trial Lawyers of America (Member, Railroad Law Section). ***PRACTICE AREAS:*** Federal Employers Liability Act (FELA); Personal Injury; Railroad Law; Litigation; Labor and Employment. ***Email:*** athompson@stege-law.com

OF COUNSEL

DEBORAH A. WAINEY, born Cleveland, Ohio, March 5, 1959; admitted to bar, 1991, Ohio; 1992, U.S. District Court, Northern District of Ohio; 1993, U.S. Court of Appeals, Sixth Circuit. *Education:* Baldwin-Wallace College (B.A., cum laude, 1987); Cleveland-Marshall College of Law (J.D., summa cum laude, 1990). Recipient: Chief Justice Samuel H. Silbert Award, Cleveland State Law Review; Outstanding Achievement Award, Cleveland State Law Review. Author: "Voluntary Active Euthanasia: The Ultimate Act of Care for the Dying," 37 Clev. St. L. Rev. 645, 1989; "Power of Attorney, Guardianship and Conservatorship," Elder Law Desk Reference, Ohio State Bar Association, Elder Law Committee, 1993; "The Role of a 'Medicaid Payback Trust' in Personal Injury Awards Granted to Disabled Persons," Ohio Lawyer (March/April 1994); "Nursing Homes: A Consumer Perspective," Ohio Lawyer (Sept./Oct. 1994). *Member:* Cuyahoga County, Ohio State and American Bar Associations; National Academy of Elder Law Attorneys. ***PRACTICE AREAS:*** Elder Law; Estate Planning; Probate; General Civil Practice. ***Email:*** dwainey@netzero.net

THOMAS C. WOOD, JR., born Toledo, Ohio, August 28, 1943; admitted to bar, 1974, Ohio; 1975, Florida. *Education:* University of Toledo (B.A., 1971; J.D., 1974). *Member:* Columbus and Ohio State Bar Associations; The Florida Bar; The Association of Trial Lawyers of America; Ohio Academy of Trial Lawyers. ***PRACTICE AREAS:*** Personal Injury; Federal Employers Liability Act (FELA); Railroad Law. ***Email:*** tomcwood@yahoo.com

ROBERT N. STEIN, CO. LPA

1450 ROCKEFELLER BUILDING
614 SUPERIOR AVENUE, N.W.
CLEVELAND, OHIO 44113
Telephone: 216-781-8040
Fax: 216-781-9091
Email: robertnsteinesq@sbcglobal.net
URL: http://www.lawyers.com/robertsteinlaw

Business Law, Contract Disputes, Corporate Law, Small Business Law, Litigation, Real Estate, Civil Trial, Personal Injury, Auto Accidents, Dog Bites, Premises Liability.

ROBERT N. STEIN, born Cleveland, Ohio, April 30, 1961; admitted to bar, 1986, Ohio; 1987, U.S. District Court, Northern District of Ohio and Western District of Michigan. *Education:* The Ohio State University (B.A., 1983); Cleveland Marshall College of Law (J.D., cum laude, 1986). *Member:* Ohio State and American Bar Associations. ***PRACTICE AREAS:*** Business Law; Corporate Law; Litigation; Real Estate; Civil Practice; Trial Practice.

MITCHELL A. STERN

55 PUBLIC SQUARE, SUITE 1717
CLEVELAND, OHIO 44113-1901
Telephone: 216-861-0006
Fax: 216-771-8404

Workers Compensation, Appeals, Personal Injury, Automobile Accidents, General Practice.

MITCHELL A. STERN, born 1952; admitted to bar, 1977, Ohio. *Education:* Miami University (B.A.); Ohio State University (J.D.). Assistant Attorney General of Ohio, 1978-1986.

STERNBERG & ZEID CO., L.P.A.

CLEVELAND, OHIO

(See Mentor)

Personal Injury, Automobile Accidents, Wrongful Death, Workers Compensation, Municipal Law, Zoning Law, Bankruptcy, Domestic Relations, Family Law, Divorce, Child Custody, Guardianship, Real Estate, Probate, Estate Planning, Trusts and Wills, Business, Corporate, Contract Law, General Civil Trial Practice in State and Federal Courts.

STEUER, ESCOVAR, BERK & BROWN CO., L.P.A.

Established in 1918

55 PUBLIC SQUARE, SUITE 1828
CLEVELAND, OHIO 44113-1977
Telephone: 216-771-8121
Fax: 216-771-8120
URL: http://www.sebblaw.com
Email: info@sebblaw.com
URL: http://www.lawyers.com/steuerescovar&berk

General Civil and Criminal Practice. Personal Injury, Negligence, Workers Compensation, Corporation, Mergers and Acquisitions, Taxation, Real Estate, Bankruptcy, Family, Probate and Commercial Law. Estate Planning, Trials and Medical Malpractice, Civil and Criminal Appellate Work, Insurance Defense, Business Law, Administrative Law.

FIRM PROFILE: Steuer, Escovar, Berk & Brown Co., L.P.A. was established in 1918 by Judge Alfred L. Steuer. The firm offers services in most areas of law including personal injury, bankruptcy, criminal law, tax, wills, workers compensation, divorce, trial, probate, corporate, D.W.I., malpractice, social security and victim of crime reparations.

(This Listing Continued)

STEUER, ESCOVAR, BERK & BROWN CO., L.P.A., Cleveland—Continued

The firm whose collective experience totals an impressive 93 years has earned the respect and confidence of three generations of Cleveland families and business. We serve all of Cuyahoga, Lake, Lorain and Medina Counties as well as the entire State of Ohio. We are able to offer the experience of a larger firm while retaining a warm, personal atmosphere.

RICHARD B. STEUER (Retired)

ALFRED L. STEUER (1892-1967)

THOMAS J. ESCOVAR, born Endicott, New York, September 5, 1940; admitted to bar, 1969, Ohio; 1971, U.S. District Court, Northern District of Ohio; 1982, U.S. Tax Court; 1984, U.S. Supreme Court. *Education:* Niagara University (B.A., 1963); Cleveland Marshall College of Law (J.D., 1968). Delta Theta Phi (Tribune, 1967-1968). Member, Editorial Board, Ohio Lawyers Magazine, Ohio State Bar Association. Assistant Prosecuting Attorney, Cuyahoga County, Ohio, 1972-1974. Member, National Panel of Arbitrators, American Arbitration Association. Delegate 8th Circuit Court of Appeals Convention, 1989. Life Member, Judicial Conference of the 8th Judicial District. Member, Joint Bar Admission Appeals Committee of Cuyahoga County Bar Association and Cleveland Bar Association; Vice-Chairman and Chairman, 1991, Chairman, 2002-2003. Cuyahoga County Bar Association Admissions Committee, 1994-1997 and 1998; Former Chairman, 1995. Member: Ohio Supreme Court Rule 20 Commission on Death Penalty Cases, 2004-2008; Associate Board of Trustees for Myers University, 2003—. "Rule 20" Commission Supreme Court. *Member:* Cleveland (Former Member, Attorney/Client Compensation Committee; Former Vice Chairman, Character and Fitness Committee, 1996-1998, Chairman, 2002-2003), Cuyahoga County (President, 2003-2004; President Elect, 2002-2003; First Vice-President, 2001-2002; Second Vice-President, 2000-2001; Current Division Member; Criminal Law Committee, 1976—; Grievance Fee Committee, 1985—; Grievance Committee, 1990—; Former Lawyer/Client Relations Committee, 1992-1997; Trustee, 1991—; Life Member, Judicial Selection Committee; Mentoring Program for Young Lawyers, 1997—), Hispanic and Ohio State (Chair; Member, Judicial Administration and Legal Reform Committee; Member, Board of Delegates, 1995—; Member, Board of Governors, 2001—; Member, Board of Editors, 2001-2003; Member, 2002 and 2004 Commission on Judicial Candidates) Bar Associations; The Association of Trial Lawyers of America; Ohio Academy of Trial Lawyers; Cleveland Criminal Lawyers Association; Cuyahoga Criminal Defense Lawyers Association; Judicial Administration and Legal Reform Committee. ***PRACTICE AREAS:*** Personal Injury Law; Medical Malpractice; Corporate Law; Criminal Law; Driving While Intoxicated; Death; Penalty; Appellate Practice. ***Email:*** tescovar@sebblaw.com

GERALD A. BERK, born Cleveland, Ohio, April 8, 1943; admitted to bar, 1970, Ohio; 1973, U.S. District Court, Northern District of Ohio; 1980, U.S. Tax Court; 1984, U.S. Supreme Court. *Education:* Fenn College; The Ohio State University (B.S., 1966); Cleveland State University (J.D., 1970). Internal Revenue Agent, Internal Revenue Service, Field Audit Division, Cleveland, Ohio, 1969-1972. Member, Richmond Heights School Board, 1975-1983. Member: National Panel of Arbitrators, American Arbitration Association; Construction Panel, American Arbitration Association. *Member:* Cleveland, Cuyahoga County (Member: Committees on Tax and Bankruptcy, 1976—; Workers' Compensation Committee, 1979—), Ohio State and American (Member: Sections on Taxation; Corporation, Banking and Business Law) Bar Associations; Ohio Academy of Trial Lawyers (Member, Workers' Compensation Committee, 1981—). ***PRACTICE AREAS:*** Workers Compensation Law; Bankruptcy Law; Probate Law; Corporation Law; Business Law; Real Estate.

WILLIAM D. BROWN, born Parma, Ohio, January 7, 1965; admitted to bar, 1991, Ohio; 1992, U.S. District Court, Northern District of Ohio. *Education:* Bowling Green University (B.S., 1987); Case Western Reserve (J.D., 1991). *Member:* Cuyahoga County and Ohio State Bar Associations; Ohio Academy of Trial Lawyers. ***PRACTICE AREAS:*** Personal Injury; Domestic Relations; Business Litigation; Discrimination; Wrongful Termination. ***Email:*** wbrown@sebblaw.com

---

L. CHRISTOPHER COLEMAN, born Pikeville, Kentucky, May 19, 1977; admitted to bar, 2002, Ohio; 2003, U.S. District Court, Northern District of Ohio; U.S. Court of Appeals, Sixth Circuit. *Education:* University of Kentucky (B.A., 1999); University of Akron (J.D., 2002). Phi Delta Phi. *Member:* Cuyahoga County, Ohio State and American Bar Associations; Ohio Academy of Trial Lawyers; The Association of Trial Lawyers of America. ***PRACTICE AREAS:*** Personal Injury; Domestic Relations; Social Security; Business Litigation. ***Email:*** ccoleman@sebblaw.com

PATRICK P. MERRICK, born Warren, Ohio, July 6, 1968; admitted to bar, 2004, Ohio; 2005, U.S. District Court, Northern District of Ohio. *Education:* Youngstown State University (B.S., 1992); Case Western Reserve University (J.D., 2004). *Member:* Cuyahoga County Bar Association; The Association of Trial Lawyers of America; The Ohio Association of Trial Lawyers of America. ***PRACTICE AREAS:*** Personal Injury; Domestic Relations; Social Security. ***Email:*** pmerrick@sebblaw.com

REFERENCES: Huntington Bank; Key Bank.

STEWART AND DE CHANT CO., L.P.A.

Established in 1966

THE STANDARD BUILDING
1370 ONTARIO STREET, SUITE 1440
CLEVELAND, OHIO 44113-1701
Telephone: 216-781-2258
Fax: 216-781-8210
Email: INFO@STEWARTDECHANT.COM
URL: http://www.STEWARTDECHANT.COM

General Trial and Appellate Practice. Negligence, Products Liability, Malpractice, Medical Legal, Workers Compensation and Social Security Disability Law. Wrongful Death Law.

(This Listing Continued)

FIRM PROFILE: Stewart and De Chant Co., L.P.A. is a law firm of trial lawyers, providing legal services to anyone who has experienced injury and damage as a result of the misconduct of another person, company or corporation. Founded by Lawrence E. Stewart in 1950, the firm has consistently been devoted to the practice of plaintiffs' injury litigation since its birth. Thomas H. De Chant joined Larry Stewart in 1958 and together have provided the stability for the firm's practice for the past 52 years.

The firm's lawyers practice regularly in state and federal trial and appellate courts throughout Ohio, as well as in other states. As plaintiffs' injury trial lawyers, we take pride as ethical practitioners who are diligent, effective and compassionate.

LAWRENCE E. STEWART, born Cleveland, Ohio, March 15, 1925; admitted to bar, 1950, Ohio; 1952, U.S. District Court, Northern District of Ohio; 1957, U.S. Court of Appeals, Sixth Circuit; 1966, U.S. Supreme Court; 1980, U.S. Court of Appeals for the District of Columbia Circuit; 1986, U.S. Court of Appeals, Third and Eleventh Circuits. *Education:* Ohio University (B.S.C., with honors, 1949; Medal of Merit, Distinction in Jurisprudence, 1994); Case Western Reserve University (J.D., 1950). Society of Benchers; Phi Delta Phi; Tau Kappa Alpha. Member: National Panel of Arbitrators, American Arbitration Association, 1961-1980; Medical-Legal Committee, Cleveland Academy of Medicine, 1963-1975. Associate-In-Law, The American College of Legal Medicine, (1973—). Member: The American Society of Law and Medicine, 1976—; Advisory Committee Case Western Reserve University Law Medicine Center, 1994; American Board of Professional Liability Attorneys, 1990; Oxfords Who's Who, 1990—; The Best Lawyers in America, 1987—. Master Bencher, American Inns of Court, 1990. *Member:* Cleveland (Trustee, 1969-1972 and Chairman, Court Management Project, 1973-1975; President, 1976-1977; Chairman: Judicial Campaign Committee, 1984-1989; Co-Chair, American Inns of Court, 1988; Joint Academy of Medicine and Bar Committee, 1984 Cuyahoga County (Member, 1958-1985, Chairman, 1962-1963 and Co-Chairman, 1963, Medical Legal Committee), Ohio State and American (Delegate, House of Delegates, 1978-1980) Bar Associations; Cleveland Academy of Trial Attorneys (Trustee, 1972-1974; President, 1977-1978); Ohio Academy of Trial Lawyers (Trustee, 1973-1975; Vice President, 1976-1977); Cleveland Law Library Association (Director, 1988-1999); American Judicature Society (Director, 1986-1990); American Board of Trial Advocate (Advocate, 1989). American College of Forensic Examiners, 1995—. Fellow: American College of Trial Lawyers (Ohio Chairman, 1986-1987); International Academy of Trial Lawyers; Judicial Conference of Eighth Judicial District (Life). ***PRACTICE AREAS:*** Medical Malpractice; Personal Injury Law; Airplane Crash Litigation. ***Email:*** les@stewartdechant.com

THOMAS H. DE CHANT, born Cleveland, Ohio, November 28, 1932; admitted to bar, 1958, Ohio; 1959, U.S. District Court, Northern District of Ohio; 1971, U.S. Supreme Court. *Education:* University of Detroit (Ph.B., 1955); Western Reserve University (LL.B., 1958). Phi Delta Phi; Psi Chi. Member, Master Bencher, A.J. Celebrezze National Inns of Court (Federal). *Member:* Cleveland (Chairman, Judicial Selections Committee, 1976; Member, Grievance Committee, 1986-1987; Division of Attorney Fees) and Ohio State (Delegate, 12th District, 1987; Mediation and Arbitration Committee, 1993—) Bar Associations; Cleveland Academy of Trial Attorneys (Trustee, 1974-1977); Ohio Academy of Trial Lawyers; Judicial Conference of Eighth Judicial District (Life). Fellow, American College of Trial Lawyers. ***PRACTICE AREAS:*** Premises Liability Law; Personal Injury Law. ***Email:*** thd@stewartdechant.com

FRED WENDEL III, born Cleveland, Ohio, March 21, 1949; admitted to bar, 1974, Ohio; 1975, U.S. District Court, Northern District of Ohio. *Education:* Colgate University (B.A., 1971); Case Western Reserve University (J.D., 1974). Member, Case Western Reserve Law Review, 1973-1974. Member, Moot Court Board. Recipient, Dean's Brief Writing Award, 1972. Instructor, Research, Writing and Advocacy, Case Western Reserve University Law School, 1972-1974. *Member:* Cleveland (Board of Trustees, 1994-1997; Judicial Selection Committee, Chairman; Judicial Selection Monitoring Committee, 1997—; Secretary-Treasurer, Young Lawyers Section, 1978-1979, 1980-1981), Ohio State (District Representative, Young Lawyers Section, 1982-1984) and American (Vice-Chair, Law-Medicine Committee, Tort and Insurance Practice Section, 1995—; Member, Task Force on Auto Choice Legislation and Plaintiff's Involvement Committee) Bar Associations; The Association of Trial Lawyers of America; Ohio Academy of Trial Lawyers (Trustee, 1983-1990); Cleveland Academy of Trial Attorneys (Member, Board of Directors, 1979-1981; Treasurer, 1980-1981; Vice-President, 1981-1982; President, 1982-1983);National Institute for Trial Advocacy (Diplomate and Advanced Diplomate) Judicial Conference for the Eighth Judicial District (Life Member). ***PRACTICE AREAS:*** Medical Malpractice; Dental Malpractice; Wrongful Death Law; Personal Injury Law; Legal Malpractice. ***Email:*** fw3@stewartdechant.com

SCOTT E. STEWART, born Cleveland, Ohio, July 9, 1951; admitted to bar, 1976, Ohio; 1978, U.S. District Court, Northern District of Ohio; 1989, U.S. Court of Appeals, Sixth Circuit. *Education:* Bethany College (B.A., with senior high honors, 1973); Case Western Reserve University (J.D., 1976); Court Practice Institute (Diplomate, 1977; Advanced Diplomate, 1978); National Institute for Trial Advocacy (Diplomate, 1980; Advanced Diplomate, 1985). Phi Beta Kappa. *Member:* Cleveland (Director, Young Lawyers Section, 1984-1986; Chairman, Alternative Dispute Resolution Committee, 1993-1995; Litigation Council, 1994—), Ohio State (District Representative, 1993-2002) and American Bar Associations; Ohio Academy of Trial Lawyers; The Association of Trial Lawyers of America; Cleveland Academy of Trial Attorneys (Member, Board of Trustees, 1984-1989; Treasurer, 1985-1986; Secretary, 1986-1987; Vice President, 1987-1988; President, 1988-1989); National Organization of Social Security Claimants Representatives; American Judicature Society. American Board of Professional Liability Attorneys (Diplomate). Fellow, American Board of Trial Advocates. (Certified as a Civil Trial Advocate by the National Board of Trial Advocacy). ***PRACTICE AREAS:*** Products Liability; Legal Malpractice; Wrongful Death; Intentional Torts; Negligence. ***Email:*** scott@stewartdechant.com

SAMUEL V. BUTCHER, born Titusville, Pennsylvania, July 19, 1954; admitted to bar, 1984, Ohio; 1990, U.S. District Court, Northern District of Ohio. *Education:* Ohio Northern University (B.S., in Pharmacy, 1977); Cleveland-Marshall College of Law (J.D., 1982). Registered Pharmacist, Ohio, 1977. Recipient: The Smith Kline and French Laboratories Award for Superior Achievement in Clinical Pharmacy, 1977; Rexall Award for Outstanding Achievement, Pharmacy Graduating Class, 1977. Assistant Prosecuting Attor-

(This Listing Continued)

ney, Cuyahoga County, Ohio, 1984-1987; Associate, Judge Anthony J. Celebrezze Inn of Court, National Inns of Court Foundation, 1991-1995; Barrister, 1995—). *Member:* Cleveland and Ohio State Bar Associations; Cleveland Academy of Trial Attorneys; The Ohio Academy of Trial Lawyers; The Association of Trial Lawyers of America. ***PRACTICE AREAS:*** Medical Malpractice; Dental Malpractice; Wrongful Death; Personal Injury Law. ***Email:*** samb@stewartdechant.com

---

CINDY L. KOBAL, born Cleveland, Ohio, March 9, 1973; admitted to bar, 2000, Ohio. *Education:* University of Akron (Associate Degree, Legal Assisting Technology, with high distinction, 1993; B.S., Technical Education, magna cum laude, 1996); University of Akron School of Law (J.D., 2000). Formerly with: Bevan and Associates, LPA, Inc.; Summit County Prosecutor's Office. *Member:* Cleveland and Ohio State Bar Associations; Cleveland Academy of Trial Lawyers. ***PRACTICE AREAS:*** Workers Compensation. ***Email:*** clk@stewartdechant.com

LAWRENCE D. WILSON, born Mayfield, Ohio, May 13, 1977; admitted to bar, 1977, Ohio. *Education:* University of Virginia (B.A., 1999); Case Western Reserve University (J.D., 2003). *Member:* Cleveland Bar Association; Cleveland Academy of Trial Attorneys. ***PRACTICE AREAS:*** Personal Injury (60%); Medical Malpractice (40%). ***Email:*** lwilson@stewartdechant.com

SHERI A. SWEENEY, born Cleveland, Ohio, November 28, 1973; admitted to bar, 2002, Ohio. *Education:* Kent State University (B.A., 1997); Cleveland-Marshall College of Law (J.D., 2001). ***PRACTICE AREAS:*** Workers Compensation.

OF COUNSEL

PAUL S. SANISLO, born Cleveland, Ohio, February 8, 1927; admitted to bar, 1961, Ohio; 1964, U.S. District Court, Northern District of Ohio. *Education:* Baldwin Wallace College (B.A., 1948); Cleveland State University (J.D., 1961). Delta Theta Phi. Member, 1945— and President, 1967-1968, Hungarian Business and Tradesmen's Club. Member, 1964— and President, 1973-1976, Cleveland Association of Compensation Attorneys. Member, Cleveland City Council, 29th Ward, 1964-1967. Member, 1972-1983 and President, 1974-1983, Solon City Board of Education. Chairman, Solon Charter Review Commission, 1971 and 2000. Member, American Arbitration Association, 1972-1978. Trustee, Cleveland-Marshall Law School, 1962-1963. Trustee, Cleveland-Marshall Educational Institution, 1963-1973, President, 1970. President, Cleveland-Marshall Law School Alumni, 1968-1969. *Member:* Cleveland (Chairman, Workers Compensation Section), Cuyahoga County and Ohio State Bar Associations; Ohio Academy of Trial Attorneys. [Staff Sergeant, U.S. Army Corps. of Engineers, 1945-1946]. ***LANGUAGES:*** Hungarian. ***PRACTICE AREAS:*** Worker's Compensation Law; Personal Injury Law; Probate Law. ***Email:*** pss@stewartdechant.com

REFERENCE: Keybank (Main Office).

SULLIVAN & SULLIVAN, LTD.

25201 CHAGRIN BOULEVARD
SUITE 350
CLEVELAND, OHIO 44122
Telephone: 216-896-0001
Fax: 216-896-0002
URL: http://www.sullivanandsullivan.com

Asset Protection Planning, Asset Recovery, Debtor/Creditor, Collections, Levy, Attachment, Bankruptcy and Workouts, Estate Planning, Oil & Gas, Commercial Litigation and Appellate.

JOHN E. SULLIVAN, III, born Boston, Massachusetts, November 11, 1958; admitted to bar, 1985, Massachusetts and Illinois; 1986, Ohio and U.S. District Court, Northern District of Ohio; 1987, U.S. District Court, Northern District of Texas; 1988, U.S. Court of Appeals, Fifth Circuit; 1991, U.S. Court of Appeals, Sixth Circuit; 1995, U.S. Supreme Court; 1997, U.S. Tax Court. *Education:* Boston College (B.A., magna cum laude; Phi Alpha Theta, 1980); University of Texas (J.D., 1984). Recipient, Dean's Distinction Award for Damages Seminar. Author: "Oil and Gas Securities Litigation," 8 Eastern Min. L. Institute 16-1, 1987; "Future Creditors and Fraudulent Transfers...Important Limits to Fraudulent Transfers Law for the Asset Protection Planner," 22 Delaware J. Corp. Law 955 (1997); "Gutting the Rule Against Self-Settled Trusts: How the New Delaware Trust Law Competes With Offshore Trusts," 234 Del. J. Corp. Law 423 (1998); "The Often Overlooked Role of Disclosure in Asset Protection Planning," Ch. 19 of "Asset Protection Strategies (Planning with Domestic and Offshore Entities)" (Bove, Ed., 2002 ABA). Contributing Author, "Capital Formation and Investment Incentives Around The World," 1998-2000. Contributing Author, "International Trust Laws and Analysis." Contributing Editor, "Tax Havens of the World," 2000-2004. Member, Offshore Institute. Member, International Tax Planning Association. Member, Cleveland Estate Planning Council. *Member:* Ohio State Bar Association (Member, Creditor Access to Individual Retirement Account Committee). ***REPORTED CASES:*** Columbia Natural Resources, Inc. v. Tatum, 58 F.3d 1101 (6th Cir. 1995); Javitch v. Capwill, 284 F.Supp. 2d 848 (N.D. Ohio 2003). ***PRACTICE AREAS:*** Debtor/Creditor Law; Bankruptcy; Collections; Fraudulent Transfers; Asset Protection; Levy; Attachment; Estate Planning; Oil & Gas; Litigation. ***Email:*** jesullivan3@sullivanandsullivan.com

JULIA RYAN SULLIVAN, born Fort Worth, Texas, January 8, 1961; admitted to bar, 1986, Ohio; 1990, U.S. District Court, Northern District of Ohio; 1992, U.S. Court of Appeals, Sixth Circuit; 1993, U.S. Court of Appeals for the Federal Circuit. *Education:* University of Texas (B.A., with highest honors, 1982; J.D., 1985); Case Western Reserve University (M.B.A., 1990). Phi Beta Kappa; Beta Gamma Sigma. Contributing Editor: "International Trust Laws and Analysis;" "Tax Havens of the World." *Member:* Cleveland Bar Association. ***PRACTICE AREAS:*** Litigation; Appellate; Estate Planning; Probate. ***Email:*** jrsullivan@sullivanandsullivan.com

(This Listing Continued)

ASSOCIATE

PATRICK J. RHOA, born Cleveland, Ohio, May 30, 1960; admitted to bar, 1990, Ohio and U.S. District Court, Northern District of Ohio. *Education:* University of Cincinnati (B.S., 1984); Cleveland-Marshall College of Law (J.D., 1990). Delta Theta Phi. Judicial Clerk to the Hon. James M. Porter, Ohio Court of Appeals, Eighth District. Author: "Nursing Home Malpractice in Ohio," January 18, 2000. *Member:* Cleveland, Cuyahoga County and Ohio State Bar Associations; Lawyers Guild of the Catholic Diocese of Cleveland. ***PRACTICE AREAS:*** Creditor Representation; Debtor and Creditor; Fraudulent Transfers; Collections; Oil and Gas Law; Litigation; Appellate Practice; Commercial Litigation. ***Email:*** pjrhoa@sullivanandsullivan.com

OF COUNSEL

ROBERT J. RISCHITELLI, JR, born Cleveland, Ohio, March 3, 1970; admitted to bar, 1995, Florida and Ohio; 1996, Massachusetts. *Education:* Kent State University (B.A., magna cum laude, 1992); University of Akron School of Law (J.D., 1994); Case Western Reserve University (LL.M., Taxation, 1998). *Member:* The Florida Bar (Real Property, Probate Section). ***PRACTICE AREAS:*** Sports Law; Entertainment Law; Probate; Estate Planning; Taxation; Litigation. ***Email:*** rjrischitelli@sullivanandsullivan.com

---

SUTTER, O'CONNELL & FARCHIONE

3600 ERIEVIEW TOWER
1301 EAST NINTH STREET
CLEVELAND, OHIO 44114
Telephone: 216-928-2200
Fax: 216-928-4400
Email: LSutter@sutter-law.com
URL: http://www.sutter-law.com

Franklin, Tennessee Office: 217 Second Avenue, South, 37064-2622. Telephone: 615-791-1031. Fax: 615-791-9578.

Trial Practice in all Courts: General and Automotive Product Liability, Medical Malpractice, Trucking/Transportation, Medical Device, Material Handling, Toxic Tort, General Liability, Professional Liability, Excess Insurance, and Class Action Defense.

MEMBERS OF FIRM

LAWRENCE A. SUTTER, born Barberton, Ohio, October 24, 1963; admitted to bar, 1989, Ohio; 1990, U.S. District Court, Northern District of Ohio; 1991, U.S. Court of Appeals, Sixth Circuit; 2001, Tennessee. *Education:* Glenville State College (B.A., 1986); University of Akron School of Law (J.D., 1989). Director, Trial Advocacy, University of Akron School of Law. *Member:* Akron, Cleveland, Cuyahoga County, Ohio State and American Bar Associations; Anthony D. Celebrezze Inn of Court; International Association of Defense Counsel. (Also at Franklin, Tennessee Office). ***PRACTICE AREAS:*** Automobile Products Liability; Material Handling; Products Liability; Catastrophic Injury Litigation. ***Email:*** lsutter@sutter-law.com

MATTHEW C. O'CONNELL, born Brooklyn, New York, July 30, 1957; admitted to bar, 1983, Ohio; 1991, U.S. District Court, Northern District of Ohio and U.S. Court of Appeals, Sixth Circuit; 1995, Kentucky; 2001, U.S. District Court, Eastern and Western Districts of Kentucky; 2003, Tennessee. *Education:* University of Wisconsin-Madison (B.A., 1979); Case Western Reserve University (J.D., 1983). *Member:* Cleveland, Cuyahoga County, Kentucky, Ohio State and Federal Bar Associations; Defense Research Institute; International Association of Defense Counsel; Anthony D. Celebrezze Inn of Court. ***LANGUAGES:*** Spanish. ***PRACTICE AREAS:*** Toxic Torts; Products Liability; Insurance Defense; Insurance Coverage. ***Email:*** moconnell@sutter-law.com

JOSEPH A. FARCHIONE, JR., born Buffalo, New York, February 9, 1962; admitted to bar, 1987, Ohio and U.S. District Court, Northern District of Ohio. *Education:* State University of New York at Buffalo (B.A., 1984); Case Western Reserve University (J.D., 1987). Member, Ohio Society of Healthcare Risk Managers and American Society for Healthcare Risk Management. *Member:* Cleveland and Ohio State Bar Associations; Defense Research Institute. ***PRACTICE AREAS:*** Medical Malpractice; Products Liability. ***Email:*** jfarchione@sutter-law.com

DENISE A. DICKERSON, born Lock Haven, Pennsylvania, May 23, 1967; admitted to bar, 1995, Ohio; 1996, Kentucky and U.S. District Court, Northern District of Ohio; 1997, U.S. District Court, Eastern District of Kentucky; 2001, West Virginia, Tennessee, U.S. District Court, Western District of Kentucky and U.S. District Court, Southern District of West Virginia; 2004, U.S. District Court, Southern District of Ohio. *Education:* Temple University (BS., 1989); Cleveland Marshall College of Law (J.D., 1995). *Member:* Ohio State and American Bar Associations; Defense Research Institute. (Also at Franklin, Tennessee Office). ***PRACTICE AREAS:*** Products Liability; Toxic Torts. ***Email:*** ddickerson@sutter-law.com

JONATHAN M. MENUEZ, born Millersburg, Ohio, August 25, 1969; admitted to bar, 1995, Ohio and U.S. District Court, Northern District of Ohio. *Education:* The Ohio State University (B.S.B.A., 1992); University of Akron School of Law (J.D., 1995). *Member:* Cleveland, Ohio State and American Bar Associations; Defense Research Institute. ***PRACTICE AREAS:*** Products Liability; Medical Malpractice; Transportation. ***Email:*** jmenuez@sutter-law.com

JOY D. DAY, born Knoxville, Tennessee, August 19, 1970; admitted to bar, 1996, Ohio; 1997, Michigan and U.S. District Court, Eastern District of Michigan; 1998, Tennessee and U.S. District Court, Northern District of Ohio; 2000, U.S. District Court, Middle District of Tennessee; 2001, U.S. District Court, Eastern and Western Districts of Tennessee; 2002, Kentucky; 2003, U.S. District Court, Western District of Kentucky. *Education:* University of Tennessee (B.A., 1992); University of Tennessee School of Law; Cleveland-Marshall College of Law (J.D., magna cum laude, 1996). *Member:* Williamson County, Tennessee and Ohio State Bar Associations; State Bar of Michigan. (Resident Partner, Franklin, Tennessee Office). ***PRACTICE AREAS:*** Products Liability; Transportation; General Liability Defense. ***Email:*** jburns@sutter-law.com

(This Listing Continued)

SUTTER, O'CONNELL & FARCHIONE, Cleveland—Continued

BRANT E. POLING, born March 2, 1968; admitted to bar, 1994, Ohio and U.S. District Court, Southern District of Ohio; 2004, U.S. District Court, Northern District of Ohio. *Education:* Capital University (B.A., 1990; J.D., 1994). Capital University Law Review, 1993-1994. *Member:* Columbus and Ohio State Bar Associations; Ohio Association of Civil Trial Attorneys; Defense Research Institute. ***PRACTICE AREAS:*** Medical Malpractice; Medical Device Liability. ***Email:*** bpoling@sutter-law.com

JOHN V. JACKSON, II, born Washington, D.C., April 11, 1947; admitted to bar, 1972, Ohio. *Education:* Ohio University (B.A., 1968); Cleveland State University (J.D., 1972). *Member:* Cleveland, Cuyahoga County and Ohio State Bar Associations; Ohio Association of Civil Trial Attorneys; Defense Research Institute; Cleveland Association of Civil Trial Attorneys; Judicial Conference of the Eighth Judicial District (Life Member). ***PRACTICE AREAS:*** Medical Malpractice; Products Liability. ***Email:*** jjackson@sutter-law.com

OF COUNSEL

THOMAS H. TERRY, III, born Detroit, Michigan, August 14, 1950; admitted to bar, 1979, Ohio; 1980, U.S. District Court, Northern District of Ohio; 1981, U.S. Court of Appeals, Sixth Circuit; 1982, U.S. Court of Appeals, Seventh Circuit and U.S. Supreme Court. *Education:* Marquette University (B.A., 1972); Cleveland State University (J.D., cum laude, 1978). ***PRACTICE AREAS:*** Medical Malpractice; Products Liability. ***Email:*** tterry@sutter-law.com

ASSOCIATES

COLLEEN H. PETRELLO, born Cleveland, Ohio, June 15, 1950; admitted to bar, 1989, Ohio; 2001, U.S. Court of Appeals, Sixth Circuit. *Education:* Cleveland Metropolitan General Hospital School of Nursing (R.N., 1972); Ursuline College (B.A., 1985); Cleveland-Marshall College of Law (J.D., 1988). Member: Ohio Hospital Society of Risk Managers; Association of Hospital Risk Managers. Author: "Terminating Medical Treatment: What Risk Managers Need to Know," Perspective in Healthcare Risk Management, Fall 1991, Vol. 11, No. 4. *Member:* Cleveland and Ohio State Bar Associations. ***PRACTICE AREAS:*** Medical Malpractice; Hospital Liability; Health Care. ***Email:*** cpetrello@sutter-law.com

CHRISTINA J. MARSHALL, born Cleveland, Ohio, September 16, 1971; admitted to bar, 1998, Ohio; 2000, U.S. District Court, Northern District of Ohio and U.S. Court of Appeals, Sixth Circuit; 2002, West Virginia, U.S. District Court, Southern District of Ohio and U.S. District Court, Southern District of West Virginia. *Education:* St. Louis University (B.A., 1994); University of Akron (M.B.A., Finance, 1998; J.D., 1998). ***PRACTICE AREAS:*** Automotive Products Liability; Products Liability; Lemon Law; Automotive Warranty Law. ***Email:*** cmarshall@sutter-law.com

DAVID W. SKALL, born Cleveland, Ohio, September 3, 1970; admitted to bar, 1997, Ohio; 1998, U.S. District Court, Northern District of Ohio. *Education:* Indiana University (B.A., 1993); Case Western Reserve University (J.D., 1997). Judicial Extern to the Honorable John M. Manos, United States District Court, Northern District of Ohio, 1995. *Member:* Cleveland, Cuyahoga County and Ohio State Bar Associations. ***PRACTICE AREAS:*** Medical Malpractice; Products Liability; Insurance Defense; Professional Liability. ***Email:*** dskall@sutter-law.com

DAVID J. HUDAK, born Cleveland, Ohio, October 30, 1968; admitted to bar, 1999, Ohio; 2003, U.S. District Court, Northern District of Ohio. *Education:* Denison University (B.S., 1991); Bowling Green State University (M.S., 1993); Cleveland-Marshall College of Law (J.D., cum laude, 1998). *Member:* Cleveland, Cuyahoga County and Ohio State Bar Associations. ***PRACTICE AREAS:*** Medical Malpractice. ***Email:*** dhudak@sutter-law.com

DANIEL E. PERRICO, born Youngstown, Ohio, March 8, 1974; admitted to bar, 1999, Ohio; 2000, U.S. District Court, Northern and Southern Districts of Ohio. *Education:* Baldwin-Wallace College (B.A., 1996); University of Dayton (J.D., 1999). Adjunct Professor, Baldwin-Wallace College. *Member:* Akron (Member, Medical Society Liaison Committee), Ohio State and American Bar Associations. ***PRACTICE AREAS:*** Medical Malpractice; Medical Device Litigation; Products Liability. ***Email:*** dperrico@sutter-law.com

VICTORIA BARTO, born Lima, Ohio, December 30, 1974; admitted to bar, 1999, Ohio, U.S. District Court, Northern District of Ohio; 2003, U.S. District Court, Southern District of Ohio. *Education:* University of Akron (B.A., summa cum laude, 1995); Case Western Reserve University (J.D., 1999). *Member:* Cleveland, Ohio State, and American Bar Associations; Ohio Women's Bar Association; Defense Research Institute. ***PRACTICE AREAS:*** Products Liability; Insurance Coverage; Medical Malpractice. ***Email:*** vbarto@sutter-law.com

EDWARD H. BLAKEMORE, born Cleveland, Ohio, January 2, 1974; admitted to bar, 2000, Ohio, U.S. District Court, Southern District of Ohio and U.S. Court of Appeals, Sixth Circuit; 2001, U.S. District Court, Northern District of Ohio. *Education:* Morehouse College (B.A., magna cum laude, Phi Beta Kappa, 1995); University of Dayton School of Law (J.D., 1999). *Member:* Cleveland, Dayton and Ohio State Bar Associations; Ohio Academy of Trial Lawyers; Defense Research Institute; Norman S. Minor Bar Association; City Club of Cleveland. ***PRACTICE AREAS:*** Medical Malpractice; Professional Liability; Insurance Defense; Transportation. ***Email:*** eblakemore@sutter-law.com

JAMES M. POPSON, born East Cleveland, Ohio, July 8, 1966; admitted to bar, 2000, Ohio; 2001, West Virginia; U.S. District Court, Northern and Southern Districts of Ohio; U.S. District Court, Southern District of West Virginia. *Education:* Stephen F. Austin State University (B.S., 1988; M.Ed., 1990); University of Akron (J.D., summa cum laude, 2000). *Member:* Ohio State and West Virginia Bar Associations; Defense Research Institute. ***PRACTICE AREAS:*** Automotive Products Liability; Trucking Law; Transportation; Insurance Defense; Automotive Warranty Law. ***Email:*** jpopson@sutter-law.com

J. BRITT PHILLIPS, born Dallas, Texas, August 5, 1970; admitted to bar, 2000, Tennessee; 2003, U.S. District Court, Middle District of Tennessee; 2004, U.S. District Court, Eastern and Western Districts of Tennessee. *Education:* Louisiana Tech University, University of Tennessee (B.A., 1992); Nashville School of Law (J.D., 2000). *Member:* Williamson County and Tennessee Bar Associations. (Resident, Franklin, Tennessee Office). ***PRACTICE AREAS:*** Real Estate; Contract Litigation; Products Liability. ***Email:*** bphillips@sutter-law.com

CHRISTINA TUGGEY HIDEK, born Jacksonville, Florida, July 30, 1975; admitted to bar, 2000, Ohio; 2001, U.S. District Court, Northern District of Ohio. *Education:* University of Kentucky (B.A., 1997); Case Western Reserve University (J.D., 2000). *Member:* Cleveland and Ohio State Bar Associations; Ohio Women's Bar Association; Defense Research Institute. ***PRACTICE AREAS:*** Toxic Torts; Insurance Coverage; Automotive Warranty Law. ***Email:*** chidek@sutter-law.com

AMY K. CORRIGALL, born Toronto, Ontario, October 2, 1975; admitted to bar, 2001, Ohio. *Education:* Kent State University (B.A., summa cum laude, 1997); University of Akron School of Law (J.D., 2001). *Member:* Akron, Portage and Ohio State Bar Associations. ***PRACTICE AREAS:*** Products Liability; Transportation; General Liability Defense. ***Email:*** acorrigall@sutter-law.com

JOHN C. LEACH, born Dayton, Ohio September 17, 1952; admitted to bar, 2002, Ohio; 2003, U.S. District Court, Northern District of Ohio; 2004, Kentucky, U.S. District Court, Southern District of Ohio and U.S. District Court, Eastern District of Kentucky. *Education:* Miami University (B.A., 1974); Arizona State University (M.A., 1992); University of Akron School of Law (J.D., magna cum laude, 2002). ***PRACTICE AREAS:*** Products Liability; Automotive Warranty Law; Appellate Practice. ***Email:*** jleach@sutter-law.com

DOUGLAS R. SIMEK, born Euclid, Ohio, June 3, 1976; admitted to bar, 2003, Ohio; 2003, U.S. District Court, Northern District of Ohio. *Education:* University of Dayton (B.A., 1998); Cleveland-Marshall College of Law (J.D., 2002). Staff Attorney, Hon. Harry Hanna and Leo Spellacy, Cuyahoga County Court of Common Pleas, 2003-2005. *Member:* Ohio State, Cuyahoga County, Lake County and American Bar Associations; Cleveland Bar Association; Defense Research Institute. ***PRACTICE AREAS:*** Toxic Torts; Products Liability; Appellate Practice. ***Email:*** dsimek@sutter-law.com

MARCO G. BOCCIARELLI, born Trenton, New Jersey, March 2, 1972; admitted to bar, 2003, Ohio; 2004, Tennessee and U.S. District Court, Northern District of Ohio. *Education:* Kent State University (B.S., 2000); University of Akron School of Law (J.D., 2003). *Member:* Akron and Ohio State Bar Associations. ***PRACTICE AREAS:*** Products Liability; Medical Malpractice. ***Email:*** mbocciarelli@sutter-law.com

MARC D. AMOS, born Cleveland, Ohio, December 27, 1973; admitted to bar, 2004, Ohio. *Education:* United States Naval Academy (B.S., 1996); Thomas M. Cooley Law School (J.D., magna cum laude, 2004). *Member:* Cleveland and Ohio State Bar Associations. ***PRACTICE AREAS:*** Products Liability; Medical Malpractice. ***Email:*** mamos@sutter-law.com

ADAM W. MARTIN, born Findlay, Ohio, September 6, 1971; admitted to bar, 2004, Ohio; 2005, West Virginia. *Education:* The Ohio State University (B.A., 2000); University of Akron School of Law (J.D., 2004). ***PRACTICE AREAS:*** Products Liability; General Liability. ***Email:*** amartin@sutter-law.com

JASON P. FERRANTE, born Cleveland, Ohio, October 4, 1973; admitted to bar, 2004, Ohio. *Education:* Ohio University (B.A., 1996); Cleveland-Marshall College of Law (J.D., 2004). ***PRACTICE AREAS:*** Products Liability; Medical Malpractice; Appellate Practice. ***Email:*** jferrante@sutter-law.com

STUART D. BAKER, born Mansfield, Ohio, August 5, 1977; admitted to bar, 2004, Ohio. *Education:* Bowling Green State University (B.A., 2000); University of Akron School of Law (J.D., 2004). ***PRACTICE AREAS:*** Products Liability. ***Email:*** sbaker@sutter-law.com

SVETE, McGEE & CARRABINE CO., L.P.A.

CLEVELAND, OHIO

(See Chardon)

Insurance Defense, Personal Injury, Products Liability, Professional Malpractice, Commercial, Governmental Construction and General Negligence Litigation, Automobile Accidents, Wrongful Death, Medical Negligence, Real Estate and Zoning, Contracts, Deeds, Easements, Leases, Family Law, Divorce, Dissolution, Child Custody and Support, Paternity, Adoption, Child Abuse and Neglect, Criminal Defense, Felonies, Misdemeanors, Juvenile and Traffic Offenses, D.U.I., Wills, Probate, Estate Planning, Elder Law, Trusts, Powers of Attorney, Living Wills, Guardianships, Asset Preservation, Medicare/Medicaid Planning, Litigation, Corporate and Business Law, Partnerships, Limited Liability Companies, Buying and Selling of a Business.

SWARTZ CAMPBELL LLC

Established in 1921

55 PUBLIC SQUARE, SUITE 1120
CLEVELAND, OHIO 44113
Telephone: 216-685-9188
Fax: 216-685-9293
Email: webmaster@swartzcampbell.com
URL: http://www.swartzcampbell.com

Allentown, Pennsylvania Office: Suite 230, 5100 Tilghman Street. Telephone: 610-395-5903. Fax: 610-395-7097.

Bedminster, New Jersey Office: Bedminster Center, 90 Washington Valley Road. Telephone: 908-719-8932. Fax: 908-719-6005.

Fort Myers, Florida Office: World Plaza, 12585 New Brittany Boulevard, Suite 21E. Telephone: 239-790-7700. Fax: 239-332-5325.

Harrisburg, Pennsylvania Office: 1631 North Front Street, 2nd Floor. Telephone: 717-233-3515. Fax: 717-233-3468.

Media, Pennsylvania Office: 115 North Jackson Street. Telephone: 610-566-9222. Fax: 610-566-7351.

Mount Laurel, New Jersey Office: Bloom Court, Suite 101. 1300 Route 73. Telephone: 856-727-4777. Fax: 856-727-0464.

(This Listing Continued)

(This Listing Continued)

New York, New York Office: Suite 900, 132 Nassau Street. Telephone: 212-406-1282. Fax: 212-619-2340.
Orlando, Florida Office: Millenia Park One, 4901 Vineland Road, Suite 300. Telephone: 407-209-1000. Fax: 407-209-1001.
Philadelphia, Pennsylvania Office: 1601 Market Street, 34th Floor. Telephone: 215-564-5190. Telefax: 215-299-4301.
Pittsburgh, Pennsylvania Office: U.S. Steel Building, 47th Floor, 600 Grant Street. Telephone: 412-232-9800. Fax: 412-471-1106.
Scranton, Pennsylvania Office: Bank Towers, 11th Floor, 321 Spruce Street. Telephone: 570-343-0029. Fax: 570-343-1534.
West Chester, Pennsylvania Office: One South Church Street, Suite 400. Telephone: 610-692-9500. Fax: 610-692-4936.
Wilmington, Delaware Office: 300 Delaware Avenue, Suite 1130, P.O. Box 330. Telephone: 302-656-5935. Fax: 302-656-1434.

General Civil and Trial Practice in State and Federal Courts including Insurance, Workers Compensation, Product Liability, Toxic Torts, Medical Malpractice, Legal Malpractice, and Commercial, Bankruptcy Defense, Employment and Labor Law.

FIRM PROFILE: Founded in 1921, Swartz Campbell LLC has been providing legal service to the insurance industry for 80 years.

RESIDENT PARTNER

KENNETH F. KRAWCZAK, born Saginaw, MI, March 5, 1951; admitted to bar, 1977, Ohio. *Education:* Western College (A.B., 1974); The Ohio State University (J.D., 1976). Member, Ohio State Bar Association, 1982-2000. ***PRACTICE AREAS:*** Asbestos Defense; Workers Compensation; Personal Injury; Products Liability. ***Email:*** kkrawczak@swartzcampbell.com

ASSOCIATE

MICHELE L. LARISSEY, born St. Louis, MO, April 26, 1970; admitted to bar, 1997, Illinois; 1998, Missouri; 2001, Ohio. *Education:* University of Missouri, Columbia (B.A., Marketing, 1992); University of Denver (J.D., 1996). *Member:* Ohio State Bar Association. ***PRACTICE AREAS:*** Toxic Tort Litigation. ***Email:*** mlarissey@swartzcampbell.com

TIMOTHY F. SWEENEY, LAW OFFICE OF

Established in 1996

THE 820 BUILDING
820 WEST SUPERIOR AVENUE, SUITE 430
CLEVELAND, OHIO 44113-1800
Telephone: 216-241-5003
Fax: 216-241-3138
Email: tim@timsweeneylaw.com

Litigation, including General Civil and Criminal Litigation in State and Federal Courts at the Trial and Appellate Levels; Arbitration; Commercial Litigation; Employment Litigation and Employment Matters; Insurance and Contract Litigation; Products Liability Litigation; Construction Litigation; Bankruptcy Litigation, including representing Creditors in Bankruptcy and Related Proceedings; Workouts; Corporate and Commercial Transactions; Criminal Defense; Criminal Appeals and Post-Conviction Proceedings; Federal Death Penalty Litigation.

FIRM PROFILE: We are a small firm of two attorneys, each with almost a decade of experience practicing at one of Ohio's largest and most prestigious law firms. Now in our tenth year, we focus our practice on those litigation and other matters that can most effectively and efficiently be managed by a team of two experienced attorneys. Out clients work directly with us on their matters, not with unseasoned associates or with legal assistants. Our rates are reasonable.

TIMOTHY F. SWEENEY, born Cleveland, Ohio, October 1, 1960; admitted to bar, 1987, Ohio; 1990, U.S. District Court, Northern District of Ohio; 1995, U.S. Court of Appeals, Sixth Circuit; 2003, U.S. District Court, Southern District of Ohio. *Education:* University of Notre Dame (A.B., 1982); The Ohio State University (J.D., summa cum laude, 1987). Order of the Coif. Editor-in-Chief, Ohio State Law Journal, 1986-1987. Law Clerk to The Honorable Nathaniel R. Jones, U.S. Court of Appeals, Sixth Circuit, 1987-1988. *Member:* Cleveland, Ohio State, Federal and American Bar Associations; Defense Research Institute; National Association of Criminal Defense Lawyers. ***PRACTICE AREAS:*** Litigation; General Civil; Criminal Litigation; Commercial Disputes; Products Liability; Employment Law; Insurance Litigation; Contract Litigation; Construction Law; White Collar Criminal Defense.

LYNN ROWE LARSEN, born El Paso, Texas, 1963; admitted to bar, 1991, Ohio; 1992, U.S. District Court, Northern District of Ohio. *Education:* Hillsdale College (B.A., summa cum laude, 1985); Wake Forest University (J.D., cum laude, 1991). Fletcher Scholar. Articles Editor, Wake Forest Law Journal, 1990-1991. Benton Moot Court Team, 1989-1990. *Member:* Cleveland (Member Sections On: Commercial; Bankruptcy) Bar Association. ***PRACTICE AREAS:*** Litigation; Bankruptcy; Workouts; Corporate and Commercial Transactions; Creditors Rights. ***Email:*** lynn@timsweeneylaw.com

SYNENBERG & ASSOCIATES, LLC

55 PUBLIC SQUARE
SUITE 1200
CLEVELAND, OHIO 44113
Telephone: 216-622-2727
Fax: 216-622-2707
Email: lawoffice@synenberg.com
URL: http://www.synenberglaw.com

Federal and State Criminal Defense. White Collar Crimes, Drug Crimes, Felonies, Misdemeanors, Driving While Intoxicated.

(This Listing Continued)

ROGER M. SYNENBERG, born Cleveland, Ohio, May 1, 1949; admitted to bar, 1977, Ohio; 1978, U.S. District Court, Northern District of Ohio; 1982, U.S Court of Appeals, Sixth Circuit; 1986, U.S. Supreme Court. *Education:* American University (B.S., 1971); Cleveland Marshall College of Law (J.D., 1976). Assistant U.S. Attorney, Northern District of Ohio, 1982-1985. Life Member, United States Sixth Circuit Judicial Conference. Member, 1989-1993 and Chairman, 1993—, Cuyahoga County Board of Elections. *Member:* Cleveland (Member, Criminal Law Section; Real Estate Law Section; Chairman, Criminal Law Section, 1987-1988), Cuyahoga County, Ohio State and Federal Bar Associations; Ohio Association of Criminal Defense Lawyers; National Association of Criminal Defense Lawyers. ***PRACTICE AREAS:*** Criminal Law; Business Litigation; Commercial Litigation; Administrative Law; Municipal Law.

GREGG D. GARFINKEL, born New Hartford, New York, March 18, 1977; admitted to bar, 2004, Ohio; 2005, U.S. District Court, Northern District of Ohio. *Education:* State University of New York at Fredonia (B.A., Legal Studies and Philosophy, 2000); Cleveland-Marshall College of Law (J.D., 2003). *Member:* Cuyahoga County, Cleveland, Ohio State and American Bar Associations. ***PRACTICE AREAS:*** Criminal Law; Civil Practice. ***Email:*** ggarfinkel@synenberg.com

DOMINIC J. COLETTA, born Cleveland, Ohio, July 7, 1978; admitted to bar, 2004, Ohio; 2005, U.S. District Court, Northern District of Ohio. *Education:* Miami University (B.A., Political Science, 2001); Cleveland-Marshall College of Law (J.D., 2004). *Member:* Cuyahoga County, Cleveland, Ohio State and American Bar Associations. ***PRACTICE AREAS:*** Criminal Law; Civil Practice. ***Email:*** dcoletta@synenberg

GREGORY P. SZUTER

730 OHIO SAVINGS PLAZA
1801 EAST 9TH STREET
CLEVELAND, OHIO 44114
Telephone: 216-861-0503; 1-877-301-0332
Fax: 216-696-6653
Email: gpsz@aol.com
URL: http://www.lawyers.com/arbitration

Northbrook, Illinois Office: 500 Skokie Boulevard, Suite 350, 60062.

Alternative Dispute Resolution, Arbitration, Mediation.

FIRM PROFILE: Practice concentrated on providing services as a neutral Arbitrator or Mediator in areas of Labor, Employment, ERISA, Pension, Executive Compensation, Commercial Transactions, Health Industry and Securities.

GREGORY P. SZUTER, born Cleveland, Ohio, September 7, 1945; admitted to bar, 1973, Ohio and U.S. District Court, Northern District of Ohio; 1977, U.S. Court of Appeals, Sixth Circuit; 1985, U.S. Supreme Court. *Education:* John Carroll University (A.B., cum laude, 1967); Kent State University (M.A., magna cum laude, 1971); Case Western Reserve University (J.D., 1973). Designated Ohio Super Lawyer, 2004. *Member:* Cleveland, Ohio State and American Bar Associations; American Arbitration Association; American Health Lawyers Association; International Foundation of Employee Benefit Plans; Industrial Relations Research Association; Federal Mediation and Conciliation Service. (Certified Specialist in Labor and Employment Law, Ohio State Bar Association). ***PRACTICE AREAS:*** Arbitration; Pension; Health Care; ERISA; COBRA; Multiemployer Benefits; Deferred Compensation; Covenant not to Complete; Labor and Employment; Firefighters Labor Law; Municipal Labor Law; Police Labor Law; Alternative Dispute Resolution; Mediation; Business Arbitration; Commercial Arbitration; NASD Arbitration; Securities Arbitration; Labor Arbitration.

TAFT, STETTINIUS & HOLLISTER LLP

3500 BP TOWER
200 PUBLIC SQUARE
CLEVELAND, OHIO 44114-2302
Telephone: 216-241-2838
Facsimile: 216-241-3707
URL: http://www.taftlaw.com

Cincinnati, Ohio Office: 425 Walnut Street, Suite 1800. Telephone: 513-381-2838.
Columbus, Ohio Office: Twelfth Floor, 21 East State Street. Telephone: 614-221-2838.
Covington, Kentucky Office: 1717 Dixie Highway, Suite 340. Telephone: 859-331-2838; 513-381-2838.
Dayton, Ohio Office: 110 North Main Street, Suite 900. Telephone: 937-228-2838.

Antitrust, Bankruptcy and Debtor/Creditor Rights, Business and Finance, E-Business (Internet and E-Commerce), Employee Benefits/ERISA and Tax-Planning, Environmental Law, Family Law, Family Business Planning, Franchise, General Litigation, Health Care, Immigration, Institutional Finance, Intellectual Property and Technology Group, International, Japanese Practice, Labor and Employment, Mergers and Acquisitions, Nonprofit and Tax-Exempt Organizations, Product Liability and Personal Injury, Public Finance, Real Property, Securities, Tax, Probate and Estate Planning, Workers' Compensation.

RESIDENT MEMBERS

STEPHEN M. O'BRYAN, born Dayton, Ohio, December 9, 1944; admitted to bar, 1969, Ohio. *Education:* Bowling Green State University (B.A., 1966); Case Western Reserve University (J.D., 1969).

MARGARET ANNE CANNON, born Highland, Illinois, January 19, 1948; admitted to bar, 1973, Ohio. *Education:* Oberlin College (A.B., 1970); Case Western Reserve University (J.D., 1973).

(This Listing Continued)

TAFT, STETTINIUS & HOLLISTER LLP, Cleveland—Continued

JOHN D. BROWN, born Cleveland, Ohio, November 1, 1942; admitted to bar, 1969, Ohio. *Education:* University of Colorado (B.A., 1966); Case Western Reserve University (J.D., 1969).

JOEL A. MAKEE, born Cleveland, Ohio, May 27, 1944; admitted to bar, 1969, Ohio. *Education:* Wittenberg University (B.A., 1966); Case Western Reserve University (J.D., 1969).

THOMAS J. LEE, born Cleveland, Ohio, March 27, 1952; admitted to bar, 1977, Ohio. *Education:* Wittenberg University (B.A., 1974); Case Western Reserve University (J.D., 1977).

CARL A. MURWAY, born Lakewood, Ohio, May 6, 1958; admitted to bar, 1983, Ohio. *Education:* Oberlin College (B.A., 1980); University of Wisconsin (J.D., 1983). Fellow, American Academy of Matrimonial Lawyers.

MARK J. VALPONI, born Cleveland, Ohio, March 23, 1952; admitted to bar, 1977, Ohio. *Education:* Purdue University (B.S., 1974); Cleveland State University (J.D., 1977; M.B.A., 1981).

STEVEN A. MARRER, born Cincinnati, Ohio, March 25, 1958; admitted to bar, 1983, Ohio. *Education:* Northwestern University (B.A., 1980); Case Western Reserve University (J.D., 1983).

BRUCE L. WATERHOUSE, JR., born Pittsburgh, Pennsylvania, May 17, 1955; admitted to bar, 1982, Colorado; 1988, Ohio. *Education:* University of Michigan (B.S., 1977); American University (J.D., 1982).

ROBERT P. McMANUS, born New York, N.Y., October 15, 1953; admitted to bar, 1978, Ohio. *Education:* University of Notre Dame (B.B.A., 1975); The Ohio State University (J.D., 1978).

DAVID H. WALLACE, born Cleveland, Ohio, February 28, 1961; admitted to bar, 1986, Ohio. *Education:* Middlebury College (B.A., 1983); Case Western Reserve University (J.D., 1986).

PETER M. POULOS, born Roslyn, New York, September 3, 1965; admitted to bar, 1990, Ohio. *Education:* Washington University (B.S.E.E., 1987); Case Western Reserve University (J.D., 1990).

DONNA M. FLAMMANG, born Cleveland, Ohio, January 15, 1951; admitted to bar, 1975, Ohio. *Education:* Albion College (B.A., 1971); Cleveland State University (J.D., 1975).

MARY GRACE BALAZS, born Cleveland, Ohio, December 19, 1953; admitted to bar, 1980, Ohio. *Education:* John Carroll University (B.A., 1976); Cleveland Marshall College of Law (J.D., 1979).

GREGORY J. O'BRIEN, born Cleveland, Ohio, May 27, 1966; admitted to bar, 1994, Ohio. *Education:* University of Toledo (B.B.A., 1989); Cleveland State University (J.D., 1994).

JILL FRIEDMAN HELFMAN, born Akron, Ohio, February 20, 1962; admitted to bar, 1987, Ohio. *Education:* University of Michigan (A.B., 1984); Case Western Reserve University (J.D., 1987). Fellow, American Academy of Matrimonial Lawyers.

WILLIAM J. STAVOLE, born Parma, Ohio, March 23, 1963; admitted to bar, 1988, Ohio. *Education:* Kenyon College (B.A., 1985); The Ohio State University (J.D., 1988).

DANIEL K. WRIGHT, II, born Cleveland, Ohio, April 21, 1954; admitted to bar, 1979, Ohio. *Education:* Hillsdale College (B.L.S., 1976); Case Western Reserve University (J.D., 1979).

BRUCE J. L. LOWE, born Brighton, Sussex, England, 1949; admitted to bar, 1976, England and Wales; 1979, Ohio. *Education:* St. Edmunds Hall, Oxford University (B.A., 1972; M.A., 1976); Inns of Court School of Law, London, England (Barrister at Law, 1976).

DAVID V. ALLEN, born Fort Meade, Maryland, June 20, 1961; admitted to bar, 1987, Ohio. *Education:* Baldwin-Wallace College (B.A., 1983); Akron University Law School (J.D., 1987).

TIMOTHY L. ZIX, born Cincinnati, Ohio, July 20, 1965; admitted to bar, 1991, Ohio. *Education:* University of Dayton (B.S., 1987); Cleveland Marshall College of Law (J.D., 1991).

STEPHEN H. JETT, born Augusta, Georgia, July 2, 1962; admitted to bar, 1990, Ohio. *Education:* University of Kentucky (B.A.,1984; J.D., 1990).

CHARLES A. BOWERS, born Haverhill, Massachusetts, March 15, 1967; admitted to bar, 1994, Ohio. *Education:* Lafayette College (B.A., Government and Law, 1989); Case Western Reserve University (J.D., 1994).

OF COUNSEL

FRED J. LIVINGSTONE, born Cleveland, Ohio, February 20, 1926; admitted to bar, 1950, Ohio. *Education:* Western Reserve University; Harvard University (LL.B., 1950).

DAVID E. BURKE, born Chicago, Illinois, November 3, 1937; admitted to bar, 1964, Ohio. *Education:* University of Dayton (B.A., 1959); Case Western Reserve University (J.D., 1963).

GEORGE J. DUNN, born Cleveland, Ohio, April 29, 1935; admitted to bar, 1960, Ohio. *Education:* Yale University (B.S., 1957); Harvard University (LL.B., 1960).

RICHARD D. TOMSICK, born Euclid, Ohio, August 3, 1959; admitted to bar, 1984, Ohio. *Education:* Case Western Reserve University (B.A., 1981; J.D., 1984).

RESIDENT ASSOCIATES

CHRISTINE LEWANSKI, born Cleveland, Ohio, August 11, 1970; admitted to bar, 1996, Ohio. *Education:* Hollins College (B.A., 1992); Case Western Reserve University (J.D., 1995).

(This Listing Continued)

ROBERT B. OWEN, born Willoughby, Ohio, October 31, 1967; admitted to bar, 2000, Ohio. *Education:* Hiram College (B.A., in Business Administration, 1995); Cleveland-Marshall College of Law (J.D., 2000).

PATRICK J. KREBS, born Euclid, Ohio, June 8, 1975; admitted to bar, 2000, Ohio. *Education:* Villanova University (B.A., 1997); Case Western Reserve University (J.D., 2000).

MATTHEW T. VIOLA, born Cleveland, Ohio, November 11, 1973; admitted to bar, 2000, Ohio. *Education:* Miami University (B.S.B.A., 1996); Cleveland-Marshall College of Law (J.D., 2000).

HEATHER L. TONSING, born Cleveland, Ohio, July 29, 1972; admitted to bar, 1998, Ohio. *Education:* University of Akron (B.S., 1994); Cleveland-Marshall College of Law (J.D., 1998).

ROBERT H. FISCHER, JR., born Akron, Ohio, November 19, 1973; admitted to bar, 1999, Ohio. *Education:* Ohio University (B.A., 1996); Vanderbilt University (J.D., 1999).

MAJEED G. MAKHLOUF, born Jerusalem, West Bank, Palestine, January 2, 1977; admitted to bar, 2001, Ohio; 2003, District of Columbia. *Education:* Hiram College (B.A., 1998); The Ohio State University (J.D., 2001).

KIMBERLIE L. HUFF, born Park Ridge, Illinois, April 21, 1975; admitted to bar, 2000, Ohio; 2001, Illinois. *Education:* Valparaiso University (B.A., 1996); University of Illinois (J.D., 2000).

LAWRENCE C. DAVISON, born Alliance, Ohio, March 29, 1966; admitted to bar, 1991, Ohio. *Education:* University of Dayton (B.S.B.A., 1988); Case Western Reserve University (J.D., 1991).

PATRICIA FLEMING KREWSON, born Warren, Ohio, July 4, 1979; admitted to bar, 2003, Ohio. *Education:* Bowling Green State University (B.A., 2000); Case Western Reserve University (J.D., 2003).

ADAM D. CORNETT, born Mayfield Heights, Ohio, December 11, 1975; admitted to bar, 2004, Ohio. *Education:* College of Wooster (B.A., 1998); Cleveland-Marshall College of Law (J.D., 2004).

KRISTIN R. ERENBURG, born Springfield, Illinois, July 1, 1974; admitted to bar, 2004, Ohio. *Education:* University of Michigan (B.A., 1996); Cleveland-Marshall College of Law (J.D., 2004).

KRISTI J. KMETZ, born Youngstown, Ohio, February 6, 1977; admitted to bar, 2003, Ohio. *Education:* Youngstown State University (B.A., 1999); Ohio Northern University (J.D., 2002).

RONN J. GEHRING, born Hubbard, Ohio, November 5, 1977; admitted to bar, 2003, Ohio. *Education:* Bowling Green State University (B.A., 2000) University of Akron (J.D., 2002).

(For biographical data on all other personnel, see Cincinnati, Columbus, Dayton, Ohio and Covington, Kentucky professional biographies)

TAROLLI, SUNDHEIM, COVELL & TUMMINO, L.L.P.

LEADER BUILDING, SUITE 111
526 SUPERIOR AVENUE
CLEVELAND, OHIO 44114
Telephone: 216-621-2234
Telex: 980209 TSC CLV PAT
Facsimile: 216-621-4072
Email: tarolli@tarolli.com
URL: http://www.tarolli.com

Intellectual Property Law including Patent, Trademark, Copyright and Unfair Competition Law.

MEMBERS OF FIRM

THOMAS L. TAROLLI, born Coalport, Pennsylvania, May 29, 1935; admitted to bar, 1961, Ohio; 1962, U.S. District Court, Northern District of Ohio; 1969, U.S. Court of Appeals for the Federal Circuit; registered to practice before U.S. Patent and Trademark Office. *Education:* University of Pittsburgh (B.S., 1957); George Washington University (LL.B., 1961). Sigma Tau; Omicron Delta Kappa. Member, George Washington Law Review, 1960-1961. Examiner, U.S. Patent Office, 1957-1961. *Member:* Cleveland and American Bar Associations; Cleveland Intellectual Property Law Association; American Intellectual Property Law Association. **PRACTICE AREAS:** Patent; Trademark. ***Email:*** ttarolli@tarolli.com

ROBERT B. SUNDHEIM, born Bismarck, North Dakota, November 18, 1936; admitted to bar, 1964, Ohio; 1968, U.S. District Court, Northern District of Ohio; 1989, U.S. Court of Appeals for the Federal Circuit; registered to practice before U.S. Patent and Trademark Office. *Education:* Worcester Polytechnic Institute (B.S. in E.E., 1958); George Washington University; University of Detroit (LL.B., 1963). Gamma Eta Gamma. *Member:* Cleveland and American Bar Associations; Cleveland Intellectual Property Law Association; American Intellectual Property Law Association. ***PRACTICE AREAS:*** Patent; Trademark. ***Email:*** rsundheim@tarolli.com

CALVIN G. COVELL, born Muskegon, Michigan, January 14, 1936; admitted to bar, 1966, Illinois; 1968, Ohio; registered to practice before U.S. Patent and Trademark Office. *Education:* University of Michigan (B.S.M.E., 1959); George Washington University (M.B.A., 1961); Georgetown University (J.D., 1965). Delta Theta Phi. *Member:* Cleveland and American Bar Associations; Cleveland Intellectual Property Law Association; American Intellectual Property Law Association. **PRACTICE AREAS:** Patent; Trademark. ***Email:*** ccovell@tarolli.com

BARRY L. TUMMINO, born Cleveland, Ohio, June 5, 1950; admitted to bar, 1980, Ohio, U.S. District Court, Northern District of Ohio and U.S. Court of Appeals for the Federal Circuit; registered to practice before U.S. Patent and Trademark Office. *Education:*

(This Listing Continued)

Cleveland State University (B.E.S., 1972; M.S., 1974); Cleveland Marshall College of Law (J.D., 1979). Sigma Pi Sigma. *Member:* Ohio State and American Bar Associations; Cleveland Intellectual Property Law Association; American Intellectual Property Law Association. ***PRACTICE AREAS:*** Patent. ***Email:*** btummino@tarolli.com

JAMES L. TAROLLI, born Lakewood, Ohio, April 10, 1966; admitted to bar, 1991, Ohio; registered to practice before U.S. Patent and Trademark Office. *Education:* The Columbus Ohio State University (B.S.M.E., 1988); Case Western Reserve University (J.D., 1991). *Member:* Cleveland Intellectual Property Law Association. ***PRACTICE AREAS:*** Patent; Trademark. ***Email:*** jtarolli@tarolli.com

RICHARD S. WESORICK, born Cincinnati, Ohio, November 3, 1966; admitted to bar, 1995, Ohio; 1996, U.S. Court of Appeals for the Federal Circuit; 1998, U.S. District Court, Northern District of Ohio; registered to practice before U.S. Patent and Trademark Office. *Education:* Purdue University (B.S.M.E., 1988); University of Dayton Law School (J.D., 1995). Phi Alpha Delta. Inventor, U.S. Patent No. 5,178,003. *Member:* Cleveland Intellectual Property Law Association; American Intellectual Property Law Association. ***PRACTICE AREAS:*** Patent; Trademark. ***Email:*** rwesorick@tarolli.com

RICHARD A. SUTKUS, born Chicago, Illinois, September 29, 1969; admitted to bar, 1997, Missouri; 1999, Ohio; registered to practice before U.S. Patent and Trademark Office. *Education:* St. Louis University (B.S., 1992; M.S., 1994; J.D., 1997). *Member:* St. Louis and American Bar Associations; The Missouri Bar; American Chemical Society. ***PRACTICE AREAS:*** Patents; Trademarks. ***Email:*** rsutkus@tarolli.com

MATTHEW M. SHAHEEN, born Frankfurt, West Germany, November 30, 1968; admitted to bar, 1997, Ohio; 1998, U.S. District Court, Northern District of Ohio; registered to practice before U.S. Patent and Trademark Office. *Education:* University of Akron (B.S.M.T., 1992; J.D., 1996). *Member:* Akron, Ohio State and American Bar Associations. ***PRACTICE AREAS:*** Patents; Trademarks. ***Email:*** mshaheen@tarolli.com

GARY J. PITZER, born Solon, Ohio, May 29, 1969; admitted to bar, 1995, Florida and U.S. District Court, Middle District of Florida; 1999, Ohio; 2001, U.S. Court of Appeals for the Federal Circuit; registered to practice before U.S. Patent and Trademark Office. *Education:* The Ohio State University (B.S.E.E., 1991); University of Miami School of Law (J.D., 1995). Phi Delta Phi. *Member:* Hillsborough County (Member, Entertainment and Sports Law Section) and American (Member: Intellectual Property Law and Law Practice Management Sections) Bar Associations; The Florida Bar (Member: Business Law Section; Intellectual Property Law Committee); International Trademark Association; American Intellectual Property Law Association; Cleveland Intellectual Property Law Association. ***PRACTICE AREAS:*** Patents; Trademarks; Trade Secrets; Licensing. ***Email:*** gpitzer@tarolli.com

CHRISTOPHER P. HARRIS, born Cleveland, Ohio, July 27, 1965; admitted to bar, 1997, Ohio; 1999, U.S. District Court, Northern District of Ohio; registered to practice before U.S. Patent and Trademark Office. *Education:* California State University, Fullerton (B.S.E.E., 1987; M.B.A., 1992); Cleveland-Marshall College of Law (J.D., 1997). Recipient, Watts Hoffman Award for Best Intellectual Property Student, 1996. *Member:* Cleveland Intellectual Property Law Association; American Intellectual Property Law Association. ***PRACTICE AREAS:*** Patents; Trademarks; Copyrights; Licensing. ***Email:*** charris@tarolli.com

ASSOCIATES

ROBERT N. LIPCSIK, born Cleveland, Ohio, September 5, 1965; admitted to bar, 1996, Ohio and District of Columbia; U.S. District Court, Northern District of Ohio, U.S. Court of Appeals for the District of Columbia Circuit and U.S. Court of Appeals, Sixth Circuit; registered to practice before U.S. Patent and Trademark Office. *Education:* Case Western Reserve University (B.S.M.E., 1987); Cleveland-Marshall College of Law (J.D., 1995). Delta Theta Phi. *Member:* Ohio State and American (Member, Intellectual Property Section) Bar Associations; American Society of Mechanical Engineers; Cleveland Intellectual Property Law Association. ***PRACTICE AREAS:*** Patents; Trademarks. ***Email:*** rlipcsik@tarolli.com

BRETT A. SCHENCK, born Valparaiso, Indiana, November 8, 1964; admitted to bar, 1992, Indiana and U.S. District Court, District of Indiana; 2004, Ohio. *Education:* Purdue University (B.S., E.E., 1987); Valparaiso University (J.D., 1991); University of Akron (M.B.A., 2003). Former Member: Honda R & D America; Maytag Corporation. *Member:* Cleveland Bar Association; Cleveland Intellectual Property Law Association. ***PRACTICE AREAS:*** Patents (89%); Trademarks (10%); Copyrights (1%). ***Email:*** bschenck@tarolli.com

BRIAN W. BOLINGER, born Elyria, Ohio, October 2, 1977; admitted to bar, 2002, Ohio; registered to practice before the U.S. Patent and Trademark Office. *Education:* University of Toledo (B.S., 1999); Case Western Reserve University (J.D., 2002). *Member:* Cleveland Intellectual Property Law Association. ***PRACTICE AREAS:*** Patents. ***Email:*** bbolinger@tarolli.com

THOMPSON HINE LLP

3900 KEY CENTER
127 PUBLIC SQUARE
CLEVELAND, OHIO 44114-1291
Telephone: 216-566-5500
Fax: 216-566-5800
Telex: 980217
Cable Address: "Thomflor"
Email: info@ThompsonHine.com
URL: http://www.ThompsonHine.com

Cincinnati, Ohio Office: 312 Walnut Street, 14th Floor, 45202-4089. Telephone: 513-352-6700. Fax: 513-241-4771. Email: info@ThompsonHine.com.

Columbus, Ohio Office: 10 West Broad Street, Suite 700, 43215-3435. Telephone: 614-469-3200. Fax: 614-469-3361. Email: info@ThompsonHine.com.

Dayton, Ohio Office: 2000 Courthouse Plaza, N.E., P.O. Box 8801, 45401-8801. Telephone: 937-443-6600. Fax: 937-443-6635. Email: info@ThompsonHine.com.

(This Listing Continued)

Washington, D.C. Office: 1920 N Street, N.W., Suite 800, 20036-1600. Telephone: 202-331-8800. Fax: 202-331-8330. Email: info@ThompsonHine.com.

New York, N.Y. Office: One Chase Manhattan Plaza, 58th Floor, 10005-1401. Telephone: 212-344-5680. Fax: 212-809-6890. Email: info@ThompsonHine.com.

Brussels, Belgium Office: Avenue Louise 375 - b8, 1050 Brussels, Belgium, Telephone: 011 (32-2) 626-3280. Fax: 011 (32-2) 626-3299. Email: info@ThompsonHine.com.

Atlanta, Georgia Office: Proscenium Center, Suite 1200, 1170 Peachtree Street, 30309-7673. Telephone: 404-541-2900. Fax: 404-541-2905. Email: info@ThompsonHine.com.

Administrative Law, Admiralty and Maritime Law, Agency and Distributorships, Antitrust and Trade Regulation, Aviation and Aerospace, Bankruptcy, Banks and Banking, Biotechnology, Business Law, Business Litigation, Business Regulation, Business Transactions, Closely Held Business Law, Joint Ventures, Class Actions, Commercial Law, Commercial Real Estate, Communications and Media, FCC Regulation, Computers and Software, Construction Law, Contracts, Copyrights, Corporate Law, Corporate Finance, Corporate Litigation, Corporate Tax Controversies, Debtor and Creditor, Employee Benefits, ERISA, Energy, Energy Regulation, Environmental Law, Finance, Commercial Finance, Franchises and Franchising, General Practice, Government, False Claims Act, Qui Tam Litigation, Government Contracts, Health Care, Insurance Coverage, Insurance Regulation, Intellectual Property, International Law, International Trade, Internet Law, Labor and Employment, Life Sciences, Litigation, Complex Litigation, Medicare Fraud and Abuse, Mergers, Acquisitions and Divestitures, Natural Resources, Nonprofit and Charitable Organizations, Occupational Safety and Health, OSHA, Partnership Law, Patents, Probate, Products Liability, Product Safety, Professional Liability, Public Finance, Railroad Law, Real Estate, Regulatory Law, Drug and Medical Device Regulation, Food and Drug Regulation, International Regulatory Law, Regulated Industries, Securities, Initial Public Offerings, Public Offerings, Taxation, Tax Controversies, Toxic Torts, Trade Secrets, Trademarks, Transportation, Trusts and Estates, Unfair Competition, Utility Law, White Collar Crime, Zoning, Planning and Land Use.

FIRM PROFILE: Established in 1911, Thompson Hine today is among the nation's largest corporate law firms and was recently selected as one of the Best Corporate Law Firms in America (in a survey of 32,000 corporate directors conducted by Corporate Board Member magazine). Thompson Hine attorneys serve some of the premier businesses in the world, including:

Alltel, Anthem Blue Cross/Blue Shield, Avery Dennison, BIC Corporation, Chiquita Brands International, Eaton Corporation, Eveready (Energizer), Ford Motor Company, Ford Motor Credit, Formica Corp., Goodrich Corporation, Goodyear Tire and Rubber Co., Hartford Insurance, Intimate Brands, Inc. (Victoria's Secret, Bath & Body Works), Jo-Ann Stores, Inc., Kelly Services, Inc., KeyCorp/KeyBank, Lexis-Nexis, The Mead Corporation, Medical Mutual of Ohio, Milacron Inc., Newell Rubbermaid, Nordson Corporation, Oglebay Norton Company, Ohio Bankers Association, Omnicare, Inc., Parker Hannifin, Polyone Corporation, Procter & Gamble, S.C. Johnson & Son, Inc., Sherwin-Williams, Smythe Cramer Co., SuperValu, Time Warner Cable, Toro Company, Verizon Wireless, and Whirlpool Corporation.

Thompson Hine attorneys provide a wide range of corporate legal services, represented by the following practice groups:

BANKRUPTCY - We represent major secured and unsecured lenders, creditors" committees, credit enhancement providers, debtors and various other parties of interest in finance transactions, workouts and bankruptcy matters.

BUSINESS LITIGATION - We represent corporate clients in a wide variety of business litigation - from corporate control contests and insurance disputes, to class actions, securities fraud, and tax controversies.

BANKING & INSURANCE - Our lawyers provide recognized experience in virtually all areas of financial institutions matters. We provide regulatory, transactional, government relations and litigation services to clients on matters related to insurance. Our clients include all types of insurance companies and other financial services organizations including large, publicly held, multinational financial holding companies; banks and thrifts; investment banking organizations; securities broker-dealers; registered investment advisor organizations; mutual funds; and mortgage banking and broker organizations.

COMMERCIAL & PUBLIC FINANCE - We handle complex commercial finance transactions (including senior debt, subordinated debt and mezzanine financing transactions and private debt placements), public finance, asset securitizations and general bank regulatory law.

COMPETITION, ANTITRUST & WHITE-COLLAR CRIME - We represent clients in antitrust and competition matters, trade restraint and price discrimination issues, franchising and distribution, misappropriation of trade secrets, false advertising, enforcement of noncompetition covenants and interference with business relationships.

CONSTRUCTION - We represent owners, design professionals, construction managers, contractors and sureties in connection with all facets of the building industry and have served in the role of Project Counsel for billions of dollars of construction at sites across the United States.

CORPORATE, M&A AND SECURITIES - We represent both emerging and established businesses in their most important business transactions, from start-up through IPOs, joint ventures, mergers, acquisitions and beyond.

eBUSINESS & EMERGING TECHNOLOGIES - This group unites experienced counsel from various disciplines around one central goal: helping business realize the opportunities and manage the risks of electronic and technological commerce.

EMPLOYEE BENEFITS - We advise clients regarding qualified, non-qualified and welfare benefit plans; resolution of controversies with the IRS, DOL, PBGC and other agencies; incentive and equity-based compensation arrangements; statutory and regulatory compliance; ERISA fiduciary duties; ESOPs; multi-employer plans; and ERISA litigation.

(This Listing Continued)

THOMPSON HINE LLP, Cleveland—Continued

ENERGY - We provide a broad range of services to our clients in the energy industry, including those that: Generate and sell electric energy into the nation's wholesale and retail energy markets. Transport and sell natural gas and oil. Transmit and distribute electricity and natural gas in retail markets. Purchase natural gas, electric energy and coal. Conduct energy trading operations. Manufacture, construct and/or buy and sell facilities and assets associated with the energy industry. Undertake energy-related projects, such as distributed generation, conservation or energy management projects. Manage information used by the energy industry.

ENVIRONMENTAL - We help clients understand the environmental aspects of their business transactions, craft methods of allocating risk and counsel them on their compliance obligations under local, state and federal laws.

HEALTH CARE - We represent physician groups, hospitals, clinical laboratories, diagnostic service providers, pharmaceutical manufacturers, medical device manufacturers and health insurance providers.

INTELLECTUAL PROPERTY - We assist clients with patents, trademarks, copyrights, trade secrets, computer software, internet related issues, employment relationships and intellectual property litigation.

INTERNATIONAL - We advise clients on trade regulation issues, customs and duty matters, foreign investment and joint ventures, NAFTA matters, importing and exporting issues, intellectual property protection, and immigration matters.

LABOR & EMPLOYMENT - We represent clients in employment litigation, workers" compensation proceedings, immigration matters, collective bargaining, administrative proceedings before the Department of Labor, OSHA, EEOC, NLRB and various state agencies.

LIFE SCIENCES - We provide legal and regulatory management services to established and emerging companies in the food, pharmaceuticals, biotech, and medical device industries.

PERSONAL & SUCCESSION PLANNING - We assist clients in the management and transmission of wealth, the succession to the control of businesses and other personal and family concerns.

PRODUCT LIABILITY - We have handled thousands of product liability matters involving mechanical, chemical, electrical, medical, aerospace, automotive and other products.

REAL ESTATE - We represent clients in Real Estate Development; Corporate Real Estate; Zoning and Land Use; Real Estate Investment and Financing; and Real Estate Investment Trusts.

TAXATION - We counsel clients in business transactions and financings, tax controversy, litigation, legislative and regulatory activities, executive compensation and tax planning, international taxation, state and local taxation and foundation and exempt organization matters.

TELECOMMUNICATIONS - Our Telecommunications group provides clients with wide-ranging guidance on the regulations and laws affecting telecommunications, broadcasting and other electronic communications companies. Our representation includes transactional matters, regulatory compliance, telecommunications services contracting, licensing and legislative/regulatory advocacy. We also have experience in issues involving communications land use and environmental matters, including human exposure to electromagnetic energy.

TRANSPORTATION - One of the largest transportation practices in the United States, our team has more than 100 years of collective experience representing transportation interests. We are involved in matters relating to commercial relationships and arrangements as well as the extensive and complex structure of rights, remedies and regulatory requirements involved in the domestic and international transportation of goods by rail, motor, ship, barge, air and pipeline.

WORKERS COMPENSATION - We represent employers in workers" compensation matters before state courts and industrial commissions. We have extensive experience representing and counseling clients in the area of workers' compensation.

AMOS BURT THOMPSON (1871-1965)
CHARLES P. HINE (1877-1942)
WALTER L. FLORY (1880-1951)
MICHAEL L. HARDY (Partner-in-Charge, Cleveland)
PATRICIA MANN SMITSON (Partner-in-Charge, Cincinnati)
ANTHONY C. WHITE (Partner-in-Charge, Columbus)
ROBERT M. CURRY (Partner-in Charge, Dayton)
NICHOLAS J. DiMICHAEL (Partner-in-Charge, Washington, DC)
GEORGE J. WALSH III (Partner-in-Charge, New York City)
LUDO DEKLERCK (Partner-in-Charge, Brussels)
WALT A. LINSCOTT (Partner-in-Charge, Atlanta)

PARTNERS

THOMAS A. ALDRICH, born Sandusky, Ohio, December 1, 1956; admitted to bar, 1982, Ohio. *Education:* Ohio University (A.B., summa cum laude, 1978); Harvard Law School (J.D., cum laude, 1982). Group Leader, Corporate Transactions and Securities, 1999-2004. Presentations: "Preparing the New MD&A," RR Donnelley/Glasser LegalWorks SEC "Hot Topics" Institute, 2004; "Accelerated and Enhanced 8-K Current Disclosure," RR Donnelley/Glasser LegalWorks SEC "Hot Topics" Institute, 2004; "General Principles of Contract Drafting," Contract Preparation in Ohio Seminar, Lorman Education Services, 2004; "Director Liability: How Higher Expectations and Enhanced Scrutiny May Increase Risk," Bowne of Cleveland/American Society of Corporate Secretaries, Ohio Chapter SEC Issues Update Seminar, 2004; "New Proxy Rules and Shareholder Access," 2004 Cleveland Bar Association Securities Law Institute; "SEC Proxy Process Reform Proposals/Sarbanes-Oxley Section 307 Professional Responsibility Rules," 2003 Bowne of Cleveland/American Society of Corporate Secretaries, Ohio Chapter SEC Issues Update Seminar; "1934 Act Reporting - More Disclosure, Less Time," 2002 Bowne of Cleveland/Cleveland Bar Association Representing Corporations: Recent Developments Seminar; "Recent Developments in Securities Laws," 2002 Cleveland Bar Association Securities Law Institute; "Employee Stock Ownership Plan and Stock Option Issues/The Corporate Takeover/Ethics" 2001 Ohio Advanced Corporate Securities Law Seminar; National Business Institute, Inc.; "Audit Committee," 2000 Cleveland Bar Association Securities Law Seminar; "Aircraft Carrier Proposal - Corporate Finance," 1999 Cleveland Bar Association Securities Law Seminar; "Report and Recommendations of the Blue Ribbon Commission on Improving the Effectiveness of Corporate Audit Committees," 1999 Ohio Society of Certified Public Accountants Ohio Securities Issues Conference; "Conflict of Interest Issues in the Representation of Entrepreneurial Businesses," 1999 Cleveland Bar Association Entity Selection and Formation Seminar; 1999 Cleveland Bar Association Securities Law Back to Basics Seminar; "Structure of the Asset Purchase Agreement and Significant Representations and Warranties," 1999 Ohio State Bar Association Corporate Basics Seminar; "Due Diligence Requirements of Directors," 1996 Cleveland Bar Association Securities Law Institute; "Recent Developments in Securities Law," 1994 Cleveland Bar Association Securities Law Institute; "New Proxy Rules," 1993 Cleveland Bar Association Securities Law Institute; "Federal and State Law Defensive Strategies," 1992 Cleveland Bar Association Corporation Banking and Business Law Institute; 1985, 1986, 1989 and 1990 Cleveland Bar Association Securities Law Institute. Member, Board of Trustees, Young Audiences of Greater Cleveland, Inc., 1996-2003. Member, Board of Trustees, Great Lakes Theater Festival, 2001—. United Way Services, Children and Youth Services Allocations Panel, 1985-1993; Chair, 1992-1993. Member, Funds Distribution Committee, 1991-1994. *Member:* Cleveland Bar Association (Chair, Corporation, Banking and Business Law Section, 1998-1999; Chair, Securities Law Section, 1999-2000; Chair, Securities Law Institute, 1995). ***TRANSACTIONS:*** Mergers and Acquisitions: Sale by a NYSE-listed diversified industrial manufacturer of valve business; sale by a super-regional bank holding company of its defined contribution pension plan record-keeping business; acquisition by a NYSE-listed diversified industrial manufacturer of the industrial and hydraulic hose and tubing business of a NYSE-listed manufacturer of vehicle modules, systems and components; consolidation of a NYSE-listed polymer services company with another NYSE-listed polymer services company; sale by a Japanese chemical manufacturer of its biochemical research business; $500 million sale by a Japanese chemical manufacturer of its worldwide agricultural chemical business to a British pharmaceutical and chemical manufacturer; $50 million merger of a NASDAQ NMS-listed construction and environmental abatement company with another public company and related senior secured revolving credit facility and subordinated secured term loan; $490 million sale by a super-regional bank holding company of its mortgage servicing business. Joint Ventures: Joint ventures of national shopping center developers for development of large regional shopping centers; joint venture between a NYSE-listed diversified industrial manufacturer and a NYSE-listed heavy industrial equipment manufacturer for the manufacture of generator/paralleling switchgear and automatic transfer switches; $1 billion (book value of assets) joint venture between a NYSE-listed polymer services company and a NYSE-listed chemical company involving twelve chemical plants and related acquisition of two chemical plants. Securities: Multi-state private placements of limited liability company member interests in connection with exchange of interests in thirty regional enclosed shopping malls; $480 million public offering for NASDAQ NMS-listed medical technology company in connection with acquisition of a NYSE-listed medical technology company; $125 million public offering of senior unsecured debt for NYSE-listed specialty chemicals manufacturer; employee stock ownership plan stock purchase agreement for privately held airplane parts manufacturer; initial public offering and follow-on public offering for medical technology company. Private equity: investment in developer of high-speed data links for commercial trucks; investment in automated teller network for super-regional bank holding company. ***PRACTICE AREAS:*** Mergers and Acquisitions; Corporate Law; Securities Law. ***Email:*** Tom.Aldrich@ThompsonHine.com

JEFFREY R. APPELBAUM, born Canton, Ohio, March 9, 1952; admitted to bar, 1977, Ohio. *Education:* Cornell University (A.B., 1974; J.D., 1977). Recipient, American Arbitration Association Special Award for Dedicated Service to Alternative Dispute Resolution in the Construction Industry, 1997. Author: "Bridging the Design Gap," Communique, Winter 1996; "Building Gateway: The Role of Project Construction Counsel," Cleveland Bar Journal, July, 1994. Co-Author: "Building Gateway: Resolving Labor and Employment Issues," Cleveland Bar Journal, September, 1994; "Owner-Construction Manager Agreement," Chapter 7, *Construction Renovation Formbook*, Wiley Law Publications, 1991; "The Rights and Responsibilities of the Architect-Engineer Under Ohio Law; Cambridge Institute, 1987 and 1988 Edition; "Partnering in Construction Administration", Segment of the Central Ohio Columbus, Ohio, March, 2000. Presentations: Lectures frequently on construction, negotiation and alternate methods of resolving dispute. Topics have included: "Construction Contracts: Approaches, Pitfalls and Solutions"; Representing the Builder in the Negotiation of a Construction Contract"; The Use of Dispute Resolution to Resolve Construction Disputes"; "The Use of Arbitration to Resolve Construction Disputes". Member: United States District Court, Northern District of Ohio, ADR Panel; Cuyahoga County Common Pleas Court Mediation Panel; Leadership Cleveland Class of 1997. Board of Directors, Cleveland Foundation for Architecture. *Member:* Cleveland (Member, Fee Mediation and Arbitration Committee), Ohio State (Member, Judicial Administration and Legal Reform Committee) and American (Member, Forum Committee on Construction Industry; Insurance, Negligence and Compensation Section; Litigation Section) Bar Associations; Ohio Contractors Association; American Arbitration Association National "Blue Ribbon" Panel of Arbitrators. (Group Leader, Construction). ***PRACTICE AREAS:*** Litigation; Construction Law. ***Email:*** Jeff.Appelbaum@ThompsonHine.com

JAMES B. ARONOFF, born Cleveland, Ohio, January 31, 1959; admitted to bar, 1984, Ohio. *Education:* Bowdoin College (A.B., cum laude, 1981); Case Western Reserve University (J.D., 1984). Order of the Coif. Author: "Ohio Landlord-Tenant Law", prepared for Cleveland Bar Association Practice and Procedure Clinic; "When Are Real Estate Interests Securities?" *The Practical Real Estate Lawyer;* "Securities Law Liabilities in Real Property Transactions", prepared for American Bar Association Annual Meeting; "What's In a Name?: The Business Judgement Rule After Zapata Corp. V. Maldonado", 34 Case

(This Listing Continued)

Western Law Review 340. *Member:* Cleveland, Ohio State (Member, Board of Governors, Real Property Section) and American (Member, Real Property, Probate and Trust Law Section; Immediate Past Chair, Decisions Committee and Non-Traditional Commercial Real Estate Finance Committee) Bar Associations; Cleveland Mortgage Bankers Association; NAREIT (Member, SEC Subcommittee). ***TRANSACTIONS:*** Representation of a NYSE-listed lodging REIT in the restructuring of its $400,000,000 hotel lease portfolio pursuant to the REIT Modernization Act; Representation of an AMEX-listed lodging REIT in the acquisition of a 10 hotel portfolio located in several Southwestern states; Representation of a major foreign insurance company in a $240,000,000 sale involving 43 retail and office properties located in 14 states; Representation of a NYSE-listed REIT in a $300,000,000 acquisition of 9 regional mall properties located in 5 states; Counsel to a private developer in a $1,200,000,000 sale of 21 regional mall properties to a NYSE-listed REIT; Counsel to a national bank in the purchase of a $210,000,000 portfolio of mortgage loans for properties in 12 states; Counsel to an institutional investor in the leveraged lease sale/leaseback of 7 full-service supermarket properties located in 5 states; Lead transaction counsel for the leveraged lease sale/leaseback financing of 13 "Superstores" of a national retailer located in 9 states; Lead counsel to a Big 3 auto manufacturer in connection with the leveraged lease sale/leaseback of both a major assembly operation as well as an environmentally sensitive truck painting facility; Counsel to national retailer for leveraged lease sale/leaseback of 8 newly constructed retail properties located in 5 states, structure involved the severance of estates for years and remainder interests which enhanced the overall return to the retailer; Lead counsel in the leveraged lease financing of a major steel processing center in Northwestern Ohio; Ohio counsel, responsible for the sale/leaseback and secured lease bond financing of 36 supermarket and grocery distribution warehouse properties as part of a 127 property multi-state transaction. ***PRACTICE AREAS:*** Real Estate Law; Real Estate Securities; Partnership Law; Corporate Law; Securities. ***Email:*** Jim.Aronoff@ThompsonHine.com

NANCY M. BARNES, born Sandusky, Ohio, October 2, 1968; admitted to bar, 1994, Pennsylvania; 1996, District of Columbia; 2002, Ohio and Northern District of Ohio. *Education:* College of William & Mary (B.A., summa cum laude, 1991); University of Pennsylvania Law School (J.D., summa cum laude, 1994). Phi Beta Kappa; Order of the Coif. Gordon A. Block Award for Wills and Future Interests; M.H. Goldstein Prize for Labor Law. Presidential Scholar. Article Editor, Comparative Law Journal. Law Clerk to United States Magistrate Judge Barry L. Garber, Southern District of Florida; Law Clerk to United States District Judge Patricia A. Seitz, Southern District of Florida. Member: College of William and Mary Alumni Association, Northeast Ohio Chapter; University of Pennsylvania Law Alumni Network; Hudson Newcomers Club. Presenter: Interplay of FMLA, ADA, and Workers' Compensation Law in Ohio (September 2003—NLRB Region 8 Seminar); The Bermuda Triangle: FMLA, ADA, and Workers' Compensation (June 2003); Top 10 Mistakes Employers Make With FMLA (July 2002); Avoiding Claims of Sexual Harassment (January 1997); Update on Employment Discrimination Law (Fall 1996). Author: "Avoid Mistakes Regarding Employee Leave Law" (Crain's Cleveland Business, Jan. 6- 12, 2003); "FMLA: The 10 Most Common Mistakes Employers Make" (HR Solutions, June 2003). *Member:* Anthony J. Celebrezze Inn of Court. ***REPORTED CASES:*** Hospodor v. ARINC, 956 F. Supp. 1263 (D. Md. 1997). ***TRANSACTIONS:*** Successfully negotiated favorable settlement of ERISA and ADEA claims alleged by former Chief Executive Officer of non-profit corporation; Prevailed on behalf of close corporation in breach of fiduciary duty and tortious interference claim; Developed sexual harassment prevention policy for paper manufacturer and presented training sessions at all corporate and manufacturing locations; Obtained dismissal of potential shareholder derivative action; Prevailed on summary judgment in environmental insurance coverage matter resulting in the dismissal of millions of dollars in claims against insurer; Obtained directed verdict on age discrimination claim asserted against hospital by a former employee; Obtained voluntary dismissal of multi-count employment discrimination complaint filed against client without filing answer or motion to dismiss; Represented former general counsel in ADEA and ERISA suit against union-employer and obtained favorable settlement and dismissal of counterclaims; Obtained successful outcome in bench trial for transportation communications corporation in suit brought by former chief executive officer alleging contract and tort claims arising from his termination and alleged breach of executive compensation agreement; Advised and counseled human resource professionals on a wide variety of employment-related matters, including employee handbooks, non-competitive agreements, OFCCP compliance, EEO matters, employee discipline and discharge, affirmative action, FLSA compliance, FMLA and arbitration agreements; Assisted in obtaining favorable consent judgment on behalf of employer in suit relating to non-competition agreement; Conducted Employment Audit reviewing employment policies, practices and procedures; frequent speaker on ADA and FMLA. ***PRACTICE AREAS:*** Litigation; Labor and Employment. ***Email:*** Nancy.Barnes@ThompsonHine.com

RICHARD C. BINZLEY, born New York, N.Y., September 1, 1937; admitted to bar, 1966, Ohio; 1971, U.S. Supreme Court. *Education:* Kenyon College (A.B., 1959); Western Reserve University (J.D., 1966). Adjunct Professor of Law Cleveland State University, 1979-2001. Associate Editor, American Maritime Cases. Past President, Propeller Club of United States, Port of Cleveland. *Member:* Cleveland, Ohio State and Federal Bar Associations; Maritime Law Association (Former Member, Board of Directors); Lawyer-Pilots Bar Association. [CDR U.S. Coast Guard Reserve (RET)]. ***PRACTICE AREAS:*** Admiralty Law; Litigation; Products Liability. ***Email:*** Dick.Binzley@ThompsonHine.com

APRIL V. BOISE, born Shaker Heights, Ohio, August 27, 1968; admitted to bar, 1994, Ohio, New York, Missouri (inactive) and Kansas (inactive). *Education:* University of Michigan, School of Business Administration (B.B.A., summa cum laude, Accounting and Marketing, 1990); University of Chicago (J.D., 1994). The German Marshall Fund, American Marshall Fellow, Spring 2002. Lecturer, Securities Law Section - Introduction to Securities Transacations, Cleveland Bar Association, October 2001. Lecturer, American Society of Corporate Secretaries, Securities Law Update, January 2001. Board of Trustees: Cleveland Zoo Society, 2003—; Board of Trustees: The Cleveland Foodbank, Inc., 2000—; United Black Fund, 2000—. Executive Committee of Board of Directors, State Ballet of Missouri, 1995-1997. Board of Trustees, Volunteer Council, Science City Museum at Union Station, 1995-1997. Young Friends of Art, Nelson Atkins Museum, 1995-1997. ***PRACTICE AREAS:*** Mergers and Acquisitions; Capital Markets; Securities; Private Equity; Corporate Law. ***Email:*** April.Boise@ThompsonHine.com

(This Listing Continued)

KIP T. BOLLIN, born Toledo, Ohio, September 22, 1970; admitted to bar, 1995, Ohio; 1997, Colorado (inactive) and U.S. District Court, Northern District of Ohio; 1999, U.S. Court of Appeals, Sixth Circuit; 2002, U.S. Supreme Court. *Education:* New York University (B.A., cum laude, 1992); Georgetown University (J.D., 1995). Editor, Georgetown Journal on Poverty Law & Policy, 1991-1992. Law Clerk, the Honorable Sam H. Bell, N.D. Ohio, E.D., 1995-1997. *Member:* Ohio State and Federal Bar Associations; Defense Research Institute. ***TRANSACTIONS:*** Successfully defended at trial Fortune 100 manufacturer from claims involving closed head injury; Involved in pre-suit resolution of Qui Tam (False Claims Act) action brought by government against major supplier of product used in government construction; Defense of electronic circuit board manufacturer of assembly materials in products liability and breach of warranty claims; Defense of Fortune 100 manufacturer of construction and mining equipment in wrongful death claim; Defense of website developer in cases involving alleged breach of contract, replevin and breach of warranty; Defense of class action on behalf of major manufacturer; Defense of multiple product liability and workplace intentional tort claims involving death; Prosecution of claims on behalf of Fortune 100 company to recover millions of dollars in insurance proceeds due to business interruption; Defense of Fortune 500 appliance manufacturers in cases alleging products liability, design defect, failure to warn and negligence; Defense of Fortune 500 companies in cases arising out of fire; Pro bono appellate representation of white collar criminal conviction involving wire fraud, mail fraud and money laundering; Defense of division of Fortune 100 company from copyright infringement claim; Arbitration defense of construction contractor and successful prosecution of counterclaim for payments owed. ***PRACTICE AREAS:*** Litigation; Business Litigation; Products Liability; Premises Liability. ***Email:*** Kip.Bollin@ThompsonHine.com

DEREK D. BORK, born Monroe, Michigan, March 11, 1971; admitted to bar, 1996, Ohio. *Education:* Stanford University (A.B., 1993); Georgetown University (J.D., 1996). ***PRACTICE AREAS:*** Corporate; Mergers, Acquisitions and Divestitures; Venture Capital; Securities; Business Law. ***Email:*** Derek.Bork@ThompsonHine.com

STEPHEN L. BUESCHER, born Cleveland, Ohio, October 31, 1944; admitted to bar, 1969, Ohio; 1975, U.S. Supreme Court; 1976, U.S. Tax Court; 1977, U.S. Claims Court. *Education:* Allegheny College (B.A., 1966); Case Western Reserve University (J.D., 1969). Presentations: "E-Commerce/Sales Tax Nexus Issues," Cleveland Bar Ass'n State and Local Tax Institute, 2002; "Interest Netting," Cleveland Tax Institute, 2000; "Representing Closely Held Businesses-Traps for the Unwary," Cleveland Tax Instutute, 1999; "Conducting a Corporate Closing," Ohio CLE Institute, 1999; "Corporate Law Basics: The Organization and Sale of a Small Business," Ohio CLE Institute, 1995; "S Corporation Update, Unreasonable Corporation and Accumulated Earnings Tax, Ohio Tax Developments and Estate Planning," Firm Briefing Series for Accountants, 1992-1995; "S Corporations - A Tax & Estate Planning Primer," CLE Institute, 1991; "S Corporation Issues," Cleveland Bar Association Practice and Procedure Clinic, 1991. Frequent lecturer at Cleveland Tax Institute and State and Local Tax Institute. Member, Tax Club of Cleveland. *Member:* Ohio State and American Bar Associations. ***PRACTICE AREAS:*** Taxation Law. ***Email:*** Steve.Buescher@ThompsonHine.com

THOMAS J. CALLAHAN, born Cleveland, Ohio, January 21, 1957; admitted to bar, 1985, Ohio, U.S. District Court, Northern District of Ohio; U.S. Supreme Court; U.S. Court of Appeals for the Federal Circuit; U.S. Court of Appeals, Sixth Circuit; 1987, U.S. Tax Court and U.S. Court of Federal Claims. *Education:* Duke University (B.S., 1979); Case Western Reserve University (J.D., 1985). Lecturer: "Independence of IRS Appeals," ABA Section of Taxation (2005); "Tax Accrual Workpapers," Tax Executives Institute (2005); "Are Your Tax Accrual Workpapers Exposed?", ABA Section of Taxation (2005); "Privileged Communications and Tax Accrual Workpapers" and "Federal Tax Update," Tax Executives Institute (Cleveland Chapter)(2004); "Know When to Hold 'Em: Tax Accrual Workpapers," Tax Executives Institute (2004); "Tax Talk Today: Tax Shelter Enforcement Update," Internal Revenue Service (2004); "National Research Program Update," ABA Section of Taxation (2004); "Attorney-Client Privilege, Tax Accural Workpapers and Related Production Issues," ABA Section of Taxation (2003); "Update on IRS Appeals Following the Reorganizations," ABA Section of Taxation (2003); "Tax Accrual Workpapers 2003: What Documentation Should a Corporate Tax Department Generate," Tax Executives Institute 58th Annual Conference; "Like-Kind Exchanges of Personal Property and Multi-Asset Exchanges," Cleveland Tax Institute (2003); "New LMSB Audit Initiatives," ABA Section of Taxation (2003); "Federal Tax Aspects of Individual Bankruptcy," Cleveland Tax Institute (2002); "National Research Program," ABA Section of Taxation (2002); "Like Kind Real Estate Exchanges in Ohio," Lorman Educational Services (2002); "Disclosure of Tax Accrual Workpapers to IRS," Tax Executives Institute (Cincinnati Chapter)(2002); "Federal Tax Update," Tax Executives Institute (Cleveland Chapter) (2001 & 2002); "Redesign of the LMSB Audit Process," ABA Section of Taxation (2002); "Handling IRS Audits and Appeals," Cleveland Bar Association (2001 & 2002); "Real Estate Workouts at the Beginning of the New Millennium - Tax Issues," Cleveland Bar Association (2001); "IRS Collection Due Process - Mesa Oil v. United States," ABA Section of Taxation (2001); "IRC §6404 (e) and New Cash Bond Proposals," ABA Section of Taxation (2001); "Alternative Dispute Resolution Techniques for Issue Resolution with the Service," Cleveland Tax Institute (2000); "Accountants vs. Lawyers: The Accountant / Taxpayer Privilege," Cleveland Tax Institute (1999); "Corporate Tax Update," Tax Executives Institute (Cleveland Chapter) (1999). Articles: "Tax Accrual Workpapers: IRS Efforts to Obtain Them, Corporate Strategies to Protect Them," The Tax Executive (2003); "What Tax Lawyers Need to Know About Single Member Limited Liability Companies," The Practical Tax Lawyer (1999); "1997 Tax Law Change: Reporting of Payments to Attorneys," Cleveland Bar Journal, (1998). Listed in: *The Best Lawyers in America, Who's Who in America, Who's Who in American Law, Who's Who in Finance and Industry, Who's Who in the World, CCH Journal of Tax Practice and Procedure Advisory Board (2005) and Thompson West Publishing Tax Advisory Board (2005).* Certified Public Accountant, Ohio, 1981—. *Member:* Ohio State and American Bar Associations; American College of Tax Counsel (Regent - Sixth Circuit); American Institute of Certified Public Accountants. (Practice Group Leader (Tax)). ***TRANSACTIONS:*** Member of legal team that eliminated over $400 million in tax, penalty and interest for U.S. subsidiary of foreign corporation with respect to elimination of U.S.withholding tax on distributions to foreign parent, determination of tax basis of subsidiary stock under U.S. consolidated return regulations, reduction of excess loss account income arising from termination of U.S. consolidated group, elimination of proposed transfer pricing adjustments, and reduction of gain on sale of subsidiary stock; member of legal

(This Listing Continued)

THOMPSON HINE LLP, Cleveland—Continued

team that obtained recovery of $4.6 million in tax and interest for Fortune 500 client in settlement of U.S. Court of Federal Claims litigation concerning creditable Brazilian taxes and dividends received deduction; Member of legal team that obtained recovery of $3.4 million refund attributable to previous payment of deficiency interest by Fortune 500 client to IRS; Member of legal team that obtained favorable private letter ruling which allowed real estate client to claim $3 million of low-income housing tax credits; Member of legal team that obtained recovery of $2.5 million in tax and interest for Buckeye Power, Inc. in U.S. Court of Federal Claims litigation which confirmed Buckeye's qualification as a tax-exempt rural electric cooperative. Buckeye Power, Inc. v. U.S., 38 Fed. Cl. 154, 97-2 USTC¶ 50,580 (1997); and Buckeye Power, Inc. v U.S., 38 Fed. Cl. 283 (1997); Eliminated $1.9 million in tax, penalties and interest against client with respect to unreasonable compensation case docketed in U.S. Tax Court; Member of legal team that obtained $1 million concession in tax, penalties and interest from IRS for a client previously convicted of filing false tax returns; Member of legal team that obtained a concession from IRS of $650,000 in tax, penalties and interest for a client previously convicted of wire fraud; Eliminated over $500,000 in taxable income for a real estate developer in bankruptcy with respect to foreclosure of distressed properties; Member of legal team that eliminated $500,000 proposed assessment of accumulated earnings tax for closely held corporate client; Obtained over $250,000 concession of tax and interest in TEFRA case based on jurisdictional defense; Eliminated $200,000 in tax, penalties and interest with respect to a pension rollover; Eliminated $150,000 trust fund recovery penalty for client; Obtained $100,000 concession of tax from IRS concerning proposed liability of client for funding payroll with knowledge that vendor was unable to pay payroll taxes. Tax counsel to issuer of multi-billion dollar bank notes to the public market; Tax counsel to large real estate developer with respect to $1.2 billion sale of regional shopping center mall properties to publicly-held REIT; Tax counsel to large real estate developer with respect to income and partnership tax issues arising in connection with the formation of an UPREIT; Tax counsel to issuer of over $50 million of trust preferred securities to the public market; Tax counsel to closely-held client with respect to $50 million part sale and part redemption of its stock; Tax counsel to large publicly-held bank holding company with respect to tax-free merger of investment banking and consulting business into wholly-owned subsidiaries; Advised on tax and accounting issues with respect to synthetic lease financing of a $40 million distribution center constructed by publicly-held client; Tax counsel to the unsecured creditors committee of a large retailer concerning the preservation of substantial net operating losses and minimization of taxes in bankruptcy; Tax counsel to large publicly-held retailer with respect to income and payroll tax implications of internal restructuring; Tax counsel to numerous clients with respect to structuring taxable mergers and acquisitions and tax-free reorganizations; Acquisition by Phoenix Packaging Corporation of its principal competitor. ***PRACTICE AREAS:*** Taxation Law. ***Email:*** Tom.Callahan@ThompsonHine.com

JAMES R. CARLSON, born Arlington, Virginia, February 22, 1947; admitted to bar, 1975, Ohio. *Education:* Oberlin College (B.A., 1969); Harvard Law School (J.D., 1975). *Member:* American Bar Association; Ohio Bar Association (Tender Offer Subcommittee of Corporation Law Committee). ***TRANSACTIONS:*** The Lubrizol Corporation 2004 acquisition of Noveon International; Jo-Ann Stores, Inc. 2003 reclassification of common shares; Ohio counsel for TRW Inc. in 2002 takeover contest with Northrop Grumman; KeyCorp electronic processing card venture with NOVA International and various acquisitions; Nordson Corporation various acquisitions and mergers. ***PRACTICE AREAS:*** Corporate Law; Securities Law. ***Email:*** Jim.Carlson@ThompsonHine.com

THOMAS J. COLLIN, born Windom, Minnesota, January 6, 1949; admitted to bar, 1975, Ohio; 1977, U.S. Court of Appeals, Tenth Circuit; 1980, U.S. Supreme Court; 1981, U.S. Court of Appeals, Sixth Circuit; 1982, U.S. Court of Appeals, Eighth Circuit; 1997, U.S. Court of Appeals, Seventh Circuit; 1999, U.S. Court of Appeals, Eleventh Circuit; U.S. District Court, Northern and Southern Districts of Ohio. *Education:* University of Minnesota (B.A., 1970); Harvard University (A.M., 1972); Georgetown University (J.D., 1974). Listed in: *Who's Who in America, Who's Who in American Law* and *Who's Who in Midwest*. Author: *Ohio Business Competition Law* (Lawyers Cooperative 1994); "State Franchise Laws and the Small Business Franchise Act of 1999: Barriers to Efficient Distribution," 55 Business Lawyer 1699 (2000). Editor: *Punitive Damages and Business Torts: A Practitioner's Handbook* (American Bar Association 1998). Chair, Business Torts and Unfair Competition Committee (1995-1998), Chair, Annual Meeting Committee (2001-2002) and Chair, Distribution and Franchising Committee (2002-2005), ABA Antitrust Section. Member, Board of Governors, Antitrust Section, Ohio State Bar Association, 1989-1998. President, The Citizens League of Greater Cleveland, 1997-1999. *Member:* Ohio State (Member, Antitrust Section) and American (Member, Antitrust, Litigation and Intellectual Property Sections; Forum on Franchising) Bar Associations. (Group Leader, Competition, Antitrust and White Collar Crime). ***LANGUAGES:*** German and French. ***PRACTICE AREAS:*** Antitrust and Trade Regulation; Dealership Law; Franchise Law; Franchise Litigation; Intellectual Property Litigation; Unfair Competition. ***Email:*** Tom.Collin@ThompsonHine.com

DIANNE S. COSCARELLI, born Tiffin, Ohio, January 17, 1952; admitted to bar, 1978, Ohio. *Education:* Ohio University (A.B., 1974); University of San Francisco (J.D., 1978). Recipient, Women of Professional Excellence Award, YWCA, 1988. Director, 1988—; Secretary 1990—, Boys and Girls Clubs of Cleveland. Associate Representative, Greater Cleveland Real Estate Organizations, 1997-2000. Member, Commercial Real Estate Women of Cleveland. Trustee, 1980-1989; Vice President, 1987-1989; Secretary, 1984-1987, Legal Aid Society of Cleveland. Volunteer, 1979-1982, Guardian Ad Litem Program. *Member:* Cleveland (Chair, 1999-2000; Vice-Chair, 1998-1999, Secretary, 1997-1999, Treasurer, 1996-1997, Real Property Section; Chairperson, Legal Opinion Committee, 1994-1996), Ohio State (Chair, 2005— ,Vice Chair, 2003-2005; Member, 1998—, Board of Governors, Real Property Section) and American (Member, Real Property and Probate Section; Chair, 2000— and Vice Chair, 1997-1999, Construction Lending Committee; Member, Committee on Legal Opinions in Real Estate Transactions, 1995—) Bar Associations; American College of Real Estate Lawyers; National Association of Industrial and Office Properties (Secretary, 1996-1997; Public Affairs Chair, 1997-2000); Cleveland Mortgage Bankers Association. ***PRACTICE AREAS:*** Real Estate Law; Commercial Finance; Public Finance. ***Email:*** Dianne.Coscarelli@ThompsonHine.com

(This Listing Continued)

TIMOTHY J. COUGHLIN, born Chicago, Illinois, June 27, 1959; admitted to bar, 1984, Ohio. *Education:* University of Notre Dame (B.B.A., 1981); Case Western Reserve University (J.D., 1984). Order of the Coif. *Member:* Cleveland Bar Association (Member, Litigation Section); Defense Research Institute. ***TRANSACTIONS:*** National representation of multiple chemical companies and the industry trade association in product liability and industry wide liability claims; Representation of hand tool manufacturers in consumer class action Litigation; Representation of defendant in class action damage phase Litigation; Representation of numerous pesticide manufacturers in product liability matters arising out of chemical exposure; Representation of various medical device manufacturers in product liability cases ranging from implants to sterilizers; Representation of multi-national electronic supplier in product liability matters; Representation of multi-national chemical corporation in product liability matters resulting in wrongful death suits; National representation of an after-market automotive supplier in product liability and contractual disputes; Representation of numerous machine tool manufacturers in product liability matters; Representation of multi-national electronics entity in commercial disputes over breaches of warranty; Statewide representation of a Fortune 10 manufacturer in all premises liability matters. ***PRACTICE AREAS:*** Products Liability Law; Toxic Torts; Business Litigation; Commercial Law. ***Email:*** Tim.Coughlin@ThompsonHine.com

THOMAS J. COYNE, born Cleveland, Ohio, November 18, 1959; admitted to bar, 1985, Ohio. *Education:* Holy Cross College (B.A., Major in History, Minor in Economics and Philosophy, 1982); University of Notre Dame (J.D., 1985). Phi Beta Kappa. Recipient: Crains Cleveland Business "40 Under 40," 1995. Editorial Board Member and Book Review Editor, Notre Dame Law Review. Former Lecturer, Real Estate Law, Cleveland Marshall College of Law. Listed in: *The Best Lawyers in America*, 2003-2004 edition. Member, American College of Real Estate Attorneys. Former Board President, Family Transitional Housing, Inc. *Member:* International Council of Shopping Centers; Urban Land Institute; National Association of Real Estate Investment Trusts; Building Owners and Managers Association of Greater Cleveland. ***PRACTICE AREAS:*** Real Estate Law; Private Companies. ***Email:*** Thomas.Coyne@ThompsonHine.com

J. KURT DENKEWALTER, born Columbus, Ohio, 1956; admitted to bar, 1990, Ohio; U.S. District Court, Southern District of Ohio. *Education:* Wright State University (B.S., 1984); University of Dayton (J.D., cum laude, 1990); University of Cincinnati (M.S., 1993). Associate Editor, University of Dayton Law Review, 1988-1989. Author: "Poison Pills: Is the Flip-in Flipping Out?" University of Dayton Law Review. *Member:* Dayton, Ohio State and American Bar Associations. ***PRACTICE AREAS:*** Business Law; Corporate Law; Commercial Law; General Litigation. ***Email:*** Kurt.Denkewalter@ThompsonHine.com

FRANK R. DeSANTIS, born Erie, Pennsylvania, November 28, 1951; admitted to bar, 1980, Pennsylvania and Tax Court; 1983, Ohio; 1984, U.S. District Court, Northern District of Ohio; 1991, U.S. District Court, Western District of Pennsylvania; 1993, U.S. District Court, Northern District of Texas; 1997, U.S. Court of Appeals, Sixth Circuit; 2001, U.S. Supreme Court. *Education:* Mercyhurst College (B.A., 1973); Gannon University (M.B.A., 1977); Gonzaga University School of Law (J.D., magna cum laude, 1979). Associate Editor, Gonzaga University Law Review, 1978-1979. Office of Chief Counsel, Internal Revenue Service, 1980-1986. *Member:* Cuyahoga County Bar Association (President, 1997), Ohio State and American Bar Associations; Conference of the Eighth Judicial District (Life Member). Ohio State Bar Foundation; Cuyahoga County Bar Foundation (President, 2000—). ***PRACTICE AREAS:*** Complex Business Litigation; Tax Litigation; Professional Liability. ***Email:*** Frank.DeSantis@ThompsonHine.com

JEFFRY J. ERNEY, born Cleveland, Ohio, September 12, 1960; admitted to bar, 1988, Ohio. *Education:* Cleveland State University (B.S., 1982); Case Western Reserve University (J.D., 1988). Beta Alpha Psi. Recipient, Chief Counsel's Office, Central Division, Attorney of the Year Award, 1993; Chief Counsel's Office, National Award for Advisory Opinions, 1995; Internal Revenue Service Performance Award, 1989, 1990, 1994 and 1996. Certified Public Account, Ohio. Co-Author: "Unified Audit Procedures for Partnership & Passthrough Entities," Warren, Gorham & Lamont, 2000 Edition. Lecturer: Regulated Public Utilities Section, American Bar Association, 1992, 1994 and 1996. Business Law Instructor, Becker C.P.A. Review Course, September 1989 - December 1999. Finance Council, Member, St. Clare Church, 1993-1996. *Member:* Cleveland and American Bar Associations; Cleveland Tax Bar. ***TRANSACTIONS:*** Obtained over a $1 million concession from the Appeals Division of the IRS for a case involving incentive stock options; Sustained $1.2 million of a research credit taken by a public company; Successfully defended a refund claim in the amount of $500,000 for a research credit; Obtained a favorable ruling from IRS relating to a VEBA plan; Obtained "no change" letters for three separate clients in cases that involved substantial corporate issues; Filed numerous protests, which are currently being worked in Appeals, involving the following topics: specified liability loss pursuant to IRC § 172 (f) Foreign Sales Corporation: Captive Life Insurance; Mark to Market - IRC § 475; repairs vs. maintenance; and the "one year rule." Governmental Experience: Obtained a favorable decision from the United States Tax Court in the case of *Southwestern Energy Co. v. Commissioner*, 100 T.C. 500 (1993), involving the deductibility for repayment of overrecoveries, and the accrual of interest on convertable bonds; Received a favorable opinion from the United States Tax Court regarding built in gains - IRC § 1374. *Argo Sales v. Commissioner*, 105 T.C. 86 (1995); Established precedential law in the area of discharge of indebtedness income. *Babin v. Commissioner*, T.C. Memo 1992-673 (1992), aff'd, 23 F.3d 1032 (6th Cir. 1994), reh'g denied, 1994 U.S. App. Lexis (6th Cir. 1994), cert. denied,513 U.S. 961 (1994); Obtained a favorable decision from the United States Tax Court regarding the determination of debt vs. equity. Ginsberg v. Commissioner, T.C.M. 1992-372 (1992), aff'd in part, rev'd in part, 1993 U.S. App. Lexis 21519 96th Cir.1993); Obtained a favorable decision from the United States Tax Court in a case involving the determination of transferee liability. *Staffilino v. Commissioner*, T.C.M. 1992-706 (1992); Member of litigation team that successfully defended the IRS position relating to contributions in aid of construction - IRC § 118. *Florida Progress Corp. v. United States*, 82 A.F.T.R. 2d 5363 (1998); Member of legal team that developed IRS Coordinated Issue Paper-Utilities Specialization Program for the following issues: ITC for Transitional Property; IRC § 1341-Excess Deferred Taxes; and Decommissioning and Decontamination costs; Specialization Program for the following issues: ITC for Transitional Property; IRC

(This Listing Continued)

§ 1341-Excess Deferred Taxes; and Decommissioning and Decontamination costs. ***PRACTICE AREAS:*** Taxation; Business Litigation. ***Email:*** Jeffry.Erney@ThompsonHine.com

S. STUART EILERS, born Cleveland, Ohio, June 4, 1938; admitted to bar, 1963, Ohio. *Education:* Williams College (B.A., 1960); University of Michigan (J.D., 1963). Fellow, American College of Trial Lawyers. Master Bencher, Anthony J. Celebrezze Inns of Court. Author: "Recent Developments in Product Liability Law and Punitive Damages," Birmingham, Alabama Bar Association, 1996; "Relationship Between In-House and Outside Counsel," Minnesota Institute of Legal Education, Minnesota Products Liability Seminar, 1995. Life Member, Eighth Judicial District Conference. *Member:* Cleveland and Ohio State Bar Associations. ***PRACTICE AREAS:*** Products Liability; Business Litigation. ***Email:*** Stu.Eilers@ThompsonHine.com

ANDREW L. FABENS, III, born Washington, D.C., April 8, 1942; admitted to bar, 1967, Ohio. *Education:* Yale University (A.B., 1964); University of Chicago (J.D., 1967). Trustee, Bascom Little Fund, Cleveland Ohio, 1985—. Member since 1980, Trustee since 1991, Chairman of Board, 2001., A.M. McGregor Home, East Cleveland, Ohio, Finance Committee. Trustee, Shaker Lakes Regional Nature Center, 1983-1986. Trustee, 1975-1984, President 1978-1980, 1983-1984, Family Health Association, Cleveland, Ohio. *Member:* Cleveland (Member, Estate Planning Institute) and Ohio State (Board of Governors, Probate and Trust Law Section; Treasurer, 1997-1999; Secretary, 1999-2001; Vice Chair, 2001—) Bar Associations. Fellow, American College of Trust and Estate Counsel. ***PRACTICE AREAS:*** Estate Planning Law; Probate Law; Personal Planning; Successions. ***Email:*** Andy.Fabens@ThompsonHine.com

THOMAS L. FEHER, born Cleveland, Ohio, January 26, 1960; admitted to bar, 1987, Ohio; 1988, U.S. District Court, Northern District of Ohio; 1992, U.S. Supreme Court; 1994, U.S. Court of Appeals, 6th Circuit. *Education:* Kent State University (B.S., 1983); Cleveland Marshall College of Law (J.D., magna cum laude, 1987). Phi Alpha Delta. Research Editor, Cleveland State Law Review, 1986-1987. Author, "The Alleged Molestation Victim, the Rules of Evidence, and the Constitution: Should Children Really Be Seen and Not Heard?", 14 AmJ. Crim.L. 227, 230-33 (1988), reprinted in Towards a Critical Victimology, Fattah, E.A. (ed.), St. Martins Press, Great Britain, 1992. Member, Board of Trustees: Shaker Family Center; Cleveland Marshall Law Alumni Association. *Member:* Cleveland, Ohio State and Federal Bar Associations. ***REPORTED CASES:*** Jones v. Sumser Retirement Village, 209 F.3d 851 (2000) 10 AM. Disability Cas. (BNA 790; Boedeker v. Rogers, 136 Ohio App. 3d 425, 736 N.E. 2d 955 (1999); Schachner v. Blue Cross/Blue Shield of Ohio, 77 F.3d 889 (1996); Steiner v. Van Dorn, 104 Ohio App. 3d 51 (1995); Mackey v. Cleveland State University, 837 F. Supp. 1396, 64 Employment Practice Rep. ¶42,980 (U.S. District Court, N.D. Ohio, July 20, 1993); Record Data International, Inc. v. Record Data of Michigan, Inc., 677 F. Supp. 915 (N.D. Ohio 1988); Sedar v. Knowlton Construction Co., 49 Ohio St. 3d 193 (1990). ***PRACTICE AREAS:*** Employment Litigation; Complex Business Litigation; Fiduciary Law; Class Action Litigation; Consumer Litigation; Products Liability. ***Email:*** Tom.Feher@ThompsonHine.com

JENNIFER A. LESNY FLEMING, born Berea, Ohio, July 18, 1968; admitted to bar, 1993, Ohio; U.S. District Court, Northern District of Ohio and U.S. Court of Appeals, Sixth Circuit. *Education:* Miami University (B.A., with University Honors, Diplomacy and Foreign Affairs, German and Political Science, 1990); Vanderbilt University (J.D., 1993). Research Editor, Vanderbilt Journal of Transnational Law. Vanderbilt Moot Court Board. Outstanding Oralist, Philip C. Jessup International Moot Court Team. Adjunct Professor of Law, Focused Problem Solving, Core Lawyering Skills (CORE III) and The Lawyering Process (negotiation and client counseling), Case Western Reserve University School of Law. *Member:* Cleveland, Ohio State and American Bar Associations; Defense Research Institute; The William K. Thomas American Inn of Court. ***LANGUAGES:*** German and French. ***TRANSACTIONS:*** Obtained full defense verdict in complex breach of contract case brought by an asbestos abatement and demolition contractor against the owner of a PCB and asbestos-contaminated site for damages in excess of $1.3 million; Obtained complete dismissal of federal RICO action brought by former company officer alleging a conspiracy to deprive him of his interests in the client company; Obtained full defense verdict in a breach of contract case involving the sale of defective steel; Prevailed in representing twenty major motion picture companies in five federal copyright infringement cases to restrain video store owners from offering counterfeit videocassettes to the public; Won summary judgment in the defense of a federal case where a real estate developer alleged $50 million in damages for negligence and fraud against a major bank in connection with the bank's role as a construction lender; Prevailed in defense of mandatory arbitration in which two plaintiff employees alleged racial discrimination and breach of their respective employee contracts against their former employer; Successfully defended a nursing facility against an attempt to unionize the staff, including numerous unfair labor practices claims; Successfully defended company providing elevator and escalator maintenance services from varying product liability and/or personal injury claims. ***PRACTICE AREAS:*** Litigation; Business Law; Civil Practice; Contracts; Banks and Banking; Securities; RICO; Unfair Competition; Trade Secrets; Fraud and Deceit; Libel, Slander and Defamation; Professional Liability; Commercial Law; Real Estate; Leases and Leasing; Labor and Employment; Premises Liability; Torts; Negligence; Products Liability; Personal Injury; Construction Law; Alternative Dispute Resolution; Appellate Practice; General Practice. ***Email:*** Jennifer.Fleming@ThompsonHine.com

MARK S. FLOYD, born El Paso, Texas, 1958; admitted to bar, 1983, Ohio. *Education:* Stanford University (A.B., with honors, 1980); Columbia University (J.D., 1983). Listed in: Who's Who Among Black Americans; Who's Who in American Law. Recipient, Crain's Cleveland Business' 40 Under 40 Outstanding Young Business Leaders Award. Articles Editor, Columbia Journal of Art & The Law. Author: "Supreme Court Ruling Moved Toward Favoring Arbitration," Crain's Cleveland Business, July 9, 2001; "Written Policy Can Help Control Technology Abuse," Employee Cost Control Strategies for CEOs, Managers & Administrators, November 2000; "Discrimination Damages: Controlling The Tax Consequences For The Plaintiff," The Practical Lawyer, January 1999; "Employment at Will: Job-Related Lawsuits Rapidly Overwhelming the Courts," Kaleidoscope, April/May 2000. Co-Authored with Jim Neumeister: "Road to Becoming Law Long for OSHA, Crain's Cleveland Business, May 8, 2000 and "NLRB Ruling to Dramatically Impact Employers", Crain's Cleveland Business, August 14, 2000. Lecturer: "Confidentiality, Trade Secrets, and Covenants Not to Compete: Are They Really Enforceable," ABA - MCP 2000 Conference, Chicago, Illinois, October, 1999; "Hiring and Firing Issues," HR Star Conference, Cleveland, Ohio, July, 2000; "A Guide to Avoiding Litigation Pitfalls," HR Star Conference, Cleveland, Ohio, July, 2001; "Effective Drafting of Non-Compete Agreements," OSBA Post-Employment Litigation Conference, Cleveland, Ohio, November, 2001; "Litigation Avoidance Strategies," HR Star Conference, Cleveland, Ohio, July, 2002. Member, Board of Trustees, Cleveland Institute of Music. Former Labor Arbitration Panelist, Cleveland State University Industrial Relations Center. Former Executive Committee Member and Labor Counsel, Cleveland Ballet. Former Member of Steering Committee for Orchestra Tomorrow, Cleveland Orchestra. Former Vice President of Board and Legal Counsel, Apollo's Fire - The Cleveland Baroque Orchestra. *Member:* Cleveland (Former Member, Board of Trustees, Immigration Referral Panel), Ohio State and American Bar Associations; American Immigration Lawyers Association. ***LANGUAGES:*** Spanish. ***PRACTICE AREAS:*** Labor and Employment; Employment Litigation; Immigration Law. ***Email:*** Mark.Floyd@ThompsonHine.com

ROBERT C. FOLLAND, born Columbus, Ohio, June 23, 1970; admitted to bar, 1995, Ohio. *Education:* Bowling Green State University (B.A., Economics, summa cum laude, 1992); Ohio Northern University (J.D., with high distinction, 1995). Phi Beta Kappa. Editor, Ohio Northern Law Review, 1994-1995. Author, "Lending Under Revised Article 9 After Uniform Commercial Code," May 2001; "Boom or Bust: Managing Credit Risks in the Business Cycle, What Do You Do When?" May 1999. *Member:* Ohio State Bar Association (Member Sections on: Banking; Bankruptcy; Commercial Law; recent case law update editor); The American Bankruptcy Institute. ***PRACTICE AREAS:*** Bankruptcy; Commercial Litigation; Business Litigation. ***Email:*** Rob.Folland@ThompsonHine.com

ROBERT B. FORD, born Steubenville, Ohio, November 12, 1944; admitted to bar, 1968, Ohio; 1979, U.S. Tax Court. *Education:* Yale University (B.A., cum laude, 1965); University of Michigan (J.D., 1968). Member, Peace Corp, 1968-1970. Author: "On the Threshold of Fortune", Professional Press, 1999. Adjunct Associate Professor of Law, Retired, "Wealth Transfer Taxation" and "Estate Planning", Cleveland State University Law School. Fellow, American College of Trust and Estate Counsel. Member, Legal Education Committee of ACTEC. Member: Estate Planning Council and Estate Planners Group. ***LANGUAGES:*** Spanish and French. ***PRACTICE AREAS:*** Estate Planning Law (60%); Probate Law (20%); Personal Planning (5%); Successions (5%); Nonprofit and Charitable Organizations (10%). ***Email:*** Robert.Ford@ThompsonHine.com

HEIDI B. GOLDSTEIN, born Cleveland, Ohio, March 11, 1970; admitted to bar, 1995, Ohio. *Education:* The Ohio State University (B.S., summa cum laude, Psychology, 1992); Case Western Reserve University (J.D., summa cum laude, 1995). Phi Beta Kappa. Order of the Coif. Editor, Case Western University Law Review, Spring 1997. Member, Case Western Reserve University School of Law Alumni Committee. Author: "Chance v. BPChem., Inc.: Changing Ohio's Perception of Stigma Damages, Cleveland State Law Review, Spring 1997; "Preventing a Toxic Tort Suit," Environmental Compliance Advisor, May 18, 1998; "Bush, Gore Hold Separate Environmental Agendas," Crain's Cleveland Business, October, 2000; with Heather Austin, "Complex Regs Keeping Many From Cleaning Up Brownfields," Crain's Cleveland Business, April, 2001; Co-author: with Keely O'Bryan, "Toxic Mold Grows as Cause for Complaints," Crain's Cleveland Business, October, 2001, Vol. 22, No. 41; "What Owners Need to Know About Mold Litigation," HPAC Engineering, September 2002; "The Next Asbestos? 'Toxic Mold' Lawsuits Are Growing Like a Fungus," Insurance Insight, September 2002. Presentations: "Hot Topics in CERCLA and RCRA and an Update on VAP," Cleveland Bar Association, March, 2001; "The 'Growing' Impact of Mold Litigation on the Insurance Industry," Omniclean Seminar, March, 2002; "How Super Is It?" The Comprehensive Environmental Response Compensation and Liability Act," Ohio Bar Association, May, 2002; "Terror Toxins and Trophy Projects: The New World View of Preparedness," International Conference of Shopping Centers, Ohio, Kentucky and Indiana Retail Development and Law Symposium, June 14, 2002; "Mold Over Bagels: Managing Risks Arising From Toxic Mold in Buildings," Cleveland, OH/Columbus, OH, May 7/July 25, 2002; "Managing Risks Arising From Toxic Mold in Buildings," ACCA Seminar, July 18, 2002; "Welcome to the Mold Litigation Party: B.Y.O.C.—Bring Your Own Checkbook," AIG Environmental Seminar, November 20, 2002; "Toxic Mold: Is It Really A Growing Concern for You and Your Clients?", Cleveland Bar Association Real Estate Law Institute, October 9, 2003; "Just Add Water: The Recipe for Mold Growth in Construction Litigation," Mealy's Mold 101 Conference, April 26, 2004. Board of Trustees: The Bellflower Center for Prevention of Child Abuse; Cleveland Hearing and Speech Center. Great Strides Walkathon, Executive Committee, Cystic Fibrosis Foundation. Fundraising Committee, The Cleveland Works. *Member:* Cleveland (Executive Committee Member, Environmental Law Section) and Ohio State (Member, Environmental Law Section). ***TRANSACTIONS:*** Organized and participated in Steering Committees for various industrial clients at Superfund sites across the country; Defended chemical company in federal toxic tort class action litigation; Represented waste management company in toxic tort suit regarding the land application of biosolids; Prosecuted and defended CERCLA cost recovery and contribution cases against both the government and private parties; Counseled manufacturing companies on various environmental compliance and permitting issues; Defended government enforcement actions, particularly in connection with notices of violation for asbestos removal and Clean Air Act compliance issues; Defending vinyl chloride manufacturer in toxic tort suit that includes conspiracy allegations; defending contractor in sick building syndrome allegation relating to mold; defending manufacturer of waterproofing materials against allegations product caused mold growth. ***PRACTICE AREAS:*** Environmental; Products Liability Litigation. ***Email:*** Heidi.Goldstein@ThompsonHine.com

MICHAEL L. HARDY, born St. Louis, Missouri, August 28, 1947; admitted to bar, 1972, Ohio. *Education:* John Carroll University (A.B., magna cum laude, 1969); University of Michigan (J.D., cum laude, 1972). Partner-in-Charge, Cleveland Office. Listed in: Best Lawyers in America, Environmental and Who's Who in American Law. Chapter Author: Ohio Environmental Law, Matthew Bender Environmental Law Practice Guide, 2001; Ohio Voluntary Cleanup Program, Matthew Bender Brownfields Law and Practice, 2002. Editor, Ohio Environmental Law, 1992. Board of Advisors, The Environmental Counselor, 1989—. Editor-in-Chief, Ohio Environmental Monthly, 1989-1994. Board of Trustees, Nature Center of Shaker Lakes. Chairman, Ohio Environmental Law Committee, Ohio State Bar Association, 1987-1991. Chairman, Industrywide Litigation Committee of Defense Research Institute, 1989-1991. Co-chairman, Environmental Law Committee, United States Law Firm Group; Trustee, Nature Center of Shaker Lakes. Member, Court of Nisi Prius. Fellow, Ohio State Bar Foundation, 2000. *Member:* Cleveland (Member, Environ-

(This Listing Continued)

THOMPSON HINE LLP, Cleveland—Continued

mental Law Committee), Ohio State (Chairman, Environmental Law Committee, 1987-1991) and American (Member, Natural Resource Section) Bar Associations; Defense Research Institute (Chairman, Industry wide Litigation Committee, 1989-1991; Toxic Tort and Environmental Law Committee). Fellow, Ohio State Bar Foundation. [U.S. Army, Transportation Corps; 1969-1977; honorable discharge as Captain]. (Partner-in-Charge). ***REPORTED CASES:*** Jones v. Allercare, 203 F.R.D. 290 (N.D. Ohio 2001). ***TRANSACTIONS:*** Common counsel for industrial group defendants and superfund litigation; Defense of federal and state environmental enforcement actions; Defense of national, statewide and regional products liability, toxic tort and environmental class actions in federal and state courts; Lead counsel in new source review enforcement case, remedy phase; Jury and bench trials, including product liability, cost recovery and contribution actions; Defense of indoor air pollution, sick building and mold cases; Structuring environmental allocation and indemnity provisions in merger, acquisition and disposition agreements, real estate agreements and project financing; Due diligence and strategic counseling for corporate transactions; Counseling business entities regarding permitting and compliance requirements; and Brownfield redevelopment projects. ***PRACTICE AREAS:*** Environmental Law (60%); Products Liability (20%); Life Sciences (20%). ***Email:*** Mike.Hardy@ThompsonHine.com

LAURA A. HAUSER, born Syracuse, New York, February 22, 1964; admitted to bar, 1988, Florida and U.S. District Court, Middle District of Florida; 1989, Ohio and U.S. District Court, Northern District of Ohio; 1992, U.S. District Court, Southern District of Ohio. *Education:* University of Michigan; The Ohio State University (B.A., 1985); Case Western Reserve University (J.D., 1988). Winner, Jonathan M. Ault Moot Court Tournament Award for Best Brief, 1988. Appointed to the Board of Governors of the Ohio State Bar Association section on Women In The Profession, August 1998. Member of the Greater Cleveland Chapter of the American Red Cross Board of Directors, July 2003—; Member of the Board of Directors for Preterm; Member of the Case Western Reserve School of Law Alumni Board Of Governors, November 2002—; Contributing author of the chapter relating to Ohio law, Public Construction Source Book, Logistics Management Institute for the American Bar Association, 1999, 2000. Contributing author to "State-By-State Guide To Architect, Engineer, And Contractor Licensing," Ohio Chapter, 1999- 2003; Legal columnist for the equestrian website, "Towerheads," geared towards the hunterjumper equestrian. Legal Columnist for the national magazine, "Commercial Builder/Architect." Federal Publications, Inc., Columbus Builders' Exchange, Institute of Business Law; Program speaker on employment discrimination and sexual harassment in the workplace. Program speaker for the Ohio Continuing Legal Education Institute regarding advocacy, deposition skills, negotiation tactics, business development and networking. *Member:* Cuyahoga County and Ohio State Bar Associations; The Florida Bar; Ohio Women's Bar Association (President, 1996-1997). ***REPORTED CASES:*** Counsels individuals, small and large businesses, financial institutions and non-profit entities in transactions and litigation in their business, employment and related matters; Represents owners, contractors and engineers on issues and claims related to public and private construction projects; Represents various clients in disputes with local and state governmental authorities related to public contracting and procurement; Represented major financial institution regarding claims brought under the Americans with Disabilities Act, claims against institutional trustee, and claims arising out of lease dispute. ***PRACTICE AREAS:*** Construction Law; Business Litigation; Public Construction Contracts; Construction Contracts; Public Contract Law. ***Email:*** Laura.Hauser@ThompsonHine.com

DANIEL M. HAYMOND, born Cleveland, Ohio, September 30, 1962; admitted to bar, 1993, Ohio; U.S. District Court, Northern District of Ohio; U.S. Court of Appeals, Third and Sixth Circuits. *Education:* The Ohio State University (B.S., 1985; J.D., summa cum laude, 1993). *Member:* Cleveland, Ohio State and American (Forum on Construction Industry) Bar Associations. ***PRACTICE AREAS:*** Construction Litigation; Commercial and Business Litigation; Professional Malpractice; Litigation. ***Email:*** Dan.Haymond@ThompsonHine.com

HAROLD W. HENDERSON, born Greenville, Texas, August 18, 1948; admitted to bar, 1976, Ohio and U.S. Court of Military Appeals; 1985, U.S. Court of Appeals, Sixth Circuit; 1986, U.S. Supreme Court; 1994, U.S. Court of Appeals, Third Circuit; U.S. District Court, Northern District of Ohio and U.S. District Court, Eastern and Western Districts of Michigan. *Education:* United States Coast Guard Academy (B.S., with high honors, 1970); Cleveland State University (J.D., summa cum laude, 1975). Author: "1993 Amendments to Federal Rules of Civil Procedures," Maritime Law Association, October, 1993. Member, Propeller Club, Port of Cleveland. Adjunct Lecturer in Law (Admiralty), Cleveland State University Law School, 2001—. *Member:* Lake Carriers Association (General Counsel, 1992—). [Lieutenant Commander, U.S. Coast Guard, 1970-1982]. ***REPORTED CASES:*** Szymanski v. Columbia Transportation Co., 154 F.3d 591 (6th Cir., 1998) (en banc); Miller v. American President Lines, Ltd., 989 F. 2d 1450 (6th Cir., 1993), cert. denied 510 U.S. 915 (1993); Oglebay Norton Co. v. CSX Corp., 788 F. 2d 361 (6th Cir., 1986), cert. denied 479 U.S. 849 (1986); Kasper v. Oglebay Norton Co., 1998 A.M.C. 1158 (N.D. Ohio 1998). ***PRACTICE AREAS:*** Admiralty Law and Maritime Law; Litigation; Products Liability. ***Email:*** Hal.Henderson@ThompsonHine.com

OLIVER C. HENKEL, JR., born White Plains, New York, November 7, 1936; admitted to bar, 1964, Ohio. *Education:* Yale University (B.A., 1958; LL.B., 1964). Life Member, The Judicial Conference of the Eighth Judicial District. Director, Parkland Management Company. Trustee and Executive Committee and Founding Chairman, Playhouse Square Foundation. Trustee, Town Hall of Cleveland. Trustee and Executive Committee, Downtown Cleveland Partnership. Trustee, Woodruff Foundation. Member, Corporate Council and Planned Giving Council, The Cleveland Museum of Art. Chairman, May 1990 Special Election, Gateway to the Future Campaign Committee. President and Trustee, Cleveland Bar Foundation. Trustee, The Althans Foundation. Member: Promoting Philanthropy Committee, The Cleveland Foundation; Planned Giving Advisory Council, Musical Arts Association. *Member:* Cleveland (Former Treasurer, 1991-1993 and former Trustee, 1977-1979) and American Bar Associations. Fellow, American College of Trust and Estate Counsel. [Lieutenant Junior Grade, U.S. Navy, 1958-1961]. ***PRACTICE AREAS:*** Personal Planning (65%); Fiduciary Law (15%); Estate, Gift and Generation Skipping Transfer Taxation (10%); Private Business Law (5%); Succession (5%). ***Email:*** Oliver.Henkel@ThompsonHine.com

(This Listing Continued)

DAVID J. HOOKER, born Tiffin, Ohio, September 6, 1950; admitted to bar, 1975, Ohio; U.S. Court of Federal Claims; U.S. Court of Appeal, Second, Third, Fifth and Sixth Circuits; U.S. District Court, Northern District of Ohio. *Education:* Denison University (B.A., with highest honors, 1972); Stanford University (J.D., 1975). Member, Stanford Law Review. Fellow: American College of Trial Lawyers; Ohio State Bar Foundation. Master Bencher, Judge Anthony J. Celebrezze Inn of Court. Life Member, Judicial Conference of the Eighth Judicial District (Ohio). Trustee, 1992-1998; 1999—, President, Society of Alumni, 1985-1986, Denison University. Chair of Northeast Ohio Region, Board of Trustees, 1998-2000, Trustee, 1993—, Development Committee, Chair, 1996-1998, National Conference For Community and Justice. Director, 1999—, Greater Cleveland Growth Association. Trustee, 1998-2004, MetroHealth Foundation. Chair, Cleveland Initiative for Education, 2001—. Member and Co-chair, Finance and Audit Subcommittee, Cleveland Metropolitan School Board Bond Oversight Commission 1999-2004. Member Visiting Committee, Society of Benchers, Case Western Reserve University School of Law. Leadership Cleveland, Class of 1995. Author, "People Business," Inside the Minds: Firm Leadership, Aspatore Books, 2003. Co-Author, Architect-Engineer Liability Under Ohio Law, Cambridge Institute, 1988, 1989. *Member:* Cleveland (Chair, Juvenile Committee, 1995-1997; Trustee, 1989-1992), Ohio State (Member, Litigation Section) and American (Member, Litigation and Business Section; UCC Committee; Task Force on Suretyship; Forum on Construction Industry) Bar Associations; National Institute for Trial Advocacy (Faculty Member, Trial Skills, Advanced Deposition Skills and Deposition Skills Workshops). (Managing Partner). ***PRACTICE AREAS:*** Business Litigation; Commercial Litigation; Complex Litigation; Accounting Malpractice Law; Architectural Malpractice Law; UCC (Uniform Commercial Code Litigation); Litigation Group. ***Email:*** David.Hooker@ThompsonHine.com

LESLIE W. JACOBS, born Akron, Ohio, December 5, 1944; admitted to bar, 1968, Ohio; 1969, U.S. Court of Appeals, Sixth Circuit and U.S. District Court, Northern District of Ohio; 1970, U.S. Court of Appeals, District of Columbia Circuit, U.S. Tax Court, U.S. Court of Military Appeals and U.S. Court of Claims; 1971, U.S. Supreme Court; 1975, U.S. Court of Appeals, Third Circuit; 1980, District of Columbia, U.S. Court of Appeals, Second Circuit, U.S. District Court, District of Columbia and U.S. Court of International Trade; 1982, U.S. Court of Appeals, Fourth, Eleventh and Federal Circuits; 1983, U.S. District Court, Northern District of California; 1989, U.S. District Court, Eastern District of Michigan; 1994, U.S. Court of Appeals, Fifth Circuit; 1995, U.S. District Court, District of Arizona, U.S. Court of Appeals, First Circuit and French Order, Bar of Brussels (Belgium, Associated Member); 1999, U.S. Court of Appeals, Tenth Circuit; 2004, U.S. District Court, Southern District of Ohio. *Education:* Denison University; Northwestern University (B.S., summa cum laude, 1965); Harvard Law School (J.D., 1968). Recipient, Ohio Bar Medal, 1990; Ritter Award for Outstanding Contributions to the Administration of Justice, 1997. Listed in: International Who's Who of Competition Lawyers (all editions); Guide to the World's Leading Competition and Antitrust Lawyers (all editions); Guide to the World's Leading Competition and Antitrust Advisors (since 2000); Who's Who in America (since 1986); Who's Who in American Law (since 1977); Who's Who in Emerging Leaders in America (since 1987); Who's Who in the Midwest (since 1985); Ohio Superlawyers; Best Lawyers in America. Visiting Committee, Case Western Reserve University School of Law (1985-1991). Law Clerk to Chief Justice Kingsley A. Taft, Supreme Court of Ohio (1968-1969). Author: "Doing Business in and with the United States" (1st ed. 1999, 2d ed. 2000); "Effective Use of Expert Testimony in Defending Criminal Antitrust Cases," 13 Antitrust 48 (Spring, 1999); "International Distribution and Franchising," Corporate Counsel's Guide to Laws of International Trade (1997); "Dealing with Government Authorities During an Antitrust Investigation," White Collar Crime (1996); "Legal Remedies for Dirty Tricks: A Competitor's Response to Disparagement," ABA Section of Antitrust Law (1995); "Making Global Deals: The Art of International Business Negotiation," 5 Int'l Quarterly 1 (1993). Member, Boards of Editors: Corporate Counsel's International Advisor; Guide to the International Sale of Goods Convention. ABA Task Forces on Corporate Responsibility (2002-2003) and Sarbanes-Oxley (2002-2004). Chairman, Nominating Committee, Civil Justice Reform Act Advisory Group to the U.S. District Court, Northern District Ohio. Mediator, U.S. District Court, Northern District of Ohio. Co-Chairman, Ohio Lawyers for Bush-Cheney. Member, Ohio General Assembly Joint Commission on Judicial Compensation. Member, Court of Nisi Prius. Life Member, Judicial Conference of the Eighth Judicial District and Sixth Circuit Judicial Conference. Former Chairman, Citizens Advisory Board to the Cuyahoga County Juvenile Court. Member, Leadership Cleveland (1989). Chairman, EconomicsAmerica (1990-1994). Director, The Holden Arboretum (since 2003). Ohio Board of Bar Examiners (1990-1995). Nominating Council, Ohio Public Utilities Commission (1986-1987). *Member:* Cleveland (Former Trustee), Ohio State (Past President), American (Board of Governors) and International Bar Associations; American Law Institute; Greater Cleveland International Lawyers Group; National Conference of Bar Presidents. Life Fellow: Ohio State Bar Foundation (Former Trustee) and American Bar Foundation. [Lt. Commander, U.S. Naval Reserve (Intelligence)]. (Also at Brussels, Belgium). ***PRACTICE AREAS:*** Competition; Antitrust; International; Trade Regulation; Business Torts; Intellectual Property; Government Regulation; Complex Litigation; White Collar Criminal Defense. ***Email:*** Les.Jacobs@ThompsonHine.com

WILLIAM W. JACOBS, born Lansing, Michigan, December 19, 1951; admitted to bar, 1976, Ohio; U.S. District Court, Northern District of Ohio; 1992, U.S. Court of Appeals, 6th Circuit; U.S. Court of Appeals, 8th and 5th Circuits; U.S. Supreme Court. *Education:* Michigan State University (B.A., with honors, 1973); Case Western Reserve University (J.D., 1976). Law Clerk to Judge Corrigan, Eighth Ohio Appellate District 1976-1978. Staff Attorney, 1978-1981; Assistant Director, 1981-1984; Director, Cleveland Regional Office, Federal Trade Commission, 1984-1987. *Member:* Cleveland (Member, Litigation Section; Chair, Continuing Education Committee), Ohio State (Member, Litigation Section), Federal (Member, Antitrust and Trade Regulation Section; Board Member and Past President, Northeast Ohio Chapter) and American (Member, Sections on: Antitrust; Litigation) Bar Associations. ***PRACTICE AREAS:*** Complex Business Litigation (50%); Civil Trial (25%); Eminent Domain (15%); Antitrust Law (5%); Trade Regulation Law (5%). ***Email:*** Bill.Jacobs@ThompsonHine.com

WILLIAM E. KARNATZ, SR., born Cleveland, Ohio, October 4, 1937; admitted to bar, 1962, Ohio. *Education:* John Carroll University (B.B.A., 1959); Case Western Reserve School of Law (J.D., 1962). Alpha Sigma Nu (Jesuit Honorary). Executive Vice-President, Trust Division, Society National Bank, 1965-1994. Special Gift Division, United Way Ser-

(This Listing Continued)

vices, 1997. Chairman, Investment Committee, 1997—, University Hospital Healthcare System. Executive Committee and Trustee, 1993—, University Hospitals of Cleveland. Advisory Board, Member, Ursuline Sisters of Cleveland, 1999—. Chairman, Development Advisor Council, 1995—. Member, 1983-1992, Chairman of the Board, 1989-1992, Marymount Hospital. Member, 1977-1983, Chairman of the Board, 1981-1983, St. Augustine Manor. Trustee, 1977-1999, Finance Committee, Chairman, 1977-1999, Magnificat High School. *Member:* Cleveland (Member, Estate Planning and Probate Section) and Ohio State (Member, Estate Planning and Probate Section); Estate Planning Council of Cleveland. [U.S. Army Transportation Corps., 1963-1965, Hon. Disch., Capt.]. ***PRACTICE AREAS:*** Estate Planning; Probate and Trust Administration; Personal Planning; Successions. ***Email:*** Bill.Karnatz@ThompsonHine.com

STEVEN S. KAUFMAN, born Oceanside, New York, April 13, 1950; admitted to bar, 1975, Ohio; 1977, U.S. District Court, Northern District of Ohio and Western District of Michigan, U.S. Court of Appeals, 6th Circuit; 1978, U.S. Court of Federal Claims; 1993, U.S. District Court, Northern District of Texas; 1995, U.S. Supreme Court; 2003, U.S. Court of Appeals, 5th Circuit. *Education:* Colgate University (A.B., 1972); Case Western Reserve University (J.D., 1975). Member, The Order of Barristers. Finalist, National Moot Court Competition, 1973. Chairman, Moot Court Board, 1974-1975. Law Clerk, Hon. Jack G. Day, Ohio Court of Appeals, Eighth Appellate District, 1975-1977. President, Shaker Heights Citry School District Board of Education, 2004-2005. Special Counsel to Attorney General of Ohio, 1991-1997. Member, Judicial Review Commission for the Northern District of Ohio, 1995-1998. Member, Leadership Cleveland Class of 1999. *Member:* Cleveland Bar Association (President, 2003-2004; Board of Trustees, 1998-2004); Ohio State Bar Association; Master Bencher, Celebrezze Inn of Court; Life Member, Conference of the Eighth Judicial District, Ohio. ***REPORTED CASES:*** Arpadi v. First MSP Corporation, 68 Ohio St.3d 453, 628 N.E.2nd 1335 (1994); In re Election of November 6, 1990 for the Office of Attorney General of Ohio, 62 Ohio St.3d 1, 577 N.E.2d 343 (1991); Cleveland Bar Association v. Herzog, 87 Ohio St. 3d 215 (1999); Cleveland Bar Association v. Rossi, 81 Ohio St. 3d 195, 690 N.E.2d 501; 1998 Ohio LEXIS 558; Glaxo Wellcome, Inc., et al., v. Ben Venue Laboratories, Inc., 1998 U.S. Dist. LEXIS 19774; Interim Healthcare of Northeast Ohio, Inc., et al., v. Interim Services, Inc., et al.; 12 F. Supp. 2d 703; 1998 U.S. Dist. LEXIS 11546. ***PRACTICE AREAS:*** Complex Business Litigation; Class Action Litigation; Eminent Domain Litigation; Securities Litigation; Fiduciary Duty; Professional Liability Litigation. ***Email:*** Steve.Kaufman@ThompsonHine.com

DENA M. KOBASIC, born Lorain, Ohio, October 1, 1963; admitted to bar, 1989, Ohio. *Education:* Notre Dame College of Ohio (B.A., 1986); University of Notre Dame (J.D., 1989). *Member:* Cuyahoga County, Cleveland and Ohio State Bar Associations; Defense Research Institute; Federation of Defense and Corporate Counsel. ***PRACTICE AREAS:*** Business Litigation; Products Liability. ***Email:*** Dena.Kobasic@ThompsonHine.com

JAMES C. KOENIG, born Cleveland, Ohio, December 23, 1958; admitted to bar, 1987, Ohio. *Education:* John Carroll University (B.S., B.A., summa cum laude, 1981); Case Western Reserve University (M.B.A., summa cum laude, 1983; J.D., summa cum laude, 1987). Order of the Coif. Certified Public Accountant, Ohio. Awards/Honors: Included in the 2003- 2004 edition of The Best Lawyers in America. Co-Author: "Practical and Policy Considerations in Corporate Inversion Transactions," Corporate Business Taxation Monthly, September 2002. Co-Author: "Contingent Consideration: The Taxation of Earnouts and Escrows," Mergers and Acquisitions, July 2001. Author: "An Analysis of the Section 367(a)(3)(c) Temporary Regulations," International Tax & Business Lawyer, Summer 1987. Lecturer: Tax Shelter Disclosure Treasury Regulations, Cleveland Tax Institute, 2003; Legislation of Ethics, Cleveland State University Business School Alumni, 2003; Corporate Inversions, Cleveland Tax Institute, 2002; Sarbanes-Oxley Act, Cleveland Tax Executives Institute, 2002; Sarbanes-Oxley Act, Cleveland Tax Executives Institute, 2002; Sarbanes-Oxley Act, Cincinnati Tax Executives Institute, 2002; Planning Update: Limited Liability Companies, Cleveland Tax Club, 2002, Section 367; Outbound and Inbound Transactions, Cleveland Tax Institute, 2001; Tax Planning with Foreign LLCs, Cleveland Tax Institute, 2000; Tax Planning with Multi-member LLCs, Cleveland Tax Club, November 1999; Value Added Taxes, Cleveland Tax Institute, 1996. Member, Cleveland Tax Club. President (2002-2005), Vice President (2001-2002), Treasurer (1998-2001), and Trustee, (1998—), Family Transitional Housing Inc. Director, St. Michael Credit Union, 1995-1998. *Member:* Cleveland and American (Member, Taxation Section) Bar Associations. ***PRACTICE AREAS:*** Taxation; Nonprofit; Corporate. ***Email:*** Jim.Koenig@ThompsonHine.com

BRIAN J. LAMB, born Cleveland, Ohio, October 18, 1965; admitted to bar, 1991, Ohio, U.S. District Court, Northern District of Ohio and U.S. District Court, Eastern District of Michigan, U.S. Court of Appeals, Third and Sixth Circuits, U.S. Supreme Court. *Education:* College of Wooster (B.A., with honors, 1988); Phi Beta Kappa; Columbia University School of Law (J.D., 1991). Publications: Author: "Recent Changes to Declaratory Judgment Act Should Not Affect the Award of Attorney's Fees in Fiduciary Litigation;" Ohio Probate Law Journal; Sept./Oct. 2000; "Absence of Appellate Options Main Drawback to Arbitration;" Crain's Cleveland Business; Aug. 13-19, 2001. Presentations: Network of Business Professionals; "Litigation Update, Including Fiduciary Considerations;" 2001; Cleveland Bar Association, Business Litigation Seminar; "Complexities in Fiduciary Litigation;" 1999. Cleveland Bridge Builders (Leadership Organization), Member, Charter Class of 2000-2001. *Member:* Cleveland and Ohio State Bar Associations; Anthony J. Celebrezze Inn of Court (Barrister). ***TRANSACTIONS:*** Obtaining dismissal of securities fraud and Williams Act (tender offer) claims in the Southern District of New York; Representing a major financial institution in an ERISA class action involving a public company spin-off and consolidation of employee benefit plans; Representing a major telecommunications company in a substantial tax controversy with the IRS; Representing a Big Four accounting firm in defense of audit malpractice claims involving investments in derivative securities; Representing bank trustees, individual trustees, and beneficiaries in all manner of fiduciary disputes. ***PRACTICE AREAS:*** Business Litigation. ***Email:*** Brian.Lamb@ThompsonHine.com

ALAN R. LEPENE, born Cleveland, Ohio, October 16, 1946; admitted to bar, 1971, Ohio. *Education:* Ohio University (A.B., summa cum laude, 1968); University of Michigan (J.D., magna cum laude, 1971). Phi Beta Kappa. Order of the Coif. Listed in: *The Best Lawyers in America* (Bankruptcy); *Euromoney Guide to the Leading U.S. Insolvency Lawyers.*

(This Listing Continued)

Fellow Ohio State Bar Foundation. Author: "Assessing the Fraudulent Conveyance Risk," Insights; 1999; "Bankruptcy Acquisitions - A Secured Party's Perspective," Ohio CLE Institute Publications, 1998; "Diluted Bankruptcy Reform Act Doesn't Pack Much Wallop," Corporate Legal Times, 1995. *Member:* Cleveland, Ohio State and American Bar Associations; American Bankruptcy Institute; Turnaround Management Association. Fellow, Ohio State Bar Foundation. ***PRACTICE AREAS:*** Bankruptcy Chapter 11; Bankruptcy Law; Business Reorganization; Commercial Law; Creditor Bankruptcy; Creditors Rights Law. ***Email:*** Alan.Lepene@ThompsonHine.com

CRAIG R. MARTAHUS, born Pittsburgh, Pennsylvania, November 21, 1954; admitted to bar, 1979, Ohio. *Education:* Indiana University of Pennsylvania (B.S., magna cum laude, 1976); University of Pennsylvania (J.D., 1979). Listed in: *The Best Lawyers in America* (Banking Law). Author: "Recap ventures now reaching smaller firms," Crain's Cleveland Business, November 10, 1997. Adjunct Professor of Law, Secured Transactions and Remedies, Cleveland State University, 1989—. Chairman, Board of Trustees, George W. Codrington Foundation. *Member:* Cleveland, Ohio State and American Bar Associations. ***PRACTICE AREAS:*** Corporate Law; Securities; Commercial Law; Bankruptcy Law. ***Email:*** Craig.Martahus@ThompsonHine.com

THOMAS A. MASON, born Cleveland, Ohio, May 4, 1936; admitted to bar, 1962, Ohio. *Education:* Kenyon College (A.B., 1958); Case Western Reserve University (LL.B., 1961). Listed in: *Who's Who in America* and *The Best Lawyers in America*. Member: American College of Real Estate Lawyers; Mortgage Bankers Association of Metropolitan Cleveland. United States Law Firm Group, Inc., Real Estate Committee. Lenders Counsel Group, American Land Title Association. Advisory Board, Chicago Title Insurance Company. *Member:* Cleveland (Past Chairman, Real Property Section) and Ohio State (Member, Real Property Section) Bar Associations. ***PRACTICE AREAS:*** Real Estate. ***Email:*** Tom.Mason@ThompsonHine.com

LOUIS L. McMAHON, born Mansfield, Ohio, July 17, 1963; admitted to bar, 1996, Ohio. *Education:* John Carroll University (B.A., magna cum laude, 1985); Kent State University (M.A., 1990); Cleveland Marshall College of Law (J.D., summa cum laude, 1996). Author: "Not Yet Home on the Range: Ohio Voluntary Action Program Experiences Life as Pioneer," Cleveland Bar Journal, September, 1999; "Regulatory Update: New Nationwide Wetlands Permits," Cleveland Bar Journal, July/August 2000. Lecturer: "TMDLs: Today and Tomorrow," Ohio State Bar Association Environmental Law Committee 15th Annual Ohio Environmental Law Seminar, May, 2000; "Introduction to Clean Water Act," Cleveland Bar Association Environmental Law Symposium, March, 2000; "Environmental Issues in Real Estate Transactions," Ohio CLE Institute, July, 2000; "Introduction to Clean Water Act and Ohio Wetlands Regulations," Cleveland Bar Association Environmental Law Symposium, February, 1999. *Member:* Cleveland and Ohio State Bar Associations. ***PRACTICE AREAS:*** Environmental. ***Email:*** Louis.Mcmahon@ThompsonHine.com

DONALD H. MESSINGER, born Lyons, New York, July 1, 1943; admitted to bar, 1968, Ohio. *Education:* Colgate University (A.B., 1965); Duke University (J.D., 1968). Listed in: *Who's Who in America* and *The Best Lawyers in America*. Director and Secretary, Business Volunteers Unlimited. Director and Past President, Cleveland Hearing and Speech Center. Trustee and Past President, The Free Medical Clinic of Greater Cleveland. Trustee and Former Officer, Senior Citizen Resources. Member, Leadership Cleveland. *Member:* Cleveland (Trustee, 1975-1979; Chair, Securities Law Institute (1983) Ohio State and American Bar Associations. ***TRANSACTIONS:*** Counsels senior management and owners of several of the firm's major clients; manages large, complex acquisition, disposition, and financing transactions involving multiple operations in the United States and worldwide; represents issuers and underwriters in the public offering of securities; recent transactions have ranged in size from under $10 million to over $i.3 billion; representations include transactions for major publicly-owned and privately-held businesses, as well as newly emerging businesses, headquartered in North America and Europe; serves or has served as a director and officer of public and private corporations. ***PRACTICE AREAS:*** General Corporate; Mergers and Acquisitions; Securities. ***Email:*** Don.Messinger@ThompsonHine.com

LESLEE W. MIRALDI, admitted to bar, 1978, Ohio. *Education:* Ohio University (B.A., summa cum laude, 1973; M.A., summa cum laude, 1975); The Ohio State University (J.D., 1978). Phi Beta Kappa; Alpha Kappa Delta. Recipient: Press Person of the Year, The Press, 1997; CitiSUN of the Year, The SUN Newspapers, 1998. President, Board of Trustees, Avon School Educational Endowment Fund. Member, Board of Trustees, Avon United Methodist Church. Trustee, Erie Shores Girl Scout Council, 1994-1996. Chairperson, Avon Charter Review Committee; Chairperson, Avon Local Schools, Bond Issue Committee, 1995; Chairperson, Land Acquisition Levy Committee, 1994. Ranked as one of America's Leading Banking and Finance lawyers by Chambers USA, a multi-national research organization that publishes law firm rankings based on peer review and market recommendations. *Member:* Lorain County, Cleveland and Ohio State Bar Associations. ***PRACTICE AREAS:*** Commercial Finance; Public Finance. ***Email:*** Leslee.Miraldi@ThompsonHine.com

ROBERT D. MONNIN, born Cleveland, Ohio, October 2, 1941; admitted to bar, 1968, Ohio. *Education:* Miami University (A.B., 1963); Cleveland Marshall College of Law (J.D., cum laude, 1968). Member: Product Liability Advisory Council, Inc. Chairman of the Board, National Foundation for Judicial Excellence. *Member:* Cleveland, Ohio State and American Bar Associations; Defense Research Institute (President, 1991-1992); Internationa Association of Defense Counsel; Federation of Defense and Corporate Counsel; Association of Defense Trial Attorneys; Cleveland Association of Civil Trial Attorneys; American Bar Foundation. (Group Leader, Product Liability Litigation). ***PRACTICE AREAS:*** Business Litigation; Products Liability Litigation; Mediation Services. ***Email:*** Robert.Monnin@ThompsonHine.com

DAVID J. NAFTZINGER, born Harrisburg, Pennsylvania, October 26, 1948; admitted to bar, 1973, Ohio. *Education:* University of Pennsylvania (B.S., cum laude, 1970); Duke University (J.D., 1973). Board of Editors, Duke Law Journal. Lecturer: "The Revised Ins and Outs of Article 9 of The Uniform Commercial Code in Ohio," Independence, Ohio, May 2001; "Lending Under Revised Article 9 of The Uniform Commercial Code," Program Director and Presenter; Ohio Bankers Association/Ohio League of Financial Institutions, Akron, Columbus and Findlay, June 2001; "Educational Forum on Letter of Credit Assignments and Transfers," KeyBank National Association and Thompson Hine LLP, 1996; Member, Panel on Financial Institutions, The 2000 Securities Law Institute, Cleve-

(This Listing Continued)

THOMPSON HINE LLP, Cleveland—Continued

land Bar Association; Member, Panel on Electronic Commerce Law, 1999 William J. O'Neill Bankruptcy Institute, Cleveland Bar Association. *Member:* Ohio State and American Bar Associations. ***PRACTICE AREAS:*** Banking Law; Bankruptcy Law; Commercial Law; Public Finance. ***Email:*** David.Naftzinger@ThompsonHine.com

DAVID E. NASH, born Sandusky, Ohio, November 24, 1955; admitted to bar, 1981, Ohio; 1985, U.S. Supreme Court; 1990, U.S. Court of Appeals, Sixth Circuit. *Education:* Wake Forest University (B.A., magna cum laude, 1978); Duke University (J.D., with honors, 1981). Phi Beta Kappa. Fellow, Ohio State Bar Foundation, Class of 2001. Listed in: *The Best Lawyers in America.* Co-Author: *A Guide to EPA's Permit Application Requirements for Stormwater Discharges,* The Practical Real Estate Lawyer 13 (1991); "Superfund Site Apportionment of Liability," Natural Resources and Environment, Vol. 12, American Bar Association, Summer 1997; Ohio Environmental Law, 1992-1993. Author: "Negotiating for Protection Against Environmental Risks in Business Transactions," Cleveland Bar Journal, Vol. 68, July/August, 1997. Chapter Author: "Ohio's Voluntary Real Estate Reuse and Cleanup Program: Amended Substitute Senate Bill 221," Wiley Environmental Law Update, 1996. Lecturer: Society of Mining Engineers Annual Meeting @ Environmental Compliance Programs, Denver, Colorado, 2000; Legal Co-chair, Ohio EPA Inland Spills Conference, 1999; Ohio State Bar Associations Environmental Law Seminar, 1991, 1992, 1995, 1996, 1997, 1998, 2000-2003; "Disaster Planning and Crisis Management," The Network of Trial Law Firms, Inc., 1996; "Environmental Regulation in Ohio," The Institute of Business Law, 1993-1994; The Chemical Manufacturers Association Toxic Tort Symposium, 1993; Cleveland Bar Association Environmental Law Institutes, 1991-1996, Chair, 1997. *Member:* Cleveland (Chair, Environmental Law Section, 1997-1998) and Ohio State (Chair, Environmental Law Committee, 1999-2001) Bar Associations. ***TRANSACTIONS:*** Represents a variety of manufacturing and industrial companies in selling and acquiring businesses or plant sites; assists clients in developing and maintaining EHS Compliance programs and management systems; including corporate sustainable development programs; represents lending institutions in facility purchases and sales, commercial and real estate loans, and work outs; assists clients with regulatory counseling in solid and hazardous waste matters, and in air, water and wetland compliance issues. ***PRACTICE AREAS:*** Environmental Law; Government and Regulatory Affairs; Mediation Services; Toxic Tort Defense. ***Email:*** Dave.Nash@ThompsonHine.com

DEBORAH ZIDER READ, born Greensburg, Pennsylvania, July 22, 1957; admitted to bar, 1982, Pennsylvania; 1983, Massachusetts; 1985, District of Columbia; 1987, Ohio; 1988, U.S. Tax Court; 1989, U.S. Claims Court and U.S. Supreme Court. *Education:* Ohio University (A.B., summa cum, 1979); Boston University (J.D., 1982). Recipient: 2001 Community Honoree-Women Who Give Back; 1998 Greater Cleveland United Way Volunteer of the Year. Lecturer: "Research and Technology Transfer," American Health Lawyers Association; "Use of Compliance Plans by Healthcare Providers," Cleveland Society of Anesthesiologists; "Healthcare Law Update," Healthcare Financial Management Association of Ohio; "Limited Liability Companies and Potential Uses by Health Care Providers," National Health Lawyers Association; "Taxable Subsidiaries and Limited Liability Companies," National Health Lawyers Association; Chairperson, Exempt Organizations Session, 1996 Cleveland Tax Institute. Speaker on numerous topics for the Cleveland Tax Institute. Board of Trustees: Benjamin Rose Institute, Martha Holden Jennings Foundation, and United Way Services. Member: Nominating Committee and Executive Committee, United Way Services. Member, Community Vision Council. Co-Chair, Health and Caring for All Vision Council. *Member:* District of Columbia Bar; American Bar Association (Member, Health Law Section); American Health Lawyers Association. ***TRANSACTIONS:*** Tax and corporate planning for nonprofit and health care organizations; formation of nonprofit entities; qualification of nonprofit entities for tax exempt status; conversions to and from exempt status; corporate restructurings of nonprofit entities, physician groups, hospitals, and other health care providers; Internal Revenue Service ruling requests; tax reviews; legal structures for affiliations, ventures, and other business arrangements; mergers and other combinations; compliance with Medicare/Medicaid anti-kickback and physician self referral rules; HIPAA privacy compliance. ***PRACTICE AREAS:*** Nonprofit and Charitable Organizations; Health Care; Medicare and Medicaid; Taxation. ***Email:*** Deborah.Read@ThompsonHine.com

JAMES D. ROBENALT, born Lima, Ohio, July 11, 1956; admitted to bar, 1981, Ohio. *Education:* Miami University (A.B., 1978); Ohio State University (J.D., 1981). Phi Beta Kappa. Order of the Coif. Appointment to Merit Selection Committee by United States District Court, Northern District of Ohio, for selection of United States Magistrate Judge. Instructor, National Institute of Trial Advocacy, Deposition Skills. *Member:* Cleveland Bar Association (Vice Chair, Judicial Selection Committee); American Arbitration Association (Arbitrator). ***PRACTICE AREAS:*** Business Litigation; Professional Malpractice; Construction Law; Competition; Intellectual Property Law. ***Email:*** Jim.Robenalt@ThompsonHine.com

DAVID W. SALISBURY, born Cleveland, Ohio, September 18, 1956; admitted to bar, 1984, Ohio. *Education:* Duke University (B.A., cum laude, 1978); Vanderbilt University (J.D., 1984). Listed in: *Who's Who in American Law,* Eleventh Edition; *Who's Who in Executive and Businesses, Millenium Edition. Author:* "Perpetual Problems: Perpetuities Revisited," Ohio Lawyer's Weekly, November 30, 1998; "Smart Leasing in Smart Buildings," Crain's Cleveland Business, June 11-18, 2000; "Site Choice Hinges on Incentives," The National Law Journal, January 20, 1997; "Ruling Restricts Tax Challenge," Crain's Cleveland Business, February 9-15, 1998; "Job Creation Goal of State," Crain's Cleveland Business, February 10-14, 1997; "New LLC Rules Offer Flexibility on Land Deals," Crain's Cleveland Business, December 8-10, 1997. Lecturer: "Cleveland State Alumni Roundtable on Real Estate Issues," Cleveland State, November, 2000; "Fiduciary Liability Update," National Trust Real Estate Conference, May 1999; "Corporate Real Estate and Opinions," OSBA Institute, March 2000; "Fundamentals of a Corporate Closing," Ohio CLE Institute (Cleveland and Columbus), March 1999; "Real Estate Closing Issues," Ohio CLE Institute (Cleveland and Columbus), March 1999; "Real Estate Aspects of Corporate Transactions," Ohio CLE Institute, July 1999; "Title Law," National Business Institute, January 2000; "Leadership Lake County Government Symposium," Panelist, December, 2000; "Paperless Transactions," International Council on Shopping Centers (Midwest), April 2000; "Real Property Practice and Procedure," Cleveland Bar Association, April 1999; "Economics of Commercial Leasing," Ohio CLE Institute (Cleveland and Columbus), April 1998. Member: International Association of Attorneys and Executives in Corporate Real Estate; Greater Cleveland Mortgage Bankers Association, Outside Counsel. Course Advisor, COSE Strategic Planning, 2000. Board Member and Chairman, 1994-1999, Cystic Fibrosis Foundation. Trustee, Clean-Land, Ohio, 1994-1996. Trustee, Detroit Avenue Neighborhood Development Corporation, 1995-1997. Trustee, Cleveland Independence Day Foundation, 1990-1997. *Member:* Cleveland (Member, Real Estate Section) and Ohio State Bar Associations; Mortgage Bankers Association. ***PRACTICE AREAS:*** Real Estate Law; Corporate Law. ***Email:*** Dave.Salisbury@ThompsonHine.com

JENNIFER A. SAVAGE, born Lawrence, Kansas, January 30, 1965; admitted to bar, 1990, Ohio. *Education:* Rice University (B.A., cum laude, 1987); Case Western Reserve University (J.D., cum laude, 1990). ***PRACTICE AREAS:*** Personal and Succession Planning. ***Email:*** Jennifer.Savage@ThompsonHine.com

WILLIAM R. STEWART, born Washington, D.C., March 26, 1943; admitted to bar, 1968, Ohio; 1969, U.S. Court of Appeals, Sixth Circuit; 1978, U.S. Claims Court; 1979, U.S. Tax Court. *Education:* Yale University (B.A., 1965); Duke University (J.D., 1968). Member: Yale Alumni Scholarship Fund of Cleveland, Inc., Trustee; Yale Club of Cleveland, Trustee; Phillips Academy Andover, Alumni Representative; ideastream WVIZ/PBS WCPN 90.3, Trustee and Secretary. Lecturer: "Franchise Tax," Ohio Corporate Tax Workshop, The Ohio Society of Certified Public Accountants, July 25, 1988; "Ohio Corporation Franchise Tax," Ohio Corporate Tax Workshop, The Ohio Society of Certified Public Accountants, September 6, 1991; "Ohio Corporation Franchise Tax: Overview and Recent Developments," Ohio Corporate Tax Workshop, The Ohio Society of Certified Public Accountants, October 5, 1992; "Ohio Tax Procedures," State and Local Tax Institute, February 23, 1982; "Franchise Tax-Allocation and Apportionment Developments," State and Local Tax Institute, February 16, 1990; Ohio Corporation Franchise Tax: Overview and Recent Developments," State and Local Tax Institute, August 24, 1994; "Manufacturer Tax Credits and Other Tax Incentives," State and Local Tax Institute, February 8, 1996; "Current Ohio Franchise Tax Issues," State and Local Tax Institute, February 6, 1998; "Current Ohio Franchise Tax Issues," State and Local Tax Institute, February 10, 2000; "Current Ohio Franchise Tax Developments," State and Local Tax Institute, May 14, 2002; "Getting Down to the Basics: Fundamental Tax Issues for Rural Electric and Telephone Cooperatives," 1992 Cooperative National Tax conference, November 30-December 1, 1992; "Tax-Free Cancellations of Accrued Interest Indebtedness: Contribution to Capital triumphs Over Tax Benefit Rule - Putoma Corp. Case, "Cleveland Tax Institute, November 11, 1977; "Individual Income Tax changes," Cleveland Tax Institute, November 13 1981; "Timing and Limitation of Loss Recognition," Cleveland Tax Institute, November 13, 1982; "Corporate Transactions with Stockholders," Cleveland Tax Institute, November 19, 1983; "Leveraged Buyouts," Cleveland Tax Institute, November 8, 1984; "Sale and Leaseback Transactions," Cleveland Tax Institute, November 15, 1985; "Statutory Mergers, Consolidations and Triangular Reorganizations," Cleveland Tax Institute, November 15, 1986; "Limited Liability Companies," Cleveland Tax Institute, November 13, 1993; "State Tax Considerations in Mergers and Acquisitions," Cleveland Tax Institute, October 19, 1995; "Choice of Pass-Through Entity After Check-the-Box," Cleveland Tax Institute, October 28, 1997; "Tax Motivated Transactions and Structures," Cleveland Tax Institute, November 10, 1998; "Forward and Reverse Triangular Reorganizations," Cleveland Tax Institute, November 1, 1999; "Transactions With Disregarded Entities," Cleveland Tax Institute, October 30, 2000; "Conversions, Mergers, Single Member LLCs," Cleveland Tax Institute, November 22, 2002; "Ohio Taxation of Corporations," Cleveland Tax Institute, October 16, 2003; "Post-Enron Tax Planning," 2003 Tax Executives Institute Conference, Denver Colorado; "State Tax Consequences of Mergers and Acquisitions and Nexus Issues," 2004 Tax Executives Institute Conference, Cleveland, Ohio. (Group Leader, Tax). ***REPORTED CASES:*** Parker Hannifin Corp. v. Commissioner, 139 F.3d 1090 (6th Cir. 1998) aff'g and rev'g 72 TCM 191 (1996)(deduction of contribution to VEBA); Buckeye Power Co. v. United States, 97-2 USTC ¶50,510 (Ct. Fed. Cls. 1997) (upheld tax exempt status of rural electric cooperative under section 501 (c)(12); Parker Hannifin Corp. v. United States, unreported settlement (motion for summary judgment on refund claims for foreign tax credits and dividend received deductions); Oglebay Norton Company v. United States, 610 F.2d 715 (Ct. Cls. 1979) (investment tax credits on vessels funded under MARAD funds); Norandex v. Limbach, 69 Ohio St. 3d 26 (1994), rev'g Ohio B.T.A. (sales tax on sample products); Custom Beveridge Packers, Inc. v. Kosydar, 33 Ohio St. 2d 68 (1973) (sales tax on conveyers and packaging for soft drink processor); Noranda Aluminum Inc. v. Limbach, journal entry settlement (1998) (franchise tax doing business nexus issue); Heidelberg Harris, Inc. v. Limbach, journal entry settlement (1996) (refund of Ohio franchise tax); Society Corp. v. Limbach, B.T.A. No. 90-x-12903 (1993) (franchise tax on net worth); Bechtel Corp. v. Kosydar B.T.A. No. A-263 (1973) (sales tax on chemical plant). ***TRANSACTIONS:*** Shelf registration of $1 billion debt and equity securities of bank holding company; Registration of $750 million medium term notes of bank holding company; Registration of $1 billion debt obligation of bank; Registration of $500 million of student loans securities of bank; Auto loan securitization ($500 million) of bank; Consolidation of two Fortune 500 chemical processors; Purchase of mortgage service business; Purchase of leasing business; Tax-Free merger acquisition of investment banking and consulting business; Tax-Free B reorganization of investment advisory and mutual fund business; Tax-free merger of two bank holding companies and merger of subsidiary banks; Taxable purchase of U.S. hydraulics manufacturer with seventeen foreign subsidiaries; Tax-free merger acquisition of pump manufacturer; taxable sale of U.S. subsidiary chemical company and foreign subsidiary to U.K. purchaser; Various other taxable and tax-free acquisitions; Conversion of small FISC to large FISC; Section 482 transfer price study; Tax-free exchange of life insurance policies; Built-in grains and Section 482 loss limitation; Restructuring corporate to form holding company structure; Formation of U.S. manufacturing joint venture between U.S. and Japanese truck manufacturers; Disposition of joint venture interest in mortgage service business; Formation of chemical processing joint venture between two U.S. chemical processors; Formation of U.S. fiberboard manufacturer; Operation of U.S. iron ore mining joint venture; Formation of foreign tire manufacturing joint venture; Formation and operation of investment partnership; Retail joint venture corporation of nonprofit tax exempt corporation; Joint venture LLC to construct and operate electric generation facility; Formation and operation of joint venture LLC to purchase and sell electric power; Conversion of real estate partnerships to LLCs; Formation of UPREIT; Disposition of hotel properties to UPREIT;

(This Listing Continued)

Disposition of real estate properties to UPREIT; Formation of oil exploration and drilling joint venture. ***PRACTICE AREAS:*** Taxation. ***Email:*** William.Stewart@ThompsonHine.com

LINDA A. STRIEFSKY, born Carbondale, Pennsylvania, April 27, 1952; admitted to bar, 1977, Ohio. *Education:* Marywood College (B.A., summa cum laude, 1974); Georgetown University (J.D., 1977). Author: "Pick Your Poison: Is "Toxic" Mold or a Sick Healthcare Project Distressing Your Loan", The ACREL Papers, Fall 2003; "Acquisition, Development and Construction Loan Commitment Letters," *Construction Renovation Formbook,* (1991); "Disposition of Rents and Profits After Mortgage Default," Ohio Section, 16 Real Property, Probate and Trust Journal 835, 1981, updated 1987 and 1990 for inclusion in Dunaway, The Law of Distressed Real Estate. Lecturer: "Modern Real Estate Transactions," ALI-ABA, 1997, 1998; "Keeping Pace with New Financing Options," ICSC Ohio Law Conference, 1997; "The Effect of the Americans With Disabilities Act on Leases," Georgetown University, 1993; "Loan Documents in the 90's: Assignments of Rents and Guarantees," 1993. Co-Author, with Pamela P. Brown, "Would a Rose by Any Other Name Smell So Sweet: Is Your Lease Financeable?" International Council of Shopping Centers Law Conference, Fall 2004. American Bar Association Real Property, Probate and Trust Section, 1993. Chair, Cleveland District Council, Urban Land Institute, 1996-2000. Member, Commercial Real Estate Women. Trustee, ideastream and Musical Theater Education Programming. *Member:* Cleveland (Member, Real Property Section), Ohio State (Member, Board of Governors, Real Property Section, 1985-1997) and American (Opinions Committee) Bar Associations; American College of Real Estate Lawyers (Board of Governors, 1993-1998; Treasurer, 1998-1999); National Association of Industrial and Office Parks; International Council of Shopping Centers; American College of Mortgage Attorneys. American Bar Foundation; Urban Land Institute (Chair, Cleveland District Council, 1996-2000); Commercial Real Estate Women. ***PRACTICE AREAS:*** Real Estate Law; Commercial Finance. ***Email:*** Linda.Striefsky@ThompsonHine.com

PATRICK J. SWEENEY, born Cleveland, Ohio, July 23, 1958; admitted to bar, 1986, Ohio. *Education:* College of Wooster (B.A., 1980); Cleveland-Marshall College of Law (J.D., 1986). *Member:* Cleveland, Ohio State and American Bar Associations. ***PRACTICE AREAS:*** Construction Law; Real Estate Law. ***Email:*** Pat.Sweeney@ThompsonHine.com

BRIAN A. TROYER, born Wooster, Ohio; admitted to bar, 1992, Ohio; 1993, U.S. District Court, Northern District of Ohio; 1994 U.S. Court of Appeals, Sixth Circuit. *Education:* College of Wooster (B.A., with honors, 1989); Harvard University (J.D., magna cum laude, 1992). Phi Beta Kappa. ***PRACTICE AREAS:*** Business Litigation; Securities Litigation; Complex Litigation; Class Actions; Toxic Torts; Products Liability; Consumer Litigation. ***Email:*** Brian.Troyer@ThompsonHine.com

ROY L. TURNELL, born Manitowoc, Wisconsin, August 26, 1947; admitted to bar, 1974, Ohio and Wisconsin. *Education:* Yale University (B.A., 1969); University of Wisconsin (J.D., cum laude, 1974). *Member:* Cleveland and American (Member, Business Law Section) Bar Associations. ***PRACTICE AREAS:*** Corporate Law; Mergers and Acquisitions; Securities. ***Email:*** Roy.Turnell@ThompsonHine.com

ROBERT F. WARE JR., born Rogers City, Michigan, November 14, 1966; admitted to bar, 1991, Ohio; U.S. District Court, Northern District of Ohio; U.S. District Court, District of Colorado; U.S. District Court, Central District of Illinois; U.S. Court of Appeals, First, Sixth and Eleventh Circuits; U.S. Supreme Court. *Education:* University of Virginia (B.A., 1988); University of Michigan Law School (J.D., cum laude, 1991). Author: "Identifying and Protecting Trade Secrets"; Et al., a publication of the Deloitte & Touche Dispute Consulting Services Group, 2001. Contributing Author: "State Antitrust Practice and Statutes," 2d ed., 1999; "Trade Secrets May Enjoy Wide Legal Protection," Crain's Cleveland Business, 1997. Co-Author: "Are You a Medical Monopoly," Unique Opportunities, 1996; "Declatory Judgment Actions in Dealer Termination Cases," Private Antitrust Litigation News, 1993. Program Chair: "Competition Law Skills Workshop," Ohio State Bar Association Annual Convention, 2002; "Protecting Proprietary Information Through Litigation", Cleveland Bar Association, Intellectual Property Committee Seminar, 2002; "Antitrust Principles Governing Multi-Firm Conduct," Ohio State Bar Association Antitrust Section, Antitrust Institute, 2001; "Identifying, Protecting and Exploiting Your Company's Proprietary Information," Deloitte & Touche/Thompson Hine LLP Seminar, 2001. Lecturer: "Current Hot Issues in Antitrust and Other Complex Litigation: Joint Defense Agreements," Ohio State Bar Association Annual Convention, 2001; "Antitrust: What Every Business Lawyer Should Know," Ohio State Bar Association Annual Convention, 2000; "Copyright and E-Commerce Issues for the Design Professional," Denmark Group Annual Management Workshops, 2000; "Intellectual Property Licensing Arrangements," Ohio State Bar Association Antitrust Section, Antitrust Institute, 2000; "Copyright and E-Commerce Issues for the Design Professional," Denmark Group Annual Management Workshops, 2000; "Price-Related Distribution Practices," Ohio State Bar Association Antitrust Section, Antitrust Institute, 1999. Member, United Way Leadership Development Program, Class of 1996. *Member:* Cleveland (Member: Ethics and Professionalism Committee; Certified Grievance Committee) Ohio State (Council of Delegates, District 12 Representative; Member, Antitrust Section; Board of Governors) and American (Member, Antitrust Section) Bar Associations. ***TRANSACTIONS:*** Defense verdict for financial institution in lender liability litigation brought by Toledo developer; Jury verdict on counterclaim and rejecting plaintiff competitor's claim against national cleaning products supplier; Judgement after five-week trial dismissing claims against City of Akron by other local governments challenging its conrol of waters of the Cuyahoga River; Defense Judgment in bench trial for electromechanical parts supplier in beach of contract action brought by competing company; Representation of residential home builders and architect in copyright infringement litigation; Summary judgment in favor of major financial institution in trademark infringement litigation; Favorable settlement for real estate brokerage of civil antitrust conspiracy claim by national franchisor; Favorable settlement for software developer in arbitration against computer education franchisor; Numerous trade secret, non-competition convenant, tortious interference and other business tort cases and preliminary injunction hearings, for both plaintiffs and defendants; Regular counseling of clients concerning antitrust, intellectual property and other competition issues. ***PRACTICE AREAS:*** Competition; Antitrust; White Collar Crime; Business Litigation; Intellectual Property. ***Email:*** Rob.Ware@ThompsonHine.com

STEPHEN D. WILLIGER, born Cleveland, Ohio, 1951; admitted to bar, 1982, Ohio. *Education:* Ohio University (B.A., 1973); Case Western Reserve University (M.S.S.A., 1977); Cleveland-Marshall College of Law (J.D., 1982). Author: "Negotiating the Minefields of Electronic Discovery", University of Richmond Law Review (2004); "Health Care Entities: A World of Privilege and Immunity?", The Federal Lawyer (January 2002). Speaker, Loan Fraud Seminar, Federal Reserve Bank of Cleveland (December 2001). Author: "A Trial Lawyer's Perspective on Mental Health Professionals as Expert Witnesses", Consulting Psychology Journal: Practice and Research, Vol. 47 (1995). Keynote Speaker, Institute of Internal Auditors National Fraud Conference, Nashville, Tennessee (October 1994). Author: "Phar-Mor - A Lesson in Fraud, The Wall Street Journal (March 28, 1994); Reprinted in Jennings, "Business: Its Legal, Ethical and Global Environment", South-Western College Publishing Co. (Fourth Edition 1997). *Member:* Cleveland, Ohio State, Federal and American (Member, Business Torts and Corporate Fraud Subcommittee) Bar Associations; Anthony J. Celebrezze Inn of Court; Federal Bar Association Foundation. ***PRACTICE AREAS:*** Complex and Multi-District Litigation; Fraud and Deceit; Trade Secrets; Litigation; White Collar Crime; Unfair Competition; Entertainment and the Arts; Entertainment Contracts; Entertainment Law; Entertainment Litigation; Entertainment Liability. ***Email:*** Stephen.Williger@ThompsonHine.com

ELIZABETH B. WRIGHT, born Wheeling, West Virginia, October 14, 1959; admitted to bar, 1984, Ohio. *Education:* College of William and Mary (B.A., 1981); Duke University (J.D., 1984). Member, Anthony J. Celebrezze Inn of Court. Member: The Junior League of Cleveland, Inc.; Board of Trustees, Alzheimer's Association, 1999-2003. *Member:* Defense Research Institute. American College of Trial Lawyers. ***PRACTICE AREAS:*** Products Liability; Automotive Products Liability; Aircraft Products Liability; Consumer Products Liability; Business Litigation; Litigation. ***Email:*** Elizabeth.Wright@ThompsonHine.com

DANIEL T. YOUNG, born Akron, Ohio, August 2, 1967; admitted to bar, 1992, Ohio. *Education:* University of Pennsylvania (B.S., Econ., magna cum laude, 1989); University of California, Los Angeles (J.D., 1992). Order of the Coif. *Member:* Cleveland and Ohio State Bar Associations; National Association of Bond Lawyers. ***PRACTICE AREAS:*** Securities; Public Finance; Corporate. ***Email:*** Dan.Young@ThompsonHine.com

KAREN D. YOUNGSTROM, born Cleveland, Ohio, March 15, 1950; admitted to bar, 1976, Ohio. *Education:* Yale University (B.A., 1972); Harvard Law School (J.D., 1975). *Member:* American Bar Association; The ESOP Association; Charter Fellow, American College of Employee Benefits Counsel; Advisory Board, Ohio Employee Ownership Center. ***PRACTICE AREAS:*** Employee Benefits Law; Employee Stock Ownership Plans; ERISA; Executive Compensation; Health Care; Pension and Profit Sharing Law. ***Email:*** Karen.Youngstrom@ThompsonHine.com

RETIRED PARTNERS

DAVID L. PARHAM, born Warren, Arkansas, January 1, 1945; admitted to bar, 1974, Ohio, U.S. District Court, Northern District of Ohio; 1980, U.S. Supreme Court; U.S. Court of Appeals for the Fifth, Sixth and Federal Circuits. *Education:* Case Institute of Technology (B.S., 1967); University of Dayton (M.B.A., 1970); Case Western Reserve University (J.D., 1974). Order of the Coif. Editor, Case Western Reserve University Law Review; National Chair, Case Western Reserve University Law School Annual Fund, 2002-2004; Case Western Reserve University Law Alumni Board, 2000-2003. Case Western Reserve University, Case Advisory Board, 1978—; University Council, 1987-1992; Chairman, Visiting Committee for the Colleges, 1991-1992. Case Alumni Association, National President, 1984-1985; Executive Committee and Council, 1975—. Shaker Heights Police Review Board, 1989-2004. CLE Seminar Lecturer: Zoning Law Updates, October, 1995; Ohio Zoning Law, December, 1999; Ohio Land Use: Current Issues in Subdivision Annexation and Zoning Law, November 2001 and 2002. City Councilman, City of Shaker Heights, 1984-1988. City Planning Commission and Board of Zoning Appeals, 1980-1988. *Member:* Cleveland Bar Association(Litigation Section); Ohio State Bar Association; Federal Bar Association (National - Vice President for the Sixth Circuit 2003-2007; Local Board of Directors, Northern District of Ohio Chapter, 1998—); American Bar Association (Member, Litigation and Business Law Sections); Defense Research Institute. Foundation of the Federal Bar Association; Ohio State Bar Foundation; Cleveland Bar Foundation; Society of Benchers. [U.S. Air Force, 1967-1971]. ***PRACTICE AREAS:*** Litigation - Commercial; Zoning Law; Business Litigation; Product Liability Litigation. ***Email:*** David.Parham@ThompsonHine.com

THOMAS F. ZYCH, born Harrisburg, Pennsylvania, May 19, 1958; admitted to bar, 1983, Ohio. *Education:* Miami University (B.A., 1979); Duke University (J.D., 1983). Contributor: "Doing Business in and With the United States," 2000; "Antitrust Law Developments," 1995 Annual Review. American Bar Association Contributor, Antitrust Evidence Manual, 1990. Author: "Software Buys Need Careful Plan, Vigilant Review," Crain's Cleveland Business, 1999. Co-Author: "Protecting Your Intellectual Property Under Ohio Law," 1989; "Drafting International Technology License Agreements"; Negotiating and Structuring International Commercial Transactions, ABA. *Member:* Ohio State (Member, Board of Governors, Member, Antitrust Law Section) and American (Chair, Privacy and Information Security Committee and Member, Antitrust Law Section). Fellow, Ohio State Bar Foundation. ***TRANSACTIONS:*** Represents a leading international industrial products manufacturer in litigation against software vendor; Represents numerous publicly and privately held business entities in software acquisition and licensing; Represents B2B and B2C .com start-ups in fabricated metal products, food, media, print, construction, application services provider, medical devices, motion picture, computer hardware and other markets; Represents national law firm in domain name matters; Counsels Fortune 200, middle market and start-up companies on website design and e-commerce implementation strategies; Intellectual property litigation experience involving banking and investment services, industrial valves, software, fabrics, aircraft electronics, home decor, collectibles, lawn and tree care services, broadcast music, packaging, sports entertainment services, steel mill equipment, legal services, automotive components, surgical instruments, medical apparatus, oil and fuel additives, paints and coatings, power tools, lawn furniture, lighting fixtures and other products and services; Represents publicly held specialty retail chain in supply chain integration strategies; Civil and criminal antitrust litigation in the commercial explosives, construction, motion picture distribution, carbon black, metals, used machinery auction, concrete pipe, engineered materials, food additive, packaging, grocery store, telephone, chlorine distribution, automotive aftermarket component and other markets; Represents Canadian health care software developer in contract dispute; Represents strategic

(This Listing Continued)

(This Listing Continued)

THOMPSON HINE LLP, Cleveland—Continued

investor in syndicated sports media content site; Represents strategic partners in the formation, development and marketing of industry-wide vertical supply chain management and content sites; Represents leading specialty retailer in business integration software contract dispute; Represents leading life sciences software developer in ongoing patent litigation and in strategic technology acquisitions; Represents publicly-held national retailer in internet branding and domain name strategies and disputes; Represents major financial institutions in internet branding strategies and strategic alliances. ***PRACTICE AREAS:*** E-Business; Intellectual Property Law; Antitrust Law; Civil and Criminal Litigation; Competition; Trade and Professional Organizations; Trade Secrets; Trademarks. ***Email:*** Tom.Zych@ThompsonHine.com

ASSOCIATES

MATTHEW BRADFORD, born Akron, Ohio, January 15, 1971; admitted to bar, 2001, Ohio; 2002, U.S. District Court, Northern District of Ohio. *Education:* Case Western Reserve University (B.A., 1993); Cleveland State University (M.B.A., 1999); Cleveland-Marshall College of Law (J.D., summa cum laude, 2001). *Member:* Cleveland Bar Association; American Bar Association. ***PRACTICE AREAS:*** Corporate Transactions; Securities. ***Email:*** Matt.Bradford@ThompsonHine.com

PATRICIA A. BURGESS, admitted to bar, 2002, Ohio; U.S. District Court, Northern District of Ohio. *Education:* Ohio State University (B.S., 1969; M.C.R.P., 1979; Ph.D., 1988); Case Western Reserve University School of Law (J.D., 2002). Author: Planning for the Private Interest: Land Use Controls and Residential Patterns in Columbus, Ohio, 1900-1970 (1994); "Of Swimming Pools and Slums: Zoning and Residential Development in Post-War Columbus, Ohio," Planning the Twentieth Century City, 1996; "An Acceptable Degree of Risk: A Study of Ohio Building Standards Law," 1998. *Member:* Cleveland, Ohio State (Uniform State Laws Committee) and American Bar Associations. ***TRANSACTIONS:*** Incorporate new non-profit and charitable organizations and file for tax-exempt status with Internal Revenue Service; Handle Acquisition, Closure, and Disposition of nursing homes and long-term care facilities; Provide advice on Tax Code and Regulations governing the actions of tax-exempt entities; Provide advice on state and federal statutes and regulations for medical service providers. ***PRACTICE AREAS:*** Exempt Organizations (80%); Health Care Law (15%); Tax Law (5%). ***Email:*** Patricia.Burgess@ThompsonHine.com

ROBERT W. BURGER, born Ft. Leonard Wood, Missouri, July 29, 1963; admitted to bar, 1997, Ohio and U.S. District Court, Northern District of Ohio; 1999, U.S. District Court, Eastern District of Michigan. *Education:* Maine Maritime Academy (B.S., magna cum laude, Valedictorian, 1993); Tulane Law School (J.D., cum laude, 1997; Certificate in Maritime Law; Certificate of Advanced Study and Training in Commercial Arbitration). Editor in Chief, Tulane Maritime Law Journal, Vol. 21. U.S. Coast Guard Licence, 1987—. *Member:* United States Maritime Law Association; Propeller Club of the United States, Port of Cleveland. ***PRACTICE AREAS:*** Admiralty; Maritime Law. ***Email:*** Rob.Burger@ThompsonHine.com

JEREMY M. CAMPANA, born Louisville, Kentucky, 1973; admitted to bar, 2000, Pennsylvania; 2001, New Jersey; 2002, Ohio. *Education:* University of Rhode Island (B.A., 1997); Rutgers University School of Law, Camden (J.D., 2000). *Member:* Ohio State and Cleveland Bar Associations. ***LANGUAGES:*** Spanish. ***PRACTICE AREAS:*** Chapter 11; Debtor Representation; Debtor and Creditor. ***Email:*** Jeremy.Campana@ThompsonHine.com

ANDREW H. COX, born Burlington, Iowa, March 15, 1972; admitted to bar, 1999, Ohio. *Education:* University of Iowa (B.A., 1995); University of Iowa College of Law (J.D., with high distinction, Order of the Coif, 1999). ***PRACTICE AREAS:*** Products Liability; Business Litigation. ***Email:*** Andrew.Cox@ThompsonHine.com

ANDREA B. DALOIA, born Washington, Pennsylvania, October 14, 1974; admitted to bar, 2001, Ohio; 2002, U.S. District Court, Northern District of Ohio; 2003, Pennsylvania. *Education:* Mercyhurst College (B.A., summa cum laude, 1997); Cleveland-Marshall College of Law (J.D., summa cum laude, 2001). Managing Editor, Cleveland State Law Review. *Member:* Ohio State Bar Association. ***PRACTICE AREAS:*** Products Liability; Toxic Torts; Torts; Negligence; Litigation; Business Law; Civil Practice; Contracts. ***Email:*** Andrea.Daloia@ThompsonHine.com

C. LEANN DAVIS, born Jacksonville, Florida, April 29, 1975; admitted to bar, 2003, Florida and U.S. District Court, Northern, Middle and Southern Districts of Florida (Not admitted in Ohio). *Education:* Duke University (B.A., 1997); University of Florida (J.D., with high honors, 2002; M.A., Real Estate and Urban Analysis, 2002; M.B.A., 2003). Order of the Coif. Chair, Justice Campbell Thornal Moot Court Board, 2002. Finalist, Ruby Vale Corporate Moot Court Competition, 2002. Senior Galleys Editor, Florida Law Review, 2001-2002. *Member:* Jacksonville and American Bar Associations; The Florida Bar. ***PRACTICE AREAS:*** Real Estate. ***Email:*** LeAnn.Davis@ThompsonHine.com

RENEE L. DAVIS, born Eastlake, Ohio, 1969; admitted to bar, 2003, Ohio, U.S. District Court, Northern District of Ohio and U.S. Bankruptcy Court, Northern District of Ohio. *Education:* Lake Erie College (B.S., Accounting, summa cum laude, 1999); Cleveland-Marshall College of Law (J.D., magna cum laude, 2003). Order of the Barristers. Semi-Finalist, National Moot Court Regional Competition and First Place Respondent Brief, 2002. Chairperson, Moot Court Board of Governors, Cleveland-Marshall College of Law, 2002-2003. Editor, Cleveland State Law Review, 2001-2003. Certified Public Accountant, Ohio, 1999. Member, Willoughby Hills Board of Zoning Appeals. *Member:* Cleveland (Member, Young Lawyer Section) and Ohio State Bar Associations; American Bankruptcy Institute, Ohio Society of CPA; American Institute of Certified Public Accountants; American Association of Attorney-CPA's. ***PRACTICE AREAS:*** Bankruptcy; Business Litigation. ***Email:*** Renee.Davis@ThompsonHine.com

JENNIFER LYNN DILLMAN, born Billings, Montana, May 4, 1971; admitted to bar, 2000, Ohio. *Education:* University of Montana (B.A., 1994); University of Toledo (J.D., magna cum laude, 2000). Phi Kappa Phi. Order of the Coif. Executive Editor, University of Toledo Law Review, 1999-2000. Author: "Arkansas Educational Television Commission v. Forbes - Journalistic Editorial Discretion or Unconstitutional Prior Restraint?" University of Toledo Law Review, Volume 30, Number 2, 1999. Presentations: "Revised UCC Article 9 Secured Transactions," National Business Institute, 2004; "Update on Revised UCC Article 9," Ohio State Bar Association Annual Convention, 2002; "Overview of Article 9 Changes," 10th Annual Bradley J. Shaeffer Real Property Institute, 2002; "Lending under Revised Article 9 of the Uniform Commercial Code," Ohio Bankers Association/Ohio League of Financial Institutions. *Member:* Ohio State (Co-Chair, Secured Transactions Subcommittee and Member, Banking, Commercial and Bankruptcy Law Committee) and American Bar Associations; National Association of Bond Lawyers. ***PRACTICE AREAS:*** Commercial Law; Public Finance; Complex Commercial Finance; Banking Law; Bankruptcy Law. ***Email:*** Jennifer.Dillman@ThompsonHine.com

OLIVER J. DUNFORD, born Milwaukee, Wisconsin, 1973; admitted to bar, 2001, Ohio; 2002, U.S. District Court, Northern District of Ohio. *Education:* University of Dayton (B.A., 1995); Cleveland-Marshall College of Law (J.D., cum laude, 2001). ***PRACTICE AREAS:*** Business Litigation. ***Email:*** Oliver.Dunford@ThompsonHine.com

DAMARIS G. FISHER, admitted to bar, 2000, Ohio. *Education:* Bates College (B.A., cum laude, 1993); University of Utah (J.D., 1999). Member, Utah Law Review. Served as a Judicial Clerk to Chief Judge Dee V. Benson, of the United States District Court, District of Utah. *Member:* Ohio State (Member, Environmental Committee) and American Bar Associations. ***PRACTICE AREAS:*** Environmental Law; Toxic Torts Law; Products Liability Law. ***Email:*** Damaris.Fisher@ThompsonHine.com

SARAH C. FLANNERY, born Willoughby, Ohio; admitted to bar, 2002, Ohio; 2003, U.S. District Court, Northern District of Ohio; 2005, U.S. District Court, Northern District of Indiana. *Education:* John Carroll University (B.S., magna cum laude, 1999); Cleveland-Marshall College of Law (J.D., summa cum laude, 2002). Research Editor, Cleveland State Law Review. Author: "Extending Weingarten to the Nonunion Setting: A History of Oscillation," Cleveland State Law Review, Volume 49, Number 1. *Member:* Ohio State Bar Association. ***PRACTICE AREAS:*** Labor and Employment; Immigration. ***Email:*** Sarah.Flannery@ThompsonHine.com

ADAM D. FULLER, born Grand Rapids, Michigan; admitted to bar, 2003, Ohio; 2004, U.S. District Court, Northern District of Ohio; 2005, U.S. Court of Appeals, Sixth Circuit. *Education:* Miami University (B.S., 2000); Case Western Reserve University (J.D., cum laude, 2003). Executive Articles Editor: Case Western Reserve Journal of International Law, 2002-2003. Moot Court, Craven Team Member, 2002-2003. Extern: Judge Alice M. Batchelder, United States Court of Appeals for the Sixth Circuit, 2002. Author: "Extraterritorial Implications of the Digital Millenium Copyright Act," Case Western Reserve Journal of International Law, Winter 2003. *Member:* Cleveland and Ohio State Bar Associations. ***PRACTICE AREAS:*** Business Litigation (50%); Labor and Employment (50%). ***Email:*** Adam.Fuller@ThompsonHine.com

DENISE L. GAWLIK, born Cleveland, Ohio, November 16, 1975; admitted to bar, 2001, Ohio; 2001, U.S. District Court, Northern District of Ohio and U.S. Court of Appeals, Sixth Circuit. *Education:* Xavier University of Cincinnati, Ohio (B.A., magna cum laude, 1998); Cleveland-Marshall College of Law (J.D., magna cum laude, 2001). Managing Editor Law Review. *Member:* Cleveland Bar Association (Member, Business Litigation Section; Committee Member); Cuyahoga County Bar Association (Member: Certified Grievance Committee, Young Lawyers Section; Executive Committee); American Bar Association. ***PRACTICE AREAS:*** Complex Civil Litigation; Business Litigation. ***Email:*** Denise.Gawlik@ThompsonHine.com

GREGORY J. GAWLIK, admitted to bar, 2000, Ohio. *Education:* Bowling Green State University (B.A., summa cum laude, 1997); Cleveland-Marshall College of Law (J.D., summa cum laude, 2000). Phi Beta Kappa. Executive Editor, Cleveland State Law Review, 1999-2000. Recipient: Faculty Award, 2nd Highest GPA Class of 2000; Suggs I. Garber Award, Highest Academic GPA in Business Organization and Taxation Courses. Author: "The Politics of Religion: 'Reasonable Accommodations' and the Establishment Clause, An Analysis of the Workplace Religious Freedom Act," Cleveland State Law Review, Volume 47, Number 2, 1999. *Member:* Cleveland and American (Member, Tax Section; Member and Vice Chair, Important Developments Subcommittee of Administrative Practice Committee) Bar Associations; Tax Club of Cleveland; Cleveland Tax Institute (Chairperson, Arrangements Committee, 2002). ***PRACTICE AREAS:*** Taxation. ***Email:*** Gregory.Gawlik@ThompsonHine.com

ALEXANDRA J. GEFFERT, born Cleveland, Ohio, 1976; admitted to bar, 2003, Ohio and U.S. District Court, Northern District of Ohio. *Education:* Denison University (B.A., Biology, Honors Program, summa cum laude, Phi Beta Kappa, 1998); Case Western Reserve University School of Law (J.D., cum laude, 2003). Managing Editor, Health Matrix: Journal of Law-Medicine, 2002-2003. Recipient: CALI Excellence for the Future Award in Products Liability, 2001; CALI Excellence for the Future Award in Criminal Procedure, 2002. *Member:* Cleveland, Ohio State and American Bar Associations. ***PRACTICE AREAS:*** Litigation; Business Litigation. ***Email:*** Alexandra.Geffert@ThompsonHine.com

JONATHAN A. GOOD, born September 23, 1969; admitted to bar, 1995, Ohio; U.S. District Court, Northern District of Ohio; U.S. Court of Appeals, Sixth Circuit. *Education:* Dartmouth College (B.A., 1992); Cleveland Marshall College of Law (J.D., 1995). Recipient, Spangenberg Trial Practice Award. *Member:* Ohio State Bar Association. ***PRACTICE AREAS:*** Labor and Employment; Workers' Compensation. ***Email:*** Jonathan.Good@ThompsonHine.com

SEAN GORDON, admitted to bar, 2001, Ohio. *Education:* University of Florida (B.A., B.S., 1996); Case Western Reserve University (J.D., cum laude, 2001). *Member:* Cleveland and Ohio State Bar Associations. ***LANGUAGES:*** Japanese. ***PRACTICE AREAS:*** Bankruptcy; Business Litigation. ***Email:*** Sean.Gordon@ThompsonHine.com

TRACY HANNAN, born December 15, 1976; admitted to bar, 2003, Ohio; 2004, Illinois. *Education:* University of Michigan (B.A., in Sociology); Boston University School of Law (J.D.). *Member:* Ohio State, Illinois State and American Bar Associations. ***PRACTICE AREAS:*** Business Litigation. ***Email:*** Tracy.Hannan@ThompsonHine.com

JEFFREY R. HARTWIG, admitted to bar, 2005, Ohio and U.S. District Court, Northern District of Ohio. *Education:* San Francisco State University (B.A., 2001); University of Pittsburgh (J.D., cum laude, 2004; Certificate in International and Comparative Law, 2004). Recipient: Faculty Award for Excellence in Legal Scholarship; School of Law Community Service Award, University of Pittsburgh School of Law, 2004. Executive Editor, Journal of

(This Listing Continued)

Law and Commerce, 2003. Author, "Schmitz-Werke Gmbh & Co. v. Rockland Industries Inc. and the United Nations Convention on Contracts for the International Sale of Goods (CISG): Diffidence and Developing International Legal Norms," 22 J.L. & Com. 77 (2003). *Member:* Cleveland, Ohio State and American Bar Associations. ***LANGUAGES:*** French. ***PRACTICE AREAS:*** Litigation; Civil Litigation; Complex Litigation. ***Email:*** Jeffrey.Hartwig@ThompsonHine.com

KENNETH W. HUBBARD, born Lorain, Ohio, December 26, 1966; admitted to bar, 1996, Ohio and U.S. District Court, Northern District of Ohio. *Education:* Valparaiso University (B.A., 1989); Cleveland Marshall College of Law (J.D., magna cum laude, 1996). Member, Board of Governors, Moot Court, 1995-1996. Recipient, American Jurisprudence Award in Legal Writing, 1994. Member, Editorial Board, Cleveland Marshall Law Review, 1995-1996. *Member:* Ohio State Bar Association. ***PRACTICE AREAS:*** Business Litigation (75%); Products Liability Defense (20%); Workers Compensation Defense (5%). ***Email:*** Kenneth.Hubbard@ThompsonHine.com

WILLIAM J. HUBBARD, born Freehold, New Jersey; admitted to bar, 2003, Ohio and U.S. District Court, Northern District of Ohio. *Education:* College of Wooster (B.A.); University of Michigan (M.S.); Boston College (J.D.). ***PRACTICE AREAS:*** Product Liability Litigation. ***Email:*** Bill.Hubbard@ThompsonHine.com

EMILY S. HUGGINS, born Lexington, Kentucky, May 14, 1978; admitted to bar, 2004, Ohio. *Education:* University of Virginia (B.A., with distinction, 2000); University of Notre Dame Law School (J.D., 2004). Phi Beta Kappa. ***LANGUAGES:*** French. ***PRACTICE AREAS:*** Products Liability; Environmental Law. ***Email:*** Emily.Huggins@ThompsonHine.com

CHRISTOPHER R. JOHNSON, born Cleveland, Ohio, June 16, 1975; admitted to bar, 2000, Ohio; 2001, U.S. District Court, Northern District of Ohio; 2003, U.S. District Court, Southern District of Ohio, U.S. District Court, Northern District of Indiana and U.S. Court of Appeals, Sixth Circuit. *Education:* Case Western Reserve University (B.A., magna cum laude, 1997); George Washington University (J.D., cum laude, 2000). Author: "Protect Yourself From Risk— Put It on Paper," Crain's Cleveland Business, May 13-19, 2002; "Ratchet Up Discrimination Policies," Crain's Cleveland Business, March 14-20, 2005. Member, Board of Trustees, Delta Tau Delta Cleveland Corp. Member, CWRU Alumni Task Force. Tutor, Harvey Rice Elementary School. *Member:* Cleveland (Sections on: Labor and Employment Law; Litigation; Young Lawyers) and Ohio State and American Bar Associations. ***TRANSACTIONS:*** Counseled employers in areas including anti-discrimination/harassment policies, family and medical leave, ADA claims, employee discipline and employee discharge; Counseled and represented employers in matters involving OSHA inspections, collective bargaining and plant closings/relocations; Defended employers against allegations of employment discrimination in state and federal courts and before the Ohio Civil Rights Commission, the Equal Employment Opportunity Commission, the NLRB, and OSHA. Represent manufacturers in actions claiming injurious exposure to airborne silica. Represent manufacturers in actions claiming strict product liability and negligence. ***PRACTICE AREAS:*** Labor and Employment (70%); Litigation (30%). ***Email:*** Chris.Johnson@ThompsonHine.com

LARRY J. JONES, admitted to bar, 2002, Ohio. *Education:* Cleveland State University (B.A., 1998; M.B.A., 2002); Cleveland-Marshall College of Law (J.D., 2002). *Member:* Cleveland and Ohio State Bar Associations. ***PRACTICE AREAS:*** Business Litigation; Products Liability. ***Email:*** Larry.Jones@ThompsonHine.com

JILL M. H. KARLGAARD, born Bismarck, North Dakota, January 30, 1976; admitted to bar, 2002, Minnesota; 2005, Ohio. *Education:* University of North Dakota (B.A. & B.S., summa cum laude, 1998); University of Minnesota Law School (J.D., cum laude, 2002). ***PRACTICE AREAS:*** Products Liability (100%). ***Email:*** Jill.Karlgaard@ThompsonHine.com

AMANDA A. KESSLER, born St. Louis, Missouri, May 12, 1978; admitted to bar, 2003, Missouri; 2004, Illinois (Not admitted in Ohio). *Education:* St. Louis University (B.A., cum laude, 2000; J.D., 2003). Executive Editor, Saint Louis University Law Journal, 2002-2003. Law Clerk to the Hon. Catherine D. Perry, United States District Court, Eastern District of Missouri, 2003-2004. *Member:* Illinois State Bar Association; The Missouri Bar. ***PRACTICE AREAS:*** Business Litigation. ***Email:*** Amanda.Kessler@ThompsonHine.com

EDUARDO KIM, born Buenos Aires, Argentina; admitted to bar, 2000, Ohio. *Education:* Cornell University (B.A., history and Literature, 1996) Cornell University Law School (J.D., 2000). *Member:* Cleveland and Ohio State Bar Associations. ***LANGUAGES:*** Spanish, Korean. ***TRANSACTIONS:*** Practice focused on commercial lending; Representation of banks and other financial institutions as well as public and private companies in connection with senior and subordinated debt facilities; Extensive experience with syndicated, multi-bank senior credit facilities, asset based and structured finance facilities, acquisition financing, letter of credit facilities, foreign currency transactions and real estate financing; Representation includes loan restructuring and workouts. ***PRACTICE AREAS:*** Commercial Finance; Public Finance. ***Email:*** Eduardo.Kim@ThompsonHine.com

SHANA F. KLEIN, born Columbus, Ohio, 1976; admitted to bar, 2001, Ohio. *Education:* The Ohio State University (B.A., 1998); Northwestern University (J.D., 2001). ***PRACTICE AREAS:*** Real Estate. ***Email:*** Shana.Klein@ThompsonHine.com

KELLY A. KOSEK, born Washington, Pennsylvania, March 5, 1977; admitted to bar, 2002, Ohio; U.S. District Court, Northern District of Ohio. *Education:* Allegheny College (B.A., History and Political Science, 1999); College of William & Mary, Marshall-Wythe School of Law (J.D., 2002). *Member:* Cleveland and American Bar Associations. ***PRACTICE AREAS:*** Products Liability; Business Litigation. ***Email:*** Kelly.Kosek@ThompsonHine.com

MICHELE T. KRYSZAK, born Warren, Michigan, November 19, 1976; admitted to bar, 2003, Ohio and U.S. District Court, Northern District of Ohio. *Education:* Denison University (B.A., 1998); Case Western Reserve University School of Law (J.D., 2003); Case Western University, Weatherhead School of Management (M.B.A., 2003). Pi Beta Phi. Recipient, Paul J. Hergenroëder Award in Trial Tactics, 2003. Author: "Net Taxation: Dallas Meeting Moves Closer to a Compromise" and "Information Broker eccelerate.com Created to Facilitate Secure E-Commerce Transactions," The Internet Law Journal, www.TILJ.com, November 15, 1999. Co-Author: "Establishing Consumer Confidence and Trust in the Government Sector: An Assessment and Framework for Online Security," National E-Commerce Coordinating Council, 2001; "Lessons Learned: E-Signature Statutes," National E-Commerce Coordinating Council, 2002. Member: Cleveland Bridge Builders Flagship Program Class of 2006; The City Club of Cleveland, New Leaders. Connector and Co-Chairperson of MarCAT, Connection Series; Cleveland East Alumni Club; Young Friends of the Cleveland Museum of Art; Advisory Council, YWCA of Greater Cleveland; Women's Leadership Intiative. *Member:* Cleveland Bar Association; Ohio State Bar Association; American Bar Association. ***TRANSACTIONS:*** Litigation Experience: Successful defense of metal products processing company, resulting in voluntary dismissal by Plaintiff. Represented a major non-profit corporation in a contract dispute, resulting in a complete defense verdict at trial. Defense of a major automobile manufacturer in a personal injury action based upon alleged defects in design and manufacture. Representation of a charitable foundation in a $35 million dispute over distribution of trust assets. Successful defense of one of the country's largest private charitable foundations in an employment contract dispute. Representation of major national bank holding company in a legal malpractice action in an action where the legal advice rendered failed to identify a multi-million dollar liability. eBusiness and Emerging Technologies Experience: Advised multi-billion dollar corporation on the design and implementation of a global privacy compliance program to ensure compliance with regulations such as Graham-Leach-Bliley, USA Patriot Act, ECPA (Electronic Communications Privacy Act), FCRA (Fair Credit Reporting Act), PIPEDA (Canadian Privacy Directive), COPPA (Children's Online Privacy Protection Act), and HIPAA (Health Insurance Portability and Accountability Act), among others. Served as Co-Chairperson of National E-Commerce Coordinating Council workgroups charged with establishing standards for e-government; drafted white papers presented at annual conference, "Establishing Consumer Confidence and Trust In The Government Sector: An Assessment and Framework For Online Security" and "Lessons Learned: E-Signature Statutes". Drafted electronic contracting section of Thompson Hine publication, "Doing Business In and With the United States". Assisted in development of professional malpractice intranet site for Business Litigation practice group. ***PRACTICE AREAS:*** Business Litigation; E-Business; Emerging Technologies. ***Email:*** Michele.Kryszak@ThompsonHine.com

ROBERT S. LEWIS, born April 30, 1976; admitted to bar, 2002, Ohio and U.S. District Court, Northern District of Ohio; 2005, U.S. Court of Appeals, Sixth Circuit. *Education:* University of Detroit Mercy (B.A., 1998); Case Western Reserve University School of Law (J.D., 2002). *Member:* Cleveland, Ohio State and American Bar Associations. ***REPORTED CASES:*** RE/MAX Int'l, Inc. v. Smythe, Cramer Co., 265 F. Supp. 2d 882 (N.D. Ohio 2003); Portage Cty. Bd. of Comm'rs v. City of Akron, 156 Ohio App. 3d 657 (Portage Cty. App. 2004). ***PRACTICE AREAS:*** Construction; Litigation. ***Email:*** Robert.Lewis@ThompsonHine.com

MATTHEW E. LIEBSON, born Bristol, Pennsylvania, June 10, 1974; admitted to bar, 1999, Ohio; U.S. District Court, Northern District of Ohio 2005: Southern District of Ohio, 6th Circuit Court of Appeals. *Education:* Denison University, Ohio (B.A., summa cum laude, Phi Beta Kappa, 1996); Harvard Law School (J.D., 1999). *Member:* Cleveland, Ohio State and American (Member, Antitrust Section) Bar Associations. ***REPORTED CASES:*** RE/MAX Int'l, Inc. v. Smythe, Cramer Co., 265 F. Supp. 2d 882 (N.D. Ohio 2003) Portage Cty. Bd. of Comm'rs v. City of Akron, 156 Ohio App. 3d 657 (Portage Cty. App. 2004). ***PRACTICE AREAS:*** Antitrust and Trade Regulation; Franchises and Franchising; Intellectual Property; Civil Litigation; Unfair Competition. ***Email:*** Matthew.Liebson@ThompsonHine.com

TIMOTHY H. LINVILLE, born December 16, 1976; admitted to bar, 2003, Ohio; 2004, U.S. District Court, Northern District of Ohio. *Education:* Wheaton College (B.A., cum laude); Duke University School of Law (J.D., cum laude). *Member:* Cleveland and American Bar Associations. ***PRACTICE AREAS:*** Labor and Employment (90%); Business Litigation (10%). ***Email:*** Tim.Linville@ThompsonHine.com

CLIFFORD S. MENDELSOHN, (admission pending). *Education:* Emory University (B.B.A., 1998); The University of Michigan Law School (J.D., cum laude, 2001). Beta Gamma Sigma. *Member:* Cleveland and Ohio State Bar Associations. ***PRACTICE AREAS:*** Business Litigation; Product Liability Litigation.

HORATIO ("HARRY") G. MIHET, born Romania; admitted to bar, 2002, Ohio. *Education:* University of Florida (B.A., Political Science and Criminology, cum laude, 1999); Duke University School of Law (J.D., magna cum laude, 2002). *Member:* Cleveland, Cuyahoga County, Ohio State and American Bar Associations. ***LANGUAGES:*** Romanian, French. ***PRACTICE AREAS:*** Competition; Antitrust; White Collar Crime; Products Liability. ***Email:*** Harry.Mihet@ThompsonHine.com

CATHERINE L. MILLER, born Cleveland, Ohio, June 4, 1973; admitted to bar, 2001, Ohio. *Education:* University of Notre Dame (B.B.A., magna cum laude, 1995); Case Western Reserve University (J.D., cum laude, 2001). Health Matrix, Journal of Law-Medicine, 1999-2001. Certified Public Accountant, Illinois, 1995. *Member:* Cleveland and Ohio State Bar Associations; National Italian American Bar Association. ***PRACTICE AREAS:*** Corporate Law; Securities. ***Email:*** Catherine.Miller@ThompsonHine.com

KATHLEEN M. MINAHAN, born Cleveland, Ohio, January 7, 1970; admitted to bar, 1995, Ohio; 1996, U.S. District Court, Northern District of Ohio; 2002, U.S. District Court, Eastern District of Michigan and U.S. Court of Appeals, Sixth Circuit. *Education:* Ohio Wesleyan University (B.A., summa cum laude, 1992); Case Western Reserve University (J.D., 1995). Lecturer: "Help Us Help You: Procedures for Handling Employee Complaints, Discipline and Discharge" (July 2002); "Retaliation Claims, Whistleblowers and Public Policy" (June 2003) *Member:* Cleveland and Ohio State Bar Associations; Association of Trial Lawyers of America. ***LANGUAGES:*** French. ***PRACTICE AREAS:*** Business Litigation; Employment Litigation. ***Email:*** Kathleen.Minahan@ThompsonHine.com

JOHN R. MITCHELL, born Cleveland, Ohio; admitted to bar, 1996, Ohio; 2003, U.S. District Court, Northern District of Ohio. *Education:* Ohio State University (B.A., 1992); Capital University Law School (J.D., 1996). Member, Capital University Law Review. Author: "Attorneys Representing Death Row Clients: Client Autonomy Over Personal Opinion," 25 Cap. U. Law Rev. 3 (1996). Assistant Prosecuting Attorney, 1996-2004 and Member, Major Trials Unit, 2002-2004, Cuyahoga County. Delegate, Judicial Conference of the Eighth Judicial District. ***PRACTICE AREAS:*** Products Liability. ***Email:*** John.Mitchell@ThompsonHine.com

(This Listing Continued)

THOMPSON HINE LLP, Cleveland—Continued

JULANNE MONTVILLE, admitted to bar, 2002, Ohio and U.S. District Court, Northern District of Ohio; 2005, U.S. Court of Appeals, Sixth Circuit. *Education:* Eastern New Mexico University (B.A., English, 1993); Kent State University (M.A., English, 1997); Case Western Reserve School of Law (J.D., 2002). *Member:* Cleveland, Ohio State and American Bar Associations. ***PRACTICE AREAS:*** Litigation; Antitrust and Trade Regulation; Intellectual Property. ***Email:*** Julanne.Montville@ThompsonHine.com

JENNIFER MINGUS MOUNTCASTLE, born Lorain, Ohio, April 10, 1975; admitted to bar, 2000, Ohio; U.S. District Court, Northern District of Ohio, U.S. District Court, Eastern District of Michigan and U.S. Court of Appeals, Sixth Circuit. *Education:* Bowling Green State University (B.A., cum laude, 1997); Cleveland-Marshall College of Law (J.D., summa cum laude, 2000). Vice Chairperson, 1999-2000, Associate Member, 1998-1999. Moot Court Board of Governors. Order of the Barristers. Best Oralist: NOVA Southeastern Moot Court Competition. Best Oralist: American College of Trial Lawyers National Moot Court Competition Regionals. Member, Scribes. Executive Editor, Cleveland Marshall Law Review, 1999-2000. Author: "E-Mail: A Constitutional (and Economical) Method of Transmitting Class Action Notice," Cleveland State Law Review, Volume 47, Number 1. Volunteer, St. Patrick's Hunger Center. Judge, SCA Dance Team Competitions. *Member:* Cleveland and Ohio State Bar Associations. ***PRACTICE AREAS:*** Product Liability Litigation (75%); Business Litigation (25%). ***Email:*** Jennifer.Mountcastle@ThompsonHine.com

SAMER M. MUSALLAM, born April 27, 1977; admitted to bar, 2004, Ohio, 2005; U.S. District Court, Northern District of Ohio. *Education:* University of Toronto (B.A., with honors, 2000); Case Western Reserve University (J.D., cum laude, 2004; M.B.A., 2004). *Member:* Cleveland, Ohio State and American (Member, Antitrust Section) Bar Associations. ***Email:*** Samer.Musallam@ThompsonHine.com

JOHN DAVID MYER, born Ravenna, Ohio, January 16, 1973; admitted to bar, 2001, Ohio; 2002, U.S. District Court, Northern District of Ohio. *Education:* Oberlin College (B.A., with Honors, 1995); University of Michigan (J.D., 2001). *Member:* American Bar Association (Member, Forum on the Construction Industry); Ohio State Bar Association; Cleveland Bar Association. ***PRACTICE AREAS:*** Construction; Business Litigation; Products Liability. ***Email:*** John.Myer@ThompsonHine.com

ADAM R. NAZETTE, admitted to bar, 2003, Ohio. *Education:* Miami University (B.S., cum laude, 2000); Case Western Reserve University School of Law (J.D., cum laude, 2003); Case Western Reserve University, Weatherhead School of Management (M.B.A., 2003). *Member:* Cleveland, Ohio State and American Bar Associations; The City Club of Cleveland (New Leaders). ***PRACTICE AREAS:*** Commercial Finance; Public Finance. ***Email:*** Adam.Nazette@ThompsonHine.com

LAURA BANCROFT NEMER, admitted to bar, 1996, Illinois; 1999, Ohio. *Education:* Lake Forest College (B.A., 1991); Loyola University (J.D., magna cum laude, 1996). *Member:* Cleveland Bar Association; Defense Research Institute. ***PRACTICE AREAS:*** Products Liability; Business Litigation. ***Email:*** Laura.Nemer@ThompsonHine.com

KEELY J. O'BRYAN, born Cleveland, Ohio, February 16, 1973; admitted to bar, 1999, Ohio. *Education:* Boston College (B.A., 1995); Vermont Law School (M.S.E.L., cum laude, Environmental Law, 1999; J.D., 1999). Co-author: with Heidi Goldstein: "Toxic Mold Grows as Cause for Complaints," Crain's Cleveland Business, August 14, 2001, Vol. 22, No. 41; "The New Wave of Sick Building Syndrome Litigation: When Mold Grows Beyond Your Refrigerator". Great Strides Executive Committee Member, Cystic Fibrosis Foundation, 1999-2001. Silent Auction Committee Member, Cleveland Hearing and Speech Center, 2000. Member, MedWish International Special Events Committee, 2005. *Member:* Cleveland (Member, Environmental Law Section), Ohio State and American Bar Associations. ***TRANSACTIONS:*** Counseling clients on federal, state and local compliance and permitting requirements; environmental due diligence and counseling for corporate transactions and sales; defense of federal, state and local enforcement actions; defense of private party actions under CERCLA; toxic tort litigation. ***PRACTICE AREAS:*** Environmental Law. ***Email:*** Keely.Obryan@ThompsonHine.com

STACEY A. PALMER, admitted to bar, 2004, Ohio. *Education:* Baldwin-Wallace College (B.A., summa cum laude, 2001); Cleveland-Marshall College of Law (J.D., summa cum laude, 2004). ***PRACTICE AREAS:*** Products Liability; Business Litigation. ***Email:*** Stacey.Palmer@ThompsonHine.com

TROY S. PRINCE, admitted to bar, 2004, Ohio; registered to practice before U.S. Patent and Trademark Office. *Education:* Case Western Reserve University (B.S., cum laude, 1994; M.S., 1998); Cleveland-Marshall College of Law (J.D., summa cum laude, 2002). *Member:* The Association of the Bar of the City of New York; Cleveland (Member, Intellectual Property Section), Ohio State and American (Member, Intellectual Property Section) Bar Associations. ***PRACTICE AREAS:*** Intellectual Property. ***Email:*** Troy.Prince@ThompsonHine.com

CHRISTOPHER M. RASSI, admitted to bar, 2003, Ohio. *Education:* Case Western Reserve University (B.A., magna cum laude, 2000; M.A., 2000); Case Western Reserve University School of Law (J.D., cum laude, 2003); Case Western Reserve University, Weatherhead School of Management (M.B.A., 2003). Frederick K. Cox International Law Center Post-Graduate Fellow, clerking for Her Excellency Judge Weinberg de Roca, Appeals Chamber, International Criminal Tribunal for the Former Yugoslavia and Rwanda, 2003. Executive Symposium and Topic Development Editor, Case Western Reserve Journal of International Law. Law Clerk, Honorable Yvonne Mokgoro, Constitutional Court of South Africa, 2004. Adjunct Associate Professor of Law, Case Western Reserve School of Law. *Member:* Cleveland, Ohio State and American Bar Associations; Greater Cleveland International Lawyers Group (Vice President and Board Member); The City Club of Cleveland (New Leaders); Public International Law and Policy Group. ***LANGUAGES:*** French. ***PRACTICE AREAS:*** Commercial Finance; Public Finance. ***Email:*** Christopher.Rassi@ThompsonHine.com

HOPE E. REDMOND, born Niles, Michigan, June 4, 1976; admitted to bar, 2001, Ohio. *Education:* Grove City College (B.A., magna cum laude, 1997); University of Notre Dame (J.D., cum laude, 2001). Presidential Scholar. Author: "A Message to Sex Offenders: Sex Registration and Notification Laws Do Not Infringe Upon Your Pursuit of Happiness," Univ. of Notre Dame's Journal of Legislation, Spring 2000. Associate Board Member, Catholic Diocese of Cleveland. *Member:* Ohio State and Federal Bar Associations. ***PRACTICE AREAS:*** Toxic Tort Defense (80%); Products Liability (20%). ***Email:*** Hope.Redmond@ThompsonHine.com

JENNIFER S. ROACH, born Euclid, Ohio, March 17, 1975; admitted to bar, 2001, Ohio; 2002, U.S. District Court, Northern District of Ohio. *Education:* Duke University (A.B., cum laude, 1997); Northwestern University (J.D., 2001). *Member:* Ohio State and American Bar Associations. ***PRACTICE AREAS:*** Antitrust; Intellectual Property; Franchises and Franchising. ***Email:*** Jennifer.Roach@ThompsonHine.com

ANTHONY J. ROSPERT, born Toledo, Ohio; admitted to bar, 2003, Ohio. *Education:* John Carroll University (B.A., magna cum laude, 2000); Vermont Law School (J.D., magna cum laude, 2003). *Member:* Cleveland and Ohio State Bar Associations. ***PRACTICE AREAS:*** Environmental Law. ***Email:*** Anthony.Rospert@ThompsonHine.com

KAREN E. RUBIN, born Columbus, Ohio, September 4, 1953; admitted to bar, 1985, Ohio. *Education:* Cleveland State University (B.A., magna cum laude, 1981); Cleveland-Marshall College of Law (J.D., 1985). Author: "Can You Sue a Current Client? Maybe-...Sometimes," Ohio Legal Ethics Update, August 2002. Co-Author: "Keeping Mediation a Private Process," National Law Journal, September 22, 1997; "Does Good Faith Avoid a Breach of Mediation Confidentiality?" Alternatives, October 1999; "What You Say (And Don't Say) in ADR," For the Defense, July 2000; "Keeping the 'R' in ADR," Alternatives, December 1999. Lecturer, "Professionalism in the Law: Good for Ethics or Good for Business?" Cleveland Bar Association, April 2001; "Ethics Issues in Interviewing Employees of Adverse Entities - The 'No-Contact' Rule," August 2001; "Ethics Issues for Attorneys in Commercial Transactions: Multijurisdiction Practice, Confidentiality and Conflicts of Interest," August 2002. ***PRACTICE AREAS:*** Legal Ethics and Professional Responsibility; Professional Liability; Litigation; Business Law; Products Liability Defense; Chemical Products Liability. ***Email:*** Karen.Rubin@ThompsonHine.com

DELISA Y. RUSSELL, born September 20, 1969; admitted to bar, 2001, Ohio; 2002, Indiana. *Education:* Southern Illinois University (B.S., 1991); Indiana University School of Law (J.D., 2001). *Member:* Cleveland Bar Association; Ohio State Bar Association; American Bar Association. ***PRACTICE AREAS:*** Corporate Transactions; Securities. ***Email:*** Delisa.Springfield@ThompsonHine.com

ROBYN M. SMYERS, born Cleveland, Ohio, October 5, 1969; admitted to bar, 1998, New York; 2001, Ohio. *Education:* Harvard University (B.A., cum laude, 1991); Yale University (J.D., 1997). Earl Warren/NAACP Legal Defense Fund Scholar. Author: "High Noon in Public Housing: The Showdown Between Due Process Rights and Good Management Practices," The Urban Lawyer, Summer 1998. Trustee, Board of Directors, Karamu House, Inc. Citizen Member, Shaker Heights City Council Economic Development Committee. Advisory Committee Member, Albert A. Levin Chair of Urban Studies at The Levin College of Urban Affairs at Cleveland State University. Member of Class of 2002, Cleveland Bridge Builders. *Member:* The Association of the Bar of The City of New York (Member, Housing and Urban Development Committee, 1997-2000); Ohio State and American (Member, Real Estate Section) Bar Associations; International Council of Shopping Centers; Commercial Real Estate Women. ***PRACTICE AREAS:*** Real Estate. ***Email:*** Robyn.Smyers@ThompsonHine.com

JEREMY S. SOSIN, born Indianapolis, Indiana; admitted to bar, 1997, Connecticut; 1998, New York; 2000, U.S. District Court, Southern and Eastern Districts of New York; 2004, Ohio. *Education:* Indiana University (B.A., 1994); Valparaiso University School of Law (J.D., 1997). ***PRACTICE AREAS:*** Real Estate. ***Email:*** Jeremy.Sosin@ThompsonHine.com

RACHEL J. TATTER, born May 9, 1975; admitted to bar, 2001, Ohio. *Education:* The Ohio State University (B.A., cum laude, 1998); Georgetown University (J.D., 2001). Phi Beta Kappa. *Member:* Cleveland, Ohio State and American Bar Associations. ***PRACTICE AREAS:*** Real Estate. ***Email:*** Rachel.Tatter@ThompsonHine.com

CURTIS L. TUGGLE, born Marion, Ohio, 1977; admitted to bar, 2004, Ohio; 2005, U.S. District Court, Northern District of Ohio. *Education:* The Ohio State University (B.A., summa cum laude, 2001); The Ohio State University - Moritz College of Law (J.D., 2004). *Member:* Cleveland, Ohio State and American Bar Associations. ***PRACTICE AREAS:*** Bankruptcy; Business Litigation. ***Email:*** Curtis.Tuggle@ThompsonHine.com

ANDREW L. TURSCAK, JR., born Youngstown, Ohio, September 6, 1964; admitted to bar, 2001, Ohio; 2002, U.S. District Court, Northern District of Ohio; 2004, U.S. District Court, Southern District of Ohio. *Education:* Youngstown State University (B.A., 1988); Cleveland-Marshall College of Law (J.D., 2001). Author: "School Principals and New York Times: Ohio's Narrow Reading of Who is a Public Official or Public Figure," 48 Cleveland State Law Review 169, 2000. *Member:* Cleveland Bar Association; Ohio State Bar Association. ***PRACTICE AREAS:*** Bankruptcy (70%); Litigation (30%). ***Email:*** Andrew.Turscak@ThompsonHine.com

GARY L. WALTERS, born Monroe, Michigan, 1956; admitted to bar, 1999, Ohio; U.S. District Court, Northern District of Ohio; U.S. District Court, Eastern District of Wisconsin; U.S. Court of Appeals, Third, Sixth and Ninth Circuits. *Education:* Auburn University (B.A., with highest honors, 1988); Command and General Staff College, School of Advanced Military Studies, United States Army (M.M.A.S., 1994); Cornell University Law School (J.D., 1999). [Major, U.S. Army, 1975-1996]. ***PRACTICE AREAS:*** Business Litigation; Banking Litigation; Professional Liability Litigation; Products Liability Litigation; Tax Litigation; Class Actions; Alternative Dispute Resolution. ***Email:*** Gary.Walters@ThompsonHine.com

MARK A. WEINTRAUB, born Cleveland, Ohio; admitted to bar, 2005, Ohio and U.S. District Court, Northern District of Ohio. *Education:* Miami University (B.S., 1984); Cleveland-Marshall College of Law (J.D., cum laude, 2004). *Member:* Cleveland, Ohio State and American Bar Associations. ***PRACTICE AREAS:*** Bankruptcy. ***Email:*** Mark.Weintraub@ThompsonHine.com

KATE B. WEXLER, born Kings Lynn, Norfolk, England; admitted to bar, 2002, Ohio. *Education:* Vassar College (B.A., 1985); St. John's University (M.B.A., 1989); Case Western Reserve University School of Law (J.D., cum laude, 2002). *Member:* Cleveland and Ohio State Bar Associations. ***LANGUAGES:*** French. ***PRACTICE AREAS:*** Corporate Transactions; Securities. ***Email:*** Kate.Wexler@ThompsonHine.com

(This Listing Continued)

NICOLE K. WILSON, born Warren, Ohio, April 29, 1976; admitted to bar, 2002, Ohio and U.S. District Court, Northern District of Ohio. *Education:* Thomas Aquinas College (B.A., 1998); Duke University School of Law (J.D., 2001). ***PRACTICE AREAS:*** Business Litigation; Products Liability. ***Email:*** Nicole.Wilson@Thompsonhine.com

ROBIN M. WILSON, born East Cleveland, Ohio, March 26, 1961; admitted to bar, 1996, Ohio and U.S. District Court, Northern District of Ohio; 1998, U.S. Court of Appeals, Sixth Circuit. *Education:* Ohio University (B.S., Journalism, 1983); Cleveland Marshall College of Law (J.D., cum laude, 1996). Recipient, Burton Award for Legal Achievement, 2005. Author: "Are Cybersmear Suits Worth the Effort?" NE Ohio Crain Tech, September 10, 2002; "Employees Cyber Behavior Could Get Employer in Trouble," The Alert, Federal Bar Association, March 1998. Co-Author, "Negotiating the Minefields of Electronic Discovery," 10 RICH. J.L. & TECH. 52 (2004), http://law.richmond.edu/jolt. Contributor, "Meet the Press," Cleveland Bar Journal, September 2001. Former Assistant County Prosecutor, Civil Division, Stark County, Ohio. Life Member, Cleveland-Marshall Law Alumni Association. *Member:* Cleveland (Member, Justice for All Committee), Cuyahoga County (Member, ADR Committee) and Ohio State Bar Associations. ***LANGUAGES:*** Spanish. ***REPORTED CASES:*** State of Ohio v. McCaulley (February 3, 1997, Stark County), 1997 Ohio App. LEXIS 1045, in which the 5th District upheld a trial court decision to grant a permanent injunction for a resident's violation of zoning regulations; Kaufman & Cumberland v. Jalisi (August 8, 2002, Cuyahoga County), 2002 Ohio App. LEXIS 4252, in which the 8th District upheld the granting of a default judgment finding that the trial court had jurisdiction over the matter. ***PRACTICE AREAS:*** Business Litigation (75%); Products Liability Defense (25%). ***Email:*** Robin.Wilson@ThompsonHine.com

AUDRA J. ZARLENGA, born Youngstown, Ohio, May 1, 1970; admitted to bar, 1996, Ohio. *Education:* University of Cincinnati (B.A., 1992); Cleveland-Marshall College of Law (J.D., 1995). *Member:* Cleveland (Chairwoman, Juvenile Justice Committee), Cuyahoga County (Member, Guardian Ad Litem Advisory Council) and Ohio State (Member, Construction Law Subcommittee) Bar Associations. ***PRACTICE AREAS:*** Construction Law. ***Email:*** Audra.Zarlenga@ThompsonHine.com

OF COUNSEL

HEATHER ALEY AUSTIN, born Pittsburgh, Pennsylvania, April 28, 1968; admitted to bar, 1993, Ohio; 2000 Pennsylvania. *Education:* Allegheny College (B.A., cum laude, in Political Science, 1990); University of Pittsburgh (J.D., cum laude, 1993). Author: "Corporate Social Responsibility - New Pressures In A Sustainable Environment"; Cleveland Bar Association; April 2003; "USEPA and Ohio Compromise on Audit Privilege Law"; OSBA Corporate News; Spring 1999; "Preventing a Toxic Tort Suit"; Environmental Manager's Compliance Advisor; May 18, 1998; "EPA to Clean Up Audit Privileges"; Crain's Cleveland Business; January 12, 1998; "Lawyer Advises Caution With Ohio Audit Privilege"; Environmental Manager's Compliance Advisor; February 16, 1998; "Audit Law Amended to Suit U.S. EPA"; Crain's Cleveland Business; August 17, 1998; Co-Authored with Heidi Goldstein, "Complex Regs Keeping Many From Cleaning Up Brownfields," Crain's Cleveland Business; April 2001. Lecturer: "Environmental Issues in Commercial Transactions: Diligence and Insurance", OSBA/CLE, September 23, 2003; "Environmental Issues in Real Estate Transactions", National Business Institute's Advanced Commercial Real Estate Seminar; July 24, 2003; "Indemnification Panel: Doing the Deal, Bridging the Gap with Environmental Insurance," Cleveland Bar Association, November 14, 2001; "Buying and Selling a Business in Ohio: Bridging the Gap with Environmental Insurance," Ohio Bar Association's Environmental Law Seminar, April 29, 2001; "The Innocent Purchaser Defense in Commercial Real Estate Transactions," Inland Spills Conference, September 22, 1999; "Environmental Considerations in Commercial Real Estate Transactions," Ohio CLE Institute, July 27, 2001 and October 22, 1998; "Preparing for an Environmental Catastrophe," Planner and Moderator of Columbus Bar Association CLE, December 9, 1999; "Corporate Management of Citizens' Suits," Air and Waste Management Association, April 22, 1998; Environmental Law Expert, University for Young Americans. Chairperson, Cleveland Great Strides Walkathon, Cystic Fibrosis Foundation. Executive Committee, Cystic Fibrosis Foundation. Member, Fundraising Committee, Cleveland Works. Chair, Southminster Nursery School Board of Directors; Chair of Finance Committee and Member of Allegheny College Alumni Council. *Member:* Cleveland (Member, Environmental Law Section), Ohio State (Member, Environmental Law Committee) and Pennsylvania Bar Associations. ***LANGUAGES:*** Spanish. ***TRANSACTIONS:*** Representation of clients in the chemical, pulp and paper, aluminum, powder metal, steel, plastic, medical, food and automotive industries on all environmental aspects of the purchase, sale and post closing diligence of businesses and business assets; Representation of clients in Ohio, Pennsylvania and Michigan voluntary action programs; Representation of clients under New Jersey's Industrial Sites Recovery Cleanup Program; Representation of venture capital fund on environmental issues regardings acquisitions and investments in portfolio companies and post-closing environmental compliance; Representation of client in the chemical industry relating to SEC disclosure requirements; Representation of construction demolition debris and solid waste landfill client on all permitting, legislative and compliance issues; Representation of lending institutions on environmental issues relating to various transactions; Representation of a hospital in connection with environmental compliance and permitting issues; Representation of clients in the powder metal industry in Brownfield redevelopment projects; Representation of waste management company in a toxic tort suit regarding the land application of biosolids. ***PRACTICE AREAS:*** Environmental Law; Natural Resources; Mergers, Acquisitions and Divestitures (Environmental aspects). ***Email:*** Heather.Austin@ThompsonHine.com

MALVIN E. BANK, born Philadelphia, Pennsylvania, May 22, 1930; admitted to bar, 1957, Ohio. *Education:* Pennsylvania State University (B.A., 1952); Yale University (LL.B., 1957). Listed in: Who's Who in America; Who's Who in American Law; The Best Lawyers in America, 1985—. Editor, Yale Law Journal, 1956-1957. Former General Counsel, The Cleveland Foundation. [U.S. Army, Korea, 1952-1954; Bronze Star; Presidential Unit Citation; Commendation Ribbon]. ***PRACTICE AREAS:*** Charitable Trusts and Foundations; Federal Tax Law; Tax Planning; Tax Exempt Organizations. ***Email:*** Mal.Bank@ThompsonHine.com

BRIAN L. GAJ, born Cleveland, Ohio, December 19, 1959; admitted to bar, 1984, Michigan; 1985, Ohio. *Education:* Case Western Reserve University (B.A., 1981); Cornell University (J.D., 1984). Order of the Coif; Phi Beta Kappa. *Member:* American Bar Association. ***TRANSACTIONS:*** Advising on ERISA fiduciary issues, cash balance plans, and multiemployer withdrawal liability; drafting welfare and pension plan documents, summary plan descriptions ("SPDs"), and plan QDRO procedures; and preparing IRS determination letter filings and IRS Voluntary Compliance Program Submissions. ***PRACTICE AREAS:*** Employee Benefits Law; ERISA; Pension and Profit Sharing Law. ***Email:*** Brian.Gaj@ThompsonHine.com

WILLIAM D. GINN, born Philadelphia, Pennsylvania, December 17, 1923; admitted to bar, 1951, Ohio; 1975, U.S. Supreme Court. *Education:* Bates College (A.B., 1947); Yale University (LL.B., 1950). Phi Beta Kappa. Forum on the Construction Industry. Member, National Council of Juvenile and Family Court Judges. (Retired). ***Email:*** Bill.Ginn@ThompsonHine.com

DANIEL W. HAMMER, born Cleveland, Ohio, December 30, 1932; admitted to bar, 1959, Ohio; 1965, U.S. Supreme Court. *Education:* University of Notre Dame (B.S., 1954; LL.B., 1959). American Inns of Court. Master Bencher. Fellow: American College of Trial Lawyers; American Bar Foundation. Life Member, 6th Circuit Judicial Conference; 8th Appellate Judicial Conference. *Member:* Cleveland Bar Association (President, 1993-1994). ***PRACTICE AREAS:*** Litigation; Business and Commercial Litigation; Securities Litigation. ***Email:*** Dan.Hammer@ThompsonHine.com

KENT L. MANN, born Oklahoma City, Oklahoma, July 1, 1951; admitted to bar, 1976, Ohio; 1985, U.S. Tax Court. *Education:* Dartmouth College (A.B., magna cum laude, 1973); Duke University (J.D., with honors, 1976). Author: "Retirement Plans Available for all Stages," Crain's Cleveland Business, November 13, 1995. Lecturer: "Executive Compensation and Benefits: Beyond Qualified Retirement Plans," Cleveland Benefits Council, 2002; "Broad Based Stock Options," Ohio Employee Ownership Center Annual Conference, 2000; "Tax Issues in the Settlement of Employment Litigation," Cleveland Bar Association Labor and Employment Law Seminar, 2000; "Drafting the Employee Handbook - Benefit Policies," Ohio CLE Institute, 1997, 1999; "Taxability of Medical Negligence Verdicts and Settlements," The Ohio Academy of Trial Lawyers, 1997; "Current Developments in Employee Benefits," Cleveland Tax Institute, 1997; "Stock Ownership Plans," The Growth Association Council of Smaller Enterprises, 1996; "Executive Compensation Planning for the 21st Century," Cleveland Chapter of WEB, 1996; "Ohio Sales and Use Tax," National Business Institute, Inc., 1993; "This Distribution Is Too Much, This Distribution Is Too Little, and This Distribution Is Just Right," Cleveland Tax Institute, 1993; "Developments in Employment Tax Compliance," Ohio Hospital Association, 1993; "How an ESOP Works," National Center for Employee Ownership, 1991; "Employment Tax Matters Relating to Health Care Organizations," National Health Lawyers Association, Tax Planning for Nonprofit Health Care Organizations, 1989. Member: WEB Network of Benefit Professionals. Treasurer, 1987—, Distinguished Scholar Lecture Series. Member, Dartmouth College Alumni Council, 1988-1991. Trustee, The Garden Center of Greater Cleveland, 1989-1991. Member, Duke Law Alumni Association Board of Directors, 2000-2003. *Member:* Cleveland, Ohio State and American (Member, Tax Section) Bar Associations; The ESOP Association. ***PRACTICE AREAS:*** Taxation Law; Employee Benefits; Private Companies. ***Email:*** Kent.Mann@ThompsonHine.com

CATHY B. PANZICA, born Columbus, Ohio, 1962; admitted to bar, 1986, Ohio. *Education:* University of Michigan (B.A., with distinction, 1983); The Ohio State University, Moritz College of Law (J.D., 1986). Practiced abroad in London 1989-2002. Ordained Episcopal Priest. *Member:* Ohio State and American Bar Associations; Association of Women Lawyers in London. ***PRACTICE AREAS:*** Corporate; Mergers and Acquisitions; Information Technology. ***Email:*** Cathy.Panzica@ThompsonHine.com

PATRICK J. SACCOGNA, born Cleveland, Ohio; admitted to bar, 1990, Ohio. *Education:* Kent State University (B.B.A., summa cum laude, 1987); Case Western Reserve University (J.D., magna cum laude, 1990; LL.M., Taxation, 1999). Beta Gamma Sigma; Beta Alpha Psi; Order of the Coif. Recipient, American Jurisprudence Award, Evidence, 1989. Certified Public Accountant, Ohio, 1997. Co-Author: "It's No Longer 'Out of Sight, Out of Mind' in Ohio: House Bill 73, A First Step Toward Relaxing Ohio's Residency Requirements While Strengthening Ohio's Nonprofits and Bolstering Ohio's Coffers," Probate Law Journal of Ohio, July/August 2005. Author: "The CARE Act: Does Congress Care Enough?" Leave A Legacy News, Summer 2005; "Estate Tax Repeal: A Glimpse of the Future?" Crain's Cleveland Business, November 12, 2001; "Gifting Programs: Advantages and Disadvantages," Crain's Cleveland Business, November 13, 2000; "The Most Common Family Business Mistakes Can Be Avoided," Family Business Journal, Winter 1999; "The Family Business: Why It's A Brand New Ballgame!" Crain's Cleveland Business, November 22, 1999; "The Five Most Common Family Business Mistakes," Crain's Cleveland Business, November 2, 1998; "Looking to the Future: What Changes Might Be In Store for Estate and Gift Taxes," Family Business Journal, Summer 1998. Speaker: "Bailouts From Sales to Defective Grantor Trusts," Cleveland Bar Association Estate Planning Institute, 2004; "Exploring the Universe of Business Succession Planning Options," Cleveland Bar Association, 2003; "Federal Taxation Update," Ohio State Bar Association Annual Convention, 2002; "Planning Opportunities and Challenges Under the 2001 Tax Act," Northern Ohio Planned Giving Council, 2001; "Making Financial Sense-Tax Cuts, Credits and Savings," The Cleveland Museum of Art Planned Giving Council, 2001; "Estate Planning With Real Estate," Cleveland Bar Association Real Estate Law Institute, 2000; "Federal Developments-Highlights," Cleveland Bar Association Estate Planning Institute, 1999; "Recent Developments in the Family Limited Partnership and Valuation Areas," Akron Estate Planning Council, 1999; "The Installment Sale to a Defective Grantor Trust," North Central Ohio Estate Planning Council, 1999; "Business Succession Planning," Tax Club of Cleveland, 1999; "Valuation Issues Regarding Family Limited Partnerships," Toledo Bar Association Annual Probate Seminar, 1998; "The Final GST Tax Regulations," Estate Planning Council of Cleveland, 1996. Ohio Society of Certified Public Accountants Annual Accounting Shows, 1996-2000; National Business Institutes, 1996-1999. Member, Planned Giving Council, The Cleveland Museum of Art. Member, Estate Planning Discussion Group. *Member:* Cleveland Bar Association (Vice-Chair, 2005— and Member, Council of Delegates, 2003—, Section on: Estate Planning, Probate, and Trust Law); Northern Ohio Planned Giving Council (Secretary, 2003—; Member, Board of Trustees, 2001—); Estate Planning Council of Cleveland (President, 2001-2002; Member, Board of Trustees, 1997-2002). ***PRACTICE AREAS:*** Estate Planning; Business Succession Planning; Estate, Gift and Generation Skipping Transfer Taxation; Probate. ***Email:*** Patrick.Saccogna@ThompsonHine.com

(This Listing Continued)

(This Listing Continued)

THOMPSON HINE LLP, Cleveland—Continued

SENIOR ATTORNEYS

SUSAN L. BELMAN, born Hartford, Connecticut, September 10, 1951; admitted to bar, 1977, Ohio; U.S. District Court, Northern District of Ohio. *Education:* Princeton University (B.A., cum laude, 1973); Columbia University (M.A., 1974); Case Western Reserve University (J.D., 1977). Order of the Coif. *Member:* Cleveland and Ohio State Bar Associations. ***PRACTICE AREAS:*** Business Law; Commercial Litigation; Product Liability. ***Email:*** Susan.Belman@ThompsonHine.com

DIANE S. LEUNG, born Akron, Ohio; admitted to bar, 1992, Ohio. *Education:* College of Wooster (B.A., 1978); Phi Beta Kappa; Kent State University (M.L.S., 1985); Cleveland Marshall College of Law (J.D., summa cum laude, 1992). Lecturer: "The Lender/Tenant Relationship," Ohio CLE Institute: Commercial Real Estate, Buying, Selling or Leasing, July 26, 2000, October 22, 1998 and April 30, 1998. Board Member, Living in Cleveland Center, 1996—. Honoree, YWCA Women of Professional Excellence, 1999 and 2000. Member, Commercial Real Estate Women. Member, Planning Committee and Moderator, 1997, 1998, 1999, 2000 and 2001 Institutes, Cleveland Bar Association Real Estate Law Institute. Member, Genealogical Committee, 1998—, Western Reserve Historical Society. Member, 1998—, Reporting Secretary, 1999-2001, North Royalton High School Band Boosters. *Member:* Cleveland Bar Association (Member, Real Estate Section). ***TRANSACTIONS:*** Representation of national commercial lender in connection with the issuance of letters of credit as credit enhancement for financing for numerous low income multifamily housing tax credit projects in Alabama, Arkansas, Arizona, California, Florida, Nevada, Tennessee and the State of Washington; Representation of national commercial lender in connection with a pool of securitized loans; Representation of national developer in connection with the full and partial defeasances of securitized loans; Representation of borrowers and lenders, as local Ohio counsel, in multi-state financing transactions; Representation of local lender in connection with more than 125 loans to refinance apartment complexes in Ohio, Michigan, Pennsylvania, West Virginia and Kentucky; Representation of life insurance company in connection with loans for Ohio shopping centers and office buildings; Representation of local nonprofit lender in its issuance of loans for various rehabilitation or new construction projects in the City of Cleveland; Representation of seller in connection with $250,000,000 sale of its multi-state portfolio of radio stations; Representation of client in its acquisition and later sale of 175 communications towers located throughout the United States; Representation of a national jewelry store tenant in negotiating mall leases; Representation of a national records management firm in its acquisition of Ohio facilities; Representation of the owner of a medical office building in drafting and negotiating physician leases; Representation of a national wireless communications company in negotiating and preparing ground leases for the placement of communications towers. ***PRACTICE AREAS:*** Real Estate. ***Email:*** Diane.Leung@ThompsonHine.com

PAMELA ZARLINGO, born Youngstown, Ohio, October 27, 1950; admitted to bar, 1989, Ohio; 1990, District of Columbia. *Education:* Westminster College (B.A., 1985); Case Western Reserve University (J.D., 1988). *Member:* Cleveland Bar Association; Maritime Law Association. ***PRACTICE AREAS:*** Admiralty Law; Products Liability; Litigation. ***Email:*** Pam.Zarlingo@ThompsonHine.com

STAFF ATTORNEYS

BYRON J. HORN, born Columbus, Ohio, April 27, 1964; admitted to bar, 1989, Ohio. *Education:* Kenyon College (B.A., 1986); Case Western Reserve University (J.D., 1989). ***PRACTICE AREAS:*** Products Liability; Litigation. ***Email:*** Byron.Horn@ThompsonHine.com

LORI A. PITTMAN, born Athens, Ohio; admitted to bar, 2004, Ohio. *Education:* Youngstown State University (B.S., B.A., 1997); Akron University Law School (J.D., 2004). *Member:* Cleveland (Member, Real Estate Section), Ohio State and American (Member, Real Property, Probate and Trust Law Section) Bar Associations; Commercial Real Estate Women - CREW (Member, Cleveland Chapter). ***PRACTICE AREAS:*** Real Estate (90%). ***Email:*** Lori.Pittman@ThompsonHine.com

LEGAL SUPPORT PERSONNEL

STEVEN M. MAURO. *Education:* Boston College (B.A.); Villanova University (M.B.A.); Widener University School of Law (J.D.). Certified Public Accountant, New Jersey. ***Email:*** Steve.Mauro@ThompsonHine.com

(For complete biographical data on Lawyers in Offices other than Cleveland, see Professional Biographies at the Respective Office Location)

THORMAN & HARDIN-LEVINE

1220 WEST 6TH STREET, SUITE 307
CLEVELAND, OHIO 44113
Telephone: 216-621-9767
Fax: 216-621-3422
URL: http://www.thllaw.com
Email: plevine@thllaw.com
Email: cthorman@thllaw.com
URL: http://www.lawyers.com/christopherthorman

Employment Law, Civil Rights, Discrimination, Harassment, Job Termination.

MEMBERS OF FIRM

CHRISTOPHER P. THORMAN, born Cincinnati, Ohio, October 24, 1963; admitted to bar, 1991, Ohio and U.S. District Court, Northern and Southern Districts of Ohio; 1996, U.S. Court of Appeals, Sixth Circuit; 1997, U.S. Supreme Court. *Education:* Kenyon College (A.B., with high honors and distinction, 1986); Columbia University (M.A., 1986); Case Western Reserve University (J.D., cum laude, 1991). Executive Notes Editor, 1990-1991 and Member, 1989-1990, Case Western Reserve Law Review. Law Clerk to Judge Ann Aldrich, U.S. District Court, Northern District of Ohio, 1994-1996. Assistant Regional Attorney, Office for Civil Rights, U.S. Department of Education, 1993-1994. *Member:* Cleveland, Cuyahoga and Ohio State Bar Associations; The Association of Trial Lawyers of America; Ohio Academy of Trial Lawyers; National and Ohio Employment Lawyer's Association. ***PRACTICE AREAS:*** Employment Law; Discrimination; Civil Rights; Harassment; Employment Termination. ***Email:*** cthorman@thllaw.com

PETER S. HARDIN-LEVINE, born Cleveland, Ohio, January 15, 1959; admitted to bar, 1984, Ohio and U.S. District Court, Northern and Southern Districts of Ohio; 2000, Michigan. *Education:* Northwestern University (B.A., with honors, 1981); University of Michigan (J.D., 1984). Associate, Benesch, Friedlander, Coplan & Aronoff, 1984-1985. Trial Attorney, Equal Employment Opportunity Commission, 1985-1988. Law Professor, Case Western Reserve University, 1988-1990. Counsel, Senior Counsel, VP and Assistant General Counsel, TRW Inc., 1990-2001. Partner, Baker & Hostetler, 2002-2004. *Member:* Cleveland, Cuyahoga County, Ohio State and American Bar Associations. ***PRACTICE AREAS:*** Employment Law; Business. ***Email:*** plevine@thllaw.com

RYAN A. SOBEL, born Highland Park, Illinois; admitted to bar, 2004, Ohio; 2005, U.S. District Court, Northern District of Ohio. *Education:* Miami University (B.A., 2001); Case Western Reserve University (J.D., magna cum laude, 2004) Order of the Coif. Phi Delta Phi (Magister, 2003-2004). Member, National Moot Court Team, 2003-2004. Recipient: Paul J. Hergenroeder Award for Trial Advocacy; CALI Award in Product Liability, Admiralty, Complex Litigation, Trial Tactics and Lawyering Process. ***PRACTICE AREAS:*** Labor and Employment; Civil Rights. ***Email:*** rsobel@thllaw.com

TIPPING CO., L.P.A.

A LEGAL PROFESSIONAL ASSOCIATION

CLEVELAND, OHIO

(See Akron)

General Civil Trial and Appellate Practice, Negligence, Personal Injury, Business, Commercial, Corporate, Probate, Workers Compensation, Administrative, Insurance, Real Estate, Bankruptcy, Estate Planning, Labor/Employment, Zoning, Municipal Law and Social Security Disability Law.

TOEREK CO., LPA

29525 CHAGRIN BOULEVARD, SUITE 208
CLEVELAND, OHIO 44122
Telephone: 216-360-9919
Fax: 216-360-7450

Copyrights, Trademarks, Business Law.

SHARON L. TOEREK, born Lakewood, Ohio, August 19, 1963; admitted to bar, 1991, Ohio. *Education:* Cleveland State University (B.A., Political Science, 1985); Cleveland Marshall College of Law (J.D., 1991). Recipient: Rising Star Award and Networking Award, National Association of Women Business Owners; New Member of the Year Award, Women's City Club. Judicial Extern to Honorable Alvin I. Krenzier, U.S. District Court, Northern District of Ohio. Seminar Speaker, Akron Advertising Association. Founding Partner, Mcedonio, Toerek & Box, PLL (nks Toerek Co. LPA). Formerly with Thompson, Hine and Flory, 1985-1993. Member, Northeast Ohio Software Association. Volunteer Attorney, Adult Guardianship Services. Guardian Ad Litem, Cuyahoga County Juvenile Court. Board Director, Greater Cleveland Partnership's Council of Small Enterprises. *Member:* Cleveland (Vice Chair, 2000 and Chair, 2001, Intellectual Property Committee) and Ohio State Bar Associations; National Association of Women Business Owners (President, Cleveland Chapter); Growth Association Council of Smaller Enterprises (Board Member). ***PRACTICE AREAS:*** Copyrights; Trademarks; Intellectual Property Law; Business Law. ***Email:*** sltoerek@ameritech.net

TORRES WILLIAMS CO. LPA

75 PUBLIC SQUARE, SUITE 800
CLEVELAND, OHIO 44113
Telephone: 216-771-6303
Fax: 216-771-6993
URL: http://www.torreswilliams.com

Family Law, Divorce, Child Support, Immigration Law, Business Dissolutions, Business Successions, Personal Injury, Creditors Rights, Bankruptcy, Litigation, Wills, Probate, Trusts and Estates, Estate Planning, Criminal Law.

JOSE A. TORRES-RAMIREZ, born Mayaguez, Puerto Rico, January 13, 1966; admitted to bar, 1994, Ohio and Puerto Rico. *Education:* Interamerican University of Puerto Rico (B.A., 1988); Pontifical Catholic University (J.D., 1993). *Member:* Puerto Rico and Ohio State Bar Associations. ***LANGUAGES:*** Spanish, Italian and French. ***PRACTICE AREAS:*** Family Law; Divorce; Immigration Law; Business Dissolutions; Personal Injury. ***Email:*** jtorres@torreswilliams.com

KATHRYN A. WILLIAMS, born Detroit, Michigan, February 22, 1970; admitted to bar, 1998, Ohio; 1999, U.S. District Court, Northern District of Ohio. *Education:* University of Pennsylvania (B.A., 1992; M.G.A., 1994); Case Western Reserve University (J.D., 1997). Delta Sigma Theta. Member, International Women's Insolvency and Restructuring Confederation. Member, Bankruptcy Court Strategic Planning Committee, Northern District of Ohio. *Member:* Cleveland Bar Association; Norman S. Minor Bar Association; William K. Thomas Inn of Court; International Women's Insolvency and Restructuring Confederation (WIRC) (Member, Network Steering Committee). ***LANGUAGES:*** Spanish. ***PRACTICE AREAS:*** Creditors Rights; Bankruptcy; Family Law; Child Support; Litigation; Wills; Probate; Trusts and Estates; Estate Planning; Business Successions; Commercial Litigation; Contracts. ***Email:*** kwilliams@torreswilliams.com

(This Listing Continued)

TRIVERS & DICKERSON, LLC

55 ERIEVIEW PLAZA, SUITE 220
CLEVELAND, OHIO 44114
Telephone: 216-696-5444
Fax: 216-696-3937
URL: http://www.triversanddickersonlaw.com

Criminal Law, Family Law, Personal Injury, Divorce.

OSCAR TRIVERS, born Birmingham, Alabama, February 2, 1934; admitted to bar, 1960, Ohio. *Education:* Hiram College (B.A., 1956); Case Western Reserve University (J.D., 1960).

EMMANUEL EUGENE DICKERSON (1919-2003)

ATTORNEYS

EDWIN KELLY, born Cleveland, Ohio, October 5, 1948; admitted to bar, 1986, Ohio. *Education:* Ohio University (B.S.ED., 1970); Baldwin-Wallace College (M.B.A., 1980); Cleveland-Marshall College of Law (J.D., 1986).

REGINALD MAXTON, born Cincinnati, Ohio, December 5, 1948; admitted to bar, 1993, Ohio. *Education:* Antioch College (B.A., 1976); Cleveland-Marshall College of Law (J.D., 1993). ***PRACTICE AREAS:*** Criminal Law; Family Law; Personal Injury.

ULMER & BERNE LLP

Established in 1908

SKYLIGHT OFFICE TOWER
1660 WEST 2ND STREET, SUITE 1100
CLEVELAND, OHIO 44113-1448
Telephone: 216-583-7000
Fax: 216-583-7001
Email: infocleveland@ulmer.com
URL: http://www.ulmer.com

Columbus, Ohio Office: 88 East Broad Street, Suite 1600. Telephone: 614-229-0000. FAX: 614-229-0001.

Cincinnati, Ohio Office: 600 Vine Street, Suite 2800. Telephone: 513-698-5000. FAX: 513-698-5001.

Chicago, Illinois Office: One North Franklin Street, Suite 1825. Telephone: 312-324-8000. FAX: 312-324-8001.

Antitrust; Banking and Commercial Lending; Broker/Dealer and Securities Litigation; Business Law; Business Litigation; Business Restructuring; Class Action Defense; Construction Law; Corporate Finance; Corporate Restructuring and Creditors' Rights; Corporate Succession Planning; Emerging Businesses; Employee Benefits; Employment and Labor; Environmental; Fair Housing; Financial Institution Compliance; General Counsel Services; Health Care; Income Tax; Insurance Coverage; Intellectual Property and Technology; Joint Ventures; Liability Defense; Mass Torts; Mergers, Acquisitions and Divestitures; Nonprofit; OSHA; Pharmaceutical; Product Liability; Public Law; Real Estate; Securities; Securities Regulatory Compliance; Subrogation; Tax; Technology Transactions; Toxic Tort Defense; Trade Secrets/ Unfair Competition; Trusts and Estates; Venture Capital; Workers' Compensation; Trial and Appellate Practice in All Courts.

FIRM PROFILE: Ulmer & Berne LLP, established in 1908, is one of Ohio's largest law firms, as well as one of its fastest growing. The firm has doubled in size in the last five years and tripled in size in the last 10. In the last 18 months alone, the firm has added 47 new lawyers. A full-service firm with over 185 attorneys in Cleveland, Columbus, Cincinnati and Chicago, Ulmer & Berne represents publicly traded and privately held companies, financial institutions, pharmaceutical companies, family businesses, international joint ventures and affiliations, investor groups, start-ups and emerging businesses, public bodies and nonprofit organizations. For more information, visit www.ulmer.com.

LAW FIRM ALLIANCES/ASSOCIATIONS: ***LAWYERS ASSOCIATED WORLDWIDE (L.A.W.)***

BUSINESS COUNSEL, INC.

PARTNERS

JENNIFER LAWRY ADAMS, born July 23, 1970; admitted to bar, 1996, Ohio. *Education:* Georgetown University (B.A., 1992); Case Western Reserve University (J.D., cum laude, 1996). ***PRACTICE AREAS:*** Business Law; Corporate Law; Finance; Mergers, Acquisitions and Divestitures; Securities. ***Email:*** jadams@ulmer.com

STEVEN W. ALBERT, born December 13, 1946; admitted to bar, 1971, Ohio. *Education:* American University (B.A., 1968); University of Toledo (J.D., 1971). ***PRACTICE AREAS:*** Professional Liability Defense; Business Litigation; Products Liability Defense. ***Email:*** salbert@ulmer.com

THOMAS H. BARNARD, born September 5, 1939; admitted to bar, 1964, Ohio; 1970, District of Columbia. *Education:* University of Puget Sound (B.A., 1961); Columbia University (LL.B., 1964); Case Western Reserve University (LL.M., 1970). With Office of the Solicitor, U.S. Department of Labor, 1968-1971. Deputy Counsel for Litigation, Division of Labor-Management Laws, 1970. Special Assistant, Division of Labor Relations and Civil Rights, 1971. Chair, Labor and Employment Law Section, Ohio State Bar Association, 1998-2000. Labor and Employment Law Specialty Board, Ohio State Bar Association, 1997—. Fellow, College of Labor and Employment Lawyers. (Chair, Employment & Labor Law Group). ***PRACTICE AREAS:*** Labor and Employment; Trial Practice. ***Email:*** tbarnard@ulmer.com

LEWIS T. BARR, born August 9, 1942; admitted to bar, 1967, Ohio. *Education:* University of Pennsylvania (B.S., 1964); University of Michigan (J.D., 1967). Author: "Tax Management Portfolio #780-3rd, Net Operating Losses," BNA. *Member:* American Law Institute. American College of Trust and Estate Counsel; American College of Tax Counsel. ***PRACTICE AREAS:*** Taxation; Trusts and Estates; Real Estate; Corporate Law. ***Email:*** lbarr@ulmer.com

BARTON A. BIXENSTINE, born January 8, 1950; admitted to bar, 1981, Ohio. *Education:* Kent State University (B.A., 1971); Indiana University (M.A., 1973; Ph.D., 1977); University of Chicago (J.D., 1981). (Certified Specialist in Labor & Employment Law, Ohio State Bar Association). ***PRACTICE AREAS:*** Employment Law; Civil Rights; Immigration and Naturalization; Alternative Dispute Resolution; Public Construction Law. ***Email:*** bbixenstine@ulmer.com

KENNETH A. BRAVO, born July 27, 1942; admitted to bar, 1967, Ohio and District of Columbia. *Education:* Rutgers University (B.S., 1964); The Ohio State University (J.D., cum laude, 1967). Trial Attorney, Criminal Division, U.S. Department of Justice, 1967-1979. Member: Ohio State Bar Association Council of Delegates, 1992—; Board of Governors, 2001-2004. ***PRACTICE AREAS:*** Complex Litigation; Securities Litigation; White Collar Criminal Defense; Financial Services Regulation; Aviation Law. ***Email:*** kbravo@ulmer.com

JOSEPH A. CASTRODALE, born March 3, 1958; admitted to bar, 1983, Ohio. *Education:* Youngstown State University (A.B., summa cum laude, 1980); Harvard University (J.D., magna cum laude, 1983). Co-Author: "Interference with Contractual, Business Prospective and Employment Relations and Opportunities," Chapters 11-14, Business Torts (c) Matthew Bender & Co., 1989. ***PRACTICE AREAS:*** Litigation. ***Email:*** jcastrodale@ulmer.com

INAJO DAVIS CHAPPELL, born September 30, 1960; admitted to bar, 1988, Ohio. *Education:* Yale University (B.A., with distinction in major, 1982); Columbia University (J.D., 1985). (Chair, Nonprofit Group). ***PRACTICE AREAS:*** Business Law; Corporate Law; Commercial Real Estate; Construction Law; Education Law; Government; Nonprofit and Charitable Organizations; Public Finance; Real Estate. ***Email:*** ichappell@ulmer.com

ROBERT E. CHUDAKOFF, born September 21, 1962; admitted to bar, 1987, Ohio. *Education:* Miami University (B.A., 1984); Case Western Reserve University (J.D., 1987). ***PRACTICE AREAS:*** Intellectual Property; Trademarks; Copyrights; Internet Law; Property Insurance Defense; Arson and Insurance Fraud; Insurance Bad Faith Defense. ***Email:*** rchudakoff@ulmer.com

GEORGE S. CRISCI, born May 30, 1958; admitted to bar, 1983, Ohio. *Education:* College of Wooster (B.A., with honors, Phi Beta Kappa, 1980); Case Western Reserve University (J.D., 1983). Order of the Coif. (Certified Specialist in Labor and Employment Law, Ohio State Bar Association). ***PRACTICE AREAS:*** Labor and Employment; Education Law; Public School Law; School Tenure; Teachers Credentials; Title IX Discrimination; Civil Rights; Civil Rights Defense; Civil Rights Section 1983; Discrimination; Race Discrimination; Sex Discrimination; Disabilities; Americans with Disabilities Act; Disability Discrimination; Government; Political Subdivision Liability. ***Email:*** gcrisci@ulmer.com

MARIA DEL MONACO, born November 16, 1961; admitted to bar, 1987, New York; 1988, Massachusetts; 1990, Michigan; 1997, Ohio. *Education:* Tufts University (B.A., summa cum laude, 1983); Harvard Law School (J.D., cum laude, 1986). ***PRACTICE AREAS:*** Complex Litigation; Commercial Litigation; Securities Litigation; RICO; Contract Litigation; Antitrust Law. ***Email:*** mdelmonaco@ulmer.com

TIMOTHY J. DOWNING, born June 2, 1963; admitted to bar, 1988, Pennsylvania; 1989, Ohio. *Education:* Allegheny College (B.A., with honors, 1985); Case Western Reserve University (J.D., 1988). Member, Board of Directors, Human Rights Campaign, 2003—. President, Board of Directors, Cleveland Film Society, 2002-2004. Member, Board of Trustees, Great Lakes Theater Festival, 2005—. *Member:* Ohio State Bar Association (Member, Council of Delegates). ***PRACTICE AREAS:*** Employment Law; Commercial Litigation; Nonprofit Organizations Law; Gay and Lesbian Rights. ***Email:*** tdowning@ulmer.com

JEFFREY S. DUNLAP, born August 17, 1963; admitted to bar, 1989, Illinois; 1997, Ohio. *Education:* Cornell University (B.S., with distinction, 1986); Harvard Law School (J.D., 1989). ***PRACTICE AREAS:*** Complex Litigation; Employment Law; Commercial Torts; Securities Litigation; Financial Services Regulation. ***Email:*** jdunlap@ulmer.com

WILLIAM D. EDWARDS, born July 25, 1967; admitted to bar, 1994, Ohio. *Education:* Wittenberg University (B.A., cum laude, 1989); Case Western Reserve University (J.D., 1993). Member, National Multi-Housing Council. (Chair, Fair Housing Group). ***PRACTICE AREAS:*** Employment and Labor Law; Employment Defense; Fair Housing Defense. ***Email:*** wdedwards@ulmer.com

ROBERT A. FEIN, born February 5, 1946; admitted to bar, 1970, Ohio. *Education:* The Ohio State University (B.S., 1967); Cleveland State University (J.D., cum laude, 1970). Law Review Editorial Board, 1970. (Member, Firm Management and Financial Committees). ***PRACTICE AREAS:*** Real Estate; Corporate Law; Business Law; Securities. ***Email:*** rfein@ulmer.com

HAROLD E. FRIEDMAN, born April 7, 1934; admitted to bar, 1959, Ohio. *Education:* The Ohio State University (B.Sc., 1956); Western Reserve University (LL.B., 1959). Order of the Coif. ***PRACTICE AREAS:*** Real Estate; Corporate Law; Health Law. ***Email:*** hfriedman@ulmer.com

BILL J. GAGLIANO, born July 6, 1955; admitted to bar, 1980, Ohio. *Education:* John Carroll University (B.S.B.A., 1977); Case Western Reserve University (J.D., 1980). American Bar Association Forum on Affordable Housing; American Red Cross National Board of Governors. (Chair, Real Estate Group). ***PRACTICE AREAS:*** Real Estate; Property Tax Appeals; Construction. ***Email:*** bgagliano@ulmer.com

JOHN C. GOHEEN, born March 17, 1951; admitted to bar, 1979, Wisconsin; 1983, Ohio. *Education:* Dartmouth College (A.B., magna cum laude, 1974); Georgetown University Law Center (J.D., cum laude, 1979). (Chair, Income Tax Group). ***PRACTICE AREAS:*** Taxation; Business Law; Corporate Law; Partnership Law; Trusts and Estates. ***Email:*** jgoheen@ulmer.com

FRANCES FLORIANO GOINS, born January 30, 1950; admitted to bar, 1977, Ohio; 1979, New York. *Education:* Cleveland Institute of Music (B.Mus., 1971); Case Western Reserve University (M.Mus., 1973; J.D., 1977). Order of the Coif. Recipient, Society of Benchers Award. Editor-in-Chief, Case Western Reserve University Law Review, 1976-

(This Listing Continued)

ULMER & BERNE LLP, Cleveland—Continued

1977. Member, Federal Court Panel of Alternative Dispute Resolution Neutrals. (Co-Chair, Financial Institutions, Securities & Broker-Dealer Group). *Member:* Cleveland (Member, Judicial Selection Committee) and American (Member: Business Law Section; Business and Corporate Litigation Subcommittee; SEC Enforcement Subcommittee; Corporate Governance Subcommittee) Bar Associations; Ohio Women's Bar Association; William K. Thomas American Inn of Court (Master of the Bench; Past President). ***PRACTICE AREAS:*** Banking Litigation; Takeovers; Proxy Contests; Corporate Governance; Securities Litigation; SEC Enforcement; Complex Business Litigation; Fiduciary Law; Insurance; Commercial Litigation; Civil Appeals. ***Email:*** fgoins@ulmer.com

JAMES A. GOLDSMITH, born April 10, 1955; admitted to bar, 1980, Ohio; 1981, Florida. *Education:* University of Denver (B.S.B.A., 1977); Case Western Reserve University (J.D., 1980). Past President, Estate Planning, Probate and Trust Law Section, Cleveland Bar Association. Fellow, American College of Trusts and Estates Counsel. (Chair, Trusts & Estates Group). ***PRACTICE AREAS:*** Trusts and Estates; Probate. ***Email:*** jgoldsmith@ulmer.com

HOWARD M. GROEDEL, born April 17, 1957; admitted to bar, 1982, District of Columbia; 1989, Maryland; 1992, Ohio. *Education:* Miami University (B.A., 1979); George Washington University Law School (J.D., 1982). ***PRACTICE AREAS:*** Securities Regulation; Corporate Law; Mergers and Acquisitions; Franchise Law. ***Email:*** hgroedel@ulmer.com

NEIL W. GURNEY, born June 4, 1952; admitted to bar, 1978, Ohio. *Education:* The Ohio State University (B.A., summa cum laude, 1974; J.D., 1977); University of Michigan (Danforth Fellow, School of Philosophy, 1975). ***PRACTICE AREAS:*** Corporate Law; Venture Capital; Commercial Finance; Real Estate; Estate Planning. ***Email:*** ngurney@ulmer.com

JOHN J. HAGGERTY, born March 3, 1967; admitted to bar, 1992, Pennsylvania and New Jersey; 2003, Ohio. *Education:* Franklin and Marshall College (B.A., cum laude, 1989); Temple University Law School (J.D., cum laude, 1992). ***PRACTICE AREAS:*** Litigation; Products Liability; Toxic Torts; Commercial Law; Intellectual Property. ***Email:*** jhaggerty@ulmer.com

RICHARD G. HARDY, born October 29, 1953; admitted to bar, 1978, Ohio. *Education:* University of Iowa (B.A., 1975); Case Western Reserve University (J.D., 1978). (Chair, Corporate Restructuring & Creditors' Rights Group). (Certified in Business Bankruptcy Law by the American Board of Certification). ***PRACTICE AREAS:*** Bankruptcy Reorganization; Commercial Workouts; Secured Creditors Rights; Bankruptcy Litigation. ***Email:*** rhardy@ulmer.com

RONALD H. ISROFF, born May 11, 1943; admitted to bar, 1967, Ohio. *Education:* Boston University (B.S., 1964); The Ohio State University (J.D., 1967). (Chair, Business Litigation Group; Member, Firm Management Committee). Member, Board of Trustees, Cleveland Bar Association, 1995-1998. ***PRACTICE AREAS:*** Complex Litigation; Employment Litigation; Covenants Not To Compete; Noncompete Litigation; Trade Secrets. ***Email:*** risroff@ulmer.com

RONALD L. KAHN, born November 5, 1946; admitted to bar, 1973, Ohio. *Education:* University of Pennsylvania (B.S., 1968); University of Michigan (J.D., 1973). Member, Employee Plans Panel of Great Lakes TE/GE IRS Advisory Council. ***PRACTICE AREAS:*** Employee Benefits; Health Care; Corporate Law; Business Law; Taxation; Nonprofit and Charitable Organizations; Trusts and Estates. ***Email:*** rkahn@ulmer.com

MARVIN L. KARP, born June 12, 1934; admitted to bar, 1958, Ohio. *Education:* Yale University (B.A., summa cum laude, 1955; LL.B., 1958). Life Member: Judicial Conference, U.S. Court of Appeals, Sixth Circuit. President, 1988-1989 and Member, Board of Trustees, 1981-1984, 1994—, Cleveland Bar Association. Chair, Section of Tort and Insurance Practice, 1990-1991; Chair, Standing Committee on Ethics and Professional Responsibility, 2001—2004, American Bar Association. Member, American Bar Association House of Delegates, 1992—. President, Federation of Defense and Corporate Counsel, 1994-1995. Fellow, American College of Trial Lawyers, International Academy of Trial Lawyers and American Bar Foundation. ***PRACTICE AREAS:*** Civil Litigation; Complex Litigation; Federal Litigation; Defense Litigation. ***Email:*** mkarp@ulmer.com

MARK D. KATZ, born April 26, 1949; admitted to bar, 1974, Ohio. *Education:* State University of New York at Buffalo (B.A. cum laude, 1970); Case Western Reserve University (J.D., 1974). ***PRACTICE AREAS:*** Occupational Safety and Health; Labor and Employment; Wage and Hour Law. ***Email:*** mkatz@ulmer.com

JAMES N. KLINE, born October 29, 1959; admitted to bar, 1984, Ohio. *Education:* University of Michigan (B.A., with honors, 1981); The Ohio State University (J.D., with honors, 1984). ***PRACTICE AREAS:*** First and Third Party Insurance Defense; Toxic Tort Defense; Products Liability Defense; Premises Liability Defense; Casualty Insurance Defense; Automobile Insurance Defense. ***Email:*** jkline@ulmer.com

STUART A. LAVEN, born February 13, 1943; admitted to bar, 1970, Ohio. *Education:* University of Pennsylvania (B.A., 1965); Case Western Reserve University (J.D., 1970). ***PRACTICE AREAS:*** Business Law; Real Estate; Securities; Corporate Law. ***Email:*** slaven@ulmer.com

MURRAY K. LENSON, born July 24, 1942; admitted to bar, 1968, Ohio. *Education:* Miami University (B.A., 1965); University of Toledo (J.D., 1968). Articles Editor, Toledo Law Review, 1967-1968. ***PRACTICE AREAS:*** Medical Malpractice Defense; Legal Malpractice Defense; Products Liability; Employment Defense. ***Email:*** mlenson@ulmer.com

DAVID L. LESTER, born October 9, 1958; admitted to bar, 1983, Ohio; 1989, California. *Education:* The Colorado College (B.A., 1980); Case Western Reserve University (J.D., 1983). ***PRACTICE AREAS:*** Insurance Coverage Defense; Insurance First Party Defense; Appellate Practice. ***Email:*** dlester@ulmer.com

BRUCE P. MANDEL, born March 16, 1951; admitted to bar, 1976, Ohio. *Education:* The Ohio State University (B.S., summa cum laude, 1973); Case Western Reserve University (J.D., 1976). (Chair, Toxic Tort Defense Group). ***PRACTICE AREAS:*** Products Liability Defense; Asbestos Defense; Silicosis Litigation; Business Litigation; Construction Litigation; Personal Injury. ***Email:*** bmandel@ulmer.com

(This Listing Continued)

STEPHEN A. MARKUS, born March 14, 1954; admitted to bar, 1979, Ohio. *Education:* Case Western Reserve University (B.A., cum laude, 1976; J.D., 1978). ***PRACTICE AREAS:*** Labor and Employment; Collective Bargaining; Corporate Law; Mergers, Acquisitions and Divestitures. ***Email:*** smarkus@ulmer.com

CRAIG A. MARVINNEY, born December 11, 1957; admitted to bar, 1982, Ohio. *Education:* Case Western Reserve University (B.A., cum laude, 1979; J.D., 1982). Recipient, Student of the Year, Environmental Law Awards. ***PRACTICE AREAS:*** Complex Litigation; Intellectual Property Litigation; Insurance Litigation. ***Email:*** cmarvinney@ulmer.com

CHRISTOPHER C. McCRACKEN, born December 18, 1951; admitted to bar, 1977, Ohio. *Education:* Bowling Green State University (B.A., 1973); Case Western Reserve University (J.D., 1977). Chairman, Lawyers Associated Worldwide. Chair, Non Profit Corporation Law Subcommittee, Corporation Law Committee, Ohio State Bar Association. ***PRACTICE AREAS:*** Business Law; Finance; Mergers, Acquisitions and Divestitures; Securities; Nonprofit and Charitable Organizations; Public Finance. ***Email:*** cmccracken@ulmer.com

STEPHEN C. MERRIAM, born April 19, 1957; admitted to bar, 1985, Ohio. *Education:* Brown University (A.B., 1979); Case Western Reserve University (J.D., 1985). ***PRACTICE AREAS:*** Drug and Medical Device Litigation; Toxic Tort Defense; Products Liability Defense. ***Email:*** smerriam@ulmer.com

CRAIG S. MILLER, born April 6, 1945; admitted to bar, 1971, District of Columbia; 1977, Ohio. *Education:* Duke University (B.A., 1967); George Washington University (J.D., with honors, 1971). (Chair, Public Law Group). ***PRACTICE AREAS:*** Local Government Law; Real Estate; Public-Private Development; Zoning Law; Nonprofit Organizations Law. ***Email:*** cmiller@ulmer.com

MATTHEW J. MORELLI, born May 17, 1969; admitted to bar, 1994, Ohio; 1995, Illinois. *Education:* Bowling Green State University (B.A., 1991); Case Western Reserve University (J.D., cum laude, 1994). ***PRACTICE AREAS:*** Civil Litigation; Noncompete Litigation; Theft of Trade Secrets; Broker-Dealer Arbitration; Employment Law. ***Email:*** mmorelli@ulmer.com

BRIAN M. O'NEILL, born August 11, 1961; admitted to bar, 1987, Ohio; 1988, Florida. *Education:* The Ohio State University (B.S., 1983); Cleveland Marshall College of Law (J.D., cum laude, 1987). (Chair, Business/Tax Department and Business Law Group). ***PRACTICE AREAS:*** Banks and Banking; Business Law; Commercial Law; Commercial Real Estate; Construction Law; Corporate Law; Finance; Mergers, Acquisitions and Divestitures; Real Estate; Loan Restructuring; Loan Syndication; Loan Workouts; Closely Held Business Law; Family Business Successions; Joint Ventures; Strategic Alliances; Commercial Real Estate Development; Shopping Center Acquisitions; Shopping Center Development; Leases and Leasing. ***Email:*** boneill@ulmer.com

THOMAS W. OSTROWSKI, born May 16, 1966; admitted to bar, 1993, Ohio; 1994, New York. *Education:* State University of New York at Buffalo (B.A., 1989); Cleveland-Marshall College of Law (J.D., 1993). ***PRACTICE AREAS:*** Commercial Banking; Commercial Loans; Letters of Credit; Loan Restructuring; Loan Syndication; Loan Workouts; Secured Lending; Commercial Real Estate Finance; Corporate Finance; Secured Creditors Rights; Asset Based Finance; Structured Finance; Secured Finance. ***Email:*** tostrowski@ulmer.com

LAWRENCE D. POLLACK, born May 22, 1964; admitted to bar, 1989, Ohio. *Education:* Miami University (B.A., 1986); The Ohio State University (J.D., with honors, 1989). ***PRACTICE AREAS:*** Business Litigation; Subrogation; Property Subrogation; Fire Insurance Subrogation; Products Liability; Products Subrogation; Fire Litigation. ***Email:*** lpollack@ulmer.com

BRIAN N. RAMM, born May 19, 1962; admitted to bar, 1987, Ohio. *Education:* Miami University (B.A., 1984); University of Toledo (J.D., 1987). ***PRACTICE AREAS:*** Products Liability; Law Enforcement; Medical Malpractice; Negligence; Torts; Personal Injury. ***Email:*** bramm@ulmer.com

HAROLD (KIP) READER, born March 10, 1949; admitted to bar, 1974, Ohio. *Education:* Brown University (A.B., 1971); Case Western Reserve University (J.D., 1974). Chair, Tort and Insurance Practice Section, 1998-1999; Chair, Property Insurance Law Committee, 1987-1988; Member of Council, 1993-1996, American Bar Association. (Firm Managing Partner). ***PRACTICE AREAS:*** Complex Litigation; Civil Litigation; Insurance Coverage. ***Email:*** kreader@ulmer.com

PETER A. ROME, born May 28, 1959; admitted to bar, 1984, Ohio; 1989 District of Columbia (inactive). *Education:* Tufts University (B.A., magna cum laude, 1981); George Washington University (J.D., with high honors, 1984). Order of the Coif. Chair, Securities Law Section, Cleveland Bar Association, 1997-1998. (Chair, Corporate Finance & Securities Group; Chair, Mergers & Acquisitions Group; Marketing Partner). ***PRACTICE AREAS:*** Corporate Law; Mergers, Acquisitions and Divestitures; Finance; Venture Capital; Securities. ***Email:*** prome@ulmer.com

RICHARD E. RUBINSTEIN, born July 3, 1939; admitted to bar, 1963, New York; 1964, Ohio. *Education:* Brooklyn College (B.A., cum laude, 1960); Columbia University (L.L.B., 1963). (Chair, Subrogation Group). ***PRACTICE AREAS:*** Insurance Litigation; Subrogation; Civil Litigation; Products Liability; Real Estate Tax Appeals. ***Email:*** rrubinstein@ulmer.com

ALAN W. SCHEUFLER, born May 25, 1958; admitted to bar, 1983, Ohio; 1984, U.S. District Court, Northern District of Ohio. *Education:* Miami University (B.A., 1980); Case Western Reserve University (J.D., 1983). (Chair, Banking and Commercial Lending Group). ***PRACTICE AREAS:*** Banks and Banking; Corporate Law; Mergers, Acquisitions and Divestitures; Leases and Leasing; Finance. ***Email:*** ascheufler@ulmer.com

ISAAC SCHULZ, born October 10, 1941; admitted to bar, 1971, Ohio; 1984, Michigan. *Education:* University of Michigan (B.A., 1968; J.D., cum laude, 1970). Life Member, Judicial Conference, 8th District. Chair, Health Law Section, 1989-1990. Chair, Professional Ethics Committee, 1985-1986. Trustee, 1992-1995; Executive Committee, 1994-1995, and President, 2001-2002, Cleveland Bar Association. (Chair, Health Care Group).

(This Listing Continued)

PRACTICE AREAS: Complex Litigation; Antitrust Litigation; Health Care Litigation; Business Transactions; Health Law; Mergers and Acquisitions. ***Email:*** ischulz@ulmer.com

FRED SELEMAN, born January 13, 1968; admitted to bar, 1993, Indiana; 1997, Ohio. *Education:* Indiana University (B.A., 1990); Case Western Reserve University (J.D., cum laude, 1993). Phi Beta Kappa. Law Review Associate, Case Western Reserve University. Member, Board of Directors, Singers' Club of Cleveland. (Certified Specialist in Labor and Employment Law, Ohio State Bar Association). ***PRACTICE AREAS:*** Labor and Employment; Litigation. ***Email:*** fseleman@ulmer.com

DOUGLAS K. SESNOWITZ, born October 14, 1969; admitted to bar, 1994, Ohio. *Education:* Washington University (B.A., magna cum laude, 1991); Ohio State University (J.D., with honors, 1994). ***PRACTICE AREAS:*** Business Law; Finance. ***Email:*** dsesnowitz@ulmer.com

PATRICIA A. SHLONSKY, born May 13, 1959; admitted to bar, 1984, Ohio. *Education:* Miami University (B.A., 1981); The Ohio State University (J.D., with honors, 1984). (Chair, Employee Benefits Group). ***PRACTICE AREAS:*** Employee Benefits. ***Email:*** pshlonsky@ulmer.com

MICHAEL D. STOVSKY, born March 10, 1964; admitted to bar, 1991, Ohio. *Education:* Northwestern University (B.A., 1986); University of Pennsylvania (J.D., 1991). Chair, Technology Committee, Cleveland Bar Association, 1998-1999. (Chair, Intellectual Property & Technology Group). ***PRACTICE AREAS:*** Corporate; Finance; Securities; Trademark Licensing; Technology Licensing; Intellectual Property; Internet; Computers and Software; Information and Privacy; Technology Transactions; Life Sciences; Data Security. ***Email:*** mstovsky@ulmer.com

RICHARD D. SWEEBE, born August 13, 1951; admitted to bar, 1979, Ohio. *Education:* Kent State University (B.A., cum laude, 1975); University of Akron (J.D., 1979). (Chair, Insurance Coverage Group). ***PRACTICE AREAS:*** Property Insurance Defense; Arson and Insurance Fraud; Insurance Bad Faith Defense; Insurance Coverage Defense; Fire Litigation. ***Email:*** rsweebe@ulmer.com

STEPHANIE DUTCHESS TRUDEAU, admitted to bar, 1982, Ohio. *Education:* University of Toledo (B.A., magna cum laude and with College Honors, 1978); DePaul University College of Law (J.D., 1982). Chair, Labor and Employment Section of the Cleveland Bar Association, 1996-1997. Vice-Chair, Employer-Employee Relations Committee, Torts and Insurance Practice Section, American Bar Association, 1997—. American Arbitration Association's National Roster of Neutrals. (Certified Specialist in Labor and Employment Law, Ohio State Bar Association). ***PRACTICE AREAS:*** Business Litigation; Employment Law; Employment Litigation; Employer Rights; Sexual Harassment. ***Email:*** strudeau@ulmer.com

MICHAEL S. TUCKER, born May 31, 1961; admitted to bar, 1986, Ohio. *Education:* Miami University (B.A., 1983); Case Western Reserve University (J.D., 1986). Past Chair, Bankruptcy and Commercial Law Section, Cleveland Bar Association. (Certified in Business Bankruptcy Law by the American Board of Certification). ***PRACTICE AREAS:*** Bankruptcy; Debtor and Creditor. ***Email:*** mtucker@ulmer.com

MICHAEL N. UNGAR, born June 5, 1959; admitted to bar, 1984, Ohio. *Education:* Boston University (B.A., cum laude, 1981; J.D., 1984). (Chair, Litigation Department; Co-Chair, Financial Institutions, Securities & Broker-Dealer Group; Member, Management Committee). ***PRACTICE AREAS:*** Securities Litigation; Unfair Competition; Trade Secrets; Business Litigation; Complex Litigation; Financial Services Regulation. ***Email:*** mungar@ulmer.com

JEFFREY W. VAN WAGNER, born November 18, 1953; admitted to bar, 1979, Ohio. *Education:* John Carroll University (B.A., magna cum laude, 1975); Case Western Reserve University (J.D., 1979). Order of the Coif. ***PRACTICE AREAS:*** Medical Malpractice Defense; Professional Liability Defense; Nursing Home Liability; Insurance Coverage Defense; Drug and Medical Device Defense. ***Email:*** jvanwagner@ulmer.com

F. THOMAS VICKERS, born July 22, 1955; admitted to bar, 1983, Ohio. *Education:* Loyola of Montreal, Montreal, Quebec (B.A., cum laude, 1977); Cleveland State University (J.D., 1983). President/Master of the Bench, American Inns of Court, William K. Thomas Chapter. Construction Arbitrator, American Arbitration Association. Member, The American Institute of Architects. (Chair, Construction Litigation Group). ***PRACTICE AREAS:*** Construction Litigation; Unfair Competition Litigation; Health Care Litigation; Business Litigation. ***Email:*** tvickers@ulmer.com

FREDERICK N. WIDEN, born August 28, 1954; admitted to bar, 1981, Ohio. *Education:* Cleveland State University (B.B.A., summa cum laude, 1975); Cleveland-Marshall College of Law (J.D., magna cum laude, 1981). Certified Public Accountant, Ohio, 1976. ***PRACTICE AREAS:*** Taxation Law; Business Law; Estate Planning Law; Health Care Law. ***Email:*** fwiden@ulmer.com

DAVID D. YEAGLEY, born September 9, 1963; admitted to bar, 1989, Ohio. *Education:* Ohio Northern University (B.S.B.A., with distinction, 1986; J.D., with distinction, 1989). ***PRACTICE AREAS:*** Class Actions; Complex Litigation; Environmental Litigation; Toxic Tort Litigation; Business and Commercial Litigation; Warranty Litigation; Real Estate Litigation; Investment Fraud Litigation; Shareholder Rights Litigation; Consumer Litigation; Consumer Fraud; Financial Services Litigation; Construction Litigation. ***Email:*** dyeagley@ulmer.com

LEONARD D. YOUNG, born 1943; admitted to bar, 1975, Ohio. *Education:* Miami University (B.S., 1967); Cleveland State University (J.D., 1974). Member: Board of Directors, Cleveland-Cuyahoga County Port Authority, 2002—; Cleveland Council on World Affairs, 1999—; American Society for Corporate Secretaries, 1997. Former Chairman, Visiting Committee, Cleveland-Marshall College of Law, Cleveland State University, 1996-2002. Member, Council of Chief Legal Officers, Conference Board. (Chair, General Counsel Services Group). [Capt. U.S. Air Force, 1967-1972]. ***PRACTICE AREAS:*** Corporate Law; Mergers and Acquisitions; International Business Law. ***Email:*** lyoung@ulmer.com

OF COUNSEL

CHARLES A. CREHORE, born September 15, 1946; admitted to bar, 1976, Ohio; registered to practice before U.S. Patent and Trademark Office. *Education:* Wittenberg University (B.A., cum laude, 1968); University of Akron (J.D., 1976). ***PRACTICE AREAS:*** Trademark Registration; Chemical Patents; Intellectual Property Licensing; Copyright Registration. ***Email:*** ccrehore@ulmer.com

C. REYNOLDS KELLER, born New York, New York, March 23, 1938; admitted to bar, 1963, Ohio; 1974, California. *Education:* Phillips Exeter Academy; Princeton University (A.B., cum laude, 1960); University of Michigan (J.D., LL.B., 1963). Phi Delta Phi. *Member:* Cleveland (Chairman, Federal Courts Committee, 1977) and Ohio State Bar Associations; State Bar of California; Cleveland Association of Civil Trial Attorneys. Fellow, American College of Trial Lawyers. ***PRACTICE AREAS:*** Products Liability; Insurance Law; Banks and Banking; Environmental Law; Construction Law. ***Email:*** crkeller@ulmer.com

WILLIAM K. SMITH, born February 10, 1953; admitted to bar, 1978, Georgia (inactive); 1981, Ohio. *Education:* Washington & Lee University (B.A., magna cum laude, 1975) Phi Beta Kappa; University of Virginia (J.D., 1978). ***PRACTICE AREAS:*** Real Property; Real Property Finance. ***Email:*** wsmith@ulmer.com

SENIOR COUNSEL

CHARLES R. OLSAVSKY, JR., born December 20, 1956; admitted to bar, 1987, Ohio and Florida. *Education:* Youngstown State University (B.E., cum laude, 1979); University of Akron (J.D., cum laude, 1987). ***REPORTED CASES:*** Silver v. Franklin Township, 966 F.2d 1031 (Sixth Cir. 1992); Weiss v. Thomas & Thomas Development Company, 79 Ohio St.3d 274 (1997); Zell v. Aetna Casualty & Surety Ins. Company, 114 Ohio App. 3d 677 (Cuyahoga Cty. 1996); Collova v. Matousek, 85 Ohio App.3d 440 (Cuyahoga Cty. 1993). ***PRACTICE AREAS:*** Construction Law; Intellectual Property. ***Email:*** colsavsky@ulmer.com

SENIOR ATTORNEYS

THOMAS L. ANASTOS, born January 8, 1959; admitted to bar, 1989, Ohio. *Education:* Case Western Reserve University (B.A., summa cum laude, 1981); Yale University (Ph.D., 1986); Harvard Law School (J.D., cum laude, 1989). Phi Beta Kappa. ***PRACTICE AREAS:*** Civil Litigation; Commercial Litigation; Business Litigation; Antitrust; Local Government Law. ***Email:*** tanastos@ulmer.com

BARI E. GOGGINS, born September 3, 1949; admitted to bar, 1980, Ohio. *Education:* Central State University (B.A., 1972); Cleveland State University (J.D., 1980). (Certified Specialist in Labor and Employment Law, Ohio State Bar Association). ***PRACTICE AREAS:*** Labor and Employment; Workers Compensation. ***Email:*** bgoggins@ulmer.com

ASSOCIATES

JOHN M. ALTEN, born October 2, 1972; admitted to bar, 1999, Ohio. *Education:* Northwestern University (B.S., Journalism, 1994); Case Western Reserve University (J.D., magna cum laude, 1999). Order of the Coif. ***PRACTICE AREAS:*** Business Litigation; Complex Litigation; Products Liability; Alternative Dispute Resolution; Securities Litigation. ***Email:*** jalten@ulmer.com

MICHELLE R. ARENDT, born October 13, 1972; admitted to bar, 1998, Ohio. *Education:* University of Dayton (B.A., summa cum laude, 1994); Case Western Reserve University (J.D., cum laude, 1998). ***PRACTICE AREAS:*** Labor and Employment. ***Email:*** marendt@ulmer.com

YELENA BOXER, born June 10, 1971; admitted to bar, 1999, Ohio. *Education:* Miami University (B.Phil., magna cum laude, 1993); Case Western Reserve University (J.D., magna cum laude, 1999). Order of the Coif. *Member:* Cuyahoga County Bar Association (Member, Judicial Review Committee). ***PRACTICE AREAS:*** Civil Litigation; Commercial Litigation; Labor and Employment. ***Email:*** yboxer@ulmer.com

MARIA A. CITERONI, born December 25, 1967; admitted to bar, 2001, Ohio. *Education:* Johnson & Wales University (B.S., cum laude, 1990); Cleveland-Marshall College of Law (J.D., summa cum laude, 2001). ***PRACTICE AREAS:*** Civil Litigation; Complex and Multi-District Litigation; Drug and Medical Device Litigation; Vaccine Injury; Welding Products Liability; Contract Litigation; Copyright Litigation. ***Email:*** mciteroni@ulmer.com

JAMES M. CRANE, born October 19, 1967; admitted to bar, 1998, Massachusetts; 1999, New York; 2004, Ohio. *Education:* University of Rhode Island (B.A., 1992); Case Western Reserve University School of Law (J.D., cum laude, 1998). ***PRACTICE AREAS:*** Business Law; Private Equity; Venture Capital; Emerging Growth Companies; Mergers and Acquisitions; Technology Transfers. ***Email:*** jcrane@ulmer.com

ELIZABETH M. DeRIENZO, born July 16, 1978; admitted to bar, 2004, Ohio. *Education:* The Ohio State University (B.S.B.A., 2000); Cleveland-Marshall College of Law (J.D., 2004). ***PRACTICE AREAS:*** Financial Institutions Litigation; Business Litigation. ***Email:*** ederienzo@ulmer.com

SUZANNE DUDDY, born August 3, 1975; admitted to bar, 2000, Ohio. *Education:* Miami University (B.A., 1997); The Ohio State University (J.D., 2000). Member, Moot Court National Team. ***PRACTICE AREAS:*** Complex Commercial Litigation; Securities Class Actions; Civil Appeals; Business Litigation; Banking Litigation. ***Email:*** sduddy@ulmer.com

ISAAC J. EDDINGTON, born June 23, 1973; admitted to bar, 2000, Ohio. *Education:* Brigham Young University (B.A., magna cum laude, 1996); Harvard University (J.D., cum laude, 2000). ***PRACTICE AREAS:*** Business Litigation; Employment Litigation. ***Email:*** ieddington@ulmer.com

BRIAN P. FARNAN, born August 21, 1976; admitted to bar, 2002, Ohio. *Education:* Purdue University (B.S., Mgmt., 1998); St. John's University School of Law (J.D., cum laude, 2002). ***PRACTICE AREAS:*** Business Law; Mergers and Acquisitions; Commercial Lending; Capital Formation. ***Email:*** bfarnan@ulmer.com

CHRISTOPHER P. FISHER, born January 22, 1960; admitted to bar, 1997, Ohio. *Education:* College of William & Mary (B.S., 1982); Northeastern University (M.B.A., 1991); University of Texas at Austin (J.D., 1997). [LT. U.S. Coast Guard, 1982-1986]. ***PRACTICE AREAS:*** Business Litigation. ***Email:*** cfisher@ulmer.com

(This Listing Continued)

ULMER & BERNE LLP, Cleveland—Continued

ARLISHEA L. FULTON, born March 8, 1971; admitted to bar, 1999, Ohio. *Education:* Florida A & M University (B.S., magna cum laude, 1994); Case Western Reserve University (J.D., 1999). ***PRACTICE AREAS:*** Corporate. ***Email:*** afulton@ulmer.com

GARY T. GARDNER, born May 22, 1958; admitted to bar, 1997, Ohio. *Education:* Kent State University (B.B.A., 1982; M.B.A., 1988); University of Akron School of Law (J.D., 1996). ***PRACTICE AREAS:*** Real Estate Law; Construction Law. ***Email:*** ggardner@ulmer.com

GARY S. GREENLEE, born August 23, 1959; admitted to bar, 1997, Ohio. *Education:* Bowling Green State University (B.A., 1981; M.A., 1983); Case Western Reserve University (J.D., 1997). ***PRACTICE AREAS:*** Insurance Coverage; Insurance Litigation. ***Email:*** ggreenlee@ulmer.com

MICHAEL A. GROSS, born October 2, 1974; admitted to bar, 2000, Ohio. *Education:* University of Pennsylvania (B.A., cum laude, 1997); Case Western Reserve University (J.D., cum laude, 2000). ***PRACTICE AREAS:*** Business Litigation; Securities; Broker-Dealer. ***Email:*** mgross@ulmer.com

MICHAEL J. HALL, born December 16, 1973; admitted to bar, 2004, Ohio. *Education:* Cedarville College (B.A., 1996); Washington University (J.D., 2004). ***PRACTICE AREAS:*** Business Law; Real Estate. ***Email:*** mhall@ulmer.com

ELIZABETH A. HARVEY, born December 27, 1960; admitted to bar, 1992, Michigan; 1996, Ohio. *Education:* Alma College (B.A., 1983); Thomas M. Cooley Law School (J.D., cum laude, 1992). Member, Board of Examiners, Supreme Court of Ohio. ***PRACTICE AREAS:*** Litigation; Civil Appeals. ***Email:*** eharvey@ulmer.com

JASON S. HOLLANDER, born October 11, 1974; admitted to bar, 1999, Ohio. *Education:* Washington University (B.A., 1996); Case Western Reserve University (J.D., 1999). ***PRACTICE AREAS:*** Commercial Litigation; Banking Litigation. ***Email:*** jhollander@ulmer.com

SALLY A. JAMIESON, born May 25, 1963; admitted to bar, 2000, Ohio; 2001, District of Columbia. *Education:* John Carroll University (B.A., 1985); Cleveland-Marshall College of Law (J.D., cum laude, 2000). ***PRACTICE AREAS:*** Products Liability; Drug and Medical Device Litigation; Mass Torts. ***Email:*** sjamieson@ulmer.com

ELIZABETH A. JERDONEK, born March 12, 1972; admitted to bar, 1997, Ohio. *Education:* Baldwin-Wallace College (B.A., 1994); Cleveland-Marshall College of Law (J.D., cum laude, 1997). ***PRACTICE AREAS:*** Securities; NASD Arbitration; New York Stock Exchange Arbitration; Broker-Dealer Arbitration. ***Email:*** ejerdonek@ulmer.com

STEPHANIE E. KENNEDY, born January 5, 1973; admitted to bar, 1998, Ohio. *Education:* University of Colorado (B.A., magna cum laude, 1995); Case Western Reserve University (J.D., cum laude, 1998). ***PRACTICE AREAS:*** Labor and Employment. ***Email:*** skennedy@ulmer.com

ANNE M. KLEPACH, born November 5, 1977; admitted to bar, 2003, Ohio. *Education:* Miami University (B.S., cum laude, 1999); The Ohio State University Moritz College of Law (J.D., 2003). ***PRACTICE AREAS:*** Business Litigation. ***Email:*** aklepach@ulmer.com

TRISH D. LAZICH, born July 26, 1963; admitted to bar, 1991, Ohio. *Education:* Kent State University (B.S., 1985); Capital University (J.D., 1991). ***PRACTICE AREAS:*** Business Law; Bankruptcy. ***Email:*** tlazich@ulmer.com

STEVEN D. McGREW, born 1958; admitted to bar, 2001, Ohio. *Education:* Bowling Green State University (B.A., 1980); University of California, Los Angeles (M.F.A., 1982); Case Western Reserve University School of Law (J.D., cum laude, 2001). ***PRACTICE AREAS:*** Real Estate Law; Construction Litigation; Environmental Law. ***Email:*** smcgrew@ulmer.com

STACEY L. McKINLEY, born January 31, 1960; admitted to bar, 1997, Ohio. *Education:* Ohio Wesleyan University (B.A., magna cum laude, 1982); Cleveland-Marshall College of Law (J.D., summa cum laude, 1997). ***PRACTICE AREAS:*** Business Law; Real Estate; Mergers and Acquisitions; Emerging Business Law; Nonprofit Organizations Law; Real Estate Development; Real Estate Finance. ***Email:*** smckinley@ulmer.com

CASH H. MISCHKA, born August 13, 1963; admitted to bar, 1991, Ohio. *Education:* Columbia University (B.A., 1985); Case Western Reserve University (J.D., 1990). ***PRACTICE AREAS:*** Workers' Compensation Defense; Intentional Torts. ***Email:*** cmischka@ulmer.com

SUZANN R. MOSKOWITZ, born January 6, 1977; admitted to bar, 2004, Ohio. *Education:* Cornell University (B.S., Policy Analysis, 1998); Stanford University (J.D., 2003). ***PRACTICE AREAS:*** Intellectual Property; Business Law; Corporate Finance; Technology Transfers. ***Email:*** smoskowitz@ulmer.com

ADRIENNE L. RAPP, born August 3, 1978; admitted to bar, 2004, Ohio. *Education:* Miami University (B.A., 2000); Ohio State University (J.D., 2004). ***PRACTICE AREAS:*** Litigation. ***Email:*** arapp@ulmer.com

JODI B. RICH, born March 2, 1975; admitted to bar, 2000, Ohio. *Education:* George Washington University (B.A., cum laude, 1996); Case Western Reserve University (J.D., magna cum laude, 2000). Order of the Coif. ***PRACTICE AREAS:*** Real Estate; Corporate Law. ***Email:*** jrich@ulmer.com

DONALD J. RICHARDSON, born January 15, 1967; admitted to bar, 1997, Ohio. *Education:* Oberlin College (B.A., 1989); University of Pennsylvania (M.G.A., 1992); Case Western Reserve University (J.D., 1997). ***PRACTICE AREAS:*** Defense Litigation; Civil Litigation; Products Liability; Drug and Medical Device Defense; Business Litigation; Medical Malpractice. ***Email:*** drichardson@ulmer.com

NITA KAY RICHARDSON, born August 27, 1969; admitted to bar, 1994, Ohio. *Education:* H. Sophie Newcomb College, Tulane University of Louisiana (B.A., 1991); Case Western Reserve University (J.D., 1994). ***REPORTED CASES:*** Chambers v. St. Mary's School, 82 Ohio St. 3d 563 (1998); Livingston v. Diocese of Cleveland, 126 Ohio App. 3d 299 (1998). ***PRACTICE AREAS:*** Commercial Litigation; General Litigation; Broker-Dealer Arbitration. ***Email:*** nrichardson@ulmer.com

(This Listing Continued)

MEGAN K. ROBERTS, born June 6, 1975; admitted to bar, 2002, Ohio. *Education:* Baldwin-Wallace College (B.A., 1997); Cleveland-Marshall College of Law (J.D., 2002). ***PRACTICE AREAS:*** Real Estate; Business Law. ***Email:*** mroberts@ulmer.com

LYNNETTE L. RODGERS, born December 28, 1970; admitted to bar, 2001, Tennessee; 2003, Ohio. *Education:* Cleveland State University (B.A., cum laude, 1995); Maxine Goodman Levine College of Urban Affairs, Cleveland State University (M.P.A., Management Concentration, 2000); Cleveland-Marshall College of Law (J.D., 2000). ***PRACTICE AREAS:*** Labor and Employment; Workers Compensation; Food Products Liability; Premises Liability. ***Email:*** lalshidhani@ulmer.com

ELIZABETH S. RUDNICK, born October 22, 1972; admitted to bar, 1998, Maryland; 1999, Ohio. *Education:* University of Pennsylvania (B.A., magna cum laude, 1995); Case Western Reserve University (J.D., 1998). ***PRACTICE AREAS:*** Labor and Employment; Civil Rights; Fair Housing. ***Email:*** erudnick@ulmer.com

KATE E. RYAN, admitted to bar, 1997, Ohio. *Education:* Bowling Green State University (B.S., 1990); Cleveland-Marshall College of Law (J.D., 1997). ***PRACTICE AREAS:*** Litigation; Medical Malpractice; Products Liability Defense. ***Email:*** kryan@ulmer.com

RICHIK SARKAR, born May 24, 1971; admitted to bar, 1998, Ohio. *Education:* University of Michigan (B.A., with honors, 1993; M.S., Social Welfare Administration & Policy Planning, 1994); Case Western Reserve University School of Law (J.D., 1998). *Member:* American Bar Association (Young Lawyers Division: District 18 Representative; Co-Chair, Business Law Committee; Judicial Division: Member, Executive Committee; Member, Lawyers Conference). ***PRACTICE AREAS:*** Administrative Law; Appellate Practice; Banking Litigation; Class Actions; Complex Business Litigation; Complex Commercial Litigation; Commercial Real Estate Litigation; Complex and Multi-District Litigation; Consumer Law; Corporate Litigation; Historic Preservation; Litigation; Civil RICO; Money Laundering; Securities Litigation. ***Email:*** rsarkar@ulmer.com

WAYNE M. SERRA, born March 30, 1967; admitted to bar, 1997, Massachusetts; 2002, Ohio. *Education:* University of Massachusetts (B.S., magna cum laude, 1994); Boston University School of Law (J.D., cum laude, 1997). ***PRACTICE AREAS:*** Computer and Software Patents; Medical Patents; Business Method Patents; Internet Patents; Patent Litigation; Patent Prosecution; Computer Software Law; Trade Secrets; Copyrights; Trademarks.

KURT S. SIEGFRIED, born October 9, 1968; admitted to bar, 1994, Ohio. *Education:* Youngstown State University (B.A., cum laude, 1991); Cleveland State University (J.D., 1994). ***PRACTICE AREAS:*** Civil Litigation; Toxic Tort Defense; Asbestos Defense; Silicosis Litigation. ***Email:*** ksiegfried@ulmer.com

EDWARD P. SIMMS, born June 23, 1971; admitted to bar, 1998, Ohio. *Education:* Kent State University (B.A., summa cum laude, 1993); Cleveland State University (J.D., summa cum laude, 1997). ***PRACTICE AREAS:*** Business Litigation; Commercial Litigation; Contract Litigation. ***Email:*** esimms@ulmer.com

JOSEPH S. SIMMS, born June 23, 1971; admitted to bar, 1996, Ohio. *Education:* The Ohio State University (B.A., 1993); Cleveland Marshall College of Law (J.D., 1996). ***PRACTICE AREAS:*** Broker-Dealer Liability Defense; Securities Litigation; Business Litigation; Domestic Relations. ***Email:*** jsimms@ulmer.com

ALICEIA J. SMITH, born January 19, 1978; admitted to bar, 2004, Ohio. *Education:* Case Western Reserve University (B.A., 2000); Case Western Reserve University School of Law (J.D., 2003). ***PRACTICE AREAS:*** Business Litigation. ***Email:*** asmith@ulmer.com

LINDA DELACOURT SUMMERS, born October 19, 1968; admitted to bar, 1996, Ohio. *Education:* University of North Carolina (B.S.B.A., 1990); Case Western Reserve University (J.D., cum laude, 1996). ***PRACTICE AREAS:*** Trusts and Estates; Wills; Federal Estate and Gift Taxation; Estate Planning; Decedents Estates; Estate Administration; Trust Planning; Living Trusts; Trust Administration. ***Email:*** ldelacourt@ulmer.com

MAX W. THOMAS, born September 14, 1966; admitted to bar, 2003, Ohio. *Education:* Case Western Reserve University (B.A., summa cum laude, 1988; M.A., 1989); University of Pennsylvania (Ph.D., 1993); Case Western Reserve University (J.D., 2003). ***PRACTICE AREAS:*** Business Litigation; Appellate Practice; Financial Institutions; Class Actions. ***Email:*** mthomas@ulmer.com

MICHAEL D. TODD, born October 3, 1974; admitted to bar, 2005, Ohio. *Education:* United States Military Academy (B.S., 1999); Case Western Reserve University School of Law (J.D., cum laude, 2005). ***PRACTICE AREAS:*** Litigation. ***Email:*** mtodd@ulmer.com

PATRICK J. TULLEY, born March 26, 1958; admitted to bar, 1994, Ohio. *Education:* The Ohio State University (B.A., 1988); Cleveland Marshall College of Law (J.D., cum laude, 1994); Case Western Reserve University (L.L.M., in Taxation, 2001). ***PRACTICE AREAS:*** Estate Planning; Family Business Successions; Federal Estate and Gift Taxation; Probate Administration; Probate Litigation; Trust Law; Wills. ***Email:*** ptulley@ulmer.com

KRISTIN M. WALKER, born December 14, 1974; admitted to bar, 2001, Ohio. *Education:* Baldwin-Wallace College (B.A., magna cum laude, 1997); Case Western Reserve University (M.B.A., 2001; J.D., 2001). *Member:* Cleveland, Ohio State and American Bar Associations. ***PRACTICE AREAS:*** Business Law; Real Estate. ***Email:*** kwalker@ulmer.com

JANE F. WARNER, born April 16, 1964; admitted to bar, 2002, Ohio. *Education:* Ursuline College (B.S.N., cum laude, 1986); Cleveland-Marshall College of Law (J.D., magna cum laude, 2002). ***PRACTICE AREAS:*** Liability Defense. ***Email:*** jwarner@ulmer.com

ELIZABETH M. WIDMAN, born March 27, 1979; admitted to bar, 2004, Ohio. *Education:* Ohio University (B.A., 2001); University of Akron School of Law (J.D., 2004). ***PRACTICE AREAS:*** Intellectual Property; Trademarks; Domain Name Infringement; Patents. ***Email:*** ewidman@ulmer.com

TANYA L. WILLIAMS, born September 8, 1979; admitted to bar, 2004, Ohio. *Education:* University of North Carolina at Chapel Hill (B.S., 2001; J.D., 2004). ***PRACTICE AREAS:*** Litigation. ***Email:*** twilliams@ulmer.com

(This Listing Continued)

JAKE P. YANCHAR, born July 11, 1974; admitted to bar, 2001, New York (Not admitted in Ohio). *Education:* Pennsylvania State University (B.S., 1997); Vermont Law School (J.D., cum laude, 2001). ***PRACTICE AREAS:*** Litigation. ***Email:*** jyanchar@ulmer.com

ELIN B. YOUNG, born July 12, 1973; admitted to bar, 1998, Ohio. *Education:* University of Pennsylvania, The Wharton School (B.S.E, magna cum laude, 1995); University of Michigan (J.D., 1998). ***PRACTICE AREAS:*** Securities Arbitration; Securities Litigation; Business Litigation; NASD Arbitration; New York Stock Exchange Arbitration. ***Email:*** eyoung@ulmer.com

MELISSA L. ZUJKOWSKI, born December 30, 1978; admitted to bar, 2004, Ohio. *Education:* Northwestern University (B.A., 2001); Ohio State University (J.D., cum laude, 2004). ***PRACTICE AREAS:*** Litigation. ***Email:*** mzujkowski@ulmer.com

ROBERT E. ZULANDT III, born August 17, 1973; admitted to bar, 1999, Ohio. *Education:* Allegheny College (B.A., 1995); Cleveland-Marshall College of Law (J.D., 1999). ***PRACTICE AREAS:*** Products Liability; Toxic Tort. ***Email:*** rzulandt@ulmer.com

URBAN & POZZUTO LLC

600 STANDARD BUILDING
1370 ONTARIO STREET
CLEVELAND, OHIO 44113
Telephone: 216-241-4244
Fax: 216-241-1677
URL: http://www.urbanfamilylaw.com
Email: brian@urbanfamilylaw.com
URL: http://www.lawyers.com/urbanfamilylaw

Domestic Relations, Family Law, Divorce, Child Custody, Child Support, Premarital Agreements.

FIRM PROFILE: Provides legal services to clients who desire experienced, personalized assistance in divorce, dissolution, custody and support matters. One firm member (Brian M. Urban) is a Certified Family Relations Law Specialist, has been selected by Inside Business Magazine as one of the leading lawyers in Northeastern Ohio, 2001-2003, and has been selected by Law & Politics magazine as an Ohio Super Lawyer for 2004-2005. The other firm member (Bridgette D. Pozzuto) has been selected by Law & Politics magazine as an Ohio Super Lawyer-Rising Star for 2005. Both attorneys belong to the Center for Principal Family Advocacy.

BRIAN M. URBAN, born Cleveland, Ohio, May 4, 1954; admitted to bar, 1979, Ohio; 2001, U.S. Supreme Court. *Education:* John Carroll University (B.A., magna cum laude, 1976); Cleveland State University (J.D., cum laude, 1979). Bar Register of Preeminent Lawyers in America, 2004-2005, Leading Lawyers in Northeastern Ohio, 2001-2005, and Ohio Super Lawyers, 2004-2006. Associate Professor, Business Law, Cleveland State University, 1984-1986. *Member:* Cleveland, Cuyahoga County (Chairman, 1997-1998, Executive Committee Officer, 1990-1992, 1994-1997, Family Law Section), Ohio State and American Bar Associations. (Certified Specialist in Family Relations Law, Ohio State Bar Association). ***PRACTICE AREAS:*** Domestic Relations; Family Law; Divorce; Child Custody; Child Support; Premarital Agreements; Collaborative Family Law. ***Email:*** brian@urbanfamilylaw.com

BRIDGETTE D. POZZUTO, born Cleveland, Ohio, December 26, 1968; admitted to bar, 1994, Ohio; 1995, Pennsylvania; 2001, U.S. Supreme Court. *Education:* Ohio Wesleyan University (B.A., summa cum laude, 1991); Temple University (J.D., 1994). Ohio Super Lawyers - Rising Stars (2005). Phi Beta Kappa. *Member:* Cleveland and Cuyahoga Bar Associations. ***PRACTICE AREAS:*** Domestic Relations; Family Law; Divorce; Child Custody; Child Support; Premarital Agreements; Collaborative Family Law. ***Email:*** bpozzuto@urbanfamilylaw.com

---

JACOB M. FIGELMAN, born Aurora, Colorado, 1978; admitted to bar, 2004, Ohio. *Education:* University of Maryland (B.A., 2000); Case Western Reserve University (J.D., 2004). ***PRACTICE AREAS:*** Family Law; Divorce; Domestic Relations; Child Custody; Child Support. ***Email:*** jfigelman@urbanfamilylaw.com

VICKERS, DANIELS & YOUNG

CLEVELAND, OHIO

(See Fay, Sharpe, Fagan, Minnich & McKee, LLP)

VORYS, SATER, SEYMOUR AND PEASE LLP

Established in 1909
2100 ONE CLEVELAND CENTER
1375 EAST NINTH STREET
CLEVELAND, OHIO 44114-1724
Telephone: 216-479-6100
Facsimile: 216-479-6060
URL: http://www.vssp.com

Columbus, Ohio Office: 52 East Gay Street, P.O. Box 1008, 43216-1008. Telephone: 614-464-6400. Facsimile: 614-464-6350.
Cincinnati, Ohio Office: Suite 2000, Atrium Two, 221 East Fourth Street, P.O. Box 0236, 45201-0236. Telephone: 513-723-4000. Facsimile: 513-723-4056.
Washington, D.C. Office: Suite 1111, 1828 L Street, N.W., 20036-5104. Telephone: 202-467-8800. Facsimile: 202-467-8900.
Alexandria, Virginia Office: 277 South Washington Street, Suite 310, 22314. Telephone: 703-837-6999. Facsimile: 703-549-4492.

(This Listing Continued)

Akron, Ohio Office: First National Tower, 106 South Main Street, Suite 1100, 44308. Telephone: 330-208-1000. Facsimile: 330-208-1001.

Civil Litigation, Commercial Transactions/Bankruptcy, Environmental, International, Labor and Employment, Product Liability, Workers Compensation.

PARTNERS

JOHN WINSHIP READ, born Pittsburgh, Pennsylvania, September 5, 1947; admitted to bar, 1972, Colorado and Washington; 1976, Pennsylvania; 1985, Ohio. *Education:* Northwestern University (B.A., 1969); University of Washington (J.D., 1972). ***PRACTICE AREAS:*** Litigation. ***Email:*** jwread@vssp.com

ANTHONY J. O'MALLEY, born Cleveland, Ohio, 1958; admitted to bar, 1984, Ohio. *Education:* John Carroll University (A.B., cum laude, 1980); Case Western Reserve University (J.D., 1984). Articles Editor, Case Western Reserve Law Review, 1984. Co-Author, "Corporate Communications: Problems, Pitfalls and Practical Pointers." Instructor, Deposition Skills Program, National Institute for Trial Advocacy. Life Member, Judicial Conference for Ohio's Eighth Appellate Judicial District. *Member:* Federal Bar Association (Former Director, Cleveland Chapter). Master Bencher, Anthony J. Celebrezze Inn of Court. ***PRACTICE AREAS:*** Litigation; Health Care Litigation; Business Litigation. ***Email:*** ajomalley@vssp.com

DREW T. PAROBEK, born Lorain, Ohio, October 22, 1957; admitted to bar, 1984, Ohio; U.S. District Court, Northern and Southern Districts of Ohio; U.S. Court of Appeals, Sixth Circuit. *Education:* Vanderbilt University (B.A., summa cum laude, 1980); Vanderbilt University School of Law (J.D., 1984). Phi Beta Kappa. Associate Editor, Vanderbilt Law Review, 1984. Judicial Clerk for the Honorable J. Craig Wright, Supreme Court of Ohio, 1985. Member, State of Ohio Board of Bar Examiners. Cleveland Zoological Society; Bay Soccer Club; Contemporary Youth Orchestra. *Member:* Cleveland (Former Trustee; Member: Executive Committee; Bankruptcy and Commercial Law Section; Chair, Continuing Legal Education Committee), Lorain County and Ohio State (CLE Institute) Bar Associations; Turnaround Management Association. ***PRACTICE AREAS:*** Bankruptcy Law; Commercial Law; Collections; Banking Law. ***Email:*** dtparobek@vssp.com

JOHN M. SAGANICH, born Warren, Ohio, March 15, 1957; admitted to bar, 1984, Texas; 1998, Ohio. *Education:* Case Western Reserve University (B.A., 1979; J.D., 1984). Order of the Coif. ***PRACTICE AREAS:*** Corporate; Securities. ***Email:*** jmsaganich@vssp.com

DAVID J. TOCCO, born Detroit, Michigan, December 29, 1960; admitted to bar, 1986, Ohio; 1988, U.S. District Court, Northern District of Ohio. *Education:* University of Michigan (B.B.A., magna cum laude, 1983); Case Western Reserve (J.D., cum laude, 1986). ***PRACTICE AREAS:*** Professional Liability; Business Litigation; Construction Litigation. ***Email:*** djtocco@vssp.com

AMANDA MARTINSEK, born Carbondale, Illinois, May 10, 1962; admitted to bar, 1992, Ohio; U.S. District Court, Northern District of Ohio; U.S. Court of Appeals, Sixth Circuit. *Education:* Oberlin College (B.A., cum laude, 1985); New York University School of Law (J.D., magna cum laude, 1991). Order of the Coif. *Member:* Cleveland, Ohio State and American Bar Associations. ***Email:*** amartinsek@vssp.com

LISA BABISH FORBES, born Cleveland, Ohio, July 26, 1963; admitted to bar, 1992, Ohio and U.S. District Court, Northern District of Ohio; 1998, U.S. Court of Appeals, Sixth Circuit; 2004, U.S. District Court, Southern District of Ohio. *Education:* Cornell University (B.S., 1985); Case Western Reserve University (J.D., summa cum laude, 1992). Order of the Coif. Executive Notes Editor, Case Western Reserve Law Review. Member, Case Western Reserve Law Review. Law Clerk to Judge Frank J. Battisti, U.S. District Court, Northern District of Ohio, Eastern Division. Author: "Federal Election Regulation and the States: An Analysis of the Minnesota and New Hampshire Attempts to Regulate Congressional Elections" published in Volume 42 of the Case Western Reserve Law Review. Eighth District Trustee, 1999-2002, Programming Co-Chair, 2002-2003 and Member, Newsletter Committee, 2002-2003, Ohio Women's Bar Association. *Member:* Ohio State Bar Association; Cleveland Bar Association; Ohio Women's Bar Association. ***PRACTICE AREAS:*** Commercial Litigation. ***Email:*** lbforbes@vssp.com

DAVID A. CAMPBELL III, born Canton, Ohio, March 12, 1971; admitted to bar, 1996, Ohio. *Education:* The Ohio State University (B.S.B.A., cum laude, 1993; J.D., summa cum laude, 1996). Order of the Coif. Member, Ohio State Law Journal, 1994-1996. Elected to the Prevent Blindness Ohio Board of Directors. ***PRACTICE AREAS:*** Labor; Employment; Non-Compete Litigation; ERISA. ***Email:*** dacampbell@vssp.com

SENIOR ATTORNEY

MARGARET DODANE EVERETT, born Dayton, Ohio, May 14, 1960; admitted to bar, 1985, Ohio. *Education:* Miami University (A.B., 1982); Case Western Reserve University (J.D., 1985). *Member:* Ohio State Bar Association. ***PRACTICE AREAS:*** Workers Compensation; Litigation. ***Email:*** mdeverett@vssp.com

ASSOCIATES

MICHAEL SCOT GORDON, born Washington, D.C.; admitted to bar, 1986, Ohio. *Education:* University of Virginia (B.A., with high distinction, 1978); National Law Center, George Washington University (J.D., 1986); The Judge Advocate General's School, United States Army (LL.M., 1990); University of Virginia School of Law (LL.M., 1995). *Member:* Ohio State Bar Association. ***PRACTICE AREAS:*** Civil Litigation; Criminal Litigation. ***Email:*** msgordon@vssp.com

MARCEL C. DUHAMEL, born Providence, Rhode Island, March 4, 1968; admitted to bar, 1993, Ohio; 1995, U.S. District Court, Northern District of Ohio; 1996, U.S. Court of Appeals, Sixth Circuit. *Education:* Case Western Reserve University (B.A., summa cum laude, 1990); University of Chicago (J.D., 1993). *Member:* Ohio State and Federal Bar Associations. ***PRACTICE AREAS:*** Litigation. ***Email:*** mcduhamel@vssp.com

ANTHONY O. CALABRESE III, born Cleveland, Ohio, June 29, 1972; admitted to bar, 1997, Ohio. *Education:* Georgetown University (B.A., magna cum laude, 1994); Case Western Reserve University (J.D., 1997). Member, National Moot Court Team. Semifinalist, Dunmore Moot Court Competition. Justinian Forum. Author, "Business Law Update,"

(This Listing Continued)

VORYS, SATER, SEYMOUR AND PEASE LLP, Cleveland—Continued

Ohio CLE Institute 1999 Coursebook. Member: Board of Directors, Hawken School Alumni Association; Alumni of Georgetown University (1994 B.A.); Alumni of Case Western Reserve University School of Law (1997 J.D.); National Organization of Italian Americans; Justinian Forum. *Member:* National Association of Bond Lawyers. ***PRACTICE AREAS:*** Corporate. ***Email:*** aocalabrese@vssp.com

MATTHEW D. ENGLISH, born Cleveland, Ohio, July 15, 1972; admitted to bar, 1999, Ohio. *Education:* Michigan State University (B.A., with high honor, 1994); Case Western Reserve University (J.D., cum laude, 1999). Phi Beta Kappa; Order of the Coif. ***PRACTICE AREAS:*** Commercial Law; Real Estate; Bankruptcy. ***Email:*** mdenglish@vssp.com

JAMES A. HOGAN, born Sodus, New York, January 6, 1972; admitted to bar, 1999, Ohio and U.S. District Court, Northern District of Ohio. *Education:* University of Notre Dame (B.A., 1994); University of Cincinnati (J.D., 1999). Recipient: Order of the Coif; Judge John W. Peck Trial Practice Award. Articles and Senior Articles Editor, Human Rights Quarterly. Judicial Extern for the Honorable Sandra Beckwith, U.S. District Court, Southern District of Ohio. *Member:* Ohio State and Federal Bar Associations. Fellow, Arthur Russel Morgan, Urban Morgan Institute for Human Rights. ***PRACTICE AREAS:*** Civil Litigation. ***Email:*** jahogan@vssp.com

BRYAN J. FARKAS, born Skokie, Illinois; admitted to bar, 2000, Ohio. *Education:* University of California, San Diego (B.A., with honors, 1994); Heiden Torah Institute, Jerusalem, Israel, 1994-1997; Case Western Reserve University School of Law (J.D., cum laude, 2000). ***Email:*** bjfarkas@vssp.com

MARQUETTES D. ROBINSON, born Cleveland, Ohio; admitted to bar, 2001, Ohio. *Education:* Harvard University (B.A., 1998; J.D., 2001). ***Email:*** mdrobinson@vssp.com

ELIA O. WOYT, born Parma, Ohio; admitted to bar, 2001, Ohio. *Education:* Canisius College (B.A., summa cum laude, 1998); Columbia University (J.D., 2001). Harlan Fiske Stone Scholar. Managing Editor, Journal of East European Law, 2000-2001. ***LANGUAGES:*** Ukrainian. ***PRACTICE AREAS:*** Commercial Law; Banking Law. ***Email:*** eowoyt@vssp.com

CARRIE M. CALDWELL, born Jamestown, New York, March 13, 1977; admitted to bar, 2002, Ohio; U.S. District Court, Northern District of Ohio. *Education:* University of Virginia (B.A., 1999; J.D., 2002). Member, Virginia Tax Review, 2000-2002. *Member:* Cleveland and Ohio State Bar Associations. ***PRACTICE AREAS:*** Bankruptcy; Commercial Litigation; Debtor and Creditor; Creditors Rights; Banking Law; Financial Law. ***Email:*** cmcaldwell@vssp.com

JOHN GERAK, born Youngstown, Ohio, January 6, 1970; admitted to bar, 2002, Ohio. *Education:* Pennsylvania State University (B.S., 1992); University of Pittsburgh (J.D., 2002). ***Email:*** jgerak@vssp.com

ELIZABETH A. RATLIFF, born Columbus, Ohio, December 5, 1977; admitted to bar, 2002, Ohio. *Education:* College of William & Mary (B.A., 1999); University of Virginia (J.D., 2002). Phi Beta Kappa. ***PRACTICE AREAS:*** Litigation. ***Email:*** earatliff@vssp.com

CARRIE DUNN, born Fairfax, Virginia, November 10, 1977; admitted to bar, 2003, Ohio. *Education:* The Ohio State University (B.A., 2000); University of Pittsburgh (J.D., 2003). Order of the Coif; Order of Barristers. ***Email:*** cmdunn@vssp.com

LORI L. FAUVIE, born Warren, Ohio, January 30, 1974; admitted to bar, 2003, Ohio. *Education:* Ohio University (B.S., summa cum laude, 1997); Cleveland-Marshall College of Law (J.D., summa cum laude, 2003). Managing Editor, Law Review, 2002-2003. Senior Advisor, Journal of Law and Health, 2002-2003. ***LANGUAGES:*** Spanish. ***Email:*** llfauvie@vssp.com

JOCELYN N. PREWITT-STANLEY, born Garfield Heights, Ohio, January 20, 1977; admitted to bar, 2003, Ohio. *Education:* Grinnell College (B.A., 1999); University of Iowa College of Law (J.D., 2003). *Member:* Ohio State and National Bar Associations. ***PRACTICE AREAS:*** Litigation. ***Email:*** jnprewitt@vssp.com

RACHEL J. GRABOW, born Cleveland, Ohio, October 23, 1970; admitted to bar, 1997, Ohio; 1998, District of Columbia; 1999, U.S. District Court, Northern District of Ohio. *Education:* College of the Holy Cross (B.A., 1992); Jagiellonian University Law School, Cracow, Poland (International Business and Trade Law Program, 1995); Catholic University of America (J.D., with Certificate in Comparative and International Law, 1997). Lead Articles Editor, Catholic University Law Review. Author: "McIntyre v. Ohio Elections Commission: Protecting the Freedom of Speech or Damaging the Electoral Process?" 46 Catholic University Law Review 565, 1997. *Member:* Cleveland and Ohio State Bar Associations; The District of Columbia Bar. ***PRACTICE AREAS:*** Corporate; International; Mergers and Acquisitions; Financial Institutions; Securities. ***Email:*** rjgrabow@vssp.com

MATTHEW D. BESSER, born 1973; admitted to bar, 2004, Ohio; 2005, U.S. Court of Appeals, Third Circuit. *Education:* George Washington University (B.A., 2001); The Ohio State University Moritz College of Law (J.D., summa cum laude, 2004) Order of the Coif. Recipient: Donald S. Teller Memorial Award; Judge Joseph H. Harter Memorial Award. Author: "May I Be Recused? The Tension Between Judicial Campaign Speech and Recusal After Republican Party of Minnesota v. White," 64 Ohio St. L.J. 1197 (2003). ***PRACTICE AREAS:*** Labor and Employment; Appeals; Litigation. ***Email:*** mdbesser@vssp.com

OF COUNSEL

JAMES J. McMONAGLE, born Cleveland, Ohio, October 1, 1944; admitted to bar, 1970, Ohio; U.S. District Court, Northern District of Ohio. *Education:* Georgetown University (B.S./B.A., 1966); Cleveland Marshall College of Law (J.D., 1970). Author: numerous Reported Decisions. Judge, Cuyahoga County Common Pleas Court, 1978-1990. General Counsel, University Hospitals Health System, Cleveland Ohio 1990-2003. Judge, Cuyahoga County Common Pleas Court (Cleveland) 1978-1990. *Member:* Cleveland (Trustee, 1991-1992) and Ohio State (Member, House of Delegates, 1985-1993) Bar Associations. ***Email:*** jjmcmonagle@vssp.com

THOMAS J. ONUSKO, born Warren, Ohio, October 17, 1952; admitted to bar, 1977, Ohio. *Education:* University of Notre Dame (B.A., magna cum laude, 1974); Cornell University (J.D., 1977). Author: "Medical Staff Conflict of Interest Policies: The Rationale for Restructuring Hospital Privileges of Competing Physicians," 75 Cleveland Bar Journal 5, March 2004; "The Impact of HIPPA Privacy Regulations on Physicians," Physician Magazine, October 2001; Chapter 5, "Hospital-Physician Integration: Strategies for Success," in Legal Issues in Hospital-Group Practice Affiliations, American Hospital Publishing, Inc., September 1994; "The Right to Refuse Medical Treatment in Ohio After Cruzan: The Need for a Comprehensive Legislative Solution," 5 Journal of Law & Health 35, 1990-1991. Adjunct Professor in Health Care Law, Case Western Reserve University School of Law and Cleveland State University School of Business. Listed in Best Lawyers in America, 2003-2004 edition. *Member:* Cleveland and Ohio State Bar Associations; American Health Lawyers Association; Ohio Society of Hospital Attorneys; National Association of Bond Lawyers; Healthcare Financial Managers Association. ***PRACTICE AREAS:*** Health Care. ***Email:*** tjonusko@vssp.com

STAFF ATTORNEYS

JEROME C. WEBBS, born Cleveland, Ohio, November 30, 1955; admitted to bar, 1980, Ohio; U.S. District Court, Northern and Southern Districts of Ohio. *Education:* Oberlin College (A.B., 1977); Case Western Reserve University (J.D., 1980). ***PRACTICE AREAS:*** Workers Compensation; Litigation. ***Email:*** jcwebbs@vssp.com

MARY EILEEN PURCELL, born Washington, D.C.; admitted to bar, 1994, Ohio; U.S. District Court, Northern District of Ohio. *Education:* Bowling Green State University (B.S., Pre-Law, with honors, 1990); University of Toledo, College of Law (J.D., 1993). (Certified Specialist in Workers' Compensation Law, Ohio State Bar Association). ***PRACTICE AREAS:*** Labor and Employment; Workers' Compensation. ***Email:*** mepurcell@vssp.com

KENNETH A. STUMP, born Peoria, Illinois, March 6, 1969; admitted to bar, 1994, Ohio. *Education:* Boston University (B.S.B.A., 1991); Cleveland-Marshall College of Law (J.D., 1994). *Member:* Medina County, Cleveland and Ohio State Bar Associations. ***PRACTICE AREAS:*** Labor Law. ***Email:*** kastump@vssp.com

CHARLES A. LoPRESTI, born Cleveland, Ohio, 1971; admitted to bar, 1996, Ohio; 2000, U.S. District Court, Northern District of Ohio, U.S. Court of Appeals, Sixth Circuit, U.S. Court of Federal Claims and U.S. Supreme Court and U.S. Tax Court. *Education:* Cleveland State University (B.A., Political Science, cum laude, 1993); University of Toledo (J.D., 1996); Case Western Reserve University (LL.M., Taxation, 1997); Cleveland State University (M.P.A., 2001; M.B.A., 2003). Beta Gamma Sigma. Member, Justinian Forum. *Member:* Cleveland, Ohio State, Federal and American Bar Associations. ***PRACTICE AREAS:*** Business Litigation; Commercial Litigation; Civil Litigation. ***Email:*** calopresti@vssp.com

WELDON H. RICE, born Cincinnati, Ohio; admitted to bar, 2003, Ohio. *Education:* Marietta College (B.A., 1993); Cleveland-Marshall College of Law (J.D., 2002). *Member:* Ohio State Bar Association. ***PRACTICE AREAS:*** Workers Compensation; Litigation. ***Email:*** whrice@vssp.com

REPRESENTATIVE CLIENTS: Abercrombie & Fitch; Airborne Express, Inc.; American Showa; Bob Evans Farms, Inc.; Cardinal Health; Columbus Blue Jackets; Consolidated Stores Corp.; Dominion Homes; Eaton Corporation; Greif Bros.; Honda of America Mfg., Inc.; Insurance Federation of Ohio; M/I Homes; Martin Marietta Energy Systems; National City Bank; Fraternal Order of Police; Ohio Casualty Corporation; Ohio League of Financial Institutions; R.G. Barry Corp.; Showa Aluminum Corporation; Techneglas; The Children's Hospital; The Limited, Inc.; The Ohio State University; The Scotts Company; Value City Department Stores; Filene's Basement; DSW; Wendy's International, Inc.; Worthington Industries, Inc.; Hamilton County.

LOCAL COUNSEL: Abbott Laboratories; American Telephone & Telegraph Co.; Anheuser-Busch, Inc.; Ashland Oil, Inc.; B.F. Goodrich Co.; BP America; Emerson Electric; General Electric Company; General Motors Corp.; Goodyear Tire & Rubber; Household Finance Corp.; Mac Tools, Inc.; Navistar International; The Kroger Co.; United States Playing Card Co.; Waste Management; Western Southern Life Insurance Company.

(For Complete Biographical Data on all Personnel, see Professional Biographies at Columbus, Ohio)

(This Listing Continued)

WALLACE W. WALKER, JR.

7774 OAKHURST CIRCLE
P.O. BOX 470340
CLEVELAND, OHIO 44147-0340
Telephone: 440-526-4244
Fax: 440-526-8511
Email: wwwalker@adelphia.net

Bankruptcy, Commercial Law, Debtors' Rights.

WALLACE W. WALKER, JR., born Akron, Ohio, May 3, 1941; admitted to bar, 1966, Ohio and U.S. District Court, Northern District of Ohio; 1982, U.S. Court of Appeals, Sixth Circuit; 1990, Florida. *Education:* Ohio Wesleyan University (B.A., 1963); Case Western Reserve University (J.D., 1966). Listed: "The Best Lawyers in America" in Bankruptcy Law; Ohio Super Lawyers, 2004. ***PRACTICE AREAS:*** Bankruptcy; Commercial Law; Debtors Rights; Bankruptcy Reorganization; Bankruptcy Litigation; Debtor and Creditor Reorganization.

WALTER & HAVERFIELD LLP

Established in 1932

THE TOWER AT ERIEVIEW
1301 EAST NINTH STREET, SUITE 3500
CLEVELAND, OHIO 44114
Telephone: 216-781-1212
Fax: 216-575-0911
Email: law@walterhav.com
URL: http://www.walterhav.com

General Practice (State and Federal Courts). Antitrust and Trade Regulation, Banking Law, Business Acquisitions, Commercial Law, Constitutional Law, Construction Law, Corporate Financing, Corporation Law, Employee Benefits, Employment Discrimination, Environmental

(This Listing Continued)

Law, Estate Planning, Wills and Probate Law, Health Care, Labor Relations, Legislative Practice, Libel, Media Law, Municipal, Public Contract, School, Zoning and Related Public Law, Lender's Counsel, Products Liability, Property, Public Employment Relations and Related Labor Law, Real Estate Development, Taxation, Cable Television/Telecommunications and Related Business Law, International Business.

LAW FIRM ALLIANCES/ASSOCIATIONS: ***GREAT LAKES LAW***

MANAGING PARTNER

RALPH E. CASCARILLA, born August 6, 1949; admitted to bar, 1976, Ohio; 1981, Florida. *Education:* University of Notre Dame (B.A., 1971); T.M. Cooley Law School (J.D., 1976). Former Assistant U.S. Attorney, Northern District of Ohio, 1978-1984. Member, Advisory Committee, U.S. District Court. Life Member, 8th District Judicial Conference. *Member:* Cleveland Inns of Court XXI (Master Burcher). ***PRACTICE AREAS:*** General Civil and Commercial Litigation; White Collar Criminal Law; Environmental Law; Construction/Real Estate Litigation; Antitrust Litigation. ***Email:*** rcascarilla@walterhav.com

PARTNERS OF FIRM

PAUL W. WALTER (1907-1992)

D. RUSK HAVERFIELD (1907-1993)

ANTHONY J. VIOLA, born March 14, 1932; admitted to bar, 1957, Ohio. *Education:* Case Western Reserve University (B.A., 1954; LL.B., 1956). ***LANGUAGES:*** Italian. ***PRACTICE AREAS:*** Corporate and Business Counseling; Estate Planning; Real Estate. ***Email:*** aviola@walterhav.com

RUSSELL C. SHAW, born March 19, 1940; admitted to bar, 1965, Ohio; 1968, U.S. Supreme Court. *Education:* Ohio State University (B.S. in B.A., 1962; J.D., 1965). Member, IRS Employee Plans Ad Hoc Committee, 1989-1990; Midwest Pension Conference; Ohio Advisory Council for the Aging (Vice Chairman, 1992-1993; Chairman, 1993-1999). Delegate, 1995 White House Conference on Aging. [Capt., JAGC, U.S. Army, 1965-1969]. ***PRACTICE AREAS:*** Employee Benefits Law; Pension and Profit Sharing Law. ***Email:*** rshaw@walterhav.com

ROBERT J. CRUMP, born May 18, 1943; admitted to bar, 1968, Ohio. *Education:* Ohio Wesleyan University (B.A., 1965); Case Western Reserve University (J.D., 1968). Editor, Case Western Reserve Law Review, 1967-1968. *Member:* American Health Lawyers Association. ***PRACTICE AREAS:*** Business Law; Corporate Contracts; Health Care; Mergers and Acquisitions; Physician Contracts. ***Email:*** rcrump@walterhav.com

MICHAEL McMENAMIN, born November 11, 1943; admitted to bar, 1968, Ohio; 1981, U.S. Supreme Court. *Education:* Case Western Reserve University (B.A., 1965); University of Pennsylvania (LL.B., 1968). Omicron Delta Kappa. Contributing Editor, *Reason Magazine,* (1983—) and *Finest Hour,* (1998—). Trustee, 1978-1986 and President, 1982-1985, Board of Trustees, Fairmount Montessori Association. Trustee, Institute for Child Advocacy, 1976-1981. *Member:* Cleveland (Employment Law Section), Ohio State (Employment Law and Media Law Sections), and American (Antitrust, Employment Law and Litigation Sections) Bar Associations. ***PRACTICE AREAS:*** Litigation; Employment Law; First Amendment Law; Media Law; Antitrust and Trade Regulation. ***Email:*** mmcmenamin@walterhav.com

CHARLES R. SCHAEFER, born December 7, 1943; admitted to bar, 1969, Ohio; 1977, Florida. *Education:* Lehigh University (B.A., 1966); Case Western Reserve University (J.D., 1969). Order of the Coif. Editor, Case Western Reserve Law Review, 1968-1969. Law Clerk, Ohio Supreme Court, 1969-1970. ***PRACTICE AREAS:*** Closely Held Businesses; Corporate Law; Business Acquisitions. ***Email:*** cschaefer@walterhav.com

ROBERT S. HORBALY, born August 15, 1945; admitted to bar, 1970, Ohio. *Education:* The Ohio State University (B.S., 1967); University of Toledo (J.D., 1970). Member, University of Toledo Law Review, 1969-1970. ***PRACTICE AREAS:*** Probate Administration; Trust Administration; Estate Planning; Estate and Gift Taxation. ***Email:*** rhorbaly@walterhav.com

CHARLES T. RIEHL, III, born November 14, 1944; admitted to bar, 1971, Ohio. *Education:* Colgate University (B.A., 1966); Case Western Reserve University (J.D., 1971). Order of the Coif. Research Editor, Case Western Reserve Law Review, 1970-1971. Trustee, Meridia Suburban Hospital, 1987-1997. Member, Cuyahoga County Board of Health, 2002—. ***PRACTICE AREAS:*** Municipal Law; Construction Law; Litigation; Real Estate. ***Email:*** criehl@walterhav.com

HERBERT L. BRAVERMAN, born April 24, 1947; admitted to bar, 1972, Ohio. *Education:* University of Pennsylvania, Wharton School of Finance (B.S., cum laude, 1969); Harvard Law School (J.D., 1972). Beta Gamma Sigma. Fellow, American College of Trust and Estate Counsel. *Member:* Cleveland (Section Chair, 1992), Ohio State and American Bar Associations; Estate Planning Council of Cleveland. ***PRACTICE AREAS:*** Estate Planning and Taxation; Probate Administration; Business Succession. ***Email:*** hbraverman@walterhav.com

JOHN H. GIBBON, born November 27, 1943; admitted to bar, 1972, Ohio. *Education:* Oberlin College (B.A., 1967); Case Western Reserve University (J.D., 1972). Law Director, City of Cleveland Heights, 1987—. Member, International Municipal Lawyers Association; National Association of Telecommunications Officers and Advisors. *Member:* American Bar Association. ***PRACTICE AREAS:*** Litigation; Municipal Law; Cable Television and Telecommunications. ***Email:*** jgibbon@walterhav.com

MICHAEL A. CYPHERT, born January 15, 1948; admitted to bar, 1973, Ohio. *Education:* Case Western Reserve University (B.A., 1970); Case Western Reserve University School of Law (J.D., 1973). Phi Delta Phi, Order of the Coif, Society of Benchers. Adjunct Lecturer, Energy & Environmental Law, Case Western Reserve University School of Law, 1976-1990. *Member:* American Bar Association (Member, Litigation, Environmental, Energy and Resources Sections); Federal Bar Association (Member, Environmental Law Section); Ohio State Bar Association (Member, Environmental Law Committee); Cleveland Bar Association (Member, Environmental Law Section). ***TRANSACTIONS:*** Specific Industry Experience: appliance manufacturing, automotive, bakeware, building products, chemicals, construction, highway construction, construction and demolition debris disposal, environmental consultants, foundries, metal working, solid waste disposal, secondary magnesium, primary aluminum, aluminum rolling and manufacturing, pesticide application, primary titanium, titanium manufactured products, rubber products, rubber recycling, ferrous and non-ferrous metal recycling, reinforced plastic composites, steel, waste management, waste water treatment. ***PRACTICE AREAS:*** Environmental Law; Litigation. ***Email:*** mcyphert@walterhav.com

JAMES P. CONROY, born September 8, 1949; admitted to bar, 1974, Ohio. *Education:* The Ohio State University (B.A., cum laude, 1971; J.D., 1974). Phi Beta Kappa. ***PRACTICE AREAS:*** Corporate Law; Commercial Law; Mergers and Acquisitions; Closely Held Corporations. ***Email:*** jconroy@walterhav.com

DAVID W. WELTY, born June 9, 1949; admitted to bar, 1974, Ohio; 1983, U.S. Tax Court. *Education:* Denison University; Miami University (B.S., 1971); Case Western Reserve University (J.D., 1974). Phi Delta Phi. Instructor, Federal Income Taxation Law, Retirement Planning, Estate Planning, Cleveland State University, 1991—. ***PRACTICE AREAS:*** Corporation Law; Mergers and Acquisitions Law; Estate Planning Law. ***Email:*** dwelty@walterhav.com

JAMES M. MACKEY, born December 17, 1949; admitted to bar, 1974, Ohio; 1975, Pennsylvania. *Education:* John Carroll University (B.A., 1971); Cleveland State University (J.D., 1974). *Member:* Cleveland, Ohio State and American (Member, Sections on: Business Tax; Real Property, Probate and Trust Law) Bar Associations. ***PRACTICE AREAS:*** Corporate Law; Estate Planning. ***Email:*** jmackey@walterhav.com

CHRISTOPHER L. GIBBON, born October 9, 1950; admitted to bar, 1977, Ohio. *Education:* Carleton College (B.A., 1973); Cleveland-Marshall College of Law (J.D., 1977). Law Director: City of Pepper Pike, 1989—; Village of Moreland Hills, 1989-1995. *Member:* Cuyahoga County Law Directors Association. ***PRACTICE AREAS:*** Real Estate Transactions; Real Estate Litigation; Land Use Litigation; Corporations; Municipal Law. ***Email:*** cgibbon@walterhav.com

JOHN W. WALDECK, JR., born May 3, 1949; admitted to bar, 1977, Ohio. *Education:* John Carroll University (B.S., 1973); Cleveland-Marshall College of Law, Cleveland State University (J.D., summa cum laude, 1977). Chairman, Bainbridge Township Board of Zoning Appeals, 1984-1992. Chair, Geauga County Mental Health Board, 1995-1997. ***PRACTICE AREAS:*** Real Estate; Banking; Corporate/Business. ***Email:*** jwaldeck@walterhav.com

MICHAEL J. JORDAN, born January 1, 1954; admitted to bar, 1979, Ohio; 1980, Michigan. *Education:* Kalamazoo College; Ohio Wesleyan University (B.A., with highest distinction, 1976); George Washington University (J.D., 1979). Phi Beta Kappa; Omicron Delta Kappa; Pi Sigma Alpha. Member, George Washington Law Review, 1978-1979. Acting Judge, Shaker Heights Municipal Court, 1994. Rotary Club President, 2001-2002. *Member:* Cleveland, Ohio State and American Bar Associations; State Bar of Michigan; Panel of Arbitrators; American Arbitration Association; American Health Lawyers Association. ***PRACTICE AREAS:*** Health Care Litigation; General Civil and Commercial Litigation; Arbitration. ***Email:*** mjordan@walterhav.com

GARY A. ZWICK, born July 7, 1954; admitted to bar, 1980, Ohio and U.S. Tax Court. *Education:* Kent State University (B.B.A., Accounting and Finance, 1976); Cleveland-Marshall College of Law (J.D., 1980); Georgetown University Law Center (LL.M., Taxation, 1982). Certified Public Accountant, Ohio, 1981. (Certified Specialist in Tax Law, Ohio State Bar Association). ***PRACTICE AREAS:*** Tax Law; Estate Planning; ERISA; Family Business Law; International Taxation; Closely Held Business Law. ***Email:*** gzwick@walterhav.com

NANCY A. NOALL, born May 5, 1957; admitted to bar, 1981, Ohio; U.S. Supreme Court. *Education:* John Carroll University (B.A., magna cum laude, 1977) Alpha Sigma Nu; Case Western Reserve University (J.D., 1981). Order of the Coif. ***PRACTICE AREAS:*** Labor Law; Employment Law; Employment Discrimination. ***Email:*** nnoall@walterhav.com

FREDERICK W. WHATLEY, born August 4, 1949; admitted to bar, 1981, Ohio; 1982, U.S. District Court, Northern District of Ohio; 1984, U.S. Court of Appeals, Sixth Circuit; 1987, U.S. Supreme Court; 1990, U.S. Court of Appeals, Fourth Circuit; 1994, U.S. Court of Appeals, Eighth Circuit. *Education:* Wright State University (B.A., 1974); Cleveland-Marshall College of Law (J.D., cum laude, 1981). Former Lecturer in Law, First Amendment Rights, Cleveland-Marshall College of Law. ***PRACTICE AREAS:*** First Amendment Law; Local Government Law; Business Litigation Law. ***Email:*** fwhatley@walterhav.com

JONATHAN D. GREENBERG, born May 7, 1957; admitted to bar, 1983, Ohio and U.S. District Court, Northern District of Ohio; 1984, U.S. Court of Appeals, Sixth Circuit. *Education:* Macalester College (B.A., 1980); Case Western Reserve University (J.D., 1983). ***PRACTICE AREAS:*** White Collar Criminal Law; Commercial and Employment Litigation; Health Care Litigation; Municipal Law. ***Email:*** jgreenberg@walterhav.com

R. TODD HUNT, born February 2, 1954; admitted to bar, 1984, Ohio; U.S. District Court, Northern District of Ohio; U.S. Court of Appeals, 6th Circuit; U.S. Supreme Court. *Education:* Case Western Reserve University (M.S.S.A., 1984; J.D., 1984). Law Director, City of Richmond Heights, 1995—. Assistant Solicitor, City of Hudson, 1994—. Former Assistant Director of Law, Cities of Cleveland and Cleveland Hts. ***PRACTICE AREAS:*** Land Use; Zoning Law; Public Law; Cable TV; Civil Rights Defense; Tort Defense; Public Sector Employment Law; Telecommunications Law. ***Email:*** rthunt@walterhav.com

KENNETH A. ZIRM, born August 6, 1957; admitted to bar, 1984, Ohio; U.S. District Court, Northern District of Ohio; U.S. Court of Appeals, Third, Fourth and Sixth Circuits. *Education:* Bethany College (B.A., magna cum laude, 1979); Cleveland-Marshall College of Law (J.D., cum laude, 1984). *Member:* Cleveland, Ohio State (Member, Media Law Committee) and American (Member, Forum on Communications Law) Bar Associations. ***PRACTICE AREAS:*** Media and First Amendment; Privacy and Publicity; Copyright and Trademark; Trade Secrets; Commercial Litigation Law. ***Email:*** kzirm@walterhav.com

PATRICIA F. WEISBERG, born August 8, 1959; admitted to bar, 1985, Ohio. *Education:* University of Wisconsin-Madison (B.A., 1981); Cleveland-Marshall College of Law (J.D., 1985). ***PRACTICE AREAS:*** Employment Law and Litigation; Labor Law; General Civil Litigation; Human Resources Consultation and Compliance; Workers Compensation; Unemployment Compensation. ***Email:*** pweisberg@walterhav.com

(This Listing Continued)

WALTER & HAVERFIELD LLP, Cleveland—Continued

RANDAL G. AMMONS, born May 7, 1967; admitted to bar, 1992, Ohio. *Education:* University of Miami (B.S., 1989); Tulane University (J.D., 1992). *Member:* Cleveland (Member, Labor and Employment Section, 1992—), Ohio State and American Bar Associations; Great Lakes Law Employment Group (Chairman, 2000-2001). ***PRACTICE AREAS:*** Employment; Labor; Litigation; Immigration Law. ***Email:*** rammons@walterhav.com

SOPHIA M. DESERAN, born April 28, 1957; admitted to bar, 1992, Ohio. *Education:* College of Wooster (B.A., 1979); Cleveland-Marshall College of Law (J.D., cum laude, 1991). Articles Editor, Law Review, 1990-1991. *Member:* Cleveland Real Estate Women (CREW); Greater Cleveland Mortgage Bankers Association (Membership Chair; Trustee). ***LANGUAGES:*** German. ***PRACTICE AREAS:*** Real Estate; Lender Law. ***Email:*** sdeseran@walterhav.com

SUSAN M. ZIDEK, born May 18, 1967; admitted to bar, 1992, Ohio. *Education:* Wittenberg University (B.A., 1989); The American University National Government Program (1987); The Ohio State University (J.D., with honors, 1992). Judicial Clerk, Hon. William H. Harsha, Fourth District Court of Appeals, 1992-1995. Member, William K. Thomas Inn of Court. *Member:* Cleveland, Ohio State and American Bar Associations; Ohio State Women's Bar Association. ***PRACTICE AREAS:*** Litigation; Labor and Employment; College and University Law; Appellate Practice. ***Email:*** szidek@walterhav.com

JOHN W. MONROE, born July 24, 1968; admitted to bar, 1993, Ohio. *Education:* Fairfield University (B.A., 1990); George Washington University (J.D., 1993). *Member:* Cleveland and Ohio State Bar Associations. ***PRACTICE AREAS:*** Real Estate; Municipal Law; Corporate. ***Email:*** jmonroe@walterhav.com

AMY LEOPARD, born June 26, 1960; admitted to bar, 1996, Ohio; 1997, West Virginia. *Education:* Auburn University (B.S., 1981); University of Alabama at Birmingham (M.S., Hospital and Health Administration, 1983); Case Western Reserve University (J.D., cum laude, 1995). Internship, Antitrust Division, U.S. Department of Justice, 1995-1996. Former Vice President, West Virginia University Hospitals, 1985-1992. Member, AHLA. *Member:* Cleveland, Ohio, West Virginia and American Bar Associations. ***PRACTICE AREAS:*** Health Care; Corporate Law; Business Acquisitions. ***Email:*** aleopard@walterhav.com

DARRELL A. CLAY, born March 21, 1968; admitted to bar, 1994, Louisiana; 1997, Ohio. *Education:* University of South Florida (B.A., 1989; M.A., 1991); Tulane University (J.D., magna cum laude, 1994). Order of the Coif. Managing Editor, 1993-1994, Tulane Law Review. National Editor, 1993, Federalist Society Symposium, Harvard Journal of Law and Public Policy. *Member:* Cleveland, Ohio and American Bar Associations. ***PRACTICE AREAS:*** First Amendment and Media Law; Antitrust Law; Commercial Litigation; White Collar Criminal Defense. ***Email:*** dclay@walterhav.com

WILLIAM R. HANNA, born February 5, 1965; admitted to bar, 1997, Ohio. *Education:* Miami University (A.B., 1988); Cleveland-Marshall College of Law (J.D., 1997). Member, Cleveland State Law Review. Assistant Director of Law, City of Cleveland Heights, Ohio, 1997—. *Member:* Cleveland and Ohio State Bar Associations; Cuyahoga County Law Directors Association. ***PRACTICE AREAS:*** Public Law; Litigation; Telecommunications; Employment Law; Equal Employment Opportunity Law; Employment Discrimination; Cable TV. ***Email:*** whanna@walterhav.com

MIA M. MOUNTS, born May 14, 1973; admitted to bar, 1998, Ohio; 2000, U.S. Tax Court. *Education:* University of Akron (B.A., cum laude, 1995); University of Akron School of Law (J.D., 1998); Case Western Reserve School of Law (LL.M. in Taxation, 1999). *Member:* Cleveland, Ohio State and American Bar Associations; Cleveland Tax Club. ***PRACTICE AREAS:*** Tax Law; Tax Controversy; Corporate Law; Mergers and Acquisitions; Business Planning; Estate Planning; Real Estate Law. ***Email:*** mmounts@walterhav.com

LARRY E. KLAYMAN, born July 20, 1951; admitted to bar, 1977, Florida; 1980, District of Columbia; 1989, Pennsylvania (Not admitted in Ohio). *Education:* Duke University (A.B., with honors, 1973); Hague Academy of International Law, The Hague, Netherlands; Emory University School of Law (J.D., 1977). Member: National Press Club; Council for National Policy; National Religious Broadcasters Association. *Member:* Pennsylvania Bar Association; The Florida Bar; The District of Columbia Bar. ***PRACTICE AREAS:*** Business Law; International Law; Governmental Law; Public Policy. ***Email:*** lklayman@walterhav.com

ASSOCIATES

JOHN E. SCHILLER, born June 14, 1957; admitted to bar, 1984, Ohio; 1985, U.S. District Court, Northern District of Ohio; 1988, U.S. District Court, Eastern District of Michigan; 1992, U.S. Court of Appeals, Fourth and Sixth Circuits. *Education:* University of Virginia (B.A., 1979); Case Western Reserve University School of Law (J.D., 1984). *Member:* Cleveland and Ohio State Bar Associations. ***LANGUAGES:*** Spanish. ***PRACTICE AREAS:*** Health Care; Litigation; Entertainment Law. ***Email:*** jschiller@walterhav.com

JANET L. ALTER, born September 29, 1956; admitted to bar, 1990, Ohio. *Education:* University of Cincinnati (B.A., 1979); University of Cincinnati School of Law (J.D., 1990). *Member:* Cleveland and Ohio State Bar Associations; National Association of Telecommunications Officers and Advisors, Ohio Chapter. ***PRACTICE AREAS:*** Public Law; Telecommunications. ***Email:*** jalter@walterhav.com

JOHN A. HEER, born September 7, 1965; admitted to bar, 1991, Ohio. *Education:* Indiana University (B.A., 1987); Case Western Reserve University (J.D., cum laude, 1991). Recipient, Lewis F. Powell, Jr. Excellence in Advocacy Award, 1990. *Member:* Cleveland, Ohio State and American Bar Associations; Harold Burton Inn of Court (Barrister). ***PRACTICE AREAS:*** Litigation; Environmental Litigation; Environmental Compliance. ***Email:*** jheer@walterhav.com

KATHERINE A. FRIEDELL, born April 15, 1945; admitted to bar, 1992, Ohio. *Education:* University of Michigan (B.A., 1967); Case Western Reserve University (M.A., 1968; J.D., cum laude, 1992). *Member:* Cleveland, Cuyahoga County and Ohio State Bar Associations. ***PRACTICE AREAS:*** Domestic Relations; Child Custody; Post-Divorce Litigation; Employment Discrimination; Sexual Harassment; Commercial Litigation. ***Email:*** kfriedell@walterhav.com

BONNIE S. FINLEY, born December 18, 1969; admitted to bar, 1995, Ohio. *Education:* Duke University (B.A., 1992); Washington University School of Law (J.D., 1995). Member, Law Review. ***PRACTICE AREAS:*** Litigation. ***Email:*** bfinley@walterhav.com

MORRIS L. HAWK, born November 4, 1967; admitted to bar, 1995, Ohio. *Education:* Ohio University (B.A., summa cum laude, 1990); Case Western Reserve University School of Law (J.D., 1995). *Member:* Cleveland and Ohio State Bar Associations. ***PRACTICE AREAS:*** Labor and Employment; Litigation. ***Email:*** mhawk@walterhav.com

T. CHRISTOPHER BROWN, born February 15, 1971; admitted to bar, 1997, Ohio. *Education:* University of Michigan (B.A., with distinction, 1993); The Ohio State University (J.D., 1997). *Member:* Ohio State Bar Association; Leadership Heights (Member); Home Repair Resource Center (Trustee). ***PRACTICE AREAS:*** Business Services; Lender's Counsel; Real Estate. ***Email:*** cbrown@walterhav.com

AIMEE W. LANE, born March 4, 1974; admitted to bar, 1999, Ohio. *Education:* Marietta College (B.A., magna cum laude, 1996); Case Western Reserve University School of Law (J.D., 1999). *Member:* Cleveland, Ohio State and American Bar Associations; Cuyahoga Soil and Water Conservation District (Board Member). ***PRACTICE AREAS:*** Public Law. ***Email:*** alane@walterhav.com

LESLIE G. WOLFE, born November 22, 1971; admitted to bar, 2000, Ohio. *Education:* Miami University (B.A., cum laude, 1994); Case Western Reserve University School of Law (J.D., cum laude, 2000). *Member:* Cleveland and Ohio State Bar Associations; Anti-Defamation League, Cleveland Region (Civil Rights Committee Member). ***PRACTICE AREAS:*** Litigation; Environmental; White Collar Criminal Defense. ***Email:*** lwolfe@walterhav.com

ERIC J. HALL, born April 29, 1973; admitted to bar, 2001, Ohio; 2003, Florida. *Education:* University of Florida (B.A., with honors, 1997); University of Florida School of Law (J.D., with honors, 2000). *Member:* Ohio State and American (Member, Tax Section) Bar Associations. ***PRACTICE AREAS:*** Tax Law; Employee Benefits; Estate Planning. ***Email:*** ehall@walterhav.com

TODD E. GONYER, born November 9, 1972; admitted to bar, 1998, Kansas; 1999, Missouri; 2002, Ohio. *Education:* Ohio University (B.A., 1995); University of Kansas School of Law (J.D., 1998). *Member:* Cleveland and Ohio State Bar Associations; Greater Cleveland Ohio University Alumni Association (Board of Directors Member and Committee Chair). ***PRACTICE AREAS:*** Litigation. ***Email:*** tgonyer@walterhav.com

SARAH L. IDDINGS, born March 21, 1978; admitted to bar, 2003, Ohio. *Education:* Ohio University (B.A., magna cum laude, 2000); Case Western Reserve University School of Law (J.D., 2003). *Member:* Cleveland, Cuyahoga County, Ohio State and American Bar Associations; Ohio Association of Civil Trial Lawyers; Defense Research Institute. ***PRACTICE AREAS:*** Labor and Employment; Litigation. ***Email:*** siddings@walterhav.com

SUSANNE DE GENNARO, born May 2, 1968; admitted to bar, 2004, Ohio. *Education:* Cleveland Institute of Art (B.F.A., 1991); Maxine Levin College of Urban Affairs, Cleveland State University (M.M.A., 1997); Cleveland-Marshall College of Law (J.D., cum laude, 2003). *Member:* Cleveland and Ohio State Bar Associations. ***PRACTICE AREAS:*** Telecommunications Law; Real Estate; Zoning Law. ***Email:*** sdegennaro@walterhav.com

BRADLEY J. KLINK, born July 29, 1979; admitted to bar, 2004, Ohio. *Education:* University of Dayton (B.A., cum laude, 2001); Case Western Reserve University (J.D., 2004). *Member:* Cleveland, Akron and American Bar Associations. ***PRACTICE AREAS:*** Business Services; Real Estate Law. ***Email:*** bklink@walterhav.com

JAMIE F. GINSBERG, born December 11, 1972; admitted to bar, 2005, Ohio. *Education:* University of Michigan (B.A., 1994); Cleveland-Marshall College of Law (J.D., 2004). *Member:* Cleveland and American Bar Associations. ***PRACTICE AREAS:*** Estate Planning; Tax Planning; Tax Exempt Organizations. ***Email:*** jginsberg@walterhav.com

JONATHAN R. GOODMAN, born January 29, 1974; admitted to bar, 1998, Maryland and New Jersey; 2002, Virginia; 2003, District of Columbia; 2005, Ohio. *Education:* University of Michigan (B.A., 1994); Catholic University of America, Columbus School of Law (J.D., 1998). [Lieutenant, Judge Advocate General's Corps, U.S. Navy, Appellate Defense Counsel, 1999-2001]. ***PRACTICE AREAS:*** Litigation; Health Care. ***Email:*** jgoodman@walterhav.com

W. CLIFFORD MULL, born April 23, 1978; admitted to bar, 2005, Ohio. *Education:* DePauw University (B.A., 2001); Case Western Reserve University (J.D., M.A. in Bioethics, 2005). *Member:* Cleveland and American Bar Associations. ***PRACTICE AREAS:*** Health Care. ***Email:*** cmull@walterhav.com

OF COUNSEL

ARTHUR P. STEINMETZ, born November 18, 1925; admitted to bar, 1951, Ohio. *Education:* Adelbert College, Western Reserve University (B.A., 1949); Western Reserve University (LL.B., 1951). ***LANGUAGES:*** German. ***PRACTICE AREAS:*** Corporate Law; Estate Planning Law; Taxation Law. ***Email:*** asteinmetz@walterhav.com

SHELDON M. YOUNG, born August 27, 1926; admitted to bar, 1951, Ohio. *Education:* The Ohio State University (B.A., 1948; J.D., 1951); Case Western Reserve University (LL.M., 1962). Member, Treasury Department Ad Hoc TRA86 Committee, 1989; Charter Fellow of American College of Employee Benefits Council. *Member:* American Bar Association (Tax Section; Task Force Chair, Employee Benefits Committee). [U.S. Navy, 1945]. ***LANGUAGES:*** Spanish, French. ***PRACTICE AREAS:*** Employee Benefits.

THOMAS C. SCHRADER, born March 8, 1940; admitted to bar, 1966, Michigan; 1968, Ohio. *Education:* University of Detroit (Classical B.A., 1962); University of Detroit (J.D., 1966). *Member:* Cleveland and American Bar Associations; Association of Trial Lawyers of America; Brecksville Planning Commission; Brecksville Towne Center, Inc. (Director and Founding Member); Fairlawn Country Club (Board Member and Former President). ***PRACTICE AREAS:*** Litigation; Labor and Employment.

DAVID D. NOBLE, born October 28, 1941; admitted to bar, 1967, District of Columbia and Ohio. *Education:* College of Wooster (B.A., 1963); Duke University (LL.B., 1966).

(This Listing Continued)

Phi Alpha Delta; Order of the Coif. Member, Duke Law Journal Editorial Board, 1966. *Member:* Ohio Oil & Gas Association. ***PRACTICE AREAS:*** Pipeline Law; Oil and Gas Law; Underground Gas Storage Law; RICO. ***Email:*** dnoble@walterhav.com

JAMES E. BETTS, born January 14, 1933; admitted to bar, 1976, Ohio. *Education:* Ohio University (B.S., in Comm., 1954); Cleveland-Marshall College of Law, Cleveland State University (J.D., 1976). State Representative, 1975-1980. ***PRACTICE AREAS:*** Administrative Law; Health Care Law; State Government Relations Law. ***Email:*** betts@netwalk.com

MARK D. WELLER, born February 21, 1956; admitted to bar, 1982, Ohio. *Education:* Pennsylvania State University (B.A., 1978); Cleveland State University (M.B.A., 1981); Cleveland-Marshall College of Law (J.D., 1982). Beta Gamma Sigma. *Member:* American Corporate Counsel Association. (Also General Counsel, Linde Gas, Inc.)

LEGAL SUPPORT PERSONNEL

JOHN B. ELDRED, born July 23, 1932. *Education:* Miami University (B.S., Accounting, 1954). Internal Revenue Service Agent and Chief, Technical Staff, Employee Plans and Exempt Organizations, 1955-1990; Enrolled to practice before Internal Revenue Service, 1990. Employee Benefits Consultant. Chairman, Avon Planning Commission, 1964-1968; 1972-1991. ***Email:*** jeldred@walterhav.com

REPRESENTATIVE CLIENTS: 20th Century Fox; A.J. Rose Manufacturing Co.; Andrews Moving & Storage Company; Applied Medical Technology, Inc.; The Associated Press; Beverly Enterprises, Inc.; Braden Sutphin Ink Co.; Cities of Cleveland, Cleveland Heights, Hudson and Pepper Pike; Cooper Tire & Rubber Company; Edgepark Surgical, Inc.; Flair Corporation; Land O' Lakes; Linde Gas, Inc.; Morse Diesel International; Nevada Energy Company; Oberlin Farms Dairy, Inc.; Paramount Distillers; Park Corporation; Playhouse Square Foundation; The Sherwin Williams Company; University Manor Health Care Center, Inc.; WJW-TV (Cleveland).

WATTS HOFFMANN CO., L.P.A.

DIAMOND BUILDING
1100 SUPERIOR AVENUE EAST
SUITE 1750
CLEVELAND, OHIO 44114-2518
Telephone: 216-241-6700
Facsimile: 216-241-8151

Intellectual Property Law including Patent, Trademark, Copyright and Unfair Competition Law. Trials and Appeals.

BLYTHE D. WATTS (1888-1984)
DANIEL J. SAMMON (1934-1991)
JAMES T. HOFFMANN (1900-2002)
THOMAS E. FISHER (1926-2005)

JOHN R. HLAVKA, born Cleveland, Ohio, June 15, 1949; admitted to bar, 1976, Ohio; 1981, U.S. District Court, Northern District of Ohio; registered to practice before U.S. Patent and Trademark Office. *Education:* Case Western Reserve University (B.S.M.E., with honors, 1971); Cleveland Marshall College of Law (J.D., magna cum laude, 1976). *Member:* Cleveland, Lake County and American Bar Associations; Cleveland and American Intellectual Property Law Associations. ***PRACTICE AREAS:*** Intellectual Property; Patents; Trademarks; Copyrights; Litigation. ***Email:*** hlavka@apk.net

STEPHEN J. SCHULTZ, born Frewsburg, New York, September 21, 1950; admitted to bar, 1977, Wisconsin and U.S. District Court, Northern District of Ohio; 1978, Ohio; 1981, New York; 1986, U.S. Court of Appeals, Federal Circuit; registered to practice before U.S. Patent and Trademark Office. *Education:* State University of New York at Fredonia (B.S., magna cum laude, 1972); University of Wisconsin-Madison (M.S., 1973; J.D., 1977); Cleveland State University (M.C.I.S., 1994). *Member:* Cleveland and American Intellectual Property Law Associations. ***PRACTICE AREAS:*** Intellectual Property; Patents; Trademarks; Copyrights; Computers and Software. ***Email:*** sschultz@wattshoff.com

GEORGE L. PINCHAK, JR., born Cleveland, Ohio, July 28, 1956; admitted to bar, 1991, Ohio; 1992, U.S. District Court, Northern District of Ohio; 1996, U.S. Court of Appeals for the Federal Circuit; registered to practice before U.S. Patent and Trademark Office. *Education:* Cleveland State University (B.I.E., summa cum laude, 1978); Case Western Reserve University (M.B.A., 1981); Cleveland Marshall College of Law (J.D., magna cum laude, 1991); Cleveland State University (B.S.E.E.T., summa cum laude, 1998). Tau Beta Pi; Beta Gamma Sigma. Recipient: Charles Auerbach Memorial Award in Evidence; Federal Bar Association Award in Constitutional Law. Executive Editor, Cleveland State Law Review, 1990-1991. *Member:* Lake County Bar Association; Cleveland and American Intellectual Property Law Associations. ***PRACTICE AREAS:*** Intellectual Property; Patents; Trademarks; Copyrights; Litigation. ***Email:*** gpinchak@wattshoff.com

---

JENNIFER NOCK HINTON, born Dayton, Ohio, June 25, 1966; admitted to bar, 1998, Ohio; registered to practice before U.S. Patent and Trademark Office. *Education:* University of Cincinnati (B.S.E.E., 1989); University of Dayton (M.S.E.E., 1995); Case Western Reserve University (J.D., magna cum laude, Order of the Coif, 1998). *Member:* Cleveland Intellectual Property Law Association. ***PRACTICE AREAS:*** Intellectual Property; Patents; Trademarks; Copyrights; Computers and Software. ***Email:*** jhinton@wattshoff.com

JOHN A. YIRGA, born January 9, 1969; admitted to bar, 2003, Ohio; U.S. District Court, Northern District of Ohio and U.S. Court of Appeals, Federal Circuit; registered to practice before U.S. Patent and Trademark Office. *Education:* University of Toledo (B.S., Mechanical Engineering, 1992); Indiana University (M.B.A., 1998); Cleveland-Marshall College of Law (J.D., magna cum laude, 2002). Golden Key National Honor Society. Moot Court Board of Governors, Cardozo College of Law Intellectual Property Competition. Recipient: Watts, Hoffmann, Fisher & Heinke Co. Award for Intellectual Property; ABA-BNA Award for Excellence in the Study of Intellectual Property Law; CALI Excellence for the Future Award, Copyright, Patent and Trademark Law; Cleveland-Marshall Law Alumni Association Scholarship. Professional Engineering FE/EIT Registration. Executive Editor, Law Journal. ***PRACTICE AREAS:*** Intellectual Property; Patents; Trademarks; Copyrights; Litigation. ***Email:*** jyirga@wattshoff.com

(This Listing Continued)

WAXMAN BLUMENTHAL LLC

29225 CHAGRIN BOULEVARD
SUITE 350
CLEVELAND, OHIO 44122
Telephone: 216-514-9400
Fax: 216-514-9401
URL: http://www.waxmanblumenthal.com

Construction Law, Corporate Law, Environmental Law, General Civil, Trial and Appellate Practice, OSHA Law, Real Estate Development, Real Estate Finance, Real Estate Leasing, Zoning Law, Redevelopments and Brownfields.

DAVID B. WAXMAN, born Toledo, Ohio, August 29, 1958; admitted to bar, 1986, Ohio; 1991, U.S. District Court, Northern District of Ohio. *Education:* The Ohio State University (B.A., 1982); University of Toledo (J.D., 1986). Phi Alpha Delta. City Councilman, South Euclid, Ohio (Ward 4), 1996-1999 (Chair, Legislative Committee; Member, Planning and Zoning Committee). Member, Zoning Board of Appeals, South Euclid, Ohio, 1996. Former General Counsel, Consolidated Management, Inc. *Member:* Cleveland (Chairman, Real Estate Section, 2001-2002; Co-Chairman, Real Estate Law Institute, 1997 and 1998; Member, Real Estate Law Section) and American (Member, Sections on: Real Property, Probate and Trust Law; Business Law) Bar Associations; National Association of Office and Industrial Properties; International Council of Shopping Centers. ***PRACTICE AREAS:*** Construction Law; Corporate Law; Real Estate Development; Real Estate Finance; Real Estate Leasing; Zoning Law. ***Email:*** dwaxman@waxmanblumenthal.com

MICHAEL R. BLUMENTHAL, born Cleveland, Ohio, October 28, 1959; admitted to bar, 1989, Ohio; 1993, U.S. District Court, Southern District of Ohio; 1995, U.S. District Court, Northern District of Ohio and U.S. Supreme Court. *Education:* Ohio State University (B.S., 1984); Cleveland Marshall College of Law (J.D., 1988). Assistant Attorney General, State of Ohio, 1989-1992. Contributing Author: "The Administrative Regulations for the Petroleum Underground Storage Tank Release Compensation Board (PETRO Board)," Anderson Publishing Company, 1992; "The Bureau of Underground Storage Tank Regulations," ("BUSTR"), Anderson Publishing Company, 1990. Co-Author: "The Underground Storage Tank Manual," Hemisphere Corporation, 1994. Legal Columnist, "The Underground Storage Tank Digest," Maxicom Publications, 1993-1995. *Member:* Cleveland, Ohio State (Environmental Law Committee) and American (Section on: Natural Resources Energy and Environmental Law) Bar Associations. ***REPORTED CASES:*** Amoco Oil Co. v. Petroleum Underground Storage Tank, 89 Ohio St.3d 477 (2000); Davis v. Sun Oil Company, United States Court of Appeals, 148 F. 3d 606 (6th Cir. 1998); Sun Co. Inc. v. Petroleum Underground Storage Tank, 133 Ohio App. 3d 449 (1999); Davis v. Sun Refining & Marketing Co., 109 Ohio App. 3d 42 (1996). ***PRACTICE AREAS:*** Construction Claims; Construction Litigation; Environmental Compliance and Litigation; CERCLA; Resource Conservation and Recovery Act (RCRA); Underground Storage Tank Regulation; Solid and Hazardous Waste; Federal Insecticide, Fungicide and Rodenticide (FIFRA); Environmental Cost Recovery; Wetlands Regulation; Safe Drinking Water Act; Brownfields Redevelopment; Mold Litigation; Oil Pollution; OSHA Compliance and Litigation; Asbestos Defense; Land Use Regulation. ***Email:*** mblumenthal@waxmanblumenthal.com

OF COUNSEL

FRANK MOSS, born Cleveland, Ohio, January 7, 1927; admitted to bar, 1957, Ohio and U.S. District Court, Northern District of Ohio. *Education:* Columbia University (B.A., 1949; LL.B., 1951). Attorney, Port of New York Authority, 1951-1956. In-House Legal Counsel, Forest City Enterprises, Inc. 1957-1965. Private Practice, 1965—. Past Member and Legal Counsel, Homebuilders Association of Greater Cleveland. Member, Columbia College and Columbia Law School Alumni Associations. Past Member and Officer, Beachwood Civic League and Beachwood Council on Community Affairs. *Member:* Cuyahoga County (Member, Real Property Law Section), Cleveland (Member, Sections on: Real Estate Law; Environmental Law; Co-Chairman, Real Estate Law Institute, 1986) and Ohio State (Member, Sections on: Real Property Law; Probate and Trust Law) Bar Associations. ***PRACTICE AREAS:*** Real Estate Law; Construction Law; Corporate Law; Real Estate Development; Subdivisions; Zoning Law; Condominium Law; Real Estate Leasing; Real Estate Finance. ***Email:*** fmoss@waxmanblumenthal.com

REPRESENTATIVE CLIENTS: Omni Realty Companies; Skye Development Company; National City Bank; LaSalle Bank; Renal Care Group, Inc.; First Interstate Properties, Ltd.; Conway Transportation, Inc.; Developers Diversified Realty Corporation; The Finch Company; BP, Chevron Texaco Corporation; Rysar Properties, Inc.; Rite Aid Corporation; Marathon Ashland Petroleum LLC; Tops Markets, LLC; Ohio Savings Bank; Sunoco; Emery Worldwide; Avis Rent-A-Car; CNF; Duke-Weeks Realty; Prima Energy Corporation; Sherwin-Williams Company; Heritage Development Company; Simon Property Group.

WEGMAN, HESSLER & VANDERBURG

A LEGAL PROFESSIONAL ASSOCIATION
6055 ROCKSIDE WOODS BOULEVARD, SUITE 200
CLEVELAND, OHIO 44131
Telephone: 216-642-3342
Fax: 216-642-8826

General Civil Practice in all Courts. Corporate, Labor/Employment, Personal Injury, Products Liability, Real Estate, Probate, Domestic Relations, Trials and Business and Estate Planning, Intellectual Property.

MARTIN J. WEGMAN (1918-1977)

DAVID J. HESSLER, born Wyandotte, Michigan, June 21, 1943; admitted to bar, 1968, Ohio; 1983, U.S. Supreme Court. *Education:* Valparaiso University (B.A., 1965; J.D.,

(This Listing Continued)

WEGMAN, HESSLER & VANDERBURG, A LEGAL PROFESSIONAL ASSOCIATION, Cleveland—Continued

1968). Pi Sigma Alpha; Delta Theta Phi. Assistant Law Director, North Olmsted, 1974-1979. *Member:* Cleveland, Ohio State and American Bar Associations. ***PRACTICE AREAS:*** Corporate. ***Email:*** djhessler@wegmanlaw.com

KEITH A. VANDERBURG, born Luverne, Minnesota, October 18, 1953; admitted to bar, 1978, Indiana and Ohio; 1982, U.S. Court of Appeals, Sixth Circuit; 1992, U.S. Supreme Court. *Education:* Dordt College (B.A., 1975); Valparaiso University (J.D., cum laude, 1978). Co-Recipient, Outstanding Legal Scholarship Award, Valparaiso University School of Law, 1977-1978. Listed, Ohio List of Super Lawyers, Cincinnati Magazine, 2004. *Member:* Cleveland, Ohio State and Indiana State Bar Associations; Christian Legal Society. ***PRACTICE AREAS:*** Commercial Transactions; Commercial Litigation. ***Email:*** kavanderburg@wegmanlaw.com

PETER A. HESSLER, born Manistee, Michigan, February 20, 1953; admitted to bar, 1978, Ohio; 1979, U.S. District Court, Northern District of Ohio; 1992, U.S. Supreme Court. *Education:* Valparaiso University (B.A., cum laude, 1975; J.D., with distinction, 1978). Pi Sigma Alpha; Omicron Delta Epsilon. Co-recipient, Outstanding Legal Scholarship Award, Valparaiso University School of Law, 1977-1978. *Member:* Cleveland, Ohio State and American Bar Associations; The Association of Trial Lawyers of America. ***PRACTICE AREAS:*** Litigation; Nonprofit Corporations. ***Email:*** pahessler@wegmanlaw.com

DAVID R. KNOWLES, born Cleveland, Ohio, September 28, 1947; admitted to bar, 1974, Ohio; 1980, U.S. Supreme Court and U.S. Court of Appeals, First Circuit; 1981, New York and U.S. Court of Appeals, Fifth, Eighth and Eleventh Circuits; 1983, U.S. Court of Appeals, Sixth Circuit; 1986, U.S. Court of Appeals, Fourth Circuit. *Education:* Cleveland State University (B.B.A., 1970); Cleveland-Marshall College of Law (J.D., 1973). Listed, Ohio List of Super Lawyers, Cincinnati Magazine, 2004. Instructor of Labor Law, Cuyahoga County Community College, 1977-1987. Trial Attorney, National Labor Relations Board, 1975-1977. *Member:* Cleveland (Member and Past Chair, Labor and Employment Law Section), Ohio State (Member, Labor and Employment Law Section), New York State and American (Member, Labor and Employment Law Section) Bar Associations. (Certified Specialist in Labor & Employment Law, Ohio State Bar Association). ***PRACTICE AREAS:*** Labor and Employment Law. ***Email:*** drknowles@wegmanlaw.com

JOHN D. KEDZIOR, born Cleveland, Ohio, September 10, 1955; admitted to bar, 1981, Ohio; 1983, U.S. District Court, Northern District of Ohio and U.S. Court of Appeals, Sixth Circuit. *Education:* Cleveland State University (B.A., 1978); Cleveland-Marshall College of Law (J.D., 1981). *Member:* Cleveland, Ohio State (Member, Estate Planning, Trust and Probate and Trust Law) and American (Member, Real Property, Probate and Trust Law) Bar Associations. ***PRACTICE AREAS:*** Probate Law; Trust Law; Estate Planning; Litigation; Taxation. ***Email:*** jdkedzior@wegmanlaw.com

STEVEN E. PRYATEL, born Cleveland, Ohio, March 18, 1960; admitted to bar, 1986, Ohio; 1989, U.S. District Court, Northern District of Ohio; 2002, U.S. Supreme Court. *Education:* Xavier University (B.S., magna cum laude, 1982); Cleveland-Marshall College of Law (J.D., 1985). Spangenberg Award for Outstanding Student in Trial Practice and Procedure. *Member:* Ohio State (Member, Corporate and Business Law Sections) and Federal Bar Associations. ***PRACTICE AREAS:*** Corporate; Real Estate. ***Email:*** sepryatel@wegmanlaw.com

RICHARD T. COYNE, born Cleveland, Ohio, September 25, 1964; admitted to bar, 1989, Ohio and U.S. District Court, Northern and Southern Districts of Ohio. *Education:* University of Dayton (B.A., 1986); Case Western Reserve University (J.D., 1989). *Member:* Ohio State and American Bar Associations; Trial Attorneys of America; Defense Research Institute. ***REPORTED CASES:*** Juan Cortez vs. MTD Products Inc, et al., In the United States District Court, Northern District of California, Case No. C-95-0990 WDB, 927 F.Supp. 386 (N.D.Cal., 1996). ***PRACTICE AREAS:*** Products Liability Law; Insurance Law; Litigation. ***Email:*** rtcoyne@wegmanlaw.com

LAWRENCE S. CROWTHER, born Cleveland, Ohio, April 5, 1958; admitted to bar, 1984, Ohio and U.S. District Court, Northern District of Ohio; 1989, U.S. Court of Appeals, Sixth Circuit; 2003, U.S. District Court, Southern District of Ohio. *Education:* St. Lawrence University (B.A., cum laude, 1980); Washington & Lee University (J.D., 1984). St. Lawrence University, Economics Honor Society. *Member:* Cleveland (Member, Corporate, Banking and Business Law Section) and Ohio State (Member, Corporate Counsel Section) Bar Associations. ***PRACTICE AREAS:*** Business Law; Real Estate; Creditors Rights; Commercial Litigation. ***Email:*** lscrowther@wegmanlaw.com

BRUCE E. PEACOCK, born Philadelphia, Pennsylvania, November 23, 1950; admitted to bar, 1975, Pennsylvania; 1988, Ohio; registered to practice before U.S. Patent and Trademark Office. *Education:* Philadelphia College of Textiles and Sciences (B.S., cum laude, 1972); University of Toledo (J.D., 1975). Recipient: Toledo Patent Law Scholarship Award, 1975; American Jurisprudence Book Award in Patent Law, Trust Law, and Copyright Law. Listed, Ohio List of Super Lawyers, Cincinnati Magazine, 2004. Adjunct Professor, University of Dayton Law School, 1990-1995. *Member:* American Bar Association; American Intellectual Property Law Association; Dayton Intellectual Property Law Association (Former President, 1999-2001); Cleveland Intellectual Property Law Association. ***PRACTICE AREAS:*** Intellectual Property. ***Email:*** bepeacock@wegmanlaw.com

JEFFREY W. KRUEGER, born Galesburg, Illinois, 1960; admitted to bar, 1985, Ohio and U.S. District Court, Northern District of Ohio; 1986, U.S. District Court, Southern District of Ohio; 1990, U.S. Court of Appeals, Sixth Circuit; 2002, U.S. Supreme Court; 2003, U.S. District Court, Eastern District of Michigan and U.S. District Court, Western District of Pennsylvania. *Education:* Bowling Green State University (B.S., 1982); Case Western Reserve University (J.D., 1985). *Member:* Medina County, Ohio State and Federal Bar Associations. ***PRACTICE AREAS:*** Commercial Litigation; Appellate Practice; Creditors Rights; Business Law. ***Email:*** jwkrueger@wegmanlaw.com

CHRISTOPHER A. HOLECEK, born Cleveland, Ohio, June 14, 1961; admitted to bar, 1988, Ohio; 1990, U.S. District Court, Northern District of Ohio; 2002, U.S. Supreme Court; U.S. Court of Appeals, Sixth Circuit. *Education:* John Carroll University (B.A., Economics, 1983); Cleveland-Marshall College of Law (J.D., 1988). Assistant Director of Law, City of Cleveland, 1988-1992. *Member:* Cleveland, Ohio State and Federal Bar Associations; Ohio Association of Civil Trial Attorneys. ***REPORTED CASES:*** Presrite v. Commercial Union Insurance Company (1996), 113 Ohio App. 3d 38; Burns v. Presrite Corporation (1994), 97 Ohio App. 3d 377; Phillips v. Garfield Heights (1992), 85 Ohio App. 3d 413; Cleveland Industrial Square v. Cleveland Bd. of Zoning Appeals (1992), 83 Ohio App. 3d 301. ***PRACTICE AREAS:*** Civil Litigation; Employment Litigation; Products Liability; Personal Injury; Appellate Practice. ***Email:*** caholecek@wegmanlaw.com

DAVID W. HERRINGTON, born Cleveland, Ohio, October 13, 1960; admitted to bar, 1986, Ohio; 1987, U.S. District Court, Northern District of Ohio. *Education:* Clemson University (B.A., summa cum laude, 1982); The Ohio State University (J.D., 1986). *Member:* Cleveland, Geauga County, and Ohio State Bar Associations; Defense Research Institute. ***PRACTICE AREAS:*** Product Liability; Litigation. ***Email:*** dwherrington@wegmanlaw.com

ANTOINETTE F. GIDEON, born Canton, Ohio, October 26, 1961; admitted to bar, 1987, Ohio; 1988, U.S. District Court, Northern District of Ohio; 1989, U.S. Court of Appeals, Sixth Circuit; 1990, U.S. District Court, Southern District of Ohio. *Education:* University of Dayton (B.A., 1983); University of Toledo (J.D., 1987). Author: "Workplace Surveillance," Ohio Lawyer, Jan/Feb 1991. *Member:* Cleveland (Member, Labor & Employment Section) and Ohio State Bar Associations. ***REPORTED CASES:*** Giambrone v. Spalding & Evenflo, 79 Ohio App. 3d 308 (1992); EEOC v. Ohio Edison, 7 F 3d 541 (6th Cir. 1993). ***PRACTICE AREAS:*** Labor Law; Employment Law. ***Email:*** afgideon@wegmanlaw.com

DAVID R. BUTTON, born Cleveland, Ohio, December 23, 1966; admitted to bar, 1992, Ohio. *Education:* The Ohio State University (B.S.B.A., 1988; J.D., 1992). ***PRACTICE AREAS:*** Real Estate; Estate Planning; Probate; Creditors Rights; Litigation. ***Email:*** drbutton@wegmanlaw.com

TANJA M. HOLECEK, born Cambridge, Ohio, November 6, 1964; admitted to bar, 1989, Ohio. *Education:* John Carroll University (B.S., 1986); Cleveland-Marshall College of Law (J.D., 1989). *Member:* Geauga County, Portage County and Ohio State Bar Associations; Center for Principled Family Advocacy. ***PRACTICE AREAS:*** Domestic Relations. ***Email:*** tmholecek@wegmanlaw.com

---

NATHAN E. HESSLER, born Cleveland, Ohio, August 29, 1970; admitted to bar, 1995, Ohio. *Education:* Valparaiso University (B.A., 1992; J.D., 1995). *Member:* Cleveland and Ohio State Bar Associations. ***Email:*** nehessler@wegmanlaw.com

SIMON P. DEMIAN, born Pembury, England, January 26, 1966; admitted to bar, 1992, Ohio; 1993, U.S. District Court, Northern District of Ohio. *Education:* Franklin & Marshall College (B.A., 1988); Cleveland-Marshall College of Law (J.D., 1992). Articles Editor, Journal of Law & Health. *Member:* Cleveland, Ohio State and American Bar Associations. ***PRACTICE AREAS:*** Corporate Law. ***Email:*** spdemian@wegmanlaw.com

DONNA M. DRESP, born Cleveland, Ohio, March 26, 1961; admitted to bar, 1995, Ohio. *Education:* Baldwin-Wallace College (B.A., summa cum laude, 1990); Cleveland-Marshall College of Law (J.D., 1994). ***PRACTICE AREAS:*** Probate (75%); Medicaid Planning (10%); Estate Planning (10%); Tax (5%). ***Email:*** dmdresp@wegmanlaw.com

KARL ROBERT WETZEL, born Cleveland, Ohio, May 6, 1958; admitted to bar, 1984, Ohio; 1996, U.S. District Court, District of Ohio; 1999, U.S. Supreme Court. *Education:* Bowling Green State University (B.A., cum laude, 1980); John Marshall Law School (J.D., 1984). Cuyahoga Assistant City Prosecutor, 1986-1995. Ohio Assistant Attorney General, 1995-1999. *Member:* Cleveland, Ohio State and American Bar Associations. ***PRACTICE AREAS:*** Litigation; Criminal; Antitrust; Environmental Law; Construction Law; Commercial Transactions. ***Email:*** krwetzel@wegmanlaw.com

JENNIFER A. CORSO, born Cleveland, Ohio, October 11, 1968; admitted to bar, 1994, Ohio. *Education:* Eastern Michigan University (B.S., 1990); Cleveland-Marshall College of Law (J.D., 1993). *Member:* Cleveland Bar Association; Ohio Women's Bar Association; Public Sector Labor Relations Association; Industrial Relations Resources Association. ***PRACTICE AREAS:*** Employment Law; Labor Law. ***Email:*** jacorso@wegmanlaw.com

LESLEY A. WEIGAND, born Barberton, Ohio, March 26, 1971; admitted to bar, 1996, Ohio and U.S. District Court, Northern District of Ohio; 1998, U.S. Tax Court; 2003, U.S. District Court, Southern District of Ohio and U.S. Court of Appeals, Federal Circuit; 2004, U.S. District Court, Western District of Pennsylvania. *Education:* Miami University (B.S., 1993); University of Akron (J.D., M.Tax, 1996). ***LANGUAGES:*** German. ***Email:*** laweigand@wegmanlaw.com

CHRISTOPHER A. CORPUS, born Cleveland, Ohio, January 6, 1970; admitted to bar, 2000, Ohio. *Education:* Ashland University (B.S., cum laude, 1993); Case Western Reserve University, Franklin Thomas Bakus School of Law (J.D., 2000). Member, Chamber of Commerce, Westshore, 2000—. *Member:* Ohio State and American Bar Associations. ***LANGUAGES:*** English. ***PRACTICE AREAS:*** Products Liability Litigation; Civil Litigation; Corporate Transactional; Business Litigation. ***Email:*** cacorpus@wegmanlaw.com

ANGELA MARIE PRIVITERA, born Buffalo, New York, 1972; admitted to bar, 1998, Ohio; 1999, U.S. District Court, Northern District of Ohio; 2000, U.S. Court of Appeals, Sixth Circuit. *Education:* State University of New York at Buffalo (B.A., 1994); Cleveland-Marshall College of Law (J.D., 1998). Member: Women's City Club of Cleveland, 1999—; Justinian Forum, 2000—. ***LANGUAGES:*** Italian. ***Email:*** amprivitera@wegmanlaw.com

ANDREW C. LAKE, born Cleveland, Ohio, September 21, 1964; admitted to bar, 1999, Ohio; registered to practice before U.S. Patent and Trademark Office. *Education:* College of Wooster (B.A., 1986); John Carroll University (M.B.A., 1993); University of Akron law School (J.D., 1999); Cleveland State University (B.A., Physics, 2002). Recipient: Anderson Publishing Scholastic Achievement Award; CALI Excellence for the Future Award. Member: Scanlon Inn of Court, 1998-1999; American Institute of Physics, 2001—; Institute of Electrical & Electronics Engineers, 2001—. ***PRACTICE AREAS:*** Intellectual Property. ***Email:*** alake@wegmanlaw.com

(This Listing Continued)

DANIELLE A. SKOCZEN, born Parma, Ohio, October 4, 1973; admitted to bar, 1999, Ohio; registered to practice before U.S. Patent and Trademark Office. *Education:* Ohio Northern University (B.S.M.E., 1996); Cleveland-Marshall College of Law (J.D., 1999). *Member:* Ohio State and American Bar Associations; Cleveland Intellectual Property Law Association; American Intellectual Property Law Association. ***PRACTICE AREAS:*** Intellectual Property. **Email:** daskoczen@wegmanlaw.com

JEFFREY S. ELLSWORTH, born Santa Barbara, California, 1968; admitted to bar, 2000, California; 2002, Missouri (Not admitted in Ohio). *Education:* Brigham Young University (B.S., Civil Engineering, 1991; J.D., 2000). [Lt., U.S. Navy, 1990-1997]. ***LANGUAGES:*** Portuguese. ***PRACTICE AREAS:*** Patents. **Email:** jsellsworth@wegmanlaw.com

CHRISTOPHER W. KRAUSE, born Parma, Ohio, January 23, 1962; admitted to bar, 1993, Ohio. *Education:* Baldwin-Wallace College (B.A., magna cum laude, English and Political Science, 1990); Ohio State University (J.D., 1993). Phi Sigma Alpha. *Member:* Cleveland, Lorain County and Ohio State Bar Associations; Estate Planning Council of Cleveland; National Association of Elder Law Attorneys. ***PRACTICE AREAS:*** Estate Planning; Wills; Trusts and Estates; Administrative Law; Guardianship; Conservatorship; Elder Law; Business Law; Corporate Law. **Email:** cwkrause@wegmanlaw.com

REFERENCE: Key Bank of Cleveland.

KEITH D. WEINER & ASSOCIATES CO., L.P.A.

Established in 1989

75 PUBLIC SQUARE
FOURTH FLOOR
CLEVELAND, OHIO 44113
Telephone: 216-771-6500
Fax: 216-771-6540
Email: collections@weinerlaw.com
URL: http://www.weinerlaw.com

Collections, Bankruptcy, Foreclosures, Evictions, Replevins, Mechanic Liens, Commercial Litigation, Post Judgment Collections.

FIRM PROFILE: Our practice is limited to representing creditors in the debt collection arena. We handle secured and unsecured claims. In addition to attorneys we are staffed with debt collectors, paralegals & support staff. We offer competent personalized service on a contingency or hourly basis.

KEITH D. WEINER, born New York, N.Y., February 8, 1957; admitted to bar, 1982, Ohio; 1983, U.S. District Court, Northern and Eastern Districts of Ohio; 2000, U.S. District Court, Southern District of Ohio. *Education:* State University of New York at Buffalo (B.A., 1979); Cleveland State University (J.D., 1982). Special Counsel to Ohio Attorney General's Office. *Member:* Cleveland, Cuyahoga County and Ohio State Bar Associations. ***PRACTICE AREAS:*** Retail Collections; Commercial Collections; Post Judgment Remedies; Replevins; Real Estate Foreclosures; Bankruptcy; Mechanical Liens; Creditors Rights; Evictions. **Email:** kweiner@weinerlaw.com

---

KIM M. HAMMOND, born Augusta, Georgia, August 22, 1967; admitted to bar, 1993, Ohio. *Education:* State University of New York at Buffalo (B.A., 1990); Cleveland-Marshall College of Law (J.D., 1993). *Member:* Cleveland Bar Association. ***PRACTICE AREAS:*** Real Estate Foreclosures; Real Estate Title Claims; Real Estate Litigation. **Email:** khammond@weinerlaw.com

GILBERT E. BLOMGREN, born Cleveland, Ohio, March 24, 1969; admitted to bar, 1995, Ohio; 1996, U.S. District Court, Northern District of Ohio; 1997, U.S. District Court, Southern District of Ohio. *Education:* Kenyon College (B.A., 1991); Case Western Reserve University (J.D., 1995). *Member:* Cuyahoga County Bar Association. ***PRACTICE AREAS:*** Civil Litigation; Collections; Foreclosures; Contracts; Replevins. **Email:** gblomgren@weinerlaw.com

LEONARD A. CUILLI, born Cleveland, Ohio, October 12, 1966; admitted to bar, 1997, Ohio. *Education:* Ohio State University (B.A., English, 1990); Cleveland-Marshall College of Law (J.D., 1996). Formerly with Carlisle, McNellie, Rini, Kramer and Ulrich. ***PRACTICE AREAS:*** Foreclosures. **Email:** lcuilli@weinerlaw.com

SUZANA KRASNICKI, born Euclid, Ohio, December 21, 1974; admitted to bar, 2001, Ohio. *Education:* Mercyhurst College (B.A., 1997); Cleveland-Marshall College of Law (J.D., 2000). Author: "Accidental Release Prevention on a General Duty Clause Discussed," The Air and Waste Management Association Newsletter, Northern Chapter, Volume 12, Number 1, April 1990. Legal Defender, Legal Defender's Office, 2001-2002. *Member:* Women's Bar Association. ***PRACTICE AREAS:*** Civil Litigation; Collections; Criminal Law. **Email:** skrasnicki@weinerlaw.com

TODD A. BOBKA, born 1973; admitted to bar, 1999, Ohio; 2002, U.S. District Court, Northern District of Ohio; 2003, U.S. District Court, Southern District of Ohio. *Education:* Ohio University (B.B.A., cum laude, 1996); Cleveland-Marshall College of Law (J.D., 1999). Former Associate, Rauser & Associates. *Member:* Ohio State Bar Association. ***PRACTICE AREAS:*** Bankruptcy. **Email:** tbobka@weinerlaw.com

MATTHEW P. CURRY, born Marion, Ohio, November 11, 1974; admitted to bar, 2004, Ohio. *Education:* Youngstown State University (B.A., M.A., 2001); Cleveland-Marshall College of Law (J.D., 2004). ***PRACTICE AREAS:*** Foreclosures; Litigation; Collections. **Email:** mcurry@weinerlaw.com

REPRESENTATIVE CLIENTS: State of Ohio; Citifinancial Mortgage Company; HSBC pka; Household Finance Corporation; Beneficial Financial Corporation; Litton Loan Servicing; Accredited Loan Lenders; SN Servicing Corp.; Ohio Machinery Co.; Ohio Savings Bank; Kaiser Peramente; Management Recruiters International.

WELTMAN, WEINBERG & REIS CO., L.P.A.

323 W. LAKESIDE AVENUE, SUITE 200
CLEVELAND, OHIO 44113
Telephone: 216-685-1000
Fax: 216-363-4121
Email: wwr@weltman.com
URL: http://www.weltman.com

Burlington, New Jersey Office: Telephone: 609-914-0437.
Chicago, Illinois Office: Telephone: 312-782-9676.
Cincinnati, Ohio Office: Telephone: 513-723-2200.
Columbus, Ohio Office: Telephone: 614-228-7272.
Deerfield, Illinois Office: Telephone: 847-940-9812
Philadelphia, Pennsylvania Office: Telephone: 215-599-1500.
Pittsburgh, Pennsylvania Office: Telephone: 412-434-7955.
Troy, Michigan Office: Telephone: 248-362-6100.

Creditors Rights, Collections, Creditor Bankruptcy, Foreclosure/Eviction, Title Insurance Law, Fair Debt Collections Practices Act, Probate/Deceased Collections, Subrogation, Credit Union Law, Banks and Banking, Creditor Defense, Complex Consumer and Commercial Litigation, Real Estate Title & Closing Services.

FIRM PROFILE: WWR is the largest creditors' rights law firm in the country based on revenues and placements according to Collections & Credit Risk magazine. Our clients include banks, financial institutions, auto financers, mortgage companies, credit unions, service organizations, government entities, insurance companies, utility companies and corporations. We provide traditional collection agency services nationally and direct legal representation with in-house attorneys in Illinois, Indiana, Kentucky, Michigan, New Jersey, Ohio and Pennsylvania. WWR takes an active role working with clients in order to implement new strategies and programs, and partner with them to offer solutions to daily concerns that affect profitability. See individual listings in each city.

Alliances/Associations: American Collectors Association; Commercial Law League of America; National Association of Retail Collectors; attorneys certified as Creditors Rights Specialists by American Board of Certification.

ROBERT B. WELTMAN, born Cleveland, Ohio, December 23, 1937; admitted to bar, 1965, Ohio; U.S. District Court, Northern District of Ohio; U.S. Supreme Court. *Education:* The Ohio State University (B.B.A., 1959); The Ohio State University (M.A. in Finance, 1962); Case Western Reserve University School of Law (LL.B., 1965). Recipient, Ernst & Young Entrepreneur of The Year Award for the Service Industry Category in Northeast Ohio, 2003. Instructor, Cleveland Bar Association Continuing Education, 1986—. Director, Ohio Credit Union League, 1982-1990. Treasurer, Menorah Federal Credit Union, 1965-1985. Past President, Menorah Federal Credit Union. Established scholarship fund in honor of Maurice Weltman at the Cleveland-Marshall College of Law, Cleveland State University. Ohio Super Lawyer (2004, 2005). *Member:* Cleveland (Member, Municipal Court Committee), Cuyahoga County, Ohio and American Bar Associations; National Association of Retail Collection Attorneys; Northern Ohio Credit Association. [Ohio National Guard, 1959-1962]. ***PRACTICE AREAS:*** Creditors Rights; Collection, Banking Law; Commercial and Consumer Litigation; Complex Litigation; Collection Services. **Email:** rweltman@weltman.com

ALAN H. WEINBERG, born Boston, Massachusetts, March 8, 1950; admitted to bar, 1974, Ohio; 1975, U.S. District Court, Northern District of Ohio; 1999, U.S. Supreme Court. *Education:* Boston University (B.A., Mathematics, magna cum laude, 1971) Phi Beta Kappa; Case Western Reserve University School of Law (J.D., 1974). Phi Beta Kappa; Phi Delta Phi (Vice-President, 1973-1974). Lecturer: Debt Collection, Ohio CLE Institute, 1994-2002; Ohio Magistrates Association, 1996; AIC Conference, Inc., 1997; Debt Collection, National Business Institute, 2004-2005. Ohio Clerk of Courts Association, 1999-2000, Garnishment, Ohio State Bar Association 2005. Managing Partner of Weltman, Weinberg & Reis Co., L.P.A., 1996—. *Member:* Cleveland (Member, Bankruptcy and Commercial Law Sections) and Ohio State Bar Associations; Ohio Creditors Attorneys Association (Educational Chairperson); Commercial Law League of America; Northern Ohio Credit Association (Past President). [U.S. Army Finance Corps, 1971-1979; Distinguished Graduate Army Finance School, 1974]. (Certified as Creditors' Rights Specialist by the American Board of Certification). ***PRACTICE AREAS:*** Commercial and Consumer Litigation; Creditors Rights; Litigation and Defense. **Email:** aweinberg@weltman.com

LARRY R. ROTHENBERG, born Cleveland, Ohio, September 18, 1953; admitted to bar, 1978, Ohio and U.S. District Court, Northern District of Ohio; 1986, U.S. Court of Appeals, Sixth Circuit. *Education:* The Ohio University (B.B.A., summa cum laude, 1975); The Ohio State University Michael E. Moritz College of Law (J.D., 1978). Author: Ohio Jurisdictional Summary for "The Law of Distressed Real Estate," Clark Boardman Callaghan. Served on Executive Committee of National Association of Foreclosure Professionals (now known as American Legal and Financial Network); Past President, Mortgage Servicing Society of Northeast Ohio; Past Chairman, Cleveland Bar Association, Real Estate Section and Foreclosure Procedures Committee; Past Chairman, Real Estate Law Institute; Past Chairman, Cuyahoga County Bar Association, Real Property Section. *Member:* Cleveland, Cuyahoga County and Ohio State Bar Associations. (Certified as Creditors' Rights Specialist by the American Board of Certification). ***PRACTICE AREAS:*** Foreclosure/Evictions; Real Estate; Title Insurance; Creditors Rights. **Email:** lrothenberg@weltman.com

CHARLES G. PONA, born Cleveland, Ohio, April 13, 1960; admitted to bar, 1987, Ohio; 1988, U.S. District Court, Northern District of Ohio; 1998, Pennsylvania. *Education:* Bowling Green State University (B.S., magna cum laude, 1982); Cleveland State University, Cleveland-Marshall College of Law (J.D., 1986). *Member:* Ohio State Bar Association; Northern Ohio Credit Association; Commercial Law League of America; National Association of Retail Collection Attorneys (Immediate Past President). ***PRACTICE AREAS:*** Creditors Rights; Collection Services; Commercial Law. **Email:** cpona@weltman.com

ALAN C. HOCHHEISER, born Brooklyn, New York, May 1, 1963; admitted to bar, 1989, Ohio, U.S. District Court, Northern District of Ohio and U.S. Court of Appeals, Sixth

(This Listing Continued)

WELTMAN, WEINBERG & REIS CO., L.P.A., Cleveland—Continued

Circuit; 1995, U.S. District Court, Western District of Pennsylvania. *Education:* State University of New York at Albany (B.A., cum laude, 1985); Case Western Reserve University School of Law (J.D., 1988). Phi Delta Phi. *Member:* Cleveland (Member, Sections on: Bankruptcy Law; Commercial Law) and Ohio State Bar Associations; Northern Ohio Credit Association; American Bankruptcy Institute (Consumer Committee Member); National Association of Ch. 13 Trustees (Member, Creditors' Auxiliary); Commercial Law League of America; National Association of Bankruptcy Trustees (Associate Member). ***PRACTICE AREAS:*** Creditors Rights; Bankruptcy Law. **Email:** ahochheiser@weltman.com

SCOTT S. WELTMAN, born Cleveland, Ohio, June 29, 1964; admitted to bar, 1989, California and U.S. District Court, Central District of California; 1990, Ohio; 2001, U.S. Supreme Court. *Education:* University of Southern California (B.S., magna cum laude, 1986); University of Southern California, The Law School (J.D., 1989). Phi Kappa Phi; Beta Gamma Sigma; Order of the Coif. *Member:* American, Cuyahoga County, Cleveland and Ohio State Bar Associations; State Bar of California. ***PRACTICE AREAS:*** Creditors Rights; Commercial Litigation; Consumer and Commercial Collection Law; Commercial Collections; Probate Law; Nursing Home Collections; Collection Services. **Email:** sweltman@weltman.com

ROSEMARY TAFT-MILBY, born Louisville, Kentucky, December 4, 1957; admitted to bar, 1983, Kentucky; 1984, U.S. District Court, Eastern District of Kentucky; 1991, Ohio and U.S. District Court, Northern District of Ohio; 1995, U.S. Supreme Court; 1997, U.S. Court of Appeals, Sixth Circuit; 2004, U.S. Court of Federal Claims; 2005, U.S. District Court, Western District of Kentucky. *Education:* University of Louisville (B.A., with honors, 1978); The Louis D. Brandeis School of Law at University of Lousiville (J.D., 1983). Phi Alpha Delta; Ohio Super Lawyer (2004, 2005); YMCA Woman of Professional Excellence (2004). *Member:* Cleveland (Member, Commission on Women in the Law), Ohio State (Member, Sections on: Women in the Profession; Litigation), Kentucky, American and Ohio Women's Bar Associations. (Certified as Creditors' Rights Specialist by the American Board of Certification). ***PRACTICE AREAS:*** Commercial and Consumer Litigation; Creditors Rights; Litigation and Defense. **Email:** rtaftmilby@weltman.com

THERESA A. FORTUNATO, born Cleveland, Ohio, December 9, 1967; admitted to bar, 1992, Ohio and U.S. District Court, Northern District of Ohio. *Education:* John Carroll University (B.A., cum laude, 1989); Case Western Reserve University School of Law (J.D., 1992). Phi Alpha Delta (Alumni Advisor). Law Clerk to Hon. Carolyn B. Friedland and Hon. Frank D. Celebrezze, Jr., Cuyahoga County Court of Common Pleas, 1993-1995. Treasurer, Northern Ohio Credit Association. *Member:* Cleveland and Ohio State Bar Associations; Ohio Women's Bar Association; National Association of Retail Collection Attorneys; Debt Buyer's Association; Justinian Forum. ***PRACTICE AREAS:*** Commercial and Consumer Litigation; Creditors Rights; Legal Action Recovery. **Email:** tfortunato@weltman.com

DONALD A. MAUSAR, born Cleveland, Ohio, August 1, 1963; admitted to bar, 1995, Ohio; 1998, U.S. District Court, Northern District of Ohio. *Education:* Cleveland State University (B.A., cum laude, 1991); Cleveland State University, James J. Nance College of Business (M.B.A., with honors, 1995); Cleveland State University, Cleveland-Marshall School of Law (J.D., cum laude, 1995). *Member:* Cuyahoga County and Cleveland Bar Associations; Northern Ohio Credit Association. ***PRACTICE AREAS:*** Creditors Rights; Commercial and Consumer Litigation; Collection Services. **Email:** dmausar@weltman.com

ROBERT W. RUTKOWSKI, born Washington, D.C., May 13, 1966; admitted to bar, 1991, Ohio; 1992, U.S. District Court, Northern District of Ohio. *Education:* University of Akron (B.A., cum laude, 1988); Case Western Reserve University School of Law (J.D., 1991). Lake County Educational Federal Credit Union (former Board President, Board of Directors); Lecturer for CUNA, CUES, NAFCU, The Ohio Credit Union System, The Pennsylvania Credit Union Association, The New Jersey Credit Union League, The Indiana Credit Union League, The Illinois Credit Union League, Lorman and NBI; published in Credit Union Magazine, CUES Management Magazine and The Cleveland Bar Journal. *Member:* Cleveland (Trustee, 2001-2004; Professional Ethics, 1999-2000; Unauthorized Practice Law Committee, 1999-2000; Technology Committee, 2000-2002), Lake County, Ohio State and American Bar Associations. ***PRACTICE AREAS:*** Credit Union Law; Regulatory Compliance; Employment Law; Contracts; Creditors; Real Estate. **Email:** rrutkowski@weltman.com

GEORGE R. HICKS, JR., born Cleveland, Ohio, June 9, 1954; admitted to bar, 1988, Ohio; 1989, U.S. District Court, Northern District of Ohio; 1992, U.S. Supreme Court; 1998, U.S. District Court, District of Arizona. *Education:* United States Naval Academy (B.S., 1976); Cleveland State University, Cleveland-Marshall College of Law (J.D., 1987). Lectures: Equal Credit Opportunity Act. *Member:* American, Ohio State and Cleveland Bar Associations. [Capt., USNR, Ret]. ***LANGUAGES:*** French. ***PRACTICE AREAS:*** Creditors Rights; Litigation and Defense. **Email:** ghicks@weltman.com

SARA M. DONNERSBACH, born New Washington, Ohio, August 26, 1972; admitted to bar, 1998, Ohio and U.S. District Court, Northern District of Ohio. *Education:* Heidelberg College (B.S., 1994); Cleveland State University (M.B.A., 1998); Cleveland Marshall College of Law (J.D., 1998). *Member:* American, Ohio State and Cuyahoga County Bar Associations; Northern Ohio Creditors' Association; Cleveland Professional 20/30 Club; Cleveland-Marshall College of Law Alumni Association. ***PRACTICE AREAS:*** Creditors Rights; Commercial Litigation; Collection Services; Complex Litigation. **Email:** sdonnersbach@weltman.com

EILEEN M. BITTERMAN, born Cleveland, Ohio, July 18, 1969; admitted to bar, 1997, Ohio; 2003, U.S. District Court, Northern District of Ohio. *Education:* University of Dayton (B.A., 1991); Cleveland-Marshall College of Law (J.D., 1997). Lectures, FDCPA CLE Seminars for: Ohio State Bar Association; Judicial College; NBI. Member: American Collectors Association, Member's Attorney Program (MAP); Northern Ohio Credit Association. *Member:* Cleveland Bar Association (Member: Joint Committee on Bar Admissions; Appeals Committee); Cuyahoga County Bar Association (Member: Joint Committee on Bar Admissions; Appeals Committee); Ohio State Bar Associations. (Compliance Officer). ***PRACTICE AREAS:*** Creditors Rights; Fair Debt Collection Practices Act Compliance; Employment Law; Collections; Compliance/Training. **Email:** ebitterman@weltman.com

---

A. ELIZABETH CARGLE, born Ravenna, Ohio, November 23, 1968; admitted to bar, 1998, Ohio and U.S. District Court, Northern District of Ohio; 2003, U.S. Court of Appeals, Sixth Circuit. *Education:* Kent State University (B.A., 1994); University of Akron School of Law (J.D., 1998); Tiffin University (M.B.A.). *Member:* Akron, Ohio State and American Bar Associations; Women's Bar Association. ***PRACTICE AREAS:*** Litigation and Defense; Creditors Rights; Intellectual Property; Corporate Law. **Email:** ecargle@weltman.com

JAMES M. DORAN, born New Liskeard, Ontario, Canada, April 5, 1973; admitted to bar, 1998, Ohio and U.S. District Court, Northern District of Ohio. *Education:* Miami University (B.S., 1995);Cleveland-Marshall College of Law (J.D., 1998). Beta Alpha Psi; Golden Key National Honor Society. President, 2003— and Member, Deerfield Meadows Home Owners Association, Inc. *Member:* Ohio State, Cuyahoga County and Cleveland Bar Associations. ***PRACTICE AREAS:*** Commercial Litigation; Consumer Litigation; Creditors Rights; Collection Services; Credit Union Law; Bankruptcy Law. **Email:** jdoran@weltman.com

STEVEN EMERY, born Haverhill, Massachusetts; admitted to bar, 2002, Ohio; 2003, U.S. District Court, Northern District of Ohio. *Education:* Tufts University (B.A., cum laude, 1995); Case Western Reserve University School of Law (J.D., 2000). *Member:* Ohio State and Cleveland Bar Associations. ***PRACTICE AREAS:*** Creditors Rights; Bankruptcy. **Email:** semery@weltman.com

SCOTT D. FINK, born New York, New York, January 16, 1972; admitted to bar, 1998, Ohio and U.S. District Court, Northern, District of Ohio; 2000, U.S. District Court, Southern District of Ohio. *Education:* Miami University (B.A., 1993); Case Western Reserve University School of Law (J.D., 1997). *Member:* Cleveland, Cuyahoga County and Ohio State Bar Associations. ***PRACTICE AREAS:*** Bankruptcy; Creditors Rights. **Email:** sfink@weltman.com

STANLEY GREEN, born Montreal, Quebec, Canada, November 11, 1943; admitted to bar, 1969, Ohio; 1970, U.S. District Court, Northern District of Ohio; 1985, U.S. Court of Appeals, Sixth Circuit and U.S. Supreme Court; 1997, Michigan; 1998, U.S. District Court, Eastern District of Michigan. *Education:* Miami University (B.S., 1966); University of Akron School of Law (J.D., 1969). Member, American Collectors Association. *Member:* Cleveland, Cuyahoga County and Ohio State Bar Associations. ***PRACTICE AREAS:*** Creditors Rights; Commercial Litigation; Collection Services; Complex Litigation. **Email:** sgreen@weltman.com

DAVID A. HEAD, born Dover, Ohio, July 17, 1977; admitted to bar, 2002, Ohio. *Education:* Ashland College (B.A., cum laude, 1999); Cleveland State Unviersity, Cleveland-Marshall College of Law (J.D., magna cum laude, 2002). Member, Northern Ohio Credit Association. *Member:* Ohio State Bar Association. ***PRACTICE AREAS:*** Collection Services; Commercial Law; Consumer Law; Debtor and Creditor; Litigation. **Email:** dhead@weltman.com

BENJAMIN N. HOEN, born Cleveland, Ohio, June 1, 1976; admitted to bar, 2004, Ohio. *Education:* Tomchei Tmimim Lubavitz, First Rabbinical Degree, Central Yeshiva; Cleveland State University, Cleveland-Marshall College of Law (J.D., cum laude, 2004). Member, Moot Court Board of Governors, Cleveland State University Cleveland-Marshall College of Law, 2002-2003. *Member:* Ohio State and Cleveland Bar Associations. ***PRACTICE AREAS:*** Foreclosure/Evictions; Creditors Rights; Real Estate. **Email:** bhoen@weltman.com

AMY CLUM HOLBROOK, born Indianapolis, Indiana, November 8, 1972; admitted to bar, 2002, Ohio. *Education:* Ohio Northern University (B.A., 1995); University of Akron Law School (J.D., 2002). *Member:* American, Ohio State and Cleveland Bar Associations. ***PRACTICE AREAS:*** Legal Action Recovery; Creditors Rights. **Email:** aholbrook@weltman.com

BRYAN T. KOSTURA, born Bedford, Ohio, June 5, 1978; admitted to bar, 2005, Ohio. *Education:* John Carroll University (B.A., 2001); Cleveland State University, Cleveland-Marshall College of Law (J.D., 2004). *Member:* American Bar Association. ***PRACTICE AREAS:*** Bankruptcy; Creditors Rights. **Email:** bkostura@weltman.com

LUCILLE MARKOWSKI, born Cleveland, Ohio, June 24, 1948; admitted to bar, 1989, Ohio and U.S. District Court, Northern District of Ohio. *Education:* Myers University (B.S., cum laude, 1985); Cleveland State University, Cleveland-Marshall College of Law (J.D., 1988). Business Law Lecturer, Myers University. Member, Myers University Paralegal Advisory Board Program. *Member:* Cleveland and Ohio State Bar Associations. ***PRACTICE AREAS:*** Legal Action Recovery; Creditors Rights. **Email:** lmarkowski@weltman.com

JENNIFER M. MONTY, born Cleveland, Ohio, June 20, 1978; admitted to bar, 2003, Ohio; 2004, U.S. District Court, Northern District of Ohio. *Education:* DePauw University (B.A., cum laude, 2000); The Ohio State University, Michael E. Moritz College of Law (J.D., 2003). Delta Theta Phi. Participant, Ohio State Moot Court Competition. Member and Regional Semi-Finalist, National Moot Court Team. Recipient: John E. Hallen Memorial Award; CALI Award of Excellence in Torts. *Member:* Cuyahoga County and Ohio State Bar Associations. ***PRACTICE AREAS:*** Creditors Rights; Litigation and Defense. **Email:** jmonty@weltman.com

CHRISTOPHER E. OLSZTYN, born Detroit, Michigan, May 14, 1977; admitted to bar, 2004, Ohio. *Education:* University of Michigan (B.A., 1999); Case Western Reserve University School of Law (J.D., 2003). *Member:* American and Ohio State Bar Associations. ***LANGUAGES:*** Polish. ***PRACTICE AREAS:*** Creditors Rights; Real Estate; Foreclosure/Evictions. **Email:** colsztyn@weltman.com

DANIELLE PECENKA CULLEN, born Fairview Park, Ohio, June 25, 1973; admitted to bar, 1998, Ohio; 1999, U.S. District Court, Northern District of Ohio. *Education:* The Ohio State University (B.A., 1995); Capital University Law School (J.D., 1998). Member, Young Directors of the Center for Families and Children. *Member:* Cleveland and Ohio

(This Listing Continued)

State Bar Associations. ***PRACTICE AREAS:*** Commercial Law; Contract Litigation; Creditors Rights; Torts; Municipal Law; Litigation and Defense. ***Email:*** dpecenkacullen@weltman.com

JOHN B. C. PORTER, born Evanston, Illinois, August 12, 1976; admitted to bar, 2002, Ohio; 2003, U.S. District Court, Northern District of Ohio. *Education:* Wittenberg University (B.A., magna cum laude, with honors, 1999); The Ohio State University, Michael E. Moritz College of Law (J.D., 2002). Phi Beta Kappa. Recipient, CALI Award for Pre-Trial Litigation, 2001. Finalist, National Moot Court Competition, 2002. Author: "Regulation CC & Deposits Into Share Accounts," Summer 2003; "Recent Trends in Courtesy Pay or Bounced-Check Protection Programs," Summer 2004; "Credit Union Mergers Implicate Burdensome and Onerous Reporting Requirements," Spring 2005; "Amendments to Truth in Savings Act Target Courtesy Pay Programs," Fall 2005. *Member:* Cleveland and Ohio State Bar Associations. ***PRACTICE AREAS:*** Credit Union Representation; Banks and Banking; Commercial Law; Creditors Rights; Litigation. ***Email:*** jporter@weltman.com

MARIA A. ROWAN, born Painesville, Ohio, March 5, 1976; admitted to bar, 2003, Ohio. *Education:* Ohio University (B.A., 1999); Case Western Reserve University School of Law (J.D., 2002). Phi Delta Phi Legal Ethics Fraternity. *Member:* The Ohio State Bar Association; The American Bar Association. ***PRACTICE AREAS:*** Commercial Collections; Probate; Creditors Rights. ***Email:*** mrowan@weltman.com

WILLIAM M. SHACKELFORD, born Warren, Ohio, October 31, 1961; admitted to bar, 1996, Ohio; 1997, U.S. District Court, Northern District of Ohio. *Education:* Mount Vernon Nazarene University (B.A., 1983); University of Akron School of Law (J.D., with honors, 1996). *Member:* Trumbull and Ohio State Bar Associations. ***PRACTICE AREAS:*** Collection Services; Creditors Rights. ***Email:*** wshackelford@weltman.com

DEAN S. TALAGANIS, born New Castle, Pennsylvania, 1962; admitted to bar, 1989, Ohio; 1990, U.S. Claims Court and U.S. District Court, Southern District of Ohio; 1999, U.S. District Court, Northern District of Ohio. *Education:* Youngstown State University (B.S.B.A., 1986); Capital University Law School (J.D., 1989). Phi Kappa Tau (Former Trustee, Alumni Association). Former Trustee, Pinegate Homeowner's Association (three terms). Licensed Title Insurance Agent, Ohio and Michigan. *Member:* Lake County and Ohio State Bar Associations; Northern Ohio Credit Association (Director & Former President); Ohio Land Title Association. ***PRACTICE AREAS:*** Creditors Rights; Foreclosure/Evictions; Real Estate; Title Insurance. ***Email:*** dtalaganis@weltman.com

JULIE A. VACCARELLI MUSSMAN, born Buffalo, New York, May 17, 1977; admitted to bar, 2003, Ohio. *Education:* State University of New York College at Buffalo (B.A., 1999); Cleveland State University, Cleveland-Marshall College of Law (J.D., 2003). *Member:* Cleveland and Ohio State Bar Associations. ***PRACTICE AREAS:*** Creditors Rights; Legal Action Recovery. ***Email:*** jvaccarelli@weltman.com

HEATHER R. BALDWIN VLASUK, born Erie, Pennsylvania, August 25, 1977; admitted to bar, 2004, Ohio. *Education:* Bowling Green State University (B.A., cum laude, 1999); Cleveland State University, Cleveland-Marshall College of Law (J.D., cum laude, 2003). *Member:* Ohio State Bar Associations. ***PRACTICE AREAS:*** Compliance/Training. ***Email:*** hbaldwinvlasuk@weltman.com

ANDREW C. VOORHEES, born Cleveland, Ohio, March 17, 1978; admitted to bar, 2004, Ohio. *Education:* University of Akron (B.A., 2001); University of Akron School of Law (J.D., cum laude, 2004). *Member:* Ohio State and American Bar Associations. ***PRACTICE AREAS:*** Collection Services; Creditors Rights. ***Email:*** avoorhees@weltman.com

STACIE H. WITTENBERG, born Royal Oak, Michigan, January 25, 1975; admitted to bar, 2000, Ohio; 2001, U.S. District Court, Northern District Court; 2005, U.S. Court of Appeals, Sixth Circuit. *Education:* University of Michigan (B.A., 1997); University of Toledo College of Law (J.D., 2000). *Member:* Toledo, Cleveland and Ohio State Bar Associations. ***PRACTICE AREAS:*** Creditors Rights; Bankruptcy. ***Email:*** swittenberg@weltman.com

MATTHEW M. YOUNG, born Akron, Ohio, June 19, 1976; admitted to bar, 2002, Ohio. *Education:* Ohio University (B.A., magna cum laude, 1999); The Ohio State University, Michael E. Moritz College of Law (J.D., 2002). *Member:* Cleveland and Ohio State Bar Associations. ***PRACTICE AREAS:*** Litigation; Creditors Rights; Banks and Banking; Commercial Law; Credit Union Representation. ***Email:*** myoung@weltman.com

AMANDA YURECHKO, born Canton, Ohio, May 2, 1975; admitted to bar, 2000, Ohio. *Education:* Miami University (B.A., 1997); University of Akron School of Law (J.D., cum laude, 2000). *Member:* Cleveland and Ohio State Bar Associations. ***PRACTICE AREAS:*** Creditors Rights; Collection Services. ***Email:*** ayurechko@weltman.com

(For complete biographical data on other personnel, see Professional Biographies at other locations)

WESTON HURD LLP

Established in 1925

THE TOWER AT ERIEVIEW
1301 EAST 9TH STREET, SUITE 1900
CLEVELAND, OHIO 44114-1882
Telephone: 216-241-6602;
Ohio Toll Free: 800-336-4952
FAX: 216-621-8369
URL: http://www.westonhurd.com

General Civil Practice in State and Federal Courts. Appellate, Banking and Finance, Bankruptcy, Business Law, Civil Litigation, Commercial Law, Commercial Litigation, Corporate Law, Construction Law, Creditors' Rights, Domestic Relations, Environmental Law, Family Law, Government Relations, Health Care, Insurance, Intellectual Property, Labor and Employment, Litigation, Long Term Care, Medical Malpractice, Mergers, Acquisitions and Divestitures, Municipal Law, Nonprofit and Charitable Organizations, Nursing Home Litigation, Probate, Products Liability, Professional Liability Defense, Real Estate, Securities, Taxation, Toxic Torts, Trademarks and Copyrights, Trusts and Estates.

(This Listing Continued)

FIRM PROFILE: The lawyers at Weston Hurd LLP have provided superior legal services for more than 80 years. Weston Hurd counsels local and national clients in all legal specialities. The firm represents corporations, insurance companies, governmental bodies, non-profit enterprises, health care providers, real estate entities, other unincorporated businesses, partnerships and individuals.

LAW FIRM ALLIANCES/ASSOCIATIONS: **MSI LEGAL & ACCOUNTING NETWORK WORLDWIDE**

S. BURNS WESTON (1904-1994)

FRANK SETH HURD (1913-1990)

HAROLD FALLON (1910-1989)

LOUIS PAISLEY (1922-2002)

LEE C. HOWLEY (1910-1983)

MEMBERS OF FIRM

DAVID ARNOLD, admitted to bar, 1966, Ohio. *Education:* Ohio University (B.A., 1963); The Ohio State University (J.D., 1966). ***PRACTICE AREAS:*** Family Law; Business Transactions; Commercial Litigation. ***Email:*** DArnold@westonhurd.com

JAMES S. AUSSEM, admitted to bar, 1975, Ohio. *Education:* Baldwin-Wallace College (B.A., 1971); Cleveland-Marshall College of Law (J.D., 1975). ***PRACTICE AREAS:*** Mergers and Acquisitions; Business; Corporate; Successions; Estate Planning; Estate Administration. ***Email:*** JAussem@westonhurd.com

CAROLYN M. CAPPEL, admitted to bar, 1977, Ohio. *Education:* Indiana University (B.A., 1974); Cleveland-Marshall College of Law (J.D., 1977). ***PRACTICE AREAS:*** Products Liability; Construction Law. ***Email:*** CCappel@westonhurd.com

ANGELA G. CARLIN, admitted to bar, 1955, Ohio. *Education:* Bowling Green State University (A.B., 1952); Case Western Reserve University (J.D., 1955). ***PRACTICE AREAS:*** Probate Law; Trust Law; Estate Planning Law. ***Email:*** ACarlin@westonhurd.com

KAREN A. DAVEY, admitted to bar, 1980, Ohio. *Education:* John Carroll University (A.B., 1977); Cleveland-Marshall College of Law (J.D., 1980). ***PRACTICE AREAS:*** Probate Law; Trusts and Estates; Litigation. ***Email:*** KDavey@westonhurd.com

CHRISTOPHER M. ERNST, admitted to bar, 1991, Ohio. *Education:* Tufts University (B.A., 1988); Case Western Reserve University (J.D., 1991). ***PRACTICE AREAS:*** Civil Litigation; Corporate Commercial Law; Electronic Commerce. ***Email:*** CErnst@westonhurd.com

JOHN G. FARNAN, admitted to bar, 1987, Ohio. *Education:* Georgetown University (B.A., 1984); Notre Dame Law School (J.D., 1987). ***PRACTICE AREAS:*** Insurance Defense; Personal Injury; Insurance Coverage. ***Email:*** JFarnan@westonhurd.com

JEFFREY D. FINCUN, admitted to bar, 1973, Ohio. *Education:* Bucknell University (B.S., 1968); Case Western Reserve University (J.D., 1973). ***PRACTICE AREAS:*** Disability Insurance; Life and Health Insurance; ERISA Litigation. ***Email:*** JFincun@westonhurd.com

ADAM H. GIMBEL, admitted to bar, 1995, Illinois; 2001, Ohio. *Education:* Indiana University (B.S., 1991); University of Miami (J.D., 1995). ***PRACTICE AREAS:*** Insurance Litigation; Business Litigation; Legal Malpractice Defense. ***Email:*** AGimbel@westonhurd.com

JAY S. HANSON, admitted to bar, 1985, Ohio. *Education:* Baldwin-Wallace College (B.A., 1982); Cleveland-Marshall College of Law (J.D., 1985). ***PRACTICE AREAS:*** Insurance Defense; Insurance Coverage; Subrogation. ***Email:*** JHanson@westonhurd.com

BEVERLY A. HARRIS, admitted to bar, 1978, Ohio. *Education:* Children's Hospital School of Nursing (Diploma, 1965); Ursuline College (B.A., 1975); Cleveland-Marshall College of Law (J.D., 1978). ***PRACTICE AREAS:*** Medical Malpractice Defense. ***Email:*** BHarris@westonhurd.com

DEIRDRE G. HENRY, admitted to bar, 1977, Ohio. *Education:* Bowling Green State University (B.S., 1974); University of Toledo (J.D., 1977). ***PRACTICE AREAS:*** Medical Malpractice; Nursing Home Litigation; Workers Compensation. ***Email:*** DHenry@westonhurd.com

TODD G. JACKSON, admitted to bar, 1985, Ohio. *Education:* Kent State University (B.B.A., 1982); Cleveland-Marshall College of Law (J.D., 1985). ***PRACTICE AREAS:*** Business Transactions; Securities; Construction Law. ***Email:*** TJackson@westonhurd.com

JOHN W. JEFFERS, admitted to bar, 1964, Ohio. *Education:* Harvard University (A.B., 1958); University of Pennsylvania (J.D., 1964). ***PRACTICE AREAS:*** Medical Malpractice; Hospital Defense; Drug and Medical Device Defense. ***Email:*** JJeffers@westonhurd.com

GARY W. JOHNSON, admitted to bar, 1979, Ohio. *Education:* Georgetown University (B.S.B.A., 1976); University of Toledo (J.D., 1979). ***PRACTICE AREAS:*** Business Transactions; Business Litigation; Environmental Law. ***Email:*** GJohnson@westonhurd.com

TIMOTHY D. JOHNSON, admitted to bar, 1974, Ohio. *Education:* Loyola University-Rome (1968); Xavier University (B.S.B.A., 1970); Case Western Reserve University (J.D., 1974). ***PRACTICE AREAS:*** Insurance Coverage; Complex Litigation; Professional Malpractice. ***Email:*** TJohnson@westonhurd.com

WILLIAM R. JOSEPH, admitted to bar, 1972, Ohio. *Education:* Columbia University (A.B., 1968; J.D., 1972). ***PRACTICE AREAS:*** Nonprofit and Charitable Organizations; Government Relations. ***Email:*** WJoseph@westonhurd.com

KURT KARAKUL, admitted to bar, 1979, Ohio. *Education:* Kenyon College (B.A., 1973); Case Western Reserve University (J.D., 1979). ***PRACTICE AREAS:*** Real Estate; Trusts and Estates; Business Law. ***Email:*** KKarakul@westonhurd.com

(This Listing Continued)

WESTON HURD LLP, Cleveland—Continued

JOHN S. KLUZNIK, admitted to bar, 1977, Ohio. *Education:* Ohio University (B.A., 1972; M.A., 1974); Yale University (J.D., 1977). ***PRACTICE AREAS:*** Employment Law; Civil Rights; Copyrights. ***Email:*** JKluznik@westonhurd.com

PAMELA E. LOESEL, admitted to bar, 1995, Ohio. *Education:* Valparaiso University (B.A., 1976); University of Akron (M.A., 1985; J.D., 1995). ***PRACTICE AREAS:*** Medical Malpractice Defense; First and Third Party Insurance Defense; Nursing Home Litigation. ***Email:*** PLoesel@westonhurd.com

SHAWN W. MAESTLE, admitted to bar, 1994, Ohio. *Education:* Cleveland State University (B.A., 1990); Ohio Northern University (J.D., 1994). ***PRACTICE AREAS:*** Appellate Practice; Commercial Litigation; Estate Planning. ***Email:*** SMaestle@westonhurd.com

PATRICK J. McINTYRE, admitted to bar, 1989, Ohio. *Education:* Pennsylvania State University (B.A., 1974); Cleveland-Marshall College of Law (J.D., 1988). ***REPORTED CASES:*** United States vs. Pretty Products, 780 F.Supp. 1488, 22 ELR 20725. ***PRACTICE AREAS:*** Business; Corporate; Environmental; Labor and Employment; Real Estate. ***Email:*** PMcIntyre@westonhurd.com

GREGORY E. O'BRIEN, admitted to bar, 1986, Ohio. *Education:* Walsh College (B.A., 1983); The Ohio State University (J.D., 1986). ***PRACTICE AREAS:*** Insurance Coverage; Bad Faith Litigation; Appellate Practice; Real Estate Law. ***Email:*** GOBrien@westonhurd.com

MARK O'NEILL, admitted to bar, 1952, Ohio. *Education:* Harvard College (A.B., 1949); Harvard Law School (J.D., 1952). ***PRACTICE AREAS:*** Professional Malpractice; Complex Litigation. ***Email:*** MONeill@westonhurd.com

DANIEL A. RICHARDS, admitted to bar, 1992, Ohio. *Education:* Miami University (B.S., 1989); Cleveland-Marshall College of Law (J.D., 1992). ***PRACTICE AREAS:*** Appellate Practice; Insurance Coverage; Commercial Litigation; Medical Malpractice Defense. ***Email:*** DRichards@westonhurd.com

RONALD A. RISPO, admitted to bar, 1967, Ohio. *Education:* College of the Holy Cross (A.B., 1964); University of Michigan (J.D., 1967). ***PRACTICE AREAS:*** Insurance Coverage; Medical Malpractice; Products Liability. ***Email:*** RRispo@westonhurd.com

TIMOTHY P. RISTAU, admitted to bar, 1966, Ohio. *Education:* Bradley University (B.A., 1963); Case Western Reserve University Law School (J.D., 1966). ***PRACTICE AREAS:*** Litigation; Business Planning; Trusts and Estates. ***Email:*** TRistau@westonhurd.com

DANA A. ROSE, admitted to bar, 1984, Ohio; 1986, California. *Education:* Georgetown University (B.S.F.S., 1981); Case Western Reserve University (J.D., 1984). ***PRACTICE AREAS:*** Real Estate; Business Transactions; Nonprofit Organizations Law. ***Email:*** DRose@westonhurd.com

WARREN ROSMAN, admitted to bar, 1976, Ohio. *Education:* Johns Hopkins University (B.A., 1973); Case Western Reserve University (J.D., 1976). ***PRACTICE AREAS:*** Insurance Coverage Defense; Tort Defense; Appellate Practice. ***Email:*** WRosman@westonhurd.com

HARRY SIGMIER, admitted to bar, 1980, Ohio. *Education:* Fordham University (B.A., 1977); Case Western Reserve University (J.D., 1980). ***PRACTICE AREAS:*** Products Liability; Insurance Coverage; Construction Litigation. ***Email:*** HSigmier@westonhurd.com

SCOTT C. SMITH, admitted to bar, 1987, Michigan; 1988, Ohio. *Education:* Albion College (B.A., 1984); Case Western Reserve University (J.D., 1987). ***PRACTICE AREAS:*** Business Litigation; Nursing Home Litigation; Professional Malpractice. ***Email:*** SSmith@westonhurd.com

JOSEPH B. SWARTZ, admitted to bar, 1970, Ohio. *Education:* Middlebury College (A.B., 1963); Cornell University (J.D., 1970). ***PRACTICE AREAS:*** Labor and Employment; Trusts and Estates; Federal Estate and Gift Taxation. ***Email:*** JSwartz@westonhurd.com

JEFFREY L. TASSE, admitted to bar, 1981, Ohio. *Education:* Miami University (B.A., 1978); Case Western Reserve University (J.D., 1981). ***PRACTICE AREAS:*** Products Liability; Corporate Litigation; Complex and Multi-District Litigation; Insurance Defense. ***Email:*** jtasse@westonhurd.com

HILARY S. TAYLOR, admitted to bar, 1977, Ohio. *Education:* Central State University (B.S., 1967); Cleveland-Marshall College of Law (J.D., 1977). ***PRACTICE AREAS:*** Governmental Law; Toxic Torts; Medical Malpractice. ***Email:*** HTaylor@westonhurd.com

KENNETH A. TORGERSON, admitted to bar, 1966, Ohio. *Education:* Dartmouth College (B.A., 1963); Northwestern University (J.D., 1966). ***PRACTICE AREAS:*** Complex Business Litigation; Medical Malpractice; Complex Commercial Litigation. ***Email:*** KTorgerson@westonhurd.com

HERNAN N. VISANI, admitted to bar, 1986, Ohio. *Education:* Andrews University (B.S.B.A., 1982); University of Michigan (J.D., 1986). ***PRACTICE AREAS:*** Business Law; Commercial Law; Construction Law. ***Email:*** HVisani@westonhurd.com

STEPHEN D. WALTERS, admitted to bar, 1968, Ohio; 1970, Massachusetts. *Education:* Georgetown University (A.B., 1965); The Ohio State University (J.D., 1968). ***PRACTICE AREAS:*** Medical Malpractice; Complex Litigation; Corporate Litigation. ***Email:*** SWalters@westonhurd.com

OF COUNSEL

JOHN M. BAKER, admitted to bar, 1967, Ohio. *Education:* John Carroll University (B.A., cum laude, 1964); Boston College (J.D., 1967). ***PRACTICE AREAS:*** Medical Malpractice; Legal Malpractice; Higher Education Law; Mediation. ***Email:*** JBaker@westonhurd.com

JASON C. BLACKFORD, admitted to bar, 1964, Ohio. *Education:* Denison University (B.A., 1960); Yale University (LL.B., 1963). ***PRACTICE AREAS:*** Business Law; Securities; Antitrust. ***Email:*** JBlackford@westonhurd.com

HERBERT BUCKMAN, admitted to bar, 1940, Ohio. *Education:* Yale University (A.B., 1936; LL.B., 1939). ***PRACTICE AREAS:*** Corporate Law; Trusts and Estates; Real Estate. ***Email:*** HBuckman@westonhurd.com

JAMES T. MILLICAN II, admitted to bar, 1967, Ohio. *Education:* Wabash College (B.A., 1964); Case Western Reserve University (J.D., 1967). ***PRACTICE AREAS:*** Insurance Coverage; Products Liability; Toxic Tort. ***Email:*** JMillican@westonhurd.com

ASSOCIATES

VICTOR T. DI MARCO, admitted to bar, 2000, Ohio. *Education:* Baldwin-Wallace College (B.S., 1995); Cleveland-Marshall College of Law (J.D., 1999). ***PRACTICE AREAS:*** Insurance Defense; Personal Injury; Products Liability; Nursing Home Litigation. ***Email:*** VDimarco@westonhurd.com

ROBERT E. GOFF, JR., admitted to bar, 1998, Ohio. *Education:* University of Dayton (B.S., 1995); Cleveland-Marshall College of Law (J.D., 1998). ***PRACTICE AREAS:*** Internet Law; E-Commerce Law; Products Liability; Appellate Practice; Premises Liability. ***Email:*** RGoff@westonhurd.com

JOHN M. JANUSZ, admitted to bar, 1998, Ohio. *Education:* State University of New York at Buffalo (B.A., 1995); Cleveland-Marshall College of Law (J.D., 1998). ***PRACTICE AREAS:*** Probate; Trusts and Estates; Litigation. ***Email:*** JJanusz@westonhurd.com

JEFFREY R. LANG, admitted to bar, 2002, Ohio. *Education:* University of Dayton (B.A., 1998); Cleveland-Marshall College of Law (J.D., 2001). ***PRACTICE AREAS:*** Insurance Coverage; Insurance Defense. ***Email:*** JLang@westonhurd.com

CAROL K. METZ, admitted to bar, 2000, Ohio. *Education:* University of Akron (B.S.B.A., 1992); Case Western Reserve University (J.D., 2000). ***PRACTICE AREAS:*** Insurance Coverage; Uninsured and Underinsured Motorists; Medical Malpractice. ***Email:*** CMetz@westonhurd.com

JEFFREY G. PALMER, admitted to bar, 1999, Ohio. *Education:* Valdosta State University (B.A., 1995); Gonzaga University (J.D., cum laude, 1999). ***PRACTICE AREAS:*** Civil Litigation; Insurance Coverage; Insurance Bad Faith Defense. ***Email:*** JPalmer@westonhurd.com

JILL S. PATTERSON, admitted to bar, 1998, Ohio. *Education:* John Carroll University (B.A., 1995); Cleveland-Marshall College of Law (J.D., 1998). ***PRACTICE AREAS:*** Litigation; Civil Rights; Governmental Law; Insurance Defense; Insurance Coverage. ***Email:*** JPatterson@westonhurd.com

JENNIFER A. RIESTER, admitted to bar, 1999, Ohio. *Education:* Cleveland State University (B.A., 1994); Cleveland-Marshall College of Law (J.D., 1999). ***PRACTICE AREAS:*** Asbestos Defense; Insurance Coverage; Medical Malpractice Defense. ***Email:*** JRiester@westonhurd.com

BRIAN P. RILEY, admitted to bar, 2000, Ohio. *Education:* State University of New York at Brockport (B.S., 1996); Cleveland-Marshall College of Law (J.D., 2000). ***PRACTICE AREAS:*** Litigation. ***Email:*** BRiley@westonhurd.com

ANDREW STIENECKER, admitted to bar, 2000, Ohio. *Education:* The Ohio State University (B.S., 1995); Ohio Northern University (J.D., 2000). ***PRACTICE AREAS:*** Civil Litigation; Medical Malpractice Defense; Insurance Coverage Defense. ***Email:*** AStienecker@westonhurd.com

RANDY L. TAYLOR, admitted to bar, 1998, Ohio. *Education:* James Madison University (B.A., 1994); Cleveland-Marshall College of Law (J.D., 1998). ***PRACTICE AREAS:*** Litigation; Insurance; Premises Liability. ***Email:*** RTaylor@westonhurd.com

WICKENS, HERZER, PANZA, COOK & BATISTA

A LEGAL PROFESSIONAL ASSOCIATION

CLEVELAND, OHIO

(See Avon)

General Civil Practice. Corporate, Taxation, Professional Corporations, Pension, Profit Sharing, Employee Benefits, ERISA, Partnership, Real Estate, Environmental, Labor and Employment Relations; Health Care and Hospital, Public Law, Municipal Bonds, Libel and Media Law, Probate and Estate Planning Law, Insurance Defense, Trials and Appeals, Banking, Bankruptcy.

WILLIAMS, SENNETT & SCULLY CO., L.P.A.

Established in 1993

113 ST. CLAIR AVENUE N.E., SUITE 430
CLEVELAND, OHIO 44114-1214
Telephone: 216-771-8660
Fax: 216-771-8831
Email: attorneys@wsslaw.com
URL: http://www.wsslaw.com

Twinsburg, Ohio Office: 2241 Pinnacle Parkway. Telephone: 330-405-5061. Fax: 330-405-5586.

General Civil Trial and Appellate Practice in all Courts. Insurance, Casualty and Surety, Life, Accident and Health, Negligence Litigation, Medical-Legal, Products Liability, Labor and Employment Law and Commercial Litigation, Toxic Tort and Environmental Law, Professional Liability Defense.

WILLIAM F. SCULLY, JR., born Bayshore, New York, July 10, 1950; admitted to bar, 1975, Ohio; 1980, U.S. District Court, Northern District of Ohio and U.S. Court of Appeals, Sixth Circuit. *Education:* University of Notre Dame (B.A., 1972); Case Western Reserve University (J.D., 1975). *Member:* Cleveland, Ohio State and American Bar Associations; Ohio Association of Civil Trial Attorneys. (Also Practicing Individually). ***PRAC-***

(This Listing Continued)

TICE AREAS: Civil Litigation; Insurance Defense; Product Liability; Insurance Coverage; Medical-Legal; Toxic Tort; Environmental; Professional Liability Defense; Commercial Litigation; Labor and Employment Law. ***Email:*** wfs@wsslaw.com

(For Complete Biographical Data on all personnel see Biographies at Twinsburg)

WILSMAN & SCHOONOVER, L.L.C.

Established in 1993
THE TOWER AT ERIEVIEW, SUITE 1420
1301 EAST 9TH STREET
CLEVELAND, OHIO 44114
Telephone: 216-589-9600
Fax: 216-589-9800
Email: wslegal@sbcglobal.net

Family Law, General and Commercial Litigation, Credit Union Law, Manufacturers' Agents Law.

FIRM PROFILE: Wilsman & Schoonover, L.L.C., established in 1993, is a highly rated firm listed in Martindale-Hubbell's Bar Register of Preeminent Lawyers. The firm specializes in Family Law, General and Commercial Litigation, Credit Union Law and Manufacturers' Agents Law.

JAMES M. WILSMAN, born Port Huron, Michigan, October 7, 1939; admitted to bar, 1964, Ohio. *Education:* Hiram College (B.A., 1961); University of Michigan (J.D., 1964). Member, Garfield Society. President, Hiram College Alumni Association, 1971-1973. *Member:* Cleveland (Chairman, Family Law Section, 1988-1989; Member, Lawyers Assistance Committee, 1987—; Member, Board of Trustees, 1973-1976), Cuyahoga County, Ohio State (Member, Assistance to Lawyer's Committee, 1987—) and American Bar Associations. (Certified Specialist in Family Law, Ohio State Bar Association). ***PRACTICE AREAS:*** Family Law; Credit Union Law; Litigation. ***Email:*** jmwilsman@sbcglobal.net

JOHN E. SCHOONOVER, born Cincinnati, Ohio, October 2, 1958; admitted to bar, 1984, Ohio; 1985, U.S. District Court, Northern District of Ohio; 1986, U.S. Court of Appeals, Sixth Circuit. *Education:* Oberlin College (A.B., 1981); Case Western Reserve University School of Law (J.D., 1984). Trustee, Center for Principled Advocacy, 2002—. *Member:* Cleveland, Cuyahoga County (Chair, Family Law Section, 2001-2002), Ohio State and American (Council Member, General Practice Section, 1994-1995; Membership Chair, Ohio, 1993-1997; Director, Young Lawyers Division, 1993-1994; Executive Council Coordinator, Young Lawyers Division, 1991-1992; Chair, Litigation Committee, Young Lawyers Division, 1990-1991; District Representative for District 12 (Ohio) Young Lawyers Division, 1989-1991) Bar Associations. (Certified Specialist in Family Law, Ohio State Bar Association). ***PRACTICE AREAS:*** Family Law; Litigation; Manufacturers' Agents Law. ***Email:*** jschoonover@sbcglobal.net

ASSOCIATES

SCOTT S. ROSENTHAL, born Cleveland, Ohio, February 13, 1971; admitted to bar, 1998, Ohio. *Education:* Miami University (B.S., 1993); Cleveland Marshall College of Law (J.D., 1997). Order of Barristers. *Member:* Cleveland, Cuyahoga County, Ohio State and American Bar Associations. ***PRACTICE AREAS:*** Family Law; Litigation. ***Email:*** srosenthal@sbcglobal.net

MOIRA A. WOPERSHALL, born Cleveland, Ohio, November 17, 1974; admitted to bar, 2000, Ohio; 2001, U.S. District Court, Northern District of Ohio. *Education:* Ohio University (B.A., summa cum laude, 1997); Cleveland-Marshall College of Law (J.D., cum laude, 2000). Phi Alpha Delta. *Member:* Cleveland, Cuyahoga County, Ohio State and American Bar Associations. ***PRACTICE AREAS:*** Family Law; Business Law; Corporate Law; Litigation. ***Email:*** moiramcandrew@sbcglobal.net

OF COUNSEL

KEITH W. KERN, born Cleveland, Ohio, November 3, 1951; admitted to bar, 1975, Ohio. *Education:* Michigan State University (B.S., 1972); The Ohio State University (J.D., 1975). *Member:* Cleveland, Lake County, Ohio State and American Bar Associations. ***PRACTICE AREAS:*** Corporate; Business; Estate Planning; Federal, State and Local Tax Law; Probate; Real Estate. ***Email:*** kwkern@sbcglobal.net

MICHAEL J. CONNICK, born Cleveland, Ohio, July 20, 1957; admitted to bar, 1990, Ohio, U.S. District Court, Northern District of Ohio and U.S. Court of Appeals, Sixth Circuit. *Education:* John Carroll University (B.S.B.A., 1987); Cleveland Marshall College of Law (J.D., cum laude, 1990). *Member:* Cleveland and Ohio State (Litigation Section) Bar Associations. [U.S.M.C., 1975-1979]. ***PRACTICE AREAS:*** Civil Litigation; Criminal Law. ***Email:*** mconnick@sbcglobal.net

DOUGLAS A. ANDREWS, born Massapequa, New York, May 7, 1956; admitted to bar, 1984, Ohio and U.S. District Court, Northern District of Ohio; U.S. Court of Appeals, Sixth Circuit. *Education:* Washington University in St. Louis (B.A., summa cum laude, 1978; M.A., 1980); Case Western Reserve University (J.D., 1984). *Member:* Cleveland and Ohio State Bar Associations. ***PRACTICE AREAS:*** Litigation; Business Law; Employment Law; ERISA. ***Email:*** daandrews@sbcglobal.net

JAMES D. WILSON, LLC

75 PUBLIC SQUARE, SUITE 1100
CLEVELAND, OHIO 44113
Telephone: 216-861-6393
Fax: 216-861-6394
Email: jwilson@wilsonlawyers.com

Creditors Rights, Commercial Litigation, Bankruptcy, Construction Litigation, Creditors Bankruptcy.

(This Listing Continued)

JAMES D. WILSON, born Sharon, Pennsylvania, February 23, 1962; admitted to bar, 1987, Pennsylvania; 1989, Ohio. *Education:* Catholic University of America (B.A., magna cum laude, 1984); Georgetown University (J.D., cum laude, 1987). Phi Beta Kappa. ***PRACTICE AREAS:*** Creditors Rights; Commercial Litigation; Bankruptcy; Construction Litigation.

REPRESENTATIVE CLIENTS: ABC Supply Co., Kaplan Trucking Co.; Horizon Freight System, Inc.; Wholesale Builders Supply Co.; Linde Gas; GE Commercial Finance Business Property Corporation; Warner-Kingwood Nurseries.

DAVID WIRTH

CLEVELAND, OHIO

(See Columbus)

Insurance Law, Negligence, Legal Malpractice, Subrogation, Personal Injury, Probate.

WOLF AND AKERS

A LEGAL PROFESSIONAL ASSOCIATION
1717 EAST NINTH STREET, SUITE 1515
CLEVELAND, OHIO 44114
Telephone: 216-623-9999
Fax: 216-623-0629

Practice Limited to Domestic Relations Law.

MARSHALL J. WOLF, born Cleveland, Ohio, November 20, 1941; admitted to bar, 1967, Ohio; 1970, U.S. District Court, Northern District of Ohio. *Education:* Miami University (B.A., 1964); Case Western Reserve University (J.D., 1967). Tau Epsilon Rho. Member: Best Lawyers in America, 1983-2002; Who's Who in American Law, 1977—. Co-editor: "Managing Clients and Cases: Procedures and Systems for the Family Lawyer," ABA Press, 1986. Co-Author: "Books Can Help," Family Advocate, Vol. 1, No. 2; "Dealing With Divorce: Books to Help Families Make the Best of It," Family Advocate, Vol. 6, No. 4, 1986; "Disqualification," Family Advocate, Vol. 9, No. 3, 1987. Law Clerk, Court of Common Pleas, Cuyahoga County, Ohio, 1967-1969. Principal, Metzenbaum, Gaines & Stern Co., L.P.A., 1975-1981, Associate, 1969-1975. Principal, Schwarzwald, Robiner, Wolf & Rock, Co., L.P.A., 1981-1987. Chief U.S. Delegate, 1st World Congress on Family Law & Rights of Children, Sydney, Australia, 1993. *Member:* Cuyahoga County (Chairman, Domestic Relations Committee, 1980-1982; Chairman, Family Law, 1984-1985; Member, Judicial Selection Committee, 1982-1983; Member, Grievance Committee, 1988-1993), Ohio State (Member, Family Law Committee, 1975—) and American (Section of Family Law; Executive Committee, 1988-1994, 2000-2002; Chairman, 1992-1993; Chairman Elect, 1991-1992; Vice Chairman, 1990-1991; Faculty Member, Family Law Advocacy Institute, 1987-1990, 1995; Section Delegate, ABA House of Delegates, 2000-2002) Bar Associations; Ohio Academy of Trial Lawyers (Chairman, Family Law Section, 1976-1977; Recipient, Distinguished Service Award, 1977); The Association of Trial Lawyers of America. Fellow, International Academy of Matrimonial Lawyers; American Academy of Matrimonial Lawyers (Ohio Chapter, President, 1984-1987). ***PRACTICE AREAS:*** Family Law.

DEBORAH AKERS-PARRY, (FORMERLY DEBORAH ROWLEY AKERS), born Troy, New York, April 27, 1949; admitted to bar, 1976, Ohio. *Education:* Washington University (A.B., 1971); Cleveland Marshall College of Law (J.D., 1976). Fellow: American Academy of Matrimonial Lawyers; American Bar Foundation. Listed in: Best Lawyers in America, 1987— Who's Who in American Law, 1990—; Ohio Super Lawyers; Top 50 Women Lawyers; Law Politics/Cincinnati Magazine, January 2004, 2005. Co-Author: "Disqualification," Family Advocate, Vol. 9, No. 3, 1987. Author: "The Valuation of Stock Options in Divorce and Dissolution Cases," and "The Valuation of Limited Partnerships in Divorce and Dissolution Cases," ABA Family Law Section Compendium, 1990. Lecturer: Property Division and Spousal Support in Ohio; Divorce Taxation; Venue and Jurisdiction in Divorce Actions; Valuation of Stock Options and Limited Partnership Interests; Wiretapping in Domestic Relations Cases; New Property Division and Spousal Support Statutes; Real Estate Valuation; Lecture and Trial Demonstration; House Bill 514 and Senate Bill 3; Alimony; Pension Evaluation; Valuation of Stock Options in Divorce and Dissolution Cases; Family Law Update; Child Custody; Fundamentals of Litigation; Qualified Medical Child Support Orders; Property Division and Valuation Issues; Bridge the Gap; Demystifying the Divorce Process; Tax Issues-The Marital Residence; Valuation of Social Security Benefits. Primary Draftsman: Ohio House Bill 514 (ORC 3105.171 and 3105.18); Opinion No. 89-3, "Representing the Mentally Disabled Client," The Cleveland Bar Journal, November, 1989 (as corrected at page 190, April 1990). Member, Editorial Advisory Board, The Domestic Relations Journal of Ohio. Faculty, American Bar Association, Family Law Trial Advocacy Institute, 1992-1994, 1997; Ohio Supreme Court Judicial College Teleconference, 1991. Principal, 1979 and Associate, 1976-1978, Manlove, Manlove, Rowley and Fuhry Co., L.P.A. Sole Practitioner, 1979-1984. Trial Referee, Medina County Court of Common Pleas, 1983-1984. Associate, Schwarzwald, Robiner, Wolf & Rock, L.P.A., 1984-1988. Principal, Wolf and Akers, L.P.A., 1988—. Trustee, Cleveland-Marshall College of Law Alumni Association, 1991-1996. Appointee: Bench Bar Conference, 1990, 1994, 2002. Life Member, Eighth Ohio Appellate District Judicial Conference. *Member:* Cleveland (Member, Family Law Section; Chair, 1989-1990; Professional Ethics Committee, 1987-1993); Cuyahoga County (Trustee, 1992-1995; Family Law Section; Chair, 1992-1993; Chair, Trial Advocacy Institute, 1990-1991, 1993; Certified Grievance Committee, 1986-1996); Ohio State (Delegate to Council of Delegates, 1990—; Family Law Committee; Chair, 1994-1996; Legislative Drafting Sub-Committee: Chair, 1989-1994; Family Law Specialty Certification Board, 1999-2002; Specialization Committee: Chair, 2001-2003); American (Member, Family Law Section: Financial Officer, 2004—; Publications Board, 2000—; Member, Litigation Section) Bar Associations. ***PRACTICE AREAS:*** Family Law.

MARGARET W. WONG & ASSOCIATES CO., LPA

Established in 1979

3150 CHESTER AVENUE
CLEVELAND, OHIO 44114
Telephone: 216-566-9908
Fax: 216-566-1125
URL: http://www.lawyers.com/wonglaw
Email: wong@imwong.com
URL: http://www.imwong.com

Columbus, Ohio Office: 470 Olde Worthington Road, Suite 200, (Westerville, Ohio) 43082. Telephone: 614-221-8892.
Detroit, Michigan Office: 11201 Conner Avenue, 48213. Telephone: 313-527-9989.

Immigration and Naturalization Law, H-1B, Work Visas, Labor Certifications, L-1A, L-1B, O-1, F-1, R-1, Criminal Aliens, Criminal Law, Removal Defense, Student, Business, Visa, Asylum, Amnesty, 245(i), Green Card, Family-based Immigration.

FIRM PROFILE: Margaret W. Wong & Associates Co., LPA is a nationally and internationally renowned immigration and naturalization law firm. The firm services clients from every country, from governmental and corporate entities to ordinary individuals. The staff is multilingual. The firm brings its extensive experience to consular law, employment visas, family immigration, investor visas, removal defense and business immigration cases.

MARGARET W. WONG, born Hong Kong, July 27, 1950; admitted to bar, 1977, New York and Ohio; 1978, District of Columbia; 1980, U.S. District Court, Northern District of Ohio, U.S. Court of Appeals, Sixth Circuit and U.S. Supreme Court. *Education:* Western Illinois University (B.S, 1973); State University of New York at Buffalo (J.D., 1976). Charter Member and Member, Racial Task Force, Ohio Supreme Court Continuing Legal Education Commission. *Member:* Cuyahoga County, Cleveland, Columbus, Sixth Judicial Circuit, Eighth Judicial District, Ohio State and Federal (President, Cleveland Chapter, 1994-1995) Bar Associations; Asian Bar Association; American Immigration Lawyers Association. ***LANGUAGES:*** Chinese, Filipino, French, Mandarin, Russian, Slovak, Spanish, Taiwanese, Ukrainian. ***PRACTICE AREAS:*** Immigration and Naturalization. ***Email:*** wong@imwong.com

Languages: Chinese, Filipino, French, Mandarin, Russian, Slovak, Spanish, Taiwanese, Ukrainian.

REPRESENTATIVE CLIENTS: Cleveland Clinic; Dix & Eaton; Keithley Instruments; Manco Inc.; Master Builders; Mitsubishi Caterpillar Forklift; Ohio State Colleges & Universities; Progressive Insurance.
REFERENCE: National City Bank.

WULIGER, FADEL & BEYER

THE BROWNELL BUILDING
1340 SUMNER COURT
CLEVELAND, OHIO 44115
Telephone: 216-781-7777
Fax: 216-781-0621
Email: WFBLaw@wfblaw.com

General Civil, Labor and Criminal Trial Appellate Practice in all State and Federal Courts. General Corporate, Partnership and Business Law, Domestic Relations Law, Personal Injury and Probate.

MEMBERS OF FIRM

WILLIAM I. FADEL, born Cleveland, Ohio, June 23, 1943; admitted to bar, 1969, Ohio; 1972, U.S. District Court, Northern District of Ohio; U.S. Court of Appeals, Sixth Circuit; U.S. Supreme Court. *Education:* Western Reserve University (B.A., 1965); Case Western Reserve University (J.D., 1969). Phi Delta Phi. Member, International Union of Operating Engineers, Local 18. Labor Representative, Ohio State Construction Compliance Council, 1988—. *Member:* Ohio State (Member, Labor Section; AFL-CIO Labor Lawyers Coordinating Committee) and Cleveland (Chair, Labor and Employment Section, 1999) Bar Associations. ***SPECIAL AGENCIES:*** International Union of Operating Engineers, Locals 18, 18D, 18S; Bakery, Confectionary, Tobacco Workers and Grain Millers International Union AFL-CIO, CLC. ***REPORTED CASES:*** Murphy vs. International Union of Operating Engineers, Local 18, 744 F.2d 114 (6th Cir. 1985); Shimman vs. Grothaus, 633 F.2d 468 (6th Cir. 1980); Deczon Inc. vs. Carpenters District Council, Its Affiliates and Successors, 295 NLRB 19 (1989). ***PRACTICE AREAS:*** Labor Law; Employment Law; General Litigation. ***Email:*** WFadel@wfblaw.com

WILLIAM D. BEYER, born Lakewood, Ohio, June 28, 1944; admitted to bar, 1969, Ohio; 1970, U.S. District Court, Northern District of Ohio and U.S. Court of Appeals, Sixth Circuit; 1983, U.S. Supreme Court; 1987, U.S. Court of Appeals, District of Columbia Circuit; 2005, U.S. District Court, Eastern District of Michigan. *Education:* Ohio Wesleyan University (B.A., 1966); Case Western Reserve University (J.D., 1969). Assistant Public Defender, Cuyahoga County, 1969-1971. Assistant U.S. Attorney, Northern District of Ohio, 1972-1977; Chief Criminal Section, 1974-1977; U.S. Attorney: Northern District of Ohio, 1977-1978; Jones, Day, Reavis & Pogue, 1978-1980. Adjunct Faculty, Cleveland State University John Marshall College of Law, 1980-1981. *Member:* Cleveland and American Bar Associations; The Association of Trial Lawyers of America. ***REPORTED CASES:*** Rockey vs. 84 Lumber Co., 66 Ohio St. 3d 221 (1993); Olle, Jr. vs. Henry & Wright Corp., 910 F.2d 357 (6th Cir. 1990); Warren vs. Society Natl. Bank, 905 F.2d 975 (6th Cir. 1990); U.S. vs. Friedrick, 842 F.2d 382 (D.C. Cir. 1988) Surace vs. Wuliger, 25 Ohio St. 3d 229 (1986); Shimola vs. Nationwide Ins., 25 Ohio St. 3d 84 (1986); Cafferkey vs. Turner Construction, 21 Ohio St.3d 110 (1986); Williams vs. U.S., 582 F.2d 1039 (6th Cir. 1978); U.S. vs. Callahan, 579 F.2d 398 (6th Cir. 1978); U.S. vs. Lee, 575 F.2d 1184 (6th

(This Listing Continued)

Cir. 1978); U.S. vs. Payner, 572 F.2d 144 (6th Cir. 1977); U.S. vs. John Doe, 556 F.2d 391 (6th Cir. 1977). ***PRACTICE AREAS:*** Trial Litigation; White Collar Criminal Defense; Business Litigation; Probate Law. ***Email:*** wbeyer@wfblaw.com

JOAN E. PETTINELLI, born Lorain, Ohio, May 15, 1964; admitted to bar, 1990, Ohio; 1994, U.S. District Court, Northern District of Ohio; 1994, U.S. Court of Appeals, 6th Circuit; 2005, U.S. District Court, Eastern District of Michigan. *Education:* North Carolina State University (B.A., 1986); University of North Carolina (J.D., 1990). Gamma Beta Phi Honor Society. Law Clerk to Honorable Thomas D. Lambros, Chief Judge, Northern District of Ohio, 1991-1994. Member, Criminal Justice Act Panel of the U.S. District Court for the Northern District of Ohio. *Member:* Cleveland and Ohio State Bar Associations; Cleveland Academy of Trial Attorneys. ***PRACTICE AREAS:*** General Civil Litigation; Federal Criminal Law; Criminal Defense; Criminal Appeals; Business Litigation. ***Email:*** joanepettinelli@wfblaw.com

OF COUNSEL

WILLIAM T. WULIGER, born Cleveland, Ohio, February 15, 1944; admitted to bar, 1969, Ohio; 1970, U. S. District Court, Northern District of Ohio; 1973, U.S. Court of Appeals, Sixth Circuit; 1984, U.S. Supreme Court; U.S. Court of Appeals, Third Circuit. *Education:* Miami University (B.A., 1965); Case Western Reserve (J.D., 1969). Editor-in-Chief of Exeter Jurist, 1968. 1st Assistant Legal Aid Public Defender's Office, 1973-1975. Recipient: Certificate of Merit, Cleveland Bar Association; Claude E. Clarke Award, Legal Aid Society. *Member:* Cleveland Bar Association; The Association of Trial Lawyers of America. ***PRACTICE AREAS:*** Personal Injury; Commercial Litigation; Matrimonial; Criminal Law. ***Email:*** wtwuliger@core.com

MATTHEW D. GREENWELL, born Cleveland, Ohio, September 27, 1977; admitted to bar, 2004, Ohio. *Education:* University of Toledo (B.S., 1999); Cleveland-Marshall College of Law (J.D., cum laude, 2004). ***PRACTICE AREAS:*** Personal Injury; Matrimonial Law; Commercial Litigation. ***Email:*** mgreenwell@core.com

RICHARD G. ROSS, born New York, New York, February 17, 1958; admitted to bar, 1983, Ohio; 1984, U.S. District Court, Northern District of Ohio. *Education:* University of Rochester (B.A., 1980); Case Western Reserve University (J.D., 1983). Clinton Dewitt Scholar. Lecturer, Case Western Reserve Law School. *Member:* Cleveland (Member, 1983— and Chairman, 1987-1988, Labor Law Committee), Ohio State and American Bar Associations; Federal Court Advisory Group. ***PRACTICE AREAS:*** Labor and Employment; General Practice; Civil Litigation; Administrative Law. ***Email:*** Rross@wfblaw.com

REFERENCE: National City Bank.

YORMICK & ASSOCIATES CO., L.P.A.

Established in 1995

KEY TOWER -- 52ND FLOOR
127 PUBLIC SQUARE
CLEVELAND, OHIO 44114
Telephone: 216-928-3474
Facsimile: 216-566-0857
URL: http://www.yormicklaw.com

Agency and Distributorship Law, Arbitration, Business and Corporate Law, Business and Commercial Litigation, Commercial Collections, Cross-border Business, Customs Law, European Union Law, Export Law, Immigration, International Arbitration and Litigation, International Trade, NAFTA Law, Transportation Law.

FIRM PROFILE: Recognizing the changing global economy, our growth has focused on representing and advising clients involved in International Trade and Transactions, including Business Immigration. These practice areas distinguish Yormick & Associates Co., L.P.A. from other Ohio-based law firms.

SHAREHOLDER

JON P. YORMICK, born Buffalo, New York, November 7, 1965; admitted to bar, 1990, Ohio; 1992, Maryland; 1993, District of Columbia, U.S. District Court, Northern District of Ohio, U.S. District Court, Eastern District of Michigan and U.S. Court of Appeals, Sixth Circuit; 1994, U.S. District Court, District of Maryland; 1995, Michigan; 2000, U.S. Court of International Trade. *Education:* Canisius College (B.A., cum laude, History, 1987); Case Western Reserve University (J.D., 1990). Member, World Trade Center-Cleveland, 1999—. Advisor, Corporate College. Chair, Ohio Partnership for Excellence, 2005—. *Member:* The District of Columbia Bar (International Law Section); State Bar of Michigan (International Law Section); Customs and International Trade Bar Association; German American Chamber of Commerce of the Midwest, Ohio Chapter (Director, 2001-2003); Greater Cleveland International Lawyers Group; International Trade and Customs Broker Association, Inc. (Director, 2001-2005). (Also Of Counsel, Blanco & Associates, P.C., Troy, Michigan). ***PRACTICE AREAS:*** International Business Law; International Trade; Customs Law; Business Litigation; Commercial Litigation.

Languages: Spanish, Indonesian and Polish.

REPRESENTATIVE CLIENTS: ACE USA Insurance Group; AGS Custom Graphics; A & S Precision Manufacturing, Inc.; American Medical Response; Arrow International, Inc.; Atlantic Bingo Supply Company; Bison Wealth Management, Inc.; The Bivings Group, Inc.; cab Produkttechnik GmbH & Co. KG; Consumers Energy Company; Craig International, Inc.; EPCOM International, Ltd.; ERIE Insurance Group; Integrated Services Network; InteliTool Manufacturing Services, Inc.; Interoil Services, LLC; Less Sweat Products, Ltd.; Maple Oak, LLC; Mary Coyne Investments, LLC; Neighborhood Leadership Institute; Pearlessence, Ltd.; PLIDCO, Inc. dba The Pipeline Development Company; Reader Roofing, Co.; Speed Strength Systems, Inc.; Targett Plastics International, Inc.; Targett Motorsports, Ltd.; Targett Racing, Ltd.; USG Holdings, Ltd.; The Warren Trustees Group, Ltd.

THE LAW OFFICES OF DAVID A. YOUNG LLC

700 W. ST. CLAIR AVENUE
SUITE 316
CLEVELAND, OHIO 44113
Telephone: 216-621-5100
Fax: 216-621-7810
Email: dyoung@davidyounglaw.com
URL: http://www.davidyounglaw.com

Employment, Sexual Harassment, Sexual Discrimination, Age Discrimination, Racial Discrimination, Disability, Wrongful Termination.

DAVID A. YOUNG, born Cleveland, Ohio, September 24, 1970; admitted to bar, 1995, Ohio; 1996, U.S. District Court, Northern District of Ohio. *Education:* Miami University (B.A., cum laude, 1992); Cleveland Marshall College of Law (J.D., cum laude, 1995). Recipient, Spangenberg Award for Excellence in Trial Advocacy, 1994. Member, Board of Editors, Cleveland Marshall Law Review, 1993-1994. Member, Cleveland Marshall Law Alumni Association, 1995—. *Member:* Cleveland, Portage County, Ohio State and American Bar Associations; Association of Trial Lawyers of America; Ohio Academy of Trial Lawyers; National Employment Lawyers Association; Cleveland Employment Lawyers Association; Ohio Employment Lawyers Association. ***PRACTICE AREAS:*** Employment Law. ***Email:*** dyoung@davidyounglaw.com

YOUNG, GUIDUBALDI & SUCHER, P.L.L.

55 PUBLIC SQUARE, SUITE 1020
CLEVELAND, OHIO 44113
Telephone: 216-623-1123
Fax: 216-623-1124
Email: cmy1ooo@aol.com
URL: http://www.sygslaw.com

Personal Injury, Medical Malpractice, Auto Accidents, Products Liability, Legal Malpractice, Commercial Litigation.

MEMBERS OF FIRM

CHARLES M. YOUNG, born New Brighton, Pennsylvania, May 18, 1947; admitted to bar, 1974, Ohio and U.S. District Court, Northern District of Ohio; 1975, U.S. Court of Appeals, Sixth Circuit; 1987, U.S. Supreme Court. *Education:* Geneva College (B.A., 1969); Cleveland State University (J.D., 1973). Editor, 1971-1973 and Issue Editor, 1972-1973, Cleveland Marshall Law Review. *Member:* Greater Cleveland, Cuyahoga County and Ohio State Bar Associations; Cleveland Academy of Trial Lawyers; The Ohio Academy of Trial Lawyers; The Association of Trial Lawyers of America. (Certified as Civil Trial Advocate by the National Board of Trial Advocacy). ***Email:*** cmy1ooo@aol.com

DAVID J. GUIDUBALDI, born Youngstown, Ohio, February 26, 1945; admitted to bar, 1972, Ohio; 1973, U.S. District Court, Northern District of Ohio and U.S. Court of Appeals, Sixth Circuit; 1979, U.S. Supreme Court. *Education:* Youngstown State University (B.S., 1968); Cleveland State University (J.D., cum laude, 1972). Member, Moot Court Board. *Member:* Cleveland, Cuyahoga County, Ohio State and American Bar Associations; The Association of Trial Lawyers of America; Ohio Academy of Trial Lawyers; Cleveland Academy of Trial Lawyers. ***Email:*** djgatty@aol.com

DANIEL M. SUCHER, born Youngstown, Ohio, February 21, 1966; admitted to bar, 1991, Ohio; 1992, U.S. District Court, Northern District of Ohio. *Education:* John Carroll University (B.A., 1988); Cleveland Marshall College of Law (J.D., 1991). Phi Alpha Theta. Associate, Cleveland Marshall Law Review, 1989-1990; Editor, Cleveland Marshall Law Review, 1990-1991. *Member:* Cleveland, Ohio State and American Bar Associations; The Ohio Academy of Trial Lawyers; The Cleveland Academy of Trial Lawyers; The Association of Trial Lawyers of America; First Amendment Lawyers Association. (Certified as Civil Trial Advocate by the National Board of Trial Advocacy). ***Email:*** sucherdan@hotmail.com

JAMES P. BOYLE, born Cleveland, Ohio, June 8, 1966; admitted to bar, 1991, Ohio. *Education:* Miami University (B.A., 1988); Case Western Reserve University (J.D., 1991). Attorney, Cuyahoga County Prosecutor's Office, 1992-1997. Councilman, City of South Euclid, Ohio, 1998—. *Member:* Cleveland and Ohio State Bar Associations; Ohio Academy of Trial Attorneys; National Employment Lawyers Association; The Cleveland Academy of Trial Lawyer. ***Email:*** mr1jpb@aol.com

ANTHONY N. PALOMBO, born Cleveland, Ohio, April 28, 1965; admitted to bar, 1995, Ohio; 1998, U.S. District Court, Northern District of Ohio. *Education:* Kent State University (B.A., 1988); Cleveland Marshall School of Law (J.D., 1994). Member, Ohio Academy of Trial Lawyers, Justnian Forum. Staff Counsel, Ohio Turnpike Commission, 1995-1998. Assistant Law Director, City of Cleveland, 1998-1999. *Member:* Cleveland, Ohio and American Bar Associations. ***Email:*** tonybash@sbcglobal.net

REFERENCES: First Merit; Fidelity Investments.

ZASHIN & RICH CO., L.P.A.

55 PUBLIC SQUARE, 4TH FLOOR
CLEVELAND, OHIO 44113-1901
Telephone: 216-696-4441
Fax: 216-696-1618
Email: email@zrlaw.com
URL: http://www.zrlaw.com

Columbus, Ohio Office: Fifth Third Center, Suite 1900, 21 East State Street, 43215. Telephone: 614-224-4411. Fax: 614-224-4433.

Domestic Relations, Labor and Employment, Corporate Law, Real Estate, Civil Litigation.

(This Listing Continued)

FIRM PROFILE: Zashin & Rich Co., L.P.A., founded in 1981, practices law throughout the state of Ohio. The firm's primary practice areas are family law and employment and labor law.

Zashin & Rich Co., L.P.A is well known for handling large and complicated domestic relations cases. The family law practice area includes: divorce, dissolution, child custody, domestic violence, support issues, marital settlement agreements and equitable property divisions. The firm regularly handles these matters in the common pleas and appellate courts of Ohio and the Ohio Supreme Court. Robert I. Zashin, a founding partner of Zashin & Rich, has been recognized in domestic relations in every edition of the Best Lawyers in America since the publication's inception.

Zashin & Rich also has a comprehensive labor and employment practice. The firm represents employers in lawsuits under all federal and state anti-discrimination statutes. The firm also represents employers before all employment related administrative agencies. Zashin & Rich handles matters involving alleged violations of anti-discrimination statutes including, but not limited to, Title VII of the Civil Rights Act of 1964, state discrimination laws, the Americans with Disabilities Act, the Age Discrimination in Employment Act and the Family and Medical Leave Act.

In labor relations, Zashin & Rich regularly negotiates and counsels clients on the administration of collective bargaining agreements. In addition, the firm represents employers in grievance and arbitration proceedings and in litigation matters arising out of collective bargaining agreements.

Further, the firm counsels clients on the preparation and administration of employment policies and procedures and reviews them for legal compliance.

ROBERT I. ZASHIN, born 1940; admitted to bar, 1968, Ohio and New York. *Education:* Rutgers University (B.A., 1962; M.A., Education, 1966); Cleveland Marshall College of Law (J.D., 1967). Frequent Lecturer: Cleveland Marshall College of Law; Ohio Academy of Matrimonial Lawyers. Appointed, Committee on Child Support Guidelines, Ohio Supreme Court. Life Member and Honorary Trustee, Cleveland Marshall College of Law. Listed in every edition of "The Best Lawyers in America." Recognized as one of Cleveland's Top 10 Lawyers. *Member:* Cleveland, Cuyahoga County (Member, Character and Fitness and Judicial Selection Committee) and Ohio State Bar Associations; Ohio (Past President), American and International Academies of Matrimonial Lawyers. ***PRACTICE AREAS:*** Domestic Relations; Divorce; Child Custody; Child Support; Domestic Violence. ***Email:*** riz@zrlaw.com

ANDREW A. ZASHIN, born Cleveland, Ohio, February 7, 1968; admitted to bar, 1993, Ohio; 1994, Florida; 1995, District of Columbia. *Education:* Brown University (A.B., 1990); Case Western Reserve University (J.D., 1993). Notes Editor, Case Western Reserve Law Review. Adjunct Assistant Professor of Law, Case Western Reserve University. Lecturer, Domestic Violence, Ohio State Bar Association (OSBA CLE Institute). *Member:* Cuyahoga County (Member, Certified Grievance Committee; Vice Chair, Family Law Section) and Ohio State Bar Associations. (Certified Specialist in Family Relations Law, Ohio State Bar Association). ***PRACTICE AREAS:*** Domestic Relations; Divorce; Child Custody; Child Support. ***Email:*** aaz@zrlaw.com

STEPHEN S. ZASHIN, born Cleveland, Ohio, December 24, 1969; admitted to bar, 1995, Ohio. *Education:* University of Pennsylvania (B.S., cum laude, 1991); Case Western Reserve University (J.D.; M.B.A., 1995). Phi Delta Phi. Recipient, Dean's Academic Achievement Award. Member, Case Western Reserve University Law Review, 1993-1994. Author: "Bodyslam From the Top Rope: Unequal Bargaining Power and Professional Wrestling's Failure to Unionize," 12 University of Miami, Entertainment and Sports Law Review 1, 1995. *Member:* Cleveland, Ohio State and American Bar Associations. (Certified Specialist in Labor and Employment Law, Ohio State Bar Association). ***SPECIAL AGENCIES:*** EEOC; OCRC. ***PRACTICE AREAS:*** Employment Law; Equal Employment Opportunity Law; Employment Discrimination; Labor Relations; Civil Litigation. ***Email:*** ssz@zrlaw.com

JONATHAN A. RICH, born 1966; admitted to bar, 1993, Ohio. *Education:* Ohio State University (B.S., cum laude, Business Administration, 1989); Cleveland Marshall College of Law (J.D., 1992). *Member:* Cuyahoga County and Ohio State Bar Associations. ***PRACTICE AREAS:*** Real Estate; Domestic Relations; Civil Litigation. ***Email:*** jar@zrlaw.com

OF COUNSEL

LAWRENCE J. RICH, born 1941; admitted to bar, 1967, Ohio. *Education:* Ohio State University (B.S., 1963); Cleveland Marshall College of Law (J.D., 1967). Instructor, Real Estate Law, Cuyahoga Community College. Deputy Cuyahoga County Auditor. President, Cleveland-Marshall's Law Alumni Association, 1980-1981. ***PRACTICE AREAS:*** Domestic Relations; Business Law; Real Estate. ***Email:*** ljr@zrlaw.com

DEANNA LYNN DI PETTA, born Cleveland, Ohio, April 23, 1958; admitted to bar, 1987, Ohio. *Education:* Cleveland State University (B.A., 1980); Cleveland Marshall College of Law (J.D., 1986). Tau Epsilon Rho. Blue Key. Adjunct Professor, Domestic Relations Law, Notre Dame College of Ohio, 2002. Member, Make-a-Wish Foundation and Ronald McDonald House. *Member:* Cuyahoga County Bar Association (Past Member, Domestic Relations Court's Local Rules Committee; Trustee, Cuyahoga County Bar Association). ***LANGUAGES:*** French. ***PRACTICE AREAS:*** Domestic Relations; Divorce; Child Custody; Child Support. ***Email:*** dld@zrlaw.com

LOIS A. GRUHIN, born 1947; admitted to bar, 1971, New Jesey and Kentucky; 1972, New York; 1973, Ohio. *Education:* Rutgers University (B.A., 1968); University of Louisville (J.D., magna cum laude, 1971). Recipient: Louis D. Brandeis Scholarship; Carl Mann Scholarship; West Publishing Company Award for Highest Scholastic Average in the Freshman Class; Phi Alpha Delta Robert B. Linton Award; American Law Book Company Award; Kappa Beta Pi Award for Outstanding Third Year Woman. Executive Editor, Journal of Family Law, 1970-1971. General Counsel and Secretary, Schottenstein Stores Corporation. ***PRACTICE AREAS:*** Employment Law; Employment Discrimination; Domestic Relations; Civil Litigation. ***Email:*** lag@zrlaw.com

(This Listing Continued)

ZASHIN & RICH CO., L.P.A., Cleveland—Continued

ROBERT M. FERTEL, born 1947; admitted to bar, 1972, Ohio. *Education:* Ohio State University (B.A., 1969; J.D., 1972). ***REPORTED CASES:*** Cleveland Board of Education v. Loudermill, 470 U.S. 532 (1985). ***PRACTICE AREAS:*** Domestic Relations; Employment Law; Complex Civil Litigation; Appellate Practice. ***Email:*** rmf@zrlaw.com

JENNIFER SUE SVEC, born 1974; admitted to bar, 1999, Ohio. *Education:* Walsh College (B.A., magna cum laude, History, 1996); Cleveland-Marshall College of Law (J.D., 1999). *Member:* Cleveland, Ohio State and American Bar Associations. ***PRACTICE AREAS:*** Domestic Relations; Divorce; Child Support; Spousal Support; Property Division; Child Custody. ***Email:*** jss@zrlaw.com

MICHELE L. JAKUBS, born Portsmouth, Virginia, September 30, 1970; admitted to bar, 1999, Ohio. *Education:* Ohio State University (B.S., 1992); Cleveland-Marshall College of Law (J.D., magna cum laude, 1999). *Member:* Ohio State and American Bar Association. ***PRACTICE AREAS:*** Labor Relations; Equal Employment Opportunity Law; Employment Discrimination; Torts. ***Email:*** mlj@zrlaw.com

HELENA J. OROZ, admitted to bar, 2002, Ohio. *Education:* Denison University (B.A., 1998); Cleveland-Marshall College of Law (J.D., 2002). *Member:* Cleveland and Ohio State Bar Associations. ***PRACTICE AREAS:*** Employment Discrimination; Equal Employment Opportunity Law; Labor Relations; COBRA; ERISA; Health Insurance Portability and Accountability Act (HIPAA). ***Email:*** hjo@zrlaw.com

ROBERT W. HARTMAN, born Baltimore, Maryland, January 12, 1977; admitted to bar, 2004, Ohio. *Education:* Allegheny College (B.A., cum laude, 1999); Case Western Reserve University School of Law (J.D., cum laude, 2004). *Member:* Ohio State Bar Association. ***PRACTICE AREAS:*** Labor Relations; Employment Discrimination; Equal Employment Opportunity Law; Alternative Dispute Resolution. ***Email:*** rwh@zrlaw.com

RYAN L. LONG, born 1979; admitted to bar, 2004, Ohio. *Education:* Ohio University (B.A., Sociology/Pre-Law, 2001); Case Western Reserve University School of Law (J.D., 2004). *Member:* Cuyahoga County and Ohio State Bar Associations. ***PRACTICE AREAS:*** Domestic Relations; Divorce; Child Support; Spousal Support; Marital Property Distribution; Child Custody. ***Email:*** rll@zrlaw.com

ZIEGLER, METZGER & MILLER LLP

Established in 1952

2020 HUNTINGTON BUILDING
925 EUCLID AVENUE
CLEVELAND, OHIO 44115-1441
Telephone: 216-781-5470
Fax: 216-781-0714;
Toll Free: 800-528-3300

Painesville, Ohio Office: 152 Main Street, 44077. Telephone: 440-352-3003. Fax: 440-354-3299.

Pepper Pike, Ohio Office: 29525 Chagrin Boulevard, Suite 310. Telephone: 216-360-9000. Fax: 216-360-0303.

General Civil Practice. Trials and Appeals in all Courts. Commercial, Personal Injury and General Litigation. Corporation, Estate Planning, Real Estate, Probate, Taxation, International and Insurance Law.

FIRM PROFILE: Our firm was founded in 1952 when Harold O. Ziegler and Roger L. Metzger began practicing law together in what was then the Union Commerce Building (now the Huntington Building). Prior to that time, the two had been in the law departments of different Cleveland banks.

The shared background of the founders is reflected today in both our practice and quarters. Our clients include many of the region's leading companies, and our offices have remained at the same location in the heart of the city's historic legal and financial district.

An emphasis on the special individual continues to be the basis of our firm's success. Whether distinguished by exceptional academic achievement, unique talent, or extraordinary motivation, our partners and associates are truly capable of the firm's mission: to be quality counsel of good value.

There is a bonus in having extraordinary people work together...giving each other the advantage of their specialized skills...giving each client the benefit of multi-faceted experience...giving our practice an effective synergy.

HAROLD O. ZIEGLER (1899-1980)

ROGER L. METZGER (1908-1981)

MEMBERS OF FIRM

ROBERT L. METZGER, born Cleveland, Ohio, July 8, 1937; admitted to bar, 1962, Ohio. *Education:* University of Michigan (A.B., 1959; LL.B., 1962). *Member:* Cleveland, Ohio State and American Bar Associations. ***PRACTICE AREAS:*** Estate Planning; Probate Law; Tax Law.

WILLIAM L. SPRING, born Newark, Ohio, December 31, 1942; admitted to bar, 1967, Ohio and U.S. Tax Court. *Education:* Denison University (B.A., 1964); Case Western Reserve University (J.D., 1967). Phi Alpha Delta. *Member:* Cleveland, Ohio State and American Bar Associations. ***PRACTICE AREAS:*** Estate Planning; Estate Administration; International Estate Planning. ***Email:*** bspring@zieglermetzger.com

STEPHEN M. DARLINGTON, born Lancaster, Pennsylvania, October 23, 1942; admitted to bar, 1967, Ohio. *Education:* Denison University (B.A., 1964); Case Western Reserve University (J.D., 1967). Phi Delta Phi. Chairman, Moot Court Board, Case Western Reserve University, 1966-1967. Special Agent, F.B.I., 1967-1970. *Member:* Cleveland and Ohio State Bar Associations. (Board Certified - Creditors' Rights Law - American Board of Certification). ***PRACTICE AREAS:*** Civil Trials; Commercial Law; Bankruptcy; Banking; Corporate Transactions. ***Email:*** sdarlin@zieglermetzger.com

RICHARD T. SPOTZ, JR., born Johnstown, Pennsylvania, February 26, 1948; admitted to bar, 1973, Ohio; 1980, U.S. Supreme Court. *Education:* Miami University (B.S., 1970); Cleveland State University (J.D., 1973). *Member:* Cleveland, Lake County (President, 1988-1989), Ohio State, and American Bar Associations. Fellow: Ohio State Bar Foundation and American Bar Association. ***PRACTICE AREAS:*** Probate; Trusts and Estates; Tax Law. ***Email:*** rspotz@zieglermetzger.com

PAUL S. KLUG, born Cleveland, Ohio, February 4, 1950; admitted to bar, 1975, Ohio; 1976, U.S. District Court, Northern District of Ohio. *Education:* Allegheny College (B.A., cum laude, 1972); Case Western Reserve University (J.D., 1975). *Member:* Greater Cleveland, Ohio State and American (Member, Sections of: Real Property, Probate and Trust Law; Family Law) Bar Associations; Estate Planning Council of Cleveland. ***PRACTICE AREAS:*** Corporate Law; Probate; Trusts and Estates; Business Succession Planning; Domestic Relations; Commercial Law. ***Email:*** pklug@zieglermetzger.com

STEPHEN M. BALES, born Stuttgart, West Germany, October 3, 1957; admitted to bar, 1983, Ohio and U.S. District Court, Northern District of Ohio; 1986, U.S. Court of Appeals, Sixth Circuit; 1987, U.S. Supreme Court; 1998, U.S. District Court, Eastern and Western Districts of Wisconsin; 2001, U.S. District Court, Southern District of Ohio. *Education:* Rockford College (B.A., cum laude, 1979); Cleveland State University (J.D., 1983). Articles Editor, Cleveland State Law Review, 1982-1983. *Member:* Cleveland, Geauga County and Ohio State Bar Associations. ***PRACTICE AREAS:*** Arbitration; Commercial Law; Commercial Bankruptcy; Employment Law; Appeals; Securities Litigation. ***Email:*** sbales@zieglermetzger.com

JOHN E. REDEKER, born Cleveland, Ohio, June 18, 1949; admitted to bar, 1974, Ohio; 1975 U.S. District Court, Northern District of Ohio. *Education:* Denison University (B.S., 1971); Cleveland Marshall College of Law (J.D., 1974). *Member:* Cleveland and Ohio State Bar Associations. ***PRACTICE AREAS:*** Real Estate Transactions; Corporate Transactions; Succession Planning; Real Estate Law; Receiverships; Business. ***Email:*** jredeker@zieglermetzger.com

JOSEPH W. KAMPMAN, born Cleveland, Ohio, January 18, 1954; admitted to bar, 1980, Ohio. *Education:* Cleveland State University (B.B.A., 1977; M.B.A., 1980); Cleveland Marshall College of Law (J.D., 1980). *Member:* Cuyahoga County, Lake County and Ohio State (Probate Section) Bar Associations. ***PRACTICE AREAS:*** Estate Planning; Estate Administration; Business Succession Planning. ***Email:*** jkampman@zieglermetzger.com

ASSOCIATES

HOWARD E. HENDERSHOTT, JR., born Cleveland, Ohio, November 22, 1926; admitted to bar, 1953, Ohio. *Education:* Massachusetts Institute of Technology (B.S., 1949); Case Western Reserve University (J.D., 1953). Delta Theta Phi. Member, Board of Education, Hudson Local School District, 1979-1997. [with U.S. Navy, 1944-1946]. (Resident, Pepper Pike Office). ***PRACTICE AREAS:*** Commercial Real Estate; Estate Planning; Financial Planning; Corporate Law; Business Law. ***Email:*** hehzmmppo@aol.com

JEFFREY L. KOBERG, born Westlake, Ohio, March 30, 1965; admitted to bar, 1990, Ohio, U.S. District Court, Northern District of Ohio and U.S. Court of Appeals, Sixth Circuit. *Education:* Indiana University (B.S., 1987); Case Western Reserve University (J.D., 1990). *Member:* Cleveland, Ohio State and American Bar Associations; Ohio Academy of Trial Lawyers; Commercial Law League of America. ***PRACTICE AREAS:*** Creditor Rights; Civil Trials; Real Estate Law. ***Email:*** jkoberg@zieglermetzger.com

CHRISTOPHER E. SOUKUP, born Detroit, Michigan, July 1, 1948; admitted to bar, 1975, Ohio. *Education:* The Ohio State University (B.A., 1970); Case Western Reserve University (J.D., 1975). *Member:* Cleveland and Ohio State Bar Associations. ***PRACTICE AREAS:*** Commercial Real Estate; Land Conservation; Residential Real Estate; Corporate Law; Business Law. ***Email:*** csoukup@zieglermetzger.com

GLEN H. GARRETT, born Toledo, Ohio, October 18, 1969; admitted to bar, 1995, Ohio and U.S. District Court, Northern District of Ohio; 2000, U.S. Court of Appeals, Sixth and Third Circuits; 2001, U.S. District Court, Southern District of Ohio. *Education:* Ohio University (B.B.A., Accounting, 1992); Cleveland State University (J.D., 1995). Articles Editor, Cleveland State Law Review, 1995. *Member:* Cleveland and Ohio State Bar Associations; Ohio Academy of Civil Trial Attorneys; Defense Research Institute. ***PRACTICE AREAS:*** Commercial Law; Banking Law; Insurance Coverage; Insurance Bad Faith; Subrogation; Civil Litigation. ***Email:*** ggarrett@zieglermetzger.com

LISA J. ROTH, born Norwalk, Ohio, August 2, 1972; admitted to bar, 2001, Ohio. *Education:* Bowling Green State University (B.A., 1993); Cleveland-Marshall College of Law (J.D., 2000). *Member:* Cleveland and Ohio State Bar Associations. ***PRACTICE AREAS:*** Probate; Estate Planning; Taxation; Elder Law; Real Estate; Civil Practice. ***Email:*** lroth@zieglermetzger.com

SCOTT A. NORCROSS, born Sumter, South Carolina, October 12, 1974; admitted to bar, 2001, Ohio; 2003, U.S. District Court, Northern District of Ohio. *Education:* University of Miami (B.A., 1997); University of Toledo (J.D., 2000). Formerly with Strachan Miller Oleander & Roessler. *Member:* Cleveland and Ohio State Bar Associations. ***PRACTICE AREAS:*** Commercial Law; Civil Practice; Foreclosures; Subrogation; Criminal Law. ***Email:*** norcross@zieglermetzger.com

LORI KILPECK, born Euclid, Ohio, July 15, 1975; admitted to bar, 2002, Ohio. *Education:* Cleveland State University (B.A., 1998); Cleveland-Marshall College of Law (J.D., 2002). Acting Magistrate, Willoughby Municipal Court, 2003-2004. *Member:* Lake County (Member, Probate and Young Lawyer Committee) and Ohio State Bar Associations. ***PRACTICE AREAS:*** Probate; Estate Planning; Guardianship. ***Email:*** lrk@zieglermetzger.com

KATHLEEN A. McLAUGHLAN, born Cleveland, Ohio, September 20, 1979; admitted to bar, 2004, Ohio. *Education:* Fordham University (B.A., 2001); Case Western Re-

(This Listing Continued)

serve University (J.D., 2004). *Member:* Cleveland and Ohio State Bar Associations. ***PRACTICE AREAS:*** Real Estate; Estate Planning; Estate Administration; Corporate Law; Civil Practice. ***Email:*** kmadigan@zieglermetzger.com

OF COUNSEL

JOHN J. REIDY, JR., born Youngstown, Ohio, September 21, 1932; admitted to bar, 1957, Ohio. *Education:* University of Notre Dame (A.B., 1954); Case Western Reserve University (LL.B., 1957). *Member:* Cleveland and Lake County Bar Associations. ***PRACTICE AREAS:*** Estate Planning; Estate Administration; Probate; Trusts; Taxation. ***Email:*** jreidy@zieglermetzger.com

LEGAL SUPPORT PERSONNEL

MARGARET E. MENDENHALL, born Fairmont, West Virginia, February 23, 1950. *Education:* West Virginia University (B.S.N., R.N., 1973); Case Western Reserve University (M.N.O., 1995). Client Care Manager. ***PRACTICE AREAS:*** Elder Care Assistance; Care Giver Education/Advocacy; Crisis Intervention. ***Email:*** mmenden@zieglermetzger.com

P. THOMAS AUSTIN, born Indianapolis, Indiana, October 10, 1926. *Education:* Central Michigan University; Miami University (B.S., 1947); University of Michigan (M.B.A., 1949); American College (M.S.F.S., 1986); Cambridge University, Cambridge, England. CPA, 1952. (Consultant). ***PRACTICE AREAS:*** Estate Planning; Compensation Planning; Tax Planning. ***Email:*** taustin@zieglermetzger.com

TIMOTHY RESOR, born Elyria, Ohio, July 17, 1955. *Education:* Academy of Court Reporting-Paralegal Division (A.A., 1989); Cleveland State University (1989-1995). Enrolled Agent, IRS. ***PRACTICE AREAS:*** Estate and Trust Accounting; Preparation of Income Tax Returns (Individual and Fiduciary); Federal and State Estate Tax Returns. ***Email:*** tresor@zieglermetzger.com

REPRESENTATIVE CLIENTS: Action Collectors; Air Services of Cleveland, Inc.; Air-Temp Climate Control, Inc.; American Tank and Fabricating Company; Automated Valve & Equipment Co.; Bank One, Cleveland N.A.; C.B. Richard Ellis Inc.; Dollar Bank; Dun & Bradstreet; Fidelity Home Loans Corp.; The Financial Group, LLC; Forest Corp.; Hartford Insurance Co.; Heartland Home Finance Co.; Hudson & Keyse; Hummer Whole Health Management, Inc.; Huntington National Bank; Key Bank; Koll Bren Schreiber Realty Advisors, Inc.; Merrill Lynch Business Financial Services, Inc.; Merrill Lynch, Pierce, Fenner & Smith Inc.; Metallic Resources, Inc.; Milliken & Michaels; The Money Store, Inc.; National City Bank; Nationwide Insurance Co.; Ohio Clear Title Agency, Inc.; Ohio Gear & Transmission, Inc.; Ohio Pipe, Valves & Fittings, Inc.; The Osborn Engineering Co.; Pumphrey Marketing Inc.; Technitronics, Inc.; Travelers Insurance; Watts Industrial Tyres, Ltd. (U.K.); West Environmental, Inc.; Western Reserve Historical Society; D.E. Williams Electric, Inc.; Wilson Mill Foods, Inc.

ZIPKIN WHITING CO., L.P.A.

CLEVELAND, OHIO

(See Beachwood)

Age Discrimination, Bankruptcy, Discrimination, Race Discrimination, Sex Discrimination, Criminal Law, Disability Discrimination, Americans With Disabilities Act, Family Law, Divorce, Consumer Violations, Nursing Home Abuse and Neglect, Employment Law, Employment Age Discrimination, Employment Disability Discrimination, Employment Discrimination, Harassment, National Origin Discrimination, Negligent Hiring, Retaliatory Discharge, Sexual Harassment, Title VII Discrimination, Wrongful Termination, Medical Malpractice, Personal Injury, Accidents, Automobile Accidents and Injuries, Wrongful Death.

ZUKERMAN, DAIKER & LEAR, CO., L.P.A.

2000 EAST NINTH STREET, SUITE 700
CLEVELAND, OHIO 44115
Telephone: 216-696-0900
Fax: 216-696-8800
Email: lwz@duiohio.com
URL: http://www.duiohio.com

White Collar Criminal Defense, Attorney Discipline, Personal Injury, Domestic Relations, Internet Law, Computer Crime, Drug Law Violations, DUI.

LARRY WILLIAM ZUKERMAN, born Pittsburgh, Pennsylvania, November 11, 1960; admitted to bar, 1985, Ohio; 1986, U.S. District Court, Northern District of Ohio; 1988, U.S. Court of Appeals, Sixth Circuit; 1993, U.S. Supreme Court; 2003, U.S. District Court, Southern District of Ohio and Eastern District of Michigan. *Education:* Washington & Jefferson College (A.B., 1982); Case Western Reserve University (J.D., 1985). Adjunct Professor of Law, Case Western Reserve University School of Law. Law Director, Village of Moreland Hills, 1996-1998. Life Member, The Judicial Conference of the Eighth Judicial District, Cuyahoga County, Ohio. *Member:* Cleveland (Chairman, 1994-1995, Criminal Law Division; Professional Ethics Committee, 1987-1991; Vice Chairman, 1991-1992, Chairman, 1992-1993, Chairman, Criminal Trial Walkthrough, 1988-1992 and 1994-1998; Division of Fees/Mediation Vice Chairman, 1993-1999; Trustee, 1999-2002), Cuyahoga County (Member, Grievance Committee, 1988-1994; Chairman, Law School Liaison Committee; Member, Judicial Selection Committee, 1992-2001) and Ohio State (Council of Delegates, 1994-2000; Member, Criminal Justice Committee, 1989-2000) Bar Associations; National Association of Criminal Defense Lawyers; Ohio Association of Criminal Defense Lawyers (Charter Member, Board of Directors; Vice President); Cuyahoga Criminal Defense Lawyers Association (President, 1999-2000; Vice President, 1998-1999; Board of Directors, 1987-1989, 1992-1995; Membership Chairman, 1986-1992; Treasurer, 1989-1992). ***REPORTED CASES:*** State Ex. Rel. Corn v. Russo 90 Ohio St 3d 551: 700 NE2d 265 (2001). ***PRACTICE AREAS:*** White Collar Criminal Defense; Internet Law; Computer Law; Attorney Discipline; Driving While Intoxicated. ***Email:*** lwz@duiohio.com

PAUL B. DAIKER, born Oxford, Ohio, November 6, 1967; admitted to bar, 1993, Ohio; 1996, U.S. District Court, Northern District of Ohio and U.S. Court of Appeals, Sixth Circuit; 2003, U.S. District Court, District of Colorado. *Education:* Vanderbilt University (B.A., 1990); Cleveland-Marshall College of Law (J.D., 1993). Member, Cleveland State Law Review. Prosecutor, Village of Moreland Hills, 1996-2000. *Member:* Cleveland (Member: Young Lawyers Section; Executive Council, 1996-2000; Criminal Law Division, 1997-2003; Speaker and Panel Member, Criminal Trial Walkthrough, 1998-2001; Certified Grievance Committee, 1997-2001; Professional Ethics Committee, 1997-2003; Chairman, 2003-2004. Legal Fee Dispute Resolution Committee, 1997—) and Ohio State Bar Associations; Cuyahoga Criminal Defense Lawyers Association (Secretary, 2003-2004); Ohio Association of Trial Lawyers; National Association of Criminal Defense Lawyers. ***PRACTICE AREAS:*** Criminal Defense; Personal Injury; Civil Litigation; Family Law; Divorce; Domestic Relations; Appellate Practice; Driving While Intoxicated. ***Email:*** pbd@duiohio.com

S. MICHAEL LEAR, born Cleveland, Ohio, December 31, 1962; admitted to bar, 1989, Ohio; 1991, U.S. District Court, Northern District of Ohio; U.S. Court of Appeals, Sixth Circuit. *Education:* Ohio State University (B.A., 1985); Case Western Reserve University (J.D., 1988). *Member:* Cuyahoga County Bar Associations; Criminal Defense Lawyers Association. ***REPORTED CASES:*** State Ex Rel. Koren v. Grogan, 68 Ohio St. 3d 590, 629 N.E.2d 446 (1994); State Ex Rel. Corn v. Russo, 90 Ohio St. 3d 551, 740 N.E. 2d 265 (2001); State v. Othman, 149 Ohio App 3d 82, 775 N.E. 2d 903 (2002); Disciplinary Counsel v. Pollock, 100 Ohio St. 3d 280, 798 N.E. 2d 594 (2003); State ex rel. Ministerial Day Care Assn. v. Montgomery, 100 Ohio St.3d 343, 800 N.E. 2d 18 (2003); State ex rel Ministerial Day Care Assn. v Zelman, 100 Ohio St.3d 347, 800 N.E.2d 21 (2003); Cleveland v. Haffey, 94 Ohio Misc. 2d79, 703 N.E. 2d 380 (1998). ***PRACTICE AREAS:*** Criminal Defense; Personal Injury; Civil Litigation; Appellate Practice; Collections; Municipal Law; Attorney Discipline. ***Email:*** mlear@duiohio.com

LAW OFFICES OF MARK S. FISHMAN

CLEVELAND HEIGHTS, OHIO

(See Cleveland)

Personal Injury, Automobile Accidents, Worker's Compensation, Dog Bites, Insurance Law.

ROTH, BLAIR, ROBERTS, STRASFELD & LODGE, L.P.A.

COLUMBIANA, OHIO

(See Youngstown)

General Civil Practice in all State and Federal Courts, Banking, Commercial, Corporate, Partnership, and General Business Law, Education Law, Employee Benefits and ESOP's, Estate Planning and Administration, Family Law, Employment Law, Management and Labor Relations, Insurance Defense, Mergers and Acquisitions, Pension, Profit Sharing and Retirement Plans, Personal Injury, Probate, Product Liability, Commercial, Industrial and Residential Real Estate, School Law, Securities, Trials, Venture Capital, Workers Compensation.

ABRAMSON & O'CONNELL, LLC

695 BRYDEN ROAD
COLUMBUS, OHIO 43205
Telephone: 614-461-6066
Fax: 614-461-4524
URL: http://www.lawyers.com/abramson&oconnell

Personal Injury, Wrongful Death, Medical Malpractice, Hospital Negligence, Professional Negligence, Premises Liability, Automobile Accidents.

LAWRENCE D. ABRAMSON, born Wooster, Ohio, March 13, 1952; admitted to bar, 1978, Ohio; 1980, U.S. District Court, Southern District of Ohio. *Education:* Boston University (B.A., magna cum laude, with distinction in Political Science, 1973); University of Cincinnati (J.D., 1978). Member: The Order of Barristers. Special Assistant on Legislative Matters, Ohio Department of Industrial Relations, 1973-1975. *Member:* Columbus, Ohio State Bar Association; Franklin County Trial Lawyers Association; Ohio Academy of Trial Lawyers (Board Member); The Association of Trial Lawyers of America. ***PRACTICE AREAS:*** Personal Injury; Medical Malpractice; Hospital Negligence; Wrongful Death; Professional Negligence; Automobile Accidents and Injuries. ***Email:*** larry@aolawfirm.com

THOMAS J. O'CONNELL, born Kettering, Ohio, December 5, 1959; admitted to bar, 1985, Ohio; 1986, U.S. District Court, Southern and Northern Districts of Ohio and U.S. Court of Appeals, Sixth Circuit. *Education:* Ohio State University (B.S., 1982); University of Dayton (J.D.,1985). Legislation Note Editor, University of Dayton Law Review, 1984-1985; Co-Author with A. Tolnitch, "Ohio's Attempts to Halt the Medical Malpractice Crisis: Effective or Meaningless?" University of Dayton Law Review, Vol. 9, No. 2, 1984. Assistant Attorney General, State of Ohio, 1986-1991. *Member:* Columbus and American Bar Associations; Ohio Academy of Trial Lawyers; Franklin County Trial Lawyers Association; The Association of Trial Lawyers of America. ***PRACTICE AREAS:*** Personal Injury; Medical Malpractice Law; Wrongful Death; Professional Negligence; Premises Liability; Automobile Accidents and Injuries. ***Email:*** tom@aolawfirm.com

ALAN S. ACKER

145 EAST RICH STREET, FOURTH FLOOR
COLUMBUS, OHIO 43215
Telephone: 614-220-8877
Facsimile: 614-220-8876
Email: alansacker@aol.com
URL: http://www.lawyers.com/alanacker

Estate Planning, Family Wealth Transfer, Estate Administration, Gift and Estate Taxation, Charitable Giving, and Income Taxation of Trusts and Estates.

(This Listing Continued)

ALAN S. ACKER, Columbus—Continued

ALAN S. ACKER, born Chicago, Illinois, March 14, 1953; admitted to bar, 1977, Illinois; 1986, Virginia; 1990, Ohio. *Education:* University of Illinois (B.S., 1974); Chicago-Kent College of Law (J.D., 1977). Author: Estate Planners' Guide to Income in Respect of a Decedent, CCH Tax and Accounting; Income Taxation of Trusts and Estates, Tax Management Portfolio #852-2d; "Income in Respect of a Decedent," Tax Management Portfolio, #B62-1st "Estate and Trust Administration - Tax Planning," BNA Tax Management Portfolio #855-1st; "Administrative Powers," Tax Management Portfolio #B 20-1st; "Income Taxation of Estates and Trusts," 20 Tax Management Estates, Gifts and Trusts Journal No. 2, 1995; "Sections 2703 and 2704 of the Internal Revenue Code (or, if you are not winning, try changing the rules)," 19 Tax Management Estates, Gifts and Trusts Journal Number 6, November 1994; "Death Bed Tax Planning," 17 Tax Management Estates, Gift and Trust Journal No. 2, 1992; "Death Bed and Post-Mortem Tax Planning," Columbus Tax Conference, 1991; "Added Dimensions: The Allocation of GST," Trusts and Estates (1991); "Crummey Trusts: Better than Ever," Estate Planning and Administration Service, Warren, Gorham & Lamont, 1989. Adjunct Professor, Income Taxation of Trusts and Estates, Capital Law School, Columbus, Ohio, 1992-2003. *Member:* Columbus, Ohio State, Illinois State, Virginia and American Bar Associations; American Institute and Ohio Society of Certified Public Accountants. Fellow: American College of Trusts and Estates Counsel.

ALBER CRAFTON, PSC

501 W. SCHROCK ROAD, SUITE 104 (WESTERVILLE)
COLUMBUS, OHIO 43081
Telephone: 614-890-5632
Fax: 614-890-5638
URL: http://www.albercrafton.com

Troy, Michigan Office: 2301 West Big Beaver Road, Suite 300, 48054. Telephone: 248-822-6190. Fax: 248-822-6191.
Louisville, Kentucky Office: Hurstbourne Place, Suite 1300, 9300 Shelbyville Road, 40222. Telephone: 502-815-5000. Fax: 502-815-5005.

Fidelity Surety Law, Construction Law, Directors & Officers and Errors & Omissions Litigation, Insurance Defense and Policy Litigation, Workers Compensation, Transportation Litigation, Commercial Litigation, Mediation, Arbitration.

LEE M. BREWER, born Akron, Ohio, September 21, 1954; admitted to bar, 1989, Ohio. *Education:* University of Tennessee (B.S., 1978); Capital University (M.B.A., 1982; J.D., cum laude, 1989). *Member:* American Bar Association (Member: Tort and Insurance Practice Section; Fidelity and Surety Law Committee; Forum Committee on Construction Industry); National Bond Claims Association (Director; Member, 1980—); Ohio Surety Association. ***PRACTICE AREAS:*** Fidelity and Surety Law; Construction Law; Probate. ***Email:*** lbrewer@albercrafton.com

DOUGLAS M. BEARD, born Wausau, Wisconsin, August 2, 1974; admitted to bar, 2001, Ohio; 2002, U.S. District Court, Southern District of Ohio. *Education:* The E.W. Scripps School of Journalism at Ohio University (B.S.J., summa cum laude, 1997); The Ohio State University College of Law (J.D., 2001). Member, Golden Key National Honor Society. *Member:* Ohio State and American Bar Associations. ***PRACTICE AREAS:*** Fidelity and Surety; Insurance Litigation; Construction Litigation; Transportation Law; Commercial Law. ***Email:*** dbeard@albercrafton.com

(For complete biographical data on other personnel, see Professional Biographies at those locations)

LAW OFFICES OF
JOHN L. ALDEN

Established in 1972
ONE EAST LIVINGSTON AVENUE
COLUMBUS, OHIO 43215-5700
Telephone: 614-221-1306
614-221-3551
Email: JAlden@AldenLaw.net
Email: BEdwards@AldenLaw.net
URL: http://www.aldenlaw.net

Transportation Law, Motor Carrier and Interstate Commerce Law, Traffic Law, Litigation, Business and Corporate Law, Public Utilities Law, Warehousing Law, Real Estate, Environmental Law, Mergers and Acquisitions and Employment Law.

JOHN L. ALDEN, born Olean, New York, May 16, 1941; admitted to bar, 1972, Ohio and U.S. District Court, Southern District of Ohio. *Education:* Ohio University (B.B.A., 1966; M.B.A., 1967); The Ohio State University (J.D., 1972). Phi Delta Phi; Beta Alpha Psi; Delta Nu Alpha. *Member:* Columbus and Ohio State (Member, Public Utilities Committee) Bar Associations; Transportation Lawyers Association; Association for Transportation Law; Logistics and Policy; Conference of Freight Counsel; Dump Truck Carriers Conference. ***PRACTICE AREAS:*** Transportation Law; Interstate Commerce Law; Public Utility Law; Warehousing Law; Business Law; Traffic Law.

ASSOCIATE

R.D. BENJAMIN EDWARDS, born Columbus, Ohio, December 21, 1973; admitted to bar, 2000, Ohio; 2005, U.S. District Court, Southern District of Ohio. *Education:* The Ohio State University (B.A., 1997; J.D., 2000). Law Clerk, Ohio Court of Claims, 1999-2000. *Member:* Columbus and Ohio State Bar Associations; Transportation Lawyers Association. ***PRACTICE AREAS:*** Transportation; Corporate Law; Business Law; Employment Law; Real Estate.

OF COUNSEL

JOHN E. BREEN, born Dayton, Ohio, November 1, 1956; admitted to bar, 1982, Ohio; 1986, U.S. District Court, Southern District of Ohio. *Education:* Miami University (B.A., 1979); Harvard University, Ohio Northern University (J.D., 1982). Member: National Moot Court Team; Mock Trial Team; Law Review, Georgetown Law Center, 1982. Assistant Attorney General, Ohio, 1983-1986. Formerly with: Chester, Wilcox & Saxbe, 1986-1991; General Counsel, Terminix, 1992-2000; Breen Law Offices, 2000—. *Member:* Ohio State Bar Association. ***PRACTICE AREAS:*** Civil Litigation; Appellate Practice; Corporate Law; Business Law; Real Estate.

DAVID L. McCLURE, born Columbus, Ohio, September 13, 1939; admitted to bar, 1964, Ohio. *Education:* The Ohio State University (B.S., 1961; J.D., 1964). *Member:* Ohio State Bar Association. ***PRACTICE AREAS:*** Transportation; Corporate Law; Business Law; Real Estate; Environmental Law; Mergers and Acquisitions; Employment Law.

REPRESENTATIVE CLIENTS: Arrow Concrete Co.; BNSF Railway Co.; Cavalier Coach Corp.; Certified Oil Company; The Cleveland Coca-Cola Bottling Co.; Columbus Regional Airport Authority; Corporate Transit of America, Inc.; Covenant Transport, Inc.; Diamond Logistics, Inc.; The Mason and Dixon Lines, Inc.; National Star Route Mail Contractors Assn.; Quickway Carriers, Inc.; Parsec, Inc.; Pre-Paid Legal Services, Inc.; Specialized Transportation, Inc.; Transport Network, LLC; United Dairy Farmers Transit, Inc.

(This Listing Continued)

ALLEN, KUEHNLE & STOVALL LLP

21 WEST BROAD STREET, SUITE 400
COLUMBUS, OHIO 43215
Telephone: 614-221-8500
Fax: 614-221-5988
URL: http://www.akslaw.net

Bankruptcy, Debtor and Creditor Rights, Insolvency and Workouts, Commercial Law, Real Estate, Condominium Law, Commercial Leasing, Litigation, Alternative Dispute Resolution.

MEMBERS OF THE FIRM

THOMAS R. ALLEN, born Cleveland, Ohio, May 31, 1956; admitted to bar, 1981, Ohio; 1982, U.S. District Court, Southern District of Ohio; 1988, U.S. Court of Appeals, Sixth Circuit; 1990, U.S. Court of Appeals, Fourth Circuit; 1993, U.S. District Court, District of Arizona; 1997, U.S. Court of Appeals, Fifth Circuit; 2001, U.S. District Court, Northern District of Ohio. *Education:* Miami University (B.S., 1978); The Ohio State University (J.D., 1981). Thomas R. Allen has achieved the highest rating possible by Martindale-Hubbell. Listed in: Best Lawyers in America; Ohio Super Lawyers. Speaker: "What's New in Healthcare Workouts, Restructurings and Bankruptcies," The Association of Insolvency and Restructuring Advisors; "Revised Article 9," Ohio Bankers Association; "Planning and the Effect of Bankruptcy on Pending State and Federal Court Litigation," Columbus Bar Association; "Not Your Ordinary Bankruptcy," Ohio Continuing Legal Education Institute; "Selected Assumption and Assignment Issues Arising with the Sale of Leases," International Council of Shopping Centers Ohio, Indiana and Kentucky Law Symposium; "Addressing the Problems of the Financially Distressed Small Business," Ohio Continuing Legal Education Institute. Speaker and Co-Author: "Foreclosure and Repossession," National Business Institute; "How to Collect a Judgment: A Primer," Lorman Education Services; "Protection of Secured Interests in Bankruptcy in Ohio," National Business Institute; "Basic Bankruptcy in Ohio," National Business Institute. Speaker and Contributing Author, "Special Problems Affecting Ohio Commercial Real Estate," Professional Educational Systems, Inc. *Member:* Columbus (Member, Bankruptcy Section) and Ohio State Bar Associations; Columbus Bar Foundation; American Bankruptcy Institute. ***PRACTICE AREAS:*** Bankruptcy Law; Commercial Law. ***Email:*** allen@akslaw.net

KENTON L. KUEHNLE, born Chicago, Illinois, November 10, 1945; admitted to bar, 1970, Ohio. *Education:* Augustana College (B.A., 1967); Duke University (J.D., 1970). Listed in: Best Lawyers in America; Ohio Super Lawyers. Lead Author, West Group's 3-Volume Treatise, "Ohio Real Estate Law," Kuehnle and Levy. Author: "Ohio Condominium Law," West, 2005, by Kuehnle & Williams. Lecturer, Ohio State Bar Association: "Condominium Law" and "Commercial Real Estate Contacts;" Columbus Bar Association: "Condominium Law"; "Commercial Leasing" and "Title Insurance"; National Business Institute: "Foreclosure Law," Title Insurance," "Commercial Leasing" and "Condominium Law;" Lorman Education Services: "Condominium Law" and "Law of Easements". Instructor, Capital University Law School Paralegal Program, 1998-2001. *Member:* Columbus (Member, Real Property Committee, 1980—), Ohio State (Member, Board of Governors, 1990— and Chairman, 1997-1999, Real Property Section and Real Estate Specialization Certification Board) and American (Member, Committee on Condominiums, Cooperative and Homeowner Associations, Real Property Section, 1980—) Bar Associations; American College of Real Estate Lawyers (Vice-Chair, Title Insurance Committee, 2005—). ***PRACTICE AREAS:*** Real Estate Law. ***Email:*** kuehnle@akslaw.com

RICHARD K. STOVALL, born Dayton, Ohio, September 11, 1960; admitted to bar, 1985, Ohio; 1986, U.S. District Court, Southern District of Ohio; 1991, U.S. Court of Appeals, Sixth Circuit; 2001, U.S. District Court, Northern District of Ohio. *Education:* Bowling Green State University (B.A., 1982); University of Toledo College of Law (J.D., 1985). Contributing Author and Speaker: "Bankruptcy in Ohio," Lorman Education Services, 2005; "Selling Distressed Businesses," Ohio State Bar Association, Annual Convention, 2003; "Chapter 11 Asset Sales," Bankruptcy Law Institute, Columbus Bar Association, 2003; "How to Collect A Judgment; A Primer," Lorman Education Services; "Caught in the Bankruptcy Whirlpool," Ohio Continuing Legal Education Institute; "Solving Practical Problems in Business Bankruptcies," Ohio Continuing Legal Education Institute; "Basics of Chapter 11 Practice," Ohio Continuing Legal Education Institute. Board Member, S.O.S. Respite, Worthington, Ohio, 1997—. Member, Turnaround Management Association, Ohio Chapter. *Member:* Columbus (Member, Bankruptcy Committee) and Ohio State Bar Associations; American Bankruptcy Institute. ***PRACTICE AREAS:*** Bankruptcy Law; Commercial Law; Business Litigation. ***Email:*** stovall@akslaw.net

(This Listing Continued)

J. MATTHEW FISHER, born Lima, Ohio, September 28, 1969; admitted to bar, 1996, Ohio; 1997, Colorado; 1999, U.S. District Court, Southern District of Ohio. *Education:* Wittenberg University (B.A., 1992); Ohio Northern University (J.D., with distinction, 1996). Staff Editor, Ohio Northern University Law Review, 1994-1996. Author: Dalton vs. Specter: The Supreme Court Precludes Judicial Review of Decisions Made Pursuant to the Defense Base Closure and Realignment Act of 1990, 21 Ohio N.U.L.Rev. 1257 (1995). *Member:* Columbus and Ohio State Bar Associations. ***PRACTICE AREAS:*** Bankruptcy; Business Law; Civil Litigation. ***Email:*** fisher@akslaw.net

OF COUNSEL

LISA L. NORRIS, born Warren, Ohio, July 31, 1966; admitted to bar, 1993, Ohio; 1994, U.S. District Court, Southern District of Ohio; 1996, U.S. Court of Appeals, Sixth Circuit. *Education:* Kent State University (B.B.A., magna cum laude, 1988); The Ohio State University (M.A., Economics, 1989; J.D., 1993). Order of the Coif. Recipient: Business First Forty Under 40 Awards, 2000. Member, Ohio State Law Journal, 1993. Author: "Alterative Dispute Resolution in Bankruptcy" Rule 9019 and Bankruptcy Mediation Programs," 68 Am. Bankr. L.J. 55, Winter, 1994. Speaker, Construction Disputes: "Can This Job be Saved?" Cleveland, Ohio; "Collecting on a Judgment," Ohio Continuing Legal Education Institute. Member, Board of Trustees, Godman Guild Association. ***PRACTICE AREAS:*** Litigation; Alternative Dispute Resolution. ***Email:*** norris@akslaw.net

JOHN M. ALTON CO., L.P.A.

Established in 1998

175 SOUTH THIRD STREET, SUITE 360
COLUMBUS, OHIO 43215
Telephone: 614-221-6751
Fax: 614-221-6788
Email: jalton@johnalton.com
URL: http://www.johnalton.com

Medical Malpractice, Personal Injury, Wrongful Death, Automobile Accidents.

FIRM PROFILE: John M. Alton Co., L.P.A. is a full service trial law firm dedicate to providing representation and aggressive advocacy on behalf of severely injured or deceased persons and their families.

John Alton has an active trial practice offering close personal attention and seasoned trial skills to persons injured by the errors, omissions, carelessness and inattention of others.

JOHN M. ALTON, born Columbus, Ohio, March 14, 1952; admitted to bar, 1977, Ohio; 1978, U.S. District Court, Southern District of Ohio; 1988, U.S. Supreme Court. *Education:* Duke University (B.A., Psychology, cum laude, with distinction, 1974); Southern Methodist University (J.D., 1977). Robert M. Duncan Chapter, Inns of Court, Alumni Board, Columbus Academy, 1980-1982; 1990-1992. Co-Author: *Personal Injury Litigation Practice in Ohio,* National Business Institute, 1988; 1991. Author: "Attorney Malpractice in Franklin County, Ohio," Columbus Bar Association Briefs, 1978; "Ohio Evidence Rule 702-Beware," Ohio Trial Magazine, 1996; "Contingent Fee Agreements Clarified," Daily Reporter, 1996. Associate, 1977-1981 and Partner, 1982-1994, Lane, Alton & Horst. Partner: Ray, Todaro & Alton Co. L.P.A., 1994-1996; Ray, Todaro, Alton & Kirstein Co. L.P.A., 1996-1997; Ray, Alton & Kirstein Co. L.P.A., 1997-1998. Owner, John M. Alton, Co., L.P.A., 1998—. Recognition: One of eight Columbus, Ohio attorneys in Medical Negligence by Law and Politics Magazine. Member, Million Dollar Advocates Forum. Member, Ohio Supreme Court Committee on Alternative Dispute Resolution, 1996—. *Member:* Columbus (Member, Ethics Committee, 1996-1998), Ohio State and American (Member, Sections on: Litigation; Tort and Insurance Practice) Bar Associations; Franklin County Trial Lawyers Association; Ohio Academy of Trial Lawyers; The Association of Trial Lawyers of America; American Board of Trial Advocates. Fellow: American College of Trial Lawyers. (Certified, Civil Trial Specialist by the National Board of Trial Advocacy). ***PRACTICE AREAS:*** Medical Malpractice; Personal Injury; Wrongful Death. ***Email:*** jalton@johnalton.com

ANTHONY LAW OFFICES, LLC

555 SOUTH FRONT STREET
SUITE 320
COLUMBUS, OHIO 43215-5668
Telephone: 614-340-0011
Fax: 614-228-3102
URL: http://www.mjanthonylaw.com
Email: mja@mjanthonylaw.com
URL: http://www.lawyers.com/anthonylawoffices

Business and commercial law, real estate, business organization, commercial transactions, contracts, commercial leasing, limited liability company law (LLCs), joint ventures, partnership law; corporate law; liability protection law; business succession, construction, mechanic's lien law, evictions and foreclosures.

MICHAEL J. ANTHONY, born Westerville, Ohio, June 19, 1970; admitted to bar, 1996, Ohio. *Education:* Cedarville College (B.A., 1993); Capital University Law School (J.D., cum laude, 1996). *Member:* Columbus Bar Association (Real Property Law, Construction Law and Business Tax Law Committees); Ohio State Bar Association (Corporate Law Committee). ***PRACTICE AREAS:*** Business Law; Commercial and Real Property Law. ***Email:*** mja@mjanthonylaw.com

JAVIER H. ARMENGAU

857 S. HIGH STREET
COLUMBUS, OHIO 43206
Telephone: 614-443-0516
URL: http://www.armengaulaw.com

Criminal Litigation in all Federal and State Courts.

JAVIER H. ARMENGAU, born Buenos Aires, Argentina, April 14, 1962; admitted to bar, 1998, Ohio; 1999, U.S. District Court, Northern District of Ohio; 2000, U.S. Court of Appeals, Sixth Circuit. *Education:* Hofstra University (B.A., 1985); Capital University (J.D., 1998). *Member:* Columbus, Cleveland, Marion County New York State, Federal and American Bar Associations; Ohio Association of Trial Lawyers; Association of Trial Lawyers of America; Ohio Academy of Trail Lawyers; National Association of Criminal Defense Lawyers; Ohio Association of Criminal Defense Lawyers; New York State Association of Criminal Defense Lawyers. ***LANGUAGES:*** Spanish. ***PRACTICE AREAS:*** Criminal Law; Personal Injury.

ARNEBECK LAW OFFICE

341 S. 3RD STREET, SUITE 10
COLUMBUS, OHIO 43215
Telephone: 614-224-8771
Fax: 614-224-8082
Email: arnebeck@aol.com
URL: http://www.lawyers.com/arnebecklaw

Civil and Federal Civil Litigation, Election Law, Fraud Litigation and Personal Injury Law.

MEMBER OF FIRM

CLIFFORD O. ARNEBECK, JR., born Washington, D.C., January 15, 1945; admitted to bar, 1970, Ohio, U.S. District Court, Southern District of Ohio and U.S. Court of Appeals, Sixth Circuit. *Education:* Wesleyan University (B.A., 1967); Harvard University (J.D., 1970). Attorney, The Ohio Bell Telephone Co., 1970-1974. General Counsel and General Attorney, Ohio Power Co., 1975-1979. General Counsel, Ohio Senate Republican Campaign Committee, 1980-1988. Partner: Jones Day Reavis & Pogue, 1980-1984; Arnebeck & Christensen, 1989-1997. Counsel, Chester Willcox & Saxbe, 1985-1988. *Member:* Ohio State Bar Association. ***Email:*** arnebeck@aol.com

OF COUNSEL

ROBERT FITRAKIS, admitted to bar, 2003, Ohio. *Education:* Ohio State University, Moritz College of Law; Ohio State University (J.D., 2003).

BABBITT & WEIS LLP

THE WORLY BUILDING
503 SOUTH FRONT STREET
SUITE 200
COLUMBUS, OHIO 43215-5666
Telephone: 614-228-4200
Fax: 614-228-4224
URL: http://www.bwfamilylaw.com
Email: BW@BWFamilyLaw.com
URL: http://www.babbittwellbaum.com

Family and Matrimonial Law, Divorce, Dissolutions, Legal Separation, Spousal Support, Property Division, Child Custody, Child Support, Pre-Marital Agreements, Divorce Arbitration.

FIRM PROFILE: Babbitt & Weis LLP is a firm dedicated to providing its clients strong, experienced representation in family and matrimonial law matters. With over thirty years of combined family and matrimonial law experience and two Ohio State Bar Association Board Certified Family Relations Law Specialists, the attorneys of Babbitt & Weis LLP represent individuals in negotiating agreed resolutions, as well as representing clients in trial and appellate proceedings, for divorce, dissolution of marriage, legal separation, spousal support, property division, 60(B) proceedings, child custody, companionship rights, child support, establishment of parentage, contempt, domestic violence, pre-marital agreements, cohabitation agreements, and step-parent adoptions.

Babbitt & Weis LLP's commitment to responding to its client's needs is instrumental in the firm's ability to consistently achieve favorable results for their clients. The firm's attorneys strive to remain on the forefront of developing trends in family and matrimonial law, frequently attending and speaking at state and national conferences and seminars. Mr. Babbitt has been a fellow in the American Academy of Matrimonial Lawyers for over seven years. The firm makes every effort to provide its clients the empathy and compassion which is so often needed during what can be one of the most traumatic phases of an individual's life. With their excellent network of financial experts, appraisers, psychologists, and other experts, the firm offers the family and matrimonial client an entire team of professionals to effectively reach their individual goals.

GERALD J. BABBITT, born Cleveland Ohio, May 6, 1954; admitted to bar, 1979, Ohio; 1980, U.S. District Court, Southern District of Ohio. *Education:* Miami University (B.S., cum laude, 1976); The Ohio State University (J.D., 1979). Continuing Legal Education Lecturer, Family and Matrimonial Law: Ohio State Bar Association, 1987—; Columbus Bar Association, 1987—; Legal Aid Society of Columbus, 1987—; Ohio Legal Services, 1987—. Referee: Franklin County Court of Domestic Relations, 1983-1986; Franklin County Juvenile Court, 1980-1983. *Member:* Columbus (Member, Family Law Committee), Ohio State (Member, Family Law Committee) and American (Member, Family Law Section) Bar Associations; Franklin County Trial Lawyers Association (Chairman,

(This Listing Continued)

BABBITT & WEIS LLP, Columbus—Continued

Family Law Committee, 1995-1997). Fellow, American Academy of Matrimonial Lawyers (Trained as Arbitrator). (Certified Specialist in Family Relations Law, Ohio State Bar Association). ***PRACTICE AREAS:*** Family; Matrimonial Law; Divorce Arbitration. ***Email:*** gjbabbitt@bwfamilylaw.com

AMY J. WEIS, born Lima, Ohio, June 8, 1969; admitted to bar, 1996, Ohio. *Education:* The Ohio State University (B.A., 1991); Capital University (J.D., magna cum laude, 1996). Order of the Curia. Staff Member, 1994-1995; Associate Editor, 1995-1996, Capital University Law Review. Co-Author, "Using Discovery to Your Client's Advantage," The Best of Family Law, 1997, edited by Rosemary Rubin. *Member:* Columbus, Ohio State and American Bar Associations; Franklin County Trial Lawyers Association (Family Law Committee Chair, 2002-2005). (Certified Specialist in Family Relations Law, Ohio State Bar Association). ***PRACTICE AREAS:*** Family Law; Matrimonial Law. ***Email:*** aweis@bwfamilylaw.com

---

C. GUSTAV DAHLBERG, born Chillicothe, Ohio, May 2, 1975; admitted to bar, 2001, Ohio. *Education:* Ohio University (B.A., 1998); The Ohio State University (J.D., 2001). *Member:* Columbus, Ohio State and American Bar Associations; Franklin County Trial Lawyers Association. ***PRACTICE AREAS:*** Family Law. ***Email:*** gdahlberg@bwfamilylaw.com

JENNIFER BROCKMEYER, born Columbus, Ohio; admitted to bar, 2004, Ohio. *Member:* Columbus, Ohio State and American Bar Associations. ***PRACTICE AREAS:*** Family Law.

BAILEY CAVALIERI LLC

SUITE 2100, ONE COLUMBUS
10 WEST BROAD STREET
COLUMBUS, OHIO 43215-3422
Telephone: 614-221-3155
Fax: 614-221-0479
URL: http://www.baileycavalieri.com

Dayton, Ohio Office: Kettering Tower, Suite 2310, 40 North Main Street, 45423-0001. Telephone: 937-223-4701. Fax: 937-223-0170.

General Civil and Trial Practice. Director and Officer Liability, Antitrust, Banking, Bankruptcy and Commercial Transactions, Corporate, Corporate Financing, Creditors Remedies, Environmental, Employee Benefits and ERISA, Estate Planning, Trust, Probate, Intellectual Property, Internet and E-Commerce, Labor and Employment, Products Liability, Public Utility, Real Estate, Finance, Securities and Taxation Law. Appellate, Communications, Energy Deregulation, Health Care, Insurance, Mergers and Acquisitions, Professional Liability, Retail and Catalog Law, Technology and Science.

FIRM PROFILE: At Bailey Cavalieri, we realize the challenges facing today's businesses. Superior services from an experienced team of lawyers can smooth the path to help companies succeed by avoiding the many legal pitfalls that exist in today's business environment.

From offices in Columbus and Dayton, Ohio, our attorneys provide innovative and practical solutions to solve clients' challenges and help them run their businesses effectively.

We are guided by the belief that clients deserve superior service, and we strive to consistently provide that level of service to our clients. We understand the unique relationship between client and lawyer and work to exceed our clients' expectations.

As outside counsel, we bring a hard-to-find level of sophistication and knowledge of our specialty practice areas into play. In situations where the client has in-house legal staff, Bailey Cavalieri is an extension of that staff, understanding and furthering the client's objective in each transaction or litigation matter.

MEMBERS OF FIRM

WILLIAM A. ADAMS, born Columbus, Ohio, April 21, 1960; admitted to bar, 1985, Ohio and U.S. District Court, Southern District of Ohio; 1987, U.S. Court of Appeals, Sixth Circuit. *Education:* Miami University (B.A., 1982); Capital University (J.D., cum laude, 1985). Order of the Curia. Articles Editor, Capital University Law Review, 1984-1985. Author: "Legal Limitations of the ADR Process," Public Utilities Fortnightly, January 15, 1993. Law Clerk to Alan E. Norris, Judge, U.S. Court of Appeals, Sixth Circuit, 1986-1987. *Member:* Columbus, Ohio State (Member, Public Utilities Committee) and Federal Communications Bar Associations. ***PRACTICE AREAS:*** Telecommunications; Energy; Public Utilities. ***Email:*** william.adams@baileycavalieri.com

DAN A. BAILEY, born Pittsburgh, Pennsylvania, August 31, 1953; admitted to bar, 1978, Ohio. *Education:* Bowling Green State University (B.S., 1975); The Ohio State University (J.D., 1978). Co-Author: Knepper, Bailey, "Liability of Corporate Officers and Directors," 7th Edition, LexisNexis Publisher. Contributing Author: "Handbook for Corporate Directors," McGraw Hill. *Member:* Columbus, Ohio State and American Bar Associations. ***PRACTICE AREAS:*** Directors and Officers Insurance Coverage; Directors and Officers Liability. ***Email:*** dan.bailey@baileycavalieri.com

GARY S. BATKE, born Chicago, Illinois, December 13, 1959; admitted to bar, 1985, Ohio; 1987, Illinois; U.S. District Court, Southern District of Ohio; U.S. Court of Appeals, Sixth Circuit. *Education:* Elmhurst College (B.S., Accounting, high honors, 1982); Indiana University (J.D., 1985). Associate Member Indiana Law Journal, 1983-1985. Contributing Author: Ohio Public Contract Law, 3d edition, 1994. *Member:* Columbus, Ohio State, Illinois and American Bar Associations. ***PRACTICE AREAS:*** Labor and Employment Law; Litigation. ***Email:*** gary.batke@baileycavalieri.com

KATHARINE B. BOWMAN, born Dayton, Ohio, April 29, 1958; admitted to bar, 1983, Ohio; 1984, U.S. District Court, Southern District of Ohio. *Education:* The Ohio State University (B.A., summa cum laude, 1980); University of Michigan (J.D., 1983).

(This Listing Continued)

Contributing Author: Knepper, Bailey, "Liability of Corporate Officers and Directors," 7th Edition, Matthew Bender & Co. Publisher. ***PRACTICE AREAS:*** Directors and Officers Liability; Insurance; Banking Litigation. ***Email:*** kathy.bowman@baileycavalieri.com

RICHARD D. BROOKS, JR., born Daytona Beach, Florida, September 17, 1944; admitted to bar, 1972, Ohio; 1975, U.S. District Court, Southern District of Ohio; 1993, U.S. Court of Appeals, Sixth Circuit. *Education:* Marietta College (B.A., 1967); Case Western Reserve University (J.D., 1972). *Member:* Columbus, Ohio State (Member: Council of Delegates, 1976-1980; Executive Committee, 1980-1983) and American Bar Associations. Fellow: American Bar Foundation; Ohio State Bar Foundation (President, 1988). ***PRACTICE AREAS:*** Environmental Law; Litigation. ***Email:*** richard.brooks@baileycavalieri.com

D. DAVID CARROLL, born Columbus, Ohio, August 5, 1964; admitted to bar, 1990, Ohio. *Education:* The Ohio State University (B.A., 1986); Capital University (J.D., cum laude, 1990). Order of the Curia. Member, Capital University Law Review. *Member:* Columbus and Ohio State (Member, Section on Corporate Counsel) Bar Associations. ***PRACTICE AREAS:*** Corporate; Securities; Electronic Commerce and Internet. ***Email:*** david.carroll@baileycavalieri.com

NICK V. CAVALIERI, born Cleveland, Ohio, August 10, 1947; admitted to bar, 1973, Ohio; 1974, U.S. District Court, Southern District of Ohio; 1984, U.S. District Court, Northern District of Ohio; 1987, U.S. Court of Appeals, Sixth Circuit and U.S. District Court, Northern District of Texas. *Education:* The Ohio State University (B.S., 1970; B.A., 1970; J.D., 1973). *Member:* Columbus (President, 1990-1991; Member, Board of Governors, 1985-1992; Member, 1979— and Chairman, 1980-1982, Bankruptcy Committee); Ohio State (Member, Council of Delegates, 1984-2000) and American Bar Associations; Columbus Bar Foundation (Fellow, Trustee, 1997—). Fellow: American College of Bankruptcy; Legal Aid Society of Columbus (President, 1989, Board of Trustees, 1985-1989). ***PRACTICE AREAS:*** Bankruptcy; Commercial Transactions; Commercial Litigation. ***Email:*** nick.cavalieri@baileycavalieri.com

YVETTE A. COX, born Ironton, Ohio, March 2, 1948; admitted to bar, 1979, Ohio and U.S. District Court, Southern District of Ohio. *Education:* The Ohio State University (B.A., 1970; M.A., 1971); Capital University (J.D., 1979). Order of the Curia. Law Clerk to the Hon. Grady L. Pettigrew, Jr., U.S. Bankruptcy Judge, 1979-1981. *Member:* Columbus (Member, Bankruptcy Committee) and Ohio State Bar Associations. ***PRACTICE AREAS:*** Bankruptcy; Commercial Transactions. ***Email:*** yvette.cox@baileycavalieri.com

DAN L. CVETANOVICH, born Wheeling, West Virginia, October 2, 1952; admitted to bar, 1977, Ohio; 1978, U.S. District Court, Southern District of Ohio; 1980, U.S. Court of Appeals, Sixth Circuit; 1984, U.S. District Court, Northern District of Ohio; 1985, West Virginia and U.S. District Court, Southern District of West Virginia; 1986, U.S. Court of Appeals, Fourth Circuit; 1998, U.S. District Court, Western District of Texas; 2001, U.S. District Court, Northern District of West Virginia. *Education:* West Liberty State College (B.A., with highest honors, 1974); Harvard University (J.D., 1977). *Member:* Columbus, Ohio State, West Virginia and American Bar Associations. ***PRACTICE AREAS:*** Business and Commercial Litigation. ***Email:*** dan.cvetanovich@baileycavalieri.com

DONALD A. DAVIES, born Ashland, Kentucky, January 3, 1937; admitted to bar, 1962, Ohio. *Education:* Dartmouth College (A.B., 1959); The Ohio State University (J.D., 1962). *Member:* Columbus and Ohio State (Member, Health Care Law Committee) Bar Associations; American Health Lawyers Association; Catholic Health Association. ***PRACTICE AREAS:*** Health Care. ***Email:*** donald.davies@baileycavalieri.com

ROBERT R. DUNN, born Columbus, Ohio, January 16, 1966; admitted to bar, 1991, Ohio. *Education:* University of Kentucky (B.A., 1988); Vanderbilt University (J.D., 1991). Phi Delta Phi. Associate Editor, Vanderbilt Journal of Transnational Law. *Member:* Columbus, Ohio State and American Bar Associations. ***PRACTICE AREAS:*** Estate Planning; Probate; Trial Practice. ***Email:*** robert.dunn@baileycavalieri.com

ROBERT L. EBLIN, born 1963; admitted to bar, 1991, Ohio; 1992, U.S. District Court, Southern District of Ohio and U.S. Court of Appeals, Sixth Circuit; 1997, U.S. Supreme Court. *Education:* Harvard University (A.B., cum laude, 1985); The Ohio State University (J.D., summa cum laude, 1991). Order of the Coif. Managing Editor, Ohio State Law Journal. Contributing Author: Knepper, Bailey, "Liability of Corporate Officers and Directors," 7th Edition, Mathew Bender & Co., publisher. Adjunct Professor, The Ohio State University College of Law, 1997. Member, American Inns of Court, 1996-1998. Member, Professional Liability Underwriting Society. ***PRACTICE AREAS:*** Directors and Officers Liability; Employment Law; Litigation. ***Email:*** robert.eblin@baileycavalieri.com

MICHAEL R. GOODSTEIN, born Flushing, New York, May 16, 1964; admitted to bar, 1989, Maryland; 1990, District of Columbia, Virginia, U.S. District Court, District of Columbia, U.S. District Court, Eastern District of Virginia and U.S. District Court, District of Maryland; 1991, U.S. Bankruptcy Court, Eastern District of Virginia (Not admitted in Ohio). *Education:* Brandeis University (B.A., 1986); Washington College of Law (J.D., 1989). Note and Comment Editor, The Administrative Law Journal, 1988-1989. ***PRACTICE AREAS:*** Directors and Officers Liability; Litigation. ***Email:*** michael.goodstein@baileycavalieri.com

DENNIS D. GRANT, born Cleveland, Ohio, November 2, 1940; admitted to bar, 1965, Ohio. *Education:* Muskingum College (B.A., cum laude, 1962); University of Michigan (J.D., 1965). Phi Alpha Theta. Adjunct Professor, Labor Law, The Ohio State University College of Law, 1975-1977. Trustee, Muskingum College, 1972—. *Member:* Columbus, Ohio State (Member, Board of Governors, Labor Section, 1978-1984, 1987-1999) and American Bar Associations. ***PRACTICE AREAS:*** Labor and Employment Law. ***Email:*** dennis.grant@baileycavalieri.com

JAMES M. GRONER, born Warren, Ohio, February 19, 1965; admitted to bar, 1991, Ohio. *Education:* Miami University (B.S., 1987); University of Cincinnati (J.D., 1990). *Member:* Columbus, Ohio State and American Bar Associations. ***PRACTICE AREAS:*** Real Estate; Business Enterprises; Banking. ***Email:*** jim.groner@baileycavalieri.com

DANIEL R. HACKETT, born September 21, 1961; admitted to bar, 1988, Ohio. *Education:* University of Notre Dame (B.B.A., summa cum laude, 1983); The Ohio State University (J.D., summa cum laude, 1988). Order of the Coif. Member, Ohio State University

(This Listing Continued)

Law Journal, 1987-1988. Certified Public Accountant, Ohio, 1985 (non-practicing). *Member:* American Health Lawyers Association. ***PRACTICE AREAS:*** Health Care; Corporate Law. ***Email:*** dan.hackett@baileycavalieri.com

MARY JO HUDSON, born St. Marys, Ohio, January 31, 1963; admitted to bar, 1989, Ohio; 1996, U.S. District Court, Southern District of Ohio. *Education:* Miami University (B.A., 1985); University of Cincinnati (J.D., 1988). Author: Comment, "Expert Witness Fees as Taxable Costs - The Exceptions and the Rule," 55 U. Cinn. L. Rev. 1207, 1987. *Member:* Columbus, Ohio State Bar Associations; Ohio Human Rights Bar Association; American Inns of Court. ***PRACTICE AREAS:*** Trade Regulation; Commercial Lending; Insurance Regulation; Insurance Liquidation; Corporate; Liquor. ***Email:*** mj.hudson@baileycavalieri.com

DARIUS N. KANDAWALLA, born Enfield, England, July 1, 1971; admitted to bar, 1996, Ohio; 1997, U.S. District Court, Southern District of Ohio; 1998, U.S. Court of Appeals, Sixth Circuit. *Education:* Bowling Green State University (B.A., cum laude, 1993); The Ohio State University (J.D., with honors, 1996). Member, American Bar Association Moot Court Team. Member, Ohio State University Law Journal. *Member:* Columbus and Ohio State Bar Associations. ***PRACTICE AREAS:*** Director and Officer Liability; Insurance Coverage Litigation; Business Litigation. ***Email:*** darius.kandawalla@baileycavalieri.com

R. STACY LANE, born Columbus, Ohio, October 6, 1958; admitted to bar, 1989, Ohio and U.S. District Court, Southern District of Ohio. *Education:* The Ohio State University (B.S., 1981); Capital University (J.D., magna cum laude, 1989). Gamma Sigma Delta; Order of the Curia. Contributing Author: Knepper, Bailey "Liability of Corporate Officers and Directors," 7th Edition, Matthew Bender & Co. Publisher. *Member:* Columbus, Ohio State and American Bar Associations. ***PRACTICE AREAS:*** Directors and Officers Liability and Insurance; Professional Liability. ***Email:*** stacy.lane@baileycavalieri.com

MICHAEL P. MAHONEY, born Columbus, Ohio, October 26, 1945; admitted to bar, 1972, Ohio, U.S. District Court, Southern and Northern Districts of Ohio, U.S. Court of Appeals, Sixth Circuit, U.S. Tax Court and U.S. Supreme Court. *Education:* The Ohio State University (B.S., 1967; J.D., summa cum laude, 1972). Order of the Coif. Member, Board of Editors, Ohio State Law Journal, 1971-1972. *Member:* Columbus, Ohio State and American Bar Associations. ***PRACTICE AREAS:*** Corporate; ERISA; Business Planning. ***Email:*** michael.mahoney@baileycavalieri.com

NANCY J. MANOUGIAN, born La Salle, Illinois, March 20, 1948; admitted to bar, 1985, Ohio, U.S. District Court, Southern District of Ohio, U.S. Court of Appeals, Sixth Circuit and U.S. Supreme Court. *Education:* Monmouth College (B.A., 1970); Capital University (J.D., magna cum laude, 1985). Order of The Curia. Executive Notes Editor, Capital University Law Review, 1983-1984. *Member:* Columbus, Ohio State and American Bar Associations. ***PRACTICE AREAS:*** Appellate; Insurance; Commercial Litigation. ***Email:*** nancy.manougian@baileycavalieri.com

DONALD G. PAYNTER, born Galion, Ohio, March 5, 1946; admitted to bar, 1971, Ohio. *Education:* Miami University (B.S., 1968); The Ohio State University (J.D., cum laude, 1970). Order of the Coif. *Member:* Columbus, Ohio State and American Bar Associations. ***PRACTICE AREAS:*** Real Estate. ***Email:*** donald.paynter@baileycavalieri.com

W. EVAN PRICE, II, born Cincinnati, Ohio, December 7, 1964; admitted to bar, 1991, Ohio. *Education:* Dartmouth College (B.A., 1988); University of Florida (J.D., with honors, 1991). Recipient, American Jurisprudence Awards in Criminal Law, Contracts, Creditors Remedies and Bankruptcy. ***PRACTICE AREAS:*** Litigation. ***Email:*** evan.price@baileycavalieri.com

JAMES G. RYAN, born Painesville, Ohio, January 31, 1960; admitted to bar, 1985, Ohio. *Education:* University of Dayton (B.A., magna cum laude, 1982); The Ohio State University (J.D., cum laude, 1985). *Member:* Columbus, Ohio State and American Bar Association (Member, Business Law Section; Consumer Finance Subcommittee). ***PRACTICE AREAS:*** Commercial Lending; Mergers and Acquisitions; Consumer Protection. ***Email:*** jamie.ryan@baileycavalieri.com

DANE STINSON, born Columbus, Ohio, February 8, 1956; admitted to bar, 1981, Ohio. *Education:* The Ohio State University (B.A., 1978; J.D., 1981). *Member:* Columbus, Ohio State and Federal Communications Bar Associations. ***PRACTICE AREAS:*** Communications; Energy; Utility Regulation. ***Email:*** dane.stinson@baileycavalieri.com

OF COUNSEL

JOHN J. DILENSCHNEIDER, born 1931; admitted to bar, 1959, Ohio and U.S. District Court, Southern and Northern Districts of Ohio; 1965, U.S. Court of Appeals, 5th Circuit; 1984, U.S. District Court, Eastern District of Kentucky; 1994, U.S. Court of Appeals, 3rd Circuit. *Education:* University of Notre Dame (A.B., 1953); Northwestern University (J.D., 1959). U.S. Bankruptcy Judge, 1967-1976; Partner, Porter Wright Morris & Arthur, 1976-1986; Partner, Squire Sanders & Dempsey, 1988-1996; Counsel to the Court, Supreme Court of Ohio, 1996-2002; Fellow, American College of Bankruptcy; Associate Member, National Conference of Bankruptcy Judges; Past President, Association of Former Bankruptcy Judges; Former Member of Editorial Board, American Bankruptcy Law Journal; Former Adjunct Professor, The Ohio State University Law School; Contributing Author to Collier on Bankruptcy, 15th Ed. and Collier Bankruptcy Practice Guide; Publications: "A Close Look at the Proposed Discharge Provisions," 50 Am. Bankr. L.J. 107 (1976); "Truth in Lending Actions and the Trustee," 51 Am.Bankr. L.J. 371 (1977); "Regulation: Another Role for the Trustee," 48 Am.Bankr. L.J. 107 (1974); "Dischargeability, A Brief for the Consumer Bankrupt," 44 Ref. Journ. 83 (1970); Author and frequent lecturer on bankruptcy topics; Mississippi volunteer attorney, Lawyer's Committee for Civil Rights Under Law, 1965. ***PRACTICE AREAS:*** Bankruptcy. ***Email:*** john.dilenschneider@baileycavalieri.com

JULES L. GAREL, born Woonsocket, Rhode Island, December 22, 1930; admitted to bar, 1955, Ohio; 1956, Massachusetts; 1980, Florida. *Education:* Harvard University (A.B., 1952); Boston University (J.D., 1955). Member, Boston University Law Review. *Member:* Columbus, Ohio State and American Bar Associations; The Florida Bar. ***PRACTICE AREAS:*** Corporate; Real Estate; Business Planning. ***Email:*** jules.garel@baileycavalieri.com

(This Listing Continued)

THOMAS E. GEYER, born Columbus, Ohio, November 17, 1964; admitted to bar, 1990, Ohio; 1991, U.S. District Court, Southern District of Ohio. *Education:* University of Notre Dame (B.B.A., Finance, 1987); The Ohio State University (J.D., with honors, 1990). Recipient, Distinguished Recent Alumnus Award, The Ohio State University College of Law, 1999; Outstanding Service Award, North American Securities Administrators Association, 1999. Member, 1988-1990 and Articles Editor, 1989-1990, Ohio State Law Journal. Author: "Ohio Investment Adviser Manual," Lexis-Nexis Publishing; "Civil Liability and Remedies in Ohio Securities Transactions," 70 U.Cin.L.Rev. 939 (2002); "The Vitality of the Ohio Laws Designed to Encourage Negotiated Takeovers," 23 U.Day.L.Rev. 515 (1998). Adjunct Professor, Capital University Law School, 1998-2003. Assistant Director, Ohio Department of Commerce, 2000-2004. Commissioner, 1996-2000 and Enforcement Attorney, 1994-1996, Ohio Division of Securities. *Member:* Columbus and Ohio State (Member, Corporation Law Committee, Tender Offer Subcommittee and State Securities Regulation Subcommittee) Bar Associations. ***SPECIAL AGENCIES:*** Chair, Financial Services Modernization Project Group, North American Securities Administrators Association, 1998-2001. Member and Past Chair, Ohio Division of Securities Takeover Advisory Committee, 1996—. ***PRACTICE AREAS:*** Directors and Officers Liability; Corporate Law; Securities; Government Relations. ***Email:*** thomas.geyer@baileycavalieri.com

R. CLIFFTON GIBBS, born Fremont, Ohio, October 17, 1935; admitted to bar, 1959, Ohio; 1960, U.S. District Court, Southern District of Ohio. *Education:* The Ohio State University (B.S., 1958; J.D., 1958). Phi Delta Phi. *Member:* Columbus (Member: Real Estate Committee, 1979-1980, 1982—; Bankruptcy Committee, 1979—), Ohio State and American Bar Associations; American Judicature Society; Commercial Law League of America. ***Email:*** cliffton.gibbs@baileycavalieri.com

SARAH E. LYNN, born Dayton, Ohio, April 13, 1959; admitted to bar, 1987, Virginia; 1989, District of Columbia; 1991, Ohio. *Education:* Indiana University (B.A., 1981); George Washington University (J.D., 1987). Assistant Attorney General, Environmental Enforcement Section, State of Ohio, 1991-1994. Special Assistant U.S. Attorney, U.S. Department of Justice, 1993-1994. *Member:* Columbus, Ohio State (Member, State Environmental Law Committee) and American Bar Associations. ***PRACTICE AREAS:*** Environmental Law; Litigation. ***Email:*** sarah.lynn@baileycavalieri.com

TIMOTHY A. RIEDEL, born Cleveland, Ohio, September 26, 1960; admitted to bar, 1987, Ohio. *Education:* Kent State University (B.A., 1984); Paul Valery University, Montpellier, France; The Ohio State University (J.D., 1987). Recipient, American Jurisprudence Prize Award in International Law. ***PRACTICE AREAS:*** Bankruptcy. ***Email:*** timothy.riedel@baileycavalieri.com

ANTHONY J. SUGAR, born Columbus, Ohio, December 29, 1963; admitted to bar, 1991, Ohio. *Education:* The Wharton School, University of Pennsylvania (B.A. in Economics, 1986); University of Pennsylvania (J.D., 1991). *Member:* Columbus and Ohio State Bar Associations. ***PRACTICE AREAS:*** Corporate Law; Business Law; Commercial Loans; Private Equity; Real Estate Lending, Sales and Financing; Securities Law; Corporate Governance; Mergers and Acquisitions. ***Email:*** anthony.sugar@baileycavalieri.com

ASSOCIATES

ADAM J. BIEHL, born Carbondale, Illinois, September 12, 1969; admitted to bar, 1995, Ohio; 1996, U.S. District Court, Southern District of Ohio. *Education:* Ohio Wesleyan University (B.A., magna cum laude, 1991); The Ohio State University (J.D., 1995). Member, Mortar Board. *Member:* Columbus, Ohio State and American Bar Associations. ***PRACTICE AREAS:*** Corporate; Securities; Mergers and Acquisitions; Business Law; Internet Law; Technology Law; Commercial Transactions; Bankruptcy. ***Email:*** adam.biehl@baileycavalieri.com

MATTHEW J. BURKHART, born Columbus, Ohio, October 7, 1971; admitted to bar, 1997, Ohio. *Education:* Wittenberg University (B.A., summa cum laude, 1994); University of Virginia (J.D., 1997). Phi Beta Kappa. *Member:* Columbus, Ohio State and American Bar Associations. ***PRACTICE AREAS:*** Business Litigation; Government Affairs; General Practice. ***Email:*** matthew.burkhart@baileycavalieri.com

HARLAN S. LOUIS, born Dayton, Ohio, December 28, 1966; admitted to bar, 1994, Ohio; 1995, Florida, U.S. District Court, Southern District of Ohio and U.S. Tax Court. *Education:* Miami University (B.S., 1989); University of Dayton (J.D., cum laude, 1994); University of Florida (LL.M., Taxation, 1995). Certified Public Accountant, Ohio (Inactive). *Member:* Columbus and Ohio State Bar Associations; The Florida Bar. (Certified Specialist in Estate Planning, Trust and Probate Law, Ohio State Bar Association). ***PRACTICE AREAS:*** Estate Planning; Trusts and Estates; Business Law; Probate; Local Taxation; State Taxation; Federal Taxation. ***Email:*** harlan.louis@baileycavalieri.com

TIMOTHY B. McGRANOR, born Elyria, Ohio, January 16, 1975; admitted to bar, 2000, Ohio. *Education:* The Ohio State University (B.A., summa cum laude, 1997; J.D., 2000). Delta Theta Phi; Order of the Coif. Member, Ohio State Law Journal. ***PRACTICE AREAS:*** Business Litigation; Bankruptcy. ***Email:*** timothy.mcgranor@baileycavalieri.com

TIFFANY C. MILLER, born Columbus, Ohio, October 29, 1973; admitted to bar, 2000, Ohio; 2001, U.S. District Court, Southern District of Ohio and U.S. Court of Appeals, Sixth Circuit. *Education:* The Ohio State University (B.A., magna cum laude, Journalism, 1996; J.D., with honors, 2000). Public Service Fellow. Managing Editor, The Ohio State Journal on Dispute Resolution. Co-Coordinator, Volunteer Tax Assistance Program. Senator, Ohio State University Student Bar Association. *Member:* Columbus and Ohio State Bar Associations. ***PRACTICE AREAS:*** Business Litigation; Employment Litigation. ***Email:*** tiffany.miller@baileycavalieri.com

DAVID A. MULLER, born May 15, 1974; admitted to bar, 2000, Ohio; 2001, U.S. District Court, Northern and Southern Districts of Ohio. *Education:* The Ohio State University (B.A., Political Science, magna cum laude, 1996); The Moritz College of Law at The Ohio State University (J.D., 2000). *Member:* The Franklin American Inns of Court. ***PRACTICE AREAS:*** Directors and Officers Liability. ***Email:*** david.muller@baileycavalieri.com

AMANDA MUSIC, born Rochester, New York, September 23, 1977; admitted to bar, 2003, Ohio. *Education:* University of Toledo (B.A., International Relations, 2000); Uni-

(This Listing Continued)

BAILEY CAVALIERI LLC, Columbus—Continued

versity of Toledo College of Law (J.D., summa cum laude, 2003). *Member:* Columbus and Ohio State Bar Associations. ***PRACTICE AREAS:*** Director and Officer Liability. ***Email:*** amanda.music@baileycavalieri.com

RITA A. PEREZ, born Canton, Ohio, September 25, 1979; admitted to bar, 2004, Ohio. *Education:* Capital University (B.A., Business Management and Finance, 2001); University of Akron (J.D., magna cum laude, 2004). *Member:* Columbus and Ohio State Bar Associations. ***PRACTICE AREAS:*** Director and Officer Liability; Health Care. ***Email:*** rita.perez@baileycavalieri.com

TODD J. SAMPLES, born Columbus, Ohio, May 5, 1975; admitted to bar, 2001, Ohio. *Education:* The Ohio State University (B.A., Political Science, 1997); Capitol University (J.D., summa cum laude, 2001). ***PRACTICE AREAS:*** Corporate Law; Commercial Transactions. ***Email:*** todd.samples@baileycavalieri.com

MATTHEW T. SCHAEFFER, born Troy, Ohio, July 28, 1970; admitted to bar, 1996, Ohio; 1997, U.S. District Court, Northern and Southern Districts of Ohio. *Education:* The Ohio State University (B.A., 1993); Capital University (J.D., cum laude, 1996). Order of the Curia. Author: "The Waiver Provisions of the OWBPA," 24 Capital University Law Review 257; "The Fundamentals of Bankruptcy Law and Procedure in Ohio," National Business Institute, 1998; "Judgment Enforcement in Ohio," Lorman, 2000. *Member:* Columbus Bar Association (Member: Bankruptcy Committee, 1997—. ***PRACTICE AREAS:*** Bankruptcy; Commercial Transactions; Commercial Litigation. ***Email:*** matthew.schaeffer@baileycavalieri.com

JAMEEL S. TURNER, born June 14, 1977; admitted to bar, 2004, Ohio. *Education:* University of Toledo (B.A., cum laude, 2000); The Ohio State University (J.D., 2004). *Member:* Columbus and Ohio State Bar Associations. ***PRACTICE AREAS:*** Corporate; Business. ***Email:*** jameel.turner@baileycavalieri.com

JON C. WALDEN, born Bowling Green, Kentucky, January 19, 1968; admitted to bar, 1994, Ohio; 1995, U.S. District Court, Southern District of Ohio; 1996, U.S. District Court, Northern District of Ohio; 1997, U.S. Supreme Court. *Education:* University of Michigan (B.G.S., 1990); The Ohio State University (J.D., with honors, 1994). ***PRACTICE AREAS:*** Directors and Officers Liability. ***Email:*** jon.walden@baileycavalieri.com

BAKER & HOSTETLER LLP

Established in 1916

CAPITOL SQUARE, SUITE 2100
65 EAST STATE STREET
COLUMBUS, OHIO 43215-4260
Telephone: 614-228-1541
Telecopier: 614-462-2616
To contact an attorney on the Internet use first initial and surname followed by @bakerlaw.com
URL: http://www.bakerlaw.com

In Cleveland, Ohio: 3200 National City Center, 1900 East Ninth Street. Telephone: 216-621-0200.
In Cincinnati, Ohio: 312 Walnut Street, Suite 3200. Telephone: 513-929-3400.
In Costa Mesa, California: 600 Anton Boulevard, Suite 900. Telephone: 714-754-6600.
In Denver, Colorado: 303 East 17th Avenue, Suite 1100. Telephone: 303-861-0600.
In Houston, Texas: 1000 Louisiana, Suite 2000. Telephone: 713-751-1600.
In Los Angeles, California: 333 South Grand Avenue, Suite 1800. Telephone: 213-975-1600.
In Orlando, Florida: SunTrust Center, Suite 2300, 200 South Orange Avenue. Telephone: 407-649-4000.
In Washington, D. C.: Washington Square, Suite 1100, 1050 Connecticut Avenue, N.W. Telephone: 202-861-1500.
In New York, N.Y.: 666 Fifth Avenue. Telephone: 212-589-4200.

General Practice.

EXECUTIVE PARTNERS

ALEC WIGHTMAN, born Cleveland, Ohio, January 23, 1951; admitted to bar, 1975, Ohio; 1982, U.S. Tax Court. *Education:* Duke University (A.B., cum laude, 1972); The Ohio State University (J.D., cum laude, 1975). ***PRACTICE AREAS:*** Business Law; Bankruptcy Law. ***Email:*** awightman@bakerlaw.com

R. STEVEN KESTNER, born August 6, 1954; admitted to bar, 1979, Ohio. *Education:* Ohio Wesleyan University (B.A., cum laude, 1976); The Ohio State University (J.D., 1979). Pi Mu Epsilon (Mathematics); Omicron Delta Epsilon (Economics); Omicron Delta Kappa (Leadership). Member, 1977-1979, Issue Planning Editor, 1978-1979, Ohio State Law Journal. Member, Firm's Policy Committee. Firmwide Group Chair, Business Group Practice Area. *Member:* Cleveland (Member, Sections of: Securities Law; Corporations, Banking and Business Law), Ohio State and American Bar Associations (Member, Business Law Section). (Resident at Cleveland Office). ***PRACTICE AREAS:*** Mergers and Acquisitions; Private Equity; Venture Capital; Securities Law. ***Email:*** skestner@bakerlaw.com

OFFICE MANAGING PARTNER

GEORGE W. HAIRSTON, born Ironton, Ohio, August 1, 1942; admitted to bar, 1968, Ohio. *Education:* University of Cincinnati; Southern Methodist University (B.B.A., 1965); The Ohio State University (J.D., cum laude, 1968). Order of the Coif; Beta Gamma Sigma. Associate Editor, 1967 and Comment Editor, 1968, Ohio State Law Journal. ***PRACTICE AREAS:*** Litigation. ***Email:*** ghairston@bakerlaw.com

PARTNERS

M.J. ASENSIO, III, born Madrid, Spain, February 27, 1961; admitted to bar, 1985, Ohio. *Education:* University of Michigan (B.A., 1982); Indiana University (J.D., cum laude, 1985). *Member:* Columbus, Ohio State and American (Member, Labor and Employment Law Section) Bar Associations. ***PRACTICE AREAS:*** Employment Law; Labor Relations; Labor Negotiations; Employment Litigation. ***Email:*** masensio@bakerlaw.com

OTTO BEATTY, III, born Columbus, Ohio, February 2, 1969; admitted to bar, 1994, Ohio. *Education:* Morehouse College (B.A., 1991); University of Michigan (J.D., 1993). Law Clerk to Hon. Peggy Bryant, Ohio Court of Appeals, 1994-1995. *Member:* American and National Bar Associations. ***PRACTICE AREAS:*** Commercial Law; Bankruptcy; Creditors Rights. ***Email:*** obeatty@bakerlaw.com

EDWARD J. BERNERT, born Steubenville, Ohio, June 7, 1952; admitted to bar, 1977, Ohio. *Education:* Ohio Northern University (B.A., cum laude, 1974); The Ohio State University (J.D., 1977). Chief Editor, Ohio Tax Review, Capital University Law Center, 1987. Adjunct Professor, Capital University Law and Graduate Program. *Member:* Ohio State Bar Association (Former Chairman, Taxation Committee); Ohio Manufacturers Association (Member, Taxation Committee). ***PRACTICE AREAS:*** Tax. ***Email:*** ebernert@bakerlaw.com

JACK A. BJERKE, born Buffalo, New York, July 23, 1945; admitted to bar, 1970, Ohio. *Education:* Wittenberg University (B.S., 1967); Case Western Reserve University (J.D., 1970). ***PRACTICE AREAS:*** Securities Law; Auto Racing Law; Oil and Gas Law; Corporation Law. ***Email:*** jbjerke@bakerlaw.com

JOSEPH P. BOECKMAN, born St. Marys, Ohio, November 26, 1959; admitted to bar, 1987, Ohio. *Education:* University of Cincinnati (B.B.A., cum laude, 1982); The Ohio State University (J.D., with Honors, 1987). Order of the Coif. *Member:* Columbus, Ohio State and American Bar Associations. ***PRACTICE AREAS:*** Corporate; Securities; Mergers and Acquisitions; Private Capital; Insurance. ***Email:*** jboeckman@bakerlaw.com

MICHAEL D. BRIDGES, born Tiffin, Ohio, January 10, 1965; admitted to bar, 1993, Ohio; 1994, U.S. District Court, Southern District of Ohio. *Education:* Miami University (B.A., cum laude, Phi Beta Kappa, 1987); Capital University (J.D., magna cum laude, 1992). *Member:* Columbus and Ohio State Bar Associations. ***PRACTICE AREAS:*** Business; Real Estate; Corporate Law; Commercial Finance. ***Email:*** mbridges@bakerlaw.com

JOHN H. BURTCH, born Columbus, Ohio, August 14, 1948; admitted to bar, 1974, Ohio. *Education:* Denison University (B.A., 1970); The Ohio State University (J.D., summa cum laude, 1974). Order of the Coif. Member, Ohio State Law Journal, 1973-1974. ***PRACTICE AREAS:*** Litigation. ***Email:*** jburtch@bakerlaw.com

JOSEPH C. DEVINE, born Syracuse, New York, December 15, 1966; admitted to bar, 1991, Maryland; 1995, Ohio; U.S. District Court, Southern District of Ohio and U.S. Court of Appeals, Sixth and District of Columbia Circuits. *Education:* St. John's University (B.A., 1988); George Washington University, The National Law Center (J.D., 1991). ***PRACTICE AREAS:*** Labor and Employment. ***Email:*** jdevine@bakerlaw.com

MICHAEL D. DORTCH, born Columbus Ohio, February 8, 1958; admitted to bar, 1990, Ohio. *Education:* Ohio State University (B.A., 1986); Capital University (J.D., summa cum laude, 1990). Order of the Curia. Member, Capital U. Law Review, 1989-1990. Author: Comment, "Punitive Damages and the Constitution," 18 Cap. U. L. Rev. 545. ***PRACTICE AREAS:*** Litigation; Utility Law; Environmental Law. ***Email:*** mdortch@bakerlaw.com

R. CHRISTOPHER DOYLE, born Columbus, Ohio, January 16, 1954; admitted to bar, 1979, Ohio. *Education:* Ohio Dominican College (B.A., 1976); The Ohio State University (J.D., 1979). Industrial Commission of Ohio - District Hearing Officer, 1980-1983, Staff Hearing Officer, 1983-1985, Chief Staff Attorney, 1985-1989. ***PRACTICE AREAS:*** Employment Law; Workers' Compensation Law. ***Email:*** cdoyle@bakerlaw.com

SANDRA PARKS FAULKNER, born Hialeah, Florida, September 20, 1969; admitted to bar, 1993, Ohio. *Education:* Florida State University (B.S., 1990); The Ohio State University (J.D., 1993). ***Email:*** sfaulkner@bakerlaw.com

ANDREW M. FERRIS, born Columbus, Ohio, August 12, 1968; admitted to bar, 1995, Ohio; 1996, U.S. District Court, Southern District of Ohio. *Education:* Miami University (B.S., 1990); University of Cincinnati College of Law (J.D., 1995). ***PRACTICE AREAS:*** Tax Law; State Tax; Local Tax; Tax Exempt Organizations. ***Email:*** aferris@bakerlaw.com

CHRISTOPHER D. FIDLER, born Shelby, Ohio, March 3, 1964; admitted to bar, 1992, Ohio. *Education:* The Ohio State University (B.A., 1986); Capital University Law School (J.D., 1992). Certified Public Accountant, Ohio, 1990 (holds nonpracticing license). *Member:* Ohio State and Columbus Bar Associations. ***PRACTICE AREAS:*** Trusts and Estates; Estate Planning. ***Email:*** cfidler@bakerlaw.com

ELLEN J. GARLING, born Ashland, Ohio, April 6, 1959; admitted to bar, 1989, Ohio; U.S. District Court, Northern and Southern Districts of Ohio and U.S. Court of Appeals, Sixth Circuit. *Education:* The Ohio State University (B.A., 1986); Capital University Law School (J.D., cum laude, 1989). Delta Theta Phi; Order of the Curia; Moot Court Board (Chief Justice). *Member:* Columbus and Ohio State Bar Associations; Women Lawyers of Franklin County. ***PRACTICE AREAS:*** Labor and Employment Law. ***Email:*** egarling@bakerlaw.com

JEANNE A. GRIFFIN, born Richland, Washington, October 25, 1955; admitted to bar, 1984, Wisconsin; 1991, Ohio; 2003, U.S. Court of Appeals, Sixth Circuit and U.S. District Court, Eastern District of Michigan. *Education:* Washington State University (B.A., 1977; M.A., 1979); University of Minnesota (J.D., 1984). Author, Note: "President Clinton's Pension Simplification Initiative," 1995; "Plan Administration Correction Strategies," 2000. *Member:* State Bar of Wisconsin; Columbus Bar Association. ***PRACTICE AREAS:*** Employee Benefits; ERISA Compliance. ***Email:*** jgriffin@bakerlaw.com

MARY C. PELINI GRILLO, born Youngstown, Ohio, February 3, 1959; admitted to bar, 1994, Ohio. *Education:* Washington University (B.S., 1981); The Ohio State University (J.D., 1994). ***PRACTICE AREAS:*** Business Law; Commercial Law; Licensing; Technology Law. ***Email:*** mgrillo@bakerlaw.com

DANIEL J. GUNSETT, born Van Wert, Ohio, October 8, 1948; admitted to bar, 1974, Ohio; 1975, U.S. District Court, Southern District of Ohio; 1979, U.S. District Court, Northern District of Ohio; 1998, U.S. Court of Appeals, Fifth Circuit. *Education:* University of Michigan (B.S., Chemical Engineering, 1971); University of North Carolina (J.D., 1974). *Member:* American Bar Association (Member, Section of Natural Resources, Energy and Environmental Law); Ohio State Bar Association (Member, Environmental Law

(This Listing Continued)

Committee); Columbus Bar Association (Member, Environmental and Real Estate Committees); Electric Cooperative Bar Association. ***PRACTICE AREAS:*** Business Law; Energy; Environmental Law; Environmental Litigation; Real Estate Litigation; Class Actions. ***Email:*** dgunsett@bakerlaw.com

DANIEL J. GUTTMAN, born Toledo, Ohio, February 17, 1972; admitted to bar, 1997, Ohio; U.S. District Court, Southern District of Ohio and U.S. Court of Appeals, Sixth Circuit. *Education:* Indiana University (B.A., with honors, 1994); Ohio State University College of Law (J.D., 1997). Blue Key; Gold Key; Pi Sigma Alpha. Managing Editor, Ohio State Journal on Dispute Resolution. Recipient, Outstanding Managing Editor Award. Author: "Alternatives to Traditional Adversarial Litigation," 12 Ohio State Journal on Dispute Resolution 175 (1996). *Member:* Columbus, Ohio State and American Bar Associations. ***PRACTICE AREAS:*** Employment Litigation; Labor Arbitration; Employment Contracts; Executive Employment Law; Employment Law; Business Law. ***Email:*** dguttman@bakerlaw.com

ELIZABETH L. HENDERSHOT, born Columbus, Ohio, May 16, 1970; admitted to bar, 1995, Ohio; 1996, U.S. District Court, Southern District of Ohio and U.S. Court of Appeals, Sixth Circuit. *Education:* Ohio Wesleyan University (B.A., summa cum laude, 1992), Phi Beta Kappa; Ohio State University (J.D., summa cum laude, 1995). Order of the Coif. Author: "Constitutional Gag Orders Restricting Trial Participants' Speech," 57 Ohio St. Law Journal. ***PRACTICE AREAS:*** General Litigation. ***Email:*** ehendershot@bakerlaw.com

CHARLES H. HIRE, born Xenia, Ohio, September 16, 1941; admitted to bar, 1966, Ohio. *Education:* Denison University (A.B., 1963); The Ohio State University (J.D., 1966). Phi Delta Phi. *Member:* Columbus, Ohio State and American Bar Associations. ***PRACTICE AREAS:*** Securities Law; General Corporate Law; Investment Company Law. ***Email:*** chire@bakerlaw.com

MARK A. JOHNSON, born Marysville, Ohio, June 5, 1960; admitted to bar, 1985, Ohio and U.S. District Court, Southern District of Ohio; 1987, U.S. Court of Appeals, Sixth Circuit; 1991, U.S. District Court, Northern District of Ohio; 1998, U.S. Court of Appeals, Fifth Circuit. *Education:* Otterbein College (B.A., summa cum laude, 1982); The Ohio State University (J.D., with honors, 1985). Order of the Coif. Author: Case Comment, "*Littlefield v. Pillsbury Co.:* A Turn to the Left in Workers' Compensation," 46 Ohio St. L. J. 411 (1985). Articles Editor, Ohio State Law Journal, 1985. ***PRACTICE AREAS:*** Litigation; Class Action. ***Email:*** mjohnson@bakerlaw.com

ROBERT M. KINCAID, JR., born Columbus, Ohio, May 10, 1952; admitted to bar, 1977, Ohio and U.S. District Court, Northern and Southern Districts of Ohio; 1986, U.S. Supreme Court, U.S. Court of Appeals, Sixth Circuit and U.S. District Court, Eastern District of Michigan; 1991, U.S. Tax Court and U.S. Court of Appeals, Fifth and Seventh Circuits; 2000, U.S. Court of Appeals, Second Circuit. *Education:* University of Notre Dame (B.A., cum laude, 1974); St. Louis University (J.D., cum laude, 1977). Student Writings Editor, St. Louis University Law Journal, 1976-1977. Member, The Million Dollar Advocates Forum. *Member:* American, Ohio State, Columbus and Federal Bar Associations. ***PRACTICE AREAS:*** Business Litigation; Fiduciary, Probate and Trust Litigation; Employment Litigation. ***Email:*** rkincaid@bakerlaw.com

SHERRI BLANK LAZEAR, born Cleveland, Ohio, July 22, 1958; admitted to bar, 1985, Ohio. *Education:* The Ohio State University (B.A., 1981; J.D., Honors in Law, 1985). Articles Editor, Ohio State Law Journal, 1985. ***PRACTICE AREAS:*** Litigation; Construction Law; Bankruptcy. ***Email:*** slazear@bakerlaw.com

DAVID C. LEVINE, born Detroit, Michigan, July 5, 1952; admitted to bar, 1989, Ohio; U.S. Supreme Court, U.S. Court of Appeals, Sixth Circuit, U.S. District Court, Southern and Northern Districts of Ohio and U.S. District Court, Eastern District of Michigan. *Education:* Oakland University (B.A., 1973); Wayne State University (M.A., 1976); The Ohio State University (J.D., with honors, 1989). Managing Editor, The Ohio State Law Journal. ***PRACTICE AREAS:*** Medical Malpractice Defense; Commercial Foreclosure; Real Estate Litigation; Business Litigation. ***Email:*** dlevine@bakerlaw.com

RONALD G. LINVILLE, born Youngstown, Ohio, October 28, 1954; admitted to bar, 1980, Ohio; 1994, U.S. Supreme Court. *Education:* Wittenberg University (B.A., cum laude, 1977); Capital University (J.D., summa cum laude, 1980). *Member:* American (Member, Labor and Employment Law Section), Ohio State and Columbus Bar Associations. ***PRACTICE AREAS:*** Labor and Employment; Labor Litigation Defense; Labor Negotiation; Labor Arbitration. ***Email:*** rlinville@bakerlaw.com

THOMAS L. LONG, born Mansfield, Ohio, May 30, 1951; admitted to bar, 1976, Ohio and U.S. District Court, Southern District of Ohio; 1977, U.S. District Court, Northern District of Ohio; 1981, U.S. Court of Appeals, Sixth Circuit; 1986, U.S. District Court, Eastern District of Michigan. *Education:* University of Notre Dame (B.A., magna cum laude, 1973); The Ohio State University (J.D., cum laude, 1976). Phi Delta Phi. *Member:* Federal Bar Association. ***PRACTICE AREAS:*** Litigation. ***Email:*** tlong@bakerlaw.com

ELIZABETH A. McNELLIE, born Lodi, Ohio, February 2, 1964; admitted to bar, 1990, Ohio, U.S. District Court, Northern and Southern Districts of Ohio and U.S. Court of Appeals, Federal, Fourth, Sixth and Eighth Circuits. *Education:* Miami University (B.Phil., 1986); Columbia University (J.D., 1989). Articles Editor, Columbia Law Review, 1988-1989. Author: "The Use of Extrinsic Aids in the Interpretation of Popularly Enacted Legislation," 89 Columbia L. Rev. 157, Vol. 89, no. 1, 1989. *Member:* American Bar Association. ***PRACTICE AREAS:*** Litigation. ***Email:*** emcnellie@bakerlaw.com

MICHAEL E. MINISTER, born Athens, Ohio, February 14, 1944; admitted to bar, 1974, Ohio. *Education:* The Ohio State University (B.S., 1966); Capital University (J.D., 1974). Director of Administration, City of Worthington, 1970-1973. City Manager, City of Worthington, 1974. Director of Law, City of Worthington, 1975—. [LTJG, U.S. Navy, 1967-1969]. ***PRACTICE AREAS:*** Business. ***Email:*** mminister@bakerlaw.com

HENRY P. MONTGOMERY, born Redwood City, California, May 30, 1954; admitted to bar, 1979, Ohio. *Education:* Bowling Green State University (B.S., magna cum laude, 1976); The Ohio State University (J.D., 1979). Beta Gamma Sigma; Omicron Delta Kappa. *Member:* Columbus, Ohio State and American Bar Associations. ***PRACTICE AREAS:*** Business Acquisitions; Private Equity; Debt Finance; Commercial Real Estate. ***Email:*** hmontgomery@bakerlaw.com

(This Listing Continued)

GEORGEANN G. PETERS, born Cincinnati, Ohio, January 14, 1952; admitted to bar, 1983, Ohio. *Education:* Denison University (B.S., 1974); Capital University (J.D., summa cum laude, 1983). Member: Order of the Curia; Mortar Board. Recipient, National Merit Scholar. Member, Capital University Law Review, 1980-1981. ***PRACTICE AREAS:*** Employee Benefits and Compensation; Tax; ERISA. ***Email:*** gpeters@bakerlaw.com

BEN L. PFEFFERLE, III, born Columbus, Ohio, May 3, 1954; admitted to bar, 1979, Ohio; 1980, U.S. District Court, Southern District of Ohio. *Education:* Miami University (B.S.B.A., 1976); Capital University (J.D., 1979). Listed in: *Who's Who in American Law.* Author: "SEC Disclosure: The Environmental Foray Into Corporate Practice," Environmental Law Journal of Ohio, (January 1992); "Consensus Building: Key to Successful Superfund Negotiations," Bureau of National Affairs Toxics Law Reporter, 1995; "Admissibility of Governmental Reports: Unreliable Hearsay or an Exception Under Evidence Rule 803(8)(c)", Chemical Waste Regulation Reporter, 1999; "Ohio's Environmental Requirements Are Explicit When it Comes to Plant Closings," The Daily Reporter, 1997; "Petroleum Underground Storage Tanks - A Trap for the Unwary," The Daily Reporter, 1996; "Key Issues in Wetlands Regulation in Ohio," National Business Institute, 1995; "Regulation by Policy: An End to a Means," Environmental Law Journal of Ohio, 1990. Environmental Seminar, Committee Mid-Year Meeting and the Ohio State Bar Association, 1999. Lecturer: "Clear Air Update: EPA's Economic Benefit Model," American Bar Association Environmental Enforcement Conference, 1998; "Key Zoning and Environmental Issues," Ohio CLE Institute, 1997; "Continuing Evolution of Title V and the Any Credible Evidence Rule," Manufacturer's Education Council and the Ohio Cast Metals Association, 1996, 1997, 1998; "Legal Considerations in Developing Risk Management Plans Under the Clean Air Act," Ohio Chemical Council and the National Architectural Spray Coaters Association, 1996, 1997; "Preparing for an Environmental Inspection from the Government," Manufacturer's Education Council, 1995; "Superfund Private Cost Recovery," American Bar Association Environmental Litigation. Member, Ohio Chemical Council. Former Counsel for the Director of the Ohio EPA, 1980-1985. Associate General Counsel, Mead Corporation, 1988-1991. Director and Chairperson, Make A Wish Foundation of Greater Ohio and Kentucky. Environmental Law Committee, American Paper Institute, 1988-1993. Editorial Board, *Environmental Law Journal of Ohio,* 1989-1995. *Member:* Columbus (Chairman, Environmental Law Committee, 1993-1995, 1998-2000), Ohio State (Member, Environmental Law Committee; Chairman, Brownfield Litigation Subcommittee, 2001—) and American (Member, Litigation Section; Environmental Committee; Section of Natural Resources, Energy and Environmental Law) Bar Associations. Fellow, Columbus Bar Foundation. ***PRACTICE AREAS:*** Environmental Compliance; Environmental Regulation; Environmental Litigation; Complex and Multi-District Litigation; Business Litigation.

HARLAN W. ROBINS, born Columbus, Ohio, April 15, 1963; admitted to bar, 1988, Georgia; 1992, Ohio. *Education:* University of Michigan (B.A., with highest distinction, 1985); Emory University (J.D., summa cum laude, 1988). Phi Beta Kappa; Order of the Coif. Member, Emory Law Journal, 1987-1988. ***PRACTICE AREAS:*** Commercial Real Estate; Financing. ***Email:*** hrobins@bakerlaw.com

BARRY R. ROBINSON, born Dover, Ohio, December 8, 1946; admitted to bar, 1972, Ohio. *Education:* Princeton University (B.A., 1969); The Ohio State University (J.D., cum laude, 1972). *Member:* Columbus, Ohio State and American Bar Associations. Fellow, American College of Trust and Estate Counsel. ***PRACTICE AREAS:*** Trusts and Estates. ***Email:*** brobinson@bakerlaw.com

ROBERT K. RUPP, born Omaha, Nebraska, March 13, 1957; admitted to bar, 1982, Ohio, U.S. District Court, Southern District of Ohio and U.S. Tax Court. *Education:* Walsh College (B.A., Accounting and History, summa cum laude, 1979); The Ohio State University (J.D., summa cum laude, 1982). Order of the Coif. Member, Ohio State Law Journal, 1980-1982. ***PRACTICE AREAS:*** Business; Corporate; Securities; Mergers and Acquisitions. ***Email:*** rrupp@bakerlaw.com

MARK D. SENFF, born Wooster, Ohio, August 13, 1945; admitted to bar, 1971, Ohio. *Education:* The Ohio State University (B.S., 1968; J.D., summa cum laude, 1971). Order of the Coif. Member, Editorial Staff, 1969-1970 and Editor-in-Chief, 1970-1971, Ohio State Law Journal. ***PRACTICE AREAS:*** Trusts and Estates; Political Subdivisions; Health Care. ***Email:*** msenff@bakerlaw.com

WILLIAM B. SHEARER, born Santa Ana, California May 15, 1964; admitted to bar, 1994, Ohio. *Education:* Clemson University (B.A., 1986; M.A., 1989); University of North Carolina (J.D., 1994). *Member:* Ohio State and American Bar Associations. ***PRACTICE AREAS:*** Business. ***Email:*** wshearer@bakerlaw.com

AMY M. SHEPHERD, born Columbus, Ohio, February 7, 1964; admitted to bar, 1989, Ohio. *Education:* The Ohio State University (B.A., 1986; J.D., 1989). ***PRACTICE AREAS:*** Securities; Corporate; Franchising. ***Email:*** ashepherd@bakerlaw.com

RICHARD W. SIEHL, born Dayton, Ohio, September 12, 1952; admitted to bar, 1977, Ohio; 1979, Florida; 1987, West Virginia. *Education:* Miami University (B.A., magna cum laude, 1974); University of Illinois (J.D., 1977). Phi Beta Kappa; Phi Kappa Phi; Phi Delta Phi. Assistant Franklin County Prosecuting Attorney, 1977-1978. Minority Counsel, Ohio House of Representatives, 1979-1980. Deputy Director, Ohio Department of Administrative Services, 1980-1982. *Member:* Columbus Bar Association (Former Chairman, Health Law Committee); American Health Lawyers Association; The Society of Ohio Hospital Attorneys. (Board Certified Health Law Lawyer, Florida Bar Board of Legal Specialization and Education). ***PRACTICE AREAS:*** Health Law; Insurance Law. ***Email:*** rsiehl@bakerlaw.com

J. STEPHEN VAN HEYDE, born Columbus, Ohio, May 22, 1943; admitted to bar, 1968, Ohio. *Education:* University of Notre Dame (B.B.A., magna cum laude, 1965); The Ohio State University (J.D., cum laude, 1968). Beta Gamma Sigma; Beta Alpha Psi; Phi Delta Phi. Member: Board of Governors, 1989-1990, Columbus Bar Association. ***PRACTICE AREAS:*** Business; Intellectual Property; Finance; Trade Associations. ***Email:*** svanheyde@bakerlaw.com

GARY A. WADMAN, born New Castle, Indiana, May 7, 1957; admitted to bar, 1985, Ohio. *Education:* Ball State University (B.S., summa cum laude, 1978); Indiana University (J.D., cum laude, 1985). ***PRACTICE AREAS:*** Business, Computer Law. ***Email:*** gwadman@bakerlaw.com

(This Listing Continued)

BAKER & HOSTETLER LLP, Columbus—Continued

DAVID A. WHITCOMB, born San Antonio, Texas, July 14, 1966; admitted to bar, 1991, Illinois; 1992, Ohio; 1994, U.S. District Court, Western District of Michigan; 1995, U.S. District Court, Eastern District of Michigan; 1998, U.S. District Court, Southern and Northern Districts of Ohio; 1999, U.S. Court of Appeals, Sixth Circuit. *Education:* Ohio State University (B.A., cum laude, 1988); University of Michigan (J.D., 1991). Law clerk for the Honorable Gordon J. Quist, U.S. District Judge for the Western District of Michigan, 1992; law clerk for the Honorable Wendell A. Miles, U.S. District Judge for the Western District of Michigan, 1993; Trial Attorney, U.S. Equal Employment Opportunity Commission, 1994-1998. ***PRACTICE AREAS:*** Employment Law; Employment Litigation. ***Email:*** dwhitcomb@bakerlaw.com

JEFFREY T. WILLIAMS, born Columbus, Ohio, April 17, 1959; admitted to bar, 1988, Ohio and U.S. District Court, Southern District of Ohio; 2002, U.S. Court of Appeals, Sixth Circuit and U.S. District Court, Northern District of Ohio. *Education:* University of Utah (B.S. in Accounting, 1984; J.D., 1988). Staff Member, University of Utah Journal of Contemporary Law, 1986-1987. Leary Scholar. ***PRACTICE AREAS:*** Employment Litigation; Corporate Governance and Control; Probate Litigation; Commercial Contract; Construction Litigation; Products Liability; Personal Injury Defense. ***Email:*** jwilliams@bakerlaw.com

BARRY H. WOLINETZ, born Cleveland, Ohio, October 27, 1944; admitted to bar, 1971, Ohio. *Education:* The Ohio State University (B.A., 1967; J.D., 1971). Tau Epsilon Phi; Tau Epsilon Rho; Pi Sigma Alpha. Lecturer, Capital University Law School, 1990-1995. Member, Panel of Arbitrators, American Arbitration Association. *Member:* Columbus, Ohio State and American Bar Associations; National College of Advocacy (Advocate); Franklin County Trial Lawyers Association; Ohio Academy of Trial Lawyers; The Association of Trial Lawyers of America; National Association of Securities Dealers, Inc. (Member, Board of Arbitrators, 1990—). ***PRACTICE AREAS:*** Commercial Litigation; Civil Litigation; Family Law. ***Email:*** bwolinetz@bakerlaw.com

ASSOCIATES

ERIC R. BARNETT, admitted to bar, 1999, California; 2004, Ohio. *Education:* Northwestern University (B.S., 1994); Stanford University (M.S., 1995; J.D., 1999). ***PRACTICE AREAS:*** Corporate Law; Securities; Transactions. ***Email:*** ebarnett@bakerlaw.com

KIRSTEN L. BARTHOLOMEW, born Washington, D.C.; admitted to bar, 2004, Ohio; 2005, U.S. District Court, Southern District of Ohio. *Education:* The Ohio State University (B.A., 1999); Capital University (J.D., summa cum laude, 2004). *Member:* Columbus and Ohio State Bar Associations. ***PRACTICE AREAS:*** General Practice; Business; Litigation. ***Email:*** kbartholomew@bakerlaw.com

LETITIA S. BRYANT, admitted to bar, 2004, Ohio; 2005, U.S. District Court, Southern District of Ohio. *Education:* Miami University (B.A., cum laude, 2001); The Ohio State University, Moritz College of Law (J.D., 2004). Alpha Kappa Alpha. *Member:* Columbus, Ohio State and American Bar Associations; John Mercer Langston Bar Association. ***PRACTICE AREAS:*** General Practice. ***Email:*** lbryant@bakerlaw.com

RODGER L. ECKELBERRY, born Zanesville, Ohio, February 23, 1969; admitted to bar, 1999, Ohio. *Education:* State University of New York at Albany (B.S., 1995); University of Cincinnati College of Law (J.D., 1999). Co-Author, "Initial Interview of the Commercial Plaintiff, Litigation Basics 99," published by Ohio State Bar Association CLE Course Book. [STG 2 (SW), U.S. Navy, 1986-1995]. ***PRACTICE AREAS:*** Civil Litigation; General Practice. ***Email:*** reckelberry@bakerlaw.com

TARA M. FERRELL, admitted to bar, 2003, Ohio; 2004, U.S. District Court, Southern District of Ohio. *Education:* Ohio University (B.S., Journalism, summa cum laude, 1996); The Ohio State University Moritz College of Law (J.D., with honors, 2003). Order of the Coif. *Member:* Columbus, Ohio State (Member, Labor and Employment Section) and American Bar Associations. ***PRACTICE AREAS:*** Labor and Employment. ***Email:*** tferrell@bakerlaw.com

SEAN P. FLYNN, admitted to bar, 2001, Ohio; 2002, U.S. District Court, Northern and Southern Districts of Ohio. *Education:* The College of Wooster (B.A., 1995); University of South Carolina (M.E.R.M., 1998); The Ohio State University College of Law (J.D., with honors, 2001). Order of the Coif. ***PRACTICE AREAS:*** Environmental Law; Commercial Litigation. ***Email:*** sflynn@bakerlaw.com

JOHN J. FROST, admitted to bar, 2003, Ohio; 2004, U.S. District Court, Southern District of Ohio. *Education:* Western Michigan Univeristy (B.A., Political Science, summa cum laude, 2000) Phi Beta Kappa; University of Michigan Law School (J.D., 2002). *Member:* Columbus, Ohio State and American Bar Associations. [U.S. Navy, 1993-1998]. ***PRACTICE AREAS:*** Litigation. ***Email:*** jfrost@bakerlaw.com

MATTHEW W. HOYT, born Flint, Michigan, January 9, 1974; admitted to bar, 2000, Ohio; 2002, U.S. District Court, Northern and Southern Districts of Ohio; 2004, U.S. Courts of Appeals, Sixth Circuit. *Education:* Michigan State University (B.A., 1996); University of Notre Dame (J.D., 2000). Member, Golden Key National Honor Society. *Member:* Columbus, Ohio State and American Bar Associations; American Immigration Lawyers Association. ***PRACTICE AREAS:*** Employment Law; Immigration Law. ***Email:*** mhoyt@bakerlaw.com

JANINE HANCOCK JONES, born Albany, New York; admitted to bar, 2001, Ohio; 2002, U.S. District Court, Southern District of Ohio. *Education:* Spelman College (B.A., with honors, 1997); Howard University School of Law (J.D., cum laude, 2000). *Member:* Columbus (Co-Chair, Martin Luther King Jr. Committee) and Ohio State Bar Associations; John Mercer Langston Bar Association (Secretary). ***PRACTICE AREAS:*** Labor and Employment; Employment Litigation. ***Email:*** jjones@bakerlaw.com

RICHARD EUGENE KOZLOWSKI, born Port Chester, New York, December 14, 1967; admitted to bar, 1998, Ohio. *Education:* Beijing Capital Teachers University (1988); Providence College (B.A., 1989); Taiwan Normal University, Mandarin Training Center (1990); University of Hawaii at Manoa (M.A., 1993); Vanderbilt University (J.D., 1998). ***LANGUAGES:*** Mandarin Chinese, Polish. ***PRACTICE AREAS:*** Business. ***Email:*** rkozlowski@bakerlaw.com

(This Listing Continued)

MARCELLA L. LAPE, admitted to bar, 2004, Ohio; 2005, U.S. District Court, Southern District of Ohio. *Education:* Ohio Northern University (B.S., International Business and Economics, with high distinction, 2001; B.A., Spanish, with high distinction, 2001); Ohio State University (J.D., with honors, 2004). Order of the Coif. ***PRACTICE AREAS:*** General Practice. ***Email:*** mlape@bakerlaw.com

SUSAN NOLAN LUBOW, born Nashville, Tennessee, January 9, 1968; admitted to bar, 1995, Ohio. *Education:* Oberlin College (B.A./B.M., 1990); Harvard Law School (J.D., 1995). *Member:* Columbus, Ohio State and American Bar Associations. ***PRACTICE AREAS:*** Employee Benefits; Compensation. ***Email:*** slubow@bakerlaw.com

FRANK C. MILLER, born Columbus, Ohio, February 15, 1974; admitted to bar, 1999, Ohio; 2000, U.S. District Court, Southern District of Ohio. *Education:* Miami University (B.A., cum laude, 1996); Case Western Reserve University (J.D., 1999). *Member:* Columbus, Ohio State and American Bar Associations. ***LANGUAGES:*** French. ***PRACTICE AREAS:*** Health Law; Medicare and Medicaid; Privacy; Insurance; Local Taxation. ***Email:*** fmiller@bakerlaw.com

DEBORAH A. PICKREL, admitted to bar, 2004, Ohio; 2005, U.S. District Court, Southern District of Ohio. *Education:* Villanova University (B.A., magna cum laude, 1997) Phi Beta Kappa; The Ohio State University Moritz College of Law (J.D., with honors, 2004). *Member:* American, Ohio State and Columbus Bar Associations. ***PRACTICE AREAS:*** General Practice. ***Email:*** dpickrel@bakerlaw.com

WILLIAM R. POST, born Columbus, Ohio; admitted to bar, 2000, Ohio; 2002, U.S. District Court, Southern District of Ohio; 2004, U.S. District Court, Northern District of Ohio. *Education:* Miami University (A.B., cum laude, 1997); Case Western University (J.D., cum laude, 2000). Alpha Lambda Delta. *Member:* Columbus, Ohio State and American Bar Associations. ***PRACTICE AREAS:*** Employment Discrimination; Labor Arbitration. ***Email:*** wpost@bakerlaw.com

SOMMER L. SHEELY, born Youngstown, Ohio, June 13, 1977; admitted to bar, 2002, Pennsylvania; 2003, Ohio and U.S. District Court, Western District of Pennsylvania; 2005, U.S. District Court, Southern District of Ohio. *Education:* Ohio Wesleyan University (B.A., magna cum laude, 1999); The Ohio State University, Michael E. Moritz College of Law (J.D., with honors, 2002). *Member:* Columbus, Ohio State, Pennsylvania and American (Member, Civil Litigation Section) Bar Associations; American Inns of Court. ***PRACTICE AREAS:*** Litigation; Employment Litigation. ***Email:*** ssheely@bakerlaw.com

LISA R. STARK, admitted to bar, 2002, Ohio; 2003, U.S. District Court, Northern and Southern Districts of Ohio. *Education:* Oklahoma Baptist University (B.A., magna cum laude, 1998); The Ohio State University (J.D., with honors, 2002). Order of the Coif. *Member:* Columbus, Ohio State and American Bar Associations. ***PRACTICE AREAS:*** Employment Law.

STACY E. WILHITE, admitted to bar, 1998, Ohio; 2004, Missouri. *Education:* Miami University (B.S., Accountancy and Business Economics, cum laude, 1995); University of Dayton School of Law (J.D., cum laude, 1998). *Member:* The Missouri Bar; American Bar Association. ***PRACTICE AREAS:*** Employee Benefits. ***Email:*** swilhite@bakerlaw.com

LEIGH ANN WILSON, born Youngstown, Ohio, September 2, 1959; admitted to bar, 1999, Ohio. *Education:* Mount Union College (B.A., magna cum laude, 1981); Capital University (J.D., cum laude, 1999); John Marshall Law School (LL.M., with honors, 2000). Pi Gamma Mu; Blue Key. Member, Order of the Curia. *Member:* Columbus (Member, Employee Benefits Committee), Ohio State and American Bar Associations; International Society of Certified Employee Benefits Specialists. ***PRACTICE AREAS:*** Employee Benefits. ***Email:*** lwilson@bakerlaw.com

JULIE M. WOOLLEY, born Parkersburg, West Virginia, December 28, 1977; admitted to bar, 2003, Ohio; 2004, U.S. District Court, Southern District of Ohio. *Education:* Washington & Jefferson College (B.A., Political Science and History, cum laude, 2000); The Ohio State University (J.D., Certificate in Dispute Resolution, 2003). *Member:* Columbus, Ohio State and American Bar Associations; Electric Cooperative Bar Association. ***PRACTICE AREAS:*** General Business; Transactions; Municipal Law; Cooperative Law. ***Email:*** jwoolley@bakerlaw.com

ROSANNE T. YANG, born Columbus, Ohio; admitted to bar, 1999, Ohio; 2000, U.S. District Court, Northern and Southern Districts of Ohio. *Education:* The Ohio State University (B.A., 1996; J.D., 1999). Phi Beta Kappa. Author: Ohio State Journal on Dispute Resolution, Vol. 14, Issue 1. *Member:* American (Member, Intellectual Property Section), Ohio State (Member, Intellectual Property Section)and Columbus (Member, Intellectual Property Section) Bar Associations; International Trademark Association. ***PRACTICE AREAS:*** Intellectual Property; Cyberlaw. ***Email:*** ryang@bakerlaw.com

STAFF ATTORNEYS

DAVID R. FUNK, born New Albany, Ohio, March 11, 1974; admitted to bar, 1998, Ohio, U.S. District Court, Southern and Northern Districts of Ohio and Eastern District of Michigan and U.S. Court of Appeals, Sixth Circuit. *Education:* Otterbein College (B.A., 1995); Capital University Law School (J.D., cum laude, 1998). Order of the Curia. *Member:* Columbus, Ohio State and American Bar Associations; Franklin County Trial Lawyers Association. ***REPORTED CASES:*** State ex rel. The Ryant Committee v. Lorain County Board of Elections, 86 Ohio St. 3d 107 (1999). ***PRACTICE AREAS:*** Consumer Litigation. ***Email:*** dfunk@bakerlaw.com

M. ELIZABETH GILL, born Honolulu, Hawaii, October 22, 1962; admitted to bar, 1988, Ohio. *Education:* Ohio Dominican University; University of Cincinnati (B.A., with honors, 1984); Ohio State University (J.D., 1987). Phi Alpha Delta. *Member:* Columbus and Ohio State Bar Associations; Ohio Academy of Trial Lawyers; Franklin County Trial Lawyers Association. ***PRACTICE AREAS:*** Family Law. ***Email:*** egill@bakerlaw.com

MARY ARENS HALE, born Canton, Ohio, November 19, 1971; admitted to bar, 1996, Ohio; 2000, U.S. District Court, Southern District of Ohio. *Education:* University of Notre Dame (B.A., 1993); The Ohio State University (J.D., 1996). *Member:* Columbus, Ohio State and American Bar Associations. ***PRACTICE AREAS:*** Consumer Litigation. ***Email:*** mhale@bakerlaw.com

KAREN E. SHEFFER, born Winchester, Indiana, May 4, 1953; admitted to bar, 1979, Ohio; 1983, U.S. District Court, Northern District of Ohio; 1984, U.S. Supreme Court;

(This Listing Continued)

1998, U.S. District Court, Southern District of Ohio. *Education:* Ohio Northern University (B.A., 1975); University of Cincinnati (J.D., 1979). Phi Alpha Theta; Phi Kappa Phi. Assistant County Prosecutor, Crawford County, Ohio, 1979-1983. Prosecutor, Worthington, Ohio, 1986—. **PRACTICE AREAS:** Litigation; Workers Compensation. **Email:** ksheffer@bakerlaw.com

All Partners, Of Counsel and Associates are Members of the Columbus, Ohio State and American Bar Associations.

BALL & TANOURY

700 ACKERMAN ROAD, SUITE 450
COLUMBUS, OHIO 43202
Telephone: 614-447-8550
Fax: 614-447-1673

Civil Trial and Appellate Practice, Construction Contract Law, Business and Commercial Litigation, Liquor, State Boards and Agencies, Business Organizations and Planning, Real Estate Law, ERISA, Zoning and Land Development, Probate.

MEMBERS OF FIRM

STEVEN L. BALL, born Dayton, Ohio, September 24, 1946; admitted to bar, 1974, Ohio; 1975, U.S. District Court, Southern District of Ohio; 1997, U.S. District Court, Northern District of Ohio; 2001, U.S. Court of Appeals, 6th Circuit. *Education:* Ohio State University (B.Sc.Ed., 1968); University of Toledo (J.D., 1973). Note and Comment Editor, University of Toledo Law Review, 1972-1973. Member, Ohio Waterway Safety Council, 1987—. Assistant Attorney General, Ohio, 1974-1977; Chief Court of Claims Section, 1976-1977. Special Counsel to the Ohio Attorney General, 1977-1995. Neutral, State Employee Relations Board, 1997—. *Member:* Columbus and Ohio State Bar Associations; Franklin County Trial Lawyers Association (President, 1986-1987). **REPORTED CASES:** Tony Zumbo and Son Construction Co. vs. Ohio Department of Transportation 22 Ohio app. 3d 141; John P. Novatny Electric Co. vs. State, 46 O.app. 2d 255; Harris vs. University of Akron, 46 O. Misc. 29, 7500 2d 126. **PRACTICE AREAS:** General Civil Litigation; State Boards and Agencies; Business and Commercial Law; ERISA; Probate. **Email:** sball@gabrielmail.com

JOHN L. TANOURY, born Zanesville, Ohio, December 10, 1951; admitted to bar, 1977, Ohio and U.S. District Court, Southern District of Ohio. *Education:* The Ohio State University (B.S.Ed., 1974); Capital University (J.D., 1977). Recipient, Administrative Law Scholar Award. Assistant Attorney General, 1977-1983. Administrative Law Judge, State of Ohio, 1984-1996. *Member:* Columbus and Ohio State Bar Associations. **PRACTICE AREAS:** Construction Contract Law (Private and Public); Administrative Law; Liquor Law; Business Litigation; Health Care; ERISA; Zoning Law; Land Use. **Email:** jtanoury@gabrielmail.com

REPRESENTATIVE CLIENTS: Midwestern Medical Company; Hoster Brewing Co.; Polis and Simon Realty Co.; P.D.K. Construction Co.; Chesrown Oldsmobile-GMC, Inc.; Dave Gill Pontiac-GMC Truck, Inc.; Coughlin Automotive Group; Barrett Mortgage Co.; Ohio Laborer's Fringe Benefits Funds; Crossmann Communities of Ohio; Deluxe Homes; Ohio Laborers' Training Fund; Ohio Laborers' District Council - Ohio Contractors Association Education and Cooperation Fund.
REFERENCES: US Bank; Huntington National Bank.

BARAN, PIPER, TARKOWSKY, FITZGERALD & THEIS CO., L.P.A.

6877 NORTH HIGH STREET, SUITE 105
COLUMBUS, OHIO 43085
Telephone: 614-436-0539
Fax: 614-436-1713
URL: http://www.baranlaw.com

General Civil Practice. Trials in all Courts. Insurance Defense, Corporate, Family Law, Estate Planning, Personal Injury, Products Liability and Construction Law. Commercial Litigation. Suretyship. Environmental and Governmental Liability. Professional Liability, Worker's Compensation.

(For Complete list of all Personnel and Biographical data, see Professional Biographies at Mansfield, Ohio)

ROBERTA J. BARBANEL

1799 W. 5TH AVENUE, SUITE 143
COLUMBUS, OHIO 43212
Telephone: 614-221-5824
Fax: 614-621-9109

Commercial Real Estate, Commercial Leasing, Corporate Law, LLC, Contracts, Business Litigation, Contract Disputes, Real Estate, Buying and Selling a House, Residential Real Estate Closings.

ROBERTA J. BARBANEL, born Salem, Massachusetts, February 13, 1958; admitted to bar, 1985, Connecticut; 1988, Kentucky; 2002, Ohio. *Education:* Brandeis University; University of Louisville (B.A., 1980); Yale Law School; University of Louisville, School of Law (J.D., 1985). *Member:* Cincinnati, Kentucky and Ohio State Bar Associations. **PRACTICE AREAS:** Commercial Real Estate; Commercial Leasing; Corporate Law.

BARREN & MERRY CO., L.P.A.

COLUMBUS, OHIO

(See Westerville)

Creditors Rights, Workouts, Bankruptcy Law, Banking and Finance, Commercial Law, Breach of Contracts, Business Litigation.

KAREN H. BAUERNSCHMIDT CO., LPA

COLUMBUS, OHIO

(See Cleveland)

Real Estate Tax, Litigation, Appellate Practices and Procedure.

BEERY & SPURLOCK CO., L.P.A.

Established in 1972
275 EAST STATE STREET
COLUMBUS, OHIO 43215
Telephone: 614-228-8575
FAX: 614-228-1408
Email: law@beeryspurlock.com
URL: http://www.beeryspurlock.com

Transportation Law, Administrative Law, Litigation, Business Law, Corporate Law, Antitrust and Trade Regulation, Labor and Employment, Taxation, Workers Compensation, Environmental Law, Business Litigation.

PAUL F. BEERY (1931-2002)

MICHAEL SPURLOCK, born Dayton, Ohio, October 17, 1949; admitted to bar, 1974, Ohio, U.S. District Court, Southern and Northern Districts of Ohio and U.S. Court of Appeals, 3rd, 6th, 7th and 9th Circuits. *Education:* The Ohio State University (B.S., 1971; J.D., cum laude, 1974). Phi Delta Phi; Beta Gamma Sigma; Beta Alpha Psi (President, 1970-1971). Recipient, Outstanding Senior in Accounting Scholarship, Awarded by Marathon Oil Company, 1971. Member, Moot Court Team, The Ohio State University College of Law, 1973. *Member:* The Columbus and Ohio State Bar Associations; Association for Transportation Law, Logistics and Policy (Former President, Columbus Chapter, 1987-1988); Transportation Lawyers Association (Member, Executive Committee, 1999-2001); Conference of Freight Counsel. **REPORTED CASES:** In re Lower Lake Erie Iron Ore Antitrust Litigation (MDL 587) 998 F.2d 1144 (3rd. Cir. 1993). **PRACTICE AREAS:** Transportation Law; Litigation; Corporate Law; Antitrust and Trade Regulation; Labor and Employment Law; Business Law; Taxation; Workers Compensation; Environmental Law; Administrative Law; Public Utility Law. **Email:** mspurlock@beeryspurlock.com

ERIC W. BEERY, born Columbus, Ohio, September 25, 1963; admitted to bar, 1996, Ohio, U.S. District Court, Southern District of Ohio and U.S. Court of Appeals, 7th and 9th Circuits. *Education:* Valparaiso University (B.S., 1987); Thomas M. Cooley Law School (J.D., 1995). *Member:* Columbus Bar Association; Columbus Transportation Club; Transportation Lawyers Association; Conference of Freight Counsel. **REPORTED CASES:** The Baldewein Company v. Tri-Clover, Inc., 606 N.W.2d 124 (Wisconsin Supreme Court 1999). **PRACTICE AREAS:** Transportation Law; Litigation; Corporate Law; Antitrust and Trade Regulation; Labor and Employment Law; Administrative Law; Taxation; Public Utility Law. **Email:** ebeery@beeryspurlock.com

REPRESENTATIVE CLIENTS: APX Central, Inc.; The Branson Corporation, d/b/a Brewster Travel; Bulk Transit Corp.; DAP Inc.; Dart Trucking Co., Inc.; Dunbar Armored, Inc.; Falcon Transport Co.; Golden Hawk Transportation, Inc.; Kennedy Freight Lines, Inc.; Kuhnle Brothers, Inc.; Matesich Distributing Co.; Priority Dispatch, Inc.; RPM, Inc.; SPX Corporation; Steubenville Transfer Co.; Top Line Express, Inc.
OHIO COUNSEL FOR: ABF Freight Systems, Inc.; Greyhound Lines, Inc.; Superior Carriers, Inc.; Triad Transport, Inc.; U.S. Xpress Enterprises, Inc.; Werner Enterprises, Inc.
REFERENCE: Bank One of Columbus, N.A.

BELL, ROYER & SANDERS CO., L.P.A.

Established in 1968
33 SOUTH GRANT AVENUE
COLUMBUS, OHIO 43215-3900
Telephone: 614-228-0704
FAX: 614-228-0201

General Civil Trial and Appellate Practice. Utilities, Taxation, Telecommunications, Municipal, Corporation, Motor Carrier, Environmental, Labor and Administrative Law.

LANGDON D. BELL, born Cleveland, Ohio, May 17, 1939; admitted to bar, 1963, Ohio. *Education:* Miami University (B.A., 1960); The Ohio State University (J.D., 1963). Phi Delta Phi. Administrative Law Judge, 1963-1966 and Chief Counsel, 1966-1969, Public Utilities Commission of Ohio. Assistant Attorney General, 1966-1969. Member, Panel of Arbitrators, American Arbitration Association. *Member:* Ohio State Bar Association; Federal Mediation and Conciliation Service; Ohio Motor Carrier Lawyers Association. **PRACTICE AREAS:** Energy; Telecommunications; Labor; Legislative Law. **Email:** lbell33@aol.com

BARTH E. ROYER, born Mechanicsburg, Ohio, July 5, 1947; admitted to bar, 1972, Ohio. *Education:* Harvard University (A.B., 1969); University of Michigan (J.D., 1972). Assistant Attorney General, 1972-1973; Chief Attorney Examiner, 1973-1978 and Deputy Legal Director, 1986-1989, Public Utilities Commission of Ohio. *Member:* Ohio State Bar Association. **PRACTICE AREAS:** Utility Law; Energy; Telecommunications Law. **Email:** barthroyer@aol.com

JUDITH B. SANDERS, born Chicago, Illinois, February 15, 1952; admitted to bar, 1977, Ohio. *Education:* Wittenberg University (B.A., cum laude, 1974); The Ohio State University (J.D., 1977). Assistant Attorney General, State of Ohio and Counsel, Public Utilities Commission of Ohio, 1977-1981. *Member:* Columbus and Ohio State Bar Associations. **PRACTICE AREAS:** Utility; Telecommunications; Motor Carrier. **Email:** jsand21552@aol.com

REPRESENTATIVE CLIENTS: ALC Communications Corp. (Allnet); United Communications, Inc.; Davis Trucking Co.; Ohio Motor Bus Assn.; Ohio State Taxicab Owners Association. PPG Industries, Inc.; Pattersonville Telephone Co.; Vanlue Telephone Co.
REFERENCE: The Huntington National Bank.

JOHN T. BELTON

Established in 1977

2066 W. HENDERSON ROAD, SUITE 102
COLUMBUS, OHIO 43220
Telephone: 614-457-2034
Fax: 614-457-0311
Email: Beltonlaw@aol.com

Civil Practice, Trial Practice, Criminal Law, Federal Criminal Law, Criminal Defense, Personal Injury, Driving While Intoxicated, Domestic Relations, Real Estate, Construction Litigation.

JOHN T. BELTON, born Yonkers, New York, February 24, 1947; admitted to bar, 1977, Ohio and U.S. District Court, Southern District of Ohio; 1985, U.S. Claims Court; 1987, U.S. Court of Appeals, Federal Circuit; 1997, U.S. Supreme Court. *Education:* The Ohio State University (B.A., 1972); Xavier University (M.B.A., 1973); Ohio Northern University (J.D., 1976). Phi Alpha Delta. Omicron Delta Kappa. Order of Barristers. Member, National Moot Court Team. Listed Who's Who in American Law, 1987—. Appointed Special Counsel to Attorney General, State of Ohio, 2003—. *Member:* Columbus, Ohio State (Member, Criminal Law Section) and American (Member, Litigation Section) Bar Associations; Ohio Academy of Trial Lawyers; The Association of Trial Lawyers of America; The Ohio Association of Criminal Defense Lawyers; U.S. Claims Court Bar Association. [E-5, USAF, 1968-1971]. ***LANGUAGES:*** Italian.

BENESCH, FRIEDLANDER, COPLAN & ARONOFF LLP

Established in 1938

88 EAST BROAD STREET
SUITE 900
COLUMBUS, OHIO 43215-3506
Telephone: 614-223-9300
Facsimile: 614-223-9330
URL: http://www.bfca.com

Cleveland, Ohio Office: 2300 BP Tower, 200 Public Square, 44114-2378. Telephone: 216-363-4500. Facsimile: 216-363-4588.

Bankruptcy, Bankruptcy Reorganization, Banks and Banking, Business Law, Casino and Gambling, Class Actions, Collections, Commercial Law, Commercial Real Estate, Complex and Multi-District Litigation, Construction Law, Consumer Law, Contracts, Copyrights, Corporate Law, Debtor and Creditor, Election Campaign and Political Law, Electronic Commerce, Employee Benefits, Environmental Law, Finance, Health Care, Immigration Law, Intellectual Property, Internet and Technology, Labor and Employment, Leases and Leasing, Mergers, Acquisitions, Divestitures, Mortgages, Patent, Probate, Product Liability, Real Estate, Resort and Leisure, Securities, Taxation, Trademarks, Transportation, Trusts and Estates, Wills, Workers Compensation, Zoning, Planning and Land Use.

LAW FIRM ALLIANCES/ASSOCIATIONS: ***TERRALEX, THE WORLDWIDE NETWORK OF INDEPENDENT LAW FIRMS***

MEMBERS OF FIRM

MARC S. BLUBAUGH, born Cleveland, Ohio, 1971; admitted to bar, 1997, Ohio. *Education:* Case Western Reserve University (B.A., magna cum laude, 1994); The Ohio State University (J.D., with honors, 1997). Order of the Coif; Phi Beta Kappa. Associate Editor, The Ohio State University Law Journal. ***PRACTICE AREAS:*** Transportation; Long Term Care; Commercial Law. ***Email:*** mblubaugh@bfca.com

FRANK W. CARSONIE, born Youngstown, Ohio, 1965; admitted to bar, 1992, Ohio. *Education:* Wittenberg University (B.A., 1987); Capital University (J.D., magna cum laude, 1992). *Member:* Columbus, Ohio State and American Bar Associations; American Health Lawyers Association; Society of Ohio Hospital Attorneys. ***PRACTICE AREAS:*** Health Care; Health Care Fraud; Managed Care Contracts; Business Law; Corporate Law; Securities. ***Email:*** fcarsonie@bfca.com

ORLA ELLIS COLLIER, III, born Detroit, Michigan, 1949; admitted to bar, 1975, Ohio; 1975, U.S. District Court, Southern District of Ohio; 1992, U.S. Supreme Court and U.S. Court of Appeals, Sixth Circuit. *Education:* The Ohio State University (B.A., 1971); Ohio Northern University (J.D., 1975). Phi Kappa Phi; Willis Society. Recipient, American Jurisprudence Awards in Contracts, Procedure, Constitutional Law and Sales. Issue Editor, Ohio Northern University Law Review, 1974-1975. Assistant Legal Director, Office of the Consumers' Counsel, State of Ohio, 1977-1981. Hearing Examiner, Public Utilities Commission, State of Ohio, 1975-1977. *Member:* Ohio Academy of Trial Lawyers (Special Counsel to Ohio Attorney General). ***PRACTICE AREAS:*** Public Utility Law; Environmental Law; Insurance Regulation; Class Actions; Business Torts; Unfair Competition; Health Care Law; Administrative Law. ***Email:*** ocollier@bfca.com

JANET K. FELDKAMP, born Jefferson City, Missouri, 1956; admitted to bar, 1990, Ohio. *Education:* University of Missouri (B.S. N., magna cum laude, 1978); St. Louis University (J.D., cum laude, 1990). Registered Nurse, Missouri, 1978-1992; Ohio, 1989—. Licensed Nursing Home Administrator, Missouri, 1982—. Co-Author: "The Law of Medical Practice In Ohio," Lawyers Cooperative Publishing, 1996; "The Long Term Care Handbook: Regulatory, Operational and Financial Guideposts" (second edition), American Health Lawyers Association, 2000. ***PRACTICE AREAS:*** Health Care; Health Care Fraud; Long Term Care; Nursing Home Regulation; Nursing Law. ***Email:*** jfeldkamp@bfca.com

N. VICTOR GOODMAN, born Columbus, Ohio, 1936; admitted to bar, 1961, Ohio; 1964, U.S. Supreme Court. *Education:* Yale University (B.A., magna cum laude, 1957); Harvard University (J.D., 1961). Pi Sigma Alpha. Associate Editor, "The Developing Labor Law," The Bureau of National Affairs, 1973-1978. Appointed as Member, Federal Service Impasses Panel, 1982-1987; reappointed, 1987, 1992. Member, Committee on Development of the Law under the National Labor Relations Act, 1969—. Member, Board of Regents, State of Ohio, 1976-1990. Member and Chairman, Rickenbacker Port Authority, 1985—. Trustee, Ohio University, 1995—. ***PRACTICE AREAS:*** Administrative Law; Labor Law; Legislative Practice. ***Email:*** vgoodman@bfca.com

(This Listing Continued)

C. DAVID PARAGAS, born Cleveland, Ohio, 1961; admitted to bar, 1990, Ohio; 1991, Illinois. *Education:* Ohio Wesleyan University (B.A., 1983); University of Madrid, Torreon De Soto; Capital University (J.D., 1989). ***PRACTICE AREAS:*** Immigration Law; Legislative Practice; International Law; Health Care; Insurance. ***Email:*** dparagas@bfca.com

ROGER L. SCHANTZ, born Lima, Ohio, 1966; admitted to bar, 1991, Ohio. *Education:* Ohio Northern University (B.S.B.A., with high distinction, 1988); The Ohio State University (J.D., with honors, 1991). Member, The Ohio State Law Journal, 1990-1991. ***Email:*** rschantz@bfca.com

JOHN F. STOCK, born Columbus, Ohio, 1956; admitted to bar, 1981, Ohio. *Education:* The Ohio State University (B.A., 1978; J.D., with honors, 1981). ***PRACTICE AREAS:*** Litigation; Employment Law; Intellectual Property. ***Email:*** jstock@bfca.com

MARK D. TUCKER, born Logan, Ohio, 1960; admitted to bar, 1986, Ohio. *Education:* The Ohio State University (B.A., cum laude with honors, 1983; J.D., with honors, 1986). Phi Beta Kappa; Phi Kappa Phi. Clerk to Hon. Robert B. Krupansky, U.S. Court of Appeals, Sixth Circuit, 1986-1988. ***PRACTICE AREAS:*** Civil Appeals; Election, Campaign and Political Law; Voting Rights; Prevailing Wage Litigation. ***Email:*** mtucker@bfca.com

THOMAS C. WASHBUSH, born Neenah, Wisconsin, 1957; admitted to bar, 1991, Ohio; 1995, District of Columbia. *Education:* Capital University (B.A., 1986; J.D., 1989). ***PRACTICE AREAS:*** Banks and Banking; Business Law; Commercial Law; Corporate Law; Finance; Public Finance; Mergers, Acquisitions and Divestitures. ***Email:*** twashbush@bfca.com

ASSOCIATES

LYLE B. BROWN, born Columbus, Ohio, 1970; admitted to bar, 1998, Ohio; 1999, U.S. District Court, Southern District of Ohio. *Education:* Haverford College (B.A., with honors, 1993); The Ohio State University (J.D., with honors, 1998). Phi Beta Kappa. Managing Editor, The Ohio State Law Journal, 1997-1998. ***Email:*** lbrown@bfca.com

J. ALLEN JONES, III, born 1973; admitted to bar, 2000, Ohio. *Education:* Wheaton College (B.A., 1996); Capital University (J.D., magna cum laude, 2000). Member, Capital University Law Review. ***Email:*** ajones@bfca.com

DONALD M. KELLER, born Sandusky, Ohio, 1974; admitted to bar, 2004, Ohio. *Education:* The Ohio State University (B.S., 1996); Capital University (J.D., summa cum laude, 2004). ***Email:*** dkeller@bfca.com

BENJAMEN E. KERN, admitted to bar, 2003, Ohio. *Education:* Denison University (B.S., with honors, 1996); The Ohio State University (M.S., 1999); Capital University Law School (J.D., summa cum laude, 2003). ***Email:*** bkern@bfca.com

JENNIFER M. TURK, born Chicago, Illinois, 1971; admitted to bar, 2001, Ohio. *Education:* Marquette University (B.A., 1992); The Ohio State University (J.D., 2001). Member, The Ohio State Law Journal. ***Email:*** jturk@bfca.com

GARY G. YASHKO, admitted to bar, 1997, Ohio; 1998, U.S. District Court, Southern District of Ohio; 1999, U.S. Court of Appeals, Sixth Circuit. *Education:* The Ohio State University (B.A., 1992; J.D., 1997). ***Email:*** gyashko@bfca.com

OF COUNSEL

JAMES F. DELEONE, born Akron, Ohio, 1926; admitted to bar, 1951, Ohio. *Education:* The Ohio State University (B.S.B.A., 1949; J.D., 1951). Author: "The New Ohio Workmen's Compensation Act," 16 Ohio State Law Journal, No. 4. Assistant Attorney General of Ohio, 1951-1954; 1957-1959. Acting Chief Counsel, Attorney General of Ohio, 1957. Counsel, Public Utilities Commission of Ohio, 1957-1959. Life Member, Sixth Circuit Judicial Conference, 1978—. Chairman, Board of Bar Examiners, 1991-1992; Member, Board of Bar Examiners, 1981-1984; 1987—. ***PRACTICE AREAS:*** Alcoholic Beverages; Litigation; Sports Law; Labor and Employment. ***Email:*** jdeleone@bfca.com

RONALD L. HOUSE, born Alliance, Ohio, 1958; admitted to bar, 1986, Ohio. *Education:* Miami University (B.S., 1980); The Ohio State University (J.D., with honors, 1986). ***Email:*** rhouse@bfca.com

FRANK J. REED, JR., born Columbus, Ohio, 1965; admitted to bar, 1991, Ohio; 1992, U.S. District Court, Southern District of Ohio; 1998, U.S. District Court, Northern District of Ohio and U.S. Court of Appeals, 6th Circuit; 2000, U.S. Court of Appeals, District of Columbia Circuit; 2001, U.S. Supreme Court. *Education:* The Ohio State University (B.A., with honors, 1988); Capital University (J.D., 1991). *Member:* Columbus (Member: Environmental Law Committee; Board of Governors, 2000—) and Ohio State (Member, Environmental Law Committee) Bar Associations. ***PRACTICE AREAS:*** Public Law; Environmental Law. ***Email:*** freed@bfca.com

MARTHA J. SWETERLITSCH, born Canton, Ohio, 1945; admitted to bar, 1983, Ohio. *Education:* Northwestern University; The Ohio State University (B.A., 1967; J.D., 1983). Legal Committee, American Association of Homes, Housing and Services for Aging, 1990-2001. *Member:* Ohio State Bar Association (Chair, 1990-2001, Elder Law Committee). ***PRACTICE AREAS:*** Certificates of Need; Long Term Care; Tax Exempt Organizations. ***Email:*** msweterlitsch@bfca.com

(For complete biographical data on other personnel, see Professional Biographies at Cleveland, Ohio)

MICHAEL E. BENSON

109 TOWN STREET
COLUMBUS, OHIO 43230
Telephone: 614-418-4740
Fax: 614-418-5045
Email: mb007@columbus.rr.com
URL: http://www.michaelbensonlaw.com

Bankruptcy Law, Foreclosures, Debtor and Creditor, Real Estate, Landlord and Tenant, Buying and Selling, Wills, Living Wills, Healthcare, Powers of Attorney.

MICHAEL E. BENSON, born Akron, Ohio, 1969; admitted to bar, 1997, Ohio; 1998, U.S. District Court, Southern District of Ohio; 2004, U.S. District Court, Northern District of Ohio. *Education:* University of Akron (B.A., 1991); Capital University (J.D., 1997). Volunteer Attorney, Ohio Legal Assistance Foundation. *Member:* Columbus Bar Association. ***LANGUAGES:*** Spanish and Russian. ***PRACTICE AREAS:*** Bankruptcy Law; Real Estate; Wills; Probate; Living Wills.

BLAUGRUND, HERBERT & MARTIN

INCORPORATED

COLUMBUS, OHIO

(See Dublin)

Administrative Law, Bankruptcy, Civil Rights Litigation, Civil Service, Commercial Collections, Corporate Law, Debtor-Creditor Law, Disability Law, Employment Discrimination, Employment Law, Estate Administration, Estate Planning, General Civil Practice, Labor Relations, Limited Liability Companies, Limited Liability Partnerships, Liquor Law, Litigation, Motor Vehicle Law, Non-profit Corporation Law, Probate, Real Estate and Construction Law, State and Local Government Law, Trade Association Law, UCC, Workers Compensation, Zoning, Planning and Land Use, Alternative Dispute Resolution, Appellate Practice and Administrative Appeals.

BLUE, WILSON & BLUE, L.L.C.

471 EAST BROAD STREET, SUITE 1100
COLUMBUS, OHIO 43215
Telephone: 614-224-6969
Toll Free: 1-877-543-BLUE (2583)
Fax: 614-224-6999
URL: http://www.bluewilsonbluelaw.com
Email: mailbox@bluewilsonbluelaw.com
URL: http://www.lawyers.com/bwblaw

Medical and Dental Malpractice, Personal Injury and Products Liability Law, Wrongful Death, Automobile Accidents, Industrial Accidents, Airplane Crash Litigation, Nursing Home Litigation, Automobile Insurance. Civil and Appellate Practice in State and Federal Courts.

FIRM PROFILE: Blue, Wilson & Blue represents hundreds of Ohioans each year in personal injury, wrongful death, traffic and work-related accident claims and medical malpractice cases.

JASON A. BLUE, born Carey, Ohio, August 2, 1939; admitted to bar, 1964, Ohio. *Education:* The Ohio State University (B.S., 1961; J.D., 1964). Assistant Attorney General, State of Ohio, 1964-1966. President, Lawyers Club of Columbus, 1975-1976. Member, Ohio Supreme Court Committee on Substance Abuse, 1994. *Member:* Columbus (Member, Board of Governors, 1982-1986), Ohio State (Member, Council of Delegates, 1975—; Chairman, Litigation Section, 1987—) and American Bar Associations; Franklin County Trial Lawyers Association (President, 1973-1974), Ohio Academy of Trial Lawyers (Member, Board of Trustees, 1973—; President, 1979-1980); The Association of Trial Lawyers of America (State Committeeman, 1981, Board of Governors, 1982-1985); American Board of Trial Advocates (President, Ohio Chapter, 1987-1989; Member, National Board of Directors 1990—). ***REPORTED CASES:*** Morgan V. Children's Hospital (1985) 18 Ohio St. 3d 185, 480 N.E. 2d 464. ***PRACTICE AREAS:*** Medical Malpractice; Personal Injury. ***Email:*** jason@bluewilsonbluelaw.com

MARK R. WILSON, born Charleston, West Virginia, May 18, 1957; admitted to bar, 1982, Ohio. *Education:* Wright State University (B.A., summa cum laude, 1979); The Ohio State University (J.D., 1982). Teacher for the American Institute for Paralegal Studies Inc., 1988. *Member:* Columbus and Ohio State Bar Associations; Ohio Academy Trial Lawyers; The Association of Trial Lawyers of America; Franklin County Trial Lawyers Association. ***PRACTICE AREAS:*** Personal Injury Law. ***Email:*** mark@bluewilsonbluelaw.com

DOUGLAS J. BLUE, born Columbus, Ohio, July 1, 1966; admitted to bar, 1992, Ohio. *Education:* Wittenberg University (B.A., 1988); Vermont Law School (J.D.; M.S.L., magna cum laude, 1991). Phi Alpha Delta (President, 1991). Thomas DeBevois Moot Court. *Member:* Columbus, Ohio State and American Bar Associations; Ohio Academy of Trial Lawyers; Franklin County Trial Lawyers; The Association of Trial Lawyers of America. ***PRACTICE AREAS:*** Personal Injury; Medical Malpractice. ***Email:*** douglas@bluewilsonbluelaw.com

REFERENCE: Bank One of Columbus, N.A.

SEAN O. BOYLE

580 SOUTH HIGH STREET
SUITE 200
COLUMBUS, OHIO 43215-5644
Telephone: 614-457-7219
Fax: 614-538-2905
Email: sboyle@macb-law.com
URL: http://www.lawyers.com/seanboyle

State and Federal Criminal Defense, Felonies and Misdemeanors, Juvenile Law.

(This Listing Continued)

SEAN O. BOYLE, born Columbus, Ohio, March 7, 1961; admitted to bar, 1988, Ohio, U.S. District Court, Southern District of Ohio and U.S. Tax Court. *Education:* Ohio State University (B.A., 1985); Capital University (J.D., 1987). *Member:* Ohio Association of Criminal Defense Lawyers; Central Ohio Association of Criminal Defense Lawyers. ***PRACTICE AREAS:*** Criminal Defense; Felonies; Misdemeanors; Juvenile Law; Drug Crimes; Sexual Assault; Domestic Violence; Driving While Intoxicated; Traffic Violations.

BRENNER, BROWN, GOLIAN & McCAFFREY CO., L.P.A.

2109 STELLA COURT
COLUMBUS, OHIO 43215
Telephone: 614-258-6000
Telecopier: 614-258-6006
Email: pbrown@rrcol.com
URL: http://www.lawyers.com/bbgm

ERISA, Life, Health and Disability Defense, Liability Defense and Insurance Coverage. Business and Corporate Law, General Civil Litigation, Motor Carrier Law.

FIRM PROFILE: The attorneys of Brenner, Brown, Golian & McCaffrey Co., L.P.A., manage a civil trial practice with a special emphasis in liability insurance, ERISA, individual and group health and disability insurance defense, motor carrier, special risks and commercial litigation.

The firm is listed in the Bar Register of Preeminent Lawyers.

PHILIP F. BROWN, born Berea, Ohio, November 2, 1955; admitted to bar, 1985, Ohio and U.S. District Court, Southern District of Ohio; 1990, U.S. District Court, Northern District of Ohio; 1991, U.S. District Court, Eastern District of Michigan; U.S. Court of Appeals, Sixth Circuit; 1992, U.S. Supreme Court; 1993, U.S. District Court, Western District of Michigan; U.S. Court of Appeals, Fourth Circuit; 1997, U.S. Court of Appeals, Eighth Circuit. *Education:* The Ohio State University (B.A., 1979); Capital University Law School (J.D., 1985). *Member:* Columbus and Ohio State Bar Associations; Defense Research Institute. ***REPORTED CASES:*** Tri-State Machine v. Nationwide Life Insurance Co. 33 F.3d. 309 (4th Cir. 1994); Fugarino v. Hartford Life & Accident Insurance Co., 969 F.2d 178 (6th Cir. 1993); Brown v. Seitz Food Disability Plan, 140 F.3d 1198 (8th Cir. 1998). ***PRACTICE AREAS:*** Individual and Group Insurance Defense; ERISA Defense; Liability Insurance; General Civil Litigation. ***Email:*** pbrown@rrcol.com

JOSEPH J. GOLIAN, born Johnstown, Pennsylvania, October 4, 1960; admitted to bar, 1985, Ohio and U.S. District Court, Southern District of Ohio; U.S. Court of Appeals, Fifth and Sixth Circuits; 1986, U.S. District Court, Southern District of Ohio and U.S. Court of Appeals, Fourth Circuit; 1990, U.S . District Court, Northern District of Ohio; 1994, U.S. District Court, Southern District of Texas. *Education:* Washington & Jefferson College (B.A., Economics, 1982); American University; Capital University (J.D., 1985). *Member:* Columbus Bar Association; American Trucking Association; Trucking Insurance Defense Association (TIDA); National Association of Railroad Trial Counsel. ***PRACTICE AREAS:*** Individual Life Disability; Insurance Defense; General and Civil Litigation; FELA; Railroad Liability; Longshore and Harbor Workers Compensation Act; Trucking Law; Amusement Park Liability; Motor Carrier; Insurance Coverage. ***Email:*** jgolian@rrcol.com

TODD AUSTIN BRENNER, born Canton, Ohio, July 10, 1965; admitted to bar, 1991, Ohio and U.S. District Court, Southern District of Ohio; 1992, U.S. District Court, Western District of Michigan and U.S. District Court, Northern District of Ohio; 1996, U.S. District Court, Northern District of Texas; 1997, U.S. Court of Appeals, Eighth Circuit; 1998, North Carolina; 2000, U.S. Court of Appeals, Fourth Circuit; 2002, U.S. Court of Appeals, Sixth Circuit. *Education:* Capital University (B.A., 1987; J.D., 1990). Delta Theta Phi. Notes Editor, Law Review. Author: "Legalization of Drugs: For and Against," Open Court Publishing, 1992. *Member:* Columbus and Ohio Bar Associations; Defense Research Institute. ***REPORTED CASES:*** Brown v. Seitz Foods Disability Plan, 140 F.3d 1198 (8th Cir. 1998); Bond v. Cerner Corporation, 309 E.3d 1064 (8th Cir. 2002). ***PRACTICE AREAS:*** Insurance Litigation; ERISA Defense; General Civil Litigation; General Business; Insurance Claims Defense. ***Email:*** tbrenner@rrcol.com

PATRICK McCAFFREY, JR., born Canonsburg, Pennsylvania, August 30, 1960; admitted to bar, 1985, Texas; 1996, Ohio. *Education:* Washington & Jefferson College (B.A., cum laude, 1982); University of Texas (J.D., with honors, 1985). *Member:* Houston, Federal and American Bar Associations; State Bar of Texas; Texas Association of Defense Council; Defense Research Institute. (Board Certified, Personal Injury Trial Law, Texas Board of Legal Specialization). ***PRACTICE AREAS:*** Motor Carrier; Insurance Defense Law; Coverage Law; ERISA. ***Email:*** patmc@rrcol.com

MICHAEL E. HEFFERNAN, born Detroit, Michigan, February 14, 1971; admitted to bar, 1998, Ohio; 1999, U.S. District Court, Southern District; 2000, U.S. District Court, Western District of Pennsylvania, U.S. District Court, Northern and Central Districts of Illinois and U.S. Court of Appeals, Sixth and Seventh Circuits; 2001, U.S. District Court, Northern District of Ohio, U.S. District Court, Northern and Southern Districts of Indiana; 2002, U.S. District Court, Eastern District of Wisconsin. *Education:* Georgetown University (B.S., 1993); Ohio State University (J.D., 1998). Member, Ohio State Journal on Dispute Resolution. *Member:* Columbus, Ohio State and American Bar Associations; Defense Research Institute. ***PRACTICE AREAS:*** ERISA; Insurance Defense; Civil Litigation. ***Email:*** mheff@rrohio.com

AUDREY E. VARWIG, born Toledo, Ohio, December 4, 1974; admitted to bar, 2001, Ohio; 2002, U.S. District Court, Southern and Northern Districts of Ohio and U.S. Court of Appeals, Sixth Circuit. *Education:* Bowling Green State University (B.S.B.A., cum laude, 1997); The Ohio State University (J.D., 2000). Member, Moot Court. ***PRACTICE AREAS:*** Litigation. ***Email:*** avarwig@rrcol.com

(This Listing Continued)

BRENNER, BROWN, GOLIAN & McCAFFREY CO., L.P.A., Columbus—Continued

JEFFERY S. MAYNARD, born Columbus, Ohio, January 30, 1968; admitted to bar, 2001, Ohio. *Education:* The Ohio State University (B.S., Criminology, 1995); Capital University (J.D., 2001). ***PRACTICE AREAS:*** Tort Defense; Insurance. ***Email:*** jmaynard@rrohio.com

SHANNON K. BENTON, born Bellefontaine, Ohio, March 8, 1975; admitted to bar, 2000, Ohio; 2001, U.S. District Court, Northern and Southern Districts of Ohio and U.S. Court of Appeals, Sixth Circuit. *Education:* The Ohio State University (B.A., 1996); The Ohio State University, Moritz College of Law (J.D., 2000). Member, Jessup International Law Moot Court Team. Public Events Editor, 1999-2000 and Member, Ohio State Law Journal. *Member:* Columbus and Ohio State Bar Association; Women Lawyers of Franklin County. ***PRACTICE AREAS:*** Litigation. ***Email:*** sbenton@rrohio.com

MELISSA M. PRENDERGAST, born Detroit, Michigan, September 30, 1975; admitted to bar, 2002, Ohio; U.S. District Court, Northern and Southern Districts of Ohio, U.S. District Court, Eastern and Western Districts of Michigan, U.S. District Court, Northern District of Indiana and U.S. District Court, Northern and Central Districts of Illinois. *Education:* Miami University (B.Phil., 1997); The Ohio State University, Moritz College of Law (J.D., 2002). Member, Moot Court. ***PRACTICE AREAS:*** Litigation. ***Email:*** mprendergast@rrohio.com

---

BRICKER & ECKLER LLP

Established in 1944

100 SOUTH THIRD STREET
COLUMBUS, OHIO 43215-4291
Telephone: 614-227-2300
Fax: 614-227-2390
Email: info@bricker.com
URL: http://www.bricker.com

Cleveland, Ohio Office: 1375 East Ninth Street, Suite 1500, 44114-1718. Telephone: 216-523-5405. Fax: 216-523-7071.

Antitrust and Competitive Business Practices, Banking, Bankruptcy, Commercial, Construction, Corporate Governance, Corporation and Partnership, Cyberlaw, Creditor-Debtor, Education, Emerging Business, Employment Relations, Entertainment/Sports, Environmental, Federal Taxation, Governmental Agencies and Legislative Law, Health Care, Insurance, Intellectual Property, International Transactions, Litigation, Mental Retardation and Developmental Disabilities, Mergers and Acquisitions; Mortgage Lending, Pension and Employee Benefits, Public Finance, Public Utilities, OSHA, Real Estate, Securities, State and Local Taxation, Trusts and Estates, Workers' Compensation.

FIRM PROFILE: Bricker & Eckler LLP is one of Ohio's leading law firms. Located in Columbus and Cleveland, the firm represents individuals as well as corporations, nonprofit organizations, government agencies, health care facilities, school districts and municipalities.

Dedicated to comprehensive client service, Bricker & Eckler offers services focused on both industry sectors and traditional practice areas. Bricker & Eckler LLP was founded in 1944 by John W. Bricker, a three-term Ohio governor, two-term Ohio senator, and a former candidate for vice president of the United States. Today, we continue our founder's tradition of public service by placing our clients and our communities first.

LAW FIRM ALLIANCES/ASSOCIATIONS: ***LEGALINK***

PARTNERS

JOHN W. BRICKER (1893-1986)

JOHN ECKLER (1913-1994)

EDWARD A. MATTO, born Toronto, Ohio, July 21, 1941; admitted to bar, 1966, Ohio; 1967, Florida. *Education:* The Ohio State University (B.S., 1963; J.D., 1966). ***PRACTICE AREAS:*** Antitrust; Unfair Business Practices; Complex Litigation; International Law. ***Email:*** ematto@bricker.com

MICHAEL F. SULLIVAN, born Hartford, Connecticut, April 7, 1942; admitted to bar, 1967, Ohio. *Education:* Yale University (B.A., 1964); University of Chicago (J.D., 1967). ***PRACTICE AREAS:*** Corporate Law; Mergers, Acquisitions and Divestitures; Corporate Control Contests; Corporate Investigations; Shareholder Rights. ***Email:*** msullivan@bricker.com

SALLY W. BLOOMFIELD, born Columbus, Ohio, July 20, 1943; admitted to bar, 1969, Ohio; 1970, New York and U.S. Tax Court; 1971, U.S. District Court, Southern District of Ohio. *Education:* Ohio Wesleyan University; St. Louis University (B.A., 1965); The Ohio State University (J.D., 1969). ***PRACTICE AREAS:*** Public Utility Law; Energy Facility Siting; Energy; Telecommunications Law. ***Email:*** sbloomfield@bricker.com

NICHOLAS A. PITTNER, born Ottoville, Ohio, March 14, 1942; admitted to bar, 1970, Ohio; 1971, U.S. District Court, Southern District of Ohio; 1973, U.S. District Court, Northern District of Ohio and U.S. Court of Appeals, Sixth Circuit; 2003, U.S. Supreme Court. *Education:* The Ohio State University (B.A., 1964); Capital University (J.D., 1970; Doctor of Laws, Honoris Causa, 2001). ***PRACTICE AREAS:*** Education Law; Labor and Employment; Public Finance; Computers and Software; Public Construction Law. ***Email:*** npittner@bricker.com

RICHARD F. KANE, born New York, N.Y., May 18, 1943; admitted to bar, 1971, Ohio. *Education:* City College of the City University of New York (B.E., Elect. Eng., 1965); Columbia University (M.B.A., 1966); Capital University (J.D., 1971). ***PRACTICE AREAS:*** Municipal Bonds; Municipal Bonds Taxation; Municipal Finance; Municipal Securities; Tax Increment Finance. ***Email:*** rkane@bricker.com

(This Listing Continued)

JOHN F. BIRATH, JR., born Youngstown, Ohio, December 8, 1946; admitted to bar, 1971, Ohio. *Education:* Miami University (B.A., 1968); Washington University (J.D., 1971). ***PRACTICE AREAS:*** Civil Litigation; Commercial Litigation; Personal Injury; Health Care; Professional Liability Litigation. ***Email:*** jbirath@bricker.com

MICHAEL S. HOLMAN, born Columbus, Ohio, December 6, 1942; admitted to bar, 1972, Ohio. *Education:* United States Naval Academy (B.S., with distinction, 1964); The Ohio State University (J.D., summa cum laude, 1971). ***PRACTICE AREAS:*** Construction Law; Occupational Safety and Health; Corporate Law. ***Email:*** mholman@bricker.com

RICHARD C. SIMPSON, born Dayton, Ohio, May 19, 1947; admitted to bar, 1972, Ohio. *Education:* Michigan State University (B.A., with honors, 1969); University of Michigan (J.D., 1972). (Managing Partner). ***PRACTICE AREAS:*** Municipal Bonds; Business; Real Estate Finance; Tax Increment Finance; Property Tax Assessments. ***Email:*** rsimpson@bricker.com

JOHN P. BEAVERS, born Toledo, Ohio, March 21, 1947; admitted to bar, 1972, Ohio; 2002, Colorado. *Education:* The Ohio State University (B.A., cum laude, 1969; J.D., cum laude, 1972). ***PRACTICE AREAS:*** Corporate Governance; Securities; Corporate Law; Mergers, Acquisitions and Divestitures; Executive Compensation. ***Email:*** jbeavers@bricker.com

DAVID G. BAKER, born Columbus, Ohio, February 4, 1947; admitted to bar, 1972, Ohio; 1975, U.S. District Court, Southern District of Ohio; 1978, U.S. Supreme Court. *Education:* Wittenberg University (B.S., 1969); University of Michigan (J.D., 1972). ***PRACTICE AREAS:*** Commercial Real Estate; Leases and Leasing; Real Estate Development; Mortgage Finance. ***Email:*** dbaker@bricker.com

JERRY E. NATHAN, born Bluefield, West Virginia, August 15, 1948; admitted to bar, 1973, Ohio. *Education:* The Ohio State University (B.S., summa cum laude, 1970); Yale University (J.D., 1973). ***PRACTICE AREAS:*** Labor and Employment; Employer Rights; Collective Bargaining; Education Law; School Law. ***Email:*** jnathan@bricker.com

MARSHALL L. LERNER, born Brooklyn, New York, August 4, 1947; admitted to bar, 1973, Ohio. *Education:* Michigan State University (B.A., 1968); Harvard University (J.D., 1973). ***PRACTICE AREAS:*** Federal Taxation Law; ERISA; Employee Benefits. ***Email:*** mlerner@bricker.com

RANDOLPH C. WISEMAN, born Staunton, Virginia, January 25, 1946; admitted to bar, 1974, Ohio. *Education:* East Tennessee State University (B.S., 1969); Capital University (J.D., 1974). ***PRACTICE AREAS:*** Complex and Multi-District Civil Litigation; ERISA Litigation; Class Action Defense; Business Torts; Environmental Litigation; Toxic Torts; Computers and Software. ***Email:*** rwiseman@bricker.com

DONALD R. KELLER, born Tiffin, Ohio, February 27, 1949; admitted to bar, 1974, Ohio; 1975, U.S. District Court, Southern District of Ohio; 1982, U.S. Supreme Court; 1985, U.S. Court of Appeals, Sixth Circuit. *Education:* Heidelberg College (B.A., 1971); The Ohio State University (J.D., 1974). ***PRACTICE AREAS:*** Management Labor Law; Collective Bargaining; Arbitration; Wrongful Discharge Litigation; Employee Discipline; Employment at Will; Employment Discrimination; Employment Disability Discrimination; Wrongful Termination; Non-Compete Litigation. ***Email:*** dkeller@bricker.com

KAREN MUELLER MOORE, born Baltimore, Maryland, April 20, 1950; admitted to bar, 1975, Ohio. *Education:* Ohio University (A.B., summa cum laude, 1972); The Ohio State University (J.D., summa cum laude, 1975). ***PRACTICE AREAS:*** Estate Planning; Trusts and Estates; Probate; Estate, Gift and Generation Skipping Transfer Taxation. ***Email:*** kmoore@bricker.com

STEVEN R. KERBER, born Sandusky, Ohio, April 10, 1951; admitted to bar, 1976, Ohio. *Education:* Bowling Green State University (B.S., cum laude, 1973); The Ohio State University (J.D., summa cum laude, 1976). ***PRACTICE AREAS:*** Corporate Law; Securities; Partnership Law; Mergers and Acquisitions. ***Email:*** skerber@bricker.com

CHARLES H. WALKER, born Columbus, Ohio, November 11, 1951; admitted to bar, 1976, Ohio; 1977, U.S. District Court, Southern District of Ohio; 1988, U.S. Court of Appeals, Sixth Circuit; 1992, U.S. District Court, Northern District of Ohio; 1995, U.S. District Court, Eastern District of Michigan; 1996, U.S. District Court, Western District of Michigan. *Education:* Tufts University (B.A., magna cum laude, 1973); Emory University (J.D., 1976). ***PRACTICE AREAS:*** Commercial Litigation; Civil Litigation; Employment Discrimination; Real Estate; Zoning Law. ***Email:*** cwalker@bricker.com

GORDON W. JOHNSTON, born Wooster, Ohio, April 28, 1951; admitted to bar, 1976, Ohio. *Education:* Wittenberg University (A.B., summa cum laude, 1973); University of Michigan (J.D., 1976). ***PRACTICE AREAS:*** Commercial Loans; Lenders' Rights; Loan Workouts; Secured Lending; Uniform Commercial Code. ***Email:*** gjohnston@bricker.com

DAVID A. ROGERS, born Montgomery, Alabama, December 11, 1952; admitted to bar, 1976, Ohio; 1977, U.S. District Court, Southern District of Ohio. *Education:* The Ohio State University (B.S., summa cum laude, 1973); Harvard University (J.D., 1976). ***PRACTICE AREAS:*** Bond Finance; Municipal Finance; Structured Finance; Project Finance; Securities; Golf Course Financing. ***Email:*** drogers@bricker.com

CHARLES H. WATERMAN III, born Rockville Centre, New York, June 29, 1951; admitted to bar, 1977, Ohio. *Education:* The Ohio State University (B.S., cum laude, 1972; B.A., cum laude, 1972; J.D., cum laude, 1977). ***PRACTICE AREAS:*** Environmental Law; Administrative Law; Civil Litigation. ***Email:*** cwaterman@bricker.com

MICHAEL K. GIRE, born San Francisco, California, January 25, 1947; admitted to bar, 1977, Ohio; 1978, District of Columbia. *Education:* The Ohio State University (B.S., 1970); American University (J.D., 1977). ***PRACTICE AREAS:*** Health Care. ***Email:*** mgire@bricker.com

JAMES A. RUTLEDGE, born Fort Polk, Louisiana, February 12, 1953; admitted to bar, 1978, Ohio; 1979, U.S. Tax Court. *Education:* University of Dayton (B.A., summa cum laude, 1974); The Ohio State University (J.D., 1977). ***PRACTICE AREAS:*** Business Law; Tax Planning; Mergers and Acquisitions; Family Partnerships; Estate and Gift Taxation. ***Email:*** jrutledge@bricker.com

DAVID C. SPIALTER, born Dayton, Ohio, May 21, 1952; admitted to bar, 1978, New York; 1979, Massachusetts; 1982, Ohio. *Education:* Harvard University (A.B., 1974); Co-

(This Listing Continued)

lumbia University (J.D., 1977). ***PRACTICE AREAS:*** Health Care; Corporate Law; Government Law; Securities; International Law; Municipal Finance. ***Email:*** dspialter@bricker.com

RANDALL EDWIN MOORE, born Columbus, Ohio, April 3, 1949; admitted to bar, 1978, Ohio. *Education:* Massachusetts Institute of Technology (B.S., 1971); The Ohio State University (J.D., summa cum laude, 1978). ***PRACTICE AREAS:*** Corporate Law; Corporate Finance; Municipal Finance. ***Email:*** rmoore@bricker.com

JOHN W. COOK, III, born Palo Alto, California, March 16, 1952; admitted to bar, 1978, Ohio. *Education:* Carleton College (B.A., cum laude, 1974); The Ohio State University (J.D., summa cum laude, 1978). ***PRACTICE AREAS:*** Mergers and Acquisitions; Insurance Mergers and Acquisitions; Corporate Law; Securitization; Securities. ***Email:*** jcook@bricker.com

CHARLES H. McCREARY, III, born Zanesville, Ohio, January 13, 1953; admitted to bar, 1978, Ohio. *Education:* Duke University (A.B., magna cum laude, 1975); Vanderbilt University (J.D., 1978). ***PRACTICE AREAS:*** Commercial Mortgage; Mortgage Finance; Real Estate Acquisitions; Real Estate Development; Real Estate Leasing. ***Email:*** cmccreary@bricker.com

JAMES P. BURNES, born Columbus, Ohio, September 15, 1951; admitted to bar, 1978, Ohio and U.S. District Court, Southern District of Ohio; 1981, U.S. District Court, Northern District of Ohio; 1983, U.S. Court of Appeals, Sixth Circuit. *Education:* Ohio Wesleyan University (B.A., 1973); Capital University (J.D., 1978). ***PRACTICE AREAS:*** School Law; Construction Law; Special Education; Title IX Discrimination; Collective Bargaining. ***Email:*** jburnes@bricker.com

ELISABETH A. SQUEGLIA, born Youngstown, Ohio, April 12, 1949; admitted to bar, 1979, Ohio and U.S. District Court, Southern District of Ohio; 1999, Colorado. *Education:* The Ohio State University (B.A., 1971; J.D., 1978). ***PRACTICE AREAS:*** Health Care; Insurance; State Legislative Practice; Lobbying; Administrative Law. ***Email:*** esqueglia@bricker.com

KENNETH C. JOHNSON, born Cleveland, Ohio, October 26, 1953; admitted to bar, 1979, Ohio. *Education:* Denison University (B.A., magna cum laude, 1976); University of Virginia (J.D., 1979). ***PRACTICE AREAS:*** Bankruptcy; Real Estate; Commercial Law. ***Email:*** kjohnson@bricker.com

MICHAEL E. FLOWERS, born Columbus, Ohio, November 20, 1953; admitted to bar, 1979, Ohio and U.S. District Court, Southern District of Ohio; 1984, U.S. Supreme Court. *Education:* Bucknell University (B.S., 1976); The Ohio State University (J.D., 1979). ***PRACTICE AREAS:*** Mergers, Acquisitions and Divestitures; Private Placement Syndications; Corporate Law. ***Email:*** mflowers@bricker.com

MARK A. ENGEL, born Mt. Clemens, Michigan, December 30, 1953; admitted to bar, 1979, Ohio; 1981, U.S. District Court, Southern District of Ohio; 1987, U.S. Supreme Court; 2004, U.S. Court of Appeals, Sixth Circuit. *Education:* St. Clair County Community College; University of Michigan (B.A., with high honors, 1976); Capital University (J.D., with high honors, 1979; LL.M., Taxation, 1990). ***PRACTICE AREAS:*** State Taxation; Local Taxation; Tax Appeals; Property Tax Abatement; Manufacturing. ***Email:*** mengel@bricker.com

DAVID K. CONRAD, born Hamilton, Ohio, February 29, 1956; admitted to bar, 1980, Ohio. *Education:* Kenyon College (A.B., summa cum laude, 1977); The Ohio State University (J.D., 1980). ***PRACTICE AREAS:*** Real Estate; Commercial Law; Mortgage Financing; Banking. ***Email:*** dconrad@bricker.com

RICHARD S. LOVERING, born Washington, D.C., July 31, 1954; admitted to bar, 1980, Ohio; 1981, U.S. District Court, Southern and Northern Districts of Ohio. *Education:* Trinity College (B.A., with honors, 1976); University of Virginia (M.B.A., 1980; J.D., 1980). ***PRACTICE AREAS:*** Commercial Litigation; Medical Malpractice; Unfair Trade; Education Law. ***Email:*** rlovering@bricker.com

REBECCA COLEMAN PRINCEHORN, born Canton, Ohio, May 6, 1957; admitted to bar, 1981, Ohio. *Education:* Otterbein College (B.A., with honors, 1978); University of Kansas (J.D., 1981; M.P.A., 1982). ***PRACTICE AREAS:*** Bond Finance; Public Finance; School Law; Local Government Law; Tax Exempt Bonds. ***Email:*** rprincehorn@bricker.com

DIANE M. SIGNORACCI, born Columbus, Ohio, May 26, 1950; admitted to bar, 1981, Ohio; 1982, U.S. District Court, Southern District of Ohio. *Education:* Franklin University (B.S., 1978); The Ohio State University (J.D., summa cum laude, 1981). ***PRACTICE AREAS:*** Computer Contracts; Health Care Fraud; Health Care Reimbursement; Health Care Contracts; Medicare and Medicaid Hearings. ***Email:*** dsignoracci@bricker.com

LUTHER L. LIGGETT, JR., born Marysville, Ohio, March 1, 1956; admitted to bar, 1981, Ohio and U.S. District Court, Southern District of Ohio; 1982, U.S. District Court, Northern District of Ohio; 1996, U.S. Supreme Court. *Education:* George Washington University (B.A., with distinction, 1978; J.D., 1981). ***PRACTICE AREAS:*** Legislative Lobbying; Mortgage Banking; Construction Litigation; Public Policy; Government Agency Practice. ***Email:*** lliggett@bricker.com

MARTHA POST BAXTER, born Fremont, Ohio, September 14, 1950; admitted to bar, 1982, Ohio; 1982, U.S. District Court, Southern District of Ohio; 1996, Montana. *Education:* The Ohio State University (B.S., 1972); University of Iowa (M.S., 1976); University of Richmond (J.D., 1981). ***PRACTICE AREAS:*** Health Care; Hospital Law. ***Email:*** mbaxter@bricker.com

GRETCHEN A. McBEATH, born Akron, Ohio, August 20, 1944; admitted to bar, 1982, Ohio. *Education:* The Ohio State University (B.A., 1966); Capital University (J.D., summa cum laude, 1982). ***PRACTICE AREAS:*** Health Care. ***Email:*** gmcbeath@bricker.com

CRAIG A. HADDOX, born Columbus, Ohio, 1957; admitted to bar, 1982, Ohio; 1983, U.S. District Court, Southern District of Ohio. *Education:* Duke University (B.A., magna cum laude, 1979); University of Michigan (J.D., 1982). ***PRACTICE AREAS:*** Real Estate; Telecommunications Leasing and Site Management; Real Estate Transfers; Real Estate Development; Commercial Leasing. ***Email:*** chaddox@bricker.com

(This Listing Continued)

SUSAN BEALE GREENBERGER, born Santa Monica, California, January 26, 1952; admitted to bar, 1979, Wisconsin; 1980, U.S. District Court, Western District of Wisconsin; 1981, U.S. District Court, Eastern District of Wisconsin; 1983, Ohio. *Education:* University of California, Berkeley (A.B., with great distinction, 1973); University of Wisconsin-Madison (M.S.S.W., 1975; J.D., summa cum laude, 1979). ***PRACTICE AREAS:*** School Law, public school representation; County Boards of MR/DD; Local Governments and Consortia; First Amendement; Telecommunications Site Leases; Civil Litigation. ***Email:*** sgreenberger@bricker.com

WILLIAM T. CONARD, II, born Columbus, Ohio, May 6, 1958; admitted to bar, 1983, Ohio. *Education:* Otterbein College (B.A., with honors, 1980); The Ohio State University (J.D., with honors, 1983). ***PRACTICE AREAS:*** Public Finance; Municipal Finance; Finance; Taxation; Securities. ***Email:*** wconard@bricker.com

ROBERT C. RAFFERTY, born Canton, Ohio, May 12, 1953; admitted to bar, 1984, Ohio. *Education:* Grove City College (B.A., cum laude, 1975); Western Kentucky University (M.Ed., 1977); Capital University (J.D., cum laude, 1984). ***PRACTICE AREAS:*** Estate Planning; Estate and Gift Taxation; Trusts and Estates Taxation; Probate; Ancillary Probate. ***Email:*** rrafferty@bricker.com

JERRY O. ALLEN, born Cleveland, Ohio, December 16, 1953; admitted to bar, 1984, Ohio. *Education:* Capital University (B.A., 1975; J.D., cum laude, 1984); New York University (LL.M., Taxation, 1987). ***PRACTICE AREAS:*** Federal Taxation; State Taxation; Local Taxation. ***Email:*** jallen@bricker.com

H. RANDY BANK, born New Haven, Connecticut, October 4, 1956; admitted to bar, 1984, Ohio; 1987, U.S. District Court, Northern District of Ohio. *Education:* Kenyon College (B.A., 1979); The Ohio State University (J.D., 1984). ***PRACTICE AREAS:*** School Law; Public Sector Employment Law; County Government Law; Mental Disability Law; Collective Bargaining. ***Email:*** rbank@bricker.com

ANNE MARIE SFERRA VORYS, born Youngstown, Ohio, July 11, 1960; admitted to bar, 1985, Ohio; 1986, U.S. District Court, Southern District of Ohio. *Education:* Bowling Green State University (B.S., magna cum laude, 1982); The Ohio State University (J.D., 1985). ***PRACTICE AREAS:*** Civil Litigation; Employment Litigation; Appellate Practice; Asbestos; Tort Reform; Ballot Initiatives. ***Email:*** asferra@bricker.com

CATHERINE M. BALLARD, born Coronado, California, September 24, 1952; admitted to bar, 1985, Ohio; 1987, U.S. District Court, Southern District of Ohio; 1988, U.S. Court of Appeals, Sixth Circuit; 1990, U.S. Supreme Court. *Education:* University of Louisville (B.A., 1975); The Ohio State University (J.D., summa cum laude, 1985). ***PRACTICE AREAS:*** Health Care; Civil Litigation; Hospital Law; Medicare and Medicaid; Administrative Law. ***Email:*** cballard@bricker.com

GORDON F. LITT, born New Concord, Ohio, December 18, 1957; admitted to bar, 1985, Ohio. *Education:* Muskingum College (B.A., summa cum laude, 1980); The Ohio State University (J.D., with honors, 1985). ***PRACTICE AREAS:*** Closely Held Business Estate Planning; Limited Liability Company Law; Partnership Taxation; Family Trusts; Conservation Easements. ***Email:*** glitt@bricker.com

SUE WYSKIVER YOUNT, born Logan, Ohio, March 7, 1960; admitted to bar, 1986, Ohio; 1987, U.S. District Court, Southern District of Ohio; 1988, U.S. Court of Appeals, Sixth Circuit; 1995, U.S. District Court, Northern District of Ohio. *Education:* Ohio University (B.B.A., summa cum laude, top business graduate, 1983); The Ohio State University (J.D., summa cum laude, 1986). ***PRACTICE AREAS:*** Education Law; Special Education; Labor and Employment; Public Sector Collective Bargaining; Public Sector Employment Law. ***Email:*** syount@bricker.com

JAMES J. HUGHES, III, born South Bend, Indiana, November 6, 1958; admitted to bar, 1986, Ohio; U.S. Court of Appeals, Fourth and Sixth Circuits; U.S. District Court, Southern District of Ohio. *Education:* Union College (B.A., with honors, 1980); Capital University (J.D., with honors, 1986). ***PRACTICE AREAS:*** Commercial Litigation; Corporate Law; Environmental Law; Environmental Compliance; Health Care Litigation. ***Email:*** jjhughes@bricker.com

FRANK L. MERRILL, born Circleville, Ohio, October 15, 1958; admitted to bar, 1987, Ohio. *Education:* Dartmouth College (B.A., 1981); University of Cincinnati (J.D., 1987). ***PRACTICE AREAS:*** Environmental Law; Environmental Real Estate; Wetlands Regulation; Hazardous Waste Liability; Clean Water Act. ***Email:*** fmerrill@bricker.com

KURTIS A. TUNNELL, born North Platte, Nebraska, October 1, 1960; admitted to bar, 1987, Ohio. *Education:* Hastings College (B.A., magna cum laude, 1983); University of Toronto (M.A., 1985); The Ohio State University (J.D., with honors, 1987). ***PRACTICE AREAS:*** State Legislative Practice; Life and Health Insurance; Election and Campaign Finance; Lobbying; Public Policy; Manufacturing Representation. ***Email:*** ktunnell@bricker.com

BETSY A. SWIFT, born Warren, Ohio, August 12, 1954; admitted to bar, 1988, Ohio and U.S. District Court, Southern District of Ohio; 1989, U.S. Court of Appeals, Sixth Circuit. *Education:* Miami University (B.S., Education, 1976); The Ohio State University (J.D., with honors, 1988). ***PRACTICE AREAS:*** Labor and Employment. ***Email:*** bswift@bricker.com

JACK R. ROSATI, JR., born Morgantown, West Virginia, April 28, 1958; admitted to bar, 1989, Ohio. *Education:* The Ohio State University (B.S., Pharmacy, 1981; J.D., 1989). ***PRACTICE AREAS:*** Litigation; Construction Law. ***Email:*** jrosati@bricker.com

SUSAN E. GEARY, born Kittanning, Pennsylvania, January 17, 1956; admitted to bar, 1989, Ohio. *Education:* Indiana University of Pennsylvania (B.S., in Education, 1976); Bowling Green University (M.Ed., 1979); Capital University (J.D., summa cum laude, 1989). ***PRACTICE AREAS:*** School Law. ***Email:*** sgeary@bricker.com

SYLVIA LYNN GILLIS, born San Benito, Texas, September 11, 1954; admitted to bar, 1989, Ohio, U.S. District Court, Southern and Northern Districts of Ohio and U.S. Court of Appeals, Sixth Circuit. *Education:* Northern Arizona University (B.A., magna cum laude, 1976); University of Washington (M.A., 1980); The Ohio State University (J.D., with honors, 1989). ***PRACTICE AREAS:*** Construction law. ***Email:*** sgillis@bricker.com

JAMES F. FLYNN, born South Bend, Indiana, December 18, 1964; admitted to bar, 1990, Ohio; 1991, U.S. District Court, Southern District of Ohio; 1996, U.S. District Court, Northern District of Ohio; 1997, U.S. Court of Appeals, Sixth and Seventh Circuits; 2000,

(This Listing Continued)

BRICKER & ECKLER LLP, Columbus—Continued

U.S. Supreme Court. *Education:* University of Notre Dame (B.A., 1987; J.D., 1990). ***PRACTICE AREAS:*** Hospital Law; Health Care; Medicare and Medicaid; Administrative Law; Litigation. ***Email:*** jflynn@bricker.com

PRICE D. FINLEY, born Tacoma, Washington, November 21, 1963; admitted to bar, 1990, Ohio. *Education:* Capital University (B.A., magna cum laude, 1986); The Ohio State University (M.B.A., 1989; J.D., 1990). ***PRACTICE AREAS:*** Public Finance; Municipal Bonds; Tax Exempt Bonds; Tax Increment Finance; Economic Development. ***Email:*** pfinley@bricker.com

HARRY WRIGHT, IV, born Columbus, Ohio, March 17, 1958; admitted to bar, 1990, Ohio; 1991, U.S. District Court, Southern and Northern Districts of Ohio; 1992, U.S. Court of Appeals, Sixth Circuit. *Education:* Washington & Lee University (B.A., 1980); Memphis Theological Seminary; Emory University (J.D., with distinction, 1990). ***PRACTICE AREAS:*** Medicare and Medicaid Compliance; Medicare Fraud and Abuse; Health Care Insolvency; Bankruptcy; Foreclosures; Consumer Law. ***Email:*** hwright@bricker.com

DREW H. CAMPBELL, born Los Angeles, California, April 19, 1958; admitted to bar, 1990, Ohio; 1992, U.S. District Court, Southern District of Ohio and U.S. Court of Appeals, Sixth Circuit. *Education:* Boston University (B.F.A., 1981); The Ohio State University (J.D., 1990). ***PRACTICE AREAS:*** Commercial Litigation; Business Torts; Fraudulent Conveyance; Federal Civil Practice; Civil Appeals. ***Email:*** dcampbell@bricker.com

STEPHEN C. GRAY, born Milwaukee, Wisconsin, February 23, 1965; admitted to bar, 1991, Wisconsin; 1993, U.S. District Court, Eastern and Western Districts of Wisconsin; 1996, U.S. Court of Appeals, Seventh Circuit; 1997, Ohio, U.S. District Court, Northern District of Ohio and U.S. Court of Appeals, Sixth Circuit; 1998, U.S. District Court, Southern District of Ohio. *Education:* University of Wisconsin-Madison (B.S., 1987); The Ohio State University (J.D., 1991). ***PRACTICE AREAS:*** Business Litigation; Commercial Litigation; Computer Law; Contract Litigation; Information Technology; Intellectual Property Litigation. ***Email:*** sgray@bricker.com

KAREN D. SMITH, born Marietta, Ohio, November 21, 1952; admitted to bar, 1991, Ohio. *Education:* Ohio University (B.S.N., 1984); The Ohio State University (M.S., 1988); University of Cincinnati (J.D., 1991). ***PRACTICE AREAS:*** Hospital Law; Health Law; Medicare and Medicaid; Regulatory; Administrative Proceedings. ***Email:*** ksmith@bricker.com

JAMES G. PETRIE, born New York, N.Y., December 14, 1965; admitted to bar, 1992, Ohio; 1994, U.S. District Court, Southern District of Ohio; 1996, U.S. District Court, Northern District of Ohio and U.S. Court of Appeals, Sixth Circuit. *Education:* Miami University (B.A., with honors, 1988); The Ohio State University (J.D., 1992). ***PRACTICE AREAS:*** Employment Defense; Employment Discrimination; Wrongful Termination Defense; Noncompetition and Non-Solicitation; Wage and Hour Law. ***Email:*** jpetrie@bricker.com

STEPHEN INTIHAR, born Cleveland, Ohio, May 19, 1966; admitted to bar, 1993, Ohio; 1994, U.S. District Court, Southern District of Ohio. *Education:* Brown University (Sc.B, 1988); The Ohio State University (J.D., with honors, 1993). ***PRACTICE AREAS:*** Real Estate; Commercial Real Estate Finance; Commercial Real Estate Acquisitions; Commercial Leasing; Commercial Real Estate Development. ***Email:*** sintihar@bricker.com

T. EARL LeVERE, born Raleigh, North Carolina, May 11, 1969; admitted to bar, 1994, Ohio; 1995, U.S. District Court, Southern District of Ohio; 1998, U.S. Court of Appeals, Sixth Circuit; 2002, U.S. Court of Appeals, Federal Circuit. *Education:* Capital University (B.A., summa cum laude, 1990); The Ohio State University (J.D., cum laude, 1994). ***LANGUAGES:*** French. ***PRACTICE AREAS:*** Litigation; Intellectual Property; Computers and Software; Entertainment Law; Copyrights; Patent Litigation; Trademarks. ***Email:*** elevere@bricker.com

BOBBIE S. SPRADER, born Bowling Green, Ohio, September 9, 1969; admitted to bar, 1994, Ohio. *Education:* Bowling Green State University (B.S.B.A., 1991); The Ohio State University (J.D., 1994). ***PRACTICE AREAS:*** Hospital Liability Defense; Medical Malpractice Defense; Dental Malpractice Defense; Workers Compensation Defense; Personal Injury Defense. ***Email:*** bsprader@bricker.com

KIMBERLY J. BROWN, born Bellaire, Ohio, March 27, 1969; admitted to bar, 1995, Ohio. *Education:* Otterbein College (B.A., magna cum laude, with honors, 1991); Capital University (J.D., summa cum laude, 1995). ***PRACTICE AREAS:*** OSHA; Construction Law; Eminent Domain; Medical Malpractice. ***Email:*** kbrown@bricker.com

FAITH M. WILLIAMS, born Lawrence, Massachusetts, March 12, 1958; admitted to bar, 1993, Maryland; 1996, Ohio. *Education:* American University (B.S., 1979); Georgetown University (J.D., cum laude, 1993). ***PRACTICE AREAS:*** Insurance Regulation; Insurance Investigations; Life Insurance; Health Insurance; Long Term Care; Lobbying; Manufacturing. ***Email:*** fwilliams@bricker.com

CHRISTINE M. POTH, born Lexington, Kentucky, November 1, 1969; admitted to bar, 1995, Ohio. *Education:* University of Cincinnati (B.A., summa cum laude, 1992); The Ohio State University (J.D., 1995). ***PRACTICE AREAS:*** Employee Benefits; Taxation; ERISA; Executive Compensation; Non-Qualified Benefits. ***Email:*** cpoth@bricker.com

LAURA GREENBERG ANTHONY, born Cleveland, Ohio, September 9, 1970; admitted to bar, 1995, Ohio. *Education:* The Ohio State University (B.A., summa cum laude, with honors, 1992; J.D., 1995). ***PRACTICE AREAS:*** School Law; Labor and Employment; Family and Medical Leave Act; Special Education; Appellate Practice. ***Email:*** lanthony@bricker.com

NELSON M. REID, born Kettering, Ohio, July 24, 1972; admitted to bar, 1997, Ohio; 1998, U.S. District Court, Southern and Northern Districts of Ohio; 1999, U.S. Court of Appeals, Sixth Circuit. *Education:* Dartmouth College (B.A., 1994); Duke University (J.D., 1997). ***PRACTICE AREAS:*** Trial Practice; Federal Civil Practice; Commercial Litigation; Contract Litigation; Appellate Practice. ***Email:*** nreid@bricker.com

(This Listing Continued)

SENIOR ATTORNEYS

WARREN I. GRODY, born Springfield, Ohio, July 11, 1960; admitted to bar, 1993, Ohio; 1995, U.S. District Court, Southern District of Ohio; 1996, U.S. Court of Appeals, Sixth Circuit. *Education:* Wright State University (B.A., magna cum laude, 1987); Capital University (J.D., summa cum laude, 1993). ***PRACTICE AREAS:*** Education; MRDD; Federal Procurement; Public Contracts; Copyrights; Open Meetings; Public Records. ***Email:*** wgrody@bricker.com

AMY STRAKER BARTEMES, born Steubenville, Ohio, July 17, 1968; admitted to bar, 1993, Ohio; 1996, U.S. District Court, Southern District of Ohio and U.S. Court of Appeals, Sixth Circuit; 1997, U.S. District Court, Northern District of Ohio. *Education:* Purdue University (B.A., 1990); L'Université de Strasbourg (Certificate of Proficiency in French, 1989); Oxford University, Institute on International and Comparative Law (Magdalen College, 1991); Vanderbilt University (J.D., 1993). ***LANGUAGES:*** French. ***PRACTICE AREAS:*** Litigation; Public Utility Law. ***Email:*** abartemes@bricker.com

SUSAN L. OPPENHEIMER, born Rochester, New York, September 3, 1962; admitted to bar, 1987, Pennsylvania and U.S. District Court, Eastern District of Pennsylvania; 1988, U.S. District Court, Middle District of Pennsylvania; 1994, Ohio and U.S. District Court, Southern District of Ohio. *Education:* Williams College (B.A., cum laude, 1984); University of Chicago (J.D., 1987). ***PRACTICE AREAS:*** School Law; Labor and Employment Law; Employer Rights; Collective Bargaining; First Amendment Law. ***Email:*** soppenheimer@bricker.com

KATHERINE SPIES GIUMENTI, born Dover, Ohio, August 18, 1964; admitted to bar, 1989, Ohio and U.S. District Court, Southern District of Ohio; 1993, U.S. Court of Appeals, Sixth Circuit; 1997, U.S. District Court, Northern District of Ohio. *Education:* The Ohio State University (B.A., cum laude, 1986; J.D., with honors, 1989). ***PRACTICE AREAS:*** Employment Litigation; Employment Discrimination; Sexual Harassment; Title VII Discrimination; Defense Litigation. ***Email:*** kgiumenti@bricker.com

MAUREEN P. TAYLOR, born Aurora, Illinois, May 24, 1942; admitted to bar, 1989, Kentucky and U.S. District Court, Western District of Kentucky; 1990, U.S. District Court, Eastern District of Kentucky and U.S. Court of Appeals, Sixth Circuit; 1997, Ohio and U.S. District Court, Southern District of Ohio. *Education:* University of Michigan, Flint (A.B., with high honors, 1963); Michigan State University (M.A., 1964); Western Michigan University (Ed.D., 1978); University of Michigan, Ann Arbor (J.D., cum laude, 1989). ***PRACTICE AREAS:*** Construction Claims; Government Agency Practice; Civil Appeals; Arbitration; Public Contract Law. ***Email:*** mtaylor@bricker.com

---

C. ALLEN SHAFFER, born Columbus, Ohio, January 21, 1956; admitted to bar, 2004, Ohio. *Education:* Ohio State University (Ph.D., 1999; J.D., 2004). ***PRACTICE AREAS:*** Education.

GREGORY T. PARKS, born Columbus, Ohio, June 21, 1965; admitted to bar, 1995, Ohio; 1996, U.S. District Court, Southern District of Ohio. *Education:* The Ohio State University (B.S., 1990); Capital University (J.D., 1995). ***PRACTICE AREAS:*** Construction Law. ***Email:*** gparks@bricker.com

MARIA J. ARMSTRONG, born Canton, Ohio, July 21, 1962; admitted to bar, 1987, Ohio. *Education:* The Ohio State University (B.A., 1984; J.D., 1987). ***PRACTICE AREAS:*** Government Affairs; Construction; Environmental; Election, Campaign and Political Law, Ballot Initiatives; Public Contracting and Public Contract Litigation. ***Email:*** marmstrong@bricker.com

EMMETT M. KELLY, born Syracuse, New York, August 19, 1967; admitted to bar, 1999, Ohio. *Education:* Hobart and William Smith College (B.A., 1993); Capital University (J.D., magna cum laude, 1999). ***PRACTICE AREAS:*** Public Finance; Public Law. ***Email:*** ekelly@bricker.com

ALEXANDER M. BROWN, born Covina, California, September 8, 1974; admitted to bar, 1999, Ohio. *Education:* University of California, Berkeley (B.A., with distinction, 1996); University of Virginia (J.D., 1999). ***PRACTICE AREAS:*** Corporate Law; Computers and Software; Intellectual Property; Internet Law. ***Email:*** abrown@bricker.com

MATTHEW L. STOUT, born Columbus, Ohio, September 19, 1971; admitted to bar, 1999, Ohio. *Education:* University of Michigan (B.B.A., 1995); The Ohio State University (J.D., 1999; M.B.A., 1999). ***PRACTICE AREAS:*** Bond Finance; Public Finance; Public Law. ***Email:*** mstout@bricker.com

ALLEN R. KILLWORTH, born Falls Church, Virginia, March 7, 1972; admitted to bar, 1997, Ohio and U.S. District Court, Southern District of Ohio. *Education:* Vanderbilt University (B.A., 1994); The Ohio State University (J.D., 1997). ***PRACTICE AREAS:*** Healthcare. ***Email:*** akillworth@bricker.com

VLADIMIR P. BELO, born Lansing, Michigan, February 9, 1971; admitted to bar, 1997, California; 1999, Ohio; U.S. District Court, Southern and Northern Districts of Ohio, U.S. District Court, Eastern and Central Districts of California and U.S. Court of Appeals, Sixth, Ninth and District of Columbia Circuits. *Education:* University of California, Berkeley (B.A., with distinction, 1992); Hastings College of the Law, University of California (J.D., magna cum laude, 1997). ***PRACTICE AREAS:*** Litigation; Labor and Employment; Appellate Practice; Asbestos; Tort Reform. ***Email:*** vbelo@bricker.com

JAMES S. GRAY, born Hamilton, Ohio, October 10, 1973; admitted to bar, 2000, Ohio. *Education:* The Ohio State University (B.A., 1996; J.D., 2000). ***PRACTICE AREAS:*** Real Estate Acquisitions; Real Estate Finance; Real Estate Leasing; Real Estate Secured Lending; Telecommunications Leasing and Site Management. ***Email:*** jgray@bricker.com

JOHN F. FURNISS III, born Lancaster, Ohio, September 3, 1975; admitted to bar, 2000, Ohio; 2001, U.S. District Court, Southern District of Ohio, U.S. Court of Appeals, Sixth Circuit and U.S. Tax Court; 2003, U.S. District Court, Northern District of Ohio. *Education:* Kenyon College (A.B., magna cum laude, 1997); University of Virginia (J.D., 2000). ***PRACTICE AREAS:*** Probate; Trusts and Estates; Estate Planning; Estate and Gift Taxation; Family Wealth Transfer. ***Email:*** jfurniss@bricker.com

(This Listing Continued)

JAMES P. SCHUCK, born Findlay, Ohio, February 20, 1975; admitted to bar, 2000, Ohio; 2001, U.S. District Court, Southern District of Ohio; 2002, U.S. Court of Appeals, Sixth Circuit; 2004, U.S. District Court, Northern District of Ohio. *Education:* Bowling Green State University (B.A., 1997); Capital University (J.D., magna cum laude, 2000). ***PRACTICE AREAS:*** Litigation; Trial Practice; Federal Civil Practice; Commercial Litigation; Contract Litigation; Business Torts; Insurance; Appellate Practice. ***Email:*** jschuck@bricker.com

MIRANDA CREVISTON MOTTER, born Springfield, Ohio, April 25, 1974; admitted to bar, 2001, Ohio. *Education:* Anderson College (B.A., cum laude, 1996); Capital University (J.D., magna cum laude, 2001). ***PRACTICE AREAS:*** Insurance Services including Property and Casualty; Financial Services Law; Government Relations; Election, Campaign and Political Law; Asbestos; Tort Reform. ***Email:*** mmotter@bricker.com

MARK E. EVANS, P.E., born Dayton, Ohio, August 14, 1970; admitted to bar, 2001, Ohio. *Education:* The Ohio State University (B.S.C.E., 1995); Capital University (J.D., 2001). ***PRACTICE AREAS:*** Construction Law; Utilities Law. ***Email:*** mevans@bricker.com

TERRENCE O'DONNELL, born Rocky River, Ohio, April 11, 1976; admitted to bar, 2001, Ohio. *Education:* Miami University (B.A., 1997); University of Notre Dame (J.D., 2001). ***PRACTICE AREAS:*** Public Policy; Government Affairs; Litigation; Election, Campaign and Political Law; Mortgage Banking. ***Email:*** todonnell@bricker.com

JAMES R. BERENDSEN, born Cleveland, Ohio, August 26, 1942; admitted to bar, 1971, Ohio and U.S. District Court, Southern District of Ohio. *Education:* Ohio University (B.B.A., 1964); Capital University (J.D., 1971). ***REPORTED CASES:*** Luper v. Columbia Gas of Ohio, 91 F 3d 811 (6th Circuit); Commerce and Industry v. City of Toledo and VColumbia Gas of Ohio 45 Ohio St 3d 96 (Supreme Court of Ohio); Higgins v. Columbia Gas of Ohio 136 Ohio App. 3d 198 (Ohio Court of Appeals). ***PRACTICE AREAS:*** Tort Litigation; Bankruptcy; Commercial Litigation; Negligence. ***Email:*** jberendsen@bricker.com

THEODORE J. GALLAGHER, born Bay City, Michigan, May 23, 1962; admitted to bar, 1991, Ohio; 1994, U.S. District Court, Southern District of Ohio; 1998, U.S. District Court Northern District of Ohio; 2003, Pennsylvania. *Education:* University of Toronto (B.A., 1986); University of Toledo (J.D., 1991). ***REPORTED CASES:*** Reeves v. Columbia Gas of Ohio (In re Reeves), 265 B.R. 766 (Bankr. N.D. Ohio 2001); Luper v. Columbia Gas (In re Carled) 91 F. 3d 811 (6th Cir. 1996). ***PRACTICE AREAS:*** Litigation; Labor and Employment; Bankruptcy; Tort Litigation. ***Email:*** tgallagher@bricker.com

ALAN D. DUFFY, born Cleveland, Ohio, August 27, 1976; admitted to bar, 2002, Ohio. *Education:* Kenyon College (B.A., 1998); The Ohio State University (J.D., with honors, 2001); New York University (LL.M., 2002). ***PRACTICE AREAS:*** Federal Taxation; Employee Benefits. ***Email:*** aduffy@bricker.com

CHRISTOPHER N. SWANK, born Troy, Ohio, October 19, 1976; admitted to bar, 2002, Ohio. *Education:* Miami University (B.A., 1999); The Ohio State University (J.D., 2002). ***PRACTICE AREAS:*** Commercial Real Estate. ***Email:*** cswank@bricker.com

ELIZABETH C. STOCK, born Sao Paulo, Brazil, September 17, 1976; admitted to bar, 2002, Ohio; 2003, U.S. District Court, Southern District of Ohio. *Education:* Miami University (B.A., 1998); The Ohio State University (J.D., 2002). ***LANGUAGES:*** Portuguese. ***PRACTICE AREAS:*** Labor and Employment; Litigation. ***Email:*** estock@bricker.com

NATALIE C. TRISHMAN, born Columbus, Ohio, May 20, 1978; admitted to bar, 2002, Ohio and U.S. District Court, Southern District of Ohio; 2003, U.S. District Court, Northern District of Ohio. *Education:* The Ohio State University (B.A., 1999); Capital University (J.D., summa cum laude, 2002). ***Email:*** ntrishman@bricker.com

SEAN M. McGLONE, born Rochester, New York, September 8, 1974; admitted to bar, 2002, Ohio. *Education:* Wittenberg University (B.A., 1996); The Ohio State University (J.D., 2002). ***PRACTICE AREAS:*** Health Care. ***Email:*** smcglone@bricker.com

JUSTIN W. RISTAU, born Cambridge, Ohio, July 11, 1977; admitted to bar, 2002, Ohio; 2003, U.S. District Court, Southern District of Ohio. *Education:* Hobart College (B.A., 1999); University of Cincinnati (J.D., 2002). ***Email:*** jristau@bricker.com

ROBERT B. HOLODNAK, born Sharon, Pennsylvania, April 8, 1961; admitted to bar, 1989, Ohio and U.S. District Court, Southern District of Ohio. *Education:* Ohio State University (B.A., 1984); Capital University (J.D., 1988; LL.M., Business Law and Taxation, 1995). ***PRACTICE AREAS:*** Tax Exempt Financing; Securities; Commercial Lending; Real Estate; Tax. ***Email:*** rholodnak@bricker.com

PHILLIP H. LEE, born Dayton, Ohio, August 15, 1971; admitted to bar, 2000, California (Not admitted in Ohio). *Education:* Dartmouth College (B.A., 1993; M.S., 1994); University of Michigan (J.D., 1999). ***PRACTICE AREAS:*** Real Estate; Banking; Corporate; Insurance. ***Email:*** phlee@bricker.com

BECKY L. RAMSEYER, born Fairview Park, Ohio, November 14, 1977; admitted to bar, 2003, Ohio; 2004, U.S. District Court, Southern District of Ohio. *Education:* Ohio University (B.S., summa cum laude, 2000); University of Cincinnati (J.D., 2003). ***PRACTICE AREAS:*** Labor and Employment Law; Worker's Compensation. ***Email:*** bramseyer@bricker.com

MAGGIE F. WEBER, born Elizabeth, New Jersey, February 15, 1976; admitted to bar, 2003, Ohio; U.S. District Court, Southern District of Ohio. *Education:* Wittenberg University (B.A. in English, 1997); American University, Washington College of Law (J.D., 2003). ***PRACTICE AREAS:*** General Practice. ***Email:*** mweber@bricker.com

HOPE M. SHARETT, born Youngstown, Ohio, May 11, 1977; admitted to bar, 2003, Ohio. *Education:* Vanderbilt University (B.A., 1999); The Ohio State University (J.D., 2003). ***PRACTICE AREAS:*** Public Law; Bond Finance. ***Email:*** hsharett@bricker.com

JOHN A. ENSIGN, born Huntington, West Virginia, May 10, 1972; admitted to bar, 2003, Ohio. *Education:* Miami University (B.S., 1994); Capital University Law School (J.D., magna cum laude, 2003; LL.M., 2005). ***PRACTICE AREAS:*** Corporate Law; Securities; Mergers and Acquisitions. ***Email:*** jensign@bricker.com

(This Listing Continued)

KEVIN M. KINROSS, born Cincinnati, Ohio, November 25, 1974; admitted to bar, 2000, Ohio; 2001, U.S. District Court, Southern District of Ohio. *Education:* Indiana University (B.S., Finance, 1997); Capital University (J.D., cum laude, 2000). ***PRACTICE AREAS:*** General Practice. ***Email:*** kkinross@bricker.com

STEPHANIE T. GREENE, born Aiken, South Carolina, August 15, 1978; admitted to bar, 2004, New York (Not admitted in Ohio). *Education:* Emory University (B.A., 2000); New York University (J.D., 2003). ***PRACTICE AREAS:*** Real Estate. ***Email:*** sgreene@bricker.com

SEAN A. MENTEL, born Columbus, Ohio, June 23, 1973; admitted to bar, 2004, Ohio. *Education:* Michigan State University (B.A., 1995); Capital University (J.D., magna cum laude, 2004). ***PRACTICE AREAS:*** Government Relations; Real Estate Law; Land Use. ***Email:*** smentel@bricker.com

KARL J. SILVERBERG, born Long Beach, New York, October 22, 1969; admitted to bar, 2003, New Jersey; 2004, New York and Ohio. *Education:* Rensselaer Polytechnic Institute (B.S., 1991); Rutgers University (M.S., Civil Engineering, 1994); St. John's University Law School (J.D., 2003). ***PRACTICE AREAS:*** Construction Law. ***Email:*** ksilverberg@bricker.com

JENNIFER M. NELSON CARNEY, born Landstuhl, Germany, February 8, 1975; admitted to bar, 2004, Ohio. *Education:* The Ohio State University (B.A., 1998; B.S., 1998; J.D., 2004). ***PRACTICE AREAS:*** Health Care.

DOUG L. SHEVELOW, born Steubenville, Ohio, December 28, 1966; admitted to bar, 2004, Ohio. *Education:* The Ohio State University (B.S.C.E., 1990); Capital University (J.D., 2004). ***PRACTICE AREAS:*** Construction Law. ***Email:*** dshevelow@bricker.com

CHRISTOPHER N. SLAGLE, born Livonia, Michigan, October 28, 1971; admitted to bar, 2004, Ohio. *Education:* Miami University (B.A., 1995); Capital University (J.D., 2004). ***Email:*** cslagle@bricker.com

SCOTT W. DAVIS, born Cleveland, Ohio, June 26, 1976; admitted to bar, 2004, Ohio. *Education:* University of Cincinnati (B.S., 1999); The Ohio State University (J.D., 2004). ***PRACTICE AREAS:*** General Practice. ***Email:*** sdavis@bricker.com

MATTHEW A. RICH, born Covington, Kentucky, November 1, 1978; admitted to bar, 2004, Ohio. *Education:* Bellarmine University (B.A., 2000); Cornell University (J.D., 2004). ***Email:*** mrich@bricker.com

CHUAN SUN, born Wuhu, Anhui, P.R. China, January 23, 1973; admitted to bar, 2004, Ohio. *Education:* Peking University (B.A., 1996); Northwestern University School of Law (J.D., 2004). ***Email:*** csun@bricker.com

CHRISTOPHER L. McCLOSKEY, born 1972; admitted to bar, 2000, Ohio; 2002, Florida. *Education:* The Ohio State University (B.S.L.E., 1996); Capital University (J.D., 2000).

CAVETT R. KREPS, born 1977; admitted to bar, 2003, Ohio. *Education:* Miami University (B.A., 1999; B.S., 1999); The Ohio State University (J.D., 2002).

JENNIFER ANN FLINT, born Columbus, Ohio, November 5, 1965; admitted to bar, 1992, Ohio and U.S. District Court, Southern District of Ohio. *Education:* The Ohio State University (B.A., 1988); Capital University (J.D., cum laude, 1992). ***PRACTICE AREAS:*** Education Law; Litigation. ***Email:*** jflint-gonzales@bricker.com

DANE A. GASCHEN, born Harrisburg, Pennsylvania, August 23, 1957; admitted to bar, 1994, Ohio; 1995, U.S. Court of Appeals, Sixth Circuit; 1996, U.S. District Court, Southern District of Ohio; 1998, U.S. Supreme Court; 2004, U.S. District Court, Northern District of Ohio. *Education:* University of Virginia (B.A., with distinction, 1979); University of Michigan (M.B.A., with honors, 1981); The Ohio State University (J.D., 1994). ***PRACTICE AREAS:*** Education Law. ***Email:*** dgaschen@bricker.com

CATHERINE J. BAIRD-VELEY, born Columbus, Ohio, February 27, 1972; admitted to bar, 2004, Ohio. *Education:* The Ohio State University (B.A.); Capital University Law School (J.D., 2004). ***PRACTICE AREAS:*** Real Estate.

SARAH E. HURST, born Wooster, Ohio, January 22, 1973; admitted to bar, 2002, Ohio and U.S. District Court, Southern District of Ohio; 2003, U.S. District Court, Northern District of Ohio. *Education:* Kenyon College (B.A., 1995); The Ohio State University, Moritz College of Law (J.D., 2002). ***PRACTICE AREAS:*** Litigation.

OF COUNSEL

JAMES J. HUGHES, born Columbus, Ohio, September 9, 1936; admitted to bar, 1962, Ohio; 1975, U.S. Supreme Court; 1987, West Virginia. *Education:* University of Notre Dame (A.B., 1959); Georgetown University (J.D., 1962). ***PRACTICE AREAS:*** Health Care; Corporate Law; Health Care Fraud; Health Care Mergers and Acquisitions; Health Care Reimbursement; Integrated Health Care Delivery Systems. ***Email:*** jhughes@bricker.com

THOMAS R. SANT, born Middletown, Ohio, October 7, 1943; admitted to bar, 1973, Ohio; 1974, U.S. District Court, Southern District of Ohio. *Education:* Kenyon College (A.B., 1966); Ohio Northern University (J.D., 1973). ***PRACTICE AREAS:*** Workers' Compensation; Litigation. ***Email:*** tsant@bricker.com

ROBERT H. KATZ, born Washington, Pennsylvania, June 1, 1945; admitted to bar, 1975, Ohio. *Education:* Youngstown State University (B.S.B.A., 1972); The Ohio State University (J.D., 1975). ***PRACTICE AREAS:*** Insurance Regulation; Government Agency; Administrative Law; Corporate Law. ***Email:*** rkatz@bricker.com

KIMBALL H. CAREY, born Columbus, Ohio, August 10, 1952; admitted to bar, 1979, Ohio. *Education:* Wittenberg University (B.A., magna cum laude, 1974); The Ohio State University (J.D., 1979). ***PRACTICE AREAS:*** Education Law. ***Email:*** kcarey@bricker.com

THOMAS J. O'BRIEN, born Danville, Illinois, June 28, 1960; admitted to bar, 1986, Illinois; 1996, Ohio. *Education:* DePauw University (B.A., 1982); Southern Illinois University (J.D., 1986). ***PRACTICE AREAS:*** Energy; Telecommunications; Water. ***Email:*** tobrien@bricker.com

G. SAMUEL WAMPLER, born Troy, Ohio, August 13, 1947; admitted to bar, 1978, California and U.S. District Court, Southern District of California; 2002, Ohio and U.S.

(This Listing Continued)

BRICKER & ECKLER LLP, Columbus—Continued

District Court, Northern and Southern Districts of Ohio. *Education:* Western State University (B.S.L.); The Ohio State University (J.D., with honors, 2001). ***PRACTICE AREAS:*** Construction; Alternative Dispute Resolution. ***Email:*** swampler@bricker.com

RETIRED

BRUCE G. LYNN, born Columbus, Ohio, December 16, 1916; admitted to bar, 1941, Ohio; 1977, U.S. Supreme Court. *Education:* The Ohio State University (B.A., 1938); Harvard University (J.D., 1941). ***Email:*** blynn@bricker.com

RICHARD C. PICKETT, born Columbus, Ohio, January 21, 1926; admitted to bar, 1955, Ohio. *Education:* The Ohio State University (B.S. in B.A., 1948; J.D., 1954). ***Email:*** rpickett@bricker.com

WILLIAM H. LEIGHNER, born Pittsburgh, Pennsylvania, December 8, 1929; admitted to bar, 1958, Ohio. *Education:* Northwestern University (B.S., 1952); University of Michigan (J.D., 1958). ***Email:*** wleighner@bricker.com

JAMES S. MONAHAN, born Akron, Ohio, November 9, 1933; admitted to bar, 1962, Ohio; 1963, U.S. District Court, Southern District of Ohio; 1967, U.S. Court of Appeals, Sixth Circuit; 1972, U.S. Supreme Court. *Education:* University of Akron (B.A., 1956); Case Western Reserve University (J.D., 1962). ***PRACTICE AREAS:*** Medical-Legal Professional Liability; Alternative Dispute Resolution. ***Email:*** jmonahan@bricker.com

ELBERT J. KRAM, born Frankfort, Indiana, March 28, 1941; admitted to bar, 1966, Ohio, U.S. District Court, Southern District of Ohio; 1977, U.S Supreme Court; 1983, U.S. Court of Appeals, Sixth Circuit. *Education:* Indiana University (B.S., 1963); University of Chicago (J.D., 1966); Capital University (LL.M., 1997). ***PRACTICE AREAS:*** Civil Litigation; Construction Law; Eminent Domain; Railroad Law; Alternative Dispute Resolution. ***Email:*** ekram@bricker.com

REPRESENTATIVE CLIENTS: American Insurance Association; Association of Ohio Life Insurance Companies; Bank One Corp.; CEMEX, Inc.; City of Columbus; County of Franklin; Dayton City School District; Dublin City School District; Duke Energy Corporation; Fairfield Medical Center; Fifth Third Bank; General Motors Corporation; Kenyon College; The McGraw-Hill Companies, Inc.; MetLife Auto & Home; Morgan Stanley Dean Witter/Discover Financial Services, Inc.; Nationwide Insurance Enterprise; New Par/Verizon Wireless; Ohio Hospital Association; OhioHealth Corp.; Ohio Manufacturers' Association; PhRMA; The Ohio State University; Turner Construction Company; U.S. Bridge; Von Roll America, Inc.; Westfield Insurance Group; Whirlpool Corporation.

BRICKER & MAXFIELD, L.L.C.

EASTON TOWN CENTER
4100 REGENT STREET, SUITE T
COLUMBUS, OHIO 43219
Telephone: 614-269-4900
Fax: 614-269-4901
URL: http://www.brickermaxfield.com

Labor and Employment, Workers Compensation Defense, OSHA, Products Liability, Intentional Torts.

MEMBERS OF FIRM

DOUGLAS M. BRICKER, born Cincinnati, Ohio, April 1, 1942; admitted to bar, 1969, Ohio. *Education:* Eastern Kentucky University (B.A., 1964); University of Kentucky (M.S., L.S., 1966; J.D., 1969). Order of the Coif. Editor in Chief, Kentucky Law Journal, 1969. *Member:* Columbus and Ohio State Bar Associations; Central Ohio Self Insured Association; International Association of Defense Counsel. ***PRACTICE AREAS:*** Workers' Compensation; OSHA; Litigation. ***Email:*** dbricker@brickermaxfield.com

MICHAEL L. MAXFIELD, born Cincinnati, Ohio, January 24, 1959; admitted to bar, 1984, Ohio and U.S. District Court, Southern District of Ohio. *Education:* The Ohio State University (B.S., Architecture, 1981); University of Toledo (J.D., 1984). *Member:* Columbus (Member, Committees on: Workers' Compensation; Product Liability; Negligence; Personal Injury) and Ohio State Bar Associations; Central Ohio Self Insured Association; Defense Research Institute. ***PRACTICE AREAS:*** Workers' Compensation; Product Liability. ***Email:*** mmaxfield@brickermaxfield.com

ASSOCIATE

SHANE M. DAWSON, born Huron, Ohio, May 10, 1970; admitted to bar, 1996, Ohio; 1999, U.S. District Court, Southern and Northern Districts of Ohio. *Education:* The Ohio State University (B.S., 1992); Capital University Law School (J.D., 1996). *Member:* Columbus (Member, Labor and Employment; Workers' Compensation Committees), Delaware County and Ohio State Bar Associations. ***PRACTICE AREAS:*** Workers' Compensation Defense; Labor and Employment Litigation. ***Email:*** sdawson@brickermaxfield.com

BRISCOE & WEBBER

500 SOUTH FRONT STREET, SUITE 125
COLUMBUS, OHIO 43215
Telephone: 614-224-4149
Fax: 614-224-0738
URL: http://www.briscoelaw.com

Family Law, Divorce, Child Custody, Child Support, Child Support Mediation, Visitation Rights, Premarital Agreements.

COLLEEN H. BRISCOE, born Steubenville, Ohio, February 21, 1952; admitted to bar, 1977, Ohio; 1980, U.S. District Court, Southern District of Ohio. *Education:* Miami University (B.A., 1974); Capital University (J.D., 1977). Office of the Franklin County Prosecuting Attorney, Franklin County, 1975-1977. Referee, Domestic Relations Court, 1977-1981. Former Member, Ohio Supreme Court Joint Task Force on Gender Bias; Former Member, Ohio Child Support Task Force; Mayor, New Albany, 1996—. *Member:* Columbus (Board of Governors), Ohio State (Member, Family Law Section) and American Bar Associations. ***PRACTICE AREAS:*** Family Law; Children.

(This Listing Continued)

MARCI L. WEBBER, born Columbus, Ohio, June 18, 1970; admitted to bar, 1997, Ohio and U.S. District Court, Southern District of Ohio. *Education:* The Ohio State University (B.S.B.A., 1992); Capital University (J.D., 1997). Phi Delta Phi; Order of the Curia. *Member:* Columbus, Ohio State and American (Member, Sections on: Family Law; Labor and Employment Law) Bar Associations. ***PRACTICE AREAS:*** Domestic Relations; Family Law; Employment Law; Real Estate; Litigation.

C. WILLIAM BROWNFIELD & ASSOCIATES

Established in 1972
2661CHARING ROAD
COLUMBUS, OHIO 43221
Telephone: 614-464-2201
Fax: 614-486-6492
Email: brownfieldlaw@msn.com
Email: brownfieldlaw@usa.net
URL: http://www.brownfieldlawfirm.com

Business Litigation, Securities Litigation and Arbitration, Corporate Law, International Business Law.

FIRM PROFILE: Mr. Brownfield concentrates on complex litigation, including trials, arbitrations, and appeals, related to claims in professional/business malpractice, fraud claims and defenses, securities litigation and arbitration, business litigation, injunction actions, and SEC enforcement action defenses.

C. WILLIAM BROWNFIELD, born Columbus, Ohio, March 30, 1941; admitted to bar, 1971, Ohio; 1972, U.S. District Court, Southern District of Ohio; 1974, U.S. Court of Appeals, Sixth Circuit; 1975, U.S. Supreme Court; 1980, U.S. District Court, Northern District of Ohio; 1981, District of Columbia and U.S. Court of Appeals, First Circuit. *Education:* Miami University (B.A., in Economics, 1964); The National Law Center, George Washington University (J.D., cum laude, 1971). Phi Delta Phi. Member, Moot Court Honor Board. Editor-in-Chief, 5 Journal of International Law and Economics, 1971. Author: Note, "Who Represents the Interests of the Shareholder in an International Corporation? Belgium v. Spain," 5 Journal of International Law and Economics 239, National Law Center, George Washington University. Assistant Prosecuting Attorney, Franklin County, Ohio, 1971-1973. Member, Ohio Elections Commission, 1976. Special Counsel to the Attorney General of the State of Ohio. Member, Advisory Committee on Local Federal Rules, U.S. District Court, Southern District of Ohio, 1990-2003. Special Master, U.S. District Court, Southern District of Ohio. *Sustaining Member:* Columbus, Ohio State (Member, Federal Courts and Practice Committee) and American (Member, Sections on: International Law; Corporation, Banking and Business Law) Bar Associations; Ohio Academy of Trial Lawyers (Chairman, Commercial Litigation Section, 1974-1976); The Association of Trial Lawyers of America; American Society of International Law; American Inns of Court (Master Lawyer, Central Ohio Chapter). ***LANGUAGES:*** Spanish. ***PRACTICE AREAS:*** Business Litigation; Securities Litigation and Arbitration; SEC Defense; Corporate Law; International Business Law.

BROWNING & MEYER CO., LPA

Established in 1985
8101 NORTH HIGH STREET, SUITE 370
COLUMBUS, OHIO 43235
Telephone: 614-471-0085
Fax: 614-430-8132
URL: http://www.elderlaw.us
URL: http://www.lawyers.com/bmslaw

Elder Law, Estate Planning, Administration and Litigation, Trusts and Estates, Wills and Probate, Medicare and Medicaid, Medicaid Hearings, Guardianship and Conservatorship, Asset Protection, Charitable Giving, Estate and Gift Taxation, Family Business Succession Planning, Small Business Planning, Taxation.

WILLIAM J. BROWNING, born Columbus, Ohio, April 26, 1957; admitted to bar, 1983, Ohio; 1984, U.S. District Court, Southern District of Ohio; 1985, U.S. Tax Court; 1996, U.S. Court of Appeals, Sixth Circuit. *Education:* Capital University (B.A., 1979; J.D., 1983). Author: "Impact of Retirement Plans on Medical Eligibility," Estate Planning Magazine, November 1992; "Medicaid Treatment of Retirement Plans Revisited," NAELA Quarterly, Spring 1995; "Trusts and the Young Case, Planning for Disabled Beneficiaries," Ohio Lawyer, Nov. 1997; USA Today Counterpoint, July 7, 2003. *Member:* Columbus and Ohio State (Former Chair: Disability Law Committee; Elder Law Committee)Bar Associations ; National Elder Law Foundation (Certified Elder Law Attorney). Fellow, National Academy of Elder Law Attorneys (Past-President). ***REPORTED CASES:*** Young v. Ohio Department of Human Services, 76 OS 3rd 640 (1996); Kimnach v. Ohio Department of Human Services, 95 OH APP 3rd 640 (1994); Gruber v. Ohio Department of Human Services, 98 OH APP 3rd 72 (1994); Chambers v. Ohio Department of Human Services (1998). ***PRACTICE AREAS:*** Elder Law; Wills; Probate; Estate Planning; Asset Protection; Trusts and Estates; Medicaid Planning; Medicaid Hearings; Wealth Preservation. ***Email:*** wbrowning@elderlaw.us

RICHARD F. MEYER, born Springfield, Ohio, May 15, 1955; admitted to bar, 1980, Ohio, U.S. District Court, Southern District of Ohio and U.S. Court of Appeals, Sixth Circuit. *Education:* Marietta College (B.A., cum laude, 1977); Capital University (J.D., 1980). Member, Ohio State Council Knights of Columbus; Ohio Charity Foundation Knights of Columbus. *Member:* Columbus, Ohio State and American Bar Associations; Columbus Bar Association Foundation; National Academy of Elder Law Attorneys. (Certified Specialist in Estate Planning, Trust and Probate Law, Ohio State Bar Association). ***PRACTICE AREAS:*** Trust Administration; Estate Administration; Guardianship; Estate Planning;

(This Listing Continued)

Wealth Preservation; Asset Protection; Probate Administration; Wills. ***Email:*** rmeyer@elderlaw.us

BUCKINGHAM, DOOLITTLE & BURROUGHS, LLP

Established in 1989

191 WEST NATIONWIDE BOULEVARD

COLUMBUS, OHIO 43215-3506

Telephone: 614-221-8448; Toll Free: 1-888-686-2825

Fax: 614-221-8590

Email: bdb@bdblaw.com

URL: http://www.bdblaw.com

Akron, Ohio Office: 50 South Main Street, P.O. Box 1500, 44309-1500. Telephone: 330-376-5300. Toll Free: 800-686-2825. Fax: 330-258-6559.

Canton, Ohio Office: 4518 Fulton Drive Northwest, P.O. Box 35548, 44735-5548. Telephone: 330-492-8717. Toll Free: 800-811-2825. Fax: 330-492-9625.

Cleveland, Ohio Office: 1375 East Ninth Street, Suite 1700, 44114. Telephone: 216-621-5300. Toll Free: 888-843-2825. Fax: 216-621-5440.

Boca Raton, Florida Office: 2500 North Military Trail, Suite 480, 33431. Telephone: 561-241-0414. Toll Free: 800-682-2825. Fax: 561-241-9766.

Appellate, Closely Held Companies, Commercial Law and Litigation, Computer and Technology, Construction Law, Copyrights, Corporate and Business, Creditors Rights/Bankruptcy, Criminal Law, Employment Law, Environmental, Estate Planning, Family Law, Finance and Public Law, Franchise, Health Care, Immigration Law, Insurance Defense, Intellectual Property, Labor and Employment, Land Use and Zoning, Medical Malpractice Defense, Mergers and Acquisitions, Patents, Probate, Publicly Held Companies, Real Estate, School Law, Securities, Succession Planning, Taxation and Employee Benefits, Toxic Tort/Complex Litigation, Trademarks/Service Marks, Trade Secrets, Trial, Trusts and Estates, Venture Capital/Emerging Companies, Workers' Compensation.

FIRM PROFILE: Established in 1913, Buckingham, Doolittle & Burroughs, LLP is a full-service law firm with offices in Akron, Cleveland, Canton and Columbus, Ohio and Boca Raton, Florida. Its attorneys represent clients from the sole proprietor to multinational corporations, tax-exempt organizations, governmental bodies, charities, foundations and public organizations.

The focus of the Firm's corporate practice is on legal issues affecting closely held businesses including start-up joint ventures, agreements among shareholders, corporate reorganization and business contracts. Buckingham attorneys have expertise in mergers and acquisitions, intellectual property, succession planning and related areas of significance to rapidly expanding business organizations and also provide trusts and estates and probate services to individual clients.

The Litigation Practice of Buckingham, Doolittle & Burroughs, LLP has steadily grown to meet the increasingly complex legal demands of the Firm's clients. Areas of focus include appellate, commercial law and litigation, construction, domestic relations, employment, school law, medical malpractice and workers' compensation. The Firm is committed to finding innovative solutions to clients' legal problems. The breadth of its practice in all forums often enables the Firm to avoid disputes by providing legal guidance before problems arise.

Buckingham's clients are representative of virtually every industry and trade, including transportation, food production, chemical manufacturing and distribution, rubber and tire manufacturing, technology, automotive, steel, agriculture and horticulture, financial and banking, insurance and medical, accounting and other professional practices.

MANAGING PARTNER

DONALD B. LEACH, JR., born Ohio, August 9, 1954; admitted to bar, 1982, Ohio; U.S. District Court, Southern District of Ohio. *Education:* Union College (B.A., cum laude, 1976); The Ohio State University College of Law (J.D., 1982). Member and Past President, Builders Exchange of Central Ohio. Listed in The Best Lawyers in America, 2003-2006. Listed in Chambers USA America's Leading Business Lawyers 2002-2005 Editions (Construction). Listed in Ohio's Super Lawyers, 2004-2005 (Construction and Top 50 Lawyers in Columbus (2004)). Member: Associated General Contractors; Associated Builders and Contractors. Professional Member, Ohio Structural Steel & Architectural Metals Association. Member, The Million Dollar Advocates Forum; Member and Vice-Chair, American Arbitration Association Construction Advisory Council. Chair, Upper Arlington Parks & Recreation Advisory Board. Member, Upper Arlington Area Chamber of Commerce Board of Trustees. Treasurer, Columbus and Upper Arlington School Levy Campaign Committees. *Member:* Columbus (Member and Past Chair, Construction Law Committee and Real Property Institute), Ohio State (Member: Construction Law Committee; Real Property Section; Council of Delegates, District 7) and American (Member: Forum on the Construction Industry, Past Member, Division 2 Steering Committee; Real Property Section) Bar Associations. Columbus Bar Association. ***REPORTED CASES:*** Sherman R. Smoot Co. v. Ohio Dept. Adm. Serv (2000), 136 Ohio App.3d 166; Cleveland Construction Inc v. Ohio Dept. Adm. Serv. (1997), 121 Ohio App.3d 372. ***PRACTICE AREAS:*** Construction Law; Real Estate; Commercial Law. ***Email:*** dleach@bdblaw.com

SHAREHOLDERS

DONALD A. ANTRIM, born Philadelphia, Pennsylvania, June 13, 1947; admitted to bar, 1974, Ohio; 1977, U.S. Supreme Court and U.S. District Court, Northern and Southern Districts of Ohio; U.S. Circuit Court of Appeals, Fifth and Sixth Circuits. *Education:* Pennsylvania State University (B.A., 1969); The Ohio State University (M.A., 1971); Capital University (J.D., 1974). Listed in The Best Lawyers in America, 1991 through 2006. Recognized as one of Ohio's Super Lawyers in the 2004 and 2005 Cincinnati Magazine, as voted by his peers. Lecturer: "An Overview of Health Care Regulations and Managed Care" (Weatherhead School of Business, Case Western Reserve University); "The Regulation of Healthcare" (Columbus Bar Association Bed Rock Series); "Managed Care and Provider Contracting" (The Ohio State University, College of Medicine); "Professional Employment Agreements and Provider Contracting" (The Ohio State University, College of Optometry); "Specialty Hospitals After the Moratorium: Where Are We Now" (Professional Education Systems); "Retaliation Suits - What Do I Do" (Medical Group Management Association); "Update: Nursing Home Litigation" (Ohio Healthcare Association); "HIPAA: Privacy Rule Compliance" (Practice Management University; Ohio Optometric Association); "Legal Issues in Eye Care" (Columbus Ophthalmology Associates, LLC - Annual Seminar on Eyecare); "Antitrust and The Regulation of Health Care" (National Business Institute); "Health Care Corporate Compliance Programs in Ohio" (Lorman Education Services). Author: "Giving In America" A Study of Charitable Giving (Ohio Attorney General's Report to Congress). Member: Ohio Optometric Foundation; Trout Unlimited; Mad River Steering Committee; Central Ohio Fly Fishers. *Member:* Columbus (Former Chair, Health Care Law Committee), Ohio State (Health Care Law Committee, Licensure Subcommittee) and American Bar Associations; American Lawyers Association; American Health Lawyers Association. ***PRACTICE AREAS:*** Health Care Corporate Law; Managed Care; Nursing Home Regulation. ***Email:*** dantrim@bdblaw.com

THOMAS J. BONASERA, born Warren, Ohio, June 14, 1948; admitted to bar, 1975, Ohio. *Education:* Ohio State University (B.S., 1970); Capital University (J.D., 1975). Order of the Curia. Recipient, Capital University Law School Alumni Association Professionalism Award, 1996. Speaker and Regular Guest, "You and the Law" series, WOSU Radio. Board Member: American Red Cross of Greater Columbus; Franklin County Alcohol, Drug Addiction & Mental Health Services Board (ADAMH); Legal Aid Society of Columbus; Alzheimer's Association of Central Ohio. Officer and Board Member, Ronald McDonald House Charities of Columbus, Inc. Past Board Member and Past Chair, Board of Trustees, St. Vincent Family Centers. Past Board Member, Ohio Bar Liability Insurance Co., 1998-2000. Member, Panel of Arbitrators: National Association of Securities Dealers; American Arbitration Association. Past Special Magistrate, Franklin County Probate Court, Mental Illness and Mental Patient Cases. *Member:* Columbus (President, 1993-1994; Pas Chair, Probate Court Committee and Member, 1980-1993, Securities Law Committee; Member: Board of Governors, 1986-1995; Professionalism Committee), Ohio State (District 7 Delegate, 1988—; Member: Elder Law Committee; Board of Governors, Proabte and Trust Law Section, 1997-2000; Board Member, Estate Planning, Trust and Probate Section, 1997-2001; Member, 1996-1998, President-Elect, 1998-1999 and President, 1999-2000, Board of Governors) and American (Law School Accreditation Site Evaluation Team Member) Bar Associations; Ohio Academy of Trial Lawyers; Franklin County Trial Lawyers Association. Fellow: Columbus Bar Foundation; Ohio State Bar Foundation; American College of Trust and Estate Counsel. ***Email:*** tbonasera@bdblaw.com

JAN E. HENSEL, born Kent, Ohio, April 5, 1961; admitted to bar, 1988, Ohio; U.S. District Court, Southern District of Ohio; U.S. District Court, Northern District of Ohio and U.S. Court of Appeals, Sixth Circuit. *Education:* The Ohio State University (B.A., 1983; J.D., with honors, 1988). Author: "Supreme Court Rules on 'Constructive Discharge'" Employment Law Supplement to Ohio Lawyer's Weekly, July 19, 2004; "U.S. Supreme Court Narrows, OSC Expands Age Bias Claims," Ohio Lawyer's Weekly, May 2004. Named "Attorney of the Year" 1999 by Ohio Lawyer's Weekly. Accepted as life member of the National Registry of Who's Who, published in the 2000 Edition. Board Member, The Interprofessional Commission of Ohio. *Member:* American Bar Association (Member, Labor and Employment Law Section); Ohio State Bar Association (Member, Labor and Employment Law Section); Columbus Bar Association (Member, Labor and Employment Law Section). Fellow, Columbus Bar Foundation. ***PRACTICE AREAS:*** Employment Law. ***Email:*** JHensel@bdblaw.com

RICHARD A. HERNANDEZ, born Youngstown, Ohio, June 6, 1961; admitted to bar, 1986, Ohio; 1988, Florida. *Education:* The Ohio State University (B.A., 1983); Capital University Law School (J.D., 1986). *Member:* Columbus, Ohio State (Workers' Compensation Specialist) and American Bar Associations; The Florida Bar. ***PRACTICE AREAS:*** Workers Compensation. ***Email:*** RHernandez@bdblaw.com

THOMAS W. HESS, born Portsmouth, Ohio, March 13, 1951; admitted to bar, 1976, Ohio; 1980, U.S. Supreme Court; U.S. Court of Appeals, Sixth Circuit; U.S. District Court, Northern and Southern Districts of Ohio. *Education:* Ohio University (B.S., Ed., cum laude, 1973); Capital University (J.D., 1976). Member, Editorial Advisory Board, Health Law Journal of Ohio, 1989-1995. Listed in: "The Best Lawyers in America," 1995-2006; "Ohio Super Lawyers," 2004-2005. Speaker: "Confidentiality of Medical Records," Lorman Education Services; "How to Survive the Nursing Home Survey Process," Autumn Enterprises; "Conducting Abuse/Neglect Investigations," Ohio Health Care Association; "What to do in a Medicaid Audit," Ohio Association of Medical Equipment Services; "Nursing Home Litigation - Case Management from Investigation to Trial," National Business Institute; "Nursing Home Litigation Update," Ohio Health Care Association; "Nursing Home Survey Process," Autumn Enterprises; "Fraud & Abuse Update," Ohio Health Care Association; "Nursing Home Negligence Seminar," Professional Education Systems; "Liability Insurance and Nursing," National Business Institute; "DNR: Your Questions Answered," Ohio Health Care Association; "Quality Assurance: Protecting Your Quality," Ohio Health Care Association; "The Role of Accounting Firms in Nursing Home Representation," The Leading Edge Symposium; "Top Ten Items Not to Release to Nursing Home Surveyors," Ohio Health Care Association; "Nursing Home Malpractice in Ohio: Successful Case Management from Investigation to Trial," National Business Institute, "Conducting Abuse/Neglect Investigations (AOPHA). *Member:* Columbus, Ohio State and American Bar Associations; American Health Lawyers Association. ***SPECIAL AGENCIES:*** Member, Ohio Board of Examiners of Nursing Home Administrators. ***PRACTICE AREAS:*** Health Law; Administrative Law. ***Email:*** THess@bdblaw.com

BRETT L. MILLER, born Cambridge, Ohio, January 10, 1956; admitted to bar, 1981, Ohio. *Education:* Miami University (A.B., 1978); The Ohio State University (J.D., 1981). Phi Alpha Delta. Listed in The Best Lawyers in America, 2003-2004, 2005-2006. Recognized as one of Ohio's Super Lawyers in the 2004 and 2005 Cincinnati Magazine, as voted by his peers. Workers' Compensation Trustee, Builders Exchange of Central Ohio. Member, Steering Committee, Stefanie's Champions. *Member:* Columbus, Ohio State and American Bar Associations. (Certified Specialist in Workers' Compensation Law, Ohio State Bar Association). ***PRACTICE AREAS:*** Workers Compensation; Labor and Employment. ***Email:*** BMiller@bdblaw.com

ANDREW W. OWEN, born York, Pennsylvania, January 25, 1967; admitted to bar, 1992, Ohio; U.S. District Court, Northern and Southern Districts of Ohio; U.S. Court of

(This Listing Continued)

BUCKINGHAM, DOOLITTLE & BURROUGHS, LLP, Columbus—Continued

Appeals, 6th Circuit. *Education:* University of Virginia (B.A., 1989); George Washington University (J.D., 1992). Articles Editor, The George Washington University Law Review. Author: "Note, Toward a New Functional Methodology in Appointments Clause Analysis," 60 George Washington Law Review 536, 1992. *Member:* Ohio Association of Civil Trial Attorneys; Defense Research Institute; Ohio State Bar Foundation. ***PRACTICE AREAS:*** Litigation; Bankruptcy Chapter 11; Bank Foreclosures; Commercial Real Estate Foreclosure. ***Email:*** AOwen@bdblaw.com

BRENT D. ROSENTHAL, born Columbus, Ohio, March 15, 1955; admitted to bar, 1984, Ohio and U.S. District Court, Southern District of Ohio. *Education:* The Ohio State University (B.A., 1977; M.C.R.P., 1980; J.D., with honors, 1984). Order of the Coif. Assistant District Governor, Rotary International District 6690. Co-Chair, Foundation Committee, Rotary District 6690. Past President, 2001-2002 and Committee Chair, Board of Directors, The Rotary Club of Westerville. Vice President and Member, Board of Trustees, Westerville Area Chamber of Commerce, 1995-1998. Member and Chair, Board of Zoning Appeals, City of Westerville, 1988-1996. Member, Westerville Zoning Code Review Commission, 1990-1994. Trustee, Lost and Found Ministries, Columbus, Ohio, 1995-1997. Recipient: President's Awards, Westerville Area Chamber of Commerce; Westerville Rotary Club; Commendations, Westerville City Council. Member and Former Deacon, 1985-2000, Christian Assembly Church, Columbus, Ohio. Speaker, "Drafting Operating Agreements with Business Succession in Mind" (NBI Seminar). *Member:* Columbus (Member and Chair, Real Property Law Committee), Ohio State (Member, Former District 7 Representative - Real Property Law Section Board of Governors) and American (Member: Real Property Probate and Trust Committee; Business Law Committee) Bar Associations. (Certified Specialist in Business, Commercial and Industrial Real Property Law, Ohio State Bar Association). ***LANGUAGES:*** French. ***PRACTICE AREAS:*** Business Law; Business Transactions; Commercial Real Estate; Contracts; Commercial Law; Franchises and Franchising; Zoning, Planning and Land Use. ***Email:*** BRosenthal@bdblaw.com

THOMAS J. SIGMUND, born Cleveland, Ohio, 1954; admitted to bar, 1978, Ohio, U.S. Tax Court and U.S. District Court, Southern District of Ohio. *Education:* The Ohio State University (B.A., cum laude, 1975; J.D., 1978). Listed Best Lawyers in America (1997 through 2006). Recognized as one of Ohio's Super Lawyers in 2004 Cincinnati Magazine, as voted by his peers. Member, The Columbus Foundation, Legal Advisory Committee. Adjunct Professor, Executive Compensation, LL.M. Program, Capital Law School. Member, Board of Directors: Columbus Chapter, The Society of Financial Service Professionals; Ohio Reads Program. Chairman, Columbus Estate Planning Council II. Member, Governing Board, ATHENA PowerLink. *Member:* American, Ohio State and Columbus Bar Associations. Columbus Bar Foundation. ***PRACTICE AREAS:*** Estate Planning; ERISA. ***Email:*** tsigmund@bdblaw.com

CHARLES E. TICKNOR, III, born Mansfield, Ohio, January 28, 1963; admitted to bar, 1989, Ohio. *Education:* Ohio State University (B.A., 1986; J.D., 1989). *Member:* Columbus and Ohio State Bar Associations. ***Email:*** cticknor@bdblaw.com

MICHAEL L. WILLIAMS, born Mt. Clemens, Michigan, September 21, 1967; admitted to bar, 1992, Ohio and U.S. District Court, Northern District of Ohio. *Education:* Capital University (B.A., magna cum laude, 1989); The Ohio State University College of Law (J.D., 1992). *Member:* Columbus, Ohio State (Workers' Compensation Specialist) and American Bar Associations; Central Ohio Self Insured Association. ***PRACTICE AREAS:*** Workers Compensation; Litigation. ***Email:*** MWilliams@bdblaw.com

PARTNERS

DAVID M. ABROMOWITZ, admitted to bar, 1990, Ohio; 1992, U.S. District Court, Southern District of Ohio. *Education:* Washington & Jefferson College (B.A., with honors, 1987); University of Dayton (J.D., 1990). Speaker: "Legal Considerations and Contract Negotiations," Ohio State University, October 18, 2002; "Protecting Physician Assets in Medical Malpractice Litigation," Principle Financial Group, October 9, 2001; "Legal Considerations and Contract Negotiations," Ohio State University, October 18, 2000; "Legal Considerations and Contract Negotiations," Ohio State University, March 31, 1999; "Medicare/Medicaid Legal Issues and Other Responsibilities," St. Elizabeth Health Center, January 26, 1999; "Protecting Physician Assets in Medical Malpractice Litigation," Principle Financial Group, October 8, 1998. Member, Columbus Metropolitan Club. Development Board Member, Heinzerling Foundation. Medical Advisory Board Member, HCR Manor Care. *Member:* Columbus, Ohio State and American Bar Associations; American Health Lawyers Association. ***PRACTICE AREAS:*** Health and Medicine; Business Law; Corporate Law. ***Email:*** dabromowitz@bdblaw.com

MICHAEL F. COPLEY, born Columbus, Ohio, January 1, 1960; admitted to bar, 1986, Ohio; 1999, U.S. District Court, Southern District of Ohio; U.S. District Court, Eastern District of Michigan; U.S. Court of Federal Claims. *Education:* Troy State University (B.S., Business Administration, 1982); Capital University (J.D., 1986). Member: Associated Builders and Contractors, National Mold Task Force; Ceilings & Interior Systems Contruction Association, Mold Task Force; Member, Board of Trustees, Ohio Military Hall of Fame Foundation. Member, Board of Trustees and Assistant Tresurer, United Way Young Leadership Group. Lecturer, Builders Exchange of Central Ohio. *Member:* Columbus, Ohio State and American (Member, Forum Construction Industry) Bar Associations. [Lt. Col., Ohio Air National Guard Judge Advocate, 1991—; Active Duty, Air Force 1978-1982; 1986-1991]. ***REPORTED CASES:*** Appeal of Grumman Aerospace, ASBCA Nos. 46834, 480006, 51526 (March 14, 2003). ***PRACTICE AREAS:*** Real Estate Title; Construction Law; Toxic Tort Defense; Business Litigation. ***Email:*** mcopley@bdblaw.com

ROBERT C. PRESTON, born Columbus, Ohio, 1934; admitted to bar, 1958, Ohio; 1990, U.S. Supreme Court, U.S. District Court, Southern District of Ohio and U.S. Tax Court. *Education:* The Ohio State University (B.S., 1956; J.D., 1958). *Member:* Columbus and Ohio State Bar Associations; American Health Lawyers Association. ***PRACTICE AREAS:*** Business; Health Care; Estates and Trust. ***Email:*** rpreston@bdblaw.com

SUSAN G. SHERIDAN, born Niles, Michigan, April 21, 1964; admitted to bar, 1989, Ohio and U.S. District Court, Southern District of Ohio. *Education:* The Ohio State University (B.A., with honors, 1986; J.D., 1989). Author, "Judicial Participation in Settlement: Pattern, Practice and Ethics," 4 Ohio St. J. Dis. 81, 1988. *Member:* Columbus and Ohio State Bar Associations. ***PRACTICE AREAS:*** Business Law; Finance; Public Law; Securities Law; Real Estate. ***Email:*** SSheridan@bdblaw.com

OF COUNSEL

KENNETH A. FISHER, JR., born Lima, Ohio, June 23, 1966; admitted to bar, 1995, Ohio; 1997, U.S. District Court, Southern District of Ohio and U.S. Court of Appeals, Sixth Circuit. *Education:* The Ohio State University (B.S., Architecture, 1990); Capital University Law School (J.D., 1995). Order of the Curia. Recipient: American Jurisprudence Award for Business Associations; Harter Award for Academic Achievement; Student Bar Association's Student Service Award. Published Member, Capital University Law Review. Registered Architect, Ohio, 1995. *Member:* Columbus, Ohio State and American Bar Associations. ***PRACTICE AREAS:*** Construction Law. ***Email:*** kfisher@bdblaw.com

MICHAEL A. RENNE, born St. Louis, Missouri, January 17, 1962; admitted to bar, 1987, Ohio. *Education:* Kenyon College (B.A., magna cum laude, 1984); Case Western Reserve University (J.D., cum laude, 1987). Law Clerk to Justice Herbert Brown, Ohio Supreme Court, 1988-1989. Trustee, New Life Nurse-Midwifery Care.*Member:* Ohio State Bar Association. ***Email:*** mrenne@bdblaw.com

ASSOCIATES

PRIYA J. BATHIJA, admitted to bar, 2004, Ohio. *Education:* The Ohio State University (B.S.B.A., Finance and Economics, 2001; J.D., 2004). Delta Theta Phi; Delta Phi Epsilon. Editor, Buckingham, Doolittle & Burroughs, LLP, Health and Medicine Reporter. *Member:* Columbus, Ohio State and American Bar Associations. ***PRACTICE AREAS:*** Health Law; Medical Law. ***Email:*** pbathija@bdblaw.com

MICHAEL D. BONASERA, born Columbus, Ohio, December 12, 1975; admitted to bar, 2003, Ohio. *Education:* Ohio University (B.S., 1998); Capital University (J.D., 2002). Member, National Mock Trial Team, 2002. Lecturer, eBusiness and Emerging Technologies Law. *Member:* Columbus (Member: Ethics and Professionalism Committee; Probate Committee; Technology Law Committee), Ohio State and American Bar Associations; Franklin County Trial Lawyers Association. ***Email:*** mbonasera@bdblaw.com

JANICE E. CASANOVA, born 1973; admitted to bar, 2002, Ohio; U.S. District Court, Southern District of Ohio. *Education:* Wake Forest University (B.S., 1996); The Ohio State University (J.D., 2002). Judicial Law Clerk, Tenth Circuit Court of Appeals, Franklin County, Ohio. *Member:* Columbus and Ohio State Bar Associations. ***PRACTICE AREAS:*** Construction Law; Real Estate. ***Email:*** jcasanova@bdblaw.com

KIMBERLY COCROFT, born Columbus, Ohio, March 1, 1973; admitted to bar, 2000, Ohio 2003, U.S. District Court, Southern District of Ohio. *Education:* The Ohio State University (B.A. in Psychology, 1995; M.A. in Sports Management, 1997); The Ohio State University Moritz College of Law, Columbus, Ohio (J.D., 2000). Member, Barrister Leaders Program. State Judicial Assistant and Coordinator, Buckeye Girls. Director, The Education Ministry for Triedstone Missionary Baptist Church. Associate Justice, Moot Court Governing Board. President, Black Law Students Association. Assistant Director, Appellate Advocacy Council. Recipient: Outstanding Senior Finalist; Athena Award for Leadership Among Women; Achievement Award for Campus and Community Participation. *Member:* Columbus, Ohio State and American Bar Associations. ***PRACTICE AREAS:*** Litigation; Labor and Employment. ***Email:*** kcocroft@bdblaw.com

JOSEPH E. EZZIE, born Canton, Ohio, 1977; admitted to bar, 2002, Ohio; 2003, U.S. District Court, Northern District of Ohio; U.S. District Court, Southern District of Ohio and U.S. Court of Appeals, Sixth Circuit. *Education:* Miami University (B.S., Business Economics, cum laude); The Ohio State University, Moritz College of Law (J.D., cum laude, with honors). Member, Franklin American Inn of Court; Board Member, City Year Service Alliance. *Member:* Columbus, Ohio State and American Bar Associations. ***PRACTICE AREAS:*** Litigation; Commercial Litigation; Patent Litigation; Civil Defense. ***Email:*** jezzie@bdblaw.com

PETER W. HAHN, born Michigan, April 26, 1973; admitted to bar, 1998, Ohio; 1999, District of Columbia and U.S. District Court, Southern District of Ohio; 2003, U.S. District Court, Northern District of Ohio; U.S. Court of Appeals, Sixth Circuit. *Education:* College of Wooster (B.A., with honors, 1995); Washington University, St. Louis (J.D., 1998). Author: "Personal Technology for Lawyers," CBA Briefs (2005); "Long-Term Care Liability for Pressure Ulcers," Journal of the American Geriatrics Society (2005); "Long-Term Care Liability for Pressure Ulcers," Journal of the American Geriatrics Society (2005); "Recognizing the Disability: Extending the (Tenuous) Rights of English Language Deficient Students in the Public Schools," 53 Wash. Univ. J. Urb. and Contemp. L. 271 (1998); "The Effects of Attorney Presentation Style, Attorney Gender, and Juror Gender on Juror Decisions," 20 Law and Human Behavior 533 (1996). Member: Leadership Columbus, Class of 2001-2002; College of Wooster Scots-in Service Leader. Board Member, Kids Voting Central Ohio. *Member:* Columbus (Member, Bar Admission Committee), Ohio State (Member, Legal Ethics & Professional Conduct Committee) and American (Member: Forum Committee on Communications Law; Sections on: Intellectual Property Law; Litigation) Bar Associations. ***PRACTICE AREAS:*** Intellectual Property Licensing; Intellectual Property Litigation; Litigation. ***Email:*** phahn@bdblaw.com

KERRY McCONAGHY MACKIN, admitted to bar, 2002, Ohio. *Education:* Saint Norbert College (B.A., English and Education, cum laude); Capital University Law School (J.D., cum laude, 2002). *Member:* Columbus, Ohio State and American Bar Associations. ***PRACTICE AREAS:*** Workers Compensation. ***Email:*** kmackin@bdblaw.com

FRANK SCHUCKMANN, born Duesseldorf, Germany; admitted to bar, 1997, Ohio; 1998, Pennsylvania. *Education:* University of Akron (B.S., Industrial Management, cum laude, 1993; M.B.A., 1996; J.D., 1996). Member: Columbus Venture Network; German American Chamber of Commerce, New York. *Member:* Columbus, Ohio State and American Bar Associations; American Health Lawyers Association. ***LANGUAGES:*** German. ***PRACTICE AREAS:*** Business Law; Health and Medicine. ***Email:*** fschuckmann@bdblaw.com

REPRESENTATIVE CLIENTS: Columbus Eye Surgery Center; Columbus Public Schools; Columbus Regional Airport Authority; Danis Building Construction Company; Liberty Township; Ohio Association of Medical Equipment Services; Ohio Health Care Association; Ohio

(This Listing Continued)

Optometric Association; Ohio Optometric Foundation; Promo West Pavilion; Smoot Construction Company; Wendy's International.

BUCKLEY KING

A LEGAL PROFESSIONAL ASSOCIATION

ONE COLUMBUS
10 WEST BROAD STREET, SUITE 1300
COLUMBUS, OHIO 43215-3419
Telephone: 614-461-5600
Toll Free: 877-266-6625
Email: bkb-columbus.com
URL: http://www.buckleyking.com

Cleveland, Ohio Office: 1400 Fifth Third Center. Telephone: 216-363-1400. Telecopier: 216-579-1020.

Cincinnati, Ohio Office: 1420 PNC Center, 201 East Fifth Street. Telephone: 513-412-5400. Telecopier: 513-412-5401.

Atlanta, Georgia Office: Suite 1220 Lennox Building, 3399 Peachtree Road. Telephone: 404-816-7791. Telecopier: 404-816-9786.

Corporate, Litigation, Commercial, Estate Planning, Banking, Real Estate, Merger and Acquisition, Appellate, Bankruptcy, Professional and Executive (Directors and Officers) Liability, Insurance Law, Products Liability, Health Care, Hospital Law, Medical Malpractice Defense, Immigration/Naturalization, Toxic and Hazardous Materials, ERISA, Taxation, Environmental, Labor, Public Employment Relations, Employee Benefits. Workers Compensation and NLRB Matters, Patent and Trademark.

FIRM PROFILE: Founded in 1983, Buckley King has established itself as a leading full service business and commercial law firm with offices in Cleveland, Columbus, Cincinnati and Atlanta. The attorneys at Buckley King are dedicated to delivering creative, efficient and precise legal solutions for businesses and individuals.

The Firm's clients include individuals, closely-held businesses, Fortune companies, financial institutions, insurance companies, and governmental entities. Each client is highly-valued, and the preservation of long-standing client relationships is every bit as important to us as fostering new relationships.

Client service is the single most important goal of Buckley King. As a mid-sized firm, Buckley King delivers legal services with the depth, agility and resources necessary for timely and practical legal advice. Individualized attention and interactive communication with our clients is vital to our client relationships.

Because the Firm carefully chooses each of its attorneys, our clients receive the highest quality legal product from a skilled, innovative legal team. Although our attorneys may have different resident offices, Buckley King's success is providing solutions, analysis and advice from a range of complementary practice areas through its practice groups.

We take great pride in our ability to respond immediately to any situation, whether to an emergency court hearing, a critical incident, a client crisis, or to a complex and volatile legal situation requiring thoughtful and effective solutions. Even when our counsel is sought due to urgent, complex, or unique circumstances, we react with clear, focused and strategic advice and options.

When your legal or business needs require insight, clarity, focus and strategic direction, contact us.

We intend to exceed your expectations.

THOMAS I. BLACKBURN, born Columbus, Ohio, May 4; admitted to bar, 1979, Ohio. *Education:* The Ohio State University (B.S., 1972; J.D., with honors, 1979). ***PRACTICE AREAS:*** Insurance Defense Law; Bankruptcy Law; Debt Reorganization; Corporate. ***Email:*** blackburn@bucklaw.com

RICHARD D. BROWN, born Ironton, Ohio, March 18; admitted to bar, 1981, Ohio. *Education:* University of Cincinnati (B.A., summa cum laude, 1978); The Ohio State University (J.D., 1981). ***PRACTICE AREAS:*** Litigation; Insurance Defense Law; Oil and Gas Law. ***Email:*** brown@bucklaw.com

GARY A. GILLETT, born Cincinnati, Ohio, April 4; admitted to bar, 1985, Ohio. *Education:* Vanderbilt University (B.A., magna cum laude, 1982); The Ohio State University (J.D., with honors, 1985). ***PRACTICE AREAS:*** Litigation; Insurance Defense Law. ***Email:*** gillett@bucklaw.com

DONELL R. GRUBBS, born Bellefontaine, Ohio, September 6; admitted to bar, 1986, Ohio. *Education:* Ohio Northern University (B.A., with distinction, 1983); Ohio State University (J.D., 1986). ***PRACTICE AREAS:*** Litigation; Commercial Law; Class Actions; Environmental Law. ***Email:*** don@shaynegreenwald.com

JAMES E. MELLE, born Cleveland, Ohio, October 29; admitted to bar, 1971, Ohio; 1976, U.S. Supreme Court. *Education:* John Carroll University (B.S.B.A., 1967); Cleveland State University (J.D., magna cum laude, 1971). ***PRACTICE AREAS:*** Litigation; Labor Law. ***Email:*** melle@bucklaw.com

ROBERT J. WALTER, born Cleveland, Ohio, September 14; admitted to bar, 1972, Ohio. *Education:* Miami University (B.A., 1969); The Ohio State University (J.D., 1972). ***PRACTICE AREAS:*** Business Law; Labor and Employment; Real Estate. ***Email:*** walter@bucklaw.com

---

PHILIP L. JUDY, born Columbus, Ohio, May 27; admitted to bar, 1997, Ohio. *Education:* Ohio State University (B.F.A., 1988); Capital University (J.D., 1997). ***PRACTICE AREAS:*** Insurance Defense; Personal Injury; Torts; Civil Litigation. ***Email:*** judy@bucklaw.com

(For complete biographical data on all personnel, see Professional Biographies at Cleveland, Ohio)

BURMAN & ROBINSON

Established in 1979

601 SOUTH HIGH STREET
COLUMBUS, OHIO 43215-5695
Telephone: 614-221-8900
Fax: 614-221-8912

Commercial and Business Litigation, Creditors Rights, Collections, Corporate Law, Matrimonial Law.

FIRM PROFILE: For more than two decades Burman & Robinson has provided aggressive, result-oriented representation of middle market and institutional clients. Our practice is statewide in all courts. We successfully combine the cost-effective, personalized advantages of a small firm with the quality, experience, and sophistication of a large one.

MEMBERS OF FIRM

ROBERT N. BURMAN, born Steubenville, Ohio, February 18, 1948; admitted to bar, 1973, Ohio, U.S. District Court, Southern District of Ohio and U.S. Supreme Court. *Education:* Bowling Green State University (B.S., 1970); Capital University Law School (J.D., 1973). Phi Alpha Delta. Member, National Panel of Arbitrators, American Arbitration Association. *Member:* Columbus (Member, Common Pleas Court Committee, 1983—; Municipal Court Committee, 1978—), Ohio State and American Bar Associations. ***PRACTICE AREAS:*** Business and Commercial Litigation; Corporate Planning Law; Business Acquisitions; Construction Law; Matrimonial Law. ***Email:*** rnburman@ameritech.net

RANDAL D. ROBINSON, born Newark, Ohio, April 2, 1949; admitted to bar, 1975, Ohio and U.S. District Court, Southern District of Ohio; 1983, U.S. Court of Appeals, Sixth Circuit. *Education:* Denison University (B.A., 1971); Capital University (J.D., 1975). Listed in: Who's Who in American Law, 11th Edition, 2000. Lecturer, Family Law, Columbus Bar Association Legal Assistants Program, 1980—. Lecturer, Franklin County Trial Lawyers Association, 1985. Instructor, Business Law, Columbus Technical Institute, 1983—. Member, National Panel of Arbitrators, American Arbitration Association. *Member:* Columbus, Ohio State and American Bar Associations; Commercial Law League of America (Member, Creditors Rights Section). Fellow, Columbus Bar Foundation. ***PRACTICE AREAS:*** Business and Commercial Litigation; Creditors Rights; Matrimonial Law. ***Email:*** rrobinsonesq@ameritech.net

CALFEE, HALTER & GRISWOLD LLP

1100 FIFTH THIRD CENTER
21 EAST STATE STREET
COLUMBUS, OHIO 43215-4228
Telephone: 614-621-1500
Telecopier: 614-621-0010
URL: http://www.calfee.com

Cleveland, Ohio Office: 1400 McDonald Investment Center, 800 Superior Avenue. Telephone: 216-622-8200. Telecopier: 216-241-0816.

General Practice and Litigation.

PARTNERS

P. MICHAEL DeANGELO, born Youngstown, Ohio, 1944; admitted to bar, 1969, Ohio. *Education:* John Carroll University (B.A., 1966); Case Western Reserve University (J.D., 1969). Assistant Attorney General, 1971-1975. Deputy Attorney General, 1975-1979. ***PRACTICE AREAS:*** Government Relations; Legislative Practice; Public Law; Public Finance. ***Email:*** pdeangelo@calfee.com

STEVEN C. KARZMER, born Youngstown, Ohio, 1963; admitted to bar, 1989, New York; 1992, Massachusetts; 2001, Ohio. *Education:* The Ohio State University (B.A., with honors, 1985); New York University (J.D., 1988). ***Email:*** skarzmer@calfee.com

ALBERT J. LUCAS, born Cleveland, Ohio, 1959; admitted to bar, 1984, Ohio. *Education:* John Carroll University (B.S.B.A., magna cum laude, 1981); Case Western Reserve University (J.D., 1984). Order of the Coif. ***PRACTICE AREAS:*** Litigation. ***Email:*** alucas@calfee.com

DOUGLAS S. MORGAN, born Youngstown, Ohio, 1956; admitted to bar, 1982, Ohio. *Education:* Harvard University (B.A., cum laude, 1978); The Ohio State University (J.D., with honors, 1982). Order of the Coif. Member, Ohio State Law Journal. *Member:* Columbus, Ohio State and American Bar Associations. ***PRACTICE AREAS:*** Corporate Law; Mergers and Acquisitions; Private Finance; Partnership Law. ***Email:*** dmorgan@calfee.com

THOMAS E. O'CONNOR, JR., born Bellefontaine, Ohio, 1941; admitted to bar, 1967, Ohio and U.S. District Court, Northern and Southern Districts of Ohio; U.S. Court of Appeals, Fifth and Federal Circuits; registered to practice before U.S. Patent and Trade mark Office. *Education:* University of Notre Dame (B.A., 1963; B.S., 1964); University of Michigan (J.D., 1966). Tau Beta Pi. Member, National Engineering Honor Society. Jones, Day, Reavis & Pogue (Associate, 1967-1973; Partner, 1974; Of Counsel, 1986-1987). Judge, Logan County Municipal Court. President, Logan County Bar Association, 1980. *Member:* Columbus and Ohio State Bar Associations; American Intellectual Property Law Association; International Trade Commission Trial Lawyers Associations. ***PRACTICE AREAS:*** Intellectual Property. ***Email:*** toconnor@calfee.com

LEAH PAPPAS, born Barberton, Ohio, 1966; admitted to bar, 1993, Ohio. *Education:* Miami University (B.A., 1988); Capital University School of Law (J.D., 1992). *Member:* Columbus Bar Association. ***PRACTICE AREAS:*** Government Relations; Legislative Practice; College and University Law; Public Law; Public Finance; Partnership Law. ***Email:*** lpappas@calfee.com

KRISTOPHER WAHLERS, born Toledo, Ohio, 1963; admitted to bar, 1991, Ohio. *Education:* University of Georgia (A.B., 1985); University of Michigan (M.A., 1987; J.D.,

(This Listing Continued)

CALFEE, HALTER & GRISWOLD LLP, Columbus—Continued

1990). *Member:* Columbus and Ohio State Bar Associations; National Association of Bond Lawyers; American Health Lawyers Association. ***PRACTICE AREAS:*** Commercial Finance; Public Law; Public Finance. ***Email:*** kwahlers@calfee.com

SENIOR ATTORNEYS

CHRISTOPHER JONES, born Newton, Massachusetts, 1957; admitted to bar, 1990, Ohio; U.S. District Court, Southern District of Ohio and U.S. Court of Appeals, Sixth Circuit. *Education:* Ohio Wesleyan University (B.A., 1979); Georgetown University (J.D., 1990). *Member:* Columbus and Ohio State Bar Associations. ***PRACTICE AREAS:*** Environmental Law; Regulatory Law; Government Relations. ***Email:*** cjones@calfee.com

ERIN E. KARZMER, born Schnectady, New York, 1963; admitted to bar, 1990, New York; 1992, Massachusetts; 2001, Ohio. *Education:* University of Notre Dame (B.S., summa cum laude, 1985); New York University (J.D., 1989). Phi Beta Kappa. ***PRACTICE AREAS:*** Corporate Law; Private Equity; Securities. ***Email:*** ekarzmer@calfee.com

ASSOCIATES

JOAN N. DREW, born Butte, Montana, 1979; admitted to bar, 2001, Ohio; registered to practice before U.S. Patent and Trademark Office. *Education:* Montana College of Mineral Science and Technology (B.S., Chemistry, with honors, 1998); University of Dayton (J.D., summa cum laude, 2001). *Member:* Columbus and American Bar Associations; American Intellectual Property Law Association. ***PRACTICE AREAS:*** Intellectual Property. ***Email:*** jdrew@calfee.com

MARK A. LOSEY, born Bellefontaine, Ohio, 1968; admitted to bar, 1994, Ohio. *Education:* Miami University (B.A., 1990); Case Western Reserve University (J.D., 1994). Delta Theta Phi. Assistant Prosecuting Attorney: Logan County, 1995-1996; Champaign County, 1997. Formerly with Arter & Hadden LLP, 1997-2001. *Member:* American Intellectual Property Law Association; Columbus Intellectual Property Law Association; Columbus Bar Association; Ohio State Bar Association; American Bar Association. ***PRACTICE AREAS:*** Intellectual Property; Business Litigation. ***Email:*** mlosey@calfee.com

WILLIAM J. MICHAEL, born Mt. Clemens, Michigan, 1973; admitted to bar, 1999, Ohio; 2000, U.S. District Court, Northern District of Ohio; 2004, U.S. District Court, Southern District of Ohio. *Education:* Ohio State University (B.A. in Economics, summa cum laude, with honors, 1996); Ohio State University Law School (J.D., 1999). Listed in International Who's Who of Professionals. *Member:* American, Federal, Cleveland, Columbus and Ohio State (Member, Appellate Law Committee) Bar Associations; American Agricultural Law Association. ***PRACTICE AREAS:*** Antitrust and Trade Regulation; Litigation; Agricultural Law; Municipal Law. ***Email:*** wmichael@calfee.com

COURTNEY J. MILLER, born Columbus, Ohio, 1966; admitted to bar, 1999, Ohio. *Education:* College of Wooster (B.A., 1989); Capital University (J.D., 1998; LL.M., 2002). Member, Association of University Technology Managers. *Member:* Columbus, Ohio State and American Bar Associations; American Intellectual Property Law Association; Columbus Intellectual Property Law Association. ***PRACTICE AREAS:*** Information Technology; Intellectual Property. ***Email:*** cmiller@calfee.com

SEAN C. MYERS-PAYNE, born Cincinnati, Ohio, 1967; admitted to bar, 2001, Virginia; 2002, District of Columbia; registered to practice before the U.S. Patent and Trademark Office (Not admitted in Ohio). *Education:* Ohio Wesleyan University (B.A., 1990); University of Cincinnati (Ph.D., 1995); George Mason University (J.D., cum laude, 2001). ***PRACTICE AREAS:*** Patent Law; Intellectual Property. ***Email:*** smyers-payne@calfee.com

DANIEL A. REINHARD, born Bucyrus, Ohio, 1974; admitted to bar, 2002, Ohio. *Education:* The Ohio State University (B.S., 1997); Capital University Law School (J.D., 2001). *Member:* Columbus, Ohio State and American Bar Associations; Ohio State Lobbying Associations. ***PRACTICE AREAS:*** Government Relations and Legislation; Public Utility Law; Government Contracts; Government Procurement; Public Bidding; Gaming Law; Election, Campaign and Political Law; Administrative Lobbying; Campaign Ethics; Election and Campaign Finance; Election Law; Executive Lobbying; Legislative Lobbying; Legislative Redistricting; Lobbying; Government Affairs; Government Ethics; Government Relations; Initiative and Referendum; Legislative Practice; Local Government Relations; State Legislative Practice; Tax Legislation. ***Email:*** dreinhard@calfee.com

PETER A. ROSATO, born Danbury, Connecticut, December 11, 1970; admitted to bar, 1997, Ohio. *Education:* Western Connecticut State University (B.A., magna cum laude, 1993); The Ohio State University College of Law (J.D., with honors, 1997). *Member:* Columbus, Ohio State and American Bar Associations. ***PRACTICE AREAS:*** Commercial Litigation; ERISA; Industrial Injury Defense; Public Utility Law. ***Email:*** prosato@calfee.com

CHRISTOPHER M. WARD, born Canton, Ohio, 1978; admitted to bar, 2003, Ohio; 2004, U.S. District Court, Southern District of Ohio. *Education:* University of Dayton (B.A., summa cum laude, with honors, 2000); The Ohio State University, Moritz College of Law (J.D., 2003). *Member:* Columbus, Ohio State and American Bar Associations. ***PRACTICE AREAS:*** Business Litigation; Commercial Litigation; Environmental Litigation; Civil Litigation; Complex Litigation; Federal Civil Litigation; Federal Litigation; Workers Compensation Defense. ***Email:*** cward@calfee.com

STEPHEN C. WILEY, born Columbus, Ohio, 1960; admitted to bar, 1997, Ohio. *Education:* Otterbein College (B.A., 1984); Capital University Law School (J.D., cum laude, 1997). *Member:* Columbus, Ohio State and American Bar Associations. ***PRACTICE AREAS:*** Corporate Law; Mergers and Acquisitions; Commercial Business; Finance; Real Estate. ***Email:*** swiley@calfee.com

STAFF ATTORNEYS

LORI HANNAN, born Akron, Ohio, 1971; admitted to bar, 1998, Ohio. *Education:* Ohio State University (B.S., Psychology, 1993); Michigan State University College of Law (J.D., cum laude, 1998). *Member:* Columbus, Ohio State and American Bar Associations. ***PRACTICE AREAS:*** Corporate Law; Commercial Law. ***Email:*** lhannan@calfee.com

(This Listing Continued)

ANNE E. WILL, born Columbus, Ohio, 1977; admitted to bar, 2003, Ohio. *Education:* The Ohio State University (B.A., cum laude, with honors, 1999; J.D., 2003). *Member:* Columbus, Ohio State and American Bar Associations. ***PRACTICE AREAS:*** Litigation; Public Law; Public Finance; Finance. ***Email:*** awill@calfee.com

SENIOR COUNSEL

STANLEY J. DOBROWSKI, born Cleveland, Ohio, 1951; admitted to bar, 1976, Ohio; 1982, U.S. District Court, Southern District of Ohio; 1990, U.S. Court of Appeals, Sixth Circuit. *Education:* University of Notre Dame (B.A., 1973); The Ohio State University (J.D., 1976). Assistant Attorney General, 1983-1987. *Member:* Columbus, Ohio State and American Bar Associations; National Association of Bond Lawyers; Ohio Council of School Board Attorneys; American Arbitration Association (Member, Central Ohio Construction Advisory Council); Builders Exchange of Central Ohio Law Group. ***PRACTICE AREAS:*** Construction Law; Public Law; Public Finance. ***Email:*** sdobrowski@calfee.com

OF COUNSEL

RICHARD H. FINAN, born 1934; admitted to bar, 1959, Ohio; 1960, U.S. District Court, Southern District of Ohio; 1961, U.S. District Court, Eastern District of Kentucky; 1968, U.S. Supreme Court. *Education:* University of Dayton (B.S., 1954); University of Cincinnati (J.D., 1959); Xavier University (Honorary Degree, 2000). Member: Anderson Township Business Association; Sharonville, Blue Ash, Reading, Montgomery, Hamilton County, Anderson Township and Sycamore Township Republican Clubs. *Member:* Cincinnati Bar Association. [G-2 Intelligence Division, U.S. Army, 1954-1956]. ***PRACTICE AREAS:*** Government Relations and Legislation. ***Email:*** rfinan@calfee.com

J. TROY TERAKEDIS, born Dennison, Ohio, 1969; admitted to bar, 1996, Ohio. *Education:* Kenyon College (B.A., cum laude, 1991); Case Western Reserve University (M.B.A., 1995; J.D., cum laude, 1995); University of Miami (LL.M., Taxation, 1996). *Member:* Columbus, Ohio State and American Bar Associations; Columbus Estate Planning Council. ***PRACTICE AREAS:*** Tax Law; Estate Planning; Corporate Successions; Corporate Law; Asset Protection; Business Law. ***Email:*** tterakedis@calfee.com

(For Complete Biographical Data on all Personnel, see Professional Biographies at Cleveland, Ohio)

CALIG & HANDELMAN, LPA

854 EAST BROAD STREET
COLUMBUS, OHIO 43205
Telephone: 614-252-4885; 1-800-633-5000
URL: http://www.chohiolawyers.com

Newark, Ohio Office: 29 S. Park Place, 43055. Telephone: 740-349-8581. Fax: 740-345-4101.

Lancaster, Ohio Office: 204 N. Columbus Street, 43130. Telephone: 740-653-4400. Fax: 740-653-0037.

Marion, Ohio Office: 274 S. Main Street, 43302. Telephone: 740-375-5051.

Bankruptcy, Personal Injury, Probate, Real Estate, Social Security, Social Security Disability, Medical Malpractice, Wrongful Death, Civil Litigation, Domestic Relations Law.

SAMUEL L. CALIG, admitted to bar, 1974, Ohio; 1975, Florida. *Education:* The Ohio State University (B.A., 1968); Ohio Northern University (J.D., 1974). *Member:* Ohio State Bar Association. ***LANGUAGES:*** Spanish. ***PRACTICE AREAS:*** Bankruptcy; Personal Injury.

ROBERT B. HANDELMAN, born New York, N.Y., September 1, 1951; admitted to bar, 1976, Ohio; 1978, U.S. District Court, Southern District of Ohio; 1980 U.S. District Court, Northern District of Ohio. *Education:* Franklin & Marshall College (B.A., Government and Philosophy, 1973); Cleveland-Marshall College of Law (J.D., cum laude, 1976). *Member:* Licking County (Co-Chair, Mediation Committee) and Ohio State (Member, Family Law Committee, 1983-1986) Bar Associations; Ohio Academy of Trial Lawyers (Trustee, 1996-1997). ***PRACTICE AREAS:*** Personal Injury; Bankruptcy; Probate; Real Estate; Social Security.

TERRY V. HUMMEL, born Jacksonville, North Carolina, May 23, 1955; admitted to bar, 1982, Ohio and U.S. District Court, Southern and Northern Districts of Ohio. *Education:* Capital University (B.A., 1978; J.D., 1982). ***PRACTICE AREAS:*** Personal Injury; Medical Malpractice; Wrongful Death; Civil Litigation. ***Email:*** terryhummel_law@hotmail.com

KENNETH P. KARLOCK, born Pittsburgh, Pennsylvania, September 21, 1968; admitted to bar, 1993, Ohio. *Education:* Ohio State University (B.A., 1990); Case Western Reserve University (J.D., 1993). *Ohio Academy of Trial Lawyers; Franklin County Trial Lawyers; National Organization of Social Security Claimants Representatives.* ***PRACTICE AREAS:*** Social Security Disability; Personal Injury.

LEE A. THOMPSON, born Cleveland, Ohio, September 14, 1952; admitted to bar, 1983, Ohio and U.S. District Court, Northern District of Ohio. *Education:* Ohio State University; Kent State University (B.S., 1976); University of Akron (J.D., 1983). *Member:* Fairfield County, Ohio State and American Bar Associations; The Association of Trial Lawyers of America; Ohio Trial Lawyers Association. ***PRACTICE AREAS:*** Domestic Relations Law; Personal Injury; Bankruptcy.

CARLILE PATCHEN & MURPHY LLP

Established in 1967

366 EAST BROAD STREET
COLUMBUS, OHIO 43215
Telephone: 614-228-6135
Fax: 614-221-0216
Email: CPM@cpmlaw.com
URL: http://www.cpmlaw.com

Business Law; Corporate; Commercial; Banking; Civil Trial; Appellate Practice; Legislative and Administrative; Real Estate; Zoning, Planning and Land Use; Probate and Estate Planning; Securities; Mergers, Acquisitions and Divestitures; Municipal Bonds and Tax-Exempt

(This Listing Continued)

Financing; Financial Services Regulations; Taxation; Partnership Law; Insurance; Contracts; Construction; Creditor's Rights; Collections; Family Law; Wills; Labor and Employment; Employment Relations; Trademarks; Bankruptcy; Franchising; Intellectual Property; Public Law; International Law; Transportation Regulations; Telecommunications; and Public Utility Regulations.

FIRM PROFILE: Carlile Patchen & Murphy LLP is a full-service law firm with practice groups concentrating in all major areas of the law. Our firm represents a wide range of commercial and financial enterprises, including large corporations and small and medium-size businesses. We also provide legal services to individuals, frequently the owners, managers and employees of our business clients.

MEMBERS OF FIRM

HUNTINGTON CARLILE (1924-1990)

RICHARD V. PATCHEN, born Steubenville, Ohio, August 21, 1935; admitted to bar, 1959, Ohio. *Education:* Franciscan University of Steubenville (B.A., cum laude, 1957); The Ohio State University (J.D., 1959). Member, Editorial Board, Ohio State Law Journal, 1956-1959. Member, 1977-1981 and Chairman, 1980-1981, Board of Bar Examiners, Supreme Court of Ohio. Chairman, Board of Advisors, Capital University Legal Assistant Program, 1984-1989. *Member:* Columbus (Board of Governors, 1986-1990; Counsel, 1992—; Investment Committee, 1990-1999), Ohio State (Fellow) and American Bar Associations. ***PRACTICE AREAS:*** Business Law; Estate Planning; Tax; Real Estate. ***Email:*** RVP@cpmlaw.com

CRAIG M. STEWART, born Coshocton, Ohio, March 25, 1943; admitted to bar, 1967, Ohio. *Education:* The Ohio State University (B.S., 1964; J.D., 1967). Phi Delta Phi (Treasurer, 1966; President, 1967). *Member:* Columbus (Member, Real Property and Bankruptcy Committees, 1972—) and Ohio State (Member, Real Property Section) Bar Associations. [Capt., U.S. Army, 1968-1970]. ***PRACTICE AREAS:*** Commercial Law; Real Estate Law; Creditors Rights Law. ***Email:*** CMS@cpmlaw.com

JAMES R. MOATS, born Lima, Ohio, September 7, 1944; admitted to bar, 1969, Ohio; 1982, U.S. Supreme Court. *Education:* Denison University (B.A., 1966); The Ohio State University (J.D., 1969). Special Agent, Federal Bureau of Investigation, 1969-1973. Panel of Arbitrators, American Arbitration Association. *Member:* Columbus (Member, Business Law, Nonprofit Law and Real Property Committees), Ohio State and American (Member, Business Law) Bar Associations. ***PRACTICE AREAS:*** Business Law; Commercial; Nonprofit Tax Law. ***Email:*** JRM@cpmlaw.com

DENNIS J. CONCILLA, born Erie, Pennsylvania, September 22, 1951; admitted to bar, 1979, Ohio. *Education:* University of Pittsburgh (B.A., 1963); Capital University (J.D., 1979). Assistant Attorney General, 1979-1980. District Director, U.S. Congress, 1980-1982. Legal Counsel, State Senate Majority, 1982-1985. *Member:* Columbus, Ohio State and American Bar Associations; Securities Industry Association, Law and Compliance Division. ***PRACTICE AREAS:*** Broker Dealer Law; Securities Law; Business Litigation. ***Email:*** DJC@cpmlaw.com

CAROL A. SHEEHAN, born Lowell, Massachusetts, January 19, 1953; admitted to bar, 1978, Ohio. *Education:* University of Michigan (B.A., with distinction, 1975); The Ohio State University (J.D., cum laude, 1978). *Member:* Columbus (Member: Real Property and Tax Committee) Ohio State and American (Member, Sections on: Affordable Housing, Corporate, Banking, Taxation and Business Law) Bar Associations. ***PRACTICE AREAS:*** Taxation Law; Corporate Law; Real Estate Law; Affordable Housing Law. ***Email:*** CAS@cpmlaw.com

MICHAEL H. IGOE, born Columbus, Ohio, September l, 1950; admitted to bar, 1975, Ohio; U.S. Supreme Court. *Education:* University of Notre Dame (B.B.A., 1972); University of Toledo (J.D., 1975). Editor, Banks-Baldwin Ohio Revised Code, 1985. Special Counsel: Ohio Attorney General, 1987— City of Columbus, 1998—. Member, Ohio Elections Commission, 1989-1993. *Member:* Columbus (Governmental Agency and Common Pleas Court Committees), Ohio State and American Bar Associations; Ohio Academy of Trial Lawyers; Franklin County Trial Lawyers Association; The Association of Trial Lawyers of America. ***PRACTICE AREAS:*** Litigation; Government Relations; Construction Law. ***Email:*** MHI@cpmlaw.com

ROBERT B. BARNETT, JR., born Cleveland, Ohio, July 24, 1949; admitted to bar, 1975, Ohio. *Education:* The Ohio State University (B.S., 1971; J.D., cum laude, 1975). *Member:* Columbus (Chairman, Taxation Committee, 1984-1985; Chairman, Estate and Gift Tax Section, 1982-1984; Chairman, Columbus Tax Conference, 1986; Chairman, Probate Court Committee, 2001-2003. Member, Estate and Gift Tax and Probate Court Committees, 1979—), Ohio State and American (Member, Sections on: Real Property, Probate and Trust Law) Bar Associations. Fellow, The American College of Trust and Estate Counsel. ***PRACTICE AREAS:*** Family Business Law; Closely Held Business Law; Taxation; Estate Planning; Probate; Employee Benefits. ***Email:*** RBB@cpmlaw.com

BRYAN K. HOGUE, born Danville, Kentucky, February 16, 1959; admitted to bar, 1985, Ohio. *Education:* Wittenberg University (B.A., 1981); Capital University (J.D., 1985). Order of the Curia. *Member:* Columbus (Business Law, Probate Court, Taxation Committees), Ohio State (Corporate Counsel, Estate Planning Trust and Probate Committees) and American (Business Law, Real Property, Probate and Trust, and Tax Committees) Bar Associations. ***PRACTICE AREAS:*** Taxation; Probate; Estate Planning. ***Email:*** BKH@cpmlaw.com

MICHAEL A. SMITH, born Parkersburg, West Virginia, June 6, 1957; admitted to bar, 1982, Ohio. *Education:* Kenyon College (A.B., in Psychology, with honors, 1979); The Ohio State University (J.D., with honors, 1982). Sigma Xi Society. *Member:* Columbus (Past Chairman, Business Law Committees; Member: Corporate and Securities Law Committee; Ohio Division on Securities Takeover Advisory and Negotiated Acquisitions Committee), Ohio State and American (Member, Corporate Law Section) Bar Associations. ***PRACTICE AREAS:*** Business Law; Employment Law; Intellectual Property; Securities. ***Email:*** MAS@cpmlaw.com

JOHN P. WILKERSON, JR., born Memphis, Tennessee, June 26, 1954; admitted to bar, 1981, Ohio; 1982, U.S. District Court, Southern District of Ohio. *Education:* The Ohio State University (B.S., 1976); Capital University (J.D., 1981). Delta Theta Phi. Instructor: Institute of Financial Education, 1986-1988; Lecturer for Columbus and Ohio State Bar Association on Real Estate and Lender's Counsel Issues. *Member:* Columbus (Financial Institutions; Real Property and Environmental Law Committees), Ohio State and American Bar Associations; Ohio Land Title Association; Mid-Ohio Lender's Counsel Attorneys Association; Ohio Presbyterian Retirement Services Real Estate Advisory Committee. ***PRACTICE AREAS:*** Real Estate Law; Banking Law. ***Email:*** JPW@cpmlaw.com

JOSEPH M. PATCHEN, born Columbus, Ohio, December 27, 1961; admitted to bar, 1987, Ohio. *Education:* Boston College (A.B., magna cum laude, 1984); The Ohio State University (J.D., 1987). Phi Beta Kappa. *Member:* Columbus (Member, Sections on: Business Law, Bankruptcy Law, Real Property Law), Ohio State and American Bar Associations; Mid-Ohio Lender's Counsel Association. ***PRACTICE AREAS:*** Corporate Law; Commercial Law; Real Estate Law. ***Email:*** JMP@cpmlaw.com

SCOTT R. MERGENTHALER, born Alliance, Ohio, September 25, 1956; admitted to bar, 1981, Ohio and U.S. District Court, Northern District of Ohio; 1991, U.S. District Court, Southern District of Ohio; 1992, U.S. Court of Appeals, Sixth Circuit. *Education:* University of Akron (B.A., cum laude, 1978); Cleveland Marshall College of Law (J.D., 1981). Assistant Prosecutor, City of Dublin, Ohio, 1991-1998. Member: Knights of Columbus, Council No. 11445; Optimist Club of Columbus. *Member:* Columbus and Ohio State Bar Association; Defense Research Institute. ***PRACTICE AREAS:*** Civil Litigation; Criminal Defense; Traffic Violations; Workers Compensation Defense. ***Email:*** SRM@cpmlaw.com

MARIE-JOËLLE C. KHOUZAM, born Jeddah, Saudi Arabia, February 27, 1963; admitted to bar, 1991, Ohio; 1992, U.S. District Court, Southern District of Ohio; 2004, U.S. District Court, Northern District of Ohio. *Education:* Bowling Green State University (B.A., cum laude, 1985); Universität Salzburg, Salzburg, Austria; Universität Innsbruck, Innsbruck, Austria; University of Toledo (J.D., 1991). Phi Alpha Delta. Order of Barristers. Member, University of Toledo Law Review, 1990-1991. Semi-finalist, Moot Court National Trial Team. Recipient Alumni Law Scholarship; Fulbright Fellowship. *Member:* Columbus (Chair, Labor and Employment Law Committee, 2003-2005; Community Service Committee, 1995-1997), Ohio State and American Bar Associations; American Inns of Court; Ohio Management Lawyers Association. ***LANGUAGES:*** French and German. ***PRACTICE AREAS:*** Labor and Employment Law; Litigation; Workers Compensation. ***Email:*** JCK@cpmlaw.com

ANTHONY DELLIGATTI, JR., born Connellsville, Pennsylvania, December 13, 1943; admitted to bar, 1972, Ohio; 1973, U.S. District Court, Southern District of Ohio; 1975, U.S. Supreme Court. *Education:* The Ohio State University (B.A., 1965); Capital University (J.D., 1972). *Member:* Columbus, Ohio State and American Bar Associations; Franklin County Trial Lawyers Association; Ohio Academy of Trial Lawyers; The Association of Trial Lawyers of America. ***PRACTICE AREAS:*** Litigation; Domestic Relations; Personal Injury; Business Law.

H. RITCHEY HOLLENBAUGH, born Shelby, Ohio, November 12, 1947; admitted to bar, 1973, Ohio; 1978, U.S. Supreme Court. *Education:* Kent State University (B.A., 1969); Capital University (J.D., 1973). Capital University Law School, Board of Visitors, 1998—. Commissioner, Ohio Public Defender Commission, 1988-1996. Special Prosecutor, 1991-1992. Ohio Legal Assistance Foundation, 1999—; Treasurer, The Governor's Committee, 1987-1996. Trustee, Ohio CLE Institute, 1994-1996. *Member:* Columbus (President, 1987-1988; Board of Governors, 1982-1985; Bar Service Medal, 1997), Ohio State (President, 1992-1993; Council of Delegates, 1985—; Member, Board of Governors, 1989-1994; Liaison, Litigation Section; Liaison, Labor and Employment Law Committee; Member, Criminal Law Committee; Advisor, Section on Women in the Profession, 1993-1999; Member, Supreme Court of Ohio Ukraine Delegation, 1994) and American (Chair, ABA Commission on Advertising, 1993-1997; Strategic Communications, 1997-2000; National Conference of Lawyers and Representatives of the Media, 2000—, Chair, 2001—; House of Delegates, 1993—; Consortium on Legal Services and the Public, 1993-1997; National Conference of Bar Presidents; Member, Sections on: Criminal Justice; Litigation) Bar Associations; National Association of Criminal Defense Lawyers. ***PRACTICE AREAS:*** Civil Litigation; White Collar Criminal Defense; Employment Litigation. ***Email:*** HRH@cpmlaw.com

WILLIAM RICHARD YOST, born Alliance, Ohio, 1946; admitted to bar, 1972, Ohio; 1978, U.S. Supreme Court. *Education:* The Ohio State University (B.S., 1968); Capital University (J.D., 1972). *Member:* Columbus and Ohio State Bar Associations. ***PRACTICE AREAS:*** Collections; Commercial Litigation. ***Email:*** WRY@cpmlaw.com

DAVID A. ONEGA, born Montclair, New Jersey, January 21, 1969; admitted to bar, 1998, Ohio. *Education:* Ohio University (B.B.A., 1991); University of Dayton (M.B.A., 1997); Capital University (J.D., 1998). Member, Executive Board, Capital University Law Review, 1998. Author, "Hegel's Hobbled Heritage: The Ohio Supreme Court's Use of the Doctrine of Ademption to Prey on the Incompetent," Capital University Law Review, 1997, republished in Ohio Probate Law Journal, 1997.*Member:* Columbus and Ohio State Bar Associations. ***PRACTICE AREAS:*** Estate Planning; Tax Law; Business Law. ***Email:*** DAO@cpmlaw.com

OF COUNSEL

ANDREW J. FEDERICO, born Cleveland, Ohio, June 13, 1950; admitted to bar, 1978, Ohio. *Education:* Ohio Wesleyan University (B.A., 1972); Capital University (J.D., 1978). Staff Attorney, Ohio Department of Commerce, Division of Securities, 1978-1980. *Member:* Columbus (Member, Securities Law Committee), Ohio State and American (Member, Corporation, Banking and Business Law Section) Bar Associations; National Association of Bond Lawyers. ***PRACTICE AREAS:*** Corporate Law; Municipal Bond Law; Securities Law. ***Email:*** AJF@cpmlaw.com

THOMAS M. BOLON, born Wheeling, West Virginia, October 25, 1933; admitted to bar, 1964, Ohio and U.S. District Court, Southern District of Ohio. *Education:* Ohio University; Lafayette College (B.A., 1955); The Ohio State University (J.D., 1963). *Member:* Columbus (Member: Board of Governors, 1976-1980; Family Law Committee, 1966-1976 and 1980-1999) and Ohio State Bar Associations; Franklin County Trial Lawyers Association; City of Bexley Civil Service Commission; Bexley Historical Society (Board Member). ***PRACTICE AREAS:*** Domestic Relations; Family Law; Family Mediation.

(This Listing Continued)

CARLILE PATCHEN & MURPHY LLP, Columbus—Continued

LEON FRIEDBERG, born Bensheim, Germany, February 16, 1947; admitted to bar, 1979, Ohio; 1980, U.S. Claims Court and U.S. Tax Court; 1982, Florida and U.S. Supreme Court; U.S. District Court, Northern District of Ohio; U.S. District Court, Southern District of Ohio; U.S. Court of Appeals, Sixth Circuit. *Education:* DePauw University (B.M., 1969); Miami University (M.M., 1972); Capital University (J.D., 1979). Order of the Curia. *Member:* Columbus (Chairman: Notaries Public Committee, 1987-1988, 1993—; Common Pleas Court Committee, 1985-1987; Member, Bankruptcy Committee), Ohio State and American Bar Associations. (Also practicing individually). ***PRACTICE AREAS:*** Bankruptcy; Commercial Litigation; Commercial Law; Real Estate; Civil Practice; Trial Practice; Appellate Practice. ***Email:*** LXF@cpmlaw.com

STEPHEN D. ENZ, born Columbus, Ohio, August 13, 1942; admitted to bar, 1967, Ohio; 1968, U.S. District Court, Southern District of Ohio. *Education:* University of Wyoming; The Ohio State University (B.A., 1964; J.D., 1967). *Member:* Columbus Bar Association (Member, Admissions to the Bar Committee, 1974-1979); Sports Lawyers Association. ***PRACTICE AREAS:*** Corporate Law; Real Estate Law; Estate Planning Law; Tax Law. ***Email:*** SDE@cpmlaw.com

RICHARD L. BIBART, born Newark, Ohio, April 10, 1942; admitted to bar, 1967, Ohio and U.S. Tax Court; 1969, U.S. District Court, Southern District of Ohio. *Education:* Harvard University (A.B., 1964); University of Michigan (J.D., 1966). Author: "Partnership Taxation," 40 U. of Cinn. L.R. 3, 1971. ***PRACTICE AREAS:*** Business Law; Federal Tax Law. ***Email:*** RLB@cpmlaw.com

DANIEL G. ROHLETTER, born Columbus, Ohio, September 3, 1959; admitted to bar, 1986, Ohio; 1987, U.S. District Court, Southern District of Ohio and U.S. Tax Court. *Education:* Capital University (B.A., magna cum laude, 1982; J.D., 1986). Member, Order of the Curia. *Member:* Columbus and Ohio State Bar Associations. ***PRACTICE AREAS:*** Corporate; Commercial Law; Lender Law; Real Estate; Probate; Tax Law. ***Email:*** dgr@cpmlaw.com

ASSOCIATES

DAVID S. JACKSON, born Winchester, Virginia, October 3, 1966; admitted to bar, 1998, Ohio. *Education:* University of Georgia (B.A., 1988); Capital Law School (J.D., summa cum laude, 1998). Order of the Curia. Member, Law Review Executive Board. Author: "Privacy and Ohio's Public Records Act," 26 Cap.U.L.Rev. 107 (1997). Co-Author: "History of the YMCA Night Law Schools," 26 Cap.U.L.Rev. 235 (1998). *Member:* Columbus, Ohio State and American Bar Associations; Franklin Ohio Inn, American Inns of Court. [Sgt., US Army, 1981-1995]. ***PRACTICE AREAS:*** Corporate Law; Taxation; Business Planning. ***Email:*** DSJ@cpmlaw.com

THOMAS H. WALLACE, born Milwaukee, Wisconsin, September 1, 1964; admitted to bar, 1990, Ohio. *Education:* Bowling Green State University (B.S., 1987); Capital University (J.D., 1990). *Member:* Columbus, Ohio State and American Bar Associations. ***PRACTICE AREAS:*** Business Planning. ***Email:*** THW@cpmlaw.com

JANE A. HIGGINS MARX, born Sandusky, Ohio, November 6, 1975; admitted to bar, 2000, Ohio. *Education:* Denison University (B.A., cum laude, 1997); The Ohio State University (J.D., 2000). Member, Editorial Board, Ohio State Journal on Dispute Resolution. *Member:* Columbus, Ohio State and American Bar Associations. ***PRACTICE AREAS:*** Estate Planning. ***Email:*** JAH@cpmlaw.com

DOUGLAS R. JENNINGS, born Sacramento, California, November 26, 1962; admitted to bar, 1989, Ohio, U.S. District Court, Southern District of Ohio and U.S. Court of Appeals, Sixth Circuit. *Education:* The Ohio State University (B.A., 1986; J.D., with honors, 1989). Contributing Author: "Sowald Morganstern Domestic Relations Law," Banks-Baldwin Law Publishing Co., 1997. *Member:* Columbus, Ohio State and American Bar Associations. ***PRACTICE AREAS:*** Civil Litigation; Securities Litigation; Family Law. ***Email:*** DRJ@cpmlaw.com

NECOL D. RUSSELL-WASHINGTON, born Columbus, Ohio, August 30, 1966; admitted to bar, 2001, Ohio. *Education:* Franklin University (B.S., 1996); The Ohio State University (J.D., 2000). *Member:* Columbus and Ohio State Bar Associations. [U.S. Army Active, 1994-1996; U.S. Army Reserve, 1986-1995]. ***LANGUAGES:*** English. ***PRACTICE AREAS:*** Business Litigation. ***Email:*** NRW@cpmlaw.com

STEPHANIE D. CHAMP, born Logan, Ohio, April 10, 1968; admitted to bar, 2002, Ohio. *Education:* The Ohio State University (B.A., 1991; J.D., 2002). Member, 1st Amendment Moot Court Team. Member, Executive Board, Pro Bono Research Group. *Member:* Columbus and Ohio State Bar Associations; International Womens Insolvency and Restructuring Confederation. ***PRACTICE AREAS:*** Commercial Law; Bankruptcy; Business Law. ***Email:*** SDC@cpmlaw.com

CHRISTOPHER A. RINEHART, born Parkersburg, West Virginia, November 25, 1971; admitted to bar, 1999, Ohio; 2000, West Virginia. *Education:* Wittenberg University (B.S., 1994); Ohio State University (J.D., 1997). ***PRACTICE AREAS:*** Business Law. ***Email:*** car@cpmlaw.com

CHRISTOPHER J. DUSSEAU, born Columbus, Ohio, December 6, 1976; admitted to bar, 2003, Ohio. *Education:* University of Notre Dame (B.A., 1999); University of Oregon School of Law (J.D., 2003). *Member:* Columbus and Ohio State Bar Associations. ***PRACTICE AREAS:*** Litigation. ***Email:*** CJD@cpmlaw.com

JOSEPH M. GILLOTTI, born Lima, Ohio, November 6, 1966; admitted to bar, 1996, Ohio. *Education:* The Ohio State University (B.S., 1990); Capital University (J.D., 1995). Order of the Curia. Certified Public Accountant, 1991. *Member:* Columbus, Ohio State Bar Associations. ***PRACTICE AREAS:*** Probate (33%); Taxation (33%); Business Law (33%). ***Email:*** jmg@cpmlaw.com

MARY G. MENKEDICK, born Cincinnati, Ohio, November 5, 1971; admitted to bar, 1999, Ohio; 2000, U.S. District Court, Southern District of Ohio; 2001, U.S. Court of Appeals, Sixth Circuit. *Education:* The Ohio State University (B.S., 1995; J.D., 1999). Managing Editor, Law Journal Ohio State University, 1999. *Member:* Columbus Bar Association. ***PRACTICE AREAS:*** Labor and Employment Law; ERISA. ***Email:*** mgm@cpmlaw.com

(This Listing Continued)

BRIAN T. JOHNSON, born Flint, Michigan, April 16, 1967; admitted to bar, 1995, Ohio and U.S. District Court, Northern District of Ohio; 1999, U.S. District Court, Southern District of Ohio. *Education:* Wheaton College (B.A. in History, 1989); Trinity Evangelical Divinity School (M.Div., 1992); University of Notre Dame (J.D., cum laude, 1995). *Member:* Columbus, Ohio State and American Bar Associations. ***PRACTICE AREAS:*** Business Litigation; Construction Litigation; Alternative Dispute Resolution. ***Email:*** btj@cpmlaw.com

JOHN LEWIS EINSTEIN, IV, born Huntington, West Virginia, July 31, 1968; admitted to bar, 1996, West Virginia; 2000, Ohio; 2001, U.S. Tax Court. *Education:* Emory and Henry College (B.A., 1990); University of Dayton (J.D., magna cum laude, 1996). Recipient, American Jurisprudence Awards in Legal Research and Writing I & II. Best Oralist, Walter H. Rice Moot Court Competition. Associate Editor, University of Dayton Law Review, 1995-1996. ***PRACTICE AREAS:*** Taxation; Commercial Transactions; Business Law. ***Email:*** jle@cpmlaw.com

EMILY A. SMITH, born Des Moines, Iowa, 1976; admitted to bar, 2002, Ohio. *Education:* Miami University of Ohio (B.A., 1999); The Ohio State University, Moritz College of Law (J.D., 2002). *Member:* Columbus and Ohio State Bar Associations. ***PRACTICE AREAS:*** Civil Litigation. ***Email:*** eas@cpmlaw.com

REPRESENTATIVE CLIENTS: Advest, Inc.; American Ceramic Society; Central Ohio Transit Autority; City of Columbus; Delaware County Bank; Future Communications; U.S. Bank, N.A.; General Motors Acceptance Corp.; George Byers & Sons; Homesteaders Life Insurance Co.; J.A. Croson Co.; Kansas City Life Insurance Co.; National City Bank, Columbus; Ohio State Life Insurance; The Provident Bank; Prudential Securities; Steiner+ Associates; Team Rahal, Inc.; Yerke Mortgage Co.
APPROVED ATTORNEYS FOR: Chicago Title Insurance Co.
REFERENCE: Commerce National Bank.

CARPENTER & LIPPS LLP

Established in 1994

280 PLAZA, SUITE 1300
280 NORTH HIGH STREET
COLUMBUS, OHIO 43215
Telephone: 614-365-4100
Facsimile: 614-365-9145
URL: http://www.carpenterlipps.com

General Civil Trial, Appellate and Federal Practice. Banking. Business. Commercial. Franchise Law, Employment, Media, First Amendment, Health Care, Libel, Communications Law, Products Liability, Professional Liability, Sports Law, Complex, Class Action and Multi-District Litigation.

FIRM PROFILE: Carpenter & Lipps LLP was established in 1994 by eight lawyers from the Columbus office of Jones, Day, Reavis & Pogue. The Firm is a litigation boutique with an emphasis on class action and complex litigation primarily in the areas of business and commercial law, banking and consumer finance, First Amendment, health care, libel, marketing and franchise law, professional liability defense, products liability, and sports law.

The firm's lawyers have been recognized as comprising one of Ohio's outstanding litigation firms by various publications such as Martindale-Hubbell's Bar Register of Preeminent Lawyers (areas: banking law; civil trial practice; commercial litigation; communication law; employment benefits law; franchise law; products liability law; professional liability); Chambers USA America's Leading Lawyers for Business; The Best Lawyers in America and Ohio's Super Lawyers.

MEMBERS OF FIRM

MICHAEL H. CARPENTER, born Huntington, West Virginia, March 3, 1953; admitted to bar, 1977, Ohio. *Education:* The Ohio State University (B.A., summa cum laude, 1974; J.D., cum laude, 1977). Phi Beta Kappa; Order of the Coif. ***Email:*** carpenter@carpenterlipps.com

JEFFREY A. LIPPS, born Painesville, Ohio, August 23, 1956; admitted to bar, 1981, Ohio. *Education:* University of Cincinnati (B.A., summa cum laude, 1978; J.D., 1981). Phi Beta Kappa; Order of the Coif. Student Articles Editor and Chairperson, University of Cincinnati Law Review, 1980-1981. ***Email:*** lipps@carpenterlipps.com

DAVID A. WALLACE, born Pittsburgh, Pennsylvania, March 24, 1959; admitted to bar, 1985, Ohio; 1991, District of Columbia. *Education:* University of Rochester (B.A., cum laude, 1981); George Washington University (J.D., 1985). Notes Editor, The George Washington Journal of International Law & Economics, 1983-1985. Law Clerk to Hon. David D. Dowd, U.S. District Court, Northern District of Ohio, 1985-1987. ***Email:*** wallace@carpenterlipps.com

TIMOTHY R. BRICKER, born Salem, Ohio, December 20, 1965; admitted to bar, 1993, Ohio. *Education:* University of Akron (B.S. cum laude, 1989); Ohio State University (J.D., with honors, 1993). Member, Ohio State Journal of Dispute Resolution, 1992-1993. ***Email:*** bricker@carpenterlipps.com

DANIEL R. MORDARSKI, born Cleveland, Ohio, November 22, 1968; admitted to bar, 1994, Ohio. *Education:* Bowling Green State University (B.A., cum laude, 1991); Cleveland-Marshall College of Law (J.D., magna cum laude, 1994). Articles Editor, Cleveland State Law Review, 1993-1994. ***Email:*** mordarski@carpenterlipps.com

ANGELA M. PAUL, born Ravenna, Ohio, June 11, 1972; admitted to bar, 1997, Ohio. *Education:* University of Chicago (B.A., with honors, 1993); University of Texas (J.D., 1997). Recent Developments Editor, Journal of Business Law, 1996-1997. ***Email:*** paul@carpenterlipps.com

ASSOCIATES

SHANNON M. SHOAFF, born Akron, Ohio, July 3, 1976; admitted to bar, 2001, Ohio. *Education:* University of Toledo (B.A., 1998; J.D., magna cum laude, 2001). Order of the Coif. ***Email:*** shoaff@carpenterlipps.com

(This Listing Continued)

MONIQUE A. HALL, born Canton, Ohio, February 5, 1977; admitted to bar, 2002, Ohio. *Education:* The Ohio State University (B.A., summa cum laude, 1999; J.D., 2002). ***Email:*** hall@carpenterlipps.com

KATHERYN M. LLOYD, born Brandy Station, Virginia, June 25, 1976; admitted to bar, 2002, Ohio. *Education:* The Ohio State University (B.A., summa cum laude, 1999); Duke University School of Law (J.D., magna cum laude, 2002). Phi Beta Kappa. Editor, The Duke Journal of Comparative and International Law, 2000-2001. ***Email:*** lloyd@carpenterlipps.com

SHANA O. SEE, born Fairfax, Virginia, February 23, 1976; admitted to bar, 2002, Illinois; 2004, Ohio. *Education:* Kenyon College (B.A., with highest honors, 1998); Duke University (J.D., 2002); Northwestern University (LL.M., Taxation, 2003). ***Email:*** ortiz@carpenterlipps.com

DANIEL M. MASSEY, born Columbus, Ohio, November 6, 1976; admitted to bar, 2003, Ohio. *Education:* Boston College (B.A., 1999); Wake Forest University (J.D., 2002). ***Email:*** massey@carpenterlipps.com

JOEL E. SECHLER, born Johnstown, Pennsylvania, November 12, 1977; admitted to bar, 2003, Ohio. *Education:* Susquehanna University (B.A., summa cum laude, 2000); The Ohio State University (J.D., with honors, 2003). Associate Editor, The Ohio State Journal on Dispute Resolution, 2001-2003. ***Email:*** sechler@carpenterlipps.com

CAROLINE D. IMHOFF, born Wooster, Ohio, January 29, 1979; admitted to bar, 2004, Ohio. *Education:* University of Akron (B.A., magna cum laude, 2001); Wake Forest University School of Law (J.D., 2004). ***Email:*** imhoff@carpenterlipps.com

JOSEPH L. BRUEMMER, born Cincinnati, Ohio, June 5, 1980; (admission pending); admitted to bar, admission pending, Ohio. *Education:* Xavier University (B.S.B.A., 2002); The Ohio State University, Moritz College of Law (J.D., with honors, 2005). Associate Editor, Ohio State Journal of Dispute Resolution, 2003-2005. ***Email:*** brueummer@carpenterlipps.com

ANNE M. ZEHR, born Columbus, Ohio, October 24, 1979; (admission pending). *Education:* Miami University (B.A., with honors, 2002); The Ohio State University, Moritz College of Law (J.D., 2005). Member, National Moot Court Team. Articles Editor, The Ohio State Law Journal, 2003-2005. ***Email:*** zehr@carpenterlipps.com

KAREN M. CADIEUX, born Batavia, New York, July 5, 1979; (admission pending). *Education:* The Ohio State University (B.A., 2002); Capital University Law School (J.D., summa cum laude, 2005). Order of the Curia. Research Editor, Capital University Law Review, 2004-2005. ***Email:*** cadieux@carpenterlipps.com

OF COUNSEL

MICHAEL N. BEEKHUIZEN, born Dayton, Ohio, May 10, 1969; admitted to bar, 1995, Ohio. *Education:* Oberlin College (B.A., 1991); The Ohio State University (J.D., 1995). Order of the Coif. Articles Editor, Ohio State Law Journal, 1994-1995. Law Clerk to Hon. Monroe G. McKay, U.S. Court of Appeals, Tenth Circuit, 1995-1996. ***Email:*** beekhuizen@carpenterlipps.com

REPRESENTATIVE CLIENTS: American Express Co.; American Honda Motor Co.; Associates Financial Services, Inc.; Banc One Corporation; Bank of America; Bell Sports, Inc.; Charter One Bank; Chelsea Title; Countrywide Mortgage; Credit Suisse First Boston LLC; Curtis 1000, Inc.; Daewoo Motor America, Inc.; Developer Finance Corporation; DirecTV, Inc.; Evenflo Company, Inc.; Fairbanks Capital Corporation; Federal Express Corporation; First American Real Estate Services, Inc.; First American Title Insurance Company, Inc.; General Motors Acceptance Corporation; General Motors Corporation; GMAC Commercial Mortgage Corporation; Green Mountain Energy Co.; Harley-Davidson Motor Company; Health Alliance Plan; Homecomings Financial Network; Isuzu Motors America, Inc.; Kawasaki Motors Corp., Limited Brands; Marubeni America Corp.; Massey Enterprises, Inc.; McDonald's Corporation; Meijer, Inc.; Mitsui & Co. (U.S.A.), Inc.; Nations Standard Mortgage Corporation; New United Motor Manufacturing, Inc.; Nissan Motor Corp.; Paramount Financial Group; Physician Weblink, Inc.; Residential Funding Corporation; RFC Capital Corporation; Select Portfolio Servicing, Inc.; Syntiro Healthcare Services, Inc.; Takata Corporation; Textron Financial Corporation; 3M Company; Toyota Motor Sales, U.S.A., Inc.; Volvo Cars of North America, Inc.

TIMOTHY G. CHASSER

2109 WEST FIFTH AVENUE, SUITE A
COLUMBUS, OHIO 43212-1976
Telephone: 614-777-7610
Fax: 614-777-7620
URL: http://www.chasserlawoffice.com
URL: http://www.lawyers.com/chasserlaw

Civil Practice. Personal Injury, Workers Compensation and Social Security Disability Law.

TIMOTHY G. CHASSER, born Cleveland, Ohio, June 4, 1949; admitted to bar, 1976, Ohio. *Education:* University of Dayton (B.A., 1971); Cleveland State University (J.D., 1975). *Member:* Columbus (Member, Workers Compensation Section), Ohio State (Member, Workers Compensation Section) and American Bar Associations; The Association of Trial Lawyers of America; Franklin County Trial Lawyers Association; The Ohio Academy of Trial Lawyers.

CHEEK & ZEEHANDELAR, LLP

471 EAST BROAD STREET, 12TH FLOOR
P.O. BOX 15069
COLUMBUS, OHIO 43215-3872
Telephone: 614-229-3888; 1-800-689-6677
Fax: 614-241-5865
Email: czlaw@czlaw.com

Collections, Subrogation, and Creditors Rights.

(This Listing Continued)

MEMBERS OF FIRM

EMERSON CHEEK, III, born Columbus, Ohio, February 5, 1944; admitted to bar, 1970, Ohio; 1971, U.S. District Court, Southern District of Ohio; 1985, U.S. Court of Appeals, Sixth Circuit. *Education:* Ohio Northern University (B.A., with distinction, 1967; J.D., with distinction, 1970). Phi Alpha Delta (Student District Justice, 1969-1970). Member, Willis Society. *Member:* Columbus, Ohio State and American Bar Associations; American Alliance of Creditor Attorneys (Member, Board of Directors, 1994—; Chairman of Board, 1996-1999; President, 1994-1996; Treasurer, 1993-1994); National Association of Retail Collection Attorneys (NARCA); American Collector Association (Member, Attorney Program). ***PRACTICE AREAS:*** Creditors' Rights. ***Email:*** echeek@czlaw.com

STEVEN J. ZEEHANDELAR, born Cincinnati, Ohio, December 29, 1954; admitted to bar, 1982, Ohio and U.S. District Court, Southern District of Ohio. *Education:* University of Cincinnati (B.A., History, with honors, 1977); The Ohio State University (J.D., 1981). *Member:* Columbus and Ohio State Bar Associations. ***PRACTICE AREAS:*** Personal Injury; Collections; Insurance Subrogation. ***Email:*** szeehandelar@czlaw.com

ASSOCIATES

ALESSANDRO SABATINO, born Yonkers, New York, July 1, 1968; admitted to bar, 1993, Ohio. *Education:* Fordham University (B.A., 1990); University of Dayton (J.D., 1993). *Member:* Columbus and Ohio State Bar Associations. [U.S.M.C., 1990-1994; First Lt.; Judge Advocate General, 1992]. ***PRACTICE AREAS:*** Debtor and Creditor; Insurance Subrogation. ***Email:*** asabatino@czlaw.com

JAMES C. ZURY, born Kew Gardens, New York, March 25, 1968; admitted to bar, 1995, Ohio. *Education:* University of Akron (B.S., Natural Science, 1988); Capital University (J.D., 1995). *Member:* Columbus and Ohio State Bar Associations. ***PRACTICE AREAS:*** Insurance Litigation; Personal Injury. ***Email:*** jzury@czlaw.com

MATTHEW WARNER, born Dunkirk, New York, July 21, 1976; admitted to bar, 2002, Ohio. *Education:* State University of New York at Fredonia (B.A., 1997); Capital University Law School (J.D., 2000). Pi Sigma Alpha. *Member:* Columbus, Ohio State and American Bar Associations. ***PRACTICE AREAS:*** Subrogation (60%); Creditors Rights (40%). ***Email:*** mwarner@czlaw.com

JON S. DOYLE, born Winfield, Illinois, May 16, 1967; admitted to bar, 2003, Ohio. *Education:* Ohio State University (B.A., 1989); Capital University Law School (J.D., 2000). *Member:* Columbus and Ohio State Bar Associations. ***PRACTICE AREAS:*** Subrogation; Creditors Rights; Personal Injury.

KRISHNA K. VELAYUDHAN, born Saskatoon, Saskatchewan, Canada, July 10, 1975; admitted to bar, 2002, Ohio. *Education:* College of Wooster (B.A., Biology/History, 1997); Capital University Law School (J.D., 2000). *Member:* Ohio State and Columbus Bar Associations. ***PRACTICE AREAS:*** Creditors Rights; Subrogation; Personal Injury. ***Email:*** kvelayudhan@czlaw.com

REPRESENTATIVE CLIENTS: State Farm Insurance Co.; AT&T Universal Card; Huntington National Bank; Grange Mutual Casualty Co.; Citicorp Mortgage, Inc.; National City Bank; Motorists Insurance Co.; Fidelity Financial Services; Central Ohio Credit Corp.; Elsea Mobile Homes; Controlled Credit Corp.; Ameritech.

CHESTER, WILLCOX & SAXBE LLP

Established in 1884
65 EAST STATE STREET, SUITE 1000
COLUMBUS, OHIO 43215-3413
Telephone: 614-221-4000
Fax: 614-221-4012
URL: http://www.cwslaw.com

Administrative, Bankruptcy, Business, Corporation, Education Law, Employment Law, Estate Planning, Family Law, General Practice, Intellectual Property Law, International Law, Legislative, Municipal, Oil and Gas, Probate, Public Utilities, Real Estate, Taxation, Trial and Appeals.

FIRM PROFILE: Chester, Willcox & Saxbe LLP is a full-service law firm with a business orientation designed to meet the varied needs of its individual and corporate clients, regardless of their size.

Over the course of more than 100 years of practice, the firm has produced many leaders in the law, civil affairs, and public service.

PARTNERS

ANDREW J. ART, born Columbus, Ohio, July 7, 1962; admitted to bar, 1990, Ohio. *Education:* Bob Jones University (B.A., 1984); Capital University (J.D., 1990). General Referee and Special Magistrate, Franklin County Probate Court, Ohio, 1990-1991. *Member:* Columbus (Member, Admissions Committee, 2003), Ohio State and American Bar Associations. ***PRACTICE AREAS:*** Probate Law; Estate Planning Law. ***Email:*** aart@cwslaw.com

JOHN W. BENTINE, born Huntington, West Virginia, July 27, 1947; admitted to bar, 1975, Ohio and U.S. District Court, Southern District of Ohio. *Education:* Marshall University (B.B.A., 1970); The Ohio State University (J.D., cum laude, 1975). Listed in, Best Lawyers, Public Utility Law. Senior Assistant City Attorney, City of Columbus, 1978-1980. Assistant Attorney General and Counsel, Public Utilities Commission of Ohio, 1975-1978. Member, Ohio Telecommunications Advisory Board, 1984-1986. Member, Ohio Veterinary Medical Licensing Board, 2004—. Listed in Ohio Super Lawyers, Utilities. *Member:* Columbus (Founding Chairman, Public Utilities Committee, 1993-1994), Ohio State (Chairman, Public Utilities Committee, 1994-1996) and American Bar Associations. ***PRACTICE AREAS:*** Regulated Industries; Local Government Law; Mediation; Litigation. ***Email:*** jbentine@cwslaw.com

APRIL R. BOTT, born Salem, Ohio, April 7, 1972; admitted to bar, 1996, Ohio; 1997, U.S. District Court, Southern and Northern Districts of Ohio; 1998, U.S. Court of Appeals, District of Columbia and Sixth Circuits. *Education:* Youngstown State University (B.A.,

(This Listing Continued)

CHESTER, WILLCOX & SAXBE LLP, Columbus—Continued

1992); The Ohio State University (J.D., 1996). Adjunct Professor, Environmental Law, Columbus State Community College, 1998-2002. Listed, 2005 "Ohio Rising Star", Law & Politics magazine. *Member:* Columbus (Member, Environmental Committee), Ohio State and American Bar Associations. ***TRANSACTIONS:*** Defend clients in complex state and federal enforcement actions, including federal New Source Review look-back air litigation; Counsel clients on proactive facility-wide compliance with federal and state environmental and safety laws and regulations; Represent national manufacturing and utilities clients with all aspects of state and federal air permitting matters including prevention of significant deterioration permits, non-attainment area permits, synthetic minor permits, Title V permits and federally enforceable state operating permits; Counsel clients with respect to federal and state rule-making proceedings; Representation industry sectors include: power generation, chemical, manufacturing, plating operations, automotive parts manufacturing, foundries, medical, mining, pulp & pepper and metal part manufacturing. ***PRACTICE AREAS:*** Environmental Law; Energy. ***Email:*** abott@cwslaw.com

DONALD C. BREY, born Columbus, Ohio, August 31, 1955; admitted to bar, 1981, Ohio; U.S. District Court, Southern District of Ohio; U.S. Court of Appeals, Sixth Circuit. *Education:* Ohio Wesleyan University (B.A., summa cum laude, 1977); Yale University (J.D., 1981). Phi Beta Kappa. Contributor, *Ohio Administrative Law Guide and Directory*, 1993—. Rules Advisory Committee, Supreme Court of Ohio (Member, 1997-2001; Chair, 1999-2000). Listed in Ohio Super Lawyers, General Practice. *Member:* Columbus and Ohio State Bar Associations; Federalist Society (Member, Free Speech and Election Law and Religious Liberties Practice Groups); Christian Legal Society; National Lawyers Association; American Inns of Court (President, Duncan Chapter, 1998-1999). ***PRACTICE AREAS:*** General Civil Law; Election Law; Litigation. ***Email:*** dbrey@cwslaw.com

DAVID J. BUTLER, born Columbus, Ohio, May 30, 1972; admitted to bar, 1997, Ohio, U.S. District Court, Southern and Northern Districts of Ohio; 1998, U.S. Court of Appeals, 6th Circuit; U.S. Supreme Court. *Education:* University of Notre Dame (B.B.A., cum laude, 1994; J.D., cum laude, 1997). Listed as a 2005 "Ohio Rising Star," Law & Politics. *Member:* Columbus, Ohio State and American Bar Associations; American Inns of Court, Franklin Inn Chapter. ***PRACTICE AREAS:*** Civil Litigation. ***Email:*** dbutler@cwslaw.com

JAMES J. CHESTER, born Columbus, Ohio, April 22, 1962; admitted to bar, 1987, Ohio and U.S. Court of Appeals, Sixth Circuit; 1988, U.S. District Court, Southern District of Ohio; 1994, Wyoming. *Education:* Amherst College (B.A., cum laude, 1984); Case Western Reserve University (J.D., 1987). Member and Chairman, City of Columbus License Appeals Board, 1990—. *Member:* Columbus, Ohio State and American Bar Associations; American Judicature Society. ***PRACTICE AREAS:*** Corporate Law; Business Law; Real Estate Law. ***Email:*** jimchester@cwslaw.com

JOHN J. CHESTER, born Columbus, Ohio, July 13, 1920; admitted to bar, 1948, Ohio. *Education:* Amherst College (B.A., cum laude, 1942); Yale Law School (J.D., 1948); Capital University (Honorary LL.D.). Adjunct Professor, Ohio State University, Moritz College of Law. Listed: Best Lawyers, Business Litigation; Ohio Super Lawyers, General Litigation. Representative, Ohio General Assembly, 1953-1958. Special Counsel to the President of the United States, 1974. *Member:* Columbus (Recipient, Professionalism Award, 2000), Ohio State and American (Member, Sections of General Practice; Litigation) Bar Associations; American Judicature Society; American Board of Trial Advocates. Fellow, American College of Trial Lawyers. [Lt. USNR, 1942-1946]. ***PRACTICE AREAS:*** General Civil Law; Trial Practice. ***Email:*** jackchester@cwslaw.com

JOHN J. CHESTER, JR., born Columbus, Ohio, June 9, 1960; admitted to bar, 1989, Ohio. *Education:* Ohio State University (B.A., 1983); Capital University (J.D., 1989). *Member:* Columbus, Ohio State and American Bar Associations. ***PRACTICE AREAS:*** Real Estate Law; Litigation. ***Email:*** jchesterjr@cwslaw.com

J. RICHARD EMENS, born Jackson, Michigan, May 3, 1934; admitted to bar, 1959, Michigan; 1964, Ohio; 1968, U.S. Supreme Court. *Education:* DePauw University (B.A., 1956); University of Michigan (J.D., 1959). Phi Delta Phi Honor Society; Phi Beta Kappa. Co-Author: "Mergers and Acquisitions, Tender Offers and Limited Partnership Rollups -- Applicable Securities Laws," Proceedings of Ninth Annual Institute, Eastern Mineral Law Foundation, 1988; "Family Business Basics: The Guide to Family Business Financial Success," 2000. Named, Best Lawyers in America, Corporate Law and Natural Resources Law. Listed, Ohio Super Lawyers, General Business. President, 1982 and Trustee, 1980—, Energy and Mineral Law Foundation. *Member:* Columbus, Ohio State (Member, Corporation Law Committee) and American (Member, Sections of: Corporation, Banking and Business Law; Natural Resources Law; International, Business Law and Energy and Natural Resources Law) Bar Associations; State Bar of Michigan; International Bar Association. ***PRACTICE AREAS:*** Corporation Law; Oil and Gas Law; Family Business Law. ***Email:*** demens@cwslaw.com

STEPHEN C. FITCH, born Portsmouth, Ohio, September 18, 1948; admitted to bar, 1973, Ohio and U.S. District Court, Southern District of Ohio; 1977, U.S. Supreme Court; 1978, U. S. Court of Appeals, Sixth, Eighth and Tenth Circuits. *Education:* Ohio State University (B.A., 1970; J.D., 1973). Listed in, Best Lawyers, Business Litigation. Assistant Ohio Attorney General, 1973-1979. Listed, Ohio Super Lawyers, Business Litigation. *Member:* Columbus (Member, Board of Governors, 1989-1996; President, 1994-1995), Ohio State (Member, Council of Delegates, 1990—), Federal (Member, Columbus Chapter) and American (Member, Litigation Section) Bar Associations; Franklin Inn, American Inns of Court. Fellow, Columbus Bar Foundation (Member, Board of Trustees, 1996—; President, 2003-2004). ***PRACTICE AREAS:*** Litigation. ***Email:*** sfitch@cwslaw.com

GARY B. GITLITZ, born Chicago, Illinois, May 17, 1951; admitted to bar, 1976, Ohio. *Education:* University of Arizona (B.A., 1973); University of Toledo School of Law (J.D., 1976). Former General Counsel to Glimcher Realty Trust, a New York Stock Exchange Real Estate Investment Trust, specializing in development of commercial real estate. *Member:* Columbus and Ohio State Bar Associations; International Council of Shopping Centers. ***PRACTICE AREAS:*** Commercial Law; Real Estate Law. ***Email:*** ggitlitz@cwslaw.com

GUY R. HUMPHREY, born Burton, Ohio, April 20, 1960; admitted to bar, 1984, Ohio and U.S. District Court, Southern and Northern Districts of Ohio; U.S. Court of Appeals, Sixth and Eighth Circuits. *Education:* Kent State University (B.S., magna cum laude, 1981); Ohio State University (J.D., with honors, 1984). Listed, Turnaround Management Association. *Member:* Columbus (Bankruptcy Committee); Federal, Ohio State and American Bar Associations; Commercial Law League of America. ***PRACTICE AREAS:*** Commercial Debtor/Creditor; Bankruptcy Representation; Litigation. ***Email:*** ghumphrey@cwslaw.com

J. ANTHONY KINGTON, born Cleveland, Ohio, December 13, 1953; admitted to bar, 1980, Ohio. *Education:* Columbus International College (A.A., 1974); The Ohio State University (B.A., 1977; J.D., 1979). Listed, Best Lawyers in America, Mergers and Acquisitions, Securities Law. *Member:* Columbus (Member and Past Chairman: Estate and Gift Tax Subcommittee), Ohio State and American Bar Associations. ***PRACTICE AREAS:*** Corporate Law; Real Estate Law; Federal Income Tax Law; Estate and Gift Tax Law. ***Email:*** tkington@cwslaw.com

EUGENE B. LEWIS, born Columbus, Ohio, September 8, 1957; admitted to bar, 1982, Ohio; U.S. District Court, Southern District of Ohio. *Education:* Wittenberg University (B.A., 1979); University of Cincinnati (J.D., 1982). Listed in: Best Lawyers, Family Law; Ohio Super Lawyers, Family Law. *Member:* Columbus, Ohio State and American Bar Associations. (Certified Specialist in Family Relations Law, Ohio State Bar Association). ***PRACTICE AREAS:*** General Civil Practice; Litigation; Family Law. ***Email:*** glewis@cwslaw.com

JAMES V. MANIACE, born Lima, Ohio, 1956; admitted to bar, 1981, Ohio; 1983, U.S. District Court, Southern District of Ohio; 1984, U.S. Court of Appeals, Sixth Circuit. *Education:* University of Notre Dame (B.A., with honors, 1978); Duke University (J.D., 1981). Author, "Avoiding Copyright Infringement in a Multi-Vendor Environment," The Newsletter of the Federal Bar Association's Corporate and Association Counsel's Division, Vol. 4, No. 3, September, 1999. Chairman, City of Columbus, Board of Zoning Adjustment, 1998—. *Member:* Columbus, Ohio State and American Bar Associations; Building Owners and Managers' Association (Member, Columbus Chapter). ***PRACTICE AREAS:*** Real Estate; Intellectual Property; Business Law.

SARAH D. MORRISON, born Lufkin, Texas, November 12, 1970; admitted to bar, 1997, Ohio; 1998, U.S. District Court, Southern District of Ohio and U.S. Court of Appeals, Sixth Circuit. *Education:* Ohio State University (B.A., 1992); Capital University Law School (J.D., magna cum laude, 1997). Order of the Curie. Staff, 1995-1996 and Associate Editor, 1996-1997, Capital University Law Review. *Member:* Columbus, Ohio State, Federal and American Bar Associations; American Inns of Court (Member, Franklin Inn). ***PRACTICE AREAS:*** Litigation; Elections Law; Legislative Practice. ***Email:*** smorrison@cwslaw.com

CRAIG B. PAYNTER, born Detroit, Michigan, February 19, 1957; admitted to bar, 1982, Ohio; 1983, U.S. District Court, Southern District of Ohio; 1984, U.S. Court of Appeals, Sixth Circuit; 1993, U.S. Supreme Court. *Education:* Denison University (B.A., 1979); University of Akron (J.D., 1982). Member, The University of Akron Law Review, 1981-1982. Assistant Prosecuting Attorney, 1983-1987. Former Special Counsel to Ohio Attorney General. Hearing Examiner, Ohio Department of Commerce. *Member:* Columbus (Chairman, Construction Law Committee, 2002-2004), Ohio State and American (Member, Forum on the Construction Industry 2003-2005) Bar Associations. ***REPORTED CASES:*** Matz v. Ohio Dept. of Human Services (2001) 145 Ohio App. 3d 304; GTE Wireless of the Midwest Inc. v. Anderson Township (1999), 134 Ohio App. 3d 352; Chambers v. Stevenson (1991) 71 Ohio App. 3d 566 - Co-Counsel; James v. Franklin County Sheriff (1990) 52 Ohio st 3d 40 - Trial Counsel; Beeler v. Franklin County Sheriff (1990), 67 Ohio App. 3d 748 Trial Counsel. ***PRACTICE AREAS:*** Construction Law (60%); Government (25%); Municipal Law (5%); Zoning, Planning and Land Use (5%); Litigation (5%). ***Email:*** cpaynter@cwslaw.com

CHARLES R. SAXBE, born Urbana, Ohio, November 2, 1946; admitted to bar, 1975, Ohio; U.S. District Court, Southern District of Ohio; U.S. Court of Appeals, Sixth Circuit; U.S. Supreme Court. *Education:* Southern Methodist University (B.A., 1969); The Ohio State University (J.D., 1975). Phi Delta Phi. Listed in, Best Lawyers, Business Litigation. Member, Ohio House of Representatives, 1975-1982. *Member:* Columbus, Champaign County, Ohio State and American Bar Associations. [Capt., USMC, 1969-1972]. ***PRACTICE AREAS:*** Litigation; General Law; Legislative Practice. ***Email:*** rsaxbe@cwslaw.com

ELIZABETH M. STANTON, born Lansdale, Pennsylvania, April 12, 1947; admitted to bar, 1979, Texas; 1980, U.S. District Court, Southern District of Texas; 1982, Ohio; 1983, U.S. District Court, Southern District of Ohio; 1986, U.S. Court of Appeals, Sixth Circuit; 1990, U.S. Supreme Court; 1992, U.S. Court of Appeals, Third Circuit. *Education:* Drexel University (B.S., Bus. Ad., 1969); University of Houston (J.D., magna cum laude, 1979). Phi Kappa Phi; Beta Gamma Sigma; Alpha Sigma Alpha. Member, Barons Scholastic Honor Society. Chair, State and Local Government Committee, 2004. *Member:* Columbus (Chair, Labor and Employment Law Section, 1996-1998), Ohio State (Chair, Government, Education and Construction Law Committee, 2003); American (Member, Labor and Employment Law Section) Bar Associations; State Bar of Texas; Ohio Women's Bar Association (Founding Member; Board Member, 1994-1997); National Association of Women Lawyers; Women Lawyers of Franklin County, Inc. (Treasurer, 1989-1990; Board Member, 1990-1992); Ohio Management Lawyers Association. (Certified Specialist in Labor and Employment Law, Ohio State Bar Association). ***PRACTICE AREAS:*** Labor and Employment Law; University Law; Annexation; Civil Trial and Appellate Practice; Mediation; Zoning Law. ***Email:*** estanton@cwslaw.com

ELIZABETH J. WATTERS, born Columbus, Ohio, July 3, 1965; admitted to bar, 1990, Connecticut; 1991, Ohio, New York and District of Columbia; U.S. District Court, Southern District of Ohio, Southern and Eastern Districts of New York and District of Connecticut; 1992, U.S. Court of Appeals, Sixth Circuit; 1993, U.S. Court of Appeals, Second Circuit; 1995, U.S. Supreme Court. *Education:* The Ohio State University (B.A., cum laude, 1987; J.D., 1990). Phi Kappa Phi. Managing Editor, Ohio State Law Journal, 1988-1990. Member, National Council The Ohio State University Moritz College of Law, 1993—. Past President, OSU College of Law Alumni Society. Past President, Women Lawyers of Franklin County. Past Chair, Common Pleas Court Committee. *Member:* Columbus (Member, Board of Governors, 2003—); Judiciary Committee, 2000-2002), Ohio State,

(*This Listing Continued*)

Federal and American Bar Associations; Columbus Bar Foundation. ***PRACTICE AREAS:*** Litigation; General Civil Law; Employment Law; Bankruptcy Law. ***Email:*** ewatters@cwslaw.com

RODERICK H. WILLCOX, born Columbus, Ohio, January 10, 1934; admitted to bar, 1958, Ohio. *Education:* Williams College (B.A., 1955); University of Michigan (LL.B., 1958). Listed in *Best Lawyers in America* Corporate Law, 2001-2002. *Member:* Columbus, Ohio State and American (Member, Section of Business Law and Section of Taxation) Bar Associations; Columbus Bar Foundation (Chairman, Legal Advisory Committee). ***PRACTICE AREAS:*** Corporate Law; Estate and Gift Taxation; Business Law; Real Estate Law. ***Email:*** rwillcox@cwslaw.com

BEATRICE E. WOLPER, born New Haven, Connecticut, November 28, 1945; admitted to bar, 1978, Ohio and U.S. District Court, Southern District of Ohio. *Education:* University of Cincinnati (B.S., cum laude, 1974); Salmon P. Chase College of Law (J.D., 1978). Editor-in-Chief, 1977-1978, Northern Kentucky Law Review. Co-Author: "Mergers and Acquisitions, Tender Offers and Limited Partnership Rollups -- Applicable Securities Laws," Proceedings of Ninth Annual Institute, Eastern Mineral Law Foundation, 1988; "Profits, Survival and Sales of the Family Owned Business"; "Corporate Restructuring as an Estate Planning Tool." Co-Author: "Family Business Basics: The Guide to Family Business Financial Success," 2000." Author: "Start-up Financing," Small Business Administration, 1991; 1993 Entrepreneur of the year (Support Category), Columbus Region; 1993 Columbus YWCA Woman of Achievement." State of Ohio delegate to 1995 White House Conference on Small Business. President, Ohio International Women's Forum, 1990—. *Member:* Columbus (Member, Committees on: Corporate Counsel, 1980—; Securities Law, 1981—; Chairman, 1987-1989), Ohio State (Member: Corporation Law Committee, 1985—; Corporate Governance Sub-Committee, 1986—) and American (Member: Corporation, Banking and Business Law Section; Small Business Committee; Securities Regulation and Financing Subcommittees, 1986—) Bar Associations; Attorney for Family-Held Enterprises; Director, 1997-2000. ***PRACTICE AREAS:*** Mergers and Acquisitions Law; Family-Held Business Law; Estate Planning; International Law; Corporate Law. ***Email:*** bwolper@cwslaw.com

ASSOCIATES

JAMES D. ABRAMS, born Stockton, California, May 18, 1945; admitted to bar, 2003, Ohio; U.S. District Court, Southern District of Ohio; U.S. Court of Appeals, Sixth Circuit. *Education:* San Francisco State University (B.A., 1967); California State University (M.B.A., 1973); Capital University Law School (J.D., summa cum laude, 2003). Phi Alpha Delta. Member, Law Review. Certified Public Accountant, California. Author: A Missed Opportunity: Medical Use of Marijuana is Defensible. Case Note: U.S. v. Oakland Cannabis, Capital U.L.R. 31 Vol. 4. *Member:* Columbus, Ohio State, American and Federal Bar Associations; American Inns of Court. [E-5, U.S. Army, 1968-1970]. ***PRACTICE AREAS:*** Litigation; Employment. ***Email:*** jabrams@cwslaw.com

W. TRAVIS GARRISON, born Altoona, Pennsylvania, February 9, 1970; admitted to bar, 2003, Ohio; U.S. District Court, Southern District of Ohio; U.S. Court of Appeals, Sixth Circuit. *Education:* Indiana University of Pennsylvania (B.S., 1992); Ohio State University (J.D., 2003); Marshall University (M.B.A., 1999). *Member:* Columbus, Ohio State and American Bar Associations. ***PRACTICE AREAS:*** Bankruptcy; Creditors Rights; Corporate Law; Litigation. ***Email:*** tgarrison@cwslaw.com

GERHARDT A. GOSNELL II, born Saginaw, Michigan, November 4, 1967; admitted to bar, 1995, Ohio. *Education:* Capital University (B.A., summa cum laude, 1990); Ohio State Law School (J.D., 1995). Law Clerk to Hon. Judge Cynthia Lazarus, Tenth Judicial District, Ohio Court of Appeals, 1997-2001. Listed, 2005 "Ohio Rising Star", Law & Politics magazine. *Member:* Ohio State and Columbus Bar Associations; American Inns of Court; Franklin Inn. ***PRACTICE AREAS:*** Litigation. ***Email:*** ggosnell@cwslaw.com

TIMOTHY S. HORTON, born Columbus, Ohio, February 20, 1970; admitted to bar, 1996, Ohio; U.S. District Court, Southern District of Ohio; U.S. Court of Appeals, Sixth Circuit. *Education:* Boston University (B.A., 1992); Ohio State University College of Law (J.D., 1995). Listed, 2005 "Ohio Rising Star", Law & Politics magazine. Member, John Mercer Langston Association. *Member:* Columbus and Ohio State Bar Associations. ***PRACTICE AREAS:*** Civil Litigation; Employment Law; Sports and Entertainment; Business Law. ***Email:*** thorton@cwslaw.com

LARK T. MALLORY, born Warren, Ohio, July 9, 1969; admitted to bar, 1998, Maryland; 1999, District of Columbia; 2005, Ohio. *Education:* Ohio State University (B.S.B.A., 1991); Ohio State University College of Law (J.D., 1997); University of Florida College of Law, Graduate Tax Program (LL.M., 1998). ***PRACTICE AREAS:*** Tax Law; Estates. ***Email:*** lmallory@swslaw.com

JOSEPH C. PICKENS, born Cleveland, Ohio; admitted to bar, 2003, Ohio. *Education:* Duke University (B.A., Environmental Science and Policy, 1995); Ohio State University (J.D., 2002). *Member:* Columbus, Ohio State and American Bar Associations. ***PRACTICE AREAS:*** Environmental Law. ***Email:*** jpickens@cwslaw.com

TODD M. RODGERS, born Columbus, Ohio, May 27, 1968; admitted to bar, 1993, Ohio; 1995, U.S. District Court, Southern District of Ohio. *Education:* Miami University (B.A., Business, 1990); University of Cincinnati (J.D., 1993). ***PRACTICE AREAS:*** Municipal Law; Utilities Law. ***Email:*** trodgers@cwslaw.com

JESSICA A. SHANKLE, born Westerville, Ohio, 1974; admitted to bar, 2001, Ohio; 2004, California; U.S. District Court, Southern District of Ohio; U.S. District Court, Southern District of California. *Education:* Bowling Green State University (B.S., Criminal Justice, 1996); Capital University (J.D., 2001). Order of Curie. Author: "Social Security Benefits - Clarified by the Supreme Court," Columbus Bar Briefs, April 2005. ***PRACTICE AREAS:*** Family Law; General Practice; Civil Litigation; Real Estate; Criminal Defense. ***Email:*** shankle@cwslaw.com

BOBBY SINGH, born Poona, India, November 27, 1969; admitted to bar, 2000, Ohio. *Education:* Pennsylvania State University (B.S., Engineering, 1993); Capital University Law School (J.D., summa cum laude, 2000). Order of the Curia. Associate Notes Editor, 1999-2000 and Staff Member, 1998-1999, Capital University Law Review. Author: "Miller v. Albright: The Denial Of Equal Protection Through A Lethal Combination Of Stereotyping And Misapplied Deference," 28 Cap. U.L. Rev 1 (1999). *Member:* Columbus and Ohio State Bar Associations. ***PRACTICE AREAS:*** Energy; Utility Law. ***Email:*** bsingh@cwslaw.com

TODD A. WEBER, born Barnesville, Ohio, April 6, 1971; admitted to bar, 1996, Ohio; 1998, U.S. District Court, Southern District of Ohio. *Education:* Wake Forest University (B.S., 1993); Capital University Law School (J.D., 1996). *Member:* Columbus, Ohio State and American Bar Associations. ***PRACTICE AREAS:*** Estate Planning; Probate; Taxation; Corporate. ***Email:*** tweber@cwslaw.com

OF COUNSEL

WILLIAM B. SAXBE, born Mechanicsburg, Ohio, June 24, 1916; admitted to bar, 1948, Ohio (inactive); 1976, District of Columbia. *Education:* The Ohio State University (B.A., 1940; LL.B., 1948). Member, Ohio House of Representatives, 1947-1954. Majority Leader, 1951-1952; Speaker, 1953-1954; Ohio Attorney General, 1957-1958; 1963-1968. U.S. Senator, 1969-1974. U.S. Attorney General, 1974-1975. U.S. Ambassador to India, 1975-1977.

REPRESENTATIVE CLIENTS: American Municipal Power-Ohio, Inc.; Franklin County Convention Facilities Authority; Hill Distributing Co.; Association of Municipal and County Judges of Ohio, Inc.; Interstate Gas Supply, Inc.; Kenneths Hair Salons and Day Spas, Inc.; Marion Steel Company; Ohio Auto Auction; Ohio Federation of Business & Professional Women; Ricart Automotive; Scioto Downs, Inc.; State of Ohio; Tee Jaye's Country Place Restaurants; United States Trotting Association.

(This Listing Continued)

CLARK & HEDIEN

2000 BETHEL ROAD

COLUMBUS, OHIO 43220-5610

Telephone: 614-538-5381; 538-5382

Fax: 614-538-5380

Civil Litigation, Corporate, Securities, Immigration.

MEMBERS OF THE FIRM

R. MICHAEL CLARK, born Springfield, Ohio, March 9, 1967; admitted to bar, 1992, Ohio; 1993, U.S. District Court, Southern District of Ohio; 1994, U.S. Court of Appeals, Sixth Circuit. *Education:* Boston University (B.A., 1989; M.A., 1989); Georgetown University Law Center (J.D., 1992). Associate, Thompson Hine, Columbus, Ohio, 1992-1995. *Member:* Ohio State Bar Association; Columbus Bar Association; Ohio Academy of Trial Lawyers. ***PRACTICE AREAS:*** Corporate and Securities; Commercial Litigation; General Litigation. ***Email:*** mclark@clark-hedien.com

MARK J. HEDIEN, born Evanston, Illinois, December 30, 1966; admitted to bar, 1992, District of Columbia; 1995, Ohio; 1996, U.S. District Court, Southern District of Ohio; 2004, U.S. Court of Appeals, Sixth Circuit. *Education:* Stanford University (B.A., 1989); Georgetown University (J.D., 1992). Associate, Winston & Strawn, Washington, D.C., 1992-1994. *Member:* Ohio State Bar Association; Columbus Bar Association; American Immigration Lawyers Association. ***LANGUAGES:*** German. ***PRACTICE AREAS:*** Litigation; Immigration. ***Email:*** mhedien@clark-hedien.com

---

CLARK, PERDUE, ARNOLD & SCOTT CO, LPA

Established in 1986

471 EAST BROAD STREET

SUITE 1400

COLUMBUS, OHIO 43215-3853

Telephone: 614-469-1400

Fax: 614-469-0900

URL: http://www.cpaslaw.com

URL: http://www.lawyers.com/cpas

Personal Injury, Products Liability, Wrongful Death, Medical Malpractice, Insurance Law, Aviation Law, Railroad Law, Professional Negligence, Traumatic Brain Injury, Nursing Home Torts, Intentional Torts, Complex Civil and Commercial Litigation, Probate Litigation, Probate Administration, Estate Planning and Trusts.

FIRM PROFILE: Clark, Perdue, Arnold & Scott Co., L.P.A., is an aggressive trial practice firm devoted to the representation of victims of serious injury and death as well as complex financial and commercial litigation. The Firm also has a Statewide practice in the area Probate and Estate Planning, including Probate Litigation. The firm's trial attorneys maintain a statewide practice in all Ohio courts with capabilities for litigation in all states. The firm's extensive network of investigators and experts allows it to respond to new cases or litigation crises with impressive immediacy. All attorneys are members of the Ohio Bar. Two partners are past presidents of the Ohio Academy of Trial Lawyers and all partners are listed in "Best Lawyers in America". REPORTED CASES: Brookover v. Flexmag Ind., Inc., 2002-Ohio-2004; 2404; Griffith v. Wausau Bus. Ins. Co., 2003-Ohio-955; Simpson v. Big Bear Stores Co. (1995), 73 Ohio St. 3d 130; Scott v. Yates (1994), 71 Ohio St. 3d 219; Hillman v. Hastings Mut. Ins. Co. (1994), 69 Ohio St. 3d 1203; Hicks v. Consolidated Rail Corp. (1993), 92 Ohio App. 3d 636; Woods vs Cincinnati Ins. Co., 63 Ohio St. 3d 639 (1992); Ross vs Nationwide Mut. Ins. Co., 63 Ohio St. 3d 33, 1992; Senig vs. Nationwide Mut. Ins. Co., 76 Ohio App. 3d 565 (1992); Buckeye Fed. Savings & Loan Assn. vs Guirlinger, 62 Ohio St. 3d 312 (1991); Adkins vs Republic Franklin Ins. Co., 76 Ohio App. 3d 611 (1991); Nationwide Mu. Ins. Co. vs Chivington, 72 Ohio App. 3d 700; Demetry vs Kim, 72 Ohio App. 3d 692 (1991); Barr vs Ins. Co. of North America, 72 Ohio App. 3d 595 (1991); Stonerock vs Miller Bros. Paving, Inc., 72 Ohio App. 3d 123 (19991); Tritt vs Judd's Moving & Storage, Inc., 62 Ohio App. 3d 206 (1990); Omni-Food and Fashion, Inc. vs Smith, 38 Ohio St. 3d 385 (1988); Tardy v. Norfolk S. Corp., 103 Ohio App. 3d 372, 1995; Truck Ins. Exchange v. Superior Court (1998) 67 Cal App. 4th 142.

(This Listing Continued)

CLARK, PERDUE, ARNOLD & SCOTT CO, LPA, Columbus—Continued

DALE K. PERDUE, born Columbus, Ohio, March 22, 1950; admitted to bar, 1980, Ohio; 1981, U.S. District Court, Southern District of Ohio; 1987, Pennsylvania. *Education:* Ohio Northern University (B.A., 1972); Miami University (M.A., 1974); Ohio State University (J.D., 1980). Author: "Restoring Justice: The Constitutional Victory Over Tort Reform," Ohio Trial, Spring, 1995. Lecturer: "Techniques for Effective Voir Dire: How to Level the Playing Field," OATL Negligence Law Seminar, 1999; "Taking Your Case to the Next Level: Maximizing Your Effectiveness Through Jury Research," Utah Trial Lawyers Association, 2000; "Presenting the TBI Case at Trial: Proven Techniques for Maximum Effectiveness," BIA, 2000; "The TBI Jury: Strategy and Voir Dire," Utah Trial Lawyers Association, 2000; "Conducting Informal Discovery," ATLA, 2000; "Taking Your Case to the Next Level: Maximizing Results through Focus Groups," ATLA, 2001.*Member:* Columbus and Ohio State Bar Associations; Franklin County Trial Lawyers Association (President, 1995-1996); Ohio Academy of Trial Lawyers (President, 1996-1997); Association of Trial Lawyers of America; Brain Injury Association of Ohio; Brain Injury Association; Million Dollar Advocates Forum. Listed in The Best Lawyers in America; American Board of Trial Advocates. (Certified as a Civil Trial Specialist by the National Board of Trial Advocacy). ***PRACTICE AREAS:*** Personal Injury; Products Liability; Wrongful Death; Insurance; Traumatic Brian Injury Litigation; Nursing Home Torts. ***Email:*** dperdue@cpaslaw.com

PAUL O. SCOTT, born Cambridge, Ohio, November 4, 1948; admitted to bar, 1974, Ohio; 1975, Florida and U.S. District Court, Southern and Northern Districts of Ohio; 1978, U.S. Supreme Court; 1980, U.S. Court of Appeals, Sixth Circuit. *Education:* Ohio Northern University (B.A., 1970); Capital University (J.D., 1974). Phi Alpha Theta; Omicron Delta Kappa; Pi Kappa Delta. Member, Order of the Curia. Frequent Author, including "Referral Fees," Malpractice Alert! Ohio Bar Liability Insurance Co., January 1996. Frequent Lecturer, including "Advanced Trial Techniques," Ohio Legal Center, 1997. Listed in: The Best Lawyers in America. *Member:* Columbus, Ohio State and American Bar Associations; Franklin County Trial Lawyers Association (President, 1981); Ohio Academy of Trial Lawyers (President, 1991-1992); The Association of Trial Lawyers of America; American Board of Trial Advocates. Fellow, American College of Trial Lawyers. (Certified as a Civil Trial Specialist by the National Board of Trial Advocacy). ***PRACTICE AREAS:*** Personal Injury; Products Liability; Wrongful Death; Insurance; Aviation; Railroad; Professional Negligence. ***Email:*** pscott@cpaslaw.com

JAMES E. ARNOLD, born Boston, Massachusetts, December 1, 1956; admitted to bar, 1987, Ohio, U.S. District Court, Southern and Northern Districts of Ohio, U.S. Court of Appeals, Sixth Circuit and U.S. Supreme Court. *Education:* Ohio State University (B.S., 1979); Capital University Law School (J.D., cum laude, 1987). Order of the Curia; Order of the Barristers. Oralist, National Moot Court Team. Member, Capital University Law Review, 1986-1987. Lecturer, Trial Skills Seminar, Ohio State Bar Association, 1995, 1998. Listed in, "The Best Lawyers in America," "Ohio Super Lawyers," and "Columbus Top Lawyers." *Member:* Columbus, Ohio State and American Bar Associations; Franklin County Trial Lawyers Association; Ohio Trial Lawyers Association; The Association of Trial Lawyers of America; Million Dollar Advocates Forum. ***PRACTICE AREAS:*** Wrongful Death; Medical Malpractice; Personal Injury; Products Liability; Business Torts; Complex Commercial Litigation; Class Actions. ***Email:*** jarnold@cpaslaw.com

D. ANDREW LIST, born Newark, Ohio, July 14, 1965; admitted to bar, 1991, Ohio; 1993, U.S. District Court, Southern District of Ohio; 2000, U.S. District Court, Northern District of Ohio and U.S. Supreme Court. *Education:* Wake Forest University (B.A., cum laude, 1987); The Ohio State University, Moritz College of Law (J.D., 1990). Listed: *Best Lawyers in America,* 2005-2006; *Ohio Super Lawyers,* 2004-2005; *Business First Top Lawyers in Columbus,* 2004-2005. Honors: Franklin County Trial Lawyer's Association President's Award, 1994, 1999; Million Dollar Advocates Forum; Distinguished Service Award, 125th General Assembly of Ohio. Lecturer: Strategies for Handling Vioxx Litigation (Charleston, Columbus, Indianapolis, Louisville, Nashville, Washington, Pa., 2004-2005); Mass Tort and Class Action Litigation (Columbus, 2004); Voir Dire in the Anti-Lawsuit Era (Ohio Attorney General, 2004; Franklin County Trial Lawyers Association, 2003); Long-Term Care Litigation: Representing the Elderly Client (Bucyrus, 2005; Columbus, 2004; Strongsville, 2003; Canton, Cleveland, Columbus, Dayton, Toledo, 2002); Litigation After Tort Reform in Ohio (Beachwood, Cincinnati, Columbus, 2003). Author: *The Vioxx Debate,* Columbus Bar Association, *Columbus Bar Briefs* (2005); *Representing the Neglected Nursing Home Resident,* Columbus Bar Association, *Columbus Bar Briefs* (2003). *Member:* Franklin County Trial Lawyers Association (President, 2002-2003; Board of Trustees, 1996-2003); Ohio Academy of Trial Lawyers; Association of Trial Lawyers of America. ***PRACTICE AREAS:*** Mass Torts; Class Actions; Long Term Care Litigation; Products Liability; Commercial Litigation. ***Email:*** alist@cpaslaw.com

DAVID E. KAUFFMAN, born Lancaster, Ohio, October 4, 1968; admitted to bar, 1995, Ohio; 2000, U.S. District Court, Southern District of Ohio; 2004, U.S. Tax Court. *Education:* Capital University (B.A., cum laude, 1991); The Ohio State University (J.D., 1995). Recipient, American Jurisprudence Award Trial Practice, Conflicts of Law. Contributing Author: "Giving: Philanthropy for Everyone," Quantum Press, 2002. Author: "Code Section 419 Plans: What are they and who needs them," Journal of Practical Estate Planning, Commerce Clearing House, 2001; "Planning for Client's with Special Needs Children," Journal of Practical Estate Planning Commerce Clearing House, 2000; "Transformational Dialectic; Philosophical and Practical Implementation," Journal of Practical Estate Planning, Commerce Clearing House, 2000; "Transformational Dialectic Part One," Journal of Practical Estate Planning, Commerce Clearing House, 1999. Lecturer: "Drafting Wills and Trusts," Ohio State Bar Association, 2003-2004, 2005; "Charitable Planning Strategies," Ohio Bar Association, 2004; "Business Succession Planning," Ohio Lumberman's Association, 2003-2004; "Estate Planning for Business Owners," Ohio Veterinary Association, 2003; "Economic Growth and Tax Relief Reconciliation Act," Financial Planning Association of Central Ohio, 2003; "Charitable Giving," Ohio Catholic Foundation, 2003; "Working with Not-for-Profit Organizations," National Network of Estate Planning Attorneys, Reno, NV, 2000; Estate Planning: Basics and Beyond," Martin County Florida Estate Planning Council, 2000; "Implementing Charitable Giving into your Estate Planning Practice," National Network of Estate Planning Attorneys, Chicago, IL, 1999; "Non-Profit Organizations," National Network Estate Planning Attorneys, Nashville, TN, 1999; "Charitable Giving," Mercy Hospital Foundation, 1999; "Estate Planning Practice Management Round Table," National Network Estate Planning Attorneys, Seattle WA, 1998. Commerce Clearing House, *Journal of Practical Estate Planning* Advisory Board, 1991-2001. *Member:* Columbus and Ohio State Bar Associations; Wealth Council L.L.C.; Tri-County Estate Planning Council (President, 1999); Ohio Forum of Estate Planning Attorneys. ***PRACTICE AREAS:*** Estate Planning; Probate; Trust Administration; Probate Litigation; Special Needs Trusts Planning; Elder Law. ***Email:*** dkauffman@cpaslaw.com

GLEN R. PRITCHARD, born Lawton, Oklahoma, November 5, 1962; admitted to bar, 1988, Ohio; 1992, U.S. District Court, Southern District of Ohio. *Education:* Denison University (B.A., 1985); Ohio State University (J.D., 1988). Recipient: Ohio Academy of Trial Lawyers Amicus Curiae Award, 1994; Franklin County Trial Lawyers President's Award, 1994. Lecturer: "Getting by the Gate-Keeper—Making Sense of Daabert v. Merrell Dow," Seneca County Bar Association, June 2001; Allen County Bar Association, May 2000; Mahoning County Bar Association, May 2000. *Member:* Columbus and Ohio State Bar Associations; Ohio Academy of Trial Lawyers (Member, Editorial Board, Ohio Trial Magazine, 2000—; Member, Technology Committee, 2000—); Franklin County Trial Lawyers Association (Co-Editor, Quarterly Comment Newsletter, 1994-1995; Editor, Quarterly Comment Newsletter, 1995-1996; Chair, Negligence Law Committee, 2000-2001); Association of Trial Lawyers of America. ***PRACTICE AREAS:*** Personal Injury; Wrongful Death; Insurance; Product Liability; Professional Negligence. ***Email:*** gpritchard@cpaslaw.com

BRANDI LASER SESKES, born Akron, Ohio, April 21, 1975; admitted to bar, 2004, Ohio. *Education:* University of Akron (B.A., 1998); Capital University Law School (J.D., 2004). *Member:* Columbus and Ohio State Bar Associations; The Association of Trial Lawyers of America; Franklin County Trial Lawyers Association; Ohio Academy of Trial Lawyers; The Association of Trial Lawyers of America; Ohio Women's Bar Association; Women Lawyers of Franklin County. ***PRACTICE AREAS:*** Wrongful Death; Medical Malpractice; Personal Injury; Products Liability. ***Email:*** bseskes@cpaslaw.com

SCOTT J. STITT, born Parma, Ohio, May 1, 1972; admitted to bar, 2001, Ohio; 2002, U.S. District Court, Southern District of Ohio. *Education:* Boston University (B.A., 1995); The Ohio State University College of Law (J.D., with honors, 2001). National Moot court Team (National Quarterfinalist: first Place in Regional VI). Managing Editor, Ohio State Law Journal. National Trial Team. Author: "Tort Reform—Did H.B. 215 Resurrect Any of the Provisions of H.B. 350?", Ohio Trial, Spring 2000. Presentations: "Fix It or Fight It—Principles for Fighting Malicious Peer Review and for Fixing a system that just Doesn't Work," Semmelweis Society Int'l, 2005. *Member:* Columbus Bar Associations; Franklin Inn of Court. ***PRACTICE AREAS:*** Commercial Litigation; ERISA Litigation; Employment Law; Health Care Litigation; Securities Litigation; Shareholder Litigation; Personal Injury; Wrongful Death; Medical Malpractice. ***Email:*** sstitt@cpaslaw.com

Representative Clients furnished upon request.

LORA H. CLEARY

1500 WEST THIRD AVENUE, SUITE 127
COLUMBUS, OHIO 43212
Telephone: 614-487-8210
Fax: 614-487-8212
Email: lcleary@aol.com
URL: http://www.lawyers.com/lcleary

Family Law, Litigation, Mediation, Collaborative Law.

LORA H. CLEARY, born Chillicothe, Ohio, June 28, 1966; admitted to bar, 1991, Ohio. *Education:* Capital University (B.A., magna cum laude, 1988; J.D., 1991). Phi Beta. *Member:* Columbus (Member, Family Law Committee), Ohio State and American (Member, Child Support Committee) Bar Associations; Collaborative Law Council. ***PRACTICE AREAS:*** Family Law; Divorce; Separation Agreements; Alimony; Child Custody; Child Support; Visitation Rights; Paternity; Mediation; Collaborative Law; Guardian Ad Litem.

RICHARD A. CLINE & CO., LLC

580 S. HIGH STREET, SUITE 200
COLUMBUS, OHIO 43215
Telephone: 614-224-4114
Fax: 614-224-3804
Email: rcline@attorneycline.com
URL: http://www.lawyers.com/richardcline

Criminal Law, DUI, Traffic Tickets, Appellate, Misdemeanor Defense, Professional, License Defense, Medical and Legal License Defense.

MEMBER

RICHARD A. CLINE, born Columbus, Ohio, October 1, 1955; admitted to bar, 1981, Ohio and U.S. District Court, Southern District of Ohio; 1983, U.S. Court of Appeals, Sixth Circuit; 1985, U.S. Supreme Court. *Education:* Kent State University (B.A., Political Science, with honors, 1977; B.S., Criminal Justice, with honors, 1977); Ohio State University (J.D., 1981). *Member:* Ohio State Bar Association (Member, Criminal Law Committee); National Ohio Association of Criminal Defense Lawyers; Association of Criminal Defense Lawyers; Central Ohio Association of Criminal Defense Lawyers. [Retired Major, Ohio National Guard, JAG.]. ***PRACTICE AREAS:*** Criminal Law; Civil Litigation; Administrative Law; Criminal Defense. ***Email:*** rcline@attorneycline.com

(This Listing Continued)

RICHARD D. COLBY

169 EAST LIVINGSTON AVENUE
COLUMBUS, OHIO 43215
Telephone: 614-461-1516
Fax: 614-461-1520
Email: colbylaw@aol.com
URL: http://www.lawyers.com/richardcolbylaw

Civil and Criminal Trials, Family Law, Divorce, Child Custody, Child Support, Visitation Rights, Securities Litigation, Securities Fraud, Small Business Law, Real Estate and Corporate Law.

RICHARD D. COLBY, born Columbus, Ohio, August 31, 1949; admitted to bar, 1974, Ohio; 1975, U.S. District Court, Southern District of Ohio. *Education:* Ohio State University (B.A., 1971); Capital University (J.D., 1974). Phi Alpha Delta. Adjunct Instructor, Medical-Legal Issues, School of Allied Medicine, The Ohio State University, 1985—. *Member:* Columbus and American (Member, Domestic Relations and Litigation Sections) Bar Associations; Franklin County Trial Lawyers Association. ***LANGUAGES:*** Spanish. ***PRACTICE AREAS:*** Family Law; Child Custody; Child Support; Visitation Rights; Small Business Law; Real Estate; Residential Real Estate; Corporate; Litigation; Securities; Investments; Criminal Defense; Driving While Intoxicated; Traffic Violations.

COLLEY SHROYER & ABRAHAM CO., L.P.A.

Established in 1977
HOSTER AND HIGH BUILDING
536 SOUTH HIGH STREET
COLUMBUS, OHIO 43215-5674
Telephone: 614-228-6453
Fax: 614-228-7122
Email: csa@ee.net
URL: http://www.colleyshroyerabraham.com

Civil Trial Practice. Personal Injury, Medical Malpractice, Automobile Accidents, Wrongful Death, Railroad Accidents, Slip and Fall, Negligence, Product Liability and Toxic Torts.

FIRM PROFILE: The firm was founded in 1977 by Michael F. Colley. The firm's practice is limited to representing plaintiffs statewide in personal injury, medical malpractice, products liability and class action cases. Members of the firm regularly participate as lecturers in trial practice seminars nationwide and are active in professional associations and civic affairs.

MICHAEL F. COLLEY, born Youngstown, Ohio, October 26, 1936; admitted to bar, 1961, Ohio; U.S. District Court, Southern and Northern Districts of Ohio; U.S. Court of Appeals, 6th Circuit. *Education:* The Ohio State University (B.A., 1958; J.D., 1961). Phi Delta Phi. Author: "Defective Products: Post Sale Duty to Warn and to Remedy," ATLA, 1977; "Persuasion: First Impressions Really Count," ABA Litigation Journal, Summer, 1977; "Principles of Direct Examination," Trial Diplomacy Journal, Spring, 1979; "Friendly Persuasion," Trial Magazine, August, 1981; "Proof of Defect," Trial Magazine, October, 1981; "Design Defects in Products Liability," SMU Center for Advanced Professional Development, 1980; "Opening Statement in the Products Liability Case," SMU Center for Advanced Professional Development, 1981; Co-Author: "Anatomy of a Trial 2nd," ATLA, 1982"; "Style, Structure and Semantics," Trial Magazine, August, 1983; "Picking a Damage Jury in a Mild Head Trauma Case," Trial Diplomacy Journal, Fall, 1992; "Re-creating Mom in the Courtroom," The Trial Lawyer, October, 1999. Lecturer: Association of Trial Lawyers of America; Ohio Academy of Trial Lawyers; Franklin County Trial Lawyers Association; Ohio State Bar Association; Ohio State University College of Law; Capital University Law School; Kansas Trial Lawyers Association; Mississippi Trial Lawyers Association; North Carolina Trial Lawyers Association; South Carolina Trial Lawyers Association; Kentucky Trial Lawyers Association; Tennessee Trial Lawyers Association; West Virginia Trial Lawyers Association; Oklahoma Trial Lawyers Association; Alaska Trial Lawyers Association; Arkansas Bar Association; The Belli Seminar; National Head Injury Foundation, Inc.; Annual Trial Lawyers Seminar, 1990-1993. Chairman, Board of Editors Trial Diplomacy Journal, 1979-1984. Assistant City Attorney, City of Columbus, 1962-1964. Special Counsel to Attorney General of Ohio, 1963-1964. Who's Who in American Law, First and Second Editions. Selected as one of the outstanding trial lawyers in the United States, Town and Country Magazine, 1985. *Member:* Columbus, Ohio State, American and International Bar Associations; Franklin County Trial Lawyers Association (President, 1968-1969); Ohio Academy of Trial Lawyers (President, 1971-1972); The Association of Trial Lawyers of America (National Secretary, 1975-1976; National Vice President, 1976-1977; President-Elect, 1977-1978; President, 1978-1979); Roscoe Pound-American Trial Lawyers Foundation (President, 1982-1985); American Board of Trial Advocates (Ohio Chapter, President, 1991-1992, National Vice-President, President-Elect and President, 1995-1997); Diplomate, American Board of Professional Liability Attorneys. ***REPORTED CASES:*** Temple v. Wean United, 50 Ohio St. 2d 317 (1977) (adopted Section 402(A) of the "Restatement of Torts"), Morgan v. Biro Manufacturing 15 Ohio St. 3d 339 (1984) (adopted to the "Restatement of Torts" for conflict of law issues), Allenius v. Thomas, M.D., et al, 42 Ohio St. 3d 131 (1989) (defined the statute of limitations in medical negligence cases). ***PRACTICE AREAS:*** Products Liability Law; Malpractice Law; Negligence and Commercial Law; Personal Injury Law. ***Email:*** mfcolley@rrcol.com

DAVID I. SHROYER, born Middletown, Ohio, June 2, 1955; admitted to bar, 1980, Ohio; 1982, U.S. District Court, Southern District of Ohio. *Education:* Ohio State University (B.S., 1977); Capital University (J.D., 1980). Author: Monograph "Mastering the Principles of Trial Advocacy," 1988. Adjunct Professor, Capital University, Trial Advocacy, 1985—. Instructor, U.S. Attorney Generals Advocacy Institute, 1987-1989. Assistant U.S. Attorney, U.S. Attorney's Office, 1982-1989. Assistant Franklin County Prosecutor, 1980-1982. Member, Supreme Court Rules Advisory Committee (1997—). *Member:* American Bar Association; Ohio Academy of Trial Lawyers (Member, Negligence Law Subcommittee, 1989—); Franklin County Trial Lawyers Association. ***PRACTICE AREAS:*** Medical Malpractice; Personal Injury.

(This Listing Continued)

DANIEL N. ABRAHAM, born Nelsonville, Ohio, May 2, 1956; admitted to bar, 1982, Ohio; 1991, U.S. Supreme Court and U.S. Court of Appeals, Sixth Circuit; 1994, U.S. District Court, Southern District of Ohio; 1995, U.S. District Court, Northern District of Ohio. *Education:* West Liberty State College (B.S., 1978); Capital University (J.D., 1981). Director, Economic Crime Unit, Franklin County Prosecutors Office, 1980-1990. Adjunct Professor, Trial and Evidence, Columbus State Community College, 1992—. *Member:* Columbus, Ohio State and American Bar Associations; The Association of Trial Lawyers of America; Franklin County Trial Lawyers Association. ***PRACTICE AREAS:*** Products Liability Law; Personal Injury Law. ***Email:*** dnabraham@ee.net

---

ROGER GARCIA, admitted to bar, 1996, Ohio. *Education:* Ohio University (D.O., 1983); Capital University (J.D., 1996). Member, Ohio College Osteopathic Emergency Physicians. Fellow, American College Legal Medicine. ***PRACTICE AREAS:*** Medical Malpractice.

REFERENCE: Bank One of Columbus, NA.

JEFFREY P. COMPTON

COLUMBUS, OHIO
(See Grove City)

Personal Injury, Automobile Accidents, Insurance, Medical Malpractice, Wrongful Death, Slip and Fall, Family Law, Divorce, Child Custody, Child Support, Visitation Rights, Real Estate, Buying or Selling, Business Formation, Buying and Selling of Businesses, Small Business Law, Partnerships, Limited Liability Companies, Corporate, Contracts, Bankruptcy, Wills and Probate, Estate Administration, Powers of Attorney and Health Care documents, Consumer Law, IRS Negotiations.

CONNOR BEHAL, LLP

501 SOUTH HIGH STREET
COLUMBUS, OHIO 43215
Telephone: 614-464-2025
Fax: 614-224-8708
URL: http://www.connorbehal.com
URL: http://www.lawyers.com/ddconnorlaw

Civil and Criminal Litigation, Driving While Intoxicated, Criminal Defense, DUI, White Collar Crimes, Professional Licenses, Workers Compensation, Business Law, Tax Planning, Family Law, Divorce, Probate and Estate Planning, Personal Injury, Automobile Accidents, Negligence, Social Security, Disability.

FIRM PROFILE: Connor Behal LLP was founded in 1998, by attorneys Daniel D. Connor and Robert J. Behal who merged two diverse law practices of long-standing duration. Mr. Connor began his private practice as a solo practitioner in 1971 and gradually grew his practice into a three lawyer firm by 1995 practicing in the areas of DUI, workers' compensation, personal injury, social security, and defending persons charged with crimes (mostly in the white collar area) or the loss of their professional license. Mr. Behal commenced his general practice in 1977. In 1988, he became a partner in a large Columbus law firm where he focused on business representation including litigation, business planning and formation, contract work and transactions. Behal continued his practice in those areas as well as the areas of probate and estate planning, domestic relations and personal injury litigation.

The members of this law firm have written and spoken extensively in their various areas of practice and have had a great deal of involvement in various government and community activities. An extremely competent support staff as well as the latest office technology enable the firm to deliver the best possible legal services to its clients in the most efficient manner. One block away from the court house in downtown Columbus, our firm also regularly represents clients in Fairfield, Licking, Pickaway, Madison, Union and Delaware counties as well as Zanesville, Marion, Springfield, Chillicothe and the surrounding areas of Central Ohio.

DANIEL D. CONNOR, born Columbus, Ohio, June 14, 1939; admitted to bar, 1968, Ohio. *Education:* University of Dayton; The Ohio State University (B.S., 1961; J.D., 1967). Author: "Testing For Alcohol or Drug Intoxication," Ohio Legal Center Institute, 1983; "Ohio Drunk Driving Law," 4th Edition, Professional Education Systems, Inc., 1986; "Winning Strategies in Per Se Cases," Capital Law School Continuing Legal Education Program, 1984. President, Columbus Civil Service Commission, 1984-1994. *Member:* Ohio State Bar Association; Franklin County Trial Lawyers Association (Chairman, Workers Compensation Committee, 1982-1984; Member, Board of Trustees, 1984-1989); Ohio Academy of Trial Lawyers (Seminar Lecturer, Criminal Law - Driving Under Influence, 1982-1983); National Association of Criminal Defense Lawyers; Ohio Association of Criminal Defense Lawyers (Member, Board of Directors, 1988-1990; Seminar Lecturer, Voir Dire Examination and Opening Statements in DWI Cases, 1989-1990). [Lt., U.S. Navy, 1962-1965]. ***REPORTED CASES:*** Columbus Bar Association v. Harris, 1 Ohio St. 3d 33 (1982); Varnacini v. Registrar, 59 Ohio App. 3d 28 (1991); Major v. Lincoln National Life Insurance Co., 84 Ohio App. 3d 219 (1993); The State ex rel. Waddle v. Industrial Comm. of Ohio, et al., 67 Ohio St. 3rd 452 (1993); The State ex. rel. Patterson v. Industrial Commission of Ohio, 77 Ohio St. 3rd 201 (1996); The State ex. rel. Waugh v. Industrial Commission of Ohio, 77 Ohio St. 3rd 453 (1997). ***PRACTICE AREAS:*** Driving While Intoxicated; Criminal Trial Practice; White Collar Crime; Juvenile Law; Negligence; Workers Compensation; Professional Licensing. ***Email:*** dconnor@connorbehal.com

ROBERT J. BEHAL, born Columbus, Ohio, September 10, 1953; admitted to bar, 1977, Ohio; 1978, U.S. District Court, Southern District of Ohio; 2002, U.S. Court of Appeals, 6th Circuit. *Education:* The Ohio State University (B.A., 1974; J.D., 1977). Member, Board of Zoning Adjustment, City of Columbus, 1988-1998. *Member:* Columbus, Ohio State and American Bar Associations; Ohio Academy of Trial Lawyers; Franklin County Trial Lawyers Association (President, 1993-1994). ***PRACTICE AREAS:*** Business Plan-

(This Listing Continued)

CONNOR BEHAL, LLP, Columbus—Continued

ning; Contracts; Transactions; Business Litigation; Family Law; Divorce; Tax Planning; Probate; Estate Planning; Personal Injury; Automobile Accidents. ***Email:*** rbehal@connorbehal.com

DENNIS P. EVANS, born Columbus, Ohio, June 21, 1953; admitted to bar, 1985, Ohio; U.S. Supreme Court; U.S. District Court, Southern District of Ohio. *Education:* Ohio State University (B.S., 1975); Capital University (J.D., magna cum laude, 1985). Order of the Curia. Inn of Court (Fellow). Member, Capital University Law Review, 1984-1985. Columbus Police Officer, 1978-1986. Seminar Lecturer, "Drink and Drive," Ohio Association of Criminal Defense Lawyers Seminar, March 31, 1985; "Hot Issues in DUI Litigation," August 25, 1995; "OMVI Law Update," President's Seminar, Franklin County Trial Lawyers Association, December 1, 1995; "Strategies in Handling DWI and DUI Cases in Ohio" November, 1999 and November 2000; Case Law Update, CBA Criminal Law Seminar, December 1999, December 2000 and December 2001; Advanced DUI Seminar, April 2000 and February 2002; Ohio State Bar Association DUI Seminar, December 2001; Lorman DUI Update Seminar, May 2003 and 2004. *Member:* Columbus and Ohio State Bar Associations; Franklin County Trial Lawyers Association; The Ohio Academy of Trial Lawyers; Ohio Association of Criminal Defense Lawyers; National Association of Criminal Defense Lawyers. ***REPORTED CASES:*** Buchanan v. Registrar, 85 Ohio App. 3d 263, 619 N.E. 2d 523 (1993); State v. Marryott, 85 Ohio App. 3d 601, 620 N.E. 2d 891 (1993); Hudson v. Brown, 82 Ohio App. 3d 574, 612 N.E. 2d 817 (1993); State v. Lamm, 80 Ohio App. 3d 510, 609 N.E. 2d 1286 (1992); Columbus v. Watson, 64 Ohio App. 3d 6, 580 N.E. 494 (1989); Columbus v. Forest, 36 Ohio App. 3d 169, 522 N.E. 2d 52 (1987). ***PRACTICE AREAS:*** Driving While Intoxicated; Criminal Trial Practice; Personal Injury. ***Email:*** devans@connorbehal.com

KENNETH S. HAFENSTEIN, born Topeka, Kansas, January 1, 1969; admitted to bar, 1994, Ohio. *Education:* Wittenberg University (B.A., summa cum laude, 1991); The Ohio State University (J.D., 1994). *Member:* Columbus and Ohio State Bar Associations. (Certified Specialist in Workers Compensation Law, Ohio State Bar Association). ***PRACTICE AREAS:*** Worker's Compensation. ***Email:*** khafenstein@connorbehal.com

DANIEL JOSEPH FUSCO, born Mansfield, Ohio, January 3, 1969; admitted to bar, 1999, Ohio; 2000, U.S. District Court, Southern District of Ohio. *Education:* Ashland University (B.S., 1992); Capital University (J.D., 1999). *Member:* Columbus and Ohio State Bar Associations. ***PRACTICE AREAS:*** Corporate Law; Estate Planning; Probate Administration. ***Email:*** dfusco@connorbehal.com

JOHN P. JOHNSON, born Columbus, Ohio, August 6, 1964; admitted to bar, 1993, Ohio; 1998, U.S. District Court, Southern District of Ohio. *Education:* Ohio Wesleyan University (B.A., 1986); Capital University (J.D., 1993). Assistant Attorney General, State of Ohio, 1994-1995. *Member:* Columbus Bar Association (Member: Family Law Committee, 1999—; Municipal Court Committee, 2000—). ***PRACTICE AREAS:*** Domestic Relations; Family Law; Criminal Defense; Traffic Violations; Litigation. ***Email:*** jjohnson@connorbehal.com

GARY P. MARTIN, born Barberton, Ohio, July 16, 1970; admitted to bar, 1996, Ohio; 2001, U.S. District Court, Southern District of Ohio. *Education:* The Ohio State University (B.A., 1992; J.D., 1995). *Member:* Columbus and Ohio State Bar Associations. ***PRACTICE AREAS:*** Workers Compensation; Social Security Disability; Personal Injury. ***Email:*** gmartin@connorbehal.com

LEGAL SUPPORT PERSONNEL

Rita Tobias ***Terri McQuaid***
Judy Lund ***Justine Maag***
Christine Kramer ***Diane Koscho***
Wendy Bayless ***Jenica Ballard***
Melissa Altman ***Deanna DeGraffinreed***
Cathy Baker

REFERENCE: Key Bank National Association.

CRABBE, BROWN & JAMES LLP

Established in 1915

500 SOUTH FRONT STREET, SUITE 1200
COLUMBUS, OHIO 43215
Telephone: 614-228-5511
Fax: 614-229-4559
Email: info@cbjLawyers.com
URL: http://www.cbjLawyers.com

Cincinnati, Ohio Office: 30 Garfield Place, Suite 740, 45202. Telephone: 513-784-1525. Fax: 513-784-1250.
Cleveland, Ohio Office: 1280 W. Third Street. Telephone: 216-574-9312.
Lancaster, Ohio Office: 111 South Broad Street, Suite 209, 43130. Telephone: 740-689-1743. Fax: 740-689-1746.
Urbana, Ohio Office: 118 Scioto Street. Telephone: 937-652-4000.

General Insurance Defense, Product Liability, Professional Malpractice, Premises Liability, Environmental and Toxic Tort Claims, Employment and Labor Law, Tax Matters, General Business and Corporate Law and Litigation, Banking and Securities, Real Estate, Probate and Estate Planning, Criminal Law, Administrative, Regulatory and Governmental Law, Workers Compensation, Intellectual Property, Fire, Arson and Fraud, Fidelity and Surety Life, Accident and Health, Insurance Coverage Law, Construction Claims, Health and Hospital Law, Oil, Gas and Energy Law, Transportation Law, Automobile Dealer Law, Zoning, International Practice and Domestic Law, Land Use Planning, and Eminent Domain.

(This Listing Continued)

FIRM PROFILE: Crabbe, Brown & James has been a member of the legal community serving Ohio and surrounding states for more than 75 years with offices in Columbus, Cincinnati and Lancaster. We are also a member of the American Law Firm Association which has one member firm in every major city in the country. Our diverse clientele includes major U.S. companies, financial institutions, public utilities, smaller corporations, partnerships and individuals as well as associations and community organizations. Superior service and performance is a tradition with Crabbe, Brown & James -- A tradition built upon the emphasis of responsiveness, trust, and respect for the individual client.

VINCENT J. LODICO, born New York, N.Y., February 7, 1948; admitted to bar, 1973, Ohio. *Education:* Fordham University (B.A., 1969; J.D., 1973). Phi Alpha Delta. ***PRACTICE AREAS:*** Healthcare; Medical Malpractice; Insurance Defense; Products Liability Defense; Transportation. ***Email:*** VLodico@cbjLawyers.com

STEVEN B. AYERS, born Williamston, North Carolina, November 21, 1948; admitted to bar, 1975, Ohio. *Education:* University of North Carolina at Chapel Hill (B.S., 1971; J.D., 1975). Beta Gamma Sigma. ***PRACTICE AREAS:*** Professional Negligence; Products Liability; Personal Injury; Commercial Litigation. ***Email:*** SAyers@cbjLawyers.com

JEFFREY M. BROWN, born Columbus, Ohio, July 4, 1953; admitted to bar, 1979, Ohio. *Education:* Wittenberg University (B.A., cum laude, 1975); The Ohio State University (J.D., 1979). Delta Theta Phi. Listed in: Who's Who in American Law. Ohio Supreme Court Board of Commissioners on Grievances and Discipline, 1994-1998. City of Columbus Development Commission, 1990-1991; Columbus Apartment Association. *Member:* Ohio Association of Civil Trial Attorneys; Columbus Defense Association; Columbus Claims Association; United States Trademark Association; Computer Law Association. ***PRACTICE AREAS:*** Corporate Law; Commercial Law; Insurance Defense; Labor and Employment; Litigation; Zoning Law. ***Email:*** JBrown@cbjLawyers.com

LARRY H. JAMES, born Elyria, Ohio, December 26, 1951; admitted to bar, 1977, Ohio. *Education:* Wittenberg University (B.A., 1974); Cleveland State University (J.D., 1977). Assistant Director of Law, Cleveland, Ohio, 1977-1978. Assistant Director of Law, Columbus, Ohio, 1978-1981. Chairman, Ohio Elections Commission, 1985-1989. Member, Advisory Committee on Local Rules, U.S. District Court, Southern District of Ohio, 1990-1992. Supreme Court of Ohio Board of Bar Examiners, 1989-1992. Board of Trustees, Columbus Museum of Art, 1992-2002. President, Board of Trustees for The Martin Luther King Jr. Center for Performing and Cultural Arts, 1986-1990 and 1997—. Past General Counsel of Columbus NAACP and Columbus Urban League. General Counsel of the National Fraternal Order of Police, 2001—. Long Range Planning Committee, 1982-1985; Ethics Committee, 1979-1983; Chairperson, Unauthorized Practice of Law Committee, 1981-1983; Council of Delegates, 1982-1985. *Member:* Columbus, Ohio State and American Bar Associations. ***PRACTICE AREAS:*** Labor and Employment; Government Practice; Administrative Hearings and Appeals; Civil Rights Litigation; Attorney Discipline; General Litigation; General Corporate and Business Practice. ***Email:*** LJames@cbjlawyers.com

RICHARD D. WETZEL, JR., born Pittsburgh, Pennsylvania, October 7, 1957; admitted to bar, 1982, Ohio; U.S. District Court, Southern District of Ohio; U.S. Court of Appeals, Sixth Circuit; U.S. Court of International Trade; U.S. Supreme Court. *Education:* Ohio University (B.A., History, summa cum laude, 1979); Dickinson School of Law (J.D., 1982). Phi Beta Kappa; Omicron Delta Kappa; Pi Gamma Mu; Phi Kappa Phi. *Member:* Ohio State and American Bar Associations; Customs and International Trade Bar Association; Ohio Oil and Gas Association. ***LANGUAGES:*** Portuguese, Spanish and French. ***PRACTICE AREAS:*** Corporate Law; Commercial Law; International Law; Probate; Estate Planning; Real Estate; Oil and Gas Law. ***Email:*** RWetzel@cbjLawyers.com

LUIS M. ALCALDE, born Havana, Cuba, March 17, 1954; admitted to bar, 1980, Ohio; 1981, U.S. Court of Military Appeals; 1984, U.S. District Court, Southern District of Ohio; 1992, U.S. Court of Appeals, Sixth Circuit. *Education:* The Ohio State University (B.A., 1977; J.D., 1980). Assistant Attorney General, State of Ohio, 1984-1987. *Member:* Columbus and Ohio State Bar Associations; Computer Law Association. [Capt., U.S. Army JAG Corps, 1981-1984]. ***LANGUAGES:*** Spanish. ***PRACTICE AREAS:*** Cable; Telecommunications; Computer Law; Corporate Law; Commercial Law; Intellectual Property; International Law; Litigation; Municipal Law; Governmental Law; Professional Liability; Taxation. ***Email:*** LAlcalde@cbjLawyers.com

JOHN C. ALBERT, born Columbus, Ohio, August 25, 1955; admitted to bar, 1981, Ohio; 1983, U.S. District Court, Southern District of Ohio; 1992, U.S. Court of Appeals, Sixth Circuit; 1993, U.S. District Court, Northern District of Ohio. *Education:* Otterbein College; Ohio State University (B.S., Finance, 1977); Capital University (J.D., 1981). Staff Counsel and Ohio Legislative Agent, Ohio State Medical Board, 1982-1984. Assistant Attorney General, Ohio, 1984-1987. Special Counsel to the Attorney General's Office, 1987-1988. *Member:* Columbus, Ohio State and American Bar Associations; Columbus Claims Association; Ohio Counsel of School Board Attorneys; Federation of Insurance and Corporate Counsel; Ohio Association of Civil Trial Attorneys. ***PRACTICE AREAS:*** Labor and Employment; Litigation; Governmental Law; Professional Liability; Real Estate; Workers Compensation; School Law; Products Liability; Discrimination; Automobile Liability. ***Email:*** JAlbert@cbjLawyers.com

GEORGE R. McCUE, III, born Lorain, Ohio, April 6, 1956; admitted to bar, 1981, Ohio and U.S. District Court, Southern District of Ohio; 1982, U.S. District Court, Northern District of Ohio. *Education:* The Ohio State University (B.S.B.A., Finance, 1978; J.D., 1981). Phi Kappa Phi; Beta Gamma Sigma; Phi Alpha Kappa. John Phahl Honorarium. *Member:* Columbus, Ohio State and American Bar Associations. ***PRACTICE AREAS:*** Municipal Law; Government Relations; Administrative Litigation; Zoning. ***Email:*** GMccue@cbjLawyers.com

MICHAEL R. HENRY, born Chillicothe, Ohio, March 17, 1957; admitted to bar, 1985, Ohio. *Education:* Miami University (B.S., 1980); Capital University (J.D., cum laude, 1985). *Member:* Ohio State Bar Association; Ohio Association of Civil Trial Attorneys; Defense Research Institute; Columbus Association of Civil Trial Attorneys. ***PRACTICE AREAS:*** Insurance; Litigation; Government Immunity; General Litigation. ***Email:*** MHenry@cbjLawyers.com

(This Listing Continued)

ROBERT C. BUCHBINDER, born Jersey City, New Jersey, August 13, 1958; admitted to bar, 1988, Ohio and U.S. District Court, Southern District of Ohio. *Education:* Bethany College (B.A., 1980); Louisiana State University; Capital University (J.D., 1987). Assistant City Prosecutor, 1987-1988. *Member:* Columbus, Ohio State and American Bar Associations; Defense Research Institute; Ohio Association of Civil Trial Attorneys; Columbus Claims Association. ***PRACTICE AREAS:*** Insurance Defense; Litigation; Transportation; Trucking Law. ***Email:*** RBuchbinder@cbjLawyers.com

STEVEN A. DAVIS, born Lancaster, Ohio, October 19, 1963; admitted to bar, 1991, Ohio. *Education:* University of Arizona (B.A., 1990); University of Texas (J.D., 1991). Chairman, Fairfield County Republican Party, 2004—. *Member:* Fairfield County and Ohio State Bar Associations; Lancaster City Council. (Resident, Lancaster Office). ***PRACTICE AREAS:*** Corporate Law; Commercial Law; Insurance Defense; Litigation; Municipal Law; Premises Liability; Governmental Law; Civil Litigation; Personal Injury Defense; Products Liability. ***Email:*** SDavis@cbjLawyers.com

JOHN P. KENNEDY, born New Brunswick, New Jersey, September 4, 1953; admitted to bar, 1978, Ohio. *Education:* University of Bridgeport (B.S., cum laude, 1975); Ohio Northern University (J.D., 1978). President, Zoning and Finance Committee, Columbus City Council, 1988-1999. Judge Tenth District Court of Appeals, State of Ohio, 1999-2002. Member, Ohio Real Estate Commission, 2004—. *Member:* Columbus, Ohio State and American Bar Associations. ***PRACTICE AREAS:*** Government Affairs; Zoning Law; Real Estate Development; Real Property. ***Email:*** JKennedy@cbjLawyers.com

MICHAEL T. SHANNON, born Columbus, Ohio, May 30, 1957; admitted to bar, 1983, Ohio. *Education:* Ohio Dominican College (B.A., cum laude, 1979); Capital University (J.D., 1982). Labor Relations Administrator, City of Columbus, 1984-1988. Development Regulations Administrator, City of Columbus, 1988-1992. Member, Whitehall City Council, 2001—. ***LANGUAGES:*** French and Latin. ***PRACTICE AREAS:*** Real Estate Development; Commercial Real Estate; Land Use Planning; Zoning; Constitutional Law. ***Email:*** MShannon@cbjLawyers.com

CHRISTINA L. CORL, born Goshen, Indiana, April 25, 1969; admitted to bar, 1995, Michigan and U.S. District Court, Eastern District of Michigan; 1997, Ohio; 1999, Georgia. *Education:* Western Michigan University (B.S., Phil., 1991); Thomas M. Cooley Law School (J.D., summa cum laude, 1994). Member, Capital University Mentor Program, Columbus Claims Association. ***PRACTICE AREAS:*** Labor and Employment Law; Products Liability; General Negligence Defense. ***Email:*** CCorl@cbjLawyers.com

DANIEL J. HURLEY, born Cleveland, Ohio, November 19, 1961; admitted to bar, 1986, Ohio and U.S. District Court, Northern and Southern Districts of Ohio. *Education:* Xavier University (B.A., cum laude, 1983); Cleveland-Marshall College of Law (J.D., 1986). *Member:* Columbus and Ohio State Bar Associations; Ohio Association of Civil Trial Attorneys. ***REPORTED CASES:*** Gayheart v. Doe(2001), 143 OhioApp.3d 692;Carmen v. Link(1997),119 OhioApp.3d 244;Brown v. Allstate(1991),81 OhioApp.3d 87. ***PRACTICE AREAS:*** General Insurance Defense; Premises and Products Liability. ***Email:*** DHurley@cbjLawyers.com

LAURA MACGREGOR COMEK, born Youngstown, Ohio, December 13, 1971; admitted to bar, 1999, Ohio; 2000, U.S. District Court, Southern District of Ohio. *Education:* Youngstown State University (B.S.B.A., 1994); Capital University (J.D., 1999). *Member:* Columbus, Ohio State and American Bar Associations. ***Email:*** LComek@cbjLawyers.com

ASSOCIATES

STEVEN E. MILLER, born Columbus, Ohio, January 27, 1970; admitted to bar, 1996, Ohio. *Education:* Ohio Dominican College (B.A., 1992); Capital University (J.D., 1996). *Member:* Columbus and Ohio State Bar Associations. ***Email:*** SMiller@cbjLawyers.com

PHILLIP A. TEMPLETON, born Bartlesville, Oklahoma, January 19, 1966; admitted to bar, 1992, Ohio; 1999, U.S. District Court, Southern District of Ohio. *Education:* Marietta College (B.A., 1988); Capital University (J.D., 1992). Former Franklin County Assistant Public Defender with experience in both Municipal and Common Pleas Court. *Member:* Columbus, Ohio State and American Bar Associations; Ohio Association of Criminal Defense Lawyers. ***Email:*** PTempleton@cbjLawyers.com

JAMES L. ERVIN, JR., born Los Angeles, California, August 5, 1970; admitted to bar, 1996, Ohio. *Education:* University of Arizona (B.A., 1993); Capital University (J.D., 1996). Chairperson, Board on the Unauthorized Practice of the Law, Supreme Court of Ohio. Board Member: Columbus Metropolitan Housing Authority; NeverQuit USA, Inc. ***PRACTICE AREAS:*** Business Litigation; Government Relations; Lobbying; Litigation; Criminal Defense. ***Email:*** JErvin@cbjLawyers.com

AMANDA C. BAKER, born Columbus, Ohio, February 15, 1975; admitted to bar, 2000, Ohio; 2002, U.S. District Court, Southern District of Ohio. *Education:* Miami University (B.S., cum laude, 1997); Capital University (J.D., 2000). Order of the Curia. ***Email:*** ABaker@cbjLawyers.com

MATTHEW R. PLANEY, born Youngstown, Ohio, July 9, 1967; admitted to bar, 1996, Ohio; 1997, U.S. District Court, Northern District of Ohio; 1998, U.S. Court of Appeals, Sixth Circuit. *Education:* Youngstown State University (B.A., magna cum laude, 1993); University of Toledo (J.D., cum laude, 1996). *Member:* Ohio State and American Bar Associations. ***Email:*** MPlaney@cbjLawyers.com

JEFFREY D. HOUSER, born Centerville, Ohio, August 8, 1978; admitted to bar, 2003, Ohio; 2004, Indiana. *Education:* Miami University (B.A., cum laude, 2000); Ohio State University (J.D., 2003). ***PRACTICE AREAS:*** Litigation; Corporate Law. ***Email:*** JHouser@cbjLawyers.com

EILEEN R. BOWER, born Saginaw, Michigan, December 28, 1965; admitted to bar, 1995, Ohio. *Education:* De La Salle University (B.A., 1985); Ateneo de Manila University (J.D., 1989); Capital University (LL.M., Taxation, 1998). ***PRACTICE AREAS:*** Tax Matters; Estate Planning.

STEPHEN D. BROWN, born Lancaster, Ohio, December 27, 1963; admitted to bar, 1998, Ohio; 2000, U.S. District Court, Southern District of Ohio; 2003, U.S. District Court, Northern District of Ohio. *Education:* Ohio University (B.B.A., 1986); Capital University Law School (J.D., 1998). *Member:* Columbus, Fairfield County, Ohio State and American Bar Associations. (Resident, Lancaster Office). ***Email:*** sbrown@cbjlawyers.com

(This Listing Continued)

OF COUNSEL

WILLIAM A. GOLDMAN (Also Member, Goldman & Braunstein, LLP)

MICHAEL BRAUNSTEIN (Also Member, Goldman & Braunstein, LLP)

ANDY DOUGLAS, born Toledo, Ohio, July 5, 1932; admitted to bar, 1960, Ohio. *Education:* University of Toledo (J.D., 1959). Instructor: University of Toledo Community & Technical College, 1980-1984; Ohio Dominican College, 1992-1995. Toledo City Counsel, 1961-1980. Judge, Ohio Sixth District Court of Appeals, 1981-1984. Justice, Ohio Supreme Court, 1985-2002. *Member:* Toledo, Lucas County and Ohio State Bar Associations; American Judicature Society. [1st Lt., Army Infantry and Signal Corps, 1954-1956.]. ***PRACTICE AREAS:*** General Practice; Labor and Employment; Government Service. ***Email:*** ADouglas@cbjLawyers.com

MARK E. KERNS, born Urbana, Ohio, July 7, 1955; admitted to bar, 1980, Ohio. *Education:* Bowling Green State University (B.S., 1977); University of Dayton (J.D., 1980). Special Counsel to the State of Ohio through the Attorney General. *Member:* Columbus, Clark County, Champaign County and Ohio State Bar Associations. (Resident, Urbana Office). ***PRACTICE AREAS:*** Medical Malpractice; Personal Injury; Wrongful Death; Probate; Estate Planning. ***Email:*** MKerns@cbjLawyers.com

BRIAN R. MCGRAW, born Madison, Wisconsin, August 23, 1957; admitted to bar, 1986, Ohio. *Education:* Kenyon College (A.B., 1979); Cleveland-Marshall College of Law (J.D., 1986). *Member:* Ohio State Bar Association; Cleveland Association of Civil Trial Attorneys; Cuyahoga County Criminal Defense Lawyers Association. (Resident, Cleveland Office). ***PRACTICE AREAS:*** Criminal Law; Personal Injury. ***Email:*** bmcgraw@cbjlawyers.com

REPRESENTATIVE CLIENTS: Allstate Insurance Co.; American Guernsey Assn.; AIG; Autozone; Burger King Corp.; Caronia Corporation; Central Ohio Transit Authority; Chemcote, Inc.; Clear Channel Entertainment; Columbus Internatonal Airport; Con-Way Transportation Services Inc.; Corning Glass Works; Crum & Foster Managers Corp.; Dayton International Airport; Dominion Homes; Electronics Automation Corp.; Erie Insurance Co.; Farmers Insurance Co.; Federal Express; Firemans Fund Insurance; First Financial Ins. Co.; First Securities Corp.; Gallagher-Bassett; Grove Worldwide; Hartland Express; InPhyNet; ITT Hartford Specialty Risks, Inc.; Kemper Group; Liberty Mutual; Lifestyles Communities; Medical Protective; National Cablevision Network; National Energy Explorations; National Fraternal Order of Police; Nationwide Insurance Companies; Ohio Fair Plan; Ohio Hospital Insurance Co.; Ohio Medical Professional Liability Underwriters Assn.; Old Dominion Freight Lines; Pharmacists Mutual Ins. Co.; Peabody Coal Co.; Polycel, Inc.; Progressive Ins. Co.; Prudential/LMI; SAFCO Life Ins. Co.; Ricart Automotive; Sandstone Resources; Select Sires, Inc.; Solid Waste Authority of Central Ohio; Spectrum Emergency Care, Inc.; Sperry New Holland; The Coleman Co.; Travelers Insurance Co.; United Dairy Farmers; United Parcel Service; U.S. Gypsum; Weyerhauser/Tacoma Credit Union; World Wide Insurance Group.
REFERENCE: Fifth Third Bank.

(For biographical data on other personnel, see Professional Biographies at Cincinnati, Ohio)

DENMEAD LAW OFFICE

37 WEST BROAD STREET, SUITE 1100-B
COLUMBUS, OHIO 43215
Telephone: 614-228-5271
Fax: 614-228-7624
Email: cdenmead@sbcglobal.net
URL: http://www.denmeadlaw.com

Civil Trial and Appellate Practice and Personal Injury, Traumatic Brain Injury (TBI), Professional Negligence and Complex Litigation including Class Actions, Patents, Civil Rights, Civil Litigation, RICO, Employment and Political Subdivision Liability issues.

CRAIG DENMEAD, born Columbus, Ohio, July 30, 1947; admitted to bar, 1972, Ohio; 1975, U.S. District Court, Southern District of Ohio; 1990, Pennsylvania, U.S. Supreme Court and U.S. Court of Appeals, Sixth Circuit. *Education:* The Ohio State University (B.S., 1969; J.D., cum laude, 1972). Author: "The Death of Medical Necessity," *TBI Challenge,* Winter 1993, Issue 1, Number 1, published by the National Head Injury Foundation. Co-Author: "A Bright 'IDEA' for the Student with Traumatic Brain Injury," a chapter from *Analysis, Understanding and Presentation of Cases Involving Traumatic Brain Injury,* published by the National Head Injury Foundation, 1994. Assistant Prosecutor, Franklin County, 1972-1974. *Member:* Columbus, Ohio State, American and Federal Bar Associations; Federation of Insurance and Corporate Counsel. ***REPORTED CASES:*** Florence County School District Four v. Carter, (1993) 510 U.S. 7, Counsel for Amicus Curiae, National Head Injury Foundation; Firestone v. Galbreath, (6th Cir. 1994) 25 F.3d 323, Counsel of Record for one of the Defendants-Appellees; Forest Hills Util. Co. v. City of Heath (6th Cir. 1982), 701 F.2d 177, Counsel of Record for Defendant-Appellee; Buchel v. Prentice (6th Cir. 1977), 572 F.2d 141, Counsel of Record for Defendant-Appellees; Firestone v. Galbreath (6th Cir. 1992), 976 F.2d 279, Counsel of Record for one of the Defendants-Appellees; Firestone v. Galbreath (U.S.D.C. S.D. Ohio 1990), 747 Fed.Supp. 1556, Counsel of Record for one of the Defendants-Appellees; Firestone v. Galbreath (1993), 67 Ohio St. 3d 87, Counsel of Record for one of the Respondents; Rockey v. 84 Lumber Co. (1993), 66 Ohio St. 3d 221, Counsel of Record for Amicus Curiae; Cook v. Naveau (1993), 66 Ohio St. 3d 227, Counsel of Record for Plaintiff-Appellant; Hutchinson v. J.C. Penny Casualty Ins. Co. (1985), 17 Ohio St. 3d 195.

M. SHAWN DINGUS

Established in 2003

1141 S. HIGH STREET

COLUMBUS, OHIO 43206

Telephone: 614-542-0220

Fax: 614-542-0230

Email: sdingus@dinguslaw.com

URL: http://www.dinguslaw.com

Personal Injury, Wrongful Death, Civil Litigation, Criminal Law, Juvenile Law and Family Law.

M. SHAWN DINGUS, born Ashland, Kentucky, June 19, 1972; admitted to bar, 1998, Ohio; 2001, U.S. District Court, Southern District of Ohio and U.S. Court of Federal Claims; 2003, U.S. Court of Appeals, Federal Circuit. *Education:* Morehead State University (B.A., 1994); Akron University Law School (J.D., cum laude, 1998). Omicron Delta Kappa. President, Phi Delta Phi, 1997-1998. *Member:* Columbus and Ohio State Bar Associations; Association of Trial Lawyers of America; Ohio Association of Trial Lawyers; Franklin County Trial Lawyers Association; Ohio Association of Criminal Defense Lawyers.

DINSMORE & SHOHL LLP

10TH FLOOR, 175 SOUTH THIRD STREET

COLUMBUS, OHIO 43215-5134

Telephone: 614-628-6880

FAX: 614-628-6890

Email: info@dinslaw.com

URL: http://www.dinslaw.com

Cincinnati, Ohio Office: 255 East Fifth Street, Suite 1900, 45202-4700. Telephone: 513-977-8200. FAX: 513-977-8141.

Dayton, Ohio Office: One Dayton Centre, One South Main Street, Suite 1300, 45402. Telephone: 937-449-6400. FAX: 937-449-6405.

Lexington, Kentucky Office: Lexington Financial Center, 250 West Main Street, Suite 1400, 40507. Telephone: 859-425-1000. FAX: 859-425-1099.

Louisville, Kentucky Office: 1400 PNC Plaza, 500 West Jefferson Street, 40202. Telephone: 502-540-2300. FAX: 502-585-2207.

Pittsburgh, Pennsylvania Office: The Grant Building, 330 Grant Street, Suite 2415, 15219. Telephone: 412-281-5000. FAX: 412-281-5055.

Charleston, West Virginia Office: 900 Lee Street, Huntington Square, Suite 600, 25301. Mailing Address: P.O. Box 11887, 25339. Telephone: 304-357-0900. FAX: 304-357-0919.

Appellate Practice; Bankruptcy; Banks and Banking; Business Law; Commercial Real Estate; Construction Law; Contracts; Corporate Law; Education Law; Environmental Law; General Practice; Labor & Employment; Leases and Leasing; Litigation; Medical Malpractice; Mortgages; Probate; Real Estate; Taxation; Trusts & Estates; Wills; Workers' Compensation; Zoning, Planning and Land Use.

FIRM PROFILE: Our Foundation

For over 95 years, Dinsmore & Shohl LLP has been providing quality legal counsel to our clients. In recent years, our practice has grown to include seven offices and taken on national and international clients. Today's full-service practice with more than 260 attorneys continues to live up to the ideals set in 1908 by Frank F. Dinsmore and Walter M. Shohl: efficient, cost-effective and comprehensive solutions for every client.

Our Service

At Dinsmore & Shohl LLP, we put our clients first in every element of our full-service practice. The Firm's commitment to quality service extends from our highly-skilled attorneys to our experienced professional staff. By establishing client relationships based on trust, communication and responsiveness, we listen to our clients' concerns and expectations while refining our service to ensure that these needs are met. We recognize that service begins with accessibility and ends with fulfilled expectations.

Our Clients

With over 35 practice areas, Dinsmore & Shohl LLP has the experience and variety to meet your legal needs. Our clients range from public and private corporations to charitable organizations and encompass healthcare providers, local and state governments, financial institutions, real estate developers, franchisors and distributors and pharmaceutical companies.

Our Technology

By embracing and utilizing the latest technology, our efficiencies are passed on to clients. We continuously assess and update our case management systems, intranet, extranets, billing systems, document management systems, and other practice-specific software to ensure our work product can be leveraged and measured. In addition, our legal library uses technology to keep important, up-to-date information close at hand. These combined resources help us strategize, plan, develop and integrate our practice to meet your business needs.

Our Innovation

Our commitment to client service extends to our growing subsidiaries: DinsNet Technologies LLC, Great Water Capital Partners, LLC, and Mercantile Title Agency, Inc. which provide various portals for client collaboration. These unique services help optimize e-business, business intelligence and knowledge management solutions for clients.

Our Future

(This Listing Continued)

Utilizing the latest technology and resources, we embrace the future today while maintaining our historical values. With attorneys and staff skilled in a broad range of legal and ancillary subjects, we will continue to offer the knowledge and experience needed to maintain our strict standard of excellence. This commitment has continued to drive our growth and will sustain our foundation into the future.

RICK A. LAVINSKY, born New Rochelle, New York, October 9, 1944; admitted to bar, 1969, Ohio; U.S. District Court, Southern District of Ohio; U.S. Court of Military Appeals. *Education:* Hobart College (B.A., 1966); Northwestern University (J.D., 1969). Pi Gamma Mu. Author: "Representing the Seller; Representing the Seller as Lender," Real Estate Bedrock Series, Ohio Legal Center Institute, 1975; Chapter, "Condominiums," Principles of Ohio Real Estate Titles, Ohio Land Title Association textbook published, 1984 and Second edition, 2000. *Member:* Columbus and Ohio State Bar Associations; Ohio Land Title Association (Former Member, Board of Trustees). ***LANGUAGES:*** French. ***PRACTICE AREAS:*** Commercial Real Estate; Condominium Law; Community Association Law; Corporate Law; Banking Law. ***Email:*** rick.lavinsky@dinslaw.com

WAYNE A. JENKINS, born Euclid, Ohio, July 11, 1953; admitted to bar, 1978, Ohio; U.S. District Court, Southern District of Ohio; U.S. Tax Court. *Education:* Denison University (B.A., magna cum laude, 1975); The Ohio State University (J.D., 1978). *Member:* Columbus and Ohio State Bar Associations. Fellow, American College of Trust and Estate Counsel. ***PRACTICE AREAS:*** Estate Planning; Probate; Tax; Corporate. ***Email:*** wayne.jenkins@dinslaw.com

MICHAEL L. SQUILLACE, born Hackensack, New Jersey, June 24, 1955; admitted to bar, 1980, Ohio; U.S. District Court, Northern and Southern Districts of Ohio; U.S. Court of Appeals, Sixth Circuit. *Education:* University of Notre Dame (B.A., 1977); University of Toledo School of Law (J.D., cum laude, 1980). Associate Editor, University of Toledo Law Review, 1978-1979. Assistant Attorney General, State of Ohio, 1980-1991. (Certified Specialist in Workers Compensation Law, Ohio State Bar Association). ***PRACTICE AREAS:*** Workers Compensation Law. ***Email:*** mike.squillace@dinslaw.com

MARILENA R. WALTERS, born Noepoli, Potenza, Italy, May 12, 1954; admitted to bar, 1984, Ohio. *Education:* Ohio State University (B.S., Pharm., 1978; J.D., 1984). Member, Rho Chi Pharmaceutical Honorary Society. Registered Pharmacist, Ohio, 1978—. Listed in: Strathmore's Who's Who; International Who's Who of Professionals. *Member:* Ohio State Bar Assocoation; The Association of Trial Lawyers of America; Ohio Association of Civil Trial Attorneys; Defense Research Institute. ***LANGUAGES:*** Italian. ***PRACTICE AREAS:*** Litigation; Hospital Negligence; Products Liability Defense; Medical Negligence. ***Email:*** walters@dinslaw.com

WILLIAM M. MATTES, born Easton, Pennsylvania, June 6, 1963; admitted to bar, 1988, Ohio; 1994, U.S. District Court, Southern District of Ohio; 1998, U.S. Court of Appeals, Sixth Circuit; 2003, U.S. District Court, Northern District of Ohio. *Education:* Southern Connecticut State (B.S., 1985); Ohio Northern University (J.D.,1988). Member, Moot Court. Member, Ohio Northern University Law Review. *Member:* Columbus and Ohio State Bar Associations. ***REPORTED CASES:*** Disciplinary Counsel v. Ball (1999), 85 Ohio St. 3d 393; DeRolph v. State (1997), 78 Ohio St. 3d 419; DeRolph v. State (1997), 78 Ohio St. 3d 193; Elliott v. Ohio Department of Insurance (1993), 88 Ohio App. 3d 1; Whirlpool Corp. v. Industrial Commission (1991), 61 Ohio St. 3d 719; Anderson v. Ohio Department of Insurance (1991), 58 Ohio St. 3d 215; Sorrentino v. Ohio National Guard (1990), 53 Ohio St. 3d 214; CSX Transportation, Inc. v. Public Utilities Commission (1989), 64 Ohio App. 3d 10. ***PRACTICE AREAS:*** Construction Litigation; Commercial Litigation; Employment Litigation; Franchise Law; School Law. ***Email:*** bill.mattes@dinslaw.com

KIRK M. WALL, born Loveland, Colorado, September 21, 1967; admitted to bar, 1993, Ohio; U.S. Court of Appeals, Sixth and Seventh Circuits; U.S. District Court, Northern and Southern Districts of Ohio. *Education:* The Ohio State University (B.A., 1989); Capital University School of Law (J.D., magna cum laude, 1993). Member, Board of Trustees, Project EAR. Member, Ohio Public Transit Authorities. *Member:* Columbus, Ohio State and American Bar Associations. ***PRACTICE AREAS:*** Employment Litigation; Labor and Employment; Litigation; National Labor Relations Act. ***Email:*** kirk.wall@dinslaw.com

ASSOCIATES

JOHN D. JOLLEY, born Columbus, Ohio, December 9, 1967; admitted to bar, 1996, Michigan; 1997, Ohio; U.S. District Court, Eastern District of Michigan. *Education:* The Ohio State University (B.A., 1991); University of Detroit, Mercy School of Law (J.D., 1995); The George Washington University Law School (LL.M., Environmental Law, 1997). Member, University of Detroit Mercy Law Review, 1994-1995. Author: Comment, "Death by Right: A Call for Change to Michigan's Healthcare Decisions Law," 72 U.Det. Mercy L. Rev. 927 (1995). LL.M. Advisory Editor, The Environmental Lawyer, 1995-1996. *Member:* Columbus (Member, Real Estate Committee and Environmental Law Committee) and Ohio State (Member, Real Property Law Section) Bar Associations; State Bar of Michigan. [U.S. Army (National Guard), 1986-1994]. ***PRACTICE AREAS:*** Corporate Law; Real Estate; Environmental Law. ***Email:*** john.jolley@dinslaw.com

MICHAEL J. KING, born Toledo, Ohio, February 10, 1971; admitted to bar, 2000, Ohio; U.S. District Court, Northern and Southern Districts of Ohio; U.S. Court of Appeals, Sixth Circuit. *Education:* The Ohio State University (B.A., 1997; J.D., 2000). Law Clerk to the Hon. Lisa L. Sadler, Court of Common Pleas of Franklin County, Ohio, 2000-2002. *Member:* Columbus and Ohio State Bar Associations. ***PRACTICE AREAS:*** Litigation; Commercial Litigation; Products Liability; Appellate Practice. ***Email:*** michael.king@dinslaw.com

KELLY L. KAUFFMAN, born St. Louis, Missouri, November 17, 1971; admitted to bar, 1999, Ohio and U.S. Court of Appeals, Sixth Circuit; 2000, U.S. District Court, Southern District of Ohio; 2002, U.S. District Court, Northern District of Ohio. *Education:* Illinois Wesleyan University (B.A., magna cum laude, 1994); University of Illinois (J.D., magna cum laude, 1998). Order of the Coif. Articles Editor and Notes Editor, 1997-1998 and Member, University of Illinois Law Review. Law Clerk to the Hon. Alice M. Batchelder,

(This Listing Continued)

U.S. Court of Appeals, Sixth Circuit, 1998-1999. *Member:* Ohio State Bar Association. ***PRACTICE AREAS:*** Labor and Employment. **Email:** kelly.kauffman@dinslaw.com

REPRESENTATIVE CLIENTS: Capital Lighting, Inc.; Buckeye Ford-Mercury, Inc.; Central Ohio Transit Authority; Ohio Lake Communities Association; Worthington Mall; Levis Commons Mall; Capital Plus, Inc.; University Hospital; Alliance Primary Care; Christ Hospital; Kindred Healthcare, Inc; Extendicare, Inc.; Laurels Healthcare, Inc.; Bank One Trust Co., N.A.; FirstMerit Bank, N.A.; CAMCO Financial Corporation; Huntington National Bank; Bartlett Farmers Bank; Interstate Cold Storage, Inc.; Ohio State University; Perpetual Federal Savings Bank.

DREHER LANGER & TOMKIES L.L.P.

2250 HUNTINGTON CENTER
41 SOUTH HIGH STREET
COLUMBUS, OHIO 43215
Telephone: 614-628-8000
Facsimile: 614-628-1600
Email: ddreher@dltlaw.com
URL: http://www.dltlaw.com

Banking and Consumer Financial Services. Regulation of Banks and Other Financial Institutions, Credit Cards, Mortgages and Other Consumer Finance Products, Debt Collection, Bankruptcy, Insurance, Reinsurance, Privacy and E-Commerce.

FIRM PROFILE: Dreher Langer & Tomkies L.L.P. concentrates its practice in the area of banking and financial services law. The Firm's practice encompasses all aspects of financial services to consumers and includes strategic and corporate planning, lending program development, internet lending, forms preparation and review, federal and multistate regulation and compliance, chartering and licensing, insurance, reinsurance, regulatory and legislative counseling and representation, creditor representation in bankruptcy and litigation, and acquisition counseling and support. The Firm's clients include banks, and bank holding companies, diversified companies, finance companies, credit and charge card issuers, insurance companies, mortgage bankers, student loan providers, retailers, manufacturers, investment bankers, industry and trade associations, and coalition and issue groups.

MEMBERS OF FIRM

DARRELL L. DREHER, admitted to bar, 1974, Ohio. *Education:* The Ohio State University (B.A., 1966); George Washington University (J.D., with honors, 1973). Order of the Coif. Founding Fellow and Member of Board of Regents, American College of Consumer Financial Services Lawyers; Chairman of Conference on Consumer Finance Law. ***PRACTICE AREAS:*** Banking and Finance; Consumer Finance; Mortgages; Credit Card Law. **Email:** ddreher@dltlaw.com

JEFFREY I. LANGER, admitted to bar, 1980, Illinois; 1990, Ohio; 1996, U.S. Supreme Court. *Education:* University of Illinois (A.B., summa cum laude, 1977); Northwestern University (J.D., 1980). Phi Beta Kappa. Founding Member and Fellow, American College of Financial Services Lawyers. *Member:* American Bar Association (Vice-Chair, Consumer Financial Services Committee, Business Law Section, 2000-2003). ***PRACTICE AREAS:*** Banking Regulation; Consumer Banking; Consumer Credit; Credit Card Law. **Email:** jlanger@dltlaw.com

MICHAEL C. TOMKIES, admitted to bar, 1986, Ohio; 1988, District of Columbia. *Education:* Hampden-Sydney College (B.A., summa cum laude, 1983); Harvard University (J.D., 1986). Phi Beta Kappa. Fellow, American College of Financial Services Lawyers. ***PRACTICE AREAS:*** Financial Institutions; Consumer Finance; Debt Collection Regulation. **Email:** mtomkies@dltlaw.com

JUDITH M. SCHEIDERER, admitted to bar, 1991, Ohio. *Education:* The Ohio State University (B.A., 1967; M.S., 1973; J.D., summa cum laude, 1991). Order of the Coif. **Email:** jscheiderer@dltlaw.com

MARGARET M. STOLAR, admitted to bar, 1990, Pennsylvania; 1991, New York; 1993, Ohio. *Education:* Allegheny College (B.S., cum laude, 1985); University of Pittsburgh (J.D., magna cum laude, 1990). Order of the Coif. **Email:** mstolar@dltlaw.com

SENIOR COUNSEL

ELIZABETH L. ANSTAETT, admitted to bar, 1991, Ohio. *Education:* The Ohio State University (B.A., 1985; J.D., summa cum laude, 1991). Order of the Coif. Law Clerk to Hon. John D. Holschuh, Chief Judge, U.S. District Court, Southern District of Ohio, 1991-1993. **Email:** eanstaett@dltlaw.com

ASSOCIATES

CHARLES VICTOR GALL, admitted to bar, 1999, Ohio. *Education:* The Ohio State University (B.A., 1996; J.D., with honors, 1999). **Email:** cgall@dltlaw.com

VANESSA A. NELSON, admitted to bar, 2000, Ohio. *Education:* Princeton University (A.B., 1993); Case Western Reserve University (J.D., cum laude, 2000). **Email:** vnelson@dltlaw.com

OF COUNSEL

ROBIN RONQUILLO DE LEO, admitted to bar, 1990, Louisiana (Not admitted in Ohio). *Education:* Michigan State University (B.A., 1987); Tulane University of Louisiana (J.D., cum laude, 1990). ***PRACTICE AREAS:*** Bankruptcy; Consumer Finance; Banking. **Email:** robin@dreher-la.com

ROBERT J. KAPITAN, admitted to bar, 1964, Ohio. *Education:* John Carroll University (B.S.S., magna cum laude, 1959); Cleveland-Marshall College of Law (J.D., cum laude, 1964). ***PRACTICE AREAS:*** Consumer Finance; Mortgage Lending. **Email:** bob@bobkapitan.com

REPRESENTATIVE CLIENTS: Alliance Data Systems Corporation; American Express Company; American Financial Services Association; American General Finance, Inc.; AmeriCredit Corp.; Aon Corporation; Associates First Capital Corporation; Bank One Corporation; BankAmerica Corp.; Berkshire Hathaway; BMW Financial Services NA, LLC; Bombardier Capital Inc.; Bridgestone/Firestone, Inc.; Capital One Financial Corporation; Central States Health and Life Co. of Omaha; ChevronTexaco Corporation; The CIT Group, Inc.; CitiGroup, Inc.; Community Loans of America, Inc.; CompuCredit Corporation; Countrywide Home Loans, Inc.; Credit Industry Research Council; Credit Suisse Group; Deutsche Bank AG; DaimlerChrysler Corporation; Dillard Department Stores, Inc.; E*Trade Finance Group, Inc.; Employers Reinsurance Company; First Nationwide Bank; Ford Motor Credit Corporation; Friedman's Inc.; Gateway, Inc.; GMAC Mortgage Corp.; GE Capital Consumer Card Co.; General Electric Capital Corporation; General Motors Acceptance Corporation; Goldman Sachs & Co.; Harland Financial Solutions; Household International, Inc.; Huntington Bancshares Incorporated; J.P. Morgan Chase Corp.; Kennedy-Western University; KeyCorp; Knight-Ridder, Inc.; M&I Bank; MBNA Corporation; Mellon Financial Corporation; Merrill Lynch & Co., Inc.; Monogram Credit Card Bank of Georgia; Morgan Stanley, Dean Witter & Co.; National Australian Bank; National City Corporation; National Premium Finance Association; Nationwide Mutual Insurance Company; Nordstrom, Inc.; Ohio Bankers League; Ohio Financial Services Association; Ohio Premium Finance Association; Ohio Savings Bank; Porsche Business Services, Inc.; Primus Venture Partners, Inc.; Providian Financial Corporation; Scott Fetzer Company; Student Loan Target Corporation; TCF Financial Corp.; Toyota Motor Credit Corporation; Transamerica Corporation; Volkswagen of America, Inc.; The Volvo Group; VW Credit, Inc.; Wachovia Corporation; Warburg Pincus LLC; Washington Mutual, Inc.; Wells Fargo & Co.; World Financial Network National Bank; Zale Corporation.

(This Listing Continued)

WILLIAM SIDNEY DRUEN

85 EAST DESHLER AVENUE
COLUMBUS, OHIO 43230
Telephone: 614-444-7655
Fax: 614-444-7655
Email: druens@gmail.com
URL: http://www.williamsidneydruen.com

Corporation Law, Real Estate, Securities Law, Finance Law.

WILLIAM SIDNEY DRUEN, born 1942; admitted to bar, 1968, Virginia; 1970, Ohio. *Education:* Hampden-Sydney College (A.B., 1964); University of Virginia (LL.B., 1968). *Member:* Virginia State Bar. ***PRACTICE AREAS:*** Corporation Law; Real Estate; Securities Law; Finance Law.

VINCENT A. DUGAN, JR.

500 SOUTH FOURTH STREET
COLUMBUS, OHIO 43206
Telephone: 614-222-8200
Fax: 614-222-8100
Email: vadmrlaw@sbcglobal.net

Family Law, Divorce, Child Custody, Child Support, Adoption Law, Visitation Rights, Real Estate, Small Business Law, Traffic Violations.

VINCENT A. DUGAN, JR., born Pittsburgh, Pennsylvania, 1955; admitted to bar, 1983, Ohio. *Education:* Duquesne University (B.A., 1977); Capital University School of Law (J.D., 1982). *Member:* Columbus and Ohio State Bar Associations; Ohio Academy of Trial Lawyers. (Certified Specialist in Family Relations Law, Ohio State Bar Association)

KEVIN DURKIN

471 EAST BROAD STREET, SUITE 1100
COLUMBUS, OHIO 43215
Telephone: 614-884-1551
Fax: 614-884-1550
Email: info@atd-law.com
URL: http://www.lawyers.com/atd-law

Civil and Criminal Trial and Appellate Practice in State and Federal Courts. Administrative Law, Business Litigation, Criminal Defense, Taxation.

KEVIN PATRICK DURKIN, born Cleveland, Ohio, September 27, 1955; admitted to bar, 1980, Ohio; 1981, U.S. District Court, Southern District of Ohio; 1987, U.S. Court of Appeals, Sixth Circuit; 2000, U.S. Supreme Court; 2003, U.S. District Court, Northern District of Ohio. *Education:* Youngstown State University (A.B., magna cum laude, 1977); Ohio State University (J.D., 1980). Special Prosecutor, City of Whitehall, Ohio, 1984-1990. State Hearing Officer, 1991—. Member, State Public Defenders Commission (Governor's Appointee). *Member:* Columbus Bar Association (Chairperson, Juvenile Law Committee, 1994-1995); Central Ohio Association of Juvenile Lawyers (Past President); Central Ohio Association of Criminal Defense Lawyers. ***PRACTICE AREAS:*** Criminal Trial Practice; Civil Trial Practice; Appellate Practice; Juvenile Law; Business Litigation; Criminal Defense. **Email:** kd@tayloranddurkin.com

EARL, WARBURTON, ADAMS & DAVIS

A LEGAL PROFESSIONAL ASSOCIATION
136 WEST MOUND STREET
COLUMBUS, OHIO 43215
Telephone: 614-464-2392
Telecopier: 614-464-0754

General Trial and Appellate Practice. Insurance, Negligence, Products Liability, Medical and Professional Malpractice, Premises Liability, Workers Compensation, Corporate, Toxic Torts, Real Estate, Aviation and Probate Law.

FIRM PROFILE: Established in 1970, our firm represents the interests of individuals, as well as local and national corporate clients throughout the state of Ohio.

TED EARL, born Chillicothe, Ohio, February 9, 1934; admitted to bar, 1960, Ohio; 1961, U.S. District Court, Southern District of Ohio; 1977, U.S. District Court, Northern District of Ohio; 1980, U.S. District Court, Eastern District of Kentucky and U.S. Court of Appeals, Sixth Circuit; 1985, U.S. Supreme Court. *Education:* Miami University (B.A., 1956); The Ohio State University (LL.B., 1960). Phi Delta Phi; Omicron Delta Kappa.

(This Listing Continued)

EARL, WARBURTON, ADAMS & DAVIS, A LEGAL PROFESSIONAL ASSOCIATION, Columbus—Continued

Member, National Panel of Arbitrators, American Arbitration Association, 1971—. *Member:* Columbus (Member, 1974-1979 and Chairman, 1976-1977, Common Pleas Court Committee), Ohio State and American Bar Associations; International Association of Defense Counsel; Ohio Association of Civil Trial Attorneys; Defense Research Institute. ***Email:*** tearl@ohiodefensecounsel.com

DICK M. WARBURTON, JR., born Akron, Ohio, October 22, 1935; admitted to bar, 1961, Ohio and U.S. District Court, Southern District of Ohio; 1981, U.S. District Court, Northern District of Ohio. *Education:* Kent State University (B.A., 1957); The Ohio State University (LL.B., 1960). Phi Delta Phi. Member, Panel of Arbitrators, American Arbitration Association. *Member:* Columbus (Member, Admissions Committee, 1964-1979), Ohio State and American Bar Associations; Ohio Association of Civil Trial Attorneys; Defense Research Institute. ***Email:*** dickw@ohiodefensecounsel.com

ANDREW S. ADAMS, born Portsmouth, Ohio, October 26, 1946; admitted to bar, 1975, Ohio; 1976, U.S. District Court, Southern District of Ohio. *Education:* Ohio University (B.S.Ed., 1970); Capital University (J.D., 1975). *Member:* Columbus, Ohio State and American Bar Associations. ***Email:*** doublea@ohiodefensecounsel.com

THOMAS L. DAVIS, born Columbus, Ohio, August 26, 1956; admitted to bar, 1982, Ohio; 1983, U.S. District Court, Southern District of Ohio and U.S. Court of Appeals, Sixth Circuit. *Education:* The Ohio State University (B.A., 1978); Capital University (J.D., cum laude, 1982). Delta Theta Phi. Member, Order of the Curia. Recipient, American Jurisprudence Award for Contracts and Criminal Procedure. Author: Note, 10 Capital University Law Review 909, 1981; Note, "Michael M. v. Superior Court of Sonoma County: Supreme Court Reopens Confusion Concerning Constitutionality of Gender Based Classifications," ll Capital University Law Review 135, 1981. *Member:* Columbus, Ohio State and American Bar Associations; International Association of Defense Counsel; Defense Research Institute. ***Email:*** tldavis@ohiodefensecounsel.com

STEVEN A. HATTEN, born Columbus, Ohio, February 17, 1953; admitted to bar, 1978, Ohio and U.S. District Court, Southern District of Ohio. *Education:* Ohio State University (B.S., 1975); Capital University (J.D., 1978). Assistant Franklin County Prosecuting Attorney, 1978-1979. Deputy Assistant to Governor, 1979-1982. Member, Industrial Commission of Ohio, 1982-1985. *Member:* Columbus and Ohio State Bar Associations. ***Email:*** shatten@ohiodefensecounsel.com

GRIER D. SCHAFFER, born Pottstown, Pennsylvania, June 14, 1961; admitted to bar, 1988, Ohio, U.S. District Court, Southern and Northern Districts of Ohio; 1993, U.S. Court of Appeals, Sixth Circuit. *Education:* LaSalle University (B.A., History, Political Science, 1983); Capital University Law School (J.D., 1987). Judicial Law Clerk, Court of Common Pleas, Franklin County, Ohio, 1989; Resch & Root Attorneys at Law; Earl, Warburton, Adams & Davis. Member, Board of Construction Appeals, City of Dublin, 1990-1997. *Member:* Columbus (Member, Insurance Law Committee), Ohio State (Member, Ohio Jury Instruction Committee) and American Bar Associations; Defense Research Institute (Committee Member, Medical Liability); Ohio Academy of Trial Lawyers. ***Email:*** gschaffer@ohiodefensecounsel.com

BRUCE L. HIRSCH, born Bowling Green, Ohio, November 15, 1951; admitted to bar, 1979, Ohio and U.S. District Court, Northern District of Ohio; 1982, U.S. District Court, Southern District of Ohio. *Education:* Bowling Green State University (B.A., 1973); Ohio Northern University (J.D., 1979). *Member:* Columbus (Member, Probate, Workers Compensation and Gift and Estate Tax Committee) and Ohio State (Member, Probate and Trust Section) Bar Associations; Ohio Academy of Trial Lawyers (Member, Social Security Disability Committee, Workers' Compensation Section, 1980—). ***Email:*** bhirsch@ohiodefensecounsel.com

CHRISTOPHER R. WALSH, born Xenia, Ohio, October 12, 1958; admitted to bar, 1995, Ohio and U.S. District Court, Northern District of Ohio; 1996, U.S. District Court, Southern District of Ohio. *Education:* The Ohio State University (B.A., History, 1992); Dayton Law School (J.D., 1995). ***Email:*** cwalsh@ohiodefensecounsel.com

MARK CHUPARKOFF, born November 5, 1972; admitted to bar, 2000, Ohio; 2001, Florida. *Education:* Miami University (B.A., 1995); University of Toledo School of Law (J.D., 1999). ***PRACTICE AREAS:*** Criminal Law; Civil Litigation; Personal Injury; Medical Malpractice; Contracts.

REPRESENTATIVE CLIENTS: Ohio Casualty Insurance Co.; Royal Globe Insurance Cos.; The Hartford; Ace USA; ESIS; Harleysville Ins. Cos.; United States Aviation Underwriters, Inc.; Permanent General Assurance Co.; Vision Insurance Group; Podiatry Ins. Co. of America; Universal Underwriters Group; Trinity Health; Ohic Insurance Co.; Victoria Fire and Casualty Co.; MSI Insurance Co.; Matsushita Electric Corp. of America; Volvo Trucks North America; Mettler Toledo, Inc.; Lane Aviation Corp.
REFERENCES: National City Bank; Key Bank.

EASTMAN & SMITH LTD.

Established in 1844

100 EAST BROAD STREET, SUITE 1300
COLUMBUS, OHIO 43215
Telephone: 614-280-1770
Fax: 614-280-1777
URL: http://www.eastmansmith.com

Toledo, Ohio, Office: One Seagate, Twenty-Fourth Floor, P.O. Box 10032, 43699-0032. Telephone: 419-241-6000. Fax: 419-247-1777.
Findlay, Ohio Office: 725 South Main Street, 45840. Telephone: 419-424-5487. Fax: 419-424-9860.

General Civil Practice: Corporate, Business, Banking, Taxation, Real Estate, Securities, Antitrust, Environmental, Public, Labor and Employment, Civil Rights, Employee Benefits, Insurance, Hospital and Health Care, Estate Planning, Pension and Estate Planning, Probate, Workers Compensation, Commercial Litigation, Litigation, Immigration and Naturalization.

(For complete biographical data on all personnel, see Professional Biographies at Toledo, Ohio)

SUSAN GARNER EISENMAN

336 SOUTH HIGH STREET
COLUMBUS, OHIO 43215
Telephone: 614-222-0540
Fax: 614-222-0543
Email: ADOPTOHIO@aol.com
URL: http://www.adoptohiolaw.com

Adoption Law (Private, Interstate, International and Stepparent).

SUSAN GARNER EISENMAN, born Newark, Ohio, May 3, 1950; admitted to bar, 1974, Ohio; 1976, U.S. District Court, Northern District of Ohio; 1977, U.S. District Court, Southern District of Ohio. *Education:* The Ohio State University (B.A., 1971; J.D., cum laude, 1974). Lecturer: Adoption, Legal Institute, Inc., 1989, 1999, 2000; Ohio CLE Institute, 1990, 1992, 1995, 1996 and 2001; North American Council for Adoptable Children, 2000 and 2001; National Association for Open Adoption Education, 1992, 1997 and 2000. Chairman, Ohio Adoption Law Roundtable, 2002—. *Member:* Columbus (Member, Juvenile Law Committee) and Ohio State Bar Associations; American Academy of Adoption Attorneys (Trustee); National Federation for Open Adoption Education. Fellow, Ohio State Bar College; Fellow, Columbus Bar Foundation; Fellow, Ohio State Bar Foundation. ***PRACTICE AREAS:*** Adoption Law; Juvenile; Child Custody; Mediation.

ELK & ELK CO., L.P.A.

FIFTH THIRD CENTER
CAPITAL SQUARE
21 EAST STATE STREET, SUITE 320
COLUMBUS, OHIO 43215
Telephone: 1-888-ELK-OHIO
Email: kthompson@elkandelk.com
URL: http://www.elkandelklaw.com

Cleveland, Ohio Office: Landerhaven Corporation Center, 6100 Parkland Boulevard, 44124-4187. Telephone: 888-355-6446.

Automobile Accidents, Product Defects, Nursing Home Neglect, Medical Malpractice, Personal Injury.

(For complete biographical data on all personnel, see Professional Biographies at Cleveland, Ohio)

JOHN H. ENGLE
ATTORNEY AND COUNSELOR AT LAW

COLUMBUS, OHIO

(See Cincinnati)

Insurance Defense, Arson, Insurance Fraud, Personal Injury, Subrogation, Construction, Casualty Insurance and Commercial Litigation.

FARLOW & ASSOCIATES LLC

COLUMBUS, OHIO

(See Dublin)

Family Law, Divorce, Child Custody, Child Support, Premarital Agreements, Post-Decree Enforcements, Employment Law, School Law, Personal Injury.

JOSEPH F. FRASCH, JR.

1550 OLD HENDERSON ROAD
SUITE N-130
P.O. BOX 20387
COLUMBUS, OHIO 43220
Telephone: 614-326-5544
Fax: 614-457-4151
Email: jfrasch@ix.netcom.com
URL: http://www.lawyers.com/frasch

Trusts and Estates, Wills, Probate, Estate Planning, Taxation, Estate and Gift Taxation, Income Tax, Real Estate.

JOSEPH F. FRASCH, JR., born Columbus, Ohio, March 21, 1948; admitted to bar, 1974, Ohio; 1977, U.S. Tax Court; 1979, U.S. Supreme Court; 1986, U.S. District Court, Southern District of Ohio. *Education:* Capital University (B.A., magna cum laude, 1970; J.D., cum laude, 1974). Order of the Curia; Phi Alpha Delta. General Counsel and Adjunct Professor, Franklin University. *Member:* Columbus (Member, Probate Court Committee), Ohio State and American Bar Associations. ***PRACTICE AREAS:*** Probate Administration; Estate Planning; Income Tax; Real Estate.

FREUND, FREEZE & ARNOLD

A LEGAL PROFESSIONAL ASSOCIATION

CAPITOL SQUARE BUILDING
65 EAST STATE STREET
SUITE 800
COLUMBUS, OHIO 43215
Telephone: 614-827-7300
Telecopier: 614-827-7303
Email: ffalawco@ffalaw.com
URL: http://www.ffalaw.com

Dayton, Ohio Office: One Dayton Centre, One South Main Street, Suite 1800, 45402-2017. Telephone: 937-222-2424. Telecopier: 937-222-5369. Email: ffalawda@ffalaw.com.

(This Listing Continued)

Cincinnati, Ohio Office: Fourth and Walnut Centre, 105 East Fourth Street, Suite 1400, 45202-4006. Telephone: 513-665-3500. Telecopier: 513-665-3503. Email: ffalawci@ffalaw.com.

Covington, Kentucky Office Suite: RiverCenter, 50 East RiverCenter Boulevard, Suite 408, 41011. Telephone: 859-292-2088. Telecopier: 859-292-2514. Email: ffalawky@ffalaw.com

Civil Litigation including Commercial Litigation, Employment Defense, Professional Malpractice Defense, Employer Intentional Torts, Construction Litigation, Civil Rights Defense, Local Government Defense, Nursing Home Defense, Environmental Litigation and Insurance Defense.

FIRM PROFILE: Freund, Freeze & Arnold is a full service litigation firm, with offices in Dayton, Cincinnati, Columbus and Covington, Kentucky. The firm's practice emphasizes civil litigation including commercial litigation, employment litigation, municipal government defense, malpractice defense of doctors, lawyers, realtors, insurance agents and other professionals; civil rights defense; employer intentional torts defense; nursing home defense; environment litigation and insurance defense. The firm holds the highest rating given by Martindale-Hubbell and is listed in the Bar Register of Preeminent Lawyers. The firm is an equal opportunities employer. The attorneys in the firm are active in community and professional groups, including local, state and national bar associations. They also have enjoyed strong academic backgrounds.

Geographic area of practice: The firm represents clients in Ohio, southeastern Indiana, and Kentucky, handling an extensive amount of cases in the cities of Dayton, Cincinnati, and Columbus, in the surrounding Ohio counties of Darke, Shelby, Miami, Clark, Champaign, Logan, Madison, Greene, Preble, Butler, Warren, Clermont, Clinton and Franklin, the Kentucky counties of Boone, Kenton and Campbell, and the Indiana counties of Clark, Dearborn, Decatur, Delaware, Franklin, Henry, Jennings, Ohio, Randolph, Ripley, Rush, Scott, Switzerland, Union and Wayne. The firm practices in the local, state and federal courts of northern Kentucky, southeastern Indiana and southern and central Ohio, including Columbus and Franklin County. The firm has offices in Dayton, Cincinnati, Columbus and Covington, Kentucky. The firm's central location in southwestern Ohio allows it to efficiently and economically serve its clients in all of southwestern Ohio and surrounding areas. Dayton, Springfield, Columbus and Indianapolis are closely linked by Interstate 70. Dayton, Cincinnati and Covington are closely linked by Interstate 75. All four offices are at the junction of the area's major highways.

STEPHEN C. FINDLEY, born Cincinnati, Ohio, February 9, 1949; admitted to bar, 1980, Ohio; 1983, U.S. District Court, Southern District of Ohio. *Education:* University of Cincinnati (B.B.A., 1974); Chase College of Law (J.D., 1980). *Member:* Columbus and Ohio State Bar Associations; Ohio Association of Civil Trial Attorneys; Defense Research Institute. [USMC, 1968-1970]. ***Email:*** sfindley@ffalaw.com

MARK L. SCHUMACHER, born Toledo, Ohio, January 1, 1953; admitted to bar, 1981, Ohio; 1982, U.S. District Court, Northern District of Ohio; 1994, U.S. District Court, Southern District of Ohio; 1995, U.S. Court of Appeals, Sixth Circuit; 1997, U.S. District Court, Western District of Pennsylvania; 1998, Pennsylvania. *Education:* Loyola University; University of Toledo (B.A., 1976; J.D., 1981). *Member:* Columbus, Dayton and Ohio State Bar Associations; Society of Ohio Hospital Attorneys; Ohio Association of Civil Trial Attorneys; Defense Research Institute; American Board of Trial Advocates. ***PRACTICE AREAS:*** Medical Malpractice; Professional Malpractice Defense; Products Liability. ***Email:*** mschumac@ffalaw.com

CARL A. ANTHONY, born Detroit, Michigan, 1962; admitted to bar, 1991, Ohio and U.S. District Court, Southern District of Ohio; 2002, U.S. District Court, Eastern District of Michigan. *Education:* Central Michigan University (B.A., 1986); The Ohio State University (J.D., 1991). *Member:* Columbus and Ohio State Bar Associations; Ohio Association of Civil Trial Attorneys; Defense Research Institute. ***PRACTICE AREAS:*** Insurance Defense; Complex and Multi-District Litigation; Class Actions; Appellate Practice; Litigation. ***Email:*** canthony@ffalaw.com

W. FREDERICK FIFNER, born Lakewood, Ohio, March 7, 1948; admitted to bar, 1973, Ohio; 1974, U.S. District Court, Northern District of Ohio; 1975, U.S. Court of Appeals, Sixth Circuit; 1976, Texas. *Education:* Florida Southern College (A.B., 1970); Cleveland State University (J.D., 1973). Law Clerk to the Hon. Robert B. Krupansky, U.S. District Judge, Northern District of Ohio, 1973-1975. *Member:* Columbus and Ohio State Bar Associations; Defense Research Institute; Ohio Association of Civil Trial Lawyers Attorneys. ***Email:*** ffifner@ffalaw.com

---

JENNIFER L. HILL, born Gallipolis, Ohio, 1974; admitted to bar, 1999, Ohio and U.S. District Court, Southern District of Ohio; 2000, U.S. Court of Appeals, Sixth Circuit; 2005, U.S. District Court, Northern District of Ohio. *Education:* University of Dayton (B.S., Crinimal Justice, 1996; B.A., Psychology, magna cum laude, 1996); University of Dayton School of Law (J.D., 1999). *Member:* Dayton, Columbus, Ohio State and American Bar Associations; Defense Research Institute; Ohio Association of Civil Trial Attorneys. ***PRACTICE AREAS:*** Business Litigation; Commercial Litigation; Personal Injury Defense; Domestic Relations. ***Email:*** jhill@ffalaw.com

SANDRA R. McINTOSH, born Cleveland, Ohio, March 7, 1978; admitted to bar, 2004, Ohio and U.S. District Court, Southern District of Ohio. *Education:* Miami University (B.S., Business Administration, 1999); Capital University (J.D., cum laude, 2004). Judicial Extern to Hon. James L. Graham, U.S. District Court, Southern District of Ohio, 2003. Member, Compliance Work Group, Standards Subcommitte, Supreme Court of Ohio Advisory Committee on Technology and the Court, 2004. *Member:* Columbus and Ohio State Bar Associations; Ohio Association of Civil Trial Attorneys. ***PRACTICE AREAS:*** Personal Injury Defense; Medical Malpractice Defense; Workers Compensation; Probate. ***Email:*** smcintos@ffalaw.com

KEVIN E. HESS, born Ashland, Ohio, February 24, 1979; admitted to bar, 2004, Ohio; U.S. District Court, Northern and Southern Districts of Ohio. *Education:* Messiah College (B.A., History, 2001); University of Dayton (J.D., 2004). *Member:* Columbus, Dayton and Ohio State Bar Associations; Ohio Association of Civil Trial Attorneys. ***PRACTICE AREAS:*** Medical Malpractice Defense; Personal Injury Litigation. ***Email:*** khess@ffalaw.com

LOCAL COUNSEL FOR: Special Trial Counsel: City of Dayton; Miami Valley Hospital; Children's Medical Center; Dayton Power & Light Company; Commercial Clients: Bottlers Services, Inc.; Lutheran Social Services. Insurance Company Clients: Auto-Owners Insurance Company; Cincinnati Ins. Co.; CNA Insurance Company; Erie Insurance Group; Farmers Insurance Group; Government Employees Ins. Co.; GRE Insurance Group; Great American Insurance Company; Kemper Group; Media/Professional Insurance, Inc.; Motorists Insurance Company; OHIC Insurance Co.; St. Paul Fire & Marine Insurance Co.; State Auto Insurance Co.; State Farm Mutual Automobile Insurance Company; Liberty Mutual Ins. Co.; Indiana Ins. Co.; Met Life; GE Medical Protective Ins. Co.; American Empire Group.

(For Complete Biographical Data on Dayton and Cincinnati, Ohio Personnel, See Professional Biographies at Dayton and Cincinnati, Ohio)

THOMAS E. FRIEDMAN

Established in 1977

502 SOUTH THIRD STREET
COLUMBUS, OHIO 43215
Telephone: 614-224-3814
Fax: 614-221-7745
Email: tefriedman@thomasefriedman.com
URL: http://www.thomasefriedman.com

Family Law, Domestic Relations Law, Divorce, Child Custody, Child Support, Visitation Rights, Premarital Agreements, Juvenile Law, Professional and Commercial Collections.

FIRM PROFILE: I am an independent Civil Litigator who focuses primarily on all aspects of family law and civil trials and appeals. I also do professional and commercial collections and practice throughout Central Ohio. I am a Board Certified Family Relations Law Specialist.

THOMAS E. FRIEDMAN, admitted to bar, 1974, Ohio; 1975, U.S. District Court, Southern District of Ohio; 1987, U.S. Northern District of Ohio. *Education:* Miami University (A.B., 1968); Ohio State University (J.D., 1974). Omicron Delta Kappa. Assistant Attorney General of Ohio, 1974-1976. Member: Governors Commission on Child Support, 1984-1985; State Child Support Guideline Review Commission, 1996-1997. *Member:* Columbus (Chairman, Family Law Committee, 1984-1986), Ohio State (Chairman, Family Law Committee, 1996-1998; Member, Family Law Committee, 1985—) and American Bar Association; The Association of Trial Lawyers of America; Ohio Academy of Trial Lawyers; Franklin County Trial Lawyers Association. (Certified Specialist in Family Relations Law, Ohio State Bar Association). ***REPORTED CASES:*** Pacht v. Jadd 13 Ohio App. 3d 363 (1983).

REPRESENTATIVE CLIENTS: Great American Trucking Co., Inc.; Nash-Wilson Associates, Inc.; Threshold Audio.
REFERENCE: National City Bank.

FRIEDMAN & MIRMAN CO., L.P.A.

Established in 1973

THE WORLY BUILDING
503 SOUTH FRONT STREET
SUITE 250
COLUMBUS, OHIO 43215-5666
Telephone: 614-221-0090
Fax: 614-221-7213
URL: http://www.friedmanmirman.com
URL: http://www.lawyers.com/friedmanmirman

Family Relations Law, Divorce.

FIRM PROFILE: Friedman & Mirman Co., L.P.A.'s strength and expertise results from their experience in practicing only family and matrimonial law. The firm's participation in local, state and national educational programs in family law as well as their appearance in Ohio family law courts on a daily basis, not only keeps the firm abreast of recent developments in family and matrimonial legislation but also keeps them at the forefront of developing trends in Ohio's family court system.

The firm's dedication to working with their clients is largely responsible for their success in achieving favorable results. Friedman & Mirman Co., L.P.A. strives to be compassionate and responsive to their clients' concerns and works hard to involve their clients in every stage of their representation. The firm has developed a strong and diverse network of accountants, appraisers, business evaluators, psychologists, actuaries and other professionals whom they can enlist, when appropriate, to assist in the effective preparation of their clients' cases. By carefully matching the specific needs of each client's case with the individual strengths of the firm's attorneys and the professional resources available to them, Friedman & Mirman Co., L.P.A. assembles a team to work with each client in reaching that client's individual goals.

WILLIAM S. FRIEDMAN, born Springfield, Ohio, March 19, 1941; admitted to bar, 1966, Ohio; 1969, U.S. Supreme Court. *Education:* University of Dayton (B.A., 1963); University of Cincinnati (J.D., 1966). Co-Author: "Baldwins Ohio Domestic Relations Law," Banks-Baldwin, 1984. Instructor, Capital University Para Legal Program, Domestic Relations Law, 1986-1990. Lecturer: Family Law, Ohio State Bar Association, 1986—. Listed in: "Best Lawyers in America (Family Law)," 1987-2005; Ohio Super Lawyers, 2004; among Top Lawyers Business First Verdict, 2004. Assistant Attorney General of Ohio, 1966. Assistant to Governor of Ohio, 1969. Member, Governors Task Force for Domestic Relations Law, 1986-1991. *Member:* Columbus (Member, Family Law Committee), Ohio State (Member, Family Law Committee) and American (Member, Family Law Committee) Bar Associations. Fellow: American Academy of Matrimonial Lawyers (Member: Board of Governors, 1987-1991; Chairman, Long Range Planning Committee, 1989-1990; Chairman, Site Selection Committee, 1991-1992, and Public Relations Committee, 1991-1992; President, Ohio Chapter, 1987). Fellow: International Academy of Matrimonial Law-

(This Listing Continued)

FRIEDMAN & MIRMAN CO., L.P.A., Columbus—Continued

yers. Trained both as Mediator (American Bar Association) and Arbitrator (American Academy of Matrimonial Lawyers). (Certified Specialist in Family Relations Law, Ohio State Bar Association). ***PRACTICE AREAS:*** Family; Matrimonial Law; Divorce; Arbitration; Child Custody. ***Email:*** wfriedman@friedmanmirman.com

DENISE M. MIRMAN, born Toledo, Ohio, July 24, 1958; admitted to bar, 1982, Ohio. *Education:* The Ohio State University (B.A., 1979; J.D., 1982). Member: Order of the Barristers; National Moot Court Team (Best Oralist and Best Petitioner Brief, 1981, Regional Competition). Lecturer, Ohio Legal Center Institute, 1989—. Chair, Family Law Section, The Association of Trial Lawyers of America, 1990-1991. *Member:* Columbus Bar Association (Chair, Family Law Committee, 1992-1993; Member, Professional Ethics and Grievances Committee, 1993-1999); American Academy of Matrimonial Lawyers (Fellow, 1994—). (Certified Specialist in Family Relations Law, Ohio State Bar Association). ***PRACTICE AREAS:*** Domestic Relations; Family Law; Divorce; Child Custody. ***Email:*** dmirman@friedmanmirman.com

SCOTT N. FRIEDMAN, born Columbus, Ohio, April 29, 1971; admitted to bar, 1998, Ohio; 1999, Florida. *Education:* Miami University (B.A., 1993); Capital University (J.D., 1998). *Member:* Columbus, Ohio State and American (Member, Section: Family Law; Co-Chair, Continuing Legal Education Committee, 2005-2006; Council Member, 2002—) Bar Associations. ***PRACTICE AREAS:*** Family Law; Matrimonial Law; Divorce; Child Custody; Spousal Support. ***Email:*** sfriedman@friedmanmirman.com

---

KENNETH R. KLINE, born Youngstown, Ohio, April 27, 1975; admitted to bar, 2001, Ohio; 2002, U.S. District Court, Northern District of Ohio. *Education:* Indiana University-Bloomington, Kelley School of Business (B.S., Accounting, 1998; M.B.A., Taxation, 2001); Indiana University-Bloomington School of Law (J.D., 2001). Phi Eta Sigma; Alpha Lambda Delta; Golden Key. Ohio Super Lawyer-Rising Star-Cincinnati Magazine, 2005. Member: Business and Law Society, 1999-2001; Trumbull County Bar Association, 2001-2002. *Member:* American, Columbus (Member, Family Law Committee, 2003—) and Ohio State Bar Associations; Ohio Academy of Trial Lawyers. ***PRACTICE AREAS:*** Matrimonial Law; Family Law; Juvenile Law; Divorce; Child Custody; Spousal Support. ***Email:*** kkline@friedmanmirman.com

HEATHER R. GALL, born Wheeling, West Virginia, September 13, 1974; admitted to bar, 1999, Ohio; 2001, U.S. District Court, Southern District of Ohio. *Education:* The Ohio State University (B.A., summa cum laude, 1996; J.D., with honors, 1999). Adjunct Professor, Legal Writing, Ohio State University College of Law, 2001-2004. *Member:* Columbus (Family Law Committee), Ohio State and American Bar Associations. ***PRACTICE AREAS:*** Family Law; Divorce; Child Custody; Child Support; Paternity; Visitation Rights. ***Email:*** hgall@friedmanmirman.com

REFERENCE: Bank One.

FROST BROWN TODD LLC

ONE COLUMBUS
10 WEST BROAD STREET
COLUMBUS, OHIO 43215-3467
Telephone: 614-464-1211
Telecopier: 614-464-1737
Email: info@fbtlaw.com
URL: http://www.frostbrowntodd.com

Cincinnati, Ohio Office: 2200 PNC Center, 201 East Fifth Street, 45202-4182. Telephone: 513-651-6800. Telecopier: 513-651-6981.
Middletown, Ohio Office: 300 North Main Street, Suite 200, 45042-1919. Telephone: 513-422-2001. Telecopier: 513-422-3010.
Lexington, Kentucky Office: 250 West Main Street, Suite 2700, 40507-1742. Telephone: 859-231-0000. Telecopier: 859-231-0011.
Louisville, Kentucky Office: 400 West Market Street, 32nd Floor, 40202-3363. Telephone: 502-589-5400. Telecopier: 502-581-1087.
Nashville, Tennessee Office: 424 Church Street, Suite 1600, 37219-2308. Telephone: 615-251-5550. Telecopier: 615-251-5551.
New Albany, Indiana Office: 120 West Spring Street, Suite 400, 47150-3655. Telephone: 812-948-2800. Telecopier: 812-948-7994.

Alternative Dispute Resolution, Bankruptcy and Reorganization, Business Acquisitions, Business and Corporate, Commercial Finance, Commercial Litigation, Commercial/Real Estate, Construction, Copyright, Corporate Responsibility and Defense, Employee Benefits, Energy and Natural Resources, Entrepreneurial, Environmental, Equine, Estate Planning and Administration, Financial Institutions, Fire and Explosion, Health Care, Immigration, International, Intellectual Property, International Business, Internet and Electronic Commerce, Labor and Employment Law, Litigation, Media, Mold and Water Intrusion, Multi-District Litigation, Patent Litigation, Personal Planning and Family Business, Privacy and Information Security, Product Liability, Public Finance, Securities, Tax, Tort & Insurance Law, Trademark, Venture Capital, General Trial Practice in all State and Federal Courts.

FIRM PROFILE: Frost Brown Todd LLC is the result of the November 1, 2000 merger of Frost & Jacobs LLP and Brown, Todd & Heyburn PLLC. This super-regional law firm of approximately 370 attorneys has seven offices in Cincinnati, Columbus and Middletown, Ohio; Louisville and Lexington, Kentucky; Nashville, Tennessee; and New Albany, Indiana. The increased breadth of practice experience, combined with the depth of service and expanded geographic scope, allows the combined firm to effectively serve the growing and changing needs of its institutional, commercial and individual clients at the local, regional, national and international level.

MEMBERS

JOHN I. CADWALLADER, born Toledo, Ohio, March 25, 1952; admitted to bar, 1978, Ohio; 1979, Florida. *Education:* Denison University (B.A., cum laude, 1974); University of Chicago (M.A., 1975); The Ohio State University (J.D., 1978). Fellow, Rockefeller Foundation. Co-Author: "Renovating and Expanding Existing Regional Shopping Centers," International Council of Shopping Centers (ICSC), 1999 ICSC National Law Conference; "Retooling REA's: Evaluation of the Critical Elements of the Typical REA," 2001 ICSC Regional Law Conference; "Expansions: Breathing New Life into Old Shopping Centers," 2003 ICSC Regional Law Conference. Contributing Author: "Crafting Lease Clauses, Volume III," ICSC, 2003. Member, International Council of Shopping Centers. Listed in "The Best Lawyers in America". *Member:* Columbus (Member, Real Property and Business Law Committees), Ohio State (Member, Board of Governors for the Real Property Law Section; Real Property Law and Corporate Counsel Sections) and American (Member, Real Property, Probate and Trust Law Section) Bar Associations; The Florida Bar (Member, Real Property, Probate and Trust Law Section); American College of Real Estate Lawyers. ***PRACTICE AREAS:*** Commercial Real Estate; Corporate; Mergers and Acquisitions. ***Email:*** jcadwallader@fbtlaw.com

STEVEN J. ELLCESSOR, born Columbus, Ohio, May 21, 1952; admitted to bar, 1977, Ohio. *Education:* Miami University (A.B., summa cum laude, 1974); Harvard Law School (J.D., cum laude, 1977). Phi Beta Kappa. Member, American Society of Corporate Secretaries. *Member:* Columbus, Ohio State and American Bar Associations. ***PRACTICE AREAS:*** Corporate Law; Securities; Mergers, Acquisitions and Divestitures; Food and Agriculture. ***Email:*** sellcessor@fbtlaw.com

TERRENCE M. FAY, born Cleveland, Ohio, 1953; admitted to bar, 1978, Ohio. *Education:* Baldwin-Wallace College (B.S., cum laude, 1974; B.A., cum laude, 1975); The Ohio State University (J.D., cum laude, 1978). Phi Alpha Theta; Omicron Delta Kappa; Phi Kappa Delta; Psi Chi. Assistant Attorney General, Ohio Attorney General's Office, 1978-1988. *Member:* Columbus (Member, Environmental Law Committee), Ohio State (Member, Environmental Law Committee) and American (Member, Environmental Law Committee) Bar Associations. ***PRACTICE AREAS:*** Environmental Law; Public Law; Public Contract Law; Litigation. ***Email:*** tfay@fbtlaw.com

JEFFREY N. LINDEMANN, born Ann Arbor, Michigan, May 4, 1966; admitted to bar, 1991, Ohio. *Education:* University of Michigan (A.B., with highest distinction, 1987; J.D., cum laude, 1990). ***PRACTICE AREAS:*** Labor Law; Employment Law; Employment Litigation; Workers' Compensation. ***Email:*** jlindemann@fbtlaw.com

THOMAS V. WILLIAMS, born Lima, Ohio, May 7, 1951; admitted to bar, 1977, Ohio. *Education:* University of Cincinnati (B.B.A., magna cum laude, 1974); University of Toledo (J.D., cum laude, 1977). ***PRACTICE AREAS:*** Labor Law; Employment Law; Employment Litigation. ***Email:*** twilliams@fbtlaw.com

MICHAEL K. YARBROUGH, born Jeffersonville, Indiana, July 7, 1948; admitted to bar, 1976, Ohio. *Education:* University of Notre Dame (B.A., magna cum laude, 1970); Northwestern University (J.D., cum laude, 1976). ***PRACTICE AREAS:*** Civil Litigation; Chemical Exposure; Product Liability. ***Email:*** myarbrough@fbtlaw.com

SENIOR ASSOCIATE

NOEL C. SHEPARD, born Alliance, Ohio, November 22, 1970; admitted to bar, 1996, Ohio, U.S. District Court, Southern and Northern Districts of Ohio and U.S. Court of Appeals, Sixth Circuit. *Education:* Mount Union College (B.A., 1993); Capital University Law School (J.D., 1996). *Member:* Columbus and Ohio State (Member, Workers Compensation Committee) Bar Associations. ***REPORTED CASES:*** State ex rel. Akers V. Robertshaw Controls (2002), 94 Ohio St.3d 36; State ex rel. Gauvey v. Indus. Comm. (2002), 94 Ohio St.3d 38; State ex rel. Wells v. Indus. Comm. (2001 WL 1607340, 10th Dist. Ct. App.); State ex rel. Continental Hose v. Swartz (2001), 92 Ohio St.3d 27; State ex rel. Sears Logistics Services, Inc. v. Cope (2000), 89 Ohio St. 3d 393. ***PRACTICE AREAS:*** Labor and Employment; Workers Compensation. ***Email:*** nshepard@fbtlaw.com

ASSOCIATES

WILLIAM M. HARTER, born Kansas City, Missouri, July 29, 1975; admitted to bar, 1999, West Virginia; 2000, Ohio; U.S. District Court, Northern and Southern District of West Virginia and U.S. District Court, Northern and Southern Districts of Ohio. *Education:* The Ohio State University (B.A., 1996; J.D., 1999). Public Service Fellow. Reader, Ohio Board of Bar Examiners. *Member:* Columbus, Ohio State, West Virginia State and American Bar Associations. ***PRACTICE AREAS:*** Litigation; Extra Contractual Insurance Claims; Insurance Coverage Disputes; Insurance Defense. ***Email:*** wharter@fbtlaw.com

KIMERA J. KING, born Indianapolis, Indiana, 1980; (admission pending). *Education:* Michigan State University (B.A., high honors, 2001); University of Notre Dame (J.D., 2005). *Member:* American Bar Association (Member, Business Law Section). ***LANGUAGES:*** Spanish. ***PRACTICE AREAS:*** Business Law; Corporate Law. ***Email:*** kking@fbtlaw.com

CHRISTINE L. ROBEK, born Youngstown, Ohio, December 24, 1978; admitted to bar, 2004, Ohio; 2005, U.S. District Court, Southern and Northern Districts of Ohio. *Education:* Youngstown State University (B.A., summa cum laude, 2001); Ohio State University (J.D., with honors, 2004). Order of the Coif. Managing Editor, Ohio State Law Journal, 2003-2004. *Member:* Columbus, Ohio State and American (Member, Sections on: Labor and Employment; Young Lawyers) Bar Associations. ***PRACTICE AREAS:*** Labor and Employment. ***Email:*** crobek@fbtlaw.com

JEFFREY G. RUPERT, born Lima, Ohio, July 15, 1969; admitted to bar, 1995, Ohio; 1996, Illinois. *Education:* Northwestern University (B.A., 1991); The Ohio State University (J.D., with honors, 1995). ***PRACTICE AREAS:*** Litigation. ***Email:*** jrupert@fbtlaw.com

KEVIN T. SHOOK, born Cleveland, Ohio, November 22, 1972; admitted to bar, 2001, Ohio and U.S. District Court, Southern District of Ohio; 2003; U.S. Court of Appeals, Sixth Circuit. *Education:* Denison University (B.A., cum laude, 1995); The Ohio State University (J.D., 2001). Author: "State Sponsors of Terrorism Are Persons Too," The Ohio Law Journal. Member: Franklin Park Association; Advertising Federation of Columbus. *Member:* Columbus and Ohio State Bar Associations. ***PRACTICE AREAS:*** Media Law; Products Liability; Commercial Litigation; Construction Law. ***Email:*** kshook@fbtlaw.com

(This Listing Continued)

REPRESENTATIVE CLIENTS: AAF-McQuay Inc.; AEGON USA Realty Advisors, Inc.; AIG Insurance Group; AK Steel Corporation; Anthem Health Plans; Broadwing Inc.; Brown & Williamson Tobacco Corporation; Catholic Healthcare Partners; Central Bank & Trust Company; Chapelthorp plc; Chiquita Brands International; ClubLink Corporation; Convergys Corporation; Coolmore Castlehyde and Associated Stud Farms; Federated Department Stores, Inc.; FieldTurf, Inc.; Firstar/U.S. Bank; Taco Bell Franchise Management Advisory Council (FRANMAC); General Electric Company; ICI Paints World Group; Jewish Hospital HealthCare Services, Inc.; LensCrafters, Inc.; Lexis-Nexis; LG&E Energy Corp.; Liberty Mutual Insurance Group; Lightyear Communications, Inc.; MidAmerica Bancorp; New Horizon Resources, Inc.; NTS Development Company; OneBeacon Insurance Group; Progressive Insurance Company; PNC Bank Corp. and PNC Bank; Res-Care, Inc.; The Rouse Companies, LLC; Services Net Incorporated; Smithkline Beecham Clinical Lab; Terex Corporation; Turner Construction Company; Unified Foodservice Purchasing Co-op, LLC; United Parcel Service; Vincor International Inc.; Waste Management of North America; Western Southern Life Insurance Company.

(For complete biographical data on all personnel, see Professional Biographies at Cincinnati, Ohio)

FROST & JACOBS LLP

COLUMBUS, OHIO

(See Frost Brown Todd LLC)

PHILIP J. FULTON LAW OFFICE

89 EAST NATIONWIDE BOULEVARD, SUITE 300
COLUMBUS, OHIO 43215-2554
Telephone: 614-224-3838
Fax: 614-224-3933
URL: http://www.ohiocompensationlawyer.com
Email: phil@fultonlaw.com
URL: http://www.philipfultonlaw.com

Workers Compensation, Social Security Disability, Administrative Law, Civil Litigation, Legislative and Appellate Practice.

FIRM PROFILE: Philip J. Fulton Law Office is dedicated to representing only plaintiffs in matters of workers compensation, social security disability and personal injury throughout most of the state. Philip Fulton is the author of "Ohio Workers Compensation Law," Anderson Publishing Company.

PHILIP J. FULTON, born Columbus, Ohio, March 8, 1955; admitted to bar, 1980, Ohio; 1982, U.S. District Court, Southern District of Ohio. *Education:* The Ohio State University (B.A., 1977); Capital University (J.D., 1980). Member, Order of the Curia. Author: Ohio Workers Compensation Law, Anderson Publishing, 1991, 1998. Elected, Ohio Academy of Trial Lawyers Workers Compensation Section Hall of Fame. Listed in: "The Best Lawyers in America," Woodward/White, Inc. (1995-2004); Ohio Super Lawyers, 2004; Law and Politics Magazine. *Member:* Columbus, Ohio State and American Bar Associations; Ohio Academy of Trial Lawyers (President-Elect, 2004-2005; Vice President; Secretary, 2002—; Treasurer, 2001-2002; Chair, Workers Compensation Section, 1995, 2000); Franklin County Trial Lawyers (Past Chair Person, Workers Compensation Section); The Association of Trial Lawyers of America (Board Member, Workplace Injury Litigation Group); National Organization of Social Security Claimants Representatives. ***PRACTICE AREAS:*** Workers Compensation; Social Security Disability; Appellate Practice.

WILLIAM A. THORMAN III, born Cincinnati, Ohio, September 19, 1962; admitted to bar, 1988, Ohio and U.S. District Court, Southern District of Ohio; 1992, U.S. Supreme Court and U.S. Court of Veteran Appeals. *Education:* Lawrence University (B.A., 1984); The Ohio State University (J.D., 1988). Member, The Ohio State University Law Journal. Assistant Attorney General, 1994-1996. Member, Board of Directors, Access Center for Independent Living, 1992-1995. *Member:* Columbus and American Bar Associations. ***PRACTICE AREAS:*** Workers Compensation; Social Security Disability.

LORI BURNS PAINTER, born Columbus, Ohio, December 4, 1963; admitted to bar, 1992, Ohio. *Education:* University of Colorado at Boulder (B.S., Journalism, 1987); Capital University (J.D., 1992). Order of the Barristers. Jessup International Moot Court Team. *Member:* Columbus and Ohio State Bar Associations. ***PRACTICE AREAS:*** Workers Compensation; Social Security Disability; Appellate Practice.

DAVID B. BARNHART, born Greenville, Pennsylvania, July 12, 1956; admitted to bar, 1981, Ohio. *Education:* Westminster College (B.A., cum laude, 1978); Capital University (J.D., 1981). Elected, Ohio Academy of Trial Lawyers Workers Compensation Section Hall of Fame. *Member:* Columbus and Ohio State Bar Associations; Ohio Academy of Trial Lawyers; Franklin County Trial Lawyers Association (Member, Chairman, 1991-1992, 1992-1993, Workers Compensation Committee). (Certified Specialist in Workers Compensation Law, Ohio State Bar Association). ***PRACTICE AREAS:*** Workers Compensation Law; Personal Injury Law.

JACOB DOBRES, born 1972; admitted to bar, 1999, Ohio. *Education:* Ohio State University (B.A., 1995; J.D., summa cum laude, 1999). Assistant Ohio Attorney General, Workers Compensation Section, 1999-2004. *Member:* Ohio State Bar Association. ***PRACTICE AREAS:*** Workers Compensation.

ALLISON A. CLARK, born Columbus, Ohio, March 4, 1979; admitted to bar, 2004, Ohio. *Education:* University of Dayton (B.A., 2001; J.D., 2004). *Member:* Ohio State Bar Association. ***PRACTICE AREAS:*** Workers Compensation. **Email:** allison@fultonlaw.com

GARVIN & HICKEY, LLC

181 EAST LIVINGSTON AVENUE
COLUMBUS, OHIO 43215
Telephone: 614-225-9000
Fax: 614-225-9080
Email: wclaw@garvin-hickey.com
URL: http://www.garvinhickey.com

Labor and Employment, Workers Compensation Defense and Intentional Torts.

FIRM PROFILE: Garvin & Hickey, LLC focuses on helping employers reduce their workers compensation claims through preventative measures as well as representation in all stages of the claim process. Both partners have maintained this focus throughout their entire legal careers and have been recognized by Best Lawyers in America in workers compensation law.

MEMBERS OF FIRM

PRESTON J. GARVIN, born Wilmington, Delaware, 1949; admitted to bar, 1974, Ohio. *Education:* University of Delaware (B.A., 1971); University of Akron (J.D., 1974). *Member:* Columbus (Member, Workers Compensation Committee) and Ohio State (Member, Workers Compensation Committee) Bar Associations. ***PRACTICE AREAS:*** Labor and Employment Law; Workers Compensation; Intentional Torts.

MICHAEL J. HICKEY, born Columbus, Ohio, 1942; admitted to bar, 1968, Ohio. *Education:* The Ohio State University (B.A., 1965; J.D., 1968). Member, Columbus Bar Foundation. *Member:* Columbus (Member, Workers Compensation Committee) and Ohio State (Member, Workers Compensation Committee) Bar Associations. ***PRACTICE AREAS:*** Labor and Employment Law; Workers Compensation; Intentional Torts.

DANIEL M. HALL, born Columbus, Ohio, October 27, 1966; admitted to bar, 1993, Ohio; 1994, U.S. District Court, Southern District of Ohio; 1995, U.S. Court of Appeals, Sixth Circuit; 1996, U.S. Supreme Court. *Education:* Ohio University (B.Sc., 1989); Capital University (J.D., 1993). Order of the Curia. Assistant Attorney General, Workers' Compensation Section, 2000-2002. *Member:* Columbus (Member, Unauthorized Practice of Law Committee; Workers' Compensation Committee) and Ohio State (Member, Workers' Compensation Committee; Board of Governors, Young Lawyers Section). ***PRACTICE AREAS:*** Workers Compensation; Torts.

PAUL JOSEPH HESS, JR., born Cincinnati, Ohio, 1956; admitted to bar, 1981, Ohio; 1988, U.S. District Court, Southern District of Ohio; U.S. Court of Appeals, Fourth Circuit. *Education:* University of Notre Dame (B.A., 1978); The Ohio State University (J.D., 1981). *Member:* Columbus and Ohio State Bar Associations. ***PRACTICE AREAS:*** Workers Compensation; Social Security Disability; Entertainment and the Arts; Sports Law.

OF COUNSEL

KATHRYN A. CHUBB, born Cleveland, Ohio, August 1, 1948; admitted to bar, 1991, Ohio. *Education:* Dyke College (B.S., 1983); Cleveland State University (J.D., 1990). Attorney, Ohio Bureau of Workers Compensation, 1992-1995. *Member:* Ohio State and American Bar Associations; National Association of Female Executives. ***PRACTICE AREAS:*** Workers Compensation Defense; Child Advocacy.

SANDEE E. RIEM, born Cleveland, Ohio, October 30, 1971; admitted to bar, 1998, Ohio. *Education:* University of Dayton (B.S., 1994); Georgetown University (J.D., 1998). *Member:* Columbus, Ohio State and American Bar Associations. ***PRACTICE AREAS:*** Workers Compensation.

WILLIAM L. GEARY

SUITE 101 WATERFORD TOWER
155 WEST MAIN STREET
COLUMBUS, OHIO 43215-5000
Telephone: 614-228-1968
Fax: 614-228-7630
Email: gearylawoffices@aol.com
URL: http://columbusfamilylawyer.com

Family Law, Divorce, Separation Agreements, Child Custody, Child Support, Visitation Rights, Alimony.

WILLIAM L. GEARY, born Portsmouth, Ohio, July 17, 1952; admitted to bar, 1978, Ohio; 1979, U.S. District Court, Southern District of Ohio. *Education:* The Ohio State University (B.A., 1974); Shawnee State College; Ohio Northern University (J.D., 1978). Delta Theta Phi. Recipient: American Jurisprudence Book Awards; Contracts, Secured Transactions; Products Liability; International Law. Licensed Real Estate Broker, Ohio, 1975. Instructor, Business Law, Portsmouth Interstate Business College, 1975-1976. Member: Community Faculty Member Marion Technical College, 1994-1995. Franklin County Family Law Committee; Board of Directors, Community Mediation Services of Central Ohio, 1993-1996; Franklin County Common Pleas Court, Domestic Division, Mediator Accreditation Advisory Committee, 1993-1996. *Member:* Columbus and Ohio State Bar Associations. (Also Of Counsel, Edwin J. Hollern Co., LPA). ***PRACTICE AREAS:*** Family Law; Divorce; Child Custody; Child Support; Visitation Rights; Spousal Support.

GERTNER & GERTNER

Established in 1935

199 SOUTH FIFTH STREET, SUITE 302
COLUMBUS, OHIO 43215
Telephone: 614-463-9393
Fax: 614-463-9669
Email: gertnerlaw@aol.com
URL: http://www.michaelgertner.com

Trials, Appeals, Personal Injury, Automobile Accidents and Injuries, Construction Site Accidents, Wrongful Death, Nursing Home Negligence, Premises Liability, Insurance Law, Medical Negligence, Criminal Law, White Collar Crimes, Business Litigation, Breach of Contract, Lawsuits, Securities Arbitration, Securities Fraud, Stockbroker Disputes, Investments, Police Misconduct, Employment Law, Sexual Assault/Rape Victims, Civil Litigation, Probate Litigation, Contested Wills, Contested Guardianships.

FIRM PROFILE: Abraham Gertner founded the firm in 1935 and retired after 55 years of practice. He earned his Ph.D. in Political Science at Yale University in 1934 and graduated Summa Cum Laude from Ohio State University Law School in 1935. He was a Cowles fellow while at Yale and a member of Phi Beta Kappa while earning his undergraduate degree at Ohio State University. While at Ohio State University Law School he was Order of the Coif. His distinguished career included serving as United States Administrative Law Judge, Office of Hearings and Appeals, from 1972 to 1979, and directing the A.B. Gertner Bar Review School from 1936 to 1961. He also was national President of Tau Epsilon Law Fraternity in 1962 and member of the Board of Governors of the Columbus Bar Association.

Michael H. Gertner is a trial attorney dedicated to the aggressive but thoughtful representation of his clients. Mr. Gertner primarily represents individuals who have been injured by others in automobile accidents and by medical negligence. He has been successful in representing women who have been raped due to the negligence of employers and property owners. As a former prosecutor, he also represents persons accused of criminal conduct, especially white-collar crime. Mr. Gertner personally handles all civil, criminal and business cases to achieve optimum results for each individual client while upholding the highest standards of the legal profession.

MEMBERS OF FIRM

ABRAHAM GERTNER (1909-1996)

MICHAEL H. GERTNER, born Columbus, Ohio, August 26, 1941; admitted to bar, 1966, Ohio, 1971, U.S. Supreme Court; 1971, U.S. District Court, District of Columbia; 1973, U.S. Claims Court; 1974, U.S. Court of Appeals for the District of Columbia Circuit; 1979, U.S. District Court, Northern and Southern Districts of Ohio; 1983, U.S. Court of Appeals, Sixth Circuit and U.S. Court of Appeals for the Federal Circuit. *Education:* The Ohio State University (B.A., cum laude, 1963; J.D., 1966). Phi Beta Kappa; Phi Eta Sigma; Eta Sigma Phi; Pi Sigma Alpha; Tau Epsilon Rho. Member, National Institute of Trial Advocacy. Faculty: Seminar on Negotiations, University of North Carolina School of Law, 1989 and 1990. Law Clerk to Hon. Louis J. Schneider, Jr., Supreme Court of Ohio, 1966-1968. Legislative Assistant to Senator William B. Saxbe, 1969-1974. Attorney Advisor to Office of Attorney General of the United States and Special Assistant to U.S. Attorney for District of Columbia, January-April, 1974. Assistant U.S. Attorney for District of Columbia, April, 1974-1976. Former President, American Inns of Court, Robert M. Duncan Chapter, 1997. *Member:* Columbus and Ohio State Bar Associations; Franklin County Trial Lawyers Association; National Association of Criminal Defense Lawyers; Ohio Academy of Trial Lawyers; The Association of Trial Lawyers of America; Ohio Association of Criminal Defense Lawyers; Central Ohio Association of Defense Lawyers; National Organization of Social Security Claimants Representatives (NOSSCR). ***PRACTICE AREAS:*** Civil Litigation; Personal Injury Law; Automobile Accidents and Injuries; Medical Malpractice; Criminal Law; Drug Crimes; Premises Liability; Rape Victims; Workplace Violence; Employment Law; Sexual Harassment; Sexual Assault; Social Security Disability; Police Misconduct; Business Litigation; Securities Arbitration.

GOLDMAN & ROSENTHAL

5350 EAST MAIN STREET
COLUMBUS, OHIO 43213
Telephone: 614-864-4359
Fax: 614-864-2818
URL: http://www.goldmanrosenthal.com

Personal Injury, Family Law, Real Estate, Commercial Leasing, Construction and Mechanics Lien Law, Collections, Estate Planning and Probate, Corporate, Juvenile Law, Criminal. Civil and Criminal Trials in all Courts.

JEROME S. GOLDMAN, born Brooklyn, New York, July 17, 1948; admitted to bar, 1973, Ohio; 1977, U.S. District Court, Southern District of Ohio; 1978, U.S. Supreme Court. *Education:* Hofstra University (B.A., 1970); Capital University (J.D., 1973). Phi Alpha Delta. *Member:* Columbus (Member, Municipal Court Committee, 1979—) and Ohio State Bar Associations. ***PRACTICE AREAS:*** Commercial Leasing Law; Personal Injury Law; Automobile Accidents and Injuries; Wrongful Death; Slip and Fall; Dog Bites; Criminal Law; Traffic Violations; Driving While Intoxicated. ***Email:*** jgoldman@goldmanrosenthal.com

LEE S. ROSENTHAL, born Columbus, Ohio, October 10, 1957; admitted to bar, 1982, Ohio; 1984, U.S. District Court, Northern District of Ohio and U.S. Court of Appeals, Sixth Circuit; 1988, U.S. District Court, Southern District of Ohio. *Education:* The Ohio State University (B.A., 1979; J.D., 1982). Law Clerk to the Hon. Earle E. Wise, Ohio Fifth District Court of Appeals, 1983-1984. Vice-Chairperson, City of Gahanna Cable Advisory Board, 1991—. *Member:* Columbus (Member, Family Law and Negligence Law Committee) and Ohio State Bar Associations; Franklin County Trial Lawyers Association. ***PRACTICE AREAS:*** Family Law; Divorce; Child Custody; Child Support; Visitation Rights; Domestic Violence; Construction Law; Mechanics Lien Law; Personal Injury; Civil Litigation; Real Estate; Estate Planning; Probate; Corporate. ***Email:*** lrosenthal@goldmanrosenthal.com

(This Listing Continued)

DAVID A. GOLDSTEIN, CO., L.P.A.

529 S. THIRD STREET
COLUMBUS, OHIO 43215
Telephone: 614-222-1889
Fax: 614-222-1899
Email: dgoldstein@dgoldsteinlaw.com
URL: http://www.davidagoldstein.com

Insurance Law, Insurance Coverage, Professional Liability, Legal Malpractice, Personal Injury, Products Liability, Wrongful Death, Automobile Accidents.

DAVID A. GOLDSTEIN, born Columbus, Ohio, December 19, 1968; admitted to bar, 1995, Ohio; 1997, U.S. District Court, Northern and Southern Districts of Ohio. *Education:* The Ohio State University (B.A., 1991); Capital University (J.D., 1994). *Member:* Columbus and Ohio State Bar Associations. (Also Of Counsel to Edwin J. Hollern Co., LPA). ***PRACTICE AREAS:*** Insurance Defense; Litigation; Personal Injury; Automobile Accidents and Injuries; Insurance Coverage; Products Liability; Professional Negligence.

SETH KLEINMAN, born 1973; admitted to bar, 2002, Ohio; U.S. District Court, Southern District of Ohio. *Education:* The Ohio State University (B.A., 1997; J.D., 2000).

REPRESENTATIVE CLIENTS: Safe Auto Insurance Co.; Great American Insurance Co.; Capital Bonding; Leader/Infinity Insurance Company; Sagamore Insurance Co.

GORDON LAW FIRM CO., LPA

FIFTH THIRD CENTER
21 EAST STATE STREET, SUITE 1700
COLUMBUS, OHIO 43215
Telephone: 614-228-0888
Fax: 614-228-0850
Email: jgordon@rrcol.com
URL: http://www.jameshgordon.com

General Civil Trial and Appellate Practice, Real Estate, Small Business, Buying and Selling of Businesses, Business Formation, Partnerships, Limited Liability Company Law, Business Litigation, Contract Law, Collections, Corporate, Construction Litigation, Probate.

JAMES H. GORDON, born Southampton, New York, November 28, 1942; admitted to bar, 1974, Ohio; 1976, U.S. District Court, Southern District of Ohio. *Education:* College of Wooster (B.A., 1963); Ohio University (M.Ed., 1965; Ph.D., 1969); The Ohio State University (J.D., cum laude, 1974). Lecturer, "Legal Aspects of Higher Education," Department of Education, Faculty of Special Services, The Ohio State University, 1976, 1977 and 1979. *Member:* Columbus, Ohio State and American Bar Associations. ***REPORTED CASES:*** In re Marriage of Stearns, (1993) 88 Ohio App.3d 264; 623 N.E. 2d 711; 1993 Ohi App. Lexis 3081, June 15, 1993, Pended; Biomedical Innovation v. McLaughlin, (1995) 103 Ohio App. Lexis 1655, April 20, 1995, Pended.

REPRESENTATIVE CLIENTS: Star Leasing Co.; G.E. Capital Corporation; Becraft & Sons General Contractors, Ltd; U.S. Retail Flowers Ohio, Inc.; G&S Diversified, LLC
REFERENCE: Fifth Third Bank

TERRENCE A. GRADY & ASSOCIATES CO., L.P.A.

100 EAST BROAD STREET, SUITE 2310
COLUMBUS, OHIO 43215
Telephone: 614-849-0378
Fax: 614-849-0379
Email: tgrady@tgradylaw.com
URL: http://www.tgradylaw.com

Civil and Criminal Tax Litigation in State and Federal Courts. Federal Criminal Tax and Federal White Collar Crime Defense, Tax Controversies, Substantive Federal Tax Planning; Complex IRS Collection Matters; Corporate and Small Business Services, Estate and Asset Protection Planning.

TERRENCE A. GRADY, born Columbus, Ohio, 1954; admitted to bar, 1982, Ohio; 1983, U.S. Tax Court; 1984, U.S. District Court, Southern District of Ohio; 1987, U.S. Supreme Court and U.S. Court of Federal Claims; U.S. Court of Appeals, Sixth Circuit. *Education:* Capital University (B.A., 1977; J.D., 1982); Georgetown University (LL.M., Taxation, 1988). Certified Public Accountant (CPA) Ohio, 1984 (Inactive). Listed in, The Best Lawyers in America, Tax Law Section, 1995—. Author: "IRS Attacks on Nontaxpayers-Fraudulent Conveyances and Other Third-Party Liability Theories: When You Might Want to Look a Gift Horse In the Mouth," Journal of Tax Practice and Procedures, 2001. Adjunct Professor, Civil and Criminal IRS Tax Controversies Practicium, Capital University Law School, Master's in Tax Law Program, 1990—. Member, Order of the Curia. Certified Public Accountant, Ohio, 1984. Prosecutor's Division, 1982-1983 and Civil Division, 1984, Columbus City Attorney's Office. Trial Attorney, U.S. Department of Justice, Tax Division, Criminal Tax Section, 1985-1988. *Member:* Columbus (Chairman: Business Tax Subcommittee, 1991-1993; Taxation Committee, 1994-1995), Ohio State and American (Committee Member, Criminal and Tax Penalties) Bar Associations; Ohio Society of Certified Public Accountants.

GROSSMAN LAW OFFICES

Established in 1972

32 WEST HOSTER STREET
COLUMBUS, OHIO 43215
Telephone: 614-221-7711
Fax: 614-221-7145
Email: lawyers@grossman-law.com
URL: http://www.grossmanlawoffices.com

Family Law, Matrimonial Law, Child Custody, Divorce, Domestic Violence, Premarital Agreements, Child Support, Visitation Rights, Trial and Appellate Practice.

FIRM PROFILE: Grossman Law Offices is a legal professional association practicing exclusively in the field of matrimonial and family law. The firm consists of five attorneys and numerous in-house support personnel. In addition, the firm has developed an outstanding relationship with numerous specialists in related fields including pension experts, certified public accountants, real estate and business appraisers. Established to meet the many complex financial and personal needs of clients involved in marriage breakdowns, the practice has extensive experience in successfully conducting difficult legal cases and settlement negotiations.

JEFFREY A. GROSSMAN, born Columbus, Ohio, November 23, 1946; admitted to bar, 1972, Ohio; 1977, U.S. Supreme Court. *Education:* Ohio University (B.S.J., 1968); Capital University (J.D., 1972). Listed in "Best Lawyers in America," 1988-2002. Lecturer on Family Law for the Columbus, Ohio State and American Bar Associations and for the American Academy of Matrimonial Lawyers. *Member:* Columbus (Member, Family Law Committee), Ohio State and American Bar Associations. Fellow: American Academy of Matrimonial Lawyers (President, Ohio Chapter, 1994-1995); International Academy of Matrimonial Lawyers. (Certified Specialist in Family Relations Law, Ohio State Bar Association). ***PRACTICE AREAS:*** Divorce; Child Custody; Visitation Rights; Child Support; Spousal Support; Family Law. ***Email:*** jag@grossman-law.com

THOMAS J. JEDINAK, born Cleveland, Ohio, June 17, 1947; admitted to bar, 1974, Ohio; 1978, U.S. Supreme Court. *Education:* Miami University (B.S., 1968); Capital University (J.D., 1974). Chief Referee, Franklin County Court of Common Pleas, Division of Domestic Relations, 1979-1987. *Member:* Columbus, Ohio State and American Bar Associations. (Certified Specialist in Family Relations Law, Ohio State Bar Association). ***Email:*** tjj@grossman-law.com

ANTHONY R. AUTEN, born Minneapolis, Minnesota, March 11, 1947; admitted to bar, 1972, Ohio. *Education:* Bowling Green State University (B.S. in B.A., 1969); College of William & Mary (J.D., 1972). Assistant Law Director, Ashland, Ohio, 1972-1973. Prosecuting Attorney, Ashland County, Ohio, 1973-1977. *Member:* Columbus, Ashland County (President, 1978), Ohio State and American Bar Associations. (Certified Specialist in Family Relations Law, Ohio State Bar Association). ***Email:*** ara@grossman-law.com

ANDREW SCOTT GROSSMAN, born Columbus, Ohio, December 9, 1970; admitted to bar, 1996, Ohio; 1997, District of Columbia. *Education:* University of Kansas (B.A., English, 1993); Capital University (J.D., 1996). *Member:* Columbus (Member, Family Law Section), Ohio State and American (Member, Family Law Section) Bar Associations; Ohio Academy of Trial Lawyers. (Certified Specialist in Family Relations Law, Ohio State Bar Association). ***LANGUAGES:*** French. ***Email:*** asg@grossman-law.com

ALYSON B. MILLER, born Columbus, Ohio; admitted to bar, 2004, Ohio. *Education:* Miami University (B.A., Political Science, 2001); University of Maryland (J.D., 2004). Phi Delta Phi. Member, Miami University Mock Trial Team, 1997-2001; All-American Witness, All American Attorney-Mock Trials, 1998-2001; University of Maryland National Trial Team, 2002-2004. National Champion, National Collegiate Mock Trial Competition, 2001. *Member:* Columbus, Ohio State and American Bar Associations. ***PRACTICE AREAS:*** Domestic Relations (50%); Family Law (50%). ***Email:*** abm@grossman-law.com

JULIA L. LEVERIDGE, born Somerset, Kentucky, November 27, 1974; admitted to bar, 2000, Ohio. *Education:* University of Kentucky (B.A., 1997); Capital University Law School (J.D., 2000). Phi Alpha Delta (Treasurer, 1998-1999). Order of the Curia. *Member:* Columbus (Member, Family Law Committee), Ohio State and American Bar Associations. ***PRACTICE AREAS:*** Domestic Relations; Employment Law; Real Estate; Civil Litigation; Estate Planning. ***Email:*** jll@grossman-law.com

HABASH, REASONER & FRAZIER LLP

471 EAST BROAD STREET, SUITE 800
COLUMBUS, OHIO 43215-3844
Telephone: 614-221-9400
Fax: 614-221-1214
URL: http://www.lawyers.com/hrf-law

Employment Law, Labor Relations and Workers' Compensation.

STEPHEN J. HABASH, born Steubenville, Ohio, December 25, 1951; admitted to bar, 1978, Ohio. *Education:* The Ohio State University (B.A., cum laude, 1974; J.D., 1978). Phi Beta Kappa. Adjunct Professor of Law, The Capital University Law and Graduate Center, 1992-1996. *Member:* Defense Research Institute (Member, National Workers' Compensation Committee, Chairperson, 1999-2001; Ohio State Liaison, 1999—). ***PRACTICE AREAS:*** Employment Law; Disability Law; Workers' Compensation. ***Email:*** shabash@hrf-law.com

W. IRL REASONER, III, born Hamilton, Ohio, December 24, 1951; admitted to bar, 1978, Ohio. *Education:* Indiana University (B.A., 1974); University of South Carolina (J.D., cum laude, 1978). Member, 1976-1978 and Articles Editor, 1977-1978, South Carolina Law Review. Recipient, Cy Young Award, 1977. ***PRACTICE AREAS:*** Employment Law. ***Email:*** ireasoner@hrf-law.com

(This Listing Continued)

JEAN M. FRAZIER, born Elizabethtown, Kentucky, September 8, 1962; admitted to bar, 1987, Ohio. *Education:* Indiana University (B.S., 1984; J.D., 1987). Member, National Moot Court Team. ***PRACTICE AREAS:*** Employment Law; Labor Law; Litigation. ***Email:*** jfrazier@hrf-law.com

TRACY L. TURNER, born Toledo, Ohio, November 29, 1972; admitted to bar, 1998, Ohio; 1999, U.S. District Court, Southern District of Ohio; 1999, U.S. District Court, Northern District of Ohio. *Education:* Miami University (B.A., 1995); The Ohio State University (J.D., 1998). Member, 1996-1998 and Managing Editor, Ohio State Law Journal. ***PRACTICE AREAS:*** Employment Law; Labor Law; Workers Compensation. ***Email:*** tturner@hrf-law.com

ASSOCIATE

MATTHEW C. McNEIL, (admission pending). *Education:* Taylor University (B.A., 1998); The Ohio State University, Moritz College of Law (J.D., 2005). Articles Editor, Ohio Law Journal. ***PRACTICE AREAS:*** Employment Law; Labor Law; Workers Compensation. ***Email:*** mmcneil@hrf-law.com

OF COUNSEL

JEAN M. LUCZKOWSKI, born Lorain, Ohio, October 5, 1951; admitted to bar, 1978, Ohio. *Education:* John Carroll University (B.A., 1974); Ohio State University (J.D., 1978). Alpha Sigma Nu. ***PRACTICE AREAS:*** Workers' Compensation. ***Email:*** jluczkowski@hrf-law.com

HAHN LOESER & PARKS LLP

Established in 1920

65 EAST STATE STREET, SUITE 1400
COLUMBUS, OHIO 43215
Telephone: 614-221-0240
FAX: 614-221-5909/1-877-HAHNLAW
URL: http://www.hahnlaw.com

Cleveland, Ohio Office: 3300 BP Tower, 200 Public Square, 44114-2301. Telephone: 216-621-0150. Fax: 216-241-2824.
Akron, Ohio Office: One Gojo Plaza, Suite 300, 44311-1076. Telephone: 330-864-5550. Fax: 330-864-7986.
Naples, Florida Office: 3301 Bonita Beach Road, Suite 308, Bonita Springs, 34134. Telephone: 239-949-6989. Fax: 239-949-6687.

Business, Corporate and Securities, Litigation, Taxation and Employee Benefits, Estate Planning, Probate, Real Estate, Labor, Creditors Rights, Reorganization and Bankruptcy, Intellectual Property and Technology, Environmental, Patent, Trademark and Copyright Law, Telecommunications Law, Government Relations, Public Utility and Regulatory Law, Health Care, Construction Law.

FIRM PROFILE: Hahn Loeser & Parks LLP . . . Dedicated, diverse legal counsel serving businesses, industries, institutions and individuals since 1920. We deliver sophisticated and innovative counseling to a wide spectrum of clients from our offices in Cleveland, Columbus and Akron, Ohio, and Bonita Springs and Naples, Florida.

RESIDENT MEMBERS

STEPHEN E. CHAPPELEAR, born Columbus, Ohio, December 25, 1952; admitted to bar, 1977, Ohio; 1978, U.S. Tax Court. *Education:* The Ohio State University (B.A., 1974; J.D., 1977). Order of the Barristers. Member: National Moot Court Team; Moot Court Governing Board, 1976-1977. President: National Caucus, Metro Bar Leaders, 2001-2002; Executive Council, National Conference of Bar Presidents, 1998-2000. Listed in Best Lawyers in America - Business Litigation, 2003-2004, 2005-2006. *Member:* Columbus (President, 1995-1996; Member, Board of Governors, 1987-1991, 1992-1997), Ohio State (President, 2002-2003, Member, Board of Governors, 1998-2004; Council of Delegates, 1991—; Litigation Section, Board of Governors, 2000—) and American (Chair, Real Estate Litigation Committee, Litigation Section; Member, Tort Trial and Insurance Practice Section, Vice Chair, Trial Techniques Committee, Member, Ethics and Professionalism Committee) Bar Associations; Million Dollar Advocates Forum; American Inns of Court, Franklin Chapter (President, 1994-1995, 2005-2006; Master Lawyer); Fellow, American Bar Foundation, Ohio State Bar Foundation and Columbus Bar Foundation. ***PRACTICE AREAS:*** Business Litigation; Complex Litigation; Patent Infringement; Trademark Infringement; Personal Injury; Probate Litigation; Product Defects. ***Email:*** sechappelear@hahnlaw.com

MARC J. KESSLER, born Neptune, New Jersey, 1966; admitted to bar, 1992, Ohio; 1993, U.S. Court of Appeals, Sixth Circuit and U.S. District Court, Nothern and Southern Districts of Ohio. *Education:* Dickinson College (B.A., cum laude, 1989); Capital University (J.D., 1992). Principal Author: Ohio's Athelete-Agent Registration (March 2001). Adjunct Professor, Professional Sports Law, Capital University School of Law. Certified Player's Representative: National Football League Players' Association; National Basketball Players' Association; Women's National Basketball Players' Association. *Member:* Sports Lawyer's Association. ***PRACTICE AREAS:*** Complex Commercial Litigation; Business Law; Sports Law; Trial Practice; Appellate Practice; Business Litigation; Products Liability; Real Estate; Sports Facilities; Construction; Insurance; Health Care; Aviation. ***Email:*** mjkessler@hahnlaw.com

THOMAS J. RILEY, born Columbus, Ohio, June 18, 1944; admitted to bar, 1969, Ohio; 1974, U.S. Tax Court. *Education:* The Ohio State University (B.A., 1966; J.D., 1969); New York University (LL.M. in Taxation, 1970). ***PRACTICE AREAS:*** Business Law; Corporate Law; Taxation; Tax Law; Estate Planning; Trusts and Estates. ***Email:*** tjriley@hahlaw.com

ARLAND T. STEIN, born November 19, 1938; admitted to bar, 1965, Pennsylvania; 1966, Ohio; 1999, Indiana; U.S. Supreme Court; U.S. Court of Appeals for the Federal Circuit; U.S. Court of Appeals, Second, Third, Fourth, Sixth, Seventh and Ninth Circuits; U.S. Court of Appeals for the District of Columbia Circuit; U.S. District Court, Eastern and

(This Listing Continued)

HAHN LOESER & PARKS LLP, Columbus—Continued

Western Districts of Pennsylvania; U.S. District Court, Southern District of Indiana; U.S. District Court, Northern and Southern Districts of Ohio; U.S. District Court, Eastern and Western Districts of Michigan; U.S. District Court, Eastern and Western Districts of Wisconsin; registered to practice before U.S. Patent and Trademark Office; registered to practice before Canadian Patent Office. *Education:* Purdue University (B.S., 1961); University of Virginia (LL.B., 1965; J.D., 1965). ***PRACTICE AREAS:*** Intellectual Property; Litigation; Administrative Law; Appellate Practice; Computer Law; Copyrights; Mergers, Acquisitions and Divestitures; Patents; Trademarks. ***Email:*** astein@hahnlaw.com

JEFFREY W. STILTNER, born Cleveland, Ohio, July 11, 1970; admitted to bar, 1995, Ohio. *Education:* John Carroll University (B.A., cum laude, 1992); Capital University (J.D., cum laude, 1995; LL.M., Taxation, 2002). Member, 1993-1994 and Associate Editor, 1994-1995, Capital University Law Review. ***PRACTICE AREAS:*** Business Law; Corporate Law; Real Estate; Commercial Litigation. ***Email:*** jwstiltner@hahnlaw.com

RESIDENT ASSOCIATES

JULIE E. BRIGNER, born Columbus, Ohio, October 22, 1970; admitted to bar, 1996, Ohio and U.S. District Court, Southern District of Ohio; 2000, U.S. Court of Appeals, Sixth Circuit; 2001, U.S. District Court, Northern District of Ohio; 2005, U.S. Court of Appeals, Federal Circuit. *Education:* Northwestern University (B.A., 1993); Ohio State University (J.D., with honors, 1996). ***PRACTICE AREAS:*** Litigation; Creditors Rights; Bankruptcy; Patent Litigation. ***Email:*** jebrigner@hahnlaw.com

DAWN-RAE GRAUEL, born May 24, 1972; admitted to bar, 2001, Ohio. *Education:* Youngstown State University (B.A., summa cum laude, 1996); The Ohio State University (J.D., 2001). [U.S. Army, 1991-1993]. ***PRACTICE AREAS:*** Labor and Employment; Litigation. ***Email:*** drgrauel@hahnlaw.com

ANTHONY J. MILLER, born Lima, Ohio, May 7, 1971; admitted to bar, 2000, Ohio. *Education:* The Ohio State University (B.S., 1994); Capital University (J.D., 2000). ***PRACTICE AREAS:*** Construction Litigation; Litigation. ***Email:*** amiller@hahnlaw.com

ERICA K. WILLIAMS, born Albany, New York, June 11, 1970; admitted to bar, 1996, Ohio. *Education:* Fordham University (B.A., 1992); Case Western Reserve University (J.D., 1996). ***PRACTICE AREAS:*** Estate Planning; Trusts and Estates; Probate; Taxation. ***Email:*** ewilliams@hahnlaw.com

JEFFREY A. YEAGER, born Toledo, Ohio, December 8, 1970; admitted to bar, 1997, Ohio; 1998, U.S. District Court, Southern District of Ohio and U.S. Court of Appeals, Sixth Circuit. *Education:* Bowling Green State University (B.S., cum laude, 1993); The Ohio State University College of Law (J.D., with honors, 1997). ***PRACTICE AREAS:*** Litigation. ***Email:*** jyeager@hahnlaw.com

REPRESENTATIVE CLIENTS: Commerce National Bank; HFI, Inc.; Ohio State Medical Association; Ohio Transmission Corp.; The Media Group, Inc.

(For Complete Biographical Data on all Personnel, see Professional Biographies at Cleveland, Ohio)

HALLIBURTON-COHEN LAW OFFICE

1776 WEST LANE AVENUE, SUITE B
COLUMBUS, OHIO 43221-3363
Telephone: 614-486-2600
Fax: 614-486-2609
Email: kmh-c@halliburton-cohen.com
URL: http://www.halliburton-cohen.com

Family Law, Divorce, Child Custody, Child Support, Visitation Rights, Adoptions.

KIM M. HALLIBURTON-COHEN, born St. Louis, Missouri, December 19, 1957; admitted to bar, 1982, Ohio. *Education:* Denison University (B.A., 1979); The Ohio State University (J.D., 1982). Assistant Franklin County Prosecutor, 1982-1984. Chief Counsel, Franklin County Children Services, 1989-1990. Sisterhood President and Executive Board Member, Congregation Beth Tikvah, 1994—. *Member:* Columbus Bar Association (Sustaining Member; Member, Family Law, Professionalism, Small Firm and Solo Practitioner Committees). ***PRACTICE AREAS:*** Family Law; Divorce; Child Custody; Child Support; Visitation Rights; Spousal Support; Marital Property Distribution.

KAREN E. HAMILTON ATTORNEY AT LAW INC.

Established in 1999

31 E. WHITTIER STREET
COLUMBUS, OHIO 43206
Telephone: 614-443-7920; 1-800-774-8544
Fax: 614-443-7922
Email: khamiltonlaw@sbcglobal.net
URL: http://www.khamiltonlaw.com

Bankruptcy Law, Debtor and Creditor Law, Estate Planning, Revocable Trusts, Living Trusts, Charitable Giving, Elder Law, Medicaid Planning.

KAREN E. HAMILTON, born Travis Air Force Base, California, March 31, 1962; admitted to bar, 1995, Ohio and U.S. District Court, Northern District of Ohio; 1999, U.S. District Court, Southern District of Ohio; 2000, U.S. Supreme Court. *Education:* Franklin University (B.S., magna cum laude, 1992); Cleveland-Marshall College of Law (J.D., cum laude, 1995). Delta Theta Phi National Officer; Member, Moot Court Team. Member, Board of Trustees, Cleveland-Marshall Law Alumni, 1995—. *Member:* Ohio State Bar Association (Member: Elder Law Committee; Credit Education Coalition). ***PRACTICE AREAS:*** Bankruptcy; Trusts and Estates; Wills; Probate; Estate Planning; Elder Law.

REPRESENTATIVE CLIENT: Firstmerit Bank.

HAMMOND, SEWARDS & WILLIAMS

556 EAST TOWN STREET
COLUMBUS, OHIO 43215
Telephone: 614-228-6061
Fax: 614-228-5883

Medical Malpractice Defense, Nursing Home Defense, Insurance, Personal Injury, Litigation.

MEMBERS OF THE FIRM

GARY W. HAMMOND, born Youngstown, Ohio, March 29, 1951; admitted to bar, 1980, Ohio; 1981, U.S. District Court, Southern District of Ohio; 1982, U.S. Court of Appeals, Sixth Circuit; 1993, U.S. Supreme Court. *Education:* Miami University (B.A., 1974); Capital University (J.D., 1980). *Author:* "Ohio Courtroom Evidence," (Privileges Section) Parker & Son Publications, Inc., 1981; "Damages Covered by Uninsured and Underinsured Motorist Insurance," Professional Education Systems, Inc., 1986, 1988 and 1990; "Settling Personal Injury Insurance Claims in Ohio - The Defense Perspective," Professional Education Systems, Inc., 1987; "Ohio Insurance Law," National Business Institute, 1994; "Punitive Damages in Ohio and Bad Faith," National Business Institute, 1993. *Speaker/Author:* "Insurance Law, Personal Injury Actions, Comparative Negligence, Uninsured Motorists Law and Orthopedics for Lawyers," Continuing Legal Education, Professional Education Systems, Inc., 1986; "Evaluation of Orthopedic Injury for Lawyers," Professional Education Systems, 1988; "Recovery and Avoidance of Prejudgment Interest," Physicians Insurance Company of Ohio Seminar, 1989; Ohio Insurance Law," National Business Institute, Inc., 1994; "Auto Litigation and Insurance Law," Lorman Education Service, 1996; Advanced Trial Techniques, Ohio State Bar Association continuing legal education, 1997; "Obtaining and Using Medical Record," Ohio State Bar Association, 1999. *Member:* Columbus and Ohio State Bar Associations; Columbus Claims Association; Ohio Association of Civil Trial Attorneys. ***REPORTED CASES:*** Supreme Court: Nationwide Mut. Ins. Co. v. Ferrin (1986), 21 Ohio St.3d 43; Schaefer v. Allstate 63 Ohio St.3d 708 (1992); Lovewell v. Satayathum, 79 Ohio St.3d 143 (1997); Family Medicine Foundation Inc. v. Bright, 96 Ohio St.3d 183, 2002-Ohio-4034. ***PRACTICE AREAS:*** Medical Malpractice Defense; Insurance Law; Business Litigation; Commercial Litigation; Seed Law. ***Email:*** ghammond@hammondandsewards.com

FREDERICK A. SEWARDS, born Newark, Ohio, May 15, 1965; admitted to bar, 1990, Ohio; 1991, U.S. District Court, Southern District of Ohio; 1994, U.S. Court of Appeals, Sixth Circuit; 1999, U.S. Supreme Court. *Education:* The Ohio State University (B.A., 1987; J.D., 1990). Delta Theta Phi. Speaker: "Medical Malpractice in Ohio, April 2001; "Medical Malpractice: Obtaining and Using Medical Records," Ohio State Bar Association CLE Institution, April 2000; "Using Medical Records to Win Your Case in Ohio," Institute for Paralegal Education, April 2001. *Member:* Columbus and Ohio State Bar Associations; Ohio Association of Civil Trial Attorneys; Defense Research Institute. ***REPORTED CASES:*** Wireman v. Keneco Distributors, Inc., (1996) 75 Ohio St.3d 103, 661 N.E.2d 744. ***PRACTICE AREAS:*** Medical Malpractice Defense; Nursing Home Litigation; Litigation. ***Email:*** fsewards@hammondandsewards.com

SCOTT E. WILLIAMS, born Columbus, Ohio, February 24, 1956; admitted to bar, 1992, Ohio; 1999, U.S. District Court, Southern District of Ohio. *Education:* The Ohio State University (B.S., 1978); Capital University (J.D., 1992). Member, Capital University Law Review, 1990. Order of the Curia. *Member:* Columbus and Ohio State Bar Associations. ***PRACTICE AREAS:*** Insurance Law; Insurance Defense Law; Business and Commercial Litigation; Personal Injury; Medical Malpractice Defense. ***Email:*** swilliams@hammondandsewards.com

ASSOCIATES

JAMES M. McGOVERN, born Parma, Ohio, October 17, 1966; admitted to bar, 1993, Ohio and U.S. District Court, Northern District of Ohio; 1994, U.S. District Court, Southern District of Ohio; 1996, U.S. Court of Appeals, Sixth Circuit. *Education:* Miami University (B.A., 1989); The Ohio State University (J.D., 1993). Assistant Ohio Attorney General, 1993-1999; Counsel, Ohio Department of Human Services, 1993-1996; Counsel, State Medical Board of Ohio (Prosecuting Disciplinary Cases against Physicians), 1996-1999. *Member:* Columbus and Ohio State Bar Associations. ***REPORTED CASES:*** Chambers v. Ohio Dept. of Human Services (C.A.6, 1998), 145 F.3d 793, certiorari denied (1998), 119 S.Ct. 408. ***PRACTICE AREAS:*** Administrative Law; Professional Discipline; Professional Licensing; Insurance Defense; Medical Malpractice Defense. ***Email:*** jmcgovern@hammondandsewards.com

LAURA FOLKERTH COOK, born Columbus, Ohio, May 14, 1969; admitted to bar, 1999, Ohio. *Education:* The Ohio State University (B.S., 1993); University of Michigan (J.D., 1999). *Member:* Columbus and Ohio State Bar Associations. ***PRACTICE AREAS:*** Insurance Defense; Medical Malpractice Defense. ***Email:*** lcook@hammondandsewards.com

R. CHRIS HARBOLD AND ASSOCIATES

500 S. FRONT STREET, SUITE 1140
COLUMBUS, OHIO 43215
Telephone: 614-255-1140
Fax: 614-255-1141
Email: lawyers@harboldlaw.com
URL: http://www.lawyers.com/rcharboldlaw

Family and Matrimonial Law including Divorce, Dissolution, Legal Separation, Annulment, Allocation of Parental Rights and Responsibilities (including child support and parenting time), Spousal Support, Antenuptial Agreements, Step-Parent Adoption, Civil Domestic Violence, Post-Decree Enforcement and Modification.

FIRM PROFILE: Mr. Harbold has concentrated his practice in the area of family law since 1982. He is board certified as a specialist in family relations law by the Ohio State Bar Association. The firm is also included in the family law section of the Bar Register of Preeminent Lawyers. Mr. Harbold has also been listed as an Ohio Super Lawyer.

(This Listing Continued)

R. CHRIS HARBOLD, born Columbus, Ohio, November 27, 1948; admitted to bar, 1975, Ohio; 1976, U.S. District Court, Southern District of Ohio. *Education:* Ohio University (B.B.A., cum laude, 1970); Capital University (J.D., 1975). Member, Order of the Curia. Lecturer, Family Law Seminars. *Member:* Columbus (Member, Committees on: Family Law, 1980—); Ohio State (Member, Family Law Section) and American (Member, Committees on: Family Law) Bar Associations; Franklin County Trial Lawyers Association; Ohio Academy of Trial Lawyers. (Certified Specialist in Family Relations Law, Ohio State Bar Association). ***PRACTICE AREAS:*** Family Law; Divorce; Child Custody; Child Support; Spousal Support; Visitation Rights; Premarital Agreements.

ASSOCIATES

AMY M. McKINLAY, born Columbus, Ohio, February 20, 1971; admitted to bar, 1996, Ohio; 1997, U.S. District Court, Southern District of Ohio. *Education:* Otterbein College (B.A., summa cum laude, 1992); Capital University (J.D., magna cum laude, 1996). Phi Alpha Delta; Order of the Curia; Law Review. Ohio Super Lawyer Rising Star (Law & Politics). *Member:* Columbus (Member, Family Law Section) and American (Member, Family Law Committee) Bar Associations. ***PRACTICE AREAS:*** Family Law; Divorce; Child Custody; Child Support; Spousal Support; Visitation Rights.

CHAD KRISTIAN HEMMINGER, born Shelby, Ohio, December 19, 1977; admitted to bar, 2004, Ohio. *Education:* The Ohio State University (B.A., 2001); Cleveland-Marshall College of Law, Cleveland State University (J.D., 2004). Delta Theta Phi. Recipient: Joel Jay Finer Award for Outstanding Student in the Field of Criminal Procedure (Cleveland Marshall College of Law, 2002-2003). *Member:* Columbus (Member, Family Committee), Ohio State (Member, Family Law Section) and American (Member, Family Law Committee) Bar Associations.

REFERENCE: Bank One.

HARRIS, McCLELLAN, BINAU & COX, P.L.L.

NINTH FLOOR, HUNTINGTON PLAZA
37 WEST BROAD STREET
COLUMBUS, OHIO 43215
Telephone: 614-464-2572
Fax: 614-464-2245
URL: http://www.hmbc.com

General Civil Practice. Corporation, Taxation, Securities, Creditors' Rights; Bankruptcy, Banking Law, Real Estate, Zoning, Shopping Center Law, Administrative, Civil Litigation, Criminal, Immigration, International Law, Family Law. Construction Law, Insurance Defense, Estate Planning and Probate. Trials in all Courts.

FIRM PROFILE: HMB&C is a medium-sized general practice law firm emphasizing attentive and personal service to its clients. Although the firm does have large corporate clients, the majority of the firm's clients consist of individuals and small to medium-sized businesses.

Members of the firm are particularly experienced in civil litigation in all courts, business and corporate law, tax and estate planning, probate, securities and franchising, real estate, construction law and litigation, creditors' rights, banking, and bankruptcy. In addition, certain members of the firm emphasize administrative law, immigration and naturalization, criminal, employment and family law.

HMB&C is proud of the close working relationship it establishes with its clients. HMB&C is large enough to handle the legal needs of its clients but not so large that close personal contact is lost.

While each of the HMB&C attorneys has areas of professional emphasis, each attorney has the depth of experience and resources within the firm to offer the client comprehensive and sophisticated legal representation.

MEMBERS OF FIRM

CURTIS H. PORTER (1920-1993)

JOHN H. KOZICH, born Lorain, Ohio, August 18, 1949; admitted to bar, 1975, Ohio; 1976, U.S. District Court, Southern District of Ohio. *Education:* Kent State University (B.A., 1971); Ohio State University (J.D., 1975). Certified Public Accountant, Ohio, 1976. *Member:* Columbus Bar Association. ***PRACTICE AREAS:*** Business Law; Taxation Law; Real Estate. ***Email:*** jkozich@hmbc.com

DAN J. BINAU, born Tiffin, Ohio, September 14, 1950; admitted to bar, 1976, Ohio; 1978, U.S. District Court, Southern District of Ohio. *Education:* Ohio Northern University and The Ohio State University (B.S., 1973); Capital University (J.D., 1976). Member, Moot Court Board, 1974-1976. Member, National Panel of Arbitrators, American Arbitration Association. *Member:* Columbus and Ohio State Bar Associations; Franklin County Trial Lawyers (President, 1992-1993). ***PRACTICE AREAS:*** Civil Litigation; Corporate Litigation; Shopping Center Law. ***Email:*** dbinau@hmbc.com

JAMES B. HARRIS, born Wilkes-Barre, Pennsylvania, November 6, 1950; admitted to bar, 1976, Ohio and U.S. District Court, Southern District of Ohio; 1977, U.S. Tax Court. *Education:* Wilkes College (B.A., 1972); Villanova University (M.A., 1973); Capital University (J.D., 1976). Order of the Barristers. Associate Justice, 1974-1975, and Chief Justice, 1975-1976, Moot Court Board. *Member:* Columbus and Ohio State Bar Associations; Franklin County Trial Lawyers Association; Ohio Academy of Trial Lawyers. ***PRACTICE AREAS:*** Immigration Law; Construction Law; Corporate Law; Business Litigation; Family Law. ***Email:*** jharris@hmbc.com

SCOTT R. MOTE, born Troy, Ohio, January 20, 1950; admitted to bar, 1977, Ohio; 1978, Florida and U.S. District Court, Southern District of Ohio; 1979, U.S. District Court, Northern District of Ohio; 1987, U.S. Supreme Court. *Education:* Bowling Green State University; Wright State University (B.A., cum laude, 1972); University of Dayton (M.A., 1973); Stetson University College of Law; Capital University (J.D., 1977). Delta Theta Phi. Guest Lecturer, Capital University Law School, Professionalism, 1991—. Member, 1985— and Treasurer, 1988-1995, President, 1995, Board of Directors, Ohio Legal Services Fund, Inc. Member, Capital Law Alumni Governing Board, 1989—. *Member:* Columbus and Ohio State Bar Associations; The Florida Bar; Franklin County Trial Lawyers Association; Columbus Bar Foundation. ***PRACTICE AREAS:*** Civil Litigation; Family Law; Probate. ***Email:*** smote@hmbc.com

GARTH G. COX, born Washington C.H., Ohio, February 15, 1956; admitted to bar, 1981, Ohio; 1989, U.S. District Court, Southern District of Ohio; 1990, U.S. Supreme Court; 1993, U.S. Court of Appeals, Sixth Circuit; U.S. District Court, Northern District of Ohio. *Education:* Ohio State University (B.A., 1978); Capital University (J.D., 1981). Guest Advocate, Ohio State Highway Patrol Academy, 1985—. Certified by National Football League Players Association as Player Agent. Registered Player Agent with NCAA. *Member:* Columbus, Ohio State and American Bar Associations; Ohio Association of Criminal Defense Attorneys. ***PRACTICE AREAS:*** Civil Litigation; Criminal Defense Law; Business Litigation. ***Email:*** gcox@hmbc.com

RALPH E. DILL, born Celina, Ohio, September 4, 1950; admitted to bar, 1975, Ohio; 1976, U.S. District Court, Southern District of Ohio; 1978, U.S. Court of Appeals, Sixth Circuit. *Education:* Capital University (B.A., summa cum laude, 1972); The Ohio State University (J.D., cum laude, 1975). Order of the Coif. Member, Ohio State Law Journal, 1974-1975. *Member:* Columbus Bar Association. ***PRACTICE AREAS:*** Bankruptcy Law; Commercial Law; Commercial and Business Litigation; Civil Litigation; Criminal Law. ***Email:*** rdill@hmbc.com

MARK S. COCO, born Alliance, Ohio, November 1, 1952; admitted to bar, 1977, Ohio; 1978, U.S. District Court, Southern District of Ohio; 1981, U.S. District Court, Northern District of Ohio and U.S. Court of Appeals, Sixth Circuit. *Education:* The Ohio State University (B.A., cum laude, 1974; J.D., summa cum laude, 1977). Phi Eta Sigma; Order of the Coif. Editor, Issue Planning, Ohio State Law Journal, 1976-1977. Author: Note, "The Right to Defend Pro Se in Criminal Proceedings," 37 Ohio St. L.J. 220 (1976). *Member:* Columbus (Member, Committees on: Common Pleas; Trial Practice; Labor Law; Federal Court), Ohio State (Member, Committees on: Litigation; Labor Law) and American (Member, Litigation and Labor Law Committees) Bar Associations. ***REPORTED CASES:*** Mers v. Dispatch Printing Co., 19 Ohio St. 3d 100 (1985). ***PRACTICE AREAS:*** Business Litigation; Employment Litigation. ***Email:*** mcoco@hmbc.com

STEPHEN H. DODD, born Columbus, Ohio, May 30, 1959; admitted to bar, 1985, Ohio. *Education:* Villanova University; The Ohio State University (B.S., 1982; J.D., 1985). Phi Alpha Kappa; Phi Eta Sigma; Alpha Lambda Delta. *Member:* Columbus, Ohio State and American Bar Associations. ***PRACTICE AREAS:*** Litigation; Real Estate; Employment Law. ***Email:*** sdodd@hmbc.com

MICHAEL A. COLEMAN, born Williamsport, Pennsylvania, October 3, 1960; admitted to bar, 1986, Ohio. *Education:* Dickinson College (B.A., 1982); Capital University (J.D., 1986). *Member:* Columbus and Ohio State Bar Associations. ***PRACTICE AREAS:*** Real Estate; Business Law; Commercial Law. ***Email:*** mcoleman@hmbc.com

OF COUNSEL

JOHN D. HVIZDOS, born Cleveland, Ohio, November 27, 1947; admitted to bar, 1975, Ohio; 1976, U.S. District Court, Southern District of Ohio; 1982, U.S. Tax Court. *Education:* Ohio State University (B.A., cum laude, 1972; J.D., cum laude, 1975). Articles, Editor, Ohio State Law Journal, 1974-1975. *Member:* Columbus, Ohio State and American Bar Associations. ***PRACTICE AREAS:*** Corporate Law; Securities Law; Business Litigation. ***Email:*** jhvizdos@hmbc.com

EDWARD T. McCLELLAN, born Lansing, Michigan, June 15, 1947; admitted to bar, 1975, Ohio. *Education:* University of Munich, Germany (1967-1968); Ohio Wesleyan University (B.A., 1969); The Ohio State University (J.D., cum laude, 1975). Phi Delta Phi. *Member:* Columbus and Ohio State Bar Associations. ***LANGUAGES:*** German. ***PRACTICE AREAS:*** Bankruptcy Law; Real Estate Law; Zoning Law; Computer Law. ***Email:*** tmcclellan@ohiorealestate.law.pro

REPRESENTATIVE CLIENTS: The Olen Corp.; Choices for Victims of Domestic Violence; Concessions by Cox, Inc.; Donatos Pizza, Inc.; Don M. Casto Organization; Equitable Life Assurance Society of America; The Pontifical College Josephinum; The Erie Group of Companies; Town and Country Shopping Center; Great Western Shopping Center; Graceland Shopping Center; University City Shopping Center; Country Fair Shopping Center; Indian Valley Plaza; United Ohio Insurance Co.; Ohio Mutual Insurance Co.; J.C. Penny Casualty Insurance Co.; Refrigeration Systems, Inc.; Shimizu Group, Inc.; Steego Auto Parts; Tanishi Corp.; Sterling Paper Co.; R & F. Coal Co.; Simco Control, Inc.; Broad Street Oil and Gas; Star Bank, N.A.; Society National Bank; Complete Resources Company; Ohio Rifle & Pistol Association; Glasfloss Industries, Inc.; Columbus Hi-Lo, Inc.; Vietnam Veterans of America, Inc.; Lightning Rod Insurance; Harleyville Insurance; Western Reserve Mutual Insurance Co.

HECKERT & HOCKENSMITH CO., L.P.A.

Established in 2002

495 SOUTH HIGH STREET, SUITE 220
COLUMBUS, OHIO 43215
Telephone: 614-224-7700
Fax: 614-224-7766
Email: info@heckerthockensmith.com
URL: http://www.heckerthockensmith.com

General Civil and Criminal Litigation in all Courts. Personal Injury, Automobile Accidents, Criminal Defense, Felonies, Misdemeanors, Drug Crimes, Sexual Assault, Parole and Probation, Driving While Intoxicated, Traffic Violations, Juvenile Law, Family Law, Divorce, Child Custody, Child Support, Visitation Rights, Spousal Support, Domestic Violence, Wills and Probate.

FIRM PROFILE: When you face a legal situation you want a law firm committed to serving your needs. Heckert & Hockensmith Co., L.P.A. is a law firm that will provide immediate and personalized service one would expect from a friend. We are a general practice firm dedicated to serving the needs of the everyday person. Through our experience and knowledge of the law, we intend to provide innovative and creative solutions to our client's needs, thereby not only meeting by attempting to surpass our clients' expectations.

(This Listing Continued)

HECKERT & HOCKENSMITH CO., L.P.A., Columbus—Continued

Whether an individual, corporation, or organization, we will work in an aggressive and conscientious manner to provide the best possible result. Heckert & Hockensmith offers services in the areas of: Criminal Law, DUI/OMVI, Traffic Violations, Personal Injury (Auto accidents, medical malpractice), Family Law (Divorce, dissolution, custody, visitations, wills).

CHRIS E. HECKERT, born Dallas, Texas, June 29, 1972; admitted to bar, 2000, Ohio and U.S. District Court, Southern District of Ohio. *Education:* University of Alabama (B.A., Political Science, 1995); Capital University (J.D., 1999). Pi Sigma Alpha. Vice President, Criminal Justice Student Association, 1993-1994. Formerly with Franklin County Public Defender Office, 1999-2002. *Member:* Columbus and Ohio State Bar Associations; National Association of Criminal Defense Lawyers. ***PRACTICE AREAS:*** Criminal Law; Felonies; Misdemeanors; Drug Crimes; Driving While Intoxicated; Domestic Violence; Juvenile Law; Personal Injury. ***Email:*** ceheckert.hhlaw@rrohio.com

MARK L. HOCKENSMITH, born Youngstown, Ohio, August 28, 1972; admitted to bar, 1997, Ohio. *Education:* Miami University (B.A., History, 1994); University of Dayton (J.D., 1997). Phi Alpha Theta; Delta Kappa Epsilon; Phi Alpha Delta (Treasurer, 1997). Formerly with Franklin County Public Defenders Office, 1999-2002. *Member:* Columbus, Ohio State and American Bar Associations. ***PRACTICE AREAS:*** Criminal Law; Felonies; Misdemeanors; Driving While Intoxicated; Traffic Violations; Personal Injury; Automobile Accidents and Injuries; Slip and Fall; Products Liability; Lemon Law. ***Email:*** mlhocken.hhlaw@rrohio.com

JENNIFER M. RILEY, born Mentor, Ohio, May 22, 1976; admitted to bar, 2002, Ohio; 2003, U.S. District Court, Southern District of Ohio. *Education:* Miami University (B.S., 1998); Capital University (J.D., 2002). Phi Alpha Delta. Law Clerk, Public Defenders Office, Franklin County, 2002. *Member:* Columbus and American Bar Associations. ***PRACTICE AREAS:*** Criminal Defense; Driving While Intoxicated; Traffic Violations; Juvenile Law; Family Law; Divorce; Child Custody; Child Support; Visitation Rights; Wills. ***Email:*** hhlaw@rrohio.com

HOCKSTAD LAW OFFICE, LTD.

471 E. BROAD STREET, SUITE 800
COLUMBUS, OHIO 43215
Telephone: 614-224-1727
Fax: 614-463-1296
Email: khockstad@hockstadlaw.com
URL: http://www.hockstadlaw.com

Business Law, Business Formation, Joint Ventures, Strategic Alliances, Limited Liability Companies, Partnerships, Family Business Law, Closely Held Businesses, Small Business Law, Business Planning, Franchise Law, Commercial Leasing, Business Litigation, Mergers and Acquisitions, Taxation, Tax Planning, Labor and Employment, Employment Contracts, Personnel Policies, Human Resources.

FIRM PROFILE: Ms. Hockstad serves as outside General Counsel for a variety of small business and corporate clients.

She has extensive experience with corporate planning, employment related issues, including non-competes, tax controversy work at both the State and Federal levels, and business-related litigation.

KAREN S. HOCKSTAD, born Traverse City, Michigan, June 4, 1965; admitted to bar, 1992, Michigan; 1993, Ohio; U.S. District Court, Southern District of Ohio; U.S. Court of Appeals, Sixth Circuit. *Education:* University of Michigan (B.A., 1987); Detroit College of Law at Michigan State University (J.D., magna cum laude, 1992); Capital University Law School (LL.M., Taxation, 1994). Tax Fellow, Capital University, 1992-1993. Managing Editor and Notes and Comment Editor, Detroit College of Law Review. National Moot Court Competition. Author: "Tax Executives Institute, Inc.," Ohio Tax Review, Vol. 7.1, Winter, 1993. Recipient: Business First Forty under Forty Award. Trustee, Safety Council of Central Ohio. Member and Past President, Children's Hospital Development Board. *Member:* Columbus, Ohio State, Federal and American Bar Associations; State Bar of Michigan. Fellow, Columbus Bar Foundation. ***PRACTICE AREAS:*** Business Law; Taxation; Employment Law; Complex Commercial Litigation; Tax Planning; Complex Business Litigation; Corporate Law; Small Business Law; Distribution; Franchise Law; Local Taxation.

EDWIN J. HOLLERN CO., LPA

77 NORTH STATE STREET
COLUMBUS, OHIO 43081
Telephone: 614-839-5700
Fax: 614-839-4200
Email: ehollern@ejhlaw.com
URL: http://www.ejhlaw.com

Product Liability, Professional Liability, Insurance Coverage, Insurance Defense, Civil Litigation.

EDWIN J. HOLLERN, born Columbus, Ohio, August 21, 1955; admitted to bar, 1988, Ohio; 1989, U.S. District Court, Northern and Southern Districts of Ohio; 1989, U.S. Court of Appeals, Sixth Circuit; 1994, U.S. Supreme Court. *Education:* The Ohio State University (B.A., 1976); Capital University (J.D., 1988). *Member:* Columbus and Ohio State Bar Associations; DRI. ***PRACTICE AREAS:*** Trial and Appellate Practice; Insurance Coverage. ***Email:*** ehollern@ejhlaw.com

(This Listing Continued)

KEVIN J. ZIMMERMAN, born Lima, Ohio, October 15, 1971; admitted to bar, 1999, Ohio; 2000, U.S. District Court, Southern and Northern Districts of Ohio. *Education:* Bowling Green State University (B.S., 1994); Capital University (J.D., 1999). Member: Law Review, 1994-1996; Moot Court, 1994-1996. *Member:* Columbus and Ohio State Bar Associations; Ohio Association of Civil Trial Attorneys (OACTA). ***PRACTICE AREAS:*** Insurance; Insurance Defense; Negligence Defense; Premises Liability.

ROMINA P. NEWSOME, born Cleveland, Ohio, March 10, 1978; admitted to bar, 2003, Ohio. *Education:* Capital University (B.A., 2000; J.D., 2003). ***PRACTICE AREAS:*** Insurance Defense; Litigation; Personal Injury.

REPRESENTATIVE CLIENTS: Allstate Insurance Co.; American National Property Casualty; Alphavision Insurance Group; Auto Owners Insurance Co.; Encompass Insurance Co.; Mitsui Marine; Wendy's International Inc.; Seibels' Bruce Group; Taylor Dunn Manufacturing; BP Products, Inc.; Simplex Grinnell; Grocers' Insurers Group.

LEANNE HOLMES

338 SOUTH HIGH STREET
COLUMBUS, OHIO 43215
Telephone: 614-679-9618
Fax: 614-481-8048
URL: http://www.leannecollaw.com

Bankruptcy, Domestic Relations, Child Custody, Child Support, Family Law, Juvenile Law.

LEANNE M. HOLMES, born Columbus, Ohio, November 30, 1975; admitted to bar, 2003, Ohio; 2004, U.S. District Court, Southern District of Ohio. *Education:* The Ohio State University (B.A., Criminology, 1998); Capital University Law School (J.D., 2003). *Member:* Columbus, Ohio State and American Bar Associations. ***PRACTICE AREAS:*** Bankruptcy; Domestic Relations; Child Custody; Child Support; Family Law; Juvenile Law.

DWIGHT I. HURD CO., LPA

Established in 1999
4235 WESTLETON COURT
COLUMBUS, OHIO 43221-4930
Telephone: 614-876-0480
Fax: 614-876-0565
Email: hurdlaw@columbus.rr.com
URL: http://www.hurdlawoffice.com

Elder Law, General Business and Corporate Law, Estate Administration, Trusts and Estates, Business Succession and Small Business.

FIRM PROFILE: Dwight Hurd practices in the areas of elder law, estate planning and administration, and business law with emphasis on closely held businesses and business succession planning. He is a member of the Ohio and Columbus Bar Associations. Mr. Hurd is also a member of the National Academy of Elder Law Attorneys and is active in the planning of estates for elder persons, including living trusts, wills, powers of attorney and related documents for the protection of assets. He is a member of the Columbus Rotary Club and has been active in various local community affairs, including serving as an original member of the Columbus Capital Square Commission.

DWIGHT I. HURD, born Columbus, Ohio, June 1, 1932; admitted to bar, 1959, Ohio; U.S. District Court, Southern District of Ohio; 1964, U.S. Tax Court. *Education:* The Ohio State University (B.B.A., 1957; J.D., 1959). Author: "Ohio Limited Partnerships-Business Use and Effect"; "Managing Stock In a Closely-Held Business"; "One Time Business Decisions". Lecturer, Ohio Entrepreneurship Seminars. Various CLE Seminars. *Member:* Columbus (Member, Board of Governors, 1968-1972) and Ohio State Bar Association; National Academy of Elder Law Attorneys. ***PRACTICE AREAS:*** Business Law; General Practice; Elder Law. ***Email:*** hurdlaw@columbus.rr.com

REPRESENTATIVE CLIENTS: Available Upon Request.

ISAAC, BRANT, LEDMAN & TEETOR LLP

Established in 1936
THE MIDLAND BUILDING
250 EAST BROAD STREET
COLUMBUS, OHIO 43215-3742
Telephone: 614-221-2121
Fax: 614-365-9516
Email: mail@isaacbrant.com
URL: http://www.isaacbrant.com

Civil Trial and Appellate Practice in all State and Federal Courts, Medical Malpractice, General Business, Corporate, Intellectual Property, Taxation, Estate Planning, Probate, Guardianship, Real Estate, Political Subdivisions, Employment, Family, Negligence, Personal Injury, Civil Arson, Insurance Defense, Insurance, Professional Malpractice, Premises Liability, Products Liability, Carrier Liability and Motor Sports Law, Commercial, including Banking, OSHA and Securities Litigation, Mediation, Arbitration.

FIRM PROFILE: Isaac, Brant, Ledman & Teetor LLP is a full service law firm that has been representing a wide range of clients since 1936. Our diverse clientele range from multinational corporations to family owned businesses to individuals. Our litigation department has taken plaintiffs' cases to verdicts as large as $12 million, and numerous defense cases to defense verdicts. We also represent a wide range of governmental entities including county commissioners, sheriffs, trustees, engineers, and other county agencies. Our business department

(This Listing Continued)

regularly handles issues involving corporate law, commercial litigation and intellectual property. In addition, we have an established family law practice group along with a probate and estate planning practice.

We offer our clients an experienced support staff, effective use of paralegals to reduce costs and expenses, and a state-of-the-art computer network which includes cost-effective desk top CD-ROM and on-line research for all our attorneys and support staff. We are the only mid-sized Columbus law firm listed among America's top law firms. Our lawyers are listed in America's Who's Who in American Law, America's Best Attorneys, and Who' Who in the Law.

To learn more about Isaac, Brant, Ledman & Teetor LLP, please visit our website at www.isaacbrant.com.

SOL MORTON ISAAC (1911-1995)
DAVID H. MEADE (1957-1994)

MEMBERS OF FIRM

CHARLES E. BRANT, born Dayton, Ohio, March 6, 1930; admitted to bar, 1959, Ohio; 1973, U.S. Supreme Court. *Education:* University of Dayton (B.A., 1952); The Ohio State University (J.D., 1959); Northwestern University (LL.M., 1960). Phi Alpha Delta; Alpha Sigma Tau. Author: "A Practitioners Guide to Comparative Negligence in Ohio," Ohio State Law Journal, Vol. 41, No. 3, 1980; "Slip, Trip & Fall," Ohio Lawyer, June, 1988. *Member:* Columbus (Chairman, Insurance Committee, 1974-1975; Vice Chairman, Ethics Committee, 1977-1979), Ohio State (Chairman, Negligence Law Committee, 1976-1980), Federal and American (Member, Tort and Insurance Practice Section) Bar Associations; Judge Advocates Association; Ohio Association of Civil Trial Attorneys; Defense Research Institute, Inc.; The Association of Trial Lawyers of America; American Board of Trial Advocates. [Colonel, JAGC, AUS Ret.]. ***PRACTICE AREAS:*** Litigation; Insurance Law; Products Liability Law; Mediation; Arbitration. ***Email:*** charlesbrant@isaacbrant.com

JAMES H. LEDMAN, born Ashland, Ohio, February 1, 1940; admitted to bar, 1965, Ohio. *Education:* Duke University (B.A., 1961); The Ohio State University (J.D., 1965). Phi Delta Phi. Author: "Ohio Taxation, Update '80," The Ohio Legal Center Institute, 1980. *Member:* Columbus and Ohio State Bar Associations; National Arbitration Forum. ***PRACTICE AREAS:*** Insurance Coverage Law; Litigation; State and Local Taxation Law; Mediation; Arbitration. ***Email:*** jamesledman@isaacbrant.com

FREDERICK M. ISAAC, born Columbus, Ohio, March 5, 1941; admitted to bar, 1966, Ohio. *Education:* Yale University (B.A., 1963); Vanderbilt University (LL.B., 1966). Phi Alpha Delta. Author: "Enforcement of Orders from the Domestic Relations Court," Ohio Legal Center Institute, 1982. Member, Supreme Court Advisory Committee on Child Support Guidelines. Secretary, The Columbus Association for the Performing Arts, 1972-1978; 1979-1989. Recipient, Columbus Bar Association Community Service Award, 1972 and 1982. Trustee, 1968-1986 and President, 1982-1984, The Columbus Symphony Orchestra. Treasurer, National Conference on Social Welfare, 1977-1980. Vice Chairman, The Columbus Urban League, 1980-1981. *Member:* Columbus (Chairman, Ethics Committee, 1976-1978; Member, Board of Governors, 1978-1982), Ohio State (Member, Council of Delegates, 1978-1980) and American Bar Associations. ***PRACTICE AREAS:*** Civil Practice; Litigation; Family Law. ***Email:*** fredisaac@isaacbrant.com

DENNIS R. NEWMAN, born Toledo, Ohio, August 24, 1943; admitted to bar, 1968, Ohio. *Education:* Ohio Wesleyan University (B.A., 1965); The Ohio State University (J.D., cum laude, 1968). Omicron Delta Kappa; Pi Sigma Alpha. *Member:* Columbus, Ohio State and American Bar Associations; Lawyers Council of the Direct Selling Association. ***PRACTICE AREAS:*** Small Business Law; Real Estate Law. ***Email:*** dennisnewman@isaacbrant.com

J. STEPHEN TEETOR, born Marion, Ohio, December 24, 1951; admitted to bar, 1977, Ohio; 1979, District of Columbia. *Education:* The Ohio State University (B.S., 1974); Capital University (J.D., 1977). *Member:* Columbus and Ohio State Bar Associations; American Board of Trial Advocates. ***PRACTICE AREAS:*** Litigation; Insurance Law; Professional Liability. ***Email:*** steveteetor@isaacbrant.com

STEVE M. SOLTIS, born Connellsville, Pennsylvania, March 18, 1940; admitted to bar, 1967, West Virginia; 1968, Ohio; 1975, U.S. District Court, Southern District of Ohio. *Education:* West Virginia University (B.S., 1962; J.D., 1967). *Member:* Columbus and Ohio State Bar Associations. ***PRACTICE AREAS:*** Probate Law; Estate Planning; Business Law; Real Estate. ***Email:*** stevesoltis@isaacbrant.com

RANDY S. KUREK, born Oklahoma City, Oklahoma, January 7, 1954; admitted to bar, 1979, Ohio, U.S. District Court, Southern District of Ohio and U.S. Court of Appeals, Sixth Circuit. *Education:* DePauw University (B.A., 1976); The Ohio State University (J.D., 1979). Trustee, 1979-1989, Vice President, 1984-1986 and President, 1986-1989, Directions For Youth. Trustee, Hugh O'Brian Youth Leadership Foundation, 1988-2004. *Member:* Columbus and Ohio State Bar Associations. ***PRACTICE AREAS:*** Family Law; General Civil Practice. ***Email:*** randykurek@isaacbrant.com

DONALD L. ANSPAUGH, born Marion, Ohio, July 2, 1955; admitted to bar, 1980, Ohio; U.S. Supreme Court, U.S. Court of Appeals, Sixth Circuit; U.S. District Court, Southern District of Ohio. *Education:* Bowling Green State University (B.A., summa cum laude, 1977); The Ohio State University (J.D., 1980). *Member:* Columbus and Ohio State Bar Associations; Defense Research Institute, Ohio Association of Civil Trial Attorneys. ***PRACTICE AREAS:*** Insurance Defense Law; Motor Sports Law; General Negligence Law; Trials and Appeals. ***Email:*** donanspaugh@isaacbrant.com

MARK LANDES, born Columbus, Ohio, June 20, 1956; admitted to bar, 1982, Kentucky and Ohio; 1987, U.S. Court of Appeals, 9th Circuit; U.S. District Court, Northern and Southern District of Ohio; 1988, U.S. Court of Appeals, Sixth Circuit; 1991, U.S. Supreme Court. *Education:* Johns Hopkins University (B.A., 1978); The Ohio State University (J.D., 1982). President, City Council, London, Ohio, 1980-1982. Adjunct Assistant Professor, Legal Writing, Ohio State College of Law, 1988. Member, Ohio Jury Instructions Drafting Committee (Employment Discrimination). Member, Ohio State Dental board, 2003-2005. *Member:* Columbus (Chair, Labor and Employment, 2000-2001), Ohio State (Chair, Federal Courts, 2003-2004) and Federal (President, Columbus Chapter, 1997-1998) Bar Associations. [Capt., 2002-2003, U.S. Army Judge Advocate General's Corps, 1982-1987; Lieutenant Colonel, Judge Advocate General's Corps, USAR (Ret.)]. ***PRACTICE AREAS:*** Trial Practice; Local Government Law; Employment Law. ***Email:*** marklandes@isaacbrant.com

(This Listing Continued)

STEVEN G. LAFORGE, born Waukegan, Illinois, September 12, 1959; admitted to bar, 1986, Ohio. *Education:* University of Illinois (B.A., 1981); The Ohio State University (J.D., 1986). Member, Jessup International Moot Court Team, 1985, 1986. Member, The Ohio State University Journal on Dispute Resolution, 1986. Speaker, Selected Issues in Insurance Law, Ohio Continuing Education Institute, 1988-1994. Member, State of Ohio Board of Orthotics, Prosthetics and Pedorthics, 2000—. Speaker, Insurance Litigation in Ohio, Lorman Education Services, 1998-2003. *Member:* Columbus, Ohio State and American Bar Associations; The Ohio Association of Civil Trial Attorneys. ***PRACTICE AREAS:*** Tort Law; Insurance Defense Law; Municipal Liability. ***Email:*** stevelaforge@isaacbrant.com

TIMOTHY E. MILLER, born Cincinnati, Ohio, July 9, 1961; admitted to bar, 1986, Ohio; U.S. District Court, Northern and Southern Districts of Ohio; U.S. Court of Appeals, Sixth Circuit; U.S. Supreme Court. *Education:* Purdue University (B.S., 1983); Capital University (J.D., 1986). Order of the Curia. Member, Capital Law Review, 1986. *Member:* Columbus and Ohio State Bar Associations. ***PRACTICE AREAS:*** Business Law; Commercial Litigation. ***Email:*** timmiller@isaacbrant.com

JAMES M. ROPER, born Youngstown, Ohio, February 4, 1959; admitted to bar, 1987, Ohio, U.S. District Court, Southern and Northern Districts of Ohio, U.S. Court of Appeals, Sixth Circuit and U.S. Supreme Court. *Education:* Mount Union College (B.S., 1981); Capital University (J.D., 1987). Member, Capital University Law Review, 1986. Member, Order of the Curia. Recipient, American Jurisprudence Award in Evidence. Author: Note, "Smith v. VanGorkom, A Narrow Interpretation of the Business Judgment Rule," 15 Capital University Law Review, Summer 1986. Listed in Who's Who in American Law, 1996. Trustee, Perry Township. *Member:* Columbus, Ohio State and American Bar Associations. ***PRACTICE AREAS:*** Professional Negligence; Medical Malpractice; Insurance Litigation; Civil Trials and Appeals. ***Email:*** jimroper@isaacbrant.com

DOUGLAS J. SUTER, born Wheeling, West Virginia, September 30, 1962; admitted to bar, 1988, Ohio, U.S. District Court, Southern District of Ohio and U.S. Court of Appeals, Sixth Circuit. *Education:* West Liberty State College (B.S., Business Administration, with honors, 1985); Capital University Law School (J.D., cum laude, 1988). Phi Alpha Delta. Member, 1986-1987 and Articles Editor, 1987-1988, Capital University Law Review. Member, Order of the Curia. Recipient, American Jurisprudence Award in Contracts and Antitrust. Listed in Who's Who in American Law 1990, 1991, 1998. Listed in Business First as One of Best Attorneys in Central Ohio. *Member:* Columbus, Ohio State and American (Member, Government Litigation and Labor and Employment Law Sections; Appointed to Occupational Safety & Health Law Committee) Bar Associations; International Association of Arson Investigators. ***PRACTICE AREAS:*** Litigation; Insurance Defense Law; Labor Law; Civil Rights Law; OSHA Litigation; Governmental Law. ***Email:*** douglassuter@isaacbrant.com

DAVID G. JENNINGS, born North Kingstown, Rhode Island, September 27, 1958; admitted to bar, 1988, Ohio; U.S. Supreme Court, U.S. District Court, Southern and Northern Districts of Ohio; U.S. Court of Appeals, Sixth Circuit. *Education:* Wittenberg University (B.A., 1980); The Ohio State University (J.D., with honors, 1988). *Member:* Columbus and Ohio State Bar Associations. ***PRACTICE AREAS:*** Litigation; Insurance Defense Law; Product Liability; Tort Law. ***Email:*** davidjennings@isaacbrant.com

DOUGLAS CRAIG BOATRIGHT, born Barberton, Ohio, October 7, 1957; admitted to bar, 1989, Ohio; 1990, U.S. District Court, Northern and Southern Districts of Ohio and U.S. Court of Appeals, Sixth Circuit; 1994, U.S. Supreme Court; 1997, Pennsylvania; 1999, West Virginia and U.S. District Court, Southern District of West Virginia; 2000, U.S. District Court, Northern District of West Virginia. *Education:* University of Akron (B.S.B.A., 1981; A.A.S., 1984; J.D., summa cum laude, 1989). Phi Alpha Delta. Registered Respiratory Therapist, Ohio, 1984. Ohio Assistant Attorney General, 1989-1991. *Member:* Columbus, Franklin County and Ohio State Bar Associations; West Virginia State Bar. ***PRACTICE AREAS:*** Administrative Law; Litigation; Civil Rights Defense. ***Email:*** douglasboatright@isaacbrant.com

PAUL A. MACKENZIE, born Gallipolis, Ohio, December 19, 1966; admitted to bar, 1992, Ohio; 1993, West Virginia and U.S. District Court, Southern District of Ohio and U.S. Court of Appeals, Sixth Circuit; U.S. Supreme Court. *Education:* Miami University (B.A., 1989); The Ohio State University (J.D., with honors, 1992). *Member:* Columbus, Ohio State and American Bar Associations; West Virginia State Bar; Ohio Association of Civil Trial Attorneys. ***PRACTICE AREAS:*** Civil Trials; Insurance Law; Commercial Litigation; Municipal Law. ***Email:*** paulmackenzie@isaacbrant.com

JOANNE S. PETERS, born Milford, Massachusetts, July 23, 1968; admitted to bar, 1994, Ohio and U.S. District Court, Northern and Southern Districts of Ohio; U.S. Court of Appeals, Sixth Circuit; U.S. Supreme Court. *Education:* University of Wisconsin (B.B.A., with honors, 1991); The Ohio State University College of Law (J.D., 1994). *Member:* Columbus and Ohio State and Bar Associations. ***PRACTICE AREAS:*** Commercial Litigation; Trademark Litigation; Copyright Litigation; Employment Litigation. ***Email:*** jsp@isaacbrant.com

PATRICK M. PICKETT, born Sandusky, Ohio, November 5, 1963; admitted to bar, 1989, Ohio; 1990, U.S. District Court, Northern District of Ohio; 1991, District of Columbia; 1993, Virginia, U.S. Court of Appeals, District of Columbia and Fourth Circuits and U.S. District Court, District of Columbia and Eastern District of Virginia; 1997, U.S. District Court, Southern District of Ohio; 1998, U.S. Supreme Court; 1999, U.S. Court of Appeals, Sixth Circuit. *Education:* Bowling Green State University (B.S., cum laude, 1986); Ohio Northern University (J.D., with high distinction, 1989). Phi Alpha Delta. Editor-in-Chief, Ohio Northern University Law Review, 1988-1989. *Member:* Columbus and Ohio State Bar Associations. ***PRACTICE AREAS:*** Business Law; Real Estate; Construction Law; Commercial Litigation. ***Email:*** patrickpickett@isaacbrant.com

DANIEL T. DOWNEY, born Youngstown, Ohio, November 26, 1968; admitted to bar, 1994, Ohio and U.S. District Court, Northern and Southern Districts of Ohio; U.S. Court of Appeals, Sixth Circuit. *Education:* Youngstown State University (B.A., 1991); Ohio State

(This Listing Continued)

ISAAC, BRANT, LEDMAN & TEETOR LLP, Columbus—Continued

University (J.D., 1994). *Member:* Columbus, Ohio State and Federal Bar Associations; Defense Research Institute. ***PRACTICE AREAS:*** Civil Rights Litigation; Insurance Law. ***Email:*** danieldowney@isaacbrant.com

MARIBETH DEAVERS, born Niles, Ohio, April 30, 1959; admitted to bar, 1991, Ohio; 1992, U.S. District Court, Southern District of Ohio; registered to practice before U.S. Patent and Trademark Office. *Education:* Miami University (B.A., 1982); Capital University (J.D., cum laude, 1991). Order of the Curia. Recipient, American Jurisprudence Awards for Decedents Estates and Secured Transactions. Member and Notes Editor, Capital Law Review. Member, Capital University Moot Court Team. Magistrate, Delaware County, Ohio Juvenile Court, 1996-1999. Author, Civil Service Law in Ohio, West Publishing, Banks Baldwin, 1993. *Member:* Columbus, Delaware County and Ohio State (Member, Board of Governors, 1998-2002) Bar Associations. ***PRACTICE AREAS:*** Business Law; Commercial Litigation; Patents; Intellectual Property; Labor and Employment. ***Email:*** maribethdeavers@isaacbrant.com

ASSOCIATES

DANIELLE MARIE CARTER, born Toledo, Ohio, November 3, 1973; admitted to bar, 1999, Ohio; 2000, U.S. District Court, District of Ohio. *Education:* Miami University (B.A., 1996); Capital University (J.D., cum laude, 1999). Phi Alpha Delta. Order of the Curia. Member, Capital University Law Review, 1998-1999. *Member:* Columbus and Ohio State Bar Associations. ***PRACTICE AREAS:*** Domestic Relations; Adoption Law; Litigation. ***Email:*** daniellecarter@isaacbrant.com

JOHN E. VINCENT, JR., born Livonia, Michigan, September 30, 1971; admitted to bar, 1999, Ohio. *Education:* Western Michigan University (B.B.A., 1993); Capital University (J.D., 1999). Phi Alpha Delta. ***PRACTICE AREAS:*** Insurance Defense; Civil Litigation; Political Subdivision Liability; Commercial Litigation; Business Litigation. ***Email:*** johnvincent@isaacbrant.com

JEFFREY A. STANKUNAS, born Akron, Ohio. *Education:* Bowling Green State University (B.A., 1997); The Ohio State University (J.D., 2000). *Member:* Ohio State and Columbus Bar Associations. ***PRACTICE AREAS:*** Civil Defense Litigation; Employment Law; Corporate Law; Government Law; Civil Plaintiffs Litigation. ***Email:*** jeffreystankunas@isaacbrant.com

MICHAEL V. PASSELLA, born Youngstown, Ohio, July 1, 1974; admitted to bar, 2000, Ohio and U.S. District Court, Southern Districts of Ohio; 2001, U.S. District Court, Northern District of Ohio; 2002, U.S. Court of Appeals, Sixth Circuit; 2004, U.S. Supreme Court. *Education:* The Ohio State University (B.A., 1996); Capital University (J.D., 2000). Order of the Curia. *Member:* Ohio State, Columbus, American and Federal Bar Associations. ***PRACTICE AREAS:*** Litigation; Insurance Defense; Political Subdivision Liability; Negligence; Personal Injury; Commercial Litigation. ***Email:*** michaelpassella@isaacbrant.com

J. ERIC HOLLOWAY, born Fairfax, Virginia, January 11, 1968; admitted to bar, 1994, Ohio and U.S. Court of Appeals, Sixth Circuit; 1995, U.S. District Court, Northern District of Ohio; 1996, U.S. District Court, Southern District of Ohio. *Education:* College of William and Mary (B.A., 1990); University of Akron (J.D., 1994). Phi Alpha Delta. *Member:* Stark County, Ohio State, American and Federal Bar Associations. ***PRACTICE AREAS:*** Civil Rights Defense; Negligence Defense; Tort Defense; Wrongful Death; Construction Litigation. ***Email:*** ericholloway@isaacbrant.com

SCYLD D. ANDERSON, born Framingham, Massachusetts, August 6, 1963; admitted to bar, 1995, Ohio. *Education:* Ohio State University (B.S.E.P., 1986; J.D., 1995). *Member:* Columbus and Ohio State Bar Associations. ***PRACTICE AREAS:*** Litigation; Insurance; Personal Injury; General Civil Litigation.

JESSICA K. WALLS, born Painesville, Ohio, June 26, 1978; admitted to bar, 2003, Ohio and U.S. District Court, Southern District of Ohio; U.S. Court of Appeals, Sixth Circuit. *Education:* Miami University (B.S., 2000); The Ohio State University (J.D., 2003). ***PRACTICE AREAS:*** Civil Litigation; Civil Rights Defense; Commercial Litigation. ***Email:*** jkw@isaacbrant.com

JEFFERY J. SNIDERMAN, born Iowa City, Iowa, March 6, 1969; admitted to bar, 1995, Ohio; 1997, Kentucky; 1998, District of Columbia. *Education:* University Rochester (B.A., 1991); University of Akron School of Law (J.D., 1995). Phi Delta Phi (Vice President). *Member:* Kentucky Bar Association; The District of Columbia Bar. ***REPORTED CASES:*** Federal Ins. v. HPG Int'l., Inc., 143 Ohio App.3d 450 (2001); Freeman v. Brooks, 154 Ohio App.3d 371 (2003). ***PRACTICE AREAS:*** Commercial Litigation; Business Litigation; Insurance Defense. ***Email:*** jjs@isaacbrant.com

MARK H. TROUTMAN, born Sandusky, Ohio, May 19, 1978; admitted to bar, 2003, Ohio; 2004, U.S. District Court, Middle and Southern Districts of Ohio; 2005, U.S. Court of Appeals, Sixth Circuit. *Education:* The Ohio State University (B.A., summa cum laude, 2000; J.D., 2003). Phi Kappa Phi; Golden Key. Who's Who in America's Colleges. Formerly, Ohio Attorney General, Health and Human Services Section. *Member:* Columbus, Ohio State and American Bar Associations. ***LANGUAGES:*** English. ***REPORTED CASES:*** Almendares v. Palmer, 222 F.R.D.324 (N.D.Ohio 2004). ***PRACTICE AREAS:*** Civil Litigation; Insurance Defense; Government; Personal Injury. ***Email:*** marktroutman@isaacbrant.com

JERRY L. KALTENBACH, born Columbus, Ohio, February 17, 1977; admitted to bar, 2002, Ohio; 2003, U.S. District Court, Southern and Northern Districts of Ohio and U.S. Court of Appeals, Sixth Circuit. *Education:* Ohio University (B.A., 199); Capital University Law School (J.D., 2002). Member, Capital University Law Review. Law Clerk: Franklin County Prosecuting Attorney's Office, Criminal Division, 2001; Brooks & Wilburn Co., L.P.A., 2002. Legal Intern, Judge Daniel T. Hogan, Franklin County Court of Common Pleas, 2002. Maguire & Schneider, L.L.P., 2002—. *Member:* Columbus, Ohio State and American Bar Associations. ***PRACTICE AREAS:*** Civil Litigation; Commercial Litigation; Insurance Defense. ***Email:*** jlk@isaacbrant.com

BRANDI L. DORGAN, born Royal Oak, Michigan, December 2, 1977; admitted to bar, 2003, Ohio; 2004, U.S. District Court, Southern District of Ohio. *Education:* Michigan State University (B.A., magna cum laude, 2000); The Ohio State University, Moritz College of Law (J.D., 2003). *Member:* Columbus, Ohio State and American Bar Associations. ***PRACTICE AREAS:*** General Litigation; Insurance Defense; Commercial Litigation. ***Email:*** brandidorgan@isaacbrant.com

OF COUNSEL

MARK R. WEAVER, born Philadelphia, Pennsylvania, January 9, 1961; admitted to bar, 1989, Pennsylvania; 1992, District of Columbia; 1995, Ohio. *Education:* Kutztown University (B.S., 1983; M.P.A., 1985); Widener University (J.D., 1989). Adjunct Professor of Law, Ohio State University, 1996—. Deputy Attorney General, Ohio, 1995-1999. Assistant Director of Public Affairs, U.S. Department of Justice, 1988-1989. Assistant County Prosecutor, 2001—. Ohio Mayor's Court Magistrate, Hilliard, 2005—. ***PRACTICE AREAS:*** General Practice. ***Email:*** markweaver@isaacbrant.com

REPRESENTATIVE CLIENTS: ALD Concrete & Grading Co.; Alternative Service Concepts; Amanda Bent Bolt Co.; American International Group; American Pavements; American Risk Pooling Consultants (ARPCO); American Select Insurance Co.; American Specialty Insurance Services, Inc.; Arch Insurance Company; Architecture! Ohio Incorporated; Alternate Service Concepts; Auditor of State; The Barcus Company; BKW Drywall Supply, Blaney Logging, Inc.; Celina Mutual Insurance Co.; Central Ohio Risk Management Association (CORMA); Century Insurance Company; Cincinnati Inquirer, City Sandusky; City of Whitehall; Colonial Heating & Cooling Co., Inc.; Colonial Insurance of California; Commercial Movers, Inc.; Continental Building Systems; Contract Sweepers and Equipment Company; County Commissioner Assn. of Ohio; County Risk Sharing Authority, Inc. (CORSA); Crawford and Company; Custom Drywall, Inc.; Dairyland Insurance Co.; Dayton Alloy Wheel Corp.; Deshler Group; Duffy Homes; Duron Paint & Wall Coverings; ERX Logistics, Inc.; Exciton, Inc.; Fifth-Third Bank; Forma Scientific, Inc.; Gay & Taylor, Inc.; Gerling America Ins. Co.; Greenlawn Transit, Inc.; Gutnecht Construction; Harleysville Insurance Companies; Heritage Marble of Ohio; Highlights-Jigsaw Toy Factory, Ltd.; K & K Insurance, Inc.; Lang Masonry; Lexington Insurance Co.; Markel Insurance Company; Medscan Open MRI of Middletown; Mendoza Company; Met Life; Mid America Waste Corp.; Midwest Claims Service; Modular Design Technology; National Union Fire Insurance Co.; New Hampshire Insurance Group; North American Specialty Insurance Co.; Nourse Family of Dealerships; Ohio Attorney General; Ohio Bar Title Insurance Co.; The Ohio Department of Insurance; The Old Bag of Nails; Olympus Homes, Inc.; Pete Miller, Inc.; Pioneer Pipe, Inc.; Prestige Claims Service; Property One, Inc.; RJF International, Inc.; RWS Building Co.; Range Kleen Manufacturing; Safway Steel Products, Inc.; Secor International; Seneca Insurance Co.; Sentry Insurance Group; Schools of Ohio Risk Sharing Authority (SORSA); Shelby Insurance Company; The Shelly Co.; Shelly and Sands, Inc.; Seville Sand & Gravel; Sharon Speedway; TIG Insurance Company; Touchmark CounselingTransmanagement, Inc.; Tri-Modal Services; Trucco Concrete; Trucco Construction; Village of Ashville; Vista Industrial Packaging; The Wasserstrom Co.; Wesam Construction; Westfield Companies; Wide Open West Holdings, LLC.

LAW OFFICES OF
KATRYNA JOHNSON LLC

2525 TILLER LANE, SUITE 104
COLUMBUS, OHIO 43231
Telephone: 614-895-1722
Fax: 614-895-1322
Email: katryna@katrynalaw.com
URL: http://www.katrynalaw.com

Family Law, Divorce, Consumer Law, Internet Law, Estate Planning, Wills, Probate, Trusts and Estates.

KATRYNA L. JOHNSON, born McDowell, Kentucky, November 30, 1961; admitted to bar, 1999, Ohio; 2000, U.S. District Court, Southern District of Ohio. *Education:* The Ohio State University (B.A., 1984); Capital University (J.D., 1999). *Member:* Columbus, Ohio (Member, Computer Law Section) and American Bar Associations. ***PRACTICE AREAS:*** Family Law; Divorce; Consumer Law; Internet Law; Estate Planning; Wills; Probate; Trusts and Estates.

JOHRENDT, COOK & EBERHART

A LEGAL PROFESSIONAL ASSOCIATION

471 EAST BROAD STREET, SUITE 800
COLUMBUS, OHIO 43215
Telephone: 614-464-0082
Fax: 614-463-1296

Tax, Business, Estate Planning and Probate, Corporate, Partnership, Business Acquisitions, ERISA, Real Estate, Business, Tax and Securities Litigation.

MICHAEL J. JOHRENDT, born Columbus, Ohio, April 18, 1953; admitted to bar, 1977, Ohio; 1978, U.S. Tax Court and U.S. District Court, Southern District of Ohio; 1983, U.S. Court of Appeals, Sixth Circuit; 1992, U.S. District Court, Northern District of Ohio. *Education:* The Ohio State University (B.A., 1974; J.D., 1977). Special Counsel to the Ohio Attorney General. Author: "Current Status of IRS Tax Shelter Attack," The Ohio Public Accountant, November, 1982. Lecturer: 21st Annual Federal Tax Conference, Ohio Legal Center Institute, 1981; 27th Annual Federal Tax Seminar, Ohio Society of Public Accountants, 1989; Internal Revenue Service, Appellate Division, Central Region, Practitioner's Panel, 1991. *Member:* Columbus (Member, Tax and Real Estate Committees) and Ohio State Bar Associations. ***REPORTED CASES:*** Edward A. Kemmler Memorial Foundation v. 691/733 East Dublin-Granville Road Company, 62 Ohio St. 3d 494 (1992) (partnership obligations). ***PRACTICE AREAS:*** Tax Law; Business Litigation; Tax Litigation; Estate Litigation; Legal Malpractice; Accountants Malpractice.

JOHN W. COOK, born Columbus, Ohio, July 16, 1952; admitted to bar, 1977, Ohio; 1978, U.S. District Court, Southern District of Ohio and U.S. Tax Court; 1987, U.S. Court of Appeals, Sixth Circuit. *Education:* Miami University (B.S., cum laude, 1974); Ohio State University (J.D., cum laude, 1977). Lecturer: 20th Annual Federal Tax Conference, Ohio Legal Center Institute, 1980; 27th Annual Federal Tax Seminar, Ohio Society of Public Accountants, 1989. *Member:* Columbus (Member, Taxation and Probate Committees) and Ohio State Bar Associations. ***PRACTICE AREAS:*** Taxation; Buying and Selling of Businesses; ERISA; Commercial Real Estate; Trusts and Estates. ***Email:*** jcook@jcelaw.com

(This Listing Continued)

ROBERT L. EBERHART, born Findlay, Ohio, October 30, 1939; admitted to bar, 1964, Ohio; 1972, U.S. District Court, Southern District of Ohio; 1976, U.S. Tax Court; 1994, U.S. Court of Appeals, Sixth Circuit. *Education:* The Ohio State University (B.A., 1961; J.D., 1964). Author: "Planning the Capital Structure of a Corporation," 14th Annual Federal Taxation Conference, Ohio Legal Center Institute, 1973. Lecturer, Tax and Business Planning for the Small Business, Columbus Bar Association and Capital University Law School, 1979. Guest Lecturer, Federal Taxation, Capital University Law School, 1978-1981. Member, Ohio Board of Tax Appeals, 2003—. *Member:* Columbus (Member, Taxation and Probate Committees), Ohio State (Member, Estate Planning, Trust and Probate Law Section) and American (Member, Taxation Section) Bar Associations. ***PRACTICE AREAS:*** Federal and State Taxation; Tax Litigation; Estate Planning, Probate and Trusts; General Business. ***Email:*** rleberhart@aol.com

REFERENCES: The Huntington National Bank; Key Bank.

JONES DAY

325 JOHN H. MCCONNELL BOULEVARD
SUITE 600
COLUMBUS, OHIO 43215
Telephone: 614-469-3939
Telecopier: 614-461-4198
Email: counsel@jonesday.com
URL: http://www.jonesday.com

In Cleveland, Ohio: North Point, 901 Lakeside Avenue. Telephone: 216-586-3939. Telecopier: 216-579-0212.
In Atlanta, Georgia: 1420 Peachtree Street, N.E., Suite 800. Telephone: 404-521-3939. Telecopier: 404-581-8330.
In Beijing, China: 3201 China World Tower 1, No. 1 Jianguomenwai Avenue. Telephone: 86-10-5866-1111. Telecopier: 86-10-5866-1122.
In Brussels, Belgium: Boulevard Brand Whitlocklaan 165, 1200 Brussels. Telephone: 32-2-645-14-11. Telecopier: 32-2-645-14-45.
In Chicago, Illinois: 77 West Wacker. Telephone: 312-782-3939. Telecopier: 312-782-8585.
In Dallas, Texas: 2727 North Harwood Street. Telephone: 214-220-3939. Telecopier: 214-969-5100.
In Frankfurt, Germany: Hochhaus am Park, Grüneburgweg 102, 60323 Frankfurt am Main. Telephone: 49-69-9726-3939. Telecopier: 49-69-9726-3993.
In Hong Kong, China: 31st Floor, Edinburgh Tower, The Landmark, 15 Queen's Road, Central. Telephone: 852-2526-6895. Telecopier: 852-2868-5871.
In Houston, Texas: 717 Texas, Suite 3300. Telephone: 832-239-3939. Telecopier: 832-239-3600.
In Irvine, California: 3 Park Plaza, Suite 1100. Telephone: 949-851-3939. Telecopier: 949-553-7539.
In London, England: 21 Tudor Street. Telephone: 44-20-7039-5959. Telecopier: 44-20-7039-5999.
In Los Angeles, California: 555 South Flower Street, Fiftieth Floor. Telephone: 213-489-3939. Telecopier: 213-243-2539.
In Madrid, Spain: Velázquez 51, 4th Floor. Telephone: 34-91-520-39-39. Telecopier: 34-91-520-39-38.
In Menlo Park, California: 2882 Sand Hill Road, Suite 240. Telephone: 650-739-3939. Telecopier: 650-739-3900.
In Milan, Italy: Via Turati, 16/18. Telephone: 39-02-7645-4001. Telecopier: 39-02-7645-4400.
In Moscow, Russia: Smolenskaya Square 3, 9th Floor, 121099 Moscow. Telephone: 7-095-980-6769. Telecopier: 7-095-980-6765.
In Munich, Germany: Prinzregentenstr. 11, 80538 Munich. Telephone: 089-20 60 42-200. Telecopier: 089-20 60 42-293.
In New York, New York: 222 East 41st Street. Telephone: 212-326-3939. Telecopier: 212-755-7306.
In Paris, France: 120, rue du Faubourg Saint-Honoré. Telephone: 33-1-56-59-39-39. Telecopier: 33-1-56-59-39-38.
In Pittsburgh, Pennsylvania: 500 Grant Street, One Mellon Bank Center, 31st Floor. Telephone: 412-391-3939. Telecopier: 412-394-7959.
In San Diego, California: 12750 High Bluff Drive, Suite 300. Telephone: 858-314-1200. Telecopier: 858-314-1150.
In San Francisco, California: 555 California Street, 26th Floor. Telephone: 415-626-3939. Telecopier: 415-875-5700.
In Shanghai, China: 30th Floor, Shanghai Kerry Centre, 1515 Nanjing Road West. Telephone: 86-21-2201-8000. Telecopier: 86-21-5298-6569.
In Singapore, Singapore: 30 Cecil Street, #29-01 Prudential Tower. Telephone: 65 6 538 3939. Telecopier: 65 6 536 3939.
In Sydney, Australia: Australia Square, Level 38, 264-278 George Street. Telephone: 61-2-8272-0500. Telecopier: 61-2-8272-0599.
In Taipei, Taiwan: 6th Floor, 2 Tun Hwa South Road, Section 2. Telephone: (886-2) 2704-6808 or (886-2) 7712-3399. Telecopier: (886-2) 2704-6791.
In Tokyo, Japan: Shiroyama MT Building, 6th Floor, 1-17 Toranomon 4-chome, Minato-ku, Tokyo 105-0001. Telephone: 81-3-3433-3939. Telecopier: 81-3-5401-2725.
In Washington, D.C.: 51 Louisiana Avenue, N.W. Telephone: 202-879-3939. Telecopier: 202-626-1700.

Full-Service Civil Practice, Antitrust and Competition Law, Business Restructuring and Reorganization, Capital Markets, Complex Commercial and Multrijurisdictional Litigation, Corporate Criminal Investigations, Employee Benefits and Executive Compensation, Energy Delivery and Power, Government Regulation, Health Care, Intellectual Property and Technology, International Litigation and Arbitration, Issues and Appeals, Labor and Employment, Lending/Structured Finance and Derivatives, Life Sciences, Mergers and Acquisitions, Oil and Gas, Private Equity, Products Liability, Personal Injury Torts and Health Litigation, Real Estate and Environment, Securities and Shareholder Litigation, Tax.

(This Listing Continued)

MEMBERS OF FIRM IN COLUMBUS

J. KEVIN COGAN, born Chicago, Illinois; admitted to bar, 1978, Ohio; 1979, Florida. *Education:* DePauw University (B.A., 1975); Case Western Reserve University (J.D., 1978). Phi Beta Kappa; Order of the Coif. ***PRACTICE AREAS:*** Litigation; Complex Commercial Litigation; Corporate Control Contests; Insurance Coverage. ***Email:*** jcogan@jonesday.com

COLLEEN A. DEEP, born Pittsburgh, Pennsylvania; admitted to bar, 1993, Ohio. *Education:* University of Alabama (B.S., 1989); The Ohio State University (J.D., 1993). Phi Beta Kappa. ***PRACTICE AREAS:*** Labor and Employment. ***Email:*** cadeep@jonesday.com

JOSEPH R. DREITLER, born December 19, 1950; admitted to bar, 1979, Ohio. *Education:* University of Cincinnati (B.S., 1973); Salmon P. Chase College of Law (J.D., 1978). Secretary, 1997, Board of Governors, 1997 and Vice-Chair, 2000, Intellectual Property Law Section, Ohio State Bar Association. ***PRACTICE AREAS:*** Intellectual Property; Intellectual Property Licensing; Trademarks. ***Email:*** jrdreitler@jonesday.com

THOMAS E. DUTTON, born Marysville, Ohio; admitted to bar, 1983, Ohio. *Education:* Washington and Lee University (B.A., 1980); Northwestern University (J.D., 1983). Phi Beta Kappa. ***PRACTICE AREAS:*** Health Care Mergers and Acquisitions; Integrated Health Care Delivery Systems. ***Email:*** tedutton@jonesday.com

MARLENE P. FRANK, born Dayton, Ohio; admitted to bar, 1982, Ohio. *Education:* The Ohio State University (B.A., 1979; J.D., 1982). Order of the Coif. ***PRACTICE AREAS:*** Employee Benefits; Deferred Compensation; Health Benefits. ***Email:*** mpfrank@jonesday.com

MARYANN BAKER GALL, born Cleveland, Ohio; admitted to bar, 1970, Ohio. *Education:* The Ohio State University (B.A., 1967; J.D., 1970). Assistant Attorney General, 1971-1974; Attorney, Chief Taxation Section, 1974-1975; Chief Counsel, 1975-1976, Office of the Attorney General, State of Ohio. ***PRACTICE AREAS:*** Taxation; State Taxation. ***Email:*** mbgall@jonesday.com

GREGORY A. GOROSPE, born Youngstown, Ohio; admitted to bar, 1993, Ohio. *Education:* The Ohio State University (B.S., 1989; J.D., 1993). ***PRACTICE AREAS:*** Real Estate. ***Email:*** ggorospe@jonesday.com

KELLEY M. GRIESMER, born Akron, Ohio; admitted to bar, 1993, Ohio. *Education:* Indiana University (B.A., 1990); The Ohio State University (J.D., 1993). Phi Beta Kappa. Law Clerk to: Judge Cook, Ninth District Court of Appeals of Ohio, 1993-1994; Justice Cook, Supreme Court of Ohio, 1995. ***PRACTICE AREAS:*** General Litigation. ***Email:*** kmgriesmer@jonesday.com

ROBERT W. HAMILTON, born Lafayette, Indiana; admitted to bar, 1987, Ohio. *Education:* Northwestern University (B.S., 1981); Harvard University (J.D., 1984). ***PRACTICE AREAS:*** Litigation; Complex Commercial Litigation; Bankruptcy Litigation; First Amendment Law. ***Email:*** rwhamilton@jonesday.com

FORDHAM E. HUFFMAN, born Hilliard, Ohio; admitted to bar, 1980, Georgia; 1984, Ohio. *Education:* The Ohio State University (B.A., 1977; J.D., 1980). Law Clerk to Judge Rosenn, U.S. Court of Appeals, Third Circuit, 1980-1981. ***PRACTICE AREAS:*** Litigation; Bankruptcy Litigation; Insurance Insolvency; Insurance Regulation. ***Email:*** fehuffman@jonesday.com

JEFFREY J. JONES, born Toledo, Ohio; admitted to bar, 1985, Ohio. *Education:* University of Kentucky (B.B.A., 1981); Harvard University (J.D., 1985). ***PRACTICE AREAS:*** Litigation; Products Liability. ***Email:*** jjjones@jonesday.com

MATTHEW A. KAIRIS, born Chicago, Illinois; admitted to bar, 1991, Ohio. *Education:* University of Notre Dame (B.A., 1988); Harvard University (J.D., 1991). ***PRACTICE AREAS:*** Litigation; First Amendment Law; Complex Business Litigation. ***Email:*** makairis@jonesday.com

JEFFREY L. KAPP, born Ypsilanti, Michigan; admitted to bar, 1993, Ohio. *Education:* Miami University (B.A., 1990); The Ohio State University (J.D., 1993). Phi Beta Kappa. ***PRACTICE AREAS:*** Mergers and Acquisitions. ***Email:*** jlkapp@jonesday.com

ELIZABETH P. KESSLER, born Columbus, Ohio; admitted to bar, 1993, Ohio. *Education:* University of Michigan (B.S., 1990); The Ohio State University (J.D., 1993). ***PRACTICE AREAS:*** General Litigation. ***Email:*** ekessler@jonesday.com

G. ROGER KING, born Ashland, Ohio; admitted to bar, 1971, Ohio; 1972, District of Columbia. *Education:* Miami University (B.S., 1968); Cornell University (J.D., 1971). Legislative Assistant to U.S. Senator Robert Taft, Jr., 1971-1973. Professional Staff Counsel, Labor and Human Resources Committee, U.S. Senate, 1973-1974. ***PRACTICE AREAS:*** Labor and Employment; National Labor Relations Act; Equal Employment Opportunity Law; Collective Bargaining. ***Email:*** gking@jonesday.com

JAMES R. KING, born Geneva, Illinois; admitted to bar, 1974, Ohio. *Education:* Miami University (B.A., 1968); The Ohio State University (J.D., 1974). Order of the Coif. ***PRACTICE AREAS:*** Taxation; Federal Income Tax; Tax Controversies. ***Email:*** jrking@jonesday.com

MATTHEW W. LAMPE, born Silver Spring, Maryland; admitted to bar, 1989, Ohio. *Education:* Kenyon College (B.A., 1986); Cornell University (J.D. 1989). Phi Beta Kappa; Order of the Coif. ***PRACTICE AREAS:*** Labor and Employment; Employment Litigation; Employment Class Actions; Employment Breach of Contract. ***Email:*** mwlampe@jonesday.com

KEVIN D. LYLES, born Portsmouth, Ohio; admitted to bar, 1986, Ohio. *Education:* The Ohio State University (B.S., 1983; J.D., 1986). Order of the Coif. ***PRACTICE AREAS:*** Health Care Mergers and Acquisitions; Health Care Fraud; Health Maintenance Organizations; Technology Contracts. ***Email:*** kdlyles@jonesday.com

DOUGLAS M. MANSFIELD, born Berkeley, California; admitted to bar, 1994, Ohio. *Education:* Stanford University (B.A., 1988); University of Cincinnati (J.D., 1994). ***LANGUAGES:*** Chinese (Mandarin). ***PRACTICE AREAS:*** General Litigation. ***Email:*** dmansfield@jonesday.com

(This Listing Continued)

JONES DAY, Columbus—Continued

WILLIAM E. NAKASIAN, born Cleveland, Ohio; admitted to bar, 1990, Ohio. *Education:* Case Western Reserve University (B.S., 1987); The Ohio State University (J.D., 1990). ***PRACTICE AREAS:*** Real Estate; Real Estate Development; Real Estate Finance. ***Email:*** wenakasian@jonesday.com

CHARLES M. OELLERMANN, born Grant, Nebraska; admitted to bar, 1991, Ohio. *Education:* University of Nebraska (B.S., 1980); Purdue University (M.S., 1981; Doctor of Philosophy, 1985); Harvard University (J.D., 1991). ***PRACTICE AREAS:*** Bankruptcy; Bankruptcy Chapter 11; Insolvency. ***Email:*** coellermann@jonesday.com

MICHAEL K. ORDING, born Troy, Ohio; admitted to bar, 1980, Ohio; 1982, Texas. *Education:* Ohio Northern University (B.A., 1977); The Ohio State University (J.D., 1980). Order of the Coif. ***PRACTICE AREAS:*** Real Estate; Real Estate Investment Trusts; Real Estate Finance. ***Email:*** mkording@jonesday.com

SHAWN J. ORGAN, born Dearborn, Michigan; admitted to bar, 1989, Ohio. *Education:* Miami University (B.S., 1986); University of Cincinnati (J.D., 1989). Law Clerk to Judge George C. Smith, U.S. District Court, Southern District of Ohio, 1990-1992. Adjunct Professor of Law, The Ohio State University, 1991-1992. ***PRACTICE AREAS:*** Litigation; Bankruptcy Litigation; Complex Commercial Litigation. ***Email:*** sjorgan@jonesday.com

GAYLE E. PARKHILL-KREIN, born Colville, Washington; admitted to bar, 1983, Ohio. *Education:* Miami University (B.A., 1980); The Ohio State University (J.D., 1983). Order of the Coif. ***LANGUAGES:*** French. ***PRACTICE AREAS:*** Health Care Corporate Law; Health Care Mergers and Acquisitions; Integrated Health Care Delivery Systems. ***Email:*** geparkhill@jonesday.com

TODD L. SARVER, born Lancaster, Ohio; admitted to bar, 1993, Ohio. *Education:* Ohio Northern University (B.S., 1990); The Ohio State University (J.D., 1993). ***PRACTICE AREAS:*** Labor and Employment. ***Email:*** tlsarver@jonesday.com

BRIAN G. SELDEN, born Great Lakes, Illinois; admitted to bar, 1995, Ohio. *Education:* Princeton University (A.B., 1992); University of Michigan (J.D., 1995). Order of the Coif. Law Clerk to Judge Kinneary, U.S. District Court, Southern District of Ohio, 1995-1997. ***PRACTICE AREAS:*** Complex Litigation; Class Action Defense; Corporate Governance. ***Email:*** bgselden@jonesday.com

TODD SHAWN SWATSLER, born Lima, Ohio; admitted to bar, 1981, Ohio. *Education:* The Ohio State University (B.A., 1978; J.D., 1981). Order of the Coif. ***PRACTICE AREAS:*** Litigation; Complex Commercial Litigation; Corporate Control Contests; Tax Litigation. ***Email:*** toddsswatsler@jonesday.com

RANDALL M. WALTERS, born Columbus, Ohio; admitted to bar, 1978, Ohio; 1979, Illinois; 1982, Texas. *Education:* The Ohio State University (B.S., 1975; J.D., 1978). ***PRACTICE AREAS:*** Capital Markets; Mergers and Acquisitions; Corporate Governance. ***Email:*** rmwalters@jonesday.com

COUNSEL

MARGARET L. GRAMANN, born Dallas, Texas; admitted to bar, 1985, Ohio. *Education:* Hollins College (B.A., 1976); University of Virginia (J.D., 1980). Phi Beta Kappa. ***LANGUAGES:*** Spanish. ***Email:*** mgramann@jonesday.com

HELEN L. LIEBMAN, born Philadelphia, Pennsylvania; admitted to bar, 1974, Ohio. *Education:* Barnard College (B.A., 1971); Boston College (J.D., 1974). Order of the Coif. Administrative Law Judge, 1975-1983 and Legal Director, 1983-1986, Public Utilities Commission of Ohio. Chair, Public Utilities Committee, Ohio State Bar Association, 1996-1998. ***Email:*** hlliebman@jonesday.com

JOSEPH M. WITALEC, born Newark, Ohio; admitted to bar, 1994, Ohio. *Education:* The Ohio State University (B.S.B.A., 1991); Harvard University (J.D., 1994). ***Email:*** jmwitalec@jonesday.com

ASSOCIATES

CANDACE A. BANKOVICH, born Johnstown, Pennsylvania; admitted to bar, 1996, Indiana; 1999, Pennsylvania; 2002, Ohio. *Education:* Northwestern State University of Louisiana (B.A., 1991); Indiana University (J.D., 1996). ***Email:*** cabankovich@jonesday.com

DAVID A. BECK, born Marietta, Georgia; admitted to bar, 2000, Ohio. *Education:* Kenyon College (B.A., 1997); University of Virginia (J.D., 2000). Phi Beta Kappa. ***Email:*** dabeck@jonesday.com

TONYA BLOSSER BRAUN, born Toledo, Ohio; admitted to bar, 2002, Ohio. *Education:* Duke University (B.A., 1994); Ohio University (M.S.A., 1997); The Ohio State University (J.D., 2002). Order of the Coif. ***Email:*** tbraun@jonesday.com

BRIGETTE A. BURNELL, born Willard, Ohio; admitted to bar, 2002, Ohio. *Education:* Massachusetts Institute of Technology (B.S., 1998); The Ohio State University (M.B.A., 2002; J.D., 2002). Tau Beta Pi; Order of the Coif. ***LANGUAGES:*** Spanish. ***Email:*** baburnell@jonesday.com

SEAN P. BYRNE, born Portchester, New York; admitted to bar, 1997, Michigan and Illinois; 2004, Ohio. *Education:* University of Richmond (B.A., 1994); University of Michigan (J.D., 1996). ***Email:*** spbyrne@jonesday.com

JOHN C. CAMILLUS, born Cambridge, Massachusetts; admitted to bar, 2004, Ohio. *Education:* Ohio Wesleyan University (B.A., 1998); Yale University (J.D., 2002). Phi Beta Kappa. Law Clerk to Judge Cole Jr., U.S. Court of Appeals, Sixth Circuit, 2002-2003. ***Email:*** jccamillus@jonesday.com

MATTHEW C. CORCORAN, born Hessen, Germany; admitted to bar, 2004, Ohio. *Education:* University of Michigan (B.A., 2000); The Ohio State University (J.D., 2004). Order of the Coif. ***Email:*** mccorcoran@jonesday.com

BRIAN JAMES DOWNEY, born Santa Fe, New Mexico; admitted to bar, 1996, Virginia; 1998, Ohio. *Education:* University of California, Santa Barbara (B.A., 1991); George Mason University (J.D., 1996). ***Email:*** bjdowney@jonesday.com

(This Listing Continued)

MEGHAN E. DOYLE, born Detroit, Michigan; admitted to bar, 2001, Ohio. *Education:* The Ohio State University (B.S.B.A., B.A., 1998; J.D., 2001). Order of the Coif. ***LANGUAGES:*** Spanish. ***Email:*** medoyle@jonesday.com

JENNIFER L. FATE, born Columbus, Ohio; admitted to bar, 1997, Ohio. *Education:* Miami University (B.S., 1990); The Ohio State University (J.D., 1997). Order of the Coif. Certified Public Accountant, Indiana, 1994. ***Email:*** jlfate@jonesday.com

MARC FULKERT, born Columbus, Ohio; admitted to bar, 2003, Ohio. *Education:* Marietta College (B.A., 2000); University of Cincinnati (J.D., 2003). Order of the Coif. ***Email:*** mfulkert@jonesday.com

ERICK D. GALE, born Sandusky, Ohio; admitted to bar, 2002, Ohio. *Education:* College of Wooster (B.A., 1999); The Ohio State University (J.D., 2002). Phi Beta Kappa; Order of the Coif. Law Clerk to Judge Carr, U.S. District Court, Northern District of Ohio, 2002-2003. ***Email:*** edgale@jonesday.com

RICK J. GIBSON, born Elmhurst, Illinois; admitted to bar, 1996, Ohio. *Education:* Loyola University, Chicago (B.B.A., 1991; M.B.A., 1994); University of Pittsburgh (J.D., 1996). Order of the Coif. ***Email:*** rjgibson@jonesday.com

BRIAN L. GIFFORD, born Beaufort, South Carolina; admitted to bar, 1997, Ohio. *Education:* Denison University (B.A., 1991); The Ohio State University (J.D., 1997). Order of the Coif. ***Email:*** blgifford@jonesday.com

MICHAEL R. GLADMAN, born Columbus, Ohio; admitted to bar, 1992, Ohio. *Education:* The Ohio State University (B.S., 1988; J.D., 1992). Principal Attorney/Assistant Attorney General, Ohio Attorney General's Office, 1998-2003. ***Email:*** mrgladman@jonesday.com

CHRISTOPHER M. GLAROS, born Cincinnati, Ohio; admitted to bar, 2003, Ohio. *Education:* Columbia University (B.A., 1996); Stanford University (J.D., 2001). Law Clerk to Judge Marbley, U.S. District Court, Northern District of Ohio, 2001-2002. ***Email:*** cmglaros@jonesday.com

KERRY RENKER GREEN, born Stuttgart, Germany; admitted to bar, 2002, Ohio. *Education:* The Ohio State University (B.S., 1996); University of Akron (J.D., 2002). ***Email:*** krgreen@jonesday.com

JANICE L. GRESKO, born Youngstown, Ohio; admitted to bar, 1996, Ohio. *Education:* Hiram College (B.A., 1993); Ohio Northern University (J.D., 1996). Phi Beta Kappa. ***Email:*** jlgresko@jonesday.com

EVA U. GUNASEKERA, born Melbourne, Australia; admitted to bar, 2004, Ohio. *Education:* Ohio University (B.A., M.A., 2001); Georgetown University (J.D., 2004). ***Email:*** eugunasekera@jonesday.com

REBECCA J. HARRISON, born Dayton, Ohio; admitted to bar, 1997, Ohio. *Education:* Ohio University (B.B.A., 1994); University of Cincinnati (J.D., 1997). ***Email:*** rjharrison@jonesday.com

THOMAS J. HERSCH, born Columbus, Ohio; admitted to bar, 2001, Ohio. *Education:* The Ohio State University (B.A., 1998); University of Virginia (J.D., 2001). Phi Beta Kappa. ***Email:*** tjhersch@jonesday.com

KASEY T. INGRAM, born Georgetown, Ohio; admitted to bar, 2002, Ohio. *Education:* United States Naval Academy (B.S., 1994); University of Cincinnati (J.D., 2002). Order of the Coif. Law Clerk to Chancellor Chandler, Delaware Court of Chancery, 2002-2003. ***Email:*** ktingram@jonesday.com

DANIEL N. JABE, born Woodhaven, Michigan; admitted to bar, 2001, California; 2003, Ohio. *Education:* University of Michigan (A.B., 1998); Harvard University (J.D., 2001). Phi Beta Kappa. ***Email:*** djabe@jonesday.com

JUNXIA T. JERNEJCIC, born Hubei, China; admitted to bar, 2002, Ohio. *Education:* Hunan Medical University (B.M., 1994); Case Western Reserve University (J.D., 2002). Order of the Coif. Law Clerk to Judge Lesley Brooks Wells, U.S. District Court, Northern District of Ohio, 2002-2004. ***LANGUAGES:*** Chinese (Mandarin). ***Email:*** jjernejcic@jonesday.com

J. TODD KENNARD, born Pittsburgh, Pennsylvania; admitted to bar, 1997, Ohio. *Education:* United States Military Academy (B.S., 1988); Harvard University (Master in Public Policy, 1994; J.D., 1997). ***Email:*** jtkennard@jonesday.com

LAURA A. KULWICKI, born Canton, Ohio; admitted to bar, 1987, Ohio. *Education:* The Ohio State University (B.A., 1984; J.D., 1987); Case Western Reserve University (M.A., 2000). Order of the Coif. ***Email:*** lakulwicki@jonesday.com

RODD B. LAPE, born Columbus, Ohio; admitted to bar, 1996, Ohio. *Education:* The Ohio State University (B.A., 1991; J.D., 1996). Phi Beta Kappa; Order of the Coif. ***Email:*** rlape@jonesday.com

RONALD E. LAYMON, born Muskogee, Oklahoma; admitted to bar, 1997, Ohio. *Education:* Brooklyn College of the City University of New York (B.A., 1965); University of Chicago (M.A., 1967; Ph.D., 1975; J.D., 1997); Yale University (M.S.L., 1992). ***Email:*** relaymon@jonesday.com

JUSTIN C. LETTS, born Columbus, Ohio; admitted to bar, 2005, Ohio. *Education:* Morehouse College (B.A., 2001); Duke University (J.D., 2004). ***Email:*** jcletts@jonesday.com

JEFFREY D. LITLE, born Pittsburgh, Pennsylvania; admitted to bar, 1999, Ohio. *Education:* Miami University (B.S., 1996); Duke University (J.D., 1999). Phi Beta Kappa. ***Email:*** jdlitle@jonesday.com

ROBERT H. MILLER, born Chillicothe, Ohio; admitted to bar, 2003, Ohio. *Education:* Vanderbilt University (B.A., 2000); Harvard University (J.D., 2003). ***Email:*** rhmiller@jonesday.com

CHAD A. READLER, born Pontiac, Michigan; admitted to bar, 1997, Ohio. *Education:* University of Michigan (B.A., 1994; J.D., 1997). Law Clerk to Judge Norris, U.S. Court of Appeals, Sixth Circuit, 1997-1998. ***Email:*** careadler@jonesday.com

(This Listing Continued)

E. MICHAEL ROSSMAN, born Louisville, Kentucky; admitted to bar, 1998, Ohio. *Education:* University of Michigan (B.S., 1994; J.D., 1998). Order of the Coif. Law Clerk to Judge Cole, Jr., U.S. Court of Appeals, Sixth Circuit, 1998-1999. ***Email:*** emrossman@jonesday.com

HOLLY H. SAIGO, born Madison, Wisconsin; admitted to bar, 2001, Ohio. *Education:* University of Florida (B.A., 1997); Johns Hopkins University (M.P.H., 2001); Georgetown University (J.D., 2001). Phi Beta Kappa. Law Clerk to Judge T. John Ward, U.S. District Court, Eastern District of Texas, 2002-2003. ***Email:*** hhsaigo@jonesday.com

ANDREA L. SEIDT, born Columbus, Ohio; admitted to bar, 1998, Ohio. *Education:* The Ohio State University (B.A., 1994; J.D., 1998). ***Email:*** alseidt@jonesday.com

MATTHEW R. SHURTE, born Cincinnati, Ohio; admitted to bar, 1998, Ohio. *Education:* The Ohio State University (B.S.B.A., 1994); Tulane University of Louisiana (J.D., 1998). Order of the Coif. ***Email:*** mrshurte@jonesday.com

KERSTIN SJOBERG-WITT, born Dayton, Ohio; admitted to bar, 2003, Ohio. *Education:* The Ohio State University (B.A., 1998; J.D., 2003). Phi Beta Kappa; Order of the Coif. Law Clerk to Judge John D. Holschuh, U.S. District Court, Southern District of Ohio, 2003-2004. ***Email:*** ksjoberg-witt@jonesday.com

DENISE L. SKINGLE, born Cleveland, Ohio; admitted to bar, 1996, Ohio. *Education:* The Ohio State University (B.A., 1993; J.D., 1996). Phi Beta Kappa; Order of the Coif. ***Email:*** dskingle@jonesday.com

ROGER A. STALNAKER, born Charleston, West Virginia; admitted to bar, 2004, Ohio. *Education:* Marshall University (B.B.A., 2001); University of Virginia (J.D., 2004). ***Email:*** rastalnaker@jonesday.com

KELLI JONES STILES, born St. Marys, Ohio; admitted to bar, 2003, Ohio. *Education:* The Ohio State University (B.A., 2000; J.D., 2003). Order of the Coif. ***Email:*** kjstiles@jonesday.com

JONATHAN K. STOCK, born Middletown, Ohio; admitted to bar, 1995, Ohio. *Education:* Dartmouth College (B.A., 1992); Harvard University (J.D., 1995). Phi Beta Kappa. ***Email:*** jkstock@jonesday.com

MARY E. TAIT, born Lawrence, Kansas; admitted to bar, 1999, Ohio. *Education:* University of Nebraska (B.A., 1979; M.A., 1981); Edinburgh University (Ph.D., 1991); Northwestern University (J.D., 1999). ***Email:*** metait@jonesday.com

TRACY C. TATE, born Detroit, Michigan; admitted to bar, 2003, Ohio. *Education:* Central Michigan University (B.S., 1998); University of Michigan (J.D., 2002). ***Email:*** tctate@jonesday.com

MARY R. TRUE, born Niagara Falls, New York; admitted to bar, 1990, Ohio. *Education:* University of Cincinnati (B.M., 1978; B.A., 1978; M.M., 1984; J.D., 1990). ***Email:*** mrtrue@jonesday.com

SHAWN M. TURNER, born Springfield, Illinois; admitted to bar, 2004, Ohio. *Education:* Hanover College (B.A., 2000); Case Western Reserve University (M.B.A., J.D., 2004). Order of the Coif. ***Email:*** snturner@jonesday.com

SETH J. TUROFF, born Shelby, Ohio; admitted to bar, 2004, Ohio. *Education:* Ashland University (B.A., 1998); University of Virginia (J.D., 2004). ***Email:*** sjturoff@jonesday.com

JONATHAN M. VAAS, born Sandusky, Ohio; admitted to bar, 2004, Ohio. *Education:* The Ohio State University (B.A., 2000); Harvard University (J.D., 2004). ***Email:*** jmvaas@jonesday.com

SCOTT C. WALKER, born Detroit, Michigan; admitted to bar, 1994, Ohio. *Education:* Kent State University (B.A., 1991); Cleveland State University (J.D., 1994). Administrative Law Attorney, 1995; Claims Judge Advocate, 1995-1996; Trial Counsel, 1996-1997; Post Tax Officer, 1997-1998; Federal Tort Claims Attorney, 1998; Judge Advocate General's Corps, U.S. Army. ***Email:*** scwalker@jonesday.com

MARK A. WHITT, born Alliance, Ohio; admitted to bar, 1997, Ohio. *Education:* University of Akron (B.S., 1993; J.D., 1997). ***Email:*** mawhitt@jonesday.com

MATTHEW R. WILSON, born Circleville, Ohio; admitted to bar, 2000, Ohio. *Education:* Denison University (B.A., 1997); University of Virginia (J.D., 2000). Phi Beta Kappa. ***Email:*** mrwilson@jonesday.com

JEFFREY D. WINCHESTER, born Baltimore, Maryland; admitted to bar, 1997, Ohio. *Education:* University of Arizona (B.A., 1981); Temple University (M.Ed., 1990); Cornell University (J.D., 1997). Law Clerk to Judge Ebel, U.S. Court of Appeals, Tenth Circuit, 1997-1998. ***LANGUAGES:*** Japanese. ***Email:*** jdwinchester@jonesday.com

ISAAC S. WOFFORD, born Denton, Texas; admitted to bar, 2002, Ohio. *Education:* University of Illinois (B.A., 1999; J.D., 2002). Order of the Coif. ***Email:*** iswofford@jonesday.com

MARY BETH YOUNG, born Elizabethtown, Kentucky; admitted to bar, 2001, Ohio. *Education:* University of Kentucky (B.S., 1990); Georgia Institute of Technology (M.S., 1993); University of Chicago (J.D., 1998). Phi Beta Kappa. Order of the Coif. Law Clerk to: Judge Sentelle, U.S. Court of Appeals, District of Columbia Circuit, 1998-1999; Justice Scalia, U.S. Supreme Court, 1999-2000. ***Email:*** mbyoung@jonesday.com

STAFF ATTORNEYS

AshLee M. Hamilton-McGranor ***Phyllis J. Shambaugh***

Languages: Chinese (Mandarin), French, Japanese, and Spanish.

GARY L. JONES CO., L.P.A.

175 SOUTH THIRD STREET, SUITE 800
COLUMBUS, OHIO 43215
Telephone: 614-221-2300
Fax: 614-221-8428
URL: http://www.garyljonescolpa.com
URL: http://www.joneslaw-firms.com

General Civil Practice. Administrative, Alcoholic Beverages, Liquor and Licensing Law, Real Estate Taxation and Appeals.

(This Listing Continued)

GARY L. JONES, born Middletown, Ohio; admitted to bar, 1966, Ohio. *Education:* Ohio State University (B.S., 1960); Capital University (J.D., 1966); Ohio State University (M.S., 1978). Editor, Title 43 "Liquor," Baldwins Ohio Revised Code. Author: "Ohio Department of Liquor Control Commission", Chapter 15, Ohio Administrative Law Book. Chief, Permit Division, Ohio Department of Liquor Control, 1971-1974. *Member:* Columbus and Ohio State Bar Associations. ***PRACTICE AREAS:*** Administrative; Liquor Law; Alcoholic Beverages; Liquor Licensing. ***Email:*** lawglj@aol.com

ROBYN R. JONES, born Middletown, Ohio, February 22, 1951; admitted to bar, 1989, Ohio; 1990, U.S. District Court, Southern District of Ohio. *Education:* Ohio University (B.S., 1973); Capital University (J.D., 1989). Assistant Administrator, Ohio Department of Taxation, 1989-2002. *Member:* Columbus Bar Association. ***PRACTICE AREAS:*** Alcoholic Beverages; Real Estate Taxation; Property Tax Appeals; Property Valuation. ***Email:*** lawrrj@aol.com

REPRESENTATIVE CLIENTS: Applebee's Restaurants ; ARA Leisure Services, Inc.; Benson's Catering, Inc.; Brinker Restaurant Corp.; Cameron Mitchell Restaurants; Cassano's Pizza Restaurants; Chi-Chi's, Inc.; Chuck E. Cheese Pizza Restaurants; City Barbecue; Columbus Brewing Co. Inc.; Damon's Restaurants, Inc.; Donatos Pizzeria Corp.; Gilbert-Robinson, Inc.; Ground Round Restaurants; Harry Buffalo Restaurants; Hooters Restaurants; J. Alexander's Restaurant; The Kroger Company; Morton's of Chicago, Inc.; New Albany Country Club; Ohio Valley AFM. Inc.; Quality Dining, Inc.; Ruby Tuesday Resturaants; Speedway-SuperAmerican LLC; Tumbleweed Restaurants; Texas Roadhouse Restaurants; Yucatan Columbus.

JOHN S. JONES

COLUMBUS, OHIO

(See Worthington)

Estate Planning, Estate Administration, Wills, Trusts, Probate, Estates, Elder Law, Real Estate.

JONES, TROYAN, PAPPAS & PERKINS

A LEGAL PROFESSIONAL ASSOCIATION
1472 MANNING PARKWAY
COLUMBUS, OHIO 43065
Telephone: 614-888-8500
Fax: 614-888-2560
URL: http://www.jonestroyan.com

Business Organization, Planning and Transactions; Estate Planning; Retirement Plans; Real Estate; Employment Law; Probate; Federal Income, Estate and Gift Taxation.

JAMES P. JONES (1927-1991)

GARY M. TROYAN, born Cleveland, Ohio, August 18, 1953; admitted to bar, 1978, Ohio; 2003, Wyoming. *Education:* Bethany College (B.A., summa cum laude, 1975); The Ohio State University (J.D., 1978). *Member:* Columbus, Ohio State and American Bar Associations. ***PRACTICE AREAS:*** Tax and Business Planning; Retirement Plans; Estate Planning. ***Email:*** gtroyan@jonestroyan.com

ROBERT T. PAPPAS, born Charlotte, North Carolina, June 23, 1959; admitted to bar, 1984, Ohio. *Education:* Carleton College (B.A., cum laude, 1981); Ohio State University (J.D., with honors, 1984). Senior Staff Member, Ohio State Law Journal, 1983-1984. *Member:* Columbus, Ohio State and American Bar Associations. ***REPORTED CASES:*** Spencer v. Commissioner, 75 AFTR2d 95-380 (6th Cir., 1995). ***PRACTICE AREAS:*** Business Planning; Estate Planning; Probate; Taxation. ***Email:*** rpappas@jonestroyan.com

JOHN R. PERKINS, JR., born Boardman, Ohio, June 9, 1959; admitted to bar, 1984, Ohio. *Education:* Miami University (B.A., 1981); University of Cincinnati (J.D., 1984). Staff Member, University of Cincinnati Law Review, 1982-1983. Assistant Attorney General, State of Ohio, 1984-1986. *Member:* Columbus, Ohio State and American Bar Associations. ***REPORTED CASES:*** Worthinglen Condominium Unit Owners Assn. v. Brown, 57 Ohio App. 3d 73; Wide Scope, Inc. v. Freedom Federal Savings & Loan Assn., 35 Ohio Misc. 2d 25. ***PRACTICE AREAS:*** Business Planning; Real Estate; Employment Law. ***Email:*** jperkins@jonestroyan.com

REPRESENTATIVE CLIENTS: APCO Industries, Inc.; AquaTech Environmental Laboratories, Inc.; Raymond Barry, Inc.; BBS Corporation; Floyd Browne Group; Victor J. Cook, Jr., Inc.; Creative Child Care, Inc.; William R. Hague, Inc.; Newark Anesthesia, Inc.; Roger C. Perry & Co.; Physician's, Inc.; R.D. Zande & Associates, Inc.; Richards Farms, Inc.; Ruscilli Construction Co.; Strait & Lamp Lumber Co.; Wirthman Brothers, Inc.
REFERENCE: National City Bank, Columbus, Ohio.

JOSEPH & JOSEPH

Established in 1992
931 SOUTH FRONT STREET
COLUMBUS, OHIO 43206
Telephone: 614-449-8282
FAX: 614-449-8287
URL: http://www.josephandjosephlaw.com
Email: johnjoseph@josephandjoseph.com
URL: http://www.josephandjoseph.com

General Civil Trial Practice. Real Estate, Corporate, Domestic and Family Law, Employment, Banking and Commercial Law.

FIRM PROFILE: Joseph & Joseph is a firm which has obtained Martindale-Hubbell's highest rating with a concentration in general civil litigation, banking, contracts, real estate, corporations, domestic relations, employment, commercial law and estate planning. The firm represents a wide range of commercial and financial enterprises, including large corporations and small to medium-size companies, many of which are located outside the state of Ohio. The firm is also proud to provide services to individuals and families.

(This Listing Continued)

JOSEPH & JOSEPH, Columbus—Continued

MEMBERS OF FIRM

JOHN J. JOSEPH, born Owen Sound, Ontario, Canada, July 10, 1953; admitted to bar, 1981, Ohio. *Education:* The Ohio State University (B.S., summa cum laude, 1978; J.D., cum laude, 1981). Listed in Best Lawyers in America, 1993—. Recipient, Judge Joseph M. Harter Memorial Award. Listed in Ohio Super Lawyers. *Member:* Columbus (Member, Committees on: Real Property and Financial Institutions, 1985—; Chairman, Real Property Law Institute, 1989-1990; Chairman, Real Property Committee, 1991, 1992), Ohio State (Member, Real Property Section) and American (Member: Sections on: Real Property, Probate and Trust Law, Corporation, Banking and Business Law) Bar Associations. ***PRACTICE AREAS:*** Civil Litigation; Real Estate; Banking; Commercial. ***Email:*** johnjoseph@josephandjoseph.com

JENNIFER J. JOSEPH, born Highland Park, Illinois, July 17, 1953; admitted to bar, 1991, Ohio. *Education:* Lake Forest College; Loyola University (B.A., 1976); The Ohio State University (J.D., 1991). Recipient, John R. Moats Memorial Award. Appointed to Joint Task Force on Gender Fairness of the Supreme Court of Ohio, 1993. Member, Professionalism Committee, Delaware and Columbus. Frequent Lecturer: Columbus Bar Association; National Business Institute; CLE, Inc. *Member:* Delaware, Madison County, Columbus (Member, Family Law and Professionalism Committee), Ohio State and American (Member, Divorce Law, Family Law, Principles, Ethics, Domestic Violence Committees) Bar Associations; The Association of Trial Lawyers of America (Member, Family Law Network); St. Croix Environmental Association; St. Croix Landmarks Society. Fellow, Columbus Bar Foundation. ***LANGUAGES:*** French and Spanish. ***PRACTICE AREAS:*** Civil Litigation; Domestic Relations/Family Law; Divorce; Child Custody; International Custody; Employment; Corporate. ***Email:*** jenniferjoseph@josephandjoseph.com

ASSOCIATES

DENNIS E. HORVATH, born South Bend, Indiana; admitted to bar, 2001, Ohio. *Education:* Indiana University (B.S., 1997); Capital University Law School (J.D., 2000). Delta Theta Phi (Social Chairman, 1998-1999). *Member:* Columbus (Member: Young Lawyers Association; Family Law Committee), and Ohio State Bar Associations. Fellow, Columbus Bar Foundation. ***PRACTICE AREAS:*** Civil Litigation; Real Estate; Commercial Law; Family Law; Landlord Tenant. ***Email:*** dennishorvath@josephandjoseph.com

DEBORAH L. McNINCH, born Warren, Ohio, April 6, 1966; admitted to bar, 1991, Ohio; 1995, U.S. Supreme Court; U.S. District Court, Southern and Northern Districts of Ohio; U.S. Court of Appeals, Sixth Circuit. *Education:* The Ohio State University (B.A., with honors, Liberal Arts, 1988; J.D., 1991). *Member:* Columbus and Ohio State Bar Associations. ***PRACTICE AREAS:*** Domestic Relations; Real Estate; Employment Law; Personal Injury; Civil Litigation. ***Email:*** deborahmcninch@josephandjoseph.com

Languages: Spanish and French.

GLENNON J. KARR, LLC

1328 OAKVIEW DRIVE
COLUMBUS, OHIO 43235
Telephone: 614-848-3100
Fax: 614-848-3160
Email: gkarr@karrlaw.com
URL: http://www.lawyers.com/karrlaw

Health Care and Insurance Regulation Law, Employment Law, Employee Benefits, Business and Corporate Law.

GLENNON J. KARR, born Trenton, New Jersey, July 21, 1947; admitted to bar, 1974, Ohio; 1979, U.S. District Court, Southern District of Ohio. *Education:* Wake Forest University Law School (B.A., in Law, 1969); Capital University (J.D., 1974). Order of the Curia. Babcock Scholar. Named One of Ten Outstanding Young Citizens by Columbus Jaycees, Columbus, Ohio, 1978. Adjunct Professor, The Regulation of Insurance, Capital University Law School, 1989-1993. *Member:* Columbus (Chair, Corporate Counsel Committee, 1976-1978; Member, Employment Law Committee), Ohio State and American (Member, Tort and Insurance Practice) Bar Associations; Federation of Regulatory Counsel, Inc.; American Health Lawyers Association. [Former 1st Lt., Office of Special Investigation, U.S. Air Force]. ***PRACTICE AREAS:*** Insurance Regulation; Health Care Law; Employment Law; Employee Benefits; Business Law; Corporate Law; Professional Licensing. ***Email:*** gkarr@karrlaw.com

REPRESENTATIVE CLIENT: Mount Aloysius, Corp.

KAYNE LAW GROUP, CO., P.A.

Established in 2002
2461 EAST MAIN STREET
COLUMBUS, OHIO 43209
Telephone: 614-236-9900
Fax: 614-559-6768
Email: dkayne@kaynelaw.com
URL: http://www.kaynelaw.com

Charlotte, North Carolina Office: 521 E. Morehead Street, Suite 100, 28202. Telephone: 704-370-0031. Fax: 614-559-6768.

Commercial Real Estate, Real Estate Development, Retail Acquisition and Leasing, Finance, Commercial Leasing, Environmental Issues, Zoning and Land Use, Business Law, Closely Held Companies, Business Formation, Business Planning, Wills, Trusts and Estate Planning.

DANIEL J. KAYNE, born Columbus, Ohio, 1951; admitted to bar, 1976, Ohio; 1978, U.S. Court of Military Appeals. *Education:* University of Pennsylvania (B.A., cum laude, 1973); University of Chicago (M.B.A., 1985); University of Cincinnati (J.D., 1976). *Member:* Ohio State, Columbus and American Bar Associations; International Council of Shopping Centers. [Lt., USNR, JAGC, 1977-1980]. (Managing Partner). ***LANGUAGES:*** Hebrew. ***PRACTICE AREAS:*** Real Estate Development; Commercial Real Estate; Commercial Leasing; Business Law; Trusts and Estates. ***Email:*** dkayne@kaynelaw.com

LISA J. BERGER, born Philadelphia, Pennsylvania, 1970; admitted to bar, 1998, Ohio. *Education:* Princeton University (A.B., 1991); The Ohio State University (J.D., 1998). ***PRACTICE AREAS:*** Real Estate Development; Commercial Real Estate; Commercial Leasing; Retail Acquisition; Financing; Leasing. ***Email:*** lberger@kaynelaw.com

LEGAL SUPPORT PERSONNEL

TINA BECKETT, (admission pending), *Member:* Columbus Bar Association; Paralegal Association of Central Ohio; National Notary Association. ***Email:*** tbeckett@kaynelaw.com

KEGLER, BROWN, HILL & RITTER

Established in 1964
CAPITOL SQUARE
SUITE 1800
65 EAST STATE STREET
COLUMBUS, OHIO 43215-4294
Telephone: 614-462-5400
Telecopier: 614-464-2634
Cable Address: "Law KBHR"
Telex: 246671
Email: info@keglerbrown.com
URL: http://www.keglerbrown.com

Marion, Ohio Office: 250 Executive Drive, Suite B, P.O. Box 919. Telephone: 740-387-1120. Facsimile: 740-387-3630.

Administrative Law/Governmental Relations; Banking; Bankruptcy and Creditor's Rights; Business, Corporations and Partnerships; Commercial; Construction; Energy; Estate Planning; Franchise; Gaming Law; Health Care; International; Labor and Employee Relations; Litigation; Mergers and Acquisitions; Oil and Gas; Patent, Trademark and Copyright Law; Probate; Professional Responsibility; Public Utilities; Real Estate; Securities; Tax.

FIRM PROFILE: Our more than 60 lawyers are strategically located directly across the street from the Ohio Capitol Building and the Ohio Supreme Court and only three blocks from the Federal District Court, County Courts and the other major state offices. Our attorneys practice in nearly all business-oriented disciplines, as well as in government and regulatory affairs. Kegler, Brown represents clients throughout the Midwest, varying from Fortune 500 companies to small business enterprises.

LAW FIRM ALLIANCES/ASSOCIATIONS: **STATE CAPITAL GLOBAL LAW FIRM GROUP:** *Member firms of the State Capital Law Firm Group practice independently and not in a relationship for the joint practice of law.*

JOHN P. BRODY, born Cleveland, Ohio, June 16, 1953; admitted to bar, 1979, Ohio; 1980, U.S. District Court, Southern District of Ohio and U.S. Tax Court; 1983, U.S. Court of Appeals, Sixth Circuit. *Education:* The Ohio State University (B.A., summa cum laude, 1976); Case Western Reserve University (J.D., 1979). *Member:* Columbus (Member, Bankruptcy Committee, 1982—), Ohio State and American (Member, Section of Litigation) Bar Associations. ***PRACTICE AREAS:*** Bankruptcy Law; Insurance Liquidation. ***Email:*** jbrody@keglerbrown.com

ROBERT GARRETT COHEN, born Columbus, Ohio, July 23, 1963; admitted to bar, 1989, Ohio; U.S. District Court, Northern and Southern Districts of Ohio; U.S. Court of Appeals, Sixth Circuit; U.S. Supreme Court. *Education:* University of Michigan (B.A., 1985); The Ohio State University College of Law (J.D., 1988). Phi Delta Phi. Member of the Board of Governors of the Ohio State Bar Association, Antitrust Section, 1999—. Commissioner, Powell Planning and Zoning Commission, 1999—. *Member:* Columbus, Ohio State and American Bar Associations. ***PRACTICE AREAS:*** Litigation; Antitrust. ***Email:*** rcohen@keglerbrown.com

KENNETH R. COOKSON, born Bluffton, Ohio, November 8, 1951; admitted to bar, 1977, Ohio; U.S. Court of Appeals, Sixth Circuit, U.S. District Court, Northern and Southern Districts of Ohio and U.S. Tax Court. *Education:* Kalamazoo College (B.A., 1974); University of Toledo (J.D., 1977). Member, Toledo Law Review. Law Clerk to U.S. District Judge Don. J. Young, Toledo, 1977-1979. Member, City of Columbus Downtown Commission; President, Friends of WOSU Board, 1999-2001; Member, Franklin County Public Defender Commission; Founding Trustee and Initial President, Discovery District Development Corporation. *Member:* Columbus and Ohio State Bar Associations. (Resident, Columbus, Ohio Office). ***PRACTICE AREAS:*** Banking and Commercial Lending; Business; Tax; Securities; Creditor's Rights; Bankruptcy; Real Estate; Financing. ***Email:*** kcookson@keglerbrown.com

LAWRENCE F. FEHELEY, born Philadelphia, Pennsylvania, October 9, 1946; admitted to bar, 1973, Ohio; 1974, U.S. District Court, Southern District of Ohio; 1980, U.S. Court of Appeals, Sixth Circuit; 1993, U.S. Supreme Court; 1996, U.S. District Court, Northern District of Ohio. *Education:* Cornell University (A.B., 1969; J.D., with distinction, 1973). Order of the Coif. Adjunct Professor, Franklin University, Legal Aspects of Human Resources Management, 2000—. *Member:* Columbus (Member, Labor Law Committee, 1981—), Ohio State (Member: Board of Governors, Labor and Employee Relations Law Section, Law 1980—; Program Committee, 1989—) and American (Member, Sections of: Labor Relations Law and Affordable Housing) Bar Associations. ***PRACTICE AREAS:*** Management Labor Law; Employment Law; Employment Discrimination; Public Housing; Wrongful Termination Defense. ***Email:*** lfeheley@keglerbrown.com

DONALD W. GREGORY, born San Diego, California, January 12, 1957; admitted to bar, 1982, Ohio; 1999, Wyoming. *Education:* Miami University (B.A., cum laude, 1979); Ohio State University (J.D., 1982). Phi Beta Kappa; Phi Kappa Phi. Author: "The New Me-

(This Listing Continued)

chanic's Lien Law and Prompt Payment Act," Ohio Lawyer 1992; "Fairness in Construction Contracting Act," Ohio Lawyer, 1998. President's Award, American Subcontractors Association, 1999. *Member:* Columbus, Madison County, Ohio State and American (Member, Forum on the Construction Industry) Bar Associations. ***PRACTICE AREAS:*** Construction Arbitration; Construction Claims; Construction Contracts; Construction Litigation; Mechanics Liens; Construction Mediation; Public Construction Law; Trial Practice. ***Email:*** dgregory@keglerbrown.com

ALLEN L. HANDLAN, born Parkersburg, West Virginia, October 10, 1947; admitted to bar, 1972, Ohio; 1974, U.S. District Court, Southern District of Ohio. *Education:* Ohio University (B.A., 1969); University of Virginia (J.D., 1972). Phi Beta Kappa. *Member:* Columbus (Member, Committees on: Real Property and Business Law, 1979—), Ohio State (Member: Banking Committee; Commercial Law and Bankruptcy Law Committee, Real Property; Natural Resources Law Committee, 1983—) and American (Member, Business Law) Bar Associations; National Association of Industrial and Office Parks (NAIOP). [1st Lt., USAR, 1971-1981]. ***TRANSACTIONS:*** Glimcher Realty Trust - IPO. ***PRACTICE AREAS:*** Banks and Banking; Commercial Real Estate; Corporate Law; Real Estate Law; Business Law. ***Email:*** ahandlan@keglerbrown.com

PAUL R. HESS, born Centerville, Ohio, October 29, 1960; admitted to bar, 1986, Ohio. *Education:* University of Michigan (A.B., with highest distinction, 1983; J.D., magna cum laude, 1986). Order of the Coif. *Member:* Columbus, Ohio State and American Bar Associations. ***PRACTICE AREAS:*** Corporation Law; Securities Law. ***Email:*** phess@keglerbrown.com

THOMAS W. HILL, born Canton, Illinois, May 23, 1945; admitted to bar, 1970, Ohio; 1972, U.S. District Court, Southern District of Ohio; U.S. Court of Appeals, Fifth, Sixth and Seventh Circuits. *Education:* Grinnell College (A.B., 1967); Cornell University (J.D., 1970). Listed in: The Best Lawyers in America; Who's Who in American Law. Fellow, American College of Trial Lawyers. *Member:* Columbus, Ohio State, Federal and American (Member, Section of Litigation) Bar Associations. ***PRACTICE AREAS:*** Trial Practice; Appellate Practice. ***Email:*** thill@keglerbrown.com

CHARLES J. KEGLER, born Buffalo, New York, January 18, 1942; admitted to bar, 1968, Ohio; 1970, U.S. Tax Court; 1972, U.S. Supreme Court. *Education:* Xavier University; The Ohio State University (B.S., summa cum laude, 1965; J.D., summa cum laude, 1968). Beta Gamma Sigma. Author: "Life Insurance: How Do We Answer the 10 Most Important Questions Our Clients Ask?" Columbus Tax Conference, 1995. *Member:* Columbus (Member, Committees on: Taxation; Business Law), Ohio State and American (Member, Sections of: Taxation; Corporation, Banking and Business Law) Bar Associations. ***PRACTICE AREAS:*** Taxation Law; Corporation Law; Estate Planning Law. ***Email:*** ckegler@keglerbrown.com

TODD M. KEGLER, born Columbus, Ohio, 1968; admitted to bar, 1994, North Carolina; 1997, Ohio. *Education:* DePauw University (B.A., summa cum laude, 1991); Vanderbilt University (J.D., 1994). Phi Beta Kappa. Associate Editor, Vanderbilt Law Review. *Member:* Columbus (Member, Business Taxation and Estate and Gift Taxation Committees), Ohio State and American Bar Associations. ***PRACTICE AREAS:*** Business Law; Corporate Law; Probate, Trusts and Estate Planning Law; Tax Law. ***Email:*** tkegler@keglerbrown.com

R. KEVIN KERNS, born Urbana, Ohio, July 22, 1952; admitted to bar, 1983, Ohio. *Education:* Marymount College of Kansas (B.A., Sociology, 1974); University of Dayton (M.P.A., 1976); Capital University (J.D., 1983). *Member:* Columbus and Ohio State Bar Associations. ***PRACTICE AREAS:*** Trial Practice; Administrative Law; Municipal Law. ***Email:*** kkerns@keglerbrown.com

HELEN MAC MURRAY, born Somers Point, New Jersey, October 1, 1960; admitted to bar, 1987, Ohio and U.S. District Court, Southern District of Ohio; 1999, U.S. District Court, Northern District of Ohio. *Education:* Stockton State College (B.A., 1984); University of Toledo (J.D., 1987). Recipient, American Jurisprudence Award. Former Chief of Consumer Protection, Ohio Attorney General's Office (1995-2001). Member, Bexley City Council (2000—). *Member:* Columbus and Ohio State Bar Associations; Ohio Women's Bar Association; Women Lawyers of Franklin County, Ohio. ***PRACTICE AREAS:*** Governmental Relations; Federal Regulatory; Consumer Regulatory. ***Email:*** hmacmurray@keglerbrown.com

DAVID M. McCARTY, born Akron, Ohio, November 19, 1963; admitted to bar, 1992, Ohio and U.S. District Court, Northern District of Ohio. *Education:* Columbia University (B.A., 1986); The Ohio State University (J.D., with honors, 1992). *Member:* Columbus and Ohio State Bar Associations. ***PRACTICE AREAS:*** Workers Compensation Appeals; Workers' Compensation Defense; Workers Compensation Subrogation. ***Email:*** dmccarty@keglerbrown.com

LARRY J. McCLATCHEY, born Huntingburg, Indiana, May 1, 1951; admitted to bar, 1975, Ohio; 1976, U.S. District Court, Northern District of Ohio; 1978, U.S. District Court, Southern District of Ohio; 1984, U.S. Supreme Court. *Education:* Indiana University (B.A., 1972; J.D., 1975). *Member:* Columbus (Member, Bankruptcy Committee) and Ohio State (Member, Banking, Commercial and Bankruptcy Law Committee) Bar Associations; National Association of Bankruptcy Trustees; Commercial Law League; American Agricultural Law Association. [Lt. (JG) USNR 1974-1980]. ***SPECIAL AGENCIES:*** Panel Trustee, U.S. Bankruptcy Court, Southern District of Ohio (1988—). ***PRACTICE AREAS:*** Bankruptcy Law; Creditors Rights Law; Commercial Law; Agricultural Law. ***Email:*** lmcclatchey@keglerbrown.com

PAUL D. RITTER, JR., born Columbus, Ohio, December 28, 1930; admitted to bar, 1956, Ohio; 1962, California. *Education:* Princeton University (A.B., 1953); The Ohio State University (J.D., 1956). Phi Delta Phi. Attorney, Office of Chief Counsel, Internal Revenue Service, 1956-1962. *Member:* Columbus and Ohio State Bar Associations; National Diocesan Attorneys Association. ***PRACTICE AREAS:*** Taxation Law; Employee Benefits Law. ***Email:*** pritter@keglerbrown.com

RICHARD W. SCHUERMANN, JR., born Cincinnati, Ohio, October 6, 1957; admitted to bar, 1983, Ohio; 1984, U.S. District Court, Southern District of Ohio. *Education:* University of Dayton (B.A., 1979; J.D., 1982). *Member:* Columbus, Ohio State and American Bar Associations. ***SPECIAL AGENCIES:*** Ohio Senate board appointee to Ohio Legal Rights Service Commission. ***TRANSACTIONS:*** Special Counsel for Ohio Department of Insurance Re: Insurance Company Insolvencies; General Counsel to the Butler County and Hamilton County, Ohio Transportation Improvement Districts. ***PRACTICE AREAS:*** Insurance Law; Public Law; Governmental Relations and Administrative Law; Business Law; Criminal Law Litigation. ***Email:*** rschuermann@keglerbrown.com

ROBERT G. SCHULER, born Marion, Ohio, August 15, 1961; admitted to bar, 1987, Ohio; 1988, U.S. District Court, Southern District of Ohio; 1993, U.S. Court of Appeals for the Federal Circuit. *Education:* University of Dayton (B.A., magna cum laude, 1983); University of Illinois (J.D., magna cum laude, 1987). Order of the Coif. *Member:* Columbus and Ohio State Bar Associations. ***PRACTICE AREAS:*** Intellectual Property Law; Trial Practice; Appellate Practice. ***Email:*** rschuler@keglerbrown.com

S. MARTIJN STEGER, born Jakarta, Java, Indonesia, June 1, 1956; admitted to bar, 1983, Ohio; 1985, U.S. District Court, Southern District of Ohio; 1986, U.S. Court of Appeals, Sixth Circuit; 1991, U.S. District Court, Eastern District of Michigan. *Education:* Miami University (B.Phil, summa cum laude, 1978); University of Sheffield Faculty of Law, Sheffield, England; The Ohio State University (J.D., 1983). Phi Beta Kappa. Rotary International Graduate Fellow, 1978-1979. *Member:* Columbus, Ohio State, American and International Bar Associations; Inter-Pacific Bar Association. ***PRACTICE AREAS:*** International Law; International Trade; Intellectual Property; Investments; Dispute Resolution. ***Email:*** msteger@keglerbrown.com

GEOFFREY STERN, born Columbus, Ohio, November 29, 1942; admitted to bar, 1968, Ohio. *Education:* The Ohio State University (B.A., cum laude, 1965; J.D., summa cum laude, 1968). Disciplinary Counsel of the Supreme Court of Ohio, 1993-1997. Phi Beta Kappa; Order of the Coif. Recipient: American Jurisprudence Evidence Award; Columbus Bar Association Liberty Bell Award for Community and Professional Service, 1998; Ohio State Bar Association Salute for Volunteer Activities, 2001. Lecturer: on Legal Ethics, and on Litigation Management and Legal Ethics. Speaker, ABA Commission on Impaired Attorneys. Special Investigator, Ohio Supreme Court, Board of Commissioner on Character and Fitness. Member: Ohio Special Commission on Legal Education, 1995-1997; Bell Commission on Disciplinary Rules, 1995-1997. Fellow: American Bar Foundation; Ohio Bar Foundation; Columbus Bar Foundation. *Member:* Columbus (Member, Legal Ethics Committee), Ohio State and American (Member: Center for Professional Responsibility; Association of Professional Responsibility Lawyers) Bar Associations. ***PRACTICE AREAS:*** Professional Responsibility; Legal Malpractice; Litigation Management; Appellate Practice. ***Email:*** gstern@keglerbrown.com

ROGER P. SUGARMAN, born Cleveland, Ohio, June 16, 1950; admitted to bar, 1975, Ohio; 1977, U.S. District Court, Southern District of Ohio; 1980, U.S. Supreme Court. *Education:* Vanderbilt University (B.A., 1972); University of Toledo (J.D., cum laude, 1975). Assistant Attorney General, 1976-1979 and Section Chief, Financial Institutions Section, 1979-1982, Ohio Attorney General's Office. *Member:* Columbus (Securities Law Committee), Ohio State and American Bar Associations. ***PRACTICE AREAS:*** Trial Practice; Securities Litigation; White Collar Criminal Defense; Telephone Utility Regulation. ***Email:*** rsugarman@keglerbrown.com

KEVIN L. SYKES, born Lima, Ohio, August 28, 1948; admitted to bar, 1979, Ohio; 1980, U.S. District Court, Southern District of Ohio. *Education:* American University of Beirut, Beirut, Lebanon; Beloit College (B.A., summa cum laude, 1970); University of Chicago (M.A., 1973); The Ohio State University (J.D., 1979). Phi Eta Sigma; Phi Beta Kappa. *Member:* Columbus, Ohio State (Member, 1980—, Natural Resources Law Committee) and American Bar Association; Energy & Mineral Law Foundation (Member, 1983—); Federal Bar Association. ***PRACTICE AREAS:*** Commercial Law; Computers and Software; Finance; Health Care; Natural Resources; Real Estate. ***Email:*** ksykes@keglerbrown.com

JOHN R. THOMAS, born Springfield, Ohio, October 28, 1942; admitted to bar, 1968, Ohio. *Education:* The Ohio State University (B.A., 1965; J.D., cum laude, 1968). *Member:* Columbus, Ohio State and American Bar Associations. ***PRACTICE AREAS:*** Corporation Law; Mergers and Acquisitions; Securities Law. ***Email:*** jthomas@keglerbrown.com

TIMOTHY T. TULLIS, born Ashland, Ohio, June 27, 1963; admitted to bar, 1989, Ohio; 1993, U.S. Court of Appeals, Sixth Circuit; 1994, U.S. Supreme Court; 1998, U.S. District Court Southern District of Ohio. *Education:* College of Wooster (B.S., 1985); The Ohio State University (J.D., 1989). Phi Delta Phi. Recipient: Harry J. Levey Memorial Scholarship in Law; Jurisprudence Award. *Member:* Columbus and Ohio State Bar Associations; American Trial Lawyers Association; Million Dollar Advocates Forum. ***PRACTICE AREAS:*** Trial Practice; Appellate Practice; Medical Malpractice; Personal Injury. ***Email:*** ttullis@keglerbrown.com

CHRISTOPHER J. WEBER, born Parma, Ohio, December 18, 1966; admitted to bar, 1992, Ohio; 1993, U.S. District Court, Southern District of Ohio. *Education:* John Carroll University (B.A., cum laude, 1989); University of Toledo (J.D., cum laude, 1992). Order of the Coif. *Member:* Columbus, Ohio State and American Bar Associations. ***SPECIAL AGENCIES:*** Member of Board of Trustees, Columbus Catholic Social Services. ***REPORTED CASES:*** Cleveland Construction v. State of Ohio, Dept. of Admin. Services, 121 Ohio App.3d 372 (1997); State Savings Bank v. Gunthor, Union County App. No. 14-97-33, 41 (April 23, 1998). ***PRACTICE AREAS:*** Construction Law; Medical Malpractice Defense; Personal Injury Defense; Commercial Litigation. ***Email:*** cweber@keglerbrown.com

MELVIN D. WEINSTEIN, born Dayton, Ohio, September 20, 1947; admitted to bar, 1973, Ohio; 1976, U.S. Court of Appeals, Sixth Circuit; 1979, U.S. District Court, Southern District of Ohio and U.S. Supreme Court; 1987, U.S. Court of Appeals, Fifth Circuit. *Education:* The Ohio State University (B.A., 1969); University of Cincinnati (J.D., 1973). Assistant Attorney General, 1973-1981 and Assistant Chief, Court of Claims Defense Section, 1979-1981, Office of the Attorney General of Ohio. *Member:* Columbus (Member: Federal Court Committee, 1986—), Ohio State and American (Member: Trial Practice Committee, 1986—; Litigation Section) Bar Associations. ***PRACTICE AREAS:*** Trial Practice; Appellate Practice. ***Email:*** mweinst@keglerbrown.com

MICHAEL E. ZATEZALO, born Steubenville, Ohio, June 23, 1949; admitted to bar, 1975, Ohio; 1977, California; 1980, U.S. District Court, Southern District of Ohio. *Education:* West Virginia University (B.S., A.E., 1972); The Ohio State University (J.D., cum laude, 1975). Sigma Gamma Tau; Phi Delta Phi. Assistant Attorney General, 1976-1979 and Section Chief, Consumer Frauds and Crimes Section, 1979-1980, Ohio Attorney Gen-

(This Listing Continued)

KEGLER, BROWN, HILL & RITTER, Columbus—Continued

eral's Office. *Member:* Columbus and Ohio State Bar Associations; State Bar of California; Ohio Land Title Association; International Council of Shopping Centers. ***TRANSACTIONS:*** Glimcher Realty Trust - IPO. ***PRACTICE AREAS:*** Real Estate Law; Corporate Law; Gaming Law; Administrative Law. ***Email:*** mzatezalo@keglerbrown.com

COUNSEL

CHARLES R. DYAS, JR., born Cleveland, Ohio, December 15, 1956; admitted to bar, 1986, Ohio; U.S. District Court, Northern and Southern Districts of Ohio; U.S. Court of Appeals, Sixth and District of Columbia Circuits; U.S. Supreme Court. *Education:* Ohio University (B.A., 1981); Capital University School of Law (J.D., 1986). Assistant Attorney General, State of Ohio, 1986-1990. *Member:* Columbus (Member, Environmental Law Committee), Ohio State (Secretary, Environmental Law Committee) and American Bar Associations. ***PRACTICE AREAS:*** Insurance Liquidation; Environmental Law; Litigation. ***Email:*** cdyas@keglerbrown.com

THOMAS D. KITCH, born Wichita, Kansas, February 15, 1944; admitted to bar, 1969, Kansas; 1997, Ohio. *Education:* Yale University (A.B.); University of Chicago (J.D.). Editor, University of Chicago Law Review, 1967-1969. *Member:* Wichita, Kansas and American Bar Associations. (Also Member, Fleeson, Gooing, Coulson & Kitch, L.L.C., Wichita, Kansas). ***PRACTICE AREAS:*** Complex Business Litigation; Litigation; Banking Law; Commercial Law; Corporate Law. ***Email:*** tkitch@keglerbrown.com

ROBERT D. MAROTTA, born Brooklyn, New York, May 18, 1946; admitted to bar, 1975, Ohio. *Education:* University of Notre Dame (A.B., 1968); Illinois Institute of Technology, Chicago-Kent College of Law (J.D., 1974). *Member:* Columbus, Ohio State and American Bar Associations; National Health Lawyers Association; American Managed Care Pharmacy Association. ***PRACTICE AREAS:*** Health Care Law. ***Email:*** rmarotta@keglerbrown.com

TED M. McKINNISS, born Marion, Ohio, November 21, 1950; admitted to bar, 1976, Ohio; 1977, U.S. District Court, Northern District of Ohio. *Education:* Miami University (A.B., 1973); Ohio Northern University (J.D., with distinction, 1976). Phi Kappa Phi; Delta Theta Phi. Special Counsel, Ohio Attorney General, 1981. Member, Marion City Board of Education, 1984—. *Member:* Marion County, Ohio State and American Bar Associations. (Resident, Marion Office). ***PRACTICE AREAS:*** Business Litigation; Commercial Real Estate; Commercial Law; Corporate Law; Trusts and Estates; Probate. ***Email:*** tmckinniss@keglerbrown.com

RANDALL W. MIKES, born Athens, Ohio, October 3, 1963; admitted to bar, 1990, Ohio. *Education:* Kenyon College (B.A., cum laude, 1986); Ohio State University College of Law (J.D., with honors, 1990). *Member:* Ohio State and Columbus (Member, Workers' Compensation Committee) Bar Associations. ***PRACTICE AREAS:*** Litigation; Workers' Compensation; Labor and Employment; Employer Intentional Torts. ***Email:*** rmikes@keglerbrown.com

S. MICHAEL MILLER, born Huntington, West Virginia, November 2, 1938; admitted to bar, 1963, Ohio; 1968, U.S. District Court, Northern and Southern Districts of Ohio; 1969, U.S. Court of Appeals, Sixth Circuit; 1970, U.S. Supreme Court. *Education:* The Ohio State University (B.S., Bus. Ad., 1960; J.D., 1963). Judge, Franklin County Municipal Court, 1977-1980; Franklin County Prosecuting Attorney, 1980-1996. *Member:* Columbus and Ohio State Bar Associations. ***PRACTICE AREAS:*** Criminal Law. ***Email:*** millersm@keglerbrown.com

MICHELE ANN SHUSTER, born Cincinnati, Ohio, January 31, 1967; admitted to bar, 1993, Ohio and U.S. District Court, Northern and Southern Districts of Ohio. *Education:* University of Cincinnati (B.A., 1989); Golden Gate University (J.D., 1993). Delta Theta Phi. Former Sr. Deputy Attorney General, Ohio Consumer Protection Section of Attorney General's Office. Former Assistant Section Chief, Crime Victims Section of Ohio Attorney General's Office. Legislative Director, American Teleservices Association. *Member:* Columbus, Ohio State and American Bar Associations; Ohio Women's Bar Association (10th District Trustee). ***PRACTICE AREAS:*** Administrative Law; Government Affairs; Regulatory Affairs; National Regulatory Affairs. ***Email:*** mshuster@keglerbrown.com

PATSY A. THOMAS, born Columbus, Ohio, March 24, 1960; admitted to bar, 1994, Ohio; U.S. District Court, Southern District of Ohio. *Education:* Franklin University (B.A., Computer Science, 1989); Capital University Law School (J.D., 1994). Formerly with Columbus City Attorney's Office. Former Assistant Attorney General, Workers Compensation Section. Founding Member, John Mercer Langston Bar Association, Columbus Affiliate Chapter for the National Bar Association. Chairwoman, Columbus Area Salvation Army Program Committee. *Member:* Columbus (Member, Committees on: Community Service; Minorities in the Law; Martin Luther King), Ohio State and American Bar Associations. ***PRACTICE AREAS:*** Government Affairs; Regulatory Affairs; Labor Relations; Employee Relations; Litigation. ***Email:*** pthomas@keglerbrown.com

ASSOCIATES

STEPHEN C. BARSOTTI, born Pittsburgh, Pennsylvania, November 1, 1976; admitted to bar, 2002, Ohio; 2003, U.S. Court of Appeals, Sixth Circuit and U.S. District Court, Southern District of Ohio. *Education:* Wake Forest University (B.S., magna cum laude, 1999); Ohio State University (J.D., 2002). *Member:* Columbus and Ohio State Bar Associations. ***PRACTICE AREAS:*** Business; Corporate; Litigation; Intellectual Property; Tax; Securities. ***Email:*** sbarsotti@keglerbrown.com

MARY F. BRENNING, born Columbus, Ohio, August 4, 1971; admitted to bar, 1996, Ohio; 1997, U.S. District Court, Southern District of Ohio. *Education:* Wittenberg University (B.S., cum laude, 1993); Capital University (J.D., 1996). Phi Alpha Delta. Order of the Curia. *Member:* Columbus (Member, Community Service Committee), and Ohio State Bar Associations. ***PRACTICE AREAS:*** Health Care Law; Commercial Transactions; Uniform Commercial Code. ***Email:*** mbrenning@keglerbrown.com

STEWART H. CUPPS, born New York, N.Y., January 27, 1970; admitted to bar, 1999, Ohio; U.S. Court of Appeals, Sixth Circuit; U.S. District Court, Northern and Southern Districts of Ohio. *Education:* Ohio State University (B.S., 1993); University of Dayton School of Law (J.D., 1999). Author: Recent Developments - Section 523 - Exception to Discharge,

(This Listing Continued)

and Recent Developments - Section 727, The Global Denial of Discharge, Norton's Annual Survey of Bankruptcy Law, 2004; Reclamation of Goods in Bankruptcy Under Section 526(C) - Will Reclamation Procedures Orders be Permitted to Deny Creditors Substantive Rights? Cincinnati Bar Assoc., presented June, 2003; Remedies Under Revised Article 9, Allen County Bar Association, 2001. *Member:* Columbus and Ohio State (Member, Committee on Uniform State Laws) Bar Associations; American Bankruptcy Institute. ***PRACTICE AREAS:*** Bankruptcy; Litigation. ***Email:*** scupps@keglerbrown.com

E. ROD DAVISSON, born Columbus, Ohio, October 26, 1970; admitted to bar, 2002, Ohio; U.S. District Court, Northern District of Ohio; U.S. District Court, Southern District of Ohio. *Education:* Franklin University (B.S.B.A., cum laude, 1997); Capital University (J.D., 2002). Order of the Curia. *Member:* Columbus, Ohio State and American Bar Associations. [Hospital Corpsman, U.S. Naval Reserve, 1989-1997]. ***PRACTICE AREAS:*** Construction; Litigation. ***Email:*** rdavisson@keglerbrown.com

EVE M. ELLINGER, born Orrville, Ohio, July 9, 1976; admitted to bar, 2001, Ohio; 2003, U.S. District Court, Southern District of Ohio. *Education:* The Ohio State University (B.S., Special Education, magna cum laude, 1998); Capital University Law School (J.D., cum laude, 2001). *Member:* Columbus and Ohio State Bar Associations. ***PRACTICE AREAS:*** Litigation. ***Email:*** eellinger@keglerbrown.com

LORIANN E. FUHRER, born Massillon, Ohio, June 21, 1966; admitted to bar, 1997, Ohio; 1998, U.S. District Court, Southern District of Ohio and U.S. Court of Appeals, Sixth Circuit. *Education:* Mount Union College (B.A., magna cum laude, 1988); University of Toledo (M.A., 1990); The Ohio State University (J.D., with honors, 1997). *Member:* Columbus, Ohio State and American Bar Associations. ***PRACTICE AREAS:*** Litigation; Appeals. ***Email:*** lfuhrer@keglerbrown.com

DAVID T. GRAHAM, born Fairview Park, Ohio, March 15, 1973; admitted to bar, 1998, Ohio; U.S. District Court, Southern District of Ohio; U.S. District Court, Northern District of Ohio. *Education:* Bowling Green State University (B.S.B.A., Finance, cum laude, 1994); The Ohio State University Moritz College of Law (J.D., cum laude, 1998). Public Service Fellow, The Ohio State University. *Member:* Columbus, Ohio State and American Bar Associations. ***PRACTICE AREAS:*** Commercial Real Estate; Real Estate Development; Leasing; Finance; Business Law. ***Email:*** dgraham@keglerbrown.com

STUART W. HARRIS, born Toronto, Canada, June 13, 1962; admitted to bar, 1992, Illinois; 1994, U.S. Court of Appeals, Seventh Circuit; 1995, U.S. Court of Appeals, Sixth Circuit and U.S. District Court, Southern District of Illinois; 1996, Ohio; 1997, U.S. Supreme Court; 1998, U.S. District Court, Northern District of Illinois. *Education:* Miami University (B.A., Political Science and History, 1980); John Marshall Law School(J.D., 1992). Assistant Chief, Ohio Attorney General, Corrections Litigation Section, 1998-2002. *Member:* Columbus (Chair, Government Agencies Committee) and Ohio State Bar Associations. ***REPORTED CASES:*** Rhodes v. Brigano, 91 F.3d 803 (6th Circ. 1996); Hill v. Brigano, 199 F.3d 833 (6th Circ. 1999); Boggs v. Collins, 226 F.3d 728 (6th Circ. 2000); McMeans v. Brigano, 228 F.3d 674 (6th Circ. 2000); Mitzel v. Tate, 267 F.3d 524 (6th Circ. 2001). ***PRACTICE AREAS:*** Business Litigation; Construction Litigation; Medical Malpractice; Workers Compensation. ***Email:*** sharris@keglerbrown.com

RASHEEDA Z. KHAN, born Columbus, Ohio, September 9, 1968; admitted to bar, 2002, Ohio; U.S. District Court, Southern District of Ohio. *Education:* The Ohio State University (B.S., Biology, 1992); The Ohio State University College of Law (J.D., 2002). Recipient: Clinical Programs Award; Medal for Excellence in Advocacy, 2002. The Association of Trial Lawyers of America Trial Team. *Member:* Columbus and Ohio State Bar Associations; American College of Trial Lawyers. ***PRACTICE AREAS:*** Litigation; Criminal Law. ***Email:*** rkhan@keglerbrown.com

JENNIFER L. MACKANOS, born Cleveland, Ohio, September 25, 1964; admitted to bar, 2002, Ohio; 2003, U.S. District Court, Southern District of Ohio. *Education:* University of Notre Dame (B.A., Psychology and Business Administration, 1986); Capital University Law School (J.D., summa cum laude, 2002). Order of the Curia. *Member:* Columbus, Ohio State and American (Member, Sections on: Business Law; Litigation) Bar Associations. ***PRACTICE AREAS:*** Litigation. ***Email:*** jmackanos@keglerbrown.com

TRACI A. McGUIRE, born Schaumburg, Illinois, July 28, 1972; admitted to bar, 1999, Ohio; U.S. District Court, Southern District of Ohio; 2001, U.S. Court of Appeals, Sixth Circuit. *Education:* Miami University, Oxford, Ohio (B.A., magna cum laude, 1995; M.A., 1996); Ohio State University College of Law (J.D., 1999). Phi Beta Kappa. *Member:* Columbus, Ohio State and American Bar Associations. ***PRACTICE AREAS:*** Labor and Employment; Medical Malpractice; Litigation. ***Email:*** tmcguire@keglerbrown.com

VINITA MEHRA, born Mumbai (Bombay) India, October 1, 1976; admitted to bar, 1995, Ohio. *Education:* Mumbai University of India, Government Law College (L.L.B., 2000). *Member:* Columbus and Ohio State Bar Associations; Bar Association of Maharasthra and Goa, India. ***PRACTICE AREAS:*** International Law; Insurance; Insurance Liquidation. ***Email:*** vmehra@keglerbrown.com

CAMILLE A. MILLER, born Cincinnati, Ohio, January 5, 1979; admitted to bar, 2004, Ohio. *Education:* Smith College (B.A., 2001); The Ohio State University College of Law (J.D., 2004). *Member:* Columbus and Ohio State Bar Associations. ***PRACTICE AREAS:*** Litigation. ***Email:*** cmiller@keglerbrown.com

JAYME P. MOORE, born Columbus, Ohio, August 25, 1976; admitted to bar, 2003, Ohio. *Education:* University of Notre Dame (B.S., 1998); The Ohio State University Moritz College of Law (J.D., 2003). Public Service Fellow, Ohio State University. *Member:* Columbus and Ohio State Bar Associations. ***PRACTICE AREAS:*** Government; Regulatory Affairs; Labor; Employee Relations. ***Email:*** jmoore@keglerbrown.com

ANGELA GUGLE PARSONS, born Columbus, Ohio, September 5, 1972; admitted to bar, 1997, Ohio. *Education:* University of Notre Dame (B.B.A., Finance, 1994); The Ohio State University (J.D., 1997). Board Member: Junior League of Columbus; Columbus Foundation Professional Advisors Board. *Member:* Columbus Bar Association. ***PRACTICE AREAS:*** Estate Planning; Probate; Business; Tax. ***Email:*** aparsons@keglerbrown.com

JEFFREY D. PORTER, born Coshocton, Ohio, October 13, 1970; admitted to bar, 1996, Ohio; U.S. Court of Appeals for Sixth Circuit; U.S. District Court, Southern District. *Education:* Muskingum College (B.A., History, cum laude, 1993); Capital University (J.D., 1996). Order of the Curia. Assistant City Attorney,City of Columbus 1997-2002. *Member:*

(This Listing Continued)

Columbus and Ohio State Bar Associations. **REPORTED CASES:** City of Columbus v. New Plan Realty Trust, 94 Ohio St. 3d 193. **PRACTICE AREAS:** Creditors Rights; Bankruptcy; Administrative Law; Gaming Law. **Email:** jporter@keglerbrown.com

ANNE D. POUGET, born Royal Oak, Michigan, August 21, 1975; admitted to bar, 2003, Ohio. *Education:* Georgetown University (B.S., 1997); The Ohio State University Moritz College of Law (J.D., 2003). Omicron Delta Epsilon. *Member:* Columbus and Ohio State Bar Associations. **PRACTICE AREAS:** Business; Tax; Real Estate; Financing. **Email:** apouget@keglerbrown.com

REBECCA RODERER PRICE, born Dayton, Ohio, April 13, 1976; admitted to bar, 2001, Ohio. *Education:* The Ohio State University (B.S., 1998; J.D., 2001). Member, Ohio State Journal of Dispute Resolution. *Member:* Columbus and Ohio State Bar Associations. **PRACTICE AREAS:** Litigation. **Email:** rprice@keglerbrown.com

MARK R. REITZ, born St. Petersburg, Florida, August 15, 1967; admitted to bar, 1996, Ohio and U.S District Court, Southern District of Ohio. *Education:* Franklin University (B.S., 1990); Capital University (J.D., 1996). *Member:* Columbus and Ohio State Bar Associations. **PRACTICE AREAS:** Probate; Trust Law; Estate Planning. **Email:** mreitz@keglerbrown.com

ERIC B. TRAVERS, born Prince George, British Columbia, Canada, 1972; admitted to bar, 1998, Virginia; 1999, Maryland; 2005, Ohio. *Education:* Lake Forest College (B.A., English and Political Science, cum laude, 1995); George Washington University Law School (J.D., 1998). Phi Delta Phi. *Member:* Columbus, Ohio State and American Bar Associations. **REPORTED CASES:** R.W. Granger & Sons, Inc. v. J & S Insulation, Inc.; USF&G, 435 Mass. 66, 754 N.E.2d 668 (2001); Gelles & Sons General Contracting, Inc. v. Jeffrey Stack, Inc., 264 Va. 285, 569 S.E.2d 406 (2002); Kohl's Department Stores, Inc. v. Target Stores, Inc., 214 F.R.D 406 (E.D. VA. 2003). **PRACTICE AREAS:** Construction Law; Litigation. **Email:** etravers@keglerbrown.com

STEPHANIE P. UNION, born Cleveland, Ohio, September 10, 1974; admitted to bar, 1999, Ohio and U.S. District Court, Northern and Southern Districts of Ohio. *Education:* Miami University, Oxford, Ohio (B.S., International Studies, Political Science, 1996); University of Cincinnati (J.D., 1999). *Member:* Columbus and Ohio State Bar Associations. **PRACTICE AREAS:** Creditors Rights; Bankruptcy. **Email:** sunion@keglerbrown.com

NICHOLAS E. WILKES, born Burlington, Vermont, May 24, 1970; admitted to bar, 1995, Ohio. *Education:* Ohio University (B.A., 1992); The Ohio State University (J.D., 1995). *Member:* Columbus, Ohio State and American Bar Associations. **PRACTICE AREAS:** Commercial Real Estate Conveyancing; Commercial Real Estate Acquisitions; Information Technology Contracts; Commercial Mortgages; Real Estate Leasing; Real Estate Taxation. **Email:** wilkesne@keglerbrown.com

MICHELE SELIG WOROBIEC, born Canton, Ohio, December 28, 1966; admitted to bar, 1996, Ohio; 1999, U.S. District Court, Southern District of Ohio. *Education:* The Ohio State University (B.S., summa cum laude, with honors in the liberal arts, 1989); The Ohio State University College of Law (J.D., 1996). Board Member: Marion County Free Medical Clinic; Women's Business Council; Central Ohio Women's Guild. *Member:* Marion County, Columbus and Ohio State Bar Associations; American Health Lawyers Association. (Resident, Marion Office). **PRACTICE AREAS:** Business Formation; Closely Held Corporations; Employment Contracts; Real Property; Estate Planning. **Email:** mworobiec@keglerbrown.com

REPRESENTATIVE CLIENTS: American Subcontractors Association; Artic Express, Inc.; Ashland Chemical Co.; Associated Builders & Contractors, Inc.; AT&T Wireless; BancFirst Ohio Corp.; Bank One, NA; Battelle Memorial Institute; Butler County Transportation District; Ceilings & Interior Systems Construction Association; Central States Southeast and Southwest Areas Health and Welfare and Pension Funds; Columbus Metropolitan Housing Authority; Danis Industries; Diocese of Columbus; Donato's Pizzeria, LLC; Farmers Insurance Group; The Fishel Co.; George J. Igel Co.; Homewood Corp.; Independent Insurance Agents of Ohio; The Kemper Group; Lincoln Construction, Inc.; Merck & Co., Inc.; Merck-Medco Managed Care; Ohio Counsel for Home Care; The Ohio State University Hospital; S.G. Loewendick & Sons, Inc.; Spenley Newspapers, Inc.; State Teachers Retirement System of Ohio; Telesis Technologies, Inc.; Time Warner Communications; United McGill Corp.; West Publishing, Inc.

RUSSELL A. KELM

SUITE 860
37 WEST BROAD STREET
COLUMBUS, OHIO 43215
Telephone: 614-246-1000
Fax: 614-246-8110
Email: kelm@kelmlawfirm.com

Litigation in the areas of Corporate, Securities, Commercial, Employment, Construction and Computer Law.

RUSSELL A. KELM, born Rochester, New York, August 28, 1946; admitted to bar, 1971, Ohio and Michigan. *Education:* State University of New York at Buffalo (B.A., 1968); University of Toledo (J.D., 1971). Justice, Phi Alpha Delta; Order of the Barristers. Member, 1975-1983 and President, 1978-1979, Board of Trustees, The Legal Aid Society of Columbus. Former Partner, Schwartz, Kelm, Warren & Ramirez, 1977-1995. *Member:* Columbus (Member: Federal Courts, Common Pleas Courts and Labor Law Committee), Ohio State (Member, Federal Courts Committee) and American (Member: Class Actions and Derivative Suits Committee; Chairman, State Class Action Subcommittee, 1994-1997; Securities Litigation Committee and Employment and Labor Relations Law Committee, Litigation Section) Bar Associations; National Employment Lawyers Association; Ohio Employment Lawyers Association; Ohio Academy of Trial Lawyers; Association of Trial Lawyers of America. [Capt., U.S. Army Res., 1970-1978]. **PRACTICE AREAS:** Litigation.

JOANNE WEBER DETRICK, born Columbus, Ohio, November 18, 1957; admitted to bar, 1989, Ohio. *Education:* The Ohio State University (B.A., 1980); University of Toledo (J.D., 1988). Editor, University of Toledo Law Review. Member: Admissions Committee, Columbus and Ohio State Bar Associations. **PRACTICE AREAS:** Litigation; Commercial; Employment; Corporate and Construction Law. **Email:** detrick@kelmlawfirm.com

CYNTHIA L. DAWSON, born Terre Haute, Indiana, May 9, 1967; admitted to bar, 1998, Ohio. *Education:* Indiana University (B.S., 1989); University of Delaware (M.A., 1993); The Ohio State University (J.D., 1998). *Member:* Columbus and Ohio State Bar Associations. **PRACTICE AREAS:** Litigation; Commercial; Employment; Corporate and Construction Law. **Email:** dawson@kelmlawfirm.com

KENNEDY REEVE & KNOLL

98 HAMILTON PARK
COLUMBUS, OHIO 43203
Telephone: 614-228-2050
Facsimile: 614-228-3320
URL: http://www.krkattorneys.com/

Cleveland, Ohio Office: 75 Public Square, Suite 1300, 44113. Telephone: 216-771-5511. Facsimile: 216-771-5511.

Sexual Harassment, Americans with Disability Act, Age Discrimination in Employment Act, Title VII Race and Gender Discrimination, Family Medical Leave Act, National Origin Discrimination, Civil Service, State and Federal Civil Rights Litigation, Religion Discrimination, Representation to the Equal Employment Opportunity Commission and Ohio Civil Rights Commission, Administrative Law, Unemployment, Worker's Compensation Retaliation, Whistleblower Statute, Intentional Tort, Equal Protection and Due Process Violations, Employee Benefits, Wrongful Termination, Public Policy, Severance Package Review and Negotiation, Contract Review, Negotiation and Litigation, Small Business Start-Up and Consulting.

MEMBERS OF FIRM

LAREN ELIZABETH KNOLL, born Lexington, Kentucky, September 04, 1968; admitted to bar, 1999, Ohio and U.S. District Court, Southern District of Ohio; 2000, U.S. Court of Appeals, Sixth Circuit; 2004, U.S. Supreme Court. *Education:* Emory and Henry College (B.A., 1990); University of Tennessee at Knoxville (M.S.S.W., 1994); Ohio Northern University (J.D., 1998). **PRACTICE AREAS:** Sexual Harassment; Americans with Disabilities Act; Age Discrimination; Title VII Discrimination; Family and Medical Leave Act; National Origin Discrimination; Civil Service; Civil Rights; Federal Civil Litigation; Equal Employment Opportunity Law; Administrative Law; Unemployment Law; Workers Compensation; Whistleblower Litigation; Intentional Torts; Employee Benefits; Wrongful Termination; Public Policy; Contracts; Litigation; Small Business Law; Juvenile Law. **Email:** lknoll@kennedyknoll.com

GARY A. REEVE, born Cleveland, Ohio, October 15, 1956; admitted to bar, 1995, Ohio and U.S. District Court, Southern District of Ohio; 1998, U.S. Court of Appeals, Fourth Circuit; 1999, U.S. Court of Appeals, Sixth Circuit; 2000, U.S. District Court, Northern District of Ohio. *Education:* The Ohio State University (B.S.E.D., 1980; J.D., 1995). Member, Robert S. Duncan Inns of Court, 1996-1998. *Member:* Columbus (Member, Labor and Employment Section), Union County, Ohio State (Member, Sections on: Labor and Employment; General Practice) and American (Member, Sections on: Labor and Employment; General Practice; Litigation) Bar Associations; National Employment Lawyers Association; Ohio Employment Lawyers Association; Columbus Employment Lawyers Association. **PRACTICE AREAS:** Employment; Labor; ERISA and Benefits Law; Contracts.

NICHOLAS EDWARD KENNEDY, born 1973; admitted to bar, 1998, Ohio and U.S. Court of Appeals, Sixth Circuit. *Education:* Bowling Green State University (B.S., 1995); Ohio Northern University (J.D., 1998). *Member:* Columbus and Ohio State Bar Associations; Ohio Employment Lawyers Association; National Employment Lawyers Association. **PRACTICE AREAS:** Sexual Harassment; Americans with Disabilities Act; Age Discrimination; Family and Medical Leave Act; National Origin Discrimination; Civil Service; Civil Rights; Federal Civil Litigation; Equal Employment Opportunity Law; Administrative Law; Unemployment Law; Workers Compensation; Whistleblower Litigation; Intentional Tort; Employee Benefits; Wrongful Termination; Public Policy; Contracts; Litigation; Small Business Law; Noncompetition and Non-Solicitation Agreements. **Email:** nkennedy@kennedyknoll.com

ASSOCIATES

BRAD E. BENNETT, born Lancaster, Ohio, August 16, 1973; admitted to bar, 2003, Ohio. *Education:* Ohio University (B.S., 1997); Capital University (J.D., cum laude, 2003). **PRACTICE AREAS:** Sexual Harassment; Americans with Disabilities Act; Age Discrimination in Employment; Title VII Discrimination; Family and Medical Leave Act; National Origin Discrimination; Civil Service; Civil Rights; Federal Civil Litigation; Equal Employment Opportunity Law; Administrative Law; Unemployment; Workers Compensation Retaliation; Whistleblower Litigation; Intentional Torts; Equal Protections and Due Process Violation; Employee Benefits; Wrongful Termination; Public Policy; Severance Package Review and Negotiation; Contract Negotiation; Business Start-Ups and Consulting. **Email:** bbennett@kennedyknoll.com

PATRICK M. WATTS, admitted to bar, 2002, Ohio. *Education:* The Ohio State University (J.D., 2004). (Resident, Cleveland Office)

SUSAN KENNEY-PFALZER

P.O. BOX 30466
COLUMBUS, OHIO 43230
Telephone: 614-337-2722
Fax: 614-418-0528
Email: skplaw@sbcglobal.net
URL: http://www.skpfamilylaw.com

Family Law, Divorce, Dissolution, Child Custody, Spousal and Child Support, Visitation Rights, Adoptions, Paternity, Juvenile Law, Collaborative Law, Restraining Orders.

(This Listing Continued)

SUSAN KENNEY-PFALZER, Columbus—Continued

FIRM PROFILE: Caring representation with personal attention in all areas of family law.

SUSAN KENNEY-PFALZER, born Bay Village, Ohio, June 13, 1971; admitted to bar, 2003, Ohio. *Education:* The Ohio State University (B.F.A., 1995; J.D., with honors, 2002). Member, Law Review, 2000-2002. Court Appointed Special Advocate, 1999-2002. Treasurer, New Roots Adoption Support Group, 2001—. Former Board Member, Resolve of Ohio. Board Member, Ohio Dance. *Member:* Columbus (Member, Family Law Committee; Chair, Ad Litem Subcommittee), Ohio State and American Bar Associations; Women Lawyers of Franklin County (Secretary). ***PRACTICE AREAS:*** Adoption Law; Family Law; Divorce; Child Custody; Child Support; Visitation Rights; Domestic Violence; Restraining Orders; Collaborative Family Law; Domestic Relations; Paternity; Post Divorce Modification; Spousal Support; Separation Agreements.

ROBERT W. KERPSACK CO., L.P.A.

FIFTH THIRD CENTER
21 EAST STATE STREET, SUITE 300
COLUMBUS, OHIO 43215
Telephone: 614-242-1000
Fax: 614-242-4180
URL: http://www.rwklaw.com
Email: info@rwklaw.com
URL: http://www.lawyers.com/kerpsacklaw

Personal Injury, Wrongful Death, Professional Malpractice, Products Liability, Consumer Class Action.

ROBERT W. KERPSACK, born Frederick, Maryland, June 15, 1961; admitted to bar, 1989, Ohio; 1990, U.S. District Court, Southern District Ohio; 1993, U.S. District Court, Northern District of Ohio and U.S. Supreme Court. *Education:* Ohio State University (B.S., 1983); Capital University (J.D., 1987). Beta Theta Pi. National Institute of Trial Advocacy, 1994. *Member:* Columbus and Ohio State Bar Associations; Association of Trial Lawyers of America (Sustaining Member; Advocate, National College of Advocacy, 1995; Chair, Insurance Law Section, 2000); Ohio Academy of Trial Lawyers (Member, Advocates Circle, Board of Trustees, 1995—; Insurance Law Section, Chair, 1998-1999); Franklin County Trial Lawyers Association; Million Dollar Advocates Forum. (Certified as a Civil Trial Advocacy Specialist by the National Board of Trial Advocacy)

KESSLER & BALLENGER CO., L.P.A.

Established in 1990
7650 RIVERS EDGE DRIVE
COLUMBUS, OHIO 43235
Telephone: 614-888-3185
Fax: 614-433-0964
Email: kballenger@kb-law.net
Email: rkessler@kb-law.net
URL: http://www.lawyers.com/kessler

Estate Planning and Probate. General Business and Corporate Law. Federal, State and Local Taxes, Real Estate, Taxation, Trusts and Estates, Wills and Probate, Contracts, Elder Law, Professional Liability, Business Law, Employee Benefits.

RUSSELL W. KESSLER, born Columbus, Ohio, August 26, 1954; admitted to bar, 1979, Ohio; 1981, U.S. Tax Court; 2004, New York. *Education:* Miami University (B.S., 1976); Capital University (J.D., 1979; LL.M., Taxation, 1990). Certified Public Accountant, Ohio, 1978. Ohio State Bar Association Certified Specialist in Federal Taxation Law, 2002. *Member:* Columbus, Ohio State and American Bar Associations; American Institute of Certified Public Accountants; Ohio Society of Certified Public Accountants. (Certified Specialist in Federal Tax and Estate Planning, Trust and Probate Law, Ohio State Bar Association). ***PRACTICE AREAS:*** Real Estate; Taxation; Estate and Gift Taxation; Corporate Law; Partnership Taxation; Income Tax; Property Tax; Divorce Taxation; Wills; Trusts and Estates; Asset Protection; Charitable Giving; Will Contests; Estate Planning; Guardianship; Probate; Business Law; Buying and Selling of Businesses; Family Business Law; Limited Liability Company Law; Partnership Law; Professional Practices; Small Business Law; Premarital Agreements; Elder Law; Professional Liability; Employee Benefits. ***Email:*** rkessler@kb-law.net

KATHLEEN A. BALLENGER, born Columbus, Ohio, April 7, 1947; admitted to bar, 1979, Ohio. *Education:* The Ohio State University (B.S., 1970); Capital University (J.D., 1979; LL.M., Taxation, 1989). Certified Public Accountant, Ohio, 1986. *Member:* Columbus (Member, Subcommittees on: Estate and Gift Tax; Business Tax), Ohio State (Board Member, Federal Taxation Specialty) and American Bar Associations; Women Lawyers of Franklin County; Estate Planning Council I (Project Chairperson 1988-1989; President 1989-1990); American Institute of Certified Public Accountants. (Certified Specialist in Federal Tax Law and Estate Planning, Trust and Probate Law, Ohio State Bar Association). ***PRACTICE AREAS:*** Probate; Taxation; Estate and Gift Taxation; Partnership Taxation; Income Tax; Property Tax; Divorce Taxation; Wills; Trusts and Estates; Asset Protection; Charitable Giving; Estate Planning; Guardianship; Premarital Agreements; Qualified Domestic Relations Orders (QDROs); Elder Law. ***Email:*** kballenger@kb-law.net

KETCHAM & KETCHAM

Established in 1981
755 SOUTH HIGH STREET
COLUMBUS, OHIO 43206
Telephone: 614-444-3900
Fax: 614-444-9086
Email: rsketch@msn.com
Criminal Trial and Appellate Practice.
(This Listing Continued)

MEMBERS OF FIRM

VICTOR A. KETCHAM (1913-2003)

RICHARD S. KETCHAM, born Columbus, Ohio, January 8, 1948; admitted to bar, 1974, Ohio; 1975, U.S. District Court, Southern District of Ohio. *Education:* Bowling Green State University (B.S., 1970); Capital University (J.D., cum laude, 1974). Order of the Curia. Senior Assistant Prosecuting Attorney, Criminal Trial Staff, Franklin County, 1975-1984. Member, Governors Task Force on Domestic Violence, 1984-1988. *Member:* Columbus (Co-Chairman, Criminal Law Committee, 1995-1996) and Ohio State Bar Associations; Lawyers Club of Columbus; Franklin County Trial Lawyers Association; Ohio Association of Criminal Defense Lawyers (Director, 1989—; Past Secretary, Past Vice President); National Association of Criminal Defense Lawyers; Central Ohio Association of Criminal Defense Lawyers (Founding Member; President, 1994-1995; Board of Directors, 2001—). ***PRACTICE AREAS:*** Criminal Law. ***Email:*** rsketch@msn.com

REFERENCE: Key Bank.

KILLWORTH, GOTTMAN, HAGAN & SCHAEFF, L.L.P.

COLUMBUS, OHIO

(See Dinsmore & Shohl LLP)

KINCAID, RANDALL & CRAINE

2201 RIVERSIDE DRIVE
COLUMBUS, OHIO 43221
Telephone: 614-224-7193
Fax: 614-586-4051
URL: http://www.lawyers.com/kincaidrandallcraine-law

Probate Law, Estate Planning, Wills and Trusts, Estate Administration, Will or Trust Contests, Probate Litigation, Special Needs or Medicaid Payback Trusts, Living Wills, Power of Attorneys, Estate Planning for Parents of Disabled Children, Guardianship, Conservatorship, Elder Law, Business Law, Business Formation, Business Incorporation and General Practice.

SAMUEL B. RANDALL, born Dennison, Ohio, August 12, 1926; admitted to bar, 1951, Ohio. *Education:* The Ohio State University (B.A., 1948; J.D., 1951). Phi Delta Phi; Order of the Coif. Adjunct Professor, The Ohio State University School of Law, 1967-1968. Assistant City Attorney, Columbus, Ohio, 1952-1954. *Member:* Columbus and Ohio State Bar Associations. ***PRACTICE AREAS:*** Probate Law; Banking Law; Business Law.

KEVIN A. CRAINE, born Columbus, Ohio, July 23, 1956; admitted to bar, 1982, Ohio. *Education:* Ohio Northern University (B.A., 1978); Capital University (J.D., 1982). Referee, Franklin County Probate Court, 1982. Member: Franklin County Board of Mental Retardation and Developmentally Disabled (Past President and Member); Northwest Counseling Services-Older Adults Advisory Committee, OCAPS (Ohio Coalition of Adult Protective Services); Franklin County Forum (Vice President); Agonis Club of Columbus; Downtown Lions Club (Past President); PLANCO (Planned Lifetime Assistance Network of Columbus, Ohio); Aging Solutions One; Ohio Human Services Training Program (trainer); Ohio Physicians' Elder Abuse Prevention Project (contributor). *Member:* Columbus (Chair, Committee on Mental Law and Disabilities, 1982) and Ohio State (Member, Section on, Trust and Probate) Bar Associations; Alzheimer's Association of Columbus (Board Member and President); National Alzheimer's Association (Board Member). ***PRACTICE AREAS:*** Probate Law; Estate Planning; Wills and Trusts; Estate Administration; Will or Trust Contests; Probate Litigation; Special Needs Trusts; Living Wills; Powers of Attorney; Guardianship; Conservatorship; Elder Law; Business Law; General Practice. ***Email:*** kacraine@krc-law.com

S. BREWSTER RANDALL, II, born Columbus, Ohio, May 20, 1968; admitted to bar, 1993, Ohio. *Education:* Denison University (B.A., 1990); Capital University (J.D., cum laude, 1993). Committee Member, Probate Estate and Gift Tax. *Member:* Columbus and Ohio (Member, Probate and Estate Tax Committees) State Bar Associations. ***PRACTICE AREAS:*** Probate Law; Estate Planning; Wills and Trusts; Estate Administration; Will or Trust Contests; Probate Litigation; Special Needs Trusts; Living Wills; Powers of Attorney; Guardianship; Conservatorship; Elder Law; Business Formation; Business Incorporation; General Practice. ***Email:*** sbr2@krc-law.com

KISOR & WINKLER, LLC

Established in 2004
555 CITY PARK AVENUE
COLUMBUS, OHIO 43215
Telephone: 614-559-3841
Fax: 614-559-3846
URL: http://www.columbuscounsel.com

Complex and Commercial Litigation, Appeals, Corporate Law, Admiralty, Business Law Negotiation, Banking and Securities Law.

FIRM PROFILE: Kisor & Winkler, LLC focuses on Complex and Commercial Litigation and Negotiation. Referrals by other firms both locally and out of state are the primary source of its work.

JOHN F. WINKLER, born Gallipolis, Ohio, May 26, 1946; admitted to bar, 1983, Ohio; 1984, U.S. District Court, Southern District of Ohio; 1988, U.S. Court of Appeals, Third and Sixth Circuits and U.S. Court of Federal Claims; 1992, U.S. Supreme Court. *Education:* Yale University (B.A., 1968); McGill University (M.A., 1972); Harvard University (M.A., 1973); The Ohio State University (J.D., 1982). Articles Editor, The Ohio State Law Journal, 1981-1982; National Institute of Trial Advocacy, 1986. Lecturer: Ohio Judicial College, Ohio CLE Institute; Professional Education Systems, Inc. Adjunct Professor, Capital University Law School, 1987—. Co-Author: *The History of Ohio Law,* 2004. Au-

(This Listing Continued)

thor: "Roman Law in Anglo-Saxon England," 13 Journal of Legal History 29, 1992; "The Probate Jurisdiction of the Federal Courts," 13 Probate Law Journal 77, 1997; "The Probate Courts of Ohio," 28 University of Toledo Law Review 563, 1997. Counsel, Appellate Rules, Rules Advisory Committee, Ohio Supreme Court. *Member:* Columbus, Ohio State and Federal Bar Associations; American Inns of Court. ***REPORTED CASES:*** Galbreath v. del Valle, 91 Ohio App.3d 829 (1993); Firestone v. Galbreath, 67 Ohio St.3d 87 (1993). ***PRACTICE AREAS:*** Business Litigation; Civil Litigation; Probate Litigation; Litigation; Commercial Litigation; Insurance. ***Email:*** jwinkler@columbuscounsel.com

JOHN C. DEAL, born Kenton, Ohio, January 5, 1947; admitted to bar, 1974, Ohio; 1977, U.S. District Court, Northern and Southern Districts of Ohio; 1979, U.S. Court of Appeals, District of Columbia Circuit; 1980, U.S. District Court, Eastern District of Kentucky; 1983, U.S. Court of Appeals, Sixth Circuit; 1988, U.S. Court of Appeals, Eighth Circuit and U.S. Supreme Court; 1990, U.S. Court of Appeals, Fourth and Fifth Circuits; 1993, U.S. Court of Federal Claims. *Education:* Centre College; Ohio State University (B.S., 1969; J.D., cum laude, 1974). Author: *Baldwin's Ohio Practice, Commercial Code* (vol. 3) (1996) (with Kevin L. Sykes); "Capital Punishment: The Death of Limited Liability for Shareholders of Federally Regulated Financial Institutions," 24 Cap. U.L. Rev. 67 (1995) (with Bob F. Thompson and Bennett L. Ross) "Banking Law is Not for Sisses: Judicial Review of Capital Directives," 12 J.L. & Com. 185, 1993; "Bank Director Liability: Some Issues of Federalism," 1987 Mississippi Law Institute 201; "Regulation of Bank Subsidiaries: The FDIC Stakes a Claim," 7 J.L. & Com. 1 (1987); "Bank Regulatory Enforcement, 1985 Developments," 42 Bus. Law. 145 (1986); "Bank Regulatory Enforcement, Some New Dimensions," 40 Bus. Law. 1319 (1985); "Liability of Bank Directors," 39 Bus. Law. 1033 (1984). Regional Counsel, Federal Deposit Insurance Corporation, 1976-1985. *Member:* Columbus, Ohio State (Chair, Banking, Commercial and Bankruptcy Law Committee, 1992-1994) and American (Member, Business Law Section; Chair, Regulatory Enforcement and Director, Liability Subcommittee of Committee on Banking Law, 1985-1990) Bar Associations. ***REPORTED CASES:*** *FDIC v. D'Annunzio,* 524 F. Supp. 694 (N.D. W. Va. 1981) (first Change in Bank Control Act injunction case); *Fitzpatrick v. FDIC,* 765 F.2d 569 (6th Cir. 1985) (first banking agency civil penalty case); *First State Bank of Wayne County v. FDIC,* 770 F.2d 81 (6th Cir. 1985); *Central Kentucky Production Credit Ass'n v. United States,* 846 F.2d 1460 (D.C. Cir. 1988); *Production Credit Ass'n of Northern Ohio v. Farm Credit Administration,* 846 F.2d 373 (6th Cir.) *cert. denied,* 488 U.S. 851 (1988); *Curtin v. FDIC* 866 F.2d 255 (8th Cir. 1989); *CIBA-GEIGY Corp. v. Flo-Lizer (in Re Flo-Lizer),* 100 Bankr. 341 (Bankr. S.D. Ohio 1989), *aff'd,* 121 Bankr. 324 (S.D. Ohio 1990), *aff'd,* 946 F.2d 1237 (6th Cir. 1991); *Buckeye Production Credit Ass'n. v. United States,* 792 F. Supp. 827 (D.D.C. 1990); *FDIC v. Bank of Coushatta,* 930 F.2d 1122 (5th Cir.), *cert. denied,* 502 U.S. 857 (1991) (first capital directive case); *Wachtel v. Office of Thrift Supervision,* 982 F.2d 581 (D.C. Cir. 1993); *Doolin Security Savings Bank, F.S.B. v. FDIC,* 53 F.3d 1395 (4th Cir.), *cert denied,* 116 S.Ct. 475 (1995) (risk-based deposit insurance case); *Doolin Security Savings Bank, F.S.B. v. Office of Thrift Supervision,* 139 F.3d 203 (D.C. Cir. 1998) (Vacancies Act cease-and-desist case); Landry v. FDIC, 204 F.3d 1125 (D.C. Cir. 2000), cert denied, 121 S. Ct. 298 (2000) (Appointment Clause removal case); In re Nowak, 104 Ohio St.3d 466 (2004). ***PRACTICE AREAS:*** Banking Law; Litigation; Securities Law; Business Law. ***Email:*** jdeal@columbuscounsel.com

GEOFFREY T. KISOR, born Portsmouth, Ohio, October 13, 1957; admitted to bar, 1990, Ohio; 1992, U.S. District Court, Southern District of Ohio and U.S. Court of Appeals, Sixth Circuit; 1993, Colorado. *Education:* Ohio University (A.B., History, summa cum laude, 1979); Capital University (J.D., summa cum laude, 1990). Phi Beta Kappa. Phi Delta Phi (Vice President, 1989-1990). Law Clerk: Hon. J. D. Holschuh, U.S. District Court for the Southern District of Ohio, 1990-1992, 1993-1994; Hon. Barbara J. Sellers, U.S. Bankruptcy, 1989-1990; 1994-2005. ***REPORTED CASES:*** Springfield Armory Inc. v. Columbus 29 F.3d 250 (6th Cir. 1994) Ziegler v. Wendal Poultry Svc. Inc. 67 Ohio St.3d 10. 615 NE.2d 1022 (1993). ***PRACTICE AREAS:*** Bankruptcy; Civil Litigation. ***Email:*** tkisor@columbuscounsel.com

Languages: Italian and French.

ROBERT A. KOBLENTZ

35 EAST LIVINGSTON AVENUE
COLUMBUS, OHIO 43215
Telephone: 614-461-6666
Fax: 614-461-4666
Email: rk@rkoblaw.com
URL: http://www.lawyers.com/koblentzlaw

Family and Matrimonial Law, Divorce, Child Custody, Child Support, Spousal Support, Property Law, Premarital Agreements. Trials and Appellate Practice. Family Law Arbitration. Collaborative Law.

FIRM PROFILE: Certified Specialist in Family Relations Law. Listed as Ohio Super Lawyer in Law and Politics Magazine and as one of Central Ohio's Best Lawyers in Columbus Business First Magazine.

ROBERT A. KOBLENTZ, born Columbus, Ohio, August 20, 1946; admitted to bar, 1970, Ohio; 1972, U.S. District Court, Southern District of Ohio; 1992, U.S. Supreme Court. *Education:* The Ohio State University (B.A., 1967; J.D., 1970). Phi Delta Phi. Author: "Law You Can Use," Ohio State Bar Association, 1996 and 1997. Lecturer on Family Law, Columbus Bar Association Continuing Legal Education Series, 1976 and 1979 and 1984. Member, Collaborative Family Law Committee of Central Ohio. *Member:* Columbus (Chairman, Family Law Committee, 1976-1978), Ohio State (Delegate, Family Law Committee, 1979—; Lecturer, Family Law, CLE, 1989) and American (Member, Family Law Section) Bar Associations; Franklin County Trial Lawyers Association (Trustee, 1981-1982; Vice President and President Elect, 1984-1985; President, 1985-1986; Lecturer on Family Law, 1984); Ohio Academy of Trial Lawyers (Chairman, Family Law Committee, 1982-1983, Lecturer on Family Law, 1989). (Certified Specialist in Family Relations Law, Ohio State Bar Association)

RONALD J. KOCH

4200 REGENT STREET, SUITE 200
COLUMBUS, OHIO 43219
Telephone: 614-288-4740
Fax: 866-255-6793
Email: ronaldkoch@earthlink.net
URL: http://www.kochattorneys.com

Litigation, Copyrights, Trademarks, Patents, Intellectual Property, Contracts, Forensic Science, Engineering, Juvenile, Criminal, Patent Law.

RONALD J. KOCH, born Akron, Ohio, December 19, 1964; admitted to bar, 2003, Ohio; registered to practice before U.S. Patent and Trademark Office in patent matters. *Education:* Ohio State University (B.S.E.E., 1989); Capital University (J.D., 2002). Licensed Professional Engineer. Licensed Patent Attorney. Certified Energy Manager. *Member:* Columbus Bar Association; American Intellectual Property Law Association. ***PRACTICE AREAS:*** Patents; Litigation; Copyrights; Trademarks; Intellectual Property; Contracts; Forensic Science; Juvenile Law; Criminal Law; Family Law; Divorce; Post Divorce Modification; Uncontested Divorce; Spousal Support; Separation Agreements; Restraining Orders.

THE KOKENSPARGER LAW OFFICE

471 E. BROAD STREET, SUITE 2001
COLUMBUS, OHIO 43215
Telephone: 614-232-0424
Fax: 614-280-9675
Email: steve@kokensparger.com
URL: http://www.kokensparger-law.com

Domestic Relations, Divorce, Dissolution, Legal Separation, Child Custody, Paternity, Family Law.

STEVEN J. KOKENSPARGER, born Zanesville, Ohio, August 7, 1969; admitted to bar, 1994, Ohio. *Education:* Ohio University (B.A., 1991); The Ohio State University (J.D., 1994). *Member:* Columbus and Ohio State Bar Associations; Franklin County Trial Lawyers Association. (Certified Specialist in Family Relations Law, Ohio State Bar Association). ***LANGUAGES:*** English. ***PRACTICE AREAS:*** Family Law.

KRAVITZ, GATTERDAM & BROWN, LLC

145 EAST RICH STREET
COLUMBUS, OHIO 43215
Telephone: 614-464-2000
Fax: 614-464-2002
Email: mkravitz@kgbllc.com
URL: http://www.kgbllc.com

Federal and State Criminal Defense, Criminal Appeals, Post-Conviction and Federal Habeas, Criminal and Civil Asset Forfeiture, Equine and Administrative Law, International Criminal Law.

MAX KRAVITZ, born Cleveland, Ohio, November 2, 1946; admitted to bar, 1973, Ohio. *Education:* The Ohio State University (B.A., Economics, 1969); Capital University (J.D., 1973). Author: Kravitz, "Due Process in Ohio for the Delinquent and Unruly Child," 2 Cap.U.L.Rev. 53 (1973); "Ohio's Administrative License Suspension: A Double Jeopardy and Due Process Analysis," 29 Akron L.Rev. 123 (1996). Professor of Law: Criminal Law, Criminal Procedure, Advanced Criminal Procedure, Federal Criminal Law, International Criminal Law, Clinical Education, Capital University Law School, Columbus, Ohio, 1976—. Member, Ohio Criminal Sentencing Commission (Appointed by Governor Voinovich as the Ohio State Bar Association Representative, 1993—; Ohio Supreme Court Commission on Professionalism, 1997-1999 (Appointment by Court); Rule 65 Committee on the Appointment of Counsel for Indigent Defendants in Capital Cases, Ohio Supreme Court, 1987-1993. *Member:* Columbus, Ohio State (Chair, Criminal Justice Committee, 1993-1995; President's Award) and American Bar Associations; National Association of Criminal Defense Lawyers; Ohio Association of Criminal Defense Lawyers (President, 1990). Fellow and Board of Governors, American Board of Criminal Lawyers. ***REPORTED CASES:*** Smith v. Ohio, 494 U.S. 541 (1990) (stop and search violated the 4th Amendment); Lockett v. Ohio, 438 U.S. 586 (1978) (Ohio's capital sentencing scheme held unconstitutional). ***PRACTICE AREAS:*** Civil Litigation; Criminal Litigation; Forfeiture; White Collar.

JANET E. KRAVITZ, born Cleveland, Ohio, August 25, 1952; admitted to bar, 1987, Ohio. *Education:* Ohio State University (B.S., 1981); Capital University School of Law (J.D., magna cum laude, 1987). Order of the Curia. Notes Editor, 1986-1987 and Staff Member, 1985-1986, Capital University Law Review. Author: Comment: "The I.R.S.'s Computer Generated Assessments and Notices--Are They Valid?" 16 Capital University Law Review 87, 1986. *Member:* Columbus, Ohio State and American Bar Associations. ***PRACTICE AREAS:*** Criminal Litigation; Forfeiture; White Collar Crime.

KREMBLAS, FOSTER, PHILLIPS & POLLICK

COLUMBUS, OHIO

(See Reynoldsburg)

Patent, Trademark, Copyright and Intellectual Property Law. Foreign Patent and Trademarks Law. Litigation. Licensing.

KRUPMAN, GOLDEN, MEIZLISH, MARKS & WITTENBERG, LLP

923 EAST BROAD STREET
COLUMBUS, OHIO 43205-1101
Telephone: 614-258-1983
Fax: 614-253-5071
URL: http://www.kgmmw.com

Business and Corporate Law, Business Planning, Buying or Selling a Business, Computers and Software, Entertainment and Publishing Law, Franchise Law, Commercial Law, Federal Civil and Criminal Practice, Construction Law, Limited Liability Companies, Collections, Estate Planning, Wills, Probate, Guardianships, Trusts, Family Law, Divorce, Child Custody, Visitation Rights, Personal Injury, Automobile Accidents, Insurance Coverage, Dental Malpractice, Commercial and Residential Real Estate.

VICTOR S. KRUPMAN, born Cleveland, Ohio, 1934; admitted to bar, 1959, Ohio. *Education:* Amherst College (B.A., 1956); University of Michigan (J.D., 1959). Phi Delta Phi. *Member:* Columbus Bar Association. ***PRACTICE AREAS:*** Litigation; Real Estate; Probate; Wills; Trusts. ***Email:*** vsk@kgmmw.com

KEITH E. GOLDEN, born Providence, Rhode Island, 1952; admitted to bar, 1984, Ohio; U.S. Supreme Court; U.S. Court of Appeals, Second, Third, Fourth, Fifth, Sixth, Seventh, Eighth, Ninth and Eleventh Circuits; U.S. District Court, Southern and Northern Districts of Ohio. *Education:* Ohio State University (B.S., 1974); Capital University (J.D., 1982). Past President, Capital University Law School Alumni Association Governing Board. *Member:* Columbus, Ohio State and American Bar Associations; Franklin County Trial Lawyers Association; National Association of the Deaf. ***PRACTICE AREAS:*** Business; Corporate Law; Family Law; Collections; Personal Injury; Federal Criminal Defense; Post-Conviction Remedies; Entertainment Law. ***Email:*** keg@kgmmw.com

JODIE KAY MEIZLISH, born Columbus, Ohio, 1955; admitted to bar, 1987, Ohio, U.S. Supreme Court and U.S. District Court, Southern District of Ohio. *Education:* Kent State University (B.A., 1976; M.Ed., 1978); The Ohio State University (J.D., 1986). *Member:* Columbus, Ohio State and American Bar Associations. ***PRACTICE AREAS:*** Family Law; Personal Injury; Dog Bites; Dental Malpractice; URESA and Title IVD; Construction Disputes; Real Estate; Consumer Law. ***Email:*** jkm@kgmmw.com

IRVING B. (BUDDY) MARKS, born Cleveland, Ohio, 1945; admitted to bar, 1971, Ohio. *Education:* The Ohio State University (B.S., 1967); Cleveland State University (J.D., 1970). Assistant Attorney General of Ohio, 1971-1972; 1973-1976. First Deputy Superintendent of Banks and Counsel, Division of Banks, State of Ohio, 1972-1973. *Member:* Columbus and Ohio State Bar Associations. ***PRACTICE AREAS:*** Business Law; Commercial Real Estate; Construction Law; Banking Law; Finance; Debtor and Creditor Law. ***Email:*** bmarks@kgmmw.com

ERIC J. WITTENBERG, born Philadelphia, Pennsylvania, 1961; admitted to bar, 1987, Ohio and U.S. District Court, Southern District of Ohio; 1989, U.S. District Court, Northern District of Ohio and U.S. Court of Appeals, Sixth Circuit. *Education:* Dickinson College (B.A., 1983); University of Pittsburgh (M.A., Public and International Affairs, 1987; J.D., 1987). Phi Alpha Delta. Head Notes and Comments Editor, Journal of Law and Commerce, 1986-1987. Author: "The State of Lost Profits & Punitive Damages for Breach of Contract in Pennsylvania," 6 Journal of Law and Commerce 531, 1986; "The Arms Export Control Act of 1976; An Arms Export Regulation that Failed," 10 American Society Of International Law Students International Law Journal, 1986; "The Practitioner's Guide to Ohio Covenant Not to Compete and Trade Secret Law in the Post-Employment Context," 18 Ohio Number Law Review 833, 1992. *Member:* Columbus, Ohio State and American Bar Associations. ***PRACTICE AREAS:*** Litigation; Commercial Law; Corporate Law; Business Law; Collections; Real Estate; Construction Law; Publishing Law; Computers and Software. ***Email:*** eric@kgmmw.com

LAW OFFICE OF GUNTHER K. LAHM, LLC

SUITE 101, WATERFORD TOWER
155 WEST MAIN STREET
COLUMBUS, OHIO 43215-5063
Telephone: 614-222-0963
Fax: 614-228-7630
Email: guntherlahm@aol.com
URL: http://www.lawyers.com/guntherlahm

Professional Negligence, Insurance Bad Faith, Personal Injury, Automobile Accidents, Wrongful Death.

GUNTHER K. LAHM, born Salzburg, Austria, May 3, 1948; admitted to bar, 1987, Ohio; 1988, U.S. District Court, Northern and Southern Districts of Ohio and U.S. Court of Appeals, Sixth Circuit; 2000, North Carolina. *Education:* Wittenberg University (B.A., 1972); Capital University Law School (J.D., 1987). Delta Phi Alpha. Member, Order of the Curia. Recipient, American Jurisprudence Book Awards for Excellence in Agency/Partnership and Trial Advocacy. *Member:* Columbus, Ohio State and American (Member, Committees on: Medical-Legal; General Practice; Economics) Bar Associations; Franklin County Trial Lawyers Association; Ohio Academy of Trial Lawyers; Association of Trial Lawyers of America; Million Dollar Advocates Forum. ***LANGUAGES:*** German. ***PRACTICE AREAS:*** Civil Litigation; Personal Injury; Wrongful Death; Professional Negligence; Insurance Bad Faith. ***Email:*** guntherlahm@aol.com

LAMKIN, VAN EMAN, TRIMBLE, BEALS & DOUGHERTY, LLC

500 SOUTH FRONT STREET, SUITE 200
COLUMBUS, OHIO 43215-5671
Telephone: 614-224-8187
Fax: 614-224-4943
URL: http://www.lvtbd.com
URL: http://www.lawyers.com/lvtbd

Personal Injury, Medical Malpractice, Products Liability, Negligence, Insurance Coverage, Stockbroker Malpractice & Fraud. Litigation and Trial Practice.

FIRM PROFILE: For more than a quarter century, the law firm of Lamkin, Van Eman, Trimble, Beals & Dougherty has led a winning campaign to achieve fair compensation for the people we represent. By combining a seasoned mastery of trial practice with an aggressive approach, our firm has achieved a significant number of large settlements and verdicts.

Most of our clients have suffered severe-often tragic-injuries. Our mission is to help them receive fair compensation for their damages and losses. We believe our clients have the right to return to living as normal a life as possible, as soon as possible.

We are dedicated to assuring that our clients receive what they deserve under the law. Negligent defendants usually have powerful corporations or insurance companies on their side. Our firm stands ready to commit the necessary resources on behalf of our clients to help ensure they achieve just results.

MEMBERS OF FIRM

WILLIAM W. LAMKIN, born Yazoo City, Mississippi, April 22, 1934; admitted to bar, 1965, Mississippi and U.S. District Court, Southern District of Ohio; 1966, Ohio. *Education:* The Ohio State University (B.A., 1963); University of Mississippi (J.D., 1965). Phi Delta Phi. *Member:* Columbus, Ohio State and American Bar Associations; Ohio Academy of Trial Lawyers; The Association of Trial Lawyers of America; Franklin County Trial Lawyers Association. Advocate, American Board of Trial Advocates. ***PRACTICE AREAS:*** Personal Injury; Negligence; Products Liability; Medical Malpractice; Trial Practice.

TIMOTHY L. VAN EMAN, born Columbus, Ohio, August 19, 1955; admitted to bar, 1981, Ohio and U.S. District Court, Southern District of Ohio; 1982, Michigan and U.S. District Court, Eastern District of Michigan; 1987, U.S. Supreme Court. *Education:* Ohio Dominican University (B.A., 1977); Capital University (J.D., 1981). Author: "Ohio's Assumption of Risk: The Deafening Silence," Capital University Law Review, Vol. 11, Page 661, Summer 1982. *Member:* Columbus and Ohio State Bar Associations; State Bar of Michigan; Ohio Academy of Trial Lawyers; The Association of Trial Lawyers of America; Franklin County Trial Lawyers Association; Michigan Trial Lawyers Association; NASD Arbitrator. ***PRACTICE AREAS:*** Personal Injury; Negligence; Products Liability; Medical Malpractice; Insurance Disputes; Fraud; Trial Practice. ***Email:*** tvaneman@lvtbd.com

THOMAS W. TRIMBLE, born Rochester, Pennsylvania, March 4, 1954; admitted to bar, 1983, Ohio and U.S. District Court, Northern and Southern Districts of Ohio; 1987, U.S. Supreme Court. *Education:* Bowling Green State University (B.S., 1976; M.A., 1977); Capital University (J.D., 1983). Notes Editor, Capital University Law School Law Review, 1982. Note Published at 11 Capital University Law Review 111, 1981. *Member:* Columbus, Ohio State and American Bar Associations; The Association of Trial Lawyers of America; Franklin County Trial Lawyers Association; Ohio Academy of Trial Lawyers (Trustee). ***PRACTICE AREAS:*** Personal Injury; Negligence; Products Liability; Medical Malpractice; Insurance Coverage; Trial Practice. ***Email:*** ttrimble@lvtbd.com

DAVID A. BEALS, born Newburgh, New York, July 6, 1943; admitted to bar, 1987, Ohio. *Education:* George Washington University (B.A., 1971); Ohio University (M.A., 1972); Capital University (J.D., 1987). Instructor, Political Science, Ohio University, 1977-1985. Member, Athens, Ohio, City Council, 1979-1985. YMCA Man of the Year, 1972. *Member:* Columbus, Franklin County and Ohio State Bar Associations; Ohio Trial Lawyers Association; The Association of Trial Lawyers of America. ***PRACTICE AREAS:*** Personal Injury; Negligence; Products Liability; Trial Practice. ***Email:*** dbeals@lvtbd.com

KATHY A. DOUGHERTY, born Columbus, Ohio, May 1, 1955; admitted to bar, 1992, Ohio. *Education:* The Ohio State University (B.S., 1989; J.D., 1992). Registered Nurse, Ohio, 1986. *Member:* Columbus and Ohio State Bar Associations; Ohio Academy of Trial Lawyers. ***PRACTICE AREAS:*** Medical Malpractice; Personal Injury. ***Email:*** kdougherty@lvtbd.com

KERI N. YAEGER, born Columbus, Ohio, March 12, 1974; admitted to bar, 2001, Ohio and U.S. District Court, Southern District of Ohio. *Education:* Kent State University (B.B.A., 1996); The Ohio State University (J.D., with honors, 2001). Order of the Coif. *Member:* Columbus and Ohio State Bar Associations; Ohio Academy of Trial Lawyers. ***PRACTICE AREAS:*** Personal Injury; Negligence; Medical Malpractice; Products Liability; Trial Practice. ***Email:*** kyaeger@lvtbd.com

REFERENCE: Commerce National Bank.

LANE, ALTON & HORST LLC

Established in 1929
175 SOUTH THIRD STREET
COLUMBUS, OHIO 43215-5100
Telephone: 614-228-6885
Fax: 614-228-0146
Email: Lane@lah4law.com
URL: http://www.lah4law.com

Business Litigation, Construction Law, Employment Law, Family and Juvenile Law, Immigration Law, Legal and Judicial, Medical and Products Liability Law.

(This Listing Continued)

FIRM PROFILE: Lane, Alton & Horst LLC, located in Columbus, Ohio, is engaged in the general practice of law. Its litigation practice is extensive, including the defense of professional liability claims against physicians and hospitals, lawyers, judges, accountants, architects and engineers. Its lawyers are highly experienced in product liability law, insurance coverage and insurance fraud, employment discrimination, white collar crime, premises liability, personal injury, domestic relations, criminal law and commercial and business litigation.

Lane, Alton & Horst also represents clients in commercial transactions, business associations, banking, environmental law, administrative law, trusts, probate and estate planning. The firm's excellent reputation in the central Ohio legal community was built on more than seven decades' work in civil litigation.

MEMBERS OF FIRM

JACK R. ALTON, born Columbus, Ohio, December 17, 1925; admitted to bar, 1950, Ohio; 1953, U.S. District Court, Southern and Northern Districts of Ohio and U.S. Court of Appeals, 6th Circuit; 1960, U.S. Supreme Court. *Education:* The Ohio State University (B.A., 1948; J.D., 1949). Delta Theta Phi. Associate Editor, The Ohio State Law Journal, 1949. Author: "Special Verdicts," Ohio State Bar, 1953 and 1957; "Special Verdicts in the State Courts," Insurance Counsel Journal, 1960; "Settlement Negotiations," Insurance Counsel Journal, 1961. Contributing Author: "Personal Injury Litigation in Ohio," with the chapter on "Special Verdicts, Interrogatories and Instructions," 1965; "Law and Order in our 101st Year," Ohio State Bar, 1969; "Interrogatory Practice in Ohio," Ohio State Bar, 1975. Adjunct Professor, Ohio State College of Law, 1972-1980. Recipient of Ohio Bar Medal, 1989, and the American Judicature Society Herbert Harley Award, 1989. *Member:* Columbus (President, 1969-1970), Ohio State and American Bar Associations; Ohio State Bar Foundation; International Association of Defense Counsel (Chairman, Medical Malpractice Committee, 1981-1982). Fellow, American College of Trial Lawyers; Columbus Bar Foundation. ***PRACTICE AREAS:*** Medical Malpractice; Legal Malpractice; Products Liability Defense; Personal Injury Defense; Insurance Coverage Defense. ***Email:*** Lane@lah4law.com

MARY BARLEY-McBRIDE, born North Canton, Ohio, July 9, 1961; admitted to bar, 1986, Ohio; 1987, U.S. District Court, Southern District of Ohio; 1992, U.S. Court of Appeals, 6th Circuit. *Education:* The Ohio State University (B.A., 1983); University of Toledo (J.D., cum laude, 1986). Order of the Coif. Member, University of Toledo Law Review. Clerk to the Hon. Norah McCann King, U.S. Magistrate Judge, 1986-1987. Author: "Trilogy for Small Business Owners," Columbus CEO Magazine, Sept. 1997. *Member:* Columbus (Member, Construction Law Committee), Ohio State and American Bar Associations; Ohio Builders Exchange; Ohio Association of the Associated General Contractors; International Association of Defense Counsel; Defense Research Institute. Associate Member, Ohio Health Care Association. ***PRACTICE AREAS:*** Medical Malpractice; Pharmacy Law; Construction Litigation; Architectural and Engineering Law; Products Liability; Torts. ***Email:*** MBarley-McBride@lah4law.com

BELINDA S. BARNES, born Miami, Florida, October 7, 1963; admitted to bar, 1987, Ohio and U.S. District Court, Southern District of Ohio. *Education:* The Ohio State University (B.S., summa cum laude, 1984; J.D., with honors, 1987). Beta Gamma Sigma. *Member:* Columbus, Ohio State and American Bar Associations. ***PRACTICE AREAS:*** Insurance Defense; Commercial Insurance Defense; Litigation Defense. ***Email:*** BBarnes@lah4law.com

JOHN C. BARNO, born Lorain, Ohio, November 12, 1968; admitted to bar, 1994, Ohio; 2002, U.S. District Court, Southern District of Ohio. *Education:* Heidelberg College (B.A., cum laude, 1991); Ohio State University (J.D., 1994). Former Assistant Attorney General, Workers' Compensation Section. *Member:* Columbus (Member, Workers Compensation and Labor and Employment Committees) and Ohio State (Member, Worker's Compensation Committee) Bar Associations; Workers' Compensation Forum; Ohio Academy of Civil Trial Attorneys; Defense Research Institute. ***REPORTED CASES:*** Reynolds v. Wal-Mart Stores, 1999 OH Wrk. Comp. LEXIS 66 - March 23, 1999. ***PRACTICE AREAS:*** Workers Compensation Defense; Insurance Defense; Administrative Law; Litigation. ***Email:*** JBarno@lah4law.com

JOSHUA R. BILLS, born Urbana, Ohio, November 17, 1973; admitted to bar, 1999, Ohio; 2003, U.S. District Court, Southern District of Ohio. *Education:* Miami University (B.A., 1996); Toledo College of Law (J.D., cum laude, 1999). Associate, Reminger & Reminger Co., L.P.A., 1999-2002. *Member:* Columbus, Ohio State and American Bar Associations; Columbus Claims Association. ***REPORTED CASES:*** State ex. rel. ABF Freight Systems, Inc. v. Industrial Comm., 96 Ohio St.3d 80. ***PRACTICE AREAS:*** Products Liability; Personal Injury; Litigation; Malpractice. ***Email:*** JBills@lah4law.com

MATTHEW S. BROWN, born Findlay, Ohio, 1972; admitted to bar, 2004, Ohio. *Education:* Bowling Green State University (B.S., 1994); University of Toledo, College of Law (J.D., magna cum laude, 2004). Order of the Coif. Assistant Managing Editor, University of Toledo Law Review, 2003-2004. Author: "Zelman v. Simmons-Harris: A World of Opportunities Created for Parents, Children and Legislators, but at the cost of a Lemon," 35 U. Tol. L. R. 485 (2004). *Member:* Columbus and Ohio State Bar Associations. ***PRACTICE AREAS:*** Insurance Defense; Civil Litigation. ***Email:*** MBrown@lah4law.com

JAMES C. CARPENTER, born Louisville, Kentucky, November 20, 1949; admitted to bar, 1975, Ohio. *Education:* Ohio University (B.A., summa cum laude, 1972); The Ohio State University (J.D., 1974). Phi Beta Kappa. Administrative Assistant to U.S. Representative Robert N. Shamansky, 12th District, Ohio, 1981-1982. Secretary, Franklin Chapter, American Inns of Court, 1994-1997. Member, Panel of Arbitrators, American Arbitration Association. *Member:* Columbus (Member, Common Pleas and Federal Court Committees), Ohio State (Member, Litigation Committee) and American (Member, Litigation Section) Bar Associations; Defense Research Institute. ***PRACTICE AREAS:*** Commercial Litigation; Banking Litigation; Professional Negligence; Construction Litigation. ***Email:*** JCarpenter@lah4law.com

DAVID G. COX, born Columbus, Ohio, January 20, 1958; admitted to bar, 1989, Ohio; 1990, U.S. District Court, Southern District of Ohio. *Education:* The Ohio State University (B.A., 1982); Capital University (J.D., 1989). Order of the Curia. Former Senior Assistant Attorney General, State of Ohio, Environmental Enforcement Section, August, 1989 - June, 2003. *Member:* Columbus and Ohio State Bar Associations. ***PRACTICE AREAS:*** Environment (100%, 65); General Litigation; Toxic Torts; Agricultural; Asbestos Litigation. ***Email:*** DCox@lah4law.com

CLAUDIA L. DAVIS, born Tucson, Arizona, 1956; admitted to bar, 1982, California; 2002, Ohio. *Education:* University of California, Riverside (B.A., 1974); Southwestern University School of Law (J.D., 1981). Gamma Phi Beta. Member, Junior League. *Member:* Columbus, Ohio State and American Bar Associations; State Bar of California; American Board of Trial Advocates; Association of Trial Lawyers of America; Southern California Defense Counsel. ***PRACTICE AREAS:*** Torts; Insurance Defense; Litigation. ***Email:*** CDavis@lah4law.com

AMY J. ERVIN, born Newark, Ohio, May 19, 1971; admitted to bar, 1996, Ohio and U.S. District Court, Southern District of Ohio; 2001, U.S. Court of Appeals, Sixth Circuit. *Education:* University of Dayton (B.A., 1993); Capital University (J.D., 1996). Order of the Curia. Recipient, American Jurisprudence Award for Personal Property, 1994. Former Staff Attorney, The Honorable John Connor, Franklin County Court of Common Pleas, 1997-1999. *Member:* Columbus and Ohio State Bar Associations; Association of Trial Lawyers of America; Defense Research Institute; NITA Advocates Association. ***PRACTICE AREAS:*** Medical Malpractice; Litigation; Insurance Defense. ***Email:*** AErvin@lah4law.com

SCOTT A. FENTON, born Columbus, Ohio, 1967; admitted to bar, 1997, Ohio. *Education:* Bowling Green State University (B.A., 1989); Capital University Law School (J.D., 1997). Order of the Curia. Member, Capital University Law Review, 1996-1997. Author: Comment, "School Voucher Programs: An Idea Whose Time Has Arrived," 26 Cap. U. L. Rev. 645, 1997. *Member:* Columbus and Ohio State Bar Associations. ***PRACTICE AREAS:*** Business Litigation; Construction and Real Estate Litigation. ***Email:*** SFenton@lah4law.com

MELISSA M. FERGUSON, born Columbus, Ohio, May 22, 1973; admitted to bar, 1998, Ohio and U.S. District Court, Southern District of Ohio. *Education:* Indiana University (B.S., 1995); Capital University (J.D., 1998). *Member:* Columbus and Ohio State Bar Associations. ***PRACTICE AREAS:*** Litigation; Insurance Defense. ***Email:*** MFerguson@lah4law.com

CURTIS F. GANTZ, born Castalia, Ohio, August 25, 1943; admitted to bar, 1968, Ohio; 1973, U.S. District Court, Southern District of Ohio and U.S. Court of Appeals, 6th Circuit. *Education:* Heidelberg University (B.A., 1965); American University; The Ohio State University (J.D., 1968). Assistant Prosecutor, Franklin County, 1971-1972. Senior Assistant, Columbus City Attorney, 1978-1981. First Assistant City Attorney, 1982-1985. *Member:* Columbus, Ohio State and American Bar Associations; Inns of Court (Master, 1990-1992). Fellow, Columbus Bar Foundation. ***PRACTICE AREAS:*** Civil Rights; Civil Litigation; Business Litigation; Commercial Litigation; Personal Injury; Criminal Law. ***Email:*** CGantz@lah4law.com

JOSEPH A. GERLING, born Dayton, Ohio, February 25, 1952; admitted to bar, 1977, Ohio; 1978, U.S. District Court, Southern District of Ohio; 1984, U.S. Court of Appeals, 6th Circuit; 1996, U.S. District Court, Northern District of Ohio. *Education:* University of Notre Dame (B.S., cum laude, in Chemical Engineering, 1974); The Ohio State University (J.D., cum laude, 1977). Tau Beta Pi. *Member:* Columbus, Ohio State and American (Member, Sections of: Litigation; Tort and Insurance Practice; Member, Environmental Law Committee, 1979-1981) Bar Associations; Ohio Association of Civil Trial Attorneys; Columbus Defense Association (Past President); International Association of Defense Counsel; Defense Research Institute. ***PRACTICE AREAS:*** Products Liability Defense; Medical Malpractice; Personal Injury Defense; Insurance Coverage Defense; Construction Law; Professional Liability. ***Email:*** JGerling@lah4law.com

MELISSA A. GURILE, born Columbus, Ohio, February 20, 1974; admitted to bar, 2004, Ohio. *Education:* University of Massachusetts, Amherst (B.A., 1996); University of Dayton (J.D., 2004). Member, University of Dayton Law Review. Member, Philip C. Jessup International Law Moot Court Team. *Member:* Columbus and Ohio State Bar Associations. ***PRACTICE AREAS:*** Civil Litigation. ***Email:*** MGurile@lah4law.com

JEFFREY B. HARTRANFT, born Columbus, Ohio, August 31, 1971; admitted to bar, 1997, Ohio; 1999, U.S. District Court, Southern District of Ohio. *Education:* Harvard University (B.A., 1994); The Ohio State University (J.D., 1997). *Member:* Columbus Bar Association. ***PRACTICE AREAS:*** Workers Compensation; Litigation. ***Email:*** JHartranft@lah4law.com

VINCENT I. HOLZHALL, born Chicago Heights, Illinois, April 29, 1965; admitted to bar, 1994, Illinois; 2002, Ohio. *Education:* University of Notre Dame (B.A., 1987); Columbia University (M.A., 1988; M.Phil., 1991); University of Illinois (J.D., magna cum laude, 1994). Law Clerk, Hon. Benjamin K. Miller, Justice, Supreme Court of Illinois. *Member:* Columbus and Ohio State Bar Associations; Defense Research Institute. ***PRACTICE AREAS:*** Commercial Litigation. ***Email:*** VHolzhall@lah4law.com

EDWARD G. HUBBARD, born Columbus, Ohio, August 31, 1966; admitted to bar, 1997, Ohio. *Education:* Miami University (B.A., 1988); Case Western Reserve University (J.D., 1996). Recipient, Stanley I. and Hope S. Adelstein Environmental Law Award. *Member:* Columbus and Ohio State Bar Associations. ***PRACTICE AREAS:*** Litigation; Personal Injury Defense; Professional Liability Defense; Business Litigation. ***Email:*** EHubbard@lah4law.com

JEFFREY W. HUTSON, born New London, Connecticut, July 19, 1941; admitted to bar, 1966, Ohio; 1970, Hawaii; 1971, U.S. District Court, Southern and Northern Districts of Ohio and U.S. Court of Appeals, 6th and 9th Circuits. *Education:* University of Michigan (A.B., 1963; LL.B., 1966). Phi Delta Phi. Author: Case Notes, The Construction Lawyer, Summer, 1981-1982. Member, Ohio Supreme Court Committee on Creeds and Professionalism, 1989-1990. Member, National Panel of Arbitrators (Commercial), American Arbitration Association. *Member:* Columbus (Chairman: Judiciary Committee, 1979-1981; Professional Economics Committee, 1981-1983; Construction Law Committee, 2004—), Ohio State (Chairman, Litigation Section, 1986-1987; Member, Special Committee on Tort Reform, 1995) and American Bar Associations; Ohio Association of Civil Trial Attorneys (Member, Board of Governors, 1979-1984; President, 1982-1983); International Association of Defense Counsel (Chairman, Architectural and Engineering and Construction Law Committee, 1987-1989); Defense Counsel Trial Academy (Faculty, 1991); Columbus De-

(This Listing Continued)

LANE, ALTON & HORST LLC, Columbus—Continued

fense Association; Defense Research Institute (Regional Vice President, 1991-1993). American College of Trial Lawyers (Member, State Committee, 1990-1994); Columbus Bar Foundation; Ohio State Bar Foundation; American Bar Foundation. [U.S. Navy, Judge Advocate, 1967-1971]. ***REPORTED CASES:*** Hocking Conservancy Dist. v. Dodson-Lindblom Assoc., Ohio Supreme Court, Cite: (1980) 62 Ohio St. 2d 195 (architect malpractice, statute of limitations); SÆ Constructs, Inc. v. City of Columbus, Court of Appeals Case, 10th Appellate District. Cite: 1981 Ohio App. LEXIS 14347, affirmed at (1982) 70 Ohio St. 3d 69 (construction disclaimer); Willoughby Hills v. Cincinnati Ins. Co., Ohio Supreme Court Case Cite: (1984)9 Ohio St. 3d 177 (insurance coverage); Kemmerer v. Waste Management, Court of Appeals Case, 5th Appellate District, Cite: 1997 Ohio App. LEXIS 3259 (premises liability); City of Columbus v. Alden E. Stilson & Assocs., Court of Appeals, 10th Appellate District, Cite: (1993) 90 Ohio App. 3d 608, mco (1994) 68 Ohio St.3rd 1461 (indemnity); Bishop v. Waterbeds 'n Stuff, Court of Appeals, 10th Appellate District, Cite: 2002 Ohio App. LEXIS 2426 (intentional tort); Shoedinger v. Hess, Court of Appeals, 10th Appellate District, Cite: 2000 Ohio App. LEXIS 2409 (engineering malpractice). ***PRACTICE AREAS:*** Alternative Dispute Resolution; Construction Law; Insurance; Insurance Defense. ***Email:*** JHutson@lah4law.com

LESLIE S. JOHNSON, born Dayton, Ohio, November 15, 1970; admitted to bar, 1997, Ohio. *Education:* The Ohio State University (B.A., 1993); Capital University (J.D., 1997). Phi Alpha Delta. Member, Central Ohio Land Title Association (Secretary/Treasurer). *Member:* Columbus (Member, Committees on: Real Estate; Probate; Young Lawyers) and Ohio State Bar Associations. ***PRACTICE AREAS:*** Real Estate; Business Law; Probate; Immigration. ***Email:*** LJohnson@lah4law.com

JEFFREY J. JURCA, born Cleveland, Ohio, December 26, 1954; admitted to bar, 1979, Ohio; 1981, U.S. District Court, Southern District of Ohio; 1982, U.S. District Court, Northern District of Ohio; 1984, U.S. Court of Appeals, 6th Circuit. *Education:* Kenyon College (A.B., 1976); The Ohio State University (J.D., 1978). Assistant Attorney General, 1979-1986. *Member:* Columbus (Chairman, Governmental Agencies Committee, 1985-1986), Ohio State and American Bar Associations. Fellow, Columbus Bar Foundation. ***PRACTICE AREAS:*** Medical Malpractice; Product Liability; Administrative Law; Trucking Law; Employment Law. ***Email:*** JJurca@lah4law.com

WILLIAM M. LANE, born Columbus, Ohio, September 15, 1935; admitted to bar, 1960, Ohio; 1961, U.S. District Court, Southern District of Ohio; 1971, U.S. Supreme Court. *Education:* Amherst College (B.A., 1957); University of Michigan (J.D., 1960). Phi Delta Phi. Village Solicitor, Village of Canal Winchester, 1961-1966. Special Counsel, Superintendent of Insurance of Ohio, 1970-1976. *Member:* Columbus (Member: Real Estate Law Committee; Taxation Committee, Estate and Gift Tax Section; Probate Committee), Ohio State (Member: Probate and Real Property Law Section; Probate Committee; Agricultural Law Committee) and American (Member, Sections on: Real Property, Probate and Trust Law; Business Law; Taxation) Bar Associations; Estate Planning Council II; Ohio Land Title Association. Fellow, Columbus Bar Foundation. ***PRACTICE AREAS:*** Business Associations; Non-profit Organizations; Commercial Leasing; Estate Planning; Probate. ***Email:*** WLane@lah4law.com

BETH ANNE LASHUK, born Bronx, New York, March 4, 1965; admitted to bar, 1994, Ohio; 1996, U.S. District Court, Southern District of Ohio; 2000, U.S. Court of Appeals, Sixth Circuit; 2001, U.S. District Court, Northern District of Ohio. *Education:* Denison University (B.A., 1987); Capital University (J.D., 1993). *Member:* Columbus and Ohio State Bar Associations; Defense Research Institute. ***PRACTICE AREAS:*** Insurance Defense; Litigation. ***Email:*** BLashuk@lah4law.com

WILLIAM SCOTT LAVELLE, born Athens, Ohio, December 20, 1955; admitted to bar, 1980, Ohio; 1981, U.S. District Court, Northern and Southern Districts of Ohio. *Education:* Ohio University (B.S., Journalism, 1977); The Ohio State University (J.D., 1980). Assistant Attorney General of Ohio, 1980-1981, 1983-1990; Administrative Agencies Section, 1983-1987; Chief, Charitable Foundations Section, 1987-1990. *Member:* Columbus and Ohio State Bar Associations; Ohio Association of Civil Trial Attorneys; Defense Research Institute. ***PRACTICE AREAS:*** Civil Litigation; Personal Injury; Premises Liability; Insurance Coverage; Insurance Bad Faith; Nonprofit Corporations Litigation; Professional Licensing; Administrative Law. ***Email:*** WLavelle@lah4law.com

BARBARA K. LETCHER, born Pittsburgh, Pennsylvania, November 14, 1957; admitted to bar, 1990, Ohio, U.S. District Court, Southern and Northern Districts of Ohio, U.S. Court of Appeals, Sixth Circuit and U.S. Supreme Court. *Education:* The Ohio State University (B.S., 1979; J.D., 1990); The Moritz College of Law. Delta Theta Phi. Member, ABA Moot Court Team, 1989-1990. Recipient: American Jurisprudence Award for Moot Court Participation, 1990. Adjunct Professor, Appellate Advocacy, The Ohio State University, 1999-2001. *Member:* Columbus, Ohio State and American Bar Associations. (Certified Specialist in Labor and Employment Law, Ohio State Bar Association). ***PRACTICE AREAS:*** Employment Law; Litigation. ***Email:*** BLetcher@lah4law.com

JAMES W. LEWIS, born Columbus, Ohio, October 31, 1947; admitted to bar, 1975, Ohio; 1978, U.S. District Court, Southern District of Ohio; 1979, U.S. Supreme Court; 1982, U.S. Court of Appeals, 6th Circuit; 1990, U.S. District Court, Northern District of Ohio. *Education:* George Washington University; The Ohio State University (B.A., 1969); Capital University (J.D., cum laude, 1975). Phi Alpha Delta. Member, Order of the Curia. Notes Editor, Capital University Law Review, 1974-1975. Assistant Prosecuting Attorney, 1975-1977. Senior Assistant Prosecuting Attorney, 1977-1979. Director, Economic Crime Unit, Franklin County, 1979-1980. Special Counsel to the Franklin County Prosecuting Attorney, 1980, 1983-1987; to the Noble County Prosecuting Attorney, 1988-1991. Counsel to Investigative Sub-committee on Ohio Medicaid Health Maintenance Organizations, Ohio Senate, 1986-1988. *Member:* Columbus (Member: Admission to the Bar Committee, 1978-1980; Professional Ethics and Grievance Committee, 1980-1987; Judiciary Committee, 1988-1994, Chairman, 1992-1994; Chairman, Law Day Committee, 1985) and Ohio State Bar Associations. [U.S. Army, 1st Lieutenant, Field Artillery (Panama Canal Zone, 1969-1972)]. ***LANGUAGES:*** Spanish. ***PRACTICE AREAS:*** Arson and Insurance Fraud; Fire Insurance Defense; First Party Insurance Defense; Property Insurance Defense; Insurance Bad Faith Defense; International Business Law. ***Email:*** JLewis@lah4law.com

(This Listing Continued)

RICK E. MARSH, born Columbus, Ohio, December 29, 1936; admitted to bar, 1960, Ohio. *Education:* The Ohio State University (B.A., cum laude, 1958; J.D., cum laude, 1959). Order of the Coif; Phi Beta Kappa. Member, Teaching Faculty, Capital University Law School, Certified Legal Assistant Program, 1982-1988. *Member:* Columbus, Ohio State and American Bar Associations; International Association of Defense Counsel; Ohio Association of Civil Trial Attorneys; Defense Research Institute. Fellow: The American College of Trial Lawyers; American Board of Trial Advocate. ***PRACTICE AREAS:*** Accident Insurance; Automobile Insurance; Insurance Bad Faith; Uninsured Motorists Coverage; Legal Malpractice. ***Email:*** RMarsh@lah4law.com

ALVIN E. MATHEWS, JR., born Lake Worth, Florida, August 11, 1962; admitted to bar, 1987, Ohio; 1988, U.S. District Court, Southern District of Ohio; 1998, U.S. Court of Appeals, Sixth Circuit. *Education:* Miami University (A.B., 1984); Ohio Northern University (J.D., 1987). Author: "Legal Malpractice in Ohio: The Defense Perspective," Ohio Association of Civil Trial Attorneys Quarterly Review, 2002. Assistant Prosecutor, Montgomery County, Ohio, 1987-1990. Assistant Attorney General, Ohio, 1990-1992. Assistant Disciplinary Counsel, Ohio, 1992-1997. *Member:* Columbus (Chair, Martin Luther King Committee, 2001-2003; Member, Professionalism Committee; Member, Judicial Screening Committee), Ohio State (Council of Delegates) and American (Member, Litigation Section) Bar Associations; Association of Professional Responsibility Lawyers. ***REPORTED CASES:*** Disciplinary Counsel v. Mills, 93 Ohio St. 3d 407 (2001); Columbus Bar Association v. Winkfield, 91 Ohio St. 3d 364 (2001); Chirila v. Chiropractice Board, 145 Ohio App. 3d 589 (2001). ***PRACTICE AREAS:*** Civil Litigation; Professional Liability Defense; Administrative Law; Legal Ethics; Professional Responsibility Defense. ***Email:*** AMathews@lah4law.com

THEODORE M. MUNSELL, born Dayton, Ohio, June 26, 1954; admitted to bar, 1979, Ohio and U.S. District Court, Southern District of Ohio. *Education:* Ohio Wesleyan University (B.A., 1976); Case Western Reserve University (J.D., 1979). Phi Beta Kappa; Omicron Delta Epsilon. Board of Trustees, Action for Children. *Member:* Columbus, Ohio State and American (Member, Sections of: Tort and Insurance Practice; Litigation) Bar Associations; Federation of Defense and Corporate Counsel; Defense Research Institute; Ohio Association of Civil Trial Attorneys; Columbus Defense Association. ***PRACTICE AREAS:*** Medical Malpractice; Legal Malpractice; Products Liability; Personal Injury Defense; Insurance Coverage; Business Litigation; Commercial Litigation. ***Email:*** TMunsell@lah4law.com

D. WESLEY NEWHOUSE, born Dayton, Ohio, February 8, 1958; admitted to bar, 1983, Ohio. *Education:* Ohio Northern University (B.A., 1980); The Ohio State University (J.D., 1983). Finalist, Team Member and Member, Governing Board, Moot Court. Recipient: American Jurisprudence Book Award in Criminal Law; Judge Joseph M. Harter Memorial Award. Author: "Are You Covered? Sexual Harassment Decisions Change Insurance Coverage for Employment Claims," The Ohio Lawyer, May/June 1999; "Asbestos Litigation in our Schools," The Ohio Lawyer, Jan/Feb 1989. *Member:* Columbus (Member, Labor and Employment Law Committee), Ohio State and American (Member, Labor and Employment Law Section) Bar Associations. Fellow, Columbus Bar Foundation. ***PRACTICE AREAS:*** Employment Discrimination; Business Litigation; Business Law; Environmental Law. ***Email:*** WNewhouse@lah4law.com

CHRISTOPHER T. O'SHAUGHNESSY, born Princeton, New Jersey, January 19, 1971; admitted to bar, 1998, Ohio and U.S. District Court, Northern and Southern Districts of Ohio. *Education:* The Ohio State University (B.A., 1993); Capital University (J.D., 1997). Phi Alpha Delta. Listed in: Who's Who in American Law Students, 1995-1997; Who's Who in American Law, 2003—; Who's Who in America, 2004. *Member:* Columbus and Ohio State Bar Associations; Builders Exchange; Defense Research Institute; Franklin American Inns of Court. ***PRACTICE AREAS:*** Litigation; Construction Law; Products Liability; Insurance Defense; Medical Malpractice. ***Email:*** CO'Shaughnessy@lah4law.com

JEFFERY M. POTH, born Toledo, Ohio, March 26, 1968; admitted to bar, 1993, Florida; 1996, Ohio, U.S. District Court, Southern District of Ohio and U.S. Court of Appeals, Sixth Circuit. *Education:* Miami University (B.S., Finance, 1990); The Ohio State University (J.D., 1993). Former Assistant State Attorney, Felony Division, Miami, Florida, 1993-1996. Assistant Attorney General, Health Care Fraud Section, 1996-1998, Ohio. *Member:* Columbus and Ohio State Bar Associations; The Florida Bar. ***PRACTICE AREAS:*** Business Litigation; White Collar Crime; Health Care Fraud; Health Care Litigation; Health Care Licensing; Real Estate Litigation. ***Email:*** JPoth@lah4law.com

WILLIAM H. PROPHATER, JR., born Cleveland, Ohio, March 5, 1968; admitted to bar, 1998, Ohio and U.S. Court of Appeals, Sixth Circuit; U.S. District Court, Southern District of Ohio. *Education:* Providence College (B.S., cum laude, 1990); University of Dayton (J.D., 1993). Recipient, American Jurisprudence Award in Labor Law. *Member:* Columbus and Ohio State Bar Associations. ***PRACTICE AREAS:*** Employment Law; Labor Law; Administrative Law; Litigation; Workers' Compensation Defense. ***Email:*** WProphater@lah4law.com

GREGORY D. RANKIN, born Columbus, Ohio, March 17, 1952; admitted to bar, 1977, Ohio and U.S. District Court, Southern and Northern Districts of Ohio; U.S. Supreme Court. *Education:* Albion College (B.A., magna cum laude, 1974); The Ohio State University (J.D., 1977). Phi Beta Kappa; Omicron Delta Kappa; Psi Chi. *Member:* Columbus, Ohio State and American Bar Associations; Ohio Association of Civil Trial Attorneys (Member, Executive Committee, 1988-1992); Defense Research Institute. ***PRACTICE AREAS:*** Medical Malpractice; Legal Malpractice; Property Insurance Coverage; Arson and Insurance Fraud; Products Liability Defense; Personal Injury Defense. ***Email:*** GRankin@lah4law.com

JAMES K. REUSS, born Chicago, Illinois, February 26, 1952; admitted to bar, 1979, Ohio and U.S. District Court, Southern District of Ohio. *Education:* Miami University (B.A., 1975); The Ohio State University (J.D., with honors, 1979). Phi Beta Kappa. *Member:* Columbus, Ohio State and American Bar Associations; Ohio Association of Civil Trial Attorneys. ***PRACTICE AREAS:*** Products Liability Defense; Personal Injury Defense; Insurance Coverage Defense; Arson and Property Litigation. ***Email:*** JReuss@lah4law.com

KAREN KRISHER ROSENBERG, born Baltimore, Maryland, March 8, 1959; admitted to bar, 1984, Ohio. *Education:* Wittenberg University (B.A., 1981); The Ohio State University (J.D., 1984). The Ohio State Law Journal. Recipient: American Jurisprudence

(This Listing Continued)

Award, Torts; John E. Hollen Memorial Award. Author: "Jones v. Barnes, The Sixth and Fourteenth Amendments: Whose Appeal Is It, Anyway?", 47 Ohio State Law Journal, 179 (1986). Adjunct Assistant Professor, Legal Research and Writing, The Ohio State University College of Law, 1988-1992. *Member:* Columbus, Ohio State and American Bar Associations; Defense Research Institute; Ohio Association of Civil Trial Attorneys. Fellow, Columbus Bar Foundation. ***PRACTICE AREAS:*** Insurance Coverage; First and Third Party Insurance Defense; Premises Liability Defense. ***Email:*** KRosenberg@lah4law.com

CORINNE N. RYAN, born Washington, D.C., December 8, 1970; admitted to bar, 1996, Ohio. *Education:* John Carroll University (B.A., Arts, 1993); Capital University (J.D., 1996). *Member:* Columbus and Ohio State Bar Associations. ***PRACTICE AREAS:*** Family Law; Domestic Relations Law; Juvenile Law; Adoption Law. ***Email:*** CRyan@lah4law.com

KIMBERLY M. SCHELLHAAS, born Worcester, Massachusetts, January 31, 1968; admitted to bar, 1993, Ohio; 1996, Commonwealth of Massachusetts. *Education:* Michigan State University (B.A., 1990); Capital University (J.D., 1993). *Member:* Columbus and Ohio State Bar Associations. ***PRACTICE AREAS:*** Insurance Defense; Litigation; Medical Malpractice; Leasing. ***Email:*** KSchellhaas@lah4law.com

DOUGLAS J. SCHOCKMAN, born Coldwater, Ohio, April 28, 1969; admitted to bar, 1994, Ohio. *Education:* University of Toledo (B.S., 1991); Capital University (J.D., 1994). Order of Curia. *Member:* Columbus and Ohio State Bar Associations; Defense Research Institute. ***PRACTICE AREAS:*** Litigation. ***Email:*** DSchockman@lah4law.com

THOMAS E. SWITZER, born Columbus, Ohio, November 3, 1970; admitted to bar, 1997, Ohio and U.S. District Court, Northern District of Ohio. *Education:* Capital University (B.A., 1993); Ohio Northern University (J.D., 1996). Member, Administrative Law Moot Court Team, 1995. *Member:* Columbus and Ohio State Bar Associations; National Society of Professional Insurance Investigators (NSPII); International Association of Arson Investigators (IAAI). ***PRACTICE AREAS:*** Insurance Subrogation; First Party Property Insurance; Insurance Fraud; Civil Litigation. ***Email:*** TSwitzer@lah4law.com

MONICA L. WALLER, born Findlay, Ohio, January 18, 1974; admitted to bar, 1999, Ohio; 2000, U.S. District Court, Southern District of Ohio. *Education:* Ohio State University (B.A., 1996; J.D., 1999). *Member:* Columbus and Ohio State Bar Associations. ***PRACTICE AREAS:*** Litigation; Insurance Defense; Employment Law. ***Email:*** MWaller@lah4law.com

RICHARD O. WUERTH, born Cleveland, Ohio, November 12, 1946; admitted to bar, 1973, Ohio; 1975, U.S. District Court, Southern District of Ohio; U.s. Court of Appeals, Sixth Circuit; U.S. Supreme Court. *Education:* Wittenberg University (B.A., 1968); Washington University (J.D., 1973). Topic Editor, Washington University Law Quarterly, 1972-1973. Member: Violet Township, Fairfield County, Ohio Zoning Board. *Member:* Columbus, Ohio State and American (Member, Business Law Section) Bar Associations. ***PRACTICE AREAS:*** Banking Litigation; Business Litigation; Zoning Law; Eminent Domain; Legal Malpractice; Accountants Malpractice; Finance; Securities Litigation; Bankruptcy Litigation. ***Email:*** RWuerth@lah4law.com

STEPHEN B. YURIK, born Detroit, Michigan, November 3, 1958; admitted to bar, 1985, Michigan; 1990, Arizona; 1996, Ohio. *Education:* Michigan State University (B.A., 1982); Wayne State University (J.D., 1985). *Member:* Columbus, Ohio State and American Bar Associations; Defense Research Institute; American Immigration Lawyers Association. [Capt., U.S. Army Judge Advocate General Counsel, 1986-1994]. ***PRACTICE AREAS:*** Medical Malpractice Defense; Immigration and Naturalization; Professional Discipline. ***Email:*** SYurik@lah4law.com

REPRESENTATIVE CLIENTS: Allstate Insurance Company; American International Group; Amerisure Insurance Company; Auto Owners Insurance Co./Owners Insurance Co.; Bank One; Burgess & Niple Engineers and Architects; Cantwell Machinery Co.; Chubb Group of Insurance Cos.; CIGNA; Cincinnati Insurance Company; CNA Insurance; Cooper Foods; Crawford and Company; Dominos Pizza, Inc.; Frontier Insurance; Gandee & Associates, Inc.; GEICO (Government Employees Insurance Company); GRE Insurance Group; Great West Casualty Company; Heritage Insurance Company; ITT Hartford; Kellam and Associates, Inc.; Keller Industries, Inc.; KinderCare Learning Centers, Inc.; Kroger Company; MMI; Mathews Click & Associates; Medical Protective Company; Meridian Mutual Insurance; Michigan Miller; Midwestern Indemnity Co.; Motorists Mutual Insurance Company; National City Bank; National Youth Advocate Program; Nations Banc; NBBJ; Ohio Bar Liability Insurance Company; Royal Insurance Company; Ruscilli Construction Company; SAFECO Ins. Co.; St. Paul Companies; State Farm Insurance Companies; USF&G Insurance Co.; Vesta Insurance Group; Westfield; White Consolidated.

LARRIMER & LARRIMER

165 N. HIGH STREET
COLUMBUS, OHIO 43215-2486
Telephone: 614-221-7548
Fax: 614-221-8659
URL: http://www.larrimer.com

Employment Law and Workers Compensation.

FIRM PROFILE: Practice consists of exclusively representing injured workers before the Ohio Bureau of Workers' Compensation and Industrial Commission of Ohio.

Helping injured workers since 1928.

TERRENCE W. LARRIMER, born Columbus, Ohio, December 4, 1947; admitted to bar, 1972, District of Columbia; 1972, Ohio. *Education:* Princeton, University (B.A., 1969); University of Michigan (LL.B., 1972). *Member:* Columbus and Ohio State Bar Associations. ***PRACTICE AREAS:*** Workers Compensation.

GAVIN R. LARRIMER, born Columbus, Ohio, November 24, 1936; admitted to bar, 1961, Ohio. *Education:* The Ohio State University (B.S., Business Administration, 1959; J.D., 1961). *Member:* Columbus and Ohio State Bar Associations. ***PRACTICE AREAS:*** Workers Compensation.

JOSEPH F. NAVIN, born New York, NY, March 3, 1960; admitted to bar, 1988, Ohio. *Education:* The Ohio State University (B.A., 1984); Capital University (J.D., 1987). *Member:* Muskingum County and Ohio State Bar Associations. ***PRACTICE AREAS:*** Workers Compensation.

DARLA E. KAIKIS, born Columbus, Ohio, November 23, 1963; admitted to bar, 1992, Ohio. *Education:* The Ohio State University (B.S., Allied Health Professions, 1987); Capital University (J.D., 1992). *Member:* Columbus and Ohio State Bar Associations; American Society of Radiologic Technologies. ***PRACTICE AREAS:*** Workers Compensation (100%).

COURTNEY ANN LARRIMER, born Columbus, Ohio, April 13, 1971; admitted to bar, 1996, Ohio. *Education:* Miami University (B.S., Finance, 1993); Capital University (J.D., 1996). *Member:* Columbus and Ohio State Bar Associations. ***PRACTICE AREAS:*** Workers Compensation.

JOHN H. LARRIMER, born Columbus, Ohio, November 8, 1968; admitted to bar, 1997, Ohio. *Education:* Lafayette College (B.A., 1991); Cleveland Marshall College of Law (J.D., 1997). *Member:* Columbus, Ohio State and American Bar Associations. ***PRACTICE AREAS:*** Workers Compensation.

KEVIN J. LARRIMER, born Columbus, Ohio, October 31, 1969; admitted to bar, 1997, Ohio. *Education:* University of Michigan (B.A., 1993); Capital University (J.D., 1997). *Member:* Columbus and Ohio State Bar Associations. ***PRACTICE AREAS:*** Workers Compensation.

CRAIG E. LARRIMER, born Columbus, Ohio, November 18, 1969; admitted to bar, 1997, Ohio. *Education:* Duke University (B.A., 1992); The Ohio State University (J.D., with honors, 1997). *Member:* Columbus and Ohio State Bar Associations. ***PRACTICE AREAS:*** Workers Compensation.

(This Listing Continued)

RICHARD L. LEVINE CO., L.P.A.

460 EAST MAIN STREET
COLUMBUS, OHIO 43215-5344
Telephone: 614-227-0300
Fax: 614-227-6060
Email: richard@levinepa.com
URL: http://www.richardllevine.com

Commercial Real Estate, Real Estate Development, Real Estate Finance, Commercial Leasing, Construction Law, Commercial Law, Mechanics Liens, Entity Formation, Corporate Law, Partnerships, Limited Liability Companies.

RICHARD L. LEVINE, born Columbus, Ohio, February 12, 1958; admitted to bar, 1984, Ohio, U.S. District Court, Southern and Northern Districts of Ohio, U.S. District Court, Northern District of Georgia and U.S. Court of Appeals, 11th Circuit. *Education:* Indiana University (B.A., 1980); Emory University (J.D., 1984). *Member:* Columbus and Ohio State Bar Associations. ***LANGUAGES:*** Hebrew. ***PRACTICE AREAS:*** Real Estate Law; Commercial Law; Construction Law. ***Email:*** richard@levinepa.com

YALE R. LEVY

903 EASTWIND DRIVE
COLUMBUS, OHIO 43081
Telephone: 614-898-5200
Fax: 614-898-5230
Email: ylevy@popelevy.com

Collections, Creditor Representation, Bankruptcy, Corporate Law, Estate Planning, Structured Settlement Transfers.

YALE R. LEVY, born Youngstown, Ohio, June 6, 1970; admitted to bar, 1995, Ohio; U.S. Supreme Court; U.S. Court of Appeals, Sixth Circuit; U.S. District Court, Northern and Southern Districts of Ohio and U.S. Bankruptcy Court, Southern District of Ohio. *Education:* Indiana University (B.S., Accounting, 1992); The Ohio State University (J.D., 1995). *Member:* Columbus and Ohio State Bar Associations; ACA International General Bar; National List of Attorneys; American Lawyers Quarterly; The Columbia Law List; National Association of Retail Collection Attorneys. (Also with Pope & Levy). ***PRACTICE AREAS:*** Collections; Estate Planning; Corporate Law; Business Law; Consumer Law.

REPRESENTATIVE CLIENTS: JG Wentworth; Garden City Boxing Club; Physicians Credit Bureau; Delphi Capital; Wells Fargo; OSI Outsourcing Services, Inc.; NationsRent; CitiBank; Consumer Credit Counseling Service of the Midwest; Riverside Methodist Hospital; Grant Hospital; Doctors Hospital; Upper Valley Medical Center; Hocking Valley Community Hospital; Mercedes Benz Credit Corporation; Frigidaire Financial Corporation.

GREGG R. LEWIS

Formerly Harry Lewis Co., L.P.A.
625 CITY PARK AVENUE
COLUMBUS, OHIO 43206-1003
Telephone: 614-221-3938
Fax: 614-221-3713
Email: glewislaw@aol.com
URL: http://www.gregglewislaw.com

Family Law, Matrimonial Law and Civil Litigation.

FIRM PROFILE: The firm concentrates in all aspects of family and matrimonial law, including among other areas, divorce, custody and child support. We are attentive to each client. The firm has an excellent legal support staff as well as an established network of professionals in related fields to meet the many needs of our clients in complex personal circumstances.

GREGG R. LEWIS, born Columbus, Ohio, August 27, 1963; admitted to bar, 1989, Ohio. *Education:* Ohio State University (B.S., Marketing, Mathematics, 1986) Phi Delta Theta; Somerville College, Oxford, England (1988); Capital Law School (J.D., 1989) Delta Theta Phi. Assistant Prosecutor, Franklin County Prosecutors Office, 1988-1990. *Member:* Columbus (Family Law Committee; Business Law Committee) and Ohio State (Young Lawyers Committee) Bar Associations; Ohio Academy of Trial Lawyers (Chairman, Family

(This Listing Continued)

GREGG R. LEWIS, Columbus—Continued

Law Committee, 1998—); Franklin County Trial Lawyers Association; The Association of Trial Lawyers of America. ***PRACTICE AREAS:*** Family Law; Divorce; Child Custody; Child Support; Visitation Rights; Premarital Agreements; Post Decree Matters; Domestic Violence; Civil Litigation; Criminal Law; Felonies; Misdemeanors; Driving While Intoxicated.

HARRY LEWIS (1925-1995)

ERIC E. WILLISON, born Columbus, Ohio, August 31, 1966; admitted to bar, 1996, Ohio. *Education:* Ohio State University (B.A., 1992); Capital University (J.D., 1996). ***PRACTICE AREAS:*** Family Law; General Civil Litigation; Criminal Law.

ROXI A. LIMING

1989 WEST FIFTH AVENUE
COLUMBUS, OHIO 43212
Telephone: 614-488-2053
Fax: 614-488-2069
Email: roxil@roxiliming.com
URL: http://www.roxiliming.com

Immigration Law, Visas, Naturalization, H1-B Visas, Green Cards, Financé Visas, Investor Visas, Investor Green Cards, Labor and Employment, Wage and Hour Violations, Wrongful Discharge, Employment Discrimination, Americans with Disabilities Act, Sexual Harassment, Family and Medical Leave Act, Employment Contracts, Severance Package Negotiation, Personnel Policies.

ROXI A. LIMING, born Bucyrus, Ohio, August 13, 1952; admitted to bar, 1998, Ohio; 2001, U.S. District Court, Southern District of Ohio; 2003, U.S. District Court, Northern District of Ohio; 2004, U.S. Court of Appeals, 6th Circuit. *Education:* The Ohio State University (B.A., 1975); Capital University (J.D., 1998). Order of the Curia. *Columbus and Ohio State (Member, Sections on:* Labor and Employment; Solo and Small Firms) Bar Associations; American Immigration Lawyers Association. ***PRACTICE AREAS:*** Immigration Law; Visas; Employment Law; Discrimination; Alternative Dispute Resolution; Disabilities; Family and Medical Leave Act; Sexual Harassment; Wrongful Termination; Employment Contracts; Personnel Policies.

LITTLER MENDELSON

A PROFESSIONAL CORPORATION
Established in 1942
FIFTH THIRD CENTER
21 EAST STATE STREET
SUITE 1600
COLUMBUS, OHIO 43215
Telephone: 614-463-4201
Fax: 614-221-3301
Email: info@littler.com
URL: http://www.littler.com

Offices located in: Phoenix, Arizona; California -- Fresno, Los Angeles, Sacramento, San Diego, San Francisco, San Jose, Santa Maria, Stockton and Walnut Creek; Denver, Colorado; Washington, D.C.; Miami, Florida; Atlanta, Georgia; Chicago, Illinois; Boston, Massachusetts; Minneapolis, Minnesota; Reno and Las Vegas, Nevada; Newark, New Jersey; New York, New York; Charlotte, North Carolina; Philadelphia and Pittsburgh, Pennsylvania; Dallas and Houston, Texas; Seattle, Washington.

Employment and Labor Law; Affirmative Action; Age Discrimination in Employment Civil Service; Collective Bargaining; Confidentiality Agreements; Covenants Not To Compete; Employee Drug Testing; Employee Privacy; Employer Liability; Employment Arbitration; Employment Breach of Contract; Employment Civil Rights; Employment Class Actions; Employment Discrimination; Employment Litigation; Equal Employment Opportunity Law; Fair Labor Standards; Family and Medical Leave Act; Harassment; Labor Relations; Labor Strikes; National Labor Relations Act; Noncompete Litigation; Noncompetition and Non-Solicitation Agreements; Personnel Policies; Prevailing Wage Litigation; Reductions in Force; Restrictive Covenants; Sexual Harassment; Title VII Discrimination; Unfair Labor Practices; Union Contract Negotiations; Union Elections; Union Organization; Wage and Hour Law; WARN Act; Whistleblower Litigation; Workplace Violence; Wrongful Termination; Wrongful Termination Defense.

FIRM PROFILE: Littler Mendelson, a Professional Corporation, is the largest law firm in the United States engaged exclusively in the practice of employment and labor law. The firm has 400 attorneys in 28 offices nationwide who represent and advise management in all major subspecialties of employment and labor law including wrongful termination; sex, race, and age discrimination; wage and hour law; NLRB cases and collective bargaining; workers' compensation; unemployment benefits; workplace violence; substance abuse; employee privacy rights; occupational safety and health; the ADA; FMLA; ERISA; employee benefits; tax issues and immigration.

JAMES M. L. FERBER, born New York, N.Y., July 21, 1947; admitted to bar, 1971, Pennsylvania; 1974, Ohio, U.S. Supreme Court and U.S. Court of Appeals, Third, Fourth, Sixth, Seventh and Tenth Circuits. *Education:* Pennsylvania State University (B.A., 1968); Temple University (J.D., 1971). Tau Epsilon Rho. Recipient, American Jurisprudence Award in Labor Law. Attorney, National Labor Relations Board, Pittsburgh Regional Office, 1971-1973. Assistant Editor: "The Developing Labor Law," Bureau of National Affairs, 1986-1987, 2003. Adjunct Professor of Labor Law, Capital University Law School, Tokyo, Japan, 1987. Author and Lecturer: "The Pretext-Mixed Motive Dichotomy in

(This Listing Continued)

Wright Line Cases," and "Levitz Furniture And The Never-Ending Changing Landscape of the Withdrawal of Recognition Doctrine," American Bar Association, Labor Law Section, Committee on Development of Law Under National Labor Relations Act. Author: "Development of the Alter-Ego Doctrine," 1 Midwest Labor and Employment Law Journal 1, 1983. Co-author: "Withdrawal of Recognition: The Impact of Allentown Mack and Lee Lumber," 14 The Labor Law. 339 (1998). Special Labor Counsel, City of Columbus, Ohio, 1984-1986. Listed in Best Lawyers in America. *Member:* Columbus, Ohio State (Member, Labor Law Section, 1976—), Pennsylvania and American (Member, Committee on Development of Law under National Labor Relations Act, and International Labor Law Committee, Labor Law Section, 1973-) Bar Associations. Fellow, College of Labor and Employment Lawyers. ***PRACTICE AREAS:*** Labor and Employment. ***Email:*** jferber@littler.com

DAVID A. KADELA, born Detroit, Michigan, April 17, 1956; admitted to bar, 1982, Virginia, U.S. District Court, Eastern and Western Districts of Virginia and U.S. Court of Appeals, 4th Circuit; 1986, Ohio; 1987, U.S. District Court, Northern and Southern Districts of Ohio and U.S. Court of Appeals, Sixth Circuit; 1992, U.S. Court of Appeals, Eleventh Circuit. *Education:* University of Michigan (A.B., with distinction, 1978); University of Detroit (J.D., magna cum laude, 1981). Member, Frank Murphy Honor Society. Contributor, University of Detroit Law Review, 1980-1981. Assistant Editor, "How To Take A Case Before the NLRB," 7th ed., Bureau of National Affairs. *Member:* Columbus, Ohio State, Virginia and American (Member, Labor and Employment Law and Litigation Sections; Committee on Practice and Procedure Under NLRA) Bar Associations. ***PRACTICE AREAS:*** Labor and Employment. ***Email:*** dkadela@littler.com

ROBERT C. LONG, born 1953; admitted to bar, 1979, Illinois (Not admitted in Ohio). *Education:* Knox College (B.A., magna cum laude, 1975); Harvard University (J.D., 1979). (Also at Chicago, Ohio). ***PRACTICE AREAS:*** Labor and Employment. ***Email:*** rlong@littler.com

THOMAS M. L. METZGER, born West Palm Beach, Florida, December 13, 1966; admitted to bar, 1992, Ohio; 1993, U.S. District Court, Southern District of Ohio and U.S. Court of Appeals, Sixth Circuit; 1996, U.S. Supreme Court; 1999, U.S. District Court, Northern District of Ohio. *Education:* Washington University (B.A., magna cum laude, 1989); University of Pittsburgh (J.D., 1992). Order of the Barristers. Dean's Scholarship. "FDIC Capital Directive Procedures: The Unacceptable Risk of Bias," 110 Banking Law Journal 237. *Member:* Columbus, Ohio State (Board of Governors, Labor and Employment Law Section, 1998—) and American (Member: Labor and Employment Law; Subcommittees: Labor Arbitration and The Law of Collective Bargaining; State Labor Law Development) Bar Associations. ***PRACTICE AREAS:*** Labor and Employment Law; Employment Discrimination; Labor Relations; Employee Rights. ***Email:*** tmetzger@littler.com

DANIEL W. SRSIC, admitted to bar, 1994, Ohio. *Education:* Indiana University of Pennsylvania (B.A., 1991); University of Pennsylvania Law School (J.D., 1994). Associate Editor: Comparative Labor Law Journal, 1992-1993. *Member:* Columbus, Ohio State and American Bar Associations. ***LANGUAGES:*** Spanish. ***PRACTICE AREAS:*** Labor and Employment. ***Email:*** dsrsic@littler.com

---

Margaret C. Bettendorf; Wendy Clary; Alison M. Day; Christa S. Fossee (Not admitted in OH); ***Cheryl R. Hankerson; Jeffrey S. Hiller*** (Not admitted in OH); ***Tracy Stott Pyles.***

(For biographical data on personnel at other locations, see Professional Biographies at those cities).

LIVORNO & ARNETT CO., LPA

Established in 1986
280 N. HIGH STREET
SUITE 1410
COLUMBUS, OHIO 43215
Telephone: 614-224-7771
Fax: 614-224-7775
Email: livorno@megapathdsl.net
URL: http://www.livornoarnett.com

Workers Compensation, Labor and Employment, Discrimination, Americans with Disabilities Act, Sexual Harassment, Employment Contracts, Wrongful Termination, Civil Service, Government Agency Practice, Union Labor Law, Bankruptcy.

JOHN F. LIVORNO, born Wheeling, West Virginia, November 23, 1946; admitted to bar, 1972, Ohio; 1976, U.S. District Court, Southern District of Ohio and U.S. Supreme Court. *Education:* The Ohio State University (B.S., 1968; J.D., 1971). Listed, Who's Who in Law, Business First, Workers Compensation, Columbus. Assistant Attorney General, 1971. *Member:* Columbus and Ohio State Bar Associations. [First Lieut., U.S. Army, 1968-1976]. ***REPORTED CASES:*** State, Ex Rel. Miller v. Indus. Comm., 26 Ohio St. 3d 110 (1986); State Ex Rel. Tumbleson v. Eaton Corp., 87 Ohio St. 3d 140 (1999). ***PRACTICE AREAS:*** Workers Compensation; Labor and Employment. ***Email:*** jflivorno@megapathdsl.net

HENRY A. ARNETT, born Sidney, Ohio, April 24, 1951; admitted to bar, 1976, Ohio; 1977, U.S. District Court, Southern District of Ohio; 1980, U.S. Supreme Court; 1982, U.S. District Court, Northern District of Ohio and U.S. Court of Appeals, Sixth Circuit. *Education:* Bowling Green State University (B.L.S., 1973); The Ohio State University (J.D., summa cum laude, 1976). Assistant Attorney General, State of Ohio, 1976-1982. *Member:* Columbus (Government Agencies, Labor Law Committees) and Ohio State Bar Associations. ***REPORTED CASES:*** Portsmouth v. International Association of Fire Fighters, Local 512, 139 Ohio App. 3d 621 (2000); State Employment Relations Board v. Pierce Township, 155 Ohio App.3d 68 (2003); Kettering v. State Employment Relations Board, 26 Ohio St.3d 21 (1986); State Ex Rel. Demint v. Chillicothe, 76 Ohio App.3d 315 (1991). ***PRACTICE AREAS:*** Labor and Employment; Employment Contracts; Discrimination; Americans with Disabilities Act; Family and Medical Leave Act; Workers Compensation; Bankruptcy. ***Email:*** henryarnett@megapathdsl.net

(This Listing Continued)

CHARLES W. KRANSTUBER, born Cleveland, Ohio, July 27, 1954; admitted to bar, 1979, Ohio; 1980, U.S. District Court, Southern District of Ohio. *Education:* The Ohio State University (B.A., 1976); University of San Diego (J.D., 1979). Member, Dublin City Council, 1991-2003. Hearing Officer, Ohio Industrial Commission, 1979-1982. Mayor of Dublin, 1995-2001. Member, Dublin City Council, 1991-2003. ***REPORTED CASES:*** State, Ex. Rel. Kegley v. Indus. Comm., 82 Ohio St.3d 379 (1998). ***PRACTICE AREAS:*** Workers Compensation; Labor and Employment. ***Email:*** cwkrans@megapathdsl.net

REPRESENTATIVE CLIENTS: Ohio Association of Professional Fire Fighters; Paper, Allied-Industrial, Chemical and Energy Workers International Union; Fraternal Order of Police; Retail, Wholesale and Department Store Union.
REFERENCE: Bank One of Columbus.

LOVELAND & BROSIUS

Established in 1980

50 WEST BROAD STREET, SUITE 3300
COLUMBUS, OHIO 43215
Telephone: 614-464-3563
Fax: Available Upon Request
Email: admin@lblaw.net

General Practice. Business, Real Estate, Condominium, Local Government, Land Use, Construction and Business Litigation, Estate Planning.

RICHARD L. LOVELAND, born Warren, Pennsylvania, November 16, 1930; admitted to bar, 1957, Ohio. *Education:* Miami University (B.S., 1952); The Ohio State University (J.D., summa cum laude, 1957). Order of the Coif; Phi Alpha Delta. Member, Ohio State Law Journal, 1956-1957. Adjunct Professor, The Ohio State University College of Law, 1963-1969, 1975-1976 and 1985. *Member:* Columbus (Board of Governors, 1984-1988; Chairman: Notary Public Committee, 1959-1960; Real Property Committee, 1966-1968 and 1982-1983; Legal Economics Committee, 1983-1984; Investment Committee, 1987-1988), Ohio State (Chairman: General Practice Section, 1987-1989) and American Bar Associations; Columbus Bar Fondation (President, 1995-1996. ***PRACTICE AREAS:*** Real Estate; Condominium Law; Business. ***Email:*** rloveland@lblaw.net

DONALD F. BROSIUS, born Altoona, Pennsylvania, June 16, 1954; admitted to bar, 1980, Ohio. *Education:* Juniata College (B.S., 1976); Capital University (J.D., magna cum laude, 1980). Delta Theta Phi. Member, Order of the Curia. Member, Capital University Law Review, 1979-1980. *Member:* Columbus, Ohio State and American Bar Associations. ***PRACTICE AREAS:*** Labor; Local Government; Land Use; Business. ***Email:*** dbrosius@lblaw.net

WILLIAM L. LOVELAND, born Columbus, Ohio, January 9, 1955; admitted to bar, 1982, Ohio. *Education:* Denison University (B.A., 1977); The Ohio State University (J.D., with honors, 1982). *Member:* Columbus (Chairman, Litigation Practice Institute, 1994-1995), Ohio State and American Bar Associations; The Association of Trial Lawyers of America. ***PRACTICE AREAS:*** Civil Litigation; Real Estate; Land Use; Condominium Law. ***Email:*** wloveland@lblaw.net

CALVIN T. JOHNSON, JR., born South Charleston, West Virginia, December 4, 1969; admitted to bar, 1995, Ohio. *Education:* Marshall University (B.A., 1992); Capital University (J.D., 1995). Phi Alph Delta (Barrister, 1993-1994); Order of the Curia. *Member:* Columbus, Ohio State and American Bar Associations. ***PRACTICE AREAS:*** Real Estate; Condominium Law; Land Use. ***Email:*** tjohnson@lblaw.net

ASSOCIATES

HELEN M. QUENEMOEN, born Cleveland, Ohio, October 20, 1941; admitted to bar, 1985, Ohio. *Education:* Carlton College (B.A., magna cum laude, 1964); University of Minnesota (M.A., 1966); The Ohio State University (J.D., with honors, 1985). Phi Beta Kappa. Member, Mortar Board. Member, Ohio State Law Journal, 1983-1984. *Member:* Columbus, Ohio State and American Bar Associations. ***PRACTICE AREAS:*** Estate Planning; General Practice; Local Government. ***Email:*** hquenemoen@lblaw.net

PETER N. GRIGGS, born Mansfield, Ohio, May 19, 1972; admitted to bar, 2001, Ohio; 2002, U.S. District Court, Southern District of Ohio. *Education:* The Ohio State University (B.A., 1995); University of Akron (J.D., cum laude, 2001). Member, Akron Law Review. Formerly with Martin McCarty Wright Roach Co LPA. *Member:* Columbus and Ohio State Bar Associations. ***PRACTICE AREAS:*** General Practice. ***Email:*** pgriggs@lblaw.net

JONATHAN E. ADKINS, born Weirton, West Virginia, November 4, 1977; (admission pending). *Education:* West Virginia University (B.S.B.A., 2000; M.P.A., 2001); The Ohio State University (J.D., 2004). ***Email:*** jadkins@lblaw.net

REPRESENTATIVE CLIENTS: Dominion Homes, Inc.; Epcon Group, Inc.; The Fritsche Corp.; Hamilton Township; Perry Township; Prairie Township.

LUCAS, PRENDERGAST, ALBRIGHT, GIBSON & NEWMAN

600 SOUTH HIGH STREET
COLUMBUS, OHIO 43215
Telephone: 614-228-5711
Telecopier: 614-228-0982
URL: http://www.lpagnlaw.com

General Civil Practice. Corporation, Wills, Probate, Taxation, Real Estate, Zoning, Public Utilities, Labor and Health Law. Estate Planning. Trials and Appeals.

FIRM PROFILE: Our Civil Litigation Firm has had a tradition of providing personal, Quality Legal Representation since it's inception in 1910. Today, the firm practices statewide, consists of five attorneys and has an excellent legal support staff.

(This Listing Continued)

MEMBERS OF FIRM

RALPH M. LUCAS (1880-1967)

R. RUSH WARREN (1917-1967)

JOHN A. BROWN (1926-1980)

ARTHUR J. PRENDERGAST, JR. (1923-1987)

RALPH W. LUCAS (1920-1993)

ROBERT E. ALBRIGHT, born Greenville, Ohio, November 7, 1921; admitted to bar, 1950, Ohio; 1951, Michigan. *Education:* Oberlin College; University of Michigan (A.B., 1947; J.D., 1950). ***PRACTICE AREAS:*** Real Estate; Business Law; Probate. ***Email:*** ralbright@lpagn.com

WILLIAM F. NEWMAN, born Wellston, Ohio, June 7, 1929; admitted to bar, 1955, Ohio. *Education:* Ohio University (B.Sc., cum laude, 1950); The Ohio State University (J.D., 1954). Associate Editor, Ohio State Law Journal, 1954. *Member:* Columbus, Ohio State and American Bar Associations. ***PRACTICE AREAS:*** Real Estate Law; Probate Law; Business Law. ***Email:*** wnewman@lpagn.com

JOHN C. LUCAS, born Columbus, Ohio, April 20, 1951; admitted to bar, 1976, Ohio. *Education:* Miami University (B.S., 1973); Case Western Reserve University (J.D., 1976). Beta Alpha Psi. Certified Attorney Specialist, Federal Taxation Law. *Member:* Columbus (Member, Committees on: Taxation Law; Probate Law), Ohio State (Member, Committee on Taxation Law) and American (Member, Committee on Taxation Law) Bar Associations. ***PRACTICE AREAS:*** Business Law; Partnership Law; Probate; Real Estate; Taxation; Trusts and Estates; Wills. ***Email:*** jlucas@lpagn.com

TONDA L. MOORE, born Columbus, Ohio, September 4, 1968; admitted to bar, 1995, Ohio and U.S. District Court, Northern and Southern Districts of Ohio. *Education:* Tarkio College (B.A., 1989); Cleveland-Marshall College of Law (J.D., 1994). *Member:* Columbus and Ohio State Bar Associations; Trial Lawyers Association. ***PRACTICE AREAS:*** Civil Litigation; Trial Practice; Domestic Relations; Appellate Practice; Criminal Law; Juvenile Law; Guardian Ad Litem; Zoning, Planning and Land Use; Real Estate. ***Email:*** tmoore@lpagn.com

STACEY L. WIDEMAN, born Springfield, Ohio, January 21, 1977; admitted to bar, 2003, Ohio. *Education:* University of Cincinnati (B.S., 1999); Capital University (J.D., 2003). *Member:* Columbus and Ohio State Bar Associations. ***PRACTICE AREAS:*** Business Law; Civil Litigation; Real Estate; Zoning, Planning and Land Use. ***Email:*** swideman@lpagn.com

REPRESENTATIVE CLIENTS: Anderson Concrete Corp.; Archer-Meeks-Weiler Insurance Agency; Architectural Systems; Ludo Bevilacqua Builders; Claggett Electric Company, Inc.; Columbus Paper Box Company; Commonwealth Land Title Insurance Company; Cooker Restaurant Corp.; Creative Housing, Inc.; Davis & Son, Inc.; Delaware County Bank; Dublin Manor Corp., Inc.; Financial Land Corporation; Jeg's Automotive, Inc.; Kurtz Bros., Inc.; McNally Lumber Company; Mid-City Electric Company; Miller Cabinet Company; New Albany Company; N.P. Limited Partnership; Oxford Cleaners, Inc.; Potter Homes Company; R.J. Solove & Associates Management, Inc.; Roofing Wholesale, Inc.; Triangle Real Estate Services, Inc.; The Robert Weiler Company; WM. J. Shaffer Associates.
AGENT FOR: Commonwealth Land Title Insurance Co.
REFERENCE: Bank One of Columbus.

MAGUIRE & SCHNEIDER LLP

Established in 1993

250 CIVIC CENTER DRIVE, SUITE 500
COLUMBUS, OHIO 43215
Telephone: 614-224-1222
Fax: 614-224-1236
URL: http://www.maguire-schneider.com

Cleveland, Ohio Office: 1370 Ontario Street, Suite 1700, 44113. Telephone: 800-600-1222. Fax: 216-274-9808.

Business Litigation, Labor and Employment, Insurance Defense, Directors Liability Errors and Omissions Defense, Real Estate Malpractice Claims, Real Estate, Corporate, Commercial Litigation, Health Care Law, Health Care Fraud and Abuse, Banking Law, Probate and Estate Planning, Family Law, Adoptions, Mediation, White Collar Crime, Criminal Defense, Consumer Law, Administrative Law, Creditor's Rights Law, Financial Institution Law, Intellectual Property, Internet Law, Lemon Law, Product Liability, and Worker's Compensation.

PARTNERS OF FIRM

PATRICK D. MAGUIRE, born Cleveland, Ohio, June 8, 1951; admitted to bar, 1976, Ohio; 1978, U.S. District Court, Southern District of Ohio; 1992, U.S. Court of Appeals, Sixth Circuit. *Education:* Wittenberg University (B.A, 1973); Ohio Northern University (J.D, 1976). Recipient, Outstanding Young Men of America, 1980. Instructor, Business Law, Advanced Litigation for Paralegals, Columbus State Community College, 1979-1989. Lecturer: "How to Avoid Bad Faith Exposure," 1990; Insurance Fraud Seminar, 1994. Director, 1977-1978, Child Support Enforcement Division, Senior Assistant Prosecuting Attorney, 1979-1982, Felony Trial Staff, Franklin County Prosecuting Attorney Office. Managing Attorney, Frutig, Travis & Zapka, Columbus Office, 1988-1991. Managing Partner, Maguire & Schneider, LLP, 1993—. *Member:* Columbus (Member, Managing Partners Group) and Ohio State Bar Associations. ***PRACTICE AREAS:*** Civil Litigation; Personal Injury; Insurance Defense. ***Email:*** pmaguire@ms-lawfirm.com

KARL H. SCHNEIDER, born Columbus, Ohio, May 10, 1957; admitted to bar, 1982, Ohio; 1983, U.S. District Court, Southern District of Ohio; 1990, U.S. Court of Appeals, Sixth Circuit and U.S. Supreme Court; 1995, U.S. District Court, Northern District of Ohio. *Education:* Denison University (B.A., 1979); Capital University (J.D., 1982). Lecturer: To Real Estate Brokers and Trade Associations on subject of Real Estate Malpractice and Directors and Officers Liability. Appointed, Commissioner of the Ohio Court of Claims, 1987. *Member:* Columbus, Ohio State and American Bar Associations. ***PRACTICE***

(This Listing Continued)

MAGUIRE & SCHNEIDER LLP, Columbus—Continued

AREAS: Professional Liability Defense; Real Estate Brokers Malpractice; Commercial Litigation; Banking Litigation; Construction Law; White Collar Crime. ***Email:*** khschneider@ms-lawfirm.com

KEITH W. SCHNEIDER, born Columbus, Ohio, November 19, 1962; admitted to bar, 1989, Ohio; 1991, U.S. District Court, Southern District of Ohio; 1993, Florida; 2003, U.S. Supreme Court. *Education:* Miami University (B.A., 1985); Capital University (J.D., 1989). Order of the Curia. Judicial Law Clerk, Honorable Richard B. Metcalf, Franklin County Probate Court, 1986-1988; Senior Judicial Law Clerk, Honorable George C. Smith, U.S. District Court for the Southern District of Ohio, Eastern Division, 1989-1991. Appointed: Special Master, Federal District Court, Southern District, 1995-2002; Special Counsel, by the Honorable Betty D. Montgomery, Attorney General, 2000-2002; Special Counsel, by the Honorable Jim Petro, Ohio Attorney General, 2002—; The Ohio State University; Ohio University; Lima Technical College nka James A. Rhodes College Bureau of Workers' Compensation; The Rehabilitation Services Commission and Ohio Department of Mental Health; Treasurer's Counsel, by the Honorable Joseph T. Deters, 1998—. Instructor, Paralegal Probate and Practice Course, Columbus State Community College. Speaker, General Litigation Principles and Employment Law, Columbus Bar Association Continuing Legal Education Seminars. Former Associate, Vorys, Sater, Seymour & Pease, Columbus, Ohio. Maguire & Schneider, L.L.P., 1995—. *Member:* American and Ohio State Bar Associations; The Florida Bar; Columbus Bar Association. ***REPORTED CASES:*** Mallory v. Ohio University, 76 Fed.Appx. 634, 181 Ed. Law Rep. 428 (6th Cir. 2003); Das v. Ohio State University, 115 F.Supp.2d 885, 84 Fair Emp.Prac.Case. (BNA) 691, 79 Empl. Prac. Dec. P 40,322; 147 Ed. Law Rep. 975, (2000 S.D. Ohio); Thomson v. Ohio State University Hosp., 5 F.Supp.2d 574, 4 Wage & Hour Cas.2d (BNA) 1139 (1998 S.D. Ohio); Johari v. Big Easy Restaurants, Inc., et al., 78 Fed. Appx. 546 (6th Cir. 2003). ***PRACTICE AREAS:*** Litigation; Complex Litigation; Federal Litigation; Labor and Employment; Employment Litigation; Liquidations; Class Actions; White Collar Crime; Banking Law; Municipal Law; Probate; Real Estate; Administrative Law. ***Email:*** kwschneider@ms-lawfirm.com

BRIAN E. DICKERSON, born Galesburg, Illinois, January 21, 1971; admitted to bar, 1997, Florida and Illinois; 1998, Ohio, U.S. District Court, Middle District of Florida and U.S. District Court, Southern and Northern Districts of Ohio; 2004, U.S. District Court, Northern District of Illinois and Northern and Southern Districts of Indiana and U.S. Supreme Court; 2005, District of Columbia. *Education:* MacMurray College (B.S., 1993); Capital University (J.D., 1996); Ohio University (M.S.A., 1996). Author: "The Evolution of Free Agency in the National Football League: Collective Bargaining Restrictiveness," The Sports Lawyers Journal, 1996. Co-Author: "Corporate Compliance for Handling Litigation Claims," National Food Processors Association Journal, January 2003. Instructor: Seminars on The Admissibility of Evidence, Internet and The Law, Nursing Home Negligence, and White Collar Crime. Formerly with, Florida's 20th Circuit State Attorney's Office, 1996-1998. With, Maguire & Schneider L.L.P., 1998—. *Member:* The Florida Bar; Illinois State, Ohio State, Columbus and American Bar Associations. ***REPORTED CASES:*** In re National City Financial Enterprises, Inc, an Ohio Corporation, Debtors, 292 B.R. 850, 2003 Bankr. LEXIS 442 (S.D. Ohio, 2003); Nike v. Tomba, 8 No. 24 Andrews Intell. Prop. Litig. Rep. 4 Maitland v. Ford Motor Co., 153 Ohio App. 3d 161, 2003 Ohio 3009, 792 N.E.2d 207, 2003 Ohio App. LEXIS 2690 (10th Ohio App. 2003); The Evolution of Free Agency in the National Football League: Collective Bargaining Restrictiveness, The Sports Lawyers Journal, 1996. ***PRACTICE AREAS:*** Litigation; Trademarks; White Collar Crime; Products Liability; Tax Evasion; Money Laundering; RICO; Securities; Fraud. ***Email:*** bdickerson@ms-lawfirm.com

WAYNE HASSAY, born Youngstown, Ohio, February 13, 1967; admitted to bar, 1991, Ohio; 1992, U.S. District Court, Northern District of Ohio and U.S. Court of Appeals, Sixth Circuit. *Education:* Youngstown State University (B.A., 1988); University of Akron (J.D., 1991). Attorney, Chuparkoff & Associates, 1991-1995; Betras & Dann, 1995-1998. Maguire & Schneider, 1998—. Commentator, Personal Injury and Tort Matters, WKBN Radio and Television, 1995-1998. *Member:* Columbus and Ohio State Bar Associations. ***REPORTED CASES:*** Herald v. Hood, 70 Ohio St.3d 1210, 639 N.E.2d 109 (Ohio, 1994). ***PRACTICE AREAS:*** Personal Injury; Torts; Products Liability; Civil Litigation. ***Email:*** whassay@ms-lawfirm.com

BRADLEY D. BARBIN, born Johnstown, Pennsylvania, February 2, 1957; admitted to bar, 1983, Pennsylvania; 1998, Ohio; 2000, Florida. *Education:* Randolph-Macon College (B.A., 1979); The University of Akron School of Law (J.D., 1983). Former AUSA, Pittsburgh, Pennsylvania and Columbus, Ohio, 1984-1995. Criminal Justice Director to Ohio Attorney General Betty D. Montgomery, 1995-2000. Former Special Counsel to Florida Attorney Generals Robert Butterworth and Charlie Crist. Part-time Special Counsel to Florida Attorney General Charlie Crist. *Member:* Columbus, Cambria County (Pennsylvania), Ohio State and Federal (Member, Columbus Chapter; Former President, Columbus Chapter) Bar Associations. ***PRACTICE AREAS:*** Business Law; Labor and Employment; Insurance Defense; Real Estate; Corporate Law; Commercial Litigation; Health Care Fraud; Banks and Banking; Probate; Family Law; White Collar Crime; Criminal Defense; Consumer Law; Administrative Law; Creditors Rights; Financial Institutions Law; Intellectual Property; Internet Law; Products Liability; Workers Compensation; Directors Liability Errors and Omissions Defense; Adoption. ***Email:*** bbarbin@ms-lawfirm.com

ASSOCIATES

GARY D. ANDORKA, born Lorain, Ohio, July 22, 1961; admitted to bar, 1986, Ohio; 1987, U.S. District Court, Southern District of Ohio; 1987, U.S. District Court, Northern District of Ohio; 1988, U.S. Court of Appeals, Sixth Circuit. *Education:* University of Toledo (B.A., 1983); The Ohio State University (J.D., 1986). Formerly with: Gary D. Andorka, Attorney at Law, 1987; The Ohio Attorney General's Office, Federal Litigation/Criminal Justice/Corrections Litigation Section, 1988-1996; Franklin County Public Defender's Office, 1996-1997; Maguire & Schneider, L.L.P., 1997—. *Member:* Columbus Bar Association. ***PRACTICE AREAS:*** Civil Litigation; Criminal Defense; Traffic Violations; Law Enforcement; Civil Rights; Family Law. ***Email:*** gandorka@ms-lawfirm.com

DONALD SCOTT ANDREWS, born Defiance, Ohio, 1971; admitted to bar, 1998, Ohio. *Education:* University of Toledo (B.B.A, Accounting, 1993); Capital University (J.D., 1998; LL.M., Taxation, 1999). Formerly with, Deloitte & Touche, 1999-2000. *Member:* Columbus and Ohio State Bar Associations. ***PRACTICE AREAS:*** Tax Law; Small Business Law; Landlord and Tenant Law; General Practice. ***Email:*** dandrews@ms-lawfirm.com

(This Listing Continued)

NIVITA BHALLA, born Sioux Falls, South Dakota, April 16, 1974; admitted to bar, 2000, Illinois; 2003, Ohio. *Education:* The Ohio State University (B.B.A., Business Administration, 1996); John Marshall Law School (J.D., 1999). ***LANGUAGES:*** Hindi. ***PRACTICE AREAS:*** Contracts; Consumer Finance; Business; White Collar Crime. ***Email:*** nbhalla@ms-lawfirm.com

CHRISTOPHER G. BLACK, admitted to bar, 1997, Ohio; U.S. District Court, Southern and Northern Districts of Ohio. *Education:* Capital University (B.A., 1993); Capital University Law School (J.D., 1997). Purcell & Scott Co., LPA, 1998-2001. Maguire & Schneider, L.L.P., 2001—. *Member:* Columbus, Ohio State and American Bar Associations. ***PRACTICE AREAS:*** Mergers and Acquisitions; Corporate Law; Secured Transactions; Real Property; Trademarks; Copyrights; Litigation. ***Email:*** cblack@ms-lawfirm.com

SHARLENE I. CHANCE, born Georgetown, Guyana, South America, January 21, 1972; admitted to bar, 1999, Ohio; 2000, U.S. District Court, Southern District of Ohio. *Education:* Capital University (B.A., Political Science and Criminology, 1994); Capital University Law School (J.D., 1999). Judicial Law Clerk to The Honorable Cynthia C. Lazarus, 10th District Court of Appeals, 2001-2005. Assistant City Attorney, Environmental Division, Franklin County Municipal Court, 1999-2001. *Member:* Columbus (CBA) and National (Member, Columbus Affiliate Chapter) Bar Associations; John Mercer Langston Bar Association (JMLBA). [U.S. Army Reserve, Honorable Discharge, 1997]. ***PRACTICE AREAS:*** Business Litigation; Labor and Employment; Insurance Defense; Real Estate; Corporate Law; Commercial Litigation; Health Care; Health Care Fraud; Banks and Banking; Probate; Family Law; Criminal Defense; Consumer Law; Administrative Law; Creditors Rights; Financial Institutions Law; Intellectual Property; Internet Law; Products Liability; Workers Compensation; Directors Liability Errors and Omissions Defense; Adoption; Lemon Law. ***Email:*** schance@ms-lawfirm.com

TRICIA L. CLARKE, born Dayton, Ohio, November 21, 1977; admitted to bar, 2004, Ohio. *Education:* The Ohio State University (B.A., Sociology and Criminology, 2001); Capital University Law School (J.D., 2004). Order of the Curia. Magistrate, Morrow County Municipal Court. *Member:* Columbus and Ohio State Bar Associations. ***PRACTICE AREAS:*** Business Litigation; Labor and Employment; Insurance; Real Estate; Corporate Law; Commercial Litigation; Health Care; Health Care Fraud; Banks and Banking; Probate; Family Law; White Collar Crime; Intellectual Property; Internet Law; Products Liability; Workers Compensation; Directors Liability Errors and Omissions Defense; Adoption; Administrative Law. ***Email:*** tclark@ms-lawfirm.com

KATHLEEN A. DEYOUNG, born Detroit, Michigan, February 7, 1960; admitted to bar, 1999, Ohio. *Education:* University of Detroit Mercy (B.A., 1984; J.D., 1987). Nationwide Insurance Company, Oh., 1999-2001; Maguire & Schneider, L.L.P., 2001—. *Member:* Ohio State and Columbus Bar Associations. ***PRACTICE AREAS:*** Consumer Law; Finance; Collections; Landlord and Tenant Law; Traffic Violations. ***Email:*** kdeyoung@ms-lawfirm.com

WILLIAM C. DONAHUE, born Youngstown, Ohio, November 10, 1943; admitted to bar, 1970, Ohio; 1979, U.S. District Court, Southern District of Ohio; 1984, Texas. *Education:* Denison University (B.A., 1966); The Ohio State University (J.D., 1969; M.S., 1974). Squire, Sanders & Dempsey, 1974-1982; Houston Lighting & Power Company, 1982-1991; Trans American Natural Gas Corporation, 1992-1994; Mazer & Company, 1995-1997. With, Maguire & Schneider, L.L.P., 1997—. *Member:* Ohio State Bar Association; State Bar of Texas. ***LANGUAGES:*** French. ***PRACTICE AREAS:*** Commercial Litigation; Personal Injury; Workers Compensation; Employment Law; Professional Malpractice; Public Utility Law; Oil and Gas Litigation. ***Email:*** wdonahue@ms-lawfirm.com

JODI L. DOZER, born Columbus, Ohio, September 1, 1972; admitted to bar, 1997, Ohio. *Education:* Franklin University (B.S., 1994); Capital University Law School (J.D., 1997). Instructor, Business Law I and II, Torts and Insurance Law, Real Estate Transactions for the Paralegal, Zane State College. Employment: Ohio Civil Rights Commission, 1995; Maguire & Schneider, L.L.P., 1996—. *Member:* Columbus Bar Association. ***PRACTICE AREAS:*** Personal Injury; General Practice; Probate. ***Email:*** jdozer@ms-lawfirm.com

YSIDRO EDWARD DURAN, born Toledo, Ohio, September 6, 1960; admitted to bar, 1986, Ohio; 1987, U.S. District Court, Northern District of Ohio; 2001, U.S. District Court, Southern District of Ohio. *Education:* University of Toledo (B.A., cum laude, 1982); University of Notre Dame (J.D., M.B.A., 1986). Employment: Sole Practitioner, 1986-1989; Toledo Legal Aid Society, 1989-1990; GM-UAW Legal Services Plan, 1990-1999; Maguire & Schneider, L.L.P., 2000—. ***LANGUAGES:*** Spanish. ***PRACTICE AREAS:*** Domestic Relations; Wills; Probate; Traffic Violations; General Practice. ***Email:*** eduran@ms-lawfirm.com

THOMAS S. ERLENBACH, born Helena, Montana, August 7, 1935; admitted to bar, 1960, Ohio; 1963, U.S. District Court, Southern District of Ohio. *Education:* Ohio Wesleyan University (B.A., 1957); Ohio Northern University (J.D., 1960). Instructor, Columbus Police Academy. Private Practice, 1960-1964 and 1972-1997. Prosecutor, Columbus City, 1964-1972; Maguire & Schneider, L.L.P., 1997—. *Member:* Columbus and Ohio State Bar Associations. ***PRACTICE AREAS:*** Criminal Defense; Traffic Violations; Workers Compensation; Personal Injury. ***Email:*** terlenbach@ms-lawfirm.com

THOMAS J. GALLAGHER, born Cleveland, Ohio, March 29, 1951; admitted to bar, 1985, Ohio; 1990, U.S. District Court, Northern District of Ohio; 1994, U.S. District Court, Southern District of Ohio. *Education:* Miami University (B.A., 1973; MEn., 1977); University of Idaho (J.D., 1985). Author, "Gambling with Financial Assurance," Environmental Law Journal of Ohio. Lecturer, "Underground Storage Tank Regulations," for Ohio State Bar Association, Ohio, West Virginia and Kentucky Chambers of Commerce and Ohio Society of CPAs, 1988-1991. Instructor, Environmental Regulations and Hazardous Waste Management, Columbus State Community College. Employment: Ohio Attorney General, 1986-1991; Private Practice, 1992-1997; Maguire & Schneider, L.L.P., 1997—. ***PRACTICE AREAS:*** Probate; Estate Planning; Real Estate; Environmental Law; Zoning, Planning and Land Use; Administrative Law. ***Email:*** tgallagher@ms-lawfirm.com

(This Listing Continued)

RICHARD S. GERBER, born Victoria, Texas, December 4, 1954; admitted to bar, 1984, Ohio; U.S. Tax Court; U.S. Court of Appeals, Sixth Circuit; U.S. District Court, Northern and Southern Districts of Ohio. *Education:* The Ohio State University (B.S., Business Administration., 1979); Capital University Law School (J.D., 1984; LL.M. in Taxation, 1988). Chair, Business Transactional Group. *Member:* Columbus, Ohio State and American (Member, Tax Section) Bar Associations. ***PRACTICE AREAS:*** Business Litigation; Labor and Employment; Insurance Defense; Real Estate; Corporate Law; Commercial Litigation; Health Care; Health Care Fraud; Banks and Banking; Probate; Family Law; White Collar Crime; Criminal Defense; Consumer Law; Administrative Law; Creditors Rights; Financial Institutions Law; Intellectual Property; Internet Law; Products Liability; Workers Compensation; Directors Liability Errors and Omissions Defense; Adoption. ***Email:*** rgerber@ms-lawfirm.com

ROBERT H. GRIFFIN, JR., born Philadelphia, Pennsylvania, March 8, 1960; admitted to bar, 1985, Ohio and U.S. Court of Appeals, Sixth Circuit; 1986, U.S. District Court, Southern District of Ohio. *Education:* Miami University (A.B., 1982); Capital University (J.D., 1985). Phi Alpha Delta. Business Manager, Capital University Law Review, 1984-1985. Associate, Fry & Waller Co., L.P.A., Columbus, Oh., 1985-1986. Formerly with, Meridian Reserve, Inc., Columbus, Oh., 1986-1987. General Counsel, AEI Holdings, Inc., Columbus, Oh., 1989-1992. Private Practice, 1993-1996. Maguire & Schneider, L.L.P., 1996—. *Member:* Columbus, Ohio State (Member, Corporation Law Committee) and American Bar Associations. ***PRACTICE AREAS:*** Small Business Law; Estate Planning; Probate; Real Estate; Business Law; Business Formation; Business Organization; Business Planning; Business Start-Ups; Business Transfers; Commercial Law; Commercial Transactions. ***Email:*** rgriffin@ms-lawfirm.com

JOHN H. HIX, born Springfield, Ohio, June 16, 1945; admitted to bar, 1970, Ohio. *Education:* University of Chicago (B.A., 1967); University of Illinois (J.D., 1970). Assistant County Prosecutor, Marion County, 1972-1976. Acting Municipal Judge, Marion Municipal Court, 1980-1988. City Law Director, Marion, 1988-1992. Administrative Law Judge, SPBR, 1992-1993. Deputy Director, ODMRDD, 1993-1996. Formerly with Department of Agriculture (Ohio), 1996-2005. Retired from state service, 2005. *Member:* Columbus Bar Association. [U.S. Air Force, 1971-1972]. ***PRACTICE AREAS:*** Business Litigation; Labor and Employment; Insurance Defense; Real Estate; Corporate Law; Commercial Litigation; Health Care; Health Care Fraud; Banks and Banking; Probate; Family Law; White Collar Crime; Criminal Defense; Consumer Law; Administrative Law; Creditors Rights; Financial Institutions Law; Intellectual Property; Internet Law; Products Liability; Workers Compensation; Directors Liability Errors and Omissions Defense; Adpotion; Lemon Law. ***Email:*** jhix@ms-lawfirm.com

D. TIMOTHY HUGHES, born Newark, Ohio, February 19, 1955; admitted to bar, 1984, Ohio and Colorado (inactive); 1992, U.S. District Court, Northern District of Ohio. *Education:* Kent State University (B.B.A., 1978); Cleveland Marshall College of Law (J.D., 1983). Author: "The UN Convention on the International Sale of Goods: A Comparison with the Uniform Commercial Code," Business Laws, Inc. (1988); "Application and Exceptions to the UCC Statute of Frauds," Electronic Commerce Magazine (1992). Instructor, Presented more than 300 one and two day seminars for major corporations. *Member:* American Bar Association. ***PRACTICE AREAS:*** Commercial Transactions; Consumer Law; Small Business Law; Technology Law; Intellectual Property Rights; Construction Law; Insurance; Real Estate; Corporate Law; Internet Law; Employment Law; Franchise Law. ***Email:*** thughes@ms-lawfirm.com

STEVEN R. HUGHES, born Mount Vernon, Ohio, November 24, 1952; admitted to bar, 1983, Ohio and U.S. District Court, Southern District of Ohio; 1984, California; 1986, Nevada and U.S. District Court, Central District of California; 1987, U.S. Court of Appeals, Ninth Circuit; 1988, U.S. Supreme Court. Private Practice, 1983-1985, 1994-1995. Formerly with, Law Offices of Michael Singer, 1985-1994.; Childers & Dickerson, 1990-1993. Judge Pro Tem, Los Angeles Municipal Court, 1988-1994. With, Maguire & Schneider, L.L.P., 1995—. ***PRACTICE AREAS:*** General Practice; Consumer Law; Criminal Law. ***Email:*** shughes@ms-lawfirm.com

DAVID G. KORN, born Columbus, Ohio, May 14, 1951; admitted to bar, 1976, Ohio; 1980, U.S. District Court, Southern District of Ohio; 1998, U.S. District Court, Northern District of Ohio. *Education:* Miami University (B.A., with honors, 1973); University of Cincinnati (J.D., 1976). Publications: "How to get Results in Collection of Delinquent Debts in Ohio" (N.B.I. 1996); "Complying with the Fair Debt Collection Practices Act in Ohio" (N.B.I. 1997); "Bankruptcy Update" (Lorman Education Services, 1997); "How to Get Results in Collection of Delinquent Debts in Ohio" (N.B.I. 1997); "Ohio Bankruptcy Update" (Lorman Education Services, 1999); "How to Get Results in Collection of Delinquent Debts in Ohio" (N.B.I. 2000). Assistant Prosecuting Attorney, Franklin County, 1976-1981. Formerly with: Weltman, Weinberg and Associates Company, L.P.A., 1981; M.D. Cohen Company, L.P.A., 1981-1983. Sole Practitioner, 1983-2000. Assistant General Counsel, Value Recovery Group, 2000-2001. Maguire & Schneider, L.L.P., 2001—. *Member:* Columbus and Ohio State Bar Associations. ***PRACTICE AREAS:*** Bankruptcy; Debtor and Creditor; Finance; Real Estate. ***Email:*** dkorn@ms-lawfirm.com

EMERY J. LEUCHTAG, born Cleveland, Ohio, May 4, 1944; admitted to bar, 1983, Ohio; 1989, U.S. District Court, Northern District of Ohio. *Education:* University of Akron (B.S., cum laude, 1965); Indiana University School of Medicine, Department of Pharmacology and Toxicology (Graduate School Research and Studies in Toxins), 1967; University of Bologna School of Medicine (M.D., summa cum laude, 1980); University of Akron (J.D., 1983). Guest Lecturer: "Medical/Legal Issues in Family Law," University of Akron School of Law, 1983-1986. Hanover Lectures, "Medical/Legal Issues, Good Faith Claims Handling," 1986-1989. Sponsor and Participant, Seminar: "Good Faith Claims Practices," May 1990; "Medical Ethics and Euthanasia, Sierra Club, 1993. Formerly with, Ferrari Corporation, Ferrara, Italy, 1969-1980. Assistant Team Physician, Bologna Soccer Club, 1980. Private Practice, 1983-1986. Casualty/Litigation Manager, Beacon/American Insurance Company, 1986-1989. Gallagher, Sharpe, Fulton and Norman, 1989-1992; Zapka and Leuchtag, 1992-1997; Maguire & Schneider, L.L.P., 1997—. *Member:* Federal Bar Association; Cleveland Association of Civil Trial Attorneys. ***PRACTICE AREAS:*** Personal Injury Litigation; Insurance; Casualty Insurance; Medical Malpractice; Bankruptcy. ***Email:*** eleuchtag@ms-lawfirm.com

ANDREA E. MARTIN, born Belvedere, Illinois, October 2, 1956; admitted to bar, 1982, Ohio. *Education:* Ohio State University (B.A., 1978); Capital Law School (J.D., 1982). Instructor, Academy of Court Reporting, 1996-2001. Sole Practitioner, 1982-2001. With, Maguire & Schneider, L.L.P., 2001—. ***PRACTICE AREAS:*** Family Law; Real Estate; Consumer Law; Small Business Law. ***Email:*** amartin@ms-lawfirm.com

MATTHEW F.G. MARTIN, born Haddonfield, New Jersey, 1963; admitted to bar, 1991, Ohio; 1994, U.S. District Court, Southern District of Ohio. *Education:* Ohio State University (B.A., 1985); Case Western Reserve University (J.D., 1991). Law Clerk, Ward & Associates, 1989-1991; Instructor and Dean of Legal Studies, The Academy of Court Reporting, 1992-1997; Private Practice, Martin Law Offices, 1991-1997; Associate Attorney, Maguire & Schneider, L.L.P., 1997—. *Member:* Columbus Bar Association. ***PRACTICE AREAS:*** Bankruptcy; Consumer Law; Business Law; Commercial Law; Internet Law. ***Email:*** mmartin@ms-lawfirm.com

TED P. McCLATCHEY, born Columbus, Ohio, December 7, 1952; admitted to bar, 1994, Ohio; 1995, U.S. District Court, Southern District of Ohio. *Education:* The Ohio State University (B.S., 1980); Capital University Law School (Paralegal Certificate, 1983; J.D., 1993). Private Practice, 1994-1995. Formerly with, Calig & Handelman, Attorneys at Law, 1995-1997; U.A.W. Legal Services, 2000-2001; Weltman, Weinberg & Reis, 2001-2002. With, Maguire & Schneider, L.L.P., 1997-2000 and 2002—. ***REPORTED CASES:*** In re Ashworth, 227 B.R. 801 (S.D. Ohio 1998); In re Reaster, 242 B.R. 423 (S.D. Ohio 1999). ***PRACTICE AREAS:*** Bankruptcy; Consumer Law; Domestic Relations; Creditors Rights. ***Email:*** tmcclatchey@ms-lawfirm.com

PATRICIA L. MOORE, born Newark, Ohio, January 16, 1957; admitted to bar, 1991, Ohio; 1992, U.S. District Court, Southern District of Ohio. *Education:* The Ohio State University (B.S.L.H.R., 1982); Capital University (J.D., 1990). Participant, Judge in State Final Moot Court Competitors; Staff and Managing Attorney, Central Ohio Legal Aid Society, Newark, Lancaster and Logan offices, 1991-1998. Maguire & Schneider, L.L.P., 1998—. *Member:* Licking County and Hocking County Bar Associations. ***PRACTICE AREAS:*** Family Law; Bankruptcy; Traffic Violations; Consumer Law. ***Email:*** pmoore@ms-lawfirm.com

BRICE O. RECKER, born Lima, Ohio, December 31, 1948; admitted to bar, 1990, Ohio and U.S. District Court, Northern District of Ohio; 1991, U.S. Claims Court; 1992, U.S. District Court, Southern District of Ohio. *Education:* Bluffton College (B.A., 1980); Case Western Reserve University, Weatherhead School of Management (M.B.A., 1986); Ohio Northern University, Claude W. Pettit College of Law (J.D., 1990). Adjunct Instructor: Business and Management, Northwestern College; Management Information Systems, Tiffin University. Private Solo Practice, 1990-1997. Maguire & Schneider, L.L.P., 1997—. ***PRACTICE AREAS:*** General Practice; Bankruptcy; Consumer Law.

MANBIR S. SANDHU, admitted to bar, 2000, Ohio and U.S. District Court, Northern District of Ohio. *Education:* University of Akron (B.A., 1995); Thomas M. Cooley Law School (J.D., 2000). *Member:* Cleveland, Cuyahoga County and Ohio State Bar Associations. ***PRACTICE AREAS:*** Foreclosures; Collections; Bankruptcy; Creditors Rights; Evictions; Litigation. ***Email:*** msandhu@ms-lawfirm.com

JONATHAN R. SECREST, born Columbus, Ohio, July 27, 1976; admitted to bar, 2002, Ohio; 2003, U.S. District Court, Southern District of Ohio and U.S. Court of Appeals, Sixth Circuit. *Education:* DePauw University (B.A., 1999); Capital University (J.D., 2002). Order of the Curia. Maguire & Schneider, L.L.P., 2002—. *Member:* Columbus, Ohio State (Member, Sections on: Litigation; Labor and Employment) and American Bar Associations. ***REPORTED CASES:*** Johari v. Big Easy Restaurants, Inc., et al., 78 Fed. Appx. 546 (6th Cir. 2003). ***PRACTICE AREAS:*** Labor and Employment; Litigation; Administrative Law; Products Liability; General Practice. ***Email:*** jsecrest@ms-lawfirm.com

TRICIA A. SPRANKLE, born Sugarcreek, Ohio, December 30, 1969; admitted to bar, 1999, Ohio; 2000, West Virginia and U.S. District Court, Southern District of West Virginia; 2001, U.S. Tax Court; 2002, U.S. District Court, Southern District of Ohio. *Education:* Wittenberg University (B.A., 1992); Capital University Law School (J.D., 1999; LL.M, 1999). *Member:* Columbus, Ohio State (Member, Unauthorized Practice of Law Committee) and American (Member, Taxation Section) Bar Associations. ***PRACTICE AREAS:*** Federal Taxation; State Taxation; Local Taxation; Estate Planning; Corporate Litigation; Tax Exempt Organizations. ***Email:*** tsprankle@ms-lawfirm.com

JAMES G. VARGO, born Youngstown, Ohio, August 25, 1969; admitted to bar, 1997, Ohio; 1998, U.S. District Court, Northern District of Ohio; 1999, U.S. District Court, Southern District of Ohio; 2004, U.S. Court of Appeals, Sixth Circuit. *Education:* Youngstown State University (B.S., 1992); University of Akron School of Law (J.D., magna cum laude, 1997). Baker & Hostetler, LLP, 1998-2002; Private Practice, 2002-2003. Maguire & Schneider, L.L.P., 2003—. *Member:* Ohio State and Akron Bar Associations. ***PRACTICE AREAS:*** Business Litigation; Criminal Defense; Consumer Law; Eminent Domain; Appellate Practice; Personal Injury. ***Email:*** jvargo@ms-lawfirm.com

PHILLIP LAWRENCE WRIGHT, JR., born Nashville, Tennessee, December 20, 1969; admitted to bar, 2000, Ohio and U.S. District Court, Southern District of Ohio. *Education:* University of California at Los Angeles (B.A., 1994); Capital University (J.D., 1999). Case Law Summaries Editor, Lexis Nexis, 1999-2000; Assistant Attorney General, State of Ohio, 2000-2004; Maguire & Schneider, 2004—. *Member:* Columbus and Ohio Bar Associations. ***PRACTICE AREAS:*** Civil Litigation; Labor and Employment; Sports Law; Entertainment Law; Workers Compensation. ***Email:*** pwright@ms-lawfirm.com

OF COUNSEL

ROBERT CARL SCHULER, born Cincinnati, Ohio, June 25, 1963; admitted to bar, 1990, Ohio; 1993, U.S. District Court, Southern District of Ohio and U.S. Court of Appeals, Sixth Circuit. *Education:* Miami University (B.A., 1985); Capital University (J.D., 1990). *Member:* Columbus, Cincinnati, Ohio State and American Bar Associations. ***PRACTICE AREAS:*** Litigation; Government Relations; Administrative Law; Telecommunications Law. ***Email:*** rschuler@ms-lawfirm.com

MARK W. KOEHLER, born Columbus, Ohio, June 8, 1959; admitted to bar, 1993, Ohio. *Education:* Franklin University (B.S. in Business Administration, 1982); Capital University Law School (J.D., 1992). Certified Public Accountant, 1987. Senior Financial Analyst, Ross Laboratories, 1987-1995. Private Practice, 1994. *Member:* Ohio State Bar

(This Listing Continued)

MAGUIRE & SCHNEIDER LLP, Columbus—Continued

Association; National Academy of Elder Law Attorneys. ***PRACTICE AREAS:*** General Practice; Estate Planning; Elder Law; Probate; Trust Law; Small Business Law; Tax Law; Medicaid Planning. ***Email:*** mkoehler@ms-lawfirm.com

ROBERT P. FREED, born Akron, Ohio, February 25, 1957; admitted to bar, 2003, Ohio. *Education:* Ohio State University and Mt. Vernon Nazarene University (B.B.A., 1998); The American College (M.S., 1998); Capital University Law School (J.D., 2003). Certified Employee Benefit Specialist (CEBS), The Wharton School of Business. McCloy Financial Services, 1981—. Of Counsel, Maguire & Schneider, 2004—. *Member:* Columbus and American Bar Associations. ***PRACTICE AREAS:*** Employee Benefits; ERISA; Estate Planning; Probate. ***Email:*** bfreed@ms-lawfirm.com

MALEK & MALEK

1227 SOUTH HIGH STREET
COLUMBUS, OHIO 43206
Telephone: 614-444-7440
Fax: 614-444-8836
URL: http://www.maleklawoffice.com

Workers Compensation, Personal Injury, Railroad Accidents and Injuries, Automobile Accidents and Injuries, Wrongful Death, Dog Bites.

FIRM PROFILE: Experienced workers compensation attorneys, with over 40 years combined experience representing injured workers.

EDWIN LeROY MALEK, born 1939; admitted to bar, 1969, Ohio. *Education:* Capital University (J.D., 1969). *Member:* Columbus Bar Association. ***PRACTICE AREAS:*** Workers Compensation; Personal Injury; Railroad Accidents and Injuries; Automobile Accidents and Injuries; Wrongful Death; Dog Bites. ***Email:*** ed@maleklawfirm.com

JAMES EDWIN MALEK, born 1965; admitted to bar, 1995, Ohio. *Education:* Cleveland State University (J.D., 1995). *Member:* Columbus Bar Association. ***PRACTICE AREAS:*** Workers Compensation; Personal Injury; Railroad Accidents and Injuries; Automobile Accidents and Injuries; Wrongful Death; Dog Bites. ***Email:*** jim@maleklawfirm.com

MANLEY • DEAS • KOCHALSKI LLC

495 SOUTH HIGH STREET, SUITE 300
COLUMBUS, OHIO 43215
Telephone: 614-220-5611
Fax: 614-220-5613
URL: http://www.mdk-llc.com

Real Estate, Mortgages, Foreclosures, Loss Mitigation, Creditors Rights, Bankruptcy, Evictions, Landlord and Tenant Law, Title Service, Mortgage Servicing, Real Estate Development Closings.

FIRM PROFILE: Manley Deas Kochalski LLC an Ohio limited liability company, represents banks, savings and loan companies, mortgage servicing companies, and other lenders. We focus exclusively on residential real estate foreclosures and related bankruptcy and title matters and practice exclusively in this area so that we can dedicate our resources to your foreclosure and bankruptcy portfolios and your legal needs.

MEMBERS OF THE FIRM

THEODORE K. MANLEY, born Richmond, Virginia, April 26, 1964; admitted to bar, 1992, Ohio; 1995, U.S. District Court, Southern District of Ohio; 1998, Kentucky and U.S. District Court, Northern District of Ohio; 1999, U.S. District Court, Eastern and Western Districts of Kentucky; 2000, West Virginia and U.S. District Court, Southern District of West Virginia. *Education:* Kenyon College (A.B., cum laude, History, 1986); The Ohio State University College of Law (J.D., 1992). Member, Creditor Education Soalition. *Member:* Columbus (Member, Bankruptcy Law Committee), Ohio State (Member, Continuing Legal Education Faculty) and Kentucky Bar Association; Mortgage Bankers Association. ***PRACTICE AREAS:*** Bankruptcy; Foreclosures; Consumer Lending; Litigation; Creditors Rights. ***Email:*** tkm@mdk-llc.com

BRIAN T. DEAS, born Daytona Beach, Florida, April 16, 1966; admitted to bar, 1993, Ohio. *Education:* Miami University (B.S., Accounting, 1988); The Ohio State University (J.D., with honors, 1993). Editor in Chief, The Ohio State Law Journal. Certified Public Accountant. Law Clerk: Honorable J. Craig Wright, Justice of the Supreme Court of Ohio; Honorable John D. Holschuh, United States District Court, Southern District of Ohio. *Member:* Columbus, Ohio State and American Bar Associations; Mortgage Bankers Association. ***PRACTICE AREAS:*** Real Estate Litigation; Foreclosures; Creditors Rights; Finance; Mortgage Banking Law. ***Email:*** btd@mdk-llc.com

EDWARD M. KOCHALSKI, born Buffalo, New York, June 8, 1950; admitted to bar, 1975, Ohio. *Education:* State University of New York at Buffalo (B.A., Speech Communication, 1972); University of Toledo College of Law (J.D., 1975). Licensed Title Agent. Former Senior Counsel, Lawyers Title Insurance Company. *Member:* Columbus (Member, Real Property Committee) and Ohio State (Member, Real Property Committee) Bar Associations; Mortgage Bankers Association. ***PRACTICE AREAS:*** Complex Real Estate Litigation; Foreclosures; Real Estate. ***Email:*** emk@mdk-llc.com

LAURA L. DRAKE, born Des Moines, Iowa, January 24, 1970; admitted to bar, 1997, Indiana; 1998, Ohio; 1999, Illinois; 2000, Kentucky; U.S. District Court, District of Ohio. *Education:* Indiana University, Bloomington (B.A., 1992); Institut International des Etudes Français, Strasbourg, France (Premier Degré, 1991); University of Minnesota School of Law (J.D., cum laude, 1997). Recipient: Young Leader Award, AAUW/Ohio, 2003-2004. Volunteer, Board of Directors: Cincinnati Brand; Ohio State Board of the American Association of University Women. *Member:* Louisville, Cincinnati, Kentucky, Indiana State and Ohio State Bar Associations. ***LANGUAGES:*** French and German. ***PRACTICE AREAS:*** Creditors Rights; Bankruptcy; Real Estate; Foreclosures; Evictions. ***Email:*** lld@mdk-llc.com

HOLLY N. WOLF, born Dayton, Ohio, December 10, 1971; admitted to bar, 1997, Ohio; 1998, U.S. District Court, Northern and Southern Districts of Ohio. *Education:* University of Dayton (B.A., magna de latta, Political Science, Spanish, 1994); The Ohio State University College of Law (J.D., 1997). Member, Michael F. Colley National Mock Trial Team. *Member:* Columbus and Ohio State (Member, Bankruptcy Committee) Bar Associations. ***LANGUAGES:*** Spanish. ***PRACTICE AREAS:*** Bankruptcy; Real Estate Litigation; Litigation; Creditors Rights; Foreclosures; Commercial Collections; Consumer Collections.

RACHEL A. LEIER, born Worcester, Massachusetts, May 8, 1971; admitted to bar, 1999, Ohio; 2000, U.S. District Court, Southern District of Ohio; 2004, U.S. District Court Northern District of Ohio. *Education:* The Ohio State University (B.A., Anthropology, 1994; J.D., 1999). Recipient: Best Oralist Award, National Juvenile Law moot Court Competition, Costa Mesa, California. *Member:* Columbus and Ohio State Bar Associations. ***PRACTICE AREAS:*** Real Estate Litigation; Commercial Collections; Consumer Collections; Bankruptcy; Foreclosures; Consumer Loans; Litigation; Creditors Rights.

KEVIN LANE WILLIAMS, born Wooster, Ohio, January 6, 1961; admitted to bar, 1993, Ohio; 1994, U.S. District Court, Southern District of Ohio. *Education:* Kenyon College (A.B., magna cum laude, English, 1983); Ohio State University College of Law (J.D., with honors, 1993). Managing Editor, Ohio State Law Journal. Law Clerk: Honorable Sandra S. Beckwith, United States District Judge, Southern District of Ohio; Honorable Thomas J. Moyer, Chief Justice, Ohio Supreme Court. Former Assistant Disciplinary Counsel. *Member:* Columbus and Ohio State Bar Associations. ***PRACTICE AREAS:*** Real Estate; Litigation; Foreclosures; Creditors Rights; Mortgage Banking Law. ***Email:*** williamk@sconet.state.oh.us

DAVID F. HANSON, born Chagrin Falls, Ohio, February 14, 1965; admitted to bar, 1992, Ohio; 1994, U.S. District Court, Southern and Northern Districts of Ohio; 1996, U.S. Supreme Court. *Education:* Kenyon College (B.A., with distinction, 1987); Ohio State University College of Law (J.D., 1992). Adjunct Professor, Wilmington College. *Member:* Ohio State Bar Association (Member, Federal Courts Committee). ***PRACTICE AREAS:*** Civil Litigation; Federal Practice.

REPRESENTATIVE CLIENTS: Ameriquest; Centex; CitiCorp; CitiFinancial Mortgage, Inc.; Eastern Savings Bank; EMC Mortgage; Fidelity; Fifth Third; East Horizon; First Tennessee; GMAC Mortgage, Inc.; Green Tree Servicing; Homecomings; HomEq; Huntington; JP Morgan Chase; KeyBank; National City Mortgage; National City Home Loans; NovaStar; Ocwen; Saxon; Select Portfolio Servicing; Washington Mutual; Wendover.

MARQUARDT & WHITE CO., LPA

COLUMBUS, OHIO

(See Dublin)

Personal Injury, Automobile Accidents, Negligence, Wrongful Death, Motorcyle Accidents, Dog Bites, Slip and Fall, Medical Malpractice, Wills and Trusts.

MASON LAW FIRM CO., L.P.A.

425 METRO PLACE NORTH, SUITE 620
COLUMBUS, OHIO 43017
Telephone: 614-734-9450
Fax: 614-734-9451
Email: rmason@maslawfirm.com
URL: http://www.maslawfirm.com

Representing and Advising Management in Labor and Employment Law, including Wrongful Termination, Employment Discrimination, Sexual Harassment, Americans with Disabilities Act, Family and Medical Leave Act, Wage and Hour Law, NLRB cases and Collective Bargaining, Unemployment Benefits, Employee Privacy Rights, OSHA, Railroad Law.

RONALD L. MASON, born Huntington, West Virginia, May 16, 1951; admitted to bar, 1978, Ohio; 1979, U.S. District Court, Southern and Northern Districts of Ohio; 1982, Georgia and U.S. District Court, Southern, Middle and Northern Districts of Georgia; 1994, U.S. Supreme Court and U.S. Court of Appeals, Fourth, Sixth and Eleventh Circuits. *Education:* Ohio Dominican College (B.A., 1975); University of Dayton (J.D., summa cum laude, 1978); Georgetown University (LL.M., in Labor Law, 1981). Author: "The Non-Board Settlement Agreement: An Analysis of the Power of the General Counsel to Reinstate a Withdrawn Charge," 31 Case Western Reserve Law Review 509, 1981, reprinted in 33 Labor Law Journal 328, 1982; "Collective Bargaining Agreements Without Arbitration Clauses: Does the Finality Doctrine Bar Section 301 Suits?" 7 University of Dayton Law Review 387, 1982. Attorney: Montgomery County Prosecutor's Office, Dayton, Ohio, 1978-1980; National Labor Relations Board, 1980-1982. *Member:* Columbus, Ohio State (Member, Labor and Employment Law Section) and American (Member, Committee on Practice and Procedure Under the National Labor Relations Act) Bar Associations; State Bar of Georgia. ***PRACTICE AREAS:*** Management Labor Law; Employment Law. ***Email:*** rmason@maslawfirn.com

OF COUNSEL

DAVID S. TIMMS, born Akron, Ohio; admitted to bar, 1999, Ohio; U.S. District Court, Southern and Northern Districts of Ohio; U.S. Court of Appeals, Third, Sixth and Tenth Circuits. *Education:* University of Akron (B.A., magna cum laude, 1995); Georgetown University (J.D., 1999). Ohio Assistant Attorney General, 1999-2002. *Member:* Columbus, Ohio State and American Bar Associations. ***PRACTICE AREAS:*** Management Labor Law; Employment Law; Litigation; Constitutional Law. ***Email:*** dtimms@maslawfirm.com

(This Listing Continued)

NICOLE FLYNN, born Monroe, Michigan, July 1, 1976; admitted to bar, 2001, Ohio; U.S. District Court, Southern and Northern Districts of Ohio. *Education:* Western Michigan University (B.A., Finance, magna cum laude, 1998); The Ohio State University (J.D., 2001). Formerly with, Kegler, Brown, Hill & Ritter, 2001-2003. *Member:* Columbus, Ohio State and American Bar Associations. ***PRACTICE AREAS:*** Management Labor Law; Employment Law; Litigation. ***Email:*** nflynn@maslawfirm.com

REPRESENTATIVE CLIENTS: Associated Builders and Contractors, Inc.; Anderson Concrete Corp.; Accurate Electric Construction; Brush Contractors, Inc.; Crown Equipment Corp.; Crawford Mechanical Services, Inc.; Ellis Brothers Concrete; Columbus Limestone, Inc.; Converse Electric, Inc.; DeFabco, Inc.; Forum Manufacturing, Inc.; Jess Howard Electric Co.; National Stair Corp.; Oberfield's, Inc.; Ohio Central Railroad System; The Columbus & Ohio River Rail Road Co.; Youngstown & Austintown, Inc.; Ohio Southern Railroad, Inc.; Ohio & Pennsylvania Railroad Co.; The Warren & Trumbull Railroad Co.; Pittsburgh & Ohio Central Railroad, Co.; The Youngstown Belt Railroad Co.; Mahoning Valley Railway Co.; Pike Community Hospital; Pierce Township; State-Wide Concrete Pumping; The Shelly Company; Palmer Donavin Manufacturing, Inc.; Ross-Co Redi-Mix Co., Inc.; Sandel Corp.; Stoneco, Inc.; Jones Fuel Co.; Oldcastle Materials, Inc.; Oldcastle APG Midwest, Inc.

MASON, SCHILLING & MASON CO., L.P.A.

Established in 1973

460 EAST MAIN STREET
COLUMBUS, OHIO 43215-5398
Telephone: 513-489-0829
1-800-840-3514
Fax: 513-489-0834
Email: msm@mason-law.com
URL: http://www.mason-law.com

Covington, Kentucky Office: Heritage International, Suite 203, P.O. Box 2158. Telephone: 513-489-0829. Fax: 513-489-0834.
Cincinnati Office: 11340 Montgomery Road, Suite 210. Telephone: 513-489-0829, 800-840-3514. Fax: 513-489-0834.
Dayton Office: 319 Liberty Tower. Telephone: 513-489-0829. Fax: 513-489-0834.
Lima Office: P.O. Box 937. Telephone: 513-489-0829. Fax: 513-489-0834.
Madison, Indiana Office: 201 East Main Street. Telephone: 513-489-0829. Fax: 513-489-0834.

Commercial, Creditors Rights, Bankruptcy, Collection, Banking and Financial Institution Law, Civil Litigation, Federal Consumer Law Litigation, Foreclosures, Automobile Deficiencies, Credit Cards, Medical Debts, Bad Checks, Business Loans/Commercial Debt, Vehicle and Property Repossessions, Landlord Representation/Evictions/Lease Litigation, Equipment Leasing.

FIRM PROFILE: Mason, Schilling & Mason Co., L.P.A., since its founding over 30 years ago, exclusively concentrates in the areas of creditor representation, in all aspects of commercial litigation, banking law, leasing law, bankruptcy law, and creditors' rights law.

We have developed a full service staff of attorneys in all aspects of representation to the credit granting community. Our legal services concentrate exclusively on representing creditors in all facets of legal representation concerning credit management and credit granting, commercial law, and bankruptcy law on behalf of the credit management community.

Further, of particular attention, is the providing of legal services to the banking and credit management community throughout the entire States of Ohio and Kentucky. Our attorneys appear in all State and federal courts in both states.

The value of our law firm rests with the dependable level of service that we provide to all creditor-clients. We pride ourselves in the personalized service and the conscientious follow through that has been a trade mark throughout over three decades of providing legal services to our creditor and banking clients.

(For Complete Biographical Data on all Personnel, see Professional Biographies at Cincinnati, Ohio)

MATAN, GEER & WRIGHT

Established in 1973

261 SOUTH FRONT STREET
COLUMBUS, OHIO 43215
Telephone: 614-228-2678
Fax: 614-228-6122
URL: http://www.mgwlawoffice.com
URL: http://www.mgwlawfirm.com

General Trial and Appellate Practice. Commercial, Negligence, Personal Injury, Automobile Accidents, Products Liability, Medical Malpractice, Wrongful Death, Corporation, Family, Divorce, Child Custody, Child Support, Premarital Agreements, Insurance, Wills and Probate, Criminal Defense, Driving While Intoxicated and Employment Discrimination.

MEMBERS OF FIRM

EUGENE L. MATAN, born Chicago, Illinois, 1931; admitted to bar, 1958, Ohio; 1959, U.S. Tax Court and U.S. District Court, Southern District of Ohio; 1961, U.S. Court of Appeals, Sixth Circuit; 1980, U.S. Supreme Court; 1988, Florida. *Education:* The Ohio State University (B.A., 1953; J.D., summa cum laude, 1958). Phi Alpha Delta; Phi Alpha Theta. Associate Editor, The Ohio State University Law Journal, 1957-1958. Lecturer in Evidence and Negligence Law. *Member:* Columbus, Ohio State and American Bar Associations; The Florida Bar; The Association of Trial Lawyers of America; Ohio Academy of Trial Lawyers; Franklin County Trial Lawyers Association; American Society of Law and Medicine; American College of Forensic Examiners; American Board of Professional Liability Attorneys (Board Certified Diplomate). Fellow: Ohio State Bar Foundation; Columbus Bar Foundation. (Certified as a Civil Trial Advocate by the National Board of Trial Advocacy). ***PRACTICE AREAS:*** Trial Practice; Appellate Practice; Medical Malpractice; Products Liability Law; Personal Injury; Civil Practice. ***Email:*** ematan@mgwlaw.com

CHRISTOPHER J. GEER, born Topeka, Kansas, 1948; admitted to bar, 1978, Ohio; 1979, U.S. Court of Appeals, Sixth Circuit. *Education:* The Ohio State University (B.A., Education, 1977); Capital University (J.D., 1977). Co-Author: "Family Law Practice in Ohio." *Member:* Columbus, Ohio State and American Bar Associations; Franklin County Trial Lawyers Association; The Association of Trial Lawyers of America. ***PRACTICE AREAS:*** Domestic Relations; Family Law; Probate Administration; Trial Practice. ***Email:*** cgeer@mgwlaw.com

SCOTT E. WRIGHT, born Columbus, Ohio, August 25, 1962; admitted to bar, 1989, Ohio, U.S. District Court, Southern District of Ohio and U.S. Court of Appeals, Sixth Circuit; 1990, District of Columbia; 1994, U.S. Supreme Court. *Education:* The Ohio State University (B.S., 1984); Capital University (J.D., 1989). *Member:* Columbus, Licking County, Ohio State and American Bar Associations; The District of Columbia Bar; Ohio Academy Trial Lawyers; Franklin County Trial Lawyers; American Agricultural Law Institute; The Association of Trial Lawyers of America. ***PRACTICE AREAS:*** Personal Injury Law; Medical Malpractice; General Practice; Civil Litigation; Products Liability Law. ***Email:*** swright@mgwlaw.com

ROBERT DEAN NOBLE, born Columbus, Ohio, September 18, 1963; admitted to bar, 1988, Ohio. *Education:* The Ohio State University (B.A., 1985); University of Toledo (J.D., 1987). *Member:* Columbus Bar Association; Ohio Association of Criminal Defense Lawyers; National Association of Criminal Defense Lawyers. ***PRACTICE AREAS:*** Trial Practice; Appellate Practice; Personal Injury; Domestic Relations; Criminal Defense; Administrative Law; Employment Law. ***Email:*** rnoble@mgwlaw.com

REPRESENTATIVE CLIENTS: Available Upon Request.

MAZANEC, RASKIN & RYDER CO., L.P.A.

SUITE 400
250 CIVIC CENTER DRIVE
COLUMBUS, OHIO 43215
Telephone: 614-228-5931
Fax: 614-228-5934
Email: mrrlaw.com
URL: http://www.mrrlaw.com

Cleveland, Ohio Office: 100 Franklin's Row, 34305 Solon Road 44139. Telephone: 440-248-7906. Fax: 440-248-8861.

Civil Litigation, Insurance Defense, Construction Law, Negligence, Professional Negligence, Municipal Law, Civil Rights, Real Estate, Business Law, Probate, Estate Planning.

ROBERT H. STOFFERS, born San Francisco, California, June 29, 1957; admitted to bar, 1982, Ohio; 1985, U.S. District Court, Northern District of Ohio; 1989, Illinois and U.S. District Court, Southern District of Ohio; 1994, U.S. Court of Appeals, Sixth Circuit and U.S. Supreme Court. *Education:* Otterbein College (B.A., 1979); University Of Toledo College of Law (J.D., 1982). *Member:* Cleveland, Ohio State and American Bar Associations; Ohio Association of Civil Trial Attorneys; Defense Research Institute. ***REPORTED CASES:*** Freas v. Prater Constr. Corp., Inc. (1991), 60 Ohio St. 3d 61; Didler v. Johns (1996), 114 Ohio App. 3d 746; Arthur Young & Co. v. Kelly (1990), 68 Ohio App. 3d 287; Korodi v. Minot (1987), 40 Ohio App. 3d 1; State v. Berger (1984), 17 Ohio App. 3d 8. ***PRACTICE AREAS:*** Construction Law; Insurance; Insurance Defense; Litigation; Negligence; Products Liability; Professional Liability; Torts; Transportation. ***Email:*** rstoffers@mrrlaw.com

DAVID K. FRANK, born Piqua, Ohio, December 25, 1948; admitted to bar, 1974, Ohio; 1975, U.S. District Court, Southern District of Ohio, U.S. Court of Military Appeals and U.S. Tax Court; 1976, U.S. Supreme Court; 1983, U.S. Supreme Court; 1986, U.S. Court of Appeals, Sixth Circuit; 1995, U.S. District Court, Northern District of Ohio; 2002, U.S. Court of Appeals for Veteran's Claims. *Education:* Miami University (B.A., cum laude, 1971); The Ohio State University (M.A., Public Administration, 1974; J.D., 1974). *Member:* Columbus and Ohio State Bar Associations; Franklin County Trial Lawyers Association; American Health Lawyers Association; The Association of Trial Lawyers of America. [USAF and USAFR, 1973-1997, retired as Lt. Col., Staff Judge Advocate, 910th Airlift Wing]. ***REPORTED CASES:*** *U.S. Supreme Court:* Zauderer v. Disciplinary Counsel of the Supreme Court of Ohio, 471 U.S. 626 (1985) [a landmark case involving commercial speech]. *Ohio Supreme Court:* Horton v. Harwick Chem. Corp., 73 Ohio St. 3d 679 (1995). *Ohio Court of Appeals:* American Modern Homes Ins. Co. v. Hagopian, 2003-OHIO-342 (3 Dist.); Bennett v. Pullins, 2002-OHIO-3560 (2 Dist.); Midwestern Indemnity Co. v. Savage, 149 Ohio App.3d 596 (2002); Shannon v. Johnson & Hughes Excavating Co., 2002-OHIO-7350 (10 Dist.); Bayes v. Knudson, 95 LW 0351 (1995); Midwestern Indemnity Co. v. Craig, 106 Ohio App.3d 158 (1995); Tonti v. Mar-Kett 91 LW 1813 (10 Dist. 1991). ***PRACTICE AREAS:*** Appellate Practice; Complex Litigation; Class Action Litigation; Disability Insurance; Administrative Law; Constitutional Law. ***Email:*** dfrank@mrrlaw.com

---

CARL E. CORMANY, born Massillon, Ohio, November 16, 1954; admitted to bar, 1980, Ohio; 1983, U.S. District Court, Northern District of Ohio; 1985, U.S. Court of Appeals, Sixth Circuit; 1986, U.S. Court of Appeals, Seventh Circuit. *Education:* Miami University (A.B., cum laude, 1977); University of Michigan Law School (J.D., 1980). ***PRACTICE AREAS:*** Civil Litigation; Insurance Defense; Labor and Employment; Municipal Law; Appellate Practice. ***Email:*** ccormany@mrrlaw.com

MICHAEL S. LOUGHRY, born Houston, Texas, April 2, 1969; admitted to bar, 2001, Ohio. *Education:* University of Texas at Austin (B.A., 1991); Capital University Law School (J.D., 2001). ***Email:*** mloughry@mrrlaw.com

(For complete biographical data personnel, at Cleveland, see that location)

(This Listing Continued)

JOHN J. McCARROLL

COLUMBUS, OHIO

(See Cleveland)

Victims Rights, Personal Injury, Bankruptcy, Business Law, Probate, Criminal Defense, Immigration Law.

McDONALD HOPKINS CO., LPA

Established in 1921

41 SOUTH HIGH STREET, SUITE 3650
COLUMBUS, OHIO 43215
Telephone: 614-458-0025
Fax: 614-458-0028
Email: info@mcdonaldhopkins.com
URL: http://www.mcdonaldhopkins.com

West Palm Beach, Florida Office: McDonald Hopkins Co., PA, One Clearlake Centre, 250 Australian Avenue S., Suite 700, 33401-5007. Telephone: 561-472-7510. Fax: 561-472-2975.

Dennis, Massachusetts Office: 956 Main Street, 02638. Telephone: 508-385-5227. Fax: 508-385-4355.

Cleveland, Ohio Office: 600 Superior Avenue, E., Suite 2100, 44114-2653. Telephone: 216-348-5400. Telecopier: 216-348-5474.

General Civil Trial and Appellate Practice. Corporate, Taxation, Pension and Profit Sharing, Professional Corporations, Insurance, Securities, Estate Planning, Probate, Real Estate, Family Law, Banking, Partnership, Employment and Labor Relations, Equipment Leasing, Bankruptcy, Communications, Computer Law, Health and Hospital Law.

Richard C. Farrin
Thomas M. Zaino

STEPHEN K. HALL, born Columbus, Ohio, 1971; admitted to bar, 1997, Ohio. *Education:* The Ohio State University (B.A., 1993; J.D., 1997); Capital University (LL.M., Taxation, 2000). ***PRACTICE AREAS:*** State Taxation. ***Email:*** shall@mcdonaldhopkins.com

VINCENT J. NARDONE, born Monghela, Pennsylvania, 1970; admitted to bar, 1996, Ohio; U.S. District Court, Southern District of Ohio, U.S. Court of Appeals, Sixth Circuit, U.S. Tax Court and U.S. Supreme Court. *Education:* Duquesne University (B.S., Business Administration, 1993); Capital University (J.D., cum laude, 1996; LL.M., Taxation, 1997). ***PRACTICE AREAS:*** Tax Controversies; Nonprofit Organizations Law; Corporate Governance; Corporate Investigations. ***Email:*** vnardone@mcdonaldhopkins.com

(For complete biographical data on all personnel, see Professional Biographies at Cleveland, Ohio)

McFADDEN WINNER AND SAVAGE

175 SOUTH THIRD STREET, SUITE 210
COLUMBUS, OHIO 43215-5134
Telephone: 614-221-8868
Telecopier: 614-221-3985

Business and Commercial Litigation, Bankruptcy, Employment, Discrimination, Tax and White Collar Criminal Defense, Appellate Advocacy, Complex Personal Injury.

FIRM PROFILE: McFadden Winner and Savage concentrates on providing cost-effective litigation services to publicly and privately-held corporate clients. The firm has extensive experience at all levels of the Ohio courts system as well as in the United States District and Bankruptcy Courts for the Southern District of Ohio and the Sixth Circuit Court of Appeals. Since its inception in 1990, McFadden, Winner and Savage has prided itself on providing the quality of service expected from the largest firms with the responsive and cost-effective service that characterizes the best small law firms. References will be provided upon request.

MEMBERS OF FIRM

MARY JANE McFADDEN, born Columbus, Ohio, November 18, 1950; admitted to bar, 1974, Ohio; 1977, U.S. District Court, Southern District of Ohio; 1978, U.S. Court of Appeals, Sixth Circuit; 1986, U.S. Tax Court and U.S. Supreme Court. *Education:* The Ohio State University (B.A., 1971); University of Virginia (J.D., 1974). Trial Attorney, Antitrust Division, U.S. Department of Justice, 1974-1976. Assistant U.S. Attorney, Southern District of Ohio, 1977-1980. Special Assistant U.S. Attorney, Northern District of California, 1980-1981. Ohio Elections Commissioner, 1988-1989. Member, Judicially Appointed Committee to Revise Local Rules of the Southern District of Ohio, 1985-1997. *Member:* Columbus, Ohio State and Federal (President, Columbus Chapter, 1995-1996) Bar Associations; Million Dollar Advocates Forum. ***REPORTED CASES:*** In re special Grand Jury Investigation Concerning Organic Technologies, 84 Ohio St. 3d 304 (1999); State v. Conrad, 50 Ohio St. 3d 1 (1989); Ohio Dental Hygienists v. Ohio State Dental Board, 21 Ohio St. 2nd 321 (1986). ***PRACTICE AREAS:*** Commercial Litigation; White Collar Criminal Defense; Administrative Law; Civil Rights; Employment Discrimination; Sexual Harassment Law. ***Email:*** m_mcfadden@earthlink.net

JOSEPH C. WINNER, born Circleville, Ohio, September 7, 1949; admitted to bar, 1976, Ohio; 1977, U.S. District Court, Southern District of Ohio; 1980, U.S. Court of Appeals, Sixth Circuit. *Education:* Purdue University (B.S., Ch.E., with highest distinction, 1971); The Ohio State University (J.D., summa cum laude, 1976). *Member:* Columbus (Member, Bankruptcy Committee) and Ohio State (Member, Banking, Commercial and

(This Listing Continued)

Bankruptcy Law Committee) Bar Associations. ***REPORTED CASES:*** Master Consolidated Corp. v. BancOhio National Bank, 61 Ohio St. 3d 570 (1991). ***PRACTICE AREAS:*** Bankruptcy Law; Commercial Litigation. ***Email:*** jcwinner@earthlink.net

JAMES S. SAVAGE, III, born Pittsburgh, Pennsylvania, 1956; admitted to bar, 1981, Ohio, U.S. District Court, Southern District of Ohio; 1982, U.S. District Court, Northern District of Ohio; 1984, U.S. Court of Appeals, Sixth Circuit. *Education:* Duke University (B.A., magna cum laude, 1978); Washington University (J.D., 1981). *Member:* Columbus (Member, Court of Common Pleas, Committees; Construction), Ohio State (Member, Construction Subcommittee) and American (Member, Construction Litigation) Bar Associations; Million Dollar Advocates Forum. ***REPORTED CASES:*** Royal Electric Construction Corp. v. Ohio State University, 73 Ohio St. 3d 110 (1995). ***PRACTICE AREAS:*** Commercial Litigation; Construction Law; Wrongful Death Law. ***Email:*** jssavage@earthlink.net

ASSOCIATE

DOUGLAS JAY SEGERMAN, born Cincinnati, Ohio, March 23, 1970; admitted to bar, 1995, Ohio, U.S. District Court, Southern District of Ohio. *Education:* University of Cincinnati (B.B.A., cum laude, 1992; J.D., 1995). *Member:* Columbus (Construction Law Committee), Ohio State (Construction Law Subcommittee) and American Bar Associations; American Institute of Certified Public Accountants. ***PRACTICE AREAS:*** Commercial Litigation; Construction Law. ***Email:*** djsegerman@earthlink.net

REPRESENTATIVE CLIENTS: Cryobiology, Inc.; John Deere Company; Deere Credit Services, Inc.; Dick Masheter Ford, Inc.; DMF of Ohio, Inc.; Fields Excuvating, Inc.; The Ohio Dental Hygienist Association, Inc.; McDaniel's Construction Corp.; McGinnis & Associates, Inc.; Orkin Exterminating Company, Inc.; Real Property Management, Inc.; Reproductive Diagnostics; The Guernsey Bank.

McGRATH & BREITFELLER, LLP

Established in 1985

140 EAST TOWN STREET, SUITE 1070
COLUMBUS, OHIO 43215
Telephone: 614-464-4201
Facsimile: 614-464-0572
Email: trmcgrath@attymail.com

Real Estate Title Insurance, Real Estate Litigation, Federal State and Local Taxation, Tort Liability, Business Litigation, Corporate Litigation, Health Care Law, Pharmacy Law, Antitrust, Contract Litigation, Employment Law, Creditors Rights, Probate Administration and Estate Planning. Civil Litigation and Civil Appeals. General Practice in State and Federal Courts.

FIRM PROFILE: McGrath & Breitfeller, LLP concentrates in the area of general litigation. The firm practices in all Courts in the State offering an array of legal services, including local appellate and federal litigation practice.

THOMAS R. McGRATH, born Columbus, Ohio; admitted to bar, 1974, Ohio, U.S. District Court, Northern and Southern Districts of Ohio, U.S. Tax Court, U.S. Court of Appeals, Sixth Circuit and U.S. Supreme Court. *Education:* Ohio State University (B.A., 1969); Capital University School of Law (J.D., 1974). *Member:* Columbus, Ohio State and American (Member, Sections on: Title Insurance Committees of Real Property; Torts and Insurance Practices) Bar Associations; Ohio State Bar Association College. ***PRACTICE AREAS:*** Civil Litigation; Real Estate Litigation; Real Estate Title Insurance; Corporate Litigation; Contract Litigation. ***Email:*** trmcgrath@attymail.com

RALPH E. BREITFELLER, born Columbus, Ohio, November 7, 1953; admitted to bar, 1978, Ohio; 1979, U.S. District Court, Southern District of Ohio; 1984, U.S. District Court, Northern District of Ohio. *Education:* Providence College (B.A., cum laude, 1975); Georgetown University (J.D., 1978). Assistant Attorney General, Antitrust Section, Ohio Attorney General's Office, 1978-1983. Assistant Chief, Antitrust Section, Ohio Attorney General's Office, 1981-1983. *Member:* Columbus (Chairman, Federal Court Committee, 1991-1992), Ohio State (Chairman, Federal Court Committee, 1995-1997; Member, Board of Governors, Antitrust Section, 2000—) and Federal (President, Columbus Chapter, 1994-1995) Bar Associations. ***PRACTICE AREAS:*** Litigation; Antitrust; Employment Law; Health Care Law; Pharmacy Law. ***Email:*** rbreitfeller@ee.net

REPRESENTATIVE CLIENTS: First American Title Insurance Co.; LandAmerica Company; Fidelity National Title Insurance Co.; Chicago Title Insurance Co.; T.A. Title Insurance Co.; Columbus Micro Systems, Inc.
REFERENCES: National City Bank; Park National Bank.

LAW OFFICES OF CHARLES A. McKINNEY

141 EAST TOWN STREET, SUITE 102
COLUMBUS, OHIO 43215
Telephone: 614-460-9000
Fax: 614-460-9001
Email: camlaw@woh.rr.com

Dayton, Ohio Office: 20 West Monument Avenue, 45402. Telephone: 937-461-9000. Fax: 937-461-9640.

Corporate Law, Business Planning, Contracts, Insurance, Lawsuits, Labor (Management) Law, Personal Injury Law, Automobile Accidents, Dog Bites, Sexual Abuse, Slip and Fall, Trusts and Estates, Estate Planning Law, Guardianship, Wills and Probate, Wrongful Death, Civil Litigation, Buying or Selling a Business, Formation, Closely Held Business, Limited Liability Companies, Partnerships, Small Business, Employment Law, Disability Accommodations, Discrimination, Sexual Harassment, Wrongful Termination.

(For complete biographical data on all personnel, see Professional Biographies at Dayton, OH)

WAYMON B. McLESKEY II

Established in 1997

FIVE EAST LONG STREET, SUITE 405
COLUMBUS, OHIO 43215
Telephone: 614-232-9132
Fax: 614-232-9135
Email: mcleskeylaw@aol.com
URL: http://www.mcleskeylaw.com

Creditor Bankruptcy, Foreclosures, Workouts, Collections, Replevins, Creditor Rights, Commercial Litigation.

FIRM PROFILE: Waymon B. McLeskey II is an attorney with more than twenty two years experience concentrating in the Creditors Rights field. He has substantial experience in Creditor Bankruptcy, Replevins, Collections (both Commercial and Consumer), Workouts and Commercial Litigation for financial institutions, finance companies and other corporations. He is licensed to practice in all Ohio Courts, The United States District Courts for the Northern and Southern Districts of Ohio, The United States Bankruptcy Court in each district, and the Sixth Circuit Court of Appeals. He is a third generation attorney in Columbus and often makes seminar presentations in Commercial Law, Creditors Rights, Bankruptcy and related topics. Each client receives personal attention and can expect their concerns to be handled in a prompt and professional manner.

WAYMON B. McLESKEY, II, born Columbus, Ohio, December 17, 1953; admitted to bar, 1981, Ohio; 1982, U.S. District Court, Southern District of Ohio; 1990, U.S. District Court, Northern District of Ohio; 2001, U.S. Court of Appeals, Sixth Circuit; 2004, U.S. District Court, Eastern and Western Districts of Kentucky, Kentucky Supreme Court. *Education:* Yale University (B.A., 1976); Brown University (A.M., 1977); Emmanuel College, Cambridge University (University of Richmond); Ohio Northern University (J.D., 1981). Former Attorney, Porter, Wright, Morris & Arthur, 1984-1997. *Member:* Columbus (Member, Bankruptcy, Professionalism and Small Firms Committees), Ohio State (Member, Banking, Commercial and Bankruptcy Law Committee) and American (Member, Business Law Section) Bar Associations. ***REPORTED CASES:*** Huntington National Bank v. Elkins, 43 Ohio App.3d 64 (Franklin County, 1987); Bank One, Dayton N.A., v. Doughman, 59 Ohio App.3d 60 (Hamilton County, 1988); Logan v. Bank America Housing Services (In Re DeLong), 273 B.R. 141 (Bkrtcy. S.D. Ohio, 2001); Huntington National Bank v. Hall, 1985 Ohio App. LEXIS 8805 (Franklin County Ct. App. 1985). ***PRACTICE AREAS:*** Creditor Bankruptcy; Foreclosures; Workouts; Collections; Replevins; Creditor Rights; Commercial Litigation.

McNAMARA AND McNAMARA, L.L.P.

Established in 1948

SUITE 1250, 88 EAST BROAD STREET
COLUMBUS, OHIO 43215-3558
Telephone: 614-228-6131
FAX: 614-228-6126
Email: mcnamaralaw@mcnamaralaw.us

General Civil and Trial Practice. Fidelity and Surety, Insurance, Negligence, Products Liability, Construction, Administrative, Appellate Practice, Business Law, Probate and Real Estate Law.

FIRM PROFILE: Founded in 1948 by J. Paul McNamara, Our firm was built on the tradition of providing the highest quality legal representation for our clients and that is a tradition that we uphold today. We focus primarily in the areas of Insurance, Fidelity and Surety, Negligence and Products Liability, and our practice has a large geographic scope.

MEMBERS OF FIRM

J. PAUL McNAMARA (1908-1994)

WILLIAM H. WOODS, born Toledo, Ohio, May 30, 1946; admitted to bar, 1973, Ohio. *Education:* The Ohio State University (B.S., 1968; J.D., cum laude, 1973). Author: "Conditions to Recovery: Notice Proof of Loss and Timeliness of Filing Suit," Bankers and Other Financial Institution Blanket Bonds, American Bar Association, 1979; "Defenses Based Upon Contractual Requirements for Timely Filling of Suit in Fidelity Cases," 17 Forum 1291, 1982; "Defenses and Remedies of the Financial Institution Bond Surety in the 1980's," Financial Institution Bond Litigation, American Bar Association, 1988; "Conditions to Recovery: Notice, Proof of Loss and Timeliness of Filing Suit," Financial Institution Bonds, American Bar Association, 1st. ed., 1992, 2nd ed. 1998; "Historical Development of Suretyship," American Bar Association, 1st. ed., 1993, 2nd ed., 2000. *Member:* Columbus, Ohio State and American (Member, Sections of: Tort and Insurance Practice; Vice Chairman, Fidelity and Surety Law Committee, 1986-1991, 1993-1998) Bar Associations. ***PRACTICE AREAS:*** Litigation; Fidelity and Surety; Insurance; Directors and Officers Liability; Construction.

DENNIS D. LISTON, born Hawarden, Iowa, February 24, 1944; admitted to bar, 1974, Ohio and U.S. District Court, Southern and Northern Districts of Ohio; 1982, U.S. Court of Appeals, Sixth Circuit. *Education:* University of Iowa (B.A., 1965); The Ohio State University (J.D., cum laude, 1973). Member, Ohio State Law Journal, 1972-1973. *Member:* Columbus, Ohio State and American (Member, Section of Tort and Insurance Practice) Bar Associations. [Capt., USAF, 1966-1971]. ***PRACTICE AREAS:*** Fidelity and Surety; Insurance; Negligence; Products Liability; Construction.

JONATHAN M. BRYAN, born Canfield, Ohio, August 25, 1970; admitted to bar, 1995, Ohio; 1996, U.S. District Court, Northern and Southern Districts of Ohio; 2001, U.S. Court of Appeals, Sixth Circuit. *Education:* Youngstown State University (B.A., magna cum laude, 1992); The Ohio State University (J.D., with honors, 1995). Adjunct Professor, Legal Writing Program, Ohio State University College of Law, 1999-2002. *Member:* Columbus, Ohio State and American Bar Associations. ***PRACTICE AREAS:*** Fidelity and Surety; Insurance; Business; Civil Practice.

(This Listing Continued)

OF COUNSEL

KEITH McNAMARA, born Upper Sandusky, Ohio, October 12, 1928; admitted to bar, 1953, Ohio. *Education:* Amherst College (B.A., 1950); The Ohio State University (J.D., 1953). Member, House of Representatives, Ohio General Assembly, 1961-1972. Member, Board of Directors, State Justice Institute, 1990—. Chairman, Ohio Board of Bar Examiners, 1994-1995; Member, Franklin County Board of Elections, 1993-2003. Chairman, Ohio Liquor Control Commission, 2003-2009. *Member:* Columbus, Ohio State (Member, Legal Ethics Committee, 1966—) and American Bar Associations. ***PRACTICE AREAS:*** Legislation; Appellate; Trade Associations.

JOHN L. MILLER, born Akron, Ohio, August 13, 1934; admitted to bar, 1963, Ohio. *Education:* Harvard College (A.B., 1956); The Ohio State University (J.D., 1963). Phi Delta Phi. ***PRACTICE AREAS:*** Negligence; Products Liability; Insurance.

SCOTT F. STURGES, born Rockville Centre, New York, June 9, 1951; admitted to bar, 1982, Ohio and U.S. District Court, Southern District of Ohio; 1995, U.S. Tax Court; 1999, U.S. Court of Appeals, Sixth Circuit. *Education:* Ohio Wesleyan University (B.A., 1973); Miami University (M.A., 1980); The Ohio State University (J.D., 1982). *Member:* Columbus, Ohio State and American Bar Associations; Lawyer-Pilots Bar Association. ***PRACTICE AREAS:*** Administrative Law; Appellate Practice; Aviation Law; Business Law; Fidelity and Surety; Labor Law.

MICHAEL R. SZOLOSI, SR., born Toledo, Ohio, November 30, 1944; admitted to bar, 1969, Ohio; 1971, U.S. District Court, Southern District of Ohio and U. S. Court of Appeals, Sixth Circuit; 1977, U.S. Supreme Court; 1979, U.S. District Court, Northern District of Ohio. *Education:* University of Toledo (B.A., 1966); Ohio State University (J.D., 1968). *Member:* Columbus, Ohio State and American Bar Associations. ***PRACTICE AREAS:*** Civil Business Litigation. ***Email:*** mrs@mcnamaralaw.us

REPRESENTATIVE CLIENTS: Cincinnati Insurance Co.; Cumis Insurance Society, Inc.; Firemans Fund Insurance Cos.; Hartford Accident & Indemnity Co.; Kemper Insurance Group; Ohio Casualty Insurance Co.; The Safeco Cos.; St. Paul Fire & Marine Insurance Co.; Travelers Insurance Co.; The Westfield Cos.; Zurich North America.

McNEES WALLACE & NURICK LLC

FIFTH THIRD CENTER, 17TH FLOOR
21 EAST STATE STREET
COLUMBUS, OHIO 43215-4228
Telephone: 614-469-8000
Fax: 614-469-4653
Email: info@mwn.com
URL: http://www.mwn.com

Harrisburg, Pennsylvania Office: 100 Pine Street, P.O. Box 1166, 17108. Telephone: 717-232-8000. Fax: 717-237-5300.
Washington, D.C. Office: Suite 401, 777 North Capitol, N.E., 20002. Telephone: 202-898-5700. Fax: 202-898-0688.
Hazleton, Pennsylvania Office: 1 South Church Street, Suite 302, 18201. Telephone: 570-455-8300. Fax: 570-455-8390.
State College, Pennsylvania Office: 1600 University Drive, 16801. Telephone: 814-867-8500. Fax: 814-867-6200.
Lancaster, Pennsylvania Office: 180 Good Drive, 17603. Telephone: 717-291-1177. Fax: 717-291-2186.

Energy Law, Communications Law, Utility Law, Government Relations.

FIRM PROFILE: McNees Wallace & Nurick, established in 1935, is a firm of over 100 attorneys headquartered in Harrisburg, Pennsylvania. While based in the capital city, our practice represents clients which operate locally, regionally and nationally. With additional offices in Columbus, Ohio, Hazelton, PA, State College, PA, Lancaster, PA and Washington, DC, the practice includes all areas of commercial practice and civil litigation. Our attorneys represent businesses, banks, insurance companies, trade associations, hospitals, public and private nonprofit institutions and individuals.

MEMBER OF THE FIRM

SAMUEL C. RANDAZZO, born 1949; admitted to bar, 1975, Ohio and U.S. District Court, Southern District of Ohio; 1976, U.S. Court of Appeals for the District of Columbia Circuit; 1987, U.S. Supreme Court. *Education:* University of Akron (B.S., 1971); Capital University (J.D., 1975). (Resident). ***PRACTICE AREAS:*** Communications Law; Energy Law; Public Utility Law. ***Email:*** srandazzo@mwncmh.com

RESIDENT OF COUNSEL

THOMAS L. FROEHLE, admitted to bar, 1993, Ohio. *Education:* Ohio Dominican College (B.A., 1989); Capital University (J.D., 1993). ***PRACTICE AREAS:*** Government Relations; Energy; Communications Law; Utility Law. ***Email:*** tfroehle@mwncmh.com

GRETCHEN J. HUMMEL, born 1947; admitted to bar, 1979, Ohio. *Education:* Ohio University (A.B., 1968; M.A., 1973); Capital University (J.D., 1979). ***PRACTICE AREAS:*** Utility Regulation; Energy Deregulation; Energy Marketing. ***Email:*** ghummel@mwncmh.com

ASSOCIATES

LISA G. McALISTER, admitted to bar, 2002, Ohio. *Education:* Elon University (B.A., magna cum laude, 1999); Michael E. Moritz College of Law, The Ohio State University (J.D., 2002). Delta Theta Phi. ***PRACTICE AREAS:*** Energy; Utility Law; Communications Law; Regulatory Energy Practice. ***Email:*** lmcalister@mwncmh.com

DANIEL J. NEILSEN, admitted to bar, 2003, Ohio. *Education:* University of Maryland (B.S., 1999); The Ohio State University (J.D., 2003). (Resident). ***PRACTICE AREAS:*** Energy; Communications; Utility Law. ***Email:*** dneilsen@mwncmh.com

MEANS, BICHIMER, BURKHOLDER & BAKER CO., L.P.A.

Established in 1962

2006 KENNY ROAD
COLUMBUS, OHIO 43221-3502
Telephone: 614-485-2010
Fax: 614-485-2019
Email: mail@mbbblaw.com

Antitrust, Estate Planning, Probate, Trust, Pension and Profit Sharing, Taxation, Corporate, Creditor's Rights, Insurance, Real Estate, Construction Litigation, Labor, Employment, Civil Rights, and School Law.

ROBERT G. STAFFORD, born Columbus, Ohio, December 30, 1938; admitted to bar, 1968, Ohio; 1971, U.S. Tax Court; 1978, U.S. Supreme Court. *Education:* The Ohio State University (B.E.E., 1961); Capital University (J.D., 1968). Phi Eta Sigma. Member, Order of The Curia. Member, Adjunct Faculty, Capital University Law School, 1973-1980. *Member:* Columbus and Ohio State Bar Associations; Ohio Society of Professional Engineers (Recipient of Outstanding Service Award, 1977); National Society of Professional Engineers. ***PRACTICE AREAS:*** Probate; Corporate; Insurance; Pension and Profit Sharing; Estate Planning.

CRAIG D. LEISTER, born Alliance, Ohio, December 25, 1949; admitted to bar, 1974, Ohio; 1975, U.S. Court of Appeals, Sixth Circuit; 1976, U.S. District Court, Southern District of Ohio; 1977, U.S. District Court, Northern District of Ohio; 1978, U.S. Supreme Court; 1986, U.S. Tax Court. *Education:* Bowling Green State University (B.S., cum laude, 1971); Duke University (J.D., 1974). Beta Gamma Sigma; Phi Kappa Phi. Lecturer, Columbus Tax Conference. *Member:* Columbus (Member: Taxation Committee; Probate Committee) and Ohio State (Member, Probate and Trust Law Section) Bar Associations. [Lt., JAGC, USNR, 1973-1974]. ***PRACTICE AREAS:*** Probate; Corporate; Insurance; School; Estate Planning; Business Planning.

ROBERT M. MORROW, born Jackson, Ohio, January 21, 1957; admitted to bar, 1983, Ohio and U.S. District Court, Southern District of Ohio; 1987, U.S. District Court, Northern District of Ohio; 1989, U.S. Court of Appeals, Sixth Circuit; 1997, U.S. Supreme Court. *Education:* Ohio State University (B.S., 1979); Capital University (J.D., 1983). Delta Theta Phi; Order of Curia, 1983; Articles Editor, Capital University Law Review, 1981-1983. Law Clerk to the Honorable J. Craig Wright, Franklin County Common Pleas Court, 1982-1983. Member, State of Ohio Board of Bar Examiners, 1996-2001. Assistant Reader for Bar Examination Appointed by Supreme Court of Ohio, 1995-1996, 2001—. *Member:* Columbus (Real Property, Probate and Common Pleas Court Committees), Ohio State and American Bar Associations. ***PRACTICE AREAS:*** Estate Planning; Corporate; Business; Litigation; Commercial; School; Real Estate.

RICHARD W. ROSS, born Coshocton, Ohio, June 26, 1953; admitted to bar, 1978, Ohio and U.S. District Court, Northern District of Ohio; 1979, U.S. District Court, Southern District of Ohio and U.S. Court of Appeals, Sixth Circuit. *Education:* Ohio State University (B.A., 1975); Georgetown University Law Center (J.D., 1978). Assistant Attorney General, State of Ohio, 1978-1987. Section Chief, Charitable Foundations Section, 1985-1987. Member, Grandview Heights City Board of Health (1992—). *Member:* Columbus (Member, Committees on: Labor and Employment Law; Federal Courts), Ohio State and American (Member, Sections on: Litigation and Health Law) Bar Associations; Ohio Council of School Board Attorneys (Member, Executive Committee). ***PRACTICE AREAS:*** Labor; School; Litigation.

DENNIS J. MORRISON, born Buffalo, New York, April 28, 1954; admitted to bar, 1983, Ohio and U.S. District Court, Southern District of Ohio; 1988, U.S. Supreme Court; 1989, New York. *Education:* State University of New York at Buffalo (B.S., 1976); Capital University (J.D., 1982). Order of the Curia. Member, New York State Bar Association, 1989-1992. *Member:* Columbus (Member, Sections on: Real Property; Construction; Bankruptcy Committee) and Ohio State Bar Associations. ***PRACTICE AREAS:*** Creditor's Rights; Real Estate; Construction Law; Litigation; Adoptions.

NICOLE M. DONOVSKY, born Zanesville, Ohio, August 7, 1973; admitted to bar, 2000, Ohio; 2001, U.S. District Court, Southern District of Ohio; 2005, U.S. District Court, Northern District of Ohio. *Education:* Capital University (B.A., 1995; J.D., 2000). *Member:* Columbus Bar Association; Ohio Council of School Board Attorneys; Franklin Inn of Court. ***PRACTICE AREAS:*** School Law; Labor and Employment.

LISA M. McCLURE, born Columbus, Ohio, November 1, 1970; admitted to bar, 2001, Ohio; 2003, U.S. District Court, Southern District of Ohio. *Education:* Ohio Wesleyan University (B.A., 1992); Capital University Law School (J.D., 1997). *Member:* Columbus and Ohio State Bar Associations; Ohio Council of School Board Attorneys. ***PRACTICE AREAS:*** School Law; Labor and Employment; Collective Bargaining Litigation.

ELIZABETH L. MILLER, born Dillsburg, Pennsylvania, August 13, 1975; admitted to bar, 2001, Ohio; 2002, U.S. Court of Appeals, Sixth Circuit and U.S. Tax Court. *Education:* Grove City College (B.A., 1997); Pennsylvania State University, Dickinson School of Law (J.D., 2000). Notes Editor, Dickinson Journal of International Law, 1999-2000. Author: "Sound the Trumpets! Quebec is Shouting, 'Victory!' Despite the Canadian Supreme Court's Denial of Unilateral Secession," 17 Dick. J. Int'l L. 505, Spring 1999. Member: Women's Law Caucus, 1998-1999; Junior League of Columbus, 2003-2005; Barrister's Leadership Program, 2002-2003. *Member:* Columbus and Ohio State Bar Associations. ***PRACTICE AREAS:*** Probate; Estate Planning; Trust Administration.

JOHN F. KIRTLEY II, born Royal Oak, Michigan, February 25, 1977; admitted to bar, 2004, Ohio; 2005, U.S. District Court, Southern District of Ohio. *Education:* Northern Kentucky University (B.A., 1999); Capital University Law School (J.D., 2004). ***PRACTICE AREAS:*** Creditors Rights; Business Litigation; Commercial Litigation.

GENERAL COUNSEL: Accent on Management, Inc. (Management of Trade Associations); Associations, Conventions, Tradeshows, Inc.; Kerr Companies, Athens, Ohio; Ohio Association of Insurance and Financial Advisors; Ohio Society of Professional Engineers; Ohio State Mortgage, Inc.; Professional Insurance Agents Association of Ohio; L. Frank Wilson Trucking, Inc.; Professional Land Surveyors of Ohio; VNC Bearing, Inc.; TechDisposal.com, Inc.

SPECIAL COUNSEL: Bellefontaine City School District; Celina Group; Unizan Bank, National Association; The Mortgage Banc; Bank One, Columbus, N.A.; Kin Properties, Inc.; Complete Property Resources; HER, Inc.; Buckeye Local School District; Chillicothe City School District; Delaware Area Career Center; Grandview Heights City School District; Greene County Career Center; Olentangy Local School District; Stark County Schools; Ohio Attorney General for Jefferson Community College and North Central Technical College; Springfield City School District; Clark-Shawnee Local School District.

R. WILLIAM MEEKS

Established in 1975

511 SOUTH HIGH STREET
COLUMBUS, OHIO 43215
Telephone: 614-228-4141
Fax: 614-228-0899

Criminal Trial and Appellate Practice in all State and Federal Courts.

FIRM PROFILE: I practice exclusively in the area of Criminal Defense. I have an excellent support staff and utilize investigators and other professionals of the highest quality to achieve the best result for each client.

R. WILLIAM MEEKS, born Columbus, Ohio, April 26, 1947; admitted to bar, 1975, Ohio; 1976, U.S. District Court, Southern District of Ohio; 1978, U.S. District Court, Northern District of Ohio; 1979, U.S. Court of Appeals, Sixth Circuit; 1980, U.S. District Court, Eastern District of Kentucky and U.S. Supreme Court; 1982, U.S. District Court, Middle District of Florida; 1988, U.S. District Court, Eastern District of Michigan. *Education:* University of Cincinnati (B.S., 1969); Capital University (J.D., 1975). Special Counsel to Ohio Attorney General, 1978-1979. *Member:* Columbus, Ohio State and American (Member, Criminal Justice Section) Bar Associations; National Association of Criminal Defense Lawyers; Ohio Association of Criminal Defense Lawyers (Director, 1987—). ***REPORTED CASES:*** Berkemer v. McCarty (extended Miranda warnings to misdemeanor defendants); State v. Smith (imposed limitations on similar acts evidence). ***PRACTICE AREAS:*** Criminal Defense.

REFERENCE: Bank One of Columbus, Ohio.

FREDERICK MEISTER

Established in 1988

150 EAST MOUND STREET, SUITE 200
COLUMBUS, OHIO 43215-5429
Telephone: 614-221-1644
Fax: 614-221-1696
Email: fmeister2@aol.com
URL: http://www.lawyers.com/meisterlaw

Family Law, Divorce, Dissolution, Legal Separation, Child Custody, Child Support, Visitation, Family Mediation, Matrimonial Arbitration, Premarital Agreements.

FREDERICK MEISTER, born Karlsruhe, Baden, Germany, October 5, 1946; admitted to bar, 1980, Ohio. *Education:* The Ohio State University (B.S., in Ed., 1968; M.A., 1972; J.D., 1980). *Member:* Columbus (Member, 1980— and Chair, 1995-1997, Family Law Committee; Member, Alternative Dispute Resolution Committee), Ohio State and American (Member, Sections on: Family Law; Alternative Dispute Resolution) Bar Associations; Association for Conflict Resolution; Supreme Court Task Form on Family and Children (Member, 1998-2001); National Association of Counsel for Children. (Certified Specialist, Family Relations Law, Ohio State Bar Association). ***PRACTICE AREAS:*** Domestic Relations; Matrimonial Law; Family Law; Family Mediation; Matrimonial Arbitration.

DAVID P. MEYER CO., L.P.A.

Established in 2000

401 NORTH FRONT STREET, SUITE 350
COLUMBUS, OHIO 43215
Telephone: 614-224-6000
Toll Free: 866-827-6537
Fax: 614-224-6066
Email: dmeyer@dmlaws.com
URL: http://www.dmlaws.com

Securities Consumer Arbitration, Securities Arbitration, Stockbroker Fraud and Misconduct, Securities Class Actions, Business Torts, Consumer Class Action.

FIRM PROFILE: Representing individuals investors and consumers against corporate misconduct.

DAVID P. MEYER, born Charleston, West Virginia, April 13, 1970; admitted to bar, 1995, Ohio; 1996, U.S. District Court, Southern District of Ohio. *Education:* Ohio University (B.B.A., with honors, 1992); Capital University Law School (J.D., 1995; LL.M., 1996). *Member:* Columbus, Ohio State and American Bar Associations; Association of Trial Lawyers of America; Franklin County Trial Lawyers Association; Public Investors Arbitration Bar Association. ***Email:*** dmeyer@dmlaws.com

---

PATRICK G. WARNER, born Columbus, Ohio, January 10, 1966; admitted to bar, 1995, Ohio. *Education:* The Ohio State University (B.S., 1990); Capital University (J.D., 1995, Order of the Curia). ***REPORTED CASES:*** Cope, et al. v. Metro Life Ins. Co., 82 Ohio St.3d 426 (1998); Byrnes, et al. v. LCI Communications, et al., 77 Ohio St.3d 125

(This Listing Continued)

(1996); Drage v. Procter & Gamble, 119 Ohio App.3d 19 (1997). ***PRACTICE AREAS:*** Class Actions; Commercial Litigation; Consumer Protection; Securities; Consumer Arbitration; Business Torts. ***Email:*** pwarner@dmlaws.com

MARNIE C. LAMBERT, born Salt Lake City, Utah, March 31, 1967; admitted to bar, 1993, California (inactive) and U.S. District Court, Central District of California; 2000, Ohio; 2003, U.S. District Court, Southern District of Ohio. *Education:* Miami University (B.A., 1989); Pepperdine University School of Law (J.D., 1992). *Member:* Columbus and Ohio State Bar Associations; The Association of Trial Lawyers of America; Franklin County Trial Lawyers; Ohio Women's Bar Association; Women Lawyers of Franklin County; Public Investors Arbitration Bar Association. ***REPORTED CASES:*** Truck Ins. Exchange v. Superior Court (Park Northridge HOA), 67 Cal.App. 4th 142 (1998). ***PRACTICE AREAS:*** Commercial Litigation; Securities; Consumer Protection; Consumer Arbitration; Business Torts; Insurance; Class Actions. ***Email:*** mlambert@dmlaws.com

BRIAN G. MILLER CO., L.P.A.

326 SOUTH HIGH STREET, SUITE 500
COLUMBUS, OHIO 43215
Telephone: 614-221-4035
Fax: 614-222-1899
Email: bgm@bgmillerlaw.com
URL: http://www.bgmillerlaw.com

Personal Injury, Employer Intentional Tort, Workplace Injuries, Premises Liability, Slip and Fall, Wrongful Death, Automobile Accidents, Motorcycle Accidents, Third Party Negligence, Torts, Civil Litigation.

BRIAN G. MILLER, born Plainfield, New Jersey, June 10, 1969; admitted to bar, 1994, Ohio; 1995, U.S. District Court, Southern District of Ohio; 1998, U.S. District Court, Northern District of Ohio. *Education:* The Ohio State University (B.S., summa cum laude, 1991; J.D., 1994). Phi Beta Kappa. Assistant Prosecuting Attorney, Franklin County, Ohio, 1994-1998. Ohio Super Lawyer, Rising Star, 2005. *Member:* Columbus, Ohio State and American Bar Associations; The Association of Trial Lawyers of America; Ohio Academy of Trial Lawyers (Member, Ohio Supreme Court Candidate Screening Committee, 2004); Franklin County Trial Lawyers Association; National Institute of Trial Advocacy (Graduate). ***PRACTICE AREAS:*** Personal Injury; Wrongful Death; Employer Intentional Torts; Negligence; Products Liability. ***Email:*** bgm@bgmillerlaw.com

REPRESENTATIVE CLIENTS: Columbus Clippers Baseball Organization; International League of Professional Baseball Clubs.

MILLISOR & NOBIL

A LEGAL PROFESSIONAL ASSOCIATION
Established in 1975
300 EAST BROAD STREET, SUITE 190
COLUMBUS, OHIO 43215
Telephone: 614-221-2234; 800-800-8807
Fax: 614-221-1278
Email: laborlaw@millisor.com
URL: http://www.millisor.com

Cleveland, Ohio Office: 9150 South Hills Boulevard, Suite 300, 44147-3599. Telephone: 440-838-8800. Telefax: 440-838-8805.
Canton, Ohio Office: 4117 Whipple Avenue NW, 44718. Telephone: 330-493-8525; 888-867-6869. Telefax: 330-493-8606.

Employment Law including Labor Relations, Equal Employment Opportunity, Public Sector, OSHA, Arbitration Law, Litigation, Workers Compensation Law, Human Resources Consulting and Employee Benefit Law.

All Personnel are Members of Ohio State and American Bar Associations.

(For complete biographical data on all personnel, see Professional Biographies at Cleveland, Ohio)

MOOTS, CARTER & HOGAN

A Legal Professional Association
3600 OLENTANGY RIVER ROAD
COLUMBUS, OHIO 43214-3913
Telephone: 614-459-4140
FAX: 614-459-4503

Private and Public Sector Labor and Employment Law. College and University Law, Township and Annexation Law, Non-Profit, Mediation, Administrative, Civil Trial and Appellate Practice.

PHILIP R. MOOTS, born Bellefontaine, Ohio, June 10, 1940; admitted to bar, 1965, Ohio; 1966, U.S. District Court, Southern District of Ohio; 1980, U.S. Supreme Court. *Education:* The Ohio State University (B.A., cum laude, 1962); Harvard University (J.D., 1965); West Virginia Wesleyan College (LL.D., honorary, 1978). Phi Beta Kappa; Phi Alpha Theta. Author: "A Fresh Look At Your Bylaws," AGB Reports, 1991; "Candor on the Campus," Synthesis, 1991; "Civility: A Critical Issue in Faculty Evaluation," Outside Council, Summer 2000. Adjunct Professor, The Ohio State University College of Law, 1972-1977. Executive Assistant to the Governor of Ohio, 1972-1975. Director, 1977-1981 and Chair of the Advisory Board, 1981-1985, Center for Constitutional Studies, University of Notre Dame Law School. Board of Directors, Chair, Executive Committee, Community Mutual Insurance Company, 1981-1992. Chair, Legal Services Review Panel, National Association of Independent Colleges and Universities, 1990—. Member, Board of Directors, The Ohio State University Managed Health Care Systems, Inc., 2004—. Board of Directors, Executive Committee, Legal Aid Society of Columbus, 2002—. Named to Best Lawyers in America, 2005. *Member:* Columbus (Member, Agency Board, 1997—); Ohio State and American Bar Associations; National Association of College and University Attorneys. ***PRACTICE AREAS:*** College and University Law; Labor and Employment Law; Mediation. ***Email:*** pmoots@mchlaw.us

WANDA L. CARTER, born Dayton, Ohio, June 19, 1948; admitted to bar, 1982, Ohio; 1984, U.S. District Court, Southern District of Ohio; 1988, U.S. Court of Appeals, Sixth Circuit; 1990, U.S. Supreme Court; 2005, U.S. District Court, Northern District of Ohio. *Education:* Bowling Green State University (B.S., 1970); The Ohio State University (M.S., 1977; J.D., summa cum laude, 1982). Order of the Coif. Associate Editor, Ohio State University Law Journal, 1980-1982. Recipient: C. Simeral Bunch Award for Academic Excellence in the Study of Law, 1981; Donald B. Becker Memorial Award, 1981. Judicial Clerk to the Honorable John D. Holschuh, United States District Court, Southern District of Ohio, 1982-1984. Named to Best Lawyers in America, 2005. *Member:* Columbus, Ohio State (Board of Governors, Labor and Employment Section), Federal and American Bar Associations; Ohio Women's Bar Association; Ohio Higher Education Facilities Commission; Upper Arlington Public Library Board of Trustees. ***PRACTICE AREAS:*** Employment Law; College and University Law; Township and Annexation Law; Civil Trial and Appellate Practice; Mediation. ***Email:*** wcarter@mchlaw.us

CHRISTOPHER E. HOGAN, born Iowa City, Iowa, August 11, 1968; admitted to bar, 1998, Ohio and U.S. District Court, Southern District of Ohio; 1999, U.S. Court of Appeals, Sixth Circuit; 2004, U.S. Supreme Court; 2005, U.S. District Court, Northern District of Ohio. *Education:* The Ohio State University (B.A., Philosophy, summa cum laude, 1995; J.D., 1998). Recipient: 1998, University of Minnesota National Civil Rights Moot Court Champion (Best Oralist and Best Brief); George R. Beneman Memorial Award for Outstanding Performance in the Moot Court Program, 1998; Albert A. Levin Memorial Award for Professional Responsibility, 1997; Corpus Juris Secundum Award for Scholastic Excellence in Torts, 1995-1996. Author: "The 11th Amendment: A Primer for the Employment Lawyer," *Labor and Employment News* (2003); "Eleventh Amendment Challenge to Family-Care Provision of FMLA Rejected," *Labor and Employment News* (2003). Contributor: *Legal Deskbook for Administrators of Independent College and Universities* (Revised 2nd Edition). *Member:* Columbus, Ohio State, Federal and American Bar Associations. (Certified Specialist in Labor and Employment Law, Ohio State Bar Association). ***PRACTICE AREAS:*** Labor and Employment Law; College and University Law; Nonprofit and Charitable Corporations; Civil Litigation; Appellate Practice. ***Email:*** chogan@mchlaw.us

REPRESENTATIVE CLIENTS: The Ohio State University; Capital University; Ohio Wesleyan University; Marietta College; University of Dayton; Ohio Dominican University; Otterbein College; Columbus State Community College; Ohio Association of Independent Colleges and Universities; East Central Colleges; Methodist Theological School in Ohio; West Virginia Wesleyan College; Benedictine University; Defiance College; DeVry Institute of Technology; Cornell College; Northland College; Urbana University; Transportation Research Center of Ohio; The West Ohio Annual Conference of the United Methodist Church; Kripalu Center for Yoga & Health; Superior Fibers, Inc.; Miami, Butler, Washington and Jefferson Townships, Montgomery County; Union, Monroe and Bethel Townships, Miami County; Spring Valley, Beavercreek, Xenia and Sugarcreek Townships, Greene County; Violet Township, Fairfield County; Carryall Township, Paulding County; Insight Communications of Central Ohio, LLC; C.M. Media, Inc.

MICHAEL R. MORAN CO., L.P.A.

181 GRANVILLE STREET
P.O. BOX 307437
COLUMBUS, OHIO 43230-7437
Telephone: 614-476-6453
Fax: 614-476-4157
Email: MRMoran@MRMoran.com
URL: http://www.MRMoran.com

Administrative Law, Occupational and Professional Licensing, Health Law, Personal Injury, Municipal Law, Privacy and Freedom of Information, Government Law, White Collar Crime, Fraud, Corporate Compliance and Legislation, Trial Practice and Appeals, Firearm and 2nd Amendment Law.

MICHAEL R. MORAN, born Toledo, Ohio, October 3, 1967; admitted to bar, 1994, Ohio and U.S. Court of Appeals, Sixth Circuit; 1995, U.S. District Court, Southern and Northern Districts of Ohio; 1997, District of Columbia and U.S. Court of Appeals for the Armed Forces; 2001, U.S. Supreme Court. *Education:* Marietta College (B.A., 1990); Capital University (J.D., 1994). Phi Delta Phi. Co-Author: "Ohio Administrative Law Handbook & Agency Directory," 1995-2006 editions. Solicitor & Prosecuting Attorney, Village of Hartford, 1996—. Special Prosecutor: Miami County, 1997; Shelby County, 1997; City of Newark, 1997-1998; City of Columbus, 1999. Hearing Examiner, Ohio Board of Nursing. Executive Director/Counsel, State Chiropractic Board, 1997-2000; Chairman, Gahanna Board of Zoning & Building Appeals. Ohio Insurance Fraud Taskforce. *Member:* Columbus, Ohio State and Federal Bar Associations; American Health Lawyers Association; Million Dollar Advocates Forum; Association of Certified Fraud Examiners; Judge Advocate Association; Association of Inspectors General. [Major, Ohio Military Reserve, JAGC, 2001—]. ***PRACTICE AREAS:*** Administrative Law; Professional Licensing; Health Law; Personal Injury; Municipal Law; Freedom of Information; Government; White Collar Crime; Fraud.

THOMAS EVAN MORGAN & ASSOCIATES

A LEGAL PROFESSIONAL ASSOCIATION
906 EAST BROAD STREET
COLUMBUS, OHIO 43205
Telephone: 614-258-1133; Toll Free: 800-948-6200
Fax: 614-258-3344
Email: info@thomasevanmorgan.com

Workers' Compensation and Social Security Disability Law.

THOMAS EVAN MORGAN, born Columbus, Ohio, August 31, 1949; admitted to bar, 1975, Ohio; 1976, U.S. District Court, Southern District of Ohio; 1997, U.S. Supreme Court. *Education:* Ohio University (B.B.A., 1971); Ohio Northern University (J.D., 1975).

(This Listing Continued)

THOMAS EVAN MORGAN & ASSOCIATES, A LEGAL PROFESSIONAL ASSOCIATION, Columbus—Continued

Member: Columbus, Ohio State and American Bar Associations; Franklin County Trial Lawyers Association; Ohio Academy of Trial Lawyers; The Association of Trial Lawyers of America; National Organization of Social Secretary Claimants Representatives. ***PRACTICE AREAS:*** Workers' Compensation Law; Social Security Disability. ***Email:*** tmorgan@thomasevanmorgan.com

ASSOCIATE

STEWART JUSTICE, III, born Charleston, West Virginia, February 27, 1973; admitted to bar, 2001, Ohio. *Education:* West Virginia State College (B.S., 1996); Capital University Law School (J.D., 2001). Phi Alpha Delta. Law Clerk, Chief Justice Elliot Maynard, West Virginia Supreme Court of Appeals, 2000. *Member:* Columbus and Ohio State Bar Associations; Ohio Trial Lawyers Association; Franklin County Trial Lawyers Association. ***PRACTICE AREAS:*** Workers Compensation; Social Security Disability; Personal Injury. ***Email:*** sjustice@thomasevanmorgan.com

WILLIAM A. MORSE

A LEGAL PROFESSIONAL ASSOCIATION

COLUMBUS, OHIO

(See Worthington)

Estate Planning, Probate, Small Business and Non-Profit Corporations.

MOWERY & YOUELL, LTD.

COLUMBUS, OHIO

(See Dublin)

General Trial including Federal Practice, Labor, Employment Discrimination, Sexual Harassment, Americans With Disabilities Act, Family and Medical Leave Act, Corporate, Business, Real Estate and Family Law.

MUELLER AND SMITH

A LEGAL PROFESSIONAL ASSOCIATION

Established in 1980

MUELLER-SMITH BUILDING
7700 RIVERS EDGE DRIVE
COLUMBUS, OHIO 43235-1355
Telephone: 614-436-0600
Telecopier: 614-436-0057
Email: patents@muellersmith.com
URL: http://www.lawyers.com/muellerandsmith

Intellectual Property Law including Patents, Trademarks, Copyrights, Licensing, Computer Law, Unfair Competition and International Patent Law. Trial and Appellate Practice in all Courts.

JERRY K. MUELLER, JR., born El Paso, Texas, July 19, 1948; admitted to bar, 1973, Ohio; 1979, U.S. District Court, Southern District of Ohio; 1982, U.S. Court of Appeals for the Federal Circuit; 1985, U.S. Court of Federal Claims; 1986, U.S. Court of Appeals, Sixth Circuit; registered to practice before U.S. Patent and Trademark Office. *Education:* Case Institute of Technology (B.S., Chem. Eng., 1970); The Ohio State University (J.D., 1973). Adjunct Professor of Law, Capital U., 1985-1999. *Member:* Columbus and American Bar Associations; American Intellectual Property Law Association; Columbus Intellectual Property Law Association (President, 1982-1983). ***PRACTICE AREAS:*** Intellectual Property Law; Computer Law. ***Email:*** smueller@muellersmith.com

GERALD L. SMITH, born Columbus, Ohio, February 11, 1934; admitted to bar, 1964, Maryland; 1970, Massachusetts; 1976, Ohio; 1977, U.S. District Court, Southern District of Ohio; 1982, U.S. Court of Appeals for the Federal Circuit; 1985, U.S. Court of Federal Claims; 1986, U.S. Court of Appeals, Sixth Circuit; registered to practice before U.S. Patent and Trademark and Canadian Patent Offices. *Education:* The Ohio State University (B.E. and M.S., 1957); University of Maryland (J.D., 1964). Tau Beta Pi; Delta Theta Phi. Licensed Professional Engineer, Ohio, 1961. Special Counsel to the Attorney General of Ohio, 1992. *Member:* Columbus (Member, Planning Committee, Computer Law Institute, 1982—) and American Bar Associations; American Intellectual Property Law Association; Columbus Intellectual Property Law Association (President, 1979-1980); Computer Law Association. ***PRACTICE AREAS:*** Intellectual Property Law; Computer Law. ***Email:*** jsmith@muellersmith.com

DIANE E. BURKE, born Milton, Florida, August 1, 1973; admitted to bar, 1998, Ohio; 2000, U.S. Court of Appeals, Federal Circuit; registered to practice before U.S. Patent and Trademark Office. *Education:* Wake Forest University (B.S., Physics, 1995; J.D., 1998). Sigma Pi Sigma. *Member:* Columbus and American Bar Associations; American Intellectual Property Law Association. ***PRACTICE AREAS:*** Intellectual Property Law; Computer Law. ***Email:*** dburke@muellersmith.com

JOHN J. OKULEY, born Napoleon, Ohio, September 11, 1962; admitted to bar, 2003, Ohio. *Education:* The Ohio State University (B.S., Crop Science, with Distinction, 1984; Ph.D., Molecular Genetics, 1991; J.D., 2003). Gamma Sigma Delta; Sigma Xi. ***PRACTICE AREAS:*** Intellectual Property; Biotechnology. ***Email:*** jokuley@muellersmith.com

REPRESENTATIVE CLIENTS: Ashland Chemical Co.; R.H. Burton Co.; Calfacior Corp.; Container Associates, Inc.; Damon's International, Inc.; Dynelec Corp.; Fficiency Software, Inc.; Hague Quality Water International; Infosight Corp.; Intek, Inc.; La Chatelaine French Cafe and Bakery; Liebert Corp.; Ferguson Beauregard/Logic Controls; Multi-Plastics, Inc.; Neoprobe Corp.; Neothermia, Inc.; Nucon International, Inc.; OCLC Online Computer Library Center, Inc.; Quadrant Systems, Inc.; Transdata, Inc.; United McGill Corp.; The Edward Orton, Jr. Ceramic Foundation; The Ohio State University; Tracewell Systems, Inc.; IT Centrix, Inc.; MD Systems, Inc
REFERENCE: Bank One of Columbus.

NELSON LEVINE DE LUCA & HORST, LLC

280 NORTH HIGH STREET, SUITE 920
COLUMBUS, OHIO 43215
Telephone: 614-228-1398
Fax: 614-221-7529
URL: http://www.nldhlaw.com

Blue Bell, Pennsylvania Office: 4 Sentry Parkway, Suite 300, 19422. Telephone: 610-862-6500. Fax: 614-862-6501.

Princeton, New Jersey Office: 212 Carnegie Center, Suite 206, 08540. Telephone: 609-919-6320. Fax: 609-520-1863.

Antitrust Litigation, Appellate Practice, Bad Faith Consulting and Litigation, Class Action Litigation, Construction Law, Insurance Regulatory, Consulting and Litigation, Large Loss Property and Workers' Compensation Subrogation.

FIRM PROFILE: NLdH provides sophisticated and innovative legal services with an understanding of the business of insurance. NLdH helps develop and protect the insurance industry's business practices so that clients can successfully manage their enterprise. Together, NLdH and its clients identify issues before they become legal problems and integrate risk management throughout the decision-making process. It is NLdH's mission to enable clients to evaluate risks and make informed, proactive choices.

NLdH has transformed the way insurers use legal teams—proactive prevention when possible and aggressive litigation when required. Our attorneys understand the architecture of the insurance industry and are therefore able to zealously defend its systems and methods. Clients can expect NLdH to have the courage to make hard decisions, to have a passion for achieving their goals and to have the dedication to deliver excellence.

(For complete biographical data on all personnel, see Professional Biographies at Blue Bell, Pennsylvania)

JOHN C. NEMETH AND ASSOCIATES

21 EAST FRANKFORT STREET
COLUMBUS, OHIO 43206-1069
Telephone: 614-443-4866
Fax: 614-443-4860
URL: http://www.nemethlaw.com
Email: nemeth@nemethlaw.com
URL: http://www.lawyers.com/nemeth

General Negligence Trials. Trials and Appeals. Insurance Defense, Medical/Legal Malpractice, Toxic Torts, Products Liability, Asbestos Litigation, Aviation, Complex and Multi-District Litigation, Arson, Premises Liability, Fraud Defense and Insurance Law.

JOHN C. NEMETH, born Cleveland, Ohio, June 24, 1945; admitted to bar, 1971, Ohio and U.S. District Court, Southern District of Ohio; 1972, U.S. Court of Appeals, Sixth Circuit; 1979, Florida and U.S. Supreme Court; 1985, U.S. District Court, Northern District of Ohio; 1992, Colorado. *Education:* Kent State University (B.A., 1967); The Ohio State University (J.D., 1970). Listed in: Who's Who in American Law; Who's Who in America. Author: "Personal Injury Litigation in Ohio," 1984, Ohio Legal Center Institute, 1984—; "Legal Malpractice," Ohio Association of Civil Trial Attorneys, Volume 25 Winter, 1990. Co-Author: "Ohio Preparing and Trying the Automobile Accident Case, Professional Education Systems, Inc., 1990; "Legal Malpractice in Ohio," 40 Clev. St. L. Rev., 1991. Lecturer, Ohio Legal Center Institute, 1984-2000; Ohio Judicial College, 1986-1996; Ohio Association of Civil Trial Attorneys, 1989-1999; Professional Education Systems, Inc., 1990—. Member, Million Dollar Advocacy Forum, 1997. Board Certified by the American Board of Professional Liability Attorneys. Member, Board of Directors, American Board of Trial Advocacy, 2001—. *Member:* Columbus (Member, Negligence & Professionalism Committee), Ohio State (Member, Specialization Committee, 1999-2003), Colorado, Federal and American Bar Associations; The Florida Bar (Member, Out of State Membership Committee); Ohio Association of Civil Trial Attorneys; Defense Research Institute, Inc.; International Association of Insurance Defense Counsel (Member: Legal Malpractice Committee; Products Liability Committee); American Board of Trial Advocates. Diplomate, National Board of Trial Advocacy (Civil). (Certified as a Civil Trial Specialist by the National Board of Trial Advocacy). ***REPORTED CASES:*** In re Complaint Against Harper (1996), 77 Ohio St 3d 211;Erie Ins. Group v. Fisher, Ohio, 474 NE 2d, 15 Ohio St 3d 380; Brinkman v. Ross, 68 Ohio St 3d 82; Hillman v. Hastings Mut. Ins. Co., 68 Ohio St. 3d 238; Selander v. Erie Insurance Exchange, 85 Ohio St 3d St 3d 541 (1999). ***PRACTICE AREAS:*** Personal Injury; Automobile Accidents and Injuries; Insurance Defense Law; Toxic Tort; Product Liability Law; Professional Negligence; Medical Legal Malpractice. ***Email:*** jnemeth@columbus.rr.com

ASSOCIATES

DAVID A. HERD, born Newport News, Virginia, August 5, 1967; admitted to bar, 1992, Ohio. *Education:* College of William and Mary (B.A., 1989); The Ohio State University (J.D., 1992). Delta Theta Phi. Recipient, Lawyers Cooperative Publishing Award (Conflict of Laws), 1991; The Ohio State University African Studies Center Award, International Law, 1991. ***PRACTICE AREAS:*** Insurance Defense Law; General Negligence Law.

MICHAEL J. COLLINS, born Portsmouth, Virginia, September 30, 1969; admitted to bar, 1994, Ohio. *Education:* Alma College (B.A., 1991); Ohio State University (J.D., 1994). *Member:* Columbus and Ohio State Bar Associations. ***PRACTICE AREAS:*** Insurance Defense; General Negligence.

(This Listing Continued)

MATTHEW E. ICE, born Buffalo, New York, August 19, 1970; admitted to bar, 1996, Ohio; 1997, U.S. District Court, Southern District of Ohio. *Education:* Ohio State University (B.A., magna cum laude, 1992; J.D., 1996). *Member:* Ohio State Bar Association. ***PRACTICE AREAS:*** Insurance Defense; General Negligence; Legal Malpractice.

NOBILE, NEEDLEMAN & THOMPSON, LLC

Established in 2001

5300 E. MAIN STREET, SUITE 109
COLUMBUS, OHIO 43213
Telephone: 614-575-1188
Fax: 614-575-1186
Email: jenobile@n-n-t.com
URL: http://www.n-n-t.com

West Office: 4511 Cemetery Road, Suite B, Hilliard, Ohio 43026. Telephone: 614-529-8600. Fax: 614-529-8656.

Bankruptcy Chapter 7, Bankruptcy Chapter 13, Bankruptcy Chapter 11, Bankruptcy Litigation, Bankruptcy Reorganization, Consumer Bankruptcy, Creditor Bankruptcy, Debtor Bankruptcy, Foreclosures, Insolvency, Liquidations, Personal Bankruptcy, Criminal Law, Juvenile Criminal Law, Assault and Battery, Burglary, Criminal Defense, Drivers License Suspensions, Driving While Intoxicated, Drug Crimes, Felonies, Misdemeanors, Traffic Violations, Consumer Law, Consumer Litigation, Consumer Rights, Fair Credit Reporting Act, Debtor Rights, Lemon Law, Wills, Estate Planning, Real Estate.

MEMBERS OF FIRM

JAMES E. NOBILE, born Columbus, Ohio, November 13, 1965; admitted to bar, 1992, Ohio; 1993, U.S. District Court, Southern District of Ohio; 1996, U.S. Court of Appeals, Sixth Circuit. *Education:* The Ohio State University (B.A., 1988); Capital University (J.D., 1992). Law Clerk to Hon. Barbara J. Sellers, U.S. Bankruptcy Judge, 1992-1993. Board Trustee for Creditor Education Coalition. *Member:* Columbus and Ohio State Bar Associations. ***Email:*** jenobile@n-n-t.com

SCOTT R. NEEDLEMAN, born Cleveland, Ohio, November 15, 1956; admitted to bar, 1991, Ohio; 1992, U.S. District Court, Southern District of Ohio. *Education:* Ohio State University (B.A., 1986); Capital University (J.D., 1991). *Member:* Columbus Bar Association. ***Email:*** srneedleman@n-n-t.com

MATTHEW J. THOMPSON, born Reynoldsburg, Ohio, March 29, 1963; admitted to bar, 1988, Ohio; 1990, U.S. District Court, Southern District of Ohio; 1999, U.S. District Court, Northern District of Ohio. *Education:* The Ohio State University (B.A., 1985; J.D., 1988). Former President, Creditor Education Coalition. *Member:* Columbus and Ohio State (Bankruptcy Law, Judicial Liaison Committees) Bar Associations. ***REPORTED CASES:*** In re Wagner 200 B.R. 160 (Bkrptcy. N.D. Ohio 1996); In re Cobb, 188 B.R. 22 (Bkrptcy N.D. Ohio 1995); Weethee v. Boso, 64 Ohio App: 3d 532, 582 N.E. 2d 19 (1989); In re Gammoh, 174 B.R. 707, (Bkrptcy N.D. Ohio (1994). ***Email:*** mjthompson@n-n-t.com

OGNE, ALBERTS & STUART, P.C.

COLUMBUS, OHIO

(See Troy, Michigan)

General Civil Litigation Practice in State and Federal Courts. Insurance Defense, General Negligence, Product Liability, Employment and Commercial Litigation, Worker's Compensation, Professional Negligence and Aviation Law. Trials and Appeals, Business Law, Wills, Trusts & Estates, Probate, Criminal Law.

OLIVER LAW OFFICE

471 E. BROAD STREET, SUITE 1303
COLUMBUS, OHIO 43215
Telephone: 614-220-9100
Fax: 614-242-3948
Email: joliver@jamioliver.com
URL: http://www.jamioliver.com

Products Liability, Personal Injury, Wrongful Death, Latex Allergy Litigation, Medical Malpractice, Vioxx Litigation, Automobile Accidents, Insurance Law, Employment Discrimination.

JAMI S. OLIVER, born Galion, Ohio, January 11, 1968; admitted to bar, 1993, Ohio; 1995, U.S. District Court, Southern and Northern Districts of Ohio; 2004, U.S. Supreme Court. *Education:* Ohio Northern University (B.A., high distinction, 1990), Ohio State University (J.D., 1993). Consumer Education: Summertime Fun Can Be Dangerous, WCVO, 104.9 FM, "Everybody's Talking" (July 6, 1995). Lecturer: 2004 Trial Strategies Seminar, "Trial Advocacy Tactics" and Panel Question and Answer, Franklin County Trial Lawyers Association, Columbus, Ohio (October 19, 2004); Successful Handling of Wrongful Death Cases in Ohio, "Simplifying Complicated Issues in Wrongful Death Cases," Lorman Education Services, Worthington, Ohio (March 12, 2004); PI Guerilla Seminar, "Common Problems Lawyers Face and How to Solve Them," Franklin County Trial Lawyers Association, Columbus, Ohio (January 21, 2003); Proof of Damages, "Plaintiff's Perspective on Developing and Proving Damages," and "Plaintiff's Perspective on Arguing Damages at Trial," PESI, Columbus, Ohio (November 29, 2000); The Woman Advocate, "The Woman Lawyer in the Courtroom," Ohio State Bar Association and CLE Institute, Columbus, Ohio (September 7, 2000); Faculty, Trial Advocacy Seminar, Ohio Academy of Trial Lawyers, Columbus, Ohio (annually, 2000 to present); How to Get and Work with Attorneys, Solidarity '99, Columbus, Ohio (May 24, 1999); "Complex Litigation and Discovery Abuse: What Do I Do Now?", Advanced Discovery Seminar, Ohio Academy of Trial Lawyers, Strongsville, Ohio (March 5, 1999); Co-Chair of the 1999 Discovery/Evidence Seminars, "Forms, Motions and Experts after Kuhmo Tire," Ohio Academy of Trial Lawyers, Strongsville and Columbus, Ohio (September 10 and 17, 1999); Discovery in Complex Litigation, Ohio Academy of Trial Lawyers, New Lawyer's Seminar, 41st Annual Con-

(This Listing Continued)

vention, Cincinnati, Ohio (May 21, 1998); Latex Glove Allergies, Association of Trial Lawyers of America 1997 Annual Convention, San Diego, California (July 21, 1997); Attorneys and Disability Rights, Solidarity '97, Columbus, Ohio (May 29, 1997); Latex Allergies, Ohio Academy of Trial Lawyers, Litigation at Sunrise, 40th Annual Convention, Cleveland, Ohio (April 25, 1997); Patients' Responsibilities, Prescriptions for Pharmacist Liability, Ohio Pharmacists Association (1995). Distinctions: Million Dollar Advocate's Forum, 2005; Ohio Super Lawyers Rising Stars, Top Lawyers under 40, 2005. *Member:* Ohio Women's Bar Association (President, 1999-2000; President-Elect, 1998-1999; Vice-President, 1997-1998; Chairperson, Legislative Committee, 1995-1998; Chairperson, Membership Committee, 1998-1999); Ohio Academy of Trial Lawyers (Board of Trustees, 2000-current; Chairperson, Employment Law, 2002-2003; Membership Committee, 1994-1996; Chairperson, 1999-2000); Association of Trial Lawyers of America (Chairperson, New Lawyers Division, Public Image Committee, 1997-1998; Ohio Delegate for Women's Caucus, 1999-2000); Franklin County Trial Lawyers Association (Board of Trustees, 1999—; President, 2005-2006, Vice-President, 2004-2005, Secretary, 2003-2004, Treasurer, 2002-2003; Chairperson, Newsletter Committee, 1998-1999; Chairperson, Membership Committee, 1996-1997); Columbus Bar Association; Ohio State Bar Association; Women Lawyers of Franklin County. ***LANGUAGES:*** Spanish. ***REPORTED CASES:*** Incarnato v. Metropolitan Prop. and Cas. Ins. Co. (1996), 668 N.E.2d 920, 76 Ohio St. 3d 562; Hamlin v. Motel Six, et al., (2000), Ohio App. LEXIS 2439; Perrine v. MPW Industrial Serv., 213 F. Supp.2d 835 (S.D. Ohio 2002). Notable Verdicts and Accomplishments: The Estate of Roger Ferguson, Deceased, v. Suzuki Motor Corp., et al. (Case No. 00CVB06-5541), Franklin County Common Pleas Court, Judge Hogan, Jury Verdict $4.5 million, February 4, 2003; participated in the Multidistrict Litigation (MDL) in the Eastern District of Pennsylvania for Latex Glove Litigation (1996-2004); Co-counsel in prospective class action involving violations of the Fair Labor Standards Act and wage and hour laws in Landsberg v. Acton Enterprises, Inc., Case Number 2:05-cv-00500, Southern District of Ohio; Co-counsel in prospective class action involving government employees subject to unreasonable medical examinations and violations of Constitutional rights in Cramblit v. City of Columbus Case numbers 2:05 cv 00301; 2:05 cv 00413, So. District of Ohio; currently involved in litigation against Merck arising out of the drug Vioxx (r) in State and Federal courts. ***PRACTICE AREAS:*** Plaintiff's Products Liability Law; Plaintiff's Pharmaceutical and Drug Litigation; Class Actions; Personal Injury; Wrongful Death; Medical Malpractice; Vioxx Litigation; Insurance; Employment Law; Wrongful Termination; Whistleblower Litigation. ***Email:*** joliver@jamioliver.com

ONDA, LaBUHN & RANKIN CO., LPA

Established in 1991

266 NORTH FOURTH STREET, SUITE 100
COLUMBUS, OHIO 43215-2511
Telephone: 614-716-0500
Fax: 614-716-0511
URL: http://www.olr-law.com

Business Formation, Buying and Selling of Businesses, Business Law, Federal Tax Controversies, Commercial and General Litigation, Real Estate, Zoning, Land Use, Tax Deferred Exchanges, Estate and Gift Taxation, Estate Planning, Wills and Probate, Tax Planning, Mechanic's Lien Law, Construction Law, Criminal Defense, Banking Law, Finance, Lender and Borrower Representation, Employment, Representing Professionals in Administrative Proceedings.

FIRM PROFILE: Onda, LaBuhn & Rankin Co., LPA is a diverse general practice law firm that represents clients ranging from large corporate clients to individuals. The primary focus of the firm is a wide variety of business transactional related items such as real estate, land use, 1031 tax deferred exchanges, general to complex business transactions, general counseling to businesses, tax and business litigation.

ROBERT J. ONDA, born Gary, Indiana, March 27, 1957; admitted to bar, 1983, Ohio; 1984, Florida and U.S. Tax Court. *Education:* University of Notre Dame (B.B.A., cum laude, 1979); Washington and Lee University (J.D., cum laude, 1983); University of Florida (LL.M., 1984). Certified Public Accountant, Illinois, 1980. Author: "Self-Cancelling Installment Sales, An Income Tax and Estate Planning Evaluation," 36, University of Florida Law Review, No. 5, 1984. Speaker and Author: "Sophisticated Section 1031 Transactions in Ohio," National Business Institute, March 2004; "Ohio Tax Strategies Using Like Kind Exchanges," PESI, August 2003; "Section 1031 Planning Opportunities," Ohio State Bar Association, August, 2003; "Section 1031 Exchanges of Investment Properties in Ohio," National Business Institute, June 2003, August 2002 and July 2001; "The Nuts and Bolts of Like Kind Exchanges," Ohio State Bar Association, May 1998; "Death and Taxes: an Overview of How to Avoid One of the Two Certainties of Life (At Least Temporarily)," Columbus Bar Association, Bankruptcy Law Institute, May, 1993; "Selected Tax Issues," Columbus Bar Association, Real Property Law Institute, February 1992. Co-Author: "Negligence/Substantial Understatement and Valuation Penalties," ALI-ABA Course of Study, April, 1989; "Hidden Penalties," ALI-ABA Course of Study, April, 1987; 1988. Adjunct Professor, Capital University Graduate Tax Program, 1986—. *Member:* Columbus, Ohio State and American Bar Associations; The Florida Bar. ***PRACTICE AREAS:*** Estate and Gift Taxation; Federal Tax Controversies; Tax Deferred Exchanges; Business Law; Business Formation; Buying and Selling of Businesses; Tax Planning. ***Email:*** rjo@olrlaw.com

MATTHEW A. LaBUHN, born Oregon, Ohio, March 4, 1970; admitted to bar, 1996, Ohio; 1997, U.S. District Court, Northern and Southern Districts of Ohio and U.S. Tax Court. *Education:* Capital University (B.A., magna cum laude, 1992); The Ohio State University (J.D., with honors, 1996). Author: "Agricultural Law Update," General Practice Update for Ohio Continuing Legal Education Institute, 1999, 2000, 2001 and 2002. Author and Speaker: "Variances," Advanced Real Estate Topics, Ohio Continuing Legal Education Institute, March 2001; "Ohio Like-Kind Real Estate Exchanges," Lorman Education Services, September, 2001; "1031 Tax Deferred Exchanges - Update," Advanced Real Estate Topics, Ohio Continuing Legal Education Institute, August 2002; "1031 Like-Kind Exchanges," Ohio Continuing Legal Education Institute Online Seminar, 2002; "1031 Real Estate Exchanges," OSBA Continuing Legal Education Institute, August, 2003; "1031 Exchange Planning Opportunities," Columbus Board of Realtors, October 2003; "Real Estate

(This Listing Continued)

ONDA, LaBUHN & RANKIN CO., LPA, Columbus—Continued

Tax Valuations and Appeals," Columbus Board of Realtors, November, 2003. Faculty, Ohio Continuing Legal Education Institute. *Member:* Columbus (Member, Real Estate Section) and American (Member, Business Law and Real Property and Probate Law Sections) Bar Associations; Ohio State Bar Association (Member, Agricultural Law and Real Estate Sections). ***PRACTICE AREAS:*** Real Estate; Zoning, Planning and Land Use; Tax Deferred Exchanges; Real Estate Foreclosure; Mechanics Liens; Construction Law; Commercial Loans; Agricultural Law. ***Email:*** mal@olrlaw.com

TIMOTHY S. RANKIN, born Columbus, Ohio, August 17, 1965; admitted to bar, 1992, Ohio, U.S. District Court, Southern and Northern Districts of Ohio and U.S. Court of Appeals, Sixth Circuit. *Education:* The Ohio State University (B.A., Chem., 1988; J.D., 1992). Delta Theta Phi. Order of the Curia. Assistant City Attorney and City Prosecutor for Whitehall, Ohio, 1992-1995. Councilman, City of Upper Arlington, Ohio, 2000—. *Member:* Columbus and Ohio State Bar Associations. ***PRACTICE AREAS:*** General Practice; Civil Litigation; Administrative Law; Zoning Law; Land Use; Employment Law. ***Email:*** tsr@olrlaw.com

PATRICK H. BOGGS, born Columbus, Ohio; admitted to bar, 1985, Ohio. *Education:* University of Notre Dame (B.B.A., 1980); Capital University (J.D., cum laude, 1985). Order of the Curia. Member, Board of Editors, Capital University Law Review, 1984-1985. Author: "Lemon Laws in Ohio Turn Sour for the Dealers," 13 Capital University Law Review, Winter 1984. *Member:* Columbus and Ohio State Bar Associations; Ohio Association of Civil Trial Attorneys. ***PRACTICE AREAS:*** Litigation; Business Law; Construction Law; Commercial Law. ***Email:*** phb@olrlaw.com

---

ROBERT E. BOYD, III, born Columbus, Ohio, February 4, 1951; admitted to bar, 1979, Ohio; 1980, U.S. District Court, Southern District of Ohio. *Education:* Ohio University (B.G.S., 1973); Cleveland State University (J.D., 1979). *Member:* Columbus and Ohio State Bar Associations. ***PRACTICE AREAS:*** Business Law; Corporate; Real Estate; Zoning Law; Land Use; Contracts; Probate. ***Email:*** reb@olrlaw.com

TODD A. ERNSBERGER, admitted to bar, 2004, Ohio. *Education:* The Ohio State University (B.A., Economics, 2000); Capital University (J.D., cum laude, 2003; LL.M., 2004). Business Editor, Capital University Law Review, 2003. *Member:* Columbus and Ohio State Bar Associations. ***PRACTICE AREAS:*** Business; Taxation; Real Estate; Tax Deferred Exchanges. ***Email:*** tae@olrlaw.com

BENJAMIN W. OGG, born Portsmouth, Ohio; admitted to bar, 2003, Ohio and U.S. District Court, Southern District of Ohio. *Education:* Capital University (B.A., summa cum laude, 2000); The Ohio State University (J.D., 2003). Intern, Hon. Howard H. Haracha III, Portsmouth Municipal Courthouse, 1995-1996. Research Assistant, Prof. Mary Ellen O'Connell, Ohio State University Moritz College of Law, May 2001-December 2001. *Member:* Columbus and Ohio State Bar Associations. ***PRACTICE AREAS:*** Commercial Litigation; Construction Law; Mechanics Liens; Civil Litigation; Zoning Law. ***Email:*** bwo@olrlaw.com

BRIAN M. GARVINE, admitted to bar, 1997, Ohio; U.S. District Court, Northern and Southern Districts of Ohio. *Education:* The Ohio State University (B.A., 1992); University of Toledo (J.D., 1997). Former Associate with: Connelly, Jackson & Collier, Toledo, Ohio, 1997-2000; Colley, Shroyer & Abraham, Columbus, Ohio, 2000-2001; Law Offices of Russell A. Kelm, Columbus, Ohio, 2001-2003; Lane Alton & Horst, Columbus, Ohio, 2003-2005. *Member:* Columbus and Ohio State Bar Associations; The Association of Trial Lawyers of America. ***PRACTICE AREAS:*** Litigation; Business Law; Construction Law; Mechanics Liens. ***Email:*** bmg@olrlaw.com

ELIZABETH M. KELLY, born Columbus, Ohio, August 3, 1964; admitted to bar, 1994, Ohio; 1995, U.S. District Court, Southern District of Ohio. *Education:* The Ohio State University (B.A., 1987); Capital University (M.B.A., 1993; J.D., 1994). Member, Capital University Law Review. President, Commercial Real Estate Women, Columbus, 2005. *Member:* Columbus and Ohio State Bar Associations. ***PRACTICE AREAS:*** Real Estate; Commercial Lending; Zoning, Planning and Land Use. ***Email:*** bethk@olrlaw.com

JACQUELINE A. FERRIS, admitted to bar, 2004, Ohio. *Education:* The Ohio State University (B.A., 2001); Capital University (J.D., 2004). Phi Alpha Delta. Order of the Curia. Speaker: "Ohio Equine Liability Law: Ohio Equine Affaire," April, 2005. *Member:* Columbus and Ohio State Bar Associations. ***PRACTICE AREAS:*** Civil Litigation; General Business; Real Estate; Estate Planning; Probate; Equine Law. ***Email:*** jaf@olrlaw.com

REPRESENTATIVE CLIENTS: Midwest Business Capital; The Arlington Bank; Realty Options, Inc.; Re/Max Capital Centre; Hondros College; Home Savings Bank; M.E. Companies, Inc.; KNG Energy, Inc.; Equity Real Estate; Leslie Development Company; ALD Concrete and Grading Co., Inc., Fiserv Health, Inc.

LARISSA OSBORN

454 EAST MAIN STREET
COLUMBUS, OHIO 43215
Telephone: 614-538-9202
Fax: 614-267-8092
Email: larissaoh1@yahoo.com
URL: http://www.larissaohlaw.com

Litigation, Products Liability, Aviation Law, Business Litigation.

LARISSA D. OSBORN, born Lima, Ohio, November 22, 1973; admitted to bar, 2001, Ohio; 2002, U.S. District Court, Northern and Southern Districts of Ohio. *Education:* Ohio University (B.B.A., summa cum laude, 1996); Capital University (J.D., magna cum laude, 2001). Member, Capital University Law Review. *Member:* Columbus, Ohio State and American Bar Associations. ***PRACTICE AREAS:*** Litigation; Products Liability; Aviation Law; Business Litigation. ***Email:*** larissaoh1@yahoo.com

ROBERT GRAY PALMER, CO., LPA

140 EAST TOWN STREET, SUITE 1200
COLUMBUS, OHIO 43215
Telephone: 614-484-1200
Fax: 614-484-1201
Email: bob@rgpalmerlaw.com
URL: http://www.rgpalmerlaw.com

Bad Faith Insurance, Personal Injury, Wrongful Death, Malpractice.

FIRM PROFILE: Plaintiff's tort litigation, including bad faith insurance practices, patient advocacy, insurance disputes, aviation law, professional malpractice, personal injury (including traumatic brain injury), sex abuse, breach of fiduciary duty and will contests.

ROBERT G. PALMER, born Columbus, Ohio, September 4, 1945; admitted to bar, 1970, Missouri; 1971, U.S. Court of Military Appeals; 1976, Ohio and U.S. District Court, Southern District of Ohio; 1985, U.S. Court of Appeals, Sixth Circuit; 1987, U.S. Court of Appeals, Fourth Circuit; 1990, U.S. Claims Court; 1998, U.S. Supreme Court; 2001, U.S. District Court, Northern District of Ohio. *Education:* DePauw University (B.A., 1967); Washington University (J.D., 1970). Author: "Altered and "Lost" Medical Records," Trial Magazine, May, 1999; "Proving Damages," *Civil Litigation in Ohio, CLIO,* 1992; "Section 23 Housing: Low Rent Housing and Private Accommodations," 48 Journal of Urban Law 255, 1970. Faculty: National College of Advocacy, 1981—; National Institute for Trial Advocacy, 1993, 1994; Ohio CLE, 1982-1996. Trustee (President, 1996-1997) Columbus Bar Foundation, 1993-1999. *Member:* Columbus, Ohio State (Chairman, Negligence Law Committee, 1986-1990; 1998-2000) and American Bar Associations; Franklin County Trial Lawyers Association; Ohio Academy of Trial Lawyers (Chairman, Insurance Law Section, 1987-1989); The Association of Trial Lawyers of America (Chairman, Federal Tort Liability and Military Advocacy, 1994-1995, 1999-2000). Fellow, American College of Trial Lawyers. [Capt., JAG, USAF, 1970-1975]. ***REPORTED CASES:*** Dardinger v. Anthem Insurance Companies, Inc. 98 Ohio St. 3d 77, 2002-Ohio-7113; Schaefer v. Allstate Ins. Co., 63 Ohio St. 3d 708 (1992); Schaefer v. Allstate Ins. Co., 79 Ohio St. 3d 553 (1996). ***PRACTICE AREAS:*** Insurance Bad Faith; Personal Injury; Professional Negligence. ***Email:*** bob@rgpalmerlaw.com

---

CARMA R. PAUSCH

7100 N. HIGH STREET, SUITE 307
COLUMBUS, OHIO 43085-2361
Telephone: 614-880-2303
URL: http://www.lawyers.com/carmarpausch

State and Federal Criminal Defense, Appellate Practice, Civil Litigation.

CARMA R. PAUSCH, born Newark, Ohio, July 6, 1964; admitted to bar, 1994, Ohio. *Education:* The Ohio State University (B.A., 1986); Capital University (J.D., 1994). *Member:* Columbus, Ohio State and American Bar Associations. ***PRACTICE AREAS:*** Criminal Defense; Appellate Practice; Civil Litigation.

PECK, SHAFFER & WILLIAMS LLP

175 SOUTH THIRD STREET, SUITE 600
COLUMBUS, OHIO 43215
Telephone: 614-224-5205; 888-900-5205
Telecopier: 614-224-0069
Email: lawinfo@peck-shaffer.com
URL: http://www.peck-shaffer.com

Atlanta, Georgia Office: Peck, Shaffer & Williams LLP, Atlanta Financial Center, Suite M20, 3353 Peachtree Road, N.E. Telephone: 404-995-3850. Fax: 404-995-3851.
Chicago, Illinois Office: Peck, Shaffer & Williams LLP, 11 South LaSalle Street, Suite 2100. Telephones: 312-372-6060; 877-372-6060. Fax: 312-372-6085.
Cincinnati, Ohio Office: Peck, Shaffer & Williams LLP, 201 E. 5th Street, Suite 900. Telephones: 513-621-3394; 800-927-2663. Telecopier: 513-621-3813.
Covington, Kentucky Office: Peck, Shaffer & Williams LLP, 118 West 5th Street. Telephones: 859-431-7000; 888-431-7511. Telecopier: 859-431-0673.
Denver, Colorado Office: Peck, Shaffer & Williams LLP, 555 17th Street, Suite 845 South, 80202. Telephone: 303-296-3996; 877-296-0333. Fax: 303-296-0344.
Louisville, Kentucky Office: Peck, Shaffer & Williams LLP, 239 S. Fifth Street, Suite 1603. Telephone: 502-561-0054. Telecopier: 502-561-0058.

Public Finance, Municipal Bonds, Municipal Bond Taxation, Municipal Securities. Tax Exempt Bonds, Housing and Urban Development, Health Care Finance, Tax Increment Finance, Municipal Leasing, Public Finance Taxation, Securities Finance, Blue Sky Law, Low Income Housing, Industrial Development Bonds, Municipal Bankruptcy, Public Construction Law.

FIRM PROFILE: Peck, Shaffer & Williams LLP (PS&W) is a law firm with the experience, knowledge and creativity to guide its clients (hundreds of municipalities, counties, school districts, townships, special districts and underwriters) in issuing bonds and other debt instruments. The capital improvements financed with the proceeds of this debt include traditional governmental projects, such as roads, sewers, water systems, all types of public buildings, public infrastructure facilities, such as stadiums, convention centers and single-, multifamily and public housing; facilities for 501(c)(3) organizations, such as hospitals, university and long term care facilities and "exempt facilities" for industrial and commercial users, such as factories, waste recovery plants and port facilities. PS&W's expertise also extends to lease transactions and public construction counsel matters and has helped finance thousands of low-income housing projects in virtually every state.

MEMBERS OF FIRM

RICHARD A. CARDWELL, born Ironton, Ohio, August 30, 1963; admitted to bar, 1991, Ohio. *Education:* The Ohio State University (B.A., 1986); Capital University Law School (J.D., 1990). ***PRACTICE AREAS:*** Municipal Contracts; Construction Contracts; Public Construction Law. ***Email:*** rcardwell@peck-shaffer.com

(This Listing Continued)

EDWARD CAVEZZA, born Scranton, Pennsylvania, March 28, 1957; admitted to bar, 1982, Ohio; 1983, U.S. District Court, Southern District of Ohio. *Education:* University of Scranton (B.S., summa cum laude, 1979); University of Notre Dame (J.D., cum laude, 1982). ***PRACTICE AREAS:*** Municipal Bonds; Tax Exempt Bonds; Public Finance. ***Email:*** ecavezza@peck-shaffer.com

MARY S. DUFFEY, born Columbus, Ohio, July 4, 1957; admitted to bar, 1987, Ohio; 1988, U.S. District Court, Southern District of Ohio and U.S. Court of Appeals, Sixth Circuit. *Education:* University of Michigan (B.A., 1983); The Ohio State University (J.D., with honors, 1987). ***PRACTICE AREAS:*** Municipal Bonds; Tax Exempt Bonds; Public Finance. ***Email:*** mduffey@peck-shaffer.com

STEPHEN P. GRASSBAUGH, born Mount Vernon, Ohio, December 2, 1951; admitted to bar, 1984, Ohio. *Education:* The Ohio State University (B.S.B.A., 1973); Case Western Reserve University (J.D., 1984). ***PRACTICE AREAS:*** Municipal Bonds; Tax Exempt Bonds; Tax Exempt Finance. ***Email:*** sgrassbaugh@peck-shaffer.com

MICHAEL J. MELLIERE, born St. Paul, Minnesota, 1967; admitted to bar, 1991, Indiana; 1997, Ohio. *Education:* Purdue University (B.S., 1988); University of Michigan - Ann Arbor (J.D., 1991). ***PRACTICE AREAS:*** Structured Finance; Health Care Finance; Municipal Securities; Public Finance Taxation; Asset Based Finance. ***Email:*** mmelliere@peck-shaffer.com

GLENDON B. PRATT, born Cincinnati, Ohio, September 11, 1957; admitted to bar, 1982, Ohio. *Education:* Miami University (B.A., magna cum laude, 1978); University of Michigan (J.D., 1982). ***PRACTICE AREAS:*** Municipal Bonds; Tax Exempt Bonds; Industrial Development Bonds. ***Email:*** gpratt@peck-shaffer.com

DENNIS G. SCHWALLIE, born Cincinnati, Ohio, April 27, 1953; admitted to bar, 1978, Ohio; 1980, U.S. District Court, Southern District of Ohio. *Education:* University of Cincinnati (B.B.A., with honors, 1975); The Ohio State University (J.D., 1978). ***PRACTICE AREAS:*** Municipal Bonds; Tax Exempt Bonds; Public Finance. ***Email:*** dschwallie@peck-shaffer.com

THOMAS A. WILSON, born Port Huron, Michigan, January 13, 1960; admitted to bar, 1985, Michigan; 1990, Ohio. *Education:* Albion College (A.B., magna cum laude, with honors in Philosophy, 1982); Georgetown University (J.D., 1985). ***PRACTICE AREAS:*** Municipal Bonds; Tax Exempt Bonds; Public Finance. ***Email:*** twilson@peck-shaffer.com

ASSOCIATES

JENNIFER R. BLASER, born Akron, Ohio, December 1, 1973; admitted to bar, 1999, Ohio. *Education:* Ohio University (B.A., Finance, 1996); The Ohio State University (J.D., 1999). ***PRACTICE AREAS:*** Municipal Bonds; Tax Exempt Bonds; Public Finance. ***Email:*** jblaser@peck-shaffer.com

JASON L. GEORGE, born Waukegan, Illinois, December 8, 1972; admitted to bar, 1998, Ohio. *Education:* DePauw University (B.A., 1995); Indiana School of Law-Bloomington (J.D., 1998). ***PRACTICE AREAS:*** Municipal Bonds; Tax Exempt Bonds; Municipal Bankruptcy. ***Email:*** jgeorge@peck-shaffer.com

MARC KAMER, born Columbus, Ohio, November 28, 1972; admitted to bar, 1998, Ohio. *Education:* The Ohio State University (B.A., Liberal Arts, summa cum laude, with honors, 1995; J.D., with honors in Law, 1998). ***PRACTICE AREAS:*** Public Construction Law; Municipal Bonds; Tax Exempt Bonds; Tax Exempt Finance. ***Email:*** mkamer@peck-shaffer.com

NICOLLE STALLWORTH, born 1974; admitted to bar, 2004, New York and New Jersey (Not admitted in Ohio). *Education:* Hampton University (B.S., Marketing, 1996); Fordham Law School (J.D., 2003). *Member:* Ohio State and New York State Bar Associations. ***PRACTICE AREAS:*** Tax Exempt Bonds; Municipal Bonds; Public Finance. ***Email:*** nstallworth@peck-shaffer.com

CHARLES H. WATERMAN, IV, born Columbus, Ohio, March 4, 1974; admitted to bar, 2001, Ohio. *Education:* University of Arizona (B.A., 1996); The Ohio State University College of Law (J.D., with honors, 2001). ***PRACTICE AREAS:*** Muncipal Bonds; Tax Exempt Bonds; Public Finance; Economic Development. ***Email:*** cwaterman@peck-shaffer.com

(For Additional Biographical Data on all Personnel, see Professional Biographies at http.www.peck-shaffer.com)

PICKREL, SCHAEFFER & EBELING

COLUMBUS, OHIO

(See Dayton)

Banking, Civil, Corporate, General Business, Commercial Lending, Mergers and Acquisitions, Insurance, Labor and Employment, Healthcare, Municipal and Zoning, Personal Injury and Products Liability, Probate, Trust and Estate Planning, Construction, Computer, Real Estate, Environmental, Workers' Compensation Defense, Immigration, Bankruptcy and Tax Law. Trials and Appeals, School Law and Title Insurance.

PLANK & BRAHM

A LEGAL PROFESSIONAL ASSOCIATION
145 EAST RICH STREET
SUITE 400
COLUMBUS, OHIO 43215-5240
Telephone: 614-228-4546
Fax: 614-228-1472
Email: email@plankbrahm.com

Civil Litigation, Trial Practice and Civil Appeals. Real Estate Development and Zoning Law. Construction Law, Corporate and General Business Law. Banking and Securities Law. Municipal Law. Land Annexation, Eminent Domain, Personal Injury and Negligence Law.

(This Listing Continued)

FIRM PROFILE: Plank & Brahm was formed by a small group of experienced attorneys with a singular purpose: to provide our clients with the highest quality legal service in the most cost effective manner. Our lawyers have excellent academic credentials and a broad range of experience in both the public and private sectors. We are a general practice law firm with special emphasis on real estate matters, including acquisition, financing, annexation, zoning, platting, permitting and subdivision work; business transactions, including the formation and continuing representation of large and small businesses, and sophisticated financing and securities matters; civil and business litigation and appeals in all courts in commercial disputes, contract claims, negligence actions, including insurance defense, and eminent domain proceedings. Above all, we pride ourselves on being honest, ethical and hard-working attorneys committed to serving the needs of our clients.

DONALD T. PLANK, born Columbus, Ohio January 3, 1952; admitted to bar, 1979, Ohio. *Education:* Ohio State University (B.S., cum laude, Phi Alpha Kappa, 1975); Capital University (J.D., 1979). Chief Real Estate Attorney, City of Columbus, Ohio, 1983-1987. *Member:* Columbus and American (Member, Real Property and Probate Section) Bar Associations. ***PRACTICE AREAS:*** Real Estate; Zoning, Planning and Land Use; Eminent Domain; Municipal Law. ***Email:*** dplank@plankbrahm.com

RICHARD C. BRAHM, born Cincinnati, Ohio, January 29, 1945; admitted to bar, 1970, Ohio. *Education:* University of Cincinnati (B.S., 1967; J.D., 1970). Phi Delta Phi. Assistant General Counsel, U.S. Department of Agriculture, 1970-1971. Assistant Attorney General, State of Ohio, 1971-1974. Ohio Attorney General, Chief Court of Claims Defense Section, 1974-1976. *Member:* Columbus and Ohio State Bar Associations. ***PRACTICE AREAS:*** Real Estate Law; Corporate Law; Civil Practice; Appellate Practice; Trial Practice; Zoning Law; Annexation Law. ***Email:*** rbrahm@plankbrahm.com

MARK A. PETERSON, born Columbus, Ohio, May 15, 1962; admitted to bar, 1989, Ohio. *Education:* The Ohio State University (B.S.B.A., 1985); Case Western Reserve University (J.D., 1989). *Member:* Columbus, Ohio State and American Bar Associations. ***PRACTICE AREAS:*** Corporate Law; Business Law; Securities Law; Real Estate Law. ***Email:*** mpeterson@plankbrahm.com

---

MICHAEL F. RYAN, born Zanesville, Ohio, April 3, 1945; admitted to bar, 1988, Ohio; 1989, U.S. District Court, Southern District of Ohio; 1993, U.S. Supreme Court. *Education:* Ohio Dominican College (B.A., 1983); Capital University (J.D., 1987). *Member:* Columbus, Ohio State and American Bar Associations. ***PRACTICE AREAS:*** Personal Injury; Accidents; Insurance Subrogation; Civil Litigation; Trial Practice; Personal Injury Defense. ***Email:*** mryan@plankbrahm.com

FRANKLIN E. ECK, JR., born White Plains, New York, May 15, 1964; admitted to bar, 1989, Ohio; 1990, U.S. District Court, Southern District of Ohio; 1992, U.S. Court of Appeals, 6th Circuit; 1993, U.S. Supreme Court. *Education:* John Carroll University (B.A., 1986); Notre Dame Law School (J.D., 1989). *Member:* Columbus, Ohio State and American Bar Associations. ***PRACTICE AREAS:*** Civil Practice; Trial Practice; Appellate Practice; Foreclosure Law; Real Estate; Insurance Subrogation; Annexation Law; Municipal Law. ***Email:*** feck@plankbrahm.com

CATHERINE A. CUNNINGHAM, born Columbus, Ohio, October 28, 1958; admitted to bar, 1983, Ohio; 1984, U.S. District Court, Southern District of Ohio. *Education:* Allegheny College (B.A., cum laude, 1980); University of Exeter, Exeter England (1978-1979); The Ohio State University (J.D., 1983). Director of Law, City of Hilliard, Ohio, 1996-2000; Solicitor, Village of New Concord, Ohio, 1987-1991. *Member:* Columbus, Ohio State and American Bar Associations. ***PRACTICE AREAS:*** Real Property; Zoning Law; Annexation; Land Use Law; Municipal Law; Business Law; Civil Trial; Appellate Practice. ***Email:*** ccunningham@plankbrahm.com

DAVID WATKINS, born Oceanside, New York, July 24, 1955; admitted to bar, 1992, Ohio and U.S. District Court, Southern District of Ohio; 2000, U.S. Tax Court. *Education:* Beloit College (B.A., magna cum laude, 1976); Capital University (J.D., 1992). Phi Beta Kappa; Omicron Delta Kappa. Order of Curia. *Member:* Columbus and Ohio State Bar Associations. ***PRACTICE AREAS:*** Civil Litigation; Trial Practice; Civil Appeals; Business Law; Agricultural Law. ***Email:*** dwatkins@plankbrahm.com

JILL STEMEN TANGEMAN, born Columbus, Ohio, April 11, 1971; admitted to bar, 1996, Ohio. *Education:* Denison University (B.A., 1993); The Ohio State University (J.D., 1996). *Member:* Columbus, Ohio State and American Bar Associations. ***PRACTICE AREAS:*** Zoning Law; Land Use; Land Sales and Acquisitions; Real Estate Litigation; Eminent Domain. ***Email:*** jtangeman@plankbrahm.com

REPRESENTATIVE CLIENTS: Central Ohio Contractors; C.V. Perry & Co. Development; Donald W. Kelley and Associates; Dominion Homes; Diyanni Homes, Inc.; Rockford Homes; Triangle Properties; Homewood Corp.; The Edwards Land Company; F.W. Sloter, Inc.; Hamilton Parker; Huntington National Bank; Mid-City Electric Co.; Personal Service Insurance Co.; S.G. Loewewdick & Sons, Inc.;The Computer Group, Inc.; Creative Child Care, Inc.
SPECIAL COUNSEL TO: City of Centerville; City of Columbus; City of Dayton; City of Gahanna; City of Grove City; City of Middletown; City of Pickerington; City of Union; City of Westerville; Franklin County Convention Facilities Authority; Rickenbacker Port Authority.
LOCAL COUNSEL FOR: B.P. Oil Co.; Centex Homes, Ohio Division; Lamar Outdoor Advertising; Martin Marietta Materials; United Dairy Farmers, Inc.

PLUNKETT & COONEY, P.C.

Established in 2002
300 EAST BROAD STREET, SUITE 590
COLUMBUS, OHIO 43215
Telephone: 614-629-3000
Fax: 614-629-3019
Email: plunkettinfo@plunkettcooney.com
URL: http://www.plunkettcooney.com

Offices also at: Detroit, Bloomfield Hills, Flint, Grand Rapids, Kalamazoo, East Lansing, Marquette, Mount Clemens and Petoskey, Mi.

(This Listing Continued)

PLUNKETT & COONEY, P.C., Columbus—Continued

Alternative Dispute Resolution, Banking Law and Commercial Loans, Bankruptcy, Business Law, Construction Law, Corporate Law, Criminal Law, Debtor's Rights and Creditor's Rights, Environmental Law, Estate Planning, Food Service and Hospitality Law, Franchise Law, General Business and Civil Practice, Government Law, Health Care, Insurance, Intellectual Property Law, Labor and Employment Law, Legal Malpractice, Medical Malpractice, Municipal Law, Products Liability, Professional Liability, Real Estate Law, Securities, Taxation, Telecommunications Law, Trials in all Federal and State Courts and Worker's Compensation.

AMELIA BOWER, born Indianapolis, Indiana, October 15, 1954; admitted to bar, 1984, Ohio; 1985, U.S. District Court, Northern District of Ohio; 1990, U.S. Supreme Court; 2002, U.S. District Court, Southern District of Ohio. *Education:* Miami University (B.A., 1977); Cleveland Marshall College of Law (J.D., 1984). Member, 1992-2002 and Former Chair, Certified Grievance Committee, Cleveland Bar Association. Member, Bar Admissions Committee, 1990-2002 and Joint Bar Admissions Appeals Sub Committee, 1993-2002, Cuyahoga County/Cleveland Bar Associations. Speaker: Mastering Real Estate Title and Title Insurance in Ohio, 2001-2004; Advanced Principles of Title Insurance, 2002-2004. Co-Editor: Merrick Rippner Ohio Probate Law (4th ed.); Ohio Real Estate Law and Practice, 2003. *Member:* Cleveland, Columbus (Member, Real Estate Law Section) and Ohio State (Member, Committees on: Legal Ethics and Professionalism; Insurance Staff Counsel) Bar Associations. ***REPORTED CASES:*** David O. Simon v. Chase Manhattan Bank (In re Zaptocky), 250 F. 2d 1020; Treinish v. Norwest Bank Minnesota (In re Periandri), 266 B.R. 651. ***PRACTICE AREAS:*** Title Insurance Defense; Real Estate Law; Professional Liability; Foreclosure; Escrow agent and title company liability. ***Email:*** abower@plunkettcooney.com

TODD A. COOK, born Lima, Ohio, January 31, 1966; admitted to bar, 1991, Ohio; 1997, U.S. Supreme Court; 2003, U.S. District Court, Northern District of Ohio and U.S. Court of Appeals, Sixth Circuit. *Education:* University of Toledo (B.A., 1988); Ohio Northern University (J.D., 1991). *Member:* Columbus, Ohio State and American (Member, Sections on: Litigation; Torts; and Insurance) Bar Associations; Defense Research Institute (Member: Toxic Torts and Environmental Law Committee; Medical Liability Committee); Ohio Association of Civil Trial Attorneys; Columbus Claims Association; American Health Lawyers Association. ***REPORTED CASES:*** Armentrout v. Anthem Cas. Ins. Co., No. 01-296, Supreme Court of Ohio, 92 Ohio St. 3d 88; 2001 Ohio 153; 748 N.E.2d 534; 2001 Ohio LEXIS 1675, May 30, 2001; 2. Dycoco v. Guernsey Mem. Hosp., Case Nos. 99CA06, 99CA10, Court of Appeals of Ohio, Fifth Appellate District, Guernsey County, 2000 Ohio App. LEXIS 2306, May 15, 2000; 3. Lovewell v. Physicians Ins. Co., NO. 68542, Court of Appeals of Ohio, Eighth Appellate District, Cuyahoga County, 1995 Ohio App. LEXIS 4606, October 19, 1995. ***PRACTICE AREAS:*** Complex Litigation; Toxic Torts; Environmental Litigation; Banking Litigation; Commercial Litigation; Product Liability Litigation; Insurance Law; Professional Liability; Medical Malpractice; Health Care Law. ***Email:*** tcook@plunkettcooney.com

JACK S. LEVEY, born Chicago, Illinois, May 16, 1950; admitted to bar, 1978, Minnesota; 1983, Ohio. *Education:* University of Wisconsin-Madison (B.A., 1972); University of Minnesota (J.D., magna cum laude, 1978). Author: "Beginner's Guide to the Commitment for Owner's Title Insurance," Probate & Property, May/June 2000; "Title Insurance and the LLC," Probate and Property, Jan./Feb. 1995; "Don't Sell or Die Without the Landlord's Permission," Practical Real Estate Lawyer, Januar, 1999. Co-Author: with Kenton L. Kuehnle, *Ohio Real Estate Law,* West Publishing Company; "Non-Tax Aspects of Income Tax Driven LLCs and LLPs," Practical Real Estate Lawyer, July 1998; "Title Examination in Ohio," Lorman Education Services; "The Commercial Property Lease," American Bar Association. *Member:* Columbus, Ohio State and American (Member: Real Property, Probate and Trust Law Section; Commercial Leasing Group; Vice Chairman, Title Insurance Committee, 1995-2002) Bar Associations. ***TRANSACTIONS:*** Ground lease for Nationwide Arena. ***PRACTICE AREAS:*** Commercial Real Estate; Commercial Law; Business Law; Wills; Contracts; Construction Law. ***Email:*** jlevey@plunkettcooney.com

SENIOR ASSOCIATE

PAUL E. PERRY, born May 4, 1951; admitted to bar, 1976, Ohio; 1991, Tennessee; 1998, Michigan. *Education:* The Ohio State University (B.A., 1973; J.D., 1976). *Member:* Columbus, Ohio State and American Bar Associations; State Bar of Michigan; American Bankruptcy Institute. ***PRACTICE AREAS:*** Commercial Real Estate Workouts; Bankruptcy; Creditors Rights; Real Estate Title Insurance; Real Estate. ***Email:*** pperry@plunkettcooney.com

ASSOCIATE

DAVID L. VAN SLYKE, born Conneaut, Ohio, December 17, 1978; admitted to bar, 2004, Ohio; U.S. Court of Appeals, 6th Circuit; U.S. District Court, Northern District of Ohio. *Education:* Baldwin Wallace (B.A., magna cum laude, 2001); Cleveland State University (J.D., magna cum laude, 2004). Cleveland State Law Review, 2002-2004. Member, Cleveland Marshall College of Law Student Bar Association, 2003-2006. ***PRACTICE AREAS:*** Title Insurance; Litigation; White Collar Crime. ***Email:*** dvanslyke@plunkettcooney.com

THE PLYMALE PARTNERSHIP LLP

495 SOUTH HIGH STREET, SUITE 400
COLUMBUS, OHIO 43215
Telephone: 614-221-1166; 614-LAW-8000; 800-221-6675
Fax: 614-221-6633
URL: http://www.lawyers.com/protectingohio
Email: help@plymalelaw.com
URL: http://www.protectingohio.com

Personal Injury, Products Liability, Wrongful Death, Medical Malpractice, Professional Negligence, Traumatic Brain Injury, Automobile Accidents, Nursing Home Torts, Civil Litigation.

(This Listing Continued)

FIRM PROFILE: The Plymale Partnership in an aggressive trial practice firm devoted to the representation of victims of serious injury and death. The firm's trial attorneys litigate in all Ohio courts. For over thirty years, the firm has leveraged their reputation for the benefit of victims in serious injury, wrongful death and professional negligence.

MEMBERS OF FIRM

ANDREW W. CECIL, born Louisville, Kentucky, February 8, 1960; admitted to bar, 1986, Ohio and U.S. District Court, Southern and Eastern Districts of Ohio. *Education:* Eastern Kentucky University (B.S., Police Administration, with high honors, 1982); University of Louisville (J.D., 1985). *Member:* Columbus and Ohio State Bar Associations; Franklin County Trial Lawyers Association; Ohio Academy of Trial Lawyers (Trustee, 1999); National College of Advocacy (Associate, 1995); The Association of Trial Lawyers of America; San Antonio Trial Lawyers Association; Million Dollar Advocates Forum. (Board Certified Civil Trial Specialist by the National Board of Trial Advocacy). ***REPORTED CASES:*** Olander v. Nationwide Mut. Ins. Co., 76 Ohio St.3d 229 (Aug. 7, 1996); Horvath v. Nationwide Mut. Fire Ins. Co., 108 Ohio App.3d 732 (Jan. 25, 1996); Huffer v. Cicero, 107 Ohio App.3d 65 (Nov. 3, 1995); Mayes v. Columbus, 105 Ohio App.3d 728 (Aug. 17, 1995); Thornton v. Parker, 100 Ohio App.3d 743 (Jan. 31, 1995); Senig v. Nationwide Mut. Ins. Co., 76 Ohio App.3d 565 (July 23, 1992); Ross v. Nationwide Mut. Ins. Co., 63 Ohio St.3d 33 (Feb. 19, 1992); James v. Wright, 76 Ohio App.3d 493 (Dec. 5, 1991); Cox v. Nationwide Mut. Ins. Co., 76 Ohio App.3d 398 (Nov. 26, 1991); Casto v. State Farm Mut. Auto. Ins. Co., 72 Ohio app.3d 410 (Feb. 7, 1991); State Farm Fire & Cas. Co. v. Chrysler Corp., 37 Ohio St.3d 1 (May 18, 1988); Bogan v. Progressive Cas. Ins. Co., 36 Ohio St.3d 22 (Mar. 30, 1988); Bob-Boyd Lincoln Mercury v. Hyatt, 32 Ohio St.3d 300 (Sep. 9, 1987); Jewett v. Owners Ins. Co., 82 Ohio St.3d 1224, 696 N.E.2d 598 (Ohio, July 22, 1998); Columbus Bar Assn. v. Dye, 82 Ohio St.3d 64, 694 N.E.2d 440 (Ohio, June 3, 1998); Mayes v. Columbus, 124 Ohio App.3d 411, 706 N.E.2d 402 (Ohio App.10 Dist., Dec 11, 1997-No. 97APE05-597); Quappe v. Ohio Dept. of Pub. Safety, 84 Ohio Misc.2d 74, 679 N.E. 755 (Ohio CtCl., Jan 09, 1997-No. 95-09485). ***PRACTICE AREAS:*** Personal Injury; Civil Practice; Legal Ethics and Professional Responsibility; Professional Discipline; Wrongful Death; Insurance Coverage. ***Email:*** acecil@plymalelaw.com

MICHAEL KEITH GEISER, born Columbus, Ohio, August 9, 1964; admitted to bar, 1991, Ohio and U.S. Court of Appeals, Sixth Circuit; 1993, U.S. District Court, Southern District of Ohio; 1994, U.S. Supreme Court. *Education:* The Ohio State University (B.A., Political Science, 1987); Capital University (J.D., 1990). *Member:* Columbus and Ohio State Bar Associations; Ohio Academy of Trial Lawyers; The Association of Trial Lawyers of America; Franklin County Trial Lawyers Association. ***PRACTICE AREAS:*** Negligence; Personal Injury; Premises Liability; Insurance Contracts; Civil Practice. ***Email:*** mgeiser@plymalelaw.com

ASSOCIATES

J. SCOTT BOWMAN, born Wheeling, West Virginia, January 29, 1970; admitted to bar, 1998, Ohio. *Education:* Ohio State University (B.S., Environmental Science, cum laude, 1992; J.D., 1998). *Member:* Franklin County Trial Lawyers Association; Columbus Bar Association; Ohio Academy of Trial Lawyers; Association of Trial Lawyers of America; Ohio State Bar Association. ***PRACTICE AREAS:*** Personal Injury; Wrongful Death; Insurance Coverage; Civil Litigation. ***Email:*** sbowman@plymalelaw.com

EUGENE R. CRITCHETT, born Des Moines, Iowa, October 25, 1975; admitted to bar, 2001, Ohio. *Education:* Ithaca College (B.A., Spanish, cum laude, 1997); The Ohio State University College of Law (J.D., 2001). *Member:* Columbus, Ohio State and American Bar Associations; Franklin County Trial Lawyers Association; Ohio Academy of Trial Lawyers. ***LANGUAGES:*** Spanish. ***PRACTICE AREAS:*** Personal Injury; Wrongful Death; Insurance Coverage; Civil Litigation. ***Email:*** rcritchett@plymalelaw.com

C. MICHAEL WISE, born Columbus, Ohio, November 29, 1959; admitted to bar, 1988, Ohio. *Education:* Ohio State University (B.A., with honors in Liberal Arts and with distinction in English, 1984; J.D., 1988). *Member:* Columbus Bar Association; Franklin County Bar Association; Ohio State Bar Association; Franklin County Trial Lawyers Association; Ohio Academy of Trial Lawyers. ***PRACTICE AREAS:*** Personal Injury; Wrongful Death; Civil Litigation.

SYDNEY D. STEIN, born Cincinnati, Ohio, September 2, 1978; admitted to bar, 2003, Ohio. *Education:* The Ohio State University (B.A., English, 2000); Capital University Law School (J.D., 2003). *Member:* Columbus Bar Association; Franklin County Trial Lawyers Association; Ohio Academy of Trial Lawyers; Ohio State Bar Association. ***PRACTICE AREAS:*** Personal Injury; Wrongful Death; Insurance Coverage; Civil Litigation.

OF COUNSEL

RONALD E. PLYMALE, born Huntington, West Virginia, September 16, 1941; admitted to bar, 1968, Ohio, U.S. District Court, Southern District of Ohio, U.S. Court of Appeals, Sixth Circuit and U.S. Supreme Court. *Education:* The Ohio State University (B.A., 1963; J.D., 1968). Member, Million Dollar Advocates Forum. Listed in Who's Who in American Business: Strathmore. Law Director, Grove City, Ohio, 1971-1979. Lifetime Fellow, Roscoe Pound American Trial Lawyers Foundation. *Member:* Columbus and Ohio State Bar Associations; The Association of Trial Lawyers of America; Ohio Academy of Trial Lawyers; Franklin County Trial Lawyers Association (Secretary, 1977-1978; Vice-President, 1978-1979; President, 1979-1980). (Board Certified Civil Trial Specialist by the National Board of Trial Advocacy). ***REPORTED CASES:*** Anderson v. Ruoff, 100 Ohio App.3d 601 (Mr. 9, 1995); Thronton v. Parker, 100 Ohio App.3d 743 (Jan. 31, 1995); Frericks-Rich v. Zengarelli, 94 Ohio App.3d 357 (Apr. 24, 1994); Grossman v. Hawkes Hosp. of Mount Carmel, 52 Ohio St.3d 87 (June 27, 1990); Marion v. Baker, 42 Ohio App.3d 151 (Oct. 6, 1987); Hull v. Baltimore & Ohio R. Co., 37 Ohio App.3d 94 (Mar. 31, 1987); Pond v. Carey Corp., 34 Ohio App.3d 109 (June 12, 1986); Nationwide Mut. Ins. Co. v. Ferrin, 21 Ohio St.3d (Jan. 2, 1986); Miller v. Levy, 60 Ohio App.2d 78 (Aug. 15, 1978). ***PRACTICE AREAS:*** General Negligence; Medical Malpractice; Legal Malpractice; Wrongful Death; Products Liability. ***Email:*** rplymale@plymalelaw.com

ROSEMARY EBNER POMEROY

Established in 1993

120A NORTHWOODS BOULEVARD
COLUMBUS, OHIO 43235
Telephone: 614-885-2101
Fax: 614-885-1783
Email: ebnerpom@netwalk.com
URL: http://www.lawyers.com/rosemaryebnerpomeroylaw

Adoption, Estate Planning and Administration, Guardianships, Elder Law, Real Estate.

ROSEMARY EBNER POMEROY, born Detroit, Michigan, December 1, 1955; admitted to bar, 1988, Ohio and U.S. District Court, Southern District of Ohio. *Education:* Michigan State University (B.A., 1977); Institute for Paralegal Training (Litigation Certificate, 1980); Detroit College of Law (J.D., 1986). Founder, Worthington Area Business and Professional Women. *Member:* Columbus, Ohio and American Bar Associations; Women Lawyers of Franklin County (President, 1992-1993); American Academy of Adoption Attorneys. ***PRACTICE AREAS:*** Adoption Law; Wills; Trusts; Probate; Guardianship; Real Estate.

PORTER WRIGHT MORRIS & ARTHUR LLP

Established in 1846

41 SOUTH HIGH STREET
COLUMBUS, OHIO 43215-6194
Telephone: 614-227-2000; (800-533-2794)
Fax: 614-227-2100
Email: columbus@porterwright.com
URL: http://www.porterwright.com

Cincinnati, Ohio Office: 250 E. Fifth Street, Suite 2200, 45202-5117. Telephones: 513-381-4700; (800-582-5813). Fax: 513-421-0991. Internet: cincinnati@porterwright.com.

Cleveland, Ohio Office: 925 Euclid Avenue, Suite 1700, 44115-1483. Telephones: 216-443-9000; (800-824-1980). Fax: 216-443-9011. Internet: cleveland@porterwright.com.

Dayton, Ohio Office: One Dayton Centre, One South Main Street, Suite 1600, 45402-2028. Telephones: 937-449-6810; (800-533-4434). Fax: 937-449-6820. Internet: dayton@porterwright.com.

Naples, Florida Office: 5801 Pelican Bay Boulevard, Suite 300, 34108-2709. Telephones: 239-593-2900; (800-876-7962). Fax: 239-593-2990. Internet: naples@porterwright.com.

Washington, D.C. Office: 1919 Pennsylvania Avenue, N.W., Suite 500, 20006-3434. Telephones: 202-778-3000; (800-456-7962). Fax: 202-778-3063. Internet: washington@porterwright.com.

Alternative Dispute Resolution, Agricultural Law, Antitrust and Trade Regulation, Business and Corporate, Complex Litigation, Construction, Employee Benefits, Energy and Utilities, Environment, Federal Administrative Law, Federal Contracting and Procurement, Financial Institutions, General Practice, Governmental Affairs, Health Care, Insurance, Intellectual Property, International Business, Labor and Employment, Litigation, Public Law, Public Finance, Real Estate, Securities, Taxation, Technology, Trusts and Estates.

FIRM PROFILE: Porter Wright Morris & Arthur LLP is a nationally known business law firm delivering creative solutions for large, mid-size and entrepreneurial businesses. The Firm, which traces its origins to 1846, has more than 250 lawyers practicing in Cincinnati, Cleveland, Columbus, and Dayton, Ohio; Washington, D.C.; and Naples, Florida. The Firm provides legal services to a worldwide base of clients in the areas of business and finance, commercial litigation, financial institutions law and regulation, commercial and personal lending, bankruptcy, government affairs, environmental law, personal injury and tort litigation, insurance, health care, employee benefits, labor and employment, real estate, federal and state tax, trusts and estates, probate proceedings and litigation, federal procurement and contracting, utility regulation, international and intellectual property, securities and technologies.

PARTNERS COLUMBUS, OHIO OFFICE

JON M. ANDERSON, born Rio Grande, Ohio, January 10, 1937; admitted to bar, 1961, Ohio. *Education:* Ohio University (A.B., 1958); Harvard Law School (J.D., cum laude, 1961). Law Clerk to Hon. Kingsley A. Taft, Supreme Court of Ohio, 1961-1962. Member, 1970-1975 and Chairman, 1974-1975, Ohio State Board of Bar Examiners. Adjunct Professor of Law, The Ohio State University Law School, 1975-1983. *Member:* Columbus, Ohio State and American Bar Associations. ***PRACTICE AREAS:*** Estate Planning; Probate Administration; Business Law; Tax. ***Email:*** janderson@porterwright.com

EDWIN M. BARANOWSKI, born Utica, New York, January 26, 1947; admitted to bar, 1972, New York; 1973, U.S. District Court, Southern District of New York; 1976, U.S. Court of Appeals, Second Circuit; 1982, Ohio, U.S. District Court, Southern District of Ohio and U.S. Court of Appeals for the Federal Circuit; 1983, U.S. Court of Appeals, Sixth Circuit; registered to practice before U.S. Patent and Trademark Office. *Education:* Hamilton College (B.A., 1968) Charles A. Dana Scholar; University of Virginia (J.D., 1971). Special Patent Counsel, City of Columbus (1986-2005); Inventor, 11 U.S. Letters Patent. *Member:* The Association of the Bar of the City of New York; American Bar Association (Subcommittee Chairman and Editor and Co-Author of Intellectual Property Section Subcommittee Reports: Preliminary Injunctions in Patent Litigation and Survey of Law on Comparative and False Advertising); Columbus Intellectual Property Law Association (President and Officer, 1983-1987). ***PRACTICE AREAS:*** Patents, Trademarks and Copyrights; Litigation; Technology. ***Email:*** ebaranowski@porterwright.com

PHILLIP H. BARRETT, born Detroit, Michigan, May 7, 1943; admitted to bar, 1968, Ohio. *Education:* The Ohio State University (B.Sc., 1965; J.D., 1968). *Member:* Columbus,

(This Listing Continued)

Ohio State and American Bar Associations. ***PRACTICE AREAS:*** Business Law; Real Estate; Financing; Mergers and Acquisitions; Health Care; Non-Profits; Financial Institutions. ***Email:*** pbarrett@porterwright.com

SCOTT E. BAUGHMAN, born Cleveland, Ohio, March 23, 1967; admitted to bar, 1992, Ohio. *Education:* The Ohio State University (B.A., 1989); The University of Toledo (J.D., 1992). Moot Court Board. National Moot Court. Chief Counsel, 1993-1998 and Co-Chief of Staff, 1998, The Ohio House of Representatives. Chair, Legislative Task Force on Redistricting. Secretary and Counsel, Ohio Public Expenditure Council. Special Counsel, Ohio Attorney General. ***PRACTICE AREAS:*** State and Federal Government Relations. ***Email:*** sbaughman@porterwright.com

JOHN C. BEELER, born Indianapolis, Indiana, December 3, 1951; admitted to bar, 1976, Ohio. *Education:* Dartmouth College (A.B., magna cum laude, 1973); Duke University (J.D., with distinction, 1976). Phi Beta Kappa. Adjunct Professor, Capital University Law School, 2000—. *Member:* Columbus, Ohio State (Chair, International Committee, 2000-2001) and American (Section on Business Law, Forum on Affordable Housing) Bar Associations. ***PRACTICE AREAS:*** Business Planning; International Law; Immigration; Affordable Housing; Real Estate; Tax. ***Email:*** jbeeler@porterwright.com

JAMES P. BOTTI, born Columbus, Ohio, December 30, 1956; admitted to bar, 1982, Ohio; 1983, U.S. District Court, Southern District of Ohio. *Education:* The Ohio State University (B.A., cum laude, 1979; J.D., with honors, 1982). Author: Ohio Creditor's Rights and Volume 6 of Ohio Civil Practice, Anderson Publishing Co., 1993. Co-author: Representing Creditors in Ohio, Professional Education Systems, Inc., 1990, 1992. Frequent lecturer: Creditor's Rights and Loan Documentation Issues. *Member:* Columbus (Board of Governors, 1997-2001; Professional Ethics Committee; Bankruptcy Committee; Financial Institutions Committee; Chair, Law School Liaison Committee, 2002—, Vice-Chair, 2005—) and Ohio State (Member, Banking, Commercial and Bankruptcy Law Committee; Chair, Secured Transactions Subcommittee, 1991-1994; Ohio Supreme Court Joint Commission on the Education of Lawyers, 1995-1996) Bar Associations. ***PRACTICE AREAS:*** Bankruptcy Law; Commercial Law; Creditors; Finance; Commerce. ***Email:*** jbotti@porterwright.com

JOHN E. BRADY, born Paulding, Ohio, June 23, 1945; admitted to bar, 1970, Ohio. *Education:* The Ohio State University (B.S., 1967; J.D., cum laude, 1970). Phi Delta Phi. *Member:* Columbus, Ohio State and American Bar Associations. ***PRACTICE AREAS:*** Real Estate; Business; Securities. ***Email:*** jbrady@porterwright.com

ROBERT L. BRUBAKER, born Louisville, Kentucky, May 22, 1947; admitted to bar, 1972, Ohio; 1973, U.S. District Court, Southern District of Ohio; 1975, U.S. Court of Appeals, Sixth Circuit; 1979, U.S. Court of Appeals, D.C. Circuit and U.S. Supreme Court; 1995, U.S. Court of Appeals, Third, Fourth and Seventh Circuits. *Education:* Earlham College (B.A., 1969); University of Chicago (J.D., 1972). Editor, Ohio Environmental Law Handbook, Government Institutes, 1990. Author: "Deposition, Strategy, Law and Forms: Environmental Law," Matthew Bender, 1981, 1983. Assistant Attorney General, 1972-1976 and Assistant Chief, Environmental Law Section, Office of Ohio Attorney General. Chairman, East Central Section of Air and Waste Management Association, 1991-1992. Member, National Coal Council, 1998—. *Member:* Columbus, Ohio State and American (Chair, Environment Committee, Section of Public Utilities, Communications, and Transportation Law, 2003—) Bar Associations. ***PRACTICE AREAS:*** Environmental Law. ***Email:*** rbrubaker@porterwright.com

BRIAN L. BUZBY, born Columbus, Ohio, March 26, 1949; admitted to bar, 1974, Ohio. *Education:* The Ohio State University (B.A., 1971; J.D., cum laude, 1974). Member: Moot Court Governing Board, 1973-1974; National Moot Court Team, 1973-1974. Councilman, Grove City, Ohio, 1988-1993 (Chairman, Safety Committee, 1988-1990, Chairman, Finance Committee, 1990-1992; President, 1992-1993). Member, Panel of Arbitrators, American Arbitration Association (Commercial, Construction, Accident Claims). *Member:* Columbus, Ohio State and American (Member, Litigation Section; Construction Law Forum) Bar Associations. ***PRACTICE AREAS:*** Construction Law; Public Utility Law; Trial Practice; Business; Securities; Real Estate. ***Email:*** bbuzby@porterwright.com

CRAIG R. CARLSON, born White Plains, New York, October 4, 1966; admitted to bar, 1991, Ohio; 1992, U.S. District Court, Southern District of Ohio; 1994, U.S. Court of Appeals, Sixth Circuit; 1998, U.S. District Court, Eastern District of Michigan; 1999, U.S. District Court, Northern District of Ohio; 2001, U.S. District Court, Western District of Michigan and Eastern District of Wisconsin. *Education:* Duke University (A.B., 1988); Capital University (J.D., magna cum laude, 1991). Delta Theta Phi. Member: Order of the Curia; Capital University Law Review, 1989-1990. *Member:* Columbus and Ohio State Bar Associations; Defense Research Institute; National Association of Railroad Trial Counsel. ***PRACTICE AREAS:*** Life Insurance Defense; Commercial Litigation; Tort Defense; Utility Law; Railroad Liability; Professional Liability Defense; Employee Benefits. ***Email:*** ccarlson@porterwright.com

THOMAS C. COADY, born Salem, Ohio, August 20, 1938; admitted to bar, 1964, Ohio. *Education:* The Ohio State University (B.I.E., 1961; J.D., 1964). Member, Board of Editors, Ohio State Law Journal, 1963-1964. *Member:* Columbus and Ohio State (Chair, Corporation Law Committee, 2001-2003) Bar Associations; National Association of Bond Lawyers. ***PRACTICE AREAS:*** Business; Securities; Financial Institutions; Finance; Commerce. ***Email:*** tcoady@porterwright.com

ROBERT H. COHEN, born Erie, Pennsylvania, September 13, 1951; admitted to bar, 1976, Ohio and U.S. District Court, Northern District of Ohio; 1977, U.S. District Court, Southern District of Ohio; 1979, U.S. Court of Appeals for the Sixth Circuit. *Education:* Miami University (A.B., 1971); University of Cincinnati (J.D., 1976). *Member:* Columbus, Ohio State and American Bar Associations; American Immigration Lawyers Association (Chair, Ohio Chapter, 2003—). ***PRACTICE AREAS:*** Immigration and Nationality. ***Email:*** rcohen@porterwright.com

DANIEL R. CONWAY, born Chicago, Illinois, November 3, 1955; admitted to bar, 1980, Ohio; 1981, U.S. District Court, Southern District of Ohio; 1996, U.S. Court of Appeals, Sixth Circuit. *Education:* Miami University (B.S., cum laude, 1977); University of Michigan (J.D., 1980). Phi Beta Kappa. *Member:* Columbus, Ohio State and American Bar Associations. ***PRACTICE AREAS:*** Telecommunications; Energy; Administrative Hearings and Appeals. ***Email:*** dconway@porterwright.com

(This Listing Continued)

PORTER WRIGHT MORRIS & ARTHUR LLP, Columbus—Continued

S. RONALD COOK, JR., born Valparaiso, Indiana, February 19, 1945; admitted to bar, 1970, Ohio; 1971, U.S. Court of Military Appeals; 1975, U.S. District Court, Southern District of Ohio; 1977, U.S. District Court, Northern District of Ohio; 1978, U.S. Court of Appeals, Sixth Circuit; 1994, U.S. Supreme Court. *Education:* The Ohio State University (B.A., 1967; J.D., summa cum laude, 1970). Order of the Coif. Associate Editor, The Ohio State Law Journal, 1969-1970. *Member:* Columbus, Ohio State and American Bar Associations. ***PRACTICE AREAS:*** Banking and Failed Financial Institutions; Breach of Contract; Lender Liability; Commercial Banking; Fair Lending; Letters of Credit; Fraud; Computer Law; Contracts; High Technology. ***Email:*** rcook@porterwright.com

DANIEL W. COSTELLO, born New York, N.Y., April 19, 1952; admitted to bar, 1980, Ohio; 1982, U.S. District Court, Southern District of Ohio; 1984, U.S. Court of Appeals, Sixth Circuit; 1989, U.S. District Court, Northern District of Ohio; 1995, U.S. District Court, Eastern District of Michigan; 2003, U.S. Court of Appeals for the District of Columbia. *Education:* Xavier University (A.B., 1973; M.A., 1973); The Ohio State University (J.D., 1980). ***PRACTICE AREAS:*** Litigation. ***Email:*** dcostello@porterwright.com

JAMES D. CURPHEY, born Toledo, Ohio, September 29, 1958; admitted to bar, 1983, Ohio. *Education:* The Ohio State University (B.S., 1980); Case Western Reserve University (J.D., 1983). *Member:* Columbus (Chair, Committee on Law Firm and Fee Disputes, 1994—), Ohio State and American Bar Associations. ***PRACTICE AREAS:*** Commercial Litigation. ***Email:*** jcurphey@porterwright.com

LLOYD G. DePEW, JR., born Dayton, Ohio, October 18, 1952; admitted to bar, 1981, Ohio. *Education:* The Ohio State University (B.S.B.A., 1975); Capital University (J.D., 1981). Board Member, Central Ohio Chapter of Arthritis Foundation. Board Member, Godman Guild Association. Board Member, Northside Community Development Corporation. Trustee, Aviation Safety Institute. *Member:* Ohio State and American Bar Associations; American Health Lawyers Association. ***PRACTICE AREAS:*** Health Law; Business Law; Employee Benefits. ***Email:*** ldepew@porterwright.com

JOYCE D. EDELMAN, born Wheeling, West Virginia, April 26, 1957; admitted to bar, 1982, West Virginia; 1983, Ohio and U.S. District Court, Southern and Northern Districts of Ohio; U.S. Court of Appeals, Sixth Circuit. *Education:* Indiana University (B.A., 1979); West Virginia University (J.D., 1982). ***PRACTICE AREAS:*** Drug and Medical Device Litigation; Product Liability Litigation; Blood Bank Litigation. ***Email:*** jedelman@porterwright.com

JOSEPH F. ELLIOTT, born Pawtucket, Rhode Island, December 1, 1956; admitted to bar, 1982, Ohio. *Education:* Boston College (B.A., summa cum laude, 1979); University of Virginia (J.D., 1982). Phi Beta Kappa. ***PRACTICE AREAS:*** Litigation. ***Email:*** jelliott@porterwright.com

MASON EVANS, IV, born Evanston, Illinois, September 26, 1952; admitted to bar, 1977, Ohio; 1978, U.S. District Court, Southern District of Ohio. *Education:* Miami University (B.A., 1974); George Washington University (J.D., with high honors, 1977). Order of the Coif. *Member:* Ohio State and American Bar Associations; Columbus Defense Association; Ohio Association of Civil Trial Attorneys (Legislative Chairman, 1983-1984; Executive Committee, 1985-1987). ***PRACTICE AREAS:*** Litigation. ***Email:*** mevans@porterwright.com

R. LELAND EVANS, born Pittsburgh, Pennsylvania, May 7, 1957; admitted to bar, 1983, Ohio and U.S. District Court, Northern District of Ohio; 1988, U.S. District Court, Southern District of Ohio. *Education:* The Ohio State University (B.S., 1979); Case Western Reserve University (J.D., 1983). *Member:* Columbus Bar Association; Defense Research Institute; Ohio Association of Civil Trial Attorneys; National Association of Railroad Trial Counsel. ***PRACTICE AREAS:*** Products Liability; Toxic Torts; Railroad Law; Transportation Law; Environmental Law; Litigation. ***Email:*** revans@porterwright.com

LLOYD E. FISHER, JR., born Medina, Ohio, October 23, 1923; admitted to bar, 1950, Ohio. *Education:* The Ohio State University (B.Sc., 1948; J.D., summa cum laude, 1949). Phi Delta Phi; Order of the Coif. Editor-in-Chief, Ohio State Law Journal, 1949. Adjunct Professor, Ohio State University College of Law, 1967-1969, 1984-1991. *Member:* Columbus (Chairman, Probate Court Committee, 1974-1975; Board of Governors, 1980-1984), Ohio State and American Bar Associations. Fellow, American College of Trust and Estate Counsel. ***PRACTICE AREAS:*** Estate Planning; Probate Law; Trust and Estates. ***Email:*** lfisher@porterwright.com

THEODORE G. FISHER, born Columbus, Ohio, February 24, 1944; admitted to bar, 1969, Ohio; 1971, U.S. District Court, Southern District of Ohio. *Education:* The Ohio State University (B.A., 1966); University of New Mexico (J.D., 1969). Recipient, American Jurisprudence Award for Excellence in Corporations. Adjunct Faculty, Ohio State University School of Social Work, 1978-1981. *Member:* Columbus Bar Association. ***PRACTICE AREAS:*** Business; Securities. ***Email:*** tfisher@porterwright.com

MARC L. FLEISCHAUER, born Columbus, Ohio, November 19, 1965; admitted to bar, 1991, Florida, U.S. District Court, Middle District of Florida; 1994, U.S. District Court, Northern District of Ohio; 1995, Ohio; 1997, U.S. District Court, Southern District of Ohio; 1999, U.S. Court of Appeals, Sixth Circuit; 2001, U.S. Court of Appeals for Veterans Claims and U.S. Court of Appeals, Federal Circuit. *Education:* College of Wooster (B.A., honors, 1988); Florida State University (J.D., 1991). Associate Editor, Florida State University Law Review, 1990-1991. Author: "Teeth for a Paper Tiger: A Proposal to Add Enforceability to Florida's Hates Crimes Act," Florida State University Law Review, 1990. Society for Human Resource Management, 1999. Fellow, Florida Supreme Court Dispute Resolution Center, 1989-1991. Adjunct Instructor and Professional Fellow, Ashland University, 2000—. *Member:* Columbus (Labor and Employment Section) and Ohio State (Labor Law Section) Bar Associations. ***PRACTICE AREAS:*** Labor and Employment Law; Employment Discrimination Law; Wage and Hour Law; Employee Benefits. ***Email:*** mfleischauer@porterwright.com

GREGORY B. FOLIANO, born Dayton, Ohio, December 30, 1962; admitted to bar, 1990, Ohio; 1993, U.S. District Court, Southern District of Ohio. *Education:* Miami University (B.A., 1986); Cleveland-Marshall College of Law (J.D., 1990). ***PRACTICE AREAS:*** Medical Malpractice Defense; Litigation. ***Email:*** gfoliano@porterwright.com

RALPH F. GILDEHAUS, born Tulsa, Oklahoma, December 7, 1960; admitted to bar, 1990, Ohio; 1991, U.S. Court of Federal Claims; 1992, U.S. District Court, Southern District of Ohio; 1993, U.S. District Court, Northern District of Ohio; U.S. Court of Appeals for the Federal Circuit. *Education:* Amherst College (B.A., cum laude, 1983); George Washington University (J.D., with honors, 1990). Law Clerk to Judge Lawrence Margolis, U.S. Claims Court, 1990-1991. ***PRACTICE AREAS:*** Civil Litigation; Intellectual Property; Labor and Employment. ***Email:*** rgildehaus@porterwright.com

TIMOTHY E. GRADY, born Belvidere, Illinois, March 23, 1950; admitted to bar, 1979, Ohio. *Education:* Bradley University (B.A., magna cum laude, 1972); Northern Arizona University (M.A., 1973); University of Illinois (J.D., cum laude, 1979). Managing Editor, University of Illinois Law Review, 1978-1979. *Member:* Ohio State (Banking, Commercial and Bankruptcy Committee) and American (Member, Committee on Commercial Financial Services) Bar Associations. ***PRACTICE AREAS:*** Asset-Based Lending; Senior Debt Financing; Loan Workouts and Bankruptcy. ***Email:*** tgrady@porterwright.com

CONSTANCE M. GREANEY, born Boston, Massachusetts, July 21, 1963; admitted to bar, 1992, Ohio, U.S. District Court, Northern and Southern Districts of Ohio and U.S. Court of Appeals, Sixth Circuit; 1994, Wisconsin; 1995, Illinois and U.S. District Court, Western District of Wisconsin. *Education:* Mount Holyoke College (B.A., 1986); Case Western Reserve University (J.D., cum laude, 1992). Recipient, American Jurisprudence Award for Excellence in Torts. Fellow: American Inns of Court; Thomas E. Fairchild Inn. ***PRACTICE AREAS:*** Civil Litigation; Employment Law; Employee Benefits. ***Email:*** cgreaney@porterwright.com

KEVIN E. GRIFFITH, born Dayton, Ohio, February 23, 1960; admitted to bar, 1986, Ohio. *Education:* University of Notre Dame (B.A., 1982; J.D., 1986). ***PRACTICE AREAS:*** Labor and Employment Law; Business Litigation; Covenants Not To Compete; Trade Secrets. ***Email:*** kgriffith@porterwright.com

JAMES B. HADDEN, born Columbus, Ohio, May 4, 1967; admitted to bar, 1992, Ohio; 1994, U.S. District Court, Southern District of Ohio. *Education:* Miami University (B.A., 1989); The Ohio State University College of Law (J.D., 1992). Law Clerk: Honorable Norah McCann King, United States Magistrate Judge; Honorable Edmund A. Sargus, United States District Judge, Southern District of Ohio. ***PRACTICE AREAS:*** Commercial Litigation. ***Email:*** jhadden@porterwright.com

BRIAN D. HALL, born Brooklyn, New York, September 17, 1960; admitted to bar, 1985, Ohio; 1986, U.S. Court of Appeals, Sixth Circuit and U.S. District Court, Southern District of Ohio; 1993, U.S. Court of Appeals, Fourth Circuit; 2001, U.S. District Court, Northern District of Ohio. *Education:* State University of New York at Albany (B.S., cum laude, 1982); University of North Carolina (J.D., 1985). *Member:* Columbus, Ohio State and American Bar Associations. ***PRACTICE AREAS:*** Labor and Employment Law; Workers Compensation Law; Employee Benefits; Intellectual Property; Litigation. ***Email:*** bhall@porterwright.com

PAUL A. HANKE, born Cleveland, Ohio, June 2, 1936; admitted to bar, 1961, Ohio. *Education:* College of Wooster (B.A., 1958); University of Michigan (J.D., with distinction, 1961). Assistant Editor, Michigan Law Review, 1960-1961. Trustee, The Paul G. Duke Foundation. Trustee, The College of Wooster, 2001-2004. *Member:* Columbus and Ohio State Bar Associations. ***PRACTICE AREAS:*** ERISA; Employee Benefits. ***Email:*** phanke@porterwright.com

POLLY J. HARRIS, born Cleveland, Ohio, November 16, 1960; admitted to bar, 1985, Ohio. *Education:* Miami University (B.A., with honors, 1982); The Ohio State University (J.D., with honors, 1985). ***PRACTICE AREAS:*** Banking Law; Bankruptcy Law; Commercial Law; Employee Benefits; Finance; Commerce. ***Email:*** pharris@porterwright.com

JOHN C. HARTRANFT, SR., born Fostoria, Ohio, September 15, 1942; admitted to bar, 1967, Ohio. *Education:* Harvard University (A.B., 1964); University of Michigan (J.D., 1967). Adjunct Professor of Law: Capital University Law School, 1972-1974; The Ohio State University College of Law, 1975, 1978. Member, Ohio Supreme Court Board of Commissioners on the Unauthorized Practice of Law, 1985-1987. Co-author: *Ohio Secured Transactions Under Revised Article 9 of the Uniform Commercial Code:* Forms and Practice Manual, Data Trace Publishing Co., 2002. *Member:* Columbus (President, 1999-2000; Board of Governors, 1993-2001; Chairman, Unauthorized Practice of Law Committee, 1983-1985), Ohio State (Council of Delegates, 1997—; Chairman, Banking, Commercial and Bankruptcy Law Committee, 1979-1981) and American Bar Associations. ***PRACTICE AREAS:*** Banking Law; Banking and Failed Financial Institutions; Commercial Law; Creditors Rights Law; UCC. ***Email:*** jhartranft@porterwright.com

JEFFREY T. HAYES, born Aurora, Illinois, February 22, 1948; admitted to bar, 1979, Ohio. *Education:* United States Naval Academy (B.S., 1970); University of Illinois (J.D., magna cum laude, 1979). Order of the Coif. *Member:* Columbus, Ohio State and American Bar Associations. ***PRACTICE AREAS:*** Business; Securities. ***Email:*** jhayes@porterwright.com

RICHARD J. HELMREICH, born Canton, Ohio, May 6, 1964; admitted to bar, 1989, Ohio, U.S. District Court, Southern District of Ohio. *Education:* Bowling Green State University (B.S., Business Accounting, 1986); The Ohio State University (J.D., 1989). *Member:* Columbus (Chair, Employee Benefits Committee, 1999-2001) and Ohio State Associations. ***PRACTICE AREAS:*** Employee Benefits; Executive Compensation; Federal Tax. ***Email:*** rhelmreich@porterwright.com

HARRY L. HENNING, admitted to bar, 1971, Ohio; 1994, Florida. *Education:* University of Notre Dame (B.B.A., cum laude, 1960; J.D., magna cum laude, 1971). Articles Editor, Notre Dame Lawyer, 1970-1971. Adjunct Professor of Law, Capital University Law School, 1972-1984. Co-author: Ohio Limited Liability Company Forms and Practice Manual, Data Trace Publishers, 1994—. Best Lawyers in America, Corporate Law. *Member:* Columbus (Chair, Business Law Committee, 1983-1984), Ohio State and American (Chair, Small Business Committee, 1993-1997; Member of Council, Section of Business Law, 1997-2001; Program Chair, Venture Capital Committee, 2002-2005) Bar Associa-

(This Listing Continued)

(This Listing Continued)

tions. (Also at Naples, Florida Office). ***PRACTICE AREAS:*** Corporate Finance; Financial Restructuring; Corporate Governance; Business; Securities; Litigation. ***Email:*** hhenning@porterwright.com

C. ANDREW IRETON, JR., born Dayton, Ohio, June 21, 1948; admitted to bar, 1973, Ohio. *Education:* Xavier University; University of Notre Dame (B.B.A., cum laude, 1970); The Ohio State University (J.D., 1973). Beta Gamma Sigma; Beta Alpha Psi; Phi Delta Phi. *Member:* Columbus (Chairman, Probate Court Committee, 1989-1991; Taxation Committee), Ohio State and American Bar Associations. ***PRACTICE AREAS:*** Estate Planning; Guardianship Law; Probate Law; Trust Law. ***Email:*** aireton@porterwright.com

LAURIE N. JACQUES, born McKeesport, Pennsylvania, July 25, 1958; admitted to bar, 1990, Ohio; 1991, U.S. District Court, Southern District of Ohio; 1997, U.S. District Court, Northern District of Ohio; registered to practice before U.S. Patent and Trademark Office. *Education:* Allegheny College (B.S., cum laude, 1978); Case Western Reserve University (M.S., 1987); The Ohio State University (J.D., with honors, 1990). Order of the Coif. Managing Editor, Ohio State Law Journal, 1989-1990. Member, American Bar Association Moot Court Team, 1990. ***PRACTICE AREAS:*** Patent, Trademark and Copyright Law; Intellectual Property Law. ***Email:*** ljacques@porterwright.com

DONALD W. JORDAN, born Princeton, Indiana, January 15, 1947; admitted to bar, 1976, Ohio. *Education:* University of Illinois (B.A., 1969; J.D., with honors, 1976). Order of the Coif. Managing Editor, University of Illinois Law Review, 1975-1976. *Member:* Columbus and Ohio State Bar Associations. ***PRACTICE AREAS:*** Real Property Law; Title Insurance; Finance; Commerce. ***Email:*** djordan@porterwright.com

WILLIAM J. KELLY, JR., born Columbus, Ohio, June 15, 1951; admitted to bar, 1976, Ohio; 1982, District of Columbia. *Education:* The Ohio State University (B.A., cum laude, 1973; J.D., summa cum laude, 1976). Phi Beta Kappa. Phi Delta Phi. Order of the Coif. Associate Editor, Ohio State Law Journal, 1975-1976. Ohio Public Expenditure Council, Vice Chair, 1991-1992; Secretary, 1992-1998; Trustee, 1990-1998. Listed in: The Best Lawyers in America, Corporate, Mergers & Acqusitions, and Securities Laws. *Member:* Columbus (Chair, Securities Law Committee, 1991-1992), Ohio State (Member, Corporation Law Committee, Vice Chair, Legislation Subcommittee) and American (Business Law Section, Venture Capital and Private Equity and State Regulation of Securities Committees) Bar Associations; The District of Columbia Bar. ***PRACTICE AREAS:*** Securities; Securities Regulation Law (Blue Sky Law); Corporate Law; Mergers and Acquisitions; Technology; Business Law. ***Email:*** wjkelly@porterwright.com

ROBERT C. KIGER, born Lakewood, Ohio, August 3, 1933; admitted to bar, 1960, Ohio. *Education:* Miami University (A.B., 1955); The Ohio State University (J.D., 1960). Phi Delta Phi. *Member:* Columbus and Ohio State Bar Associations. ***PRACTICE AREAS:*** Finance and Commerce; Real Estate. ***Email:*** rkiger@porterwright.com

LORI-LOU KIMM, born Hartford, Connecticut, October 21, 1962; admitted to bar, 1990, Ohio. *Education:* Wittenberg University (B.A., 1984); University of Denver College of Law (M.S.J.A., 1985); Capital University (J.D., cum laude, 1990). ***PRACTICE AREAS:*** Estate Planning; Estate and Trust Administration. ***Email:*** lkimm@porterwright.com

JAMES A. KING, born Huntington, West Virginia, October 19, 1962; admitted to bar, 1988, Ohio. *Education:* University of Michigan (B.A., 1985); The Ohio State University (J.D., 1988). Phi Beta Kappa. Order of the Coif. Managing Editor, 1987-1988, Ohio State Law Journal. Assistant to the General Counsel of the Army, 1988-1992. ***PRACTICE AREAS:*** Litigation. ***Email:*** jking@porterwright.com

MARK B. KOOGLER, born Dayton, Ohio, November 14, 1954; admitted to bar, 1980, Ohio. *Education:* The Ohio State University (B.S., 1977); University of Dayton (J.D., 1980). Associate Editor, University of Dayton Law Review, 1979-1980. Vice President and Associate General Counsel, Nationwide Insurance Co. *Member:* Columbus, Ohio State and American Bar Associations; Association of Life Insurance Counsel. ***TRANSACTIONS:*** Handled over 30 acquisitions and divestitures of insurance companies, including tender offers and IPOs. ***PRACTICE AREAS:*** Mergers and Acquisitions; Insurance; Financial Services Law; General Corporate; Business; Securities. ***Email:*** mkoogler@porterwright.com

CURTIS A. LOVELAND, born Youngstown, Ohio, October 19, 1946; admitted to bar, 1973, Ohio; 1977, U.S. Supreme Court. *Education:* Ohio University (B.B.A., cum laude, 1968); The Ohio State University (J.D., summa cum laude, 1973). Phi Delta Phi. Order of the Coif. Associate Editor, Ohio State Law Journal, 1972-1973. Best Lawyers in America, Corporate Law. *Member:* Columbus (Securities Law Committee), Ohio State and American (Section of Business Law) Bar Associations. ***PRACTICE AREAS:*** Corporate Law; Corporate Finance; International Investment; Business Acquisitions. ***Email:*** cloveland@porterwright.com

JOHN F. MARSH, born Washington, D.C., March 25, 1963; admitted to bar, 1990, New York; 1995, Ohio. *Education:* John Carroll University (B.A., cum laude, 1986); Vanderbilt Law School (J.D., 1989). ***PRACTICE AREAS:*** Business; Securities; Finance; Commerce; Litigation. ***Email:*** jmarsh@porterwright.com

DANIEL J. MASSEY, born Chicago, Illinois, May 22, 1943; admitted to bar, 1970, Ohio; 1971, U.S. District Court, Southern District of Ohio. *Education:* Capital University (B.A., 1966; J.D., 1970). Phi Alpha Delta. Assistant Attorney General of Ohio, 1971-1973; 1975-1982. ***Email:*** dmassey@porterwright.com

JAMES M. MATTIMOE, born Toledo, Ohio, March 27, 1963; admitted to bar, 1989, Ohio. *Education:* The University of Virginia (B.S., 1985); The Ohio State University (J.D., with honors, 1988). Order of the Coif. ***PRACTICE AREAS:*** Tax Law; Business; Securities; Real Estate. ***Email:*** jmattimoe@porterwright.com

ALVIN J. McKENNA, born New Orleans, Louisiana, August 17, 1943; admitted to bar, 1966, New York; 1967, Ohio. *Education:* Canisius College (A.B., 1963); University of Notre Dame (J.D., 1966). Senior Editorial Staff Member, Notre Dame Law Review, 1965-1966. Law Clerk to the Hon. Joseph P. Kinneary, U.S. District Judge, Southern District of Ohio, 1966-1968. Assistant U.S. Attorney, Southern District of Ohio, 1968-1970. Member, 1972-1980; 1982-1984 and President, 1973, Gahanna City Council. Member: Committee for Revision of Rules of Practice, U.S. District Court, Southern District of Ohio, 1973-1974, Chairperson, 1980-1981; Bar Examination Committee, U.S. District Court, Southern District of Ohio, 1973-1976, 1981-2003. *Member:* Columbus (Chairperson: Federal Court Committee, 1972-1973; Member, Labor Law Committee), Ohio State (Labor Law Section), Federal (President, Columbus Chapter, 1972-1973) and American (Labor Relations Law Section) Bar Associations. ***PRACTICE AREAS:*** Labor and Employment Law; Mining Law; Federal Litigation; Appellate Practice; Trusts and Estates. ***Email:*** amckenna@porterwright.com

(This Listing Continued)

J. JEFFREY McNEALEY, born Cincinnati, Ohio, February 8, 1944; admitted to bar, 1969, Ohio; 1972, U.S. District Court, Southern District of Ohio; 1976, U.S. Court of Appeals, Sixth Circuit; 1978, U.S. Supreme Court; 1979, U.S. Court of Appeals for the District of Columbia Circuit; 1987, U.S. Court of Appeals, Fourth Circuit; 1992, U.S. District Court, Northern District of Ohio. *Education:* Cornell University (B.A., 1966); The Ohio State University (J.D., 1969). *Member:* Columbus, Ohio State and American Bar Associations. ***PRACTICE AREAS:*** Environmental Law; Zoning Law; Business; Securities; Real Estate. ***Email:*** jmcnealey@porterwright.com

RICHARD C. McQUOWN, born Youngstown, Ohio, May 21, 1958; admitted to bar, 1986, Ohio. *Education:* The Ohio State University (B.A., 1980); Capital University (J.D., magna cum laude, 1986). Order of the Curia; Order of Barristers. Member, National Moot Court Team, 1984-1985. Co-Author: Ohio Limited Liability Company Forms and Practice Manual, Data Trace Publishers, 1994. ***PRACTICE AREAS:*** Securities; Corporate Law; Business Acquisitions; Asset Based Lending; Finance; Commerce. ***Email:*** rmcquown@porterwright.com

MARK K. MERKLE, JR., born Columbus, Ohio, November 13, 1944; admitted to bar, 1970, Ohio. *Education:* Villanova University (B.A., 1967); The Ohio State University (J.D., 1970). *Member:* Columbus, Ohio State and American Bar Associations; Franklin County Trial Lawyers Association; Ohio Academy of Trial Lawyers; The Association of Trial Lawyers of America. ***PRACTICE AREAS:*** Litigation. ***Email:*** mmerkle@porterwright.com

RICHARD M. MESCHER, born Dayton, Ohio, January 12, 1960; admitted to bar, 1993, Ohio; registered to practice before U.S. Patent and Trademark Office, 1994. *Education:* The Ohio State University (B.S.M.E., 1982); University of Dayton School of Law (J.D., magna cum laude, 1993). Author: "Patent Law: Best Mode Disclosure — Genetic Engineers Get Their Trade Secret and Their Patent Too?" Amgen v. Chugai Pharmaceutical, 18 University of Dayton Law Review 177, 1992. Adjunct Professor of Law, Case Western Reserve University School of Law, 1997-1999. *Member:* Cleveland Intellectual Property Law Association; American Intellectual Property Law Association; Columbus Intellectual Property Law Association. ***PRACTICE AREAS:*** Patent Prosecution; Intellectual Property Litigation; Intellectual Property Licensing; Trademark Registration; Technology Contracts. ***Email:*** rmescher@porterwright.com

ROBERT A. MEYER, JR., born Pittsburgh, Pennsylvania, July 13, 1953; admitted to bar, 1978, Ohio and U.S. District Court, Southern District of Ohio; 2005, Kentucky. *Education:* Indiana University (B.S., 1975); The Ohio State University (J.D., 1978). *Member:* Columbus (Chairman, Environmental Law Committee, 1986-1988), Ohio State, Kentucky and American Bar Associations. ***PRACTICE AREAS:*** Zoning, Planning and Land Use; Environmental Law; Real Estate. ***Email:*** rmeyer@porterwright.com

KATERINA EFTIMOFF MILENKOVSKI, born Columbus, Ohio, May 18, 1967; admitted to bar, 1994, Ohio; 1995, U.S. District Court, Southern District of Ohio. *Education:* The Ohio State University (B.S., 1989); Capital University Law School (J.D., summa cum laude, 1994). ***LANGUAGES:*** French and Macedonian. ***PRACTICE AREAS:*** Environmental Law; Litigation. ***Email:*** kmilenkovski@porterwright.com

DIXON F. MILLER, born Columbus, Ohio, March 11, 1948; admitted to bar, 1976, Ohio; 1996, Florida. *Education:* Wesleyan University (B.A., 1969); Bowling Green State University (M.Ed., 1973); Case Western Reserve University (J.D., 1976). Order of the Coif. Kappa Delta Pi. *Member:* The Florida Bar; Columbus, Ohio State and American (Antitrust and International Law Sections) Bar Associations. ***LANGUAGES:*** German. ***PRACTICE AREAS:*** Antitrust and Trade Regulation; International Business. ***Email:*** dmiller@porterwright.com

TERRANCE M. MILLER, born Fostoria, Ohio, January 13, 1947; admitted to bar, 1972, Ohio. *Education:* Hobart College (B.A., 1969); University of Virginia (LL.B., 1972). Author: Products Liability Depostions, Juris Publishing, 2003. Co-Author: Deposition Strategy, Law and Forms: Products Liability, Matthew Bender, 1981. *Member:* Columbus and Ohio State Bar Associations; Federation of Insurance and Corporate Counsel; Defense Research Institute (State Chairman, 1993-1998; Board of Directors, 1999-2002); Product Liability Advisory Council; Ohio Association of Civil Trial Attorneys (Legislative Chairman, 1981-1983, Executive Committee, 1982-1985; President, 1988-1989); Columbus Defense Association (President, 1982-1983); American Board of Trial Advocates (Secretary, Ohio Chapter, 2005—). American College of Trial Lawyers. ***PRACTICE AREAS:*** Litigation; Products Liability; Torts. ***Email:*** tmiller@porterwright.com

JENNIFER T. MILLS, born Washington, D.C., June 13, 1950; admitted to bar, 1983, Ohio; 1984, U.S. District Court, Southern District of Ohio; 1988, U.S. Court of Appeals, Sixth Circuit; 1994, U.S. Supreme Court; 2003, U.S. District Court, Northern District of Ohio. *Education:* Ohio Wesleyan University (B.A., 1979); Ohio State University (J.D., summa cum laude, 1983). Order of the Coif. Articles Editor, Ohio State Law Journal, 1983. Lecturer, The Ohio State University College of Law, Commercial Paper, 1995-1996. *Member:* Ohio State and American Bar Associations. ***PRACTICE AREAS:*** Commercial Litigation; Financial Institutions; Commercial Law. ***Email:*** jmills@porterwright.com

SCOTT E. NORTH, born Dayton, Ohio, September 12, 1958; admitted to bar, 1983, Illinois and U.S. District Court, Northern District of Illinois; 1984, Ohio; 1986, U.S. District Court, Southern District of Ohio; 1990, U.S. Court of Appeals, Seventh Circuit; 1993, District of Columbia, U.S. District Court for the District of Columbia and U.S. District Court, Northern District of Ohio. *Education:* University of Michigan (A.B., with distinction and honors in Economics, 1980); University of Virginia (J.D., 1983). ***PRACTICE AREAS:*** Litigation; Employee Benefits; Financial Institutions. ***Email:*** snorth@porterwright.com

ADELE E. O'CONNER, born Cincinnati, Ohio, April 22, 1951; admitted to bar, 1976, Ohio. *Education:* University of Cincinnati (B.A., magna cum laude, 1973); The Ohio State University (J.D., cum laude, 1976). Phi Beta Kappa. *Member:* Columbus (Member, Labor Law Committee), Ohio State (Labor Law Section; Civil Rights Committee; Workers Com-

(This Listing Continued)

PORTER WRIGHT MORRIS & ARTHUR LLP, Columbus—Continued

pensation Committee) and American (Labor and Employment Law Section) Bar Associations. ***PRACTICE AREAS:*** Labor and Employment Law; Workers' Compensation; Litigation Defense. ***Email:*** aoconner@porterwright.com

JAMES S. OLIPHANT, born Evanston, Illinois, April 17, 1945; admitted to bar, 1971, Ohio. *Education:* Northwestern University (B.A., 1967); The Ohio State University (J.D., 1971). Adjunct Professor of Law, The Ohio State University College of Law, 1981-1984, 1989. *Member:* Columbus, Ohio State and American Bar Associations; International Association of Defense Counsel; Federation of Insurance and Corporate Counsel; Defense Research Institute (Member, Board of Directors, 1988-1991; Vice President, 1991-1993; President, 1994-1995; Immediate Past President, 1995-1996); Lawyers for Civil Justice (Member, Board of Directors, 1993-1995; Member of the Ohio Supreme Court's Special Committee on Alternative Dispute Resolution, 1991-1993); Ohio Association of Civil Trial Attorneys (President, 1984-1985); Columbus Defense Association (President, 1978-1979). Advocate, American Board of Trial Advocates. Fellow, American College of Trial Lawyers. ***PRACTICE AREAS:*** Products Liability; Professional Liability; Toxic Exposure; Complex Litigation. ***Email:*** joliphant@porterwright.com

JACK R. PIGMAN, born Fostoria, Ohio, June 5, 1944; admitted to bar, 1969, Ohio; 1970, U.S. Court of Military Appeals. *Education:* University of Notre Dame (B.A., 1966); The Ohio State University (J.D., cum laude, 1969). Order of the Coif. Phi Delta Phi. Managing Editor, Ohio State Law Journal, 1968-1969. Law Clerk to Hon. Thomas M. Herbert, Supreme Court of Ohio, 1969-1970. *Member:* Columbus (Chairman, Bankruptcy Committee, 1982-1984) and Ohio State (Banking, Commercial and Bankruptcy Law) Bar Associations. ***PRACTICE AREAS:*** General Business; Creditors Rights and Bankruptcy Law; Commercial Litigation; Banks and Banking; Finance; Commerce. ***Email:*** jpigman@porterwright.com

ERIC J. PLINKE, born Janesville, Wisconsin, December 28, 1966; admitted to bar, 1992, Ohio; 1997, U.S. District Court, Northern District of Ohio; 1998, U.S. District Court, Southern District of Ohio. *Education:* Hanover College (B.A., 1989); University of Toledo College of Law (J.D., 1992). Attorney, State Medical Board of Ohio, 1993-1996. ***PRACTICE AREAS:*** Health Care Law; Professional Licensing; Litigation; Business; Securities. ***Email:*** eplinke@porterwright.com

SAMUEL H. PORTER, born Columbus, Ohio, July 5, 1927; admitted to bar, 1953, Ohio; 1955, U.S. District Court, Southern District of Ohio; 1977, U.S. Supreme Court; 1978, U.S. Court of Appeals, Sixth Circuit; 1993, Colorado, U.S. District Court, Northern District of Ohio and U.S. District Court, District of Colorado; 1975, U.S. Court of Appeals for the District of Columbia Circuit. *Education:* Amherst College (A.B., 1950); The Ohio State University (J.D., 1952). Member, 1995—, American Arbitration Association's Commercial Panel of Arbitrators and Mediators and Large Complex Case Panel. Panel Member, International Institute for Conflict Prevention and Resolution. *Member:* Columbus (Board of Governors, 1972-1973), Ohio State (Chair, Public Utilities Law Committee, 1984-1985; Counsel of Delegates, 1975-1979) and American (Member: House of Delegates, 2002—; Section on Dispute Resolution; Chair, Section of Public Utility, Communications and Transportation Law, 1998-1999) Bar Associations; Sixth Circuit Judicial Conference of the United States (Life Member); American College of Trial Lawyers. ***PRACTICE AREAS:*** Litigation; Utility Law; Energy; Arbitration; Mediation. ***Email:*** sporter@porterwright.com

FRED G. PRESSLEY, JR., born Bronx, New York, June 19, 1953; admitted to bar, 1978, Ohio. *Education:* Union College (B.A., cum laude, 1975); Northwestern University (J.D., 1978). *Member:* American Bar Association (Section on Labor and Employment Law). ***PRACTICE AREAS:*** Labor Law (Management); Housing Discrimination; Employment Discrimination; Litigation. ***Email:*** fpressley@porterwright.com

JAMES H. PRIOR, born Bradford, Pennsylvania, December 23, 1959; admitted to bar, 1985, Ohio; 1986, U.S. District Court, Southern District of Ohio; 1994, U.S. District Court, Northern District of Ohio. *Education:* Pennsylvania State University (B.A., with highest distinction, 1981); University of Virginia (J.D., 1985). Phi Beta Kappa. ***PRACTICE AREAS:*** Employee Benefits; Finance; Commerce; Financial Institutions. ***Email:*** jprior@porterwright.com

W. JOHN PRITCHARD, born Milwaukee, Wisconsin, July 18, 1947; admitted to bar, 1972, Wisconsin and U.S. District Court, Eastern and Western Districts of Wisconsin; 1992, Ohio and Colorado. *Education:* University of Wisconsin-Madison (B.B.A., 1969; J.D., 1972); Marquette University (M.B.A., 1973). ***PRACTICE AREAS:*** Business; Securities; Finance; Commerce; Real Estate; Tax. ***Email:*** wjpritchard@porterwright.com

DIANE C. REICHWEIN, born Philadelphia, Pennsylvania, December 6, 1952; admitted to bar, 1983, Ohio. *Education:* University of Pittsburgh (B.A., cum laude, 1974); Ohio State University (J.D., cum laude, 1982). *Member:* Columbus, Ohio State and American Bar Associations; Women Lawyers of Franklin County. ***PRACTICE AREAS:*** Labor and Employment Law; Workers Compensation Law; Litigation. ***Email:*** dreichwein@porterwright.com

JOHN B. ROHYANS, born Lafayette, Indiana, June 15, 1944; admitted to bar, 1969, Ohio. *Education:* Miami University (B.S., 1966); The Ohio State University (J.D., 1969). *Member:* Columbus and Ohio State Bar Associations. ***PRACTICE AREAS:*** Finance; Commerce; Real Estate. ***Email:*** jrohyans@porterwright.com

DONNA M. RUSCITTI, born Cleveland, Ohio, September 30, 1952; admitted to bar, 1986, Ohio; 1987, U.S. District Court, Southern District of Ohio. *Education:* College of Wooster (B.A., magna cum laude, 1974); Capital University (J.D., 1986). Phi Beta Kappa. Editor-in-Chief, Capital University Law Review. 1985-1986. ***PRACTICE AREAS:*** Corporation Law; Computer Technology; Intellectual Property; Construction Law; Business; Securities. ***Email:*** druscitti@porterwright.com

CHRISTOPHER C. RUSSELL, born New Haven, Connecticut, May 31, 1963; admitted to bar, 1988, Ohio; 1989, U.S. District Court, Southern District of Ohio; 1993, U.S. Court of Appeals, Sixth Circuit; 1994, U.S. District Court, Northern District of Ohio; 1997, U.S. District Court, Central District of Illinois. *Education:* Kenyon College (B.A., magna cum laude, 1985); The Ohio State University (J.D., 1988). Phi Beta Kappa. ***PRACTICE AREAS:*** Labor and Employment Law; Workers Compensation Law; Litigation. ***Email:*** crussell@porterwright.com

JOSEPH W. RYAN, JR., born Philadelphia, Pennsylvania, June 24, 1948; admitted to bar, 1978, Ohio. *Education:* St. Joseph's College (A.B., 1970); Villanova University (M.A., 1971); University of Virginia (J.D., 1978). Recipient, National Law Journal's Recognition for the Most Significant Defense Verdict of 2002: Ching Lung Chang v. The Cleveland Clinic Foundation, et. al., Cuyahoga County Ohio Court of Common Pleas, Case No. 403722. Author: "Use of Demonstrative, Documentary and Physical Evidence at Trial," Ohio Legal Center Institute, 1984. Associate Editor, "Litigation News," 1986—. *Member:* Columbus, Ohio State and American Bar Associations; Defense Research Institute; Ohio Association of Civil Trial Attorneys (Legislative Chairperson, 1989-1990); International Association of Defense Counsel (Trial Academy Faculty, 1994). ***PRACTICE AREAS:*** Intellectual Property; Litigation; Labor and Employment. ***Email:*** jryan@porterwright.com

CHRISTOPHER R. SCHRAFF, born Cleveland, Ohio, July 19, 1947; admitted to bar, 1972, Ohio; 1973, U.S. District Court, Northern and Southern Districts of Ohio; 1974, U.S. Court of Appeals, Sixth Circuit. *Education:* John Carroll University (A.B., 1969); University of Notre Dame (J.D., 1972). Assistant Section Chief, Office of Attorney General of Ohio, Environmental Law Section, 1972-1976. Adjunct Professor of Law, Capital University Law School, 1977—. Co-Author: "RCRA and Superfund: A Practice Guide with Forms," 1988. *Member:* Columbus, Ohio State and American Bar Associations. ***PRACTICE AREAS:*** Environmental Law. ***Email:*** cschraff@porterwright.com

EDWARD M. SEGELKEN, born Cleveland, Ohio, October 3, 1958; admitted to bar, 1984, Ohio; 1985, U.S. District Court, Southern District of Ohio. *Education:* Wabash College (A.B., summa cum laude, 1981); University of Michigan (J.D., magna cum laude, 1984). Phi Beta Kappa; Order of the Coif. Fellow, American College of Trust and Estate Counsel. *Member:* Columbus, Ohio State and American Bar Associations. ***PRACTICE AREAS:*** Estate Planning; Tax Exempt Organizations; Estate and Gift Tax. ***Email:*** esegelken@porterwright.com

MARTIN S. SELTZER, born Brooklyn, New York, April 8, 1937; admitted to bar, 1977, Ohio. *Education:* New York University (B.Eng., 1958); Yale University (D.Eng., 1962); The Ohio State University (J.D., 1977). Editor: "Ohio Environmental Law Letter." Counsel to Ohio Chemical Council. Member, Ohio Chamber of Commerce Energy and Environment Executive Committee. *Member:* Ohio State Bar Association. ***PRACTICE AREAS:*** Administrative Hearings and Appeals; Water Pollution; Environmental Law; Hazardous Materials Law; Solid and Hazardous Waste. ***Email:*** mseltzer@porterwright.com

DARRELL R. SHEPARD, born Lincoln, Nebraska, August 14, 1941; admitted to bar, 1981, Ohio, U.S. District Court, Southern District of Ohio and U.S. Court of Appeals, Sixth Circuit. *Education:* University of Nebraska (B.A., 1962; Ph.D., 1967); Indiana University (J.D., magna cum laude, 1980). Phi Beta Kappa; Order of the Coif. ***PRACTICE AREAS:*** Workers Compensation Law; Insurance Litigation. ***Email:*** dshepard@porterwright.com

DAVID P. SHOUVLIN, born Cambridge, Massachusetts, May 15, 1952; admitted to bar, 1979, North Carolina; 1983, U.S. District Court, Middle District of North Carolina; 1990, Massachusetts; U.S. District Court, District of Massachusetts; 1996, Ohio and U.S. District Court Court, Northern District of Ohio; 1997, U.S. District Court, Southern District of Ohio. *Education:* Wake Forest University (B.A., 1974); Wake Forest University School of Law (J.D., 1979); Weston School of Theology, Cambridge, MA, Harvard Law School. *Member:* Columbus, Ohio and American Bar Associations. ***PRACTICE AREAS:*** Litigation; Antitrust and Trade Regulation; Intellectual Property. ***Email:*** dshouvlin@porterwright.com

BRADD N. SIEGEL, born Ithaca, New York, March 31, 1952; admitted to bar, 1977, Virginia; 1978, Ohio; 1979, U.S. District Court, Southern District of Ohio; 1980, District of Columbia, U.S. District Court, Northern District of Ohio and U.S. Court of Appeals, Sixth Circuit. *Education:* Cornell University (A.B., with distinction, 1974); George Washington University (J.D., with honors, 1977); Georgetown University (LL.M., 1978). George Washington University Law Review, 1975-1977. Co-author: Ohio Employment Practices Law: A Practical Guide for Employers and Their Legal Counsel, Thomson-West, 1991-2005 eds. Co-editor, Ohio Employment Law Letter. *Member:* Ohio State (Labor and Employment Law Section, Chair, 2002-2004; Vice-Chair, 2000-2002; Secretary-Treasurer, 1998-2000; Board of Governors, 1991—; Civil Rights Committee; Chairman, 1987-1989, Employment-at-Will Subcommittee; Chairman, 1989—, Wrongful Discharge Committee) and American (Committee on Equal Employment Opportunity Law, Labor and Employment Law Section, 1979—; Litigation Section, 1984—; ABA/EEO Committee Co-liaison with EEOC for Central Ohio, 1984—) Bar Associations. College of Labor and Employment Lawyers; Ohio State Bar Foundation; Columbus Bar Foundation. ***PRACTICE AREAS:*** Employment Discrimination; Wrongful Termination-Employment at Will; Labor Law (Management); OSHA; Employee Benefits; Litigation. ***Email:*** bsiegel@porterwright.com

ERIN F. SIEGFRIED, born Dayton, Ohio, May 16, 1971; admitted to bar, 1996, Ohio; 1997, U.S. District Court, Southern District of Ohio. *Education:* Duke University (A.B., 1993); The Ohio State University College of Law (J.D., 1996). ***PRACTICE AREAS:*** Corporate Law; Securities Law; Business; Securities. ***Email:*** esiegfried@porterwright.com

MARK S. STEMM, born Dowagiac, Michigan, January 10, 1959; admitted to bar, 1984, Ohio; U.S. District Court, Southern District of Ohio; U.S. Court of Appeals, Sixth Circuit; 2002, U.S. District Court, Northern District of Ohio; 2003, U.S. Supreme Court. *Education:* Michigan State University (B.S., with honors, Mech. Eng., 1981); The Ohio State University (J.D., with honors, 1984). ***PRACTICE AREAS:*** Employment Law; Fair Housing; Litigation; Employee Benefits; Environmental Law. ***Email:*** mstemm@porterwright.com

JOHN M. STEPHEN, born Mt. Vernon, Ohio, November 19, 1954; admitted to bar, 1979, Ohio; 1980, U.S. District Court, Southern District of Ohio; 1981, U.S. Court of Appeals, Sixth Circuit; 1982, U.S. District Court, Northern District of Ohio; 1984, U.S. District Court, Eastern District of Kentucky; 1986, U.S. District Court, Eastern District of Michigan; 1990, U.S. Supreme Court; 1996, U.S. District Court, Western District of Michigan; 1997, U.S. District Court, Southern District of Indiana and Central District of Illinois; 1998, U.S. Court of Appeals, Second Circuit; 2003, U.S. Court of Appeals, Third Circuit. *Education:* DePauw University (B.A., cum laude, 1976); The Ohio State University (J.D.,

(This Listing Continued)

1979). Adjunct Professor, Capital University Law Center. Co-Author: Ohio Employment Practices Law: A Practical Guide for Employers and Their Legal Counsel, Thomson-West, 1991-2005 eds. Best Lawyers in America, Labor and Employment Law. ***PRACTICE AREAS:*** Labor and Employment Law. ***Email:*** jstephen@porterwright.com

H. GRANT STEPHENSON, born Jacksonville, Florida, September 11, 1949; admitted to bar, 1979, Ohio; 1980, U.S. District Court, Southern District of Ohio; 1983, U.S. District Court, Northern District of Ohio; 1990, U.S. Supreme Court. *Education:* Ohio University (B.A., summa cum laude, 1971); The Ohio State University (J.D., 1979). Phi Beta Kappa; Omicron Delta Kappa; Phi Kappa Phi. *Member:* Columbus, Ohio State and American Bar Associations. ***PRACTICE AREAS:*** Financial Institutions; Business Law; Securities; Corporate Law; Commercial and Bankruptcy Law; Equipment Leasing; Technology. ***Email:*** gstephenson@porterwright.com

KARL J. SUTTER, born Shelby, Ohio, February 2, 1957; admitted to bar, 1982, Ohio; 1984, U.S. District Court, Northern District of Ohio; 1986, U.S. District Court, Southern District of Ohio. *Education:* Ohio University (B.S., cum laude, 1979); University of Toledo (J.D., 1982). ***PRACTICE AREAS:*** Workers Compensation; Consumer Law; Injury; Insurance Defense; Litigation. ***Email:*** ksutter@porterwright.com

ROBERT J. TANNOUS, born Amman, Jordan, June 4, 1962; admitted to bar, 1987, Ohio. *Education:* The Ohio State University (B.S., cum laude, 1984; J.D., with honors, 1987). Co-author: "Coal Supply Contracts and Proposed Clean Air Act Amendments," Proceeding of Eleventh Annual Institute, Eastern Mineral Law Foundation, 1990. *Member:* Columbus, Ohio State and American Bar Associations. ***PRACTICE AREAS:*** Securities Law; Mergers and Acquisitions Law; Corporation Law; Business; Securities. ***Email:*** rtannous@porterwright.com

RICHARD G. TERAPAK, born Columbus, Ohio, October 28, 1946; admitted to bar, 1972, Ohio; 1973, U.S. District Court, Southern District of Ohio. *Education:* The Ohio State University (B.A., 1968; J.D., 1971). Executive Director, Ohio Ethics Commission, 1976-1981. *Member:* American Bar Association; American Health Lawyers Association. ***PRACTICE AREAS:*** Health Care; Banking Law. ***Email:*** rterapak@porterwright.com

JEAN YINGLING TETERIS, admitted to bar, 1975, Ohio. *Education:* The Ohio State University (B.A., cum laude, 1961; J.D., summa cum laude, 1975). Phi Beta Kappa; Order of the Coif. Articles Editor, Ohio State Law Journal, 1974-1975. *Member:* Columbus, Ohio State and American Bar Associations. ***PRACTICE AREAS:*** Antitrust Law; Trade Regulation Law; Distribution Law; Business; Securities; Finance; Commerce. ***Email:*** jteteris@porterwright.com

KATHLEEN McMANUS TRAFFORD, born Syracuse, New York, January 16, 1949; admitted to bar, 1979, Ohio and U.S. District Court, Southern District of Ohio; 1984, U.S. District Court, Northern District of Ohio; 1986, U.S. Supreme Court; 1988, U.S. Court of Appeals, Sixth Circuit. *Education:* Nazareth College of Rochester (B.A., 1970); Kent State University (M.A., 1971); Capital University Law School (J.D., cum laude, 1979). Member, Ohio Board of Bar Examiners, 1990-1995. ***PRACTICE AREAS:*** Litigation. ***Email:*** ktrafford@porterwright.com

ROBERT W. TRAFFORD, born Homestead, Florida, December 1, 1951; admitted to bar, 1977, Ohio and U.S. District Court, Southern District of Ohio; 1982, U.S. Court of Appeals, Sixth Circuit; 1987, U.S. District Court, Northern District of Ohio and U.S. District Court, Eastern District of Michigan; 1991, U.S. Court of Appeals, Fourth Circuit; 1992, U.S. District Court, Northern District of Texas; 1993, U.S. Supreme Court. *Education:* The Ohio State University (B.A., with distinction, 1974; J.D., 1977). Managing Editor, Ohio State Law Journal, 1976-1977. *Member:* Columbus, Ohio State and American (Member, Sections on: Litigation; Business Law) Bar Associations; Defense Research Institute (Chairman, Business Litigation Committee, 1991-1994). Fellow, American College of Trial Lawyers. ***PRACTICE AREAS:*** Complex Litigation; Securities Litigation; Director and Officer Liability; Constitutional Law; Intellectual Property. ***Email:*** rtrafford@porterwright.com

DAVID A. TUMEN, born Cincinnati, Ohio, December 30, 1955; admitted to bar, 1981, Ohio. *Education:* Washington and Lee University (B.A., cum laude, 1978); University of Cincinnati (J.D., 1981); New York University (LL.M., in Taxation, 1983). Adjunct Professor, Capital University Law School, 1993. *Member:* Columbus (Chairman, Business Tax Committee, 1988-1989) and American Bar Associations. ***PRACTICE AREAS:*** Federal Tax; Executive Compensation; Low Income Housing Tax Credits; Estate and Business Succession Planning; Historic Tax Credits; Real Estate. ***Email:*** dtumen@porterwright.com

MICHAEL J. UNDERWOOD, born Pittsburgh, Pennsylvania, May 5, 1954; admitted to bar, 1980, Ohio; 1981, U.S. District Court, Southern District of Ohio. *Education:* University of Pittsburgh (B.A., cum laude, 1976; J.D., cum laude, 1980). *Member:* Columbus (Chairperson, Labor and Employment Law Committee, 1990-1992), Ohio State and American Bar Associations. ***PRACTICE AREAS:*** Labor and Employment Law. ***Email:*** munderwood@porterwright.com

CHARLES C. WARNER, born Cambridge, Massachusetts, June 19, 1942; admitted to bar, 1970, Ohio. *Education:* Yale University (B.A., 1964); The Moritz College of Law at The Ohio State University (J.D., cum laude, 1970). Recipient: Frank Hurd Award from Ohio Association of Civil Trial Attorneys; The Ohio State University Distinguished Service Award; Columbus Bar Association Community Service Award; Harrison Tweed Award for Best Brief in National Moot Court Competition. Chief Justice, Moot Court Program, The Moritz College of Law. *Member:* Columbus (Chair: Law Institute Committee, 1979-1981; Labor Law Committee, 1981-1982; President, 1991-1992; Member, Board of Governors, 1982-1987; 1988-1993), Ohio State (Chair, Federal Courts Committee, 1992-1994; Council of Delegates, 1993—), Federal and American (Labor and Employment Law Section, EEO Committee, Co-chair, 2000-2002; Executive Committee, National Metropolitan Bar Leaders Caucus, 1992-1994; Chairman, State and Local Bar Committee, Dispute Resolution Section, 1995-1997) Bar Associations; Ohio Metropolitan Bar Association (President, 1991-1992); Ohio Association of Civil Trial Attorneys (Legislative Chairman, 1978-1980; Chairman, Corporate Employment Law Committee, 1986-1998; Executive Committee, 1988-1998); Ohio Management Lawyers Association (Co-founder, Chair, 2004—). College of Labor and Employment Lawyers; American, Ohio State and Columbus Bar Foundations. ***PRACTICE AREAS:*** Employment Discrimination Law; Employment Law; Civil Trial; Legal Malpractice Law. ***Email:*** cwarner@porterwright.com

(This Listing Continued)

FRANCK G. WOBST, born Lynchburg, Virginia, July 12, 1958; admitted to bar, 1983, Ohio. *Education:* Universitat Freiburg; Trinity College (B.A., 1980); Washington & Lee University (J.D., 1983). ***LANGUAGES:*** German. ***PRACTICE AREAS:*** Labor (Management) Law; Wrongful Termination-Employment at Will; Employment Law; Employee Benefits; Litigation. ***Email:*** fwobst@porterwright.com

NANCY B. YOUNG, born Chillicothe, Ohio, November 5, 1952; admitted to bar, 1977, Ohio. *Education:* Bowling Green State University (B.A., cum laude, 1974); The Ohio State University (J.D., cum laude, 1977). Alpha Lambda Delta; Order of the Coif. Member, Mortar Board. *Member:* Ohio State Bar Association. ***PRACTICE AREAS:*** Real Estate and Commercial Finance. ***Email:*** nyoung@porterwright.com

THOMAS A. YOUNG, born Columbus, Ohio, March 30, 1947; admitted to bar, 1973, Ohio. *Education:* The Ohio State University (B.S., 1969); Capital University (J.D., magna cum laude, 1973). Notes Editor, Capital University Law Review, 1972-1973. Law Clerk to Chief Justice C. William O'Neill, Supreme Court of Ohio, 1973-1974. Acting Clerk of the Court of Claims of Ohio, 1975. *Member:* Columbus and Ohio State Bar Associations. ***PRACTICE AREAS:*** Employee Benefits; Litigation; Real Estate. ***Email:*** tyoung@porterwright.com

ASSOCIATES COLUMBUS, OHIO OFFICE

JULIE L. ATCHISON, born Wooster, Ohio, February 11, 1972; admitted to bar, 1998, Ohio, U.S. District Court, Southern District of Ohio and U.S. Court of Appeals, Sixth Circuit. *Education:* The Ohio State University (B.A., summa cum laude, 1995); Northwestern University (J.D., cum laude, 1998). Phi Beta Kappa. *Member:* Columbus, Ohio State and American Bar Associations. ***PRACTICE AREAS:*** Litigation. ***Email:*** jatchison@porterwright.com

CARL A. AVENI II, born Melrose, Massachusetts, July 29, 1969; admitted to bar, 1996, New Jersey and U.S. District Court, District of New Jersey; 1997, Pennsylvania and U.S. District Court, Eastern District of New Jersey; 1999, Ohio. *Education:* American University (B.A., 1991); Boston University (J.D., cum laude, 1996). Editor, 1995-1996 and Member, 1994-1995, Boston University Law Review. ***PRACTICE AREAS:*** Litigation. ***Email:*** caveni@porterwright.com

BRADLEY K. BAKER, born Denver, Colorado, April 5, 1950; admitted to bar, 1991, Ohio and U.S. District Court, Southern District of Ohio; 1992, Colorado; 1993, California; 1998, U.S. District Court, Northern District of Ohio. *Education:* University of Colorado (B.A., 1986); Capital University (J.D., 1991). Phillip Jessup International Moot Court Team, Order of Barristers. ***PRACTICE AREAS:*** Commercial Law; Creditors' Rights; Bankruptcy Law; Art Law; Finance; Commerce; Financial Institutions; Litigation. ***Email:*** bbaker@porterwright.com

KATHRYN S. BALTES, born Dayton, Ohio, July 22, 1977; admitted to bar, 2002, Oregon (Not admitted in Ohio). *Education:* The Ohio State University (B.A., 1999; J.D., 2002). Order of the Coif. *Member:* Multnomah County and American Bar Associations; Oregon State Bar. ***LANGUAGES:*** German. ***PRACTICE AREAS:*** International Law; Business Law; Real Estate; Immigration. ***Email:*** kbaltes@porterwright.com

JENNIFER E. BEALE, born Galion, Ohio; admitted to bar, 2001, Ohio. *Education:* Ohio State University (B.S.B.A., 1988); West Virginia University (M.S.I.L.R., 1991); Capital University (J.D., summa cum laude, 2001). Author: "Comment: Affirmative Action and Violation of Union Contracts: The EEOC's New Requirements under the Americans with Disabilities Act," 29 Cap.Univ. Law Review 811, 2002. Labor and Employment Law Association, Capital University (Vice President, 2000). *Member:* Columbus and Ohio State (Member, Labor and Employment Section) Bar Associations. ***PRACTICE AREAS:*** Labor and Employment. ***Email:*** jbeale@porterwright.com

DAVID S. BLOOMFIELD, JR., born Columbus, Ohio, October 7, 1972; admitted to bar, 1997, Ohio; 1999, U.S. District Court, Northern and Southern Districts of Ohio and U.S. Court of Appeals, Sixth Circuit; 2003, U.S. Court of Appeals, Third Circuit. *Education:* London School of Economics (1993); Haverford College (B.A., 1994); Ohio State University (J.D., 1997). Order of the Coif. Articles Editor, 1996-1997 and Staff Member, 1995-1996, Ohio State Journal on Dispute Resolution. *Member:* Columbus and Ohio State Bar Associations. ***PRACTICE AREAS:*** Litigation. ***Email:*** dbloomfield@porterwright.com

ANDREW M. BOJKO, born Le Sueur, Minnesota, July 24, 1970; admitted to bar, 1998, Ohio. *Education:* Princeton University (A.B., 1993); University of Notre Dame (J.D., 1998). ***PRACTICE AREAS:*** Financial Institutions; Business; Securities; Real Estate. ***Email:*** abojko@porterwright.com

STACEY GARBER BOROWICZ, born Massillon, Ohio, February 3, 1970; admitted to bar, 2003, Ohio. *Education:* The Ohio State University (B.S., 1992); Medical College of Ohio (M.S., 1996); Capital University (J.D., summa cum laude, 2003). Order of the Curia. Recipient, Dean's Award, Medical College of Ohio. Associate Editor, Capital University Law Review, 2002-2003. Author: "Cox v. Miller: The Clergy Privilege and Alcoholics Anonymous," 31 Capital Univ. L. Rev. 917, 2003. ***PRACTICE AREAS:*** Health Care Law; Business Law; Antitrust and Trade Regulation; Business; Securities. ***Email:*** sborowicz@porterwright.com

TIMOTHY J. CAHILL, born Cincinnati, Ohio, March 23, 1972; admitted to bar, 2003, Ohio. *Education:* The Ohio State University (B.S., 1996); University of Cincinnati (J.D., 2003). Associate Member, 2001-2002 and Student Articles Editor, 2002-2003, University of Cincinnati Law Review. Law Clerk, Honorable Sylvia H. Rambo, U.S. District Court, Middle District of Pennsylvania, 2003-2005. ***PRACTICE AREAS:*** Health Care. ***Email:*** tcahill@porterwright.com

JOHN PATRICK CARNEY, born Fairview, Ohio, March 28, 1976; admitted to bar, 2001, Ohio. *Education:* The Ohio State University (B.A., Criminology, 1998; J.D., 2001). Member, Mortar Board. ***PRACTICE AREAS:*** Health Care; Business Law; Labor and Employment. ***Email:*** jcarney@porterwright.com

LORI A. CLARY, born Chillicothe, Ohio, October 4, 1967; admitted to bar, 1996, Ohio; 1997, U.S. District Court, Southern District of Ohio. *Education:* Ohio University

(This Listing Continued)

PORTER WRIGHT MORRIS & ARTHUR LLP, Columbus—Continued

(B.S., with high honors, 1990); The The Ohio State University (J.D., summa cum laude, 1996). *Member:* Columbus and Ohio State Bar Associations. ***PRACTICE AREAS:*** Labor and Employment; Litigation. ***Email:*** lclary@porterwright.com

MOLLY S. CRABTREE, born Kettering, Ohio, October 9, 1975; admitted to bar, 2001, Ohio. *Education:* The Ohio State University (B.S., Zoology, cum laude with honors, 1997); Case Western Reserve University (J.D., magna cum laude with honors, 2001). Member, Law Review, Case Western Reserve University. ***LANGUAGES:*** Spanish. ***PRACTICE AREAS:*** Litigation. ***Email:*** mcrabtree@porterwright.com

KYSHA L. CURRENCE, born New Castle, Pennsylvania; admitted to bar, 2002, Ohio. *Education:* The Ohio State University (B.S.B.A., 1999); George Washington University (J.D., 2002). ***PRACTICE AREAS:*** Business Law. ***Email:*** kcurrence@porterwright.com

JAIME ALLISON DANSA, born Cleveland, Ohio, September 13, 1976; admitted to bar, 2002, Ohio. *Education:* Ohio Northern University (B.S.B.A. with high distinction, 1998); Capital University Law School (J.D., summa cum laude, 2002). ***PRACTICE AREAS:*** Business Law; Employee Benefits. ***Email:*** jdansa@porterwright.com

GREG M. DAUGHERTY, born Sandusky, Ohio, April 24, 1979; admitted to bar, 2004, Ohio. *Education:* Miami University (B.S., summa cum laude, 2001); The Ohio State University (J.D., with honors, 2004). Articles Editor, Ohio State Law Journal, 2002-2004. Executive Director, Ohio State University Pro Bono Research Group, 2002-2004. ***PRACTICE AREAS:*** Corporate Law; Business Law; Securities; Taxation; Employee Benefits. ***Email:*** gdaugherty@porterwright.com

AARON A. DRYER, born Coshocton, Ohio, September 26, 1971; admitted to bar, 1998, Ohio. *Education:* The Ohio State University (B.S.B.A., with honors, 1995); Case Western Reserve University (J.D., with honors, 1998). ***PRACTICE AREAS:*** Business Law; Mergers and Acquisitions; Federal Tax. ***Email:*** adryer@porterwright.com

ROBERT W. EDMUND, born Biloxi, Mississippi, July 9, 1973; admitted to bar, 1998, Ohio and U.S.District Court, Southern District of Ohio; 1999, Florida, U.S. Court of Appeals, Sixth Circuit and U.S. District Court, Northern District of Ohio. *Education:* The Ohio State University (B.A., summa cum laude, 1995); Harvard University (J.D., cum laude, 1998). Phi Beta Kappa. *Member:* Columbus, Ohio State, Federal and American Bar Associations. ***PRACTICE AREAS:*** Labor and Employment. ***Email:*** redmund@porterwright.com

JENNIFER E. EDWARDS, born Akron, Ohio, September 16, 1977; (admission pending). *Education:* American University (B.A., cum laude, 1999); University of Texas (J.D., 2005). ***PRACTICE AREAS:*** Labor and Employment. ***Email:*** jedwards@porterwright.com

TAHEERAH K. EL-AMIN, admitted to bar, 2002, Ohio; 2003, U.S. District Court, Southern District of Ohio. *Education:* Dartmouth College (A.B., 1998); University of Illinois (J.D., 2002). *Member:* American Bar Association. ***PRACTICE AREAS:*** Litigation; Finance; Commerce; Financial Institutions. ***Email:*** telamin@porterwright.com

ANDREW C. EMERSON, born Toledo, Ohio, August 9, 1971; admitted to bar, 1999, Ohio. *Education:* DePaul University (B.A., 1993); The Ohio State University (J.D., 1999). *Member:* Columbus, Ohio State and American Bar Associations. ***PRACTICE AREAS:*** Telecommunications Law; Energy; Public Utilities. ***Email:*** aemerson@porterwright.com

ROBERT ESKRIDGE III, born Columbus, Ohio, July 27, 1980; (admission pending). *Education:* Morehouse College (B.A., 2002); Boston College (J.D., 2005). ***PRACTICE AREAS:*** Commercial Law; Real Estate; Trusts and Estates. ***Email:*** reskridge@porterwright.com

BRYAN R. FALLER, born Celina, Ohio, September 14, 1974; admitted to bar, 2000, Ohio and U.S. District Court, Southern District of Ohio. *Education:* Ohio University (B.S., Communication, 1997); The Ohio State University College of Law (J.D. with honors, 2000). Managing Editor, Ohio State Law Journal, 1999-2000. Law Clerk, Honorable James L. Graham, U.S. District Judge, Southern District of Ohio, 2000-2002. Author: "The 1998 Amendment to the Roving Wiretap Statute: Congress 'could have' done better," 60 Ohio State Law Journal 2093 (1999). ***PRACTICE AREAS:*** Litigation. ***Email:*** bfaller@porterwright.com

DAVID C. FAURE, born Columbus, Ohio, April 3, 1969; admitted to bar, 1996, Ohio; 1998, U.S. District Court, Southern District of Ohio; 1999, U.S. District Court, Northern District of Ohio. *Education:* The Ohio State University (B.A., 1991; M.A., 1993; J.D., 1996). Order of the Coif. Law Clerk to: Hon. Joseph P. Kinneary, U.S. District Court, Southern District of Ohio, 1996-1998; Hon. Edmund A. Sargus, Jr., U.S. District Court, Southern District of Ohio, 2000-2001. *Member:* Columbus, Federal and American Bar Associations. ***PRACTICE AREAS:*** Employment Law; Litigation; Labor Law. ***Email:*** dfaure@porterwright.com

M. THERESA FINNERAN, born Columbus, Ohio, September 15, 1951; admitted to bar, 1989, Ohio. *Education:* The Ohio State University (B.A., 1972); Capital University (J.D., 1989). ***PRACTICE AREAS:*** Employee Benefits. ***Email:*** tfinneran@porterwright.com

ERIC BENJAMIN GALLON, born 1975; admitted to bar, 1999, Ohio; 2000, U.S. District Court, Southern District of Ohio and U.S. Court of Appeals, 6th Circuit. *Education:* The Ohio State University (B.A., 1996); The University of Chicago (J.D., 1999). ***PRACTICE AREAS:*** Litigation. ***Email:*** egallon@porterwright.com

CHRISTOPHER R. GEIDNER, born Bethesda, Maryland, September 28, 1977; (admission pending). *Education:* American University, 1995-1998; Youngstown State University (B.S., 2001); The Ohio State University (J.D., 2005). *Member:* Columbus and Ohio State Bar Associations. ***PRACTICE AREAS:*** Litigation. ***Email:*** cgeidner@porterwright.com

JACK GRAVELLE, born Columbus, Ohio, April 19, 1980; (admission pending). *Education:* Ohio University (B.A., 2001); The Ohio State University (J.D., 2005). Order of the Coif. ***PRACTICE AREAS:*** Business Law. ***Email:*** jgravelle@porterwright.com

(This Listing Continued)

KAREN K. HAMMOND, born Columbus, Ohio, February 8, 1967; admitted to bar, 1994, Ohio; 1995, U.S. District Court, Southern District of Ohio. *Education:* The Ohio State University (B.S.B.A., 1989); Capital University Law and Graduate Center (J.D., 1994). ***PRACTICE AREAS:*** Trademark Prosecution; Trademark Litigation; Copyright Prosecution; Copyright Litigation; Trademark Licensing; Copyright Licensing; Software Licensing; Technology Licensing; Computer Law; General Corporate Law. ***Email:*** khammond@porterwright.com

ELIZABETH A. HARTMAN, born Sandusky, Ohio, May 21, 1977; admitted to bar, 2004, Ohio. *Education:* The Ohio State University (B.A., summa cum laude, 1999); University of Notre Dame (J.D., magna cum laude, 2004). Managing Editor, Notre Dame Law Review, 2003-2004. ***PRACTICE AREAS:*** Real Estate ***Email:*** ehartman@porterwright.com

JAY HARTRANFT, born Columbus, Ohio, April 22, 1969; admitted to bar, 2000, Ohio. *Education:* Albion College (B.A., 1992); Capital University (J.D., 2000). ***PRACTICE AREAS:*** Business Law; Tax. ***Email:*** jayhartranft@porterwright.com

MICHAEL E. HEINTZ, born Cuyahoga Falls, Ohio, January 6, 1977; admitted to bar, 2003, Ohio. *Education:* Purdue University (B.S., 1999); Indiana University (J.D., 2003; M.S., 2003). Senior Notes and Comments Editor, Federal Communications Law Journal, 2001-2002. Author: "The Digital Divide and Courtroom Technology: Can David Keep Up With Goliath?" 54 Federal Communicatons Law Journal 567, 2001. *Member:* Ohio State and American Bar Associations. ***PRACTICE AREAS:*** Environmental Law; Litigation. ***Email:*** mheintz@porterwright.com

KATHLEEN BLICKENSTAFF HILL, born Greenville, Ohio, October 24, 1950; admitted to bar, 1998, Ohio. *Education:* The Ohio State University (B.S.N., cum laude, 1972; M.S., 1973); Capital University (J.D., 1998). Registered Nurse, Ohio, 1972. Professor, Capital University, 1989—. *Member:* Columbus (Member, Health Law Committee), Ohio State (Member, Disability and Health Law Committees, 1998—) and American (Member, Health Law Section) Bar Associations; American Health Lawyers Association. ***PRACTICE AREAS:*** Health Care Law; Business Law; Corporate Law. ***Email:*** khill@porterwright.com

J.H. HUEBERT, born Salem, Ohio, June 14, 1979; admitted to bar, 2004, Ohio and U.S. Court of Appeals, Sixth Circuit. *Education:* Grove City College (B.A., 2001); University of Chicago (J.D., 2004). John M. Olin Student Fellow in Law and Economics. Law Clerk Extern to the Hon. John W. Darrah, U.S. District Court, Northern District of Illinois, 2002-2003. Law Clerk to the Hon. Deborah L. Cook, U.S. Court of Appeals, Sixth Circuit, 2004-2005. *Member:* American Bar Association. ***PRACTICE AREAS:*** Litigation; Intellectual Property; International Business Law; White Collar Crime. ***Email:*** jhuebert@porterwright.com

ANNE M. HUGHES, born Columbus, Ohio, December 1, 1976; admitted to bar, 2001, Ohio; 2002, U.S. District Court, Southern and Northern Districts of Ohio. *Education:* Bob Jones University (B.A., cum laude, 1998); Capital University (J.D., summa cum laude, 2001). *Member:* Columbus and Ohio State Bar Associations; Defense Research Institute. ***PRACTICE AREAS:*** Litigation; Employee Benefits. ***Email:*** ahughes@porterwright.com

LAWRENCE BRADFIELD HUGHES, born Dayton, Ohio, January 25, 1972; admitted to bar, 1999, Ohio; 2001, U.S. District Court, Southern District of Ohio; 2002, U.S. Court of Appeals, Sixth Circuit. *Education:* Kenyon College (B.A., Political Science, summa cum laude, 1994); University of Dayton (J.D., magna cum laude, 1999). Phi Beta Kappa. ***PRACTICE AREAS:*** Litigation; Appellate Practice. ***Email:*** bhughes@porterwright.com

PATRICK IAN JACKSON, born Memphis, Tennessee, January 28, 1970; admitted to bar, 2002, Ohio. *Education:* Harvard University (B.A., 1992); University of Wisconsin-Madison (J.D., 2001). ***PRACTICE AREAS:*** Health Care Contracts; Health Care Corporate Law; Health Care Fraud; Health Care Regulation; Health Law; Physicians Contracts; Business Formation; Business Transactions; Limited Liability Company Law. ***Email:*** pjackson@porterwright.com

BERNARD JONES, born Oklahoma City, Oklahoma, January 20, 1979; admitted to bar, 2004, Ohio. *Education:* Southern Methodist University (B.A., 2001), University of Notre Dame (J.D., 2004). ***PRACTICE AREAS:*** Litigation. ***Email:*** bjones@porterwright.com

JENNIFER L. JUNG, born Cincinnati, April 26, 1974; admitted to bar, 2000, Ohio. *Education:* Ohio University (B.S., in Journalism, summa cum laude, 1995); Capital University (J.D., summa cum laude, 2000). Order of the Curia. Author, "Restrictions on the Representation of Indigent Communities in Public Interest and Law School Clinic Practice in Louisiana," 28 Capital University Law Review 873, Fed. Leg. & State Jud. *Member:* Columbus Bar Association. ***PRACTICE AREAS:*** Labor and Employment. ***Email:*** jjung@porterwright.com

AKIHIKO KITAGUCHI, admitted to bar, 1999, Japan (Not admitted in the United States). *Education:* The University of Tokyo (Law Degree, 1994; LL.B., 1997); New York University (LL.M., 2004). *Member:* Japanese Federation of Bar Associations. ***PRACTICE AREAS:*** Business; Securities; Immigration. ***Email:*** akitaguchi@porterwright.com

KYLE A. KNAPP, born Mansfield, Ohio, January 15, 1973; admitted to bar, 1998, Ohio; 1999, Florida. *Education:* Ohio State University (B.A., summa cum laude, 1994); Capital University (J.D., magna cum laude, 1998). Phi Beta Kappa. Author: Comment, "One Cannot Serve Two Masters," 26 Capital University Law Rev. 141, 1997. *Member:* Columbus Bar Association; American Immigration Lawyers Association. ***LANGUAGES:*** German. ***PRACTICE AREAS:*** Business Immigration; Family Immigration. ***Email:*** kknapp@porterwright.com

KATHRYN KRISHER, born Dayton, Ohio, July 15, 1979; (admission pending). *Education:* Ohio University (B.S., 2002); The Ohio State University (J.D., 2005). Order of the Coif. Managing Editor, The Ohio State Journal on Dispute Resolution, 2004-2005. ***PRACTICE AREAS:*** Labor and Employment. ***Email:*** kkrisher@porterwright.com

(This Listing Continued)

ROBERT J. KRUMMEN, born Columbus, Ohio, March 20, 1979; admitted to bar, 2003, Ohio. *Education:* The Ohio State University (B.A., 2000); Harvard University (J.D., 2003). [U.S. Coast Guard, 1997-1998]. ***PRACTICE AREAS:*** Litigation. ***Email:*** rkrummen@porterwright.com

MONIQUE B. LAMPKE, born McAllen, Texas, December 27, 1971; admitted to bar, 1997, Ohio; 1998, U.S. District Court, Northern and Southern Districts of Ohio. *Education:* Stanford University (B.A., 1994); The Ohio State University (J.D., 1997). *Member:* Ohio State and Federal Bar Associations; Women Lawyers of Franklin County; Ohio Women's Bar Association. ***PRACTICE AREAS:*** Litigation. ***Email:*** mlampke@porterwright.com

JAIME TARYN LANDRUM, born Jackson, Ohio, November 12, 1977; admitted to bar, 2003, Ohio. *Education:* The Ohio State University (B.S., 2000); Capital University (J.D., summa cum laude, 2003). National Moot Court Team, 2001-2003. Managing Editor, Capital Law Review, 2002-2003. *Member:* American Bar Association. ***PRACTICE AREAS:*** Labor and Employment. ***Email:*** jlandrum@porterwright.com

CHRISTINE D. LI, born Columbus, Ohio; admitted to bar, 2004, Ohio. *Education:* The Ohio State University (B.S., 2001); University of Virginia (J.D., 2004). ***LANGUAGES:*** Mandarin Chinese. ***PRACTICE AREAS:*** Business Law; Taxation; Securities. ***Email:*** cli@porterwright.com

SHAWN G. LISLE, admitted to bar, 1994, Pennsylvania; 2001, Ohio; 2003, U.S. Tax Court. *Education:* Westminster College (B.A., Economics, cum laude, 1989); University of Akron School of Law (J.D., summa cum laude, 1993). Phi Alpha Delta. University of Akron Law Review. Trial Attorney, U.S. Department of Justice, Tax Division, Civil Tax Section,1998-2000. Special Assistant U.S. Attorney, District of Hawaii, 1995-1997. *Member:* Ohio State and American Bar Associations. [Lt., U.S. Navy Reserve, JAGC, 1993-2001; Major, U.S. Air Force Reserve, JAGC, 2001—]. ***PRACTICE AREAS:*** ERISA; Employee Benefits; Executive Compensation; Federal Tax Controversies and Litigation; Commercial Transactions. ***Email:*** slisle@porterwright.com

HAIMA VATHI VARADAN MARLIER, born Columbus, Ohio, August 8, 1979; admitted to bar, 2004, Ohio. *Education:* Pennsylvania State University (B.A., 2001); Boston College (J.D., 2004). ***PRACTICE AREAS:*** Litigation. ***Email:*** hmarlier@porterwright.com

COLLEEN L. MARSHALL, born Dunbar, Pennsylvania, July 6, 1956; admitted to bar, 2004, Ohio. *Education:* Point Park University (B.A., 1978); Capital University (J.D., 2004). Member, Captial University Law Review, 2002-2004. *Member:* Ohio State Bar Association. ***PRACTICE AREAS:*** Litigation. ***Email:*** cmarshall@porterwright.com

MELANIE MARTIN-JONES, born Union City, Indiana, August 9, 1955; admitted to bar, 1999, Ohio and U.S. District Court, Southern District of Ohio; 2001, U.S. Court of Appeals, Sixth and Federal Circuits; 2003, U.S. Supreme Court; registered to practice before U.S. Patent and Trademark Office. *Education:* The Ohio State University (B.S., 1977; M.S., 1993); Capital University (J.D., 1999). Vice President, Havenswood Homeowners Association. Prevent Blindness Ohio, Development Committee. Presentations: "Assignment and Confidentiality Agreements," Columbus Business Technology Center, 2003; "Overview of Intellectual Property Law," Columbus Bar Association, 2003; "Can a Copyright Byte?," Columbus Bar Association, 2004; "Fair Use: BetaMax v. Grokster," Capital University Law School, 2004; "Trademark Practice in the U.S. Under the Madrid Protocol," Columbus Intellectual Property Association, 2005; "U.S. FDA Approval Process," and "U.S. Intellectual Property Protection," (taped presentations), Doing Business in USA-Ohio, Shanghai, China, 2005. *Member:* Columbus (Chair, Technology and the Law Committee, 2005—) and Ohio State Bar Associations; Columbus Intellectual Property Association (Secretary, 2000-2001; President, 2001-2002); American Intellectual Property Association (2000—). ***PRACTICE AREAS:*** Intellectual Property; Technology Transfers; Corporate Law. ***Email:*** mmartin-jones@porterwright.com

KRISTIN E. MATISZIW, born Marshall, Missouri, December 19, 1975; admitted to bar, 2004, Ohio. *Education:* University of Missouri (B.A., 1999); Capital University (J.D., summa cum laude, 2004). Notes and Comments Editor, Capital University Law Review, 2003-2004. ***PRACTICE AREAS:*** Health Care; Business; Securities. ***Email:*** kmatisziw@porterwright.com

ANTHONY R. McCLURE, born Columbus, Ohio, January 17, 1973; admitted to bar, 2003, Ohio. *Education:* Miami University, Oxford, Ohio (B.S., magna cum laude, 1995); Chicago-Kent College of Law (J.D., Order of the Coif, valedictorian, 2001). ***PRACTICE AREAS:*** Litigation. ***Email:*** amcclure@porterwright.com

MYRA L. McKENZIE, born Biloxi, Mississippi, September 2, 1977; admitted to bar, 2002, Ohio and U.S. District Courts, Southern and Northern Districts of Ohio. *Education:* Spelman College (B.A., cum laude, 1999); University of Notre Dame Law School (J.D., 2002). Phi Beta Kappa. *Member:* Columbus, Ohio State, American and National Bar Associations. ***PRACTICE AREAS:*** Labor and Employment. ***Email:*** mmckenzie@porterwright.com

TRACY L. MERRILL, born Warwick, Rhode Island, February 21, 1975; admitted to bar, 2001, Ohio, Florida and U.S. District Court, Southern District of Ohio. *Education:* Emory University (B.A., 1997); Georgetown University (J.D., 2000). *Member:* Ohio State and American Bar Associations; The Florida Bar; American Immigration Lawyer's Association. ***PRACTICE AREAS:*** Labor and Employment; Immigration Law. ***Email:*** tmerrill@porterwright.com

ROBERT JAMES MORGAN, born Dayton, Ohio, September 16, 1975; admitted to bar, 2001, Ohio. *Education:* University of Kentucky (B.A., English, 1998); The Ohio State University (J.D., 2001). Phi Beta Kappa. Member, Golden Key. *Member:* Ohio State Bar Association. ***PRACTICE AREAS:*** Trademarks; Copyrights; Intellectual Property Licensing; Technology; Litigation. ***Email:*** rmorgan@porterwright.com

ERIC C. MYERS, born Wheeling, West Virginia, September 5, 1976; admitted to bar, 2002, Ohio. *Education:* University of Notre Dame (B.B.A., Finance and Business Economics, 1999); The Ohio State University (J.D., 2002). ***PRACTICE AREAS:*** Labor and Employment; Litigation. ***Email:*** emyers@porterwright.com

(This Listing Continued)

MITCHELL A. NAUMOFF, JR., born Barberton, Ohio, September 17, 1976; admitted to bar, 2004, Ohio. *Education:* Case Western Reserve University (B.S., cum laude, 1999); George Washington University (J.D., with honors, 2004). ***PRACTICE AREAS:*** Financial Institutions; Corporate Law. ***Email:*** mnaumoff@porterwright.com

JANICE A. NELSON, born Medina, Ohio, October 2, 1937; admitted to bar, 1992, Ohio. *Education:* The Ohio State University (B.S., 1959; M.A., 1969); Capital University (J.D., 1992). ***PRACTICE AREAS:*** Corporate Law; Affordable Housing; Private Placement Securities Law; Business; Securities; Real Estate. ***Email:*** jnelson@porterwright.com

DAVID KEVIN ORENSTEN, born Duluth, Minnesota, August 19, 1976; admitted to bar, 2002, Ohio and U.S. District Court, Southern District of Ohio. *Education:* Indiana University (B.S., Public Policy, 1999); The Ohio State University College of Law (J.D., 2002). ***PRACTICE AREAS:*** Litigation. ***Email:*** dorensten@porterwright.com

CHRISTINA A. PATE, born Harvey, Illinois, September 6, 1977; admitted to bar, 2004, Ohio. *Education:* Marietta College (B.A., 1995); Georgetown University (J.D., 2004). ***PRACTICE AREAS:*** Labor and Employment. ***Email:*** cpate@porterwright.com

ANDREW R. POST, born Columbus, Ohio, August 1, 1978; admitted to bar, 2003, Ohio. *Education:* DePauw University (B.A., 2000); Capital University (J.D., 2003). ***PRACTICE AREAS:*** Business Law. ***Email:*** apost@porterwright.com

NICOLE S. RANDALL, born Las Cruces, New Mexico, November 8, 1973; admitted to bar, 2000, Ohio; 2001, U.S. District Court, Southern District of Ohio. *Education:* The Ohio State University (B.A., 1995; J.D. 2000). ***PRACTICE AREAS:*** Litigation; Environmental Compliance. ***Email:*** nrandall@porterwright.com

TRACIE RANSOM, born Natchez, Mississippi, January 4, 1979; admitted to bar, 2004, Ohio; 2005, U.S. District Court, Southern District of Ohio. *Education:* University of Alabama (B.S., cum laude, 2001); University of Illinois (J.D., cum laude, 2004). ***PRACTICE AREAS:*** Litigation. ***Email:*** transom@porterwright.com

PAUL G. ROZELLE, born Philadelphia, Pennsylvania, November, 17, 1972; admitted to bar, 1999, Massachusetts; 2001, U.S. District Court, District of Massachusetts; 2003, Ohio. *Education:* University of Pennsylvania (B.A., cum laude, 1994); University of North Carolina (M.A., 1996); Duke University (J.D., magna cum laude, 1999). Order of the Coif. Co-Author: "The Independent Counsel Statute: A Legal History," 62 Law & Contemporary Problems 5, 1999. *Member:* Boston and American Bar Associations. ***PRACTICE AREAS:*** Litigation. ***Email:*** prozelle@porterwright.com

AMANDA L. SCHERMER, born Granite City, Illinois, April 27, 1978; (admission pending). *Education:* University of Illinois (B.S., 2000; J.D., cum laude, 2005). ***PRACTICE AREAS:*** Litigation. ***Email:*** aschermer@porterwright.com

ROBERT J. SCHMIDT, born Cleveland, Ohio, September 22, 1967; admitted to bar, 1993, Ohio; 1999, U.S. District Court, Southern District of Ohio. *Education:* University of Virginia (B.A., 1990; J.D., 1993). Author, "International Negotiations Paralyzed by Domestic Politics: Two-Level Source Theory and the Problem of the Pacific Salmon Commission," Environmental Law, 1996. Assistant Attorney General, Ohio, 1996-2000. *Member:* Columbus (Co-Chair, Environmental Law Committee, 1996-2000) and Ohio State Bar Associations. ***PRACTICE AREAS:*** Environmental Law; Real Estate. ***Email:*** rschmidt@porterwright.com

LINDSAY M. SESTILE, born Mountain View, California, April 13, 1977; admitted to bar, 2002, Ohio; 2003, U.S. District Court, Southern District of Ohio. *Education:* Albion College (B.A., magna cum laude, 1999); University of Notre Dame (J.D., 2002). Phi Beta Kappa. Mortar Board. *Member:* Columbus, Ohio State and American Bar Associations. ***LANGUAGES:*** French. ***PRACTICE AREAS:*** Litigation. ***Email:*** lsestile@porterwright.com

AARON M. SHANK, born Rochester, New York, November 4, 1971; admitted to bar, 1998, Ohio and U.S. District Court, Southern District of Ohio. *Education:* Wittenberg University (B.A., 1993); The Ohio State University (J.D., 1998). *Member:* Columbus (Member, Young Lawyers) and Ohio State Bar Associations. ***PRACTICE AREAS:*** Litigation; Complex Litigation; Environmental Litigation. ***Email:*** ashank@porterwright.com

KYLE T. SHAW, born Detroit, Michigan, July 5, 1975; admitted to bar, 2003, Wisconsin; 2004, Ohio. *Education:* University of Michigan (B.A., 1997); University of Wisconsin (J.D., 2003). ***PRACTICE AREAS:*** Litigation. ***Email:*** kshaw@porterwright.com

RYAN PATRICK SHERMAN, born Columbus, Ohio, October 24, 1976; admitted to bar, 2002, Ohio. *Education:* The Ohio State University (B.A., magna cum laude, 1999; J.D., with honors, 2002). ***PRACTICE AREAS:*** Litigation. ***Email:*** rsherman@porterwright.com

JEREMY DAVID SIEGFRIED, born Harvard, Massachusetts, June 7, 1974; admitted to bar, 1999, Ohio. *Education:* University of North Carolina (A.B., 1996); Ohio State University College of Law (J.D., 1999). Delta Theta Phi. ***PRACTICE AREAS:*** Securities; Corporate Law; Business Law. ***Email:*** jsiegfried@porterwright.com

ALLISON K. SLAGLE, born Ironton, Ohio, July 31, 1980; (admission pending). *Education:* Miami University (B.S., 2002); Capital University (J.D., magna cum laude, 2005). Order of the Curia. Managing Editor, Capital University Law Review, 2004-2005. Author: "Nevada Department of Human Resources v. Hibbs:. ***Email:*** aslagle@porterwright.com

MARK A. SNIDER, born Olean, New York, July 5, 1979; admitted to bar, 2004, Ohio. *Education:* Denison University (B.S., summa cum laude, 2001); Washington & Lee University (J.D., magna cum laude, 2004). Phi Beta Kappa. Senior Articles Editor, Washington & Lee Law Review, 2003-2004. ***PRACTICE AREAS:*** Tax Law; Business Law; Real Estate. ***Email:*** msnider@porterwright.com

JENNY T. SWINERTON, born Columbus Grove, Ohio, April 29, 1976; admitted to bar, 2004, Ohio. *Education:* University of Toledo (B.A., 1998); Capital University (J.D., summa cum laude, 2004). ***PRACTICE AREAS:*** Labor and Employment; Litigation. ***Email:*** jswinerton@porterwright.com

HEATHER N. TAYLOR, born Cincinnati, Ohio, April 27, 1977; admitted to bar, 2003, Ohio. *Education:* Hanover College (B.A., magna cum laude, 1999); Indiana Univer-

(This Listing Continued)

PORTER WRIGHT MORRIS & ARTHUR LLP, Columbus—Continued

sity-Bloomington (J.D., 2002). Federal Communications Law Journal, 2000-2002. ***PRACTICE AREAS:*** Business Law; Securities Law; Real Estate. ***Email:*** htaylor@porterwright.com

M. TODD TAYLOR, born Columbus, Ohio, January 26, 1973; admitted to bar, 2000, New York and Ohio; 2002, Paris. *Education:* Bucknell University (B.A., magna cum laude, French, with honors, 1995); Cornell Law School (J.D., 1999); Université de Paris I, Panthéon-Sorbonne (Maîtrise en droit, 1999). Mortar Board, Bucknell University. *Member:* Columbus, Paris, New York State (Member, Sections on: International Law; Young Lawyers), American and International Bar Associations. ***LANGUAGES:*** French. ***PRACTICE AREAS:*** Corporate Organization; Securities Regulation; International Comparative Law; Commercial Transactions; Immigration Law; Business; Securities. ***Email:*** ttaylor@porterwright.com

JOHN KENNETH THIEN, born 1957; admitted to bar, 1999, Ohio; 2000, U.S. District Court, Southern and Northern Districts of Ohio; 2004, U.S. Court of Appeals, Sixth Circuit. *Education:* Cedarville College (B.A., 1982); University of Virginia School of Law (J.D., 1999). ***PRACTICE AREAS:*** Litigation. ***Email:*** kthien@porterwright.com

TERRY L. THOMSON, born Olney, Illinois, November 20, 1965; admitted to bar, 2003, Ohio. *Education:* Northwest Christian College (B.A., 1999); Indiana University (J.D., cum laude, 2003). *Member:* Columbus and American Bar Associations. ***PRACTICE AREAS:*** Finance; Financial Institutions. ***Email:*** tthomson@porterwright.com

BRETT P. THORNTON, born Cincinnati, Ohio, April 2, 1975; admitted to bar, 2001, Ohio. *Education:* The Ohio State University (B.S., Business Administration, 1997); George Washington University (J.D., 2001). Member, Golden Key. ***PRACTICE AREAS:*** Corporate Law; Business; Securities. ***Email:*** bthornton@porterwright.com

AARON T. TULENCIK, admitted to bar, 2000, Ohio. *Education:* Malone College (B.A., Law and Society, 1997); Oklahoma City University (J.D., 2000). *Member:* Columbus and Ohio State Bar Associations. ***PRACTICE AREAS:*** Litigation. ***Email:*** atulencik@porterwright.com

DARIN L. VAN VLERAH, born Defiance, Ohio, May 15, 1973; admitted to bar, 2003, Ohio. *Education:* The Ohio State University (B.S., magna cum laude, 1996); Boston University (J.D., 2003). *Member:* Columbus Bar Association. ***PRACTICE AREAS:*** Labor and Employment.

KENDALL S. VERRETT, born Dayton, Ohio, August 2, 1978; admitted to bar, 2003, Ohio. *Education:* Denison University (B.A., cum laude, 2000); University of Cincinnati (J.D., 2003). Student Articles Editor, University of Cincinnati Law Review, 2002-2003. Author: "Ohio's Immunity Challenge: Statutory Immunity from Medical Malpractice for Dually-Employed Physicians," 71 University of Cincinnati Law Rev. 279, 2002. *Member:* Ohio State Bar Association. ***PRACTICE AREAS:*** Litigation. ***Email:*** kverrett@porterwright.com

JAY A. YURKIW, born Cleveland, Ohio, January 24, 1972; admitted to bar, 1997, Ohio; 2000, U.S. District Court, Southern District of Ohio. *Education:* University of Notre Dame (B.A., magna cum laude, 1994); The Ohio State University (J.D., with honors, 1997). Pi Sigma Alpha. Author, "Recent Development Note: Allied-Bruce Terminix Cos., Inc. v. Dobson," 12 Ohio St. J. on Disp. Resol. 223, 1997. *Member:* Cleveland, Columbus, Cuyahoga County, Ohio State and American (Member, Litigation Section) Bar Associations. ***PRACTICE AREAS:*** Litigation. ***Email:*** jyurkiw@porterwright.com

OF COUNSEL COLUMBUS, OHIO OFFICE

WILLIAM E. ARTHUR, born Columbus, Ohio, January 13, 1929; admitted to bar, 1953, Ohio. *Education:* The Ohio State University (B.S. in B.A., 1950; J.D., 1953). Phi Delta Phi. *Member:* Columbus, Ohio State and American Bar Associations. ***PRACTICE AREAS:*** Mergers, Acquisitions and Divestitures; Business Planning; Corporate Finance; Real Estate Development; Business Syndications; Financial Institutions; Tax. ***Email:*** warthur@porterwright.com

DONALD L. BECKETT, born Akron, Ohio, 1931; admitted to bar, 1957, Ohio. *Education:* Heidelberg College (A.B., 1954); The Ohio State University (J.D., 1957). *Member:* Columbus, Ohio State and American Bar Associations. (Also Member of Robins, Beckett, Hammond & Sewards). ***PRACTICE AREAS:*** Probate; Trusts and Estates. ***Email:*** dbeckett@porterwright.com

ANDREW S. BERGMAN, born Philadelphia, Pennsylvania, October 4, 1957; admitted to bar, 1986, Minnesota; 1988, U.S. District Court, District of Minnesota; 1991, Ohio; U.S. Supreme Court; U.S. Court of Appeals, District of Columbia and Sixth Circuits; U.S. District Court, Southern and Northern Districts of Ohio. *Education:* Grinnell College (B.A., with honors, 1979); University of Minnesota Law School (J.D . cum laude, 1986); Humphrey Institute of Public Affairs, University of Minnesota (M.A., 1987). Attorney, Federal Reserve Bank of Minneapolis, 1987-1990. Assistant Attorney General, Chief Counsel's Staff, 1992-1996, Assistant Attorney General, Environmental Enforcement Section, 1996-2000 and Assistant State Solicitor, Major Appeals Group, 1999-2000, Ohio Attorney General's Office. Assistant State. ***PRACTICE AREAS:*** Clean Air Act; Air Pollution; Environmental Compliance; Environmental Administrative Law; Water Pollution. ***Email:*** abergman@porterwright.com

HOWARD P. FINK, born Rochester, New York, March 4, 1933; admitted to bar, 1958, New York; 1962, Connecticut; 1970, Ohio; 1980, U.S. Supreme Court. *Education:* Cornell University (B.S., 1955); Yale University (LL.B., 1958). Professor of Law, Ohio State University, 1965—. ***PRACTICE AREAS:*** Civil Procedure; Federal Practice. ***Email:*** hfink@porterwright.com

RALPH K. FRASIER, born September 16, 1938; admitted to bar, 1965, North Carolina; 1976, Ohio. *Education:* North Carolina Central University (B.Sc., 1963; J.D., magna cum laude, 1965). Past Counsel and Secretary, Huntington Bancshares Incorporated. Chairman, Ohio Board of Regents and Community Mutual Insurance Company. Board Member: Huntington National Bank, Ohio Health Corporation; North Carolina Central University; National Judicial College. *Member:* North Carolina State Bar. (Also of Counsel, Frasier & Alston, P.A., Durham, North Carolina). ***PRACTICE AREAS:*** Finance; Commerce; Financial Institutions. ***Email:*** rfrasier@porterwright.com

(This Listing Continued)

KEVIN HAWLEY, born Binghamton, New York, October 31, 1958; admitted to bar, 1983, District of Columbia (Not admitted in Ohio). *Education:* Syracuse University (B.A., summa cum laude, 1980); Duke University (J.D., 1983). ***PRACTICE AREAS:*** Civil and Appellate Litigation; Regulated Industries; Litigation. ***Email:*** khawley@porterwright.com

CHARLES J. KURTZ, III, born Columbus, Ohio, May 13, 1940; admitted to bar, 1965, Ohio; 1967, District of Columbia and U.S. District Court, Southern District of Ohio; 1976, U.S. District Court, Northern District of Ohio; 1993, U.S. Court of Appeals, Sixth Circuit. *Education:* Williams College (B.A., 1962); The Ohio State University (J.D., 1965). Phi Delta Phi. Law Clerk to the Hon. John Marshall Matthias, Justice, Supreme Court of Ohio, 1965-1967. Member, of Faculty, Ohio CLE Institute, 1970—. Member, Panel of Commercial Arbitrators, American Arbitration Association. *Member:* Columbus, Ohio State (Workers Compensation Committee) and American (Litigation Committee) Bar Associations. ***PRACTICE AREAS:*** Litigation; Contracts; Workers' Compensation; Business; Securities; Labor and Employment. ***Email:*** ckurtz@porterwright.com

WAYMAN C. LAWRENCE, III, born Columbus, Ohio, March 28, 1931; admitted to bar, 1959, Ohio. *Education:* Princeton University (A.B., 1953); The Ohio State University (J.D., cum laude, 1959). Order of the Coif; Phi Delta Phi. Editor-in-Chief, Ohio State Law Journal, 1958-1959. *Member:* Columbus, Ohio State and American Bar Associations. ***PRACTICE AREAS:*** Estate Planning; Probate; Trust Administration; Business; Securities. ***Email:*** wlawrence@porterwright.com

FRANK R. MORRIS, JR., born Jackson, Michigan, July 1, 1929; admitted to bar, 1958, Ohio. *Education:* Yale University (B.A., 1952); University of Michigan (J.D., with distinction, 1957). Phi Delta Phi. Member, New York Stock Exchange Legal Advisory Committee, 1983-1986. Editor, The Business Lawyer, 1983-1984. *Member:* Columbus, Ohio State (Chairman, Corporation Law Committee, 1974-1976) and American (Member, House of Delegates, 1991—; Chairman, Section of Business Law, 1985-1986; Chairman, Committee on Corporate Laws, 1988-1992) Bar Associations. Fellow: American Bar Foundation; Ohio State Bar Foundation; Columbus Bar Foundation. ***PRACTICE AREAS:*** Corporate Law; Business Law; Financial Institutions Law; Tax; Trusts and Estates. ***Email:*** fmorris@porterwright.com

ROBERT J. NORDSTROM, born Cadillac, Michigan, May 14, 1924; admitted to bar, 1949, Rhode Island; 1956, Ohio. *Education:* Western Michigan University (A.B., 1948); University of Michigan (J.D., 1949). Order of the Coif. Associate Editor, University of Michigan Law Journal. Co-author: *Commercial Paper*, West Publishing, 1972; *Sales*, West Publishing, 1982; *Secured Transactions*, West Publishing, 1986; *Sales and Leases of Goods*, Aspen Law & Business, 2000. Professor, The Ohio State University College of Law, 1951-1976. Board of Trustees, Ohio Legal Center Institute, 1961-1977. *Member:* Columbus and Ohio State Bar Associations; American Law Institute. ***PRACTICE AREAS:*** Business Law; Franchise Law; International Law. ***Email:*** rnordstrom@porterwright.com

DAVID E. NORTHROP, born Pittsburgh, Pennsylvania, June 11, 1948; admitted to bar, 1973, Ohio and U.S. District Court, Southern District of Ohio; 1977, U.S. Supreme Court and U.S. Court of Appeals, Sixth Circuit; 1979, U.S. District Court, Northern District of Ohio and U.S. District Court, Eastern District of Kentucky. *Education:* Allegheny College (B.A., 1970); Ohio State University (J.D., summa cum laude, 1972). Order of the Coif. Member, Editorial Staff, Ohio State University Law Review, 1971-1972. Author: "Obscenity--Injunctive Proceedings Against the Display or Sale of Obscene Materials," 33 Ohio State Law Journal 236, 1972. Co-Author: with Robert L. Brubaker, "Appellate Review of Administrative Rule Making in Ohio-Prospects for Revival," 37 Ohio State Law Journal 471, 1976. Assistant Attorney General, Ohio, 1973-1987. Chief, Environmental Law Section, 1979-1983. Deputy Chief Counsel, 1983-1987. *Member:* Columbus and Ohio State Bar Associations. ***PRACTICE AREAS:*** Environmental Law; Litigation. ***Email:*** dnorthrop@porterwright.com

PATRICK J. SMITH, born Raleigh, North Carolina, December 18, 1939; admitted to bar, 1965, Ohio. *Education:* Bowling Green State University (B.Sc., 1961); The Ohio State University (J.D., 1965). Phi Alpha Delta. Note Editor, Ohio State Law Journal, 1964-1965. *Member:* Columbus, Ohio State, Federal and American Bar Associations; National Association of Railroad Trial Counsel; Ohio Association of Civil Trial Attorneys. ***PRACTICE AREAS:*** Environmental Law; Litigation. ***Email:*** psmith@porterwright.com

GEORGE E. ZOLA, born Chicago, Illinois, 1954; admitted to bar, 1985, Ohio; 1986, Florida. *Education:* Ohio State University (B.S., 1976); College of St. Thomas (M.B.A., 1980); Capital University (J.D., 1985). *Member:* Columbus and Ohio State Bar Associations; The Florida Bar. ***PRACTICE AREAS:*** Estate Planning; Probate. ***Email:*** gzola@porterwright.com

COUNSEL TO THE FIRM

LISA L. ESCHLEMAN, born Ashland, Ohio, October 12, 1959; admitted to bar, 1987, Ohio. *Education:* Indiana University (B.S.P.A., 1981); Capital University (J.D., magna cum laude, 1987). Order of the Curia. ***PRACTICE AREAS:*** Commercial Litigation; Professional Malpractice; Products Liability. ***Email:*** leschleman@porterwright.com

(See Listings at Dayton, Cincinnati and Cleveland, Ohio, Washington, D.C. and Naples, Florida for professional biographies on attorneys resident in those offices)

CHARLES C. POSTLEWAITE

3040 RIVERSIDE DRIVE, SUITE 122
COLUMBUS, OHIO 43221
Telephone: 614-486-2111
Fax: 614-486-8943
Email: ccpostlaw@aol.com
URL: http://www.lawyers.com/p&jlaw

Business, Corporation and Commercial Law, Family/Domestic Law, Collections, Construction Law, Mechanics Liens, Real Estate, Probate and Estate Planning, Personal Injury, Civil and Criminal Litigation in all State and Federal Courts.

(This Listing Continued)

CHARLES C. POSTLEWAITE, born Columbus, Ohio, February 14, 1955; admitted to bar, 1982, Ohio; 1983, U.S. District Court, Southern District of Ohio; 1986, U.S. Supreme Court; 1991, U.S. Court of Appeals, Sixth Circuit. *Education:* Williams College (B.A., 1977); Ohio Northern University (J.D., 1982). The Willis Society; Phi Kappa Phi. *Member:* Columbus, Ohio State and American Bar Associations. ***PRACTICE AREAS:*** Business Law; Corporate Law; Commercial Law; Family Law; Domestic Law; Collections; Construction Law; Mechanics Liens; Real Estate; Probate; Estate Planning; Personal Injury; Civil Litigation; Criminal Litigation.

FRANK A. RAY CO., L.P.A.

Established in 1983

SUITE 1000
65 EAST STATE STREET
COLUMBUS, OHIO 43215
Telephone: 614-221-7791
Fax: 614-221-4012
Email: far@raylaw.com

Civil Trial and Appellate Practice in Personal Injury and Wrongful Death. Automobile Accidents, Negligence, Products Liability, Employer Intentional Tort, Business Litigation and Sports Law.

FIRM PROFILE: Since 1983, the law firm has provided aggressive, thoughtful counsel to hundreds of people, many of whom could not otherwise obtain or afford it. The firm represents people who have been injured in automobile accidents, by faulty products or on unsafe premises. It also handles insurance, commercial and business litigation cases. The firm's small size means clients receive close, personal attention. Its academic focus keeps lawyers knowledgeable in the latest developments of challenging legal fields that require innovation and flexibility.

FRANK A. RAY, born Lafayette, Indiana, January 30, 1949; admitted to bar, 1973, Ohio; 1975, U.S. District Court, Southern District of Ohio; 1976, U.S. Supreme Court; 1977, U.S. Tax Court and U.S. Court of Appeals, Sixth Circuit; 1980, U.S. District Court, Northern District of Ohio; 1983, U.S. District Court, Eastern District of Michigan; 1987, U.S. Court of Appeals, First Circuit. *Education:* The Ohio State University (B.A., 1970; J.D., 1973). Recipient, National Award of Distinctive Service, National District Attorneys Association, 1977; Professionalism Award, Columbus Bar Association, 1997. Co-Author: *Personal Injury Litigation Practice in Ohio,* National Business Institute, Inc., 1988, 1991. Board of Editors, *Manual for Complex Litigation, 4th Ed.*Federal Judicial Center, 2004. Director: Economic Crime Unit, Assistant Prosecuting Attorney, Franklin County, Ohio, 1973-1975; Economic Crime Project, National District Attorneys Association, Washington, D.C., 1975-1976. Chief Counsel, Civil Division, Office of the Franklin County Prosecuting Attorney, 1976-1977, 1978. Associate: Brownfield, Kosydar, Bowen, Bally & Sturtz, 1977-1978; Michael F. Colley Co., L.P.A., 1979-1983. Owner, Frank A. Ray Co., L.P.A., 1983-1993 and 1998—; Ray & Todaro Co., L.P.A., 1993-1994; Ray, Todaro & Alton Co., L.P.A., 1994-1996; Ray, Todaro, Alton & Kirstein Co., L.P.A., 1996-1997; Ray, Alton & Kirstein Co., L.P.A., 1997-1998. *Member:* Columbus (President, 2001-2002), Ohio State (Member, Negligence Law Committee, 1989-1998; Board of Editors, Jury Instructions Committee, 2003—), American (Member, Special Committee on Economic Crime, Criminal Justice Section, 1976-1977) Bar Associations; Franklin County Trial Lawyers Association (President, 1987-1988); Ohio Academy of Trial Lawyers (President, 1989-1990); The Association of Trial Lawyers of America (State Delegate, Ohio, 1990-1992); American Inns of Court (President, Robert M. Duncan Chapter, 1992-1993); American Board of Trial Advocates (Ohio Chapter, President, 2004); Million Dollar Advocates Forum; Board of Bar Examiners, Ohio Supreme Court, 1992-1995; Rules Advisory Committee, Ohio Supreme Court, 1995-1999. Fellow: American College of Trial Lawyers; Roscoe Pound Foundation; Ohio Academy of Trial Lawyers; Ohio State Bar Foundation; Columbus Bar Foundation; International Society of Barristers. (Certified as a Civil Trial Specialist by the National Board of Trial Advocacy). ***PRACTICE AREAS:*** Personal Injury; Wrongful Death; Negligence; Products Liability; Business Litigation. ***Email:*** far@raylaw.com

JANICA A. PIERCE, born Dayton, Ohio, July 26, 1977; admitted to bar, 2002, Ohio. *Education:* University of Tennessee at Knoxville (B.A., 1999); The Ohio State University, Moritz College of Law (J.D., 2002). Member, Golden Key International Honour Society. *Member:* Columbus and Ohio State Bar Associations; Franklin County Trial Lawyers Association; Ohio Academy of Trial Lawyers. ***PRACTICE AREAS:*** Personal Injury; Intentional Torts; Products Liability; Contracts. ***Email:*** jap@raylaw.com

OF COUNSEL TO

CHESTER, WILLCOX & SAXBE LLP

REPRESENTATIVE CLIENTS: Columbus Clippers Baseball Organization; Franklin County Stadium, Inc.; International League of Professional Baseball Clubs.
REFERENCES: National City Bank; Diamond Hill Management.

RICH, CRITES & DITTMER, LLC

300 EAST BROAD STREET, SUITE 300
COLUMBUS, OHIO 43215-3452
Telephone: 614-228-5822
Telecopier: 614-540-7476
URL: http://www.RichCrites.com

Delaware, Ohio Office: 25 West Central Avenue, 43015-8340. Telephone: 740-363-1931; 800-619-5780. Fax: 740-363-4594.

Galena, Ohio Office: 21 Middle Street, P.O. Box 248, 43021-0248. Telephone: 740-965-3900. Fax: 740-965-2718.

(This Listing Continued)

Corporate, Commercial, Real Estate, Zoning and Land Use, Family, Creditors Rights, Entertainment Law, Franchise, Tax, Bankruptcy, Administrative Law, General Civil Practice, Estate Planning, Administrative, Complex Litigation, Aviation Law, Personal Injury, Medical Malpractice, Automobile Accidents, Products Liability, Aviation Law, School and Municipal Law, White Collar Crime, Health Care Fraud, Government Law and Governmental Relations.

FIRM PROFILE: Any undertaking that requires legal work involves important decisions for a client. The first one is choosing the right law firm to handle your work. That decision should be an informed one. Established in 1946, Rich, Crites & Dittmer, LLC has 14 attorneys, well trained paraprofessionals and an extensive clerical and support staff. We offer clients careful attention, combined with excellent legal knowledge and vast experience in a broad range of legal areas.

A collective pool of practical experience is a valuable resource in the handling of many client problems. Although knowledge of the law is fundamental, an understanding of how the judicial, administrative and legislative processes work can produce results that legal knowledge alone cannot. Our lawyers participate in continuing legal education programs, focusing on their specialty areas. Some are instructors and speakers and have written extensively in professional and business publications.

We strive to render professional services of uncompromising quality, while also recognizing our responsibilities to the community and to society. This is reflected in the varied activities of each of our attorneys.

MEMBERS OF FIRM

JEFFREY A. RICH, born Cleveland, Ohio, July 10, 1945; admitted to bar, 1970, Ohio; 1973, U.S. District Court, Southern and Northern Districts of Ohio, U.S. Tax Court, U.S. Court of Appeals, Sixth Circuit and U.S. Supreme Court; 1985, Florida; 1994, Arizona. *Education:* The Ohio State University (B.A., with distinction, 1967); Cleveland State University Law School (J.D., 1970). Editor-in-Chief, Cleveland State Law Review, 1969-1970. Author: "Valuation," Ohio Taxation, Matthew Bender, Chapter 87, 1985; "Administrative Remedies and Appeals," Chapter 90, 1985. Of Counsel, Rose Law Group, Scottsdale, Arizona. Member: Committee to Establish a Client Security Fund, 1984-1986; Ohio Board of Bar Examiners, 1985-1987, Ohio Supreme Court. *Member:* Columbus, Franklin County, Ohio State and American Bar Associations; The Florida Bar; State Bar of Arizona. ***PRACTICE AREAS:*** Public and Governmental Law; Entertainment Law; Accident and Personal Injury Law; Administrative Law; Federal, State and Local Tax Law; Appellate Practice; Property Tax Abatement Law; School Law; Complex Business Litigation; Zoning Law; Real Estate. ***Email:*** jrich@RichCrites.com

D. MICHAEL CRITES, born Bluffton, Ohio, June 16, 1948; admitted to bar, 1978, Ohio; 1979, U.S. District Court, Northern and Southern Districts of Ohio, U.S. Court of Appeals, Sixth Circuit and U.S. Supreme Court. *Education:* The United States Naval Academy (B.S., 1970); Ohio Northern University College of Law (J.D., 1978). Member: Willis Honor Society; Delta Theta Phi (President, 1977-1978); Ohio Veterans Hall of Fame. Adjunct Professor: The Ohio State University, College of Law, 1996. Law Director/Prosecutor, Granville, Ohio, 2000— and Pataskala, Ohio, 2003—, Harrisburg, Ohio, 2003—, Commercial Point, Ohio, 2004— and Hillard, Ohio, 2003-2004. Special Counsel to Galena, Ohio and Powell, Ohio, 2003—. First Assistant Prosecuting Attorney, Delaware County, Ohio, 1993. United States Attorney, Southern District of Ohio, 1986-1993. Assistant United States Attorney, Southern District of Ohio, 1983-1986. Assistant Prosecuting Attorney, Allen County, Ohio, 1979-1983. City Prosecutor, Lima, Ohio, 1979. Member: Olentangy Local School District Board of Education, 1993-1997; President, 1995-1997; Vice-President, 1994-1995. Chairman, Ohio Board of Building Appeals, 2002—. President, Greater Powell Veterans Memorial Foundation, 2004—. Trustee, University of Rio Grande, 2004—. *Member:* Delaware County, Licking County, Columbus, Ohio State and American Bar Associations; Defense Research Institute; National Association of Former U.S. Attorneys. [Captain, U.S. Naval Reserve, Retired]. ***PRACTICE AREAS:*** Litigation; Public Law. ***Email:*** mcrites@RichCrites.com

JEFFREY A. DITTMER, born Lorain, Ohio, April 18, 1962; admitted to bar, 1989, Ohio and U.S. District Court, Southern District of Ohio. *Education:* Ohio State University (B.A., 1984); Capital University (J.D., 1988). Bailiff, Franklin County Common Pleas Court, 1987-1989. *Member:* Delaware County, Columbus (Member, Admissions Committee, 2003—) and Ohio State Bar Associations; Franklin County Trial Lawyers Association; Ohio Association of Criminal Defense Lawyers. ***PRACTICE AREAS:*** Personal Injury Litigation; Commercial Litigation; Business Litigation; Products Liability; Products Liability Defense; Criminal Trial Law; General Defense; Employment Law. ***Email:*** jdittmar@RichCrites.com

ASSOCIATES

MARK H. GILLIS, born Modesto, California, September 16, 1966; admitted to bar, 1996, Ohio and U.S. District Court, Southern District of Ohio. *Education:* Ohio University (B.B.A., with high honors, 1993); Whittier College School of Law (J.D., cum laude, 1996). *Member:* Columbus, Ohio State and American Bar Associations. ***PRACTICE AREAS:*** Real Estate Taxation; Administrative Law; Appellate Practice. ***Email:*** mgillis@RichCrites.com

BRANDY M. MAAS, born Columbus, Ohio, December 29, 1974; admitted to bar, 2001, California and U.S. District Court, Central District of California; 2003, Ohio. *Education:* Eastern New Mexico University (B.S., History, Political Science, 1997); Rutgers University Law School (J.D., 2000). Assistant Law Director/Prosecutor, Granville, Pataskala and Harrisburg, Ohio, 2004—. *Member:* Columbus and Ohio State Bar Associations. ***PRACTICE AREAS:*** Litigation; Public Law; Family Law; Real Estate Taxation. ***Email:*** bmaas@RichCrites.com

JOSEPH E. SCHMANSKY, born Toledo, Ohio, July 22, 1967; admitted to bar, 2000, Ohio. *Education:* The Ohio State University (B.A., 1991); Capital University Law School (J.D., 2000). Order of the Curia. Formerly with Court of Common Pleas, Delaware County, 2000-2005. *Member:* Delaware and Ohio State Bar Associations. ***PRACTICE AREAS:*** Litigation; Administrative Law. ***Email:*** jschmansky@RichCrites.com

(This Listing Continued)

RICH, CRITES & DITTMER, LLC, Columbus—Continued

OF COUNSEL

E. JOEL WESP, born Atlantic City, New Jersey, January 12, 1946; admitted to bar, 1970, Ohio; 1973, U.S. District Court, Southern District of Ohio and U.S. Court of Appeals, Sixth Circuit. *Education:* Wabash College (B.A., 1967); Case Western Reserve University (J.D., 1970). Order of the Coif. Editor, Law Review. *Member:* Columbus Bar Association (Member, Professional Ethics and Grievance Committee, 1991-1995). Columbus Bar Foundation (Board of Trustees, 2000—). ***PRACTICE AREAS:*** Business Litigation; Commercial Litigation; Employment Litigation; Professional Associations; Corporate Law; Closely Held Corporations; Noncompete Litigation; Trade Secrets; Biotechnology. ***Email:*** ejwesp@wesplaw.com

ROSEMARY SOVA, born Cincinnati, Ohio, July 20, 1950; admitted to bar, 1984, Ohio; 1985, U.S. District Court, Southern District of Ohio. *Education:* The Ohio State University (B.S., 1972); Capital University Law School (J.D., 1984). Order of the Barrister. Member: Capital University Law Review, 1982-1983; National Moot Court Team, 1982-1984; National Semi-finalist; American Bar Association National Appellate Advocacy Competition. Judicial Clerk to the Honorable Alba L. Whiteside, Tenth District Court of Appeals of Ohio, 1984-1986. Adjunct Professor, The Ohio State University College of Law, 1986-1987. *Member:* Columbus (Chairman: Young Lawyers Committee, 1987-1988; Member, Family Law and Probate Committees) and Ohio State Bar Associations. ***PRACTICE AREAS:*** Family Law; Probate. ***Email:*** rosemarysova@hotmail.com

JAMES R. GORRY, born Columbus, Ohio, February 21, 1947; admitted to bar, 1972, Ohio and U.S. District Court, Southern District of Ohio; 1994, Arizona. *Education:* Miami University of Ohio (B.A., with honors, 1969); University of Michigan Law School (J.D., 1972). Author: Ohio Taxation, Matthew Bender, 1985. Staff Counsel, Ohio House, Judiciary Committee, Legislative Ethics Committee. Chief Legal Counsel, Ohio Department of Tax Equalization. *Member:* Columbus and Ohio State Bar Associations; State Bar of Arizona. ***PRACTICE AREAS:*** Administrative Law; Government Law; Zoning; Business Taxation. ***Email:*** jgarry@RichCrites.com

R. LAMONT KAISER, born New Philadelphia, Ohio, September 6, 1944; admitted to bar, 1969, Ohio. *Education:* Ohio State University (B.A., 1966; J.D., cum laude, 1969). Managing Editor, Ohio State Law Journal, 1967-1968. *Member:* Delaware County (Member, Probate Law Committee), Ohio State (Member, Board of Governors, Estate Planning, Trust and Probate Law Section) and American Bar Associations. [Captain, U.S. Air Force JAG, 1969-1972]. (Resident, Delaware Office). ***PRACTICE AREAS:*** Estate Planning; Probate Law; Mental Health Law; Administrative Law; Corporate Law; Residential Real Estate; Commercial Real Estate Law; Litigation; Business Law; School Law. ***Email:*** kaiserlaw2@aol.com

LEON D. BASS, born Cincinnati, Ohio, October 22, 1972; admitted to bar, 1998, Ohio; 1999, U.S. District Court, Southern District of Ohio. *Education:* Michigan State University (B.A., 1995); The Ohio State University (J.D., 1998). Delta Theta Phi; Alpha Phi Omega. Golden Key National Honor Society. President, Ohio State Sports and Entertainment Law Association, 1997-1998. Member: Rotary International, 2000—; Columbus Community Festival. Author: "From the High Courts," Free Press, 1999; "Will Ya Face the Music?" Music Download 101, 2004. *Member:* Columbus and Ohio State Bar Associations. ***PRACTICE AREAS:*** Entertainment and the Arts; Business; Corporate; Trademark; Copyright; Civil Litigation. ***Email:*** idb@lawbass.com

MARK E. PHILLIPS, born Steubenville, Ohio, September 20, 1954; admitted to bar, 1984, Ohio; 1985, U.S. District Court, Southern District of Ohio; 1986, West Virginia and U.S. District Court, Southern District of West Virginia; 1989, U.S. Tax Court; 1991, U.S. Court of Appeals, Sixth Circuit. *Education:* The Ohio State University (B.S.B.A., 1976); Capital University Law School (J.D., 1984). Associate Professor, Columbus State, 1991-1992. *Member:* Columbus and Ohio State Bar Associations. ***PRACTICE AREAS:*** Business Law; Real Estate; Probate; Estate Planning. ***Email:*** lawyermark1@msn.com

KENNETH J. MOLNAR, born Cleveland, Ohio, July 31, 1946; admitted to bar, 1974, Ohio; 1975, U.S. District Court, Southern District of Ohio. *Education:* University of Dayton (B.A., 1968); Capital University (J.D., 1974). Solicitor: Galena, Ohio, 1984—; Powell, Ohio, 1985—. *Member:* Columbus, Delaware County (President, 1987-1988) and Ohio State Bar Associations. (Resident, Galena Office; Also practicing individually). ***Email:*** kmolnar@columbus.rr.com

GREGORY P. BARWELL, born Amherst, New York, June 11, 1970; admitted to bar, 1999, Ohio. *Education:* University of Buffalo (B.S., 1994); Ohio Northern University (J.D., 1998). Vice-President, Criminal Law Society, 1996-1998. Member: Moot Court Board of Advocates, 1996-1998; Ohio Courts of Appeals Judges Association, 1999-2001; Ohio Association of Magistrates, 1999-2001; Ohio Jury Instruction Committees, 1999-2003; Ohio Court Security Committee, 1998-2001. ***PRACTICE AREAS:*** Business Law; Litigation; Administrative Law. ***Email:*** barwellg@yahoo.com

JEFFREY H. JORDAN, born Columbus, Ohio, October 2, 1963; admitted to bar, 1990, Ohio; 1992, U.S. District Court, Southern District of Ohio; 1995, U.S. Court of Appeals, Sixth Circuit. *Education:* The Ohio State University (B.A., 1986); Moritz College of Law, The Ohio State University (J.D., 1990). *Member:* Columbus, Delaware County and Ohio State Bar Associations. ***LANGUAGES:*** French. ***REPORTED CASES:*** Columbus Show Case Company v. Cee Contracting, Inc., 75 Ohio App., 3d 559, 599 N.E. 2d 881, 1992. ***PRACTICE AREAS:*** Creditors Rights; Commercial Litigation; Landlord and Tenant Law. ***Email:*** lawoffice@lawofficejhj.com

REPRESENTATIVE CLIENTS: Bexley, Cambridge, Chillicothe, Columbus, Dublin, Kettering, Vandlia-Butler, West Carrollton, Worthington, Zaneville, Huber Heights, Licheing Heights, Northridge, Gahanna, Granville, Hilliard, Hamilton Local, Health, Lancaster City; Olentangy Local, Plain Local, Southwestern City; Groveport Madison, Westerville City, Wooster, School Districts, Knox County, Miami County, Wayne County; Tuscarawas County Boards of Revision; Village of Granville; City of Pataskala; City of Hilliard; City of Powell; Zivena, Inc.; Thomson Multimedia, Inc.; Arena One, Inc.; Signature Medical Direct; W.P. Baker & Sons Builders, Inc.; Riley Homes, Ltd.; Valley View Homes, Inc.; Adkins Productions, Inc.; Rain & Hail Insurance; Avonlca Homes, Ltd.; Allstate Financial, Inc.; Surgery and Gynecology, Inc.; McNeilus Truck and Manufacturing, Inc.; McNeilus Financial Services, Inc.; Kelly Services; Novamedix, Ltd.; Harrison Restaurants, Inc.; MAPSYS, Inc.; Motion Picture Association of America; Bow Wow; Fatty Koo.
REFERENCES: Huntington National Bank, N.A.; KeyBank.

(This Listing Continued)

MELISSA K. RIGGINS
ATTORNEY AT LAW

Established in 1995

118 E. MAIN STREET
COLUMBUS, OHIO 43215
Telephone: 614-228-6625
Fax: 614-228-6640
URL: http://www.rigginscriminallaw.com

Criminal Law, Felonies, Misdemeanors, Traffic Violations, Drug Crimes, Driving While Intoxicated, Domestic Violence and Drivers License Law.

MELISSA K. RIGGINS, born 1963; admitted to bar, 1988, Ohio; 1995, U.S. District Court, Southern District of Ohio. *Education:* Bowling Green State University (B.A., cum laude, 1985); University of Akron (J.D., 1988). Delta Theta Phi-Dean, Tribune. Law Clerk, Lorain County Court of Common Pleas, 1988-1991. Assistant Prosecutor, City of Columbus, 1991-1995. *Member:* Ohio State Bar Association (Member, Sections on: Criminal Law; Traffic Law); Central Ohio Association of Criminal Defense Lawyers; Ohio Association of Criminal Defense Lawyers. ***PRACTICE AREAS:*** Criminal Defense; Misdemeanors; Felonies; Driving While Intoxicated; Traffic Violations; Drug Crimes; Domestic Violence; Assault; Drivers License Suspension.

ROBOL LAW OFFICE LPA

Established in 2004

555 CITY PARK AVENUE
COLUMBUS, OHIO 43215
Telephone: 614-737-3739
Toll Free: 877-580-6859
Fax: 614-737-3756
Email: rrobol@robollaw.com
URL: http://www.robollaw.com

Civil Litigation, Trials and Appeals, Business Organizations, International, Admiralty and Maritime.

RICHARD T. ROBOL, born Norfolk, Virginia, February 8, 1952; admitted to bar, 1979, Virginia; 1991, District of Columbia; 1996, Ohio; U.S. Court of Appeals, Fourth, Sixth, Ninth and Eleventh Circuits; U.S. Supreme Court. *Education:* University of Virginia (B.A., 1974); University of Pavia, Pavia, Italy; Harvard University (J.D., 1978). Phi Beta Kappa. Fulbright Scholar. Managing Editor, Harvard International Law Journal, 1977-1978. Law Clerk to the Hon. John A. Mackenzie, U. S. District Court, Eastern District of Virginia, 1978-1979. International Law Section, Virginia State Bar, 1982-1983. *Member:* Bar Association of the District of Columbia; Virginia State Bar; Maritime Law Association of the United States. ***LANGUAGES:*** French and Italian. ***PRACTICE AREAS:*** Civil Litigation; Trial Practice; Appellate Practice; Business Organization; International Law; Admiralty and Maritime Law.

OF COUNSEL

LORI E. SHAW, born May 14, 1961; admitted to bar, 1987, Ohio and U.S. District Court, Southern District of Ohio. *Education:* University of Dayton (B.S., Finance, summa cum laude); University of Dayton School of Law (J.D., summa cum laude). Casenote Editor, University of Dayton Law Review. ***PRACTICE AREAS:*** Litigation.

L. LEAH REIBEL, born Philadelphia, Pennsylvania, October 10, 1959; admitted to bar, 1991, Pennsylvania; 1992, District of Columbia; 1996, Ohio and U.S. District Court, Southern District of Ohio. *Education:* The Ohio State University (B.A., 1989); District of Columbia School of Law (J.D., cum laude, 1991). *Member:* District of Columbia Bar Association; American Bar Association. ***PRACTICE AREAS:*** Employment Law; Litigation; Legislative Practice.

ASSOCIATE

KIMBERLY EDELSTEIN, admitted to bar, 2002, Ohio. *Education:* University of Findlay (B.A., magna cum laude); University of Akron (M.A.); Albany Law School of University of Findlay (J.D.). ***PRACTICE AREAS:*** Business Organization; Corporate Law; Litigation.

Languages: Italian and French.

ROETZEL & ANDRESS

A LEGAL PROFESSIONAL ASSOCIATION

Established in 1876

NATIONAL CITY CENTER
155 EAST BROAD STREET, 12TH FLOOR
COLUMBUS, OHIO 43215
Telephone: 614-463-9770
Telecopier: 614-463-9792
Email: inquiries@ralaw.com
URL: http://www.ralaw.com

Akron, Ohio Office: 222 South Main Street. Telephone: 330-376-2700. Telecopier: 330-376-4577.
Naples, Florida Office: 850 Park Shore Drive, Trianon Centre, 3rd Floor. Telephones: 239-649-6200; 800-535-7239. Telecopier: 239-261-3659.

(This Listing Continued)

Cleveland, Ohio Office: One Cleveland Center, 1375 East Ninth Street, 9th Floor. Telephone: 216-623-0150. Telecopier: 216-623-0134.

Cincinnati, Ohio Office: 250 East Fifth Street, 310 Chiquita Center. Telephone: 513-361-0200. Telecopier: 513-361-0335.

Fort Myers, Florida Office: 2320 First Street, Suite 1000. Telephone: 239-337-3850. Telecopier: 239-337-0970.

Toledo, Ohio Office: One SeaGate, 9th Floor. Telephone: 419-242-7985. Facsimile: 419-242-0316.

Tallahassee, Florida Office: 225 South Adams Street, Suite 250, P.O. Box 10369. Telephone: 850-222-7718. Telecopier: 850-222-8222.

Washington, D.C. Office: 1025 Connecticut Avenue, NW, Suite 220. Telephone: 202-625-0600. Telecopier: 202-338-6340.

General Corporate and Business Law, Banking and Finance, Mergers, Acquisitions and Divestitures, Securities Law, Real Estate Law, Real Estate Development/Syndication/Condominium Law, Tax Law, Intellectual Property Law, Computer Law, Hospital and Health Care Law, Public Law and Finance, Governmental Relations, School Law, Commercial/Bankruptcy Law, Employment Law, Pension, Employee Benefits, Workers' Compensation, OSHA, Business and Commercial Litigation, Complex and Multidistrict Litigation, Antitrust Law, RICO, Federal Court Practice, Product Liability, Environmental Law/Toxic Torts, Insurance Law, Information Technology Law, Medical Malpractice Defense, Asbestos Litigation, Construction Law, 1st Amendment/Media Law, White Collar Criminal Defense, Railroad and FELA, Trucking and Transportation Law, Probate and Estate Planning, Utility Law, International Law, Trial and Appellate Practice.

FIRM PROFILE: Founded in 1876, Roetzel & Andress is one of the largest and fastest growing full-service, corporate law firms with nine offices throughout Ohio, Florida, and Washington, D.C. Roetzel & Andress represents a wide range of clients from individuals and closely-held businesses to multi-national corporations, financial institutions, and government entities. Our lawyers serve as general counsel to many clients, and many of those relationships have existed for much of our history. Our lawyers provide a broad range of legal services to clients on a local, national, and international basis.

PARTNERS

DAVID J. DEMERS, born 1965; admitted to bar, 1991, Ohio; 1992, U.S. Court of Appeals, Sixth Circuit and U.S. District Court, Southern District of Ohio; 1994, Indiana and U.S. District Court, Northern District of Ohio; 2000, U.S. District Court, Northern District of Indiana; 2003, U.S. District Court, Western District of Pennsylvania; 2004, U.S. District Court, Southern District of Indiana. *Education:* Mount Union College (B.S., History and Political Science, cum laude, 1988); University of Toledo College of Law (J.D., 1991). Pi Gamma Mu. Recipient, Herschel Kreger Award. *Member:* Indiana State, Ohio State and American Bar Associations. ***PRACTICE AREAS:*** Bankruptcy; Defense Litigation; Products Liability; Risk Management. ***Email:*** ddemers@ralaw.com

THOMAS A. DILLON, born Champaign, Illinois, November 4, 1945; admitted to bar, 1974, Ohio, U.S. District Court, Southern District of Ohio and U.S. Court of Appeals, Sixth Circuit. *Education:* Western Michigan University; Taylor University (B.S., 1968); The Ohio State University (J.D., 1973). ***PRACTICE AREAS:*** Medical Malpractice Defense; Products Liability Defense; Personal Injury Defense; Insurance Coverage; Business Litigation; Legal Malpractice Defense. ***Email:*** tdillon@ralaw.com

JEFFREY E. FROMSON, born Boise, Idaho, July 24, 1944; admitted to bar, 1969, Ohio; 1984, Massachusetts. *Education:* Miami University (B.A., 1966); The Ohio State University (J.D., cum laude, 1969). Tau Epsilon Rho. Associate Editor, Ohio State Law Journal, 1968-1969. *Member:* Columbus and Ohio State Bar Associations. ***PRACTICE AREAS:*** Corporate; Mergers and Acquisitions; Business; Securities; Franchising; International. ***Email:*** jfromson@ralaw.com

ROBERT B. GRAZIANO, born McKeesport, Pennsylvania, December 6, 1964; admitted to bar, 1991, Ohio. *Education:* Duquesne University (B.A., 1987); Case Western Reserve University (J.D., 1990). Kappa Tau Alpha; Delta Theta Phi. Member: Mock Trial Team; Moot Court Board, 1989-1990. *Member:* Columbus, Ohio State and American Bar Associations; Ohio Association of Civil Trial Attorneys; Defense Research Institute; Columbus Claims Association. ***PRACTICE AREAS:*** Litigation; Medical Malpractice; Personal Injury; Products Liability. ***Email:*** rgraziano@ralaw.com

ERIKA L. HAUPT, born Canton, Ohio, December 13, 1968; admitted to bar, 1994, Ohio; 1996, U.S. District Court, Northern District of Ohio; 1999, U.S. Tax Court. *Education:* Miami University, Oxford, Ohio (B.S.B., 1991); The Ohio State University College of Law (J.D., 1994). Recipient, Joseph J. Harter Memorial Award for Excellence in Trial Practice, 1994. Managing Editor, Ohio State Law Journal, 1993-1994. Author: "For Better, For Worse, For Richer, For Poorer: Premarital Agreement Case Studies," 37 Real Prop., Prob. & Tr. J. 29 (2002); "Brady v. Safety-Kleen Corp.: Tipping Ohio's Workers' Compensation Scale in Favor of the Employee," 54 Ohio St. L.J. 837 (1993). Greater Columbus Salvation Army Advisory Board: Member; Resource Development Chair, 2005—; Secretary, 2003-2005. Member: Leadership Columbus Class of 2000; Miami University Alumni Association Recruitment Network; Ohio Pet Fund Board of Directors. *Member:* Columbus (Member, Business Tax and Estate and Gift Tax Committees) and Ohio State (Member, Estate Planning, Trust and Probate Law Section) Bar Associations. ***PRACTICE AREAS:*** Estate Planning; Tax; Business Law; Charitable Organizations; Probate. ***Email:*** ehaupt@ralaw.com

EDWARD C. HERTENSTEIN, born Columbus, Ohio, August 25, 1951; admitted to bar, 1976, Ohio; 1978, U.S. District Court, Southern District of Ohio; 1979, U.S. Tax Court; 1980, U.S. Supreme Court. *Education:* Southern Methodist University (B.B.A., 1973; J.D., 1976). Phi Delta Phi. Editor, Journal of Air Law and Commerce, 1975-1976. Law Clerk to Associate Justice, Supreme Court of Ohio, 1976-1977. Commissioner, Supreme Court of Ohio, 1977-1978. Author: "Interest-Free Loans," 1983 Columbus Tax Conference Manual; "Estate Freezes: Maintaining After Tax Values," 1985 Columbus Tax Conference Manual; "Estate Planning Implications of The Tax Reform Act of 1986," 1986, Columbus Tax Conference Manual; "Life Insurance for the Business Owner: Income and Estate Tax Planning to Reduce Cost," 1987 Columbus Tax Conference Manual; "GRITs, GRATs and GRUTs, and How to Use Them," 1993 Columbus Tax Conference Manual and Passing the Buck! A Guide to Flow-Through Entities in the Context of Wealth Transfer for Families," 1995 Wealth Transfer Conference Reference Manual, Volume 95-07; "GRAT-itude: Effective Use of GRATs and Other Techniques -- The Alchemy of Leveraged Giving," 1996 Wealth Transfer Conference Manual, Volume 1996—; "Some Thoughts on Installment Sales to Grantor Trusts: A GRAT Alternative," 2000 Wealth Transfer Conference Manual, Volume 2000—. *Member:* Columbus (Member, Committee on: Taxation, 1978—; Chairman, 1985-1986), Ohio State and American (Member, Section of Taxation) Bar Associations. Fellow, The American College of Trust and Estate Counsel. (Certified Specialist in Federal Tax Law, Ohio State Bar Association). ***PRACTICE AREAS:*** Taxation Law (40%); Trusts and Estates (40%); Corporate Law (20%). ***Email:*** ehertenstein@ralaw.com

DANIEL G. HILSON, born 1959; admitted to bar, 1986, Ohio; U.S. District Court, Northern District of Ohio. *Education:* Loyola University, Rome, Italy, 1981; John Carroll University (B.A., Political Science, 1982); Capital University Law School (J.D., with honors, 1986). Order of the Barrister. Order of the Curia. Recipient, Alumni Service Medal, John Carroll University, 2000. Recognized as a Ohio Super Lawyer by Law and Politics Magazine. Author: "Lobbying, PACS and Campaigning Finance," 50 State Handbook, Ohio Chapter, West Publishing Company, 1994-2004. Majority Legal Counsel to Ohio Senate, 1990-1993. *Member:* Columbus and American Bar Associations. Fellow, Columbus Bar Foundation. ***PRACTICE AREAS:*** Government Relations; Public Law and Finance; Health Care Facility Licensing; Health Care Legislation; Home Health Care; Pharmacy Law. ***Email:*** dhilson@ralaw.com

STEPHEN D. JONES, born Cincinnati, Ohio, June 5, 1953; admitted to bar, 1981, Ohio; U.S. Court of Appeals, Federal Circuit; U.S. Supreme Court. *Education:* Otterbein College (B.A., 1975); University of Michigan (M.S.W., 1977); Capital University (J.D., 1980). Frequent Lecturer throughout Ohio and the U.S. on Discovery of Electronic Evidence, Internet and e-Commerce issues. President, Franklin County Chapter, Mothers Against Drunk Driving. Public Policy Director, MADD Ohio. *Member:* Columbus and Ohio State (Chair, Computer Law Committee, 2001-2003) Bar Associations; Association of Defense Trial Attorneys. ***REPORTED CASES:*** CompuServe v. Patterson, 89 F.3d 1257 (1996); Ohio Edison v. Parrott, 73 O. St. 3d 70J (1995); Wheeling Corporation v. Columbus and Ohio River Railroad, et al., 147 Ohio App.3d 460 (2001). ***PRACTICE AREAS:*** Business Litigation; Medical Malpractice Defense; UCC Warranty Litigation; Government Contracts; Government Litigation; Real Estate Litigation; Technology Litigation; Employment Law Litigation. ***Email:*** sjones@ralaw.com

DOUGLAS M. KENNEDY, born Columbus, Ohio, October 11, 1954; admitted to bar, 1980, Ohio; 1981, U.S. District Court, Southern District of Ohio; 1993, U.S. Court of Appeals, Sixth Circuit. *Education:* Ohio Wesleyan University (B.A., 1977); University of Toledo (J.D., 1980). Member and Associate Editor, University of Toledo Law Review, 1979-1980. Speaker: Professional Educations Systems, Inc: "Ohio Uninsured and Underinsured Motorist Coverage Issues," 1990; "Orthopedics For Lawyers," 1991. Assistant Attorney General, State of Ohio, 1980-1985. *Member:* Columbus and Ohio State Bar Associations; Ohio Association of Civil Trial Attorneys; Defense Research Institute; Columbus Defense Association. ***PRACTICE AREAS:*** Employment Law; Workers' Compensation; Litigation. ***Email:*** dkennedy@ralaw.com

JUDITH D. LEVINE, born New York, N.Y., September 2, 1950; admitted to bar, 1975, Colorado; 1979, Ohio; 1982, New York. *Education:* Kirkland College (B.A., 1972); University of Denver (J.D., 1975). Order of St. Ives. Editor, Denver Law Journal, 1974-1975. Member, Board of Directors, CREW Network, 2001-2002. Member. Board of Trustees, CREW Foundation, 2005. Chair, Subcommittee on Mortgage Loan Commitments for Lenders and Borrowers, American Bar Association, 1987-1991. ***PRACTICE AREAS:*** Real Estate; Financial Services; Restructuring; Commercial Law; Corporate. ***Email:*** jlevine@ralaw.com

RICHARD S. MULLIGAN, born Yonkers, New York, April 18, 1951; admitted to bar, 1979, Ohio and U.S. District Court, Southern District of Ohio; 1983, U.S. Tax Court. *Education:* Kenyon College (A.B., cum laude, 1973); Capital University (J.D., cum laude, 1979). Order of the Curia. Law Clerk to Justice William B. Brown, Ohio Supreme Court, 1979-1981. *Member:* Columbus, Ohio State and American Bar Associations. ***PRACTICE AREAS:*** Corporate; Business; Mergers and Acquisitions; Real Estate; Franchising; Estate Planning; Probate. ***Email:*** rmulligan@ralaw.com

KEVIN J. OSTERKAMP, born Anamosa, Iowa, January 29, 1949; admitted to bar, 1974, Ohio and U.S. District Court, Southern District of Ohio; 1985, U.S. Court of Appeals, Sixth Circuit; 2005, U.S. District Court, Northern District of Ohio. *Education:* University of Iowa (B.B.A., cum laude, 1971); The Ohio State University (J.D., cum laude, 1974). Beta Gamma Sigma; Phi Delta Phi. Administrative Law Judge, Rate Section, Public Utilities Commission of Ohio, 1974-1978. *Member:* Columbus (Member, Business and Administrative Law Section), Ohio State and American (Member, Business Law Section) Bar Associations. ***REPORTED CASES:*** Penn. Traffic v.AIU Ins. Co. et al 99 Ohio St.3rd 227, 203-3373. ***PRACTICE AREAS:*** Business Litigation (60%); Construction Litigation (20%); Administrative Law (20%). ***Email:*** kosterkamp@ralaw.com

MICHAEL A. POE, born Greenville, Mississippi, October 26, 1953; admitted to bar, 1978, Mississippi and Ohio. *Education:* University of Mississippi (B.A., 1975; J.D., 1978). *Member:* Columbus and Ohio State Bar Associations. ***PRACTICE AREAS:*** Corporate Law; Personal Planning; Successions; Estate Planning Law; Probate Law. ***Email:*** mpoe@ralaw.com

THOMAS L. ROSENBERG, born 1955; admitted to bar, 1983, Ohio; U.S. Court of Appeals, Sixth Circuit; U.S. District Court, Northern District of Ohio; U.S. District Court, Southern District of Ohio. *Education:* Ohio Wesleyan University (B.A., 1977); Capital University (J.D., 1983). *Member:* Columbus, Ohio State and American Bar Associations. ***PRACTICE AREAS:*** Business Litigation; Construction Law; Government Relations; Regulatory Compliance. ***Email:*** trosenberg@ralaw.com

CHARLES D. SMITH, born New York, N.Y., July 24, 1958; admitted to bar, 1983, Ohio and U.S. District Court, Southern District of Ohio. *Education:* Ohio Wesleyan University (B.A., 1980); Capital University (J.D., 1983). Order of the Curia. Judicial Clerk to Judge Dean Strausbaugh, Tenth District Court of Appeals, Ohio, 1983-1984. *Member:* Columbus and Ohio State and American Bar Associations. ***PRACTICE AREAS:*** Civil Litigation; Workers' Compensation. ***Email:*** csmith@ralaw.com

(This Listing Continued)

ROETZEL & ANDRESS, A LEGAL PROFESSIONAL ASSOCIATION, Columbus—Continued

BRADLEY L. SNYDER, born Shelby, Ohio, September 28, 1956; admitted to bar, 1981, Ohio; 1982, U.S. District Court, Southern District of Ohio and U.S. Court of Appeals, Sixth Circuit; 1983, Florida and U.S. District Court, Northern District of Ohio. *Education:* The Ohio State University (B.S., cum laude, 1978); Capital University (J.D., with honors, 1981). Order of the Curia. *Member:* Columbus and Ohio State Bar Associations; Defense Research Institute; Ohio Association of Civil Trial Attorneys; Transportation Lawyers Association; Central Ohio Civil War Roundtable. (Board Certified in Civil Trial Advocacy by the National Board of Trial Advocacy). ***PRACTICE AREAS:*** Trucking Litigation; Insurance Coverage Litigation; Product Liability and Personal Injury Defense; Employment Litigation; Civil Rights Litigation. ***Email:*** bsnyder@ralaw.com

MICHAEL S. YASHKO, born Wintersville, Ohio, December 2, 1961; admitted to bar, 1987, Ohio; 2003, Florida; U.S. Court of Appeals, Sixth Circuit; U.S. District Court, Southern and Northern Districts of Ohio; U.S. Tax Court. *Education:* The Ohio State University (B.S.B.A., cum laude, 1984); Northwestern University (J.D., cum laude, 1987). Co-Author: "A Positive Theory of the Attorney-Client Privilege," The Journal of Legal Studies, June 1990. Member, Board of Directors, Accelerated Cure Project for Multiple Sclerosis. *Member:* Columbus, Lee County and Ohio State Bar Associations; The Florida Bar; Urban Land Institute; International Council of Shopping Centers; Associated General Contractors. (Chair of Real Estate, Construction and Environmental Law Group) (Also at Fort Myers, Florida Office). ***PRACTICE AREAS:*** Real Estate; Construction; Business Law. ***Email:*** myashko@ralaw.com

---

RYAN E. BONINA, (admission pending). *Education:* Oberlin College (B.A., 2000); University of Pittsburgh School of Law (J.D., 2005). ***PRACTICE AREAS:*** Labor and Employment. ***Email:*** rbonina@ralaw.com

JEFFREY S. BRAUN, born June 14, 1975; admitted to bar, 2002, Ohio. *Education:* Albion College (B.A., cum laude, 1997); The Ohio State University (J.D., 2002). *Member:* Columbus and Ohio State Bar Associations. ***PRACTICE AREAS:*** Corporate Law. ***Email:*** jbraun@ralaw.com

ERIC S. BRAVO, born Columbus, Ohio, April 12, 1965; admitted to bar, 1990, Ohio; 1991, U.S. District Court, Northern District of Ohio. *Education:* Northwestern University (B.A., 1987); Ohio State University (J.D., 1990). *Member:* Columbus and Ohio State Bar Associations. ***PRACTICE AREAS:*** Workers Compensation (100%). ***Email:*** ebravo@ralaw.com

SHARON CASON-ADAMS, admitted to bar, 1997, Ohio; 1999, U.S. District Court, Southern District of Ohio; 2001, U.S. District Court, Northern District of Ohio; 2002, U.S. Supreme Court. *Education:* Franklin University (B.S., 1991); Capital University (J.D., 1997). *Member:* Columbus, Ohio State (Member, Labor and Employment Law Section) and American Bar Associations; Society of Human Resources Management. [With, Ohio Air National Guard, 1983-1991]. ***PRACTICE AREAS:*** Employment Litigation; Insurance Coverage; Labor and Employment; Risk Management; Workers Compensation. ***Email:*** sadams@ralaw.com

SCOT C. CROW, born Bergholz, Ohio, April 30, 1972; admitted to bar, 1997, Ohio; 1998, U.S. District Court, Southern District of Ohio; 1999, U.S. Tax Court. *Education:* Franciscan University of Steubenville (B.S., Business Administration, 1994); Capital University (J.D., 1997; LL.M., in Taxation, 1997). Order of the Curia. *Member:* Columbus (Member, Business Taxation and Estate and Gift Taxation Committees), Ohio State and American Bar Associations. ***PRACTICE AREAS:*** Taxation; Business Law; Estate and Gift Taxation; Trusts and Estates Taxation; Estate Planning. ***Email:*** scrow@ralaw.com

MELISSA R. HOEFFEL, admitted to bar, 2003, Ohio. *Education:* The College of Wooster (B.A., 1995); Capital University Law School (J.D., 2003). Associate Editor, Capital University Law Review. *Member:* Columbus and Ohio State Bar Associations. ***PRACTICE AREAS:*** Government Relations; Public Law and Finance. ***Email:*** mhoeffel@ralaw.com

JAMISON S. SPEIDEL, born 1970; admitted to bar, 2001, Ohio; 2002, District of Columbia; 2003, West Virginia and U.S. District Court, Northern and Southern Districts of West Virginia; 2005, U.S. Court of Appeals, Sixth and Fourth Circuits and U.S. District Court, Northern and Southern Districts of Ohio. *Education:* The Ohio State University (B.S.B.A., 1993); Wheeling Jesuit University (M.B.A., 1998); University of Dayton School of Law (J.D., 2001). Phi Delta Phi (Treasurer, 2000-2001). Member, MENSA 1997—. *Member:* Columbus, Ohio State, West Virginia and American Bar Associations; District of Columbia Bar. ***PRACTICE AREAS:*** Banking and Finance; Creditor Bankruptcy; Business Tort and Contract Litigation; Condominium, Associations, and Homeowners Law; Estate Planning; Probate and Estate Administration. ***Email:*** jspeidel@ralaw.com

VINCENT J. SQUILLACE, III, born Columbus, Ohio, July 10, 1975; admitted to bar, 2002, Ohio; 2002, District of Columbia. *Education:* University of Notre Dame (B.A., 1998); Capital University (J.D., 2002). *Member:* Columbus and Ohio State Bar Associations; Ohio Lobbying Association. ***PRACTICE AREAS:*** Government; Government Contracts; Federal Government Law; Federal Legislative Practice; Government Affairs; Government Agency Practice; Government Ethics; Government Relations; Governmental Law; Legislative Practice; Local Government Law; Local Government Relations; Public Policy; State Government Law; State Legislative Practice. ***Email:*** vsquillace@ralaw.com

BRIAN A. TARIAN, born Columbus, Ohio, July 31, 1955; admitted to bar, 1982, Ohio. *Education:* Georgetown University (B.A., 1977); University of Akron (J.D., 1982). *Member:* Columbus and Ohio State Bar Associations. ***PRACTICE AREAS:*** Workers Compensation. ***Email:*** btarian@ralaw.com

TARA L. VAN HO, (admission pending). *Education:* Marietta College (B.A., English); University of Cincinnati College of Law (J.D., 2005). Corporate Law Fellow, University of Cincinnati College of Law. ***PRACTICE AREAS:*** Corporate and Business Services. ***Email:*** tvanho@ralaw.com

(This Listing Continued)

REPRESENTATIVE CLIENTS: Advanced Elastomer Systems, Inc.; Akron General Medical Center; Atlantic Tool & Die; Automobilia Lamborghini; Babcock & Wilcox, a McDermott Company; Bank One; Barberton Citizens Hospital; Beacon Journal Publishing Company; BP America; Burger Iron Company; Catholic Healthcare Partners; City of Akron; The Cleveland Clinic Foundation; CSX Transportation; Dart Industries, Inc.; Doctors Hospital; Edward J. Debartolo Corp.; F.E. Myers; FirstEnergy; Ford Motor Company; General Motors Corporation; Grant/Riverside Methodist Hospitals; Honeywell, Inc.; Lloyd's of London; Louisiana Pacific Corporation; Marathon Oil Company; Marriott Corporation; Medtronic, Inc.; MRK Technologies; National City Bank; National Railroad Passenger Corporation (AMTRAK); Norfolk Southern Corporation; Ohio Health Corporation; Ohio Rail Commission; OHM Remediation Services; Pentair, Inc.; PPG Industries, Inc.; Pulte Homes Corporation; Rite-Aid; Seaman Corporation; State of Ohio; Summa Health System; Summit County; The University of Akron; Waste Management, Inc.; Western Parcel Express.

(For complete biographical data on all personnel, see Professional Biographies at Akron, Ohio)

ROURKE & BLUMENTHAL, LLP

495 SOUTH HIGH STREET, SUITE 450
COLUMBUS, OHIO 43215
Telephone: 614-220-9200
Toll Free: 866-257-9200
Fax: 614-220-7900
URL: http://www.randbllp.com
URL: http://www.rourkeblumenthal.com

Personal Injury, Negligence, Products Liability, Medical Malpractice, Nursing Home Litigation, Wrongful Death, Intentional Tort, Insurance Disputes, Automobile Accidents, Civil Trial Practice, Aviation, Professional Liability.

MICHAEL J. ROURKE, born Huntington, West Virginia, October 8, 1955; admitted to bar, 1981, Ohio and U.S. District Court, Northern and Southern Districts of Ohio; 1988, U.S. Court of Appeals, Sixth Circuit. *Education:* The Ohio State University (B.A., summa cum laude, with distinction in History, 1978); Harvard Law School (J.D., cum laude, 1981). Phi Kappa Phi. Author: Personal Injury Litigation in Ohio, Chapter on "Investigation of Physical Evidence," Ohio Legal Center Institute, 1984. Adjunct Assistant Professor, Ohio State Law School, 1984-1987. *Member:* Columbus, Ohio State and American Bar Associations; Franklin County Trial Lawyers Association; Ohio Academy of Trial Lawyers; The Association of Trial Lawyers of America. ***PRACTICE AREAS:*** Personal Injury; Negligence; Products Liability; Aviation Law; Professional Liability; Motor Vehicle Accidents and Injuries; Wrongful Death; Medical Malpractice; Civil Trial Practice; Intentional Torts. ***Email:*** mrourke@randbllp.com

KENNETH S. BLUMENTHAL, born New York, N.Y., March 5, 1951; admitted to bar, 1983, Ohio; 1984, U.S. District Court, Southern District of Ohio; 1989, U.S. Supreme Court. *Education:* Marietta College (B.A., 1973); Capital University (J.D., cum laude, 1983). Order of the Curia. Selected, "The Best Lawyers in America." *Member:* Ohio State Bar Association; Franklin County Trial Lawyers Association; Ohio Academy of Trial Lawyers; The Association of Trial Lawyers of America. ***PRACTICE AREAS:*** Medical Malpractice; Products Liability; Personal Injury; Civil Trial; Intentional Torts; Nursing Home Litigation. ***Email:*** kblumenthal@randbllp.com

---

ROBERT P. MILLER, born Columbus, Ohio, November 27, 1974; admitted to bar, 2000, Ohio. *Education:* Wittenberg University (B.A., 1997); Pennsylvania State University (J.D., 2000). Delta Theta Phi; Corpus Juris Society. Member, Moot Court Trial Advocacy Team. *Member:* Columbus, Ohio State and American Bar Associations; Defense Research Institute; Ohio Association of Civil Trial Attorneys; Franklin American Inns of Court. ***PRACTICE AREAS:*** Litigation; Medical Malpractice; Personal Injury; Products Liability; Trademarks; Intentional Torts. ***Email:*** rmiller@randbllp.com

---

DANIEL R. RUBIN

4930 REED ROAD
COLUMBUS, OHIO 43220
Telephone: 614-457-7700
Fax: 614-457-7878
Email: sandz10@yahoo.com
URL: http://www.danielrubinlaw.com

Breach of Contract, Enforcement of Judgments, Business Formation and Termination, Business Start-Ups, Small Business Law, Creditors Rights, Commercial Law, Civil Litigation, Contracts.

DANIEL R. RUBIN, born South Bend, Indiana, December 16, 1957; admitted to bar, 1984, Ohio; 1985, U.S. District Court, Southern District of Ohio; 1989, U.S. Supreme Court. *Education:* Indiana University (B.A., 1980); The Capital University (J.D., 1984). *Member:* Columbus and Ohio State Bar Associations; Commercial Law League of America.

SUZANNE KAY SABOL

820 SOUTH HIGH STREET
COLUMBUS, OHIO 43206
Telephone: 614-445-0793
Fax: 614-445-7948
Email: s.sabol@gte.net
URL: http://www.suzannekaysabol.com

Family Law and Domestic Relations.

SUZANNE KAY SABOL, born Union City, Pennsylvania, October 7, 1953; admitted to bar, 1983, Ohio; 1985, U.S. District Court, Southern District of Ohio. *Education:* Edinboro University (B.S., 1975); Gannon University (M.Ed., 1978); Capital University (J.D., 1982). *Member:* Columbus (Member, Family Law Section), Ohio State and American Bar

(This Listing Continued)

Associations; Franklin County Trial Lawyers Association. ***PRACTICE AREAS:*** Family Law; Divorce; Child Custody; Child Support; Visitation Rights; Parental Rights.

ROBERT B. ST. CLAIR

580 SOUTH HIGH STREET, SUITE 200
COLUMBUS, OHIO 43215-5644
Telephone: 614-224-4114
Fax: 614-224-3804
Email: rstclair@macb-law.com
URL: http://www.stclairlaw.com

Trusts and Estates, Wills, Probate, Elder Law, Estate Planning, Estate Administration.

ROBERT B. ST. CLAIR, born Columbus, Ohio, October 16, 1948; admitted to bar, 1977, Ohio and U.S. District Court, Southern District of Ohio. *Education:* Ohio Northern University (B.A., 1970; J.D., 1976). *Member:* National Academy of Elder Law Attorneys; American Bar Association; Ohio State Bar Association (Estate Planning, Trust and Probate Law Section); Columbus Bar Association (Probate Court and Trust and Estate Planning Committees); Columbus Bar Foundation (Fellow). [Colonel, U.S. Marine Corps Reserves, 1968-1996]. ***PRACTICE AREAS:*** Trusts and Estates; Wills; Probate; Elder Law; Estate Planning; Estate Administration.

HARVEY M. SAMUELS

500 SOUTH FRONT STREET, SUITE 1150
COLUMBUS, OHIO 43215
Telephone: 614-221-2580
Fax: 614-221-2575

Family Law, Divorce, Domestic Relations, Subrogation.

HARVEY M. SAMUELS, born Paducah, Kentucky, April 13, 1949; admitted to bar, 1974, Ohio. *Education:* Syracuse University (B.A., magna cum laude, 1971); University of Kentucky (J.D., 1974). Phi Beta Kappa. Member, Moot Court. *Member:* Columbus and Ohio State Bar Associations; Franklin County Trial Lawyers Association; Ohio Academy of Trial Lawyers. ***PRACTICE AREAS:*** Family Law; Collections.

REPRESENTATIVE CLIENTS: Phillips Oil Company, Inc. of Ohio; Safeco Insurance Co.; Trinity Insurance Co.; CNA Insurance.
REFERENCE: Key Bank.

SCHERNER, HANSON & CORNWELL, LLC

130 NORTHWOODS BOULEVARD
COLUMBUS, OHIO 43235-4725
Telephone: 614-431-7200
Fax: 614-431-7262

Delaware, Ohio Office: 5300 David Road. Telephone: 740-595-3366.
Lima, Ohio Office: 714 West North Street. Telephone: 419-222-1155. Fax: 419-227-3131.

Civil Trial and Appellate Litigation in State and Federal Courts. Medical Malpractice and other Professional Liability, Personal Injury, Product Liability, Commercial, Corporate, Fraud and other Civil Litigation.

HANS SCHERNER, born Mülheim/Ruhr, Germany, April 15, 1942; admitted to bar, 1979, Ohio; 1980, U.S. District Court, Southern District of Ohio; 1981, U.S. District Court, Northern District of Ohio, U.S. Court of Claims and U.S. Court of Appeals, Sixth Circuit; 1983, U.S. Supreme Court; 1993, Wisconsin and U.S. District Court, Eastern District of Wisconsin. *Education:* Harvard University (A.B., 1964); Oberlin Graduate School of Theology and Wittenberg University (M.Div., 1978); Ohio Northern University (J.D., with distinction, 1979). *Member:* Columbus, Ohio State and American Bar Associations; State Bar of Wisconsin; Franklin County Trial Lawyers Association; Ohio Academy of Trial Lawyers; The Association of Trial Lawyers of America; Christian Legal Society. Fellow, American College of Trial Lawyers. ***LANGUAGES:*** German. ***PRACTICE AREAS:*** Civil Trial and Appellate Litigation in State and Federal Courts; Medical Malpractice and other Professional Liability; Personal Injury; Product Liability; Commercial; Corporate; Fraud and other Civil Litigation. ***Email:*** hans@hansscherner.com

SCHOTTENSTEIN LAW OFFICES

BANK ONE BUILDING
SUITE 1400
100 EAST BROAD STREET
COLUMBUS, OHIO 43215
Telephone: 614-462-2266; 1-800-437-3757
Telecopier: 614-462-2406
Email: schott100@sbcglobal.net

Personal Injury Law, Automobile Accidents, Workers Compensation, Wrongful Death, Medical Malpractice.

FIRM PROFILE: Mr. Schottenstein has been practicing for over 25 years. He is a member of the Bar Register of Preeminent Lawyers and emphasizes Personal Injury, Medical Malpractice and Workers Compensation and is a member of the Million Dollar Advocates Forum.

EDWIN E. SCHOTTENSTEIN, born Columbus, Ohio, May 19, 1940; admitted to bar, 1965, Kentucky; 1982, Ohio. *Education:* The Ohio State University (B.A., 1961); University of Louisville (J.D., 1965). Phi Alpha Delta. Co-Editor and Chief, Louisville Lawyer, 1964-1965. Author, Article, "Criminal Lawyers Disagree," Louisville Lawyer, 1964. Adjunct Professor, University of Kentucky, Department of Communications, 1977-1982. Member of County Bench and Jefferson County Juvenile Court Judge, 1969-1970. Member, Commission on Higher Education, Commonwealth of Kentucky, 1970-1973. President, Secretary and Vice President, Law Alumni Foundation, University of Louisville School of Law, 1970-1973. *Member:* Louisville Bar Association (Secretary, 1972-1973; Vice President, 1973-1974); Columbus Bar Association (Chairman, Lawyer Legal Assistant Committee, 1986-1988); Kentucky Bar Association (Chairman, General Law Day, 1975-1976); Ohio State Bar Association; American Bar Association (Member, Juvenile Delinquency Committee, 1970-1982); Million Dollar Advocates Forum (Member, 2001—). ***LANGUAGES:*** English. ***PRACTICE AREAS:*** Personal Injury Law; Automobile Accidents; Workers Compensation; Wrongful Death; Medical Malpractice. ***Email:*** schott100@sbcglobal.net

SCHOTTENSTEIN LEGAL SERVICES

Established in 1974
341 SOUTH THIRD STREET, SUITE 300
COLUMBUS, OHIO 43215-5444
Telephone: 614-464-1880
Fax: 614-464-3004
URL: http://www.schottensteinlaw.com
Email: jim@schottensteinlaw.com
URL: http://www.lawyers.com/schottensteinlaw

Business Litigation, Business Law, Limited Liability Companies, Buying and Selling of Businesses, Business Formation, Corporate Law, Partnership Law, Commercial Real Estate, Commercial Leasing, Taxation, Trusts and Estates, Wills, Estate Planning, Employment Discrimination, Sexual Harassment.

FIRM PROFILE: Schottenstein Legal Services concentrates in the areas of small business formation, planning and development, business litigation and commercial real estate. It helps clients solve problems from general business disputes to tax, estate planning, property and business acquisitions. The Firm also represents individuals who have been victims of sexual harassment and employment discrimination.

JAMES M. SCHOTTENSTEIN, born Columbus, Ohio, February 8, 1947; admitted to bar, 1972, Ohio; 1973, Florida; 1975, U.S. District Court, Southern District of Ohio and U.S. Tax Court. *Education:* University of Wisconsin (B.B.A., 1969); The Ohio State University (J.D., 1972); New York University (LL.M. in Taxation, 1974). Assistant Attorney General, Ohio, 1973. Special Counsel to Attorney General, Ohio, 1976-1982. *Member:* Columbus, Ohio State and American Bar Associations; The Florida Bar. ***PRACTICE AREAS:*** Commercial Real Estate; Business Litigation; Business Formation; Small Business Law; Taxation; Estate Planning; Employment; Discrimination; Sexual Harassment. ***Email:*** jim@schottensteinlaw.com

RADHA SUBRAMANIAM, born Bangalore, India, August 12, 1966; admitted to bar, 2001, Ohio. *Education:* The Ohio State University (B.A., 1996; J.D., 2001). *Member:* Columbus and Ohio State Bar Associations. ***LANGUAGES:*** Tamil. ***PRACTICE AREAS:*** Labor and Employment; Sexual Harassment; Estate Planning; Corporate Law; Business Law; Buying and Selling of Real Estate; Consumer Fraud. ***Email:*** radha@schottensteinlaw.com

SCHOTTENSTEIN ZOX & DUNN CO., LPA

Established in 1966
250 WEST STREET
COLUMBUS, OHIO 43215-2538
Telephone: 614-462-2700
Telecopier: 614-462-5135
Telex: 650 24 444 365
Email: info@szd.com
URL: http://www.szd.com
Mailing Address: P.O. Box 165020, Columbus, OH 43216

Cincinnati, Ohio Office: Bank One Towers, 8044 Montgomery Road, Suite 630, 45236-2926. Telephone: 513-792-0792. Fax: 513-792-0803.
Cleveland, Ohio Office: USBank Centre, 1350 Euclid Avenue, Suite 1400, 44115. Telephone: 216-621-6501. Fax: 216-621-6502.

Business (Corporate, Banking and Lending, Real Estate/Land Use, General Tax, State and Local Tax, Employee Benefits, Estate Planning, White Collar Crime, E-Commerce, Intellectual Property/Technology Protection, International); Labor and Employment Law, Litigation, Health Law, Construction Law, Bankruptcy Law, Environmental Law, Debtor/Creditor Rights, Workers' Compensation, Municipal Law, Government Affairs.

FIRM PROFILE: Since its founding in 1966, Schottenstein Zox & Dunn has grown from four lawyers to over 100. The firm is dedicated to viewing the law from varied perspectives for the variety of local, regional and national clients it represents as either general counsel or in one or more of the above practice areas. Schottenstein Zox & Dunn is a complete law firm offering comprehensive services to businesses, governmental entities and individuals. Our position in the marketplace combined with the experience of our lawyers enables us to provide our clients with the responsive answers they need to succeed.

DANIEL M. ANDERSON, born Tulsa, Oklahoma, 1968; admitted to bar, 1993, California; 1996, Ohio. *Education:* University of Michigan (A.B., 1990); University of California at Berkeley (J.D., 1993). ***PRACTICE AREAS:*** Debtor and Creditor Rights; Commercial Litigation; Business Litigation; Bankruptcy. ***Email:*** danderson@szd.com

RANDALL S. ARNDT, born Columbus, Ohio, 1956; admitted to bar, 1981, Ohio. *Education:* Northwestern University (B.A., with honors, 1978); George Washington University (J.D., 1981). ***PRACTICE AREAS:*** Real Estate Development; Retail Leasing; Commercial Leasing; Shopping Center Acquisition; Shopping Center Leasing; Shopping Center Development. ***Email:*** rarndt@szd.com

(This Listing Continued)

SCHOTTENSTEIN ZOX & DUNN CO., LPA, Columbus—Continued

MITCHELL H. BANCHEFSKY, born New York, N.Y., 1953; admitted to bar, 1983, Ohio and U.S. District Court, Southern District of Ohio. *Education:* Ohio State University (B.A., 1976); Capital University (J.D., 1983). Assistant Law Director and Prosecutor, City of Dublin, 1984—. ***PRACTICE AREAS:*** Municipal Law; Environmental Law. ***Email:*** mbanchefsky@szd.com

WILLIAM J. BARATH, born Gary, Indiana, 1960; admitted to bar, 1987, Illinois and U.S. District Court, Northern District of Illinois; 1989, Ohio and U.S. District Court, Southern District of Ohio; 1995, U.S. Court of Appeals, Sixth Circuit; 2005, U.S. District Court, Northern District of Ohio. *Education:* Indiana University (B.A., 1983); Valparaiso University (J.D., 1987). ***PRACTICE AREAS:*** Labor Law; Employment Law; Workers Compensation; Employment Litigation; Personnel Policies. ***Email:*** wbarath@szd.com

RICHARD A. BARNHART, born Youngstown, Ohio, 1953; admitted to bar, 1979, Ohio. *Education:* Youngstown State University (B.S.B.A., cum laude, 1976); The Ohio State University (J.D., with honors, 1978). ***PRACTICE AREAS:*** Securities Offerings Law; Federal Income Tax; Estate and Gift Taxation; Business Law; Banking Law. ***Email:*** rbarnhart@szd.com

PAUL L. BITTNER, born Columbus, Ohio, 1968; admitted to bar, 1993, Ohio; 1994, U.S. District Court, Southern District of Ohio; 1995, U.S. District Court, Northern District of Ohio and U.S. Court of Appeals, Sixth circuit; 2000, District of Columbia, West Virginia and U.S. District Court, Southern District of West Virginia. *Education:* Capital University (B.A., 1990); The Ohio State University (J.D., 1993). ***PRACTICE AREAS:*** Management Labor Law; Management Employment Law; Title VII Discrimination; Americans with Disabilities Act; Family and Medical Leave Act; Fair Labor Standards; Employment Law. ***Email:*** pbittner@szd.com

COREY V. CROGNALE, born Warren, Ohio, 1954; admitted to bar, 1980, Ohio; 1981, U.S. District Court, Northern District of Ohio; 1988, U.S. District Court, Southern District of Ohio. *Education:* Marietta College (B.A., 1976); Capital University (J.D., 1980). ***PRACTICE AREAS:*** Labor and Employment; Workers Compensation; Securities. ***Email:*** ccrognale@szd.com

JAMES E. DAVIDSON, born New York, N.Y., 1956; admitted to bar, 1980, Ohio; 1981, U.S. District Court, Southern District of Ohio and U.S. Court of Appeals, Sixth Circuit. *Education:* Northwestern University (B.A., with honors, 1977); Ohio State University (J.D., 1980). Assistant Attorney General, Office of the Attorney General of Ohio in Antitrust Enforcement and Court of Claims Defense, 1980-1984. ***PRACTICE AREAS:*** Commercial Litigation; Employment Litigation; Business Litigation; Complex Business Litigation; Construction Litigation. ***Email:*** jdavidson@szd.com

KRIS M. DAWLEY, born Columbus, Ohio, 1960; admitted to bar, 1985, Ohio; 1988, U.S. District Court, Southern District of Ohio; 1989, U.S. District Court, Northern District of Ohio. *Education:* Wittenberg University (B.A., 1982); Capital University (J.D., cum laude, 1985). Order of the Curia. ***PRACTICE AREAS:*** Commercial Litigation; Administrative Litigation; Health Care; Health Care Litigation. ***Email:*** kdawley@szd.com

PATRICK A. DEVINE, born Marysville, Ohio, 1955; admitted to bar, 1980, Ohio; 1981, U.S. District Court, Northern District of Ohio; 1982, U.S. District Court, Southern District of Ohio and U.S. Court of Appeals, Sixth Circuit; 1985, U.S. Supreme Court. *Education:* Wittenberg University (B.S., 1977); Capital University (J.D., 1980). ***PRACTICE AREAS:*** Employment and Construction Law; Workers Compensation; Administrative Law; Employment Litigation; Construction Labor Law. ***Email:*** pdevine@szd.com

JAY R. DINGLEDY, born Youngstown, Ohio, 1947; admitted to bar, 1972, Ohio; 1980, Florida; U.S. District Court, Northern District of Ohio. *Education:* Ohio University (B.B.A., 1969); The Ohio State University (J.D., summa cum laude, 1971). Order of the Coif. ***PRACTICE AREAS:*** Business Law; Corporate Law; Banking Law; Lender Liability; Financial Institutions Law. ***Email:*** jdingledy@szd.com

CATHERINE T. DUNLAY, born Cincinnati, Ohio, 1958; admitted to bar, 1984, Ohio. *Education:* University of Cincinnati (B.A., summa cum laude, 1981); The Ohio State University (J.D., summa cum laude, 1984). Order of the Coif. ***PRACTICE AREAS:*** Health Law; Business; Securities; Health Care; Hospital Law; Health Maintenance Organizations; Integrated Health Care Delivery Systems. ***Email:*** cdunlay@szd.com

GREGORY J. DUNN, born Youngstown, Ohio, 1953; admitted to bar, 1978, Ohio. *Education:* Davidson College (B.A., 1975); Capital University (J.D., 1978). ***PRACTICE AREAS:*** Cable Television; Telecommunications Law. ***Email:*** gdunn@szd.com

HARVEY DUNN, born Rochester, New York, 1938; admitted to bar, 1966, Ohio. *Education:* University of Cincinnati (B.B.A., 1962); Salmon P. Chase College of Law (J.D., 1966). Member, Order of the Curia. ***PRACTICE AREAS:*** Tax Controversies; Individual Taxation; Business Taxation; Business Law; White Collar Crime; Tax Litigation; Criminal Taxation; Criminal Tax Audits; Income Tax; Local Taxation; Tax Audits; Tax Appeals. ***Email:*** hdunn@szd.com

MATTHEW L. FORNSHELL, born Kettering, Ohio, 1967; admitted to bar, 1993, Ohio; U.S. District Court, Northern and Southern Districts of Ohio and U.S. Court of Appeals, Sixth Circuit. *Education:* Ohio University (B.B.A., cum laude, 1990); Valparaiso University (J.D., 1993). ***PRACTICE AREAS:*** Litigation; Bankruptcy. ***Email:*** mfornshell@szd.com

M. COLETTE GIBBONS, born Cleveland, Ohio, 1951; admitted to bar, 1976, Ohio; 1977, U.S. District Court, Southern District of Ohio. *Education:* John Carroll University (A.B., cum laude, honors program, 1973); Cleveland-Marshall College of Law, Cleveland State University (J.D., 1976). (Resident, Cleveland Office). ***PRACTICE AREAS:*** Bankruptcy; Litigation. ***Email:*** cgibbons@szd.com

ROGER A. GILCREST, born Springfield, Ohio, 1955; admitted to bar, 1985, Ohio; 1986, California; U.S. District Court, Northern and Southern Districts of Ohio; U.S. Court of Appeals, Sixth Circuit; registered to practice before U.S. Patent and Trademark Office. *Education:* College of Wooster (B.A. in Chemistry, 1979); University of San Diego (J.D., 1984); University of Cincinnati (M.S. in Chemistry, 1991). Special Counsel to the Attorney

(This Listing Continued)

General of the State of Ohio. ***LANGUAGES:*** German. ***PRACTICE AREAS:*** E-Commerce; Intellectual Property; Technology Protection; Litigation. ***Email:*** rgilcrest@szd.com

JOHN P. GILLIGAN, born Cincinnati, Ohio, 1949; admitted to bar, 1977, California and U.S. District Court, Northern District of California; 1981, Ohio and U.S. District Court, Southern District of Ohio. *Education:* Dartmouth College (B.A., magna cum laude, 1971); University of California Boalt Hall School of Law (J.D., 1977). ***PRACTICE AREAS:*** Commercial Litigation; Unfair Competition; Trade Secrets; Government Contracts; Construction Litigation; Banking Litigation; Torts. ***Email:*** jgilligan@szd.com

HERBERT R. GODBY, born Cincinnati, Ohio, 1946; admitted to bar, 1973, Ohio. *Education:* Ohio University (B.B.A., 1968); University of Michigan (J.D., 1973). ***PRACTICE AREAS:*** Real Estate; Real Estate Development; Real Estate Syndication; Real Estate Banking Law. ***Email:*** hgodby@szd.com

LISA GE SHANG HAN, born Taiwan, Republic of China, 1962; admitted to bar, 1993, Ohio. *Education:* Ohio State University (J.D., 1992); University of Pennsylvania (LL.M., 1998). ***PRACTICE AREAS:*** Corporate Health Care Law; International Law. ***Email:*** lhan@szd.com

PHILIP K. HARTMANN, born Columbus, Ohio, 1966; admitted to bar, 1992, Ohio. *Education:* Capital University (B.A., 1989); The Ohio State University (J.D., 1992). ***PRACTICE AREAS:*** Municipal Law. ***Email:*** phartmann@szd.com

RAYMOND C. HEADEN, born Cleveland, Ohio, 1960; admitted to bar, 1987, Ohio. *Education:* Williams College (B.A., 1982); University of Pennsylvania Law School (J.D., 1987). ***PRACTICE AREAS:*** Banking; Finance; Corporate; Public Law. ***Email:*** rheaden@szd.com

RICHARD W. HOLZ, born Bridgeport, Connecticut, 1960; admitted to bar, 1985, Ohio. *Education:* Ohio Northern University (B.S., 1982); The Ohio State University (J.D., 1985). Order of the Coif. ***PRACTICE AREAS:*** Trusts and Estates; Estate Planning; Retirement Tax Planning; Tax Law; Corporate Law; Family Wealth Transfer; Business Estate Planning. ***Email:*** rholz@szd.com

E. JAMES HOPPLE, born Cleveland, Ohio, 1936; admitted to bar, 1963, Ohio; 1965, U.S. District Court, Southern District of Ohio; 1972, U.S. Court of Appeals, Sixth Circuit. *Education:* Bowling Green State University (B.A., 1958); The Ohio State University (LL.B., 1963). ***PRACTICE AREAS:*** Bankruptcy Law; Business Law; Creditor Rights; Business Reorganization; Commercial Bankruptcy; Debtor and Creditor Workouts. ***Email:*** jhopple@szd.com

MICHAEL S. JORDAN, born Kettering, Ohio, 1971; admitted to bar, 1997, Ohio. *Education:* Washington University (B.A., 1994); Capital University (J.D., magna cum laude, 1997). Order of Curia; Order of Barristers. ***LANGUAGES:*** Spanish. ***PRACTICE AREAS:*** Corporate Law; Securities. ***Email:*** mjordan@szd.com

JOSEF KEGLEWITSCH, born Chicago, Illinois, 1971; admitted to bar, 1996, Ohio. *Education:* Kalamazoo College (B.A., magna cum laude, 1993); Case Western Reserve University (J.D., cum laude, 1996). ***PRACTICE AREAS:*** Business Law; Corporate Law; Securities. ***Email:*** jkeglewitsch@szd.com

STEPHEN R. KLEINMAN, born Bethesda, Maryland, 1969; admitted to bar, 1995, Ohio; 1996, West Virginia. *Education:* Cornell University (B.S., 1991); Ohio State University (J.D., with honors, 1995). ***PRACTICE AREAS:*** Health Care. ***Email:*** skleinman@szd.com

JOHN J. KRIMM, JR., born Philadelphia, Pennsylvania, 1960; admitted to bar, 1987, Ohio, U.S. District Court, Southern District of Ohio and U.S. Court of Appeals, Sixth Circuit; 1990, U.S. District Court, Northern District of Ohio. *Education:* University of Notre Dame (B.A., magna cum laude, 1982); Tulane Law School (J.D., magna cum laude, 1987). ***PRACTICE AREAS:*** Labor and Employment Law; Litigation. ***Email:*** jkrimm@szd.com

RUSSELL J. KUTELL, born New York, N.Y., 1967; admitted to bar, 1992, New Jersey; 1993, New York; 1997, Ohio. *Education:* University of Pennsylvania (B.A., 1989); Georgetown University (J.D., 1992). ***PRACTICE AREAS:*** Commercial Litigation. ***Email:*** rkutell@szd.com

JOHN M. LATSKO, born Sharon, Pennsylvania, 1946; admitted to bar, 1973, Pennsylvania; 1975, Alabama; 1981, Ohio. *Education:* Michigan State University (B.A., 1968); University of Pittsburgh (J.D., 1973). ***PRACTICE AREAS:*** Health Care; Health Law; Hospital Law; Health Maintenance Organizations; Managed Care; Integrated Health Care Delivery Systems. ***Email:*** jlatsko@szd.com

MARIE A. MALLOY, born New Jersey, 1966; admitted to bar, 1991, Ohio. *Education:* The Ohio State University (B.A., 1988; J.D., 1991). ***PRACTICE AREAS:*** Corporate Law; Banking; Real Estate. ***Email:*** mmalloy@szd.com

KEVIN R. McDERMOTT, born Youngstown, Ohio, 1952; admitted to bar, 1977, Ohio. *Education:* Miami University (A.B., 1974); The Ohio State University (J.D., cum laude, 1977). Order of the Coif. ***PRACTICE AREAS:*** Commercial Litigation; Product Liability; Constitutional Law; Trade Secrets; Business Torts; Construction Litigation; Business Litigation; Complex Business Litigation. ***Email:*** kmcdermott@szd.com

JOHN C. McDONALD, born Columbus, Ohio, 1936; admitted to bar, 1961, Ohio; 1965, U.S. District Court, Southern District of Ohio; 1973, U.S. Tax Court; 1974, U.S. Court of Appeals, Sixth Circuit; 1974, U.S. Supreme Court; 1991, U.S. Court of Appeals, Federal Circuit. *Education:* Denison University (A.B, with honors, 1958); The Ohio State University (J.D., summa cum laude, 1961). Order of the Coif. ***PRACTICE AREAS:*** Appellate Practice; Trial Practice; Commercial Litigation; Construction Litigation; Business Litigation; Complex Business Litigation. ***Email:*** jmcdonald@szd.com

CHRISTOPHER L. MILLER, born Kettering, Ohio, 1967; admitted to bar, 1994, Ohio. *Education:* Miami University (B.A., 1990); Capital University (J.D., 1994). ***PRACTICE AREAS:*** Telecommunications Law; Cable Television. ***Email:*** cmiller@szd.com

KEVIN L. MURCH, born Pittsfield, Massachusetts, 1969; admitted to bar, 1996, Ohio and U.S. District Court, Southern District of Ohio; 1997, U.S. Court of Appeals, Sixth Circuit. *Education:* The Ohio State University (B.A., 1993); Capital University (J.D., cum laude, 1996). ***PRACTICE AREAS:*** Litigation. ***Email:*** kmurch@szd.com

(This Listing Continued)

MARCIA J. MYERS, born Salem, Ohio, 1959; admitted to bar, 1985, Ohio. *Education:* Bowling Green State University (B.A., magna cum laude, 1982); The Ohio State University (J.D., 1985). (Resident, Cincinnati Office). ***PRACTICE AREAS:*** Health Law; Corporate Law; Hospital Law. ***Email:*** mmyers@szd.com

ANGELIQUE PAUL NEWCOMB, born Columbus, Ohio, 1969; admitted to bar, 1997, Ohio; 1998, U.S. District Court, Southern District of Ohio. *Education:* Columbia University (B.A., 1991); Ohio State University (J.D., 1997). ***PRACTICE AREAS:*** Labor Law; Employment Law. ***Email:*** anewcomb@szd.com

ROBERT H. NICHOLS, born Columbus, Ohio, 1960; admitted to bar, 1988, Texas; 1992, Ohio; U.S. District Court, Southern District of Ohio and Texas. *Education:* Ohio State University (B.S.B.A., Accounting Honors Program, 1982); University of Texas (J.D., with honors, 1987). ***PRACTICE AREAS:*** Litigation; Business Litigation; Construction Litigation; Commercial Litigation; Product Liability Defense. ***Email:*** rnichols@szd.com

ROBERT R. OUELLETTE, born Highland Park, Michigan, 1965; admitted to bar, 1991, Ohio. *Education:* University of Michigan (A.B., 1987; J.D., 1991). Omicron Delta Epsilon; James B. Angell Scholar. ***PRACTICE AREAS:*** Mergers and Acquisitions; Corporate Finance; Corporate Governance. ***Email:*** rouellette@szd.com

THOMAS A. PAMPUSH, born Cleveland, Ohio, 1968; admitted to bar, 1993, Ohio; U.S. District Court, Northern and Southern Districts of Ohio; U.S. Court of Appeals, Sixth Circuit. *Education:* The Ohio State University (B.S., 1990; J.D., 1993). ***PRACTICE AREAS:*** Corporate Law. ***Email:*** tpampush@szd.com

PETER A. PAVARINI, born New York, N.Y., 1952; admitted to bar, 1977, Massachusetts; 1979, District of Columbia; 1981, Ohio. *Education:* State University of New York at Albany (B.A., summa cum laude, 1973); Boston College Law School (J.D., 1977). ***PRACTICE AREAS:*** Health Law; Hospital Law; Corporate Compliance; Managed Care Law; Biotechnology Law. ***Email:*** peter.pavarini@szd.com

SUSAN PORTER, born Grand Rapids, Michigan, 1961; admitted to bar, 1986, Ohio. *Education:* University of Michigan (A.B., 1983); Boston University School of Law (J.D., 1986). ***PRACTICE AREAS:*** Labor Law; Employment Law; Health Law; Family and Medical Leave Act; Sexual Harassment; Employment Litigation; Employment Termination; Management Labor Law; Personnel Policies. ***Email:*** sporter@szd.com

VICTORIA E. POWERS, born Ann Arbor, Michigan, 1959; admitted to bar, 1987, California; 1991, Ohio. *Education:* University of Michigan; Mount Holyoke College (B.A., 1981); Hastings College of the Law, University of California (J.D., 1987). ***PRACTICE AREAS:*** Debtors Rights; Creditors Rights; Commercial Litigation; Health Law; Commercial Law; Bankruptcy; Business Law; Commercial Bankruptcy; Commercial Insolvency. ***Email:*** vpowers@szd.com

BRYAN K. PROSEK, born Zanesville, Ohio, 1966; admitted to bar, 1991, Ohio. *Education:* Ohio State University (B.S.B.A., 1988; J.D., cum laude, 1991). ***PRACTICE AREAS:*** Corporate Law. ***Email:*** bprosek@szd.com

JENNIFER DUTEY READLER, born Ironton, Ohio, 1971; admitted to bar, 1997, Ohio. *Education:* Marshall University (B.B.A., summa cum laude, 1994); The Ohio State University (J.D., 1997). ***PRACTICE AREAS:*** Municipal Law. ***Email:*** jreadler@szd.com

SUSAN D. RECTOR, born Wilmington, Delaware, 1959; admitted to bar, 1984, Ohio. *Education:* Wake Forest University (B.A., magna cum laude, with honors, 1981); University of North Carolina (J.D., 1984). ***PRACTICE AREAS:*** Business Law; Securities; Intellectual Property; Closely Held Business Law; Limited Liability Company Law; Intellectual Property Infringement; Trademarks; Copyrights. ***Email:*** srector@szd.com

JOSEPH M. REIDY, born Cleveland, Ohio, 1955; admitted to bar, 1985, Ohio and U.S. District Court, Southern District of Ohio; 1993, U.S. District Court, Northern District of Ohio and U.S. Court of Appeals, Fourth Circuit. *Education:* University of Cincinnati (B.S., Biology, 1977); DePauw University (M.A., Zoology, 1979); Capital University (J.D., 1985). Order of the Curia. ***PRACTICE AREAS:*** Environmental Law; Workers Compensation Law; Civil Litigation; Arbitration; Mediation. ***Email:*** jreidy@szd.com

ROBERT M. ROBENALT, born Lima, Ohio, 1959; admitted to bar, 1989, Ohio. *Education:* Miami University (B.S., 1982); Cleveland-Marshall College of Law (J.D., 1989). ***PRACTICE AREAS:*** Labor Law; Environmental Law; Commercial Litigation; Employment Law; Management Labor Law. ***Email:*** rrobenalt@szd.com

JOHN D. ROBINETT, born Columbus, Ohio, 1956; admitted to bar, 1982, Ohio and U.S. District Court, Northern District of Ohio. *Education:* Muskingum College (B.A., cum laude, 1979); Case Western Reserve University (J.D., 1982). ***PRACTICE AREAS:*** Commercial Banking Law; Corporate Law; Business Law; Loans; Banking Law; Lender Liability; Financial Institutions Law. ***Email:*** jrobinett@szd.com

DAVID J. ROBINSON, born Columbus, Ohio, 1966; admitted to bar, 1992, Ohio. *Education:* Bowling Green State University (B.A., magna cum laude, 1989); The Ohio State University College of Law (J.D., 1992). ***PRACTICE AREAS:*** Government Contracts; Bond Finance; Business Regulation; Constitutional Law; Economic Development; Legislative Practice; Telecommunications Law; E-Commerce; Zoning Law. ***Email:*** drobinson@szd.com

H. ALAN ROTHENBUECHER, born Akron, Ohio, 1964; admitted to bar, 1989, Ohio; 1990, Florida; 1991, District of Columbia; U.S. District Court, Northern District of Ohio, U.S. District Court, Middle District of Florida, U.S. District Court, Northern District of Illinois, U.S. Court of Appeals, Sixth Circuit and U.S. Supreme Court. *Education:* University of Michigan (A.B., 1985); Case Western Reserve University (J.D., 1989). *Member:* Akron Bar Association (Fellow); Federal Bar Association. (Resident, Cleveland Office). ***LANGUAGES:*** German. ***PRACTICE AREAS:*** Intellectual Property; Litigation; Business Immigration.

ROGER L. SABO, born Newark, Ohio, 1943; admitted to bar, 1968, Maryland and District of Columbia; 1971, Ohio; U.S. Supreme Court; U.S. Court of Appeals, Sixth Circuit. *Education:* The Ohio State University (B.A., 1965); Georgetown Law Center (J.D., 1968). ***PRACTICE AREAS:*** Occupational Safety and Health; Management Labor Law; Equal Employment Opportunity Law; Arbitration; Construction Litigation; Construction Law; Construction Labor Law; Construction Arbitration; Mechanics Liens. ***Email:*** rsabo@szd.com

(This Listing Continued)

STEPHEN P. SAMUELS, born Ann Arbor, Michigan, June 28, 1948; admitted to bar, 1975, Massachusetts and Ohio; 1976, U.S. District Court, Southern District of Ohio; 1980, U.S. Supreme Court; 1982, U.S. District Court, Northern District of Ohio; 1989, U.S. Court of Appeals, Sixth Circuit. *Education:* University of Michigan at Ann Arbor (B.A., cum laude, 1970); Northeastern University (J.D., 1974). ***PRACTICE AREAS:*** Environmental Law; Alternative Dispute Resolution. ***Email:*** ssamuels@szd.com

MELVIN L. SCHOTTENSTEIN (1932-1993)

ANTHONY D. SHAFFER, born Peoria, Illinois, February 15, 1963; admitted to bar, 1995, Ohio and U.S. District Court, Southern District of Ohio. *Education:* Ohio University (B.A., cum laude, 1985); Capital University (J.D., summa cum laude, 1995). ***PRACTICE AREAS:*** Health Care; Corporate Law. ***Email:*** ashaffer@szd.com

STEPHEN J. SMITH, born Toledo, Ohio, 1946; admitted to bar, 1971, Ohio; 1973, U. S. Supreme Court and U.S. District Court, Southern District of Ohio. *Education:* University of Toledo (B.A., 1968); Ohio State University (J.D., 1971). ***PRACTICE AREAS:*** Municipal Law; Zoning; Litigation. ***Email:*** ssmith@szd.com

ALAN G. STARKOFF, born Cleveland, Ohio, 1950; admitted to bar, 1975, Ohio, U.S. District Court, Northern District of Ohio and Florida; 1981, Pennsylvania. *Education:* Ohio State University (B.S., 1972); Cleveland State University (J.D., 1975). ***PRACTICE AREAS:*** Business Law; Business Litigation; Labor and Employment. ***Email:*** astarkoff@szd.com

ROBERT M. STEFANCIN, born Uniontown, Pennsylvania, 1965; admitted to bar, 1990, Ohio; 1991, U.S. District Court, Northern District of Ohio and U.S. Court of Appeals, Sixth Circuit; 2000, U.S. Tax Court. *Education:* Washington & Jefferson College (B.A., cum laude, 1987); Case Western Reserve University (J.D., cum laude, 1990). *Member:* Akron Bar Association. (Resident, Cleveland Office). ***PRACTICE AREAS:*** Bankruptcy; Litigation. ***Email:*** rstefancin@szd.com

MATTHEW J. STOCKSLAGER, born Greenville, Ohio, April 2, 1966; admitted to bar, 1992, Ohio; U.S. District Court, Northern District of Ohio. *Education:* The Ohio State University (B.S., 1989); University of Akron (J.D., cum laude, 1992). *Member:* Akron Bar Association. (Resident, Cleveland Office). ***PRACTICE AREAS:*** Corporate Law; Health Care; Real Estate. ***Email:*** mstockslager@szd.com

DANIEL R. SWETNAM, born Columbus, Ohio, 1957; admitted to bar, 1982, Ohio. *Education:* The Ohio State University (B.A., 1979); University of Cincinnati (J.D., 1982). Order of the Coif. ***PRACTICE AREAS:*** Commercial Litigation; Debtor and Creditor Rights; Commercial Law; Bankruptcy; Business Law; Commercial Bankruptcy; Commercial Insolvency. ***Email:*** dswetnam@szd.com

MICHAEL D. TARULLO, born Louisville, Kentucky, 1949; admitted to bar, 1989, Ohio; U.S. District Court, Southern District of Ohio; U.S. Federal Claims Court. *Education:* University of Louisville (B.S., 1972); Capital University (J.D., 1989). ***PRACTICE AREAS:*** Construction Law; Construction Arbitration; Mechanics Liens; Construction Contracts; Construction Litigation. ***Email:*** mtarullo@szd.com

JOHN TERAKEDIS, JR., born Dennison, Ohio, 1945; admitted to bar, 1970, Ohio, U.S. Supreme Court and U.S. Tax Court. *Education:* Baldwin-Wallace College (B.S., 1967); Harvard University (J.D., 1970). ***PRACTICE AREAS:*** Business Law; Taxation; Pension and Profit Sharing Plans; Executive Compensation; Estate Planning; Corporate Tax Planning; Employee Benefits; ERISA; COBRA; Retirement Benefit Plans; Deferred Compensation; Fringe Benefits; Flexible Benefits Plans; Health Benefits; Employee Stock Ownership Plans. ***Email:*** jterakedis@szd.com

FELIX C. WADE, born Charleston, South Carolina, 1949; admitted to bar, 1977, Ohio. *Education:* Indiana University (B.A., 1971); Chase College of Law (J.D., 1977). ***PRACTICE AREAS:*** Management Labor Law; Employment Discrimination Law; Occupational Safety and Health Law. ***Email:*** fwade@szd.com

ROBERT D. WEISMAN, born Cleveland, Ohio, 1948; admitted to bar, 1975, Ohio. *Education:* George Washington University; Case Western Reserve University (B.A., summa cum laude, 1970); Cleveland State University (J.D., summa cum laude, 1975). ***PRACTICE AREAS:*** Labor Law; Employment Law; Workers Compensation Defense; Collective Bargaining; Family and Medical Leave Act; Management Labor Law; Labor Relations; Labor Strikes; National Labor Relations Act; Union Contract Negotiations; Employment Contracts; Public Sector Employment Law; Public Sector Labor Relations; Public Sector Collective Bargaining. ***Email:*** rweisman@szd.com

---

ALAN J. ARVILLE, admitted to bar, 2003, Ohio. *Education:* University of Dayton (B.A., 2000);Georgetown University Law Center (J.D., cum laude, 2003). ***PRACTICE AREAS:*** Health Law. ***Email:*** aarville@szd.com

GREGORY S. BAKER, born Ravenna, Ohio, 1971; admitted to bar, 1998, Ohio. *Education:* University of Wisconsin (B.S., 1994); The Ohio State University (J.D., 1998). ***PRACTICE AREAS:*** Corporate Law; Real Estate. ***Email:*** gbaker@szd.com

VALERIE T. BARNETT, admitted to bar, 1999, California; 2004, Ohio. *Education:* University of California, Irvine (B.A., with honors, 1996); Cornell University Law School (J.D., cum laude, 1999). ***PRACTICE AREAS:*** Bankruptcy; Corporate; Securities. ***Email:*** vbarnett@szd.com

KRISTEN E. BRADEN, born 1976; (admission pending). *Education:* Vanderbilt University (Bachelor of Engineering, Civil Engineering and Mathematics, 1998); University of Texas (Master of Science, Construction Engineering and Project Management, 2000); University of Cincinnati (J.D., 2005). ***PRACTICE AREAS:*** Construction Law. ***Email:*** kbraden@szd.com

SARA F. BUSCHUR, born 1979; (admission pending). *Education:* University of Dayton (B.S., magna cum laude, 2002; M.B.A, 2002); Wake Forest University School of Law (J.D., 2005). ***PRACTICE AREAS:*** Corporate Law. ***Email:*** sbuschur@szd.com

J. COREY COLOMBO, born Columbus, Ohio, 1975; admitted to bar, 2000, Ohio; 2001, U.S. District Court, Southern District of Ohio and U.S. Court of Appeals, Sixth Cir-

(This Listing Continued)

SCHOTTENSTEIN ZOX & DUNN CO., LPA, Columbus—Continued

cuit; 2004, U.S. District Court, Northern District of Ohio. *Education:* Miami University (B.A., Political Science and History, 1997); Capital University (J.D., 2000). ***PRACTICE AREAS:*** Public Law. ***Email:*** jcolombo@szd.com

TYSON A. CRIST, born Towson, Maryland, 1973; admitted to bar, 1999, Ohio. *Education:* The College of Wooster (B.A., 1996); The Ohio State University College of Law (J.D., 1999). ***PRACTICE AREAS:*** Bankruptcy; Debtor and Creditor. ***Email:*** tcrist@szd.com

KELLY K. CURTIS, born 1977; (admission pending). *Education:* Saint Mary's College (B.A., 1999); The Ohio State University Moritz College of Law (J.D., 2005). ***PRACTICE AREAS:*** Labor and Employment. ***Email:*** kcurtis@szd.com

ELAINE DARR, born Silver Springs, Maryland, 1975; admitted to bar, 2001, Ohio. *Education:* The Ohio State University (B.S.B.A., Marketing, 1998); Capital University (J.D., 2001). ***PRACTICE AREAS:*** Real Estate Law. ***Email:*** edarr@szd.com

JENNIFER L. FEWELL, admitted to bar, 2003, Ohio. *Education:* Ohio University (B.S., cum laude, 2000); The Ohio State University, Moritz College of Law (J.D., 2003). ***PRACTICE AREAS:*** Labor and Employment; Workers Compensation. ***Email:*** jfewell@szd.com

STEVEN D. FORRY, born Indianapolis, Indiana, 1975; admitted to bar, 2002, Ohio. *Education:* Miami University (B.A., 1997); Indiana University School of Law (J.D., 2002). ***PRACTICE AREAS:*** Litigation. ***Email:*** sforry@szd.com

LINDA S. GEMIND, born Detroit, Michigan, April 6, 1958; admitted to bar, 1990, Florida (inactive) and U.S. District Court, Middle District of Florida; 1991, Ohio and U.S. Tax Court; 2003, Pennsylvania. *Education:* Kent State University (B.A., cum laude, 1979); University of Florida College of Law (J.D., with honors, 1989). (Resident, Cleveland Office). ***LANGUAGES:*** German. ***PRACTICE AREAS:*** Immigration and Naturalization; Corporate Law; Securities. ***Email:*** lgemind@szd.com

AARON L. GRANGER, born Rochester, New York, 1970; admitted to bar, 1997, Ohio. *Education:* Ohio Wesleyan University (B.A., 1993); Ohio State University College of Law (J.D., 1996). ***PRACTICE AREAS:*** Labor and Employment. ***Email:*** agranger@szd.com

JEREMY GRAYEM, born 1974; admitted to bar, 2000, Ohio. *Education:* Miami University, Ohio (B.A., summa cum laude, Political Science and History, 1996); The Ohio State University College of Law (J.D., 2000). ***PRACTICE AREAS:*** Litigation. ***Email:*** jgrayem@szd.com

MATTHEW T. GREEN, born Cambridge, Ohio, 1977; admitted to bar, 2002, Ohio and U.S. District Court, Northern District of Ohio. *Education:* The Ohio State University (B.S.B.A., 1999); The Ohio State University College of Law (J.D., summa cum laude, 2002). ***PRACTICE AREAS:*** Commercial Litigation; Appellate Litigation. ***Email:*** mgreen@szd.com

CHAD W. HELMICK, born 1981; (admission pending). *Education:* Hillsdale College (B.S., summa cum laude, 2002); Wake Forest University School of Law (J.D., 2005). ***PRACTICE AREAS:*** Health Care. ***Email:*** chelmick@szd.com

KEVIN M. HILVERT, born Cincinnati, Ohio, 1974; admitted to bar, 2002, Ohio. *Education:* Wittenberg University (B.A., cum laude, 1997); The Ohio State University (J.D., cum laude, 2002). ***PRACTICE AREAS:*** Health Law; Government Affairs. ***Email:*** khilvert@szd.com

ELIZABETH KASTNER, born Memphis, Tennessee, September 3, 1975; admitted to bar, 2001, Ohio. *Education:* Indiana University (B.A., 1998); The Ohio State University (J.D., 2001). ***PRACTICE AREAS:*** Health Law. ***Email:*** ekastner@szd.com

JAY E. KRASOVEC, born Cleveland, Ohio, 1970; admitted to bar, 1998, Ohio and U.S. District Court, Northern District of Ohio; 2003, U.S. District Court, Northern District of Illinois. *Education:* University of Akron (B.A., cum laude, 1995; J.D., cum laude, 1998). (Resident, Cleveland Office). ***PRACTICE AREAS:*** Intellectual Property; Litigation. ***Email:*** jkrasovec@szd.com

MELISSA C. LLOYD, born Columbus, Ohio, 1973; admitted to bar, 1999, Ohio. *Education:* University of Arizona (B.A., cum laude, 1994); Ohio State University (J.D., with honors, 1999). ***PRACTICE AREAS:*** Health Law. ***Email:*** mlloyd@szd.com

MEGHAN D. MAJERNIK, born Cleveland, Ohio, 1978; admitted to bar, 2002, Ohio. *Education:* Baldwin-Wallace College (B.A., summa cum laude, 1999); Cleveland-Marshall College of Law (J.D., summa cum laude, 2002). (Resident, Cleveland Office). ***PRACTICE AREAS:*** Labor and Employment; Workers Compensation. ***Email:*** mmajernik@szd.com

KATHERINE G. MANGHILLIS, born Cleveland, Ohio, August 14, 1978; admitted to bar, 2004, Ohio and U.S. District Court, Northern District of Ohio; 2005, District of Columbia. *Education:* College of Wooster (B.A., 2000); Akron University Law School (J.D., 2004). (Resident, Cleveland Office). ***PRACTICE AREAS:*** Bankruptcy; Litigation. ***Email:*** kmanghillis@szd.com

JENNIFER K. MASON, born Wheeling, West Virginia, 1971; admitted to bar, 1996, Ohio and U.S. District Court, Northern and Southern Districts of Ohio. *Education:* Northwestern University (B.A., 1993); The Ohio State University (J.D., 1996). ***PRACTICE AREAS:*** Workers Compensation; Employment Law; Litigation. ***Email:*** jmason@szd.com

JENNIFER M. McDANIEL, born Gallipolis, Ohio, 1977; admitted to bar, 2002, Ohio. *Education:* Capital University (B.A., cum laude, 1998); The Ohio State University (J.D., 2002). ***PRACTICE AREAS:*** Workers Compensation. ***Email:*** jmcdaniel@szd.com

PHILIP R. MIELE, born Niles, Ohio, 1957; admitted to bar, 1984, Ohio. *Education:* Bowling Green State University (B.A., 1980); Ohio Northern University (J.D., 1983). ***PRACTICE AREAS:*** Public Law. ***Email:*** pmiele@szd.com

MIRANDA MORGAN, born 1979; (admission pending). *Education:* The Ohio State University (B.A., summa cum laude, 2001); The Ohio State University Moritz College of Law (J.D., 2005). ***PRACTICE AREAS:*** Taxation. ***Email:*** mmorgan@szd.com

(This Listing Continued)

KEVIN M. MUELLER, born 1973; admitted to bar, 2002, Ohio. *Education:* The Ohio State University (B.S., 1997); The Ohio State University, Moritz College of Law (J.D., 2002). ***PRACTICE AREAS:*** Corporate Law. ***Email:*** kmueller@szd.com

JOHN H. OBERLE, born 1970; admitted to bar, 2001, Ohio. *Education:* Ohio Wesleyan University (B.S., 1993); Capital University (J.D., 2000). ***PRACTICE AREAS:*** Governmental Law; Banking Regulation. ***Email:*** joberle@szd.com

ANDRE T. PORTER, born 1979; (admission pending). *Education:* Capital University (B.A., 2002); The Ohio State University Moritz College of Law (J.D., 2005). ***PRACTICE AREAS:*** Government Affairs. ***Email:*** aporter@szd.com

HANSEL H. RHEE, born Seoul, South Korea, 1970; admitted to bar, 1995, Maryland; 1996, U.S. District Court, District of Maryland; 1998, District of Columbia, Virginia, U.S. Court of Appeals, Eastern District of Virginia and U.S. Court of Appeals, Fourth Circuit; 1999, U.S. District Court, District of Columbia and U.S. Court of Federal Claims; 2003, Ohio. *Education:* Wittenberg University (B.A., 1992); Syracuse University (J.D., 1995). ***PRACTICE AREAS:*** Construction Litigation; Commercial Litigation. ***Email:*** hrhee@szd.com

MICHAEL T. SHORT, born Napolean, Ohio, 1973; admitted to bar, 1998, Ohio; 1999, U.S. District Court, Northern and Southern Districts of Ohio. *Education:* Miami University (B.S., 1995); The Ohio State University (J.D., 1998). ***PRACTICE AREAS:*** Labor Law; Employment Law; Litigation. ***Email:*** mshort@szd.com

DENISE R. SLAZYK, born Saskatoon, Saskatchewan, 1969; admitted to bar, 1998, Saskatchewan; 2001, Ohio. *Education:* University of Saskatchewan (B.Com., 1992; LL.B., 1997). ***PRACTICE AREAS:*** Corporate Law; Banking Law; Finance. ***Email:*** dslazyk@szd.com

ADAM L. SMITH, born Bowling Green, Ohio, 1970; admitted to bar, 1999, Ohio. *Education:* The Ohio State University (B.S., Business Administration, 1995); Ohio State University College of Law (J.D., 1999). ***PRACTICE AREAS:*** Real Estate; Business Law; Tax Law; Estate Planning. ***Email:*** asmith@szd.com

STEPHEN JENNINGS SMITH, born Columbus, Ohio, 1973; admitted to bar, 1999, Ohio. *Education:* Miami University (B.A., 1995); Capital University (J.D., summa cum laude, 1999). ***PRACTICE AREAS:*** Public Law. ***Email:*** sjsmith@szd.com

JOSHUA N. STINE, admitted to bar, 2003, Ohio. *Education:* Indiana University (B.A., summa cum laude, 2000); The Ohio State University, Moritz College of Law, (J.D., with honors, 2003). ***PRACTICE AREAS:*** Litigation. ***Email:*** jstine@szd.com

ERIC M. STOLLER, born Canton, Ohio, 1974; admitted to bar, 1999, Ohio. *Education:* Ohio University (B.B.A., 1996); The Ohio State University College of Law (J.D., 1999). ***PRACTICE AREAS:*** Bankruptcy. ***Email:*** estoller@szd.com

CATHERINE L. STRAUSS, born Toledo, Ohio, 1975; admitted to bar, 2000, Ohio. *Education:* The Ohio State University (B.A., 1997); George Washington University School of Law (J.D., 2000). ***PRACTICE AREAS:*** Commercial Litigation. ***Email:*** cstrauss@szd.com

MALINDA L. SUSALLA, admitted to bar, 1995, Maryland; 1996, Indiana; 2001, Ohio. *Education:* Michigan State University (B.S., 1984); Oakland University (M.B.A., 1992); The George Washington University Law School (J.D., with high honors, 1995); Georgetown University Law School (LL.M., Taxation, 2003). ***PRACTICE AREAS:*** Tax. ***Email:*** msusalla@szd.com

EVAN R. WEIDENHAMER, born Ashland, Ohio, 1973; admitted to bar, 1999, Ohio. *Education:* Ashland College (B.S., cum laude, 1996); The Ohio State University (J.D., with honors, 1999). ***PRACTICE AREAS:*** Real Estate. ***Email:*** eweidenhamer@szd.com

TAYLOR M. WESLEY, born 1980; (admission pending). *Education:* Dickinson College (B.A., 2002); Case Western Reserve University School of Law (J.D., 2005). (Resident, Cleveland Office). ***PRACTICE AREAS:*** Bankruptcy. ***Email:*** twesley@szd.com

AMANDA L. WICKLINE, admitted to bar, 2003, Ohio. *Education:* Denison University (B.A., cum laude, 2000); Wake Forest University School of Law (J.D., 2003). ***PRACTICE AREAS:*** Labor and Employment; Litigation; Workers Compensation. ***Email:*** awickline@szd.com

STEPHEN WITHEE, born Omaha, Nebraska, 1969; admitted to bar, 1995, West Virginia and U.S. District Court, Southern District of West Virginia; 1998, Ohio and U.S. District Court, Southern District of Ohio. *Education:* Miami University (A.B., 1992); Washington & Lee University (J.D., 1995). ***PRACTICE AREAS:*** Construction; Commercial Litigation. ***Email:*** swithee@szd.com

AIMEE A. ZALESKI, admitted to bar, 1998, Ohio. *Education:* Wilkes University (B.A., magna cum laude, 1990); The Ohio State University College of Law (J.D., with honors, 1998). ***PRACTICE AREAS:*** Intellectual Property; Copyrights; Trademarks; Corporate Law. ***Email:*** azaleski@szd.com

BRIAN M. ZETS, born Youngstown, Ohio, July 3, 1971; admitted to bar, 1996, Ohio and U.S. District Court, Northern District of Ohio; 1997, U.S. District Court, Southern District of Ohio and U.S. Court of Appeals, Sixth Circuit. *Education:* The Ohio State University (B.S., 1993); University of Toledo (J.D., 1996). ***PRACTICE AREAS:*** Public Law; Municipal Law; Litigation. ***Email:*** bzets@szd.com

OF COUNSEL

NANCY A. BRIGNER, born Columbus, Ohio, 1967; admitted to bar, 1992, Ohio. *Education:* Northwestern University (B.A., 1989) Phi Beta Kappa; University of Michigan (J.D., 1992). ***PRACTICE AREAS:*** Hospital Law; Health Maintenance Organizations; Integrated Health Care Delivery Systems. ***Email:*** nbrigner@szd.com

ROBERT J. COCHRAN, born Cleveland, Ohio, July 26, 1966; admitted to bar, 1991, Ohio; U.S. District Court, Southern District of Ohio. *Education:* Miami University (B.A., 1988); The Ohio State University (J.D., magna cum laude, 1991). ***PRACTICE AREAS:*** Health Care; Criminal Law; Environmental Law. ***Email:*** rcochran@szd.com

MARY FRANCES GESWEIN, born Youngstown, Ohio, 1969; admitted to bar, 1994, Ohio. *Education:* University of Notre Dame (B.A., 1991); The Ohio State University (J.D., 1994). ***PRACTICE AREAS:*** Commercial Litigation. ***Email:*** mgeswein@szd.com

(This Listing Continued)

JEFFREY A. PERLMUTER, born Cleveland, Ohio, 1949; admitted to bar, 1975, Ohio. *Education:* Tulane University (B.A., 1972); The American University (J.D., 1975); Georgetown University (LL.M., 1979). (Resident Cleveland Office). ***PRACTICE AREAS:*** Estate Planning; Employee Benefits. ***Email:*** jperlmuter@szd.com

CHARLES SAUNDERS, JR., admitted to bar, 1972, Ohio. *Education:* Ohio State University (B.S., 1968); The Ohio State University School of Law (J.D., 1972). ***PRACTICE AREAS:*** Corporate; Labor and Employment. ***Email:*** csaunders@szd.com

ELIZABETH E. TULMAN, admitted to bar, 1982, Ohio; U.S. District Court, Southern and Northern Districts of Ohio; U.S. Court of Appeals, Sixth Circuit. *Education:* Emory University (B.A., 1978); University of Cincinnati College of Law (J.D., 1982). ***PRACTICE AREAS:*** Litigation. ***Email:*** etulman@szd.com

BENJAMIN L. ZOX, born Des Moines, Iowa, 1937; admitted to bar, 1962, Ohio. *Education:* Williams College (A.B., 1959); The Ohio State University (J.D., 1962). ***PRACTICE AREAS:*** Arbitration; Mediation; Business Dispute Resolution; Business Law; Real Estate Law. ***Email:*** bzox@szd.com

MELISSA L. ZOX, born Columbus, Ohio, 1964; admitted to bar, 1990, Ohio, U.S. District Court, Southern District of Ohio and U.S. District Court, Northern District of Illinois. *Education:* Northwestern University (B.S., 1986); The Ohio State University (J.D., 1990). ***PRACTICE AREAS:*** Labor Law; Employment Law. ***Email:*** mzox@szd.com

All of the firm's attorneys are members of the Columbus, Ohio State and American Bar Associations.

REPRESENTATIVE CLIENTS: America Showa, Inc.; Apex M&P; Ashland Inc.; Associated General Contractors of Ohio; Bank One, N.A.; Belmont Bancorp; Benjamin Steel Company; Big Lots Inc.; City of Dublin, Ohio; Clermont County; Columbus Medical Association & Foundation; Continental Real Estate Co.; Corna - Kokosing Construction; Decker Construction Company; Diamond Hill Investment Group, Inc.; Dynalectric; Elford Development Co.; Fairfield County; Franklin County; GE Capital Consumer Card Co.; Genesis Health Care System; Huntington National Bank; JPMorgan Chase Bank; JPMorgan Trust Company; JWF, Ohio Municipal Insurance Pool; Lake Hospital System, Inc.; Midwest Acoust-A-Fiber, Inc.; Morning Pride Manufacturing LLC; NP Ltd.; Nationwide Mutual Insurance Company and Affiliated Companies; Nationwide Realty Investors; Nestle R and D; OARnet; Ohio Contractors Association; Performance Site Management; Pinnacle Data Systems, Inc.; Retail Ventures Inc.; Reynoldsburg City Schools; Rural/ Metro Corporation; Schneller; Schottenstein Management Company; Solid Waste Authority of Central Ohio; South-Western City Schools; State of Ohio Bond Counsel; Summa Health System (Akron City Hospital, SummaCare); The Honeybaked Ham Company; Tosoh America, Inc.; Tosoh SMD, Inc.; TriHealth, Inc. (Good Samaritan and Bethesda Hospitals); Village of New Albany, Ohio.

JOHN SCOTT

4719 REED STREET, SUITE 146
COLUMBUS, OHIO 43220
Telephone: 614-267-5354
Fax: 614-267-8092
Email: backinthesaddle9@yahoo.com
URL: http://www.johnscottlawfirm.com

Criminal Law, Driving While Intoxicated, Drug Crimes, Felonies, Assault, Misdemeanor, Traffic Violations, White Collar Crimes, Forgery.

JOHN SCOTT, born Louisville, Kentucky, 1964; admitted to bar, 1998, Ohio. *Education:* University of Louisville (B.S., 1992); University of Cincinnati (J.D., 1997). ***PRACTICE AREAS:*** Criminal Law; Driving While Intoxicated; Drug Crimes; Felonies; Assault; Misdemeanors; Traffic Violations; White Collar Crime; Forgery.

SCOTT, SCRIVEN & WAHOFF LLP

Established in 1995

2600 LEVEQUE TOWER
50 WEST BROAD STREET
(FRANKLIN COUNTY)
COLUMBUS, OHIO 43215
Telephone: 614-222-8686
Fax: 614-222-8688
URL: http://www.lawyers.com/scottscriven&wahoff

Representation of Public and Private Sector Employers in Labor and Employment Law Matters. Collective Bargaining, Arbitration, Employment Discrimination, Workers' Compensation, OSHA, ADA, Intentional Tort Defense and Education Law.

MEMBERS OF FIRM

GREGORY B. SCOTT, born Peoria, Illinois, 1951; admitted to bar, 1976, Ohio. *Education:* University of Illinois (B.A., 1973; J.D., 1976). Order of the Coif. Editor-in-Chief, University of Illinois Law Forum. Clerk, U.S. Circuit Judge Walter P. Gewin, Fifth Circuit, 1976-1977. *Member:* Columbus and Ohio State Bar Associations. ***PRACTICE AREAS:*** Employment Law; Wage and Hour; Private Business Law; Public Sector; Labor Law. ***Email:*** gregory@sswlaw.com

DONALD C. SCRIVEN, born Grants Pass, Oregon, 1948; admitted to bar, 1974, Ohio. *Education:* Andrews University (B.A., 1969); Tulane University (J.D., 1974). Articles Editor, Tulane Law Review. Co-Author: *Ohio School Law,* Banks-Baldwin, 1994. ***PRACTICE AREAS:*** Private and Public Sector Labor and Employment Law; Education Law.

WILLIAM J. WAHOFF, born Ashland, Kentucky, 1956; admitted to bar, 1982, Ohio. *Education:* Miami University (A.B., with honors, 1978); The Ohio State University (J.D., with honors, 1982). Issue Planning Editor, *Ohio State Law Journal. Member:* Cincinnati (Member, Workers' Compensation Committee), Columbus (Member, Workers' Compensation Committee), Ohio State (Member: Workers' Compensation, Labor and Employment Law Committee) and American (Member, Sections on: Employment and Labor Law; Litigation) Bar Associations; Defense Research Institute. ***PRACTICE AREAS:*** Employment Law; Workers' Compensation; OSHA. ***Email:*** bill@sswlaw.com

(This Listing Continued)

JAMES K. STUCKO, JR., born Chicago, Illinois, 1963; admitted to bar, 1988, Illinois; 1993, Ohio. *Education:* Denison University (B.A., with honors, 1985); University of Notre Dame (J.D., 1988). Co-author: "Privatization: A Management Perspective," Illinois Public Employee Relations Report, Vol. 6, No. 2, Spring, 1989; "ADA: Is Your District Complying?" OASBO Business Chronicle, Vol. 23, Issue 2, 1993-1994. *Member:* Columbus (Labor Law Committee) and Ohio State (Labor and Employment Law Committee) Bar Associations. ***PRACTICE AREAS:*** Labor and Employment Law; Public Sector Labor Relations. ***Email:*** jim@sswlaw.com

TIMOTHY E. COWANS, born Columbus, Ohio, 1963; admitted to bar, 1988, Ohio. *Education:* Ohio Dominican College (B.A., summa cum laude, 1985); The Ohio State University (J.D., with honors, 1988). Member, Ohio State Law Journal. Co-Author: "Prevent Personnel Problems," Unique Opportunities, November/December, 1993. *Member:* Columbus (Workers' Compensation Committee) and Ohio State (Workers' Compensation Committee) Bar Associations. ***PRACTICE AREAS:*** Labor and Employment Law; Workers' Compensation; Public Sector Labor Relations. ***Email:*** tim@sswlaw.com

RICHARD GOLDBERG, born Brooklyn, New York, 1958; admitted to bar, 1983, Ohio; 1992, U.S. Supreme Court. *Education:* Rutgers College (B.A., 1980); Ohio State University (J.D., 1983). *Member:* Columbus (Workers' Compensation Law Committee), Ohio State (Workers' Compensation Committee) and American (Employment and Labor Law Section) Bar Associations. ***LANGUAGES:*** German. ***PRACTICE AREAS:*** Workers' Compensation; Employment Law. ***Email:*** rich@sswlaw.com

JULIE C. MARTIN, born Columbus, Ohio, 1965; admitted to bar, 1991, Ohio. *Education:* The Ohio State University (B.S., summa cum laude, 1987); Harvard University (J.D., cum laude, 1991). Editor, Harvard Human Rights Journal. *Member:* Columbus and Ohio State Bar Associations; Ohio Council of School Board Attorneys. ***PRACTICE AREAS:*** Labor and Employment Law; Education Law. ***Email:*** julie@sswlaw.com

ASSOCIATES

EDWARD L. OSTROWSKI, JR., born Youngstown, Ohio, 1958; admitted to bar, 1995, Ohio. *Education:* The Ohio State University (B.S., 1981; M.L.H.R., 1983); Capital University (J.D., 1995). *Member:* Columbus (Labor Law Committee) and Ohio State (Labor and Employment Law Committee) Bar Association. ***PRACTICE AREAS:*** Private Business Law; Public Sector Labor Relations; Employment Law; Workers' Compensation. ***Email:*** ed@sswlaw.com

KARLA S. SOARDS, born West Union, Ohio, 1969; admitted to bar, 1998, Ohio. *Education:* Ohio University (B.A., 1991); Capital University (J.D., 1997). *Member:* Columbus and Ohio State Bar Association. ***PRACTICE AREAS:*** Workers' Compensation. ***Email:*** karla@sswlaw.com

JODIE M. TAYLOR, born Hamilton, Ohio, 1969; admitted to bar, 1995, Ohio. *Education:* Miami University (B.A., 1991); University of Akron School of Law (J.D., 1995). University of Akron School of Law, Legal Writing and Oral Advocacy, 1995-1997. *Member:* Columbus and Ohio State Bar Association. (Certified Specialist in Worker's Compensation Law, Ohio State Bar Association). ***PRACTICE AREAS:*** Workers' Compensation. ***Email:*** jodie@sswlaw.com

MELISSA C. BONDY, born Laredo, Texas, 1971; admitted to bar, 1996, Ohio and U.S. District Court, Northern and Southern Districts of Ohio; 1997, District of Columbia; 2002, U.S. Court of Appeals, Sixth Circuit. *Education:* The Ohio State University (B.A., summa cum laude, 1993); University of Notre Dame (J.D., 1996). *Member:* Columbus and Ohio State Bar Associations. ***PRACTICE AREAS:*** Labor and Employment Law; Education Law. ***Email:*** melissa@sswlaw.com

LACEY L. CAIN, born Port Jefferson, New York, 1975; admitted to bar, 2000, Ohio and U.S. District Court, Southern District of Ohio. *Education:* Ohio Wesleyan University (B.A., 1997); Capital University Law School (J.D., 2000). *Member:* Columbus Bar Association. ***PRACTICE AREAS:*** Workers' Compensation. ***Email:*** lacey@sswlaw.com

KATHLEEN V. DAVIS, born Cincinnati, Ohio, 1977; admitted to bar, 2003, Ohio. *Education:* Miami University (B.A., magna cum laude, 2000); Ohio State University (J.D., with honors, 2003). Order of the Coif. *Member:* Columbus and Ohio State Bar Associations; Ohio Council of School Board Attorneys. ***PRACTICE AREAS:*** Labor and Employment; Education Law. ***Email:*** kate@sswlaw.com

C. BRADLEY HOWENSTEIN, born St. Louis, Missouri, 1967; admitted to bar, 1991, Ohio. *Education:* University of Illinois (B.A., 1988); The Ohio State University (J.D., 1991). Phi Beta Kappa. Edmund James Honors Program. Recipient: American Jurisprudence Award. Member, Central Ohio Self- Insurer's Association. *Member:* Ohio State (Worker's Compensation Committee) and Columbus Bar Associations (Worker's Compensation Committee). ***PRACTICE AREAS:*** Workers Compensation; Labor Law. ***Email:*** brad@sswlaw.com

SAMUEL H. SHAMANSKY CO., LPA

511 SOUTH HIGH STREET
COLUMBUS, OHIO 43215
Telephone: 614-228-4141
Fax: 614-228-0899
Email: sshamansky@hotmail.com

Criminal Trial and Appellate Practice in State and Federal Courts.

SAMUEL H. SHAMANSKY, born Columbus, Ohio, May 28, 1960; admitted to bar, 1985, Ohio; 1986, U.S. District Court, Northern and Southern Districts of Ohio and U.S. Court of Appeals, 4th and 6th Circuits. *Education:* The Ohio State University (B.A., 1982); Capital University (J.D., cum laude, 1985). Order of the Curia, Capital Law Review. Listed, "The Best Lawyers in America," and "Ohio Super Lawyers - Cincinnati Magazine" for Criminal Defense. *Member:* Columbus, Ohio State and American Bar Associations.

SHARMA LAW OFFICES, LLC

Established in 1989

853 PIPESTONE DRIVE
COLUMBUS, OHIO 43235
Telephone: 614-436-1240
614-436-3874
Fax: 614-436-0220
Email: csharma@sharmalawoffices.com
URL: http://www.sharmalawoffices.com

Trusts and Estates, Wills, Probate, Guardianship and Conservatorship, Probate litigation, Estate Planning for Parents of Handicapped Children, Estate Planning for the Elderly, Special Needs Trusts, Taxation, Business Law, Business Formation, Limited Liability Companies, Business Immigration, Tax-Exempt Organization Law.

FIRM PROFILE: Our firm focuses on representing individuals and families, as well as privately held and publicly-traded businesses and non-profit organizations in the following areas:1) estate planning and probate; 2) business law; 3) immigration law; 4) tax-exempt organization law. Prior to establishing her own law firm in 1989, Constance Sharma had served in the trust industry for over ten years as Trust and Tax Counsel for a nationally-recognized premier bank, headquartered in Columbus, Ohio. Mrs. Sharma and her staff are dedicated to providing clients with personalized and unpretentious quality legal services. Constance Sharma carries the highest legal ability rating in Martindale-Hubbell.

CONSTANCE L. SHARMA, born Chicago, Illinois, June 18, 1948; admitted to bar, 1978, Ohio; 1979, U.S. District Court, Northern District of Ohio; 2000, U.S. Court of Appeals, Sixth Circuit. *Education:* The Ohio State University (B.A., summa cum laude, 1974; J.D., 1978). *Member:* Columbus, Ohio State (Member, Probate and Trust Law Committees) and American (Member, Real Property, Probate and Trust-Income Taxation of Trust and Estate and Tax Sections) Bar Associations; Ohio Bankers Association Trust Tax Committee (Past Chairman and Member); American Immigration Lawyers Association; Association of Trial Lawyers of America. ***LANGUAGES:*** Czech, German and Hindi. ***PRACTICE AREAS:*** Trusts; Wills; Estate Planning; Probate; Special Needs Trusts; Medicaid Planning; Business Law; Immigration Law; Tax Exempt Organizations. ***Email:*** csharma@sharmalawoffices.com

Languages: Hindi, Czech, German.

REPRESENTATIVE CLIENTS: Aviat Aircraft, Inc.; Auddino's Italian Bakery; Cable Link, Inc.; Data Link, Inc.; Dublin Womens' Club, Inc.; Comfort Inns; FST Logistics; Huntington Bank; U.S. Bank; Fifth Third Bank; Ohio Credit Union League; Intech Technology Services, Inc.; Yau's Kitchen, LLC; Wholly Joe's Chicago Eatery; URS Corporation.

MELISSA J. SHAW

COLUMBUS, OHIO

(See Gahanna)

Business Law, Business Planning and Formation, Contracts, Corporate, Partnership, Family Business, Wills, Trusts and Estates, Contested Wills, Estate and Gift Taxation, Estate Planning, Living Wills, Powers of Attorney, Probate, Elder Law, Guardianship, Medicaid Eligibility.

TERRY K. SHERMAN

Established in 1978

52 WEST WHITTIER STREET
COLUMBUS, OHIO 43206-2503
Telephone: 614-444-8800
Fax: 614-445-9487
Email: ofc43206@aol.com
URL: http://www.terrysherman-law.com

Practice Limited to Criminal Defense in both State and Federal Courts.

FIRM PROFILE: Mr. Sherman concentrates in criminal defense work. Mr. Sherman has taken over 200 jury trials to conclusion. All types of offenses including criminal IRS cases, white collar, crime and criminal environmental law. Mr. Sherman has taken 20 capital murder cases to trial. Frequent lecturer at Ohio State Association Seminars.

TERRY K. SHERMAN, born Cleveland, Ohio, October 20, 1946; admitted to bar, 1971, Ohio; 1978, U.S. District Court, Southern District of Ohio; 1987, U.S. Court of Appeals, Sixth Circuit. *Education:* Ohio University (B.A., 1968); Ohio State University (J.D., cum laude, 1971). Nominated: "The Best Lawyers in America," 2003, 2004, 2005; "Ohio Super Lawyer," 2005. Assistant Franklin County Prosecutor, 1972-1978. Law Clerk, Judge William K. Thomas, U.S. District Court, Northern Division, 1971-1972. *Member:* Columbus (Chairman, Criminal Law Committee, 1992-1993) and Ohio State Bar Associations; National Association of Criminal Defense Lawyers; Ohio Association of Criminal Defense Lawyers; Central Ohio Association of Criminal Defense Lawyers. ***PRACTICE AREAS:*** Criminal Law; Traffic Law; Juvenile Law.

GUS M. SHIHAB

65 E. STATE STREET, SUITE 1550
COLUMBUS, OHIO 43215
Telephone: 614-224-2428
Fax: 614-224-5080
Email: info@shihab.net
URL: http://www.lawyers.com/eminentdomainohio

Eminent Domain, Zoning, Planning and Land Use.

GUS M. SHIHAB, born April 25, 1961; admitted to bar, 1993, Ohio; U.S. District Court, Southern and Northern Districts of Ohio; U.S. Court of Appeals, Sixth Circuit; U.S.

(This Listing Continued)

Supreme Court. *Education:* Ohio State University (B.S. CE., 1983); Capital University (J.D., 1993). Licensed Professional Engineer, Ohio, 1990. Ohio Department of Transportation, 1985-1994. Chairperson, Planning Committee, Ohio's Safety Management System, 1994-1995. Member and Chairperson, Legislative Committee, Institute of Transportation Engineers, 1995-1997. *Member:* Columbus, Cleveland, Ohio State and American Bar Associations; American Immigration Lawyers Association. (Also partner, Shihab & Associates, Columbus & Cleveland and Washington, D.C.). ***LANGUAGES:*** Arabic. ***PRACTICE AREAS:*** Eminent Domain.

OF COUNSEL

ROBERT J. MANN, born Euclid, Ohio, January 16, 1963; admitted to bar, 1988, Ohio; 1989, U.S. District Court, Southern District of Ohio. *Education:* Miami University (B.A., 1985); Ohio State University (J.D., with honors, 1988). Member, Strathmore's and the National Registry's Who's Who in the field of Eminent Domain. *Member:* Columbus, Ohio State and American Bar Associations; The Association of Trial Lawyers of America. ***PRACTICE AREAS:*** Eminent Domain.

SHIHAB & ASSOCIATES

Established in 1995

65 EAST STATE STREET, SUITE 1550
COLUMBUS, OHIO 43215
Telephone: 614-224-2428
Fax: 614-224-5080
Email: info@shihab.net
URL: http://www.shihab.net

Cleveland, Ohio Office: 600 Superior Avenue East, Suite 1300, 44114. Telephone: 216-479-7670. Fax: 216-479-7671.
Washington, DC Office: 1725 I Street NW, Suite 300, 2006. Telephone: 202-373-1535. Fax: 800-878-9405.

Immigration and Nationality Law, Business Immigration, Citizenship, Deportation, Employment Immigration, Family Immigration Law, Investor Visas, Labor Certification, Political Asylum, Eminent Domain, Zoning Planning and Land Use, Real Estate, Construction Law, Litigation.

FIRM PROFILE: The law firm of Shihab & Associates Co., LPA focuses primarily in the areas of Immigration, Land Use, Zoning and Eminent Domain Law.

Gus and Sam Shihab, who are licensed professional engineers, represent clients in a broad spectrum of fields, including IT, health care, government, engineering, agriculture and architecture for both immigrants and non-immigrant visas.

GUS M. SHIHAB, born April 25, 1961; admitted to bar, 1993, Ohio; U.S. District Court, Southern and Northern Districts of Ohio; U.S. Court of Appeals, Sixth Circuit; U.S. Supreme Court. *Education:* Ohio State University (B.S. CE., 1983); Capital University (J.D., 1993). Licensed Professional Engineer, Ohio, 1990. Ohio Department of Transportation, 1985-1994. Chairperson, Planning Committee, Ohio's Safety Management System, 1994-1995. Member and Chairperson, Legislative Committee, Institute of Transportation Engineers, 1995-1997. *Member:* Columbus, Cleveland, Ohio State and American Bar Associations; American Immigration Lawyers Association. ***LANGUAGES:*** Arabic. ***PRACTICE AREAS:*** Immigration Law; Eminent Domain; Zoning Law; Land Use; Construction Law; Litigation. ***Email:*** gus@shihab.net

SAM M. SHIHAB, born March 18, 1962; admitted to bar, 1994, Ohio; U.S. District Court, Southern District of Ohio; U.S. Supreme Court. *Education:* The Ohio State University (B.S.C.E., 1984); Capital University (J.D., 1994). Licensed Professional Engineer, Ohio, 1990. *Member:* Columbus, Cleveland, Ohio State and American Bar Associations; American Immigration Lawyers Association. ***LANGUAGES:*** Arabic. ***PRACTICE AREAS:*** Immigration Law; Land Use; Real Estate; Right of Way Easements; Litigation. ***Email:*** sam@shihab.net

ASSOCIATES

KIMBERLY E. HARRISON, born Parma, Ohio, September 3, 1977; admitted to bar, 2003, Ohio. *Education:* Valparaiso University (B.S., 1999); The Ohio State University (J.D., 2003); Fisher College of Business, The Ohio State University (M.B.A., 2003). *Member:* Columbus, Cleveland, Ohio State and American Bar Associations; American Immigration Lawyers Association. ***PRACTICE AREAS:*** Immigration Law. ***Email:*** kharrison@shihab.net

NOURE ALO, born Barberton, Ohio, June 5, 1978; admitted to bar, 2004, Ohio. *Education:* University of Toledo (B.A., cum laude, 2001); The Ohio State University, Moritz College of Law (J.D., 2004). Recipient: Thomas Hart Memorial Scholar Award, 1999; Margaret Patterson Scholar Award, 2000; Merit Scholar, 2001. FLAS (Foreign Language and Area Studies) Fellow, 2002. *Member:* Columbus and Ohio State Bar Associations; American Immigration Lawyers Association. ***LANGUAGES:*** Arabic. ***PRACTICE AREAS:*** Immigration Law; Business Litigation; Eminent Domain; Medical Services Contract Review. ***Email:*** nalo@shihab.net

LIOUHUV SELIOVSKI, born Tomsk, Russia; admitted to bar, 2003, Ohio. *Education:* Tomsk State University Law School, Tomsk, Russia (J.D., 1996); Capital University Law School (J.D., 2003). *Member:* Columbus and Ohio State Bar Associations. ***LANGUAGES:*** Russian and English. ***PRACTICE AREAS:*** Immigration Law; Business Litigation.

LEGAL SUPPORT PERSONNEL

BRET GILMORE, (Accounting)
KEVIN DAGOSTINO, (Information Technology)
BEN HARRIS, (Marketing)
CHUMKI BAGCHI, (Foreign Legal Consultant)

(This Listing Continued)

LIE JOHN, (Paralegal)

Languages: Arabic, Spanish, Portuguese, Hindi.

REPRESENTATIVE CLIENTS: Affordable Housing Associates; Ambassador Homes; Bell Homes, Inc.; Borror Corp.; Buckeye Management; Condelco Development; Dan Tobin Pontiac; Dehlendorf & Co.; Deltar Corp.; Edwards Land Co.; Englefield Oil Co.; Epler Development; Franklin Homes Builders, Inc.; Homewood Corp.; Land Network; Layman Homes, Inc.; M/I Schottenstein Homes; Massa Development and Realty; Mobley Homes of Columbus, Inc.; Parkmead Corp.; Ricart Ford, inc.; Rockford Homes, Inc.; Royal Crown Homes; Stor-All; The Jacobs Co.; The Robert Weiler Co.; Tiger Oil, Inc.; Today Homes; Tom Gill Oldsmobile; Triangle Properties, Inc.

SHOEMAKER, HOWARTH & TAYLOR, LLP

471 E. BROAD STREET, SUITE 2001
COLUMBUS, OHIO 43215
Telephone: 614-469-0100
Telecopy: 614-280-9675
URL: http://www.midohiolaw.com

Business Litigation, Corporate Law, Legislative Practice and Government Relations, Real Estate, Probate Litigation and Civil Litigation, Trial and Appellate Practice.

KEVIN L. SHOEMAKER, born Chillicothe, Ohio, November 28, 1953; admitted to bar, 1979, Ohio; 1980, U.S. District Court, Southern District of Ohio; 1984, U.S. Tax Court and U.S. Court of Appeals, Sixth Circuit; 1989, U.S. Supreme Court. *Education:* Otterbein College; University of Cincinnati (B.A., magna cum laude, 1976; J.D., 1979). *Member:* Columbus, Ohio State and American Bar Associations. ***PRACTICE AREAS:*** Business Litigation; Administrative Law; Legislative Practice. ***Email:*** tmills@midohiolaw.com

ROBERT F. HOWARTH, born Newark, Ohio, July 1, 1944; admitted to bar, 1970, Ohio; 1971, U.S. District Court, Southern District of Ohio; 1972, U.S. Court of Appeals, Sixth Circuit; 1973, U.S. Supreme Court; 1976, U.S. District Court, Northern District of Ohio. *Education:* Denison University (B.A., 1966); The Ohio State University (J.D., 1969). President, Ohio State Controlling Board; Assistant Director, Ohio Office of Budget & Management, 1975-1979. Executive Assistant, Governor of Ohio, 1979-1983. Member, Gubernatorial Transition Committees, 1982 and 1990. Regent, Ohio Board of Regents, 1982-1987. Member, Columbus Mayoral Transition Committees, 1992 &2000. Member, Board of Examiners, Supreme Court of Ohio, 1993-1998. Chairman, City of Columbus Charter Review Committee, 1998 and 1999. [U.S. Air Force Reserve and Ohio Air National Guard, Brig. Gen. (Ret.)]. ***PRACTICE AREAS:*** Business Law; Government Relations. ***Email:*** bobhowarth@aol.com

ROBERT H. TAYLOR, born Pittsburgh, Pennsylvania, October 14, 1944; admitted to bar, 1974, Ohio. *Education:* John Carroll University (A.B., 1966); Kent State University (M.Ed., 1968); The Ohio State University (J.D., cum laude, 1974). Phi Delta Phi. Prosecutor, City of Worthington, 1976-1978. Member, Arbitration Panel, National Association of Securities Dealers. ***PRACTICE AREAS:*** Real Property Law; Business Law. ***Email:*** rtaylor@midohiolaw.com

OF COUNSEL

DAVID A. TURANO, born Ashtabula, Ohio, September 9, 1946; admitted to bar, 1971, Ohio; 1972, U.S. District Court, Southern District of Ohio; 2002, U.S. Court, Northern District of Ohio. *Education:* Kent State University (B.S., 1968); The Ohio State University (J.D., 1971). Phi Delta Phi. Examiner, Public Utilities Commission of Ohio, 1971-1972. *Member:* Columbus and Ohio State Bar Associations; Transportation Lawyers Association. ***PRACTICE AREAS:*** Transportation Law; Telecommunications Law; Business Law; Business Litigation; Civil Litigation. ***Email:*** dturano@midohiolaw.com

SHUMAKER, LOOP & KENDRICK, LLP

HUNTINGTON CENTER
41 SOUTH HIGH STREET, SUITE 2400
COLUMBUS, OHIO 43215
Telephone: 614-463-9441
Fax: 614-463-1108

Toledo, Ohio Office: North Courthouse Square, 1000 Jackson, 43624-1573. Telephone: 419-241-9000. Fax: 419-241-6894.

Tampa, Florida Office: 101 East Kennedy Boulevard, Suite 2800, 33602-5151. Telephone: 813-229-7600. Fax: 813-229-1660.

Charlotte, North Carolina Office: 128 South Tryon Street, Suite 1800, 28202. Telephone: 704-375-0057. Fax: 704-332-1197.

Administrative Law; Advertising and Marketing; Agency and Distributorships; Agricultural Law; Alternative Dispute Resolution; Antitrust and Trade Regulation; Appellate Practice; Bankruptcy; Banks and Banking; Business Law; Business Crimes; Business Torts; Civil Rights; Commercial Law; Commercial Litigation; Commercial Real Estate; Communications and Media; Complex and Multi-District Litigation; Computers and Software; Construction Law; Contracts; Copyrights; Corporate Law; Federal Criminal Law; Debtor and Creditor; Domestic Relations; Education Law; Employee Benefits; Entertainment Law; Environmental Law; Fidelity and Surety; Finance; Franchises and Franchising; Health Care; Hospital Law; Immigration and Naturalization; Intellectual Property; International Law; Labor and Employment; Leases and Leasing; Litigation; Media Law; Medicare and Medicaid; Mergers, Acquisitions and Divestitures; Nonprofit and Charitable Organizations; Patent Litigation; Personal Injury; Probate; Products Liability; Professional Liability; Public Finance; Real Estate; Securities; Sports Law; Taxation; Torts; Trade Secrets; Trademarks; Trusts and Estates; Unfair Competition; Wills; Zoning, Planning and Land Use.

FIRM PROFILE: Shumaker, Loop & Kendrick, LLP is a full service law firm whose practice includes civil litigation, corporate, tax, securities, banking and commercial law, creditors' rights, real property, employment relations, employee benefits, estate planning and probate, health, domestic relations, environmental, immigration and administrative law. Our practice areas are organized into the following departments: litigation, corporate, health law, real estate, trusts and estates, taxation, employment law, environmental law and intellectual property. The firm is located in four cities -- Toledo and Columbus, Ohio, Charlotte, North Carolina, and Tampa, Florida.

We represent a wide variety of business, institutional, governmental and individual clients including manufacturers, banks and other financial institutions, insurance companies, contractors, broadcasters, accounting firms, real estate developers and brokers, public utilities, transportation companies, health care providers, trade associations and various public bodies and agencies.

LAW FIRM ALLIANCES/ASSOCIATIONS: ***TOLEDO CONFERENCE GROUP***

RESIDENT PARTNERS

MICHAEL E. BORN, born Huntington, West Virginia, February 17, 1963; admitted to bar, 1988, Ohio, U.S. Court of Appeals, Sixth Circuit and U.S. District Court, Northern and Southern Districts of Ohio. *Education:* Grand Valley State University (B.S., 1985); University of Michigan (J.D., 1988). *Member:* Columbus, Ohio State and American Bar Associations. ***PRACTICE AREAS:*** Environmental Law; Administrative Law. ***Email:*** mborn@slk-law.com

JOHN E. HALLER, born Mt. Vernon, Ohio, February 24, 1954; admitted to bar, 1980, Indiana and U.S. District Court, Southern District of Indiana; 1986, Ohio; 1987, U.S. District Court, Southern District of Ohio; 1989, U.S. District Court, Northern District of Ohio and U.S. Court of Appeals, Sixth Circuit. *Education:* Grace College (B.A., cum laude, 1976); Indiana State University (M.S., 1977); Indiana University (J.D., cum laude, 1980). *Member:* Columbus, Ohio State and American (Member, Litigation Section) Bar Associations. ***PRACTICE AREAS:*** Commercial Litigation; Business Litigation. ***Email:*** jhaller@slk-law.com

MICHAEL J. O'CALLAGHAN, born Detroit, Michigan, December 2, 1963; admitted to bar, 1990, Ohio; U.S. Court of Appeals, Sixth, Seventh and District of Columbia Circuits and U.S. District Court, Northern and Southern Districts of Ohio. *Education:* University of Michigan (A.B., 1986); University of Detroit (J.D., 1989). *Member:* Toledo, Ohio State and American Bar Associations. ***PRACTICE AREAS:*** Environmental Law; Administrative Law; Litigation; Intellectual Property. ***Email:*** mocallaghan@slk-law.com

LOUIS E. TOSI, born Martins Ferry, Ohio, April 22, 1949; admitted to bar, 1974, Ohio. *Education:* The Ohio State University (B.A., cum laude, 1971; J.D., cum laude, 1974). Phi Beta Kappa. *Member:* Toledo, Ohio State (Chairman, Committee on Environmental Law, 1984-1988) and American (Member, Sections on: Natural Resources Law; Administrative Law; Past Vice Chair, Air Quality Committee) Bar Associations. (Resident, Toledo, Ohio Office). ***PRACTICE AREAS:*** Environmental Law; Litigation Defense. ***Email:*** ltosi@slk-law.com

RESIDENT ASSOCIATES

MICHAEL A. SNYDER, born North Canton, Ohio, January 8, 1973; admitted to bar, 1998, Ohio; 1999, U.S. District Court, Northern and Southern Districts of Ohio and U.S. Court of Appeals, Sixth Circuit. *Education:* Ohio University (B.A., cum laude, 1995); Capital University (J.D., magna cum laude, 1998). Order of the Curia. Capital University Law Review, 1997-1998. *Member:* Columbus, Ohio State, Federal, and American Bar Associations. ***PRACTICE AREAS:*** Environmental Law; Litigation; Administrative Law; Regulatory Litigation. ***Email:*** msnyder@slk-law.com

KATIE L. TOURNOUX, admitted to bar, 2002, Ohio. *Education:* Saint Mary's College (B.A., cum laude, 1999); Ohio State University Moritz College of Law (J.D., 2002). ***PRACTICE AREAS:*** Litigation. ***Email:*** ktournoux@slk-law.com

OF COUNSEL

WALTER W. RECKLESS, born Nashville, Tennessee, September 12, 1936; admitted to bar, 1969, Ohio; U.S. District Court, Southern and Northern Districts of Ohio and U.S. Court of Appeals, Sixth Circuit. *Education:* The Ohio State University (B.S., 1959; J.D., 1969). Lecturer, Personal Injury Litigation and How to Take a Case to Federal Court, Ohio Legal Center Institute. Member, Examination and Admission Committee, U.S. District Court, Southern District of Ohio, 1977—. *Member:* Columbus (Chairman, Federal District Committee, 1974-1976), Ohio State, Federal and American Bar Associations; Franklin Inns of Court. (Also practicing Individually, Columbus Ohio). ***PRACTICE AREAS:*** Trial Practice; Personal Injury; Products Liability; Professional Negligence; Medical Negligence; Professional Malpractice; Medical Malpractice; Employment Law; White Collar Criminal Defense. ***Email:*** wreckless@slk-law.com

REPRESENTATIVE CLIENTS: AVAILABLE UPON REQUEST.

(For complete biographical data on all personnel, see Professional Biographies at Toledo, Ohio)

SLOWIK & ROBINSON, LLC

250 E. BROAD STREET, SUITE 250
COLUMBUS, OHIO 43215
Telephone: 614-884-4800
Facsimile: 614-884-4801
URL: http://www.s-r-law.com/

Labor and Employment Law, Immigration Law, Small Business Law, Alternative Dispute Resolution, Business Formations.

MEMBERS OF FIRM

DONALD C. SLOWIK, born Cleveland, Ohio, November 9, 1952; admitted to bar, 1980, Ohio. *Education:* Duke University (B.A., magna cum laude, with distinction in philosophy, 1975); Ohio State University (J.D., 1980). Author: "How to Avoid the Employment Verification Form I-9 Pitfalls," Labor and Employment News, Ohio State Bar Association, Vol. 13, Issue 2, Spring 2003. Minority Counsel, Ohio House of Representatives, Columbus, Ohio, 1981-1983. Porter, Wright, Morris & Arthur, Columbus, Ohio, 1983-1992.

(This Listing Continued)

SLOWIK & ROBINSON, LLC, Columbus—Continued

Member: Columbus, Ohio State (Member: Dispute Resolution Committee; Labor and Employment Law Section) and American Bar Associations; American Immigration Lawyers Association. ***PRACTICE AREAS:*** Labor Law; Employment Law; Employment Discrimination; Small Business Law; Professional Practices; Immigration Law; Visas; Mediation. ***Email:*** dslowik@s-r-law.com

KENNETH J. ROBINSON, born Cincinnati, Ohio, May 4, 1972; admitted to bar, 1998, Ohio. *Education:* Miami University (B.A., cum laude, 1994); Ohio State University (J.D., 1998). Adjunct Professor, Paralegal Program, Capital University, 2003—. Harvard Law School, Mediation Workshop, 1991. Author: "Genocide in Cambodia: Documents from the Trial of Pol Pot and Leng Sary," University of Penn. Press, April, 2000. Special Counsel to the State of Ohio, Attorney General's Office, on Immigration Matters". Named: "Ohio Rising Star Super Lawyer for 2005" by Law and Politics (top 2.5% of attorneys practicing 10 years or less, under the age of 40). *Member:* Columbus and Ohio State Bar Associations; American Immigration Lawyers Association. ***LANGUAGES:*** French. ***PRACTICE AREAS:*** Immigration and Naturalization; Business Law; Corporate Law. ***Email:*** krobinson@s-r-law.com

ASSOCIATES

INNA SIMAKOVSKY, born St. Petersburg, Russia, February 15, 1971; admitted to bar, 1998, Washington (Not admitted in Ohio). *Education:* University of Cincinnati (B.A., 1993); The Ohio State University College of Law (J.D., 1998). ***LANGUAGES:*** Russian. ***PRACTICE AREAS:*** Immigration Law. ***Email:*** isimakovsy@s-r-law.com

JULIE C. NEMECEK, born Cincinnati, Ohio, October 25, 1976; admitted to bar, 2004, Ohio. *Education:* The Ohio State University (B.A., 1999); National Taiwan Normal University (1997-1998); The Ohio State University, Moritz College of Law (J.D., 2003). ***LANGUAGES:*** Mandarin Chinese. ***Email:*** jnemecek@s-r-law.com

OF COUNSEL

ANDREW P. SAGARTZ, born Fort Madison, Iowa, February 15, 1967; admitted to bar, 1998, Ohio; 1999, Illinois. *Education:* Lesley College (B.S., Asian Studies, 1992); Thunderbird, The American Graduate School of International Management (M.B.A., with honors, 1995); The Ohio State University (J.D., with distinction, 1998). ***LANGUAGES:*** Japanese and Spanish.

SMITH & COLNER

Established in 1994

261 SOUTH FRONT STREET
COLUMBUS, OHIO 43215
Telephone: 614-228-6040
Fax: 614-228-6099
Email: SmithandColner@aol.com

General Trial and Appellate Practice. Commercial, Negligence, Products Liability, Corporation and Insurance Law.

FIRM PROFILE: Civil litigation practice focuses on business and personal injury with increased concentration on commercial creditors' representation.

MEMBERS OF FIRM

STEVEN LEE SMITH, born Hamilton, Ohio, 1946; admitted to bar, 1973, Ohio and U.S. District Court, Southern District of Ohio; 1980, U.S. Supreme Court. *Education:* Ball State University (B.S., 1968); The Ohio State University (J.D., 1972). *Member:* Columbus and Ohio State Bar Associations; Defense Research Institute; Ohio Academy of Trial Lawyers; Commercial Law League of America. ***PRACTICE AREAS:*** Commercial Law; Insurance Law; Trial Practice.

JAMES D. COLNER, born Cleveland, Ohio, 1953; admitted to bar, 1979, Ohio, U.S. District Court, Southern District of Ohio and U.S. Court of Appeals, Sixth Circuit; U.S. Supreme Court. *Education:* Ohio State University (B.A., 1975); Capital University (J.D., 1979). *Member:* Columbus and Ohio State Bar Associations; Franklin County Trial Lawyers Association; Ohio Academy of Trial Lawyers; The Association of Trial Lawyers of America; American Board of Professional Liability Attorneys; American Board of Trial Advocates. (Certified as a Civil Trial Advocate by the National Board of Trial Advocacy). ***REPORTED CASES:*** Moss v. Nationwide Mutual Ins. Co., (1985) 24 Ohio App. 3d 145; Sedgewick v. Kawasaki Cycleworks, (1997) 71 Ohio App. 3d 117. ***PRACTICE AREAS:*** Civil Trial Law; Business Litigation; Personal Injury. ***Email:*** jdcolner@rrohio.com

LAW OFFICES OF NANCY L. SPONSELLER

COLUMBUS, OHIO

(See Dublin)

Franchise Law, Small Business Law, Divorce Dissolutions, Pre-Marital Agreements, Child Custody, Child Support, Family Law, Estate Planning, Wills and Probate.

SQUIRE, SANDERS & DEMPSEY L.L.P.

1300 HUNTINGTON CENTER
41 SOUTH HIGH STREET
COLUMBUS, OHIO 43215-6197
Telephone: 614-365-2700
Fax: 614-365-2499
URL: http://www.ssd.com

REVISOR OF THE OHIO AND TEXAS LAW DIGESTS FOR THIS DIRECTORY

(This Listing Continued)

The Americas Offices: Cincinnati, Cleveland, Houston, Los Angeles, Miami, New York, Palo Alto, Phoenix, San Francisco, Tallahassee, Tampa, Tysons Corner, Washington DC, West Palm Beach, Caracas, Santo Domingo, Rio de Janeiro.
European Offices: Bratislava, Brussels, Budapest, London, Madrid, Milan, Moscow, Prague, Warsaw.
Asia Offices: Beijing, Hong Kong, Shanghai, Tokyo.
Associated Offices: Bucharest, Dublin, Kyiv, Buenos Aires, Santiago.

Bankruptcy and Reorganization, Chemicals, Communications, Construction and Engineering, Corporate Transactions and Securities Regulation, E-Commerce, Economic Regulation, Education, Energy, Environmental, Health and Safety, Financial Institutions and Services, Financial Services, Gaming and Casinos, Government and Administrative Agencies, Health Care and Hospitals, Health Sciences, Hospitality and Recreation, Insurance, Intellectual Property, International Dispute Resolution, Labor and Employment, Life Sciences, Litigation, Manufacturing, Media and Entertainment, Private Equity, Project Finance, Public Finance, Real Estate, Real Estate and Hospitality, Sports, Steel, Taxation, Technology, Transportation and Utilities.

FIRM PROFILE: As the firm's second largest office, the Columbus office of Squire, Sanders & Dempsey L.L.P. provides a full range of legal services essential for keeping businesses competitive in today's global marketplace while continuing to remain focused on sound business practices and compliance with existing and emerging law. Particular strengths include longstanding practices in corporate, litigation, environmental, public law, labor and employment, real estate, financial services, health care, tax, and estate planning and administration. Growing practices include e-commerce and intellectual property, international, pharmaceuticals, insurance, retail, sports and entertainment law.

The Columbus office provides strategic business counsel to a number of large corporations headquartered throughout the U.S. Midwest and also represents numerous Asia businesses with Ohio operations. Lawyers also counsel clients on the legislative process and assist them in business regulatory matters affecting their industries.

PARTNERS

COLUMBUS OFFICE

DAVID W. ALEXANDER, born Springfield, Ohio, 1952; admitted to bar, 1978, New Hampshire (Inactive); U.S. Court of Appeals, First Circuit; Ohio and U.S. District Court, Southern District of Ohio; U.S. Court of Appeals, Sixth Circuit; U.S. Court of Appeals, Ninth Circuit; U.S. Court of Appeals, Tenth Circuit; U.S. Court of Appeals, Fifth Circuit; U.S. District Court, Northern District of Ohio. *Education:* Wittenberg University (B.A., cum laude, 1974); The Ohio State University (J.D., with honors, 1978). *Member:* Columbus (Civility Program Chair) and Ohio State Bar Associations; Columbus Bar Foundation, Fellow. ***PRACTICE AREAS:*** Arbitration; Complex Commercial Litigation; Insurance Coverage Litigation; International Dispute Resolution; Trademark and Intellectual Property Litigation. ***Email:*** dalexander@ssd.com

VINCENT ATRIANO, born Pescara, Italy, 1963; admitted to bar, 1988, Ohio; U.S. District Court, Southern District of Ohio; U.S. Court of Appeals, Sixth Circuit; U.S. District Court, Northern District of Ohio; U.S. Court of Appeals, Seventh Circuit. *Education:* The Ohio State University (B.A., with honors and distinction, 1985); University of Michigan (J.D., cum laude, 1988). *Member:* Ohio State Bar Association (Member, Environmental Law Committee). ***PRACTICE AREAS:*** Advocacy; Government Litigation; Toxic Tort Litigation; Environmental Health and Safety Litigation. ***Email:*** vatriano@ssd.com

D. LEWIS CLARK, JR., born Dover, Ohio, 1965; admitted to bar, 1990, Ohio; 2002, New York; U.S. District Court, Southern District of Ohio; U.S. Court of Appeals, Sixth Circuit; U.S. District Court, Northern District of Ohio; U.S. Supreme Court; U.S. District Court, Eastern District of Michigan; U.S. District Court, Northern District of Indiana; U.S. Court of Appeals, Fourth Circuit; U.S. Court of Appeals, Eleventh Circuit. *Education:* The University of Akron (B.A., cum laude, 1987); The Ohio State University (J.D., 1990). ***PRACTICE AREAS:*** Labor and Employment. ***Email:*** lclark@ssd.com

TIMOTHY J. COSGROVE, born Cleveland, Ohio, 1961; admitted to bar, 1987, Ohio. *Education:* Cleveland State University (B.A., 1983; J.D., 1987). Director of Legislation and Policy, Office of the Governor, State of Ohio, 1991-1993. Member and Chair: Board of Trustees, Cleveland State University; Chair, Board of Directors, Northeast Midwest Institute; Public Affairs Committee, Greater Cleveland Partnership; Public Affairs Committee, Ohio Chamber of Commerce. *Member:* Ohio State Bar Association; Ohio Lobbying Association. ***PRACTICE AREAS:*** Public Law; Public Finance. ***Email:*** tcosgrove@ssd.com

PHILOMENA M. DANE, born Miami, Florida, 1955; admitted to bar, 1990, Ohio; U.S. Court of Appeals, Sixth Circuit; U.S. District Court, Southern District of Ohio; U.S. Court of Appeals, Fourth Circuit. *Education:* St. Norbert College (B.A., 1977); Western Michigan University (M.A., 1978); The Ohio State University (J.D., summa cum laude, 1989). ***PRACTICE AREAS:*** Litigation; Insurance Litigation; Environmental; Institutional Law; Media Law; Sports Law; First Amendment Law; Commercial Litigation. ***Email:*** pdane@ssd.com

SUSAN M. DiMICKELE, born Canton, Ohio, 1970; admitted to bar, 1995, Ohio; U.S. Court of Appeals, Sixth Circuit; U.S District Court, Southern and Northern Districts of Ohio. *Education:* Miami University (B.A., summa cum laude, 1991); The Ohio State University (J.D., with honors, 1995). ***PRACTICE AREAS:*** Labor and Employment. ***Email:*** sdimickele@ssd.com

PATRICK J. DUGAN, born Lima, Ohio, 1957; admitted to bar, 1982, Ohio. *Education:* Bowling Green State University (B.S., B.A., cum laude, 1979); The Ohio State University (J.D., with honors, 1982). Beta Alpha Psi. Order of the Coif. Included in The Best Lawyers in America, 2006 edition. Member, Board of Directors, Ariel Corporation. Board of Trustees, Raymond E. Mason Foundation. ***PRACTICE AREAS:*** Corporate Law; Financial Services; Capital Markets. ***Email:*** pdugan@ssd.com

CHRISTOPHER J. FRANZMANN, born Indianapolis, Indiana, 1965; admitted to bar, 1991, Indiana (inactive); 1998, Ohio. *Education:* Indiana University (B.S., 1988; J.D., summa cum laude, 1991). *Member:* National Association of Bond Lawyers; Ohio Govern-

(This Listing Continued)

ment Finance Officers Association (Board of Trustees, Education Committee). ***PRACTICE AREAS:*** Tax-Exempt Finance; Economic Development; Project Finance; Public Finance. ***Email:*** cfranzmann@ssd.com

JOHN R. GALL, born San Francisco, California, 1945; admitted to bar, 1971, Ohio; U.S. Court of Appeals, Sixth Circuit; U.S. District Court, Southern District of Ohio; U.S. Supreme Court; U.S. District Court, Northern District of Ohio; U.S. Court of Appeals, Third Circuit; U.S. Court of Appeals, Ninth Circuit; U.S. District Court, Eastern District of Michigan; U.S. Court of Appeals, Federal Circuit; U.S. Court of Appeals, Tenth Circuit; U.S. Court of Appeals, Fourth Circuit; U.S. District Court, Northern District of California. *Education:* Miami University (B.A., 1967); The Ohio State University (J.D., 1970). Trustee, Columbus Marathon, Inc. Anti-Doping Review Board Panel Member, International Tennis Foundation, Association of Tennis Professionals; Women's Tennis Association. Anti-Doping Review Board Panel Member, United States Anti-Doping Agency. *Member:* Columbus, Federal, Ohio State and International Bar Associations; International Association of Defense Counsel. ***PRACTICE AREAS:*** Trial and Appellate Practice; Business Litigation; Contract Litigation; Employment Litigation; Restrictive Covenants; Proprietary Information; Trademark; Copyright; Trade Secret; Professional Liability; Public Contracts; Public Finance. ***Email:*** jgall@ssd.com

DAVID W. GRAUER, born Marysville, Kansas, 1954; admitted to bar, 1985, Ohio. *Education:* University of Kansas (B.S. Pharmacy, 1977); The Ohio State University (M.B.A., 1982); Capital University (J.D., 1984). ***PRACTICE AREAS:*** Corporate; Healthcare; Mergers and Acquisitions; Integrated Healthcare Delivery Systems; Joint Ventures; Medicare and Medicaid. ***Email:*** dgrauer@ssd.com

HOLLY H. HEER, born Columbus, Ohio, 1967; admitted to bar, 1993, Ohio; U.S. Court of Appeals, Sixth Circuit; U.S. District Court, Southern District of Ohio. *Education:* Wellesley College (B.A., 1989); University of Virginia (J.D., 1993). ***PRACTICE AREAS:*** Real Estate; Corporate Law; Housing Law. ***Email:*** hheer@ssd.com

DONALD W. HUGHES, born Lima, Ohio, 1960; admitted to bar, 1997, Ohio. *Education:* Bowling Green State University (B.S., 1982); Morehead State University (M.B.A., 1983); Ohio Northern University (J.D., with distinction, 1997). ***PRACTICE AREAS:*** Corporate Law; Health Care; Mergers and Acquisitions; Corporate Governance. ***Email:*** dhughes@ssd.com

JOHN M. KIRSNER, born Cincinnati, Ohio, 1966; admitted to bar, 1992, Ohio. *Education:* University of Michigan (B.A., 1989); The Ohio State University (J.D., honors, 1992). *Member:* Ohio State Bar Association (Health Law Committee, Chair, 2004-2006; Vice Chair, 2002-2004; Secretary, 2000-2002). ***PRACTICE AREAS:*** Health Insurance; Health Care; Corporate. ***Email:*** jkirsner@ssd.com

STEVEN M. LOEWENGART, born Cincinnati, Ohio, 1953; admitted to bar, 1987, Ohio, U.S. District Court, Northern District of Ohio; U.S. District Court, Southern District of Ohio. *Education:* Northwestern University (B.M., summa cum laude, 1975; M.M., magna cum laude, 1976); University of Cincinnati (J.D., 1987). *Member:* Columbus, Ohio State and American Bar Associations; Central Ohio Self-Insurers Association. ***LANGUAGES:*** German. ***PRACTICE AREAS:*** Labor and Employment Law; General Litigation; Workers; Intentional Torts; Personal Injury Law; Workers Compensation. ***Email:*** sloewengart@ssd.com

DANIEL M. MAHER, born Jacksonville, Florida, 1945; admitted to bar, 1972, Ohio. *Education:* United States Merchant Marine Academy (B.S., 1967); University of Virginia (J.D., 1972). Order of the Coif. *Member:* Columbus (Member, Business Law Committee), Ohio State (Member, Corporate Counsel Section) and American Bar Associations. ***PRACTICE AREAS:*** Corporate; Mergers and Acquisitions; Licensing; Trademarks. ***Email:*** dmaher@ssd.com

STEVEN F. MOUNT, born Nelsonville, Ohio, 1953; admitted to bar, 1979, Massachusetts; 1982, New York; 1986, Ohio. *Education:* Muskingum College (B.A., summa cum laude, 1976); Harvard University (J.D., cum laude, 1979). Author: Mount, 742 T.M. *Real Estate Investment Trusts; Tax Checklist for Formation of* UPREIT, 35 Tax Management Memorandum, No. 3, Feb. 7, 1994; *The Tax Equity and Fiscal Responsibility Act of* 1982--*Safe Harbor Lease Provisions Corralled, But Still Alive and Kicking,* TAXES 707, October 1982. ***PRACTICE AREAS:*** Taxation; Corporate. ***Email:*** smount@ssd.com

WILLIAM A. NOLAN, born Bloomington, Indiana, 1962; admitted to bar, 1989, Ohio; U.S. District Court, Southern District of Ohio; U.S. Court of Appeals, Seventh Circuit; U.S. Court of Appeals, Sixth Circuit. *Education:* Cornell University (B.A., magna cum laude, 1984); Harvard University (J.D., cum laude, 1989). ***PRACTICE AREAS:*** Employment Law; Covenants Not To Compete; College and University Law; Information and Privacy; School Law. ***Email:*** wnolan@ssd.com

MICHAEL R. REED, born Meadville, Pennsylvania, 1962; admitted to bar, 1994, Ohio; U.S. District Court, Northern District of Ohio; U.S. District Court, Southern District of Ohio; U.S. Court of Appeals, Sixth Circuit; U.S. Supreme Court; U.S. Court of Appeals, Eleventh Circuit. *Education:* Allegheny College (B.A., 1984); The Ohio State University (J.D., 1994). ***PRACTICE AREAS:*** Litigation. ***Email:*** mreed@ssd.com

RICHARD W. RUBENSTEIN, born Albany, New York, 1944; admitted to bar, 1969, New York; 1980, Ohio. *Education:* Amherst College (B.A., 1966); New York University (J.D., 1969). ***PRACTICE AREAS:*** Real Estate; Real Estate Finance; Corporate; Mergers and Acquisitions. ***Email:*** rrubenstein@ssd.com

MICHAEL D. SAAD, born Zanesville, Ohio, 1941; admitted to bar, 1966, Ohio. *Education:* University of Dayton; The Ohio State University (B.S., 1963; J.D., summa cum laude, 1966). Order of the Coif. Note Editor, Ohio State University Law Journal. Law Clerk, Chief Justice, Ohio Supreme Court. Member, National Council of State Housing Agencies. *Member:* Columbus (Financial Institutions, Real Estate and Bankruptcy Committees), Ohio State and American Bar Associations; Ohio Housing Council (Board Member). ***PRACTICE AREAS:*** Real Estate; Workouts; Bankruptcy; Limited Partnerships; Corporate; Real Estate Syndication; Tax Credit Syndication. ***Email:*** msaad@ssd.com

PAUL F. SEFCOVIC, born Cleveland, Ohio, 1946; admitted to bar, 1971, Ohio. *Education:* University of Dayton (B.S., 1968); University of Michigan (J.D., cum laude, 1971). ***PRACTICE AREAS:*** Public Law; Corporate; Public Finance; Health Care; Underwriters. ***Email:*** psefcovic@ssd.com

(This Listing Continued)

ALEX SHUMATE, born De Kalb, Mississippi, 1950; admitted to bar, 1975, Ohio; U.S. District Court, Northern and Southern Districts of Ohio; U.S. Supreme Court. *Education:* Ohio Wesleyan University (B.A., 1972); University of Akron (J.D., 1975). (Managing Partner, Columbus Office). ***PRACTICE AREAS:*** Public Law; Legislative Counseling; Administrative Law. ***Email:*** ashumate@ssd.com

KEITH SHUMATE, born Portsmouth, Ohio, 1966; admitted to bar, 1991, Ohio; U.S. Court of Appeals, Sixth Circuit; U.S. District Court, Southern District of Ohio. *Education:* University of Akron (B.A., 1988); The Ohio State University (J.D., 1991). ***PRACTICE AREAS:*** Civil Litigation; Complex Commercial Litigation; Business Litigation; Products Liability Defense; Health Care Litigation. ***Email:*** kshumate@ssd.com

FREDRIC L. SMITH, born Dearborn, Michigan, 1938; admitted to bar, 1963, Ohio. *Education:* Michigan State University (B.A., 1959); University of Michigan (J.D., 1963). ***PRACTICE AREAS:*** Corporate; Tax; Estates and Trusts. ***Email:*** fsmith@ssd.com

GREGORY W. STYPE, born Wooster, Ohio, 1955; admitted to bar, 1982, Ohio. *Education:* College of Wooster (B.A., 1977); The Ohio State University (J.D., 1982). ***PRACTICE AREAS:*** Public Law; Public Finance; Economic Development. ***Email:*** gstype@ssd.com

WILLIAM M. TODD, born Cleveland, Ohio, 1952; admitted to bar, 1976, Ohio; U.S. District Court, Southern District of Ohio; U.S. Supreme Court; U.S. District Court, Northern District of Ohio and U.S. Court of Appeals, Sixth Circuit. *Education:* University of Notre Dame (B.A., with honors, 1973); The Ohio State University (J.D., cum laude, 1976). ***PRACTICE AREAS:*** Health Care; Civil Litigation; Legislative Practice; Election, Campaign and Political Law. ***Email:*** wtodd@ssd.com

BRYAN J. VENESY, born Evanston, Illinois, 1963; admitted to bar, 1988, Ohio. *Education:* Ohio Wesleyan University (B.A., 1985); University of Cincinnati (J.D., 1988). *Member:* Columbus, Ohio State and American Bar Associations. ***PRACTICE AREAS:*** Real Estate; Finance; Corporate. ***Email:*** bvenesy@ssd.com

LEE A. WENDEL, born Van Wert, Ohio, 1962; admitted to bar, 1987, Ohio. *Education:* Ohio Wesleyan University (B.A., 1984); University of Michigan (J.D., cum laude, 1987). *Member:* Columbus (Estate and Gift Tax Committee), Ohio State (Estate Planning, Trust and Probate Section) and American (Real Property, Probate and Trust Law Section) Bar Associations; American College of Trust and Estate Counsel (Fellow). ***PRACTICE AREAS:*** Trusts and Estates; Business Law; Taxation. ***Email:*** lwendel@ssd.com

KAREN A. WINTERS, born Washington, D.C., 1956; admitted to bar, 1981, Ohio, U.S. Court of Appeals, Sixth Circuit; U.S. District Court, Northern District of Ohio; U.S. District Court, Southern District of Ohio. *Education:* Bowling Green State University (B.A., 1978); University of Akron (J.D., 1981). *Member:* Ohio State Bar Association (Board of Governors, Section on Women in the Profession, Environmental Law Committee); Columbus Bar Association (Environmental Law Committee); Ohio Chamber of Commerce (Executive Committee, Energy and Environment Committee). ***PRACTICE AREAS:*** Environmental Law; Litigation. ***Email:*** kwinters@ssd.com

C. CRAIG WOODS, born Laredo, Texas, 1956; admitted to bar, 1981, Ohio; U.S. District Court, Southern District of Ohio; U.S. Court of Appeals, Sixth Circuit; U.S. Supreme Court; U.S. District Court, Northern District of Ohio; U.S. District Court, District of Maryland. *Education:* Dartmouth College (B.A., magna cum laude, 1978); University of Virginia (J.D., 1981). ***PRACTICE AREAS:*** Civil Litigation; Commercial Litigation; Environmental Litigation; Professional Liability Litigation; Product Liability Litigation; Tort Litigation. ***Email:*** cwoods@ssd.com

COUNSEL

COLUMBUS OFFICE

ROBERTA L. FISHER, born Cleveland, Ohio, 1952; admitted to bar, 1976, Ohio. *Education:* The Ohio State University (B.A., summa cum laude, with distinction in Linguistics, 1973); Harvard University (J.D., 1976). *Member:* Ohio State Bar Association. ***LANGUAGES:*** French. ***PRACTICE AREAS:*** Public Securities; Public Finance. ***Email:*** rfisher@ssd.com

RICHARD R. MURPHEY JR., born Athens, Ohio, 1925; admitted to bar, 1950, Ohio. *Education:* University of Pennsylvania; Washington University (A.B., 1947); Harvard University (LL.B., 1950). *Member:* Columbus and Ohio State Bar Associations; Columbus Bar Foundation; American Judicator Society. ***PRACTICE AREAS:*** Corporate. ***Email:*** rmurphey@ssd.com

FRED A. SUMMER, born Columbus, Ohio, 1946; admitted to bar, 1974, Ohio; U.S. District Court, Southern District of Ohio. *Education:* Harvard University (A.B., cum laude, 1968); University of Michigan (J.D., magna cum laude, 1973). Order of the Coif. Member, University of Michigan Journal of Law Reform. *Member:* Columbus (Securities Law Committee), Ohio State (Member, Corporation Law Committee) and American (Member: Federal Regulation of Securities Committee) Bar Associations. ***PRACTICE AREAS:*** Corporate; Securities. ***Email:*** fsummer@ssd.com

OF COUNSEL

COLUMBUS OFFICE

H. CORT DOUGHTY, JR., born Charleston, West Virginia, 1939; admitted to bar, 1965, West Virginia; 1966, Ohio; U.S. District Court, Southern District of Ohio. *Education:* Xavier University (B.A., 1961); West Virginia University (LL.B., 1965). *Member:* Columbus Bar Association (Real Estate Committee); Columbus Bar Foundation. ***PRACTICE AREAS:*** Real Estate Development; Real Estate Acquisitions; Corporate Real Estate; Construction Law. ***Email:*** hdoughty@ssd.com

MICHAEL B. GARDINER, born Columbus, Ohio, 1967; admitted to bar, 1992, Illinois; 2005, Ohio. *Education:* Northwestern University (B.A., 1989); The Ohio State University (J.D., cum laude, 1992); University of Chicago (M.B.A., with high honors, 2003). ***PRACTICE AREAS:*** Corporate Law; Mergers, Acquisitions and Divestitures; Finance. ***Email:*** mgardiner@ssd.com

KIM A. RIECK, born Youngstown, Ohio, 1952; admitted to bar, 1977, Ohio; U.S. District Court, Southern District of Ohio. *Education:* Case Western Reserve University (B.A.,

(This Listing Continued)

SQUIRE, SANDERS & DEMPSEY L.L.P., Columbus—Continued

1974); The Ohio State University (J.D., 1977). *Member:* International Council of Shopping Centers. ***PRACTICE AREAS:*** Real Estate Development; Corporate Real Estate; Real Estate Acquisitions; Real Estate Finance. ***Email:*** krieck@ssd.com

TIM J. ROBINSON, born Bexley, Ohio, 1962; admitted to bar, 1990, Ohio; U.S. District Court, Southern District of Ohio; U.S. Court of Appeals, Sixth Circuit. *Education:* Ohio State University (B.S., 1985); University of San Diego School of Law Institute on International & Comparative Law, London, England (Cert., 1988); Northeastern University (J.D., 1990). Intern, Hon. Dolores K. Sloviter, Chief Judge, U.S. Court of Appeals, Third Circuit, 1989. Law Clerk, Hon. Rosemary Gambardella, U.S. Bankruptcy Court, District of New Jersey, 1990-1991. *Member:* Cincinnati and Columbus Bar Associations. ***PRACTICE AREAS:*** Bankruptcy Law; Reorganization. ***Email:*** tjrobinson@ssd.com

JAMES E. P. SISTO, born Phoenixville, Pennsylvania, 1959; admitted to bar, 1984, Ohio. *Education:* Ohio Wesleyan University (B.A., 1981); Capital University (J.D., 1984); Georgetown University (LL.M., 1988). Adjunct Professor of Law, Capital University Law School and Ohio State University Law School. Former Deputy Director, Ohio Department of Development, International Trade Division, 1993-2000. Secretary to the Board, International Development Organizations, Inc. Past Chair, International Trade and Investment Committee, National Association of State Development Agencies, Inc. *Member:* Columbus Bar Association; Northern Ohio District Export Council; Southern Ohio District Council (Past Chair, International Finance Committee). ***PRACTICE AREAS:*** Business Law; Commercial Law; Corporate Law; International Trade Law; International Law; Government; Public Finance. ***Email:*** jsisto@ssd.com.

SENIOR COUNSEL

COLUMBUS OFFICE

DAVID J. YOUNG, born Troy, Ohio, 1932; admitted to bar, 1955, Ohio; 1997, North Carolina; U.S. District Court, Northern and Southern Districts of Ohio; U.S. Supreme Court; U.S. Court of Appeals, Sixth Circuit. *Education:* University of Dayton; The Ohio State University (J.D., 1955). ***PRACTICE AREAS:*** Litigation; Complex Litigation; Health Care; Antitrust; RICO; Legal Malpractice. ***Email:*** djyoung@ssd.com

SENIOR ATTORNEY

COLUMBUS OFFICE

CRAIG A. STURTZ, born Columbus, Ohio, 1967; admitted to bar, 1992, Ohio and U.S. District Court, Northern District of Ohio; U.S. District Court, Southern District of Ohio; U.S. Court of Appeals, Sixth Circuit. *Education:* Indiana University (B.S., 1989); Capital University (J.D., cum laude, 1992). ***PRACTICE AREAS:*** Environmental Law; Administrative Law; Commercial Real Estate; Economic Regulation; Government and Administrative Agency; Manufacturing. ***Email:*** csturtz@ssd.com

ASSOCIATES

COLUMBUS OFFICE

LAING P. AKERS, born Columbus, Ohio, 1971; admitted to bar, 2000, Ohio. *Education:* Wittenberg University (B.A., summa cum laude, 1994); Capital University (J.D., summa cum laude, 2000). Order of the Curia. ***PRACTICE AREAS:*** Corporate Law; Real Estate. ***Email:*** lakers@ssd.com

TARA ASCHENBRAND, born Cincinnati, Ohio, 1977; admitted to bar, 2002, Ohio; U.S. District Court, Southern District of Ohio. *Education:* The Ohio State University (B.S.B.A., summa cum laude, 1999; J.D., with honors, 2002). ***PRACTICE AREAS:*** Labor and Employment.

BETH C. BOLYARD, born Toledo, Ohio, 1974; admitted to bar, 2001, Ohio. *Education:* Ohio Northern University (B.A., 1997); Capital University (J.D., cum laude, 2001). Order of the Curia. ***PRACTICE AREAS:*** Real Estate. ***Email:*** bbolyard@ssd.com

KRISTEN J. BROWN, born Pittsburgh, Pennsylvania, 1963; admitted to bar, 1990, Ohio; U.S. Court of Appeals, Sixth Circuit; U.S. District Court, Southern and Northern Districts of Ohio. *Education:* The Ohio State University (B.A., 1986); Capital University (J.D., cum laude, 1990). ***PRACTICE AREAS:*** Litigation. ***Email:*** kbrown@ssd.com

PATRICK D. CORNELIUS, born Columbus, Ohio, 1970; admitted to bar, 1997, Ohio. *Education:* University of Notre Dame (B.A., with high honors, 1993); University of Virginia (J.D., 1997). ***LANGUAGES:*** Japanese, Portuguese. ***PRACTICE AREAS:*** Corporate Law. ***Email:*** pcornelius@ssd.com

KELLY T. CUSTER, born Columbus, Ohio, 1970; admitted to bar, 2005, Ohio. *Education:* Miami University (B.S., magna cum laude, 2001); Duke University (J.D., 2004). Beta Gamma Sigma. ***LANGUAGES:*** Spanish. ***PRACTICE AREAS:*** Litigation. ***Email:*** kcuster@ssd.com

GREGORY R. DANIELS, born Traverse City, Michigan, 1976; admitted to bar, 2001, Ohio; U.S. District Court, Southern District of Ohio. *Education:* The Ohio State University (B.A., magna cum laude, with honors, 1998); University of Michigan (J.D., 2001). Phi Beta Kappa. ***PRACTICE AREAS:*** Public Finance. ***Email:*** gdaniels@ssd.com

JESSICA E. DeMONTE, born Milton, Florida, 1975; admitted to bar, 2000, Ohio; U.S. District Court, Southern District of Ohio. *Education:* The Ohio State University (B.A., summa cum laude, 1997; J.D., 2000). ***LANGUAGES:*** Spanish. ***PRACTICE AREAS:*** Environmental Law. ***Email:*** jdemonte@ssd.com

RYAN G. EASTHAM, born Dayton, Ohio, 1967; admitted to bar, 1997, Ohio. *Education:* Ohio University (B.B.A., summa cum laude, 1990); University of Dayton (M.B.A., 1992); The Ohio State University (J.D., 1997). ***PRACTICE AREAS:*** Taxation.

JESSICA D. GOLDMAN, born Columbus, Ohio, 1977; admitted to bar, 2003, Ohio; U.S. District Court, Southern District of Ohio. *Education:* Kenyon College (B.A., magna cum laude, 2000); Vanderbilt University (J.D., 2003). Phi Beta Kappa. ***PRACTICE AREAS:*** Litigation. ***Email:*** jgoldman@ssd.com

(This Listing Continued)

KYU CHANG HAN, born Seoul, Korea, 1966; admitted to bar, 2004, Ohio. *Education:* Seoul National University (B.A., cum laude, 1988); Ohio State University (J.D., with honors, 2004). ***PRACTICE AREAS:*** Corporate Law.

AMY RUTH ITA, born Cleveland, Ohio, 1976; admitted to bar, 2001, Ohio; U.S. Court of Appeals, Sixth Circuit; U.S. District Court, Northern District of Ohio; U.S. District Court, Southern District of Ohio; U.S. Court of Appeals, Eleventh Circuit. *Education:* George Washington University (B.A., cum laude, 1998); The Ohio State University (J.D., cum laude, 2001). ***PRACTICE AREAS:*** Labor and Employment. ***Email:*** aita@ssd.com

CORIE MARTY JUDGE, born Wheeling, West Virginia, 1972; admitted to bar, 1998, Ohio; U.S. District Court, Northern and Southern Districts of Ohio; U.S. Court of Appeals, Sixth Circuit. *Education:* Denison University (B.A., cum laude, 1994); The Ohio State University (J.D., with honors, 1998). ***PRACTICE AREAS:*** Labor and Employment; Education Law; Workers Compensation. ***Email:*** cjudge@ssd.com

GRETA M. KEARNS, born Murphysboro, Illinois, 1971; admitted to bar, 1997, Ohio; U.S. District Court, Southern District of Ohio. *Education:* University of Kansas (B.A., with highest distinction, 1993); University of Iowa (J.D., with distinction, 1997). ***PRACTICE AREAS:*** Labor and Employment. ***Email:*** gkearns@ssd.com

RAYMOND C. KEYSER, born Steubenville, Ohio, 1973; admitted to bar, 2002, Ohio; 2004, Pennsylvania. *Education:* Mount Vernon Nazarene College (B.A., summa cum laude, 1995); The Ohio State University (J.D., with honors, 2002) Order of the Coif. Associate Editor, The Ohio State Law Journal. ***PRACTICE AREAS:*** Real Estate.

THOMAS F. KIBBEY, born Wilmington, Ohio, 1964; admitted to bar, 2002, Ohio. *Education:* University of South Florida (B.A., summa cum laude, 1999); The Ohio State University (J.D., summa cum laude, 2002). ***PRACTICE AREAS:*** Real Estate. ***Email:*** tkibbey@ssd.com

JILL S. KIRILA, born Sharon, Pennsylvania, 1972; admitted to bar, 1997, Ohio; U.S. Court of Appeals, Sixth Circuit; U.S. District Court, Northern District of Ohio; U.S. District Court, Southern District of Ohio. *Education:* The Ohio State University (B.A., summa cum laude, 1994); Georgetown University (J.D., 1997). ***LANGUAGES:*** Spanish. ***PRACTICE AREAS:*** Labor and Employment. ***Email:*** jkirila@ssd.com

TIFFANY L. KOMASARA, born Warren, Michigan, 1971; admitted to bar, 2001, Ohio; U.S. District Court, Southern District of Ohio; U.S. Court of Appeals, Sixth Circuit; U.S. Court of Appeals, Fourth District. *Education:* Capital University (B.Mus., magna cum laude, 1993; J.D., magna cum laude, 2001). ***PRACTICE AREAS:*** Labor and Employment. ***Email:*** tkomasara@ssd.com

ANECA E. LASLEY, born Sidney, Ohio, 1975; admitted to bar, 2000, Ohio; U.S. District Court, Southern District of Ohio. *Education:* Ohio Northern University (B.A., cum laude, 1997); The Ohio State University (J.D., with honors, 2000). Member and Managing Editor, The Ohio State Law Journal. ***PRACTICE AREAS:*** Litigation; Adoption Law. ***Email:*** alasley@ssd.com

T. BENNETT LITLE, born Zanesville, Ohio, 1975; admitted to bar, 2002, Massachusetts (inactive); 2004, Ohio. *Education:* Miami University (B.A., cum laude, 1998); Duke University (J.D., 2001). ***PRACTICE AREAS:*** Public Securities. ***Email:*** blitle@ssd.com

MARY C. MERTZ, born Dayton, Ohio, 1965; admitted to bar, 2002, Ohio; U.S. District Court, Northern District of Ohio; U.S. District Court, Southern District of Ohio. *Education:* The American University (B.S., 1987); George Washington University (M.A., 1990); Ohio State University (J.D., summa cum laude, 2002). Order of the Coif. ***PRACTICE AREAS:*** Litigation. ***Email:*** mmertz@ssd.com

J. SETH METCALF, born Columbus, Ohio, 1979; admitted to bar, 2004, Ohio. *Education:* Ohio State University (B.A., cum laude, 2001); Cornell University (J.D., 2004). ***PRACTICE AREAS:*** Public Securities. ***Email:*** smetcalf@ssd.com

ANDREW D. M. MILLER, born Dayton, Ohio, 1975; admitted to bar, 2002, Ohio; U.S. Court of Appeals, Fifth Circuit; U.S. District Court, Southern District of Texas; U.S. District Court, Southern District of Ohio. *Education:* Ohio University (B.B.A., magna cum laude, 1998); Ohio State University (J.D., summa cum laude, 2001). Order of the Coif. ***PRACTICE AREAS:*** Litigation. ***Email:*** amiller@ssd.com

MATTHEW J. MILLER, born Columbus, Ohio, 1978; admitted to bar, 2003, Ohio. *Education:* Ashland University (B.A., 2000); Capital University (J.D., 2003); Ohio University (M.S.A., 2003). ***PRACTICE AREAS:*** Public Securities. ***Email:*** mjmiller@ssd.com

ROBERT D. NAUMAN, born Mansfield, Ohio, 1971; admitted to bar, 2002, Ohio. *Education:* The Ohio State University (B.A., 1994); Capital University (J.D., summa cum laude, 2002). Order of the Curia. ***PRACTICE AREAS:*** Health Care. ***Email:*** rnauman@ssd.com

KEELY J. RHODES, born South Bend, Indiana, 1977; admitted to bar, 2003, Ohio. *Education:* Princeton University (A.B., 1999); University of Michigan (J.D., 2002). ***PRACTICE AREAS:*** Real Estate. ***Email:*** krhodes@ssd.com

KRISTIN E. RICHNER, born Canton, Ohio, 1975; admitted to bar, 2000, California (inactive), U.S. District Court, Central District of California; 2004, Ohio; U.S. District Court, Southern District of California; U.S. District Court, Northern District of California; U.S. Court of Appeals, Ninth Circuit. *Education:* Denison University (B.A., summa cum laude, 1997); University of California, Los Angeles (J.D., 2000). Order of the Coif. ***PRACTICE AREAS:*** Bankruptcy. ***Email:*** krichner@ssd.com

ERIK J. RICKARD, born Wilmington, Ohio, 1972; admitted to bar, 1997, Ohio. *Education:* Denison University (B.A., summa cum laude, 1994); Duke University (J.D., cum laude, LL.M., 1997). ***PRACTICE AREAS:*** Real Estate; Real Estate and Hospitality. ***Email:*** erickard@ssd.com

ETHAN E. RII, born South Korea, 1974; admitted to bar, 2002, Michigan (Not admitted in Ohio). *Education:* University of Michigan (B.A., 1997); University of Minnesota (J.D., 2002). ***LANGUAGES:*** Korean. ***PRACTICE AREAS:*** Health Care.

EMILY E. ROOT, born Troy, Ohio, 1976; admitted to bar, 2003, Ohio; U.S. District Court, Southern District of Ohio; U.S. Court of Appeals, Sixth Circuit. *Education:* Ohio State University (B.A., summa cum laude, 1998; J.D., summa cum laude, 2003). Phi Beta Kappa. Order of the Coif. ***PRACTICE AREAS:*** Litigation. ***Email:*** eroot@ssd.com

(This Listing Continued)

MATTHEW L. SAGONE, born Columbus, Ohio, 1968; admitted to bar, 1994, Ohio; U.S. Court of Appeals, Sixth Circuit; U.S. District Court, Southern District of Ohio. *Education:* The Ohio State University (B.A., cum laude, with honors, 1991); Capital University (J.D., 1994). ***PRACTICE AREAS:*** Construction Law; Real Estate. ***Email:*** msagone@ssd.com

AARON A. SEAMON, born Gallipolis, Ohio, 1973; admitted to bar, 1999, Ohio. *Education:* Wittenberg University (B.A., 1996); University of Dayton (J.D., magna cum laude, 1999). ***PRACTICE AREAS:*** Corporate Law. ***Email:*** aseamon@ssd.com

P. BRIAN SEE, born Cleveland, Ohio, 1975; admitted to bar, 2000, Ohio; U.S. District Court, Southern District of Ohio. *Education:* Yale University (B.A., 1997); Duke University (J.D., 2000). ***PRACTICE AREAS:*** Litigation. ***Email:*** bsee@ssd.com

KENDRA S. SHERMAN, born Edmonton, Alberta, Canada, 1970; admitted to bar, 1997, Ohio, U.S. District Court, Southern and Northern Districts of Ohio; U.S. Court of Appeals, Eleventh Circuit. *Education:* Stanford University (B.A., 1992); The Ohio State University (J.D., 1997). ***PRACTICE AREAS:*** Environmental Law. ***Email:*** ksherman@ssd.com

JULIE B. SMITH, born Columbus, Ohio, 1979; admitted to bar, 2004, Ohio. *Education:* Bowling Green State University (B.A., cum laude, 2001); Northwestern University (J.D., 2004). Phi Beta Kappa. ***PRACTICE AREAS:*** Labor and Employment.

HEATHER L. STUTZ, born Steubenville, Ohio, 1980; admitted to bar, 2004, Ohio; U.S. District Court, Southern District of Ohio; U.S. Court of Appeals, Sixth Circuit. *Education:* Ohio Northern University (B.A., summa cum laude, 2001; J.D., summa cum laude, 2004). ***PRACTICE AREAS:*** Litigation.

JOHNATHAN E. SULLIVAN, born Columbus, Ohio, 1973; admitted to bar, 2000, Ohio; U.S. District Court, Southern District of Ohio; U.S. Court of Appeals, Sixth Circuit; U.S. Court of Appeals, Eleventh Circuit; U.S. District Court, Northern District of Ohio and U.S. District Court, Eastern District of Michigan; U.S. District Court, Northern District of Indiana. *Education:* The Ohio State University (B.A., summa cum laude, 1996; J.D., 2000). Order of the Coif. ***Email:*** jsullivan@ssd.com

PAMELA HACKES THURSTON, born Washington, D.C., 1953; admitted to bar, 1978, District of Columbia; 1982, Virginia; 1987, Ohio; U.S. Court of Appeals, District of Columbia, Federal, Fourth, Ninth and Sixth Circuits. *Education:* Wellesley College (B.A., with honors, 1974); Georgetown University (J.D., 1978). ***PRACTICE AREAS:*** Complex Litigation. ***Email:*** pthurston@ssd.com

JEFFREY R. WAHL, born Marion, Indiana, 1976; admitted to bar, 2002, Ohio; U.S. District Court, Southern District of Ohio; U.S. District Court, Northern District of Ohio; U.S. Court of Appeals, Sixth Circuit. *Education:* Ohio Northern University (B.A., high distinction, 1998; J.D., high distinction, 2002). ***PRACTICE AREAS:*** Corporate Law. ***Email:*** jwahl@ssd.com

GREG R. WEHRER, born Washington, Pennsylvania, 1972; admitted to bar, 1997, Ohio; U.S. District Court, Northern and Southern Districts of Ohio; U.S. Court of Appeals, Sixth Circuit. *Education:* Bowling Green State University (B.A., cum laude, 1993); Vanderbilt University (J.D., 1997). ***PRACTICE AREAS:*** Litigation. ***Email:*** gwehrer@ssd.com

PHILIP R. WESTERMAN, born Marshall, Michigan, 1967; admitted to bar, 1996, Indiana (inactive); 1998, Ohio. *Education:* Wabash College (B.A., magna cum laude, 1989); The Ohio State University (J.D., with honors, 1996). ***PRACTICE AREAS:*** Real Estate. ***Email:*** pwesterman@ssd.com

LORI MAIORCA ZANCOURIDES, born Youngstown, Ohio, 1978; admitted to bar, 2003, Ohio; U.S. District Court, Southern District of Ohio. *Education:* Capital University (B.A., summa cum laude, 2000); The Ohio State University (J.D., with honors, 2003). Order of the Coif. ***PRACTICE AREAS:*** Labor and Employment. ***Email:*** lzancourides@ssd.com

REVISOR OF THE OHIO AND TEXAS LAW DIGESTS FOR THIS DIRECTORY

(For Biographical Data on Cincinnati and Cleveland, Ohio, Miami and Tampa, Florida, Houston, Texas, New York, New York, Phoenix, Arizona, Washington, D.C., Los Angeles, Palo Alto and San Francisco, California, Tysons Corner, Virginia, Rio de Janeiro, Brazil, Bratislava, Slovak Republic, Brussels, Belgium, Budapest, Hungary, London, England, Madrid, Spain, Milan, Italy, Moscow, Russian Federation, Prague, Czech Republic, Warsaw, Poland, Beijing and Hong Kong, China and Tokyo, Japan Personnel, see Professional Biographies at those Points Respectively).

STEBELTON, ARANDA & SNIDER

A LEGAL PROFESSIONAL ASSOCIATION

COLUMBUS, OHIO

(See Lancaster)

Personal Injury, Automobile Accidents and Injuries, Wrongful Death, Medical Malpractice, Civil Litigation, Business and Tax Planning and Corporations, Family Law, Divorce, Child Custody, Child Support and Adoptions, Residential and Commercial Real Estate, Probate, Elder Law, Estate Planning and Employment Law.

STANLEY R. STEIN

280 NORTH HIGH STREET
SUITE 220
COLUMBUS, OHIO 43215
Telephone: 614-224-7077
Fax: 614-224-5519
Email: stanstein@ssatty.ldmi.net
URL: http://www.stansteinlaw.com

Workers Compensation (Defense/Claimant), Social Security Disability, Civil Litigation.

STANLEY R. STEIN, born Cleveland, Ohio, August 11, 1945; admitted to bar, 1971, Ohio; 1972, U.S. District Court, Southern District of Ohio; 1977, U.S. Court of Appeals, Sixth Circuit. *Education:* Ohio University (B.B.A., 1967); Cleveland Marshall College of Law (J.D., 1971). Assistant Attorney General, Ohio, 1971-1974. *Member:* Columbus (Member, Workers' Compensation Committee) and Ohio State (Member, Workers Compensation Committee, Chairman, 1989-1991) Bar Associations; Ohio Academy of Trial Lawyers. ***PRACTICE AREAS:*** Workers Compensation Law; Social Security Disability; Civil Litigation.

STRIP, HOPPERS, LEITHART, McGRATH & TERLECKY CO., LPA

Established in 1960

575 S. 3RD STREET
COLUMBUS, OHIO 43215
Telephone: 614-228-6345
Fax: 614-228-6369
URL: http://www.columbuslawyer.net
Email: jwh@columbuslawyer.net
URL: http://www.lawyers.com/shlmtlpa

Business Matters, Corporations, Limited Liability Companies, Insolvency, Receivership, Bankruptcy, Construction, Probate, Personal Injury, Estate Planning, Professional Associations, Ethics Representation, Civil Litigation, Family Law, Real Estate, Trusts and Wills, Elder Law, Zoning and Acquisition, Tax Planning, Discrimination.

FIRM PROFILE: Strip, Hoppers, Leithart, McGrath & Terlecky Co. LPA has experience helping individuals and businesses sort through the complexities of the legal system and achieve their goals. Whether it's tax advice, litigation, or estate and business planning, we have the knowledge, experience and dedication you expect from a law firm.

Founded in 1960, Strip, Hoppers, Leithart, McGrath & Terlecky Co. LPA is committed to providing clients with dependable, affordable legal advice in all business, financial and personal matters. Our goal is to make certain our clients receive quality advice, value for the dollar and the peace of mind that comes from knowing that caring, experienced professionals are working for you.

A. C. STRIP, born Antwerp, Belgium, April 13, 1936; admitted to bar, 1960, Ohio; 1966, U.S. Supreme Court. *Education:* The Ohio State University (B.A., 1957; J.D., 1960). *Member:* Columbus and Ohio State Bar Associations. [With U.S. Army, O.C.S., 1960-1961]. ***LANGUAGES:*** French. ***PRACTICE AREAS:*** Business Law; Corporate Law; Insolvency. ***Email:*** acs@columbuslawyer.net

JOHN WM. HOPPERS, born Wheeling, West Virginia, November 23, 1939; admitted to bar, 1968, Ohio and U.S. District Court, Southern District of Ohio; U.S. Supreme Court. *Education:* West Liberty State College (B.A., 1962); The Ohio State University (J.D., 1968). *Member:* Columbus, Ohio State and American Bar Associations. ***PRACTICE AREAS:*** Business Planning; Business Formation; Estate Planning; Receiverships; Probate. ***Email:*** jwh@columbuslawyer.net

PAUL W. LEITHART, born Columbus, Ohio, May 18, 1955; admitted to bar, 1981, Ohio. *Education:* Hillsdale College (B.A., 1977); Capital University (J.D., 1981). Phi Alpha Theta; Delta Theta Phi. Author, Case Note, "Workers Compensation—Appeal Claim," Capital University Law Review, Summer 1980 issue. Safety Director, City of Gahanna, 1988. *Member:* Columbus (Member, Committees on Workers Compensation, Municipal Court and Criminal Law), Ohio State and American Bar Associations. ***PRACTICE AREAS:*** Civil Practice; Personal Injury; Family Law. ***Email:*** pwl@columbuslawyer.net

TIMOTHY J. McGRATH, born Columbus, Ohio, May 24, 1943; admitted to bar, 1969, Ohio; 1974, U.S. District Court, Southern District of Ohio. *Education:* The Ohio State University (B.S. in Bus. Adm., 1965; J.D., cum laude, 1969). Instructor, Business Law, Capital University, Graduate School of Administration, 1987 and 1988. *Member:* Columbus (Member, 1974-1978 and Chairman, 1976-1978, Interprofessional Committee; Member, Real Property Law Committee, 1972—; Member, 1976— and Chairman, 1979-1981, Lawyer Referral Service Committee), Ohio State and American Bar Associations. ***PRACTICE AREAS:*** Real Property; Business Law; Probate; Estate Planning. ***Email:*** tjm@columbuslawyer.net

MYRON N. TERLECKY, born Youngstown, Ohio, July 9, 1959; admitted to bar, 1984, Ohio; 1985, U.S. District Court, Southern District of Ohio. *Education:* John Carroll University (B.A., 1981); Capital University (J.D., 1984). Recipient, Dean's Award for Outstanding Service, 1984. President, Capital University Student Bar Association, 1984. *Member:* Columbus, Ohio State and American Bar Associations. ***PRACTICE AREAS:*** Bankruptcy; Business Law. ***Email:*** mnt@columbuslawyer.net

NELSON E. GENSHAFT, admitted to bar, 1973, Ohio. *Education:* Wharton School of Finance and Commerce, University of Pennsylvania (B.S., 1970); Case Western Reserve University School of Law (J.D., 1973). *Member:* Columbus Bar Association (Member, Board of Governors, 2001—; Chair, Professional Ethics Committee, 1994-1998). ***PRACTICE AREAS:*** Business Litigation; Professional Responsibility; Regulatory Law; Administrative Agency Law. ***Email:*** neg@columbuslawyer.net

KEN GOLDBERG, born Rockville, Maryland; admitted to bar, 1992, Ohio; 1993, U.S. District Court, Northern and Southern Districts of Ohio; 1994, Maryland. *Education:* College of William & Mary (B.A., 1987); Capital University (J.D., 1992). *Member:* Columbus (Member, Domestic Relations and Business Law Committee) and Ohio State Bar Associations; Franklin County Trial Lawyers Association. ***PRACTICE AREAS:*** Civil Litigation; Domestic Relations; Family Law; Divorce; Business Law; Insurance Litigation. ***Email:*** krg@columbuslawyer.net

AARON C. FIRSTENBERGER, born Columbus, Ohio; admitted to bar, 2000, Ohio. *Education:* Otterbien College (B.A., 1992); Capitol University (J.D., cum laude, 2000). *Member:* Columbus and Ohio State Bar Associations. ***PRACTICE AREAS:*** Real Estate; Estate Planning; General Practice. ***Email:*** acf@columbuslawyer.net

(This Listing Continued)

STRIP, HOPPERS, LEITHART, McGRATH & TERLECKY CO., LPA, Columbus—Continued

ANDREW C. HALL, born Columbus, Ohio; admitted to bar, 1996, Ohio; 1998, U.S. District Court, Northern and Southern Districts of Ohio and U.S. Court of Appeals, Sixth Circuit. *Education:* Otterbein College (B.A., 1989); Capital University (J.D., 1996). *Member:* Columbus Bar Association. ***PRACTICE AREAS:*** Estate Planning; Probate; Business; Real Estate; Domestic Relations; Divorce. ***Email:*** ach@columbuslawyer.net

JERRY E. PEER, JR., born Columbus, Ohio; admitted to bar, 2002, Ohio. *Education:* Ohio Dominican College (B.A., 1995); Capital University (J.D., 2002). *Member:* Columbus, Ohio State and American Bar Associations. ***PRACTICE AREAS:*** Business Litigation; Insolvency; Estate Planning. ***Email:*** jep@columbuslawyer.net

REBECCA J. STUMLER

1500 W. 3RD AVENUE, SUITE 127
COLUMBUS, OHIO 43212
Telephone: 614-487-8210
Fax: 614-487-8212
Email: rjstumler@aol.com
URL: http://www.stumlerlaw.com

Family Law, Divorce, Child Custody, Child Support, Visitation Rights, Adoption Law, Paternity, Domestic Violence, Bankruptcy Law, Civil Litigation.

REBECCA J. STUMLER, born Louisville, Kentucky, April 6, 1961; admitted to bar, 1990, Ohio and U.S. District Court, Southern District of Ohio. *Education:* University of Louisville (B.A., 1986); Capital University (J.D., 1990). Magistrate, Knox County, Court of Common Pleas, 2003. *Columbus (Member, Family Law Section) and Ohio State Bar Associations.* ***PRACTICE AREAS:*** Family Law; Divorce; Child Custody; Child Support; Visitation Rights; Adoption Law; Paternity; Domestic Violence; Bankruptcy; Civil Litigation.

IRA B. SULLY

844 SOUTH FRONT STREET
COLUMBUS, OHIO 43206
Telephone: 614-443-3930
Fax: 614-443-7463
URL: http://www.lawyers.com/irasullylaw

Real Estate, Business and Commercial Law. Commercial Collections, Contracts, Small Business Law, Wills and Probate, Trusts and Estate Planning.

FIRM PROFILE: As a sole practitioner, I have primarily focused my practice on business, commercial, real estate and probate matters since 1981. Having previously been with a large firm, as well as having been in-house counsel for a large corporation, I can provide the same level of sophisticated services as a large firm at a more economic rate.

IRA B. SULLY, born Columbus, Ohio, June 3, 1947; admitted to bar, 1974, Ohio; 1975, U.S. District Court, Southern District of Ohio. *Education:* The Ohio State University (B.A., cum laude, 1969; J.D., summa cum laude, 1974). Phi Beta Kappa; Order of the Coif. Listed in Who's Who in American Law, 1990—. Instructor, Real Property Law, Columbus State Community College, 1982-1987. Special Counsel to Attorney General of Ohio, 1983-1994. *Member:* Columbus, Ohio State and American Bar Associations. [E4, U.S. Army Reserves, 1975-1980]

REPRESENTATIVE CLIENTS: Borden, Inc.; Caravan Trailer Park, Inc.; Thomas Fortin Realtors; Star Time Video; Badurina Construction Co., Inc.; Barnes Stucco, Inc.
APPROVED AGENT FOR: Ohio Bar Title Insurance Co.; First American Title Insurance Co.
LOCAL COUNSEL FOR: Central Ohio Chapter, Video Software Dealers Assn.

TAFT, STETTINIUS & HOLLISTER LLP

Established in 1885
TWELFTH FLOOR
21 EAST STATE STREET
COLUMBUS, OHIO 43215-4221
Telephone: 614-221-2838
Facsimile: 614-221-2007
URL: http://www.taftlaw.com

Cincinnati, Ohio Office: 425 Walnut Street, Suite 1800. Telephone: 513-381-2838
Covington, Kentucky Office: 1717 Dixie Highway, Suite 340. Telephone: 859-331-2838; 513-381-2838.
Cleveland, Ohio Office: 3500 BP Tower, 200 Public Square. Telephone: 216-241-2838.
Dayton, Ohio Office: 110 North Main Street, Suite 900. Telephone: 937-228-2838.

Antitrust, Bankruptcy and Debtor/Creditor Rights, Business and Finance, E-Business (Internet and E-Commerce), Employee Benefits/ERISA and Tax-Planning, Environmental Law, Family Law, Family Business Planning, Franchise, General Litigation, Health Care, Immigration, Institutional Finance, Intellectual Property and Technology Group, International, Japanese Practice, Labor and Employment, Mergers and Acquisitions, Nonprofit and Tax-Exempt Organizations, Product Liability and Personal Injury, Public Finance, Real Property, Securities, Tax, Probate and Estate Planning, Workers' Compensation.

MEMBERS OF FIRM

DAVID L. JOHNSON, born Lima, Ohio, September 23, 1946; admitted to bar, 1971, Ohio; 1973, Hawaii. *Education:* Ohio Wesleyan University (B.A., 1968); Harvard Law School (J.D., 1971).

LAWRENCE D. WALKER, born Syracuse, New York, July 10, 1948; admitted to bar, 1973, Ohio. *Education:* Fordham University (B.A., 1970); Northwestern University (J.D., 1973).

(This Listing Continued)

TIMOTHY P. NAGY, born Elyria, Ohio, April 18, 1949; admitted to bar, 1974, Ohio. *Education:* Wake Forest College; The Ohio State University (B.A., 1971); Capital University (J.D., 1974).

MICHAEL A. BYERS, born Columbus, Ohio, October 20, 1953; admitted to bar, 1978, Ohio. *Education:* The Ohio State University (B.A., 1975); University of Akron (J.D., 1978).

ROBERT W. McADAMS, JR., born Bradford, Pennsylvania, November 9, 1954; admitted to bar, 1987, Ohio. *Education:* University of Dayton (B.S., 1976); University of Virginia (M.B.A., 1980); University of California, Hastings College of the Law (J.D., 1986).

TIMOTHY B. MITCHELL, born Dallas, Texas, January 5, 1956; admitted to bar, 1982, Ohio. *Education:* The Ohio State University (B.A., 1979); Capital University Law School (J.D., 1982).

JOHN P. CURP, born Dayton, Ohio, February 17, 1970; admitted to bar, 1995, Ohio. *Education:* Miami University (B.S., 1992); Indiana University (J.D., 1995).

JAMES B. FARMER, born Corpus Christi, Texas, May 5, 1949; admitted to bar, 1976, Ohio. *Education:* Cornell University (B.A., 1971); The Ohio State University (M.C.R.P., 1976; J.D., 1976).

OF COUNSEL

FRANK A. TITUS, born Gallipolis, Ohio, June 28, 1946; admitted to bar, 1979, Ohio. *Education:* The Ohio State University (B.A., 1970; M.A., 1973); Capital University Law School (J.D., 1979).

DIANE D. REYNOLDS, born Akron, Ohio, 1959; admitted to bar, 1985, Ohio. *Education:* The Ohio State University (B.A., 1982); Capital University (J.D., 1985); University of Chicago (M.B.A., 1999).

RESIDENT ASSOCIATES

SHELLI TURNER CLARK, born Westerville, Ohio, December 3, 1974; admitted to bar, 2000, Ohio. *Education:* Wittenberg University (B.A., 1997); The Ohio State University (J.D., 2000).

BENJAMIN J. PARSONS, born Columbus, Ohio, February 16, 1978; admitted to bar, 2003, Ohio. *Education:* Miami University (B.A., 1999); The Ohio State University (J.D., 2003).

BARBARA A. McNEIL, born Buffalo, New York, July 19, 1948; admitted to bar, 1980, Ohio. *Education:* The Ohio State University (B.S.S.W., 1970); Capital University (J.D., 1979).

(For biographical data on all other personnel, see Cleveland, Cincinnati, Dayton, Ohio and Covington, Kentucky Professional Biographies)

J. PATRICK THOMAS

211 EAST LIVINGSTON AVENUE
COLUMBUS, OHIO 43215
Telephone: 614-221-2331
Fax: 614-221-4125
Email: pat@jpthomaslaw.com
URL: http://www.jpthomaslawfirm.com

Collections, Credit Union Law, Hospital Collections, Creditors Rights, Mechanics Liens, Construction Law, Real Estate, Contracts, Probate; Probate Law, Creditors Bankruptcy, Commercial and Consumer Collections, Secured Collections, Replevin, Leases and Leasing.

J. PATRICK THOMAS, born Columbus, Ohio, July 16, 1951; admitted to bar, 1978, Ohio and U.S. District Court, Southern District of Ohio. *Education:* Denison University; Ohio State University (B.A., summa cum laude, 1973; J.D., cum laude, 1977). Member, Lawyers for Justice Program. *Member:* Columbus (Member, Construction Committee) and Ohio State (Member, Real Property Section) Bar Associations; Credit Union Attorney's Legal Society. ***PRACTICE AREAS:*** Collections; Credit Union Law; Hospital Collections; Creditors Rights; Mechanics Liens; Construction Law; Real Estate; Contracts; Probate.

THOMAS LAW GROUP

COLUMBUS, OHIO

(See Dublin)

Family Law, Divorce, Child Custody, Child Support, Visitation Rights, Business Litigation, Corporate, Small Business Law, Business Formation, Partnerships, Limited Liability Companies, Buying and Selling of Businesses, Contracts, Personal Injury, Automobile Accidents, Wrongful Death, Medical Malpractice, Estate Planning, Wills and Probate, Trusts and Estates, Estate Administration.

THOMPSON HINE LLP

10 WEST BROAD STREET, SUITE 700
COLUMBUS, OHIO 43215-3435
Telephone: 614-469-3200
Fax: 614-469-3361
Email: info@ThompsonHine.com
URL: http://www.ThompsonHine.com

Cleveland, Ohio Office: 3900 Key Center, 127 Public Square, 44114-1291. Telephone: 216-566-5500. Fax: 216-566-5800. Email: info@ThompsonHine.com.
Cincinnati, Ohio Office: 312 Walnut Street, 14th Floor, 45202-4089. Telephone: 513-352-6700. Fax: 513-241-4771. Email: info@ThompsonHine.com.

(This Listing Continued)

Dayton, Ohio Office: 2000 Courthouse Plaza, N.E., P.O. Box 8801, 45401-8801. Telephone: 937-443-6600. Fax: 937-443-6637, 937-443-6635. Email: info@ThompsonHine.com.
Washington, D.C. Office: 1920 N Street, N.W., Suite 800, 20036-1600. Telephone: 202-331-8800. Fax: 202-331-8330. Email: info@ThompsonHine.com.
New York, N.Y. Office: One Chase Manhattan Plaza, 58th Floor, 10005-1401. Telephone: 212-344-5680. Fax: 212-809-6890. Email: info@ThompsonHine.com.
Brussels, Belgium Office: Avenue Louise 375 - b8, 1050 Brussels, Belgium, Telephone: 011 (32-2) 626-3280. Fax: 011 (32-2) 626-3299. Email: info@ThompsonHine.com.
Atlanta, Georgia Office: Proscenium Center, Suite 1200, 1170 Peachtree Street, 30309-7673. Telephone: 404-541-2900. Fax: 404-541-2905. Email: info@ThompsonHine.com.

Administrative Law, Admiralty and Maritime Law, Agency and Distributorships, Antitrust and Trade Regulation, Aviation and Aerospace, Bankruptcy, Banks and Banking, Biotechnology, Business Law, Business Litigation, Business Regulation, Business Transactions, Closely Held Business Law, Joint Ventures, Class Actions, Commercial Law, Commercial Real Estate, Communications and Media, FCC Regulation, Computers and Software, Construction Law, Contracts, Copyrights, Corporate Law, Corporate Finance, Corporate Litigation, Corporate Tax Controversies, Debtor and Creditor, Employee Benefits, ERISA, Energy, Energy Regulation, Environmental Law, Finance, Commercial Finance, Franchises and Franchising, General Practice, Government, False Claims Act, Qui Tam Litigation, Government Contracts, Health Care, Insurance Coverage, Insurance Regulation, Intellectual Property, International Law, International Trade, Internet Law, Labor and Employment, Life Sciences, Litigation, Complex Litigation, Medicare Fraud and Abuse, Mergers, Acquisitions and Divestitures, Natural Resources, Nonprofit and Charitable Organizations, Occupational Safety and Health, OSHA, Partnership Law, Patents, Probate, Products Liability, Product Safety, Professional Liability, Public Finance, Railroad Law, Real Estate, Regulatory Law, Drug and Medical Device Regulation, Food and Drug Regulation, International Regulatory Law, Regulated Industries, Securities, Initial Public Offerings, Public Offerings, Taxation, Tax Controversies, Toxic Torts, Trade Secrets, Trademarks, Transportation, Trusts and Estates, Unfair Competition, Utility Law, White Collar Crime, Zoning, Planning and Land Use.

FIRM PROFILE: Established in 1911, Thompson Hine today is among the nation's largest corporate law firms and was recently selected as one of the Best Corporate Law Firms in America (in a survey of 32,000 corporate directors conducted by Corporate Board Member magazine). Thompson Hine attorneys serve some of the premier businesses in the world, including:

Alltel, Anthem Blue Cross/Blue Shield, Avery Dennison, BIC Corporation, Chiquita Brands International, Eaton Corporation, Eveready (Energizer), Ford Motor Company, Ford Motor Credit, Formica Corp., Goodrich Corporation, Goodyear Tire and Rubber Co., Hartford Insurance, Intimate Brands, Inc. (Victoria's Secret, Bath & Body Works), Jo-Ann Stores, Inc., Kelly Services, Inc., KeyCorp/KeyBank, Lexis-Nexis, The Mead Corporation, Medical Mutual of Ohio, Milacron Inc., Newell Rubbermaid, Nordson Corporation, Oglebay Norton Company, Ohio Bankers Association, Omnicare, Inc., Parker Hannifin, Polyone Corporation, Procter & Gamble, S.C. Johnson & Son, Inc., Sherwin-Williams, Smythe Cramer Co., SuperValu, Time Warner Cable, Toro Company, Verizon Wireless, and Whirlpool Corporation.

Thompson Hine attorneys provide a wide range of corporate legal services, represented by the following practice groups:

BANKRUPTCY - We represent major secured and unsecured lenders, creditors" committees, credit enhancement providers, debtors and various other parties of interest in finance transactions, workouts and bankruptcy matters.

BUSINESS LITIGATION - We represent corporate clients in a wide variety of business litigation - from corporate control contests and insurance disputes, to class actions, securities fraud, and tax controversies.

BANKING & INSURANCE - Our lawyers provide recognized experience in virtually all areas of financial institutions matters. We provide regulatory, transactional, government relations and litigation services to clients on matters related to insurance. Our clients include all types of insurance companies and other financial services organizations including large, publicly held, multinational financial holding companies; banks and thrifts; investment banking organizations; securities broker-dealers; registered investment advisor organizations; mutual funds; and mortgage banking and broker organizations.

COMMERCIAL & PUBLIC FINANCE - We handle complex commercial finance transactions (including senior debt, subordinated debt and mezzanine financing transactions and private debt placements), public finance, asset securitizations and general bank regulatory law.

COMPETITION, ANTITRUST & WHITE-COLLAR CRIME - We represent clients in antitrust and competition matters, trade restraint and price discrimination issues, franchising and distribution, misappropriation of trade secrets, false advertising, enforcement of noncompetition covenants and interference with business relationships.

CONSTRUCTION - We represent owners, design professionals, construction managers, contractors and sureties in connection with all facets of the building industry and have served in the role of Project Counsel for billions of dollars of construction at sites across the United States.

CORPORATE, M&A AND SECURITIES - We represent both emerging and established businesses in their most important business transactions, from start-up through IPOs, joint ventures, mergers, acquisitions and beyond.

eBUSINESS & EMERGING TECHNOLOGIES - This group unites experienced counsel from various disciplines around one central goal: helping business realize the opportunities and manage the risks of electronic and technological commerce.

(This Listing Continued)

EMPLOYEE BENEFITS - We advise clients regarding qualified, non-qualified and welfare benefit plans; resolution of controversies with the IRS, DOL, PBGC and other agencies; incentive and equity-based compensation arrangements; statutory and regulatory compliance; ERISA fiduciary duties; ESOPs; multi-employer plans; and ERISA litigation.

ENERGY - We provide a broad range of services to our clients in the energy industry, including those that: Generate and sell electric energy into the nation's wholesale and retail energy markets. Transport and sell natural gas and oil. Transmit and distribute electricity and natural gas in retail markets. Purchase natural gas, electric energy and coal. Conduct energy trading operations. Manufacture, construct and/or buy and sell facilities and assets associated with the energy industry. Undertake energy-related projects, such as distributed generation, conservation or energy management projects. Manage information used by the energy industry.

ENVIRONMENTAL - We help clients understand the environmental aspects of their business transactions, craft methods of allocating risk and counsel them on their compliance obligations under local, state and federal laws.

HEALTH CARE - We represent physician groups, hospitals, clinical laboratories, diagnostic service providers, pharmaceutical manufacturers, medical device manufacturers and health insurance providers.

INTELLECTUAL PROPERTY - We assist clients with patents, trademarks, copyrights, trade secrets, computer software, internet related issues, employment relationships and intellectual property litigation.

INTERNATIONAL - We advise clients on trade regulation issues, customs and duty matters, foreign investment and joint ventures, NAFTA matters, importing and exporting issues, intellectual property protection, and immigration matters.

LABOR & EMPLOYMENT - We represent clients in employment litigation, workers" compensation proceedings, immigration matters, collective bargaining, administrative proceedings before the Department of Labor, OSHA, EEOC, NLRB and various state agencies.

LIFE SCIENCES - We provide legal and regulatory management services to established and emerging companies in the food, pharmaceuticals, biotech, and medical device industries.

PERSONAL & SUCCESSION PLANNING - We assist clients in the management and transmission of wealth, the succession to the control of businesses and other personal and family concerns.

PRODUCT LIABILITY - We have handled thousands of product liability matters involving mechanical, chemical, electrical, medical, aerospace, automotive and other products.

REAL ESTATE - We represent clients in Real Estate Development; Corporate Real Estate; Zoning and Land Use; Real Estate Investment and Financing; and Real Estate Investment Trusts.

TAXATION - We counsel clients in business transactions and financings, tax controversy, litigation, legislative and regulatory activities, executive compensation and tax planning, international taxation, state and local taxation and foundation and exempt organization matters.

TELECOMMUNICATIONS - Our Telecommunications group provides clients with wide-ranging guidance on the regulations and laws affecting telecommunications, broadcasting and other electronic communications companies. Our representation includes transactional matters, regulatory compliance, telecommunications services contracting, licensing and legislative/regulatory advocacy. We also have experience in issues involving communications land use and environmental matters, including human exposure to electromagnetic energy.

TRANSPORTATION - One of the largest transportation practices in the United States, our team has more than 100 years of collective experience representing transportation interests. We are involved in matters relating to commercial relationships and arrangements as well as the extensive and complex structure of rights, remedies and regulatory requirements involved in the domestic and international transportation of goods by rail, motor, ship, barge, air and pipeline.

WORKERS COMPENSATION - We represent employers in workers" compensation matters before state courts and industrial commissions. We have extensive experience representing and counseling clients in the area of workers' compensation.

AMOS BURT THOMPSON (1871-1965)
CHARLES P. HINE (1877-1942)
WALTER L. FLORY (1880-1951)
MICHAEL L. HARDY (Partner-in-Charge, Cleveland)
PATRICIA MANN SMITSON (Partner-in-Charge, Cincinnati)
ANTHONY C. WHITE (Partner-in-Charge, Columbus)
ROBERT M. CURRY (Partner-in Charge, Dayton Office)
NICHOLAS J. DiMICHAEL (Partner-in-Charge, Washington, D.C.)
GEORGE J. WALSH III (Partner-in-Charge, New York City)
LUDO DEKLERCK (Not admitted in Ohio; Partner-in-Charge, Brussels)
WALT A. LINSCOTT (Partner-in-Charge, Atlanta)

PARTNERS

JAMES H. BALTHASER, born Columbus, Ohio, October 7, 1954; admitted to bar, 1978, Ohio; 1984, U.S. Tax Court. *Education:* The Ohio State University (B.A., summa cum laude, 1975; J.D., with honors, 1978). Listed in: *Who's Who in America,*2000—. Certified Public Accountant, Ohio, 1980. Columbus Zoo and Aquarium, Trustee, 1995—; Chair of Audit, Finance and Investment Committee, 2004—; Participant in annual campaign, 1995—. Lecturer: "Advanced Wealth Transfer Techniques - Strategies, Issues and Opportunities," Midwest Trust Schools, June 2003; "Charitable Gifts of Real Property,"

(This Listing Continued)

THOMPSON HINE LLP, Columbus—Continued

Central Ohio Planned Giving Council, 2003; "Nonqualified Deferred Compensation Under 2004 Tax Refund Act," Tax Executives Institute, October 2004; "Sales of Businesses by Estates," Ohio Society of CPA's Personal Financial Planning Committee, November 2004. *Member:* Columbus and Ohio State Bar Associations; American Institute of Certified Public Accountants. ***TRANSACTIONS:*** Business Transactions: Represent heirs of a founder of a national business in the sale of their interests in the business to other family members. Resolve complex fiduciary and tax planning concerns. Lead acquisition of a business from a financially distressed public company. Assist with structuring pre- and post- acquisition business relations with strategic partner. Represent owners of a privately held automobile dealership in the sale of their business to a public company (NYSE) for cash. Address tax and non-tax legal issues, including due diligence, representations and warranties, indemnification and long term lease of facilities and land to purchaser. Negotiate employment agreements and equity based compensation packages for individuals joining publicly traded companies in senior management roles. Tax Planning and Controversies: Obtain >$1 million Ohio personal property tax refund for publicly traded (NYSE), multi-national retailer. Obtain favorable treatment in "bonus depreciation" regulations (published September 2003) and "Blue Book" (issued by the Joint Committee on Taxation) for nationally recognized company serving a niche market. Develop and implement plan for international lessor of specialized assets in response to 2002 changes in Ohio sales and use tax law. Defend federal income tax returns, as filed, by various entrepreneurs and business owners. Issues addressed include: active/passive gains and losses, investment interest expense, and ordinary/capital gain concerns. Represent numerous retailers, manufacturers and telephone companies in Ohio sales and use tax and personal property tax cases. Defend over 200 similarly situated executives of a public company (NYSE) against a City of Columbus assessment related to equity based compensation. Develop and implement streamlined approach to addressing common issues of law and fact. Estate Planning and Administration: Integrate estate planning and business succession goals of owners and senior executives of public and private companies. Develop buy-sell strategies and management succession plans. Create special purpose entities. Represent affluent families with complex personal and financial circumstances, including highly appreciated, illiquid assets (real estate, concentrated equity positions, etc.), non-pro rata asset allocation desires (arising from multiple marriages or other business/personal situations); Develop and implement strategies to facilitate administration of trusts and estates holding significant wealth. Methodology reflects each family's unique circumstances, including asset identification, centralization of personal financial management duties and responsibilities, financial reporting strategies, periodic conferences among family members and counselors, and preparation and defense of complex income, gift and estate tax returns. ***PRACTICE AREAS:*** Corporate Law; Taxation; Trusts and Estates; Wills. ***Email:*** Jim.Balthaser@ThompsonHine.com

ALAN F. BERLINER, born Columbus, Ohio, February 26, 1951; admitted to bar, 1976, Ohio. *Education:* Case Western Reserve University (B.A., magna cum laude, 1973); The Ohio State University College of Law (J.D., cum laude, 1976). Interim Director, Assistant Director and Chief Legal Counsel, Ohio Department of Insurance, 1997-1999. Federation of Regulatory Counsel. Special Counsel, Attorney General to the State of Ohio, Ohio Department of Insurance, 2000. Board of Trustees: Ohio State Bar Insurance Agency; Employment for Seniors. Graduate, Leadership Columbus Program. *Member:* Columbus (Member, Insurance Committee; Chairman, 1983-1984; Member, Government Agencies), Ohio State (Member, Insurance) and American (Member, Section on Tort and Insurance Practice) Bar Associations; Ohio Lobbying Association. ***REPORTED CASES:*** Jump v. Goldenhersh, No. 79-1734, (8th Cir. 1980) 619 F.2d 11; Manchester Premium Budget Corp. v. Manchester Ins. & Indem. Co. (8th Cir. 1980) 612 F.2d 389; Ratchford v. Manchester Life & Casualty Management Corp., Nos. 81-1974, 81-2012 (8th Cir.) 679 F.2d 741, 1982 U.S. App. LEXIS 18750; Paul Revere Life Ins. Co. v. Brock, Nos. 92-4227, 92-4228, (6th Cir.) 28 F.3d 551, 1994 FED App. 0228P; Newark Orthopedics v. Brock, No. 95APE03-246 (1995 Ohio App.) LEXIS 4423, October 5, 1995; Arthur Young & Co. v. Kelly, No. 92AP-1332, 88 Ohio App. 3d 343, 623 N.E.2d 1303; Covington v. Am. Chambers Life Ins. Co., No. 01AP-1338 (Ohio App.) 119 Ohio App. 3d 199, 2002 Ohio 6165, 779 N.E.2d 833. ***TRANSACTIONS:*** Representation of life insurance company on formation and approval from the Ohio Department of Insurance of mutual holding company; representation of purchasers of an insurance company regarding concerns of the Ohio Department of Insurance with respect to financial issues and risk based capital requirements; representation of several reinsurance companies with respect to disputes with the Ohio Department of Insurance regarding an insolvent insurance company; representation of a group of community banks purchasing a controlling interest in an excess and surplus lines insurer the Gramm Leach Bliley Act; representation of the Ohio Department of Insurance as special counsel in connection with the sale of an under capitalized Ohio insurance company; legislative lobbyist for national trade association regarding change in Ohio insurance statutes relating to reinsurance. Advised a large Ohio-based financial institution on the formation and contractual relationships of a captive private mortgage insurance reinsurance company. Advised a major Ohio-domiciled life insurance company on its formation and approval from the Ohio Department of Insurance of a Mutual Holding Company. Advised a group of Ohio and Indiana community banks in conjunction with a ground-breaking acquisition of a collective 50% interest in an excess and surplus lines insurer under the Gramm-Leach- Bliley Act. Negotiated with the Ohio Department of Insurance on behalf of a large multi-line insurer on the timing and terms of liquidation proceedings against its insolvent subsidiary. Advised a national multi-line insurance carrier regarding regulatory issues with the Ohio Department of Insurance due to liquidity problems caused by the insolvency of an Ohio-domiciled insurance company. Obtained approval from the Ohio Department of Insurance of both the corporate reorganization of an HMO and the corresponding major modification of its operation. Advised the Ohio Department of Insurance as "special counsel" in conjunction with the planned sale of an undercapitalized small Ohio personal lines insurer. Advised a national insurer regarding negotiation of its dispute over reinsurance treaties with an Ohio-domiciled insurer under the supervision of the Ohio Department of Insurance. Conducted a reinsurance arbitration on behalf of a ceding company against the reinsurer. Represented two insurance trade organizations with respect to their discussions with the Ohio Department of Insurance on desired amendments to the Ohio Insurance and Reinsurance Statutes. Advised the Board of Directors of a publicly held financial institution with respect to continuation of Directors and Officers insurance coverage in conjunction with a merger transaction. Advised a number of insurance companies and financial institutions considering their options and opportunities under the Gramm-Leach-Bliley Act and related matters. Represented an insurance company, state agency and an insurance agency in different insurance insolvencies regarding disputes with the Liquidators as to classification of their claims. Advised three reinsurance companies regarding disputes as to amounts due the Liquidator of an insolvent insurance company. Advised a trade association of termination of a sponsored MEWA. ***PRACTICE AREAS:*** Insurance Regulation; Insurance Litigation; Government Affairs; Regulatory Law; Arbitration. ***Email:*** Alan.Berliner@ThompsonHine.com

SCOTT A. CAMPBELL, born October 30, 1962; admitted to bar, 1995, Ohio; 1996, U.S. District Court, Southern District of Ohio; 1998, U.S. Court of Appeals, Sixth Circuit; United States Supreme Court, 2004. *Education:* Harvard University (A.B., Psychology and Social Relations, 1985); Ohio State University (J.D., 1995). Order of the Coif. Managing Editor, Ohio State Law Journal, 1994-1995. Member, American Inns of Court, Franklin Inn (Programming Chair). Leadership Columbus, Class of 2001. Comment," *United States v. Ferguson:* The Sixth Circuit Adds a Third Test for Pretextual Police Conduct," Ohio State Law Journal, 1995. *Member:* Columbus, Ohio State and American Bar Associations. ***REPORTED CASES:*** Thornton v. Salak, 2005 Ohio App. LEXIS 1558 (5th Dist. Mar. 28, 2005); Welsh v. Indiana Insurance Co., 2005 Ohio App. LEXIS 1116 (5th Dist. Mar. 7, 2005); RFC Capital Corp. v. EarthLink, Inc., 2004 Ohio App. LEXIS 6507 (10th Dist. Dec. 23, 2004); In Re: Petition to Annex 100.642 Acres, 2004 Ohio App. LEXIS 6576 (5th Dist. Dec. 20, 2004); CitiFinancial Mortgage Company v. Carson, 2004 Ohio App. LEXIS 5874 (10th Dist. Dec. 2, 2004); Hayman v. DiLoretto, 2004 Ohio App. LEXIS 2995 (7th Dist. June 21, 2004); Solove v. Westerville City Council, 2002 Ohio App. LEXIS 2926 (Ohio App. 10th Dist. June 13, 2002); Schutte v. Danis Cos., 141 Ohio App. 3d 824 (2001); Shanker v. Columbus Warehouse Ltd. Partnership, 2000 Ohio App. LEXIS 2391 (Ohio App. 10th Dist. June 6, 2000); Bauer v. Huntington National Bank, 2000 Ohio App. LEXIS 412 (Ohio App. 10th Dist. Feb. 10, 2000); Jackson v. Columbus, 194 F.3d 737 (6th Cir. 1999); Chicago Title Ins. Co. v. Huntington National Bank, 87 Ohio St. 3d 270 (1999); Charvat v. Colorado Prime, 1998 Ohio App. LEXIS 4292 (Ohio App. 10th Dist. Sept. 17, 1998); Brooks v. Ohio State Anesthesia Corp., 1996 Ohio App. LEXIS 3662 (Ohio App. 10th Dist. Aug. 29, 1996). ***PRACTICE AREAS:*** Business Litigation; Products Liability Litigation. ***Email:*** Scott.Campbell@ThompsonHine.com

WILLIAM R. CASE, born Akron, Ohio, October 8, 1948; admitted to bar, 1973, Ohio; 1977, Florida. *Education:* University of Akron (B.A., 1970); Ohio Northern University (J.D., 1973). Co-author, "Settlement Pitfalls - Recent cases and legislation create new dangers for settling clients," Ohio Lawyer, 2000; "Wrongful Cutting of Trees: A Shifting Measure of Damages," Ohio Lawyer, 1993; "Pitfalls Are Everywhere," Ohio Lawyer, 1989. Member, International Counsel of Shopping Centers. Board of Trustees, Opera Columbus. *Member:* Ohio State (Chair, Litigation Section, 1994-1996; Board of Governors; Business Courts Subcommittee, 1994) and Federal Bar Associations; Defense Research Institute. ***PRACTICE AREAS:*** Utility Liability Litigation; Product Liability Litigation; Commercial and Shopping Center Litigation; Labor and Employment. ***Email:*** William.Case@ThompsonHine.com

MICHAEL W. CURRIE, born Circleville, Ohio, April 20, 1957; admitted to bar, 1983, Ohio and U.S. District Court, Southern and Northern Districts of Ohio. *Education:* The Ohio State University (B.S., cum laude, 1980; J.D., cum laude, 1983). Co-Author and Editor: *Ohio Public Contract Law and Construction Claims,* 3rd edition, 1994. Named as one of the Best Lawyers in America in the 10th edition by Woodward/White. Member: The Best Lawyers in America, 2004; Columbus Top Lawyers, 2004. Recognized by Chambers as one of the Top Construction Lawyers in the State of Ohio. Speaker: "Construction Contracting for Public Owners, "Lorman, 1997-1999; "Construction Project Management/ Proving Claims and Resolving Disputes, "The Cambridge Institute, 1999; Construction Industry Panel Member, American Arbitration Association; Program speaker for Professional Education Systems, Inc. on Ohio Construction Law; Frequent speaker on Construction Law, Ohio Contractors Association. Member, Builders Exchange, 1987—. Arbitrator and Mediator, Construction, American Arbitration Association. *Member:* Columbus (Past Chairman, Construction Law Committee, 1990-1991), Ohio State and American (Member, Forum Committees on: Construction; Suretyship) Bar Associations; Ohio Contractors Association; Associated General Contractors; Central Ohio Builders Exchange. ***REPORTED CASES:*** Gesco v. Warden Electric (General Electric Supply Co. v. Warden Electric, Inc. (1988), 38 Ohio St. 3d 378, 528 N.E. 2d 195); Cedar Bay v. City of Fremont, 50 Ohio St. 3d 19 (Complete Gen. Constr. Co. v. Ohio Dept. of Transportation (2002), 94 Ohio St. 3d 54. ***PRACTICE AREAS:*** Construction Law; Commercial Litigation. ***Email:*** Mike.Currie@ThompsonHine.com

WILLIAM S. FEIN, born Chicago, Illinois, January 17, 1947; admitted to bar, 1971, Ohio and U.S. District Court, Southern District of Ohio; 1973, U.S. Court of Appeals, 6th Circuit; 1976, U.S. Tax Court. *Education:* Washington University (A.B., 1968); University of Michigan (J.D., 1971). *Member:* Columbus, Ohio State and American Bar Associations. ***PRACTICE AREAS:*** Closely Held Business Organization; Business Succession; Closely Held Business Estate Planning; Health Care Regulation; Health Care Licensing; Health Care Privacy Law; Health Plan Administration; Contested Trusts and Estates; Decedents Estates; Estate Administration; Estate Litigation; Estate Planning; Estate Planning for Parents of Handicapped Children; Estate Planning for the Disabled; Estate Planning for the Elderly; Estate Planning for Unmarried Couples; Estate Settlements; Family Trusts; Family Wealth Transfer; Fiduciary Law; Fiduciary Liability; Fiduciary Litigation; Living Trusts; Personal Planning; Probate Court Practice; Trust Administration; Trust Law; Trust Litigation; Trust Planning; Wealth Preservation. ***Email:*** Bill.Fein@ThompsonHine.com

CHARLES F. FREIBURGER, IV, admitted to bar, 1970, Ohio. *Education:* Miami University (B.S., 1966); The Ohio State University (J.D., 1970). Columbus Zoo Trustee. *Member:* Ohio State Bar Association. ***PRACTICE AREAS:*** Environmental and Corporate Transactions and Securities. ***Email:*** Chuck.Freiburger@ThompsonHine.com

KURT P. HELFRICH, born Hinsdale, Illinois, July 6, 1967; admitted to bar, 1997, Ohio. *Education:* University of Virginia (B.A., 1992); The Ohio State University (J.D., with honors, 1997); Order of the Coif. Order of the Coif. Recipient, Judge William M. Drennen Award. Member, Ohio State Journal on Dispute Resolution, 1996-97. *Member:* Columbus, Ohio State, American (Member, Sections on: Business Law; Public Utility), Energy and Electric Cooperative Bar Associations. ***TRANSACTIONS:*** Representation of electric

(This Listing Continued)

generation and transmission cooperative (G & T) in transactional, regulatory, corporate governance, tax, litigation and other matters, including in connection with the acquisition, construction, operation, maintenance, fuel supply, siting, and permitting of electric generating facilities and interests in electric generating facilities; financings and refinancings, including from the Rural Utilities Service; wholesale rates and power contracts with G & T members; open access transmission service from regional transmission organizations, including PJM; Federal Energy Regulatory Commission proceedings; and cooperative taxation. Representation of electric distribution cooperatives in transactional, regulatory, corporate governance, tax, litigation and other matters, including in connection with financings and refinancings; large retail power sales contracts; distributed generation and PURPA requirements; territorial protection and disputes; state public utility commission proceedings; annual meetings of members; capital credits and cooperative taxation. Representation of statewide association of electric distribution cooperatives, including in connection with the evaluation of state and federal legislative activities relating to electric cooperatives. ***PRACTICE AREAS:*** Corporate Law; Finance; Energy; Utility Law. ***Email:*** Kurt.Helfrich@ThompsonHine.com

THOMAS E. LODGE, born La Canada, California, July 14, 1956; admitted to bar, 1981, Ohio. *Education:* Ohio State University (B.A., cum laude, 1978); Case Western Reserve University (J.D., 1981). Order of the Coif. *Member:* Columbus (Member, Public Utilities Committee) and Ohio State (Past Chair, Public Utilities Committee) Bar Associations; Federal Communications Bar Association. ***PRACTICE AREAS:*** Telecommunications Law; Public Utilities Law; Commercial Law; Competition; Government Affairs; Regulatory Law. ***Email:*** Tom.Lodge@ThompsonHine.com

BOYD K. MOEHRING, born Columbus, Ohio, February 23, 1962; admitted to bar, 1989, Ohio. *Education:* Capital University (B.A., magna cum laude, 1984); The Ohio State University (J.D., 1989). ***PRACTICE AREAS:*** Business; Real Estate; Imports; Customs. ***Email:*** B.Moehring@ThompsonHine.com

ROBERT P. MONE, born Columbus, Ohio, July 23, 1934; admitted to bar, 1959, Ohio; 1968, U.S. Supreme Court. *Education:* University of Dayton (B.A., 1956); University of Notre Dame (J.D., 1959). Lawyers Subcommittee, Founder and First Chairman of National Generation and Transmission Managers Technical Advisory Committee, 1990—. Lawyers Committee, National Rural Electric Cooperative Association. Founder and First President, National Generation and Transmission Cooperative Lawyers Association. Member, Rotary International. *Member:* Columbus, Ohio State (Member, Public Utility Committee), American (Member, Public Utility Committee) and Energy Bar Associations. ***PRACTICE AREAS:*** Corporate Law; Securities; Public Utilities Law. ***Email:*** Robert.Mone@ThompsonHine.com

WILLIAM C. MOUL, born Columbus, Ohio, January 12, 1940; admitted to bar, 1964, Ohio; U.S. Court of Appeals, 6th, 3rd and 2nd Circuits. *Education:* Miami University (B.A., 1961); Ohio State University (J.D., 1964). Order of the Coif. Member, Lawyers Club of Columbus. Author: "Probable Cause", Ohio State Law Journal, 1964. *Member:* Columbus (Member, Arbitration Committee, Labor Law Committee) and Ohio State (Labor Section) Bar Associations; Industrial Relations Research Association. (Group Leader, Labor and Employment). ***TRANSACTIONS:*** Multiple representations of clients in complex collective bargaining, including hundreds of separate bargaining units, along with regular counseling, arbitration, litigation, and administrative agency appearances associated with the employment relationship. ***PRACTICE AREAS:*** Labor and Employment; Administrative Law. ***Email:*** Bill.Moul@ThompsonHine.com

JANIS B. ROSENTHAL, born New York, N.Y., September 15, 1953; admitted to bar, 1981, Ohio. *Education:* Indiana University (B.A., 1974); University of Cincinnati (J.D., 1981). Phi Beta Kappa. Speaker: Ohio Employment and Labor Law, Professional Development Institute; Employment Regulations in Ohio, Institute of Business Law; Labor Law Seminar, National Business Institute. Speaker for various other organizations, including Ohio State Bar Association State Convention, Ohio State Bar Association, 1999—. Seminar in Mexico, Central Ohio Self Insurers, Northern Ohio Self Insurers, Project Head Start Coordinators, Columbus Bar Association; Southwest Ohio Self Insurers and Ohio Self Insurers Schools. *Member:* Columbus and Ohio State Bar Associations; Self Insurers Association (Central Ohio). ***LANGUAGES:*** Spanish and French. ***PRACTICE AREAS:*** Workers' Compensation Law; Labor and Employment. ***Email:*** Janis.Rosenthal@ThompsonHine.com

O. JUDSON SCHEAF III, born Seattle, Washington, November 30, 1958; admitted to bar, 1988, Ohio; 1989, U.S. Court of Appeals, Fourth, Fifth and Sixth Circuits; U.S. District Court, Southern District of Ohio; 1996, U.S. District Court, Northern District of Ohio; U.S. Supreme Court. *Education:* Utah State University; Franklin University (B.P.A., summa cum laude, 1985); Capital University (J.D., summa cum laude, 1988). Order of the Curia. Recipient, American Jurisprudence Awards for Constitutional Law, Property, Contracts, Secured Transactions, Business Associations, Oil and Gas, Civil Procedure, Remedies and Insurance Law. Member, Capital University Law Review, 1986-1987. Law Clerk for the Honorable Alan E. Norris, U.S. Circuit Judge, Sixth Circuit Court of Appeals, 1988-1989. Co-Author, Opening Statements, Lawyers Cooperative Federal Practice Guide. *Member:* Columbus and Ohio State Bar Associations. ***PRACTICE AREAS:*** Trial Practice; Appellate Practice; Construction Law; Business Litigation. ***Email:*** Jud.Scheaf@ThompsonHine.com

JEFFERY E. SMITH, born Toledo, Ohio, April 27, 1953; admitted to bar, 1979, Ohio; 1991, Indiana. *Education:* University of Toledo (B.A., 1975; J.D., 1978). Co-author: "Financial Institutions Director Liabilities and Responsibilities" (AFSI 2000); "Corporate Governance Reform: Sarbanes-Oxley and Banking Organizations" (AFSI 2004); "BHC Formation under the Community Development Banking Act," The Banking Law Journal, Warren, Gorham & Lamont (1995). Author: "New Law Modernizes Financial Practices," OSBA "law you can use" (2000). Lecturer: "Corporate Governance for Community Banks," Midwest Bank Regulators Conference, August, 2004; "Bank Regulatory Enforcement Actions: An Overview," multistate webcast, February, 2004; "Corporate Governance for Community Bank Directors," multistate webcast, June, 2003; "Banking Law Update," Community Bankers Association of Ohio, June, 2003; "Bank Corporate Governance," Ohio Bankers League, February, 2003; "Financial Institutions Update," Ohio State Bar Association Banking Committee Fall Institute, September 1999; "Lending Under Revised Article 9 of the Uniform Commercial Code," Ohio Bankers Association and Ohio League of Financial Institutions, June 2001; "Developing and Implementing a Privacy Policy," Ohio

(This Listing Continued)

Bankers Association, June 2000; "Banking Law Update," Ohio State Bar Association CLE Institute, June 1999. Previous Employment: Trustcorp Inc., General Counsel and Secretary; Lincoln Financial Corporation, General Counsel and Secretary; Bank One Corporation, Counsel. Trustee, Olentangy Pride Foundation. *Member:* Toledo, Ohio State (Chair, Financial Institutions Subcommittee, 1998—), Indiana State and American (Member, Business Law Section; Subcommittees on Banking Law and Bank Holding Company Acquisitions and Divestitures) Bar Associations. ***TRANSACTIONS:*** Representation of small, regional and multi-national financial institution holding companies in numerous significant merger, acquisition, reorganization and divestiture transactions involving both cash and stock structures; divestiture of over 275 operating branch banking offices by large financial institution; affiliation transactions involving banking entities and insurance entities; formation of banks and other financial services organizations; extensive legislative and regulatory relations and compliance matters for financial institutions and financial institutions management; extensive disclosure issues for publicly-held entities; representation of trade associations; extensive "troubled company" representation with respect to corporate and regulatory enforcement and related issues; Riegle-Neal interstate branching preemption; acquisition of corporate trust business. ***PRACTICE AREAS:*** Corporate Law; Mergers and Acquisitions; Financial Institutions Law; Regulatory Law. ***Email:*** Jeff.Smith@ThompsonHine.com

JOHN T. SUNDERLAND, born Kansas City, Missouri, May 12, 1954; admitted to bar, 1983, Ohio. *Education:* Kenyon College (A.B., cum laude, 1976); Capital University (J.D., summa cum laude, 1983). Member: Columbus Area International Program; Mid-Ohio Scottish Heritage Association. Trustee, Scottish American Cultural Society of Ohio. *Member:* Columbus, Ohio State and Federal Bar Associations; Defense Research Institute. ***PRACTICE AREAS:*** Business Litigation; Labor and Employment; Product Liability Litigation. ***Email:*** John.Sunderland@ThompsonHine.com

JERRY VANDE WERKEN, born Chicago, Illinois, May 13, 1950; admitted to bar, 1974, Ohio; 1976, U.S. Tax Court. *Education:* Hope College (B.A., cum laude, 1971); Ohio State University (J.D., cum laude, 1974). Adjunct Professor, Pension and Profit Sharing Plan, Capital University Law School, 1989-1994. Lecturer: "Creative Pension Strategies"; "Designing Key Employee Distribution Plans"; "Avoiding Unexpected Violations of Fiduciary and Investment Rules"; "Retirement Plans - Participant Loans". *Member:* Columbus and Ohio State Bar Associations. ***PRACTICE AREAS:*** Employee Benefits Law; Personal and Business Succession Planning Law; Closely Held Business Law. ***Email:*** Jerry.Vandewerken@ThompsonHine.com

PETER D. WELIN, born Denver, Colorado, November 22, 1956; admitted to bar, 1988, Ohio. *Education:* Iowa State University (B.S.C,E, 1979); The Ohio State University (J.D., 1988). Co-author and Editor: *Ohio Public Contract Law and Construction Claims,* third ed., 1994. Speaker: "Litigation of Construction Claims," Lorman Education Services, 1997; "Construction Payment Remedies In Ohio," National Business Institute, 1998; "Ohio Construction Contracting for Public Entities," Lorman, 1999; "Mechanics' Lien Law and Strategies in Ohio," National Business Institute, 1999; "Construction Project Management: Proving Claims, Resolving Disputes," Cambridge University Institute, 1999; "Architect/Engineer Liability and Practice in Ohio," Lorman Education Services, 2000; "Understanding Construction Delay and Disruption Claims: Being Proactive Toward Resolution," Lorman Education Services Claims, 2000; "Ohio Construction Claims and Mechanics' Lien Law," Lorman Education Services, 1996; "Law for Design Professionals," Lorman Education Services, 2002. Construction Industry Panel Member, American Arbitration Association. Past Chairman, Dublin, Ohio Construction Appeals Board. Trustee, Dublin Soccer League. *Member:* Columbus (Member, Construction Law Committee), Ohio State (Member, Government Contracts Committee) and American (Member, Construction Industry Forum; Public Contract Section) Bar Associations; Associated General Contractors of Ohio; The Builders Exchange of Central Ohio. ***PRACTICE AREAS:*** Construction; Government Procurement Law. ***Email:*** Peter.Welin@ThompsonHine.com

ANTHONY C. WHITE, admitted to bar, 1993, Ohio. *Education:* The Ohio State University (B.S., 1989); Northwestern University School of Law (J.D., 1993). *Member:* Columbus, Ohio State and American Bar Associations. (Partner-in-Charge). ***PRACTICE AREAS:*** Business Litigation; Construction; Labor and Employment. ***Email:*** Tony.White@ThompsonHine.com

WILLIAM C. WILKINSON, born Cambridge, Ohio, October 25, 1947; admitted to bar, 1976, Ohio. *Education:* University of Akron (B.A., cum laude, 1971; J.D., 1976). *Seminar Presentations:* "Antitrust Law Issues for Purchasing Professionals," 2002; "Special Issues in Cross-Examination of Witnesses," 2002; "Taking and Defending Effective Depositions," 2001; "Television Coverage of The Legal Process," 2000; "Limiting The Liability of Design Professionals," 2000; "Issues of Style & Presentation in the Federal Courts," 1999; "Conducting Effective Depositions," 1999; "Federal Appellate Practice," 1998; "Developments in Ohio Corporate Takeover Laws"; 1997; "Resolving Complex Trust and Estate Disputes," 1997; "Implementing the New Fraud Auditing Standard," 1996; "Presenting Expert Testimony," 1996; "Dealing With Hardball Trial Tactics and Difficult Judges," 1993; "Statutory Interpretation," 1992; "Pleading Under the Ohio Rules of Civil Procedure," 1991. Industry Seminar: "Prevention of Accountant Malpractice Claims," 1995; "Limiting the Liability of Design Professionals," 2000; "Trade Secrets and the Employment of Technical Personnel," 1989; "The Right of Privacy of Hotel Guests," 1988. Lecturer: "Judicial Interpretation of Ohio's Control Share Acquisition Act," Cleveland Bar Association, 1996; "Media Relations in High Profile Cases," Inns of Court, 1997; "Television Coverage of The Legal Process," Ohio State Bar Foundation, 2000; "Industry vs. The Media," Panel Discussion, Ohio State University School of Journalism, 1991. Legal Advisory Board, Planned Parenthood of Central Ohio, Inc. Past Chairman, Board of Trustees, Junior Baseball and Softball Leagues of Westerville, Ohio. *Member:* Columbus, Ohio State and American (Member, Litigation Section) Bar Associations. ***PRACTICE AREAS:*** Trial and Appellate Practice; Administrative Hearings and Appeals; Complex Business Litigation; Complex and Multi-District Litigation; Insurance Regulation; Professional Liability Law; Construction, Intellectual Property and Securities Litigation; Commercial Litigation and Arbitration. ***Email:*** William.Wilkinson@ThompsonHine.com

OF COUNSEL

BRADFORD L. TAMMARO, born 1954; admitted to bar, 1985, Ohio. *Education:* Jacksonville University (B.S., 1976); University of Dayton (J.D., 1985). Assistant Attorney

(This Listing Continued)

THOMPSON HINE LLP, Columbus—Continued

General, Ohio Attorney General's Office. *Member:* Ohio State Bar Association. [Col., JAC, USAF, Reserves]. ***PRACTICE AREAS:*** Environmental; White Collar Crime. ***Email:*** Brad.Tammaro@ThompsonHine.com

MICHAEL V. WIBLE, born Dayton, Ohio, September 15, 1962; admitted to bar, 1987, Maryland; 1988, District of Columbia; 2004, Ohio. *Education:* Miami University (B.A., cum laude, 1983); American University, Washington College of Law (J.D., cum laude, 1987). Phi Beta Kappa. Attorney-Adviser, Office of Administrative Law Judges, U.S. Department of Labor, 1987-1989. Special Counsel, Office of Insurance Products, Division of Investment Management, U.S. Securities and Exchange Commission, 1989-1994. Counsel, Bank One, 1994-2003. *Member:* District of Columbia Bar; Ohio State, Maryland State and American Bar Associations. ***SPECIAL AGENCIES:*** U.S. Securities and Exchange Commission. ***PRACTICE AREAS:*** Investment Company Law; Investment Management; Mutual Funds; Broker-Dealer Regulation. ***Email:*** Michael.Wible@ThompsonHine.com

ASSOCIATES

CRAIG A. CALCATERRA, born Flint, Michigan, July 14, 1973; admitted to bar, 1998, Ohio; 1999, U.S. District Court, Southern District of Ohio. *Education:* The Ohio State University (B.A., magna cum laude,Phi Beta Kappa, 1995); The George Washington University Law School (J.D., 1998). *Member:* Columbus and Ohio State Bar Association. ***PRACTICE AREAS:*** Litigation. ***Email:*** Craig.Calcaterra@ThompsonHine.com

DANIEL F. EDWARDS, born Columbus, Ohio, March 6, 1967; admitted to bar, 1992, Ohio. *Education:* Miami University (B.S., cum laude, 1987); Georgetown University (J.D., 1992). *Member:* Columbus (Member, Construction Law Committee) and Ohio State (Member, Construction Law Subcommittee) Bar Associations; Builders Exchange of Central Ohio (Member, Law Group). [Capt., USAFR]. ***PRACTICE AREAS:*** Litigation; Construction Law; Government Affairs; Government Regulations. ***Email:*** Dan.Edwards@ThompsonHine.com

CAROLYN S. FLAHIVE, born West Palm Beach, Florida; admitted to bar, 2000, Ohio and U.S. District Court, Southern District of Ohio. *Education:* The Ohio State University (B.A., 1979); Capital University Law School (J.D., magna cum laude, 2000). Author: "A Study of Federal Preemption and Its Impact on the Wireless Communications Industry - What Did Congress Really Have in Mind?", Capital University Law Review; 1999-2000. *Member:* Columbus and Ohio State Bar Associations; Ohio Women's Bar Association. ***PRACTICE AREAS:*** Regulatory Law; Utility Law. ***Email:*** Carolyn.Flahive@ThompsonHine.com

PAUL GIORGIANNI, born Cleveland, Ohio, March 26, 1965; admitted to bar, 1995, Ohio, U.S. District Court, Northern and Southern Districts of Ohio; U.S. Court of Appeals, Sixth Circuit. *Education:* University of Notre Dame (B.A., 1987); Indiana University (M.B.A., 1989); The Ohio State University (J.D., 1995). Member, Executive Committee, Franklin American Inn of Court, 1995-2003. Law Clerk to Judge Cynthia Lazarus of the Ohio Court of Appeals, Tenth District, 1995-1997. Editor: "Guide to the Courts of Central Ohio," Columbus Bar Association, 1997-2000. Author: "The Small Preference Exception of Bankruptcy Code Section 547(c)," Ohio State Law Journal, 1995. *Member:* Columbus (Member, Judiciary Committee, 2002—; Chair, Appellate Courts Committee, 1997-1999; Jury Management Task Force, Reporter, 1999; Bedrock CLE Series, Coordinator, 1997) and Ohio State Bar Associations. ***PRACTICE AREAS:*** Business Litigation; Products Liability; Administrative Law. ***Email:*** Paul.Giorgianni@ThompsonHine.com

HEATHER D. GREGG, admitted to bar, 2001, Ohio. *Education:* The Ohio State University (B.A., 1997); Capital University Law School (J.D., summa cum laude, 2001). Associate Editor, Capital University Law Review. *Member:* Columbus and Ohio State Bar Associations; Ohio Women's Bar Association (Member, 10th District Trustee, Commercial Real Estate Women). ***PRACTICE AREAS:*** Real Estate. ***Email:*** Heather.Gregg@ThompsonHine.com

JOSEPH J. HUPRICH, born Marysville, Ohio, 1969; admitted to bar, 1998, California (Not admitted in Ohio). *Education:* University of Southern California (B.A., 1993); University of San Diego School of Law (J.D., 1997). *Member:* Los Angeles County and American Bar Associations; National Association of Realtors; California Department of Real Estate (Broker). ***PRACTICE AREAS:*** Construction. ***Email:*** Joe.Huprich@ThompsonHine.com

MELISSA L. KIDD, born Mansfield, Ohio, April 25, 1971; admitted to bar, 1999, Ohio. *Education:* University of Michigan (B.A., with honors in African/African-American Studies, English and Spanish, 1993); Case Western Reserve University School of Law (J.D., 1998); Capital University Law School (LL.M., Business and Taxation, 2004). *Member:* Columbus, Ohio State and American Bar Associations. ***PRACTICE AREAS:*** Trusts and Estates; Corporate Law. ***Email:*** Melissa.Kidd@ThompsonHine.com

JOHN B. KOPF, III, born July 3, 1975; admitted to bar, 2002, Ohio; 2003, U.S. District Court, Southern District of Ohio. *Education:* The Ohio State University (B.A., 1998); Capital University Law School (J.D., summa cum laude, 2002). ***PRACTICE AREAS:*** Business Litigation (70%); Bankruptcy Litigation (30%). ***Email:*** John.Kopf@ThompsonHine.com

W. BLAIR LEWIS, born Columbus, Ohio, August 14, 1960; admitted to bar, 1998, Ohio. *Education:* The Ohio State University (B.S.C.E., 1984); Miami University (Masters of Architecture, 1987); Capital University (J.D., 1998). Registered Architect, Ohio, 1992. Professional Engineer, Ohio, 1992. *Member:* Columbus, Ohio and American Bar Associations; American Institute of Architects; Builders Exchange of Central Ohio; Design Build Institute of America; Construction Specification Institute. ***PRACTICE AREAS:*** Construction Law. ***Email:*** Blair.Lewis@ThompsonHine.com

ROBERT W. MYERS, born Camden, New Jersey, June 26, 1961; admitted to bar, 1988, Ohio; 1992, U.S. Court of Appeals, Sixth Circuit and U.S. District Court, Northern and Southern Districts of Ohio. *Education:* Ohio State University (B.A., 1984); Cleveland-Marshall College of Law (J.D., 1987). Assistant Ohio Attorney General, 1992-1996. Co-Author: "Settlement Pitfall - Recent cases and legislation create new dangers for settling clients," Ohio Lawyer, April, 2000. *Member:* Ohio State Bar Association (Member, Workers' Compensation Committee). ***PRACTICE AREAS:*** Workers' Compensation; Labor and Employment; Litigation. ***Email:*** Robert.Myers@ThompsonHine.com

(This Listing Continued)

MICHELE L. NOBLE, admitted to bar, 2000, Ohio. *Education:* Ohio State University (B.A., magna cum laude, 1997); Capital University (J.D., summa cum laude, 2000). Executive Articles Editor, 1999-2000; Law Review Staff Member, 1998-1999, Capital Univeristy Law Review. *Member:* Columbus Bar Association. ***PRACTICE AREAS:*** Litigation; Municipal Law; Civil Rights; Products Liability. ***Email:*** Michele.Noble@ThompsonHine.com

MARK A. NOEL, born Harrodsburg, Kentucky, May 17, 1978; admitted to bar, 2003, Ohio. *Education:* University of Kentucky (B.A., magna cum laude, 2000); University of Kentucky College of Law (J.D., 2003). *Member:* Columbus and Ohio State Bar Associations. ***PRACTICE AREAS:*** Business Litigation; Labor and Employment. ***Email:*** Mark.Noel@ThompsonHine.com

JUNE M. OSHIMA, born Cleveland, Ohio, October 9, 1955; admitted to bar, 1989, California, 1998, Ohio. *Education:* Harvard University (A.B., magna cum laude, 1977); Dartmouth College (M.B.A., 1980); Columbia University (J.D., 1989). *Member:* Columbus, Ohio State and American Bar Associations; State Bar of California. ***PRACTICE AREAS:*** Personal Planning; Successions. ***Email:*** June.Oshima@ThompsonHine.com

THOMAS W. PALMER, born Cleveland, Ohio, February 15, 1969; admitted to bar, 2001, Ohio and U.S District Court, Northern and Southern Districts of Ohio, U.S. Court of Appeals, Sixth Circuit. *Education:* Ohio State University (B.A., 1993; J.D., 2000);. ***LANGUAGES:*** French. ***PRACTICE AREAS:*** Business Litigation; Products Liability; Environmental Litigation. ***Email:*** Thomas.Palmer@ThompsonHine.com

AKHIL PATEL, admitted to bar, 2000, Ohio. *Education:* The Ohio State University (B.A., 1996); University of Cincinnati (M.A., 1998); University of Cincinnati College of Law (J.D., 2000). *Member:* Columbus and Ohio State Bar Association. ***PRACTICE AREAS:*** Bankruptcy. ***Email:*** Akhil.Patel@ThompsonHine.com

GABE J. ROEHRENBECK, born 1979; admitted to bar, 2004, Ohio. *Education:* Texas Christian University (B.A., cum laude, 2001); Capital University Law School (J.D., summa cum laude, 2004). *Member:* Columbus and Ohio State Bar Associations.

JENNIFER E. SHORT, born Gainesville, Florida, April 15, 1972; admitted to bar, 1998, Ohio; 1999, U.S. District Court, Southern District of Ohio. *Education:* University of Washington (B.A., 1994); Seattle University School of Law (J.D., cum laude, 1998). Director, Corporate Boards: Fox Chase, Inc.; S&K Development, Inc. ***PRACTICE AREAS:*** Business Litigation; Products Liability. ***Email:*** Jennifer.Short@ThompsonHine.com

MARTHA S. VAN HOY, born 1977; admitted to bar, 2004, Ohio and U.S. District Court, Southern District of Ohio. *Education:* Georgetown University (B.A., cum laude, 1999); University of Virginia School of Law (J.D., 2004). *Member:* Columbus, Ohio State and American Bar Associations; Ohio Women's Bar Association. ***PRACTICE AREAS:*** Litigation. ***Email:*** Martha.VanHoy@ThompsonHine.com

GLEN A. VARCHETTI, admitted to bar, 1999, Ohio. *Education:* Michigan State University (B.A., with honors, 1995); Ohio State University College of Law (J.D., with honors, 1999). *Member:* Columbus and Ohio State Bar Associations. ***PRACTICE AREAS:*** Corporate Law; Securities; Insurance Regulation. ***Email:*** Glen.Varchetti@ThompsonHine.com

SENIOR ATTORNEY

PHILIP B. COCHRAN, born Columbus, Ohio, February 13, 1952; admitted to bar, 1981, Ohio. *Education:* Ohio State University (B.A., 1974); Thomas M.Cooley Law School (J.D., 1980). ***PRACTICE AREAS:*** Labor and Employment; Workers' Compensation Law; Litigation. ***Email:*** Phil.Cochran@ThompsonHine.com

(For complete biographical data on Lawyers in Offices other than Columbus, see Professional Biographies at the Respective Office Location)

TODARO & WAGONER

471 EAST BROAD STREET, SUITE 1303
COLUMBUS, OHIO 43215
Telephone: 614-242-4333; 1-800-510-4680
Telecopier: 614-242-3948
Email: bob@todarolaw.com
Email: frank@todarolaw.com
URL: http://www.lawyers.com/todaro-law

Civil Trial and Appellate Practice in Medical and Legal Malpractice, Personal Injury, Wrongful Death. Negligence, Products Liability, Business and Insurance Law.

MEMBERS OF FIRM

FRANK E. TODARO, born Jamestown, New York, December 5, 1957; admitted to bar, 1987, Ohio and U.S. District Court, Southern District of Ohio. *Education:* State University of New York College at Brockport (B.A., 1981); Capital University Law School (J.D., 1987). Recipient: Distinguished Service Award, 1995 and 1996 and Amicus Curiae Award, 1993-1994, Ohio Academy of Trial Lawyers. Author: "State Farm v. Alexander - Evidence of the Supreme Court's Growing Support of Statutorily Mandated UM/UIM Coverage," Ohio Trial, Fall, 1993, Vol. 4, Issue 4; "The John Doe Loop Hole," Ohio Trial, Summer 1995, Vol. 6, Issue 3; "Traditional Approach to Establishing a Law Practice," Bar Briefs, Columbus Bar Association, Fall, 1995; "Workers Compensation Subrogation - Timing is Everything," Ohio Trial, February, 1996, Vol. 7, Issue 1; "Product Non-Liability Statute H.B. 350," Ohio Trial, November 1996, Vol. 7, Issue 4. Co-Author: "Anesthesia Malpractice," Proof of Facts American Jurisprudence, 1989. Listed: Best Lawyers in America, 2001—. *Member:* Columbus (Member: Doctor/Lawyer Committee, 1990-1991; Insurance Law Committee, 1994-1998; Chairperson, Trial Advocacy Committee, 1989-1991), Ohio State and American Bar Associations; Ohio Academy of Trial Lawyers (Chairperson, Computer Services Committee, 1988-1991; Chairperson, Brief Bank Committee, 1989-1991; Home Office Committee, 1991-1992; Board Member at Large, 1992-1993; Co-Chair, Insurance Law Section, 1993-1994; Chair, Membership Committee, 1994; Chair, Insurance Law Section 1994-1997; Executive Committee Member, 1997-2003 and Vice President, 2000-2001, President, 2002-2003, A.D.O.P.T. Political Action Committee; Chair, 1994-2004; Treasurer, 1998-1999, Secretary, 1999-2000); The Association of Trial Lawyers of

(This Listing Continued)

America (Member, Young Lawyers Advisory Committee, 1991-1993; Member, Product Liability Section 1996-2004); Franklin County Trial Lawyers Association (Member, Negligence Law Committee, 1988-1990; Presidents Award, 1991; Newsletter Editor, 1990-1992; Chairperson Trial Advocacy Committee, 1989-1991; Trustee, 1992-1994; Chair Administrative Oversight Committee, 1994; Treasurer, 1995; Vice President, 1996; President, 1997); American Board of Trial Advocates, ABOTA (Member, 2004—). (Board Certified as a Civil Trial Advocate by the National Board of Trial Advocacy). ***PRACTICE AREAS:*** Medical Malpractice; Personal Injury Law; Wrongful Death Law; Negligence Law; Insurance Law; Railroad Law; Products Liability Law; Automobile Accidents and Injuries. ***Email:*** Frank@todarolaw.com

ROBERT J. WAGONER, born Wrangell, Alaska, October 14, 1972; admitted to bar, 1998, Ohio and U.S. District Court, Northern and Southern Districts of Ohio. *Education:* John Carroll University (B.S., Economics, 1994); Capital University (J.D., 1997). *Member:* Columbus and Ohio State Bar Associations; Franklin County Trial Lawyers Association (Chairperson, Membership Committee, 2002-2004; President's Award, 2003; Board Member, 2004—); The Ohio Academy of Trial Lawyers; The Association of Trial Lawyers of America. ***PRACTICE AREAS:*** Personal Injury; Products Liability; Wrongful Death; Medical Malpractice; Insurance Law; Litigation. ***Email:*** bob@todarolaw.com

LISA M. TOME

511 SOUTH HIGH STREET
COLUMBUS, OHIO 43215
Telephone: 614-228-4141
Fax: 614-228-0899
URL: http://www.lawyers.com/lisatome

Criminal Defense, Driving While Intoxicated, Traffic Violations, Juvenile Law, Appellate Practice.

LISA M. TOME, born Warren, Pennsylvania, December 20, 1972; admitted to bar, 2001, Ohio. *Education:* Allegheny College (B.A., 1995); University of Pittsburgh (J.D., 2001). Order of the Coif. *Member:* Columbus and Ohio State Bar Associations. ***PRACTICE AREAS:*** Criminal Defense; Driving While Intoxicated; Traffic Violations; Criminal Appeals.

RICHARD D. TOPPER

1500 WEST THIRD AVENUE, SUITE 400
COLUMBUS, OHIO 43212
Telephone: 614-486-4805
Fax: 614-481-7905
Email: rictopper@aol.com
URL: http://www.lawyers.com/topperlaw

Plaintiff's Medical Malpractice, Personal Injury, Automobile Accidents and Injuries, Wrongful Death, Insurance Law, Products Liability and Negligence.

RICHARD D. TOPPER, admitted to bar, 1979, Ohio. *Education:* Miami University (B.S., 1976); University of Toledo (J.D., 1979). Recipient: Presidents Award, Franklin County Trial Lawyers' Association, 1992 and 1993; Distinguished Service Award, Ohio Academy of Trial Lawyers, 1994 and 1999 . *Member:* Columbus and Ohio State Bar Associations; Ohio Academy of Trial Lawyers (Board of Trustees, 1991-1998; 2000-2004); Franklin County Trial Lawyers (Board of Trustees, 1993-1999; President, 1998-1999); The Association of Trial Lawyers of America; American Board of Trial Advocates. (Certified as a Civil Trial Advocate by the National Board of Trial Advocacy)

CRAIG P. TRENEFF LAW OFFICE

Established in 2001
555 SOUTH FRONT STREET, SUITE 320
COLUMBUS, OHIO 43215-5668
Telephone: 614-228-3715
Fax: 614-228-3102
URL: http://www.treneff.com
Email: ctreneff@treneff.com
URL: http://www.lawyers.com/treneffIaw

Family Law, Divorce, Dissolution, Child Custody, Child Support, Premarital Agreements, Real Estate Taxation.

CRAIG P. TRENEFF, born Columbus, Ohio, July 16, 1952; admitted to bar, 1981, Ohio; 1982, U.S. District Court, Southern District of Ohio. *Education:* The Ohio State University (B.A., 1974); Capital University (J.D., 1981). Staff Member, Capital University Law School Law Review, 1979-1981. Legislative Assistant, Ohio House of Representatives, 1975-1981. Law Clerk to Justice William B. Brown, Ohio Supreme Court, 1981-1983. Special Counsel to Ohio Attorney General, 1983-1990. Member, Westerville Board of Zoning Appeals, 1990-1994, 1996. Chairman, Westerville Planning Commission, 1996-2004; Member, Westerville City Council, 2004—. *Member:* Columbus, Ohio State and American Bar Associations; Fellow, American Academy of Matrimonial Lawyers. (Certified Specialist in Family Relations Law, Ohio State Bar Association). (Also Of Counsel, Flanagan/Bilton, Chicago, Illinois). ***REPORTED CASES:*** Heritage Hills, Ltd. v. Deacon (1990), 49 Ohio St. 3d 80; Bd. of Edu. of Worthington S.D. v. Bd. of Revision of Franklin Cty., (1999) 85 Ohio St. 3d 156. ***PRACTICE AREAS:*** Family Law; Divorce; Dissolution; Child Custody; Child Support; Premarital Agreements; Tax Appeals. ***Email:*** ctreneff@treneff.com

TWYFORD & DONAHEY, P.L.L.

Established in 1968
BREWERY DISTRICT
495 SOUTH HIGH STREET
COLUMBUS, OHIO 43215-5058
Telephone: Toll Free: 1-800-686-1699
Fax: 614-849-0475
Email: help@twyforddonahey.com
URL: http://www.twyforddonahey.com

Circleville, Ohio Office: 214 South Court Street, 43113. Telephone: Toll Free: 1-800-686-1699. Email: help@twyforddonahey.com.
Delaware, Ohio Office: 163 N. Sandusky Street, Suite 103, 43015. Telephone: Toll Free: 1-800-686-1699. Email: help@twyforddonahey.com.
Lancaster, Ohio Office: 3794 Old Columbus Road, N.W., 43130. Telephone: Toll Free: 1-800-686-1699. Email: help@twyforddonahey.com.
Newark, Ohio Office: 137 West Main Street, Suite C, 43025. Telephone: Toll Free: 1-800-686-1699. Email: help@twyforddonahey.com.
London, Ohio Office: 25 West Fifth Street, 43140. Telephone: Toll Free: 1-800-686-1699. Email: help@twyforddonahey.com.

Personal Injury Litigation, Wrongful Death, Medical Malpractice, Products Liability, Automobile Accidents, Trucking Accidents, Head and Spinal Injuries, Motorcycle Accidents and Injuries, Uninsured Motorists, Insurance Law, Airplane Crash Litigation, Railroad Accidents, Slip and Fall, Dog Bites, Work Related Injuries, Birth Injuries, Nursing Home Abuse and Neglect.

FIRM PROFILE: Tom Twyford and Dick Donahey have been partners since 1968 and have practiced exclusively in the areas of personal injury, medical malpractice and products liability law. We have never represented insurance companies! In recent years, we have obtained some of the largest verdicts in Franklin County. We have purposely remained small in order to concentrate on a limited number of cases. We have six offices and will handle cases in any part of the state of Ohio.

SENIOR PARTNERS

THOMAS L. TWYFORD, born Steubenville, Ohio, 1935; admitted to bar, 1965, Ohio; 1969, U.S. District Court, Southern District of Ohio; 1971, U.S. Supreme Court. *Education:* Ohio State University (B.A., 1964; J.D., 1966). Phi Delta Phi. *Member:* Columbus and Ohio State Bar Associations; Ohio Academy of Trial Lawyers; The Association of Trial Lawyers of America; Franklin County Trial Lawyers Association. ***PRACTICE AREAS:*** Personal Injury Law; Medical Malpractice.

RICHARD S. DONAHEY, born Cincinnati, Ohio, 1941; admitted to bar, 1968, Ohio; 1969, U.S. Court of Appeals, Sixth Circuit and U.S. District Court, Southern District of Ohio; 1971, U.S. Supreme Court. *Education:* The Ohio State University (B.C.E., 1965; J.D., 1967). *Member:* Columbus and Ohio State Bar Associations; Ohio Academy of Trial Lawyers; The Association of Trial Lawyers of America; Franklin County Trial Lawyers Association. ***PRACTICE AREAS:*** Personal Injury Law; Medical Malpractice.

MARK E. DEFOSSEZ, born New York, N.Y., February 2, 1957; admitted to bar, 1985, Massachusetts; 1991, Ohio. *Education:* Northwestern University (B.S., 1979); Boston College (J.D., cum laude, 1984). ***PRACTICE AREAS:*** Personal Injury; Medical Malpractice.

ASSOCIATES

T. JEFFERY BEAUSAY, born Toledo, Ohio; admitted to bar, 1987, Ohio. *Education:* Ohio State University (B.A., 1984); University of Toledo (J.D., 1987). Author: "Insurance: The 'Each Person/Each Accident' Issue," Journal of the Ohio Association of Civil Trial Attorneys, Vol. 28, Issue 2, Spring 1992; "Uninsured/Underinsured Motorist Coverage: The 'Sexton' Issue," Journal of the Ohio Association of Civil Trial Attorneys, Vol. 28, Issue 4, Summer 1993. *Member:* Columbus, Ohio State and American Bar Associations. ***PRACTICE AREAS:*** Medical Malpractice; Personal Injury; Uninsured and Underinsured Motorists; Insurance; Civil Litigation.

GORDON D. EVANS, II, born Cincinnati, Ohio; admitted to bar, 2001, Ohio; 2002, U.S. District Court, Southern District of Ohio. *Education:* Kentucky Wesleyan College (B.A., 1997); Capital University Law School (J.D., cum laude, 2001). Order of the Barristers. Adjunct Professor, Trial Advocacy, Capital University Law School, 2002—. Formerly with Reminger & Reminger. *Member:* Ohio State and American Bar Associations; The Association of Trial Lawyers of America; Columbus Bar Association. ***PRACTICE AREAS:*** Medical Malpractice; Wrongful Death; Nursing Home Abuse and Neglect; Personal Injury. ***Email:*** Gevans@twyfordanddonahey.com

REBEKAH G. WEISS, born Columbus, Ohio, 1978; admitted to bar, 2004, Ohio and U.S. District Court, Southern District of Ohio. *Education:* The Ohio State University (B.A., 2001); Capital University (J.D., cum laude, 2004). Order of the Curia; Delta Theta Phi (Social Chair, 2001-2002; Treasurer, 2002-2003; Member, 2003-2004). Associate Editor, Capital University Law Review, 2003-2004. President, Environmental Law Society, 2002-2004. Recipient: Trustee's Scholarship; Justin S. Morrill Grant; Mike Begeny Memorial Scholarship; CALI Award for Property, 2002. Teaching Assistant, First Year Property, 2002-2004. ***PRACTICE AREAS:*** Litigation; Motor Vehicle Accidents; Personal Injury.

REFERENCES: The Huntington National Bank; Bank One of Columbus; BancOhio National Bank.

TYACK, BLACKMORE & LISTON CO., L.P.A.

536 SOUTH HIGH STREET
COLUMBUS, OHIO 43215
Telephone: 614-221-1341
Fax: 614-228-0253
URL: http://www.tblattorneys.com
URL: http://www.lawyers.com/tyackblackmore&liston

General Criminal, Civil Trial and Appellate Practice in all State and Federal Courts. Negligence, Medical Malpractice, Personal Injury, Automobile Accidents, Family Law, Divorce, Child Custody, Adoption Law, Juvenile Law.

(This Listing Continued)

TYACK, BLACKMORE & LISTON CO., L.P.A., Columbus—Continued

THOMAS M. TYACK, born Columbus, Ohio, June 20, 1940; admitted to bar, 1965, Ohio; 1970, U.S. Court of Appeals, Sixth Circuit; 1972, U.S. District Court, Southern District of Ohio; 1974, U.S. Supreme Court; U.S. Claims Court. *Education:* The Ohio State University (B.A., 1962; J.D., 1965). Order of the Coif; Phi Beta Kappa. Adjunct Professor, Family Law, Ohio State University Law School, 1969. Member, Board of Bar Examiners, State of Ohio, 1975-1980. Instructor: Criminal Procedure, Capital University Law School, Certified Legal Assistant Program, 1979-1990; Civil Trial Advocacy Institute, 1978, 1980-1982. *Member:* Columbus (Member: Board of Governors, 1990-1992; Ethics Committee, 1985-1990; 1992-1996), Ohio State and American (Member, Family Law Section) Bar Associations; Franklin County Trial Lawyers Association; Ohio Academy of Trial Lawyers; The Association of Trial Lawyers of America; Ohio Association of Criminal Defense Lawyers; National Association of Criminal Defense Lawyers. Fellow, American College of Trial Lawyers. ***PRACTICE AREAS:*** Personal Injury Law; Medical Malpractice; Criminal Law; Family Law; Divorce; Child Custody.

MARGARET L. BLACKMORE, born Columbus, Ohio, July 27, 1951; admitted to bar, 1981, Ohio; 1984, U.S. District Court, Southern District of Ohio; 1987, U.S. Supreme Court; U.S. Claims Court. *Education:* Stephens College (A.A., 1971); The Ohio State University (B.S., 1973); University of Exeter, Exeter, England; Capital University (J.D., 1981). Instructor, Legal Writing, Ohio State University Law School, 1987. *Member:* Columbus (Member, Family Law Committee), Ohio State and American (Member, Family Law Section) Bar Associations; Franklin County Trial Lawyers Association (Chairman, Family Law Committee, 1992-1993; Trustee, 1993-1996; Secretary, 1996-1997; Treasurer, 1997-1998; Vice President, 1998-1999; President, 1999-2000); The Association of Trial Lawyers of America; Ohio Academy of Trial Lawyers; American Academy of Adoption Attorneys. ***PRACTICE AREAS:*** Family Law; Adoption Law; Divorce; Child Custody; Personal Injury Law; Medical Malpractice.

JEFFERSON E. LISTON, born Troy, Ohio, April 11, 1954; admitted to bar, 1978, Ohio; 1983, U.S. District Court, Southern District of Ohio; 1987, U.S. Supreme Court. *Education:* Otterbein College (B.A., 1975); Case Western Reserve University (J.D., 1978). Phi Eta Sigma. Torch & Key. Member, Moot Court Board, Case Western Reserve University. Referee, Franklin County Court of Common Pleas, Domestic Relations Division, Juvenile Branch, 1985-1990. Founding President, Ohio Association of Court Referees. Founding President: Central Ohio Association of Juvenile Lawyers, 1996-1997. *Member:* Columbus (Chairperson: Juvenile Law Committee, 1986-1988; Law Day Committee, 1988-1989), Ohio State and American Bar Associations; Franklin County Trial Lawyers Association; National Association of Criminal Defense Lawyers; Ohio Association Criminal Defense Lawyers (President, 2001-2002); The Association of Trial Lawyers of America. ***PRACTICE AREAS:*** Criminal Law; Juvenile Law; Family Law; Divorce; Child Custody; Personal Injury Law.

JONATHAN T. TYACK, born Columbus, Ohio, April 26, 1971; admitted to bar, 1996, Ohio and U.S. Court of Appeals, Sixth Circuit; 1998, U.S. District Court, Southern District of Ohio. *Education:* Denison University (B.A., cum laude, 1993); The Ohio State University (J.D., with honors, 1996). Phi Beta Kappa; Order of the Coif. Member, Moot Court, 1995. Member, Law Journal, The Ohio State University, 1994-1996. National Finalist, NCTL Mock Trial Competition, 1996. Recipient, Judge Harter Award for Trial Practice, 1996. *Member:* Columbus, Ohio State and American Bar Associations; Ohio Academy of Trial Lawyers; The Association of Trial Lawyers of America; Franklin County Trial Lawyers Association; National Association of Criminal Defense Lawyers; Ohio Association of Criminal Defense Lawyers. ***PRACTICE AREAS:*** Personal Injury; Medical Malpractice; Criminal Defense; Family Law; Labor and Employment.

JAMES P. TYACK, born Columbus, Ohio, June 28, 1975; admitted to bar, 2000, Ohio; 2001, U.S. District Court, Southern District of Ohio and U.S. Court of Appeals, Sixth Circuit. *Education:* Denison University (B.A., History, 1997); The Ohio State University (J.D., 2000). *Member:* Columbus, Ohio State and American Bar Associations; Ohio Academy of Trial Lawyers; The Association of Trial Lawyers of America; Franklin County Trial Lawyers Association; National Association of Criminal Defense Lawyers; Ohio Association of Criminal Defense Lawyers. ***PRACTICE AREAS:*** Criminal Defense; Personal Injury; Medical Malpractice; Civil Litigation.

REFERENCES: US Bank, NA; Bank One of Columbus, NA.

ULMER & BERNE LLP

Established in 1908

88 EAST BROAD STREET, SUITE 1600
COLUMBUS, OHIO 43215
Telephone: 614-229-0000
FAX: 614-229-0001
Email: infocolumbus@ulmer.com
URL: http://www.ulmer.com/

Cleveland, Ohio Office: Skylight Office Tower, 1660 West 2nd Street, Suite 1100. Telephone: 216-583-7000. FAX: 216-583-7001.

Cincinnati, Ohio Office: 600 Vine Street, Suite 2800. Telephone: 513-698-5000. FAX: 513-698-5001.

Chicago, Illinois Office: One North Franklin Street, Suite 1825. Telephone: 312-324-8000. FAX: 312-324-8001.

Antitrust; Banking and Commercial Lending; Broker/Dealer and Securities Litigation; Business Law; Business Litigation; Business Restructuring; Class Action Defense; Construction Law; Corporate Finance; Corporate Restructuring and Creditors' Rights; Corporate Succession Planning; Emerging Businesses; Employee Benefits; Employment and Labor; Environmental; Fair Housing; Financial Institution Compliance; General Counsel Services; Health Care; Income Tax; Insurance Coverage; Intellectual Property and Technology; Joint Ventures; Liability Defense; Mass Torts; Mergers, Acquisitions and Divestitures; Nonprofit; OSHA; Pharmaceutical; Product Liability; Public Law; Real Estate; Securities; Securities Regulatory Compliance; Subrogation; Tax; Technology Transactions; Toxic Tort Defense; Trade Secrets/ Unfair Competition; Trusts and Estates; Venture Capital; Workers' Compensation; Trial and Appellate Practice in All Courts.

FIRM PROFILE: Ulmer & Berne LLP, established in 1908, is one of Ohio's largest law firms, as well as one of its fastest growing. The firm has doubled in size in the last five years and tripled in size in the last 10. In the last 18 months alone, the firm has added 47 new lawyers. A full-service firm with over 185 attorneys in Cleveland, Columbus, Cincinnati and Chicago, Ulmer & Berne represents publicly traded and privately held companies, financial institutions, pharmaceutical companies, family businesses, international joint ventures and affiliations, investor groups, start-ups and emerging businesses, public bodies and nonprofit organizations. For more information, visit www.ulmer.com.

LAW FIRM ALLIANCES/ASSOCIATIONS: **LAWYERS ASSOCIATED WORLDWIDE (L.A.W.)**

BUSINESS COUNSEL, INC.

PARTNERS

ALEXANDER M. ANDREWS, born August 27, 1956; admitted to bar, 1981, Ohio. *Education:* Boston University (B.A., 1978); Case Western Reserve University (J.D., 1981). (Partner-in-Charge, Columbus Office). (Partner-in-Charge). ***PRACTICE AREAS:*** Complex Litigation; Business Litigation; Commercial Litigation. ***Email:*** aandrews@ulmer.com

TIMOTHY M. FOX, born June 27, 1962; admitted to bar, 1987, Ohio. *Education:* Kenyon College (B.A., 1984); Case Western Reserve University (J.D., 1987). ***PRACTICE AREAS:*** Toxic Tort; Products Liability Defense; Asbestos Litigation; Complex Litigation; Aviation Litigation. ***Email:*** tfox@ulmer.com

ROBERT J. KARL, born April 29, 1959; admitted to bar, 1984, Ohio. *Education:* Wright State University (B.A., 1982); Vermont Law School (J.D., 1989). (Chair, Environmental Law Group). *Member:* Columbus Bar Association (Co-Chair, Environmental Section). ***PRACTICE AREAS:*** Agricultural Law; Environmental Law; Natural Resources; Toxic Torts; Real Estate; Business Law; Business Litigation; Complex Litigation; Administrative Law. ***Email:*** bkarl@ulmer.com

REX A. LITTRELL, born September 9, 1964; admitted to bar, 1989, Ohio. *Education:* John Carroll University (B.A., magna cum laude, 1986); The Ohio State University (M.A., Public Administration with Specialty in Law, 1989; J.D., 1989). General Counsel, Ohio Manufactured Homes Association. ***PRACTICE AREAS:*** Diet Drug Litigation; Mobile Home Law; Defense Litigation; State Legislative Practice. ***Email:*** rlittrell@ulmer.com

OF COUNSEL

MARTYN T. BRODNIK, born June 26, 1951; admitted to bar, 1980, Ohio and U.S. District Court, Northern and Southern Districts of Ohio. *Education:* Cleveland State University (B.S., 1973); Cleveland-Marshall College of Law (J.D., 1980). Delta Theta Phi. Instructor, Ohio State University, 1977—. Co-Author, *Ohio Environmental Law,* Hardy Banks Baldwin, 1992. Assistant Ohio Attorney General, 1980-1986. ***PRACTICE AREAS:*** Environmental Law; Administrative Law; Natural Resources; Business Law; Real Estate; Mergers and Acquisitions. ***Email:*** mbrodnik@ulmer.com

GREGORY A. LOWE, born June 18, 1959; admitted to bar, 1993, Ohio. *Education:* The Ohio State University (B.S., 1984); Capital University (J.D., 1993). ***PRACTICE AREAS:*** Commercial Real Estate; Contracts; Banks and Banking; Business Law; Construction Contracts; Construction Finance; Assett Based Finance; Commercial Finance; Equity Finance; Commercial Mortgages; Mortgage Finance; Real Estate; Zoning, Planning and Land Use. ***Email:*** glowe@ulmer.com

SENIOR ATTORNEYS

CHARLES R. (BOB) JANES, born April 20, 1952; admitted to bar, 1977, Ohio. *Education:* The Ohio State University (B.A., cum laude, 1974; J.D., 1977). ***PRACTICE AREAS:*** Products Liability Defense; Drug and Medical Device Defense; Toxic Tort Defense; Asbestos Defense; Medical Negligence; Legal Malpractice Defense; Insurance Litigation; Insurance Coverage; Insurance Defense. ***Email:*** cjanes@ulmer.com

J. GREGORY SMITH, born August 19, 1967; admitted to bar, 1993, Ohio. *Education:* Northwestern University (B.A., 1989); Ohio State University (J.D., 1993). *Member:* Columbus Bar Association (Co-Chair, Environmental Law Committee, 2004-2005). ***PRACTICE AREAS:*** Environmental Law; Natural Resources; Administrative Law; Real Estate; Business Law; Business Litigation. ***Email:*** gsmith@ulmer.com

ASSOCIATES

DAVID L. EIDELBERG, born September 20, 1963; admitted to bar, 1988, Ohio. *Education:* Oberlin College (B.A., 1985); Case Western Reserve University (J.D., cum laude, 1988). President, 2001-2002 and Board Member, 2002-2003, National Society of Professional Insurance Investigators - Ohio Chapter. ***PRACTICE AREAS:*** Civil Litigation; First Party Insurance; Fire Loss; Insurance Bad Faith; Property Insurance; Insurance Coverage; Commercial Landlord and Tenant Law; Workers Compensation. ***Email:*** deidelberg@ulmer.com

REBECCA B. JACOBS, born December 19, 1973; admitted to bar, 1997, Ohio; 2001, California. *Education:* University of California, Santa Cruz (B.A., Economics, 1994); Vanderbilt University (J.D., 1997). Dean's List. Phi Beta Kappa; Phi Alpha Delta. ***PRACTICE AREAS:*** Labor and Employment; Litigation; Civil Litigation; Business Litigation; Fair Housing. ***Email:*** rjacobs@ulmer.com

MATTHEW C. KREJCI, born March 29, 1977; admitted to bar, 2002, Ohio. *Education:* Miami University (B.S., 1999); Capital University Law School (J.D., 2002). Order of the Curia. ***PRACTICE AREAS:*** Products Liability; Liability Defense; Business Litigation; Construction Litigation. ***Email:*** mkrejci@ulmer.com

(This Listing Continued)

SHERRY L. MOWRY, born March 31, 1976; admitted to bar, 2001, Ohio. *Education:* Massachusetts Institute of Technology (B.S., 1998); The Ohio State University Moritz College of Law (J.D., 2001). ***PRACTICE AREAS:*** Environmental Law; Real Estate; Business Litigation; Business Law; Construction Law. ***Email:*** smowry@ulmer.com

CHRISTINE E. WATCHORN, born March 25, 1972; admitted to bar, 2003, Ohio. *Education:* Ohio Wesleyan University (B.A., cum laude, 1994); Capital University (J.D., summa cum laude, 2003). ***PRACTICE AREAS:*** Complex Commercial Litigation; Business Litigation; Construction Litigation. ***Email:*** cwatchorn@ulmer.com

VAN KLEY & WALKER, LLC

132 NORTHWOODS BOULEVARD, SUITE C-1
COLUMBUS, OHIO 43235
Telephone: 614-431-8900
Fax: 614-431-8905
Email: jvankley@vankleywalker.com
URL: http://www.vankleywalker.com

Dayton Office: 137 North Main Street, Suite 316, 45402. Telephone: 937-226-9000. Fax: 937-226-9002.

Air Pollution, Brownfields Redevelopment, Environmental Administrative Law, Environmental Auditing, Environmental Cost Recovery, Environmental Cleanup, Environmental Due Diligence, Environmental Legislative Practice, Environmental Permitting, Hazardous Waste, Nuclear Waste, Sick Building Syndrome, Solid Waste, Superfund, Underground Storage Tanks, Water Pollution, Wetlands Regulation.

JACK A. VAN KLEY, born Rensselaer, Indiana, February 14, 1954; admitted to bar, 1979, Ohio. *Education:* Valparaiso University (B.A., 1976); George Washington University (J.D., 1979). Former Chief, Environmental Enforcement Section, Ohio Attorney General's Office. ***PRACTICE AREAS:*** Environmental Law. ***Email:*** jvankley@vankleywalker.com

VOLKEMA, THOMAS, MILLER, BURKETT, SCOTT & MERRY

A LEGAL PROFESSIONAL ASSOCIATION
Established in 1988
140 EAST TOWN STREET, SUITE 1100
COLUMBUS, OHIO 43215
Telephone: 614-221-4400
Telecopier: 614-221-6010
URL: http://www.volkemathomas.com
Email: attorneys@vt-law.com
URL: http://www.vt-law.com

Cincinnati, Ohio Office: 700 Walnut Street, Suite 400. 45202-2015. Telephone: 513-651-4400. Fax: 513-651-4405.

Civil State and Federal Trial and Appellate Practice. Personal Injury. Malpractice, Nursing Home Negligence, HMO Liability, Class Actions, Wrongful Death, Automobile Accidents, Product Liability, Employee Benefits, Insurance Bad Faith, Aviation and Tort Law, ERISA, Qui Tam (Whistleblower), False Claims Act.

FIRM PROFILE: A Plaintiff Tort Litigation Firm.

ELIZABETH SCHORPP BURKETT, born Cleveland, Ohio, June 20, 1960; admitted to bar, 1986, Ohio. *Education:* The Ohio State University (B.S., cum laude, 1982; J.D., with honors in Law, 1986). Member, The Ohio State Law Journal, 1985-1986. Recipient: Summa Award, 1979; President's Scholarship Award, 1982; Mildred E. Newton Scholarship, 1980-1982; John E. Hallen Memorial Award, 1984; Soroptimist Scholarship Award, 1985; Le Tourneau Award (American College of Legal Medicine), 1986. Adjunct Professor, Ohio State University College of Law, 1988-1989. *Member:* The Columbus, Ohio State and American Bar Associations; Ohio Academy of Trial Lawyers; Association of Trial Lawyers of America. ***PRACTICE AREAS:*** Medical Malpractice; Nursing Home Negligence; Insurance Coverage; Insurance Bad Faith. ***Email:*** eburkett@vt-law.com

JEFFREY L. MALOON, born Columbus, Ohio, May 14, 1958; admitted to bar, 1983, Ohio; 1987, U.S. Supreme Court. *Education:* Ball State University (B.S., 1980); Capital University (J.D., 1983). Order of the Curia; Blue Key. Fellow, Roscoe Pound Foundation, 2000—. Law Clerk for the Hon. Robert E. Holmes of the Ohio Supreme Court, 1983-1985. Board of Commissioners on the Unauthorized Practice of Law, 1988-1994. Editorial Board, *Ohio Trial,* 1991-1993; Editor, *Ohio Trial,* 1993-1994. Member, Martindale-Hubble Bar of Preeminent Lawyers, 2001. *Member:* Columbus (Member, Doctor-Lawyer Committee, 1985—), Ohio State and American (Member, Tort Insurance Practice Committee, 1985—) Bar Associations; Ohio Academy of Trial Lawyers; Franklin County Trial Lawyers Association; The Association of Trial Lawyers of America; Ohio Academy of Trial Lawyers (Vice-Chair, Medical Negligence Section, 1991-1996; Chair, Medical Negligence Section, 1996—; Member, Board of Trustees, 1992—; Executive Committee, 1993-1994); American Board of Trial Advocacy. ***REPORTED CASES:*** Hardy v. VerMeulen (1987), 32 Ohio St. 3d 45; Morgan v. Fairfield Family Counseling Cir. (1977), 77 Ohio St.3d 284. ***PRACTICE AREAS:*** Medical Negligence; Personal Injury; Products Liability. ***Email:*** jmaloon@vt-law.com

TONY C. MERRY, born Dell Rapids, South Dakota, October 16, 1951; admitted to bar, 1989, Ohio and U.S. District Court, Southern District of Ohio; 1991, U.S. Court of Appeals, Sixth Circuit. *Education:* Sioux Falls College (B.A., 1973); Harvard University (J.D., cum laude, 1989). Lecturer: "Procedural and Jurisdictional Issues under ERISA," Columbus Bar Association, December 1991; "Qualified Domestic Relations Orders," Columbus Bar Association, February 1992; "Identifying ERISA Issues," Columbus Bar Association, December 1993; "Fiduciary Duty and Benefits Discrimination," Duquesne University Benefits Institute, Pittsburgh, Pennsylvania, 1994. Chief of Staff to the Governor of South Dakota, 1983-1986. *Member:* Columbus, Ohio State and American Bar Associations. ***REPORTED CASES:*** Eichner v. Celtic Life Insurance Company, 73 Ohio App.3d 281 (1991); Chroma Studios Insurance v. Community Mutual Insurance Company, 91 Ohio App.3d 422 (1993a); Byrd v. Faber, 57 Ohio St. 3d 56 (1991); Producers Service Corporation v. Limbach, 80 Ohio App.3d 613 (1992); Hubbard Press v. Tracy, 67 Ohio St.3d 564 (1993); Astor v. International Business Machines Corporation, 7 F.2d 533 (6th Cir. 1993); Tregoning v. American Community Mutual Insurance Company, 12 F.3d 79 (6th Cir. 1993); Branham v. Cigna Healthcare of Ohio, Inc., 81 Ohio St. 3d 388 (1988). ***PRACTICE AREAS:*** ERISA; Insurance Bad Faith; Compensation and Benefits; Employment Law; Appellate Practice. ***Email:*** tmerry@vt-law.com

(This Listing Continued)

MICHAEL S. MILLER, born Cincinnati, Ohio, May 12, 1958; admitted to bar, 1984, Ohio. *Education:* University of Cincinnati (B.A., high honors in Political Science, magna cum laude, 1981); Ohio State University College of Law (J.D., summa cum laude, 1984). Phi Beta Kappa; The Order of the Coif. Member Staff, 1982-1983 and Issue Planning Editor, Ohio State Law Journal, 1983-1984. Author: Comment, "Redefining Underinsured Motorist Coverage in Ohio," 44 Ohio State Law Journal 771-795, 1983; "The Impact of Amended Substitute Senate Bill Number 20 upon Savioe and Other Cases," Ohio Trial, Vol. 5, No. 4 (1994); "HB 350: A Comprehensive Overview," Ohio Trial, Vol. 7, No. 4 (1996); "The Use of Learned Treatises and Newly Enacted Rule 706 of the Ohio Rules of Evidence," Ohio Trial, Vol. 9, No. 3 (1998); "The Exhaustion Requirement and Underinsured Motorists Coverage," Ohio Trial, Vol. 10, No. 4 (2000); "Joint Tortfeasors and UM/UIM Coverage," Ohio Trial, Vol. 11, Nos. 2 and 3 (2000). *Member:* Columbus and Ohio State Bar Associations; Franklin County Trial Lawyers Association (Chair, Negligence Law Committee, 1995-1997; Trustee, 1999-2002; President, 2004-2005); Ohio Academy of Trial Lawyers (Member, Board of Trustees, 1996—; Chair of Constitutional Challenge Committee, 1997—; Board of Editors, 1997— and Editor, 1999, Ohio Trial Magazine; Editor, Ohio Advisory, 1998—); The Association of Trial Lawyers of America. ***REPORTED CASES:*** Fulmer v. Insura Prop. S Cas. Co. (2002); 94 Ohio St. 3d 85 (American Brief for Academy of Trial Lawyers); Morgan v. Fairfield Family Counseling Ctr. (1997), 77 Ohio St.3d 248, 673 N.E.2d 1311 (Amicus Brief for Academy of Trial Lawyers): Schaefer v. Allstate Ins. Co. (1996), 76 Ohio St.3d 553, 668 N.E.2d 913; Duckworth v. Creative Interglobal, Inc. (1995), 74 Ihio St. 3d 12, 665 N.E.2d 1299 (Amicus Brief for Academy of Trial Lawyers); Pond v. Leslein (1995), 72 Ohio St. 3d 50, 647 N.E.2d 477; Stinson v. England (1994), 69 Ohio St.3d 451, 633 N.E.2d 532; Clark v. Southview Hosp. & Family Health Ctr. (1994), 68 Ohio St.3d 435, 628 N.E.2d 46 (Amicus Brief for The Ohio Academy of Trial Lawyers for which received The Academic Amicus Curiae Award, 1993-1994 from the Ohio Academy of Trial Lawyers); Ramage v. Central Ohio Emergency Serv., Inc. (1992), 64 Ohio St.3d 97, 592 N.E.2d 828; Skaggs v. Lima Memorial Hospital (1991), 62 Ohio St.3d 296, 581 N.E.2d 1085; Morris v. Savoy (1991), 61 Ohio St.3d 684, 576 N.E.2d 765 (Amicus Brief for Ohio Academy of Trial Lawyers); Fyffe v. Jeno's Inc. (1991), 59 Ohio St.3d 115, 570 N.E.2d 1108; Lane v. Grange Mutual Insurance Company (1989), 45 Ohio St.3d 63, 543 N.E.2d 488; Jewell v. Holzer Hospital (Sixth Cir., 1990), 899 F.2d 1507; Nestor v. Lima Mem. Hosp. (2000), 139 Ohio App. 3d 188; Limle v. Lab. Corp. of Am. (2000), 137 Ohio App. 3d 434, 738 N.E.2d 890; Orvets v. National City Bank (1999), 131 Ohio App. 3d 180, 722 N.E.2d 114; Taulbee v. Adience, Inc. (1997), 120 Ohio App. 3d 11, 696 N.E.2d 625; Gregory v. Bureau of Workers' Compensation (1996), 115 Ohio App.3d 798, 686 N.E.2d 347; Frazee v. Ellis Bros., Inc. (1996), 113 Ohio App.3d 828, 682 N.E.2d 676; Wiltberger v. Davis (1996), 110 Ohio App.3d 46, 673 N.E.2d 628; Loura v. Adler (1995), 105 Ohio App. 3d 634, 664 N.E.2d 1002; In Re Estate of Shepherd (1994), 97 Ohio App. 3d 280, 646 N.E.2d 561; Kitts v. U.S. Health Corp. (1994), 97 Ohio App.3d 271, 646 N.E.2d 555; Miller v. Paulson (1994), 97 Ohio App. 3d 217, 646 N.E.2d 521; Shoemaker v. Crawford (1991), 78 Ohio App.3d 53, 603 N.E.2d 1114; Canady v. Central Benefits (1991), 71 Ohio App. 3d 363, 594 N.E.2d 37 Mulloy v. Longaberger, Inc. (1989), 47 Ohio App.3d 77, 547 N.E.2d 411. ***PRACTICE AREAS:*** Appellate Practice; Medical Malpractice; Legal Malpractice; Uninsured and Underinsured Motorists; Automobile Accidents and Injuries; Personal Injury. ***Email:*** mmiller@vt-law.com

FREDERICK M. MORGAN, JR., born Wheeling, West Virginia, September 19, 1956; admitted to bar, 1983, Ohio; 1997, U.S. Court of Appeals, Fifth, Sixth, Tenth and Eleventh Circuits and U.S. Supreme Court. *Education:* Denison University (B.A., 1978); University of Cincinnati (J.D., 1983). Co-Author, "The Last Privateers Encounter Sloppy Seas: Inconsistent Original Source Jurisprudence Under the Federal False Claims Act," 24 Ohio N.U.L. Rev. 163 (1998). Law Clerk to the Honorable David S. Porter, U.S. Senior District Judge, Southern District of Ohio, 1983-1985. Trial Attorney, Federal Programs Branch, Civil Division, U.S. Department of Justice, Washington, D.C., 1985-1989. *Member:* Cincinnati and American Bar Associations; The Association of Trial Lawyers of America. Member Emeritus: The Charles Fahy American Inn of Court; Potter Stewart Inn of Court. ***Email:*** rmorgan@vt-law.com

CRAIG P. SCOTT, born Columbus, Ohio, April 27, 1961; admitted to bar, 1989, Ohio and U.S. District Court, Southern District of Ohio. *Education:* The Ohio State University (B.A., 1984); Capital University (J.D., 1989). Clerk, The Supreme Court of Ohio, 1984-1986. *Member:* Columbus and Ohio State Bar Associations; Franklin County Trial Lawyers Association; Ohio Academy of Trial Lawyers; The Association of Trial Lawyers of America. ***PRACTICE AREAS:*** Products Liability; Personal Injury; Medical Malpractice. ***Email:*** cscott@vt-law.com

WARNER M. THOMAS, JR., born Charlottesville, Virginia, November 12, 1949; admitted to bar, 1979, Ohio; 1983, U.S. District Court, Southern District of Ohio; 1987, U.S. Court of Appeals, Sixth Circuit and U.S. Supreme Court; 1989, Kentucky. *Education:* Bethune-Cookman College (B.S., magna cum laude, 1974); University of Scranton; Ohio Northern University (J.D., 1978). Pi Gamma Mu. Assistant City Attorney, Criminal Division, Columbus, Ohio, 1980-1982. Selected to Who's Who in Law, 1994. *Member:* Columbus, Ohio State and Kentucky Bar Associations; The Association of Trial Lawyers of America; Ohio Academy of Trial Lawyers; Franklin County Trial Lawyers Association; Kentucky Academy of Trial Lawyers. ***PRACTICE AREAS:*** Personal Injury; Wrongful Death; Medical Negligence; Legal Negligence; Insurance; Automobile Accidents and Injuries; Product Liability. ***Email:*** jrthomas@vt-law.com

JENNIFER M. VERKAMP, born Cincinnati, Ohio, August 9, 1970; admitted to bar, 1996, Ohio and U.S. Court of Appeals, Sixth and Eleventh Circuits. *Education:* Xavier University (B.S., 1992); Georgetown University (J.D., 1996). Recipient, BNA Legal Scholar Award. Co-Author, "Notes From the Field: Practicalities of the Qui Tam 'Working Partner-

(This Listing Continued)

VOLKEMA, THOMAS, MILLER, BURKETT, SCOTT & MERRY,
A LEGAL PROFESSIONAL ASSOCIATION, Columbus—Continued

ship' Under the 1986 False Claims Act Amendments," 29 False Claims Act and Qui Tam Quarterly Review 31 (2003). *Member:* Cincinnati Bar Association; Cincinnati Academy of Leadership for Lawyers. **Email:** jverkamp@vt-law.com

DANIEL R. VOLKEMA, born Miami, Florida, September 9, 1953; admitted to bar, 1979, Ohio; 1980, U.S. District Court, Southern and Northern Districts of Ohio; 1985, U.S. Court of Appeals, Third and Sixth Circuits; U.S Supreme Court. *Education:* Western Washington University (B.A., 1975); Ohio Northern University (J.D., 1978). Lecturer: "Opening Statement," Ohio Legal Center Institute, 1986-2004; "Underinsurance in Ohio," Ohio Academy of Trial Lawyers, November, 1983; "Ohio Civil Rule 35," Ohio Academy of Trial Lawyers, October, 1986; "Tort Reform and the New Collateral Source Rule," Ohio Academy of Trial Lawyers, August, 1987; "Evaluation of Medical Claims," Ohio Legal Center Institute, 1993; "Claims Against Insurance Agents," Ohio Academy of Trial Lawyers, 1994; Best of Bridge The Gap Ohio CLE Institute, 2000. *Member:* Columbus and Ohio State (Member, New Lawyer Training) Bar Associations; Ohio Academy of Trial Lawyers (Producer and Director, 2001); The Association of Trial Lawyers of America. ***REPORTED CASES:*** Huth v. State, 64 Ohio St. 2d.143 (1980); Winters v. Beitler, 21 Ohio Op 3d 459 (1980); Woods v. Columbus, 23 Ohio App. 3d 163 (1985); Beshara v. Schindler, 74 Ohio St. 3d 1209 (1995); Ingram v. Adena Health System, 144 Ohio (2001). ***PRACTICE AREAS:*** Personal Injury; Malpractice; Insurance Bad Faith; Product Liability. ***Email:*** dvolkema@vt-law.com

---

JANET L. LARKIN, born Youngstown, Ohio, November 25, 1966; admitted to bar, 2001, Ohio. *Education:* The Ohio State University (B.S., 1991); Capital University (J.D., 2001). *Member:* Columbus, Struthers, Ohio State and American Bar Associations; Ohio Association of Trial Lawyers; Association of Trial Lawyers of America. ***PRACTICE AREAS:*** Plaintiffs Personal Injury Litigation; ERISA; Employee Benefits; Employment Discrimination; Insurance Bad Faith. ***Email:*** jlarkin@vt-law.com

REFERENCE: Huntington National Bank.

VORYS, SATER, SEYMOUR AND PEASE LLP

Established in 1909
52 EAST GAY STREET
P.O. BOX 1008
COLUMBUS, OHIO 43216-1008
Telephone: 614-464-6400
Facsimile: 614-464-6350
URL: http://www.vssp.com

Washington, D.C. Office: 1828 L Street, N.W., 20036-5109. Telephone: 202-467-8800. Facsimile: 202-467-8900.

Cleveland, Ohio Office: 2100 One Cleveland Center, 1375 East Ninth Street, 44114-1724. Telephone: 216-479-6100. Facsimile: 216-479-6060.

Cincinnati, Ohio Office: Atrium Two, Suite 2000, 221 East Fourth Street, P.O. Box 0236, 45201-0236. Telephone: 513-723-4000. Facsimile: 513-723-4056.

Alexandria, Virginia Office: 277 South Washington Street, Suite 310, 22314. Telephone: 703-837-6999. Facsimile: 703-549-4492.

Akron, Ohio Office: First National Tower, 106 South Main Street, Suite 1100, 44308. Telephone: 330-208-1000. Facsimile: 330-208-1001.

Alternative Dispute Resolution, Antitrust, Trade Regulation, Customs, Banks and Banking, Finance, Bankruptcy, Biotechnology, Business Law, Civil Rights, Debtors and Creditors Rights, Computers and Software, Congressional Investigations, Construction Law, Contracts, Copyrights, Disabilities, Election, Campaign and Political Law, Employee Benefits, Environmental Law, Probate, Guardianship and Conservatorship, General Practice, Health Care, Labor, Employment, Occupational Safety and Health, Workers Compensation, Corporate Law, Securities, Energy, Natural Resources, Franchises and Franchising, Government Contracts, Hospital Law, Immigration and Naturalization, Insurance, Intellectual Property, International Law, International Trade, Legal Ethics and Professional Responsibility, Litigation, Media Law, Medicare and Medicaid, Mergers, Acquisitions and Divestitures, Municipal Law, Telecommunications, Personal Injury, Products Liability, Railroad Law, Real Estate, RICO, Sports Law, Taxation, Technology and Science, Torts, Toxic Torts, Trade Secrets, Transportation, Trusts and Estates, Unfair Competition, Utility Law, White Collar Defense, Wills, Zoning, Planning and Land Use.

ARTHUR I. VORYS (1856-1933)
LOWRY F. SATER (1867-1935)
AUGUSTUS T. SEYMOUR (1873-1926)
EDWARD L. PEASE (1873-1924)

PARTNERS

JAMES R. BEATLEY, JR., born Columbus, Ohio, January 2, 1941; admitted to bar, 1965, Ohio. *Education:* The Ohio State University (B.A., 1962; J.D., 1965). Order of the Coif; Phi Delta Phi. Member, Board of Editors, Ohio State Law Journal, 1964-1965. Law Clerk, U.S. District Court, Northern District of Illinois, 1965-1967. ***PRACTICE AREAS:*** Mergers and Acquisitions Law; Corporate Law; Business Law; Insurance. ***Email:*** jrbeatley@vssp.com

THOMAS B. RIDGLEY, born Columbus, Ohio, April 29, 1940; admitted to bar, 1965, Pennsylvania; 1968, Ohio; U.S. District Court, Northern and Southern Districts of Ohio, U.S. Court of Appeals, Third, Sixth and Tenth Circuits and U.S. Supreme Court. *Education:* Princeton University (A.B., magna cum laude, 1962); University of Michigan (J.D., with distinction, 1965). Assistant Editor, Michigan Law Review, 1964-1965. *Member:* Columbus, Cincinnati, Ohio State and American Bar Associations. Fellow, American College

(This Listing Continued)

of Trial Lawyers. ***PRACTICE AREAS:*** Civil Litigation; Corporate Litigation; Labor and Employment Litigation; Environmental Litigation; Product Liability Litigation. ***Email:*** tbridgley@vssp.com

ROBERT W. WERTH, born Clyde, Ohio; admitted to bar, 1965, Ohio. *Education:* The Ohio State University (B.A., 1962; J.D., summa cum laude, 1965). Phi Delta Phi; Order of the Coif. Associate Editor, Ohio State Law Journal, 1964-1965. Law Clerk to Hon. Kingsley A. Taft, Chief Justice, Ohio Supreme Court, 1965-1966. President, Columbus Law Library Association, 1975—. Member, Board of Directors, Greater Columbus Chamber of Commerce, 1993-2001 and 2004—. Member, Board of Directors, Columbus Technology Leadership Council, 2000—. Member, Ohio Business Roundtable, 1994—. National Council, The Ohio State University Moritz College of Law, 1995—. President, Columbus Law Library Association, 1968—. Member, Greater Columbus Sports Commission Advisory Council, 2004—. *Member:* Columbus, Ohio State and American (Member, Business Bankruptcy Committee, 1981—) Bar Associations; Ohio State Bar Foundation; American Bar Foundation; American College of Mortgage Attorneys. (Managing Partner). ***PRACTICE AREAS:*** Financial Institutions Law; Real Estate; Bankruptcy. ***Email:*** rwwerth@vssp.com

DAVID S. CUPPS, born Pittsburgh, Pennsylvania, October 25, 1936; admitted to bar, 1966, New York; 1972, Ohio; 1979, District of Columbia. *Education:* Harvard College (A.B., 1958); The Ohio State University (J.D., summa cum laude, 1965). Order of the Coif. Mershon Fellowship, 1964-1965. Editor, Ohio State Law Journal, 1964-1965. Fellow, American College of Trial Lawyers and Regent, 1997-2001. ***PRACTICE AREAS:*** Professional Malpractice; Securities Litigation; Complex Litigation. ***Email:*** dscupps@vssp.com

JAMES H. GROSS, born Springfield, Ohio, September 21, 1941; admitted to bar, 1966, Ohio; 1975, District of Columbia. *Education:* The Ohio State University (B.A., summa cum laude, 1963); Harvard University (LL.B., 1966). Phi Beta Kappa. City Attorney, Bexley, Ohio, 1985—. ***PRACTICE AREAS:*** Corporate Law; Mergers and Acquisitions Law; Securities Regulation. ***Email:*** jhgross@vssp.com

GEORGE L. JENKINS, born Cadiz, Ohio; admitted to bar, 1966, Ohio; 1967, U.S. District Court, Southern District of Ohio; 1970, U.S. Court of Appeals, Sixth Circuit; 1971, U.S. Supreme Court. *Education:* Kent State University (A.B., magna cum laude, 1963; National Political Science and National Social Science Honoraries, Blue Key); University of Michigan (J.D., with distinction, 1966). First Assistant Attorney General, Ohio, 1971-1975. Member, President's National Commission on Employment Policy, 1979-1982. Appointed by Gov. Bob Taft as Member, Kent State University Board of Trustees. ***PRACTICE AREAS:*** Business Acquisitions; Administrative Law; Corporate Law; Real Estate Development; Economic Development Incentives. ***Email:*** gljenkins@vssp.com

ROBERT J. SIDMAN, born Cleveland, Ohio, August 4, 1943; admitted to bar, 1968, Ohio; 1970, U.S. Court of Appeals, Sixth Circuit; 1972, U.S. Tax Court and U.S. Supreme Court; 1990, U.S. Court of Appeals, Fourth Circuit; 1993, U.S. Court of Appeals, Third Circuit. *Education:* St. Benedict's College (B.A., magna cum laude, 1965); University of Notre Dame (J.D., 1968). Law Clerk to Judge Joseph P. Kinneary, U.S. District Court, Southern District of Ohio, 1968-1970. United States Bankruptcy Judge, Southern District of Ohio, 1975-1982. Member: Board of Advisors, Annual Survey of Bankruptcy Law, 1980-1982; Advisory Board, American Bankruptcy Law Journal, 1982. Adjunct Professor, Ohio State University School of Law, 1984-1987. *Member:* Columbus and Ohio State Bar Associations; American Bar Association (Member, Section of Corporation, Banking and Business Law); Association of Former Bankruptcy Judges (Charter Member and Advisory Committee; President, 1988-1989); National Conference of Bankruptcy Judges (Member, 1975-1982 and Associate Member, 1982—, Board of Governors; 6th Circuit Representative, 1981-1982; Chairman, Associates Committee, 1983-1984); American Bankruptcy Institute. ***PRACTICE AREAS:*** Bankruptcy; Debtor Creditor Law; Commercial Law. ***Email:*** rjsidman@vssp.com

MICHAEL G. LONG, born Columbus, Ohio, February 27, 1944; admitted to bar, 1969, Ohio. *Education:* Ohio Wesleyan University (B.A., 1966); The Ohio State University (J.D., cum laude, 1969). Member, Board of Editors, Ohio State Law Journal, 1968-1969. *Member:* Ohio Association of Civil Trial Attorneys; Defense Research Institute. ***PRACTICE AREAS:*** Trial Practice; Appellate Practice; Commercial Litigation; Employment Litigation. ***Email:*** mglong@vssp.com

WILLIAM S. NEWCOMB, JR., born Columbus, Ohio; admitted to bar, 1969, Ohio. *Education:* The Ohio State University (B.S., 1965; J.D., 1968). Legal Director, Ohio EPA, 1976. Commissioner, 1977-1980 and Chairman, 1980-1981, Ohio Public Utilities Commission. Chairman, Committee on Administration, 1979-1981 and Member, Executive Committee, 1980-1981, National Association of Regulatory Utility Commissioners. Commissioner, Mid-Ohio Regional Planning Commission, 1992-2000; Commissioner, Ohio Public Works Commission, 1991-1995. *Member:* Columbus (Chairman: Judiciary Committee, 1982-1983; Energy Committee, 1983-1984) and Ohio State (Chairman, Public Utilities Committee, 1992—) Bar Associations. ***PRACTICE AREAS:*** Public Utility Law; Telecommunications Law; Common Carrier Law; Legislative Practice. ***Email:*** wsnewcomb@vssp.com

DANIEL H. SCHOEDINGER, born Elgin Field Air Force Base, Florida, September 5, 1944; admitted to bar, 1969, Ohio. *Education:* Lehigh University (B.S., 1966); University of Denver (J.D., 1969). Phi Alpha Delta. Member, Order of St. Ives. Member, Denver Law Journal, 1968-1969. Law Clerk to Hon. C. William O'Neil, Chief Justice, Ohio Supreme Court, 1969-1971. Councilman, City of Columbus, 1972-1979. ***PRACTICE AREAS:*** Real Estate; Zoning Law; Tax Exempt Finance. ***Email:*** dschoedinger@vssp.com

THOMAS M. TARPY, born Columbus, Ohio, January 4, 1945; admitted to bar, 1969, Ohio. *Education:* John Carroll University (A.B., 1966); The Ohio State University (J.D., 1969). Phi Delta Phi. Columbus Graphics Commission (Member, 1977-1980; Chairman, 1980). Listed in The Best Lawyers in America. *Member:* Ohio State and American (Member, Labor Law Section) Bar Associations. The College of Labor and Employment Lawyers. ***PRACTICE AREAS:*** Employment Law; Labor Law; Litigation; ERISA Law; Business Law. ***Email:*** tmtarpy@vssp.com

SUSAN E. BROWN, born Youngstown, Ohio, April 19, 1946; admitted to bar, 1971, Ohio. *Education:* Georgetown University; The Ohio State University (B.A., summa cum laude and with distinction, 1968; J.D., summa cum laude, 1971). Phi Beta Kappa; Tau Ep-

(This Listing Continued)

silon Rho. Recipient, Moritz Law Community Service Award, 2003. Adjunct Professor of Regulation of Securities Distribution, The Ohio State University College of Law, 1989. ***PRACTICE AREAS:*** Corporate Law; Securities Regulation; Mergers and Acquisitions. ***Email:*** sebrown@vssp.com

RICHARD P. FAHEY, born Oakland, California, November 2, 1944; admitted to bar, 1971, New Mexico and U.S. District Court, District of New Mexico; 1972, U.S. Court of Appeals, Tenth Circuit; 1973, Ohio and U.S. District Court, Northern and Southern Districts of Ohio; 1975, U.S. Supreme Court. *Education:* San Francisco State University (B.A., 1966); Northwestern University (J.D., 1971). Phi Sigma Alpha. Author: "The Enforcement of the Illinois Felony Marijuana Law in Chicago," Washington University Law Quarterly 281-308, 1971; "The Poro As a System of Judicial Administration in Northwest Liberia," 4 African Law Studies 1-25, 1971; "Native American Justice: The Courts of the Navajo Nation," 59 Judicature 1, 10-17, 1975. Co-Author: "An Inquest On the Cook County Coroner," 19 Crime and Delinquency 19-32, 1973; "Killings by Chicago Police," 46 Southern California Law Review 284-315, 1973; "Groundwater Law in Ohio Past and Future," 14 Capital University Law Review 43-80, 1984; "Underground Storage Tanks: The New Federal Regulatory Program," ABA Natural Resources Monograph Series, 1989, 2nd edition, 1995; Chapter 2, "Underground Storage Tank Program," Ohio Environmental Law, Banks-Baldwin, 1992. Adjunct Professor: Environmental Law, Natural Resources Law, Capital University Law School, 1976-1986; Environmental Law, The Ohio State University Law School, 1986-1987. Assistant Attorney General, Environmental Law Section, State of Ohio, 1973-1975. Special Assistant Attorney General for Environmental Affairs, State of West Virginia, 1984-1985. General Counsel, Ohio Savings and Loan Assurance Corporation, 1985-1990. Chairman, Ohio Oil and Gas Regulatory Review Commission, 1986-1987. Member, 1986-1994 and President, 1989-1990, Columbus Public Schools Board of Education. Member, Columbus Charter Review Committee, 1998. President, National Audubon Society Ohio, 1999. . *Member:* Columbus, Ohio State and American (Vice Chair, Water Quality Committee, Section on Natural Resources, Energy and Environmental Law, 1993-1995) Bar Associations; State Bar of New Mexico. ***PRACTICE AREAS:*** Environmental Law. ***Email:*** rpfahey@vssp.com

C. WILLIAM O'NEILL, born Marietta, Ohio, June 4, 1946; admitted to bar, 1971, Ohio. *Education:* Princeton University (A.B., cum laude, 1968); University of Michigan (J.D., cum laude, 1971). Associate Editor, Michigan Law Review, 1969-1971. ***PRACTICE AREAS:*** Libel and Slander; Products Liability; Litigation. ***Email:*** cwoneill@vssp.com

DOUGLAS L. ROGERS, born White Plains, New York, October 9, 1946; admitted to bar, 1971, Ohio; 1978, District of Columbia. *Education:* Cornell University (B.A., 1968); Yale University (J.D., 1971). Director: Ohio Legal Rights Service, 1975-1980; Legal Aid Society of Columbus, 1980-1982. *Member:* Columbus, Ohio State and American Bar Associations. ***PRACTICE AREAS:*** Litigation; Antitrust; Computer Law; Copyright; Disabilities. ***Email:*** dlrogers@vssp.com

MICHAEL J. CANTER, born Cincinnati, Ohio, June 28, 1947; admitted to bar, 1972, Ohio. *Education:* Ohio University (B.B.A., cum laude, with honors in Business, 1969); Northwestern University (J.D., cum laude, 1972). Pi Gamma Mu. Lecturer, Ohio Continuing Legal Education Institute. Member, Board of Trustees, Wexner Center Foundation, 2003. *Member:* American Bar Association (Member, Sections on: Antitrust Law; Litigation; Vice Chair, Private Litigation Section). ***PRACTICE AREAS:*** Antitrust; Litigation; Administrative Law. ***Email:*** mjcanter@vssp.com

RUSSELL M. GERTMENIAN, born New York, N.Y., July 22, 1947; admitted to bar, 1972, Ohio. *Education:* Rutgers University (A.B., 1969); Columbia University (J.D., 1972). *Member:* United States Trademark Association. ***PRACTICE AREAS:*** Business Law; Corporate Law; Trademarks. ***Email:*** rmgertmenian@vssp.com

JOSEPH D. LONARDO, born Cleveland, Ohio, October 15, 1947; admitted to bar, 1972, Ohio. *Education:* Georgetown University (A.B., 1969); University of Michigan (J.D., cum laude, 1972). *Member:* American Bar Association (Member, Section of: Environment, Energy and Resources); Defense Research and Trial Lawyers Association; International Association of Defense Counsel (Member, Toxic/Hazardous Substances Litigation Committee). (Resident, Washington, D.C. Office). ***PRACTICE AREAS:*** Litigation; Trial Practice; Environmental Law. ***Email:*** jdlonardo@vssp.com

ALAN T. RADNOR, born Cleveland, Ohio, March 10, 1946; admitted to bar, 1972, Ohio. *Education:* Kenyon College (A.B., 1967); The Ohio State University (M.S., in Anatomy, 1969; J.D., cum laude, 1972). Order of the Coif. Member, Ohio State Law Journal, 1971-1972. Adjunct Professor, Trial Advocacy, The Ohio State University College of Law, 1979-1999. Fellow, American College of Trial lawyers. ***PRACTICE AREAS:*** Trial Practice; Medical-Legal Law; Medical Malpractice. ***Email:*** atradnor@vssp.com

RONALD L. ROWLAND, born Columbus, Ohio, November 15, 1947; admitted to bar, 1972, Ohio; 1973, Florida. *Education:* Wittenberg University (B.A., cum laude, 1969); The Ohio State University (J.D., summa cum laude, 1972); University of Florida (LL.M. in Taxation, 1976). Pi Sigma Alpha; Order of the Coif. Adjunct Professor of Law, Capital University, Graduate Tax Program, 1988. Chairman, Taxation Committee, Ohio Oil and Gas Association, 1984-1998. Member, Executive Committee, Columbus Investment Interest Group (Chairman, 1993-1995). Chairman, Cost and Availability of Capital Committee, Ohio Small Business and Entrepreneurship Council, 1991-1995. Trustee and Secretary, Industrial and Technology Council. Member, Graduate Tax Council, Capital University, 1991-1994. Member: Charitable Giving and Tax Advisory Committee of the Foundation of the Catholic Diocese of Columbus; Legal Advisory Committee of the Columbus Foundation. *Member:* Columbus (Chairman, Tax Committee, 1981-1983), Ohio State and American (Member of Partnership Committee of Taxation) Bar Associations; The Florida Bar. ***PRACTICE AREAS:*** Federal Income Tax; Estate and Gift Taxation Law; Partnership Law; Business Planning. ***Email:*** rlrowland@vssp.com

W. JONATHAN AIREY, born Loma Linda, California, December 23, 1944; admitted to bar, 1973, Ohio; 1974, California. *Education:* Loma Linda University (B.A., with honors, 1967); University of California at Los Angeles (J.D., 1973). Member, U.C.L.A. Law Review, 1971-1973. Author: "Transportation of Natural Gas," 5 Proceedings of Eastern Mineral Laws Foundation, Matthew Bender, 1984. Trustee, Eastern Mineral Law Foundation, 1980—; Chairman, Oil and Gas Law Committee, 1985, 1989. *Member:* Ohio State (Member, Natural Resources Committee, 1977—; Chairman, 1982-1985) and American (Member, Natural Resources Law) Bar Associations; State Bar of California; Independent

(This Listing Continued)

Petroleum Association of America (Chairman, Law Committee, 1989—). ***PRACTICE AREAS:*** Oil and Gas Law; Federal Gas Law; Gas Contract Litigation. ***Email:*** wjairey@vssp.com

G. ROSS BRIDGMAN, born New Haven, Connecticut, December 27, 1947; admitted to bar, 1973, Ohio. *Education:* Yale University (B.A., cum laude, 1970); Northwestern University (J.D., 1973). Member, Editorial Board, Northwestern Law Review, 1972-1973. Listed in The Best Lawyers in America. *Member:* Columbus, Ohio State and American (Member: Labor and Employment Law Section; Federal Labor Standards Legislation Committee) Bar Associations; The National Association of College and University Attorneys. Fellow, College of Labor & Employment Lawyers, Inc. ***PRACTICE AREAS:*** Management Labor Law; Employment Discrimination; Education Law; College and University Law; Behavioral Law. ***Email:*** grbridgeman@vssp.com

CHARLES S. DeROUSIE, born Adrian, Michigan, May 24, 1947; admitted to bar, 1973, Ohio. *Education:* Oakland University (B.A., magna cum laude, 1969); University of Michigan (J.D., magna cum laude, 1973). Order of the Coif. *Member:* American Bar Association (Member: Business Law Section; Banking and Health and Biotechnology Committees, 1982—). ***PRACTICE AREAS:*** Health Care Law; Banking Law; Bank Holding Company Regulation; Business Law; Corporate Law. ***Email:*** csderousie@vssp.com

MARY ELLEN FAIRFIELD, born Pittsburgh, Pennsylvania, January 4, 1949; admitted to bar, 1973, Ohio. *Education:* Purdue University (B.A., cum laude, 1970); The Ohio State University (J.D., cum laude, 1972). Phi Delta Phi. Articles Editor, Ohio State Law Journal, 1972. Adjunct Faculty, Trial Practice, The Ohio State University College of Law, 1984-1995. Ohio State Bar Examiner, 1975. *Member:* Columbus, Ohio State and American Bar Associations; Defense Research Institute. Fellow, American College of Trial Lawyers. ***PRACTICE AREAS:*** Employment Discrimination; Trial Practice; Products Liability; Federal and Appellate Practice. ***Email:*** mefairfield@vssp.com

ROBERT E. TAIT, born Lima, Ohio, September 3, 1946; admitted to bar, 1973, Ohio. *Education:* Kenyon College (B.A., cum laude, 1968); University of Michigan (J.D., cum laude, 1973). Phi Kappa Sigma. Staff Counsel, Select Committee for the Investigation and Prevention of Industrial Accidents, 1977-1978. Advocate of the American Board of Trial Advocates. *Member:* Columbus, Ohio State (Member, Workers' Compensation Committee, 1982—) and American Bar Associations; Association of Defense Trial Attorneys (Treasurer, 2002—; Member: Executive Committee, 1991-1994); Defense Research Institute (Member, Workers' Compensation Committee, 1987—); Federation of Defense and Corporate Counsel (Member, Toxic Tort Committee, 2002—). ***PRACTICE AREAS:*** Workers Compensation; Trial Practice; Toxic Torts. ***Email:*** retait@vssp.com

JAMES M. BALL, born Plymouth, Indiana, April 3, 1949; admitted to bar, 1974, Ohio. *Education:* Miami University (B.A., 1971); University of Chicago (J.D., 1974). Phi Eta Sigma; Phi Beta Kappa. *Member:* Columbus (Member, Financial Institution Committee, 1983—), Ohio State (Member, Banking, Commercial and Bankruptcy Law Committee, 1985—) and American (Member, Corporate, Banking and Business Law Section) Bar Associations. ***PRACTICE AREAS:*** Financial Institutions Law; Secured Finance; Consumer Law; Real Estate Law. ***Email:*** jmball@vssp.com

PHILIP A. BROWN, born Gettysburg, Pennsylvania, June 12, 1949; admitted to bar, 1974, Ohio. *Education:* George Washington University (B.A., 1971); University of Michigan (J.D., 1974). Phi Beta Kappa. *Member:* Columbus, Ohio State and American Bar Associations. ***PRACTICE AREAS:*** Securities Litigation; Complex Litigation. ***Email:*** pabrown@vssp.com

STEPHEN R. BUCHENROTH, born Bellefontaine, Ohio, February 8, 1948; admitted to bar, 1974, Ohio. *Education:* Wittenberg University (A.B., cum laude, 1970); University of Chicago (J.D., 1974). Pi Sigma Alpha. Chairman, Ohio Supreme Court Commission on Continuing Education, 1999. *Member:* Columbus (Member, Board of Governors, 1986-1994; President, 1992-1993), Ohio State (Member: Council of Delegates, 1986-1988, 1991—; Real Property Section, Board of Governors, 1990—; Chair, Real Property Section, 2003-2005; Member, Real Property Specialty Board, 2003—); and American (Member: Sections on: Antitrust Law; Business Law, Chairman, Franchising Subcommittee of Small Business Committee, 1991-1992; Real Property, Probate and Trust Law; Forum on Franchising) Bar Associations; American College of Real Estate Lawyers. ***PRACTICE AREAS:*** Real Estate; Foreclosure; Franchise Law. ***Email:*** srbuchenroth@vssp.comom

M. HOWARD PETRICOFF, born Cincinnati, Ohio, December 22, 1949; admitted to bar, 1974, Ohio; U.S. Court of Appeals, Sixth, Tenth and District of Columbia Circuits and U.S. Supreme Court. *Education:* American University (B.S., 1971); University of Cincinnati (J.D., 1974); Harvard University (M.P.A., 1981). Adjunct Professor, Capital University Law School, 1992—. Assistant Attorney General, 1977-1982 and Special Assistant Attorney General, 1983—, State of Ohio. *Member:* Ohio State Bar Association (Chair, Committee of Natural Resources, 2003-2004); Ohio State Bar Foundation. ***SPECIAL AGENCIES:*** Member, Oil and Gas Commission. ***PRACTICE AREAS:*** Oil and Gas Law; Public Utility Law; Administrative Law; Administrative Hearings and Appeals; Administrative Adjudications; Contracts; Education Law; Energy; Environmental Law; Natural Resources. ***Email:*** mhpetricoff@vssp.com

SUZANNE K. RICHARDS, born Akron, Ohio, May 19, 1947; admitted to bar, 1974, Ohio. *Education:* St. Mary's College (B.A., summa cum laude, 1969); The Ohio State University (J.D., summa cum laude, 1974). Member, Order of the Coif. Law Clerk to Hon. Robert Duncan, Judge, U.S. District Court, Southern District of Ohio, 1974-1976. Board of Commissioners on Character and Fitness for the Supreme Court of Ohio, 1988—(Chair, 1991-1993). Member, Board of Directors, CASA of Franklin County (President, 2002-2003). *Member:* Columbus, Ohio (Chair, Legal Assistants Committee, 1991-1993 and American (Chair, Standing Committee on Legal Assistants1997-2000) Bar Associations. ***PRACTICE AREAS:*** Commercial Litigation; Federal Practice; Employment Discrimination; Alternative Dispute Resolution; Directors' and Officers' Liability. ***Email:*** skrichards@vssp.com

FREDERICK L. RANSIER, III, born Brooklyn, New York, 1949; admitted to bar, 1974, Ohio and U.S. District Court, Northern District of Ohio; 1975, U.S. District Court, Southern District of Ohio and U.S. Court of Appeals, Sixth Circuit. *Education:* Central State University (B.A., 1971); The Ohio State University (J.D., 1974). Recipient: Community Service Award, Columbus Bar Association, 1990; Minority Business Advocate Award, Society National Bank, 1993; Presidental Citation, National Association for Equal Oppor-

(This Listing Continued)

VORYS, SATER, SEYMOUR AND PEASE LLP, Columbus—Continued

tunity in High Education, 1999; Central State University Alumni Association Alumnus of the Year Award, 1999; Columbus Urban League Equal Opportunity Day Award of Excellence, 1998; The Ohio State University College of Law Alumni Community Service Award, 2002. Founder: Ransier & Ransier, Attorneys at Law, February, 1976. Chapter 7 Bankruptcy Panel Trustee, 1988—. Former President, City of Columbus Municipal Civil Service Commission. Former Member, Columbus City Council. Member and Former Chair, Board of Trustees, Central State University. Member, Board of Directors, Columbus College of Art and Design, 2000. Chair, Board of Unauthorized Practice of Law of the Supreme Court of Ohio. Trustee, The Ohio State University Hospitals Development Board. Former Law Director, Village of Urbancrest. Former Chair, Broad Brunson Condominium Association and Columbus Work. Former Trustee, Marbury Academy, Association for the Developmentally Disabled and The Legal Aid Society of Columbus. Former Assistant Attorney General, State of Ohio, Criminal Activities Section. Former Member, Bankruptcy Court Judicial Liaison Committee. Former Member, Bankruptcy Trustee Advisory Committee. Member and Treasurer of the Board of Directors, Columbus College of Art and Design; Member and Treasurer of the Franklin Park Conservatory Joint Recreation District; Member, The Ohio State University Hospitals East Board of Directors; Member, The Ohio State University Alumni Association Advisory Council. Panel of Arbitrators and Former Member, American Arbitration Association. Member: Board of Directors, KidsOhio.org; Experience Columbus. *Member:* Columbus (Member, Judicial Advertising Committee), Ohio State, American and National Bar Associations; National Association of Bankruptcy Trustees. ***PRACTICE AREAS:*** Administrative; Civil and Trial Practice; Bankruptcy; Business Law; Housing Law; Real Estate. ***Email:*** flransier@vssp.com

KATHLEEN H. RANSIER, born Huntington, West Virginia, 1947; admitted to bar, 1974, Ohio; 1975, U.S. District Court, Southern District of Ohio; 1984, U.S. Court of Appeals, Federal Circuit. *Education:* Western College for Women (B.A., 1969); The Ohio State University (J.D., 1974). Recipient: Constance Baker Motley Award, NAACP Legal Defense and Education Fund, Inc., 1974; Community Service Award, Columbus Bar Association, 1990; Minority Business Advocate Award, Society National Bank, 1993; Community Service Award, OSU Michael E. Moritz College of Law, 2002; YWCA "Women of Achievement" Award, 2004. Founder: Ransier & Ransier, LLP, Attorneys at Law, February, 1976. Current Director, Huntington Bancshares Incorporated; Director, Moody-Nolan, Inc.; Chair, Columbus Regional Airport Authority; President, Women's Fund of Central Ohio, Inc.; Director, Capital South Community Urban Redevelopment Corporation; Director, Capital Club. Former Chair: Franklin County Board of Mental Retardation and Developmental Disabilities; Greater Columbus Arts Council; Friends of the Libraries, The Ohio State University. Former Trustee: Western College Alumnae Association, Inc.; The African American Breast Cancer Alliance; Minority Business Board; Center for New Direction; St. Vincent Children's Center; Private Industry Council; Central Community House; Children's Hospital Guidance Centers; Columbus Bar Foundation; Special Ties, Inc.; YWCA Housing Corporation; State Savings Bank Community Panel; Creative Housing, Inc.; YWCA of Columbus, Ohio. Former Commissioner: Ohio Court of Claims. Former Special Counsel, Ohio Attorney General; Franklin County Probate Court. Former Staff Attorney, Ohio Department of Commerce, Division of Securities; 2004-2006, The Columbus Foundation's Legal Advisory Committee. *Member:* Columbus (Former Member, Board of Governors; Chair, Grievance Mediation Committee, 2003-2004) Ohio State (Former Member, Council of Delegates), American and National Bar Associations. ***PRACTICE AREAS:*** Corporate. ***Email:*** khransier@vssp.com

JOHN K. KELLER, born East Orange, New Jersey, March 21, 1950; admitted to bar, 1975, Ohio. *Education:* Indiana University (A.B., 1971); Duke University (J.D., 1975). *Member:* Ohio State (Member, Natural Resources Committee, 1978—; Chairman, 1996-1998) Bar Association; Eastern Mineral Law Foundation (Trustee and Chairman, Oil and Gas Subcommittee, 1995-1997; Executive Committee, 1998-2002); Mountain States Legal Foundation (Board of Litigation, 2003—). ***PRACTICE AREAS:*** Natural Resources Law; Litigation; Real Estate Law; Secured Transactions. ***Email:*** jkkeller@vssp.com

TERRY M. MILLER, born Columbus, Ohio, March 11, 1947; admitted to bar, 1975, Ohio; 1980, U.S. Supreme Court. *Education:* The Ohio State University (B.S., 1969; J.D., summa cum laude, 1975). Editor, Ohio State Law Journal, 1974-1975. Assistant Attorney General, State of Ohio, 1975-1977. ***PRACTICE AREAS:*** Bankruptcy; Franchise Litigation; Commercial Litigation. ***Email:*** tmmiller@vssp.com

ROBERT A. MINOR, born Washington, D.C., October 20, 1948; admitted to bar, 1975, Ohio; 1979, District of Columbia. *Education:* Duke University (A.B., 1970); The Ohio State University (J.D., cum laude, 1975). Phi Delta Phi. *Member:* Columbus and Ohio State Bar Associations. ***PRACTICE AREAS:*** Workers' Compensation; Employer Liability; Employment Relations Law (Management). ***Email:*** raminor@vssp.com

JAMES E. PHILLIPS, born New York, N.Y., August 30, 1949; admitted to bar, 1975, Ohio; 1979, U.S. District Court, Southern District of Ohio and U.S. Supreme Court; 1983, U.S. Court of Appeals, Tenth Circuit and U.S. District Court, Northern District of Ohio. *Education:* Boston University (B.A., cum laude, 1971); Case Western Reserve University (J.D., 1975). General Counsel and National Legal Advisor, National Fraternal Order of Police, 1987-1995. Member, National Law Enforcement Certification Board. Founder, President, Ohio Center for Law Related Education, 1981-1995; Trustee, 1981-2003. Listed in Who's Who in America and Who's Who in American Law (9th Edition). *Member:* Columbus (Chairman, Publications Committee, 1988-1990; Editor, Bar Briefs, 1988-1990; Chairman, Committee on Law Related Education, 1978-1980; Professional Ethics Committee, 2002—; Committee on the Judiciary, 2003—), Ohio State (Chairman, Committee on Law Related Education, 1980-1985, 1990-1996) and American (Special Committee on Youth Education For Citizenship, 1989-1993; Member, Criminal Justice Section, White Collar Crime Committee) Bar Associations; Ohio Association of Criminal Defense Lawyers (Board of Trustees, 2000—); National Association of Criminal Defense Lawyers. Fellow: Ohio State Bar Foundation; Columbus Bar Foundation. ***LANGUAGES:*** Spanish. ***PRACTICE AREAS:*** Criminal Defense; Litigation. ***Email:*** jephillips@vssp.com

SANDRA J. ANDERSON, born Greenfield, Ohio, August 2, 1951; admitted to bar, 1976, Ohio. *Education:* Ohio University (B.S.C., summa cum laude, 1973); Northwestern University (J.D., magna cum laude, 1976). Member, Order of the Coif. Recipient, Justice Alice Robie Resnick Award of Distinction, Ohio Women's Bar Association, 2004. Notes and Comments Editor, Northwestern University Law Review, 1972-1973. Member, National Moot Court Team. Law Clerk to the Hon. George Edwards, U.S. Court of Appeals, Sixth Circuit, 1976-1977. Faculty, National Institute for Trial Advocacy, 1983—. Adjunct Professor: The Ohio State University, College of Law, 2001—; Capital University Law School, 1999. Member, Advisory Committee on Local Rules, U.S. District Court for the Southern District of Ohio, 1990—. Member, Ohio Supreme Court Board of Commissioners, Grievances and Discipline, 2002—. *Member:* Columbus (President, 1996-1997), Ohio State, (Member, Council of Delegates, 1990—) and American Bar Associations. Fellow: American Bar Foundation; American College of Trial Lawyers. ***PRACTICE AREAS:*** Litigation; Products Liability; Workers Compensation. ***Email:*** sjanderson@vssp.com

GARY E. DAVIS, born Dayton, Ohio, November 11, 1947; admitted to bar, 1976, Ohio. *Education:* Dartmouth College (A.B., magna cum laude, 1970); University of Michigan (J.D., cum laude, 1976). Phi Beta Kappa. *Member:* Columbus, Ohio State and American Bar Associations; Columbus Bar Foundation. ***PRACTICE AREAS:*** Commercial Leasing; Mortgage Law; Real Estate; Property Management Law; Title Insurance. ***Email:*** gedavis@vssp.com

DAVID W. HARDYMON, born Columbus, Ohio, August 22, 1949; admitted to bar, 1976, Ohio; 1977, U.S. District Court, Southern District of Ohio; 1980, U.S. Supreme Court; 1983, U.S. Court of Appeals, Sixth Circuit; 1999, Kentucky, Reciprocity and MPRE Exam; U.S. District Court, Northern District of Ohio; 2000, West Virginia, Reciprocity with Kentucky; U.S. District Court, Southern District of West Virginia; 2001, U.S. Court of Appeals, Fourth Circuit; 2002, U.S. District Court, Northern District of West Virginia. *Education:* Bowling Green State University (B.A., 1971); Capital University (J.D., 1976). Assistant Prosecuting Attorney, Franklin County, Ohio, 1976-1981. ***PRACTICE AREAS:*** Litigation; Products Liability; Criminal Law; Environmental Liability. ***Email:*** dwhardymon@vssp.com

JONATHAN M. NORMAN, born Coshocton, Ohio, October 7, 1951; admitted to bar, 1976, Ohio. *Education:* Ohio University (A.B., summa cum laude, 1973); The Ohio State University (J.D., summa cum laude, 1976). Order of the Coif; Phi Beta Kappa. ***PRACTICE AREAS:*** Labor Relations; Employment Discrimination; Litigation. ***Email:*** jmnorman@vssp.com

AARON P. ROSENFELD, born Des Moines, Iowa, March 14, 1951; admitted to bar, 1976, Ohio. *Education:* University of Iowa (B.B.A., summa cum laude, 1973); The Ohio State University (J.D., summa cum laude, 1976). Order of the Coif. Editor, Ohio State Law Journal, 1975-1976. Trial Attorney, Department of Justice, Tax Division, 1976-1980. *Member:* Columbus, Ohio State and American (Member, Sections of Litigation and Taxation) Bar Associations. ***PRACTICE AREAS:*** Tax; ERISA; Commercial Litigation. ***Email:*** aprosenfeld@vssp.com

F. JAMES FOLEY, born Youngstown, Ohio, April 29, 1952; admitted to bar, 1977, Ohio; 1981, U.S. Supreme Court. *Education:* University of Notre Dame (B.A., magna cum laude, 1974; J.D., 1977). Member, National Moot Court Team, 1976-1977. Trial Attorney, U.S. Department of Justice, Washington, D.C., 1979-1982. Board Member, Ohio Legal Rights Service Commission, 1987-1993. Adjunct Professor, The Ohio State University Law School, 1993-2000. Member, The Legal Committee of The National Conference of Insurance Guaranty Funds, 1997— (Chair, Coordination of Litigation Subcommitttee). *Member:* Columbus and Ohio State Bar Associations. ***PRACTICE AREAS:*** Litigation. ***Email:*** fjfoley@vssp.com

ROBERT J. STYDUHAR, born Sharon, Pennsylvania, February 9, 1949; admitted to bar, 1977, Maryland; 1979, Ohio; U.S. District Court, Southern District of Ohio; U.S. Court of Appeals, District of Columbia. *Education:* Case Western Reserve University (B.S.C.E., with honors, 1971; J.D., 1977). Maryland Assistant Attorney General, 1978-1979; Ohio Assistant Attorney General, 1979- 1983; Legal Advisor, Ohio EPA, 1983-1984; ChemLawn Services Corporation, 1984-1987. Member, Ohio Chamber of Commerce Environmental Committee; Member, Greater Columbus Chamber of Commerce Infrastructure Committee. *Member:* Ohio State Bar Association (Real Property Section, Environmental Committee). ***PRACTICE AREAS:*** Eminent Domain; Boundary Litigation; Environmental Law. ***Email:*** rjstyduhar@vssp.com

JAMES A. YANO, born Pittsburgh, Pennsylvania, December 19, 1951; admitted to bar, 1977, Ohio. *Education:* Pennsylvania State University (B.S., summa cum laude, 1973); University of Virginia (J.D., 1977). ***PRACTICE AREAS:*** Insurance; Corporate Law; Regulatory Law; Mergers, Acquisitions and Divestitures. ***Email:*** jayano@vssp.com

DAVID F. AXELROD, born Cincinnati, Ohio, November 8, 1953; admitted to bar, 1978, Ohio and U.S. Court of Appeals, Sixth Circuit; 1982, New York; 1983, New Jersey and U.S. Court of Appeals, Second Circuit; 1996, U.S. Court of Appeals, Eleventh Circuit; U.S. District Court, Southern and Eastern Districts of New York; U.S. District Court, Southern District of Ohio. *Education:* University of Cincinnati (B.A., with honors, 1975); American University (J.D., 1978). Senior Editor, 1977-1978 and Staff Member, 1976-1977, American University Law Review. Assistant United States Attorney, Southern District of Florida, 1987-1991. Trial Attorney, U.S. Department of Justice, Tax Division, Criminal Section 1984-1987. Law Clerk for United States District Judge David S. Porter, Southern District of Ohio, 1978-1980. Listed in Who's Who in American Law (9th Edition). Member, United States Sentencing Commission Practitioners Advisory Group, 1992—. *Member:* American Bar Association (Chair, Subcommittee on Document Retention and E-Policy, Business Law Section Ad Hoc Committee on Corporate Compliance; Member: Tax Section; Committee on: Civil and Criminal Tax Penalties; Chair, 1999-2001; Vice-Chair, 1997-1999; Chair, Monetary Violations and Forfeitures Subcommittee, 1993-1997; Criminal Justice Section, White Collar Crime Committee, 1986—; Litigation Section; Chairman, Young Lawyers Division Committee on Criminal Justice, 1986-1988); National Association of Criminal Defense Lawyers. ***PRACTICE AREAS:*** White Collar Criminal Defense; Criminal Tax; Corporate Compliance; Civil Litigation. ***Email:*** dfaxelrod@vssp.com

IVERY D. FOREMAN, born Wilson, North Carolina, November 11, 1951; admitted to bar, 1978, Ohio. *Education:* Tufts University (B.A., magna cum laude, 1974); Northwestern University (M.B.A., 1978; J.D., 1978). Adjunct Professor, The Ohio State University College of Law, 1996-1997; Capital University Law School, 1991-1996. *Member:* Columbus (Member: Securities Law Committee, 1984; Ethics Committee, 1993-1994), American (Member, Business Law Section) and National Bar Associations; John Mercer Langston

(This Listing Continued)

Bar Association. ***PRACTICE AREAS:*** Corporate Law; Partnership Law; Securities Law; Antitrust Regulatory Law; Mergers, Acquisitions and Divestitures. ***Email:*** idforeman@vssp.com

BRUCE L. INGRAM, born Memphis, Tennessee, August 25, 1953; admitted to bar, 1978, Ohio. *Education:* The Ohio State University (B.A., summa cum laude, 1975); University of Michigan (J.D., cum laude, 1978). Phi Beta Kappa; Phi Kappa Phi; Phi Eta Sigma. ***PRACTICE AREAS:*** Litigation; Products Liability. ***Email:*** blingram@vssp.com

LAURA G. KUYKENDALL, born Alexandria, Virginia, May 6, 1953; admitted to bar, 1978, Ohio. *Education:* University of Virginia (B.A, with highest distinction, 1975; J.D., 1978). Phi Beta Kappa. Member, Raven Society. Author, OSBA CLE Institute, Litigation Basics textbook, Satisfaction of Judgment. Faculty and Contributing Author, OSBA CLE Institute, Litigation Basics, Dealing with the Difficult Lawyer. Author, ABA Section of Antitrust Law, Corporate Counseling Report: "A Preventative Approach to Protecting Trade Secrets". Contributing Author: NITA, Commentaries to the Federal Rules of Civil Procedure. Faculty, National Institute for Trial Advocacy, 1994—. Faculty, OSBA CLE Institute, Evidence, Laying Proper Foundation. Faculty, NITA, Great Lakes Deposition Program. Faculty, Ohio CLE Institute, Direct and Cross Examination Skills Training Workshop. Faculty, PESI, Dealing with Hardball Trial Tactics and Difficult Judges. Faculty, Ohio CLE Institute, Deposition Skills Workshop. Faculty, CBA, Litigation Management Series, Depositions. Faculty, Ohio CLE Institute, Bridge the Gap: Trial Advocacy Courtroom Techniques and Procedures discussed and demonstrated. Faculty, PESI, Ohio Evidence Workshop. Faculty, ABA Section of Litigation, Trial Practice Committee, Direct and Cross-Examination of Experts. Faculty, Ohio CLE Institute, 23rd Annual Antitrust Institute: Application of Antitrust Laws to Regulated Industries, Antitrust Immunities and Exemptions. Faculty, Ohio CLE Institute, The Woman Advocate. Faculty, Ohio Attorney General, Inhouse Training Discovery Practicum. Faculty, Ohio CLE Institute, Basics of Antitrust Law. Contributing Author: "Antitrust Counseling and Litigation Techniques" (General Editor, Van Kalinowski). Adjunct Professor, Capital University Law School, 2001—. Presiding Judge, OSU College of Law, Colley Trial Competition. *Member:* Columbus, Ohio State (Member, Antitrust Section and Co-Editor, Antitrust Newsletter, 1985-1987) and American (Member, Antitrust Law and Litigation Sections) Bar Associations. ***PRACTICE AREAS:*** Litigation; Antitrust Law; Complex Litigation; Tender Offers. ***Email:*** lgkuykendall@vssp.com

DAVID A. SWIFT, born Piqua, Ohio, November 4, 1952; admitted to bar, 1978, Ohio; 1979, U.S. District Court, Southern District of Ohio. *Education:* Miami University (A.B., magna cum laude, 1975); The Ohio State University (J.D., summa cum laude, 1978). Phi Eta Sigma; Phi Beta Kappa. Member, Order of the Coif. Member, 1976-1978 and Associate Editor, 1977-1978, The Ohio State Law Journal. Fellow, American College of Trust and Estate Counsel. ***PRACTICE AREAS:*** Probate; Estate Planning. ***Email:*** swiftda@vssp.com

RAYMOND D. ANDERSON, born Canton, Ohio, May 6, 1947; admitted to bar, 1979, Ohio. *Education:* Marietta College (B.A., 1969); The Ohio State University (J.D., 1979). Omicron Delta Kappa. Former Editor of Ohio Tax Review Published by Capital University, 1987-1998. *Member:* Columbus (Chairman, Ohio Tax Section, 1982-1984) and Ohio State (Member, Taxation Committee; Chairman, 1991-1993) Bar Associations. ***PRACTICE AREAS:*** State Taxation; Local Taxation; Litigation. ***Email:*** rdanderson@vssp.com

MICHAEL A. CLINE, born Shelby, Ohio, April 13, 1954; admitted to bar, 1979, Ohio. *Education:* University of Toledo (B.A., cum laude, 1976; J.D., magna cum laude, 1978). Attorney-Advisor, 1979-1981 and Branch Chief, 1981-1982, Securities and Exchange Commission, Washington, D.C. *Member:* Columbus (Securities Law Committee; Chairman, 1992-1993) and Ohio State (Corporation Law Committee) Bar Associations. ***PRACTICE AREAS:*** Corporate Law; Mergers and Acquisitions; Securities. ***Email:*** macline@vssp.com

ROBERT G. DYKES, born Canton, Ohio, July 16, 1950; admitted to bar, 1979, Wisconsin; 1980, Florida; 1981, Ohio. *Education:* Dickinson College (B.A., 1972); University of Virginia (M.B.A., 1979; J.D., 1979). Phi Beta Kappa. *Member:* Ohio State Bar Association (Past Chairman, Estate Planning, Trust and Probate Law Section). Fellow, American College of Trust and Estate Counsel. ***PRACTICE AREAS:*** Estate Planning; Probate; Taxation. ***Email:*** rgdykes@vssp.com

GERALD P. FERGUSON, born Teaneck, New Jersey, October 17, 1951; admitted to bar, 1979, Ohio. *Education:* Fairleigh Dickinson University (B.A., cum laude, 1974); Capital University (J.D., magna cum laude, 1979). National Institute of Trial Advocacy, 1983. Member, Order of the Curia. *Member:* Columbus, Ohio State (Member, Federal Courts and Practice Committee, 1988—) and American (Member, Sections on: Intellectual Property; Litigation) Bar Associations. ***PRACTICE AREAS:*** Commercial Litigation; Intellectual Property Litigation; Complex Litigation. ***Email:*** gpferguson@vssp.com

BRUCE R. HENKE, born Sidney, Ohio, July 21, 1950; admitted to bar, 1979, Ohio. *Education:* Miami University (B.A., magna cum laude, 1972); Georgetown University (J.D., 1979). Phi Beta Kappa; Omicron Delta Kappa. Assistant Minority Counsel, Interstate & Foreign Committee, U.S. House of Representatives, 1975-1978. Member: Board of Trustees, Gladden Community House; Japan America Society of Central Ohio. *Member:* Columbus, Ohio State and American Bar Associations; Ohio State Bar Foundation; National Association of Bond Lawyers. ***PRACTICE AREAS:*** Corporate Law; Corporate Finance; Tax Exempt Bonds; Taxable Bond Finance; Joint Ventures; International Business Law. ***Email:*** brhenke@vssp.com

J. SCOTT JAMIESON, born Columbus, Ohio, December 30, 1953; admitted to bar, 1979, Ohio. *Education:* Miami University (B.S., magna cum laude, 1976); The Ohio State University (J.D., with honors, 1979). Phi Beta Kappa; Order of the Coif. ***PRACTICE AREAS:*** Litigation; Products Liability; Medical Malpractice; Workers Compensation. ***Email:*** jsjamieson@vssp.com

PAUL J. COVAL, born Johnstown, Pennsylvania, June 6, 1949; admitted to bar, 1979, Ohio; 1980, U.S. District Court, Southern District of Ohio. *Education:* Ohio Dominican College (B.A., magna cum laude, 1976); Capital University (J.D., cum laude, 1979). Order of the Curia. Recipient, American Jurisprudence Award for Constitutional Law. Instructor, Criminal and Constitutional Law, Ohio Dominican College, 1981-1983. Ohio Assistant Attorney General, 1979-1989. [Petty Officer, 3rd Class, USN, 1969-1972]. ***PRACTICE AREAS:*** Criminal Law; Environmental Law; Health Care; Fraud and Abuse. ***Email:*** pjcoval@vssp.com

ROGER E. LAUTZENHISER, born Portland, Indiana, February 24, 1954; admitted to bar, 1979, Ohio. *Education:* Stanford University (A.B., with distinction, 1976); University of California at Los Angeles (J.D., 1979). Phi Beta Kappa. (Resident, Cincinnati Office). ***PRACTICE AREAS:*** Corporate Law; Securities Regulation; Business Law. ***Email:*** relautzenhiser@vssp.com

JOHN P. WELLNER, born Butler, Pennsylvania, March 14, 1951; admitted to bar, 1979, Ohio. *Education:* Indiana University of Pennsylvania (B.S., 1973); The Ohio State University (J.D., with honors, 1979). Member, Order of the Coif. Administrative Partner, Firm's Real Estate, Commercial and Bankruptcy Group. Member: ICSC; ULI; NAIOP. *Member:* Columbus (Member, Real Estate Section) and Ohio State (Member, Real Estate Section) Bar Associations. ***PRACTICE AREAS:*** Real Estate; General Practice. ***Email:*** jpwellner@vssp.com

JOSEPH A. BRUNETTO, born Columbus, Ohio, March 5, 1951; admitted to bar, 1980, Ohio. *Education:* University of Cincinnati (B.A., 1973); Capital University (J.D., magna cum laude, 1980). Member, Order of the Curia. Executive Notes Editor, Capital University Law Review, 1979-1980. ***PRACTICE AREAS:*** Litigation; Workers Compensation; Products Liability; Construction Law; Insurance Agents and Brokers Errors and Omissions. ***Email:*** jabrunetto@vssp.com

REGINALD W. JACKSON, born Philadelphia, Pennsylvania, August 24, 1955; admitted to bar, 1980, Ohio. *Education:* Cornell University (B.A., 1977); University of Pennsylvania (J.D., 1980). Executive Editor, ABI Journal. President, Ohio State Bar Foundation, 2001. *Member:* Columbus (Chairman, Bankruptcy Law Committee, 1990-1992), Ohio State (District 7 Representative, Board of Governors) and American (Member, Business Law Committee) Bar Associations; American Bankruptcy Institute (Board of Trustees, Executive Committee of Board; Chair, Environmental Subcommittee); American College of Bankruptcy. ***PRACTICE AREAS:*** Bankruptcy; Creditors Rights; Workouts. ***Email:*** rwjackson@vssp.com

CHRIS J. NORTH, born Winchester, Massachusetts, November 2, 1949; admitted to bar, 1980, Ohio. *Education:* University of Cincinnati (B.S.M.E., 1973; M.B.A., 1977); The Ohio State University (J.D., summa cum laude, 1980). Delta Mu Delta; Order of the Coif. *Member:* Columbus (Member, Labor Law Committee, 1982—), Ohio State and American (Member, Section of Labor and Employment Law) Bar Associations. ***PRACTICE AREAS:*** Labor Law; Employment Litigation. ***Email:*** cjnorth@vssp.com

CARL D. SMALLWOOD, born Thessaloniki, Greece, June 15, 1956; admitted to bar, 1980, Ohio. *Education:* The Ohio State University (B.S., 1977; J.D., 1980). *Member:* Columbus (President, 2000-2001; Board of Governors, 1999-2002); Ohio State (Member: Council of Delegates, District VII; Board of Governors, Litigation Section) and American (Member, House of Delegates Board, Metropolitan Bar Caucus) Bar Associations; Columbus Defense Association (President, 1986-1987); Defense Research Institute. ***PRACTICE AREAS:*** Litigation; Professional Malpractice; Workers Compensation. ***Email:*** cdsmallwood@vssp.com

JOHN C. VORYS, born Columbus, Ohio, May 5, 1953; admitted to bar, 1980, Ohio. *Education:* Williams College (B.A., cum laude, 1975); Capital University (J.D., magna cum laude, 1980). Order of the Curia. *Member:* Columbus, Ohio State and American Bar Associations. ***PRACTICE AREAS:*** Corporate Law; Securities Regulation; Financial Institutions Law. ***Email:*** jcvorys@vssp.com

JONATHAN D. ITEN, born Orrville, Ohio, April 6, 1957; admitted to bar, 1981, Ohio. *Education:* Bowling Green State University (B.A., magna cum laude, 1978); Stanford University (J.D., 1981). Delta Phi Alpha. Article Editor, Stanford Journal of International Law, 1979-1981. *Member:* Ohio State and American Bar Associations; Computer Law Association. ***PRACTICE AREAS:*** Computer Law; Copyrights. ***Email:*** jditen@vssp.com

JOHN J. KULEWICZ, born Indianapolis, Indiana, March 22, 1954; admitted to bar, 1981, Ohio. *Education:* The Ohio State University (B.A., 1976); Yale Law School (J.D., 1979). Editor, Yale Law Journal, 1978-1979. Law Clerk to Hon. Gilbert S. Merritt, U.S. Court of Appeals, 6th Circuit, 1979-1980. Author: "The History of One-Subject Rule of the Ohio Constitution," 45 Clev. St. L. Rev. 591, 1997; "Equal Representation of Party Members on Political Party Central Committees," 88 Yale L. J. 167, 1978; "Relationship Between Military and Civil Power in Ohio," 28 Clev. St. L. Rev. 611, 1979; "Agent Orange: The States Fight Back," 44 Ohio St. L.J. 691, 1983; "Reinventing the Governor: A History of Executive Power Under Ohio Law (in The History of Ohio Law)," Ohio University Press, 2004. Recipient: Certificat Pratique de Francais Commercial et Economique; Ten Outstanding Young Citizens, 1988. *Member:* Columbus, Ohio State, American and Federal (President, 2004-2005, local chapter) Bar Associations. ***PRACTICE AREAS:*** Litigation. ***Email:*** jjkulewicz@vssp.com

RICHARD D. SCHUSTER, born Mt. Clemens, Michigan, March 28, 1954; admitted to bar, 1981, Ohio; 1982, U.S. District Court, Southern District of Ohio and U.S. Court of Appeals, Sixth Circuit; 1995, U.S. District Court, Northern District of Ohio. *Education:* Miami University (B.A., 1976); Ohio State University (J.D., with honors, 1981). Member, Ohio State University Law Journal, 1980-1981. Law Clerk to Hon. John D. Holschuh, U.S. District Court Judge, Southern District of Ohio. ***PRACTICE AREAS:*** General Civil Trial Practice; Toxic Torts; Products Liability; Class Actions. ***Email:*** rdschuster@vssp.com

ANKER M. BELL, born Painesville, Ohio, February 16, 1953; admitted to bar, 1982, Ohio. *Education:* The Ohio State University (B.A., cum laude, 1975; M.A., 1977); University of Michigan (J.D., 1981). *Member:* American Bar Association (Member, Intellectual Property Law Section); Computer Law Association. ***PRACTICE AREAS:*** Computer Law; Technology Law. ***Email:*** ambell@vssp.com

BENITA A. KAHN, born Akron, Ohio, April 28, 1949; admitted to bar, 1982, Ohio. *Education:* University of Akron (B.A., cum laude, 1970); The Ohio State University (J.D., summa cum laude, 1982). Order of the Coif. Member, Ohio Oil and Gas Commission, 1990—. *Member:* Columbus and Ohio State Bar Associations; Ohio Oil and Gas Association; Eastern Mineral Law Foundation (President, 1996-1997; Trustee, 1990-1996). ***PRACTICE AREAS:*** Telecommunications Law; Privacy Law; Energy; Historic Preservation; Oil and Gas Law. ***Email:*** bakahn@vssp.com

(This Listing Continued)

VORYS, SATER, SEYMOUR AND PEASE LLP, Columbus—Continued

ELIZABETH TURRELL FARRAR, born Steubenville, Ohio, May 22, 1957; admitted to bar, 1982, Ohio and U.S. District Court, Southern District of Ohio. *Education:* Smith College (B.A., magna cum laude, 1979); University of Virginia (J.D., 1982). Phi Beta Kappa. Moot Court Board, 1981-1982; Dillard Fellow, 1981-1982. *Member:* Columbus (Member, Securities Law Committee, 1988—), Ohio State (Member, Corporation Law Committee, 1991—) and American (Member, Business Law Section, 1988—) Bar Associations. ***PRACTICE AREAS:*** Securities Regulation; Corporate Law; Mergers and Acquisitions; Banking Law. ***Email:*** etfarrar@vssp.com

THOMAS O. RUBY, born Mount Vernon, Ohio, May 21, 1957; admitted to bar, 1982, Ohio. *Education:* Davidson College (A.B., 1979); Harvard University (J.D., 1982). Phi Beta Kappa. ***PRACTICE AREAS:*** Uniform Commercial Code; Secured Transactions; Letters of Credit; Commercial Paper; Aircraft Sales; Aircraft Finance and Leasing; Contracts. ***Email:*** toruby@vssp.com

THOMAS E. SZYKOWNY, born Cleveland, Ohio, January 2, 1957; admitted to bar, 1982, Ohio. *Education:* Denison University (B.A., summa cum laude, 1979); The Ohio State University (J.D., 1982). Phi Beta Kappa. Member, Board of Editors, Ohio State Law Journal, 1981-1982. ***PRACTICE AREAS:*** Corporate Law; Insurance. ***Email:*** teszykowny@vssp.com

JONATHAN R. VAUGHN, born Ann Arbor, Michigan, June 29, 1957; admitted to bar, 1982, Ohio. *Education:* Duke University (B.S., 1979); Vanderbilt University (J.D., 1982). ***PRACTICE AREAS:*** Labor Law; Employment Law. ***Email:*** jrvaughn@vssp.com

ANTHONY C. CIRIACO, born Jersey City, New Jersey, April 26, 1958; admitted to bar, 1983, Ohio. *Education:* University of Virginia (B.S., with distinction, in Accounting, 1980); University of North Carolina (J.D., 1983). Beta Gamma Sigma; Beta Alpha Psi. Former Member: Board of Trustees, The Buckeye Ranch; Board of Governors, Gladden Community House. *Member:* Columbus (Former Chairman, Executive and Employee Benefits Committee) and Ohio State Bar Associations. ***PRACTICE AREAS:*** Employee Benefits. ***Email:*** acciriaco@vssp.com

SHAWN M. FLAHIVE, born Delaware, Ohio, April 24, 1959; admitted to bar, 1984, Ohio. *Education:* University of Notre Dame (B.A., with high honors, 1981); Georgetown University (J.D., cum laude, 1984). Phi Beta Kappa; Omicron Delta Epsilon. ***PRACTICE AREAS:*** Corporate Law; Securities; Insurance. ***Email:*** smflahive@vssp.com

WILLIAM G. PORTER II, born Columbus, Ohio, May 29, 1956; admitted to bar, 1984, Ohio; 1985, U.S. District Court, Southern District of Ohio; 1988, U.S. Court of Appeals, Sixth Circuit. *Education:* Amherst College (B.A., cum laude, 1978); Case Western Reserve University (J.D., 1984). Chair, Firm Litigation Practice Group, Columbus office. Recipient: American College of Trial Lawyers Medal for Excellence in Advocacy; International Academy of Trial Lawyers Commendation for Distinguished Achievement in Advocacy. *Member:* International Association of Defense Counsel (Chair, Employment Law Committee; Member, National Jury Trial Innovation Program Committee). ***PRACTICE AREAS:*** General Commercial and Business Litigation; Eminent Domain; Zoning and Land Use Litigation; Construction and Design Professional Litigation; Tort Litigation; Professional Malpractice; Catastrophic Injury or Death Litigation. ***Email:*** wgporter@vssp.com

ANDREW C. SMITH, born Gary, Indiana, May 28, 1958; admitted to bar, 1984, Ohio; 1985, U.S. District Court, Southern District of Ohio; 1988, U.S. Court of Appeals, Sixth Circuit; 1993, U.S. District Court, Northern District of Ohio; 2001, U.S. Court of Appeals, Fifth Circuit; 2002, U.S. Court of Appeals, Eleventh Circuit. *Education:* College of Wooster (B.A., 1980); University of Pittsburgh (J.D., 1984). Phi Beta Kappa. *Member:* Columbus, Ohio State and American (Member, Labor Section) Bar Associations. ***PRACTICE AREAS:*** Labor and Employment; Employment Litigation. ***Email:*** acsmith@vssp.com

ELIZABETH T. SMITH, born Evansville, Indiana, September 16, 1959; admitted to bar, 1984, Ohio; 1985, U.S. District Court, Southern District of Ohio; 1997, U.S. District Court, Northern District of Ohio; 1998, U.S. Court of Appeals, Sixth Circuit; 2004, U.S. Supreme Court. *Education:* Heidelberg College (B.A., magna cum laude, 1981); Ohio State University (J.D., 1984). Member, 1997-2002 and Vice-Chair, 2001-2002, Board of Commissioners, Columbus Metropolitan Housing Authority. Member, 1997—, Vice-Chair, 2000-2001 and Chair, 2001—, Judicial Screening Committee and Elected Member, Franklin County Republican Committee. Chief Counsel, Ohio Attorney General, 2003-2005. *Member:* Columbus (Chair, Common Pleas Committee, 1997-1999), Ohio State (Chair, 1997-1999 and Member, Federal Courts and Practice Committee), Federal (Vice-President, 2002-2003; President, 2003-2004) and American (Member, Litigation Section) Bar Associations. ***PRACTICE AREAS:*** Litigation; Employment Litigation; Business Litigation; Securities Litigation; Commercial Arbitration; Public Law. ***Email:*** etsmith@vssp.com

THOMAS R. WINTERS, born Columbus, Ohio, March 12, 1950; admitted to bar, 1984, Ohio; 1987, U.S. Supreme Court. *Education:* Ohio Dominican College (A.B., 1972); Capital University (J.D., 1984). House Majority Counsel, 1984-1986, Clerk of the Ohio House of Representatives, 1975-1978, 1982-1984. Member, Ohio Ballot Board, 1985—. Board of Trustees, Shawnee State University, 1988-1996. Member, Board of Trustees, Ohio Dominican University, 2003—. ***PRACTICE AREAS:*** Administrative Law; Legislative Practice. ***Email:*** trwinters@vssp.com

DAN L. JAFFE, born Cincinnati, Ohio, July 22, 1959; admitted to bar, 1985, New York; 1986, U.S. Tax Court and U.S. Claims Court; 1990, Ohio. *Education:* Cornell University (A.B., cum laude, 1981); Stanford University (J.D., 1984); New York University (LL.M. in Taxation, 1989). Listed in The Best Lawyers in America. Managing Editor, Stanford Journal of International Law, 1983-1984. *Member:* Columbus (Member, Business Tax Subcommittee), Ohio State (Member, Federal Taxation Committee) and American (Member, Section of Taxation) Bar Associations. ***LANGUAGES:*** French. ***PRACTICE AREAS:*** Taxation; Acquisitions and Divestitures Law; Corporate Law; Limited Liability Company Law; Partnership Law. ***Email:*** dljaffe@vssp.com

WEBB I. VORYS, born Columbus, Ohio, March 13, 1958; admitted to bar, 1985, Ohio; 1986, U.S. District Court, Southern District of Ohio; U.S. Court of Appeals, Federal Circuit.

(This Listing Continued)

Education: Dartmouth College (B.A., 1980); Ohio State University (J.D., 1985). Member, 1983-1985 and Executive Editor, 1984-1985, The Ohio State Law Journal. Recipient, 1985 Denis B. Eastman Memorial Award for Law Journal. Member: Board of Trustees, Children's Hospital; Advisory Board, Prevent Child Abuse Ohio; Jefferson Township Civic Association. President and Member, Board of Trustees, Green Lawn Cemetery. Commissioner, Franklin County Hospital Commission. *Member:* Columbus, Ohio State and American Bar Associations. ***PRACTICE AREAS:*** Commercial Law; Real Estate; Business Law. ***Email:*** wivorys@vssp.com

ROBERT N. WEBNER, born Akron, Ohio, April 20, 1957; admitted to bar, 1985, Ohio. *Education:* The Ohio State University (B.A., 1980); Georgetown University (J.D., magna cum laude, 1985). Managing Editor, The Georgetown Law Journal, Vol. 72, 1984-1985. Law Clerk, U.S. District Judge Oliver Gasch, United States District Court for the District of Columbia, 1985-1986. ***PRACTICE AREAS:*** Commercial Litigation; Employment Litigation; Constitutional Law; ERISA Litigation. ***Email:*** rnwebner@vssp.com

JOHN B. WEIMER, born Lake Forest, Illinois, May 3, 1959; admitted to bar, 1985, Texas (inactive); 1989, Ohio. *Education:* Miami University (B.A., 1981); Southern Methodist University (J.D., M.B.A., 1985). *Member:* Columbus, Ohio State (Member, Banking, Commercial and Bankruptcy Law Committee) and American (Member, Real Property, Probate and Trust Committee) Bar Associations; State Bar of Texas (Inactive Member). ***PRACTICE AREAS:*** Commercial Finance; Business Law; Real Estate; Commercial Law. ***Email:*** jbweimer@vssp.com

JAMES A. WILSON, born New Castle, Pennsylvania, June 27, 1960; admitted to bar, 1985, Ohio and U.S. District Court, Southern District of Ohio. *Education:* Miami University (A.B., magna cum laude, 1982); Columbia University (J.D., 1985). Phi Beta Kappa. Managing Editor, Columbia Journal of Law and Social Problems, 1984-1985. Law Clerk, Hon. Walter H. Rice, Southern District of Ohio, 1985-1987. Delegate, Anti-Trust Section of the American Bar Association, ABA House of Delegates, 2004—. ***PRACTICE AREAS:*** Litigation; Antitrust. ***Email:*** jawilson@vssp.com

SCOTT M. DORAN, born Trenton, New Jersey, June 13, 1957; admitted to bar, 1986, Ohio; U.S. District Court, Southern District of Ohio. *Education:* Miami University (B.A., 1979; M.S., 1983); University of Cincinnati (J.D., 1986). Order of the Coif. *Member:* Columbus (Chairman, Environmental Law Committee, 1992-1994) and Ohio State Bar Associations. ***PRACTICE AREAS:*** Environmental Law. ***Email:*** smdoran@vssp.com

GAIL C. FORD, born Reading, Pennsylvania, January 14, 1946; admitted to bar, 1986, Ohio and U.S. District Court, Southern District of Ohio; 1987, U.S. Court of Appeals, Sixth Circuit. *Education:* The Ohio State University (B.Sc., 1968; M.S., 1977; J.D., with honors, 1986). Member, The Ohio State Law Journal, 1984-1986. *Member:* Columbus, Ohio State and American Bar Associations. ***PRACTICE AREAS:*** Business Litigation; Toxic Torts; Class Action and Complex Litigation; Products Liability; Litigation. ***Email:*** gcford@vssp.com

SHEILA NOLAN GARTLAND, born Dayton, Ohio, January 24, 1961; admitted to bar, 1986, Ohio, U.S. District Court, Southern District of Ohio and U.S. Supreme Court. *Education:* University of Dayton (B.S., cum laude, 1983); University of Toledo (J.D., 1986). The Order of the Barristers. Member, National Moot Court Team. *Member:* Columbus and Ohio State (Real Property Section Board of Governors) Bar Associations; Network of Commercial Real Estate Women (NNCREW); Cystic Fibrosis Foundation. ***PRACTICE AREAS:*** Commercial Law; Real Estate; Mortgage Lending. ***Email:*** sngartland@vssp.com

KENNETH A. GOLONKA, JR., born Cleveland, Ohio, July 25, 1961; admitted to bar, 1986, Ohio. *Education:* University of Notre Dame (B.A., with honors, 1983); The Ohio State University (J.D., with honors, 1986). Pi Sigma Alpha. Solicitor, Village of Riverlea, Ohio, 1988-1994. Member, Columbus City Graphics Commission, 1988—. ***PRACTICE AREAS:*** Real Property; Commercial Law. ***Email:*** kagolonka@vssp.com

BRADLEY K. SINNOTT, born Nelsonville, Ohio, May 4, 1961; admitted to bar, 1986, Ohio; U.S. District Court, Southern and Northern Districts of Ohio; U.S. Court of Appeals, Sixth Circuit; U.S. Supreme Court. *Education:* Ohio State University (B.A., cum laude, 1982); Capital University (J.D., summa cum laude, 1986). Phi Kappa Phi. Order of the Curia. Former Public Member of the State Medical Board of Ohio. Chairman, Franklin County Republican Party Central Committee. *Member:* Columbus (Chairman, Workers' Compensation Committee, 1993-1995) and Ohio State Bar Associations. ***PRACTICE AREAS:*** Workers Compensation; Employment Law; Administrative Adjudications; Administrative Hearings and Appeals; Civil Rights; Election, Campaign and Political Law; Labor and Employment. ***Email:*** bksinnott@vssp.com

SUSAN A. COHEN, born Altoona, Pennsylvania, August 9, 1962; admitted to bar, 1987, Ohio; 1988, Pennsylvania. *Education:* Washington and Jefferson College (B.A., cum laude, 1984); University of Pittsburgh (J.D., magna cum laude, 1987). Order of the Coif. *Member:* Ohio State and American (Member, Labor and Employment Law Section) Bar Associations. ***PRACTICE AREAS:*** Labor and Employment Law. ***Email:*** sacohen@vssp.com

ANTHONY L. EHLER, born Sidney, Ohio, March 23, 1962; admitted to bar, 1987, Ohio; 1988, U.S. District Court, Northern District of Ohio and U.S. Tax Court. *Education:* University of Notre Dame (B.A., 1984); Wake Forest University (J.D., 1987). *Member:* Ohio State Bar Association (Chair, Taxation Committee, 2003-2004). ***PRACTICE AREAS:*** State Taxation; Local Taxation. ***Email:*** alehler@vssp.com

RANDALL D. LATOUR, born Columbus, Indiana, January 26, 1954; admitted to bar, 1987, Ohio. *Education:* Ohio State University (B.A. with honors in Liberal Arts and Distinction in American Studies, 1977); Ohio State University College of Law (J.D., with honors, 1987). Phi Alpha Delta. ***PRACTICE AREAS:*** Bankruptcy; Commercial Law; Real Estate Law. ***Email:*** rdlatour@vssp.com

DOUGLAS R. MATTHEWS, born Massachusetts, September 10, 1962; admitted to bar, 1987, Ohio and U.S. District Court, Southern District of Ohio. *Education:* University of Virginia (B.A., 1984); Ohio State University (J.D., magna cum laude, 1987). Order of the Coif. Law Clerk: Hon. Joseph P. Kinneary, U.S. District Court, Southern District of Ohio; Hon. Alan E. Norris, U.S. Court of Appeals, Sixth Circuit. ***PRACTICE AREAS:*** Litigation. ***Email:*** drmatthews@vssp.com

(This Listing Continued)

RUSSELL R. ROSLER, born Toledo, Ohio, May 27, 1962; admitted to bar, 1987, Ohio; 1988, U.S. District Court, Southern District of Ohio. *Education:* Washington & Lee University (B.A., magna cum laude, 1984); Cornell University (J.D., 1987). Phi Beta Kappa; Phi Eta Sigma. ***PRACTICE AREAS:*** Corporate Law; Limited Liability Company Law; Business Law; Mergers, Acquisitions and Divestitures; Contract Law. ***Email:*** rrrosler@vssp.com

MARK E. VANNATTA, born Mt. Vernon, Ohio, August 5, 1962; admitted to bar, 1987, Ohio and U.S. Tax Court. *Education:* Bowling Green State University (B.S., cum laude, 1984); Ohio State University (J.D., with honors, 1987). Order of the Coif; Phi Alpha Delta. ***PRACTICE AREAS:*** Federal Estate and Gift Taxation; Estate and Gift Administration; Tax Exempt Organizations; Charitable Trusts and Foundations. ***Email:*** mevannatta@vssp.com

DAVID W. COOK, born Pocatello, Idaho, August 6, 1962; admitted to bar, 1988, Ohio. *Education:* Brigham Young University (B.A., 1985); University of Washington (J.D., 1988). Phi Delta Phi. *Member:* American Bar Association; American Immigration Lawyers Association. ***LANGUAGES:*** Japanese. ***PRACTICE AREAS:*** Immigration; Business Law; Corporate Law. ***Email:*** dwcook@vssp.com

PHILIP F. DOWNEY, born Trenton, New Jersey, August 22, 1963; admitted to bar, 1988, Ohio. *Education:* Rutgers University (B.A., 1985); Ohio State University (J.D., 1988). Phi Beta Kappa; Order of the Coif. ***PRACTICE AREAS:*** Litigation. ***Email:*** pfdowney@vssp.com

ANTHONY J. GIULIANI, born Columbus, Ohio, November 2, 1962; admitted to bar, 1988, Ohio. *Education:* The Ohio State University (B.A., with honors, 1985; J.D., 1988). Pi Sigma Alpha. Ohio State University Representative to the 1984 Air Force Academy Conference. ***PRACTICE AREAS:*** Environmental; Energy Law. ***Email:*** ajgiuliani@vssp.com

ALLEN S. KINZER, born Euclid, Ohio, February 22, 1963; admitted to bar, 1988, Ohio; 1989, U.S. District Court, Southern District of Ohio; 1991, U.S. Court of Appeals, Sixth and Tenth Circuits; 1995, U.S. District Court, Northern District of Ohio; 1996, U.S. District Court, Eastern District of Michigan; 1999, U.S. District Court, Western District of Wisconsin. *Education:* Vanderbilt University (B.A., summa cum laude, 1985); University of North Carolina (J.D., with honors, 1988). Phi Beta Kappa. Member, University of North Carolina Law Review, 1987-1988. *Member:* Columbus, (Member, Labor Law Committee), Ohio State (Member, Labor and Employment Law Committee) and American (Member, Labor and Employment Law Section) Bar Associations. ***PRACTICE AREAS:*** Labor Law; Employment Law. ***Email:*** askinzer@vssp.com

WILLIAM D. KLOSS, JR., born Nelsonville, Ohio, August 22, 1963; admitted to bar, 1988, Ohio. *Education:* Miami University (B.S., 1985); University of Cincinnati (J.D., 1988). Order of the Coif. Member, University of Cincinnati Law Review, 1986-1987. Author: "Mistaken Payment and Restitutionary Principles Under the Uniform Commercial Code," 56 U.C.L. Rev. (1988). *Member:* Columbus and Ohio State Bar Associations. ***PRACTICE AREAS:*** Trial Practice; Catastrophic Personal Injury; Commercial Litigation; Franchise Litigation; Reinsurance; Reinsurance Litigation. ***Email:*** wdklossjr@vssp.com

WILLIAM J. POHLMAN, born Columbus, Ohio, April 20, 1960; admitted to bar, 1988, Ohio; 1990, Pennsylvania. *Education:* Oberlin College (B.A., 1982); Ohio State University (J.D., with honors, 1988). Law Clerk for the Hon. James P. Churchill, U.S. District Court, Eastern District of Michigan, 1988-1990. *Member:* Pennsylvania, Ohio State and American Bar Associations. ***PRACTICE AREAS:*** Commercial Litigation; Insurance Law. ***Email:*** wjpohlman@vssp.com

BRENT C. TAGGART, born Omaha, Nebraska, December 14, 1961; admitted to bar, 1988, Ohio; 1989, U.S. District Court, Southern District of Ohio; 1990, U.S. District Court, Northern District of Ohio; 1995, U.S. Court of Appeals, Sixth Circuit; 1996, U.S. Supreme Court. *Education:* Cornell University (A.B., magna cum laude, with distinction in all subjects, 1984); University of Michigan (J.D., cum laude, 1988; M.A., 1989). Member: League of Women Voters of Columbus, Ohio; Leadership Council, Southern Poverty Law Center; Partners Council, Habitat for Humanity. *Member:* Ohio State Bar Association. ***PRACTICE AREAS:*** Litigation; Alternative Dispute Resolution; Arbitration; Mediation; Civil Rights; Discrimination; Race Discrimination; Sex Discrimination; Employment Discrimination; Employment Law; Wrongful Termination; Sexual Harassment; Complex Litigation; Federal Litigation; Class Actions; Toxic Torts; Asbestos Litigation; Chemical Exposure. ***Email:*** bctaggart@vssp.com

JOHN L. LANDOLFI, born Niles, Ohio, November 15, 1963; admitted to bar, 1989, Ohio. *Education:* Westminster College (B.A., magna cum laude, 1986); Ohio State University (J.D., with honors, 1989). Omicron Delta Kappa; Omicron Delta Epsilon; Phi Alpha Delta. Member, Order of the Barristers. ***PRACTICE AREAS:*** Litigation. ***Email:*** jllandolfi@vssp.com

KRISTIN L. WATT, born Everett, Washington, August 14, 1963; admitted to bar, 1989, Ohio; U.S. Court of Appeals, Sixth Circuit; U.S. District Court, Northern and Southern Districts of Ohio. *Education:* Ohio State University (B.S.B.A., cum laude, 1986; J.D., with honors, 1989). Member, National Council, Ohio State University College of Law Alumni Association. Trustee, Opera Columbus. *Member:* Columbus and Ohio State Bar Associations. ***PRACTICE AREAS:*** Environmental Law; Administrative Law. ***Email:*** klwatt@vssp.com

GARY J. SAALMAN, born Coldwater, Ohio, July 20, 1962; admitted to bar, 1989, Ohio; 1990, U.S. Court of Appeals, Sixth Circuit and U.S. District Court, Southern District of Ohio; 1995, Texas. *Education:* Miami University (B.S., 1984); University of Notre Dame (J.D., magna cum laude, 1989). Alumni Merit Scholar, Miami University. Executive Articles Editor, Notre Dame Law Review, Vol. 64. Judicial Clerk, Hon. Alan E. Norris, U.S. Court of Appeals, 1989-1990. Certified Public Accountant, Ohio, 1986. ***PRACTICE AREAS:*** Litigation. ***Email:*** gjsaalman@vssp.com

KEVIN M. CZERWONKA, born Madison, Wisconsin, September 27, 1965; admitted to bar, 1990, Ohio and Wisconsin. *Education:* University of Wisconsin (B.A., with distinction, 1987; J.D., 1990). Member, Tax Committee and Participant, Ohio Chamber of Commerce. *Member:* Columbus Bar Association. ***PRACTICE AREAS:*** Taxation. ***Email:*** kmczerwonka@vssp.com

(This Listing Continued)

HERBERT A. HEDDEN, born Charlotte, North Carolina, December 22, 1956; admitted to bar, 1990, Ohio. *Education:* University of North Carolina (B.S., 1979); Harvard University, John F. Kennedy School of Government (M.P.P., 1981); George Washington University National Law Center (J.D., with honors, 1990). Phi Beta Kappa. *Member:* Columbus (Chairman, Franchise and Distribution Law Committee, 1994-1996), Ohio State (Member: Banking, Commercial and Bankruptcy Law Committee; Chairman, Uniform State Laws Committee, 1995-1997 and 1999-2001) and American (Member: Section on Business Law; Forum Committee on Franchising) Bar Associations. ***PRACTICE AREAS:*** Franchise and Distribution; Commercial Law. ***Email:*** hahedden@vssp.com

RONALD A. ROBINS, JR., born Columbus, Ohio, November 19, 1963; admitted to bar, 1990, Ohio and New York. *Education:* Duke University (B.A., summa cum laude, 1985) Phi Beta Kappa; Harvard Law School (J.D., cum laude, 1989). Law Clerk to the Hon. Milton Pollack, U.S. District Court, Southern District of New York. Co-Author: "Uses and Abuses of Proxy Contests," 1988 P.L.I. Journal (20th Annual Institute on Securities Regulation), 223. ***PRACTICE AREAS:*** Corporate Law; Securities; Mergers and Acquisitions. ***Email:*** rarobins@vssp.com

TRAVIS J. WAHL, born Tulsa, Oklahoma, January 13, 1963; admitted to bar, 1990, Texas; 1997, New York; 2000, Ohio. *Education:* Texas A&M University (B.A., Finance, 1985); University of Houston (J.D., cum laude, 1990); Columbia University (LL.M., 1996). Harlan Fiske Stone Scholar. ***PRACTICE AREAS:*** Commercial Finance. ***Email:*** tjwahl@vssp.com

D. MICHAEL SCHIRA, born Van Wert, Ohio, September 9, 1956; admitted to bar, 1990, Ohio. *Education:* The Ohio State University (B.S.C.E., 1979); University of Texas at Austin (J.D., with honors, 1990). Order of the Coif. Professional Engineer, Illinois, 1985. *Member:* Columbus Bar Association. ***PRACTICE AREAS:*** Real Property Law; Commercial Leasing. ***Email:*** dmschira@vssp.com

SUZANNE J. SCRUTTON, born Dearborn, Michigan, December 4, 1963; admitted to bar, 1990, Ohio. *Education:* Albion College (B.A., cum laude, with honors, 1986); Capital University (J.D., 1989). Mortar Board. Executive Articles Editor, Capital University Law Review. Chief Legal Counsel, Ohio Department of Alcohol and Drug Addiction Services, 1994-1997. Assistant Legal Counsel, Ohio Office of Budget and Management, 1989-1994. *Member:* Columbus Bar Association; Ohio Human Rights Bar Association (President, 1997-1999). ***PRACTICE AREAS:*** Health Care. ***Email:*** sjscrutton@vssp.com

JACKLYN J. FORD, born Ft. Belvoir, Virginia, 1961; admitted to bar, 1991, Ohio. *Education:* Oberlin College (A.B., 1983); Case Western Reserve University (J.D., magna cum laude, 1991). Order of the Coif. Member, Board of Directors, Columbus Speech and Hearing Center, 2003-2004. *Member:* Columbus, Ohio State and American Bar Associations. ***PRACTICE AREAS:*** Labor and Employment; Workers Compensation; Privacy Rights. ***Email:*** jjford@vssp.com

MICHAEL D. MARTZ, born Charleston, South Carolina, September 3, 1963; admitted to bar, 1991, Ohio and Wisconsin. *Education:* University of Nebraska at Lincoln (B.S., 1987); University of Wisconsin (J.D., 1991). ***PRACTICE AREAS:*** Corporate Law. ***Email:*** mdmartz@vssp.com

THEODORE P. MATTIS, born Columbus, Ohio, May 25, 1966; admitted to bar, 1991, Ohio. *Education:* The Ohio State University (B.A., cum laude, 1988; J.D., with honors, 1991). Member, Ohio State University Law Review, 1990-1991. Vice-President and Member, Board of Trustees, National Kidney Foundation of Ohio. Member, Ohio League of Conservation Voters. *Member:* Columbus, Ohio State and American Bar Associations. ***PRACTICE AREAS:*** Litigation; Employment Law; Medical Malpractice; Labor Law; Government Relations; Civil Rights; Workers Compensation. ***Email:*** tpmattis@vssp.com

ROBERT A. HARRIS, born Brooklyn, New York, April 12, 1965; admitted to bar, 1992, Ohio. *Education:* Kenyon College (B.A., magna cum laude, 1987); The Ohio State University (M.B.A., with honors, 1992; J.D., with honors, 1992). Order of the Coif. Member, Ohio State Law Journal, 1990-1992. *Member:* Columbus Bar Association; American Immigration Lawyers Association. ***PRACTICE AREAS:*** Labor and Employment; Litigation; Immigration Law. ***Email:*** raharris@vssp.com

D. SCOTT POWELL, born Canton, Ohio, March 18, 1966; admitted to bar, 1992, Ohio. *Education:* The Ohio State University (B.A., summa cum laude, with distinction, 1989); Northwestern University (J.D., 1992). Phi Beta Kappa. Articles Editor, Northwestern University Journal of International Law and Business. *Member:* Columbus and American Bar Associations. ***PRACTICE AREAS:*** Federal Taxation; International; Excise Tax; Income Tax. ***Email:*** dspowell@vssp.com

LISA PIERCE REISZ, born West Lafayette, Indiana, May 12, 1967; admitted to bar, 1992, Ohio; U.S. District Court, District of Ohio; U.S. Court of Appeals, Sixth Circuit. *Education:* Harvard University (B.A., cum laude, 1989); The Ohio State University (J.D., summa cum laude, 1992). Order of the Coif. Staff Member, 1990-1991 and Managing Editor, 1991-1992, Ohio State Law Journal. *Member:* Columbus, Ohio State and American Bar Associations. ***PRACTICE AREAS:*** Litigation. ***Email:*** lpreisz@vssp.com

GREGORY D. RUSSELL, born Albany, New York, January 16, 1966; admitted to bar, 1992, Ohio; 1993, U.S. District Court, Southern District of Ohio; U.S. Court of Appeals, Sixth Circuit; U.S. Supreme Court. *Education:* Washington & Lee University (B.A., summa cum laude, 1988) Valedictorian, University Scholar; TH Darmstadt, W. Germany, Mathematics (Fulbright Grant, 1988-1989); Harvard Law School (J.D., 1992). Phi Beta Kappa; Omicron Delta Kappa. *Member:* Ohio State Bar Association. ***PRACTICE AREAS:*** Environmental Law; Energy Law; Public Utilities Law. ***Email:*** gdrussell@vssp.com

NINA I. WEBB-LAWTON, admitted to bar, 1992, California; 1996, Ohio. *Education:* Oberlin College (B.A., 1987); Boalt Hall School of Law, University of California at Berkeley (J.D., 1992). Law Clerk: Hon. William A. Ingram, U.S. District Court, Northern District of California; Hon. Susan J. Dlott, U.S. District Court, Southern District of Ohio. *Member:* State Bar of California; Columbus and Ohio State Bar Associations. ***PRACTICE AREAS:*** Litigation (100%). ***Email:*** niwebb@vssp.com

STEPHEN D. BROWNING, born Northampton, Massachusetts, June 15, 1966; admitted to bar, 1993, Ohio. *Education:* Williams College (B.A., 1987); Boston College Law School (J.D., cum laude, 1993). Executive Editor, Boston College Law Review, 1992-1993. Author: "The Misguided Application of the Sherman Act to Colleges and Universities in the

(This Listing Continued)

VORYS, SATER, SEYMOUR AND PEASE LLP, Columbus—Continued

Context of Sharing Financial Aid Information," Boston College Law Review, Vol XXXIII No. 4, July 1992. Member, Board of Trustees, Friends of the Columbus Metropolitan Library, 2002-2004. *Member:* Columbus (Chairperson, Real Property Committee, 2003-2005) and Ohio State Bar Associations. ***PRACTICE AREAS:*** Commercial Finance; Real Estate. ***Email:*** sdbrowning@vssp.com

MELINDA R. McAFEE, born Willard, Ohio, July 20, 1970; admitted to bar, 1995, Ohio; 1996, U.S. District Court, Southern and Northern Districts of Ohio; U.S. Court of Appeals, Sixth Circuit; 1999, U.S. District Court, Western District of Pennsylvania; 2000, U.S. Supreme Court. *Education:* Ohio Wesleyan University (B.A., summa cum laude, 1992); Georgetown University (J.D., magna cum laude, 1995). Phi Beta Kappa. Recipient, John F. Kennedy Labor Law Award; Henry Kaiser Memorial Labor Scholarship. *Member:* Ohio State and American Bar Associations. ***PRACTICE AREAS:*** Labor and Employment. ***Email:*** mrmcafee@vssp.com

ADAM K. BRANDT, born Cleveland, Ohio, November 30, 1970; admitted to bar, 1996, Ohio. *Education:* Williams College (B.A., cum laude, 1993); Ohio State University (J.D., with honors, 1996). Order of the Coif. Secretary, Board of Directors, Big Brothers Big Sisters of Central Ohio, 2003-2005. Member, Advisory Council, Center of Science and Industry - COSI Columbus. *Member:* Columbus Bar Association. ***PRACTICE AREAS:*** Corporate; Finance. ***Email:*** akbrandt@vssp.com

TIMOTHY J. DOBYNS, born Columbus, Ohio, April 7, 1971; admitted to bar, 1996, Ohio. *Education:* Miami University (B.A., summa cum laude, 1993); The Ohio State University College of Law (J.D., with honors, 1996). Phi Beta Kappa. Order of the Coif. ***PRACTICE AREAS:*** Corporate; Finance. ***Email:*** tjdobyns@vssp.com

MARK A. KNUEVE, born Columbus, Ohio, October 30, 1970; admitted to bar, 1996, Ohio and U.S. District Court, Southern District of Ohio; 1997, U.S. Court of Appeals, Sixth, Eighth and Eleventh Circuits; U.S. District Court, Western District of Wisconsin. *Education:* University of Virginia (B.S., 1993; J.D., 1996). Member, The Salvation Army Adult Rehabilitation Center. *Member:* Columbus and American Bar Associations. ***PRACTICE AREAS:*** Employment Litigation; Labor Law. ***Email:*** maknueve@vssp.com

CRAIG R. AUGE, born Fort Madison, Iowa, October 29, 1965; admitted to bar, 1997, Ohio; 1998, U.S. District Court, Southern District of Ohio. *Education:* Bowling Green State University (B.A., summa cum laude, 1988); University of Notre Dame (M.A., 1990); Georgetown University (J.D., 1997). Phi Beta Kappa. *Member:* Computer Law Association. ***PRACTICE AREAS:*** Computer Law; Copyrights. ***Email:*** crauge@vssp.com

MARY L. GARCEAU, born Nashua, New Hampshire, December 6, 1972; admitted to bar, 1997, Ohio. *Education:* University of New Hampshire (B.A., summa cum laude, 1994); Vanderbilt University (J.D., 1997). Phi Beta Kappa. Associate Justice, Vanderbilt Moot Court Board, 1996-1997. ***PRACTICE AREAS:*** Corporate; Federal Securities; Mergers, Acquisitions and Divestitures. ***Email:*** mlgarceau@vssp.com

SUSAN BARRETT HARTY, born Indianapolis, Indiana, August 9, 1966; admitted to bar, 1991, Ohio. *Education:* University of Dayton (B.A., 1988; J.D., summa cum laude, 1991). Order of Barristers. Member, National Moot Court Team. Staff Member and Associate Editor, University of Dayton Law Review, 1989-1991. ***PRACTICE AREAS:*** Litigation; Employment; Commercial; Products Liability Class Actions. ***Email:*** sbharty@vssp.com

KIMBERLY WEBER HERLIHY, born Belleville, New Jersey, March 4, 1971; admitted to bar, 1997, Ohio; 1998, U.S. District Court, Southern District of Ohio. *Education:* Boston College (B.A., magna cum laude, 1993); Georgetown University Law Center (J.D., magna cum laude, 1997). Order of the Coif; Phi Beta Kappa. Law Clerk to the Honorable James G. Carr, United States District Court for the Northern District of Ohio, 1997-1998. *Member:* Columbus Bar Association. ***PRACTICE AREAS:*** Litigation. ***Email:*** kwherlihy@vssp.com

JOSEPH R. MILLER, born Elgin, Illinois, February 13, 1972; admitted to bar, 1997, Ohio; 1998, U.S. District Court, Southern District of Ohio; 1999, U.S. Court of Appeals, Sixth Circuit. *Education:* The Ohio State University (B.A., summa cum laude, 1994); Harvard University (J.D., cum laude, 1997). Phi Beta Kappa. ***PRACTICE AREAS:*** Litigation. ***Email:*** jrmiller@vssp.com

SCOTT J. ZIANCE, born Fort Belvoir, Virginia, December 10, 1970; admitted to bar, 1997, Ohio. *Education:* Bowling Green State University (B.A., magna cum laude, 1993); Harvard University (J.D., cum laude, 1997). Phi Beta Kappa. Author, "Making Economic Development Incentives More Efficient," The Urban Lawyer, Winter 1998. Member, Bowling Green City Council, 1992-1993. *Member:* Columbus and Ohio State (Member, Taxation Committee; Chair, Economic Development Incentives Subcommittee) Bar Associations; Federalist Society for Law and Public Policy. ***PRACTICE AREAS:*** State and Local Taxation; Economic Development Incentives; Escheat (Unclaimed Funds). ***Email:*** sjziance@vssp.com

SENIOR ATTORNEYS

TIMOTHY J. BECHTOLD, born Cincinnati, Ohio, October 9, 1950; admitted to bar, 1978, Ohio. *Education:* Xavier University (B.S., magna cum laude, 1972); The Ohio State University (J.D., 1978). Member: Ohio Society of Association Executives; Ohio Lobbying Association; Board of Directors, Upper Arlington Civic Association. *Member:* Columbus and Ohio State Bar Associations. ***PRACTICE AREAS:*** Regulatory Law; Liquor Law; Liquor Licensing; Alcoholic Beverages. ***Email:*** tjbechtold@vssp.com

CAROL MAHAFFEY, born Columbus, Ohio, October 2, 1950; admitted to bar, 1983, Ohio and U.S. District Court, Southern District of Ohio. *Education:* Ohio State University (B.A., 1972); Capital University (J.D., 1983). Administrator, Ohio Department of Taxation, Tax Equalization Division, 1986-1988. *Member:* Columbus (Chair) and Ohio State (Member, State and Local Taxation Subcommittee, 1988-1989) Bar Associations. ***PRACTICE AREAS:*** Ohio State and Local Taxation Law; Ad Valorem Tax; Administrative Law; Tax Litigation; Administrative Adjudications. ***Email:*** cmahaffey@vssp.com

(This Listing Continued)

KAREN A. CINCIONE, born St. Louis, Missouri, December 30, 1963; admitted to bar, 1989, Ohio and U.S. District Court, Northern District of Ohio; 1990, U.S. District Court, Southern District of Ohio; 1994, U.S. Court of Appeals, Sixth Circuit. *Education:* Miami University (B.A., cum laude, 1986); University of North Carolina at Chapel Hill (J.D., 1989). Chief Counsel, Ohio Department of Alcohol and Drug Addiction Services. Assistant Attorney General, Ohio Attorney General's Office. *Member:* Columbus and Ohio State Bar Associations. ***PRACTICE AREAS:*** Health Care. ***Email:*** kacincione@vssp.com

RICHARD T. MILLER, born Columbus, Ohio, May 26, 1953; admitted to bar, 1991, Ohio; 1992, Colorado. *Education:* Kenyon College; University of Colorado at Boulder (B.A., 1979); University of Denver (J.D., 1987). ***PRACTICE AREAS:*** Labor and Employment; Disability Discrimination. ***Email:*** rtmiller@vssp.com

ANTHONY SPINA, born Akron, Ohio, 1971; admitted to bar, 1998, Ohio. *Education:* University of Akron (B.S., Financial and Business Administration, 1993); Capital University (J.D., cum laude, 1998). Order of the Curia. Law Clerk to Judge David W. Fais, Franklin County Court of Common Pleas, 1998-2000. *Member:* Ohio State Bar Association. ***PRACTICE AREAS:*** Insurance Law; Corporate Law. ***Email:*** aspina@vssp.com

ASSOCIATES

MELISSA J. MITCHELL, born Houston, Texas, August 30, 1956; admitted to bar, 1983, Ohio. *Education:* Denison University (B.A., 1978); Case Western Reserve University (J.D., 1982). *Member:* Columbus Bar Association. ***Email:*** mjmitchell@vssp.com

MICHAEL C. GRIFFATON, born New Hyde Park, New York, February 7, 1968; admitted to bar, 1993, Ohio; 1998, U.S. District Court, Southern District of Ohio; 2000, U.S. District Court, Northern District of Ohio; 2004, U.S. Court of Appeals, Sixth Circuit. *Education:* Ohio Wesleyan University (B.A., magna cum laude, 1990); Case Western Reserve University (J.D., magna cum laude, 1993). Phi Beta Kappa. Order of the Coif. Executive Notes Editor, Case Western Reserve Law Review. Co-Author: (with W. Porter II) "Between the Devil and the Deep Blue Sea: Charting a Course for Monitoring the Electronic Workplace and Handling the Information Received," 70 Defense Counsel Journal 65 (January 2003); (with W. Porter II) "Using NonCompete Agreements to Protect Legitimate Business Interests," Defense Counsel Journal, April 2002; (with W. Porter II) "Identifying and Protecting Employers' Interests in Trade Secrets and Other Proprietary Information," Defense Counsel Journal, October 2001. Author: "State-Level Initiatives and Campus Crime," Campus Crime: Legal, Social and Policy Issues, May 1995; "Forewarned is Forearmed: The Crime Awareness and Campus Security Act of 1990," Case W. Res. L. Rev. 525, December 1993; "Personnel Records, Pedophiles, and Priests: An Addendum to Discovery in Sexual Abuse Cases," with W. Porter II, in International Association of Defense Counsel, Privacy Project (2004). *Member:* Columbus and Ohio State Bar Associations. ***PRACTICE AREAS:*** Labor and Employment Law. ***Email:*** mcgriffaton@vssp.com

MICHAEL F. O'BRIEN, born Cleveland, Ohio, July 16, 1957; admitted to bar, 1993, Ohio; 1994, U.S. District Court, Northern District of Ohio; 1998, U.S. District Court, Southern District of Ohio; 1999, U.S. District Court, Western District of Wisconsin; 2003, U.S. Court of Appeals, Sixth Circuit. *Education:* Holy Cross College (B.A., 1979); Cleveland-Marshall (J.D., magna cum laude, 1993). Research Editor, Cleveland State Law Review. Author: "Operation Rescue and the Misuse of 42 U.S.C. §1985(3)," 41 Clev. St. L. Rev. 145 (1993). *Member:* Ohio State Bar Association. ***PRACTICE AREAS:*** Labor and Employment; School Law; Age Discrimination in Employment; Employment Contracts; Employment Disability Discrimination; Employment Law; Family and Medical Leave Act; Labor Law; Sexual Harassment; Unfair Labor Practices; Wage and Hour Law; WARN Act; Wrongful Termination. ***Email:*** mfobrien@vssp.com

KYONG W. NAHM WAHL, admitted to bar, 1993, Ontario; 1997, New York; 2000, Ohio. *Education:* McMaster University (B.A.Sc., summa cum laude, 1988); Osgoode Hall Law School (LL.B., 1991); Columbia University School of Law (LL.M., 1996). Former Adjunct Professor, Paralegal Program, Capital University Law School. *Member:* Law Society of Upper Canada. ***PRACTICE AREAS:*** Mergers and Acquisitions; Corporate Finance; Corporate Law; Securities. ***Email:*** knwahl@vssp.com

NELSON D. CARY, born Battle Creek, Michigan, July 13, 1968; admitted to bar, 1994, Virginia; 1995, District of Columbia; 2001, Ohio. *Education:* Albion College (B.A., summa cum laude, 1990); Washington & Lee University (J.D., summa cum laude, 1994). Order of the Coif. Law Clerk, Chief Judge Jackson L. Kiser, Western District of Virginia. Contributor, Washington & Lee Law Review. *Member:* Virginia State Bar. ***PRACTICE AREAS:*** Labor and Employment.

TIFFANY STRELOW COBB, born Oakland, California, June 11, 1968; admitted to bar, 1994, Missouri; 1995, Illinois; 1997, Ohio. *Education:* The Principia College (B.A., with highest honors, 1990); Washington University (J.D., 1994). Phi Beta Kappa. *Member:* Columbus Bar Association. ***PRACTICE AREAS:*** Litigation; Bankruptcy. ***Email:*** tscobb@vssp.com

PERRY W. DORAN II, born Columbus, Ohio, October 9, 1968; admitted to bar, 1994, Florida; 1995, U.S. District Court, Middle District of Florida and U.S. Court of Appeals, Eleventh Circuit; 2000, Ohio; 2001, U.S. District Court, Southern District of Ohio. *Education:* University of Florida (B.S., 1990; J.D., 1993). Beta Gamma Sigma; Phi Kappa Phi. *Member:* The Florida Bar; Columbus, Ohio State and American Bar Associations; Ohio Trial Lawyers Association. ***PRACTICE AREAS:*** Civil Litigation; Trial Practice. ***Email:*** pdoran@vssp.com

DAVID A. FROLING, born Livingston, New Jersey, November 15, 1966; admitted to bar, 1995, Ohio. *Education:* The Ohio State University (B.S., B.A., 1990); Capital University (L.L.M. Taxation, 1995; J.D., 1995). Formerly with Bath & Body Works and KPMG LLP. *Member:* Columbus and Ohio State Bar Associations. ***PRACTICE AREAS:*** State and Local Taxation. ***Email:*** dafroling@vssp.com

KELLY JENNINGS YEOMAN, born Pittsburgh, Pennsylvania, August 19, 1971; admitted to bar, 1996, Maryland and U.S. District Court, District of Maryland; 2000, District of Columbia; 2004, Ohio. *Education:* Denison University (B.A., 1993); George Washington University (J.D., 1996). ***PRACTICE AREAS:*** Labor and Employment. ***Email:*** ksjennings@vssp.com

(This Listing Continued)

LYNNE M. FROLING, born Detroit, Michigan, June 26, 1971; admitted to bar, 1997, Michigan; 2003, Ohio and U.S. District Court, District of Ohio. *Education:* Western Michigan University (B.B.A., magna cum laude, 1993); University of Detroit Mercy (M.B.A.and J.D., 1996); Wayne State University (L.L.M., 1999). Mortar Board Society, Western Michigan University. Managing Editor, Michigan Business Law Journal, 1995-1996. *Member:* Detroit, Columbus and Ohio State Bar Associations; State Bar of Michigan (Member, Taxation Section). ***PRACTICE AREAS:*** State and Local Tax. ***Email:*** lmfroling@vssp.com

MATTHEW D. GOTTSCHALL, born Dayton, Ohio; admitted to bar, 1997, Ohio. *Education:* Miami University (B.A., 1994); University of Cincinnati (J.D., summa cum laude, 1997). Phi Beta Kappa. Member, University of Cincinnati Law Review. *Member:* Ohio State and American Bar Associations. ***PRACTICE AREAS:*** Commercial Real Estate. ***Email:*** mdgottschall@vssp.com

RODNEY A. HOLADAY, born Findlay, Ohio, November 3, 1971; admitted to bar, 1997, Ohio; 1998, U.S. District Court, Southern District of Ohio; 2001, U.S. District Court, Northern District of Ohio. *Education:* Miami University (B.S., with honors, 1994); The Moritz College of Law, The Ohio State University (J.D., with honors, 1997). Order of the Coif. Former Extern, Supreme Court of Ohio. Former Intern, State of Ohio Attorney General's Office. *Member:* Columbus and Ohio State Bar Associations. ***PRACTICE AREAS:*** Alternative Dispute Resolution; Appellate Practice; Business Law; Commercial Litigation; Intentional Tort Litigation; Toxic Tort Litigation. ***Email:*** raholaday@vssp.com

JOSEPH B. MANN, born Marion, Ohio, August 3, 1970; admitted to bar, 1997, New York (Not admitted in Ohio). *Education:* Case Western Reserve University (B.S., 1992); Columbia University (J.D., 1996). *Member:* New York State Bar Association. ***PRACTICE AREAS:*** Taxation. ***Email:*** jbmann@vssp.com

MAGGIE O'SHAUGHNESSY, born Columbus, Ohio; admitted to bar, 1997, Ohio. *Education:* University of Notre Dame (B.A., 1994); The Ohio State University (J.D., 1997). ***PRACTICE AREAS:*** Litigation. ***Email:*** moshaughnessy@vssp.com

NICOLE J. PAPA, born Baltimore, Maryland, April 4, 1970; admitted to bar, 1997, Maryland; 2005, Ohio. *Education:* University of Virginia (B.A., 1992); University of Baltimore (J.D., cum laude, 1996). Lecturer: Modern Real Estate Transactions, Maryland Institute for Continuing Professional Education for Lawyers, 1999-2001; "How to Conduct a Successful Closing," Lorman Institute, 2001. Formerly with Ballard, Spahr, Andrews & Ingersoll, LLP. Member, Commercial Real Estate Women - CREW Columbus. *Member:* Columbus, Maryland State and Ohio State Bar Associations. ***PRACTICE AREAS:*** Commercial Real Estate; Commercial Transactions; Condominium Law; Banking Law; Financial Law; Real Estate; Business Transactions.

ALYCIA N. BROZ, born Cleveland, Ohio, May 25, 1971; admitted to bar, 1998, Ohio. *Education:* Marquette University (B.S., magna cum laude, 1993); Northwestern University (J.D., 1998). Beta Gamma Sigma. Named Outstanding Senior of the Year, College of Business Administration, Marquette University, 1993. Law Clerk to The Honorable Algenon L. Marbley, U.S. District Court, Southern District of Ohio, 1999-2001. Vice-Chair, 2003, Chair, 2004 and Board Member, 2001-2005, Kaleidoscope Youth Coalition. Member, Young Professionals Executive Committee, 2002-2003 and Member, City Year Columbus. Member, Education Vision Council, United Way of Central Ohio. *Member:* Columbus Bar Association. ***Email:*** anbroz@vssp.com

VICTOR J. FERGUSON, born Akron, Ohio, October 5, 1971; admitted to bar, 1998, Ohio. *Education:* Wittenberg University (B.A., 1994); University of Akron (J.D., magna cum laude, 1998). Editor-in-Chief, Akron Law Review. ***PRACTICE AREAS:*** Federal Estate and Gift Taxation; Estate Administration; Estate Planning; Nonprofit and Charitable Organizations. ***Email:*** vferguson@vssp.com

PETER A. LUSENHOP, admitted to bar, 1998, Ohio. *Member:* Columbus and Ohio State Bar Associations. ***PRACTICE AREAS:*** Litigation. ***Email:*** palusenhop@vssp.com

ALLEN L. RUTZ, born Gallipolis, Ohio, October 11, 1961; admitted to bar, 1998, Ohio and U.S. District Court, Southern District of Ohio; 1999, District of Columbia and U.S. Court of Appeals, Sixth Circuit; registered to practice before the U.S. Patent and Trademark Office. *Education:* University of Cincinnati (B.S.M.E., magna cum laude, 1984) Ohio State University (M.S.M.E., 1989); Capital University Law School (J.D., summa cum laude, 1998). Tau Beta Pi; Pi Tau Sigma. Order of the Barrister; Order of the Curia. Recipient, American College of Trial Lawyers Medal for Excellence in Advocacy, 1996. Staff Member, Capital University Law Review, 1996-1997. Author: "After the Meter: Energy Products Liability in a Deregulated Environment," 26 Capital U.L. Rev. 421, 1997. Professional Engineer, Ohio. *Member:* Columbus and Ohio Bar Associations; Columbus Intellectual Property Law Association. ***PRACTICE AREAS:*** Litigation; Products Liability; Construction Litigation; Intellectual Property. ***Email:*** alrutz@vssp.com

J. THEODORE SMITH, born Bellefontaine, Ohio, May 8, 1970; admitted to bar, 1998, Ohio. *Education:* Purdue University (B.S., Civil Engineering, 1992); University of Illinois (J.D., magna cum laude, 1998). Chi Epsilon; Phi Delta Phi. Author: "1-800-ripoffs: Internet Domain Names Are the Telephone Numbers of Cyberspace," University of Illinois Law Review, 1997. Member, 1996-1997 and Administrative Editor, 1997-1998, University of Illinois Law Review. *Member:* Columbus and Ohio State (Member and Newsletter Editor, Real Property Law Section) Bar Associations. ***PRACTICE AREAS:*** Commercial Real Estate; Condominium; Commercial Transactions. ***Email:*** jtsmith@vssp.com

CARTER M. STEWART, born Boston, Massachusetts, 1969; admitted to bar, 1998, California; U.S. District Court, Northern District of California; U.S. Court of Appeals, Ninth Circuit (Not admitted in Ohio). *Education:* Stanford University (B.A., Political Science, 1991); Columbia University (M.A., Education, 1994); Harvard Law School (J.D., 1997). Adjunct Professor, Education Law, Lincoln School of San Jose, 2003. Member, Bar Association of San Francisco, 1999-2002. *Member:* Santa Clara County Bar Association. ***PRACTICE AREAS:*** Commercial Litigation; Antitrust; White Collar Defense. ***Email:*** cmstewart@vssp.com

MEREDITH K. KNUEVE, born Canton, Ohio, September 14, 1973; admitted to bar, 1999, Ohio. *Education:* The Ohio State University (B.S., 1995; M.Ed., 1996; J.D., 1996). Delta Theta Phi. *Member:* Columbus and Ohio State Bar Associations. ***PRACTICE AREAS:*** Estate Planning; Probate; Federal Taxation. ***Email:*** mkknueve@vssp.com

BRIAN J. LALIBERTE, born Youngstown, Ohio, March 8, 1974; admitted to bar, 1999, Ohio; 2000, U.S. District Court, Northern District of Ohio; 2001, U.S. District Court, Southern District of Ohio. *Education:* University of Michigan (B.A., 1996); Case Western Reserve University (J.D., 1999). Law Clerk to U.S. District Judge Peter C. Economus, Northern District of Ohio, 1999-2001. *Member:* Columbus, Ohio State and American Bar Associations. ***PRACTICE AREAS:*** Litigation. ***Email:*** bjlaliberte@vssp.com

SEBASTIAN E. PROELS, born Erlangen, West Germany, January 14, 1967; admitted to bar, 1999, Ohio. *Education:* University of Chicago (B.A., 1989: M.D, 1994); Case Western Reserve University (J.D., 1999). Author: "Medical-Legal Internet Research: Finding Reliable Information," The Trial Lawyer Volume 23 Number 2, March-April, 2000. ***PRACTICE AREAS:*** Litigation. ***Email:*** seproels@vssp.com

BLAKE A. SNIDER, born Columbus, Ohio, August 6, 1974; admitted to bar, 1999, Ohio. *Education:* The Ohio State University (B.S., 1996); Harvard Law School (J.D., 1999). *Member:* Columbus and Ohio State Bar Associations. ***PRACTICE AREAS:*** State and Local Taxation. ***Email:*** basnider@vssp.com

ANTHONY D. WEIS, born Toledo, Ohio, April 19, 1974; admitted to bar, 1999, Ohio. *Education:* Bowling Green State University (B.S.B.A., summa cum laude, 1996); The Ohio State University (J.D., summa cum laude, 1999). Order of the Coif. Author: "Striking an Imbalance: The Interpretation of Section 21D (b)(2) of the Securities Exchange Act of 1934 in Siticon Graphics," 59 Ohio St. L.J. 1741 (1998). *Member:* Columbus and Ohio State Bar Associations. ***PRACTICE AREAS:*** Corporate Law. ***Email:*** adweis@vssp.com

HEIDI L. YURKIW, born Toledo, Ohio, January 16, 1974; admitted to bar, 1999, Ohio; 2000, U.S. District Court, Southern District of Ohio and U.S. Court of Appeals, Sixth Circuit. *Education:* Ohio University (B.S., summa cum laude, 1996); Ohio State University (J.D., 1999). Member, The National Moot Court Team. Member, The Ohio State Law Journal. Law Clerk, The Honorable Joseph R. Kinneary, Southern District of Ohio. *Member:* Columbus Bar Association (Member, Barrister Leader Program, 2001-2002). ***PRACTICE AREAS:*** Litigation. ***Email:*** hlyurkiw@vssp.com

ROBERT A. BELL, JR., born Lanham, Maryland; admitted to bar, 2000, Ohio. *Education:* Miami University (B.S., 1992); University of Dayton School of Law (J.D., magna cum laude, 2000). Managing Editor, University of Dayton Law Review. Certified Public Accountant. *Member:* Columbus Bar Association. ***Email:*** rabell@vssp.com

JOHN N. BOYER, born Ft. Belvoir, Virginia, December 3, 1974; admitted to bar, 2000, Ohio. *Education:* Cornell University (B.S., 1997); Harvard Law School (J.D., 2000). *Member:* Ohio State Bar Association. [Captain, U.S. Army, 2000-2004]. ***PRACTICE AREAS:*** Litigation.

JASON C. ELVERS, born Bellevue, Washington; admitted to bar, 2000, Ohio. *Education:* The Ohio State University (B.A., 1997); Vanderbilt University School of Law (J.D., 2000). *Member:* Columbus and American Bar Associations; Computer Law Association. ***Email:*** jcelvers@vssp.com

MICHAEL J. HAUSWIRTH, born Columbus, Ohio, April 14, 1971; admitted to bar, 2000, Illinois (Not admitted in Ohio). *Education:* Northwestern University (B.A., 1993); Duke University (M.A., 1997); Harvard Law School (J.D., 2000). ***LANGUAGES:*** German. ***PRACTICE AREAS:*** Taxation.

JOLIE N. HAVENS, born Minford, Ohio; admitted to bar, 2000, Ohio; U.S. District Court, Southern District of Ohio. *Education:* Ohio Wesleyan University (B.A., Political Science and History, magna cum laude, 1997); The Ohio State University College of Law (J.D., with honors, 2000). Member: The Ohio State University Center for Law and Social Policy; The Godman Guild; Arthritis Foundation; Ohio Parents for Drug Free Youth (Board Member). ***Email:*** jnhavens@vssp.com

STACIA M. JONES, born Columbus, Ohio; admitted to bar, 2000, Ohio. *Education:* The Ohio State University (B.A., magna cum laude, 1997); The Ohio State University College of Law (J.D., with honors, Certificate of Alternative Dispute Resolution, 2000). Article and Symposium Editor, Ohio State Journal on Dispute Resolution. Board Member, Columbus Women's Auxiliary Club. ***Email:*** smjones@vssp.com

SCOTT A. KOSSOUDJI, born Dayton, Ohio; admitted to bar, 2000, Ohio. *Education:* Navy Dive School; Naval Explosive Ordinance Disposal School (Honor Graduate, 1992); Army Airborne Jump School; The Ohio State University (B.A., summa cum laude, 1997); The Ohio State University College of Law (J.D., with honors, 2000). *Member:* Ohio State and American Bar Associations. [E-5, U.S. Navy 1988-1995]. ***Email:*** sakossoudji@vssp.com

JUDITH L. MARSH, born Albion, Michigan; admitted to bar, 2000, Ohio. *Education:* Albion College (B.A., summa cum laude, 1994); The Ohio State University (J.D., 2000). Order of the Coif. *Member:* Ohio State and Columbus Bar Associations. ***Email:*** jlmarsh@vssp.com

JEFFREY ALLEN MILLER, born Mt. Vernon, Ohio; admitted to bar, 2000, Ohio. *Education:* The Ohio State University (B.S., summa cum laude, 1997); The Ohio State University College of Law (J.D., 2000). Naval Nuclear Power Program, 1986-1988. *Member:* Ohio State Bar Association. ***PRACTICE AREAS:*** Taxation. ***Email:*** jamiller2@vssp.com

WILLIAM A. SIECK, born Madison, Wisconsin; admitted to bar, 2000, Ohio. *Education:* The University of Chicago (B.A., cum laude, 1991); University of Pennsylvania Law School (J.D., cum laude, 1999). *Member:* Columbus and Ohio State Bar Associations. ***Email:*** wasieck@vssp.com

JENNIFER M. BURKE, born Kent, Ohio, July 14, 1970; admitted to bar, 2001, Ohio. *Education:* John Carroll University (B.A., cum laude, 1996); Boston College Law School (J.D., magna cum laude, 2001). Recipient, David Bonnot Book Award for Scholarship in the Humanities, John Carroll University. Staff Writer and Editor, Boston College Law School Environmental Affairs Law Review, 1999-2001. ***Email:*** jmburke@vssp.com

TRISHA M. CORBIN, born Findlay, Ohio, April 15, 1976; admitted to bar, 2001, Ohio; 2002, U.S. District Court, Southern District of Ohio. *Education:* Hiram College (B.A., summa cum laude, 1998); University of Cincinnati (J.D., cum laude, 2001). Phi Beta Kappa; Phi Gamma Mu. Listed in Who's Who Among American Law Students, 2001. Congressional Intern to Rep. Michael G. Oxley (R-OH). *Member:* Columbus and Ohio State Bar Associations. ***Email:*** tmcorbin@vssp.com

(This Listing Continued)

VORYS, SATER, SEYMOUR AND PEASE LLP, Columbus—Continued

THOMAS H. FUSONIE, born Greenfield, Massachusetts; admitted to bar, 2001, Ohio; 2002, U.S. District Court, Southern District of Ohio. *Education:* Hamilton College (B.A., magna cum laude, 1998); Vanderbilt University (J.D., 2001). Student Writing Editor, Journal of Transnational Law, Vanderbilt School of Law. *Member:* Columbus Bar Association. ***Email:*** thfusonie@vssp.com

JENNIFER NAUMOFF, born Rochester, New York, December 12, 1971; admitted to bar, 2001, Ohio. *Education:* Miami University (B.S., 1994); Ohio State University (J.D., 2001). Associate Editor, Ohio State Journal on Dispute Resolution, 2000-2001. Member, Board of Trustees, Children's Hospital Black Tie Ball. Volunteer, German Village Society. *Member:* Columbus Bar Association. ***PRACTICE AREAS:*** Real Estate; Commercial Law; Technology Law; Software Licensing. ***Email:*** janaumoff@vssp.com

ANGELA K. REITLER, born Charleston, South Carolina, September 23, 1972; admitted to bar, 2001, Tennessee; 2003, Ohio and U.S. District Court, Eastern District of Tennessee; 2004, U.S. District Court, Southern District of Ohio. *Education:* University of Cincinnati (B.S., magna cum laude, 1994; M.S., summa cum laude, 1995); Ohio Northern University (J.D., 2001). *Member:* Columbus and Federal Bar Associations. ***PRACTICE AREAS:*** Litigation. ***Email:*** akreitler@vssp.com

JEFFREY D. ROBERTS, born Oxford, Ohio, November 4, 1973; admitted to bar, 2001, Ohio. *Education:* Miami University (B.S., 1996); University of Virginia (J.D., 2001). ***Email:*** jdroberts@vssp.com

MICHAEL J. SETTINERI, born Midland, Michigan, September 6, 1967; admitted to bar, 2001, Ohio. *Education:* University of Michigan (B.S., Chemical Engineering, 1989); Capital University (J.D., 2001). Order of the Curia. ***Email:*** mjsettineri@vssp.com

CHRISTOPHER A. SNYDER, born Youngstown, Ohio; admitted to bar, 2001, Florida; 2002, U.S. Court of Appeals, Eighth Circuit (Not admitted in Ohio). *Education:* Ohio University (B.A., B.B.A., 1996); The Ohio State University College of Law (J.D., 2000). Editor-in-Chief, Ohio State Law Journal. Law Clerk: Hon. Lavenski R. Smith, Eighth Circuit Court of Appeals, 2002-2003; Hon. Jose A. Gonzalez, Jr., Southern District of Florida, 2000-2002. Adjunct Professor, University of Arkansas at Little Rock, Bowen School of Law, 2003. ***LANGUAGES:*** Spanish. ***Email:*** casnyder@vssp.com

WENDY M. SWARY, born Columbus, Ohio, December 20, 1972; admitted to bar, 2001, New York (Not admitted in Ohio). *Education:* Duke University (B.A., Public Policy Studies, 1995); Ohio State University (J.D., with honors, 2000). ***PRACTICE AREAS:*** Labor and Employment; ERISA. ***Email:*** wmswary@vssp.com

DANIEL J. CLARK, born Scranton, Pennsylvania, February 8, 1977; admitted to bar, 2002, Ohio. *Education:* Wittenberg University (B.A., summa cum laude, 1999); The Ohio State University (J.D., with honors, 2002). Phi Beta Kappa. ***Email:*** djclark@vssp.com

ELIZABETH A. FOX, born Fremont, Ohio, January 26, 1975; admitted to bar, 2002, Ohio. *Education:* University of Toledo (B.A., 1998; J.D., summa cum laude, 2002). ***PRACTICE AREAS:*** Litigation. ***Email:*** eafox@vssp.com

DAREN S. GARCIA, born Youngstown, Ohio, June 23, 1976; admitted to bar, 2002, Florida; 2003, Ohio. *Education:* The Ohio State University (B.A., cum laude, 1998); Emory University (J.D., 2002). ***LANGUAGES:*** Spanish. ***PRACTICE AREAS:*** Litigation. ***Email:*** dsgarcia@vssp.com

TIMOTHY D. HUDOK, born Meadville, Pennsylvania, April 1, 1977; admitted to bar, 2002, Ohio. *Education:* Bowling Green State University (B.A., 1999); Oxford University Faculty of Law, Oxford, England; The Ohio State University College of Law (J.D., 2002). Board Member, Camp Mary Orton. ***PRACTICE AREAS:*** Commercial Real Estate. ***Email:*** tdhudok@vssp.com

ALBERT G. LIN, born Cleveland, Ohio, April 7, 1973; admitted to bar, 2002, California; 2003, Ohio. *Education:* The Ohio State University (B.A., summa cum laude, 1996); Stanford University Law School (J.D., 2000). Phi Beta Kappa. President, Asian Pacific Islander Law Student Association. Publishing Chair, Stanford Journal of International Law, 1999-2000. Law Clerk to Judge R. Guy Cole, Jr., U.S. Court of Appeals, Sixth Circuit, 2004-2005. Steering Committee, Ohio for Howard Dean, 2003-2004. Law Clerk to Judge Ann Aldrich, U.S. District Court, 2000-2001. Cambodia Defender's Project, Summer 1998, Phnom Penh, Cambodia. English Teacher, Yantai University, 1996-1997, Yantai, Shandong Province, People's Republic of China. ***PRACTICE AREAS:*** Litigation; Securities Litigation; Intellectual Property. ***Email:*** aglin@vssp.com

BRUCE P. PAIGE, born Akron, Ohio, July 6, 1976; admitted to bar, 2002, Ohio. *Education:* Ohio University (B.A., summa cum laude, 1998); The Ohio State University (J.D., 2002). Phi Beta Kappa. Associate Editor, Ohio State University Law Journal. *Member:* Columbus and Ohio State Bar Associations. ***PRACTICE AREAS:*** Closely Held Business Law; Limited Liability Company Law; Business Reorganization; Contracts; Business Formation; Mergers, Acquisitions and Divestitures. ***Email:*** bppaige@vssp.com

GINA R. RUSSO, born Cincinnati, Ohio, September 29, 1977; admitted to bar, 2002, Ohio. *Education:* Bowling Green University (B.A., summa cum laude, 1999); Wake Forest Law School (J.D., 2002). Phi Beta Kappa. Order of the Barristers. Member: National Moot Court Team, 2001-2002; Jessup Moot Court Team, 2000-2001. ***Email:*** grrusso@vssp.com

ALEXANDRA T. SCHIMMER, born Philadelphia, Pennsylvania; admitted to bar, 2002, Ohio. *Education:* Princeton University (A.B., 1998); Yale University (J.D., 2002). *Member:* Ohio State Bar Association.

CHRISTOPHER E. SUMI, born Lawrence, Kansas, March 6, 1977; admitted to bar, 2002, Ohio. *Education:* Ohio State University (B.A., 1999; J.D., 2002). Phi Beta Kappa. *Member:* Columbus Bar Association. ***PRACTICE AREAS:*** Corporate and Finance; Intellectual Property; Tax and Probate. ***Email:*** cesumi@vssp.com

BETHANY R. THOMAS, born Lima, Ohio, January 7, 1978; admitted to bar, 2002, Ohio. *Education:* Miami University (B.A., 1999); The Ohio State University (J.D., 2002). ***Email:*** brthomas@vssp.com

(This Listing Continued)

TAMARA J. WATTS, born Defiance, Ohio, November 6, 1976; admitted to bar, 2002, Ohio. *Education:* Defiance College (B.S., 1999); The Ohio State University (J.D., 2002). Managing Editor, Ohio State Journal on Dispute Resolution. ***PRACTICE AREAS:*** Litigation. ***Email:*** tjwatts@vssp.com

MICHAEL G. BERNER, born Buffalo, New York, June 8, 1978; admitted to bar, 2003, Ohio. *Education:* St. Lawrence University (B.A., summa cum laude, 2000); Syracuse University-Maxwell School of Public Administration (M.P.A., 2003); Syracuse University College of Law (J.D., summa cum laude, 2003). *Member:* Ohio State Bar Association. ***Email:*** mgberner@vssp.com

P. JASON DEJELO, born Cleveland, Ohio, December 15, 1977; admitted to bar, 2003, Ohio. *Education:* University of Pennsylvania (B.A., cum laude, 2000); The Ohio State University (J.D., cum laude, 2003). *Member:* Ohio State and American Bar Associations. ***Email:*** pjdejelo@vssp.com

GRETCHEN JEFFRIES, born Columbus, Ohio, November 27, 1975; admitted to bar, 2003, Ohio. *Education:* Ohio State University (B.A., 1999); University of Texas at Austin (J.D., 2003). ***Email:*** gdjeffries@vssp.com

DARRELL A. H. MILLER, born Anderson, Indiana; admitted to bar, 2003, Ohio; 2003, U.S. District Court, Southern District of Ohio and U.S. Court of Appeals, Sixth Circuit. *Education:* Anderson University (B.A., 1994); Oxford University, England (B.A., 1997; M.A., 2002); Harvard Law School (J.D., 2001). British Marshall Scholar. *Member:* Columbus Bar Association. ***Email:*** dahmiller@vssp.com

MATTHEW J. RICHARDSON, born Cincinnati, Ohio, November 4, 1968; admitted to bar, 2003, Ohio. *Education:* Stanford University (A.B., 1992); The Ohio State University (M.A., 1994; Ph.D., 2001; J.D., 2003). Editor-in-Chief, Ohio State Law Journal, 2002-2003. Law Clerk to the Hon. Howell Cobb, Eastern District of Texas, 2003-2004. *Member:* Columbus and Ohio State Bar Associations. ***LANGUAGES:*** French and German.

BENJAMIN J. RICKERT, born Green Bay, Wisconsin, January 30, 1977; admitted to bar, 2003, Ohio. *Education:* Ashland College (B.A., summa cum laude, 1999); University of Wisconsin-Madison (M.A., Latin American, Iberian and Caribbean Studies, 2003; J.D., cum laude, 2003). Author, "Data Privacy and Institutional Decision Makers," Tilburg Foreign Law Review, Vol. II, Issue 1. ***LANGUAGES:*** Spanish and Portuguese. ***PRACTICE AREAS:*** Privacy Law; Technology Law; Intellectual Property (50%); Litigation (30%); Labor and Employment (20%). ***Email:*** bjrickert@vssp.com

JENNIFER S. RUSIE, born Jonesboro, Arkansas, January 3, 1977; admitted to bar, 2003, Ohio. *Education:* Vanderbilt University (B.A., 1999); New York University (J.D., 2003). *Member:* Columbus and Ohio State Bar Associations. ***PRACTICE AREAS:*** Litigation. ***Email:*** jsrusie@vssp.com

MICHAEL J. RUSIE, born Martinsville, Indiana, April 5, 1977; admitted to bar, 2003, Ohio. *Education:* DePauw University (B.A., 1999); Washington University - St. Louis (J.D., 2002). *Member:* Columbus and Ohio State Bar Association. ***Email:*** mjrusie@vssp.com

CHELSEY M. VASCURA, born Columbus, Ohio, June 6, 1978; admitted to bar, 2003, Ohio. *Education:* Bethany College (B.A., cum laude, 2000); Ohio State University (J.D., cum laude, 2003). Order of the Coif. ***Email:*** cmvascura@vssp.com

NATHAN J. WAUTIER, born Green Bay, Wisconsin, July 4, 1974; admitted to bar, 2003, Ohio; 2004, Wisconsin; U.S. District Court, Southern District of Ohio. *Education:* University of Chicago (B.A., cum laude, 1997); University of Wisconsin (J.D., cum laude, 2003). Volunteer, U.S. Peace Corps, Momostenango, Guatemala. *Member:* Columbus Bar Association. ***LANGUAGES:*** Spanish. ***PRACTICE AREAS:*** Bankruptcy; Commercial Finance; Real Estate. ***Email:*** njwautier@vssp.com

MARJORIE F. AMERINE, born Shreveport, Louisiana, June 13, 1979; admitted to bar, 2004, Ohio. *Education:* Hendrix College (B.A., 2001); Washington University (J.D., 2004).

ROBERT W. CONLEY, born Monroeville, Pennsylvania, April 28, 1979; admitted to bar, 2004, Ohio. *Education:* University of Michigan (B.M., Voice Performance, with honors, 2001); University of Pittsburgh (J.D., 2004). Articles Editor, Pittsburgh Tax Review, 2003-2004. Board Member: Columbus Operrazzi, 2005; Sterling Condominium Association, 2005. ***PRACTICE AREAS:*** Labor and Employment.

CHRIS L. CONNELLY, born Dayton, Ohio, April 17, 1975; admitted to bar, 2004, Ohio. *Education:* The Ohio State University (B.S., 1997); University of Dayton (J.D., 2004).

MONICA GRANDE, born March 28, 1979; admitted to bar, 2004, Ohio. *Education:* The Ohio State University (B.S.B.A., magna cum laude, 2001; J.D., with honors, 2004). ***PRACTICE AREAS:*** Corporate Law.

SARAH L. HERBERT, born Youngstown, Ohio; admitted to bar, 2004, Ohio. *Education:* The Ohio State University (B.S.B.A., summa cum laude, 2000); Cornell University (J.D., cum laude, 2004).

DAVID J. KAUFMAN, born Columbus, Ohio, July 29, 1978; admitted to bar, 2004, Ohio and U.S. District Court, Southern District of Ohio. *Education:* Georgetown University (B.A., Comparative Government, 2000); Emory University (J.D., 2004). *Member:* Columbus and American Bar Associations. ***PRACTICE AREAS:*** Labor and Employment.

CHRISTINA M. LYONS, born East Liverpool, Ohio; admitted to bar, 2004, Ohio. *Education:* The Ohio State University (B.S.N., 1995); Capital University Law School (J.D., magna cum laude, 2004). Delta Theta Phi. Order of the Curia. *Member:* Ohio State Bar Association. ***PRACTICE AREAS:*** Corporate Law; Finance. ***Email:*** cmlyons@vssp.com

ANNA KATHREEN NUBER, born Sandusky, Ohio, April 8, 1979; admitted to bar, 2004, Ohio; 2005, U.S. District Court, Southern District of Ohio. *Education:* Ohio Northern University (B.S.B.A., 2001); The Ohio State University (J.D., 2004). *Member:* Columbus and Ohio State Bar Associations. ***PRACTICE AREAS:*** Litigation.

JODY GILKEY SHAFFER, born Dunedin, Florida, November 21, 1978; admitted to bar, 2004, Ohio. *Education:* Ohio Northern University (B.S.B.A., 2001); The Ohio State University (J.D., 2004). Member, Ohio State Law Journal.

(This Listing Continued)

TODD A. WALTER, born Columbus, Ohio, October 12, 1977; admitted to bar, 2004, Ohio. *Education:* Miami University (B.S., with honors, 2000); Georgetown University (J.D., 2004).

ROBIN G. WYCKOFF, born Canton, Ohio, December 14; admitted to bar, 2004, Ohio. *Education:* The Ohio State University (B.A., 1999; J.D., 2004). Author, "Recent Development: Mayo v. Dean Witter Reynolds, Inc., 19 Ohio St. J. On Disp. Resol. 749," 2004.

PEARL CHIN, born Jersey City, New Jersey; admitted to bar, 2005, Ohio and U.S. District Court, Southern District of Ohio. *Education:* Yale University (B.A., 1996); University of Illinois (J.D., 2004). Author, "Payday Loans: The Case for Federal Legislation," University of Illinois Law Review, No. 3, 2004. ***Email:*** pchin@vssp.com

OF COUNSEL

RICHARD HEER OMAN, born Columbus, Ohio, January 4, 1926; admitted to bar, 1951, Ohio. *Education:* The Ohio State University (B.A., 1948; LL.B., 1951). Phi Delta Phi. Listed in: Who's Who in America; The Best Lawyers in America; Who's Who in American Law. Secretary and Director, 1955-1977 and Counsel, 1955—, The Columbus Foundation. Trustee: Reinberger Foundation, Cleveland. *Member:* Columbus, Ohio State and American Bar Associations. Fellow: American College of Trust and Estate Counsel; Ohio State Bar Foundation. ***PRACTICE AREAS:*** Estate Planning; Estate and Gift Taxation; Non-Profit Organizations Law; Charitable Trusts and Foundations. ***Email:*** rhoman@vssp.com

NORTON R. WEBSTER, born Cleveland, Ohio, December 23, 1928; admitted to bar, 1952, Ohio; 1960, U.S. District Court, Southern District of Ohio. *Education:* The Ohio State University (B.A., 1949; LL.B., 1952). Phi Delta Phi. Recipient: Ohio State University Distinguished Affirmative Action Award, 1989; Columbus Bar Association Community Service Award, 1980; Columbus Bar Association Bar Service Medal, 1994. Recipient, Justice Blackmon Bill of Rights Award by Columbus Bar Association and Anti-Defamation League (1996). Member, Board of Commissioners on Grievances and Discipline, 1970-1975 and Chairman, 1975, Supreme Court of Ohio. Member, Ohio Elections Commission, 1996-2002. *Member:* Columbus (Member, Board of Governors, 1962-1966), Ohio State (Member, Executive Committee, 1960-1963; 1967; Chairman, Legal Ethics and Professional Conduct Committee, 1963-1966; President, 1967-1968) and American (Member, 1968-1973; State Delegate, 1973-1982, House of Delegates; Member, Board of Editors, ABA Journal, 1988-1994) Bar Associations; American Judicature Society (Member, Board of Directors, 1986-1990); Columbus Barrister's Club (President, 1960-1961). Fellow, American Bar Foundation. ***PRACTICE AREAS:*** Business Law; General Practice. ***Email:*** nrwebster@vssp.com

RICHARD G. ISON, born Columbus, Ohio, June 19, 1927; admitted to bar, 1953, Ohio. *Education:* Ohio Wesleyan University (A.B., 1950); The Ohio State University (J.D., 1953). Order of the Coif; Phi Delta Phi. Member, Board of Editors, Ohio State Law Journal, 1952-1953. Co-Author of Ohio's Open-end Mortgage Law, 1967 and Original Condominium Act, 1963. ***PRACTICE AREAS:*** Business Law; Partnership Law; Real Estate Law. ***Email:*** rgison@vssp.com

EDGAR A. STRAUSE, born Burlington, Iowa, April 18, 1927; admitted to bar, 1953, Iowa; 1954, Ohio. *Education:* State University of Iowa (B.A., 1950); University of Michigan (J.D., with distinction, 1953). Phi Delta Phi. Assistant Editor, Michigan Law Review, 1952-1953. *Member:* Columbus, Ohio State and American Bar Associations; Association of Defense Attorneys; International Association of Defense Counsel. Fellow: American College of Trial Lawyers: International Academy of Trial Lawyers. ***PRACTICE AREAS:*** Civil Litigation; Products Liability; Aviation Litigation; Class Actions; Toxic Torts. ***Email:*** eastrause@vssp.com

WILLIAM D. KLOSS, born Columbus, Ohio, May 1, 1931; admitted to bar, 1958, Ohio. *Education:* The Ohio State University (B.S., 1953; J.D., 1958). Phi Delta Phi. Faculty, Department of Business Law, Ohio University, 1958-1968, Chairman and Associate Professor, 1963-1968. *Member:* Columbus, Ohio State and American Bar Associations. ***PRACTICE AREAS:*** Insurance; Legislative Practice; Administrative Law; Business Law; Election and Campaign Finance Law. ***Email:*** wdkloss@vssp.com

COLBORN M. ADDISON, born Columbus, Ohio, September 23, 1932; admitted to bar, 1960, Ohio. *Education:* Dartmouth College (A.B., cum laude, 1954); University of Michigan (J.D., 1960). *Member:* Columbus and Ohio State Bar Associations. ***PRACTICE AREAS:*** Estate Planning; Probate; Estate and Gift Taxation. ***Email:*** cmaddison@vssp.com

LESTER S. LASH, born Massillon, Ohio, November 9, 1931; admitted to bar, 1961, Ohio. *Education:* Ohio Wesleyan University (B.A., 1953); The Ohio State University (J.D., 1960). *Member:* Columbus (Member, Labor Law Committee), Ohio State (Member, Labor Law Section) and American (Member, Labor Relations Law Section) Bar Associations. ***PRACTICE AREAS:*** Employment Discrimination; Management Labor Law. ***Email:*** lslash@vssp.com

EDWARD A. SCHRAG, JR., born Milwaukee, Wisconsin, March 27, 1932; admitted to bar, 1961, Ohio. *Education:* Wharton School, University of Pennsylvania (B.S. in Econ., 1954); Harvard University (J.D., 1960). Beta Gamma Sigma; Phi Sigma Alpha; Pi Gamma Mu. Member, Takeover Advisory Committee, Ohio Division of Securities, 1980—. *Member:* Columbus, Ohio State (Corporation Law Committee, Chairman, 1986-1989; Chairman, Securities Regulation Subcommittee, 1979—; Member, Board of Governors; Corporate Counsel Section, Chairman, 1991-1993; Member, Committee on Business Courts, 1994—) and American Bar Associations. ***PRACTICE AREAS:*** Business Law; Corporate Law. ***Email:*** easchrag@vssp.com

ROBIN R. OBETZ, born Columbus, Ohio, February 8, 1938; admitted to bar, 1964, Ohio. *Education:* Deerfield Academy; The Ohio State University (A.B., 1960); Ohio Northern University (J.D., 1964). Delta Theta Phi. Member, 1969-1972 and Chairman, Columbus Regional Board of Review, Bureau of Workers' Compensation. Member, Board of Trustees, Doctor of Laws, Ohio Northern University, 1974-2004. Adjunct Professor of Law, Ohio Northern University College of Law. Executive Secretary, Ohio Self-Insurers Association, 1974—. Member, State of Ohio Workers' Compensation Advisory Council, 1977-1990. Vice President, National Council of Self-Insurers. Chairman, U.S. Chamber of Commerce, Council on Workers Compensation, 1982-1992, Member, Labor Committee, 1993—. *Member:* Columbus, Ohio State (Member and Chairman, 1983-1985, Workers Compensation and Unemployment Compensation Law Committee, 1982—) and American (Member, Workers Compensation and Employers Liability Committee, 1972—) Bar Associations. ***PRACTICE AREAS:*** Workers' Compensation; Employment Law. ***Email:*** rrobetz@vssp.com

DUKE W. THOMAS, born Scuddy, Kentucky; admitted to bar, 1964, Ohio. *Education:* The Ohio State University (B.S., Business Administration, 1959; J.D., 1964). *Member:* Columbus (Member, Executive Committee, 1975-1979; President, 1977-1978), Ohio State (Member, Executive Committee, 1981-1987; President, 1985-1986) and American (Member, Board of Governors, 1995-1998; State Delegate, 1990-1995) Bar Associations. Fellow: American College of Trial Lawyers; International Society of Barristers. ***PRACTICE AREAS:*** Trial Practice; State Appellate Practice; Business Litigation. ***Email:*** dwthomas@vssp.com

THOMAS M. TAGGART, born Sioux City, Iowa, February 22, 1937; admitted to bar, 1965, Ohio; 1967, U.S. District Court, Southern District of Ohio; 1981, U.S. District Court, Northern District of Ohio. *Education:* Dartmouth College (B.A., cum laude, 1959); Harvard University (LL.B., 1965). Member, Board of Trustees, Columbus Legal Aid and Defender Society, 1969-1970. Instructor, Capital University Law Center, 1984-1991. *Member:* Columbus (Member, Board of Governors, 1983-1991; Secretary/Treasurer, 1987-1988; President, 1989-1990; Chairman, Doctor/Lawyer Committee, 1982), Ohio State (Member: Board of Governors, 1991-1999; President, 1998-1999; Workers Compensation Law Committee, 1970-1999) and American Bar Associations; American Board of Trial Advocates (Member, 2004); Columbus Defense Association (President, 1979-1980). ***PRACTICE AREAS:*** Professional Malpractice Law; Workers Compensation Law; Trial Practice. ***Email:*** tmtaggart@vssp.com

PHILIP C. JOHNSTON, born Wheeling, West Virginia, August 24, 1943; admitted to bar, 1968, Ohio. *Education:* Colgate University (A.B., magna cum laude, 1965); Harvard Law School (LL.B., 1968). Phi Beta Kappa. *Member:* National Association of Bond Lawyers. ***PRACTICE AREAS:*** Corporate Law; Finance. ***Email:*** pcjohnston@vssp.com

FREDERICK E. MILLS, born Fostoria, Ohio, February, February 17, 1947; admitted to bar, 1973, Ohio. *Education:* The Ohio State University (B.S., Business Administration, 1969); Capital University (J.D., 1973). Legislative Assistant to Governor, 1975-1979. State Superintendent of Banks, 1979-1982. Clerk, Ohio House, 1995-1998. Chief-of-Staff Ohio House, 1996-2000. Majority Counsel, Ohio House, 1999-2000. *Member:* Columbus and Ohio State Bar Associations. ***PRACTICE AREAS:*** Legislative Law; Administrative Law. ***Email:*** femills@vssp.com

RONALD A. KLADDER, born Flint, Michigan, September 22, 1947; admitted to bar, 1974, Pennsylvania; 1979, Ohio. *Education:* Oakland University (B.A., 1968); University of Michigan (J.D., 1974). *Member:* Columbus Bar Association. ***PRACTICE AREAS:*** Executive Compensation; Employee Benefits. ***Email:*** rakladder@vssp.com

STEPHEN M. HOWARD, born Columbus, Ohio, December 29, 1951; admitted to bar, 1976, Ohio. *Education:* Capital University (B.A., 1973; J.D., 1976). Attorney Examiner, Public Utilities Commission of Ohio, 1976-1985. Appointed by the Governor as Member, Ohio Telecommunications Advisory Board, June 1992-January, 1995. ***PRACTICE AREAS:*** Public Utility Law. ***Email:*** smhoward@vssp.com

MICHAEL R. THOMAS, born Flint, Michigan, September 22, 1951; admitted to bar, 1976, Michigan; 1983, Ohio; U.S. Court of Appeals, Sixth Circuit. *Education:* University of Michigan (B.A., with high honors, 1973; J.D., 1975); The Ohio State University (M.A., with high honors, 1983). Adjunct Professor, Sociology of Law and Judicial Decision-making, Ohio State University, 1984-1987. Legal Research and Writing, The Ohio State University Law School, 1985-1988. ***PRACTICE AREAS:*** Litigation; Appellate Practice. ***Email:*** mrthomas@vssp.com

LINDA R. MENDEL, born Cincinnati, Ohio, February 28, 1956; admitted to bar, 1981, Ohio. *Education:* Kent State University (B.B.A., magna cum laude, 1978); The Ohio State University (J.D., with honors, 1981). Author: Articles, "Cash or Deferred Arrangements," Section 401(k), S.M. Young, Matthew Bender, 1992; "Coverage," Sections 5.13, 5.14 410(b); "Pension and Profit Sharing Plans," Section 3A.05. Co-Author: "State Income Tax Withholding on Qualified Plan Distributions," Tax Mgmt. Comp. Plan J., 1987. *Member:* Columbus (Chairman, Executive and Employee Benefits Committee, 1992-1994) and American Bar Associations. ***PRACTICE AREAS:*** Labor and Employment. ***Email:*** lrmendel@vssp.com

ROBERT C. MITCHELL, born Oak Park, Illinois, March 6, 1955; admitted to bar, 1981, Indiana; 1990, Ohio; 1992, Illinois; 1981, U.S. District Court, Southern District of Indiana; 1985, U.S. District Court, Southern District of Illinois; 1988, U.S. District Court, Northern District of Indiana; 1992, U.S. District Court, Northern District of Illinois; 1989, U.S. Court of Appeals, Third Circuit; 1990, U.S. Court of Appeals, Tenth Circuit; 1990, U.S. Court of Appeals, Ninth Circuit; 1993, U.S. Court of Appeals, Seventh Circuit; 2000, U.S. Court of Appeals, Sixth Circuit. *Education:* Denison University (B.A., History and Political Science, 1977); University of Cincinnati College of Law (J.D., 1981). Member, Indiana Industrial Board, 1982—. Associate, Fine & Hatfield, Evansville IN, 1981-1986; Partner, Kahn, Dees, Donovan & Kahn, Evansville IN, 1986-1988; Senior Counsel, North American Van Lines Inc., Ft. Wayne IN, 1988-1991; Litigation Counsel, Morton International Inc., Chicago IL, 1991-1997; Director, Litigation & Insurance, Owens Corning, Toledo, OH, 1997-2001; In-house Counsel, The Goodyear Tire & Rubber Co., Akron, OH, 2001-2003. ***PRACTICE AREAS:*** Litigation; Toxic Torts; Insurance Coverage. ***Email:*** rcmitchell@vssp.com

SHERYL CLARK STOLL, born Waterloo, Iowa, March 7, 1948; admitted to bar, 1981, Iowa; 1985, Pennsylvania; 1998, Ohio. *Education:* Cornell College (B.A., magna cum laude, 1970); University of Iowa (J.D., with high distinction, 1981). Phi Beta Kappa. Mortar Board, Order of the Coif. Recipient, National ATHENA Award, 1991. Member, Board of Directors, International ATHENA Foundation (Secretary; Executive Committee), 1993-2000. Member, Board of Trustees and Officer, Executive Committee, The Wesley Institute, Pittsburgh, Pennsylvania, 1986-1997. Member, Board of Trustees of Cornell College. U.S. Secretary of Commerce appointment to U.S. Delegation, International Proprietary Rights Committee for Collaborative Research, 1993-1995. *Member:* Computer Law Association. ***PRACTICE AREAS:*** Computer; Internet; Technology Law; Licensing; Copyright; General Commercial.

(This Listing Continued)

VORYS, SATER, SEYMOUR AND PEASE LLP, Columbus—Continued

JEFFREY H. TOUR, born New York, N.Y., October 8, 1957; admitted to bar, 1982, Georgia; 1984, District of Columbia; 1993, Ohio. *Education:* Syracuse University (B.A., cum laude, 1979); George Washington University National Law Center (J.D., with honors, 1982). Author: "Overview of Proposed Regulations on Single Employer Plan Terminations Under SEPPAA," Tax Management Compensation Planning Journal, November 1987; "Plan Termination Update: Impact of Pension Protection Act of 1987," Tax Management Compensation Planning Journal, May 1988; "Complex Temporary Regulations Cover Plan Compensation," The Journal of Taxation, May 1988; "Early Retirement Window Benefits Under Final Section 401 (a)(4) Regulations," Maxwell-MacMillan Pension and Profit Sharing Bulletin, September 20, 1991. Contributing Author: "Plan Terminations and Mergers," BNA Tax Management Portfolio 357. *Member:* The District of Columbia Bar; State Bar of Georgia; American Bar Association (Member, Sections on: Taxation; Business Law; Committee on Employee Benefits). ***PRACTICE AREAS:*** Labor and Employment. ***Email:*** jhtour@vssp.com

A. BRIAN DENGLER, born Cleveland, Ohio, October 26, 1953; admitted to bar, 1985, Ohio; 1986, U.S. District Court, Southern District of Ohio and U.S. Court of Appeals, Sixth Circuit; 1987, U.S. District Court, Northern District of Texas; 1993, U.S. Court of Appeals for the Federal Circuit. *Education:* Kent State University (B.A., magna cum laude, 1976); Capital University Law School (J.D., summa cum laude, 1985). Order of the Curia. Editor, Law Review Symposium, 1985. Best Oralist, Moot Court Competition, 1982. Recipient, Alumni Achievement Award, 2003, Kent State University. Co-Author: *Electronic and Software Patents Law and Practice,* Bureau of National Affairs, 2000; *Internet and Online Law,* 3d ed. (1998 Law Journal Seminar Press); *Bankers and Thrift, Government Enforcement and Receivership,* Matthew Bender, 1991. Author: "UCC Article 2B on the Fast Track," The Intellectual Property Strategist, January, 1997; "Article 2B: Taking the UCE Into the 21st Century," Multimedia Law and Technology Licensing Journal, June 1996; "The Information Theory for Defamation Privilege in Ohio," Ohio Northern Law Review, Vol. 12, No. 3, Fall, 1986. Faculty Member, Advanced Electronics Commerce Institute for the Georgetown University Law Center's Continuing Legal Education Division. Board of Advisors, College of Communications at Kent State University. Member: Board of Advisors, Columbus Symphony Youth Orchestras; Trustee's Circle for the Columbus Symphony Orchestra; Corporate Council for the Cleveland Orchestra; Board of Trustees, Westerville Symphony Orchestra. *Member:* American Bar Association (Vice President, Subcommittee on Information Licensing, Business Law Section). ***PRACTICE AREAS:*** Commercial Law; E-Commerce. ***Email:*** abdengler@vssp.com

THEODORE A. BOGGS, born Covington, Ohio, June 29, 1955; admitted to bar, 1986, Ohio and U.S. District Court, Southern District of Ohio. *Education:* Bowling Green State University (B.S., 1977); Miami University (M.En., Applied Ecology, 1979); Capital University (J.D., 1986). ***PRACTICE AREAS:*** Environmental Law; Health and Safety Law; Administrative Law; Water Quality Law; Environmental Protection; OSHA Compliance. ***Email:*** taboggs@vssp.com

KEVIN R. CONNERS, born San Diego, California, October 27, 1959; admitted to bar, 1989, Ohio; U.S. District Court, Southern District of Ohio; U.S. Court of Appeals, Sixth Circuit. *Education:* University of California at Berkeley (B.A., 1985); The Ohio State University College of Law (J.D., 1989). Phi Beta Kappa. Assistant United States Attorney, Southern District of Ohio, 1989-1994. *Member:* American Bar Association. ***PRACTICE AREAS:*** White Collar Criminal Defense; Corporate Law; Corporate Investigations. ***Email:*** krconners@vssp.com

NATHAN C. HAMILTON, born Marysville, Ohio, October 7, 1963; admitted to bar, 1989, Ohio. *Education:* Ohio Wesleyan University (B.A. 1986); Vanderbilt University (J.D., 1989). ***PRACTICE AREAS:*** Probate; Tax. ***Email:*** nchamilton@vssp.com

BRADLEY A. SMITH, born Wyandotte, Michigan, 1958; admitted to bar, 1990, Ohio. *Education:* Kalamazoo College (B.A., cum laude, 1980); Harvard Law School (J.D., cum laude, 1990). Author: "Unfree Speech: The Folly of Campaign Finance Reform," Princeton University Press (2001); "Faulty Assumptions & Undemocratic Consequences of Campaign Finance Reform," 105 Yale L.J. 1049 (1996); "A Toothless Anaconda: Innovation, Impotence & Over-Enforcement at the Federal Election Commission," 1 Journal of Election Law 145 (2002). Adjunct Professor of Law, George Mason University School of Law, 2002-2004. Professor of Law, Capital University Law School, 1993-2000, 2005—. Commissioner, 2000-2005, Chairman, 2004 and Vice Chairman, 2003, Federal Election Commission. *Member:* American Bar Association (Advisory Board to the Standing Committee on Election Law); Ohio State Bar Association. ***LANGUAGES:*** Spanish. ***PRACTICE AREAS:*** Election, Campaign and Political Law; Administrative Law; Constitutional Law. ***Email:*** basmith@vssp.com

JAMES P. KENNEDY, born St. Louis, Missouri; admitted to bar, 1960, Ohio. *Education:* Washington University, St. Louis, Missouri (A.B., 1954; B.S.B.A., 1954); University of Michigan (J.D., with distinction, 1959). Omicron Delta Kappa; Beta Gamma Sigma. Faculty Member, The Intensified Antitrust Law Course, Ohio Legal Center Institute, 1983-1996. Member, Committee of Visitors, 1983—, University of Michigan Law School. *Member:* Columbus, Ohio State (Chairman, Antitrust Section, Board of Governors, 1979-1981) and American (Chairman, Criminal Practice and Procedure Committee, Section of Antitrust Law, 1982-1985; Council Member, Section of Antitrust Law, 1985-1988; Vice-Chair, Continuing Legal Education Committee, Section of Antitrust Law, 1992-1993; Chair, Continuing Legal Education Committee, Section of Antitrust Law, 1993-1994) Bar Associations. Fellow, American College of Trial Lawyers. ***PRACTICE AREAS:*** Litigation; Antitrust; White Collar Crime. ***Email:*** jpkennedy@vssp.com

STAFF ATTORNEYS

DONALD A. BROWN, born New Kensington, Pennsylvania, October 15, 1938; admitted to bar, 1977, Ohio. *Education:* Indiana University of Pennsylvania (B.S.Ed., 1962); University of Toledo (J.D., 1976). ***PRACTICE AREAS:*** Insurance. ***Email:*** dabrown@vssp.com

(This Listing Continued)

JONATHAN P. BECK, born Liberty, New York, 1956; admitted to bar, 1981, Ohio. *Education:* Ithaca College (B.S., 1978); University of Dayton School of Law (J.D., 1981). *Member:* Columbus Bar Association (Member, Employee Benefits Committee, 2003-2004). ***PRACTICE AREAS:*** Labor and Employment. ***Email:*** jpbeck@vssp.com

GREGORY J. ZELASKO, born Alliance, Ohio, December 21, 1956; admitted to bar, 1981, Ohio. *Education:* Mount Union College (B.S., cum laude, 1978); Capital University (J.D., 1981). Order of the Curia. Attorney Inspector, Ohio Division of Securities, 1987. ***PRACTICE AREAS:*** Securities Law; Corporate Law; Insurance Law; Limited Liability Company Law; Limited Partnerships. ***Email:*** gjzelasko@vssp.com

BRENDA K. BOWERS, born Lima, Ohio, October 17, 1964; admitted to bar, 1990, Ohio. *Education:* Ohio Northern University (B.A., 1987); The Ohio State University (J.D., 1990). Former Law Clerk, Honorable Donald E. Calhoun, Jr., U.S. Bankrupty Court, Southern District of Ohio, Eastern Division. Member, Ohio State University Advocates Board Program. *Member:* Columbus (Member, Bankruptcy Committee, 1996—), Ohio State and American Bar Associations; International Women's Insolvency and Restructuring Confederation (Membership Services Director, 2004—; Program Director, 2002-2004); Central Ohio International Women's Insolvency and Restructuring Confederation (Newsletter Editor, 1997-2000, Chairperson, 1998-2000); American Bankruptcy Institute. ***PRACTICE AREAS:*** Bankruptcy Law; Collections; Evictions; Foreclosures. ***Email:*** bkbowers@vssp.com

CORRINE S. CARMAN, born Wheeling, West Virginia, September 22, 1967; admitted to bar, 1992, Ohio; 1993, U.S. District Court, Southern District of Ohio. *Education:* West Virginia University (B.A., 1989); Capital University (J.D., 1992). Delta Theta Phi. Capital University Law Review, Member and Notes Editor. Moot Court Board Member. ***PRACTICE AREAS:*** Workers' Compensation; Employment Litigation. ***Email:*** cscarman@vssp.com

STEPHEN CRAIG MUSILLI, born Wheeling, West Virginia, November 2, 1968; admitted to bar, 1994, West Virginia; 2002, Ohio; U.S. District Court, Northern and Southern Districts of West Virginia; U.S. District Court, Northern and Southern Districts of Ohio. *Education:* Hampden-Sydney College (B.A., cum laude, 1991); West Virginia University (J.D., 1994). Omicron Delta Kappa. *Member:* Columbus, Ohio State and American Bar Associations; West Virginia State Bar. ***PRACTICE AREAS:*** Toxic Tort; Asbestos Defense. ***Email:*** scmusilli@vssp.com

KELLY A. BOGGS, born Greenville, Pennsylvania, February 20, 1970; admitted to bar, 1998, Ohio; 1999, U.S. District Court, Southern District of Ohio. *Education:* The Ohio State University (B.A., cum laude, 1992); DePaul University (J.D., 1998). Order of the Coif. Adjunct Instructor, Moritz College of Law, The Ohio State University. Former Member, Board of Directors, YWCA of Columbus, 1999-2004. ***LANGUAGES:*** Japanese. ***PRACTICE AREAS:*** Labor and Employment Law Litigation. ***Email:*** kaboggs@vssp.com

ELIZABETH HANNING SMITH, born Columbus, Ohio, February 3, 1976; admitted to bar, 2003, Ohio. *Education:* Mount Holyoke College (B.A., 1998); The Ohio State University, Moritz College of Law (J.D., 2003). ***PRACTICE AREAS:*** Litigation; Toxic Torts.

REPRESENTATIVE CLIENTS: Abercrombie & Fitch; Airborne Express, Inc.; American Showa; Bob Evans Farms, Inc.; Cardinal Health; Columbus Blue Jackets; Consolidated Stores Corp.; Dominion Homes; Eaton Corporation; Greif Bros.; Honda of America Mfg., Inc.; Insurance Federation of Ohio; M/I Homes; Martin Marietta Energy Systems; National City Bank; Fraternal Order of Police; Ohio Casualty Corporation; Ohio League of Financial Institutions; R.G. Barry Corp.; Showa Aluminum Corporation; Techneglas; The Children's Hospital; The Limited, Inc.; The Ohio State University; The Scotts Company; Value City Department Stores; Filene's Basement; DSW; Wendy's International, Inc.; Worthington Industries, Inc.; Hamilton County.
LOCAL COUNSEL: Abbott Laboratories; American Telephone & Telegraph Co.; Anheuser-Busch, Inc.; Ashland Oil, Inc.; B.F. Goodrich Co.; BP America; Emerson Electric; General Electric Company; General Motors Corp.; Goodyear Tire & Rubber; Household Finance Corp.; Mac Tools, Inc.; Navistar International; The Kroger Co.; United States Playing Card Co.; Waste Management; Western Southern Life Insurance Company.

GEOFFREY E. WEBSTER

Established in 1979

SUITE 310, TWO MIRANOVA PLACE
COLUMBUS, OHIO 43215-3413
Telephone: 614-461-1156
Fax: 614-461-7168
Email: gewebster@gewebster.com
URL: http://www.lawyers.com/gewlaw

Health Care Administration, Facility Licensing, Facility Regulation, Contracts and Finance, Long Term Care, Nursing Home Regulation, Patients Rights and Pharmacy Law. Health Care Mergers and Acquisitions Regulation and Reimbursement, and Civil Litigation.

GEOFFREY E. WEBSTER, born Dalhart, Texas, January 19, 1948; admitted to bar, 1975, Ohio and U.S. District Court, Northern and Southern Districts of Ohio; 1978, U.S. Supreme Court; 1984, U.S. Court of Appeals, Sixth Circuit. *Education:* Ohio State University (B.S., 1970); Capital University (J.D., magna cum laude, 1975). Order of the Coif; Archons. Member, Office of the Attorney General, 1971-1976. Member, Victorian Village Commission, 1985. Member, Alumni Board of Trustees, Delta Chi Fraternity, Ohio State Chapter, 1990-1999. Elder, Liberty Presbyterian Church, 1994-2004;. Development Board, Catholic Social Services, Columbus, Ohio, 1997-2000. Member, Development Board, Columbus Symphony Orchestra, 2000-2004. Participant, Oxford Round Table, Oxford University, U.K., April, 2001. *Member:* Columbus, Ohio State and American Bar Associations; American Health Lawyers Association. [With U.S. Army Reserves, 1970-1976]. ***REPORTED CASES:*** Ohio Academy of Nursing Homes, Inc. v. Barry (1994), 71 Ohio St 3d 5; Ohio Academy of Nursing Homes, Inc. v. Barry (1990), 56 Ohio St. 3d 120; Elder v. Fischer (1998), 129 Ohio App. 3d 209; Drake Center Inc. v. Department of Human Services (1998), 125 Ohio App 3d 678; In re St. John Medical Center (1993), 91 Ohio App 3d, 310, 632NE 2d 595; In re Deaconess Hospital (1992), 83 Ohio App 3d 1, 613NE 2d 1049; Buckeye Quality Care Centers, Inc. v. Fletcher (1988), 48 Ohio App. 3d 150, m. to certify den'd., 39 Ohio St. 2d 703; State ex rel. Avon Convalescent Center v. Bates (1976), 45 Ohio St. 2d 53; Westchester Management Corp. v. HHS (CA 6, 1991), 948 F. 2d 279; State Bd. of Phar-

(This Listing Continued)

macy v. Weinstein (1987), 33 Ohio Misc. 2d 25. **PRACTICE AREAS:** Health Care; Long Term Care; Health Care Mergers and Acquisitions; Health Care Facility Licensing; Health Care Facility Regulation; Health Care Administration; Contracts and Finance.

ASSOCIATES

J. RANDALL RICHARDS, born Gallipolis, Ohio, June 30, 1961; admitted to bar, 1993, Ohio; 1995, U.S. District Court, Southern District of Ohio. *Education:* Ohio Wesleyan University (B.A., 1984); Capital University Law and Graduate Center (J.D., cum laude, 1993). Order of the Curia. Member, (1991-1992) and Articles Editor (1992-1993), Capital University Law Review. Coordinator, Marketing Administration, United Health-Care Corporation of Ohio, Inc. (1988-1993); Law Clerk, The Honorable J. Craig Wright, The Supreme Court of Ohio (1993-1994). *Member:* Columbus, Ohio State and American Bar Associations. **PRACTICE AREAS:** Health Care; Health Care Regulation; Patients Rights; Health Care Reimbursement.

ERIC B. HERSHBERGER, born Philadelphia, Pennsylvania, November 20, 1965; admitted to bar, 1991, Ohio; 1994, U.S. District Court, Southern District of Ohio; 1996, U.S. Court of Appeals, Sixth Circuit. *Education:* Miami University (B.A., 1988); The Ohio State University (J.D., 1991). Member, American Bar Association, 1994-1997. *Member:* Columbus and Ohio State Bar Associations. **REPORTED CASES:** 96 Ohio App. 3d 764, 645 N.E.2d 1320, McKee v. Gilg (1994) 1994 Ohio App. Lexis 3982; 87 Ohio App. 3d 214, 621 N.E.2d 1365, Rinehart v. Board of Educ. (1993) 1993 Ohio App. Lexis 2147. **PRACTICE AREAS:** Business Litigation; Insurance Defense.

PAUL V. DISANTIS, born Cleveland, Ohio, October 23, 1970; admitted to bar, 1996, Ohio; 1998, U.S. District Court, Northern District of Ohio; 1999, U.S. District Court, Southern District of Ohio. *Education:* Bowling Green State University (B.S., 1993); Capital University (J.D., 1996). *Member:* Columbus and Ohio State Bar Associations; Ohio Academy of Trial Lawyers. [Captain, U.S. Army Reserve, 1999—]. **PRACTICE AREAS:** Health Care; Administrative Law; Litigation. **Email:** pvdisantis@juno.com

REPRESENTATIVE CLIENTS: The Ohio Academy of Nursing Homes, Inc.; Suburban Nursing & Mobile Homes, Inc.; Mother Angeline McCrory Manor; CommuniCare Health Services, Inc.; Soroka Telle & Associates, Inc.; Marketing Services by Vectra, Inc.; Ohio Full Court Press, Ltd.; Oscar Jarnicki, Inc.; Cedar Village; Lancia Nursing Homes, Inc.; Omnilife Systems, Inc.; Carington Health Systems; Strategic Nursing Systems, Inc.

WEGMAN, HESSLER & VANDERBURG

A LEGAL PROFESSIONAL ASSOCIATION

COLUMBUS, OHIO

(See Cleveland)

General Civil Practice in all Courts. Corporate, Labor/Employment, Personal Injury, Products Liability, Real Estate, Probate, Domestic Relations, Trials and Business and Estate Planning, Intellectual Property.

SAMUEL B. WEINER CO., L.P.A.

Established in 1978

743 SOUTH FRONT STREET
COLUMBUS, OHIO 43206
Telephone: 614-443-6581
Fax: 614-443-9978
Email: sbwesq@ameritech.net
URL: http://www.samuelbweinerlawcolpa.com

Criminal Trial and Appellate Practice, Felonies and Misdemeanors in all State and Federal Courts. White Collar Crime, Arson.

FIRM PROFILE: Mr. Weiner concentrates in the area of criminal defense. He has over 300 jury trials to conclusion, in all types of felonies, misdemeanors and traffic offenses. He also specializes in white collar criminal cases in both federal and state court. Mr. Weiner has extensive trial experience in state and federal courts throughout the United States.

SAMUEL WEINER, born Columbus, Ohio, November 18, 1943; admitted to bar, 1973, Ohio; 1975, U.S. District Court, Southern District of Ohio; 1978, U.S. Supreme Court; 1981, Florida; 1982, U.S. Court of Appeals, Sixth Circuit; 1991, U.S. District Court, Southern and Middle Districts of Florida and U.S. Court of Appeals, Eleventh Circuit; 1992, U.S. Tax Court. *Education:* Miami University; The Ohio State University (B.A., 1965); Capital University (J.D., 1973). Recipient: Earl F. Morris Professionalism Award, 1995; Capital University Law School Alumni Association Professionalism Award, 1997. Listed in: Best Lawyers in America, 1989—; Martindale-Hubbell Bar Register of Preeminent Lawyers, 1994—. Member: Franklin County Public Defender's Commission, 1984—; Governors Task Force on Indigent Defense, 1992; State of Ohio Public Defender's Commission, 1993-1995. Member, American Inns of Court, Robert M. Duncan Chapter, 1992—. *Member:* Columbus (Chairman, Criminal Law Committee, 1987-1989; District 7 Delegate, Ohio State Bar Council of Delegates, 1994—; Board of Governors, 1997—; President, 2003-2004) and Ohio State (Member, Criminal Law Section, 1995—; Member, Specialization Committee) Bar Associations; The Florida Bar; Franklin County Trial Lawyers Association (President, 1982-1983); Ohio Association of Criminal Defense Lawyers (President, 1994-1995); National Association of Criminal Defense Lawyers. Fellow: Ohio State Bar Foundation; Columbus Bar Foundation; American College of Trial Lawyers. Certified as a Criminal Trial Advocate by the National Board of Trial Advocacy. **Email:** sbwesq@ameritech.net

REFERENCE: The Fifth Third Bank.

WELTMAN, WEINBERG & REIS CO., L.P.A.

175 SOUTH 3RD STREET, SUITE 900
COLUMBUS, OHIO 43215
Telephone: 614-228-7272
Fax: 614-222-2193
Email: wwr@weltman.com
URL: http://www.weltman.com

Burlington, New Jersey Office: Telephone: 609-914-0437.
Chicago, Illinois Office: Telephone: 312-786-9676.
Cincinnati, Ohio Office: Telephone: 513-723-2200.
Cleveland, Ohio Office: Telephone: 216-685-1000.
Deerfield, Illinois Office: Telephone: 847-940-9812.
Philadelphia, Pennsylvania Office: Telephone: 215-599-1500.
Pittsburgh, Pennsylvania Office: Telephone: 412-434-7955.
Troy, Michigan Office: Telephone: 248-362-6100.

See Firm Profile and Statement of Practice under Cleveland, Ohio Listing.

ALLEN J. REIS, born Cleveland, Ohio, March 7, 1951; admitted to bar, 1976, Ohio and U.S. District Court, Northern District of Ohio; 1980, U.S. District Court, Southern District of Ohio. *Education:* The Ohio State University (B.A., 1973); The Ohio State University Michael E. Moritz College of Law (J.D., 1976). Phi Alpha Theta. President, Cols Dispatch Credit Union, 1987-1988. Member, Board of Directors of Columbus Chapter of Credit Unions, 1988-1997. Member, Board of Directors of the Ohio Credit Union League, 1990-1994. Secretary, Executive Committee of the Ohio Credit Union League, 1992. Member, Civil Service Commission, City of Gahanna, 1990-1997. *Member:* Columbus (Member, Committees on: Financial Institutions; Municipal Court), Ohio State and American Bar Associations. **PRACTICE AREAS:** Creditors Rights; Real Estate; Banking Law; Legal Action Recovery. **Email:** areis@weltman.com

STEPHEN A. SANTANGELO, born Wooster, Ohio, June 27, 1953; admitted to bar, 1978, Ohio; 1979, U.S. District Court, Northern and Southern Districts of Ohio; 1982, U.S. Court of Appeals, Sixth Circuit. *Education:* College of Wooster (B.A., 1975); Case Western Reserve University School of Law (J.D., 1978). President of Creditor Education Coalition, 1993-1995. *Member:* Columbus and Ohio State Bar Associations; Commercial Law League of America. **PRACTICE AREAS:** Litigation and Defense; Creditors Rights. **Email:** ssantangelo@weltman.com

TERRENCE R. HEFFERNAN, born Cincinnati, Ohio, October 12, 1951; admitted to bar, 1982, Ohio; 1983, U.S. District Court, Southern District of Ohio; 1992, U.S. Court of Appeals, Sixth Circuit. *Education:* The Ohio State University (B.S.S.W., 1979); Capital University Law School (J.D., 1982). Member, American Association of Medical Society Executives, 1988. *Member:* Columbus and Ohio State (District 7 Representative to Real Property Section, Board of Governors, 2002-2004) Bar Associations; Creditors International; Community Bankers Association of Ohio. [U.S. Army, Security Agency, 1973-1977]. **PRACTICE AREAS:** Creditors Rights; Real Estate; Foreclosure/Evictions. **Email:** theffernan@weltman.com

---

MONETTE W. COPE, born Salem, Ohio; admitted to bar, 1988, Illinois; 1990, U.S. District Court, Northern District of Illinois; 1997, Ohio; 1998 U.S. District Court, Southern District of Ohio. *Education:* The Ohio State University (B.A., cum laude, 1979); The Ohio State University, Michael E. Moritz College of Law (J.D., 1988). Delta Theta Phi (President, 1987-1988; Exchequer, 1986-1987). *Member:* Columbus and Ohio State Bar Associations; Credit Education Coalition (Board Member, 1998—); Ohio Creditors' Attorney Association (Secretary). **PRACTICE AREAS:** Creditors Rights; Bankruptcy. **Email:** mcope@weltman.com

ANGELA CORIELL, born Columbus, Ohio, April 3, 1976; admitted to bar, 2003, Ohio. *Education:* The Ohio State University (B.A., 1998); Capital University Law School (J.D., cum laude, 2003). Order of the Coif. *Member:* American Bar Association; Columbus Bar Association; Ohio State Bar Association. **PRACTICE AREAS:** Creditors Rights; Foreclosure/Evictions. **Email:** acoriell@weltman.com

DOUGLAS M. DAHMER, born Chicago, Illinois, June 23, 1952; admitted to bar, 1986, Illinois and U.S. District Court, Northern District of Illinois; 1989, New Jersey and U.S. District Court, District of New Jersey; 1993, Ohio; 1997, U.S. District Court, Southern District of Ohio. *Education:* Northern Illinois University (B.S., 1974); Northern Illinois University (M.A., 1975); Roosevelt University (M.P.A., 1980); Chicago-Kent College of Law, Illinois Institute of Technology (J.D., 1986). *Member:* Columbus and Ohio State (Member: Banking, Commercial and Bankruptcy Law Committee) Bar Associations. **PRACTICE AREAS:** Creditors Rights; Legal Action Recovery. **Email:** ddahmer@weltman.com

JAMES G. KOZELEK, born Columbus, Ohio, September 30, 1967; admitted to bar, 2001, Ohio, U.S. Bankruptcy Court and U.S. District Court, Southern District of Ohio. *Education:* The Ohio State University (B.A., 1997); Capitol University Law School (J.D., cum laude, 2001). Order of the Curia. *Member:* Columbus, Ohio State and American Bar Associations. **PRACTICE AREAS:** Collection Services; Creditors Rights. **Email:** jkozelek@weltman.com

JOSEPH M. McCANDLISH, born Columbus, Ohio, May 21, 1971; admitted to bar, 2001, Ohio; 2002, U.S. District Court, Southern District of Ohio. *Education:* The Ohio State University (B.S. in Finance, 1994); Capital University Law School (J.D., 2001). *Member:* Columbus and Ohio State Bar Associations; The Federalist Society (Columbus Lawyers Chapter). **PRACTICE AREAS:** Creditors Rights; Collection Services. **Email:** jmccandlish@weltman.com

RAYMOND F. MOATS, born San Diego, California, November 4, 1963; admitted to bar, 1993, California and U.S. District Court, Southern District of California; 2000, Ohio. *Education:* University of California, Irvine (B.A., 1987); Golden Gate University School of Law (J.D., 1992). *Member:* Columbus and Ohio State Bar Associations. **PRACTICE AREAS:** Creditors Rights; Collection Services. **Email:** rmoats@weltman.com

(This Listing Continued)

WELTMAN, WEINBERG & REIS CO., L.P.A., Columbus—Continued

RONALD B. NOGA, born Cleveland, Ohio, December 12, 1946; admitted to bar, 1974, Ohio; 1977, U.S. District Court, Southern District of Ohio; 1980, U.S. Supreme Court; 1991, U.S. Court of Appeals, Sixth Circuit. *Education:* The Ohio State University (B.S., 1968); The Ohio State University Michael E. Moritz College of Law (J.D., 1974). *Member:* Columbus and Ohio State Bar Associations. [Army-Infantry, 1968-1970, 1st Lt.]. ***PRACTICE AREAS:*** Creditors Rights; Litigation and Defense. ***Email:*** rnoga@weltman.com

GEOFFREY J. PETERS, born Cleveland, Ohio, September 1, 1969; admitted to bar, 1994, Ohio; 1995, U.S. District Court, Northern District of Ohio; 2001, U.S. District Court, Southern District of Ohio; 2004, New York and U.S. District Court, Southern District of New York; 2005, U.S. District Court, Northern, Eastern and Western Districts of New York. *Education:* Kent State University (B.B.A., summa cum laude, 1991); Case Western Reserve University School of Law (J.D., 1994). Beta Gamma Sigma; Golden Key. *Member:* Ohio State Bar Association; American Bankruptcy Institute. ***REPORTED CASES:*** In re: Stewart, 96 Ohio St.3d 67 (2002) In re: Stump, 280 B.R. (Bkrtcy S.D. Ohio 2002). ***PRACTICE AREAS:*** Bankruptcy; Creditors Rights. ***Email:*** gpeters@weltman.com

BRIAN D. WOOD, born Cleveland, Ohio, October 4, 1976; admitted to bar, 2002, Ohio and U.S. District Court, Northern District of Ohio; 2004, U.S. District Court, Southern District of Ohio. *Education:* The Ohio State University (B.A., 1999); Capital University School of Law (J.D., 2002). *Member:* Columbus and Ohio State Bar Associations. ***PRACTICE AREAS:*** Creditors Rights; Bankruptcy. ***Email:*** bdwood@weltman.com

(For complete biographical data on other personnel, see Professional Biographies at other locations)

EDWARD F. WHIPPS & ASSOCIATES

500 SOUTH FRONT STREET, SUITE 860
COLUMBUS, OHIO 43215
Telephone: 614-461-6006
Fax: 614-461-6010
URL: http://www.efwhipps.com
Email: efwhipps@efwhipps.com
URL: http://www.lawyers.com/efwhipps

Dublin, Ohio Office: 555 Metro Place North, Suite 100, 43017. Telephone: 614-461-6007. Fax: 614-461-6010.

Family, Matrimonial and Domestic Relations Law, Divorce Taxation, Child Custody, Visitation Rights, Premarital Agreements.

EDWARD F. WHIPPS, born Columbus, Ohio, December 17, 1936; admitted to bar, 1961, Ohio; U.S. Supreme Court; U.S. Court of Appeals, Sixth Circuit; U.S. District Court, Southern and Northern Districts of Ohio; U.S. District Court, Northern District of Mississippi; U.S. Court of Federal Claims. *Education:* Ohio Wesleyan University (B.A., 1958); The Ohio State University (J.D., 1961). Omicron Delta Kappa; Delta Sigma Rho; Phi Mu Alpha. Listed in: Martindale-Hubbell Bar Register of Preeminent Lawyers, Family Law, 1992-1998; Who's Who in America, 1988—; Who's Who in American Law, 1980—. Member, Editorial Staff, Ohio State Law Journal, 1960-1961. Principal, Edward F. Whipps & Associates, 1993—. Partner, Thompson, Hine & Flory, 1980-1992. President, 2001-2002; Member, 1992-2002, Ohio State Board of Psychology. President, 1975; Vice President, 1974; Member, 1971-1980, Upper Arlington Board of Education. Member, Board of Alumni Directors, Ohio Wesleyan University, 1975-1979. Creative Living, Inc. (Founder and Trustee, 1972—, President, 1975); Founder and Trustee, Unverferth House, 1978-1982. *Member:* Columbus (Common Pleas Court Committee; Municipal Court Committee, Chair, 1974; Family Law Committee, Member, 1975—), Ohio State (Family Law Committee, 1982—) and American (Member, Section on Family Law) Bar Associations; Ohio Academy of Trial Lawyers; Franklin County Trial Lawyers Association. ***PRACTICE AREAS:*** Family Law; Matrimonial Law; Domestic Relations Law; Divorce Taxation; Child Custody; Visitation Rights; Premarital Agreements.

ASSOCIATE

BOBBIE CORLEY O'KEEFE

WHITE & FISH, L.P.A., INC.

Established in 1969
1335 DUBLIN ROAD
SUITE 201 (C)
COLUMBUS, OHIO 43215
Telephone: 614-485-9300
Fax: 614-485-9462
URL: http://www.whiteandfish.com
Email: wflpa@centralohioattorneys.com
URL: http://www.centralohioattorneys.com

Civil Litigation, Bankruptcy, Workouts, Chapter 11, Collections, Corporate Law, Small Business Law, Commercial, Family Law, Divorce, Personal Injury, Real Estate, Estate Litigation, Employment Contracts, Wrongful Termination.

ARNOLD S. WHITE, born Columbus, Ohio, October 7, 1944; admitted to bar, 1969, Ohio. *Education:* The Ohio State University (B.A., 1966); American University (J.D., 1969). Phi Alpha Delta. Instructor, Bankruptcy and Repossession Seminars, National Business Institute and Lorman Seminars, 2003—. Lecturer, Real Estate Law, Ohio Legal Center Institute, 1982. Chief, Legal Services, Ohio Department of Economic & Development, 1971-1974. Columnist, Bankruptcy and Related Topics, Business First, 2001—. Special Counsel to Ohio Attorney General, 1974-1994. Law Director, Gahanna, Ohio, 1976-1979. President, Voices of Hope, Inc. *Member:* Association of Trial Lawyers of America; Columbus (Member, Bankruptcy Committee, 1986—) and Ohio State Bar Associations; National Association of Bankruptcy Trustees. ***REPORTED CASES:*** In Re Creditors Service Corp., 195 Bankr. 680 (BKNY S.D.OH, 1996). ***PRACTICE AREAS:*** Bankruptcy; Workouts; Personal Injury; Automobile Accidents; Sexual Abuse; Slip and Fall; Wrongful Death; Small Business Law; Business Formation; Business Planning; Partnerships; Limited Liability Company Law; Zoning, Planning and Land Use; Buying and Selling of Businesses; Commercial Law; Collections; Debtor and Creditor; Real Estate; Buy-Sell Agreements; Commercial Leasing; Mortgages; Commercial Litigation. ***Email:*** awhite@centralohioattorneys.com

JEFFREY D. FISH, born Portsmouth, Ohio, October 1, 1965; admitted to bar, 1991, Ohio. *Education:* University of Tennessee; Ohio State University (B.S.B.A., 1988); Capital University (J.D., 1991). *Member:* Columbus (Member, Family Law Committee) and Ohio State Bar Associations; Association of Trial Lawyers of America. (Certified Specialist in Family Relations Law, Ohio State Bar Association). ***PRACTICE AREAS:*** Civil Litigation; Family Law; Divorce; Juvenile Law; Child Custody; Visitation Rights; Adoptions; Spousal Support; Premarital Agreements; Domestic Violence; Dissolution; Child Support; Bankruptcy; Personal Injury; Construction Accidents; Construction Defects; Wills; Probate; Guardianship and Conservatorship. ***Email:*** jfish@centralohioattorneys.com

REPRESENTATIVE CLIENTS: Sonitrol of Central Ohio Corp.; DR Grading & Excavating, Inc.; C & L Ventures, LLC; CCAE, Inc. (Consumer Electronics); Ash Machine Co.
AGENT FOR: Stewart Title Guaranty; White Title Agency, Inc.

WILES, BOYLE, BURKHOLDER & BRINGARDNER CO., L.P.A.

Established in 1940
300 SPRUCE STREET, FLOOR 1
COLUMBUS, OHIO 43215
Telephone: 614-221-5216
Fax: 614-221-5692; 221-0624
Email: mail@wileslaw.com
URL: http://www.wileslaw.com

General Practice, Insurance Defense, Medical Legal, Products Liability, Aviation, Motor Carrier, Business, Corporate, Municipal, Construction, Real Estate, Commercial Leasing, Hospitality and Restaurant, Estate Planning Law, Trusts, Wills and Probate, Taxation, Trial, and Appellate Practice, Bankruptcy, Foreclosure and Debtor-Creditor Law.

FIRM PROFILE: Founded in 1940, the firm is engaged in a civil, corporate, real estate, home building, restaurant and defense-oriented practice and serves clients statewide. The firm's attorneys are active in numerous bar associations, as well as the International Association of Defense Counsel, The Ohio Association of Civil Trial Attorneys, and the Defense Research Institute. The firm is comprised of 24 attorneys.

DANIEL G. WILES, born Columbus, Ohio, April 23, 1941; admitted to bar, 1966, Ohio. *Education:* The Ohio State University (B.S., 1963); Ohio Northern University (J.D., 1966). Delta Theta Phi. *Member:* Columbus (Member: Common Pleas Court Committee, 1983; Doctor-Lawyer Committee), Ohio State and American Bar Associations; Defense Research and Trial Lawyers Association; Ohio Association of Civil Trial Attorneys; Columbus Defense Association (Member, Judiciary Committee). ***PRACTICE AREAS:*** Medical-Legal Law; Products Liability Law; Insurance Defense; Civil Litigation. ***Email:*** dwiles@wileslaw.com

JAMES W. WHEELER, born Bellefontaine, Ohio, June 15, 1943; admitted to bar, 1968, Ohio; 1972, U.S. District Court, Southern District of Ohio; 1984, U.S. District Court, Northern District of Ohio. *Education:* Muskingum College; The Ohio State University (B.A., 1965; J.D., 1968). Phi Delta Phi. Assistant Attorney General, State of Ohio, 1968-1970. Instructor: Real Estate Law, Columbus Paraprofessional Institute; Institute of Financial Education; American Institute for Paralegal Studies; National Business Institute. *Member:* Columbus (Member: Real Property Law Committee; Committee on Fee Arbitration; Bankruptcy Law Committee; Financial Institutions Committee), Ohio State (Member, Real Property Law Section) and American (Member, Real Property Special Committee on Foreclosures) Bar Associations; Mid Ohio Lenders Counsel Association; Central Ohio Land Title Underwriters Association. ***PRACTICE AREAS:*** Creditor Bankruptcy Law; Creditor Rights Law; Foreclosure Law; Real Estate Law; Title Insurance Law. ***Email:*** jwheeler@wileslaw.com

JAMES M. WILES, born Columbus, Ohio, June 21, 1945; admitted to bar, 1970, Ohio. *Education:* Xavier University (B.S., 1967); Ohio Northern University (J.D., 1970). Phi Alpha Delta. *Member:* Columbus, Ohio State and American Bar Associations; Ohio Association of Civil Trial Attorneys; American Board of Trial Advocates; Defense Research Institute; Federation of Insurance and Corporate Counsel; Loss Executives Association. ***PRACTICE AREAS:*** Negligence Law; Products Liability Law; Aviation Law; Construction Law; Commercial Law; Business Law; Motor Carrier Law. ***Email:*** jwiles@wileslaw.com

MARK J. SHERIFF, born Columbus, Ohio, November 6, 1945; admitted to bar, 1970, Ohio; 1972, District of Columbia. *Education:* The Ohio State University (B.A., 1967); University of Cincinnati (J.D., 1970). Order of the Coif. Former Member, Luper, Sheriff and Naidanthal. Member, Upper Arlington Board of Education, 1984-2000. *Member:* Commercial Law League of America. [Captain, U.S. Army, 1971-1973]. (Board Certified, Creditors Rights Law, Commercial Law League of America Academy of Commercial and Bankruptcy Law Specialists). ***PRACTICE AREAS:*** Commercial Litigation; Creditors Rights; Collections; Civil Litigation; Corporate Finance. ***Email:*** msheriff@wileslaw.com

THOMAS E. BOYLE, born Elmira, New York, November 15, 1947; admitted to bar, 1972, Ohio. *Education:* The Ohio State University (B.S., 1969; J.D., cum laude, 1972). *Member:* Columbus (Member: Doctor-Lawyer Committee; Common Pleas Court Committee; Judicial Committee), Ohio State and American (Member: Litigation Section; Tort & Insurance Practice Section) Bar Associations; Ohio Association of Civil Trial Attorneys; Defense Research Institute; International Association of Defense Counsel; National Society of Professional Insurance Investigators. ***PRACTICE AREAS:*** Civil Litigation; Neg-

(This Listing Continued)

ligence Law; Products Liability Law; Professional Liability Law; Commercial Litigation; Insurance Contracts; Construction Litigation; Trucking Law; Arson and Insurance Fraud. ***Email:*** tboyle@wileslaw.com

MICHAEL L. CLOSE, born Columbus, Ohio, July 23, 1944; admitted to bar, 1975, Ohio; 1976, Florida; 1979, U.S. Supreme Court. *Education:* The Ohio State University (B.S., 1967); Capital University (J.D., 1975). Law Director, City of Hilliard, 1978-1983. City Council, City of Dublin, 1984-1989. Mayor, City of Dublin, 1986-1989. Judge: Franklin County Common Pleas Court, 1989-1992; Court of Appeals of Ohio, 10th District, 1993-1998. *Member:* Columbus and Ohio State Bar Associations; The Florida Bar. ***PRACTICE AREAS:*** Civil Litigation; Arbitration; Mediation; Appellate Practice. ***Email:*** mclose@wileslaw.com

RICHARD D. BRINGARDNER, born Columbus, Ohio, September 18, 1953; admitted to bar, 1978, Ohio; 1979, U.S. District Court, Southern and Northern Districts of Ohio. *Education:* Ashland University (B.S., 1975); Capital University (J.D., 1978). Member, Order of the Curia. *Member:* Columbus (Member: Real Property Law Committee; Bankruptcy Committee; Probate Committee; Estate and Gift Tax Committee), Ohio State (Member, Sections on: Estate Planning; Trust and Probate Law; Real Estate Law) and American (Member, Sections on: Corporation, Banking and Business Law; Real Property, Probate and Trust Law) Bar Associations. ***PRACTICE AREAS:*** Real Estate Law; Estate Planning; Bankruptcy Law; Business Law; Creditors Rights. ***Email:*** rbringardner@wileslaw.com

DANIEL E. BRINGARDNER, born Columbus, Ohio, September 18, 1953; admitted to bar, 1978, Ohio; 1979, U.S. District Court, Southern District of Ohio; 1988, U.S. Tax Court. *Education:* Ashland College (B.S. in Business Admin., cum laude, 1975); Capital University Law School (J.D., 1978). *Member:* Columbus (Member: Admissions, Business Tax, Construction, Estate and Gift Tax, Probate Court and Real Property Committees) and Ohio State (Member, Sections on: Estate Planning, Trust and Probate Law; and Real Estate Law) Bar Associations. ***PRACTICE AREAS:*** Real Estate; Estate Planning; Probate; Business and Commercial; Taxation. ***Email:*** dbringardner@wileslaw.com

STEVEN P. ELLIOTT, born Columbus, Ohio, August 27, 1953; admitted to bar, 1979, Ohio. *Education:* Miami University (B.A., cum laude, 1975); The Ohio State University (J.D., with honors, 1979). *Member:* Columbus (Member, Real Property Law Committee), Ohio State (Member, Real Property Law Committee) and American (Member, Business Section) Bar Associations. ***PRACTICE AREAS:*** Real Estate Law; Construction Law; Corporate Law. ***Email:*** selliott@wileslaw.com

BRUCE H. BURKHOLDER, born Mansfield, Ohio, July 7, 1955; admitted to bar, 1980, Ohio; 1981, U.S. District Court, Southern District of Ohio. *Education:* Bowling Green State University (B.S., 1977); Capital University (J.D., 1980). Member, Ohio Home Builders Association (Member, Executive Committee). *Member:* Columbus (Member: Real Property Law Committee, Chairman, 1993-1995), Ohio State and American Bar Associations. ***PRACTICE AREAS:*** Real Estate Law; Construction Law; Corporate Law. ***Email:*** bburkholder@wileslaw.com

DALE D. COOK, born Cleveland, Ohio, December 19, 1956; admitted to bar, 1982, Ohio; 1985, U.S. District Court, Southern District of Ohio; 2000, U.S. Court of Appeals, Sixth Circuit. *Education:* Trinity College (B.A., 1979); Duke University (J.D., 1982). Pi Gamma Mu; Phi Beta Kappa. *Member:* Columbus and Ohio State Bar Associations. ***PRACTICE AREAS:*** Litigation; Insurance Coverage; Products Liability. ***Email:*** dcook@wileslaw.com

MARY TEN EYCK TAYLOR, born Morristown, New Jersey, September 9, 1953; admitted to bar, 1985, Ohio. *Education:* Russell Sage College (B.A., magna cum laude, 1975); Capital University (J.D., with honors, 1985). Member, Parks and Recreation Commission, Powell, Ohio. Formerly with: Kegler, Brown Hill Ritter; Bank One Ohio Trust Company; Merrill Lynch Trust; The Ohio Company. *Member:* Columbus (Business, Probate and Tax Committee), Ohio State and American Bar Associations. ***PRACTICE AREAS:*** Estate Planning Law; Tax Law; Probate; Trust Law; Fiduciary Law; Fiduciary Litigation; Retirement Planning; Business Law; Elder Care. ***Email:*** mtaylor@wileslaw.com

JAY B. EGGSPUEHLER, born Champaign, Illinois, November 12, 1957; admitted to bar, 2002, U.S. Supreme Court; 1986, New York; 1987, U.S. District Court, Southern and Eastern Districts of New York; 1988, District of Columbia and U.S. District Court, Western District of New York; 1990, Ohio; 1991 U.S. District Court, Northern and Southern Districts of Ohio; 1996, U.S. Court of Appeals, Sixth Circuit. *Education:* The Ohio State University (B.S.B.A., 1982); Ohio Northern University (J.D., 1985). *Member:* Columbus, Ohio State, New York State, and American Bar Associations; District of Columbia Bar; Lawyer-Pilot Bar Association; National Transportation Safety Board Bar Association; Defense Research Institute; Ohio Association of Civil Trial Attorneys; Central Ohio Association of Civil Trial Attorneys; Trucking Industry Defense Association; Helicopter Association International. ***PRACTICE AREAS:*** Litigation; Products Liability; Negligence; Aviation; Motor Carrier; Insurance Defense; Business/Commercial; Construction; Administrative. ***Email:*** jeggspuehler@wileslaw.com

EUGENE L. HOLLINS, born Orange, Texas, February 21, 1962; admitted to bar, 1988, Ohio. *Education:* Vanderbilt University (B.A., 1983); The Ohio State University (J.D., 1988). Order of the Coif. Articles Editor, Ohio State Law Journal. *Member:* Columbus (Member, Real Property Law Committee), Ohio State and American Bar Associations; Ohio Municipal Attorneys Association; International Municipal Lawyers Association. ***PRACTICE AREAS:*** Municipal Government; Local Government; Real Property; Zoning and Land Use.

WILLIAM B. BENSON, born Chillicothe, Ohio, May 20, 1965; admitted to bar, 1990, Ohio. *Education:* Miami University (B.A., 1987); Capital University (J.D., 1990). Delta Theta Phi. Executive Notes Editor, Capital University Law Review, 1989-1990. *Member:* Columbus, Ohio State and American Bar Associations; Ohio Association of Civil Trial Attorneys. ***PRACTICE AREAS:*** Litigation; Products Liability; Negligence; Aviation; Motor Carrier; Insurance; Construction; Commercial Litigation. ***Email:*** wBenson@wileslaw.com

SAMUEL M. PIPINO, born Niles, Ohio, August 1, 1968; admitted to bar, 1993, Ohio; 1994, Pennsylvania and U.S. District Court, Southern District of Ohio; 1998, U.S. District Court, Northern District of Ohio. *Education:* Oberlin College (B.A., 1990); The Ohio State University (J.D., 1993). Articles Editor, Ohio State University. Author: "In Whose Best Interest? Exploring the Continuing Viability of the Parental Immunity Doctrine," 53 Ohio State Law Journal 1111. *Member:* Columbus, Ohio State and Pennsylvania Bar Associations; Ohio Association of Civil Trial Attorneys; Defense Research Institute. ***PRACTICE AREAS:*** Insurance Coverage; Insurance Defense; Civil Litigation; Products Liability. ***Email:*** spipino@wileslaw.com

(This Listing Continued)

C. WILLIAM KLAUSMAN, born Columbus, Ohio, January 19, 1968; admitted to bar, 1994, Ohio and U.S. District Court, Southern District of Ohio. *Education:* Hanover College (B.A., 1990); Capital University (J.D., 1994; LL.M., Taxation, 1995). *Member:* Columbus, Ohio State and American Bar Associations. ***PRACTICE AREAS:*** General Business/Corporate Law; Estate Planning; Taxation; Real Estate. ***Email:*** wklausman@wileslaw.com

JAMES M. HUGHES, born Columbus, Ohio, September 17, 1964; admitted to bar, 1994, Ohio and U.S. District Court, Southern District of Ohio. *Education:* The Ohio State University (B.S.B.A., 1987); Capital University (J.D, 1994). State Representative, Ohio, 2000—. *Member:* Columbus and Ohio State Bar Associations. ***PRACTICE AREAS:*** Probate; Estate Planning; Contracts; Real Estate; Business; Torts. ***Email:*** jhughes@wileslaw.com

MARK C. MELKO, born Delaware, Ohio, June 2, 1972; admitted to bar, 1998, Ohio, 1999, U.S. District Court, Southern District of Ohio; 2000, U.S. District Court, Northern District of Ohio. *Education:* Miami University (B.A., 1994); Capital University (J.D., magna cum laude, 1998). Recipient, Corpus Juris Secundum Award. Member, Capital University Law Review. *Member:* Columbus, Ohio State and American Bar Associations. ***PRACTICE AREAS:*** Civil Litigation; Aviation; Administrative; Products Liability; Negligence. ***Email:*** mmelko@wileslaw.com

KERRY T. BOYLE, born Columbus, Ohio, May 22, 1973; admitted to bar, 2000, Ohio; 2001, U.S. District Court, Southern District of Ohio. *Education:* Ohio University (B.S., 1995); Capital University (J.D., 2000). *Member:* Columbus (Member: Young Lawyers Committee; Construction Committee) and Ohio State Bar Associations. ***PRACTICE AREAS:*** Business Law; Construction Law; Real Estate; Litigation. ***Email:*** kboyle@wileslaw.com

CHRISTOPHER G. PHILLIPS, born Toledo, Ohio, February 2, 1976; admitted to bar, 2001, Ohio. *Education:* University of Toledo (B.A., 1998); Thomas Jefferson School of Law (J.D., 2001). *Member:* Columbus and Ohio State Bar Associations. ***PRACTICE AREAS:*** Creditors Rights; Creditor Bankruptcy Law; Foreclosure Law; Real Estate Law. ***Email:*** cphillips@wileslaw.com

LAUREN S. BRILL, born Warren, Ohio, March 6, 1978; admitted to bar, 2003, Ohio. *Education:* Ohio Wesleyan University (B.A., Zoology, cum laude, 2000); Capital University Law School (J.D., magna cum laude, 2003). Order of the Curia. Member, Capital University Law Review, 2002-2003. ***PRACTICE AREAS:*** Civil Litigation; Insurance Defense; Aviation Law.

NEIL C. SANDER, born Bowling Green, Ohio, January 6, 1978; admitted to bar, 2004, Ohio. *Education:* The Ohio State University (B.S., 2001); Capital University (J.D., 2004). *Member:* Columbus and Ohio State Bar Associations. ***PRACTICE AREAS:*** Creditors Rights; Civil Litigation; Collections.

JENNIFER B. CASTO, born 1969; admitted to bar, 2005, Ohio. *Education:* Otterbein College (B.A., 2001); Capital University (J.D., cum laude, 2005). Order of the Curia. *Member:* Columbus, Ohio State and American Bar Associations. ***PRACTICE AREAS:*** Litigation. ***Email:*** jcasto@wileslaw.com

REPRESENTATIVE INSURANCE CLIENTS: Aetna Life Insurance Company; AIG Claim Service; American Hardware Mutual Ins. Co.; American International Group, Inc.; Auto Owners Insurance Co.; Capital Enterprise Ins. Group; CNA Insurance Company; Central Mutual Insurance Co.; Connecticut Specialty Ins. Group; Continental Loss Adjusting Co.; Detroit Auto Inter-Ins. Exchange; Electric Mutual Insurance Co.; Gulf Insurance Company; Investors Heritage Life; Insurance Claim Service; Lightning Rod Mutual Insurance; Lincoln General Insurance Company; Maryland Casualty; Mead Reinsurance Company; Michigan Mutual Insurance Company; Planet Insurance Company; Professional Mutual Insurance Company; Professional Underwriters Agency, Inc.; Reliance Insurance Company; State Auto Insurance Company; The Blackmoor Group; Travel Air Insurance Company; Travelers Property and Casualty Company; Underwriters at Lloyds of London; United States Aviation Underwriters, Inc.; Victoria Fire & Casualty; Worldwide Insurance Group; Zurich Insurance Company.
REPRESENTATIVE CORPORATE CLIENTS: Architectural Alliance Ltd.; Ashland Oil; Beulah Park Jockey Club; Building Industry Association; Burlington Motor Carriers, Inc.; The Cessna Aircraft Company; Cameron Mitchell Restaurants; Coca-Cola Bottling Company; Contract Freighters, Inc.; C.V. Perry & Co.; Damons Restaurants; Davidson Phillips, Inc.; Deere & Company; Fairfax Properties, LLC; Firestone Tire & Rubber Company; General Electric Household Finance Corporation; Image Hotel Management Corporation; Leviton Manufacturing Company, Ltd.; LDA Investments, LLC; McNaughton-McKay Electric Company; Mercedes-Benz of North America, Inc.; Ohio Automobile Dealers Association; Palmer-Donavin Manufacturing Co.; Physicians Weight Loss Centers; Piper Aircraft Corporation; Raytheon Aircraft Company; Roosters Restaurants; Ryder Truck Lines; Ryder Truck Rental; Sarang Corporation; The Daimler Group, Inc.; The Truberry Group, Inc.; Tradesmen International, Inc.; USAir, Inc.; U.S. Truck Lines; The Valvoline Company; Victorian Community Developers; WWCD Radio Station.

WILLI LAW OFFICES

COLUMBUS, OHIO

(See Westerville)

Estate Planning, Business Succession Planning, Tax Planning, Small Business Law, Business Start-Ups, Real Estate, Trust Administration, Asset Protection, Charitable Giving, Guardianships, Premarital Agreements, Trusts and Estates, Probate.

WILLIAMS & PETRO CO., L.L.C.

Established in 1998

338 SOUTH HIGH STREET, 2ND FLOOR
COLUMBUS, OHIO 43215-4546
Telephone: 614-224-0531
Fax: 614-224-0553
URL: http://www.williamspetro.com
Email: generalcounsel@wplaw.org
URL: http://www.wplaw.org

Insurance Defense, Personal Injury, Automobile Accidents, Wrongful Death, Municipal Law, Construction Law, Employment Law, Business Representation, Estate Planning and Administration, Probate Administration, Advisory/Coverage Opinions, Family Law.

FIRM PROFILE: William & Petro Co., L.L.C. was founded by Richard A. Williams and John P. Petro in June 1998 to provide outstanding legal services at reasonable costs to its clients. We are fortunate to have a group of attorneys with strong level of academic achievement combined with the talent and experience necessary to maintain a successful civil practice. The diverse backgrounds of the men and women in our office enables us to serve our clients in all litigation services, from trial through the appellate process, to fit the specific needs of our clients. Ultimately, we strive to provide each of our clients with the highest level of quality legal services in a cost-effective manner.

RICHARD A. WILLIAMS, born Cleveland, Ohio, April 8, 1957; admitted to bar, 1982, Ohio; 1986, U.S. District Court, Northern District of Ohio and U.S. Court of Appeals, Sixth Circuit; 1991, U.S. District Court, Southern District of Ohio; 1994, U.S. Supreme Court. *Education:* Miami University, Ohio (B.S., 1979); University of Toledo College of Law (J.D., 1982). Member, Moot Court Competition and National Moot Court Coordinator. Former Partner, Mazanec Raskin & Ryder Co., Columbus, Ohio. *Member:* Columbus and Ohio State Bar Associations. ***PRACTICE AREAS:*** Insurance Defense; Personal Injury; Municipal Law; Employment Law. ***Email:*** rwilliams@wplaw.org

JOHN P. PETRO, born Columbus, Ohio, February 22, 1967; admitted to bar, 1992, Ohio; 1993, U.S. District Court, Southern District of Ohio. *Education:* Miami University, Ohio (B.A., cum laude, political science/history, 1989); The Ohio State University College of Law (J.D., 1992). Phi Beta Kappa. Former Staff Attorney for: The Honorable William L. Millard and The Honorable Tommy Thompson, Franklin County Common Pleas Court. Former Associate, Mazanec, Raskin & Ryder Co., L.P.A. Former Speaker, "Insurance Coverage Law in Ohio", National Business Institute. Arbitrator, Franklin County Court of Common Pleas. *Member:* Columbus, Ohio State and American Bar Associations. ***PRACTICE AREAS:*** Insurance Defense; Employment Litigation; Municipal Law; Civil Litigation; Personal Injury Litigation; Construction Law. ***Email:*** jpetro@wplaw.org

---

LORREE L. DENDIS, born Geneva, New York, October 31, 1974; admitted to bar, 2000, Ohio and U.S. District Court, Northern District of Ohio; 2001, U.S. District Court, Southern District of Ohio and U.S. Court of Appeals, Sixth Circuit. *Education:* William Smith College (B.A., summa cum laude, Economics and East Asian Studies, 1996); Ohio State University College of Law (J.D., 2000). Phi Beta Kappa; Omicron Delta Epsilon. Member, Franklin American Inn of Court. *Member:* Columbus, Ohio State and American Bar Associations. ***PRACTICE AREAS:*** Insurance Litigation; Insurance Defense; Municipal Law. ***Email:*** ldendis@wplaw.org

SUSAN S.R. PETRO, born Columbus, Ohio, December 14, 1964; admitted to bar, 1990, Ohio. *Education:* The Ohio State University (B.A., cum laude, 1987); University of North Carolina at Chapel Hill (J.D., 1990). Volunteer, The Legal Aid Society of Columbus, 1992-1993. ***PRACTICE AREAS:*** Family Law; Divorce; Child Custody; Child Support; Visitation Rights; Insurance Defense. ***Email:*** spetro@wplaw.org

JOSH L. SCHOENBERGER, born Upper Sandusky, Ohio, November 13, 1978; admitted to bar, 2004, Ohio. *Education:* University of Findlay (B.A., summa cum laude, Political Science, 2001); The Ohio State University, Moritz College of Law (J.D., 2004). Delta Theta Phi. *Member:* Columbus and Ohio State Bar Associations. ***PRACTICE AREAS:*** Insurance Defense; Insurance Litigation; Personal Injury. ***Email:*** JSchoenberger@WPlaw.org

OF COUNSEL

JOHN J. PETRO, born Elyria, Ohio, November 7, 1937; admitted to bar, 1962, Ohio. *Education:* The Ohio State University (B.A., 1959; J.D, 1962). Phi Delta Phi. *Member:* Columbus, Ohio State and American (Member, Sections of: Public Contract Law; Tort and Insurance Practice; Chairman, Fidelity and Surety Law Committee, 1979-1980) Bar Associations; Federation of Insurance and Corporate Counsel. ***PRACTICE AREAS:*** Fidelity and Surety; Negligence; Products Liability; Construction; Insurance.

WINTERS & MERKLE

Established in 1982

500 SOUTH FRONT STREET, SUITE 900
COLUMBUS, OHIO 43215
Telephone: 614-228-0068
FAX: 614-228-1660
URL: http://www.wintersmerkle.com

Civil and Criminal Trial and Appellate Practice in all State and Federal Courts, Business and White Collar Crimes, Environmental Crimes, Health Care Fraud, Grand Jury Investigations, Personal Injury. Business and Commercial Litigation. Insurance Coverage and Bad Faith Litigation.

DAVID C. WINTERS, born Fort Wayne, Indiana, April 14, 1944; admitted to bar, 1975, Ohio; 1979, U.S. District Court, Southern District of Ohio and U.S. Supreme Court; 1983, U.S. Court of Appeals, Sixth Circuit; 1992, U.S. District Court, District of Arizona.

(This Listing Continued)

Education: Ohio State University (B.A., 1966; J.D., 1975). Lecturer, Criminal Law Update, Ohio Legal Center Institute, 1983; Developments in Criminal Enforcement of Environmental Laws, 15th Annual Inland Spills Conference, 1991; Search and Seizure in Environmental Crimes, Ohio State Bar Association, Environmental Section, 1993. Assistant Prosecuting Attorney, Franklin County, 1975-1978. Senior Assistant Prosecuting Attorney, Franklin County, 1978-1982. Listed in Who's Who in Criminal Law in Central Ohio, 1994. Adjunct Professor, Trial Practice, Ohio State University, College of Law, 1999—. *Member:* Columbus (Member: Criminal Law Committee, 1982—; Common Pleas Committee, 1986—; Judiciary Committee, 1988-1989), Ohio State and American (Member: Criminal Justice Section; White Collar Crime Committee) Bar Associations; Franklin County Trial Lawyers Association (Chairman, Criminal Law Committee, 1984, 1986-1990); Ohio Academy of Trial Lawyers; Ohio Association of Criminal Defense Lawyers (Director, 1987—); National Association of Criminal Defense Lawyers (Member, Environmental Crimes Committee). ***PRACTICE AREAS:*** Business Crimes; White Collar Crime; Environmental Criminal Law; Criminal Defense; Federal Criminal Law; Complex Civil Litigation. ***Email:*** dcw@wintersmerkle.com

H. TIM MERKLE, born Columbus, Ohio, April 12, 1952; admitted to bar, 1979, Ohio; 1980, U.S. District Court, Southern District of Ohio; 1991, U.S. District Court, Northern District of Ohio; 1994, U.S. Court of Appeals, Sixth Circuit. *Education:* Hope College (B.A., 1974); Capital University (J.D., 1979). Lecturer, Testifying as an Expert Witness, Ohio Arson School, 1991; Prosecuting and Defending Civil Arson Cases, Ohio State Fire Marshall Seminar, 1994, 1995; Bad Faith Law in Ohio, 1999. Assistant Prosecuting Attorney, Franklin County, 1979-1990. Senior Assistant Prosecuting Attorney, Franklin County, 1984-1990. *Member:* Columbus, Ohio and American Bar Associations. ***PRACTICE AREAS:*** White Collar Criminal Defense; Health Care Fraud; Grand Jury Practice; Federal Criminal Law; Personal Injury; Business Litigation; Commercial Litigation; Insurance Coverage; Insurance Bad Faith Litigation. ***Email:*** htm@wintersmerkle.com

REFERENCE: National City Bank.

DAVID WIRTH

829 BETHEL ROAD
COLUMBUS, OHIO 43214
Telephone: 614-267-5354
Fax: 614-875-6606
Email: wirthman@hotmail.com

Insurance Law, Negligence, Legal Malpractice, Subrogation, Personal Injury, Probate.

DAVID S. WIRTH, born Cincinnati, Ohio, May 23, 1975; admitted to bar, 2001, Ohio; 2002, U.S. District Court, Southern District of Ohio. *Education:* University of Cincinnati (B.A., cum laude, 1996; J.D., 2000). *Member:* Columbus, Ohio State and American Bar Associations. ***PRACTICE AREAS:*** Insurance; Negligence; Legal Malpractice; Subrogation; Personal Injury; Probate.

WOLSKE & BARCLAY

A LEGAL PROFESSIONAL ASSOCIATION

Established in 1968

580 SOUTH HIGH STREET
COLUMBUS, OHIO 43215-5672
Telephone: 614-221-6969
800-862-6969
Fax: 614-228-4367
URL: http://www.wolskeandbarclay.com
Email: Firm@wolskeandbarclay.com
URL: http://www.lawyers.com/wolskeandbarclay

Civil and Appellate Practice in State and Federal Courts. Medical and Dental Malpractice, Nursing Home Negligence, Personal Injury and Products Liability Law, Worker's Compensation and Industrial Accidents, Automobile Accidents, Airplane Crash Litigation.

FIRM PROFILE: Wolske & Barclay is one of Ohio's most recognized and trusted plaintiff's personal injury firms. In the course of its thirty-year history, Wolske & Barclay has handled several cases that shaped tort law in Ohio. Today the firm represents hundreds of Ohioans each year in traffic and work-related accident claims, medical malpractice cases and nursing home negligence cases.

WALTER J. WOLSKE, JR., born Columbus, Ohio, September 1, 1932; admitted to bar, 1956, Ohio; 1982, U.S. Supreme Court; 1989, Kentucky. *Education:* The Ohio State University (B.S., 1954; J.D., 1956). President, Lawyers Club of Columbus, 1972-1973. *Member:* Columbus and Ohio State Bar Associations; Franklin County Trial Lawyers Association (President, 1967-1968); Ohio Academy of Trial Lawyers; The Association of Trial Lawyers of America (Member, Board of Education, 1983-1984); American Board of Trial Advocates (Advocate, State Representative to the Board of Directors, 1987-1989 and Treasurer, Ohio Chapter, 1991-1992). Certified as a Civil Trial Advocate by the National Board of Trial Advocacy. ***REPORTED CASES:*** Hensley V. Henry (1980) 61 Ohio St. 2d 277; Morgan V. Children's Hospital (1985), 480 N.E., 2d 464; Beard V. Investors (1985) 21 Ohio App. 3d 219, 486 N.E., 2d 1255; Karam V. Allstate Insurance Company (1985) 27 Ohio App. 3d 137, 500 N.E., 2d 358; Humphry V. Riverside Methodist Hospital (1986) 22 Ohio St. 3d 94, 488 N.E., 2d 877; Mulloy V. Longaberger Basket Company (1989) 47 Ohio App. 3d 77, 547 N.E. 2d 411. ***PRACTICE AREAS:*** Medical Malpractice; Dental Malpractice; Personal Injury; Airplane Crash Litigation; Automobile Accidents and Injuries.

CRAIG D. BARCLAY, born Zanesville, Ohio, October 19, 1948; admitted to bar, 1973, Ohio. *Education:* The Ohio State University (B.S., magna cum laude, 1970; J.D., cum laude, 1973). Phi Delta Phi. *Member:* Columbus, Ohio State and American Bar Associations; Advocate, American Board of Trial Advocates (Ohio Chapter President, 1990); Ohio

(This Listing Continued)

Academy of Trial Lawyers; Franklin County Trial Lawyers Association; The Association of Trial Lawyers of America. ***PRACTICE AREAS:*** Medical Malpractice; Personal Injury; Nursing Home Negligence. ***Email:*** craigb@wolskeandbarclay.com

---

DAVID A. ROSCOE, born Pittsburgh, Pennsylvania, July 12, 1966; admitted to bar, 2001, Ohio and U.S. District Court, Southern District of Ohio. *Education:* Gannon University (B.S., Physical Science, 1988; M.S., Health Service Administration, 1993); Capital University (J.D., 2000). *Member:* Ohio State Bar Association. [Major, United States Army Reserve.]. ***PRACTICE AREAS:*** Medical Malpractice; Personal Injury; Nursing Home Litigation. ***Email:*** daver@WolskeandBarclay.com

SARAH J. WOLSKE-DONALDSON, born Columbus, Ohio, September 10, 1968; admitted to bar, 2001, Ohio and U.S. District Court, Southern District of Ohio. *Education:* Sarah Lawrence College (B.A., 1990); Capital University (J.D., 2000). *Member:* Columbus and Ohio State Bar Associations; Franklin County Trial Lawyers Association; The Ohio Academy of Trial Lawyers. ***PRACTICE AREAS:*** Medical Malpractice; Personal Injury; Nursing Home Litigation. ***Email:*** sarahd@wolskeandbarclay.com

JASON K. WRIGHT, born Columbus, Ohio, July 31, 1970; admitted to bar, 2001, Ohio and U.S. District Court, Southern District of Ohio. *Education:* Ohio University (B.A., Political Science, 1992); Capital University (J.D., 2000). Order of Curia. *Member:* Columbus and Ohio State Bar Associations; Franklin County Trial Lawyers Association; The Ohio Academy of Trial Lawyers. ***PRACTICE AREAS:*** Medical Malpractice; Personal Injury; Nursing Home Litigation. ***Email:*** jasonw@wolskeandbarclay.com

REFERENCE: Bank One of Columbus, N.A.

WOOD, HERRON & EVANS, L.L.P.

COLUMBUS, OHIO

(See Cincinnati)

Intellectual Property and Related Litigation; Computer Law, Patents, Trademarks and Copyrights.

YAVITCH & PALMER CO., L.P.A.

Established in 1997

511 SOUTH HIGH STREET
COLUMBUS, OHIO 43215
Telephone: 614-224-6142
Facsimile: 614-228-6078
Email: spalmer@yp-lawyers.com
URL: http://www.yp-lawyers.com

Criminal Defense, Appellate Practice, Post-Conviction Remedies, and Trial Practice in All State and Federal Courts.

ERIC J. YAVITCH, born Columbus, Ohio, March 19, 1969; admitted to bar, 1995, Ohio and U.S. District Court, Southern District of Ohio; 1998, U.S. Court of Appeals, Sixth Circuit. *Education:* Baldwin-Wallace College (B.A., 1991); Capital University (J.D., 1994). *Member:* Columbus and Ohio Bar Associations; Ohio Association of Criminal Defense Lawyers; Central Ohio Association of Criminal Defense Lawyers; National Association of Criminal Defense Lawyers. ***PRACTICE AREAS:*** Criminal Defense; Driving While Intoxicated; Traffic Violations; Drug Crimes; Felonies; White Collar Crime. ***Email:*** eyavitch@yp-lawyers.com

STEPHEN E. PALMER, born Columbus, Ohio, May 5, 1970; admitted to bar, 1995, Ohio; 1996, U.S. District Court, Southern District of Ohio; 1998, U.S. Court of Appeals, Sixth Circuit; 2002, U.S. Supreme Court. *Education:* College of Wooster (B.A., History, 1992); Capital University (J.D., magna cum laude, 1995). Order of the Curia. Law Review, Capital University, 1994-1995. Co-Author: "Ohio Courtroom Evidence", Third Edition, Lexis Law Publishing, 1998; "State v. Vega and Ohio's Operating Motor Vehicle While Intoxicated (OMVI) Law: per se Unconstitutional?", Capital University Law Review, No. 3, Vol., 24, 1995. *Member:* Columbus, Ohio State and American (Member, Criminal Section) Bar Associations; National Association of Criminal Defense Lawyers. ***PRACTICE AREAS:*** Criminal Defense; Appellate Practice; White Collar Crime; Driving While Intoxicated; Traffic Violations; Drug Crimes; Felonies; Homicide; Misdemeanors; Parole and Probation; Sexual Assault. ***Email:*** spalmer@yp-lawyers.com

---

KEITH A. YEAZEL

Attorney at Law

Established in 1990

65 SOUTH FIFTH STREET
COLUMBUS, OHIO 43215
Telephone: 614-228-7005
Fax: 614-224-2347
Email: yeazel@netwalk.com

Federal and White Collar Criminal Defense, U.S. Guideline Sentencing Litigation.

FIRM PROFILE: Mr. Yeazel provides the quality of service expected from a large law firm with the responsive and cost-effective service that characterizes the best solo-practitioners. His background and experience enable him to provide knowledgeable and dependable representation in Federal Court.

KEITH A. YEAZEL, born Fayetteville, North Carolina, February 14, 1956; admitted to bar, 1989, Ohio and U.S. District Court, Southern District of Ohio; 1990, U.S. Court of Appeals, Sixth Circuit; 1992, U.S. Supreme Court; 1998, U.S. District Court, Northern District of Ohio. *Education:* Ohio State University (B.A., 1983); Capital University (J.D., 1989). Order of the Curia. Law Clerk, U.S. District Judge George Smith, 1989. *Member:* Columbus and Ohio State Bar Associations; Ohio Association of Criminal Defense Lawyers (Member, Board of Directors); National Association of Criminal Defense Lawyers. ***PRACTICE AREAS:*** Criminal Law; Litigation; White Collar Crime.

(This Listing Continued)

ZEIGER & CARPENTER

COLUMBUS, OHIO

(See Carpenter & Lipps, LLP)

ZEIGER, TIGGES & LITTLE LLP

3500 HUNTINGTON CENTER
41 SOUTH HIGH STREET
COLUMBUS, OHIO 43215
Telephone: 614-365-9900
Fax: 614-365-7900
Email: zeiger@lithohio.com
URL: http://www.litohio.com

FIRM PROFILE: A litigation boutique founded in 1994 by the then Senior Litigation Partner of the Columbus Office of Jones Day. The Firm is regarded as one of the premier commercial litigation firms in Ohio by publications such as Chambers USA America's Leading Business Lawyers. The Firm's practice focuses on complex litigation primarily in the areas of corporate and commercial disputes, First Amendment and media law, and professional liability defense of law firms.

JOHN W. ZEIGER, born Akron, Ohio, June 27, 1947; admitted to bar, 1972, Ohio. *Education:* The Ohio State University (B.S., cum laude, 1969; J.D., summa cum laude, 1972). Order of the Coif. Commissioner, The Supreme Court of Ohio Clients' Security Fund, 1995-1997. Bar Examiner, Board of Examiners of the Supreme Court of Ohio, 1997-1998. ***PRACTICE AREAS:*** Media Law; Complex Litigation; Class Action Defense. ***Email:*** zeiger@litohio.com

STEVEN W. TIGGES, born Toledo, Ohio, June 26, 1952; admitted to bar, 1981, Ohio. *Education:* University of Toledo (B.S., cum laude, 1975); The Ohio State University (J.D., summa cum laude, 1981). Order of the Coif. Editor-in-Chief, The Ohio State Law Journal, 1980-1981. ***Email:*** tigges@litohio.com

MARION H. LITTLE, JR., born Columbus, Ohio, July 27, 1964; admitted to bar, 1989, Ohio. *Education:* The Ohio State University (B.A., 1986; J.D., summa cum laude, 1989). Order of the Coif. Articles Editor, The Ohio State Law Journal, 1987-1989. Law Clerk to Hon. Joseph P. Kinneary, Senior Judge, U.S. District Court, Southern District of Ohio, 1989-1991. ***Email:*** little@litohio.com

STUART G. PARSELL, born Upper Sandusky, Ohio, July 7, 1969; admitted to bar, 1994, Ohio. *Education:* Oral Roberts University (B.A., summa cum laude, 1991); University of Notre Dame (J.D., summa cum laude, 1994). Research and Projects Editor, Notre Dame Law Review, 1993-1994. Law Clerk to Hon. J. Craig Wright, Associate Justice, Ohio Supreme Court, 1994-1995. ***Email:*** parsell@litohio.com

---

BRADLEY T. FERRELL, born Wheeling, West Virginia, March 1, 1974; admitted to bar, 1999, Ohio. *Education:* Ohio University (B.A., summa cum laude, 1996); The Ohio State University (J.D., summa cum laude, 1999). Phi Beta Kappa. Order of the Coif. Articles Editor, The Ohio State Law Journal, 1998-1999. Law Clerk to Hon. George C. Smith, U.S. District Court, Southern District of Ohio, 1999-2000. ***Email:*** ferrell@litohio.com

MATTHEW S. ZEIGER, born Columbus, Ohio, October 25, 1976; admitted to bar, 2002, Ohio. *Education:* Rhodes College (B.A., 1999); St. John's University (J.D., 2002). ***Email:*** zeigerm@litohio.com

KRIS BANVARD, born Los Angeles, California, March 23, 1957; admitted to bar, 2003, Ohio. *Education:* University of Oregon (B.A., 1978); Capital University Law School (J.D., summa cum laude, 2003). Order of the Curia. ***Email:*** banvard@litohio.com

DARREN L. NEALY, born Dayton, Ohio, October 27, 1976; admitted to bar, 2001, Ohio. *Education:* University of Dayton (B.A., magna cum laude, 1998); University of Virginia School of Law (J.D., 2001). ***Email:*** nealy@litohio.com

AIMEE PIRONE KEANE, born Boardman, Ohio; admitted to bar, 2004, Ohio. *Education:* Ohio State University (B.A., magna cum laude, 2001; J.D., magna cum laude, with honors, 2004). Associate Editor, The Ohio State Law Journal, 2003-2004. ***Email:*** pirone@litohio.com

OF COUNSEL

DANIEL R. FREYTAG, born Napoleon, Ohio, July 27, 1949; admitted to bar, 1975, Ohio. *Education:* Wittenberg University (B.A., cum laude, 1971); The Ohio State University (J.D., summa cum laude, 1974). ***Email:*** freytag@litohio.com

REPRESENTATIVE CLIENTS: America Online, Inc.; American Electric Power; American Share Insurance; Banc One Corporation; Borden Chemical, Inc.; CareWorks of Ohio Ltd.; Citigroup; The Columbus Dispatch; CompuServe Incorporated; CompuServe Interactive Services; Dispatch Broadcast Group; Fifth Third Bank; ING Americas; Merrill Lynch & Co., Inc.; Nationwide Arena LLC; State Automobile Insurance Company; Textron Financial; The Scotts Company; Stonehenge Financial Holdings; United Healthcare of Ohio; WBNS Radio; WBNS-TV.

DAVID J. GORNIK

7103 BRIGHTWOOD DRIVE
CONCORD, OHIO 44077
Telephone: 440-392-9580
Fax: 440-392-9155
Email: david@davidgornik.com
URL: http://www.davidgornik.com

Corporate Law, Real Estate Law, International Business Law, Business Law, Intellectual Property Licensing, Commercial Litigation, Employment Law, Mergers and Acquisitions, Employment Contracts, Business Planning, Joint Ventures, Limited Liability Companies, Partnerships, Energy Law, Landlord Tenant, Strategic Alliances, Commercial Leasing, Consumer Law, Contracts, Buying and Selling Business.

DAVID J. GORNIK, born Eastlake, Ohio, April 11, 1954; admitted to bar, 1990, Ohio. *Education:* Cleveland State University (B.A., cum laude, 1986; M.B.A., 1989); Cleveland Marshall College of Law (J.D., magna cum laude, 1989). *Member:* Ohio State Bar Association. ***REPORTED CASES:*** United States v. Gresser, 935 F.2d 96 (6th Circuit). ***TRANSACTIONS:*** Power purchase agreement with Caribbean Basin Utilities; Non-Traditional Sources for financing offshore transactions.

CARL McCOY
ATTORNEY AT LAW

COSHOCTON, OHIO

(See Newark)

Criminal Law, Divorce, Family Law, Medical Malpractice, Personal Injury, Automobile Accidents, Child Custody, Child Support, General Practice, Trusts and Estates, Wills and Probate Law, Driving While Intoxicated, Drug Crimes, Elder Law, Estate Planning, Insurance, Slip and Fall, Traffic Violations, Wrongful Death, Dog Bites, Domestic Violence, Parole and Probation, Visitation Rights, White Collar Crime, Automobile Insurance, Automotive Products Liability, Felonies, Misdemeanors, Premarital Agreements, Sexual Assault, Spousal Support and Motorcycle Accidents.

DAVID WIRTH

COSHOCTON, OHIO

(See Columbus)

Insurance Law, Negligence, Legal Malpractice, Subrogation, Personal Injury, Probate.

SHRYOCK & MORRISON

CUYAHOGA FALLS, OHIO

(See Wickliffe)

Family Law, Domestic Relations, Mediation, Juvenile Law, Criminal Law, Traffic Violations, Personal Injury.

ABRAMSON & O'CONNELL, LLC

DAYTON, OHIO

(See Columbus)

Personal Injury, Wrongful Death, Medical Malpractice, Hospital Negligence, Professional Negligence, Premises Liability, Automobile Accidents.

ALTICK & CORWIN CO., L.P.A.

Established in 1853

1700 ONE DAYTON CENTRE
ONE SOUTH MAIN STREET
DAYTON, OHIO 45402
Telephone: 937-223-1201
Fax: 937-223-5100
Email: info@altickcorwin.com
URL: http://www.altickcorwin.com

General Practice. Administrative, Bankruptcy, Business, Collections, Condominium, Creditors' Rights, Criminal, Commercial Law, Decedent's Estates, Employee Benefits, Elder Law, Employment, Estate Planning, Family Law, Immigration and Naturalization, Insurance Defense, Labor Relations, Local Government, Military Law, Municipal, Personal Injury, Probate, Products Liability, Real Estate, Social Security, Taxation, Workers' Compensation, Zoning.

FIRM PROFILE: ALTICK & CORWIN CO., L.P.A. is a results-oriented, full-service law firm with deep roots in the history of southwestern Ohio. Our present organization is the successor to an unbroken series of partnerships which began serving the Dayton area in 1853. The firm is currently comprised of 21 attorneys and an excellent support staff.

Sound advice and exceptional legal services since 1853.

HUGH H. ALTICK (1905-1990)

ROBERT K. CORWIN (1913-1998)

ROBERT N. FARQUHAR, born Dayton, Ohio, April 23, 1936; admitted to bar, 1961, Ohio; 1963, U.S. District Court, Southern District of Ohio; 1966, U.S. Court of Appeals, Sixth Circuit; 1978, U.S. Supreme Court; 1994, Michigan. *Education:* Kenyon College (A.B., 1958); Cornell Law School (J.D., 1961). Phi Delta Phi. Municipal Attorney, City of Centerville, Ohio, 1969-2004. Law Director, City of Oakwood, Ohio, 1998-2004. Secretary, Miami Conservancy District, 1990-2004. Trustee, 1974—and President of Board, 1982-1987, Dayton Law Library Association. Member, 1988-1994 and 1997-2003 and Chairman, 1999-2001, Commission on Character and Fitness, Ohio State Supreme Court. *Member:* Dayton (Member, Executive Committee, 1982-1986; President, 1984-1985), Ohio State (Chairman, Committee on Legal Ethics and Professional Conduct, 1982-1986; Member, Executive Committee, 1988-1991 and Council of Delegates, 1988—) and American (Member, House of Delegates, 2001-2004) Bar Associations. ***PRACTICE AREAS:*** Corporate Law; Local Government Law. ***Email:*** farquhar@altickcorwin.com

MARSHALL D. RUCHMAN, born Fort Wayne, Indiana, March 6, 1934; admitted to bar, 1964, Indiana and Ohio. *Education:* Indiana University (B.S., 1955; LL.B., 1964; J.D., 1967). Phi Delta Phi. *Member:* Dayton, Ohio State (Member, Board of Governors, Estate Planning, Trust and Probate Sections), Indiana State and American Bar Associations. ***PRACTICE AREAS:*** Corporate Law; Wills; Trusts and Estates; Business Law; Employee Benefits. ***Email:*** ruchmanm@altickcorwin.com

DENNIS J. ADKINS, born Dayton, Ohio, January 26, 1955; admitted to bar, 1986, Ohio and U.S. District Court, Southern District of Ohio; 1987, U.S. Court of Appeals, Sixth Circuit. *Education:* University of Dayton (B.S., 1981); Salmon P. Chase College of Law (J.D., 1986). *Member:* Dayton (Chair, Criminal Law Committee, 1999), Ohio State and American Bar Associations; Ohio Academy of Trial Lawyers; The Association of Trial Lawyers of America; Ohio Association of Criminal Defense Lawyers. ***PRACTICE AREAS:*** Litigation; Criminal Law; Negligence Law; Personal Injury; Products Liability; Medical Malpractice. ***Email:*** adkinsd@altickcorwin.com

PHILIP B. HERRON, born Athens, Ohio, November 25, 1939; admitted to bar, 1966, Ohio; 1975, U.S. District Court, Southern District of Ohio and U.S. Court of Appeals, Sixth Circuit; 1981, U.S. Court of Military Appeals. *Education:* Ohio Wesleyan University (B.A., 1962); The Ohio State University (J.D., 1965). Phi Delta Phi. Law Director: City of Moraine, 1977-1985, 1986-1993, 2000-2001; City of Riverside, 1994—; City of Trotwood, 1998-2004. *Member:* Dayton and Ohio State Bar Associations. [Maj. U.S. Air Force, 1966-1975, Military Judge USAF Trial Judiciary]. ***PRACTICE AREAS:*** Municipal Law; Zoning, Planning and Land Use; Eminent Domain. ***Email:*** herronp@altickcorwin.com

DEBORAH J. ADLER, born Bowling Green, Ohio, November 12, 1956; admitted to bar, 1982, Ohio and U.S. District Court, Southern District of Ohio. *Education:* University of Dayton (B.S., 1978; J.D., 1981). Certified Ohio Workers' Compensation Specialist. *Member:* Dayton and Ohio State Bar Associations; Miami Valley Trial Lawyers Association (Board Member, 1999—); Ohio Academy of Trial Lawyers (Board Member, 1997-1999); American Trial Lawyers Association; National and Ohio Employment Lawyers Association; Dayton Employment Lawyers Association. ***REPORTED CASES:*** State Ex rel Smith v. Industrial Comm., 98 Ohio State 3d 16, 2003. ***PRACTICE AREAS:*** Workers Compensation Law; Social Security Disability; Employment Litigation; Discrimination; Civil Practice; Trial Practice. ***Email:*** adlerd@altickcorwin.com

STEPHEN M. McHUGH, born Dayton, Ohio, March 31, 1953; admitted to bar, 1979, Ohio, U.S. District Court, Southern District of Ohio and U.S. Court of Appeals, Sixth Circuit. *Education:* Ohio Northern University (B.A., 1975; J.D., 1978). Law Director: City of Oxford, Ohio, 1989—; City of Beavercreek, Ohio, 1998—; Miami Conservancy District, 2004—; City of Trotwood, 2004—. *Member:* Dayton and Ohio State Bar Associations (Member and Chair, 1996-1998, State of Ohio, Local Government Law Committee; Judges' Committee on Notary Public). ***PRACTICE AREAS:*** Municipal Law; Zoning Law; Trusts and Estates; Corporate Law. ***Email:*** mchughs@altickcorwin.com

SCOTT A. LIBERMAN, born Knoxville, Tennessee, January 19, 1966; admitted to bar, 1992, Ohio and U.S. District Court, Southern District of Ohio; 2004, U.S. District Court, Northern District of Ohio. *Education:* Indiana University at Bloomington (B.S., 1988); University of Dayton (J.D., 1991). Phi Alpha Delta. Interim Municipal Attorney, City of Centerville, Ohio, 2004—. Board of Zoning Appeals, Washington Township, Ohio, 1997-2004. *Member:* Dayton (Member, Judges' Committee on Notaries Public) and Ohio State Bar Associations; Commercial Law League of America. ***PRACTICE AREAS:*** Creditors' Rights; Collections; Civil Trial; Real Estate; Municipal Law; Corporate Law; Fair Debt Collection Practices Act Defense. ***Email:*** liberman@altickcorwin.com

DONALD K. SCOTT, born Oakland, California, September 19, 1951; admitted to bar, 1986, Ohio and U.S. District Court, Southern District of Ohio. *Education:* Wright State University (B.A., cum laude, 1979); Salmon P. Chase College of Law (J.D., 1986). Certified Ohio Workers' Compensation Specialist. *Member:* Dayton and Ohio State Bar Associations; Ohio Academy of Trial Lawyers. ***PRACTICE AREAS:*** Workers Compensation; Social Security; Wrongful Termination; Employment Discrimination; Personal Injury. ***Email:*** scottd@altickcorwin.com

DALMA C. GRANDJEAN, admitted to bar, 1977, Ohio and U.S. District Court, Southern District of Ohio; 1980, U.S. Court of Appeals, Sixth Circuit; 1988, U.S. Court of Appeals, Federal Circuit. *Education:* University of Dayton (B.A., 1967; J.D., summa cum laude, 1977). City Attorney, City of Oakwood, Ohio, 2004—. Assistant Law Director, Trotwood, Ohio. Cooperating Attorney, Montgomery County Fair Housing Center. *Member:* Dayton (Chair, Family Law Committee; Fee Dispute Arbitration), Greene County, Ohio State and American (Member: Trial Practice Committee; Family Law Committee; International Law Committee; Local and State Government Law Committee; Sections on: Family Law; Litigation) Bar Associations; Association of Trial Lawyers of America; Ohio Academy of Trial Lawyers; Miami Valley Trial Lawyers; Miami Valley Family Law Forum (President); International Child Abduction Attorney Network. ***LANGUAGES:*** Hungarian. ***PRACTICE AREAS:*** Family Law; Employment Law; Municipal Law; Fair Housing; Wills; Divorce; Dissolution of Marriage; Child Custody; Child Support; Alimony; Domestic Violence; Visitation Rights; Military Divorce; Premarital Agreements; Cohabitation Agreements; Hague Convention Proceedings; International Child Abduction; Juvenile Law. ***Email:*** grandjed@altickcorwin.com

PETER R. CERTO, born Mineola, New York, March 13, 1952; admitted to bar, 1979, Ohio and U.S. District Court, Southern District of Ohio. *Education:* University of Dayton (B.S., 1973; J.D., 1978). Acting Municipal Judge, Dayton, Ohio, 1991-2003. Adjunct Professor, Criminal Procedure, University of Dayton, 1985-1986. *Member:* Dayton (Chairman, Criminal Law Section, 1991-1993 and 1995-1997) and Ohio State Bar Associations; Ohio Association of Criminal Defense Lawyers; Miami Valley Trial Lawyers Association; Family Law Forum (President, 2001-2002). ***PRACTICE AREAS:*** Criminal Law; Probate; Domestic Relations; Personal Injury; DWI. ***Email:*** certop@altickcorwin.com

(This Listing Continued)

JONATHAN B. FREEMAN, born Dayton, Ohio, March 15, 1968; admitted to bar, 1997, Ohio and U.S. District Court, Southern District of Ohio. *Education:* Washington and Jefferson College (B.A., 1990); University of Massachusetts (M.S., 1992); University of Dayton School of Law (J.D., 1996). *Member:* Dayton, Ohio State and American Bar Associations; The Association of Trial Lawyers of America. ***PRACTICE AREAS:*** Insurance Defense; Criminal; Personal Injury; Civil Litigation. ***Email:*** freemanj@altickcorwin.com

MATTHEW D. STOKELY, born St. Louis, Missouri, December 27, 1960; admitted to bar, 1986, Connecticut; 1987, New York; 1993, Ohio. *Education:* Fairfield University (B.A., 1983); University of Bridgeport School of Law (J.D., 1986). Member, 1983-1984, Research Editor, 1984-1985, University of Bridgeport Law Review. *Member:* Dayton, Ohio State and American (Member, Labor and Employment Law Sections) Bar Associations. ***PRACTICE AREAS:*** Labor and Employment; Employee Benefits; Workers Compensation; Municipal Law. ***Email:*** stokelym@altickcorwin.com

---

DAVID E. LARSON, born Dayton, Ohio, February 9, 1945; admitted to bar, 1979, Ohio; 1980, U.S. District Court, Southern District of Ohio. *Education:* Wittenberg University (B.A., 1967); University of North Carolina (M.P.A., 1974); Ohio State University (J.D., 1979). U.S. Peace Corps Volunteer, Turkey, 1967-1969; U.S. Department of Housing and Urban Development, 1971-1979. *Member:* Dayton (Chair of Debtor Creditor Committee, 1993-1994; Vice Chair, 2004-2005) and Ohio State Bar Associations; American Immigration Lawyers Association. ***LANGUAGES:*** Turkish. ***PRACTICE AREAS:*** Immigration Law; Personal Bankruptcy. ***Email:*** larsond@altickcorwin.com

BRENT A. CRANE, born Norman, Oklahoma; admitted to bar, 1995, Ohio; 2000, U.S. District Court, Southern District of Ohio, U.S. Court of Appeals, Sixth Circuit and U.S. Supreme Court. *Education:* Wright State University (B.A., 1991); Capital Univserity (J.D., 1995). *Member:* Dayton and Ohio State Bar Associations. ***PRACTICE AREAS:*** Probate; Estate Planning; Trust Law; Small Business Law; Real Estate. ***Email:*** craneb@altickcorwin.com

JULIE COPE HAMMOND, born Louisville, Kentucky, November 29, 1973; admitted to bar, 2000, Ohio and U.S. District Court, Southern District of Ohio; registered to practice before U.S. Patent and Trademark Office. *Education:* Hanover College (B.A., 1995); University of Dayton (J.D., 2000). *Member:* Dayton, Ohio State and American Bar Associations. ***PRACTICE AREAS:*** Employment Law; Workers Compensation; Social Security Disability. ***Email:*** hammondj@altickcorwin.com

LYNNE M. FLEMING, born Medford, Massachusetts, October 13, 1960; admitted to bar, 1997, New Jersey and Pennsylvania; 1998, U.S. District Court, District of New Jersey and U.S. District Court, Eastern District of Pennsylvania; 2004, Ohio; 2005, U.S. District Court, Southern District of Ohio. *Education:* Rowan University (B.A., 1993); Widener University (J.D., 1997). *Member:* Dayton and Ohio State Bar Associations. ***PRACTICE AREAS:*** Criminal Law; Civil Litigation. ***Email:*** flemingl@altickcorwin.com

OF COUNSEL

DAVID L. HALL, born Akron, Ohio, October 12, 1940; admitted to bar, 1968, Ohio; 1974, U.S. Supreme Court; 1980, U.S. District Court, Southern District of Ohio, U.S. Court of Appeals, Sixth Circuit, U.S. Claims Court and U.S. Supreme Court. *Education:* Wilmington College (A.B., 1965); Case Western Reserve University (J.D., 1968). Phi Alpha Theta. Law Clerk to Judge David S. Porter, U.S. District Court, Southern District of Ohio, 1968-1969. *Member:* Dayton, Greene County, Clinton County and Ohio State Bar Associations. ***LANGUAGES:*** Russian, German and Spanish. ***PRACTICE AREAS:*** Labor and Employment; Business Law; Corporate Law; Commercial Law; Computers and Software Law; General Practice; Litigation. ***Email:*** halld@altickcorwin.com

ADELE M. RILEY, born New Britain, Connecticut, April 3, 1947; admitted to bar, 1982, Ohio and U.S. District Court, Southern District of Ohio. *Education:* Boston University (B.S., 1969); University of Dayton (M.S., 1979; J.D., 1981). Member, Judicial Council, (President), Thurgood Marshall Law Society. *Member:* Dayton (Chair and President, Diversity Issues, 1995-1997; Secretary/Treasurer, Inn of Court, 1999—), Ohio State, American and National Bar Associations. ***PRACTICE AREAS:*** Alternative Dispute Resolution; Government; Probate; Real Estate; Federal Practice. ***Email:*** riley@altickcorwin.com

REPRESENTATIVE CLIENTS: City of Centerville; City of Oxford; City of Riverside; City of Beavercreek; City of Trotwood; City of Riverside; City of Oakwood; Electra Form, Inc.; Formex, Inc.; Kettering Civil Service Commission; The Miami Conservancy District; Miami Valley Cable Council; Woodland Cemetery Assn.; Daytronic Corp.; Realmark Properties; Anchor Fabricators, Inc.
SPECIAL COUNSEL: City of Kettering; Dayton Board of Education.

THOMAS M. BAGGOTT

130 WEST SECOND STREET, SUITE 2103
DAYTON, OHIO 45402
Telephone: 937-461-8800
Fax: 937-461-8818
Email: tom@baggottlaw.com
URL: http://www.baggottlaw.com

Wills, Probate, Trusts and Estates, Estate Planning, Guardianship, Adoption Law, Conservatorship, Small Business Corporations Law.

THOMAS M. BAGGOTT, born Dayton, Ohio, February 10, 1943; admitted to bar, 1971, Ohio and U.S. District Court, Southern District of Ohio; 1997, U.S. Supreme Court. *Education:* Ohio University; The Ohio State University (B.A., 1967); Ohio Northern University (J.D., 1971). Phi Alpha Delta. General Referee, 1971-1973, Special Referee, 1981-1992, Magistrate, 2000-2003. Montgomery County Probate Court. Prosecutor, City of Vandalia, 1973-1974. Adjunct Professor: Capital University School of Law, 2005—. *Member:* Dayton (Treasurer, 1985-1986; Member, 1986—and Chairman, 1996-1997, Committee on Grievances and Discipline) and Ohio State Bar Associations; Ohio Academy of Trial Lawyers (Trustee, 1977-1984); The Association of Trial Lawyers of America; Ohio Association of Magistrates (Chairman, Probate Committee; Member, Board of Trustees, 2000-2003).

(This Listing Continued)

PRACTICE AREAS: Wills; Trusts and Estates; Probate; Estate Planning; Guardianship; Conservatorship; Adoption Law; Small Business Corporations.

BAILEY CAVALIERI LLC

KETTERING TOWER
SUITE 2310, 40 NORTH MAIN STREET
DAYTON, OHIO 45423-0001
Telephone: 937-223-4701
Fax: 937-223-0170
URL: http://www.baileycavalieri.com

Columbus, Ohio Office: Suite 2100, One Columbus, 10 West Broad Street. 43215-3422. Telephone: 614-221-3155. Fax: 614-221-0479.

General Civil and Trial Practice. Director and Officer Liability, Antitrust, Banking, Bankruptcy and Commercial Transactions, Corporate, Corporate Financing, Creditors Remedies, Environmental, Employee Benefits and ERISA, Estate Planning, Trust, Probate, Intellectual Property, Internet and E-Commerce, Labor and Employment, Products Liability, Public Utility, Real Estate, Finance, Securities and Taxation Law. Appellate, Communications, Energy Deregulation, Health Care, Insurance, Mergers and Acquisitions, Professional Liability, Retail and Catalog Law, Technology and Science.

FIRM PROFILE: At Bailey Cavalieri, we realize the challenges facing today's businesses. Superior services from an experienced team of lawyers can smooth the path to help companies succeed by avoiding the many legal pitfalls that exist in today's business environment.

From offices in Columbus and Dayton, Ohio, our attorneys provide innovative and practical solutions to solve clients' challenges and help them run their businesses effectively.

We are guided by the belief that clients deserve superior service, and we strive to consistently provide that level of service to our clients. We understand the unique relationship between client and lawyer and work to exceed our clients' expectations.

As outside counsel, we bring a hard-to-find level of sophistication and knowledge of our specialty practice areas into play. In situations where the client has in-house legal staff, Bailey Cavalieri is an extension of that staff, understanding and furthering the client's objective in each transaction or litigation matter.

PRINCIPAL OF FIRM

ROBERT B. BERNER, born Dayton, Ohio, February 15, 1959; admitted to bar, 1984, Ohio, U.S. District Court, Southern District of Ohio and U.S. Court of Appeals, Sixth Circuit. *Education:* Indiana University (B.S., 1981); Capital University (J.D., 1984). *Member:* Dayton and Ohio State Bar Associations; American Bankruptcy Law Forum. ***PRACTICE AREAS:*** Bankruptcy; Commercial; Real Estate; Cemetery Law; Municipal Law. ***Email:*** robert.berner@baileycavalieri.com

(For complete biographical data on other personnel, see Professional Biography at Columbus, Ohio)

THOMAS D. BERRY

1839 EAST STROOP ROAD
DAYTON, OHIO 45429
Telephone: 937-294-7398
Fax: 937-294-6812
Email: 110968@msn.com
URL: http://www.daytonbankruptcylawyer.com

Probate, Wills, Bankruptcy, Consumer Bankruptcy, Chapter 7 and Chapter 13.

THOMAS D. BERRY, born El Paso, Texas, February 6, 1950; admitted to bar, 1978, California; 1983, Ohio; 1986, U.S. District Court, Southern District of Ohio. *Education:* Wright State University; Ohio State University (B.Sc., 1972; J.D., 1974). *Member:* Montgomery County and Ohio State Bar Associations. ***PRACTICE AREAS:*** Probate; Domestic Relations; Bankruptcy.

BIESER, GREER & LANDIS, LLP

400 NATIONAL CITY CENTER
6 NORTH MAIN STREET
DAYTON, OHIO 45402-1908
Telephone: 937-223-3277
Fax: 937-223-6339
Email: biesergreer.com
URL: http://www.biesergreer.com

General Civil Practice, Trial Practice, Business Litigation, Professional Liability Defense, Personal Injury Defense, Products Liability Defense, Corporate Law, Employment Law, Commercial Law, Probate, Tax Law, White Collar Criminal Defense, Arbitration, Mediation.

FIRM PROFILE: A firm with roots in Dayton going back to 1854, Bieser, Greer & Landis addresses legal problems with modern insights and current technologies. The members of the firm prepare and try complex cases in such areas as business and corporate disputes, intellectual property, construction, employment, professional liability, environmental, white-collar criminal charges and personal injury claims.

Bieser, Greer & Landis complements a strong emphasis on litigation with general practice services in the fields of real estate, estate planning and administration, and small business and professional organizations. The firm is medium sized by design, so as to be large enough to bring needed resources and expertise to complex matters, yet small enough to mandate effi-

(This Listing Continued)

BIESER, GREER & LANDIS, LLP, Dayton—Continued

cient handling of those matters. Two of the firm's partners are Fellows of the American College of Trial Lawyers, six are listed in Best Lawyers in America, and nine of the firm's partners carry the highest eligibility rating in Martindale-Hubbell.

MEMBERS OF FIRM

IRVIN G. BIESER (1902-1989)

ROWAN A. GREER, JR. (1907-1967)

ROBERT K. LANDIS (1915-1991)

CHARLES D. SHOOK, born Dayton, Ohio, August 14, 1927; admitted to bar, 1952, Ohio. *Education:* University of Chicago (A.B., 1947); The Ohio State University (LL.B., 1952). Member, Editorial Board, Ohio State Law Journal, 1951-1952. *Member:* Dayton (Treasurer, 1971-1972), Ohio State and American Bar Associations. ***PRACTICE AREAS:*** Commercial Banking; Lender Law; Real Estate; Estate Planning; Probate. ***Email:*** cds@biesergreer.com

EDWARD L. SHANK, born Dayton, Ohio, January 6, 1929; admitted to bar, 1956, Ohio; 1957, Michigan. *Education:* Miami University (B.S., 1950); University of Michigan (J.D., 1956); Georgetown University Law Center (LL.M., 1957). Listed under Real Estate Practice in Best Lawyers in America; Listed under Estate Planning/Trusts Practice in Ohio Super Lawyers, 2005. *Member:* Dayton, Ohio State and American Bar Associations. ***PRACTICE AREAS:*** Trusts and Estates; Wills; Probate. ***Email:*** els@biesergreer.com

DAVID C. GREER, born Dayton, Ohio, February 14, 1937; admitted to bar, 1962, Ohio. *Education:* Yale University (B.A., 1959; LL.B., 1962). Phi Delta Phi; Order of the Coif; Phi Beta Kappa. Member, Editorial Board, Yale Law Review, 1961-1962. Life Member, Sixth Circuit Judicial Conference. Listed in Best Lawyers in America. Ranked first among all lawyers in Ohio Super Lawyers 2004, 2005. Listed in Dayton Business Journal Best of the Bar, 2005. *Member:* Dayton (President, 1981-1982), Ohio State and American Bar Associations. Fellow, American College of Trial Lawyers. ***PRACTICE AREAS:*** Complex Litigation; Business Litigation; Commercial Litigation; Personal Injury Defense; Professional Liability Defense. ***Email:*** dcg@biesergreer.com

IRVIN G. BIESER, JR., born Dayton, Ohio, June 17, 1941; admitted to bar, 1966, Ohio. *Education:* Harvard University (A.B., magna cum laude, 1963; LL.B., 1966). Author: "Drugs & the Law," Cincinnati Law Review, Vol. 36, No. 1, 1967. Instructor of Law, University of Liberia School of Law, Monrovia, Liberia, 1967-1968. *Member:* Dayton, Ohio State and American Bar Associations. ***PRACTICE AREAS:*** Estate Planning; Trust Planning; Estate Administration; Nonprofit and Charitable Organizations; Charitable Trusts and Foundations; Business Law. ***Email:*** igb@biesergreer.com

LEO F. KREBS, born Botkins, Ohio, June 9, 1937; admitted to bar, 1966, Ohio. *Education:* University of Dayton (B.A., 1959); Georgetown University (J.D., 1965). Phi Delta Phi. Associate Editor, Georgetown Law Review, 1964-1965. Legal Deputy, Montgomery County Probate Court, 1966-1968. Listed in Best Lawyers in America. Listed in Ohio Super Lawyers 2004. *Member:* Dayton, Ohio State and American Bar Associations. Fellow, American College of Trial Lawyers. ***PRACTICE AREAS:*** Products Liability Defense; Personal Injury Defense; Professional Liability Defense; Insurance Defense; Medical Malpractice Defense. ***Email:*** lfk@biesergreer.com

HOWARD PENN KRISHER, II, born Dayton, Ohio, September 19, 1947; admitted to bar, 1975, Ohio. *Education:* Princeton University (A.B., magna cum laude, 1969); The Ohio State University (J.D., cum laude, 1974). Listed in Best Lawyers in America. Listed in Ohio Super Lawyers 2004. *Member:* Dayton, Ohio State and American Bar Associations. ***PRACTICE AREAS:*** Medical Malpractice Defense; Personal Injury Defense; Hospital Law; Law Enforcement Liability; Business Litigation; Commercial Litigation. ***Email:*** hpk@biesergreer.com

MICHAEL W. KRUMHOLTZ, born Dayton, Ohio, December 3, 1953; admitted to bar, 1979, Ohio. *Education:* Denison University (B.A., 1976); University of Cincinnati (J.D., 1979). Moot Court. Assistant Prosecutor, Montgomery County, 1979-1981. Recipient, Eugene Weir Award for Ethics and Professionalism, Ohio State Bar Association. Adjunct Professor, University of Dayton School of Law, Trial Practice/Evidence, 2000-2002. Listed in Best Lawyers in America. Listed in Ohio Super Lawyers 2004, 2005; Listed in Dayton Business Journal Best of the Bar, 2004. *Member:* Dayton (Bar Counsel, 1997-2001), Ohio State and American Bar Associations; American Bar Foundation. ***PRACTICE AREAS:*** Personal Injury Defense; Business Litigation; Commercial Litigation; Professional Liability Defense; Products Liability Defense; White Collar Criminal Defense; Business Crimes; Arbitration; Mediation. ***Email:*** mwk@biesergreer.com

JOHN F. HAVILAND, JR., born Clifton, New Jersey, October 14, 1959; admitted to bar, 1985, Ohio. *Education:* University of Dayton (B.S., cum laude, 1982; J.D., cum laude, 1985). Phi Alpha Delta. Managing Editor, University of Dayton Law Review, 1984-1985. *Member:* Dayton, Ohio State and American Bar Associations. ***PRACTICE AREAS:*** Medical Malpractice Defense; Personal Injury Defense; Business Litigation; Commercial Litigation; Intellectual Property Litigation. ***Email:*** jfh@biesergreer.com

DAVID P. WILLIAMSON, born Camden, New Jersey, July 2, 1953; admitted to bar, 1978, Ohio. *Education:* Ohio University (B.A., summa cum laude, 1975); The Ohio State University (J.D., 1978). Phi Beta Kappa. Moot Court; The Order of Barristers. Adjunct Professor, University of Dayton School of Law, Remedies/Administrative Law, 1999—. Magistrate, Montgomery County Common Pleas Court, 1983-1988. President, Ohio Metro Bar Association, 2000-2001. Listed in Best Lawyers in America. Listed in Ohio Super Lawyers 2004, 2005. Listed in Dayton Business Journal Best of the Bar, 2004. *Member:* Dayton (President, 2000-2001), Ohio State and American Bar Associations. ***PRACTICE AREAS:*** Business Litigation; Commercial Litigation; Construction Litigation; Governmental Law; White Collar Criminal Defense; Business Crimes; Arbitration; Mediation. ***Email:*** dpw@biesergreer.com

JAMES H. GREER, born Dayton, Ohio, April 27, 1964; admitted to bar, 1990, Ohio. *Education:* Indiana University (B.A., 1986); University of Dayton (J.D., 1990). *Member:* Dayton, Ohio State and American Bar Associations. ***PRACTICE AREAS:*** Personal Injury Defense; Professional Liability Defense; Business Litigation; Commercial Litigation; Products Liability Defense; Construction Litigation. ***Email:*** jhg@biesergreer.com

CHARLES F. SHANE, born Washington, D.C., July 7, 1967; admitted to bar, 1993, Ohio. *Education:* Miami University (B.S., 1990); University of Dayton (J.D., cum laude, 1993). Member, University of Dayton Law Review, 1992-1993. *Member:* Dayton, Ohio State and American Bar Associations. ***PRACTICE AREAS:*** Complex Business Litigation; Commercial Litigation; Products Liability Defense; Construction Litigation; Personal Injury; Small Business Law; Business Counseling. ***Email:*** cfs@biesergreer.com

JOSEPH C. OEHLERS, born St. Paul, Minnesota, April 13, 1965; admitted to bar, 1995, Ohio. *Education:* Harvard University (B.A., 1987); University of Dayton (J.D., cum laude, 1995). Adjunct Professor, Trial Practice/Evidence, University of Dayton School of Law, 2000-2002. Member: St. Joseph Children's Treatment Center Board of Trustees; Dayton Metro Library Board of Directors. Member, Board of Trustees, United Rehabilitation Service. President, Harvard Club of Dayton. Chair, Harvard Club Schools Committee. *Member:* Dayton (Member, Certified Grievance Committee), Ohio State and American Bar Associations. ***PRACTICE AREAS:*** Business Litigation; Commercial Litigation; Tax Litigation; Personal Injury Defense; Products Liability Defense; White Collar Criminal Defense. ***Email:*** jco@biesergreer.com

CARLA J. MORMAN, born Oswego, New York, June 12, 1970; admitted to bar, 1996, Ohio. *Education:* Pennsylvania State University (B.A., 1992); University of Dayton (J.D., 1996). Phi Beta Kappa. Adjunct Professor, Legal Writing/Appellate Advocacy, University of Dayton School of Law, 2000-2002. *Member:* Dayton, Ohio State and American Bar Associations. ***PRACTICE AREAS:*** Business Litigation; Commercial Litigation; Medical Malpractice Defense; Insurance Defense; Employment Law. ***Email:*** cjm@biesergreer.com

JAMES P. FLEISHER, born Xenia, Ohio, October 12, 1966; admitted to bar, 1992, Ohio. *Education:* University of Notre Dame (B.A., 1989); University of Cincinnati (J.D., 1992). *Member:* Dayton, Ohio State and Federal (President, Dayton Chapter, 2004—) Bar Associations. [Captain, USAF, JAGC, 1993-1997]. ***PRACTICE AREAS:*** Business Litigation; Commercial Litigation; Personal Injury Defense; White Collar Criminal Defense; Military Law; Asset Forfeiture. ***Email:*** jpf@biesergreer.com

KAREN T. DUNLEVEY, born Philadelphia, Pennsylvania, October 22, 1970; admitted to bar, 1996, Ohio. *Education:* Clarion University of Pennsylvania (B.S., magna cum laude, 1992); University of Dayton (J.D., 1996). Editor, University of Dayton Law Review. *Member:* Dayton, Ohio State and American Bar Associations. (Certified Specialist in Labor and Employment Law, Ohio State Bar Association). ***PRACTICE AREAS:*** Employment Law; Employment Litigation; Commercial Litigation; Professional Malpractice. ***Email:*** ktd@biesergreer.com

ASSOCIATES

JOSEPH L. FELLER, born Gibson City, Illinois, November 25, 1972; admitted to bar, 1998, Ohio; U.S. District Court, Southern District of Ohio. *Education:* University of Notre Dame (B.B.A., Accounting, 1995); University of Dayton (J.D., 1998). Assistant Prosecutor, Montgomery County, 1998-2001. *Member:* Dayton, Ohio State, Federal and American Bar Associations. ***PRACTICE AREAS:*** Medical Malpractice Defense; Hospital Law; Business Litigation; Commercial Litigation; Criminal Defense. ***Email:*** jlf@biesergreer.com

GRETCHEN M. TREHERNE, born Cincinnati, Ohio, April 1, 1976; admitted to bar, 2001, Ohio and U.S. District Court, Southern District of Ohio. *Education:* Spring Hill College (B.A., summa cum laude, 1998); University of Dayton (J.D., cum laude, 2001). Member, Moot Court. Editor, University of Dayton Law Review. *Member:* Dayton, Ohio State and American Bar Associations. ***PRACTICE AREAS:*** Business Litigation; Commercial Litigation; Personal Injury Defense. ***Email:*** gmt@biesergreer.com

JENNIFER L. STUEVE, born Dayton, Ohio, July 22, 1977; admitted to bar, 2002, Ohio and U.S. District Court, Southern District of Ohio. *Education:* Miami University (B.S., 1999); University of Dayton (J.D., 2002). Member, Moot Court. *Member:* Dayton, Ohio State and American Bar Associations. ***PRACTICE AREAS:*** Business Litigation; Commercial Litigation; Domestic Relations; Employment Law. ***Email:*** jls@biesergreer.com

JOHN D. BODIN, born Cincinnati, Ohio, September 10, 1978; admitted to bar, 2003, Ohio. *Education:* Wittenberg University (B.A., 2000); University of Toledo (J.D., cum laude, 2003). Member, Moot Court Honor Board. *Member:* Dayton, Ohio State and American Bar Associations. ***PRACTICE AREAS:*** Business Litigation; Commercial Litigation; Personal Injury Defense. ***Email:*** jdb@biesergreer.com

REPRESENTATIVE CLIENTS: National City Bank, Dayton; Consolidated Rail Corp.; Columbia Gas Transmission Corp.; The Dayton Foundation; Greater Dayton Public Television, Inc.; Miami Valley Regional Transit Authority; Ohio Transit Risk Pool; Kettering Medical Center Network; Good Samaritan Hospital; Miami Valley Hospital; Stewart Title Guaranty Co.; Ohio Bar Liability Co.; Medical Protective Co.; Motorists Insurance Cos.; National Casualty Co.; St. Paul Insurance Cos.; Travelers Insurance Co.; United States Fidelity & Guaranty Co.; Cofap of America, Inc.; Leisure Lawn; Crawford & Company; Western Heritage Ins. Co.; Purity Foods, Inc.; Miller Valentine; Price WaterHouse-Coopers; Deloitte & Touche; United Technologies; Premier Integrated Medical Associates, LLC; Dayton Water Systems; Stone Center; Boeing Corp.; Victoria Theatre Association; EvenFlo; Vectren Energy Delivery of Ohio; Beerman Realty; Summit Solutions; Mead Corp.; Carrier, Inc.; GE Lighting, Inc.
REFERENCES: Bank One, Dayton, NA; National City Bank; Key Bank, NA.

ROGER E. BLOOMFIELD

P.O. BOX 9218
DAYTON, OHIO 45409-9218
Telephone: 937-438-5310
Email: bloomfield_law@att.net

Business Law, Nonprofit and Charitable Organizations, Taxation, Trusts and Estates, Wills and Probate, Real Estate.

ROGER E. BLOOMFIELD, born Lakewood, Ohio, December 31, 1945; admitted to bar, 1974, Ohio; 1977, U.S. Tax Court; 1979, U.S. Supreme Court; 1986, Arizona. *Education:* Wittenberg University (B.S.B.A., 1967); Case Western Reserve University (J.D.,

(This Listing Continued)

1974). Omicron Delta Kappa. Member, Case Western Reserve Law Review, 1968-1969. Fellow, Ohio State Bar Foundation. *Member:* Dayton, Ohio State (Corporation Law Committee, 1977—) and American Bar Associations; State Bar of Arizona.

REFERENCE: Fifth Third Bank.

BOGIN PATTERSON ELLIS SLATON & STUMP LLP

Established in 1977

1200 TALBOTT TOWER
131 NORTH LUDLOW STREET
DAYTON, OHIO 45402-1135
Telephone: 937-226-1200
FAX: 937-226-1625
Email: bp@bpess.com

Secured Creditors, Bankruptcy and Reorganization (Creditors), General Litigation, Arbitration, Real Estate Law, General Business Law, Non-Profit Corporation Law, Computer Law, Construction Law.

MEMBERS OF FIRM

DENNIS L. PATTERSON, born Dayton, Ohio, January 30, 1939; admitted to bar, 1964, Ohio; 1969, U.S. Supreme Court. *Education:* University of Miami; Case Western Reserve University (B.B.A., 1961; J.D., 1964). Phi Delta Phi. Listed in The Best Lawyers in America, 1989-2005. Member, Clayton Community Improvement Corp. *Member:* Dayton, Ohio State and American Bar Associations; The Association of Trial Lawyers of America. ***PRACTICE AREAS:*** Secured Creditors Rights; Bankruptcy; Litigation; Construction Litigation. ***Email:*** dpatterson@bpess.com

JAMES C. ELLIS, born Dayton, Ohio, August 30, 1956; admitted to bar, 1981, Ohio; 1983, U.S. District Court, Southern District of Ohio. *Education:* University of Dayton (B.A., magna cum laude, 1978); The Ohio State University (J.D., 1981). Elected, Huber Heights, Ohio City Council, 2003. Acting Judge, Montgomery County District Court, 1999-2001. Lecturer of Law, "Ethical Considerations in Practice of Bankruptcy Law," American Bankruptcy Forum, 1993; "Ohio Foreclosure and Repossession," National Business Institute, Inc. Member: American Bankruptcy Law Forum, 1992-1996; Advisory Council for Montgomery Developmental Center, 1997-2003. *Member:* Montgomery County, Ohio State (Member, Probate and Trust Law Section) and American Bar Associations; The Association of Trial Lawyers of America. ***PRACTICE AREAS:*** Secured Creditors Rights; Bankruptcy; Real Estate; Nonprofit Corporations; Litigation; Construction Litigation; Domestic Relations. ***Email:*** jellis@bpess.com

CURTIS F. SLATON, born Dayton, Ohio, July 22, 1960; admitted to bar, 1986, Ohio and U.S. District Court, Southern District of Ohio. *Education:* Wright State University (B.A., 1983); University of Dayton (J.D., cum laude, 1986). Member, Moot Court Team, 1985-1986. Member, University of Dayton Law Review, 1984-1985. Chairman, Butler Township Board of Zoning Appeals. Member, School of Law Alumni Board, University of Dayton. *Member:* Dayton, Ohio State and American Bar Associations; Ohio Academy of Trial Lawyers. ***PRACTICE AREAS:*** Secured Creditors Rights; Creditor Bankruptcy; Litigation; Business Law; Real Estate; Nonprofit Corporations; Computer Law. ***Email:*** cslaton@bpess.com

RANDALL L. STUMP, born Dayton, Ohio, July 20, 1959; admitted to bar, 1984, Ohio and U.S. Court of Appeals, Sixth Circuit. *Education:* University of Dayton (B.A., 1981; J.D., 1984). *Member:* Dayton, Ohio State and American Bar Associations. ***PRACTICE AREAS:*** Criminal Law; Civil Litigation; Personal Injury; Litigation; Employment Law; Creditor Bankruptcy; Juvenile Law; Domestic Relations.

ASHER BOGIN, born New York, N.Y., April 23, 1927; admitted to bar, 1950, New York; 1953, Ohio; 1967, U.S. Supreme Court; 1968, U.S. Tax Court. (Retired)

REPRESENTATIVE CLIENTS: City of Dayton; CityWide Development Corp.; United Way of the Greater Dayton Area, Inc.; Huber Heights Jaycees; Riverside Jaycees; Korie Investments, LLC; Belton, Inc.; Prosthetic Design, Inc.; Unsecured Creditors' Committee, U.S. Aeroteam, Inc. (Chap. 11); Unsecured Creditors' Committee; Allied Technology, Inc. (Chap. 11); Unsecured Creditors' Committee; Lima Distributors, Inc. (Chap. 11); Unsecured Creditors' Committee, Replicap Products, Inc. (Chap 11); Unsecured Creditors' Committee, Trinity Plastics, Inc. (Chap. 7); Unsecured Creditors' Committee; Kruse & Co., Inc. (Chap. 11); Unsecured Creditors' Committee Cassano's Inc. (Chap. 11); Area Agency on Aging PSA2; Lewis & Michael Moving & Storage; Certifichecks, Inc.; West Dayton Steel Service.
LOCAL COUNSEL FOR: American General Life and Accident Insurance Co.; Citibank/Citicorp; Signet Bank/Maryland; First National Bank of Commerce; TCF Financial, Inc.; Navistar Financial Corp.; 1st Source Bank; ITC Acceptance Co.; ING (U.S.) Capital; Times Publishing Co.; Southland Publishing Co., Inc.; Wayne Bank; First Bank of Richmond; Kowa Co., Ltd.; Mid-Atlantic Finance; Homeland Financial Group; Small Business Loan Source.

KAREN DENISE BRADLEY

130 WEST 2ND STREET, SUITE 1818
DAYTON, OHIO 45402
Telephone: 937-226-1212
Fax: 937-226-1224
Email: bradlw@main-net.com
URL: http://www.karenlawfirm.com

Immigration Law.

KAREN DENISE BRADLEY, born Belize City, Belize, April 26, 1964; admitted to bar, 1996, Ohio. *Education:* Fordham University (B.A., 1990); University of Dayton (J.D., 1994). Phi Alpha Delta. *Member:* Dayton and Ohio State Bar Associations; American Immigration Lawyers Association. ***LANGUAGES:*** Spanish. ***PRACTICE AREAS:*** Immigration.

BRANNON & ASSOCIATES

130 WEST SECOND STREET, SUITE 900
DAYTON, OHIO 45402-1590
Telephone: 937-228-2306
Fax: 937-228-8475
Email: dbrannon@branlaw.com
URL: http://www.branlaw.com

Personal Injury, Complex Litigation, Commercial Litigation, Medical Malpractice, Criminal Litigation and Appellate Practice Law, Matrimonial Law.

DWIGHT D. BRANNON, born Jamestown, Tennessee, March 30, 1948; admitted to bar, 1974, Ohio; 1975, U.S. District Court, Southern District of Ohio; 1981, U.S. Supreme Court; 1982, U.S. Court of Appeals, Sixth Circuit; 1985, Florida and U.S. District Court, Eastern District of Kentucky; 1999, U.S. District Court, Eastern District of Wisconsin. *Education:* University of Dayton (B.S., cum laude, 1970); Salmon P. Chase College of Law (J.D., with honors, 1974). Order of the Curia. Law Review. Research Editor, Chase Law Forum, 1973-1974. Former Law Director, Village of New Lebanon, Ohio. Former Assistant City of Dayton Prosecutor. Fellow: American Trial Lawyers, National College of Advocacy. *Member:* Dayton, Ohio State and American Bar Associations; Miami Valley Trial Lawyers Association; Ohio Association of Trial Lawyers; Association of Trial Lawyers of America. (Board Certified Civil Trial Advocate by the National Board of Trial Advocacy). ***REPORTED CASES:*** Newton v. Ohio Univ. Sch. of Osteopathic Med. (1993), 91 Ohio App. 3d 703; Quill v. R.A. Investment Co., 124 Ohio App. 3d 653 (1997); Disciplinary Counsel v. Holzer (1997), 78 Ohio St. 3d 309; State ex. rel. Bloomingdale v. Fairborn (1983), 20 Ohio St. 3d 142; State ex. rel. FOP v. Dayton, 49 Ohio St. 2d 219 (1977); State v. Mundy (1994), 99 Ohio App. 3d 275; State ex. rel.. Crossman v. Greene County Bd. of Elections (1999), 87 Ohio St. 3d 132. ***PRACTICE AREAS:*** Personal Injury; Medical Malpractice; Wrongful Death; Criminal Defense; Products Liability; Administrative Law; Appellate Practice; Complex Litigation; Contracts; Employment Law; Labor Law; Economic Development; General Practice; Business Litigation.

REPRESENTATIVE CLIENTS: Ascent Solutions, Inc. (ASI); Neoworx, Inc.; Dayton Power and Light; Employment Organizations (i.e. S.O.L.I.D.).

BUECHNER, HAFFER, O'CONNELL, MEYERS, HEALEY & KOENIG CO., L.P.A.

DAYTON, OHIO

(See Cincinnati)

General Practice. Estate and Gift Taxation, Probate, Family Law, Corporate, Negligence, Medical Legal Products Liability, Real Estate, Construction, Land Use, Zoning and Eminent Domain Law. Trials and Appeals, Pension and Profit Sharing, Federal Income.

BURDGE LAW OFFICE CO., LPA

Established in 1982

2299 MIAMISBURG-CENTERVILLE ROAD
DAYTON, OHIO 45459-3817
Telephone: 937-432-9500
Fax: 937-432-9503
Toll Free: 888-331-6422
URL: http://www.ohioconsumerlaw.com
Email: Ron@OhioLemonLaw.com
URL: http://www.OhioLemonLaw.com

Consumer Law, Lemon Law, Class Actions, Consumer Fraud, Consumer Protection, Warranty Law, Ohio Consumer Sales Practices Act, Fair Credit Reporting.

FIRM PROFILE: Burdge Law Office is known throughout Ohio as a leading consumer law practice representing consumers for more than 26 years. This law practice is dedicated to fighting for the rights of consumers in the areas of lemon law, auto fraud, mortgage fraud, and fair credit reporting.

RONALD L. BURDGE, born Dayton, Ohio, June 25, 1948; admitted to bar, 1978, Ohio; 1979, U.S. District Court, Southern District of Ohio; 1982, U.S. Court of Appeals, Sixth Circuit; 1989, U.S. Supreme Court; 2004, U.S. District Court, Northern and Southern Districts of Indiana; 2005, Kentucky. *Education:* Merced College (A.A., 1973); San Diego State University (B.A., 1975); University of Dayton (J.D., 1978). Named: 2004 Consumer Law Trial Attorney of the Year; 2005 Ohio Super Lawyer, National Association of Consumer Advocates. *Member:* Dayton, Cincinnati, Butler County, Greene County and Ohio State Bar Associations; The Association of Trial Lawyers of America; Ohio Academy of Trial Lawyers; National Association of Consumer Advocates; Consumers for Auto Reliability and Safety. Certified by the National Board of Trial Advocacy. ***REPORTED CASES:*** Bolt v. Yamaha (2004) 2004-Ohio 1205, 2004 App. LEXIS 1052; Abel v. Keybank USA (2004), 2004 U.S. Dist. LEXIS 4601; Cincinnati ex rel Ritter v. Cincinnati REds LLC (2002) 2002-Ohio 2078, 150 Ohio App.3d 728; Boyle v. Daimler Chrysler Corp. (2002); 2002-Ohio 4199, 2002 Ohio App. LEXIS 4367, 2002-2 Trade Cas. (CCH) p. 73, 774; Bryant v. Walt Sweeney Automotive, Inc. (2002) 2002-Ohio 2577, 2002 Ohio App. LEXIS 2657, 02-LW-1985; Turner v. Bob Ross Buick, Inc. (1993), 629 N.E.2d 1372, 1993 WL 485256, Cert. Denied 69 Ohio St.3d 1410; State v. Rose Chevrolet, Inc. (1993), 622 N.E.2d 543, 1993 WL 229392, Cert. Denied 67 Ohio St.3d 1506; Sprovach v. Bob Ross Buick, Inc. (1993), 628 N.E.2d 82; Bittner v. Tri-County Toyota, Inc. (1991), 58 Ohio St.3d 143; Einhorn v. Beau Townsend Ford, Inc. (1990), 48 Ohio St.3d 27; Brown v. Liberty Clubs (1989), 45 Ohio St.3d 191; Rose Chevrolet, Inc. v. Adams (1988), 36 Ohio St.3d 17; Hardeman v. Wheels, Inc. (1988), 56 Ohio App.3d 142; Crull v. Maple Park Body Shop (1987), 36 Ohio App.3d 153; Thomas v. Hurst Lincoln-Mercury, Inc. (SD Ohio 1987), 72 Bankr. R.747; Brooks v. Hurst Buick-Pontiac-Olds-GMC, Inc. (1985), 23 Ohio App.3d. ***PRACTICE AREAS:*** Consumer Law; Lemon Law; Automobile Fraud; Fair Credit Reporting Act. ***Email:*** Ron@OhioLemonLaw.com

(This Listing Continued)

BURDGE LAW OFFICE CO., LPA, Dayton—Continued

AMY L. WELLS, born Middletown, Ohio, June 27, 1973; admitted to bar, 2004, Ohio. *Education:* University of Dayton (M.B.A.; J.D., 2004). Member, Moot Court. Listed in Who's Who Among Law School Students. Teaching Assistant, Legal Writing. Vice President, Womens Caucus, 2003-2004. Justice for Interschool Competition, 2003-2004. Inn of Court Representative, 2003-2004. ***PRACTICE AREAS:*** Consumer Law; Lemon Law. ***Email:*** Amy@OhioLemonLaw.com

ELIZABETH A. WELLS, born Toledo, Ohio, November 16, 1977; admitted to bar, 2004, Ohio and U.S. District Court, Southern District of Ohio. *Education:* Clemson University (B.A., English, cum laude, 2000); University of Toledo College of Law (J.D., cum laude, 2004). Associate, 2002-2003 and Note and Comment Editor, 2002-2004, University of Toledo Law Review. Author: "Warrantless Traffic Stops: A Suspension of Constitutional Guarantees in Post September 11th America," 34 U. Tol. L. Rev. 899. *Member:* Ohio State and American Bar Associations. ***PRACTICE AREAS:*** Consumer Protection Litigation; Lemon Law. ***Email:*** Beth@LemonLaw.com

CASPER AND CASPER

Established in 1936

FIRST NATIONAL PLAZA BUILDING
130 WEST SECOND STREET, SUITE 1950
DAYTON, OHIO 45402
Telephone: 937-224-1122

Middletown, Ohio Office: Gas and Electric Building, One North Main Street, P.O. Box: 510, 45042. Telephone: 513-424-2401.
Cincinnati, Ohio Office: 119 East Court Street, Fourth Floor, Suite 410, 45202. Telephone: 513-381-7096.
Hamilton Office: 2 South 3rd Street, Suite 360, 45011. Telephone: 513-892-2560.

Personal Injury, Workers Compensation and Social Security Disability Law. Products Liability Litigation. Trials.

REFERENCES: First National Bank of S.W. Ohio; Bank One of Middletown, Ohio.

(For complete biographical data on all personnel, see Professional Biographies at Middletown, Ohio)

CHERNESKY, HEYMAN & KRESS P.L.L.

Established in 1988

10 COURTHOUSE PLAZA, SW, SUITE 1100
DAYTON, OHIO 45402
Telephone: 937-449-2800
Facsimile: 937-449-2821
URL: http://www.chklaw.com

Mailing Address: P.O. Box 3808, Dayton, OH 45401-3808

General Business, General Litigation, Taxation, Corporate and Real Estate Practice. Partnerships, Mergers and Acquisitions, Syndications, Antitrust, Zoning, Banking, Securities Regulation, Estate Planning, Probate, Trust and Charitable Organization, Employment, Products Liability and Health Care Law.

FIRM PROFILE: Chernesky, Heyman & Kress P.L.L. is a firm which focuses its practice in corporate, securities, antitrust, tax, employee benefits, estate planning, real estate, bankruptcy, employment, products liability, partnerships, general litigation, banking law matters, and health care law.

The firm services a variety of clients, from the closely held corporations and their owners to publicly held companies.

The firm engages in a substantial transactional-based practice, representing clients on such matters as acquisitions, dispositions, restructurings, financings, syndications, and so on. In addition, the "general counsel" practice is substantial, and includes SEC compliance and proxy work, annual reports, filings, insider trading, executive compensation, antitrust, product distribution, franchising, real estate transactions and development, estate planning and business succession planning, complex corporate tax questions and a variety of other matters. The firm also has a substantial practice in the employment law and products liability areas and has general and commercial litigation capabilities.

The firm has an affiliation with "The Law Firm Alliance.".

PARTNERS OF FIRM

KAREN R. ADAMS, born Cincinnati, Ohio, 1959; admitted to bar, 1991, Ohio. *Education:* Butler University (B.S., cum laude 1981); Xavier University (M.B.A., 1986); University of Dayton (J.D., summa cum laude, 1991). Executive Editor, Law Review 1990-1991. *Member:* Dayton, Ohio State (Member, Real Property Specialty Board) and American Bar Associations. ***PRACTICE AREAS:*** Real Estate; Business; Employment Law. ***Email:*** kra@chklaw.com

RICHARD A. BROOCK, born Dayton, Ohio, 1946; admitted to bar, 1972, Ohio. *Education:* University of Michigan (A.B., 1968; J.D., cum laude, 1971). *Member:* Dayton, Ohio State and American Bar Associations. ***PRACTICE AREAS:*** Business Law; Corporate Law; Mergers and Acquisitions; Corporate Finance Law. ***Email:*** rab@chklaw.com

FREDERICK J. CASPAR, born Fort Thomas, Kentucky, 1955; admitted to bar, 1981, Pennsylvania; 1985, Ohio. *Education:* Wright State University (B.S., summa cum laude, 1977); The Ohio State University (J.D., summa cum laude, 1980). Order of the Coif; Beta Gamma Sigma. Member, Ohio State Law Journal, 1979-1980. *Member:* Dayton (Chair, Committee on Taxation, 1990-1991), Ohio State and American (Chair, S Corporation Proposed Regulations Sub-Committee, 1994-1999, Tax Section) Bar Associations. ***PRACTICE AREAS:*** Taxation Law; Estate Planning; Partnership Law; Transactional Business Matters. ***Email:*** fjc@chklaw.com

RICHARD J. CHERNESKY, born Scranton, Pennsylvania, 1939; admitted to bar, 1966, Ohio. *Education:* Michigan State University and The Ohio State University (B.A., 1963); The Ohio State University (J.D., 1966). Case Note Editor, Ohio State Law Journal, 1965-1966. *Member:* Dayton and Ohio State (Member, Corporation Law Committee) Bar Associations; National Lawyers Association. ***PRACTICE AREAS:*** Business Law; Corporate Law; Mergers and Acquisitions Law; Strategic Alliances; Public Utility Law. ***Email:*** rjc@chklaw.com

ANDREW K. CHERNEY, born Hamilton, Ohio, 1947; admitted to bar, 1973, Ohio. *Education:* University of the South (B.A., 1970); The Ohio State University (J.D., summa cum laude, 1973). Order of the Coif. Member, Ohio State Law Journal, 1972-1973. *Member:* Dayton, Ohio State and American Bar Associations. ***PRACTICE AREAS:*** Mergers and Acquisitions Law; Corporate Finance Law; Banking Law. ***Email:*** akc@chklaw.com

THOMAS L. CZECHOWSKI, admitted to bar, 1974, Ohio, U.S. District Court, Southern and Northern Districts of Ohio and U.S. Court of Appeals, 6th Circuit. *Education:* Randolph-Macon College (B.A., 1965); Tulane University School of Law (J.D., 1974). President, Dayton Urban Ministry Center. *Member:* Dayton and Ohio State Bar Associations; Defense Research Institute; Ohio Association of Civil Trial Attorneys. ***PRACTICE AREAS:*** Civil Litigation; Products Liability; Toxic Torts; Employment Litigation. ***Email:*** tlc@chklaw.com

BRADLEY W. EVERS, born Philadelphia, Pennsylvania, 1955; admitted to bar, 1980, Virginia, U.S. District Court, Eastern District of Virginia and U.S. Court of Appeals, Fourth Circuit; 1985, Ohio. *Education:* James Madison University (B.S., 1977); Marshall-Wythe School of Law (J.D., 1980). Co-Author, with Hon. F. Bruce Bach: "Effective Assistance of Counsel in Criminal Cases," 4 George Mason University Law Review, Fall, 1981. Law Clerk to the Judges of the Circuit Court of Fairfax County, Virginia, 1980-1981. Dynalectric Company, McLean, Virginia, Associate Corporate Counsel, 1983-1985; Price Brothers Company, Vice President-Legal, Secretary and General Counsel, 1985-1996. *Member:* Dayton, Ohio State and American Bar Associations. ***PRACTICE AREAS:*** Business Law; Corporate Law; Limited Liability Company Law; Partnership Law; Finance; Mergers, Acquisitions and Divestitures; Nonprofit Organizations Law; Contracts; Construction Law; Port Authority Law. ***Email:*** bwe@chklaw.com

MARK S. FEUER, born Dayton, Ohio, 1952; admitted to bar, 1978, Ohio and U.S. Tax Court; 1982, U.S. District Court, Southern District of Ohio. *Education:* Yale University (B.A., 1974); University of Dayton (J.D., summa cum laude, 1978). Senior Attorney, Office of Chief Counsel, Internal Revenue Service, 1978-1984. Adjunct Faculty, Masters in Tax Program, University of Cincinnati, Ohio, 1988-1989. *Member:* Cincinnati, Dayton, Ohio State and American (Member, Tax and Business Law Sections) Bar Associations. ***PRACTICE AREAS:*** Taxation; Tax Litigation; Business Law; Partnership Law; Corporate Law; Employee Benefits; ERISA. ***Email:*** msf@chklaw.com

RALPH E. HEYMAN, born Cincinnati, Ohio, 1931; admitted to bar, 1956, Ohio; 1957, Illinois. *Education:* Dartmouth College (A.B., magna cum laude, 1953); Harvard University (LL.B., cum laude, 1956); University of Cincinnati (LL.M., 1957). Author: "Estate Planning and Conflict of Laws," University of Cincinnati Law Review. Member, Committees on Partnerships, Real Estate Tax Problems, Probate and Estate Planning, Section of Taxation, American Bar Association. *Member:* Dayton, Cincinnati and Ohio State Bar Associations. ***PRACTICE AREAS:*** Business Law; Corporate Law; Partnership Law; Tax Law; Real Estate Development and Syndications Law; Estate Planning Law; Financing Law; Restructuring; Mergers and Acquisitions Law. ***Email:*** reh@chklaw.com

EDWARD M. KRESS, born Dayton, Ohio, 1949; admitted to bar, 1974, Ohio. *Education:* Miami University (B.S., 1971); The Ohio State University (J.D., cum laude, 1974). *Member:* Dayton, Ohio State and American Bar Associations. ***PRACTICE AREAS:*** Business Law; Corporate Law; Estate Planning Law; Mergers and Acquisitions Law; Syndications Law; Real Estate Development Law; Probate Law. ***Email:*** emk@chklaw.com

WILLIAM J. LEIBOLD, born Dayton, Ohio, 1957; admitted to bar, 1982, Ohio. *Education:* University of Dayton (B.A., summa cum laude, 1979); The Ohio State University (J.D., summa cum laude, 1982). Order of the Coif. *Member:* Dayton, Ohio State and American Bar Associations. ***PRACTICE AREAS:*** Business Law; Corporate Law; Antitrust and Trade Regulation Law. ***Email:*** wjl@chklaw.com

LISA S. PIERCE, born Tunkhannock, Pennsylvania, 1968; admitted to bar, 1995, Ohio and U.S. District Court, Southern District of Ohio. *Education:* Kenyon College (B.A., magna cum laude, 1990); University of Cincinnati (J.D., 1995). Phi Beta Kappa; Order of the Coif. Author: "Making Aid without Lemon?" Zobrest v. Catalina Foothills School District, Vol. 63, University of Cincinnati Law Review. *Member:* Dayton, Ohio State and American Bar Associations. ***PRACTICE AREAS:*** Business Law; Corporate Law; Securities Regulation Law; Mergers and Acquisitions; Corporate Finance. ***Email:*** lsp@chklaw.com

DONNA S. TWEEL, born Huntington, West Virginia, 1960; admitted to bar, 1990, Ohio; 1994, U.S. District Court, Southern District of Ohio. *Education:* Marshall University (B.A., 1982); University of Dayton Law School (J.D., cum laude, 1990). Carl D. Kessler Inn of Court, 1993-1996. Member, University of Dayton Law Review. Listed in: Who's Who Among Rising Young Americans, 1992; Marquis' Who's Who in American Law, 11th Edition. Staff Attorney, State of Ohio Second District Court of Appeals. Council Member, Village of Waynesville, 1994-1996. Member, Board of Education, Wayne Local School District. *Member:* Dayton, Ohio and American Bar Associations; Ohio Women's Bar Association; Dayton Women's Bar Association (Board Member). ***PRACTICE AREAS:*** Corporate Law; Business Law; Mergers and Acquisitions; Captive Insurance. ***Email:*** dst@chklaw.com

STEVEN R. WATTS, born Toledo, Ohio, 1955; admitted to bar, 1981, Ohio. *Education:* The Ohio State University (B.A., 1978); University of Dayton (J.D., summa cum laude, 1981). *Member:* Dayton, Ohio State and American Bar Associations. ***PRACTICE AREAS:*** Business Law; Corporate Law; Securities Regulation Law; Mergers and Acquisitions. ***Email:*** srw@chklaw.com

THOMAS P. WHELLEY II, born Saranac Lake, New York, 1949; admitted to bar, 1977, Ohio and U.S. District Court, Southern District of Ohio. *Education:* Kings College

(This Listing Continued)

(B.A., 1972); University of Dayton (J.D., 1977). Editor-in-Chief of the University of Dayton Law Review. Adjunct Professor of Law, Civil Trial Practice and Evidence, The University of Dayton Law School, 1987—. President, University of Dayton School of Law Advisory Counsel. Member and Past President, Board of Trustees, Legal Aid Society of Dayton. Member, Board of LAWO. *Member:* Dayton, Ohio State and American Bar Associations; Ohio Civil Trial Lawyers Association; Defense Research Institute. Master, Inn of Court. ***PRACTICE AREAS:*** Litigation: Business; Product Liability; Employment Law; Employment Law Management. ***Email:*** tpw@chklaw.com

DAVID R. WICKHAM, born Loudonville, Ohio, 1958; admitted to bar, 1983, Ohio; 1984, U.S. Tax Court. *Education:* The Ohio State University (B.A., cum laude, 1979; J.D., 1983); Washington University (LL.M., 1984). Order of the Coif. Visiting Professor, Ohio Northern University School of Law, 1987-1988. Adjunct Professor, University of Dayton School of Law, 1991. *Member:* Dayton, Ohio State and American (Member, Tax Section and Property Probate and Trust Section) Bar Associations. ***PRACTICE AREAS:*** Federal Income, Estate and Gift Taxation Law; Charitable Trusts and Foundations Law; Probate Law. ***Email:*** drw@chklaw.com

PHILIP A. ZUKOWSKY, born Chicago, Illinois, 1955; admitted to bar, 1980, Illinois; 1981, U.S. District Court, Central District of Illinois; 1985, Ohio and U.S. Tax Court. *Education:* Loyola University (A.B., 1977; J.D., 1980); New York University (LL.M., Taxation, 1984). Assistant Illinois Attorney General, 1981-1983. Officer of Cleveland Tax Institute, 1990-1991. Adjunct Professor of Corporate Tax, Cleveland State University Law School, 1991. ***LANGUAGES:*** Hebrew. ***PRACTICE AREAS:*** Taxation; Transactional Business Matters. ***Email:*** paz@chklaw.com

---

CHRISTOPHER M. BROWN, admitted to bar, 2003, Ohio. *Education:* Cedarville College (B.A., 1999); University of Dayton School of Law (J.D., 2003). Omicron Delta Kappa. Author: University of Dayton Law Review. *Member:* American, Ohio State and Dayton Bar Associations. ***LANGUAGES:*** Japanese. ***PRACTICE AREAS:*** Commercial Litigation; Employment Law; Labor and Employment. ***Email:*** cmb@chklaw.com

ANTHONY E. BRUZZESE, admitted to bar, 2003, Ohio. *Education:* Miami University (B.S., 1998); University of Dayton School of Law (J.D., 2003). Member, Ohio Society of Certified Public Accountants. *Member:* American, Ohio State and Dayton Bar Associations. ***PRACTICE AREAS:*** Corporate Law; Partnership Law; Corporate Partnerships; Mergers and Acquisitions. ***Email:*** aeb@chklaw.com

TODD E. BRYANT, born Dayton, Ohio, 1974; admitted to bar, 2000, Ohio. *Education:* Grace College (B.A., 1997); University of Dayton (J.D., 2000). *Member:* Dayton Bar Association; Ohio State Bar. ***PRACTICE AREAS:*** Corporate; Litigation. ***Email:*** teb@chklaw.com

CARRIE E. HERMAN, born Bellbrook, Ohio, 1973; admitted to bar, 1999, Massachusetts; 2003, Ohio. *Education:* The Ohio State University (B.S., 1996; B.S.B.A., 1996); Boston University School of Law (J.D., 1999). Author: "Opting-Out: Implications of Denmark's Self-Imposed Exile from Euroland," 19 Annual Rev. Banking L. 581 (2000). *Member:* American, Boston and Ohio State Bar Associations. ***PRACTICE AREAS:*** Corporate; Banking; Securities; Real Estate; Mergers and Acquisitions; Business Planning; Business Formation. ***Email:*** ceh@chklaw.com

RACHAEL L. RODMAN, born Chillicothe, Ohio; admitted to bar, 2001, Ohio; 2003, U.S. District Court, Southern District of Ohio and U.S. Court of Appeals, Sixth Circuit. *Education:* University of Cincinnati (B.A., cum laude, 1998; J.D., 2001). Order of the Coif. *Member:* American, Ohio State and Dayton Bar Associations. ***PRACTICE AREAS:*** Business Litigation; Appellate Practice; Labor and Employment; Litigation. ***Email:*** rlr@chklaw.com

KEVIN V. SIMON, born Cincinnati, Ohio, November 5, 1969; admitted to bar, 1994, Illinois; 1996, Ohio; 1998, U.S. Court of Appeals, Sixth Circuit; 2001, U.S. Tax Court. *Education:* University of Dayton (B.A., 1990); Vanderbilt University (J.D., 1994); New York University (LL.M. in Taxation, 2001). ***PRACTICE AREAS:*** Taxation; Estate Planning; Corporate Law. ***Email:*** kvs@chklaw.com

SUSAN D. SOLLE, born Dayton, Ohio, 1968; admitted to bar, 1999, Ohio. *Education:* Oglethorpe University (B.A., 1994); University of Dayton (J.D., 1999). Member, University of Dayton Moot Court Team. University of Dayton Law Review. Author, "Sibling Relationships Should Not Be Denied by Formalistic Judges," 23 University of Dayton Law Review 659, Spring 1998. Formerly with, Second District Court of Appeals. *Member:* Dayton and Ohio State Bar Associations. ***PRACTICE AREAS:*** Commercial Litigation; Employment Law. ***Email:*** sds@chklaw.com

OF COUNSEL

L. DOUGLAS KNEISLY, born 1936; admitted to bar, 1962, Ohio. *Education:* University of Cincinnati (B.B.A., 1960; LL.B., 1962). ***Email:*** ldk@chklaw.com

JAMES DAVID RUFFNER, II, born Dayton, Ohio, 1958; admitted to bar, 1994, Ohio and U.S. District Court, Southern District of Ohio; 2000, U.S. Court of Appeals, Sixth Circuit. *Education:* Wright State University (B.S., summa cum laude, 1983); University of Dayton (J.D., 1994). Outside Articles Editor, Executive Board of Editors, University of Dayton Law Review, 1993-1994. Certified Public Accountant, Ohio. Arbitrator, Montgomery County Common Pleas Court Arbitration Program. Member, Board of Trustees, Senior Resource Connection, Dayton, Ohio. Past President, Board of Trustees, Epilepsy Foundation of Western Ohio. *Member:* Dayton, Ohio State and American Bar Associations; American Institute of Certified Public Accountants; Ohio Society of Certified Public Accountants (Dayton Chapter); American Health Lawyers Association. ***PRACTICE AREAS:*** Corporate Law; Business Law; Taxation; Health Care; Mergers and Acquisitions; Real Estate; Tax Exempt Organizations; Nonprofit and Charitable Organizations. ***Email:*** jdr@chklaw.com

GAIL H. LITTLEJOHN, born Oberlin, Ohio; admitted to bar, 1983, Ohio. *Education:* Ohio Northern University (B.A., 1970); University of Dayton School of Law (J.D., 1982). Member, Dayton Board of Education, 2002—. *Member:* Ohio State and Dayton Bar Associations. ***PRACTICE AREAS:*** Public Policy. ***Email:*** ghl@chklaw.com

(This Listing Continued)

JAMES R. MITCHELL, admitted to bar, 2003, Ohio. *Education:* University of Tennessee (B.A., 1969); University of Cincinnati (J.D., 1972). *Member:* American, Ohio State and Dayton Bar Associations. ***PRACTICE AREAS:*** Real Estate Finance; Small Business Law. ***Email:*** jrm@chklaw.com

Languages: Hebrew, Japanese.

REPRESENTATIVE CLIENTS: AAA Miami Valley; Architectural Resources Corporation; Aristocrat Products Mfg. Co., Inc.; Audi of America, Inc.; Better Business Bureau of Dayton/Miami Valley, Inc.; BriLyn, Inc.; CSA Nutrition Services, Inc.; Day International, Inc.; Digitron Inc.; Dolly, Inc.; Exciton, Inc.; Fifth Third Bank; Hills Developers; International Display Systems, Inc.; Jewish Federation of Greater Dayton, Inc.; K.K. Motorcycle Supply, Inc.; Lewis & Michael, Inc.; Lutheran School of the Miami Valley; Miami Valley School; Miller-Valentine Group; North American Nutrition Companies, Inc.; North Dayton Ob-Gyn Associates; Price Brothers Company; R & M Materials Handling, Inc.; REX Stores Corporation; Reynolds & Reynolds Company; RG Properties, Inc.; Riverain Group, Inc.; SEI & Development Corporation; Senior Resource Connection; St. Mary Development Corporation; Temple Israel; The Berry Company; The Connor Group; The Dayton Heart Center, Inc.; The Dayton-Montgomery County Port Authority; The F.A. Requarth Company; The Iams Company; The Sportsman's Guide, Inc.; Temple Israel Foundation; Towne Properties, Ltd.; Vernay Laboratories, Inc.; VocaLink, Inc.; Volkswagon of America, Inc.; Weaver Bros., Inc.

CICERO & KOLLIN PLL

500 EAST 5TH STREET
DAYTON, OHIO 45402
Telephone: 937-424-5390
Fax: 937-424-5393
URL: http://www.cicerokollinfirm.com
Email: cicero@woh.rr.com
URL: http://www.cicero-kollin.com

Criminal Defense, Personal Injury, Family Law.

ANTHONY R. CICERO, born Racine, Wisconsin, April 18, 1970; admitted to bar, 1995, Ohio; 2001, U.S. Supreme Court; 2002, U.S. District Court, Southern District of Ohio. *Education:* University of Wisconsin (B.A., 1992); University of Dayton School of Law (J.D., 1995). *Member:* Dayton, Ohio State and Federal Bar Associations; Ohio Association of Criminal Defense Lawyers (Board Member); National Association of Criminal Defense Lawyers. (Board Certified Criminal Trial Advocacy Specialist by the National Board of Trial Advocacy). ***PRACTICE AREAS:*** Criminal Defense; Civil Rights; Personal Injury. ***Email:*** cicero@woh.rr.com

THOMAS M. KOLLIN, born Sacramento, California, February 4, 1968; admitted to bar, 1996, Ohio. *Education:* Ohio University (B.S., 1991); University of Dayton School of Law (J.D., 1996). *Member:* Dayton Bar Association. ***PRACTICE AREAS:*** Personal Injury; Criminal Defense; Family Law.

COOLIDGE, WALL, WOMSLEY & LOMBARD

A LEGAL PROFESSIONAL ASSOCIATION
SUITE 600
33 WEST FIRST STREET
DAYTON, OHIO 45402-1289
Telephone: 937-223-8177
Fax: 937-223-6705
URL: http://www.coollaw.com

Corporate, Partnerships, Securities, International Transactions, Antitrust, Tax, Labor, Employment, Employment Immigration, Employee Benefits, Banking, Real Estate, Municipal, Zoning, Environmental, Commercial Transactions, Bankruptcy, Health Care, Civil and Criminal Trials and Appeals, Commercial Litigation, Personal Injury, Products Liability, Workers Compensation, Insurance Defense, Estate and Financial Planning, Probate and Trust Law.

FIRM PROFILE: Coolidge, Wall, Womsley & Lombard is one of the oldest law firms in Ohio, with a continuous existence since 1853. Our practice is business-oriented and we offer a full line of legal services as listed above. Our clients include publicly-owned national corporations, some of whose stocks are listed on the New York Stock Exchange. In addition, we serve as counsel for numerous large and small closely-held corporations, financial institutions, individuals, partnerships, trusts and non-profit and charitable organizations. Our clients engage in a wide range of businesses locally, nationally and internationally.

JOHN C. LOMBARD, admitted to bar, 1959, Massachusetts; 1964, Ohio. *Education:* Harvard University (A.B., 1950); Boston College (LL.B., 1959). Contributing Attorney, 1972-1987, Assistant Editor, 1988-1996, "The Developing Labor Law". ***PRACTICE AREAS:*** Health Care and Hospital. ***Email:*** lombard@coollaw.com

RONALD S. PRETEKIN, admitted to bar, 1966, Ohio. *Education:* University of Oklahoma (A.B., 1963); University of Michigan (LL.B., 1966). Member, Panel for Merit Selection of Bankruptcy Judges, Southern District of Ohio, 1992-1993; Chairman, 1995-1996; Trustee, American Bankruptcy Law Forum, 1992-1994. *Member:* Dayton and Ohio State Bar Associations. Certified in Business Bankruptcy Law by the American Board of Certification. ***PRACTICE AREAS:*** Bankruptcy; Banking; Commercial Law. ***Email:*** pretekin@coollaw.com

JONAS J. GRUENBERG, admitted to bar, 1970, Ohio. *Education:* University of Pennsylvania (B.S., 1967); Vanderbilt University (J.D., 1970). Member, Vanderbilt University Law Review. ***PRACTICE AREAS:*** Business Planning; Estate Planning; Real Estate Development and Syndications. ***Email:*** gruenberg@coollaw.com

MERLE F. WILBERDING, admitted to bar, 1969, Iowa and District of Columbia; 1973, Ohio. *Education:* St. Mary's University, Minnesota (B.A., cum laude, 1966); University of Notre Dame (J.D., 1969); George Washington University (LL.M. in Taxation, 1972); University of Dayton (M.B.A., 1975). Member, International Council of Shopping Centers. [U.S. Army, Captain, JAGC, 1969-1973]. ***PRACTICE AREAS:*** Business Planning; Taxation; Real Estate; Shopping Centers Law; Zoning Law. ***Email:*** wilberding@coollaw.com

(This Listing Continued)

COOLIDGE, WALL, WOMSLEY & LOMBARD, A LEGAL PROFESSIONAL ASSOCIATION, Dayton—Continued

GLENN L. BOWER, admitted to bar, 1977, Ohio; 1991, Maryland. *Education:* Pennsylvania State University (B.A., with high distinction, 1974); Harvard Law School (J.D., 1977). Phi Beta Kappa. ***PRACTICE AREAS:*** Mergers and Acquisitions; Strategic Alliances; Technology; Health Care. ***Email:*** bower@coollaw.com

J. STEPHEN HERBERT, admitted to bar, 1978, Ohio. *Education:* Yale University (B.A., 1974); University of Virginia (J.D., 1978). Member, Virginia Law Review, 1976-1978. ***PRACTICE AREAS:*** Real Estate; Financing Transactions; Franchise. ***Email:*** herbert@coollaw.com

FRED A. UNGERMAN, JR., admitted to bar, 1980, Ohio. *Education:* Grove City College (A.B., magna cum laude, 1977); Duke University (J.D., 1980). ***PRACTICE AREAS:*** Labor and Employment; Construction. ***Email:*** ungerman@coollaw.com

R. SCOTT BLACKBURN, admitted to bar, 1977, Pennsylvania; 1979, Ohio. *Education:* Ohio University (B.B.A., BSIT, 1972); University of Cincinnati (M.B.A., 1974); University of Toledo (J.D., 1977). ***PRACTICE AREAS:*** Estate Planning; Probate. ***Email:*** blackburn@coollaw.com

RICHARD A. SCHWARTZ, admitted to bar, 1978, Ohio. *Education:* University of Toledo (B.A., 1970); The Ohio State University (J.D., with honors, 1977). [U.S. Army, Capt., 1970-1975]. ***PRACTICE AREAS:*** Securities Regulations; Mergers and Acquisitions; Partnerships; Limited Liability Companies; Corporate and Business; Health Care. ***Email:*** schwartz@coollaw.com

SAM WARWAR, admitted to bar, 1981, Ohio and Florida. *Education:* The Ohio State University (B.A., 1977); University of Dayton (J.D., cum laude, 1980); University of Florida (LL.M., Taxation, 1981). ***PRACTICE AREAS:*** Taxation. ***Email:*** warwar@coollaw.com

TERENCE L. FAGUE, admitted to bar, 1978, Ohio. *Education:* Wilmington College (A.B., cum laude, 1972); The Ohio State University (J.D., 1978). Assistant Prosecuting Attorney, Montgomery County, Ohio, 1979-1981. Special Prosecutor, Montgomery County, 1990-1992. ***PRACTICE AREAS:*** Business Litigation; Employment Litigation. ***Email:*** fague@coollaw.com

TIMOTHY D. HOFFMAN, admitted to bar, 1981, Ohio; 1982, U.S. District Court, Southern District of Ohio; 1988, U.S. District Court, Northern District of Ohio. *Education:* Capital University (B.A., cum laude, 1978; J.D., 1981). Environmental Counsel, Dayco Corporation, Dayton, Ohio, 1982-1986. *Member:* Ohio State and American Bar Associations (Member, Committees on: Solid and Hazardous Waste, 1986—; Environmental Crimes and Enforcement Committee Newsletter Reporter for USEPA Region V; Sections on: Natural Resources, Energy and Environmental Law; Administrative Law). ***PRACTICE AREAS:*** Environmental; Environmental Criminal Defense; Administrative Law; Regulatory; Alternative Dispute Resolution. ***Email:*** hoffman@coollaw.com

JOHN C. CHAMBERS, admitted to bar, 1985, Ohio. *Education:* Ohio University (B.A., cum laude, 1971); University of Michigan (M.P.P., 1975); University of Dayton (J.D., magna cum laude, 1985). City Manager, Springboro, Ohio, 1978-1982. Law Director, Huber Heights, Ohio, 1991-2003; Law Director, Yellow Springs, Ohio, 2003—. *Member:* Dayton, Ohio State and American Bar Associations; National Association of Industrial and Office Properties. ***PRACTICE AREAS:*** Real Estate; Municipal. ***Email:*** chambers@coollaw.com

JANICE M. PAULUS, admitted to bar, 1985, Ohio; 1986, U.S. District Court, Southern District of Ohio; 1991, U.S. Supreme Court; 1992, U.S. Court of Appeals, Sixth Circuit. *Education:* The Ohio State University (B.A., 1980); University of Dayton (J.D., summa cum laude, 1985). Society of Professional Journalists Award, Best Defense of the First Amendment (2001, co-recipient). Member, Clayton Council, 1998-2003. *Member:* Dayton (Judiciary Committee, 1991-1997; Chair, 1995-1997), Ohio State and American Bar Associations; Carl D. Kessler, American Inn of Court (1992—). ***PRACTICE AREAS:*** Commercial Litigation; Complex and Multi-District Litigation; Tax; Securities and Antitrust Litigation; Employment Litigation; White Collar Criminal Defense. ***Email:*** paulus@coollaw.com

JEFFREY A. MULLINS, admitted to bar, 1990, Ohio. *Education:* University of Dayton (B.A., magna cum laude, 1986; J.D., summa cum laude, 1990). Contributing Attorney, "The Developing Labor Law," 1993. ***PRACTICE AREAS:*** Labor; Employment; Health Care and Hospital. ***Email:*** mullins@coollaw.com

RICHARD A. TALDA, admitted to bar, 1982, Ohio; 1984, U.S. District Court, Southern District of Ohio; 1986, U.S. Tax Court; 1991, U.S. Supreme Court; 1994, U.S. Court of Appeals, Sixth Circuit. *Education:* Ohio University; Wittenberg University (B.A., with honors, 1979); University of Toledo (J.D., 1982). Phi Alpha Delta. *Member:* Dayton, Ohio State and American Bar Associations. ***PRACTICE AREAS:*** Commercial Litigation; Employment Litigation. ***Email:*** talda@coollaw.com

DAVID N. REED, admitted to bar, 1991, Ohio. *Education:* Dartmouth College (B.A., 1988); University of Notre Dame (J.D., 1991). Phi Delta Phi. *Member:* Dayton, Ohio State and American Bar Associations. ***PRACTICE AREAS:*** Real Estate; Environmental; Corporate. ***Email:*** reed@coollaw.com

R. BRENT GAMBILL, admitted to bar, 1979, Indiana; 1997, Ohio. *Education:* DePauw University (B.A., summa cum laude, 1976); Indiana University School of Law (J.D., magna cum laude, 1979). Phi Beta Kappa. Senior Corporate Counsel, Cinergy Corp., 1979-2001. *Member:* Dayton, Indiana State, Ohio State and American Bar Associations. ***PRACTICE AREAS:*** Employee Benefits; Labor and Employment Law. ***Email:*** gambill@coollaw.com

M. SHANNON MARTIN, admitted to bar, 1993, Ohio. *Education:* John Carroll University (B.A., 1990); Cleveland-Marshall (J.D., 1993). *Member:* Dayton, Greene County, Ohio State and American Bar Associations. ***PRACTICE AREAS:*** Real Estate; Public Sector; Financing Transactions. ***Email:*** martin@coollaw.com

LANCE A. GILDNER, admitted to bar, 1991, Ohio. *Education:* Indiana University (B.A., 1988); University of Dayton (J.D.,1991). *Member:* Dayton, Ohio State (Member, Federal Taxation Committee, 2000—) and American (Member, Committee on Partnerships Taxation Section, 2000—) Bar Associations. (Certified Specialist in Federal Tax Law, Ohio State Bar Association). ***PRACTICE AREAS:*** Taxation. ***Email:*** gildner@coollaw.com

NICHOLAS E. DAVIS, JR., admitted to bar, 1990, Ohio. *Education:* Kent State University (B.A., 1986); University of Dayton (J.D., 1990). Attorney Advisor to Hon. J. Michael O'Neill, Office of Administrative Law Judges, U.S. Department of Labor, 1991-1992. *Member:* Dayton, Ohio State and American Bar Associations. ***PRACTICE AREAS:*** Workers' Compensation Law; Labor Law. ***Email:*** davis@coollaw.com

KRISTIN A. FINCH, admitted to bar, 1995, Ohio. *Education:* Wright State University (B.S., Accounting and Finance, 1991); University of Cincinnati (J.D., 1995). Order of the Coif. Recipient, American Jurisprudence Award in Real Estate Transactions. *Member:* Dayton, Ohio State and American Bar Association. ***PRACTICE AREAS:*** Corporate; Real Estate; Computer Law. ***Email:*** finch@coollaw.com

DAVID P. PIERCE, admitted to bar, 1993, Ohio, U.S. District Court, Southern District of Ohio and U.S. Court of Appeals, Sixth Circuit. *Education:* Vanderbilt University (B.A., cum laude, 1990); University of Cincinnati (J.D., 1993). Phi Alpha Delta. *Member:* Dayton, Ohio State and American Bar Associations; Ohio Association of Civil Trial Attorneys; Carl D. Kessler Inn of Court. ***PRACTICE AREAS:*** General Litigation; Commercial Litigation; Employment Litigation. ***Email:*** pierce@coollaw.com

LOWELL T. WOODS, JR., admitted to bar, 1994, Indiana and U.S. District Court, Southern and Northern Districts of Indiana; 1997, Ohio, U.S. District Court, Southern District of Ohio and U.S. Court of Appeals, Sixth and Seventh Circuits. *Education:* Indiana University (B.A., 1986; J.D., magna cum laude, 1994). Published, Indiana Law Review. *Member:* Dayton, Ohio State and American Bar Associations; Defense Research Institute; Construction Financial Management Association. ***PRACTICE AREAS:*** Construction Law; Labor and Employment Law; Civil Litigation. ***Email:*** woods@coollaw.com

---

C. MARK KINGSEED, admitted to bar, 1979, Illinois; 1985, Ohio. *Education:* Miami University (A.B., cum laude, 1976); Georgetown University (J.D., cum laude, 1979). Member, Board of Directors, Ohio Chamber of Commerce, 1999 —. *Member:* Dayton, Ohio State and American Bar Associations. ***PRACTICE AREAS:*** Employment Law; Labor Law; Litigation; Alternative Dispute Resolution. ***Email:*** kingseed@coollaw.com

DAVID C. KORTE, admitted to bar, 1980, Ohio; 1981 Kentucky. *Education:* Miami University (A.B., 1977); University of Cincinnati (J.D., 1980). Phi Alpha Delta. *Member:* Dayton (Workers' Compensation Law Committee), Cincinnati, Kentucky, Ohio State and American Bar Associations. (Certified Specialist in Workers Compensation Law, Ohio State Bar Association). ***PRACTICE AREAS:*** Workers Compensation Defense. ***Email:*** korte@coollaw.com

JOHN L. GREEN, admitted to bar, 1982, Ohio. *Education:* Alma College (A.B., 1977); Ohio Northern University (J.D., 1981). *Member:* Dayton and Ohio State Bar Associations; American Health Lawyers Association; Society of Ohio Hospital Attorneys. ***PRACTICE AREAS:*** Health Care; Business Law. ***Email:*** green@coollaw.com

MARY L. WISEMAN, admitted to bar, 1988, Arkansas; 1991, Ohio; U.S. District Court, Southern District of Ohio; U.S. District Court, Western District of Michigan; U.S. Court of Appeals, Sixth, Seventh, Eighth and Ninth Circuits; U.S. Supreme Court. *Education:* Ball State University (B.S., 1984); University of Arkansas at Little Rock (J.D., with honors, 1988). *Member:* Dayton, Ohio State and American Bar Associations; Dayton Intellectual Property Law Association; Carl D. Kessler Inn of Court. ***PRACTICE AREAS:*** Litigation; Antitrust; Zoning; Class Actions; Intellectual Property; Environmental Litigation. ***Email:*** mwiseman@coollaw.com

DAVID M. RICKERT, admitted to bar, 1978, Ohio; 1995, U.S. Tax Court. *Education:* Northern Illinois University (B.A., summa cum laude, 1975); University of Chicago (J.D., 1978). *Member:* Ohio State and Dayton Bar Associations. ***LANGUAGES:*** American Sign Language. ***PRACTICE AREAS:*** Litigation. ***Email:*** rickert@coollaw.com

EDIE ENGLAND CRUMP, admitted to bar, 1991, Ohio. *Education:* Stephens College; University of Missouri-Columbia (B.S., 1986); University of Louisville (J.D., 1990); Emory University (LL.M., Taxation, 1991). Brandeis Society. Journal of Family Law. Journal of Law and Education. *Member:* Dayton and Ohio Bar Associations. ***PRACTICE AREAS:*** Employment Benefits. ***Email:*** crump@coollaw.com

DINA M. CARY, admitted to bar, 1997, Ohio and U.S. District Court, Southern District of Ohio; 1999, U.S. Court of Appeals, Sixth Circuit. *Education:* Ohio State University (B.A., 1994); University of Dayton (J.D., 1997). *Member:* Dayton, Ohio State and American Bar Associations. ***PRACTICE AREAS:*** Civil Litigation. ***Email:*** cary@coollaw.com

SHANNON L. COSTELLO, admitted to bar, 1998, Ohio and U.S. District Court, Southern District of Ohio. *Education:* The Ohio State University (B.A., summa cum laude, with honors, 1995); University of Cincinnati (J.D., 1998). *Member:* Dayton, Ohio State and American Bar Associations. ***PRACTICE AREAS:*** Real Estate; Environmental Law. ***Email:*** costello@coollaw.com

CHRISTOPHER R. CONARD, admitted to bar, 1988, Ohio and U.S. District Court, Southern District of Ohio. *Education:* University of Dayton (B.A., History, 1984; J.D., 1987). Adjunct Professor, University of Dayton, 1990-2000; Adjunct Professor, University of Dayton School of Law, 2003—. Allbery, Cross & Turner, 1988-1989. Assistant Montgomery County Public Defender, 1989-1997. Deputy Director of the Montgomery County Public Defender, 1997-2000. *Member:* Dayton, Ohio State, Federal and American Bar Associations; Carl D. Kessler Inn of Court. ***PRACTICE AREAS:*** Commercial Litigation; General Litigation; White Collar Criminal Defense; Criminal Defense. ***Email:*** conard@coollaw.com

ARBUTUS LIKENS CARLISLE, admitted to bar, 1994, Illinois; 2003, North Carolina; 2004, Ohio. *Education:* Columbia Union College (B.A., summa cum laude, 1971); Andrews University (M.A., 1973); Chicago Kent College of Law (J.D., 1994). *Member:* Dayton, Ohio State and American Bar Associations; American Health Lawyers Association; Society of Ohio Hospital Attorneys. ***PRACTICE AREAS:*** Health Care. ***Email:*** carlisle@coollaw.com

GREGORY M. EWERS, admitted to bar, 1996, Illinois; 1997, Ohio. *Education:* Miami University (B.S., 1992); John Marshall Law School (J.D., magna cum laude, 1996);

(This Listing Continued)

New York University (LL.M. in Corporate Law, 1999). *Member:* Dayton, Ohio State and American Bar Associations. ***PRACTICE AREAS:*** Corporate; Securities. ***Email:*** ewers@coollaw.com

JILL A. MAY, admitted to bar, 2000, Ohio. *Education:* Adrian College (B.A., Communications, summa cum laude, 1997); University of Toledo (J.D., magna cum laude, Class Valedictorian, 2000). Honors, Adrian College: Mortar Board National College Senior Honor Society; Alpha Chi National College Honor Scholarship Society; Phi Eta Sigma, Honor Society; University of Toledo: Order of the Coif; Corpus Juris Secondum Awards in Civil Procedure, Property; Anderson Publishing Book Award, 1998-1999. *Member:* Dayton, Ohio State and American Bar Associations. ***PRACTICE AREAS:*** Labor and Employment. ***Email:*** may@coollaw.com

ALLISON D. MICHAEL, admitted to bar, 1999, Ohio and U.S. District Court, Southern District of Ohio. *Education:* Wright State University (B.A., Spanish, 1996); University of Dayton (J.D., cum laude, 1999). Recipient: Walter H. Rice Moot Court Competition Best Appellate Brief Award, 1997; Michael & Elissa Cohen Best Student Note Award, 1998; CALI Excellence for the Future Awards in Constitutional Law I and Criminal Procedure. *Member:* Dayton (Member, Board of Trustees; Chair, New Lawyers Committee, 2002-2003), Ohio State and American Bar Associations. ***PRACTICE AREAS:*** Labor and Employment. ***Email:*** michael@coollaw.com

SYLVIE J. DERRIEN, admitted to bar, 2000, Ohio. *Education:* University of Paris, Sorbonne; University of Cincinnati (B.A., summa cum laude, 1997); University of Cincinnati College of Law (J.D., 2000). Assistant Secretary of the French American Trade Council. *Member:* Dayton, Cincinnati and Ohio State Bar Associations; Alliance of Française of Greater Cincinnati. ***PRACTICE AREAS:*** Bankruptcy; Immigration; Trademarks; Copyrights. ***Email:*** derrien@coollaw.com

MICHELLE D. BACH, admitted to bar, 1995, Ohio. *Education:* Miami University (B.A., magna cum laude, 1992); University of Pittsburgh (J.D., cum laude, 1995). (Certified Specialist in Workers Compensation Law, Ohio State Bar Association). ***PRACTICE AREAS:*** Workers Compensation Defense. ***Email:*** bach@coollaw.com

DOUGLAS C. ANSPACH, admitted to bar, 2001, Ohio. *Education:* University of Notre Dame (B.A., Psychology, cum laude, 1998); College of William and Mary (J.D., 2001). *Member:* Dayton and Ohio State Bar Associations. ***PRACTICE AREAS:*** Labor and Employment; Immigration Law. ***Email:*** anspach@coollaw.com

CHAD D. HANSEN, admitted to bar, 1997, Idaho; 2002, Ohio. *Education:* Utah State University (B.A., Accounting, 1994); University of Idaho (J.D., 1997); University of Florida (LL.M., Taxation, 2001). Law Clerk to Honorable Jim D. Pappas, United States Bankruptcy Court for the District of Idaho, 1997-2000. *Member:* Dayton, Ohio State and American (Member: Taxation Section; Committee on Partnerships and LLC's and Committee on Corporate Tax, Taxation Section) Bar Associations; Idaho State Bar. ***LANGUAGES:*** Swedish. ***PRACTICE AREAS:*** Taxation. ***Email:*** hansen@coollaw.com

STEVEN M. WACHSTEIN, admitted to bar, 2001, Ohio; 2002, U.S. District Court, Southern District of Ohio. *Education:* Miami University (B.A., 1997); University of Cincinnati (J.D., 2001). *Member:* Dayton and Ohio State Bar Associations; American Bankruptcy Institute; American Bankruptcy Law Forum. ***PRACTICE AREAS:*** Bankruptcy; Commercial Law. ***Email:*** wachstein@coollaw.com

LISA K. WISEMAN, admitted to bar, 2001, Ohio. *Education:* Wright State University (B.A., summa cum laude, 1998); University of Dayton (J.D., magna cum laude, 2001). Member, University of Dayton Law Review. Member, Miami Valley Select Advisors Group. Board Member, Greater Dayton Planned Giving Council. *Member:* Dayton (Assistant Committee Chair), Ohio State and American Bar Associations; Dayton Trust & Estate Planning Group; Estate Planning Council of the Miami Valley. ***PRACTICE AREAS:*** Estate Planning; Probate. ***Email:*** wiseman@coollaw.com

ANIRUDDHA D. BHAT, admitted to bar, 2001, Ohio. *Education:* University of Michigan (B.A., 1997); Case Western Reserve University (J.D., 2001). *Member:* Dayton and Ohio State Bar Associations. ***PRACTICE AREAS:*** Corporate Law; Business Law; Securities; Intellectual Property. ***Email:*** bhat@coollaw.com

JUSTIN D. BRINKMAN, admitted to bar, 2003, Ohio. *Education:* University of Michigan (B.A., 2000); University of Illinois (J.D., 2003). *Member:* Dayton, Ohio State and American Bar Associations. ***PRACTICE AREAS:*** Real Estate. ***Email:*** brinkman@coollaw.com

MY'CHAEL D. JEFFERSON, admitted to bar, 2003, Ohio. *Education:* University of Richmond, (B.A., cum laude, 2000); University of Dayton (J.D., 2003). *Member:* Dayton, Ohio State and American Bar Associations. ***PRACTICE AREAS:*** Litigation. ***Email:*** jefferson@coollaw.com

PETER L. JENKINS, admitted to bar, 2003, Ohio. *Education:* Denison University (B.A., 2000); University of Cincinnati (J.D., 2003). Order of the Coif. ***PRACTICE AREAS:*** Corporate; Health Care. ***Email:*** jenkins@coollaw.com

MATTHEW D. AUSTIN, admitted to bar, 2003, Ohio. *Education:* The Ohio State University (B.A., magna cum laude, 1999); University of Dayton School of Law (J.D., 2002). *Member:* Dayton, Ohio State and American Bar Associations; Defense Research Institute. ***PRACTICE AREAS:*** Labor and Employment; Construction Law; Litigation. ***Email:*** austin@coollaw.com

BRIAN M. WAKEFIELD, admitted to bar, 2004, Ohio. *Education:* Embry-Riddle Aeronautical University (B.S., 1997); Park University (B.S., 1999); Chapman University (M.S., 1999); Ohio Northern University (J.D., 2004). *Member:* Dayton, Ohio State and American Bar Associations. [Chief Master Sergeant, U.S. Air Force, 1976-2000]. ***PRACTICE AREAS:*** Labor and Employment. ***Email:*** wakefield@coollaw.com

JOSHUA R. LOUNSBURY, admitted to bar, 2004, Ohio; 2005, U.S. District Court, Southern District of Ohio. *Education:* Michigan State University (B.A., with high honors, 2001); University of Texas School of Law (J.D., 2004). *Member:* Dayton, Ohio State and American Bar Associations. ***PRACTICE AREAS:*** Workers Compensation. ***Email:*** lounsbury@coollaw.com

References provided on request.

COOPER & GENTILE CO.

A LEGAL PROFESSIONAL ASSOCIATION

Established in 2000

TALBOTT TOWER, SUITE 850
118 WEST FIRST STREET
DAYTON, OHIO 45402
Telephone: 937-224-5300
Fax: 937-224-5301
Email: dlgentile@cooperandgentile.com
URL: http://www.lawyers.com/cooperandgentile

General Practice.

FIRM PROFILE: Representing employers, school districts and municipalities in the areas of employment and labor, school law, special education, general civil litigation and workers' compensation.

JANET K. COOPER, born Marion, Ohio, March 14, 1946; admitted to bar, 1978, Ohio and U.S. District Court, Southern District of Ohio. *Education:* Wichita State University (B.A., 1969); University of Tulsa (J.D., 1978). Special Counsel to Attorney General of Ohio, 1992—. *Member:* Dayton and Ohio State Bar Associations. ***PRACTICE AREAS:*** School and Special Education Law; Labor and Employment. ***Email:*** jkcooper@cooperandgentile.com

DIANE L. GENTILE, born Fort Dix, New Jersey, April 4, 1956; admitted to bar, 1986, Ohio, U.S. District Court, Southern District of Ohio and U.S. Court of Appeals, Sixth Circuit. *Education:* University of Dayton (B.A., 1977; J.D., 1986). Law Clerk: Montgomery County, Ohio Common Pleas Court, 1984-1986; U.S. Magistrate Robert A. Steinberg, Southern District of Ohio, 1986-1988. Special Counsel for the Ohio Attorney General, 1995-2003. Member, Advisory Board, Dayton Mediation Center, 1994—. *Member:* Dayton (Member, Board of Trustees, 2000-2003), Ohio State and American Bar Associations; Dayton Women's Bar Association (President, 1995-1996). ***PRACTICE AREAS:*** Civil Litigation; Commercial and Employment Litigation; School Law; Appellate Practice; Mediation. ***Email:*** dlgentile@cooperandgentile.com

---

COWDEN, PFARRER, CREW & BECKER

DAYTON, OHIO

(See Crew & Buchanan)

CREW & BUCHANAN

Established in 1912

Formerly Cowden, Pfarrer, Crew & Becker

2580 KETTERING TOWER
DAYTON, OHIO 45423-2580
Telephone: 937-223-6211
Facsimile: 937-223-7631
Email: office@crewbuchanan.com

General Civil Practice. Corporate, Employment, Employment Intentional Tort, Labor, Personal Injury, Probate, Real Estate, Tax and Workers' Compensation Defense Law. Trials.

MEMBERS OF FIRM

CHARLES A. CRAIGHEAD (1857-1926)
ROBERT E. COWDEN (1886-1954)
ROBERT E. COWDEN, JR. (1910-1968)
CHARLES P. PFARRER (1905-1984)
PHILIP ROHRER BECKER (1905-1989)

ROBERT B. CREW, born Miamisburg, Ohio, March 1, 1912; admitted to bar, 1936, Ohio; 1946, U.S. Supreme Court. *Education:* Northwestern University (B.S., 1933; J.D., 1936). Phi Alpha Delta. *Member:* Dayton (Past President), Ohio State and American Bar Associations. ***PRACTICE AREAS:*** Probate; Tax; Real Estate. ***Email:*** rcrew@crewbuchanan.com

JOSEPH P. BUCHANAN, born Dayton, Ohio, March 13, 1929; admitted to bar, 1956, Ohio. *Education:* Occidental College; Miami University (B.S., 1951); The Ohio State University (LL.B., 1956). Phi Delta Phi. *Member:* Dayton (Past President), Ohio State and American Bar Associations. ***PRACTICE AREAS:*** Labor; Employment; Corporate; Workers Compensation Defense; Civil Litigation. ***Email:*** jbuchanan@crewbuchanan.com

JEFFREY A. SWILLINGER, born Cincinnati, Ohio, August 13, 1952; admitted to bar, 1979, Ohio; 1980, U.S. District Court, Southern District of Ohio. *Education:* Boston University (B.A., magna cum laude, 1974); Franklin Pierce Law Center (J.D., 1978). *Member:* Dayton (President, 2005-2006), Ohio State and American Bar Associations; Thurgood Marshall Law Society. ***PRACTICE AREAS:*** Labor and Employment; Corporate Law; Real Estate; Civil Litigation; Personal Injury. ***Email:*** jswillinger@crewbuchanan.com

ROBERT J. DAVIDEK, born Chicago, Illinois, August 24, 1956; admitted to bar, 1981, Ohio; 1984, U.S. District Court, Southern District of Ohio; 1986, U.S. Supreme Court. *Education:* The Ohio State University (B.A., 1976); University of Toledo (J.D., 1981). Phi Alpha Delta. Board of Editors, University of Toledo Law Review, 1980-1981. Hearing Officer, Industrial Commission of Ohio, 1981-1984. Contributor: *Manual for The Lawyer's Assistant,* West Publishing, 2000. Certified Specialist, Ohio Workers' Compensation Law. *Member:* Columbus (Member, Workers' Compensation Committee), Dayton (Member, Workers' Compensation Committee and Past Chair, 1988-1989, 1992-1993, 1995-1996) and Ohio State (Member, Workers' Compensation Committee) Bar Associations; Defense Research Institute (Member, Workers' Compensation Committee); The

(This Listing Continued)

CREW & BUCHANAN, Dayton—Continued

Ohio Association of Civil Trial Attorneys; Southwestern Ohio Self-Insurers Association. ***PRACTICE AREAS:*** Workers Compensation Defense; Employment Intentional Torts; Retaliatory Discharge. ***Email:*** rdavidek@crewbuchanan.com

ASSOCIATE

JENNIFER HANN HARRISON, born Kettering, Ohio, December 12, 1969; admitted to bar, 1996, Ohio. *Education:* West Chester University (B.A., magna cum laude, 1992); Dickinson School of Law of the Pennsylvania State University (J.D., 1995). Delta Theta Phi. *Member:* Dayton (Co-Chair, Certified Grievance Committee), Ohio State and American Bar Associations; The Ohio Academy of Trial Lawyers; Dayton Women's Bar Association (Treasurer, 1999-2001; President, 2003-2004); Southwestern Ohio Self Insurers Association. ***PRACTICE AREAS:*** Workers Compensation Defense; Civil Litigation; Employer Intentional Torts. ***Email:*** jhann@crewbuchanan.com

REPRESENTATIVE CLIENTS: Airway Billiards, Inc.; Bauers Trenching and Excavating; Brookside Homeowners Association, Inc.; Buckeye Lawn and Landscaping; Cal-Maine Foods, Inc.; Columbia Sussex, Corp.; Copper and Brass Sales, Inc.; DaimlerChrysler A.G.; Danis Environmental Industries, Inc.; Delphi, Inc.; Denlinger Landscaping, LLC; Diamond Tool & Die Co.; File Sharpening Co.; Foxtronix, Inc.; General Motors Corp.; Grandview/Southview Hospitals; Green Tokai Co., Ltd.; GZK, Inc.; High Performance Results, Inc.; The Holland Group; Horizon Properties, Inc.; Hunters Glen Apts., Inc.; HVR Limited Partnership; L.B. Robinson, Inc.; Martin Chevrolet-Oldsmobile; Mars Properties, LLC; Mays-Shedd Sales Co.; Waxco International, Inc.; Planet Ford; Process Equipment Co.; Proto Fabrication, Inc.; The Rodgers Pontiac Co.; Saturn of Dayton, Inc.; Schu-Fly, LLC; Schumacher Crane Rental, Inc.; Serra Chevrolet, Inc.; Siebenthaler Co.; Speedway SuperAmerica, L.L.C.; Torok Kennels, Inc.; U.S. Xpress Enterprises, Inc.; Vandalia Auto Clinic, Inc.; Witt Plastics, Inc.; W.R. Hackett, Inc.; Yowell Transportation, Inc.

DENMEAD LAW OFFICE

DAYTON, OHIO

(See Columbus)

Civil Trial and Appellate Practice and Personal Injury, Traumatic Brain Injury (TBI), Professional Negligence and Complex Litigation including Class Actions, Patents, Civil Rights, Civil Litigation, RICO, Employment and Political Subdivision Liability issues.

DAVID M. DEUTSCH CO., L.P.A.

THE POLLACK HOUSE
208 WEST MONUMENT AVENUE
DAYTON, OHIO 45402
Telephone: 937-223-7170
Facsimile: 937-223-7180
Email: groundcrew@deutsatlaw.com
URL: http://www.deutschlawoffice.com

Personal Injury, Product Liability, Wrongful Death, Medical Malpractice.

FIRM PROFILE: Having spent many years with a large law firm, David Deutsch established his practice to provide high-quality, efficient and more responsive legal service on a personalized basis with his clients. He engages in matters relating to all aspects of liability and injury, from medical devices to machinery, from small to significant cases. Mr. Deutsch believes in leveling the playing field for the common man, and he is often referred to as "David who takes on Goliath".

DAVID M. DEUTSCH, born Dayton, Ohio, July 28, 1943; admitted to bar, 1969, Ohio; 1970, U.S. District Court, Southern District of Ohio and U.S. Court of Appeals, Fourth and Sixth Circuits; 2000, U.S. Court of Appeals, Eleventh Circuit. *Education:* The Ohio State University (B.S., 1965); Cumberland School of Law of Samford University (J.D., 1969). Phi Alpha Delta. President, Government Affairs Committee of Ohio Jewish Communities, 1986-1988. Member, Board of Directors, Greater Dayton Jewish Federation, 1982-1988. Chairman, Community Relations Council, Greater Dayton Jewish Federation, 1982-1987. Member, Board of Directors and Vice President, Temple Israel, 1989-1991. Member, Miami Valley Hospital Head Injury Re-Entry Program Advisory Board, 1991—. Member, 1994-1999 and Chairman, 1997, The Supreme Court of Ohio Commission on Continuing Legal Education. *Member:* Dayton and Ohio State (Secretary, 1981-1982) Bar Associations; Ohio Academy of Trial Lawyers (Governing Trustee, 1984-1990); Miami Valley Trial Lawyers Association (President, 1986-1987). ***PRACTICE AREAS:*** Personal Injury Law; Product Liability; Medical Malpractice. ***Email:*** david@deutschatlaw.com

DINSMORE & SHOHL LLP

ONE DAYTON CENTRE
ONE SOUTH MAIN STREET, SUITE 1300
DAYTON, OHIO 45402
Telephone: 937-449-6400
FAX: 937-449-6405
Email: info@dinslaw.com
URL: http://www.dinslaw.com

New address effective April 1, 2004: One Dayton Centre, One South Main Street, Suite 1300, 45402.

Cincinnati, Ohio Office: 255 East Fifth Street, Suite 1900, 45202-4700. Telephone: 513-977-8200. FAX: 513-977-8141.
Columbus, Ohio Office: 10th Floor, 175 South Third Street, 43215-5134. Telephone: 614-628-6880. FAX: 614-628-6890.
Lexington, Kentucky Office: Lexington Financial Center, 250 West Main Street, Suite 1400, 40507. Telephone: 859-425-1000. FAX: 859-425-1099.
Louisville, Kentucky Office: 1400 PNC Plaza, 500 West Jefferson Street, 40202. Telephone: 502-540-2300. FAX: 502-585-2207.

(This Listing Continued)

Pittsburgh, Pennsylvania Office: The Grant Building, 330 Grant Street, Suite 2415, 15219. Telephone: 412-281-5000. FAX: 412-281-5055.
Charleston, West Virginia Office: 900 Lee Street, Huntington Square, Suite 600, 25301. Mailing Address: P.O. Box 11887, 25339. Telephone: 304-357-0900. FAX: 304-357-0919.

General Practice.

FIRM PROFILE: Our Foundation

For over 95 years, Dinsmore & Shohl LLP has been providing quality legal counsel to our clients. In recent years, our practice has grown to include seven offices and taken on national and international clients. Today's full-service practice with more than 260 attorneys continues to live up to the ideals set in 1908 by Frank F. Dinsmore and Walter M. Shohl: efficient, cost-effective and comprehensive solutions for every client.

Our Service

At Dinsmore & Shohl LLP, we put our clients first in every element of our full-service practice. The Firm's commitment to quality service extends from our highly-skilled attorneys to our experienced professional staff. By establishing client relationships based on trust, communication and responsiveness, we listen to our clients' concerns and expectations while refining our service to ensure that these needs are met. We recognize that service begins with accessibility and ends with fulfilled expectations.

Our Clients

With over 35 practice areas, Dinsmore & Shohl LLP has the experience and variety to meet your legal needs. Our clients range from public and private corporations to charitable organizations and encompass healthcare providers, local and state governments, financial institutions, real estate developers, franchisors and distributors and pharmaceutical companies.

Our Technology

By embracing and utilizing the latest technology, our efficiencies are passed on to clients. We continuously assess and update our case management systems, intranet, extranets, billing systems, document management systems, and other practice-specific software to ensure our work product can be leveraged and measured. In addition, our legal library uses technology to keep important, up-to-date information close at hand. These combined resources help us strategize, plan, develop and integrate our practice to meet your business needs.

Our Innovation

Our commitment to client service extends to our growing subsidiaries: DinsNet Technologies LLC, Great Water Capital Partners, LLC, and Mercantile Title Agency, Inc. which provide various portals for client collaboration. These unique services help optimize e-business, business intelligence and knowledge management solutions for clients.

Our Future

Utilizing the latest technology and resources, we embrace the future today while maintaining our historical values. With attorneys and staff skilled in a broad range of legal and ancillary subjects, we will continue to offer the knowledge and experience needed to maintain our strict standard of excellence. This commitment has continued to drive our growth and will sustain our foundation into the future.

MEMBERS OF FIRM

RICHARD J. BECKMANN, born Cincinnati, Ohio, 1948; admitted to bar, 1974, Ohio. *Education:* University of Cincinnati (B.B.A., cum laude, 1971); George Washington University (J.D., cum laude, 1974). [1st Lieutenant, U.S. Army Reserve, 1973-1981]. ***PRACTICE AREAS:*** Corporate Law; Mergers, Acquisitions and Divestitures; Agency and Distributorships; Antitrust and Trade Regulation; International Law. ***Email:*** richard.beckmann@dinslaw.com

LAURA GOEHRING HARRELSON, born Staunton, Virginia, March 31, 1957; admitted to bar, 1983, Ohio. *Education:* The Ohio State University (B.A., 1979); Capital University (J.D., 1982). ***PRACTICE AREAS:*** Labor; Workers Compensation. ***Email:*** harrelso@dinslaw.com

MERIDETH A. TROTT, born Glendale, California, September 9, 1949; admitted to bar, 1975, Ohio and U.S. District Court, Southern District of Ohio. *Education:* Andrews University (B.A., 1970); Claremont Graduate University (M.A., 1971); University of Southern California (J.D., 1974). *Member:* Dayton, Ohio State and American Bar Associations. ***PRACTICE AREAS:*** Real Estate; Corporate. ***Email:*** merideth.trott@dinslaw.com

NICHOLAS C. HOLLENKAMP, born Covington, Kentucky, May 4, 1937; admitted to bar, 1964, Ohio. *Education:* Xavier University (B.S., 1959); Indiana University (M.B.A., 1961); University of Cincinnati (J.D., 1964). Member, Board of Editors, Cincinnati Law Review, 1963-1964. *Member:* Dayton, Ohio State and American Bar Associations. Fellow, Ohio Bar Foundation. ***PRACTICE AREAS:*** Business Law; Civil Litigation; Mergers & Acquisitions. ***Email:*** nicholas.hollenkamp@dinslaw.com

AMES GARDNER, JR., born Dayton, Ohio, April 8, 1940; admitted to bar, 1965, Ohio. *Education:* Princeton University (B.A., 1962); University of Virginia (LL.B., 1965). *Member:* Dayton, Ohio State and American Bar Associations. ***PRACTICE AREAS:*** Estate Planning; Probate. ***Email:*** ames.gardner@dinslaw.com

WAYNE H. DAWSON, born Dayton, Ohio, October 24, 1942; admitted to bar, 1967, Ohio. *Education:* Wittenberg University (B.A., 1964); University of Cincinnati (J.D., 1967). Order of the Coif. Member, Board of Editors, Cincinnati Law Review, 1966-1967. *Member:* Dayton, Ohio State and American Bar Associations. [Lt., US Navy, JAGC, 1968-1972]. ***PRACTICE AREAS:*** Banking Law; Business Law; Corporate Law. ***Email:*** wayne.dawson@dinslaw.com

JAMES E. BEYER, born Cleveland, Ohio, September 5, 1967; admitted to bar, 1995, Ohio and U.S. District Court, Southern District of Ohio; registered to practice before the U.S. Patent and Trademark Office. *Education:* University of Cincinnati (B.S., Physics,

(This Listing Continued)

1990); American University (J.D., 1995). *Member:* Dayton, Ohio State and American Bar Associations; American Intellectual Property Law Association (Member: Patent Litigation Committee; Trade Secret Law Committee); Dayton Intellectual Property Law Association; Leadership Dayton Association; i-Zone Knowledge Network Service Provider; Intellectual Property Owners Association. ***SPECIAL AGENCIES:*** Patent Examiner, U.S. Patent and Trademark Office, 1990-1995 (Masters Certification, 1995). ***PRACTICE AREAS:*** Intellectual Property; Patent Law; Licensing; Litigation; Trademark Law; Copyright Law. ***Email:*** james.beyer@dinslaw.com

KIMBERLY GAMBREL, born Cincinnati, Ohio, December 13, 1960; admitted to bar, 1988, Ohio; U.S. District Court, Southern District of Ohio. *Education:* Miami University (B.A., Diplomacy and Foreign Affairs, 1983; M.A., Political Science, 1985); University of Cincinnati (J.D., 1988). *Member:* Dayton, Ohio State and American Bar Associations; American Intellectual Property Law Association; Ohio Women's Bar Association; Dayton Women's Bar Association; Dayton Intellectual Property Law Association. ***PRACTICE AREAS:*** Copyrights (20%); Trademarks (75%); Trade Secrets (5%). ***Email:*** kimberly.gambrel@dinslaw.com

JAMES F. GOTTMAN, born Xenia, Ohio, April 7, 1946; admitted to bar, 1974, Ohio; U.S. Court of Appeals for the Federal Circuit; U.S. District Court, Southern District of Ohio; registered to practice before U.S. Patent and Trademark Office. *Education:* University of Cincinnati (B.S.E.E., with honors, 1969); Georgetown University (J.D., 1974). Tau Beta Pi. Patent Examiner, U.S. Patent and Trademark Office, 1969-1974. *Member:* Dayton (Co-Chair, Ethics Committee), Ohio State and American Bar Associations; American Intellectual Property Law Association. (Managing Partner, Dayton, Ohio Office) (Chair, Intellectual Property Practice Group). ***PRACTICE AREAS:*** Computer and Software; Copyrights; Intellectual Property; Licensing; Patents. ***Email:*** james.gottman@dinslaw.com

TIMOTHY W. HAGAN, born Newark, Ohio, December 20, 1949; admitted to bar, 1976, Maryland; 1978, Ohio; U.S. District Court, Southern District of Ohio and U.S. Court of Appeals for the Federal Circuit; registered to practice before U.S. Patent and Trademark Office. *Education:* Cornell University (B.S., Chemical Engineering, 1972); Georgetown University (J.D., 1976). Recipient, Robert C. Watson Award, 1976. Editor, Law and Policy in International Business, 1975. Adjunct Professor of Law, University of Dayton, 1982-1997. Patent Examiner, U.S. Patent and Trademark Office, 1972-1976. Law Clerk, U.S. Court of Customs and Patent Appeals, 1976-1978. *Member:* Dayton, Federal Circuit, Ohio State and American Bar Associations; American Intellectual Property Law Association; International Trade Commission Trial Lawyers Association; AIPPI-US. ***SPECIAL AGENCIES:*** U.S. Patent and Trademark Office; United States International Trade Commission. ***REPORTED CASES:*** In re Pleuddemann, 910 F.2d 823 (Fed. Cir. 1990). ***PRACTICE AREAS:*** Intellectual Property; Patents; Trade Secrets; Trademarks; Copyrights. ***Email:*** timothy.hagan@dinslaw.com

RICHARD A. KILLWORTH, born Fort Wayne, Indiana, April, 24, 1943; admitted to bar, 1970, Virginia; 1973, Ohio; U.S. Court of Appeals, Sixth Circuit; U.S. Court of Appeals for the Federal Circuit; U.S. District Court, Southern District of Ohio; registered to practice before U.S. Patent and Trademark Office. *Education:* Purdue University (B.S., Chemistry, 1965; M.A., 1966); George Washington University Law School (J.D., 1970; LL.M., 1972). *Member:* Dayton, Ohio State and American Bar Associations; Sixth Circuit Judicial Conference (Life Member); American Law Institute; American Intellectual Property Law Association; Licensing Executives Society; The Carl D. Kessler Inn of Court. ***PRACTICE AREAS:*** Intellectual Property; Litigation; Patents. ***Email:*** richard.killworth@dinslaw.com

B. JOSEPH SCHAEFF, born Dayton, Ohio, 1950; admitted to bar, 1975, Ohio and U.S. District Court, Southern District of Ohio; 2005, U.S. District Court, Northern District of Ohio. *Education:* University of Dayton (B.A., 1972); The Ohio State University (J.D., cum laude, 1975). Adjunct Professor of Law: University of Dayton, 1983-1997; The Ohio State University College of Law, 2003. *Member:* Dayton, Ohio State and American Bar Associations; American Intellectual Property Law Association; International Trademark Association. ***PRACTICE AREAS:*** Trademarks; Copyrights; Intellectual Property. ***Email:*** joseph.schaeff@dinslaw.com

ASSOCIATES

THERESA M. MUHIC, born Bellefontaine, Ohio, May 13, 1963; admitted to bar, 1988, Ohio; U.S. District Court, Southern District of Ohio. *Education:* University of Dayton (B.A., cum laude, 1985; J.D., 1988). *Member:* Dayton, Ohio State and American Bar Associations. (Certified Specialist in Workers' Compensation Law, Ohio State Bar Association). ***PRACTICE AREAS:*** Workers Compensation. ***Email:*** theresa.muhic@dinslaw.com

MICHAEL G. FREY, born Cincinnati, Ohio, February 6, 1970; admitted to bar, 1998, Ohio and U.S. District Court, Southern District of Ohio. *Education:* College of Mount St. Joseph-on-the-Ohio (B.A., 1990); University of Cincinnati (J.D., 1998). Order of the Coif. Member, Editorial Board, University of Cincinnati Law Review, 1998. ***PRACTICE AREAS:*** Intellectual Property; Licensing; Trademarks; Copyrights. ***Email:*** michael.frey@dinslaw.com

WILLIAM A. JIVIDEN, born Port Jefferson, New York, February 3, 1967; admitted to bar, 1999, Ohio; registered to practice before U.S. Patent and Trademark Office. *Education:* United States Naval Academy (B.S., 1989); George Washington University (M.S., 1995); Franklin Pierce Law Center (J.D./M.I.P., 1999). *Member:* Dayton Bar Association; American Intellectual Property Law Association; Dayton Intellectual Property Law Association. [Lieutenant, U.S. Navy, 1989-1996]. ***PRACTICE AREAS:*** Computers and Software; Intellectual Property; Patents. ***Email:*** william.jividen@dinslaw.com

JOHN D. REED, born Philadelphia, Pennsylvania, October 26, 1959; admitted to bar, 1997, Ohio and U.S. District Court, Southern District of Ohio. *Education:* University of Cincinnati (B.S, Nuclear Engineering, 1983); University of Dayton (M.S., Mechanical Engineering, 1990); Salmon P. Chase College of Law (J.D., 1997). Patent Examiner, U.S. Patent and Trademark Office, 1998-2000. *Member:* Dayton and Ohio State Bar Associations; American Intellectual Property Law Association; Dayton Intellectual Property Law Association. ***PRACTICE AREAS:*** Intellectual Property; Litigation; Patents. ***Email:*** john.reed@dinslaw.com

(This Listing Continued)

KRISTINA E. SWANSON, born Lansing, Michigan, February 26, 1968; admitted to bar, 2002, California; 2004, Ohio; U.S. District Court, Southern District of Ohio; registered to practice before U.S. Patent and Trademark Office. *Education:* University of Michigan (B.S., Electrical Engineering, 1990); University of Virginia (M.E., Biomedical Engineering, 1992); University of Pittsburgh (J.D., 2002). *Member:* Dayton, Ohio State and American Bar Associations; State Bar of California; American Intellectual Property Law Association. ***PRACTICE AREAS:*** Intellectual Property; Litigation; Patents. ***Email:*** kristina.swanson@dinslaw.com

PAUL M. ULRICH, born Dayton, Ohio, April 26, 1967; admitted to bar, 1999, Ohio; U.S. District Court, Southern District of Ohio; registered to practice before U.S. Patent and Trademark Office. *Education:* University of Cincinnati (B.S., Mechanical Engineering, 1990); University of Dayton School of Law (J.D., 1999). *Member:* Dayton Bar Association; Dayton Intellectual Property Law Association. ***PRACTICE AREAS:*** Intellectual Property; Litigation; Patents. ***Email:*** paul.ulrich@dinslaw.com

GREGORY M. KASKEY, born Aurora, Ohio, October 27, 1975; admitted to bar, 2001, Ohio; U.S. District Court, Southern District of Ohio. *Education:* Ohio University (B.B.A., cum laude, 1998); University of Dayton School of Law (J.D., cum laude, 2001). Recipient, CALI Awards in: Basic Real Estate Transactions, 2001; Commercial & Business Drafting, 2001; UCC-I (Sales), 2001; UCC-III (Commercial Paper), 2000; UCC-II (Secured Transactions), 1999; Administrative Law, 1999; Constitutional Law, 1999. Research Editor, 2000-2001 and Associate Editor, 1999-2000, University of Dayton Law Review, 2000-2001. *Member:* Dayton and Ohio State Bar Associations. ***PRACTICE AREAS:*** Real Estate; Corporate Law; Commercial Law; Construction Law; Mergers and Acquisitions. ***Email:*** gregory.kaskey@dinslaw.com

MATTHEW A. MOLLOY, born Philadelphia, Pennsylvania, January 18, 1977; admitted to bar, 2004, Ohio and U.S. District Court, Southern District of Ohio; registered to practice before U.S. Patent and Trademark Office. *Education:* University of Pennsylvania (B.S., Chemical Engineering, 1999); University of Dayton School of Law (J.D., 2004). *Member:* Dayton and Ohio State Bar Associations; American Intellectual Property Law Association; Dayton Intellectual Property Law Association. ***PRACTICE AREAS:*** Intellectual Property; Patents; Trademarks. ***Email:*** matthew.molloy@dinslaw.com

KEVIN P. BRAIG, born Cincinnati, Ohio, October 6, 1967; admitted to bar, 1993, Ohio and U.S. District Court, Southern District of Ohio; 1995, U.S. Court of Appeals, Sixth Circuit. *Education:* Ohio University (B.S., Journalism, summa cum laude, 1989); University of Cincinnati (J.D., 1993). Recipient, American Jurisprudence Award in Constitutional Law. *Member:* Dayton, Ohio State and American Bar Associations; Potter Stewart American Inn of Court. ***PRACTICE AREAS:*** Agricultural Law; Environmental Law; Litigation. ***Email:*** kevin.braig@dinslaw.com

OF COUNSEL

PATRICIA L. PRIOR, born Cleveland, Ohio, March 4, 1959; admitted to bar, 1986, Ohio; U.S. District Court, Southern District of Ohio and U.S. Court of Appeals for the Federal Circuit; registered to practice before the U.S. Patent and Trademark Office. *Education:* University of Notre Dame (B.S., Chemical Engineering, 1981); The Ohio State University (J.D., summa cum laude, 1986); New York University (LL.M., Trade Regulation, 1998). Order of the Coif. Law Clerk to the Honorable Edward S. Smith, U.S. Court of Appeals for the Federal Circuit, 1986-1988. Adjunct Professor of Law, The Ohio State University, 1996—; Capital University, 2000; Adjunct Assistant Professor of Law, New York University, 1998. *Member:* American Bar Association (Member, Intellectual Property Section); Columbus Intellectual Property Law Association; American Intellectual Property Law Association. ***SPECIAL AGENCIES:*** U.S. Patent and Trademark Office. ***PRACTICE AREAS:*** Intellectual Property; Patents. ***Email:*** patricia.prior@dinslaw.com

DAVID A. SHOUGH, born Royal Oak, Michigan, July 25, 1954; admitted to bar, 1985, Ohio, U.S. District Court, Southern and Northern Districts of Ohio and U.S. Court of Appeals, Sixth and Federal Circuits. *Education:* University of Michigan (B.Mus., with distinction, 1976; M.A., 1977); Case Western Reserve University (J.D., magna cum laude, 1985). *Member:* Dayton, Ohio State and American (Member, Sections on: Litigation; Patent, Trademark and Copyright Law) Bar Associations. ***PRACTICE AREAS:*** Commercial Litigation; Litigation; Patents; Trademarks; Copyrights. ***Email:*** david.shough@dinslaw.com

REPRESENTATIVE CLIENTS: Arbogast Buick-Pontiac-GMC Truck, Inc.; AT&T Wireless; Dayton Bag & Burlap Co.; Ernie Green Industries, Inc.; Florida Production Engineering, Inc.; Franciscan Medical Center-Dayton Campus; Huffy Corporation; Key Bank; Marion Industries, Inc.; Mayals Corporation; NCR Corporation; The Reynolds and Reynolds Company; Richmond Foundry Co.; John Q. Sherman Trusts; The Standard Register Co.; Voss Auto Network; YSI, Incorporated.

DUNGAN & LEFEVRE

A LEGAL PROFESSIONAL ASSOCIATION

DAYTON, OHIO

(See Troy)

General Civil and Criminal Trial Practice, including Medical Malpractice, Personal Injury, Wrongful Death, Products Liability, Insurance Defense, Wrongful Discharge Defense, Business Law and Commercial Litigation in all Courts, Real Estate, Condominium, Banking, Insurance, Corporate and Business, Wills and Probate, Trusts and Estates, Estate Planning, Family and Domestic Relations, Driving While Intoxicated, Tax, Bankruptcy, Municipal, Zoning and Planning and Collection Law. Appeals in all Courts.

DUNLEVEY, MAHAN & FURRY

A LEGAL PROFESSIONAL ASSOCIATION

Established in 1985

110 NORTH MAIN STREET, SUITE 1000
DAYTON, OHIO 45402-1738
Telephone: 937-223-6003
Fax: 937-223-8550
URL: http://www.dmfdayton.com

Business Law, Labor and Employment Law, Workers' Compensation, OSHA, Government Contracts, Securities, Mergers and Acquisitions, Real Estate and Construction Law, Environmental, Litigation and Appeals, Estate Planning and Administration.

FIRM PROFILE: The firm provides personalized services in complex areas of the law to national, regional and local clients.

ROBERT T. DUNLEVEY, JR., born Dayton, Ohio, June 25, 1947; admitted to bar, 1973, Ohio. *Education:* The Ohio State University (B.A., 1969); University of Cincinnati (J.D., 1972). *Member:* Dayton (Chairman, Labor Relations Section, 1980-1981); Ohio State (Member, Labor Law Section); and American (Member: Labor and Employment Law Section, Forum Committee on the Construction Industry) Bar Associations. ***PRACTICE AREAS:*** Management Employment Law; Employment Discrimination Law; Litigation; Construction Law. ***Email:*** rtd@dmfdayton.com

CHARLES W. MAHAN, born St. Louis, Missouri, December 27, 1945; admitted to bar, 1971, Ohio. *Education:* University of Illinois (B.S., in General Engineering, 1968); The Ohio State University (J.D., 1970). *Member:* Dayton, Greene County, Ohio State (Chair, Construction and Government Contracts Committee, 1996-1998; Member, Real Property and Probate Sections) and American (Member: Public Contract Law Section; Forum Committee on the Construction Industry) Bar Associations; Boards of Contract Appeals Bar Association. [JAG USAF, 1971-1975, JAGDR USAFR, 1975-1992]. ***PRACTICE AREAS:*** Construction Claims; Government Contracts; Real Estate; Business Planning; Probate; Estate Planning. ***Email:*** cwm@dmfdayton.com

STEPHEN A. WATRING, born Ashland, Ohio, November 10, 1954; admitted to bar, 1981, Ohio. *Education:* Wright State University (B.A., cum laude, 1977); University of Dayton (J.D., magna cum laude, 1981). *Member:* Dayton (Chairman, Labor Law Committee, 2002-2003), Ohio State (Member, Labor Law Section) and American (Member, Labor and Employment Law Section and Law Practice Management Section) Bar Associations. ***PRACTICE AREAS:*** Labor and Employment Law; Employment Discrimination; Employment and Business Litigation. ***Email:*** saw@dmfdayton.com

GARY W. AUMAN, born West Reading, Pennsylvania, 1947; admitted to bar, 1976, Ohio. *Education:* University of Louisville (B.E.E., 1969); The Ohio State University (J.D., summa cum laude, 1976). *Member:* Dayton (Chairman, Workers' Compensation Committee, 1985-1986, 1991-1992), Ohio State and American Bar Associations; Defense Research Institute (Member, Workers' Compensation Committee); Ohio Association of Civil Trial Attorneys. [USAF, 1969-1973]. ***PRACTICE AREAS:*** OSHA Compliance and Litigation; Workers; Environmental Litigation. ***Email:*** gwa@dmfdayton.com

GARY T. BRINSFIELD, born Lima, Ohio, February 20, 1942; admitted to bar, 1968, Ohio. *Education:* Miami University (B.S., 1965); Ohio Northern University (J.D., 1968). Instructor: Constitutional Law, Sinclair College, 1972-1973; Evidence, University of Dayton, 1974. Assistant United States Attorney, Southern District of Ohio, 1969-1973. Member, U.S. Department of Justice, Attorney General's Honors Program, Civil Rights Division, 1968-1969. *Member:* Dayton (Chairman, Workers' Compensation Committee, 1993; Bar Briefs) and Ohio State Bar Associations; Defense Research Institute; Ohio Association of Civil Trial Attorneys. ***PRACTICE AREAS:*** Workers' Compensation; Business Litigation; Employment Discrimination; Intentional Torts; Negligence/Personal Injury Defense. ***Email:*** gtb@dmfdayton.com

WILLIAM H. BARNEY, III, born Baltimore, Maryland, December 15, 1951; admitted to bar, 1977, Ohio. *Education:* Trinity College (B.A., 1974); University of Dayton (J.D., 1977). *Member:* Dayton (Chairman, Member, Workers' Compensation Committee, 2002), and Ohio State Bar Associations. ***PRACTICE AREAS:*** Workers Compensation Defense; Intentional Torts; Tort Defense; Environmental Litigation. ***Email:*** whb@dmfdayton.com

RICHARD L. CARR, JR., born Defiance, Ohio, April 4, 1959; admitted to bar, 1984, Ohio. *Education:* Michigan State University (B.A., 1981); Boston College (J.D., 1984). Phi Beta Kappa; Phi Kappa Phi. *Member:* Dayton and Ohio State Bar Associations; Federalist Society; Construction Finance Management Association. ***PRACTICE AREAS:*** Business Law; Construction Law; Litigation; Business Planning; Computer Law; Estate Planning. ***Email:*** rlc@dmfdayton.com

---

DONALD B. RINEER, born Fairborn, Ohio, August 26, 1974; admitted to bar, 1999, Ohio; 2000, Indiana; U.S. District Court, Northern and Southern Districts of Indiana; 2001, U.S. District Court, Southern District of Ohio. *Education:* University of Cincinnati (B.A., 1996); University of Dayton (J.D., cum laude, 1999). Pi Sigma Alpha; Sigma Phi Epsilon. Member, University of Dayton Law Review. *Member:* Dayton, Indiana State, Ohio State and American (Member, Business Law Section; Construction Law Forum) Bar Associations. ***PRACTICE AREAS:*** Corporate; Mergers and Acquisitions; Contracts; Internet Law; Computer Law; Real Estate; Business Law; Construction; Mechanics Liens; Estate Planning; Business Litigation. ***Email:*** dbr@dmfdayton.com

AMY C. MITCHELL, born Dayton, Ohio, June 27, 1973; admitted to bar, 1998, Ohio. *Education:* University of Dayton (B.A., 1995); University of Cincinnati (J.D., 1998). Order of the Coif. *Member:* Dayton, Ohio State and American Bar Associations. ***Email:*** acm@dmfdayton.com

LAURIE A. DENDWICK-GORDON, born Vancouver, British Columbia, January 18, 1973; admitted to bar, 2002, Ohio. *Education:* University of North Dakota (B.A., summa cum laude, 1998); University of Dayton (J.D., 2002). Psi Chi. Dean's List. *Member:* Dayton, Ohio State and American Bar Associations. ***PRACTICE AREAS:*** Workers Compensation; OSHA. ***Email:*** lag@dmfdayton.com

(This Listing Continued)

OF COUNSEL

RICHARD L. FURRY, born Chicago, Illinois; admitted to bar, 1950, Illinois; 1964, Ohio. *Education:* University of Chicago (Ph.B., 1944; J.D., 1950). *Member:* Dayton (Past Chairman, Business Law Committee) and Ohio State Bar Associations. ***PRACTICE AREAS:*** Business Law; Securities Law; Mergers, Acquisitions, and Divestitures; Estate Planning. ***Email:*** rlf@dmfdayton.com

REPRESENTATIVE CLIENTS: SUPERVALU Holdings, Inc.; United Way of the Greater Dayton Area; Continental Airlines; The Dayton Power & Light Company; Sysco, Inc.; Miami Valley Hospital; Good Samaritan Hospital; Crown Services; Ohio Roofing Contractors Assn.; Dayton Tooling & Manufacturing Association; Meijer Stores; Construction Employers Association of North Central W. VA.; Summit Land Title Agency, Inc.; Oakwood Board of Education; Dayton Legal Blank, Inc.; PMI Food Equipment Group; Ohio State Plumbing, Heating & Cooling Contractors Assn.; Paper Systems, Incorporated; Gayston Corp.; MacAulay-Brown, Inc; Sheet Metal & Roofing Contractors Assn. of Miami Valley; NCR Corp.; National Insulation Assn. (NIA); Lamar Corporation; Midwest Insulation Contractors Assn., (MICA); National Frame Builders Assn. (NFBA); Montgomery County Medical Society; Sterling Rubber Products Co.; STC Broadcasting, Inc. (WDTN); American Subcontractors Association; The Connor Group of Miami Valley; Miami Valley Uno's; Foreside Fund Services; Bainbridge Capital Management, LLC; Greene Memorial Hospital, Inc.; Dayton Builders' Exchange; Farmers & Merchants Bank.

DYER, GAROFALO, MANN & SCHULTZ

A LEGAL PROFESSIONAL ASSOCIATION

TALBOTT TOWER
131 NORTH LUDLOW STREET
SUITE 1400
DAYTON, OHIO 45402
Telephone: 937-223-8888
Fax: 937-223-0127
URL: http://www.dgmslaw.com
URL: http://www.lawyers.com/dgmslaw

Springfield, Ohio Office: 1714 Valley Loop Road, 45504. Telephone: 937-324-1440. Fax: 937-327-0488.
Middletown, Ohio Office: 1420 South Breiel Boulevard, 45044. Telephone: 513-727-3580. Fax: 513-727-3584.
Piqua, Ohio Office: 308 Looney Road, Suite E, 45356. Telephone: 937-778-9966. Fax: 937-778-2380.
Huber Heights, Ohio Office: 4420 Taylorsville Road, 45424. Telephone: 937-235-1229. Fax: 937-727-3584.
Lima, Ohio Office: 2727 Harding Highway, P.O. Box 1569, 45802. Telephone: 419-224-8564. Fax: 419-224-0287.
Bellefontaine, Ohio Office: 1709 South Main Street, 43311. Telephone: 937-599-1300. Fax: 937-599-1306.
Wilmington, Ohio Office: 712 South Street, 45177. Telephone: 937-283-9300. Fax: 937-283-9303.
Richmond, Indiana Office: 3733 National Road East, 47374. Telephone: 765-983-3500.
Troy, Ohio Office: 1850 W. main Street, 45373. Telephone: 937-440-9414.
Xenia, Ohio Office: 547 W. Second Street, 45385. Telephone: 937-223-8888.

Plaintiffs Personal Injury, Medical Malpractice, Products Liability.

FIRM PROFILE: This Firm, a member of the Bar Register of Preeminent Lawyers, offers extensive knowledge and experience in personal injury, product liability and medical malpractice. The Firm receives referrals from approximately 200 lawyers in their practice areas. In addition to fourteen lawyers, the Firm offers an experienced support staff of 60, including three full-time investigators/adjustors. The Firm has taken a leadership role in bar association activities and regularly authors legal articles and lectures to state, regional and local trial associations.

MICHAEL E. DYER, born Atlanta, Georgia, April 23, 1953; admitted to bar, 1980, Ohio and U.S. District Court, Southern District of Ohio. *Education:* Furman University (B.A., 1975); University of Dayton (J.D., 1980). *Member:* Dayton, Ohio State and American Bar Associations; Association of Trial Lawyers of America; Ohio Academy of Trial Lawyers (Board of Trustees, 1995—); Miami Valley Trial Lawyers. ***PRACTICE AREAS:*** Personal Injury (100%). ***Email:*** Mdyer@dgmslaw.com

CARMINE M. GAROFALO, born Steubenville, Ohio, August 15, 1948; admitted to bar, 1974, Ohio; 1975, U.S. District Court, Southern District of Ohio; 1986, U.S. Court of Appeals, Sixth Circuit; 1990, U.S. Supreme Court. *Education:* Ohio University (B.B.A., summa cum laude, honors in general studies, 1971); The Ohio State University (J.D., cum laude, 1974). *Member:* Dayton, Ohio State and American Bar Associations; Ohio Academy of Trial Lawyers; Association of Trial Lawyers of America; Miami Valley Trial Lawyers Association. ***PRACTICE AREAS:*** Plaintiffs Personal Injury (100%). ***Email:*** Cgarofalo@dgmslaw.com

DOUGLAS A. MANN, born Dayton, Ohio, August 3, 1959; admitted to bar, 1984, Ohio; 1986, U.S. District Court, Southern District of Ohio; 1987, U.S. Court of Appeals, 6th and 4th Circuits. *Education:* Bowling Green State University (B.S., 1981); University of Toledo (J.D., 1984). Delta Theta Phi. *Member:* Dayton, Ohio State and American Bar Associations; Ohio Academy of Trial Lawyers; Association of Trial Lawyers of America; Miami Valley Trial Lawyers Association. ***PRACTICE AREAS:*** Plaintiff's Personal Injury (100%). ***Email:*** Dmann@dgmslaw.com

RONALD E. SCHULTZ, born Hillsdale, Michigan, May 11, 1942; admitted to bar, 1967, Ohio; 1969, U.S. District Court, Southern District of Ohio; 1972, U.S. Supreme Court; 1978, U.S. District Court, Eastern District of Kentucky and U.S. Court of Appeals, Sixth Circuit. *Education:* The Ohio University (B.S., 1964); The Ohio State University (J.D., 1967). Author: "Ohio Sovereign Immunity: Long Lives The King," Ohio State Law Journal, 1967; "In the Pipeline," Ohio Trial (Quarterly Article); "Cross Examining the Defense Medical Expert," Ohio Trial, Fall 1992. *Member:* Dayton (Chairman, Civil Trial Practice Committee), Ohio State (Member, Negligence Law Committee) and American (Member, Litigation Section) Bar Associations; Ohio Academy of Trial Lawyers (Board of Trust-

(This Listing Continued)

ees, 1988—); The Association of Trial Lawyers of America; Montgomery County Trial Lawyers Association (President, 1988-1990; Vice President, 1985-1987). ***PRACTICE AREAS:*** Personal Injury; Medical Malpractice.

JOHN A. SMALLEY, born Louisville, Kentucky, September 30, 1959; admitted to bar, 1985, Ohio; 1986, Kentucky and U.S. District Court, Southern District of Ohio. *Education:* University of Kentucky (B.A., 1981); University of Dayton (J.D., cum laude, 1985). Symposium Editor, 1984 and Research Editor, 1984-1985, University of Dayton Law Review. *Member:* Dayton, Louisville, Ohio State, Kentucky and American Bar Associations; Defense Research Institute; American Trial Lawyers Association; Ohio Trial Lawyers Association. ***PRACTICE AREAS:*** Plaintiff Personal Injury. ***Email:*** Jsmalley@dgmslaw.com

KENNETH J. IGNOZZI, born Natrona Heights, Pennsylvania, January 31, 1967; admitted to bar, 1991, Ohio and U.S. District Court, Southern District of Ohio; 1992, Pennsylvania. *Education:* Allegheny College (B.S., 1988); University of Dayton School of Law (J.D., 1991). *Member:* Dayton, Ohio State, Pennsylvania and American Bar Associations; Defense Research Institute. ***PRACTICE AREAS:*** Personal Injury; Insurance Law; Professional Liability; Employment. ***Email:*** Kignozzi@dgmslaw.com

---

DIANE E. HANSON, born Williamsburg, Ohio, February 9, 1953; admitted to bar, 1993, Ohio. *Education:* University of Connecticut (B.A. cum laude with honors, 1982; M.A., 1983); University of Dayton (J.D., 1993). Phi Alpha Theta. *Member:* Dayton and Ohio State Bar Associations; Ohio Academy of Trial Lawyers; The Carl D. Kessler Inn of Court, 1994. ***PRACTICE AREAS:*** Personal Injury; Medical Malpractice. ***Email:*** Dhanson@dgmslaw.com

HENRY HYDE, III, born Olney, Maryland, December 26, 1967; admitted to bar, 1994, Ohio. *Education:* Villanova University (B.A., 1990); University of Dayton (J.D., 1994). *Member:* Dayton Bar Association; Ohio Academy of Trial Lawyers. ***PRACTICE AREAS:*** Plaintiffs Personal Injury.

DAVID W. MARQUIS, born Albany, New York, May 8, 1963; admitted to bar, 1991, Ohio; 1992, Pennsylvania and U.S. District Court, Southern District of Ohio. *Education:* Trenton State College (B.S., 1985); Dayton Law School (J.D., 1990). Delta Theta Phi. Staff Attorney, Second District Court of Appeals, Dayton, 1990-1992. *Member:* Ohio State Bar Association; Ohio Association of Trial Lawyers. ***PRACTICE AREAS:*** Personal Injury; Probate. ***Email:*** Dmarquis@dgmslaw.com

MATTHEW D. BRUDER, born Rogers City, Michigan, August 1, 1973; admitted to bar, 1998, Ohio. *Education:* Adrian College (B.A., 1995); University of Akron (J.D., 1998). *Member:* Ohio Academy of Trial Lawyers; Association of Trial Lawyers of America. ***PRACTICE AREAS:*** Personal Injury (100%). ***Email:*** Mbruder@dgmslaw.com

KEVIN W. ATTKISSON, born St. Petersburg, Florida, September 1, 1964; admitted to bar, 1997, Ohio. *Education:* University of South Florida (B.A., 1994); Dayton Law School (J.D., 1997). ***PRACTICE AREAS:*** Personal Injury. ***Email:*** Kattkisson@dgmslaw.com

F. MARK MAIER, born Bellefontaine, Ohio, June 1, 1949; admitted to bar, 1981, Ohio; 1983, U.S. District Court, Northern and Southern Districts of Ohio. *Education:* The Ohio State University (B.A., 1972; M.B.A., 1978); University of Toledo (J.D., 1981). Recipient, American Juris Award, Top Student, Trusts and Estates. Former Member: Toledo Bar Association, 1986-1992, 2001; Columbus Bar Association, 1993-1997; Delaware County Bar Association, 1993-1997; Marion County Bar Association, 1993-1997. *Member:* Ohio State Bar Association (Member: 1982-1992, 1996, 2002). ***PRACTICE AREAS:*** Negligence; Personal Injury. ***Email:*** Fmaier@dgmslaw.com

EDWARD C. YIM, born Los Angeles, California, August 27, 1971; admitted to bar, 1996, Ohio; 2002, California. *Education:* University of California at Los Angeles (B.A., 1993); University of Dayton School of Law (J.D., 1996). *Member:* Dayton and American Bar Associations; American Trial Lawyers Association. ***PRACTICE AREAS:*** Personal Injury; Plaintiffs Personal Injury. ***Email:*** Eyim@dgmslaw.com

ROBERT A. BURKE, born Scranton, Pennsylvania, March 23, 1952; admitted to bar, 1979, Ohio; 1981, Pennsylvania; 1986, New York; 1996, Kentucky. *Education:* University of Scranton (B.S., 1970); University of Dayton (J.D., 1978); Capital University (LL.M., 1988). *Member:* Dayton, Kentucky and American Bar Associations. ***PRACTICE AREAS:*** Personal Injury Litigation. ***Email:*** Rburke@dgmslaw.com

DOUGLAS RAY MILEY, born Washington, D.C., December 25, 1968; admitted to bar, 1993, Ohio. *Education:* University of Maryland (B.A. in Economics, 1990); University of Dayton (J.D., 1993). Assistant Prosecuting Attorney, Montgomery County, Ohio, 1995-2001. *Member:* Dayton and Ohio State Bar Associations; Ohio Association of Trial Lawyers. ***PRACTICE AREAS:*** Personal Injury. ***Email:*** Dmiley@dgmslaw.com

JASON SALDANHA, born Bombay, India, July 15, 1978; admitted to bar, 2003, Ohio. *Education:* The Ohio State University (B.A., summa cum laude, 2000; J.D., 2003). Member, Ohio State Journal on Dispute Resolution, 2003-2004. *Member:* Ohio State Bar Association; Ohio Academy of Trial Lawyers. ***PRACTICE AREAS:*** Personal Injury. ***Email:*** jsaldanha@dgmslaw.com

JEFFREY CHINAULT, born Bluefield, West Virginia, April 3, 1978; admitted to bar, 2003, Ohio and U.S. District Court, Southern District of Ohio; 2004, U.S. District of Court, Northern District of Ohio. *Education:* Virginia Polytechnic Institute and State University (B.S., Psychology, 2000); University of Dayton School Law (J.D., 2003). *Member:* Ohio State and American Bar Associations; American Trial Lawyers of America; Ohio Association of Trial Lawyers. ***PRACTICE AREAS:*** Personal Injury. ***Email:*** jchinault@dgmslaw.com

J. PIERRE TISMO, born Wilmington, Delaware, May 11, 1966; admitted to bar, 1991, Illinois; 1997, Ohio and Kentucky; U.S. District Court, Eastern District of Kentucky; 2000, U.S. Court of Appeals, Sixth Circuit. *Education:* University of Dayton (B.A., Communication Management, 1988; J.D., 1991). Phi Alpha Delta, President, 1989-1991. Recipient: American Jurisprudence Award, Civil Trial Practice, 1990; Banks-Baldwin Award, Outstanding Clinical Law Student, 1991-1997. Adjunct Professor, 2004, Assistant Instructor, Mock Trial Team, Trial Practice, 2003, Salmon P. Chase College of Law, Northern Kentucky University. Member, 1997—, Board of Governors, 2003-2004, 2004-2005, Chair, Professional Development, 2004, Kentucky Academy of Trial Attorneys. Participant, Three-Day Trial Training Course, National Institute of Trial Advocacy, 1992, 1997. Assistant Prosecutor, Cook County State's Attorney's Office, Chicago, Illinois, 1991-1997, 1997-2004. Barrister, Salmon P. Chase Inn of Court, 1997—. Member, Prosecutor's Bar Association, 1994-1997. CLE Speaker, Kentucky Bar Association. *Member:* Cincinnati and Northern Kentucky (Moderator, Annual Personal Injury Seminar) Bar Associations; Kentucky Academy of Trial Attorneys (Speaker, Continuing Legal Education; Member, Board of Governors, 2004); Ohio Academy of Trial Lawyers (Speaker, Continuing Legal Education); The Association of Trial Lawyers of America; Kentucky Association of Criminal Defense Lawyers; Greater Cincinnati Criminal Defense Lawyers. ***PRACTICE AREAS:*** Civil Trial Practice; Medical Malpractice; Wrongful Death; Products Liability; Personal Injury; Criminal Defense.

(This Listing Continued)

FALKE & DUNPHY, LLC

Established in 1992

30 WYOMING STREET
DAYTON, OHIO 45409
Telephone: 937-222-3000; 800-322-1410
Fax: 937-222-1414
URL: http://www.ohiolawyers.cc

Personal Injury, Complex Litigation, Divorce, Probate Law, Will Contests, Estate Planning, Living Trusts, Real Estate and Corporation. General, Civil and Trial Practice.

FIRM PROFILE: Founded in 1992 by Lee C. Falke. Mr. Falke served as Prosecuting Attorney for Montgomery County for 28 years. Our size, focus and personal attention, combined with our experience and abilities allow us to provide cost-effective and results-oriented representation.

LEE C. FALKE, born Dayton, Ohio, June 21, 1930; admitted to bar, 1955, Ohio; 1957, U.S. District Court, Southern District of Ohio; 1967 U.S. Supreme Court. *Education:* The Ohio State University (B.S.; 1952; J.D., 1955). Phi Delta Phi. Member, American Judicature Society. Montgomery County Prosecutor, 1965-1992. Member, 1965-1992 and President, 1978-1979, National District Attorneys Association. Member, 1965-1992 and President, 1971, Ohio Prosecuting Attorneys Association. Member, Democratic State Central Committee, 1993—. *Member:* Dayton, Ohio State and American Bar Associations; Ohio Trial Lawyers Association; National Trial Lawyers Association. ***PRACTICE AREAS:*** Personal Injury; Wrongful Death; Medical Malpractice; Birth Trauma; Litigation; Estate Planning; Estate Administration; Living Trusts; Wills; Probate. ***Email:*** leefalke@ohiolawyers.cc

PATRICK K. DUNPHY, born Barre, Vermont, September 12, 1957; admitted to bar, 1982, Ohio and U.S. District Court, Southern District of Ohio; 1991, U.S. Court of Appeals, Sixth Circuit; 1992, U.S. Supreme Court. *Education:* St. Michael's College (B.A., 1979); University of Cincinnati (J.D., 1982). City Prosecutor: Huber Heights, Ohio, 1987-1990; Oakwood, Ohio, 1988-1994. *Member:* Dayton and Ohio State Bar Associations. ***PRACTICE AREAS:*** Civil Practice; Insurance Defense; Personal Injury. ***Email:*** pkdunphy@ohiolawyers.cc

MEMBERS

GREGORY P. SPEARS, born Bowling Green, Ohio, May 16, 1956; admitted to bar, 1982, Ohio, U.S. District Court, Northern and Southern Districts of Ohio. *Education:* Bowling Green State University (B.L.S., 1978); University of Toledo (J.D., 1982). Assistant Montgomery County Prosecutor, 1989—. *Member:* Ohio State Bar Association. ***PRACTICE AREAS:*** Personal Injury; Divorce; Driving While Intoxicated; Probate; Condominium Law. ***Email:*** gregspears@ohiolawyers.cc

SUSAN M. BRASIER, born Dayton, Ohio, 1959; admitted to bar, 1986, Michigan and U.S. District Court, Eastern District of Michigan; 1987, U.S. District Court, Western District of Michigan; 1988, Ohio and U.S. District Court, Southern District of Ohio. *Education:* Miami University (B.Phil., 1982); University of Dayton (J.D., 1986). Member, University of Dayton Law Review, 1984-1986. Prosecutor, City of Riverside, Ohio, 1994—. *Member:* Dayton, Ohio and American Bar Associations. ***PRACTICE AREAS:*** Litigation; Estate Planning; Probate; Family Law; Divorce; Child Custody; Premarital Agreements. ***Email:*** brasier@ohiolawyers.cc

THOMAS J. INTILI, born Cleveland, Ohio, October 2, 1959; admitted to bar, 1986, Ohio; 1987, Florida and U.S. District Court, Southern District of Ohio; 1988, U.S. District Court, Middle District of Florida; 1997, U.S. Court of Appeals, Sixth Circuit; 2001, U.S. court of Appeals, Third Circuit. *Education:* Indiana University of Pennsylvania (B.A., 1982); Case Western Reserve University (J.D., 1986). Recipient, International Academy of Trial Lawyers Award for the Outstanding Student in Trial Advocacy. Member, Law Alumni Association Board, Case Western Reserve University School of Law. *Member:* Dayton, Cleveland (Member, Executive Council, Young Lawyers Section, 1991-1992), Ohio State (Member, Judicial Administration and Legal Reform Comm., 1991—) and American (Member, Litigation Section and Construction Industry Forum) Bar Associations; Association of Trial Lawyers of America. ***PRACTICE AREAS:*** Complex Litigation. ***Email:*** intili@ohiolawyers.cc

---

ROBERT J. HOWARD, born Xenia, Ohio, November 17, 1973; admitted to bar, 2002, Ohio and U.S. District Court, Southern District of Ohio and Eastern District of Wisconsin. *Education:* Wright State University (B.S., Biology, 1996); University of Dayton School of Law (J.D., 2001). Formerly with Stukey & Associates, Dayton Ohio. President, Christian Legal Society, 1999-2001. *Member:* Ohio State Bar Association. ***PRACTICE AREAS:*** Medical Negligence; Wills; Trusts and Estates; Probate; General Practice; Personal Injury. ***Email:*** rjhoward@ohiolawyers.cc

(This Listing Continued)

FALKE & DUNPHY, LLC, Dayton—Continued

REPRESENTATIVE CLIENTS: Nationwide Mutual Insurance Company; Wausau Insurance Companies; Hamilton Mutual Insurance Company; Beau Townsend Ford, Inc.; Re-Max Professional Realty, Inc.; Miami Valley Synthetics, Inc.; Protel Software, Inc.

FARUKI IRELAND & COX P.L.L.

Established in 1989

500 COURTHOUSE PLAZA, S.W.
10 NORTH LUDLOW STREET
DAYTON, OHIO 45402
Telephone: 937-227-3700
Fax: 937-227-3717
Email: admin@ficlaw.com
URL: http://www.ficlaw.com

Civil and Criminal Trial and Appellate Practice in all Courts. Business and Commercial Litigation, Environmental Litigation, White Collar Criminal Defense, Governmental Investigations, Intellectual Property Litigation, Products Liability Defense, Bankruptcy Litigation.

FIRM PROFILE: Started in August 1989 after a team of nine business litigators left a much larger firm, Faruki Ireland & Cox P.L.L., is a dynamic firm of 32 trial lawyers, most of whom are former members of their law reviews, former judicial clerks, or both. Its trial practice is comprised of general, commercial and business litigation including antitrust, securities, RICO, environmental, ERISA, bankruptcy, class action, and intellectual property litigation, products liability defense, white collar criminal matters and administrative agency litigation.

The firm's partners and associates participate in continuing legal education seminars, professional association activities, pro bono publico work and civic affairs.

MEMBERS OF FIRM

CHARLES J. FARUKI, born Bay Shore, Long Island, N.Y., 1949; admitted to bar, 1974, Ohio. *Education:* University of Cincinnati (B.A., summa cum laude, 1971); The Ohio State University (J.D., cum laude, 1973). Associate Editor, Ohio State Law Journal, 1973. Author: "Litigation Involving Trademarks: Preparing the Trademark Case for Trial," 16 U. Dayton L. Rev. 85 (1990); "Clear Openings in the Business Case," 10 Litig. 29, No. 4, American Bar Association (1984); "The Defense of Terminated Dealer Litigation: A Survey of Legal and Strategic Considerations," 46 Ohio State L.J. 925 (1985); "The Practical Use of Motions to Structure a Complex Civil Case," 41 Ohio State L.J. 107 (1980). *Member:* Dayton (Vice President, 1993-1995; President, 1995-1996), Ohio State (Member, Board of Governors, Antitrust Law Section), Federal Circuit, Federal (Dayton Chapter Secretary, 1989-1990; Vice President, 1990-1991; President, 1991-1992) and American (Member, Sections on: Antitrust; Business; Litigation; Public Utilities; Tort and Insurance Practice) Bar Associations; Defense Research Institute. Fellow: American College of Trial Lawyers (Member, Complex Litigation Committee, 1996-1999; State Chair, 2004-2005); American Bar Foundation. ***PRACTICE AREAS:*** Business Litigation; Antitrust; Intellectual Property; Products Liability Defense. ***Email:*** cfaruki@ficlaw.com

D. JEFFREY IRELAND, born Dayton, Ohio, 1954; admitted to bar, 1980, Ohio; 1988, U.S. Supreme Court. *Education:* Denison University (B.A., 1976); University of Dayton (J.D., 1980). Special Projects Editor, University of Dayton Law Review, 1979-1980. Member, Oakwood City Council, 1984-1996; Mayor, 1986-1996. *Member:* Ohio State (Member, Board of Governors, Antitrust Law Section), Federal and American (Member, Sections on: Antitrust; Litigation; Business; Environmental; Public Utilities) Bar Associations; Ohio Municipal League (Member, Environmental Committee). ***PRACTICE AREAS:*** Business Litigation; Antitrust; False Advertising; Environmental Law. ***Email:*** djireland@ficlaw.com

PAUL L. HORSTMAN, born Dayton, Ohio, 1942; admitted to bar, 1967, Ohio. *Education:* University of Dayton (B.A., cum laude, 1964); University of Cincinnati (J.D., 1967). Law Clerk to Judge Carl A. Weinman, U.S. District Court, Southern District of Ohio, 1967-1973. Member, Board of Directors, Kettering YMCA, 1992-1998. *Member:* American Bar Association (Member, Sections on: Antitrust; Litigation; Public Utility). ***PRACTICE AREAS:*** Business Litigation; Employment Law; Public Utility Law. ***Email:*** phorstman@ficlaw.com

JEFFREY T. COX, born Richmond, Indiana, May 30, 1960; admitted to bar, 1991, Ohio; 1995, U.S. Supreme Court. *Education:* Miami University (B.A., 1982); University of Dayton (J.D., 1991). Editor-in-Chief, University of Dayton Law Review, 1990-1991. Author, Essay: "A Call to Lead-Educating Ethical, Moral Legal Professionals," 25 U. Dayton L. Rev. XV (2000). Author, Comment: "Industrial Property Transactions and Hazardous Waste Cleanup in America: An Analysis of State Innovations," 15 U. Dayton L. Rev. 471 (1990). Member, Oakwood City Council, 1996-1999. *Member:* Federal and American (Member, Sections on: Tort and Insurance Practice; Litigation) Bar Associations. ***PRACTICE AREAS:*** Complex Litigation; Business Litigation; Intellectual Property; Products Liability Defense. ***Email:*** jcox@ficlaw.com

THOMAS R. KRAEMER, born Baltimore, Maryland, June 20, 1961; admitted to bar, 1990, Pennsylvania; 1992, Ohio. *Education:* University of Virginia (B.A., 1983); University of Pittsburgh (J.D., magna cum laude, 1990). Order of the Coif; Order of the Barristers. Member, University of Pittsburgh Law Review. Law Clerk to U.S. District Judge Walter H. Rice, Southern District of Ohio, 1990-1992. Adjunct Professor, University of Dayton School of Law, 2000—. ***PRACTICE AREAS:*** Litigation. ***Email:*** tkraemer@ficlaw.com

LAURA A. SANOM, born Detroit, Michigan, 1962; admitted to bar, 1987, Ohio; 1993, New Jersey; 1998, Michigan. *Education:* Kalamazoo College (B.A., 1984); George Washington University National Law Center (J.D., 1987). Adjunct Professor, University of Dayton School of Law, Negotiation, 1991-1992. Member, National Board of Directors, Federal Bar Association Younger Lawyers Division, 1991-1995. President Elect, Board of Directors, YWCA, 1991-1992. *Member:* State Bar of Michigan; New Jersey State, American (Member, Litigation and Antitrust Sections) and Federal Bar Associations. ***PRACTICE AREAS:*** Business Litigation; Antitrust. ***Email:*** lsanom@ficlaw.com

(This Listing Continued)

RONALD I. RAETHER, JR., born Whittier, California, June 15, 1969; admitted to bar, 1997, Minnesota and Ohio. *Education:* The Ohio State University (B.A., cum laude, 1992); University of Dayton (J.D., magna cum laude, 1996). Associate Editor, University of Dayton Law Review, 1995-1996. Law Clerk to: Judge Adele M. Riley, Montgomery County Court of Common Pleas, Dayton, Ohio, 1995-1996; Judge John Meagher, Montgomery County Court of Common Pleas, Dayton, Ohio, 1995-1996. Author: "Getting Over Y2k Computer Rough Spots: Litigate, Settle or Ignore," Business Law Today, (September/October 2000); "E-Mail Maelstorm: Electronic Documents Must be Managed," Business Law Today (September/October 2003). Adjunct Professor, Trademark Trial Practice, University of Dayton School of Law (2001—). Trustee, Kettering Center, Wright State University (2003—); Camp Kern, YMCA (2004—). ***PRACTICE AREAS:*** Business Litigation; Technology and Science; Antitrust; Privacy Law; E-Commerce. ***Email:*** rraether@ficlaw.com

JEFFREY S. SHARKEY, born Dayton, Ohio, June 5, 1967; admitted to bar, 1997, Ohio. *Education:* University of Dayton (B.S., 1992); The Ohio State University (J.D., summa cum laude, 1996). Order of the Coif. Ohio State Law Journal, 1994-1996. Law Clerk to the Hon. Thomas Meskill, U.S. Court of Appeals, Second Circuit, 1996-1997. ***PRACTICE AREAS:*** Civil Litigation; Complex Litigation. ***Email:*** jsharkey@ficlaw.com

COUNSEL

ROBERT P. BARTLETT, JR., born Marietta, Ohio, February 27, 1938; admitted to bar, 1964, Ohio. *Education:* Denison University (B.A., 1960); University of Virginia; The Ohio State University (J.D., 1963). Phi Delta Phi. Lecturer, Libel and Privacy Law, National Business Institute and Ohio State Bar Association Media Law Seminars. Bar Examiner, U.S. District Court, Southern District of Ohio, 1978—. Life Member Delegate, Sixth Circuit Judicial Conference. Chair, Merit Selection Panel for Selection of Magistrate Judge for U.S. District Court, Southern Division, Ohio, 2002. *Member:* International Association of Defense Counsel (Member, Business Litigation, Product Liability and Reinsurance Committees); Defense Research Institute; Ohio Trial Lawyers Association; Ohio State Bar Association (Member, Media Law Committee; Chair, 2004— and Negligence Law Committee); National Freedom of Information Coalition. Fellow, American College of Trial Lawyers. Winner, Ohio Society of Journalists 2000 Award for Best Defense of the First Amendment. ***PRACTICE AREAS:*** Commercial Litigation; Employment Law; Insurance; Libel. ***Email:*** rbarttett@ficlaw.com

BRADLEY D. ANDERSON, born St. Paul, Minnesota, December 13, 1965; admitted to bar, 1993, Ohio; 1994, U.S. Court of Appeals for the Armed Forces and U.S. Air Force Court of Criminal Appeals. *Education:* College of Wooster (B.A., with departmental honors, 1988); University of Michigan Law School (J.D., 1992). Phi Beta Kappa. Associate Editor, University of Michigan Journal of Law Reform, 1991-1992. [Major, U.S. Air Force, 1994-2002]. ***PRACTICE AREAS:*** Litigation. ***Email:*** banderson@ficlaw.com

ERIN A. BAIR, born Dayton, Ohio, November 24, 1978; admitted to bar, 2004, Ohio. *Education:* The Ohio State University (B.S., Chemistry, magna cum laude, 2000; J.D., with honors, 2004). Order of the Coif. University Scholar. Member, National Society of Collegiate Scholars. Recipient: Academic Leader Scholarship; CALI Award for Patent Law, Patent Litigation, Patent Prosecution and Trademark. ***Email:*** ebair@ficlaw.com

JACQUELINE V. BROWN, born Kansas City, Missouri, August 20, 1979; admitted to bar, 2004, Ohio. *Education:* DePauw University (B.A., 2001); Indiana University School of Law (J.D., 2004). Pi Sigma Alpha. Order of Barristers. Member, Mortar Board. ***Email:*** jbrown@ficlaw.com

CHAD E. BURTON, born Youngstown, Ohio, February 8, 1979; admitted to bar, 2004, Ohio. *Education:* Miami University (B.A., 2001); Case Western Reserve University (J.D., cum laude, 2004). Phi Delta Phi. Member, National Moot Court Team. Author: "EECO v. Waffle House--Employers Win, Again," Defense Counsel Journal Vol. 71, No. 1 (Jan. 2004). ***Email:*** cburton@ficlaw.com

DONALD E. BURTON, born Toledo, Ohio, October 21, 1963; admitted to bar, 1988, Ohio. *Education:* University of Toledo (B.A., 1985); The Ohio State University (J.D., 1988). Order of the Coif. Participant, Moot Court National Competition, 1988. Member, Ohio State Law Journal, 1987-1988. Law Clerk to Judge Peggy Bryant, Ohio Court of Appeals, Tenth District, 1988-1990. ***PRACTICE AREAS:*** Corporate Litigation; Intellectual Property Litigation. ***Email:*** dburton@ficlaw.com

MELINDA K. BURTON, born Indianapolis, Indiana, September 22, 1968; admitted to bar, 1995, Ohio. *Education:* Vanderbilt University (B.A., summa cum laude, 1990); University of Miami (J.D., magna cum laude, 1994). Phi Beta Kappa. University of Miami Law Review, 1993-1994. ***LANGUAGES:*** Spanish. ***Email:*** mburton@ficlaw.com

JOHN A. FISCHER, born Dayton, Ohio, July 13, 1968; admitted to bar, 1997, Ohio. *Education:* Wright State University (B.A., summa cum laude, 1993); The Ohio State University (J.D., with honors, 1997). Law Clerk, Judge Clair Dickinson, 1997-1999 and Judge Beth Whitmore, 1999, Ohio Court of Appeals, Ninth District, Akron, Ohio. ***PRACTICE AREAS:*** Litigation. ***Email:*** jfischer@ficlaw.com

MARTIN A. FOOS, born Tiffin, Ohio, January 16, 1970; admitted to bar, 1995, Ohio; 1996, Indiana. *Education:* University of Notre Dame (B.A., magna cum laude, 1992; J.D., 1995). Lead Articles Editor, Notre Dame Journal of Law, Ethics and Public Policy, 1994-1995. Law Clerk to Judge Theresa L. Springmann, U.S. District Court, Northern District of Indiana, 1995-1997 and Magistrate Judge Christopher A. Nuechterlein, U.S. District Court, Northern District of Indiana, 2001-2002. ***PRACTICE AREAS:*** Complex Commercial Litigation; Securities Litigation; Intellectual Property Litigation; Class Action Defense. ***Email:*** mfoos@ficlaw.com

R. HOLTZMAN HEDRICK, born Owensboro, Kentucky, February 27, 1979; admitted to bar, 2004, Ohio. *Education:* Indiana University (B.A., highest distinction, 2001); Indiana University School of Law (J.D., cum laude, 2004). Phi Beta Kappa. Recipient, Ford C. Hope Award for Most Outstanding Student in the Department of Political Science. Executive Competition Coordinator, Moot Court Board. Quarterfinalist, Moot Court. ***PRACTICE AREAS:*** Commercial Litigation. ***Email:*** rhedrick@ficlaw.com

(This Listing Continued)

ROBERT W. KIEFABER, born Portland, Maine, August 26, 1976; admitted to bar, 2002, Wisconsin and Ohio. *Education:* Kenyon College (B.S., 1999); Marquette University Law School (J.D., cum laude, 2002). Executive Editor, Marquette University Law School Sports Law Review, 2000-2002. ***Email:*** ekiefaber@ficlaw.com

ANDREW D. LeMAR, born Minneapolis, Minnesota, October 29, 1977; admitted to bar, 2003, Ohio. *Education:* Indiana University (B.A., with honors, History, 2000; J.D., cum laude, 2003). Blue Key; Golden Key; Mortar Board; Order of Omega. Editor-in-Chief, Indiana Law Journal, 2002-2003. Author, "War Powers: What are They Good For?: Congressional Disapproval of the President's Military Actions and the Merits of a Congressional Suit Against the President," 78 Ind. L.J. 1045 (2003). ***Email:*** alemar@ficlaw.com

MICHELE A. MURPHY, born Ann Arbor, Michigan, March 3, 1955; admitted to bar, 1985, Ohio. *Education:* Georgetown University (B.S., 1978); University of Cincinnati (J.D., 1985). Phi Beta Kappa. *Member:* Cincinnati Bar Association. ***Email:*** mmurphy@ficlaw.com

TIMOTHY G. PEPPER, born Rantoul, Illinois, August 1, 1969; admitted to bar, 1999, Ohio. *Education:* The Ohio State University (B.S., summa cum laude, 1996; J.D., summa cum laude, 1999). Phi Beta Kappa; Order of the Coif. Member, Ohio State Law Journal, 1997-1999. Author: "Beyond Inherent Powers: A Constitutional Basis for *In re Tutu Wells Contamination Litigation,*" 59 Ohio St. L.J. 1777 (1998); "Maintaining Confidentiality," *In Planning Mediation Programs: A Deskbook for Common Pleas Judges,* 2000. [U.S. Navy, 1987-1991]. ***PRACTICE AREAS:*** Commercial Litigation; Employment Litigation. ***Email:*** tpepper@ficlaw.com

K. LYNN PRESTON, born Virginia Beach, Virginia, January 10, 1979; admitted to bar, 2004, Ohio. *Education:* University of Virginia (B.A., 2001); University of Dayton (J.D., 2004). Staff Writer, 2002-2003 and Executive Editor for Publication, 2003-2004, University of Dayton Law Review. Member, 2002-2003, and Coach, 2003-2004, University of Dayton Moot Court. Co-Author: "The Death Penalty Experiment: The Facts Behind the Conclusion," Volume 29, Number 2, University of Dayton Law Review. ***PRACTICE AREAS:*** Business Litigation. ***Email:*** lpreston@ficlaw.com

ANDREW J. REITZ, born Portland, Indiana, January 12, 1978; admitted to bar, 2003, Ohio. *Education:* Wabash College (A.B., magna cum laude, 2000); Indiana University School of Law (J.D., 2003). Phi Beta Kappa. Order of Barristers. Executive Editor, Indiana Journal of Global Legal Studies, 2002-2003. Top Oralist, Sherman Minton Moot Court, 2001. Member Trial Team, 2000-2003. ***Email:*** areitz@ficlaw.com

ANGELA M. SINKOVITS, born Naperville, Illinois, July 21, 1968; admitted to bar, 2003, Ohio. *Education:* University of Central Florida (B.A., 2000); University of Virginia (J.D., 2003). [Army, 1986-1989, E-4.]. ***LANGUAGES:*** German. ***Email:*** asinkovits@ficlaw.com

NICHOLAS M. SMITH, born Charleston, West Virginia, April 27, 1978; admitted to bar, 2003, Ohio. *Education:* Ohio University (B.S., Journalism, 2000); The Ohio State University (J.D., 2003). Delta Theta Phi. Managing Editor, Ohio State Law Journal, 2002-2003. ***Email:*** nsmith@ficlaw.com

ERIN E. STEFANEC, born Guantanamo Bay, Cuba, November 5, 1979; admitted to bar, 2004, Ohio. *Education:* Miami University (B.A., Political Science, 2001); University of Dayton (J.D., 2004). Recipient, Presidential Scholarship, University of Dayton School of Law. Member, University of Dayton Law Review. ***Email:*** estefanec@ficlaw.com

IAN A. TARONJI, born Washington, D.C., December 14, 1971; admitted to bar, 2000, Michigan; 2003, Ohio. *Education:* University of Michigan (B.A., 1994); Wayne State University Law School (J.D., 2000). Member, Moot Court, 1998-2000. Recipient, Menendez-Diaz Scholarship, 1999. *Member:* Dayton Bar Association (Chair, Diversity Committee, 2004—); State Bar of Michigan. ***LANGUAGES:*** Spanish. ***Email:*** itaronji@ficlaw.com

ERIC P. VOIGT, born Plainfield, New Jersey, January 29, 1978; admitted to bar, 2003, Ohio. *Education:* University of North Carolina at Chapel Hill (B.A., Economics, with honors, 2000) Phi Beta Kappa; Indiana University (J.D., magna cum laude, 2003). Order of the Coif. Notes and Comments Editor, Indiana Law Journal. Author: "Note: Reconsidering the Mythical Advantages of Cohabitation: Why Marriage Is More Efficient Than Cohabitation," 78 Indiana Law Journal 1069 (2003). ***Email:*** evoigt@ficlaw.com

KATRINA L. WAHL, born Troy, Ohio, April 8, 1976; admitted to bar, 2003, Ohio. *Education:* DePauw University (B.A., 1998); University of Notre Dame (M.A., 2002; J.D., cum laude, 2003). Executive Articles Editor, Journal of College and University Law. *Member:* Miami County and Federal Bar Associations. ***Email:*** kwahl@ficlaw.com

BRIAN D. WRIGHT, born Syracuse, New York, January 20, 1977; admitted to bar, 2002, Ohio. *Education:* Baldwin-Wallace College (B.A., summa cum laude, 1999); Case Western Reserve University (J.D., 2002). ***Email:*** bwright@ficlaw.com

JULIE E. ZINK, born Dayton, Ohio, August 28, 1973; admitted to bar, 1999, Ohio; 2000, Virginia; 2001, District of Columbia. *Education:* Wright State University (B.A., cum laude, 1996); University of Dayton (J.D., 1999). Member, Golden Key National Honor Society. Recipient, President's Scholarship. Champion, Walter H. Rice Moot Court, 1997. Member, 1998 and Coach, 1999, Moot Court Team. *Member:* Virginia Bar Association; American Intellectual Property Law Association; Dayton Intellectual Property Law Association; Association of Trial Lawyers of America. ***PRACTICE AREAS:*** Intellectual Property Litigation. ***Email:*** jzink@ficlaw.com

(All Attorneys are Members of the Dayton, Ohio State and American Bar Associations.)

FOX & ASSOCIATES CO., L.P.A.

1344 WOODMAN DRIVE
SUITE F
DAYTON, OHIO 45432
Telephone: 937-258-3668
Fax: 937-258-3098
Email: cfoxlaw@aol.com
URL: http://www.foxassociatescolapa.com

Bankruptcy, Chapter 7, Chapter 13, Foreclosures, Divorce, Adoptions, Child Custody, Visitation Rights, Estate Planning, Wills and Trusts, Driving While Intoxicated and Traffic Violations.

(This Listing Continued)

CHARLES B. FOX, born Dayton, Ohio, December 29, 1931; admitted to bar, 1958, Ohio, U.S. District Court, Southern District of Ohio, U.S. Court of Appeals, Sixth Circuit and U.S. Supreme Court. *Education:* The Ohio State University (B.S.B.A., Business Law and Administration, 1952; J.D., 1954). [with U.S. Air Force, 1954-1956]. ***PRACTICE AREAS:*** Bankruptcy Law; Domestic Relations; Probate; Estate Planning Law. ***Email:*** cfoxlaw@aol.com

---

NATE EICHELMAN, born Dayton, Ohio, July 6, 1975; admitted to bar, 2003, Ohio and U.S. District Court, Southern District of Ohio. *Education:* Wright State University (B.S., 1999); University of Dayton (J.D., summa cum laude, 2002). Phi Kappa Phi. Member, American Bankruptcy Law Forum, 2004-2005. ***PRACTICE AREAS:*** Bankruptcy Law; Domestic Relations; Estate Planning Law; Probate. ***Email:*** neichelman@aol.com

WILLIAM S. RUSSELL, born Cincinnati, Ohio, February 17, 1980; admitted to bar, 2004, Ohio and U.S. District Court, Southern District of Ohio. *Education:* Xavier University (B.S., 2001); Dayton Law School (J.D., 2004). ***PRACTICE AREAS:*** Family Law; Criminal Law; Traffic Violations; Estate Planning Law. ***Email:*** wscottrussell@hotmail.com

---

FREUND, FREEZE & ARNOLD

A LEGAL PROFESSIONAL ASSOCIATION

Established in 1984

ONE DAYTON CENTRE, SUITE 1800
ONE SOUTH MAIN STREET
DAYTON, OHIO 45402-2017
Telephone: 937-222-2424
Telecopier: 937-222-5369
Email: ffalawda@ffalaw.com
URL: http://www.ffalaw.com

Cincinnati, Ohio Office: Fourth and Walnut Centre, 105 East Fourth Street, Suite 1400, 45202-4006. Telephone: 513-665-3500. Telecopier: 513-665-3503. Email: ffalawci@ffalaw.com.

Columbus, Ohio Office: Capitol Square Office Building, 65 East State Street, Suite 800, 43215. Telephone: 614-827-7300. Telecopier: 614-827-7303. Email: ffalawco@ffalaw.com.

Covington, Kentucky Office Suite: RiverCenter, 50 East RiverCenter Boulevard, Suite 408, 41011. Telephone: 859-292-2088. Telecopier: 859-292-2514. Email: ffalawky@ffalaw.com

Civil Litigation including Commercial Litigation, Employment Defense, Professional Malpractice Defense, Employer Intentional Torts, Construction Litigation, Civil Rights Defense, Local Government Defense, Nursing Home Defense, Environmental Litigation and Insurance Defense.

FIRM PROFILE: Freund, Freeze & Arnold is a full service litigation firm, with offices in Dayton, Cincinnati, Columbus and Covington, Kentucky. The firm's practice emphasizes civil litigation including commercial litigation, employment litigation, municipal government defense, malpractice defense of doctors, lawyers, realtors, insurance agents and other professionals; civil rights defense; employer intentional torts defense; nursing home defense; environment litigation and insurance defense. The firm holds the highest rating given by Martindale-Hubbell and is listed in the Bar Register of Preeminent Lawyers. The firm is an equal opportunities employer. The attorneys in the firm are active in community and professional groups, including local, state and national bar associations. They also have enjoyed strong academic backgrounds.

Geographic area of practice: The firm represents clients in Ohio, southeastern Indiana, and Kentucky, handling an extensive amount of cases in the cities of Dayton, Cincinnati, and Columbus, in the surrounding Ohio counties of Darke, Shelby, Miami, Clark, Champaign, Logan, Madison, Greene, Preble, Butler, Warren, Clermont, Clinton and Franklin, the Kentucky counties of Boone, Kenton and Campbell, and the Indiana counties of Clark, Dearborn, Decatur, Delaware, Franklin, Henry, Jennings, Ohio, Randolph, Ripley, Rush, Scott, Switzerland, Union and Wayne. The firm practices in the local, state and federal courts of northern Kentucky, southeastern Indiana and southern and central Ohio, including Columbus and Franklin County. The firm has offices in Dayton, Cincinnati, Columbus and Covington, Kentucky. The firm's central location in southwestern Ohio allows it to efficiently and economically serve its clients in all of southwestern Ohio and surrounding areas. Dayton, Springfield, Columbus and Indianapolis are closely linked by Interstate 70. Dayton, Cincinnati and Covington are closely linked by Interstate 75. All four offices are at the junction of the area's major highways.

NEIL F. FREUND, born McHenry, Illinois, February 16, 1945; admitted to bar, 1970, Ohio; 1971, U.S. District Court, Southern District of Ohio; 1976, U.S. Supreme Court; 1980, U.S. Court of Appeals, Sixth Circuit; 1991, Kentucky. *Education:* University of Dayton (B.A., 1967); Ohio Northern University (J.D., 1970). Phi Alpha Delta. Member, Moot Court, 1969-1970. *Member:* Dayton (President, 1985-1986), Ohio State and Kentucky Bar Associations; International Association of Insurance Counsel; Federation of Insurance Counsel; Defense Research Institute; Ohio Association of Civil Trial Attorneys (President, 1992-1993); American Board of Trial Advocates (Ohio Chapter President, 1995); Society of Ohio Hospital Attorneys; American Arbitration Association. American College of Trial Lawyers. ***PRACTICE AREAS:*** Commercial Litigation; Professional Liability Defense; Employment Defense Litigation; Municipal Defense; Civil Rights Defense; Product Liability; White Collar Criminal Defense. ***Email:*** nfreund@ffalaw.com

STEPHEN V. FREEZE, born Dayton, Ohio, December 28, 1948; admitted to bar, 1974, Ohio; 1974, U.S. District Court, Southern District of Ohio; 1982, U.S. Supreme Court; 1987, U.S. Court of Appeals, Sixth Circuit; 1991, Kentucky. *Education:* St. Joseph College (B.S., valedictorian, 1971); Case Western Reserve University (J.D., 1974). *Member:* Dayton, Butler County, Ohio State and Kentucky Bar Associations; Defense Research

(This Listing Continued)

FREUND, FREEZE & ARNOLD, A LEGAL PROFESSIONAL ASSOCIATION, Dayton—Continued

Institute; Ohio Association of Civil Trial Attorneys (Vice-President, 2004-2005); American Board of Trial Advocates; Defense Research Institute. ***PRACTICE AREAS:*** Civil Litigation; Professional Malpractice Defense; Local Government Defense; School Board Defense; Construction Litigation. ***Email:*** sfreeze@ffalaw.com

GORDON D. ARNOLD, born Cincinnati, Ohio, March 13, 1950; admitted to bar, 1975, Ohio; 1976, U.S. District Court, Southern District of Ohio; 1987, U.S. Court of Appeals, Sixth Circuit; 2004, U.S. District Court, Northern District of Ohio. *Education:* Miami University (B.A., 1972); University of Akron (J.D., 1975). Editor-in-Chief, Akron Law Review, 1974-1975. Member, Panel of Arbitrators, American Arbitration Association. *Member:* Dayton, Greene County, Ohio State and American Bar Associations; American Society of Writers on Legal Subjects-Scribes; American Board of Trial Advocates; Defense Research Institute; Ohio Association of Civil Trial Attorneys; Editorial Advisory Board of Ohio Civil Practice Journal (Banks-Baldwin Law Publishing Co., 1989-1992). ***PRACTICE AREAS:*** Civil Litigation; Construction; Commercial Litigation; Product Liability; Insurance Defense. ***Email:*** garnold@ffalaw.com

PATRICK J. JANIS, born Maple Heights, Ohio, March 14, 1957; admitted to bar, 1982, Ohio and U.S. District Court, Southern District of Ohio; 1993, U.S. Court of Appeals, Sixth Circuit. *Education:* Wittenberg University (B.A., magna cum laude, 1979); The Ohio State University (J.D., 1982). Omicron Delta Kappa; Pi Sigma Alpha. Member: National Moot Court Team; Moot Court Governing Board. *Member:* Dayton and Ohio State Bar Associations; Carl D. Kessler Inns of Court; Ohio Association of Civil Trial Attorneys. ***PRACTICE AREAS:*** Civil Trial; Commercial Litigation; Product Liability; Insurance Defense. ***Email:*** pjanis@ffalaw.com

ROBERT N. SNYDER, born Canton, Ohio, July 30, 1955; admitted to bar, 1985, Ohio; 1986, U.S. District Court, Southern District of Ohio and U.S. Court of Appeals, Sixth Circuit. *Education:* The Ohio State University (B.A., 1979); University of Dayton (J.D., 1985). Law Clerk to the Honorable Herman J. Weber, U.S. District Court, Southern District of Ohio, 1985-1986. *Member:* Dayton and Ohio State Bar Associations; Ohio Association of Civil Trial Attorneys; Society of Ohio Hospital Attorneys. ***Email:*** rsnyder@ffalaw.com

CHRISTOPHER W. CARRIGG, born Steubenville, Ohio, December 2, 1953; admitted to bar, 1983, Maryland, U.S. District Court, District of Maryland and U.S. Court of Appeals, Fourth Circuit; 1985, Ohio and U.S. District Court, Southern District of Ohio; 2004, U.S. Court of Appeals, Sixth Circuit. *Education:* Franciscan University of Steubenville (B.A., 1978); University of Dayton (J.D., 1982). *Member:* Dayton and Ohio State Bar Associations; Ohio Association of Civil Trial Attorneys. ***Email:*** ccarrigg@ffalaw.com

SUSAN BLASIK-MILLER, born Pittsburgh, Pennsylvania, December 14, 1959; admitted to bar, 1984, Ohio and U.S. District Court, Southern District of Ohio. *Education:* University of Dayton (B.A., magna cum laude, 1981; J.D., magna cum laude, 1984). Editor, University of Dayton Law Rev., 1983-1984. *Member:* Dayton (President, 2004-2005) and Ohio State Bar Associations; American Board of Trial Advocates; Society of Ohio Hospital Attorneys; Dayton Women's Bar; Ohio Association of Civil Trial Attorneys. American College of Trial Lawyers. ***PRACTICE AREAS:*** Civil Litigation; Medical Malpractice Defense; Legal Malpractice Defense; Professional Liability Defense; Nursing Home Defense; Commercial Litigation. ***Email:*** sblasikm@ffalaw.com

WAYNE E. WAITE, born Canton, New York, April 8, 1957; admitted to bar, 1982, Ohio and U.S. District Court, Southern District of Ohio; 1985, U.S. Court of Appeals, Sixth Circuit; 1987, U.S. Supreme Court. *Education:* State University of New York at Potsdam (B.A., cum laude, 1979); University of Dayton (J.D., cum laude, 1982). *Member:* Dayton and Ohio State Bar Associations; National Association of Hospital Attorneys; Society of Ohio Hospital Attorneys; Nation Health Lawyers Association; Ohio Association of Civil Trial Attorneys. ***Email:*** wwaite@ffalaw.com

CHRISTOPHER F. JOHNSON, born Oak Ridge, Tennessee, October 12, 1953; admitted to bar, 1980, Ohio; 1984, U.S. District Court, Southern District of Ohio; 1985, U.S. Court of Appeals, Sixth Circuit. *Education:* College of Wooster (B.A., 1975); University of Akron (J.D., 1979); McGill University, Montreal, Canada (LL.M., 1981). Phi Beta Kappa. *Member:* Dayton and Ohio State Associations; Ohio Association of Civil Trial Attorneys; Defense Research Institute. ***PRACTICE AREAS:*** Insurance Defense; Product Liability; Employment Law; Construction Law; Transportation. ***Email:*** cjohnson@ffalaw.com

SHAWN M. BLATT, born Dayton, Ohio, March 7, 1964; admitted to bar, 1991, Ohio and U.S. District Court, Southern District of Ohio. *Education:* Auburn University (B.S., 1986); University of Dayton (J.D., magna cum laude, 1991). Production Editor, University of Dayton Law Review, 1990-1991. Author. Comment, "Section 523(A)(6): Willful and Malicious Exception From Discharge: The 'Implied Malice' Standard", 16 U. Dayton L. Rev. 155 (1990). Member, National Association of the Remodeling Industry, Miami Valley Chapter. *Member:* Dayton and Ohio State Bar Associations; Ohio Association of Civil Trial Attorneys; Defense Research Institute. ***PRACTICE AREAS:*** Insurance Defense; Creditor; Construction Law; Civil Rights; Commercial Litigation; Lender Liability; Municipal Liability and Zoning law; Architect/ Engineer Malpractice. ***Email:*** sblatt@ffalaw.com

RAY C. FREUDIGER, born Cincinnati, Ohio, June 12, 1960; admitted to bar, 1991, Ohio; 1993, U.S. District Court, Southern District of Ohio. *Education:* University of Cincinnati (B.B.A., 1982; J.D., with honors, 1991). *Member:* Cincinnati, Dayton and Ohio State Bar Associations; Ohio Association of Civil Trial Attorneys; Defense Research Institute; Association of Trial Lawyers of America. ***PRACTICE AREAS:*** Commercial Litigation; Product Liability; Insurance Defense; Corporate; Real Estate Errors and Omissions; Premises Liability; Landlord and Tenant Law. ***Email:*** rfreudig@ffalaw.com

KEVIN C. CONNELL, born Morgantown, West Virginia, July 16, 1969; admitted to bar, 1994, Ohio; 1995, U.S. District Court, Southern District of Ohio; 2004, U.S. District Court, Northern District of Ohio. *Education:* Miami University (B.A., 1991); West Virginia University (J.D., 1994). Phi Delta Phi. Order of Barristers. Barrister, Carl D. Kessler Inn of Court. Recipient, Ohio Association of Civil Trial Attorneys, Distinguished Service Award, 2002. Author: "Premises Liability in the Context of the Landlord-Tenant Relationship," OACTA Quarterly, Winter 1999. Speaker: "Prejudgment Interest For Tort Claims in Ohio," OSBA, Cleveland, May 1999; "Using Daubert as a Sword: Challenging Expert Testimony in Ohio State Courts," OSBA, Dayton, May 2001; "Preparation of the Responsive Pleading," Dayton Bar Association; "Complaint to Verdict" seminar, December 2003; Faculty, Ohio Judicial Conference, "Measure of Damages", Columbus, 2004. *Member:* Dayton (Chair, Civil Trial Practice Committee, 2003-2004) and Ohio State (Chair, Insurance Law Committee, 2002-2004; Jury Instructions Committee) Bar Associations; Ohio Association of Civil Trial Attorneys (Member, Board of Trustees); Transportation Lawyers Association (Member: Casualty Litigation Committee; Motor Carrier Transportation Committee; Freight Claims Committee). Fellow, Ohio State Bar Foundation. ***PRACTICE AREAS:*** Civil Trial; Transportation Law; Product Liability; Insurance Defense; Real Estate Litigation. ***Email:*** kconnell@ffalaw.com

T. ANDREW VOLLMAR, born Cincinnati, Ohio, July 22, 1969; admitted to bar, 1994, Ohio and U.S. District Court, Southern District of Ohio. *Education:* Xavier University (B.A., 1991); University of Dayton (J.D., 1994). *Member:* Dayton, Butler County and Ohio State Bar Associations; Ohio Association of Civil Trial Attorneys; Defense Research Institute. ***PRACTICE AREAS:*** Litigation; Commercial Litigation; Employment Litigation; Insurance Defense. ***Email:*** avollmar@ffalaw.com

ROBERT W. YOUNG, born Mansfield, Ohio, November 18, 1968; admitted to bar, 1995, Ohio; 1996, U.S. District Court, Southern District of Ohio; 2001, U.S. Court of Appeals, Sixth Circuit. *Education:* Ohio State University (B.A., 1992); Capital University (J.D., cum laude, 1995). *Member:* Dayton and Ohio State Bar Associations; Ohio Association of Civil Trial Attorneys. ***PRACTICE AREAS:*** Litigation; Insurance Defense; Business Litigation. ***Email:*** ryoung@ffalaw.com

LEONARD J. BAZELAK, born Cleveland, Ohio, March 5, 1966; admitted to bar, 1994, Ohio; 1995, U.S. District Court, Southern District of Ohio; 2003, U.S. Court of Appeals, Sixth Circuit. *Education:* Dartmouth College (A.B., 1988); University of Dayton (J.D., 1994). *Member:* Dayton and Ohio State Bar Associations; Ohio Association of Civil Trial Attorneys. ***Email:*** lbazelak@ffalaw.com

---

JOHN G. WITHERSPOON, JR., born Santa Barbara, California, February 1, 1952; admitted to bar, 1983, Ohio and U.S. District Court, Southern District of Ohio; 1984, U.S. Court of Appeals, Sixth Circuit. *Education:* University of Utah (B.A., History, 1979; B.A., Latin, 1979); University of Virginia (J.D., 1982). *Member:* Dayton and Ohio State Bar Associations; Ohio Association of Civil Trial Attorneys; Defense Research Institute. ***PRACTICE AREAS:*** Civil Litigation; Construction Litigation; Commercial Litigation; Insurance Defense. ***Email:*** jwithers@ffalaw.com

LISA A. HESSE, born Lehighton, Pennsylvania, February 18, 1964; admitted to bar, 1989, Ohio and U.S. District Court, Southern District of Ohio; 1992, U.S. Court of Appeals, Sixth Circuit; 1996, U.S. Supreme Court. *Education:* Washington University (B.A., 1986; M.A., 1986); University of Dayton (J.D., magna cum laude, 1989). Member, Dayton Law Review. *Member:* Dayton and Ohio State Bar Associations; Ohio Association of Civil Trial Attorneys; Defense Research Institute. ***PRACTICE AREAS:*** Civil Rights; Employment Defense; Municipal Defense. ***Email:*** lhesse@ffalaw.com

CINAMON S. HOUSTON, born Lake Jackson, Texas; admitted to bar, 1997, Ohio and U.S. District Court, Southern District of Ohio; 2002, Indiana and U.S. District Court, Southern and Northern Districts of Indiana; 2003, Kentucky. *Education:* University Of Illinois, Chicago (B.S., Biochemistry, 1993); University of Dayton (J.D., magna cum laude 1997). Iota Sigma Pi. *Member:* Dayton, Ohio State, Indiana State and Kentucky Bar Associations, Defense Research Institute; Ohio Association of Civil Trial Attorneys. ***PRACTICE AREAS:*** Workers; Employment Law; First and Third Party Insurance Defense; Construction Law. ***Email:*** chouston@ffalaw.com

MICHELE L. KING, born Lima, Ohio, March 8, 1963; admitted to bar, 1991, Massachusetts; 1999, Ohio. *Education:* Boston University (B.L.S., 1986); Suffolk University Law School (J.D., 1991). Assistant Attorney General, Commonwealth of Massachusetts, 1992-1993. *Member:* Dayton and Ohio State Bar Associations; Ohio Association of Civil Trial Attorneys. ***PRACTICE AREAS:*** Workers Compensation Defense. ***Email:*** mking@ffalaw.com

NICOLE A. MITCHELL, born Zanesville, Ohio, March 27, 1972; admitted to bar, 1997, Ohio and U.S. District Court, Southern District of Ohio. *Education:* Miami University (B.A., magna cum laude, 1994); University of Cincinnati (J.D., 1997). Phi Beta Kappa. Member, University of Cincinnati Law Review. *Member:* Dayton, Cincinnati, Butler County and Ohio State Bar Associations; Ohio Association of Civil Trial Attorneys. ***PRACTICE AREAS:*** Insurance Law; Litigation. ***Email:*** nmitchell@ffalaw.com

MATTHEW D. DICICCO, born Clovis, New Mexico, January 1, 1975; admitted to bar, 2000, Ohio. *Education:* Gannon University (B.A., Psychology, cum laude, 1997); University of Dayton (J.D., cum laude, 2000). Member and President, 1999, Carl Kessler Inn of Court. *Member:* Dayton and Ohio State Bar Associations; Ohio Association of Civil Trial Attorneys. ***PRACTICE AREAS:*** Insurance Defense; Medical Malpractice Defense; Commercial Litigation; Personal Injury Defense.

HEATHER M. LORIDAS, born Agana, Guam, June 3, 1976; admitted to bar, 2001, Ohio and U.S. District Court, Southern District of Ohio. *Education:* University of Dayton (B.A., 1998); University of Dayton School of Law (J.D., 2001). Phi Alpha Delta; Golden Key Honor Society; Moot Court Honor Society, Finalist in Corporate Law Competition. Teaching Assistant, Legal Profession III, 2000-2001. Member, Associate Board, Dayton Area Chapter of the American Red Cross, 2001—. *Member:* Dayton and Ohio State Bar Associations; Dayton Womans Bar Association (Secretary, 2004-2005); Ohio Association of Civil Trial Attorneys. ***PRACTICE AREAS:*** Medical Malpractice. ***Email:*** hloridas@ffalaw.com

JASON E. TREHERNE, born Dayton, Ohio, June 14, 1976; admitted to bar, 2001, Ohio. *Education:* The Ohio State University (B.A., summa cum laude, 1998); University of Dayton (J.D., summa cum laude, 2001). Recipient, Highest Academic Average Award, University of Dayton. *Member:* Ohio State and Dayton Bar Associations; Ohio Association of Civil Trial Attorneys. ***Email:*** jtreherne@ffalaw.com

VASEEM S. HADI, born Levittown, Pennsylvania, September 8, 1975; admitted to bar, 2002, Ohio and U.S. District Court, Southern District of Ohio; 2004, U.S. Court of Appeals, Sixth Circuit. *Education:* Wright State University (B.A., Political Science, cum

(This Listing Continued)

laude, 1998); University of Dayton School of Law (J.D., cum laude, 2002). Research Editor, University of Dayton Law Review, 2001-2002. Moot Court Corporate Law Team Member, 2002. Author: Comment: "Ending the 180-Day Waiting Game: An Examination of the Courts' Duty to Short-Circuit the EEOC Backlog Through the Power of Judicial Review," 16 U. Dayton L. Rev. 53, Fall 2001. *Member:* Dayton (Member, Bar Exam and Qualifications Subcommittee) and Ohio State Bar Associations; Ohio Association of Civil Trial Attorneys; Defense Research Institute. ***PRACTICE AREAS:*** Commercial Litigation; Employment Disputes; Insurance Coverage; Insurance Defense; Medical Malpractice; Alternative Dispute Resolution; Administrative Law. ***Email:*** vhadi@ffalaw.com

JAMEY T. PREGON, born Des Moines, Iowa, July 20, 1973; admitted to bar, 1999, Iowa; 2002, Ohio. *Education:* University of Iowa (B.A., 1996); Drake University (J.D., with honors, 1999). *Member:* Dayton, Butler County, Iowa State and Ohio State Bar Associations; Ohio Association of Civil Trial Attorneys. ***Email:*** jpregon@ffalaw.com

BRYAN J. MAHONEY, born Islip, New York, 1974; admitted to bar, 1999, Ohio; 2004, U.S. District Court, Southern District of Ohio. *Education:* University of Dayton (B.A., 1996); St. John's University (J.D., cum laude, 1999). *Member:* Dayton and Ohio State Bar Associations; Ohio Association of Civil Trial Attorneys. ***PRACTICE AREAS:*** Civil Litigation; Insurance Law; Criminal Defense. ***Email:*** bmahoney@ffalaw.com

KIMBERLY S. KISLIG, born Burbank, California, 1963; admitted to bar, 2003, Ohio and U.S. District Court, Southern District of Ohio; 2005, U.S. Court of Appeals, Sixth Circuit. *Education:* University of San Diego (B.B.A., Business Departmental honors, 1986); Ohio Northern University (J.D., high distinction, 2003). Phi Kappa Phi, Honor Society. Judicial Scholarship, 2000-2003. Dean's List, 2000-2003. Staff-Editor (by invitation) and Elected to Editorial Board, Law Review. Recipient: Outstanding Academic Achievement Award, 2000-2003; ONU Secretaries Association Award, Spring, 2002; Public Interest Stipend Award, Summer, 2002; Outstanding Female Graduate, May, 2003, National Association of Women Lawyers (NAWL); Book Awards: Contracts, Legal Research and Writing, Property, Evidence, International Law, Legal Profession and Transition to Ohio Practice. Member, Innocence Project, 30 Pro Bono Hours. *Member:* Dayton and Ohio State Bar Associations; Dayton Women's Bar Association; Ohio Association of Civil Trial Attorneys; Christian Legal Society. ***LANGUAGES:*** Swiss German, German and Spanish. ***PRACTICE AREAS:*** Insurance Defense; Litigation. ***Email:*** kkislig@ffalaw.com

MICHAEL N. RHINEHART, born Newton, Iowa, May 29, 1978; admitted to bar, 2003, Ohio and U.S. District Court, Southern District of Ohio; 2005, Kentucky. *Education:* University of Louisville (B.A., 2000); Dayton Law School (J.D., 2003). *Member:* Dayton, Kentucky and Ohio State Bar Associations; Ohio Association of Civil Trial Attorneys. ***Email:*** mrhineha@ffalaw.com

JULIA A. TURNER, born Dayton, Ohio; admitted to bar, 2003, Ohio and U.S. District Court, Southern District of Ohio. *Education:* Uversity of Cincinnati (B.S.N., 1996); Capital University Law School (J.D., 2003). *Member:* Dayton and Ohio State Bar Associations; Ohio Association of Civil Trial Attorneys. ***PRACTICE AREAS:*** Medical Malpractice. ***Email:*** jturner@ffalaw.com

JUSTIN D. HARRIS, born Sandusky, Ohio, March 21, 1979; admitted to bar, 2004, Ohio and U.S. District Court, Southern District of Ohio. *Education:* Bowling Green State University (B.S., Applied Health Science, 2001); The Ohio State University (J.D., 2004). *Member:* Dayton, Ohio State, and American Bar Associations; Ohio Association of Civil Trial Attorneys. ***PRACTICE AREAS:*** Construction Law; Commercial Litigation; Insurance Defense; Real Estate Law; Personal Injury Defense; Premises Liability Defense; Product Liability Defense. ***Email:*** jharris@ffalaw.com

LINDSAY M. JOHNSON, born Dayton, Ohio, December 15, 1978; admitted to bar, 2004, Ohio; 2005, U.S. District Court, Southern District of Ohio. *Education:* University of Dayton (B.A., English and Philisophy, cum laude, 2001); The Ohio State University (J.D., 2004). *Member:* Dayton and Ohio State Bar Associations; Dayton Women's Bar Association; Ohio Association of Civil Trial Attorneys. ***PRACTICE AREAS:*** Business Litigation; Commercial Litigation; Medical Malpractice; Municipal Law. ***Email:*** ljohnson@ffalaw.com

JESSE R. LIPCIUS, born Tallahassee, Florida, December 5, 1977; admitted to bar, 2004, Ohio; 2005, U.S. District Court, Southern District of Ohio. *Education:* George Mason University (B.S., Psychology, 2001); University of Dayton (J.D., 2004). *Member:* Dayton, Ohio State and American Bar Associations; Ohio Association of Civil Trial Attorneys; Association of Trial Lawyers of America. ***PRACTICE AREAS:*** Construction Law; Premises Liability; Subrogation; Commercial Litigation; Personal Injury Litigation; Insurance Coverage. ***Email:*** jlipcius@ffalaw.com

THOMAS P. SULLIVAN, born Fairbanks, Alaska, January 29, 1969; admitted to bar, 2004, Ohio. *Education:* University of Alaska, Fairbanks (B.A., Criminal Justice, 1991); University of Toledo (J.D., 2004). Member, University of Toledo Law Review. President, University of Toledo Federalist Society. *Member:* Dayton, Ohio State and American Bar Associations; Ohio Association of Civil Trial Attorneys. ***PRACTICE AREAS:*** Personal Injury Litigation; Premises Liability Litigation; Construction Law; Insurance Coverage Disputes. ***Email:*** tsulliva@ffalaw.com

JENNIFER M. WHITE, born Milwaukee, Wisconsin, January 27, 1979; admitted to bar, 2004, Ohio; U.S. District Court, Southern District of Ohio. *Education:* Furman University (B.A., Political Science and Spanish, 2001); University of Dayton (J.D., magna cum laude, 2004). *Member:* Dayton and Ohio State Bar Associations; Ohio Association of Civil Trial Attorneys. ***PRACTICE AREAS:*** Personal Injury Litigation; Premises Liability Litigation; Construction Law; Workers Compensation Litigation. ***Email:*** jwhite@ffalaw.com

RORY E. GARRITY, born Panama City, Panama, May 10, 1979; admitted to bar, 2004, Ohio; 2005, U.S. District Court, Southern District of Ohio. *Education:* University of Colorado (B.A., Studio Art, Painting Emphasis, 2000); University of Dayton (J.D., cum laude, 2004). *Member:* Dayton, Ohio State and American Bar Associations; Ohio Association of Civil Trial Attorneys. ***PRACTICE AREAS:*** Personal Injury Litigation. ***Email:*** rgarrity@ffalaw.com

LOCAL COUNSEL FOR: Special Trial Counsel: City of Dayton; Miami Valley Hospital; Children's Medical Center; Dayton Power & Light Company; Commercial Clients: Bottlers Services, Inc.; Lutheran Social Services. Insurance Company Clients: Auto-Owners Insurance Company; Cincinnati Ins. Co.; CNA Insurance Company; Erie Insurance Group; Farmers Insurance Group; Government Employees Ins. Co.; GRE Insurance Group; Great American Insurance Company; Kemper Group; Media/Professional Insurance, Inc.; Motorists Insurance Company; OHIC Insurance Co.; St. Paul Fire & Marine Insurance Co.; State Auto Insurance Co.; State Farm Mutual Automobile Insurance Company; Liberty Mutual Ins. Co.; Indiana Ins. Co.; Met Life; GE Medical Protective Ins. Co.; American Empire Group.

(This Listing Continued)

(For Complete Biographical Data on Cincinnati and Columbus, Ohio Personnel, See Professional Biographies at Cincinnati, Ohio and Columbus, Ohio)

FROELICH LAW OFFICE LPA

Established in 1978

1812 KETTERING TOWER
40 N. MAIN STREET
DAYTON, OHIO 45423-1812
Telephone: 937-226-1776
Fax: 937-226-1945
Email: froelich4law@aol.com
URL: http://www.lawyers.com/froelichlaw

General Business Practice. Trials. Probate, Trust, Estate Planning, Corporation, Negligence, Business Litigation, Real Estate, Employment, Administrative Law.

FIRM PROFILE: The firm is listed in the Martindale-Hubbell Bar Register of Preeminent Lawyers.

GARY L. FROELICH, born Benton Harbor, Michigan, June 29, 1943; admitted to bar, 1968, Ohio; 1970, U.S. District Court, Southern District of Ohio. *Education:* Miami University (B.A., 1965); The Ohio State University College of Law (J.D., 1968). Editor, Ohio Real Estate Law Instructors Manual, 1977. Assistant Montgomery County Prosecutor, 1971-1974. Chairman, Dayton Board of Income Tax Appeals, 1973-1978. Adjunct Faculty, Real Estate Law, Sinclair College, 1973—. Special Counsel, Ohio Attorney General, 1974-1995. Chairman of Board, Children's Medical Center, 1992-1993. Board Chair, United Health Services, 1997-1998. Trustee, Chamber of Commerce and Philharmonic Orchestra. *Member:* Dayton, Ohio State and American Bar Associations; Computer Law Association. [With JAGC, USAR, 1968-1974]. ***PRACTICE AREAS:*** Real Estate Law; Business Law; Intellectual Property. ***Email:*** froelich4law@aol.com

REFERENCE: Key Bank, N.A. of Dayton, Ohio.

E. S. GALLON & ASSOCIATES

40 WEST FOURTH CENTRE
SUITE 2200
DAYTON, OHIO 45402
Telephone: 937-586-3100; 800-998-4374
Fax: 937-586-3200
URL: http://www.esgallon.com

Personal Injury, Defective Product Liability, Workers' Compensation, Social Security Disability, Trials and Appeals, General Practice, Divorce, DWI, DUI, Traffic Violations, Family Law, Adoptions, Child Custody, Automobile Accidents, Slip and Fall, Child Support, Premarital Agreements, Nursing Home Litigation.

FIRM PROFILE: E.S. Gallon & Associates is the leading firm in the southwestern Ohio region that devotes itself exclusively to the representation of injured victims within the above enumerated areas of concentration. Our many attorneys utilize a large support staff which includes paralegals and others who have demonstrated a commitment and dedication which has carried on since the founding of the firm over forty years ago.

The attorneys of the firm enjoy statewide and national reputations for excellence and are active members as well as leaders in state and local bar associations, trial organizations and community activities.

Currently, the firm employs over thirty concerned, caring individuals with offices in downtown Dayton. Our attorneys are actively engaged in the practice of law not only in southwestern Ohio but also throughout the state.

MEMBERS OF FIRM

DAVID A. SAPHIRE, born Cleveland, Ohio, January 19, 1944; admitted to bar, 1970, Ohio and U.S. District Court, Southern District of Ohio. *Education:* The Ohio State University (B.A., 1967; J.D., 1970). Phi Delta Phi. Assistant Attorney General, State of Ohio, 1971-1973. Chief Arbitrator, Montgomery County Common Pleas Court, General Division, 1989—. Member, Past-Chair, Executive Committee, Montgomery County Board of Mental Health, 1978-1986. Member, Ohio Attorney General's Workers' Compensation Advisory Counsel, 1993-1994. *Member:* Dayton (Ethics Committee, 1973—), Columbus (Ethics Committee, 1971-1973), Ohio State (Chair, Workers' Compensation Committee, 1995-1997) and American Bar Associations; Miami Valley Trial Lawyers Association; The American Society of Law and Medicine, Inc.; The Ohio Academy of Trial Lawyers (Member, Executive Committee Workers' Compensation Section); The Association of Trial Lawyers of America. [Capt., U.S. Army, 1970, Retired]. (Certified Specialist in Workers' Compensation Law, Ohio State Bar Association). ***LANGUAGES:*** French. ***REPORTED CASES:*** State, ex rel. Eltra Corp., v. Indus. Comm., (1973), Ohio St. 2d 96; 304 N.E.2d 239, 65 Ohio Op. 2d 245; McIntyre v. Kuhns Bros. Co., (1977), Ohio App. 2d 131, 375 N.E.2d 1264; 8 Ohio Op.3d 245. ***PRACTICE AREAS:*** Workers' Compensation. ***Email:*** dasapphire@getgallon.com

JOSEPH R. EBENGER, born Cleveland, Ohio, January 8, 1950; admitted to bar, 1977, Ohio; U.S. District Court, Southern District of Ohio. *Education:* St. Bonaventure University (B.A., cum laude, 1972); University of Dayton (J.D., 1977). Phi Alpha Theta. *Member:* Dayton, Ohio State and American Bar Associations; The Association of Trial Lawyers of America; Miami Valley Trial Lawyers Association. (Certified Specialist in Workers' Compensation Law, Ohio State Bar Association). ***REPORTED CASES:*** Thomas v. Conrad, 81 Ohio St.3d 475 (1998); Douglas v. Ohio Bur. of Worker's Comp., 105

(This Listing Continued)

E. S. GALLON & ASSOCIATES, Dayton—Continued

Ohio App.3d 454 (1995); Frazier v. Mayfield, 64 Ohio App.3d 605, 582 N.E.2d 620 (Montgomery, 1989); Schmidt v. Mayfield, 39 Ohio App.3d 157, 530 N.E.2d 1331 (1987). ***PRACTICE AREAS:*** Workers' Compensation. ***Email:*** JREbenger@getgallon.com

JOAN B. BRENNER, born Willard, Ohio, July 12, 1954; admitted to bar, 1981, Ohio and U.S. District Court, Southern District of Ohio. *Education:* Miami University (B.S. in Education, magna cum laude, 1976); The Ohio State University (J.D., 1981). *Member:* Dayton and Ohio State Bar Associations; Miami Valley Trial Lawyers Association; Ohio Academy of Trial Lawyers; The Association of Trial Lawyers of America; National Association for Female Executives. (Certified Specialist in Workers' Compensation Law, Ohio State Bar Association). ***PRACTICE AREAS:*** Workers Compensation Law. ***Email:*** JBBrenner@getgallon.com

JAMES R. PIERCY, born Sharon, Pennsylvania, April 9, 1948; admitted to bar, 1973, Ohio. *Education:* Pennsylvania State University (B.A., 1970); Case Western Reserve University (J.D., 1973). Phi Alpha Theta. Lecturer, Ohio Continuing Legal Education Institute. Ohio Assistant Attorney General, 1973-1979. Member, City of Vandalia, Ohio, Planning Commission, 1992—. *Member:* Dayton (Past Chairman, Workers' Compensation/Social Security Committee, 1996-1997) and Ohio State (Member, Workers' Compensation Committee) Bar Associations; Ohio Academy of Trial Lawyers; Miami Valley Trial Lawyers Association. ***REPORTED CASES:*** State Ex. Rel. Gassman v. Indus. Comm., 41 Ohio St.2d 64, 322 N.E.2d 660 (1975); State Ex. Rel. General Motors Corp. v. Indus. Comm., 42 Ohio St.2d 278, 328 N.E.2d 387 (1975); State Ex. Rel. Geauga Industries v. Indus. Comm., 60 Ohio St.2d 109, 397 N.E.2d 1202 (1979); Price v. Daugherty, 5 Ohio App.3d 157, 450 N.E.2d 296 (1982); Alcorn v. Spaulding & Evenflo Corp., 79 Ohio App.3d 561, 607 N.E.2d 904 (1992); Henry v. Mayfield, 62 Ohio App.3d 814, 577 N.E.2d 689 (1989); Lewis v. Trimble, 79 Ohio St.3d 231 (1997). ***PRACTICE AREAS:*** Workers' Compensation. ***Email:*** Jrpiercy@getgallon.com

RICHARD M. MALONE, born Columbus, Ohio, February 28, 1951; admitted to bar, 1977, Ohio. *Education:* The Ohio State University (B.A., 1973); Capital University (J.D., cum laude, 1977); University of Dayton (M.B.A., 1986). Instructor, Sinclair Community College Legal Assisting Program. *Member:* Dayton and Ohio State Bar Associations. (Certified Specialist in Workers' Compensation Law, Ohio State Bar Association). ***REPORTED CASES:*** State ex rel. Mann v. Industrial Comm'n of Ohio, No. 95-1173, Supreme Court of Ohio (1998); State ex rel. Noland v. Industrial Comm'n of Ohio, No. 95-856, Supreme Court of Ohio, 79 Ohio St.3d 480, 683 N.E.2d 1142 (1997); State ex rel. Lawrence, No. 87-1529, Supreme Court of Ohio, 40 Ohio St.3d 321, 533 N.E.2d 344 (1988); State ex rel. Walters, No. 85-26, Supreme Court of Ohio, 20 Ohio St.3d 71, 486 N.E.2d 94 (1985); State ex rel. Burdette v. Dayton Walther Corp., No. 84-694, Supreme Court of Ohio, 14 Ohio St.3d 29, 470 N.E.2d 897 (1984); State ex rel. Dillon v. Dayton Press, Inc., No. 82-1442, Supreme Court of Ohio, 6 Ohio St.3d 295, 453 N.E.2d 566 (1983); State ex rel. Woodard, No. 84-1294, Supreme Court of Ohio, 18 Ohio St.3d 110, 480 N.E.2d 403 (1985); State ex rel. Mead Digital Sys. v. Jones, No. 94-2036, Supreme Court of Ohio, 77 Ohio St.3d 30, 670 N.E.2d 995 (1996); State ex rel. Kettering Med. Ctr. v. Wallace, No. 93-914, Supreme Court of Ohio, 68 Ohio St.3d 588, 629 N.E.2d 444 (1994); State ex rel. Copeland Corp., No. 89-241, Supreme Court of Ohio, 53 Ohio St.3d 238, 559 N.E.2d 1310 (1990); State ex rel. R.E.H. CO. v. Industrial Comm'n. of Ohio, No. 94-2503, Supreme Court of Ohio, 79 Ohio St.3d 352, 681 N.E.2d 928 (1997). ***PRACTICE AREAS:*** Workers Compensation. ***Email:*** RMMalone@getgallon.com

ASSOCIATES

DAVID R. SALYER, born Barquisimeto, Venezuela, South America, January 28, 1959; admitted to bar, 1991, Ohio and U.S. District Court, Southern District of Ohio. *Education:* William Jennings Bryan College (B.A., 1981); University of Dayton (J.D., 1990). Recipient, American Jurisprudence Award, Criminal Procedure. *Member:* Dayton and Ohio State Bar Associations; Miami Valley Trial Lawyers Association; Ohio Academy of Trial Lawyers; ATLA. ***LANGUAGES:*** Spanish. ***PRACTICE AREAS:*** Personal Injury Law; Defective Product Liability. ***Email:*** Drsalyer@getgallon.com

MARTIN L. MALLOY, born Cleveland, Ohio, October 22, 1949; admitted to bar, 1977, Ohio. *Education:* University of Dayton (B.A., 1971; J.D., 1977). Instructor, Criminal Law, University of Dayton, 1978-1980. ***PRACTICE AREAS:*** Domestic Relations (50%); Probate (15%); Driving While Intoxicated (10%); Traffic Violations (10%); Civil Litigation (15%). ***Email:*** mlmalloy@getgallon.com

GREGORY C. GIBSON CO., L.P.A.

Established in 2000

40 NORTH MAIN STREET
SUITE 2810
DAYTON, OHIO 45423
Telephone: 937-643-0600
Fax: 937-586-9495
Email: ggibson@gibsoncolpa.com
URL: http://www.ggibsoncolpa.com

Medical Malpractice, Serious Personal Injury, Wrongful Death.

FIRM PROFILE: Our firm is devoted to representing those individuals who have suffered injury or death as a result of medical negligence. Additionally, we represent individuals who have suffered serious personal injury or wrongful death as a result of the negligence of another party. We are experienced trial lawyers with a strong history of successful results for our clients.

GREGORY C. GIBSON, born New York, N.Y., September 27, 1947; admitted to bar, 1977, Ohio and U.S. District Court, Southern District of Ohio. *Education:* Gettysburg College (B.A., 1969); Princeton Theological Seminary (M.Div., 1973); University of Dayton (J.D., magna cum laude, 1977). Adjunct Professor of Law, Law and Medicine, University of Dayton, 1980-1985; 1996-2001. Ordained Presbyterian Minister. *Member:* Dayton, Ohio State and American Bar Associations; Ohio Association of Civil Trial Attorneys; The Association of Trial Lawyers of America; Ohio Trial Lawyers Association; American Board of Trial Advocates. ***PRACTICE AREAS:*** Medical Malpractice; Personal Injury; Nursing Home Negligence. ***Email:*** ggibson@gibsoncolpa.com

STEPHEN P. O'KEEFE, born Dayton, Ohio, September 22, 1969; admitted to bar, 1995, Ohio; 1996, U.S. District Court, Southern District of Ohio. *Education:* Miami University (B.A., 1992); Cleveland-Marshall College of Law (J.D., cum laude, 1995). *Member:* Dayton, Ohio State Bar Associations; Ohio Association of Civil Trial Attorneys; The Association of Trial Lawyers of America. ***PRACTICE AREAS:*** Medical Malpractice; Nursing Home Negligence; Personal Injury. ***Email:*** sokeefe@gibsoncolpa.com

CAMILLE LOUISE HARLAN, born Dayton, Ohio, May 7, 1957; admitted to bar, 1994, Ohio. *Education:* Wright State University (B.A., 1986); University of Dayton (J.D., 1994); Gerry Spence's Trial Lawyers College, (1996). Merit Scholar. Certified Mediator. *Member:* Dayton, Darke County, Ohio State Bar Associations. ***PRACTICE AREAS:*** Medical Malpractice; Wrongful Death; Personal Injury. ***Email:*** charlan@gibsoncolpa

GOTTSCHLICH & PORTUNE, LLP

Established in 1997

THE HISTORIC ARMORY
201 E. SIXTH STREET
DAYTON, OHIO 45402-2836
Telephone: 937-913-0200
Fax: 937-824-2818
URL: http://www.gplawdayton.com
Email: dsmith@gplawdayton.com
URL: http://www.gplawoffices.com

Administrative Law, Business Planning, Business Transactions, Commercial Law, Construction Law, Franchise Law, Labor and Employment, Media Law, First Amendment Law, Mergers and Acquisitions, Municipal Law, Real Estate and Leasing, Zoning, Commercial, Fiduciary, Professional Malpractice and Personal Injury Litigation.

FIRM PROFILE: Gottschlich & Portune, LLP, was formed in 1997 by Gary W. Gottschlich and Robert E. Portune, former partners in a large multi-state firm, and John R. Mohr, former Senior Vice President and General Counsel of Ponderosa, Inc. (a New York Stock Exchange listed company). The firm is located in its own building in downtown Dayton and offers a wide range of legal services to its business, municipal and individual clients.

MEMBERS OF FIRM

GARY W. GOTTSCHLICH, born Dayton, Ohio, August 27, 1946; admitted to bar, 1971, Ohio and U.S. District Court, Southern District of Ohio; 1985, U.S. Court of Appeals, Sixth Circuit. *Education:* University of Dayton (B.S., 1968); University College, London University, London, England; University of Notre Dame (J.D., 1971). Assistant Prosecuting Attorney, Montgomery County, 1971-1973. Arbitrator, AAA, NASD and NYSE Panels. *Member:* Dayton (Chairman: Judiciary Committee, 1978-1980; Treasurer, 1981-1982), Ohio State (Member, Board of Governors, Litigation Section, 1984-1998) and American (Member, Trial Evidence Committee, Litigation Section, 1980-1990) Bar Associations; The Association of Trial Lawyers of America; Ohio Academy of Trial Lawyers; Miami Valley Trial Lawyers Association (Founding Member). ***PRACTICE AREAS:*** Commercial Law; Fiduciary Law; Medical Malpractice; Personal Injury; Business Litigation. ***Email:*** gary@gplawdayton.com

ROBERT E. "BUZZ" PORTUNE, born Dayton, Ohio, June 5, 1948; admitted to bar, 1973, Ohio and U.S. District Court, Northern District of Ohio; 1975, U.S. District Court, Southern District of Ohio and U.S. Court of Appeals, Sixth Circuit. *Education:* Miami University (B.A., cum laude, 1970); Duke University (J.D., 1973). Phi Beta Kappa. Member, St. Andrew Society Pipes and Drums. *Member:* Dayton and Ohio State (Member, Media Law Committee) Bar Associations. ***PRACTICE AREAS:*** Municipal Law; Zoning Law; Media Law; First Amendment Law; Construction Law; Labor and Employment. ***Email:*** buzz@gplawdayton.com

JOHN R. MOHR, born Hillsboro, Ohio, July 16, 1947; admitted to bar, 1972, Ohio and U.S. District Court, Southern District of Ohio. *Education:* The Ohio State University (B.S.B.A., 1969; J.D., 1972). Former Senior Vice-President, General Counsel and Secretary, Ponderosa, Inc., a NYSE company. *Member:* Dayton, Miami County, Ohio State and American Bar Associations; American Society of Corporate Secretaries. [Capt., U.S. Army Reserve (Field Artillery)]. ***PRACTICE AREAS:*** Business Law; Mergers and Acquisitions; Franchise Law; Real Estate; Commercial Real Estate; Leasing. ***Email:*** jmohr@gplawdayton.com

MARY E. LENTZ, born Columbus, Ohio, July 8, 1961; admitted to bar, 1990, Ohio and U.S. District Court, Southern District of Ohio. *Education:* Ohio State University (B.S., 1983); Capital University (J.D., 1990). Order of Curiae. Author: "A Post Mortem of the Postpartum Psychosis Defense," Capital Law Review Volume 18:4. *Member:* Dayton and Ohio State (Member, Negligence Committee) Bar Associations; Ohio Association of Trial Lawyers; Ohio Association of Civil Trial Attorneys. ***PRACTICE AREAS:*** Personal Injury; Commercial Litigation. ***Email:*** mlentz@gplawdayton.com

ASSOCIATES

JEFFREY R. MYERS, born Kettering, Ohio, June 17, 1972; admitted to bar, 1999, Ohio. *Education:* Earlham College (B.A., 1995); University of Dayton School of Law (J.D., 1999). Assistant Montgomery County Prosecuting Attorney, 1999-2001. *Member:* Ohio State Bar Association. ***Email:*** jmyers@gplawdayton.com

BENJAMIN K. McCOMAS, born Marysville, Ohio, March 7, 1978; admitted to bar, 2004, Ohio; 2005, U.S. District Court, Southern District of Ohio. *Education:* Cedarville University (B.A., 2000); University of Michigan (J.D., 2003). *Member:* Dayton and Ohio

(This Listing Continued)

State Bar Associations. ***REPORTED CASES:*** 158 OH App.3d 98. ***PRACTICE AREAS:*** Business Litigation; Contracts; Collections; Labor and Employment. ***Email:*** bmccomas@gplawdayton.com

OF COUNSEL

WILLIAM J. BROWN, born Buffalo, New York, June 16, 1947; admitted to bar, 1973, Tennessee; 1982, Ohio; 1989, U.S. Court of Appeals, Sixth Circuit. *Education:* University of Dayton (B.A., 1970); University of Tennessee (J.D., 1973). Former General Counsel: Bell South; Berry Network. *Member:* Dayton, Ohio State and American Bar Associations; American Corporate Counsel Association.

GUMP LAW OFFICE

2541 SHILOH SPRINGS ROAD
DAYTON, OHIO 45426-2197
Telephone: 937-854-4900
Fax: 937-854-0320
Email: gump@gumplaw.com
URL: http://www.lawyers.com/gumplawoffice

Family Law, Adoption Law, Divorce, Child Custody, Child Support, Wills and Probate, Trusts and Estates, Personal Injury, Automobile Accidents, Criminal Defense, Traffic Violations, Social Security, Workers Compensation.

DENNIS E. GUMP, born Dayton, Ohio, June 24, 1944; admitted to bar, 1969, Ohio. *Education:* Ohio University (B.B.A., 1966); Ohio Northern University (J.D., 1969). Assistant Prosecuting Attorney, 1969-1972. Special Counsel to the Ohio Attorney General, 1970—. Acting Judge: Montgomery County Courts, 1976—; Kettering Municipal Court, 1989—. Past President, Ohio Academy of Criminal Defense Lawyers. Past President, Trotwood Chamber of Commerce. Past Business Leader of the Year. Life Member, Who's Who in American Law. Charter Member, Salem Mall Optimist and Trotwood Madison Rotary. Member, Dayton Chamber of Commerce and Kettering-Oakwood Chamber of Commerce. *Member:* Dayton, Ohio State and Federal Bar Associations. ***Email:*** gump@gumplaw.com

HALL & MUELLER

A LEGAL PROFESSIONAL ASSOCIATION
Established in 1932
51 IRONGATE PARK DRIVE
DAYTON, OHIO 45459
Telephone: 937-912-8910
Facsimile: 937-912-8920
URL: http://www.hallmuellerlaw.com

Fairborn, Ohio Office: 3040 Presidential Drive, Suite 222, 45324. Telephone: 937-912-8910. Facsimile: 937-912-6920.

General Business Practice. Corporation, Labor and Employment Law, Banking, Commercial Collections, Taxation, Probate, Estate Planning, Real Estate Law. Trials and Appeals.

DENNIS L. HALL, born Cincinnati, Ohio, July 8, 1944; admitted to bar, 1969, Ohio. *Education:* University of Cincinnati (B.A., 1966; J.D., 1969). Associate Editor, University of Cincinnati Law Review, 1968-1969. *Member:* Dayton and Ohio State Bar Associations. ***PRACTICE AREAS:*** Business Law; Banking Law; Real Estate Law; Employment Law. ***Email:*** dlhall_911@msn.com

CAROLYN L. MUELLER, born Mineola, New York, November 4, 1946; admitted to bar, 1995, Ohio. *Education:* Queens College of the City University of New York (B.A., 1968); University of Dayton (J.D., 1995). Associate Editor, University of Dayton Law Review, 1994-1995. *Member:* Dayton, Ohio State and American Bar Associations. ***PRACTICE AREAS:*** Business Law; Banking Law; Real Estate Law; Employment Law; Wills; Trust Law; Probate. ***Email:*** chm_cmueller@worldnet.att.net

ANDREW P. CONLEY, born Kettering, Ohio, April 2, 1976; admitted to bar, 2003, Ohio; 2004, U.S. District Court, Southern District of Ohio. *Education:* Indiana University (B.S., 1998); Case Western Reserve University (J.D., 2001). *Member:* Dayton, Ohio State and American Bar Associations. ***PRACTICE AREAS:*** Business Law; Commercial Law; Banking Law; Real Estate.

OF COUNSEL

STEVEN C. KATCHMAN, born Dayton, Ohio, May 28, 1960; admitted to bar, 1989, Ohio. *Education:* University of Cincinnati (B.A., 1982); University of Dayton (J.D., 1987). *Member:* Dayton and Ohio State Bar Associations. ***PRACTICE AREAS:*** Debtor-Creditor Law; Consumer Collections; Commercial Collections; Bankruptcy.

REPRESENTATIVE CLIENTS: Wright-Patt Credit Union, Inc.; GZK, Inc. (Arby's, Lee's Famous Recipe Country Chicken area Franchisee); B&L Packaging, Inc.; Butler Asphalt Co.; The Hallmark Title Agency, Inc.; Medical Management Technology Corporation; KMH Systems Inc.; Moyer Industries Inc.; BCS, Inc.; Dayton ADI Co-Op, Inc.; Nolba Realty, Inc.; Wright-Patt Financial Group, Ltd.; Cooperative Business Services, LLC.

KAREN E. HAMILTON
ATTORNEY AT LAW INC.

DAYTON, OHIO

(See Columbus)

Bankruptcy Law, Debtor and Creditor Law, Estate Planning, Revocable Trusts, Living Trusts, Charitable Giving, Elder Law, Medicaid Planning.

ANNE CATHERINE HARVEY

Established in 1991
5335 FAR HILLS AVENUE, SUITE 313
DAYTON, OHIO 45429
Telephone: 937-439-5708
Fax: 937-439-5710
Email: lawyeranneharvey@yahoo.com
URL: http://www.lawfirmanneharvey.com

Cincinnati Office: Tri-State Building, 432 Walnut Street, Suite 1001, 45202. Telephone: 513-721-2960. Fax: 513-621-3017.

Trials, Appeals, Federal, State and Municipal Criminal Defense, Divorce, Dissolution, Child Custody, Military Domestic Relations Law.

FIRM PROFILE: One attorney and staff; Independent Association of 2 attorneys.

ANNE CATHERINE HARVEY, born Dayton, Ohio, January 26, 1961; admitted to bar, 1985, Texas; 1991, Ohio; Federal Circuit Court of Appeals, Sixth Circuit; U.S. District Court, Southern District of Ohio; U.S. District Court, Northern District of Texas. *Education:* University of Dayton (B.S., 1981; J.D., 1985). Psi Chi. Member, University of Dayton Law Review, 1984-1985. Author: "Negligent Infliction of Emotional Distress," University of Dayton Law Review, Fall Ed., 1983. Teaching Assistant, Legal Research and Writing, University of Dayton, 1984-1985. Montgomery County Assistant Public Defender, 2001-2003. Acting Judge, Miamisburg Municipal Court, 1997-2003. Member, Greene County Ethics Committee, 2000-2002. Dayton Volunteer Lawyer's Project, 1991-2000. Civilian Trial Attorney, Wright Patterson Air Force Base, 1989-1991. *Member:* Greene County, Dayton, Ohio State, American and Federal Bar Associations; Family Law Forum, Dayton, Ohio. ***LANGUAGES:*** American Sign Language. ***PRACTICE AREAS:*** Criminal Defense; Divorce; Child Custody.

Languages: Sign Language.

HEDRICK & JORDAN CO.

A LEGAL PROFESSIONAL ASSOCIATION
SUITE 300
124 EAST THIRD STREET
DAYTON, OHIO 45402
Telephone: 937-228-3889
Fax: 937-223-3848

Real Estate Development, Leasing, Financing, Business Formation and Collections.

JAMES E. HEDRICK, born Manila, Philippine Islands, January 20, 1954; admitted to bar, 1978, Ohio. *Education:* Andrews University (B.A., 1975); University of Michigan (J.D., magna cum laude, 1977). *Member:* Dayton, Ohio State and American Bar Associations. ***PRACTICE AREAS:*** Real Estate Development; Real Estate Finance; Real Estate Title Insurance. ***Email:*** jhedrick@hedrickjordan.com

APRIL ANN JORDAN, born Madison, Wisconsin, February 8, 1961; admitted to bar, 1987, Ohio. *Education:* Indiana State University (B.S., magna cum laude, 1983); University of Dayton (J.D., cum laude, 1987). *Member:* Dayton. Ohio State and American Bar Associations. ***PRACTICE AREAS:*** Real Estate Finance; Leasing; Commercial Real Estate Development. ***Email:*** ajordan@hedrickjordan.com

JOHN G. JANSING, born Cincinnati, Ohio, August 8, 1963; admitted to bar, 1988, Ohio. *Education:* University of Cincinnati (B.A., cum laude, 1985); University of Dayton School of Law (J.D., 1988). Phi Alpha Delta; Order of the Barristers. Law Clerk to the Hon. Mike Fain, Court of Appeals of Ohio, Second Appellate District, 1988-1990. *Member:* Dayton and Ohio State Bar Associations. ***PRACTICE AREAS:*** Bankruptcy; Creditors Rights; Real Estate. ***Email:*** jjansing@hedrickjordan.com

REPRESENTATIVE CLIENTS: Fidelity Commonwealth Land Title Agency; R.G. Properties, Inc.; Lawyers Title Agency of Dayton; General Motors Acceptance Corporation; Miami Valley Management Services, Inc.; CB Partners; Bank One, NA; Fifth Third Bank (Western Ohio); Nuvell Credit Corporation; DayMet Credit Union; Republic Development Corporation.

DEAN EDWARD HINES

5335 FAR HILLS AVENUE, SUITE 313
DAYTON, OHIO 45429
Telephone: 937-439-5708
Fax: 937-439-5710
Email: hineslpa@ameritech.net

Taxation, Business Taxation, Estate and Gift Taxation, Property Tax Appeals, IRS Audits, Domestic Relations, Family Law, Divorce, Child Custody, Domestic Violence, Child Custody, Visitation Rights, Adoption Law, Alimony.

DEAN EDWARD HINES, born Cincinnati, Ohio, January 19, 1962; admitted to bar, 1994, Ohio, U.S. District Court, Southern District of Ohio and U.S. Tax Court. *Education:* Eastern Michigan University (B.B.A., 1991); University of Cincinnati (J.D., 1993). Recipient, American Jurisprudence Award in Estate Planning. Member, Domestic Relations Law Forum. *Member:* Ohio, Federal and American Bar Associations; The Trial Lawyers Association of America.

HOCHMAN & PLUNKETT

Established in 1979

SUITE 650 TALBOTT TOWER
DAYTON, OHIO 45402
Telephone: 937-228-2666
Fax: 937-228-0508
URL: http://www.hochmanplunkett.com

Personal Injury, Automobile Accidents, Workers' Compensation and Social Security Disability Law. General Civil and Criminal Practice in all Courts.

JAMES B. HOCHMAN, born Springfield, Ohio, March 4, 1941; admitted to bar, 1966, Ohio. *Education:* The Ohio State University (B.S., 1963; J.D., 1965). Tau Epsilon Rho. Assistant Attorney General, State of Ohio, 1966. Assistant City Attorney, City of Dayton, 1966-1969. Special Counsel to Ohio Attorney General, 1967-1972. Appointed Montgomery County Court Judge, 1970. Elected County Court Judge, 1972-1986; 1980-1986. Member, State Unemployment Compensation Board of Review, 1987-1990. *Member:* Dayton, Ohio State (Member, Workers' Compensation Committee, 1978—) and American Bar Associations; Ohio Trial Lawyers Association (Member, Workers' Compensation Committee, 1980—); The Association of Trial Lawyers of America; Academy of Trial Lawyers of America; Secretary, Miami Valley Trial Lawyers Association. ***PRACTICE AREAS:*** Personal Injury Law; Workers' Compensation Law; Litigation. ***Email:*** jimhochman@hochmanplunkett.com

GARY D. PLUNKETT, born New York, New York, April 11, 1964; admitted to bar, 1990, Ohio. *Education:* Siena College (B.S., 1986); University of Dayton (J.D., cum laude, 1990). Executive Editor, University of Dayton Law Review, 1989-1990. Author: "Punitive Damages, Bad Faith Breach of an Insurance Contract, and the Excessive Fines Clause of the Eighth Amendment," 14 U. Dayton Law Review 657, 1989; "Unknown Effects of Wood v. Shepard on Uninsured and Underinsured Motorist Coverage in Ohio," 39 Clev. St. Law Review 49 (1991). Law Clerk to the Hon. John M. Meagher, Common Pleas Court, Montgomery County, 1988-1990. *Member:* Dayton, Ohio State and American Bar Associations; The Association of Trial Lawyers of America; Ohio Academy of Trial Lawyers. [First Lt., U.S.A.R., Airborne, 1986-1995]. (Certified Specialist in Workers' Compensation Law, Ohio State Bar Association). ***PRACTICE AREAS:*** Personal Injury Law; Worker's Compensation Law; Litigation. ***Email:*** garyplunkett@hochmanplunkett.com

---

JEFFREY D. SNYDER, born Youngstown, Ohio, June 30, 1968; admitted to bar, 1994, Ohio; 1997, U.S. District Court, Southern District of Ohio. *Education:* Wittenberg University (B.A., 1990); University of Cincinnati (J.D., 1993). Prosecutor, Hamilton County. Assistant Attorney General, State of Ohio. *Member:* Dayton and Ohio State Bar Associations. (Certified Specialist in Workers' Compensation Law, Ohio State Bar Association). ***PRACTICE AREAS:*** Workers Compensation; Labor Law. ***Email:*** jeffreysnyder@hochmanplunkett.com

CARLA J. LAUER, born Detroit, Michigan, September 22, 1951; admitted to bar, 1988, Nevada; 1989, California; 1992, Ohio. *Education:* Westminster College (B.A., 1973); University of Nevada (M.A., 1975); Santa Clara University (J.D., 1988). Pi Sigma Alpha. Law Clerk to Judge Deborah Agosti, District Court, State of Nevada. *Member:* Ohio State and American Bar Associations; State Bar of Nevada; State Bar of California; Ohio Academy of Trial Lawyers; National Organization of Social Security Claimant's Representatives. ***PRACTICE AREAS:*** Workers Compensation Law; Social Security. ***Email:*** carlalauer@hochmanplunkett.com

TODD T. MILLER, born Toledo, Ohio, October 3, 1968; admitted to bar, 1994, Ohio. *Education:* Miami University (B.S., 1991); University of Toledo (J.D., 1994). Member, University of Toledo Law Review. *Member:* Dayton and Ohio State Bar Associations; Ohio Trial Lawyers Association. (Certified Specialist in Workers' Compensation Law, Ohio State Bar Association). ***PRACTICE AREAS:*** Workers Compensation. ***Email:*** toddmiller@hochmanplunkett.com

JOHN A. CERVAY, born Dayton, Ohio, June 2, 1943; admitted to bar, 1968, Ohio; 1969, U.S. District Court, Southern District of Ohio; 1975, U.S. Court of Appeals, 6th Circuit. *Education:* University of Dayton (B.A., 1965); The Ohio State University (J.D., 1968). *Member:* Dayton and Ohio State Bar Associations; National Organization of Social Security Claimants Representatives. ***PRACTICE AREAS:*** Social Security Disability; Workers Compensation; Disability Insurance. ***Email:*** jackcervay@hochmanplunkett.com

BRETT R. BISSONNETTE, admitted to bar, 2003, Ohio and U.S. Tax Court; 2004, U.S. District Court, Southern District of Ohio. *Education:* Kennesaw State University (B.B.A., 1998); Ohio Northern University - Pettit College of Law (J.D., with honors, 2003). Member, American Institute of Certified Public Accountants. *Member:* Ohio State Bar Association. ***PRACTICE AREAS:*** Personal Injury; Workers Compensation; Bankruptcy; Tax Law.

A list of Representative Clients will be furnished upon request.
REFERENCE: Society Bank, N.A.

VICTOR A. HODGE

Established in 1982

130 WEST SECOND STREET, SUITE 810
DAYTON, OHIO 45402
Telephone: 937-461-0009; 898-4632
Fax: 937-461-1639
Email: attyhodge@sbcglobal.net
URL: http://www.lawyers.com/hodgelaw

Criminal Defense, Family Law, Personal Injury, Probate, Divorce, Custody, Support, Paternity, Felonies, Misdemeanors, Driving While Intoxicated. Civil Appeals, Trial and Appellate Practice.

(This Listing Continued)

FIRM PROFILE: Trial and Appellate Practice with over 23 years experience in criminal and traffic matters, including capital cases, felonies, misdemeanors and D.U.I. cases; divorce, custody, support and visitation; personal injury cases, including traffic accident, dog bite and gas explosion; probate matters, including wills, estates, guardianships and adoptions; and in various real estate, contract and other matters.

VICTOR A. HODGE, born Louisville, Kentucky, April 4, 1947; admitted to bar, 1981, Ohio; 1982, Florida and U.S. District Court, Southern District of Ohio. *Education:* Bellarmine College (B.A., 1969); University of Dayton (J.D., cum laude, 1981). Phi Alpha Delta. Forensic Chemist, 1973-1980. *Member:* Dayton (Chairman: Criminal Law Committee, 1986-1987; Appellate Law Committee, 2001-2002) and Ohio State Bar Associations; Ohio Association of Criminal Defense Lawyers; Miami Valley Trial Lawyers Association. [U.S. Army, 1969-1971, Sgt. E5]. ***REPORTED CASES:*** Trussell v. GMC (1990), 53 Ohio St. 3d 142, 559 NE 2d 732; State ex rel Bloomingdale v. Fairborn (1983), 2 Ohio St. 3d 142, 443 NE 2d 181; State v. Brown (1996), 116 Ohio App 3d 389, 688 N.E. 2d 295; State v. Fleming (1996), 114 Ohio App. 3d 294, 683 N.E. 2d 79; City of Dayton v. Whiting (1996), 110 Ohio App. 3d 115, 673 N.E. 2d 671; State v. Collins (1993), 88 Ohio App. 3d 291, 623 N.E. 2d 1269; Brooks v. City of Dayton (1990), 70 Ohio App. 3d 722, 591 N.E. 2d 1352; State v. Cunningham (1990), 67 Ohio App. 3d 366, 587 N.E. 2d 310; In re Appeal of Moreo (1983), 13 Ohio App. 3d 22, 13 Ohio B. Rep. 24; State v. Sims (1998), 127 Ohio App. 3d 603, 713 N.E. 2d 513; State v. Delemos 140 Ohio App. 3d 512, 748 N.E.2d 129 (2000).

HOLZFASTER, CECIL, McKNIGHT & MUES

A LEGAL PROFESSIONAL ASSOCIATION

Established in 1940

1105 WILMINGTON AVENUE
DAYTON, OHIO 45420-4108
Telephone: 937-293-2141
FAX: 937-293-0914
Email: hcmm@hcmmlaw.com
URL: http://www.hcmmlaw.com

General Civil Practice. Corporate, Wills and Probate, Trusts & Estates, Asset Protection, Charitable Giving, Estate Litigation, Estate Planning, Guardianship and Conservatorship, Personal Injury Law, Motor Vehicle Accidents and Injuries, Dog Bites, Slip and Fall, Medical Malpractice, Domestic Relations, Divorce and Custody, Adoptions, Child Support, Domestic Violence, Premarital Agreements, Spousal Support, Insurance and Real Estate, Buying and Selling of Businesses, Family Business Law, Limited Liability Company Law, Partnership Law, Small Business Law, Driving While Intoxicated, Juvenile Law, Misdemeanors, Education Law, School Law, Elder Law.

FIRM PROFILE: Holzfaster, Cecil, McKnight & Mues' roots reach back through a number of predecessor firms to the early 1940's when founder, Byron E. Holzfaster, entered the practice of law. Byron E. Holzfaster, Thomas C. Cecil and Daniel H. McKnight have retired, but Attorney Robert L. Mues and his colleagues continue to conduct a diversified general practice with particular emphasis in estate administration and planning, business law, personal injury litigation and matrimonial law. The attorneys, along with a support staff of 13, are dedicated to providing the highest quality legal services, coupled with sensitivity to the client's individualized needs. The firm has successfully pursued cases through the various state and appellate courts as well as the Ohio Supreme Court resulting in precedent setting decisions. Firm members are active in professional organizations including local, state and national bar associations.

MEMBERS OF THE FIRM

ROBERT L. MUES, born Summit, New Jersey, April 14, 1954; admitted to bar, 1978, Ohio and U.S. District Court, Southern District of Ohio. *Education:* Wittenberg University (B.A, 1975); University of Dayton (J.D., 1978). *Member:* Dayton, Ohio State and American Bar Associations; Ohio Academy of Trial Lawyers; Association of Trial Lawyers of America; Miami Valley Trial Lawyers Association. ***PRACTICE AREAS:*** Separation and Divorce; Child Custody; Child Support; Family Law; Personal Injury Law; Wrongful Death; Auto Accidents. ***Email:*** mues@hcmmlaw.com

JOSEPH E. BALMER, III, born Xenia, Ohio, July 13, 1963; admitted to bar, 1989, Ohio; 1991, U.S. District Court, Southern District of Ohio. *Education:* Emory University (B.A., 1985); Ohio State University (J.D., 1989; M.B.A., 1989). Recipient, Emory University National Merit Scholarship. *Member:* Dayton (Member, Probate Law Section) and Ohio State Bar Associations. ***PRACTICE AREAS:*** Corporate and Business Law; Real Estate; Estate Planning; Probate; Wills; Trust Law; Elder Law; Estate Administration; General Litigation. ***Email:*** balmer@hcmmlaw.com

R. ANNE SHALE, born Meyersdale, Pennsylvania, January 14, 1946; admitted to bar, 1988, Ohio. *Education:* West Virginia University (B.S.N., 1967); Wright State University (M.S., 1983); University of Dayton (J.D., 1987). Sigma Theta Tau. Member, Mortar Board. Registered Nurse, Ohio, 1981. *Member:* Dayton (Family Law Committee) and Ohio State (Member, Family Law Forum) Bar Associations. ***PRACTICE AREAS:*** Family Law; Juvenile Law; Probate; Wills; Trust Law; Estate Administration. ***Email:*** shale@hcmmlaw.com

ASSOCIATE

TAMMY C. NORTMAN, born 1974; admitted to bar, 2001, Ohio. *Education:* Miami University (B.A., 1996); Loyola University Chicago School of Law (J.D., 2001). President, Women's Law Society, 1999-2000. Recipient, Entrance Scholarship. *Member:* Dayton and Ohio State Bar Associations; Dayton Women's Bar Association. ***PRACTICE AREAS:*** Family Law; Divorce; Childrens Rights; Juvenile Law; Civil Litigation; Criminal Defense; Estate Planning; Traffic Violations; Driving While Intoxicated. ***Email:*** nortman@hcmmlaw.com

REPRESENTATIVE CLIENTS: Cumis Insurance Society Inc.; Cuna Mutual Insurance Society.
REFERENCE: KeyBank, N.A.

JABLINSKI, FOLINO, ROBERTS & MARTIN

A LEGAL PROFESSIONAL ASSOCIATION

Established in 1961

HISTORIC HUFFMAN HOUSE
214 W. MONUMENT AVENUE
P.O. BOX 10068
DAYTON, OHIO 45402-7068
Telephone: 937-461-5980
Fax: 937-461-4139
Email: sean@jfrmlaw.com
URL: http://www.jfrmlaw.com

Personal Injury, Probate, Estate Planning, Corporation, Real Estate, Family, Commercial and Bankruptcy Law. Trials and Appeals. General Civil Practice.

THOMAS P. MARTIN, born Dayton, Ohio, November 20, 1949; admitted to bar, 1975, Ohio; 1976, U.S. District Court, Southern District of Ohio. *Education:* University of Dayton (B.S., 1972); Ohio Northern University (J.D., 1975). Instructor: Master's Degree Program, American College of Life Underwriters. *Member:* Dayton and Ohio State Bar Associations. ***PRACTICE AREAS:*** Federal Taxation; Estate and Gift Tax; Business Law; Estate Planning.

BRIAN M. ROBERTS, born Dayton, Ohio, May 28, 1957; admitted to bar, 1982, Ohio; 1983, U.S. District Court, Southern District of Ohio; 1984, U.S. Court of Appeals, Sixth Circuit; 1988, U.S. Supreme Court. *Education:* Miami University (B.S., 1979); University of Dayton (J.D., 1982). *Member:* Dayton and Ohio State Bar Associations. ***PRACTICE AREAS:*** Business Law; Estate Planning; Probate Law; Employment Law.

DAVID S. JABLINSKI, born Dayton, Ohio, February 7, 1959; admitted to bar, 1985, Ohio and U.S. District Court, Southern District of Ohio; 1986, U.S. Court of Appeals, Sixth Circuit. *Education:* University of Dayton (B.S., 1981; J.D., 1985). *Member:* Dayton, Ohio State and American Bar Associations. ***PRACTICE AREAS:*** Family Law; General Practice; Trial Practice; Bankruptcy; DUI.

JOHN H. STACHLER, born Cincinnati, Ohio, August 25, 1967; admitted to bar, 1994, Ohio. *Education:* Xavier University (B.S.B.A., 1990); University of Dayton (J.D., 1994). *Member:* Dayton, Cincinnati and Ohio State Bar Associations. ***PRACTICE AREAS:*** Commercial Litigation; Personal Injury; Civil Trial Practice.

SEAN H. HARMON, born South Bend, Indiana, June 30, 1970; admitted to bar, 1997, Ohio and U.S. Tax Court; 1998, U.S. District court, Southern District of Ohio. *Education:* University of Notre Dame (B.A., 1992); University of Dayton (J.D., magna cum laude, 1997). *Member:* Dayton and Ohio State Bar Associations. ***PRACTICE AREAS:*** Business Law; Estate Planning; Probate.

JEFFREY R. HELMS, born Cincinnati, Ohio, May 1, 1976; admitted to bar, 2002, Ohio. *Education:* Xavier University (B.A., 1998); University of Dayton (J.D., 2002). *Member:* Dayton and Ohio State Bar Associations. ***PRACTICE AREAS:*** Domestic Relations; Juvenile Law; Criminal Law. ***Email:*** jeffh@jfrmlaw.com

OF COUNSEL

EUGENE A. JABLINSKI (Retired)
SHEARL J. ROBERTS (Retired)
THOMAS F. FOLINO (1928-2002)

JENKS, PYPER & OXLEY CO., L.P.A.

Established in 2003

COURTHOUSE PLAZA SW, SUITE 901
10 N. LUDLOW STREET
DAYTON, OHIO 45402
Telephone: 937-223-3001
Fax: 937-223-3103
Email: lawyers@jpolawyers.com
URL: http://www.jpolawyers.net

General Liability, Property, Workers Compensation, Bad Faith, First Party Coverage, Third Party Coverage, Construction Defect, Environmental, Toxic Tort, Employment Practices, SUI, PIP/Med Pay, Inland Marine, Intellectual Property, Sexual Harassment, Subrogation, Professional Liability, including Accountants, Real Estate, Architects & Engineers, D&O and Agents E&O, Professional Malpractice, including Dental, Attorney and Medical.

FIRM PROFILE: Jenks, Pyper & Oxley Co., L.P.A. represents individuals, businesses, governmental entities, real estate agencies and insurers. We have substantial experience in handling litigation involving a variety of claims and in counseling clients in matters which may result in potential liability. Through the management of complex, high-exposure matters as well as relatively simple, general liability claims, the firm has developed that level of expertise and understanding which is necessary for both the expedient and economic resolution of legal problems and the avoidance of such situations. We are acutely aware of the expense which is typically involved in civil tort litigation and we are actively engaged in working with clients in risk management, prevention oriented areas and the use of alternative dispute resolutions. Nevertheless, we recognize when some legal claims are made, a vigorous and thorough defense must be developed and presented for those cases that ultimately proceed to trial. We are dedicated to providing quality legal services that are expected by our clients and which must be furnished in order to maintain a satisfactory attorney/client relationship.

THOMAS E. JENKS, born Dayton, Ohio, May 31, 1929; admitted to bar, 1953, Ohio; 1961, U.S. District Court, Southern District of Ohio; 1971, U.S. Supreme Court; 1985, U.S.

(This Listing Continued)

Court of Appeals, Sixth Circuit. *Education:* Miami University; The Ohio State University (J.D., cum laude, 1953). Phi Delta Phi; Order of the Coif. Listed: Best Lawyers in America; Ohio Super Lawyer 2004. Past President, Kettering, Ohio Chamber of Commerce. *Member:* Dayton (President, 1978-1979), Ohio State (Member, Board of Governors, Litigation Section, 1985-1998) and American (Member, House of Delegates, 1984-1987) Bar Associations; International Association of Defense Counsel; Ohio Association of Civil Trial Attorneys. Fellow: American College of Trial Lawyers; American Bar Foundation; Ohio Bar Foundation. Advocate: American Board of Trial Advocates; Dayton Lawyers Club (President, 1999-2002). [1st Lt., USMC, Trial and Defense Counsel, 1953-1955]. ***PRACTICE AREAS:*** Medical Malpractice; Business Litigation. ***Email:*** tjenks@jpolawyers.com

THOMAS H. PYPER, born Dayton, Ohio, October 16, 1956; admitted to bar, 1981, Ohio. *Education:* Ohio University (B.A., summa cum laude, 1978); University of Cincinnati (J.D., 1981). Phi Beta Kappa; Phi Kappa Phi. Member, 1980-1981 and Student Articles Editor, 1981, University of Cincinnati Law Review. *Member:* Dayton, Ohio State and American Bar Associations; Defense Research Institute; Ohio Association of Civil Trial Attorneys. ***PRACTICE AREAS:*** Insurance Defense; Consumer Litigation; Personal Injury; Contractors Liability; Professional Negligence. ***Email:*** tpyper@jpolawyers.com

SCOTT G. OXLEY, born Ashland, Ohio, September 25, 1962; admitted to bar, 1987, Ohio and U.S. District Court, Southern District of Ohio; 1989, U.S. Court of Appeals, Sixth Circuit; 2001, U.S. District Court, Northern District of Ohio. *Education:* Miami University (B.A., 1984); University of Cincinnati College of Law (J.D., 1987). *Member:* Dayton and Ohio State Bar Associations; Defense Research Institute; Ohio Association of Civil Trial Attorneys. ***PRACTICE AREAS:*** Insurance Defense; Consumer Litigation; Personal Injury Litigation; Contractors Liability Litigation. ***Email:*** soxley@jpolawyers.com

---

P. CHRISTIAN NORDSTROM, born Xenia, Ohio, June 10, 1970; admitted to bar, 1995, Ohio; 1996, U.S. District Court, Southern District of Ohio and U.S. Court of Appeals, Sixth Circuit; 1997, U.S. District Court, Northern District of Ohio; 2002, U.S. Supreme Court. *Education:* Duke University (B.S., 1992); Washington University (J.D., 1995). *Member:* Dayton and Ohio State Bar Associations; Ohio Association of Civil Trial Attorneys; Carl D. Kessler Inn of Court. ***PRACTICE AREAS:*** Insurance Defense; Insurance Litigation; Advertising Law; Consumer Banking. ***Email:*** pcnordstrom@jpolawyers.com

MARK ENGLING, born Wichita Falls, Texas, June 11, 1974; admitted to bar, 1999, Ohio and U.S. District Court, Southern District of Ohio. *Education:* University of Dayton (B.A., 1996); Cleveland-Marshall College of Law (J.D., 1999). Moot Court; Delta Theta Phi; Carl D. Kessler Inn of Court. *Member:* Dayton and Ohio State Bar Associations. ***PRACTICE AREAS:*** Civil Litigation; Insurance Litigation; Contractors Liability; Personal Injury. ***Email:*** mengling@jpolawyers.com

CHAD M. KOHLER, born Sidney, Ohio, May 22, 1976; admitted to bar, 2001, Ohio and U.S. District Court, Southern District of Ohio. *Education:* University of Dayton (B.A., cum laude, 1998); Case Western Reserve University (J.D., 2001). Phi Delta Phi; Moot Court; Dean Dunmore Distinguished Advocate. *Member:* Dayton and Ohio State Bar Associations. ***PRACTICE AREAS:*** Litigation. ***Email:*** ckohler@jpolawyers.com

REPRESENTATIVE CLIENTS: Ace Westchester Specialty Insurance; American International Group (AIG); American States Insurance, Co.; Aon Technical Insurance Services; Bristol West Casualty Insurance Co.; Buckeye State Mutual Insurance; Cashland, Inc.; Chicago Insurance Co.; Clark, Schaefer, Hackett & Co.; CNA Real Estate Claims; Coldwell Banker Heritage Realtors; Great West Casualty Insurance Co.; Harleysville Insurance Co.; Hastings Mutual Insurance Co.; K&K Insurance Group; Kemper Insurance; Keyes Gateway, Inc.; Lancer Claims Services, Inc.; Miami Mutual Insurance Co.; National Waterworks, Inc.; Occidental Fire & Casualty Co.; Prudential Residenz Realtors; Quintessential Advisors, Ltd.; Safeco Insurance Co.; The St. Paul Companies; TIG Insurance Co.; USF&G; Western Reserve Group; Wilshire Insurance Co.

KILLWORTH, GOTTMAN, HAGAN & SCHAEFF, L.L.P.

DAYTON, OHIO

(See Dinsmore & Shohl LLP)

JAMES R. KIRKLAND & ASSOCIATES, CO., L.P.A.

ONE ELEVEN WEST FIRST STREET
SUITE 518
DAYTON, OHIO 45402-1131
Telephone: 937-223-0697
Fax: 937-223-5318
Email: kirkland@sbcglobal.net
URL: http://www.lawyers.com/kirklandlaw

Family, Custody, Divorce and Juvenile Law. Civil Trials. Probate.

JAMES R. KIRKLAND, born 1944; admitted to bar, 1969, Ohio. *Education:* Ohio Wesleyan University (B.A.); The Ohio State University (J.D.). Listed: Best Lawyers in America; Ohio Super Lawyer, 2004, 2005. Author: Ohio Domestic Relations, Marital Property Rights, Marital Obligation, West Publishing, 1987-2005; Ohio Domestic Relations Journal, 1987-2003. Lecturer: "Family Law," Ohio State Bar Association, 1984-2004; Law Education Institute, Vail, Colorado, 1987-1988. *Member:* Dayton Bar Association (Chair, Family Law Committee, 2003-2004). Fellow, American Academy of Matrimonial Lawyers. (Certified Specialist, Family Relations Law, Ohio State Bar Association). ***PRACTICE AREAS:*** Family Law. ***Email:*** kirkland@sbcglobal.net

KOVERMAN & SMITH

1300 LIBERTY TOWER
DAYTON, OHIO 45402
Telephone: 937-222-6926
Fax: 937-222-6901

General Civil Practice. Business, Probate, Domestic Relations, Personal Injury, Estate Planning, Real Estate, Zoning Law, and Litigation.

ROBERT J. STOECKLEIN (1917-1990)

JOHN R. KOVERMAN, JR., born Dayton, Ohio, February 29, 1932; admitted to bar, 1959, Ohio; 1960, U.S. District Court, Southern District of Ohio; 1971, U.S. Tax Court; 1987, U.S. Court of Appeals, Sixth Circuit. *Education:* University of Dayton (B.A., 1954); The Ohio State University (J.D., 1958). *Member:* Dayton and Ohio State Bar Association. [First Lieut., Infantry, U.S. Army 1954-1956]. ***PRACTICE AREAS:*** Real Estate; Zoning; Business Law; Civil Litigation; Estate Planning; Wills; Trusts; Probate. **Email:** jkovlaw@yahoo.com

PATRICK K. SMITH, born Dayton, Ohio, November 10, 1952; admitted to bar, 1978, Ohio; 1979, U.S. District Court, Southern District of Ohio; 1988, U.S. Court of Appeals, Sixth Circuit; 1990, U.S. Court of Claims; 1995, California. *Education:* Centre College of Kentucky (B.A., 1975); University of Dayton (J.D., 1978). *Member:* Dayton and Ohio State Bar Associations; State Bar of California. (Also Member, Yanny & Smith, Los Angeles, California). ***PRACTICE AREAS:*** Business Law; Civil Litigation; Domestic Relations; Probate; Estate Planning; Trust Law; Mergers and Acquisitions. **Email:** pkslaw@ameritech.net

REFERENCE: National City Bank, Dayton, Ohio.

LAW OFFICE OF SCOTT A. KRAMER, LLC

130 W. SECOND STREET, SUITE 924
DAYTON, OHIO 45402
Telephone: 937-222-1700
Fax: 937-224-0420
Email: scottakramer@sbcglobal.net

SCOTT A. KRAMER, born Fort Knox, Kentucky, March 30, 1962; admitted to bar, 2000, Ohio. *Education:* San Francisco State University (B.A., 1986); University of Dayton (J.D., 1999). *Member, Dayton, Ohio State and American Bar Associations.* ***PRACTICE AREAS:*** Bankruptcy; Consumer Bankruptcy; Foreclosures; Workouts; Out of Court Debt Restructuring.

LAMKIN, VAN EMAN, TRIMBLE, BEALS & DOUGHERTY, LLC

DAYTON, OHIO
(See Columbus)

Personal Injury, Medical Malpractice, Products Liability, Negligence, Insurance Coverage, Stockbroker Malpractice & Fraud. Litigation and Trial Practice.

LEPPLA ASSOCIATES

Established in 1978
2100 S. PATTERSON BOULEVARD
DAYTON, OHIO 45409
Telephone: 937-294-5959
Fax: 937-294-4411
Email: gjleppla@LepLaw.com
URL: http://www.LepLaw.com

Civil Litigation, Personal Injury, Medical Malpractice, Insurance, Zoning Law, Land Use, Wills and Probate, Legal Malpractice and Ethics.

FIRM PROFILE: Leppla Associates has represented family and business clients in commercial and personal litigation for almost 25 years. The firm handles probate matters as well as malpractice, injury and contract claims in Ohio and Florida. Offices are located on the edge of downtown Dayton adjacent to Carillon Historical Park, just south of NCR World Headquarters.

MEMBERS OF FIRM

GARY J. LEPPLA, born Cleveland, Ohio, October 5, 1953; admitted to bar, 1978, Ohio and U.S. District Court, Southern District of Ohio; 1985, U.S. District Court, Northern District of Ohio; 1986, U.S. Supreme Court; 1989, U.S. Court of Appeals, Sixth Circuit; 1990, Florida, 1990, U.S. District Court, District of Arizona. *Education:* The Ohio State University (B.A., 1975; J.D., 1978). Phi Beta Kappa.; The Florida Bar, Designated Reviewer, Statewide Advertising Committee; CLE Speaker: Ohio Academy of Trial Lawyers, Ohio State Bar Association, The Florida Bar, Dayton Bar Association. Chair, Campaign for Equal Justice, 2005. Co-Chair, Voters Protection Coalition, 2004. *Member:* Dayton (President, 1997-1998; Chair, Ethics Committee, 1989-1991) and Ohio State (Member, Professional Ethics Committee, 1992—) Bar Associations; The Florida Bar (President, Out of State Practitioners Division, 1994-95; Member, Board of Governors, 1998-2000; 2003—; Chair, Bd Rev. Committee on Profession Ethics, 2004-2005); Ohio Academy of Trial Lawyers; Academy of Florida Trial Lawyers; Association of Trial Lawyers of America. ***REPORTED CASES:*** Campbell v. Great Miami Aerie (1984) 15 Ohio St. 3d 74; Pence v. Darst (1989), 62 Ohio App. 3d 32; Campbell v. Burton (2001), 92 Ohio St. 3d 336. ***PRACTICE AREAS:*** Civil Litigation; Commercial Litigation; Medical Malpractice; Personal Injury; Probate; Ethics. **Email:** gjleppla@LepLaw.com

(This Listing Continued)

ERIC S. THOMPSON, born St. Louis, Missouri, March 30, 1974; admitted to bar, 1999, Ohio; 2001, U.S. District Court, Northern District of Ohio. *Education:* The Ohio State University (B.A., Philosophy, cum laude, with honors, 1996); Case Western Reserve University (J.D., 1999). ***PRACTICE AREAS:*** Personal Injury; Criminal Law. **Email:** ericthompson@leplaw.com

OF COUNSEL

JAY M. SIMPSON, born Dayton, Ohio, January 28, 1952; admitted to bar, 1981, Ohio and U.S. District Court, Southern District of Ohio. *Education:* Wright State University (B.A., 1975); University of Dayton (J.D., 1981).

VALERIE STOCKLIN, born Chillicothe, Ohio, November 17, 1945; admitted to bar, 1981, Ohio and Maryland. *Education:* University of Toledo (B.A., 1968); University of Dayton (J.D., cum laude, 1981).

REPRESENTATIVE CLIENTS: Voss Auto Network; Dayton Amateur Softball Commission; Campbell Realtors; Crews Custom Design Homes, Inc.; Creative Land Development, Inc.; Township Hall & Opera House Restoration Co., Ltd.

LOPEZ, SEVERT & PRATT CO., L.P.A.

DAYTON, OHIO
(See Troy)

Civil Litigation, Personal Injury, Automobile Accidents, Truck Accidents, Slip and Fall, Wrongful Death, Commercial Litigation, Criminal Law, Drug Crimes, DUI/DWI/ Juvenile Law, Traffic Violations, Family Law, Divorce, Adoptions, Child Custody, Child Support, Visitation Rights, Business Law, Business Contracts, Business Litigation, Business Enterprises, Business Formation, Buying and Selling a Business, Construction Law, Contracts, Medical Malpractice, Real Estate, Estate Planning, Trusts and Estates, Resorts and Leisure Law, Wills and Probate.

MASON, SCHILLING & MASON CO., L.P.A.

Established in 1973
319 LIBERTY TOWER
120 WEST SECOND STREET
DAYTON, OHIO 45402
Telephone: 513-489-0829
800-840-3514
Fax: 513-489-0834
Email: msm@mason-law.com
URL: http://www.mason-law.com

Covington, Kentucky Office: Heritage International, Suite 203, P.O. Box 2158. Telephone: 513-489-0829. Fax: 513-489-0834.
Columbus Office: 460 E. Main Street. Telephone: 513-489-0829. Fax: 513-489-0834.
Cincinnati Office: 11340 Montgomery Road, Suite 210. Telephone: 513-489-0829. Fax: 513-489-0834.
Lima Office: P.O. Box 937. Telephone: 513-489-0829. Fax: 513-489-0834
Madison, Indiana Office: 201 East Main Street. Telephone: 513-489-0829. Fax: 513-489-0834.

Commercial, Creditors Rights, Bankruptcy, Collection, Banking and Financial Institution Law, Civil Litigation, Federal Consumer Law Litigation, Foreclosures, Automobile Deficiencies, Credit Cards, Medical Debts, Bad Checks, Business Loans/Commercial Debt, Vehicle and Property Repossessions, Landlord Representation/Evictions/Lease Litigation, Equipment Leasing.

FIRM PROFILE: Mason, Schilling & Mason Co., L.P.A., since its founding over 30 years ago, exclusively concentrates in the areas of creditor representation, in all aspects of commercial litigation, banking law, leasing law, bankruptcy law, and creditors' rights law.

We have developed a full service staff of attorneys in all aspects of representation to the credit granting community. Our legal services concentrate exclusively on representing creditors in all facets of legal representation concerning credit management and credit granting, commercial law, and bankruptcy law on behalf of the credit management community.

Further, of particular attention, is the providing of legal services to the banking and credit management community throughout the entire States of Ohio and Kentucky. Our attorneys appear in all State and federal courts in both states.

The value of our law firm rests with the dependable level of service that we provide to all creditor-clients. We pride ourselves in the personalized service and the conscientious follow through that has been a trade mark throughout over three decades of providing legal services to our creditor and banking clients.

(For Complete Biographical Data on all Personnel, see Professional Biographies at Cincinnati, Ohio)

MAURER LAW OFFICES, LLC

DAYTON, OHIO
(See Centerville)

Criminal Law, Driving While Intoxicated, Drug Crimes, Traffic Violations, White Collar Crime, Insurance, Personal Injury, Automobile Accidents and Injuries, Dog Bites, Sexual Abuse, Slip and Fall, Wrongful Death, Family Law, Divorce, Child Custody, Child Support, Domestic Violence, Visitation Rights, Employment Law, Disabled Access, Discrimination, Sexual Harassment, General Practice.

McCULLOCH, FELGER, FITE & GUTMANN CO., L.P.A.

DAYTON, OHIO

(See Piqua)

General Civil Practice. Corporation, Insurance, Taxation, Labor and Employment, Trust and Estate Administration, Estate Planning, Commercial, Real Estate, Pension and Profit Sharing, Family and Domestic Relations, Personal Injury Law, Litigation and Civil Trials.

LAW OFFICES OF CHARLES A. McKINNEY

20 WEST MONUMENT AVENUE
DAYTON, OHIO 45402
Telephone: 937-461-9000
Fax: 937-461-9640
Email: camlaw@woh.rr.com
URL: http://www.charlesamckinney.com

Columbus, Ohio Office: 141 East Town Street, Suite 102, 43215. Telephone: 614-460-9000. Fax: 614-460-9001.

Corporate Law, Business Planning, Contracts, Insurance, Lawsuits, Labor (Management) Law, Personal Injury Law, Automobile Accidents, Dog Bites, Sexual Abuse, Slip and Fall, Trusts and Estates, Estate Planning Law, Guardianship, Wills and Probate, Wrongful Death, Civil Litigation, Buying or Selling a Business, Formation, Closely Held Business, Limited Liability Companies, Partnerships, Small Business, Employment Law, Disability Accommodations, Discrimination, Sexual Harassment, Wrongful Termination.

CHARLES A. McKINNEY, born Dinkins, South Carolina, 1955; admitted to bar, 1980, Wisconsin; 1987, Ohio. *Education:* Wilberforce University (B.A., magna cum laude, 1978); University of Notre Dame (J.D., 1980).

MILLER & LURING

DAYTON, OHIO

(See Troy)

General and Trial Practice, Collections, Estate Planning, Bankruptcy, Personal Injury, Civil, Family/Domestic Relations, Corporation, Negligence, Tax, Municipal, Probate and Real Estate.

LAW OFFICES OF L. PATRICK MULLIGAN & ASSOCIATES L.P.A. CO.

28 N. WILKINSON STREET
DAYTON, OHIO 45402
Telephone: 937-228-9790
Fax: 937-228-9788
Email: acquit1@woh.rr.com
URL: http://www.daytoncriminallaw.com

Criminal Defense, Family Law.

L. PATRICK MULLIGAN, born Somerville, New Jersey, July 30, 1959; admitted to bar, 1984, Ohio; 1985, U.S. District Court, Southern District of Ohio; 1992, U.S. Court of Appeals, Sixth Circuit; 1993, U.S. Supreme Court. *Education:* King's College (B.A., 1981); University of Cincinnati (J.D., 1984). *Member:* Dayton, Ohio State and American Bar Associations. (Certified as a Criminal Trial Advocacy Specialist by the National Board of Trial Advocacy). ***PRACTICE AREAS:*** Criminal Defense (85%); Family Law.

ASSOCIATE

ADRIENNE D. BROOKS, born Dayton, Ohio, April 5, 1979; admitted to bar, 2004, Ohio. *Education:* University of Dayton (B.A., 2001); Tulane University School of Law (J.D., 2004). *Member:* Dayton, Ohio State and American Bar Associations. ***PRACTICE AREAS:*** Criminal Law; Domestic Relations; Juvenile Law.

OF COUNSEL

GEORGE A. KATCHMER, born Spangler, Pennsylvania, August 13, 1948; admitted to bar, 1981, Ohio. *Education:* Millersville University of Pennsylvania (B.A., 1973); University of Dayton (J.D., 1981). ***PRACTICE AREAS:*** Criminal Defense; Civil Litigation; Real Estate; Securities.

MYERS & FRAYNE CO., L.P.A.

Established in 1992

18 WEST FIRST STREET, SUITE 200
DAYTON, OHIO 45402
Telephone: 937-224-0076
Fax: 937-224-5782
Email: annefrayne@myersandfrayne.com
URL: http://www.myersandfraynelaw.com

Business, Corporations, Real Estate, Creditors Rights, Commercial Planning, Estate Planning, Probate, Chapter 11 Reorganizations, and Litigation.

FIRM PROFILE: The firm performs services for business, real estate, estate planning, probate, and chapter 11 clients. The firm prides itself on its creative solutions to sophisticated issues and to be able to provide litigation support in all of those areas.

(This Listing Continued)

JACOB A. MYERS, born Youngstown, Ohio, May 31, 1935; admitted to bar, 1959, Ohio, U.S. District Court, Southern District of Ohio and U.S. Supreme Court. *Education:* The Ohio State University (B.S., 1957; J.D., 1959). Member, Ohio State Law Review, 1958-1959. Fellow, American Bar Foundation. ***REPORTED CASES:*** Woodby v. Immigration and Naturalization Service, U.S. Supreme Court; U.S. v. Duberstein, U.S. Supreme Court; Zavakos v. Zavakos Enterprises, Inc., Ohio Supreme Court; Dayton Inv. Group 5 v. Speedy Muffler King Inc., Ohio Court of Appeals, Second Circuit. ***PRACTICE AREAS:*** Business; Corporate; Real Estate Development and Rezoning; Mergers and Acquisitions; Estate Planning; Commercial Litigation. ***Email:*** jacobmyers@myersandfrayne.com

ANNE M. FRAYNE, born Springfield, Ohio, 1954; admitted to bar, 1979, Ohio; 1980, U.S. District Court, Southern District of Ohio; 2000, U.S. Supreme Court; 2001, U.S. District Court, Northern District of Ohio. *Education:* The Ohio State University (B.S., summa cum laude, 1976; J.D., with honors, 1979). Order of the Coif; Phi Beta Kappa. Author: "Ethical Issues and Real Estate Lawyers," Practical Legal Ethics, 1996. Seminars and Speeches: "Commercial Real Estate Leasing in Ohio" (1990); "Ethics: Rules and the Corporate Lawyer" (1991); "Commercial Loan Documentation in Ohio - Handling Problem Loans" (1992); " New Mechanics' Lien Law in Ohio" (1992); "Preferences in Bankruptcy and Uniform Fraudulent Conveyances" (1992); "Key Issues in Real Estate Transactions" (1993); "Succession Planning" (1994); "Professional Ethics" (2004). ***REPORTED CASES:*** Dayton Title Agency, Inc. v. The White Family Companies, U.S. Bankruptcy Court (S.D. Ohio). ***PRACTICE AREAS:*** Business Law; Corporate Law; Real Estate; Creditors Rights; Bankruptcy Reorganization; Mergers and Acquisitions; Commercial Law; Estate Planning; Probate. ***Email:*** annefrayne@myersandfrayne.com

SUE SEEBERGER, born Dayton, Ohio, December 16, 1956; admitted to bar, 1992, Ohio and U.S. District Court, Southern District of Ohio. *Education:* Wright State University (B.A., summa cum laude, 1979); University of Iowa; University of Dayton (J.D., 1992). Order of the Barristers. Finalist, Honorable Walter Rice Moot Court Competition. Member, National Trial Practice Team and Semifinalist, Region VI 1992 National Trial Competition. Member, University of Dayton Law Review. Staff Attorney to the Honorable Mike Fain, Ohio Court of Appeals, Second Appellate District, 1994-1996. Author: "Partners in Crime: RICO Associations in Fact and Pinkerton Liability," American Bar Association Complex Crimes Journal 191 (1992). ***PRACTICE AREAS:*** Civil and Commercial Litigation; Appellate Practice. ***Email:*** sueseeberger@myersandfrayne.com

FREDERICK B. HATTON, born Dayton, Ohio, September 22, 1972; admitted to bar, 2000, Ohio. *Education:* Wright State University (B.S., magna cum laude, 1994); University of Dayton School of law (J.D., magna cum laude, 2000). ***PRACTICE AREAS:*** Business Law; Corporate Law; Real Estate; Estate Planning. ***Email:*** fredhatton@myersandfrayne.com

OF COUNSEL

ALAN I. BROWN, born Philadelphia, Pennsylvania, September 8, 1954; admitted to bar, 1979, Ohio. *Education:* Indiana University (B.A., 1976); The Ohio State University (J.D., 1979). ***PRACTICE AREAS:*** Taxation.

REPRESENTATIVE CLIENTS: Adena Tool Corp.; All World Travel Service, Inc.; American Woodwork Specialty Co., Inc.; Bi-Tech; Brinkman Tool & Die, Inc.; Crowe Manufacturing Services, Inc.; Dayton Investment Group; Dublin Pub; General Mortgage, LLC; Hooven-Dayton Corporation; McLen Funeral Hone, Inc.; Midwest Financial & Mortgage; Noman Spencer McKernan Agency, Inc.; Precision Manufacturing; Prime Controls, Inc.; St. Josephs Solutions, LLC; Town & Country Animal Clinic; Vaper Systems Technologies, Inc.; Weber Jewelers, Inc.; Zavakes Enterprises, Inc.

NOLAN, SPROWL, SMITH & FINKE

Established in 1946

1812 KETTERING TOWER
40 NORTH MAIN STREET
DAYTON, OHIO 45423
Telephone: 937-228-7104
Fax: 937-226-1945

General Civil Practice. Bankruptcy, Creditors Rights, Commercial, Collections, Real Estate, Taxation, Estate Planning, Probate, Corporation, Business Law, Family Practice.

MEMBERS OF FIRM

NICHOLAS F. NOLAN (1946-1982)

MILTON L. SPROWL (Retired)

R. PETER FINKE, born Dayton, Ohio, December 18, 1937; admitted to bar, 1968, Ohio. *Education:* University of Notre Dame (B.S., cum laude, 1959); Xavier University (M.B.A., 1963); Salmon P. Chase College of Law (J.D., 1968). Member, Order of the Curia; Certified Public Accountant, Ohio, 1960. Member, Ohio Society of Certified Public Accountants. Member, Miami Valley Estate Planning Council; Planned Giving Council of Greater Dayton. *Member:* Dayton and Ohio State Bar Associations. ***PRACTICE AREAS:*** Probate and Estate Planning; Taxation; Business Law.

EDWARD M. SMITH, born Dayton, Ohio, May 9, 1948; admitted to bar, 1973, Ohio; 1974, U.S. Court of Military Appeals; 1975, U.S. District Court, Northern District of Texas; 1978, U.S. District Court, Southern District of Ohio; 1983, U.S. Court of Appeals, Sixth Circuit. *Education:* University of Notre Dame (A.B., cum laude, 1970; J.D., cum laude, 1973). Staff Member, 1971-1972 and Note and Comment Editor, 1972 and 1973, Notre Dame Lawyer. *Member:* Dayton (Member, Committee on Probate and Estate Planning, 1979—) and Ohio State (Member, Committee on Legal Ethics and Professional Conduct, 1990—) Bar Associations. [Capt., JAGC, USAF, 1974-1978]. (Certified Specialist in Estate Planning, Trust and Probate Law, Ohio State Bar Association). ***PRACTICE AREAS:*** Probate Law; Estate Planning; Commercial Law; Bankruptcy Law; Business Law; Family Law; Wills; Trusts.

REFERENCES: Key Bank, N.A.; Bank One, N.A.

PETERSON & PETERSON

DAYTON, OHIO

(See Xenia)

Automobile and Motorcycle Accidents, Workers Compensation, Job-Related Injuries, Wrongful Death, Bus and Truck accidents, Negligence Claims, Insurance Claims, Probate, Estates, Wills, Living Trust, Guardianship, Power of Attorney, Real Estate, Contracts, Deeds, Evictions, Family Law, Divorce, Custody, Visitation, Domestic Violence, Criminal, Traffic Violations, Felonies, Misdemeanors, DUI, License Suspension, Juvenile, Bankruptcy.

STEPHEN M. PFARRER

Established in 1967

SUITE 2100, FIRST NATIONAL PLAZA
130 WEST SECOND STREET
DAYTON, OHIO 45402-1502
Telephone: 937-228-0894
Fax: 937-461-2923
Email: pfarrer@smpfarrerlawyer.com
URL: http://www.lawyers.com/stephanmpfarrer

Civil Litigation, Corporate Law, Construction, Health Care, Employment Law, Commercial Law.

FIRM PROFILE: Small business practice with related civil litigation.

STEPHEN M. PFARRER, born Dayton, Ohio, May 25, 1941; admitted to bar, 1967, Ohio; 1977, Oregon. *Education:* Lawrence University (B.A., 1963); Case Western Reserve University (J.D., 1967). *Member:* Dayton and Ohio State Bar Associations; Oregon State Bar; Ohio Civil Trial Lawyers Association; American Academy of Hospital Attorneys. [U.S. Marine Corps., 1967-1971]. ***PRACTICE AREAS:*** Civil Litigation; Corporate Law; Construction; Health Care; Commercial Law; Hospital Law.

REPRESENTATIVE CLIENTS: Extermital Termite Service; Buckey Electric Co.; Grandview Hospital & Medical Center; Dayton Wire Products; Submarine House Franchises; Dalton Maintenance, Inc.; Accuracy Products; Unifirst Corp.

PICKREL, SCHAEFFER & EBELING

Established in 1915

2700 KETTERING TOWER
DAYTON, OHIO 45423-2700
Telephone: 937-223-1130
Facsimile: 937-223-0339
URL: http://www.pselaw.com

Banking, Civil, Corporate, General Business, Commercial Lending, Mergers and Acquisitions, Insurance, Labor and Employment, Healthcare, Municipal and Zoning, Personal Injury and Products Liability, Probate, Trust and Estate Planning, Construction, Computer, Real Estate, Environmental, Workers' Compensation Defense, Immigration, Bankruptcy and Tax Law. Trials and Appeals, School Law and Title Insurance.

FIRM PROFILE: Pickrel, Schaeffer and Ebeling is a Dayton legal tradition founded in 1915. Our staff of legal professionals, paralegals and administrative specialists create a team approach which provides depth of experience and a broad range of skills and expertise.

Our full service firm is organized in four practice groups: General Business, Litigation, Labor and Employment Law and Probate and Estate Planning. We serve a broad client base of individuals, entrepreneurs and corporations throughout Ohio and the United States.

WILLIAM G. PICKREL (1931-1966)

VIRGIL SCHAEFFER (1932-1958)

PHILIP C. EBELING (1931-1963)

BRADLEY J. SCHAEFFER (1935-1992)

PAUL J. WINTERHALTER, born Toledo, Ohio, August 14, 1941; admitted to bar, 1966, Ohio and U.S. District Court, Southern District of Ohio. *Education:* University of Dayton (B.A., 1963); University of Cincinnati (J.D., 1966). Phi Alpha Delta. Member, University of Cincinnati Law Review. *Member:* Dayton and Ohio State Bar Associations. ***PRACTICE AREAS:*** Insurance Defense Litigation; Family Law; Civil Litigation; Personal Injury. ***Email:*** pwinterhalter@pselaw.com

PAUL E. ZIMMER, born Dayton, Ohio, January 29, 1948; admitted to bar, 1973, Ohio. *Education:* University of Notre Dame (B.A., magna cum laude, 1970); Duke University (J.D., 1973). *Member:* Dayton (Member and Past Chairman, Business and Taxation Law Committee), Ohio State (Member, Corporation Law Committee) and American (Member: Business Law Section; Forum on Health Law) Bar Associations. ***PRACTICE AREAS:*** Corporate Law; Mergers and Acquisitions; Commercial and Banking Transactions; Medical-Legal; Health Care Law; Security Law (Private Placements). ***Email:*** pzimmer@pselaw.com

ALAN B. SCHAEFFER, born Dayton, Ohio, November 24, 1946; admitted to bar, 1974, Ohio. *Education:* Hillsdale College (B.A., 1968); The Ohio State University (J.D., 1973). Past Director, The Ohio Bar Title Insurance Company. Member: National Association of Industrial and Office Parks; Urban Land Institute. Chair, General Business Practice Group. *Member:* Dayton (Real Property Committee), Ohio State (Member, Board of Governors, Real Property Section; Chair, 1996—) and American (Member, Forum Committee on Construction Law) Bar Associations. [U.S. Army, 1968-1970]. ***PRACTICE AREAS:*** Real Estate; Zoning Law; Construction; Land Use; Land Development. ***Email:*** aschaeffer@pselaw.com

ANDREW C. STORAR, born Dayton, Ohio, August 11, 1952; admitted to bar, 1981, Ohio. *Education:* Wright State University (B.A., magna cum laude, 1978); University of Dayton (J.D., magna cum laude, 1981). Pi Sigma Alpha; Phi Delta Phi. Member, The Order of Barristers. *Member:* Dayton (Member, Board of Trustees, 1995-1997) and Ohio State (Member, Council of Delegates, 1997—) Bar Associations. ***PRACTICE AREAS:*** Insurance Defense Litigation; Civil Litigation; Personal Injury; Corporate Litigation; Commercial Litigation; Appellate Advocacy; Media Representation. ***Email:*** astorar@pselaw.com

JON M. ROSEMEYER, born Libertyville, Illinois, August 20, 1954; admitted to bar, 1984, Ohio. *Education:* University of Illinois (B.A., 1979); University of Dayton (J.D., summa cum laude, 1984). Managing Editor, University of Dayton Law Review, 1983-1984. Agent for Chicago Title Insurance Company. *Member:* Dayton, Ohio State and American Bar Associations. ***PRACTICE AREAS:*** Business Transactions; Commercial Lending; Mergers and Acquisitions; Real Estate Lending; Real Estate Purchasing and Leasing; Corporate Law; Securities Law; Private Placement; Real Estate; Real Estate Title Insurance; Nonprofit Companies. ***Email:*** jrosemeyer@pselaw.com

JAMES W. KELLEHER, born West Point, New York, July 9, 1950; admitted to bar, 1979, Ohio and U.S. District Court, Southern District of Ohio; U.S. Court of Appeals, Sixth Circuit. *Education:* University of Dayton (B.A., 1972; J.D., 1979). Municipal Prosecutor, Village of New Lebanon, Ohio, 1979-1981. Adjunct Professor of Products Liability Law, University of Dayton, School of Law, 1988—. Trustee, Greater Dayton Volunteer Lawyers Project, 2004—. *Member:* Dayton (Member, 1981—; Chairman, Professional Ethics (Certified Grievance) Committee, 1986-1988; Executive Committee, 1988-1990; Chair, Constitution Review Committee, 1990; Member, Civil Trial Practice & Understanding with Physicians Committee; Co Chair, Diversity Issues Committee, 2001-2002) and Ohio State (Member, Committees on: Negligence Law; Ad Hoc Products Liability; Tort Reform Legislation) Bar Associations; Miami Valley Trial Lawyers Association (Trustee, 1988—; President, 2000-2002); Ohio Academy of Trial Lawyers (Seminar Lecturer); The Association of Trial Lawyers of America (Trial Lawyers Care Pro Bono Attorney for September 11 Family); DBA Inns of Court (President, 1999-2001). [Lieut. Col., U.S. Army Retired]. ***PRACTICE AREAS:*** Plaintiff Personal Injury; Defective Product Liability; Appellate; Civil Litigation. ***Email:*** jkelleher@pselaw.com

JAMES L. JACOBSON, born Baltimore, Maryland, January 27, 1952; admitted to bar, 1978, Ohio and U.S. District Court, Southern District of Ohio; 1979, Florida. *Education:* University of Michigan (B.S., 1974); The Ohio State University (J.D., 1977). *Member:* Dayton (Former Chairman, Estate Planning Trust and Probate Law Committee) and Ohio State Bar Associations; The Florida Bar. (Certified Specialist in Estate Planning, Trust and Probate Law, Ohio State Bar Association). ***PRACTICE AREAS:*** Estate Planning; Trust Law; Probate; Business and Real Estate. ***Email:*** jjacobson@pselaw.com

JEFFREY S. SENNEY, born Lakewood, Ohio, October 11, 1954; admitted to bar, 1986, Ohio and U.S. District Court, Northern and Southern Districts of Ohio; U.S. Tax Court; U.S. Court of Appeals, Sixth Circuit. *Education:* Bowling Green State University (B.S.B.A., 1976; M.A., 1979); University of Dayton (J.D., magna cum laude, 1986). Editor, University of Dayton Law Review, 1985-1986. Certified Public Accountant, Ohio, 1981. *Member:* Dayton, Ohio State and American Bar Associations; Ohio Society of CPA's; American Business Club; American Association of Attorneys-CPA's. ***PRACTICE AREAS:*** Federal and State Tax; ERISA and Employee Benefits; Mergers and Acquisitions; Corporate Law; Business Law. ***Email:*** jsenney@pselaw.com

L. MICHAEL BLY, born Danville, Pennsylvania, July 29, 1963; admitted to bar, 1989, Ohio and U.S. District Court, Southern District of Ohio; U.S. Supreme Court. *Education:* Bloomsburg University (B.S., 1985); University of Dayton School of Law (J.D., 1989). Order of Barristers. Member, National Product Liability Moot Court. Intern/Law Clerk, Montgomery County Common Pleas Court, 1989. Pennsylvania State Teaching Certificate, Secondary Education, Earth/Space Science, 1985. Instructor: Safety and Sports Law, University of Dayton, 1992—. *Member:* Dayton, Ohio State and American Bar Associations. ***PRACTICE AREAS:*** Civil Litigation; Personal Injury; Corporate Litigation; Commercial Litigation; Appellate Advocacy. ***Email:*** mbly@pselaw.com

MICHAEL W. SANDNER, born Charleston, West Virginia, July 22, 1969; admitted to bar, 1994, Ohio; 1995, U.S. District Court, Southern District of Ohio; 1998, U.S. Court of Appeals, Sixth Circuit; 1999, U.S. Supreme Court. *Education:* Connecticut College (B.A., 1991); University of Dayton (J.D., cum laude, 1994). Law Clerk, Montgomery County Court of Common Pleas, 1993-1994; Law Clerk, Ohio Second District Court of Appeals, 1994-1995. *Member:* Dayton, Ohio State and American Bar Associations; Ohio Association of Civil Trial Attorneys; Defense Research Institute. ***PRACTICE AREAS:*** Insurance Defense Litigation; Consumer Litigation; Commercial Litigation; Construction Litigation. ***Email:*** msandner@pselaw.com

GREGORY S. PAGE, born Dayton, Ohio, August 19, 1969; admitted to bar, 1995, Ohio and U.S. District Court, Southern District of Ohio; 1997, Kentucky; 1999, U.S. Supreme Court. *Education:* University of Cincinnati (B.A., 1991); University of Toledo (J.D., cum laude, 1995). Member, University of Toledo Law Review; Member, University of Toledo Moot Court Board; Recipient, American Jurisprudence Award for Academic Excellence in Civil Procedure and Legal Research and Writing; Recipient, Order of Barrister. *Member:* Cincinnati, Dayton, Kentucky, Ohio State and American Bar Associations; Home Builders Association of Dayton and the Miami Valley; Cincinnati Claims Association; American Subcontractors Association (Cincinnati Chapter, 1997-1998); Ohio Association of Civil Trial Attorneys. ***PRACTICE AREAS:*** Insurance Defense; Construction Law; Personal Injury; Commercial Litigation; Employment Litigation. ***Email:*** gpage@pselaw.com

DAVID H. MONTGOMERY, born Dayton, Ohio, March 3, 1972; admitted to bar, 1998, Ohio and U.S. District Court, Southern District of Ohio. *Education:* Miami University (B.A., 1994); University of Dayton School of Law (J.D., 1998). Phi Alpha Delta. University of Dayton Moot Court Board; Walter Rice Moot Court Champion, 1996. Member: Order of Barristers; National Environmental Law Moot Court; National Criminal Law Moot Court. Teaching Assistant, Legal Research and Writing, University of Dayton School of Law, 1997-1998. *Member:* Dayton, Ohio State and American Bar Associations. ***PRACTICE AREAS:*** Business Law; Corporate Law; Real Estate; Zoning Law; Land Use; Municipal Law; Construction Law; Land Development. ***Email:*** dmontgomery@pselaw.com

R. JOSEPH WESSENDARP, born Cincinnati, Ohio, May 3, 1954; admitted to bar, 1980, Ohio; U.S. District Court, Southern and Northern Districts of Ohio; U.S. District Court, Eastern District of Wisconsin; U.S. District Court, Eastern District of Missouri and

(This Listing Continued)

U.S. Court of Appeals, Sixth Circuit. *Education:* University of Cincinnati (B.A., magna cum laude, 1976); University of Detroit (J.D., 1979). Order of Barristers. Recipient, James Procter Memorial Scholarship, 1975-1976, University of Cincinnati. Vice-Chairman, University of Detroit Moot Court Board of Directors, 1978-1979. Associate Editor, University of Detroit, Journal of Urban Law, 1977-1979. Assistant Editor, Corporation, Finance and Business Law Journal, 1978-1979. Author: "The Good Faith Defense Under the Fair Labor Standards Act," published in 1978 in the Corporation, Finance and Business Law Journal; "Preferential Transfers: Current Law and Recent Changes," published in 1979 in the Corporation, Finance and Business Law Journal. Visiting Professor of Law, University of Cincinnati College of Law, 1979-1980. Law Clerk, U.S. District Court, Eastern District of Michigan, 1980-1982. ***PRACTICE AREAS:*** Labor and Employment; Workers Compensation; Business Law; School Law; Education Law; Civil Litigation. ***Email:*** jwessendarp@pselaw.com

GERALD LOUIS McDONALD, born Jackson, Michigan, February 5, 1962; admitted to bar, 1993, Michigan; 1994, Florida; 2004, Ohio. *Education:* Michigan State University (B.A., 1984); Stetson University (J.D., cum laude, 1993). Formerly with: Grua Jamo & Young, P.L.C., Lansing, Michigan. *Member:* State Bar of Michigan; The Florida Bar; Ohio State Bar Association. ***PRACTICE AREAS:*** Business; Corporate; Real Estate; Municipal. ***Email:*** gmcdonald@pselaw.com

MATTHEW T. JEWSON, born Dayton, Ohio; admitted to bar, 1994, Ohio. *Education:* Ohio University (B.B.A., 1991); The Ohio State University (J.D., 1994). ***PRACTICE AREAS:*** Criminal Defense; Civil Litigation; Domestic Relations. ***Email:*** mjewson@pselaw.com

SALVATORE A. GILENE, born Cincinnati, Ohio, July 1, 1977; admitted to bar, 2002, Ohio. *Education:* University of Notre Dame (B.A., magna cum laude, 1999); University of Dayton (J.D., 2002). Member, University of Dayton Law Review, 2000-2003. *Member:* Dayton and Ohio State Bar Associations. ***PRACTICE AREAS:*** Workers Compensation Defense.

SUZANNE P. BRUMBAUGH, born New Castle, Pennsylvania, May 1, 1977; admitted to bar, 2002, Florida; 2004, Ohio and U.S. District Court, Southern District of Ohio. *Education:* Indiana University of Pennsylvania (B.S., magna cum laude, 1999); University of Dayton (J.D., 2002). Moot Court Team. *Member:* Dayton, Ohio State and American Bar Associations. ***PRACTICE AREAS:*** Litigation. ***Email:*** sbrumbaugh@pselaw.com

OF COUNSEL

DONALD G. SCHWELLER, born Dayton, Ohio, October 13, 1930; admitted to bar, 1957, Ohio. *Education:* University of Dayton (B.A., 1952); University of Cincinnati (J.D., 1957); New York University (LL.M. in Taxation, 1958). *Member:* Dayton and Ohio State (Chairman, Probate and Trust Section, 1984-1986) Bar Associations. Fellow, American College of Trust and Estate Counsel. ***PRACTICE AREAS:*** Probate; Estate Planning. ***Email:*** dschweller@pselaw.com

THOMAS J. HARRINGTON, born Springfield, Ohio, December 17, 1935; admitted to bar, 1960, Ohio. *Education:* Xavier University; University of Cincinnati (B.B.A., 1958; J.D., 1960). Phi Delta Phi; Beta Alpha Psi. Associate Editor, University of Cincinnati Law Review, 1959-1960. Attorney, National Labor Relations Board, St. Louis, Missouri, 1960-1964. Trustee, 1985-1993, Vice President, 1988-1989 and President, 1989-1993, Ohio CLE Institute. Director, Ohio Bar Title Insurance Company, 1988-1997. *Member:* Dayton (Member: Executive Committee, 1979-1981; Fee Dispute Resolution Committee, 1996—; Bar Admissions Committee, 1998—), Ohio State (Executive Committeeman, District II, 1981-1984; Member, Council of Delegates, 1979—; Chairman, Labor Law Section, 1979-1981; Member: School Law Committee, 1976-1989; Presidents Task Force, 1989-1991; Judicial Selection Screening Committee, 1985-1991) and American (Labor and Employment Law Section: Member, 1960—; Chairman, Committee on State Labor Law and Public Employee Labor Relations, 1988; Committee on Practice and Procedure before the National Labor Relations Board, 1981-2003; Management Co-Chair, Midwest Region, 1992-1994) Bar Associations; Diocesan Attorneys Association; Ohio Council of School Board Attorneys. Fellow: Ohio State Bar Foundation (President, 1990; President Elect, 1989; Director, 1985-1991). Life Fellow, 1990; Honorary Life Fellow, 1992; American Bar Foundation Fellow, 1981—. ***PRACTICE AREAS:*** Labor Law; Public School Law; Private Education Law; Management Labor and Employment Law; Business Law.

IRA H. THOMSEN, born New York, N.Y., April 5, 1954; admitted to bar, 1979, Ohio and U.S. District Court, Southern District of Ohio. *Education:* Cornell University (B.A., 1976); Drake University School of Law (J.D., 1979). Member, American Bankruptcy Law Forum, 1993—. *Member:* Dayton, Ohio State and American Bar Associations. ***PRACTICE AREAS:*** Creditors Rights; Bankruptcy Law.

AGENT FOR: Chicago Title Insurance Co.
JON M. ROSEMEYER IS AGENT FOR: Chicago Title Insurance Co.
REPRESENTATIVE CLIENTS: WDTN-TV2; Beavercreek Board of Education; Archdiocese of Cincinnati; Sinclair Community College; Woolpert Consultants; Adams Robinson Construction Co.; Dayton Area Auto Dealers; Meijer, Inc.; The Maria Joseph Center; Lofino's, Inc.; Prudential-Residence Realty; Connor & Murphy Ltd.; Arnold Enterprises, Inc.; Midmark; Giddings & Lewis; Sofco Erectors, Inc.; Tecom, Inc.; Bridgestone/Firestone; Zumstein, Inc.; Valley Pathologists, Inc.; Dayton Foods, d/b/a/ Cub Foods; KMART; Coldwell Banker; Heritage Realtors; Provident Bank; Miami Valley Cardiologists, Inc.; Delta Airlines; Schottensteins; Towne Properties; Singer Properties.
INSURANCE COMPANY CLIENTS: Allstate Insurance Co.; American Mutual Liability Co.; Church Mutual Insurance Co.; Grange Mutual Insurance Co.; Grange Mutual; Metropolitan Property & Casualty Insurance Co.; Transport Insurance Co.; Western Reserve Mutual; Wausau Insurance Cos.; Amerisure Cos; Castle Insurance Co.; Prudential Insurance Company of America; Horace Mann Insurance Co.; MIC General Insurance Co.; Western World Insurance.

PORTER WRIGHT MORRIS & ARTHUR LLP

Established in 1846

ONE DAYTON CENTRE
ONE SOUTH MAIN STREET, SUITE 1600
DAYTON, OHIO 45402-2028
Telephone: 937-449-6810; (800-533-4434)
Fax: 937-449-6820
Email: dayton@porterwright.com
URL: http://www.porterwright.com

Columbus, Ohio Office: 41 South High Street, 43215-6194. Telephones: 614-227-2000; (800-533-2794). Fax: 614-227-2100. Internet: columbus@porterwright.com.
Cincinnati, Ohio Office: 250 E. Fifth Street, Suite 2200, 45202-5117. Telephones: 513-381-4700; (800-582-5813); Fax: 513-421-0991. Internet: cincinnati@porterwright.com.
Cleveland, Ohio Office: 925 Euclid Avenue, Suite 1700, 44115-1483. Telephones: 216-443-9000; (800-824-1980). Fax: 216-443-9011. Internet: cleveland@porterwright.com.
Washington, D.C. Office: 1919 Pennsylvania Avenue, N.W., Suite 500, 20006-3434. Telephones: 202-778-3000; (800-456-7962). Fax: 202-778-3063. Internet: washington@porterwright.com.
Naples, Florida Office: 5801 Pelican Bay Boulevard, Suite 300, 34108-2709. Telephones: 239-593-2900; (800-876-7962). Fax: 239-593-2990. Internet: naples@porterwright.com.

Alternative Dispute Resolution, Agricultural Law, Antitrust and Trade Regulation, Business and Corporate, Complex Litigation, Construction, Employee Benefits, Energy and Utilities, Environment, Federal Administrative Law, Federal Contracting and Procurement, Financial Institutions, General Practice, Governmental Affairs, Health Care, Insurance, Intellectual Property, International Business, Labor and Employment, Litigation, Public Law, Public Finance, Real Estate, Securities, Taxation, Technology, Trusts and Estates.

FIRM PROFILE: Porter Wright Morris & Arthur LLP is a nationally known business law firm delivering creative solutions for large, mid-size and entrepreneurial businesses. Porter Wright's Dayton presence traces to 1920, and emphasizes a commitment to downtown Dayton and the greater Dayton business community. The attorneys in Porter Wright's Dayton office concentrate in business and finance, commercial lending, commercial litigation, labor and employment law, government contracting law, real estate law, constitutional law, bankruptcy and workouts, and estate planning and probate. The Firm, which traces its origins to 1846, has over 280 lawyers practicing in Cincinnati, Cleveland, Columbus, and Dayton, Ohio; Washington, D.C.; and Naples, Florida.

RESIDENT PARTNERS

WILLIAM G. DEAS, born Cincinnati, Ohio, November 8, 1947; admitted to bar, 1972, Ohio. *Education:* The Ohio State University (B.S., 1969); University of Cincinnati (J.D., 1972). Member, Board of Editors, University of Cincinnati Law Review, 1971-1972. *Member:* Dayton and Ohio State Bar Associations. ***PRACTICE AREAS:*** Finance; Commerce; Real Estate. ***Email:*** wdeas@porterwright.com

CAROLINE H. GENTRY, born Atlanta, Georgia, February 23, 1970; admitted to bar, 1996, Ohio and U.S. District Court, Southern District of Ohio. *Education:* Kalamazoo College (B.A., magna cum laude, 1992); Yale University (J.D., 1995). Phi Beta Kappa. Senior Editor, The Yale Law Journal, 1994-1995. Author: "Preparing Today will Pay Off Tomorrow: Getting Clients Ready for Electronic Discovery," IP Litigator (February, 2003). *Member:* Dayton (Chair, Federal Practice Committee, 2001-2003), Ohio State and American Bar Associations. ***PRACTICE AREAS:*** Commercial Litigation; Intellectual Property Litigation; Class Actions; ERISA Litigation. ***Email:*** cgentry@porterwright.com

PAUL G. HALLINAN, born Cleveland, Ohio, 1953; admitted to bar, 1980, Ohio and U.S. District Court, Southern District of Ohio; 1983, U.S. Court of Appeals, Sixth Circuit; 1996, U.S. Court of Appeals, Federal Circuit; 1997, U.S. Supreme Court; 2002, U.S. Court of Appeals, Seventh Circuit. *Education:* University of Notre Dame (A.B., 1973); University of Dayton (M.B.A., 1977; J.D., magna cum laude, 1980). Editor-in-Chief, University of Dayton Law Review, 1979-1980. Law Clerk to the Hon. Walter H. Rice, U.S. District Court, Southern District of Ohio, 1980-1981. *Member:* Dayton, Ohio State and American (Member, Litigation Section) Bar Associations. ***PRACTICE AREAS:*** Business Litigation; Construction Litigation; Intellectual Property Litigation; Antitrust; Employment Litigation. ***Email:*** phallinan@porterwright.com

JOHN J. HERON, born Steubenville, Ohio, November 6, 1940; admitted to bar, 1965, Ohio. *Education:* The Ohio State University (B.S. in B.A., 1962; J.D., 1964). Phi Delta Phi. Member: Kettering Civil Service Commission, 1978-1979; Ohio Association of School Board Attorneys, 1983-1985; Ohio Public Employer's Association, 1983-1986; The Ohio State College of Law, National Council, 1984—. Referee, Ohio Department of Education, teacher dismissal cases, 2003. *Member:* Ohio State Bar Association (Board of Governors, Labor & Employment Law Section). ***PRACTICE AREAS:*** Employment Law; Employment at Will; Equal Employment Opportunity Affirmative Action Law; Labor Relations Law. ***Email:*** jheron@porterwright.com

THOMAS A. HOLTON, born Dayton, Ohio, November 22, 1941; admitted to bar, 1967, Ohio. *Education:* The Ohio State University (B.S., 1964); University of Detroit (J.D., 1967). *Member:* Dayton, Ohio State and American Bar Associations. ***PRACTICE AREAS:*** Corporation Law; Employment Law; Succession Planning; Business. ***Email:*** tholton@porterwright.com

C. TERRY JOHNSON, born Bridgeport, Connecticut, September 24, 1937; admitted to bar, 1964, Ohio. *Education:* Trinity College (B.A., 1960); Columbia University (J.D., 1963). Fellow, American College of Trust and Estate Counsel. Fellow, Ohio State Bar Foundation. Best Lawyers in America, Trusts & Estates, 1987—. Editorial Advisory Board, Probate Law Journal of Ohio, 1992—. Ohio State Bar Foundation Award for Outstanding Research or Service in Law or Government, 1993. Author: "The Impact of H.B. 85 upon the Allowance of Support to a Surviving Spouse," Probate Law Journal of Ohio, 2003; "The

(This Listing Continued)

PORTER WRIGHT MORRIS & ARTHUR LLP, Dayton—Continued

Dying Client Drill: Last Minute Estate Planning Advice for the Terminally Ill Client," Probate Law Journal of Ohio, 2000. Ohio State Bar Association,. *Member:* Dayton (Chair, Probate Committee, 1979, 1993) and Ohio State (Chair, Board of Governors, Estate Planning, Trust & Probate Law Section, 1993-1995) Bar Associations; Ohio CLE Institute Board of Trustees (Chair, 1998-1999); Ohio State Bar Foundation Board of Trustees (1995-2000). (Certified Specialist in Estate Planning, Trust and Probate Law, Ohio State Bar Association). ***PRACTICE AREAS:*** Estate Planning; Probate Law; Living Trust Law. ***Email:*** cjohnson@porterwright.com

CHARLES Y. KIDWELL, JR., born Toledo, Ohio, July 1, 1958; admitted to bar, 1985, Ohio and U.S. District Court, Southern District of Ohio; 1986, Georgia. *Education:* Miami University (B.S., 1980; M.B.A., 1981); University of Dayton (J.D., 1985). Certified Public Accountant, Ohio, 1987. *Member:* National Health Lawyers Association. ***PRACTICE AREAS:*** Corporation Law; Health Care Law; Taxation Law; Business; Securities; Employee Benefits. ***Email:*** ckidwell@porterwright.com

WALTER REYNOLDS, born Atlanta, Georgia, February 2, 1953; admitted to bar, 1979, Ohio. *Education:* Wilberforce University (B.A., 1975); University of Dayton (J.D., 1978). Part-time Professor, Sinclair Community College, 1989-1991. Arbitrator, Montgomery County Common Pleas Court, 1989—. Acting Judge, Dayton Municipal Court, Civil Division, 1989— and American Arbitration Association. *Member:* Dayton, Ohio State and American Bar Associations; Thurgood Marshall Law Society; American Bankruptcy Law Forum. ***PRACTICE AREAS:*** Commercial Litigation; Bankruptcy Law; Banking; Finance; Commerce. ***Email:*** wreynolds@porterwright.com

R. BRUCE SNYDER, born Dayton, Ohio, December 7, 1945; admitted to bar, 1973, Ohio. *Education:* Yale University (B.A., cum laude, 1968); The Ohio State University (J.D., summa cum laude, 1973). Order of the Coif. *Member:* Dayton, Ohio State and American Bar Associations. ***PRACTICE AREAS:*** Employment Discrimination; Employment Relations; Handicapped Right Law; Workers Compensation Law; Litigation.

RESIDENT ASSOCIATES

JOHN F. BENNETT, born Seattle, Washington, June 26, 1972; admitted to bar, 2002, Ohio. *Education:* University of St. Thomas (B.A., Political Science, cum laude, 1996); University of Cincinnati College of Law (J.D., 2001). ***PRACTICE AREAS:*** Litigation. ***Email:*** jbennett@porterwright.com

ANDREW J. GOTTMAN, born Washington, D.C., February 2, 1974; admitted to bar, 1999, Ohio. *Education:* University of Virginia (B.A., 1996); Washington & Lee University (J.D., summa cum laude, 1999). Order of the Coif. Senior Articles Editor, Washington & Lee University Law Review, 1998-1999. ***PRACTICE AREAS:*** Litigation. ***Email:*** agottman@porterwright.com

TAMI L. HART, born Cincinnati, Ohio, August 26, 1979; admitted to bar, 2004, Ohio. *Education:* University of Cincinnati (B.S., magna cum laude, 2001); University of Dayton (J.D., cum laude, 2004). Publications Editor, University of Dayton Law Review, 2003-2004. *Member:* Ohio State and American Bar Associations. ***PRACTICE AREAS:*** Bankruptcy; Commercial Litigation; Banking Law; Commercial Transactions; Finance; Commerce. ***Email:*** thart@porterwright.com

CRAIG A. HOFFMAN, born Cincinnati, Ohio, September 14, 1977; admitted to bar, 2002, Ohio. *Education:* University of Cincinnati (B.A., 1999; J.D., 2002). Judicial Clerk, U.S. Department of Labor Administrative Law Judge Thomas F. Phalen, Jr., 2003-2004. *Member:* Cincinnati and Ohio State Bar Associations. ***PRACTICE AREAS:*** Litigation. ***Email:*** choffman@porterwright.com

SCOTT K. JONES, born Cincinnati, Ohio, September 17, 1972; admitted to bar, 1998, Ohio. *Education:* Miami University (B.S.B.A., Finance, 1995); University of Dayton (J.D., 1998). Member, 1996-1997 and Associate Editor, 1997-1998, University of Dayton Law Review. *Member:* Carl D. Kessler Inn of Court (Associate). ***PRACTICE AREAS:*** Litigation. ***Email:*** sjones@porterwright.com

PHILIP E. KESSLER, born 1970; admitted to bar, 1999, Ohio. *Education:* University of Toledo (B.A., 1994); University of Dayton (J.D., 1999). ***PRACTICE AREAS:*** Estate Planning; Trust and Estates; Probate Law; Trust Litigation; Estate Litigation; Business Law; Technology. ***Email:*** pkessler@porterwright.com

H. JOHN PROUD, born Cincinnati, Ohio, October 28, 1948; admitted to bar, 2004, Ohio. *Education:* University of Dayton (B.A., 1970; J.D., 2004). University of Dayton Law Review, 2004. Trustee, University of Datyon, 1999-2001, 2004—. *Member:* Dayton and Ohio State Bar Associations. [Ohio Army of the National Guard, 1970-1976]. ***PRACTICE AREAS:*** Business Law; Labor and Employment; Tax. ***Email:*** jproud@porterwright.com

ROBIN D. RYAN, born Grand Forks, North Dakota, February 23, 1973; admitted to bar, 2001, Ohio. *Education:* Ohio University (B.A., 1995); University of Dayton (J.D., 2001). Member, University of Dayton Law Review. Author, "The Criminalization of Trade Secret Theft Under the Economic Espionage Act of 1996: An Evaluation of United States v. Hsu, 40 F.Supp.2d 623 (E.D.Pa. 1999)," University of Dayton Law Rev., Vol. 25, No. 2, p. 243-262, 2000. ***PRACTICE AREAS:*** Litigation. ***Email:*** rryan@porterwright.com

OF COUNSEL

ROLAND F. EICHNER, born Columbus, Ohio, June 3, 1930; admitted to bar, 1958, Ohio. *Education:* Xavier University (B.S. in B.A., 1958); University of Cincinnati (J.D., 1958). Phi Delta Phi. Assistant Attorney General, State of Ohio, 1958-1959. Law Director, City of Kettering, Ohio, 1959-1961. Adjunct Professor, University of Dayton Law School, 1977. *Member:* Dayton, Ohio State (Member, Board of Governors, Real Property Section, 1977-1982) and American Bar Associations. ***PRACTICE AREAS:*** Real Estate Law; Zoning Law; Easements; Annexation; Foreclosure Law; Title Insurance. ***Email:*** reichner@porterwright.com

JEFFREY W. MORRIS, born Providence, Rhode Island, October 1, 1952; admitted to bar, 1977, Georgia (inactive); 1993, Ohio. *Education:* Providence College (B.A., 1974); Washington & Lee University (J.D., 1977). Executive Editor, Washington & Lee Law Review, 1976-1977. Author: Problems & Materials on Debtor-Creditor Law, Aspen Law and Business Publishing, 1998 ed., 2005 (Third Edition); Chapter 13 Practice & Procedures, Shepards/McGraw-Hill, 1983 Chapter 12 Farm Reorganizations, Shepards/McGraw-Hill, 1987. Member, 1993—, and Secretary, 1995-2004, National Bankruptcy Conference. Professor of Law, University of Dayton School of Law, 1981—. Editorial Advisory Board, American Bankruptcy Law Journal, 2004—. Reporter, Advisory Committee on Bankruptcy Rules, U.S. Judicial Conference, 1998—. *Member:* State Bar of Georgia. American College of Bankruptcy (Regent at Large). ***PRACTICE AREAS:*** Commercial Bankruptcy; Consumer Bankruptcy; Commercial Transactions; Finance; Commerce. ***Email:*** jmorris@porterwright.com

(See Listings at Cincinnati, Cleveland and Columbus, Ohio, Washington, D.C. and Naples, Florida for Professional Biographies on attorneys resident in those offices)

RIESER & ASSOCIATES LLC

1520 FIRST NATIONAL BANK PLAZA
130 WEST SECOND STREET
DAYTON, OHIO 45402-1519
Telephone: 937-224-4128
Fax: 937-224-3090

West Palm Beach, Florida Office: Phillips Point, 777 S. Flagler Drive, Suite 800-West Tower, 33401-6161. Telephone: 561-515-6019. Fax: 561-515-6119.

General Civil Practice. Litigation, Corporate, Commercial and Complex Litigation, Business Planning and Transactions, Bankruptcy, Workouts and Reorganization, Estate Planning. Trust/Estate Litigation. Trials and Appeals in all Courts.

MANAGING MEMBER

JOHN PAUL RIESER, born Homestead, Pennsylvania, September 24, 1956; admitted to bar, 1981, Ohio; 1998, Florida. *Education:* Northwestern University (B.A., with distinction, 1978); Pushkin Institute of Russian Language, Moscow, U.S.S.R. (Certificate, 1978); Harvard University (J.D., cum laude, 1981). Notes and Comments Editor, Harvard International Law Journal, 1980-1981. Author: "Diplomatic Immunity-The Diplomatic Relations Act," 19 Harv. Int'l. L.J. 1019, 1978; Chapter 7, Bankruptcy Panel Trustee, 1989—. Lecturer in Business Law at Sinclair Community College, 1983—; Bankruptcy and Environmental Law, Dayton and Ohio State Bar Associations, 1994—. Arbitrator, Montgomery County, Ohio Civil Arbitration Panels, 1983—. Member, Rules Committee, U.S. Bankruptcy Court, Southern District of Ohio, 2001—. *Member:* Dayton, Palm Beach County and Ohio State Bar Associations; The Florida Bar; American Bar Association; American Bankruptcy Law Forum; American Registry of Arbitrators. ***LANGUAGES:*** Russian. ***PRACTICE AREAS:*** Business and Commercial Litigation; Business Planning and Transactions; Bankruptcy; Reorganization; Workouts; Asset Protection; Estate Planning; Trusts and Estates; Estate Litigation; Trial Practice; Appellate Practice. ***Email:*** jrieser@rieserlaw.com

ASSOCIATES

PATRICIA JEAN FRIESINGER, admitted to bar, 2000, Ohio and U.S. District Court, Southern District of Ohio; 2001 U.S. Circuit Court. *Education:* University of Toledo (B.A., 1997; J.D., 2000). ***PRACTICE AREAS:*** Civil Litigation; Bankruptcy; Bankruptcy Litigation. ***Email:*** pfriesinger@rieserlaw.com

RION, RION & RION, L.P.A. INC.

Established in 1938
SUITE 2150, ONE FIRST NATIONAL PLAZA
130 WEST SECOND STREET
P.O. BOX 10126
DAYTON, OHIO 45402
Telephone: 937-223-9133
Fax: 937-223-7540
Email: info@rionlaw.com
URL: http://www.lawyers.com/rionlaw

Criminal Law. Felonies, Misdemeanors, Drug Crimes, DUI, Murder, Manslaughter, Death Penalty. Family Law, Divorce, Child Custody.

JOHN H. RION, born Dayton, Ohio, August 4, 1943; admitted to bar, 1970, Ohio. *Education:* Ohio State University (B.A., Philosophy, 1965); University of Toledo (J.D., 1969). Listed in Best Lawyers in America, Criminal Law (1981—). Co-Chairman, Rule 65 Committee prescribing qualifications for attorneys in Death Penalty cases. Listed in, "Ohio Super Lawyers," in 2004. *Member:* Dayton and Ohio State (Chairman, Ohio Criminal Justice Committee, 1989-1991 Member, Setting Standards for Board Certification Committee, 1999) Bar Associations; California Defense Lawyer's Association; Ohio Association of Criminal Defense Lawyers (Life Member; President, 1989; Chairman, 1990); Montgomery County Trial Lawyers Association (Vice-President, 1989-1990; Member, Board of Trustees, 1990); National Association of Criminal Defense Lawyers (Life Member). Certified as a Criminal Trial Advocate by the National Board of Trial Advocacy. ***REPORTED CASES:*** State vs. Carter, 69 Ohio St. 3D 57., et al. ***PRACTICE AREAS:*** Criminal Law; Domestic Relations; Felonies; Murder; Drug Crimes; Misdemeanors. ***Email:*** info@rionlaw.com

JON PAUL RION, admitted to bar, 1996, Ohio; 1998, District of Columbia. *Education:* George Washington University (Philosophy and Religion, 1993); Dayton Law School (J.D., 1996). *Member:* Dayton and Ohio State Bar Associations; Life Member, National Association of Criminal Defense Lawyers; Ohio Association of Criminal Defense Lawyers (Director, 1997); Federal Bar Association. Certified as a Criminal Trial Advocate by the National Board of Trial Advocacy. ***PRACTICE AREAS:*** Criminal Defense; Felonies; Death Penalty; Violent Crimes; Federal Crimes; Domestic Relations; Misdemeanors. ***Email:*** info@rionlaw.com

KEVIN L. LENNEN, admitted to bar, 1987, Ohio. *Education:* Bowling Green State University (B.L.S., 1983); Cleveland Marshall College of Law, Cleveland State University

(This Listing Continued)

(J.D., 1987). ***PRACTICE AREAS:*** Criminal Defense; Domestic Relations; Misdemeanors; Felonies; Driving While Intoxicated; Divorce; Spousal Support. ***Email:*** info@rionlaw.com

STEVEN T. PIERSON, admitted to bar, 1984, Ohio. *Education:* Ohio University (B.S., Education, 1978); Eastern Kentucky University (M.A., 1980); University of Cincinnati (J.D., 1983). ***PRACTICE AREAS:*** Criminal Defense; Domestic Relations; Divorce; Driving While Intoxicated. ***Email:*** info@rionlaw.com

---

KERI E. FARLEY, born Toledo, Ohio, August 1, 1978; admitted to bar, 2003, Ohio and U.S. District Court, Southern District of Ohio. *Education:* University of Dayton (B.A., Music, 2000); Dayton Law School (J.D., 2003). ***PRACTICE AREAS:*** Criminal Law; Domestic Relations. ***Email:*** kfarley@rionlaw.com

MATTHEW J. BARBATO, born Port Chester, New York, September 11, 1975; admitted to bar, 2003, Ohio and U.S. District Court, Southern District of West Ohio. *Education:* Xavier University (B.A., 1998); University of Dayton (J.D., 2003). *Member:* Ohio State Bar Association. ***PRACTICE AREAS:*** Criminal Law; Domestic Relations. ***Email:*** info@rionlaw.com

OF COUNSEL

MATTHEW H. WILSON, born Piqua, Ohio, October 30, 1952; admitted to bar, 1984, Ohio. *Education:* Miami University (B.A., 1975); University of Dayton (J.D., 1984).

ROGERS & GREENBERG, L.L.P.

2160 KETTERING TOWER
DAYTON, OHIO 45423
Telephone: 937-223-8171
Fax: 937-223-1649
URL: http://www.rogersgreenberg.com

General Practice. Corporation, Tax, Labor, Estate Planning and Probate Law, Family Law, Employee Benefits/ERISA. Trials.

MEMBERS OF FIRM

WILLIAM A. ROGERS, JR., born Dayton, Ohio, April 28, 1934; admitted to bar, 1960, Ohio. *Education:* Harvard College (B.A., 1956); Harvard Law School (LL.B., 1959). *Member:* Dayton (President, 1980-1981), Ohio State and American Bar Associations. ***PRACTICE AREAS:*** Business Planning Law; Business Transactions; Estate Planning Law; Estate Administration; Trust Administration; Professional Corporations Law.

STANLEY Z. GREENBERG (1939-2003)

JOHN M. CLOUD, born Cincinnati, Ohio, January 17, 1951; admitted to bar, 1976, Ohio. *Education:* University of Notre Dame; Xavier University (B.A., summa cum laude, 1973); University of Cincinnati (J.D., cum laude, 1976). *Member:* Dayton, Ohio State and American Bar Associations. (Certified Specialist in Estate Planning, Trust and Probate Law, Ohio State Bar Association). ***PRACTICE AREAS:*** Business Planning; Business Transactions; Estate Planning Law; Estate Administration; Trust Administration; Pension and Profit Sharing Law; Professional Corporations. ***Email:*** jcloud@rogersgreenberg.com

BARRY W. MANCZ, born Dayton, Ohio, July 29, 1952; admitted to bar, 1977, Ohio. *Education:* Wright State University (B.S., summa cum laude, 1974); University of Colorado (J.D., 1977). *Member:* Dayton, Ohio State and American Bar Associations. ***PRACTICE AREAS:*** Real Estate Law; Litigation; Creditors Rights Law. ***Email:*** bmancz@rogersgreenberg.com

KEITH R. KEARNEY, born Pittsburgh, Pennsylvania, October 19, 1956; admitted to bar, 1984, Ohio. *Education:* Indiana University, Pennsylvania (B.A., 1980); University of Dayton School of Law (J.D., cum laude, 1984). Production Editor, University of Dayton Law Review, 1983-1984. *Member:* Dayton and Ohio State Bar Associations. ***PRACTICE AREAS:*** Family Law; Pension and Profit Sharing Law; Litigation.

JAMES G. KORDIK, born Elgin, Illinois, July 18, 1957; admitted to bar, 1983, Ohio. *Education:* Wright State University (B.S., 1980); Dayton Law School (J.D., 1983). Certified Public Accountant, Ohio, 1987. *Member:* Dayton and Ohio State Bar Associations; Ohio Society of Certified Public Accountants. ***PRACTICE AREAS:*** Taxation Law; Business Planning; Business Transactions; Corporate Law; Estate Planning Law; Estate Planning; Estate Administration; Trust Administration; Real Estate; Real Estate Transactions. ***Email:*** jkordik@rogersgreenberg.com

L. ANTHONY LUSH, born Chicago, Illinois, September 25, 1960; admitted to bar, 1990, Ohio. *Education:* Purdue University (B.S., 1986); University of Dayton (J.D., 1990). *Member:* Dayton, Ohio State and American Bar Associations; Association of Trial Lawyers of America. ***PRACTICE AREAS:*** Family Law; Litigation. ***Email:*** tlush@rogersgreenberg.com

MICHELLE S. VOLLMAR, born San Diego, California, January 12, 1970; admitted to bar, 1995, Ohio and U.S. District Court, Southern District of Ohio. *Education:* Miami University (B.S., Accounting, 1992); University of Dayton School of Law (J.D., magna cum laude, 1995). Phi Alpha Delta. Moot Court, Law Review. Member, Order of the Barristers, 1995. Author, "The Religious Freedom Restoration Act of 1993: Restoring Religious Freedom After the Destruction of the Free Exercise Clause," 20 Univ. Dayton Law Rev. 383 (1994). *Member:* Dayton, Ohio State and American Bar Associations. ***PRACTICE AREAS:*** Estate Planning; Estate and Trust Administration; Business Planning; Business Transactions. ***Email:*** mvollmar@rogersgreenberg.com

---

AMY R. BLAIR, born Kettering, Ohio, November 30, 1975; admitted to bar, 2001, Ohio; 2003, U.S. District Court, Southern District of Ohio. *Education:* Miami University (B.A., magna cum laude, 1998); The Ohio State University (J.D., with honors, 2001). Phi Beta Kappa. Business Editor, The Ohio State Journal on Dispute Resolution, 2001. Member, Juvenile Law Moot Court Team (Second Place Best Brief). *Member:* Dayton and Ohio State Bar Associations. ***PRACTICE AREAS:*** Family Law; Corporate Law; General Practice. ***Email:*** ablair@rogersgreenberg.com

(This Listing Continued)

LAURA C. DeSIO, born Colorado Springs, Colorado, June 18, 1972; admitted to bar, 1999, Maryland; 2004, Ohio and U.S. District Court, Southern District of Ohio. *Education:* Bowling Green State University (B.A.C., 1994); Akron University (M.P.A., 1996); The Ohio State University (J.D., 1999). *Member:* Dayton, Ohio State and American Bar Associations; American Trial Lawyers Association. ***PRACTICE AREAS:*** Business Law; Litigation; General Practice. ***Email:*** ldesio@rogersgreenberg.com

MARIAH D. BUTLER, born Zanesville, Ohio, February 8, 1978; admitted to bar, 2003, Ohio. *Education:* Mary Washington College (B.S., 2000); University of Dayton School of Law (J.D., 2003). *Member:* Dayton, Ohio State and American Bar Associations; Carl D. Kessler Inn of Court. ***Email:*** mbutler@rogersgreenberg.com

GENERAL COUNSEL FOR: App Architects, Inc.; Becker Electric Co.; Butt Construction Co., Inc.; Columbia Industrial Equipment Co.; Dayton Aerospace Associates, Inc.; Dayton Regional Dialysis, Inc.; Daniel S. German Enterprises; Harlow Marketing, Inc.; Harvest Info, Inc.; Heartland Federal Credit Union; I.A.P. Research, Inc.; J.S. Davis Co.; Lapp Roofing & Sheetmetal Co.; McGregor & Associates, Inc.; McLaughlin, Inc.; Midwest Graphic Supply Co.; Montgomery Iron & Paper Co., Inc.; Moraine Materials Co.; National Management Association; Nature's Way; New Carlisle Chrysler Dodge; Orthopedic Associates of SW OH, Inc.; Precision Machining, Inc.; Schear Financial Services; South Dayton Acute Care Consultants; Talon Group-First America Title Agency; Washington Township Park District; Trophy Nut Company; Victory Wholesale Grocers.
REFERENCE: Key Bank, N.A., Dayton, Ohio.

BARBARA L. SAGER, CO., LPA

120 WEST 2ND STREET, SUITE 1111
DAYTON, OHIO 45402
Telephone: 937-443-0295
Fax: 937-443-0457
Email: bsager@bsager.com
URL: http://www.bsager.com

Mergers and Acquisitions, Securities Regulations, Venture Capital, Corporate Law.

BARBARA L. SAGER, born Cincinnati, Ohio, June 30, 1956; admitted to bar, 1986, New York; 1987, District of Columbia; 1995, Ohio. *Education:* University of Cincinnati (B.A., summa cum laude, 1982); Harvard University (J.D., 1985). Phi Beta Kappa. *Member:* District of Columbia Bar; New York and Ohio State Bar Associations. ***PRACTICE AREAS:*** Mergers and Acquisitions; Securities Regulations; Venture Capital; Corporate Law.

SCHNEBLE, CASS & ASSOC. CO., L.P.A.

Established in 2000
11 WEST MONUMENT AVENUE, SUITE 402
DAYTON, OHIO 45402
Telephone: 937-222-1232
Fax: 937-222-5622
Email: Schneble-Cass-and-Assoc.com
URL: http://www.awslawoffice.com

Civil Litigation, Corporate Law, Contract Litigation, Medical and Legal Malpractice, Personal Injury, Liquor Licensing, Tax Appeals and Court, Bankruptcy Reorganizations, Bankruptcy Litigation, Real Estate, Domestic Relations, Probate and Criminal Law.

FIRM PROFILE: Alfred Wm. Schneble III incorporated his law practice in 1986 after operating as a sole practitioner since 1983. Alfred Wm. Schneble III spent his first two years of practice in a small firm doing a general tax, real estate and corporate practice. He then incorporated his law practice in 1986 (Alfred Wm. Schneble III Co., L.P.A.) which operated until April, 2000 whereupon this firm was established with Mr. Cass. William O. Cass, Jr. joined Alfred Wm. Schneble III Co., L.P.A. as an associate in 1994 while continuing his employment at the Montgomery County Prosecutor's Office; he became full-time February 1997. The firm services the Dayton metropolitan area, including the seven adjacent counties to Dayton's Montgomery County (Greene, Miami, Warren, Preble, Darke, Shelby, Clark), although the practice does provide Statewide services as well as cases in Florida courts.

ALFRED WM. SCHNEBLE III, born Dayton, Ohio, November 4, 1956; admitted to bar, 1981, Ohio; 1982, U.S. District Court, Southern District of Ohio; 1983, Florida; 1985, U.S. Court of Appeals, Sixth Circuit; 1994, U.S. Tax Court. *Education:* Marquette University (B.S., 1978); Ohio Northern University (J.D., 1981). *Member:* Dayton (Member, Grievance Committee, 2004—) and Ohio State Bar Associations; The Florida Bar; Ohio Academy of Trial Lawyers; Association of Professional Responsibility Lawyers. ***PRACTICE AREAS:*** Civil Litigation; Corporate Law; Contract Litigation; Medical Malpractice; Legal Malpractice; Personal Injury; Liquor Licensing; Tax Appeals; Bankruptcy Reorganization; Bankruptcy Litigation; Real Estate; Probate; Divorce. ***Email:*** bud.schneble@schneble-cass-and-assoc.com

WILLIAM O. CASS, JR., born Oakwood, Ohio, October 15, 1956; admitted to bar, 1986, Ohio; 1987, U.S. District Court, Southern District of Ohio. *Education:* University of Cincinnati (B.S., 1982); Ohio Northern University (J.D., 1986). Assistant Montgomery County Prosecutor, 1986-1997. *Member:* Dayton Bar Association. ***PRACTICE AREAS:*** General Civil Practice and Litigation; Bankruptcy Chapter 7; Personal Injury; Medical Malpractice; Legal Malpractice; Probate; Family Law; Real Estate; Criminal Law; Traffic Law; Driving Under the Influence. ***Email:*** bill@schneble-cass-and-assoc.com

LEGAL SUPPORT PERSONNEL

TRESA L. ORICK, born Scott County, Tennessee, November 10, 1963. *Education:* Rets Tech Center (Paralegal Degree, 1997-1998). Completion of pleadings for Bankruptcies Chapter 7 and 11 along with pleadings associated with bankruptcy litigation, corporate documents, probate filings and real estate documents with direct client contact via corre-

(This Listing Continued)

SCHNEBLE, CASS & ASSOC. CO., L.P.A., Dayton—Continued

spondence, telephone and personal interviews. (Paralegal). ***PRACTICE AREAS:*** Bankruptcy Chapter 7; Bankruptcy Chapter 11; Bankruptcy Litigation; Corporate Law; Real Estate; Probate. ***Email:*** tresa@schneble-cass-and-assoc.com

PATTY R. NISWONGER, born Annandale, Virginia, November 24, 1969. Preparation for trials, exhibits pleadings, file organization, correspondence, discovery, schedules depositions. ***PRACTICE AREAS:*** Medical Malpractice; Legal Malpractice; Personal Injury. ***Email:*** patty@schneble-cass-and-assoc.com

NICOLE D. VIOLETTE, born Pleasant Hill, Ohio, July 22, 1984. *Education:* Edison Community College (Paralegal degree, 2002-2004). Prepare pleadings, correspondence drafting, involved in discovery process, client contact in Domestic Relations, Criminal Law and Traffic Law. ***PRACTICE AREAS:*** Domestic Relations; Criminal Law; Traffic Law. ***Email:*** nicole@schneble-cass-and-assoc.com

REPRESENTATIVE CLIENTS: Delphi Automotive Systems; Travelers Casualty & Surety Co. of America; TRW Real Estate Loan Services; GMAC Mortgage Corp.; Provident Bank Mortgage Services; Strategic Mortgage Services; First Mortgage Banc Corp.; American Way Van and Storage, Inc.; Countrywide Moving and Storage, Inc.; National Van Lines; Morgantown & Indianapolis Freight; Jamestown Thermoset Plastics, Inc.; General Data; Paramount Plastics, Inc.; Paramount Replay, Ltd.; Paramount Racing, Ltd.; Acu-Rite Mold & Tool, Inc.; "Roosters" Restaurants; Routsong Funeral Homes; Food Service Consultants, Inc.; R&R Restaurants; Scot Business Systems; Ashton Pumpmatic, Inc.; Ashton Industrial Sales, Inc.; Ashton Medical Supply, Inc.; Ashton Investments, Inc.; Budulator Corporation, Inc.; National Real Estate Loan Services, Inc.; Century 21 Research Park Realty, Inc.; Diet Workshop; Zimmerman Realty; Balmorhea Kennels; Shannon & Co. CPAs; Kettering Real Estate Equities, Inc.; Root & Co. CPAs.; School of Advertising Art, Inc.; Midwest Behavioral Care, Ltd.; Cottman Transmission Services LLC; MJM Restaurants, Inc. dba Burger King/Bellfontaine; Holland Excavating, Inc.; Hughes Supply, Inc.; A.I.M. Inc.; Investors Development, Inc.; Mainland Industrial Coatings, Inc.; Adams Roofing; Hawpe Construction, Inc.; Simple Soft Solutions; International Content Liquidators, Inc.; G.L. Dart General Contracting Co.; Village Automotive, LLC.
REFERENCES: Bank One; Root & Co. CPAs.

SEBALY, SHILLITO & DYER

A LEGAL PROFESSIONAL ASSOCIATION

Established in 1986

1900 KETTERING TOWER
DAYTON, OHIO 45423
Telephone: 937-222-2500
Telefax: 937-222-6554; 222-8279
URL: http://www.ssdlaw.com

Business, Business Litigation, Government Contracts Law, Health Care, Labor and Employment, Workers Compensation, Commercial and Creditor Rights, Antitrust, Real Estate, Securities, Technology, Products Liability, Construction Law, Probate, Trust and Estate Planning, Insurance and ERISA.

FIRM PROFILE: Established in 1986 by former members of a regional law firm, Sebaly, Shillito & Dyer provides the quality of a large firm practice with the cohesiveness, flexibility, and client responsiveness of a smaller firm. Our attorneys are dynamic, creative, and entrepreneurial. We employ the latest office technology to facilitate communication and efficient handling of client matters. Clients include small and large closely-held companies as well as publicly-owned national and international corporations. Our practice is fully integrated and includes all of the legal services listed above. The firm is a member of Meritas, an international network of independent law firms providing legal services to business clients worldwide. We have significant experience in corporate restructuring and refinancing, mergers and acquisitions, real estate transactions, securities, and technology/intellectual property matters. The firm's litigation department is well positioned to handle all levels of dispute resolution, from probate and employment cases to the most sophisticated, complex commercial litigation. The firm is also a member of the Association of Legal Administrators.

LAW FIRM ALLIANCES/ASSOCIATIONS: **MERITAS:** *A worldwide alliance of independent business law firms.*

MARTIN A. BEYER, born Saginaw, Michigan, March 24, 1966; admitted to bar, 1992, Ohio and U.S. District Court, Southern District of Ohio. *Education:* Hillsdale College (B.A., Economics, cum laude, 1988); University of Dayton (J.D., 1992). *Member:* Dayton, Ohio State and American Bar Associations. ***PRACTICE AREAS:*** Business Litigation; Commercial Litigation. ***Email:*** mbeyer@ssdlaw.com

MICHAEL A. BOOTH, born Cincinnati, Ohio, May 15, 1967; admitted to bar, 1995, Ohio. *Education:* Miami University (B.S., 1989); University of Cincinnati (J.D., 1995). Moot Court Board. Order of the Coif. Order of the Barristers. *Member:* Dayton, Ohio State and American Bar Associations. ***PRACTICE AREAS:*** Corporate Law. ***Email:*** mbooth@ssdlaw.com

JAMES A. DYER, born Atlanta, Georgia, May 9, 1956; admitted to bar, 1980, Ohio; 1981, U.S. District Court, Southern District of Ohio; 1985, Georgia; 1991, U.S. Court of Appeals, Sixth Circuit; 1997, U.S. District Court, Northern District of Ohio. *Education:* Duke University (B.A., magna cum laude, 1977; J.D., with distinction, 1980). Order of the Coif. *Member:* Dayton, Ohio State (Member, Committee on Antitrust and Litigation) and American (Member, Antitrust Law, Litigation and Forum Committee on Health Law) Bar Associations; State Bar of Georgia; American Academy of Hospital Attorneys; American Society of Association Executives (Member, Legal Section). ***PRACTICE AREAS:*** Business Litigation; Commercial Litigation; Antitrust; Health Care; Labor and Employment. ***Email:*** jdyer@ssdlaw.com

GALE S. FINLEY, born Zanesville, Ohio, January 17, 1952; admitted to bar, 1981, Ohio and U.S. District Court, Southern District of Ohio; 1986, U.S. Court of Appeals, Sixth Circuit. *Education:* The Ohio, State University (B.A., 1977); University of Dayton (J.D., 1981). Author: *Assigning Retirement Benefits in Divorce, Second Edition,* American Bar Association, 1999. Legislation Note Editor, University of Dayton Law Review, 1980-1981. *Member:* Dayton, Ohio State (Member, Corporate Counsel Section) and American (Member, Business Law Section) Bar Associations. ***PRACTICE AREAS:*** Corporate Law; Corporate Finance; ERISA; Mergers and Acquisitions. ***Email:*** gfinley@ssdlaw.com

JOHN R. GLANKLER, born Cincinnati, Ohio, June 19, 1957; admitted to bar, 1988, Ohio. *Education:* Duke University (B.A., 1979); University of Cincinnati (J.D., 1988). Staff Member, University of Cincinnati Law Review, 1987-1988. *Member:* Dayton, Ohio State and American Bar Associations. ***PRACTICE AREAS:*** Corporate Law; Securities. ***Email:*** jglankler@ssdlaw.com

DEBORAH D. HUNT, born Marietta, Ohio, July 15, 1951; admitted to bar, 1988, Ohio and U.S. District Court, Southern District of Ohio. *Education:* West Virginia University (B.A., cum laude, 1973); Wright State University (M.B.A., 1985); University of Dayton (J.D., summa cum laude, 1988). *Member:* Dayton and Ohio State Bar Associations; Dayton Women's Bar Association; Ohio Women's Bar Association. ***PRACTICE AREAS:*** Estate Planning. ***Email:*** dhunt@ssdlaw.com

MICHAEL P. MOLONEY, born Troy, Ohio, May 1, 1952; admitted to bar, 1980, Ohio and U.S. District Court, Southern District of Ohio; 1982, Florida; 1984, U.S. Supreme Court; 1985, U.S. Court of Appeals, Sixth Circuit. *Education:* Miami University (B.A., 1974); The Ohio State University College of Law (J.D., with honors, 1980). *Member:* Dayton, Ohio State and American (Member, Real Property, Probate and Trust Law Sections) Bar Associations; The Florida Bar; Dayton Trust and Estate Planning Group. ***PRACTICE AREAS:*** Estate Planning; Probate; Corporate Law; Real Estate. ***Email:*** mmoloney@ssdlaw.com

JON M. SEBALY, born Kalamazoo, Michigan, February 10, 1936; admitted to bar, 1965, Ohio; 1966, U.S. District Court, Southern District of Ohio; 1967, U.S. Court of Appeals, Sixth Circuit, U.S. Supreme Court and U.S. Tax Court. *Education:* University of Michigan (B.A., 1958; M.A., Economics, 1960; LL.B., 1964). Regents Scholar. *Member:* Dayton, Ohio State and American (Member, Litigation and Antitrust Law Sections; Board of Governors Antitrust Section) Bar Associations; National Health Lawyers Association; Hospital Lawyers Association; American Academy of Hospital Attorneys. ***PRACTICE AREAS:*** Corporate Law; Business Litigation; Commercial Litigation; Antitrust; Health Care. ***Email:*** jsebaly@ssdlaw.com

BEVERLY F. SHILLITO, born Cincinnati, Ohio, July 11, 1953; admitted to bar, 1978, Ohio. *Education:* University of Cincinnati (B.A., Political Science, summa cum laude, 1975); Stanford University (J.D., 1978). Phi Beta Kappa. *Member:* Dayton, Ohio State and American (Member, Business Law Section) Bar Associations. ***PRACTICE AREAS:*** Corporate Law; Mergers and Acquisitions; Securities; Technology Law. ***Email:*** bshillito@ssdlaw.com

JEFFREY B. SHULMAN, born Dayton, Ohio, May 17, 1938; admitted to bar, 1963, Ohio; 1964, U.S. District Court, Southern District of Ohio; 1966, U.S. Court of Appeals, Sixth Circuit; 1972, U.S. Tax Court; 1977, U.S. Supreme Court. *Education:* Williams College (B.A., 1960); University of Michigan (J.D., 1963). *Member:* Dayton (Chairman, Labor Law Committee, 1975-1976; 1979-1980), Ohio State and American Bar Associations. ***PRACTICE AREAS:*** Corporate Law; Business Litigation; Estate Planning; Labor and Employment Law; Probate; Real Estate. ***Email:*** jshulman@ssdlaw.com

KARL R. ULRICH, born Chicago, Illinois, August 6, 1961; admitted to bar, 1986, Missouri and U.S. District Court, Western District of Missouri; 1988, U.S. Court of Appeals, Tenth Circuit; 1990, U.S. District Court, District of Arizona and U.S. Court of Appeals, Eighth Circuit; 1991, Ohio; 1992, U.S. District Court, Southern District of Ohio and U.S. Court of Appeals, Sixth Circuit; 1997, U.S. District Court, Northern District of Ohio. *Education:* Lakeland College (B.A., summa cum laude, 1983); University of Notre Dame (J.D., 1986). Associate Editor, Journal of Legislation, 1985-1986. *Member:* Dayton, Ohio State and American Bar Associations; The Missouri Bar. ***LANGUAGES:*** German. ***PRACTICE AREAS:*** Labor and Employment Law; Insurance Coverage Disputes; Business Litigation. ***Email:*** kulrich@ssdlaw.com

OF COUNSEL

BARBARA A. DUNCOMBE, born Camden, New Jersey, March 13, 1952; admitted to bar, 1980, District of Columbia; 1981, U.S. Court of Federal Claims; 1999, Ohio. *Education:* American University, School of International Service (B.A., 1974); George Washington University (J.D., with honors, 1980). *Member:* Dayton, Ohio State and American Bar Associations. ***LANGUAGES:*** French. ***PRACTICE AREAS:*** Government Contracts Law; Construction Law. ***Email:*** bduncombe@ssdlaw.com

DIANNE F. MARX, born Hamilton, Ohio, November 22, 1956; admitted to bar, 1982, Ohio and U.S. District Court, Southern District of Ohio; 1998, U.S. Court of Appeals, Sixth Circuit. *Education:* Miami University (A.B., magna cum laude, 1979); University of Notre Dame (J.D., 1982). Phi Beta Kappa. *Member:* Dayton, Ohio State and American Bar Associations; Dayton Women's Bar Association; Thurgood Marshall Law Society; Ohio Association of Trial Attorneys. ***PRACTICE AREAS:*** Business Litigation; Commercial Litigation; Products Liability. ***Email:*** dmarx@ssdlaw.com

---

CARISSA E. CLAWSON, born Dayton, Ohio, December 30, 1977; admitted to bar, 2003, Ohio. *Education:* Wright State University (B.A., magna cum laude, 2000); The Ohio State University (J.D., 2003). *Member:* Dayton, Ohio State and American Bar Associations. ***PRACTICE AREAS:*** Corporate Law; Health Care. ***Email:*** cclawson@ssdlaw.com

DANYELLE S.T. COLEMAN, born Dayton, Ohio, 1971; admitted to bar, 2000, Ohio. *Education:* Cornell University (B.A., 1993); Ohio State University (J.D., 1999). *Member:* Dayton and Ohio State Bar Association. ***PRACTICE AREAS:*** Litigation; Employment Law; Corporate Law; Business Law. ***Email:*** dcoleman@ssdlaw.com

SCOTT S. DAVIES, born Washington, D.C., August 17, 1975; admitted to bar, 2003, Ohio. *Education:* American University (B.S.B.A., 1997); University of Dayton (J.D., cum laude, 2003). *Member:* Dayton, Ohio State and American Bar Associations. ***PRACTICE AREAS:*** Business Litigation; Commercial Litigation. ***Email:*** sdavies@ssdlaw.com

KATHERINE L. EARLY, born Springfield, Ohio, May 30, 1976; admitted to bar, 2002, Ohio and U.S. District Court, Southern District of Ohio. *Education:* George Wash-

(This Listing Continued)

ington University (B.A., 1998); The Ohio State University (M.B.A., 2002; J.D., 2002). *Member:* Dayton, Ohio State and American Bar Associations. ***LANGUAGES:*** French, Russian. ***PRACTICE AREAS:*** Business Litigation; Commercial Litigation. ***Email:*** kearly@ssdlaw.com

ROBERT G. HANSEMAN, born Sacramento, California, March 3, 1969; admitted to bar, 1995, Maryland; 2000, Ohio. *Education:* The Ohio State University (B.A., Political Science, cum laude, 1992; B.A., Journalism, cum laude, 1992); George Washington University (J.D., 1995). *Member:* Ohio State Bar Association. ***PRACTICE AREAS:*** Business Litigation; Commercial Litigation. ***Email:*** rhanseman@ssdlaw.com

TOBY K. HENDERSON, born Tipton, Indiana, June 9, 1970; admitted to bar, 1999, Ohio. *Education:* Ball State University (B.S., magna cum laude, 1996); University of Dayton School of Law (J.D., 1999). *Member:* Dayton, Ohio State, and American Bar Associations. ***PRACTICE AREAS:*** Business Litigation; Commercial Litigation. ***Email:*** thenderson@ssdlaw.com

CHANDA L. LYNCH, born Dayton, Ohio, 1975; admitted to bar, 2000, Ohio. *Education:* Wright State University (B.A., summa cum laude, 1997); University of Notre Dame (J.D., 2000). *Member:* Dayton, Ohio State and American Bar Associations. ***PRACTICE AREAS:*** Corporate Law; Health Care Law. ***Email:*** clynch@ssdlaw.com

TODD E. ROBENSON, born Louisville, Kentucky, February 4, 1974; admitted to bar, 2000, Maryland; 2003, District of Columbia; 2004, Ohio. *Education:* Indiana University (B.S., 1996); American University, Washington College of Law (J.D., 2000); Georgetown University Law Center (L.L.M., with distinction, 2002). *Member:* Dayton and Ohio State Bar Associations. ***PRACTICE AREAS:*** Corporate Law. ***Email:*** trobenson@ssdlaw.com

SUZANNE SUMNER, born Charleston, South Carolina, May 6, 1968; admitted to bar, 1993, Colorado; 2001, U.S. Supreme Court; 2003, Alaska (Not admitted in Ohio). *Education:* University of Nevada, Las Vegas (B.A., 1990); University of Denver (J.D., 1993). *Member:* Dayton, Ohio State and American Bar Associations. ***PRACTICE AREAS:*** Labor and Employment Law; Business Litigation; Commercial Litigation. ***Email:*** ssumner@ssdlaw.com

HEATHER DUFFEY WELBAUM, born Troy, Ohio, October 30, 1974; admitted to bar, 1999, Ohio; 2000, U.S. District Court, Southern District of Ohio. *Education:* University of Dayton (B.A., summa cum laude, 1996; J.D., summa cum laude, 1999). Editor in Chief, University of Dayton Law Review, 1998-1999.*Member:* Dayton, Ohio State and American Bar Associations. ***PRACTICE AREAS:*** Estate Planning; Probate; Corporate Law. ***Email:*** hwelbaum@ssdlaw.com

REPRESENTATIVE CLIENTS: Advanced Composites, Inc.; AFC Tool, Inc.; Angell Manufacturing Co.; Banc One Corporation; Barsplice Products, Inc.; Bowling Green State University; Chisano Marketing Communications, Inc.; City of Dayton; Danis Building Construction Company; Dayton Newspapers, Inc.; Dayton Power and Light Company; Dayton Speedometer Service, Inc.; DMAX, Ltd.; Eaton*form*, Inc.; Excellence in Motivation, Inc.; GMP and Employers Pension Fund; Jackson Products, Inc.; Kuhns Mold and Tool Co.; LexisNexis; Manufactured Assemblies Corporation; Miami University; National City Bank; NCR Corporation; Orion Specialty Insurance Company; Piqua Technologies, Inc.; Rack Processing Co., Inc.; Real Art Design Group; School & Home Office Products Association (SHOPA); Shumsky Enterprises, Inc.; Smedley Chevrolet Sales, Inc.; Venture Manufacturing Co.; Whiteford Foods Venture, L.P.; Win Wholesale Companies; Williams Scotsman, Inc.; Wright State University.

SHERRETS LAW OFFICES, LLC

DAYTON, OHIO

(See Kettering)

SHIPMAN, DIXON & LIVINGSTON CO., L.P.A.

DAYTON, OHIO

(See Troy)

Civil Trials in all Courts. Personal Injury, Environmental, Corporation, Real Estate, Insurance Defense Law, Probate and Estate Planning, Social Security, Municipal and Zoning. General Practice. Civil Rights Defense Law.

JEFFREY M. SILVERSTEIN AND ASSOCIATES

627 S. EDWIN C. MOSES BOULEVARD
SUITE 2-C
DAYTON, OHIO 45408
Telephone: 937-228-3731
Fax: 937-228-2252
Email: jeff@silversteinlaw.com
URL: http://www.lawyers.com/silversteinlaw

Employment and Labor Law.

JEFFREY M. SILVERSTEIN, born Philadelphia, Pennsylvania, April 8, 1955; admitted to bar, 1980, Ohio and U.S. District Court, Southern District of Ohio; 1985, U.S. District Court, Northern District of Ohio; 1986, U.S. Court of Appeals, Sixth Circuit; 1992, U.S. Supreme Court; 1999, U.S. District Court of Appeals, Federal Circuit. *Education:* Boston University (B.A., 1976); University of Dayton (J.D., 1980). Phi Delta Phi. Assistant Prosecutor, Montgomery County, 1980-1982. Administrative Law Judge, State Personnel Board of Review, Ohio, 1982-1983. *Member:* Dayton, Ohio State and American Bar Associations; National Employment Lawyers Association; Miami Valley Trial Lawyers Association. (Certified Specialist in Labor & Employment Law, Ohio State Bar Association). ***PRACTICE AREAS:*** Litigation; Labor and Employment; Civil Rights; Contracts; Discrimination; Arbitration; Administrative Law; Personal Injury; Probate.

SLOWIK & ROBINSON, LLC

DAYTON, OHIO

(See Columbus)

Labor and Employment Law, Immigration Law, Small Business Law, Alternative Dispute Resolution, Business Formations.

PAUL H. SPAETH CO., L.P.A.

130 WEST 2ND STREET, SUITE 450
DAYTON, OHIO 45402
Telephone: 937-223-1655
Fax: 937-223-1656
Email: pspaeth@phslaw.com
URL: http://www.phslaw.com

Bankruptcy (Chapters 7, 11, 13, Business Reorganizations), Collections, Debtor and Creditor Rights, Business Law, Business Formations, Bankruptcy Litigation.

PAUL H. SPAETH, born Cleveland, Ohio, June 5, 1957; admitted to bar, 1983, Ohio and U.S. District Court, Southern District of Ohio; 2002, U.S. Court of Appeals, Sixth Circuit. *Education:* Miami University (B.A., cum laude, 1979); The Ohio State University College of Law (J.D., 1982). Chapter 7 Panel Trustee, Dayton, Ohio, 1997—. Author and Lecturer, Bankruptcy and Creditors' Rights Topics, National Business Institute, 1994, 1996 and 1997. Author of articles on creditors' rights topics, Dayton Business Reporter, 1996. Member, American Bankruptcy Law Forum. *Member:* Dayton (Chairman, Debtor/Creditor/Bankruptcy Committee, 1994-1995), Ohio State (Member, Bankruptcy Subcommittee) and American Bar Associations; Commercial Law League of America; National Association of Bankruptcy Trustees. ***Email:*** pspaeth@bizwoh.rr.com

STANDLEY LAW GROUP LLP

DAYTON, OHIO

(See Dublin)

Domestic and Foreign Intellectual Property Law, including Patent, Trademark, Copyright, Unfair Competition and Trade Secret Law and related Litigation, Licensing, International Trade Matters, related Antitrust, Computer and other Technology Law.

STATMAN, HARRIS, SIEGEL & EYRICH, LLC

FIFTH THIRD STREET
110 NORTH MAIN STREET
SUITE 1520
DAYTON, OHIO 45402
Telephone: 937-222-1090
Fax: 937-222-1046

Cincinnati, Ohio Office: 2900 Chemed Center, 255 East Fifth Street, 45202-2912. Telephone: 513-621-2666. Telecopier: 513-621-4896.
Chicago, Illinois Office: 333 West Wacker Drive, Suite 1710, 60606. Telephone: 312-263-1070. Fax: 312-263-1201.

General Civil Trial and Appellate Practice in Federal and State Courts. Commercial Litigation, Bankruptcy, Banking, Personal Injury and Family Law. Corporate Acquisitions, Dispositions, Spin-Offs, Corporate Formation, Financings, Real Estate, Banking and Commercial Law, Reorganizations, Restructurings, Bankruptcy, Civil Litigation, General Business, Intellectual Property, Taxation, Estate Planning.

MEMBER OF FIRM

THOMAS R. NOLAND, born Tipp City, Ohio, September 20, 1945; admitted to bar, 1970, Ohio and U.S. District Court, Southern District of Ohio, U.S. Court of Appeals, Sixth Circuit, and U.S. Supreme Court. *Education:* Ohio Wesleyan University (B.A., 1967); University of Cincinnati (J.D., 1970). *Member:* Dayton and Ohio State Bar Associations; American Bankruptcy Law Forum; American Bankruptcy Institute; Commercial Law League of America; National Association of Bankruptcy Trustees. (Certified in Business Bankruptcy Law, Consumer Bankruptcy Law by the American Board of Certification). ***REPORTED CASES:*** U.S. v. Noland 517 US 535. ***PRACTICE AREAS:*** Bankruptcy Workouts; Commercial Law; Litigation. ***Email:*** trnoland@shsedayton.com

ASSOCIATES

PAUL H. SHANEYFELT, born Troy, Ohio, June 18, 1968; admitted to bar, 1995, Ohio. *Education:* Columbia University (B.A., 1990); Case Western Reserve University (J.D., 1995). Adjunct Professor, Business Law, Edison Community College, 1994. *Member:* Dayton Bar Association; American Bankruptcy Law Forum. ***PRACTICE AREAS:*** Bankruptcy; Banking Law; Corporate Law. ***Email:*** phshaneyfelt@shsedayton.com

TINA F. WOODS, born Greensboro, North Carolina, May 25, 1968; admitted to bar, 1994, Indiana; 1997, Ohio. *Education:* North Carolina State University (B.A., magna cum laude, 1990); Indiana University (J.D., cum laude, 1994). Administrative Law Judge, OSHA, Indiana, 1995-1996. ***PRACTICE AREAS:*** Creditors Rights; Commercial Litigation; Bankruptcy. ***Email:*** tfwoods@shsedayton.com

PATRICIA L. HILL, born Dayton, Ohio, March 10, 1974; admitted to bar, 2000, Ohio. *Education:* University of Dayton (B.C.E., 1997; J.D., 2000). *Member:* Dayton and Ohio State Bar Associations; America Bankruptcy Institute. ***PRACTICE AREAS:*** Creditors Rights; Labor and Employment; Workers Compensation; Banking Law; Commercial Litigation. ***Email:*** plhill@shsedayton.com

(This Listing Continued)

STATMAN, HARRIS, SIEGEL & EYRICH, LLC, Dayton—Continued

OF COUNSEL

ROBERT F. COWDREY, born Dayton, Ohio, July 23, 1949; admitted to bar, 1975, Ohio, U.S. District Court, Southern District of Ohio and U.S. Court of Appeals, Sixth Circuit. *Education:* University of Colorado; University of Cincinnati (B.A., 1971; J.D., 1975). *Member:* Dayton and Ohio State Bar Associations; Ohio Association of Civil Trial Attorneys; Defense Research Institute; Diplomate, Court Practice Institute, 1981. ***PRACTICE AREAS:*** Insurance Defense; Medical Malpractice; Business Law. ***Email:*** rfcowdrey@shsedayton.com

STEVENS & SHOWALTER, L.L.P.

7019 CORPORATE WAY
DAYTON, OHIO 45459-4238
Telephone: 937-438-6848
Fax: 937-438-2124
Email: ssllp@speakeasy.net

Intellectual Property, Patents, Trademarks, Copyright and Unfair Competition.

RICHARD C. STEVENS, born Columbus, Ohio, 1945; admitted to bar, 1977, Illinois; 1982, Ohio; registered to practice before U.S. Patent and Trademark Office. *Education:* The Ohio State University (B.E.E., cum laude, 1968; M.S.E.E., 1969); Illinois Institute of Technology, Chicago-Kent College of Law (J.D., with high honors, 1977). Eta Kappa Nu; Tau Beta Pi. *Member:* Dayton, Ohio State and American Bar Associations; American Intellectual Property Law Association; Dayton Intellectual Property Law Association (President, 1995-1997); Institute of Electrical and Electronics Engineers. (Also Of Counsel, Stockwell & Associates, Lexington, Kentucky). ***PRACTICE AREAS:*** Intellectual Property; Patents. ***Email:*** rcstevens@speakeasy.net

ROBERT L. SHOWALTER, born Louisville, Kentucky, 1960; admitted to bar, 1989, Ohio; 2000, Kentucky. *Education:* University of Kentucky (B.S., Mech. Eng., 1983); American University Washington College of Law (J.D., cum laude, 1989). U.S. Patent Examiner, U.S. Patent and Trademark Office, 1984-1989. *Member:* Ohio State Bar Association; Dayton Intellectual Property Law Association; American Intellectual Property Law Association. (Also Of Counsel, Stockwell & Associates, Lexington, Kentucky). ***PRACTICE AREAS:*** Intellectual Property; Patents. ***Email:*** Showalter@speakeasy.net

THOMAS E. LEES, born Newark, Ohio, January 3, 1968; admitted to bar, 1998, Ohio; 2002, U.S. District Court, Southern District of Ohio; registered to practice before the U.S. Patent and Trademark Office. *Education:* The Ohio State University (B.S.E.E., 1992); Capital University (J.D., 1998). *Member:* Ohio State and American (Member, Intellectual Property Section) Bar Associations; American Intellectual Property Law Association; Dayton Intellectual Property Law Association (Treasurer, 2003—). ***PRACTICE AREAS:*** Patents. ***Email:*** thomas.lees@speakeasy.net

OF COUNSEL

MICHAEL D. FOLKERTS, born Phoenix, Arizona, February 12, 1958; admitted to bar, 1989, Ohio; registered to practice before U.S. Patent and Trademark Office. *Education:* Arizona State University (B.S. in M.E., 1980); George Mason University (J.D., 1989). Patent Examiner, U.S. Patent Office, 1984-1989. *Member:* Ohio State Bar Association; American Intellectual Property Law Association; Dayton Intellectual Property Law Association. (Also Of Counsel to Stockwell & Associates, Lexington, Kentucky). ***PRACTICE AREAS:*** Patents; Intellectual Property. ***Email:*** mfolkerts@speakeasy.net

CHARLENE L.H. STUKENBORG, born Dayton, Ohio, September 17, 1966; admitted to bar, 1995, Ohio; registered to practice before U.S. Patent and Trademark Office. *Education:* Ohio State University (B.S.E.E., 1989); University of Dayton (J.D., summa cum laude, 1995). ***PRACTICE AREAS:*** Intellectual Property; Patents. ***Email:*** ssllp@speakeasy.net

SUBASHI, WILDERMUTH & BALLATO

Established in 1997

THE OAKWOOD BUILDING
2305 FAR HILLS AVENUE
DAYTON, OHIO 45419
Telephone: 937-534-0500
Fax: 937-534-0505
Email: lawoffices@swbohiolaw.com
URL: http://www.swbohiolaw.com

Insurance Defense, Insurance Coverage, Professional Liability, School Law, Governmental Immunities, Civil Rights, Employment Law, Civil Litigation, Medical Malpractice.

FIRM PROFILE: Subashi, Wildermuth & Ballato is a firm of civil trial lawyers who concentrate their practice primarily in the defense of individuals, corporations and governmental entities. The attorneys of the firm handle a wide variety of litigation including employment law, civil rights, school law, insurance coverage, professional liability, commercial litigation, product liability, nursing homes, employer intentional torts, and insurance defense. The firm holds the highest rating given by Martindale-Hubbell.

Although the firm is located in Dayton, Ohio, the attorneys of the firm represent clients involved in litigation in most of Ohio's major cities and counties in both state and federal court. The attorneys of Subashi, Wildermuth & Ballato are very goal-oriented and they are dedicated to promptly resolving the cases which should be settled, and aggressively trying the cases which should be tried.

In addition to the firm's eight attorneys, the firm is fully supported by five paralegals and by six other clerical/administrative professionals. All of the firm's members believe strongly in client-service and in the importance defending and protecting their clients' interests above all else.

NICHOLAS E. SUBASHI, born Ridley Park, Pennsylvania, May 15, 1954; admitted to bar, 1980, Pennsylvania; 1986, Ohio; 1981, U.S. District Court, Middle District of Pennsylvania; 1985, U.S. District Court, Eastern District of Pennsylvania; 1986, U.S. Court of Appeals, Third Circuit; 1987, U.S. District Court, Southern District of Ohio; 1987, U.S. Court of Appeals, Sixth Circuit; 1992, U.S. Supreme Court. *Education:* University of Delaware (A.B., cum laude, 1977); Dickinson School of Law (J.D., 1980). Phi Beta Kappa. Master Emeritus, Carl D. Kessler Inn of Courts. Recipient: Frank S. Hurd Member of the Year Award, Ohio Association of Civil Trial Attorneys, 1995; Defense Research Institute Exceptional Performance Citation, 2002. Named: "Best of the Bar," 2004 Dayton Business Journal; Ohio Super Lawyer 2005, 2006. Deputy District Attorney, Dauphin County, Pennsylvania, 1981-1983. Litigation Counsel, Nationwide Insurance Company, 1983-1987. Member: Council of School Attorneys, National and Ohio School Boards Association; Associate Member, Dayton Claims Adjusters Association. President, OACTA, 2000-2001. *Member:* Dayton, Ohio State and American Bar Associations; Ohio Association of Civil Trial Attorneys (Member, Past President); Defense Research Institute; International Association of Defense Counsel. American Bar Foundation (Life Fellow); Ohio State Bar Foundation. (Certified as a Civil Trial Advocacy Specialist by the National Board of Trial Advocacy). ***PRACTICE AREAS:*** Insurance Defense; Insurance Coverage; Professional Liability Defense; School Law; Governmental Immunity; Civil Rights; Employment Law; Medical Malpractice. ***Email:*** nsubashi@swbohiolaw.com

BRIAN L. WILDERMUTH, born Wapakoneta, Ohio, March 5, 1970; admitted to bar, 1996, Ohio and U.S. District Court, Southern District of Ohio; 2001, U.S. Court of Appeals, 6th Circuit; 2002, U.S. District Court, Northern District of Ohio. *Education:* Miami University (B.A., 1992); University of Toledo College of Law (J.D., magna cum laude, 1996). Order of the Coif. Note and Comment Editor, Law Review, University of Toledo College of Law, 1994-1996. Barrister, Carl D. Kessler Inn of Courts. Author: "In re Lee: Tithing as Grounds for Dismissal Under Section 707(b) of the Bankruptcy Code," 26 University of Toledo Law Review 725. Co-author, with Nicholas E. Subashi: "Bad Faith Since Zoppo," OACTA Quarterly, Winter 1997.*Member:* Dayton (Member at-large, Board of Trustees, 2003—), Ohio State and American Bar Associations; Ohio Association of Civil Trial Attorneys; Defense Research Institute; Ohio Council of School Law Attorneys. ***PRACTICE AREAS:*** Insurance Defense; Professional Liability Defense; Insurance Coverage; Governmental Immunity. ***Email:*** bwildermuth@swbohiolaw.com

LYNNETTE PISONE BALLATO, born Pittsburgh, Pennsylvania, March 22, 1970; admitted to bar, 1995, Ohio and U.S. District Court, Southern District of Ohio; 1998, U.S. Court of Appeals, 6th Circuit; 2001, U.S. District Court, Northern District of Ohio; 2003, U.S. Supreme Court. *Education:* Allegheny College (B.A., cum laude, 1992); Ohio Northern University (J.D., 1995). Member, Board of Advocate, Ohio Northern University Moot Court, 1993-1995. Managing Editor, Journal of Pharmacy & Law, 1994-1995. Author: Walls v. Armour: Upholding the Principles of Liability, 30 OHIO N.U.J. Pharmacy & L.225, 1994; The Political Debate Concerning Discriminating Pricing Practices within Health Care Reform, 40 OHIO N.U.J. Pharmacy & L.63, 1995. Public Defender, Clark County, 1995-1997. *Member:* Dayton, Ohio State and American Bar Associations; Ohio Association of Civil Trial Attorneys; Defense Research Institute. ***LANGUAGES:*** French. ***PRACTICE AREAS:*** Civil Rights Defense; School Law; Local Government Defense; Professional Liability Defense; Insurance Defense. ***Email:*** lballato@swbohiolaw.com

TABITHA JUSTICE, born Gallipolis, Ohio, July 23, 1976; admitted to bar, 2002, Ohio; U.S. District Court, Southern District of Ohio; U.S. Court of Appeals, Sixth Circuit and U.S. Supreme Court. *Education:* Ohio University (B.A., Political Science, 1998); University of Dayton (J.D., 2002). Moot Court. *Member:* Dayton, Ohio State and American Bar Associations; Ohio Association of Civil Trial Attorneys; Defense Research Institute. [Ohio Army National Guard, 1996-2002]. ***PRACTICE AREAS:*** Insurance Defense; Professional Liability Defense; Insurance Coverage; Government Immunity. ***Email:*** tjustice@swbohiolaw.com

JOSHUA EPLING, born Huntington, West Virginia, May 12, 1977; admitted to bar, 2002, Kentucky (Not admitted in Ohio). *Education:* Marshall University (B.A., Business, Marketing, magna cum laude, 1999); Dayton Law School (J.D., 2002). Delta Theta Pi. *Member:* Kentucky and American Bar Associations. ***PRACTICE AREAS:*** Insurance Defense; Professional Liability Defense; Insurance Coverage; Government Immunity. ***Email:*** jepling@swbohiolaw.com

HEATHER R. ZILKA, born North Charleroi, Pennsylvania, September 9, 1973; admitted to bar, 1999, Ohio. *Education:* Washington & Jefferson College (B.A., 1995); Capital University (J.D., 1998). *Member:* Dayton, Ohio State and American Bar Associations; Ohio Association of Civil Trial Attorneys; Defense Research Institute. ***PRACTICE AREAS:*** Insurance Defense; Professional Liability; Insurance Coverage; Government Immunity. ***Email:*** hzilka@swbohiolaw.com

ANNE P. KEETON, born Lexington, Kentucky, September 19, 1978; admitted to bar, 2003, Ohio and U.S. District Court, Southern District of Ohio. *Education:* University of Virginia (B.A., 2000); University of Kentucky (J.D., 2003). *Member:* Dayton, Ohio State and American Bar Associations; Ohio Association of Civil Trial Attorneys; Defense Research Institute. ***PRACTICE AREAS:*** Insurance Defense; Professional Liability Defense; Insurance Coverage; Government Immunity. ***Email:*** akeeton@swbohiolaw.com

JEFFREY P. NODZAK, born Kettering, Ohio, July 24, 1980; (admission pending). *Education:* University of Dayton (J.D., 2005). *Member:* Dayton, Ohio State and American Bar Associations; Ohio Association of Civil Trial Attorneys; Defense Research Institute. ***PRACTICE AREAS:*** Insurance Defense; Professional Liability Defense; Insurance Coverage; Government Immunity. ***Email:*** jnodzak@swbohiolaw.com

REPRESENTATIVE CLIENTS: Nationwide Insurance Co.; Farmland Insurance Co.; Scottsdale Insurance Co.; Western Heritage Insurance Co.; Motorists Insurance Co.; Hylant Administrative Service; Erie Insurance Group; Beavercreek City Schools.; Dayton Public Schools; Tipp City Local School District; Miami Valley Risk Management Association; Southwest Ohio Educational Purchasing Cooperative Insurance Program; Allied Insurance Co.;

(This Listing Continued)

Ohio Transit Risk Pool; Safeco Insurance Co.; Guide One Insurance Co.; Progressive Insurance Co.

LAW OFFICES OF SURDYK, DOWD & TURNER, CO., L.P.A.

KETTERING TOWER 1610
40 NORTH MAIN STREET
DAYTON, OHIO 45423
Telephone: 937-222-2333
Fax: 937-222-1970

ROBERT J. SURDYK, born Dayton, Ohio, April 27, 1947; admitted to bar, 1972, Ohio, U.S. District Court, Southern District of Ohio and U.S. Court of Appeals, Sixth Circuit. *Education:* University of Notre Dame (B.A., 1969); University of Cincinnati (J.D., 1972). Assistant Prosecuting Attorney, Montgomery County, 1972-1976. Law Director, Washington Township, Montgomery County, Ohio, 1992—. *Member:* Dayton (Member, Executive Committee, 1982-1983; President, 2003-2004) and Ohio State Bar Associations; Ohio Association of Civil Trial Attorneys. Fellow, Ohio Bar Foundation; American Bar Foundation; Defense Research Institute. Diplomate, Court Practice Institute, 1981. ***PRACTICE AREAS:*** Insurance Defense; Professional Liability; Local Government Law; Zoning; Administrative Hearings and Appeals; Litigation. ***Email:*** rsurdyk@sdtlawyers.com

EDWARD J. DOWD, born Niagara Falls, New York, December 11, 1957; admitted to bar, 1983, Ohio and U.S. District Court, Southern District of Ohio; 1985, New York; 1993, U.S. Court of Appeals, Sixth Circuit and U.S. Supreme Court. *Education:* University of Notre Dame (B.A., 1980); University of Dayton (J.D., 1983). Associate Editor, University of Dayton Law Review, 1982-1983. Law Clerk, Ohio Second District Court of Appeals, 1983-1984. Assistant Attorney General, Environmental Enforcement Section, Ohio Attorney General's Office, 1984-1985. *Member:* Dayton and Ohio State Bar Associations; Ohio Association of Civil Trial Attorneys; Defense Research Institute. ***REPORTED CASES:*** UFCW Local 1099 v. City of Sidney, 367 F.3d 738 (6th Cir. 2004). ***PRACTICE AREAS:*** Employers Liability; Product Liability; Insurance Defense; Local Government Law. ***Email:*** edowd@sdtlawyers.com

JEFFREY C. TURNER, born Hamilton, Ohio, September 27, 1961; admitted to bar, 1994, Ohio, U.S. District Court, Southern District of Ohio; U.S. District Court, Northern District of Ohio; 1995, U.S. Court of Appeals, Sixth Circuit and U.S. Supreme Court. *Education:* Xavier University (B.S., 1990); University of Dayton School of Law (J.D., cum laude, 1994). Associate Editor, University of Dayton Law Review, 1993-1994. *Member:* Dayton, and Ohio State Bar Associations; Ohio Association of Civil Trial Attorneys; Defense Research Institute; ACA International. ***PRACTICE AREAS:*** Civil Rights; Local Government Law; Consumer Litigation; Professional Liability; FDLPA Defense; FCRA Defense. ***Email:*** jturner@sdtlawyers.com

---

BOYD W. GENTRY, born Dayton, Ohio, February 14, 1974; admitted to bar, 1999, Ohio and U.S. District Court, Southern District of Ohio; 2000, Kentucky; 2001, U.S. District Court, Northern District of Ohio; U.S. Court of Appeals, Sixth Circuit. *Education:* Capital University (B.A., 1996); University of Toledo (J.D., magna cum laude, 1999). Order of the Coif. *Member:* Kentucky Bar Association; Ohio State Bar Association. ***REPORTED CASES:*** UFCW Local 1099 v. City of Sidney, 367 F.3d 738 (6th Cir. 2004); Kiser v. Lowe, 236 F.Supp.2d 872 (S.D. Ohio 2002). ***PRACTICE AREAS:*** Defense Litigation. ***Email:*** bgentry@sdtlawyers.com

REBEKAH NEUHERZ, born Philadelphia, Pennsylvania, May 24, 1973; admitted to bar, 1999, Pennsylvania; 2000, Ohio and U.S. District Court, Northern District of Ohio; U.S. District Court, Southern District of Ohio; U.S. Court of Appeals, Sixth Circuit. *Education:* Lycoming College (B.A., 1995); Case Western Reserve University (J.D., 1999). ***PRACTICE AREAS:*** Domestic; Employment; Business; Probate; Family Law; Insurance Defense. ***Email:*** rnevherz@sdtlawyers.com

DAWN M. FRICK, born Bangor, Maine, February 29, 1968; admitted to bar, 1998, Ohio, U.S. District Court, Southern District of Ohio and U.S. Court of Appeals, Sixth Circuit. *Education:* The Ohio State University (B.S., 1990; J.D., 1997). *Member:* Dayton, Ohio State and American Bar Associations. ***PRACTICE AREAS:*** Insurance Defense; Employment Law. ***Email:*** dfrick@sdtlawyers.com

KEVIN A. LANTZ, born Columbus, Ohio, June 29, 1957; admitted to bar, 1994, Ohio and U.S. District Court, Southern District of Ohio. *Education:* John Brown University (B.S., Broadcasting, summa cum laude, 1979); University of Dayton (J.D., summa cum laude, 1994). Alpha Chi. Member, National Moot Court Team, University of Dayton School of Law, 1993. Finalist, Hon. Walter H. Rice Moot Court Competition, 1992. Recipient: Cohen Award for Excellence in Law Review Writing, 1993; American Jurisprudence Awards for Evidence, Legal Research and Writing II & III. Author: "The Princess and the 'Rock': Minnesota Declines to Extend 'Plain View' to 'Plain Feel' - State v. Dickerson, 481 N.W.2d 840 (Minn.), cert. granted, 113 S.CT. 53, (1992)," 18 University of Dayton Law Review 539, 1993. Staff Attorney, Court of Appeals, of Ohio, Second District, 1994-1996. *Member:* Montgomery County and Ohio State Bar Associations. ***PRACTICE AREAS:*** Insurance Defense; Business Litigation. ***Email:*** klantz@sdtlawyers.com

MICHAEL F. ARNOLD, born Houston, Texas, April 12, 1968; admitted to bar, 2003, Ohio; 2004, U.S. District Court, Southern District of Ohio. *Education:* University of Maryland, College Park (B.S., 2000); St. John's University (J.D., 2003). *Member:* Dayton and Ohio State Bar Associations. [Cpl., USMC, 1986-1990]. ***Email:*** marnold@sdtlawyers.com

TAFT, STETTINIUS & HOLLISTER LLP

Established in 1885
110 NORTH MAIN STREET, SUITE 900
DAYTON, OHIO 45402-1786
Telephone: 937-228-2838
Facsimile: 937-228-2816
URL: http://www.taftlaw.com

Columbus, Ohio Office: Twelfth Floor, 21 East State Street. Telephone: 614-221-2838.
Covington, Kentucky Office: 1717 Dixie Highway, Suite 340. Telephone: 859-331-2838; 513-381-2838.
Cleveland, Ohio Office: 3500 BP Tower, 200 Public Square. Telephone: 216-241-2838.
Cincinnati, Ohio Office: 425 Walnut Street, Suite 1800. Telephone: 513-381-2838

Antitrust, Bankruptcy and Debtor/Creditor Rights, Business and Finance, E-Business (Internet and E-Commerce), Employee Benefits/ERISA and Tax-Planning, Environmental Law, Family Law, Family Business Planning, Franchise, General Litigation, Health Care, Immigration, Institutional Finance, Intellectual Property and Technology Group, International, Japanese Practice, Labor and Employment, Mergers and Acquisitions, Nonprofit and Tax-Exempt Organizations, Product Liability and Personal Injury, Public Finance, Real Property, Securities, Tax, Probate and Estate Planning, Workers' Compensation.

RESIDENT MEMBERS

J. STEVEN JUSTICE, born Dayton, Ohio, December 2, 1958; admitted to bar, 1994, Ohio. *Education:* Anderson University (B.A., 1981); Southern Baptist Theological Seminary (M.Div., 1987); University of Cincinnati (J.D., 1994).

HUGH E. WALL, III, born Dayton, Ohio, November 5, 1946; admitted to bar, 1972, Ohio. *Education:* College of St. Thomas (B.A., 1968); University of Cincinnati (J.D., 1972).

ASSOCIATES

LISA L. PATTERSON, born Niagara Falls, New York, 1968; admitted to bar, 1996, Ohio. *Education:* University of Toronto (B.A., 1990); Capital University (J.D., 1995).

MATTHEW J. WILES, born Akron, Ohio, March 26, 1977; admitted to bar, 2002, Ohio. *Education:* Bowling Green State University (B.S., 1999); Dayton Law School (J.D., 2002).

GREGORY TURNER, born Harlan, Kentucky, May 15, 1964; admitted to bar, 2001, Ohio. *Education:* University of Dayton (B.S., 1986; J.D., 2001).

(For biographical data on all other personnel, see Covington, Kentucky, Cincinnati, Columbus and Cleveland, Ohio professional biographies)

TALBOT & DUCKER

903 KEY BANK BUILDING
DAYTON, OHIO 45402
Telephone: 937-224-1006
Fax: 937-224-1009
Email: Ttalbotjr@aol.com

Mailing Address: P.O. Box 384, Wright Bros. Station, Dayton, OH 45409

General Civil Practice. Commercial Collections, Commercial Law, Bankruptcy, Liens, Corporation, Probate Law and Mechanics' Liens. Trials.

FIRM PROFILE: Talbot & Ducker has for over fifty years engaged in the commercial practice of law. The firm handles creditor commercial collection problems involving accounts, contracts, leases, and insurance and freight claims in state, federal, and bankruptcy courts.

MEMBERS OF FIRM

THOMAS B. TALBOT, JR., born Dayton, Ohio, March 11, 1949; admitted to bar, 1974, Ohio. *Education:* Centre College of Kentucky (B.A., 1971); University of Cincinnati (J.D., 1974); Xavier University (M.S., 1988). State Senator, Ohio Sixth Senatorial District, 1984. *Member:* Dayton and Ohio State Bar Associations. ***PRACTICE AREAS:*** Commercial Law; Commercial Collections; Bankruptcy Law; Creditors Law; Lien Law.

JOHN T. DUCKER, born Louisville, Kentucky, December 5, 1931; admitted to bar, 1958, West Virginia; 1967, Ohio. *Education:* Hampden-Sydney College (A.B., 1953); West Virginia University (LL.B., 1958). Phi Delta Phi. *Member:* Dayton, Ohio State and West Virginia Bar Associations; West Virginia State Bar. (Retired)

REFERENCE: Fifth Third Bank.

THOMPSON AND DEVENY CO., L.P.A.

1340 WOODMAN DRIVE
DAYTON, OHIO 45432
Telephone: 937-252-2030
Fax: 937-252-9425
Email: info@thompsonanddeveny.com
Bankruptcy Law, Divorce, Child Custody, Child Support.

LESTER R. THOMPSON, born Dayton, Ohio, 1949; admitted to bar, 1974, Ohio. *Education:* Bowling Green State University (B.S.B.A., 1971); Ohio Northern University (J.D., 1974). *Member:* Dayton Bar Association. ***PRACTICE AREAS:*** Bankruptcy Law.

DAIN N. DEVENY, born 1948; admitted to bar, 1974, Ohio. ***PRACTICE AREAS:*** Domestic Relations Law; Divorce; Criminal Law.

CHARLES J. ROEDERSHEIMER, born Dayton, Ohio, 1942; admitted to bar, 1967, West Virginia; 1968, Ohio. *Education:* Wheeling Jesuit College (B.S., 1964); Cincinnati,

(This Listing Continued)

THOMPSON AND DEVENY CO., L.P.A., Dayton—Continued

University of (J.D., 1967). ***PRACTICE AREAS:*** Employment Law; Divorce; Bankruptcy. ***Email:*** charles@thompsonanddeveny.com

THOMPSON HINE LLP

2000 COURTHOUSE PLAZA, N.E.
P.O. BOX 8801
DAYTON, OHIO 45401-8801
Telephone: 937-443-6600
Fax: 937-443-6635
Email: info@ThompsonHine.com
URL: http://www.ThompsonHine.com

Cleveland, Ohio Office: 3900 Key Center, 127 Public Square, 44114-1291. Telephone: 216-566-5500. Fax: 216-566-5800. Email: info@ThompsonHine.com.
Cincinnati, Ohio Office: 312 Walnut Street, 14th Floor, 45202-4089. Telephone: 513-352-6700. Fax: 513-241-4771. Email: info@ThompsonHine.com.
Columbus, Ohio Office: 10 West Broad Street, Suite 700, 43215-3435. Telephone: 614-469-3200. Fax: 614-469-3361. Email: info@ThompsonHine.com.
Washington, D.C. Office: 1920 N Street, N.W., Suite 800, 20036-1600. Telephone: 202-331-8800. Fax: 202-331-8330. Email: info@ThompsonHine.com.
New York, N.Y. Office: One Chase Manhattan Plaza, 58th Floor, 10005-1401. Telephone: 212-344-5680. Fax: 212-809-6890. Email: info@ThompsonHine.com.
Brussels, Belgium Office: Avenue Louise 375 - b8, 1050 Brussels, Belgium, Telephone: 011 (32-2) 626-3280. Fax: 011 (32-2) 626-3299. Email: info@ThompsonHine.com.
Atlanta, Georgia Office: Proscenium Center, Suite 1200, 1170 Peachtree Street, 30309-7673. Telephone: 404-541-2900. Fax: 404-541-2905. Email: info@ThompsonHine.com.

Administrative Law, Admiralty and Maritime Law, Agency and Distributorships, Antitrust and Trade Regulation, Aviation and Aerospace, Bankruptcy, Banks and Banking, Biotechnology, Business Law, Business Litigation, Business Regulation, Business Transactions, Closely Held Business Law, Joint Ventures, Class Actions, Commercial Law, Commercial Real Estate, Communications and Media, FCC Regulation, Computers and Software, Construction Law, Contracts, Copyrights, Corporate Law, Corporate Finance, Corporate Litigation, Corporate Tax Controversies, Debtor and Creditor, Employee Benefits, ERISA, Energy, Energy Regulation, Environmental Law, Finance, Commercial Finance, Franchises and Franchising, General Practice, Government, False Claims Act, Qui Tam Litigation, Government Contracts, Health Care, Insurance Coverage, Insurance Regulation, Intellectual Property, International Law, International Trade, Internet Law, Labor and Employment, Life Sciences, Litigation, Complex Litigation, Medicare Fraud and Abuse, Mergers, Acquisitions and Divestitures, Natural Resources, Nonprofit and Charitable Organizations, Occupational Safety and Health, OSHA, Partnership Law, Patents, Probate, Products Liability, Product Safety, Professional Liability, Public Finance, Railroad Law, Real Estate, Regulatory Law, Drug and Medical Device Regulation, Food and Drug Regulation, International Regulatory Law, Regulated Industries, Securities, Initial Public Offerings, Public Offerings, Taxation, Tax Controversies, Toxic Torts, Trade Secrets, Trademarks, Transportation, Trusts and Estates, Unfair Competition, Utility Law, White Collar Crime, Zoning, Planning and Land Use.

FIRM PROFILE: Established in 1911, Thompson Hine today is among the nation's largest corporate law firms and was recently selected as one of the Best Corporate Law Firms in America (in a survey of 32,000 corporate directors conducted by Corporate Board Member magazine). Thompson Hine attorneys serve some of the premier businesses in the world, including:

Alltel, Anthem Blue Cross/Blue Shield, Avery Dennison, BIC Corporation, Chiquita Brands International, Eaton Corporation, Eveready (Energizer), Ford Motor Company, Ford Motor Credit, Formica Corp., Goodrich Corporation, Goodyear Tire and Rubber Co., Hartford Insurance, Intimate Brands, Inc. (Victoria's Secret, Bath & Body Works), Jo-Ann Stores, Inc., Kelly Services, Inc., KeyCorp/KeyBank, Lexis-Nexis, The Mead Corporation, Medical Mutual of Ohio, Milacron Inc., Newell Rubbermaid, Nordson Corporation, Oglebay Norton Company, Ohio Bankers Association, Omnicare, Inc., Parker Hannifin, Polyone Corporation, Procter & Gamble, S.C. Johnson & Son, Inc., Sherwin-Williams, Smythe Cramer Co., SuperValu, Time Warner Cable, Toro Company, Verizon Wireless, and Whirlpool Corporation.

Thompson Hine attorneys provide a wide range of corporate legal services, represented by the following practice groups:

BANKRUPTCY - We represent major secured and unsecured lenders, creditors" committees, credit enhancement providers, debtors and various other parties of interest in finance transactions, workouts and bankruptcy matters.

BUSINESS LITIGATION - We represent corporate clients in a wide variety of business litigation - from corporate control contests and insurance disputes, to class actions, securities fraud, and tax controversies.

BANKING & INSURANCE - Our lawyers provide recognized experience in virtually all areas of financial institutions matters. We provide regulatory, transactional, government relations and litigation services to clients on matters related to insurance. Our clients include all types of insurance companies and other financial services organizations including large, publicly held, multinational financial holding companies; banks and thrifts; investment banking organizations; securities broker-dealers; registered investment advisor organizations; mutual funds; and mortgage banking and broker organizations.

COMMERCIAL & PUBLIC FINANCE - We handle complex commercial finance transactions (including senior debt, subordinated debt and mezzanine financing transactions and private debt placements), public finance, asset securitizations and general bank regulatory law.

(This Listing Continued)

COMPETITION, ANTITRUST & WHITE-COLLAR CRIME - We represent clients in antitrust and competition matters, trade restraint and price discrimination issues, franchising and distribution, misappropriation of trade secrets, false advertising, enforcement of noncompetition covenants and interference with business relationships.

CONSTRUCTION - We represent owners, design professionals, construction managers, contractors and sureties in connection with all facets of the building industry and have served in the role of Project Counsel for billions of dollars of construction at sites across the United States.

CORPORATE, M&A AND SECURITIES - We represent both emerging and established businesses in their most important business transactions, from start-up through IPOs, joint ventures, mergers, acquisitions and beyond.

eBUSINESS & EMERGING TECHNOLOGIES - This group unites experienced counsel from various disciplines around one central goal: helping business realize the opportunities and manage the risks of electronic and technological commerce.

EMPLOYEE BENEFITS - We advise clients regarding qualified, non-qualified and welfare benefit plans; resolution of controversies with the IRS, DOL, PBGC and other agencies; incentive and equity-based compensation arrangements; statutory and regulatory compliance; ERISA fiduciary duties; ESOPs; multi-employer plans; and ERISA litigation.

ENERGY - We provide a broad range of services to our clients in the energy industry, including those that: Generate and sell electric energy into the nation's wholesale and retail energy markets. Transport and sell natural gas and oil. Transmit and distribute electricity and natural gas in retail markets. Purchase natural gas, electric energy and coal. Conduct energy trading operations. Manufacture, construct and/or buy and sell facilities and assets associated with the energy industry. Undertake energy-related projects, such as distributed generation, conservation or energy management projects. Manage information used by the energy industry.

ENVIRONMENTAL - We help clients understand the environmental aspects of their business transactions, craft methods of allocating risk and counsel them on their compliance obligations under local, state and federal laws.

HEALTH CARE - We represent physician groups, hospitals, clinical laboratories, diagnostic service providers, pharmaceutical manufacturers, medical device manufacturers and health insurance providers.

INTELLECTUAL PROPERTY - We assist clients with patents, trademarks, copyrights, trade secrets, computer software, internet related issues, employment relationships and intellectual property litigation.

INTERNATIONAL - We advise clients on trade regulation issues, customs and duty matters, foreign investment and joint ventures, NAFTA matters, importing and exporting issues, intellectual property protection, and immigration matters.

LABOR & EMPLOYMENT - We represent clients in employment litigation, workers" compensation proceedings, immigration matters, collective bargaining, administrative proceedings before the Department of Labor, OSHA, EEOC, NLRB and various state agencies.

LIFE SCIENCES - We provide legal and regulatory management services to established and emerging companies in the food, pharmaceuticals, biotech, and medical device industries.

PERSONAL & SUCCESSION PLANNING - We assist clients in the management and transmission of wealth, the succession to the control of businesses and other personal and family concerns.

PRODUCT LIABILITY - We have handled thousands of product liability matters involving mechanical, chemical, electrical, medical, aerospace, automotive and other products.

REAL ESTATE - We represent clients in Real Estate Development; Corporate Real Estate; Zoning and Land Use; Real Estate Investment and Financing; and Real Estate Investment Trusts.

TAXATION - We counsel clients in business transactions and financings, tax controversy, litigation, legislative and regulatory activities, executive compensation and tax planning, international taxation, state and local taxation and foundation and exempt organization matters.

TELECOMMUNICATIONS - Our Telecommunications group provides clients with wide-ranging guidance on the regulations and laws affecting telecommunications, broadcasting and other electronic communications companies. Our representation includes transactional matters, regulatory compliance, telecommunications services contracting, licensing and legislative/regulatory advocacy. We also have experience in issues involving communications land use and environmental matters, including human exposure to electromagnetic energy.

TRANSPORTATION - One of the largest transportation practices in the United States, our team has more than 100 years of collective experience representing transportation interests. We are involved in matters relating to commercial relationships and arrangements as well as the extensive and complex structure of rights, remedies and regulatory requirements involved in the domestic and international transportation of goods by rail, motor, ship, barge, air and pipeline.

WORKERS COMPENSATION - We represent employers in workers" compensation matters before state courts and industrial commissions. We have extensive experience representing and counseling clients in the area of workers' compensation.

AMOS BURT THOMPSON (1871-1965)
CHARLES P. HINE (1877-1942)
WALTER L. FLORY (1880-1951)
MICHAEL L. HARDY (Partner-in-Charge, Cleveland)
PATRICIA MANN SMITSON (Partner-in-Charge, Cincinnati)

(This Listing Continued)

ANTHONY C. WHITE (Partner-in-Charge, Columbus)

ROBERT M. CURRY (Partner-in Charge, Dayton)

NICHOLAS J. DiMICHAEL (Partner-in-Charge, Washington, DC)

GEORGE J. WALSH III (Partner-in-Charge, New York City)

LUDO DEKLERCK (Partner-in-Charge, Brussels)

WALT A. LINSCOTT (Partner-in-Charge, Atlanta)

PARTNERS

STEPHEN J. AXTELL, born Rochester, New York, February 16, 1963; admitted to bar, 1988, Ohio; 1990, District of Columbia. *Education:* St. Bonaventure University (B.S., cum laude, in Biology, 1985); State University of New York at Buffalo (J.D., 1988). Author: "Securing an Evidentiary Hearing After Puerto Rico Aqueduct & Sewer: Is Overcoming the Summary Judgment Hurdle a New Obstacle?" 4 EPA Administrative Law Reporter 731 (1994); "Contaminated Shellfish: A Problem in the Stream of Interstate Commerce," Journal of Environmental Health, October, 1987. *Member:* Cincinnati (Member, Environmental Law Committee), Dayton (Member, Environmental Law Committee), Ohio (Member, Environmental Law Committee) and American (Member, Natural Resources and Environmental Law Section) Bar Associations. ***PRACTICE AREAS:*** Environmental Law; Occupational Safety and Health; Administrative Law. ***Email:*** Steve.Axtell@ThompsonHine.com

J. WRAY BLATTNER, born Princeton, New Jersey, June 23, 1955; admitted to bar, 1980, Ohio. *Education:* Denison University (B.A., 1977); Georgetown University (J.D., 1980). Phi Beta Kappa. Co-Author: *The Clean Air Act Compliance Handbook,* Executive Enterprises, 1992; "Environmental Crime Prevention," Chemical Engineering, 1994; "Ohio's Title V Operating Permits," Thompson Publishing Group, 1994; "Clean Water Act Update," 1987. Lecturer: "Air Regulatory Developments," Ohio State Bar Association Annual Environmental Law Seminar, Panel Discussion, 2000; "Title V and Enforcement," Air & Waste Management Association, 1995; "A Practical Guide to Environmental Regulation in Ohio," National Business Institute, 1995. Member, Dayton Art Institute Associates Board. Environmental Sciences Advisory Board, Wright State University. Past Chair, Environmental Committee, Dayton Chamber of Commerce. *Member:* Dayton (Former Chair, Environmental Law Committee), Ohio State (Member, Environmental Law Committee) and American (Member, Natural Resources Section) Bar Associations. ***PRACTICE AREAS:*** Environmental Law. ***Email:*** Wray.Blattner@ThompsonHine.com

BARRY M. BLOCK, born Dayton, Ohio, January 26, 1949; admitted to bar, 1975, Ohio. *Education:* Princeton University (A.B., 1971); University of Michigan (J.D., magna cum laude, 1974). Order of the Coif. Member, Michigan Law Review. Contributor: Proving Antitrust Damages, Legal and Economic Issues, ABA, Section of Antitrust Law, 1996. Lecturer: "Franchising and Related Business Strategies," Dayton Convention Center, 2002; "Distributor Terminations," Dayton Bar Association Corporate Counsel Committee, 1997; "Acquisitions Under the Antitrust Laws: Substantive Analysis and Premerger Reporting," Ohio State Bar Association Annual Convention, 1996; "International Licensing of Intellectual Property: European Law Developments," Dayton Intellectual Property Law Association, 1992; "Overview of U.S. Law Affecting International Business Transactions," Miami Valley International Trade Association Seminar, 1991; "Current Developments Report to Robinson-Patman Act Committee," American Bar Association, Antitrust Law Section, 1991. Co-Chair, 28th Annual Antitrust Law Institute, Ohio State Bar Association, Distribution, Marketing and Franchising, 1994. *Member:* Dayton, Ohio State (Chair, Antitrust Law Section, 1995-1997) and American (Member, Business Law Section, Forum on Franchising and Antitrust Law Section) Bar Associations. Ohio State Bar Foundation. ***PRACTICE AREAS:*** Franchise Law; Mergers and Acquisitions; Corporate Law; Antitrust Law. ***Email:*** Barry.Block@ThompsonHine.com

ROBERT J. BROWN, born Celina, Ohio, March 28, 1942; admitted to bar, 1968, Ohio and U.S. Supreme Court; U.S. Court of Appeals, Sixth, Fourth and Eleventh Circuits. *Education:* Ohio State University (B.A., 1965); Ohio Northern University (J.D., 1968). Board Member, The Partnership for Youth, Inc. Listed in, The Best Lawyers in America (Management, Labor and Employment). *Member:* Dayton, Ohio State (Member, Labor Law Section) and American (Member, Labor Law Section) Bar Associations. ***PRACTICE AREAS:*** Labor Law; Employment Law. ***Email:*** Bob.Brown@ThompsonHine.com

LAWRENCE T. BURICK, born Dayton, Ohio, May 15, 1943; admitted to bar, 1968, Ohio. *Education:* Miami University (B.A., cum laude, 1965); Northwestern University (J.D., 1968). Phi Beta Kappa. Listed in: *Best Lawyers in America,* Banking Section; various *Who's Who* directories. Author: "The Undersecured Creditor's Adequate Protection Rights in the Single Asset Arena: Did the 1994 Bankruptcy Code Amendments Redress Lender Grievances?" Commercial Law Journal, Winter 1995; Chapter on Mechanic's Liens, Curry and Durham Ohio Real Property (5th Edition), 1996; "Ohio Construction Law: What Do You Do When?", National Business Institute, 1987, 1990. Co-Author, Garnishment Proceedings in Ohio: A Manual for Employers, Thompson Hine publication. Lecturer: "Boom or Bust: Managing Credit Risks in the Business Cycle / What Do You Do When?" Thompson Hine presentation to credit managers, 1999; Revised Article 9 presentations to Lorman, Dayton Bar Association, American Bankruptcy Law Forum, Ohio Banker's Association, 2001-2002; "Confirmation Issues," American Bankruptcy Law Forum, 1996; Presentation, "Bankruptcy Sales: Understanding 11 U.S.C. Section 363(f)" to American Bankruptcy Law Forum, 2003; "Current Bankruptcy Issues," Client presentation, 1996; "What's New?" Robert Morris Associates, Dayton Chapter, 1996; "The Single-Asset Case: New Developments as to Adequate Protection, Bad Faith, Stay Relief and Confirmation Issues," Dayton Bar Association, 1994; "Preferences Under the Bankruptcy Code: A Current Overview," Dayton Bar Association, 1991; American Bankruptcy Law Forum, 1994; "Cash Collateral and Financing Orders Under the Bankruptcy Code: A Creditor's Perspective," Robert Morris Associates, Dayton Chapter, 1990, American Bankruptcy Law Forum, 1991. President, 1989-1993; Board Member, 1976-2003; United Jewish Campaign, Chairman, 1997-1998, Jewish Federation of Greater Dayton. Assistant Treasurer, 1996; Vice-President, 1998—; Board Member, 1993—. Board Member, Beth Abraham Synagogue, 1997—. Board Member, 1997-2003; Chair, 2002-2004, The National Conference for Community and Justice, Dayton Region. *Member:* Dayton and Ohio State Bar Associations; American Bankruptcy Law Forum; American Bankruptcy Institute. ***PRACTICE AREAS:*** Creditors Rights Law; Bankruptcy Law; Business Litigation. ***Email:*** Larry.Burick@ThompsonHine.com

(This Listing Continued)

RICHARD F. CARLILE, born Los Angeles, California, April 3, 1941; admitted to bar, 1969, Ohio. *Education:* Ohio University (B.B.A., cum laude, 1963); University of Michigan (J.D., 1969). Trust Committee Member, Miriam Rosenthal Memorial Trust Fund. Trustee Emeritus: The Ohio University Foundation. Former Trustee: Oakwood Schools Education Foundation and Culture Works. Former Member, Advisory Council, University of Dayton School of Law. Former Chairman: Dayton Area Chamber of Commerce Tax Committee, Miami Valley Hospital Foundation and City of Oakwood Environmental Committee. Former Secretary: Dayton Council on World Affairs. *Member:* Dayton (Former Chairman of Taxation Committee), Ohio State (Member, Estate Planning, Trust and Probate Law Section) and American (Member, Tax, Real Property and Trust Law Section) Bar Associations. [U.S. Army Artillery, Lt., 1963-1965]. ***PRACTICE AREAS:*** Business Law; Estate Planning Law; Business Succession Planning. ***Email:*** Rick.Carlile@ThompsonHine.com

MARK A. CONWAY, born Dayton, Ohio, December 13, 1957; admitted to bar, 1983, District of Columbia and U.S. Tax Court; 1988, California; 1991, Ohio. *Education:* Denison University (B.A., 1980); California Western School of Law (J.D., 1983); Georgetown University (LL.M. in Taxation, 1984). Recipient: Burton Achievement, 2002; American Jurisprudence Award, International Law. Author: "New Required Minimum Distribution Rules," Banking Law Journal, March 2001. Lecturer: "Current Issues in Business Succession Planning", Ohio State Bar Association, 2003; "Top Ten Charitable Giving Vehicles (Strategies) in the New Millennium", Ohio Society of CPAs, 2002; "Choosing Among a Private Foundation and the Alternatives: the Supporting Organization and Donor Advised Fund", Planned Giving Council of Dayton, 2001; "Charitable Giving Strategies Using Subchapter S Corporations", Planned Giving Council of Dayton, 2000; "The Family Owned Business Deduction (Exemption)" Dayton Bar Association, 1998; "Funding and Drafting Considerations in the Creation of Family Limited Partnerships", Ohio CLE Institute, 1998; "Current Charitable Giving Strategies", Kentucky CLE Institute and Kentucky Society of CPAs, 1997; "Advanced Charitable Tax Planning", Northern Ohio Planned Giving Council, 1997; "Qualified Domestic Trusts/Marital Planning for the Non-U.S. Citizen Spouse", Dayton Bar Association, 1995; "Qualified Personal Residence Trusts", Dayton and Hamilton Bar Associations, 1994, 1995; "Using Business Organizations in Estate Planning", Cleveland Estate Planning Group, 1994; "Use of 'Defective' Grantor Trusts to Save Estate Taxes", Ohio CLE Institute and Ohio Society of CPAs, 1994. *Member:* Ohio State and American (Member, Real Property, Probate and Trust Law Section); State Bar of California; District of Columbia Bar. Fellow American College of Trust and Estate Counsel. ***PRACTICE AREAS:*** Domestic and International Estate Planning; Personal Planning; Business Succession Planning; Tax Law; Charitable Planning; Exempt Organizations. ***Email:*** Mark.Conway@ThompsonHine.com

ROBERT M. CURRY, born Cleveland, Ohio, June 5, 1953; admitted to bar, 1978, Ohio. *Education:* Miami University (B.A., magna cum laude, 1975); Ohio State University (J.D., with honors, 1978). Phi Beta Kappa; Order of the Coif. Associate Editor, Ohio State Law Review, 1977-1978. Co-Author: "Ohio Real Property Law Practice," Vol. 1, 2, 3, 5th Ed., three volume treatise published by The Michie Company, 1996, 1997. Author: *McDermott's Ohio Real Property Law & Practice,* 4th ed. Vol. 3 (Forms), 1989. Co-Author: Ohio Land Contract Law, University of Dayton L. Rev. Vol. 19, No. 2 (Winter 1994). Lecturer: "Case Law Update," Ohio State Bar Association Convention, 2003; "Impact of Mold Concerns on Real Estate Transactions," Seminar, 2002; "Drafting and Reviewing Real Estate Documents," OSA/CLE Institute Seminar, 2001; "Ohio Agency Review," Seminar for Dayton Area Board of Realtors, 2000, 1999; "Corporate Closing Real Estate Documentation," OSBA/CLE Institute Seminar, 2000; "Conveyancing in Ohio," OSBA/CLE Institute Seminar, 1999; "Drafting Conservation Easements," Conference on Agricultural and Natural Resource Conservation Easements, 1998; "Like-Kind Exchanges," Ohio State Bar Association Convention, 1998. Counsel, Dayton Area Board of Realtors. Board Member, Downtown Dayton Partnership. Chair: City of Oakwood Board of Zoning Appeals. Member, Oakwood Schools Education Foundation. Member, Advisory Council for the University of Dayton School of Law. Counsel, Five Rivers Metroparks. *Member:* Dayton (Former Chair, Real Property Committee), Ohio State (Board of Governors, Real Property Section) and American Bar Associations; American College of Real Estate Lawyers. (Partner-in Charge). ***PRACTICE AREAS:*** Real Estate Law. ***Email:*** Bob.Curry@ThompsonHine.com

THOMAS E. DeBROSSE, born Dayton, Ohio, February 1, 1950; admitted to bar, 1980, Ohio. *Education:* Ohio State University (B.S.B.A., 1972); University of Minnesota (M.B.A., 1973); Ohio State University (J.D., 1980). Certified Public Accountant, California, 1973. Lecturer: "Strategies for Structuring Mergers and Acquisitions," Ohio Society of CPAs State and Federal Tax Forum, 2001. Past President, Dayton Association of Tax Professionals. *Member:* Ohio State and American (Member, Taxation Section) Bar Associations. ***PRACTICE AREAS:*** Taxation; Business Law. ***Email:*** Tom.DeBrosse@ThompsonHine.com

STEVEN J. ELLEMAN, born Canton, Ohio, November 30, 1970; admitted to bar, 1996, Ohio; 2005, U.S. District Court, Southern District of Ohio; registered to practice before U.S. Patent and Trademark Office. *Education:* The Ohio State University (B.S.A.A.E., cum laude, 1993; J.D., with honors, 1996). Tau Beta Pi. Author, "Problems in Patent Litigation: Mandatory Mediation May Provide Settlements and Solutions," Ohio State Journal on Dispute Resolution, 1996. Speaker, "Best Practices in Patent Prosecution for 2005". *Member:* American Bar Association; American Intellectual Property Law Association; Dayton Intellectual Property Law Association. ***PRACTICE AREAS:*** Intellectual Property; Patents; Trademarks; Intellectual Property Licensing; Unfair Competition; Trade Secrets. ***Email:*** Steve.Elleman@ThompsonHine.com

FRANCESCO A. FERRANTE, born Brooklyn, New York, February 9, 1955; admitted to bar, 1981, New York and Ohio. *Education:* St. John's University (B.A., with honors, 1976); Syracuse University (J.D., with honors, 1979); New York University (LL.M., Taxation, 1981). Adjunct Professor, University of Cincinnati Business School (Tax-Free Reorganizations) 1988, 1989, 1992. Comment on § 280G in Merger of Equals Transactions 2002 TNT 96-34, 2002 TNT 128-17, Journal of Deferred Compensation Summer 2003; Comment on IRS Notice 2001-10 involving Split Dollar Insurance Arrangements 2001

(This Listing Continued)

THOMPSON HINE LLP, Dayton—Continued

TNT 76-17; Assisted on Article regarding Tax Treatment on Employee Stock Options in Mergers and Acquisitions 2001 TNT 38-83; ABA Tax Section Comments on Open Issues in § 1031 Like-Kind Exchange 95 TNT 155-22; Comment on § 162(m) $1MM Deduction Limitation or Compensation Paid to Officers of Public Corporation 94 TNT 27-42; Comment on § 737 Effective Date Regarding Property Contributed to Partnership 92 TNT 232-23; General comment on § 280G Golden Parachute Provision (29 Comments) 89 TNT 120-30; General comment on § 280G Golden Parachute Provision regarding the priority of payments within the 2.99 limitation 89 TNT 202-39. *Member:* American Bar Association (Member, Tax Section). ***PRACTICE AREAS:*** Taxation. ***Email:*** Francesco.Ferrante@ThompsonHine.com

CHRISTINE M. HAAKER, born Dayton, Ohio, September 13, 1969; admitted to bar, 1994, Ohio; U.S. Court of Appeals, Sixth Circuit; U.S. District Court, Northern and Southern Districts of Ohio; U.S. District Court, Eastern and Western Districts of Michigan. *Education:* University of Dayton (B.S., magna cum laude, Accounting, 1991); The Ohio State University (J.D., 1994). *Member:* Dayton Bar Association. ***PRACTICE AREAS:*** Business Litigation; Competition; Intellectual Property Litigation; Trade Secrets; Contract Litigation; Employer Intentional Torts; Product Liability Litigation; Appellate Practice; Arbitration and Mediation. ***Email:*** Christine.Haaker@ThompsonHine.com

TIMOTHY J. HACKERT, born McCook, Nebraska, August 2, 1953; admitted to bar, 1980, New York; 1988, Ohio. *Education:* Harvard University (B.A., cum laude, 1975); New York University (J.D., 1979). Lecturer: "Pension Fund Investments in Real Estate," American Bar Association Spring CLE and Committee Meeting, May 1990. *Member:* Dayton, Ohio State, New York State and American (Past Chairman, 1992-1994, Pension Plan Investments Committee) Bar Associations; American Land Title Association Lenders' Counsel Group; American College of Mortgage Attorneys, Inc. ***PRACTICE AREAS:*** Real Estate Law. ***Email:*** Tim.Hackert@ThompsonHine.com

ROBERT J. HADLEY, born Wilmington, Ohio, October 27, 1938; admitted to bar, 1963, Ohio. *Education:* Ohio State University (B.A., cum laude, 1960); Harvard Law School (LL.B., 1963). Phi Beta Kappa. Recipient, Kettering Citizen of the Year, 1986. Board Member, Parish Resource Center and Ministry of Money, Washington, D.C. President, Dayton Habitat for Humanity, 1988-1989. Rotary District Governor, 1993-1994. *Member:* Dayton (Member, Ethics Committee), Ohio State and American (Member, Health Law Section and Forum on the Construction Industry) Bar Associations. ***PRACTICE AREAS:*** Real Estate; Construction Contract Law; Health Law. ***Email:*** Bob.Hadley@ThompsonHine.com

LINN S. HARSON, born Hillsboro, Ohio, September 29, 1965; admitted to bar, 1996, Ohio. *Education:* Ohio State University (B.S., 1988); University of Dayton (J.D., summa cum laude, co-valedictorian, 1996). Speaker: "NIRI Cincinnati," 2002; "Franchising and Related Business Strategies," Dayton, 2002; "Securities Institute," Dayton Bar Association CLE, 2001. *Member:* Dayton and Ohio State Bar Associations. ***PRACTICE AREAS:*** Corporate; Securities. ***Email:*** Linn.Harson@ThompsonHine.com

J. MICHAEL HERR, born Middletown, Ohio, December 12, 1943; admitted to bar, 1968, Ohio. *Education:* University of Notre Dame (B.A., 1965); Ohio State University (J.D., summa cum laude, 1967). Order of the Coif. Lecturer: "Introduction to Succession Related Issues," Dayton Bar Association; "Merger & Acquisitions: Current Issues," Ohio Corporate Counsel Institute. Trustee, Goodwill Industries of Dayton. Trustee, City Wide Development Corporation. Secretary/Treasurer, Miami Valley Research Foundation and Institute. Counsel and Secretary, Arts Center Foundation. Dayton CitiPlan 20/20, Economic Development Committee. Chairman, Thompson Hine Corporate and Securities practice areas, 1994-1998. *Member:* Dayton (Former Chair, Business Law Committee) and Ohio State (Member, Corporation Law Committee) Bar Associations. ***TRANSACTIONS:*** Lead counsel in numerous acquisitions and divestitures involving public and private companies in a broad range of industries; lead counsel in major joint venture projects; representation of borrowers in numerous financing projects; representation of emerging companies in venture capital financings and other private placements; representation of public companies in securities law compliance matters; representation of closley held companies in planning and implementing the succession of ownership and management; representation of companies and individuals in executive compensation matters. ***PRACTICE AREAS:*** Corporate Law; Mergers, Acquisitions and Divestitures; Joint Ventures; Securities; Commercial Finance; Venture Capital. ***Email:*** Mike.Herr@ThompsonHine.com

TERESA D. JONES, born Scotia, California, August 5, 1948; admitted to bar, 1988, Ohio and U.S. District Court, Southern District of Ohio; 1990, U.S. Court of Appeals, Sixth Circuit; 1992, U.S. District Court, Western District of Michigan; 1997, U.S. District Court, Northern District of Georgia; 1998, U.S. District Court, District of Colorado; 2001, U.S. District Court, Eastern District of Wisconsin. *Education:* University of Missouri (B.A., 1969); University of Dayton (J.D., cum laude, 1988). Executive Editor, University of Dayton Law Review, 1987-1988. Author: "Constitutional Law: Consent Decree - A Voluntary Agreement or a Court Order? - Local No. 93, *International Association of Fire Fighters v. City of Cleveland,*" University of Dayton Law Review. Board of Directors, Vice Chair, Eastway Corporation. Member: Marshall Jordan Diversity Committee; Artemis House Advocate. Lecturer-Client Seminars: "Hiring and Retention of Women and Minorities," April 2002; "FMLA and ADA - The Good, The Bad, The Ugly," March 2002; "Investigating and Defending Sexual Harassment Claims," January 2002; "Defending Employment Discrimination Cases," October 2001; "Reasonable Accommodation Under the Americans with Disabilities Act," September 2001; "Discrimination in Employment, Housing, and Public Accommodation," May 2001; "The ADA and Contingent Workers," May 2001; "Leased Employees - Are They the Answer?" April 2001; "FMLA - When Does the Clock Start to Run?" April 2001; "Affirmative Action Programs - Have Things Really Changed?" February 2001; "Assessing Policies and Procedures/Developing Employee Handbooks," January 2001; "ADA - What You Don't Know Can Hurt You," July 2000; "FLSA - Issues Affecting Your Work Force," June 2000; "Hostile Work Environment Harassment and Employer Liability," April 2000; "Employment Law Update - Significant Developments in EEO and the Impact on Employment Practices," February 2000; "Federal and State Record Keeping Requirements," February 2000; "ADA Decisions Affecting the Definitions of 'Disability' and 'Qualified,'" March 2000; "Practical Aspects of Implementing the FMLA," March 2000; "Recent Developments in the Law on Sexual Harassment - Preventative Actions to Mitigate Potential Exposure," March 2000; "Preparing for and Dealing with the OFCCP Onsite Review," February 2000; "Conducting Sexual Harassment Investigations," January 2000; "Myths and Realities in the Employment Setting," September 1999; "FLSA Wage-Hour Update," June 1999. *Member:* Dayton (Vice Chairman, Labor and Employment Committee), Ohio State (Labor and Employment Law Section) and American (Member, Labor and Employment Section) Bar Associations; Defense Research Institute; Ohio Management Lawyers Association. ***TRANSACTIONS:*** Represents employers in all aspects of labor and employment law, including litigation in federal and state courts for Title VII, ADA, FMLA, ADEA, FLSA, ERISA, WARN, non-competition, and wrongful discharge cases; Represents employers before administrative agencies such as the EEOC, state Civil Rights Commissions, OFCCP, and DOL; Counsels employers in union organizing campaigns and collective bargaining; Designs and assists in implementation of workplace policies, including drug and alcohol testing, medical exams, hiring protocol, severance, and reduction-in-force plans; Advises employers on compliance with affirmative action obligations, including design and drafting of affirmative action plans and defense of OFCCP compliance and glass-ceiling audits; Counsels employers concerning all aspects of employment, such as wage and hour compliance, trade secrets and competition, and disciplinary issues. ***PRACTICE AREAS:*** Labor and Employment. ***Email:*** Teresa.Jones@ThompsonHine.com

SCOTT A. KING, born Columbus, Ohio, June 29, 1961; admitted to bar, 1986, Ohio and U.S. District Court, Southern District of Ohio; 1992, U.S.Court of Appeals, Sixth Circuit; 1997, U.S. Court of Appeals, Federal Circuit; 1998, U.S. Supreme Court and U.S. District Court, Northern District of Ohio; 2000, U.S. District Court, Eastern District of Michigan; 2002, U.S. District Court, Western District of Michigan; 2004, U.S. District Court, Northern District of Indiana; 2005, U.S. Court of Appeals, Fifth Circuit. *Education:* The Ohio State University (B.A., 1983; J.D., with honors, Order of the Coif, 1986). Ohio Super Lawyer, 2004-2005. Member, Dayton Volunteer Lawyers Project. 2004 Recipient, Award of Excellence for pro bono representation. Author: "Ohio Consumer Sales Practices Act," Ohio Consumer Law for the Practitioner, PESI, 1989; "Representing a Business in Consumer Cases," Ohio Consumer Law for the Practitioner, PESI, 1989. Lecturer: "Taking and Defending Depositions," *Civil Litigation in Ohio,* Ohio CLE Institute, 1990; "Representing a Business in Consumer Cases", PESI, 1989; "Ohio Consumer Sales Practice Act," PESI, 1989. *Member:* Dayton (Committee on Civil Trial Practice and ADR, Vice Chair, 1995-1996 and Chair, 1996-1997; Bench-Bar Conference, and Ohio State Bar Associations. ***REPORTED CASES:*** Johnson v. BP Chemicals Inc., 85 Ohio St. 3d 298, 707 N.E.2d 1107 (1999); Mitchell v. Lawson Milk Co., 40 Ohio St. 3d 190, 532 N.E.2d 753 (1989); Littleton v. Good Samaritan Hospital, 39 Ohio St. 3d 86, 529 N.E.2d 449 (1988); Textile Productions v. Mead Corporation, 134 F.3d 1481 (Fed. Cir. 1998); Jordan v. Armsway Tank Transport, Inc., 2004 Ohio App. LEXIS 249 (2004); Mominey v. Union Escrow Corp., 2003 Ohio App. LEXIS 5275 (2003); GZK, Inc. v. Schumaker LP, 2003 Ohio App. LEXIS 5202 (2003); McCann v. New Century Mortgage Corporation, 2003 Ohio App. LEXIS 2472 (2003); Marzluff v. Verizon Wireless, 151 Ohio App. 3d 733, 785 NE 2d 805 (2003); Bundy v. Five Rivers Metroparks, 152 Ohio App. 3d 426, 2003 Ohio App. LEXIS 1687 (2003); Moebius v. General Motors Corporation, 2002 Ohio App. LEXIS 4051 (2002) Schutte v. Danis Cos., 141 Ohio App. 3d 824 (2001); Jones v. Conrad, 2001 Ohio App. LEXIS 3897 (2001); Kain v. Conrad, 139 Ohio App. 3d 460, 744 N.E. 2d 245 (2000); Osborn v. Ohio Bureau of Workers' Comp., 134 Ohio App. 645, 731 N.E.2d 1189 (1999); Jenkins v. Fidelity Financial Services, 1999 Ohio App. LEXIS 5696 (1999); Grubbs v. Emery Air Freight Corp., 1999 Ohio App. LEXIS 6038 (1999); Builders Services v. Habitat Condo. Owners' Asso., 1999 Ohio App. LEXIS 104 (1999); Liberty Savings Bank FSB v. Sortman, 1998 Ohio App. LEXIS 1667 (1998); Hawkins Pro-Cuts v. Garcia, 1998 Ohio App. LEXIS 96 (1998); Upper Krust South v. School Employees Retirement Board, 1996 Ohio App. LEXIS 829 (1996); Nordisk Aluminum Als v. Stolle Corp., 1995 US Dist LEXIS 22179 (SD Ohio 1995); Harris v. Brown, 1995 Ohio App. LEXIS 4802 (1995); Bloom v. Third Lima Corp., 1994 Ohio App. LEXIS 4802 (1994); Star Bank N.A. v. Fisher Development Corp., 1993 Ohio App. LEXIS 2809 (1993); Star Bank NA v. Reveal, 148 B.R. 288 (SD Ohio Bankr. 1992); Centerville v. Curran, 1992 Ohio App. LEXIS 304 (1992); Anderson v. CSX Transp., 74 Ohio App. 3d 365, 599 N.E. 2d 278 (1991); Alamain v. Trombley, 1988 Ohio App. LEXIS 193 (1988); Peterson Howell & Heather v. Hughes, 1987 Ohio App. LEXIS 990 (1987). ***PRACTICE AREAS:*** Commercial Litigation; Business Litigation; Product Liability; Employer Intentional Tort. ***Email:*** Scott.King@ThompsonHine.com

DONALD J. KINLIN, born Boston, Massachusetts, November 29, 1938; admitted to bar, 1976, Nebraska; 1979, U.S. Supreme Court; 1980, U.S. Tax Court and U.S. Claims Court ; 1983, Court of Appeals for the Federal Circuit; 1984, Ohio; 1987, U.S. District Court, Southern District of Ohio. *Education:* Syracuse, University (B.S., 1968; M.B.A., 1970); University of Nebraska at Lincoln (J.D., 1975). Author: "Defective Pricing Review," NCMA Magazine, (April 1992); "Claim Certification: Who Can Certify?," NCMA Magazine; "The Program Fraud Civil Remedies Act," NCMA Magazine; "Equal Access to Justice Act," ABA Monograph; "Practitioner Comment: ASBCA Finds No Benefit to Government from Defense of Shareholder's Suite," The Government Contractor; "Current Controversies Under the Truth in Negotiations Act, Costs, Pricing and Accounting Report," Federal Publications, Inc. Chair, ABA Section of Public Contract Law, 1993-1994. Legislative Testimony: Senate Armed Services and Governmental Affairs Committees, Federal Acquisition Streamlining Act of 1994; House Armed Services Committee and Senate Governmental Affairs Committee, Truth in Negotiations Act; Senate Judiciary Committee, 1993 Amendments to the False Claim Act. Director and Fellow, National Contract Management Association. Governor, Boards of Contract Appeals Bar Association; Board of Directors, National Aviation Hall of Fame; Chair, Board of Trustees, United States Air and Trade Show. Advisory Board, Federal Publications, Inc. *Member:* Dayton, Ohio State, Federal and American (Member, Public Contract Section, Officer, Past Chair) Bar Associations; National Defense Industrial Association. Fellow, National Contract Management Association. ***PRACTICE AREAS:*** Government (Public) Contracts; Litigation; Competition; Government Affairs; Regulatory Law. ***Email:*** Don.Kinlin@ThompsonHine.com

THOMAS A. KNOTH, born Dayton, Ohio, April 23, 1959; admitted to bar, 1984, North Carolina, U.S. District Court, Eastern and Middle District of North Carolina; 1986, Ohio, U.S. District Court Southern District of Ohio; U.S. Court of Appeals, Sixth Circuit. *Education:* University of Dayton (B.S., summa cum laude, 1981); College of William & Mary (J.D., 1984). Member, William & Mary Law Review. Lecturer: Moderator, "Appellate Practice" 1996. Former Central Committee Member, Montgomery County Republican Party. Arbitrator, Montgomery County Common Pleas Court. Member, Greater Dayton

(This Listing Continued)

Area Volunteer Lawyers Project. Trustee, Dayton Bar Association, 1999-2001; Past Chair of the Substantive law Committee on Appellate Court Practice, Dayton Bar Association. Oakwood Select Basketball, Youth Coach. *Member:* Dayton, Ohio State, and North Carolina State Bar Associations. ***PRACTICE AREAS:*** Litigation; Business Litigation; Commercial Litigation; Contract Litigation; Federal Litigation; Appellate Practice; Health Care. ***Email:*** Tom.Knoth@ThompsonHine.com

MARK P. LEVY, born Columbus, Ohio, May 26, 1951; admitted to bar, 1977, Virginia; 1978, District of Columbia; 1981, Ohio and U.S. Court of Appeals for the Federal Circuit; registered to practice before U.S. Patent and Trademark Office. *Education:* University of Notre Dame (B.S., magna cum laude, 1973); George Washington University (J.D., 1977). Adjunct Professor, University of Dayton School of Law, 2000—. Lecturer: "Recent Trends in Licensing Intellectual Property," University of Dayton Licensing Program, 2001; "Negotiating Patent Licenses," University of Dayton Licensing Program, 2000; "The Impact of Post-Issue Prior Art on the Doctrine of Equivalents - NCIPLA National Inventors Hall of Fame Conference, 2000; "Patent Licensing Pitfalls," University of Dayton School of Law Licensing Program, 1999; "Officer and Director Liability for Patent Infringement," Cincinnati Intellectual Property Law Association, Dayton Intellectual Property Law Association and Dayton Bar Association, Corporate Law Section; "It is Mutiny - The Teenage Federal Circuit," NCIPLA National Inventors Hall of Fame 1999 Conference; "The Best Mode Requirement," Cincinnati Intellectual Property Law Association and Dayton Intellectual Property Law Association; "Provisional Patent Application Practice," Dayton Intellectual Property Law Association ; "Japanese Patent Flooding," Technology Transfer Society. President, Engineering and Science Hall of Fame, 1993. Commercialization Advisory Board, 1998—, Edison Materials Technology Center. *Member:* District of Columbia Bar; American Bar Association (Member, Intellectual Property Law Section); Dayton Intellectual Property Law Association (President, 1997-1999); National Council Intellectual Property Law Associations (Delegate, 1998-1999); Cincinnati Intellectual Property Law Association; American Intellectual Property Law Association. (Group Leader, Intellectual Property). ***PRACTICE AREAS:*** Intellectual Property Law; Unfair Competition Law; Licensing. ***Email:*** Mark.Levy@ThompsonHine.com

THEODORE D. LIENESCH, born Dayton, Ohio, April 20, 1951; admitted to bar, 1976, Pennsylvania; 1980, Ohio; registered to practice before the U.S. Patent and Trademark Office. *Education:* University of Michigan (B.S.M.E., cum laude, 1973); University of Cincinnati (J.D., 1976). Editorial Board, University of Cincinnati Law Review. Author: "Patentee's Threat to Discontinue Purchases Constitutes Unlawful Attempt to Monopolize," Patent Law Review, 1975. Lecturer: "Survey of International Software Protection," Cincinnati Bar Association, 1993; "Protecting Intellectual Property Internationally," Midwest International Law Conference, 2002. Executive Editor, "INTA Bulletin," 2002-2003. *Member:* Dayton Bar Association (Chairman, Unauthorized Practice of Law Committee, 1993-1994); International Trademark Association (Firm Designee, Executive Editor of the "INTA BULLETIN" 2002-2003); Dayton Intellectual Property Law Association. ***PRACTICE AREAS:*** Intellectual Property Law; Unfair Competition Law; Electronic Commerce. ***Email:*** Ted.Lienesch@ThompsonHine.com

CROFFORD J. MACKLIN, JR., born Columbus, Ohio, September 10, 1947; admitted to bar, 1977, Ohio; 1979, U.S. Tax Court. *Education:* Ohio State University (B.A., 1969); University of West Florida (B.A., summa cum laude, 1974); Ohio State University (J.D., cum laude, 1976). Listed in: *Best Lawyers in America; Who's Who in America.* Former Adjunct Professor at the University of Dayton College of Law. Counsel, Wright State University Foundation. The American College of Trust and Estate Counsel. *Member:* Dayton (Former Chair, Probate Committee), Ohio State (Former Member, Board of Governors, Probate and Trust Law Section) and American Bar Associations. [Cpt., U.S. Marine Corps, 1969-1974.]. (Group Leader, Personal and Succession Planning). ***PRACTICE AREAS:*** Estate Planning; Probate; Tax Controversies; Personal Planning; Successions. ***Email:*** Crofford.Macklin@ThompsonHine.com

DAVID A. NEUHARDT, born Sidney, Ohio, July 9, 1954; admitted to bar, 1979, Ohio. *Education:* Miami University (B.A., cum laude, 1976); Ohio State University (J.D., summa cum laude, 1979). Phi Beta Kappa; Order of the Coif. Counsel: Boys Scouts of America, Miami Valley Council; Dayton Area League of Women Voters. Trustee and Secretary, Tecumseh Land Trust. President, Yellow Springs Historical Society. *Member:* Dayton, Ohio and American Bar Associations. ***PRACTICE AREAS:*** Corporate and Securities; Partnership; Finance; Computer Law. ***Email:*** David.Neuhardt@ThompsonHine.com

SHAREN SWARTZ NEUHARDT, born Dayton, Ohio, October 16, 1951; admitted to bar, 1976, Ohio. *Education:* Northwestern University (B.A., 1973); Georgetown University (J.D., 1976). Phi Beta Kappa. Author: "Outsourcing Issues and Solutions," *Corporate Counsel's Commercial Law Advisor* (December 1993); "New Thinking Regarding Software Protection," Licensing Law and Business Report, 1990. *Member:* Dayton, Ohio State and American Bar Associations; Computer Law Association. ***PRACTICE AREAS:*** Corporate Law; Securities Law; Computer Law. ***Email:*** Sharen.Neuhardt@ThompsonHine.com

ALLEN R. NORRIS, born Dayton, Ohio, February 3, 1958; admitted to bar, 1983, Ohio; 1988, Virginia and U.S. Tax Court. *Education:* Miami University (B.A., magna cum laude, 1980); University of Cincinnati (J.D., 1983); New York University (LL.M. in Taxation, 1985). Phi Beta Kappa. Lecturer: "Employee Benefits," University of Maryland, 1989-1991; "Employee Benefits," Sinclair Community College, Instructor, 1992-1994; "Executive Compensation," Capital University College of Law, Adjunct Professor, 1999—; "Qualified Plan Distributions," 1998-2001, Midwest Trust Schools. Former Member, IRS, National Office, Employee Plans Technical and Actuarial Division, Washington D.C. *Member:* Ohio State, Virginia, Federal and American (Member, Employee Benefits Committee) Bar Associations. ***PRACTICE AREAS:*** Employee Benefits and Executive Compensation. ***Email:*** Allen.Norris@ThompsonHine.com

JOSEPH M. RIGOT, born Cleveland, Ohio, August 25, 1943; admitted to bar, 1973, Ohio. *Education:* University of Dayton (B.A., magna cum laude, 1966); University of Cincinnati (M.A., 1969); Washington University (J.D., 1973). Order of the Coif. Editor, Washington University Law Quarterly. *Member:* Dayton, Ohio and American Bar Associations; Dayton Law Library Association (Trustee and Secretary); Dayton Ballet Association (Trustee); Downtown Dayton Partnership (Trustee). ***PRACTICE AREAS:*** Corporate Law; Securities Law. ***Email:*** Joe.Rigot@ThompsonHine.com

(This Listing Continued)

JOAN H. RODDY, born Brooklyn, New York, October 15, 1953; admitted to bar, 1981, Ohio. *Education:* Wright State University (B.A., magna cum laude with special honors, 1978); University of Dayton (J.D., cum laude, 1981). Editor-in-Chief, University of Dayton Law Review, 1980-1981. Listed in: *The Best Lawyers in America.Member:* Dayton, Ohio State and American Bar Associations. ***PRACTICE AREAS:*** Real Estate. ***Email:*** Joan.Roddy@ThompsonHine.com

ARIK A. SHERK, born Panama City, Florida, June 27, 1959; admitted to bar, 1984, Ohio. *Education:* University of Michigan (B.A., with honors, 1981); George Washington University (J.D., 1984). Lecturer: "Asset-Based Lending," National Business Institute; "Multiple Bank Loans," National Business Institute; "Unauthorized Practice of Law," University of Dayton School of Law; "Revised Article 9 of the Uniform Commercial Code," Loran Education Services. Member: Miami Valley Hospital Foundation Board of Trustees and Dayton Art Institute Associates Board. *Member:* Dayton and Ohio State Bar Associations; National Association of Bond Lawyers. ***PRACTICE AREAS:*** Commercial Law; Public Finance Law; Banking Law; Bankruptcy; Real Estate Law. ***Email:*** Arik.Sherk@ThompsonHine.com

JEREMY L. TRAHAN, born Lafayette, Louisiana, August 14, 1969; admitted to bar, 1996, Ohio. *Education:* University of Southwestern Louisiana (B.S., cum laude, 1991); University of Notre Dame Law School (J.D., magna cum laude, 1996). Certified Public Accountant, Louisiana, 1995. Contributing Author, "Materials on Accounting for Lawyers," Foundation Press (the leading casebook on accounting for lawyers); "Tracking Stock," Ohio Society of CPA's 2000 SEC and Ohio Securities Conference. Member, Cleveland City Mayor-Elect Jane Campbell Transition Team, Technology. Member, Board of Directors, Big Brothers Big Sisters of Greater Cleveland. *Member:* Society of Louisiana Certified Public Accountants. ***TRANSACTIONS:*** Equity and debt financing transactions for private equity investment firms and privately held companies (start-up and later stage); General corporate and business planning counseling for early stage companies; Formation of venture capital funds, including preparation of offering materials and complex multi-tiered partnership agreements and counseling on fund structure and regulatory matters; On-going corporate representation of venture capital funds and portfolio companies; Disposition, acquisition, and merger transactions for public and private companies, including a variety of transactions involving multinational operations; Public and private company restructuring and tax planning transactions; Joint ventures and strategic integrated supply, distribution, and marketing relationships; Public company disclosure compliance and general securities law matters; Assistance to the Healthcare practice group with general corporate matters, federal and state regulation, and tax exempt issues. ***PRACTICE AREAS:*** Corporate Law; Mergers, Acquisitions and Divestitures; Securities Law. ***Email:*** Jeremy.Trahan@ThompsonHine.com

ASSOCIATES

CHARLES D. COOPER, born Dayton, Ohio, November 18, 1970; admitted to bar, 1996, Pennsylvania; 1997, New Jersey and U.S. District Court, Eastern District of Pennsylvania; 1999, U.S. Court of Appeals, Third Circuit; 2001, Ohio, U.S. District Court, Southern District of Ohio and U.S. Court of Appeals, Sixth Circuit. *Education:* Wheaton College (B.A., 1992); University of Notre Dame (J.D., 1996). Member, Pi Kappa Delta Forensics Honor Society. National Merit Scholar. Presidential Scholar. Book Review Editor, Journal of College and University Law. *Member:* Dayton and American (Member, Litigation Section) Bar Associations. ***PRACTICE AREAS:*** Business Litigation; Products Liability; Lender Liability. ***Email:*** Chad.Cooper@ThompsonHine.com

CORI R. HAPER, born Jackson, Michigan, 1976; admitted to bar, 2004, Ohio. *Education:* Union College (B.S., magna cum laude, 1999); University of Dayton (J.D., summa cum laude, 2004). Executive Editor, University of Dayton Law Review, 2003-2004. Author, "Sometimes Promising is Not So Promising: The Breakdown of the Family Resemblance Test," University of Dayton Law Review, 2003. *Member:* Ohio State and American Bar Associations. ***PRACTICE AREAS:*** Corporate Law (40%); Mergers, Acquisitions and Divestitures (30%); Franchises and Franchising (10%); Securities (20%). ***Email:*** Cori.Haper@ThompsonHine.com

NATHAN E. HOLMES, born Kettering, Ohio, November 26, 1970; admitted to bar, 2001, Ohio; 2002, U.S. District Court, Southern District of Ohio. *Education:* University of Cincinnati (B.A., 1996); University of Cincinnati College of Law (J.D., 2001); New York University School of Law (LL.M., 2003). ***PRACTICE AREAS:*** Taxation. ***Email:*** Nathan.Holmes@ThompsonHine.com

NATHAN C. HUNT, born Pittsburgh, Pennsylvania, 1974; admitted to bar, 2001, Ohio and U.S. District Court, Southern District of Ohio. *Education:* Wright State University (B.A., 1997); University of Toledo College of Law (J.D., 2001). *Member:* Dayton, Ohio State and American Bar Associations; Dayton Young Professionals Association. ***PRACTICE AREAS:*** Environmental Law. ***Email:*** Nathan.Hunt@ThompsonHine.com

JOHN F. KANE, born Dayton, Ohio, July 19, 1960; admitted to bar, 1998, Ohio; registered to practice before U.S. Patent and Trademark Office. *Education:* Wright State University (B.S., summa cum laude, 1983); University of Dayton (J.D., magna cum laude, 1998). Associate Editor, University of Dayton Law Review, 1997-1998. *Member:* Dayton Intellectual Property Law Association. ***PRACTICE AREAS:*** Intellectual Property; Patent Prosecution; Patent Applications; Patent Infringement; Patent Protection; Pharmaceutical Patents; Chemical Patent Prosecution; Chemical Patents. ***Email:*** John.Kane@ThompsonHine.com

CARL A. LUX, admitted to bar, 2004, Ohio. *Education:* Ohio State University (B.A., 1987); Wright State University (M.A., 1991); Boston University (J.D., cum laude, 1997). *Member:* Los Angeles and American Bar Associations; State Bar of California. ***PRACTICE AREAS:*** Real Estate; Finance. ***Email:*** Carl.Lux@ThompsonHine.com

JENNIFER L. MAFFETT, born September 26, 1976; admitted to bar, 2002, Ohio; 2003, U.S. District Court, Southern District of Ohio. *Education:* University of Dayton (B.A., summa cum laude, 1998); University of Dayton School of Law (J.D., summa cum laude, 2002). Ohio Rising Star, 2005. *Member:* Dayton and Ohio State Bar Associations; American Bankruptcy Law Forum (Trustee). ***PRACTICE AREAS:*** Bankruptcy; Commercial Finance. ***Email:*** Jennifer.Maffett@ThompsonHine.com

(This Listing Continued)

THOMPSON HINE LLP, Dayton—Continued

JOHN M. McCANN, admitted to bar, 2000, Ohio; 2001, District of Columbia. *Education:* Cornell University (B.A., 1997); University of Virginia (J.D., 2000). Editorial Board Member, Virginia Journal of Law and Politics, 1998-2000. Study Abroad Program, Oxford University, Pembroke College, 1995-1996. Adjunct Professor, University of Dayton School of Law. ***PRACTICE AREAS:*** Corporate Transactions; Securities.

CHRISTINE M. McLAUGHLIN, born 1980; (admission pending). *Education:* The Ohio State University (B.S., Ecology, 2002); Boston University (J.D., cum laude, 2005). ***Email:*** Christine.McLaughlin@ThompsonHine.com

JEFFREY C. METZCAR, born Springfield, Ohio, May 3, 1975; admitted to bar, 2000, Ohio; 2002, U.S. Court of Appeals, Federal Circuit. *Education:* University of Dayton (B.M.E., summa cum laude, 1997); Case Western Reserve University (J.D., magna cum laude, 2000). Author: "Raising the Defense of Procedural Default Sua Sponte: Who Will Enforce the Great Writ of Liberty?"; 50 Case W. Res. L. Rev. 869, 2000; "A Problematic Pat on the Back for the PTO: Dickinson v. Zurko", 50 Case W. Res. L. Rev. 797, 2000. ***PRACTICE AREAS:*** Patent Law; Litigation. ***Email:*** Jeff.Metzcar@ThompsonHine.com

VICTORIA L. NILLES, admitted to bar, 1998, Kansas and U.S. District Court, District of Kansas; 1999, Indiana and U.S. District Court, Northern and Southern Districts of Indiana; 2003, Ohio and U.S. District Court, Southern District of Ohio. *Education:* United States Military Academy (B.S., 1983); Washburn University School of Law (J.D., magna cum laude, 1998). *Member:* Kansas, Indiana State, Ohio State and American Bar Associations. [Capt., Military Intelligence, U.S. Army, 1983-1993]. ***PRACTICE AREAS:*** Business Litigation. ***Email:*** Victoria.Nilles@ThompsonHine.com

EDWARD C. REDDER, born Elmira, New York, August 8, 1972; admitted to bar, 1998, Ohio. *Education:* Muskingum College (B.A., summa cum laude, 1995); Ohio State University College of Law (J.D., honors, 1998). Staff Member, Journal of Dispute Resolution, 1997-1998. *Member:* Montgomery County and Ohio State Bar Associations. ***PRACTICE AREAS:*** Business Litigation; Products Liability. ***Email:*** Ed.Redder@ThompsonHine.com

JEFF C. STEWART, born Olney, Illinois, December 2, 1973; admitted to bar, 2000, Illinois; 2001, Missouri; 2002, Ohio, District of Columbia and U.S. Tax Court. *Education:* Eastern Illinois University (B.S., 1996); University of Illinois (J.D., 2000); University of Florida College of Law (LL.M., 2002). ***PRACTICE AREAS:*** Real Estate (80%); State Tax Law (10%); Like Kind Exchanges (10%). ***Email:*** Jeff.Stewart@ThompsonHine.com

SCOTT T. STIRLING, born McKeesport, Pennsylvania, January 6, 1962; admitted to bar, 1993, Ohio; 1994, U.S. District Court, Eastern District of Michigan; U.S. District Court, Northern District of Ohio; 1999, Court of Appeals for the Federal Circuit and U.S. Court of Appeals, Sixth Circuit; 2000, U.S. District Court, Southern District of Ohio. *Education:* University of Cincinnati (B.M., 1983); Temple University (M.M., 1985); University of Michigan (J.D., 1992). Judicial Clerk to the Hon. James G. Carr, 1992-1993, and the Hon. Don J. Young, 1993-1994, U.S. District Court, Northern District of Ohio. *Member:* Dayton, Ohio State and American Bar Associations. ***PRACTICE AREAS:*** Labor and Employment Law. ***Email:*** Scott.Stirling@ThompsonHine.com

VICTOR J. WASYLYNA, born Parma, Ohio, March 7, 1978; admitted to bar, 2003, Ohio; registered to practice before U.S. Patent and Trademark Office. *Education:* The Ohio State University (B.S., 2000); Case Western Reserve University School of Law (J.D., 2003). *Member:* American Intellectual Property Law Association; Dayton Intellectual Property Law Association; Ukrainian American Bar Association. ***LANGUAGES:*** Ukrainian. ***PRACTICE AREAS:*** Intellectual Property; Patent Prosecution and Litigation; Trademark Prosecution and Litigation; Biotechnology. ***Email:*** Victor.Wasylyna@ThompsonHine.com

DAVID O. ZIMMER, admitted to bar, 1995, Maryland (Inactive); 1998, District of Columbia (Inactive); 1999, Ohio. *Education:* The Ohio State University (B.A., 1989); University of Dayton (J.D., 1995). *Member:* Cleveland, Dayton and Ohio State Bar Associations. ***LANGUAGES:*** German. ***PRACTICE AREAS:*** Mergers, Acquisitions and Divestitures (80%); International Mergers and Acquisitions (20%). ***Email:*** David.Zimmer@ThompsonHine.com

SENIOR ATTORNEYS

RICHARD A. CIAMBRONE, born Red Bank, New Jersey, July 19, 1953; admitted to bar, 1980, Ohio; 1981, New Jersey. *Education:* University of Notre Dame (B.A., 1975); University of Dayton (J.D., 1980). ***PRACTICE AREAS:*** Employee Benefits (100%). ***Email:*** Richard.Ciambrone@ThompsonHine.com

STEVEN J. DAVIS, born Cleveland, Ohio, December 11, 1961; admitted to bar, 1987, Ohio. *Education:* Oberlin College (B.A., 1984); Duke University (J.D., 1987). Recipient, American Jurisprudence Awards in Labor Relations and Criminal Procedure. ***PRACTICE AREAS:*** Real Estate Law. ***Email:*** Steve.Davis@ThompsonHine.com

DOUGLAS E. ERICKSON, born Brooklyn, New York, May 25, 1943; admitted to bar, 1974, Oregon; 1989, Ohio; registered to practice before U.S. Patent and Trademark Office, 1979. *Education:* Massachusetts Institute of Technology (B.S.A.E., 1965; M.S.A.E., 1966); University of Oregon (J.D., 1974). Tau Beta Pi. Sigma Gamma Tau. ***PRACTICE AREAS:*** Intellectual Property. ***Email:*** Douglas.Erickson@ThompsonHine.com

OF COUNSEL

JOHN E. CLOUGH, born Troy, New York, August 7, 1966; admitted to bar, 1994, Ohio; 2000, U.S. Tax Court; 2004, New York. *Education:* Siena College (B.A., 1990); University of Dayton (J.D., 1994); Capital University School of Law (LL.M., Taxation, 2002). *Member:* Dayton (Member, Estate Planning, Trust and Probate Law Committee), Ohio State (Member, Estate Planning, Trust and Probate Law Section) and American (Member, Real Property, Probate and Trust Law Section) Bar Associations. ***PRACTICE AREAS:*** Probate; Estate Planning. ***Email:*** John.Clough@ThompsonHine.com

RENE M. LaFORTE, born Chicago, Illinois, November 8, 1968; admitted to bar, 1993, Ohio; 1999, District of Columbia. *Education:* The Pennsylvania State University (B.A., 1990); University of Dayton School of Law (J.D., cum laude, 1993). Recipient, American Jurisprudence Awards: Legal Research and Writing, 1991; Advanced Criminal Law, 1993. Associate Editor, University of Dayton Law Review, 1991-1993. Author, "The Constitutional Implications of Anti-Drug Loitering Ordinances in Ohio," University of Dayton Law Review, Spring 1993. Committee Member, INTA Parallel Imports Committee, 2004-2006. *Member:* District of Columbia Bar; American Bar Associations; International Trademark Association; International Trade Commission Trial Lawyers Association. ***PRACTICE AREAS:*** Trademarks; Copyrights; Intellectual Property; International Trade; Internet Law; Unfair Competition; Trade Secrets. ***Email:*** ReneLaForte@ThompsonHine.com

(For complete biographical data on Lawyers in Offices other than Dayton, see Professional Biographies at the Respective Office Location)

THORSON, SWITALA, WILKINS & SNEAD, LLP

FIRST NATIONAL PLAZA
130 WEST SECOND STREET, SUITE 1508
DAYTON, OHIO 45402
Telephone: 937-228-9000
Fax: 937-228-3550
URL: http://www.tswslaw.com

Medical Malpractice, Nursing Errors, Wrongful Death Claims, Nursing Home Negligence, Automobile Collisions, Motorcycle and Bicycle Injuries, Dog Bite Injuries, Other accidents involving serious injury or loss of life.

FIRM PROFILE: At Thorson, Switala, Wilkins & Snead, LLP, we are dedicated exclusively to representing the rights of people and families in southwestern Ohio-who have sustained serious injury or death from medical malpractice, automobile accidents, and negligence. In our more than 40 years of collective experience, we have handled thousands of cases - all types, all sizes, all with a personal touch.

Our attorneys have a strong background in protecting the rights of victims of medical negligence and those who have suffered wrongful death or serious personal injury. Our focus on medical research, our strong relationships with medical experts and our in-depth evaluation of complex medical malpractice cases enable us to handle even the most challenging cases.

JAMES M. THORSON, JR., born Zanesville, Ohio, November 6, 1964; admitted to bar, 1990, Ohio; U.S. District Court, Southern District of Ohio. *Education:* The Ohio State University (B.S., 1987); University of Dayton (J.D.,1990). *Member:* Dayton, Ohio State and American Bar Associations; Association of Trial Lawyers of America; Ohio Academy of Trial Lawyers; Miami Valley Trial Lawyers Association. ***PRACTICE AREAS:*** Personal Injury; Medical Malpractice; Wrongful Death. ***Email:*** jthorson@tswslaw.com

GILBERT B. SWITALA JR., born Pittsburgh, Pennsylvania, December 5, 1964; admitted to bar, 1991, Ohio. *Education:* University of Pittsburgh (B.A., 1987); University of Dayton (J.D., 1990). *Member:* Dayton, Ohio State and American Bar Associations; Association of Trial Lawyers of America; Ohio Academy of Trial Lawyers; Miami Valley Trial Lawyers Association. ***PRACTICE AREAS:*** Personal Injury; Wrongful Death; Medical Malpractice. ***Email:*** gswitala@tswslaw.com

LAWRENCE A. WILKINS, born Atlanta, Georgia, March 6, 1968; admitted to bar, 1995, Ohio and U.S. District Court, Southern District of Ohio. *Education:* Heidelberg College (B.S., Economics, 1991; B.S., Political Science, cum laude, 1991); Cleveland State University (J.D., with honors, 1994). Montgomery County Prosecutors Office, Assistant Prosecuting Attorney, 1995-1996. *Member:* Dayton, Ohio State and American Bar Associations; Ohio Academy of Trial Lawyers. ***PRACTICE AREAS:*** Medical Malpractice; Personal Injury; Nursing Home Negligence. ***Email:*** lwilkins@tswslaw.com

JEFFREY W. SNEAD, born Columbus, Ohio, March 28, 1968; admitted to bar, 1994, Ohio; 1996, U.S. District Court, Southern District of Ohio. *Education:* Indiana University (B.A., 1990); University of Toledo (J.D., 1994). Moot Court Board. Recipient, Barrister Award, Charles W. Fornoff Competition, 1992. Associate, Crew, Buchanan & Lowe, 1997-1999. Staff Attorney, Civil Division, Court of Claims, Ohio, 1994-1997. *Member:* Dayton and Ohio State Bar Associations; Ohio Academy of Trial Lawyers; American Trial Lawyers Association. ***PRACTICE AREAS:*** Medical Malpractice; Personal Injury; Nursing Home Negligence. ***Email:*** jsnead@tswslaw.com

JOSEPH J. MONDOCK, born Parma, Ohio, September 26, 1975; admitted to bar, 2002, Ohio and U.S. District Court, Southern District of Ohio. *Education:* Bowling Green State University (B.A., 1998); University of Dayton (J.D., 2002). *Member:* Dayton and Ohio State Bar Associations; Ohio Academy of Trial Lawyers. ***PRACTICE AREAS:*** Personal Injury; Employer Intentional Torts. ***Email:*** joemondock@tswslaw.com

TOMB LAW

DAYTON, OHIO

(See Troy)

Real Estate, Business Law, Construction Law.

TYE AND TYE

A Legal Professional Association
Established in 1978

5975 KENTSHIRE DRIVE
DAYTON, OHIO 45440
Telephone: 937-291-8646
Telecopier: 937-291-8650
URL: http://www.lawyers.com/tye&tye

Business Law, Closely Held Business Law, Residential and Commercial Real Estate, Probate, Trusts and Estates, Family Law, Funeral Directors Liability.

(This Listing Continued)

MEMBER OF FIRM

TIMOTHY N. TYE, born Dayton, Ohio, August 6, 1953; admitted to bar, 1978, Ohio. *Education:* Miami University (B.A., 1975); The Ohio State University (J.D., 1978). *Member:* Dayton (Committee on Professional Ethics, 1984-1999; Chairman, 1992-1994), Ohio State and American Bar Associations. ***PRACTICE AREAS:*** Business Law; Closely Held Business Law; Residential Real Estate; Commercial Real Estate; Probate; Trusts and Estates; Family Law; Funeral Directors Liability. ***Email:*** ttye@biegeltye.com

REFERENCES: National City Bank; Bank One, Dayton N.A.

VAN KLEY & WALKER, LLC

Established in 2005

137 NORTH MAIN STREET, SUITE 316

DAYTON, OHIO 45402

Telephone: 937-226-9000

Fax: 937-226-9002

Email: cwalker@vankleywalker.com

URL: http://www.vankleywalker.com

Columbus Office: 132 Northwoods Boulevard, Suite C-1, 43235. Telephone: 614-431-8900. Fax: 614-431-8905.

Air Pollution, Brownfields Redevelopment, Chemical Regulation, Conservation Easements, Environmental Auditing, Environmental Compliance, Due Diligence and Permitting, Environmental Dispute Resolution, Groundwater Contamination, Hazardous Materials and Substances, Hazardous Waste, National Environmental Policy Act (NEPA), Oil Pollution, Pesticide Regulation, Property Remediation, Permitting, Solid Waste, Underground Storage Tanks, Water Pollution, Wetlands Regulation.

CHRISTOPHER A. WALKER, born Dayton, Ohio, September 4, 1963; admitted to bar, 1988, Ohio; 1989, U.S. District Court, Southern District of Ohio. *Education:* University of Dayton (B.A., 1985); Vanderbilt University (J.D., 1988). Former Assistant Attorney General, Environmental Enforcement Section, Ohio. *Member:* Dayton (Past Chairman, Environmental Law Committee), Ohio State (Chairman, Environmental Law Committee; Member, Agricultural Law Committee) and American (Member, Natural Resources, Environmental and Energy Law Section). ***PRACTICE AREAS:*** Environmental Law. ***Email:*** cwalker@vankleywalker.com

WAITE, SCHNEIDER, BAYLESS & CHESLEY CO., L.P.A.

DAYTON, OHIO

(See Cincinnati)

General Civil Practice. Aviation, Antitrust Litigation, Class Action, Commercial Litigation, Complex Litigation, Corporate Law, Federal Employees Liability, General Civil Trials and Appeals in all Courts, Insurance, Labor, Consolidated and Multi-district Litigation, Products Litigation, Securities Litigation and Wrongful Death.

WHALEN & COMPTON

A LEGAL PROFESSIONAL ASSOCIATION

DAYTON, OHIO

(See Akron)

General Civil Trial and Appellate Practice. Educational and School Law, Labor Law, Management, Civil Rights and Equal Employment Law. Real Estate regarding University and School Law.

DAVID WIRTH

DAYTON, OHIO

(See Columbus)

Insurance Law, Negligence, Legal Malpractice, Subrogation, Personal Injury, Probate.

WOOD, HERRON & EVANS, L.L.P.

DAYTON, OHIO

(See Cincinnati)

Intellectual Property and Related Litigation; Computer Law, Patents, Trademarks and Copyrights.

YOUNG & ALEXANDER CO., L.P.A.

130 WEST SECOND STREET, SUITE 2000

DAYTON, OHIO 45402-7670

Telephone: 937-224-9291

Fax: 937-224-9679; 224-8977

URL: http://www.youngandalexander.com

Cincinnati, Ohio Office: 110 Boggs Lane, Suite 242. Telephone: 513-326-5555. FAX: 513-326-5550.

Business Law, Health Care, Insurance Law, Labor and Employment, Nonprofit and Charitable Organizations, Personal Injury, Products Liability, Real Estate, Toxic Torts, Trusts and Estates, Wills and Probate, Commercial Litigation.

(This Listing Continued)

FIRM PROFILE: Young & Alexander Co., L.P.A., with offices in Dayton and Cincinnati, strives to provide its clients with outstanding legal services in a variety of areas of law. The firm traces its roots back to the early 1900's. The present firm, as an ongoing entity, was an out-growth of another firm in 1940.

The firm services a variety of clients, including insurance companies, hospitals, health insuring entities, closely held corporations, shareholders and private individuals.

ROBERT F. YOUNG (1905-1978)

ROBERT C. ALEXANDER (1912-1982)

JAMES M. BRENNAN, born Dayton, Ohio, February 8, 1931; admitted to bar, 1957, Ohio. *Education:* University of Dayton; The Ohio State University (B.A., 1953; J.D., 1957). *Member:* Dayton and Ohio State Bar Associations. ***PRACTICE AREAS:*** Probate Law; Estate Planning Law; Real Estate Law.

MARK R. CHILSON, born Milwaukee, Wisconsin, April 11, 1956; admitted to bar, 1981, Ohio; U.S. Supreme Court. *Education:* University of Wisconsin-Whitewater (B.B.A., magna cum laude, 1978); University of Dayton (J.D., summa cum laude, 1981). Managing Editor, University of Dayton Law Review, 1980-1981. Selected as one of the Top Ten Lawyers in Ohio, 2000, The Ohio Lawyers Weekly. *Member:* Dayton, Ohio State and American Bar Associations; Defense Research Institute. ***PRACTICE AREAS:*** Business Law; Health Care; Insurance Law; Labor and Employment; Personal Injury; Toxic Torts; Fire Litigation. ***Email:*** mchilson@yandalaw.com

STEVEN O. DEAN, born Morristown, New Jersey, March 12, 1958; admitted to bar, 1983, Ohio. *Education:* Ohio Northern University (B.A., with high distinction, 1980; J.D., with high distinction, 1982). Member, Ohio Northern University Law Review, 1981-1982. *Member:* Dayton, Ohio State and American Bar Associations. ***PRACTICE AREAS:*** Insurance Defense Law; Litigation; Negligence Law. ***Email:*** sdean@yandalaw.com

THOMAS P. ERVEN, born Hamilton, Ohio, November 30, 1957; admitted to bar, 1983, Ohio and U.S. District Court, Southern District of Ohio. *Education:* Miami University (B.S., 1980); Ohio State University (J.D., 1983). Phi Beta Kappa; Phi Kappa Phi; Phi Delta Phi. *Member:* Cincinnati, Butler County (Secretary-Treasurer, 1985-1987), Ohio State and American Bar Associations; Ohio Association of Civil Trial Attorneys; Defense Research Institute. (Resident, Cincinnati Office) (Board Certified Civil Trial Advocacy Specialist by the National Board of Trial Advocacy). ***PRACTICE AREAS:*** Insurance Defense; Trial Practice. ***Email:*** terven@yandalaw.com

JAMES K. HEMENWAY, born Bloomington, Indiana, February 8, 1957; admitted to bar, 1988, Ohio. *Education:* Indiana University (B.S., 1980); University of Dayton (J.D., 1988). Certified Public Accountant, Ohio, 1988. *Member:* Dayton, Ohio State and American Bar Associations; American Institute of Certified Pubic Accountants; Ohio Society of Certified Public Accountants. ***PRACTICE AREAS:*** Litigation; Business Law; Insurance; Negligence; Arson; Personal Injury; Accountants Malpractice. ***Email:*** jhemenway@yandalaw.com

MARGARET R. YOUNG, born Dayton, Ohio, July 15, 1956; admitted to bar, 1984, Illinois; 1987, Ohio and U.S. District Court, Southern District of Ohio. *Education:* Mount Holyoke College (A.B., 1978); Northwestern University School of Law (J.D., 1984). *Member:* Dayton and Ohio State Bar Associations; Ohio Association of Civil Trial Attorneys; Dayton Women's Bar Association. ***PRACTICE AREAS:*** Insurance Coverage; Civil Litigation; Personal Injury.

JAMES M. BOTTOMS, born Cleveland, Ohio, December 19, 1970; admitted to bar, 2001, Ohio and U.S. District Court, Southern District of Ohio. *Education:* University of Cincinnati (B.A., 1997); University of Dayton (J.D., 2001). Pi Sigma Alpha. Member, University of Dayton Law Review, 1999. *Member:* Dayton, Ohio State and American Bar Associations. ***PRACTICE AREAS:*** Insurance Defense. ***Email:*** jbottoms@yandalaw.com

JONATHON L. BECK, born Dearborn, Michigan, January 30, 1976; admitted to bar, 2002, Florida; 2003, Ohio and U.S. District Court, Southern District of Ohio; 2005, U.S. Court of Appeals, Sixth Circuit. *Education:* Marquette University (B.A., 1999); University of Dayton (J.D., 2002). Member, Moot Court, National Trial Team. Recipient: CALI Awards for Land Use Planning; Landlord-Tenant; Criminal Procedure. *Member:* Ohio State and American Bar Associations; The Florida Bar. ***PRACTICE AREAS:*** Civil Litigation; Business Law; Health Care. ***Email:*** jbeck@yandalaw.com

C. CHRISTOPHER BENNINGTON, born Shadyside, Ohio, August 24, 1979; admitted to bar, 2004, Ohio; 2005, U.S. District Court, Southern District of Ohio. *Education:* Muskingum College (B.A., summa cum laude, 2001); The Ohio State University (J.D., with honors, 2004). *Member:* Dayton, Ohio State and American Bar Associations. ***PRACTICE AREAS:*** Civil Litigation; Business Law; Labor and Employment. ***Email:*** cbennington@yandalaw.com

COUNSEL FOR: *Health Care:* The Children's Medical Center of Dayton, Ohio; Greater Dayton Area Hospital Association; Dayton Area Health Plan, Inc., dba CareSource. *Litigation:* State Farm Mutual Automobile Insurance Company; State Farm Fire and Casualty Company; Metropolitan Life Insurance Company; Metropolitan Property and Casualty Company; Grange Mutual Casualty Company; General Electric Insurance Company; Ryder Truck and Logistics; Hertz Corporation; Fireman's Fund; ABM; Mass Mutual; New England Life; NN Investors; Prudential Property and Casualty Company. *Corporation:* Moorman Pontiac-GMC-Isuzu; Franklin Iron & Metal Corporation; Recycling Center, Inc.; Colonial Stair.

CLEMENS, KORHN, LIMING & WARNCKE, LTD.

Established in 1880

BLOCK SIX BUSINESS CENTER

419 FIFTH STREET, SUITE 2000

P.O. BOX 787

DEFIANCE, OHIO 43512

Telephone: 419-782-6055

Telecopier: 419-782-3227

Hicksville, Ohio Office: First Federal Savings & Loan Building, 201 E. High Street. Telephone: 419-542-7705.

(This Listing Continued)

CLEMENS, KORHN, LIMING & WARNCKE, LTD., Defiance—Continued

General Practice. Real Estate, Banking Law, Title Examination and Insurance, Personal Injury and Wrongful Death, Probate and Estate Planning, Insurance Defense, Corporate, Family/Domestic Relations and Municipal Law. Trials and Appeals.

FIRM PROFILE: Established in 1880, Clemens, Korhn, Liming & Warncke, Ltd. is the oldest law firm in Defiance County, and one of the oldest in Northwest Ohio. For over a century, it has provided competent, cost-effective, and practical advice and representation to its clients, and its current members are committed to maintaining those high standards. Despite its small-town location, it provides a wide range of legal services to financial institutions, insurance companies, private firms, and individuals throughout a ten county area in Northwest Ohio.

TELLIS T. SHAW (1868-1951)

DAVID W. WILLIAMS (1917-1987)

ERWIN L. CLEMENS (1910-1999)

STEPHEN F. KORHN, born Defiance, Ohio, January 31, 1947; admitted to bar, 1972, Ohio; 1973, U.S. District Court, Northern District of Ohio. *Education:* Bowling Green State University; The Ohio State University (B.S., 1969); University of Toledo (J.D., 1972). City Solicitor, Defiance, Ohio, 1976-1978. Member, Board of Trustees, Northwest Technical College, 1984-1987. *Member:* Defense Research Institute. ***PRACTICE AREAS:*** Insurance Defense Law; Probate.

JOHN M. LIMING, born Grand Rapids, Michigan, August 23, 1956; admitted to bar, 1981, Ohio; 1982, U.S. District Court, Northern District of Ohio. *Education:* Grinnell College (B.A., 1978); University of Michigan (J.D., 1981). National Merit Scholar, Grinnell College. *Member:* Ohio State Bar Association (Member, Board of Governors, Real Property Section, 1985—; Chairman, Title Standards Sub-Committee). ***PRACTICE AREAS:*** Insurance Defense Law; Real Estate Law. ***Email:*** jmllaw@defnet.com

MARC F. WARNCKE, born Toledo, Ohio, June 12, 1964; admitted to bar, 1989, Ohio and U.S. District Court, Northern District of Ohio. *Education:* Ohio State University (B.S.B.A., summa cum laude, 1986); University of Notre Dame (J.D., 1989). *Member:* Ohio State (Member, Sections on: Corporate Counsel, Estate Planning and Probate) Bar Association. ***PRACTICE AREAS:*** Civil Litigation; Real Estate; Estate Planning; Business Planning; Financial Institutions Law. ***Email:*** mfwlaw@defnet.com

TROY A. ESSEX, born Defiance, Ohio, March 24, 1975; admitted to bar, 2000, Ohio. *Education:* Ohio Northern University (B.A., with high distinction, 1997); University of Toledo (J.D., magna cum laude, 2000). Order of the Coif. Member, University of Toledo Law Review. *Member:* Ohio State Bar Association. ***Email:*** taelaw@defnet.com

REPRESENTATIVE CLIENTS: First Federal Bank of Midwest; Fifth Third Bank (Defiance Office); The State Bank & Trust Company; Farmers & Merchants State Bank (Defiance Office); Attorneys Title Agency of Northwest Ohio, Inc.; Federal Land Bank of Louisville; Norfolk & Western R.R.; Allstate Ins. Co.; Central Mutual Ins. Co.; Cincinnati Ins. Co.; Motorists Mutual Ins. Co.; State Auto. Mutual Ins. Co.; State Farm Mutual Ins. Co.; Mennonite Mutual Ins. Co.; Timcor, Inc.; Koester Corporation; Northwestern Ohio Board of Realtors.
AUTHORIZED AGENT FOR: Stewart Title Guaranty Company; First American Title Insurance Company.

STEPHEN K. SNAVELY, CO., L.P.A.

505 FOURTH STREET
P.O. BOX 759
DEFIANCE, OHIO 43512
Telephone: 419-782-8846
Fax: 419-784-5285
Email: snavely@adelphia.net
URL: http://www.snavelylaw.com

General Civil Practice. Personal Injury, Wrongful Death, Automobile Accidents, Probate, Wills, Trusts, Estate Planning, Family Law, Domestic Relations, Divorce, and Real Estate Law. Trials and Appeals.

STEPHEN K. SNAVELY, born Bluffton, Ohio, April 25, 1947; admitted to bar, 1973, Ohio and U.S. District Court, Northern District of Ohio. *Education:* Ohio Northern University (B.A., 1970); Ohio Northern University (J.D., 1973). *Member:* Defiance County (President, 1987-1989), Northwest Ohio and Ohio State Bar Associations. ***PRACTICE AREAS:*** Probate; Estate Planning; Real Estate; Civil Litigation; Personal Injury; Family Law/Domestic Relations; Divorce; Wills; Child Custody.

APPROVED ATTORNEY FOR: The Ohio Bar Title Insurance Co.
REFERENCES: Sky Bank; First Federal Bank.

BABBITT & WEIS LLP

DELAWARE, OHIO

(See Columbus)

Family and Matrimonial Law, Divorce, Dissolutions, Legal Separation, Spousal Support, Property Division, Child Custody, Child Support, Pre-Marital Agreements, Divorce Arbitration.

MICHAEL E. BENSON

DELAWARE, OHIO

(See Columbus)

Bankruptcy Law, Foreclosures, Debtor and Creditor, Real Estate, Landlord and Tenant, Buying and Selling, Wills, Living Wills, Healthcare, Powers of Attorney.

BLAUGRUND, HERBERT & MARTIN

INCORPORATED

DELAWARE, OHIO

(See Dublin)

Administrative Law, Bankruptcy, Civil Rights Litigation, Civil Service, Commercial Collections, Corporate Law, Debtor-Creditor Law, Disability Law, Employment Discrimination, Employment Law, Estate Administration, Estate Planning, General Civil Practice, Labor Relations, Limited Liability Companies, Limited Liability Partnerships, Liquor Law, Litigation, Motor Vehicle Law, Non-profit Corporation Law, Probate, Real Estate and Construction Law, State and Local Government Law, Trade Association Law, UCC, Workers Compensation, Zoning, Planning and Land Use, Alternative Dispute Resolution, Appellate Practice and Administrative Appeals.

KEITH A. BOGER

61 NORTH SANDUSKY STREET
DELAWARE, OHIO 43015
Telephone: 740-363-9412; 548-6533
Fax: 740-548-6533
Email: keithboger@yahoo.com
URL: http://www.lawyers.com/bogerlaw

General Civil and Criminal Practice. Personal Injury, Products Liability, Family/Domestic Relations, Real Estate, Probate and Estate Planning, Criminal and Traffic Law, Driving While Intoxicated, Commercial Collections.

KEITH A. BOGER, born Marion, Ohio, November 6, 1955; admitted to bar, 1981, Ohio; 1983, U.S. Court of Appeals, Sixth Circuit; 1986, U.S. District Court, Southern District of Ohio. *Education:* George Washington University (B.A., with distinction, 1978; J.D., 1981). Phi Eta Sigma; Phi Beta Kappa. Assistant City Prosecutor, Delaware, Ohio, 1983. Solicitor: Village of Ashley, 1983-1990; Village of Sunbury, 1986-1990. *Member:* Delaware County (President, 1995-1996) and Ohio State Bar Associations.

SEAN O. BOYLE

DELAWARE, OHIO

(See Columbus)

State and Federal Criminal Defense, Felonies and Misdemeanors, Juvenile Law.

CALIG & HANDELMAN, LPA

DELAWARE, OHIO

(See Columbus)

Bankruptcy, Personal Injury, Probate, Real Estate, Social Security, Social Security Disability, Medical Malpractice, Wrongful Death, Civil Litigation, Domestic Relations Law.

CHESTER, WILLCOX & SAXBE LLP

DELAWARE, OHIO

(See Columbus)

Administrative, Bankruptcy, Business, Corporation, Education Law, Employment Law, Estate Planning, Family Law, General Practice, Intellectual Property Law, International Law, Legislative, Municipal, Oil and Gas, Probate, Public Utilities, Real Estate, Taxation, Trial and Appeals.

VINCENT A. DUGAN, JR.

DELAWARE, OHIO

(See Columbus)

Family Law, Divorce, Child Custody, Child Support, Adoption Law, Visitation Rights, Real Estate, Small Business Law, Traffic Violations.

FARLOW & ASSOCIATES LLC

DELAWARE, OHIO

(See Dublin)

Family Law, Divorce, Child Custody, Child Support, Premarital Agreements, Post-Decree Enforcements, Employment Law, School Law, Personal Injury.

FRIEDMAN & MIRMAN CO., L.P.A.

DELAWARE, OHIO

(See Columbus)

Family Relations Law, Divorce.

WILLIAM L. GEARY

DELAWARE, OHIO

(See Columbus)

Family Law, Divorce, Separation Agreements, Child Custody, Child Support, Visitation Rights, Alimony.

GOLDMAN & ROSENTHAL

DELAWARE, OHIO

(See Columbus)

Personal Injury, Family Law, Real Estate, Commercial Leasing, Construction and Mechanics Lien Law, Collections, Estate Planning and Probate, Corporate, Juvenile Law, Criminal. Civil and Criminal Trials in all Courts.

DAVID A. GOLDSTEIN CO., L.P.A.

DELAWARE, OHIO

(See Columbus)

Insurance Law, Insurance Coverage, Professional Liability, Legal Malpractice, Personal Injury, Products Liability, Wrongful Death, Automobile Accidents.

JOSEPH & JOSEPH

DELAWARE, OHIO

(See Columbus)

General Civil Trial Practice. Real Estate, Corporate, Domestic and Family Law, Employment, Banking and Commercial Law.

SUSAN KENNEY-PFALZER

DELAWARE, OHIO

(See Columbus)

Family Law, Divorce, Dissolution, Child Custody, Spousal and Child Support, Visitation Rights, Adoptions, Paternity, Juvenile Law, Collaborative Law, Restraining Orders.

LAMKIN, VAN EMAN, TRIMBLE, BEALS & DOUGHERTY, LLC

DELAWARE, OHIO

(See Columbus)

Personal Injury, Medical Malpractice, Products Liability, Negligence, Insurance Coverage, Stockbroker Malpractice & Fraud. Litigation and Trial Practice.

GREGG R. LEWIS

DELAWARE, OHIO

(See Columbus)

Family Law, Matrimonial Law and Civil Litigation.

LUCAS, PRENDERGAST, ALBRIGHT, GIBSON & NEWMAN

DELAWARE, OHIO

(See Columbus)

General Civil Practice. Corporation, Wills, Probate, Taxation, Real Estate, Zoning, Public Utilities, Labor and Health Law. Estate Planning. Trials and Appeals.

MANOS, MARTIN, PERGRAM & DIETZ CO., LPA

Established in 1951

50 NORTH SANDUSKY STREET
DELAWARE, OHIO 43015-1926
Telephone: 740-363-1313
Telecopier: 740-363-1314
URL: http://www.mmpdlaw.com
Email: mail@mmpdlaw.com
URL: http://www.lawyers.com/mmpdlaw

Administrative, Appellate Practice, Litigation, Business, Contracts, Corporate, Zoning, Planning and Land Use, Real Estate, Labor and Employment, Trusts and Estates, and Wills and Probate.

PETER J. MANOS (1922-2004)

STEPHEN D. MARTIN, born Paducah, Kentucky, May 14, 1947; admitted to bar, 1974, Ohio; 1977, U.S. District Court, Southern and Northern Districts of Ohio; 1978, U.S. Supreme Court; 1982, U.S. Court of Appeals, Sixth Circuit; 1991, U.S. Tax Court; 1992, U.S. District Court, District of Arizona; 1993, U.S. Court of Appeals, Ninth Circuit. *Education:* Rutgers College (B.A., 1969); Capital University (J.D., 1973). Order of the Curia. ***PRACTICE AREAS:*** Contracts; Real Estate; Zoning, Planning and Land Use; Business Law. ***Email:*** smartin@mmpdlaw.com

DENNIS L. PERGRAM, born Tiffin, Ohio, January 24, 1947; admitted to bar, 1977, Ohio; 1979, U.S. District Court, Southern District of Ohio; 1985, U.S. Court of Appeals, 6th Circuit; 1989, U.S. Supreme Court and U.S. District Court, Northern District of Ohio. *Education:* Ohio University; Bowling Green State University; Defiance College (B.S., 1972); University of Toledo (J.D., 1976). ***PRACTICE AREAS:*** Administrative; Appellate Practice; Labor and Employment; Litigation. ***Email:*** dpergram@mmpdlaw.com

JAMES M. DIETZ, born Columbus, Ohio, October 7, 1960; admitted to bar, 1985, Ohio; 1988, U.S. District Court, Southern District of Ohio; 1993, U.S. Court of Appeals, Sixth Circuit. *Education:* Capital University (B.A., 1982); The Ohio State University (J.D., 1985). ***PRACTICE AREAS:*** Real Estate; Zoning, Planning and Land Use; Wills; Probate. ***Email:*** jdietz@mmpdlaw.com

THAYNE D. GRAY, born Columbus, Ohio, July 21, 1955; admitted to bar, 1980, Illinois; 1992, Ohio; 1993, U.S. District Court, Southern District of Ohio. *Education:* DePauw University (B.A., with honors, 1977); The Ohio State University College of Law (J.D., with honors, 1980). *Member:* Delaware County and Ohio State Bar Associations. ***PRACTICE AREAS:*** Appellate Practice; Business; Contracts; Litigation; Real Estate; Zoning, Planning and Land Use. ***Email:*** tgray@mmpdlaw.com

OF COUNSEL

LOWELL A. HEDLUND, born Jamestown, New York, August 26, 1956; admitted to bar, 1981, Ohio; 1982, U.S. Tax Court. *Education:* Wittenberg University (B.A., cum laude, 1978); The Ohio State University (J.D., with honors, 1981). Omicron Delta Kappa. ***PRACTICE AREAS:*** Business Law; Real Estate; Contracts; Corporate Law. ***Email:*** lhedlund@mmpdlaw.com

---

MELISSA K. RIGGINS ATTORNEY AT LAW

DELAWARE, OHIO

(See Columbus)

Criminal Law, Felonies, Misdemeanors, Traffic Violations, Drug Crimes, Driving While Intoxicated, Domestic Violence and Drivers License Law.

ROURKE & BLUMENTHAL, LLP

DELAWARE, OHIO

(See Columbus)

Personal Injury, Negligence, Products Liability, Medical Malpractice, Nursing Home Litigation, Wrongful Death, Intentional Tort, Insurance Disputes, Automobile Accidents, Civil Trial Practice, Aviation, Professional Liability.

SCHULZE, HOWARD & COX

DELAWARE, OHIO

(See Marysville)

Civil Trial Practice, Personal Injury, Corporate, Commercial, Probate and Trust, Real Estate Law, Estate Planning, Contract Law, Business Law, Consumer Law.

REBECCA J. STUMLER

DELAWARE, OHIO

(See Columbus)

Family Law, Divorce, Child Custody, Child Support, Visitation Rights, Adoption Law, Paternity, Domestic Violence, Bankruptcy Law, Civil Litigation.

THOMAS LAW GROUP

DELAWARE, OHIO

(See Dublin)

Family Law, Divorce, Child Custody, Child Support, Visitation Rights, Business Litigation, Corporate, Small Business Law, Business Formation, Partnerships, Limited Liability Companies, Buying and Selling of Businesses, Contracts, Personal Injury, Automobile Accidents, Wrongful Death, Medical Malpractice, Estate Planning, Wills and Probate, Trusts and Estates, Estate Administration.

TWYFORD & DONAHEY, P.L.L.

Established in 1968

163 N. SANDUSKY STREET, SUITE 103
DELAWARE, OHIO 43015
Telephone: Toll Free: 1-800-686-1699
Fax: 614-849-0475
Email: help@twyforddonahey.com
URL: http://www.twyforddonahey.com

Columbus, Ohio Office: 495 South High Street, 43215-5058. Telephone: Toll Free: 1-800-686-1699. Email: help@twyforddonahey.com.
Circleville, Ohio Office: 214 South Court Street, 43113. Telephone: Toll Free: 1-800-686-1699. Email: help@twyforddonahey.com.
Lancaster, Ohio Office: 3794 Old Columbus, N.W., 43130. Telephone: Toll Free: 1-800-686-1699. Email: help@twyforddonahey.com.
Newark, Ohio Office: 137 West Main Street, Suite C., 43025. Telephone: Toll Free: 1-800-686-1699. Email: help@twyforddonahey.com.
London, Ohio Office: 25 West Fifth Street, 43140. Telephone: Toll Free: 1-800-686-1699. Email: help@twyforddonahey.com.

(This Listing Continued)

TWYFORD & DONAHEY, P.L.L., Delaware—Continued

Personal Injury Litigation, Wrongful Death, Medical Malpractice, Products Liability, Automobile Accidents, Trucking Accidents, Head and Spinal Injuries, Motorcycle Accidents and Injuries, Uninsured Motorists, Insurance Law, Airplane Crash Litigation, Railroad Accidents, Slip and Fall, Dog Bites, Work Related Injuries, Birth Injuries, Nursing Home Abuse and Neglect.

FIRM PROFILE: Tom Twyford and Dick Donahey have been partners since 1968 and have practiced exclusively in the areas of personal injury, medical malpractice and products liability law. We have never represented insurance companies! In recent years, we have obtained some of the largest verdicts in Franklin County. We have purposely remained small in order to concentrate on a limited number of cases. We have six offices and will handle cases in any part of the state of Ohio.

(For complete biographical data on all personnel, see Professional Biographies at Columbus, Ohio.)

DAVID WIRTH

DELAWARE, OHIO

(See Columbus)

Insurance Law, Negligence, Legal Malpractice, Subrogation, Personal Injury, Probate.

WOLSKE & BARCLAY

A LEGAL PROFESSIONAL ASSOCIATION

DELAWARE, OHIO

(See Columbus)

Civil and Appellate Practice in State and Federal Courts. Medical and Dental Malpractice, Nursing Home Negligence, Personal Injury and Products Liability Law, Worker's Compensation and Industrial Accidents, Automobile Accidents, Airplane Crash Litigation.

BLACK McCUSKEY HANHART DEEDS & BAUER

A LEGAL PROFESSIONAL ASSOCIATION

130 W. THIRD STREET
DOVER, OHIO 44622
Telephone: 330-364-6553
Fax: 330-364-2739
URL: http://www.bmsa.com

Canton, Ohio Office: 220 Market Avenue South, Suite 1000, 44702. Telephone: 330-456-8341; 877-656-8341. Telecopier: 330-456-5756; 877-456-5746.

General Civil Practice in all State and Federal Courts. Administrative, Antitrust, Banking, Bankruptcy, Commercial, Construction, Corporate, Environmental, Estate Planning and Probate, Family Law, Franchising, Government, Healthcare Law, Labor, Litigation, Oil and Gas, Personal Injury, Real Estate, Securities, Taxation Law, Wrongful Death and Zoning.

(For complete biographical data on all personnel, see Black, McCuskey at Canton, Ohio)

THOMAS H. HISRICH

Established in 1966

121 WEST FOURTH STREET
DOVER, OHIO 44622-2961
Telephone: 330-343-8834
Fax: 330-343-0709

General Civil Practice. Corporation, Federal State and Local Taxation, Real Estate, Eminent Domain, Wills Probate, Estate Planning, Agriculture and Negligence Law. Personal Injury, Automobile Accidents, Medical Malpractice, Mineral and Mining Law.

THOMAS H. HISRICH, born Dover, Ohio, March 1, 1941; admitted to bar, 1966, Ohio; 1971, U.S. District Court, Northern District of Ohio. *Education:* Kent State University (B.S., B.A., 1962); Ohio State University (J.D., 1966). Ohio Assistant Attorney General, 1966-1969. City Solicitor, City of Dover, 1972-1973. Member, 1978-1983, 1988—, and Chairman, 1982-1983, 1988—, Tuscarawas County Board of Elections. Member, State of Ohio Agriculture Finance Committee, 1992-1995. *Member:* Tuscarawas County, Ohio State (Member, 1982, Secretary, 1984-1986, Vice Chairman, 1987-1988 and Chairman, 1989-1991, Agricultural Law Section) and American Bar Associations.

AGENT FOR: Ohio Bar Title Insurance Co.; Guardian Title Insurance Co.
REFERENCES: Huntington National Bank, Dover, Ohio; Bank One of Dover, N.A.

STEPHENSON, STEPHENSON & CARROTHERS

DOVER, OHIO

(See New Philadelphia)

General Civil Practice. Litigation, Appellate Practice, Business Law, Corporate Law, Hospital Law, Wills, Probate, Aged and Aging, Collections, Commercial Law, Construction Law, Consumer Law, Contacts, Eminent Domain, Environmental Law, Guardianship and Conservatorship, Insurance, Labor and Employment, Medicare and Medicaid, Nonprofit and Charitable Organizations, Personal Injury, Railroad Law, Zoning, Planning and Land Use, Mediation, Health Care, Trusts and Estate, Real Estate, Family Law.

BARRETT, EASTERDAY, CUNNINGHAM & ESELGROTH LLP

7269 SAWMILL ROAD
DUBLIN, OHIO 43016
Telephone: 614-210-1840
Facsimile: 614-210-1841
URL: http://www.ohiocounsel.com
Email: info@ohiocounsel.com
URL: http://www.lawyers.com/dbarrett

Agricultural Law, Agribusiness, Business Arbitration, Alternative Dispute Resolution, Commodities, Debtor and Creditor, Corporate Law, Commercial Law, Commercial Transactions, Antitrust, Trade Association Law, Environmental Law, Federal Civil Litigation, Commercial Litigation, Civil Litigation, Estate Planning, Estate Administration, Probate, Taxation, Real Estate Exchanges, Estate and Gift Taxation, Like Kind Exchanges, Trusts and Estates Taxation, Bankruptcy, Environmental Law.

PARTNERS

DAVID C. BARRETT, JR., born Delaware, Ohio, January 17, 1956; admitted to bar, 1981, Ohio; 1982, U.S. District Court, Northern District of Ohio; 1983, U.S. Tax Court; 1984, U.S. Court of Appeals, Sixth Circuit; 1987, U.S. Supreme Court; 1988, U.S. District Court, Southern District of Ohio; 1990, District of Columbia; 2000, U.S. District Court, Northern District of Indiana; 2004, U.S. District Court, Central District of Illinois. *Education:* The Ohio State University (B.S., Agriculture, with honors, 1978); University of Toledo (J.D., cum laude, 1981). Phi Alpha Delta; Phi Kappa Phi. Instructor of Business Law and Real Estate Law, Owens Technical College, 1982-1985. Recipient, Young Professional Achievement Award, Ohio State University College of Agriculture Alumni Association, 1985. Author: *Arbitrating Agricultural Disputes: The National Grain and Feed Association's Experience,* 68 North Dakota Law Review 539 (1992); *Hedge-to-Arrive Contracts,* 2 Drake Journal Of Agricultural Law 153 (1997). Co-Author: Agricultural Law Update 2001 and 2002, Ohio CLE Institute. National Secretary/Administrator, National Grain and Feed Association Arbitration System, 1990-2000. Active Arbitration Panelist Roster, National Futures Association, 2001—. Member, Executive Committee, Ohio Agricultural Council, 2003—. Selected by Law & Politics (R) as Ohio Super Lawyer, 2004 and 2005. *Member:* Bar Association of the District of Columbia; Ohio State (Chairman, 2005—, Agricultural Law Committee) Bar Association; American Agricultural Law Association; Columbus Bar Association; Delaware County Bar Association. ***PRACTICE AREAS:*** Agricultural Law; Agribusiness; Business Arbitration; Alternative Dispute Resolution; Bankruptcy; Commodities; Debtor and Creditor Law; Corporate Law; Commercial Law; Commercial Transactions; Antitrust; Trade Association Law; Environmental Law; Federal Civil Litigation; Commercial Litigation; Civil Litigation. ***Email:*** dbarrett@farmlawyers.com

JEFFREY A. EASTERDAY, born Delaware, Ohio, August 7, 1954; admitted to bar, 1983, Ohio; 1984, U.S. District Court, Southern District of Ohio. *Education:* The Ohio State University (B.S., 1976); Capital University (J.D., 1983). Ohio Certified General Appraisal License, 1992. *Member:* Delaware County and Ohio State Bar Associations. ***PRACTICE AREAS:*** Probate; Taxation; Real Estate Exchanges; Business Organization; Estate Planning; Estate and Gift Taxation. ***Email:*** jeasterday@ohiocounsel.com

RUSSELL N. CUNNINGHAM, born Columbus, Ohio, December 19, 1963; admitted to bar, 1989, Ohio; 1999, U.S. Court of Appeals, Sixth Circuit. *Education:* The Ohio State University (B.S., summa cum laude, 1986); Case Western Reserve University (J.D., magna cum laude, 1989). Order of the Coif. Recipient, Singer Prize for Excellence in Business and Commercial Law. Selected by Law & Politics (R) as Ohio Super Lawyer, 2005. Co-Author with James Skeeles, Estate Planning Letter Study Course, The Ohio State University Extension, 2004 Edition. (Certified Specialist in Estate Planning, Trust and Probate Law, Ohio State Bar Association). ***PRACTICE AREAS:*** Estate Planning; Estate Administration; Trust Planning; Trusts and Estates; Probate. ***Email:*** rcunningham@ohiocounsel.com

CAROLYN D. ESELGROTH, born Chillicothe, Ohio, May 11, 1958; admitted to bar, 1992, Ohio. *Education:* The Ohio State University (B.S., summa cum laude, 1980; J.D., with honors, 1992). *Member:* Columbus and Ohio State Bar Associations. ***PRACTICE AREAS:*** Real Estate; Business Law; Trusts and Estates; Agricultural Cooperatives; Nonprofit and Charitable Organizations. ***Email:*** ceselgroth@farmlawyers.com

OF COUNSEL

LARRY E. HOOVER, born Marion, Ohio, January 26, 1966; admitted to bar, 1996, Ohio. *Education:* The Ohio State University (B.S., 1993); University of Cincinnati College of Law (J.D., 1996). (Also practicing individually in Westerville). ***PRACTICE AREAS:*** Taxation; Bankruptcy; Civil Litigation. ***Email:*** lhoover@hooverlaw.org

ASSOCIATE

TROY A. CALLICOAT, born London, Ohio, September 22, 1977; admitted to bar, 2003, Ohio. *Education:* The Ohio State University (B.S., 2000); Capital University Law School (J.D., magna cum laude, 2003). Order of the Curia. Associate Editor, Capital Law Review, 2001-2003. *Member:* Columbus and Ohio State Bar Associations. ***PRACTICE AREAS:*** Agricultural Law; Environmental Law; Civil Litigation.

BLAUGRUND, HERBERT & MARTIN

INCORPORATED

5455 RINGS ROAD, SUITE 500
DUBLIN, OHIO 43017-7517
Telephone: 614-764-0681
Fax: 614-764-0774
Email: bhm@bhmlaw.com
URL: http://www.bhmlaw.com

Administrative Law, Bankruptcy, Civil Rights Litigation, Civil Service, Commercial Collections, Corporate Law, Debtor-Creditor Law, Disability Law, Employment Discrimination, Employment Law, Estate Administration, Estate Planning, General Civil Practice, Labor Rela-

(This Listing Continued)

tions, Limited Liability Companies, Limited Liability Partnerships, Liquor Law, Litigation, Motor Vehicle Law, Non-profit Corporation Law, Probate, Real Estate and Construction Law, State and Local Government Law, Trade Association Law, UCC, Workers Compensation, Zoning, Planning and Land Use, Alternative Dispute Resolution, Appellate Practice and Administrative Appeals.

FIRM PROFILE: Blaugrund, Herbert & Martin offers big firm professionalism yet is small enough to give each client focused, unpretentious service.

Since 1990, we have represented individuals, families, nonprofit organizations, governmental and independent agencies, and businesses of all sizes.

DAVID S. BLAUGRUND, born Cleveland, Ohio, February 1, 1953; admitted to bar, 1977, Ohio and U.S. District Court, Northern and Southern Districts of Ohio. *Education:* Miami University (B.A., cum laude, 1974); Ohio State University (J.D., 1976). Phi Beta Kappa; Omicron Delta Kappa; Phi Eta Sigma. Executive Secretary, Ohio State Personnel Board of Review, 1977-1980. General Counsel, CN & A, Inc., 1980-1989. *Member:* Columbus (Member, Labor Law Committee), Ohio State (Member, Labor Law Committee; Member, Board of Governors, Labor law Committee) and American (Member, Labor Law Committee) Bar Associations. ***PRACTICE AREAS:*** Labor and Employment Law; Administrative Law; Construction Law; School Law; Nonprofit Corporation Law; Disabilities Law; Motor Vehicle Law. ***Email:*** dsb@bhmlaw.com

JOHN W. HERBERT, born Wooster, Ohio, February 8, 1950; admitted to bar, 1975, Ohio; 1976, U.S. District Court, Northern District of Ohio; 1984, U.S. District Court, Western District of Tennessee; 1990, U.S. District Court, Southern District of Ohio. *Education:* The Ohio State University (B.S., cum laude, 1972; J.D., 1975). Phi Beta Kappa. *Member:* Columbus and Ohio State Bar Associations. ***PRACTICE AREAS:*** Litigation; Employment Law; UCC; Workers Compensation. ***Email:*** jwh@bhmlaw.com

DAVID S. KESSLER, born Akron, Ohio, June 2, 1964; admitted to bar, 1989, Ohio and U.S. District Court, Northern and Southern Districts of Ohio; U.S. Court of Appeals, Sixth Circuit. *Education:* University of Akron (B.S., 1986); Capital University (J.D., cum laude, 1989). Order of the Curia. Order of the Barrister. Member, International Moot Court Team. Member, Capital University Law Review. Previous Employment: Mowery & Youell; Tyack & Kessler. *Member:* Columbus and Ohio State Bar Associations. ***PRACTICE AREAS:*** Civil Litigation; Labor and Employment; Civil Rights; Collections; Shareholder Disputes. ***Email:*** dsk2@bhmlaw.com

STEVEN A. MARTIN, born Circleville, Ohio, 1953; admitted to bar, 1988, Ohio. *Education:* University of Colorado (B.S.B.A., 1981); The Ohio State University (M.B.A., 1987; J.D., 1988). Co-author: "'Check-a-box', Final Regs. Simplify Entity Classification," Taxation for Accountants, March 1997; "Limited Liability Companies and More - An Overview of Senate Bill 74," The Ohio Society of CPAs, 1996; "Proposed 'Check-a-box' Regulations, Taxation for Accountants," July 1996; "Proposed 'Check-a-box' Regulations Taxation for Lawyers," September/October 1996; " 'Check-a-box' Final Regs. Simplify Entity Classification for Tax Purposes," Warren, Gorham & Lamont, Forms of Business Manual, 1996. Author: "Senate Bill 74, Expanded Flexibility for Ohio Business and Professionals," The Ohio CPA Journal, July 1994. Co-Founder and President, MDS CPA Review Course. Assistant Professor of Law, Accounting Finance and Taxation, Capital University School of Management. Adjunct Professor of Business Law, Capital University College of Arts and Sciences. Adjunct Professor of Law, Capital University Law and Graduate Center. *Member:* Columbus and Ohio State (Past Chairman, Federal Taxation Committee; Chairman, Federal Tax Specialty Board) Bar Associations; American Institute of Certified Public Accountants; The Ohio Society of Certified Public Accountants; Colorado Society of Certified Public Accountants. [USAF, 1971-1978]. ***PRACTICE AREAS:*** Business; Tax Planning; Successions; Business Organization; Accounting Law; Trade Association Law; Tax Exempt Organizations; Campaign Ethics; Election Law. ***Email:*** sam@bhmlaw.com

SHARON L. R. MILLER, born Hicksville, Ohio, February 10, 1952; admitted to bar, 1979, Ohio; 1981, U.S. Tax Court and U.S. District Court, Southern District of Ohio; 1987, U.S. Court of Appeals, Sixth Circuit. *Education:* Kent State University (B.S., cum laude, 1974); Ohio Northern University (J.D., 1979); University of Florida (LL.M., in Taxation, 1982). Author: "'Incidents of Ownership' As It Applies To A Right Held By a Decedent To Select An Optional Mode of Settlement," 33 Case Western Law Review 51 (1982). Adjunct Professor: Capital University Law & Graduate Center, 1985—. *Member:* Columbus, Ohio State and American Bar Associations. ***PRACTICE AREAS:*** Taxation Law; Estate Planning Law; Trusts Law; Corporate Law. ***Email:*** slrm@bhmlaw.com

MARC E. MYERS, born Chillicothe, Ohio, May 14, 1951; admitted to bar, 1976, Ohio; 1977, U.S. District Courts, Southern and Northern Districts of Ohio. *Education:* Ohio University (B.A., summa cum laude, 1973); Ohio Northern University (J.D., with distinction, 1976). Phi Beta Kappa; Phi Kappa Phi. Assistant Attorney General of Ohio, 1976-1982. Chief, Liquor Section, Ohio Attorney General's Office, 1980-1982. *Member:* Columbus, Ohio State and American Bar Associations. ***REPORTED CASES:*** Our Place, Inc. v. Ohio Liquor Control Comm., 63 Ohio St. 3d 570 (1992); Mills-Jennings of Ohio, Inc. v. Department of Liquor Control, 70 Ohio St. 2d 95 (1982); Burigana v. Industrial Commission, 108 Ohio App.3d 57 (1996); Swepston v. Bd. of Tax Appeals of Ohio, 89 Ohio App. 3d 629 (1993); Summit County Bd. of Mental Retardation and Developmental Disabilities v. American Federation of State, County and Mun. Employees, 39 Ohio App. 3d 175 (1988); City of Kettering v. State Employment Relations Bd., 26 Ohio St. 3d 50 (1986); Griffith v. Department of Youth Services, 28 Ohio App. 3d 76, (1985); Blinn v. Ohio Bureau of Employment Services, 29 Ohio App. 3d 77 (1985); Foltz v. Kent State University, 52 Ohio Misc. 98 (1977); Cottrill v. Ohio Civil Service Employees Ass'n, 665 F. Supp. 525 (N.D. Ohio, 1987). ***PRACTICE AREAS:*** Labor and Employment Law; Liquor Law; Administrative Law. ***Email:*** mem@bhmlaw.com

STEPHEN P. POSTALAKIS, born Newark, Ohio, December 21, 1968; admitted to bar, 1994, Ohio; 1996, U.S. District Court, Northern and Southern Districts of Ohio. *Education:* Miami University (B.A., 1991); The Ohio State University (J.D., 1994). Phi Beta Kappa. Member, Golden Key Honor Society. *Member:* Columbus and Ohio State Bar Associations. ***PRACTICE AREAS:*** Labor and Employment; Civil Litigation; Trade and Professional Associations. ***Email:*** spp@bhmlaw.com

(This Listing Continued)

TERI G. RASMUSSEN, born Madison, Wisconsin, May 21, 1959; admitted to bar, 1984, Ohio and U.S. District Court, Southern District of Ohio; 1993, U.S. District Court, Northern District of Ohio; 1997, U.S. Court of Appeals, Sixth Circuit. *Education:* University of Iowa (B.A., with honors, 1981); University of Michigan (J.D., cum laude, 1984). Phi Beta Kappa. Member, Editorial Board, University of Michigan Journal of Law Reform, 1983-1984. *Member:* Columbus, Ohio State (Vice Chair, Subcommittee on Accounts, Payments, and Letters of Credit of Banking, Commercial and Bankruptcy Committee, 1994-1999; Chair, Financial Institutions Committee, 1997-1999) and American Bar Associations; American Bankruptcy Institute; International Women's Insolvency and Restructuring Confederation. ***PRACTICE AREAS:*** Business Law; Creditors Rights; Bankruptcy; Insolvency; Equipment Leasing; Commercial Finance; Secured Transactions; Litigation; Real Estate. ***Email:*** tgr@bhmlaw.com

---

BRET A. ADAMS, born Circleville, Ohio, May 9, 1959; admitted to bar, 1984, Ohio. *Education:* Ohio University (B.A., Political Science, 1981); Capital University (J.D., 1984). Board Member: Wendy's LPGA Championship for Children; Friends of Hoop Foundation. Advisory Board Member, Greater Columbus Sports Commission. *Member:* Columbus, Ohio State (Member, Professional Ethics and Conduct Committee) and American (Member, Entertainment and Sports Section) Bar Associations. ***PRACTICE AREAS:*** Sports Law; Entertainment Law. ***Email:*** bret.adams@bhmlaw.com

DAVID W. BABNER, born 1968; admitted to bar, 1993, Ohio and U.S. District Court, Southern District of Ohio; 1998, Massachusetts. *Education:* University of Massachusetts (B.A., 1990); Capital University (J.D., 1993). *Member:* Columbus, Ohio State, Massachusetts State and American (Member, Committee on Law of Commerce in Cyberspace, Business Law Section) Bar Associations. ***PRACTICE AREAS:*** Business. ***Email:*** davidbagner@bhmlaw.com

CHRISTOPHER T. CLINE, born Columbus, Ohio, April 14, 1950; admitted to bar, 1975, Ohio; 1976, U.S. District Court, Southern District of Ohio; 1979, U.S. Supreme Court; 1994, U.S. Army Court of Military Review. *Education:* Ohio State University (B.A., 1972); Capital University (J.D., 1975); U.S. Army War College (Masters of Strategic Studies, 2001). Certified as Military Judge, 1994. Commander, 9th Legal Support Organization, U.S. Army Reserve, 2001. Author: "Medical Operations and The Law of War," Military Review Magazine, April 1991. *Member:* Columbus and Ohio State Bar Associations. [Col., USAR, 1981—]. ***PRACTICE AREAS:*** Zoning Law; Land Use; Civil Litigation; Business Law. ***Email:*** ctc@bhmlaw.com

MARYELLEN CORNA, born Columbus, Ohio, July 30, 1957; admitted to bar, 1992, Ohio and U.S. District Court, Southern District of Ohio; 1998, U.S. Court of Appeals, Sixth Circuit. *Education:* The Ohio State University (B.A., 1989); Moritz College of Law, The Ohio State University (J.D., 1992). *Member:* Columbus (Member, Sections on: Labor and Employment; Litigation) and Ohio State (Member: Board of Governors; Labor and Employment Section) Bar Associations. ***PRACTICE AREAS:*** Labor and Employment Law; Litigation; Domestic; Business Law. ***Email:*** mec@bhmlaw.com

JONATHAN M. GABEL, born Columbus, Ohio, July 19, 1960; admitted to bar, 1985, Ohio. *Education:* Ohio State University (B.A., 1982); University of Cincinnati (J.D., 1985). Phi Alpha Theta, Zeta Chapter. *Member:* Columbus and Ohio State Bar Associations. ***PRACTICE AREAS:*** Labor and Employment; State Government Law; Local Government Law. ***Email:*** jmg@bhmlaw.net

FAZEEL S. KHAN, born Suva, Fiji Islands; admitted to bar, 2005, Ohio. *Education:* Simon Fraser University, Burnaby, B.C. (B.A., Criminology and Psychology, 1997); University of Windsor, Windsor, ON (LL.B., 2003); Case Western Reserve (LL.M., 2004). Director, AAIIL (USA), a non-profit charitable organization devoted to publishing scholary Islamic and religious studies material. Regular Panel Member: Ohio State University's Young Scholar Program; Martin W. Essex School for the Gifted annual conferences at O.S.U. *Member:* Columbus and Ohio State Bar Associations. ***LANGUAGES:*** Hindi, Urdu. ***PRACTICE AREAS:*** Labor and Employment; Consumer Protection; Debtor and Creditor Remedies. ***Email:*** fsk@bhmlaw.com

GEOFF P. SCOTT, born Columbus, Ohio, March 29, 1968; admitted to bar, 1997, Ohio. *Education:* The Ohio State University (B.S., 1990); Capital University Law School (J.D., 1997). Order of the Coif. ***PRACTICE AREAS:*** Business Law; Tax Law; Estate Planning; Probate. ***Email:*** gps@bhmlaw.com

BOBBIE J. STONEROCK, born Circleville, Ohio, November 3, 1964; admitted to bar, 1993, Ohio; U.S. District Court, Southern District of Ohio. *Education:* Ohio University (B.A., cum laude, 1990); The Ohio State University College of Law (J.D., 1993). *Member:* Columbus and Ohio State Bar Associations. ***PRACTICE AREAS:*** Litigation; Employment Law; Workers Compensation; Criminal Law; Domestic Law; Personal Injury. ***Email:*** bobbie.stonerock@bhmlaw.com

CAROLE D. WEISS, born Chattanooga, Tennessee, March 5, 1962; admitted to bar, 1986, Ohio and U.S. District Court, Southern and Northern Districts of Ohio. *Education:* The Ohio State University (B.A., 1983); University of North Carolina, Chapel Hill (J.D., 1986). Author: "General Guidelines: Gramm-Leach-Bliley Act Provisions Affecting Certified Public Accountants," 2001. *Member:* Columbus (Member, Bankruptcy Committee) and Ohio State Bar Associations. ***PRACTICE AREAS:*** Creditors Rights; Bankruptcy; Commercial Law; Secured Transactions. ***Email:*** cdw@bhmlaw.com

OF COUNSEL

FRANCIS A. KOVACS, JR., born Aquadilla, Puerto Rico, May 23, 1953; admitted to bar, 1980, Ohio; 1986, U.S. Court of Appeals, Sixth Circuit. *Education:* Ohio State University (B.A., 1975); Capital University Law School (J.D., 1980); Capital University Law School (LL.M., 1991). Adjunct Professor, Capital University Law and Graduate Center. *Member:* Columbus (Member, Employee Benefits and Executive Compensation, 1985-1988; Vice-Chairman, 1987-1988; Chairman, 1988-1989) and American (Member, Employee Benefits Committee and Important Developments and Publications Subcommittee) Bar Associations. ***LANGUAGES:*** Spanish. ***PRACTICE AREAS:*** Employee Benefits; Deferred Compensation; Non-Qualified Benefits; Estate Planning; Welfare Benefit Program; Financial Product Regulations. ***Email:*** fak@bhmlaw.com

(This Listing Continued)

BLAUGRUND, HERBERT & MARTIN, INCORPORATED, Dublin—Continued

REPRESENTATIVE CLIENTS: Ohio Association of County Boards of Mental Retardation and Developmental Disabilities; City of Bexley; Innovative Designs, Incorporated; Ohio Licensed Beverage Association; Ohio Motor Vehicle Dealers Board; City of Wilmington; Ohio Association of Elementary School Administrators; The Ohio Society of CPA'S; Ohio Soft Drink Association.

FARLOW & ASSOCIATES LLC

270 BRADENTON AVENUE
DUBLIN, OHIO 43017
Telephone: 614-734-1270
Fax: 614-923-1031
Email: bjf@farlowlaw.com
URL: http://www.lawyers.com/farlowassoc

Family Law, Divorce, Child Custody, Child Support, Premarital Agreements, Post-Decree Enforcements, Employment Law, School Law, Personal Injury.

BEVERLY J. FARLOW, born Shelbyville, Indiana, August 3, 1945; admitted to bar, 1985, Ohio and U.S. Court of Appeals, Sixth Circuit; 1986, U.S. District Court, Southern District of Ohio; 1990, U.S. Supreme Court. *Education:* Wittenberg University (B.A., 1967); The Ohio State University (M.A., 1973; J.D., 1985). Author: "A Parents Guide to Ohio School of Law;" "An Administrator's Guide to Ohio School Law." Legal Counsel for Ohio Association of Elementary School Administrators, 1998—. Legal Counsel and Associate Executive Director, Ohio Association of Secondary School Administrators, 1988-1989. Assistant Prosecutor, Columbus City Attorney, 1986-1988. Member, Governor's Youth Art Show Advisory Board, 1987—. *Member:* Columbus (Member: Family Law Committee) and Ohio State (Member, Litigation and General Practice, Board of Governors) Bar Associations; Franklin County Trial Lawyers; Education Law Association. (Certified Specialist in Family Relations Law, Ohio State Bar Association). ***LANGUAGES:*** Turkish. ***REPORTED CASES:*** Goode v. Goode, 70 Ohio App.3d 125 (1991); Douglas v. Cincinnati Bd. of Edn. 80 Ohio App.3d 173 (1992); Bechtel v. England 87 Ohio App.3d 348 (1993); Goode v. Goode, 89 Ohio App.3d 405 (1993); Smith v. Smith, 91 Ohio App.3d 248 (1993); Scott v. Borelli, 106 Ohio App.3d 449 (1995); Wiltberger v. Davis, 110 Ohio App.3d 46 (1996); Reynolds v. Whitney, Ohio 1628 (2004). ***PRACTICE AREAS:*** Family Law; Employment Law; School Law. ***Email:*** bjf@farlowlaw.com

JAMES A. BOLAND, JR., born Norfolk, Virginia, April 17, 1954; admitted to bar, 2002, Ohio; 2003, South Carolina and U.S. District Court, Southern District of Ohio; 2004, U.S. Court of Appeals, Sixth Circuit. *Education:* Furman University (B.A., 1975); Central Michigan University (M.A., Business Management, 1980); University of Maryland (German Studies, 1998); Ohio State University (J.D., 2002). Author: "Letter of the Law Regarding Military Deployments," Solo, Small Firms and General Practice Section of the Ohio State Bar Association. Airline Transport Pilot, U.S. Department of Transportation, Federal Aviation Administration, 1982—. *Member:* Ohio State and Columbus Bar Associations; South Carolina Bar; Army Aviation Association of America; Association of the United States Army; Military Officers Association of America; Disabled American Veterans; Veterans of Foreign Wars; Franklin County Trial Lawyers Association; Ohio Academy of Trial Lawyers; Association of Trial Lawyers of America. [Lieutenant Colonel, U.S. Army, 1976-1999]. ***PRACTICE AREAS:*** Personal Injury; Family Law; Criminal Defense. ***Email:*** jboland@farlowlaw.com

BARBRA BURLEIGH, born Columbus, Ohio, April 12, 1977; admitted to bar, 2004, Ohio. *Education:* Capital University (B.A., Criminology, 1999; J.D., 2003). *Member:* Columbus and Ohio State Bar Associations. ***PRACTICE AREAS:*** Family Law; Juvenile Law. ***Email:*** bburleigh@farlowlaw.com

VICKI K. JOHNSTON, born Columbus, Ohio, November 6, 1970; admitted to bar, 2004, Ohio. *Education:* Ohio State University (B.S.S.W., 1995); University of Wyoming (J.D., 2001). *Member:* Columbus, Ohio State and American Bar Associations. ***PRACTICE AREAS:*** Family Law; School Law; Juvenile Law. ***Email:*** vkjohnston@farlow.com

ROSS A. GILLESPIE, born Marietta, Ohio; admitted to bar, 2003, Ohio; 2004, U.S. District Court, Southern District of Ohio. *Education:* Ohio State University (B.A., 2000); Akron University (J.D., 2003). *Member:* Columbus and Ohio State Bar Associations; Franklin County Trial Lawyers Association. ***PRACTICE AREAS:*** Civil Litigation; Family Law; Employment Law; Medical Malpractice; Real Estate; Business Law; Corporate Law; Probate; Personal Injury. ***Email:*** rgillespie@farlowlaw.com

MICHELLE R. SAYERS, born Toledo, Ohio; admitted to bar, 2004, Ohio. *Education:* Ohio State University (B.S.B.A., 2001); Capital University (J.D., 2004). Order of the Curia. *Member:* Columbus (Member, Family Law Committee) and Ohio State (Member, Family Law Committee) Bar Associations. ***PRACTICE AREAS:*** Family Law; Juvenile Law. ***Email:*** msayers@farlowlaw.com

SUSAN KENNEY-PFALZER

DUBLIN, OHIO

(See Columbus)

Family Law, Divorce, Dissolution, Child Custody, Spousal and Child Support, Visitation Rights, Adoptions, Paternity, Juvenile Law, Collaborative Law, Restraining Orders.

MARQUARDT & WHITE CO., LPA

5455 RINGS ROAD, SUITE 100
DUBLIN, OHIO 43017
Telephone: 614-789-1622
Fax: 614-789-1623

Personal Injury, Automobile Accidents, Negligence, Wrongful Death, Motorcyle Accidents, Dog Bites, Slip and Fall, Medical Malpractice, Wills and Trusts.

(This Listing Continued)

RICHARD F. MARQUARDT, born Dayton, Ohio; admitted to bar, 2000, Ohio. *Education:* University of Alabama (B.S., 1982); University of Toledo (J.D., 1999). *Member:* Columbus and Ohio State Bar Associations; The Association of Trial Lawyers of America. ***PRACTICE AREAS:*** Personal Injury; Automobile Accidents and Injuries; Motorcycle Accidents; Wrongful Death; Dog Bites; Slip and Fall. ***Email:*** rfmarquardt@sbcglobal.net

MASON LAW FIRM CO., L.P.A.

DUBLIN, OHIO

(See Columbus)

Representing and Advising Management in Labor and Employment Law, including Wrongful Termination, Employment Discrimination, Sexual Harassment, Americans with Disabilities Act, Family and Medical Leave Act, Wage and Hour Law, NLRB cases and Collective Bargaining, Unemployment Benefits, Employee Privacy Rights, OSHA, Railroad Law.

MOWERY & YOUELL, LTD.

Established in 1983
425 METRO PLACE NORTH
SUITE 420
DUBLIN, OHIO 43017
Telephone: 614-764-1444
Fax: 614-760-8654
URL: http://www.mowery-youell.com
URL: http://www.lawyers.com/mowery&youell

General Trial including Federal Practice, Labor, Employment Discrimination, Sexual Harassment, Americans With Disabilities Act, Family and Medical Leave Act, Corporate, Business, Real Estate and Family Law.

FIRM PROFILE: Mowery & Youell is a boutique firm focusing its legal expertise in the areas of labor and employment, civil litigation and matrimonial law for a diverse group of businesses and individuals. The firm maintains a professional and conscientious staff ready to work as a team in order to respond to the most urgent and complex legal problems. Mowery & Youell, Ltd. is committed to personalized attorney-client relationships so as to assure prompt, efficient and effective legal services. The firm's labor and employment practice includes: representation of management and individuals in the areas of traditional labor relations (NLRB union elections and contract negotiations), employee benefits, ERISA, wrongful discharge, discrimination, wage and hour, human resources and tort actions.

MEMBERS OF FIRM

JAMES S. MOWERY, JR., born Circleville, Ohio, May 25, 1948; admitted to bar, 1973, Ohio and U.S. District Court, Southern and Northern Districts of Ohio; U.S. Court of Appeals, Sixth Circuit. *Education:* Ohio Wesleyan University (B.A., 1970); Harvard University; Capital University (J.D., 1973). Phi Alpha Delta. Member, Order of the Curia. Member, Robert M. Duncan Inns of Court. Member, Board of Editors, Capital University Law Review, 1972-1973. Adjunct Professor, Sociology of the Law, Ohio State University, 1979-1980. Adjunct Professor, Ohio State University Law School, Employment Litigation Clinic, 1975-1977. Special Counsel, Jefferson County, Ohio, 1982—. *Member:* Columbus (Member: Family Law Committee, 1978—; Common Pleas Court Committee, 1978—; Corporate Committee, 1982—; Corporate Counsel, 1985—; Business Law, 1985—), Ohio State and American Bar Associations; The Association of Trial Lawyers of America (Member, Labor and Family Law Sections) Franklin County Trial Lawyers Association. ***PRACTICE AREAS:*** General Trial Practice; Employment Discrimination; Family Law; Divorce; Child Custody; Child Support; Real Estate. ***Email:*** jsmowery@mowery-youell.com

SPENCER M. YOUELL, born Philadelphia, Pennsylvania, January 3, 1939; admitted to bar, 1966, Texas and U.S. District Court, Southern District of Texas; 1974, Ohio; 1982, U.S. District Court, Northern District of Ohio. *Education:* University of Houston (B.B.A., 1961; J.D., 1966). Phi Alpha Delta. Chairman, Worthington Chamber of Commerce, 1991. *Member:* Columbus, Ohio State and American (Member, Labor and Employment Law Section) Bar Associations. [Capt., USAR, 1962-1969]. ***PRACTICE AREAS:*** Labor Law; Employment Discrimination Law; Business Law. ***Email:*** smyouell@mowery-youell.com

SAMUEL N. LILLARD, born Jonesboro, Arkansas, April 29, 1963; admitted to bar, 1988, Ohio; 1990, U.S. District Court, Northern and Southern Districts of Ohio and U.S. Court of Appeals, Sixth Circuit; 1992, U.S. Supreme Court. *Education:* University of Dayton (B.A., 1985); University of Cincinnati (J.D., 1988). Member: Potter Stewart Inns of Court; Columbus Second Inns of Court; Robert M. Duncan, Inns of Court. President and Trustee, Franklin County, Ohio, CASA (Court Appointed Special Advocates), 1991-1998; Trustee, Ohio CASA, 1999—. Chair, Ohio Attorney General's Committee on Ethics and Professionalism, 1992-1993. Assistant Prosecutor, Warren County, Ohio, 1988-1989. Assistant Attorney General, Ohio, 1990-1993. (Certified Specialist in Labor and Employment Law, Ohio State Bar Association). ***PRACTICE AREAS:*** Employment Law; Labor Law Litigation; Zoning Law; General Federal and State Litigation. ***Email:*** snlillard@mowery-youell.com

JUDITH E. GALEANO, born New York, N.Y., December 27, 1965; admitted to bar, 1990, Ohio and U.S. Court of Appeals, Sixth Circuit; 1991, U.S. Claims Court; 1993, U.S. District Court, Southern District of Ohio. *Education:* University of Toledo (B.A., cum laude, 1987); The Ohio State University College of Law (J.D., 1990). Phi Alpha Delta. Member, American Inns of Court. *Member:* Columbus and Ohio State Bar Associations; Women Lawyers of Franklin County. ***PRACTICE AREAS:*** General Federal and State Litigation; Employment Discrimination Litigation; Labor Law; Domestic Relations. ***Email:*** jegaleano@mowery-youell.com

ASSOCIATES

KAREN L. POLING, born North Tonawanda, New York, March 22, 1969; admitted to bar, 1998, Ohio; 2001, U.S. District Court, Southern District of Ohio. *Education:* George-

(This Listing Continued)

town University (B.S.B.A., 1991); Ohio State University (J.D., 1998). Member, Managing Board, The Ohio State University Law Journal, 1996-1998. *Member:* Columbus, Ohio State and American Bar Associations. ***PRACTICE AREAS:*** Employment Law; Domestic Relations. ***Email:*** klpoling@mowery-youell.com

ELIZABETH J. BIRCH, born Cleveland Ohio, October 28, 1963; admitted to bar, 1989, Ohio. *Education:* Kent State University (B.S., 1986); Case Western Reserve University (J.D., 1989). Former General Counsel, The Ohio Manufactured Housing Association. Former Assistant Attorney General, State of Ohio, Employment Law Defense. Member: National Manufactured Housing Attorney's Network; National Manufactured Housing Institute Lawyers Committee. ***PRACTICE AREAS:*** Housing Law; Zoning Law; Employment Law. ***Email:*** ejbirch@mowery-youell.com

DIANNE D. EINSTEIN, born Wheeling, West Virginia, May 17, 1969; admitted to bar, 1996, West Virginia; 1997, Ohio. *Education:* Kent State University (B.S., cum laude, 1991); University of Dayton School of Law (J.D., cum laude, 1996). *Member:* Ohio State and West Virginia Bar Associations. (Resident). ***PRACTICE AREAS:*** Civil Litigation; Employment Discrimination; Labor Law; Domestic Relations. ***Email:*** ddeinstein@mowery-youell.com

MERL H. WAYMAN, born Cleveland, Ohio, February 26, 1952; admitted to bar, 1983, Ohio. *Education:* Ohio University (B.A., 1974); Cleveland-Marshall College of Law (J.D., 1982). Listed, Ohio Super Lawyer, 2005. Author: "Patient Bill of Rights: The Right to Sue Your HMO," Employee Rights Quarterly, Vol. 1, No. 1, Summer 2000; "Are Small Professional Corporations Covered Under Discrimination Laws?" Lawyers Weekly USA, Issue 2003, LWUSA 185, March 17, 2003. Member, Legal Advocacy Committee, American Diabetes Association, 1999-2002. Volunteer Mediator, Franklin County Common Please Court of Ohio. *Member:* Ohio State Bar Association; National Employment Lawyers Association; Ohio Employment Lawyers Association (Member, Executive Board, 1997-2004). (Certified Specialist in Labor & Employment Law and Workers' Compensation Law, Ohio State Bar Association). ***REPORTED CASES:*** Ford Motors v. Ohio Bureau of Employment Services (1991), 59 Ohio St.3d 188; South Ridge Baptist Church v. Industrial Commission, 91 F.3d 120/3 (1990); Woodrum v. Premier Auto Glass Co. (1995), 103 Ohio App.3d 530. ***PRACTICE AREAS:*** Employment Law (60%); Employee Benefits (20%); Civil Litigation (10%); Workers Compensation (10%). ***Email:*** mwayman@mowery-youell.com

REPRESENTATIVE CLIENTS: Lord, Sullivan & Yoder; Franklin Specialty Transport, Inc.; Ameriguard; Sutphen Corp.; Sutphen Towers, Inc.; TZT Manufacturing & Contracting, Inc.; McArthur Lumber & Post, Inc.; Seiter Electric; Festival Foods; Irrigation Systems Company, Inc.; Marion Electric Motor Service, Inc.; Crane Cor Tec; Overbrook Center, EMHT; Open Technology Group, Inc.; MAPSYS; Krema Peanut Butter; Galleria Leather, Inc.; Remax Associates, Inc.; Metal Powder Components, Inc.; Kemlite-Sequentia Inc.; Everdry, Inc.; Diversco Building Services, Inc.; Quick Solutions, Inc.; S.G. Loewendick & Sons; Ohio Manufacturing Housing Association; Wheeling Brake Block, Inc.
APPROVED ATTORNEY FOR: Ohio Bar Title Insurance Co.
REFERENCES: The Huntington National Bank; BancOne of Columbus, N.A.

BARBARA A. ROUBANES

555 METRO PLACE NORTH, SUITE 575
DUBLIN, OHIO 43017
Telephone: 614-793-8113
Fax: 614-793-8957
Email: bar@roubaneslaw.com
URL: http://www.roubaneslaw.com

Personal Injury, Automobile Accidents, Products Liability, Wrongful Death.

BARBARA A. ROUBANES, born Bedford Heights, Ohio, March 9, 1969; admitted to bar, 1997, Ohio; 1998, U.S. District Court, Northern and Southern Districts of Ohio; 1999, U.S. Court of Appeals, Sixth Circuit; 2000, U.S. District Court, Eastern District of Michigan. *Education:* Otterbein College (B.A., magna cum laude, with honors, 1991); Capital University Law School (J.D., 1997). Order of the Curia. Phi Alpha Delta. Torch & Key. Member, Mortar Board. Licensed, Pilot, single engine land. *Member:* Columbus (Member, Barrister Leader Program, 1998; New Lawyers Committee, 2000-2002), Ohio State and American Bar Associations; Franklin County Trial Lawyers Association; Ohio Academy of Trial Lawyers; The Association of Trial Lawyers of America; Women Lawyers of Franklin County (President-Elect, 2002-2003). ***PRACTICE AREAS:*** Personal Injury; Wrongful Death; Negligence; Employer Intentional Tort; Products Liability; Business Litigation.

SCHULZE, HOWARD & COX

DUBLIN, OHIO
(See Marysville)

Civil Trial Practice, Personal Injury, Corporate, Commercial, Probate and Trust, Real Estate Law, Estate Planning, Contract Law, Business Law, Consumer Law.

LAW OFFICES OF NANCY L. SPONSELLER

Established in 1984
425 METRO PLACE NORTH, SUITE 640
DUBLIN, OHIO 43017
Telephone: 614-764-0423
Fax: 614-764-2486
URL: http://www.nancysponseller.com
Email: nsponseller@netwalk.com
URL: http://www.lawyers.com/nancysponseller

Franchise Law, Small Business Law, Divorce Dissolutions, Pre-Marital Agreements, Child Custody, Child Support, Family Law, Estate Planning, Wills and Probate.

(This Listing Continued)

FIRM PROFILE: I focus my practice in three areas: 1) Family Law, 2) Probate/Estate Planning and 3) Franchise/Business.

NANCY L. SPONSELLER, born Rushsylvania, Ohio, November 15, 1951; admitted to bar, 1977, Ohio; 1978, U.S. District Court, Southern District of Ohio; 1987, U.S. Supreme Court. *Education:* The Ohio State University (B.A., summa cum laude, 1974; J.D., cum laude, 1977). Member, Editorial Staff, 1975-1976 and Associate Editor, 1976-1977, Ohio State Law Journal. President, Ohio State University College of Law Alumni Association, 1990-1991. Listed in Best Lawyers In America, 1995—. Member, National Council of the Ohio State University College of Law, 1983-1998. Member, Board of Trustees, Columbus Bar Foundation, 1991-1998. *Member:* Columbus (Member: Board of Governors, 1986-1989; Committee on: Family Law) and Ohio State Bar Associations.

REPRESENTATIVE CLIENTS: Dunkin' Brands; Countrywide Home Loans, Inc.

STANDLEY LAW GROUP LLP

Established in 1994
495 METRO PLACE SOUTH, SUITE 210
DUBLIN, OHIO 43017-5319
Telephone: 614-792-5555
Telecopier: 614-792-5536
Email: lawyers@standleyllp.com
URL: http://www.standleyllp.com

Domestic and Foreign Intellectual Property Law, including Patent, Trademark, Copyright, Unfair Competition and Trade Secret Law and related Litigation, Licensing, International Trade Matters, related Antitrust, Computer and other Technology Law.

PARTNERS OF FIRM

JEFFREY S. STANDLEY, born Springfield, Ohio, January 22, 1961; admitted to bar, 1989, Michigan, U.S. District Court, Eastern District of Michigan and U.S. Court of Appeals for the Federal Circuit; 1990, Ohio and U.S. District Court, Southern District of Ohio; registered to practice before U.S. Patent and Trademark Office. *Education:* The Ohio State University (B.S.M.E., 1983); Capital University (J.D., 1988). *Member:* State Bar of Michigan; American Intellectual Property Law Association; Columbus Intellectual Property Law Association. (Managing Partner). ***SPECIAL AGENCIES:*** U.S. Patent and Trademark Office. ***PRACTICE AREAS:*** Intellectual Property Law; Intellectual Property Litigation. ***Email:*** jstandley@standleyllp.com

CAROL G. STOVSKY, born Kalamazoo, Michigan, January 9, 1960; admitted to bar, 1994, Ohio; 1995, U.S. District Court, Southern District of Ohio; registered to practice before U.S. Patent and Trademark Office. *Education:* University of Michigan (B.S., Computer Science, 1982); Michigan State University (M.S., Computer Science, 1986); The Ohio State University (J.D., 1994). *Member:* Columbus, Ohio State and American Bar Associations; Computer Law Association. ***PRACTICE AREAS:*** Intellectual Property Law; Computer Law. ***Email:*** cstovsky@stanleyllp.com

JAMES L. KWAK, born Cleveland, Ohio, December 10, 1969; admitted to bar, 1996, Ohio; registered to practice before U.S. Patent and Trademark Office. *Education:* Purdue University (B.S.E.E., 1991); The Ohio State University (J.D., 1996). *Member:* Ohio State (Member, Committee on Computer Law) and American Bar Associations; Columbus Intellectual Property Law Association. ***SPECIAL AGENCIES:*** U.S. Patent and Trademark Office. ***PRACTICE AREAS:*** Patents; Trademarks; Copyrights; Computer Law; Telecommunications. ***Email:*** jkwak@standleyllp.com

JEFFREY C. NORRIS, born Kettering, Ohio, August 7, 1969; admitted to bar, 1996, Ohio; 1997, U.S. District Court, Southern District of Ohio; registered to practice before U.S. Patent and Trademark Office. *Education:* Purdue University (B.S.E.E., 1993); University of Dayton (J.D., 1996). *Member:* Ohio State Bar Association; American Intellectual Property Law Association; Columbus Intellectual Property Law Association. ***PRACTICE AREAS:*** Patents; Copyrights; Trademarks. ***Email:*** jnorris@standleyllp.com

ERIC M. GAYAN, born Youngstown, Ohio, June 3, 1966; admitted to bar, 1998, Ohio; registered to practice before U.S. Patent and Trademark Office. *Education:* Youngstown State University (B.S.M.E., 1990); Capital University (J.D., cum laude, 1998). *Member:* Columbus, Ohio State and American Bar Associations; American Intellectual Property Law Association; Columbus INtellectual Property Law Association. ***SPECIAL AGENCIES:*** U.S. Patent and Trademark Office. ***PRACTICE AREAS:*** Patents; Trademarks; Copyrights. ***Email:*** egayan@standleyllp.com

CHERYL S. SCOTNEY, born Grand Haven, Michigan, September 15, 1954; admitted to bar, 1998, Ohio; registered to practice before U.S. Patent and Trademark Office. *Education:* Ball State University (B.S., Chemistry, 1976); Capital University Law School (J.D., 1998; Governmental Affairs Certificate). *Member:* Ohio State (Member, Intellectual Property Law Section) and American Bar Associations; American Intellectual Property Law Association; Columbus Intellectual Property Law Association. ***SPECIAL AGENCIES:*** U.S. Patent and Trademark Office. ***PRACTICE AREAS:*** Patents; Trademarks; Copyrights. ***Email:*** cscotney@standleyllp.com

F. MICHAEL SPEED, JR., born Houston, Texas, September 20, 1965; admitted to bar, 1995, Texas; 1997, Ohio and U.S. District Court, Southern District of Ohio. *Education:* Texas A & M University (B.S., Industrial Engineering, 1988); University of Alabama (M.S.E., Industrial Engineering, 1989; Ph.D., 1993); The Ohio State University (J.D., 1995). Professor, Statistics, Texas A & M University. Manufacturing Engineer, U.S. Air Force. *Member:* Ohio State and American Bar Associations; State Bar of Texas. ***PRACTICE AREAS:*** Intellectual Property. ***Email:*** mspeed@standleyllp.com

STEPHEN L. GRANT, born Vicksburg, Mississippi, June 14, 1953; admitted to bar, 1988, Ohio, U.S. District Court, Northern District of Ohio and U.S. Court of Appeals for the Federal Circuit; registered to practice before U.S. Patent and Trademark Office. *Education:* The Ohio State University (B.S.Ch.E., 1975); University of Akron (J.D., cum laude, 1988). Adjunct Professor, University of Akron Law School. *Member:* Columbus and Ohio State

(This Listing Continued)

STANDLEY LAW GROUP LLP, Dublin—Continued

Bar Associations; Cleveland Intellectual Property Law Association; Columbus Intellectual Property Law Association. ***LANGUAGES:*** German. ***PRACTICE AREAS:*** Patents; Trademarks; Copyrights. ***Email:*** sgrant@standleyllp.com

MICHAEL R. STONEBROOK, born Canton, Ohio, November 1, 1972; admitted to bar, 2002, Ohio; 2003, U.S. District Court, Southern District of Ohio; registered to practice before the U.S. Patent and Trademark Office. *Education:* University of Akron (B.S., Chem. Eng., 1997); Capital University (J.D., 2002). *Member:* Ohio State and American Bar Associations. ***SPECIAL AGENCIES:*** U.S. Patent and Trademark Office. ***PRACTICE AREAS:*** Intellectual Property; Intellectual Property Litigation. ***Email:*** mstonebrook@ standleyllp.com

WESLY A. ALIG, born Dayton, Ohio, February 10, 1977; admitted to bar, 2002, Ohio; registered to practice before the U.S. Patent and Trademark Office. *Education:* Ashland University (B.S., Management Information Systems/Computer Science, 1999); University of Dayton (J.D., 2002). *Member:* Ohio State Bar Association; Columbus Intellectual Property Law Association. ***PRACTICE AREAS:*** Intellectual Property; Patents; Trademarks; Copyrights. ***Email:*** walig@standleyllp.com

OF COUNSEL

MICHAEL R. SZOLOSI, JR., born Columbus, Ohio, May 21, 1969; admitted to bar, 1995, Ohio; 1996, U.S. District Court, Southern District of Ohio; registered to practice before U.S. Patent and Trademark Office. *Education:* GMI Engineering and Management Institute (B.S.M.E., 1992); University of Dayton (J.D., 1995). *Member:* Columbus, Ohio State and American Bar Associations; American Society of Mechanical Engineers; Columbus Intellectual Property Law Association; American Intellectual Property Law Association. ***PRACTICE AREAS:*** Intellectual Property Litigation; Intellectual Property Licensing; Intellectual Property. ***Email:*** mszolosi@standleyllp.com

THOMAS LAW GROUP

Established in 1988

5148 BLAZER PARKWAY, SUITE A

DUBLIN, OHIO 43017

Telephone: 614-761-7701

Fax: 614-761-7703

Email: cstrehl@thomaslawgroup.com

URL: http://www.thomas-lawgroup.com

Family Law, Divorce, Child Custody, Child Support, Visitation Rights, Business Litigation, Corporate, Small Business Law, Business Formation, Partnerships, Limited Liability Companies, Buying and Selling of Businesses, Contracts, Personal Injury, Automobile Accidents, Wrongful Death, Medical Malpractice, Estate Planning, Wills and Probate, Trusts and Estates, Estate Administration.

MEMBER OF FIRM

TERRY L. THOMAS, admitted to bar, 1985, Ohio; U.S. District Court, Southern District of Ohio. *Education:* University of Cincinnati (B.S., Zoology, 1969); Ohio State University College of Dentistry (D.D.S., 1973); Capital University (J.D., cum laude, 1985). Order of the Curia. Guest Lecturer, Professional Negligence and Professional Licensing Board Enforcement Issues, Ohio State University College of Dentistry, 1988—. *Member:* Columbus Bar Association (Member, Family Law Committee). ***PRACTICE AREAS:*** Family Law; Domestic Relations; Divorce; Child Custody; Child Support; Business Formation; Business Organization; Personal Injury; Wrongful Death; Civil Litigation. ***Email:*** tthomas@thomaslawgroup.com

ASSOCIATE

CHRISTINE E. STREHL, born Pittsburgh, Pennsylvania, January 27, 1972; admitted to bar, 2004, Ohio; 2005, U.S. District Court, Southern District of Ohio. *Education:* Ohio University (B.A., summa cum laude, 1995); The Ohio State University (J.D., 2003). Public Service Fellow. *Member:* Columbus and Ohio State Bar Associations. ***PRACTICE AREAS:*** Domestic Relations; Bankruptcy; Personal Injury; Business Formation and Representation. ***Email:*** cstrehl@thomaslawgroup.com

OF COUNSEL

CHERYL H. DeVORE, born Dayton, Ohio, May 2, 1956; admitted to bar, 1991, Ohio. *Education:* The Ohio State University (B.S., Certificate in Dental Hygiene, 1978; M.S., 1986); Capital University (J.D., 1991). Order of the Curia National Honorary Legal Fraternity, 1991. Listed in Who's Who Among American Law Students, 1990. *Member:* Columbus (Member, Lawyers for Justice and Probate Law Committee), Ohio State and American Bar Associations; American Dental Education Association (Member, Legal Issues Special Interest Group). ***PRACTICE AREAS:*** Business Law; Contracts; Probate; Trusts and Estates; Estate Planning; Business Formation; Small Business Law. ***Email:*** cdevore@ thomasdevore.com

WRIGHT LAW CO. LPA

BRICKSTONE COMMONS

4266 TULLER ROAD, SUITE 101

DUBLIN, OHIO 43017-5027

Telephone: 614-791-9112

Fax: 614-791-9116

URL: http://www.lawyers.com/wright-lawco

Email: law@wright-law.net

URL: http://www.wright-law.net

Agricultural Law, Business Planning, Estate Administration, Estate Planning, Real Estate, Tax, Litigation.

(This Listing Continued)

PAUL L. WRIGHT, born Coshocton County, Ohio, August 20, 1938; admitted to bar, 1978, Ohio; 1989, U.S. District Court, Southern District of Ohio; 1997, U.S. Tax Court; 1999, U.S. Court of Appeals, Sixth Circuit;. *Education:* Ohio State University (B.S., 1960; M.S., 1970); University of Toledo (J.D., 1978). ***Email:*** plwright@wright-law.net

JAMES K. LEONARD, born Lima, Ohio, January 2, 1948; admitted to bar, 1978, Illinois (inactive); 1987, Ohio. *Education:* Princeton University (A.B., 1970); University of Denver (J.D., 1978). ***Email:*** jleonard@wright-law.net

KIMBERLY M. CUTLER, born August 2, 1978; admitted to bar, 2002, Ohio. *Education:* Ohio University (B.B.A., 1999); Capital University (J.D., 2002); Capital University (LL. M., 2003). ***Email:*** kcutler@wright-law.net

DAVID S. PENNINGTON, born December 21, 1952; admitted to bar, 1983, Ohio and U.S. Court of Appeals for the Armed Forces; 1987, Nevada and U.S. District Court, 9th Circuit. *Education:* University of Washington (B.A., 1979); Ohio State University (J.D., 1982; M.H.A., 1983). ***Email:*** dpennington@wright-law.net

BIESER, GREER & LANDIS, LLP

EATON, OHIO

(See Dayton)

General Civil Practice, Trial Practice, Business Litigation, Professional Liability Defense, Personal Injury Defense, Products Liability Defense, Corporate Law, Employment Law, Commercial Law, Probate, Tax Law, White Collar Criminal Defense, Arbitration, Mediation.

THE THOMAS LAW OFFICE

112 NORTH BARRON STREET

EATON, OHIO 45320

Telephone: 937-456-4103

Fax: 937-456-2960

Email: jthomaslaw@yahoo.com

URL: http://www.jthomaslaw.com

General Trial and Appellate Practice, Real Estate, Criminal Law including D.U.I. and Defense of Drug Cases, Domestic Relations, Personal Injury, Wrongful Death, Probate, Estate Planning, Construction Defects, Mechanics Liens, Breach of Contract, Corporate Law, Creditors Rights, Family Law, Automobile Insurance, Automobile Accidents, Wills.

JAMES W. THOMAS, born New York, New York, May 12, 1949; admitted to bar, 1974, Ohio; 1976, U.S. District Court, Southern District of Ohio. *Education:* University of Dayton (B.S., 1971); Ohio Northern University (J.D., 1974). Phi Alpha Delta. Listed in Who's Who In American Law, 1984—. Solicitor: Lewisburg, Ohio, 1977-1981; Verona, Ohio, 1979-1981. President, Rotary International, Eaton, Ohio, 1987-1988. Member, Board of Trustees, Eaton High School Academic Boosters Group, 1993. Agent, Ohio Bar Title Insurance Company. *Member:* Preble County (President, 1982-1984; Member, Board of Trustees, 1977-1984), Ohio State (Board of Governors, Solo, Small Firm and General Practice Section) and American Bar Associations; Ohio Association of Criminal Defense Lawyers. Fellow, Ohio State Bar Foundation. ***PRACTICE AREAS:*** Criminal Defense; Driving While Intoxicated; Personal Injury; Family Law; Real Estate; Probate Law.

JAMES W. THOMAS, JR., born Dayton, Ohio, 1976; admitted to bar, 2001, Ohio. *Education:* University of Dayton (B.A., 1998); Ohio Northern University (J.D., with distinction, 2001). *Member:* Preble County (Treasurer, 2005) and Ohio State Bar Associations. ***PRACTICE AREAS:*** Criminal Defense; Domestic Relations; Probate; Civil Practice.

JASON T. BAKER

ELYRIA, OHIO

(See Cleveland)

Bankruptcy, Criminal Law, DUI, Drug Crimes, Traffic Violations, Divorce, Probate, Wills, Child Custody, Child Support.

FAUVER, KEYSE-WALKER & DONOVAN

A LEGAL PROFESSIONAL ASSOCIATION

5333 MEADOW LANE COURT

ELYRIA, OHIO 44035-1469

Telephone: 440-934-3700

Telefax: 440-934-3708

URL: http://www.fkwdlaw.com

General Civil Practice. Trials and Appeals, Business Organizations, Acquisitions, Education, Probate and Estate Planning, Insurance, Taxation, Real Estate, Commercial, Employment Relations.

FIRM PROFILE: Fauver, Keyse-Walker & Donovan, a Legal Professional Association, has been serving clients in Lorain County and throughout Ohio for more than a century. We provide our clients with the highest quality legal advice and representation, combining legal expertise, personalized attention and timely and clear communication. We offer a wide variety of services to meet the needs of individuals, businesses, non-profit and tax-exempt organizations, and government entities. Our firm's services are grouped into three general areas of practice: Business Law, Civil Litigation and Estate Planning and Probate.

RETIRED PARTNER

WORTH A. FAUVER, JR., born Elyria, Ohio, April 30, 1935; admitted to bar, 1963, Ohio. *Education:* Amherst College (A.B., 1958); Western Reserve University (LL.B., 1963). Associate Editor, Western Reserve Law Review, 1962-1963. Law Director, North

(This Listing Continued)

Ridgeville, 1972-1973. *Member:* Lorain County, Ohio State and American Bar Associations. **PRACTICE AREAS:** Estate Planning Law; Probate Law; Business Organizations Law. **Email:** wfauver@fkwdlaw.com

MEMBERS OF FIRM

JOHN L. KEYSE-WALKER, born Berea, Ohio, January 2, 1956; admitted to bar, 1981, Ohio; 1983, U.S. District Court, Northern District of Ohio; 1992, U.S. Court of Appeals, Sixth Circuit. *Education:* College of Wooster (B.A., 1978); Duke University (J.D., 1981). Phi Beta Kappa. *Member:* Lorain County (Member, Executive Committee, 1992-1999; President, 1997-1998) and Ohio State Bar Associations. **PRACTICE AREAS:** Business Litigation; Commercial Litigation; Real Estate Law; Employment Relations Law; School Law. **Email:** jkeyse-walker@fkwdlaw.com

KEVIN WM. DONOVAN, born Winchester, Massachusetts, February 5, 1948; admitted to bar, 1973, Massachusetts; 1974, U.S. Court Military Appeals; 1980, Ohio, U.S. District Court, Northern District of Ohio and U.S. Tax Court; 1985, Colorado. *Education:* University of Massachusetts (B.A., cum laude, 1970); Boston University (J.D., 1973). Phi Beta Kappa. Assistant Professor of Law, USAF Academy, 1977-1979. *Member:* Lorain County (Executive Committee, 1998—; President, 2003-2004), Ohio State (Corporate Counsel Section, Board of Governors, 1995—; Chairman, 1999-2001) and American Bar Associations. [Captain, Judge Advocate, USAF, 1974-1979]. **PRACTICE AREAS:** Business Organizations Law; Business Acquisition Law; Tax Exempt Organization Law. **Email:** kdonovan@fkwdlaw.com

KURT D. ANDERSON, born Springfield, Ohio, August 18, 1965; admitted to bar, 1990, Ohio; 1991, U.S. District Court, Northern District of Ohio; 1992, U.S. Court of Appeals, Sixth Circuit; 1999, U.S. Supreme Court; 2003, U.S. District Court, Southern District of Ohio. *Education:* Cedarville College (B.A.,cum laude, 1987); Case Western Reserve University (J.D., 1990). Recipient, Distinguished Advocate Award, Case Western Reserve University. *Member:* Lorain County (Chairman: Community Relations Committee, 1998-2002; Bench Bar Committee, 2002—), Ohio State (Member, Board of Governors, Young Lawyers Section, 1994-1995) and American (Member, Litigation and Council of Appellate Lawyers Section) Bar Associations; Ohio Association of Civil Trial Attorneys (Member, Board of Trustees, 2005—). **LANGUAGES:** Portuguese. **PRACTICE AREAS:** Casualty Insurance Law; Creditors Rights; Contract Litigation; Civil Liberties Litigation; Appellate Practice. **Email:** kanderson@fkwdlaw.com

STEPHEN P. CHAVEZ, born Elyria, Ohio, March 14, 1964; admitted to bar, 1995, Ohio; 1996, U.S. District Court, Northern District of Ohio. *Education:* Kent State University (B.B.A., cum laude, 1988); University of Akron Law School (J.D., 1994); University of Florida (LL.M. in Taxation, 1995). Certified Public Accountant, 1990. *Member:* Lorain County, Ohio State and American Bar Associations. **PRACTICE AREAS:** Business Organization; Taxation; Estate Planning; Probate. **Email:** schavez@fkwdlaw.com

ASSOCIATES

BRETT D. WIEBER, born Sandusky, Ohio, December 20, 1975; admitted to bar, 2001, Ohio. *Education:* Bowling Green State University (B.A., cum laude, 1998); Akron University Law School (J.D., 2001). Recipient, Runner Up Best Oralist Jessup Moot Court, 2000. **PRACTICE AREAS:** Corporate Law; Business Law. **Email:** bwieber@fkwdlaw.com

HOWARD T. LANE, born Toledo, Ohio, August 8, 1967; admitted to bar, 1993, Ohio; 1997, U.S. District Court, Northern District of Ohio and U.S. Court of Appeals, Sixth Circuit. *Education:* Ohio Wesleyan University (B.A., 1990); Cleveland-Marshall College of Law (J.D., 1993). Assistant Law Director, City of Canton, 1998-1999. Assistant Prosecuting Attorney, Stark County, 1999-2002. *Member:* Lorain County and Ohio State Bar Associations. **PRACTICE AREAS:** Commercial Litigation; Creditors Rights; Landlord and Tenant Law. **Email:** hlane@fkwdlaw.com

KRISTINA M. KING, born Defiance, Ohio, June 18, 1975; admitted to bar, 2001, Ohio. *Education:* The Ohio State University (B.A., 1997); Cleveland-Marshall College of Law (J.D., 2000). *Member:* Lorain County and Ohio State Bar Associations. **PRACTICE AREAS:** Estate Planning; Probate Administration. **Email:** kking@fkwdlaw.com

ROBERT C. WHITE, born Willard, Ohio, September 28, 1959; admitted to bar, 1991, Ohio and U.S. District Court, Northern District of Ohio; 1997, U.S. Court of Appeals, Sixth Circuit. *Education:* Cleveland State University (B.A., 1987); Cleveland Marshall College of Law (J.D., 1991). Psi Chi. Member: Order of the Barristers. Member, Moot Court Board of Governors. Recipient: Law Alumni Association Brief Writing Award; Dean's Scholar Award. Carlisle Township Trustee, 2004—. Board of Directors, EMH Regional Medical Center, 2000—. Board of Trustees, Rural Lorain County Water Authority, 2004—. *Member:* Cleveland (Member, Corporation, Banking and Business Law Section; Labor Law Section), Lorain County and Ohio State Bar Associations. **PRACTICE AREAS:** Business Law; Labor and Employment; Workers Compensation. **Email:** rwhite@fkwdlaw.com

GENERAL COUNSEL FOR: Animal Protective League of Lorain County; A-1 Welding & Fabricating, Inc.; Freeman Manufacturing & Supply Co.; Lake Ridge Academy; Sommer's Mobile Leasing, Inc.; Modular Bulding Consultants; Village Reserve Corp.; Firelands Floors Inc.; Carpet & Tile Liquidators; Master Benefits Agency, Inc.; New Beginnings Pediatric, Inc.; Lorain County Printing & Publishing Co. (Elyria Chronicle-Telegram); Medina County Publications, Inc. (Medina County Gazette); Elyria-Lorain Broadcasting Co.; R.W. Beckett Corp.; Pikewood Manor, Inc. (Mobile Home Park); Amherst Mobile Home Park, Inc.; Amherst Village Mobile Home Park; Harbourtown Mobile Home Park; Elyria United Methodist Village; Norlake Manufacturing Co.; Mel-Ba Manufacturing, Inc.; Sliman Sales & Services, Inc.; Elyria City Board of Education; Elyria Country Club; Lorain County Title Co.; The Ridge Lumber Co.; Del Lumber Co.; United Circuits, Inc.; Circuit Solutions, Inc.; Capital Hill Development Co.; WOBL Radio, Inc.; WDLW Radio, Inc.; West Ridge Green; Rock Creek Aluminum Co.; Morris Pontiac-GMC, Inc.; Puritas Metal Products; Rhenium Alloys.

LOCAL COUNSEL FOR: Western Surety Co.; Auto-Owners Insurance; American Mutual Group; Commonwealth Title Insurance; LandAmerica Lawyers Title Insurance; Prudential Insurance Company of America; Merrill Lynch Interfunding, Inc.; Parker Hannifin Corp.; Wickes Lumber Co.; Chicago Title Insurance Company; Estes Express Lines; Sentry Insurance; TIG Insurance; OBLIC; All-American Sports (Riddell).

MARK GARDNER
ATTORNEY AND COUNSELOR AT LAW

ELYRIA, OHIO

(See Cleveland)

Criminal Law, Driving While Intoxicated, Traffic Violations, Personal Injury, Wrongful Death, Negligence, Slip and Fall, Small Business Law, Litigation.

KNEVEL & ASSOCIATES CO. LPA

ELYRIA, OHIO

(See Cleveland)

Bankruptcy.

MARILU LAUBENTHAL

Established in 1982

LAWYERS' LOFT
633 W. BROAD STREET, SUITE 200
ELYRIA, OHIO 44035
Telephone: 440-322-5505
Fax: 440-322-5509
Email: mlaubenthalesq@yahoo.com

Criminal Law, Estate Planning, Real Estate, Mediation.

FIRM PROFILE: Criminal defense, estate planning, real estate, mediation.

MARILU LAUBENTHAL, born Elyria, Ohio, November 29, 1944; admitted to bar, 1982, Ohio. *Education:* Baldwin-Wallace College (B.A., 1975); Cleveland Marshall College of Law (J.D., 1982). Phi Sigma Tau; Lambda Iota Tau; Phi Alpha Theta; Delta Theta Phi. Professional Fellow, Case-Weatherhead School of Business, 1994. Acting Judge, Avon Lake Municipal Court, 2002—. *Member:* Greater Cleveland, Lorain County (Chair, Criminal Section), Ohio State and American Bar Associations; The Association of Trial Lawyers of America. **PRACTICE AREAS:** Criminal Law; Estate Planning; Real Estate; Mediation.

LAW OFFICES OF
ROBERT E. LESSING, JR.

A LEGAL PROFESSIONAL ASSOCIATION

374 BROAD STREET, SUITE 1
ELYRIA, OHIO 44035
Telephone: 440-322-5441
Fax: 440-323-5393
Email: lesslaw@less-law.com
URL: http://www.lawyers.com/less-law

Grafton, Ohio Office: 943 Main Street, 44044. Telephone: 440-926-3818

Estate Planning, Asset Protection, Tax Planning, Guardianship, Trusts and Estates, Estate and Trust Administration, Wills and Probate, Elder Law, Small Business, Closely Held Business, LLC or Limited Liability Companies; Real Estate, Buying or Selling Home or Business; Partnerships, Business Start-Ups, Immigration.

FIRM PROFILE: Our mission is to deliver quality, ethical legal services to our clients consistent with their needs and expectations in a caring, timely and efficient manner at a reasonable cost.

ROBERT E. LESSING, JR., born Akron, Ohio, January 30, 1944; admitted to bar, 1969, Ohio. *Education:* Capital University (B.A., 1966); Valparaiso University School of Law (J.D., 1969). Recipient, Awards, Elyria Jaycees Distinguished Service Award; Who's Who in the Midwest. Recognized: Outstanding Young Men of America; Elyria Jaycees-JCI Senator; Chicago Tribune Medal of Honor. Attorney and Senior Partner at Lessing, White & Roig, Ltd. With: West, West & Sherman, Attorneys at Law, Elyria, Ohio; National City Bank, Cleveland, Ohio. Office of Counsel and the Trust Department. Member: Grafton-Midview Public Library (Board of Trustees, President for 5 terms); Vocational Guidance Services-Elyria Council, 1984—; Midview Endowment Fund (President for six terms); Eaton Township Zoning Commission (Chairman for three terms); Grafton Advisory Council for Prisons; Family Planning Services (President for two terms); Taxpayers' Committee of Eaton Township (Chairman for two terms); Kiwanis Club of Grafton-Midview; United Health Foundation (President for two terms); Elyria Board of Zoning Appeals (Chairman for two terms); Citizens Committee for Elyria Schools (Chairman); Elyria Precinct Committeeperson; Elyria Area League of Women Voters (First Male Member); Elyria Town Meeting-National Bicentennial (Chairman); Elyria Citizens for Education (Co-Chairman); and Elyria Jaycees (President 1975-1976). *Member:* Cleveland, Lorain County and Ohio State Bar Associations. **PRACTICE AREAS:** Estate Planning; Asset Protection; Tax Planning; Guardianship; Trusts and Estates; Estate Administration; Trust Administration; Wills; Probate; Elder Law; Small Business; Closely Held Business; Limited Liability Company Law; Real Estate; Buying and Selling of Homes; Buying and Selling of Businesses; Partnership Law; Business Start-Ups. **Email:** blessing@less-law.com

ASSOCIATE

ANDREA C. KRYSZAK, born Cheektowaga, New York, June 23, 1970; admitted to bar, 2003, Ohio. *Education:* State University of New York at Buffalo (B.S., 1992); Cleveland-Marshall College of Law (J.D., Magna Cum Laude, 2003). Associate, Lessing, White & Roig Ltd., Attorneys at Law. District Adjudications Officer, U.S. Immigration & Naturalization Service, Cleveland, Ohio. Immigration Inspector, U.S. Immigration and Natural-

(This Listing Continued)

LAW OFFICES OF ROBERT E. LESSING, JR. , A LEGAL PROFESSIONAL ASSOCIATION, Elyria—Continued

ization Service, Buffalo, New York. Co-Chairman, Women's Fund of The Community Foundation of Greater Lorain County. Board Member, New Riverbend Homes, Elyria, Ohio. Leadership, Lorain County's Leadership Society; Leadership Lorain County Alumni, 2005. Member, Alzheimer's Association. *Member:* Cleveland, Lorain County and Ohio State Bar Associations; The National Academy of Elder Law Attorneys, Inc. ***LANGUAGES:*** Spanish. ***PRACTICE AREAS:*** Estate Planning; Asset Protection; Tax Planning; Guardianship; Trusts and Estates; Estate Administration; Trust Administration; Wills; Probate; Elder Law; Immigration; Real Estate; Buying and Selling of Homes; Buying and Selling of Businesses; Small Business; Closely Held Business; Limited Liability Company Law; Partnership Law; Business Start-Ups. ***Email:*** akryszak@less-law.com

Languages: Spanish.

McCRAY, MUZILLA, SMITH & MEYERS CO., L.P.A.

260 BURNS ROAD, SUITE 150
ELYRIA, OHIO 44035
Telephone: 440-366-9930
Fax: 440-366-1910

General Civil Practice, Corporate, Personal Injury, Medical Malpractice, Probate and Estate Planning, Labor and Employment, Government, Real Estate, Insurance Defense, Health, Tax, Civil Litigation, Product Liability, Communications and Copyright Issues and Environment. Trial and Appellate Practice in all Courts.

THOMAS J. SMITH, born Elyria, Ohio, November 29, 1941; admitted to bar, 1966, Ohio. *Education:* Ohio University (B.S.C., 1963); The Ohio State University (J.D., 1966). Law Director, City of Avon, 1980-1989. Member: Leadership Lorain County Board, 1986-1992; Elyria Memorial Hospital Foundation Board, 1987-1998; Lorain Community College Foundation, Board of Trustees, 1987— and Community Health Partners Hospital, Board of Trustees, 2001—. *Member:* Cleveland, Lorain County, Ohio State and American Bar Associations. ***PRACTICE AREAS:*** Corporate Law; Real Estate Law; Zoning Law; Land Development; Civil Litigation; Health Law; Municipal Law. ***Email:*** tsmith@mmsmlaw.com

KIM R. MEYERS, born Lorain, Ohio, December 11, 1956; admitted to bar, 1984, Ohio; 1986, Arizona; 1991, District of Columbia; 1994, U.S. Supreme Court. *Education:* Arizona State University (B.A., 1980); University of Dayton (J.D., 1984). *Member:* Lorain County (Leadership, 1992—), Cuyahoga County, Ohio State and American Bar Associations; State Bar of Arizona; District of Columbia Bar; The Association of Trial Lawyers of America; The Ohio Trial Lawyers Association; Cleveland Academy of Trial Attorneys. ***PRACTICE AREAS:*** Personal Injury; Wrongful Death; Medical Malpractice; Civil Litigation; Insurance Law; Education Law. ***Email:*** kmeyers@mmsmlaw.com

THOMAS A. MUZILLA, born Lorain, Ohio, April 18, 1960; admitted to bar, 1986, Ohio; 1987, Illinois; 1992, U.S. District Court, Northern District of Ohio and U.S. Court of Appeals, Sixth Circuit; 1994, U.S. Supreme Court. *Education:* Ohio State University (B.S., 1982); Case Western Reserve University (J.D., 1986). Law Clerk to the Honorable Robert B. Krupansky, U.S. Court of Appeals, Sixth Circuit, 1988-1990. *Member:* Lorain County and Ohio Bar Associations; The Ohio Trial Lawyers Association. ***PRACTICE AREAS:*** Business Litigation; Labor and Employment; Product Liability. ***Email:*** tmuzilla@mmsmlaw.com

PAUL E. BLEVINS, born Oberlin, Ohio, September 10, 1965; admitted to bar, 1992, California; 1993, Ohio and U.S. District Court, Central District of California; 1997, U.S. District Court, Northern District of Ohio; 2001, U.S. Court of Appeals, Sixth Circuit. *Education:* Dartmouth College (A.B., cum laude, 1988); University of California at Los Angeles (J.D., 1992). Councilman, City of Elyria, 1999—. *Member:* Lorain County and Ohio State Bar Associations; State Bar of California. ***PRACTICE AREAS:*** Civil Litigation; Real Estate Development; Construction Law; Local Government; Municipal Law; School Law. ***Email:*** pblevins@mmsmlaw.com

PAULA A. KUHN, born Elyria, Ohio, December 14, 1959; admitted to bar, 1999, Ohio; 2001, U.S. District Court, Northern District of Ohio and U.S. Tax Court. *Education:* Ohio State University (B.S.B.A., Accounting and Finance, 1983); Cleveland-Marshall College of Law (J.D., summa cum laude, 1999). Member, Cleveland-Marshall Law Review, 1997-1999. Certified Public Accountant, Ohio, 1996. *Member:* Lorain County and Ohio State Bar Associations; Ohio Society of Certified Public Accountants; American Institute of Certified Public Accountants. ***PRACTICE AREAS:*** Estate Planning; Probate Law; Corporate Law; Civil Litigation; Tax Law. ***Email:*** pkuhn@mmsmlaw.com

LISA JANE McGUIRE, born Olmsted Falls, Ohio, July 6, 1968; admitted to bar, 2001, Ohio; 2004, U.S. District Court, Northern District of Ohio. *Education:* Cleveland State University (B.A., cum laude, 1997); Akron University Law School (J.D., magna cum laude, 2001). Member, Akron Law Review, 1999-2001. Law Clerk to the Honorable William R. Baird, Ninth District Court of Appeals of Ohio, 2001-2003. *Member:* Lorain County, Ohio State and American Bar Associations. ***PRACTICE AREAS:*** Civil Litigation; Corporate Law. ***Email:*** lmcguire@mmsmlaw.com

OF COUNSEL

J. WILLIAM McCRAY, born Pickaway County, Ohio, May 26, 1925; admitted to bar, 1950, Ohio; 1962, U.S. Supreme Court. *Education:* University of North Carolina, The Ohio State University and Ohio Wesleyan University (B.A., with honors, 1947, Phi Beta Kappa); University of Michigan (J.D., with honors, 1950). *Member:* Lorain County and Ohio State Bar Associations; Ohio Trial Lawyers Association; Defense Research and Trial Lawyers Association. ***PRACTICE AREAS:*** Civil Litigation.

(This Listing Continued)

RAYMOND A. MUZILLA, born Lorain, Ohio, November 13, 1932; admitted to bar, 1958, Ohio; 1965, U.S. Supreme Court. *Education:* Bowling Green State University (B.S.B.A., 1954); Harvard University (J.D., 1957). *Member:* Lorain County, Ohio State and American Bar Associations. ***PRACTICE AREAS:*** Corporate Law; Probate Law; Estate Planning Law; Civil Litigation. ***Email:*** rmuzilla@mmsmlaw.com

LOCAL COUNSEL FOR: The Richard E. Jacobs Group; Forest City Land Group; Browning Industries of Ohio, Inc.; KTM Sportmotorcycle AG; Emerge, Inc.; Progressive Processing, Inc.; KTM North America, Inc.; Girl Scouts of Erie Shores; Neighborhood House Association of Lorain County; American Hood Systems, Inc.; Wellington Exempted Village School District; Wellington Fire District; Sylvester Builders, Inc.; Mel-ba Manufacturing, Inc.; Nordson Corp.
GENERAL COUNSEL FOR: NorthCoast Building Industry Association; Moreland Homes, Inc.; All-Purpose Construction, Inc.; Lorain County.Com, Inc.; Lorain County Regional Airport Authority.

DAVID A. MYERS

374 BROAD STREET, SUITE 2
ELYRIA, OHIO 44035-5504
Telephone: 440-323-1111
Fax: 440-323-4284
Email: myers@aginglaw.com
URL: http://www.aginglaw.com

Elder Law.

DAVID A. MYERS, born Elyria, Ohio, October 25, 1948; admitted to bar, 1973, Ohio; 1980, U.S. Supreme Court. *Education:* John Carroll University (A.B., magna cum laude, 1970); Catholic University of America (J.D., 1973). Certified Elder Law Attorney by the National Elder Law Foundation. Member, Boards of Trustees, Lorain County Office on Aging and Long Term Care Ombudsman's Office. *Member:* Lorain County and Ohio State Bar Associations; National Academy of Elder Law Attorneys; Alzheimer's Association. ***PRACTICE AREAS:*** Elder Law (100%).

A. DALE NATICCHIA

ELYRIA, OHIO

(See Cleveland)

Driving While Intoxicated, Traffic Violations, Juvenile Law, Drivers License Suspension, DUI, Estate Planning, Wills and Probate Law, Contested Wills, Felonies and Collections.

PAGANO, WILSON, THOMARIOS, GILLISSIE & LENAHAN LLC

ELYRIA, OHIO

(See Cleveland)

Criminal Law, Employment Defense, Personal Injury, Workers Compensation, Social Security Disability, Probate, Estate Planning, Family Law, Business Law, Collections.

ST. MARIE LAW FIRM CO., L.P.A.

Established in 1976

409 EAST AVENUE, SUITE A
ELYRIA, OHIO 44035
Telephone: 440-323-1808
FAX: 440-323-6135

General Civil and Criminal Practice. Insurance, Corporate, Foreclosure, Collections, Probate and Estate Planning, Banking Law, Real Estate, Personal Injury Law, Family/Domestic Relations. Trials and Appeals.

FIRM PROFILE: St. Marie Law Firm Co., L.P.A. was formed in 1976 and has been serving Lorain County, Ohio in the general practice of law since.

The Firm provides services in a wide range of areas to meet the increasing needs of growing local companies and our other valued clients. This is accomplished by utilizing the most modern of high tech computerized approaches to the operation of our Firm. Areas of Firm concentration includes corporate representations, criminal defense, domestic relations law and personal injury.

It is the commitment of the Firm to provide the best possible representation of our clients and to keep them ever fully informed as to the status of all pending matters. Each of the Firm members has long standing ties to the community making our Firm truly aware of local needs.

THOMAS A. ST. MARIE, born Elyria, Ohio, October 23, 1946; admitted to bar, 1975, Ohio. *Education:* Loyola University, Rome, Italy; John Carroll University (B.A., cum laude, 1968); Cleveland Marshall College of Law (J.D., 1974). Assistant City Prosecutor, City of Elyria, Ohio, 1975-1976. Member: Elyria Fair Housing Board, 1986-1996; Elyria Catholic High School Endowment Committee, 1994-1997. *Member:* Lorain County (Past President), Ohio State and American Bar Associations. [1st Lt., U.S. Army, 1969-1970]. ***LANGUAGES:*** Spanish, Italian. ***PRACTICE AREAS:*** Corporate Law; Real Estate; Contract Law; Banking Law; Probate Law; Estate Planning. ***Email:*** tstmarie@stmarielawfirm.com

PAUL R. ST. MARIE, born Elyria, Ohio, February 19, 1955; admitted to bar, 1981, Ohio. *Education:* Bowling Green State University (B.A., 1978); Cleveland Marshall College of Law (J.D., 1981). *Member:* Lorain County, Ohio State and American Bar Associations; The Association of Trial Lawyers of America. ***PRACTICE AREAS:*** Personal Injury Law; Criminal Law; Civil Practice; Civil Trial; Tort Law; Domestic Relations. ***Email:*** pstmarie@stmarielawfirm.com

MARGARET A. HENDERSHOT, born Amherst, Ohio, October 20, 1973; admitted to bar, 1998, Ohio. *Education:* Ohio Northern University (B.A., 1995); Case Western Re-

(This Listing Continued)

serve University (J.D., 1998). Order of the Coif. Case Western Reserve University Law Review. *Member:* Lorain County and Ohio State Bar Associations. ***Email:*** mhendershot@stmarielawfirm.com

ASSOCIATE COUNSEL

GARY C. BENNETT, born Elyria, Ohio, 1952; admitted to bar, 1977, Ohio. *Education:* Wittenberg University (B.A., cum laude 1974); University of Notre Dame (J.D., 1977). Prosecutor, Lorain County. Law Director, Village of LaGrange, 1981- 2004. Acting Judge and Magistrate, Elyria Municipal Court. Member and Past President, Elyria City School Board. Member, Lorain County Board of Mental Retardation and Development Disabilities. Past Chairman, Lorain County Children Services Board. *Member:* Ohio State and Lorain County Bar Associations. ***PRACTICE AREAS:*** Civil Practice; Family Law; Divorce; Alimony; Uncontested Divorce; Spousal Support; Separation Agreements; Qualified Domestic Relations Orders (QDROs); Premarital Agreements; Postnuptial Agreements; Post Divorce Modification; Paternity; Restraining Orders; Name Changes; Marital Property Distribution; Marital Property Law; Marital Property Settlements; Family Mediation; Family Arbitration; Equitable Distribution; Divorce Taxation; Divorce Mediation; Divorce Arbitration; Annulment; Government Agency Practice; Trial Practice and School Law.

REPRESENTATIVE CLIENTS: Alco Manufacturing Corp.; First Merit Bank; City of Elyria; Triad Energy Corporation; Hydro-Tube Corp.; Higgins Electric Co., Inc.; Plas Brothers Paving, Inc.; Cascade Title Agency, Ltd.
APPROVED ATTORNEYS FOR: Farmers Home Administration; Ohio Bar Title Company.
REFERENCE: First Merit Bank.

STOURTON SCOTT SMITH CO., LPA

633 WEST BROAD STREET, SUITE 200
ELYRIA, OHIO 44035
Telephone: 440-284-0101
Fax: 440-322-5509
Email: stourtonsmith@sbcglobal.net
URL: http://www.aggressivelegalrep.com

Cleveland, Ohio Office: 75 Public Square, Suite 800, 44113. Telephone: 216-344-9338. Fax: 216-344-9337.

Criminal Law, DWI, Bankruptcy, Personal Injury, Divorce, Family Law.

(For complete biographical data on all personnel, see Professional Biographies at Cleveland, Ohio)

THE SPIKE & MECKLER LAW FIRM, LLP

Established in 1970
1551 WEST RIVER ROAD NORTH
ELYRIA, OHIO 44035
Telephone: 440-324-5353
Fax: 440-324-5363
URL: http://www.spikemeckler.com

General Civil Trial Practice. Personal Injury, Medical Malpractice, Family and Domestic Relations, Real Estate, Probate.

FIRM PROFILE: Spike and Meckler was founded in 1970 by Allen S. Spike and Stephen G. Meckler. The firm provides general civil services. Within the firm, however, Allen Spike limits his practice to domestic relations and family law. Allen Spike is responsible for the Ohio landmark case of Hoyt v. Hoyt, 53 03rd 177 559 NE2d 1292, which defined qualified domestic relations orders for defined benefits plans. He is a frequent lecturer locally and statewide. He has participated on the legislative drafting and legislative review subcommittees of the Family Law Committee of the Ohio State Bar Association since 1978. Stephen Meckler practices in the area of personal injury, medical negligence and general civil litigation. The firm also handles varied other civil matters including real estate and probate. Mr. Spike is active in the state bar association and was a member of the Board of Governors which is the ruling body of the Ohio State Bar Association. Mr. Meckler was active in the state level on the Negligence Law Committee and was on the State Bar Council of Delegates. Both have been very active in the local bar association activities and both have held several offices including the presidency.

MEMBERS OF FIRM

ALLEN S. SPIKE, born Elyria, Ohio, August 6, 1939; admitted to bar, 1964, Ohio; 1967 U.S. District Court, Northern District of Ohio; 1987, U.S. Supreme Court. *Education:* The Ohio State University (B.S., Psychology, 1961); Case Western Reserve University (J.D., 1964). Recipient, Distinguished Service Award, Lorain County Bar Association. Consultant to Lawyers' Co-op Publishing. Chief Editor, 4-volume set, "Ohio Family Law and Practice". Charter Member, Center for Principaled Advocacy. *Member:* Lorain County (President, 1983; Member, Executive Committee, 1978-1986) and Ohio State (Member: Family Law Committee, 1978—; Board of Governors, 1990-1993; Legislative Drafting Subcommittee; Legislative Review Subcommittee) Bar Associations; Ohio Academy of Trial Lawyers; Association of Trial Lawyers of America; Ohio Bar Foundation. ***PRACTICE AREAS:*** Domestic Relations; Family Law.

STEPHEN G. MECKLER, born Cleveland, Ohio, September 4, 1940; admitted to bar, 1965, Ohio; 1968, U.S. District Court, Northern District of Ohio. *Education:* The Ohio State University (B.S., 1962; J.D., 1965). *Member:* Lorain County (President, 1987-1988; Chairman, 1980-1987 and Member, Ethics Committee) and Ohio State (Member: Negligence Law Committee, 1978-1980, 1990-1996; Council of Delegates, 1993-1996) Bar Associations; Ohio Academy of Trial Lawyers; The Association of Trial Lawyers of America; Cleveland Academy of Trial Attorneys. ***PRACTICE AREAS:*** Negligence Law; Medical Malpractice; Dental Malpractice; Civil Litigation; Personal Injury.

DOUGLAS M. BRILL, born Philadelphia, Pennsylvania, June 12, 1952; admitted to bar, 1978, Ohio, U.S. District Court, Northern District of Ohio; 1994, U.S. Supreme Court.

(This Listing Continued)

Education: The Ohio State University (B.A., English Literature, 1975); University of Toledo (J.D., 1978). Named one of Ohio's "Super Lawyers," 2004. Lecturer: Ohio CLE Institute, 1993—; Ohio Family Law Institute. Author: "The Ohio Parenting Act: A Proposal By the Family Law Committee of the Ohio State Bar Association," Ohio Lawyer, Vol.11 No.1, Jan-Feb. 1997. Prosecutor, Cities of Avon Lake, Avon and Sheffield Village, 1984-1989. Member, Ohio Supreme Court Task Force on Family Law and Children. Charter Member, Center for Principaled Advocacy. Certified Mediator. *Member:* Lorain County and Ohio State (Member: Family Law Committee; Legislative Drafting Subcommittee; Council of Delegates, 1996—) Bar Associations. Fellow, American Academy of Matrimonial Lawyers. (Certified Specialist in Family Relations Law, Ohio State Bar Association). ***PRACTICE AREAS:*** Domestic Relations Law (95%); Juvenile Law (5%). ***Email:*** dmbrill@mediaone.net

MICHAEL D. ILLNER, born Hamilton, Ohio, November 17, 1948; admitted to bar, 1985, Ohio. *Education:* Bowling Green State University (B.S., Education, 1972); Baldwin Wallace College (M.A., Educational Administration); Akron University Law School (J.D., 1985). Assistant Prosecuting Attorney, Lorain County, 1985-1997. Former President and Chief Negotiator, Midview Educational Association. Former Counsel, Lorain County Children's Services. Certified Mediator, Domestic Relations. *Member:* Lorain County (Member, Ethics & Grievance Committee) and Ohio State (Delegate to Council of Delegates) Bar Associations. ***PRACTICE AREAS:*** Family Law; Divorce; Dissolution; Child Custody; Parenting Time; Paternal Law; Pension Plans; Domestic Violence.

JAMES R. COUCH, born Elyria, Ohio, October 18, 1947; admitted to bar, 1975, Ohio; 1977, U.S. District Court, Northern District of Ohio. *Education:* University of Dayton (B.S., Education, 1970); Cleveland State University (J.D., 1974). Assistant County Prosecutor, 1976-1978. Member: Elyria City Board of Education, 1980-1984; Board of Directors, Commerce and Industry Association of Greater Elyria, 1979-1982; Midview Board of Education, 1992-1996; Midview Sports Hall of Fame. Past Member, Board of Directors, Elyria Sports Hall of Fame. *Member:* Lorain County and Ohio State Bar Associations. ***PRACTICE AREAS:*** Domestic Relations; Commercial Litigation; Criminal Law.

ASSOCIATES

NEIL H. SPIKE, born Elyria, Ohio, October 5, 1969; admitted to bar, 1997, Ohio; 1998, Florida; U.S. District Court, Northern District of Ohio and U.S. Tax Court. *Education:* The Ohio State University (B.A., Economics, 1991); Cleveland State University (M.A., Economics, 1994); University of Toledo (J.D., 1997); University of Miami (LL.M., Estate Planning, 1998). *Member:* Cleveland, Lorain County (Chairman, Community Relations Committee), Ohio State and American Bar Associations; The Florida Bar. ***PRACTICE AREAS:*** Estate Planning; Estate Administration; Elder Law; Medicaid Planning; Asset Protection; Premarital Agreements; Real Estate; Business Law; Probate; Consumer Law; Lemon Law.

FRANK CHARLES GIAMBOI, II, admitted to bar, 1986, Ohio. *Education:* Kent State University (B.A., Economics and Political Science, 1981); Cleveland-Marshall College of Law (J.D., 1985). Family Court Magistrate, 1988-1996. *Member:* Lorain County and Ohio State Bar Associations; Ohio Trial Lawyers Association; The Association of Trial Lawyers of America. ***PRACTICE AREAS:*** Personal Injury; Domestic Relations; Juvenile Law; Civil Litigation.

MARISA A. POCCI, born March 19, 1979; (admission pending). *Education:* John Carroll University (B.A., Art History, cum laude, 2001); Loyola University; Temple University; Cleveland-Marshall College of Law (J.D., cum laude, 2004). Member, Cleveland Marshall Alumni Association. *Member:* Cleveland and Ohio State Bar Associations. ***LANGUAGES:*** Italian. ***PRACTICE AREAS:*** General Practice.

WICKENS, HERZER, PANZA, COOK & BATISTA

A LEGAL PROFESSIONAL ASSOCIATION
ELYRIA, OHIO

(See Avon)

General Civil Practice. Corporate, Taxation, Professional Corporations, Pension, Profit Sharing, Employee Benefits, ERISA, Partnership, Real Estate, Environmental, Labor and Employment Relations; Health Care and Hospital, Public Law, Municipal Bonds, Libel and Media Law, Probate and Estate Planning Law, Insurance Defense, Trials and Appeals, Banking, Bankruptcy.

E. DANIEL MAMRACK

27801 EUCLID AVENUE, SUITE 500
EUCLID, OHIO 44132-3547
Telephone: 216-261-0200 Ext. 213
Fax: 216-261-7334
Email: edmatty@amenitech.net

Collections, Creditors Rights, Real Estate and Probate Law.

E. DANIEL MAMRACK, born Cleveland, Ohio, October 1, 1954; admitted to bar, 1979, Ohio and U.S. District Court, Northern District of Ohio. *Education:* Hiram College (B.A., 1976); Cleveland Marshall College of Law (J.D., 1979). ***PRACTICE AREAS:*** Collections; Creditors Rights Law; Real Estate Law; Probate Law.

BARBARA GOLDBERG ROSMAN

EUCLID, OHIO

(See South Euclid)

Criminal Defense, Civil Practice, Family Law, Divorce, Child Custody, Health Care, Juvenile Law, Medical Collections, Collections, Medical Law, Mediation, Collaborative Law, Debt Collection, Collections, Residential Real Estate, Small Business, Contract Law.

DAMON D. ALT
ATTORNEY AT LAW, L.L.C.

612 S. MAIN STREET, SUITE 105
FINDLAY, OHIO 45840
Telephone: 419-425-0455
Fax: 419-425-0045
URL: http://www.altlawfirm.com

General Practice. Business Law, Taxation, Estate Planning and Probate Law.

DAMON D. ALT, born Tiffin, Ohio, August 1, 1977; admitted to bar, 2004, Ohio. *Education:* Eastern Michigan University (B.B.A., 1999); University of Toledo (J.D., 2003). *Member:* Ohio State and American Bar Associations. ***Email:*** damonalt@bright.net

BERNARD K. BAUER CO., L.P.A.

Established in 1988

410 WEST SANDUSKY STREET, SUITE ONE
FINDLAY, OHIO 45840
Telephone: 419-423-2673
FAX: 419-423-2127
Email: bauertrial@turbosurf.net

Civil Litigation and Appellate Practice. Personal Injury, Products Liability and Medical and Legal Malpractice.

BERNARD K. BAUER, born Cincinnati, Ohio, October 10, 1947; admitted to bar, 1972, Ohio and U.S. Court of Appeals, Sixth Circuit; 1973, U.S. District Court, Northern District of Ohio; 1975, U.S. Supreme Court. *Education:* Ohio University; Defiance College (A.B., 1969); Ohio Northern University (J.D., 1972). Phi Alpha Delta. Author: "Products Liability—The Law in Ohio," Harrison Company, 1982. Assistant Adjunct Professor of Law, Ohio Northern University, 1975-1976. Recipient, Spangenberg Award, Cleveland Academy of Trial Attorneys, 1987. Board of Commissioners on Grievances and Discipline, Member, 1998-2003; Master Commissioner, 2004—. Supreme Court Task Force on Rules of Professional Conduct, Member, 2003—. *Member:* Ohio State Bar Association; The Association of Trial Lawyers of America (Chair, State Development Fund Board, 1986; State Delegate, 1987-1989; Governor, 1989); Ohio Academy of Trial Lawyers (Member, Board of Governing Trustees, 1979—; President, 1986); American Board of Trial Advocates (President, Ohio Chapter, 2006). ***Email:*** bauertrial@turbosurf.net

GENERAL COUNSEL FOR: Ag Credit, Agricultural Credit Association.

BETTS, MILLER & RUSSO

Established in 1890

101 WEST SANDUSKY STREET
FINDLAY, OHIO 45840
Telephone: 419-422-5565
Fax: 419-423-1868
Email: mail@bmrattorneys.com

General Civil Practice. Probate and Estate Planning, Corporations, Real Estate, Insurance Defense, Personal Injury, Medical Malpractice, Family/Domestic Relations, Commercial, and Insurance Law. Trials and Appeals in all Courts.

JOHN E. BETTS (1863-1935)
RICHARD A. BETTS (1911-1996)
JACKSON E. BETTS (1904-1993)

MEMBERS OF FIRM

STEPHEN C. BETTS, born Findlay, Ohio, October 9, 1947; admitted to bar, 1973, Ohio and U.S. District Court, Northern District of Ohio; 1978, U.S. Supreme Court. *Education:* Ohio University (B.B.A., 1969); Ohio Northern University (J.D., 1973). Assistant Prosecuting Attorney, Hancock County, Ohio, 1974-1983. Interim Judge, Common Pleas Court, 1998. *Member:* Findlay/Hancock County (Secretary, 1977-1979; President, 1988-1990), and Ohio State Bar Associations. ***PRACTICE AREAS:*** Negligence Defense Law; Medical Malpractice; Probate Law; Personal Injury Law; Insurance Law. ***Email:*** sbetts@bmrattorneys.com

ROGER L. MILLER, born Dayton, Ohio, November 2, 1945; admitted to bar, 1973, Wisconsin and Indiana; 1976, Ohio and U.S. District Court, Northern District of Ohio. *Education:* Miami University (B.A., 1967); University of Wisconsin (J.D., 1973). *Member:* Findlay/Hancock County, Ohio State, Indiana State, Wisconsin State and American Bar Associations. [with U.S. Army Military Intelligence, 1968-1971]. ***PRACTICE AREAS:*** Estate Planning Law; Probate Law; Banking Law; Real Estate Law; Corporation/Partnership Law. ***Email:*** rmiller@bmrattorneys.com

RALPH D. RUSSO, born New York, New York, April 3, 1951; admitted to bar, 1978, Ohio and U.S. District Court, Northern District of Ohio. *Education:* University of Virginia (B.A., with distinction, 1973); Ohio Northern University (J.D., with distinction, 1978). Phi Kappa Phi. Research Editor, Ohio Northern University Law Review, 1976-1978. Assistant Prosecuting Attorney, 1979-1985. Acting Judge, Findlay Municipal Court. Member, Ohio Supreme Court Commission on Professionalism. *Member:* Findlay/Hancock County, Ohio State and American Bar Associations. ***PRACTICE AREAS:*** Real Estate Law; Commercial Law; Corporation Law; Construction Law. ***Email:*** rrusso@bmrattorneys.com

ASSOCIATE

ELIZABETH A. PUTNAM BEHRENDT, born Lima, Ohio, February 14, 1969; admitted to bar, 1994, Ohio. *Education:* Miami University (B.S., 1991); Case Western Reserve University (J.D., 1994). ***Email:*** ebehrendt@bmrattorneys.com

(This Listing Continued)

LOCAL COUNSEL: Motorists Mutual Insurance Co.; The Cincinnati Insurance Co.; General Casualty Insurance Co.
REPRESENTATIVE CLIENTS: The Arlington Natural Gas Co., Van Buren, Ohio; Findlay Pub. Co.; WKXA and WFIN Radio Stations; Courier Newspaper; White River Broadcasting Co.; Miami River Broadcasting Co.; Blanchard River Broadcasting Co.; Motorists Mutual Insurance Co.; Bank One, NA; Steegman-Dougherty Insurance Agency, Inc.; The Sky Bank; Alvada Const., Inc.; Findlay Machine & Tool, Inc.; Brindle's Furniture; C & S Radiator, Inc.; Wagner Lincoln-Mercury, Inc.; Warner Buick Nissan, Inc.; Kelley Chevrolet-Buick, Inc.; Findlay Inn and Conference Center; Lloyd Treadway Automobile Dealer Group; Walton Agri-Service, Inc.; Wyandot Tractor & Implement Co.; Findlay Orthopedic Associates, Inc.; Blanchard Valley OB/GYN, Inc.; Mosser Construction, Inc,; Kramer Enterprises, Inc.; Superior Trim; Tall Timbers Distribution Center, Inc.; Warner Mechanical Corporation; Great West Casualty Company; IT Corp.; Fireman's Fund Insurance Co.
APPROVED ATTORNEYS FOR: Port Lawrence Title and Trust Co.
REFERENCES: Bank One, NA; The Ohio Bank.

CONTRADA & ASSOCIATES

FINDLAY, OHIO

(See Toledo)

Plaintiff Personal Injury, Wrongful Death, Products Liability, Asbestos Litigation, Medical Malpractice, Auto Accidents.

DRAKE, PHILLIPS, KUENZLI & CLARK

Established in 1948

SUITE 3, 301 SOUTH MAIN STREET
FINDLAY, OHIO 45840
Telephone: 419-423-0242
Telecopier: 419-423-0186
URL: http://www.findlaylaw.com

General Civil and Criminal Practice. Corporation, Probate and Estate Planning, Family and Domestic Relations, Real Estate, Municipal and Creditor's Rights. Trials and Appeals.

MEMBERS OF FIRM

LLOYD D. PHILLIPS (1928-1994)

ROBERT W. DRAKE, born Wilkes-Barre, Pennsylvania, September 5, 1917; admitted to bar, 1948, Ohio; 1949, U.S. District Court, Northern District of Ohio. *Education:* Findlay College (B.A., 1939); Ohio Northern University (J.D., 1948). Delta Theta Phi. *Member:* Findlay/Hancock County (Vice President, 1967-1968) and Ohio State Bar Associations. ***PRACTICE AREAS:*** Probate and Estate Planning; Corporate Law; Business Law. ***Email:*** rdrake@findlaylaw.com

DAVID P. KUENZLI, born Upper Sandusky, Ohio, November 13, 1936; admitted to bar, 1964, Ohio; 1969, U.S. District Court, Northern District of Ohio. *Education:* Ohio University (A.B., 1958; M.A., 1958); The Ohio State University (J.D., 1964). *Member:* Findlay-Hancock County (President, 1977-1978), Ohio State and American Bar Associations. ***PRACTICE AREAS:*** Corporate Law; Business Law; Probate Law; Estate Planning; Banking Law; Real Estate; Municipal Law. ***Email:*** dkuenzli@findlaylaw.com

WILLIAM E. CLARK, born Van Wert, Ohio, September 7, 1943; admitted to bar, 1968, Ohio; 1971, U.S. District Court, Northern District of Ohio; 1986, U.S. Court of Appeals, 6th Circuit; 1991, U.S. District Court, Eastern District of Michigan. *Education:* Findlay College (B.A., 1965); Ohio Northern University (J.D., 1968). Phi Alpha Delta. Prosecutor, Findlay Municipal Court, 1969-1971. Assistant County Prosecuting Attorney, 1969-1972. *Member:* Findlay/Hancock County (President, 1980-1981) and Ohio State Bar Associations; The Association of Trial Lawyers of America; Ohio Academy of Trial Lawyers. ***PRACTICE AREAS:*** Personal Injury Law; Family Law; Commercial Litigation; Probate Law. ***Email:*** wclark@findlaylaw.com

THOMAS D. DRAKE, born Findlay, Ohio, September 1, 1952; admitted to bar, 1977, Ohio and U.S. District Court, Northern District of Ohio; 1986, U.S. Court of Appeals, 6th Circuit; 1990, Florida and Colorado. *Education:* University of Notre Dame (B.A., 1974); Ohio Northern University (J.D., 1977). Phi Kappa Phi. *Member:* Findlay/Hancock County and Ohio State Bar Associations; The Florida Bar; The Association of Trial Lawyers of America; Ohio Academy of Trial Lawyers. ***PRACTICE AREAS:*** Family Law; Civil Trial; Criminal Law; Real Estate; Banking Law; Probate Law; Estate Planning; Creditor Bankruptcy. ***Email:*** tdrake@findlaylaw.com

JOHN D. OMAN, born Hancock County, Ohio, May 9, 1957; admitted to bar, 1982, Ohio. *Education:* Ohio Northern University (B.A., 1979); Ohio State University (J.D., 1982). *Member:* Findlay/Hancock County and Ohio State Bar Associations. ***PRACTICE AREAS:*** Real Estate; Probate Law; Estate Planning; Creditor Bankruptcy. ***Email:*** joman@findlaylaw.com

PHILIP L. ROONEY, born Findlay, Ohio, July 25, 1965; admitted to bar, 1992, Ohio and U.S. District Court, Northern District of Ohio. *Education:* Ohio State University (B.S., 1988); Ohio Northern University (J.D, with high distinction, 1992). Member, Willis Society. *Member:* Findlay/Hancock County and Ohio State Bar Associations. ***PRACTICE AREAS:*** Corporate Law; Business Law; Real Estate; Municipal Law. ***Email:*** prooney@findlaylaw.com

GARTH W. BROWN, born Columbus, Ohio, February 5, 1968; admitted to bar, 1993, Ohio. *Education:* Loyola University (B.A., cum laude, 1990); Drake University (J.D., 1993). Member, Blue Key National Honor Society. Ward Councilman, Findlay City, 1996-1999. *Member:* Hancock County, Ohio State and American Bar Associations; Ohio Academy of Trial Lawyers. ***PRACTICE AREAS:*** Personal Injury; Family Law; Criminal Law; Civil Trial Practice; Landlord and Tenant Law. ***Email:*** gbrown@findlaylaw.com

CHRISTIE L. RANZAU, born Merrillville, Indiana, July 11, 1977; admitted to bar, 2002, Ohio. *Education:* Indiana University (B.A., 1999); Ohio Northern University (J.D.,

(This Listing Continued)

2002). *Member:* Hancock County, Ohio and American Bar Associations. ***PRACTICE AREAS:*** Corporate Law; Business Law; Civil Litigation; Estate Planning; Probate; Adoption Law. ***Email:*** cranzau@findlaylaw.com

OF COUNSEL

WILLIAM E. RUSE, born 1934; admitted to bar, 1972, Ohio. *Education:* Ohio Northern University (B.Sc., 1957); University of Toledo (J.D., 1972). *Member:* American Bar Association. ***PRACTICE AREAS:*** Health Care. ***Email:*** wruse@findlaylaw.com

REPRESENTATIVE CLIENTS: Acme Beverage, Inc.; Automatic Feed Company; Blanchard Valley Regional Health Center; Community Development Foundation of Hancock County; Country Club Acres, Inc.; Findlay Industries, Inc.; Grob Systems, Inc.; Jaqua's Fine Guns; Peterbilt of Northwest Ohio, Inc.
APPROVED ATTORNEYS: Lawyers Title Insurance Corp.; Old Republic National Title Insurance Company; Ticor Title Insurance Company; First American Title Ins. Co.
REFERENCES: The Fifth Third Bank of Northwestern Ohio, N.A.; Sky Bank.

EASTMAN & SMITH LTD.

Established in 1844

725 SOUTH MAIN STREET
FINDLAY, OHIO 45840
Telephone: 419-424-5847
Fax: 419-424-9860
URL: http://www.eastmansmith.com

Toledo, Ohio, Office: One Seagate, Twenty-Fourth Floor, P.O. Box 10032, 43699-0032. Telephone: 419-241-6000. Fax: 419-247-1777.
Columbus, Ohio, Office: 100 East Broad Street, Suite 1300, 43215. Telephone: 614-280-1770. Fax: 614-280-1777.

General Civil Practice: Corporate, Business, Banking, Taxation, Real Estate, Securities, Antitrust, Environmental, Public, Labor and Employment, Civil Rights, Employee Benefits, Insurance, Hospital and Health Care, Estate Planning, Pension and Estate Planning, Probate, Workers Compensation, Commercial Litigation, Litigation, Immigration and Naturalization.

(For complete biographical data on all personnel, see Professional Biographies at Toledo, Ohio)

HOWARD A. ELLIOTT

330 SOUTH MAIN STREET
FINDLAY, OHIO 45840
Telephone: 419-422-7178
Fax: 419-424-8882
Email: theboyes@aol.com

Civil Litigation, Family, Divorce, Criminal, Real Estate, Wills and Probate, Trusts and Estates, Estate Planning, Debtor and Creditor Bankruptcy.

HOWARD A. ELLIOTT, born Lima, Ohio, July 9, 1957; admitted to bar, 1986, Ohio and U.S. Tax Court; 1987, U.S. District Court, Northern District of Ohio. *Education:* Ohio Northern University (B.A., with distinction, 1979; J.D., with distinction, 1986); University of Illinois (M.S., 1983). Phi Kappa Phi; Willis Society. Member, Ohio Northern University Law Review, 1984-1986. Lecturer, Hazardous Materials Program, University of Findlay, 1989-1990. *Member:* Hancock County and Ohio State Bar Associations; Findlay Estate Planning Council.

FIRMIN, SPRAGUE & HUFFMAN CO., L.P.A.

Established in 1974

220 WEST SANDUSKY STREET
P.O. BOX 963
FINDLAY, OHIO 45839
Telephone: 419-423-4321
Fax: 419-423-8484
Email: fshlaw@fshlaw.net

General Civil Practice. Probate and Estate Planning, Corporation, Computer, Commercial, Taxation and Real Estate Law. Trials.

JOHN C. FIRMIN (1917-2005)

ROBERT F. SPRAGUE, born Chicago, Illinois, May 26, 1943; admitted to bar, 1968, Ohio; 1969, U.S. Court of Military Appeals; 1975, U.S. District Court, Northern District of Ohio; U.S. Tax Court. *Education:* Bowling Green State University (B.A., cum laude, 1965); The Ohio State University (J.D., 1968). Member, 1990-1996; Chairman, 1994, Ohio Supreme Court Commission on Continuing Legal Education. *Member:* Findlay/Hancock County, Northwestern Ohio and Ohio State Bar Associations; National Association of Estate Planning Councils. [Capt., JAGC, U.S. Army, 1969-1973]. ***PRACTICE AREAS:*** Corporate Law; Estate Planning Law; Tax Law. ***Email:*** rsprague@fshlaw.net

DOUGLAS W. HUFFMAN, born El Paso, Texas, December 13, 1951; admitted to bar, 1976, Ohio. *Education:* Purdue University (B.S., summa cum laude, 1973); University of Michigan (J.D., cum laude, 1976). Adjunct Professor of Law: Estate Planning, Ohio Northern University, 2005—. *Member:* Findlay/Hancock County, Northwestern Ohio and Ohio State (Counsel of Delegates, 1982-1985; Member, Computer Law Committee) Bar Associations; Computer Law Association; National Association of Estate Planning Councils. ***PRACTICE AREAS:*** Computer Law; Corporate Law; Estate Planning Law. ***Email:*** dhuffman@fshlaw.net

THOMAS P. KEMP, born Chicago, Illinois, September 28, 1953; admitted to bar, 1978, Ohio; 1980, U.S. District Court, Northern District of Ohio; 1983, U.S. Court of Appeals, Sixth Circuit. *Education:* University of Notre Dame (B.A., cum laude, 1975; J.D., 1978). Special Counsel to Attorney General, Ohio, 1983-1995. Member: Hancock County Board of Elections, 1983-1993; City of Findlay Civil Service Commission, 2004—. *Member:* Findlay/Hancock County, Northwestern Ohio (Secretary-Treasurer, 1989-1990; Vice President, 1990-1991; President, 1991-1992) and Ohio State (Member, Council of Delegates, 2004-2005) Bar Associations. ***REPORTED CASES:*** Krischbaum v. Dillon (1991), 58 Ohio St. 3d 58, 567 N.E.2d 1291. ***PRACTICE AREAS:*** Civil Litigation; Commercial Litigation; Family Law. ***Email:*** tkemp@fshlaw.net

STEPHEN A. ROEPKE, born Ashland, Ohio, June 22, 1957; admitted to bar, 1981, Ohio; 1982, U.S. District Court, Northern District of Ohio; 1983, U.S. Court of Appeals, Sixth Circuit. *Education:* Bowling Green State University (B.A., cum laude, 1978); Duke University (J.D., 1981). Phi Alpha Delta. *Member:* Findlay/Hancock County, Northwestern Ohio and Ohio State Bar Associations. ***REPORTED CASES:*** J.A. Industries, Inc. v. All Am. Plastics, Inc., 133 Ohio App.3d 76; Springer v. Koehler Bros., 69 Ohio App.3d 592; Frantz v. Van Gunten, 36 Ohio App.3d 96; Fenstermaker v. Elwood, 17 Ohio App.3d 520. ***PRACTICE AREAS:*** Commercial Law; Civil Litigation; Real Estate Law; Corporate Law; Taxation. ***Email:*** sroepke@fshlaw.net

ASSOCIATE

MATTHEW L. KLEIN, born Findlay, Ohio, January 3, 1971; admitted to bar, 2001, Ohio. *Education:* Bowling Green State University (B.S., cum laude, 1996); University of Notre Dame (J.D., 2001). *Member:* Findlay/Hancock County, Northwestern Ohio and Ohio State Bar Associations. ***PRACTICE AREAS:*** Corporate Law; Tax Law; Estate Planning. ***Email:*** mklein@fshlaw.net

REPRESENTATIVE CLIENTS: The National Lime & Stone Co.; MacDonald Supply, Inc.; Fornes Brake Service, Inc.; The Hercules Tire & Rubber Co.; Ridge & Associates, Inc.; Van Horn, Hoover & Associates, Inc.; Enelco, Inc.; Rader Environmental Services, Inc.; Haag Environmental Co.; Bridgestone/ Firestone, Inc.; Bridgestone APM Co.; Aviation Consultants, Inc.; Animal Care Centers of America, Inc.; Friends Service Co., Inc.; Great Lakes Conference; Church of God, General Conference; Microsoft Corp.; Schnipke Engraving Co., Inc.; Omega Mechanical Design, Inc.; Thieman Stamping Co.; Thieman Tailgates, Inc.; Richard Howard, Inc.; Copeland Financial Agency, Inc.; Aardvark Corp.; CentraComm Communications, Ltd.; Six Disciplines Corp.; MaxQ Technologies, Inc.; McClellan Health Systems, Inc.; Manor Homes, Inc.; McClellan Management, Inc.; Cornerstone Building, Ltd.; Hanco Ambulance, Inc.; TLB Foundation; Acadia Point Development, Inc.; Plumbline Solutions, Inc.; Winebrenner Theological Seminary; ObjAcct, Inc.
APPROVED ATTORNEYS FOR: Ohio Savings Bank.

FITZGERALD LAW FIRM LLC

400 SOUTH MAIN STREET
FINDLAY, OHIO 45840
Telephone: 419-420-9312
Fax: 419-420-9314
Email: fitzgerald@findlayfitzlaw.com

Personal Injury, Products Liability, Insurance, Trusts and Estates, Wills and Probate.

MEMBERS

DENNIS M. FITZGERALD, born Akron, Ohio, October 9, 1951; admitted to bar, 1976, Ohio and U.S. District Court, Northern District of Ohio; 1983, U.S. Supreme Court; 1985, U.S. Court of Appeals, 6th Circuit. *Education:* University of Notre Dame (B.A., with honors, 1973); The Ohio State University (J.D., with honors, 1976). *Member:* Findlay/Hancock County and Ohio State Bar Associations; Ohio Academy of Trial Lawyers. ***REPORTED CASES:*** Wagner v. Midwestern Indem. Co. 83 Ohio St.3d 287 (S.Ct. 1998). ***PRACTICE AREAS:*** Estate Planning Law; Insurance Defense Law; Personal Injury Law.

BRET A. SPAETH, born Findlay, Ohio, November 25, 1970; admitted to bar, 1997, Ohio. *Education:* Miami University (B.A., 1993); University of Toledo (J.D., 1997). *Member:* Findlay/Hancock County; Ohio State and American Bar Associations; Ohio Academy of Trial Lawyers. ***PRACTICE AREAS:*** Family Law; Insurance Defense; Criminal Defense; Personal Injury.

ASSOCIATE

DREW J. MIHALIK, born September 14, 1978; admitted to bar, 2004, Ohio. *Education:* University of Findlay (B.A., Political Science and International Studies, summa cum laude, 2001); University of Toledo (J.D., 2004). *Member:* Findlay-Hancock County and Ohio State Bar Associations.

REPRESENTATIVE CLIENTS: Ballinger Industries, Inc.; Blanchard Vallet Neurosurgical Associates, Inc.; Coldren-Crates Funeral Home; HealthScope Benefits, Inc.; Northwest Installations, Inc.; Ohio Bar Liability Company; Red Hawk Run Golf Course.
REFERENCE: First Federal Bank.

STEVEN C. HALES

FINDLAY, OHIO

(See Toledo)

Family Law, Divorce, Child Custody, Child Support, Visitation Rights, Business Litigation, Business Formation, Corporations, Partnerships, Limited Liability Company Law, Mergers and Acquisitions, Business Planning, Small Business Law, Business Succession Planning, Family Business Law, Contracts, Licensing Agreements, Taxation, Real Estate, Commercial Leasing, Trusts and Estates.

JOHN F. KOSTYO

1100 E. MAIN CROSS STREET, SUITE 200
FINDLAY, OHIO 45840
Telephone: 419-422-7700
Fax: 419-425-0042
Email: jfk@kostyolaw.com
URL: http://www.kostyolaw.com

Banks and Banking, Creditor Bankruptcy, Commercial Law, Civil Litigation, Contractor/Construction Law, Family Law.

(This Listing Continued)

JOHN F. KOSTYO, Findlay—Continued

JOHN F. KOSTYO, born Findlay, Ohio, February 9, 1955; admitted to bar, 1981, Ohio. *Education:* John Carroll University (B.A., magna cum laude, 1978); Case Western Reserve University (J.D., 1981). Alpha Sigma Nu; Phi Alpha Delta. ***PRACTICE AREAS:*** Banks and Banking; Creditor Bankruptcy; Commercial Law; Civil Litigation; Construction Law; Family Law.

ROXI A. LIMING

FINDLAY, OHIO

(See Columbus)

Immigration Law, Visas, Naturalization, H1-B Visas, Green Cards, Financé Visas, Investor Visas, Investor Green Cards, Labor and Employment, Wage and Hour Violations, Wrongful Discharge, Employment Discrimination, Americans with Disabilities Act, Sexual Harassment, Family and Medical Leave Act, Employment Contracts, Severance Package Negotiation, Personnel Policies.

NOGGLE LAW OFFICE, LLC

101 WEST SANDUSKY STREET, SUITE 200 C
FINDLAY, OHIO 45840
Telephone: 419-422-1887
Fax: 419-422-1830
Email: attynoggle@ameritech.net
URL: http://www.nogglelawoffice.com

Trusts and Estates, Real Estate, Business Law, Elder Law, Estate Planning.

MICHAEL C. NOGGLE, born Upper Sandusky, Ohio, August 22, 1961; admitted to bar, 1986, Ohio; 1991, U.S. District Court, Northern District of Ohio. *Education:* Bowling Green State University (B.A., 1983); University of Toledo (J.D., 1986). Delta Theta Phi. Formerly with Drake, Phillips, Kuenzli and Clark. Instructor, Real Estate Law, Real Estate Principles and Practices, University of Findlay, 2001-2003. *Member:* Findlay/Hancock County, Ohio State and American Bar Associations. ***PRACTICE AREAS:*** Trusts and Estates Law; Real Estate; Business Law; Elder Law; Estate Planning. ***Email:*** attynoggle@ameritech.net

OXLEY, MALONE, HOLLISTER, O'MALLEY & WARREN, P.L.L.

Established in 1947

301 EAST MAIN CROSS STREET
P.O. BOX 1086
FINDLAY, OHIO 45840
Telephone: 419-422-8713
Fax: 419-422-6495
Email: oxleylaw@oxleylaw.com

General Civil and Trial Practice. Probate and Estate Planning, Insurance Defense Personal Injury, Family and Domestic Relations, Bankruptcy, Real Estate, Medical Malpractice Defense, Products Liability Law and Appellate Practice.

MEMBERS OF FIRM

GARVER OXLEY (1919-1997)

MICHAEL J. MALONE, born Springfield, Ohio, December 31, 1947; admitted to bar, 1973, Ohio and U.S. District Court, Northern District of Ohio. *Education:* St. Joseph's College (B.S., cum laude, 1970); Ohio Northern University (J.D., 1973). Delta Theta Phi; Delta Epsilon Sigma. Member, Supreme Court Commission on Specialization of Attorneys. *Member:* Findlay/Hancock County, Northwestern Ohio and Ohio State (Member, Negligence, Medical Malpractice and Insurance Section; Member, Tort and Insurance Practice Section; Member, Negligence Committee; Member, Medical Malpractice Committee) Bar Associations; Ohio Association of Civil Trial Attorneys; Ohio Society of Hospital Attorneys; Defense Research and Trial Lawyers Association; Ohio State Bar College. ***PRACTICE AREAS:*** Litigation; Medical Malpractice; Personal Injury; Corporate Law; Insurance Defense; Family Law. ***Email:*** malone@oxleylaw.com

ROBERT B. HOLLISTER, born Minnehaha County, South Dakota, November 24, 1940; admitted to bar, 1977, Ohio and U.S. District Court, Northern District of Ohio; 1985, U.S. Court of Appeals, 6th Circuit. *Education:* University of South Dakota (B.S., 1962); Ohio Northern University (J.D., 1976). *Member:* Findlay/Hancock County, Ohio State and American Bar Associations; Ohio Bar Council of Delegates; Ohio Association of Civil Trial Attorneys. ***PRACTICE AREAS:*** Insurance Defense Law; Personal Injury; Bankruptcy Law; Subrogation Law; Estates Law; Farm and Utility Cooperatives; Corporate Law. ***Email:*** hollister@oxleylaw.com

MICHAEL E. O'MALLEY, born Toccoa, Georgia, December 23, 1942; admitted to bar, 1968, Ohio; U.S. District Court, Northern and Western Districts of Ohio and U.S. Court of Appeals, Sixth Circuit. *Education:* Georgetown University (A.B., 1965); Case Western Reserve University (J.D., 1968); New York University. Special Agent, Federal Bureau of Investigation, 1968-1971. Assistant Prosecuting Attorney: Cuyahoga County, Cleveland, 1971-1974; Putnam County, Ottawa, 1974-1977; Putnam County Judge, 1993—. Member, Society of Former FBI Agents. *Member:* Putnam County (President, 1991), Northwestern Ohio and Ohio State Bar Associations; Ohio Academy of Trial Lawyers. Fellow, Ohio State Bar Foundation; Ohio Land Title Association; Ohio Association of County and Municipal Judges. (Also Member, Michael E. O'Malley, LLC). ***PRACTICE AREAS:*** Estate Planning; Estate Administration; Trust Law; Real Estate; Corporate Law; Business Law; Civil Litigation; Income Tax.

(This Listing Continued)

BRADLEY S. WARREN, born Lima, Ohio, April 8, 1970; admitted to bar, 1995, Ohio. *Education:* Ohio Wesleyan University (B.A., cum laude, 1992); Ohio Northern University (J.D., 1995). *Member:* Findlay/Hancock County and Ohio State Bar Associations; Ohio Bar Council of Delegates; Ohio Academy of Trial Lawyers. ***PRACTICE AREAS:*** Personal Injury; Insurance Defense. ***Email:*** warren@oxleylaw.com

OF COUNSEL

JULIE A. DAVENPORT, born Findlay, Ohio, December 23, 1953; admitted to bar, 1979, Ohio; 1985, U.S. District Court, Northern District of Ohio and U.S. Court of Appeals, Sixth Circuit. *Education:* Bowling Green State University (B.S., magna cum laude, 1975); University of Toledo, (J.D., 1979). Mortar Board. Articles Editor, University of Toledo Law Review, 1978-1979. Judicial Clerk, Supreme Court of Ohio, Justices William B. Brown, Andrew Douglas, 1981-1984. *Member:* Ohio State Bar Association. ***PRACTICE AREAS:*** Appellate Practice; Insurance Defense Law.

REPRESENTATIVE CLIENTS: Insurance Clients: American States Insurance Co.; Auto Owners Insurance Co.; Blanchard Valley Title Agency, Inc.; Buckeye State Mutual Insurance Co.; CNA Insurance Co.; Celina Group Insurance; Chubb Insurance Co.; Cincinnati Insurance Co.; Hastings Mutual Insurance Co.; Kemper Insurance Group; Lightning Rod Mutual Insurance Co.; OHIC Insurance Co.; Safeco Insurance; State Auto Insurance Co.; Transamerica Insurance Group; Trinity Universal Insurance Co.; Wayne Insurance Co.; Western Reserve Mutual Casualty Co.; Western Surety Co. Other: Blanchard Valley Farmers Cooperative, Inc.; Hancock-Wood Electric Cooperative, Inc.; KT Rental, Inc.; Midwest Laser Systems, Inc.; Marathon Oil Co.; Miller Rigging, Inc.; Sky Financial; Hospitals: Blanchard Valley Regional Health Center; Hardin Memorial Hospital; Lima Memorial Hospital; St. Catherines Care Center; Farmers Commission Co.; Village of Jenera, Ohio; Centrex Plastics, LLC; Prism Propane LLC; Speedway Super America, LLC.
APPROVED ATTORNEYS FOR: American Realty Title Assurance Co.; Farmers Home Administration; Ohio Bar Title Insurance.
REFERENCES: Sky Financial; Marathon Oil Co.; Lima Memorial Hospital; Blanchard Valley Regional Health Center; Hardin Memorial Hospital.

RITTER, ROBINSON, McCREADY & JAMES

FINDLAY, OHIO

(See Toledo)

General Civil Practice. Insurance, Trials and Appeals, Municipal Law, Corporation, Probate, Estate Planning, Real Estate, Personal Injury, Product Liability, Labor and Employment. Federal Practice.

SPITLER, HUFFMAN, YOON & NEWLOVE, LLP

FINDLAY, OHIO

(See Bowling Green)

General Civil Practice in all Courts. Corporation, Business, Personal Injury, Wrongful Death, Product Liability, Medical Malpractice, Probate and Estate Planning, Administrative and Real Estate Law, Public Utility, Trials and Appeals, Bankruptcy, Criminal Defense, Family Law, Criminal Law.

THOMAS G. EAGLE CO., L.P.A.

FRANKLIN, OHIO

(See Lebanon)

General Civil and Criminal Trial and Appellate Practice in State and Federal Courts, in Ohio and Kentucky, including Personal Injury, Wrongful Death, Criminal Law, Civil Rights, Consumer Law, Commercial and Business Litigation, Bankruptcy, Real Estate, Family Law and others.

JOHN L. ZINKAND

THE GUSDORF BUILDING
211 SOUTH PARK AVENUE
FREMONT, OHIO 43420
Telephone: 419-332-5579
Fax: 419-332-5570
Email: zinkandlaw@aol.com

General Civil Practice. Probate, Trust and Estates, Estate Planning, Real Property, Personal Injury, Corporate, Commercial, Trials.

JOHN L. ZINKAND, born Lewiston, Idaho, October 14, 1943; admitted to bar, 1968, Ohio; U.S. District Court, Northern District of Ohio and U.S. Court of Appeals, Sixth Circuit. *Education:* Baldwin-Wallace College (A.B., 1965); The Ohio State University (J.D., 1968). *Member:* Sandusky County (President, 1982-1983; 501 (c)(3) Corp., 1999-2001), Ohio State and American Bar Associations.

AGENT FOR: Ohio Bar Title Insurance Co.
APPROVED ATTORNEY FOR: Lawyers Title Insurance Corp.; Ag Credit (ACA).

MICHAEL E. BENSON

GAHANNA, OHIO

(See Columbus)

Bankruptcy Law, Foreclosures, Debtor and Creditor, Real Estate, Landlord and Tenant, Buying and Selling, Wills, Living Wills, Healthcare, Powers of Attorney.

SUSAN KENNEY-PFALZER

GAHANNA, OHIO

(See Columbus)

Family Law, Divorce, Dissolution, Child Custody, Spousal and Child Support, Visitation Rights, Adoptions, Paternity, Juvenile Law, Collaborative Law, Restraining Orders.

MICHAEL R. MORAN CO., L.P.A.

GAHANNA, OHIO

(See Columbus)

Administrative Law, Occupational and Professional Licensing, Health Law, Personal Injury, Municipal Law, Privacy and Freedom of Information, Government Law, White Collar Crime, Fraud, Corporate Compliance and Legislation, Trial Practice and Appeals, Firearm and 2nd Amendment Law.

MELISSA J. SHAW

107 WEST JOHNSTOWN ROAD
GAHANNA, OHIO 43230
Telephone: 614-472-2529
Fax: 614-471-4581
Email: ms@shaw4law.com
URL: http://www.shaw4lawfirm.com

Business Law, Business Planning and Formation, Contracts, Corporate, Partnership, Family Business, Wills, Trusts and Estates, Contested Wills, Estate and Gift Taxation, Estate Planning, Living Wills, Powers of Attorney, Probate, Elder Law, Guardianship, Medicaid Eligibility.

MELISSA J. SHAW, born Pikeville, Kentucky, February 19, 1966; admitted to bar, 1997, Ohio. *Education:* Eastern Kentucky University (B.A., 1988; M.S., 1989); Capital University (J.D., 1997). *Member:* Columbus and Ohio State Bar Associations. ***PRACTICE AREAS:*** Business Law; Business Planning; Business Formation; Contracts; Corporate; Partnership; Family Business; Wills; Trusts and Estates; Contested Wills; Estate and Gift Taxation; Estate Planning; Living Wills; Powers of Attorney; Probate; Elder Law; Guardianship; Medicaid Eligibility.

KENNETH J. MOLNAR

21 MIDDLE STREET
P.O. BOX 248
GALENA, OHIO 43021-0248
Telephone: 740-965-3900
Fax: 740-965-2718
URL: http://www.KMolnar@columbus.rr.com
URL: http://www.molnarlaw.com

Civil Trial Practice. Municipal and Zoning, Family Law, Divorce, Child Custody, Child Support, Visitation Rights, Real Estate, Wills and Probate, Trusts and Estates, Estate Planning, Collections.

KENNETH J. MOLNAR, born Cleveland, Ohio, July 31, 1946; admitted to bar, 1974, Ohio; 1975, U.S. District Court, Southern District of Ohio. *Education:* University of Dayton (B.A., 1968); Capital University (J.D., 1974). Solicitor: Galena, Ohio, 1984—; Powell, Ohio, 1985—. *Member:* Columbus, Delaware County (President, 1987-1988) and Ohio State Bar Associations. (Also Of Counsel, Rich, Crites & Wesp, LLC)

APPROVED ATTORNEY FOR: Ohio Bar Title Insurance Co.

RICHARD M. LEWIS

GALLIPOLIS, OHIO

(See Jackson)

General Trial and Appellate Practice, Tort Law, Insurance Law, Medical Negligence, Employment Law, Personal Injury, Commercial Litigation, Domestic Relations, Corporation, Real Estate, Probate and Banking Law, Debtor-Creditor and Criminal Law.

OFFUTT, FISHER & NORD

GALLIPOLIS, OHIO

(See Huntington, West Virginia)

General Civil Trial Practice, Insurance Defense, Products Liability, Premises Liability, Asbestos Defense, Mass Tort Defense, Medical Malpractice, Legal Malpractice, Hospital Liability, Health Care Law and Commercial Litigation, Transportation Law.

JASON HENNEKES

GEORGETOWN, OHIO

(See Cincinnati)

PURDY & RING

318 WEST STATE STREET
GEORGETOWN, OHIO 45121
Telephone: 937-378-4119; 937-378-3077
Fax: 937-378-3077
Email: purdyring@siscom.net
URL: http://www.purdyandring.com

Criminal Law, DUI, Family Law, Divorce, Dissolution of Marriage, Personal Injury, Estates, Wills, Probate, Business Law, Real Estate, Appellate Practice.

MEMBERS OF FIRM

STANLEY K. PURDY, born Sardinia, Ohio, December 8, 1937; admitted to bar, 1965, Ohio; U.S. District Court, Southern District of Ohio; U.S. Court of Appeals, Sixth Circuit. *Education:* The Ohio State University (B.S., 1960; J.D., 1965). Phi Delta Phi. *Member:* Cincinnati, Brown County, Ohio State (Chairman, Young Lawyers Section, 1969; Member, Executive Committee, 1976-1979) and American Bar Associations. ***PRACTICE AREAS:*** Real Estate; Probate; Business Law. ***Email:*** stanpurdy@siscom.net

C. NICHOLAS RING, born Mariemont, Ohio, March 6, 1967; admitted to bar, 1993, Ohio; U.S. District Court, Southern District of Ohio. *Education:* University of Kentucky (B.A., 1989; J.D., 1992). Phi Delta Phi. Assistant Prosecutor, Brown County, 1993. *Member:* Cincinnati, Brown County and Ohio State Bar Associations, Ohio Association of Criminal Defense Lawyers. ***PRACTICE AREAS:*** Criminal; Traffic Violations; Domestic Relations; Family Law; Appellate Practice. ***Email:*** nickring@siscom.net

APPROVED ATTORNEYS FOR: Lawyers Title Insurance Co. (Agent); The Ohio Bar Title Insurance Co. (Agent); Farmers Home Administration; Fifth Third Bank, Ohio Valley; Brown County Title Agency.

LEPPLA ASSOCIATES

GERMANTOWN, OHIO

(See Dayton)

Civil Litigation, Personal Injury, Medical Malpractice, Insurance, Zoning Law, Land Use, Wills and Probate, Legal Malpractice and Ethics.

SUSAN KENNEY-PFALZER

GRANVILLE, OHIO

(See Columbus)

Family Law, Divorce, Dissolution, Child Custody, Spousal and Child Support, Visitation Rights, Adoptions, Paternity, Juvenile Law, Collaborative Law, Restraining Orders.

BIESER, GREER & LANDIS, LLP

GREENVILLE, OHIO

(See Dayton)

General Civil Practice, Trial Practice, Business Litigation, Professional Liability Defense, Personal Injury Defense, Products Liability Defense, Corporate Law, Employment Law, Commercial Law, Probate, Tax Law, White Collar Criminal Defense, Arbitration, Mediation.

KAREN DENISE BRADLEY

GREENVILLE, OHIO

(See Dayton)

Immigration Law.

FREUND, FREEZE & ARNOLD

A LEGAL PROFESSIONAL ASSOCIATION

GREENVILLE, OHIO

(See Dayton)

Civil Litigation including Commercial Litigation, Employment Defense, Professional Malpractice Defense, Employer Intentional Torts, Construction Litigation, Civil Rights Defense, Local Government Defense, Nursing Home Defense, Environmental Litigation and Insurance Defense.

GOUBEAUX & BRAND

Established in 1934

100 WASHINGTON AVENUE
P.O. BOX 158
GREENVILLE, OHIO 45331
Telephone: 937-548-2211
Fax: Available Upon Request

General Civil Practice. Trials. Probate and Estate Planning, Banking, Finance, Corporation and Real Estate Law.

FIRM PROFILE: The firm has worked within the Darke County and adjacent county areas for over 60 years. As the oldest firm in the county, we have a long and deep connection with the people in this part of Ohio and with state and county officials.

MEMBERS OF FIRM

EDWARD A. GOUBEAUX, JR. (1906-1964)

JEROME H. GOUBEAUX (1908-1978)

ROBERT L. MORRIS (1928-2003)

JAMES J. GOUBEAUX, born Greenville, Ohio, December 12, 1936; admitted to bar, 1961, Ohio; U.S. District Court, Southern District of Ohio; U.S. Court of Appeals, Sixth Circuit; U.S. Supreme Court. *Education:* Wabash College (A.B., magna cum laude, 1958); Harvard Law School (J.D., 1961). Phi Beta Kappa. Law Director for Villages of Burkettsville, Ansonia, 1964-1989; Yorkshire, Versailles, 1964-1976; Pittsburg, 1978-1985; North Star, 1974-1989. County Court Judge, Darke County, 1963-1978. President, Greenville Industrial Parks, Inc., 1973 and 1979. President, Greenville Community Improvement Corporation, 1974. President, 1978-1981 and Chairman, 1981-1989, The Citizens State Bank. Member, Panel of Arbitrators, American Arbitration Association. *Member:* Darke County (President, 1968), Ohio State and American Bar Associations. Fellow, Ohio State Bar Foundation. ***PRACTICE AREAS:*** Probate Law; Finance Law; Corporate Law; Litigation.

(This Listing Continued)

GOUBEAUX & BRAND, Greenville—Continued

ERIC H. BRAND, born Greenville, Ohio, September 10, 1952; admitted to bar, 1978, Ohio; 1979, U.S. District Court, Southern District of Ohio; 1980, U.S. Court of Appeals, Sixth Circuit; 1981, U.S. Supreme Court. *Education:* The Ohio State University (B.A., 1975); University of Cincinnati (J.D., 1978). City Solicitor, New Madison, Ohio, 1980—;New Weston, 1991—; Pitsburg, 2001—; Hollansburg, 2003—; Arcanum, 2004—; Ithaca, 2005—. *Member:* Darke County (President, 1983), Ohio State and American Bar Associations; Ohio Academy of Trial Lawyers. ***PRACTICE AREAS:*** Litigation; Banking Law; Municipal Law. ***Email:*** ehbrand@earthlink.net

MARK E. HEGGIE, born Detroit, Michigan, January 23, 1949; admitted to bar, 1974, Ohio. *Education:* Miami University (B.A., 1971); Ohio Northern University (J.D., 1974). Assistant Prosecuting Attorney, Darke County, 1975-1994. *Member:* Darke County, Ohio State and American Bar Associations; Ohio Prosecuting Attorney's Association; National District Attorney's Association. ***PRACTICE AREAS:*** Real Estate Law; Criminal Defense; Litigation.

GENERAL COUNSEL FOR: Second National Bank; Osgood State Bank; Fifth Third Bank; Darke Rural Electric Coop., Inc.; United Telephone Company of Ohio; Willowdell Sales Company; Walls Bros. Asphalt Co.; Greenville Industrial Park, Inc.; Greenville Community Improvement Corp.; Darke County Housing, Inc.; Greenville Federal Savings & Loan Association.
LOCAL COUNSEL FOR: Penn Central Co.; Nationwide Mutual Insurance Co.; The St. Henry Bank, St. Henry, Ohio; Ft. Recovery Banking Co., Ft. Recovery, Ohio; National Casualty Co.; New Amsterdam Casualty Co.; The Surety and Casualty Co. of New York (Aetna Group); The Automobile Club Insurance Co.; Franklin Fire & Casualty Insurance Co., Columbus, Ohio; Northwestern Mutual Life Insurance Co. (Real Estate, Mortgage Dept.); Commonwealth Life Insurance Co. of Louisville; Inmont Corp.; Greenville Technology, Inc.; Greenville Federal Savings & Loan Association.

MILLER & LURING

GREENVILLE, OHIO

(See Troy)

General and Trial Practice, Collections, Estate Planning, Bankruptcy, Personal Injury, Civil, Family/Domestic Relations, Corporation, Negligence, Tax, Municipal, Probate and Real Estate.

JEFFREY P. COMPTON

Established in 2000

4178 BROADWAY
GROVE CITY, OHIO 43123-3024
Telephone: 614-875-7233
Fax: 614-875-0480
Email: jcompton@jeffreypcompton.com
URL: http://www.jeffreypcompton.com

Personal Injury, Automobile Accidents, Insurance, Medical Malpractice, Wrongful Death, Slip and Fall, Family Law, Divorce, Child Custody, Child Support, Visitation Rights, Real Estate, Buying or Selling, Business Formation, Buying and Selling of Businesses, Small Business Law, Partnerships, Limited Liability Companies, Corporate, Contracts, Bankruptcy, Wills and Probate, Estate Administration, Powers of Attorney and Health Care documents, Consumer Law, IRS Negotiations.

FIRM PROFILE: Sole practitioner with practice emphasis on personal injuries, medical malpractice, wrongful death, bankruptcy, domestic family law, estate administration and planning, wills, power of attorney, healthcare documents, probate and IRS negotiations.

JEFFREY P. COMPTON, born Cincinnati, Ohio, November 16, 1963; admitted to bar, 1989, Ohio; 1990, U.S. District Court, Southern District of Ohio. *Education:* Ohio University (B.A., 1986); Capital University (J.D., 1989). Staff Attorney, Ohio State Medical Board, 1989-1992. Claims Attorney and Litigation/Claims Manager, Century Surety Group, 1992-1999. *Member:* Columbus, Ohio State and American Bar Associations; Ohio Academy of Trial Lawyers. ***PRACTICE AREAS:*** Personal Injury; Automobile Accidents; Insurance; Medical Malpractice; Wrongful Death; Slip and Fall; Family Law; Divorce; Child Custody; Child Support; Visitation Rights; Real Estate; Business Formation; Limited Liability Companies; Wills; Probate; Estate Administration; Powers of Attorney.

JAMES S. ARNOLD & ASSOCIATES

HAMILTON, OHIO

(See Cincinnati)

General Practice, focusing on Driving Under the Influence, Driving while Intoxicated, DUI, DWI, OVI, Personal Injury, Wrongful Death, Medical Malpractice, Real Estate, Domestic Relations, Bankruptcy and Probate.

BIESER, GREER & LANDIS, LLP

HAMILTON, OHIO

(See Dayton)

General Civil Practice, Trial Practice, Business Litigation, Professional Liability Defense, Personal Injury Defense, Products Liability Defense, Corporate Law, Employment Law, Commercial Law, Probate, Tax Law, White Collar Criminal Defense, Arbitration, Mediation.

PHYLLIS G. BOSSIN CO., L.P.A.

HAMILTON, OHIO

(See Cincinnati)

Domestic Relations and Family Law. Child Custody, Support, Divorce, Premarital Agreements.

BUECHNER, HAFFER, O'CONNELL, MEYERS, HEALEY & KOENIG CO., L.P.A.

HAMILTON, OHIO

(See Cincinnati)

General Practice. Estate and Gift Taxation, Probate, Family Law, Corporate, Negligence, Medical Legal Products Liability, Real Estate, Construction, Land Use, Zoning and Eminent Domain Law. Trials and Appeals, Pension and Profit Sharing, Federal Income.

CASPER AND CASPER

Established in 1936

2 SOUTH 3RD STREET, SUITE 360
HAMILTON, OHIO 45011
Telephone: 513-424-2401-Middletown;
937-224-1122-Dayton
513-381-7096-Cincinnati
513-892-2560-Hamilton
513-892-2560; Toll Free: 1-800-784-2889
Fax: 513-424-0622
URL: http://www.casperlaw.com

Middletown, Ohio Office: Gas and Electric Building, One North Main Street, P.O. Box: 510, 45042. Telephone: 513-424-2401.
Dayton, Ohio Office: First National Plaza Building, 130 West Second Street, Suite 1950, 45402. Telephone: 937-224-1122.
Cincinnati, Ohio Office: 119 East Court Street, Fourth Floor, Suite 410, 45202. Telephone: 513-381-7096.

Personal Injury, Workers Compensation and Social Security Disability Law. Products Liability Litigation. Trials.

REFERENCES: First National Bank of S.W. Ohio; Bank One of Middletown, Ohio.

For complete biographical data on all personnel, see Professional Biographies at Middletown, Ohio)

CONESE LAW OFFICE

Established in 1983

21 LUDLOW STREET
HAMILTON, OHIO 45011
Telephone: 513-737-7044
Fax: 513-894-1141
URL: http://www.coneselawoffice.com
Email: info@coneselawoffice.com
URL: http://www.lawyers.com/coneselawoffice

Adoption Law, Bankruptcy, Child Support, Criminal Law, Child Custody, Visitation Rights, Driving While Intoxicated, Divorce, Family Law, Probate, Estate Administration, Wills.

MARK CONESE, born 1957; admitted to bar, 1983, Ohio and U.S. District Court, Southern District of Ohio. *Education:* Miami University (B.A., Political Science, History, 1980); University of Cincinnati (J.D., 1983). ***LANGUAGES:*** English. ***Email:*** coneselaw@cinci.rr.com

VICTORIA DAIKER

FIFTH THIRD BANK BUILDING
301 HIGH STREET
HAMILTON, OHIO 45011
Telephone: 513-868-3911
FAX: 513-868-3988

General Civil and Trial Practice. Commercial Collections, Wrongful Death, Personal Injury, Probate and Estate Planning, Wills and Trusts, Juvenile Law, Domestic Relations, Spousal Support, Premarital Agreements, Domestic Violence, Adoptions, Child Custody and Support, Divorce and Dissolution, Alternative Dispute Resolution, Mediation, Collaborative Law.

VICTORIA DAIKER, born District of Columbia, July 13, 1942; admitted to bar, 1977, Ohio; 1978, U.S. District Court, Southern District of Ohio; 1982, U.S. Court of Appeals, Sixth Circuit; 1984, U.S. Supreme Court. *Education:* Manhattanville College (B.A., 1961); Indiana University (M.A., 1964); University of Cincinnati (J.D., 1977). Assistant Prosecuting Attorney, 1978-2000 and Head, Civil Division, Butler County. Special Counsel, Ohio Attorney General, 1980-1995. *Member:* Butler County and Ohio State Associations; National District Attorneys Association; Collaborative Family Law Association of Butler County.

REPRESENTATIVE CLIENTS: Cincinnati Gas & Electric; Preble County Credit Bureau; Somerville National Bank; State of Ohio (Special Counsel to Ohio Attorney General).
REFERENCES: First Financial Bank; Fifth Third Bank.

PARIS K. ELLIS

HAMILTON, OHIO

(See Middletown)

Criminal Law, Drug Crimes, Driving While Intoxicated, Alcoholic Beverages, Family Law, Divorce, Wrongful Death, Wills and Probate, Federal Criminal, White Collar Crimes, Embezzlement, Parole Violations, Sex Crimes, Rape, Murders, Juvenile Crimes, Custody, Domestic Violence, Support.

FREUND, FREEZE & ARNOLD

A LEGAL PROFESSIONAL ASSOCIATION

HAMILTON, OHIO

(See Dayton)

Civil Litigation including Commercial Litigation, Employment Defense, Professional Malpractice Defense, Employer Intentional Torts, Construction Litigation, Civil Rights Defense, Local Government Defense, Nursing Home Defense, Environmental Litigation and Insurance Defense.

LOPEZ, HODES, RESTAINO, MILMAN & SKIKOS

A LAW CORPORATION

HAMILTON, OHIO

(See Cincinnati)

Mass Tort Litigation, Medical Malpractice, Products Liability, Employment Law, Personal Injury and Elder Law.

MANLEY BURKE

A LEGAL PROFESSIONAL ASSOCIATION

HAMILTON, OHIO

(See Cincinnati)

Litigation, Local Government Law, Land Use and Zoning Law, Civil Rights, Probate. Fraternal Law. Personal Injury, Labor Law, Workers Compensation, Employee Benefits and Professional Malpractice.

McGOWAN & JACOBS, LLC

246 HIGH STREET

HAMILTON, OHIO 45011

Telephone: 513-844-2000

Fax: 513-868-1190

General Civil Practice, Insurance and Personal Injury Law, Trials and Appeals in all Courts, Products Liability, Architects, Engineers, Medical, Dental, and Legal Malpractice, Patent, Trademark and Copyright Law, Political Subdivision Liability, Land Use, Zoning and Eminent Domain Law, Fraud Investigations.

FIRM PROFILE: McGowan & Jacobs, LLC offers clients in Ohio, Kentucky and Indiana a full-service civil trial practice with appeals in state and federal courts. The firm concentrates on personal injury, malpractice and products liability, construction law, insurance defense and fraud investigations. The firm also handles patent, trademark and copyright law.

JACK C. McGOWAN, born Cincinnati, Ohio, March 26, 1947; admitted to bar, 1974, Ohio; 1975, U.S. Court of Customs and Patent Appeals; 1978, U.S. District Court, Southern District of Ohio and U.S. Supreme Court; 1995, U.S. District Court, Northern District of Ohio. *Education:* Miami University; University of Cincinnati (B.S.M.E., 1970); George Washington University (J.D., cum laude, 1974). Pi Tau Sigma; Phi Delta Phi. Patent Examiner, U.S. Patent and Trademark Office, 1970-1975. *Member:* Butler County and Ohio State Bar Associations; Ohio Association of Civil Trial Lawyers; Defense Research Institute. ***PRACTICE AREAS:*** Products Liability Law; Medical Malpractice Law; Patent Law; Trademark Law; Copyright Law; Insurance Defense Law; Personal Injury Law; School Law; Political Subdivision Liability. ***Email:*** jcm@jcmcgowan.com

MICHAEL E. JACOBS, born Madison, Wisconsin, August 14, 1969; admitted to bar, 1996, Kentucky; 1997, Ohio; 1998, U.S. District Court, Southern District of Ohio; 2001, Indiana; 2002, U.S. District Court, Southern District of Indiana. *Education:* University of Cincinnati (Design Architecture, Art & Planning, B. Arch, 1993); Southwestern University School of Law at Los Angeles, California (J.D., 1995). Vice-Chairman, 1998 and Chairman, 1999, Deerfield Township Board of Zoning Appeals, Warren County, Ohio. *Member:* Cincinnati, Kentucky, Ohio and Indiana State Bar Associations; American Institute of Architects (Cincinnati Chapter, Associate Director, 1998-2002 and Legislative and Legal Affairs Director, 2003—). ***PRACTICE AREAS:*** Construction Law; Insurance Defense; Political Subdivision Liability; Medical Malpractice; Eminent Domain; Appellate Practice. ***Email:*** michaeljacobs@jcmcgowan.com

LOCAL COUNSEL FOR: Medical Protective Co.; State Auto Mutual Insurance Co.; Ohio Bar Liability Insurance Company.
REPRESENTATIVE CLIENTS: Hamilton City School Board; Butler County Commissioners; Mid-Miami Roofing Co.
REFERENCES: First National Bank of Southwestern Ohio, Hamilton, Ohio; Fifth Third Bank, Hamilton, Ohio.

PARRISH, FRYMAN & MARCUM CO., L.P.A.

Established in 1932

FIRST FINANCIAL BANK BUILDING
300 HIGH STREET, SUITE 704
P.O. BOX 747

HAMILTON, OHIO 45012-0747

Telephone: 513-863-8270
Telecopier: 513-863-9999
Email: contact@parrishattys.com
URL: http://www.parrishattys.com

Oxford, Ohio Office: 5995 Fairfield Road, Unit One, 45056. Telephone: 513-863-8270.

(This Listing Continued)

Business, Real Estate, General Practice, Probate, Estate Planning, Banking Law and Creditor Rights.

HUNTINGTON V. PARRISH (1906-1973)

CYRUS J. FITTON (1889-1978)

FRANCIS S. BEELER (1908-1990)

LEE H. PARRISH, born Hamilton, Ohio, March 16, 1943; admitted to bar, 1968, Ohio. *Education:* Tulane University of Louisiana; The Ohio State University (B.A., 1965); University of Cincinnati (J.D., 1968). Order of the Coif. *Member:* Butler County, The Ohio State and American Bar Associations. ***PRACTICE AREAS:*** Probate; Estate Planning; Banking; Business. ***Email:*** lhp@parrishattys.com

STEPHEN S. MARCUM, born Hamilton, Ohio, October 28, 1957; admitted to bar, 1983, Ohio and U.S. District Court, Southern District of Ohio. *Education:* Vanderbilt University (B.A., cum laude, 1980); University of Dayton (J.D., 1983). Phi Alpha Delta. *Member:* Butler County, Cincinnati and The Ohio State Bar Associations. ***PRACTICE AREAS:*** Real Estate; Business; Banking; Creditors Rights. ***Email:*** stevem@parrishattys.com

SARA C. HIRKA, born Hamilton, Ohio, March 19, 1972; admitted to bar, 1997, Ohio. *Education:* Wittenberg University (B.A., cum laude, 1994); Ohio State University (J.D., 1997). *Member:* Butler County, Cincinnati and Ohio State Bar Associations. ***PRACTICE AREAS:*** Real Estate; Estate Planning; Probate; Business Law; Creditors Rights. ***Email:*** sch@parrishattys.com

CYNAMON T. TROKHAN, born Willoughby, Ohio, March 11, 1971; admitted to bar, 1996, Ohio; 2003, U.S. Tax Court; registered to practice before Patent and Trademark Office. *Education:* Case Western Reserve University (B.A., cum laude, 1993; J.D., cum laude, 1996). *Member:* Butler County and The Ohio State Bar Associations. ***PRACTICE AREAS:*** Probate; Estate Planning; Business; Taxation. ***Email:*** ctt@parrishattys.com

RETIRED

NEIL B. SMITH, born Hamilton, Ohio, September 12, 1934; admitted to bar, 1960, Ohio. *Education:* Miami University (B.S. in Bus., 1956); Salmon P. Chase College of Law (J.D., 1960). Phi Alpha Delta; Phi Beta Kappa; Beta Gamma Sigma; Phi Eta Sigma.

ROBERT E. FRYMAN, born Mt. Healthy, Ohio, March 18, 1928; admitted to bar, 1953, Ohio. *Education:* Miami University (B.S., 1950); University of Cincinnati (J.D., 1953). Phi Beta Kappa; Order of the Coif.

REPRESENTATIVE CLIENTS: First Financial Bank, N.A.; First Financial Bancorp.; U.S. Bank, N.A. (Butler County); The Great Miami Valley YMCA; Butler County United Way; Hamilton Community Foundation.
AGENTS FOR: The Ohio Bar Title Insurance Company; Stewart Title Guaranty Company; First American Title Insurance Company.

PETERSON & PETERSON

HAMILTON, OHIO

(See Xenia)

Automobile and Motorcycle Accidents, Workers Compensation, Job-Related Injuries, Wrongful Death, Bus and Truck accidents, Negligence Claims, Insurance Claims, Probate, Estates, Wills, Living Trust, Guardianship, Power of Attorney, Real Estate, Contracts, Deeds, Evictions, Family Law, Divorce, Custody, Visitation, Domestic Violence, Criminal, Traffic Violations, Felonies, Misdemeanors, DUI, License Suspension, Juvenile, Bankruptcy.

WAITE, SCHNEIDER, BAYLESS & CHESLEY CO., L.P.A.

HAMILTON, OHIO

(See Cincinnati)

General Civil Practice. Aviation, Antitrust Litigation, Class Action, Commercial Litigation, Complex Litigation, Corporate Law, Federal Employees Liability, General Civil Trials and Appeals in all Courts, Insurance, Labor, Consolidated and Multi-district Litigation, Products Litigation, Securities Litigation and Wrongful Death.

THE LAW OFFICES OF MYRON A. WOLF

Established in 1975

120 NORTH SECOND STREET
P.O. BOX 741

HAMILTON, OHIO 45012

Telephone: 513-863-0664
Fax: 513-868-1800
Email: mawolf@fuse.net
URL: http://www.mwolflaw.com

Family Law, Divorce and Custody, Insurance Defense and Criminal Law.

MYRON A. WOLF, born Cincinnati, Ohio, October 11, 1946; admitted to bar, 1975, Ohio. *Education:* Miami University (B.A., 1968); University of Cincinnati (J.D., 1975). Member of the Board of Commissioners on Grievances and Discipline for the State of Ohio. *Member:* Butler County (President, 1995-1996; Chairman, Family Law Committee, 1986-1988 and 1997—), Ohio State and American Bar Associations; Collaborative Family Law Association (Board Member). ***PRACTICE AREAS:*** Family Law; Collaborative Law; Mediation.

(This Listing Continued)

THE LAW OFFICES OF MYRON A. WOLF, Hamilton—Continued

ASSOCIATES

BARBARA L. HORWITZ, born Cleveland, Ohio, January 6, 1947; admitted to bar, 1994, Ohio. *Education:* Butler University (B.S., 1969); University of Cincinnati (J.D., 1994). *Member:* Cincinnati, Butler County, Ohio State and American Bar Associations. ***PRACTICE AREAS:*** Civil Litigation; Bankruptcy. **Email:** bhorwitz1@yahoo.com

DANIEL A. (ANDY) NASTOFF, born Atlanta, Georgia, January 10, 1966; admitted to bar, 1991, Ohio; 2000, U.S. District Court, Southern District Of Ohio. *Education:* Youngstown State University (B.A., 1988); University of Cincinnati (J.D., 1991). *Member:* Butler County and Ohio State Bar Associations. ***PRACTICE AREAS:*** Criminal Defense; Personal Injury. **Email:** danastoff2@lawyer.com

REPRESENTATIVE CLIENT: State Farm Insurance Co.

THE LAW OFFICE OF REX A. WOLFGANG

246 HIGH STREET
HAMILTON, OHIO 45011
Telephone: 513-868-2731
Fax: 513-868-1190
Email: rawolfgan@aol.com
URL: http://www.rexwolfgang.com

Civil Practice, Environmental Law, Product Liability, Personal Injury, Real Estate, Construction Law, Community Association Law.

REX A. WOLFGANG, born East Liverpool, Ohio, April 11, 1959; admitted to bar, 1988, Ohio, U.S. District Court, Southern District of Ohio and U.S. Court of Appeals, Sixth Circuit. *Education:* Xavier University (B.S., 1981); University of Cincinnati (J.D., 1988). *Member:* Butler County and Hamilton County Bar Associations; Court of Common Pleas. ***PRACTICE AREAS:*** Civil Practice; Environmental Law; Product Liability; Personal Injury; Real Estate; Construction Law; Community Association Law.

YOUNG & ALEXANDER CO., L.P.A.

HAMILTON, OHIO

(See Dayton)

Business Law, Health Care, Insurance Law, Labor and Employment, Nonprofit and Charitable Organizations, Personal Injury, Products Liability, Real Estate, Toxic Torts, Trusts and Estates, Wills and Probate, Commercial Litigation.

ZEGARSKI & ICE CO., L.P.A.

HAMILTON, OHIO

(See Cincinnati)

Bankruptcy, Consumer Bankruptcy, Foreclosures, Family Law, Adoptions, Child Custody, Child Support, Divorce, Domestic Violence, Premarital Agreements, Spousal Support, Visitation Rights, Dissolution, Modifications, Garnishments, Harassment, Lawsuits, Alimony, Paternity, Personal Injury.

BERNARD & HAFFEY CO., L.P.A.

HIGHLAND HEIGHTS, OHIO

(See Cleveland)

General Civil and Criminal Practice. Corporate, Probate, Commercial Law, Bankruptcy, Trusts and Estates, Negligence, Family Law, Divorce, Juvenile, and Real Estate. Trial and Appellate Practice, Personal Injury.

SEAN O. BOYLE

HILLIARD, OHIO

(See Columbus)

State and Federal Criminal Defense, Felonies and Misdemeanors, Juvenile Law.

BAHRET & ASSOCIATES CO., L.P.A.

Attorneys at Law
Established in 1988

7050 SPRING MEADOWS WEST
HOLLAND, OHIO 43528
Telephone: 419-861-7800
Fax: 419-861-7808

Civil Litigation and Insurance Defense Law.

ROBERT J. BAHRET, born Dayton, Ohio, October 14, 1953; admitted to bar, 1980, Ohio; 1982, Michigan; U.S. District Court, Northern District of Ohio; U.S. Court of Appeals, Sixth Circuit. *Education:* University of Cincinnati (B.A., 1975); University of Toledo (J.D., 1979). Licensed Private Pilot, Ohio.*Member:* Toledo (Member, Fee Arbitration Committee) and Ohio State Bar Associations; State Bar of Michigan; Toledo Claims Association; Ohio Association of Civil Trial Attorneys; Defense Research Institute. (Board Certified Civil Trial Specialist by the National Board of Trial Advocacy). ***PRACTICE AREAS:*** Civil Litigation; Insurance Defense Law; Aviation Law. **Email:** rbahret@bahret-law.com

(This Listing Continued)

ASSOCIATES

ANDREW J. AYERS, born Mount Vernon, Ohio, February 14, 1953; admitted to bar, 1979, Ohio and U.S. District Court, Northern District of Ohio; U.S. Court of Appeals, Sixth Circuit. *Education:* Hillsdale College (B.A., magna cum laude, 1975); University of Toledo (J.D., 1978). *Member:* Toledo, Ohio State and American Bar Associations; Ohio Association of Civil Defense Attorneys; Defense Research Institute. ***PRACTICE AREAS:*** Civil Litigation; Personal Injury; Insurance Defense; Corporate Law; Bankruptcy. **Email:** aayers@bahret-law.com

DAVID W. DOERNER, born Norwalk, Ohio, June 14, 1950; admitted to bar, 1987, Ohio and North Carolina; U.S. District Court, Northern and Southern Districts of Ohio and U.S. District Court, Eastern District of North Carolina. *Education:* Bowling Green State University (B.S., 1972); Case Western Reserve University (J.D., 1976). *Member:* Toledo and Ohio State Bar Associations; Huron County Bar Association. ***PRACTICE AREAS:*** Civil Litigation; Personal Injury; Insurance Defense.

KEVIN A. PITUCH, born Toledo, Ohio, September 17, 1956; admitted to bar, 1988, Ohio; U.S. District Court, Northern District of Ohio; U.S. Court of Appeals, Sixth Circuit. *Education:* Berklee College of Music (B.A., 1981); University of Toledo (J.D., cum laude, 1988). *Member:* Toledo and Ohio State Bar Associations. ***PRACTICE AREAS:*** Insurance Defense. **Email:** kpituch@bahret-law.com

JEFFREY B. CHARLES, born Toledo, Ohio, August 24, 1957; admitted to bar, 1995, Ohio and U.S. District Court, Northern District of Ohio; U.S. Court of Appeals, Sixth Circuit. *Education:* Bowling Green State University (B.A., 1981); University of Toledo (J.D., 1995). Adjunct Professor, Bowling Green State University. *Member:* Toledo and Ohio State Bar Associations. [U.S. Naval Reserve, LTJG, 1982-1984]. ***LANGUAGES:*** Hebrew. ***PRACTICE AREAS:*** Insurance Defense; Hospitality Law; Real Estate. **Email:** jcharles@bahret-law.com

MANDY M. GERKEN, born Lima, Ohio, September 29, 1979; admitted to bar, 2004, Ohio. *Education:* Miami University (B.A., 2001); Ohio Northern University (J.D., 2004). **Email:** mgerken@bahret-law.com

KEITH J. WATKINS, born Martin, South Dakota; admitted to bar, 1981, Ohio; 1996, Michigan, U.S. District Court, Northern District of Ohio and U.S. Court of Appeals, Sixth Circuit. *Education:* Muskingum College; University of Cincinnati (B.A., Arts, with honors, 1978); University of Toledo (J.D., with honors, 1981). Editor, University of Toledo Law Review, 1981. *Member:* Toledo and Ohio State Bar Associations; Ohio Association of Civil Trial Attorneys. ***PRACTICE AREAS:*** Civil Litigation; Insurance Defense. **Email:** kwatkins@bahret-law.com

OF COUNSEL

MARC J. MEISTER, born Cleveland, Ohio, February 9, 1954; admitted to bar, 1979, Ohio; U.S. District Court, Northern District of Ohio; U.S. Court of Appeals, Sixth Circuit. *Education:* Amherst College (B.A., 1976); University of Toledo (J.D., 1979). Recipient, American Jurisprudence Awards in Commercial Transaction I and Corporation Tax. *Member:* Toledo and Ohio State Bar Associations; National Board of Trial Advocacy; Ohio Association of Civil Trial Attorneys; Ohio Academy of Trial Lawyers; Defense Research Institute. ***PRACTICE AREAS:*** Civil Litigation; Insurance Defense. **Email:** mmeister@bahret-law.com

LEGAL SUPPORT PERSONNEL

DENISE M. SCHMIDT, born Morristown, New Jersey, February 9, 1963. *Education:* University of Toledo (A.A.B., Legal Assisting Technology, 1985). Member, Toledo Association of Legal Assistants (Past President, Past Trustee). Recipient, Legal Assistant of the Year, 1991 and 1996. Associate Member, Toledo and Ohio State (Lawyers and Paralegals Committees) Bar Associations. ***PRACTICE AREAS:*** Litigation Support. **Email:** dschmidt@bahret-law.com

ASHLEY P. BROOKS, born Haskins, Ohio, 1983. *Education:* The University of Toledo (B.S., Paralegal Studies). *Member:* Paralegal Association of Northwest Ohio.

LAURIE M. DUSA, born Toledo, Ohio, December 10, 1971. *Education:* University of Toledo (A.A.B., Legal Assisting Technology, 1992). *Member:* Toledo Association of Legal Assistants. ***PRACTICE AREAS:*** Litigation Support. **Email:** ldusa@bahret-law.com

REPRESENTATIVE CLIENTS: American Modern Homes Insurance Company; American Home Remodelers, Inc.; AIG Claims Services, Inc.; AOPA Insurance Co.; Auto-Owners Insurance Co.; CNA Insurance Co.; Central Mutual Insurance Co.; Century Surety Co.; Cincinnati Insurance Co.; Continental Western Insurance Co.; Frankenmuth Mutual Insurance Co.; General Casualty Insurance Co.; Gerkin Companies; German Mutual Insurance Co.; GuideOne Insurance; Hamilton Mutual Insurance Co.; Harco National Insurance Co.; Heritage Insurance Co.; Illinois National Insurance; Liberty Mutual Insurance Co.; Lightning Rod/Western Reserve Mutual Casualty Co.; Michigan Millers Insurance Co.; Milwaukee Insurance Co.; Motorists Mutual Insurance Co.; Ohio Farmers Insurance Co.; Pekin Insurance Co.; Permanent General; Podiatry Insurance Co. of America; Progressive Insurance Co.; Reliance Insurance Co., a Mutual Co.; Selective Insurance Co.; State Auto Insurance Co.; Titan Insurance Co.; Victoria Insurance Co.; Westfield Companies; Windsor Group, Inc.

STEUER, ESCOVAR, BERK & BROWN CO., L.P.A.

HUDSON, OHIO

(See Cleveland)

General Civil and Criminal Practice. Personal Injury, Negligence, Workers Compensation, Corporation, Mergers and Acquisitions, Taxation, Real Estate, Bankruptcy, Family, Probate and Commercial Law. Estate Planning, Trials and Medical Malpractice, Civil and Criminal Appellate Work, Insurance Defense, Business Law, Administrative Law.

DAVID G. UMBAUGH

110 W. STREETSBORO STREET, SUITE 3A
HUDSON, OHIO 44236
Telephone: 330-650-6608
Fax: 330-655-7617
URL: http://www.davidumbaugh.com
Email: umbaugh@alltel.net
URL: http://www.davidumbaugh.net

Estate Planning, Probate, Business Law, Business Law with Exit Planning, Elder Care, Trusts and Estates, Wills, Civil Practice.

DAVID G. UMBAUGH, born 1949; admitted to bar, 1974, Ohio. *Education:* Miami University (A.B., 1971); Northwestern University (J.D., 1974). Member: Wealthcounsel, National Network of Estate Planning Attorneys; Business Enterprise Institute. *Member:* Akron and Ohio State Bar Associations. ***PRACTICE AREAS:*** Trusts and Estates; Estate Planning; Asset Protection; Probate; Exit Planning for Business Owners; Small Business Law; Elder Care; Wills; Divorce; Family Law; General Practice.

THE BERNARD LAW FIRM

INDEPENDENCE, OHIO

(See Cleveland)

Complex Business Litigation, Accountants Malpractice, Stockbroker Malpractice, Banking Litigation, Employment Litigation, Personal Injury, Wrongful Termination, Employment Discrimination, Race Discrimination, Sex Discrimination, Sexual Harassment, Americans with Disabilities, Age Discrimination in Employment, Employment Termination, Family and Medical Leave Act, Breach of Contract, Contract Litigation, Insurance, Class Actions, Securities Litigation, Shareholder Derivative Actions, Lender Liability, Antitrust, Consumer Litigation, Consumer Fraud, Construction Defects, Construction Accidents, Construction Law, Automobile Accidents and Injuries, Wrongful Death, Dog Bites, Slip and Fall, Nursing Home Litigation, Products Liability.

O'ROURKE & ASSOCIATES CO., L.P.A.

2 SUMMIT PARK DRIVE, SUITE 650
INDEPENDENCE, OHIO 44131
Telephone: 216-447-9500
Fax: 216-447-9501
URL: http://www.orourke-law.com

All aspects of Construction Law including Contracts, Change Orders, Mechanic's Liens, Bond Claims, Litigation, Arbitration and Mediation.

R. RUSSELL O'ROURKE, born Cleveland, Ohio, July 27, 1955; admitted to bar, 1984, Ohio and U.S. District Court, Northern District of Ohio; 1986, Florida; 1992, U.S. Supreme Court. *Education:* University of Vermont (B.A., 1978); Cleveland State University, Cleveland-Marshall College of Law (J.D., 1984). Delta Theta Phi. Editor, Cleveland State Law Review, 1983-1984. President and Chapter Attorney, American Subcontractors Association of Northern Ohio, ASA National Attorney Council; Board Member, Ohio Subcontractors Council; National Board Member, American Subcontractors Association. Author: *Ohio Mechanics' Liens and Materialmen's Liens,* Third Edition. ***PRACTICE AREAS:*** Construction (40%); Mechanics Liens (35%); Bond Claims (10%); Commercial (5%); Arbitration and Mediation (5%); Business Law (5%). ***Email:*** rorourke@orourke-law.com

MICHAEL J. WARRELL, born Kitchener, Ontario, Canada, February 17, 1954; admitted to bar, 1980, Ohio and U.S. District Court, Northern District of Ohio. *Education:* Swarthmore College (B.A., 1976); The Ohio State University (J.D., 1980). Adjunct Professor of Law, Cleveland State University College of Law, 1985—. Member, Construction Industry Advisory Council and Commercial Advisory Council of the American Arbitration Association, 1987-1997. ***PRACTICE AREAS:*** Construction Claims (50%); Arbitration (20%); Mediation (15%); Commercial Litigation (15%). ***Email:*** mwarrell@orourke-law.com

OF COUNSEL

CHARLES A. BAKULA, born Sarajevo, Bosnia, April 14, 1964; admitted to bar, 1992, Ohio. *Education:* Cleveland State University (B.A., 1985); Cleveland-Marshall College of Law (J.D., 1991). ***LANGUAGES:*** Croatian and Serbian. ***PRACTICE AREAS:*** Construction Law (30%); Commercial Litigation (30%); Criminal Law (25%); Probate Law (15%). ***Email:*** CharlesBakula@netscape.net

MARSTELLER LAW OFFICES

IRONTON, OHIO

(See Huntington, West Virginia)

Insurance Defense Litigation, Insurance Coverage, Asbestos Litigation, Mass Litigation, Trucking Litigation, Medical Malpractice Defense, Toxic Torts, Mediation and Arbitration, Automobile Litigation, Environmental, Products Liability, Collections, Subrogation.

OFFUTT, FISHER & NORD

IRONTON, OHIO

(See Huntington, West Virginia)

General Civil Trial Practice, Insurance Defense, Products Liability, Premises Liability, Asbestos Defense, Mass Tort Defense, Medical Malpractice, Legal Malpractice, Hospital Liability, Health Care Law and Commercial Litigation, Transportation Law.

SPEARS & SPEARS

122 SOUTH FOURTH STREET
IRONTON, OHIO 45638-1520
Telephone: 740-532-5815; 740-532-6913
Fax: 740-532-5816
Email: spearslawoff@hotmail.com

General Civil Practice. Personal Injury, Workers Compensation, Social Security, Probate, Wills, Estates, Guardianships, Real Estate Law.

HAROLD D. SPEARS, born Ironton, Ohio, February 9, 1919; admitted to bar, 1948, Ohio. *Education:* Marshall University (A.B., 1941); Duke University (J.D., 1947).

DAVID R. SPEARS, born Ironton, Ohio, February 15, 1950; admitted to bar, 1978, Ohio. *Education:* Marshall University; Capital University (B.S., 1972); Thomas M. Cooley Law School (J.D., cum laude, 1978).

RICHARD M. LEWIS

295 PEARL STREET
P.O. BOX 664
JACKSON, OHIO 45640
Telephone: 740-286-0071
Telefax: 740-286-2988
URL: http://www.richardmlewis.com
Email: richard@richardmlewis.com
URL: http://www.lawyers.com/richardlewis

General Trial and Appellate Practice, Tort Law, Insurance Law, Medical Negligence, Employment Law, Personal Injury, Commercial Litigation, Domestic Relations, Corporation, Real Estate, Probate and Banking Law, Debtor-Creditor and Criminal Law.

FIRM PROFILE: The firm regularly practices in Jackson, Vinton, Pike, Gallia, Ross, Athens, Scioto and Meigs Counties. The firm serves certain clients throughout Ohio. The firm practices in the federal courts of Columbus, Cincinnati and Dayton and the U.S. Sixth Circuit Court of Appeals. Mr Lewis is admitted to practice before the United States Supreme Court.

RICHARD M. LEWIS, born Gallipolis, Ohio, December 11, 1957; admitted to bar, 1982, Ohio; 1984, U.S. District Court, Southern District of Ohio; 1986, U.S. Supreme Court; 1999, U.S. Court of Appeals, Sixth Circuit. *Education:* The Ohio State University (B.A., 1979); Capital University (J.D., 1982). Listed in: International Who's Who; Who's Who in American Law. Recipient: American Jurisprudence Book Award; OATL Distinguished Service Award, 2005. Authored and presented numerous articles at CLE seminars. NBTA Examination Writer (1994 Domestic Relations; 2004 Domestic Relations Ethics). Co-Editor: OATL Book of Complaints (2002); Big Book of Motions (2005). Former Legal Counsel, Jackson County Child Support Enforcement Agency. Expert Witness, legal issues: Ross, Pike, Jackson, Franklin, Lawrence, Washington and Stark Counties. *Member:* Jackson County (President, 1986-1988), Ohio State (Member, Committee on the Independent Judiciary and Unjust Criticism of Judges) and American Bar Associations; Ohio Bar College; Ohio Supreme Court Committee on Attorney Specialization; The Association of Trial Lawyers of America; Ohio Academy of Trial Lawyers (Member: Board of Trustees, 1993—). (Certified as a Civil Trial Advocate by the National Board of Trial Advocacy). ***REPORTED CASES:*** Akers v. Alonzo, M.D., et al (1992) 65 Ohio St. 3d 442; Gillum v. Fairgreens Country Club (Ohio App. 4th Dist.) 110 Ohio App. 3d 60. In re Caudill, 2005 Ohio 3927, Ohio App. 4th Dist., July 21, 2005. Wooten v. Kreischer, 2005 Ohio 4078, Ohio App. 5th Dist., August 3, 2005. ***PRACTICE AREAS:*** Personal Injury Law; Products Liability; Medical Malpractice; Insurance Law; Family Law; Civil Practice; Commercial Law; Employment Law; Alternative Dispute Resolution; Litigation; Libel and Slander; Defamation; Animal Law; Civil Rights.

ASSOCIATE

JILL H. SHRIVER, born Gallipolis, Ohio, March 16, 1978; admitted to bar, 2003, Ohio; 2005, U.S. District Court, Southern District of Ohio. *Education:* Ohio University (B.B.A., 2000); Capital University Law School (J.D., 2003). *Member:* Jackson County, Ohio State and American Bar Associations; Ohio Academy of Trial Lawyers. ***PRACTICE AREAS:*** Litigation; Business Law; Employment Law; Real Estate; Trusts and Estates; Probate. ***Email:*** jill@richardmlewis.com

REPRESENTATIVE CLIENTS: The Pillsbury Co.; Oak Hill Banks; Telmark, Inc.; Hon. Thos. S. DeLay; Frigid Tek, Inc.; Advanced Refrigeration Development Co.; Fleming Homes; McGraw Physical Therapy, Inc.; Martin Block Co.; A & A Truck Stop; Cotner & Cooley, CPA's; NCI Bldg Systems, LP; Marion C. Lewis Furniture Co.; Veteran Process Piping; Walnut Hills Veterinary Clinic; Dome Financial Services; Davis Broadcasting Media; CDG Management LLC; Jackson County Power; Transamerica Finance Corp.; Sterling Finance; The City of Jackson, Ohio.
REFERENCES: Oak Hill Banks; National City Banks; Morgan Stanley Dean Witter.

WARREN AND YOUNG PLL

JEFFERSON, OHIO

(See Ashtabula)

General and Trial Practice. Corporation and Business Law, Labor and Employment Law, Insurance Defense, Civil Litigation, Real Estate, Probate and Estate Planning Law.

A. DALE NATICCHIA

KENT, OHIO

(See Cleveland)

Driving While Intoxicated, Traffic Violations, Juvenile Law, Drivers License Suspension, DUI, Estate Planning, Wills and Probate Law, Contested Wills, Felonies and Collections.

SLATER, ZURZ & GILBERT

KENT, OHIO

(See Akron)

Personal Injury, Wrongful Death, Commercial Litigation, Corporate, Business, Real Estate, Business Organization, Domestic Relations, Construction Litigation.

STEPHENS & ROSENBERG

KENT, OHIO

(See Ravenna)

General Civil and Criminal Trial Practice. Personal Injury, Family, Corporate, Real Estate, Municipal, Juvenile and Probate Law.

EDWARD C. WEBER

KENT, OHIO

(See Akron)

Trials and Appeals in all Courts. Criminal, DUI, Traffic Violations, Personal Injury, Defense, Probate and Estates Drug Crimes, Assault, Domestic Violence.

WILLIAMS, WELSER & KRATCOSKI

Established in 1950

ELEVEN SOUTH RIVER STREET
P.O. BOX 396
KENT, OHIO 44240
Telephone: 330-673-3444
Tele-Fax: 330-673-6460
URL: http://www.wwklaw.com

Business Law, Corporate Law (Formation, Operation, Acquisition and Sale of Corporations, Partnerships, and Limited Liability Companies); Commercial and Residential Real Estate Law (Purchase, Sale, and Development including Condominiums, Subdivisions, and Zoning); Commercial and Residential Construction Law (including Mechanics Liens); Commercial and Residential Landlord Tenant Law; Domestic Relations Law (Divorce, Dissolution, Child Support and Custody); Estate Planning and Probate (Wills, Trusts, and Estate Administration); Traffic Law (Personal Injury, Automobile Accidents, Traffic Violations, and DUI); Criminal Law (Misdemeanors and Felonies); and Litigation Capability in all Practice Areas.

FIRM PROFILE: The firm has been providing legal services to businesses and individuals in Portage, Summit, Stark, and Geauga Counties for 50 years. By design the firm is small and made up of lawyers who focus their individual practices in differing areas of the law. The size and structure of the firm enable us to provide our clients with a variety of services ranging from proactive advice to litigation efficiently and cost effectively and enables our clients to deal directly with experienced attorneys.

MEMBERS OF FIRM

HOWARD T. WELSER, JR., born North Canton, Ohio, July 23, 1943; admitted to bar, 1969, Ohio. *Education:* Miami University (B.A., 1965); The Ohio State University (J.D., 1968). Law Director for the City of Kent, 1972-1973. *Member:* Portage County and Ohio State Bar Associations. ***PRACTICE AREAS:*** Estate Planning; Probate; Elder Law; Wills; Trusts and Estates; Real Estate. ***Email:*** twelser@wwklaw.com

DAVID E. WILLIAMS, born Akron, Ohio, October 7, 1949; admitted to bar, 1976, Ohio; 1977, U.S. District Court, Northern District of Ohio and U.S. Supreme Court. *Education:* Albion College (B.A., 1972); Capital University (J.D., 1976). *Member:* Akron (Member, Bankruptcy Section), Portage County, Ohio State and American Bar Associations. ***PRACTICE AREAS:*** Business Law; Business Formation; Partnership Law; Limited Liability Company Law; Mergers and Acquisitions; Real Estate Development; Subdivisions; Condominium Law; Zoning Law; Commercial Leasing; Secured Creditors Rights. ***Email:*** dwilliams@wwklaw.com

PETER C. KRATCOSKI, born Minneapolis, Minnesota, October 26, 1963; admitted to bar, 1988, Ohio; and U.S. District Court, Northern District of Ohio; U.S. Court of Appeals, Sixth Circuit. *Education:* Ohio State University (B.A., 1985; J.D., 1988). Phi Alpha Delta. *Member:* Akron, Portage County, Ohio State and American Bar Associations. ***PRACTICE AREAS:*** Civil Litigation; Domestic Relations Law; Commercial Collections; Real Estate; Commercial Leasing; Real Estate Litigation. ***Email:*** kratcoskip@yahoo.com

ERROL ANTHONY CAN, born North Hampton, Massachusetts, September 8, 1964; admitted to bar, 1992, Ohio. *Education:* Albion College (B.S., 1987); Thomas M. Cooley School of Law (J.D., 1991). *Member:* Portage and Ohio State Bar Associations; Ohio Association of Criminal Defense Lawyers. ***PRACTICE AREAS:*** Criminal Defense; Family Law; Personal Injury; Civil Litigation. ***Email:*** ecan@wwklaw.com

BENITO C. R. ANTOGNOLI, born Akron, Ohio, February 24, 1954; admitted to bar, 1979, Ohio; 1980, U.S. District Court, Northern District of Ohio; 1986, U.S. Court of Appeals, Sixth Circuit. *Education:* College of Wooster; University of Akron (B.A., 1976; J.D., 1979). Part-Time Instructor, Department of Criminal Justice, Kent State University, 1989-1992. Acting Judge Magistrate, Portage County Municipal Court, 1987-1992. *Member:* Portage County (President, 2002-2003), Ohio State and American Bar Associations; The Association of Trial Lawyers of America; Ohio Academy of Trial Lawyers; Summit County Trial Lawyers Association. ***PRACTICE AREAS:*** Personal Injury; Accidents; Wrongful Death; Medical Malpractice; Products Liability; Construction Litigation. ***Email:*** bantognoli@wwklaw.com

(This Listing Continued)

ASSOCIATE

JAMES E.J. ICKES, born Akron, Ohio, February 8, 1975; admitted to bar, 2000, Ohio. *Education:* Ohio University (B.B.A., summa cum laude, 1997); The Ohio State University (J.D., 2000). Phi Alpha Delta, 1994-1997. *Member:* Portage County, Ohio State and American Bar Associations. ***LANGUAGES:*** Japanese. ***PRACTICE AREAS:*** Litigation; Business Law; Domestic Relations; Personal Injury. ***Email:*** jickes@wwklaw.com

COUNSEL FOR: Huntington National Bank; Home Savings Bank; Crown Equity Mortgage Company; Kent Title Agency, Inc.; Kent Regional Business Alliance; Downtown Kent Urban Redevelopment Corporation; Hall Green Agency, Inc.; Laurenco; Dacath Development Corporation; Alar Development; Epling Contractors; Rockne's Inc.; Western Reserve Home Builders Association; Garrett-Oldsmobile Cadillac, Inc.; Havre Chevrolet Oldsmobile; Tellog Systems, Inc.; Wright Heating & Air Conditioning; Kent Credit Union; MJM Management; Century Management Company.
APPROVED ATTORNEYS FOR: Old Republic National Title Insurance Company.

OLIVER LAW OFFICE

KENTON, OHIO

(See Columbus)

Products Liability, Personal Injury, Wrongful Death, Latex Allergy Litigation, Medical Malpractice, Vioxx Litigation, Automobile Accidents, Insurance Law, Employment Discrimination.

THOMAS D. BERRY

KETTERING, OHIO

(See Dayton)

Probate, Wills, Bankruptcy, Consumer Bankruptcy, Chapter 7 and Chapter 13.

FALKE & DUNPHY, LLC

KETTERING, OHIO

(See Dayton)

Personal Injury, Complex Litigation, Divorce, Probate Law, Will Contests, Estate Planning, Living Trusts, Real Estate and Corporation. General, Civil and Trial Practice.

ANNE CATHERINE HARVEY

KETTERING, OHIO

(See Dayton)

Trials, Appeals, Federal, State and Municipal Criminal Defense, Divorce, Dissolution, Child Custody, Military Domestic Relations Law.

SHERRETS LAW OFFICES, LLC

580 LINCOLN PARK BOULEVARD, SUITE 399
KETTERING, OHIO 45429
Telephone: 937-299-9607
Fax: 937-299-9618
Email: carlsherrets@dayton-attorneys.com
URL: http://www.dayton-attorneys.com

Probate, Estate Planning, Personal Injury, Business Law, Business Planning, Real Estate, Litigation, Collections, Automobile Accidents, Guardianship, Conservatorship, Wills, Trusts and Estates, Bankruptcy, Family Law, Divorce, Domestic Relations, Child Support, Child Custody, Spousal Support.

FIRM PROFILE: Serving the entire Dayton area, including Kettering, Oakwood and Centerville.

CARL D. SHERRETS, born Dover, Ohio, January 11, 1960; admitted to bar, 1988, Ohio. *Education:* United States Military Academy; Kent State University (B.B.A., magna cum laude, 1985); University of Cincinnati (J.D., 1988). Phi Alpha Delta; Beta Gamma Sigma. *Member:* Dayton and Ohio State Bar Associations. [U.S. Army, Paratrooper, 82nd Airborne Division]. ***PRACTICE AREAS:*** Probate; Wills; Business Law; Real Estate. ***Email:*** carlsherrets@dayton-attorneys.com

ASSOCIATE

MARC N. GREENBERG, born Dayton, Ohio, March 6, 1977; admitted to bar, 2004, Ohio. *Education:* University of Dayton (B.S., cum laude, 1999; J.D., cum laude, 2003). ***PRACTICE AREAS:*** Family Law; Bankruptcy; Trusts and Estates; Criminal Law. ***Email:*** marcgreenberg@dayton-attorneys.com

---

NANCY H. CANARY PC

12500 EDGEWATER DRIVE, UNIT 1806
LAKEWOOD, OHIO 44107
Telephone: 216-226-7466
Fax: 216-266-7426
Email: nacanary@cs.com

Palm Beach, Florida Office: 125 Worth Avenue, Suite 117, 33480. Telephone: 561-833-5900. Fax: 561-833-5951.

Estate Planning Law, Probate Law, Personal Planning, Successions.

(For complete biographical data on personnel, see Professional Biographies at Palm Beach, Florida)

HUNT & COOK LLC

LAKEWOOD, OHIO

(See Westlake)

Civil Litigation and Appeals, Business and Commercial Law, Commercial Collections, Criminal Law, Divorce and Family Law, Wills and Estates, Personal Injury.

MURMAN & ASSOCIATES

Established in 1975

14701 DETROIT AVENUE, SUITE 555
LAKEWOOD, OHIO 44107
Telephone: 216-228-6996
Fax: 216-226-9011
Email: MURMANLAW@AOL.COM
URL: http://www.lawyers.com/murman&associates

Municipal Law, Probate and Estate, Professional Responsibility Legal Ethics and Criminal Law in regards to Professional Licensing.

MEMBER OF FIRM

MICHAEL E. MURMAN, born Cleveland, Ohio, August 14, 1946; admitted to bar, 1975, Ohio; 1976, Florida and U.S. District Court, Northern District of Ohio; 1979, U.S. Supreme Court; 1989, U.S. Court of Appeals, Sixth Circuit. *Education:* University of Dayton (B.A., 1968); Cleveland State University (J.D., magna cum laude, 1975). Assistant Cuyahoga County Prosecutor, 1976-1979. City Prosecutor, 1979-1990 and Director of Law, City of Lakewood, Ohio, 1991-1996. President, Cuyahoga County Law Directors Association, 1988-1989. President, Ohio Municipal Attorneys Association, 1996. Ohio Supreme Court Board of Commissioners on Grievance and Discipline, 2000-2003. Member, Board of Bar Examiners, Ohio Supreme Court, 2004—. Ohio Supreme Court Commission Certification of Attorneys as Specialists, 1997-2000. *Member:* Cleveland (Chairman, Criminal Law Section, 1989-1990), Cuyahoga County, Ohio State (Chairman, Legal Ethics and Professional Conduct Committee, 1996-1998; Bell Commission, 1995-1997; Multi Disciplinary Practice Special Committee, 1999-2000) and American Bar Associations; The Florida Bar; Cuyahoga Criminal Defense Attorneys Association; Ohio Criminal Defense Association; William K. Thomas AIC (President, 2003-2004). ***PRACTICE AREAS:*** Municipal Law; Probate; Legal Ethics and Professional Responsibility; Criminal Law; Professional Licensing. ***Email:*** murmanlaw@aol.com

ASSOCIATE

RAYMOND S. GRUSS, born Cleveland, Ohio, February 25, 1957; admitted to bar, 1991, Ohio; 1995, U.S. Supreme Court. *Education:* Mercyhurst College (B.A., 1979); Cleveland Marshall College of Law (J.D., 1990). *Member:* Cleveland, Ohio State and American Bar Associations; Cuyahoga Criminal Defense Lawyers Association. ***PRACTICE AREAS:*** Criminal Law; Probate; General Practice. ***Email:*** grusslaw@aol.com

BABBITT & WEIS LLP

LANCASTER, OHIO

(See Columbus)

Family and Matrimonial Law, Divorce, Dissolutions, Legal Separation, Spousal Support, Property Division, Child Custody, Child Support, Pre-Marital Agreements, Divorce Arbitration.

MICHAEL E. BENSON

LANCASTER, OHIO

(See Columbus)

Bankruptcy Law, Foreclosures, Debtor and Creditor, Real Estate, Landlord and Tenant, Buying and Selling, Wills, Living Wills, Healthcare, Powers of Attorney.

CALIG & HANDELMAN, LPA

204 N. COLUMBUS STREET
LANCASTER, OHIO 43130
Telephone: 740-653-4400
Fax: 740-653-0037
URL: http://www.chohiolawyers.com

Columbus, Ohio Office: 854 East Broad Street, 43205. Telephone: 614-252-4885; 1-800-633-5000.
Newark, Ohio Office: 29 S. Park Place, 43055. Telephone: 740-349-8581. Fax: 740-345-4101.
Marion, Ohio Office: 274 S. Main Street, 43302. Telephone: 740-375-5051.

Bankruptcy, Personal Injury, Probate, Real Estate, Social Security, Social Security Disability, Medical Malpractice, Wrongful Death, Civil Litigation, Domestic Relations Law.

FIRM PROFILE: Family Law, Personal Injury, Bankruptcy.

For complete biographical data on all personnel, see Professional Biographies at Columbus)

COLLEY SHROYER & ABRAHAM CO., L.P.A.

LANCASTER, OHIO

(See Columbus)

Civil Trial Practice. Personal Injury, Medical Malpractice, Automobile Accidents, Wrongful Death, Railroad Accidents, Slip and Fall, Negligence, Product Liability and Toxic Torts.

CRABBE, BROWN & JAMES LLP

111 SOUTH BROAD STREET, SUITE 209
LANCASTER, OHIO 43130
Telephone: 740-689-1743
Fax: 740-689-1746
Email: info@cbjLawyers.com
URL: http://www.cbjLawyers.com

Columbus, Ohio Office: 500 South Front Street, Suite 1200, 43215. Telephone: 614-228-5511. Fax: 614-229-4559.
Cincinnati, Ohio Office: 30 Garfield Place, Suite 740, 45202. Telephone: 513-784-1525. Fax: 513-784-1250.
Cleveland, Ohio Office: 1280 W. Third Street. Telephone: 216-574-9312.
Urbana, Ohio Office: 118 Scioto Street. Telephone: 937-652-4000.

General Insurance Defense, Product Liability, Professional Malpractice, Premises Liability, Environmental and Toxic Tort Claims, Employment and Labor Law, Tax Matters, General Business and Corporate Law and Litigation, Banking and Securities, Real Estate, Probate and Estate Planning, Criminal Law, Administrative, Regulatory and Governmental Law, Workers Compensation, Intellectual Property, Fire, Arson and Fraud, Fidelity and Surety Life, Accident and Health, Insurance Coverage Law, Construction Claims, Health and Hospital Law, Oil, Gas and Energy Law, Transportation Law, Automobile Dealer Law, Zoning, International Practice and Domestic Law, Land Use Planning, and Eminent Domain.

(For complete biographical data on all personnel, see Professional Biographies at Columbus, Ohio)

DAGGER, JOHNSTON, MILLER, OGILVIE & HAMPSON, LLP

Established in 1902

144 EAST MAIN STREET
P.O. BOX 667
LANCASTER, OHIO 43130
Telephone: 740-653-6464;
Columbus Direct Line: 614-837-1545;
For 614/740 Area Code Only: 800-339-4618
Telecopier: 740-653-8522
URL: http://www.daggerlaw.com

Thornville, Ohio Office: East Columbus Street, P.O. Box 272. Telephone: 740-246-6337.
Portsmouth, Ohio Office: 801 John Street. Telephone: 740-355-6644.

General Trial Practice. Business, Commercial, Tax, Estate Planning, Elder Law, Probate, Labor, Real Estate, Corporation, Family Law, Insurance, Personal Injury, Wrongful Death, Oil and Gas Law, Employment, Criminal Law, OMVI Law, Traffic Defense, Juvenile Law.

FIRM PROFILE: Dagger, Johnston, Miller, Ogilvie & Hampson is a law firm built on more than 100 years of collective legal experience. The firm is the result of a merger of Deffenbaugh & Miller, founded in 1902 by J. W. Deffenbaugh, and Dagger, Johnston, Ogilvie, Charles & Hampson, founded by William C. Dagger in 1946.

With clients ranging from local residents to national corporations, the firm is experienced in most areas of the law, including: Acquisitions, Adoption, Banking, Bankruptcy, Business, Civil Litigation, Commercial, Contract Disputes, Criminal Defense, Divestitures, Eminent Domain, Employment, Estate Planning, Family Law, Insurance Claims, Juvenile Defense, Labor Negotiations, Medical Malpractice, Oil and Gas, Personal Injury, Probate, Product Liability, Real Estate, Retirement Plans, Tax, Traffic Defense, Wills and Trusts and Wrongful Death.

Additionally, one of the firm's attorney is a Certified Public Accountant (INACTIVE) with a background in retirement plans, tax, and corporate planning, and tax litigation.

MEMBERS OF FIRM

ROBERT E. JOHNSTON, born Brownsville, Ohio, November 13, 1929; admitted to bar, 1954, Ohio. *Education:* Ohio Wesleyan University (B.A., 1951); University of Cincinnati (J.D., 1954). Phi Delta Phi. Assistant Editor, University of Cincinnati Law Review, 1953. *Member:* Fairfield County (President, 1971), Perry County, Ohio State and American Bar Associations. [With U.S. Army, Counter Intelligence Corp., 1954-1956]. ***PRACTICE AREAS:*** Probate; Estate Planning; Corporation; Real Estate. ***Email:*** rejohnston@daggerlaw.com

NORMAN J. OGILVIE, JR., born Santa Marie, California, June 12, 1943; admitted to bar, 1968, Ohio. *Education:* Northwestern University (B.A., 1965); The Ohio State University (J.D., 1968). Listed in: Ohio Super Lawyers, 2004 and 2005; The Best Lawyers in America, 2003-2004; Columbus Monthly "Top Lawyers: The City's Best and Brightest," Clerk, City Council, Lancaster, 1970-1974. Councilman at Large, Lancaster, 1974-1977. Chairman, Elected Official and Judicial Compensation Review Commission, State of Ohio, 1976-1978. *Member:* Fairfield County (President, 1979), Columbus and Ohio State Bar Associations; American Academy of Matrimonial Lawyers; Ohio State Bar Association Family Law Specialty Board. [With U.S. Army, 1968-1970]. (Certified Specialist in Family Relations Law, Ohio State Bar Association). ***REPORTED CASES:*** In Re Adoption of Ridenour, 61 Ohio State 3d 319 (1991). ***PRACTICE AREAS:*** Family Law; Business Litigation; Probate; Labor. ***Email:*** njogilvie@daggerlaw.com

MARK R. RIEGEL, born Lancaster, Ohio, March 22, 1951; admitted to bar, 1977, Arizona; 1985, Ohio. *Education:* Wittenberg University (B.A., magna cum laude, 1973); The Ohio State University (J.D., cum laude, 1977). Phi Delta Phi. Author: "Evaluation and Settlement of Personal Injury Claims," Personal Injury Litigation in Ohio, Revised Edition, 1989. *Member:* Fairfield County, Columbus, Ohio State and American Bar Associations; State Bar of Arizona; The Association of Trial Lawyers of America; Ohio Academy of Trial Lawyers; Million Dollar Advocates Forum. ***PRACTICE AREAS:*** Personal Injury; Insurance; General Civil Litigation; Mediation. ***Email:*** mrriegel@daggerlaw.com

(This Listing Continued)

DAGGER, JOHNSTON, MILLER, OGILVIE & HAMPSON, LLP, Lancaster—Continued

RAYMOND R. MICHALSKI, born Lorain, Ohio, July 18, 1951; admitted to bar, 1976, Ohio. *Education:* The Ohio State University (B.A., 1973); Ohio Northern University (J.D., with distinction, 1976). Phi Kappa Phi. Director, Ohio Bar Liability Insurance Company, 1993-1994. *Member:* Hocking County (Secretary-Treasurer, 1978; President, 1980 and 1981), Fairfield County, Columbus, Ohio State (President, 1994-1995; District 9 Representative, Board of Governors, 1989-1992; Council of Delegates, 1995—; Young Lawyer Representative, Board of Governors, 1985-1987; Chairman, 1983, Member, Board of Governors, 1980-1987, Young Lawyers Section; Member, Commercial, Banking and Bankruptcy Law Committee, 1981—; Real Property Section, Board of Governors, 1999—) and American (Member: House of Delegates, 1985-1986 and 1995—; Business Law Section; Real Property, Probate and Trust Law Section) Bar Associations; Ohio State Bar Foundation (Trustee, 1994-1995). ***PRACTICE AREAS:*** Real Estate; Banking; Commercial. ***Email:*** rrmichalski@daggerlaw.com

R. MARK BIBLER, born Lancaster, Ohio, April 23, 1956; admitted to bar, 1981, Ohio. *Education:* The Ohio State University (B.S., summa cum laude, 1978; J.D. with honors, 1981). Beta Alpha Psi; Beta Gamma Sigma; Phi Kappa Phi; Phi Eta Sigma. Certified Public Accountant (INACTIVE), Ohio, 1984. *Member:* Fairfield County, Columbus and Ohio State Bar Associations; The Ohio Society of Certified Public Accountants. ***PRACTICE AREAS:*** Taxation and Business Law; Retirement Planning; Probate; Estate Planning. ***Email:*** rmbibler@daggerlaw.com

RANDY L. HAPPENEY, born Circleville, Pickaway County, Ohio, September 24, 1958; admitted to bar, 1985, Ohio. *Education:* Miami University (B.A., 1981); Ohio State University (J.D., 1985). *Member:* Fairfield County and Ohio State Bar Associations; Ohio Academy of Trial Lawyers. (Certified Specialist in Family Law, Ohio State Bar Association). ***PRACTICE AREAS:*** Adoption Law; Family Law; General Civil Litigation; Personal Injury. ***Email:*** rlhappeney@daggerlaw.com

BRIAN D. SHONK, born Lancaster, Ohio, January 2, 1961; admitted to bar, 1986, Massachusetts; 1988, Ohio. *Education:* Case Western Reserve University (B.A., cum laude, 1983); Boston College (J.D., magna cum laude, 1986). Order of the Coif. Articles Editor, Boston College Law Review, 1985-1986. *Member:* Fairfield County (President, 1995-1996), Columbus, Ohio State and Massachusetts (Member, Civil Litigation and Probate Sections) Bar Associations; Commercial Law League of America. ***PRACTICE AREAS:*** Business; Banking; Commercial Litigation; Creditor Rights; Estate Planning; Probate. ***Email:*** bdshonk@daggerlaw.com

D. JOE GRIFFITH, born Mineral Wells, Texas, October 13, 1964; admitted to bar, 1991, Ohio. *Education:* Marietta College (B.A., 1987); University of Toledo (J.D., 1991). Phi Alpha Theta. Member, University of Toledo Law Review, 1989-1991. *Member:* Columbus, Fairfield County, Ohio State and American (Member, Litigation Section) Bar Associations; Ohio Academy of Trial Lawyers; The Association of Trial Lawyers of America. (Certified as a Civil Trial Advocacy Specialist by the National Board of Trial Advocacy). ***PRACTICE AREAS:*** Civil Litigation; Construction Law; Personal Injury; Legal Malpractice; Medical Malpractice. ***Email:*** djgriffith@daggerlaw.com

SCOTT P. WOOD, born Columbus, Ohio, February 20, 1968; admitted to bar, 1994, Ohio; 1995, U.S. District Court, Southern District of Ohio and U.S. Court of Appeals, Sixth Circuit; 1999, U.S. Supreme Court. *Education:* Ohio University (B.A., summa cum laude, 1990); The Ohio State University (J.D., with honors, 1994). Phi Beta Kappa; Phi Delta Phi. Member, The Ohio State Law Journal on Dispute Resolution, 1993-1994. Judicial Extern for Ohio Supreme Court Justice Craig Wright, 1994. *Member:* Fairfield County, Ohio State and American Bar Associations; Ohio Academy of Trial Lawyers; The Association of Trial Lawyers of America; National Association of Criminal Defense Lawyers; Ohio Association of Criminal Defense Lawyers; National College for DUI Defense; American Inns of Court. (Certified as a Criminal Trial Advocacy Specialist by the National Board of Trial Advocacy). ***REPORTED CASES:*** State v. Burnside (2003), 100 Ohio State 3d 152; State v. Moore (2000), 90 Ohio State 3d 47; State v. Lynn (2000), 137 Ohio App.3d 402. ***PRACTICE AREAS:*** Criminal Defense; Juvenile Defense; Traffic Defense; Civil Litigation; Personal Injury; Wrongful Death. ***Email:*** spwood@daggerlaw.com

---

AARON R. CONRAD, born Lancaster, Ohio, June 11, 1974; admitted to bar, 2002, Ohio. *Education:* University of Cincinnati (B.S., 1999); Capital University Law School (J.D., 2002). Phi Alpha Delta; Alpha Kappa Delta. Golden Key National Honor Society. *Member:* Fairfield County, Ohio State and American Bar Associations; Ohio Academy of Trial Lawyers; Association of Trial Lawyers of America. ***PRACTICE AREAS:*** Personal Injury; Juvenile Law; General Practice; Insurance; Criminal Defense. ***Email:*** arconrad@daggerlaw.com

JONATHAN C. CLARK, born Lancaster, Ohio, March 29, 1969; admitted to bar, 2002, Ohio; 2003, North Carolina. *Education:* Hillsdale College (B.A., cum laude, 1991); Capital University Law School (J.D., cum laude, 2002). Order of Curia. *Member:* Columbus, Fairfield, Ohio State and American Bar Associations. ***PRACTICE AREAS:*** Probate; Estate Planning; Real Estate; Corporate Law; Business Law; General Practice. ***Email:*** jcclark@daggerlaw.com

CARRIE S. SNOKE, born Lancaster, Ohio, February 25, 1977; admitted to bar, 2002, Ohio; 2003, U.S. District Court, Southern District of Ohio. *Education:* Ohio University (B.A., 1998); Capital University (J.D., 2002; LL.M., 2003). Delta Theta Phi. *Member:* Fairfield County and Ohio State Bar Associations. ***PRACTICE AREAS:*** Real Estate; Taxation; General Practice. ***Email:*** cssnoke@daggerlaw.com

JEFF J. SPANGLER, born Lancaster, Ohio, March 17, 1979; admitted to bar, 2004, Ohio. *Education:* University of Mississippi (B.B.A., 2001); Ohio State University (J.D., 2004). ***PRACTICE AREAS:*** Litigation; Employment Law; Commercial Litigation; Business Litigation. ***Email:*** jjspangler@daggerlaw.com

OF COUNSEL

JAMES W. MILLER, born Lancaster, Ohio, November 30, 1928; admitted to bar, 1955, Ohio. *Education:* Indiana University; The Ohio State University (B.S., 1950; J.D., 1955). Phi Delta Phi. *Member:* Fairfield County (President, 1967), Ohio State (Member: Executive Committee, 1971-1974; Council of Delegates, 1974-1980) and American Bar Associations. [1st Lieut., U.S. Army, 1951-1953]. ***Email:*** jwmiller@daggerlaw.com

---

VINCENT A. DUGAN, JR.

LANCASTER, OHIO

(See Columbus)

Family Law, Divorce, Child Custody, Child Support, Adoption Law, Visitation Rights, Real Estate, Small Business Law, Traffic Violations.

FRIEDMAN & MIRMAN CO., L.P.A.

LANCASTER, OHIO

(See Columbus)

Family Relations Law, Divorce.

GOLDMAN & ROSENTHAL

LANCASTER, OHIO

(See Columbus)

Personal Injury, Family Law, Real Estate, Commercial Leasing, Construction and Mechanics Lien Law, Collections, Estate Planning and Probate, Corporate, Juvenile Law, Criminal. Civil and Criminal Trials in all Courts.

SUSAN KENNEY-PFALZER

LANCASTER, OHIO

(See Columbus)

Family Law, Divorce, Dissolution, Child Custody, Spousal and Child Support, Visitation Rights, Adoptions, Paternity, Juvenile Law, Collaborative Law, Restraining Orders.

GREGG R. LEWIS

LANCASTER, OHIO

(See Columbus)

Family Law, Matrimonial Law and Civil Litigation.

CARL McCOY
ATTORNEY AT LAW

LANCASTER, OHIO

(See Newark)

Criminal Law, Divorce, Family Law, Medical Malpractice, Personal Injury, Automobile Accidents, Child Custody, Child Support, General Practice, Trusts and Estates, Wills and Probate Law, Driving While Intoxicated, Drug Crimes, Elder Law, Estate Planning, Insurance, Slip and Fall, Traffic Violations, Wrongful Death, Dog Bites, Domestic Violence, Parole and Probation, Visitation Rights, White Collar Crime, Automobile Insurance, Automotive Products Liability, Felonies, Misdemeanors, Premarital Agreements, Sexual Assault, Spousal Support and Motorcycle Accidents.

THE PLYMALE PARTNERSHIP LLP

LANCASTER, OHIO

(See Columbus)

Personal Injury, Products Liability, Wrongful Death, Medical Malpractice, Professional Negligence, Traumatic Brain Injury, Automobile Accidents, Nursing Home Torts, Civil Litigation.

ROURKE & BLUMENTHAL, LLP

LANCASTER, OHIO

(See Columbus)

Personal Injury, Negligence, Products Liability, Medical Malpractice, Nursing Home Litigation, Wrongful Death, Intentional Tort, Insurance Disputes, Automobile Accidents, Civil Trial Practice, Aviation, Professional Liability.

SUZANNE KAY SABOL

LANCASTER, OHIO

(See Columbus)

Family Law and Domestic Relations.

(This Listing Continued)

STEBELTON, ARANDA & SNIDER

A LEGAL PROFESSIONAL ASSOCIATION

109 NORTH BROAD STREET
LANCASTER, OHIO 43130
Telephone: 740-654-4141
Fax: 740-654-2521
Email: saslaw@sas-lawfirm.com
URL: http://www.sas-lawfirm.com

Personal Injury, Automobile Accidents and Injuries, Wrongful Death, Medical Malpractice, Civil Litigation, Business and Tax Planning and Corporations, Family Law, Divorce, Child Custody, Child Support and Adoptions, Residential and Commercial Real Estate, Probate, Elder Law, Estate Planning and Employment Law.

FIRM PROFILE: Stebelton, Aranda & Snider was founded in 1978 by Gerald L. Stebelton. The firm has a broad-based general practice serving the needs of individuals and small businesses. Members of the firm are deeply committed to their clients, community and profession. As such Stebelton, Aranda and Snider is the only local law firm to be a member of the International Society of Primerus Law Firms. Further it is the only law firm recognized by the local Chamber of Commerce as Small Business of the Year.

The firm employees nine attorneys, four paralegals and a support staff of fifteen.

GERALD L. STEBELTON, born Lancaster, Ohio, September 13, 1939; admitted to bar, 1970, Ohio; 1973, U.S. Supreme Court. *Education:* The Ohio State University (B.S. in Engr., 1963); Capital University (J.D., 1970). Phi Alpha Delta. Assistant Prosecuting Attorney, Franklin County, 1971-1972. ***REPORTED CASES:*** Kaechele v. Kaechele, 35 Ohio St. 3rd 93 (1988). ***PRACTICE AREAS:*** Personal Injury; Wrongful Death; Business Litigation; Domestic Relations. ***Email:*** glstebelton@sas-lawfirm.com

JAMES C. ARANDA, born Chicago, Illinois, June 6, 1946; admitted to bar, 1971, Ohio, Illinois and Indiana. *Education:* Xavier University (A.B., cum laude, 1968); University of Notre Dame (J.D., 1971). Alpha Sigma Nu. ***REPORTED CASES:*** In re Adoption of Ridenour, 61 Ohio St. 3d 319 (1991); In re Adoption of Zschach, 75 Ohio St. 3rd 648 (1996). ***PRACTICE AREAS:*** Elder Law; Estate Planning; Corporate Law; Adoption Law. ***Email:*** jcaranda@sas-lawfirm.com

RICK L. SNIDER, born Lancaster, Ohio, November 11, 1954; admitted to bar, 1979, Ohio. *Education:* The Ohio State University (B.A., cum laude, 1976; J.D., 1979). Phi Beta Kappa. ***PRACTICE AREAS:*** Estate Planning; Business Planning; Elder Law; Corporate Law; Taxation; Real Estate. ***Email:*** rlsnider@sas-lawfirm.com

REPRESENTATIVE CLIENTS: Ohio Attorney General; Fairfield National Division of Park National Bank; The Community Bank; First Bremen Bank; Newell Company; Taylor Dealership, Inc.; Beneficial Mortgage Company of Ohio; Lan-Fair Federal Credit Union; Fairfield Cash Register; Lowes' Home Centers, Inc.; Mid-Ohio Drywall; Sterling Grinding Co.; Office Mart, Inc.; Risch Pharmacy, Inc.; Fairfield County Alcohol Drug and Mental Health Services Board; Lancaster Country Club; Fairfield Medical Center; Lancaster Board of Realtors; Hammonds Clothiers.
APPROVED ATTORNEYS FOR: Lawyers Title Ins. Co.
REFERENCE: Fairfield National Division of Park National Bank.

REBECCA J. STUMLER

LANCASTER, OHIO

(See Columbus)

Family Law, Divorce, Child Custody, Child Support, Visitation Rights, Adoption Law, Paternity, Domestic Violence, Bankruptcy Law, Civil Litigation.

TWYFORD & DONAHEY, P.L.L.

3794 OLD COLUMBUS ROAD, N.W.
LANCASTER, OHIO 43130
Telephone: Toll Free: 1-800-686-1699
Fax: 614-849-0475
Email: help@twyforddonahey.com
URL: http://www.twyforddonahey.com

Columbus, Ohio Office: 495 South High Street, 43215-5058. Telephone: Toll Free: 1-800-686-1699. Email: help@twyforddonahey.com.
Circleville, Ohio Office: 214 South Court Street, 43113. Telephone: Toll Free: 1-800-686-1699. Email: help@twyforddonahey.com.
Delaware, Ohio Office: 163 N. Sandusky, Suite 103, 43015. Telephone: Toll Free: 1-800-686-1699. Email: help@twyforddonahey.com.
Newark, Ohio Office: 137 West Main Street, Suite C., 43025. Telephone: Toll Free: 1-800-686-1699. Email: help@twyforddonahey.com.
London, Ohio Office: 25 West Fifth Street, 43140. Telephone: Toll Free: 1-800-686-1699. Email: help@twyforddonahey.com.

Personal Injury Litigation, Wrongful Death, Medical Malpractice, Products Liability, Automobile Accidents, Trucking Accidents, Head and Spinal Injuries, Motorcycle Accidents and Injuries, Uninsured Motorists, Insurance Law, Airplane Crash Litigation, Railroad Accidents, Slip and Fall, Dog Bites, Work Related Injuries, Birth Injuries, Nursing Home Abuse and Neglect.

FIRM PROFILE: Tom Twyford and Dick Donahey have been partners since 1968 and have practiced exclusively in the areas of personal injury, medical malpractice and products liability law. We have never represented insurance companies! In recent years, we have obtained some of the largest verdicts in Franklin County. We have purposely remained small in order to concentrate on a limited number of cases. We have six offices and will handle cases in any part of the state of Ohio.

(For complete biographical data on all personnel, see Professional Biographies at Columbus, Ohio.)

DAVID WIRTH

LANCASTER, OHIO

(See Columbus)

Insurance Law, Negligence, Legal Malpractice, Subrogation, Personal Injury, Probate.

WOLSKE & BARCLAY

A LEGAL PROFESSIONAL ASSOCIATION

LANCASTER, OHIO

(See Columbus)

Civil and Appellate Practice in State and Federal Courts. Medical and Dental Malpractice, Nursing Home Negligence, Personal Injury and Products Liability Law, Worker's Compensation and Industrial Accidents, Automobile Accidents, Airplane Crash Litigation.

BIESER, GREER & LANDIS, LLP

LEBANON, OHIO

(See Dayton)

General Civil Practice, Trial Practice, Business Litigation, Professional Liability Defense, Personal Injury Defense, Products Liability Defense, Corporate Law, Employment Law, Commercial Law, Probate, Tax Law, White Collar Criminal Defense, Arbitration, Mediation.

PHYLLIS G. BOSSIN CO., L.P.A.

LEBANON, OHIO

(See Cincinnati)

Domestic Relations and Family Law. Child Custody, Support, Divorce, Premarital Agreements.

BUECHNER, HAFFER, O'CONNELL, MEYERS, HEALEY & KOENIG CO., L.P.A.

LEBANON, OHIO

(See Cincinnati)

General Practice. Estate and Gift Taxation, Probate, Family Law, Corporate, Negligence, Medical Legal Products Liability, Real Estate, Construction, Land Use, Zoning and Eminent Domain Law. Trials and Appeals, Pension and Profit Sharing, Federal Income.

CASPER AND CASPER

LEBANON, OHIO

(See Middletown)

Personal Injury, Workers Compensation and Social Security Disability Law. Products Liability Litigation. Trials.

CHALFIE & FARLEY, CO., L.P.A.

LEBANON, OHIO

(See Cincinnati)

Probate Litigation, Probate Administration, Estate Planning, Trials and Appeals, Estate and Gift Tax, Trusts, Estates, Wills, Family Law, Negligence, Wrongful Death, Will Contests, Living Trusts and Automobile Collisions.

THOMAS G. EAGLE CO., L.P.A.

Established in 1989

3386 N. STATE ROUTE 123
LEBANON, OHIO 45036
Telephone: 937-743-2545
Email: eaglelawoffice@cs.com
URL: http://www.lawyers.com/eagle

General Civil and Criminal Trial and Appellate Practice in State and Federal Courts, in Ohio and Kentucky, including Personal Injury, Wrongful Death, Criminal Law, Civil Rights, Consumer Law, Commercial and Business Litigation, Bankruptcy, Real Estate, Family Law and others.

FIRM PROFILE: The goal of this office is efficient, equitable, and successful dispute resolution without sacrifice to the quality or effectiveness of the legal representation.

THOMAS G. EAGLE, born Newhall, California, December 26, 1961; admitted to bar, 1986, Ohio and U.S. District Court, Southern District of Ohio; 1988, Kentucky; 1989, U.S. Court of Appeals, Sixth Circuit; 1990, U.S. Supreme Court and U.S. District Court, Eastern District of Kentucky. *Education:* Eastern Kentucky University (B.A., in Political Science, with high distinction, 1983); University of Kentucky (J.D., 1986). Member, Moot Court Board and National Moot Court Team. Recipient: American Jurisprudence Award in Landlord and Tenant Law; Kentucky Bar Association Continuing Legal Education Award, 1996-2000. Visiting Assistant Professor, Real Estate Law, Miami University, 1987—. Author: "The Hidden Truth in Sentencing: Getting the Best out of Ohio's New Felony Sentencing Law," OACDL Vindicator (Spring 1996); "How to Litigate Your First Civil Trial in Ohio: Ethical Considerations," National Business Institute (2004); "Achieving Favorable Settlements in Ohio: Mediation, Walking the Ethical Line and Closing the Deal," National Business Institute (2005). Presentations: "Ohio's New Felony Sentencing Law," Warren County

(This Listing Continued)

THOMAS G. EAGLE CO., L.P.A., Lebanon—Continued

Bar Association (1996); "Electronic Filing in the Federal Courts," Warren County Bar Association (2005); "Achieving Favorable Settlements in Ohio," National Business Institute (2005). Member, Warren County Law Library Board of Trustees. *Member:* Dayton, Warren County, Butler County, Ohio State, Kentucky, Federal (Dayton Chapter) and American Bar Associations; Ohio Academy of Trial Lawyers; Kentucky Academy of Trial Attorneys; The Association of Trial Lawyers of America; Ohio Association of Criminal Defense Lawyers; National Association of Criminal Defense Lawyers; Miami Valley Trial Lawyers Association. ***REPORTED CASES:*** United States vs Barrett, 982 F.2d 193 (6th Cir. 1992); Rader v. Carroll, 36 ATLA Law Reporter 135 (May 1993); Bell v. Midwestern Educational Services, Inc., 89 Ohio App. 3d. 193, 624 N.E. 2d. 386 (1993) ; State v. Feltner, 87 Ohio App 3d 279, 622 N.E. 2d 15 (1993); Moore v. Holbrook, 2 F. 3d 697 (6th Cir., 1993); State v. Crawley, 96 Ohio App. 3d 149, 644 N.E.2d 724 (1994), jurisd'l motion over'd, 71 Ohio St.3d 1420, 642 N.E.2d 386 (1994), cert. denied, 514 US 1127 (1995); Walton v. Ohio Department of Rehabilitation and Correction, 37 ATLA Law Reporter 56 (March 1994); State v. Owen, 114 Ohio App. 3d. 226, 683 N.E.2d 37 (1996); State v. Echols, 141 Ohio App.3d 556, 752 N.E.2d 314 (2001); In re Absher Children, 141 Ohio App.3d 118, 750 N.E.7d 188 (2001). ***PRACTICE AREAS:*** Personal Injury; Criminal Law; Civil Litigation; Family Law; Appellate Practice; Civil Rights; Consumer Law; Negligence; Premises Liability. ***Email:*** eaglelawoffice@cs.com

LOCAL COUNSEL FOR: Interstate Trucker, Ltd.; Trucker's Legal Services; Open Road Drivers Plan.
REPRESENTATIVE CLIENTS: Amend Center for Eye Surgery; Butler County Council for Native Americans; Franklin Emergency Squad, Inc.; Georgetowne Condominium Owner's Association; Hawkins Realtors; Robin Springs Apartments; Southwestern College of Business; Sycamore Trails Homeowner's Association.

GRAY & DUNING

Established in 1936

130 EAST MULBERRY
LEBANON, OHIO 45036
Telephone: 513-932-2871
Cincinnati: 513-398-7388
Fax: 513-932-5532
TDD: 513-932-2871
Email: duning@grayandduning.com
URL: http://www.grayandduning.com

Civil Trial Practice. Probate, Estate Planning, Family, Real Estate, Personal Injury, Juvenile, Criminal, Annexation, Zoning and Municipal Law. Trials.

MEMBERS OF FIRM

MERYL B. GRAY (1907-1989)

J. WILLIAM DUNING, born Cincinnati, Ohio, October 17, 1943; admitted to bar, 1968, Ohio. *Education:* University of Cincinnati (B.A., 1965; J.D., 1968). Assistant City Prosecutor, 1968-1970 and Assistant City Solicitor, 1970-1972, Cincinnati, Ohio. City Attorney, Lebanon, Ohio, 1974-1999. Trustee, Ohio Bar Foundation, 1987—. *Member:* Cincinnati, Warren County (President, 1988-1989), Ohio State (Member, Council of Delegates, 1978-1996 and 2000—; Commission on Judicial Candidates, 2000 and 2002; Board of Governors, 1996-1999) and American Bar Associations; Ohio Academy of Trial Lawyers (Trustee, 1981-1986); Association of Trial Lawyers of America. ***LANGUAGES:*** Sign Language for the Deaf. ***PRACTICE AREAS:*** Annexation; Family Law; Municipal Law; Personal Injury; Probate; Real Estate; Zoning. ***Email:*** duning@grayandduning.com

DONALD E. ODA, II, born Cincinnati, Ohio, April 13, 1969; admitted to bar, 1995, Ohio and U.S. District Court, Southern District of Ohio; 1996, U.S. Court of Appeals, Sixth Circuit. *Education:* The Ohio State University (B.A. in Journalism, 1991); Salmon P. Chase College of Law (J.D., 1995). *Member:* Cincinnati, Warren County and Ohio State Bar Associations; Ohio Association of Criminal Defense Lawyers. ***PRACTICE AREAS:*** Criminal Law; Family Law; Civil Trial Practice; Juvenile Law; Business Law; Estate Planning; Probate; Collections. ***Email:*** oda@grayandduning.com

LEGAL SUPPORT PERSONNEL

CARA A. McGLOTHLIN. *Education:* Mountain View College (A.A., Legal Assisting, 1990); Paralegal Specialist School (Distinguished Honor Graduate, 1988). Paralegal Specialist/Court Reporter, 9th Legal Support Organization. Legal Assistant Member, Ohio State Bar Association. [United States Army Reserve, 1987—]. (Legal Assistant). ***Email:*** mcglothlin@grayandduning.com

SPECIAL COUNSEL FOR: City of Loveland; Village of Morrow.
APPROVED ATTORNEYS FOR: Ohio Bar Title Insurance Co.

JENKS, PYPER & OXLEY CO., L.P.A.

LEBANON, OHIO

(See Dayton)

General Liability, Property, Workers Compensation, Bad Faith, First Party Coverage, Third Party Coverage, Construction Defect, Environmental, Toxic Tort, Employment Practices, SUI, PIP/Med Pay, Inland Marine, Intellectual Property, Sexual Harassment, Subrogation, Professional Liability, including Accountants, Real Estate, Architects & Engineers, D&O and Agents E&O, Professional Malpractice, including Dental, Attorney and Medical.

KAUFMAN & FLORENCE

144 EAST MULBERRY STREET
P.O. BOX 280
LEBANON, OHIO 45036
Telephone: 513-932-1515; 423-1363
Fax: 513-932-9172
Email: wkaufman@go-concepts.com

General Practice. Corporation, Probate, Insurance, Criminal, Real Estate, Family, Equine and Negligence Law, Trials, Mediation, Arbitration.

MEMBERS OF FIRM

WILLIAM H. KAUFMAN, born Dayton, Ohio, August 11, 1943; admitted to bar, 1971, Ohio. *Education:* Miami University (B.S., 1965); Salmon P. Chase College of Law (J.D., 1971). Judge, Lebanon Municipal Court, 1986-1994. Lebanon City Prosecutor, 1971-1974. *Member:* Cincinnati, Warren County (President, 1983) and Ohio State Bar Associations; American Board of Trial Advocates; American College of Trial Lawyers. ***PRACTICE AREAS:*** Personal Injury; Probate; Mediation; Arbitration; Corporate Law; Real Estate Law; Civil Practice. ***Email:*** wkaufman@go-concepts.com

MARK T. FLORENCE, born Dayton, Ohio, December 17, 1953; admitted to bar, 1980, Ohio. *Education:* Miami University (B.A., 1976); Salmon P. Chase College of Law (J.D., 1980). *Member:* Warren County and Ohio State Bar Associations. ***PRACTICE AREAS:*** Real Estate; Civil Litigation; Criminal Defense; Corporate Law; Probate Law; Arbitration.

ASSOCIATE

WM. ROBERT KAUFMAN, born Kettering, Ohio, May 7, 1972; admitted to bar, 2001, Ohio. *Education:* Miami University (B.A., 1994); University of Cincinnati (J.D., 2001). *Member:* Warren County, Cincinnati and Ohio State Bar Associations; Ohio Association of Criminal Defense Lawyers. ***PRACTICE AREAS:*** Domestic Relations; Criminal Defense; Juvenile Law; Civil Practice; Municipal Law. ***Email:*** rkaufman@go-concepts.com

REPRESENTATIVE CLIENTS: Miami Valley Trotting, Inc.; Farm Credit Services; Lebanon Raceway; Lebanon Citizens National Bank; Farmers Home Administration; Peoples Community Bank.
LOCAL COUNSEL FOR: Cincinnati Gas & Electric Co.; The Celina Mutual Insurance Co.; The Lebanon Citizens National Bank; Western Water Company.
APPROVED AGENT AND ATTORNEYS FOR: Old Republic National Title Insurance Co.; First American Title Insurance Co.

ANNE EINSPANIER KREHBIEL

Established in 1998

42 EAST MULBERRY STREET, SUITE B
LEBANON, OHIO 45036
Telephone: 513-934-3200
Fax: 513-934-3223
Email: AEKLAW@go-concepts.com

Probate, Estate Planning and Administration, Elder Law, Wills and Trusts, and Guardianship.

FIRM PROFILE: Anne Einspanier Krehbiel has been certified by the Ohio State Bar Association as a specialist in estate planning, trust and probate law.

ANNE EINSPANIER KREHBIEL, born Cincinnati, Ohio, March 23, 1955; admitted to bar, 1980, Ohio and U.S. District Court, Southern District of Ohio. *Education:* University of Kentucky (B.S., 1977); University of Cincinnati (J.D., 1980). Certified Financial Planner, 1988. Member, Lebanon Rotary Club. *Member:* Cincinnati, Warren County (Chair, Certified, Grievance Committee) and Ohio State Bar Associations. (Certified Specialist in Estate Planning, Trust and Probate Law, Ohio State Bar Association). ***PRACTICE AREAS:*** Probate; Estate Planning; Estates; Elder Law; Wills; Trusts; Guardianship Law.

LOPEZ, HODES, RESTAINO, MILMAN & SKIKOS

A LAW CORPORATION

LEBANON, OHIO

(See Cincinnati)

Mass Tort Litigation, Medical Malpractice, Products Liability, Employment Law, Personal Injury and Elder Law.

MANLEY BURKE

A LEGAL PROFESSIONAL ASSOCIATION

LEBANON, OHIO

(See Cincinnati)

Litigation, Local Government Law, Land Use and Zoning Law, Civil Rights, Probate. Fraternal Law. Personal Injury, Labor Law, Workers Compensation, Employee Benefits and Professional Malpractice.

THE LAW OFFICES OF JOHN S. MENGLE

CLARK BUILDING
42 EAST SILVER STREET
LEBANON, OHIO 45036
Telephone: 513-932-2047
Fax: 513-932-3269
Email: mengle@go-concepts.com
URL: http://www.menglelaw.com

General Civil and Criminal Trial Practice, Business Law, Negligence, Family Law, Adoptions, Child Custody, Divorce, Premarital Agreement, Wills and Probate, Trusts and Estates, Estate Planning, Equine Law, Municipal Law, Bankruptcy, Real Estate Law, Mental Health Law, Personal Injury, Dog Bites, Auto Accidents, Slip and Fall, Wrongful Death, Collaborative Law, Collections.

JOHN S. MENGLE, born Wilmington, Ohio, May 23, 1952; admitted to bar, 1978, Ohio; U.S. District Court, Southern District of Ohio. *Education:* Miami University (A.B., 1972); Edgecliff College (B.A., 1974); Salmon P. Chase College of Law (J.D., 1978). Phi Alpha Delta. *Member:* Warren County (Chairman, Certified Grievance Committee, 1994-1995; Bar Counsel, 2000—; Treasurer, 2003; President, 2004), Ohio State and American Bar Associations; The Association of Trial Lawyers of America; Southwest Ohio Collaborative Lawyers. ***REPORTED CASES:*** State ex rel. Blackman v. Hitte, 5 Ohio State 3d 156, 449 NE 2d 1279 (1983); Blanchester Lumber and Supply, Inc. v. Cardinal State Bank, 56 Ohio App. 3d 25, 564 NE 2d 1074 (1988); Bemmes v. Public Employee Retirement Board, 102 Ohio App. 3d 182 (1995); Clermont County ADAMH Board v. Hogan, 79 Ohio St. 3d 358 (1997). ***PRACTICE AREAS:*** General Practice; Personal Injury; Business Law; Family Law; Wills, Trusts and Estates; Equine Law; Municipal Law; Bankruptcy; Real Estate Law.

ASSOCIATE

JANE A. SHORT, born Wilmington, Ohio, November 30, 1972; admitted to bar, 2000, Ohio; 2001, U.S. District Court, Southern District of Ohio. *Education:* Miami University (B.Phil., 1995); University of Dayton (J.D., 1999). *Member:* Warren County and Ohio State Bar Associations. ***PRACTICE AREAS:*** General Practice; Family Law; Criminal Law; Municipal Law. ***Email:*** janeshort@hotmail.com

REPRESENTATIVE CLIENTS: Mental Health Recovery Services of Warren and Clinton Counties; The Village of Clarksville, Ohio; Southern Ohio Gun Distributors, Inc.; Bill DeLord Autocenter, Inc.

PICKREL, SCHAEFFER & EBELING

LEBANON, OHIO
(See Dayton)

Banking, Civil, Corporate, General Business, Commercial Lending, Mergers and Acquisitions, Insurance, Labor and Employment, Healthcare, Municipal and Zoning, Personal Injury and Products Liability, Probate, Trust and Estate Planning, Construction, Computer, Real Estate, Environmental, Workers' Compensation Defense, Immigration, Bankruptcy and Tax Law. Trials and Appeals, School Law and Title Insurance.

RITTGERS & RITTGERS

Established in 1994
12 EAST WARREN STREET
LEBANON, OHIO 45036
Telephone: 513-932-2115; 513-459-0355
Facsimile: 513-934-2201
Email: silfvenk@rittgers.com
URL: http://www.lawyers.com/rittgers&rittgers

Criminal Law, Family Law, Personal Injury, Civil Litigation, Insurance Law.

FIRM PROFILE: Rittgers & Rittgers is the largest firm in Lebanon, Ohio, the county seat of Warren County. The firm is dedicated to meeting the needs of its clients and in providing competent and prompt assistance to out of state and out of county practitioners in need of local counsel. Members of the firm take an active part in the local bar as members of various committees and frequently lecture at Continuing Legal Education seminars on a wide range of topics.

MEMBERS OF FIRM

CHARLES H. RITTGERS, born Hempstead, New York, February 26, 1951; admitted to bar, 1978, Ohio and U.S. District Court, Southern District of Ohio. *Education:* Miami University (B.A., 1973); Xavier University (M.S., 1978); University of Cincinnati (J.D., 1978). *Member:* Warren County (President) and Ohio State Bar Associations; Greater Cincinnati Criminal Defense Lawyers Association (Former Board Member); Ohio Association of Criminal Defense Lawyers (Former President); Association of Trial Lawyers of America; National College of DUI Defense (Founding Member). ***REPORTED CASES:*** State v. Hochhausler, et al., 76 Ohio St. 3d 455 (1996); State v. Shindler, 70 Ohio St. 3d 54 (1994); State v. Harper, 70 Ohio St. 3d 398, 639 N.E.2d 66 (1994); Nationwide Insurance Co. v. Tobler, 80 Ohio App. 3d 560, 609 N.E.2d 1318 (1992); Waynesville v. Combs, 60 Ohio App. 3d 292, 584 N.E.2d 9 (1990); Bercaw v. Bercaw, 45 Ohio St. 3d 160, 543 N.E.2d 1197 (1989); State, ex rel. Doe v. Tracy, 51 Ohio App. 3d 198, 555 N.E.2d 674 (1988); State v. Carter, 28 Ohio App. 3d 61, 501 N.E.2d 1219 (1985). ***PRACTICE AREAS:*** Criminal; Personal Injury; Driving While Intoxicated; Insurance Law. ***Email:*** silfvenk@rittgers.com

ELLEN B. RITTGERS, born Cleveland, Ohio, August 9, 1953; admitted to bar, 1979, Ohio and U.S. District Court, Southern District of Ohio. *Education:* Miami University (B.A., cum laude, 1975); University of Cincinnati (J.D., 1979). Phi Beta Kappa. Trained Collaborative Lawyer in Domestic Relations. *Member:* Cincinnati, Butler County (Member, Family Law Committee), Warren County (Member, Family Law Committee) and Ohio State Bar Associations; Ohio Family Law Forum; Southwest Ohio Collaborative Law Association. ***PRACTICE AREAS:*** Family Law; Divorce; Child Custody. ***Email:*** rittgerse@rittgers.com

JASON A. SHOWEN, born Washington Courthouse, Ohio, July 11, 1964; admitted to bar, 2000, Ohio. *Education:* University of Florida (B.S., 1987); University of Denver (J.D., 1999). Finalist, National Appellate Advocacy Competition; First Place, Hoffman Cup Trial Advocacy Competition. Trained Collaborative Lawyer in Domestic Relations. *Member:* Butler County, Warren County, Ohio State and American Bar Associations; Association of Trial Lawyers of America. ***PRACTICE AREAS:*** Family Law; Divorce; Child Custody; Juvenile Law; Trial Practice; Criminal Defense; Personal Injury. ***Email:*** showenj@rittgers.com

JAMES A. DEARIE, born Atlanta, Georgia, February 11, 1968; admitted to bar, 1993, Georgia; 2000, Ohio and U.S. District Court, Southern District of Ohio. *Education:* University of Notre Dame (B.A., cum laude, 1990); University of Georgia (J.D., cum laude, 1993). Member, Georgia Law Review, 1991-1993. Law Clerk, Honorable W. Harold Albritton, U.S. District Judge, Montgomery, Alabama, 1993-1994. *Member:* Warren County Bar Association. [Capt., JAG, U.S. Army, 1995-1999]. ***PRACTICE AREAS:*** Litigation; Criminal Defense; Driving While Intoxicated; Business Law. ***Email:*** deariej@rittgers.com

RENEE L. CRIST, born Salem, Ohio, June 23, 1971; admitted to bar, 2001, Ohio and U.S. District Court, Southern District of Ohio. *Education:* University of Kentucky (B.A., History, 1994; M.S.W., 1996); University of Dayton (J.D., 2001). Phi Alpha Mu. Trained Collaborative Lawyer in Domestic Relations. *Member:* Warren County and Ohio State Bar Associations; Southwest Collaborative Lawyers Association. ***PRACTICE AREAS:*** Family Law; Divorce; Juvenile Law; Child Custody; Probate; Criminal Law. ***Email:*** cristr@rittgers.com

REPRESENTATIVE CLIENTS: Citizens of Warren, Butler and Clinton Counties; American Mortgage Lenders, Inc.; Equitable Banc LLC; Oak & Moore Home Furnishing, Inc.; San-Tech, Inc.; Finejan Inspection Services, Inc.
LOCAL COUNSEL FOR: American Golf, Inc.

THOMPSON AND DeVENY CO., L.P.A.

LEBANON, OHIO
(See Dayton)

Bankruptcy Law, Divorce, Child Custody, Child Support.

WAITE, SCHNEIDER, BAYLESS & CHESLEY CO., L.P.A.

LEBANON, OHIO
(See Cincinnati)

General Civil Practice. Aviation, Antitrust Litigation, Class Action, Commercial Litigation, Complex Litigation, Corporate Law, Federal Employees Liability, General Civil Trials and Appeals in all Courts, Insurance, Labor, Consolidated and Multi-district Litigation, Products Litigation, Securities Litigation and Wrongful Death.

DAVID WIRTH

LEBANON, OHIO
(See Columbus)

Insurance Law, Negligence, Legal Malpractice, Subrogation, Personal Injury, Probate.

BARAN, PIPER, TARKOWSKY, FITZGERALD & THEIS CO., L.P.A.

121 WEST HIGH STREET, SUITE 905
P.O. BOX 568
LIMA, OHIO 45802
Telephone: 419-227-5858
Fax: 419-227-4569
URL: http://www.baranlaw.com

General Civil Practice. Trials in all Courts. Insurance Defense, Corporate, Family Law, Estate Planning, Personal Injury, Products Liability and Construction Law. Commercial Litigation. Suretyship. Environmental and Governmental Liability. Professional Liability, Worker's Compensation.

(For Complete List of all Personnel and Biographical data, see Professional Biographies at Mansfield, Ohio)

CORY, MEREDITH, WITTER, RUMER & CHENEY

A LEGAL PROFESSIONAL ASSOCIATION
101 N. ELIZABETH STREET
SUITE 607
P.O. BOX 1217
LIMA, OHIO 45802-1217
Telephone: 419-228-6365
Fax: 419-228-5319

General Civil Practice. Corporation, Commercial, Banking, Utilities, Negligence, Family and Domestic Relations Law, Taxation and Insurance Laws, Probate and Estate Planning, Real Property, Labor and Employment Law, Trials and Appeals in all Courts.

(This Listing Continued)

CORY, MEREDITH, WITTER, RUMER & CHENEY, A LEGAL PROFESSIONAL ASSOCIATION, Lima—Continued

FRANK B. CORY, born Lima, Ohio, March 12, 1930; admitted to bar, 1955, Ohio. *Education:* Dartmouth College (A.B., 1952); University of Michigan (LL.B., 1955). Phi Delta Phi. *Member:* Allen County (Secretary, 1960; President, 1977), Ohio State and American Bar Associations. ***PRACTICE AREAS:*** Trials and Appeals; Workers' Compensation; Employment Law; Probate. ***Email:*** fcory@corymeredithetal.com

DONALD J. WITTER, born Fremont, Ohio, September 5, 1937; admitted to bar, 1962, Ohio. *Education:* Otterbein College (B.A., 1959); University of Michigan (LL.B., 1962). Phi Delta Phi. *Member:* Allen County (President, 1990) and Ohio State Bar Associations. ***PRACTICE AREAS:*** Corporate; Estate Planning; Business Litigation; Utilities; Probate. ***Email:*** dwitter@corymeredithetal.com

MICHAEL A. RUMER, born Lima, Ohio, October 9, 1944; admitted to bar, 1970, Ohio. *Education:* Bowling Green State University (B.S., 1966); Ohio Northern University (J.D., 1970). Teacher, Bowling Green Public Schools, 1966-1967; Adjunct Professor, College of Law, Ohio Northern University, 1987-1998. Adjunct Professor, Bluffton College, 1993-1995. Private Law Practice, 1970-1981. Chief Referee and Administrative Assistant, Juvenile Court, Allen County, Ohio, 1971-1981. Judge, Common Pleas Court, Allen County, Ohio, 1981-1997. *Member:* Allen County (President, 2000), Ohio State and American Bar Associations. ***PRACTICE AREAS:*** Civil Litigation; Criminal Litigation; Alternative Dispute Resolution. ***Email:*** mrumer@corymeredithetal.com

SUMNER E. WALTERS, born Van Wert, Ohio, July 5, 1949; admitted to bar, 1974, Ohio; U.S. District Court, Northern District of Ohio. *Education:* Stanford University; Ohio Northern University (B.A., Business Administration, 1971; J.D., 1974). Private Law Practice, 1974-1982. Judge: Common Pleas Court, Van Wert County, Ohio, 1983-1999; Ohio Court of Appeals, Third District, 1999-2004. *Member:* Van Wert County (President, 1989-1991), Allen County and Ohio State (Member: Council of Delegates, 2001—; Board of Governors, 2003—) Bar Associations. ***PRACTICE AREAS:*** Appellate Practice; Alternative Dispute Resolution; Probate; Estate Planning; Corporate Law. ***Email:*** swalters@corymeredithetal.com

DAVID A. CHENEY, born Lima, Ohio, October 8, 1948; admitted to bar, 1974, Ohio. *Education:* The Ohio State University (B.S.B.A., 1971); Ohio Northern University (J.D., 1974). Phi Kappa Phi. Magistrate, Allen County Juvenile Court, 1974-1991. *Member:* Allen County and Ohio State Bar Associations. ***PRACTICE AREAS:*** Insurance Defense; Commercial Law; Domestic Relations. ***Email:*** dcheney@corymeredithetal.com

MICHAEL P. ANDERSON, born St. Marys, Ohio, April 8, 1961; admitted to bar, 1987, Ohio. *Education:* John Carroll University (B.A., 1983); Capital University (J.D., 1987). *Member:* Allen County and Ohio State Bar Associations. ***PRACTICE AREAS:*** Insurance; Social Security Disability; Litigation. ***Email:*** manderson@corymeredithetal.com

ROBERT J. MEREDITH, born Lima, Ohio, March 31, 1961; admitted to bar, 1988, Ohio. *Education:* The Ohio State University (B.S., 1983); Capital University (J.D., 1988). *Member:* Allen County, Ohio State and American (Member, Board of Governors, Probate Section, 1996-2001) Bar Associations. ***PRACTICE AREAS:*** Probate; Estate Planning; Real Estate; Corporate. ***Email:*** rmeredith@corymeredithetal.com

VICTORIA U. MAISCH, born Lima, Ohio, May 16, 1954; admitted to bar, 1994, Ohio. *Education:* Ohio Northern University (B.A., 1975; J.D., 1994); University of Dayton (M.S.Ed., 1979). *Member:* Auglaize County, Allen County, Ohio State and American Bar Associations. ***PRACTICE AREAS:*** Personal Injury; Workers Compensation; Trial Practice; Appellate Practice; Employment Law; Commercial Law. ***Email:*** vmaisch@corymeredithetal.com

J. ALAN SMITH, born Lima, Ohio, October 15, 1963; admitted to bar, 1989, Ohio; 1992, U.S. District Court, Northern District of Ohio. *Education:* Case Western Reserve University (B.S. in Business Management, 1986; J.D., 1989). *Member:* Allen and Ohio State Bar Association; Defense Research Institute; Ohio Association of Civil Trial Attorneys; American Inn of Court. ***PRACTICE AREAS:*** Insurance; Insurance Defense; Products Liability; Zoning Law; Employer Rights; Municipal Law. ***Email:*** asmith@corymeredithetal.com

GENERAL COUNSEL FOR: Univ. of Northwestern Ohio; Trisco Systems, Inc.; Northwest Title Agency Co.
LOCAL COUNSEL FOR: Huntington National Bank; Dominion East Ohio Gas Company; Bank One, Lima, N.A.; Premcor; General Dynamics; The Lima News; Superior Forge & Steel Corp.; Allstate Insurance; Auto Owners Insurance Co.; GRE America; Cincinnati Insurance; Nationwide Insurance; Travelers; Westfield Insurance Co.; Grange Insurance Co.; Motorist Insurance Co.; Ohio Bar Liability Ins., Co.;
APPROVED ATTORNEYS AND AGENTS FOR: The Ohio Bar Title Insurance Co.; Lawyers Title Insurance Corporation.

DENMEAD LAW OFFICE

LIMA, OHIO

(See Columbus)

Civil Trial and Appellate Practice and Personal Injury, Traumatic Brain Injury (TBI), Professional Negligence and Complex Litigation including Class Actions, Patents, Civil Rights, Civil Litigation, RICO, Employment and Political Subdivision Liability issues.

HUFFMAN, KELLEY, BECKER & BROCK, LLC

Established in 1963

127-129 NORTH PIERCE STREET
P.O. BOX 546
LIMA, OHIO 45802
Telephone: 419-227-3423
Fax: 419-228-1937
Email: info@hkbblaw.com
URL: http://www.hkbblaw.com

Civil Practice. Plaintiff's Personal Injury, Negligence Law, Medical Malpractice Defense, Trials and Appeals in all Courts, Family/Domestic Relations, Real Estate, Corporations, Construction Law, Probate and Estate Planning.

FIRM PROFILE: Huffman, Kelley, Becker & Brock, LLC was formed in 1963 by F.W. Gooding, John R. Evans and Lawrence S. Huffman as Gooding, Evans & Huffman. The firm is now composed of eight lawyers and offers a wide range of legal services. All attorneys participate in continuing legal education seminars, local bar activities and civic activities. The firm regularly accepts referrals from attorneys both in and outside the state of Ohio.

FRED WEMMER GOODING (1914-1972)

JOHN R. EVANS (1928-2000)

LAWRENCE S. HUFFMAN, born Tucson, Arizona, May 19, 1930; admitted to bar, 1958, Ohio; 1971, U.S. District Court, Northern District of Ohio; 1973, U.S. Supreme Court. *Education:* University of Dayton; Ohio Northern University (J.D., 1958). Assistant Director of Law, City of Lima, 1958-1960. Assistant Prosecuting Attorney, 1961-1968 and Prosecuting Attorney, 1969-1976, Allen County, Ohio. *Member:* Allen County (President, 1979) and Ohio State Bar Associations; Defense Research and U.S. Trial Lawyers Association. Fellow, American College of Trial Lawyers. ***REPORTED CASES:*** Huffman v. Pursue Ltd., 420 U.S. 592, (1975); State v. Caudill, 48 Ohio St. 2d 342, (1976); Burris v. Romaker, 71 Ohio App. 3d 772, (1991); Frysinger v. Leech, 10 Ohio App. 3d 150, (1983); White v. Soo, 65 Ohio App. 3d 731, (1989); Hale v. Rosenberg, 2004 Ohio 1204, 2004 Ohio App. Lexis 1049; Keen v. Hardin Mem. Hosp. 2003 Ohio 6707, 2003 Ohio App. Lexis 6076. ***PRACTICE AREAS:*** Civil Litigation; Medical Malpractice; Probate; Insurance Law. ***Email:*** lsh@hkbblaw.com

C. BRADFORD KELLEY, born Norwood, Massachusetts, March 6, 1952; admitted to bar, 1979, Ohio; 1982, U.S. District Court, Northern District of Ohio and U.S. Court of Appeals, Sixth Circuit; 1990, U.S. Tax Court; 2004, U.S. Supreme Court. *Education:* Ohio Wesleyan University (B.A., 1974); Ohio Northern University (J.D., 1977). *Member:* Allen County (Grievance Committee, 1995—; Executive Committee, 1995—; Vice President, 2002; President, 2003) and Ohio State Bar Associations; Ohio Academy of Trial Lawyers. ***REPORTED CASES:*** Werling v. Sandy, 17 Ohio St. 3d 45, (1985); In Re Estate of Hicks, 90 Ohio App. 3d 483 (1993); Ulery v. Ulery, 1993 Ohio App. LEXIS 5631, (Ct.App. 1993); Rehab Project, Inc. v. Sarno, 80 Ohio App. 3d 265, (Ct.App. 1992). ***PRACTICE AREAS:*** Personal Injury; Domestic Relations; Probate; Criminal Law; Civil Litigation. ***Email:*** cbk@hkbblaw.com

LAWRENCE A. HUFFMAN, born Fairborn, Ohio, July 7, 1953; admitted to bar, 1981, Ohio; 1982, U.S. District Court, Northern District of Ohio; 2000, U.S. Court of Appeals, Sixth Circuit. *Education:* Xavier University; Ohio Northern University (B.A., 1978; J.D., 1981). *Member:* Allen County (Treasurer, 1983-1989; Member, Grievance Committee, 1987-1989) and Ohio State Bar Associations. ***REPORTED CASES:*** Kleinfeld v. Link, 9 Ohio App. 3d 29 (1983); Parrish v. Mid-Atlantic Fire & Casualty Co., 63 Ohio App. 3d 1, (1989); In Re Adoption of Infant Boy, 60 Ohio App. 3d 80, (1989); State v. Hengstler, 75 Ohio App. 3d 400, (1991). ***PRACTICE AREAS:*** Personal Injury; Insurance Litigation; Probate; Civil Litigation; Domestic Relations. ***Email:*** lah@hkbblaw.com

STEPHEN L. BECKER, born Lima, Ohio, November 21, 1949; admitted to bar, 1975, Ohio; 1977, U.S. District Court, Northern District of Ohio. *Education:* University of Detroit (A.B., 1972); Ohio Northern University (J.D., 1975). Phi Alpha Delta. Recipient, American Jurisprudence Awards in Commercial Transactions and Agency. Assistant Director of Law, Lima, Ohio, 1977-1982. *Member:* Allen County and Ohio State Bar Associations; Ohio Land Title Association. ***REPORTED CASES:*** Endersby v. Schneppe, 73 Ohio App. 3d 212, (1991); Hobart Brothers Co. v. Welding Supply Svc., Inc., 21 Ohio App. 3d 142, (1985). ***PRACTICE AREAS:*** Commercial Litigation; Real Estate; Estate Planning; Personal Injury; Family Law. ***Email:*** slb@hkbblaw.com

MATTHEW C. HUFFMAN, born Lima, Ohio, April 1, 1960; admitted to bar, 1985, Ohio; 1986, U.S. District Court, Northern District of Ohio; 2000, U.S. Court of Appeals, Sixth Circuit. *Education:* St. Louis University; University of Notre Dame (B.A., 1982); University of Cincinnati (J.D., 1985). Member, Lima City Council, 1992— and President, 1998—. *Member:* Allen County and Ohio State Bar Associations. ***REPORTED CASES:*** Frysinger v. Leech, 32 Ohio St. 3d 38, 512 N.E. 2d 337 (1987); Hurst v. Ohio Dept. of Rehab. and Correction, 72 Ohio St. 3D, 325 (1995); Greenfield v. Cobb, 90 Ohio App. 3d 618, 630 N.E. 2d 66 (1993); White v. Soo, 65 Ohio App. 3d 731, 585 N.E. 2d 458 (1989); Morrison vs. Lima Radiologists, 28 Ohio St. 3d 210, 503 N.E. 2d 745 (1986); Skaggs vs. Lima Memorial Hospital, 62 Ohio St. 3d 296, 581 N.E. 2d 1085 (1991); Manley vs. Rufus Club Mozambique, 111 Ohio Ap. 3d 260, 675 N.E. 2d 1342 (1996); Hindall vs. Winterthur, 337 F.3d 680; Sheipline vs. like, 28 Ohio St. 3d, 208 (1986); Del Signore vs. Asphalt Drum Mixers, 182 F.Supp 2d (2002). ***PRACTICE AREAS:*** Civil Practice; Personal Injury; Business Litigation; Corporate; Probate; Adoption. ***Email:*** mch@hkbblaw.com

JOHN C. HUFFMAN, born Lima, Ohio, October 4, 1963; admitted to bar, 1989, Ohio; 1998, U.S. District Court, Northern District of Ohio. *Education:* Bowling Green State University (B.A., 1986); University of Toledo (J.D., 1989). Village Solicitor, Cairo, Ohio, 1990—. Legal Advisor, American Township, Ohio, 2002. *Member:* Allen County (Executive Committee, 2003—; Grievance committee, 2003—) and Ohio State Bar Associations; American Academy of Adoption Attorneys. ***REPORTED CASES:*** State ex. rel. Foltz v. Miller, 62 Ohio Misc. 2d 492, 601 N.E. 2d 681 (1992); Sherburn v. Reichert, et. al., 97 Ohio App. 3d 120, 646 N.E. 2d 255 (1994); Ricker v. Ricker, 102 Ohio App. 3d 209, 656 N.E. 2d 1337 (1995); Counsel of the Village of Cairo v. James H. Miller, et. al., 121 Ohio App. 3d

(This Listing Continued)

246; 699 N.E. 2d 571 (1997); Wise v. Brenneman, Ohio App. Lexis 4289 (1998); Paton, nka Saxton v. Paton, 91 Ohio St. 3d 94 (2001) 2001 Ohio 291; 742 N.E. 2d 619. ***PRACTICE AREAS:*** Personal Injury; Adoption; Domestic Relations; Criminal Law; Municipal Law; Civil Practice; Juvenile Law; Probate. ***Email:*** jch@hkbblaw.com

T. BLAIN BROCK, II, born Lima, Ohio, January 15, 1968; admitted to bar, 1993, Ohio. *Education:* University of Toledo (B.B.A., 1990); Ohio Northern University (J.D., 1993). Phi Delta Phi. Legal Advisor, American Township, 1995—. *Member:* Allen County and Ohio State Bar Associations; The Ohio Academy of Trial Lawyers. ***PRACTICE AREAS:*** Personal Injury; Probate; Domestic Relations; Criminal Law. ***Email:*** tbb@hkbblaw.com

CRAIG A. GOTTSCHALK, born Saint Marys, Ohio, October 23, 1971; admitted to bar, 1997, Ohio and U.S. District Court, Northern District of Ohio. *Education:* Earlham College (B.A., 1994); Ohio Northern University (J.D., 1997). Associate Editor, Ohio Northern Law Review. *Member:* Allen County and Ohio State Bar Associations. ***REPORTED CASES:*** State v. Koeppel (2002), 117 Ohio Misc. 2d 1. ***PRACTICE AREAS:*** Criminal Law; Personal Injury; Domestic Relations; Civil Litigation; Probate; Juvenile Law. ***Email:*** cag@hkbblaw.com

LEGAL SUPPORT PERSONNEL

CAROL L. SWEM, born Lima, Ohio, May 1, 1951. *Education:* Paralegal Institute, Phoenix, Arizona. (Probate Paralegal). ***PRACTICE AREAS:*** Wills; Trusts; Estate Administration; Durable Powers of Attorney; Durable Powers of Attorney for Health Care Purposes; Living Wills; Guardianships; Adoptions.

REPRESENTATIVE CLIENTS: The Medical Protective Company of Fort Wayne; The Hanson - Neely Funeral Home, Inc.; Sash & Storm, Inc.; Hamilton Mutual Insurance Co.; Bank One, Lima, Ohio; Bank One Trust Company, NA; Dayton Walls & Ceilings, Inc.; Superior Metal Products, Inc.; Spartech Corp.; Henson Garden Center; American Equity Insurance Company; Premier Health Care Services, Inc.; Shawnee Local School District; Golden Bridge Academy; Heritage Construction Company; Waterford Townhomes, LTD.; Old Republic National Title Insurance Company; Superior Federal Credit Union; John P. Timmerman Co.
AGENTS FOR: Ohio Bar Title Insurance Co.
REFERENCE: Fifth Third Bank Lima, Ohio.

HUNT & JOHNSON

400 WEST NORTH STREET
LIMA, OHIO 45801-4298
Telephone: 419-222-1040
Fax: 419-227-1826
URL: http://www.hjelawoffice.com
URL: http://www.hjelaw.com

Family Law, Adoptions, Child Custody, Child Support, Divorce, Domestic Violence, Premarital Agreements, Spousal Support, Corporate Law, Breach of Contract, Mechanics Liens, Collections, Real Estate, Commercial Real Estate, Condominium Law, Landlord and Tenant Law, Mortgages, Taxation, Estate and Gift Taxation, Income Tax, Property Tax, Trusts and Estates, Asset Protection, Charitable Giving, Estate Litigation, Estate Planning, Guardianship and Conservatorship, Wills and Probate.

MEMBERS OF FIRM

JAMES I. HUNT, born Lima, Ohio, April 28, 1914; admitted to bar, 1948, Ohio. *Education:* Ohio Northern University (J.D., 1948). *Member:* Allen County (Member, Executive Committee, 1965-1967; Vice President, 1965; President, 1966), Ohio State (Member: Board of Governors, Real Property Law Section, 1968-1974; Council of Delegates; Probate and Trust Law Section) and American Bar Associations.

JERRY M. JOHNSON, born Fort Wayne, Indiana, April 5, 1948; admitted to bar, 1975, Ohio. *Education:* Ohio Northern University (B.S., 1971; J.D., 1975). Member: Ohio Northern University Law Review, 1974-1975; The Willis Society. Phi Kappa Phi. Municipal Court Prosecutor, 1976-1978. Contributed on article publications in Hastings Law Journal. *Member:* Allen County (Secretary, 1982-1989; Executive Committee, 1982-1989; Secretary, Certified Grievance Committee, 1985-2000; Vice President, 2000-2001), Ohio State and American Bar Associations; American Academy of Adoptions Attorneys. ***PRACTICE AREAS:*** Civil Practice; Adoption Law; Family Law; Probate; Estate Planning. ***Email:*** jmj@hjelaw.com

ASSOCIATE

MARK E. G. DAVIS, admitted to bar, 1999, Ohio. *Education:* University of Wisconsin-Madison (B.A., 1994); University of Tulsa (J.D., 1997). *Member:* Allen County and Ohio State Bar Associations; National Trial Lawyers of America. ***PRACTICE AREAS:*** Collections; Real Estate; Domestic Relations; Union Contract Negotiations; Criminal Law. ***Email:*** md@hjelaw.com

OF COUNSEL

GARY R. HERMON, born Lima, Ohio, September 5, 1941; admitted to bar, 1966, Ohio; 1972, U.S. District Court, Northern District of Ohio; 1973, U.S. Supreme Court; 1974, U.S. Court of Appeals, Sixth Circuit. *Education:* Virginia Military Institute (B.A., 1963); Ohio Northern University (J.D., 1966). City Prosecutor, Lima, Ohio, 1969-1971. Assistant County Prosecutor, Lima, Ohio, 1971-1976, 1987—. *Member:* Allen County and Ohio State Bar Associations. [Capt., U.S. Army, 1967-1969]

THOMAS R. KUHN

Established in 1970

973 WEST NORTH STREET
LIMA, OHIO 45805
Telephone: 419-228-2122
Fax: 419-999-6298;
URL: http://www.kuhnlawoffice.com
Email: trkuhnatty@wcoil.com
URL: http://www.kunhlawoffice.com

Personal Injury, Wrongful Death, Criminal Law, Traffic Law, Probate, Family Law, Adoption, Wills, Domestic Relations.

THOMAS R. KUHN, born Lima, Ohio, July 17, 1945; admitted to bar, 1970, Ohio and U.S. District Court, Northern District of Ohio. *Education:* University of Notre Dame (B.A., 1967); Ohio Northern University (J.D., 1970). *Member:* Allen County (Past President) and Ohio State Bar Associations; The Association of Trial Lawyers of America; Ohio Trial Lawyers Association. ***PRACTICE AREAS:*** Personal Injury; Criminal Law; Wrongful Death; Wills; Probate; Family Law; Adoption Law.

MASON, SCHILLING & MASON CO., L.P.A.

Established in 1973

P.O. BOX 937
LIMA, OHIO 45802
Telephone: 800-840-3514
Fax: 513-489-0834
Email: msm@mason-law.com
URL: http://www.mason-law.com

Cincinnati Office: 11340 Montgomery Road, Suite 210. Telephone: 513-489-0829; 800-840-3514. Fax: 513-489-0834.
Covington, Kentucky Office: Heritage International, Suite 203, P.O. Box 2158. Telephone: 513-489-0829. Fax: 513-489-0834.
Columbus Office: 460 E. Main Street. Telephone: 513-489-0829. Fax: 513-489-0834.
Dayton Office: 319 Liberty Tower. Telephone: 513-489-0829. Fax: 513-489-0834.
Madison, Indiana Office: 201 East Main Street. Telephone: 513-489-0829. Fax: 513-489-0834.

Commercial, Creditors Rights, Bankruptcy, Collection, Banking and Financial Institution Law, Civil Litigation, Federal Consumer Law Litigation, Foreclosures, Automobile Deficiencies, Credit Cards, Medical Debts, Bad Checks, Business Loans/Commercial Debt, Vehicle and Property Repossessions, Landlord Representation/Evictions/Lease Litigation, Equipment Leasing.

FIRM PROFILE: Mason, Schilling & Mason Co., L.P.A., since its founding over 30 years ago, exclusively concentrates in the areas of creditor representation, in all aspects of commercial litigation, banking law, leasing law, bankruptcy law, and creditors' rights law.

We have developed a full service staff of attorneys in all aspects of representation to the credit granting community. Our legal services concentrate exclusively on representing creditors in all facets of legal representation concerning credit management and credit granting, commercial law, and bankruptcy law on behalf of the credit management community.

Further, of particular attention, is the providing of legal services to the banking and credit management community throughout the entire States of Ohio and Kentucky. Our attorneys appear in all State and federal courts in both states.

The value of our law firm rests with the dependable level of service that we provide to all creditor-clients. We pride ourselves in the personalized service and the conscientious follow through that has been a trade mark throughout over three decades of providing legal services to our creditor and banking clients.

(For complete Biographical Data on all Personnel, see Professional Biographies at Cincinnati, Ohio)

THE MIHLBAUGH LAW FIRM, LLP

THE MIHLBAUGH LAW BUILDING
P.O. BOX 1141
LIMA, OHIO 45802-1141
Telephone: 419-229-5886
Fax: 419-227-6445
Email: mihlbaughlawfirm@earthlink.net

Civil Litigation, General Corporate, Intellectual Property, Trademarks, Copyrights.

LESLIE K. BATTÉ, born Elmhurst, Illinois; admitted to bar, 1992, Illinois and U.S. District Court, Northern District of Illinois; 1993, U.S. Court of Appeals, Seventh Circuit; 1996, Ohio and U.S. Tax Court; 1998, U.S. Court of Appeals, Federal and Sixth Circuits; 2000, U.S. District Court, Southern and Northern Districts of Ohio; 2003, U.S. Supreme Court. *Education:* Ealing College of Higher Education, London, England, Comparative Government Studies, 1988; University of Wisconsin-Madison (B.A., Political Science, 1989); University of Notre Dame Law School (J.D., 1992); The John Marshall Law School (LL.M., Intellectual Property Law, with honors, 1996). Phi Delta Phi International Legal Fraternity. Clerk, Thomas More Inn 1991. Listed in: America's Registry of Outstanding Professionals, 2005-2006. *Member:* Federal Bar Association; International Trademark Association. ***PRACTICE AREAS:*** Corporate Law; Civil Litigation; Intellectual Property; Trademarks; Copyrights.

SCHERNER, HANSON & CORNWELL, LLC

714 WEST NORTH STREET
LIMA, OHIO 45801-3923
Telephone: 419-222-1155
Fax: 419-227-3131

Columbus, Ohio Office: 130 Northwoods Boulevard. Telephone: 614-431-7200. Fax: 614-431-7262.
Delaware, Ohio Office: 5300 David Road. Telephone: 740-595-3366.

Civil Trial and Appellate Litigation in State and Federal Courts. Medical Malpractice and other Professional Liability, Personal Injury, Product Liability, Commercial, Corporate, Fraud and other Civil Litigation, Domestic Relations, Family Law.

TED E. CORNWELL, born Springfield, Ohio, November 18, 1951; admitted to bar, 1976, Ohio; 1978, U.S. District Court, Northern District of Ohio. *Education:* The Ohio State University and Bowling Green State University (B.S., Business Administration, 1973); Ohio Northern University (J.D., 1976). Phi Alpha Delta. Assistant Prosecutor, City of Lima, 1977-1980. Referee, Lima Municipal Court, 1981-1983. *Member:* Allen County (Secretary, 1980-1982) and Ohio State Bar Associations; Ohio Academy of Trial Lawyers. ***PRACTICE AREAS:*** Civil Practice; Appellate Practice; Domestic Relations; Family Law; Personal Injury; Civil Litigation. ***Email:*** ted@watchtv.net

MARIAH M. CUNNINGHAM, born Lima, Ohio, July 4, 1977; admitted to bar, 2003, Ohio. *Education:* Bowling Green State University (B.A., Psychology, 2000); Ohio Northern University (J.D., 2003). *Member:* Allen County and Ohio State Bar Associations. ***PRACTICE AREAS:*** Civil Practice; Appellate Practice; Domestic Relations; Family Law; Personal Injury; Civil Litigation. ***Email:*** mariah@watchtv.net

(For complete Biographical Data on all personnel see Professional Biographies at Columbus, Ohio.)

NADLER NADLER & BURDMAN CO., L.P.A.

LISBON, OHIO

(See Youngstown)

General Civil Practice in all State and Federal Courts. Commercial, Creditor Rights and Collections, Bankruptcy, Reorganization, Taxation, Employment and Labor Law, Corporation, Partnership, Venture Capital, Banking, Real Estate, Shopping Center, Franchising, Environmental, Pension and Profit Sharing, Estate Planning, Probate, and Trials and Appeals.

TWYFORD & DONAHEY, P.L.L.

LOGAN, OHIO

(See Columbus)

Personal Injury Litigation, Wrongful Death, Medical Malpractice, Products Liability, Automobile Accidents, Trucking Accidents, Head and Spinal Injuries, Motorcycle Accidents and Injuries, Uninsured Motorists, Insurance Law, Airplane Crash Litigation, Railroad Accidents, Slip and Fall, Dog Bites, Work Related Injuries, Birth Injuries, Nursing Home Abuse and Neglect.

ALEITA AILES, ATTORNEY AT LAW, LLC

P.O. BOX 588
LONDON, OHIO 43140
Telephone: 740-845-0300
Fax: 740-845-0500
Email: aailes@columbus.rr.com
URL: http://www.aileslawfirm.com

Divorce, Dissolution, Separation, Child Custody, Visitation Rights, Paternity, Adoption, Real Estate, Contracts, Leases, Wills and Trusts, Business, Litigation, General Practice.

ALEITA J. AILES, born Sidney, Ohio, August 4, 1947; admitted to bar, 1972, Ohio; 1983, U.S. District Court, Southern District of Ohio; 1987, Illinois. *Education:* Ohio Northern University (B.A., 1969); Ohio State University (J.D., 1972). *Member:* Clark County, Madison County, Ohio State (Member, Board of Governors, Real Property Section) and American Bar Associations. ***Email:*** aailes@columbus.rr.com

MICHAEL E. BENSON

LONDON, OHIO

(See Columbus)

Bankruptcy Law, Foreclosures, Debtor and Creditor, Real Estate, Landlord and Tenant, Buying and Selling, Wills, Living Wills, Healthcare, Powers of Attorney.

CALIG & HANDELMAN, LPA

LONDON, OHIO

(See Columbus)

Bankruptcy, Personal Injury, Probate, Real Estate, Social Security, Social Security Disability, Medical Malpractice, Wrongful Death, Civil Litigation, Domestic Relations Law.

SHIRLEY C. HANSGEN

Established in 1920
26 SOUTH MAIN STREET
LONDON, OHIO 43140-1211
Telephone: 740-852-1576
Fax: 740-852-2760
Email: schansgen@sbcglobal.com
URL: http://www.lawyers.com/hansgenlaw

General Practice. Real Estate, Estate Planning, Probate, Personal Injury, Corporate and Family Law. Trials and Appeals, Criminal Law and Traffic Violations.

SHIRLEY C. HANSGEN, born Akron, Ohio, June 8, 1951; admitted to bar, 1979, Ohio; 1980, U.S. District Court, Southern District of Ohio; 1984, U.S. Court of Appeals, Sixth Circuit. *Education:* Miami University; Ohio University (B.S.Ed., 1973); The Ohio State University (J.D., 1979). *Member:* Madison County and Ohio State Bar Associations. ***PRACTICE AREAS:*** Domestic Relations; Divorce; Child Custody; Adoption Law; Criminal Law; Real Estate; Probate; Corporate Law.

ASSOCIATE

RENAE E. ZABLOUDIL, born Columbus, Ohio, August 25, 1976; admitted to bar, 2001, Ohio. *Education:* Otterbein College (B.S., Life Sciences/Environmental Sciences, magna cum laude, with honors, with distinction, 1998); The Ohio State University (J.D., 2001). *Member:* Madison County and Ohio State Bar Associations. ***PRACTICE AREAS:*** Domestic Relations; Criminal Law; Juvenile Law; Personal Injury; Traffic Violations; Family Law. ***Email:*** rezablou@sbcglobal.net

REPRESENTATIVE CLIENTS: Buckeye Ford/Mercury; Choctaw Lake Property Owners Association; Creative Carpet & Interiors.
APPROVED ATTORNEYS FOR: Guardian Title Insurance Co.; Ohio Bar Title Insurance Co.
REFERENCES: Huntington National Bank of London; Advantage Bank.

ROURKE & BLUMENTHAL, LLP

LONDON, OHIO

(See Columbus)

Personal Injury, Negligence, Products Liability, Medical Malpractice, Nursing Home Litigation, Wrongful Death, Intentional Tort, Insurance Disputes, Automobile Accidents, Civil Trial Practice, Aviation, Professional Liability.

TWYFORD & DONAHEY, P.L.L.

Established in 1968
25 WEST FIFTH STREET
LONDON, OHIO 43140
Telephone: Toll Free: 1-800-686-1699
Fax: 614-849-0475
Email: help@twyforddonahey.com
URL: http://www.twyforddonahey.com

Columbus, Ohio Office: 495 South High Street, 43215-5058. Telephone: Toll Free: 1-800-686-1699. Email: help@twyforddonahey.com.
Circleville, Ohio Office: 214 South Court Street, 43113. Telephone: Toll Free: 1-800-686-1699. Email: help@twyforddonahey.com
Delaware, Ohio Office: 163 N. Sandusky Street, Suite 103, 43015. Telephone: Toll Free: 1-800-686-1699. Email: help@twyforddonahey.com
Lancaster, Ohio Office: 3794 Old Columbus, N.W., 43130. Telephone: Toll Free: 1-800-686-1699. Email: help@twyforddonahey.com
Newark, Ohio Office: 137 West Main Street, Suite C., 43025. Telephone: Toll Free: 1-800-686-1699. Email: help@twyforddonahey.com

Personal Injury Litigation, Wrongful Death, Medical Malpractice, Products Liability, Automobile Accidents, Trucking Accidents, Head and Spinal Injuries, Motorcycle Accidents and Injuries, Uninsured Motorists, Insurance Law, Airplane Crash Litigation, Railroad Accidents, Slip and Fall, Dog Bites, Work Related Injuries, Birth Injuries, Nursing Home Abuse and Neglect.

FIRM PROFILE: Tom Twyford and Dick Donahey have been partners since 1968 and have practiced exclusively in the areas of personal injury, medical malpractice and products liability law. We have never represented insurance companies! In recent years, we have obtained some of the largest verdicts in Franklin County. We have purposely remained small in order to concentrate on a limited number of cases. We have six offices and will handle cases in any part of the state of Ohio.

(For complete biographical data on all personnel, see Professional Biographies at Columbus, Ohio)

COLELLA & WEIR, P.L.L.

Established in 1995
6055 PARK SQUARE DRIVE
OAK POINT PROFESSIONAL PARK
LORAIN, OHIO 44053
Telephone: 440-988-9000
Telecopier: 440-988-9002
Email: rjcolella@cnwlaw.com
URL: http://www.cnwlaw.com

Corporate, Business, Real Estate, Business and Commercial Litigation, Construction Law, Industrial Law, International Business, Corporate Financing, Business Acquisitions, Bankruptcy, Federal and State Administrative Law, Probate, Estate Planning, Licensing, Technology Law.

(This Listing Continued)

RICHARD COLELLA, born Lorain, Ohio, November 30, 1935; admitted to bar, 1960, Ohio. *Education:* Case Western Reserve University (A.B., 1958; J.D., 1960). Delta Kappa Epsilon, Delta Theta Phi. Member, Board of Directors, First Merit Corporation.*Member:* Lorain County, Ohio State, Pennsylvania (Inactive) and American Bar Associations. ***PRACTICE AREAS:*** Corporate Law; Technology Law; Construction Law; Industrial Law; International Business Law. ***Email:*** rcolella@cnwlaw.com

RICHARD J. COLELLA, born Lorain, Ohio, October 28, 1962; admitted to bar, 1987, Texas; 1993, Ohio. *Education:* Oberlin College (B.A., 1984); Wake Forest University (J.D., cum laude, 1987). Law Faculty Scholar. Member, Wake Forest Law Review, 1985-1987. Member, Board of Trustees, Lorain County Chamber of Commerce. Trustee, Lorain Foundation, Community Health Partners Foundation. *Member:* Lorain County, Ohio State and American Bar Associations. ***PRACTICE AREAS:*** Corporate Law; General Business; Estate Planning; Construction Law; Probate; Real Estate. ***Email:*** rjcolella@cnwlaw.com

JEFFREY H. WEIR II, born Jacksonville, Arkansas, February 17, 1962; admitted to bar, 1987, Texas; 1997, Ohio. *Education:* Oberlin College (B.A., 1984); University of Michigan (J.D., 1987). Phi Beta Kappa. Order of Barristers, 1986-1987. *Member:* Lorain County, Ohio State and American Bar Associations. ***PRACTICE AREAS:*** Commercial Litigation; Business Litigation; Construction Litigation; Real Estate; Bankruptcy; General Business. ***Email:*** jhweir@cnwlaw.com

---

JOSHUA LAMB, born April 2, 1978; admitted to bar, 2003, Ohio. *Education:* Bowling Green State University (B.A., 2000); University of Toledo College of Law (J.D., 2003). *Member:* Ohio State Bar Association. ***PRACTICE AREAS:*** Business Law; Banking Law. ***Email:*** joshlamb@cnwlaw.com

REPRESENTATIVE CLIENTS: United States Steel Corp.; P.C. Campana, Inc.; FirstMerit Bank, N.A.; Camp-Hill Corporation; Pro-Tec Coating Company; Exochem Corporation; Morgan Construction Company; LorMet Community Federal Union; Wallover Oil Company; The American Eagle Mortgage Corp.; Beckett Logisync LLC; CastPowder, LLC; Elyria Plastic Products; 1st Nationwide Title Agency; Banyan Technology, Inc.; Examco Title Services; Health Quest Chiropractic; Industrial Vibration; Consu Hants, Inc.
REFERENCES: FirstMerit Bank, N.A.

MARK B. FELBER

LORAIN, OHIO

(See Cleveland)

General Civil and Criminal Practice, Drug Crimes, Juvenile Crimes, Parole and Probation, Litigation, Family Law, Divorce, Child Custody, Spousal and Child Support, Domestic Violence, Visitation Rights, Personal Injury, Head and Spinal Injuries, Sexual Abuse, Slip and Fall, Trucking Accidents, Automobile Negligence, Wrongful Death, Nursing Home Litigation, Social Security Disability, Dog Bites, Workers' Compensation, Trusts and Estates, Estate Planning, Guardianship, Wills and Probate, DWI, Bankruptcy, Admiralty, Maritime Injuries, Aviation, Airplane Crashes, Consumer Law, Consumer Fraud, Lemon Law, Unsafe Products, Warranties, Education, Employment Law, Sexual Harassment, Wrongful Termination, Medical Malpractice, Products Liability, Drugs and Medical Devices, Real Estate, Buying or Selling a Home, Business Law, Debt and Credit, Collections, Creditor's Rights, Contracts, Lawsuits, Starting a Business.

GARY, NAEGELE & THEADO, LLC

446 BROADWAY
LORAIN, OHIO 44052
Telephone: 440-244-4809
Fax: 440-244-3462
Email: office@gntlaw.com
URL: http://www.gntlaw.com

Class Actions, Pension Litigation, Consumer Fraud, Employee Rights, Complex Civil Litigation, Substantial Personal Injury.

MEMBERS OF FIRM

ROBERT D. GARY, born Lorain, Ohio, June 4, 1941; admitted to bar, 1966, Ohio; 1968, U.S. Court of Appeals, Sixth Circuit and U.S. Court of Appeals for the District of Columbia Circuit; 1969, U.S. District Court, Northern District of Ohio; U.S. Tax Court and U.S. Supreme Court. *Education:* Case Western Reserve University (B.A., 1963; J.D., 1966); New York University (LL.M., 1967). Recipient, United States Department of Justice Special Achievement Award. Federal and State Court Mediator. Former Trial Attorney, United States Department of Justice; Former Deputy Chief, Organized Crime Strike Force; Former Special Assistant to the Governor of Ohio. *Member:* Lorain County and Ohio State Bar Associations. ***REPORTED CASES:*** Rybarczyk v. TRW, Inc. 235 F3d 975 (6th Cir. 2000); Ohio Civ. Rights Comm. v. Case W. Res. Univ. (1996), 76 Ohio St.3d 168; Costantino v. TRW, Inc., 13 F.3d 969 (6th Cir. 1994); Smith v. City of Elyria, 857 F.Supp. 1203 (N.D. Ohio 1994); DeSario v. Industrial Excess Landfill, Inc. (1991), 68 Ohio App.3d 117; Jacobs v. Frank (1991), 60 Ohio St.3d 111; Strock v. Pressnell (1988), 38 Ohio St.3d 207; Fine v. America Online, Inc. (2000) 139 Ohio App 3d 133. ***PRACTICE AREAS:*** Class Actions; Pension Litigation; Complex Civil Litigation. ***Email:*** rgary@gntlaw.com

JORI BLOOM NAEGELE, born Cleveland, Ohio, November 29, 1953; admitted to bar, 1980, Ohio, U.S. District Court, Northern District of Ohio; 1985, U.S. Supreme Court; 1986, Colorado; 1987, U.S. Court of Appeals, Sixth Circuit; 2002, U.S. District Court, Southern District of Ohio. *Education:* University of Cincinnati (B.A., cum laude, with honors, 1976); Case Western Reserve University (J.D., 1979). Federal and State Court Mediator; EEOC Mediator. *Member:* Lorain County Bar Association (President, 1991-1992); Ohio and National Employment Lawyers Associations; Ohio Women's Bar Association (Secretary, 1994-1995). ***REPORTED CASES:*** Rybarczyk v. TRW, Inc. 235 F3d 975 (6th Cir. 2000); Smith v. City of Elyria, 857 F.Supp. 1203 (N.D. Ohio 1994); DeSario v. Industrial Excess Landfill, Inc. (1991), 68 Ohio App.3d 117; Jacobs v. Frank (1991), 60 Ohio St.3d 111. ***PRACTICE AREAS:*** Class Actions; Pension Litigation; Complex Civil Litigation; Employment Litigation. ***Email:*** jnaegele@gntlaw.com

(This Listing Continued)

THOMAS R. THEADO, born Columbus, Ohio, December 27, 1950; admitted to bar, 1979, Ohio; 1981, U.S. District Court, Northern District of Ohio; 1993, U.S. Supreme Court; 2002, U.S. District Court, Southern District of Ohio. *Education:* Oberlin College (B.A., with honors, 1974); Case Western Reserve University (J.D., 1979). Order of the Coif. Order of Barristers. Author: "Common Fund Awards in Statutory Fee Cases," 18 Class Action Reports 83, 1995; "The Stigma Damages Rulings in DeSario v. Industrial Excess Landfill," 1996; "Class Certification In Professional Negligence Cases," 1996; "Drug and Medical Device Class Actions," 1998; "The Class Action Lawsuit in Ohio," 1999 and 2000; "Trial Advocacy in Ohio-A Plaintiff's Perspective," 2000; "The Rules of Evidence in Trial Practice," 2002; "Admissibility of Evidence and Expert Testimony in Ohio," National Business Institute, Cleveland, OH, 2004; "A Critical Update on the Class Action Fairness Act in Ohio," National Business Institute, Cleveland, OH, 2005; "Practicing Under The Class Action Fairness Act of 2005," HalfMoon Seminars, Cleveland, OH, 2005. Speaker: "Stigma Related Damages," Mealey's New Exposure's Toxic and Mass Torts Conference, 1996; "Class Action Opportunities in Professional Negligence Cases," American Board of Professional Liability Attorneys Annual Seminar, 1996; "Plaintiff Class Actions: Their Purposes, Requisites and Pathology," Oberlin College, 1997, 1998, 1999 and 2000; "Don't Overlook Class Actions," Texas Trial Lawyers Association Conference, 1998; "Litigating the Class Action Lawsuit in Ohio," National Business Institute, 1999; "How to Recognize Your Class Action Clients Before You See Them to the Door," Erie City, Pennsylvania Bar Association, 1999; "Trial Advocacy in Ohio," National Business Institute, 2000, "Class Action in Ohio," Lorain City, Ohio Bar Association, 2000; "Powerful Evidence in Ohio Civil Litigation," National Business Institute, 2002; "The Economic Principles Underlying Class Litigation," Oberlin College, Oberlin, Ohio, 2002; "Advanced Trial Advocacy in Ohio," National Business Institute, 2004; "Admissibility of Evidence and Expert Testimony in Ohio," 2004; "Introduction to The Class Action Fairness Act of 2005," 2005; "Jurisdictional Questions and Answers After The Class Action Fairness Act of 2005," 2005; "An Overview of The Class Action Fairness Act of 2005," 2005. *Member:* Lorain County, Ohio State (Member, Litigation Section) and American Bar Associations; Ohio Academy of Trial Lawyers; The Association of Trial Lawyers of America; Trial Lawyers for Public Justice. ***REPORTED CASES:*** Bd. of Ed. of the Strongsville City School Dist. v. Theado (1991), 57 Ohio St.3d 162; DeSario v. Industrial Excess Landfill, Inc. (1991) 68 Ohio App.3d 117, mot. cert. over'd (1991), 62 Ohio St.3d 1453; Turner v. Turner (1993), 67 Ohio St.3d 337; Schwochow v. Chung (1995), 102 Ohio App.3d 348; Yepko v. State Farm Mut Ins. Co. (N.D. Ohio 1998), 25 F.Supp.2d 831; Rybarczyk v. TRW Inc. (6th Cir.2000), 235 F.3d 975. ***PRACTICE AREAS:*** Class Actions; Complex Civil Litigation. ***Email:*** ttheado@gntlaw.com

THOMAS A. DOWNIE, born Pittsburgh, Pennsylvania, February 9, 1953; admitted to bar, 1978, Ohio and U.S. District Court, Northern District of Ohio; 1988, U.S. Court of Appeals, District of Columbia Circuit; 1989, U.S. Court of Appeals, Sixth Circuit; 1990, U.S. District Court, Eastern District of Michigan. *Education:* Pennsylvania State University (B.A., 1975); Cleveland-Marshall College of Law (J.D., cum laude, 1978). Editor-in-Chief, Cleveland State Law Review, 1977-1978. Co-Author: "Common Fund Awards in Statutory Fee Cases," 18 Class Action Reports 83 (1995); "Stigma Damages Rulings in DeSario v. Industrial Excess Landfill," 1996; "Class Certification in Professional Negligence Cases," 1996; "Drug and Medical Device Class Actions," 1998; "The Basics of Cross-Examination," (2001); "Federal Civil Practice: A Guide for Ohio Attorneys," (2003); "Cross-Examination in Ohio," (2003). ***REPORTED CASES:*** Rybarczyk v. TRW, Inc. 235 F.3d 975 (6th Cir. 2000); Ohio Civil Rights Comm'n v. Case Western Reserve Univ., 76 Ohio St. 3d 168 (1996). ***PRACTICE AREAS:*** Class Actions; Pension Litigation; Complex Civil Litigation. ***Email:*** tdownie@gntlaw.com

HENRETTA LAW OFFICES

LORAIN, OHIO

(See Akron)

Medical Malpractice, Legal Malpractice, Nursing Home Litigation, Insurance Litigation, Automobile Accidents and Injuries and Wrongful Death.

OBRAL & MAYS & ASSOCIATES

LORAIN, OHIO

(See Cleveland)

Personal Injury, Medical Malpractice, Automobile Accidents, Workers Compensation, Wrongful Death, Truck Accidents, Nursing Home Abuse, Products Liability, Dog Bites, Slip and Fall, Criminal Law.

STOURTON SCOTT SMITH CO., LPA

LORAIN, OHIO

(See Cleveland)

Criminal Law, DWI, Bankruptcy, Personal Injury, Divorce, Family Law.

CHALFIE & FARLEY, CO., L.P.A.

LOVELAND, OHIO

(See Cincinnati)

Probate Litigation, Probate Administration, Estate Planning, Trials and Appeals, Estate and Gift Tax, Trusts, Estates, Wills, Family Law, Negligence, Wrongful Death, Will Contests, Living Trusts and Automobile Collisions.

DOROTHEA J. KINGSBURY

5031 MAYFIELD ROAD, SUITE 230
LYNDHURST, OHIO 44124
Telephone: 216-382-5454
Email: dkingsbury@kingsburylaw.com
URL: http://www.kingsburylaw.com

Probate, Estate Planning and Corporate Law.

DOROTHEA J. KINGSBURY, born Cleveland, Ohio, September 17, 1952; admitted to bar, 1981, Ohio. *Education:* Ursuline College (A.B., summa cum laude, 1974); Cleveland Marshall College of Law (J.D., 1981). Kappa Gamma Pi. *Member:* Greater Cleveland and Ohio State Bar Associations. ***LANGUAGES:*** French. ***PRACTICE AREAS:*** Probate; Estate Planning; Corporate Law.

BARAN, PIPER, TARKOWSKY, FITZGERALD & THEIS CO., L.P.A.

3 N. MAIN STREET, SUITE 500
MANSFIELD, OHIO 44902-1725
Telephone: 419-524-6682
Fax: 419-525-4571
URL: http://www.baranlaw.com

Lima, Ohio Office: 121 W. High Street, #905, P.O. Box 568, 45802. Telephone: 419-227-5858. Fax: 419-227-4569.
Columbus, Ohio Office: 6877 North High Street, Suite 105, 43085. Telephone: 614-436-0539. Fax: 614-436-1713.
Toledo, Ohio Office: 608 Madison Avenue, Suite 1620, 43604. Telephone: 419-241-2900. Fax: 419-241-3002.
Brecksville, Ohio Office: 8748 Brecksville Road, Suite 200, 44141. Telephone: 440-746-1177. Fax: 440-746-9637.
Portsmouth Office: 633 Seventh Street, Suite A, 45662. Telephone: 740-353-4700. Fax: 740-353-4747.

General Civil Practice. Trials in all Courts. Insurance Defense, Corporate Law, Family Law, Trusts and Estates, Personal Injury, Products Liability and Construction Law. Commercial, Fidelity and Surety. Environmental Law, Governmental, Professional Liability and Worker's Compensation.

EDWARD C. BARAN, born Cleveland, Ohio, May 31, 1942; admitted to bar, 1967, Ohio; 1968, U.S. District Court, Northern District of Ohio; 1980, U.S. Court of Appeals, Sixth Circuit. *Education:* Case Western Reserve University (B.A., 1964; J.D., 1967). *Member:* Bar Association of Greater Cleveland; Richland County and Ohio State Bar Associations. ***PRACTICE AREAS:*** Products Liability; Banks and Banking; Fidelity and Surety. ***Email:*** mansfield@baranlaw.com

GREGORY G. BARAN, born Cleveland, Ohio, May 31, 1945; admitted to bar, 1970, Ohio; 1971, U.S. District Court, Northern District of Ohio; 1980, U.S. Supreme Court. *Education:* Wittenberg University (A.B., 1967); The Ohio State University (J.D., cum laude, 1970). *Member:* Bar Association of Greater Cleveland; Richland County and Ohio State Bar Associations. ***PRACTICE AREAS:*** Products Liability; Insurance; Insurance Defense. ***Email:*** ggbaran@baranlaw.com

JOHN TARKOWSKY, born Cleveland, Ohio, January 16, 1954; admitted to bar, 1978, Ohio; 1980, U.S. District Court, Northern District of Ohio and U.S. Tax Court. *Education:* Baldwin-Wallace College (B.A., 1975); Ohio Northern University (J.D., 1978). *Member:* Richland County and Ohio State Bar Associations. (Certified Specialist in Worker's Compensation, Ohio State Bar Association). ***PRACTICE AREAS:*** Workers Compensation Defense; Labor and Employment; Insurance Defense. ***Email:*** jtarkowsky@baranlaw.com

GARY A. PIPER, born Elyria, Ohio, October 18, 1949; admitted to bar, 1975, Ohio; 1976, U.S. District Court, Northern District of Ohio. *Education:* Bowling Green State University (B.S., cum laude, 1972); University of Toledo College of Law (J.D., 1975). *Member:* Richland County and Ohio State Bar Associations. ***PRACTICE AREAS:*** Insurance Law; Products Liability; Banks and Banking. ***Email:*** gapiper@baranlaw.com

ROBERT B. FITZGERALD, born Heidelberg, Germany, June 19, 1957; admitted to bar, 1982, Ohio and U.S. District Court, Northern District of Ohio; 1998, U.S. Court of Appeals, Sixth Circuit; 1997, U.S. Supreme Court. *Education:* Ohio Northern University (B.A., 1979; J.D., 1982). *Member:* Allen County, Richland County and Ohio State Bar Associations. (Resident, Lima Office). ***PRACTICE AREAS:*** Insurance Defense; Products Liability; Governmental Liability. ***Email:*** rbfitzgerald@baranlaw.com

JOHN P. CALANDRA, born Cleveland, Ohio, September 6, 1939; admitted to bar, 1964, Ohio; 1965, U.S. District Court, Northern District of Ohio; 1974, U.S. Court of Appeals, Sixth Circuit; 1980, U.S. Supreme Court. *Education:* Western Reserve University (B.A., 1961); University of Michigan (J.D., 1964). *Member:* Ohio State Bar Association. ***PRACTICE AREAS:*** Corporate Law; Trusts and Estates; Insurance Law. ***Email:*** jpcalandra@baranlaw.com

DONALD E. THEIS, born New Riegel, Ohio, February 14, 1954; admitted to bar, 1979, Ohio and U.S. District Court, Southern District of Ohio; 1981, U.S. District Court, Northern District of Ohio; 1989, U.S. Court of Appeals, 6th Circuit; 1991, U.S. Supreme Court. *Education:* Xavier University (A.B., summa cum laude, 1976); University of Michigan (J.D., 1979). *Member:* Toledo and Ohio State Bar Associations. (Resident, Toledo Office). ***PRACTICE AREAS:*** Governmental Liability; Products Liability; Banks and Banking. ***Email:*** detheis@baranlaw.com

MARK A. VAN DYNE, born Wheeling, West Virginia, March 26, 1964; admitted to bar, 1990, Ohio; 1991, West Virginia; 1994, U.S. District Court, Northern and Southern District of Ohio, Indiana and U.S. District Court, Northern and Southern Districts of Indiana and U.S. District Court, Northern District of West Virginia. *Education:* Ohio University (B.B.A., summa cum laude, 1987); Ohio Northern University (J.D., 1990). *Member:* Allen

(This Listing Continued)

County and Ohio State Bar Associations; West Virginia State Bar. (Resident, Lima Office). ***PRACTICE AREAS:*** Trusts and Estates; Debtor and Creditor; Corporate Law. ***Email:*** mvdyne@baranlaw.com

ROSE A. PATTI, born Cleveland, Ohio, November 17, 1949; admitted to bar, 1991, Ohio. *Education:* Cleveland State University (B.A., cum laude, 1975; M.B.A., 1982); Cleveland Marshall College of Law (J.D., 1991). *Member:* Cleveland and Ohio State Bar Associations. (Resident, Brecksville Office). ***LANGUAGES:*** Italian. ***PRACTICE AREAS:*** Insurance Law; Products Liability; Governmental Liability. ***Email:*** rapatti@baranlaw.com

JANET L. MIGGINS, born Akron, Ohio, January 14, 1947; admitted to bar, 1981, Ohio. *Education:* University of Akron (B.A., magna cum laude, 1969); Cleveland State University (J.D., 1981). *Member:* Cleveland and Ohio State Bar Associations. (Resident, Brecksville Office). ***PRACTICE AREAS:*** Trusts and Estates; Real Estate; Insurance Defense; Fidelity and Surety. ***Email:*** jlmiggins@baranlaw.com

RICHARD T. REESE, born Lima, Ohio, September 13, 1956; admitted to bar, 1981, Ohio; 1982, U.S. District Court, Northern District of Ohio. *Education:* Ohio Northern University (B.A., 1978; J.D., 1981). (Resident, Lima, OH Office). ***LANGUAGES:*** German. ***PRACTICE AREAS:*** Personal Injury; Domestic Relations; Family Law; Insurance Defense; Estates. ***Email:*** rtreese@baranlaw.com

KELLY L. BADNELL, born Lakewood, Ohio, June 2, 1966; admitted to bar, 1994, Ohio; 1998, U.S. District Court, Northern District of Ohio. *Education:* Washington and Jefferson College (B.A., 1988); Ohio Northern University (J.D., 1994). ***PRACTICE AREAS:*** Workers Compensation; Insurance; Employment Law; Zoning, Planning and Land Use. ***Email:*** klbadnell@baranlaw.com

MICHAEL L. JONES, born Steubenville, Ohio, May 21, 1969; admitted to bar, 1994, Ohio. *Education:* Capital University (B.A., 1991; J.D., magna cum laude, 1994). *Member:* Allen County and Ohio State Bar Associations. (Resident, Portsmouth Office). ***PRACTICE AREAS:*** Insurance Defense; Family Law; Criminal Law. ***Email:*** mljones@baranlaw.com

---

STEPHEN D. LONG, born Saint Marys, Ohio, May 19, 1964; admitted to bar, 1994, Ohio; 1996, U.S. District Court, Northern District of Ohio. *Education:* Ohio Northern University (B.A., 1987); University of Toledo (J.D., cum laude, 1994). *Member:* Toledo, Ohio State and American Bar Associations. (Resident, Toledo Office). ***PRACTICE AREAS:*** Family Law; Bankruptcy; Criminal Law; General Practice. ***Email:*** sdlong@baranlaw.com

CHAD P. HANKE, born Columbus, Ohio, August 27, 1977; admitted to bar, 2003, Ohio. *Education:* Wittenberg University (B.A., 2000); The Ohio State University (J.D., 2003). Phi Beta Kappa. *Member:* Richland County and Ohio State Bar Associations. ***PRACTICE AREAS:*** Family Law; Bankruptcy; Criminal Law; General Practice. ***Email:*** cphanke@baranlaw.com

ANGELA M. ELLIOTT, born Oregon, Ohio, August 24, 1978; admitted to bar, 2004, Ohio. *Education:* Bowling Green State University (B.A., 2000); Case Western Reserve University (J.D., 2003). *Member:* Ohio State Bar Association. (Resident, Lima Office). ***PRACTICE AREAS:*** Family Law; Criminal Law. ***Email:*** amelliott@baranlaw.com

KENNETH J. HEISELE, born 1978; admitted to bar, 2005, Ohio. *Education:* Rutgers University (B.A., 2001); Ohio Northern University (J.D., 2004). Member, Ohio Northern University Law Review. (Resident, Lima Office). ***PRACTICE AREAS:*** Probate; Insurance Defense; Civil Litigation; Criminal Law. ***Email:*** kjheisele@baranlaw.com

REPRESENTATIVE CLIENTS: Richland Trust Co.; Norfolk & Western Railroad; Terminal Transport Co.; White Consolidated Industries; Underground Utilities; Key Bank; Fifth Third Bank; Lender's Service Inc.; Brost Foundry; Lowes Inc.; Masfield Foundry Corp.; Orion Ins. Co.; Mansfield Structural & Erecting Co.
LOCAL COUNSEL FOR: Alexis Risk Management; Allied Insurance Co.; Atlanta Casualty; Allstate Insurance Co.; American-International Cos.; American Modern Home Insurance Co.; Central Mutual Insurance Co.; The CIGNA Companies; Chubb Group; Citation Corp.; Citi Financial Co., Inc.; Erie Insurance Group; Dalton Corp.; Fireman's Fund; GRE Insurance Group; Great American Insurance Co.; Guide One Insurance Group; Gulf Insurance Co.; Hamilton Mutual Insurance Co.; Hobart Corp.; Indiana Insurance Co.; K & K Claim Service; Kemper Insurance Group; Liberty Mutual Insurance Co.; Ohio Casualty Group; Ohio Farmers Insurance Co.; Ohio Mutual Insurance Co.; Omni Insurance Group; Penn Warranty; Redman Homes; Shelby Ins.Group; Therm-O-Disc; Travelers Insurance; Westfield Companies.

BROWN, BEMILLER, MURRAY, McINTYRE, VETTER & HECK, L.L.P.

Established in 1950

70 PARK AVENUE WEST
MANSFIELD, OHIO 44902
Telephone: 419-525-1611
FAX: 419-525-3810
URL: http://www.brownbemiller.com

General Civil Practice, Corporate Law, Banking, Business, Casualty and Life Insurance, Trusts and Estates, Wills and Probate, Estate Planning, Real Estate Law, Labor, Employment, Personal Injury, Medical Malpractice, Legal Malpractice. Trials and Appeals, Arbitration and Mediation.

FIRM PROFILE: The genealogy of this firm reaches to the early 1950's when it was Gongwer & Murray and served only the Mansfield area. It now covers north central Ohio from its central offices in Mansfield, offering the services set forth below.

All partners and associates are heavily involved in local and statewide professional and civic activities.

OF COUNSEL

JOHN T. BROWN, born Christiansburg, Ohio, January 23, 1931; admitted to bar, 1958, Ohio; 1960, U.S. District Court, Northern District of Ohio. *Education:* Heidelberg College; Syracuse University; The Ohio State University College of Law (J.D., 1958).

(This Listing Continued)

Member, O.S.U. College of Law National Council, 1998—. President, The Law Abstract Publishing Co., 1977-1978. Member, Ohio Supreme Court Commission on Grievances and Discipline, 1979-1983. Trustee, Ohio Legal Center Institute 1984-1988. Member, Ohio Supreme Court Visiting Judges Committee, 1987. Trustee, Mansfield Cemetery Association, 1984— President, 1997—. Vice-Chairman, Board of Directors: Ohio Bar Liability Ins. Co.; Board Member, Ohio Bar Title Ins. Co., 1988-1998. *Member:* Richland County (President, 1982) and Ohio State (Member: Negligence Law Committee, 1968-1988; Special Committee on Tort Law, 1986; Litigation Section, Board of Governors, 1985-2000; Council of Delegates, 1970-1975, 1979-1983; Commission on Judicial Candidates, 1978-1982; President's Task Force For Tomorrow; Executive Committee, 1975-1978) Bar Associations; Association of Defense Trial Attorneys: International Association of Defense Counsel; Ohio Association of Civil Trial Attorneys (Member, Executive Committee, 1981-1992; Treasurer, 1988; Vice-President, 1989; President, 1990-1991); Defense Research Institute. Fellow: Ohio State Bar Foundation (Trustee, 1983-1988; President, 1985; Recipient of the Honorary Life Fellowship Award, 1989); American College of Trial Lawyers. [with USAF, 1950-1954]. ***PRACTICE AREAS:*** Insurance Defense Law; Civil Practice; Appellate Practice. ***Email:*** JBrown@bbmmlaw.com

F. LOYAL BEMILLER, born Mansfield, Ohio, November 1, 1933; admitted to bar, 1958, Ohio; 1963, U.S. District Court, Northern District of Ohio; 1980, U.S. Tax Court. *Education:* Ohio University (A.B., 1955); University of Michigan (J.D., 1958). Delta Theta Phi; Phi Beta Kappa; Omicron Delta Kappa. Chairman, National YMCA Drug Task Force, 1972. Trustee: Richland County Regional Sewer Board, 1973-1975; Trustee/Co-Manager, the Pryor Foundation, 1980—; Mansfield-Richland County Public Library, 1982-1992; Richland County Foundation, 1984-1995; Med-Central Foundation, Chairman, 1996—; Med-Central Health System, Board of Trustees, 1980—; Director, Mansfield-Richland Educational Foundation, Inc., 1982-1995; Mansfield Chamber of Commerce, 1989-1995; Trustee, Community Health Access Program, 2001— and Johnny Appleseed Heritage Center Board, 2000—. *Member:* Richland County and Ohio State Bar Associations. [USAF, 1958-1961]. ***PRACTICE AREAS:*** Probate; Estate Planning; Corporate Business; Real Estate. ***Email:*** LBemiller@bbmmlaw.com

MEMBERS OF FIRM

D. KIM MURRAY, born Santa Barbara, California, January 17, 1945; admitted to bar, 1973, Ohio and U.S. District Court, Northern District of Ohio. *Education:* The Ohio State University (B.A., 1970); University of Akron (J.D., 1973). Phi Alpha Theta. Chairman, Mansfield Civil Service Commission, 1986-1992. *Member:* Richland County and Ohio State Bar Associations. ***PRACTICE AREAS:*** Personal Injury; Insurance Defense Law; Insurance Law; Civil Practice; Professional Liability Defense. ***Email:*** KMurray@bbmmlaw.com

WILLIAM T. McINTYRE, born Akron, Ohio, March 15, 1950; admitted to bar, 1975, Ohio. *Education:* Bowling Green State University (B.S., 1972); The Ohio State University (J.D., 1975). Beta Gamma Sigma. *Member:* Richland County (President, 1991) and Ohio State (Member, 1978—and Secretary, 1982—, Negligence Law Committee) Bar Associations; Ohio Association of Civil Trial Attorneys. ***PRACTICE AREAS:*** Insurance Defense Law; Pension and Profit Sharing Law; Labor Arbitration Law. ***Email:*** BMcintyre@bbmmlaw.com

JEFFREY MOLYET (1951-2003)

ADAM (BUD) VETTER, JR., born Decatur, Illinois, February 4, 1960; admitted to bar, 1985, Ohio and U.S. Tax Court; U.S. District Court, Northern District of Ohio. *Education:* Bowling Green State University (B.S., cum laude, 1982); Cleveland-Marshall College of Law (J.D., magna cum laude, 1985). Omicron Delta Kappa; Beta Gamma Sigma. Recipient, BGSU Male Scholar/Athlete of the Year, 1982. Participant, Varsity Tennis, 4 Letters, 1978-1982. Mortar Board (President, 1981-1982). Staff Member, 1983-1984; Editorial Board and Research Editor, 1984-1985 Executive Committee, Cleveland Marshall Law Review. *Member:* Cleveland, Richland County and Ohio State Bar Associations; Richland County Chamber of Commerce (Trustee, 1997—; Executive Committee, 2003—; Chairman Economic Development Committee, 2003—; Vice Chairman of the Board, 2003); Mansfield Metropolitan Airport and Aviation Commission (Member, 2000—; Vice Chairman, 2000—); Richland County Incubator (Trustee, 2002—). ***PRACTICE AREAS:*** Corporate Law; Real Estate; Estate Planning; Probate; Taxation. ***Email:*** BVetter@bbmmlaw.com

J. JEFFREY HECK, born Dayton, Ohio, December 4, 1959; admitted to bar, 1985, Florida; 1988, Ohio and U.S. District Court, Northern District of Ohio; U.S. Court of Appeals, Sixth and Eleventh Circuits; U.S. District Court, Middle and Southern Districts of Florida. *Education:* The Ohio State University (B.S., 1982); University of Florida (J.D., with honors, 1985). Member, Board of Education, Lexington Local Schools, 2002—; Trustee, Richland County Foundation, 1996—; Secretary, 2001—. *Member:* Richland County (Secretary, 1999—; Member: Cert. Grievance Committee, 1992-1996) and Ohio State (Member: Task Force on Sexual Harassment, 1996-1998; Federal Courts Committee, 1992-1998; Negligence Committee, 1988—; Council of Delegates, 1992—; Board of Governors, Litigation Section, 1998— Special Committee to Review the Report of the Ohio Courts Futures Commission, 1999-2001) Bar Associations; The Florida Bar; Ohio Association of Civil Trial Attorneys (Member: Executive Committee, 1997-2002; Program Chair, 1996-1997; District Director, 1990-2001); Association of Defense Trial Attorneys; Defense Research Institute. ***PRACTICE AREAS:*** Personal Injury; Insurance Defense Law; Civil Trial Practice; Commercial Litigation; Appellate Practice; Labor and Employment Law. ***Email:*** JHeck@bbmmlaw.com

JASON B. MURRAY, born Columbus, Ohio, March 3, 1970; admitted to bar, 1995, Ohio. *Education:* Ohio Wesleyan University (B.A., summa cum laude, 1992); The Ohio State University (J.D., 1995). Phi Beta Kappa. Member: Mortar Board; Phi Society. Trustee, Community Action for Capable Youth, 1997—; Trustee and Finance Co-Chairman, Mansfield Area Y, 1998—. Secretary, North Central Ohio Estate Planning Council, 2000—. *Member:* Richland County and Ohio State Bar Associations. ***PRACTICE AREAS:*** Corporate; Estate Planning; Real Estate; Probate; Taxation. ***Email:*** JMurray@bbmmlaw.com

DAVID N. HARING, born Mansfield, Ohio, March 17, 1969; admitted to bar, 1994, Ohio. *Education:* Miami University (B.A., 1991); University of Toledo College of Law (J.D., 1994). Trustee, Main Street Mansfield, 2000—. Trustee, The Red Cross, 2000—. Director: Richland County Transit Board, 2002—; Richland Alternate Program, Inc., 2001—. Trustee, The Warren G. Rupp Foundation, 2002—. *Member:* Richland County and Ohio State Bar Associations. ***PRACTICE AREAS:*** Corporate; Estate Planning; Commercial Litigation; Real Estate; Probate. ***Email:*** DHaring@bbmmlaw.com

GENERAL COUNSEL FOR: Cooper Enterprises, Inc.; Richland County Medical Society; Mansfield Brass & Aluminum Corp.; Richland County Regional Planning Commission; Mansfield Industries, Inc.; Richland County Growth Corp.; Richland Economic Development Corp.; D & S Creative ADV, Inc.; Mansfield Commerce Center, Inc.; Virtual Stores Worldwide, Inc.; Brost Foundry Co.; The Richland County Foundation; Johnny Appleseed Heritage Center; MedCentral Health Center Foundation; The Bissman Co.; Major Metals Co.; Deer Ridge Golf Club; Ohio Valley Mfg.

LOCAL COUNSEL FOR: Royal & Sun Alliance; Westfield Companies; Ohio Edison Co.; Grange Mutual Casualty Co.; Buckeye Union Insurance Co.; Shelby Insurance; Montgomery Ward & Co.; Prudential Property and Casualty Insurance Co.; C.N.A. Group; Newman Technology, Inc.; Auto Owners Ins. Co.; U.S. Life Credit Life Ins. Co.; Banque Nationale de Paris; News Journal; Hastings Mutual; Meridian Ins. Co.; Wayne Mutual Ins. Co.; Ohio Bar Liability Ins. Co.; Michigan Millers Ins. Co.; Key Bank; American National Property & Casualty; Brotherhood Mutual Insurance Co.; Interstate Insurance Co.; Dairy Mart Convenience Store, Inc.; Crawford & Company; Ideal Electric Company; AK Steel; Precision Auto Care; Hartman Electric; Gorman Rupp; Shafer Valve; Ohio American Water; General Casualty Co.; Agway Ins. Co; Roberts & Dybdahl, Inc.; Richland Bank; Sprint; German Mutual Ins. Co.; Elevators Mutual Ins. Co.; Omaha Property & Casualty Co.

(This Listing Continued)

GEORGE R. KEYSER

44 PARK AVENUE WEST
SUITE 202
MANSFIELD, OHIO 44902-1610
Telephone: 419-526-2301
Fax: 419-526-2826
Email: keysergeorge@earthlink.net
URL: http://www.keyserlaw.com

Civic and Criminal Litigation in all Courts. Personal Injury, Automobile Accidents, Slip and Fall, Products Liability, Wrongful Death, Family Law, Divorce, Child Custody, Child Support, Visitation Rights, Adoption Law, Juvenile Law, Criminal Defense, Driving While Intoxicated, Drug Crimes, Felonies, Misdemeanors.

GEORGE R. KEYSER, born 1947; admitted to bar, 1973, Ohio, Florida and U.S. District Court, Northern District of Ohio. *Education:* Florida State University; Florida Southern College (B.A.,1970); Stetson University (J.D.,1973). Phi Alpha Delta. *Member:* Richland County Bar Association; Ohio Academy of Trial Lawyers. ***PRACTICE AREAS:*** Personal Injury Law; Divorce Law; Criminal Defense.

LAMKIN, VAN EMAN, TRIMBLE, BEALS & DOUGHERTY, LLC

MANSFIELD, OHIO

(See Columbus)

Personal Injury, Medical Malpractice, Products Liability, Negligence, Insurance Coverage, Stockbroker Malpractice & Fraud. Litigation and Trial Practice.

ROXI A. LIMING

MANSFIELD, OHIO

(See Columbus)

Immigration Law, Visas, Naturalization, H1-B Visas, Green Cards, Financé Visas, Investor Visas, Investor Green Cards, Labor and Employment, Wage and Hour Violations, Wrongful Discharge, Employment Discrimination, Americans with Disabilities Act, Sexual Harassment, Family and Medical Leave Act, Employment Contracts, Severance Package Negotiation, Personnel Policies.

OLIVER LAW OFFICE

MANSFIELD, OHIO

(See Columbus)

Products Liability, Personal Injury, Wrongful Death, Latex Allergy Litigation, Medical Malpractice, Vioxx Litigation, Automobile Accidents, Insurance Law, Employment Discrimination.

THE PLYMALE PARTNERSHIP LLP

MANSFIELD, OHIO

(See Columbus)

Personal Injury, Products Liability, Wrongful Death, Medical Malpractice, Professional Negligence, Traumatic Brain Injury, Automobile Accidents, Nursing Home Torts, Civil Litigation.

POLAND, DEPLER AND SHEPHERD CO., L.P.A.

MANSFIELD, OHIO

(See Shelby)

General Civil Practice in all Courts. Real Estate, Probate and Estate Planning, Corporate, Banking, Family, Domestic Relations and Commercial Law. Trials.

ROURKE & BLUMENTHAL, LLP

MANSFIELD, OHIO

(See Columbus)

Personal Injury, Negligence, Products Liability, Medical Malpractice, Nursing Home Litigation, Wrongful Death, Intentional Tort, Insurance Disputes, Automobile Accidents, Civil Trial Practice, Aviation, Professional Liability.

SAUTER HOHENBERGER & BEDDOW

24 WEST THIRD STREET, SUITE 306
MANSFIELD, OHIO 44902
Telephone: 419-522-6242
Fax: 419-525-0258
URL: http://www.shbfirm.com

Insurance, Probate and Estate Planning, Negligence and Products Liability Law. Trials and Appeals.

MEMBERS OF FIRM

GEORGE V. SAUTER (Retired)

WAYNE P. HOHENBERGER, born Defiance, Ohio, July 3, 1946; admitted to bar, 1973, Ohio. *Education:* Bowling Green State University (B.A., 1968); The Ohio State University (J.D., 1973). Phi Delta Phi (Historian, 1973). Member, Moot Court Advisory Board. *Member:* Richland County, Ohio State and American Bar Associations; Ohio Association of Civil Trial Attorneys; Defense Research and Trial Lawyers Association. [U.S. Army, active duty, 1968-1970]. **Email:** wph@shbfirm.com

KENNETH R. BEDDOW, born Columbus, Ohio, May 9, 1956; admitted to bar, 1981, Ohio; 1982, U.S. District Court, Northern District of Ohio; 1987, U.S. Court of Appeals, Sixth Circuit. *Education:* Bowling Green State University (B.S., 1978); University of Toledo (J.D., 1981). Member, Moot Court National Trial Competition Team. Law Clerk to the Hon. Paul L. Chorpening, Ashland County Common Pleas Court, 1980. *Member:* Richland County, Ohio State (Member, Negligence Law Section) and American (Member, Litigation Section) Bar Associations; Ohio Association of Civil Trial Attorneys; Defense Research Institute. **Email:** krb@shbfirm.com

ASSOCIATE

JOSEPH P. HOERIG, born Warren, Ohio, May 31, 1967; admitted to bar, 1995, Ohio; 1998, U.S. District Court, Northern District of Ohio. *Education:* Youngstown State University (B.A., 1989); University of Akron (J.D., 1995). *Member:* Ohio State Bar Association. **PRACTICE AREAS:** Insurance Defense. **Email:** jph@shbfirm.com

GENERAL COUNSEL FOR: United Ohio Insurance Co.
REPRESENTATIVE CLIENTS: State Farm Insurance Cos.; Celina Insurance Group; Auto Owners (Mutual) Insurance Co.; Transamerica Group; St. Paul Insurance Group; Western Reserve Mutual Casualty Co.; Home Insurance Co.; Cincinnati Insurance Cos.; Aetna Casualty and Surety Co.; Pico Physicians Insurance Co.; Indiana Insurance Co.; Media Professional Ins. Inc.; Monroe Guarantee Insurance Co.
REFERENCES: Richland Bank Co.; Trust Corp.

SCHERNER, HANSON & CORNWELL, LLC

MANSFIELD, OHIO

(See Columbus)

Civil Trial and Appellate Litigation in State and Federal Courts. Medical Malpractice and other Professional Liability, Personal Injury, Product Liability, Commercial, Corporate, Fraud and other Civil Litigation.

STANDLEY LAW GROUP LLP

MANSFIELD, OHIO

(See Dublin)

Domestic and Foreign Intellectual Property Law, including Patent, Trademark, Copyright, Unfair Competition and Trade Secret Law and related Litigation, Licensing, International Trade Matters, related Antitrust, Computer and other Technology Law.

TWYFORD & DONAHEY, P.L.L.

MANSFIELD, OHIO

(See Columbus)

Personal Injury Litigation, Wrongful Death, Medical Malpractice, Products Liability, Automobile Accidents, Trucking Accidents, Head and Spinal Injuries, Motorcycle Accidents and Injuries, Uninsured Motorists, Insurance Law, Airplane Crash Litigation, Railroad Accidents, Slip and Fall, Dog Bites, Work Related Injuries, Birth Injuries, Nursing Home Abuse and Neglect.

WELDON, HUSTON & KEYSER, L.L.P.

Established in 1932
BANK ONE BUILDING
28 PARK AVE W
MANSFIELD, OHIO 44902-1692
Telephone: 419-524-9811
Fax: 419-522-5758

General Civil and Criminal Practice. Probate and Estate Planning. Business Law, Labor and Employment Law, Insurance Law, Personal Injury, Real Estate, Family/Domestic Relations, Divorce.

FIRM PROFILE: The firm of Weldon, Huston & Keyser originated as Weldon & Huston in 1932 and assumed the present name in 1946. The firm was founded as a general practice group and maintains that representation as local counsel for various industrial, banking, commercial and health care organizations. The firm has a long standing tradition of participation in charitable, governmental and educational activities as well as professional associations.

WILLIAM McE. WELDON (1868-1952)
C. H. HUSTON (1871-1957)
HENRY P. HUSTON (1903-1984)
GEORGE H. KEYSER (1917-1998)

MEMBERS OF FIRM

DAVID D. CARTO, born St. Paul, Minnesota, January 10, 1956; admitted to bar, 1981, Ohio; U.S. Supreme Court; U.S. Court of Appeals, Sixth Circuit; U.S. District Court, Northern District of Ohio. *Education:* Ohio Wesleyan University (B.A., History, 1978); Case Western Reserve University (J.D., 1981). Recipient, Student Advocacy Program Award, International Academy of Trial Lawyers, 1981. Research Editor, Case Western Reserve Journal of International Law, 1980-1981. Author: "The Monroe Doctrine in the 1980's: International Law, Unilateral Policy, or Atavistic Anachronism?" 13 Case Western Reserve Journal of International Law 203, 1981. *Member:* Richland County and Ohio State Bar Associations. **PRACTICE AREAS:** General Civil and Criminal Litigation; Employment Law; Insurance Law; Divorce. **Email:** dcarto@whkmansfield.com

RICHARD H. OTTO, born Manhasset, New York, December 7, 1954; admitted to bar, 1981, Ohio; 1983, Florida; U.S. District Court, Northern District of Ohio. *Education:* Williams College (B.A., 1976); Boston University School of Law (J.D., 1980). Referee, Richland County Domestic Relations Court, 1985-1986. *Member:* Richland County (Treasurer, 1991-1999; President, 2001) and Ohio State (Member, Family Law Committee, 1991—) Bar Associations; The Florida Bar. **PRACTICE AREAS:** Family Law/Domestic Relations; Adoptions; Juvenile Law; Civil Litigation; Divorce. **Email:** rotto@whkmansfield.com

JOHN ALLEN HOLMES, born Mansfield, Ohio, November 18, 1953; admitted to bar, 1984, California; 1994, Ohio; U.S. District Court, Northern District of Ohio. *Education:* Georgetown College, Kentucky (B.A., American Studies, magna cum laude, 1978); University of Kentucky (J.D., 1983). *Member:* Richland County and Ohio State Bar Associations. **PRACTICE AREAS:** Personal Injury Law; Civil Litigation; Consumer Law; Collections; Divorce; Wrongful Death. **Email:** jholmes@whkmansfield.com

DONALD E. HOOVER, born Mansfield, Ohio, October 5, 1954; admitted to bar, 1980, Ohio. *Education:* Ashland University (B.S., Business Administration, 1976); University of Akron School of Law (J.D., 1980). Presiding Judge, Mansfield Municipal Court, 1988-1999. *Member:* Richland County and Ohio State Bar Associations. **PRACTICE AREAS:** Business Law; Estate Planning; Probate; Corporate; Divorce. **Email:** dhoover@whkmansfield.com

ASSOCIATES

JOSEPH T. OLECKI, born Garfield Heights, Ohio, December 16, 1961; admitted to bar, 1994, Ohio; U.S. District Court, Northern and Southern Districts of Ohio. *Education:* Wesleyan University (B.A., Government, 1984); University of Virginia (J.D., 1994). *Member:* Richland County, Ohio State and American Bar Associations. **PRACTICE AREAS:** General Practice; Divorce. **Email:** jolecki@whkmansfield.com

CATHERINE D. GOLDMAN, born Marysville, Ohio, January 12, 1956; admitted to bar, 1981, Ohio; U.S. District Court, Northern District of Ohio. *Education:* University of Vermont (B.A., Sociology/Economics, cum laude, 1978); The Ohio State University College of Law (J.D., 1981). Phi Beta Kappa. First Assistant Prosecuting Attorney, 1981-1988. Magistrate: Common Pleas General Division, 1991-1996; Common Pleas Juvenile Division, 1998-2003. *Member:* Richland County Bar Association (President, 1993); Ohio State Magistrates Association. **REPORTED CASES:** State ex Rel. Jackson v. Allen (1992), 65 Ohio St. 3d 37; State v. Lewis (1993), 85 Ohio App. 3d 29. **PRACTICE AREAS:** Domestic Relations; Juvenile Law; Criminal Law; Litigation; Divorce. **Email:** cgoldman@whkmansfield.com

JEROD M. THEM, born Mansfield, Ohio, September 17, 1978; admitted to bar, 2004, Ohio. *Education:* The Ohio State University (B.S., cum laude, 2001); Capital University (J.D., cum laude, 2004). *Member:* Richland County and Ohio State Bar Associations. **PRACTICE AREAS:** Real Estate; Business Law; Estate Planning; Health Care; Probate. **Email:** jthen@whkmansfield.com

OF COUNSEL

GEORGE HALL, born Rices Landing, Pennsylvania, June 24, 1924; admitted to bar, 1952, Ohio. *Education:* University of Pittsburgh (A.B., 1949); Case Western Reserve University (LL.B., 1952). Delta Theta Phi. Member, Mansfield Board of Education, 1968-1988. *Member:* Richland County (President, 1967), Ohio State and American Bar Associations. [U.S. Army Air Force, 1943-1946]. **PRACTICE AREAS:** Real Estate Law; Probate Law; Estate Planning; Divorce. **Email:** GeoH33@aol.com

RICHARD R. FOWLER, born Philadelphia, Pennsylvania, January 30, 1928; admitted to bar, 1953, Ohio. *Education:* The Ohio State University (B.S., 1953; J.D., 1953). Phi Delta Phi. Police Prosecutor, 1953-1956. *Member:* Richland County (President, 1986) and Ohio State Bar Associations. [U.S. Marine Corps, 1946-1948]. **PRACTICE AREAS:** General Practice; Business Planning Law; Probate; Divorce.

JOHN H. SIEGENTHALER, born Mansfield, Ohio, October 12, 1939; admitted to bar, 1964, Ohio; U.S. District Court, Northern District of Ohio. *Education:* Denison University (A.B., 1961); The Ohio State University (J.D., 1964). *Member:* Richland County (President, 1988) and Ohio State Bar Associations; Ohio Society of Hospital Attorneys. **PRACTICE AREAS:** Real Estate Law; Business Law; Estate Planning and Probate Law; Divorce. **Email:** jsieg@whkmansfield.com

THOMAS L. COLE, born Waynesburg, Pennsylvania, September 22, 1937; admitted to bar, 1961, Ohio; U.S. District Court, Northern District of Ohio. *Education:* Ohio Northern University (B.A., 1959; J.D., 1961). *Member:* Richland County and Ohio State Bar Associations; Ohio Academy of Trial Lawyers. **PRACTICE AREAS:** Domestic Relations; Commercial Real Estate; Probate; Divorce. **Email:** tcole@whkmansfield.com

CHARLES M. BROWN, born Dayton, Ohio, November 1, 1943; admitted to bar, 1972, Ohio; U.S. District Court, Northern District of Ohio. *Education:* University of Dayton (B.A., 1965); Ohio Northern University (J.D., 1972). *Member:* Richland County (Presi-

(This Listing Continued)

dent, 1990) and Ohio State Bar Associations; Ohio Academy of Trial Lawyers (Trustee, 1995-1996). [U.S. Navy, 1965-1968]. ***PRACTICE AREAS:*** Personal Injury; Civil Litigation; Criminal Defense; Divorce. ***Email:*** cbrown@whkmansfield.com

REPRESENTATIVE CLIENTS: Mechanics Savings Bank; The Richland Trust Company (Richland Bank); Motorists Insurance Co.; General Motors Acceptance Corp.; Reeder Lumber Co.; Whitey's Auto Mall; North Central State College; Ohio Ski Slopes, Inc.; Milliron Industries, Inc.; Stoneridge, Inc.; Geyer's Markets, Inc.; MedCentral Health System; MT Business Technologies, Inc.; Mid-Ohio Heart Clinic; Sunset Golf, Inc.; Amerascrew, Inc.; D & S Creative Communications, Inc.

WILES, BOYLE, BURKHOLDER & BRINGARDNER CO., L.P.A.

MANSFIELD, OHIO

(See Columbus)

General Practice, Insurance Defense, Medical Legal, Products Liability, Aviation, Motor Carrier, Business, Corporate, Municipal, Construction, Real Estate, Commercial Leasing, Hospitality and Restaurant, Estate Planning Law, Trusts, Wills and Probate, Taxation, Trial, and Appellate Practice, Bankruptcy, Foreclosure and Debtor-Creditor Law.

BUELL & SIPE CO. L.P.A.

322 3RD STREET
MARIETTA, OHIO 45750
Telephone: 740-373-3219
Fax: 740-373-2892
Email: attorneys@buellsipe.com
URL: http://www.lawyers.com/buell&sipe

Personal Injury, Automobile Accidents, Wrongful Death, Civil Litigation, Estate Planning, Wills and Probate, Trusts and Estates, Employment Discrimination, Sexual Harassment, Family Law, Divorce, Child Custody, Child Support, Adoptions, Criminal Defense, Driving While Intoxicated, Traffic Violations, Appellate Law including Habeas Corpus.

MICHAEL D. BUELL, born Geneva, New York, December 29, 1952; admitted to bar, 1978, Ohio; 1979, U.S. District Court, Northern District of Ohio. *Education:* Marietta College (B.A., 1975); University of Toledo (J.D., 1978). Acting Judge, Marietta Municipal Court, 1989-1990; 1998—. *Member:* Washington County and American Bar Associations. ***PRACTICE AREAS:*** Corporate Law; Real Estate; Estate Planning; Probate; Oil and Gas; Mediation; Alternative Dispute Resolution; Domestic; Appellate; Criminal Defense. ***Email:*** mdbuell@buellsipe.com

DENNIS L. SIPE, born Lansing, Michigan, February 20, 1948; admitted to bar, 1973, Ohio; 1974, U.S. District Court, Southern District of Ohio; 1977, U.S. District Court, Northern District of Ohio and U.S. Court of Appeals, Sixth Circuit; 1980, U.S. Supreme Court. *Education:* Michigan State University (B.S., with honors, 1970); The Ohio State University (J.D., 1973). Assistant Attorney General, 1977-1982. Small Claims Referee, Marietta Municipal Court, 1983-1985. Acting Judge, Marietta Municipal Court, 1985—. *Member:* Washington County and Ohio Bar Associations; The Association of Trial Lawyers of America. ***PRACTICE AREAS:*** Personal Injury; Criminal Defense; Employment Law; Appellate Law. ***Email:*** dennis@buellsipe.com

COSENZA & MERRIMAN, PLLC

MARIETTA, OHIO

(See Parkersburg, West Virginia)

General Civil and Criminal Trial Practice. Personal Injury.

DAVIDSON, HECKLER, RIGGS & FOUSS

Established in 1958

311 FOURTH STREET
P.O. BOX 567
MARIETTA, OHIO 45750
Telephone: 740-373-7572
Fax: 740-373-7081
Email: dhrf@sbcglobal.net

General Practice in State and Federal Courts. Corporation, Small Business Law, Business Formation, Buying and Selling of Businesses, Real Estate, Probate, Trusts and Estates. Trials.

MEMBERS OF FIRM

ROLAND W. RIGGS, III, born Cleveland, Ohio, September 28, 1947; admitted to bar, 1972, Ohio; 1990, U.S. Supreme Court. *Education:* Georgetown University (B.S.F.S., 1969); Case Western Reserve University (J.D., 1972). Marietta Law Director, 1974—. *Member:* Washington County and Ohio State Bar Associations. ***PRACTICE AREAS:*** Probate Law; Estate Planning Law; Real Estate Law; Municipal Law; Commercial Law; General Practice.

DANIEL A. FOUSS, born Marietta, Ohio, November 23, 1952; admitted to bar, 1980, Ohio; 1988, West Virginia. *Education:* Ohio University (B.A., 1975); University of Toledo (J.D., 1980). *Member:* Washington County and Ohio State Bar Associations. ***PRACTICE AREAS:*** Real Estate Law; Banking Law; Commercial Law; Corporate Law; Business Law; General Practice.

REPRESENTATIVE CLIENTS: The Marietta Savings Bank; Citizens Bank Co., Beverly, Ohio; Richardson Printing Corp.; The Glass Press, Inc.; Buckeye Hills-Hocking Valley Regional Development District; Silverheels, Inc.; The Bartlett Farmers Bank; Washington County, Ohio, Community Improvement Corporation, Inc.
APPROVED ATTORNEYS FOR: Security Union Title Insurance Co.

DENMEAD LAW OFFICE

MARIETTA, OHIO

(See Columbus)

Civil Trial and Appellate Practice and Personal Injury, Traumatic Brain Injury (TBI), Professional Negligence and Complex Litigation including Class Actions, Patents, Civil Rights, Civil Litigation, RICO, Employment and Political Subdivision Liability issues.

THEISEN BROCK

A LEGAL PROFESSIONAL ASSOCIATION

424 SECOND STREET
P.O. BOX 739
MARIETTA, OHIO 45750
Telephone: 740-373-5455
Fax: 740-373-4409
Email: theisenbrock@theisenbrock.com
URL: http://www.theisenbrock.com

General Practice, Trials, Personal Injury, Insurance Law and Insurance Defense, Corporation, Partnership and Business Law, Labor and Employment Law, Probate and Estate Planning, Bankruptcy Law, Real Estate and Oil and Gas Law, Health Care Law, Export Law.

FIRM PROFILE: Theisen Brock is a full service firm established in the 1950's. We have the expertise to perform sophisticated work in diverse areas, while maintaining personal attention and service. Since its founding, the firm has fostered a tradition of high ethical standards and leadership in professional and community affairs. Our firm philosophy is straightforward: serve the client aggressively, professionally, ethically, effectively and economically. At Theisen Brock, we maintain a strong commitment to preventive law as the best way to serve our clients.

OF COUNSEL

PAUL T. THEISEN, born Athens, Ohio, February 4, 1931; admitted to bar, 1957, Ohio; 1973, West Virginia; 1990, U.S. Supreme Court. *Education:* University of Cincinnati (A.B., 1953; LL.B., 1957). Order of the Coif; Omicron Delta Kappa. Associate Editor, University of Cincinnati Law Review, 1956-1957. Member, Ohio Supreme Court Evidence Rules Advisory Committee, 1975-1979. *Member:* Washington County, Ohio State (Member, Executive Committee, 1968-1970) and American (Member, Sections on, Litigation; Labor Law) Bar Associations; West Virginia State Bar. Fellow, American College of Trial Lawyers. ***PRACTICE AREAS:*** Civil Practice; Insurance Law; Insurance Defense; Mediation; Arbitration. ***Email:*** theisen@theisenbrock.com

MEMBERS OF FIRM

JERRY A. BROCK, born Cincinnati, Ohio, February 3, 1938; admitted to bar, 1963, Ohio. *Education:* Ohio University (B.S.C., 1960); University of Cincinnati (J.D., 1963); University of Illinois (LL.M., 1964). Phi Alpha Delta; Order of the Coif. Associate Editor, University of Cincinnati Law Review, 1962-1963. Teaching Assistant, University of Illinois School of Law, 1963-1964. Trustee, Marietta College, 1984-2002. *Member:* Washington County (President, 1971-1972), Ohio State (Member: Board of Governors, 1969-1973; Real Property Section) and American Bar Associations. (Certified Specialist in Estate Planning, Trust and Probate Law, Ohio State Bar Association). ***PRACTICE AREAS:*** Corporate Law; Tax Law; Estate Planning Law; Probate Law. ***Email:*** brock@theisenbrock.com

GARY F. FRYE, born Fredericktown, Ohio, November 14, 1942; admitted to bar, 1968, Ohio. *Education:* United States Coast Guard Academy; The Ohio State University (B.A., 1965; J.D., 1967). Member, Board of Directors, Ohio Bar Liability Insurance Corporation, 1981-1990. Trustee, Ohio CLE Institute, 1990-1992. President, Ohio Land Title Association, 1994-1995. *Member:* Washington County (President, 1974-1975), Ohio State (Member: Real Property Section; Executive Committee, 1977-1980) and American Bar Associations; Ohio Land Title Association (Trustee, 1990-1993). Fellow, Ohio State Bar Foundation. ***PRACTICE AREAS:*** Probate Law; Real Estate Law. ***Email:*** frye@theisenbrock.com

JOHN E. ERB, born Marietta, Ohio, August 4, 1944; admitted to bar, 1969, Ohio. *Education:* The Ohio State University (B.SC. in Business Administration, 1966; J.D., 1968). Member, 1983— and Chairman, 1997—, Marietta Civil Service Commission. Member, 1980-1999, President, 1984, 1985, 1990, 1995, 1999, Washington County Childrens' Services Board. *Member:* Washington County, Ohio State and American Bar Associations; Ohio Association of Civil Trial Attorneys. ***PRACTICE AREAS:*** Civil Practice; General Practice; Insurance Law; Insurance Defense; Probate Law. ***Email:*** erb@theisenbrock.com

M. DALE LEEPER, born Zanesville, Ohio, October 22, 1948; admitted to bar, 1974, Ohio; 1987, West Virginia; 1990, U.S. Supreme Court. *Education:* College of Wooster (B.A., 1970); The Ohio State University (J.D., cum laude, 1974). *Member:* Washington County (President, 1985-1987), Ohio State, West Virginia and American Bar Associations. Fellow, Ohio State Bar Foundation. ***PRACTICE AREAS:*** Business Law; Commercial Law; Health Care; Export Regulation. ***Email:*** leeper@theisenbrock.com

JAMES S. HUGGINS, born Burlington, Iowa, October 4, 1956; admitted to bar, 1981, Ohio; 1984, West Virginia; 1990, U.S. Supreme Court. *Education:* The Ohio State University (B.A., cum laude, 1978; J.D., with honors, 1981). Phi Beta Kappa; Phi Kappa Phi; Phi Eta Sigma; Alpha Lambda Delta; Phi Alpha Delta. Intern for U.S. Representative John M. Ashbrook, 17th District of Ohio, 1977. Adjunct Professor of Economics, Marietta College, 1991. Lecturer: The Ohio Continuing Legal Education Institute; The Eastern Mineral Law Foundation. Special Counsel, Ohio Attorney General. Member, Commission on Continuing Legal Education, Ohio Supreme Court, 1997—. *Member:* Washington County (President, 1988-1989), Ohio State, West Virginia and American Bar Associations. ***PRACTICE AREAS:*** Tax Law; Business Law; Oil and Gas Law; Commercial Litigation; Bankruptcy. ***Email:*** huggins@theisenbrock.com

COLLEEN E. COOK, born Aurora, Illinois, January 1, 1957; admitted to bar, 1983, Ohio and West Virginia; 1990, U.S. Supreme Court. *Education:* The Ohio State University (B.A., cum laude, 1979; J.D., 1982). Phi Beta Kappa; Phi Kappa Phi; Pi Delta Phi; Phi Al-

(This Listing Continued)

THEISEN BROCK, A LEGAL PROFESSIONAL ASSOCIATION, Marietta—Continued

pha Theta. Member, Board of Directors, Ohio Bar Liability Insurance Corp, 1990-1998. Special Counsel, Ohio Attorney General. *Member:* Washington County, Ohio State (Member, Council of Delegates, 1998—), West Virginia and American Bar Associations (Member, Board of Governor's, 2001-2004; Member, Ohio Continuing Legal Education Advisory Committee, 2002—). (Certified Specialist in Labor & Employment Law, Ohio State Bar Association). ***LANGUAGES:*** French. ***PRACTICE AREAS:*** General Practice; Labor and Employment Law. ***Email:*** cook@theisenbrock.com

JOHN E. TRIPLETT, JR., born Huntington, West Virginia, September 14, 1959; admitted to bar, 1984, Ohio; 1985, Army Court of Military Review; 1990, U.S. Supreme; 1991, West Virginia. *Education:* Vanderbilt University (B.A., 1981); Ohio Northern University (J.D., with distinction, 1984). Phi Kappa Phi. Member, Order of the Barrister. *Member:* Washington County (President, 1993), Ohio State, West Virginia and American Bar Associations; Ohio Association of Civil Trial Attorneys. [Capt. U.S. Army, JAGC, 1985-1988]. ***PRACTICE AREAS:*** Civil Practice; Insurance Law; Insurance Defense; Commercial Litigation. ***Email:*** triplett@theisenbrock.com

ABE SELLERS, born Barnesville, Ohio, July 17, 1972; admitted to bar, 1997, Ohio; 1998, West Virginia, U.S. District Court, Southern District of Ohio and U.S. District Court, Southern and Northern Districts of West Virginia. *Education:* Ohio University (B.S., summa cum laude, 1994); The Ohio State University (J.D., 1997). Golden Key. *Member:* Washington County, Ohio State (Member, Board of Governors, Young Lawyers Division, 1999—) and West Virginia Bar Associations. ***PRACTICE AREAS:*** Real Estate; Labor and Employment Law; Commercial Litigation; Corporate Law; General Practice; School Law. ***Email:*** sellers@theisenbrock.com

KHADINE L. RITTER, born Panama City, Republic of Panama, March 29, 1975; admitted to bar, 2000, Ohio; 2001 West Virginia, U.S. District Court, Southern District of Ohio and U.S. District Court, Northern District of West Virginia. *Education:* Drake University (B.A., 1997); Case Western Reserve University (J.D., 2000). Member, National Political Science Honor Society; National Foreign Language Honor Society. Member, 1997-1998 and President, 1998-1999, Federalist Society. Editor in Chief, Case Western Reserve Journal of International Law, 1999-2000. ***LANGUAGES:*** Spanish, Russian, French and German. ***PRACTICE AREAS:*** Commercial Litigation; Bankruptcy; Immigration Law. ***Email:*** ritter@theisenbrock.com

MATTHEW C. CARLISLE, born Windsor, Ontario, Canada, December 18, 1971; admitted to bar, 1998, Ohio; 2001 West Virginia and U.S. District Court, Northern District of West Virginia. *Education:* Ohio University (B.B.A., 1994); The Ohio State University (J.D., 1997). *Member:* Ohio State and American Bar Associations. ***PRACTICE AREAS:*** Commercial Litigation; Insurance Defense. ***Email:*** carlisle@theisenbrock.com

---

ETHAN T. VESSELS, born Columbus, Ohio, June 20, 1973; admitted to bar, 2003, Ohio and U.S. District Court, Southern District of Ohio; 2004, West Virginia and U.S. District Court, Southern and Northern Districts of West Virginia. *Education:* United States Military Academy (B.S., 1995); The Ohio State University College of Law (J.D., with honors, 2003). Member, Ohio State Law Journal, 2001-20003. Recipient: U.S. Army Meritorious Service Medal, 2000; Judge Joseph Harter Memorial Award, 2003. Editor in Chief, U.S. Army Military Intelligence Professional Bulletin, 1998-2000. *Member:* Washington County (Secretary, 2004), Ohio State and West Virginia Bar Associations. [Captain, U.S. Army Military Intelligence, 1995-2000]. ***PRACTICE AREAS:*** Litigation; Insurance Law; Commercial Litigation; Oil and Gas Law. ***Email:*** vessels@theisenbrock.com

LEGAL SUPPORT PERSONNEL

Penny S. Biehl
Frederick C. Boyd
Karen Lynn Fortney
Mary Bennett
Joy Bowen
Bonnie Hockenberry

COUNSEL FOR: Peoples Bank; Settler's Bank; Broughton Foods Co.; Marietta College; Par Mar Oil Co. (Gasoline Distributor); Alan Stone Co. (Quarry Operation-Road and Bridge Construction); Marietta Memorial Hospital; The Airolite Co. (Industrial Louvers); Magnetic Specialty, Inc.; Rampp Company (Oil Field Supplies); Power Maintenance, Inc.; Peoples Bancorp, Inc. (Bank Holding Company); Haessly Hardwood Lumber Co.; Wetz Transportation; Pioneer Pipe; Quick Care; SportsMed; Forma Scientific Inc. (Laboratory Equipment); Analytical Products Co.; Glenwood Retirement Community; Dimex Corporation; Telepage Communication Systems, Inc.; Artex Oil Co.; Carlton Oil Corporation; Arloma Co.; Wetz Investment Company, LLC (Warehousing); NBS, Inc. (Tobacco Stores).
LOCAL COUNSEL FOR: American Municipal Power-Ohio, Inc.; Ameritech; Eramet Marietta, Inc.; Union Carbide Corp.; Allegheny Power Company; Erie Insurance Group; Motorists Mutual Insurance Co.; Nationwide Mutual Insurance Co.; State Farm Insurance Cos.; Cincinnati Insurance Co.; Chicago Title Insurance Co.; Ashland Oil; Celina Mutual Insurance Co.; Crawford & Company; Titan Indemnity Co.; Wayne Mutual Ins. Co.; Bank One; Westfield Insurance Co.

JAVIER H. ARMENGAU

MARION, OHIO

(See Columbus)

Criminal Litigation in all Federal and State Courts.

CALIG & HANDELMAN, LPA

274 S. MAIN STREET
MARION, OHIO 43302
Telephone: 740-375-5051
URL: http://www.chohiolawyers.com

Columbus, Ohio Office: 854 East Broad Street, 43205. Telephone: 614-252-4885; 1-800-633-5000.

Newark, Ohio Office: 29 S. Park Place, 43055. Telephone: 740-349-8581. Fax: 740-345-4101.

Lancaster, Ohio Office: 204 N. Columbus Street, 43130. Telephone: 740-653-4400. Fax: 740-653-0037.

Bankruptcy, Personal Injury, Probate, Real Estate, Social Security, Social Security Disability, Medical Malpractice, Wrongful Death, Civil Litigation, Domestic Relations Law.

(For complete biographical data on all personnel, see Professional Biographies at Columbus)

M. SHAWN DINGUS

MARION, OHIO

(See Columbus)

Personal Injury, Wrongful Death, Civil Litigation, Criminal Law, Juvenile Law and Family Law.

KEGLER, BROWN, HILL & RITTER

Established in 1964
250 EXECUTIVE DRIVE, SUITE B
P.O. BOX 919
MARION, OHIO 43302
Telephone: 740-387-1120
Facsimile: 740-387-3630
Email: info@keglerbrown.com
URL: http://www.keglerbrown.com

Columbus, Ohio Office: Capitol Square, Suite 1800, 65 East State Street. Telephone: 614-462-5400. Telecopier: 614-464-2634. Cable Address: "Law KBHR". Telex: 246671. Email: info@kbhr.com.

Administrative Law/Governmental Relations; Banking; Bankruptcy and Creditor's Rights; Business, Corporations and Partnerships; Commercial; Construction; Energy; Estate Planning; Franchise; Gaming Law; Health Care; International; Labor and Employee Relations; Litigation; Mergers and Acquisitions; Oil and Gas; Patent, Trademark and Copyright Law; Probate; Professional Responsibility; Public Utilities; Real Estate; Securities; Tax.

FIRM PROFILE: Our 66 lawyers are strategically located directly across the street from the Ohio Capitol Building and the Ohio Supreme Court and only three blocks from the Federal District Court, County Courts and the other major state offices. Our attorneys practice in those legal areas listed immediately preceding this paragraph. Kegler, Brown, Hill & Ritter represents clients throughout the Midwest, varying from Fortune 500 companies to small business enterprises.

COUNSEL

TED M. McKINNISS, born Marion, Ohio, November 21, 1950; admitted to bar, 1976, Ohio; 1977, U.S. District Court, Northern District of Ohio. *Education:* Miami University (A.B., 1973); Ohio Northern University (J.D., with distinction, 1976). Phi Kappa Phi; Delta Theta Phi. Special Counsel, Ohio Attorney General, 1981. Member, Marion City Board of Education, 1984—. *Member:* Marion County, Ohio State and American Bar Associations. ***PRACTICE AREAS:*** Business Litigation; Commercial Law; Corporate Law; Commercial Real Estate; Probate. ***Email:*** tmckinniss@keglerbrown.com

---

MICHELE SELIG WOROBIEC, born Canton, Ohio, December 28, 1966; admitted to bar, 1996, Ohio; 1999, U.S. District Court, Southern District of Ohio. *Education:* The Ohio State University (B.S., summa cum laude, with honors in the liberal arts, 1989); The Ohio State University College of Law (J.D., 1996). Board Member: Marion County Free Medical Clinic. Member, Women's Business Council Women's Guild *Member:* Marion County, Columbus and Ohio State Bar Associations; American Health Lawyers Association. ***PRACTICE AREAS:*** Business Formation; Closely Held Corporations; Employment Contracts; Real Property; Estate Planning. ***Email:*** mworobiec@keglerbrown.com

(For Complete Biographical Data on all Personnel see Professional Biographies at Columbus, Ohio Office)

SUSAN KENNEY-PFALZER

MARION, OHIO

(See Columbus)

Family Law, Divorce, Dissolution, Child Custody, Spousal and Child Support, Visitation Rights, Adoptions, Paternity, Juvenile Law, Collaborative Law, Restraining Orders.

LAMKIN, VAN EMAN, TRIMBLE, BEALS & DOUGHERTY, LLC

MARION, OHIO

(See Columbus)

Personal Injury, Medical Malpractice, Products Liability, Negligence, Insurance Coverage, Stockbroker Malpractice & Fraud. Litigation and Trial Practice.

ROXI A. LIMING

MARION, OHIO

(See Columbus)

Immigration Law, Visas, Naturalization, H1-B Visas, Green Cards, Financé Visas, Investor Visas, Investor Green Cards, Labor and Employment, Wage and Hour Violations, Wrongful Discharge, Employment Discrimination, Americans with Disabilities Act, Sexual Harassment,

(This Listing Continued)

(This Listing Continued)

Family and Medical Leave Act, Employment Contracts, Severance Package Negotiation, Personnel Policies.

NEMO & FRAGALE CO., L.P.A.

495 SOUTH STATE STREET
P.O. BOX 1176
MARION, OHIO 43301-1176
Telephone: 740-387-7438
Fax: 740-387-6367
Email: nemo-fragale@verizon.net

Insurance Defense, Personal Injury, Environmental, Adoption, Bankruptcy, Corporate, Criminal, Estate Planning, Family, Probate, Trials and Appeals.

ROBERT C. NEMO, born Cincinnati, Ohio, April 15, 1954; admitted to bar, 1979, Ohio; 1984, U.S. District Court, Northern and Southern Districts of Ohio. *Education:* Indiana University (B.A., 1976); University of Cincinnati (J.D., 1979). *Member:* Marion County and Ohio State (Member, Negligence Law Committee, 1983—) Bar Associations.

ROBERT D. FRAGALE, born Butler, Pennsylvania, January 13, 1956; admitted to bar, 1982, Ohio. *Education:* Butler County Community College; Slippery Rock State College (B.S., 1978); Capital University Law School (J.D., 1982). Magistrate, Marion County Common Pleas Court, Juvenile Division. Marion County Common Pleas Court Judge, May, 2004-December 2004. *Member:* Marion County (Secretary-Treasurer, 1993—) Bar Association.

REPRESENTATIVE CLIENTS: Allstate Insurance Co.; Wayne Mutual Insurance Co.; Zurich American Insurance Co.

OLIVER LAW OFFICE

MARION, OHIO
(See Columbus)

Products Liability, Personal Injury, Wrongful Death, Latex Allergy Litigation, Medical Malpractice, Vioxx Litigation, Automobile Accidents, Insurance Law, Employment Discrimination.

THE PLYMALE PARTNERSHIP LLP

MARION, OHIO
(See Columbus)

Personal Injury, Products Liability, Wrongful Death, Medical Malpractice, Professional Negligence, Traumatic Brain Injury, Automobile Accidents, Nursing Home Torts, Civil Litigation.

SCHERNER, HANSON & CORNWELL, LLC

MARION, OHIO
(See Columbus)

Civil Trial and Appellate Litigation in State and Federal Courts. Medical Malpractice and other Professional Liability, Personal Injury, Product Liability, Commercial, Corporate, Fraud and other Civil Litigation.

TWYFORD & DONAHEY, P.L.L.

MARION, OHIO
(See Columbus)

Personal Injury Litigation, Wrongful Death, Medical Malpractice, Products Liability, Automobile Accidents, Trucking Accidents, Head and Spinal Injuries, Motorcycle Accidents and Injuries, Uninsured Motorists, Insurance Law, Airplane Crash Litigation, Railroad Accidents, Slip and Fall, Dog Bites, Work Related Injuries, Birth Injuries, Nursing Home Abuse and Neglect.

DAVID WIRTH

MARION, OHIO
(See Columbus)

Insurance Law, Negligence, Legal Malpractice, Subrogation, Personal Injury, Probate.

ALLEN, YURASEK & MERKLIN

Established in 1946
233 WEST FIFTH STREET
P.O. BOX 391
MARYSVILLE, OHIO 43040-0391
Telephone: 937-642-4070
Telecopier: 937-644-4390
Email: aymucta@imetweb.net

General Civil Practice. Corporate, Probate and Estate Planning, Real Estate, and Banking Law. Trials and Appeals in all Courts.

MEMBERS OF FIRM

GWYNN SANDERS (1906-1989)

DAVID F. ALLEN, born Richwood, Ohio, 1937; admitted to bar, 1961, Ohio; U.S. District Court, Southern and Northern Districts of Ohio; U.S. Supreme Court; U.S. Tax Court; U.S. Claims Court. *Education:* The Ohio State University (J.D., 1961). *Member:* Union County, Ohio State (Board of Governors, Estate Planning, Trust and Probate Law Section; Past Chairman, 2001-2003) and American Bar Associations. Fellow, American College of Trust and Estate Counsel. ***PRACTICE AREAS:*** Corporate Law; Probate and Estate Planning. ***Email:*** allend@imetweb.net

STEPHEN J. YURASEK, born Columbus, Ohio, 1948; admitted to bar, 1979, Ohio; U.S. District Court, Northern and Southern Districts of Ohio. *Education:* The Ohio State University (B.S., cum laude, 1974; J.D., 1979). Beta Gamma Sigma. *Member:* Columbus, Union County (President, 1984) and Ohio State Bar Associations. [USAF, 1968-1971]. ***PRACTICE AREAS:*** Business; Real Estate; Probate. ***Email:*** sjyur@imetweb.net

JEFFREY A. MERKLIN, born Columbus, Ohio, 1960; admitted to bar, 1985, Ohio; U.S. District Court, Southern District of Ohio. *Education:* Muskingum College (B.A., Bus. Adm., magna cum laude, 1982); Ohio State University (J.D., with honors, 1985). *Member:* Union County, Madison County and Ohio State Bar Associations. ***PRACTICE AREAS:*** Civil Litigation; Real Estate Law; Family Law; Criminal Law. ***Email:*** merk7@imetweb.net

ASSOCIATE

TINA OWENS-RUFF, born Columbus, Ohio, 1969; admitted to bar, 1999, Ohio; U.S. District Court, Southern District of Ohio. *Education:* The Ohio State University (B.A., 1992); Ohio Northern University (J.D., 1998). *Member:* Union County and Ohio State Bar Associations. ***Email:*** owensruff@imetweb.net

GENERAL COUNSEL FOR: Ohio Grain Co.; Conklin Dairy Farms, Inc.; Ray Lewis & Son, Inc.; Richwood Banking Co.; Tuffco Sand & Gravel Co.; Community Foundation of Union County; Picklesimer Trucking, Inc.; Seed Technology, Inc.; Franke's Wood Products, Inc.; North Main Motors, Inc.
LOCAL COUNSEL FOR: John Hancock Mutual Life Insurance Co.; Farm Credit Services; Metropolitan Life Insurance Co.; Honda Federal Credit Union.

CALIG & HANDELMAN, LPA

MARYSVILLE, OHIO
(See Columbus)

Bankruptcy, Personal Injury, Probate, Real Estate, Social Security, Social Security Disability, Medical Malpractice, Wrongful Death, Civil Litigation, Domestic Relations Law.

COLLEY SHROYER & ABRAHAM CO., L.P.A.

MARYSVILLE, OHIO
(See Columbus)

Civil Trial Practice. Personal Injury, Medical Malpractice, Automobile Accidents, Wrongful Death, Railroad Accidents, Slip and Fall, Negligence, Product Liability and Toxic Torts.

FARLOW & ASSOCIATES LLC

MARYSVILLE, OHIO
(See Dublin)

Family Law, Divorce, Child Custody, Child Support, Premarital Agreements, Post-Decree Enforcements, Employment Law, School Law, Personal Injury.

SUSAN KENNEY-PFALZER

MARYSVILLE, OHIO
(See Columbus)

Family Law, Divorce, Dissolution, Child Custody, Spousal and Child Support, Visitation Rights, Adoptions, Paternity, Juvenile Law, Collaborative Law, Restraining Orders.

LAMKIN, VAN EMAN, TRIMBLE, BEALS & DOUGHERTY, LLC

MARYSVILLE, OHIO
(See Columbus)

Personal Injury, Medical Malpractice, Products Liability, Negligence, Insurance Coverage, Stockbroker Malpractice & Fraud. Litigation and Trial Practice.

GREGG R. LEWIS

MARYSVILLE, OHIO
(See Columbus)

Family Law, Matrimonial Law and Civil Litigation.

OLIVER LAW OFFICE

MARYSVILLE, OHIO
(See Columbus)

Products Liability, Personal Injury, Wrongful Death, Latex Allergy Litigation, Medical Malpractice, Vioxx Litigation, Automobile Accidents, Insurance Law, Employment Discrimination.

SCHULZE, HOWARD & COX

Established in 2005

110 S. MAIN STREET

MARYSVILLE, OHIO 43040-1552

Telephone: 937-644-3849

Fax: 937-644-1426

URL: http://www.shc-lawfirm.net

Civil Trial Practice, Personal Injury, Corporate, Commercial, Probate and Trust, Real Estate Law, Estate Planning, Contract Law, Business Law, Consumer Law.

FIRM PROFILE: Schulze, Howard & Cox is most active in Union, Delaware and Logan counties and their contiguous counties. Schulze, Howard & Cox also is one of the most active real estate practices in central Ohio.

DENNIS A. SCHULZE, born Alliance, Ohio, February 17, 1943; admitted to bar, 1968, Ohio; 1969, U.S. Court of Military Appeals. *Education:* Mount Union College (B.A., 1965); Ohio State University (J.D., 1968). Member, Real Estate Certification Committee Ohio State Bar Association. Charter Member, Union County Leadership Institute. Member, Executive Roundtable, Economic Development Action Plan Committee. Board Member, Union County Foundation. Board Member, Union County Memorial Hospital Development Council. County Public Defender Committee. Ohio Criminal Justice Services Advisory Board. *Member:* Union County (Former President), Ohio State and American Bar Associations; The Association of Trial Lawyers of America; Ohio Academy of Trial Lawyers. [Col., JAGC, 1968-1998]. ***PRACTICE AREAS:*** Estate Planning; Real Estate Law; Real Estate Development; Probate; Civil Litigation. ***Email:*** dennis@shc-law.net

FRANK HOWARD, born Columbus, Ohio, June 23, 1950; admitted to bar, 1975, Ohio; U.S. District Court, Northern District of Ohio; U.S. District Court, Southern District of Ohio; U.S. Tax Court. *Education:* Kent State University (B.S., 1972); Ohio Northern University (J.D., 1975). Phi Alpha Delta. *Member:* Union County (President, 1977) and Ohio State Bar Associations. ***PRACTICE AREAS:*** Real Estate Law; Estate Planning; Probate. ***Email:*** frank@shc-law.net

FAYE DANIELLE COX, born Lima, Ohio, January 26, 1976; admitted to bar, 2001, Ohio. *Education:* Bowling Green State University (B.A., 1998); The Ohio State University (J.D., 2001). *Member:* Union County and Ohio Bar Associations. ***PRACTICE AREAS:*** Probate; Estate Planning; Business Law; Civil Litigation; Real Estate. ***Email:*** faye@shc-law.net

LEGAL SUPPORT PERSONNEL

TAMI McFADDEN

SAUNDRA HOWARD

MELISSA HARE

REPRESENTATIVE CLIENTS: Accurate Plumbing; Ward Construction.

TWYFORD & DONAHEY, P.L.L.

MARYSVILLE, OHIO

(See Columbus)

Personal Injury Litigation, Wrongful Death, Medical Malpractice, Products Liability, Automobile Accidents, Trucking Accidents, Head and Spinal Injuries, Motorcycle Accidents and Injuries, Uninsured Motorists, Insurance Law, Airplane Crash Litigation, Railroad Accidents, Slip and Fall, Dog Bites, Work Related Injuries, Birth Injuries, Nursing Home Abuse and Neglect.

WILES, BOYLE, BURKHOLDER & BRINGARDNER CO., L.P.A.

MARYSVILLE, OHIO

(See Columbus)

General Practice, Insurance Defense, Medical Legal, Products Liability, Aviation, Motor Carrier, Business, Corporate, Municipal, Construction, Real Estate, Commercial Leasing, Hospitality and Restaurant, Estate Planning Law, Trusts, Wills and Probate, Taxation, Trial, and Appellate Practice, Bankruptcy, Foreclosure and Debtor-Creditor Law.

WOLSKE & BARCLAY

A LEGAL PROFESSIONAL ASSOCIATION

MARYSVILLE, OHIO

(See Columbus)

Civil and Appellate Practice in State and Federal Courts. Medical and Dental Malpractice, Nursing Home Negligence, Personal Injury and Products Liability Law, Worker's Compensation and Industrial Accidents, Automobile Accidents, Airplane Crash Litigation.

THE LAW OFFICES OF LYNN A. BUECKMAN

MASON, OHIO

(See Cincinnati)

Bankruptcy, Immigration, DUI, Business Law, Corporate Law, Contracts, Consumer Law.

CHALFIE & FARLEY, CO., L.P.A.

MASON, OHIO

(See Cincinnati)

Probate Litigation, Probate Administration, Estate Planning, Trials and Appeals, Estate and Gift Tax, Trusts, Estates, Wills, Family Law, Negligence, Wrongful Death, Will Contests, Living Trusts and Automobile Collisions.

JASON HENNEKES

MASON, OHIO

(See Cincinnati)

Criminal Law, Driving While Intoxicated, Felonies, Misdemeanors, Homicide, Theft, Drug crimes, Traffic Violations, Domestic Violence, Assault.

DOUGLAS D. JONES CO., LPA

MASSILLON, OHIO

(See Canton)

Wills, Probate, Trusts and Estates, Family Law, Bankruptcy, Real Estate, Property Law, Personal Injury, Torts, Automobile Accidents, Adoptions, Divorce, Child Custody, Child Support, Debtor and Creditor, Estate Planning, Medical Malpractice and Products Liabilities.

WEBER & STERLING, LLC

Established in 1990

1721 INDIAN WOOD CIRCLE, SUITE 1

MAUMEE, OHIO 43537-4065

Telephone: 419-893-3360

Fax: 419-893-7146

Email: attorneys@webersterlinglaw.com

URL: http://www.weberandsterling.com

Probate and Estate Planning, Trusts, Wills, Business Succession.

MEMBERS

ROBERT V. STERLING, born Toledo, Ohio, April 20, 1944; admitted to bar, 1971, Ohio. *Education:* Ohio Wesleyan University; University of Toledo (B.A., 1967); University of Toledo (J.D., 1971). *Member:* Toledo (Member, Probate Court Committee, 1981, 1992), Ohio State and American Bar Associations; Toledo Estate Planning Council. ***PRACTICE AREAS:*** Probate and Estate Planning; Trusts; Wills; Charitable Tax Planning; Tax Exempt Organizations. ***Email:*** bsterling@webersterlinglaw.com

DENNIS P. WILLIAMS, born Delta, Ohio, May 29, 1952; admitted to bar, 1990, Ohio; 2005, Michigan. *Education:* Bowling Green State University (B.B.A., 1974); University of Toledo (J.D., cum laude, 1989). Fellow, ACTEC. Certified Public Accountant (inactive), Ohio, 1980. *Member:* Toledo, Ohio State and American Bar Associations; Toledo Estate Planning Council. (Certified Specialist in Estate Planning, Trust and Probate Law, Ohio State Bar Association). ***PRACTICE AREAS:*** Probate, Trusts, Estate and Business Succession Planning; Tax; Charitable Tax Planning; Tax Exempt Organizations. ***Email:*** dwilliams@webersterlinglaw.com

STEPHEN S. KELLER, born Kettering, Ohio, March 6, 1973; admitted to bar, 1999, Ohio; 2000, Michigan; 2005, Florida. *Education:* University of Kentucky (B.S. Accounting, 1995); University of Toledo (J.D., 1999). Chairman, Moot Court Honor Society, University of Toledo, 1998-1999. *Member:* Toledo and Ohio State Bar Associations; State Bar of Michigan; Toledo Estate Planning Council; The Florida Bar. ***PRACTICE AREAS:*** Estate Planning; Estate and Gift Taxation; Trusts; Corporate. ***Email:*** skeller@webersterlinglaw.com

CHAD R. BAKER, born Toledo, Ohio, April 17, 1973; admitted to bar, 1999, Ohio and U.S. Tax Court; 2000, Michigan; 2005, Florida. *Education:* Ohio University (B.S.B.A., 1995); University of Toledo (J.D., 1999). *Member:* Collier County, Toledo, Ohio State and American Bar Associations; State Bar of Michigan; The Florida Bar; Toledo Estate Planning Council. ***PRACTICE AREAS:*** Estate Planning; Business Succession Planning; Estate Administration; Tax Exempt Organizations; Federal Taxation. ***Email:*** cbaker@webersterlinglaw.com

REPRESENTATIVE CLIENTS: Toledo Community Foundation; Stranahan Foundation; Toledo Museum of Art; KeyBank National Association.
REFERENCES: The Fifth Third Bank of Northwestern Ohio, N.A.; National City Bank; Mid American National Bank & Trust Co.; The Huntington Trust Company.

DAVID S. WILLEY

MAUMEE, OHIO

(See Toledo)

Plaintiffs Personal Injury, Automobile Accidents, Dog Bites, Slip and Fall, Wrongful Death.

BERNARD & HAFFEY CO., L.P.A.

MAYFIELD, OHIO

(See Cleveland)

General Civil and Criminal Practice. Corporate, Probate, Commercial Law, Bankruptcy, Trusts and Estates, Negligence, Family Law, Divorce, Juvenile, and Real Estate. Trial and Appellate Practice, Personal Injury.

DINN, HOCHMAN & POTTER, LLC

MAYFIELD HEIGHTS, OHIO

(See Cleveland)

General Civil Practice. Corporate Law, Business Law, Civil Litigation, Commercial, Real Estate, Telecommunications, Probate, Estate Planning, Family Law, Workers Compensation and Administrative Agencies.

RICHARD M. LEWIS

McARTHUR, OHIO

(See Jackson)

General Trial and Appellate Practice, Tort Law, Insurance Law, Medical Negligence, Employment Law, Personal Injury, Commercial Litigation, Domestic Relations, Corporation, Real Estate, Probate and Banking Law, Debtor-Creditor and Criminal Law.

PRAVIN S. BHAKUNI ATTORNEY AT LAW

474 SOUTH MEDINA LINE ROAD
MEDINA, OHIO 44321
Telephone: 330-607-5871
Fax: 330-668-9479
Email: bhakuni@adelphia.net

Tax, Small Business, Estate Planning, Domestic Relations, Probate.

PRAVIN S. BHAKUNI, born New Delhi, India, September 13, 1969; admitted to bar, 2002, Ohio. *Education:* University of Akron (B.S., Finance, 1992); University of Akron Law School (J.D., 2002). Instructor, Real Estate Law, Southern Ohio College, 2002-2003. *Member:* Ohio State Bar Association. [With U.S. Marine Corps, 1988-1992]. ***LANGUAGES:*** Spanish. ***PRACTICE AREAS:*** Tax; Small Business; Estate Planning; Domestic Relations; Probate.

BROWN AND AMODIO

A LEGAL PROFESSIONAL ASSOCIATION

Established in 1977

109 WEST LIBERTY STREET
MEDINA, OHIO 44256
Telephone: 330-725-8816
Fax: 330-723-5448
Email: brownlaw@zoominternet.net

Civil Trial and Appellate Practice. Negligence, Banking, Construction, Commercial, Real Estate, Business and Corporate Law, Employment, Land Use, Zoning, Bankruptcy and Probate and Estate Planning.

DAVID N. BROWN, born Cleveland, Ohio, August 6, 1944; admitted to bar, 1972, Ohio; 1975, U.S. District Court, Northern District of Ohio. *Education:* The Ohio State University (B.A., cum laude, 1968); Harvard University (J.D., 1971). Phi Beta Kappa. Author: "Notes on the Regulation of Blue Cross," 1973 Insurance Law Journal 264, 1973. Co-Author: "State Regulation of the Non-Profit Health Insurance Industry," 36 Ohio State Law Journal 17, 1975. Assistant Attorney General, Ohio, 1972-1974. *Member:* Medina County, Cleveland and American Bar Associations. ***PRACTICE AREAS:*** Civil Litigation; Real Estate; Corporate Law; Zoning Law; Land Use Law. ***Email:*** brownlaw@zoominternet.net

JAMES A. AMODIO, born South Bend, Indiana, January 20, 1952; admitted to bar, 1978, Ohio; 1979, U.S. District Court, Northern District of Ohio. *Education:* Hofstra University (B.A., magna cum laude, 1974); University of Michigan (J.D., magna cum laude, 1978). Order of the Coif. Associate, Jones, Day, Reavis & Pogue, 1978-1982. *Member:* Medina County (President, 1993), Ohio State and American Bar Associations. ***PRACTICE AREAS:*** Probate and Estate Planning; Real Estate; Corporate Law; Commercial Law; Business Law. ***Email:*** brownlaw@zoominternet.net

---

GERALD L. JEPPE, born Geneva, Ohio, December 15, 1944; admitted to bar, 1969, Ohio; 1974, U.S. District Court, District of Ohio. *Education:* Allegheny College (B.A., 1966); Case Western Reserve University (J.D., 1969). Phi Alpha Delta (President, 1968-1969). Instructor in Constitutional Law (Undergraduate), University of South Carolina, 1972. Board of Trustees, Grace Hospital, Cleveland, Ohio. *Member:* Medina County (Grievance and Judicial Review Committees) and Ohio State Bar Associations. [USAF, Judge Advocate General, 1970-1974]. ***PRACTICE AREAS:*** Civil Litigation; Commercial Litigation; Personal Injury. ***Email:*** brownlaw@zoominternet.net

MARYANN C. CHANDLER, born Cleveland, Ohio, September 1973; admitted to bar, 2004, Ohio. *Education:* Cleveland State University (B.A., magna cum laude, 2001); Cleveland-Marshall College of Law (J.D., cum laude, 2004). Judicial Law Clerk, 2002, 2003. Recipient: Academic Excellence Award, First Amendment Rights and Secured Transactions. Assistant Prosecutor, Medina County, 2004-2005. *Member:* Medina County, Ohio State and American Bar Associations. ***PRACTICE AREAS:*** Civil Litigation; Collections; Domestic Relations; Land Use; Zoning Law.

REPRESENTATIVE CLIENTS: FirstMerit Bank, N.A.; Interstate Systems, Inc.; Koppes Clay Products Co.; Virmurco Trucking, Inc.; Medina Plating Corp.; Masica Builders, Inc.; Precision Aluminum, Inc.; AFC Title Agency, Inc.; Knight Development Corp.; Seville Centrifugal Bronze, Inc.; Harbor Castings, Inc.; Computer Systems Services, Inc.; Curran Bros., Inc.; Triad Communications, Inc.; Quality Computer Specialists, Inc.; Champagne Communications, Inc.; Gonser Builders, Inc.; Brittany Homes, Inc.; Structural Grouting Systems Excavating, Inc.; Heil Process Equipment, LLC; Hillside Electric Co., Inc.; The Medina Toy & Train Museum; The Boardman Foundation.

CRITCHFIELD, CRITCHFIELD & JOHNSTON, LTD.

3985 MEDINA ROAD, SUITE 100
MEDINA, OHIO 44256
Telephone: 330-723-6404
Telecopier: 330-721-7644
URL: http://www.ccj.com

Wooster, Ohio: 225 North Market Street, P.O. Box 599, 44691-0599. Telephone: 330-264-4444.
Millersburg, Ohio: 138 E. Jackson Street, 44654. Telephone: 330-674-3055.
Mt. Vernon, Ohio: 10 South Gay Street, 43050-3546. Telephone: 740-397-4040.

General Practice in all Courts. Business, Corporate Law, Insurance, Estate Planning, Wills and Probate, Labor and Employment, ERISA, Health Care, Environmental Law, Workers Compensation, Banking, Taxation, Antitrust and Trade Regulation, Oil and Gas Law, Litigation, Debtor and Creditor, Municipal Law, School Law, Real Estate, Commercial Law, Construction Law.

ROBERT C. BERRY, born Medina, Ohio, September 10, 1966; admitted to bar, 1991, Ohio. *Education:* Ohio State University (B.S., 1988; J.D., summa cum laude, 1991). Order of the Coif. Editor, Ohio State Law Journal, 1991. ***PRACTICE AREAS:*** Corporate Law; Banking Compliance; Real Estate. ***Email:*** berry@ccj.com

AMY L. DEMLOW, born Youngstown, Ohio, February 2, 1969; admitted to bar, 1994, Ohio. *Education:* University of Akron (B.S., 1991; M.Tax, 1994; J.D., 1994). ***PRACTICE AREAS:*** Taxation; Corporate Law; Estate Planning. ***Email:*** demlow@ccj.com

REPRESENTATIVE CLIENTS: Newell Rubbermaid Inc.; The College of Wooster; Buehler Food Markets, Inc.; The Will-Burt Co.; Buckeye Feed Mills, Inc.; OEConnection LLC; Westfield Bank, FSB; Baker Sand, Inc.
TITLE POLICY ISSUING AGENTS FOR: First American Title Insurance Co.

(For complete biographical data on Wooster, Ohio personnel, see Professional Biographies at Wooster, Ohio)

DAVID V. GEDROCK

209 SOUTH BROADWAY
MEDINA, OHIO 44256
Telephone: 330-723-4947
Fax: 330-764-9739
Email: dgedrock@aol.com
URL: http://www.davidvgedrock.com

Appeals, Criminal Law, Felony, Misdemeanors, Domestic, Family Law, Child Custody, Divorce, Visitation, Support, Post Decree, Spousal Support, Debt Relief Agency, Traffic Violations, Driving Under Influence, Wills, Deeds, Civil Litigation, Personal Injury and Probate.

DAVID V. GEDROCK, born Pittsburgh, Pennsylvania, 1954; admitted to bar, 1980, Ohio and U.S District Court, Northern District of Ohio. *Education:* John Carroll University (B.A., 1976); Ohio Northern University (J.D., 1979). Second Chair Certified on Capital Cases Involving The Indigent. *Member:* Medina County and Ohio State Bar Associations; Ohio Association of Criminal Defense Lawyers. ***PRACTICE AREAS:*** Appellate Practice; Criminal Law; Felonies; Misdemeanors; Domestic Relations; Family Law; Child Custody; Divorce; Visitation Rights; Child Support; Spousal Support; Traffic Violations; Driving Under Influence; Wills; Civil Litigation; Personal Injury; Probate; Post Decree.

OBERHOLTZER, FILOUS & LESIAK

A LEGAL PROFESSIONAL ASSOCIATION

Established in 1939

39 PUBLIC SQUARE, SUITE 201
P.O. BOX 220
MEDINA, OHIO 44258-0220
Telephone: 330-725-4929
Fax: 330-723-4929
URL: http://www.lawyers.com/medinalaw
Email: counsel@medinalaw.com
URL: http://www.medinalaw.com

Civil and Criminal Trial and Appellate Practice, Banking, Business and Corporate, Negligence, Personal Injury, Commercial, Family/Domestic Relations, Real Estate, Probate and Estate Planning, Oil and Gas Law, Communications, Construction Law, Municipal and Government Law, Bankruptcy Law, Social Security Disability.

CLAYTON J. OBERHOLTZER (1913-1986)

THOMAS J. FILOUS (1948-1995)

JOHN C. OBERHOLTZER, born Cleveland, Ohio, September 11, 1942; admitted to bar, 1967, Ohio; 1979, Florida; 1981, U.S. Supreme Court; U.S. District Court, Northern District of Ohio and U.S. District Court, Middle District of Florida; 1994, Arizona and U.S. District Court, Southern District of Indiana. *Education:* College of Wooster (B.A., 1964); Case Western Reserve University (J.D., 1967). Phi Alpha Theta; Phi Alpha Delta. President, Student Bar Association, 1966-1967. Medina County Commissioner, 1971-1978. Men's Soccer Coach, Baldwin Wallace College, 1988-1996. Member, Panel of Construction Arbitrators, American Arbitration Association. *Member:* Medina County, Cuyahoga County, Southwest, Ohio State and American (Member, General Practice Section) Bar Associations; The Florida Bar; Ohio Bar College. ***PRACTICE AREAS:*** Litigation; Business Law; Construction Law; Probate and Estate Planning Law; Employment Law; Social Security Disability. ***Email:*** oberholtzer@medinalaw.com

THEODORE J. LESIAK, born Cleveland, Ohio, October 7, 1964; admitted to bar, 1989, Ohio; 1991, U.S. District Court, Northern District of Ohio; 1994, U.S. Court of Appeals, Sixth Circuit; 1995, U.S. Supreme Court; 2002, U.S. District Court, Western District of Michigan. *Education:* Ohio University (B.A., cum laude, 1986); University of Akron

(This Listing Continued)

OBERHOLTZER, FILOUS & LESIAK, A LEGAL PROFESSIONAL ASSOCIATION, Medina—Continued

(J.D., cum laude, 1989). Member, University of Akron Law Review, 1987-1988. Law Clerk to Hon. Daniel B. Quillin, Ohio Court of Appeals, Ninth District, 1989-1991. Author: "Avoiding Procedural Problems on Appeal," Ohio Lawyer, Vol. 5, No. 2, Mar./Apr. 1991. Solicitor: Village of Lodi, 1995—; Village of Seville, 2004—. Assistant Village Solicitor: Village of Seville, 1995-1996; Village of Lodi, 1994-1995. Special Medina County Prosecutor, 1996-1997. Special Village Solicitor: Village of Chippewa Lake, 2000-2001; Village of Seville, 2003. *Member:* Medina County, Ohio State and American Bar Associations. ***PRACTICE AREAS:*** Litigation; Domestic Relations; Real Estate Law; Personal Injury; Employment Law; Municipal Law; Business Law; Probate Law; Estate Planning; Criminal Appeals. ***Email:*** lesiak@medinalaw.com

JENNIFER L. HENSAL, born Barberton, Ohio, January 13, 1967; admitted to bar, 1993, Ohio; U.S. District Court, Northern District of Ohio; 2002, U.S. District Court, Western District of Michigan. *Education:* University of Akron (B.A., 1989); University of Toledo (J.D., 1993). Assistant Law Director, City of Wadsworth, 1996—. Assistant Solicitor: Village of Lodi, 1998—; Village of Seville, 2004. Prosecutor, City of Medina, 2004. *Member:* Medina County Bar Association (Treasurer, 2003). ***PRACTICE AREAS:*** Business Law; Business Litigation; Bankruptcy; Estate Planning; Collection Law; Probate; Employment Law; Personal Injury; Municipal Law; Government Law. ***Email:*** hensal@medinalaw.com

ASSOCIATES

MICHELLE L. SLIMAK, born Cleveland, Ohio, June 4, 1972; admitted to bar, 1999, Ohio; 2000, U.S. District Court, Northern District of Ohio. *Education:* Ohio University (B.A., 1994); University of Akron School of Law (J.D., 1999). *Member:* Medina County, Ohio State and American Bar Associations. ***PRACTICE AREAS:*** Domestic Relations; Business Law; Commercial Law; Mediation; Real Estate; Probate; Wills; Estate Planning. ***Email:*** slimak@medinalaw.com

ALICIA M. HATHCOCK, born Medina, Ohio, February 1, 1978; admitted to bar, 2004, Ohio; 2005, U.S. District Court, Northern District of Ohio. *Education:* Baldwin-Wallace College (B.A., magna cum laude, 1999); Cleveland State University (J.D., 2004). *Member:* Medina County, Ohio State and American Bar Associations. ***PRACTICE AREAS:*** Collections; Litigation; Estate Planning; Probate; Business Law. ***Email:*** hathcock@medinalaw.com

A. MICHELLE JACKSON, born St. Antonio, Texas, October 01, 1967; admitted to bar, 2002, Ohio; 2003, U.S. District Court, Northern District of Ohio. *Education:* Ashland College (B.A., summa cum laude, 1995); Akron University Law School (J.D., 2001). Delta Mu Delta. *Member:* Akron, Medina, Ohio and American Bar Association. [Army Specialist, 1988-1991; Sergeant, Army National Guard, 1991-1997]. ***PRACTICE AREAS:*** Bankruptcy; Criminal Law; Real Estate Law; Business Law; Probate; Wills. ***Email:*** jackson@medinalaw.com

REPRESENTATIVE CLIENTS: Mack Industries, Inc.; Pythian Sisters Home of Ohio; Plastics Consulting, Inc.; Medina Country Club; Professional Club Systems; Boss Industries; Marathon-Ashland Petroleum LLC; Horner Jones, Inc.; Home Health Care Services, Inc.; Tri-Maxx 2000, Inc.; American National Bank; Securitec, Inc.; Wise International Trucks, Inc.; Alternative Paths; Medina Home Page, LLC; Unisonal, Inc.; Medina County Mayor's Association; M.W. Meilk Co.; Mielke Development, Inc.; Swingle Mechanical Contractors, Inc.; Merrick Graphics, Inc.; CVDG Development; Pleasant Run Home Owners Association; Parker Montville Inn.
REFERENCES: National City Bank; First Merit Bank; Sky Bank, Medina, Ohio; Merrill Lynch.

OBRAL & MAYS & ASSOCIATES

MEDINA, OHIO

(See Cleveland)

Personal Injury, Medical Malpractice, Automobile Accidents, Workers Compensation, Wrongful Death, Truck Accidents, Nursing Home Abuse, Products Liability, Dog Bites, Slip and Fall, Criminal Law.

DENNIS E. PAUL

211 SOUTH COURT STREET
MEDINA, OHIO 44256
Telephone: 330-725-6082
Fax: 330-722-2534
URL: http://www.medinadivorcelaw.com

Personal Injury, Divorce, Adoption Advocate.

DENNIS E. PAUL, born Lakewood, Ohio, September 6, 1949; admitted to bar, 1975, Ohio; 1976, U.S. District Court, Northern District of Ohio; 1982, U.S. District Court, Southern and Eastern Districts of Michigan. *Education:* Ohio University (B.S., Journalism, cum laude, 1971); Ohio Northern University (J.D., 1975). Assistant Prosecutor, Medina County, 1975-1976. Medina City Prosecutor, 1976-1977. Chair, Alternative Paths, Inc. (non-profit for severely mentally disabled). *Member:* Medina County Bar Association (President, 1984); Ohio Academy of Trial Lawyers; Association of Trial Lawyers of America. [2nd Lieut., U.S. Army, 1971-1979]. ***PRACTICE AREAS:*** Personal Injury; Divorce; Adoption Law.

RICHARD LAW OFFICE, LLC

MEDINA, OHIO

(See Wooster)

Corporate, Business Law, Oil and Gas, Personal Injury, Wrongful Death, Estate Planning, Probate, Divorce, Dissolution, Real Estate, Litigation, Probate Avoidance.

DAVID S. RIEHL

MEDINA, OHIO

(See Brunswick)

Domestic Relations, Family Law, Divorce, Child Custody, Adoption Law, Premarital Agreements, Real Estate, Commercial Real Estate, Residential Real Estate, Small Business Law, Business Organization, Contracts, Probate, Estate Planning, Trust Law, Wills, Elder Care, Personal Injury, Automobile Accidents and Injuries, Negligence, Criminal Law, Driving While Intoxicated, Traffic Violations, Civil Practice.

WILLIAMS AND BATCHELDER, LLP

Established in 1880
105 WEST LIBERTY STREET
P.O. BOX 394
MEDINA, OHIO 44258-0394
Telephone: 330-725-6666;
Cleveland Direct Line: 330-225-1300
Fax: 330-723-4227
Email: wmsbatchattys@zoominternet.net

General Civil Practice in all Courts. Corporate, Banking, Probate and Estate Planning, Real Estate, Zoning and Insurance Law. Trials and Appeals.

MEMBERS OF FIRM

WILLIAM G. BATCHELDER, JR., born Cleveland, Ohio, July 30, 1914; admitted to bar, 1939, Ohio. *Education:* Ohio Wesleyan University (A.B., 1936); University of Cincinnati (J.D., 1939). Phi Beta Kappa; Delta Sigma Rho; Omicron Delta Kappa. Prosecuting Attorney, Medina County, Ohio, 1941-1953. President, Ohio State Prosecutor's Association, 1951-1952. Member, Medina City Board of Education, 1960-1964. *Member:* Greater Cleveland, Medina County and Ohio State Bar Associations. ***PRACTICE AREAS:*** Civil Litigation; Insurance Law; Probate and Estate Planning Law.

C. NEVADA JOHNSON, JR., born Cleveland, Ohio, June 24, 1938; admitted to bar, 1963, Ohio; 1964, U.S. Court of Military Appeals. *Education:* Kenyon College (A.B., 1960); Ohio Northern University (J.D., 1963). *Member:* Medina County (President, 1977) and Ohio State Bar Associations. [Capt., JAGC, U.S. Army, 1964-1967]. ***PRACTICE AREAS:*** Real Estate Law; Insurance Law; Corporate Law; Probate; Estate Planning.

ROBERT J. BUX, born Wadsworth, Ohio, February 20, 1949; admitted to bar, 1978, Ohio and U.S. District Court, Northern District of Ohio; 1984, Florida; 1986, U.S. Supreme Court. *Education:* The Ohio State University (B.S.M.E., 1971; M.S., 1973); University of Cincinnati (J.D., 1978). Pi Tau Sigma. *Member:* Medina County and Ohio State Bar Associations; The Florida Bar; American Health Lawyers Association. ***PRACTICE AREAS:*** Corporate Law; Probate and Estate Planning Law; Civil Litigation.

JEFFREY L. BRAMLEY, born Medina, Ohio, April 5, 1956; admitted to bar, 1981, Ohio; 1982, U.S. District Court, Northern District of Ohio and U.S. Court of Appeals, Sixth Circuit. *Education:* Miami University (B.S., 1978); Akron University Law School (J.D., 1981). Acting Judge, Medina Municipal Court, 1987-1997. Law Librarian, Medina County Law Library, 1983—. Assistant Solicitor, Village of Seville, 1997-2003. Member, Board of Arbitrators, Medina County Common Pleas Court, 1983—. *Member:* Medina County (President, 1989), Ohio State Bar Association. ***PRACTICE AREAS:*** Civil Litigation; Insurance Defense; Real Estate; Probate and Estate Planning Law; Corporate; Municipal Law. ***Email:*** bramleyrstar@aol.com

WILLIAM B. YOUNG, born St. Louis, Missouri, February 8, 1953; admitted to bar, 1978, Ohio and U.S. District Court, Northern District of Ohio; 1984, U.S. Supreme Court. *Education:* Manchester College (B.A., 1975); University of Cincinnati (J.D., 1978). Member, The Order of Barristers. Editor, Moot Court, 1977-1978. Law Director, City of Medina, 1995-2002. Solicitor: Village of Seville, 1981-2003; Village of Gloria Glens, 1981-1985; Village of Briarwood Beach, 1982-1997. Member, 1981— and President, 1992, Medina County Estate Planning Council. *Member:* Medina County, Ohio State and American Bar Associations. ***PRACTICE AREAS:*** Civil Litigation; Probate and Estate Planning Law; Probate Litigation; Real Estate. ***Email:*** youngwmsbatch@zoominternet.net

GREGORY A. HUBER, born Medina, Ohio, July 3, 1958; admitted to bar, 1984, Ohio; 1986, U.S District Court, Northern District of Ohio. *Education:* University of Akron (B.A., 1981); University of Akron School of Law (J.D., 1984). Solicitor, Village of Spencer, 1990—. Law Director, City of Medina, 1999—. *Member:* Medina County and Ohio State Bar Associations; Ohio Academy of Trial Lawyers; Ohio Association of Civil Trial Attorneys; Ohio Municipal Attorneys Association; Ohio Inns of Court; Medina County Estate Planning Council. ***PRACTICE AREAS:*** Civil Litigation; Insurance Defense; Municipal Law; Probate; Estate Planning. ***Email:*** ghuber7441@yahoo.com

ASSOCIATE

JONATHAN M. STEINGASS, born Elyria, Ohio, July 8, 1945; admitted to bar, 1987, Ohio. *Education:* Heidelberg College (A.B., 1967); Akron University (J.D., 1987). Phi Alpha Theta. *Member:* Medina and Ohio State Bar Associations. ***PRACTICE AREAS:*** Civil Litigation; Insurance; Probate and Estate Planning Law; Real Estate; Elder Law.

REPRESENTATIVE CLIENTS: Westfield Cos. (The Ohio Farmers Insurance Co.); Motorists Mutual Insurance Co.; Erie Insurance Co.; Auto-Owners Insurance Co.; State Auto Insurance Co.; Medina General Hospital; Aldi Inc.; Wolff Bros. Supply, Inc.; Ken Cleveland Builders, Inc.; Mack Industries, Inc.; King Drilling Co.; Armstrong Utilities, Inc; City of Medina; Village of Spencer..

CANNON, STERN, AVENI AND LOIACONO CO., L.P.A.

MENTOR, OHIO

(See Painesville)

General Civil and Criminal Practice. Corporation, Small Business, Municipal, Family, Divorce, Probate, Trust and Estate Planning, Personal Injury, Environmental Law, Real Estate Law, Litigation and Medical Malpractice.

COOPER & FORBES

MENTOR, OHIO

(See Painesville)

Commercial and Retail Collections, Commercial Law, Bankruptcy, Domestic Relations, Chapter 11, Debtors Rights, General Civil Trial Practice, Creditors Rights. Trials and Appeals in all Courts.

LEE R. KRAVITZ

MENTOR, OHIO

(See Cleveland)

Bankruptcy Law, Chapter 7, Chapter 13, Consumer Bankruptcy.

STERNBERG & ZEID CO., L.P.A.

Established in 1982

7547 MENTOR AVENUE, SUITE 301
MENTOR, OHIO 44060
Telephone: 440-942-6267
Fax: 440-942-6504
URL: http://www.sternbergzeidlaw.com
URL: http://www.sternbergandzeid.com

Personal Injury, Automobile Accidents, Wrongful Death, Workers Compensation, Municipal Law, Zoning Law, Bankruptcy, Domestic Relations, Family Law, Divorce, Child Custody, Guardianship, Real Estate, Probate, Estate Planning, Trusts and Wills, Business, Corporate, Contract Law, General Civil Trial Practice in State and Federal Courts.

DAVID J. STERNBERG, born Cleveland, Ohio, November 27, 1948; admitted to bar, 1973, Ohio; 1975, United States District Court, Northern District of Ohio; 1977, U.S. Supreme Court; 1984, U.S. District Court, Eastern District of Michigan. *Education:* Miami University (B.S., 1970); Ohio State University (J.D., 1973). Law Director, City of Willowick, 1990-2000. *Member:* Lake County, Ohio State and American Bar Associations; The Association of Trial Lawyers of America; Ohio Academy of Trial Lawyers; Cleveland Academy of Trial Lawyers. ***PRACTICE AREAS:*** Personal Injury; Automobile Accidents and Injuries; Wrongful Death; Workers Compensation; Municipal Law; Zoning Law; Bankruptcy; Domestic Relations; Divorce; Child Custody; Real Estate; Civil Trial Practice.

GARY D. ZEID, born Cleveland, Ohio, August 5, 1948; admitted to bar, 1975, Ohio; 1977, U.S. District Court, Northern District of Ohio; 1992, U.S. Supreme Court. *Education:* Cleveland State University (B.B.A., 1971); Cleveland Marshall College of Law (J.D., 1975). *Member:* Lake County and Ohio State Bar Associations; Ohio Academy of Trial Lawyers; Cleveland Academy of Trial Lawyers. ***PRACTICE AREAS:*** Personal Injury; Automobile Accidents and Injuries; Wrongful Death; Probate; Estate Planning; Family Law; Trusts; Wills; Guardianship; Domestic Relations; Divorce; Real Estate; Civil Trial Practice. ***Email:*** gzeid@aol.com

CASPER AND CASPER

Established in 1936

CINERGY BUILDING
1 NORTH MAIN STREET
5TH AND 6TH FLOORS
P.O. BOX 510
MIDDLETOWN, OHIO 45042
Telephone: 513-424-2401-Middletown;
937-224-1122-Dayton
513-381-7096-Cincinnati
513-892-2560-Hamilton
Toll Free: 1-800-784-2889
Fax: 513-424-0622
URL: http://www.casperlaw.com

Dayton, Ohio Office: First National Plaza Building, 130 West Second Street, Suite 1950, 45402. Telephone: 937-224-1122.

Cincinnati, Ohio Office: 119 East Court Street, Fourth Floor, Suite 410, 45202. Telephone: 513-381-7096.

Hamilton Office: 2 South 3rd Street, Suite 360, 45011. Telephone: 513-892-2560.

Personal Injury, Workers Compensation and Social Security Disability Law. Products Liability Litigation. Trials.

I. A. CASPER (1910-1981)

JACK A. CASPER (1912-1996)

ARTHUR BRANDEIS CASPER, born Middletown, Ohio, April 7, 1940; admitted to bar, 1967, Ohio; 1968, U.S. District Court, Southern District of Ohio and U.S. Court of Appeals, 6th Circuit. *Education:* Miami University (A.B., 1962); Harvard University; Ohio Northern University (J.D., 1967). Delta Theta Phi. *Member:* Middletown (President, 1980-1981), Butler County and Ohio State Bar Associations; Ohio Academy of Trial Lawyers; The Association of Trial Lawyers of America. ***LANGUAGES:*** French and Italian. ***PRACTICE AREAS:*** Personal Injury Law; Products Liability Litigation; Workers Compensation Law.

E. JEFFREY CASPER, born Cincinnati, Ohio, July 19, 1947; admitted to bar, 1972, Ohio and U.S. District Court, Southern District of Ohio. *Education:* University of Cincinnati (B.A., 1969; J.D., 1972). *Member:* Middletown, Butler County and Ohio State Bar Associations; The National Organization of Social Security Claimant's Representatives; Ohio Academy of Trial Lawyers. ***PRACTICE AREAS:*** Workers Compensation Law; Social Security Disability Law.

DOUGLAS W. CASPER, born Cincinnati, Ohio, April 28, 1949; admitted to bar, 1975, Ohio and U.S. District Court, Southern District of Ohio. *Education:* University of Cincinnati (B.B.A., 1971); Salmon P. Chase College of Law of Northern Kentucky University (J.D., 1975). *Member:* Middletown, Butler County and Ohio State Bar Associations; Ohio Academy of Trial Lawyers. ***PRACTICE AREAS:*** Workers Compensation Law.

SANFORD I. CASPER, born Cincinnati, Ohio, April 14, 1952; admitted to bar, 1981, Ohio and U.S. District Court, Southern District of Ohio. *Education:* Miami University (B.A., 1974); University of Dayton (J.D., 1981). *Member:* Cincinnati, Dayton, Middletown, Butler County and Ohio State Bar Associations; Ohio Academy of Trial Lawyers; The Association of Trial Lawyers of America. ***PRACTICE AREAS:*** Personal Injury Law; Workers Compensation Law.

RONALD M. KABAKOFF

REBECCA L. WILKINSON

PATRICK W. ALLEN

BARBARA L. STRADY

MARGARET HALNON McCOLLUM

MARK A. SUMMERS

MEGAN RICHARDS

WILLIAM P. ALLEN

MICHAEL J. HALLEE

STEPHEN R. FOGLE

ROBIN R. PARTIN

REFERENCES: First National Bank of S.W. Ohio; Bank One of Middletown, Ohio.

THOMAS G. EAGLE CO., L.P.A.

MIDDLETOWN, OHIO

(See Lebanon)

General Civil and Criminal Trial and Appellate Practice in State and Federal Courts, in Ohio and Kentucky, including Personal Injury, Wrongful Death, Criminal Law, Civil Rights, Consumer Law, Commercial and Business Litigation, Bankruptcy, Real Estate, Family Law and others.

PARIS K. ELLIS

1501 SOUTH BREIEL BOULEVARD
MIDDLETOWN, OHIO 45044
Telephone: 513-423-0194
Fax: 513-423-0863
Email: pkeut@aol.com
URL: http://www.lawyers.com/parisellis

Criminal Law, Drug Crimes, Driving While Intoxicated, Alcoholic Beverages, Family Law, Divorce, Wrongful Death, Wills and Probate, Federal Criminal, White Collar Crimes, Embezzlement, Parole Violations, Sex Crimes, Rape, Murders, Juvenile Crimes, Custody, Domestic Violence, Support.

PARIS K. ELLIS, born Vonore, Tennessee, September 4, 1944; admitted to bar, 1980, Ohio, U.S. District Court, Southern District of Ohio, U.S. Court of Appeals, Sixth Circuit and U.S Tax Court,. *Education:* Hiwassee College; Miami University (B.S., 1975); Salmon P. Chase College of Law, Northern Kentucky University (J.D., 1980). *Member:* Middletown, Butler County (President, 1997-1998), Warren County and Ohio State Bar Associations; Ohio Association of Criminal Defense Lawyers (President, 1996-1997); American Trial Lawyers Association; Ohio Academy of Trial Lawyers; National Association of Criminal Defense Lawyers. ***PRACTICE AREAS:*** Criminal Law; Personal Injury Law; Domestic Relations Law.

FROST BROWN TODD LLC

300 NORTH MAIN STREET, SUITE 200
MIDDLETOWN, OHIO 45042-1919
Telephone: 513-422-2001
Telecopier: 513-422-3010
Email: info@fbtlaw.com
URL: http://www.frostbrowntodd.com

Cincinnati, Ohio Office: 2200 PNC Center, 201 East Fifth Street, 45202-4182. Telephone: 513-651-6800. Telecopier: 513-651-6981.

Columbus, Ohio Office: One Columbus, 10 West Broad Street, 43215-3467. Telephone: 614-464-1211. Telecopier: 614-464-1737.

Lexington, Kentucky Office: 250 West Main Street, Suite 2700, 40507-1742. Telephone: 859-231-0000. Telecopier: 859-231-0011.

Louisville, Kentucky Office: 400 West Market Street, 32nd Floor, 40202-3363. Telephone: 502-589-5400. Telecopier: 502-581-1087.

(This Listing Continued)

FROST BROWN TODD LLC, Middletown—Continued

Nashville, Tennessee Office: 424 Church Street, Suite 1600, 37219-2308. Telephone: 615-251-5550. Telecopier: 615-251-5551.
New Albany, Indiana Office: 120 West Spring Street, Suite 400, 47150-3655. Telephone: 812-948-2800. Telecopier: 812-948-7994.

Alternative Dispute Resolution, Bankruptcy and Reorganization, Business Acquisitions, Business and Corporate, Commercial Finance, Commercial Litigation, Commercial/Real Estate, Construction, Copyright, Corporate Responsibility and Defense, Employee Benefits, Energy and Natural Resources, Entrepreneurial, Environmental, Equine, Estate Planning and Administration, Financial Institutions, Fire and Explosion, Health Care, Immigration, International, Intellectual Property, International Business, Internet and Electronic Commerce, Labor and Employment Law, Litigation, Media, Mold and Water Intrusion, Multi-District Litigation, Patent Litigation, Personal Planning and Family Business, Privacy and Information Security, Product Liability, Public Finance, Securities, Tax, Tort & Insurance Law, Trademark, Venture Capital, General Trial Practice in all State and Federal Courts.

FIRM PROFILE: Frost Brown Todd LLC is the result of the November 1, 2000 merger of Frost & Jacobs LLP and Brown, Todd & Heyburn PLLC. This super-regional law firm of approximately 370 attorneys has seven offices in Cincinnati, Columbus and Middletown, Ohio; Louisville and Lexington, Kentucky; Nashville, Tennessee; and New Albany, Indiana. The increased breadth of practice experience, combined with the depth of service and expanded geographic scope, allows the combined firm to effectively serve the growing and changing needs of its institutional, commercial and individual clients at the local, regional, national and international level.

MEMBERS

THOMAS B. ALLEN, born Middletown, Ohio, June 21, 1964; admitted to bar, 1994, Ohio and U.S. District Court, Southern District of Ohio; 2000, U.S. Court of Appeals, Sixth Circuit and U.S. Supreme Court. *Education:* The Ohio State University; Miami University (B.S., 1989) Phi Alpha Theta; University of Cincinnati (J.D., 1994). Delta Theta Phi. Member, 1992-1993, Lead Articles Chair, 1993-1994, University of Cincinnati Law Review. *Member:* Middletown Bar Association, Butler County Bar Association, Cincinnati Bar Association (Member, Labor and Employment Law Section) and Ohio State Bar Association (Member, Sections on: Litigation and Labor Law). ***REPORTED CASES:*** Lindsey v. Sinclair Broadcast Group, Inc., 2003 Ohio 6898 (2d Dist. Dec. 19, 2003); Wofford v. Middletown Tube Works, 67 Fed. App. 312, 2003 U.S. App. LEXIS 11500 (6th Cir. June 5, 2003); Lamping v. Walraven, 136 Fed. Appx. 881, 2002 U.S. App. LEXIS 4249 (6th Cir. Mar 12, 2002); Bardonaro v. General Motors Corp., 2000 Ohio App. LEXIS 3479 (2d Dist. Ct. App. Aug. 4, 2000); Day v. Middletown-Monroe City Sch. Dist., 2000 Ohio App. LEXIS 3170 (12th Dist. Ct. App., July 17, 2000); Day v. Middletown-Monroe City Sch. Dist., 2000 Ohio App. LEXIS 1868 (12th Dist. Ct. App., May 1, 2000); Carey v. AK Steel Corp., 1998 Ohio App. LEXIS 3203 (12th Dist. Ct. App. July 13, 1998); City of Oxford v. Day, 1998 Ohio App. LEXIS 1003 (12th Dist. Ct. App., Mar. 16, 1998); Brittain v. Brown's Run Country Club, 1997 Ohio App. LEXIS 725 (12th Dist. Ct. App. March 3, 1997), appeal dismissed 79 Ohio St. 3d 1445 (1997). ***PRACTICE AREAS:*** Litigation; Labor Law; Employment Law; School Law. ***Email:*** tallen@fbtlaw.com

DONALD L. CRAIN, born Hamilton, Ohio, July 7, 1948; admitted to bar, 1973, Ohio;1980,U.S.Supreme Court;1981,S.D.Ohio,U.S. Court of Appeals, Sixth Circuit. *Education:* Miami University (B.S., 1970); University of Cincinnati (J.D., 1973). Past Chairman Ohio Council of School Board Attorneys Association Board of Directors. General Counsel, Middletown City School District. Law Director, West Chester Township and Solicitor, Indian Hill, Ohio. Adjunct Faculty, Miami School of Business, coursework in Negotiations and Collective Bargaining (undergraduate and graduate). *Member:* Butler County (President, 2002-2003), Cincinnati (Twice Past Chairman, Labor and Employment Law Committee) and Ohio Bar Associations. ***PRACTICE AREAS:*** School Law (20%); Governmental Law (35%); Management Labor Law (35%); Litigation (10%). ***Email:*** dcrain@fbtlaw.com

THOMAS A. SWOPE, born Middletown, Ohio, August 26, 1948; admitted to bar, 1973, California; 1978, Ohio. *Education:* John Carroll University (A.B., 1970); University of San Francisco (J.D., 1973). ***PRACTICE AREAS:*** Employment and Labor Law; Commercial Law; Litigation. ***Email:*** tswope@fbtlaw.com

ASSOCIATES

W. JOSEPH SCHOLLER, born Bowling Green, Ohio, February 17, 1975; admitted to bar, 2000, Ohio. *Education:* Miami University (B.A., in Economics, 1997); University of Dayton (J.D., 2000). *Member:* Butler County, Ohio State and American Bar Associations. ***PRACTICE AREAS:*** Labor and Employment; Education Litigation. ***Email:*** jscholler@fbtlaw.com

REPRESENTATIVE CLIENTS: AAF-McQuay Inc.; AEGON USA Realty Advisors, Inc.; AIG Insurance Group; AK Steel Corporation; Anthem Health Plans; Broadwing Inc.; Brown & Williamson Tobacco Corporation; Catholic Healthcare Partners; Central Bank & Trust Company; Chapelthorp plc; Chiquita Brands International; ClubLink Corporation; Convergys Corporation; Coolmore Castlehyde and Associated Stud Farms; Federated Department Stores, Inc.; FieldTurf, Inc.; Firstar/U.S. Bank; Taco Bell Franchise Management Advisory Council (FRANMAC); General Electric Company; ICI Paints World Group; Jewish Hospital HealthCare Services, Inc.; LensCrafters, Inc.; Lexis-Nexis; LG&E Energy Corp.; Liberty Mutual Insurance Group; Lightyear Communications, Inc.; MidAmerica Bancorp; New Horizon Resources, Inc.; NTS Development Company; OneBeacon Insurance Group; Progressive Insurance Company; PNC Bank Corp. and PNC Bank; Res-Care, Inc.; The Rouse Companies, LLC; Services Net Incorporated; Smithkline Beecham Clinical Lab; Terex Corporation; Turner Construction Company; Unified Foodservice Purchasing Co-op, LLC; United Parcel Service; Vincor International Inc.; Waste Management of North America; Western Southern Life Insurance Company.

(For complete biographical data on all personnel, see Professional Biographies at Cincinnati, Ohio)

FROST & JACOBS LLP

MIDDLETOWN, OHIO

(See Frost Brown Todd LLC)

DON IMHOFF, JR.

2 NORTH MAIN STREET, SUITE 603
MIDDLETOWN, OHIO 45042-1975
Telephone: 513-423-3462
Fax: 513-422-5141

Wills and Probate, Estate Planning, Real Estate, Corporation Law, Business Law, Bankruptcy, Creditor and Debtor Rights and Collections, Real Estate Foreclosures, Evictions.

DON IMHOFF, JR., born Middletown, Ohio, March 4, 1947; admitted to bar, 1972, Ohio and U.S. District Court, Southern District of Ohio. *Education:* University of Cincinnati (B.A., 1969; J.D., 1972). Assistant Law Director, City of Middletown, 1978-1984. Member, Edgewood City School District Personnel Board, 1984—. *Member:* Butler County (Member, Real Estate and Probate Committees) and Ohio State Bar Associations. ***PRACTICE AREAS:*** Real Estate Law; Probate Law; Bankruptcy Law; Collections; Creditor/Debtor's Rights; Evictions.

CO-COUNSEL FOR: American Savings Bank.
REPRESENTATIVE CLIENTS: The Commercial Realty Co.; Butler Realty Co.; City of Middletown; Barbara Park Realty Co.; Beneficial Finance; Helton & Associates.
AGENT FOR: Ohio Bar Title Insurance Co.
APPROVED ATTORNEY FOR: Chicago Title Insurance Co.

PICKREL, SCHAEFFER & EBELING

MIDDLETOWN, OHIO

(See Dayton)

Banking, Civil, Corporate, General Business, Commercial Lending, Mergers and Acquisitions, Insurance, Labor and Employment, Healthcare, Municipal and Zoning, Personal Injury and Products Liability, Probate, Trust and Estate Planning, Construction, Computer, Real Estate, Environmental, Workers' Compensation Defense, Immigration, Bankruptcy and Tax Law. Trials and Appeals, School Law and Title Insurance.

WAITE, SCHNEIDER, BAYLESS & CHESLEY CO., L.P.A.

MIDDLETOWN, OHIO

(See Cincinnati)

General Civil Practice. Aviation, Antitrust Litigation, Class Action, Commercial Litigation, Complex Litigation, Corporate Law, Federal Employees Liability, General Civil Trials and Appeals in all Courts, Insurance, Labor, Consolidated and Multi-district Litigation, Products Litigation, Securities Litigation and Wrongful Death.

CRITCHFIELD, CRITCHFIELD & JOHNSTON, LTD.

Established in 1919
138 E. JACKSON STREET
MILLERSBURG, OHIO 44654
Telephone: 330-674-3055
Telecopier: 330-674-4469
URL: http://www.ccj.com

Wooster, Ohio: 225 North Market Street, P.O. Box 599, 44691-0599. Telephone: 330-264-4444.
Mt. Vernon, Ohio: 10 South Gay Street, 43050-3546. Telephone: 740-397-4040.
Medina, Ohio: 3985 Medina Road, Suite 100, 44256. Telephone: 330-723-6404.

General Practice in all Courts. Business, Corporate Law, Insurance, Estate Planning, Wills and Probate, Labor and Employment, ERISA, Health Care, Environmental Law, Workers Compensation, Banking, Taxation, Antitrust and Trade Regulation, Oil and Gas Law, Litigation, Debtor and Creditor, Municipal Law, School Law, Real Estate, Commercial Law, Construction Law.

JOHN R. WALTMAN, born Millersburg, Ohio, January 9, 1942; admitted to bar, 1970, Ohio. *Education:* Muskingum College (B.A., 1965); Ohio Northern University (J.D., 1970). Delta Theta Phi. *Member:* Ohio State Bar Foundation. ***PRACTICE AREAS:*** Probate; Estate Planning; Business Law. ***Email:*** waltman@ccj.com

DANIEL L. MATHIE, born Millersburg, Ohio, August 18, 1958; admitted to bar, 1983, Ohio. *Education:* Ohio Northern University (B.S., 1980; J.D., with high distinction, 1983). Omicron Delta Kappa; Phi Kappa Phi. Willis Society. ***PRACTICE AREAS:*** Real Estate; Banking; Business Law; Federal Income Tax; Oil and Gas Law. ***Email:*** mathie@ccj.com

STEVEN J. SHROCK, born Akron, Ohio, February 21, 1968; admitted to bar, 1992, Ohio; 1995, Colorado. *Education:* College of Wooster (B.A., 1989); University of Minnesota (J.D., magna cum laude, 1992). Phi Beta Kappa; Omicron Delta Epsilon; Order of the Coif. Member and Director, Moot Court Competition Team. *Member:* Ohio Academy of Trial Lawyers. ***PRACTICE AREAS:*** Civil Litigation; Negligence; Insurance Law; Estate Planning. ***Email:*** shrock@ccj.com

GARRETT M. ROACH, born Millersburg, Ohio, September 4, 1967; admitted to bar, 1992, Ohio. *Education:* Ohio University (B.S., summa cum laude, 1989); Cleveland-Marshall College of Law (J.D., cum laude, 1992). Member, National Moot Court Competition Team. Recipient, Hugo L. Black Oral Advocacy Award. ***PRACTICE AREAS:*** Business Law; Creditors Rights; Real Estate; Probate; Estate Planning. ***Email:*** roach@ccj.com

MARK E. LEININGER, born Millersburg, Ohio, August 8, 1969; admitted to bar, 1995, Ohio. *Education:* Ashland University (B.S., magna cum laude, 1992); Cleveland Marshall College of Law (J.D., 1995). ***PRACTICE AREAS:*** Real Estate; Probate; Oil and Gas; Business Law; Creditors Rights. ***Email:*** leininger@ccj.com

(This Listing Continued)

SEAN M. WARNER, born August 19, 1976; admitted to bar, 2002, Ohio. *Education:* Ohio State University (B.A., 1999; J.D., 2002). ***PRACTICE AREAS:*** Business Law; Corporate Law; Probate; Real Estate. ***Email:*** warner@ccj.com

GENERAL COUNSEL FOR: Multi Products Co.; Holmes-Wayne Rural Electric Coop.; Patten Drilling Co.; The Inn at Honey Run; Holmes County Education Foundation; Castle Nursing Homes, Inc.; Weaver Leather Goods, Inc.; Dutchman Hospitality Group, Inc.
LOCAL COUNSEL FOR: State Auto Insurance Co.
TITLE POLICY ISSUING AGENTS FOR: First American Title Insurance Co.

(For complete biographical data on Wooster, Ohio personnel, see Professional Biographies at Wooster, Ohio)

LOGEE, HOSTETLER, STUTZMAN & LEHMAN, LLC

MILLERSBURG, OHIO

(See Wooster)

General Practice. Insurance Law, Insurance Defense, Probate, Estate Planning, Real Estate, Corporate Law and Taxation. Trials.

STEIMEL LAW OFFICE

Established in 1986

111 SOUTH CLAY STREET
MILLERSBURG, OHIO 44654-1307
Telephone: 330-674-0001
Fax: 330-674-3985
Email: smslaw@valkyrie.net
URL: http://www.lawyers.com/steimellawoffice

General Civil Practice in all State and Federal Courts. Commercial, Corporate, Oil and Gas, Real Estate, Probate and Estate Planning, Banking Law.

SAMUEL M. STEIMEL, born Millersburg, Ohio, November 22, 1957; admitted to bar, 1983, Ohio. *Education:* College of Wooster (B.A., 1980); University of Toledo (J.D., 1983). *Member:* Holmes County (President, 1988-1989), Ohio State and American Bar Associations. ***PRACTICE AREAS:*** Probate Law; Real Estate Law; Corporate Law; Estate Planning; Banking Law.

REPRESENTATIVE CLIENTS: SMS Leasing; Holmes Cheese Co.; Millersburg Furniture; Victor Estates, Inc.; Martin Jewelers; Robison Drilling; Holmes County Title Company; Alpine Cheese Co.; Holmes Stair Parts; Hill Producing, Inc.; Southside Mo's; Loder Farms; Springhill Farms; Horse-N-Harness Pub; Holmestair, LTD.
LOCAL COUNSEL FOR: WKLM Radio FM.
APPROVED ATTORNEY FOR: Farm Credit Services; Lawyers Title Insurance Corp.

BROWN, BEMILLER, MURRAY, McINTYRE, VETTER & HECK, L.L.P.

MT. GILEAD, OHIO

(See Mansfield)

General Civil Practice, Corporate Law, Banking, Business, Casualty and Life Insurance, Trusts and Estates, Wills and Probate, Estate Planning, Real Estate Law, Labor, Employment, Personal Injury, Medical Malpractice, Legal Malpractice. Trials and Appeals, Arbitration and Mediation.

CALIG & HANDELMAN, LPA

MT. GILEAD, OHIO

(See Columbus)

Bankruptcy, Personal Injury, Probate, Real Estate, Social Security, Social Security Disability, Medical Malpractice, Wrongful Death, Civil Litigation, Domestic Relations Law.

OLIVER LAW OFFICE

MT. GILEAD, OHIO

(See Columbus)

Products Liability, Personal Injury, Wrongful Death, Latex Allergy Litigation, Medical Malpractice, Vioxx Litigation, Automobile Accidents, Insurance Law, Employment Discrimination.

AEBI LAW FIRM

111 SOUTH MULBERRY
MT. VERNON, OHIO 43050
Telephone: 740-397-8875
Fax: 740-393-0781

Personal Injury, Civil Litigation, Criminal Law, Estate Planning, Probate, Social Security Disability.

JOHN W. AEBI, born Alliance, Ohio, February 5, 1952; admitted to bar, 1978, Nevada and U.S. District Court, District of Nevada; 1979, Ohio. *Education:* Northern Illinois University (B.S., 1975); California Western School of Law (J.D., 1978). Instructor: Real Estate and Business Law, University of Nevada System, 1979-1981; Torts and Real Estate Law, Truckee Meadows Community College, 1985-1994. Chief Deputy District Attorney for Douglas County, Nevada, 1979-1981. Member, Local Rules Committee, U.S. District Court, District of Nevada, 1988-1994. *Member:* Knox County, Ohio State and American

(This Listing Continued)

Bar Associations; State Bar of Nevada; The Association of Trial Lawyers of America; National Organization of Social Security Claimants Representatives. ***PRACTICE AREAS:*** Personal Injury; Civil Litigation; Criminal Law; Estate Planning; Probate; Social Security Disability.

ROBERT E. CALESARIC ATTORNEY AT LAW

MT. VERNON, OHIO

(See Newark)

Personal Injury, Wrongful Death, D.U.I., O.V.I., O.M.V.I. and Criminal Defense.

CALIG & HANDELMAN, LPA

MT. VERNON, OHIO

(See Columbus)

Bankruptcy, Personal Injury, Probate, Real Estate, Social Security, Social Security Disability, Medical Malpractice, Wrongful Death, Civil Litigation, Domestic Relations Law.

COLLEY SHROYER & ABRAHAM CO., L.P.A.

MT. VERNON, OHIO

(See Columbus)

Civil Trial Practice. Personal Injury, Medical Malpractice, Automobile Accidents, Wrongful Death, Railroad Accidents, Slip and Fall, Negligence, Product Liability and Toxic Torts.

CRITCHFIELD, CRITCHFIELD & JOHNSTON, LTD.

10 SOUTH GAY STREET
MT. VERNON, OHIO 43050-3546
Telephone: 740-397-4040
Telecopier: 740-397-6775
URL: http://www.ccj.com

Wooster, Ohio: 225 North Market Street, P.O. Box 599, 44691-0599. Telephone: 330-264-4444.
Millersburg, Ohio: 138 E. Jackson Street, 44654. Telephone: 330-674-3055.
Medina, Ohio: 3985 Medina Road, Suite 100, 44256. Telephone: 330-723-6404.

General Practice in all Courts. Business, Corporate Law, Insurance, Estate Planning, Wills and Probate, Labor and Employment, ERISA, Health Care, Environmental Law, Workers Compensation, Banking, Taxation, Antitrust and Trade Regulation, Oil and Gas Law, Litigation, Debtor and Creditor, Municipal Law, School Law, Real Estate, Commercial Law, Construction Law.

KIM M. ROSE, born Gallipolis, Ohio, March 21, 1956; admitted to bar, 1981, Ohio. *Education:* Ohio University (B.B.A., Summa Cum Laude, 1977); Capital University (J.D., 1981); Ashland University (M.B.A., 1988). Adjunct Asst. Professor, Business Law, Mt. Vernon Nazarene College, 1982-2002. Assistant Knox County Prosecutor, 1982-1990. [USAR, JAGC, Major, 1974-1995]. ***PRACTICE AREAS:*** Corporate Law; Litigation; Probate; Estate Planning. ***Email:*** kimr@ccj.com

LAURA A. WAKEFIELD, born Bellingham, Washington, September 8, 1971; admitted to bar, 1997, Ohio. *Education:* University of Dayton (B.A., summa cum laude, 1993); Case Western Reserve University (J.D., 1997). ***PRACTICE AREAS:*** Banking; Business Law; Probate; Estate Planning; ERISA. ***Email:*** wakefield@ccj.com

JAMES R. NORRIS, born Akron, Ohio, January 27, 1950; admitted to bar, 1976, Ohio. *Education:* The Ohio State University (B.S., 1972); Capital University (J.D., 1976). ***PRACTICE AREAS:*** Real Estate; Probate; Estate Planning; Taxation. ***Email:*** norris@ccj.com

KATHY L. SWIHART, born Monroe, Michigan, June 2, 1968; admitted to bar, 1996, Ohio. *Education:* Mount Vernon Nazarene College (B.A., summa cum laude, 1989); Capital University (M.B.A., with distinction, 1996); Capital University Law School (J.D., summa cum laude, 1996). Member, Order of the Coif. Valedictorian, Mount Vernon Nazarene College. Member, Capital University Law School Law Review. ***PRACTICE AREAS:*** ERISA; Business Law; Estate Planning; Probate. ***Email:*** swihart@ccj.com

ADAM B. LANDON, born Utica, Ohio, March 20, 1975; admitted to bar, 2001, Ohio and Michigan. *Education:* Ohio State University (B.A., 1997); University of Toledo (J.D., cum laude, 2001). Member, Law Review. Recipient, American Jurisprudence Awards. *Member:* Wayne County, Ohio State and American Bar Associations. ***PRACTICE AREAS:*** Commercial Litigation; Insurance Litigation; Creditors Rights; Collections; Personal Injury; Wrongful Death. ***Email:*** landon@ccj.com

OF COUNSEL

RICHARD F. RITTER, born Hattiesburg, Mississippi, September 29, 1941; admitted to bar, 1969, Ohio. *Education:* Baldwin-Wallace College (B.A., 1963); Ohio State University School of Law (J.D., 1969). ***PRACTICE AREAS:*** Litigation; Real Estate; Estate Planning. ***Email:*** ritter@ccj.com

REPRESENTATIVE CLIENTS: Newell Rubbermaid Inc.; The College of Wooster; Buehler Food Markets, Inc.; The Will-Burt Co.; Buckeye Feed Mills, Inc.; Mt. Vernon Nazarene College; Ohio Eastern Star Home.
TITLE POLICY ISSUING AGENTS FOR: First American Title Insurance Co.

(For complete biographical data on Wooster, Ohio personnel, see Professional Biographies at Wooster, Ohio)

FARLOW & ASSOCIATES LLC

MT. VERNON, OHIO

(See Dublin)

Family Law, Divorce, Child Custody, Child Support, Premarital Agreements, Post-Decree Enforcements, Employment Law, School Law, Personal Injury.

OLIVER LAW OFFICE

MT. VERNON, OHIO

(See Columbus)

Products Liability, Personal Injury, Wrongful Death, Latex Allergy Litigation, Medical Malpractice, Vioxx Litigation, Automobile Accidents, Insurance Law, Employment Discrimination.

THE PLYMALE PARTNERSHIP LLP

MT. VERNON, OHIO

(See Columbus)

Personal Injury, Products Liability, Wrongful Death, Medical Malpractice, Professional Negligence, Traumatic Brain Injury, Automobile Accidents, Nursing Home Torts, Civil Litigation.

SCOTT A. PULLINS, LTD., LPA

110 EAST GAMBIER STREET
SUITE 5
P.O. BOX 1186
MT. VERNON, OHIO 43050
Telephone: 740-392-3505
Email: scott@pullinslaw.com
URL: http://www.pullinslaw.com

Election and Campaign Finance Law, Non-Profit Law, Business Organizations, Civil Rights, Constitutional Law, Municipal Law and Local Government Law, General Practice, Zoning, Administrative Law, Asset Protection, Business Law, Collections, Computers and Software, Consumer Law, Contracts, Copyrights, Corporate Law, Libel, Slander and Defamation, Litigation, Probate, Trusts and Estates.

SCOTT A. PULLINS, born Point Pleasant, West Virginia, January 24, 1968; admitted to bar, 2003, Ohio. *Education:* The Ohio State University (B.A., 1997); Capital University (J.D., 2003). *Member:* Knox County and Ohio State Bar Associations; Federalist Society. ***PRACTICE AREAS:*** Asset Protection; Child Advocacy; Constitutional Law; General Practice; Election and Campaign Finance; Trade Association Law; Municipal Law; Local Government Law; Collections; Business Law; Business Associations Law; Business Formation; Business Organization; Business Start-Ups; Small Business Law; Computers and Software; Consumer Law; Guardian Ad Litem; Libel, Slander and Defamation; Land Use Litigation; Zoning Law; Zoning, Planning and Land Use. ***Email:*** scott@pullinslaw.com

REBECCA J. STUMLER

MT. VERNON, OHIO

(See Columbus)

Family Law, Divorce, Child Custody, Child Support, Visitation Rights, Adoption Law, Paternity, Domestic Violence, Bankruptcy Law, Civil Litigation.

TWYFORD & DONAHEY, P.L.L.

MT. VERNON, OHIO

(See Columbus)

Personal Injury Litigation, Wrongful Death, Medical Malpractice, Products Liability, Automobile Accidents, Trucking Accidents, Head and Spinal Injuries, Motorcycle Accidents and Injuries, Uninsured Motorists, Insurance Law, Airplane Crash Litigation, Railroad Accidents, Slip and Fall, Dog Bites, Work Related Injuries, Birth Injuries, Nursing Home Abuse and Neglect.

ZELKOWITZ, BARRY & CULLERS, LTD.

121 EAST HIGH STREET
MT. VERNON, OHIO 43050
Telephone: 740-397-5262
Fax: 740-397-2682
URL: http://www.ZBCLaw.com

General Civil Practice in all Courts. Corporation, Probate and Estate Planning, Real Estate, Commercial and Banking, Insurance and Oil and Gas Law. Trials and Appeals.

MEMBERS OF FIRM

JAMES J. CULLERS, born Eaton, Ohio, April 13, 1930; admitted to bar, 1959, Ohio. *Education:* Ohio University (B.S.C., 1952); The Ohio State University (J.D., 1959). City Solicitor, Mt. Vernon, 1962-1974, Mt. Gilead, 1963-1965 and Danville, 1963-1965. Trustee, Knox Community Hospital, 1975—. Secretary, Mount Vernon Community Trust, 1977-1995. *Member:* Knox County (President, 1968) and Ohio State (Member: Oil and Gas Committee, 1965-1977; Negligence Law Committee, 1968-1976; Executive Committee, 1986-1989; Board of Governors, Probate and Trust Law Section, 1999—) Bar Associations. Fellow: Ohio State Bar Foundation (President, 1993); American College of Trust and Estate Counsel. ***PRACTICE AREAS:*** Estate Planning; Oil and Gas; Business.

DAVID E. RAILSBACK, born Wayne County, Indiana, April 27, 1942; admitted to bar, 1970, Ohio. *Education:* American University; Hanover College (A.B., 1964); The Ohio State University (J.D., 1969). Trustee and Secretary: Area Development Foundation, 1972—; YMCA, Endowment Fund, 1977-1997. Solicitor: Village of Danville, 1972-1979; Village of Fredericktown, 1974-1977. City Solicitor, Mount Vernon, 1974-1977. Trustee, Ohio State University, Newark, 1997—. *Member:* Knox County (President, 1975-1976), Ohio State (Counsel of Delegates, 2002—; Chairman, Legal Ethics and Professional Conduct Committee, 1990-1992; Bankruptcy, 1988—) and American Bar Associations. ***PRACTICE AREAS:*** Business; Bankruptcy.

ROBERT B. WESTON, born Canton, Ohio, November 30, 1946; admitted to bar, 1971, Ohio; 1972, Michigan. *Education:* Otterbein College (B.A., 1968); Ohio Northern University (J.D., 1971). Phi Alpha Delta. Solicitor, Marengo, 1976—. *Member:* Knox County (President, 1986-1987), Ohio State and American Bar Associations. ***PRACTICE AREAS:*** Estate Planning; Business; Real Estate Zoning.

LARRY J. GRINDLE, born Wadsworth, Ohio, May 21, 1961; admitted to bar, 1986, Ohio. *Education:* Ashland College (B.S.B.A., 1983); Case Western Reserve University (J.D., 1986). Certified Public Accountant, Ohio, 1986. Personal Financial Specialist, 2000. *Member:* Knox County (President, 1994-1995), Ohio State (Real Property Board of Governors, 1995—) and American (Member, Real Property Section) Bar Associations. ***PRACTICE AREAS:*** Real Estate; Business; Taxation; Estate Planning.

NOEL B. ALDEN, born Seattle, Washington, December 16, 1968; admitted to bar, 1996, Ohio and U.S. District Court, Southern District of Ohio. *Education:* Cornell University (B.S., 1991); The Ohio State University (J.D., 1996). Solicitor, Village of Canville, 2002—. *Member:* Knox County (Secretary, 2000-2001) and Ohio State Bar Associations. ***PRACTICE AREAS:*** Agriculture; Business; Real Estate; Litigation.

ASSOCIATE

WENDI M. FOWLER, born Cleveland, Ohio, October 5, 1972; admitted to bar, 2001, Ohio. *Education:* Earlham College (B.A., 1994); Case Western Reserve University (J.D., 1999). Member, Board of Directors, American Red Cross, Knox County Chapter. *Member:* Columbus, Knox County (Secretary, 2003) and Ohio State Bar Associations; American Immigration Lawyers Association. ***LANGUAGES:*** Spanish. ***PRACTICE AREAS:*** Immigration and Naturalization Law; Business Immigration; Deportation; Family Law; Business Law; Real Estate.

REPRESENTATIVE CLIENTS: The First-Knox National Bank of Mount Vernon; The Ohio Power Co.; Knox Community Hospital; AMG Industries; Kenyon College; Ariel Corp.; Wenco, Inc.; Town and Village Insurance Service; State Automobile Mutual Insurance Co.; Grange Mutual Casualty Co.; Motorists Mutual Insurance Co.; Cooper Industries; Columbia Gas of Ohio, Inc.; United Telephone Co. of Ohio; Weyerhaeusser Co.; Jeld-Wen, Inc.; Kelsey Hayes; Burrows Paper Corp.; Energy Machine, Inc.
APPROVED ATTORNEYS FOR: Ohio Bar Title Insurance Co.; Lawyers Title Insurance Corp.; Farm Credit Services of Mid-America, ACA.

MEEKISON LAW FIRM

123 WEST WASHINGTON STREET
NAPOLEON, OHIO 43545-1739
Telephone: 419-592-6801
Fax: 419-592-6944

Divorce, Family Law, Personal Injury, Probate, Estate Planning, Wills and Real Estate.

FIRM PROFILE: In 1872, David Meekison was admitted to the practice of law in Napoleon, where he also served as Probate Judge and as the U.S. Representative for the 5th Congressional District. Since that time, a Meekison has continuously practiced law in Henry County through the present day providing quality legal services to a wide cross section of clients in Henry and surrounding counties.

MEMBERS OF FIRM

DAVID MEEKISON, born Napoleon, Ohio, December 12, 1913; admitted to bar, 1936, Ohio. *Education:* Harvard College; The Ohio State University (LL.B., 1936). Phi Delta Phi. Member, 1950-1976 and Chairman, 1958-1960; 1963-1965, Henry County Election Board. *Member:* Henry County (President, 1958-1963), Northwestern Ohio, Ohio State and American Bar Associations. ***PRACTICE AREAS:*** Estate Planning; Probate Law; Real Estate Law; Negligence Law.

DAVID F. MEEKISON, born Toledo, Ohio, July 28, 1947; admitted to bar, 1972, Ohio. *Education:* University of Notre Dame (A.B., 1969; J.D., 1972). Special Counsel to Ohio Attorney General, 1972-1975. *Member:* Henry County, Stark County, Ohio State (Member, Negligence Law Committee) and American (Member, Tort and Insurance Practice Law Section) Bar Associations; Ohio Academy of Trial Lawyers; The Association of Trial Lawyers of America. ***PRACTICE AREAS:*** Personal Injury; Medical Malpractice; Insurance Coverage Disputes; Probate; Civil Litigation. ***Email:*** dm@henry-net.com

REFERENCE: National City Bank, Napoleon, Ohio.

STEPHEN K. SNAVELY, CO., L.P.A.

NAPOLEON, OHIO

(See Defiance)

General Civil Practice. Personal Injury, Wrongful Death, Automobile Accidents, Probate, Wills, Trusts, Estate Planning, Family Law, Domestic Relations, Divorce, and Real Estate Law. Trials and Appeals.

BLAUGRUND, HERBERT & MARTIN

INCORPORATED

NEW ALBANY, OHIO

(See Dublin)

Administrative Law, Bankruptcy, Civil Rights Litigation, Civil Service, Commercial Collections, Corporate Law, Debtor-Creditor Law, Disability Law, Employment Discrimination, Employment Law, Estate Administration, Estate Planning, General Civil Practice, Labor Rela-

(This Listing Continued)

tions, Limited Liability Companies, Limited Liability Partnerships, Liquor Law, Litigation, Motor Vehicle Law, Non-profit Corporation Law, Probate, Real Estate and Construction Law, State and Local Government Law, Trade Association Law, UCC, Workers Compensation, Zoning, Planning and Land Use, Alternative Dispute Resolution, Appellate Practice and Administrative Appeals.

SUSAN KENNEY-PFALZER

NEW ALBANY, OHIO

(See Columbus)

Family Law, Divorce, Dissolution, Child Custody, Spousal and Child Support, Visitation Rights, Adoptions, Paternity, Juvenile Law, Collaborative Law, Restraining Orders.

MELISSA J. SHAW

NEW ALBANY, OHIO

(See Gahanna)

Business Law, Business Planning and Formation, Contracts, Corporate, Partnership, Family Business, Wills, Trusts and Estates, Contested Wills, Estate and Gift Taxation, Estate Planning, Living Wills, Powers of Attorney, Probate, Elder Law, Guardianship, Medicaid Eligibility.

THE SWARTZ LAW FIRM

Established in 1984

220 MARKET STREET, SUITE 208
NEW ALBANY, OHIO 43054
Telephone: 614-775-5000
Fax: 614-775-1104

Personal Injury, Product Liability and Medical Negligence Litigation.

MEMBER OF FIRM

DEAN E. SWARTZ, admitted to bar, 1974, Ohio; 1976, District of Columbia; 1978, U.S. Supreme Court; 1982, Pennsylvania and Virginia. *Education:* Stanford University (A.B., 1971); University of Toledo (J.D., 1974). (Certified as a Civil Trial Advocacy Specialist by the National Board of Trial Advocacy)

OF COUNSEL

BARRY S. REED, admitted to bar, 1981, Pennsylvania; 1983, District of Columbia (Not admitted in Ohio). *Education:* University of Washington (B.A., 1967); George Washington University (M.D., 1971); Catholic University of America (J.D., 1980).

MICHAEL E. BENSON

NEWARK, OHIO

(See Columbus)

Bankruptcy Law, Foreclosures, Debtor and Creditor, Real Estate, Landlord and Tenant, Buying and Selling, Wills, Living Wills, Healthcare, Powers of Attorney.

ROBERT E. CALESARIC
ATTORNEY AT LAW

35 S. PARK PLACE
SUITE 201
NEWARK, OHIO 43055
Telephone: 740-345-6454
Fax: 740-345-0031
URL: http://www.Calesariclaw.com
Email: rcalesaric@Alltel.net
URL: http://www.calesanclawfirm.com

Personal Injury, Wrongful Death, D.U.I., O.V.I., O.M.V.I. and Criminal Defense.

ROBERT E. CALESARIC, born June 30, 1966; admitted to bar, 1994, Ohio. *Education:* Ohio State University (B.A., 1989); Capital University (J.D., 1994). Assistant County Prosecutor, 1995-2000. *Member:* Ohio State Bar Association; Ohio Association of Trial Lawyers; Ohio Association of Criminal Defense Lawyers. ***PRACTICE AREAS:*** Personal Injury; Wrongful Death; DUI; OVI; OMVI; Criminal Defense.

CALIG & HANDELMAN, LPA

29 S. PARK PLACE
NEWARK, OHIO 43055
Telephone: 740-349-8581
Fax: 740-345-4101
URL: http://www.chohiolawyers.com

Columbus, Ohio Office: 854 East Broad Street, 43205. Telephone: 614-252-4885; 1-800-633-5000.

Lancaster, Ohio Office: 204 N. Columbus Street, 43130. Telephone: 740-653-4400. Fax: 740-653-0037.

Marion, Ohio Office: 274 S. Main Street, 43302. Telephone: 740-375-5051.

Bankruptcy, Personal Injury, Probate, Real Estate, Social Security, Social Security Disability, Medical Malpractice, Wrongful Death, Civil Litigation, Domestic Relations Law.

(For complete biographical data on all personnel, see Professional Biographies at Columbus)

FRIEDMAN & MIRMAN CO., L.P.A.

NEWARK, OHIO

(See Columbus)

Family Relations Law, Divorce.

GOLDMAN & ROSENTHAL

NEWARK, OHIO

(See Columbus)

Personal Injury, Family Law, Real Estate, Commercial Leasing, Construction and Mechanics Lien Law, Collections, Estate Planning and Probate, Corporate, Juvenile Law, Criminal. Civil and Criminal Trials in all Courts.

SUSAN KENNEY-PFALZER

NEWARK, OHIO

(See Columbus)

Family Law, Divorce, Dissolution, Child Custody, Spousal and Child Support, Visitation Rights, Adoptions, Paternity, Juvenile Law, Collaborative Law, Restraining Orders.

KINCAID, TAYLOR & GEYER

NEWARK, OHIO

(See Zanesville)

Business, Banks and Banking, Health Care, Estate Planning, Estate Administration, Real Estate, Title Insurance, Environmental, Oil and Gas, Civil Litigation, Domestic Relations, Family Law, Construction, General Civil and Criminal Trial and Appellate Practice.

LAMKIN, VAN EMAN, TRIMBLE, BEALS & DOUGHERTY, LLC

NEWARK, OHIO

(See Columbus)

Personal Injury, Medical Malpractice, Products Liability, Negligence, Insurance Coverage, Stockbroker Malpractice & Fraud. Litigation and Trial Practice.

GREGG R. LEWIS

NEWARK, OHIO

(See Columbus)

Family Law, Matrimonial Law and Civil Litigation.

ROXI A. LIMING

NEWARK, OHIO

(See Columbus)

Immigration Law, Visas, Naturalization, H1-B Visas, Green Cards, Financé Visas, Investor Visas, Investor Green Cards, Labor and Employment, Wage and Hour Violations, Wrongful Discharge, Employment Discrimination, Americans with Disabilities Act, Sexual Harassment, Family and Medical Leave Act, Employment Contracts, Severance Package Negotiation, Personnel Policies.

CARL McCOY
ATTORNEY AT LAW

195 UNION STREET
NEWARK, OHIO 43055
Telephone: 740-345-4545
Fax: 740-345-3644
Email: cemccoy@alltel.net

Criminal Law, Divorce, Family Law, Medical Malpractice, Personal Injury, Automobile Accidents, Child Custody, Child Support, General Practice, Trusts and Estates, Wills and Probate Law, Driving While Intoxicated, Drug Crimes, Elder Law, Estate Planning, Insurance, Slip and Fall, Traffic Violations, Wrongful Death, Dog Bites, Domestic Violence, Parole and Probation, Visitation Rights, White Collar Crime, Automobile Insurance, Automotive Products Liability, Felonies, Misdemeanors, Premarital Agreements, Sexual Assault, Spousal Support and Motorcycle Accidents.

CARL McCOY, born Coshocton, Ohio, December 7, 1955; admitted to bar, 1982, Ohio. *Education:* Ohio University (B.S., 1978); Capital University (J.D., 1982). ***PRACTICE AREAS:*** Criminal Law; Family Law; Automobile Accidents and Injuries; Motorcycle Accidents.

MORROW & ERHARD CO., L.P.A.

Established in 1982

10 WEST LOCUST STREET

P.O. BOX 487

NEWARK, OHIO 43058-0487

Telephone: 740-349-7262

Fax: 740-345-0490

URL: http://www.morrow-erhard.com

General Practice, Corporations, Oil and Gas, Taxation, Real Estate, Probate and Estate Planning, and Insurance.

C. ARTHUR MORROW, born Newark, Ohio, June 21, 1941; admitted to bar, 1971, Ohio and U.S. District Court, Southern District of Ohio; 1978, U.S. Supreme Court. *Education:* Denison University (B.A., 1966); University of Denver (M.B.A., 1970; J.D., 1970). Omicron Delta Kappa; Phi Delta Phi. Member, 1972-1977 and Secretary, 1975-1977, Ohio Oil and Gas Board of Review. Member and Trustee, Eastern Mineral Law Foundation, 1980-2000. Member, Ohio Division of Securities Oil and Gas Advisory Committee, 1980-1989. Member, Granville Village Council, 1987-1991. *Member:* Licking County (President, 1982), Columbus and Ohio State (Member, 1974— and Chairman, 1978-1981, Natural Resources Law Committee, 1978—; Member, Probate and Trust Law Section) Bar Associations. Fellow, Ohio State Bar Foundation. [With U.S. Army, 1960-1963]. ***PRACTICE AREAS:*** Corporate Law; Probate; Insurance; Trusts and Estates. ***Email:*** amorrow@morrow-erhard.com

ROBERT T. ERHARD, born Columbus, Ohio, November 30, 1950; admitted to bar, 1977, Ohio; 1978, U.S. District Court, District of Ohio; 1979, U.S. Tax Court; 1987, U.S. Supreme Court. *Education:* Denison University (B.A., 1972); Capital University (J.D., 1977). Order of the Curia. Member, Ohio Oil and Gas Association Legal Committee, 1987. President, 1992-1993, Member, 1988-1995, Granville Exempted Village Board of Education. Chairman, 1998-1999, 2004— and Member, 1996-1999, 2003—, Granville Township Zoning Commission, 1996-1997, Chairman, 1997-1998. *Member:* Licking County and Ohio State (Member, 1979—, and Chairman, 2000, Natural Resources Law Committee; Member, Corporation Law Committee, 1982-1986) Bar Associations. ***PRACTICE AREAS:*** Oil and Gas; Real Estate. ***Email:*** rerhard@morrow-erhard.com

---

W. PRENTICE SNOW, born Murfreesboro, Tennessee, March 4, 1956; admitted to bar, 1981, Ohio, U.S. District Court, Southern District of Ohio and U.S. Tax Court; 1983, U.S. Court of Military Appeals and U.S. Court of Appeals, Sixth Circuit; 1994, U.S. Supreme Court. *Education:* Ohio State University (B.A., 1978); Capital University (J.D., 1981). *Member:* Licking County and Ohio State (Member, Sections on: Employment Law; Health Care; Insurance Law) Bar Associations. [Lt. Col. USMCR, Ret.]. ***PRACTICE AREAS:*** Litigation; Employment Law; Corporate Law; Insurance. ***Email:*** wpsnow@morrow-erhard.com

REPRESENTATIVE CLIENTS: Medical Benefits Mutual Life Insurance Co.; Reliance Energy Co.; W.E. Shrider Co.; Belden & Blake Corp.; Ohio L&M Co., Inc.; Mitchell Energy Corp.; Brown Distributing Co.; Wyeth-Scott Co.; Alliance Petroleum Corp.; Springfield Township Mutual Insurance Association; Farmers Mutual Relief Association; Leads; Washington Mutual Insurance Co.; WCLT Radio, Inc.; Velvet Ice Cream Co.; Country Mutual Insurance Co.; Claggett & Sons, Inc.; SR Door, Inc.
APPROVED AGENT FOR: Ohio Bar Title Insurance Co.; Lawyers Title Insurance Co.
REFERENCE: The Park National Bank.

MORROW, GORDON & BYRD, LTD.

33 WEST MAIN STREET

P.O. BOX 4190

NEWARK, OHIO 43058-4190

Telephone: 740-345-9611

Columbus: 614-221-4810

Fax: 740-349-9816

Email: mgblaw@nextek.net

URL: http://www.mgbohiolaw.com/

Personal Injury, Probate, Real Estate, Corporate, Eminent Domain, Taxation, Insurance and Oil and Gas Law. Trials in all Courts.

MARTIN D. ALTMAIER, admitted to bar, 1967, Ohio. *Education:* Duke University (A.B., 1964); The Ohio State University (J.D., 1967). ***PRACTICE AREAS:*** Probate; Real Estate; Oil and Gas.

GLENN A. WHITE, admitted to bar, 1969, Ohio. *Education:* DePauw University (B.A., cum laude, 1966); George Washington University (J.D., 1969). *Member:* Fellow, Ohio State Bar Foundation. ***PRACTICE AREAS:*** Insurance Defense; Probate; Products Liability; Real Estate; Litigation.

A. TERRANCE TRENEFF, admitted to bar, 1972, Ohio. *Education:* The Ohio State University (B.S., 1967); Capital University (J.D., 1972). *Member:* Fellow, Ohio State Bar Foundation. ***PRACTICE AREAS:*** Insurance Defense; Real Estate; Domestic Relations.

STEVEN T. GREENE, admitted to bar, 1973, Ohio. *Education:* Brown University (B.A., 1970); The Ohio State University (J.D., 1972). *Member:* Fellow, Ohio State Bar Foundation. ***PRACTICE AREAS:*** Insurance Defense; Civil Litigation; Criminal; Domestic Relations.

JAMES R. COOPER, admitted to bar, 1972, Ohio. *Education:* University of Notre Dame (B.B.A., cum laude, 1969); The Ohio State University (J.D., cum laude, 1972). *Member:* Fellow, Ohio State Bar Foundation. [Lieut., JAGC, USN, 1972-1976]. ***PRACTICE AREAS:*** Corporate; Taxation; Estate Planning.

ADAM K. VERNAU, admitted to bar, 1989, Ohio. *Education:* West Virginia University (B.S., 1986); Capital University (J.D., 1989). ***PRACTICE AREAS:*** Civil Litigation; Estate Planning; Probate; Domestic Relations; Taxation; Small Business.

(This Listing Continued)

CAROLYN J. CARNES, admitted to bar, 1996, Ohio. *Education:* Capital University (B.A., magna cum laude, 1993; J.D., 1996). ***PRACTICE AREAS:*** Domestic; Real Estate; Civil Litigation.

TIMOTHY M. COOPER, admitted to bar, 1998, Ohio. *Education:* University of Notre Dame (B.A., 1994); University of Toledo (J.D., 1997). ***PRACTICE AREAS:*** Bankruptcy; Business; Real Estate.

OF COUNSEL

E. Clark Morrow

L. James Gordon

GENERAL COUNSEL FOR: Denison University; Weakley Apartments, Inc.; Mid-Ohio Warehouses, Inc.; Newark Transfer, Inc.; The Murphy Group, Inc.; Licking Memorial Hospital; Jobes Henderson & Associates, Inc.; Ag & Industrial, Inc.; Mid Ohio Development Corp.; Granville Milling; Morgan-Mitchell Development Corp.; K & G Management; Gummer Wholesale Inc.; Midwest Service Management, Inc.; Ohiotelnet.com, Inc.
LOCAL COUNSEL FOR: Motorists Mutual Insurance Co.; Grange Mutual Casualty Co.; The Ohio Casualty Co.; Western Reserve Casualty Co.; Cincinnati Insurance Co.; Travelers Insurance Co.; Westfield Group; Erie Insurance Co.; Lightning Rod Mutual Insurance Co.; The Park National Bank, Granville, Ohio; American Hardware Mutual Insurance Company; National City Bank.
AGENTS FOR: Ohio Bar Title Insurance Co.; Chicago Title Insurance Co.
REFERENCES: The Park National Bank; National City Bank.

REESE, PYLE, DRAKE & MEYER, P.L.L.

36 NORTH SECOND STREET

P.O. BOX 919

NEWARK, OHIO 43058-0919

Telephone: 740-345-3431

Fax: 740-345-7302

Email: rpdm@rpdm.com

URL: http://www.rpdm.com

General Civil Practice in all Courts, State and Federal. Corporation, Banking, Insurance, Taxation, Probate and Estate Planning, Real Estate Law and Employment Law. Trials and Appeals.

MEMBERS OF FIRM

ROBERT H. FLORY (1910-1962)

WILLIAM F. FITZGIBBON (1902-1975)

JAMES W. PYLE (Retired)

J. GILBERT REESE, born Newark, Ohio, July 7, 1925; admitted to bar, 1952, Ohio. *Education:* The Ohio State University (B.A., 1949; J.D., 1952). Phi Delta Phi. Newark Law Director, 1958-1961. Chairman, National Council, Ohio State University College of Law, 1973-1979. Named Distinguished Alumnus, Ohio State University College of Law, 1979. *Member:* Licking County (President, 1969-1970), Ohio State Bar Association. [United States Army, Medical Corps, 1943-1946]. ***PRACTICE AREAS:*** Probate Law; Estate Planning Law; Corporate Law; Banking Law. ***Email:*** greese@rpdm.com

ROBERT N. DRAKE, born Waco, Texas, October 6, 1947; admitted to bar, 1972, Ohio. *Education:* College of Wooster (B.A., 1969); University of Michigan (J.D, 1972). Director of Law, Village of Granville, 1979-1987. *Member:* Licking County (President, 1995) and Ohio State Bar Associations. ***PRACTICE AREAS:*** Real Estate Law; Corporate Law; Probate Law; Estate Planning Law. ***Email:*** rndrake@rpdm.com

CHRISTOPHER R. MEYER, born Springfield, Ohio, June 18, 1952; admitted to bar, 1977, Ohio. *Education:* The Ohio State University (B.A., summa cum laude, 1974; J.D., 1977). Phi Beta Kappa. *Member:* Columbus, Licking County and Ohio State (Member: Negligence Law Committee, 1983—; Litigation Section) Bar Associations; Ohio Association of Civil Trial Attorneys; Defense Research Institute; Society of Ohio Hospital Attorneys; American Academy of Hospital Attorneys; National Association of College and University Attorneys. ***PRACTICE AREAS:*** Civil Litigation; Insurance Defense Law; Medical Malpractice; Education Law. ***Email:*** cmeyer@rpdm.com

I. RUSSELL SUSKIND, born New York, N.Y., October 21, 1943; admitted to bar, 1971, Ohio. *Education:* Bradley University (B.S., 1965); University of Michigan (J.D., 1971). Solicitor, Village of Utica, 1982-1987. *Member:* Licking County (President, 1992), Ohio State (Member, Elder Law Committee, 1986—) and American Bar Associations. [1st Lt., U.S. Army, 1966-1969]. ***PRACTICE AREAS:*** Real Estate Law; Tax Law; Elder Law; Probate. ***Email:*** rsuskind@rpdm.com

ANN MUNRO KENNEDY, born Boston, Massachusetts, April 28, 1943; admitted to bar, 1981, Ohio. *Education:* Radcliffe College, Harvard University (B.A., cum laude, 1965); The Ohio State University (J.D., with honors, 1981). Phi Delta Phi. Law Director, Village of Granville, 1987-1990. Member, Ohio Supreme Court Commission on Attorney Continuing Legal Education, 1988-1995; Vice-Chair, 1991-1992; Chair, 1993-1994. *Member:* Licking County, Ohio State and American Bar Associations. ***PRACTICE AREAS:*** Estate Planning; Probate; Nonprofit Tax Law; Family Law. ***Email:*** akennedy@rpdm.com

DAVID W. WENGER, born Akron, Ohio, January 19, 1954; admitted to bar, 1979, Ohio. *Education:* College of Wooster (B.A., 1976); The Ohio State University (J.D., 1979). Phi Beta Kappa; Delta Sigma Rho. Counsel, State Medical Board of Ohio, 1979-1982. *Member:* Columbus, Licking County and Ohio State (Member: Insurance Law Committee, 1989—) Bar Associations; Ohio Association of Civil Trial Attorneys; Defense Research Institute. ***PRACTICE AREAS:*** Civil Litigation; Personal Injury Law; Insurance Defense Law; Domestic Relations. ***Email:*** dwwenger@rpdm.com

J. ANDREW CRAWFORD, born Columbus, Ohio, March 22, 1956; admitted to bar, 1981, Ohio. *Education:* Moorhead State University (B.A., summa cum laude, 1978); Indiana University (J.D., cum laude, 1981). Recipient, American Jurisprudence Award in Creditor's Rights. Managing Editor, Indiana Law Journal, 1980-1981. *Member:* Licking County and Ohio State (Member, Litigation Section) Bar Associations; Ohio Association of Civil Trial Attorneys. ***PRACTICE AREAS:*** Civil Litigation; Business Litigation; Insurance Defense Law; Personal Injury Law. ***Email:*** acrawford@rpdm.com

(This Listing Continued)

WM. DOUGLAS LOWE, born Portsmouth, Ohio, December 2, 1959; admitted to bar, 1985, Ohio. *Education:* Ohio University (B.A., summa cum laude, 1982; M.B.A., 1982); Ohio State University (J.D., with honors, 1985). Order of the Coif; Delta Theta Phi. *Member:* Licking County, Knox County and Ohio State Bar Associations; The Association of Trial Lawyers of America; Ohio Association of Civil Trial Attorneys. ***PRACTICE AREAS:*** Civil Litigation; Business Litigation; Corporate Law; Personal Injury Law; Insurance Defense Law. ***Email:*** dlowe@rpdm.com

RODNEY A. NELSON, born Salina, Kansas, October 17, 1955; admitted to bar, 1992, Ohio. *Education:* Kansas State University (B.S., 1977; M.A., 1981) Capital University Law School (J.D., magna cum laude, 1992). Order of the Curia. Member, 1990-1991, and Notes Editor, 1991-1992, Capital University Law Review. *Member:* Licking County, Ohio State and American Bar Associations; National Association of College and University Attorneys. ***PRACTICE AREAS:*** Civil Litigation; Insurance Defense; Real Estate Foreclosure; Education Law. ***Email:*** rnelson@rpdm.com

MARY M. ALBRIGHT, born Chillicothe, Ohio, November 24, 1952; admitted to bar, 1997, Ohio. *Education:* University of Dayton (B.A., magna cum laude, 1973); The Ohio State University (M.A., 1977); Capital University (J.D., summa cum laude, 1997). Editor-in-Chief, Capital University Law Review, 1996-1997. *Member:* Licking County and Ohio State Bar Associations. ***PRACTICE AREAS:*** Estate Planning; Probate; Corporate Law; Tax Planning. ***Email:*** malbright@rpdm.com

MICHAEL H. WHITEHEAD, born Decorah, Iowa, December 19, 1972; admitted to bar, 2000, Ohio. *Education:* Miami University (B.A., magna cum laude, 1994); Ohio State University (J.D., 2000). *Member:* Licking County, Ohio State and American Bar Associations. ***PRACTICE AREAS:*** Real Estate; Estate Planning; Corporate Law. ***Email:*** mwhitehead@rpdm.com

---

BRIAN C. REED, born Newark, Ohio, September 21, 1974; admitted to bar, 2000, Ohio; 2001, Michigan and U.S. District Court, Western District of Michigan. *Education:* Wittenberg University (B.A., 1997); Ohio Northern University, Pettit College of Law (J.D., with distinction, 2000). Law Clerk to Hon. Gregory Lynn Frost, 2001-2002. *Member:* Ohio State Bar Association. ***PRACTICE AREAS:*** General Practice; Civil Litigation; Real Estate. ***Email:*** breed@rpdm.com

SIOBHAN R. CLOVIS, born Ann Arbor, Michigan, April 12, 1973; admitted to bar, 1998, Ohio. *Education:* The Ohio State University (B.A., 1995); Case Western Reserve University (J.D., cum laude, 1998). *Member:* Licking County Bar Association; Ohio State Bar Association. ***PRACTICE AREAS:*** Estate Planning; Probate; Real Estate Law; Corporate Law. ***Email:*** sclovis@rpdm.com

GENERAL COUNSEL FOR: The Park National Bank; Park Leasing Co.; First Federal Savings and Loan Association; The Thomas J. Evans Foundation; Licking County Foundation; Licking Memorial Health Systems; Newark Campus Development Fund; Licking/Knox Goodwill Industries, Inc.; Contour Forming, Inc.; Lynd Fruit Farm, Inc.; United Carriers Corp.; Able Transit, Inc.; Truck One, Inc.; Freight Service, Inc.; Lawyers Title Insurance Agency of Licking County; Central Ohio Technical College; Newark City Schools; Redskin Transport; The Shelly Company; Law General Contracting.
LOCAL COUNSEL FOR: Licking Memorial Hospital; Licking Memorial Professional Corporation; Diebold, Inc.; American Electric Power Co.; ALLTEL Ohio, Inc.; State Farm Insurance Cos.; Moundbuilders Guidance Center; American General Life & Accident Insurance Co.; Lumberman's Underwriting Alliance; Jackson National Life Insurance Company; Community Mental Health Board, Licking and Knox Counties; Bayer Corporation.
APPROVED ATTORNEYS FOR: Lawyers Title Insurance Corp.; Commonwealth Land Title Corp.

ROURKE & BLUMENTHAL, LLP

NEWARK, OHIO

(See Columbus)

Personal Injury, Negligence, Products Liability, Medical Malpractice, Nursing Home Litigation, Wrongful Death, Intentional Tort, Insurance Disputes, Automobile Accidents, Civil Trial Practice, Aviation, Professional Liability.

REBECCA J. STUMLER

NEWARK, OHIO

(See Columbus)

Family Law, Divorce, Child Custody, Child Support, Visitation Rights, Adoption Law, Paternity, Domestic Violence, Bankruptcy Law, Civil Litigation.

TWYFORD & DONAHEY, P.L.L.

137 WEST MAIN STREET, SUITE C
NEWARK, OHIO 43025
Telephone: Toll Free: 1-800-686-1699
Fax: 614-849-0475
Email: help@twyforddonahey.com
URL: http://www.twyforddonahey.com

Columbus, Ohio Office: 495 South High Street, 43215-5058. Telephone: Toll Free: 1-800-686-1699. Email: help@twyforddonahey.com.
Circleville, Ohio Office: 214 South Court Street, 43113. Telephone: Toll Free: 1-800-686-1699. Email: help@twyforddonahey.com.
Delaware, Ohio Office: 163 N. Sandusky Street, Suite 103, 43015. Telephone: Toll Free: 1-800-686-1699. Email: help@twyforddonahey.com.
Lancaster, Ohio Office: 3794 Old Columbus, N.W., 43130. Telephone: Toll Free: 1-800-686-1699. Email: help@twyforddonahey.com.
London, Ohio Office: 25 West Fifth Street, 43140. Telephone: Toll Free: 1-800-686-1699. Email: help@twyforddonahey.com.

(This Listing Continued)

Personal Injury Litigation, Wrongful Death, Medical Malpractice, Products Liability, Automobile Accidents, Trucking Accidents, Head and Spinal Injuries, Motorcycle Accidents and Injuries, Uninsured Motorists, Insurance Law, Airplane Crash Litigation, Railroad Accidents, Slip and Fall, Dog Bites, Work Related Injuries, Birth Injuries, Nursing Home Abuse and Neglect.

FIRM PROFILE: Tom Twyford and Dick Donahey have been partners since 1968 and have practiced exclusively in the areas of personal injury, medical malpractice and products liability law. We have never represented insurance companies! In recent years, we have obtained some of the largest verdicts in Franklin County. We have purposely remained small in order to concentrate on a limited number of cases. We have six offices and will handle cases in any part of the state of Ohio.

(For complete biographical data on all personnel, see Professional Biographies at Columbus, Ohio.)

VOLKEMA, THOMAS, MILLER, BURKETT, SCOTT & MERRY

A LEGAL PROFESSIONAL ASSOCIATION

NEWARK, OHIO

(See Columbus)

Civil State and Federal Trial and Appellate Practice. Personal Injury. Malpractice, Nursing Home Negligence, HMO Liability, Class Actions, Wrongful Death, Automobile Accidents, Product Liability, Employee Benefits, Insurance Bad Faith, Aviation and Tort Law, ERISA, Qui Tam (Whistleblower), False Claims Act.

WOLSKE & BARCLAY

A LEGAL PROFESSIONAL ASSOCIATION

NEWARK, OHIO

(See Columbus)

Civil and Appellate Practice in State and Federal Courts. Medical and Dental Malpractice, Nursing Home Negligence, Personal Injury and Products Liability Law, Worker's Compensation and Industrial Accidents, Automobile Accidents, Airplane Crash Litigation.

BAKER, DUBLIKAR, BECK, WILEY & MATHEWS

NEW PHILADELPHIA, OHIO

(See North Canton)

General Civil Trial and Appellate Practice in all Courts. Insurance, Products Liability, Environmental, Malpractice, Political Subdivision, Real Estate, Corporate, Commercial and Family Law.

BLACK McCUSKEY SOUERS & ARBAUGH

A LEGAL PROFESSIONAL ASSOCIATION

NEW PHILADELPHIA, OHIO

(See Canton, Ohio)

General Civil Practice in all State and Federal Courts. Administrative, Acquisitions, Antitrust, Banking, Bankruptcy, Commercial, Construction, Corporate, Divorce, Environmental, Estate Planning and Trusts, Estate Administration, Family Law, Government, Health Care Law, Insurance, Labor, Litigation, Oil and Gas, Personal Injury, Real Estate, Securities, Taxation Law, Workers' Compensation and Wrongful Death and Zoning.

FITZPATRICK, ZIMMERMAN & ROSE CO., L.P.A.

Established in 1951

140 FAIR AVENUE, N.W.
P.O. BOX 1014
NEW PHILADELPHIA, OHIO 44663-1014
Telephone: 330-364-1614
FAX: 330-343-3077
URL: http://www.fzrlaw.com

General Civil Practice. Creditors Bankruptcy, Foreclosures and Collections; Corporate-Business Planning and Litigation; Banking and Thrifts; Real Estate Conveyancing and Development; Mineral Resources Law; Estate Probating and Planning; Personal Injury, Accident and Wrongful Death Litigation in State and Federal Courts, Criminal Law.

DONALD W. ZIMMERMAN, born New Philadelphia, Ohio, September 25, 1925; admitted to bar, 1951, Ohio; 1975, U.S. District Court, Northern District of Ohio; 1986, U.S. Supreme Court. *Education:* Ohio Wesleyan University (A.B., 1949); Western Reserve University (J.D., 1951). Phi Delta Phi. Law Director: City of New Philadelphia, 1961-1967; Village of Gnadenhutten, 1969-1984. *Member:* Tuscarawas County, Ohio State and American Bar Associations. ***PRACTICE AREAS:*** Estate Planning; Probate; Business Planning; Real Estate; Elder Law. ***Email:*** dwzimmerman@fzrlaw.com

FRANK J. ROSE, JR., born Batavia, New York, August 24, 1949; admitted to bar, 1974, Ohio; 1976, U.S. District Court, Northern District of Ohio. *Education:* John Carroll University (A.B., magna cum laude, 1971); Case Western Reserve University (J.D., 1974). Assistant Professor, Real Estate Law, Kent State University, 1979-1986. *Member:* Tuscarawas County, Ohio State and American Bar Associations. [Capt., USAR, 1971-1979]. ***PRACTICE AREAS:*** Creditors Rights; Collections; Business Planning; Estate Planning; Business Litigation. ***Email:*** fjrose@fzrlaw.com

(This Listing Continued)

FITZPATRICK, ZIMMERMAN & ROSE CO., L.P.A., New Philadelphia—Continued

D. BRAD ZIMMERMAN, born New Philadelphia, Ohio, August 6, 1953; admitted to bar, 1978, Ohio; U.S. District Court, Northern District of Ohio. *Education:* Ohio Wesleyan University (B.A., 1975); Case Western Reserve University (J.D., 1978). Law Director, Village of Midvale, 1982—. *Member:* Tuscarawas County, Ohio State and American Bar Associations. ***PRACTICE AREAS:*** Real Estate; Estate Planning; Probate; Banking; Elder Law; Business Law; Litigation. ***Email:*** bzimmerman@fzrlaw.com

EUGENE H. NEMITZ, JR., born Ashtabula, Ohio, April 19, 1948; admitted to bar, 1973, Ohio and U.S. District Court, Northern District of Ohio. *Education:* Wittenberg University (B.A., 1970); Ohio State University (J.D., cum laude, 1973). City Prosecutor, City of New Philadelphia, 1977-1982. *Member:* Tuscarawas County (President, 1983), Ohio State and American Bar Associations; Ohio Academy of Trial Attorneys. ***PRACTICE AREAS:*** Litigation; Business; Insurance; Personal Injury; Probate. ***Email:*** ehnemitz@fzrlaw.com

J. GREG MILLER, born Lansing, Michigan, February 17, 1953; admitted to bar, 1990, Ohio. *Education:* Miami University (B.A., 1975); University of Akron (J.D., 1989). *Member:* Tuscarawas County, Ohio State and American Bar Associations. ***PRACTICE AREAS:*** Real Estate; Estate Planning; Banking; Probate; Elder Law. ***Email:*** jgmiller@fzrlaw.com

STEVEN A. ANDERSON, born Dover, Ohio, April 21, 1970; admitted to bar, 1996, Ohio. *Education:* Ohio State University (B.A., with honors, 1992); Capital University (J.D., magna cum laude, 1996). Phi Alpha Delta. Order of the Curia. Law Review. Recipient, Noah J. Kern Academic Scholarship; American Jurisprudence Award, Constitutional Law; CALI Award, Criminal Procedure. Solicitor: Village of Mineral City, 1999—; Village of Bolivar, 2000—. Assistant Professor, Real Estate Law, Kent State University. ***PRACTICE AREAS:*** Civil Litigation; Family Law; Collections; Real Estate; Criminal Litigation. ***Email:*** saanderson@fzrlaw.com

FRANCIS G. FITZPATRICK (Retired)

SPECIAL COUNSEL FOR: Tuscarawas County Metropolitan Sewer District; Atwood Regional Water and Sewer District; Tuscarawas County Board of Realtors.
REGIONAL COUNSEL FOR: Farm Credit Services; Bank One; United Mobile Homes, Inc.; American General Finance; Belmont National Bank.
COUNSEL FOR: Clients: Valley Mining, Inc.; Truck Sales and Service, Inc.; Peoples Satellite, Inc.; Dover Hydraulics, Inc.; Fenton Brothers Electric, Inc.; Everhart Glass Co.; Linn Hert Geib Funeral Home; Premier Land Title Co.; Tuscarawas County Title Co.; Buchanan Independent Oil Co.; Tuscarawas Schools Credit Union; Dover-Phila Federal Credit Union; Bank One N.A.; Belmont National Bank; American General Financial Services, Inc.; Farnsworth Oil & Gas, Inc.; Tipka Energy Development Co.; Express Packaging Co.; Green Valley Golf Club, Inc.; A-1 Pallet, Inc.; Village of Midvale, Ohio; TLC Travel; WTUZ Radio; Clinitec Lab; Schoenbrunn Landscaping; Commercial Roofing, Inc.; Charles G. Snyder Appraisal Co.; House of Stones Jewelers; First Federal Community Bank of Dover; Tuscarawas Ambulatory Surgery Center, LLC; Oxford Capital Enterprises, LLC.
APPROVED ATTORNEYS FOR: First American Title Insurance Co.; Old Republic National Title Insurance.

GRISI & RIEGLER

NEW PHILADELPHIA, OHIO

(See Akron)

Personal Injury, Medical Malpractice, Divorce, Probate and Estates, Municipal Zoning, Corporate.

KRUGLIAK, WILKINS, GRIFFITHS & DOUGHERTY CO., L.P.A.

158 N. BROADWAY STREET
NEW PHILADELPHIA, OHIO 44663
Telephone: 330-364-3472
Fax: 330-602-3187
Email: legal@kwgd.com
URL: http://www.kwgd.com

Canton, Ohio Office: 4775 Munson Street, N.W. Telephone: 330-497-0700. Fax: 330-497-4020.

Alliance, Ohio Office: KeyBank Building, 960 West State Street. Telephone: 330-823-9262.

Corporate Law, Mergers and Acquisitions, Labor and Employment (Private and Public Sector), Employee Benefits, Real Estate, Taxation, Complex Litigation, Contracts, Insurance Defense, Estates and Trusts, Probate, Elder Law, Commercial Litigation, Oil and Gas, Occupational Safety and Health, Environmental Law, Health Care Law, Hospital Law, Bankruptcy, Banks and Banking, Securities, Construction Law, Family Law, Education Law, Workers Compensation, Personal Injury Litigation, Collections, Debtor and Creditor, Government, Media Law and Electronic Commerce.

(For complete biographical data on all personnel, see Professional Biographies at Canton, Ohio)

MILLER & KYLER, L.P.A.

Established in 1880
405 CHAUNCEY AVENUE N.W.
P.O. BOX 668
NEW PHILADELPHIA, OHIO 44663
Telephone: 330-343-5585
Fax: 330-343-7977
URL: http://www.millerkyler.com

General Civil Practice, Corporation, Intellectual Property, Probate, Real Estate, Political Subdivisions, Personal Injury and Insurance Law. Trials and Appeals.

(This Listing Continued)

WILLIAM A. KYLER, born Jeromesville, Ohio, June 25, 1938; admitted to bar, 1964, Ohio; 1965, U.S. District Court, Northern District of Ohio and U.S. Court of Appeals, Sixth Circuit; 1977, U.S. Supreme Court. *Education:* Ohio Wesleyan University (B.A., 1960); Duke University (LL.B., 1964). *Member:* Tuscarawas County and Ohio State Bar Associations. Fellow, American College of Trial Lawyers. ***PRACTICE AREAS:*** General Litigation; Corporate Law; Estate Planning. ***Email:*** bkyler@millerkyler.com

JAMES J. PRINGLE, born Dover, Ohio, May 24, 1952; admitted to bar, 1979, Ohio; 1980, U.S. District Court, Northern District of Ohio; 1994, U.S. Court of Appeals, Sixth Circuit. *Education:* University Cincinnati (B.S. 1974; B.A., 1974; J.D., 1979). Member, Order of the Coif. Recipient, American Jurisprudence Award in Contracts. *Member:* Tuscarawas County and Ohio State Bar Associations. ***REPORTED CASES:*** Jones v. Murphy, (1984), 12 Ohio St.3d 84. ***PRACTICE AREAS:*** Political Subdivision; Corporate Law; Commercial Law; Estate Planning; Probate; Healthcare Law. ***Email:*** jpringle@millerkyler.com

GLENN G. DURMANN, born New York, N.Y., September 30, 1947; admitted to bar, 1972, Ohio; 1973, U.S. District Court, Southern District of Ohio; 1981, U.S. District Court, Northern District of Ohio. *Education:* Wittenberg University (A.B., 1969); Ohio State University (J.D., cum laude, 1972). Instructor, Real Estate Law, Kent State University. Assistant County Prosecutor, Tuscarawas County, 1981-1983. *Member:* Tuscarawas County and Ohio State (Member, Sections on: Real Property; Probate and Trust) Bar Associations. ***PRACTICE AREAS:*** Real Estate; Debtor and Creditor; Probate. ***Email:*** gdurmann@millerkyler.com

J. KEVIN LUNDHOLM, born Peoria, Illinois, November 13, 1959; admitted to bar, 1985, Ohio; 1986, U.S. District Court, Northern District of Ohio. *Education:* Blackburn College (B.A., magna cum laude, 1982); The University of Toledo (J.D., cum laude, 1985). Mediation Training, Private Adjudication Center, Duke University, 2001. *Member:* Tuscarawas County (Chair, ADR Committee) and Ohio State Bar Associations. (Certified as a Civil Trial Advocacy Specialist by the National Board of Trial Advocacy). ***PRACTICE AREAS:*** Civil Litigation; Personal Injury; Wrongful Death. ***Email:*** lundholm@millerkyler.com

---

BRENT L. MOORE, born Barberton, Ohio, July 14, 1971; admitted to bar, 1999, Ohio; 2000, U.S. District Court, Northern District of Ohio; registered to practice before U.S. Patent and Trademark Office. *Education:* University of Akron (B.S., 1996; J.D., 1999). *Member:* Tuscarawas County, Ohio State and American Bar Associations; American Intellectual Property Law Association. ***PRACTICE AREAS:*** Litigation; Intellectual Property. ***Email:*** bmoore@millerkyler.com

HARRY C.E. TOLHURST, III, born Cleveland, Ohio, March 20, 1974; admitted to bar, 2000, Ohio; 2004, U.S. District Court, Northern District of Ohio. *Education:* Southeastern College (B.A., cum laude, 1997); University of Cincinnati (J.D., 2000). Law Clerk to the Hon. David T. Evans, Fourth District Court of Appeals of Ohio, 2001-2004. ***LANGUAGES:*** Spanish. ***Email:*** htolhurst@millerkyler.com

REPRESENTATIVE CLIENTS: *Corporate:* Benchmark Construction; Hicks Roofing Co., Inc.; Marr, Knapp, Crawfis Associates, Inc.; Whitemyer Advertising, Inc.; L.J. Smith Co., Inc. *Financial:* National City Bank; Bank One, N.A.; The Commercial and Savings Bank; First Federal Savings Bank of Dover; The Huntington National Bank. *Healthcare:* Dover Orthopedic Surgeons; New Dawn Healthcare and Retirement Center; Union Hospital Association; Tuscarawas Valley Physical Therapy Clinic, Inc. *Insurance:* Gallagher Bassett Services, Inc. *Litigation:* Kimble Clay & Limestone Co.; American Electric Power. *Media:* WJER Radio, Inc. *Political Subdivision:* Muskingum Watershed Conservancy District; Tuscarawas County Port Authority; Tuscarawas County. *Real Estate:* McInturf Realty; Pissocra-Mathias Realty; Wallick Auction.
APPROVED ATTORNEYS AND AGENTS FOR: First American Title Insurance Co.; Ohio Bar Title Insurance; Old Republic National Title Insurance Company.

STEPHENSON, STEPHENSON & CARROTHERS

Established in 1887
P.O. BOX 992
NEW PHILADELPHIA, OHIO 44663-0992
Telephone: 330-339-6444
Fax: 330-339-6228
Email: lawyerssc@adelphia.net

General Civil Practice. Litigation, Appellate Practice, Business Law, Corporate Law, Hospital Law, Wills, Probate, Aged and Aging, Collections, Commercial Law, Construction Law, Consumer Law, Contacts, Eminent Domain, Environmental Law, Guardianship and Conservatorship, Insurance, Labor and Employment, Medicare and Medicaid, Nonprofit and Charitable Organizations, Personal Injury, Railroad Law, Zoning, Planning and Land Use, Mediation, Health Care, Trusts and Estate, Real Estate, Family Law.

MEMBERS OF FIRM

JAMES F. STEPHENSON (1863-1938)

ROBERT R. STEPHENSON (1897-1968)

JAMES R. STEPHENSON (1927-2003)

RICHARD L. STEPHENSON, born Cleveland, Ohio, October 19, 1933; admitted to bar, 1958, Ohio; 1966, U.S. Supreme Court and U.S. District Court, Northern District of Ohio. *Education:* Muskingum College (B.A., 1955); Ohio State University (J.D., 1958). *Member:* Bar Association of Tuscarawas County (President, 1966); Ohio State (Member, Solo-Small Firm General Practice Section; Board of Governors, 1982-2003; House of Delegates, 1972-1979; Executive Committee, 1979-1982) and American Bar Associations. ***PRACTICE AREAS:*** Business Law; Probate; Estate Planning; Real Estate; Zoning, Planning and Land Use; Mediation.

JAMES M. CARROTHERS, born Dennison, Ohio, October 20, 1946; admitted to bar, 1973, Ohio; 1975, U.S. District Court, Northern District of Ohio; 1993, U.S. Supreme Court. *Education:* University of Akron (B.S., 1968; J.D., 1973). *Member:* Tuscarawas County (President, 1979) and Ohio State (Member, Health Care Committee, 1985—) Bar Associations; American Academy of Hospital Attorneys; Ohio Society of Hospital Attor-

(This Listing Continued)

neys. **PRACTICE AREAS:** Litigation; Business Law; Health Care Law; Environmental Law; Probate; Trusts and Estates; Wills; Contracts; Commercial Law; Aged and Aging; Corporate Law; Labor and Employment; Nonprofit and Charitable Organizations; Real Estate; Railroad Law.

ROBERT R. STEPHENSON II, born Dover, Ohio, March 4, 1959; admitted to bar, 1986, Ohio; 1992, U.S. District Court, Northern District of Ohio and U.S. Court of Appeals, 6th Circuit; 1993, U.S. Supreme Court. *Education:* Ohio State University (B.S., 1982); University of Akron (J.D., 1986). *Member:* Tuscarawas County, The Ohio State and American Bar Associations; Ohio Academy of Trial Lawyers. **REPORTED CASES:** State v. Stowers (1998), 81 Ohio St. 3d 260, 690 N.E. 2d 881. **PRACTICE AREAS:** Litigation; Personal Injury; Real Estate; Family Law; Business Law; Trusts and Estates; Wills; Probate.

JAMES J. ONG, born Dennison, Ohio, February 23, 1971; admitted to bar, 1997, Ohio. *Education:* Hiram College (B.A., magna cum laude, 1993); University of Akron (J.D., cum laude, 1997). Phi Beta Kappa. *Member:* Tuscarawas County (President, 2003) and Ohio State Bar Associations. **PRACTICE AREAS:** Family Law; Business Law; Litigation; Appellate Practice; Collections; Corporate Law; Criminal Law; Education Law; Guardianship; Health Care; Insurance; Personal Injury; Probate; Trusts and Estates; Wills.

AGENTS FOR: Ohio Bar Title Insurance Company.

BAKER, DUBLIKAR, BECK, WILEY & MATHEWS

400 SOUTH MAIN STREET
NORTH CANTON, OHIO 44720
Telephone: 330-499-6000
Telecopier: 330-499-6423
URL: http://www.bakerfirm.com

General Civil Trial and Appellate Practice in all Courts. Insurance, Products Liability, Environmental, Malpractice, Political Subdivision, Real Estate, Corporate, Commercial and Family Law.

MEMBERS OF FIRM

JACK R. BAKER, born East Liverpool, Ohio, April 8, 1944; admitted to bar, 1969, Ohio. *Education:* Bowling Green University (B.A., 1966); University of Cincinnati (J.D., 1969). Phi Delta Phi; Omicron Delta Kappa. YMCA and Canton Civic Opera Boards of Trustees. *Member:* Stark County, Ohio State and American Bar Associations; Ohio Association of Civil Trial Attorneys; International Association of Insurance Counsel; Federation of Insurance and Corporate Counsel; Defense Research Institute. **PRACTICE AREAS:** Insurance Defense; Political Subdivisions; Medical Malpractice; Products Liability; Commercial Litigation; Civil Practice; General Practice. **Email:** baker@bakerfirm.com

RALPH F. DUBLIKAR, born Niles, Ohio, August 31, 1949; admitted to bar, 1974, Ohio. *Education:* Xavier University (A.B., 1971); University of Cincinnati (J.D., 1974). Author: Note, "Right to Speedy Trial, Ohio Follows the Trend," 43 University of Cincinnati Law Review 610, 1974. Clerk to U.S. District Judge Timothy S. Hogan, 1974-1976. *Member:* Stark County, Ohio State and American (Member, Torts and Insurance Practice Section) Bar Associations; American Judicature Society. **PRACTICE AREAS:** Insurance Defense; Adoptions; Health Care Litigation. **Email:** dublikar@bakerfirm.com

GREGORY A. BECK, born Akron, Ohio, February 15, 1956; admitted to bar, 1981, Ohio. *Education:* Virginia Military Institute (B.A., cum laude, 1978); University of Akron (J.D., 1981). Member, National Moot Court Team. *Member:* Stark County, Ohio State and American Bar Associations. [USAR, 1978-1986. Lt. Artillery Officer]. **PRACTICE AREAS:** Insurance Defense; Corporate; Commercial. **Email:** beck@bakerfirm.com

DONALD P. WILEY, born Wayne, Pennsylvania, June 25, 1959; admitted to bar, 1984, Ohio; 1986, U.S. District Court, Northern District of Ohio; 1987, U.S. Court of Appeals, 6th Circuit; 1993, Pennsylvania (inactive) and U.S. District Court, Southern District of Ohio. *Education:* Grove City College (B.A., 1981); University of Akron (J.D., cum laude, 1984). Phi Alpha Delta. Member, University of Akron Law Review, 1983-1984. Author: Comment, "Workers' Compensation in Ohio Scope of Employment and The Intentional Tort," 17 Akron L. Rev. 249, 1983. *Member:* Stark County, Columbus, Ohio State and American Bar Associations; Ohio Association of Civil Trial Attorneys; Defense Research Institute. **PRACTICE AREAS:** Political Subdivisions; Insurance Defense; Products Liability. **Email:** dwiley@bakerfirm.com

JAMES F. MATHEWS, born Alliance, Ohio, February 18, 1963; admitted to bar, 1988 Ohio and U.S. District Court, Northern District of Ohio; 1989, U.S. Court of Appeals, Sixth Circuit; 1996, U.S. Supreme Court. *Education:* Mount Union College (B.A., cum laude, 1985); Case Western Reserve University (J.D., cum laude, 1988). *Member:* Stark County, Ohio State and American Bar Associations; Ohio Association of Civil Trial Attorneys (Member, Environmental Law Committee); Defense Research Institute. **PRACTICE AREAS:** Environmental Law; Commercial Litigation; Insurance Coverage. **Email:** mathews@bakerfirm.com

MEL L. LUTE, JR., born Cincinnati, Ohio, July 6, 1965; admitted to bar, 1990, Ohio; 1991, U.S. District Court, Southern District of Ohio; 1993, U.S. District Court, Northern District of Ohio. *Education:* Miami University (B.A., 1987); University of Cincinnati (J.D., 1990). Phi Alpha Delta. Order of the Barristers. Member, Moot Court Board. *Member:* Stark County and Ohio State Bar Associations. **PRACTICE AREAS:** Insurance Defense; Municipal Liability; Criminal Law. **Email:** lute@bakerfirm.com

DANIEL J. FUNK, born Akron, Ohio, April 6, 1965; admitted to bar, 1994, Ohio. *Education:* Northwestern University (B.A., 1987); University of Akron (J.D., 1993). **PRACTICE AREAS:** Civil Litigation; Insurance. **Email:** funk@bakerfirm.com

JOHN B. LINDAMOOD, born Columbus, Ohio, January 18, 1941; admitted to bar, 1966, Ohio. *Education:* DePauw University (A.B., 1963); Case Western Reserve University (J.D., 1966). Phi Delta Phi. Member of Board, Western Reserve Law Review, 1965-1966. *Member:* Stark County (President, 1989-1990), Ohio State (Executive Committee, 1982-1985) and American Bar Associations; Defense Research Institute; Ohio Association of Civil Trial Attorneys. Fellow, Ohio State Bar Foundation. **Email:** johnb@bakerfirm.com

(This Listing Continued)

JAMES P. HANRATTY, born Willoughby, Ohio, March 19, 1964; admitted to bar, 1989, Ohio; 1990, Pennsylvania; 1995, West Virginia. *Education:* Walsh College (B.A., 1986); University of Akron (J.D., 1989). Member, National Moot Court Team, 1987. Author: "Discovery in a Slip/Trip and Fall Case," DACTA Quarterly Review, Vol. 33, No. 2, Spring 1998; "Brief of Amicus Curia," BACTA, Ross & Farmers Insurance Co. Speaker, Ohio Academy of Trial Lawyers' Insurance Law Seminar, 1992. Guest Speaker: University of Akron School of Law, Law Office Management, 1992 and 1995. *Member:* Stark County and Ohio State (Member: Young Lawyers Education Committee; Sports and Entertainment Law Committee) Bar Associations; Ohio Association of Civil Trial Attorneys; Defense Research Institute. [U.S. Army Reserve, 1981-1990]. **Email:** jimh@bakerfirm.com

KIMBERLY KAY WYSS, born Alliance, Ohio, April 10, 1967; admitted to bar, 1993, Ohio; U.S. District Court, Northern and Southern District of Ohio; U.S. Court of Appeals, Sixth Circuit. *Education:* University of Akron (B.A., 1990); Ohio Northern University (J.D., 1993). Phi Delta Phi. Associate Editor of Law Review; Moot Court Board of Advocates; Willis Society. *Member:* Stark County, Ohio State and American Bar Associations; Defense Research Institute; Ohio Association of Civil Trial Attorneys; National Association of Railroad Trial Counsel. **Email:** kimw@bakerfirm.com

ANTHONY E. BROWN, born Canton, Ohio, October 7, 1970; admitted to bar, 1998, Ohio, U.S. District Court, Northern District of Ohio and U.S. Tax Court. *Education:* Walsh College (B.A., 1995); University of Dayton (J.D., 1998). *Member:* Stark County and Ohio State Bar Associations. **PRACTICE AREAS:** Civil Practice; General Practice. **Email:** tonyb@bakerfirm.com

JUDE B. STREB, born Canton, Ohio, January 24, 1973; admitted to bar, 1999, Ohio; 2000, U.S. District Court, Northern District of Ohio. *Education:* University of Notre Dame (B.B.A., 1995); Case Western Reserve University (J.D., 1999). *Member:* Ohio State Bar Association. **PRACTICE AREAS:** Insurance Defense; Criminal Defense; Trusts and Estates. **Email:** judes@bakerfirm.com

ANDREA KAYE ZIARKO, born Washington, D.C., February 14, 1976; admitted to bar, 2001, Ohio. *Education:* Indiana University (B.S., 1998); The Ohio State University (J.D., 2001). *Member:* Stark County, Ohio State and American Bar Associations. **Email:** AndreaZ@bakerfirm.com

NIKI DOMENICK DI COLA, born Somerset, Pennsylvania, February 3, 1966; admitted to bar, 2003, Ohio. *Education:* Clarion University of Pennsylvania (B.A., 1988); University of Akron (J.D., 2003). *Member:* Ohio State Bar Association. **PRACTICE AREAS:** Insurance Defense (90%); Probate (3%); Real Estate (3%); Contracts (3%); Business Law (1%). **Email:** niki@bakerfirm.com

JUSTIN A. DUBLIKAR, born Canton, Ohio, June 16, 1977; admitted to bar, 2004, Ohio and U.S. District Court, Northern District of Ohio. *Education:* Marquette University (B.A., 1999); University of Cincinnati College of Law (J.D., 2002). Phi Alpha Theta National History Honor Society. Executive, Moot Court. *Member:* Stark County and Ohio State Bar Associations. **PRACTICE AREAS:** Insurance Defense (75%); Commercial Litigation (15%); Political Subdivision Liability (10%). **Email:** jdublikar@bakerfirm.com

REPRESENTATIVE CLIENTS: All Risk Claims Services, Inc.; Allstate Insurance Co.; American Family Insurance Co.; American Property & Casualty Co.; American States Insurance Co.; Auto-Owners Insurance Co.; Briggs & Stratton; Brotherhood Mutual Insurance Co.; Church Mutual Insurance Company; Cincinnati Insurance Co.; CNA Insurance Companies; Colonial Insurance Company of California; Continental Insurance Cos.; Erie Insurance Group; Grange Mutual Casualty Co.; Hamilton Mutual Insurance Co; Heritage Mutual Insurance Co.; Met Life Auto & Home; Motorists Mutual Insurance Co.; Nationwide Mutual Insurance Co.; Ohio Bar Liability Insurance Co.; Ohio Casualty Insurance Co.; Ohio Hospital Insurance Co.; Personal Service Insurance Co.; Progressive Insurance Companies; Prudential Property & Casualty Insurance Co.; Royal-Sun Alliance; Sieple Lithograph Co.; Speedway/Superamerica; State Farm Insurance Companies; Wayne Mutual Insurance Company.

STOURTON SCOTT SMITH CO., LPA

NORTH RIDGEVILLE, OHIO

(See Cleveland)

Criminal Law, DWI, Bankruptcy, Personal Injury, Divorce, Family Law.

THE SPIKE & MECKLER LAW FIRM, LLP

NORTH RIDGEVILLE, OHIO

(See Elyria)

General Civil Trial Practice. Personal Injury, Medical Malpractice, Family and Domestic Relations, Real Estate, Probate.

PARRISH, FRYMAN & MARCUM CO., L.P.A.

Established in 1932

5995 FAIRFIELD ROAD, UNIT ONE
OXFORD, OHIO 45056
Telephone: 513-863-8270
URL: http://www.parrishattys.com

Hamilton, Ohio Office: First National Bank Building, 300 High Street, Suite 704, P.O. Box 747, 45012-0747. Telephone: 513-863-8270. Telecopier: 513-863-9999.

Business, Real Estate, General Practice, Probate, Estate Planning and Banking Law.

LEE H. PARRISH, born Hamilton, Ohio, March 16, 1943; admitted to bar, 1968, Ohio. *Education:* Tulane University of Louisiana; The Ohio State University (B.A., 1965); University of Cincinnati (J.D., 1968). Order of the Coif. *Member:* Butler County, The Ohio State and American Bar Associations. **PRACTICE AREAS:** Probate; Estate Planning; Banking; Business.

CANNON, STERN, AVENI AND LOIACONO CO., L.P.A.

Established in 1975
MILBURN BUILDING
41 EAST ERIE STREET
PAINESVILLE, OHIO 44077-3983
Telephone: 440-357-5537;
Cleveland Direct Line: 440-942-5232
Telefax: 440-357-9234
URL: http://www.csalawgroup.com
Email: csal@csalawgroup.com
URL: http://www.csallaw.com

General Civil and Criminal Practice. Corporation, Small Business, Municipal, Family, Divorce, Probate, Trust and Estate Planning, Personal Injury, Environmental Law, Real Estate Law, Litigation and Medical Malpractice.

FIRM PROFILE: We are a firm of professionals whose goal is to provide excellent legal services to our clients for fair and reasonable compensation. We practice as a firm, not as individuals. Our goal is to be the best law firm possible, not necessarily the biggest or most profitable. In all matters, we shall undertake to represent each of our clients as we would want to be represented. We view our ultimate objectives as the rendering of service, and the making of profit is only a component, albeit an important component, in the pursuit of that objective.

WAYNE R. MILBURN (1910-1976)

CHARLES E. CANNON (Retired)

ANTHONY J. AVENI, born Cleveland, Ohio, August 1, 1938; admitted to bar, 1966, Ohio and U.S. District Court, Northern District of Ohio. *Education:* University of Notre Dame (B.S., 1961); Stanford University (M.S., 1962); Cleveland Marshall College of Law (J.D., 1966). Law Director: City of Eastlake, 1975; City of Mentor-on-the-Lake, 1983-1988. Assistant Law Director, City of Willowick, 2000—. Special Zoning Counsel, Village of Perry, 1999— Board Counsel to Lake County Association of Realtors, 1982—. Instructor of Real Estate Law, Lakeland Community College, 1970-2004. Member, Board of Directors, Western Reserve Counseling Service, 1973-2003. *Member:* Lake County (President, 1995-1996) and Ohio State (Member, Real Estate Board of Governors, 1984—) Bar Associations. ***PRACTICE AREAS:*** Real Estate Law; Probate Law; Alternative Dispute Resolution; Municipal Law; Zoning. **Email:** aaveni@csalawgroup.com

JAMES V. LOIACONO, born Cleveland, Ohio, August 9, 1953; admitted to bar, 1978, Ohio and U.S. District Court, Northern and Southern Districts of Ohio; U.S. Court of Appeals, Sixth Circuit. *Education:* St. Leo College (B.A., 1975); Ohio Northern University (J.D., 1978). Member, 1976-1978 and Associate Editor, 1977, Ohio Northern University Law Review. Magistrate, Painesville Municipal Court, 1984-1989, 1996— and Lake County Juvenile Court, 1999—. Solicitor, Village of North Perry, Ohio, 1990-1996. Law Director, City of Willowick, 2000—. Solicitor and Prosecutor: Village of Perry, 1998—; Solicitor and Prosecutor, Village of Fairport Harbor, 2000—. *Member:* Lake County, Ohio State and American Bar Associations; Ohio Academy of Trial Lawyers; Ohio Municipal Attorney's Association. ***PRACTICE AREAS:*** Personal Injury Law; Municipal Law; Zoning Law; Civil Litigation. **Email:** jloiacono@csalawgroup.com

TIMOTHY P. CANNON, born Painesville, Ohio, June 9, 1955; admitted to bar, 1980, Ohio and U.S. District Court, Northern District of Ohio; 1982, Florida. *Education:* John Carroll University (B.A., 1977); The Cleveland Marshall College of Law (J.D., 1980). Member: Board of Directors, First Merit Bank, 1997—; Lake County Board of Education, 1980-1994; Painesville City Prosecutor, 1989-1991; Lake County Joint Vocational School Board, 1980-1994; Board of Directors, Lake County Mental Health Center, 1980-1989; Painesville Township Board of Zoning Appeals, 1981-1985; Painesville Township Zoning Commission, 1986-1990; Leadership Lake County, 1987; Catholic Service Bureau Board of Trustees, 1980-1990. Trustee, Painesville Township, 1994-1997. Solicitor, Painesville Township, 1997—. *Member:* Lake County (Member, Executive Committee, 2001-2004; Chairman, Litigation Committee, 2003, 2004), Ohio State and American Bar Associations; The Florida Bar; Laketran Regional Transit Authority (General Counsel). ***PRACTICE AREAS:*** Personal Injury Law; Municipal Law; Insurance Law; Probate; Corporate; Business Law; Trusts and Estates; Zoning Law. **Email:** tcannon@csalawgroup.com

NICHOLAS A. D'ANGELO, born Cleveland, Ohio, February 23, 1962; admitted to bar, 1987, Ohio and U.S. District Court, Northern District of Ohio. *Education:* John Carroll University (B.A., cum laude, 1984); University of Akron (J.D., 1987). Member, Leadership Lake County, 1992. Civil Magistrate, Painesville Municipal Court.*Member:* Lake County and Ohio State Bar Associations; Ohio Academy of Trial Lawyers. ***PRACTICE AREAS:*** Personal Injury Law; Domestic Relations Law; Civil Litigation. **Email:** ndangelo@csalawgroup.com

PAUL R. MALCHESKY, born Cleveland, Ohio, August 19, 1972; admitted to bar, 1997, Ohio. *Education:* Ohio University; Cleveland State University (B.A., magna cum laude, 1994); Cleveland Marshall College of Law (J.D., 1997). Golden Key National Honor Society. Recipient, Dean's Scholarship. Acting Judge, Painesville Municipal Court, 2004—. Riverside High School Mock Trial Advisor, 2001—. *Member:* Lake County and Ohio State Bar Associations. ***PRACTICE AREAS:*** Criminal Law; Juvenile Law; Real Estate; Personal Injury Law; Contract Law. **Email:** pmalchesky@csalawgroup.com

---

BENJAMIN L. AVENI, born Cleveland, Ohio, January 10, 1967; admitted to bar, 1992, Florida; 1993, U.S. District Court, Southern District of Florida; 2003, Ohio. *Education:* Southern Methodist University (B.A., 1989); Cleveland Marshall College of Law (J.D., 1992); University of Miami (LL.M. in Real Estate Finance and Development, 1993). Member, Cleveland Marshall Law Review, 1991-1992. *Member:* Lake County, Ohio State and American Bar Associations; The Florida Bar. ***LANGUAGES:*** Spanish. ***PRACTICE AREAS:*** Real Estate; Title Insurance; General Practice; Trusts and Estates; Zoning, Planning and Land Use. **Email:** baveni@caslawgroup.com

(This Listing Continued)

GINA M. BEVACK, born Cleveland, Ohio, April 26, 1978; admitted to bar, 2003, Ohio. *Education:* John Carroll University (B.A., 2000); Cleveland-Marshall College of Law (J.D., 2003). *Member:* Lake County and Ohio State Bar Associations. ***PRACTICE AREAS:*** Probate Law; Corporate Law; Contracts; Business Law; Trusts and Estates. **Email:** gbevack@csalawgroup.com

COUNSEL FOR: Cianfaglione Builders, Inc.; Commercial Siding & Maintenance Co.; Hellrigel's Inn; Painesville Dental Group; Eye-Will Development, Inc.; Hamann Construction Co.; Equity Properties & Development Co.; Lavndero & Associates, Inc.; Falvey Realty, Inc.; Bingo Scene, Inc.; Hattendorf & Bliss, Inc.; H. D. Development Co.; Naughton Builders, Inc.; Ralph Victor Construction Co., Inc.; Farin Industries; Sunleaf Nursery; 20th Century Construction Co.; Noce Development, LLC; Harbor Credit Union; Painesville City Employees Credit Union; DDD Enterprises, Inc.; Yoe Nurseries; Walker Bros. Roofing C.; Malkamaki Builders, Inc.; Euclid Machine Co.; Lake County Association of Realtors; Little Mountain Builders, Inc.; WWA Properties, LLC; Homeowners Marketing Services; McCullough Builders, Inc.; Angeloro Construction Co.; Santee Security Co.; First Merit; Commonwealth Land Title Agency; David Knott Construction, Inc.; Knez Builders, Inc.; CDT Development, Inc.; Mrowca Realty, Inc.; JSK Inc.; Hovach Enterprise, Inc.; KOVCO, Inc.; Chemsultants International, Inc.; Quartz Scientific, Inc.; Cometic Gasket; Laketran Regional Transit Authority; Norris Garden Center, K & D Group, Inc.; Stephen M. Tokane Custom Floral & Design.
REFERENCE: First Merit Bank, N.A.

COOPER & FORBES

MAIN STREET LAW BUILDING
166 MAIN STREET
PAINESVILLE, OHIO 44077
Telephone: 440-357-6211
Cleveland Direct: 942-9027
Fax: 440-357-1634
Email: cooperandforbes@prodigy.net
URL: http://www.cooperandforbes.lawoffice.com

Commercial and Retail Collections, Commercial Law, Bankruptcy, Domestic Relations, Chapter 11, Debtors Rights, General Civil Trial Practice, Creditors Rights. Trials and Appeals in all Courts.

FIRM PROFILE: At Cooper & Forbes we are dedicated to providing high quality legal service at a reasonable cost. It is our goal to help clients attain their legal objectives. It is our policy to counsel our clients regarding the probability of obtaining their legal objectives and balancing the cost of our services against that probability.

GLENN E. FORBES, born Syracuse, New York, March 23, 1953; admitted to bar, 1979, Ohio, U.S. District Court, Northern District of Ohio, U.S. Court of Appeals, Sixth Circuit and U.S. Supreme Court. *Education:* College of Wooster (B.A., 1976); Case Western Reserve University (J.D., 1979). Instructor, Paralegal Program: Lakeland Community College; Lake Erie College. *Member:* Lake County (Member, Litigation Section), Ohio State and American (Member, Economics of Law Practice Section) Bar Associations. ***REPORTED CASES:*** Alside Supply Co. vs. Wager, 89 Ohio App. 3d 359 (1993); Ohio Department of Taxation v. Plickert, 128 Ohio App.3d 445 (1998); CMC Elec., Inc. v. OSHA, U.S. Dept. of Labor 221 F 3d 861 (2000). ***PRACTICE AREAS:*** Business Law; Contract Law; Litigation; Bankruptcy; Corporate Law; Collections. **Email:** gforbes@cooperandforbes.com

LINDA D. COOPER, admitted to bar, 1978, Ohio, U.S. District Court, Northern District of Ohio and U.S. Supreme Court. *Education:* Eastern Kentucky University (B.S., with honors, 1975); Cleveland Marshall College of Law, Cleveland State University (J.D., 1977). Member, Willoughby City Council, 1984-1986. *Member:* Cleveland, Lake County, Geauga County, Lake County (President, 2000-2001) and Ohio State Bar Associations. (Certified Specialist in Family Relations Law, Ohio State Bar Association). ***PRACTICE AREAS:*** Domestic Relations; Family Law; Divorce; Child Custody; Adoption Law; Guardianship; General Practice. **Email:** lcooper@cooperandforbes.com

ASSOCIATE

PAUL EUGENE MILLER, born 1965; admitted to bar, 1997, Ohio. *Education:* Kent State University (B.A., 1988); Cleveland-Marshall College of Law (J.D., 1997). *Member:* Lake County Bar Association (Chair, Criminal Law Committee; Member, Certified Grievance Committee); Ohio Association of Criminal Defense Lawyers. ***PRACTICE AREAS:*** Criminal Law; Family Law; Collections. **Email:** pmiller@cooperandforbes.com

---

MARK GARDNER
ATTORNEY AND COUNSELOR AT LAW

PAINESVILLE, OHIO

(See Cleveland)

Criminal Law, Driving While Intoxicated, Traffic Violations, Personal Injury, Wrongful Death, Negligence, Slip and Fall, Small Business Law, Litigation.

KLEIN & CARNEY CO., L.P.A.

PAINESVILLE, OHIO

(See Cleveland)

Personal Injury, Medical Malpractice, Insurance Law, Wrongful Death, Motor Vehicle Accidents, Nursing Home Negligence, Workers Compensation.

KNEVEL & ASSOCIATES CO. LPA

PAINESVILLE, OHIO

(See Cleveland)

Bankruptcy.

THEODORE M. MANN, JR. LAW FIRM

PAINESVILLE, OHIO

(See Cleveland)

Alternative Dispute Resolution, Mediation, Appellate Practice, Business Law, Business Litigation, Contracts, Corporate Law, Elder Law, Franchises and Franchising, Fraud, General Practice, Labor and Employment, Litigation, Negligence, Personal Injury, Probate, Real Estate, Real Estate Litigation, Residential Real Estate, Torts, Trade Secrets Trusts and Estates, Estate Planning, Trust Administration, Wills.

HEATHER L. MOSEMAN, ESQ., L.L.C.

P.O. BOX 730
PAINESVILLE, OHIO 44077
Telephone: 440-350-4779
Fax: 440-350-4613
Email: mosemanlaw@yahoo.com
URL: http://www.lawyers.com/mosemanlaw

Estate Planning, Probate, Civil Litigation, General Practice, Bankruptcy.

HEATHER L. MOSEMAN, born Lincoln, Nebraska, October 18, 1970; admitted to bar, 2003, Ohio and U.S. District Court, Northern District of Ohio. *Education:* Southwest State University (B.A., 1993); University of Akron School of Law (J.D., 2003). Phi Alpha Delta (Member, Justice of Grant Chapter, 2002-2003). *Member:* Akron, Lake County, Cleveland, Ohio State and American Bar Associations. ***LANGUAGES:*** Swedish. ***PRACTICE AREAS:*** Estate Planning; Bankruptcy; Corporate Law; Civil Litigation; Guardianship.

LAW OFFICES OF LESTER S. POTASH

PAINESVILLE, OHIO

(See Cleveland)

General Practice, Social Security, Personal Injury, Automobile Accidents, Criminal Law, Drunk Driving, Probate, Litigation, Medical Malpractice, Legal Malpractice.

SHRYOCK & MORRISON

PAINESVILLE, OHIO

(See Wickliffe)

Family Law, Domestic Relations, Mediation, Juvenile Law, Criminal Law, Traffic Violations, Personal Injury.

STERNBERG & ZEID CO., L.P.A.

PAINESVILLE, OHIO

(See Mentor)

Personal Injury, Automobile Accidents, Wrongful Death, Workers Compensation, Municipal Law, Zoning Law, Bankruptcy, Domestic Relations, Family Law, Divorce, Child Custody, Guardianship, Real Estate, Probate, Estate Planning, Trusts and Wills, Business, Corporate, Contract Law, General Civil Trial Practice in State and Federal Courts.

SVETE, McGEE & CARRABINE CO., L.P.A.

PAINESVILLE, OHIO

(See Chardon)

Insurance Defense, Personal Injury, Products Liability, Professional Malpractice, Commercial, Governmental Construction and General Negligence Litigation, Automobile Accidents, Wrongful Death, Medical Negligence, Real Estate and Zoning, Contracts, Deeds, Easements, Leases, Family Law, Divorce, Dissolution, Child Custody and Support, Paternity, Adoption, Child Abuse and Neglect, Criminal Defense, Felonies, Misdemeanors, Juvenile and Traffic Offenses, D.U.I., Wills, Probate, Estate Planning, Elder Law, Trusts, Powers of Attorney, Living Wills, Guardianships, Asset Preservation, Medicare/Medicaid Planning, Litigation, Corporate and Business Law, Partnerships, Limited Liability Companies, Buying and Selling of a Business.

MICHAEL E. BENSON

PATASKALA, OHIO

(See Columbus)

Bankruptcy Law, Foreclosures, Debtor and Creditor, Real Estate, Landlord and Tenant, Buying and Selling, Wills, Living Wills, Healthcare, Powers of Attorney.

COLLEY SHROYER & ABRAHAM CO., L.P.A.

PATASKALA, OHIO

(See Columbus)

Civil Trial Practice. Personal Injury, Medical Malpractice, Automobile Accidents, Wrongful Death, Railroad Accidents, Slip and Fall, Negligence, Product Liability and Toxic Torts.

SUSAN KENNEY-PFALZER

PATASKALA, OHIO

(See Columbus)

Family Law, Divorce, Dissolution, Child Custody, Spousal and Child Support, Visitation Rights, Adoptions, Paternity, Juvenile Law, Collaborative Law, Restraining Orders.

AGGERS, JOSEPH & CHEVERINE CO., L.P.A.

PEPPER PIKE, OHIO

(See Cleveland)

Business Law, Commercial, Admiralty and Maritime, Environmental, Contracts, Corporate, Employment Law, Construction Law, Wills, Probate, Real Estate, State and Federal Litigation.

ROSEMARY GRDINA GOLD

33000 PINE TREE ROAD
PEPPER PIKE, OHIO 44124
Telephone: 216-593-0001
Fax: 216-591-1514
Email: rggoldlaw@adelphia.net

Downtown Cleveland Office: 1140 Leader Building, 526 Superior Ave. E., Cleveland, OH 44114. Telephone: 216-696-6122.

Family Law, Civil Litigation, Divorce, and Appellate Practice.

ROSEMARY GRDINA GOLD, born Cleveland, Ohio, August 30, 1948; admitted to bar, 1982, Ohio. *Education:* Notre Dame College (B.A., magna cum laude, 1979); Cleveland State University (J.D., cum laude, 1982). *Member:* Cuyahoga County (Member, Family Law Section), Cleveland and Ohio State Bar Associations; Ohio Women's Bar Association; The Center for Principled Family Advocacy. ***PRACTICE AREAS:*** Family Law; Alimony; Collaborative Family Law; Divorce; Premarital Agreements; Post Divorce Modification; Civil Litigation; Federal Civil Litigation; Civil Appeals.

KARBERG, KURANT, WACHTER & TURNER CO., L.P.A.

PEPPER PIKE, OHIO

(See Cleveland)

Business and Corporate, Mergers and Acquisition, Employment Litigation, Real Estate, Taxation, Probate, Estate Planning, Litigation in all Courts.

MARGULIES & LEVINSON LLP

30100 CHAGRIN BOULEVARD
SUITE 250
PEPPER PIKE, OHIO 44124
Telephone: 216-514-5997
Fax: 216-514-5996
URL: http://www.ml-legal.com

Business Reorganization, Creditors' Rights, Public and Private Securities, Mergers and Acquisitions, E-Commerce, Computer Licensing, Technology Agreements, Business Law, Emerging Growth Companies.

JAMES W. MARGULIES, born New York, New York, June 8, 1964; admitted to bar, 1994, New York and Ohio. *Education:* The Ohio State University (B.S., 1986); Cleveland State University (M.B.A., 1990); Rutgers University-Newark (J.D., 1993). ***PRACTICE AREAS:*** Securities; Mergers and Acquisitions; Computer Law; Technology Law; Business Law; Emerging Growth Companies. ***Email:*** jwm@ml-legal.com

JEFFREY M. LEVINSON, born Chicago, Illinois, March 4, 1960; admitted to bar, 1990, Ohio. *Education:* University of Chicago; Northwestern University (B.S., 1987); Case Western Reserve University (J.D., cum laude, 1990). *Member:* Cleveland Bar Association (Chairman, 2004-2005, Bankruptcy and Commercial Law Section); American Bankruptcy Institute. ***PRACTICE AREAS:*** Bankruptcy; Insolvency; Creditors Rights. ***Email:*** jml@ml-legal.com

---

LEAH M. CAPLAN, born Cleveland, Ohio, December 30, 1960; admitted to bar, 1986, Ohio. *Education:* Northwestern University (B.A., 1982); Harvard University Law School (J.D., cum laude, 1986). *Member:* Cleveland Bar Association. ***PRACTICE AREAS:*** Employment Law; Corporate Law; Bankruptcy. ***Email:*** lmc@ml-legal.com

ALISA K. KHOURY, born St. Petersburg, Russia, November 8, 1971; admitted to bar, 1999, Ohio. *Education:* Case Western Reserve University (B.A., magna cum laude, 1995; J.D., cum laude, 1998). *Member:* Cleveland, Ohio State and American Bar Associations. ***PRACTICE AREAS:*** Securities Regulation; Corporate Law; Mergers and Acquisitions. ***Email:*** akk@ml-legal.com

EASTMAN & SMITH LTD.

PERRYSBURG, OHIO

(See Toledo)

General Civil Practice: Corporate, Business, Banking, Taxation, Real Estate, Securities, Antitrust, Environmental, Public, Labor and Employment, Civil Rights, Employee Benefits, Insurance, Hospital and Health Care, Estate Planning, Pension and Estate Planning, Probate, Workers Compensation, Commercial Litigation, Litigation, Immigration and Naturalization.

FRASER MARTIN BUCHANAN MILLER LLC

132 WEST SECOND STREET
PERRYSBURG, OHIO 43551-1401
Telephone: 419-874-1100
Fax: 419-874-1130
Email: firm@fmbmlaw.com

Patent Prosecution, Intellectual Property Transactions, Intellectual Property Litigation, Trademarks.

DONALD R. FRASER, born Toledo, Ohio, May 21, 1927; admitted to bar, 1957, District of Columbia; 1958, U.S. Court of Appeals for the District of Columbia Circuit; 1963, Ohio; registered to practice before U.S. Patent and Trademark Office. *Education:* The Ohio State University; University of Toledo (B.S., 1952); George Washington University (J.D., 1954). Assistant Solicitor, Patents, U.S. Department of the Interior, 1975-1976. Member, Ohio General Assembly, 1968-1972. ***PRACTICE AREAS:*** Intellectual Property. ***Email:*** Fraser@fmbmlaw.com

RICHARD G. MARTIN, born Honolulu, Hawaii, October 8, 1950; admitted to bar, 1981, Minnesota; 1990, Ohio and U.S. District Court, Northern District of Ohio; U.S. District Court, District of Minnesota and U.S. District Court, District of Hawaii. *Education:* Macalester College (B.A., 1975); William Mitchell College of Law (J.D., 1981). ***PRACTICE AREAS:*** Intellectual Property. ***Email:*** martin@fmbmlaw.com

J. MATTHEW BUCHANAN, born Toledo, Ohio, December 31, 1969; admitted to bar, 2000, Michigan and U.S. District Court, Eastern District of Michigan; registered to practice before U.S. Patent and Trademark Office (Not admitted in Ohio). *Education:* The Ohio State University (B.S., 1992); The Medical College of Ohio (M.S., 1996); University of Toledo (J.D., cum laude, 2000). Member, 1998-1999, Editor, 1999-2000, University of Toledo Law Review. Author: "Medical Device Patent Rights in The Age of FDA Modernization: The Potential Effect of Regulatory Streamlining on the Right to Exclude," University of Toledo Law Review, Winter, 1999. ***PRACTICE AREAS:*** Patent Prosecution; Intellectual Property Transactions; Intellectual Property Litigation; Trademarks. ***Email:*** buchanan@fmbmlaw.com

JAMES D. MILLER, born Mount Vernon, Ohio, October 14, 1964; admitted to bar, 2000, Ohio, U.S. District Court, Northern District of Ohio; registered to practice before U.S. Patent and Trademark Office. *Education:* University of Toledo (B.S.M.E., 1990; J.D., cum laude, 1999). Registered Professional Engineer, Ohio. ***PRACTICE AREAS:*** Intellectual Property. ***Email:*** miller@fmbmlaw.com

---

DUNGAN & LeFEVRE

A LEGAL PROFESSIONAL ASSOCIATION
111 WEST ASH STREET
P.O. BOX 1529
PIQUA, OHIO 45356
Telephone: 937-773-8054
Fax: 937-773-3379
Email: mail@dungan-lefevre.com
URL: http://www.dungan-lefevre.com

Troy, Ohio Office: 210 West Main Street. Telephone: 937-339-0511. Fax: 937-335-5802.

General Civil and Criminal Trial Practice, including Personal Injury, Wrongful Death, Medical Malpractice, Products Liability, Insurance Defense, Wrongful Discharge Defense, Business Law and Commercial Litigation in all Courts, Real Estate, Condominium, Banking, Insurance, Corporate and Business, Wills and Probate, Trusts and Estates, Estate Planning, Family and Domestic Relations, Driving While Intoxicated, Tax, Bankruptcy, Municipal, Zoning and Planning and Collection Law. Appeals in all Courts.

(For complete biographical data on all personnel, see Professional Biographies at Troy, Ohio)

McCULLOCH, FELGER, FITE & GUTMANN CO., L.P.A.

Established in 1895
FIFTH THIRD BANK BUILDING
123 MARKET STREET, SECOND FLOOR
P.O. DRAWER 910
PIQUA, OHIO 45356
Telephone: 937-773-3212
Fax: 937-773-9672; 937-773-4022
Email: mffg@wesnet.com

General Civil Practice. Corporation, Insurance, Taxation, Labor and Employment, Trust and Estate Administration, Estate Planning, Commercial, Real Estate, Pension and Profit Sharing, Family and Domestic Relations, Personal Injury Law, Litigation and Civil Trials.

FIRM PROFILE: The law firm of McCulloch, Felger, Fite & Gutmann Co., L.P.A. traces its origin to 1895, when local attorneys D.S. Lindsey and J. Harrison Smith united their law practices. Longtime senior partner, the late William M. McCulloch, served a distinguished 25 years in the United States House of Representatives and was instrumental in the passage of the Civil Rights Act of 1964. The firm presently consists of seven attorneys and an eleven member support staff and conducts a full service general practice of law. McCulloch, Felger, Fite & Gutmann represents many of the area's leading businesses, financial institutions and individuals in banking, commerce, real estate, estate planning, estate and trust administration and litigation, and has substantial practices in the areas of insurance defense, personal injury and family law. Its broad base of experience and expertise enables the firm to provide comprehensive legal services effectively and economically.

(This Listing Continued)

WILLIAM M. McCULLOCH (1901-1980)

CARL B. FELGER (1900-1984)

ROBERT P. FITE (1920-2000)

PAUL P. GUTMANN (Retired)

WILLIAM B. McNEIL, born DuBois, Pennsylvania, January 14, 1940; admitted to bar, 1964, Ohio; 1991, U.S. Tax Court; 1993, U.S. Court of Appeals, Sixth Circuit. *Education:* Pennsylvania State University (B.S., cum laude, 1961); Harvard Law School (J.D., 1964). Editorial Advisory Board, Banks Baldwin, Probate Law Journal of Ohio, 1990—. Member, 1972-1983 and President, 1977-1980, Piqua Board of Education. Listed in Best Lawyers in America, 1999-2006. *Member:* Miami County (President, 1976), Ohio State (Member: Board of Governors, Estate Planning, Trust and Probate Law Section, 1985—; Chairman, 1997-1999) and American Bar Associations. Fellow, American College of Trust and Estate Counsel; Fellow, Ohio State Bar Foundation. (Certified Specialist in Estate Planning, Trust and Probate Law, Ohio State Bar Association). ***PRACTICE AREAS:*** Estate Planning; Trusts and Estates; Pension and Profit Sharing; Probate; Estate and Gift Taxation. ***Email:*** w-mcneil@mffg.net

JACK L. NEUENSCHWANDER, born Bluffton, Ohio, January 26, 1942; admitted to bar, 1967, Ohio; 1980, U.S. District Court, Southern District of Ohio; 1989, U.S. Court of Appeals, Sixth Circuit. *Education:* Harvard University (B.A., cum laude, 1964); University of Michigan (J.D., 1967). *Member:* Miami County (President, 1979) and Ohio State (Member, Insurance Law Committee, 1985—; Chairman, 1998-2000; Member, Negligence Law Committee, 1985—; Member, Litigation Section, 1998—) Bar Associations. Fellow, Ohio State Bar Foundation. ***PRACTICE AREAS:*** Litigation; Personal Injury Law; Insurance Law; Corporate; Trusts and Estates. ***Email:*** j-neuenschwander@mffg.net

DALE G. DAVIS, born Akron, Ohio, March 6, 1951; admitted to bar, 1976, Ohio; 1981, U.S. District Court, Southern District of Ohio. *Education:* Duke University (B.A., magna cum laude, 1973); Georgetown University Law Center (J.D., 1976). *Member:* Miami County (President, 1990) and Ohio State Bar Associations. ***PRACTICE AREAS:*** Real Estate Law; Commercial Law; Labor and Employment Law; Corporate Law; Creditors Rights Law. ***Email:*** d-davis@mffg.net

MICHAEL E. GUTMANN, born Piqua, Ohio, April 14, 1959; admitted to bar, 1984, Ohio; 1985, U.S. District Court, Southern District of Ohio. *Education:* Miami University (B.S., 1981); University of Cincinnati (J.D., 1984). Recipient, Bar Foundation Award for Community Service, Ohio State Bar Association, 1997. Solicitor, Village of Bradford, 1987—. *Member:* Miami County (President, 1996), Ohio State and American Bar Associations. ***PRACTICE AREAS:*** Corporate Law; Real Estate Law; Estate Planning; Trusts; Probate; Personal Injury Law; Workers Compensation. ***Email:*** m-gutmann@mffg.net

DANIEL E. RAMER, born Dayton, Ohio, November 2, 1953; admitted to bar, 1978, Michigan; 1979, Ohio. *Education:* University of Miami (B.A., magna cum laude, 1975); The Ohio State University (J.D., 1978). *Member:* Miami County (President, 1987), Ohio State (Member, Board of Governors, Estate Planning, Trust and Probate Law Section, 1998—) and American Bar Associations. ***PRACTICE AREAS:*** Estates and Trusts; Estate Planning Law; Domestic Relations Law; Real Estate Law; Corporate Law; Commercial Law. ***Email:*** d-ramer@mffg.net

FRANK J. PATRIZIO, born Bristol, Pennsylvania, October 29, 1966; admitted to bar, 1991, Ohio. *Education:* University of Dayton (B.S., 1988); Ohio State University (J.D., 1991). *Member:* Miami County and Ohio State Bar Associations. ***PRACTICE AREAS:*** General Civil Practice; Real Estate Law; Estate Planning; Trust Law; Probate; Adoption Law; Collections; Family/Domestic Relations Law; Personal Injury Law; Corporate Law. ***Email:*** f-patrizio@mffg.net

---

LAURA HORNISH-SCHLOSSER, born Bryan, Ohio, September 24, 1974; admitted to bar, 2000, Ohio. *Education:* Adrian College (B.A., 1997); University of Toledo (J.D., 2000). *Member:* Miami County and Ohio State Bar Associations. ***PRACTICE AREAS:*** Domestic Relations; Traffic Violations; Children; Collections; Real Estate; Alternative Dispute Resolution. ***Email:*** l-hornish@mffg.net

GENERAL COUNSEL FOR: French Oil Mill Machinery Co.; Hartzell Industries, Inc.; Pioneer Rural Electric Co-op; Little Printing Co.; Dan Hemm Auto Group; Lavy Concrete Construction, Inc.; Proto Mold Products, Inc.; A.M. Leonard, Inc.; Piqua Emery Cutter and Foundry, Co.; Piqua Champion Foundry, Inc.; Tri-County Board of Recovery and Mental Health Services; Finfrock Construction Co., Inc.; Piqua Concrete Co.; Midwest Plastic System, Inc.; Gover Harley-Davidson, Inc.; Dick Lumpkin Auto Body, Inc.
ATTORNEYS FOR: Fifth Third Bank, Western Ohio; Unity National Bank; Piqua Transfer & Storage Co.; General Films, Inc.; Hartzell Propeller Inc.; Upper Valley Professional Park Development Corp.; Crane Pumps & Systems, Inc.; Piqua Family Practice, Inc.; Miami County Surgeons, Inc.
APPROVED ATTORNEYS FOR: The Ohio Bar Title Insurance Co. (Agent); Lawyers Title Insurance Corp.

MILLER & LURING

PIQUA, OHIO

(See Troy)

General and Trial Practice, Collections, Estate Planning, Bankruptcy, Personal Injury, Civil, Family/Domestic Relations, Corporation, Negligence, Tax, Municipal, Probate and Real Estate.

RICHARD M. LEWIS

POMEROY, OHIO

(See Jackson)

General Trial and Appellate Practice, Tort Law, Insurance Law, Medical Negligence, Employment Law, Personal Injury, Commercial Litigation, Domestic Relations, Corporation, Real Estate, Probate and Banking Law, Debtor-Creditor and Criminal Law.

FLYNN, PY & KRUSE

A LEGAL PROFESSIONAL ASSOCIATION
115 WEST PERRY STREET
PORT CLINTON, OHIO 43452
Telephone: 419-734-3174
Fax: 419-734-3175

Sandusky, Ohio Office: 165 East Washington Row. Telephone: 419-625-8324. Fax: 419-625-9007.

General Civil Practice. Corporation, Banking, Antitrust, Labor and Employment, Taxation, Insurance, Personal Injury, Workers Compensation, Environmental Law, Probate and Estate Planning, Commercial Litigation, Pension and Profit Sharing, Employee Benefits, Real Estate. Trials and Appeals in State and Federal Courts.

JOHN A. COPPELER, born Toledo, Ohio, June 2, 1947; admitted to bar, 1975, Ohio; 1976, U.S. District Court, Northern District of Ohio; 1984, U.S. Court of Appeals, Sixth Circuit. *Education:* The Ohio State University (B.A. in Journalism, 1970; J.D., cum laude, 1974). Phi Delta Phi. *Member:* Erie County, Ottawa County, Ohio State (Member, Litigation, Labor and Employment, and Real Property Law Sections) and American (Member, Litigation, Labor and Employment Law, and Real Property, Probate and Trust Sections) Bar Associations. ***REPORTED CASES:*** Supreme Court Cases Only: Hacker v. Dickman (1996), 75 Ohio St.3d 118; Berger v. Port Clinton (1994), 71 Ohio St.3d 1213; Manufacturer's Natl. Bank of Detroit v. Erie Cty. Road Comm. (1992), 63 Ohio St.3d 318; Gressman v. McClain (1988), 40 Ohio St.3d 359; Carney v. McAfee (1988), 35 Ohio St.3d 52; Yurista v. Nationwide Mut. Ins. Co. (1985), 18 Ohio St.3d 326; Noroski v. Fallett (1982), 2 Ohio St.3d 77; Warner v. Lindley (1982), 70 Ohio St.2d 273. ***PRACTICE AREAS:*** Personal Injury Law; Trial Practice; Business Law; Labor and Employment Law; Banking Law; Zoning and Real Estate; Township Law.

(For complete biographical data on all personnel, see Professional Biographies at Sandusky, Ohio)

KOCHER & GILLUM

101 1/2 MADISON STREET
PORT CLINTON, OHIO 43452
Telephone: 419-732-3135
Fax: 419-734-5644
Email: catherine@kochergillum.com
URL: http://www.kochergillum.com

Real Estate, Business Transactions, General Civil Litigation, Probate, Estate Planning, Construction Law.

MEMBERS OF FIRM

JOHN A. KOCHER, born Newark, Ohio, June 17, 1942; admitted to bar, 1974, Ohio. *Education:* Purdue University (B.S.C.E., 1965); Valparaiso University (J.D., 1974). Manager, Owens Corning Fiberglas, 1968-1971. *Member:* Ottawa County (President, 1978), Ohio State and American Bar Associations. [1st Lt., U.S. Army. 1965-1967]. ***PRACTICE AREAS:*** Real Estate; Business Law; Wills; Trusts and Estates. ***Email:*** john@kochergillum.com

RICHARD R. GILLUM, III, born Newport Beach, California, November 11, 1972; admitted to bar, 1998, Ohio; 2000, U.S. District Court, Northern District of Ohio. *Education:* Ohio University (B.A., 1995); The Ohio State University (J.D., 1998). Solicitor, Village of Put in Bay, Ohio, 1998—. *Member:* Ottawa County (President, 2003; Vice President, 2002), Ohio State and American Bar Associations. ***PRACTICE AREAS:*** Civil Litigation; Real Estate; Divorce; Municipal Law; Criminal Defense. ***Email:*** rich@kochergillum.com

CATHERINE EDWARDS HEIGEL, born Florence, South Carolina, July 16, 1970; admitted to bar, 1996, South Carolina and North Carolina; 1997, Georgia; 2003, Ohio. *Education:* University of South Carolina (B.A., magna cum laude, 1992); University of Amsterdam; The Ohio State University College of Law (J.D., 1995). Phi Beta Kappa. Associate Editor, The Ohio State Law Journal, 1993-1995. Author: "The Banking-Insurance War in Search of a Judicial Truce," Ohio St. L. J. Vol. 55, No. 4. Senior Counsel, Duke Energy Corporation, 1997-2002. Attorney, South Carolina Department Consumer Affairs, 1995-1996. *Member:* Ottawa County, Ohio State, North Carolina and American Bar Associations. ***PRACTICE AREAS:*** Corporate Law; Real Estate; Construction Law; Employment Law. ***Email:*** catherine@kochergillum.com

JAMES C. BARNEY, born Sandusky, Ohio, December 1, 1962; admitted to bar, 1994, Ohio; 1999, U.S. District Court, Northern District of Ohio. *Education:* University of Texas at El Paso (B.B.A. in Finance, 1990); University of Toledo (J.D., 1994). *Member:* Erie County, Ottawa County and Ohio State Bar Associations. ***PRACTICE AREAS:*** Personal Injury Law; Trial Practice; Business Law; Real Estate Law; Criminal Law; Municipal Law.

BANNON, HOWLAND & DEVER CO., L.P.A.

A LEGAL PROFESSIONAL ASSOCIATION
Established in 1827
602 CHILLICOTHE STREET, SUITE 325
P.O. BOX 1384
PORTSMOUTH, OHIO 45662-1384
Telephone: 740-353-1157
Fax: 740-353-6237
Email: bhad@bhadlaw.com

Insurance Defense, Medical Malpractice, Personal Injury, Probate, Estate Planning, Real Estate, Hospital Law, Banking, Worker's Compensation.

(This Listing Continued)

FIRM PROFILE: Bannon, Howland and Dever Co., L.P.A., was founded in 1827 by William Virgil Peck, Ohio Supreme Court Judge from 1859-1865. The firm has been practicing law for 178 years and is recognized as the first established law firm in Ohio. The firm continues to represent local and surrounding communities with an expansive range of legal services and expertise. All members of the firm are active in civic affairs and continue their professional development through participation and attendance at various seminars and professional activities.

HENRY T. BANNON (1867-1950)

LOUIS D. BANNON (1899-1991)

WILLIAM LEE HOWLAND (1916-2000)

ROBERT E. DEVER, born Portsmouth, Ohio, September 18, 1931; admitted to bar, 1956, Ohio. *Education:* Ohio University; Denison University; New York University (J.D., 1956). Phi Alpha Delta. Member, University of Cincinnati Law Review, 1953-1954. Assistant Prosecuting Attorney, Scioto County, Ohio, 1957-1967. Member of the Board, Ohio Health, 1984—. Chairman of the Board, Southern Ohio Medical Center, 1980—. President, 1980-1985 and Chairman of the Board, 1980-1995, Star Bank of South Central Ohio. *Member:* Scioto County (President, 1979-1980), Ohio State (Member, Banking and Commercial Law Committee, 1982—) and American Bar Associations; American Association of Hospital Attorneys; National Association of Railroad Trial Counsel. ***SPECIAL AGENCIES:*** Chicago Title Agency of Southern Ohio. ***PRACTICE AREAS:*** Insurance Defense; Medical Malpractice; Health and Hospital Law; Estate Planning; Probate; Corporate Financing Law; Casualty Insurance Law; Banking Law; Real Estate; Title Insurance. ***Email:*** deverre@bhadlaw.com

ROBERT R. DEVER, born New York, N.Y., June 10, 1955; admitted to bar, 1980, Ohio. *Education:* Denison University (B.A., 1977); Capital University (J.D., 1980). City Prosecutor, 1990-1992. Assistant City Solicitor, 1990-1992. *Member:* Scioto County (President, 2002) and Ohio State (Member, Board of Governors, Young Lawyers Section, 1982-1990) Bar Associations. ***PRACTICE AREAS:*** Personal Injury Law; Business; Commercial; Real Estate Law; Insurance Defense; Medical Malpractice. ***Email:*** deverrr@bhadlaw.com

STEVEN M. WILLARD, born Portsmouth, Ohio, January 24, 1962; admitted to bar, 1987, Ohio. *Education:* University of Cincinnati (B.B.A., cum laude, 1984); Capital University (J.D., magna cum laude, 1987). Member, Capital University Law Review, 1986-1987. Chairman, Green Township Board of Education. *Member:* Scioto County and Ohio State Bar Associations. ***PRACTICE AREAS:*** Insurance Defense; Medical Malpractice; Real Estate; Worker's Compensation. ***Email:*** willards@bhadlaw.com

SHERRY D. DAVIS, born Princeton, West Virginia, September 24, 1972; admitted to bar, 1997, Ohio. *Education:* Ohio Northern University (B.A., 1994); Capital University (J.D., 1997). Member, Student Bar Association. *Member:* Scioto County and Ohio State Bar Associations. ***PRACTICE AREAS:*** Juvenile Law; Real Estate; Medical Malpractice; Workers Compensation; Personal Injury; Employment Defense. ***Email:*** daviss@bhadlaw.com

DIVISION COUNSEL FOR: CSX; Norfolk Southern Corporation; Physicians Insurance Company of Ohio; St. Paul Companies.
LOCAL COUNSEL FOR: AIG Aristech Chemical Corporation; Ashland Oil Co.; Automobile Club Insurance Company; Berneal Properties, Inc.; Bluegrass LLC; Church Mutual Ins. Co.; Cigna Companies; The Cincinnati Insurance Co.; Columbia Gas of Ohio, Inc.; Continental Insurance Company; Dow Chemical Corp.; Federated Insurance Co.; Hamilton Mutual Insurance Co.; John Hancock Mutual; Head Insurance Company; INA Life Insurance Co.; The Kroger Company; W.M. Lewis & Associates Mead Corporation; Merchants Indemnity Corporation of New York; Milwaukee Insurance Co.; Mutual Assurance, Inc.; Ohio State Life Insurance Co.; Ohio Hospital Insurance Co.; Porter Township Trustees; Portsmouth Insurance Agency, Inc.; Premier Properties, Inc.; Public Entities Pool of Ohio; R.R.E., Inc.; Reinhardt Truck Sales, Inc.; Dever & Co.; Shelby Mutual Insurance Co.; Sherman Kricker Insurance Co.; Spradlin Construction Co.; Stevens Construction Co.; Tanner Stone Co.; Universal Underwriters; WXIC; Western Southern Life Insurance Co.; Zurich North America.
COUNSEL FOR: Charter One Bank; Southern Ohio Medical Center; Tri-State; US Bank.
APPROVED ATTORNEYS FOR: Lawyers Title Insurance Corp.; Ohio Bar Title Insurance Co. (Agents); Chicago Title Insurance Co. (Agents).

BARAN, PIPER, TARKOWSKY, FITZGERALD & THEIS CO., L.P.A.

633 SEVENTH STREET, SUITE A
PORTSMOUTH, OHIO 45662
Telephone: 740-353-4700
Fax: 740-353-4747
URL: http://www.baranlaw.com

General Civil Practice, Trials in all Courts, Insurance Defense, Corporate, Family Law, Personal Injury, Worker's Compensation.

REPRESENTATIVE CLIENTS: Richland Trust Co.; Norfolk & Western Railroad; Terminal Transport Co.; White Consolidated Industries; Underground Utilities; Key Bank; Fifth Third Bank; Lender's Service Inc.; Brost Foundry; Lowes Inc.; Masfield Foundry Corp.; Orion Ins. Co.; Mansfield Structural & Erecting Co.
LOCAL COUNSEL FOR: Alexis Risk Management; Allied Insurance Co.; Atlanta Casualty; Allstate Insurance Co.; American-International Cos.; American Modern Home Insurance Co.; Central Mutual Insurance Co.; The CIGNA Companies; Chubb Group; Citation Corp.; Citi Financial Co., Inc.; Erie Insurance Group; Dalton Corp.; Fireman's Fund; GRE Insurance Group; Great American Insurance Co.; Guide One Insurance Group; Gulf Insurance Co.; Hamilton Mutual Insurance Co.; Hobart Corp.; Indiana Insurance Co.; K & K Claim Service; Kemper Insurance Group; Liberty Mutual Insurance Co.; Ohio Casualty Group; Ohio Farmers Insurance Co.; Ohio Mutual Insurance Co.; Omni Insurance Group; Penn Warranty; Redman Homes; Shelby Ins.Group; Therm-O-Disc; Travelers Insurance; Westfield Companies.

(For Complete list of all Personnel and Biographical data, see Professional Biographies at Mansfield, Ohio)

COLLEY SHROYER & ABRAHAM CO., L.P.A.

PORTSMOUTH, OHIO

(See Columbus)

Civil Trial Practice. Personal Injury, Medical Malpractice, Automobile Accidents, Wrongful Death, Railroad Accidents, Slip and Fall, Negligence, Product Liability and Toxic Torts.

DENMEAD LAW OFFICE

PORTSMOUTH, OHIO

(See Columbus)

Civil Trial and Appellate Practice and Personal Injury, Traumatic Brain Injury (TBI), Professional Negligence and Complex Litigation including Class Actions, Patents, Civil Rights, Civil Litigation, RICO, Employment and Political Subdivision Liability issues.

JOHNSON & OLIVER, A LEGAL PROFESSIONAL ASSOCIATION

701 SIXTH STREET
P.O. BOX 1505
PORTSMOUTH, OHIO 45662
Telephone: 740-354-4200
Telecopier: 740-353-2413
Email: cjohnson@johnsonoliverlaw.com
Email: soliver@johnsonoliverlaw.com

General Civil Practice. Corporations, Business, Estate Planning, Real Estate, Banking, Finance and Probate Law.

C. CLAYTON JOHNSON, born Seattle, Washington, December 30, 1944; admitted to bar, 1970, Ohio and U.S. Tax Court. *Education:* Ohio Wesleyan University (B.A., 1966); University of Virginia (M.A., 1967); University of Michigan (J.D., 1970). Phi Beta Kappa; Order of the Coif. *Member:* Portsmouth, Ohio State and American Bar Associations. **PRACTICE AREAS:** Corporations; Business Planning; Estate Planning; Finance. **Email:** cjohnson@johnsonoliverlaw.com

STEPHEN L. OLIVER, born Portsmouth, Ohio, April 27, 1956; admitted to bar, 1981, Ohio and U.S. District Court, Southern District of Ohio. *Education:* Miami University (A.B., cum laude, 1977); The Ohio State University (J.D., with honors, 1981). Phi Delta Phi; Phi Beta Kappa. *Member:* Portsmouth, Ohio State and American Bar Associations. **PRACTICE AREAS:** Real Estate; Estate Administration; Probate; Corporations. **Email:** soliver@johnsonoliverlaw.com

JOSHUA D. HOWARD, born Portsmouth, Ohio, May 7, 1979; admitted to bar, 2004, Ohio. *Education:* Shawnee State University (B.S., with honors, 2001); Capital University (J.D., magna cum laude, 2004). **PRACTICE AREAS:** Real Estate (50%); Business Law (25%); Probate (15%); Estate Planning (10%). **Email:** jhoward@johnsonoliverlaw.com

REPRESENTATIVE CLIENTS:
AUTOMOTIVE: Andy's Car & Truck Center, Inc.; The Glockner Chevrolet Co.; Oberling Motor Co.; Superior Leasing, Inc.; Quality Car & Truck Leasing, Inc.
BANKING AND FINANCE: Citizens Deposit Bank and Trust; Home Federal Savings and Loan; Oak Hill Financial Inc.; Oak Hill Banks; Premier Financial Bancorp.
CONSTRUCTION: Cunningham Asphalt; Mullins Construction, Inc.; Stevens Construction, Inc.; West End Electric Co., Inc.;
EDUCATION: Portsmouth City Schools.
FAST FOOD SERVICE: Arby's of S. Ohio - N. Ky.; McDonalds Corporation; Seafood Shoppes, Inc.; Wendy's of S. Ohio-N. Ky.; Renos of Portsmouth, LLC.
MANUFACTURING: M & J Industries, Inc.; OSCO Industries, Inc.; Mitchellace, Inc.; Savory Foods, Inc.; Vinyl Kraft, Inc.
REAL ESTATE: Land America/Lawyers Title Insurance Corporation; Oak Hill Title Agency, LLC.
RETAIL: The Kroger Co.; Lewis Furniture Co.; Scioto Shoe Mart, Inc.
RIVER SERVICE: Excell Marine Corp.; McNational, Inc.; McGinnis, Inc.; National Maintenance & Repair, Inc.
WHOLESALE DISTRIBUTION: Arrick's Bottled Gas; C.G. Biscuit Company; Central Industrial Supply, Inc.; Cornett Aluminum, Inc.; Glockner Oil Co.; Lute Plumbing Supply, Inc.; Ritchie Food Distributors, Inc.; Portsmouth News Agency, Inc.; Sabina Farmers Exchange, Inc.; Valley Wholesale Foods, Inc.; Wagner Rentals, Inc.
APPROVED ATTORNEYS FOR: Land America/Lawyers Title Insurance Corporation.

KIMBLE & CLARK

Established in 1914
622 SIXTH STREET
PORTSMOUTH, OHIO 45662
Telephone: 740-354-3214
Fax: 740-353-6910
Email: kimbleandclark@hotmail.com
URL: http://www.kimbleandclarklaw.com

Real Estate, Medical Malpractice, Automobile Accidents and Injuries, Wrongful Death, Slip and Fall, Criminal Defense, Driving While Intoxicated, Drug Crimes, Felonies, White Collar Crimes, Juvenile Criminal Law, Traffic Violations, Embezzlement, Fraud.

ROGER L. CLARK, born 1940; admitted to bar, 1968, Ohio. *Education:* Ohio University (B.S.); Ohio Northern University (J.D., 1968). Selected as, "One of the Best Trial Lawyers in America," by Harvard Law School Alumni. *Member:* Ohio State Bar Association. **PRACTICE AREAS:** Real Estate; Medical Malpractice; Family Law; Automobile Accidents and Injuries; Wrongful Death; Slip and Fall; Criminal Defense; Driving While Intoxicated; Drug Crimes; Felonies; White Collar Crime; Juvenile Criminal Law; Traffic Violations; Embezzlement; Fraud. **Email:** kimbleandclark@hotmail.com

(This Listing Continued)

OF COUNSEL

DAVID B. BECK, born 1970; admitted to bar, 1997, Ohio. *Education:* Point Loma Nazarene College (B.A.); Capital University (J.D., 1997). *Member:* Ohio State Bar Association; Ohio Academy of Trial Lawyers. **PRACTICE AREAS:** Personal Injury; Wrongful Death; Medical Malpractice; Insurance; Nursing Home Negligence; Dog Bites; Civil Litigation.

JACK D. YOUNG

MILLER & RODEHEFFER

630 6TH STREET
PORTSMOUTH, OHIO 45662
Telephone: 740-354-1300
Fax: 740-354-1301
Email: srodeheffer@sciotowireless.net
URL: http://www.rodehefferlaw.com

General Practice.

MARGARET APEL MILLER, born Portsmouth, Ohio, July 8, 1964; admitted to bar, 1989, Ohio; 1996, U.S. Court of Appeals, Sixth Circuit; 1998, U.S. Supreme Court. *Education:* Ohio University (B.A.,1986); Ohio State University (J.D.,1989). Magistrate, Portsmouth Municipal Court. **PRACTICE AREAS:** Family Law; Wrongful Death; Plaintiffs Personal Injury.

STEPHEN C. RODEHEFFER, born Marietta, Ohio, January 2, 1951; admitted to bar, 1976, Ohio; U.S. District Court, Southern District of Ohio and U.S. Supreme Court. *Education:* Ohio Wesleyan University; The Ohio State University (B.A., summa cum laude, 1973); Ohio Northern University (J.D., 1976). Ohio Academy of Trial Lawyers, Past Board Member, 1979. *Member:* Scioto County (Past President) and Ohio State Bar Associations. **REPORTED CASES:** 391 N.E.2d 1026, 59 Ohio St. 2d 73 IN RE ESTATE OF STILES (S.Ct. 1979) 13 Ohio Op. 3d 62; State of Ohio v. Wilkinson 415 N.E.2d 261, 64 Ohio St. 2d 308, 18 Ohio Op. 3d 482; State of Ohio v. Keairns 460 N.E.2d 245, 9 Ohio St.3d 228, 9 Ohio B.Rep.569; State of Ohio v. Grubb 503 N.E.2d 142, 28 Ohio St. 3d 199, 28 Ohio B. Rep. 285. **PRACTICE AREAS:** Personal Injury; Products Liability; Domestic Relations; Probate; Litigation; Civil Defense and Plaintiff Work.

OFFUTT, FISHER & NORD

PORTSMOUTH, OHIO

(See Huntington, West Virginia)

General Civil Trial Practice, Insurance Defense, Products Liability, Premises Liability, Asbestos Defense, Mass Tort Defense, Medical Malpractice, Legal Malpractice, Hospital Liability, Health Care Law and Commercial Litigation, Transportation Law.

ROURKE & BLUMENTHAL, LLP

PORTSMOUTH, OHIO

(See Columbus)

Personal Injury, Negligence, Products Liability, Medical Malpractice, Nursing Home Litigation, Wrongful Death, Intentional Tort, Insurance Disputes, Automobile Accidents, Civil Trial Practice, Aviation, Professional Liability.

RUGGIERO & HAAS

600 NATIONAL CITY BANK
800 GALLIA STREET
P.O. BOX 150
PORTSMOUTH, OHIO 45662
Telephone: 740-353-9805
Telecopier: 740-353-9808
Email: info@rhlawfirm.net
URL: http://www.rhlawfirm.net

General Civil Trial Practice. Insurance Defense and Medical Malpractice Law, Personal Injury Litigation.

DANIEL P. RUGGIERO, born Fremont, Ohio, January 2, 1947; admitted to bar, 1973, Ohio. *Education:* Miami University (B.A., 1969); University of Toledo (J.D., 1973). Phi Alpha Delta. Assistant Attorney General, Ohio, 1973-1977. *Member:* Portsmouth (President, 1995), Ohio State and American Bar Associations; International Association of Defense Counsel; Ohio Association of Civil Trial Attorneys (Member, Executive Committee, 1985-1992); Defense Research Institute; American Board of Trial Advocates. **PRACTICE AREAS:** Personal Injury Law; Professional Malpractice; Trial Practice. **Email:** ruggiero@sciotowireless.net

JOHN R. HAAS, born Sumter, South Carolina, September 15, 1965; admitted to bar, 1990, Ohio; 1992, U.S. District Court, Southern District of Ohio. *Education:* Ohio State University (B.A., 1987); Capital University (J.D., 1990); Boston University (LL.M., 1991). *Member:* Portsmouth, Ohio State and American Bar Associations. **PRACTICE AREAS:** Insurance Defense; Banking Law; Personal Injury; Real Estate Transactions. **Email:** haas@rhlawfirm.net

ASSOCIATE

ANNA DAVIS, born Portsmouth, Ohio, September 21, 1964; admitted to bar, 2000, Ohio. *Education:* Ohio University (B.S.Ed., 1986); Capital University (J.D., 2000). Delta Theta Phi. Recipient, Capital Public Interest Law Scholarship, 1997. *Member:* Scioto County and Ohio State Bar Associations. **PRACTICE AREAS:** Insurance Defense; Wills; Estates; Criminal Law; Real Estate. **Email:** davis@rhlawfirm.net

(This Listing Continued)

Auto-Owners Insurance Company; American International Group; CIGNA; Gallagher Bassett; Grange Mutual Casualty Company; Medical Protective Insurance Company; National Chiropractic Mutual; Progressive Casualty Insurance Company; Prudential Casualty Co.; State Automobile Mutual Insurance Company; Portsmouth Metropolitan Housing Authority; Monroe Guaranty Insurance Co.; GRE Insurance Group; Professional Underwriters Liability Insurance Co.; Colonial Inaurance Co.; Ohio Mutual Insurance Co.; Northbrook Insurance Co.; State Farm Insurance Co.; Miami Mutual Ins. Co.; Erie Insurance Group; Pioneer Insurance Co.; Ohio Bar Liability Insurance Co.; Buckeye State Mutual Insurance Co.; Crum & Forster Insurance; Heritage Mutual Insurance Company; Victoria Insurance Co.

STEPHENSON LAW OFFICE, LLC

Established in 1992

530 SIXTH STREET
PORTSMOUTH, OHIO 45662
Telephone: 740-354-3761
Fax: 740-353-8654
Email: majdrew@bright.net
URL: http://www.marileestephenson.com

Decedents Estates, Business Law, Probate Administration, Trust Planning, Real Estate, Contracts, Asset Protection.

MARILEE STEPHENSON, admitted to bar, 1991, Ohio; 1992, U.S. Court of Appeals, Sixth Circuit. *Education:* University of Kentucky; Chase College of Law (J.D., with honors, 1991). Member, Potter Stewart Inns of Court. Listed in Who's Who in American Lawyers. Editor, Northern Kentucky Law Review, 1991. Research and Legal Writing Assistant, Chase College of Law, 1989-1991. Director, National City Bank, N.A., Portsmouth. Board Member and Music Director, Kiwanis. ***PRACTICE AREAS:*** Business Law; Trust Planning Law; Real Estate Law; Trusts and Estates; Real Estate; Probate; Personal Injury; Living Trusts; Wills; Limited Liability Company Law; Estate Settlements; Contested Trusts and Estates; Elder Law; Asset Protection; Contracts; Corporate Law; Probate Administration; Probate Taxation; Probate Litigation; Premarital Agreements; Cohabitation Agreements; Guardianship; Estate Planning for the Disabled; Estate Planning for Parents of Handicapped Children; Estate Planning; Estate Planning for the Elderly. ***Email:*** majdrew@bright.net

REPRESENTATIVE CLIENTS: Bank One, N.A. Trust Department; United States Cellular; 1st Stop, Inc.; Tao Investments, Inc.; Cantrell Oil Co.; C-Stores Realty, Inc.; Glennco Systems, Inc.; National City Bank; Falcon Technologies, Inc.; and private individuals estates and trusts.

TWYFORD & DONAHEY, P.L.L.

PORTSMOUTH, OHIO

(See Columbus)

Personal Injury Litigation, Wrongful Death, Medical Malpractice, Products Liability, Automobile Accidents, Trucking Accidents, Head and Spinal Injuries, Motorcycle Accidents and Injuries, Uninsured Motorists, Insurance Law, Airplane Crash Litigation, Railroad Accidents, Slip and Fall, Dog Bites, Work Related Injuries, Birth Injuries, Nursing Home Abuse and Neglect.

VOLKEMA, THOMAS, MILLER, BURKETT, SCOTT & MERRY

A LEGAL PROFESSIONAL ASSOCIATION

PORTSMOUTH, OHIO

(See Columbus)

Civil State and Federal Trial and Appellate Practice. Personal Injury. Malpractice, Nursing Home Negligence, HMO Liability, Class Actions, Wrongful Death, Automobile Accidents, Product Liability, Employee Benefits, Insurance Bad Faith, Aviation and Tort Law, ERISA, Qui Tam (Whistleblower), False Claims Act.

JONES, TROYAN, PAPPAS & PERKINS

A LEGAL PROFESSIONAL ASSOCIATION

POWELL, OHIO

(See Columbus)

Business Organization, Planning and Transactions; Estate Planning; Retirement Plans; Real Estate; Employment Law; Probate; Federal Income, Estate and Gift Taxation.

MANOS, MARTIN, PERGRAM & DIETZ CO., LPA

POWELL, OHIO

(See Delaware)

Administrative, Appellate Practice, Litigation, Business, Contracts, Corporate, Zoning, Planning and Land Use, Real Estate, Labor and Employment, Trusts and Estates, and Wills and Probate.

FRANK J. CIMINO

Established in 1972

250 S. CHESTNUT, #18
RAVENNA, OHIO 44266
Telephone: 330-297-5788
Fax: 330-297-7578
Email: officeF3@aol.com

Trial Practice, Appellate Practice. Personal Injury, Automobile Accidents, Corporate, Business Law, Family, Divorce, Municipal, Zoning and Land Use, Collection, Real Estate, Probate Law, Bankruptcy.

(This Listing Continued)

FRANK J. CIMINO, born Youngstown, Ohio, April 3, 1947; admitted to bar, 1972, Ohio; 1973, U.S. District Court, Northern District of Ohio. *Education:* Hiram College (B.A., 1969); University of Akron School of Law (J.D., 1972). Board of Trustees Scholarship, 1969-1972. Member, 1970-1972 and Articles Editor, 1971-1972, University of Akron Law Review. Assistant Portage County Prosecutor, 1972-1975 and Chief Prosecutor, Criminal Division, 1974-1975. Law Director, City of Ravenna, 1976— and Assistant Law Director, City of Kent, 1985-2000. *Member:* Portage County (Secretary, 1974-1975 and President, 1998-1999) and Ohio State Bar Associations. ***PRACTICE AREAS:*** Trial Practice; General Practice; Personal Injury; Real Estate; Probate Law; Bankruptcy; Zoning Law; Land Use.

REPRESENTATIVE CLIENTS: S & S Aggregate; Country Estates Mobile Home Park; Courtesy Auto World; Courtesy Chrysler, Plymouth, Dodge; Beck Sand and Gravel.
REFERENCES: Portage Community Bank.

LAW OFFICES OF KEVIN T. POLAND

240 S. CHESTNUT STREET
RAVENNA, OHIO 44266
Telephone: 330-296-9122

General Practice, Personal Injury, Criminal Law, Traffic Violations, Automobile Accidents and Injuries, Driving While Intoxicated, Probate, Family Law, Divorce, Child Custody.

KEVIN T. POLAND, born Cleveland, Ohio, May 5, 1961; admitted to bar, 1986, Ohio. *Education:* Kent State University (B.B.A., 1983); Akron University Law School (J.D., 1986). Member, National Moot Court Team. Attorney, Portage County Prosecutor's Office, 1986-1987. Councilman, Ravenna City, Ward 4, 1986-1991. President, City Council, 1991—. *Member:* Portage County and Ohio State Bar Associations. ***PRACTICE AREAS:*** General Practice; Personal Injury; Criminal Law; Traffic Violations; Automobile Accidents and Injuries; Driving While Intoxicated; Probate; Family Law; Divorce; Child Custody.

SLATER, ZURZ & GILBERT

RAVENNA, OHIO

(See Akron)

Personal Injury, Wrongful Death, Commercial Litigation, Corporate, Business, Real Estate, Business Organization, Domestic Relations, Construction Litigation.

STEPHENS & ROSENBERG

206 SOUTH MERIDIAN STREET, SUITE A
P.O. BOX 229
RAVENNA, OHIO 44266-0229
Telephone: 330-296-3434
FAX: 330-296-3435
Email: cmslaw@neo.rr.com

General Civil and Criminal Trial Practice. Personal Injury, Family, Corporate, Real Estate, Municipal, Juvenile and Probate Law.

MEMBERS OF FIRM

CRAIG M. STEPHENS, born Columbus, Kansas, July 10, 1944; admitted to bar, 1974, Ohio; 1975, U.S. District Court, Northern District of Ohio; 1980, U.S. Supreme Court. *Education:* Kent State University (B.A., 1968); Akron University Law School (J.D., 1973). Delta Theta Phi; Omicron Delta Kappa. Member, Ohio Democratic Party Executive Committee. Director of Public Safety, City of Kent, Ohio, 1966-1968. Instructor, Criminal Law, Criminal Evidence and Civil Law, Kent State University, 1975-1982. *Member:* Portage County and Ohio State Bar Associations; Ohio Association of Criminal Defense Lawyers. [Special Agent, Military Intelligence, U.S. Army, 1968-1971]. ***PRACTICE AREAS:*** Criminal Law; Personal Injury. ***Email:*** cmslaw@neo.rr.com

ROBERT E. ROSENBERG, born Cleveland, Ohio, October 24, 1962; admitted to bar, 1989, Ohio, U.S. District Court, Northern District of Ohio and U.S. Court of Appeals, 6th Circuit. *Education:* Cleveland State University (B.B.A., 1985); Cleveland-Marshall College of Law (J.D., magna cum laude, 1989). Articles Editor, Cleveland-Marshall College of Law, Law Review, 1988-1989. Law Clerk to the Honorable Leroy J. Contie, Jr., U.S. Court of Appeals, 6th Circuit, 1989-1991 and 1992-2000. Certified Mediator. *Member:* Portage County (Member, Executive Committee) and Ohio State Bar Associations. ***Email:*** RERosenberg@aol.com

REFERENCES: Portage Community Bank, Ravenna, Ohio; Ravenna Savings & Loan, Ravenna, Ohio; First Federal Savings Bank of Kent, Ohio; Key Bank, Kent, Ohio.

EDWARD C. WEBER

RAVENNA, OHIO

(See Akron)

Trials and Appeals in all Courts. Criminal, DUI, Traffic Violations, Personal Injury, Defense, Probate and Estates Drug Crimes, Assault, Domestic Violence.

WILLIAMS, WELSER & KRATCOSKI

RAVENNA, OHIO

(See Kent)

Business Law, Corporate Law (Formation, Operation, Acquisition and Sale of Corporations, Partnerships, and Limited Liability Companies); Commercial and Residential Real Estate Law (Purchase, Sale, and Development including Condominiums, Subdivisions, and Zoning); Commercial and Residential Construction Law (including Mechanics Liens); Commercial and Residential Landlord Tenant Law; Domestic Relations Law (Divorce, Dissolution, Child Sup-

(This Listing Continued)

WILLIAMS, WELSER & KRATCOSKI, Ravenna—Continued

port and Custody); Estate Planning and Probate (Wills, Trusts, and Estate Administration); Traffic Law (Personal Injury, Automobile Accidents, Traffic Violations, and DUI); Criminal Law (Misdemeanors and Felonies); and Litigation Capability in all Practice Areas.

MICHAEL E. BENSON

REYNOLDSBURG, OHIO

(See Columbus)

Bankruptcy Law, Foreclosures, Debtor and Creditor, Real Estate, Landlord and Tenant, Buying and Selling, Wills, Living Wills, Healthcare, Powers of Attorney.

KREMBLAS, FOSTER, PHILLIPS & POLLICK

7632 SLATE RIDGE BOULEVARD
REYNOLDSBURG, OHIO 43068-8159
Telephone: 614-575-2100
Fax: 614-575-2149
Email: info@ohiopatent.com
URL: http://www.ohiopatent.com

Patent, Trademark, Copyright and Intellectual Property Law. Foreign Patent and Trademarks Law. Litigation. Licensing.

MEMBERS OF FIRM

FRANK T. KREMBLAS, born Akron, Ohio, April 8, 1937; admitted to bar, 1964, Ohio and U.S. District Court, Southern District of Ohio; registered to practice before U.S. Patent and Trademark Office. *Education:* The Ohio State University (B.C.E., 1961; J.D., 1964). Special Counsel to Attorney General, State of Ohio, 1997—. *Member:* Columbus Bar Association. **Email:** fkremblas@ohiopatent.com

FRANK H. FOSTER, born Toledo, Ohio, January 31, 1940; admitted to bar, 1966, Ohio; 1967, U.S. District Court, Southern District of Ohio and U.S. Supreme Court; 1970-1982, U.S. Court of Customs and Patent Appeals; 1982, U.S. Court of Appeals for the Federal Circuit; registered to practice before U.S. Patent and Trademark Office. *Education:* The Ohio State University (B.E.E., 1963; J.D., 1966). Special Counsel to Attorney General, State of Ohio, 1983—. *Member:* Columbus Intellectual Property Law Association. **Email:** ffoster@ohiopatent.com

PATRICK P. PHILLIPS, born Traverse City, Michigan, April 28, 1955; admitted to bar, 1980, Ohio; 1981, U.S. District Court, Southern District of Ohio; 1982, U.S. Court of Appeals for the Federal Circuit. *Education:* University of Richmond (B.A., 1977); Capital University (J.D., 1980). *Member:* Columbus Intellectual Property Law Association (President, 1984-1985). ***PRACTICE AREAS:*** Patents; Trademarks; Copyrights; Unfair Competition; Intellectual Property; Litigation. **Email:** pphillips@ohiopatent.com

PHILIP J. POLLICK, (CO., L.P.A.), admitted to bar, 1987, Ohio; 1988, District of Columbia; registered to practice before U.S. Patent and Trademark Office. *Education:* University of Toledo (B.S., Chemical Engineering, 1963); Ohio State University (Ph.D., Chemistry, 1969; M.B.A., summa cum laude, 1974); Capital University (J.D., 1986). **Email:** pollick@infinet.com

JASON H. FOSTER, born Columbus, Ohio, August 29, 1968; admitted to bar, 1995, Ohio; 1996, U.S. District Court, Southern District of Ohio; 2000, U.S. Court of Appeals, Federal Circuit; 2001, District of Columbia. *Education:* The Ohio State University (B.S., 1992); Capital University (J.D., 1995). *Member:* Ohio State and American Bar Associations; Columbus Intellectual Property Law Association (President, 1999-2001). ***PRACTICE AREAS:*** Patents; Trademarks; Copyrights; Intellectual Property Litigation; Licensing. **Email:** jfoster@ohiopatent.com

EVANS, EVANS & HOFFMAN L.L.P.

15 WEST OTTAWA STREET
RICHWOOD, OHIO 43344-1138
Telephone: 740-943-2325
Fax: 740-943-2326

Banking and Lending, Business Law, Corporation Law, Estate Planning, Finance Law, Guardianships, International Law, Probate, Project Finance, Real Estate.

JEFFREY LEE EVANS, born Marion, Ohio, 1956; admitted to bar, 1981, Ohio. *Education:* Ohio Northern University (B.A., 1978; J.D., 1981). Acting Judge, Marysville Municipal Court, Union County, Ohio, 1987—. Solicitor, Village of Richwood, 1981-1997. ***PRACTICE AREAS:*** Real Estate; Estate Planning; Guardianship; Probate. **Email:** jevans@abanet.org

SCOTT L. HOFFMAN, born Marion, Ohio, 1957; admitted to bar, 1982, New York; 1988, District of Columbia; 1996, Ohio. *Education:* Ohio Northern University (B.A., with honors, 1979); Syracuse University (J.D., with honors, 1982). Author: "The Law and Business of International Project Finance" (2nd ed., 2001, Transnational Pub., Kluwer Law International); "A Practical Guide to Transactional Project Finance," 45 Business Lawyer 181 (1989). Partner, Nixon, Hargrave, Devans & Doyle, Washington, D.C., 1982-1996. Board of Trustees: Marion General Hospital, 2003— United Way of Marion County, 2005—. ***PRACTICE AREAS:*** Banking Law; Business Law; Project Finance; International Project Finance. **Email:** slhoffman@abanet.org

BATTLE & MILLER P.L.L.

Established in 1996
1340 DEPOT STREET, SUITE 100
ROCKY RIVER, OHIO 44116-1741
Telephone: 440-895-9700
Fax: 440-895-1442
Email: miller@battlemillerlaw.com
URL: http://www.lawyers.com/battle&miller

Labor Law, Employment Law, Workers Compensation, OSHA.

COLLEEN P. BATTLE, born Subiaco, Western Australia, 1945; admitted to bar, 1986, Ohio; U.S. District Court, Northern District of Ohio; U.S. Court of Appeals, Sixth Circuit. *Education:* California State University at Fullerton (B.A., 1967); University of California at Berkeley (Secondary Teaching Credential, 1968); Cleveland Marshall College of Law (J.D., cum laude, 1986). Judicial Clerk to the Honorable Robert B. Krupansky, Sixth Circuit Court of Appeals, 1985. Judicial Extern, Honorable John M. Manos, U.S. District Court, 1985. Author: "Righting the Tilted Scale: Expansion of Art Rights in the United States," Cleveland State Law Review, 1986. Associate: Squire, Sanders & Dempsey, 1986-1992; Thompson Hine LLP, 1992-1996. *Member:* Ohio State Bar Association; Self Insurers' Group of Northern Ohio. ***PRACTICE AREAS:*** Workers' Compensation; Labor and Employment. **Email:** battle@battlemillerlaw.com

SHARON L. MILLER, born Lorain, Ohio, 1962; admitted to bar, 1991, Ohio and U.S. District Court, Northern District of Ohio. *Education:* Bowling Green State University (B.S., 1985); Cleveland Marshall College of Law (J.D., 1990). Alpha Phi Sigma. National Criminal Justice Honor Society. Lorain Foundation Scholarship. Hearing Representative: Robinson Conner, 1991-1992; Spooner Incorporated, 1992-1993. Associate, Thompson Hine LLP, 1993-1996. *Member:* Cleveland (Workers' Compensation Section) and Ohio State Bar Associations; Self Insurers' Group of Northern Ohio. ***PRACTICE AREAS:*** Workers' Compensation; Labor and Employment. **Email:** miller@battlemillerlaw.com

ASSOCIATES

JAMES W. ELLIS, born Napoleon, Ohio, 1971; admitted to bar, 2000, Ohio, U.S. District Court, Northern District of Ohio and U.S. Court of Appeals, Sixth Circuit. *Education:* Bowling Green State University (B.A., 1997); Cleveland-Marshall College of Law (J.D., 2000). Judicial Extern, Honorable Solomon Oliver, Jr., U.S. District Court, 1999. Law Clerk, Joseph W. Diemart & Associates, 1999-2001. *Member:* Cleveland and Ohio State Bar Associations; Self Insurers' Group of Northern Ohio. ***PRACTICE AREAS:*** Workers' Compensation; Labor and Employment. **Email:** ellis@battlemillerlaw.com

STEVEN C. POLLY, born Detroit, Michigan, March 29, 1968; admitted to bar, 1999, Ohio and U.S. District Court, Northern and Southern Districts of Ohio; U.S. District Court, District of Colorado; U.S. Court of Appeals, Fifth Circuit. *Education:* Western Michigan University (B.S., 1991); Ohio Northern University College of Law (J.D., 1996). Associate: Webster & Webster LLP, 1999-2003; Martyn and Associates, 2003-2004. *Member:* Cuyahoga County and Ohio State Bar Associations; Self Insurer's Group of Northern Ohio. ***PRACTICE AREAS:*** Labor and Employment; Civil Litigation; Workers Compensation. **Email:** polly@battlemillerlaw.com

GRADY & ASSOCIATES

20950 CENTER RIDGE ROAD
SUITE 100
ROCKY RIVER, OHIO 44116-4307
Telephone: 440-356-7255
Fax: 440-356-7254
URL: http://www.gradyassociates.com

Banking and Securities Law.

FRANCIS X. GRADY, born Cleveland, Ohio, November 17, 1957; admitted to bar, 1984, Ohio; 1985, District of Columbia. *Education:* Georgetown University (B.S.F.S., magna cum laude, 1980); Trinity College, Dublin, Ireland (1979); College of Europe, Bruges, Belgium (Certificate of Advanced European Studies, 1981); The Ohio State University College of Law (J.D., 1984). Member, America's Community Bankers. Author: "Step-by-Step Guide Can Help Avoid Pitfalls of Buying a Branch," The American Banker, April 1, 1988; "An Internal Audit Can Help a Bank Ensure Compliance with Consumer Protection Laws," American Banker, April 9, 1991; "CRA Success Starts with a Plan," American Banker, July 30, 1991; "Steering Clear of Pollution Risk," American Banker, January 22, 1992; "Innocent Errors Create Liability Under the Truth-in-Savings Act," American Banker, March 23, 1993; "Financial Institutions Fail to Take Advantage of Dividend Reinvestment Plans," Ohio Record, Fall 1994; "Bounce Protection Overdraft Coverage: Doing It the Right Way," The Ohio Community Banker, July/August 2003; "BOLI-Financed Executive Compensation," America's Community Bankers 2003 Compensation Survey; "Bank-Owned Life Insurance Presents a Window of Opportunity," Community Banker, January 2004; "Bounce Protection Overdraft Coverage: Doing It the Right Way," Independent Banker, January 2004. Contributing Author: "Consumer Credit Law, Transaction and Forms," Matthew Bender & Co., 1988-2004; "Banking Law," Consumer Credit, Volume 7, Matthew Bender & Co., 1992-2004; "Ohio Thrift Executive Compensation," September 1989; "Ohio, Michigan and Indiana Thrift Executive Compensation," August, 1990; "Thrift Executive Compensation for Ohio, Michigan and Indiana," September 1991, September 1992; September 1993, August 1994, September 1995 and September 1996; "Bank Compensation Survey for Ohio, Michigan and Indiana," August 1994 and September 1995-1996. ***LANGUAGES:*** French and Portuguese. ***PRACTICE AREAS:*** Executive Compensation; Financial Services Law; Banking Law; Corporate Law; Securities Law. **Email:** fgrady@gradyassociates.com

(This Listing Continued)

JOSEPH A. DRAIN, born Cleveland, Ohio, April 28, 1955; admitted to bar, 1982, Ohio. *Education:* Case Western Reserve University (B.A., 1979; J.D., 1982). ***PRACTICE AREAS:*** Banking Law; Securities Law; Corporate Law. ***Email:*** jdrain@gradyassociates.com

SCOTT M. PUGLISE, born Lima, Ohio, February 25, 1970; admitted to bar, 2000, Ohio. *Education:* Wright State University (B.S., summa cum laude, 1997); Cleveland-Marshall College of Law, Cleveland State University (J.D., magna cum laude, 2000). *Member:* Ohio State and American Bar Associations. ***PRACTICE AREAS:*** Financial Services Law; Banking Law; Business Law; Corporate Law; Securities Law. ***Email:*** spuglise@gradyassociates.com

SUSAN M. GRAY

ROCKY RIVER, OHIO

(See Cleveland)

Bankruptcy, Consumer Law, Consumer Fraud, Foreclosures, Debtor and Creditor, Fair Credit Reporting Act, Fair Debt Collection Practices Act.

LINDON & LINDON, LLC

Established in 2002

1250 LINDA STREET
ROCKY RIVER, OHIO 44116
Telephone: 440-333-0011
Fax: 419-710-4925
Email: Patent@2-INVENT.COM
URL: http://www.2-INVENT.COM

All areas of Intellectual Property including Patent, Trademark, Copyright, Trade Dress, Trade Secret, and Litigation as well as Pharmacy Law.

DR. JAMES LINDON, born Cincinnati, Ohio, February, 24, 1963; admitted to bar, 1997, Ohio; 1998, U.S. District Court, Northern District of Ohio; 2000, District of Columbia; registered to practice before U.S. Patent and Trademark Office. *Education:* University of Arizona (B.S.Ph., 1987; Ph.D., 1993); Ohio Northern University (J.D., 1997). Pharmacy Licenses: Arizona, 1987; Ohio 1999. Patent Attorney. Member: American Pharmacists Association, 1986; American Society for Pharmacy Law, 1993; American Intellectual Property Law Association, 2000. *Member:* Ohio State Bar Association; The District of Columbia Bar. ***PRACTICE AREAS:*** Patents; Trademarks; Litigation; Copyrights; Trade Secrets; Pharmacy Law. ***Email:*** JLindon@LindonLaw.com

ELIZABETH ANN LINDON, born Sandusky, Ohio, December 14, 1971; admitted to bar, 1999, Ohio. *Education:* John Carroll University (B.A., 1994); Ohio Northern University (J.D., 1998). Phi Delta Phi. *Member:* Ohio State Bar Association.

MILANO WEISER

ATTORNEYS & COUNSELORS AT LAW
A LEGAL PROFESSIONAL ASSOCIATION

ROCKY RIVER, OHIO

(See Cleveland)

Criminal Defense, White Collar Crime, Wrongful Death, Medical Malpractice, Nursing Home Negligence, Internet Law, Consumer Law.

KEVIN PURCELL CO., L.P.A.

ROCKY RIVER, OHIO

(See Cleveland)

Elder Law, Trusts and Estates, Asset Protection, Estate Planning, Guardianship, Wills, Probate, Medicaid Eligibility, Revocable Trusts, Living Trusts, Charitable Giving, Living Will, Health Care Power of Attorney.

HANLON, DUFF, ESTADT & McCORMICK CO., LPA

46457 NATIONAL ROAD WEST
ST. CLAIRSVILLE, OHIO 43950-9721
Telephone: 740-695-1444
Fax: 740-695-1563
Email: hdem@localnet.com

General Civil Trial and Appellate Practice in all Courts. Corporate, Labor, Insurance, Taxation, Personal Injury, Probate, Real Estate Law. Estate Planning, Workers Compensation, Occupational Disease, Medical Malpractice Defense.

GERALD P. DUFF, born Haverhill, Massachusetts, March 5, 1947; admitted to bar, 1971, Ohio; 1972, Massachusetts; 1973, U.S. District Court, Southern District of Ohio; 1980, U.S. Court of Appeals, Sixth Circuit; 1984, U.S. Supreme Court and U.S. Court of Appeals, Third Circuit; 1995, Pennsylvania; 2001, U.S. Court of Federal Claims. *Education:* Merrimack College (B.A., 1968); University of Notre Dame (J.D., 1971). Law Clerk to Chief Judge Joseph P. Kinneary, U.S. District Court for the Southern District of Ohio, 1971-1973. Appointed, Special Counsel to Ohio Attorney General.*Member:* Belmont County, Ohio State (Member: Board of Governors, Litigation Section, 1984-2004; Workers Compensation Committee, 1984—) and Massachusetts Bar Associations. ***REPORTED CASES:*** Youghiogheny & Ohio Coal Co. v. Mayfield, Admr., 11 Ohio St. 3d 70 (1984); Ormet Primary Aluminum Corp. v. Employers Ins. Of Warsau et al. (2000), 88 Ohio St. 3d 292. ***PRACTICE AREAS:*** Insurance Defense; Medical Malpractice; Administrative Law; Workers Compensation; Labor and Employment Law; Civil Litigation. ***Email:*** hdem@localnet.com

JOHN R. ESTADT, born Zanesville, Ohio, November 7, 1950; admitted to bar, 1983, Ohio; 1984, U.S. District Court, Southern District of Ohio; 1989, U.S. Court of Appeals, Sixth Circuit and U.S. Supreme Court. *Education:* Kent State University (B.A., 1972); Ohio State University (M.S., 1979); Case Western Reserve University (J.D., 1983). Member, Estate Planning Council, Upper Ohio Valley. *Member:* Belmont County, Ohio State Bar Association (Member, Taxation Committee, 1986—; Sections on: Estate Planning; Trust and Probate Law). ***PRACTICE AREAS:*** Trusts and Estates; Wills; Probate; Taxation Law; Real Estate Law; Business Law; Corporate Law; Limited Liability Company Law; Probate Law; Estate Planning. ***Email:*** hdem@localnet.com

MICHAEL P. McCORMICK, born Barnesville, Ohio, March 6, 1959; admitted to bar, 1989, Ohio, U.S. District Court, Southern District of Ohio and U.S. Court of Appeals, Sixth Circuit; 1992, U.S. Supreme Court. *Education:* Malone College (B.A., 1984); Ohio Northern University (J.D., 1988). Councilman, Village of Bethesda, Ohio, 1989-2000. Member, Christian Legal Society, 1989—. *Member:* Belmont County (Member, Law Library Assoc. Trustee, 1997—); Ohio State (Board of Governors, 1994-1997; Real Property Section Board; Solo, Small Firms and General Practice Board; Council of Delegates, 2001-2003) Bar Associations. ***PRACTICE AREAS:*** General Civil Litigation; Real Estate Litigation; Real Estate; Probate. ***Email:*** hdem@localnet.com

ERIK ALAN SCHRAMM, born Wheeling, West Virginia, May 11, 1961; admitted to bar, 1998, West Virginia, U.S. District Court, Southern and Northern District of West Virginia; 1999, Ohio, U.S. District Court, Southern District of Ohio. *Education:* Bethany College (B.S., 1983); West Virginia University (M.B.A., 1988; J.D., 1997). Masters Certificate, Government Contracting, West Virginia University and Federal Market Institute. Estate Planning Council, Upper Ohio Valley. Member, West Virginia Board of Education, 2004—. *Member:* Belmont County, Ohio County, Ohio State, West Virginia and American Bar Associations. ***PRACTICE AREAS:*** Business Law; Civil Litigation; Estate Planning; Federal Government Contracts; Corporate Law; Limited Liability Company Law; Real Estate; Trusts and Estates; Black Lung; Workers' Compensation. ***Email:*** hdem@localnet.com

REBBECA L. BENCH, born Milwaukee, Wisconsin, April 29, 1973; admitted to bar, 2002, Ohio. *Education:* Mississippi State University for Women (B.S., 1998); Ohio Northern University (J.D., 2001). Law Clerk, Ohio Supreme Court-Criminal Sentencing Commission, 2001; Ohio Attorney General's Office-Health and Human Services Division, 2001. *Member:* Ohio State Bar Association. ***PRACTICE AREAS:*** Vaccine Injury; Civil Litigation; Domestic Relations; Insurance Defense. ***Email:*** hdem@localnet.com

OF COUNSEL

LODGE L. HANLON, born Barnesville, Ohio, April 30, 1931; admitted to bar, 1958, Ohio. *Education:* Kent State University (B.S.B.A., 1953); The Ohio State University (J.D., 1958). Phi Delta Phi. *Member:* Belmont County, Ohio State and American Bar Associations; American Institute of Certified Public Accountants. ***PRACTICE AREAS:*** Estate Planning; Taxation Law; Probate. ***Email:*** hdem@localnet.com

REPRESENTATIVE CLIENTS: Oglebay Norton Co.; The St. Paul Cos.; Consolidation Coal Co.; Wheeling-Pittsburgh Steel Corp.; The Douglas Co.; Boich Mining Co.; Panhandle Eastern Corp.; Sahara Coal Co.; Automobile Club Insurance Company; American Family Ins. Co.; State Auto Mutual Ins. Co.; State Farm Insurance Companies; General Accident Insurance Co.; Royal Insurance Company; Globe Indemnity Company; The Upper Ohio Valley Individual Practice Association, Inc.; The Health Plan of the Upper Ohio Valley, Inc.; American International Group; Pan Energy; Texas Eastern Corp.; Duke Energy; Texas Eastern Products Pipeline Co.; Nippon Steel Corp.; East Ohio Regional Hospital; Ohio Valley Health Services and Education Corporation; Tandy Corporation (Radio Shack); Kentucky National Insurance Co.; City of Wheeling, West Virginia; Daily Underwriters of America; Shelly and Sands, Inc.; The Kroger Company; Indiana Lumberman's Insurance Company; Microtel Inns; THF Realty, Inc.; New England Waste, L.L.C.; Ohio & West Virginia Insurance Guaranty Association; Monroe Guaranty Insurance Company; AEP Ohio Coal, LLC; Rock of Ages Memorials, Inc.; CENTRIA; Ameritech; IFG Companies; First Financial Insurance Company; Lowes Home Centers, Inc.; A.I. Healthcare; OMIC.
REFERENCES: Belmont National Bank, St. Clairsville, Ohio.
APPROVED ATTORNEYS FOR: Lawyers Title Insurance Company; Old Republic Title.

LANCIONE & LLOYD LAW OFFICE CO., L.P.A.

ST. CLAIRSVILLE, OHIO

(See Bellaire)

Auto Accidents, Trial Practice. Personal Injury, Medical Malpractice, Workers Compensation, Wrongful Death, Corporation Law, Insurance, Real Estate, Probate and Wills.

THORNBURG, BEAN & GLICK

113 WEST MAIN STREET
P.O. BOX 96
ST. CLAIRSVILLE, OHIO 43950
Telephone: 740-695-0532
Telefax: 740-695-8039
Email: tbean@1st.net

General Civil Practice. Corporate, Personal Injury, Probate, Insurance and Real Estate Law. Title Examinations. Trials in all Courts. Mining Law.

CARTER THORNBURG (1908-1979)

CHARLES H. BEAN, born Athens, Ohio, May 4, 1947; admitted to bar, 1972, Ohio; 1973, U.S. District Court, Southern District of Ohio; 1977, U.S. Court of Appeals, Sixth Circuit and U.S. Supreme Court. *Education:* Ohio University (A.B., cum laude, 1969); The Ohio State University (J.D., 1972). Pi Gamma Mu; Phi Delta Phi (Secretary, 1971-1972).

(This Listing Continued)

THORNBURG, BEAN & GLICK, St. Clairsville—Continued

City Solicitor, Shadyside, Ohio, 1972-1975. Solicitor, Powhatan Point, Ohio, 1992-1997. *Member:* Belmont County, Ohio State and American Bar Associations; Ohio Association of Civil Trial Attorneys; Defense Research Institute Member. Fellow, Ohio State Bar Foundation. ***PRACTICE AREAS:*** Personal Injury; Civil Litigation; Real Property; Mining Law; Insurance Defense. ***Email:*** tbean@1st.net

ELIZABETH L. GLICK, born Columbus, Indiana, September 24, 1962; admitted to bar, 1987, West Virginia and U.S. District Court, Northern and Southern Districts of West Virginia; 1988, Ohio. *Education:* Wilson College (B.A., magna cum laude, 1984); West Virginia University (J.D., 1987). Moot Court Board. Solicitor, Brilliant Water and Sewer District, 1995—. *Member:* Belmont County, West Virginia, Ohio State and American Bar Associations; West Virginia State Bar. ***PRACTICE AREAS:*** Real Property; Probate Law. ***Email:*** tbean@1st.net

LOCAL COUNSEL FOR: North American Coal Corp.; Marietta Coal Co.; Quarto Mining Co.; State Automobile Insurance Co.; Grange Mutual Casualty Co.; Ohio Edison Co.; Ohio Bell Telephone Co.; Celina Mutual Casualty Co.; Home Equity, Inc.; Republic Franklin Insurance Co.; Penn Central Transportation Co.; West American Insurance Co.; National Insurance Co.; Home Insurance Co., Inc.; South Central Power Company; Scottsdale Insurance Company; Atlantic Insurance Companies; Ohio Valley Coal Co.; Consolidated Land Co.; Consolidation Coal Co.; Consol, Inc.
REFERENCE: Belmont National Bank, St. Clairsville, Ohio.

TRIBBIE, SCOTT, PLUMMER AND PADDEN

ST. CLAIRSVILLE, OHIO

(See Cambridge)

General Civil Trial Practice. Corporation, Real Estate, Negligence, Insurance Defense, Insurance and Probate Law. Family Law, Divorce, Child Custody, Child Support.

FITCH, KENDALL, CECIL, ROBINSON & BARRY CO., L.P.A.

Established in 1950

600 EAST STATE STREET
P.O. BOX 590
SALEM, OHIO 44460-0590
Telephone: 330-337-8761
Fax: 330-337-9453
Email: FitchKendall@Compuserve.com

General Civil Trial Practice in federal and state courts and administrative agencies. Probate, Real Estate, Personal Injury, Family, Products Liability, Estate Planning, Insurance, Corporate, Taxation, Labor and Employment Law.

ALFRED L. FITCH (1913-1992)

BRYCE W. KENDALL (1923-1995)

LARRY G. CECIL, born Marietta, Ohio, May 29, 1947; admitted to bar, 1972, Ohio; 1973, U.S. Court of Military Appeals; 1977, U.S. District Court, Northern District of Ohio. *Education:* The Ohio State University (B.A., 1969; J.D., 1972). Estate Tax Agent, Ohio Department of Taxation, 1971-1973. *Member:* Columbiana County and Ohio State Bar Associations. [Capt., JAGC, U.S. Army, 1973-1976]. ***PRACTICE AREAS:*** Estate Planning; Trust Law; Probate; Corporate Law.

IAN ROBINSON, born Penkhull, Stoke-on-Trent, England, November 9, 1948; admitted to bar, 1979, Ohio; 1980, U.S. District Court, Northern District of Ohio; 2000, U.S. Supreme Court; 2001, U.S. Court of Appeals, Sixth Circuit. *Education:* Kent State University (B.G.S., summa cum laude, 1976); The Ohio State University (J.D., 1979). Licensed Title Insurance Agent, Ohio Bar Title Insurance Company. *Member:* Columbiana County, Ohio State (Member, Litigation Section; Web Site Moderator; Committees on: Negligence Law; Unauthorized Practice of Law; Member: Jury Instruction Committee; Council of Delegates; Board of Governors) and American Bar Associations; Ohio Academy of Trial Lawyers, The Association of Trial Lawyers of America. [CW3, U.S. Army, 1968-1987]. ***PRACTICE AREAS:*** Personal Injury; Products Liability; Labor and Employment; Business Litigation; Domestic Relations; Real Estate. ***Email:*** FitchKendall@Compuserve.com

TIMOTHY A. BARRY, born McKeesport, Pennsylvania, March 20, 1952; admitted to bar, 1987, Ohio; 1988, U.S. District Court, Northern District of Ohio. *Education:* Washington & Jefferson College (B.A., cum laude, 1974); Case Western Reserve University (J.D., cum laude, 1987). *Member:* Columbiana County and Ohio State Bar Associations. ***PRACTICE AREAS:*** Commercial Law; Corporate Law; Business Law; Real Estate; Commercial Litigation; Bankruptcy; Creditors Rights.

OF COUNSEL

WHITMAN ROBINSON, born Salem, Ohio, February 19, 1974; admitted to bar, 2003, Ohio; 2003, U.S. District Court, Southern District of Ohio; 2004, Colorado. *Education:* Ohio State University (B.S., Education, 1997); Capital University (J.D., 2002). *Member:* Franklin County, Columbiana County and Ohio State Bar Association; Ohio Academy of Trial Lawyers. ***PRACTICE AREAS:*** Civil Litigation.

REPRESENTATIVE CLIENTS: Eljer Mfg. Div. of Eljer Industries; Quaker City Castings, Inc.; Morris Financial Group, Inc.; Columbiana Foundry, Inc.; Hickey Metal Fabrication; Home Savings & Loan Co. of Youngstown; Farm Credit Services of Mid-America, ACA; Gordon Bros., Inc.
AGENTS FOR: Ohio Bar Title Insurance Co.; ACS Title and Closing Services.

HARRINGTON, HOPPE & MITCHELL, LTD.

2235 E. PERSHING STREET, SUITE A
SALEM, OHIO 44460
Telephone: 330-337-6586
Telefax: 330-337-6662
Email: info@hhmlaw.com
URL: http://www.hhmlaw.com

Youngstown, Ohio Office: 26 Market Street, Suite 1200, 44503-1508. Telephone: 330-744-1111. Telecopier: 330-744-2029.
Warren, Ohio Office: 108 Main Avenue, S.W., Suite 500, 44481. Telephone: 330-392-1541. Telecopier: 330-394-6890.

General Civil Trial and Equity Practice in all State and Federal Courts. Corporation, Banking, Creditors Rights and Bankruptcy, Labor, Probate, Estate Planning, Hospital and Health, Insurance Law, Real Estate Law, Commercial Law, Business Transactions.

FIRM PROFILE: The firm is the largest firm in Mahoning, Trumball and Columblana Counties of Ohio. The firm maintains offices in Youngstown, Warren and Salem, Ohio.

Harrington, Hoppe & Mitchell, Ltd. is a full service firm, organized into six general practice areas: Litigation; Business Services; Labor and Employment; Health Care Law; Public Sector Law; and Probate and Estate Planning.

HARRY R. CONN, born Lisbon, Ohio, June 4, 1941; admitted to bar, 1973, Ohio. *Education:* Ohio University (B.A., 1963); Akron University Law School (J.D., 1973). *Member:* Ohio Association of Civil Trial Attorneys; Defense Research Institute; The Association of Trial Lawyers of America. ***PRACTICE AREAS:*** Civil Litigation; Personal Injury; Insurance Defense; Probate.

SHAWNA L. ERB, born Salem, Ohio, October 4, 1970; admitted to bar, 1996, Ohio. *Education:* Mount Union College (B.A., 1993); The Ohio State University (J.D., 1996). Order of the Coif. *Member:* Columbiana County, Mahoning County and Ohio State Bar Associations. ***PRACTICE AREAS:*** Corporate Law; Real Estate; Employment Law; Business Transactions; Commercial Law. ***Email:*** SErb@hhmlaw.com

ALAN D. WENGER, born Salem, Ohio, February 19, 1952; admitted to bar, 1977, Ohio; 1978, U.S. District Court, Northern District of Ohio; 1985, U.S. Tax Court. *Education:* Youngstown State University; Eastern Mennonite College (B.A., 1974); Case Western Reserve University (J.D., 1977). Member, South Range Local School Board, 1985—. *Member:* Columbiana County, Mahoning County, Ohio State and American Bar Associations. ***PRACTICE AREAS:*** Public Utility Law; Environmental Law; Construction Law; Labor and Employment; Corporate Law. ***Email:*** awenger@hhmlaw.com

SHIRLEY J. CHRISTIAN, born Erie, Pennsylvania, July 13, 1954; admitted to bar, 1986, Ohio; 1987, Pennsylvania and U.S. District Court, Northern District of Ohio. *Education:* Edinboro University (B.S., 1976; MEd., 1977); Ohio Northern University (J.D., with distinction, 1986). Associate Editor, Ohio Northern University Law Review, 1986. Moot Court-Administrative Justice. *Member:* Mahoning County and Ohio State (Member, Board or Governors, 2002—) Bar Associations; Ohio Association of Civil Trial Attorneys; Defense Research Institute. ***PRACTICE AREAS:*** Medical Malpractice Defense; Labor and Employment. ***Email:*** SChristian@hhmlaw.com

NEIL H. MAXWELL, born Salem, Ohio, February 5, 1959; admitted to bar, 1984, Ohio. *Education:* Mount Union College (B.S., 1981); University of Akron (J.D., 1984). ***PRACTICE AREAS:*** Estate Planning; Probate. ***Email:*** NMaxwell@hhmlaw.com

LANCE A. MORRISON, born Greenville, Pennsylvania, September 23, 1966; admitted to bar, 1992, Ohio; 1998, U.S. District Court, Northern District of Ohio. *Education:* The Ohio State University (B.A., 1988; J.D., 1992). National Merit Scholar. Member, Federalist Society, 1989-1992. *Member:* Mahoning County and Ohio State Bar Associations. [Lt., U.S. Navy, JAG Corps., 1992-1997]. ***PRACTICE AREAS:*** Business Law; Corporate Law; Collections; Labor and Employment. ***Email:*** LMorrison@hhmlaw.com

CHRISTOPHER BARONZZI, born Salem, Ohio, May 10, 1978; admitted to bar, 2004, Ohio; 2005, U.S. District Court, Northern District of Ohio. *Education:* John Carroll University (B.S.E., 2001); Akron University Law School (J.D., cum laude, 2004). ABA Moot Court. Recipient, CALI Award, Antitrust Law. *Member:* Columbiana County, Ohio State and American Bar Associations. ***PRACTICE AREAS:*** General Practice. ***Email:*** cbaronzzi@hhmlaw.com

REPRESENTATIVE CLIENTS: Forum Health Hospitals and Medical Centers; Humility of Mary Healthcare; Consumers Ohio Water Company (Public Utility); City of Canfield; Beaver Township; Village of Lordstown; The City of Cortland; The Public Library of Youngstown and Mahoning County; First Energy Corp; Ohio Edison Company; ER Advanced Ceramics, Inc.; Office of Attorney General, State of Ohio; Hill, Barth & King, CPAs; Mahoning Valley Economic Development Corporation; Youngstown-Warren Regional Chamber of Commerce; A.P. O'Horo Company; Taylor Winfield Corp.; WCI Steel, Inc.; General Extrusions, Inc.; Sovereign Circuits, Inc.; Metropolitan Property & Casualty Insurance Co.; Nationwide Mutual Insurance Co.; Motorists Insurance Co.; CNA Insurance Companies; Allstate Insurance Co.; Ohio Mutual Insurance Group; American General Life and Accident Insurance Group; Coregis Insurance Company; National City Bank; Sky Bank; First Place Bank; Bank One Cleveland, N.A.; Second National Bank of Warren; V&V Real Estate Investments; Ohio Realty Company.

(For complete biographical data on personnel at Youngstown and Warren, see Professional Biographies at those locations)

FREDERIC E. NARAGON

248 EAST STATE STREET
P.O. BOX 317
SALEM, OHIO 44460-0317
Telephone: 330-337-9578
Fax: 330-337-1223
Email: frednaragon@neo.rr.com

General Civil and Criminal Practice in all Courts. Family, Corporate and Business, Commercial and Retail Collections, Negligence, Real Estate, Taxation and Probate Law, Estate Planning, Trials, Patent, Trademark and Copyright and Banking Law, Oil and Gas and Mining Law.

FREDERIC E. NARAGON, born Salem, Ohio, April 19, 1945; admitted to bar, 1971, Ohio; 1976, U.S. Supreme Court; registered to practice before U.S. Patent and Trademark Office. *Education:* Grove City College (B.S., cum laude, 1967); Case Western Reserve University (J.D., 1970). Assistant Professor, Business Law, Kent State University, 1977-2002. Columbiana County Public Defender, 1978-1993. *Member:* Columbiana County, Ohio State and American Bar Associations.

REPRESENTATIVE CLIENTS: Chappell & Zimmerman, Inc.; R.A.G. Tooling, Inc.; Peoples Lumber Co.; Stitle Construction Corp.; Taylor Pattern, Inc.; Simmons Feed & Supply, Inc.; Interstate Pump Company, Inc.; Main Street Machine, Inc.; Church Budget Envelope Co.; McDaniel's Envelope Co.; Adams Chemical and Supply; B.O.C. Water Hydraulics, Inc.; Ohio Pump Company; Interiors of Salem LLC; Advanced Equipment Manufacturing LLC; Campf's Service Company, Inc.; Axum Manufacturing, LLC; SpecEdu Konnections, LLC; Radon and Radiation Consultants, LLC; Salem Security Storage, LLC.
REFERENCES: Keybank; Bank One of Northeastern Ohio, N.A.

BUCKINGHAM, LUCAL, McGOOKEY & ZEIHER CO., L.P.A.

414 WAYNE STREET
P.O. BOX 929
SANDUSKY, OHIO 44870
Telephone: 800-410-0414; 419-627-0414
Fax: 419-627-0009
Email: attorneys@buckinghamlaw.com
URL: http://www.buckinghamlaw.com

Vermilion, Ohio Office: 1513 State Route 60, 44089. Telephone: 440-967-6136. Fax: 440-967-8541.

Trials in all State and Federal Courts. Wrongful Death, Personal Injury, Product Liability, Domestic Relations, Family Law, Corporate Law, Business Law, Banking, Real Estate Law, Employment Law, Probate, Estate Planning, Commercial, Workers Compensation, Bankruptcy Law, Criminal Defense (Felonies and Misdemeanors), Medicaid Planning.

FIRM PROFILE: Buckingham, Lucal, McGookey & Zeiher Co., L.P.A. was formed as result of the merger of long established Sandusky Law firms. The origin of the Firm dates back to the 1940's. The firm provides legal services to clients in all areas of the law in Erie, Huron, Ottawa, Sandusky, Lorain, Seneca and Crawford Counties.

The firm lists members in the American, Ohio, Erie, Huron and Lorain County Bar Associations, the American Board of Trial Advocacy, American Trial Lawyers Associations, the Ohio Academy of Trial Lawyers, and the Ohio Association of Civil Trial Attorneys.

The members of the firm are admitted to practice before all Ohio courts, the U.S. District Courts for the Northern District of Ohio, Western and Eastern Divisions, the U.S. 6th District Court of Appeals, the U.S. Supreme Court and the U.S. Court of Claims.

MAURICE L. McDERMOND, JR., born Camp Lejeune, North Carolina, June 10, 1945; admitted to bar, 1971, Ohio. *Education:* DePauw University (B.A., 1967); Indiana University (J.D., 1970). Phi Delta Phi. Assistant Law Director, City of Huron, Ohio, 1971-1994. Law Director, City of Huron, 1994—. Village Solicitor: Bayview, 1973-1978; Milan, 1974-1995; Kelleys Island, 1990-1992. *Member:* Ohio State Bar Association; Erie County Law Library and Bar Association; Ohio Association of Civil Trial Attorneys. ***REPORTED CASES:*** Burris V. Grange Mut. Cos., Ohio St.3d 84 (1989). ***PRACTICE AREAS:*** Insurance Defense Law; Personal Injury Law; Municipal Law and Zoning; Business Law; Corporate Law; Real Estate. ***Email:*** mlmcdermond@buckinghamlaw.com

JOHN D. FRANKEL, born Sandusky, Ohio, June 7, 1949; admitted to bar, 1975, Ohio; 1979, U.S. Supreme Court. *Education:* DePauw University (B.A., 1971); Capital University (J.D., cum laude, 1975). Member, Order of the Curia. *Member:* Erie County and Ohio State Bar Associations. ***PRACTICE AREAS:*** Business Law; Probate and Estate Planning; Real Estate Law; Corporation Law; Family Law. ***Email:*** jdfrankel@buckinghamlaw.com

KEVIN J. ZEIHER, born Sandusky, Ohio, February 20, 1951; admitted to bar, 1977, Ohio; 1979, U.S. Court of Appeals, 6th Circuit; U.S. District Court, Northern District of Ohio; 1998, U.S. District Court, Eastern District of Kentucky. *Education:* Miami University (B.A., 1973); University of Dayton (J.D., 1977). Special Counsel to, Attorney General, Ohio, 1983-1994 and 2001—; Erie MetroPark Board, 1980-1987; Erie Mental Health Mental Retardation Board, 1980-1986. Member, Erie MetroPark Board of Commissioners, 1987—. *Member:* Cleveland, Erie County (Member, Trial Practice Section), Ohio State (Member, Trial Advocacy Section) and American (Member, Trial Practice and Tort Sections) Bar Associations; American Board of Trial Advocates; National Board of Trial Advocacy (Civil Trial Advocate) American Academy of Trial Lawyers; Ohio Academy of Trial Lawyers; Defense Research Institute, Inc.; Ohio Association of Civil Trial Attorneys. ***REPORTED CASES:*** State v. Koontz, 65 Ohio App.2d 264, 417 N.E.2d 1272 (1979); Cuppett v. Grange, 12 Ohio App.3d 82, 466 N.E.2d 180; Koontz v. Glossa, 731 F2d 365 (CA 6 Ohio, 1984); Herman v. Veverka, 30 Ohio St.3d 41, 506 N.E.2d 218 (1987); Nobles v. Wolf, 54 Ohio St.3d 75, 562 N.E.2d 144 (1990); Landis v. Grange, 95 Ohio App.3d 422, 642 N.E.2d 679 (1994); Riedling v. Valle 132 Ohio App.3d 310 (1999). ***PRACTICE AREAS:*** Civil Practice; Construction Law; Insurance Bad Faith; Personal Injury; Accidents; Bicycle Accidents; Catastrophic Injuries; Wrongful Death; Product Liability; Medical Malpractice; Trial Practice; Workers Compensation. ***Email:*** kjzeiher@buckinghamlaw.com

(This Listing Continued)

†W. ZACK DOLYK, born Lorain, Ohio, April 2, 1953; admitted to bar, 1978, Ohio; U.S. District Court, Northern District of Ohio. *Education:* Ohio Northern University (B.A., 1975); The Ohio State University (J.D., 1978). *Member:* Erie County, Lorain County and Ohio State Bar Associations. ***PRACTICE AREAS:*** Domestic Relations; Probate and Estate Planning; Real Estate; Bankruptcy and Collections. ***Email:*** wzdolyk@buckinghamlaw.com

DANIEL L. McGOOKEY, born Sandusky, Ohio, February 5, 1953; admitted to bar, 1979, Ohio; 1980, U.S. District Court, Northern District of Ohio and U.S. Court of Appeals, Sixth Circuit. *Education:* University of Notre Dame (B.B.A., 1975); University of Toledo (J.D., 1979). *Member:* Erie County, Ohio State and American (Member, Litigation Section, 1992—, Tort and Insurance Practice Section, 1992—) Bar Associations; The Association of Trial Lawyers of America (Member, Motor Vehicle Collision, Highway and Premises Liability Section, 1992—); Ohio Academy of Trial Lawyers. ***PRACTICE AREAS:*** General Civil Litigation; Business Litigation; Commercial Law. ***Email:*** dlmcgookey@buckinghamlaw.com

DUFFIELD E. MILKIE, born Bellevue, Ohio, July 26, 1965; admitted to bar, 1991, Ohio; 1992, U.S. District Court, Northern District of Ohio. *Education:* University of Toledo (B.A., Psych., magna cum laude, 1987; J.D., 1991). Phi Beta Kappa. Paralegal Instructor, EHOVE Joint Vocational School, 1999-2001. City Prosecutor, 1994-1995 and City Law Director, 1995-1997, City of Sandusky. Village Solicitor, Bay View, Ohio, 2000-2002. Member, National Employment Lawyers Association, 2000-2003.*Member:* Erie County (Trustee) and Ohio State Bar Associations; Ohio Academy of Trial Lawyers. ***REPORTED CASES:*** Kresser v. Sandusky Board of Education, 140 Ohio App 3d 634, 748 N.E. 2d 620. ***PRACTICE AREAS:*** Business Law; Real Estate; Real Estate Development; Commercial Law. ***Email:*** demilkie@buckinghamlaw.com

TROY WISEHART, born Shelby, Michigan, September 22, 1963; admitted to bar, 1991, Ohio; 1992, U.S. District Court, Northern District of Ohio. *Education:* Michigan State University (B.A., 1986); University of Toledo (J.D., 1991). *Member:* Erie County and Ohio State Bar Associations; Ohio Academy of Trial Lawyers; Ohio Academy of Criminal Defense Attorneys; Erie County Public Defender's Board. ***PRACTICE AREAS:*** Criminal Defense; Personal Injury; Bankruptcy. ***Email:*** tdwisehart@buckinghamlaw.com

JOHN R. BALL, born Youngstown, Ohio September 2, 1961; admitted to bar, 1988, Ohio; 1990, U.S. District Court, Southern District of Ohio; 1997, U.S. Supreme Court; 1999, U.S. Court of Federal Claims. *Education:* The University of Toledo (B.A., 1984); Capital University School of Law (J.D., 1988). Recipient, American Jurisprudence Book Award for Commercial Law. Lecturer: Ohio Continuing Legal Education Institute (Estate Administration and Estate Planning Topics); Professional Education Systems Institute (Estate Planning, Medicaid and Elder Law Topics). *Member:* Erie County (Member, Probate Committee), Huron County and Ohio State (Member, Probate and Trust Law Section) Bar Associations. ***REPORTED CASES:*** In Re McPheter, 95 Ohio App.3d 440, 642 NE2d 690; In Re Tikyra A., 103 Ohio App.3d 452, 659 NE2d 867; Reidling v. Valle 132 Ohio App. 3d. 310. ***PRACTICE AREAS:*** Estate Planning; Estate Administration; Adoption Law; Guardianships; Business Law. ***Email:*** johnrball@buckinghamlaw.com

†DAVID J. CLAUS, born Sandusky, Ohio, September 20, 1972; admitted to bar, 1999, Ohio and U.S. District Court, Northern District of Ohio. *Education:* Bowling Green State University (B.A., 1995); University of Akron School of Law (J.D., 1999). Phi Delta Phi (Magister, 1998-1999). President, Sports and Entertainment Law, 1998. Treasurer, National Association of Criminal Defense Lawyers, 1999. Sgt.-at-Arms, Association of Trial Lawyers of America, 1999. Paralegal Instructor, Ehove Joint Vocational School (2001). *Member:* Erie County, Lorain County and Ohio State Bar Associations. ***PRACTICE AREAS:*** Criminal Law; Personal Injury; Domestic Relations; Collections; Products Liability; Litigation. ***Email:*** djclaus@buckinghamlaw.com

OF COUNSEL

FREDERICK D. WALDOCK

LAWRENCE H. SCHELL (Retired)

DEAN S. LUCAL (Retired)

RICHARD D. HOLZAPFEL (Retired)

ARTHUR W. ZEIHER (1920-2003)

THOMAS S. BUCKINGHAM (1926-2002)

† Sandusky and Vermilion, Ohio Offices

LOCAL COUNSEL: Attorney General's Office; Buckeye County Cablevision, Inc.; Meridian Ins. Co.
GENERAL COUNSEL: Sandusky Newspapers, Inc.; The Citizens Banking Co.; First Citizens Bank; City of Huron, Ohio; Sandusky Packaging Corp. (Paper Products); District Petroleum Products, Inc. (Petroleum Product Distributor); A.V. Lake Steel Co. (Butler-Buildings); Firelands Regional Medical Center; Jamac, Inc.; Canfield-Hartley; Windau Plumbing & Heating; Sandusky Steel-Supply Co. (Scrap Metal); Paul Motry Memorial Fund (Charitable Foundation); Sandusky Bay Development Co. (Marina and Marine Service); O.E. Meyer Co. (Liquid Gases and Welding Supplies); D & H Investments Inc.; F. Leo Groff, Inc. (Funeral Directors); Polar Pure Carbonics, Inc.; Stierhoff Bros. Moving & Cartage, Inc. (Atlas Van Lines Agent); The Lunch Box, Inc. (Restaurant); John Hancock & Associates, Inc. (Civil Engineer and Surveyor); Bores Manufacturing; Corso's Flower & Garden Center; Feick Contractors; Great Lakes Tires, Inc.; Lepley Farms; Lewco, Inc.; Put-In-Bay Township; Speer Bros., Inc. (Excavating); Lakecrest, LLC (Real Estate Development).

FLYNN, PY & KRUSE

A LEGAL PROFESSIONAL ASSOCIATION

165 EAST WASHINGTON ROW

SANDUSKY, OHIO 44870

Telephone: 419-625-8324

Fax: 419-625-9007

Port Clinton, Ohio Office: 115 West Perry Street. Telephone: 419-734-3174. Fax: 419-734-3175.

General Civil Practice. Corporation, Banking, Antitrust, Labor and Employment, Taxation, Insurance, Personal Injury, Workers Compensation, Environmental Law, Probate and Estate Planning, Commercial Litigation, Pension and Profit Sharing, Employee Benefits, Real Estate. Trials and Appeals in State and Federal Courts.

FIRM PROFILE: Flynn, Py & Kruse was founded in 1875 by Judge Edmund B. King and is one of the oldest law firms in the State of Ohio. Through both its main office in Sandusky and its branch office in Port Clinton, the firm provides legal services over a wide geographical area, including Erie, Ottawa, Sandusky, Huron, Lorain, Seneca and Lucas Counties.

JAMES F. FLYNN (1887-1963)

JOHN R. PY (1908-1969)

RICHARD R. KRUSE (1910-1997)

MELVYN J. STAUFFER, born Brookville, Ohio, October 21, 1926; admitted to bar, 1951, Ohio; 1964, U.S. Supreme Court. *Education:* The Ohio State University (A.B., 1947); University of Michigan Law School (LL.B., 1951). Delta Theta Phi. *Member:* Erie County, Cleveland, Ohio State and American (Member, Sections on: Taxation; Real Property; Labor Law) Bar Associations. ***PRACTICE AREAS:*** Business Law; Estate Planning Law; Charitable Trusts and Foundations.

GEORGE M. MUEHLHAUSER, III, born Sandusky, Ohio, January 21, 1930; admitted to bar, 1955, Ohio. *Education:* University of Michigan (A.B., 1952); The Ohio State University (J.D., 1955). Phi Delta Phi. Member, Board of Directors, 1962—, and Chairman, 1988-1989, 1992, 1993, Firelands Regional Health System. *Member:* Erie County (President, 1976) and Ohio State Bar Associations. ***PRACTICE AREAS:*** Probate and Estate Planning; Tax Law; Corporate Law; Real Estate Law. ***Email:*** gmm@flynnpykruse.com

JOHN A. COPPELER, born Toledo, Ohio, June 2, 1947; admitted to bar, 1975, Ohio; 1976, U.S. District Court, Northern District of Ohio; 1984, U.S. Court of Appeals, Sixth Circuit. *Education:* The Ohio State University (B.A. in Journalism, 1970; J.D., cum laude, 1974). Phi Delta Phi. *Member:* Erie County, Ottawa County, Ohio State (Member, Litigation, Labor and Employment, and Real Property Law Sections) and American (Member, Litigation, Labor and Employment Law, and Real Property, Probate and Trust Sections) Bar Associations. ***REPORTED CASES:*** Supreme Court Cases Only: Hacker v. Dickman (1996), 75 Ohio St.3d 118; Berger v. Port Clinton (1994), 71 Ohio St.3d 1213; Manufacturer's Natl. Bank of Detroit v. Erie Cty. Road Comm. (1992), 63 Ohio St.3d 318; Gressman v. McClain (1988), 40 Ohio St.3d 359; Carney v. McAfee (1988), 35 Ohio St.3d 52; Yurista v. Nationwide Mut. Ins. Co. (1985), 18 Ohio St.3d 326; Noroski v. Fallett (1982), 2 Ohio St.3d 77; Warner v. Lindley (1982), 70 Ohio St.2d 273. ***PRACTICE AREAS:*** Personal Injury Law; Trial Practice; Business Law; Labor and Employment Law; Banking Law; Zoning and Real Estate; Township Law.

JOHN E. ROSINO, born Sandusky, Ohio, November 1, 1951; admitted to bar, 1977, Ohio. *Education:* Ohio Wesleyan University (B.A., summa cum laude, 1974); Harvard University (J.D., 1977). Phi Beta Kappa. *Member:* Erie County, Ohio State and American (Member, Sections on: Health Law; Real Property) Bar Associations. ***PRACTICE AREAS:*** Business Law; Real Estate Law; Estate Planning Law.

JAMES W. HART, born Cleveland, Ohio, September 19, 1951; admitted to bar, 1980, Texas; 1981, Ohio. *Education:* Ohio Wesleyan University (B.A., 1973); University of Cincinnati (M.A., 1975); St. Mary's University of San Antonio (J.D., 1980). Phi Delta Phi. *Member:* Erie County and Ohio State Bar Associations; State Bar of Texas; Defense Research Institute; Ohio Association of Criminal Defense Lawyers. ***REPORTED CASES:*** Supreme Court Cases Only: Cicco v. Stockmaster (2000), 89 Ohio State 3d 95; Moore v. State Auto Mutual Insurance Co. (2000), 88 Ohio State 3d 27; Peace v. Prudential Property & Casualty Insurance Co. (1993), 68 Ohio State 3d 106. ***PRACTICE AREAS:*** Personal Injury; Criminal Law; Family Law; Civil Trial Practice; Contested Wills.

MARY JANE S. HILL, born Sandusky, Ohio, April 9, 1959; admitted to bar, 1984, Ohio. *Education:* Denison University (B.A., with honors, 1981); Case Western Reserve University School of Law (J.D., 1984). *Member:* Erie County, Ohio State and American Bar Associations. ***PRACTICE AREAS:*** Business Law; Probate; Real Estate; Estate Planning; Charitable Foundations.

CHRISTOPHER M. MARINKO, born Cleveland, Ohio, September 23, 1963; admitted to bar, 1988, Ohio. *Education:* Ohio State University (B.A., cum laude, 1985; J.D., 1988). Phi Kappa Phi; Pi Sigma Alpha. *Member:* Erie County, Ohio State and American Bar Associations; Ohio Association of Civil Trial Attorneys; Defense Research Institute. ***REPORTED CASES:*** Lemley v. Stevenson (1995), 104 Ohio App.3d 126; Russell v. Ohio Outdoor Advertising Corp. (1997), 122 Ohio App.3d 1545. ***PRACTICE AREAS:*** Insurance; Commercial Litigation; Employment Law; Mass Torts.

ERIC M. MUEHLHAUSER, born Sandusky, Ohio, October 31, 1962; admitted to bar, 1993, Ohio. *Education:* Bowling Green State University (B.S., 1985); Capital University (J.D., 1993). *Member:* Erie County and Ohio State Bar Associations. ***PRACTICE AREAS:*** Collections; Creditors Rights; Real Estate; Tax Law; Probate; Estate Planning. ***Email:*** emm@flynnpykruse.com

WM. R.S. STEUK, born Sandusky, Ohio, April 17, 1971; admitted to bar, 1996, Ohio. *Education:* University of Michigan (B.A., 1993); Ohio Northern University (J.D., 1996). *Member:* Erie County, Ohio State and American Bar Associations. ***PRACTICE AREAS:*** Corporate Law; Business Law; Real Estate; Estate Planning; Labor and Employment; Environmental Law.

(This Listing Continued)

REPRESENTATIVE CLIENTS: Barnes Nursery, Inc.; Cafaro Co.; Cedar Bay Construction, Inc.; Cedar Fair, L.P.; Cincinnati Insurance Co.; Danbury Township (Ottawa Co.); The Dorn Foundation; Erie Metropolitan Housing Authority; Executive Urology, Inc.; Extol of Ohio, Inc.; The Frohman Foundation; Fifth Third Bank; Firelands Regional Medical Center; First Energy Corp.; First National Bank of Bellevue; Flex Temp Employment Services; Foster Chevrolet Oldsmobile Cadillac, Inc.; Frost-Parker Foundation; Gannett Co., Inc.; Greater Erie Co. Marketing Group, Inc.; Herman's Furniture; Huron Lagoons Marina; J.H. Routh Packing Co.; Key Bank; Lutheran Memorial Home; Matrix Automation, Inc.; Miller Boat Line; The Mylander Foundation; Norfolk and Southern Corp.; North Coast Cancer Care Inc.; Pelz Lettering, Inc.; Perkins Township (Erie Co.); Salem Township (Ottawa Co.); Sandusky Orthopedic Surgeons, Inc.; State Automobile Mutual Insurance Co.; The Sam Stein Charitable Trusts; Telamon Construction Co.; Unimin Corp.; Vacationland Federal Credit Union; Wonderly-Horvath Funeral Home, Inc.; Young's Mobile Homes & Travel Center, Inc.

MURRAY & MURRAY CO., L.P.A.

Established in 1931

MURRAY BUILDING

111 EAST SHORELINE DRIVE

P.O. BOX 19

SANDUSKY, OHIO 44871-0019

Telephone: 419-624-3000

Fax: 419-624-0707

Email: firm@murrayandmurray.com

URL: http://www.murrayandmurray.com

General Civil and Trial Practice in all State and Federal Courts. Commercial Class Actions, Personal Injury, Products Liability, Toxic Torts and Security Litigation. Limited to Plaintiff's Trial Practice.

FIRM PROFILE: Murray & Murray represents plaintiffs, only with regard to cases which have jury trial prospects. The law firm owners now include ten Murray attorneys, and there are also nine unrelated attorneys. Established in 1931, Murray & Murray has always been a leader in the use of class action suits in Ohio and in jury trials.

EMMETT MURRAY (1903-1980)

THOMAS J. MURRAY (1907-1974)

KIRK J. DELLI BOVI (1952-1996)

DENNIS E. MURRAY, SR., born Sandusky, Ohio, June 23, 1939; admitted to bar, 1963, Michigan; 1964, Ohio; 1967, Florida; 1968, U.S. Court of Appeals, Sixth Circuit; 1971, U.S. Supreme Court and U.S. District Court, Northern and Southern Districts of Ohio. *Education:* College of the Holy Cross (B.S., 1961); University of Michigan (J.D., 1963). Supreme Court of Ohio Bar Examiner, 1983-1988. Supreme Court of Ohio Board of Commissioners on the Unauthorized Practice of Law, 1989-1992. *Member:* Erie County (President, 1983-1984) and Ohio State Bar Associations; State Bar of Michigan; The Florida Bar; The Association of Trial Lawyers of America; Ohio Academy of Trial Lawyers; American Institute of Certified Public Accountants; Ohio Society of Certified Public Accountants. ***REPORTED CASES:*** Supreme Court Cases Only: Phung v. Waste Management (1994), 71 Ohio St.3d 408; Zappo v. Homestead Insurance Company (1994), 71 Ohio St.3d 552; Leber v. Smith (1994), 70 Ohio St.3d 548; Borsick v. State Farm Fire & Cas. Co. (1994), 68 Ohio St.3d 1221; Cope v. Metro Life Ins. Co. (1998), 82 Ohio St.3d 426; Dillibovi v. Pacific Indemn. Co. (1999), 85 Ohio St.3d 343; Polikoff v. Adam (1993), 67 Ohio St.3d 100; Borsick v. State Farm Mut. Auto. Ins. Co. (1993), 68 Ohio St.3d 81; Motorist Mut. Ins. Co. v. Said (1992), 63 Ohio St.3d 690; Stepak v. Schey (1990), 51 Ohio St.3d 8; State, ex. Rel. Ohio Co. v. Maschari (1990), 51 Ohio St.3d 18; Crosby v. Beam (1989), 47 Ohio St.3d 105; Miller v. Wikel Mfg. Co., Inc. (1989), 46 Ohio St.3d 76; Digital v. Analog Design Corp. v. North Supply Co. (1989), 44 Ohio St.3d 36; Warner v. Waste Management, Inc. (1988), 36 Ohio St.3d 91; Carney v. McAfee (1988), 35 Ohio St.3d 52; Armstrong v. Marathon Oil Co. (1987), 32 Ohio St.3d 397; Phung v. Waste Management, Inc. (1986), 23 Ohio St.3d 100; Yeager v. Local Union 20 (1983), 6 Ohio St.3d 369; Ruta v. Breckenridge-Remy Co. (1982), 69 Ohio St.2d 140; Roberts v. United States Fid. & Guar. Co., 75 Ohio St. 3d 630 (1996); Weston v. Weston Paper & Meg. Co., 74 Ohio St. 3d 377 (1996). Other Federal Cases of Note: McConocha v. Blue Cross & Blue Shield Mut. of Ohio, 930 F. Supp 1182 (1996); Dowling v. Narragansett Capital Corp. (DRI 1990), 735 F.Supp. 1105. ***PRACTICE AREAS:*** Plaintiff's Trial Practice; Securities; Commercial Law; Bad Faith; Insurance Company Litigation; Toxic Tort Class Actions; Serious Personal Injury; Wrongful Death. ***Email:*** dms@murrayandmurray.com

THOMAS J. MURRAY, born Sandusky, Ohio, February 23, 1937; admitted to bar, 1965, Ohio; 1968, U.S. District Court, Northern District of Ohio and U.S. Court of Appeals, Sixth Circuit; 1971, U.S. Supreme Court. *Education:* Boston College (B.A., magna cum laude, 1959); University of Virginia (J.D., 1965). *Member:* Erie County (President, 1984-1985), Ohio State and American Bar Associations; The Association of Trial Lawyers of America; Ohio Academy of Trial Lawyers. Honorary lifetime member of the Trial Lawyers Association of British Columbia. Fellow: International Academy of Trial Lawyers; International Society of Barristers. [Lt., Military Police, 1960-1961]. (Certified as a Civil Trial Advocate by the National Board of Trial Advocacy). ***LANGUAGES:*** Russian, French and Spanish. ***REPORTED CASES:*** Supreme Court Cases Only: Wightman v. Consolidated Rail Corp. (1999), 86 Ohio St.3d 431; Lacy v. CSX (1999). Case No. 25341, Supreme Court of Appeals of West Virginia.Coleman v. Sandoz Pharmaceuticals Corp., 74 Ohio St. 3d 492 (1996); Kenty v. Transamerica Premium Ins. Co. (1995), 70 Ohio St. 3d 415; Horner v. Toledo Hospital (1994), 70 Ohio St.3d 1211; Frazier v. Depinet (1994), 69 Ohio St.3d 1211; Sorrell v. Thevenir (1994), 69 Ohio St.3d 415; Brady v. Safety-Kleen Corp. (1991), 61 Ohio St.3d 624; Schellhouse v. Norfolk & Western Ry. Co. (1991), 61 Ohio St.3d 520; Masheter v. Welschenbach (1976), 48 Ohio St.3d 8; Norfolk & Western R.R. v. Nemitz, 404 U.S. 37 (1971); Local 74 v. United Transportation Union. ***PRACTICE AREAS:*** General Negligence Law; Environmental Law; Commercial Litigation; Railroad Law; Admiralty Law; Wrongful Death Actions; Plaintiffs' Trial Practice; Product Liability; Maritime. ***Email:*** tjm@murrayandmurray.com

W. PATRICK MURRAY, born Sandusky, Ohio, September 21, 1940; admitted to bar, 1965, Ohio; 1968, U.S. District Court, Northern District of Ohio and U.S. Court of Appeals, Sixth Circuit; 1972, U.S. Supreme Court. *Education:* University of Dayton (B.A., 1962);

(This Listing Continued)

Ohio Northern University (J.D., 1965). Phi Alpha Delta. *Member:* Erie County (President, 1987-1988), Ohio State and American Bar Associations; The Association of Trial Lawyers of America; Ohio Academy of Trial Lawyers. ***REPORTED CASES:*** Supreme Court Cases Only: Hamilton mut. Ins. v. Perry (ct.App.1997), 124 Ohio App.3d147; Altvater v. Claycreft (ct.App 1994), 92 Ohio St. 3d 759; Leber v. Smith (1994), 70 Ohio St.3d 548; Freeman v. Norfolk & Western Ry. Co. (1994), 69 Ohio St.3d 611; Sanderson v. Ohio Edison Co. (1994), 69 Ohio St.3d 582; Motorists Mutual Ins. Co. v. Andrews (1992), 65 Ohio St.3d 362; Huston v. Konieczny (1990), 52 Ohio St.3d 214; Sharp v. Norfolk & Western Ry. Co. (1988), 36 Ohio St.3d 172; Viock v. Stowe-Woodward Co. (1987), 34 Ohio St.3d 602; Horman v. Veverka (1987), 30 Ohio St.3d 41; Jones v. VIP Development Co. (1984), 15 Ohio St.3d 90; Sumwalt v. Allstate Ins. Co. (1984), 12 Ohio St.3d 294; State v. Chaffin (1972), 30 Ohio St.2d 13; Brady v. Safety-Kleen Corp., 576 N.E.2d 722, 61 Ohio St. 3d 624 (S. Ct. 1991); Lang v. Colonial Manor Nursing Home, 446 N.E.2d, 4 Ohio Misc. 2d 1 (1981); Williams v. Grant, 417 N.E.2d 586, 65 Ohio App. 2d 225 (Ct. App. 1979); Stony Ridge Hill Condominium Owners Ass'n v. Auer, 410 N.E.2d 782, 64 Ohio App. (1996); Sharp v. Norfolk & W. Ry. Co., 72 Ohio St. 3d 307 (1995); Ross v. Tom Reith, Inc., 71 Ohio St. 3d 563 (1995). ***PRACTICE AREAS:*** Products Liability Law; Medical Malpractice Law; Plaintiffs' Trial Practice; Environmental Law. ***Email:*** wpm@murrayandmurray.com

JAMES T. MURRAY, born Sandusky, Ohio, September 12, 1939; admitted to bar, 1965, Ohio; 1967, U.S. District Court, Northern District of Ohio and U.S. Court of Appeals, Sixth Circuit; 1982, U.S. Supreme Court. *Education:* Boston College (B.S., 1961); Case Western Reserve University (J.D., 1965). *Member:* Erie County, Ohio State and American Bar Associations; American Judicature Society; The Association of Trial Lawyers of America. (Certified as a Civil Trial Advocate by the National Board of Trial Advocacy). ***REPORTED CASES:*** Supreme Court Cases Only: State, ex. rel. Ohio Academy of Trial Lawyers v. Sheward, 86 Ohio St.3d 451 (1999); Manufacturer's National Bank of Detroit v. Erie County Road Commission (1992), 63 Ohio St.3d 318; Burris v. Grange Mutual Companies (1989), 46 Ohio St.3d 84; Gressman v. McClain (1988), 40 Ohio St.3d 359; Noroski v. Fallet (1982), 2 Ohio St.3d 77; Chance v. BP Chemicals, Inc., 77 Ohio St. 3d 17 (1996); Landis v. Grange Mutual Ins. Co., 82 Ohio St.3d 339 (1998); Drage v. Ameritrust Corp., 49 Ohio St.3d 604 (1990); Stacy v. Nationwide Mutual Ins. Co., 85 Ohio St.3d 1203 (1999). ***PRACTICE AREAS:*** General Negligence; Will Contests; Commercial Litigation; Wrongful Death Actions; Environmental Law; Class Actions; Plaintiffs Trial Practice. ***Email:*** jitm@murrayandmurray.com

MICHAEL T. MURRAY, born Sandusky, Ohio, September 25, 1944; admitted to bar, 1970, Ohio; 1971, U.S. District Court, Northern District of Ohio; 1975, U.S. Court of Appeals, Sixth Circuit. *Education:* John Carroll University (B.S., 1966); Cleveland State University (J.D., 1970). *Member:* Erie County, Ohio State and American Bar Associations; American Judicature Society; Ohio Academy of Trial Lawyers (Member, Board of Trustees, 1975); The Association of Trial Lawyers of America. (Certified as a Civil Trial Advocacy Specialist by the National Board of Trial Advocacy). ***REPORTED CASES:*** Supreme Court Cases Only: Renfro v. Smith Labs (1990), 52 Ohio St.3d 27. State Cases: State ex. Rel. Lyons v. Zaleski, 75 Ohio St. 3d 623 (1996). ***PRACTICE AREAS:*** Products Liability Law; Wrongful Death Law; Medical Malpractice Law; Plaintiffs' Trial Practice. ***Email:*** mtm@murrayandmurray.com

JOHN T. MURRAY, born Sandusky, Ohio, September 7, 1953; admitted to bar, 1979, Ohio; 1980, U.S. District Court, Northern District of Ohio; 1988, Colorado and New York; 1990, U.S. Supreme Court. *Education:* University of Dayton (B.S., 1974); Ohio Northern University (J.D., 1979). Phi Kappa Phi; Phi Alpha Delta. *Member:* Erie County (Co-Chairman, Civil Litigation/Courts Committee, 1989-1993) and Ohio State Bar Associations; The Association of Trial Lawyers of America; Ohio Academy of Trial Lawyers; National Association of Consumer Advocates. ***REPORTED CASES:*** Supreme Court Cases: Weston v. Weston Paper & Mfg. Co., 74 Ohio St.3d 377 (1995); Kenty v. Transamerica, 72 Ohio St.3d 415 (1995); Brinkman v. Ross 68 Ohio St.3d 82 (1993); State ex rel, The Ohio Company v. Maschari, 51 Ohio St.3d 18 (1989); Stepak v. Schey (1993), 51 Ohio St.3d 8 (1989); Cope, et al. v. Metro Life Ins. Co., 82 Ohio St.3d 426 (1998); Household Credit Services, Inc. v. Pfennig, 541 US 232 (2004); Maitland v. Ford Motor Co., 1030S 3rd 463 (2004). ***PRACTICE AREAS:*** Consumer Law; Commercial Law; Class Actions; Medical Malpractice; Securities Litigation; Plaintiffs' Trial Practice; Complex Litigation; Products Liability. ***Email:*** jotm@murrayandmurray.com

DENNIS E. MURRAY, JR., born Sandusky, Ohio, May 25, 1962; admitted to bar, 1987, Ohio and U.S. District Court, Northern District of Ohio and U.S. Court of Appeals, Sixth Circuit; 1989, District of Columbia. *Education:* Georgetown University (B.A., magna cum laude, 1984; J.D., cum laude, 1987). Phi Beta Kappa. Grader, Ohio Bar Exams, 1995—. *Member:* Erie County (Member, Erie-Huron Counties Certified Grievance Committee, 1990—; Advisory Committee, U.S. District Court, Northern District of Ohio), Ohio State and American Bar Associations; The Association of Trial Lawyers of America; Ohio Academy of Trial Lawyers. ***REPORTED CASES:*** State, ex. Rel. The Ohio Company v. Maschari (1990), 51 Ohio St.3d 18; Crosby v. Beam (1989), 47 Ohio St.3d 105; Dowling v. Narragansett Capital Corp. (D.R.I. 1990), 735 F.Supp. 1105; Erebria v. Chrysler Plastic Products Corp. (6th Cir. 1989), 891 F.2d 1212; Weston v. Weston Paper & Mfg. Co., 74 Ohio St.3d 377 (1996); Shaver v. The Standard Oil Company, 135 Ohio App. 3d 242 (Huron Co. 1999); Gomez v. Towne Bancorp, 129 F.Supp.2d 1116 (N.D.Ohio 2000); Lambert v. Kazinetz, 873 F.Supp.2d — (S.D.Ohio 2003). ***PRACTICE AREAS:*** Commercial Litigation; Securities Litigation; Plaintiffs' Trial Practice. ***Email:*** dmj@murrayandmurray.com

CHARLES M. MURRAY, born Sandusky, Ohio, August 7, 1965; admitted to bar, 1991, Ohio; 1992, U.S. District Court, Northern District of Ohio; U.S. Court of Appeals, Sixth Circuit. *Education:* Xavier University (B.A., 1987); University of Dayton (J.D., 1991). Assistant Prosecuting Attorney, Adult Felony Trial Division, Erie County, 1991-1993. *Member:* Erie County and Ohio State Bar Associations; The Association of Trial Lawyers of America; Ohio Academy of Trial Lawyers; Cleveland Academy of Trial Lawyers. (Certified as a Civil Trial Advocacy Specialist by the National Board of Trial Advocacy). ***REPORTED CASES:*** Karr v. Borchardt, 88 Ohio St.3d 577 (2000). ***PRACTICE AREAS:*** Personal Injury; Wrongful Death; Medical Malpractice; Insurance Coverage; Plaintiffs' Trial Practice. ***Email:*** cmm@murrayandmurray.com

MARGARET M. MURRAY, born Sandusky, Ohio, September 6, 1970; admitted to bar, 1996, Ohio and U.S. District Court, Northern District of Ohio; 1998, U.S. Court of Appeals, Sixth Circuit; 2002, U.S. District Court, Eastern District of Michigan. *Education:* College of The Holy Cross (B.A., 1993-Sigma Tau Delta); Case Western Reserve University (J.D., 1996-Merit Scholar). Assistant Prosecuting Attorney, Erie County, 1997. *Member:* Erie County, Ohio State and American Bar Associations; The Association of Trial Lawyers of America; Ohio Academy of Trial Lawyers (Board of Trustees, 2004-2006). ***REPORTED CASES:*** Agrawal v. Paul Revere Ins., 205 F.3d 297 (CA 6, 2000) overruled by Yates v. Hendon (2004) 541 US 1.. ***PRACTICE AREAS:*** Personal Injury; Products Liability; Intentional Torts; Class Actions; Wrongful Death. ***Email:*** mmm@murrayandmurray.com

JAMES L. MURRAY, born Sandusky, Ohio, January 13, 1972; admitted to bar, 1997, Ohio. *Education:* Boston College (B.A., 1994); Case Western Reserve University (J.D., 1997). Formerly with Cuyahoga County Prosecutor's Office. *Member:* Erie County and Ohio State Bar Associations; Ohio Academy of Trial Lawyers. ***PRACTICE AREAS:*** Personal Injury; Products Liability. ***Email:*** jlm@murrayandmurray.com

WILLIAM H. BARTLE, born Torrance, California, September 24, 1949; admitted to bar, 1975, Ohio and U.S. District Court, Northern District of Ohio; 1985, U.S. Court of Appeals, Sixth Circuit; 1986, U.S. Supreme Court. *Education:* Hamilton College (A.B., 1971); Albany Law School of Union University; Case Western Reserve University (J.D., 1975). *Member:* Erie County and Ohio State Bar Associations; Ohio Academy of Trial Lawyers. ***REPORTED CASES:*** Supreme Court Cases Only: Huston vs. Konieczny (1990), 52 Ohio St.3d 214; Horman v. Veverka (1987), 30 Ohio St.3d 4; Kisil v. City of Sandusky (1984), 12 Ohio St.3d 30. State Cases: State ex. rel. Lyons v. Saleski, 75 Ohio St. 3d 623 (1996). ***PRACTICE AREAS:*** Personal Injury; Products Liability; Plaintiffs' Trial Practice; Wrongful Death; Class Actions; Employment Discrimination; Harassment; Insurance Coverage. ***Email:*** whb@murrayandmurray.com

---

STEVEN C. BECHTEL, born Sandusky, Ohio, July 14, 1958; admitted to bar, 1983, Ohio; 1989, U.S. District Court, Northern District of Ohio; 1996, U.S. Court of Appeals, Sixth Circuit. *Education:* Ohio University (B.A., summa cum laude, 1980); Ohio State University (J.D., 1983). Phi Beta Kappa; Pi Gamma Mu. Assistant Prosecuting Attorney, Franklin County, 1985-1989. Law Clerk to Honorable Earl E. Stephenson, Fourth District Court of Appeals, 1983-1984. *Member:* Erie County and Ohio State Bar Associations; Ohio Academy of Trial Lawyers. ***REPORTED CASES:*** Supreme Court Cases Only: Sanderson v. Ohio Edison Co. (1994), 69 Ohio St.3d 582; Brady v. Safety Kleen (1991), 61 Ohio St.3d 624 (amicus); Houston v. Konjieczny (1990), 52 Ohio St.3d 214; Hacker v. Dickman, 75 Ohio St. 3d 118 (1996); Sharp v. Norfolk & W. Ry. Co., 72 Ohio St. 3d 307 (1995); Ross v. Tom Reith, Inc., 71 Ohio St. 3d 563 (1995); Karr v. Borchardt, 88 Ohio St.3d 535 (2000); Littrell v. Wigglesworth (2001) 9105 3d 425; Gibson v. Drainage Products, Inc. (2002) 9505 3d; Penn Traffic Co. v. AIV Ins. Co. (2003), 99053d 227 (amicus). ***PRACTICE AREAS:*** Personal Injury Litigation; Wrongful Death; Insurance Litigation. ***Email:*** scb@murrayandmurray.com

MOLLY O'NEILL, born Cincinnati, Ohio, February 3, 1949; admitted to bar, 1977, New York; 1981, Georgia; 1997, Ohio. *Education:* Smith College (A.B., 1971); Boston University (J.D., 1976). ***Email:*** mso@murrayandmurray.com

DONNA JEAN A. EVANS, born Toledo, Ohio, July 26, 1953; admitted to bar, 2000, Ohio; 2001, U.S District Court, Northern District of Ohio. *Education:* Marian College (B.A., cum laude, 1975); Cleveland-Marshall College of Law (J.D., magna cum laude, 2000). Delta Epsilon Sigma; Alpha Psi Omega (Secretary, 1974-1975). Senior Editor, Journal of Law and Health. *Member:* Erie County, Ohio State and American Bar Associations. ***PRACTICE AREAS:*** Plaintiffs Trial Practice; Class Actions; Commercial Litigation. ***Email:*** dae@murrayandmurray.com

JAMES S. TIMMERBERG, born New Brunswick, New Jersey, November 17, 1965; admitted to bar, 1997, Ohio; 2003, U.S. District Court, Northern District of Ohio. *Education:* Earlham College (B.A., 1988); University of Wisconsin (M.A., 1990); Case Western Reserve University (J.D., 1996). Phi Beta Kappa.*Member:* Erie County and Ohio State Bar Associations. ***PRACTICE AREAS:*** Commercial Litigation. ***Email:*** jst@murrayandmurray.com

GARNETTA P. MORELAND, born Mt. Sterling, Kentucky, March 23, 1953; admitted to bar, 2002, Kentucky; 2003, Ohio and U.S. District Court, Northern District of Ohio. *Education:* Morehead State University (B.A., magna cum laude, 1999); Ohio Northern University Pettit School of Law (J.D. with distinction, 2002). *Member:* Erie County, Kentucky and Ohio State Bar Associations. ***PRACTICE AREAS:*** Class Actions; Trial Practice; Wrongful Death. ***Email:*** gpm@murrayandmurray.com

---

BRENNAN, FREDERICK, VOUROS & YARWOOD, LTD.

SEBRING, OHIO

(See Youngstown)

General Trial Practice in all Courts. Corporation and Business Law. Criminal Defense, Negligence, Family and Probate Law. Estate Planning, Personal Injury.

JOSEPH E. DOTY

23 WEST MAIN STREET
P.O. BOX 73
SEVILLE, OHIO 44273
Telephone: 330-769-4544
Fax: 330-769-4543
Email: JEDLAW69@msn.com
URL: http://www.josephdotyesq.com

Estate Planning, Probate, Guardianship, Medicaid Planning, Elder Law.

JOSEPH E. DOTY, born Glendale, West Virginia, January 5, 1969; admitted to bar, 1998, Ohio. *Education:* Muskingum College (B.A., 1992); University of Akron (M.A.,

(This Listing Continued)

JOSEPH E. DOTY, Seville—Continued

Public Administration, 1997; J.D., cum laude, 1998). *Member:* Akron (Member, Probate Section), Medina County and Ohio State (Member, Probate Section) Bar Associations.

STANLEY S. KELLER & ASSOCIATES CO., LPA

Established in 1977

5455 DETROIT ROAD
SHEFFIELD VILLAGE, OHIO 44054
Telephone: 440-930-4039
Fax: 440-934-7205
Email: keller@en.com

Cleveland, Ohio Office: Suite 330 The Hanna Building, 1422 Euclid Avenue, 44115-1901. Telephone: 216-566-7100. Fax: 216-566-5430.

FIRM PROFILE: The law firm is engaged in the practice of law with emphasis on insurance defense, insurance coverage and bad faith issues, product liability, automobile negligence, transportation companies, environmental issues, asbestos and hazardous waste litigation. In addition, our firm represents our corporate and business clients with respect to legal concerns which affect their businesses and corporations and includes corporate law, business succession planning, employment law, commercial law, real estate, commercial litigation and internet/online law.

REPRESENTATIVE CLIENTS: American International Group; Allstate Insurance Company; State Farm Insurance Company; Schneider National Carriers, Inc.; INS Insurance, Inc.; Brotherhood Mutual Insurance Company; Hartford-Omni Insurance Group; Metropolitan Property & Liability Insurance Co.; AFLAC; Infinity Insurance Company; Windsor Group; Atlanta Casualty Company; Sentry Insurance Company; Gallagher Bassett Services, Inc.; Victoria Insurance Group; CNI Claim Service; Superior Insurance Company; Admiral Insurance Company; Covenant Mutual Insurance Co.; Southeastern Fidelity Insurance Co.; O'Brien & Associates; Esis, Inc./CIGNA Cos.; Crum & Forster; Self-Insured Services Co.; C.N.A.; Capital Indemnity Co.; North American Specialty Co.; Hastings Mutual Insurance Company; Brinker International; Fortis Financial Corp.; Yellow Freight Systems; State Auto Insurance Company; Lobo Claims Management, Inc.; Watkins Motor Lines; TIG Insurance Company Environmental Claims; Tops Market, Inc.; Foremost Insurance Company; ACE USA; Continental Western Insurance Company; Roehl Transport; Merastar Insurance Company.
REFERENCE: Bank One, Cleveland.

(For complete biographical data on all personnel, see professional biographies at Cleveland, Ohio)

POLAND, DEPLER AND SHEPHERD CO., L.P.A.

Established in 1954

6 WATER STREET
SHELBY, OHIO 44875-1297
Telephone: 419-347-7421
FAX: 419-342-5116
Email: office@pds-law.com

General Civil Practice in all Courts. Real Estate, Probate and Estate Planning, Corporate, Banking, Family, Domestic Relations and Commercial Law. Trials.

G. WILLIAM DEPLER (1912-1978)

F. HERBERT POLAND (Retired)

THOMAS A. DEPLER, born Shelby, Ohio, July 25, 1949; admitted to bar, 1975, Ohio. *Education:* Bowling Green State University (B.S. in B.A., 1971); Ohio Northern University (J.D., 1975). Delta Theta Phi. *Member:* Richland County (President, 1998), Ohio State and American Bar Associations; American Judicature Society; Richland County Law Library Association (Vice President, 1997-2002; Treasurer, 2000—). ***PRACTICE AREAS:*** Probate Law; Corporate Law; Real Estate Law.

R. LEE SHEPHERD, born Shelby, Ohio, October 3, 1951; admitted to bar, 1977, Ohio. *Education:* The Ohio State University (B.S., 1973); Cleveland Marshall College of Law (J.D., 1977). Law Director, City of Shelby, 1982-1989; 1994—. *Member:* Richland County, Ohio State (Traffic Law Committee, 1989—) and American Bar Associations. ***PRACTICE AREAS:*** Family Law; Criminal Law; Administrative Law; Personal Injury.

FAULKNER, GARMHAUSEN KEISTER & SHENK

A LEGAL PROFESSIONAL ASSOCIATION

COURTVIEW CENTER, SUITE 300
100 SOUTH MAIN AVENUE
SIDNEY, OHIO 45365-2727
Telephone: 937-492-1271
Telecopier: 937-498-1306
URL: http://www.fgks-law.com

Minster, Ohio Office: 96 West Fourth Street. Telephone: 419-628-3677.
Fort Loramie, Ohio Office: 31 South Main Street, P.O. Box 320, 45845-0320. Telephone 937-295-2983. Telecopier: 937-295-3633.

General Civil and Trial Practice, Corporations, Real Estate and Development, Banking, Probate and Estate Planning, Florida Probate, Trust, Taxation, Employment and Employee Benefits, Bankruptcy and Creditor's Rights, Business Litigation, and Insurance Defense.

(This Listing Continued)

HARRY N. FAULKNER, born Richmond, Virginia, March 22, 1941; admitted to bar, 1966, Ohio. *Education:* Ohio Wesleyan University (B.A., 1963); Ohio Northern University (J.D., 1966). ***PRACTICE AREAS:*** Real Estate; Real Estate Development; Banking Law; Estate Planning; Probate. ***Email:*** hfaulkner@fgks-law.com

JOHN M. GARMHAUSEN, born Sidney, Ohio, March 29, 1948; admitted to bar, 1973, Ohio. *Education:* Ohio Wesleyan University (B.A., 1970); The Ohio State University (J.D., cum laude, 1973). ***PRACTICE AREAS:*** Corporate Law; Commercial Law; Mergers, Acquisitions and Divestitures; Real Estate; Real Estate Development; Employment Law; Employee Benefits; Banking Law. ***Email:*** jgarmhausen@fgks-law.com

RALPH F. KEISTER, born Wooster, Ohio, November 10, 1942; admitted to bar, 1967, Ohio. *Education:* The Ohio State University (B.A., 1964; J.D., 1967). ***PRACTICE AREAS:*** Taxation; Estate Planning; Trust Law; Probate. ***Email:*** rkeister@fgks-law.com

JAMES R. SHENK, born Celina, Ohio, August 12, 1949; admitted to bar, 1975, Ohio. *Education:* Miami University (B.A., cum laude, 1971); The Ohio State University (J.D., summa cum laude, 1974). ***PRACTICE AREAS:*** Corporate Law; Commercial Law; Mergers, Acquisitions and Divestitures; Employment Law; Real Estate; Real Estate Development; Banking Law; Estate Planning; Probate. ***Email:*** jshenk@fgks-law.com

MICHAEL A. STAUDT, born Akron, Ohio, April 25, 1957; admitted to bar, 1984, Ohio. *Education:* University of Akron (B.A., 1981); The Ohio State University (J.D., 1984). ***PRACTICE AREAS:*** Corporate Law; Commercial Law; Mergers, Acquisitions and Divestitures; Bankruptcy; Creditors Rights; Real Estate; Real Estate Development; Employment Law; Banking Law. ***Email:*** mstaudt@fgks-law.com

JAMES L. THIEMAN, born Coldwater, Ohio, May 16, 1955; admitted to bar, 1980, Ohio. *Education:* The Ohio State University (B.S., 1977); University of Toledo (J.D., 1980). ***PRACTICE AREAS:*** Civil Practice; Business Litigation; Commercial Litigation; Insurance Defense. ***Email:*** jthieman@fgks-law.com

THOMAS J. POTTS, born Sidney, Ohio, May 3, 1963; admitted to bar, 1988, Ohio. *Education:* Miami University (B.S.B.A., cum laude, 1985); The Ohio State University (J.D., cum laude, 1988). ***PRACTICE AREAS:*** Corporate Law; Commercial Law; Mergers, Acquisitions and Divestitures; Employment Law; Real Estate; Real Estate Development; Municipal Law. ***Email:*** tpotts@fgks-law.com

DANIEL A. BENSMAN, born Sidney, Ohio, September 22, 1965; admitted to bar, 1994, Ohio. *Education:* University of Dayton (B.S., summa cum laude, 1987); The Ohio State University (M.S., 1991); University of Virginia (J.D., 1994). ***PRACTICE AREAS:*** Corporate Law; Commercial Law; Mergers, Acquisitions and Divestitures; Real Estate; Real Estate Development; Estate Planning; Trust Law; Taxation. ***Email:*** dbensman@fgks-law.com

DAVID B. SHUFFELTON, born St. Marys, Ohio, November 18, 1944; admitted to bar, 1969, Ohio. *Education:* Miami University (A.B., 1966); Ohio Northern University (J.D., 1969). ***PRACTICE AREAS:*** Estate Planning; Trust Law; Probate; Corporate Law; Commercial Law; Real Estate; Real Estate Development. ***Email:*** dshuffelton@fgks-law.com

BRYAN A. NIEMEYER, born Columbus, Ohio, May 29, 1971; admitted to bar, 1997, Ohio. *Education:* The Ohio State University (B.A., 1994); University of Colorado, Boulder (J.D., 1997). ***PRACTICE AREAS:*** Employment Litigation; Business Litigation; Commercial Litigation; School Law. ***Email:*** bniemeyer@fgks-law.com

JOHN M. DEEDS, born Pataskala, Ohio, September 19, 1977; admitted to bar, 2003, Ohio. *Education:* Muskingum College (B.S., summa cum laude, 2000); The Ohio State University (J.D., summa cum laude, 2003). ***PRACTICE AREAS:*** Corporate Law; Commercial Law. ***Email:*** jdeeds@fgks-law.com

JOSHUA A. KOLTAK, born Columbus, Ohio, December 12, 1978; admitted to bar, 2004, Ohio. *Education:* Miami University (B.A., cum laude, 2001); The Ohio State University (J.D., 2004). *Member:* Shelby County and Ohio State Bar Associations. ***Email:*** jkoltak@fgks-law.com

REPRESENTATIVE CLIENTS: *Banking:* Community First Bank & Trust; Farm Credit Services; Fifth Third Bank (Western Ohio); Minster Bank; Osgood State Bank; Peoples Federal Savings & Loan Association of Sidney; Sky Bank-Ohio Bank Region; Unity National Bank; U.S. Bank National Association. *Industrial & Commercial:* Amos Press Inc. (Publishers of Coin World, Linn's Stamp News, Cars and Parts, Scott Stamp Monthly); Brookside Laboratories, Inc.; The Connection Co.; Fort Recovery Industries, Inc.; Freshway Foods; Hartzell Propeller, Inc.; Holloway Sportswear, Inc.; Kirk NationaLease Co.; Midmark Corp.; Paul Sherry Chevrolet, Inc.; Peerless Machinery Corp.; Purity Foods, Inc.; Sankyo America, Inc.; Schafer Oil Co.; Sidney Holiday Inn; Sidney Tool & Die, Inc.; Thor Industries, Inc. (Manufacturers of Airstream, Damon, Dutchmen, Four Winds, Keystone recreation vehicles; ElDorado and Champion buses); Wayne Trail Technologies, Inc. *Construction & Development:* Area Energy & Electric, Inc.; Bensar Developments Co.; Bruns Building & Development Corp.; Bruns General Contracting, Inc.; Buschur Electric, Inc.; Choice One Engineering Corp.; Clinton Realty; Ferguson Construction Co.; H.A. Dorsten, Inc.; Troy Land Co.; Miami River Stone Co.; Milligan Construction Co.; Piqua Lumber & Hardware Co.; Reliant Mechanical, Inc.; Robert Oldham, Ltd.; Rockford Construction Co.; Schnippel Construction, Inc.; Sidney Electric Co.; Westerheide Developers, Inc. *Insurance:* German Mutual Insurance Co.
LOCAL COUNSEL: The Dannon Company, Inc.; Honda of America Mfg., Inc.; N.K. Parts Industries, Inc.; Plastipak Packaging, Inc.
AGENTS FOR: First American Title Insurance Co.; Old Republic National Title Insurance Co.; Ohio Bar Title Insurance Co.

McCULLOCH, FELGER, FITE & GUTMANN CO., L.P.A.

SIDNEY, OHIO

(See Piqua)

General Civil Practice. Corporation, Insurance, Taxation, Labor and Employment, Trust and Estate Administration, Estate Planning, Commercial, Real Estate, Pension and Profit Sharing, Family and Domestic Relations, Personal Injury Law, Litigation and Civil Trials.

MILLER & LURING

SIDNEY, OHIO

(See Troy)

General and Trial Practice, Collections, Estate Planning, Bankruptcy, Personal Injury, Civil, Family/Domestic Relations, Corporation, Negligence, Tax, Municipal, Probate and Real Estate.

SHIPMAN, DIXON & LIVINGSTON CO., L.P.A.

SIDNEY, OHIO

(See Troy)

Civil Trials in all Courts. Personal Injury, Environmental, Corporation, Real Estate, Insurance Defense Law, Probate and Estate Planning, Social Security, Municipal and Zoning. General Practice. Civil Rights Defense Law.

TOMB LAW

SIDNEY, OHIO

(See Troy)

Real Estate, Business Law, Construction Law.

DOUGLAS R. FOUTS

Established in 1976

30575 BAINBRIDGE ROAD, SUITE 160
SOLON, OHIO 44139
Telephone: 440-248-6700
Fax: 440-248-7511
Email: dfoutslaw@sbcglobal.net
URL: http://www.lawyers.com/dfoutslaw

Probate, Estate Planning, Estate and Gift Taxation, Elder Law (including Medicaid), Trust Law, Wills, Employer/Employee, Administrative Law, Guardianship, Real Estate, Small Business Law, Corporate Law, Contract Litigation, Income & Estate Taxation, Divorce, Family Law, Domestic Relations, Personal Injury and Mold Litigation.

DOUGLAS R. FOUTS, born New Philadelphia, Ohio, January 1, 1950; admitted to bar, 1975, Ohio; 1976, U.S. District Court, Northern District of Ohio; 2001, U.S. Court of Appeals, Sixth Circuit. *Education:* Muskingum College (B.A., with honors, 1972); Cleveland Marshall College of Law (J.D., cum laude, 1975). Member, Alumni Association and Mentoring Program, Cleveland Marshall College of Law. Appraiser, Cuyahoga County Probate Court. Appointed Counsel, Cuyahoga County Probate Court Civil Commitment Hearings. President, Solon Rotary Club, 1979-1980. Director: Chagrin Valley Jaycees, 1976-1979; Director, Solon Chamber of Commerce, 1985-1989. President and Director, Master Singers, Inc., 2002-2005 (Non-Profit Corporation). *Member:* Cleveland and Ohio Bar Associations. **REPORTED CASES:** Aurora Shores Homeowners v. Hardy, 37 Oh. App. 3/169, 525 N.E. 2 26 (1987); Broska v. Henderson, 2003 U.S. App. Lexis 13450. **PRACTICE AREAS:** Probate; Elder Law; Medicaid Planning; Estate Planning; Estate and Gift Taxation; Trust Law; Wills; Employee Benefits; Administrative Law; Guardianship; Real Estate; Small Business Law; Corporate Law; Contract Litigation; Divorce; Family Law; Domestic Relations; Personal Injury; Litigation; Mold Litigation.

HARRY J. JACOB III

30405 SOLON ROAD, UNIT 14
SOLON, OHIO 44139
Telephone: 440-349-3301
Fax: 440-349-3382
Email: jacoblaw@apk.net

General Civil and Business Law, Litigation, Domestic Relations, Negligence and Personal Injury, Real Estate, Probate and Commercial Law.

FIRM PROFILE: General civil and trial practice founded in 1988. Harry Jacob has been very active in local Bar Association activities, civil affairs, sports and religious organizations.

HARRY J. JACOB, III, born Toledo, Ohio, May 8, 1956; admitted to bar, 1981, Ohio and U.S. District Court, Northern District of Ohio. *Education:* Kent State University (B.S., 1978); Case Western Reserve University (J.D., 1981). Member, Moot Court Executive Board, 1981. Legal Counsel, Ohio Department of Commerce, 1981-1983. Member, Solon, Civil Service Commission, 1988—; Chairman, 1997—. *Member:* Greater Cleveland, Cuyahoga County (Chair, Ethics Committee, 1997-2001; Member, Grievance Committee, 1997—) and Ohio State Bar Associations; The Association of Trial Lawyers of America.

KARBERG, KURANT, WACHTER & TURNER CO., L.P.A.

SOLON, OHIO

(See Cleveland)

Business and Corporate, Mergers and Acquisition, Employment Litigation, Real Estate, Taxation, Probate, Estate Planning, Litigation in all Courts.

THEODORE M. MANN, JR. LAW FIRM

SOLON, OHIO

(See Cleveland)

Alternative Dispute Resolution, Mediation, Appellate Practice, Business Law, Business Litigation, Contracts, Corporate Law, Elder Law, Franchises and Franchising, Fraud, General Practice, Labor and Employment, Litigation, Negligence, Personal Injury, Probate, Real Estate, Real Estate Litigation, Residential Real Estate, Torts, Trade Secrets Trusts and Estates, Estate Planning, Trust Administration, Wills.

PODOR & ASSOCIATES

33565 SOLON ROAD
SOLON, OHIO 44139
Telephone: 440-914-LAWS (5297)
Fax: 440-914-0377
URL: http://www.podorlaw.com

Family Law, Adoption Law, Child Support, Child Custody, Visitation Rights, Divorce, Business Law, Commercial Law, Civil Rights, Criminal Law, DUI/DWI, Discrimination, Employment Law, Insurance Law, Legal Malpractice, Pediatric Malpractice, Medical Malpractice, Motor Vehicle Accidents, Nursing Home Litigation, Plaintiffs Personal Injury, Products Liability Law, Professional Malpractice Law, Sexual Harassment, Toxic Torts, Traffic Violations, White Collar Crimes, Workers Compensation.

KENNETH C. PODOR, born Cleveland, Ohio, January 9, 1952; admitted to bar, 1978, Ohio and U.S. District Court, Northern District of Ohio. *Education:* The Ohio State University (B.A., cum laude, 1974); Cleveland Marshall College of Law (J.D., 1977). Director/ Secretary, Overdrive Systems Inc., 1988-1993. *Member:* Ohio State Bar Association. **Email:** LFarrow@podor-assoc.com

STEUER, ESCOVAR, BERK & BROWN CO., L.P.A.

SOLON, OHIO

(See Cleveland)

General Civil and Criminal Practice. Personal Injury, Negligence, Workers Compensation, Corporation, Mergers and Acquisitions, Taxation, Real Estate, Bankruptcy, Family, Probate and Commercial Law. Estate Planning, Trials and Medical Malpractice, Civil and Criminal Appellate Work, Insurance Defense, Business Law, Administrative Law.

PICKREL, SCHAEFFER & EBELING

SPRINGBORO, OHIO

(See Dayton)

Banking, Civil, Corporate, General Business, Commercial Lending, Mergers and Acquisitions, Insurance, Labor and Employment, Healthcare, Municipal and Zoning, Personal Injury and Products Liability, Probate, Trust and Estate Planning, Construction, Computer, Real Estate, Environmental, Workers' Compensation Defense, Immigration, Bankruptcy and Tax Law. Trials and Appeals, School Law and Title Insurance.

ALEITA AILES, ATTORNEY AT LAW, LLC

SPRINGFIELD, OHIO

(See London)

Divorce, Dissolution, Separation, Child Custody, Visitation Rights, Paternity, Adoption, Real Estate, Contracts, Leases, Wills and Trusts, Business, Litigation, General Practice.

ALTICK & CORWIN CO., L.P.A.

SPRINGFIELD, OHIO

(See Dayton)

General Practice. Administrative, Bankruptcy, Business, Collections, Condominium, Creditors' Rights, Criminal, Commercial Law, Decedent's Estates, Employee Benefits, Elder Law, Employment, Estate Planning, Family Law, Immigration and Naturalization, Insurance Defense, Labor Relations, Local Government, Military Law, Municipal, Personal Injury, Probate, Products Liability, Real Estate, Social Security, Taxation, Workers' Compensation, Zoning.

BIESER, GREER & LANDIS, LLP

SPRINGFIELD, OHIO

(See Dayton)

General Civil Practice, Trial Practice, Business Litigation, Professional Liability Defense, Personal Injury Defense, Products Liability Defense, Corporate Law, Employment Law, Commercial Law, Probate, Tax Law, White Collar Criminal Defense, Arbitration, Mediation.

KAREN DENISE BRADLEY

SPRINGFIELD, OHIO

(See Dayton)

Immigration Law.

COLE ACTON HARMON DUNN

A LEGAL PROFESSIONAL ASSOCIATION

Established in 1897

RIVERBEND CONDOMINIUMS
333 NORTH LIMESTONE STREET
P.O. BOX 1687
SPRINGFIELD, OHIO 45501
Telephone: 937-322-0891
Fax: 937-322-9931

General Civil Practice. Business and Corporate, Insurance, Taxation, Real Estate, Probate, Criminal Law, Family Law, Banking, Labor and Employment Law, Personal Injury Law. Litigation.

FIRM PROFILE: Cole Acton Harmon Dunn traces its roots in Springfield to the law office opened by John Cole at the turn of the 20th century.

One hundred years later, the firm consists of 10 lawyers who provide a broad range of creative, high quality legal services at fair and competitive rates. We recognize that the law is, first and foremost, a service profession. Our principal goals, day in and day out, are to provide our clients with courteous and prompt service and to find solutions to their legal problems and questions.

Cole Acton Harmon Dunn is a full service law firm, committed to meeting the varied and ever-changing needs of businesses, institutions, and individuals in central and southwest Ohio.

JOHN M. COLE (1879-1960)
ABE GARDNER (1903-1964)
FRED M. COLE (1909-1975)
GEORGE W. COLE (1914-1982)
ROBERT C. ACTON (1924-1987)
JAMES A. HARMON (Retired)

EDWARD W. DUNN, born Springfield, Ohio, September 6, 1930; admitted to bar, 1955, District of Columbia and Ohio; 1959, Minnesota. *Education:* Wittenberg College (A.B., 1952); Georgetown University (LL.B., 1955). Phi Delta Phi. Member, Board of Editors, Georgetown Law Journal, 1954-1955. *Member:* Springfield (President, 1984), Clark County and Ohio State (Member, Negligence Committee, 1963—) Bar Associations. ***PRACTICE AREAS:*** Probate.

BARRY P. REICH, born Springfield, Ohio, November 17, 1945; admitted to bar, 1970, Ohio. *Education:* Otterbein College (B.A., 1967); Georgetown University (J.D., 1970). *Member:* Springfield, Clark County and Ohio State Bar Associations. ***PRACTICE AREAS:*** Business Law; Corporate Law; Labor Law; Real Estate; Banking. ***Email:*** breich@coleacton.com

WILLIAM C. HICKS, born Lima, Ohio, December 21, 1943; admitted to bar, 1974, Ohio. *Education:* Dartmouth College (A.B., 1965); The Ohio State University (J.D., cum laude, 1973). *Member:* Springfield, Clark County and Ohio State Bar Associations. [Lieut., USNR, 1966-1978]. ***PRACTICE AREAS:*** Real Estate; Probate Law. ***Email:*** whicks@coleacton.com

JOHN R. BUTZ, born Randolph Field, Texas, September 29, 1944; admitted to bar, 1969, Ohio; 1970, U.S. District Court, Southern District of Ohio. *Education:* The Ohio State University (B.A., 1966; J.D., 1969). U.S. Bankruptcy Trustee, 1975-1995. Member of Panel, American Arbitration Association. *Member:* Springfield, Clark County, Greene County and Ohio State (Member, Board of Governors, 1992-1995; Chairman, Criminal Justice Committee, 2002-2004) Bar Associations; Ohio Society of Hospital Attorneys. ***PRACTICE AREAS:*** Criminal Law; Family Law; Medical Malpractice; Litigation; Bankruptcy. ***Email:*** jbutz@coleacton.com

JOSEPH A. DUNN, born Washington, D. C., July 8, 1955; admitted to bar, 1980, Arizona and U.S. District Court, District of Arizona; 1987, U.S. Supreme Court; 1992, Ohio; 1995, U.S. District Court, Southern District of Ohio. *Education:* Bowling Green State University (B.A., 1977); University of Notre Dame (J.D., 1980). Law Clerk to Hon. Walter E. Craig, U.S. District Judge, District of Arizona, 1980-1982. *Member:* Clark County and Ohio State Bar Associations; Million Dollar Advocates Forum (Verdict and Settlement); Ohio Academy of Trial Lawyers; The Association of Trial Lawyers of America. ***PRACTICE AREAS:*** Personal Injury; Litigation; Insurance Law. ***Email:*** jdunn@coleacton.com

TAMMI J. ANGLE, born West Reading, Pennsylvania, November 21, 1958; admitted to bar, 1994, Ohio and U.S. District Court, Southern District of Ohio. *Education:* Wittenberg University (B.M., magna cum laude, 1980); University of Wisconsin-Madison (M.M., 1982); University of Dayton (J.D., magna cum laude, 1994). Omicron Delta Kappa. Order of the Barristers. *Member:* Clark County, Springfield, Ohio State and American Bar Associations. The Association of Trial Lawyers of America. ***PRACTICE AREAS:*** Real Estate; Litigation; Labor and Employment Law. ***Email:*** tangle@coleacton.com

CYNTHIA SINGLETON BARNETT, born Dayton, Ohio, September 9, 1961; admitted to bar, 1994, Ohio. *Education:* University of Cincinnati (B.B.A., Accounting, 1984); University of Dayton (J.D., 1994). *Member:* Springfield, Clark County and Ohio State Bar Associations. ***PRACTICE AREAS:*** Probate Law; Taxation; Estate Planning; Corporate Law. ***Email:*** cbarnett@coleacton.com

PAUL J. KAVANAGH, born Homewood, Illinois, September 6, 1969; admitted to bar, 1995, Ohio; 1996, U.S. District Court, Southern District of Ohio. *Education:* University of Wisconsin-Oshkosh (B.S., 1991); Ohio Northern University (J.D., 1995). *Member:* Clark County and Ohio State Bar Associations. ***PRACTICE AREAS:*** Probate; Litigation. ***Email:*** pkavanagh@coleacton.com

(This Listing Continued)

OF COUNSEL

PHYLLIS S. NEDELMAN, born Springfield, Massachusetts, May 5, 1936; admitted to bar, 1982, Ohio. *Education:* University of Cincinnati (B.S., 1957); Ohio State University (J.D., 1982). Kappa Delta Epsilon; Phi Delta Phi; Alpha Lambda Delta. *Member:* Springfield, Clark County and Ohio State Bar Associations. ***PRACTICE AREAS:*** Family Law; Litigation.

ELIZABETH JUCIUS DUNN, born Columbus, Ohio, October 10, 1951; admitted to bar, 1976, Arizona; 1977, U.S. District Court, District of Arizona and U.S. Court of Appeals, Ninth Circuit; 1980, U.S. Supreme Court; 1992, Ohio. *Education:* Colorado College (B.A., 1972); University of Arizona (J.D., 1976). Member of Faculty, Department of Justice Civil Trial Advocacy Institute, 1984-1986. Assistant U.S. Attorney, District of Arizona, 1980-1986. Judge Pro Tem, Superior Court, Maricopa County, 1991. Law Clerk to Hon. Frank X. Gordon, Arizona Supreme Court, 1976-1977. *Member:* Maricopa County and Federal (President, Arizona Chapter, 1982-1983) Bar Associations; State Bar of Arizona; Arizona Association of Women Lawyers (Founding Member, 1977).

REPRESENTATIVE CLIENTS: KeyBank; Huntington National Bank; Home City Federal Savings Bank; Farm Credit Services; The Education Credit Union, Inc.; Navistar International; Springfield Newspapers, Inc.; Clark State Community College; Chakeres Theatres, Inc.; Springfield Metropolitan Housing Authority; Mental Health Services for Clark County, Inc.; Bobby Fisher, Inc.; Eagle Beverage Co.; Mid-Ohio Harley Davidson; Village of South Vienna, Ohio; Village of Donnelsville, Ohio; The Levine Realty Co.; Navistar Financial Corp.; Catholic Social Services of Southwest Ohio; Graphic Paper Products Corp.; Community Mercy Health Partners; Laughlin & Scanlan Construction Co., Inc.; Tool Tech, Inc.
APPROVED ATTORNEYS FOR: Stewart Title Guaranty Company; The Guarantee Title and Trust Company; Ohio Bar Title Insurance Co.

EMERICH & PEIFER

SUITE 300 THE EDISON CENTER
20 SOUTH LIMESTONE STREET
P.O. BOX 1087
SPRINGFIELD, OHIO 45501
Telephone: 937-325-7365
Fax: 937-325-9584

General Civil Practice. Corporation, Wills and Probate, Municipal, Health and Hospital, Labor Relations, Real Estate, Zoning and Annexation, Insurance and Negligence Law. Trials, Civil.

FIRM PROFILE: This firm was established in 1930. We represent a variety of clients throughout Clark and other southwestern Ohio counties, offering a civil trial practice in State and Federal courts, including personal injury, insurance defense, probate and wills, real estate and zoning.

JOHN D. EMERICH, born Cleveland, Ohio, February 20, 1939; admitted to bar, 1964, Ohio; 1971, U.S. District Court, Southern District of Ohio. *Education:* Ohio University (B.S. in Ed., 1961); Western Reserve University (J.D., 1964). Phi Delta Phi. Assistant Law Director, City of Springfield, Ohio, 1965-1966. *Member:* Springfield, Ohio State (Member, Negligence Committee, 1974—) and American Bar Associations; Ohio Association of Civil Trial Attorneys; International Association of Insurance Counsel. ***PRACTICE AREAS:*** Civil Practice; Insurance; Negligence; Probate; Wills. ***Email:*** jdemerich@yahoo.com

JAMES F. PEIFER, born Oak Park, Illinois, February 4, 1946; admitted to bar, 1972, Ohio; 1973, U.S. District Court, Southern District of Ohio. *Education:* Wittenberg University (B.A., 1968); University of Illinois (J.D., 1972). Order of the Coif. Director of Law: The City of Springfield, Ohio, 1974-1984. *Member:* Springfield (Secretary, 1974-1975), Ohio State (Council of Delegates, 1986-2001; Board of Governors, 2001-2004) and American Bar Associations. ***PRACTICE AREAS:*** Real Estate; Corporation; Probate; Zoning; Annexation. ***Email:*** jfpeifer@yahoo.com

GENERAL COUNSEL FOR: Taylor Mfg. Co.; Community Hospital of Springfield & Clark County; Monte Zinn Chevrolet Co.; Community Improvement Corp. of Springfield & Clark County, Ohio; Muncy Corp.; Village of South Charleston.
APPROVED ATTORNEYS FOR: The Ohio Bar Title Ins. Co.; First American Title Ins. Co.
COUNSEL FOR: Cincinnati Ins. Co.; Ohio Fair Plan Underwriting Association.
SPECIAL COUNSEL FOR: The City of Urbana.

FOX & ASSOCIATES CO., L.P.A.

SPRINGFIELD, OHIO

(See Dayton)

Bankruptcy, Chapter 7, Chapter 13, Foreclosures, Divorce, Adoptions, Child Custody, Visitation Rights, Estate Planning, Wills and Trusts, Driving While Intoxicated and Traffic Violations.

FREUND, FREEZE & ARNOLD

A LEGAL PROFESSIONAL ASSOCIATION

SPRINGFIELD, OHIO

(See Dayton)

Civil Litigation including Commercial Litigation, Employment Defense, Professional Malpractice Defense, Employer Intentional Torts, Construction Litigation, Civil Rights Defense, Local Government Defense, Nursing Home Defense, Environmental Litigation and Insurance Defense.

DANIEL C. HARKINS

333 NORTH LIMESTONE STREET
SUITE 203
SPRINGFIELD, OHIO 45501-1125
Telephone: 937-324-8482
Fax: 937-324-8011
Email: dch@dharkins.com

General Practice, Corporate, Taxation, Estate Planning, Probate and Health Care.

DANIEL C. HARKINS, born Akron, Ohio, August 9, 1960; admitted to bar, 1985, Ohio; 1986, District of Columbia. *Education:* College of Wooster (B.A., 1982); Case Western Reserve University (J.D., 1985); New York University (LL.M., Taxation, 1986). Treasurer, Clark County Law Library Association, 1996—. *Member:* Dayton, Clark County (Treasurer, 1993—), Medina County, Ohio State and American (Member, Sections on: Taxation; Health Law) Bar Associations; The District of Columbia Bar; American Health Lawyers Association. ***PRACTICE AREAS:*** Corporate; Taxation; Estate Planning; Probate; Health Care.

REPRESENTATIVE CLIENTS: The Ohio Masonic Home; Masonic Health Care, Inc.; Masonic Retirement Village, Inc.; The Ohio Masonic Home Benevolent Endowment Foundation, Inc.; Browning Masonic Community, Inc.; Western Rescue Masonic Community, Inc.
REFERENCE: Security National Bank and Trust Company, Springfield, Ohio.

HOCHMAN & PLUNKETT

SPRINGFIELD, OHIO

(See Dayton)

Personal Injury, Automobile Accidents, Workers' Compensation and Social Security Disability Law. General Civil and Criminal Practice in all Courts.

LAMKIN, VAN EMAN, TRIMBLE, BEALS & DOUGHERTY, LLC

SPRINGFIELD, OHIO

(See Columbus)

Personal Injury, Medical Malpractice, Products Liability, Negligence, Insurance Coverage, Stockbroker Malpractice & Fraud. Litigation and Trial Practice.

MARTIN, BROWNE, HULL & HARPER, P.L.L.

Established in 1872

ONE SOUTH LIMESTONE STREET
SUITE 800
P.O. BOX 1488
SPRINGFIELD, OHIO 45501-1488
Telephone: 937-324-5541
Fax: 937-325-5432
1-800-324-5562
Email: mbhhlaw@martinbrowne.com
URL: http://www.martinbrowne.com

General Civil Practice. Corporate, Commercial, Insurance, Insurance Defense, Litigation, Environmental, Business, Contracts, Banking, Estate Planning, Probate, Real Estate, Taxation, Education, Labor and Employment. Trials and Appeals in State and Federal Courts.

MEMBERS OF THE FIRM

OSCAR T. MARTIN (1848-1913)
PAUL C. MARTIN (1876-1939)
HOMER C. CORRY (1887-1955)
JOHN C. DURFEY (1902-1960)
ANSON E. HULL (1915-1983)
OSCAR T. MARTIN (1908-1995)
BITNER BROWNE (1914-2003)

HUGH BARNETT, born Springfield, Ohio, July 2, 1935; admitted to bar, 1962, Ohio. *Education:* Princeton University (A.B., 1957); University of Michigan (LL.B., 1962). Phi Delta Phi. *Member:* Clark County (President, 1998-1999), Ohio State and American Bar Associations. Fellow, American Bar Foundation. ***PRACTICE AREAS:*** Corporate; Probate; Estate Planning. ***Email:*** hbarnett@martinbrowne.com

ROBERT E. HARLEY, born Springfield, Ohio, March 21, 1931; admitted to bar, 1957, Ohio; 1964, U.S. Tax Court. *Education:* Bowling Green State University; The Ohio State University (B.S. and B.A., 1955; J.D., 1956); New York University (LL.M. in Taxation, 1963). *Member:* Clark County, Ohio State (Former Member, Board of Governors, Federal Taxation Law Specialty Board) and American Bar Associations; American Agricultural Law Association. ***PRACTICE AREAS:*** Corporate; Insurance; Banking; Probate; Taxation; Charitable Giving. ***Email:*** rharley@martinbrowne.com

GLENN W. COLLIER, born Lakewood, Ohio, April 30, 1940; admitted to bar, 1966, Illinois; 1968, Ohio. *Education:* Ohio Wesleyan University (B.A., 1962); Cornell University (LL.B., 1965). Chairman, Springfield-Clark County Chamber of Commerce, 1996-1998. President, Springfield-Clark County Community Improvement Corporation, 1998-2000; Springfield Museum of Art Board (1994-1996). Trustee, Wittenberg University. *Member:* Clark County, Ohio State (Member, Board of Governors, 1995-1998) and American Bar Associations. ***PRACTICE AREAS:*** Corporate; Probate; Real Estate; Taxation. ***Email:*** gcollier@martinbrowne.com

(This Listing Continued)

WALTER A. WILDMAN, born Springfield, Ohio, December 5, 1941; admitted to bar, 1968, Ohio. *Education:* College of Wooster; The Ohio State University (B.A., 1963); University of Cincinnati (J.D., 1968). Central Intelligence Agency, 1963-1965. *Member:* Clark County, Ohio State (Member, Board of Governors, 2004—) and American Bar Associations. ***PRACTICE AREAS:*** Corporate; Finance; Insurance; Banking; Transactions; Environmental Law. ***Email:*** waltwild@martinbrowne.com

DAVID A. WEAVER, born Chillicothe, Ohio, July 20, 1946; admitted to bar, 1972, Ohio, U.S. District Court, Southern District of Ohio, U.S. Court of Appeals, Sixth Circuit and U.S. Supreme Court. *Education:* Ohio University (B.B.A., cum laude, 1968); University of North Carolina (J.D., 1972). Former Member, Board of Governors, Labor and Employment Section, Ohio State Bar Association. Former Co-Chair, Labor and Employment Law Specialty Board, Ohio State Bar Association. *Member:* Clark County, Ohio State (Member, Board of Governors, Labor and Employment Law Section, 1981-1999) and American Bar Associations; National Association of College and University Attorneys; Council of School Attorneys of the National School Boards Association. ***PRACTICE AREAS:*** Corporate; Education Law; Labor and Employment; Non-Profit Organizations; Charitable Organizations Law. ***Email:*** dweaver@martinbrowne.com

WILLIAM R. GROVES, born Toledo, Ohio, July 20, 1954; admitted to bar, 1979, Ohio. *Education:* Ohio University (B.S., summa cum laude, 1976); The Ohio State University (J.D., 1979). Phi Beta Kappa. *Member:* Dayton, Clark County, Ohio State and American Bar Associations; National Association of College and University Attorneys; Ohio Council of School Board Attorneys. ***PRACTICE AREAS:*** Corporate; Insurance; Real Estate; Education Law; Non Profit Organizations; Labor and Employment. ***Email:*** bgroves@martinbrowne.com

STEVEN J. McCREADY, born Fairbanks, Alaska, September 23, 1957; admitted to bar, 1983, Ohio. *Education:* Miami University (A.B., cum laude, 1980); Ohio State University (J.D., with honors, 1983). Phi Beta Kappa. *Member:* Clark County, Ohio State and American Bar Associations. ***PRACTICE AREAS:*** Mediation; Labor and Employment; Business Law; Contracts; Civil Litigation. ***Email:*** smccready@martinbrowne.com

RICHARD F. HEIL, JR., born Lakewood, Ohio, February 4, 1952; admitted to bar, 1986, Ohio and U.S. District Court, Southern District of Ohio. *Education:* Wittenberg University (B.A., 1974); Cleveland State University (J.D., 1986). *Member:* Clark County, Ohio State and American Bar Associations; Defense Research Institute; Ohio Association of Civil Trial Attorneys. ***PRACTICE AREAS:*** General; Civil; Insurance; Banking Law; Real Estate; Probate. ***Email:*** rheil@martinbrowne.com

LAUREN M. ROSS, born Elyria, Ohio, January 16, 1959; admitted to bar, 1984, Ohio; 1985, U.S. District Court, Northern and Southern Districts of Ohio; 1987, U.S. Court of Appeals, Sixth Circuit. *Education:* Middlebury College (B.A., 1981); Case Western Reserve University (J.D., 1984). Ohio Assistant Attorney General, 1984-1997. *Member:* Clark County, Ohio State (Chief, Transportation Section; Assistant Chief, Education Section and Business and Government Regulation Section) and American (Member, Administrative Law and State and Local Government Committees) Bar Associations; National Association of College and University Attorneys. ***PRACTICE AREAS:*** Education Law; Labor and Employment Law; General Practice. ***Email:*** lmross@martinbrowne.com

R. MICHAEL OSBORN, born Chillicothe, Ohio, December 14, 1968; admitted to bar, 1995, Ohio; 1996, West Virginia and U.S. District Court, Northern and Southern Districts of West Virginia; 1999, Kentucky; 2000, U.S. District Court, Eastern and Western Districts of Kentucky. *Education:* Miami University (B.A., Political Science, 1991); University of Kentucky (J.D., 1994); Capital University (LL.M., 1995). *Member:* Ohio, West Virginia and Kentucky Bar Associations. ***PRACTICE AREAS:*** Tax Planning; Business Succession Planning; ERISA; Employee Benefits; Executive Compensation. ***Email:*** mosborn@martinbrowne.com

RETIRED PARTNER

JOHN O. HARPER

WAYNE E. SOUTHWARD, born Springfield, Ohio, March 14, 1958; admitted to bar, 1983, Ohio and U.S. District Court, Southern District of Ohio. *Education:* Wittenberg University (B.A., summa cum laude, 1980); Boston University School of Law (J.D., cum laude, 1983). Omicron Delta Kappa. Member: Federation of Exchange Accommodators; Ohio Land Title Association. President, Miami Valley Land Title Association, 1999-2000. *Member:* Clark County, Dayton and Ohio State Bar Associations. ***PRACTICE AREAS:*** Commercial Real Estate; Residential Real Estate; Tax Deferred Exchanges; Real Property; Real Estate Title Insurance. ***Email:*** wsouthward@martinbrowne.com

RANDALL M. COMER, born Springfield, Ohio, January 17, 1970; admitted to bar, 2000, Ohio and U.S. District Court, Southern District of Ohio. *Education:* College of Charleston (B.S., cum laude, 1993); University of Cincinnati College of Law (J.D., 2000). Editor-in-Chief, University of Cincinnati Law Review, 1999-2000. Greenfield Exempted Village Board of Education; Community Mercy Health Partners; Community Hospital Health Services Foundation. *Member:* Clark County, Dayton and Ohio State Bar Associations. ***PRACTICE AREAS:*** Labor and Employment; Workers Compensation; Litigation. ***Email:*** rcomer@martinbrowne.com

OF COUNSEL

KAREN W. OSBORN, born Lexington, Kentucky, August 28, 1971; admitted to bar, 1994, Kentucky; 1995, Ohio. *Education:* University of Kentucky (B.S., Accounting, 1991; J.D., 1994).

COUNSEL FOR: The Turner Foundation; Antioch University; Urbana University; Wittenberg University; Springfield City Board of Education; Washington Court House City Board of Education; City of Xenia; Ohio Prythian Home; Southbrook Care Center; Livingston Care Center; Inn at Fox Run; Cornerstone Bank; Western Ohio Financial Corporation; Aetna Building Maintenance, Inc.; Benjamin Steel Company; F.H. Bonn Company; The Champion Company; Eagle Tool & Machine, Inc.; Kapp Construction Company; Kreider Corporation; Morgal Machine Tool Co.; Morris Bean & Co.; Pentaflex, Inc.; Rawac Plating Company; Rittal Corporation; Rose City Manufacturing Corp.; Vernay Laboratories, Inc.; Woeber Mustard Company.

(This Listing Continued)

MARTIN, BROWNE, HULL & HARPER, P.L.L., Springfield—Continued

LOCAL COUNSEL FOR: National City Bank; Bridgeston APM Company; Columbia Gas of Ohio; Ohio Edison Company; Speedway SuperAmerica LLC; GRE Insurance Group; The Chubb Insurance Group; Fidelity National Title Insurance Company; Commonwealth Land Title Insurance Co.; Southward Exchange Company.

DAVID M. MARTIN CO., L.P.A.

Established in 1989
4 WEST MAIN STREET, SUITE 707
SPRINGFIELD, OHIO 45502-1316
Telephone: 937-324-5000
Telecopier: 937-322-7572
Email: davidmartin@erinet.com
URL: http://www.lawyers.com/davidmartin

General Civil and Criminal Practice. Bankruptcy, Business Law, Corporation, Collection, Debtor and Creditor, Criminal Law, Driving While Intoxicated, Family Law, Dissolution, Guardianship, Conservatorship, Children, Real Estate, Probate, Wills, Trusts and Estates.

DAVID M. MARTIN, born Springfield, Ohio, February 23, 1944; admitted to bar, 1975, Ohio, U.S. District Court, Northern and Southern Districts of Ohio and U.S. Court of Appeals, Sixth Circuit; 1976, U.S. Tax Court; 1978, U.S. Supreme Court. *Education:* Princeton University (A.B., cum laude, 1971); University of Denver (J.D., 1974). *Member:* Clark County, Ohio State (Member, Banking, Commercial Law and Bankruptcy Law Committee, 1982—) and American Bar Associations; American Judicature Society. [U.S. Air Force, 1964-1968]. ***Email:*** davidmartin@erinet.com

REPRESENTATIVE CLIENTS: National City Bank; H.S. Stevenson & Sons, Inc.; Ear, Nose & Throat of Springfield, Inc.
REFERENCE: National City Bank, Springfield, Ohio.

MYERS & FRAYNE CO., L.P.A.

SPRINGFIELD, OHIO

(See Dayton)

Business, Corporations, Real Estate, Creditors Rights, Commercial Planning, Estate Planning, Probate, Chapter 11 Reorganizations, and Litigation.

PETERSON & PETERSON

SPRINGFIELD, OHIO

(See Xenia)

Automobile and Motorcycle Accidents, Workers Compensation, Job-Related Injuries, Wrongful Death, Bus and Truck accidents, Negligence Claims, Insurance Claims, Probate, Estates, Wills, Living Trust, Guardianship, Power of Attorney, Real Estate, Contracts, Deeds, Evictions, Family Law, Divorce, Custody, Visitation, Domestic Violence, Criminal, Traffic Violations, Felonies, Misdemeanors, DUI, License Suspension, Juvenile, Bankruptcy.

THE PLYMALE PARTNERSHIP LLP

SPRINGFIELD, OHIO

(See Columbus)

Personal Injury, Products Liability, Wrongful Death, Medical Malpractice, Professional Negligence, Traumatic Brain Injury, Automobile Accidents, Nursing Home Torts, Civil Litigation.

STANDLEY LAW GROUP LLP

SPRINGFIELD, OHIO

(See Dublin)

Domestic and Foreign Intellectual Property Law, including Patent, Trademark, Copyright, Unfair Competition and Trade Secret Law and related Litigation, Licensing, International Trade Matters, related Antitrust, Computer and other Technology Law.

THORSON, SWITALA, WILKINS & SNEAD, LLP

SPRINGFIELD, OHIO

(See Dayton)

Medical Malpractice, Nursing Errors, Wrongful Death Claims, Nursing Home Negligence, Automobile Collisions, Motorcycle and Bicycle Injuries, Dog Bite Injuries, Other accidents involving serious injury or loss of life.

TWYFORD & DONAHEY, P.L.L.

SPRINGFIELD, OHIO

(See Columbus)

Personal Injury Litigation, Wrongful Death, Medical Malpractice, Products Liability, Automobile Accidents, Trucking Accidents, Head and Spinal Injuries, Motorcycle Accidents and Injuries, Uninsured Motorists, Insurance Law, Airplane Crash Litigation, Railroad Accidents, Slip and Fall, Dog Bites, Work Related Injuries, Birth Injuries, Nursing Home Abuse and Neglect.

WILLIAM WINKS ATTORNEY AT LAW

Established in 1971
SUITE 102
2525 NORTH LIMESTONE STREET
SPRINGFIELD, OHIO 45503-7100
Telephone: 937-399-7580
Fax: 937-399-7591
Email: wwinks@williamwinks.com
URL: http://www.williamwinks.com

Insurance, Civil Litigation, Civil Practice, Probate, Negligence.

FIRM PROFILE: Since 1971, William Winks has provided quality service in a variety in legal areas throughout central and southwestern Ohio. Over the course of his practice since 1971 his practice became more specialized in the area of insurance defense civil litigation, while a member of a larger law firm in Springfield, Ohio. He began his individual practice on January 1, 2000 and his current office location is ideally located for easy access to state routes and interstate routes (I-70; I-75; and I-675) to and from other cities in central and southwestern Ohio.

MR. PAUL WILLIAM WINKS, born Springfield, Ohio, September 28, 1943; admitted to bar, 1971, Ohio; 1972, U.S. District Court, Southern District of Ohio. *Education:* The Ohio State University (B.S., Dean's List Honors, 1968); University of Toledo (J.D., 1970). Delta Theta Phi; American Jurisprudence Award for Excellent Achievement in the Study of Trials. Ohio Civil Trial Practice Courts: Auglaize, Butler, Champaign, Clark, Clermont, Clinton, Darke, Fayette, Franklin, Greene, Hamilton, Hardin, Highland, Logan, Madison, Miami, Montgomery, Preble, Shelby, Union and Warren. Member, The Springfield Rotary Club (Trial Lawyer Designation). *Member:* Springfield (Secretary, 1972-1973; Member, Board of Trustees, 1975-1992), Dayton (Member, Civil Trial & Judiciary Committees), Ohio State (Member: Corporation Law Committee, 1977-1995; Negligence Law Committee, 1980—, and Insurance Committees) and American Bar Associations; Ohio Association of Civil Trial Attorneys; Defense Research and Association of Trial Lawyers of America. [Capt., US Army/Field Artillery]. ***PRACTICE AREAS:*** Insurance Defense (95%); Civil Litigation (3%); Civil Practice (1%); Probate (1%). ***Email:*** wwinks@williamwinks.com

REPRESENTATIVE CLIENTS: The State Farm Insurance Companies. Further representative clients have included: Coca Cola Bottlers Association; Ford Motor Company; Insurance Company North America; ITT; Duplex Mill and Manufacturing Company; Community Hospital of Springfield and Clark County; and The Ohio Casualty Insurance Company.

DICKIE, McCAMEY & CHILCOTE

A PROFESSIONAL CORPORATION
401 MARKET STREET , SUITE 401
STEUBENVILLE, OHIO 43952-2846
Telephone: 740-284-1682
Fax: 740-284-1692
Email: info@dmclaw.com
URL: http://www.dmclaw.com

Pittsburgh, Pennsylvania Office: Dickie, McCamey & Chilcote, P.C., Two PPG Place, Suite 400, 15222-5402. Telephone: 412-281-7272. Fax: 412-392-5367.
Camp Hill, Pennsylvania Office: Dickie, McCamey & Chilcote, P.C., 1200 Camp Hill Bypass, Suite 205, 17011-3700. Telephone: 717-731-4800. Fax: 717-731-4803.
Philadelphia, Pennsylvania Office: Dickie, McCamey & Chilcote, P.C., Public Ledger Building, Suite 901, 150 South Independence Mall, West, 19106-3409. Telephone: 215-925-2289. Fax: 215-925-0307.
Washington, D.C. Office: Dickie, McCamey & Chilcote, P.C., 1301 Pennsylvania Avenue, N.W., Suite 1000, 20004-1707. Telephone: 1-888-434-5566.
Haddonfield, New Jersey Office: Dickie, McCamey & Chilcote, P.C., 30 N. Haddon Avenue, Suite 100, 08033-2429. Telephone: 856-354-0192. Fax: 856-354-8164.
Charlotte, North Carolina Office: Dickie, McCamey & Chilcote, P.C.: 212 South Tryon Street, Suite 465, 28281-0007 Telephone: 704-334-1108. Fax: 704-334-1163.
Wheeling, West Virginia Office: Dickie, McCamey & Chilcote, L.C., 1233 Main Street, Suite 2002, 26003-2839. Telephone: 304-233-1022. Fax: 304-233-1026.

General Practice including Alternative Dispute Resolution; Appellate Advocacy; Antitrust; Asbestos; Bad Faith; Bankruptcy; Business Law; Business Torts; Civil Litigation; Class Actions; Commercial Agreements; Commercial Litigation; Commercial Transactions; Compliance Programs; Construction Law; Contract Disputes; Contract Drafting; Corporate Compliance; Computer Law; Corporate Finance; Corporate Governance; Corporate Law; Corporate Services; Creditors' Rights; Education Law; Employment Law; Environmental Law; Estate Planning and Administration; Estates and Trusts; Family Law; First Amendment/Defamation; Finance Law and Financial Institutions; Food and Beverage; General Liability; Health Law Business; Insurance Defense; Insurance Law and Litigation; Insurance and Risk Management; Intellectual Property; Labor Law; Lender Liability; Licenses; Litigation; Medical Malpractice Defense; Mergers and Acquisitions; Product Liability; Professional Liability; Real Estate Transactions; Securities; Silica; Surety; Technology Law; Technology Transfer; Telecommunications; Toxic Tort; Transportation Law; White Collar Crime; Workers' Compensation.

FIRM PROFILE: Dickie, McCamey & Chilcote is a nationally recognized litigation firm providing comprehensive legal expertise, as well as non-litigation services, in a multitude of practice areas. The firm has grown to include offices in Harrisburg (Camp Hill), Philadelphia, Washington D.C., New Jersey, North Carolina, Ohio and West Virginia to serve industry-leading clients across the country. For more information, please visit www.dmclaw.com.

SHAREHOLDERS

RICHARD C. POLLEY, admitted to bar, 1981, Pennsylvania; 1992, West Virginia; 1998, Ohio; U.S. District Court, Middle and Western Districts of Pennsylvania; U.S. Dis-

(This Listing Continued)

trict Court, Northern and Southern Districts of West Virginia; U.S. Court of Appeals, Third and Fourth Circuits; U.S. Supreme Court. *Education:* Allegheny College (B.S., cum laude, 1978); University of Pittsburgh (J.D., cum laude, 1981). Phi Beta Kappa. Comments Editor, University of Pittsburgh Law Review, 1979-1980. Comments and Notes Editor, University of Pittsburgh Journal of Law and Commerce, 1980-1981. Shareholder-in-charge, Steubenville, Ohio Office. *Member:* Allegheny County Bar Association (Member, Civil Litigation Section); Ohio County Bar Association (W. Va.); Ohio State Bar Association; Pennsylvania Bar Association; West Virginia State Bar; Defense Research Institute; Pennsylvania Defense Institute. (Also at Wheeling, West Virginia and Pittsburgh, Pennsylvania Offices). ***PRACTICE AREAS:*** Toxic Torts; Asbestos Litigation; Silicosis Litigation; Business Torts; Construction Law; Insurance Coverage Litigation. ***Email:*** RPolley@dmclaw.com

MELVIN F. O'BRIEN, admitted to bar, 1994, Ohio; 1995, West Virginia; U.S. District Court, Northern and Southern Districts of Ohio; U.S. District, Northern and Southern Districts of West Virginia. *Education:* Bowling Green State University (B.S.B.A., 1988); Cleveland-Marshall College of Law (J.D., cum laude, 1994). Executive Editor, Cleveland State University Journal of Law and Health, 1993-1994. *Member:* Ohio State Bar Association; West Virginia State Bar; West Virginia Defense Trial Counsel; Defense Research Institute; Ohio Academy of Civil Trial Attorneys. (Also at Wheeling, West Virginia Office). ***PRACTICE AREAS:*** Products Liability; Medical Malpractice Defense; Transportation Law; Insurance Coverage Litigation; Health Care Law. ***Email:*** MObrien@dmclaw.com

JOSEPH S. D. CHRISTOF, II, admitted to bar, 1974, Pennsylvania; 1993, West Virginia; 2002, Ohio; U.S. District Court, Eastern and Western Districts of Pennsylvania; U.S. District Court, Northern and Southern Districts of West Virginia; U.S. District Court, Northern District of Ohio. *Education:* College of the Holy Cross (B.A., 1970); Vanderbilt University (J.D., 1974). Listed in Best Lawyers in America. Law Clerk to the Honorable Herbert P. Sorg, Chief Judge, U.S. District Court, Western District of Pennsylvania, 1974-1975. *Member:* Allegheny County and Pennsylvania Bar Associations; West Virginia State Bar; International Association of Defense Counsel; Defense Research Institute; Pennsylvania Defense Institute. Fellow, Academy of Trial Lawyers of Allegheny County. (Also at Wheeling, West Virginia and Pittsburgh, Pennsylvania Offices). ***PRACTICE AREAS:*** Insurance Defense Litigation; Commercial Litigation; Professional Negligence; Insurance Coverage; Products Liability; Alternative Dispute Resolution. ***Email:*** JChristof@dmclaw.com

DAVID M. NEUHART, admitted to bar, 1976, Pennsylvania; 2004, Ohio, U.S. Court of Appeals, Third Circuit and U.S. Supreme Court. *Education:* University of Pittsburgh (B.A., summa cum laude, 1973; J.D., 1976). Phi Beta Kappa. *Member:* Allegheny County Bar Association; Pennsylvania Defense Institute. Fellow, Academy of Trial Lawyers of Allegheny County. (Also at Pittsburgh, Pennsylvania Office). ***PRACTICE AREAS:*** Accountants Malpractice; Family Law; Government Law; Medical Malpractice Defense. ***Email:*** DNeuhart@dmclaw.com

STEPHEN M. HOUGHTON, admitted to bar, 1978, Michigan; 1980, Pennsylvania; 1993, West Virginia; 2005, Ohio; U.S. District Court, Western District of Pennsylvania; U.S. District Court, Northern District of West Virginia; U.S. Court of Appeals, Third Circuit; U.S. Supreme Court. *Education:* University of Michigan (B.A., 1975; J.D., 1978). Phi Beta Kappa. Law Clerk to the Honorable William W. Knox, U.S. District Court, Western District of Pennsylvania, 1978-1980. *Member:* Allegheny County, Pennsylvania and American Bar Associations; State Bar of Michigan; West Virginia State Bar; National Association of Railroad Trial Counsel. Fellow, Academy of Trial Lawyers of Allegheny County. (Also at Pittsburgh, Pa. and Wheeling, W. Va. Offices). ***PRACTICE AREAS:*** Civil Litigation; Medical Malpractice Defense; Toxic Tort; Transportation Law; Personal Injury Litigation. ***Email:*** SHoughton@dmclaw.com

JOHN T. PION, admitted to bar, 1985, Pennsylvania; 1988, District of Columbia; 1999, Ohio; U.S. District Court, Eastern, Middle and Western Districts of Pennsylvania; U.S. District Court, Northern District of Ohio, U.S. Court of Appeals, Third Circuit. *Education:* University of Pittsburgh (B.A., magna cum laude, 1982); Duquesne University (J.D., 1985). Listed in Best Lawyers in America. Order of Barristers. Appellate Moot Court Board, 1985. *Member:* Allegheny County, Ohio, Pennsylvania and American Bar Associations; The District of Columbia Bar; Pennsylvania Defense Institute; National Association of Railroad Trial Counsel; Canadian Transport Lawyers Association; Pennsylvania Motor Truck Carriers Association; American Truckers Association; Trucking Industry Defense Association; Transportation Lawyers Association. (Also at Pittsburgh, Pennsylvania and Washington, D.C. Offices). ***PRACTICE AREAS:*** Litigation; Products Liability Defense; Medical Malpractice Defense; Federal Employers Liability Act (FELA); Trucking Liability Defense. ***Email:*** JPion@dmclaw.com

ASSOCIATES

DEREK M. BRONDOU, admitted to bar, 2002, Ohio; U.S. District Court, Northern and Southern Districts of Ohio. *Education:* Canisius College (B.A., 1996); University of Akron (J.D., 2000). *Member:* Ohio State Bar Association. (Also at Pittsburgh, Pennsylvania Office). ***PRACTICE AREAS:*** Insurance Defense; Toxic Torts; Workers Compensation. ***Email:*** DBrondou@dmclaw.com

PIERO P. COZZA, admitted to bar, 2000, Ohio; U.S. District Court, Northern District of Ohio; U.S. District Court, Southern District of Ohio; U.S. Supreme Court. *Education:* Kent State University (B.S., cum laude, 1994; M.S., 1996); Capital University (J.D., 2000). Order of the Curia. *Member:* Jefferson County Bar Association; Ohio State Bar Association. ***PRACTICE AREAS:*** Insurance Defense; Asbestos Defense; Silicosis Litigation; Trusts and Estates; Collections; Real Estate. ***Email:*** PCozza@dmclaw.com

KEITH R. HUNTZINGER, admitted to bar, 1995, West Virginia; 2001, Ohio; U.S. District Court, Southern District of Ohio; U.S. District Court, Northern and Southern Districts of West Virginia. *Education:* West Liberty State College (B.A., 1992); West Virginia University (J.D., 1995). *Member:* Ohio State Bar Association; West Virginia State Bar; American Bar Association. (Also at Wheeling, West Virginia Office). ***PRACTICE AREAS:*** Toxic Torts; Insurance Defense; Asbestos Litigation. ***Email:*** KHuntzinger@dmclaw.com

BRANT T. MILLER, admitted to bar, 1998, Ohio; 1999, Pennsylvania; U.S. District Court, Western District of Pennsylvania and U.S. District Court, Northern and Southern Districts of Ohio; U.S. Supreme Court. *Education:* Washington & Jefferson College (B.A.,

(This Listing Continued)

cum laude, 1995); University of Pittsburgh (J.D., 1998). *Member:* Allegheny County, Pennsylvania and Ohio State Bar Associations. (Also at Pittsburgh, Pennsylvania Office). ***PRACTICE AREAS:*** Trucking Liability Defense; Insurance Defense; Medical Malpractice Defense; Real Estate; Federal Employers Liability Act (FELA). ***Email:*** BMiller@dmclaw.com

(For complete biographical data on personnel at Pittsburgh, Camp Hill and Philadelphia, Pennsylvania; Haddonfield, New Jersey; Charlotte, North Carolina; Steubenville, Ohio; and Wheeling, West Virginia, see Professional Biographies at those locations)

ADRIAN V. HERSHEY

4110 SUNSET BOULEVARD
STEUBENVILLE, OHIO 43952
Telephone: 740-264-1651
Fax: 740-264-6720
Email: ehershey@clover.net

General Corporate Practice, Estate Planning Law, Criminal Law, Domestic Relations, Divorce Law, Personal Injury Litigation, Personal Injury Law, Probate and Estates, and Collections.

ADRIAN V. HERSHEY, born Steubenville, Ohio, December 13, 1948; admitted to bar, 1975, Ohio and U.S. District Court, Northern District of Ohio; 1976, U.S. District Court, Southern District of Ohio; 1984, U.S. Court of Appeals, Sixth Circuit. *Education:* West Liberty State College (B.A., 1972); Akron University Law School (J.D., 1975). Phi Alpha Delta. Previous Employment: Miller & Morris Co., L.P.A., Akron, 1975-1976; Mazaris, Olivito & Hershey, 1976-1978. Prosecuting Attorney, Steubenville, Ohio, 1976-1980. Assistant County Prosecutor, Jefferson County, 1980-1982. Small Claims Magistrate, Steubenville Municipal Court, 1984—. *Member:* Jefferson County (President, 1992-1993), Ohio State and American Bar Associations; Ohio Academy of Criminal Defense Lawyers; Ohio Academy of Trial Lawyers. ***REPORTED CASES:*** State v. Nemeth, 820. St. 3d 202, y N.E. 2d 1332 (1998)-Omic Leus 1699. ***PRACTICE AREAS:*** Criminal Law; Family Law; Divorce Law; Personal Injury; Probate; Trusts and Estates; Collections.

SCHRADER BYRD & COMPANION, PLLC

STEUBENVILLE, OHIO

(See Wheeling, West Virginia)

Litigation, Business and Taxation, Trusts and Estates, Banking and Real Estate, Employment, Administrative and Labor Law.

KENNETH A. BLECH COMPANY, L.P.A.

10850 PEARL ROAD, SUITE D-3
STRONGSVILLE, OHIO 44136
Telephone: 440-238-7887
Fax: 440-238-9532
URL: http://www.blechlaw.com
Email: kenblech@ameritech.com
URL: http://www.kenblech.com

Taxation Law, Probate Law, Bankruptcy Law, Real Estate, Personal Injury, Small Business Law.

KENNETH A. BLECH, born 1946; admitted to bar, 1979, Ohio; Supreme Court of Ohio; 1982, U.S. District Court, Northern District of Ohio; 1987, U.S. Tax Court. *Education:* Purdue University (B.S., 1969); Cleveland State University (J.D., 1977). Former Internal Revenue Service Agent. *Member:* Cleveland, Cuyahoga and Ohio State Bar Associations; The Association of Trial Lawyers of America. [U.S. Army Reserves, 1970-1976]

ASSOCIATE

LAUREN E. DAVIDSON, born April 7, 1974; admitted to bar, 2003, Ohio. *Education:* Michigan State University (B.A., 1996); Ohio Northern University (J.D., 1999). ***PRACTICE AREAS:*** Domestic Relationss; Probate; Bankruptcy.

DAVID S. RIEHL

STRONGSVILLE, OHIO

(See Brunswick)

Domestic Relations, Family Law, Divorce, Child Custody, Adoption Law, Premarital Agreements, Real Estate, Commercial Real Estate, Residential Real Estate, Small Business Law, Business Organization, Contracts, Probate, Estate Planning, Trust Law, Wills, Elder Care, Personal Injury, Automobile Accidents and Injuries, Negligence, Criminal Law, Driving While Intoxicated, Traffic Violations, Civil Practice.

MANOS, MARTIN, PERGRAM & DIETZ CO., LPA

SUNBURY, OHIO

(See Delaware)

Administrative, Appellate Practice, Litigation, Business, Contracts, Corporate, Zoning, Planning and Land Use, Real Estate, Labor and Employment, Trusts and Estates, and Wills and Probate.

THE McQUADES CO., L.P.A.

Established in 1937
LINCOLN AT BROADWAY
P.O. BOX 237
SWANTON, OHIO 43558
Telephone: 419-826-0055
Fax: 419-825-3871
Email: mcquadelaw@earthlink.net
URL: http://www.mcquadelaw.com

Archbold, Ohio Office: 200 N. Defiance Street. Telephone: 419-445-3755.
Whitehouse, Ohio Office: 6632 Providence Street. Telephone: 419-877-0746.

General Civil Practice. Personal Injury, Wrongful Death, Products Liability, Medical Malpractice, Real Estate, Corporate and Business Law. Probate and Estate Planning, Collections, Municipal and Zoning Law. Family Law, Criminal Law. Trials and Appellate Practice in all Courts.

RICHARD B. McQUADE, SR. (1912-1996)

DANIEL P. McQUADE, born Toledo, Ohio, July 11, 1942; admitted to bar, 1967, Ohio. *Education:* Loyola University, Chicago, Illinois (B.S., 1964); Ohio State University (J.D., 1967). Phi Delta Phi. Vice President, Student Bar Association, 1966-1967 and Law Day Chairman, 1967, Ohio State University Law School. *Member:* Toledo, Fulton County, The Ohio State and American Bar Associations; Ohio Academy of Trial Lawyers. ***PRACTICE AREAS:*** Personal Injury; Decedent's Estates; Real Estate; Criminal Defense; Domestic; Divorce.

COLIN J. McQUADE, born Toledo, Ohio, June 13, 1955; admitted to bar, 1980, Ohio. *Education:* Adrian College (B.A., magna cum laude, 1977); University of Toledo (J.D., 1980). *Member:* Fulton County, Toledo, Ohio State and American Bar Associations. ***PRACTICE AREAS:*** Municipal and Township Law; Family Law; Divorce; Probate and Estate Planning; Wills; Trusts; Real Estate; Bond Insurance Defense.

ALAN J. LEHENBAUER, born Ephrata, Washington, May 11, 1959; admitted to bar, 1984, Ohio. *Education:* University of Toledo (B.B.A., 1981; J.D., 1984). *Member:* Fulton County and Ohio State Bar Associations. ***PRACTICE AREAS:*** Personal Injury; Family Law; Divorce; Criminal Law; Bankruptcy; Probate and Estate Planning; Wills; Trusts.

APPROVED ATTORNEYS FOR: Port Lawrence Title and Trust Co.
REPRESENTATIVE CLIENTS: Swanton Welding Company; Napoleon Spring Works; Villages of Archbold, Metamora and Swanton; McNeill Chevrolet.
REFERENCE: Farmers & Merchants State Bank.

KENNEY & NIEHAUS, LTD.

Established in 1975
5470 MAIN STREET, SUITE 300
SYLVANIA, OHIO 43560
Telephone: 419-517-7000
Fax: 419-517-7001
Email: lastname@kenneyniehauslaw.com
URL: http://www.lawyers.com/kenneyniehauslaw

Corporate, Business, Securities, Banking, Estate Planning, Probate, Real Estate, Litigation.

FIRM PROFILE: A sophisticated, business-oriented practice, Kenney & Niehaus, Ltd., provides highly effective service to clients through reliable advice in all areas of business and entrepreneurial activity, counseling in personal estate planning and estate administration, and advocating when disputes arise. We approach each client relationship with the same entrepreneurial spirit as our clients and provide creative solutions tailored to each distinctive situation.

Kenney & Niehaus, Ltd. represents a broad spectrum of clients and focuses in several areas of law including: business and transactions, securities law for privately owned and public companies, banking, estate planning, probate administration, real estate, and commercial litigation.

KEVIN J. KENNEY, born Toledo, Ohio, October 12, 1955; admitted to bar, 1981, Ohio. *Education:* University of Notre Dame (B.A., 1977); University of Toledo (J.D., 1980). *Member:* Toledo, Ohio State and American Bar Associations; National Institute for Trial Advocacy; Association of Trial Lawyers of America; Ohio Association of Trial Lawyers; Public Investors Arbitration Bar Association. ***PRACTICE AREAS:*** Litigation; Securities Arbitration; Probate; Estate Planning; Real Estate; Business. ***Email:*** kenney@kenneyniehauslaw.com

CHARLES D. NIEHAUS, born Fort Thomas, Kentucky, November 27, 1959; admitted to bar, 1986, Ohio. *Education:* Lawrence Institute of Technology (B.S.C.E., 1982); University of Toledo (J.D., 1986). *Member:* Toledo, Ohio State and American Bar Associations. ***PRACTICE AREAS:*** Securities; Banking; Corporate; Civil Litigation. ***Email:*** niehaus@kenneyniehauslaw.com

ASSOCIATES

LAURIE A. SCHOONMAKER, born Toledo, Ohio, December 28, 1965; admitted to bar, 1999, Ohio. *Education:* University of Toledo (B.B.A., 1993; J.D., 1998). Board Member: Sylvania Community Services and Sylvania Chamber of Commerce. *Member:* Toledo, Lucas County and Ohio State Bar Associations; Toledo Estate Planning Council. ***PRACTICE AREAS:*** Estate Planning; Probate Administration; Corporate Law. ***Email:*** schoonmaker@kenneyniehauslaw.com

CHRISTOPHER J. HENSIEN, born Toledo, Ohio, April 16, 1952; admitted to bar, 2003, Ohio. *Education:* The Ohio State University (B.S., 1974); The American Graduate School of International Management (M.I.M., 1975); University of Toledo (J.D., 2003). Order of the Coif (Toledo Chapter). *Member:* Toledo Bar Association. ***PRACTICE AREAS:*** Corporate Law; Securities; Commercial Litigation; Real Estate. ***Email:*** hensien@kenneyniehauslaw.com

JERY E. BARTON, born Charleston, West Virginia, November 6, 1947; admitted to bar, 1972, Ohio. *Education:* Harvard University (A.B., 1969); Boston University School of Law (J.D., 1972). *Member:* Toledo and Columbus Bar Associations. ***PRACTICE AREAS:*** Securities; Corporate Law; Estate Planning. ***Email:*** barton@kenneyniehauslaw.com

REPRESENTATIVE CLIENTS: Concept Rehab, Inc.; Toledo Surgical Specialists, Inc.; UBS Financial Services, Inc.; Teleguam Holdings, LLC; Diocese of Toledo; Farmers National Bank; HCR Manor Care; Insulspan, Inc.; Plasti-Fab, Ltd.; Don's Automotive Group; Modern Builders Supply; Payak Insurance Agency, Inc.; Perstorp Polyols, Inc.; Signature Bank, N.A.

(This Listing Continued)

DAVID SIMKO

SYLVANIA, OHIO

(See Toledo)

Estate Planning, Real Estate, Small Business.

UDELL & ABRAMSON, LTD.

Established in 2000
5738 MAIN STREET
SYLVANIA, OHIO 43560
Telephone: 419-724-2600
Fax: 419-724-2601
Email: LU@ualegal.com

Business Law, Corporate and Succession Planning, Mergers and Acquisitions, ERISA, Pension and Profit Sharing Plans, Real Estate, Taxation, Tax Litigation, Nonprofit Corporations, Estate Planning and Probate, Family Law, Employment, Litigation.

LOUIS UDELL, born Youngstown, Ohio, January 26, 1958; admitted to bar, 1983, Ohio; 1997, Michigan. *Education:* Miami University (B.S., 1979); Ohio State University (J.D., 1983). CPA, Ohio, 1984. ***PRACTICE AREAS:*** Business Law; Mergers and Acquisitions; Estate Planning; Taxation; Real Estate. ***Email:*** LU@ualegal.com

MARK C. ABRAMSON, born Ft. Bragg, North Carolina, September 26, 1956; admitted to bar, 1981, Ohio. *Education:* University of Cincinnati (B.A., 1978); American University (J.D., 1981). ***PRACTICE AREAS:*** Employee Benefits Law; Family Business Law. ***Email:*** MCA@ualegal.com

OF COUNSEL

CATHERINE H. KILLAM, born Gary, Indiana, January 30, 1953; admitted to bar, 1979, Ohio. *Education:* University of Toledo (J.D., 1978). ***PRACTICE AREAS:*** Commercial Litigation; White Collar Criminal Defense; Appellate Practice; Litigation.

CONTRADA & ASSOCIATES

TIFFIN, OHIO

(See Toledo)

Plaintiff Personal Injury, Wrongful Death, Products Liability, Asbestos Litigation, Medical Malpractice, Auto Accidents.

PATINO & KNUTSON

159 S. WASHINGTON STREET
TIFFIN, OHIO 94883
Telephone: 419-455-9508
Fax: 419-455-9509

Legislative Law, Administrative Law, Bankruptcy, Domestic Relations, Juvenile Law, Education, Criminal Law, Mediation, Drainage and Levee, Probate.

MEMBERS OF FIRM

(MS) LETICIA G. PATINO, born June 17, 1953; admitted to bar, 1982, Ohio; 1987, U.S. District Court, Northern District of Ohio. *Education:* St. John College (B.S.E., 1975); Catholic University of America (J.D., 1981). Phi Alpha Delta. Member, Ohio Mediation Association. *Member:* Seneca County and Ohio State Bar Associations; National Association of Consumer Bankruptcy Attorneys. ***LANGUAGES:*** English, Spanish. ***PRACTICE AREAS:*** Bankruptcy; Mediation; Legislative Law; Domestic Relations; Juvenile Law; Education Law; Criminal Law; Administrative Law. ***Email:*** Leticia@AttorneysPK.com

(MS) ELAINE J. KNUTSON, born Charles City, Iowa, December 5, 1939; admitted to bar, 1976, Ohio; 1988, U.S. Supreme Court; 2005, U.S. District Court, Northern District of Ohio. *Education:* University of Kansas (B.A., 1966); University of Toledo (J.D., 1976). *Member:* Seneca and Ohio State Bar Associations. ***LANGUAGES:*** English. ***PRACTICE AREAS:*** Juvenile; Criminal Law; Drainage and Levee; Domestic Relations; Probate; Bankruptcy. ***Email:*** Elaine@attorneysPK.com

DYSINGER, STEWART & DOWNING, LLC

ATTORNEYS AT LAW

Established in 1981

249 SOUTH GARBER DRIVE

TIPP CITY, OHIO 45371-1183

Telephone: 937-667-4481
Facsimile: 937-667-5393
Email: info@dsdlawyers.com
URL: http://www.dsdlawyers.com

Business Law, Business Litigation, Mergers and Acquisitions, Civil Litigation, Commercial Real Estate, Corporate Law, Criminal Law, Estate Planning, Family Law, Guardianship, Litigation, Personal Injury, Probate, Real Estate, Trusts & Estates, Wills, Business Planning, Collections, Divorce, Dissolutions, Wrongful Death, Tax Planning, Medicaid Planning, Elder Law.

THOMAS E. DYSINGER, born Tipp City, Ohio, January 11, 1953; admitted to bar, 1977, Ohio and U.S. District Court, Southern District of Ohio; 1979, U.S. District Court, Northern District of Ohio. *Education:* The Ohio State University (B.S., with honors, 1974; J.D., 1977). Outstanding Young Man of Tipp City, 1985; Outstanding Citizen of the Year of Tipp City, 1997. Member: Mensa, 1992—; Tipp City Planning Board, 1981-1986; Tipp City Chamber of Commerce, 1984—, President, 1987; Tipp Improvement Corporation; Tipp City Council, 1986-1997, President, 1992-1993. Director, Unity National Bank, 2004—. *Member:* Dayton, Miami County (President, 1992) and Ohio State Bar Associations. ***SPECIAL AGENCIES:*** Agent, Ohio Bar Title Insurance Company, 1986—. ***PRACTICE AREAS:*** Business Law; Elder Law; Corporate Law; Probate; Real Estate; Trusts & Estates; Estate Planning. ***Email:*** tdysinger@dsdlawyers.com

BRYAN K. STEWART, born Springfield, Ohio, June 9, 1957; admitted to bar, 1989, Ohio and U.S. District Court, Southern District of Ohio. *Education:* Clark State College (A.S., 1983); Wright State University (B.A., magna cum laude, 1985); The Ohio State University (J.D., with honors, 1989). Member, Tipp City United Fund, 1990-2004, President, 1991-1995. Member, Tipp City Chamber of Commerce, 1989—, Board of Trustee, 1990-1993. *Member:* Miami County and Ohio State Bar Associations; The Ohio Academy of Trial Lawyers; The American Trial Lawyers Association. [2nd Class Petty Officer, U.S. Navy, 1975-1981]. ***SPECIAL AGENCIES:*** Agent, Ohio Bar Title Insurance Co., 1999—. ***PRACTICE AREAS:*** Business Law; Commercial Real Estate; Personal Injury; Family Law; Criminal Law; Litigation. ***Email:*** bstewart@dsdlawyers.com

JOSEPH A. DOWNING, born Dayton, Ohio, October 20, 1969; admitted to bar, 1996, Colorado; 1998, Ohio and U.S. District Court, Southern District of Ohio. *Education:* University of Dayton (B.A., 1992); Ohio Northern University (J.D., 1996). Member: Chamber of Commerce, 2000—; Tipp City School Board, 2002—. 2004 Dayton Bar Journal "Best of the Bar" for Business Law. *Member:* Dayton, Miami County, Ohio State and American Bar Associations. ***SPECIAL AGENCIES:*** Agent, Ohio Bar Title Insurance Company, 1999—. ***REPORTED CASES:*** In re Buechter Miami App No. 2002_CA_22, 2002_Ohio_5598, 2002WL 31341567. ***PRACTICE AREAS:*** Business Law; Corporate Law; Estate Planning; Probate; Real Estate; Litigation. ***Email:*** jdowning@dsdlawyers.com

ANDREW B. STEWART, born Pittsburgh, Pennsylvania, April 25, 1966; admitted to bar, 1999, Ohio; U.S. District Court, Southern District of Ohio. *Education:* Furman University (B.A., 1989); University of Pittsburgh (J.D., 1998). Trustee, Tipp Monroe Community Services, 2001—; President 2004—. *Member:* Dayton, Miami County and Ohio State Bar Associations. ***PRACTICE AREAS:*** Business Law; Corporate Law; Estate Planning; Litigation; Family Law; Probate. ***Email:*** astewart@dsdlawyers.com

ASSOCIATE

NICHOLAS I. ANDERSEN, born Columbus, Ohio, October 26, 1979; admitted to bar, 2004, Ohio, U.S. District Court, Southern District of Ohio. *Education:* The Ohio State University (B.S., 2001); Capital University (J.D., magna cum laude, 2004). Order of the Barristers. State Board of Registration for Professional Engineers and Surveyors of the State of Ohio. Registered Engineer Intern, 2001. *Member:* Miami County and Ohio State Bar Associations; The Ohio Academy of Trial Lawyers. ***PRACTICE AREAS:*** Personal Injury; Criminal Law; Litigation; Business Law; Family Law.

REPRESENTATIVE CLIENTS: Monroe Federal Savings & Loan Assn.; SK Mold & Tool Co.; Ishmael Precision Tool Corp.; Vital Connections Inc.; Black River Development, Inc.; Daisy Valley Gifts, Inc.; City to City Courier Service, Inc.; Wampler Plumbing, Inc.; Advanced Medical Equipment; Greene Tool Systems, Inc.; J&L Wood Products, Inc.; Tetra Mold & Tool, Inc.; Triad Fluid Power, Inc.; Pyramid Injection Molding; Magee Bros. Construction Co.; Tipp Eye Center, Inc.; Bud Polley's Floor Center, Inc.; Pak-It, Inc.; All Star Helicopters, Inc.; Hester Masonry Co., Inc.; Precision Certified Welding, Inc.; Cheng T. Pan, M.D., Inc.; Tipp City Dairy Queen, Inc.; Sidney Dairy Queen, Inc.; Borchers Construction Company; Ever-Green Lawn Care, Inc.; Hawk Construction, Inc.; Simon Ellis Superabrasives, Inc.; The Tip Top Canning Company; Specialty Packaging, Inc.; Specialty Machines, Inc.; Apex Aluminum; Steven J. Ritzi, DDS, Inc.; Freeman/Groves Insurance and Financial Services, Inc.; Unity National Bank; BK Drugs, Inc.; Wilma Mohr Farms, Ltd.; Chamberlain Farms, LLC; Corigraphics, Inc.; Exactaform Cutting Tools, LLC; Kelcor Machine and Tool, Ltd.; Wright Bros. Aero, Inc.; Don Myers Electric, Inc.; Troy Engineered Components and Assemblies Corp.; Vapor Systems Technologies, Inc.

DAMON D. ALT
ATTORNEY AT LAW, L.L.C.

TOLEDO, OHIO

(See Findlay)

ANSPACH MEEKS ELLENBERGER LLP

Established in 1986

300 MADISON AVENUE, SUITE 1600

TOLEDO, OHIO 43604-2633

Telephone: 419-246-5757
Fax: 419-321-6979
URL: http://www.anspachlaw.com

Tiffin, Ohio Office: Dell, Burtis & Anspach, L.L.P., 60 Sycamore Street, 44883. Telephone: 419-447-6181. Fax: 419-447-6332.
Buffalo, New York Office: Main Place Tower, Suite 2400, 14202-3724. Telephone: 716-856-5012. Fax: 716-852-2485.

Insurance Defense and Corporate Litigation, Railroad Defense, Employers Intentional Tort Defense, Unemployment Compensation, Environmental Law, Employment Law, Products Liability Law, Risk Management and Medical Malpractice Defense. Trials and Appeals. Probate Law, Trust Law, Real Estate Law, Banking Law.

ROBERT M. ANSPACH, born Tiffin, Ohio, February 29, 1948; admitted to bar, 1973, Ohio and U.S. District Court, Northern District of Ohio; 1976, U.S. Court of Appeals, Sixth Circuit and U.S. Supreme Court; 1985, U.S. Tax Court; 1994, Michigan; 1999, New York. *Education:* Cornell University (B.A., 1970; J.D., 1973). Co-Author: "Winning In Court: The Accountant's Role in Litigation, Arbitration and Dispute Resolution." Recipient, Ohio Legal Center Award of Merit, 1986. *Member:* Toledo (Member: Lawyer's Assistance Committee), Ohio State (Vice-Chairman, Judicial Administration and Legal Reform Committee, 1982; Member, Lawyer's Assistance Committee) and American (Member, Litigation Section) Bar Associations; National Association of Railroad Trial Counsel; Defense Research Institute. Fellow: Ohio State Bar Foundation; American Bar Foundation. ***PRACTICE AREAS:*** Railroad Law; Employment Law; Malpractice Defense; Insurance Defense; Product Liability. ***Email:*** ranspach@anspachlaw.com

MARK D. MEEKS, born Indianapolis, Indiana, July 14, 1963; admitted to bar, 1988, Ohio and U.S. District Court, Northern District of Ohio; 1993, Michigan, U.S. District Court, Eastern District of Michigan and U.S. Court of Appeals, Sixth Circuit. *Education:* Indiana Wesleyan University (B.S., cum laude, 1985); University of Toledo (J.D., 1988). *Member:* Toledo, Ohio State and Michigan State Bar Associations; National Association of Railroad Trial Counsel. ***PRACTICE AREAS:*** Railroad Law; Medical Malpractice Defense; Civil Litigation; Defense Litigation; Insurance Defense. ***Email:*** mmeeks@anspachlaw.com

RICHARD F. ELLENBERGER, born Erie, Pennsylvania, June 26, 1940; admitted to bar, 1965, Ohio, U.S. District Court, Northern District of Ohio and Eastern District of Michigan, U.S. Court of Appeals, Sixth Circuit and U.S. Supreme Court. *Education:* Ohio Wesleyan University (B.A., 1962); The Ohio State University (LL.B., 1965). *Member:* Toledo and Ohio State Bar Associations; Maritime Law Association of the United States; National Association of Railroad Trial Counsel. ***PRACTICE AREAS:*** Civil Litigation; Railroad Law; Admiralty Law; Probate Litigation. ***Email:*** rellenberger@anspachlaw.com

PAUL F. BURTIS, born Harvey, Illinois, October 2, 1962; admitted to bar, 1990, Ohio and U.S. District Court, Northern District of Ohio; 1993, Illinois and U.S. District Court, Northern District of Illinois. *Education:* Northwestern University (B.S., 1984); Indiana University (J.D., 1990). *Member:* Seneca County, Ohio State and American Bar Associations. (Resident, Tiffin, Ohio Office). ***PRACTICE AREAS:*** Civil Litigation; General Practice; Trusts and Estates; Corporate Law. ***Email:*** pburtis@bright.net

JANE C. DELL, born Tiffin, Ohio, January 21, 1964; admitted to bar, 1990, Ohio. *Education:* Georgetown University (B.S., 1987); Indiana University (J.D., 1990). Agent, Ohio Bar Title Insurance Company. *Member:* Seneca County and Ohio State Bar Associations. (Resident, Tiffin, Ohio Office). ***PRACTICE AREAS:*** Trust Law; Estate Planning; Medicaid Planning; Probate; Real Estate. ***Email:*** jdell@bright.net

KENT D. RIESEN, born Celina, Ohio, July 26, 1963; admitted to bar, 1988, West Virginia; 1989, Ohio; 1992, Michigan; 1999, New York; 2005, Pennsylvania. *Education:* Ohio Northern University (B.A., in History, 1985); University of Toledo (J.D., 1988). Phi Alpha Delta; Delta Mu Delta. Co-Author: "Repetitive Stress Injury, A Growing Threat to American Business". Former Member, Council of Delegates, American Bar Association. *Member:* Toledo and Ohio (Past Chair, CLE Committee; Past Chairperson, Young Lawyers Section) State Bar Associations; West Virginia State Bar; State Bar of Michigan. ***PRACTICE AREAS:*** Medical Malpractice; Insurance Defense; Environmental Law; Construction Law; Commercial Litigation; Nursing Home Negligence; Employment Law; Uninsured Motorists Coverage. ***Email:*** kriesen@anspachlaw.com

JOHN J. JABLONSKI, born Buffalo, New York, September 5, 1967; admitted to bar, 1994, New York, U.S. District Court, Western District of New York and U.S. Bankruptcy Court, Western District of New York. *Education:* State University of New York at Buffalo School of Law (B.S., 1989; J.D., 1993). Member, Environmental Law Journal. *Member:* Erie County, New York State and American Bar Associations; National Association of Railroad Trial Counsel; Defense Research Institute. (Resident, Buffalo, New York Office). ***PRACTICE AREAS:*** Railroad Law; Toxic Torts; Civil Litigation; Defense Litigation; Litigation. ***Email:*** jjablonski@anspachlawbuf.com

GARRICK O. WHITE, born Toledo, Ohio, October 24, 1972; admitted to bar, 1998, Ohio; 1999, Indiana; U.S. District Court, Northern District of Ohio, U.S. District Court, Eastern District of Michigan and U.S. Court of Appeals, Sixth Circuit. *Education:* Albion College (B.A., 1995); University of Toledo (J.D., 1998). Who's Who Among American Law Students, 1997 and 1998. *Member:* Toledo, Lucas County, Ohio State and Indiana State Bar Associations; Toledo Claims Association; Inns of Court (Morrison Waite Chapter); National Association of Railroad Trial Counsel (Young Lawyers' Division). ***PRACTICE AREAS:*** Railroad Law; Insurance Defense; Defense Litigation; Commercial Litigation; Medical Malpractice; Employment Law; Admiralty Law; Construction Law; Products Liability. ***Email:*** gwhite@anspachlaw.com

JAMES R. CARNES, born Toledo, Ohio, March 15, 1972; admitted to bar, 1998, Ohio; 1999, Michigan; U.S. District Court, Northern District of Ohio, Northern District of Indiana and Eastern District of Michigan; U.S. Court of Appeals, Sixth Circuit. *Education:* Eastern Michigan University (B.S., 1995); University of Toledo (J.D., cum laude, 1998).

(This Listing Continued)

ANSPACH MEEKS ELLENBERGER LLP, Toledo—Continued

Member: Toledo and Ohio State Bar Associations; National Association of Railroad Trial Counsel. ***PRACTICE AREAS:*** Railroad Law; Insurance Defense; Employment Law; Defense Litigation. ***Email:*** jcarnes@anspachlaw.com

MARJAN NECESKI, born East York, Ontario, June 28, 1968; admitted to bar, 1996, New York and U.S. District Court, Western and Northern Districts of New York; 1998, Ontario, Canada (Not admitted in Ohio). *Education:* Wilfrid Laurier University (B.A., 1992); University of Windsor (M.A., Economics, 1992); University of Toledo (J.D., 1995). *Member:* American Bar Associations; National Association of Railroad Trial Counsel. ***LANGUAGES:*** Macedonian. ***PRACTICE AREAS:*** Railroad Law; Insurance Defense; Defense Litigation. ***Email:*** mneceski@anspachlaw.com

---

DARIA A. CARR, born Salem, Massachusetts, March 13, 1973; admitted to bar, 1998, Ohio; 2004, New York; U.S. District Court, Northern District of Ohio, U.S. District Court, Northern District of Indiana and U.S. District Court, Western District of New York. *Education:* Northwestern University (B.A., 1995); Ohio Northern University (J.D., 1998). Phi Delta Phi. Author: "SEPTA: Politics of Disclosure," Journal of Pharmacy & Law, Spring, 1997. *Member:* New York State and Ohio State Bar Associations; National Association of Railroad Trial Counsel. (Resident, Buffalo, New York Office). ***LANGUAGES:*** French. ***PRACTICE AREAS:*** Defense Litigation; Railroad Law; Insurance Defense. ***Email:*** dcarr@anspachlawbuff.com

JAMES W. FRUTH, born Oberlin, Ohio, March 22, 1970; admitted to bar, 1995, Ohio. *Education:* Heidelberg College (B.A., English and Political Science, Beta Beta Beta, Sigma Tau Delta, 1992); Capital University Law School (J.D., 1995). *Member:* Seneca County and Ohio State Bar Associations. (Resident, Tiffin, Ohio Office). ***PRACTICE AREAS:*** General Practice; Real Estate Law; Probate Law; Criminal Defense; Juvenile Law. ***Email:*** jfruth@bright.net

GREGORY H. WAGONER, born Toledo, Ohio, June 27, 1974; admitted to bar, 2001, Illinois; 2002, Michigan; 2003, Ohio, U.S. District Court, Northern District of Ohio, U.S. District Court, Northern District of Illinois, U.S. District Court, Eastern and Western Districts of Michigan and U.S. District Court, Northern District of Indiana. *Education:* University of Michigan, Ann Arbor (B.A., 1997); University of Toledo (J.D., 2001). *Member:* Toledo and Ohio State Bar Associations; State Bar of Illinois; State Bar of Michigan; National Association of Railroad Trial Counsel. ***PRACTICE AREAS:*** Railroad Law; Insurance Defense; Employment Law; Business Litigation; Medical Malpractice. ***Email:*** gwagoner@anspachlaw.com

J. CHRISTINE CHIRIBOGA, born Cleveland, Ohio, September 21, 1966; admitted to bar, 1993, Ohio; 1994, New York and U.S. District Court, Western District of New York. *Education:* The Ohio State University (B.M., 1988); Cleveland Marshall College of Law (J.D., 1992). (Resident, Buffalo, New York Office). ***PRACTICE AREAS:*** Railroad Law. ***Email:*** jchiriboga@anspachlawbuf.com

STEVEN E. CARR, born Petersburg, West Virginia, August 15, 1969; admitted to bar, 1999, Ohio; 2003, U.S. District Court, Northern District of Ohio and U.S. District Court, Northern District of Indiana. *Education:* Concord College (B.A., with honors, 1996); Ohio Northern University (J.D., magna cum laude, 1999). President, Federalist Society, 1997-1999. *Member:* Toledo and Ohio State Bar Associations. (Resident, Buffalo, New York Office). ***LANGUAGES:*** Arabic. ***PRACTICE AREAS:*** Railroad Law; Employment Law; Medical Malpractice Defense; Insurance Defense; Defense Litigation; Business Litigation. ***Email:*** scarr@anspachlawbuf.com

KEVIN J. KRUPPA, born Batavia, New York, October 21, 1975; admitted to bar, 2003, New York (Not admitted in Ohio). *Education:* State University of New York at Binghamton (B.A., 1998); State University of New York at Buffalo School of Law (J.D., 2002). Publications Editor, Buffalo Law Review, 2001-2002. *Member:* Erie County and New York State Bar Associations. (Resident, Buffalo, New York Office). ***PRACTICE AREAS:*** Defense Litigation; Litigation; Railroad Law; Commercial Litigation. ***Email:*** kkruppa@anspachlawbuf.com

JESSICA W. STRAUB, born Toledo, Ohio, October 6, 1976; admitted to bar, 2003, Ohio, U.S. District Court, Northern District of Ohio. *Education:* University of Michigan, Ann Arbor (B.A., 1999); University of Toledo (J.D., cum laude, 2003). ***PRACTICE AREAS:*** Civil Litigation; Railroad Law; Insurance Defense. ***Email:*** jstraub@anspachlaw.com

J. RANDALL ENGWERT, born Fort Lauderdale, Florida, February 26, 1973; admitted to bar, 1999, Ohio; 2005, Michigan, U.S. District Court, Northern and Southern Districts of Ohio, U.S. District Court, Eastern District of Michigan, U.S. Court of Appeals, Sixth Circuit. *Education:* Ohio University (B.S., 1995); University of Toledo (J.D., 1998). Formerly with, Ohio Attorney General's Office, Environmental Enforcement Section. ***PRACTICE AREAS:*** Railroad Law; Insurance Defense; Products Liability; Environmental Law; Defense Litigation; Personal Injury. ***Email:*** rengwert@anspachlaw.com

NATHAN R. BOYD, born Zanesville, Ohio, December 27, 1975; admitted to bar, 2004, Ohio, U.S. District Court, Northern District of Ohio. *Education:* Ohio University (B.A., 1998; B.S., 1998); University of Toledo (M.B.A., 2004; J.D., magna cum laude, 2004). Assistant Management Editor, Law Review, 2003-2004. *Member:* Toledo and Ohio State Bar Associations. ***PRACTICE AREAS:*** Railroad Law; Insurance Defense; Defense Litigation. ***Email:*** nboyd@anspachlaw.com

MICHAEL W. JACKSON, born Toledo, Ohio, November 27, 1977; admitted to bar, 2003, Ohio; 2004, U.S. District Court, Northern District of Ohio. *Education:* The Ohio State University (B.S.B.A., 2000; J.D., 2003). *Member:* Toledo and Ohio State and American Bar Associations. ***PRACTICE AREAS:*** Railroad Law; Defense Litigation; Insurance Defense. ***Email:*** mjackson@anspachlaw.com

JOOHONG PARK, born Evanston, Illinois, May 12, 1979; admitted to bar, 2005, New York (Not admitted in Ohio). *Education:* Cornell University (B.S., 2001); Cornell University Law School (J.D., 2004). (Resident, Buffalo, New York Office). ***PRACTICE AREAS:*** Litigation; Railroad Law. ***Email:*** jpark@anspachlawbuf.com

(This Listing Continued)

CHERYL L. HITZEL, born Washington, DC, December 15, 1978; admitted to bar, 2004, New York. *Education:* James Madison University (B.S.W., cum laude, 2000); University of Miami School of Law (J.D., cum laude, 2003). (Resident, Buffalo, New York Office). ***PRACTICE AREAS:*** Railroad Law. ***Email:*** chitzel@anspachlawbuf.com

OF COUNSEL

JOHN R. WANICK, born Youngstown, Ohio, May 13, 1945; admitted to bar, 1970, Ohio; 1972, U.S. District Court, Northern District of Ohio; 1979, U.S. Tax Court. *Education:* Miami University (B.A., 1967); University of Toledo (J.D., 1970). Chief Deputy Clerk, Lucas County Probate Court, Toledo, Ohio, 1970-1972. Fazekas & Wanick, 1972-1974. Schnorf, Schnorf & Holmes, L.P.A., 1978-1980; Schnorf, & Schnorf, 1980-1983; Schnorf & Wanick, 1983-1985. *Member:* Lucas County, Toledo and Ohio State Bar Associations. ***PRACTICE AREAS:*** Trusts and Estates; Corporations; Real Estate. ***Email:*** jwanick@anspachlaw.com

REPRESENTATIVE CLIENTS: Whirlpool Corp.; CSX Transportation, Inc.; CNA Insurance; St. Vincent Mercy Medical Center; Farmers Insurance; Ohio Casualty Insurance; Attorneys' Liability Assurance Society; Royal Insurance Company; Buckeye State Mutual Insurance Company; Consolite Corporation; Consolidated Rail Corporation; Norfolk Southern Railway Company; Amtrak National Railroad Passanger Corp.; Seneca Insurance Company; Tri-State Insurance Company of Minnesota; Northland Insurance Company; Ameriwood Industries; Extendicare; Flying J. Travel Plaza; St. Charles Mercy Hospital; Catholic Health Partners; Chicago Insurance Company; Manufacturers & Traders Trust Company; Ohio Insurance Guaranty Association; Spieker Construction Company; Arbors Nursing Homes; Citigroup, Inc.; Citicorp Venture Capital, Ltd.; Travelers Life & Annuity Company; Travelers Insurance Company.

ARNOLD, CARUSO, GREEN & BELAZIS, LTD.

1822 CHERRY STREET
TOLEDO, OHIO 43608-2801
Telephone: 419-241-2200
Telecopier: 419-255-7623
URL: http://www.arnoldandcaruso.com

Business, Bankruptcy, Creditors Rights, Constitutional Law, Contract Law, Commercial Litigation, Federal Practice, Civil Litigation, Personal Injury, Wrongful Death, Admiralty Maritime, F.E.L.A., Municipal, Civil Rights, Employment Law, Civil Trial Practice in State and Federal Courts, Products Liability, Medical Malpractice, Professional Attorney Discipline.

MEMBERS OF FIRM

W. DAVID ARNOLD, born Houston, Texas, March 28, 1949; admitted to bar, 1974, Georgia; 1975, U.S. District Court, Northern District of Georgia; 1976, U.S. Court of Appeals, Fifth Circuit; 1979, U.S. District Court, Southern District of Georgia; 1981, U.S. District Court, Middle District of Georgia and U.S. Court of Appeals, Eleventh Circuit; 1982, U.S. District Court, Southern District of Texas; 1985, U.S. District Court, Eastern District of Texas; 1987, Ohio and U.S. District Court, Northern District of Ohio; 1989, U.S. Court of Appeals, Sixth Circuit; 1996, U.S. District Court, Western District of Michigan. *Education:* University of Michigan (B.A., with distinction, 1970; J.D., cum laude, 1974). ***PRACTICE AREAS:*** Civil Litigation; Business; Commercial; Contract Law; Creditors Rights. ***Email:*** wdarnold@arnoldandcaruso.com

PAUL T. BELAZIS, born Dayton, Ohio, April 15, 1954; admitted to bar, 1979, Ohio; 1990, New York, U.S. District Court, Northern District of Ohio and Western District of Michigan and U.S. Court of Appeals, Second and Sixth Circuits. *Education:* Denison University (B.A., 1976); University of Toledo (J.D., 1979). ***PRACTICE AREAS:*** Civil Litigation; Personal Injury; Insurance Bad Faith; Commercial Litigation; Employment Law. ***Email:*** ptbelazis@arnoldandcaruso.com

JAMES D. CARUSO, born Marion, Ohio, July 25, 1947; admitted to bar, 1978, Ohio and U.S. District Court, Northern District of Ohio; 1984, U.S. Court of Appeals, Sixth Circuit and U.S. Supreme Court; 1996, U.S. Court of International Trade. *Education:* The Ohio State University (B.A., 1970); University of Toledo (J.D., 1978). Member, Task Force Rules of Professional Conduct, 2003—. Adjunct Professor, Legal Ethics and Professionalism, University of Toledo College of Law, 1999—. *Member:* American Board of Trial Advocates. ***PRACTICE AREAS:*** Medical Malpractice; Personal Injury; Commercial Litigation; Attorney Discipline. ***Email:*** jdcaruso@arnoldandcaruso.com

MERRITT W. GREEN, III, born Toledo, Ohio, February 27, 1950; admitted to bar, 1976, Ohio and U.S. District Court, Northern District of Ohio; 1982, U.S. Court of Appeals, Sixth Circuit. *Education:* Kenyon College (B.A., 1972); University of Toledo, College of Law (J.D., 1975). *Member:* Toledo and Ohio State Bar Associations; Ohio Academy of Trial Lawyers. ***PRACTICE AREAS:*** Personal Injury; Admiralty and Maritime; FELA; Civil Litigation; General Civil Practice; Liquor Licensing. ***Email:*** mgreen@arnoldandcaruso.com

OF COUNSEL

R. MICHAEL FRANK, born January 21, 1940; admitted to bar, 1966, Connecticut and District of Columbia; 1969, U.S. District Court, Northern District of Ohio; 1970, Ohio; 1973, U.S. Court of Appeals, Sixth Circuit; 1977, U.S. Supreme Court. *Education:* University of Maryland (B.A., 1961); Cornell Law School (J.D., 1965). Member, Board of Directors, Toledo-Lucas County Port Authority. *Member:* National Employment Lawyers Association. ***PRACTICE AREAS:*** Employment Law; Municipal Law; Zoning Law. ***Email:*** rmfrank@arnoldandcaruso.com

MERRITT W. GREEN, II, born Toledo, Ohio, December 31, 1930; admitted to bar, 1956, Ohio; 1986, Michigan, U.S. District Court, Northern and Southern Districts of Ohio and District of Michigan, U.S. Court of Appeals, Sixth Circuit and U.S. Supreme Court. *Education:* University of Michigan (B.A., 1953); University of Michigan, College of Law (J.D., 1956). (Also Member, Parsons Ringsmuth PLC, Traverse City, Michigan). ***PRACTICE AREAS:*** Personal Injury; Admiralty and Maritime Law; FELA.

JAMES H. ELLIS, III, born Berwyn, Illinois, July 18, 1956; admitted to bar, 1981, California; 2000, Ohio. *Education:* Willamette University (B.S., 1978); University of San Diego (J.D., 1981; LL.M, Taxation, 1986). Recipient: James R. Webb Award; ABA/LSD

(This Listing Continued)

Board of Governor's Award. *Member:* Toledo, San Diego County, Sandusky County, Ohio State and American Bar Associations; State Bar of California. ***TRANSACTIONS:*** Coaster Rail System (San Diego). ***PRACTICE AREAS:*** Real Property; Taxation; Nonprofit Corporations; Litigation; Commercial Law; Contract Law. ***Email:*** jhellis@arnoldandcaruso.com

REPRESENTATIVE CLIENTS: The Danberry Co.; Dana Corp.; Owens Corning; Cargotec, Inc.; Signature/Oncor.
REFERENCE: Fifth Third Bank of Toledo.

BARAN, PIPER, TARKOWSKY, FITZGERALD & THEIS CO., L.P.A.

608 MADISON AVENUE, SUITE 1620
TOLEDO, OHIO 43604
Telephone: 419-241-2900
Fax: 419-241-3002
URL: http://www.baranlaw.com

General Civil Practice. Trials in all Courts. Insurance Defense, Corporate, Family Law, Estate Planning, Personal Injury, Products Liability and Construction Law. Commercial Litigation. Suretyship. Environmental and Governmental Liability, Professional Liability, Worker's Compensation.

(For Complete list of all Personnel and Biographical data, see Professional Biographies at Mansfield, Ohio)

BARBER, KAPER, STAMM & ROBINSON

TOLEDO, OHIO
(See Wauseon)

General Civil and Criminal Practice. Personal Injury, Insurance, Probate and Estate Planning, Real Estate, Title Examination, Collections, Commercial, Municipal and Banking Law. Trials and Appeals in all Courts.

CHARLES E. BOYK LAW OFFICES, LLC

502 MADISON AVENUE, SUITE 655
TOLEDO, OHIO 43604
Telephone: 419-241-1395
Fax: 419-241-8731

Personal Injury, Criminal Law.

CHARLES E. BOYK, born Toledo, Ohio, March 25, 1958; admitted to bar, 1983, Ohio. *Education:* Bowling Green State University (B.A., 1980); University of Toledo (J.D., 1983). *Member:* American Bar Association. ***PRACTICE AREAS:*** Personal Injury Law (66%); Criminal Law (34%).

BUGBEE & CONKLE

Established in 1954
SUITE 1300, NATIONAL CITY BANK BUILDING
405 MADISON AVENUE
TOLEDO, OHIO 43604
Telephone: 419-244-6788
Telefax: 419-244-7145
Email: attorneys@bugbee-conkle.com

General Civil Practice in all Courts, Corporation, Insurance, Labor and Employment, Real Estate, Personal Injury, Workers Compensation, Probate and Estate Planning and Trust Law, Taxation, Trials and Appeals.

FIRM PROFILE: Bugbee & Conkle and its predecessor firms have practiced law in Toledo, Ohio continuously since 1936. During that time the firm has served as general counsel, trial counsel and local counsel for businesses, including Fortune 500 companies, most of which have been located or doing business in Ohio.

MEMBERS OF FIRM

JOHN F. WETLI, born Toledo, Ohio, March 29, 1944; admitted to bar, 1969, Ohio; 1973, U.S. Court of Appeals, 6th Circuit; 1975, U.S. Supreme Court. *Education:* University of Notre Dame (B.A., 1966); Case Western Reserve University (J.D., 1969). Phi Delta Phi. *Member:* Toledo, Lucas County and Ohio State (Member, Probate Section) Bar Associations; Ohio Academy of Trial Lawyers. ***PRACTICE AREAS:*** Commercial Law; Litigation; Plaintiffs Personal Injury; Trusts and Estates; Business Law. ***Email:*** jwetli@bugbee.conkle.com

GREGORY B. DENNY, born Cleveland, Ohio, December 9, 1948; admitted to bar, 1973, Ohio; 1976, U.S. Court of Appeals, Sixth Circuit. *Education:* Washington University (B.S.B.A., with honors, 1970); The Ohio State University (J.D., cum laude, 1973). Delta Theta Phi. *Member:* Toledo and Ohio State (Member, Workers Compensation Section) Bar Associations. ***PRACTICE AREAS:*** Workers Compensation Defense; Intentional Tort Defense. ***Email:*** gdenny@bugbee-conkle.com

TYBO ALAN WILHELMS, born West Lafayette, Indiana, January 8, 1949; admitted to bar, 1976, Ohio; 1983, U.S. Court of Appeals, Sixth Circuit; 1987, U.S. Supreme Court. *Education:* Michigan State University (B.A., 1971); University of Toledo (J.D., 1976). Executive Editor, University of Toledo Law Review, 1975-1976. *Member:* Toledo, Ohio State (Member, Labor Law Section) and American (Member, Labor Law Section) Bar Associations. ***PRACTICE AREAS:*** Labor and Employment (Management); Federal Litigation; Appellate Practice; Commercial Litigation; Products Liability Defense. ***Email:*** twilhelms@bugbee-conkle.com

ROBERT L. SOLT, III, born Columbus, Ohio, February 23, 1959; admitted to bar, 1984, Ohio. *Education:* Miami University (B.A., 1981); University of Toledo (J.D., 1984). Delta Theta Phi. *Member:* Toledo and Ohio State Bar Associations. ***PRACTICE AREAS:*** Workers Compensation Defense; Litigation. ***Email:*** rsolt@bugbee-conkle.com

ROBERT P. KING, born Bellevue, Ohio, October 1, 1957; admitted to bar, 1983, Ohio. *Education:* Davidson College (B.A., 1980); University of Toledo (J.D., cum laude, 1983). *Member:* Toledo, and Ohio State Bar Associations. ***PRACTICE AREAS:*** Workers Compensation Defense; Litigation. ***Email:*** rking@bugbee-conkle.com

MARK S. BARNES, born Philadelphia, Pennsylvania, March 7, 1964; admitted to bar, 1995, Ohio and U.S. District Court, Northern District of Ohio. *Education:* University of Virginia (B.A., 1986); University of Maryland School of Law (J.D., 1994). Member, Board of Bar Examiners, 2001-2006. *Member:* Toledo, Ohio State and National Bar Associations; The Thurgood Marshall Law Association. ***PRACTICE AREAS:*** Workers Compensation Defense; Civil Litigation; Labor and Employment. ***Email:*** mbarnes@bugbee-conkle.com

ASSOCIATES

HARVEY C. MILLER, JR., born LaCrosse, Wisconsin, August 16 1970; admitted to bar, 1999, Ohio. *Education:* Winona State University (B.A., cum laude, 1995); Ohio Northern University (J.D., 1999). ***PRACTICE AREAS:*** Workers Compensation Defense; Domestic Relations. ***Email:*** hmiller@bugbee-conkle.com

ANDREW J. WILHELMS, born East Lansing, Michigan, October 18, 1969; admitted to bar, 1996, Ohio; 1998, U.S. District Court, Northern District of Ohio; 2000, U.S. District Court, Southern District of Ohio; 2001, U.S. District Court, Eastern District of Michigan. *Education:* Miami University (B.A., 1992); Capital University (J.D., 1995). Recipient, Ohio Academy of Trial Lawyers Distinguished Service Award, 2003. ***PRACTICE AREAS:*** Employment Litigation; Commercial Litigation; Personal Injury Litigation; Wrongful Death Litigation; Workers Compensation Litigation. ***Email:*** awilhelms@bugbee-conkle.com

JANELLE M. TROENDLE, born Toledo, Ohio, April 14, 1976; admitted to bar, 2003, Ohio. *Education:* University of Toledo (B.E., cum laude, 1999; J.D., 2002). Recipient, Dean's Merit Scholarship. *Member:* Toledo Bar Association; Ohio Trial Lawyers Association (Member, Leadership Committee, 2004-2005). ***PRACTICE AREAS:*** Workers Compensation. ***Email:*** jtroendle@busbee-conkle.com

OF COUNSEL

HARRY S. BUGBEE (1895-1982)

ALLAN J. CONKLE, born Hardin County, Ohio, March 31, 1918; admitted to bar, 1948, Ohio. *Education:* The Ohio State University (B.S., 1941; J.D., 1948). Delta Theta Phi; Order of the Coif. *Member:* Toledo (President, 1975-1976; Member, Executive Committee, 1976-1977), Ohio State and American (Member, Section of Corporation, Banking and Business Law) Bar Associations. [Lieut., USNR, 1942-1946]. ***PRACTICE AREAS:*** Business Law; Corporate Law; Trusts and Estates. ***Email:*** aconkle@bugbee-conkle.com

REPRESENTATIVE CLIENTS: Alcoa Automotive Structures, Inc.; Allied Moulded Products, Inc.; BÆ Box Co.; Bittersweet, Inc.; Blade Communications, Inc.; BP America, Inc.; Columbia Gas of Ohio, Inc.; Cooper Tire & Rubber Co.; Drivers Management, Inc.; Eaton Corporation; Erie Steel Treating, Inc.; Ford Motor Company; General Dynamics Land Systems; General Motors Corp.; Hammill Manufacturing Co.; Hecks Direct Mail & Printing Service, Inc.; Hickory Farms; I.T.T. Automotive, Inc.; Hisan, Inc.; Hospice of Northwest Ohio; Johns-Manville Corporation; Johnson Controls, Inc.; Key Bank; Kroger Company; A.C. Leadbetter & Son, Inc.; Laidlaw Transit Services; Meijer, Inc.; Ophthalmology Associates of Northwest Ohio, Inc.; Pepsi-Cola General Bottlers; Plastech Engineered Products, Inc.; Pro-Tec Coating Company; Rudolph/Libbey, Inc.; Salvation Army; Sears, Roebuck and Co.; Schutz Container Systems, Inc.; Sunoco, Inc.; Tecumseh Products; Toledo Technologies Co.; Tomco Plastics; Waste Management; Whirlpool Corporation.

BUNDA STUTZ & DeWITT, PLL

Established in 1991
ONE SEAGATE, SUITE 650
TOLEDO, OHIO 43604
Telephone: 419-241-2777
Telecopier: 419-241-4697
URL: http://www.bsd-law.com

General Civil Trial and Appellate Practice in all State and Federal Courts. Insurance Defense, Personal Injury, Toxic Torts, Product's Liability, Workman's Compensation, Corporate, Commercial and Labor Law.

FIRM PROFILE: Bunda Stutz & DeWitt, PLL offers a variety of services to businesses, individuals, financial institutions and medical groups. These services include representation involving all aspects of litigation in federal and state courts, with an emphasis on the trial and management of toxic agent, medical and product liability litigation. The firm's litigation practice is national in scope and encompasses regional and national consolidated actions and representation of coordinated multi-defendant defense groups as well as individual parties. Its litigation practice also encompasses commercial disputes, labor and personal injury actions. In addition, the firm is engaged in a general practice including probate, corporate and administrative law matters.

ROBERT A. BUNDA, born McKeesport, Pennsylvania, August 2, 1951; admitted to bar, 1977, Michigan; 1979, Ohio; U.S. Supreme Court; U.S. Court of Appeals, Sixth Circuit and U.S. District Court, Northern District of Ohio, Northern District of California, Eastern District of Wisconsin and Eastern and Western Districts of Michigan. *Education:* University of Notre Dame (A.B., magna cum laude, 1973); University of Michigan (J.D., 1976). Member, University of Michigan Journal of Law Reform, 1975. Law Clerk, Hon. Noel P. Fox, Chief Judge, U.S. District Court, Western District of Michigan, 1977-1978. Member, Ohio Supreme Court Task Force on the Unauthorized Practice of Law; Member, Civil Jus-

(This Listing Continued)

BUNDA STUTZ & DEWITT, PLL, Toledo—Continued

tice Reform Act Advisory Group for the U.S. District Court, Northern District of Ohio, 1994-1999. *Member:* Toledo (Member, Federal Courts Committee, 1989—; Chairman, Lawyers and Legal Assistants Committee, 1989-1991) and Ohio State (Member, Section on Litigation) Bar Associations; State Bar of Michigan; Ohio Association of Civil Trial Attorneys; Defense Research Institute; Toledo Association of Civil Trial Attorneys; International Association of Defense Counsel. Fellow, Ohio State Bar Foundation. ***REPORTED CASES:*** Goldman v. Johns-Manville Sales Corp., 514 N.E.2d 691, 33 Ohio St.3d 40 (1987); McGraw v. Connelly, 838 F2d 844 (6th Cir. 1989). ***PRACTICE AREAS:*** Trial Practice; Appellate Law; Toxic Torts; Products Liability Law; Pharmaceutical and Medical Services Defense. ***Email:*** rabunda@bsd-law.com

BARBARA J. STUTZ, born Toledo, Ohio, August 26, 1951; admitted to bar, 1983, Ohio; U.S. District Court, Northern District of Ohio and U.S. Tax Court. *Education:* University of Toledo (B.Ed., 1973; J.D., 1982). *Member:* Toledo (Chair, Admissions Committee, 1998-2000; Secretary, Criminal Justice Committee, 1983-1986; Member, Grievance Investigation Committee, 1987-1991), Ohio State, American and Ohio Women's Bar Associations; Toledo Women's Bar Association (President, 1987-1988; Chair, Judicial Selection Committee, 1989-1991; Member, By-Laws Committee); The Association of Trial Lawyers of America. ***REPORTED CASES:*** State of Ohio v. Gregory Esparza, 39 Ohio St. 3d 8, 529 N.E.2d 192 (1988). ***PRACTICE AREAS:*** Litigation; Products Liability Defense; Trial Practice; Appellate Practice. ***Email:*** bjstutz@bsd-law.com

THERESA R. DEWITT, born Cincinnati, Ohio, January 8, 1953; admitted to bar, 1983, Ohio; U.S. Supreme Court; U.S Court of Appeals, Sixth Circuit and U.S. District Court, Northern and Southern Districts of Ohio. *Education:* University of Michigan (B.G.S., with distinction, 1975); University of Cincinnati (J.D., 1983). *Member:* Toledo and Ohio State Bar Associations; Defense Research Institute; Toledo Women's Bar Association; Ohio Women's Bar Association (Past District Trustee). ***PRACTICE AREAS:*** Mass Tort Litigation Management; Litigation; Appellate Practice. ***Email:*** trdewitt@bsd-law.com

DAVID L. GRAY, born El Paso, Texas, March 18, 1952; admitted to bar, 1977, Indiana and U.S. District Court, Southern District of Indiana, U.S. Court of Appeals, Seventh Circuit and U.S. Supreme Court; 1998, Ohio; U.S. District Court, Northern District of Ohio. *Education:* Michigan State University (B.A., with honors, 1973); University of Michigan (J.D., 1977). Phi Delta Phi; Phi Beta Kappa. *Member:* Toledo, Ohio State, Indiana State and American (Member, Sections of: Tort and Insurance Practice; Litigation; Member, Forum Committee on the Construction Industry, 1980—) Bar Associations; Defense Research Institute. ***REPORTED CASES:*** Bemis Co. v. Rubush, 74 Ind. Dec. 364, 401 N.E.2d 48 (1980); Bemis Co. v. Rubush, 427 N.E.2d 1058 (1981); Carney v. Cummins Engine Co., 602 F.2d 763 (7th Cir. 1978); Cunningham v. Associates Capital Servs. Corp., 421 N.E.2d 681 (1981); Fenley Farms, Inc. v. Clark, 76 Ind. Dec. 228, 404 N.E.2d 1164 (1980); Monroe v. Standard Oil Co., 452 U.S. 549 (1981); South Tippecanoe Sch. Bldg. Corp. v. Shambaugh & Son, 182 Ind.App. 350, 395 N.E.2d 320 (1979). ***PRACTICE AREAS:*** Products Liability Law; Toxic Torts; Insurance; Antitrust; Litigation; Mass Tort Management. ***Email:*** dlgray@bsd-law.com

YVONNE D. BENNETT, born Waukegan, Illinois, February 5, 1962; admitted to bar, 1989, Illinois; 1992, Ohio; U.S. District Court, Northern District of Illinois; U.S. District Court, Northern District of Ohio. *Education:* Lake Forest College (B.A. in Economics, 1984); University of Michigan (J.D., 1989); Institut pour le development, language department, Brussels, Belgium, (Graduate of grand distinction, 1990); Cours de Soir de languages, Brussels, Belgium (Graduate of the highest distinction, 1990). *Member:* Toledo, Ohio State and Illinois State Bar Associations; Defense Research Institute. ***PRACTICE AREAS:*** Employment Law; Trial Practice; Appellate Practice; Mass Torts; Litigation. ***Email:*** ybennett@bsd-law.com

SUE A. SIKKEMA, born Port Huron, Michigan, March 31, 1948; admitted to bar, 1982, Ohio; U.S. District Court, Northern and Southern Districts of Ohio and Eastern District of Michigan and U.S. Court of Appeals, Sixth Circuit and U.S. Supreme Court. *Education:* University of Michigan (A.B., 1970; M.A., 1976; J.D., with honors, 1982). Associate and Contributing Editor, Michigan Law Review, 1980-1982. Law Clerk to Hon. Charles W. Joiner, U.S. District Court, E.D. Michigan, 1982-1984. *Member:* Toledo, Ohio State and American Bar Associations. ***REPORTED CASES:*** Libbey-Owens-Ford Co. v. Blue Cross & Blue Shield Mut. of Ohio, 982 F.2d 1031 (6th Cir. 1993); Toledo Edison v. G.A. Technologies, Inc., 847 F.2d 335 (6th Cir. 1988). ***PRACTICE AREAS:*** Litigation; Mass Torts Management. ***Email:*** ssikkema@bsd-law.com

REBECCA C. SECHRIST, born Lakewood, Ohio, June 8, 1961; admitted to bar, 1986, Ohio, U.S. District Court, District of Ohio and U.S. Court of Appeals, Sixth Circuit. *Education:* College of Wooster (B.A., 1983); University of Toledo (J.D., 1986). Law Clerk, Lucas County Court of Common Pleas, 1987-1989. *Member:* Toledo and Ohio State Bar Associations; Ohio Association of Civil Trial Attorneys. ***PRACTICE AREAS:*** Civil Litigation; Personal Injury; Premises Liability. ***Email:*** sechrist@bsd-law.com

---

DOUGLAS E. STALLINGS, born Tulsa, Oklahoma, February 15, 1965; admitted to bar, 1994, Ohio. *Education:* Brigham Young University (B.A., 1991); University of Toledo (J.D., 1994). Recipient: Chase National Environmental Law Moot Court Competition, Best Appellate Brief Award and Second Place Overall Team Award; American Jurisprudence Book Awards in Contracts, 1992; Legal Research, Writing and Appellate Advocacy, 1993 and Advanced Legal Writing, 1993. Adjunct Professor, University of Toledo, 1994—. *Member:* Toledo, Ohio State and American Bar Associations. (Resident). ***LANGUAGES:*** Japanese. ***PRACTICE AREAS:*** General Practice; Business Law; Real Estate; Securities; Creditor Bankruptcy. ***Email:*** dougstallings@bsd-law.com

BARBARA E. MACHIN, born Kansas City, Missouri, March 26, 1947; admitted to bar, 1978, Ohio and U.S. District Court, Northern District of Ohio; 1981, U.S. Court of Appeals, Sixth Circuit; 1987, U.S. Supreme Court. *Education:* University of Kansas (B.S., 1969; M.A., 1973); University of Toledo (J.D., 1978). Member: Law Review; Moot Court. Instructor, Research and Writing, Appellate Advocacy, 1978-1980. Author: "Corporate Takeover Statutes," 9 Univ. of Toledo L.Rev. 95 (1977). *Member:* Toledo (Chair, Federal Court Commission, 1999-2000) and Ohio State Bar Associations. ***PRACTICE AREAS:*** Employment; Education Law; Public Contract Law; Real Estate; Personal Injury. ***Email:*** bemachin@bsd-law.com

DAVID C. SHOOK, born Tiffin, Ohio, November 11, 1963; admitted to bar, 1990, Ohio; 1991, U.S. District Court, Northern District of Ohio. *Education:* University of Toledo (B.A., 1987; J.D., 1990). Phi Beta Kappa. *Member:* Toledo and Ohio State Bar Associations; Ohio Association of Civil Trial Attorneys; Defense Research Institute. ***PRACTICE AREAS:*** Civil Litigation; Personal Liability; Premise Liability; Product Liability; Toxic Torts. ***Email:*** dshook@bsd-law.com

REPRESENTATIVE CLIENTS: AC and S, Inc.; B.F. Goodrich Co.; Conoco, Inc.; DePuy, Inc.; Eagle Picher Industries, Inc.; Ethyl Corp.; The Geon Co.; Gustafson, Inc.; Hertz Claims Management Corp.; Libby-Owens-Ford; Occidental Chemical Corp.; Owens Illinois, Inc.; Phillips Petroleum; Zeneca, Inc.; R.T. Vanderbilt Co. Inc,; Shell Oil Co.; Reynolds Metals, Inc.; State Farm Insurance Companies; Smith & Nephew N.A.; Steelcase Services, Inc.; Sun Company, Inc. (R&M); Uniroyal Chemical Co.; U.S. Silica Co.; Utica Mutual Insurance Co.
REFERENCE: Charter One Bank.

FRITZ BYERS

SUITE 824, THE SPITZER BUILDING
TOLEDO, OHIO 43604
Telephone: 419-241-8013
Telecopier: 419-241-4215
Email: fbyers@accesstoledo.com

Communication Law, Constitutional Law, Health Care, Civil Trial Practice and Appellate Litigation, Labor and Employment Law.

FRITZ BYERS, born Kansas City, Missouri, May 15, 1955; admitted to bar, 1983, Texas; 1984, Ohio, U.S. Supreme Court and U.S. District Court, Northern District of Ohio; U.S. Court of Appeals, Sixth Circuit; U.S. District Court, Eastern District of Michigan; U.S. District Court, District of Columbia. *Education:* Duke University (B.A., summa cum laude, 1977); Harvard University (J.D., 1981). Phi Beta Kappa. Co- Author with John Shattuck: "An Egalitarian Interpretation of the First Amendment," Civil Rights-Civil Liberties Law Review, Vol. 15 No. 1, 1981; "Special Masters and Prison Reform: Real and Imagined Obstacles," Ohio State Journal on Dispute Resolution, Vol. 3, No. 2, Spring 1988; "Consensus Prison Reform: a Possible Dream," Impossible Jobs in Public Management, Hargrove and Glidewell, University of Kansas Press 1990. Law Clerk to the Honorable William Wayne Justice, Chief Judge, Eastern District of Texas, 1981-1982. Deputy Special Master to The Honorable Juan G. Burgiaga, U.S. District Court, District of New Mexico, 1983-1993. Monitor to the Honorable J. Owen Forester, U.S. District Court, Northern District of Georgia, 1984-1988. Member, 1987-1997 and Chairman, 1989-1991, Ohio Board of Bar Examiners. Instructor, University of Toledo College of Law, 2001—. Clinical Assistant Professor, Medical College of Ohio, Toledo, 2002—. *Member:* Toledo, Ohio State and American Bar Associations.

GENERAL COUNSEL FOR: Block Communications, Inc.; Toledo Blade Co.; Buckeye Cablevision, Inc.; Pittsburgh Post Gazette.
REFERENCE: Fifth Third.

CONNELLY, JACKSON & COLLIER LLP

Established in 1978
405 MADISON AVENUE
SUITE 1600
TOLEDO, OHIO 43604
Telephone: 419-243-2100
Fax: 419-243-7119
URL: http://www.cjc-law.com

Trial Practice.

MEMBERS OF FIRM

WILLIAM M. CONNELLY, born Toledo, Ohio, September 4, 1939; admitted to bar, 1964, Ohio; 1965, U.S. District Court, Northern District of Ohio; 1969, U.S. Court of Appeals, Sixth Circuit; 1971, U.S. Supreme Court. *Education:* John Carroll University (B.S.S., cum laude, 1961); The Ohio State University (J.D., 1964). Phi Delta Phi. Recipient, Distinguished Toledo Lawyer Award, 1995. Listed in The Best Lawyers in America, 1987—. Adjunct Professor: University of Toledo College of Law, 1968-1975; Adjunct Professor, Medical College of Ohio, 1986-1992. Assistant U.S. Attorney, Northern District of Ohio, 1969-1971. Special Attorney, U.S. Department of Justice, Internal Security Division, 1971-1972. Vice President, General Counsel, 2001-2004, Member, Board of Trustees, 1992-2001 and Chairman, 1999-2001, Medical College of Ohio. *Member:* Toledo, Ohio State and American Bar Associations; Ohio Academy of Trial Lawyers (Trustee, 1986-1988); American College of Legal Medicine (Associate Member). Fellow: American, Ohio and Toledo Bar Foundations. (Certified as a Civil Trial Advocate by the National Board of Trial Advocacy). ***PRACTICE AREAS:*** Personal Injury; Complex Business Litigation; Federal White Collar Criminal Defense. ***Email:*** wconnell@cjc-law.com

REGINALD S. JACKSON, JR., born Toledo, Ohio, October 8, 1946; admitted to bar, 1971, Ohio; 1972, U.S. District Court, Northern District of Ohio; 1976, U.S. Court of Appeals, Sixth Circuit and U.S. Supreme Court; 2003, U.S. District Court, Southern District of Ohio. *Education:* The Ohio State University (B.A., 1968; J.D., 1971). Adjunct Professor, Trial Practice, University of Toledo College of Law, 1976-1989. Assistant U.S. Attorney, Northern District of Ohio, 1976-1978. *Member:* Toledo (President, 1989-1990), Ohio State (President, 2000-2001), Federal and American (House of Delegates, 1996-1999; 2001—) Bar Associations; American Judicature Society; Association of Professional Responsibility Lawyers; American Board of Trial Advocates (Associate). Fellow: Toledo (President, 1993-1998), Ohio (Trustee, 1998—) and American Bar Foundations. (Certified as a Civil Trial Advocate by the National Board of Trial Advocacy). ***PRACTICE AREAS:*** Complex Business Litigation; Professional Liability; Federal White Collar Criminal Defense. ***Email:*** rjackson@cjc-law.com

(This Listing Continued)

(This Listing Continued)

STEVEN R. SMITH, born Findlay, Ohio, October 3, 1953; admitted to bar, 1980, Ohio; 1981, U.S. District Court, Northern District of Ohio; 1984, U.S. Court of Appeals, Sixth Circuit. *Education:* Miami University (B.A., with honors, 1975); The Ohio State University (M.A., 1977); University of Toledo (J.D., 1980). Phi Kappa Phi. Articles Editor, University of Toledo Law Review, 1979-1980. *Member:* Toledo (President, 2004-2005), Ohio State, Federal and American Bar Associations; The Association of Trial Lawyers of America; Ohio Academy of Trial Lawyers. Fellow: Toledo and Ohio Bar Foundations. ***PRACTICE AREAS:*** Complex Business Litigation; Insurance Coverage. ***Email:*** ssmith@cjc-law.com

STEVEN P. COLLIER, born Deshler, Ohio, October 4, 1955; admitted to bar, 1981, Ohio; 1982, U.S. District Court, Northern District of Ohio; 1984, U.S. Court of Appeals, Sixth Circuit. *Education:* Wittenberg University (B.A., cum laude, 1977); University of Cincinnati (J.D., 1981). Member, Moot Court. Adjunct Assistant Professor, Medical College of Ohio, 1992—. Adjunct Professor, University of Toledo College of Law, 1997—. Best Lawyers in America, Personal Injury, 1997—. Member, Ohio Medical Malpractice Commission, 2003-2005. *Member:* Toledo, Ohio State and American Bar Associations; The Association of Trial Lawyers of America; Ohio Academy of Trial Lawyers (President, 2001-2002; Fellow, 2003; Distinguished Service Awards, 1996, 2004); Toledo Trial Lawyers Association; American College of Legal Medicine (Associate Member); American Board of Trial Advocates (Associate); Ohio State Bar Foundation; Toledo Bar Foundation. (Certified as a Civil Trial Advocate by the National Board of Trial Advocacy). ***PRACTICE AREAS:*** Personal Injury; Medical Malpractice; Product Liability. ***Email:*** scollier@cjc-law.com

MICHAEL A. BONFIGLIO, born Toledo, Ohio, March 31, 1955; admitted to bar, 1985, Ohio; 1986, U.S. District Court, Northern District of Ohio; 1994, U.S. Court of Appeals, Sixth Circuit; 1996, U.S. District Court, Eastern District of Michigan. *Education:* Bowling Green State University (B.S., 1977); University of Toledo (J.D., cum laude, 1985). Assistant Lucas County Prosecutor, Criminal Division, 1987-1988. *Member:* Lucas County, Toledo, Ohio State and American Bar Associations; The Association of Trial Lawyers of America; Ohio Academy of Trial Lawyers; Toledo Trial Lawyers Association. ***PRACTICE AREAS:*** Medical Malpractice; Personal Injury. ***Email:*** bonfiglio@cjc-law.com

JANINE T. AVILA, born Perrysburg, Ohio, July 12, 1950; admitted to bar, 1991, Ohio; 1992, Michigan, U.S. District Court, Eastern District of Michigan and U.S. District Court, Northern District of Ohio; U.S. District Court, Western District of Ohio; U.S. Court of Appeals, Sixth Circuit; U.S. Supreme Court. *Education:* Miami University (B.A., cum laude, 1972); University of Toledo (J.D., summa cum laude, 1991). Phi Kappa Phi; Order of the Coif. Student Editor, Law Review, 1990-1991. *Member:* Toledo, Ohio State and American Bar Associations; The Ohio Academy of Trial Lawyers (Trustee, 2000—); The Association of Trial Lawyers of America. ***PRACTICE AREAS:*** Personal Injury; Employment Litigation; Complex Business Litigation; Insurance Coverage. ***Email:*** javila@cjc-law.com

ANTHONY E. TURLEY, born Findlay, Ohio, February 6, 1963; admitted to bar, 1998, Ohio; 1999, U.S. District Court, Northern District of Ohio and U.S. Court of Appeals, Sixth Circuit. *Education:* University of Toledo (B.S., 1995; J.D., magna cum laude, 1998). Order of the Coif. Author: "Tragedy Tomorrow, Comity Tonight," 29 U. Tol. L. Rev. 177, 1998. *Member:* Toledo, Ohio State and American Bar Associations; The Association of Trial Lawyers of America; Ohio Academy of Trial Lawyers. ***PRACTICE AREAS:*** Personal Injury; Medical Malpractice. ***Email:*** aturley@cjc-law.com

ASSOCIATES

JASON A. HILL, born Ashtabula, Ohio, April 16, 1974; admitted to bar, 2000, Ohio; 2001, U.S. District Court, Northern District of Ohio; 2004, U.S. Court of Appeals, Sixth Circuit. *Education:* Bowling Green State University (B.S., cum laude, 1996); The Ohio State University, College of Law (J.D., 2000). *Member:* Toledo, Ohio State and American Bar Associations; The Association of Trial Lawyers of America; Ohio Academy of Trial Lawyers (Toledo Bar Association Trustees Award, 2004). ***LANGUAGES:*** Spanish. ***PRACTICE AREAS:*** Complex Business Litigation; Personal Injury; Insurance Coverage; Medical Malpractice; Federal White Collar Criminal Defense; ERISA. ***Email:*** jhill@cjc-law.com

TAMMY GEIGER LAVALETTE, born Cincinnati, Ohio, November 14, 1969; admitted to bar, 1999, Ohio; 2000, U.S. District Court, Northern District of Ohio; 2001, U.S. District Court, Southern District of Ohio and U.S. Court of Appeals, Sixth Circuit. *Education:* Ohio University (B.A., cum laude, 1992); University of Toledo (J.D., magna cum laude, 1999). Order of the Coif. Member, University of Toledo Law Review, 1997-1999. *Member:* Toledo and Ohio State Bar Associations. ***PRACTICE AREAS:*** Business Litigation; Employment; Insurance. ***Email:*** tlavalette@cjc-law.com

TIMOTHY P. NACKOWICZ, born Cleveland, Ohio, November 18, 1977; admitted to bar, 2003, Ohio; 2004, U.S. District Court, Northern District of Ohio. *Education:* Miami University (B.A., International Studies, cum laude, 2000); The Ohio State University (J.D., with honors, 2003). *Member:* Toledo, Ohio State and American Bar Associations; Association of Trial Lawyers of America; Ohio Academy of Trial Lawyers. ***LANGUAGES:*** German. ***PRACTICE AREAS:*** Complex Business Litigation; Professional Liability. ***Email:*** tnackowi@cjc-law.com

REPRESENTATIVE CLIENTS: Owens Corning; Daimler/Chrysler; KeyCorp; National City Bank; Willis Day Properties, Inc.; Ohio Bar Liability Insurance Co.; Bowling Green State University; Toledo-Lucas County Port Authority; Libbey, Inc.; Chase Brass & Copper Co.; Norfolk Southern Group; Pilkington North America, Inc.; Faurecia Exhaust Systems, Inc.
REFERENCE: National City Bank,
SPECIAL COUNSEL: Attorney General of Ohio.

CONTRADA & ASSOCIATES

Established in 1990

6641 SYLVANIA AVENUE, SUITE 8
TOLEDO, OHIO 43560-3921
Telephone: 419-841-4400
Fax: 419-841-4463

Plaintiff Personal Injury, Wrongful Death, Products Liability, Asbestos Litigation, Medical Malpractice, Auto Accidents.

(This Listing Continued)

FIRM PROFILE: Contrada & Associates is an aggressive trial practice firm representing victims of serious injury and death. We practice in all counties of Northwest Ohio, and the firm has also obtained verdicts in excess of One Million Dollars in the Court of Claims and in Summit County. Charles V. Contrada, certified in the field of Civil Trial Advocacy by the National Board of Trial Advocacy, has always limited his practice to injury claims and has served as President of the Toledo Area Trial Lawyers Association. Two additional areas of extensive experience are intentional torts by employers and asbestos claims.

The firm is included in the Bar Register of Preeminent Lawyers.

CAROL A. CONTRADA, born 1951; admitted to bar, 1979, Ohio. *Education:* Denison University (B.A., cum laude, 1973); University of Toledo (J.D., 1978). ***PRACTICE AREAS:*** Products Liability Law; Asbestos Litigation; Negligence Law; Medical Malpractice. ***Email:*** carol@contrada.net

CHARLES V. CONTRADA, born Washington, D.C., August 20, 1951; admitted to bar, 1979, Ohio; 1980, Michigan. *Education:* Kenyon College (A.B., 1973); University of Toledo (J.D., 1978). *Member:* Toledo Area Trial Lawyers Association (President, 1993-1994); Toledo Law Association (Trustee, 1993—); The Association of Trial Lawyers of America; Ohio Academy of Trial Lawyers. (Certified as a Civil Trial Advocacy Specialist by the National Board of Trial Advocacy). ***REPORTED CASES:*** Callis v. Zilba, 136 Ohio App. 3d 696, 737 N.E.2d 974 (2000); Westray v. Imperial Pools & Supplies, Inc., 133 Ohio App. 3d. 426, 728 N.E.2d 431 (1999); Calmes v. Goodyear Tire & Rubber Co., 61 Ohio St. 3d 470, 575 N.E.2d 416 (1991). Kaiser v. Strall, 5 Ohio St. 3d 91, 449 N.E.2d 1 (1983). ***PRACTICE AREAS:*** Products Liability Law; Asbestos Litigation; Negligence Law; Medical Malpractice. ***Email:*** charlie@contrada.net

COOPER & WALINSKI

A LEGAL PROFESSIONAL ASSOCIATION

Established in 1969

900 ADAMS STREET
TOLEDO, OHIO 43624
Telephone: 419-241-1200
Fax: 419-242-5675
Email: toledo@cooperwalinski.com
URL: http://www.cooperwalinski.com

Ann Arbor, Michigan Office: 206 South Fifth Avenue, Suite 400. Telephone: 734-663-6535. Fax: 734-663-0996.

Business Planning, Civil Rights, Commercial Litigation, Commercial Transactions, Criminal, Employee Benefits, ERISA, Health Care, Insurance Coverage, Labor and Employment, Public Law, Probate Litigation, Product Liability, Professional Negligence, Real Estate, School Law.

FIRM PROFILE: The firm serves clients in business litigation throughout the country, and counsels business clients on a wide array of employment related issues. The firm also counsels clients in business transactions and planning. The firm has been recognized for its public service contributions, particularly in fair housing.

CARY RODMAN COOPER, born Havre de Grace, Maryland, July 10, 1942; admitted to bar, 1969, Ohio, U.S. Supreme Court and U.S. Court of Appeals, Sixth Circuit; 1970, U.S. District Court, Northern District of Ohio; 1982, U.S. Court of Appeals, Tenth Circuit; 1989, Michigan and U.S. District Court, Eastern District of Michigan. *Education:* Ohio University (B.S., 1964); University of Toledo (J.D., summa cum laude, 1969). Phi Kappa Phi. Editor, University of Toledo Law Review, 1968-1969. Lecturer, University of Toledo College of Law, 1971-1973. Life Member, U.S. Sixth Circuit Court of Appeals Judicial Conference. Law Clerk, U.S. District Court, Northern District of Ohio, 1970-1971. Special Counsel to Attorney General of Ohio, 1976-1982. Member, American Arbitration Association Panel of Commercial Arbitrators. *Member:* American Health Lawyers Association (Panel of Neutrals). ***PRACTICE AREAS:*** Civil Litigation; Appeals. ***Email:*** cooper@cooperwalinski.com

RICHARD S. WALINSKI, born Toledo, Ohio, May 1, 1943; admitted to bar, 1969, Ohio, 1973, U.S. Supreme Court and U.S. Court of Appeals, Sixth Circuit; 1982, U.S. Court of Appeals, Tenth Circuit; 1984, U.S. Court of Appeals, Fifth Circuit; 1986, U.S. Court of Appeals, Federal Circuit. *Education:* University of Toledo (B.A., magna cum laude, 1965; J.D., cum laude, 1969). Order of the Coif. Editor-in-Chief, University of Toledo Law Review, 1968-1969. Chief Counsel, Attorney General of Ohio, 1976-1978. Special Counsel to Attorney General of Ohio, 1979—. Consultant, Ohio General Assembly Select Committee on Evidence, 1979-1980. Rules Advisory Committee of the Supreme Court of Ohio, 1992-1998. ***PRACTICE AREAS:*** Civil Litigation; Appeals. ***Email:*** walinski@cooperwalinski.com

T. SCOTT JOHNSTON, born Cleveland, Ohio, October 13, 1945; admitted to bar, 1970, Ohio; 1972, District of Columbia and U.S. District Court, District of South Dakota, U.S. Court of Appeals, District of Columbia Circuit and U.S. District Court, District of Columbia; 1974, U.S. Supreme Court and U.S. District Court, Northern District of Ohio; 1978, U.S. Court of Appeals, Sixth Circuit; 1982, U.S. Court of Appeals, Tenth Circuit; 1986, U.S. District Court, Eastern District of Michigan; 1989, Michigan. *Education:* DePauw University (B.A., 1967); University of Toledo (J.D., 1970). Member, University of Toledo Law Review, 1969-1970. Trial Attorney, Department of Justice, Washington, D.C., 1970-1973. Lecturer, University of Toledo College of Law, 1974-1975. Special Counsel to Ohio Attorney General, 1977-1979; 1984-1986. Member, Panel of Commercial Arbitrators, American Arbitration Association, 1985-1999; Mediator, U.S. District Court, Northern District of Ohio, 1994-1999. ***PRACTICE AREAS:*** Civil Litigation; Products Liability; School Law. ***Email:*** johnston@cooperwalinski.com

JOHN CZARNECKI, born Toledo, Ohio, May 13, 1940; admitted to bar, 1972, Ohio, U.S. District Court, Northern District of Ohio, U.S. Court of Appeals, Sixth Circuit and U.S. Supreme Court. *Education:* University of Toledo (B.B.A., 1968; J.D., 1972). Articles Editor, University of Toledo Law Review, 1971-1972. Law Clerk, U.S. District Court, Northern District of Ohio, 1972-1974. Lecturer, University of Toledo College of Law, 1974-1978.

(This Listing Continued)

COOPER & WALINSKI, A LEGAL PROFESSIONAL ASSOCIATION, Toledo—Continued

Life Member, U.S. Sixth Circuit Court of Appeals Judicial Conference, 1977. Member: Ohio Public Defender Commission, 1990-1993; Northern District of Ohio, Criminal Justice Act Task Force, 1989-1999; Anti-Trust and Criminal Sections, American Bar Association. *Member:* Federal Bar Association; Association of Federal Defense Attorneys; National Association of Criminal Defense Lawyers. ***REPORTED CASES:*** Marshall vs. Lonberger, 459 U.S. 422 (1983). ***PRACTICE AREAS:*** Business Crimes Law; Civil Litigation; Construction Law. ***Email:*** czarnecki@cwclegal.com

JACQUELINE M. BONEY, born Toledo, Ohio, March 11, 1950; admitted to bar, 1976, Ohio and U.S. District Court, Northern District of Ohio. *Education:* University of Michigan (B.A., with honors, 1971); University of Toledo (J.D., 1976). Editor-in-Chief, University of Toledo Law Review, 1975-1976. Law Clerk, U.S. District Court, Northern District of Ohio, 1976-1978. ***PRACTICE AREAS:*** Civil Practice; Litigation. ***Email:*** boney@cooperwalinski.com

JOSEPH P. THACKER, born Toledo, Ohio, September 15, 1953; admitted to bar, 1978, Ohio; 1979, Florida and U.S. District Court, Northern District of Ohio; 1983, U.S. District Court, Northern District of Texas; 1984, U.S. Court of Appeals, Fifth Circuit; 1985, U.S. Supreme Court; 1986, U.S. Court of Appeals, Sixth Circuit; 1997, U.S. Court of Appeals, Third Circuit. *Education:* University of Toledo (B.A., cum laude, 1975; J.D., cum laude, 1978). Listed in Best Lawyers in America and Who's Who in American Law. Assistant Prosecuting Attorney, Lucas County, Ohio, 1978-1981. *Member:* The Florida Bar; Federal and American (Member, Tort and Insurance Practice Section) Bar Associations. Fellow, Ohio State Bar Foundation (the professional honorary for Ohio lawyers). ***REPORTED CASES:*** TRINOVA Corp. v. Pilkington Bros. (1994) 70 Ohio St. 3d 171. In Re Rowe, 67 Ohio St. 2d 115. ***PRACTICE AREAS:*** Indemnity Contracts; Insurance Coverage Litigation. ***Email:*** thacker@cooperwalinski.com

JOHN K. NELSON, born Toledo, Ohio, March 26, 1954; admitted to bar, 1979, Ohio; 1980, U.S. District Court, Northern District of Ohio; 1985, U.S. Supreme Court. *Education:* Miami University (B.A., cum laude, 1975); University of Toledo (J.D., magna cum laude, 1979). Note and Comment Editor, University of Toledo Law Review, 1978-1979. Law Clerk, U.S. District Court, Northern District of Ohio, 1979-1981. ***PRACTICE AREAS:*** Civil Litigation; Insurance Coverage Litigation. ***Email:*** nelson@cooperwalinski.com

JANIS E. SUSALLA FOLEY, born Detroit, Michigan, October 19, 1958; admitted to bar, 1986, Ohio and U.S. District Court, Northern District of Ohio; 1987, Michigan and U.S. Court of Appeals, Sixth Circuit; 1991, U.S. District Court, Eastern District of Wisconsin; 1993, U.S. District Court, Eastern District of Michigan; 1997, U.S. District Court, Northern District of Texas. *Education:* Western Michigan University (B.A., cum laude, 1980); University of Toledo (J.D., cum laude, 1986). Member, The Order of the Coif. Law Clerk to the Hon. Nicholas J. Walinski, U.S. District Court, Northern District of Ohio, 1986-1988. Member, Labor and Employment Law Board of Governors, Ohio State Bar Association. Member, Labor and Employment Law and Litigation Sections, American Bar Association. *Member:* Toledo Junior Bar Association (Executive Committee, 1988-1996; President, 1994-1995); Toledo Women's Bar Association; State Bar of Michigan. ***PRACTICE AREAS:*** Employment Law; Americans with Disabilities Act; Civil Litigation; Insurance Defense Law. ***Email:*** foley@cooperwalinski.com

MARGARET J. LOCKHART, born Suffern, New York, December 30, 1960; admitted to bar, 1987, New York and New Jersey; 1988, Ohio; U.S. District Court, Eastern District of Michigan; 1989, U.S. District Court, Northern District of Ohio; 1992, U.S. Court of Appeals, Sixth Circuit; 1993, U.S. Supreme Court; 1994, Michigan. *Education:* University of East Anglia, Norwich, England; College of William and Mary (B.A., 1982); Rutgers University-Newark (J.D., magna cum laude, 1986). Editor-in-Chief, Rutgers Law Review, 1985-1986. Law Clerk to the Hon. Robert DeMascio, U.S. District Court, Eastern District of Michigan, 1986-1988. Member, Labor and Employment Law Section (Board of Governors, 1992-1999), Ohio State Bar Association. Member, Labor and Employment and Litigation Sections, American Bar Association. Judge Pro Tempore, Perrysburg Municipal Court, 1994—. *Member:* New Jersey State Bar Association; State Bar of Michigan; Toledo Women's Bar Association; Ohio Association of School Board Attorneys. ***PRACTICE AREAS:*** Labor and Employment Law; Commercial Litigation; Insurance Coverage Litigation. ***Email:*** lockhart@cooperwalinski.com

WM. MILES McKEE, born Washington, D.C., February 26, 1945; admitted to bar, 1979, Michigan; 1980, Pennsylvania (inactive); 1990, Ohio; U.S. District Court, Eastern District of Michigan, Western District of Pennsylvania and Northern District of Ohio. *Education:* University of Pennsylvania (B.S., 1967); University of Michigan (M.B.A., 1968); Detroit College of Law (J.D., 1979). *Member:* State Bar of Michigan. ***PRACTICE AREAS:*** ERISA; Employee Benefits; Taxation. ***Email:*** mckee@cooperwalinski.com

JANET E. HALES, born Dubois, Pennsylvania, July 26, 1957; admitted to bar, 1991, Ohio; 1993, U.S. District Court, Eastern District of Michigan and U.S. Court of Appeals, Sixth Circuit; 1994, Michigan. *Education:* Bowling Green State University (B.Ed., 1982); University of Toledo (J.D., 1991). Editor, University of Toledo Law Review, 1991-1992. Law Clerk to The Honorable Barbara K. Hackett, U.S. District Court, Eastern District of Michigan, 1992-1994. *Member:* Toledo and Ohio State Bar Associations; State Bar of Michigan. ***PRACTICE AREAS:*** Civil Litigation; Employment Law; Fair Housing Litigation. ***Email:*** hales@cooperwalinski.com

DAVID P. STRUP, born Edgerton, Ohio, October 28, 1960; admitted to bar, 1986, Ohio. *Education:* University of Notre Dame (B.B.A., cum laude, 1983); The Ohio State University (J.D., 1986). Beta Alpha Psi (President, 1983); Delta Theta Phi. *Member:* Williams County Bar Association. ***PRACTICE AREAS:*** Civil Litigation; Commercial Torts; Insurance Coverage; Personal Injury (Plaintiff). ***Email:*** strup@cooperwalinski.com

JOEL M. SHERE, born Detroit, Michigan, April 19, 1939; admitted to bar, 1964, Michigan and U.S. District Court, Eastern District of Michigan; 1969, U.S. Court of Appeals, Sixth Circuit; 1986, U.S. Court of Appeals, Tenth Circuit. *Education:* University of Michigan (B.A., 1960); Harvard University (J.D., 1963). Phi Beta Kappa. Adjunct Professor of Law: Civil Rights Seminar, University of Detroit Law School, Summer, 1979; Criminal Procedure and Equitable Remedies, Wayne University Law School, 1980-1981. Assistant U.S. Attorney, Eastern District of Michigan, Criminal Division, 1963-1967. Chief Assistant U.S. Attorney, Eastern District of Michigan, 1982-1984. Acting U.S. Attorney, Eastern District of Michigan, 1985. *Member:* Oakland County and Federal (President, Detroit Chapter, 1992-1993); State Bar of Michigan. (Resident, Ann Arbor, Michigan Office). ***PRACTICE AREAS:*** Health Care; Nursing Home Regulatory and Administrative Defense; Commercial Litigation; White Collar Crime; Insurance Defense Law. ***Email:*** shere@cooperwalinski.com

GERALD R. KOWALSKI, born Toledo, Ohio, March 10, 1952; admitted to bar, 1980, Ohio. *Education:* University of Toledo (B.S., cum laude, 1975; J.D., 1979). Member, Order of Barristers. Author: "Penal Transfer Treaties and the Application of 'Unconstitutional Conditions' Analysis," Vol. 12, No. 1, University of Toledo Law Review, Fall 1980. Law Clerk to the Honorable Thaddeus N. Walinski, Toledo Municipal Court, 1977-1978. Law Clerk to the Honorable Francis A. Pietrykowski, Lucas County Common Pleas Court, 1977-1979. *Member:* American Inns of Court, Morris R. Waite Chapter. Fellow, American College of Trial Lawyers. ***REPORTED CASES:*** Sawicki v. Village of Ottawa Hills, 37 Ohio St. 3d 222; Fantozzi v. Sandusky Cement Products (1992) 64 O.St. 3d 601. ***PRACTICE AREAS:*** Litigation; Products Liability; Commercial Law; Professional Negligence; Probate Litigation. ***Email:*** kowalski@cooperwalinski.com

LUCY M. SNYDER, born Detroit, Michigan, November 12, 1969; admitted to bar, 1996, Ohio; 1997, Michigan and U.S. District Court, Northern District of Ohio. *Education:* Wayne State University (B.A., magna cum laude, 1991); University of Michigan (J.D., 1996). (Resident, Ann Arbor, Michigan Office). ***PRACTICE AREAS:*** Civil Litigation; Commercial Litigation; Insurance Coverage. ***Email:*** snyderl@cooperwalinski.com

DAVID RODMAN COOPER, born Toledo, Ohio, September 21, 1970; admitted to bar, 1995, Ohio; 1996, Michigan and U.S. District Court, Eastern District of Michigan; 1999, U.S. District Court, Northern District of Ohio. *Education:* Miami University, Ohio (B.A., 1992); Duke University (J.D., 1995). ***PRACTICE AREAS:*** Civil Litigation; Commercial Litigation; Insurance Coverage Litigation; Appeals. ***Email:*** cooperr@cooperwalinski.com

BETH A. WILSON, born Toledo, Ohio, April 22, 1971; admitted to bar, 1997, Ohio; 1998, Michigan, U.S. District Court, Northern and Southern Districts of Ohio. *Education:* University of Toledo (B.A., magna cum laude, 1993; J.D., magna cum laude, 1997). Phi Kappa Phi; Order of the Coif. Editor, University of Toledo Law Review, 1996-1997. Author: "Binding Arbitration of Employment Disputes: Opposing Pre-Dispute Agreements," 27 U.TOL. L.REV. 921 (1996). ***PRACTICE AREAS:*** Civil Litigation; Labor and Employment Law. ***Email:*** wilson@cooperwalinski.com

LIBBEY W. CALL BEST, born Toledo, Ohio, September 8, 1972; admitted to bar, 1997, Ohio; 1998, Michigan. *Education:* Boston University (B.A., cum laude, 1994); University of Toledo College of Law (J.D., magna cum laude, 1997). Order of the Coif. Note and Comment Editor, University of Toledo Law Review, 1996-1997. ***PRACTICE AREAS:*** Civil Litigation. ***Email:*** callbest@cooperwalinski.com

---

KIMBERLY TODD-TERPINSKI, admitted to bar, 1998, Ohio; 2000, U.S. District Court, Southern District of Ohio; 2001, U.S. District Court, Northern District of Ohio. *Education:* Bowling Green State University (B.S., 1993); University of Toledo College of Law (J.D., magna cum laude, 1998). ***PRACTICE AREAS:*** Products Liability Litigation. ***Email:*** todd-terpinski@cooperwalinski.com

MEREDITH L. MERCURIO, born Toledo, Ohio, March 23, 1974; admitted to bar, 1999, Ohio; 2001, Michigan. *Education:* University of Toledo (B.A., magna cum laude, Honors in English, 1996; J.D., magna cum laude, 1999). Order of the Coif. Executive Editor, University of Toledo Law Review, 1998-1999. Author: People v. Meyer: *Prohibiting Seventeenth Century Punishment in Twentieth Century America,* 30 U. TOL. L. REV. 97 (1998). ***PRACTICE AREAS:*** Civil Litigation; Employment Law and Litigation; Employee Benefits Law and Litigation; Fair Housing; Personal Injury; Criminal Defense. ***Email:*** mercurio@cooperwalinski.com

E. SHARON CLARK, born St. Joseph, Missouri, October 6, 1943; admitted to bar, 1981, Michigan and U.S. District Court, Eastern District of Michigan; 1991, U.S. Court of Appeals, Sixth Circuit. *Education:* William Jewell College (A.B., magna cum laude, 1966); University of Iowa (M.A., 1969); Wayne State University (J.D., 1981). Survey Editor, Wayne Law Review, 1980-1981. Author: "Diversity Jurisdiction in Direct Actions," 26 Wayne Law Review 1051 (1980); "The Supreme Court of Michigan During the Survey Period: A Statistical Analysis," 27 Wayne Law Review 511 (1981); "Federal Courts Update," Labor & Employment Lawnotes, 1995-1997. *Member:* Washtenaw County Bar Association; State Bar of Michigan (Member: Business Law, Antitrust Law and Employment and Labor Law Sections). (Resident, Ann Arbor, Michigan Office). ***Email:*** clark@cooperwalinski.com

PARISS M. COLEMAN II, born Toledo, Ohio, April 25, 1970; admitted to bar, 1996, Ohio. *Education:* Miami University (B.A., 1992); The Ohio State University (J.D., 1995). *Member:* Toledo (Member, Committees on: Lawyer Doctor; Municipal Law) and Ohio State (Member, Sports Law Section) Bar Associations. ***PRACTICE AREAS:*** Corporate Law; Real Estate; Civil Litigation. ***Email:*** coleman@cooperwalinski.com

JODI D. SPENCER, born Ashtabula, Ohio, November 6, 1974; admitted to bar, 2001, Ohio; 2002, Michigan. *Education:* Bowling Green State University (B.A., 1997); University of Toledo (J.D., 2001). ***PRACTICE AREAS:*** Civil Litigation. ***Email:*** spencer@cooperwalinski.com

MARGUERITE E. ZINZ, born Youngstown, Ohio, September 11, 1976; admitted to bar, 2001, Ohio and U.S. District Court, Northern District of Ohio; 2002, Michigan. *Education:* Westminster College (B.S., Business Administration and English, magna cum laude, 1998); Case Western Reserve University Law School (J.D., cum laude, 2001). Order of the Coif. ***PRACTICE AREAS:*** Civil Litigation. ***Email:*** zinz@cooperwalinski.com

BRAD FRANCIS HUBBELL, born Muskegon, Michigan, August 14, 1961; admitted to bar, 2002, Ohio; 2003, Michigan. *Education:* Michigan State University (B.A., English, 1990); Thomas M. Cooley Law School (J.D., magna cum laude, 2002). Editor-in-Chief, Thomas M. Cooley Law Review. National Moot Court competitor. ***PRACTICE AREAS:*** Civil Litigation. ***Email:*** hubbell@cooperwalinski.com

(This Listing Continued)

SUSAN M. HEYWOOD (MIEDLER), born Toledo, Ohio, July 3, 1976l; admitted to bar, 2002, Ohio. *Education:* University of Michigan (B.A., in History, 1998); The Ohio State University Moritz College of Law (J.D., 2002). Angell B. Scholar. ***PRACTICE AREAS:*** Civil Litigation; Medical Malpractice Litigation; Personal Injury Litigation; Commercial Litigation. ***Email:*** heywood@cooperwalinski.com

JENNIFER STEVES, born Toledo, Ohio, March 20, 1959; admitted to bar, 2002, Ohio and U.S. District Court, Northern District of Ohio. *Education:* Miami University (B.S., 1981); University of Toledo (J.D., magna cum laude, 2001). Member, The Morrison R. Waite Chapter Inns of Court. University of Toledo Law Review, 2001. *Member:* Toledo, Ohio State and American Bar Associations. ***PRACTICE AREAS:*** Civil Litigation; Products Liability; White Collar Criminal Defense; Personal Injury. ***Email:*** steves@cooperwalinski.com

GEORGE C. WARD, born Toledo, Ohio, September 8, 1949; admitted to bar, 1976, Ohio and U. S. District Court, Northern District of Ohio; 1977, Michigan. *Education:* Brown University (B.A., History, 1971); University of Toledo College of Law (J.D., 1975). *Member:* Toledo (Member, Lawyers and Doctors Committee; Judicial Candidates Committee) and Ohio State Bar Associations; State Bar of Michigan; Defense Research Institute; Ohio Association of Civil Trial Attorneys. (Retired). ***PRACTICE AREAS:*** Medical Malpractice; Insurance Coverage; Products Liability. ***Email:*** ward@cooperwalinski.com

JENNIFER S. MISTRY, born South Bend, Indiana, July 5, 1974; admitted to bar, 2000, Michigan; 2001, Ohio, U.S. District Court, Eastern District of Michigan and U.S. District Court, Northern District of Ohio. *Education:* Michigan State University (B.A., General Business Administration, with honor, 1996); University of Toledo College of Law (J.D., cum laude, 2000). Honors for Moot Court and Golden Key Honor Society. *Member:* Ohio State and American Bar Associations; State Bar of Michigan. ***PRACTICE AREAS:*** Civil Litigation. ***Email:*** mistry@cooperwalinski.com

JOSEPH V. McNAMARA, admitted to bar, 2003, Ohio; 2004, Michigan. *Education:* University of Michigan (B.A., with distinction, 1999); New York University School of Law (J.D., 2003). ***PRACTICE AREAS:*** Civil Litigation; Medical Malpractice Litigation; Products Liability Litigation; Insurance Coverage Litigation. ***Email:*** mcnamara@cooperwalinski.com

JANELLE M. ROMP, admitted to bar, 2003, Ohio; 2004, Michigan. *Education:* Bowling Green State University (B.A., cum laude, 2000); University of Cincinnati College of Law (J.D., 2003). ***PRACTICE AREAS:*** Civil Litigation. ***Email:*** romp@cooperwalinski.com

SUZI ZAZYCKI, admitted to bar, 2003, Ohio. *Education:* Miami University (B.S., cum laude, 1990); Miami University, Institute of Environmental Science (M.A., Environmental Sciences, magna cum laude, 1992); The University of Toledo College of Law (J.D., magna cum laude, 2003). Order of the Coif. Patricia Roberts Harris Fellow, Miami University, Institute of Environmental Sciences. ***PRACTICE AREAS:*** Civil Litigation; Employment Law; Medical Malpractice Litigation. ***Email:*** zazycki@cooperwalinski.com

DUSTY RENÉE TINSLEY, admitted to bar, 2000, Ohio; 2001, Michigan. *Education:* University of Rochester (B.S., 1992); Rochester Institute of Technology (B.S., Environmental Management, with honors, 1994); University of Toledo (J.D., cum laude, 2000). Member, The Morrison R. Waite Chapter Inns of Court. Managing Editor, University of Toledo Law Review, 1999-2000. *Member:* State Bar of Michigan. ***PRACTICE AREAS:*** Environmental Litigation; Insurance Litigation; Products Liability.

NICOLE K. SCHWIETERMAN, admitted to bar, 1999, Ohio; 2001, Michigan and U.S. District Court, Northern District of Ohio. *Education:* Bowling Green State University (B.S., cum laude, 1996); University of Toledo College of Law (J.D., cum laude, 1999). ***PRACTICE AREAS:*** Products Liability. ***Email:*** schwieterman@cooperwalinski.com

All Attorneys are Members of the Toledo, Ohio State and American Bar Associations.

REPRESENTATIVE CLIENTS: Ability Center of Greater Toledo; Advocates for Basic Legal Equality, Inc.; Allied Waste Ind.; American Family Insurance; Bay Park Hospital; Bostwick-Braun Company; Cooper Tire & Rubber Company; Dana Corporation; Defiance Hospital; Eaton Corporation; Flower Hospital; Harbor Capital Advisors, Inc.; HCR-Manor Care; Housing Opportunities Made Equal, Inc.; Kimble Glass, Inc.; Legal Aid of Western Ohio, Inc.; Libbey, Inc.; Lourdes College; Metropolitan Milwaukee Fair Housing Council; National Fair Housing Alliance, Inc.; Norplas Industries; Owens-Illinois, Inc.; Paramount Health Care; Penta County Vocational School District; Preferred Properties, Inc.; ProMedica Health Systems, Inc.; ProQuest Information and Learning Company; The Toledo Hospital; Toledo Fair Housing Center.

COY, KONIECZNY & PEPPEL, LLC

Established in 2005

405 MADISON AVENUE, SUITE 700

TOLEDO, OHIO 43604

Telephone: 419-724-5252

Fax: 419-724-5255

Email: gpeppel@ckp-law.com

URL: http://www.ckp-law.com

Commercial Real Estate, Corporate and Finance, Estate Planning and Probate, Commercial Litigation, Insurance Coverage Litigation.

EDWIN A. COY, born Toledo, Ohio, March 29, 1949; admitted to bar, 1974, Ohio. *Education:* Capital University (B.A., summa cum laude, 1971); The Ohio State University (J.D., summa cum laude, 1974). Order of the Coif; Best Lawyers in America; Ohio's Super Lawyers. *Member:* Toledo, Ohio State and American Bar Associations; Federation of Defense and Corporate Counsel. ***PRACTICE AREAS:*** Insurance Defense; Insurance Coverage Defense; Appellate Practice; Medical Malpractice; Personal Injury; Products Liability. ***Email:*** ecoy@ckp-law.com

TIMOTHY A. KONIECZNY, born Oak Harbor, Ohio, November 15, 1957; admitted to bar, 1982, Ohio; 1992, Michigan. *Education:* Brown University (B.A., 1979); Case Western Reserve University (J.D., 1982). Best Lawyers in America. *Member:* Toledo and Ohio State Bar Associations; State Bar of Michigan. ***PRACTICE AREAS:*** Commercial Real Estate; Corporate; Finance; Estate Planning; Probate. ***Email:*** tkonieczny@ckp-law.com

(This Listing Continued)

GREGG A. PEPPEL, born Marquette, Michigan, September 16, 1971; admitted to bar, 1999, Ohio; 2000, Michigan. *Education:* University of Toledo (B.A., 1993; J.D., 1999). Managing Editor, University of Toledo Law Review. *Member:* Toledo, Ohio State and American Bar Associations; State Bar of Michigan. ***PRACTICE AREAS:*** Commercial Litigation; Corporate; Finance; Insurance Coverage Defense; Appellate Practice. ***Email:*** gpeppel@ckp-law.com

EVY M. JARRETT, born Murray, Kentucky, April 23, 1966; admitted to bar, 1991, Kentucky; 1993, Ohio; 1994, Michigan. *Education:* Vanderbilt University (B.A., magna cum laude, 1988); Duke University (J.D., 1991); Phi Beta Kappa. *Member:* Toledo, Ohio State and American Bar Associations; State Bar of Michigan. ***PRACTICE AREAS:*** Insurance Defense; Insurance Coverage Defense; Appellate Practice. ***Email:*** ejarrett@ckp-law.com

DENMEAD LAW OFFICE

TOLEDO, OHIO

(See Columbus)

Civil Trial and Appellate Practice and Personal Injury, Traumatic Brain Injury (TBI), Professional Negligence and Complex Litigation including Class Actions, Patents, Civil Rights, Civil Litigation, RICO, Employment and Political Subdivision Liability issues.

RANDALL C. DIXON

3361 EXECUTIVE PARKWAY

TOLEDO, OHIO 43606

Telephone: 419-536-8600

Fax: 419-534-5934

Civil Litigation, Real Estate, Consumer Law.

RANDALL C. DIXON, born Ann Arbor, Michigan, 1953; admitted to bar, 1980, Ohio; 1981, Michigan. *Education:* University of Toledo (B.A., 1975; J.D., 1980). *Member:* Toledo Bar Association. (Also Member, Dixon & Hayes, Ltd.). ***PRACTICE AREAS:*** Civil Litigation; Real Estate; Consumer Law.

EASTMAN & SMITH LTD.

Established in 1844

ONE SEAGATE, TWENTY-FOURTH FLOOR

P.O. BOX 10032

TOLEDO, OHIO 43699-0032

Telephone: 419-241-6000

Fax: 419-247-1777

Email: firm@eastmansmith.com

URL: http://www.eastmansmith.com

Columbus, Ohio, Office: 100 East Broad Street, Suite 1300, 43215. Telephone: 614-280-1770. Fax: 614-280-1777.

Findlay, Ohio Office: 725 South Main Street, 45840. Telephone: 419-424-5487. Fax: 419-424-9860.

General Civil Practice: Corporate, Business, Banking, Taxation, Real Estate, Securities, Antitrust, Environmental, Public, Labor and Employment, Civil Rights, Employee Benefits, Insurance, Hospital and Health Care, Estate Planning, Pension and Estate Planning, Probate, Workers Compensation, Commercial Litigation, Litigation, Immigration and Naturalization.

FIRM PROFILE: Eastman & Smith Ltd. is the oldest firm in the Toledo, Ohio area and one of the oldest firms in the state of Ohio, having been in continuous existence through predecessor firms since 1844. We are committed to continued growth consistent with the training necessary to maintain professional standards. Our growth has been generated both internally and through merger, resulting in an expansion of capabilities which responds to our clients' needs.

MEMBERS OF FIRM

FRANK D. JACOBS, born Toledo, Ohio, December 30, 1935; admitted to bar, 1959, Ohio; 1974, U.S. Supreme Court. *Education:* University of Toledo (B.B.A., summa cum laude, 1956); University of Michigan (J.D., cum laude, 1959). Order of the Coif. Listed in: Woodward & White "The Best Lawyers in America," Tax Law and Trusts and Estates. Certified Public Accountant, Ohio, 1961 (inactive). Adjunct Professor of Law, University of Toledo College of Law, 1982. Fellow: American College of Trust and Estate Counsel. (Certified Specialist in Estate Planning, Trust and Probate Law, Ohio State Bar Association). ***PRACTICE AREAS:*** Corporate Law; Pensions Law; Estate Planning Law; Taxation Law. ***Email:*** FDJacobs@eastmansmith.com

PATRICK J. JOHNSON, born Toledo, Ohio, June 23, 1941; admitted to bar, 1967, Ohio. *Education:* Georgetown University; University of Toledo (B.S., 1963; J.D., 1967). ***PRACTICE AREAS:*** Management Labor Relations Law. ***Email:*** PJJohnson@eastmansmith.com

JAMES F. NOONEY, born Toledo, Ohio, May 18, 1941; admitted to bar, 1966, Ohio; U.S. Supreme Court; U.S. Court of Military Appeals; U.S. Court of Appeals, Sixth Circuit; U.S. District Court, Northern District of Ohio, Eastern District of Michigan and Northern District of Indiana. *Education:* Denison University (B.A., 1963); Vanderbilt University (LL.B., 1966). *Member:* Association of Defense Trial Attorneys. [JAGC, USAF, 1967-1971]. ***PRACTICE AREAS:*** Professional Liability Law; Products Liability Law; Commercial Litigation. ***Email:*** JFNooney@eastmansmith.com

BRUCE L. SMITH, born Toledo, Ohio, September 30, 1941; admitted to bar, 1966, Ohio. *Education:* The Ohio State University (B.A., 1963; J.D., 1966). [LTJG, U.S. Navy, 1967-1970]. ***PRACTICE AREAS:*** Healthcare Law; Corporate Law; Antitrust Law. ***Email:*** BLSmith@eastmansmith.com

(This Listing Continued)

EASTMAN & SMITH LTD., Toledo—Continued

MORTON BOBOWICK, born Brooklyn, New York, October 8, 1942; admitted to bar, 1966, District of Columbia and Ohio. *Education:* Brooklyn College (B.A., 1962); Harvard University (J.D., 1965). Phi Beta Kappa. ***PRACTICE AREAS:*** Estate Planning Law; Probate Law; Trust Administration Law. ***Email:*** MBobowick@eastmansmith.com

HENRY N. HEUERMAN, born Toledo, Ohio, September 1, 1945; admitted to bar, 1970, Ohio; U.S. Court of Appeals, Sixth Circuit; U.S. District Court, Northern District of Ohio; U.S. District Court, Eastern District of Michigan. *Education:* The Ohio State University (B.A., 1967; J.D., 1970). Life Fellow, Ohio State and American Bar Foundations. ***PRACTICE AREAS:*** Mergers and Acquisitions; Commercial Litigation; Secured Transactions. ***Email:*** HNHeuerman@eastmansmith.com

JOHN H. BOGGS, born Toledo, Ohio, August 13, 1946; admitted to bar, 1972, Ohio; 1985, U.S. Tax Court. *Education:* Wittenberg University (B.A., cum laude, 1968); University of Michigan (J.D., 1972). Listed in The Best Lawyers in America, Trusts and Estates, Woodward & White, 2006—. ***PRACTICE AREAS:*** Estate Planning Law; Tax Law; Corporate Law; Commercial Law. ***Email:*** JHBoggs@eastmansmith.com

JOHN T. LANDWEHR, born Toledo, Ohio, January 7, 1944; admitted to bar, 1974, Ohio and Michigan; U.S. District Court, Northern and Southern Districts of Ohio, Eastern District of Michigan and Northern District of Georgia; U.S. Court of Appeals, Sixth Circuit; U.S. Supreme Court. *Education:* Wittenberg University (B.A., 1966); University of Toledo (J.D., 1973). ***PRACTICE AREAS:*** Employment Law; Labor Law; Employment Discrimination Law; Workers Compensation Law. ***Email:*** JTLandwehr@eastmansmith.com

DAVID L. KUHL, born Dubuque, Iowa, July 25, 1950; admitted to bar, 1975, Ohio. *Education:* Loras College (B.A., maxima cum laude, 1972); University of Michigan (J.D., 1975). Author: "Business Law and Practice," chapter, Ohio State Bar Association, Lawyers' Desk Manual, 1984, 1998. ***PRACTICE AREAS:*** Corporate Law; Health Care Law. ***Email:*** DLKuhl@eastmansmith.com

RICHARD T. SARGEANT, born Norwalk, Ohio, July 14, 1947; admitted to bar, 1975, Ohio and U.S. District Court, Northern District of Ohio. *Education:* Capital University (B.S., 1969); The Ohio State University (J.D., cum laude, 1975). ***PRACTICE AREAS:*** Environmental Law; Administrative Law; Public Law. ***Email:*** RTSargeant@eastmansmith.com

KENNETH C. BAKER, born Cleveland, Ohio, September 14, 1952; admitted to bar, 1977, Ohio; 1981, U.S. District Court, Northern District of Ohio; 1988, U.S. Court of Appeals, Sixth Circuit. *Education:* Miami University (A.B., 1974); The Ohio State University (J.D., cum laude, 1976). ***PRACTICE AREAS:*** Commercial Finance; Secured Transactions; Mergers and Acquisitions; Bankruptcy Law. ***Email:*** KCBaker@eastmansmith.com

ROBERT J. GILMER, JR., born Ontonagon, Michigan, September 9, 1950; admitted to bar, 1975, Ohio; 1980, U.S. Supreme Court; 1984, U.S. Court of Appeals, Sixth Circuit; U.S. District Court, Northern and Southern Districts of Ohio and U.S. District Court, Western District of Michigan; 2002, U.S. Court of Appeals, Federal Circuit. *Education:* Ohio Northern University (A.B., 1972); University of Toledo (J.D., 1975). Assistant Prosecuting Attorney, Lucas County, Ohio, 1976-1980. Acting Judge, Perrysburg, Ohio, Municipal Court, 1997-2005. ***PRACTICE AREAS:*** Employment Litigation; Professional Liability Litigation; Environmental Litigation. ***Email:*** RJGilmer@eastmansmith.com

PETER R. CASEY, III, born Toledo, Ohio, June 5, 1944; admitted to bar, 1974, Ohio; 1983, U.S. Court of Appeals, Sixth Circuit. *Education:* Wabash College; University of Toledo (B.A., 1967; J.D., 1973). Member, The Order of Barristers. Attorney, U.S. Department of Justice, Organized Crime and Racketeering Section, Criminal Division, New England Strike Force, 1974-1978. Assistant U.S. Attorney, District of Connecticut, 1978-1981. *Member:* American Inns of Court; Ohio Association of Civil Trial Attorneys; Association of Defense Trial Attorneys. Fellow, American College of Trial Lawyers. [1st Lt., U.S. Army, 1968-1971]. ***PRACTICE AREAS:*** Professional Liability Law; Litigation. ***Email:*** PRCasey@eastmansmith.com

DAVID F. COOPER, born Miami Beach, Florida, July 25, 1945; admitted to bar, 1973, District of Columbia; 1974, Ohio; 1985, U.S. Supreme Court. *Education:* Claremont Mens College (B.A., 1966); George Washington University (J.D., 1973). Assistant County Prosecutor, Lucas County, Ohio, 1976-1980. Legal Aid Society Civil Staff and Managing Attorney, 1973-1976. [1st Lt., U.S. Army, 1966-1968]. ***PRACTICE AREAS:*** Products Liability Law; Professional Liability Law; General Personal Injury Law; Workers Compensation Litigation. ***Email:*** DFCooper@eastmansmith.com

RUDOLPH A. PECKINPAUGH, JR., born Toledo, Ohio, July 19, 1954; admitted to bar, 1980, Ohio; 1985, U.S. Court of Appeals, Sixth Circuit. *Education:* Ohio Wesleyan University (B.A., 1976); University of Toledo (J.D., 1980). ***PRACTICE AREAS:*** Professional Liability Law; General Personal Injury Law; Commercial; Probate; Insurance Litigation. ***Email:*** RAPeckinpaugh@eastmansmith.com

RONALD J. TICE, born Toledo, Ohio, March 14, 1947; admitted to bar, 1973, Ohio. *Education:* University of Vermont (B.A., 1969); University of Toledo (J.D., cum laude, 1973). Author: "10b-5: A Test for Tippee Liability," 4 University of Toledo Law Review 183, 1972-1973. ***PRACTICE AREAS:*** Mergers and Acquisitions; Business Law; Commercial Transactions. ***Email:*** RJTice@eastmansmith.com

THOMAS A. DIXON, born Chillicothe, Ohio, March 26, 1957; admitted to bar, 1982, Ohio; U.S. District Court, Northern District of Ohio; U.S. Court of Appeals, Sixth Circuit; U.S. Supreme Court. *Education:* The Ohio State University (B.S., 1979); University of Toledo (J.D., 1982). ***PRACTICE AREAS:*** Employment Law; Labor Law; Workers Compensation. ***Email:*** TADixon@eastmansmith.com

GARY M. HARDEN, born Detroit, Michigan, January 12, 1955; admitted to bar, 1980, Ohio; 1983, U.S. Tax Court. *Education:* University of Notre Dame (B.B.A. in Accounting, 1977); University of Toledo (J.D., cum laude, 1980); New York University (LL.M. in Taxation, 1981). Listed in Woodward & White, "The Best Lawyers in America," Tax Law, 1995—. Named to Law & Politics Magazine's Ohio Super Lawyers, 2004—. Special Ohio Attorney General, 2005—. Adjunct Professor of Law, University of Toledo, 1988. Member, Ohio Supreme Court Board for Certification of Specialists in Federal Taxation, 1999—. Fellow: Ohio State Bar Foundation. ***PRACTICE AREAS:*** Taxation; Employee Benefits; Business Law; Commercial Law. ***Email:*** GMHarden@eastmansmith.com

BARRY W. FISSEL, born Augusta, Georgia, October 12, 1956; admitted to bar, 1981, Ohio; 1982, U.S. District Court, Northern District of Ohio; 1984, U.S. Court of Appeals, Sixth Circuit; 1991, U.S. District Court, Eastern District of Michigan; U.S. District Court, District of Indiana. *Education:* The Ohio State University (B.A., 1978); University of Cincinnati (J.D., 1981). ***PRACTICE AREAS:*** Commercial Litigation; Noncompete Litigation; Trade Secrets Litigation; ERISA Litigation; Personal Injury Law. ***Email:*** BWFissel@eastmansmith.com

JOSEPH A. GREGG, born Bloomington, Illinois, June 1, 1956; admitted to bar, 1981, Ohio; U.S. District Court, Northern and Southern Districts of Ohio, Eastern District of Michigan and U.S. Court of Appeals, Sixth Circuit. *Education:* Miami University (A.B., with honors, 1978); University of Cincinnati (J.D., 1981). ***PRACTICE AREAS:*** Environmental Law; Administrative Law; Litigation. ***Email:*** JAGregg@eastmansmith.com

ROGER PAUL KLEE, born Detroit, Michigan, February 25, 1948; admitted to bar, 1974, Ohio; 1975, U.S. District Court, Northern District of Ohio. *Education:* Michigan State University (B.A., with high honors, 1970); University of Michigan (J.D., cum laude, 1974). ***PRACTICE AREAS:*** Commercial Law; Business Law; Civil Litigation; Eminent Domain. ***Email:*** RPKlee@eastmansmith.com

STUART J. GOLDBERG, born Toledo, Ohio, January 17, 1960; admitted to bar, 1985, Ohio; U.S. Court of Appeals, Sixth Circuit; U.S. District Court, Northern and Southern Districts of Ohio and Eastern District of Michigan. *Education:* Amherst College (B.A., cum laude, 1982); Boston University School of Law (J.D., 1985). Recipient: 2000 Toledo Bar Association Community Service Award; 1997 20 Under 40 Award. Fellow: Ohio State Bar Foundation. ***PRACTICE AREAS:*** Products Liability; Commercial Litigation; Insurance Coverage; Personal Injury Litigation. ***Email:*** SJGoldberg@eastmansmith.com

THOMAS J. GIBNEY, born Iowa City, Iowa, September 16, 1960; admitted to bar, 1985, Ohio; 1986, Michigan; U.S. Supreme Court; U.S. Court of Appeals, Sixth Circuit; U.S. District Court, Northern District of Ohio; U.S. District Court, Eastern District of Michigan. *Education:* University of Michigan (B.A., 1982; J.D., 1985). ***PRACTICE AREAS:*** Employment Discrimination; Labor Litigation; Workers' Compensation; Public Law. ***Email:*** TJGibney@eastmansmith.com

STEVEN D. REINBOLT, born Tiffin, Ohio, December 6, 1959; admitted to bar, 1985, Ohio; 1986, Michigan. *Education:* University of Toledo (B.A., summa cum laude, 1982); University of Cincinnati (J.D., 1985). ***PRACTICE AREAS:*** Real Estate; Banking; Business Law. ***Email:*** SDReinbolt@eastmansmith.com

DIRK P. PLESSNER, born Toledo, Ohio, March 17, 1952; admitted to bar, 1987, Ohio; 1989, U.S. District Court, Northern District of Ohio. *Education:* University of Toledo (B.B.A., 1984; M.B.A., 1987; J.D., cum laude, 1987). Member: Organization of Solid Waste Districts of Ohio; Solid Waste Association of North America. ***PRACTICE AREAS:*** Environmental Law; Public Law; Corporate Law. ***Email:*** DPPlessner@eastmansmith.com

JAMES L. ROGERS, born Bowling Green, Ohio, November 12, 1961; admitted to bar, 1987, Michigan and U.S. District Court, Eastern District of Michigan; 1988, Ohio; 1989, U.S. District Court, Northern District of Ohio; U.S. Court of Appeals, Sixth Circuit. *Education:* Bowling Green State University (B.S., Business Admin., 1984); University of Toledo (J.D., cum laude, 1987). ***PRACTICE AREAS:*** Commercial Litigation; Creditors Rights Litigation; Intellectual Property. ***Email:*** JLRogers@eastmansmith.com

DAVID W. NUNN, born Jacksonville, Illinois, October 31, 1958; admitted to bar, 1991, Ohio and U.S. District Court, Northern District of Ohio; U.S. District Court, Northern District of Mississippi. *Education:* Bowling Green State University (B.S., 1981); University of Toledo (J.D., magna cum laude, 1991). Order of Coif. Instructor, Environmental Law, Medical University of Ohio. *Member:* Environmental Law Institute; National Association of Environmental Professionals; Chartered Hazardous Materials Managers Association. ***PRACTICE AREAS:*** Litigation; Environmental Law; Administrative Law. ***Email:*** DWNunn@eastmansmith.com

DAVID C. KROCK, born Fremont, Ohio, May 22, 1956; admitted to bar, 1982, Ohio. *Education:* Bowling Green State University (B.S., in Business Administration, 1979); University of Toledo (J.D., 1982). Certified Public Accountant, Ohio, 1989 (inactive). ***PRACTICE AREAS:*** Estate Planning; Probate; Tax; General Corporate. ***Email:*** DCKrock@eastmansmith.com

ALBIN BAUER, II, born Groton, Connecticut, February 27, 1962; admitted to bar, 1990, Michigan and U.S. District Court, Eastern District of Michigan; 1993, Ohio and U.S. District Court, Northern District of Ohio; 1999, U.S. Court of Appeals, Sixth Circuit. *Education:* General Motors Institute (B.S., 1985); University of Toledo (J.D., cum laude, 1990). ***PRACTICE AREAS:*** Environmental; Public Law; Litigation. ***Email:*** ABauer@eastmansmith.com

PEGGY MATTIMOE STURGEON, born Toledo, Ohio, November 10, 1964; admitted to bar, 1990, Ohio and U.S. District Court, Southern District of Ohio; 1995, U.S. District Court, Northern District of Ohio; U.S. Court of Appeals, Sixth Circuit; U.S. Supreme Court. *Education:* Xavier University (B.A., summa cum laude, 1987); University of Virginia (J.D., 1990). Law Clerk to Nicholas Walinski, David D. Dowd and David A. Katz, U.S. District Court, Northern District of Ohio, 1992-1995. *Member:* Morrison R. Waite Inns of Court (Barrister). ***PRACTICE AREAS:*** Labor and Employment. ***Email:*** PMSturgeon@eastmansmith.com

LANE D. WILLIAMSON, born Toledo, Ohio, December 2, 1962; admitted to bar, 1989, Ohio and U.S. District Court, Northern District of Ohio. *Education:* Bowling Green State University (B.A., 1985); University of Toledo (J.D., 1988). ***REPORTED CASES:*** East Ohio Gas Co.v. Wood County Board of Elections: 83 Ohio St.3D 298, 699 N.E.2d 916 (1998). ***PRACTICE AREAS:*** Real Estate Law; Zoning; Planning and Land Use; Estate Planning Law; Business Law. ***Email:*** LDWilliamson@eastmansmith.com

MICHAEL W. REGNIER, born Toledo, Ohio, May 23, 1967; admitted to bar, 1993, Ohio; 1994, Michigan; U.S. District Court, Northern District of Ohio; 1995, U.S. Court of

(This Listing Continued)

Appeals, Sixth Circuit. *Education:* Hope College (B.A., 1989); University of Toledo (J.D., magna cum laude, 1993). Order of the Coif. ***PRACTICE AREAS:*** Professional Liability Law; Commercial Litigation. ***Email:*** MWRegnier@eastmansmith.com

KEVIN D. DEVANEY, born Plattsburgh, New York, October 3, 1963; admitted to bar, 1991, Ohio. *Education:* State University of New York at Buffalo (B.S., Pharmacy, 1986; M.B.A., 1987); Capital University (J.D., cum laude, 1991). Registered Pharmacist, New York (inactive). Law Clerk to the Hon. John W. Potter, U.S. District Court, Northern District of Ohio, Western Division, 1991-1993. ***PRACTICE AREAS:*** Health Care; Corporate. ***Email:*** KDDevaney@eastmansmith.com

BENNETT H. SPEYER, born Columbus, Ohio, May 23, 1960; admitted to bar, 1985, Ohio. *Education:* Miami University (B.A., 1982); University of Toledo (J.D., 1985). ***PRACTICE AREAS:*** Employee Benefits Law; Estate Planning; Taxation. ***Email:*** BHSpeyer@eastmansmith.com

AMY J. BORMAN, born Detroit, Michigan, February 7, 1954; admitted to bar, 1990, Ohio; 1991, Michigan. *Education:* Wittenberg University (B.Mus., cum laude, 1976); University of Michigan (M.Mus., magna cum laude, 1977); University of Toledo (J.D., magna cum laude, 1989). Order of the Coif. Author: "Procedural Due Process and 'The Mere Right of Reply' - Duchesne v. Williams," The University of Toledo Law Review, Sixth Circuit Review, V 20 N3 Spring 1989. ***PRACTICE AREAS:*** School Law; Real Estate; Construction; Contract Negotiations; Commercial Transactions; Corporate. ***Email:*** AJBorman@eastmansmith.com

MARCUS J. BRUBAKER, born Dayton, Ohio, March 9, 1954; admitted to bar, 1981, Ohio and U.S. District Court, Northern District of Ohio. *Education:* The Ohio State University (B.S.B.A., 1975); University of Toledo (J.D., 1980). Chief Referee, Lucas County Probate Court, 1985—1991. ***PRACTICE AREAS:*** Probate Administration Law; Guardianship Law; Estate and Fiduciary Income Tax. ***Email:*** MJBrubaker@eastmansmith.com

MATTHEW D. HARPER, born Ashland, Ohio, September 10, 1967; admitted to bar, 1992, Ohio; 1993, U.S. Court of Appeals, Sixth Circuit and U.S. District Court, Northern District of Ohio; 1995, Michigan. *Education:* Ashland University (B.A., magna cum laude, 1989); University of Toledo (J.D., magna cum laude, 1992). Order of the Coif. ***PRACTICE AREAS:*** Commercial Litigation; Real Estate Litigation. ***Email:*** MDHarper@eastmansmith.com

M. CHARLES COLLINS, born Bellefontaine, Ohio, February 13, 1964; admitted to bar, 1995, Ohio; 1996, U.S. District Court, Northern District of Ohio; 2000, U.S. Court of Appeals, Sixth Circuit; 2003, U.S. District Court, Southern District of Ohio. *Education:* Defiance College (B.S., summa cum laude, 1986); Mankato State University (M.B.A., 1989); University of Toledo (J.D., magna cum laude, 1995). Order of the Coif. Author: Note, "New Section 197 of the Internal Revenue Code: Simplifying the Amortization of Intangibles in the Wake of Newark Morning Ledger Co. v. Unites States," 25 U.Tol. Law Reiew, 815. ***PRACTICE AREAS:*** Professional Liability; Insurance; Litigation; Products Liability; Commercial Law. ***Email:*** MCCollins@eastmansmith.com

GRAHAM A. BLUHM, born Sandusky, Ohio, November 15, 1969; admitted to bar, 1995, Ohio. *Education:* Ashland University (B.S.B.A., magna cum laude, 1992); University of Toledo (J.D., magna cum laude, 1995). Order of the Coif. ***PRACTICE AREAS:*** Corporate; Commercial Transactions; Business Law. ***Email:*** GABluhm@eastmansmith.com

MICHAEL P. HENRY, born Chelsea, Massachusetts, March 1, 1969; admitted to bar, 1994, Ohio. *Education:* Marquette University (B.A., 1991); Chicago-Kent College of Law, Illinois Institute of Technology (J.D., 1994); Capital University (LL.M. in Taxation, 1998). ***PRACTICE AREAS:*** Corporate; Estate Planning; Tax. ***Email:*** MPHenry@eastmansmith.com

BRUCE D. LAZAR, born Toledo, Ohio, May 24, 1968; admitted to bar, 1995, Ohio and U.S. District Court, Northern District of Ohio. *Education:* John Carroll University (B.S.B.A., 1990); University of Toledo (M.B.A., 1992; J.D., 1995). ***PRACTICE AREAS:*** Corporate Transactions; Business; Securities; Estate Planning. ***Email:*** BDLazar@eastmansmith.com

JAMES W. MILLON, born Clarinda, Iowa, October 18, 1950; admitted to bar, 1976, Ohio. *Education:* University of Toledo (B.A. 1972; J.D. 1976). Prosecuting Attorney, City of Maumee, 1976-1979. ***Email:*** JWMillon@eastmansmith.com

JAMES B. YATES, born Cleveland, Ohio, August 19, 1965; admitted to bar, 1990, Ohio. *Education:* University of Dayton (B.A., summa cum laude, 1987); The Ohio State University (J.D., 1990). ***PRACTICE AREAS:*** Labor and Employment; Workers Compensation; Construction Law; Litigation. ***Email:*** JBYates@eastmansmith.com

MARK A. SHAW, born Chapel Hill, North Carolina, February 13, 1966; admitted to bar, 1992, Ohio; 1996, Utah. *Education:* Miami University (B.S., 1988); University of Toledo (J.D., cum laude, 1992). Order of the Coif. Author, "Institutional Academic Freedom Fails to Protect Disclosure of Peer Review Evaluations: University of Pennsylvania v. EEOC," 22 U. Tol. L. Rev. 1089. (Resident, Columbus Office). ***PRACTICE AREAS:*** Civil Litigation; Workers Compensation; Labor and Employment. ***Email:*** MAShaw@eastmansmith.com

JOHN H. KOEHLER, born Findlay, Ohio, 1950; admitted to bar, 1979, Ohio. *Education:* University of Findlay (B.S.); University of Toledo (J.D.). ***PRACTICE AREAS:*** Estate Planning; Estate Administration; Tax Planning. ***Email:*** JHKoehler@eastmansmith.com

ASSOCIATES

MARK H. BOSS, born Toledo, Ohio, April 14, 1964; admitted to bar, 1997, Ohio; 1998, Michigan. *Education:* University of Toledo (B.B.A., 1986; J.D., 1997). Order of the Coif. ***PRACTICE AREAS:*** Business; Trusts and Estates. ***Email:*** MHBoss@eastmansmith.com

MARY JO TARINI, born Columbus, Ohio, August 17, 1947; admitted to bar, 1991, Ohio, Florida and U.S. District Court, Northern District of Ohio. *Education:* The Ohio State University (B.S. in Business Administration, 1985); University of Toledo (J.D., 1991). (Certified Specialist in Estate Planning, Trust and Probate Law, Ohio State Bar Association). ***PRACTICE AREAS:*** Estate Planning; Probate; Trusts and Estates; Fiduciary Law. ***Email:*** MJTarini@eastmansmith.com

SCOTT D. NEWSOM, born Toledo, Ohio, August 12, 1971; admitted to bar, 1996, Ohio; 1997, U.S. District Court, Northern District of Ohio; 2002, Indiana and U.S. District Court, Northern and Southern Districts of Indiana; 2003, U.S. Court of Appeals, Sixth Circuit. *Education:* Kenyon College (B.A., 1993); University of Toledo (J.D., cum laude, 1996). ***PRACTICE AREAS:*** Business Law; Employee Benefits; Corporate Law. ***Email:*** SDNewsom@eastmansmith.com

GARY L. MILLER, born Butler, Pennsylvania, October 23, 1948; admitted to bar, 1999, Ohio. *Education:* Indiana University of Pennsylvania (B.S., summa cum laude, 1970); Temple University (M.M., summa cum laude, 1974); University of Toledo (J.D., cum laude, 1998). ***PRACTICE AREAS:*** Estate Planning and Probate; Elder Law; Business Law; Tax Law; Qualified Retirement Plans. ***Email:*** GLMiller@eastmansmith.com

JEFFREY M. STOPAR, born Barberton, Ohio, August 18, 1970; admitted to bar, 1996, Ohio; 2002, Indiana; 1999, U.S. District Court, Northern District of Ohio and U.S. Court of Appeals, Sixth Circuit; 2002, U.S. District Court, Northern and Southern Districts of Indiana. *Education:* University of Akron (B.A., 1992); University of Toledo (J.D., cum laude, 1996). Law Clerk to Donald R. Ford, Eleventh District Court of Appeals of Ohio, 1996-1999. ***PRACTICE AREAS:*** Litigation; Administrative Law; Public Law. ***Email:*** JMStopar@eastmansmith.com

JEFFREY D. SNAVELY, born Monroe, Michigan, November 5, 1969; admitted to bar, 1996, Ohio. *Education:* University of Toledo (B.B.A., cum laude, 1993; J.D., magna cum laude, 1996). Author: Note, "Central Bank v. First Interstate Bank: Will the Death of the Salesman Stop the Selling?" 26 U.Tol.L.Rev. 695 (1995). ***PRACTICE AREAS:*** Corporate Law; Commercial Law; Securities Law. ***Email:*** JDSnavely@eastmansmith.com

KIMBERLY S. BAKER, born Spencerville, Ohio, April 23, 1969; admitted to bar, 2000, Ohio and U.S. District Court, Northern District of Ohio. *Education:* Kansas Newman College (B.S., 1995); Ohio Northern University (J.D., with Distinction, 2000). [U.S. Air Force, 1990-1996]. ***PRACTICE AREAS:*** Environmental Law; Public Law. ***Email:*** KSBaker@eastmansmith.com

FADI VICTOR NAHHAS, born Jerusalem; admitted to bar, 2000, Ohio; 2001, U.S. District Court, Northern District of Ohio; 2003, Michigan and U.S. Court of Appeals, Sixth Circuit. *Education:* Northern Kentucky University (B.S., summa cum laude, Management and International Studies, 1993); Brigham Young University (M.A., Organizational Behavior, 1995); University of Cincinnati (J.D., 2000). Order of Barristers. Recipient: 2003 20 Under 40 Award. *Member:* American Immigration Lawyers Association. ***LANGUAGES:*** Arabic. ***PRACTICE AREAS:*** Business/Transactional; Immigration and Naturalization. ***Email:*** FVNahhas@eastmansmith.com

GENE R. ABERCROMBIE, born Toledo, Ohio, January 11, 1969; admitted to bar, 1996, Ohio. *Education:* University of Toledo (B.B.A., Finance, cum laude, 1991; J.D., cum laude, 1996). General Counsel, Cavista Corp., 1998-2000. Member, Springfield Township Board of Zoning Appeals, 1995-1997. ***PRACTICE AREAS:*** Real Estate; Corporate Law. ***Email:*** GRAbercrombie@eastmansmith.com

HEIDI N. EISCHEN, born Toledo, Ohio, July 17, 1975; admitted to bar, 2001, Ohio; 2002, U.S. Court of Appeals, Sixth Circuit and U.S. District Court, Northern District of Ohio; 2005, U.S. District Court, Southern District of Ohio. *Education:* University of Toledo (B.A., cum laude, 1998; J.D., magna cum laude, 2001). Order of the Coif. ***PRACTICE AREAS:*** Labor and Employment; Employment Discrimination; Workers Compensation. ***Email:*** HNEischen@eastmansmith.com

CARRIE L. SPONSELLER, born Bowling Green, Ohio, July 7, 1976.; admitted to bar, 2001, Ohio. *Education:* Bowling Green State University (B.A., 1998); University of Toledo (J.D., 2001). ***PRACTICE AREAS:*** Labor and Employment; Workers Compensation. ***Email:*** CLSponseller@eastmansmith.com

MICHAEL R. BARNETT, born Mansfield, Ohio, February 2, 1976; admitted to bar, 2002, Ohio; 2003, U.S. District Court, Northern District of Ohio. *Education:* Ohio Northern University (B.S., Pharmacy, 1999); University of Cincinnati (J.D., 2002). Licensed Pharmacist, Ohio. Author: Casenote, "The Admissibility Determination of Expert Testimony on Eyewitness Identification: United States v. Smithers," 70 U. Cin. L. Rev. 751. ***PRACTICE AREAS:*** Litigation; Medical Malpractice; Product Liability; Personal Injury. ***Email:*** MRBarnett@eastmansmith.com

LYNN VUKETICH LUTHER, born Oregon, Ohio, October 23, 1975; admitted to bar, 2002, Ohio and U.S. District Court, Northern District of Ohio; 2003, Michigan. *Education:* Middle Tennessee State University (B.A., 1998); University of Toledo (J.D., magna cum laude, 2002). Order of the Coif. ***PRACTICE AREAS:*** Labor and Employment; Public Law. ***Email:*** LVLuther@eastmansmith.com

PATRICK J. DOWNEY, born Charlotte, North Carolina, November 21, 1954; admitted to bar, 1993, Ohio; 1995, North Carolina; 1998, Pennsylvania and Michigan; U.S. District Court, Northern District of Ohio. *Education:* Michigan State University (B.S., 1981); University of Cincinnati (J.D., 1993); University of Florida (LL.M., Taxation, 1994). ***PRACTICE AREAS:*** ERISA; Tax; Nonprofit and Charitable Organizations; Business; Charter School Law. ***Email:*** PJDowney@eastmansmith.com

LAURIE A. WATSON, born Toledo, Ohio, July 14, 1974; admitted to bar, 2002, Ohio. *Education:* Bowling Green State University (B.S., summa cum laude, 1997); University of Toledo (J.D., summa cum Laude, 2002). Order of the Coif. ***PRACTICE AREAS:*** Estate Planning; Employee Benefits. ***Email:*** LAWatson@eastmansmith.com

RICHARD L. JOHNSON, born Lock Haven, Pennsylvania, November 21, 1957; admitted to bar, 1994, Ohio; U.S. District Court, Northern District of Ohio. *Education:* Indiana Wesleyan University (B.S., 1980); University of Toledo (J.D., cum laude, 1994). ***PRACTICE AREAS:*** Labor and Employment; Workers Compensation. ***Email:*** RLJohnson@eastmansmith.com

MARIA LIMBERT MARKAKIS, born Youngstown, Ohio, January 25, 1975; admitted to bar, 2000, Ohio. *Education:* The Ohio State University (B.S., 1997; J.D., 2000). ***PRACTICE AREAS:*** Litigation; Education Law; Public Law. ***Email:*** MLMarkakis@eastmansmith.com

(This Listing Continued)

EASTMAN & SMITH LTD., Toledo—Continued

CONNIE S. SWEMBA, born May 11, 1955; admitted to bar, 2003, Ohio and U.S. District Court, Northern District of Ohio. *Education:* University of Toledo (B.A., 2000, summa cum laude; J.D., cum laude, 2003). Phi Kappa Phi. Licensed Plumber and Steamfitter. ***PRACTICE AREAS:*** Construction Law; Civil Litigation; Personal Injury; Products Liability. ***Email:*** CSSwemba@eastmansmith.com

ALEXANDRA M. STUMP, born June 20, 1974; admitted to bar, 2003, Ohio and U.S. District Court, Northern District of Ohio. *Education:* University of Cincinnati (B.S., cum laude, 1997); University of Toledo (J.D., cum laude, 2003). Former Assistant Auditor, Ohio State Auditor's Office. ***PRACTICE AREAS:*** Business Law. ***Email:*** AMStump@eastmansmith.com

ANTHONY R. MODD, born Findlay, Ohio, March 24, 1976; admitted to bar, 2002, Ohio. *Education:* Ohio Northern University (B.A., with high distinction, 1998); The Ohio State University (J.D., 2001). "Recent Development: Fraternal Order of Police,Colorado Lodge #19 v. City of Commerce City" 16 Ohio St. J. on Disp. Resol. 425 (2001). ***PRACTICE AREAS:*** Business Law; Commercial Litigation. ***Email:*** ARModd@eastmansmith.com

A. BROOKE PHELPS, born Dayton, Ohio, May 12, 1977; admitted to bar, 2002, Ohio. *Education:* University of Toledo (B.B.A., 1999; J.D., 2002). ***Email:*** ABPhelps@eastmansmith.com

JEFFERY A. CULVER, born Saratoga Springs, New York, July 5, 1970; admitted to bar, 2002, Ohio; 2003, Michigan. *Education:* Case Western Reserve University (B.A., 1993); University of Denver (M.A., 1995); Bowling Green State University (M.P.A., 1999); University of Toledo (J.D., 2002). ***PRACTICE AREAS:*** Education Law; Environmental Law; Local Government Law. ***Email:*** JACulver@eastmansmith.com

ROY V. PITMAN, born Warner Robbins, Georgia, August 13, 1975; admitted to bar, 2004, Ohio, 2005, U.S. District Court, Northern District of Ohio. *Education:* The Ohio State University (B.S., 1998); University of Cincinnati (J.D., 2002). ***PRACTICE AREAS:*** Litigation; Medical Malpractice; Products Liability; Personal Injury. ***Email:*** RVPitman@eastmansmith.com

SHAWN M. TRACEY, born Warren, Ohio, June 2, 1971; admitted to bar, 2001, Ohio; U.S. District Court, Northern District of Ohio. *Education:* University of Toledo (B.B.A., 1997; M.B.A., 2001; J.D., 2001). ***PRACTICE AREAS:*** Real Estate; Corporate Law; Commercial Transactions. ***Email:*** SMTracey@eastmansmith.com

KIMBERLY A. STARR, born Akron, Ohio, July 4, 1971; admitted to bar, 1999, Ohio; 2000, Michigan; U.S. District Court, Northern District of Ohio. *Education:* University of Akron (B.S.B.A., 1994; M.Tax., 1998); University of Toledo (J.D., 1999). ***PRACTICE AREAS:*** Business Succession Planning; Estate Planning; Taxation. ***Email:*** KAStarr@eastmansmith.com

DENISE A. MUELLER, born Toledo, Ohio, February 13, 1972; admitted to bar, 2000, Ohio. *Education:* University of Toledo (B.A., 1994; J.D., cum laude, 2000). Assistant Prosecutor, Toledo, Ohio, 2000-2002. ***PRACTICE AREAS:*** Litigation; Misdemeanors; Traffic Violations. ***Email:*** DAMueller@eastmansmith.com

DANIEL O. CECIL, born Richmond, Indiana, September 16, 1967; admitted to bar, 2004, Ohio; 2005, U.S. District Court, Northern District of Ohio and U.S. Court of Appeals, Sixth Circuit. *Education:* Wright State University (B.A., 1991; M.B.A., 1992); Case Western Reserve University (J.D., magna cum laude, 2004). Order of the Coif. ***PRACTICE AREAS:*** Commercial Litigation; Noncompete Litigation; Trade Secrets; ERISA Litigation; Personal Injury. ***Email:*** DOCecil@eastmansmith.com

SARAH E. PAWLICKI, born Toledo, Ohio, August 3, 1974; admitted to bar, 2003, Ohio. *Education:* Miami University (B.A., 1995); University of Toledo (J.D., magna cum laude, 2003). Order of the Coif. ***PRACTICE AREAS:*** Labor and Employment; Workers Compensation Defense; Employment Litigation. ***Email:*** SEPawlicki@eastmansmith.com

ANDREA B. SMOKTONOWICZ, born Toledo, Ohio, September 28, 1978; admitted to bar, 2004, Ohio. *Education:* Ohio State University (B.A., 2001); Ohio Northern University (J.D., 2004). Author: Comment, "Federal Conservation of Wetlands Runs Amuck with Wetland Mitigation Banking," 31 Ohio N.U. L. Rev. 177; "Cases Concerning the State and Federal Constitutions: A. Fourth Amendment: State v. Weideman," 29 Ohio N.U. L. Rev. 689. ***Email:*** ABSmoktonowicz@eastmansmith.com

OF COUNSEL

HOWARD M. FRIEDMAN, born Springfield, Ohio, September 26, 1941; admitted to bar, 1965, Ohio; 1970, U.S. Supreme Court. *Education:* The Ohio State University (B.A., cum laude, 1962); Harvard University (J.D., cum laude, 1965); Georgetown University (LL.M., 1967). Phi Beta Kappa. Ohio Securities Law and Practice, Banks and Baldwin, 1987. Author: "The Trust Indenture Act of 1939," Chapter 8 in Sommer (ed) The Federal Securities Act and the Trust Indenture Act of 1939, 1984; "Securities and Commodities Enforcement: Criminal Prosecutions and Civil Injunctions," Lexington Books, 1981; "Efficient Market Theory and Rule 10b-5 Nondisclosure Claims: A Proposal for Reconciliation," 47 Missouri Law Review 745, 1982; "Some Reflections on the Corporation As Criminal Defendant," 55 Notre Dame Lawyer 173, 1979. Chairman, Ohio Bar Specialization Committee, 1991—. ***PRACTICE AREAS:*** Securities Law.

REPRESENTATIVE CLIENTS: Allstate Insurance Co.; American Empire Insurance; American International Group; Art Iron, Inc.; Black & Decker, Inc.; Boysville of Michigan, Inc.; Cargill Incorporated; Carrier Corporation; Chief Super Markets, Inc.; Cincinnati College Preparatory Academy; Clarke Power Predicts Inc.; Consolidated Biscuit Co.; DaimlerChrysler Corp.; Dana Corporation; Deerfield Manufacturing; Defiance Metal Products; EdVantages; Envirosafe Services of Ohio, Inc.; Fed Ex Ground Transportation Inc.; Glasstech, Inc.; The Hartford; Hickory Farms, Inc.; The Huntington National Bank; IMCO Carbide Tool, Inc.; Joint Solid Waste Management District of Defiance, Fulton, Paulding & Williams Counties; Lear Corporation; The Leona Group, LLC; Lloyds of London; Lucas County Educational Service Center; Lucas County Improvement Corporation; Magruder Hospital; Master Chemical Co.; Medical College of Ohio Foundation; The Medical Protective Co.; Memorial Hospital (Fremont); Miami County; NCMIC Insurance Group; North Dayton School of Discovery; North Star BlueScope Steel Ltd.; OmniSource Corporation; Pathway School of Discovery; Perry Corp.; Physicians Insurance Co. of Ohio; Pro Assurance, Inc.; Roadway Express, Inc.; Sky Financial Group; Sky Bank; Sky Insurance; Sky Trust; Solar Cells, Inc.; Solid Waste Authority of Central Ohio; Spartan Stores, Inc.; Summit Academy Management; Swanton Local School District; Tenneco Automotive; City of Toledo; The Toledo Clinic, Inc.; Toledo Engineering Co., Inc.; Toledo Radiological Associates, Inc.; Toledo School for the Arts; Toledo-Lucas County Port Authority; United Technologies Corporation; Van Wert County Hospital; Winzeler Stamping Co.; Wood County Economic Development Commission.

(This Listing Continued)

ELK & ELK CO., L.P.A.

TOLEDO, OHIO

(See Cleveland)

Automobile Accidents, Product Defects, Nursing Home Neglect, Medical Malpractice, Personal Injury.

EMCH, SCHAFFER, SCHAUB & PORCELLO CO., L.P.A.

Established in 1901

ONE SEAGATE, SUITE 1980
P.O. BOX 916
TOLEDO, OHIO 43697-0916
Telephone: 419-243-1294
Fax: 419-243-8502
URL: http://www.essp-law.com

Patent, Trademark, Copyright, Licensing, Unfair Competition and Related Litigation.

MARK C. SCHAFFER, born Toledo, Ohio, February 13, 1942; admitted to bar, 1969, Ohio and U.S. District Court, Northern District of Ohio; 1980, U.S. Supreme Court; 1982, U.S. Court of Appeals for the Federal Circuit and U.S. Claims Court. *Education:* The Ohio State University (B.A., 1964; J.D., 1969). *Member:* Toledo, Ohio State and American Bar Associations; Toledo Patent Law Association. [Engineering Officer, U.S. Navy, 1964-1966]. ***PRACTICE AREAS:*** Patent; Trademark; Copyright; Unfair Competition Litigation. ***Email:*** mschaffer@essp-law.com

CHARLES R. SCHAUB, born Toledo, Ohio, August 4, 1947; admitted to bar, 1973, Ohio and U.S. District Court, Northern District of Ohio; 1980, U.S. Supreme Court; 1982, U.S. Court of Appeals for the Federal Circuit; registered to practice before U.S. Patent and Trademark Office. *Education:* University of Toledo (B.S.M.E., 1970; J.D., 1973). Delta Theta Phi. Note and Comment Editor, University of Toledo Law Review, 1972-1973. *Member:* Toledo and Ohio State Bar Associations; Toledo Patent Law Association (President, 1984-1985). ***PRACTICE AREAS:*** Trademarks; Patents; related Business Law and Licensing. ***Email:*** crschaub@essp-law.com

JAMES F. PORCELLO, JR., born Cleveland, Ohio, October 3, 1951; admitted to bar, 1977, Ohio and U.S. District Court, Northern and Southern Districts of Ohio; 1982, U.S. Court of Appeals for the Federal Circuit and U.S. Claims Court; registered to practice before U.S. Patent and Trademark Office. *Education:* Purdue University (B.S., 1974); Capital University (J.D., 1977). Delta Theta Phi; Tau Beta Pi. *Member:* Toledo, Ohio State and American Bar Associations; Toledo Patent Law Association; American Intellectual Property Law Association; Michigan Patent Law Association. ***PRACTICE AREAS:*** Patent; Trademark; Copyright; Litigation; International Practice. ***Email:*** jporcello@essp-law.com

PHILIP M. RICE, born Toledo, Ohio, December 28, 1931; admitted to bar, 1962, Ohio; registered to practice before U.S. Patent and Trademark Office. *Education:* University of Michigan (B.S.E., 1954); University of Toledo (LL.B., 1962). Delta Theta Phi. Licensed Professional Engineer, Ohio, 1961. *Member:* Toledo, Ohio State and American (Member, Sections on: International Law, Patent, Trademark and Copyright Law) Bar Associations; Toledo Patent Law Association (President, 1974-1975); American Intellectual Property Law Association. [1st Lt., USAF, 1954-1956]. ***PRACTICE AREAS:*** Patents; Licensing; Joint Ventures. ***Email:*** price@essp-law.com

PATRICK P. PACELLA, born 1942; admitted to bar, 1968, Oklahoma; 1971, Ohio; registered to practice before U.S. Patent and Trademark Office. *Education:* The Ohio State University (B.S.E.D., 1963); University of Notre Dame (J.D., 1968). *Member:* Toledo and Ohio State Bar Associations; Toledo Patent Law Association (President, 1983-1984); American Intellectual Property Law Association; U.S. Trademark Association (Member, Board of Directors, 1983-1986). ***REPORTED CASES:*** 774 F.2d 1116. ***PRACTICE AREAS:*** Patent Law; Trademark Law; Copyright Law. ***Email:*** ppacella@essp-law.com

FECH & FECH, L.L.C.

Established in 2002

INNS OF COURT BUILDING
405 NORTH HURON STREET, SUITE 200
TOLEDO, OHIO 43604
Telephone: 419-242-0461
Fax: 419-242-0463
Email: information@fech-law.com
URL: http://www.fech-law.com

Criminal Law, Juvenile Law, Delinquency, Misdemeanors, Felonies, Driving While Intoxicated, White Collar Crimes, Traffic Violations, Family Law, Divorce, Child Custody, Visitation Rights, Child Support, Dissolution.

FIRM PROFILE: Fech & Fech, L.L.C. is a general practice firm serving their clients in several areas of law and our firm is dedicated to meeting the needs of our clients. We know how busy life can be and we accommodate our client's schedules with night and weekend appointments. We are also readily accessible to our clients, should an emergency arise.

In addition, we understand legal services are expensive and attempt to work with our clients to provide them with quality legal services at a reasonable price. We have various fee agreements, including hourly billing and flat fee representation.

These are just a few ways we guarantee our clients the legal services they deserve.

(This Listing Continued)

MEMBERS OF FIRM

MATTHEW N. FECH, born East Chicago, Indiana, October 3, 1974; admitted to bar, 2001, Ohio and U.S. District Court, Northern District of Indiana; 2002, Indiana; U.S. District Court, Northern District of Ohio. *Education:* Indiana University (B.S., with distinction, 1998); University of Toledo (J.D., 2001). *Member:* Toledo, Lucas County and Ohio State Bar Associations. ***PRACTICE AREAS:*** Criminal Law; Family Law; Civil Litigation. ***Email:*** mnf@fech-law.com

NICOLE Y. FECH, admitted to bar, 2001, Ohio; 2003, U.S. District Court, Northern District of Ohio. *Education:* Taylor University (B.S., Criminal Justice, English); University of Toledo College of Law (J.D., 2001). Member, Trial Advocacy Team, University of Toledo. *Member:* Toledo Bar Association; Women's Law Student Association; Woman's Toledo Bar Association. ***PRACTICE AREAS:*** Criminal Law; Family Law; Landlord and Tenant Law; Civil Litigation. ***Email:*** nyf@fech-law.com

FREDERICKSON, HEINTSCHEL & KING CO., L.P.A.

Established in 1991

SUITE 1212, 405 MADISON AVENUE
TOLEDO, OHIO 43604-1207
Telephone: 419-242-5100
Fax: 419-242-5556

General Civil Practice. Trial and Appellate Practice. Creditor's Rights, Bankruptcy, Corporate, Real Estate, Business, Commercial, Probate and Estate Planning Law.

CRAIG F. FREDERICKSON, born Seattle, Washington, August 14, 1946; admitted to bar, 1973, Illinois; 1975, Ohio and U.S. District Court, Northern District of Ohio. *Education:* Michigan State University (B.A., 1968); Northwestern University (J.D., 1973). Delta Theta Phi. President, Toledo Estate Planning Council, 1988-1989. Advisory Board of Probate and Trust Law Journal of Ohio, 1995—. *Member:* Toledo (Member, Board of Trustees, 1988-1996; President, 1994-1995; Chairman, Probate and Trust Law Committee, 1983-1985), Illinois State, Ohio State (Member, Board of Governors: Estate Planning, Probate and Trust Law Sections, 1989—; Member, Council of Delegates, 1998—) and American Bar Associations. Fellow: American College of Trust and Estate Counsel; American Bar Foundation; Ohio State Bar Foundation; Toledo Bar Foundation. ***PRACTICE AREAS:*** Probate; Estate Planning; Business Law; Real Estate. ***Email:*** cfrederickson@amplex.net

THOMAS W. HEINTSCHEL, born Toledo, Ohio, August 8, 1952; admitted to bar, 1978, California and U.S. District Court, Northern District of California; 1979, Ohio and U.S. District Court, Northern District of Ohio; 1986, U.S. Court of Appeals, Sixth Circuit; U.S. Court of Appeals, First Circuit. *Education:* John Carroll University (B.A., magna cum laude, 1974); University of San Francisco (J.D., with honors, 1978). Member, McAuliffe Law Honor Society. *Member:* Toledo (Member, Real Estate and Bankruptcy Committees), Ohio State (Member, Commercial, Banking and Bankruptcy Committee) and American (Member, Sections on: Business; Litigation) Bar Associations; State Bar of California. ***PRACTICE AREAS:*** Civil Litigation; Bankruptcy; Commercial Law; Business Law; Real Estate; Creditor's Rights; Appellate. ***Email:*** theintschel@amplex.net

DOUGLAS W. KING, born Toledo, Ohio, February 26, 1963; admitted to bar, 1991, Ohio; 1993, U.S. District Court, Northern District of Ohio; 1997, Michigan. *Education:* University of Toledo (B.A., with departmental honors, magna cum laude, 1985; Assoc., 1986; J.D., 1991). Phi Kappa Phi; Pi Sigma Alpha; Delta Theta Phi. Member, University of Toledo Law Review. Member: Toledo Estate Planning Council; Toledo Area Planned Giving Council. *Member:* Toledo (Chairman, Probate Court and Estate Planning, 2002-2004; Chairman, Lawyers & Life Underwriters Committee, 1995-1999) and Ohio State (Member, Section on Real Property, Probate and Trust Law) Bar Associations; State Bar of Michigan. ***LANGUAGES:*** German. ***PRACTICE AREAS:*** Probate; Estate Planning; Business Law; Real Estate; Civil Litigation. ***Email:*** dking@amplex.net

REPRESENTATIVE CLIENTS: Acute Care Services, Inc.; Scottdel, Inc.; The Whitchurst Company; Fifth Third Bank of Toledo; Keybank; Federal Deposit Insurance Corporation; Louisville Title Agency for N.W. Ohio, Inc.; Abbott Tool, Inc.; East Side Sheet Metal, Inc.; Inc.; Lawyers Title Insurance Corporation; Old Republic National Title Insurance Agency; Port Lawrence Title and Trust Co.; American 1st Title Co.; Case Credit Corp.; Catowba Cleveland Development Corp.; Catowba Island Club; World Tire Corporation; Tireman Auto Service Centers.

DAVID E. FRIEDES & ASSOCIATES

6545 W. CENTRAL AVENUE
SUITE 209
TOLEDO, OHIO 43617-1034
Telephone: 419-842-9902
Fax: 419-842-0623
Email: daveatty@buckeye-express.com
URL: http://www.toledodisabilitylaw.net

Bankruptcy, Consumer Bankruptcy, Juvenile Law, Family Law, Divorce, Personal Injury, Automobile Accidents, Dog Bites, Slip and Fall, Residential Real Estate Sales, Social Security, Social Security Disability, Workers Compensation.

DAVID E. FRIEDES, born Brooklyn, New York, July 14, 1958; admitted to bar, 1984, Ohio. *Education:* State University of New York at Buffalo (B.A., cum laude, 1980); University of Toledo (J.D., 1983). Member, National Organization of Social Security Claimant's Representatives. Frequent Lecturer, Chronic Fatigue Syndrome Issues. Counsel, Maumee Valley Save-A-Pet. *Member:* Toledo, Ohio State and American Bar Associations; Association of Trial Lawyers of America; Ohio Academy of Trial Lawyers. ***PRACTICE AREAS:*** Social Security; Social Security Disability; Supplemental Security Income Disability; Workers Compensation; Consumer Bankruptcy; Family Law; Divorce; Child Custody; Child Support; Visitation Rights; Juvenile Law; Residential Real Estate Sales; Automobile Accidents and Injuries; Personal Injury; Dog Bites.

(This Listing Continued)

FULLER & HENRY LTD

Established in 1892

ONE SEAGATE
SUITE 1700
P.O. BOX 2088
TOLEDO, OHIO 43603-2088
Telephone: 419-247-2500
Telecopier: 419-247-2665
URL: http://www.FullerHenry.com

General Civil Practice: Civil Litigation in all State and Federal Courts, Commercial, Labor and Employment, Workers' Compensation, Taxation, Estate Planning, Probate, Corporate Law, Real Estate, Health Care, Information Technology and Electronic Commerce.

MEMBERS OF FIRM

FRED E. FULLER (1901-1981)

LESLIE HENRY (1904-1976)

JAMES M. MORTON, JR., born Pontiac, Michigan, November 11, 1942; admitted to bar, 1967, Ohio. *Education:* Oakland University (B.A., 1964); University of Michigan (J.D., with distinction, 1967). ***PRACTICE AREAS:*** Corporate Law; Estate Planning; Probate and Trust Law; Taxation. ***Email:*** JMM@FULLERHENRY.COM

STEPHEN J. STANFORD, born Toledo, Ohio, July 12, 1949; admitted to bar, 1975, Ohio. *Education:* The Ohio State University (B.S., 1971; J.D., 1975). Beta Gamma Sigma. ***PRACTICE AREAS:*** Labor and Employment; Employment at Will; Employment Discrimination; Management Labor Law; Wrongful Termination Defense. ***Email:*** SJS@FULLERHENRY.COM

RAY A. FARRIS, born Fairmont, West Virginia, November 2, 1949; admitted to bar, 1975, Ohio. *Education:* The Ohio State University (B.A., 1971; J.D., summa cum laude, 1975). Order of the Coif. ***PRACTICE AREAS:*** Civil Litigation; Products Liability Law; Professional Liability Law; Insurance Defense; Commercial Law. ***Email:*** RAF@FULLERHENRY.COM

THOMAS M. GEORGE, born Toledo, Ohio, November 9, 1949; admitted to bar, 1975, Ohio. *Education:* Williams College (B.A., cum laude, 1972); Case Western Reserve University (J.D., 1975). ***PRACTICE AREAS:*** Business Law; Commercial Law; Corporate Law; Health Law; Mergers, Acquisitions and Divestitures; Hospital Law. ***Email:*** TMG@FULLERHENRY.COM

CRAIG J. VAN HORSTEN, born Waterbury, Connecticut, July 30, 1951; admitted to bar, 1976, Ohio. *Education:* Miami University (B.A., 1973); The Ohio State University (J.D., cum laude, 1976). ***PRACTICE AREAS:*** Construction Contracts; Commercial Real Estate Development; Commercial Leasing; Nonprofit Organizations Law. ***Email:*** CVH@FULLERHENRY.COM

GLENN L. RAMBO, born New Lexington, Ohio, March 28, 1951; admitted to bar, 1980, Ohio. *Education:* Ohio University (B.B.A., summa cum laude, 1973); The Ohio State University (J.D., 1980). Certified Public Accountant, Ohio, 1974. ***PRACTICE AREAS:*** Estate Planning and Administration; State and Local Taxation; Partnership, Trusts, Corporate and General Business Law. ***Email:*** GLR@FULLERHENRY.COM

DAVID R. BAINBRIDGE, born Cleveland, Ohio, January 2, 1958; admitted to bar, 1983, Ohio. *Education:* Miami University (B.S., 1980); University of Toledo (J.D., cum laude, 1983); University of Florida (LL.M., Tax, 1984). Order of the Coif. ***PRACTICE AREAS:*** Commercial Loans; Buying and Selling of Businesses; Secured Transactions; Leasing; Real Property. ***Email:*** DRB@FULLERHENRY.COM

DENNIS A. LYLE, born Akron, Ohio, May 14, 1958; admitted to bar, 1984, Ohio. *Education:* Bowling Green State University (B.B.S., 1980); University of Toledo (J.D., cum laude, 1984). ***PRACTICE AREAS:*** Products Liability; Commercial Law; Personal Injury Law; Property Tax; Class Action Litigation. ***Email:*** DAL@FULLERHENRY.COM

DANIEL T. ELLIS, born Buffalo, New York, May 2, 1957; admitted to bar, 1987, Ohio and U.S. District Court, Northern and Southern Districts of Ohio. *Education:* Canisius College (B.A., 1982); University of Toledo (J.D., cum laude, 1987). Phi Alpha Delta. ***PRACTICE AREAS:*** Complex and Multi-District Litigation; Insurance Litigation; Civil Litigation; Complex Litigation. ***Email:*** DTE@FULLERHENRY.COM

JOHN E. MAUNTLER, born Toledo, Ohio, January 16, 1962; admitted to bar, 1988, Ohio. *Education:* Capital University (BA., 1984); The Ohio State University (M.B.A., 1987; J.D., 1988). ***PRACTICE AREAS:*** Information Technology Contracts; Licensing; Electronic Commerce; Commercial Real Estate Acquisitions; Commercial Real Estate Development; Business Transactions. ***Email:*** JEM@FULLERHENRY.COM

ROBERT W. CABANSKI, born Toledo, Ohio, March 28, 1954; admitted to bar, 1979, Ohio. *Education:* University of Toledo (B.B.A., magna cum laude, 1976); University of Michigan (J.D., 1979). ***PRACTICE AREAS:*** Estate Planning; Wealth Preservation; Trusts and Estates; Estate Administration; Estate Settlements; Employee Benefits; ERISA; Estate and Gift Taxation. ***Email:*** RWC@FULLERHENRY.COM

SCOTT T. JANSON, born South Bend, Indiana, July 11, 1957; admitted to bar, 1991, Ohio. *Education:* University of Toledo (B.B.A., 1981; M.B.A., 1983; J.D., summa cum laude, 1991). Phi Kappa Phi. Order of the Coif. Chartered Financial Analyst, 1987. ***PRACTICE AREAS:*** Estate Planning; Probate Law; Trusts; Taxation; Business Transactions. ***Email:*** STJ@FULLERHENRY.COM

COUNSEL

FRED J. LANGE, JR., born Flushing, New York, February 24, 1950; admitted to bar, 1975, Ohio. *Education:* Bowling Green State University (B.S., with honors, 1972); The Ohio State University (J.D., summa cum laude, 1975). Order of the Coif; Beta Gamma Sigma. ***PRACTICE AREAS:*** Corporate Law.

(This Listing Continued)

FULLER & HENRY LTD, Toledo—Continued

HOWARD G. BRUSS, born Toledo, Ohio, November 12, 1938; admitted to bar, 1967, Ohio; registered to practice before U.S. Patent and Trademark Office. *Education:* University of Detroit (B.S.Ch.E., 1961); University of Toledo (J.D., cum laude, 1966). Legal Department, Glidden Div/SCM Corp., 1968-1972. *Member:* Toledo, Ohio State and American Bar Associations; Toledo Patent Law Association; American Patent Law Association. ***PRACTICE AREAS:*** Patents; Intellectual Property. ***Email:*** HGB@fullerhenry.com

ASSOCIATES

MELISSA M. OOSTMEYER, born Lansing, Michigan; admitted to bar, 1999, Michigan and Ohio. *Education:* Spring Arbor College (B.A., 1991); Eastern Michigan University (M.B.A., 1994); University of Detroit Mercy (J.D., 1998). ***LANGUAGES:*** Japanese. ***PRACTICE AREAS:*** Commercial Real Estate; Residential Real Estate; College and University Law; Business Transactions; Corporate Law. ***Email:*** MMO@FULLERHENRY.COM

LISA L. BOSTELMAN, born Napoleon, Ohio, February 2, 1976; admitted to bar, 2001, Ohio. *Education:* Miami University (B.A., magna cum laude, 1998); University of Toledo (J.D., 2001). ***PRACTICE AREAS:*** Civil Litigation; Labor and Employment; Workers Compensation Defense; Employment Litigation; Labor Law. ***Email:*** LLB@FULLERHENRY.COM

GALLAGHER SHARP

Established in 2004

(Formerly Hauxhurst, Sharp, Mollison & Gallagher)

420 MADISON AVENUE, SUITE 1250
TOLEDO, OHIO 43604
Telephone: 419-241-4860
Telecopier: 419-241-4866
URL: http://www.gallaghersharp.com

Cleveland, Ohio Office: Bulkley Building, Sixth Floor, 1501 Euclid Avenue, 44115. Telephone: 216-241-5310. Telecopier: 216-241-1608.

General Civil Practice. Insurance, Product Liability, Aviation, Railroad, Professional Negligence, Mass Tort, Construction, Environmental, Corporation, Securities, Probate Law, Workers' Compensation, Appellate.

FIRM PROFILE: Gallagher Sharp, in the continuous practice of law since 1912, is a trial and business practice firm serving clients throughout Ohio and the United States.

Lawyers in the Firm are active members in many professional organizations, including the Federation of Insurance and Corporate Counsel (FICC), the International Association of Defense Counsel (IADC), the Defense Research Institute (DRI), the Lawyer-Pilots Bar Association, the Ohio State Bar Association and local bar associations.

The firm has long-standing relationships with leading companies in the casualty insurance business, major airframe and engine manufacturers, pharmaceutical companies, and other product manufacturers, major health care providers, architectural, engineering and construction firms, and other large and small companies.

MEMBERS OF FIRM

THOMAS E. DOVER, born Waterloo, Iowa; admitted to bar, 1980, Ohio. *Education:* University of Dayton (B.S., summa cum laude, 1977; J.D., magna cum laude, 1980). Phi Alpha Delta. Managing Editor, University of Dayton Law Review, 1979-1980. Listed, Best Lawyers in America. *Member:* National Association of Railroad Trial Counsel (Member, Executive Committee). (Also at Cleveland Office). ***PRACTICE AREAS:*** Transportation; Mass Torts.

TIMOTHY J. FITZGERALD, born Lakewood, Ohio; admitted to bar, 1989, Ohio. *Education:* Marquette University (B.S., 1986); Cleveland Marshall College of Law (J.D., 1989). Phi Alpha Theta. (Also at Cleveland Office). ***PRACTICE AREAS:*** Business Law; Professional Liability; Appellate Practice.

ANNA S. FISTER, born Cleveland, Ohio; admitted to bar, 2003, Ohio; 2005, Michigan. *Education:* Hiram College (B.A., cum laude, 2000); University of Dayton School of Law (J.D., 2003). Staff Writer, University of Dayton Law Review, 2002-2003. Intern, The Honorable Sherrod Brown, U.S. Congress, 13th District, Ohio, 1999. (Also at Cleveland Office). ***PRACTICE AREAS:*** Transportation; Appellate Practice.

THOMAS F. NAUGHTON, born Bronx, New York; admitted to bar, 1994, Michigan; 2000, Ohio. *Education:* Ohio State University (B.A., 1989); Michigan State University College of Law (J.D., cum laude, 1994). (Also at Cleveland Office). ***PRACTICE AREAS:*** Litigation; Products Liability.

Representative Clients Available Upon Request.

STANLEY J. GARRETT

5249 SECOR ROAD, SUITE 4
TOLEDO, OHIO 43623
Telephone: 419-471-1488
Fax: 419-255-4513

Criminal Law, Traffic Violations, Misdemeanors, Felonies, Drivers License Suspension, Domestic Violence, Driving While Intoxicated, Trucking Law, Juvenile Criminal Law.

STANLEY J. GARRETT, born Ann Arbor, Michigan, March 1, 1960; admitted to bar, 1992, Ohio; 1993, Michigan and U.S. District Court, Northern District of Ohio. *Education:* Eastern Michigan University (B.S., 1988); University of Toledo (J.D., 1992). *Member:* Lucas County and Toledo Bar Associations; State Bar of Michigan. ***PRACTICE AREAS:*** Criminal Law; Traffic Violations; Misdemeanors; Felonies; Drivers License Suspension; Domestic Violence; Driving While Intoxicated; Trucking Law; Juvenile Criminal Law.

THE LAW OFFICES OF GORANSON, PARKER & BELLA

405 MADISON AVENUE
SUITE 2200
TOLEDO, OHIO 43604
Telephone: 419-244-9500
Telecopier: 419-244-9510
URL: http://www.gpblaw.com

Real Estate, Bankruptcy, Insurance Defense, Negligence Law, Civil Litigation, Construction Law, Labor and Employment, Bank Law, Probate.

ROGER W. GORANSON, born Toledo, Ohio, July 11, 1948; admitted to bar, 1976, Ohio. *Education:* Adrian College (B.A., 1970); University of Toledo (J.D., 1976). Phi Alpha Phi. *Member:* Toledo, Ohio State (Member, Real Estate and Probate Section) and American Bar Associations. ***PRACTICE AREAS:*** Real Estate; Bankruptcy. ***Email:*** rgoranson@gpblaw.com

CHRISTOPHER F. PARKER, born Toledo, Ohio, December 15, 1958; admitted to bar, 1984, Ohio; 1985, U.S. District Court, Northern District of Ohio; 1986, U.S. Court of Appeals, Sixth Circuit. *Education:* Miami University (B.A., 1980); University of Toledo (J.D., 1984). Evans Scholar. *Member:* Toledo, Lucas County, Ohio State and American Bar Associations. ***PRACTICE AREAS:*** Insurance Defense; Negligence Law; Civil Litigation; Labor and Employment; Construction Law. ***Email:*** cparker@gpblaw.com

JOHNA M. BELLA, born South Bend, Indiana, March 14, 1961; admitted to bar, 1986, Ohio; 1989, U.S. District Court, Northern District of Ohio; 1993, U.S. Court of Appeals, Sixth Circuit. *Education:* University of Notre Dame (B.A., 1983); University of Toledo (J.D., 1986). Staff Attorney, Lucas County Court of Common Pleas, 1986-1988. *Member:* Toledo Bar Association. ***PRACTICE AREAS:*** Negligence Law; Insurance Defense; Civil Litigation; Bank Law; Labor and Employment. ***Email:*** jbella@gpblaw.com

JAMES E. GORANSON, born Toledo, Ohio, May 7, 1952; admitted to bar, 1978, Ohio; 1979, Florida. *Education:* The Ohio State University (B.S., 1974); University of Toledo (J.D., 1978). *Member:* Toledo, Ohio State (Member, Real Estate and Probate Section) and American Bar Associations; The Florida Bar. ***PRACTICE AREAS:*** Real Estate; Probate. ***Email:*** jgoranson@gpblaw.com

ASSOCIATE

GRETCHEN F. WESTON, born Toledo, Ohio, March 25, 1972; admitted to bar, 2003, Ohio. *Education:* Adrian College (B.A., summa cum laude, 1994); University of Toledo (J.D., cum laude, 2003). Member, Law Review. ***LANGUAGES:*** French. ***PRACTICE AREAS:*** Foreclosures; Real Estate; Bankruptcy; Domestic Relations. ***Email:*** gweston@gpblaw.com

JOHN P GOUTTIERE CO LPA

520 MADISON AVENUE, SUITE 1026
TOLEDO, OHIO 43604-1341
Telephone: 419-242-9900
Fax: 419-244-8620
URL: http://www.lawyers.com/gouttiere
Email: johng@gouttierelaw.com
URL: http://www.gouttierelaw.com

Business, Real Estate, Creditors Rights, Bankruptcy, Estate Planning, Elder Law, Probate, General Civil Practice in all State and Federal Courts.

JOHN P GOUTTIERE, born Toledo, Ohio, March 18, 1949; admitted to bar, 1974, Ohio; 1975, U.S. District Court, Northern District of Ohio; 1997, U.S. Supreme Court; 1999, Michigan. *Education:* Bowling Green State University (B.A., 1971); Ohio Northern University (J.D., 1974). Adjunct Professor, University of Toledo College of Law, Secured Transactions. Arbitrator for National Futures Association and National Association of Securities Dealers. *Member:* Toledo, Lucas County (President, 1986) and Ohio State Bar Associations; American Bankruptcy Institute; Commercial Law League of America.

REPRESENTATIVE CLIENTS: Fifth-Third Bank; Banc One Corporation; National City Bank; Owens Illinois Inc.; Lexington Insurance Co.; Medical Value Plan HMO; GE Capital Auto Finance, Inc.; President Homes, Inc.

GRESSLEY, KAPLIN & PARKER, LLP

Established in 1980

SUITE 930, 608 MADISON AVENUE
TOLEDO, OHIO 43604-1129
Telephone: 419-244-8336
Telecopy: 419-244-1914
Email: gkp@gkplaw.net
URL: http://www.gkandp.com

Monroe, Michigan Office: 324 Washington Street. 48161. Telephone: 734-384-1021. Fax: 734-384-1021.

General Civil Practice. Corporate, Tax, Real Estate, Banking, Land Use, Zoning, Business, Business Planning, Business Litigation, Contracts, Commercial, Bankruptcy, Wills and Probate, Trusts and Estates and Estate Planning Law. Trial and Appellate Practice, Commercial Collections, Retail Collections.

(This Listing Continued)

FIRM PROFILE: The law firm of Gressley, Kaplin & Parker, LLP is a general practice law firm with special expertise in business law and sophisticated land use planning and zoning appeals. All members of the firm have large firm experience. Mr. Parker is recognized for his ability and experience as a land-use attorney. Mr. Schoenberger has had extensive experience in corporate and commercial transactional work including business bankruptcy work-outs. Mr. Conklin has more than twenty-five years of litigation and appellate practice experience. Ms. Reiser spent several years on the tax staff of a Fortune 500 Company. Mr. Hershman is widely known for his representation of financial institutions in the area of creditors' rights both in bankruptcy and collection matters. Mr. Cole has previous experience in the business group of a large firm, and spent over 12 years in-house with a large company in the service, manufacturing and specialty construction industries responsible for litigation, acquisitions, commercial real estate and general business transactions The practice is focused in Northwestern Ohio and Southeastern Michigan.

LYNN H. GRESSLEY (1913-2001)

JULIAN M. KAPLIN (1927-1995)

JEROME R. PARKER, born Toledo, Ohio, September 29, 1946; admitted to bar, 1973, Ohio and U.S. District Court, Northern District of Ohio. *Education:* University of Toledo (B.A., 1969; J.D., cum laude, 1973); University of Virginia (L.L.M., 1974). Phi Alpha Delta. Listed in "Best Lawyers in America," 1995-2005. *Member:* Toledo, Ohio State and American Bar Associations. ***PRACTICE AREAS:*** Land Use; Zoning Law; Real Estate Law; Banking Law. **Email:** jparker@gkplaw.net

BRUCE S. SCHOENBERGER, born Toledo, Ohio, June 14, 1957; admitted to bar, 1983, Ohio, U.S. District Court, Northern District of Ohio and U.S. Court of Appeals, Sixth Circuit; 1993, U.S. Supreme Court. *Education:* Miami University (B.A., 1978); Ohio State University (J.D., with honors, 1983). *Member:* Toledo, Ohio State and American Bar Associations. ***PRACTICE AREAS:*** Bankruptcy; Civil Litigation; Commercial Law; Closely Held Business Law; Real Estate Law. **Email:** bschoenberger@gkplaw.net

ROSALIND REISER, born Riverside, California, August 14, 1945; admitted to bar, 1986, Ohio; 1997, Michigan. *Education:* University of Michigan (B.S., 1967); University of Toledo (J.D., cum laude, 1985). Order of the Coif. Author: "Due Process Limitation on the Unitary Business Principle," 7 Journal of State Taxation. *Member:* Toledo, Monroe County, Lucas County, Ohio State and American Bar Associations; State Bar of Michigan. (Resident, Monroe, Michigan Office). ***PRACTICE AREAS:*** Estate Planning; Probate; Tax; Corporate. **Email:** rreiser@gkplaw.net

GEORGE J. CONKLIN, born Toledo, Ohio, December 27, 1951; admitted to bar, 1978, Ohio and U.S. District Court, Northern District of Ohio; 1988, U.S. Supreme Court. *Education:* University of Toledo (B.A., 1973; M.A., 1975; J.D., 1978). Phi Alpha Delta. Assistant Prosecutor, Lucas County, 1982-1996. *Member:* Toledo (Past Chairman, Common Pleas Court Committee; Member, Court of Appeals and Bar Admissions Committees) and Ohio State Bar Associations. ***REPORTED CASES:*** Aydin Co. Exch. v. Marting Realty (1997), 118 Ohio App.3d 274, 692 N.E. 2d 662; State v. Joy (S.Ct. 1995) 74 Ohio St. 3d 178, 657 N.E. 2d 503; Ohio Civil Rights Comm. v. Countrywide Home Loans (2003), 99 Ohio St. 3d 522, 794 NE 2d 56; Stak v. Esparza (1996), 74 Ohio St. 3d 660, 660 NE 2d 1194; State v. Tutt (1988), 44 Ohio App.3d 138, 541 NE 2d 1090. ***PRACTICE AREAS:*** Litigation; Trials; Appellate Law. **Email:** gconklin@gkplaw.net

DAVID A. COLE, born Napoleon, Ohio, September 5, 1960; admitted to bar, 1986, Ohio; U.S. District Court, Northern District of Ohio. *Education:* Miami University (B.S., 1983); Case Western Reserve University (J.D., 1986). *Member:* Toledo, Ohio State and American Bar Associations. ***PRACTICE AREAS:*** Commercial; Corporate; Product Liability; Contracts; Employment. **Email:** dcole@gkplaw.net

---

TODD J. KUHN, born Toledo, Ohio, May 13, 1976; admitted to bar, 2002, Ohio. *Education:* Bowling Green State University (B.S., honor's program, 1998); University of Toledo (J.D., 2002). Phi Alpha Theta. *Member:* Toledo, Ohio State and American Bar Associations. ***PRACTICE AREAS:*** Real Estate; Corporate Law; Closely Held Business Law; Employment Law; Intellectual Property. **Email:** tkuhn@gkplaw.net

OF COUNSEL

HOWARD B. HERSHMAN, born Toledo, Ohio, January 27, 1953; admitted to bar, 1978, Ohio and U.S. District Court, Northern District of Ohio; 1988, U.S. Court of Appeals, Sixth Circuit; 1993, Michigan. *Education:* University of Toledo (B.A., magna cum laude, 1975); The Ohio State University (J.D., 1978). Phi Kappa Phi. Order of Barristers. *Member:* Toledo and Ohio State Bar Associations. ***PRACTICE AREAS:*** Commercial Law; Bankruptcy; Collection; Civil Litigation; Banking Law. **Email:** hhershman@gkplaw.net

REPRESENTATIVE CLIENTS: Better Business Bureau Serving N.W. Ohio and S.E. Michigan, Inc.; Catawba Cleveland Development Corp.; Catawba Island Club; Cedarwood Development, Inc.; Fifth Third Bank ; Gross Electric, Inc.; Lamar Outdoor Advertising Inc.; Louisville Title Agency for N.W. Ohio, Inc.; J.A. Morrin Realty and Construction; Toledo Engineering Co., Inc.; Rudolph/Libbe Properties Inc.; CanDo Credit Union; CitiFinancial, Inc.; Citicorp Commercial Leasing and Citcorp Vendor Finance, Inc.; Sprint Spectrum L.P.; Toledo Area Community Credit Union; UT/MCO Federal Credit Union; TPS Credit Union; Focus Federal Credit Union; Mutual Federal Credit Union; Countrywide Home Loans, Inc.; C.U. Recovery, Inc.; Countrywide Credit Industries, Inc.; Port Lawrence Title and Trust Co.; Benchmark Development Corp.; Lowe's Companies, Inc.; Bottomline Ink Corporation; K-Limited Carrier Ltd.; Investek Realty; Wal-Mart Stores, Inc.; Westfield Corporation, Inc.; Wend-Toledo Realty; Shamas Urban Retreat; Union Bank Co.; J.P. Morgan Chase; Credit Adjustments Inc.; Maumee Valley Credit Union; Lakewood Acceptance / J.D. Byrider; Baywest Development Co.; Eidi Properties, LLC; Park West Development.

STEVEN C. HALES

5151 MONROE STREET, SUITE 105
TOLEDO, OHIO 43623
Telephone: 419-346-7423
Fax: 419-841-0812
Email: shalesesq@myway.net
URL: http://www.stevenhaleslaw.com

Family Law, Divorce, Child Custody, Child Support, Visitation Rights, Business Litigation, Business Formation, Corporations, Partnerships, Limited Liability Company Law, Mergers and Acquisitions, Business Planning, Small Business Law, Business Succession Planning, Family Business Law, Contracts, Licensing Agreements, Taxation, Real Estate, Commercial Leasing, Trusts and Estates.

STEVEN C. HALES, born 1960; admitted to bar, 1999, Ohio. *Education:* Heidelberg College (B.B.A., 1995); University of Toledo (J.D., 1999). *Member:* Toledo (Committee Member, Sections on: Family Law; Business Law) and Ohio State (Member, Solo and Small Firm Practice Sections) Bar Associations. ***PRACTICE AREAS:*** Divorce.

HUNTER & SCHANK CO., L.P.A.

ONE CANTON SQUARE
1700 CANTON AVENUE
TOLEDO, OHIO 43624-1378
Telephone: 419-255-4300
Fax: 419-255-9121

Business Law, Bankruptcy, Bankruptcy Litigation, Creditor's Rights, Probate, Small Business Consulting and Real Estate Law. Civil Litigation in all Federal and State Courts.

THOMAS J. SCHANK, born Tiffin, Ohio, July 5, 1950; admitted to bar, 1977, Ohio, U.S. District Court, Northern District of Ohio, U.S. District Court, Eastern and Western Districts of Michigan and U.S. Court of Appeals, Sixth Circuit. *Education:* University of Toledo (B.A., 1973; J.D., 1976). Certified in Business Bankruptcy Law, American Bankruptcy Board of Certification, 1992. Diplomate, Bankruptcy Litigation, National Institute for Trial Advocacy, 1992. ***PRACTICE AREAS:*** Bankruptcy; Business Law; Commercial Law; Contracts; Corporate Law; International Law; International Trade; Litigation; Mergers and Acquisitions. **Email:** tomschank@hunterschank.com

JOHN J. HUNTER, JR., born Toledo, Ohio, October 28, 1961; admitted to bar, 1986, Ohio and U.S. District Court, Northern District of Ohio; 1987, U.S. Court of Appeals, Sixth Circuit. *Education:* University of Toledo (B.A., 1983; J.D., 1986). Order of the Barristers. Member, Moot Court Board, National Trial Team. ***PRACTICE AREAS:*** Agricultural Law; Bankruptcy; Business Law; Commercial Law; Contracts; Corporate Law; Debtor and Creditor; Litigation. **Email:** jrhunter@hunterschank.com

KURT J. LINDOWER, born Toledo, Ohio, February 3, 1963; admitted to bar, 1990, Ohio. *Education:* Wittenberg University (B.A., cum laude, 1985); University of Cincinnati (J.D., 1990). Member, University of Cincinnati Law Review, 1989-1990. Author: Casenote, "Noerr-Pennington Antitrust Immunity and Private Standard-Setting: Allied Tube & Conduit Corp. v. Indian Head, Inc.," 58 U.Cinn.L.Rev. 341, 1989. *Member:* Toledo, Ohio State and American Bar Associations. ***PRACTICE AREAS:*** Commercial Law; Corporate Law; Products Liability; Contracts; Employment Law. **Email:** klindower@hunterschank.com

All Members of the firm are members of American, Ohio State, Toledo, Lucas and Sandusky County Bar Associations.

REPRESENTATIVE CLIENTS: ZF Friedrichshafen AG; Lemforder Corp; Ag Credit, ACA; Farm Credit Services of Mid-America, ACA; Community First Bank; ZF Industries, Inc.; Sky Bank, Mid Am Region.
REFERENCES: Community First Bank; Farm Credit Services Mid-America, ACA; Ag Credit, ACA.

JONES & SCHEICH

1600 FIFTH THIRD CENTER
608 MADISON AVENUE
TOLEDO, OHIO 43604-1117
Telephone: 419-241-6450
Telecopier: 419-241-1540
Email: j-slaw@jonesscheich.com

Civil Litigation, Real Estate, Commercial Transactions, Corporate Law, Business Law, Contracts, Creditors Rights, Bankruptcy.

CHRISTOPHER F. JONES, born Los Angeles, California, July 11, 1949; admitted to bar, 1978, Missouri; 1979, Illinois; 1987, Ohio. *Education:* University of Missouri (B.A., magna cum laude, Phi Beta Kappa, 1974); University of Missouri (J.D., 1978). Note and Comment Editor, University of Missouri Law Review, 1977-1978. *Member:* Toledo and Ohio State Bar Associations. ***PRACTICE AREAS:*** Civil Litigation. **Email:** cjones@jonesscheich.com

RICHARD A. SCHEICH, born Monroe, Michigan, September 18, 1954; admitted to bar, 1984, Ohio. *Education:* University of Michigan (B.A., 1978); University of Toledo (M.B.A., 1983; J.D., 1983). *Member:* Toledo and Ohio State Bar Associations. ***PRACTICE AREAS:*** Real Estate; Commercial Transactions; Corporate Law; Creditors Rights; Bankruptcy; Civil Litigation. **Email:** rscheich@jonesscheich.com

ASSOCIATE

CRAIG J. WAKEFIELD, born Fremont, Ohio, October 21, 1979; admitted to bar, 2004, Ohio. *Education:* Bowling Green State University (B.A., 2001); University of Toledo

(This Listing Continued)

JONES & SCHEICH, Toledo—Continued

(J.D., 2004). ***PRACTICE AREAS:*** Civil Litigation; Criminal Law; Finance; Real Estate. ***Email:*** cwakefield@jonesscheich.com

JOSEPH P. JORDAN

4127 MONROE STREET
TOLEDO, OHIO 43606
Telephone: 419-473-1300
Fax: 419-473-0329
Email: joejordan355@aol.com
URL: http://www.joejordanlaw.com

Civil and Criminal Litigation, DUI/DWI, Drug Crimes, Felonies, Juvenile Law, Misdemeanors, Parole and Probation, Traffic Violations, White Collar Crime, Zoning, Annexation, Municipal Law, Real Estate, Business Law, Personal Injury, Automobile Accidents, Dog Bites, Slip and Fall, Wrongful Death.

JOSEPH P. JORDAN, born Buffalo, New York, June 21, 1937; admitted to bar, 1962, Wisconsin and Ohio; 1963, U.S. District Court, Northern District of Ohio; 1965, U.S. Court of Appeals, Sixth Circuit; 1982, U.S. District Court, Eastern District of Michigan. *Education:* Xavier University (B.S., 1959); Marquette University (J.D., 1962). Assistant City Law Director, City of Toledo, 1965-1981. *Member:* Toledo, Lucas County and Ohio State Bar Associations.

KENNEY & NIEHAUS, LTD.

TOLEDO, OHIO

(See Sylvania)

Corporate, Business, Securities, Banking, Estate Planning, Probate, Real Estate, Litigation.

KERGER & ASSOCIATES

33 SOUTH MICHIGAN STREET, SUITE 201
TOLEDO, OHIO 43602
Telephone: 419-255-5990
Facsimile: 419-255-5997
URL: http://www.kergerkerger.com
Email: attorneys@kergerkerger.com
URL: http://www.lawyers.com/kergerkerger

Trial Practice, Appellate Practice, Criminal Law, Litigation.

RICHARD M. KERGER, born Erie, Pennsylvania, November 8, 1945; admitted to bar, 1974, Ohio. *Education:* College of Wooster; The Ohio State University (B.A., 1967; J.D., cum laude, 1974). Law Clerk to U.S. Chief District Judge Thomas D. Lambros, Northern District of Ohio, 1974-1976. Adjunct Professor, Litigation Strategy and Tactics, University of Toledo College of Law, 1987—. Life Member: U.S. Sixth Circuit Judicial Conference; Advisory Committee, Chairman, 2000-2004. *Member:* Toledo, Ohio State (Chairman, Federal Court and Practice Committee, 1985-1987; Member: Board of Governors, 1993-1996; Civil Needs Task Force) and American Bar Associations. Fellow: Ohio State Bar Foundation; American Bar Foundation; American Board of Trial Advocates; American College of Trial Lawyers; International Society of Barristers. ***PRACTICE AREAS:*** Trial Practice; Federal Criminal Law; Appellate Practice. ***Email:*** rickkerger@kergerkerger.com

ASSOCIATES

STEPHEN D. HARTMAN, born Toledo, Ohio, January 5, 1971; admitted to bar, 2002, Ohio. *Education:* University of Toledo (B.A., 1996; M.B.A., 1999; J.D., 2002). *Member:* Toledo, Ohio State and American Bar Associations. (Law Clerk). ***PRACTICE AREAS:*** Federal Criminal Law; Appellate Practice. ***Email:*** stephenhartman@kergerkerger.com

KIMBERLY A. DONOVAN, born Toledo, Ohio, November 24, 1971; admitted to bar, 2002, Ohio. *Education:* Bowling Green State University (B.S., Journalism, 1994); University of Toledo (J.D., 2001). Law Clerk to Honorable Thomas F. Bryant, Ohio court of Appeals, Third District, 2001-2003. *Member:* Ohio State and American Bar Associations. ***PRACTICE AREAS:*** Litigation; Appellate Practice. ***Email:*** kimberlydonovan@kergerkerger.com

LEGAL SUPPORT PERSONNEL

BRIGID MATTHEWS, born Toledo, Ohio. *Education:* University of Toledo (A.S., 1979). (Office Administrator). ***Email:*** brigidmatthews@kergerkerger.com

JOSEE REULING, born Middletown, Ohio, July 19, 1969. (Secretary). ***Email:*** joseereuling@kergerkerger.com

KITCH DRUTCHAS WAGNER VALITUTTI & SHERBROOK

A Professional Corporation
Attorneys and Counselors
405 MADISON AVENUE
SUITE 1500
TOLEDO, OHIO 43604-1235
Telephone: 419-243-4006
Fax: 419-243-7333
URL: http://www.kitch.com

Detroit, Michigan Office: One Woodward Avenue, Suite 2400, 48226-5485. Telephone: 313-965-7900. Fax: 313-965-7403.

(This Listing Continued)

Mount Clemens, Michigan Office: 10 South Main Street, Suite 307, 48043-7903. Telephone: 586-463-9770. Fax: 586-463-8994.
Okemos, Michigan Office: 2379 Woodlake Drive, 48864. Telephone: 517-381-4426. Fax: 517-381-4427.
Ann Arbor, Michigan Office: 303 Detroit Street, Suite 400, P.O. Box 8610, 48107-8610. Telephone: 734-994-7600. Fax: 734-994-7626.
Marquette, Michigan Office: Old City Hall, 220 West Washington, Suite 500, 49855-4344. Telephone: 906-228-0001. Fax: 906-228-0003.

General Civil and Trial Practice in all State and Federal Courts. Appellate Practice. Medical, Legal, Products Liability, Food, Drug and Cosmetic, General Negligence, Insurance Coverage, Hospital, Environmental, Toxic Torts, Professional Liability, Employment Discrimination, Wrongful Discharge and Workers Compensation, Corporate Practice, Health Care, Commercial Litigation, Estate Planning and Securities, Federal and State Taxation.

PRINCIPAL

JOHN STEPHEN WASUNG, born Detroit, Michigan, May 16, 1958; admitted to bar, 1984, Michigan and U.S. District Court, Eastern District of Michigan; 1990, U.S. District Court, Northern District of Ohio; 1991, Ohio; 1993, U.S. Supreme Court. *Education:* University of Michigan (B.A., 1981); Wayne State University (J.D., 1984). *Member:* Toledo and Ohio State Bar Associations; State Bar of Michigan; Ohio Association of Civil Trial Attorneys; Society of Ohio Hospital Attorneys; Trucking Industry Defense Association. (Principal). ***PRACTICE AREAS:*** Medical Malpractice Defense; Physicians Professional Liability; Insurance Coverage; Insurance Litigation; Trucking Liability. ***Email:*** john.wasung@kitch.com

ASSOCIATE PRINCIPAL

VALERIE A. TRUDEL, born Toledo, Ohio, April 23, 1961; admitted to bar, 1997, Ohio; 2005, Michigan. *Education:* University of Toledo (B.S., 1994; J.D., 1997). Registered Nurse, Ohio, 1984. ***PRACTICE AREAS:*** Medical Malpractice Defense. ***Email:*** valerie.trudel@kitch.com

SENIOR ASSOCIATES

ANNE M. BROSSIA, admitted to bar, 2001, Ohio; 2002, U.S. District Court, Northern District of Ohio. *Education:* Mercy School of Nursing (Nursing Diploma, 1985); Lourdes College (B.S.N., summa cum laude, 1993); University of Toledo (J.D., 2000). Sigma Theta Tau Honor Society of Nursing, Zeta Chapter (charter member). Registered Nurse, Critical Care, State of Ohio, 1985—. *Member:* Toledo and Ohio State Bar Associations; Toledo Women's Bar Association. ***PRACTICE AREAS:*** Medical Malpractice Defense; General Liability Defense; Civil RICO; Insurance Coverage. ***Email:*** anne.brossia@kitch.com

PATRICK B. CAVANAUGH, born Detroit, Michigan, February 26, 1965; admitted to bar, 2000, Ohio; 2001, U.S. District Court, Northern District of Ohio; 2003, U.S. District Court, Southern District of Ohio; 2005, U.S. Bankruptcy Court, Northern District of Ohio. *Education:* Wright State University (B.F.A., 1987); University of Toledo (Legal Assistant Certificate Program, 1995; J.D., 1999). *Member:* Toledo (Member, Attorney Grievance Investigation Committee) and Ohio State Bar Associations. ***PRACTICE AREAS:*** Medical Malpractice Defense; General Liability Defense; Insurance Bad Faith Defense; Civil Litigation. ***Email:*** patrick.cavanaugh@kitch.com

DAVID T. HENDERSON, born 1971; admitted to bar, 1996, Ohio; 1997, Michigan. *Education:* University of Michigan (B.A., 1993); University of Toledo (J.D., 1996). *Member:* Toledo, Lucas County and Ohio State Bar Associations; State Bar of Michigan. ***PRACTICE AREAS:*** Medical Malpractice Defense; Trucking Liability; Tort Defense. ***Email:*** david.henderson@kitch.com

LORI L. PERNÉ, born Lansing, Michigan, March 20, 1953; admitted to bar, 2001, Ohio. *Education:* Mount Carmel Hospital School of Nursing, Columbus, Ohio (Nursing, 1977); Lourdes College (B.I.S., 1992); University of Toledo (J.D., 2000). Registered Nurse, Minnesota, 1977; Ohio, 1986. Court Appointed Special Advocate, 1996— and Guardian Ad Litem, 2001—, Lucas County Juvenile Court. *Member:* Toledo and Ohio State Bar Associations; Bioethic Network of Ohio; The Toledo Hospital Ethics Council. ***PRACTICE AREAS:*** Medical Malpractice Defense. ***Email:*** lori.perne@kitch.com

ASSOCIATE

RYAN E. CROZIER, born Wheeling, West Virginia, November 26, 1974; admitted to bar, 2003, Ohio. *Education:* The Ohio State University (B.A., Aviation Management, 1998); Thomas Jefferson School of Law (J.D., 2003). Phi Alpha Delta; Alpha Eta Rho. Member, Thomas Jefferson School of Law Honors Advocacy Team. Winner of the 2002 Intra-school Mock Trial Competition. Recipient: CALI Excellence for the Future Award in Media Law; Witkin Award for Academic Excellence in Media Law; Jefferson Medal for Excellent Achievement in Media Law. Private Pilot. Member, American Association of Airport Executives. *Member:* Ohio State Bar Association; The Association of Trial Lawyers of America. ***LANGUAGES:*** Spanish. ***PRACTICE AREAS:*** Medical Malpractice Defense; Trucking Liability. ***Email:*** ryan.crozier@kitch.com

REPRESENTATIVE CLIENTS: INSURANCE: CNA Insurance Co.; Crawford & Company; Hanover Insurance Co.; Harco National Insurance Co.; Liberty Mutual Insurance Co.; Mackinaw Administrators, LLC; RLI/Mr. Hawley Insurance Co.; Vesta/Shelby Insurance Co.; State Farm Insurance Co. MEDICAL MALPRACTICE: American Physicians Assurance Corp.; The Bellevue Hospital; Catholic Healthcare Partners; Defiance Hospital; Fisher-Titus Medical Center; Flower Hospital; Magruder Hospital; MedCentral Health System; MHA Insurance Co.; OHIC Insurance Co.; Paulding County Hospital; ProMedica Physicians Corp.; St. Charles Mercy Hospital; St. Luke's Hospital; The Toledo Hospital; Mercy Memorial Hospital; Bixby Medical Center; Bryan Community Hospital; Memorial Hospital of Union County. CONSTRUCTION AND LITIGATION: All American Homes of Ohio, LLC.; Coachmen Industries, Inc.; Fluor Constructors International, Inc.; The Pharm. TRUCKING/TRANSPORTATION: C. R. England, Inc.; Central Refrigerated Service, Inc.; Craig Transport; Crete Carrier Corp.; Dick Simon Trucking, Inc.; Griffith Trucking; Gundrum Trucking; Old Dominion Freight Line, Inc.; P.A.M. Transport; Sharp Transport, Inc.; SNS Express; Transportation Claims, Inc.; Triton Transport Services, Inc.; Crawford & Co.; Carolina Casualty Insurance Co.

KOLB & ZIGRAY

Established in 1946

NATIONAL CITY BANK BUILDING
405 MADISON AVENUE, SUITE 2000
TOLEDO, OHIO 43604
Telephone: 419-244-3006
Fax: 419-246-4754
URL: http://www.kolbzigraylaw.com

Will Contests, Trust Contests, Will Constructions, Guardianship Disputes, Joint and Survivorship Disputes, Claims Against Estates, Claims Against Executors and other Fiduciaries, Power of Attorney Disputes, Probate Litigation, Trial and Appellate Practice.

FIRM PROFILE: The law firm of Kolb & Zigray was established by Matt Kolb in 1946 and in 1967, became a family firm for many years. This firm is now one of few firms in Ohio that focuses entirely on Will Contests and other Probate Litigation matters. Our attorneys have experience in all phases of litigation in these types of cases including trial and appellate court experience.

PARTNERS OF FIRM

RICHARD KOLB, born Toledo, Ohio, 1942; admitted to bar, 1967, Ohio; 1998, U.S. Court of Appeals, Sixth Circuit. *Education:* DePauw University (B.A., 1964); The Ohio State University (J.D., 1967). Lecturer, Ohio CLE Institute and Toledo Bar Association on Probate Litigation, 1991—. Member, Trust Department, Ohio Citizens Bank, 1968-1970. Special Counsel to Office of Ohio Attorney General, 1971-1980. *Member:* Toledo (Member: Probate Committee, 1981—), Lucas County (President, 1980) and Ohio State (Member: Board of Governors; Estate Planning, Trust and Probate Section) Bar Associations. ***REPORTED CASES:*** Holzmer v. Urbanski, 86 Ohio St. 3d 129 (1999); Redman v. Watch Tower, 69 Ohio St.3d 98 (1994); Corron v. Corron, 40 Ohio St.3d 75 (1988); Studniewski v. Krzyzanowski, 65 Ohio App.3d 628 (1989). ***PRACTICE AREAS:*** Probate Litigation; Contested Wills; Trust Litigation; Fiduciary Litigation; Guardianship; Claims Against Estates; Prenuptial Agreement Disputes; Joint and Survivorship Disputes; Probate; Trial and Appellate Practice; Estate Administration. ***Email:*** richard.kolb@kolbzigraylaw.com

DANIEL F. ZIGRAY, born Toledo, Ohio, 1962; admitted to bar, 1991, Ohio; 1992, U.S. District Court, Northern District of Ohio. *Education:* University of Toledo (B.B.A., 1986; J.D., 1991). Assistant Prosecutor: City of Rossford, OH, 1993-2003; City of Perrysburg, OH, 1998-2000. *Member:* Toledo (Member, Probate Committee, Monthly Speaker, 2002—), Lucas County, Ohio State and American Bar Associations; Ohio Academy of Trial Lawyers; The Association of Trial Lawyers of America. ***PRACTICE AREAS:*** Probate Litigation; Estate Litigation; Contested Wills; Contested Trusts and Estates; Appellate Practice. ***Email:*** daniel.zigray@kolbzigraylaw.com

---

LAVALLEY, LAVALLEY, TODAK & SCHAEFER CO., L.P.A.

Established in 1971

BUILDING F
5800 MONROE STREET
P.O. BOX 8726
TOLEDO, OHIO 43623
Telephone: 419-882-0081
FAX: 419-882-4635
Email: office@lavalley-law.com
URL: http://www.lavalley-law.com

Taxation, Probate, Estate Planning, Trust, Corporate, Partnership, Entity Formation, Mergers & Acquisitions, Corporate Finance, Real Estate, Employee Benefits.

FIRM PROFILE: Each attorney in the firm has an accounting degree in addition to a law degree. Many are Certified Public Accountants with international CPA firm experience. This education and experience enables LaValley, LaValley, Todak & Schaefer to address matters in their fields of practice efficiently in a multi-perspective manner. All attorneys are licensed in Ohio and some are also licensed in Michigan and/or Florida.

RICHARD G. LAVALLEY, JR., born 1958; admitted to bar, 1983, Ohio; 1986, Florida, and U.S. Tax Court. *Education:* University of Toledo (B.B.A., 1980; J.D., 1983). Beta Alpha Psi; Alpha Kappa Psi. *Member:* Toledo and Ohio State Bar Associations; The Florida Bar. ***PRACTICE AREAS:*** Taxation; Corporate; Mergers and Acquisitions; Probate; Estate Planning. ***Email:*** dick.lavalleyjr@lavalley-law.com

DANIEL J. LAVALLEY, born 1960; admitted to bar, 1985, Ohio; 1986, Florida and U.S. Tax Court. *Education:* University of Toledo (B.B.A., 1982; J.D., 1984). *Member:* Toledo and Ohio State Bar Associations; The Florida Bar. ***PRACTICE AREAS:*** Taxation; Real Estate; Probate; Estate Planning; Corporate. ***Email:*** dan.lavalley@lavalley-law.com

MICHAEL J. TODAK, born 1957; admitted to bar, 1982, Ohio; 1986, Michigan and U.S. Tax Court. *Education:* University of Toledo (B.B.A., 1979; J.D., 1982). Blue Key. Certified Public Accountant, Michigan, 1984. *Member:* Toledo (Treasurer, 1997-2002) and Ohio State Bar Associations; State Bar of Michigan; American Institute of Certified Public Accountants; Ohio Society of Certified Public Accountants; Toledo Estate Planning Council. ***PRACTICE AREAS:*** Taxation; Business; Estate Planning; Probate; Mergers and Acquisitions. ***Email:*** mike.todak@lavalley-law.com

JAMES E. SCHAEFER, born 1957; admitted to bar, 1982, Ohio; 1993, U.S. Tax Court. *Education:* John Carroll University (B.S.B.A., 1979); University of Toledo (J.D., 1982). Beta Gamma Sigma; Alpha Sigma Nu; Alpha Kappa Psi. Certified Public Accountant, Ohio, 1983. *Member:* Toledo and Ohio State Bar Associations; American Institute of Certified Public Accountants; Ohio Society of Certified Public Accountants; Toledo Estate Planning Council. ***PRACTICE AREAS:*** Corporate; Mergers and Acquisitions; Real Estate; Taxation; Estate Planning. ***Email:*** jim.schaefer@lavalley-law.com

(This Listing Continued)

DEIDRE A. LIEDEL, born 1969; admitted to bar, 1998, Ohio; 1999, Michigan; 2000, Florida. *Education:* University of Toledo (B.B.A., summa cum laude, 1994; J.D., magna cum laude, 1998). Beta Alpha Psi; Betta Gamma Sigma. Order of the Coif. Certified Public Accountant, Ohio 1999. *Member:* Toledo and Ohio State Bar Associations; State Bar of Michigan; The Florida Bar, Ohio Society of Certified Public Accountants; American Institute of Certified Public Accountants. ***PRACTICE AREAS:*** Taxation; Estate Planning; Probate; Business Law; Real Estate. ***Email:*** deidre.liedel@lavalley-law.com

TIMOTHY J. SEMRO, born 1973; admitted to bar, 1999, Ohio; 2000, Michigan. *Education:* Michigan State University (B.A., Accounting, with honor, 1996); University of Toledo College of Law (J.D., cum laude, 1999). Author: "Nonclaim Statute and Distributions: The Sooner the Better", Probate Law Journal of Ohio, Nov/Dec, 2002; "Ohio Enacts Income on Trusts", Ohio State Bar Association Law You Can Use, Nov., 2002. *Member:* Toledo, Ohio State and American Bar Associations; State Bar of Michigan. ***PRACTICE AREAS:*** Estate Planning; Probate; Corporate. ***Email:*** tim.semro@lavalley-law.com

OF COUNSEL

RICHARD G. LAVALLEY, born 1929; admitted to bar, 1953, Ohio; 1959, U.S. Tax Court. *Education:* University of Toledo (B.B.A., magna cum laude, 1951; J.D., summa cum laude, 1953). Phi Kappa Phi; Delta Theta Phi. Certified Public Accountant, Ohio, 1955. Instructor, Federal Income Tax, University of Toledo College of Law, 1962-1965. *Member:* Toledo, Ohio State and American Bar Associations; American Judicature Society; Ohio Society of Certified Public Accountants. [With U.S. Army, 1946-1947]. ***PRACTICE AREAS:*** Taxation; Corporate Finance; Mergers and Acquisitions; Real Estate; Estate Planning. ***Email:*** dick.lavalleysr@lavalley-law.com

REPRESENTATIVE CLIENTS: Anatrace; Bartz-Viviano Flowers & Gifts; Big Boy Restaurants; Comfort Line Inc.; Fred Christen & Sons; Dynamics Research & Development; Eric Steel, Ltd.; Floral City Beverage; Grogan's Towne Chrysler; Holiday Inn, Perrysburg; Mitchell Development; National Super Services; Pediatric Pulmonary Associates; Palmer & Associates; Gene Paul Builders; Pro-Pak Industries; Rapid Tooling Technologies; Toledo L & L Realty; Whetstone Technology; Yarder Manufacturing; Young Medical Equipment.
REFERENCES: Fifth Third Bank; Key Bank, Ohio; National City Bank.

LYDEN, LIEBENTHAL & CHAPPELL, LTD.

5565 AIRPORT HIGHWAY, SUITE 101
TOLEDO, OHIO 43615
Telephone: 419-867-8900
Fax: 419-867-8909
Email: lydenlaw.com

Business, Commercial, Corporate, Taxation, Probate and Estate Planning, Real Estate, Civil, Business and Commercial Litigation, Family Law, Labor and Employment Law.

PATRICIA G. LYDEN, born Youngstown, Ohio, January 31, 1956; admitted to bar, 1980, Ohio; 2003, Michigan. *Education:* University of Florida (B.A., 1977); University of Toledo (J.D., 1980). *Member:* Toledo, Ohio State and American Bar Associations; State Bar of Michigan; Ohio Board of Bar Examiners. ***PRACTICE AREAS:*** Real Estate; Corporate; Securities; Environmental. ***Email:*** pgl@lydenlaw.com

JON B. LIEBENTHAL, born Toledo, Ohio, May 10, 1960; admitted to bar, 1986, Ohio and U.S. District Court, Northern District of Ohio; 1987, District of Columbia; 2003, Michigan. *Education:* Miami University (B.S., 1982); University of Toledo College of Law (J.D., 1985). Certified Public Accountant, Ohio, 1987. *Member:* Toledo, Ohio State and American (Member, Section of Taxation) Bar Associations; State Bar of Michigan; District of Columbia Bar. ***PRACTICE AREAS:*** Business Planning; Federal Tax; Estate and Gift Tax; Real Estate. ***Email:*** jbl@lydenlaw.com

ERIK GRANT CHAPPELL, born Normal, Illinois, January 9, 1969; admitted to bar, 1994, Michigan and U.S. District Court, Eastern District of Michigan; 1995, U.S. District Court, Northern District of Ohio and U.S. Court of Appeals, Sixth Circuit; 1996, Ohio and U.S. District Court, Western District of Michigan; 2003, U.S. District Court, Southern District of Ohio and U.S. Court of Appeals, Tenth Circuit. *Education:* University of Michigan (B.A., 1991); University of Toledo (J.D., 1994). Recipient, American Jurisprudence Award, Civil Procedure, 1991. Member, Toledo Law Review. *Member:* Toledo, Monroe County and Ohio State Bar Associations; State Bar of Michigan. ***PRACTICE AREAS:*** Civil Litigation; Family Law; Business Litigation; Commercial Litigation; Labor and Employment Law. ***Email:*** egc@lydenlaw.com

---

BRENDA A. RAY, born Toledo, Ohio, October 17, 1969; admitted to bar, 1998, Ohio; 2002, U.S. Tax Court. *Education:* University of Toledo (B.B.A., summa cum laude, 1991); Ohio State University (J.D., 1998). Certified Public Accountant, Ohio, 1994. Author: "Home Office Deduction in Need of Repair: Applying Mixed-Use Allocation Theory to Internal Revenue Code Section 280A(c)," *The Ohio State Law Journal,* Vol. 60, pg. 199 (1999), portions reprinted by permission in 2003 tax law textbook entitled "Taxation a Skills Approach," written by Michael A. Livingston, a Tax and Business Law Professor at Rutgers School of Law, Camden. *Member:* Toledo, Ohio State (Member, Tax Committee) and American (Member, Taxation Section) Bar Associations; Ohio State Law Journal; American Institute of Certified Public Accountants; Ohio Society of Certified Public Accountants (Member, Taxation Section). ***PRACTICE AREAS:*** Business Planning; Business Formation Tax Advantage; Business Reorganization Tax Advantage; Federal Tax Controversies; State Tax Controversies; Sales and Use Tax; Estate and Gift Taxation; Charitable Organizations Law; Private Foundations; Tax Exempt Matters. ***Email:*** bar@lydenlaw.com

OF COUNSEL

MARCI L. KLUMB, born Toledo, Ohio, September 4, 1961; admitted to bar, 1987, Michigan; 1989, Ohio. *Education:* University of Michigan (B.S., with distinction, 1983); George Washington University (J.D., with high honors, 1987). Order of the Coif. Associate, George Washington Law Review, 1986-1987. Author: "Perfection of Security Interests in Intellectual Property," George Washington Law Review, Volume 57, Number 1 (1988).

(This Listing Continued)

LYDEN, LIEBENTHAL & CHAPPELL, LTD., Toledo—Continued

Member: Toledo, Ohio State and American Bar Associations; State Bar of Michigan. ***PRACTICE AREAS:*** Business; Real Estate; Real Estate Finance; Secured Transactions. ***Email:*** mklumb@lydenlaw.com

REPRESENTATIVE CLIENTS: Chempace Corporation; The Lyden Co.; OBARS Machine & Tool Co.; Reichert Stamping Co.; YZ Enterprises, Inc.; Delta Steel Products, Inc.; Advanced Rubber & Plastics, Inc.; Chardan Corp.; True North Energy, LLC; Ort Tool & Die Corporation; Sky Bank; Sky Financial Solutions, Inc.; Root Learning, Inc.; The Image Group of Toledo, Inc.; Bassett Nut Company; C.B. Richard Ellis; Dillin Development Corp.; Tri Star Energy, LLC; Toledo Area Community Credit Union.
REFERENCE: National City Bank.

R. JEFFREY LYDY

4930 HOLLAND-SYLVANIA ROAD
TOLEDO, OHIO 43560-2149
Telephone: 419-882-7100
Fax: 419-882-7201
Email: jefflydy@lydymoan.com
URL: http://www.rjeffreylydy.com

Civil Trial and Appellate Practice, Insurance Defense, Personal Injury, Negligence, Products Liability, Wrongful Death, Legal and Medical Malpractice, Civil Rights, Litigation, Business Litigation.

R. JEFFREY LYDY, born Toledo, Ohio, September 20, 1946; admitted to bar, 1972, Ohio; 1974, U.S. District Court, Northern District of Ohio; 1989, U.S. Court of Appeals, Sixth Circuit; 2002, Michigan; 2003, U.S. District Court, Southern District of Michigan. *Education:* University of Toledo (B.S., 1968; J.D., 1971). *Member:* Toledo Bar Association; Ohio Academy of Trial Lawyers. Certified as a Civil Trial Advocate by the National Board of Trial Advocacy.

REFERENCES: Mid American National Bank & Trust Co.; Charter One Bank; SKY Bank.

MALONE, AULT & FARELL

7654 WEST BANCROFT STREET
TOLEDO, OHIO 43617-1604
Telephone: 419-843-1333
Fax: 419-843-3888
Email: maf@maf-law.com

General Civil Practice in Corporate Law and Commercial Law. Real Estate, Taxation, Probate and Trusts and Estates, Civil Litigation in all State and Federal Courts.

FIRM PROFILE: Malone, Ault & Farell was founded in 1991 by Richard R. Malone and Tim A. Ault. Gregory C. Farell joined the firm in 1995. All three had formerly been associated together in practice with another Toledo firm. Malone, Ault & Farell is engaged in a diversified civil practice providing a wide range of legal services to individuals and small to medium sized businesses.

RICHARD R. MALONE, born Toledo, Ohio, April 25, 1952; admitted to bar, 1977, Ohio and U.S. District Court, Northern District of Ohio; 1979, U.S. District Court, Eastern District of Michigan. *Education:* University of Notre Dame (B.A., 1974); University of Toledo (J.D., 1977). *Member:* Toledo (Member, Board of Trustees, 1995-2001), Ohio State (Member, Board of Governors, Litigation Section, 1990-1995) and American (Member, Litigation Section) Bar Associations; Ohio Academy of Trial Lawyers; The Association of Trial Lawyers of America. ***PRACTICE AREAS:*** Civil Litigation; Commercial Law; Real Estate; Corporate Law; Labor and Employment. ***Email:*** malone@maf-law.com

TIM ALLEN AULT, born Wauseon, Ohio, March 31, 1959; admitted to bar, 1986, Ohio, U.S. District Court, Northern District of Ohio and U.S. Court of Appeals, Sixth Circuit. *Education:* Bowling Green State University (B.S. in Accounting, 1981); University of Toledo (J.D., 1986). Certified Public Accountant, Ohio, 1988. *Member:* Toledo and Ohio State Bar Associations; Ohio Society of Certified Public Accountants. ***PRACTICE AREAS:*** Taxation; Probate; Trusts and Estates; Commercial Law; Real Estate; Personal Injury. ***Email:*** ault@maf-law.com

GREGORY C. FARELL, born Toledo, Ohio, May 3, 1959; admitted to bar, 1984, Ohio, U.S. District Court, Northern District of Ohio and U.S. Court of Appeals, Sixth Circuit. *Education:* University of Toledo (B.B.A., cum laude, 1981; J.D., 1984). *Member:* Toledo, Ohio State and American Bar Associations. ***PRACTICE AREAS:*** Business Law; Corporate Law; Probate; Trusts and Estates; Commercial Law; Real Estate. ***Email:*** farell@maf-law.com

ASSOCIATES

BRADLEY R. WAUGH, born Toledo, Ohio, July 28, 1971; admitted to bar, 1999, Ohio, Michigan and U.S. District Court, Northern District of Ohio. *Education:* University of Toledo (B.S., magna cum laude, 1993; J.D., magna cum laude, 1998). Order of the Coif. Member and Editor, University of Toledo Law Review, 1997-1998. *Member:* Toledo, Ohio State, and American Bar Associations; State Bar of Michigan. ***PRACTICE AREAS:*** Business Law; Commercial Law; Real Estate; Trusts and Estates; Civil Litigation. ***Email:*** waugh@maf-law.com

MILTON E. POMMERANZ, born Toledo, Ohio, August 24, 1977; admitted to bar, 2002, Ohio; 2003, Michigan and U.S. District Court, Northern District of Ohio. *Education:* University of Toledo (B.S., Biology, cum laude, 1999; J.D., 2002). Member, Moot Court Honor Board. Student Member, The University of Toledo Board of Trustees, 1997-1999. *Member:* Toledo, Ohio State and American Bar Associations; State Bar of Michigan. ***PRACTICE AREAS:*** Civil Litigation; Trusts and Estates; Real Estate; Business Law; Labor and Employment. ***Email:*** pommeranz@maf-law.com

(This Listing Continued)

REPRESENTATIVE CLIENTS: Surface Combustion, Inc.; Transtar Electric, Inc.; Schroeder Co.; Marleau-Hercules Fence Co.; Toledo Ticket Company; Image Integration Systems, Inc.; Art Kuhn Company; Willson Builders, Inc.
REFERENCE: Signature Bank.

MARSHALL & MELHORN, LLC

Established in 1896
FOUR SEAGATE, EIGHTH FLOOR
TOLEDO, OHIO 43604
Telephone: 419-249-7100
Facsimile: 419-249-7151
Cable Address: "Patlex Toledo"
Email: attorneys@marshall-melhorn.com
URL: http://www.marshall-melhorn.com

General Civil Practice in Corporate and Commercial Law, Securities, Banking, Tax, Antitrust, Admiralty, Bankruptcy, Computer Law, Probate and Estate Planning and Administration, Real Estate, Health Services, Insurance Defense, Medical Malpractice Defense, Pension and Profit Sharing Law, Labor and Employment Law, Litigation, Patent, Trademark and Copyright Law.

MEMBERS OF FIRM

EDWIN J. MARSHALL (1873-1946)

DONALD F. MELHORN (1889-1974)

JUSTICE G. JOHNSON, JR., born Toledo, Ohio, January 2, 1939; admitted to bar, 1964, Ohio; 2003, Michigan. *Education:* Miami University (B.A., 1961); University of Michigan (J.D., 1964). Listed in *The Best Lawyers in America* in Labor and Employment Law. ***PRACTICE AREAS:*** Labor and Employment Law.

THOMAS W. PALMER, born Cincinnati, Ohio, August 13, 1947; admitted to bar, 1972, Ohio. *Education:* Ohio Wesleyan University (B.A., magna cum laude, 1969); University of Michigan (J.D., 1972). Director and Vice Chairman, Toledo Lucas County Port Authority. ***PRACTICE AREAS:*** Alternative Dispute Resolution; Litigation; Business; Corporate; Employment; Commercial; Construction.

KENNETH J. WHITE, born Bryan, Ohio, April 16, 1948; admitted to bar, 1974, Ohio. *Education:* Bowling Green State University (B.S., cum laude, 1970); University of Toledo (J.D., cum laude, 1974). ***PRACTICE AREAS:*** Medical Malpractice Defense; Alternative Dispute Resolution.

THOMAS P. KILLAM, born Toledo, Ohio, September 23, 1946; admitted to bar, 1976, Ohio. *Education:* University of Toledo (B.E., 1969; J.D., 1975). ***PRACTICE AREAS:*** Business Planning; Estate Planning.

VAUGHN A. HOBLET, born Decatur, Indiana, September 22, 1946; admitted to bar, 1974, Ohio; 1998, Michigan. *Education:* The Ohio State University (B.S., 1968); University of Toledo (J.D., cum laude, 1974); New York University (LL.M. in Taxation, 1975). ***PRACTICE AREAS:*** Bankruptcy; Commercial; Federal Income; Estate and Gift Taxation; Probate.

MICHAEL S. SCALZO, born Toledo, Ohio, March 21, 1953; admitted to bar, 1979, Ohio; 1980, Illinois; 2003, Michigan. *Education:* University of Toledo (B.S.I.E., cum laude, 1975; J.D., 1979). ***PRACTICE AREAS:*** Litigation; Employment; Products Liability; Intellectual Property; Commercial Transactions.

MARSHALL A. BENNETT, JR., born Toledo, Ohio, May 19, 1955; admitted to bar, 1980, Ohio. *Education:* Wittenberg University; University of Toledo (B.A., magna cum laude, 1977); The Ohio State University (J.D., with honors, 1980). ***PRACTICE AREAS:*** Litigation; Alternate Dispute Resolution; Antitrust and Trade Regulation; Commercial; Complex Litigation; Computers and Software; Insurance Coverage; Insurance Defense; Intellectual Property; Employment; Personal Injury; Municipal.

RUTH A. MEACHAM, born Scott City, Missouri, August 11, 1939; admitted to bar, 1981, Ohio. *Education:* Ohio State University; University of Toledo (B.A., summa cum laude, 1976 ; J.D., cum laude, 1981). ***PRACTICE AREAS:*** Labor and Employment; Health Care; Mental Health; Litigation.

LORI W. DECKER, born Cincinnati, Ohio, September 25, 1954; admitted to bar, 1978, Ohio. *Education:* University of Arizona (B.A., magna cum laude, 1975; J.D., 1978). ***PRACTICE AREAS:*** Commercial; Construction; Banking.

A. THOMAS CHRISTENSEN, born Philadelphia, Pennsylvania, January 5, 1952; admitted to bar, 1977, Ohio; 2003, Michigan. *Education:* Illinois Wesleyan University (B.A., cum laude, 1974); University of Toledo (J.D., 1977); College of William & Mary (L.L.M., 1982). ***PRACTICE AREAS:*** Corporate; Probate; Estate Planning; Tax; Employee Benefits.

NANCY D. MOODY, born Findlay, Ohio, April 16, 1946; admitted to bar, 1982, Ohio. *Education:* St. Rita's Hospital School of Nursing (R.N., 1967); Bowling Green State University (B.S.N., magna cum laude, 1977); Ohio Northern University (J.D., 1981). ***PRACTICE AREAS:*** Medical Malpractice Defense; Health Care.

GERARDO ROY ROLLISON, born Warren, Ohio, February 2, 1954; admitted to bar, 1980, Ohio; 1997, Michigan. *Education:* The Ohio State University (B.S., 1976); University of Toledo (J.D., 1980). ***PRACTICE AREAS:*** Health Care.

DAVID L. O'CONNELL, born Ithaca, New York, March 12, 1956; admitted to bar, 1984, Ohio. *Education:* Williams College (B.A., 1978); Case Western Reserve University (J.D., 1984). ***PRACTICE AREAS:*** Labor and Employment.

JENNIFER J. DAWSON, born Cumberland, Maryland, August 13, 1956; admitted to bar, 1984, Ohio. *Education:* Miami University (B.A., 1978); University of Toledo (J.D., 1984). ***PRACTICE AREAS:*** Litigation; Employment; Construction; Lender Liability; Products Liability.

JAMES H. IRMEN, born Toledo, Ohio, September 26, 1959; admitted to bar, 1986, Ohio. *Education:* University of Toledo (B.B.A., cum laude, 1981); University of Toledo College of Law (J.D., cum laude, 1985). ***PRACTICE AREAS:*** Litigation; Construction; Products Liability; Insurance Coverage; Insurance Defense.

(This Listing Continued)

D. EDWARD DOLGORUKOV, born Washington, D.C., October 28, 1944; admitted to bar, 1972, Michigan; 1993, Ohio; registered to practice before U.S. Patent and Trademark Office. *Education:* Wayne State University (B.S.I.E., 1968; J.D., 1972). ***PRACTICE AREAS:*** Intellectual Property.

MARK H. ROSE, born Toledo, Ohio, September 22, 1961; admitted to bar, 1987, Ohio; 2003, Michigan. *Education:* Indiana University (B.S., magna cum laude, 1984); Georgetown University Law Center (J.D., cum laude, 1987). ***PRACTICE AREAS:*** Bankruptcy; Real Estate; Commercial.

DONALD A. SCHURR, born Parma, Ohio, December 6, 1963; admitted to bar, 1989, Ohio; registered to practice before U.S. Patent and Trademark Office. *Education:* Case Western Reserve University (B.S., Polymer Science Engineering, with honors, 1986); University of Toledo College of Law (J.D., magna cum laude, 1989). ***PRACTICE AREAS:*** Intellectual Property.

KENNETH J. MAUER, born Toledo, Ohio, February 12, 1949; admitted to bar, 1985, Ohio; registered to practice before U.S. Patent and Trademark Office. *Education:* University of Toledo (B.S., 1971; J.D., 1985). ***PRACTICE AREAS:*** Patents; Trademarks; Licensing; Environmental.

AMY M. NATYSHAK, born Toledo, Ohio, December 17, 1965; admitted to bar, 1990, Ohio. *Education:* Bowling Green State University (B.A., magna cum laude, 1987); University of Toledo College of Law (J.D., 1989). ***PRACTICE AREAS:*** Litigation; Products Liability; Insurance Defense.

JOHN F. BODIE, JR., born Edwards Air Force Base, California, 1966; admitted to bar, 1991, Ohio. *Education:* Purdue University (B.A., 1988); University of Toledo (J.D., 1991). ***PRACTICE AREAS:*** Medical Malpractice Defense; Health Care; Litigation.

ROMAN ARCE, born Toledo, Ohio, August 16, 1967; admitted to bar, 1992, Ohio. *Education:* University of Notre Dame (B.A., 1989); University of Michigan Law School (J.D., 1992). ***PRACTICE AREAS:*** Labor and Employment; Civil Litigation.

CRAIG P. BURNS, born Marion, Indiana, November 10, 1965; admitted to bar, 1990, Ohio. *Education:* Miami University (B.A., summa cum laude, 1987); University of Virginia (J.D., 1990). ***PRACTICE AREAS:*** Business Planning; Corporate; Health Care; Federal and State Taxation.

MATTHEW J. FISCHER, born Toledo, Ohio, November 4, 1959; admitted to bar, 1991, Ohio. *Education:* University of Toledo (B.B.A., cum laude, 1984; J.D., magna cum laude, 1990). ***PRACTICE AREAS:*** Real Estate; Commercial Transactions.

ELIZABETH E. BAER, born Holland, Michigan, March 27, 1967; admitted to bar, 1995, Ohio. *Education:* Michigan State University (B.A., 1989); University of Toledo (J.D., 1994). ***PRACTICE AREAS:*** Medical Malpractice Defense; Health Care; Insurance Defense Litigation.

MICHAEL A. GONZALEZ, born Lorain, Ohio, May 14, 1972; admitted to bar, 1998, Ohio. *Education:* Bowling Green State University (B.A., 1994); University of Toledo (J.D., magna cum laude, 1998). Order of the Coif. Member, Law Review. ***PRACTICE AREAS:*** Litigation; Labor and Employment.

STEPHEN P. EVANS, born Hinsdale, Illinois, January 20, 1972; admitted to bar, 1998, Ohio; registered to practice before U.S. Patent and Trademark Office. *Education:* Ohio State University (B.S.A.A.E., 1994); University of Toledo (J.D., cum laude, 1998). Member, Law Review. ***PRACTICE AREAS:*** Intellectual Property; Litigation.

BRIDGETT J. ROOT, born Fremont, Ohio, June 11, 1973; admitted to bar, 1998, Ohio. *Education:* Ohio Northern University (B.S.B.A., 1995); University of Toledo (J.D., cum laude, 1998). ***PRACTICE AREAS:*** Estate Planning; Tax.

ASSOCIATES

MARK A. HIXON, born Lima, Ohio, August 28, 1966; admitted to bar, 1992, Ohio; registered to practice before U.S. Patent and Trademark Office. *Education:* University of Cincinnati (B.S., Chemical Engineering, 1989); Ohio Northern University (J.D., 1992). ***PRACTICE AREAS:*** Intellectual Property.

KRISTEN A. CONNELLY, born Toledo, Ohio, March 2, 1972; admitted to bar, 1998, Ohio. *Education:* University of Colorado at Boulder (B.A., 1994); University of Toledo (J.D., 1998). ***PRACTICE AREAS:*** Medical Malpractice Defense; Health Care; Litigation.

JOHN A. BORELL, JR., born Syracuse, New York, December 25, 1969; admitted to bar, 1997, Ohio. *Education:* Miami University; University of Toledo (B.B.A., 1993; J.D., 1997). ***PRACTICE AREAS:*** Commercial Litigation; Personal Injury; Medical Malpractice.

STEPHEN M. SADOWSKI, born Cincinnati, Ohio, October 23, 1970; admitted to bar, 1996, Ohio. *Education:* John Carroll University (B.S., 1993); University of Toledo College of Law (J.D., 1996). ***PRACTICE AREAS:*** Corporate Law; Business Organization; Mergers, Acquisitions and Divestitures; Residential Real Estate; Commercial Real Estate; Health Care; Securities; Contracts.

COUNSEL

DONALD F. MELHORN, JR., born Toledo, Ohio, March 20, 1935; admitted to bar, 1960, Ohio and District of Columbia. *Education:* Yale University (B.A., 1957); Harvard University (LL.B., 1960). Adjunct Professor of Law, University of Toledo College of Law, 1999—. ***PRACTICE AREAS:*** Commercial; Litigation.

PAUL M. KRAUS, born Toledo, Ohio, December 19, 1932; admitted to bar, 1957, Ohio. *Education:* University of Notre Dame (B.S.C., 1954; LL.B., 1957). ***PRACTICE AREAS:*** Estate Planning; Elder Law; Guardianship; Estate Administration; Residential Real Estate.

PHILLIP S. OBERLIN, born Toledo, Ohio, April 11, 1933; admitted to bar, 1959, Ohio; registered to practice before U.S. Patent and Trademark Office. *Education:* Purdue University (B.S., in Metallurgical Engineering, 1955); George Washington University (J.D., with honors, 1959). ***PRACTICE AREAS:*** Patents; Trademarks; Business Law; Licensing.

(This Listing Continued)

CLARE K. SMITH, born Ann Arbor, Michigan, December 26, 1968; admitted to bar, 1994, Ohio. *Education:* DePauw University (B.A., 1990); Indiana University (J.D., 1994). *Member:* Toledo Women's Bar Association (President, 1998-1999); Ohio Women's Bar Association (Trustee, 2000-2003). ***PRACTICE AREAS:*** Litigation; Employment; Business.

COUNSEL FOR: Acklin Stamping; Advanced Metal Precision Products; Aro Corporation; Auburndale Company, Inc.; Baron Drawn Steel Corp.; Bryan Custom Plastics; Camway Transportation, Inc.; Challenger Motor Freight; Children Services Board; Chubb Insurance Company; Churchill's Super Markets, Inc.; City of Bowling Green; City of Toledo; Crum & Forster Insurance Cos.; Dana Corporation; The Doctor's Company; Doehler-Jarvis/Farley Ind.; Dunbar Mechanical, Inc.; Fifth Third Bank; Finkbeiner, Pettis & Strout; General Mills, Inc.; Gerlinger Company; Great Lakes Corrugated Corp.; Hayes Wheels International, Inc.; HCR-Manor Care; Kelsey-Hayes Company; The Kiemle-Hankins Company; The Lathrop Co.; Libbey-Owens-Ford Co.; Lucas County Children Services; Lutheran Home; Meijers, Inc.; Memorial Hospital; Midwest Stamping Company; MIIX Lawrenceville Property & Casualty; Motor Carrier Service, Inc.; National Lime & Stone Co.; OHIC Insurance Company; Owens-Corning; Paben-Harlan Die Cutting and Engraving Co.; Pro Assurance; Professional Underwriters Liability Insurance Company; Professionals Advocate Insurance Company; ProMedica Health System; Ranger Insurance Company; Rescue Mental Health Services; Riverside Machine and Automation, Ltd.; Sauder Woodworking Company; Sky Bank; T.L. Industries; Teleflex, Inc.; Toledo Engineering Co.; Toledo-Lucas County Public Library; Toledo Symphony Orchestra; United Way of Greater Toledo; Visiting Nurse Service; Waste Management, Inc.; Zepf Community Mental Health Center.

McHUGH, DeNUNE & McCARTHY, LTD.

5580 MONROE STREET
TOLEDO, OHIO 43560
Telephone: 419-885-3597
Fax: 419-885-3861

Trial and Appellate Practice in Civil, Criminal and Domestic Relations Law, Employment Law, Probate and Estate Planning, Corporate and Commercial Law, Non-Profit Organizations and Real Estate.

JOHN J. McHUGH, III, born Toledo, Ohio, October 8, 1951; admitted to bar, 1976, Ohio. *Education:* University of Notre Dame (A.B., magna cum laude, 1973; J.D., 1976). Adjunct Professor, Trial Practice, University of Toledo College of Law, 1980-1986. *Member:* Toledo and Ohio State (Member, Sections on: Litigation; Tort and Insurance Practice) Bar Associations. Fellow, Ohio State Bar Foundation. ***PRACTICE AREAS:*** Civil Trial Law; Appellate Practice; Real Estate; Corporate Law; Commercial Law. ***Email:*** mchugh@mchughlaw.com

RALPH DeNUNE, III, born Toledo, Ohio, November 29, 1944; admitted to bar, 1975, Ohio; 1977, U.S. Court of Appeals, Sixth Circuit; 1981, U.S. Supreme Court. *Education:* Ohio University (B.F.A., 1966); University of Toledo (J.D., 1974). Delta Theta Phi. *Member:* Toledo and Ohio State Bar Associations; National Association of Criminal Defense Lawyers; The Association of American Trial Lawyers; American Judicature Society. ***PRACTICE AREAS:*** Civil Litigation; Business Litigation; Commercial Litigation; Receiverships; Criminal Law; Domestic Relations. ***Email:*** denune@mchughlaw.com

STEPHEN B. MOSIER, born Van Wert, Ohio, May 11, 1952; admitted to bar, 1977, Ohio and U.S. District Court, Northern District of Ohio; 1986, U.S. Court of Appeals, Sixth Circuit; 1990, U.S. District Court, Southern District of Ohio; 1994, U.S. Supreme Court. *Education:* Bowling Green State University (B.A., magna cum laude, 1974); Northwestern University (J.D., cum laude, 1977). *Member:* Ohio State (Member, Antitrust Section; Board of Governors) and American Bar Associations. (Resident). ***PRACTICE AREAS:*** Commercial Litigation; Class Action Litigation; Complex Litigation; Antitrust and Trade Regulation; Appellate Practice. ***Email:*** mosier@mchughlaw.com

KAREN J. WENSINK, born Cleveland, Ohio, February 25, 1971; admitted to bar, 2002, Ohio and U.S. District Court, Northern District of Ohio; 2003, Michigan; 2004, U.S. District Court, Eastern District of Michigan. *Education:* The Ohio State University (B.A., 1993); Bowling Green State University (B.S., 1995); University of Toledo (J.D., 2002). *Member:* Toledo and Ohio State Bar Associations; State Bar of Michigan. ***LANGUAGES:*** French.

FREDERICK E. KALMBACH, born Toledo, Ohio; admitted to bar, 2002, Ohio. *Education:* University of Toledo (B.S., Business Administration, 1968); University of Toledo College of Law (J.D., 2001). *Member:* Toledo and Ohio State Bar Associations.

OF COUNSEL

JOHN J. CALLAHAN, born Toledo, Ohio, February 5, 1922; admitted to bar, 1952, Ohio; 1966, U.S. Supreme Court and U.S. Court of Military Appeals; 1973, U.S. Court of Appeals, Sixth Circuit. *Education:* John Carroll University (A.B., 1949); University of Michigan (LL.B., 1952). *Member:* Toledo (President, 1969-1970), Ohio State (Member, 1965— and Chairman, 1976-1982, Criminal Justice Committee) and American (Member, Criminal Law Section) Bar Associations. Fellow, American College of Trial Lawyers (1982-1992).

THE McQUADES CO., L.P.A.

TOLEDO, OHIO

(See Swanton)

General Civil Practice. Personal Injury, Wrongful Death, Products Liability, Medical Malpractice, Real Estate, Corporate and Business Law. Probate and Estate Planning, Collections, Municipal and Zoning Law. Family Law, Criminal Law. Trials and Appellate Practice in all Courts.

JEFFREY P. NUNNARI

3425 EXECUTIVE PARKWAY, SUITE 111
TOLEDO, OHIO 43606
Telephone: 419-578-9246
Fax: 419-531-5675
Email: jp59691@yahoo.com

Civil Litigation, Criminal Law, Appellate Practice, Drug Crimes, Felonies, Homicide, Misdemeanors, Parole and Probation, Sexual Assault.

JEFFREY P. NUNNARI, born Dayton, Ohio, November 12, 1962; admitted to bar, 1992, Ohio. *Education:* Wright State University (B.A., 1988); University of Toledo (J.D., 1992). *Member:* Wood County, Toledo, Ohio State and American Bar Associations. ***REPORTED CASES:*** State v. Williams, 57 Ohio St.3d 24 (1991); Nickel v. Carter, 104 Ohio St. 3d 542 (2004); In re: Carlos O., 96 Ohio App.3d 252 (1994); State v. Davis, 133 Ohio App.3d 114 (1999); State v. Lyons, 138 Ohio App.3d 614 (2000); State ex rel. Wayne Cty. Child Support Enforcement Agency v. Tanner, 146 Ohio App.3d 765 (2001); State v. Perry, 147 Ohio App.3d 164 (2002); State v. Lamb, 156 Ohio App.3d 128 (2004); State v. Tyren, 91 Ohio Misc.2d 67 (1998). ***PRACTICE AREAS:*** Litigation Law.

OGNE, ALBERTS & STUART, P.C.

TOLEDO, OHIO

(See Troy, Michigan)

General Civil Litigation Practice in State and Federal Courts. Insurance Defense, General Negligence, Product Liability, Employment and Commercial Litigation, Worker's Compensation, Professional Negligence and Aviation Law. Trials and Appeals, Business Law, Wills, Trusts & Estates, Probate, Criminal Law.

SAMUEL OSNOWITZ

2727 N. HOLLAND SYLVANIA ROAD, SUITE K
TOLEDO, OHIO 43615-1800
Telephone: 419-531-1021
FAX: 419-531-1026
Email: SamOsnowitz@buckeye-express.com
URL: http://www.osnowitzlaw.com

Commercial Law, Condominium Law, Buying and Selling of Businesses, Starting a Business, Business Enterprises, Small Business, Limited Liability Company Law, Family Business, Wills and Probate, Real Estate Law.

SAMUEL OSNOWITZ, born Toledo, Ohio, December 15, 1945; admitted to bar, 1971, District of Columbia; 1973, New York; 1976, Ohio. *Education:* University of Toledo (B.B.A., 1968); George Washington University (J.D., with honors, 1971); New York University (LL.M., Taxation, 1973). *Member:* Toledo and Ohio State (Member: Probate and Trust Law Section, 1990—; Real Property Section, 1990—) Bar Associations. ***PRACTICE AREAS:*** Corporate; Contracts; Business Law; Real Estate Law; Wills; Probate; Taxation.

REFERENCE: Fifth Third Bank of Toledo, Ohio N.A.

JOHN F. POTTS

NATIONAL CITY BANK BUILDING
405 MADISON AVENUE, SUITE 1010
TOLEDO, OHIO 43604-1211
Telephone: 419-255-2800
Fax: 419-255-1105
URL: http://www.jfplain.com
Email: jfplaw@ameritech.net
URL: http://www.jfplaw.com

Criminal Defense, White Collar Criminal Defense, Criminal Forfeiture, Civil Forfeiture, Federal Criminal Law, Post-Conviction Remedies, Habeas Corpus, Business Litigation, Commercial Litigation, Civil Litigation, Trial Practice, Appellate Practice Federal Litigation.

JOHN F. POTTS, born Stamford, Connecticut, October 13, 1952; admitted to bar, 1978, Ohio and U.S. District Court, Northern District of Ohio; 1980, Michigan and U.S. Court of Appeals, 6th Circuit; 1981, U.S. District Court, Western District of Michigan; 1982, U.S. District Court, Eastern District of Michigan; 1990, U.S. Court of Appeals, 4th Circuit; 1999, U.S. Court of Appeals, 7th Circuit and U.S. District Court, Southern District of Ohio; 2001, U.S. Court of Federal Claims; 2002, U.S. Supreme Court; 2004, U.S. Court of Appeals, Tenth Circuit. *Education:* Grinnell College (B.A., 1974); University of Toledo (J.D., 1978). Member, University of Toledo Law Review. *Member:* Toledo, Ohio State, Federal and American Bar Associations; State Bar of Michigan; Sixth Circuit Judicial Conference (Life Member). ***PRACTICE AREAS:*** Criminal Defense; White Collar Criminal Defense; Criminal Forfeiture; Civil Forfeiture; Federal Criminal Law; Post-Conviction Remedies; Habeas Corpus; Business Litigation; Commercial Litigation; Civil Litigation; Trial Practice; Appellate Practice; Federal Litigation.

MARK L. POWERS

TOLEDO, OHIO

(See Wauseon)

General Civil Trial Practice in all State Courts. Personal Injury, Wills and Probate, Trusts and Estates, Estate Planning, Real Estate, Bankruptcy, Creditors Rights, Family Law, Divorce, Adoptions, Child Custody, Child Support, Domestic Relations, Collections, Commercial.

JOAN H. RIFE

TWO MARITIME PLAZA
TOLEDO, OHIO 43604
Telephone: 419-244-4000
Fax: 419-241-1900
Email: jrife4000@aol.com

Workers Compensation, Transportation, Social Security Disability.

JOAN HELEN RIFE, born Grosse Pointe, Michigan, July 28, 1957; admitted to bar, 1982, Ohio. *Education:* Adrian College (B.A., 1978); University of Toledo (J.D., 1982). Member, National Organization of Social Security Claimant's Representatives (NOSSCR). *Member:* Toledo, Ohio State and Lucas County Bar Associations; Toledo Women's Bar Association. ***PRACTICE AREAS:*** Workers Compensation; Transportation; Social Security Disability. ***Email:*** jrife4000@aol.com

RITTER, ROBINSON, McCREADY & JAMES

Established in 1927
1850 NATIONAL CITY BANK BUILDING
405 MADISON AVENUE
TOLEDO, OHIO 43604
Telephone: 419-241-3213
FAX: 419-241-4925
URL: http://www.rrmjlaw.com

General Civil Practice. Insurance, Trials and Appeals, Municipal Law, Corporation, Probate, Estate Planning, Real Estate, Personal Injury, Product Liability, Labor and Employment. Federal Practice.

FIRM PROFILE: Our firm was established in 1927 by George W. Ritter. The firm represents a variety of individual, business and government clients throughout northwestern Ohio. The firm is included in the Bar Register of Preeminent Lawyers.

MEMBERS OF FIRM

GEORGE W. RITTER (1886-1979)
MILTON C. BOESEL, SR. (1893-1993)
ELLIS F. ROBINSON (Retired)
MILTON C. BOESEL, JR. (Retired)
WILLIAM S. McCREADY (Retired)

TIMOTHY C. JAMES, born Delaware, Ohio, November 30, 1954; admitted to bar, 1980, Ohio. *Education:* Miami University (B.A., cum laude, 1977); The Ohio State University (J.D., 1980). Phi Beta Kappa; Phi Kappa Phi. Assistant Prosecutor, City of Maumee, 1981-1982. *Member:* Toledo, Ohio State and American Bar Associations; Ohio Association of Civil Trial Attorneys; Defense Research Institute. ***PRACTICE AREAS:*** Insurance; Personal Injury; Civil Litigation; Corporate. ***Email:*** james@rrmj.com

MARK P. SEITZINGER, born Youngstown, Ohio, January 29, 1963; admitted to bar, 1989, Ohio. *Education:* Kent State University (B.A., summa cum laude, 1985); The Ohio State University (J.D., 1988). Phi Alpha Delta; Phi Beta Kappa. *Member:* Portsmouth, Ohio State and American Bar Associations; Ohio Association of Civil Trial Attorneys. ***PRACTICE AREAS:*** Insurance Defense Law; Trial Practice. ***Email:*** seitzinger@rrmj.com

ASSOCIATES

SHANNON JULIENNE GEORGE, born Toledo, Ohio, April 7, 1970; admitted to bar, 1994, Michigan; 1997, Ohio. *Education:* Hillsdale College (B.A., cum laude, 1990); University of Toledo (J.D., 1993; M.A., 1995). Instructor, Department of Philosophy, University of Toledo, 1995-1996. *Member:* Toledo and Ohio State Bar Associations; State Bar of Michigan. ***PRACTICE AREAS:*** Insurance; Negligence; Premises Liability; Trial Practice; Appellate Practice. ***Email:*** dedmon@rrmj.com

VAN P. ANDRES, born Sandusky, Ohio, June 29, 1963; admitted to bar, 1989, Ohio; 1990, U.S. District Court, Northern District of Ohio. *Education:* The Ohio State University (B.A., 1985); University of Toledo (J.D., 1988). *Member:* Toledo and Ohio State Bar Associations. ***PRACTICE AREAS:*** Insurance; Negligence; Political Subdivision Liability; Workers Compensation; Premises Liability; Trial Practice; Appellate Practice. ***Email:*** andres@rrmj.com

COUNSEL FOR: Amerisure Companies; Carruth Studios, Inc.; Celina Insurance Companies; Charlie's Dodge, Incorporated; General Accident Insurance Company; Great American Insurance Companies; GRE Insurance Company; Grogan Chrysler Plymouth, Incorporated; Hall Toledo, Inc.; Midwestern Insurance Company; Ohio Casualty Insurance Companies; Personal Service Insurance Company; The Mehring Company; Toledo Auto Electric Company; Toledo Cast Tooling, Inc.; United Ohio Insurance Companies; Village of Ottawa Hills, Ohio; Westfield Insurance Companies.

ROBISON, CURPHEY & O'CONNELL

LIMITED LIABILITY COMPANY
NINTH FLOOR
FOUR SEAGATE
TOLEDO, OHIO 43604
Telephone: 419-249-7900
Telecopier: 419-249-7911
Email: firm@rcolaw.com
URL: http://www.rcolaw.com

Adrian, Michigan Office: 123 E. Maumee Street. Telephone: 517-263-8811. Fax: 517-263-8733.
Findlay, Ohio Office: 330 South Main Street. Telephone: 419-429-7900. Fax: 419-429-7911.

(This Listing Continued)

Litigation, Appellate Practice, Business Law, Corporate Law, Commercial Law, Construction Law and Probate, Commercial Real Estate, Real Estate, Health Care, Hospital Law, Insurance, Insurance Defense, Personal Injury, Labor and Employment, Medical Malpractice Defense, Bankruptcy and Creditor's Rights, Environmental Law, Employee Benefits, Railroad Law, Trusts and Estates, Estate Planning, Arbitration and Mediation.

FIRM PROFILE: Founded in 1874 as Brown and Geddes, the firm has been honored by the Ohio Senate for its 125 years of professional service. The firm actively engages in a diversified general practice in northwest Ohio and southeast Michigan from its Toledo, Ohio, Findlay, Ohio and Adrian, Michigan offices. Well into its second century of service, the firm remains dedicated to meeting both the traditional and the evolving needs of its clients.

MEMBERS OF FIRM

DOUGLAS E. METZ, born Hayesville, Ohio, December 23, 1940; admitted to bar, 1965, Ohio. *Education:* Capital University (B.A., 1962); The Ohio State University (J.D., 1965). *Member:* National Association of Estate Planning Councils. ***PRACTICE AREAS:*** Estate Planning Law; Probate Law; Trust Law; Corporate Law; Commercial Law; Real Estate Law. ***Email:*** dmetz@rcolaw.com

DAVID W. STUCKEY, born Fremont, Ohio, November 26, 1950; admitted to bar, 1975, Ohio. *Education:* Capital University (B.A., summa cum laude, 1972); The Ohio State University (J.D., cum laude, 1975). *Member:* National Association of Railroad Trial Counsel. ***PRACTICE AREAS:*** Litigation; Insurance Defense; Medical Malpractice; Railroad Law; Appellate Practice; Professional Liability Law. ***Email:*** dstuckey@rcolaw.com

TIMOTHY D. KRUGH, born Lima, Ohio, September 22, 1953; admitted to bar, 1978, Ohio. *Education:* Mount Union College (B.A., magna cum laude, 1975); University of Toledo (J.D., cum laude, 1978). *Member:* American Health Lawyers Association; Society of Ohio Healthcare Attorneys; Defense Research Institute. ***PRACTICE AREAS:*** Hospital Law; Medical Malpractice Defense; Health Care Law; Self Insured Defense; Litigation. ***Email:*** tkrugh@rcolaw.com

C. PHILIP BAITHER, III, born Toledo, Ohio, May 27, 1953; admitted to bar, 1980, Ohio; 1992, Michigan. *Education:* Yale University (B.A., 1975); University of Toledo (J.D., cum laude, 1980). *Member:* American Health Lawyers Association. (Certified Specialist in Labor and Employment Law, Ohio State Bar Association). ***PRACTICE AREAS:*** Employment Law; Health Care Law; Litigation. ***Email:*** pbaither@rcolaw.com

JAMES E. BRAZEAU, born Toledo, Ohio, October 22, 1953; admitted to bar, 1978, Ohio; 1992, Michigan. *Education:* University of Toledo (B.A., 1975; J.D., cum laude, 1978). *Member:* International Association of Defense Counsel. ***PRACTICE AREAS:*** Health Care Law; Hospital Law; Medical Malpractice; Products Liability; Litigation. ***Email:*** jbrazeau@rcolaw.com

MICHAEL S. MESSENGER, born Flint, Michigan, February 22, 1958; admitted to bar, 1983, Ohio. *Education:* Georgetown University (B.S.B.A., 1980); The Ohio State University (J.D., cum laude, 1983). ***PRACTICE AREAS:*** Corporate Law; Commercial Law; Creditors Rights; Bankruptcy. ***Email:*** mmessenger@rcolaw.com

JULIA SMITH WILEY, born Fort Jennings, Ohio, September 21, 1959; admitted to bar, 1984, Ohio. *Education:* University of Dayton (B.A., magna cum laude, 1981); The Ohio State University (J.D., cum laude, 1984). Phi Alpha Theta. *Member:* Toledo Bar Association (Secretary, 2002—; Board of Trustees, 1998-2002); National Association of Railroad Trial Counsel; Morrison R. Waite Inns of Court (Master); Defense Research Institute. Fellow: Toledo Bar Foundation. ***PRACTICE AREAS:*** Civil Litigation; Medical Malpractice Defense; Nursing Liability; Federal Employers Liability Act (FELA). ***Email:*** jwiley@rcolaw.com

THOMAS A. GIBSON, born Toledo, Ohio, April 16, 1956; admitted to bar, 1984, Kentucky 1986, Ohio. *Education:* University of Toledo (B.S.C.E., 1978; J.D., magna cum laude, 1984). Order of the Coif; Phi Kappa Phi. ***PRACTICE AREAS:*** Commercial Law; Real Estate Law; Environmental Law. ***Email:*** tgibson@rcolaw.com

JEAN ANN S. SIELER, born Toledo, Ohio, January 28, 1961; admitted to bar, 1987, Ohio; 1988, Michigan. *Education:* University of Toledo (A.S., 1981; B.S., magna cum laude, 1983; J.D., cum laude, 1986). Order of the Coif. *Member:* Forum on the Construction Industry; Defense Research Institute; Ohio Association of Civil Trial Attorneys; Michigan Defense Trial Counsel. ***PRACTICE AREAS:*** Health Care; Medical Malpractice; Commercial Litigation. ***Email:*** jsieler@rcolaw.com

KATHRYN M. MOHR, born Tecumseh, Michigan, June 5, 1962; admitted to bar, 1987, Ohio; 1988, Michigan. *Education:* Adrian College (B.A., summa cum laude, 1984); University of Toledo (J.D., cum laude, 1987). Order of the Coif. ***PRACTICE AREAS:*** Commercial Real Estate; Business Law; Wills; Corporate Law; Trust Law. ***Email:*** kmohr@rcolaw.com

THOMAS J. ANTONINI, born Toledo, Ohio, May 1, 1963; admitted to bar, 1988, Ohio. *Education:* University of Michigan; University of Notre Dame (B.A., 1985; J.D., 1988). *Member:* National Association of Railroad Trial Counsel; Defense Research Institute; Ohio Association of Civil Trial Attorneys; National Lawyers Association. ***PRACTICE AREAS:*** Litigation; Insurance Defense; Personal Injury Defense; Product Liability; Railroad Law; Business Transactions. ***Email:*** tantonini@rcolaw.com

WILLIAM V. BEACH, born Findlay, Ohio, January 3, 1962; admitted to bar, 1988, Ohio. *Education:* University of Pittsburgh (B.A., 1984); University of Toledo (J.D., 1988). ***PRACTICE AREAS:*** Employment Law; Discrimination Law. ***Email:*** wbeach@rcolaw.com

JEAN M. O'BRIEN, born Tecumseh, Michigan, August 19, 1950; admitted to bar, 1989, Ohio and Michigan. *Education:* Olivet Nazarene University (B.S.N, 1972); University of Toledo (J.D., 1988). *Member:* American Health Lawyers Association; Society of Ohio Healthcare Attorneys. ***PRACTICE AREAS:*** Hospital and Health Care Law; Medical Malpractice Defense; Physician Practices. ***Email:*** jobrien@rcolaw.com

D. CASEY TALBOTT, born Dayton, Ohio, September 25, 1964; admitted to bar, 1990, Ohio. *Education:* The Ohio State University (B.A., cum laude, 1987; J.D., 1990). *Member:* Ohio Association of Civil Trial Attorneys; National Association of Railroad Trial Counsel; Defense Research Institute. ***PRACTICE AREAS:*** Insurance; Insurance Defense; Litigation; Negligence; Personal Injury; Premises Liability; Railroad Law; Torts. ***Email:*** ctalbott@rcolaw.com

JAMES R. KNEPP, II, born Akron, Ohio, May 6, 1964; admitted to bar, 1992, Ohio; 2003, Michigan. *Education:* Mount Union College (B.A., magna cum laude, 1986); Bowling Green State University (M.A., 1987); University of Toledo (J.D., summa cum laude, 1992); Order of the Coif. *Member:* National Association of Railroad Trial Counsel; Ohio Association of Civil Trial Attorneys; Defense Research Institute; Morrison R. Waite Inn of Court. ***PRACTICE AREAS:*** Litigation; Commercial Litigation; Products Liability; Railroad Law; Medical Malpractice Defense. ***Email:*** jknepp@rcolaw.com

PETER N. LAVALETTE, born Weymouth, Massachusetts, December 29, 1963; admitted to bar, 1994, Ohio. *Education:* U.S. Coast Guard Academy (B.S., 1986); University of Toledo (J.D., 1994). *Member:* Defense Research Institute; Ohio Association of Civil Trial Attorneys. [Lt. U.S. Coast Guard, 1986-1991]. ***PRACTICE AREAS:*** Commercial Litigation; Medical Malpractice Defense; Products Liability; Insurance Coverage; Casualty Defense Litigation. ***Email:*** plavalette@rcolaw.com

SCOTT A. HASELMAN, born Lima, Ohio, October 4, 1969; admitted to bar, 1995, Ohio. *Education:* University of Toledo (B.B.A., cum laude, 1992; J.D., summa cum laude, 1995). Order of the Coif. ***PRACTICE AREAS:*** Litigation; Personal Injury; Insurance Coverage. ***Email:*** shaselman@rcolaw.com

ASSOCIATES

MICHAEL R. OLSAVER, born Adrian, Michigan, January 11, 1974; admitted to bar, 1999, Michigan (Not admitted in Ohio). *Education:* Michigan State University (B.A., 1996); DePaul University (J.D., 1999). ***PRACTICE AREAS:*** Real Estate; Trusts and Estates; Business Law; Litigation. ***Email:*** molsaver@rcolaw.com

DANIEL G. HAZARD, born St. Clair, Michigan, November 5, 1972; admitted to bar, 2001, Ohio; 2003, U.S. District Court, Northern District of Ohio. *Education:* The Ohio State University (B.A., 1996); University of Toledo (J.D., cum laude, 2001). *Member:* Defense Research Institute; Ohio Association of Civil Trial Attorneys; American Health Lawyers Association. ***PRACTICE AREAS:*** Litigation. ***Email:*** dhazard@rcolaw.com

JULIA E. BENZIGER, born Delaware, Ohio, March 31, 1972; admitted to bar, 2002, Ohio. *Education:* Ohio Northern University (B.S., Biology, 1994; B.S., Medical Technology, 1995); University of Toledo College of Law (J.D., cum laude, 2001). Member, Biology Honor Society, Ohio Northern University. Certified Medical Technologist, American Society of Clinical Pathologists, 1995. ***PRACTICE AREAS:*** Business Law; Corporate Law; Commercial Law; Mergers and Acquisitions. ***Email:*** jbenziger@rcolaw.com

KIMBERLY M. THOMAS, born Toledo, Ohio, July 26, 1977; admitted to bar, 2003, Ohio and U.S. District Court, Northern District of Ohio. *Education:* The Ohio State University (B.S.N., 1998); Ohio Northern University (J.D., 2003). Sigma Theta Tau International; Phi Kappa Phi; Order of Barristers. Registered Nurse, Ohio, 1998. *Member:* The American Association of Nurse Attorneys. ***PRACTICE AREAS:*** Medical Malpractice Defense; Insurance Coverage; Civil Practice. ***Email:*** kthomas@rcolaw.com

BRADLEY L. BLANDIN, born Toledo, Ohio, April 16, 1975; admitted to bar, 2004, Ohio. *Education:* Huntington College (B.S., magna cum laude, 1997); University of Toledo (J.D., cum laude, 2003). ***PRACTICE AREAS:*** Estate Planning; Corporate Law; Business Law; Taxation; Real Estate. ***Email:*** bblandin@rcolaw.com

MARK A. OZIMEK, born Cleveland, Ohio, June 23, 1979; admitted to bar, 2004, Ohio. *Education:* Bowling Green State University (B.A., 2001); University of Toledo (J.D., magna cum laude, 2004). ***PRACTICE AREAS:*** Civil Practice. ***Email:*** mozimek@rcolaw.com

RETIRED

JOHN M. CURPHEY, born Columbus, Ohio, June 8, 1926; admitted to bar, 1953, Ohio. *Education:* The Ohio State University (B.A., 1948; J.D., 1953). (Retired)

OF COUNSEL

MAURICE D. O'CONNELL, born Ticonderoga, New York, November 9, 1929; admitted to bar, 1956, Ohio. *Education:* Phillips Exeter Academy; Williams College (B.A., 1950); Cornell University (LL.B., 1956). Phi Delta Phi. Fellow, Ohio State Bar Foundation. ***PRACTICE AREAS:*** Corporate Law; Labor Law.

E. THOMAS MAGUIRE, born Boston, Massachusetts, January 25, 1937; admitted to bar, 1963, Ohio. *Education:* Dartmouth College (A.B., cum laude, 1958); Stanford University; The Ohio State University (J.D., 1963). Fellow: American College of Trial Lawyers; Ohio State Bar Foundation. Listed in Best Lawyers in American and Ohio Super Lawyers. *Member:* National Association of Railroad Trial Counsel (Executive Committee, 1990-1996). ***PRACTICE AREAS:*** Litigation. ***Email:*** tmaguire@rcolaw.com

JAMES J. ROBISON (1922-1986)

COUNSEL FOR: Adrian College; American Commerce Insurance Company; Buckeye Machine Fabricators; The D.S. Brown Company; CN North America; Carolina Casualty Company; Casualty Insurance Consultants; Catholic Healthcare Partners; Church Mutual Company; Community Memorial Hospital; Erie Insurance Group; Farmland Insurance Company; Fifth Third Bank; ITT Hartford; I and K Distributors, Inc.; Independent Concrete Pipe; Indiana Insurance Co.; KeyBank National Association; Lake States Insurance Company; Lakeview Farms, Inc.; Liberty Mutual Insurance Group; Medical Protective Insurance Company; The Mennel Milling Company; Mercy Health Partners; Mercy Hospital of Tiffin; Mercy Hospital of Willard; MetLife Auto and Home; Motorists Insurance Companies; Nationwide Insurance Companies; Norfolk Southern Railway; Ohio Bar Liability Insurance; OHIC Insurance; Ottawa Rubber Company; Paulding County Hospital; Preferred Professional Insurance Company; ProAssurance Insurance Company; Progressive Insurance Company; Race Spec; Rail America, Inc.; St. Anne Mercy Hospital; St.Charles Mercy Hospital; St. Paul Fire & Marine Insurance; St. Rita''s Medical Center; St.Vincent Mercy Medical Center; Scottsdale Insurance Company; Sentry Insurance Companies; The Seneca Wire & Manufacturing Company; Solvay Automotive, Inc.; VanWert County Hospital; Vreba-Hoff Dairy Development; Yoder & Frey Auctioneers, Inc.

(This Listing Continued)

ROETZEL & ANDRESS

A LEGAL PROFESSIONAL ASSOCIATION

Established in 1876

ONE SEAGATE, 9TH FLOOR
TOLEDO, OHIO 43604
Telephone: 419-242-7985
Facsimile: 419-242-0316
Email: inquiries@ralaw.com
URL: http://www.ralaw.com

Akron, Ohio Office: 222 South Main Street. Telephone: 330-376-2700. Telecopier: 330-376-4577.
Cleveland, Ohio Office: One Cleveland Center, 1375 East Ninth Street, 9th Floor. Telephone: 216-623-0150. Telecopier: 216-623-0134.
Columbus, Ohio Office: National City Center, 155 E. Broad Street, 12th Floor. Telephone: 614-463-9770. Telecopier: 614-463-9792.
Naples, Florida Office: 850 Park Shore Drive, Trianon Centre, 3rd Floor. Telephones: 239-649-6200; 800-535-7239. Telecopier: 239-261-3659.
Cincinnati, Ohio Office: 250 East Fifth Street, 310 Chiquita Center. Telephone: 513-361-0200. Telecopier: 513-361-0335.
Fort Myers, Florida Office: 2320 First Street, Suite 1000. Telephone: 239-337-3850. Telecopier: 239-337-0970.
Tallahassee, Florida Office: 225 South Adams Street, Suite 250, P.O. Box 10369. Telephone: 850-222-7718. Telecopier: 850-222-8222.
Washington, D.C. Office: 1025 Connecticut Avenue, NW, Suite 220. Telephone: 202-625-0600. Telecopier: 202-338-6340.

General Corporate and Business Law, Banking and Finance, Mergers, Acquisitions and Divestitures, Securities Law, Real Estate Law, Real Estate Development/Syndication/Condominium Law, Tax Law, Intellectual Property Law, Computer Law, Hospital and Health Care Law, Public Law and Finance, Governmental Relations, School Law, Commercial/Bankruptcy Law, Employment Law, Pension, Employee Benefits, Workers' Compensation, OSHA, Business and Commercial Litigation, Complex and Multidistrict Litigation, Antitrust Law, RICO, Federal Court Practice, Product Liability, Environmental Law/Toxic Torts, Insurance Law, Information Technology Law, Medical Malpractice Defense, Asbestos Litigation, Construction Law, 1st Amendment/Media Law, White Collar Criminal Defense, Railroad and FELA, Trucking and Transportation Law, Probate and Estate Planning, Utility Law, International Law, Trial and Appellate Practice.

FIRM PROFILE: Founded in 1876, Roetzel & Andress is one of the largest and fastest growing full-service, corporate law firms with nine offices throughout Ohio, Florida, and Washington, D.C. Roetzel & Andress represents a wide range of clients from individuals and closely-held businesses to multi-national corporations, financial institutions, and government entities. Our lawyers serve as general counsel to many clients, and many of those relationships have existed for much of our history. Our lawyers provide a broad range of legal services to clients on a local, national, and international basis.

PARTNERS

ANTHONY J. CALAMUNCI, SR., born Jamestown, New York, February 2, 1968; admitted to bar, 1994, Ohio; 1995, U.S. District Court, Northern District of Ohio; 1996, U.S. Court of Appeals, Sixth Circuit; 2002, U.S. Supreme Court. *Education:* Alfred University (B.A., 1990); Ohio Northern University (J.D., 1994). Former Assistant Lucas County Prosecuter. *Member:* Lucas County, Toledo, Ohio State and American Bar Associations. ***PRACTICE AREAS:*** Medical Law (10%); Health Care Law (5%); Civil Litigation (60%); Corporate Law (20%); Criminal Defense (5%). ***Email:*** acalamunci@ralaw.com

PATRICIA B. FUGÉE, born Oak Bluffs, Massachusetts, May 21, 1965; admitted to bar, 1991, New Jersey, New York and U.S. District Court, District of New Jersey; 1993, 1993, U.S. District Court, Southern and Eastern Districts of New York; 1998, U.S. Court of Appeals, Third Circuit; 1999, Ohio and U.S. District Court, Northern District of Ohio; 2000, Michigan and U.S. District Court, Southern District of Ohio. *Education:* Wellesley College (B.A., 1986); Rutgers University-Camden (J.D., high honors, 1990). Tax Honors Program. Member, Rutgers Law Journal, 1989-1990. Law Clerk to the Honorable John W. Bissell, U.S.D.J., Newark, New Jersey, 1990-1992. Member, New Jersey Bankruptcy Inn of Court, 1994-1998. *Member:* Toledo and Ohio State Bar Associations; State Bar of Michigan; American Bankruptcy Institute. ***PRACTICE AREAS:*** Bankruptcy; Commercial Litigation; Debtor and Creditor Law. ***Email:*** pfugee@ralaw.com

DENISE M. HASBROOK, born Livonia, Michigan, July 10, 1960; admitted to bar, 1984, Ohio and U.S. District Court, Northern District of Ohio; 1987, U.S. Court of Federal Claims; 1993, U.S. Court of Appeals, Sixth Circuit. *Education:* University of Toledo (B.A., magna cum laude, 1981; J.D., 1984). *Member:* Toledo and Ohio State Bar Associations; Toledo Women's Bar Association. ***REPORTED CASES:*** Detzel v. Brush Wellman, Inc., 141 Ohio App.3d 474, 751 N.E.2d 1067 (2001); Sopkovich v. Ohio Edison Co., 81 Ohio St.3d 628, 693 N.E.2d 233, 1998-Ohio-341 (1998); International Brotherhood of Electrical Workers, AFL-CIO, Local Union No. 245 v. FirstEnergy Corp., 233 F.Supp.2d 913 (N.D. Ohio 2001); Brush Wellman, Inc. v. Montes, et al., 288 F.Supp.2d 860 (N.D. Ohio 2003); Brush Wellman, Inc. v. Montes, et al., 295 F.Supp.2d 785 (N.D. Ohio 2003); Fillmore v. Brush Wellman, Inc., 243 F.Supp.2d 758 (N.D. Ohio 2003); Grosjean v. FirstEnergy Corporation, 349 F.3d 332 (6th Cir. 2003); Tobias v. First Energy Nuclear Operating Company, et al., 302 F.Supp.2d 849 (N.D. Ohio 2004); Yuhasz v. Brush Wellman, Inc., 181 F.Supp.2d 785 (N.D. Ohio 2001); Yuhasz v. Brush Wellman, Inc., 341 F.3d 559 (6th Cir. 2003). ***PRACTICE AREAS:*** Civil Litigation (50%); Employment Law (50%). ***Email:*** dhasbrook@ralaw.com

RUSSELL R. MILLER, born Athens, Ohio, December 7, 1949; admitted to bar, 1978, Ohio. *Education:* Ohio University (B.S.Ed., summa cum laude, 1972); Ohio Northern University (J.D., 1977). *Member:* Toledo and Ohio State Bar Associations; Toledo Estate Planning Council. [1st Lieut., U.S. Army, 1972-1975]. ***PRACTICE AREAS:*** Banking Law; Business Law; Commercial Law; Real Estate Law; Estate Planning. ***Email:*** rmiller@ralaw.com

DOUGLAS E. SPIKER, born Cadiz, Ohio, September 1, 1961; admitted to bar, 1986, Ohio and U.S. District Court, Southern District of Ohio. *Education:* Mount Union College (B.A., 1983); Ohio Northern University (J.D., 1986). *Member:* Toledo, Columbus and Ohio State (Member, Workers' Compensation Committee) Bar Associations. (Certified Specialist in Workers' Compensation, Ohio State Bar Association). ***PRACTICE AREAS:*** Workers; Litigation; Administrative Law; Workers Compensation; Workers Compensation Defense; Workers Compensation Self-Insurance; Workers Compensation Mediation; Workers Compensation Subrogation; Workers Compensation Appeals. ***Email:*** dspiker@ralaw.com

THOMAS S. ZAREMBA, born Warren, Ohio, December 20, 1951; admitted to bar, 1977, Ohio. *Education:* Hillsdale College (A.B., summa cum laude, 1974); Case Western Reserve University (J.D., summa cum laude, 1977). Order of the Coif. Author: "The C-L Cartage and Deprizio Cases," Ohio Lawyer, January, 1991; "Environmental Risks in Bankruptcy," Ohio Lawyer, July, 1991; "The 'Fair Use' of Copyrighted Materials," Ohio Lawyer, November, 1995. Appointed to Board of Editors, *Ohio Lawyer,* 1994-1996. Appointed to Industry Advisory Committee of the International Building Code Council, 1996—. *Member:* Toledo and Ohio State Bar Associations. ***PRACTICE AREAS:*** Commercial; Litigation; Bankruptcy Law; Building Codes. ***Email:*** tzaremba@ralaw.com

---

AMY L. BUTLER, born Toledo, Ohio, 1972; admitted to bar, 2002, Ohio; 2004, U.S. District Court, Northern District of Ohio. *Education:* University of Toledo (B.A., 1995; J.D., 2002); Bowling Green State University (M.Ed., 1998). Member, University of Toledo Law Review. Law Clerk to the Honorable J. Ronald Bowman, Lucas County Common Pleas Court. *Member:* Toledo and Ohio State Bar Associations. ***PRACTICE AREAS:*** Litigation. ***Email:*** abutler@ralaw.com

JULIE A. DOUGLAS, born Lima, Ohio, December 28, 1974; admitted to bar, 2001, Ohio. *Education:* University of Toledo (B.A., summa cum laude, 1997; J.D., cum laude, 2001). *Member:* Toledo and Ohio State Bar Associations. ***PRACTICE AREAS:*** Business Litigation. ***Email:*** jdouglas@ralaw.com

LISA PALM-KUEBLER, born October 11, 1973; admitted to bar, 2001, Ohio and U.S. District Court, Northern District of Ohio. *Education:* University of Toledo (B.A., 1997; J.D., 2000). *Member:* Toledo and Ohio State Bar Associations. ***PRACTICE AREAS:*** Workers Compensation; Insurance Defense; Business Litigation. ***Email:*** lpalm@ralaw.com

REPRESENTATIVE CLIENTS: Advanced Elastomer Systems, Inc.; Akron General Medical Center; Atlantic Tool & Die; Babcock & Wilcox, a McDermott Company; Bank One; Barberton Citizens Hospital; Beacon Journal Publishing Company; BP America; Burger Iron Company; Catholic Healthcare Partners; City of Akron; The Cleveland Clinic Foundation; CSX Transportation; Dart Industries, Inc.; Doctors Hospital; Edward J. Debartolo Corp.; F.E. Myers; FirstEnergy; Ford Motor Company; General Motors Corporation; Grant/Riverside Methodist Hospitals; Honeywell, Inc.; Lloyd's of London; Louisiana Pacific Corporation; Marathon Oil Company; Marriott Corporation; Medtronic, Inc.; MRK Technologies; National City Bank; National Railroad Passenger Corporation (AMTRAK); Norfolk Southern Corporation; Ohio Health Corporation; Ohio Rail Commission; OHM Remediation Services; Pentair, Inc.; PPG Industries, Inc.; Pulte Homes Corporation; Rite-Aid; Seaman Corporation; State of Ohio; Summa Health System; Summit County; The University of Akron; Waste Management, Inc.; Western Parcel Express.

(For complete biographical data on all personnel, see Professional Biographies at Akron, Ohio)

ROHRBACHERS LIGHT CRON & TRIMBLE CO., L.P.A.

405 MADISON AVENUE
TOLEDO, OHIO 43604-1243
Telephone: 419-248-2600
Fax: 419-248-2614
URL: http://www.rlct-law.com
URL: http://www.rlctlaw.com

General Civil Practice. Corporate and Business, Insurance Defense, Personal Injury, Tax, Products Liability, Real Estate, Probate and Estate Planning, Trials and Appeals, Environmental Law, Labor and Employment, Products Liability Defense, including Drug and Medical Device Defense.

FIRM PROFILE: Rohrbachers Light Cron & Trimble Co., L.P.A. was founded in 1950 as Coborn, Notnagel, Smith & Moran.

Today, Rohrbachers Light Cron & Trimble Co., L.P.A. services clients nationwide, with an emphasis on its statewide and regional practice. Our lawyers share a common goal: achieving success for clients through knowledge of the law, a commitment to legal excellence, and dedication to the highest standards of professional integrity.

VERNON E. ROHRBACHER (1920-1978)

SHAREHOLDERS

DAVID J. ROHRBACHER, born Toledo, Ohio, January 8, 1949; admitted to bar, 1975, Ohio and U.S. District Court, Northern District of Ohio; 1980, U.S. Supreme Court; 1989, U.S. Court of Appeals, Sixth Circuit; 1992, U.S. District Court, Eastern District of Michigan. *Education:* Manchester College (B.A., 1971); University of Toledo, College of Law (J.D., 1974); The Weatherhead School of Management of Case Western Reserve University (M.B.A., 1992). ***PRACTICE AREAS:*** Corporate Law; Business Law; Mergers and Acquisitions; Healthcare Law; Business Litigation. ***Email:*** drohrbacher@rlct-law.com

MATTHEW J. ROHRBACHER, born Toledo, Ohio, December 6, 1953; admitted to bar, 1980, Ohio and U.S. District Court, Northern District of Ohio. *Education:* Manchester

(This Listing Continued)

College (B.A., 1976); University of Toledo College of Law (J.D., 1979). ***PRACTICE AREAS:*** Litigation; Insurance Coverage; Products Liability. ***Email:*** mrohrbacher@rlct-law.com

C. RANDOLPH LIGHT, born Pittsburgh, Pennsylvania, May 23, 1940; admitted to bar, 1966, Ohio; 1967, U.S. District Court, Northern District of Ohio; 1973, U.S. Supreme Court; 1977, U.S. Court of Appeals, Sixth Circuit; 1979, U.S. Court of Appeals for the District of Columbia Circuit; 1998, U.S. District Court, Northern District of Illinois. *Education:* Harvard University (A.B., 1963); Northwestern University (J.D., 1966). ***PRACTICE AREAS:*** Business Transactions; Civil Litigation; Environmental Law; Labor and Employment Law. ***Email:*** crlight@rlct-law.com

NICHOLAS J. CRON, born Celina, Ohio, January 4, 1948; admitted to bar, 1974, Ohio; 1999, Florida. *Education:* St. Josephs College (B.S., 1970); University of Toledo (J.D., 1973); Wayne State University (LL.M., Taxation, 1984). ***PRACTICE AREAS:*** Business Law; Real Estate; Estate Planning; Tax; Commercial Law; Mergers and Acquisitions; Probate; Business Succession Planning. ***Email:*** ncron@rlct-law.com

J. MARK TRIMBLE, born Urbana, Ohio, January 14, 1961; admitted to bar, 1990, Ohio and U.S. District Court, Northern and Southern Districts of Ohio. *Education:* Bowling Green State University (B.S.B.A., 1983); University of Toledo (J.D., 1990). ***PRACTICE AREAS:*** Insurance Defense; Products Liability Defense; Drug and Medical Device Defense; Corporate Litigation; Construction Litigation. ***Email:*** mtrimble@rlct-law.com

TODD M. ZIMMERMAN, born Toledo, Ohio, February 23, 1972; admitted to bar, 1997, Ohio; 1998, U.S. District Court, Northern District of Ohio. *Education:* Ohio State University (B.S.B.A., 1994; J.D., 1997). ***PRACTICE AREAS:*** Civil Litigation; Insurance Defense; Appellate Practice. ***Email:*** tzimmerman@rlct-law.com

---

TRACY B. SELIS, born Lima, Ohio, July 5, 1975; admitted to bar, 2001, Ohio; 2003, U.S. District Court, Northern District of Ohio. *Education:* Bowling Green State University (B.A., 1998); University of Toledo (J.D., 2001). Order of the Coif; Phi Sigma Alpha. Technical Editor, Toledo Law Review, 1999-2001. *Member:* Toledo, Ohio State and American Bar Associations; Ohio Association of Civil Trial Attorneys. ***PRACTICE AREAS:*** Civil Litigation; Insurance Defense; Commercial Litigation; Real Estate; Business Law; General Practice. ***Email:*** tselis@rlct-law.com

JACK J. LAH, born Vienna, Ohio, September 12, 1979; admitted to bar, 2004, Ohio; 2005, U.S. District Court, Northern District of Ohio. *Education:* Hiram College (B.A., 2001); Ohio Northern University (J.D., 2004). Member: Ohio Northern University Law Review, 2002-2004; Ohio Northern University Moot Court, 2002-2004. *Member:* Toledo and Ohio State Bar Associations; Ohio Association of Civil Trial Attorneys. ***PRACTICE AREAS:*** Civil Litigation; Insurance Defense; Commercial Litigation; Business Law; General Practice. ***Email:*** jlah@rlct-law.com

OF COUNSEL

BRENT B. NICHOLSON, born Perrysburg, Ohio, March 30, 1954; admitted to bar, 1979, Ohio; 1980, U.S. District Court, Northern District of Ohio; 1984, U.S. Tax Court. *Education:* Bowling Green State University (B.S., 1976); Ohio State University (J.D., 1979). Certified Public Accountant, Ohio, 1984 (inactive). Associate. Professor, Legal Studies, Bowling Green State University, 1989—. ***PRACTICE AREAS:*** Taxation; Probate; Estate Planning. ***Email:*** bnicholson@rlct-law.com

LORI A. COYLE, born Toledo, Ohio, August 6, 1961; admitted to bar, 1998, Ohio; 2000, U.S. District Court, Northern District of Ohio; 2001, U.S. Supreme Court; 2003, Michigan. *Education:* Toledo Hospital School of Radiology (1986); University of Toledo (B.S., 1995; J.D., 1997). ***PRACTICE AREAS:*** Civil Litigation; Health Care; Business Transactions. ***Email:*** lcoyle@rlct-law.com

REPRESENTATIVE CLIENTS: Toledo Molding & Die, Inc.; Delta Motorsports Park, Inc.; Glassline Corp.; Bohl Equipment Co.; Lifestyles for Ladies, Inc.; Northwest Ohio Specialists Cooperative LLC; Midwest Terminals, Inc.; EZ Color Corp.
APPROVED COUNSEL FOR: *Insurance Companies:* Allstate Ins. Cos.; One Beacon Insurance; Fireman's Fund Insurance; Metropolitan Property & Casualty Ins. Co.; State Auto Insurance Co.; GRE Insurance Group; Liberty Mutual Insurance Co.; Prudential Property & Casualty Co.; Dorsey Pharmaceutical Co.; MedMarc; Wyeth-Ayerst Laboratories, Inc.; Novartis Pharmaceuticals Corporation.

BARRY E. SAVAGE

500 MADISON AVENUE, SUITE 315
TOLEDO, OHIO 43604
Telephone: 419-255-3557; 1-800-944-4660
Fax: 419-255-4660
Email: barsav@aol.com
URL: http://www.barsav.com

Commercial Litigation, Banking Law, Bankruptcy, Business Law, Contracts, Real Estate, Investments, Financial Services Law, Estate Planning, Trusts and Estates.

BARRY E. SAVAGE, born Jackson, Michigan, April 19, 1940; admitted to bar, 1965, Ohio; 1966, Michigan; 1968, U.S. District Court, Northern District of Ohio; 1998, South Carolina. *Education:* Denison University; University of Michigan (B.A., 1962; J.D., 1965). *Member:* Toledo and American Bar Associations; State Bar of Michigan; South Carolina Bar.

REPRESENTATIVE CLIENTS: Monroe Bank & Trust; National City Bank; High Tech Packaging, Inc.; Dunbar Mechanical, Inc.; C & W Tank Cleaning, Inc.; L & R Industries, Inc.; CSG Sales, Inc.; Perrysburg Machine & Tool, Inc.; Ohio Air Systems.

SHINDLER, NEFF, HOLMES, SCHLAGETER & MOHLER, L.L.P.

Established in 1943

1200 EDISON PLAZA
300 MADISON AVENUE
TOLEDO, OHIO 43604-1537
Telephone: 419-243-6281
Fax: 419-243-0129

FIRM PROFILE: Founded in 1943 the law firm of Shindler, Neff, Holmes, Schlageter & Mohler, L.L.P. is a full service law firm with a regional client base in Ohio, Michigan and Florida. The firm acts as general counsel and tax counsel to numerous manufacturing, distribution, medical care providers, governmental entities and closely held businesses.

The firm's practice groups have extensive experience and high professional standards in the following areas:

BUSINESS ENTITIES. Our business practice group can service corporations, partnerships and limited liability companies, including non-profit organizations and foundations, from formations to complex mergers and acquisitions. Correspondingly, we provide full service in bankruptcy and creditors rights for which one of our partners serves as a United States Bankruptcy Trustee.

TAXATION. We have tax experience in all areas relating to business entities, employment, individuals and estate planning. The firm has two partners who are former agents for the Internal Revenue Service and two partners who are certified public accountants providing extensive experience in tax audits and litigation before the United States Tax Court.

BANKRUPTCY. Our firm provides comprehensive services in all the areas of bankruptcy practice including bankruptcy litigation, motions and adversaries, creditor and debtor representation, chapter 11 committee representation and trustee representation.

PROBATE AND ESTATE PLANNING. We offer a broad and in depth level of service and experience in all aspects of estate planning, wealth transfers, trusts, taxation and probate and estate administration for the preservation of assets.

LITIGATION AND APPELLATE PRACTICE. Our litigation group has broad experience in the federal district courts in this region and the state courts of Ohio and Michigan, including all levels of appeal. We utilize the most technologically advanced research and litigation tools to ensure the best possible representation of our clients. In this connection, we have a great depth of experience in personal injury and wrongful death claims.

REAL ESTATE. Our real estate practice group is experienced in acquisitions, financing, zoning, foreclosures, workouts, condominium developments, REITS, landlord/tenant matters, construction contracting and all related areas.

LABOR RELATIONS. Our attorneys are proficient in employment related matters such as collective bargaining, employee hiring, retention and dismissal, provision of benefits and compliance issues. Skilled in the area of labor negotiations we can provide aggressive representation in collective bargaining, NLRB matters, OSHA regulations, employment discrimination, wrongful termination and workers compensation issues.

FAMILY LAW. We offer services in adoption, dissolution, divorce, legal separation, annulment and ante-nuptial agreements, juvenile abuse and neglect, providing zealous but compassionate representation to promote the welfare of our clients and their children.

HEALTH CARE FIELD. Our experience in representing both hospitals and medical staff gives our firm a competitive advantage in this field. We also provide representation of physicians and their medical practices in both professional business and individual needs.

CRIMINAL LAW. Our firm provides representation in the federal and state courts of this region and the state of Ohio, including all levels of appeal and including juvenile delinquency.

ATTORNEY DISCIPLINE/ETHICS. Our firm provides representation and consultation on grievance matters and legal ethics statewide.

MEDIATION/ARBITRATION. We provide settlement assistance in all types of disputes statewide.

PARTNERS

JAMES V. SHINDLER, JR., born Defiance, Ohio, March 28, 1939; admitted to bar, 1966, Ohio, U.S. District Court, Northern District of Ohio, U.S. Court of Appeals, Sixth Circuit and U.S. Tax Court. *Education:* The Ohio State University (B.S. in B.A., 1961); University of Toledo (J.D., 1966). Certified Public Accountant, Ohio, 1965. *Member:* Toledo, Lucas County, Ohio State and American Bar Associations; American Association of Attorney-Certified Public Accountants; U.S. Sixth Circuit Judicial Conference (Life Member). ***PRACTICE AREAS:*** Taxation; Probate; Trust Law; Estate Planning; Business Law. ***Email:*** jshindler@snhslaw.com

CARTER NEFF, born Cleveland, Ohio, August 6, 1943; admitted to bar, 1968, Ohio. *Education:* The Ohio State University (B.F.A., 1965; J.D., 1968). *Member:* Toledo, Ohio State and American Bar Associations. ***PRACTICE AREAS:*** Real Property; Probate and Estate Planning; Business Entities Law; Business Acquisitions; Construction Law. ***Email:*** pneff@snhslaw.com

MARTIN J. HOLMES, born Toledo, Ohio, February 17, 1945; admitted to bar, 1971, Ohio; 1973, U.S. District Court, Northern District of Ohio. *Education:* Marquette University (B.S., 1967); University of Toledo (J.D., 1971). *Member:* Toledo, Ohio State and American Bar Associations; The Association of Trial Lawyers of America; Ohio Academy of Trial Lawyers, Million Dollar Advocates Forum; Ohio State Bar Foundation; Toledo Bar Association Foundation. ***PRACTICE AREAS:*** Wrongful Death; Personal Injury; Matrimonial Law; Estate Planning. ***Email:*** mjhsr@snhslaw.com

(This Listing Continued)

SHINDLER, NEFF, HOLMES, SCHLAGETER & MOHLER, L.L.P., Toledo—Continued

JOHN J. SCHLAGETER, JR., born Toledo, Ohio, March 22, 1948; admitted to bar, 1973, Ohio. *Education:* Xavier University; University of Toledo (B.A., 1970; J.D., 1973). *Member:* Toledo and Ohio State Bar Associations. ***PRACTICE AREAS:*** Family; Domestic Relations; Business; Corporation; Real Estate; Probate. ***Email:*** jjsjr@snhslaw.com

MARTIN E. MOHLER, born Toledo, Ohio, April 4, 1948; admitted to bar, 1973, Ohio; U.S. District Court, Northern and Southern Districts of Ohio; U.S. Court of Appeals, Sixth Circuit; U.S. Supreme Court. *Education:* John Carroll University (B.A., English, cum laude, 1970; President, Alpha Sigma Nu); University of Toledo (J.D., 1973). Instructor in Law, Davis Junior College, 1973-1978. Adjunct Professor of Law, Siena Heights College, Adrian, Michigan, 1980. Member Board of Trustees, Toledo Legal Aid Society, 1980-1992; Legal Aid Society of NW Ohio. Member Board of Trustees, Advocates for Basic Legal Equality, 1997-2004. Member, Ohio Bar College, 1988—; National Conference of Bar Presidents, 1994—. *Member:* Toledo (President, 1993-1994; Member, Board of Trustees, 1985-1995; Officer, 1990-1993), Ohio State (Member, Council of Delegates, 1999—), American and Federal Bar Associations; National Association of Criminal Defense Lawyers; Ohio Association of Criminal Defense Lawyers; Ohio Academy of Trial Lawyers. Fellow: American Bar Association; Ohio State Bar Association; Toledo Bar Association; Life-Member, Sixth Circuit Judicial Conference. ***PRACTICE AREAS:*** Civil and Criminal Trial Practice; Corporate/Business; Personal Injury; Wrongful Death; Family/Domestic Relations; Probate; Real Estate; Attorney Discipline/Ethics; Arbitration; Mediation. ***Email:*** mmohler@snhslaw.com

CHARLES K. BOXELL, born Toledo, Ohio, September 5, 1944; admitted to bar, 1974, Ohio and U.S. District Court, Northern District of Ohio. *Education:* University of Michigan (B.B.A., 1966; M.B.A., 1967); University of Toledo (J.D., 1973). Certified Public Accountant, Ohio, 1971. ***PRACTICE AREAS:*** Corporation; Taxation; Estate Planning; Probate. ***Email:*** cboxell@snhslaw.com

DANIEL A. WORLINE, born Toledo, Ohio, August 4, 1948; admitted to bar, 1974, Ohio. *Education:* Bowling Green State University (B.S., in B.A., 1970); University of Toledo (J.D., 1974). Delta Theta Phi. *Member:* Toledo and Ohio State Bar Associations. ***PRACTICE AREAS:*** Taxation; Estate Planning; Corporation Law. ***Email:*** dworline@snhslaw.com

JOHN W. ROZIC, born Lorain, Ohio, May 8, 1951; admitted to bar, 1978, Ohio; 1982, U.S. District Court, Northern District of Ohio; 1989, U.S. Claims Court. *Education:* Case Western Reserve University (B.S., 1973); University of Toledo (J.D., 1977). ***PRACTICE AREAS:*** Estate Planning; Probate; Business; Taxation; Employee Benefits Law. ***Email:*** jrozic@snhslaw.com

JAMES F. DETTINGER, born Toledo, Ohio, March 4, 1943; admitted to bar, 1974, Ohio. *Education:* Xavier University (B.S.B.A., 1965; M.B.A., 1966); University of Toledo (J.D., 1973). *Member:* Toledo and Ohio State Bar Associations. ***PRACTICE AREAS:*** Corporations; General Business; Computer Law; Real Property; Probate and Estate Planning.

CATHERINE H. NOBLE, born Toledo, Ohio, 1944; admitted to bar, 1978, Ohio. *Education:* Notre Dame (B.A., 1962); Arkansas State University (M.S.E., 1966); University of Toledo (J.D., 1978). *Member:* Toledo (Chairman, Domestic Relations Section, 1992-1995) and Ohio State Bar Associations. ***PRACTICE AREAS:*** Domestic Relations Law; Probate.

JEFFREY J. PERKINS, born Dover, Ohio, October 4, 1953; admitted to bar, 1982, Ohio; 1983, Michigan. *Education:* Malone College (B.A., 1975); Bowling Green State University (M.A., Philosophy, 1978); University of Toledo (J.D., 1981). ***PRACTICE AREAS:*** Personal Injury; Workers Compensation; Labor and Employment Law. ***Email:*** jperkins@snhslaw.com

MARY E. SMITH, born Toledo, Ohio, June 16, 1943; admitted to bar, 1985, Ohio and U.S. District Court, Northern and Western Districts of Ohio. *Education:* Mary Manse College (B.A., 1965); University of Toledo (J.D., 1984). *Member:* National Academy of Adoption Attorneys; Toledo (Member, Domestic Relations Committee) and Ohio Bar Associations. ***PRACTICE AREAS:*** Domestic Relations; Adoption Law. ***Email:*** msmith@snhslaw.com

JAMES A. SULEWSKI, born Toledo, Ohio, February 21, 1954; admitted to bar, 1987, Ohio. *Education:* University of Toledo (B.B.A., 1977; J.D., cum laude, 1987). Order of the Coif. Special Agent, Internal Revenue Service, Criminal Investigation Division, 1977-1988. ***PRACTICE AREAS:*** Tax Law; Corporation Law. ***Email:*** jsulewski@snhslaw.com

LOUIS J. YOPPOLO, born Toledo, Ohio, September 21, 1951; admitted to bar, 1980, Ohio; 1981, U.S. District Court, Northern District of Ohio. *Education:* University of Toledo (B.A., magna cum laude, 1974); University of Toledo College of Law (J.D., 1980). ***PRACTICE AREAS:*** Bankruptcy; Banking; Commercial; Collections; Foreclosure Law. ***Email:*** lyoppolo@snhslaw.com

RICHARD L. EMERY, born Marion, Ohio, 1964; admitted to bar, 1991, Ohio; 1992, U.S. District Court, Northern District of Ohio. *Education:* Ohio Northern University (B.S.B.A, 1986); University of Toledo College of Law (J.D., 1991). *Member:* Toledo Bar Association; Ohio Academy of Trial Lawyers. ***PRACTICE AREAS:*** Personal Injury; Wrongful Death; Litigation. ***Email:*** remery@snhslaw.com

PETER A. DEWHIRST, born Ann Arbor, Michigan, October 17, 1968; admitted to bar, 1994, Ohio; 1995, Michigan. *Education:* University of Michigan (B.A., 1991); University of Toledo (J.D., 1994). Member, Toledo Law Review. *Member:* Toledo, Washtenaw County, and Ohio State Bar Associations; State Bar of Michigan. ***PRACTICE AREAS:*** Real Estate; Business Law; Corporate Law; Civil Litigation. ***Email:*** pdewhirst@snhslaw.com

MARTIN J. HOLMES, JR., born Toledo, Ohio, May 8, 1970; admitted to bar, 1995, Ohio; 1996, Michigan and U.S. District Court, Northern District of Ohio. *Education:* Harvard (B.A., 1992); University of Toledo (J.D., 1995). *Member:* Toledo Bar Association; Ohio Academy of Trial Lawyers; State Bar of Michigan. ***PRACTICE AREAS:*** Litigation; Real Estate; Probate. ***Email:*** mholmesjr@snhslaw.com

MICHAEL R. GOULDING, born Mansfield, Ohio, December 27, 1966; admitted to bar, 1996, Ohio; 1998, Florida. *Education:* Ohio State University (B.A., 1991); University of Toledo (J.D., 1995). *Member:* Toledo, Lucas County and Ohio State Bar Associations; The Florida Bar. ***PRACTICE AREAS:*** Real Estate; Probate; Litigation. ***Email:*** mgoulding@snhslaw.com

JOHN J. SCHLAGETER, III, born Toledo, Ohio, January 26, 1972; admitted to bar, 1997, Ohio; 1998, Michigan. *Education:* University of Cincinnati (B.A., 1994); University of Toledo (J.D., 1997). *Member:* Toledo Bar Association; State Bar of Michigan. ***PRACTICE AREAS:*** Real Estate; Corporate; Personal Injury; Litigation. ***Email:*** jjs3@snhslaw.com

ASSOCIATES

HEATHER J. FOURNIER, born Toledo, Ohio, April 14, 1976; admitted to bar, 2002, Ohio. *Education:* Bowling Green State University (B.Agr., 1998); Whittier College School of Law (J.D., 2002). *Member:* Toledo and Ohio State Bar Associations. ***PRACTICE AREAS:*** Domestic Relations; Juvenile Law; Personal Injury. ***Email:*** hfournier@snhslaw.com

THERESA M. NEFF, born Toledo, Ohio, June 25, 1979; admitted to bar, 2004, Ohio; 2005, U.S. District Court, Northern District of Ohio. *Education:* Bowling Green State University (B.S.B.A., cum laude, 2001); Cleveland-Marshall College of Law (J.D., cum laude, 2004). Executive Editor, Journal of Law and Health, 2003-2004. Author: "What Successful Companies Know that Law Firms Need to Know: The Importance of Employee Motivation and Job Satisfaction to Increased Productivity and Stronger Client Relationships," 17 J.L. & Health 385, 2004. *Member:* Toledo, Ohio State and American Bar Associations. ***PRACTICE AREAS:*** Civil Litigation; Business Law; Bankruptcy Law; Real Estate; Estate Planning.

(This Listing Continued)

SHUMAKER, LOOP & KENDRICK, LLP

Established in 1925

NORTH COURTHOUSE SQUARE
1000 JACKSON
TOLEDO, OHIO 43624-1573
Telephone: 419-241-9000
Fax: 419-241-6894
URL: http://www.slk-law.com

Tampa, Florida Office: 101 East Kennedy Boulevard, Suite 2800, 33602-5151. Telephone: 813-229-7600. Fax: 813-229-1660.

Charlotte, North Carolina Office: 128 South Tryon Street, Suite 1800, 28202. Telephone: 704-375-0057. Fax: 704-332-1197.

Columbus, Ohio Office: Huntington Center, 41 South High Street, Suite 2400, 43215. Telephone: 614-463-9441. Fax: 614-463-1108.

Administrative Law; Advertising and Marketing; Agency and Distributorships; Agricultural Law; Alternative Dispute Resolution; Antitrust and Trade Regulation; Appellate Practice; Bankruptcy; Banks and Banking; Business Law; Business Crimes; Business Torts; Civil Rights; Commercial Law; Commercial Litigation; Commercial Real Estate; Communications and Media; Complex and Multi-District Litigation; Computers and Software; Construction Law; Contracts; Copyrights; Corporate Law; Federal Criminal Law; Debtor and Creditor; Domestic Relations; Education Law; Employee Benefits; Entertainment Law; Environmental Law; Fidelity and Surety; Finance; Franchises and Franchising; Health Care; Hospital Law; Immigration and Naturalization; Intellectual Property; International Law; Labor and Employment; Leases and Leasing; Litigation; Media Law; Medicare and Medicaid; Mergers, Acquisitions and Divestitures; Nonprofit and Charitable Organizations; Patent Litigation; Personal Injury; Probate; Products Liability; Professional Liability; Public Finance; Real Estate; Securities; Sports Law; Taxation; Torts; Trade Secrets; Trademarks; Trusts and Estates; Unfair Competition; Wills; Zoning, Planning and Land Use.

FIRM PROFILE: Shumaker, Loop & Kendrick, LLP is a full service law firm whose practice includes civil litigation, corporate, tax, securities, banking and commercial law, creditors' rights, real property, employment relations, employee benefits, estate planning and probate, health, domestic relations, environmental, immigration and administrative law. Our practice areas are organized into the following departments: litigation, corporate, health law, real estate, trusts and estates, taxation, employment law, environmental law and intellectual property. The firm is located in four cities -- Toledo and Columbus, Ohio, Charlotte, North Carolina, and Tampa, Florida.

We represent a wide variety of business, institutional, governmental and individual clients including manufacturers, banks and other financial institutions, insurance companies, contractors, broadcasters, accounting firms, real estate developers and brokers, public utilities, transportation companies, health care providers, trade associations and various public bodies and agencies.

LAW FIRM ALLIANCES/ASSOCIATIONS: **TOLEDO CONFERENCE GROUP**

PARTNERS OF FIRM

ERIN SMITH AEBEL, born St. Petersburg, Florida, November 3, 1971; admitted to bar, 1996, Florida; 1997, U.S. District Court, Middle District of Florida. *Education:* Loyola University, New Orleans (B.A., magna cum laude, 1993; J.D., cum laude, 1996). *Member:* The Florida Bar; American Bar Association (Member, Health Law Section); American Health Lawyers Association; Suncoast Health Executives. (Board Certified Health Law Lawyer, Florida Bar Board of Legal Specialization and Education)(Resident, Tampa, Florida Office). ***LANGUAGES:*** French. ***PRACTICE AREAS:*** Health Law; Corporate Law; Commercial Litigation. ***Email:*** eaebel@slk-law.com

PETER C. ANDERSON, born Montclair, New Jersey, September 10, 1963; admitted to bar, 1992, North Carolina; 1993, District of Columbia. *Education:* Rutgers University (B.S., summa cum laude, 1986); University of Virginia (J.D., 1991). Trial Attorney, U.S. Department of Justice, Environmental Crimes Section, 1992-1994. Assistant U.S. Attorney,

(This Listing Continued)

Western District of North Carolina. Judicial Law Clerk, Hon. Graham C. Mullen, U.S. District Court, Western District of North Carolina, 1991-1992. Certified Arbitrator and Mediator, Commercial Litigation and Environmental Law. (Resident, Charlotte, North Carolina Office). ***PRACTICE AREAS:*** Commercial Litigation; Business Crimes; Environmental Law; Preventive Law; Federal Criminal Law. ***Email:*** panderson@slk-law.com

M. SCOTT AUBRY, born Toledo, Ohio, November 25, 1969; admitted to bar, 1995, Ohio; 1997, Michigan. *Education:* University of Notre Dame (B.A., cum laude, 1992); Ohio State University (J.D., 1995). *Member:* Toledo, Ohio State and American Bar Associations; State Bar of Michigan. ***PRACTICE AREAS:*** Corporate Law; Mergers, Acquisitions and Divestitures; Securities; Antitrust and Trade Regulation. ***Email:*** saubry@slk-law.com

JAIME AUSTRICH, born Baltimore, Maryland, May 13, 1971; admitted to bar, 1996, Florida; 1998, U.S. District Court, Middle District of Florida. *Education:* Florida State University (B.A., 1992); University of Florida (J.D., honors, 1996). Phi Delta Phi. (Resident, Tampa, Florida Office). ***LANGUAGES:*** Spanish. ***PRACTICE AREAS:*** Commercial Litigation; Commercial Landlord and Tenant Litigation; Contested Trusts and Estates. ***Email:*** jaustrich@slk-law.com

JOHN C. BARRON, born Howell, Michigan, September 2, 1951; admitted to bar, 1978, Ohio; 1983, Michigan. *Education:* University of Michigan (B.A., 1973); Stanford University (J.D., 1978). Phi Beta Kappa. *Member:* Toledo, Ohio State and American Bar Associations. ***PRACTICE AREAS:*** Litigation; Professional Liability; Products Liability; Hospital Law. ***Email:*** jbarron@slk-law.com

JENIFER A. BELT, born Willoughby, Ohio, November 16, 1971; admitted to bar, 1995, Ohio and Michigan. *Education:* Miami University (B.A., cum laude, 1992); University of Toledo (J.D., magna cum laude, 1995). Order of the Coif. Editor-in-Chief, University of Toledo Law Review. *Member:* Toledo, Ohio State and American Bar Associations (Member, Health Law Section); American Health Lawyers Association; Society of Ohio Healthcare Attorneys. ***PRACTICE AREAS:*** Health Law; Medicare and Medicaid; Hospital Law. ***Email:*** jbelt@slk-law.com

KATHLEEN M. BICKELHAUPT, born July 5, 1962; admitted to bar, 1987, Illinois; 1997, Florida. *Education:* Brandeis University (B.A., magna cum laude, 1984); Northwestern University (J.D., 1987). *Member:* Illinois State and American Bar Associations; The Florida Bar. (Resident, Tampa, Florida Office). ***PRACTICE AREAS:*** Mergers, Acquisitions and Divestitures; Corporate Law. ***Email:*** kbickelhaupt@slk-law.com

THOMAS C. BLANK, born Cincinnati, Ohio, February 24, 1956; admitted to bar, 1981, Ohio. *Education:* Miami University (A.B., History and Political Science, 1978); University of Toledo; Case Western Reserve University (J.D., 1981). Associate Editor, Case Western Reserve Journal of International Law, 1981. General Counsel for the Association of Independent Trust Companies, Inc., Chicago, Illinois. *Member:* Toledo, Cleveland, Ohio State and American Bar Associations. ***PRACTICE AREAS:*** Banking Law; Mergers and Acquisitions; Trust Company Law; Corporate Law; Securities Law. ***Email:*** tblank@slk-law.com

ALETA M. BONINI, born Cincinnati, Ohio, August 19, 1954; admitted to bar, 1979, Ohio. *Education:* Yale University (A.B., magna cum laude, 1976); University of North Carolina (J.D., 1979). *Member:* Toledo Bar Association; National Association of Bond Lawyers. ***PRACTICE AREAS:*** Government; Finance. ***Email:*** abonini@slk-law.com

MICHAEL E. BORN, born Huntington, West Virginia, February 17, 1963; admitted to bar, 1988, Ohio, U.S. Court of Appeals, Sixth Circuit and U.S. District Court, Northern and Southern Districts of Ohio. *Education:* Grand Valley State University (B.S., 1985); University of Michigan (J.D., 1988). *Member:* Columbus, Ohio State and American Bar Associations. (Resident, Columbus, Ohio Office). ***PRACTICE AREAS:*** Environmental Law; Administrative Law. ***Email:*** mborn@slk-law.com

MICHAEL M. BRILEY, born New York, N.Y., February 4, 1945; admitted to bar, 1969, Ohio. *Education:* Miami University (A.B., with distinction, 1966); The Ohio State University (J.D., cum laude, 1969). Phi Delta Phi. Adjunct Professor, Antitrust Law, University of Toledo, 1978-1985. Member, Ohio Board of Bar Examiners, 1998—. *Member:* Toledo, Ohio State (Former Chairman, Antitrust Law Section, Board of Governors) and American (Member, Sections of: Litigation, Antitrust Law) Bar Associations. ***PRACTICE AREAS:*** Antitrust and Trade Regulation; Commercial Litigation. ***Email:*** mbriley@slk-law.com

ERIC D. BRITTON, born Los Angeles, California, February 12, 1960; admitted to bar, 1985, California; 1986, Pennsylvania; 1992, Ohio. *Education:* Reed College (B.A., 1982); Boalt Hall School of Law (J.D., 1985). *Member:* Toledo, Ohio State and American (Member, Tax Section) Bar Associations; National Association of Stock Plan Professionals; International Foundation of Employee Benefit Plans. ***PRACTICE AREAS:*** Employee Benefits; ERISA. ***Email:*** ebritton@slk-law.com

JOHN H. BURSON, born Findlay, Ohio, June 26, 1943; admitted to bar, 1968, Ohio. *Education:* Williams College (A.B., 1965); University of Michigan (J.D., 1968); Georgetown University (LL.M. in Taxation, 1973). Phi Delta Phi. Listed in Best Lawyers in America (Trust and Estate). *Member:* Toledo and Ohio State (Member, Taxation Section) Bar Associations. Fellow, American College of Trust and Estate Counsel. ***PRACTICE AREAS:*** Estate Planning; Taxation; Corporate Law; Mergers and Acquisitions. ***Email:*** jburson@slk-law.com

C. PHILIP CAMPBELL, JR., born Boulder, Colorado, February 18, 1948; admitted to bar, 1973, Florida; 1974, U.S. District Court, Middle District of Florida; 1981, U.S. Court of Appeals, Fifth and Eleventh Circuits; 1989, U.S. Claims Court. *Education:* Rutgers University (B.A., 1970); Stetson University (J.D., 1973). *Member:* St. Petersburg, Hillsborough County (Member, Media Law Conference Committee) and American (Member: Section on Forum Committee on Communications Laws, Corporation, Banking and Business Law, 1983; Torts Litigation Committee; Contorts Subcommittee) Bar Associations; The Florida Bar (Member, Sections on: Corporation, Business and Banking Law; Sports and Entertainment Law; Trial Practice; Media and Communications Law Committees; Chairman, 1989-1990 and 1989—; Member, Legislative Committee, 1983-1984); Pinellas County Trial Lawyers Association; American Judiciary Society. (Resident, Tampa, Florida Office). ***PRACTICE AREAS:*** Communications and Media; Business Litigation; Commercial Law. ***Email:*** pcampbell@slk-law.com

(This Listing Continued)

C. GRAHAM CAROTHERS, JR., born Tallahassee, Florida, June 16, 1968; admitted to bar, 1994, Florida. *Education:* Florida State University (B.S., 1990; J.D., with honors, 1994). Phi Delta Phi. *Member:* Hillsborough County Bar Association; The Florida Bar. (Resident, Tampa, Florida Office). ***PRACTICE AREAS:*** Commercial Real Estate; Commercial Leases and Leasing; Banks and Banking. ***Email:*** ccarothers@slk-law.com

MARK A. CATCHUR, born Gary, Indiana, August 17, 1962; admitted to bar, 1993, Florida. *Education:* University of South Florida (B.A., cum laude, 1983; M.B.A., 1985); Stetson University (J.D., cum laude, 1993). Certified Public Accountant, Florida, 1985. *Member:* Hillsborough County and American Bar Associations; The Florida Bar. (Resident, Tampa, Florida Office). ***PRACTICE AREAS:*** Corporate Law; Securities; Mergers and Acquisitions. ***Email:*** mcatchur@slk-law.com

PHILIP S. CHUBB, born Key West, Florida, October 22, 1956; admitted to bar, 1982, Ohio; 1989, North Carolina. *Education:* Miami University (A.B., cum laude, 1979); University of Toledo (J.D., magna cum laude, 1982). Phi Beta Kappa; Phi Alpha Theta; Phi Kappa Phi. *Member:* Ohio State and American (Member, Sections on: Business Law; Taxation) Bar Associations; 26th Judicial District and North Carolina State Bars. (Resident, Charlotte, North Carolina Office). ***PRACTICE AREAS:*** Business Law; Mergers, Acquisitions and Divestitures; Securities Law. ***Email:*** pchubb@slk-law.com

DAVID HARRIS CONAWAY, born Augusta, Georgia, May 26, 1958; admitted to bar, 1983, North Carolina. *Education:* University of North Carolina (B.A., 1979); University of Alabama (J.D., 1982). Editor: Alabama Law Review, 1980-1982; American Journal of Tax Policy, 1981-1982. *Member:* North Carolina and American (Vice Chairman, Corporation, Business and Banking Law Committee, Young Lawyers Division, 1984-1985) Bar Associations; North Carolina State Bar; American Bankruptcy Institute. (Resident, Charlotte, North Carolina Office). ***PRACTICE AREAS:*** Bankruptcy; Commercial Law; Business Law. ***Email:*** dconaway@slk-law.com

MARK A. CONNOLLY, born Norwood, Massachusetts, November 27, 1964; admitted to bar, 1994, Florida and U.S. District Court, Middle District of Florida. *Education:* University of Florida (B.S.B.A., with honors, 1986); Stetson University College of Law (J.D., with honors, 1994). Member: Stetson Law Review, 1992-1994; Environmental Law Moot Court Team, 1994. *Member:* Hillsborough County Bar Association; The Florida Bar. (Resident, Tampa, Florida Office). ***PRACTICE AREAS:*** Commercial Litigation; Fidelity and Surety; Health Care. ***Email:*** mconnolly@slk-law.com

THOMAS A. COTTER, born Detroit, Michigan, November 27, 1962; admitted to bar, 1988, Ohio; 1990, Florida. *Education:* University of Michigan (B.A., with high distinction, 1984; J.D., cum laude, 1988). (Board Certified Wills, Trusts and Estates Lawyer, Florida Bar Board of Legal Specialization and Education). ***PRACTICE AREAS:*** Transactional and Business Tax Planning; Executive Compensation; Estate Planning; Estate and Trust Administration. ***Email:*** tcotter@slk-law.com

MARLENE (NEEMA) M. COTTRILL-BELL, born Toledo, Ohio, July 16, 1952; admitted to bar, 1987, Ohio. *Education:* Bowling Green State University (B.A., 1973; M.A., 1974); University of Toledo (J.D., 1986). Order of the Coif. Torrence R. Greene Memorial Scholarship. Judicial Clerk for the Honorable Richard B. McQuade, Jr., U.S. District Court, Northern District of Ohio. *Member:* Toledo and National Bar Associations; Thurgood Marshall Bar Association. ***PRACTICE AREAS:*** Commercial Litigation; Media Law; Civil Rights. ***Email:*** nbell@slk-law.com

DAVID J. COYLE, born Toledo, Ohio, June 24, 1960; admitted to bar, 1987, Ohio. *Education:* Ball State University (B.S., 1982); Ohio State University (J.D., 1987). *Member:* Toledo (Member, Bankruptcy Committee), Ohio State (Member, Banking, Commercial and Bankruptcy Law Committee) and American Bar Associations; American Bankruptcy Institute. ***PRACTICE AREAS:*** Bankruptcy; Creditors Rights; Commercial Litigation; Workouts; Condemnation; Government Procurement. ***Email:*** dcoyle@slk-law.com

JEFFREY S. CREAMER, born Mansfield, Ohio, December 6, 1951; admitted to bar, 1979, Ohio. *Education:* University of Dayton (B.A., 1976); Case Western Reserve University (J.D., 1979). *Member:* Toledo, Ohio State and American Bar Associations. ***PRACTICE AREAS:*** Litigation; Complex and Multi-District Litigation; Environmental Law. ***Email:*** jcreamer@slk-law.com

MARY LI CREASY, born Detroit, Michigan, March 16, 1963; admitted to bar, 1989, Louisiana; 1991, Florida. *Education:* Rhodes College (B.A., 1985); Cecil C. Humphreys School of Law, Memphis State University (J.D., with honors, 1989). Adjunct Professor, Stetson College of Law. *Member:* Hillsborough County (Chairperson, Labor and Employment Law Section, 1996-1997) and Louisiana State Bar Associations; The Florida Bar (Member, Labor and Employment Law Section); Florida Association of Women Lawyers. (Board Certified Labor and Employment Lawyer, Florida Bar Board of Legal Specialization and Education) (Resident, Tampa, Florida Office). ***PRACTICE AREAS:*** Labor and Employment. ***Email:*** mcreasy@slk-law.com

DUANE A. DAIKER, born Ridgewood, New Jersey, September 15, 1969; admitted to bar, 1994, Florida; 1995, U.S. District Court, Middle District of Florida; 1996, U.S. District Court, Southern and Northern Districts of Florida; U.S. Court of Appeals, Eleventh Circuit. *Education:* University of Florida (B.A., with high honors, 1991; J.D., with high honors, 1994). Phi Kappa Phi. Order of the Coif. Editor-in-Chief, Florida Law Review, 1994. *Member:* Hillsborough County and American Bar Associations; The Florida Bar. (Resident, Tampa, Florida Office). ***PRACTICE AREAS:*** Commercial Litigation; Fidelity and Surety; Alternative Dispute Resolution. ***Email:*** ddaiker@slk-law.com

DIANE VULICH DAVIS, born Cleveland, Ohio, September 26, 1956; admitted to bar, 1983, Ohio. *Education:* Bowling Green State University (B.L.S., magna cum laude, 1978); Case Western Reserve University (J.D., 1983). Order of the Coif. *Member:* Toledo and Ohio State Bar Associations. ***PRACTICE AREAS:*** Real Estate Finance; Health Care Finance; Commercial Real Estate; Real Estate Development. ***Email:*** ddavis@slk-law.com

TERRANCE K. DAVIS, born Detroit, Michigan, May 4, 1956; admitted to bar, 1989, Ohio and Michigan. *Education:* Oakland University (B.A., 1985); Wayne State University (J.D., cum laude, 1988). *Member:* Toledo, Ohio State and American Bar Associations. ***PRACTICE AREAS:*** Litigation. ***Email:*** tdavis@slk-law.com

SCOTT G. DELLER, born Toledo, Ohio, February 8, 1964; admitted to bar, 1990, Ohio. *Education:* University of Michigan (B.A., with distinction, 1986); Indiana University

(This Listing Continued)

SHUMAKER, LOOP & KENDRICK, LLP, Toledo—Continued

(J.D., 1990). *Member:* Toledo, Ohio State and American Bar Associations. ***PRACTICE AREAS:*** Labor and Employment; Workers Compensation. ***Email:*** sdeller@slk-law.com

GARY R. DIESING, born Detroit, Michigan, January 21, 1948; admitted to bar, 1975, Ohio; 1989, North Carolina. *Education:* University of Michigan (B.B.A., 1970; J.D., 1974). *Member:* Toledo Bar Association. ***PRACTICE AREAS:*** Employee Benefits; ERISA. ***Email:*** gdiesing@slk-law.com

THOMAS P. DILLON, born Dover, Delaware, October 4, 1965; admitted to bar, 1990, Illinois; 1992, Ohio; 1996, Michigan. *Education:* University of Michigan (B.A., 1986); University of Notre Dame (J.D., 1990). Articles Editor, University of Notre Dame Law Review, 1989-1990. ***PRACTICE AREAS:*** Commercial Litigation; Business Litigation; Real Estate Litigation. ***Email:*** tdillon@slk-law.com

JONATHAN J. ELLIS, born San Francisco, California, November 5, 1964; admitted to bar, 1990, Florida and U.S. District Court, Middle District of Florida; 1994, U.S. Court of Appeals, Eleventh Circuit; 1997, U.S. District Court, Southern District of Florida; 1999, U.S. District Court, Northern District of Florida; 2002, U.S. Supreme Court. *Education:* State University of New York at Buffalo (B.A., magna cum laude, with honors, 1987); Vanderbilt University (J.D., 1990). Phi Beta Kappa. *Member:* Hillsborough County and American Bar Associations; The Florida Bar; Tampa Bay Bankruptcy Bar Association. (Resident, Tampa, Florida Office). ***REPORTED CASES:*** City Bank & Trust Co. v. Vann (In re Vann), 67 F.3d 277 (11th Cir. 1995); Pan American World Airways v. Chiasson (In re Chiasson), 183 B.R. 293 (Bkrtcy. M.D. Fla. 1995); Southern Commerce Bank v. Katzman (In re Katzman), 207 B.R. 295 Bkrtcy. M.D. Fla. 1997). ***PRACTICE AREAS:*** Commercial Litigation; Creditors Rights; Bankruptcy; Homeowners Association Law; Condominium Association Law; Mediation; Arbitration; Professional Liability; Attorney Errors and Omissions; Accountants Liability; Agents and Brokers Liability; Securities; NASD Arbitration. ***Email:*** jellis@slk-law.com

EDWIN G. EMERSON, born Lafayette, Indiana, September 1, 1938; admitted to bar, 1966, Ohio. *Education:* Denison University (B.A., Government, 1960); University of Michigan (J.D., 1966). Phi Delta Phi. *Member:* Toledo, Ohio State and American (Member, Health Law Section) Bar Associations; American Health Lawyers Association; Society of Ohio Healthcare Attorneys. ***PRACTICE AREAS:*** Hospital Law; Health Law; Corporate Law. ***Email:*** eemerson@slk-law.com

JULIO C. ESQUIVEL, born Mexico City, Mexico, February 10, 1966; admitted to bar, 1992, Florida. *Education:* University of Florida (B.S., 1988); University of California, Boalt Hall School of Law (J.D., 1991). Attorney Advisor, Division of Corporation Finance, Securities and Exchange Commission, 1991-1992. *Member:* Hillsborough County and American Bar Associations; The Florida Bar. (Resident, Tampa, Florida Office). ***LANGUAGES:*** Spanish. ***PRACTICE AREAS:*** Corporate Law; Mergers, Acquisitions and Divestitures; Securities; Securities Regulation; Public Offerings. ***Email:*** jesquivel@slk-law.com

WILLIAM G. FISCHER, born Columbus, Ohio, January 19, 1948; admitted to bar, 1973, Ohio; 1976, U.S. Tax Court. *Education:* Bowling Green State University (B.S., 1970); The Ohio State University (J.D., 1973); Georgetown University (LL.M. in Taxation, 1976). Omicron Delta Kappa; Beta Gamma Sigma. *Member:* Toledo, Ohio State and American Bar Associations (Member, Section on Taxation). ***PRACTICE AREAS:*** Health Care Taxation; Physician Practices; Tax Exempt Organizations; Corporate Law; Income Tax. ***Email:*** wfischer@slk-law.com

VIVIAN C. FOLK, born Houston, Texas, November 13, 1951; admitted to bar, 1976, Ohio. *Education:* Ohio Wesleyan University (B.A., 1973); Case Western Reserve University (J.D., 1976). Co-Author: *The Annotated Fiduciary,*" IFEBP, 1989. Contributing Author: *Trustees' Handbook,*" IFEBP, 1990 and 1997 editions. Arbitrator, American Arbitration Association Multiemployer Pension Plan Amendments Act Panel, 1985-1988. *Member:* Toledo, Ohio State and American (Member, Corporation, Banking and Business Law Section) Bar Associations. ***PRACTICE AREAS:*** ERISA Compliance; Employee Benefits Litigation; Multi-Employer Benefits; Health Benefits; Multi-Employer Pensions. ***Email:*** vfolk@slk-law.com

JEFFREY E. FORT, born Honolulu, Hawaii, April 9, 1952; admitted to bar, 1982, Ohio. *Education:* United States Naval Academy (B.S., 1974); Ohio State University (J.D., 1982). Order of the Barristers. *Member:* Toledo Bar Association. ***PRACTICE AREAS:*** Environmental Law; Real Estate; Business Transactions. ***Email:*** jfort@slk-law.com

SHARON M. FULOP, born Toledo, Ohio, July 6, 1972; admitted to bar, 1997, Ohio. *Education:* University of Toledo (B.A., cum laude, with honors in Political Science, 1994); Ohio State University College of Law (J.D., 1997). *Member:* Toledo, Ohio State and American Bar Associations. ***PRACTICE AREAS:*** Real Estate; Finance; Construction Law; Leases and Leasing. ***Email:*** sfulop@slk-law.com

JACK G. FYNES, born Warren, Ohio, January 3, 1952; admitted to bar, 1977, Ohio. *Education:* Youngstown State University (B.A., 1974); University of Toledo (J.D., 1977). Assistant Huron County Prosecutor, 1977-1979. Solicitor, Village of Wakeman, Ohio, 1978-1979. Member: National Brain Injury Association; Ohio Brain Injury Association. Board of Directors, MADD of Greater Toledo. Consultant to: Flower Hospital Brain Injury Support Group; Medical College of Ohio Brain Injury Support Group. *Member:* Toledo and Ohio State Bar Associations; The Association of Trial Lawyers of America; Ohio Trial Lawyers Association. (Board Certified as a Civil Trial Advocate by the National Board of trial Advocacy). ***PRACTICE AREAS:*** Personal Injury. ***Email:*** jfynes@slk-law.com

BRUCE H. GORDON, born Cleveland, Ohio, November 26, 1948; admitted to bar, 1973, Ohio; 1979, Florida. *Education:* Miami University (B.S., 1970); Case Western Reserve University (J.D., 1973). *Member:* Hillsborough County, Ohio State and American (Member, Taxation Section) Bar Associations; The Florida Bar (Member: Taxation Section; Real Property, Probate and Trust Section). (Resident, Tampa, Florida Office). ***PRACTICE AREAS:*** Taxation; Trusts and Estates; Probate. ***Email:*** bgordon@slk-law.com

WILLIAM H. GOSLINE, born San Pedro, California, June 26, 1944; admitted to bar, 1970, Ohio. *Education:* Denison University (B.A., 1966); The Ohio State University (J.D., 1969). Accredited Estate Planner. *Member:* Toledo and Ohio State (Member, Real Property, Probate and Trust Law Section) Bar Associations; National Association of Estate Planners

(This Listing Continued)

and Councils. Fellow, American College of Trust and Estate Counsel. ***PRACTICE AREAS:*** Trusts and Estates; Estate Planning; Estate Administration; Trust Administration. ***Email:*** wgosline@slk-law.com

KEVIN H. GRAHAM, born Toledo, Ohio, April 15, 1952; admitted to bar, 1977, Ohio; 1979, Michigan; 1986, Florida. *Education:* Bowling Green State University (B.S., cum laude, 1974); University of Toledo (J.D., 1977). *Member:* The Florida Bar; State Bar of Michigan. (Resident, Tampa, Florida Office). ***PRACTICE AREAS:*** Commercial Litigation; Franchise Law; Debtor and Creditor. ***Email:*** kgraham@slk-law.com

DAVID M. GROGAN, born Daytona Beach, Florida, December 15, 1949; admitted to bar, 1984, Oregon; 1992, Georgia; 1993, North Carolina. *Education:* Florida State University (B.S., magna cum laude, 1971); Duke University (J.D., with honors, 1984). *Member:* North Carolina State Bar; North Carolina Bar Association; American Bankruptcy Institute. (Resident, Charlotte, North Carolina Office). ***PRACTICE AREAS:*** Commercial Bankruptcy; Insolvency; Business Reorganization. ***Email:*** dgrogan@slk-law.com

JOHN E. HALLER, born Mt. Vernon, Ohio, February 24, 1954; admitted to bar, 1980, Indiana and U.S. District Court, Southern District of Indiana; 1986, Ohio; 1987, U.S. District Court, Southern District of Ohio; 1989, U.S. District Court, Northern District of Ohio and U.S. Court of Appeals, Sixth Circuit. *Education:* Grace College (B.A., cum laude, 1976); Indiana State University (M.S., 1977); Indiana University (J.D., cum laude, 1980). *Member:* Columbus, Ohio State and American (Member, Litigation Section) Bar Associations. (Resident, Columbus, Ohio Office). ***PRACTICE AREAS:*** Commercial Litigation; Business Litigation. ***Email:*** jhaller@slk-law.com

DANIEL R. HANSEN, born Milwaukee, Wisconsin, October 3, 1967; admitted to bar, 1995, Ohio; 1996, Michigan; 1998, North Carolina. *Education:* Bowling Green State University (B.A., 1990); Case Western Reserve School of Law (J.D., 1995). Phi Beta Kappa; Phi Delta Phi (Secretary, 1994-1995). Order of the Coif. Case Western Reserve of Law Review. *Member:* Mecklenburg County, North Carolina and American Bar Associations; North Carolina State Bar. (Resident, Charlotte, North Carolina Office). ***PRACTICE AREAS:*** Commercial Litigation; Shareholder Disputes; Construction Law; Local Government Law. ***Email:*** dhansen@slk-law.com

DOUGLAS G. HAYNAM, born Canton, Ohio, December 25, 1954; admitted to bar, 1980, Ohio; 1981, Michigan. *Education:* Miami University (B.S., cum laude, 1977); The Ohio State University (J.D., with honors, 1980). Beta Gamma Sigma. *Member:* Toledo, Ohio State (Chair, Environmental Law Committee, 1995-1997), and American (Member, Sections on: Natural Resources Law; Litigation) Bar Associations; State Bar of Michigan. ***PRACTICE AREAS:*** Environmental Law; Litigation; Administrative Law; Nonprofit Organizations Law. ***Email:*** dhaynam@slk-law.com

EDWIN L. HERBERT, born Columbus, Ohio, September 12, 1950; admitted to bar, 1975, Ohio; 1995, California. *Education:* University of Notre Dame (B.A., cum laude, 1972); University of North Carolina; The Ohio State University (J.D., cum laude, 1975). *Member:* State Bar California; Ohio State Bar Association. ***PRACTICE AREAS:*** Banking Law; Mergers and Acquisition; Corporate Law; Securities Law. ***Email:*** eherbert@slk-law.com

WILLIAM H. HEYWOOD, III, born Ann Arbor, Michigan, March 3, 1944; admitted to bar, 1969, Colorado and Ohio. *Education:* Denison University (B.A., 1966); University of Denver (J.D., 1969). *Member:* Toledo, Ohio State (Member, Litigation Section) and American (Member, Litigation Section) Bar Associations. ***PRACTICE AREAS:*** Commercial Law; Construction Law; Fidelity and Surety; Intellectual Property; Tort Litigation; Trade Secret Litigation. ***Email:*** bheywood@slk-law.com

JOHN W. HILBERT, II, born Columbus, Ohio, August 3, 1946; admitted to bar, 1971, Ohio. *Education:* Ohio State University (B.A., 1968; J.D., cum laude, 1971). Order of the Coif. Articles Editor, The Ohio State Law Journal, 1969-1971. Instructor, Real Estate Law, University of Toledo, 1974-1990. Listed in, Best Lawyers in America, Banking Law, Lending, Mergers and Acquisitions, 1997, 1999, 2001. *Member:* Toledo, Ohio State (Member: Sections on, Antitrust; Banking, Commercial and Bankruptcy Law Committee, 1985—) and American (Member, Sections on: Corporation, Banking and Business Law; Antitrust Law) Bar Associations. ***PRACTICE AREAS:*** Antitrust and Trade Regulation; Business Law; Real Estate; Banks and Banking; Mergers, Acquisitions and Divestitures. ***Email:*** jhilbert@slk-law.com

CHARLES W. HILLER, born Toledo, Ohio, May 4, 1954; admitted to bar, 1986, Ohio. *Education:* Bowling Green State University (B.S., 1976); University of Toledo (J.D., summa cum laude, 1986). Order of the Coif. *Member:* Toledo, Ohio State and American (Member, Sections on: Real Property, Probate and Trust Law; Corporation, Banking and Business Law) Bar Associations. ***PRACTICE AREAS:*** Commercial Real Estate. ***Email:*** chiller@slk-law.com

WILLIAM KENT IHRIG, born Torrance, California, August 25, 1959; admitted to bar, 1984, Virginia; 1985, Florida and U.S. District Court, Middle District of Florida. *Education:* University of South Florida (B.A., magna cum laude, 1981); Washington & Lee University (J.D., 1984). (Resident, Tampa, Florida Office). ***PRACTICE AREAS:*** Institutional Lending; Commercial Real Estate; Corporate Law. ***Email:*** kihrig@slk-law.com

JOHN S. INGLIS, born Presque Isle, Maine, August 18, 1954; admitted to bar, 1985, Florida. *Education:* Colgate University (A.B., 1976); Case Western Reserve University (J.D., 1979). Editor, Case Western Reserve Law Review, 1978-1979. *Member:* Hillsborough County and American (Member, Real Property, Probate and Trust Section) Bar Associations; The Florida Bar; (Member, Sections on: Real Property, Probate and Trust; Environmental and Land Use Section). (Resident, Tampa, Florida Office). ***PRACTICE AREAS:*** Real Property; Finance; Zoning, Planning and Land Use. ***Email:*** jinglis@slk-law.com

REGINA M. JOSEPH, born Zanesville, Ohio, October 31, 1952; admitted to bar, 1979, Ohio. *Education:* The Ohio State University (B.A., with distinction, cum laude, 1976; J.D., with honors, 1979). Phi Beta Kappa. Managing Editor, Ohio State Law Journal, 1979. *Member:* Toledo (Business Law Committee, 1979—), Ohio State and American Bar Associations. ***PRACTICE AREAS:*** Business Law; Securities; Finance; Bonds; Intellectual Property. ***Email:*** rjoseph@slk-law.com

ROBERT A. KOENIG, born Lincoln, Nebraska, February 4, 1958; admitted to bar, 1983, Ohio. *Education:* Case Western Reserve University (B.A., cum laude, 1980); New

(This Listing Continued)

York Law School (J.D., 1983). Judicial Clerk to Honorable Nicholas J. Walinski, U.S. District Court, Northern District of Ohio, 1983-1985. *Member:* Toledo and American Bar Associations. ***PRACTICE AREAS:*** Construction Law; Fidelity and Surety; Computers and Software; ERISA Litigation. ***Email:*** rkoenig@slk-law.com

KATHLEEN A. KRESS, born Elmhurst, Illinois, September 5, 1958; admitted to bar, 1984, New York; 1985, Ohio. *Education:* University of Dayton (B.A., magna cum laude, 1980); Columbia University (J.D., 1983). *Member:* Toledo and Ohio State Bar Associations. ***PRACTICE AREAS:*** Business Law; Contracts; Franchises and Franchising; Intellectual Property. ***Email:*** kkress@slk-law.com

GREGORY T. LODGE, born Detroit, Michigan, September 1, 1954; admitted to bar, 1982, Ohio. *Education:* University of Toledo (B.A., cum laude, 1979); University of Notre Dame (J.D., 1982). *Member:* Toledo, Ohio State and American Bar Associations. ***PRACTICE AREAS:*** Labor and Employment. ***Email:*** glodge@slk-law.com

OKSANA M. LUDD, born Cleveland, Ohio, November 8, 1954; admitted to bar, 1980, New York, U.S. District Court, Northern District of New York and Ohio; 1982, U.S. District Court, Northern District of Ohio. *Education:* Syracuse University (B.A., 1976); University of Toledo (J.D., 1979). Member, University of Toledo Law Review, 1979. *Member:* Toledo and Ohio State Bar Associations. ***LANGUAGES:*** Ukrainian. ***PRACTICE AREAS:*** Commercial Real Estate; Finance; Leasing. ***Email:*** oludd@slk-law.com

MOSES LUSKI, born Havana, Cuba, May 23, 1953; admitted to bar, 1978, North Carolina. *Education:* Columbia University (B.A., 1975); University of North Carolina (J.D., 1978). Staff Member, North Carolina Law Review, 1976-1978. Research Assistant to Justice J. Frank Huskins, North Carolina Supreme Court, 1978-1980. *Member:* Mecklenburg County Bar Association; North Carolina State Bar. (Resident, Charlotte, North Carolina Office). ***LANGUAGES:*** Spanish. ***PRACTICE AREAS:*** Real Estate Law; Commercial Real Estate; Commercial Real Estate Finance; Leases and Leasing; Landlord and Tenant Law. ***Email:*** mluski@slk-law.com

PAUL R. LYNCH, born Denver, Colorado, September 26, 1952; admitted to bar, 1986, Colorado; 1990, Florida. *Education:* University of Denver; University of South Florida (B.A., cum laude, 1978); College of William & Mary (J.D., 1986). Order of the Coif; Phi Alpha Delta. *Member:* The Florida Bar. (Resident, Tampa, Florida Office). ***PRACTICE AREAS:*** Securities; Public Offerings; Mergers, Acquisitions and Divestitures. ***Email:*** plynch@slk-law.com

JOHN N. MACKAY, born Rome, New York, November 23, 1946; admitted to bar, 1975, Ohio. *Education:* Tulane University of Louisiana; University of Oklahoma (B.A., 1968); The Ohio State University (J.D., summa cum laude, 1975). *Member:* Toledo, Ohio State and American (Member, Sections on: Litigation; Corporation, Banking and Business Law) Bar Associations. ***PRACTICE AREAS:*** Commercial Law; Bankruptcy; Finance. ***Email:*** jmackay@slk-law.com

ERNEST J. MARQUART, born Queens, New York, October 7, 1964; admitted to bar, 1991, Florida. *Education:* Boston University (B.A., magna cum laude, 1986); University of Florida (J.D., with honors, 1991). Ralph R. Bailey Scholarship; Student Works Editor, Florida Journal of Law and Public Policy, 1990. *Member:* Hillsborough County and American Bar Associations; The Florida Bar. (Resident, Tampa, Florida Office). ***PRACTICE AREAS:*** Commercial Litigation; Business Torts Litigation; Bankruptcy; Construction Law; Transportation Law. ***Email:*** emarquart@slk-law.com

TIMOTHY C. McCARTHY, born Toledo, Ohio, December 3, 1954; admitted to bar, 1979, Ohio. *Education:* The Ohio State University (B.A., summa cum laude, 1976; J.D., with honors in Law, 1979). Order of the Coif. *Member:* Toledo, Ohio State and American Bar Associations. ***PRACTICE AREAS:*** Management Labor Law; School Law; Local Government Law. ***Email:*** tmccarthy@slk-law.com

SUSAN D. McCLAY, born Battle Creek, Michigan, March 20, 1950; admitted to bar, 1976, Ohio. *Education:* Western Michigan University (B.B.A., summa cum laude, 1972); University of Michigan (J.D., 1975). *Member:* Toledo Bar Association. ***PRACTICE AREAS:*** Employee Benefits; COBRA; ERISA; Fringe Benefits; Pension and Profit Sharing Plans; Qualified Retirement Plans; Retirement Benefit Plans. ***Email:*** smcclay@slk-law.com

OWEN P. McGILL, born Boston, Massachusetts, February 8, 1966; admitted to bar, 1994, Florida; 1995, Massachusetts. *Education:* University of Notre Dame (B.A., 1988); Boston College (J.D., 1994). Notes and Comments Editor, Boston College Law School International and Comparative Law Journal. *Member:* Hillsborough County Bar Association; The Florida Bar. (Resident, Tampa, Florida Office). ***PRACTICE AREAS:*** Commercial Litigation. ***Email:*** omcgill@slk-law.com

MICHAEL S. McGOWAN, born Toledo, Ohio, May 9, 1957; admitted to bar, 1982, Ohio. *Education:* University of Toledo (B.B.A., magna cum laude, 1978; J.D., cum laude, 1981). Certified Public Accountant, Ohio, 1979. *Member:* Toledo, Ohio State Bar Association; Ohio Society of Certified Public Accountants. ***PRACTICE AREAS:*** Mergers, Acquisitions and Divestitures; Income Tax; Partnership Law. ***Email:*** mmcgowan@slk-law.com

BRIAN N. McMAHON, born Newark, Ohio, August 21, 1952; admitted to bar, 1978, Ohio and U.S. District Court, Southern District of Ohio; 1988, U.S. District Court, Northern District of Ohio. *Education:* Ohio State University (B.A., 1974); Capital University (J.D., 1978). Member, Perrysburg Ohio Planning Committee, 1990-1991. Board of Managers, Perrysburg YMCA, 1995-2001. *Member:* Ohio State and American (Member, Forum on Franchising) Bar Associations. ***PRACTICE AREAS:*** Franchise Law; Franchise Distribution; Real Estate Finance; Real Estate Development; Business Law; Commercial Law; Intellectual Property. ***Email:*** bmcmahon@slk-law.com

WILLIAM H. McNAIR, born Winston-Salem, North Carolina, March 7, 1934; admitted to bar, 1961, North Carolina. *Education:* Davidson College (B.S., 1956); University of North Carolina (J.D., with honors, 1961). Delta Theta Phi; Order of the Coif. Associate Editor, North Carolina Law Review, 1960-1961. *Member:* Mecklenburg County and North Carolina Bar Associations; North Carolina State Bar. (Resident, Charlotte, North Carolina Office). ***PRACTICE AREAS:*** Trusts and Estates; Tax Planning; Estate and Gift Taxation; Corporate Formation; Wills; Trust Law. ***Email:*** wmcnair@slk-law.com

(This Listing Continued)

DONALD M. MEWHORT, JR., born Toledo, Ohio, October 30, 1940; admitted to bar, 1965, Ohio. *Education:* Duke University (A.B., 1962; LL.B., 1965). Phi Delta Phi. *Member:* Toledo, Ohio State and American (Member, Labor Relations Law Section) Bar Associations. ***PRACTICE AREAS:*** Labor and Employment. ***Email:*** dmewhort@slk-law.com

MICHAEL J. O'CALLAGHAN, born Detroit, Michigan, December 2, 1963; admitted to bar, 1990, Ohio; U.S. Court of Appeals, Sixth, Seventh and District of Columbia Circuits and U.S. District Court, Northern and Southern Districts of Ohio. *Education:* University of Michigan (A.B., 1986); University of Detroit (J.D., 1989). *Member:* Toledo, Ohio State and American Bar Associations. (Resident, Columbus, Ohio Office). ***PRACTICE AREAS:*** Environmental Law; Administrative Law; Litigation; Intellectual Property. ***Email:*** mocallaghan@slk-law.com

BARBARA R. PANKAU, born Miami, Florida, April 4, 1951; admitted to bar, 1975, Florida. *Education:* Tufts University (B.A., cum laude, 1972); University of Florida (J.D., cum laude, 1975). Member, University of Florida Law Review, 1973-1975. *Member:* The Florida Bar (Chairman, Health Law Committee, 1985-1987; Executive Council, Health Law Section); American Bar Association (Member, Health Law Section, 1982—; Governing Committee, 1989-1992; Chairman, Aids Task Force, 1988-1989); Florida Academy of Healthcare Attorneys (Past President; Board of Directors); American Health Lawyers Association. (Board Certified, Health Law Attorney, Florida Bar Board of Legal Specialization and Education) (Resident, Tampa, Florida Office). ***PRACTICE AREAS:*** Health Law; Physician Practices; Hospital Law. ***Email:*** bpankau@slk-law.com

WILLIAM L. PATBERG, born Elizabeth, New Jersey, June 26, 1947; admitted to bar, 1978, Ohio. *Education:* Lafayette College (B.A., 1969); University of Minnesota (J.D., magna cum laude, 1978). Order of the Coif. President, Minnesota Law Review, 1977-1978. *Member:* Toledo, Ohio State and American (Member, Section on Natural Resources Law) Bar Associations. ***PRACTICE AREAS:*** Environmental Law; Air Quality; Water Law; Administrative Law. ***Email:*** wpatberg@slk-law.com

MARY ELLEN PISANELLI, born Rutland, Vermont, February 23, 1952; admitted to bar, 1982, Ohio. *Education:* University of Vermont (B.A., cum laude, 1974); University of Chicago (M.A., 1977); Temple University (J.D., 1982). Phi Beta Kappa. *Member:* Toledo, Lucas County; Ohio State and American (Member, Sections on: Corporate, Banking and Business Law; Taxation; International Law) Bar Associations; American Immigration Lawyers Association. ***LANGUAGES:*** Italian and Modern Greek. ***PRACTICE AREAS:*** Securities; Mergers, Acquisitions and Divestitures; Immigration and Naturalization. ***Email:*** mpisanelli@slk-law.com

THOMAS G. PLETZ, born Toledo, Ohio, October 3, 1943; admitted to bar, 1971, Ohio and U.S. District Court, Northern District of Ohio; 1978, U.S. Court of Appeals, Sixth Circuit; 1985, U.S. Supreme Court. *Education:* University of Notre Dame (B.A., 1965); University of Toledo (J.D., 1971). Listed in Who's Who in America, 1997—. Acting Judge, Sylvania Municipal Court, 1990—. Life Member, Sixth Circuit Judicial Conference. Member, 1993— and Chair, 1996-1999, Ohio Board of Bar Examiners. *Member:* Toledo, Ohio State and American (Member, Insurance, Negligence and Compensation Law Section) Bar Associations. ***PRACTICE AREAS:*** Litigation; Nonprofit and Charitable Organizations; Communications and Media. ***Email:*** tpletz@slk-law.com

DAVID J. RECTENWALD, born Toledo, Ohio, April 15, 1961; admitted to bar, 1986, Ohio; 2001, North Carolina and Florida; 2002, Michigan and U.S. Tax Court. *Education:* University of Notre Dame (B.A., in English, 1983); The Ohio State University (J.D., 1986). *Member:* Toledo, Ohio State and American Bar Associations. ***PRACTICE AREAS:*** Estate Planning. ***Email:*** drectenwald@slk-law.com

CYNTHIA L. RERUCHA, born Toledo, Ohio, September 8, 1959; admitted to bar, 1984, Ohio. *Education:* University of Toledo (B.A., summa cum laude, 1980); Duke University (J.D., 1984). *Member:* Toledo, Ohio State and American Bar Associations. ***PRACTICE AREAS:*** Finance; Real Estate; Nonprofit Organizations. ***Email:*** crerucha@slk-law.com

EDWARD J. RICHARDSON, born Fort Lauderdale, Florida, November 5, 1957; admitted to bar, 1982, Florida. *Education:* University of Florida (B.A., with high honors, 1979; J.D., 1982). Certified Circuit Court Mediator. *Member:* The Florida Bar. (Resident, Tampa, Florida Office). ***PRACTICE AREAS:*** Securities; Mergers, Acquisitions and Divestitures; Business Law; Corporate Law. ***Email:*** erichardson@slk-law.com

JOSEPH A. RIDEOUT, born Toledo, Ohio, February 12, 1951; admitted to bar, 1976, Ohio. *Education:* Dartmouth College (B.A., magna cum laude, 1973); University of Virginia (J.D., 1976). Phi Beta Kappa. *Member:* Toledo, Ohio State and American (Member, Real Property, Probate and Trust Law Section and Forum on Construction Industry) Bar Associations. ***PRACTICE AREAS:*** Real Estate Finance; Real Estate Development; Construction Law; Land Use Planning; Business Law. ***Email:*** jrideout@slk-law.com

MICHAEL H. ROBBINS, born St. Petersburg, Florida, August 19, 1971; admitted to bar, 1996, Florida. *Education:* Duke University (A.B., 1993); University of Florida (J.D., with honors, 1996). Member, Justice Campbell Thornal Moot Court Team. *Member:* Hillsborough County Bar Association; The Florida Bar. (Resident, Tampa, Florida Office). ***PRACTICE AREAS:*** Securities; Corporate Law; Business Law. ***Email:*** mrobbins@slk-law.com

H. BUSWELL ROBERTS, JR., born Buffalo, New York, October 21, 1946; admitted to bar, 1975, Ohio and U.S. District Court, Northern District of Ohio; 1986, U.S. Court of Appeals, Sixth Circuit; 1995, U.S. District Court, Eastern and Western Districts of Michigan; 2000, U.S. Court of Appeals, Fourth Circuit. *Education:* State University of New York at Buffalo (B.S., 1972); University of Toledo (J.D., cum laude, 1975). Editor-in-Chief, University of Toledo Law Review, 1974-1975. Law Clerk, U.S. District Court, Northern District of Ohio, 1975-1977. Chapter 7 Panel Trustee, 1984-1996. *Member:* Toledo, Ohio State and American Bar Associations. Master of the Bench of the American Inns of Court. [With U.S. Navy, 1965-1969]. (Board Certified Business Bankruptcy Law, American Board of Certification). ***PRACTICE AREAS:*** Bankruptcy; Civil Litigation; Business Law; Commercial Law; Creditor's Rights. ***Email:*** broberts@slk-law.com

JAMES I. ROTHSCHILD, born Toledo, Ohio, December 10, 1964; admitted to bar, 1993, Ohio. *Education:* Northwestern University (B.S., 1987); University of Toledo (J.D.,

(This Listing Continued)

SHUMAKER, LOOP & KENDRICK, LLP, Toledo—Continued

1993). Order of the Coif. *Member:* Ohio State and American Bar Associations. ***PRACTICE AREAS:*** Mergers, Acquisitions and Divestitures; Securities; Public Offerings; Corporate Finance. ***Email:*** jrothschild@slk-law.com

STEPHEN A. ROTHSCHILD, born Toledo, Ohio, May 21, 1963; admitted to bar, 1988, Ohio; 1992, Michigan. *Education:* Northwestern University (B.S., 1985; J.D., cum laude, 1988). *Member:* Toledo, Ohio State and American (Member, Tort and Insurance Law Section) Bar Associations. ***PRACTICE AREAS:*** Commercial Litigation; Business Torts Litigation; Unfair Competition; Business Law. ***Email:*** srothschild@slk-law.com

MICHAEL G. SANDERSON, born Jamestown, New York, January 9, 1955; admitted to bar, 1981, Ohio. *Education:* Bowling Green State University (B.S., magna cum laude, 1978); University of Toledo (J.D., magna cum laude, 1981). *Member:* Toledo, Ohio State Bar Association. ***PRACTICE AREAS:*** Commercial Litigation; Business Torts; Insurance Coverage. ***Email:*** msanderson@slk-law.com

ROLF H. SCHEIDEL, born Cleveland, Ohio, March 2, 1940; admitted to bar, 1965, Ohio. *Education:* Case Institute of Technology (B.S., 1962); Case Western Reserve University (J.D., 1965). Order of the Coif. Assistant United States Attorney, 1967-1968. Life Member, Sixth Circuit Judicial Conference. *Member:* Toledo, Ohio State and American (Member, Section of Labor and Employment Law) Bar Associations. ***PRACTICE AREAS:*** Employment Law. ***Email:*** rscheidel@slk-law.com

STEVEN G. SCHEMBER, born Dayton, Ohio, July 7, 1945; admitted to bar, 1970, Michigan; 1979, Florida. *Education:* U.S. Coast Guard Academy (B.S., highest honors in English and History, 1967); University of Michigan (J.D., 1970). Member, Board of Directors, 1988-1992; Chairman, Commercial Litigation Section, 1988-1990; Member, 1979-1992, The Academy of Florida Trial Lawyers. Certified AAA Arbitrator, Commercial and Construction Disputes.*Member:* The Florida Bar; State Bar of Michigan; American Bar Association (Vice Chairman, Fidelity and Surety Committee, 2000—). (Board Certified Civil Trial and Business Litigation Lawyer, Florida Bar Board of Legal Specialization and Education) (Resident, Tampa, Florida Office). ***PRACTICE AREAS:*** Fidelity and Surety; Business Law; Products Liability; Construction Law; Professional Liability. ***Email:*** sschember@slk-law.com

GREGORY S. SHUMAKER, born Lakeland, Florida, August 21, 1948; admitted to bar, 1973, Ohio. *Education:* Miami University (A.B., 1970); Georgetown University Law Center (J.D., 1973). Omicron Delta Kappa. *Member:* Toledo, Ohio State and American (Member, Real Property, Probate and Trust Law Section) Bar Associations. ***PRACTICE AREAS:*** Real Estate; Commercial Real Estate; Commercial Loans; Business Law; Liquor Licensing. ***Email:*** gshumaker@slk-law.com

JOHN J. SICILIANO, born Dearborn, Michigan, August 19, 1953; admitted to bar, 1978, Ohio. *Education:* University of Michigan (B.B.A., with distinction, 1975); University of Detroit (J.D., magna cum laude, 1978). Case and Comment Editor, University of Detroit Journal of Urban Law, 1977-1978. *Member:* Toledo, Ohio State (Member, Sections on: Labor and Employment Law; Antitrust Law) and American (Member, Sections on: Litigation; Antitrust Law; Labor and Employment Law) Bar Associations; Defense Research Institute; Ohio Association of Civil Trial Attorneys. ***PRACTICE AREAS:*** Litigation; Labor and Employment; Workers Compensation. ***Email:*** jsiciliano@slk-law.com

PETER R. SILVERMAN, born Toledo, Ohio, December 26, 1955; admitted to bar, 1982, New York; 1984, Ohio; 1988, Michigan. *Education:* George Washington University (B.A., with distinction, 1977); Hebrew University; University of Michigan (J.D., cum laude, 1981). *Member:* Toledo, Ohio State and American (Member, Forum on Franchising) Bar Associations; State Bar of Michigan. ***PRACTICE AREAS:*** Complex Litigation; Arbitration; Mediation; Franchise Litigation. ***Email:*** psilverman@slk-law.com

JOSEPH S. SIMPSON, born Cincinnati, Ohio, December 28, 1962; admitted to bar, 1988, Ohio; 1989, U.S. District Court, Northern District of Ohio. *Education:* Atlantic Christian College (B.S., magna cum laude, 1985) Alpha Chi; University of Toledo College of Law (J.D., cum laude, 1988). Executive Editor, University of Toledo Law Review, 1987-1988. Author: "Unemployment Compensation and Just Cause Dismissals in Ohio: When is a Discharged Employee Entitled to Benefits," 18 University of Toledo Law Review, 1987. Law Clerk to The Hon. John W. Potter, U.S. District Judge, 1988-1990. *Member:* Toledo, Ohio State and American Bar Associations. ***PRACTICE AREAS:*** Environmental Law; Litigation; Construction Law; Civil Rights; Products Liability. ***Email:*** jsimpson@slk-law.com

DARRELL C. SMITH, born Buffalo, New York, November, 12, 1954; admitted to bar, 1982, Florida and U.S. Tax Court. *Education:* Grove City College (B.A., 1976); Capital University (J.D., 1981). *Member:* Hillsborough County and American Bar Associations; The Florida Bar (Member, Corporation Section, 1984—). (Resident, Tampa, Florida Office). ***PRACTICE AREAS:*** Securities; Business Law; Corporate Law. ***Email:*** dsmith@slk-law.com

LYMAN F. SPITZER, born Toledo, Ohio, November 20, 1949; admitted to bar, 1976, Ohio. *Education:* Williams College (B.A., magna cum laude, with highest honors in Physics, 1971); University of Michigan (J.D., magna cum laude, 1976). Phi Beta Kappa; Order of the Coif. Law Clerk to Judge Louis F. Oberdorfer, U.S. District Court, District of Columbia, 1977-1978. *Member:* Toledo and American (Member: Business Law, Intellectual Property and Science and Technology Sections) Bar Associations. ***PRACTICE AREAS:*** Business Law; Corporate Law; Mergers and Acquisitions; Securities; Intellectual Property. ***Email:*** lspitzer@slk-law.com

ANGELINA M. STAYTON, born Birmingham, Alabama, November 11, 1965; admitted to bar, 1994, Florida; 1995, Alabama; 1998, Missouri and Kansas. *Education:* University of Georgia (B.S., cum laude, 1987); University of Florida (J.D., with honors, 1994). Order of the Coif. Member, Florida Trial Team, 1992-1994. Senior Editor, 1994 and Associate Editor, 1993, Florida Law Review. *Member:* American Bar Association (Vice-Chair, Fidelity and Surety Law Committee, 1999-2000; Chair, 1999-2000 and Vice-Chair, 1998-1999, Women in the Profession Committee, Young Lawyers Division; Vice-Chair, Litigation Committee, Young Lawyers Division, 1998-1999; Member, Membership Committee,

(This Listing Continued)

Tort and Insurance Practice Section); The Florida Bar; Alabama State Bar. (Resident, Tampa, Florida Office). ***PRACTICE AREAS:*** Commercial Litigation; Construction Litigation; Employment Litigation. ***Email:*** astayton@slk-law.com

SCOTT M. STEVENSON, born Houston, Texas, July 25, 1954; admitted to bar, 1979, North Carolina; U.S. Supreme Court; U.S. Court of Appeals, Fourth Circuit; U.S. District Court, Eastern and Western Districts. *Education:* Washington & Lee University (B.A., 1976); Wake Forest University (J.D., 1979). *Member:* Mecklenburg County, North Carolina and American Bar Associations; North Carolina State Bar; Defense Research Institute; North Carolina Association of Defense Attorneys. (Resident, Charlotte, North Carolina Office). ***LANGUAGES:*** Spanish and Norwegian. ***PRACTICE AREAS:*** Medical Malpractice. ***Email:*** sstevenson@slk-law.com

MARK C. STEWART, born Norwalk, Ohio, February 7, 1947; admitted to bar, 1972, Minnesota, 1976, Ohio. *Education:* Oberlin College (B.A., 1969); University of Minnesota (J.D., 1972). *Member:* Toledo, Ohio State (Agricultural Law Committee) and American (Business Law Section) Bar Associations. ***PRACTICE AREAS:*** Agricultural Law; Cooperative Taxation. ***Email:*** mstewart@slk-law.com

JOHN L. STRAUB, born Toledo, Ohio, January 21, 1945; admitted to bar, 1970, Ohio; 1971, U.S. District Court, Northern District of Ohio; 1973, U.S. Court of Appeals, Sixth Circuit; 1985, U.S. Supreme Court. *Education:* University of Michigan (B.A., 1966); University of Toledo (J.D., 1969). Editor, University of Toledo Law Review, 1968-1969. Author: "Taxpayer Relief Act: Capital Gains, Sale of Residence, Child Credit and Family Relief Provisions," The Best of Family Law, 1997, Ohio CLE Institute Publications, 1998. Assistant Public Defender, Lucas County, 1970-1972. Member: Family Law Committee, Ohio State and American Bar Associations; Board of Trustees, Toledo Bar Association, 1981-1987. Lecturer, Legal Education Institute, Inc., 1987, 1989. Lecturer, Ohio Academy of Trial Lawyers, 1990. Lecturer, Law Education Institute, Vail, Colorado, 1994. Editorial Advisory Board, Domestic Relations Journal of Ohio, 1990-1996. ***PRACTICE AREAS:*** Domestic Relations. ***Email:*** jstraub@slk-law.com

WILLIAM H. STURGES, born Brazil, Indiana, July 24, 1953; admitted to bar, 1978, North Carolina. *Education:* Washington & Lee University (B.A., cum laude, 1975); Wake Forest University (J.D., cum laude, 1978). Recipient, Algernon Sidney Sullivan Award. Staff Member, Wake Forest Law Review, 1976-1978. Research Assistant to Chief Justice Susie Sharp, North Carolina Supreme Court, 1978-1979. Faculty Member, various programs, National Institute of Trial Advocacy. Member, 1996-2002 and Chair, 2000-2002, Charlotte Zoning Board of Adjustment. *Member:* North Carolina (Council Member, 1994-2001 and Chair, 1999-2000; Member, Sections on: Labor and Employment Law; Litigation; Environmental Law) and American (Member, Sections on: Labor and Employment Law; Litigation; Tort and Insurance Practice) Bar Associations. (Resident, Charlotte, North Carolina Office). ***PRACTICE AREAS:*** Labor and Employment Law; Commercial Litigation; Fidelity and Surety; Zoning and Land Use. ***Email:*** wsturges@slk-law.com

THEODORE C. TAUB, admitted to bar, 1960, Florida (Not admitted in Ohio). *Education:* Duke University (B.A., 1956); University of Florida College of Law (LL.B., 1960; J.D., 1967). Certified Mediator. (Board Certified Real Estate Lawyer, Florida Bar Board of Legal Specialization and Education). ***PRACTICE AREAS:*** Real Estate; Litigation. ***Email:*** ttaub@slk-law.com

W. THOMPSON THORN, III, born Coral Gables, Florida, August 23, 1947; admitted to bar, 1974, Florida; 1984, U.S. Supreme Court. *Education:* St. Andrews Presbyterian College (B.A., 1969); Stetson University (J.D., 1974). *Member:* Hillsborough County and American (Member, Business Law Section) Bar Associations; The Florida Bar (Member, Business Law Section). (Resident, Tampa, Florida Office). ***PRACTICE AREAS:*** Mergers, Acquisitions and Divestitures; Corporate Finance; Business Transactions. ***Email:*** tthorn@slk-law.com

FREDERICK M. THURMAN, JR., born Marietta, Georgia, May 3, 1970; admitted to bar, 1995, Alabama; 1999, North Carolina. *Education:* Clemson University (B.S., magna cum laude, 1992); Cumberland School of Law of Samford University (J.D., 1995). Phi Kappa Phi; Omicron Delta Kappa; Tau Beta Pi. Cordell Hull Teaching Fellow, 1993-1994. Article Editor, Cumberland Law Review, 1994-1995. *Member:* North Carolina and American Bar Associations; Alabama State Bar; North Carolina State Bar. (Resident, Charlotte, North Carolina Office). ***PRACTICE AREAS:*** Labor and Employment; Litigation. ***Email:*** fthurman@slk-law.com

J. TODD TIMMERMAN, born Tampa, Florida, July 21, 1967; admitted to bar, 1992, Florida and U.S. District Court, Middle District of Florida. *Education:* Dartmouth College (A.B., 1989); University of Florida (J.D., with honors, 1992). Member, University of Florida Trial Competition Team, 1990-1992. Author: "The European Community Trademark," The Hillsborough County Bar Association Lawyer. *Member:* Hillsborough County (Member, Section on: Business Law) and American (Member, Sections on: Business Law; Intellectual Property Law) Bar Associations; The Florida Bar (Member, Section on: Business Law); Greater Tampa Chamber of Commerce; International Trademark Association. (Resident, Tampa, Florida Office). ***PRACTICE AREAS:*** Intellectual Property; Corporate Law; Real Estate. ***Email:*** ttimmerman@slk-law.com

LOUIS E. TOSI, born Martins Ferry, Ohio, April 22, 1949; admitted to bar, 1974, Ohio. *Education:* The Ohio State University (B.A., cum laude, 1971; J.D., cum laude, 1974). Phi Beta Kappa. *Member:* Toledo, Ohio State (Chairman, Committee on Environmental Law, 1984-1988) and American (Member, Sections on: Natural Resources Law; Administrative Law; Past Vice Chair, Air Quality Committee) Bar Associations. ***PRACTICE AREAS:*** Environmental Law; Litigation Defense. ***Email:*** ltosi@slk-law.com

MICHAEL T. TROCKE, born Detroit, Michigan, April 29, 1938; admitted to bar, 1967, Florida. *Education:* Michigan State University and University of Florida (B.I.E. with honors, 1961); Stetson University (J.D., 1967). Sigma Tau; Phi Kappa Phi. Florida Certified Mediator and Arbitrator; Federal Court Mediator; AAA Arbitrator/Mediator. *Member:* Hillsborough County and American Bar Associations; The Florida Bar. (Resident, Tampa, Florida Office). ***PRACTICE AREAS:*** Fidelity and Surety; Construction Law; Corporate Law; Real Estate. ***Email:*** mtrocke@slk-law.com

BARTON L. WAGENMAN, born Toledo, Ohio, January 29, 1942; admitted to bar, 1967, Ohio. *Education:* Miami University (B.S., cum laude, 1964); Harvard Law School (LL.B., 1967). Phi Beta Kappa; Beta Gamma Sigma. *Member:* Toledo, Ohio State (Member

(This Listing Continued)

and Past Chairman and Secretary, Board of Governors, Real Property Section, 1976—) and American (Member, Sections on: Corporation, Banking and Business Law; Real Property, Probate and Trust Law) Bar Associations. ***PRACTICE AREAS:*** Real Estate; Commercial Real Estate; Real Estate Development; Corporate Law; Closely Held Corporations. ***Email:*** bwagenman@slk-law.com

ROBERT R. WARCHOLA, born Washington, Pennsylvania, July 28, 1960; admitted to bar, 1985, Florida; 1986, District of Columbia. *Education:* George Washington University (B.A., 1982); Stetson University (J.D., 1985). *Member:* Hillsborough County (Executive Council, Trial Lawyers Section) Bar Association; The Florida Bar (Chairman, Grievance Committee, 1997; Grievance Committee 13A 2000—); The District of Columbia Bar (inactive). (Resident, Tampa, Florida Office). ***PRACTICE AREAS:*** Construction Law; Business Law; Litigation. ***Email:*** rwarchola@slk-law.com

DAVID F. WATERMAN, born Columbus, Ohio, May 25, 1949; admitted to bar, 1975, Illinois; 1979, Ohio. *Education:* Princeton University (B.S.E., summa cum laude, 1971); University of Michigan Graduate School of Business; University of Michigan (J.D., cum laude, 1975). Eta Kappa Nu; Tau Beta Pi. *Member:* Toledo, Ohio State and American (Member, Sections on: Corporation, Banking and Business Law; Taxation) Bar Associations. ***PRACTICE AREAS:*** Corporate Law; Federal Taxation; Mergers, Acquisitions and Divestitures. ***Email:*** dwaterman@slk-law.com

THOMAS I. WEBB, JR., born Toledo, Ohio, September 16, 1948; admitted to bar, 1973, Ohio. *Education:* Williams College (B.A., 1970); Boston University; Case Western Reserve University (J.D., 1973). Order of the Coif. *Member:* Toledo, Ohio State and American (Member, Corporation, Banking and Business Law Section) Bar Associations. ***PRACTICE AREAS:*** Mergers, Acquisitions and Divestitures; Corporate Law; Business Law; Securities. ***Email:*** twebb@slk-law.com

MARTIN D. WERNER, born Toledo, Ohio, March 15, 1956; admitted to bar, 1981, Ohio. *Education:* Miami University; University of Toledo (B.A., 1978); Case Western Reserve University (J.D., 1981). Certified Public Accountant (inactive), Ohio, 1987. *Member:* Toledo, Ohio State and American Bar Associations. ***PRACTICE AREAS:*** Banking Law; Mergers and Acquisitions; Corporate Law; Securities Law; Tax Law. ***Email:*** mwerner@slk-law.com

DAVID W. WICKLUND, born St. Paul, Minnesota, August 7, 1949; admitted to bar, 1974, Ohio. *Education:* Williams College (B.A., cum laude, 1971); University of Toledo (J.D., cum laude, 1974). Phi Alpha Delta. *Member:* Toledo, Ohio State (Member, Antitrust Section Board of Governors) and American (Member, Litigation and Antitrust Sections) Bar Associations. ***PRACTICE AREAS:*** Complex Litigation; Antitrust and Trade Regulation; Patent Litigation; Commercial Bankruptcy. ***Email:*** dwicklund@slk-law.com

DENNIS P. WITHERELL, born Toledo, Ohio, December 15, 1951; admitted to bar, 1977, Ohio. *Education:* University of Michigan (B.A., with honors and high distinction, 1973); The Ohio State University (J.D., summa cum laude, 1977). Phi Beta Kappa; Order of the Coif. Editor-in-Chief, Ohio State Law Journal, 1976-1977. Law Clerk to Judge George Edwards, U.S. Court of Appeals, Sixth Circuit, 1977-1978. *Member:* Toledo, Ohio State and American (Member, Sections on: Antitrust, Health Law) Bar Associations; American Health Lawyers Association; Society of Ohio Healthcare Attorneys. ***PRACTICE AREAS:*** Health Law. ***Email:*** dwitherell@slk-law.com

THOMAS M. WOOD, born Lorain, Ohio, December 15, 1959; admitted to bar, 1985, Ohio (inactive); 1986, Michigan (inactive); 1994, Florida. *Education:* The Ohio State University (B.A., with honors, 1982; J.D., 1985). *Member:* Hillsborough County and American (Member, Torts and Insurance Practice Section; TIPS Fidelity and Surety Committee) Bar Associations; The Florida Bar. (Resident, Tampa, Florida Office). ***PRACTICE AREAS:*** Commercial Law; Litigation; Construction Law. ***Email:*** twood@slk-law.com

KATHRYN J. WOODWARD, born Toledo, Ohio, September 26, 1947; admitted to bar, 1987, Ohio and Michigan. *Education:* Otterbein College (B.A., 1969); University of Strasbourg; University of Toledo (J.D., 1986). *Member:* Toledo and Ohio State Bar Associations. ***LANGUAGES:*** French. ***PRACTICE AREAS:*** Trusts and Estates; Taxation. ***Email:*** kwoodward@slk-law.com

GREGORY C. YADLEY, born Tampa, Florida, January 10, 1950; admitted to bar, 1975, Florida; 1976, District of Columbia; 1981, U.S. Supreme Court. *Education:* Dartmouth College (B.A. cum laude, with highest honors in English, 1972); George Washington University (J.D., with honors, 1975). Assistant General Counsel, Federal Home Loan Mortgage Corporation, 1979-1981; Branch Chief, Securities and Exchange Commission, Division of Market Regulation, 1975-1979. *Member:* Hillsborough County and American (Chair, Securities Regulation Subcommittee, Small Business Committee, 2000—; Chair, Small Business Securities Subcommittee, 2004—) Bar Associations; The Florida Bar (Chairman: Business Law Section, 1991; Executive Council, 1984—); The District of Columbia Bar. (Resident, Tampa, Florida Office). ***LANGUAGES:*** French. ***PRACTICE AREAS:*** Securities; Mergers, Acquisitions and Divestitures; Business Law. ***Email:*** gyadley@slk-law.com

ASSOCIATES

EILEEN M. BEST, born Toledo, Ohio, May 12, 1960; admitted to bar, 1993, Ohio. *Education:* University of Toledo (B.B.A., magna cum laude, 1990; J.D., 1992). *Member:* Toledo, Ohio State and American Bar Associations. ***PRACTICE AREAS:*** Real Estate Financing. ***Email:*** ebest@slk-law.com

REBECCA A. BRIGGS, born Lowell, Massachusetts, March 19, 1965; admitted to bar, 1993, New Hampshire; 2004, Florida. *Education:* University of Lowell (B.A., History, 1988); New England School of Law (J.D., 1993). *Member:* New Hampshire Bar Association (Inactive Member); The Florida Bar (Member, Real Property, Probate and Trust Law Section). (Resident, Tampa, Florida Office). ***PRACTICE AREAS:*** Estate Planning; Living Trusts; Family Trusts; Trust Administration; Tax Planning; Family Wealth Transfer; Federal Estate and Gift Taxation; Estate Administration.

MEGAN A. FITZPATRICK BULA, born Jackson, Michigan, November 1, 1966; admitted to bar, 1998, Illinois, U.S. District Court, Northern District of Illinois; 2000, Ohio, U.S. District Court, Northern District of Ohio; 2001, Michigan. *Education:* Wayne State University (B.S., summa cum laude, 1994); University of Michigan (J.D., 1997). Phi Alpha Delta. *Member:* Toledo, Illinois State and American Bar Associations. ***PRACTICE AREAS:*** Commercial Law; Contracts; Litigation; Products Liability; Professional Liability. ***Email:*** mbula@slk-law.com

WILLIAM C. BUNTING, JR., born Garner, North Carolina, April 17, 1975; admitted to bar, 2001, North Carolina. *Education:* Appalachian State University (B.S., summa cum laude, 1997); University of North Carolina at Chapel Hill (J.D., 2001). Associate Editor, North Carolina Journal of Law and Technology, 2000-2001. *Member:* Mecklenburg County, North Carolina and American Bar Associations; North Carolina State Bar. (Resident, Charlotte, North Carolina Office). ***PRACTICE AREAS:*** Commercial Litigation; Federal Criminal Law; Business Crimes; Landlord and Tenant Law. ***Email:*** wbunting@slk-law.com

RYAN M. CARDOSO, born October 24, 1975; admitted to bar, 2003, Florida. (Resident, Tampa, Florida Office). ***PRACTICE AREAS:*** Commercial Litigation. ***Email:*** rcardoso@slk-law.com

C. CHRISTOPHER CLARK, born Roanoke, Virginia, March 10, 1971; admitted to bar, 2001, North Carolina. *Education:* Radford University (B.M., 1998); University of North Carolina (J.D., 2001). Associate Editor, North Carolina Journal of Law and Technology, 2000-2001. (Resident, Charlotte, North Carolina Office). ***PRACTICE AREAS:*** Corporate Law; Business Transactions; Entertainment Law; Intellectual Property; Internet Law. ***Email:*** cclark@slk-law.com

EDWARD J. COMEY, born St. Petersburg, Florida, August 5, 1974; admitted to bar, 2002, Florida and U.S. District Court, Middle District of Florida. *Education:* University of South Florida (B.A., magna cum laude, 1998); Florida State University (J.D., with highest honors, 2001). Order of the Coif; Articles Editor and Associate Editor, Florida State University Law Review, 2000-2001. *Member:* Hillsborough County and American Bar Associations; The Florida Bar. (Resident, Tampa, Florida Office). ***PRACTICE AREAS:*** Commercial Litigation; Fidelity and Surety; Commercial Landlord and Tenant Law. ***Email:*** ecomey@slk-law.com

STEFANIE E. DELLER, born Royal Oak, Michigan, October 22, 1974; admitted to bar, 1999, Ohio; 2000, Michigan; 2001, U.S. Court of Appeals, Sixth Circuit. *Education:* University of Michigan (B.A., 1996); Vanderbilt University (J.D., 1999). Phi Delta Phi; Gamma Sigma Alpha. Member, Gold Key. *Member:* Toledo, Ohio State and American Bar Associations; State Bar of Michigan. ***PRACTICE AREAS:*** Civil Litigation. ***Email:*** sdeller2@slk-law.com

ANDREW P. FELIX, born Pensacola, Florida; admitted to bar, 2003, Florida and U.S. District Court, Middle District of Florida. *Education:* University of Florida (B.A., 2000); University of Alabama (J.D., 2003). *Member:* Pinellas County, Hillsborough County and American Bar Associations; The Florida Bar. (Resident, Tampa, Florida Office). ***PRACTICE AREAS:*** Litigation. ***Email:*** afelix@slk-law.com

MATTHEW J. GINSBURG, born November 10, 1971; admitted to bar, 1998, Massachusetts; 2002, North Carolina (Not admitted in Ohio). *Education:* Emory University (B.A., 1994); Boston College Law School (J.D., 1998). Member, National Slavic Honor Society, 1993-1994. *Member:* Boston, Massachusetts and American Bar Associations; North Carolina State Bar. (Resident, Charlotte, North Carolina Office). ***LANGUAGES:*** Russian. ***PRACTICE AREAS:*** Commercial Litigation; Construction Litigation; Bankruptcy Litigation; Employment Litigation. ***Email:*** mginsburg@slk-law.com

NATHAN A. HALL, born Detroit, Michigan, January 11, 1978; admitted to bar, 2003, Ohio; 2004, Michigan. *Education:* Hillsdale College (B.A., 2000); University of Notre Dame (J.D., 2003). *Member:* Toledo and Ohio State Bar Associations. ***PRACTICE AREAS:*** Commercial Litigation. ***Email:*** nhall@slk-law.com

GREGORY-SCOTT R. HANEY, born New Orleans, Louisiana, August 12, 1969; admitted to bar, 1996, Florida; 1998, U.S. District Court, Northern, Middle and Southern Districts of Florida. *Education:* Louisiana State University (B.S., Finance, 1991); University of Florida (J.D., with honors, 1995). Phi Delta Phi. Recipient, Honor Scholarship, Louisiana State University. *Member:* Hillsborough County (Member, Trial Attorney Section) and American (Member, Trial Attorney Section) Bar Associations; The Florida Bar. (Resident, Tampa, Florida Office). ***PRACTICE AREAS:*** Real Estate; Bankruptcy; Construction Law; Commercial Litigation; Commercial Transactions. ***Email:*** ghaney@slk-law.com

W. REED HAUPTMAN, born Canton, Ohio, September 18, 1971; admitted to bar, 1998, Ohio; 1999, Michigan. *Education:* Miami University (B.S., 1993); Vanderbilt University (J.D., 1998). ***PRACTICE AREAS:*** Real Estate; Leases and Leasing; Zoning, Planning and Land Use. ***Email:*** rhauptman@slk-law.com

ROBIN L. HENDERSON, born Gainesville, Florida; admitted to bar, 2002, Florida and U.S. District Court, Middle District of Florida. *Education:* Furman University (B.A., 1998); University of Florida (J.D., cum laude, 2001). *Member:* Hillsborough County Bar Association; The Florida Bar. (Resident, Tampa, Florida Office). ***PRACTICE AREAS:*** Litigation. ***Email:*** rhenderson@slk-law.com

JOHN D. KOCHER, born Harrisburg, Pennsylvania, February 25, 1968; admitted to bar, 1993, New Jersey and U.S. District Court, District of New Jersey; 1994, Pennsylvania; 2000, North Carolina and U.S. District Court, Western District of North Carolina; 2001, U.S. District Court, Middle and Western Districts of North Carolina. *Education:* Pennsylvania State University (B.A., History, cum laude, 1990); Dickinson School of Law of the Pennsylvania State University (J.D., cum laude, 1993). Member: Woolack Society; The Federalist Society. *Member:* Bergen County, Mecklenburg County, North Carolina, New Jersey State and Pennsylvania Bar Associations; North Carolina State Bar; Morris Pashman Inns of Court. (Resident, Charlotte, North Carolina Office). ***PRACTICE AREAS:*** Medical Malpractice Litigation; Insurance Defense Litigation. ***Email:*** jkocher@slk-law.com

SAMUEL R. LINSKY, admitted to bar, 2002, Florida and Georgia. *Education:* University of Michigan (B.A., with distinction, 1998); University of Florida (J.D., with honors, 2001); New York University School of Law (LL.M., Taxation, 2002). *Member:* State Bar of Georgia (Member, Tax Section); The Florida Bar (Member, Tax Section); American Bar Association. (Resident, Tampa, Florida Office). ***PRACTICE AREAS:*** Tax and Benefits; Trusts and Estates. ***Email:*** slinsky@slk-law.com

KATHLEEN K. LUCCHESI, born Anderson, Indiana, September 20, 1968; admitted to bar, 1997, North Carolina. *Education:* University of Indianapolis (B.S., cum laude,

(This Listing Continued)

SHUMAKER, LOOP & KENDRICK, LLP, Toledo—Continued

1990); University of Mississippi (J.D., cum laude, 1997). Runner-Up, Ole Miss Moot Court Oral Advocacy Competition, Fall 1995. First Place, Feature Division, Indiana Associated Press Television Award, 1992. Author, "The Pros Don't Always Get Three Strikes: How Gambling Shaped the Supervisory Powers Governing Professional Sports," Gaming Law Review, Winter 1997. Instructor, Queens University Forensic Medicine Course, North Carolina Statutory Law Section, Fall 2002 and Spring 2003. Assistant District Attorney, Mecklenburg County, Charlotte, North Carolina, 1997-2003. *Member:* Mecklenburg County, North Carolina and American Bar Associations; North Carolina State Bar; North Carolina Association of Defense Attorneys; Defense Research Institute. (Resident, Charlotte, North Carolina Office). ***PRACTICE AREAS:*** Litigation; Medical Malpractice. ***Email:*** klucchesi@slk-law.com

DAVID J. MACK, born Defiance, Ohio, February 8, 1970; admitted to bar, 2000, Ohio. *Education:* University of Toledo (B.A., 1996; J.D., magna cum laude, 2000). Phi Kappa Phi; Order of the Coif. Member, Toledo Law Review. Author, "Cleansing the System: A Fresh Approach to Liability for the Negligent or Fraudulent Transmission of Sexually Transmitted Diseases," 30 U. Tol. L. Rev. 647 (1999). *Member:* Ohio State and American Bar Associations. ***PRACTICE AREAS:*** Banking Law; Regulatory Law; Securities Law; Corporate Governance; Mergers and Acquisitions. ***Email:*** dmack@slk-law.com

PATRICIA WILSON MAGEE, born Charlotte, North Carolina, January 8, 1978; admitted to bar, 2003, North Carolina. *Education:* University of North Carolina at Chapel Hill (B.A., 2000); Campbell University (J.D., 2003). Phi Alpha Delta (Chief Justice, Iredell Chapter, 2002-2003); Order of the Old Kivett. Law Clerk to the Hon. John M. Tyson, North Carolina Court of Appeals, 2003-2005. *Member:* Mecklenburg County, North Carolina and American Bar Associations; North Carolina State Bar. (Resident, Charlotte, North Carolina Office). ***PRACTICE AREAS:*** Civil Litigation. ***Email:*** tmagee@slk-law.com

NICHOLAS D. MALONE, born Toledo, Ohio, April 2, 1979; admitted to bar, 2004, Ohio. *Education:* University of Notre Dame (B.A., 2001); Indiana University (J.D., 2004). ***PRACTICE AREAS:*** Corporate Law. ***Email:*** nmalone@slk-law.com

JASON M. MANOR, born Dearborn, Michigan; admitted to bar, 2000, Michigan. *Education:* University of Michigan (B.A., with distinction, 1996); University of California School of Law, Los Angeles (J.D., 2000). *Member:* State Bar of Michigan. (Resident, Tampa, Florida Office). ***PRACTICE AREAS:*** Commercial Litigation; Toxic Torts; Construction Law; Contracts. ***Email:*** jmanor@slk-law.com

DAVID A. MATTHEWS, born Long Beach, California, 1968; admitted to bar, 1998, California; 2002, North Carolina. *Education:* Azusa Pacific University (B.A., cum laude, 1995); McGeorge School of Law (J.D., with distinction, 1998). Member, Traynor Honor Society. *Member:* Mecklenburg County, North Carolina and American Bar Associations; State Bar of California; American Bankruptcy Institute. (Resident, Charlotte, North Carolina Office). ***PRACTICE AREAS:*** Bankruptcy; Creditors Rights; Commercial Litigation. ***Email:*** dmatthews@slk-law.com

GREGORY E. MATTON, born Boston, Massachusetts, November 18, 1964; admitted to bar, 1998, California; U.S. District Court, Central District of California. *Education:* Emory University (B.A., 1988); Loyola Law School (J.D., 1998). Staff Member, 1997 and Editor-in-Chief, 1998, Loyola Law School International & Comparative Law Journal. Law Clerk to Hon. Florence-Marie Cooper, U.S. District Court, Central District of California, 1999-2000. *Member:* Los Angeles County Bar Association; State Bar of California. (Resident, Tampa, Florida Office). ***PRACTICE AREAS:*** Corporate Law; Securities; Mergers and Acquisitions; Commercial Real Estate. ***Email:*** gmatton@slk-law.com

STEVEN A. MECKLER, born Akron, Ohio, December 30, 1970; admitted to bar, 1999, North Carolina and U.S. District Court, Eastern, Middle and Western Districts of North Carolina; 2000, South Carolina and U.S. District Court, District of South Carolina. *Education:* Kent State University (B.A., 1993); Case Western Reserve University (J.D., cum laude, 1999). Member, State Liason, DRI Medical Liability and Health Care Law Committee. *Member:* Mecklenburg County (Member, Professionalism Committee, 2002—; Chair, Education Committee, 2002— and Member, Board of Directors, 2003—, Young Lawyers Division), North Carolina (Appointed Member, Bench/Bar Liason Committee, 2002—; Vice-Chairman, Litigation CLE Committee, 2003-2004) and American Bar Associations; North Carolina State Bar; South Carolina Bar; North Carolina Association of Defense Attorneys; Defense Research Institute. (Resident, Charlotte, North Carolina Office). ***PRACTICE AREAS:*** Complex Commercial Litigation; Products Liability; Medical Malpractice; Catastrophic Injury; Personal Injury; Federal Court Litigation. ***Email:*** smeckler@slk-law.com

MARK E. MERCER, born September 8, 1966; admitted to bar, 2002, Ohio. *Education:* University of Toledo (B.A., 1989; J.D., 2002). *Member:* Toledo and Ohio State Bar Associations. ***PRACTICE AREAS:*** Environmental Law; Litigation. ***Email:*** mmercer@slk-law.com

JAMES H. O'DOHERTY, born Ann Arbor, Michigan, October 9, 1973; admitted to bar, 1999, Ohio; 2000, Michigan. *Education:* University of Michigan (B.A., 1996); Duke University (J.D., 1999). *Member:* Toledo, Ohio State and American Bar Associations. ***PRACTICE AREAS:*** Litigation. ***Email:*** jodoherty@slk-law.com

W. JAN PIETRUSZKA, born Jackson, New Jersey, September 7, 1973; admitted to bar, 1999, Florida. *Education:* Catholic University of America (B.A., 1995); Stetson University College of Law (J.D., cum laude, 1999). Phi Delta Phi. *Member:* Hillsborough County Bar Association; The Florida Bar. (Resident, Tampa, Florida Office). ***PRACTICE AREAS:*** Labor and Employment; Civil Litigation. ***Email:*** jpietruszka@slk-law.com

MICHAEL J. PODOLSKY, born Pittsburgh, Pennsylvania, July 7, 1969; admitted to bar, 2002, Ohio; 2003, U.S. District Court, Northern District of Ohio; 2004, U.S. District Court, Southern District of Ohio and U.S. Court of Appeals, Sixth Circuit. *Education:* University of Pennsylvania (Ph.D., 1994); Case Western Reserve University (J.D., 2002). ***PRACTICE AREAS:*** Litigation. ***Email:*** mpodolsky@slk-law.com

MARIA C. RAMOS, born San Juan, Puerto Rico; admitted to bar, 2000, Florida; 2001, U.S. District Court, Northern, Middle and Southern Districts of Florida and U.S. Court of Appeals, Eleventh Circuit. *Education:* Yale University (B.A., 1996); University of Miami (J.D., 2000). Phi Alpha Delta. MPLE Scholar. Member, International Moot Court Board. Participant, International Moot Court Competition. Recipient, Dean's Honor Scholarship. *Member:* Hillsborough County Bar Association; The Florida Bar (Member, International Law Section). (Resident, Tampa, Florida Office). ***LANGUAGES:*** Spanish and Portuguese. ***PRACTICE AREAS:*** Labor and Employment; Commercial Litigation; Intellectual Property; Fidelity and Surety; Bankruptcy. ***Email:*** mramos@slk-law.com

DAMIAN M.P. RODGERS, born Johnstown, Pennsylvania, 1968; admitted to bar, 1994, Ohio; U.S. District Court, Northern and Southern Districts of Ohio; U.S. Court of Appeals, Sixth Circuit. *Education:* Kenyon College (B.A., with distinction, 1990); University of Toledo (J.D., 1993). Member, Moot Court Trial Team. Faculty Member, University of Toledo. *Member:* Toledo, Ohio State and American Bar Associations; American Health Lawyers Association; American Inns of Court (Morrison R. Waite Chapter). ***PRACTICE AREAS:*** Hospital Law; Health Care; Medicare and Medicaid. ***Email:*** drodgers@slk-law.com

JOSEPH J. SANTANIELLO, born Jamaica, New York, April 21, 1972; admitted to bar, 1997, North Carolina. *Education:* University of North Carolina (B.A., 1994; J.D., 1997). Phi Delta Phi. *Member:* North Carolina and American Bar Associations; North Carolina State Bar. (Resident, Charlotte, North Carolina Office). ***LANGUAGES:*** Spanish. ***PRACTICE AREAS:*** Business Law; Commercial Law; Bankruptcy. ***Email:*** jsantaniello@slk-law.com

S. ALBAN SCOTT, born Toronto, Ontario, Canada, January 19, 1977; admitted to bar, 1999, Massachusetts. *Education:* Morehouse College (B.A., 1996); New York University (J.D., 1999). Phi Beta Kappa. (Resident, Tampa, Florida Office). ***PRACTICE AREAS:*** Corporate Law; Mergers and Acquisitions; Securities. ***Email:*** sscott@slk-law.com

ROBERT E. SEARFOSS, III, born Bethesda, Maryland, March 8, 1977; admitted to bar, 2005, Ohio. *Education:* Bowling Green State University (B.S., 2000); University of Toledo (J.D., 2004). Valedictorian, University of Toledo College of Law, 2004. *Member:* Toledo, Wood County, Ohio State and American (Member, Tax Group) Bar Associations. [Reservist, U.S. Army]. ***PRACTICE AREAS:*** Taxation; Estate Planning; Trust Administration; Estate Administration; Employee Compensation; Employee Benefits. ***Email:*** rsearfoss@slk-law.com

GREGORY J. SHOPE, born Columbus, Ohio, October 8, 1973; admitted to bar, 2001, Ohio. *Education:* The Ohio State University (B.A., summa cum laude, 1996; J.D., with honors, 2001). Phi Beta Kappa. *Member:* Toledo, Ohio State and American Bar Associations. ***PRACTICE AREAS:*** Corporate Law; Mergers, Acquisitions and Divestitures; Securities. ***Email:*** gshope@slk-law.com

CHRISTOPHER M. SMITH, born Painesville, Ohio, February 22, 1972; admitted to bar, 2000, Ohio. *Education:* Kent State University (B.A., 1994); Ohio Northern University (J.D., 2000); Georgetown University (LL.M., Taxation, 2001). *Member:* Toledo and Ohio State Bar Associations. [Corporal, U.S. Army, 1992-1994]. ***PRACTICE AREAS:*** Corporate Law; Employee Benefits; Executive Compensation. ***Email:*** csmith@slk-law.com

MICHAEL A. SNYDER, born North Canton, Ohio, January 8, 1973; admitted to bar, 1998, Ohio; 1999, U.S. District Court, Northern and Southern Districts of Ohio and U.S. Court of Appeals, Sixth Circuit. *Education:* Ohio University (B.A., cum laude, 1995); Capital University (J.D., magna cum laude, 1998). Order of the Curia. Capital University Law Review, 1997-1998. *Member:* Columbus, Ohio State, Federal, and American Bar Associations. (Resident, Columbus, Ohio Office). ***PRACTICE AREAS:*** Environmental Law; Litigation; Administrative Law; Regulatory Litigation. ***Email:*** msnyder@slk-law.com

JOHN J. STALER, born Toledo, Ohio, November 21, 1971; admitted to bar, 1999, Ohio. *Education:* University of Toledo (B.A., 1995; J.D. 1998). Certified Public Accountant, Ohio. *Member:* Toledo and Ohio State Bar Associations; Ohio Society of Certified Public Accountants; American Institute of Certified Public Accountants. ***PRACTICE AREAS:*** Taxation. ***Email:*** jstaler@slk-law.com

CYNTHIA L.K. STEELE, born Toledo, Ohio, June 13, 1963; admitted to bar, 1992, California; 1994, U.S. District Court, Central District of California; 1998, Ohio. *Education:* University of Toledo (B.S.N., cum laude, 1985); University of Arizona (J.D., 1992). Phi Delta Phi. Registered Nurse: Ohio, 1985; Arizona, 1985; Texas, 1989; California, 1992 (Nursing practice featured in Spring 1988 Tucson Medical Center Foundation Journal). Author: "California Legislative Update," Cotkin & Collins Legal Update, Fall, 1994. Co-Author: "California Legislative Update," SCAHRM Forum, April, 1994. Civil Practice Internship, Office of the Attorney General, Insurance Defense Division, Tucson, State of Arizona, 1992. Judicial Clerk-Extern, Honorable Alfredo C. Marquez, U.S. District Court, District of Arizona, 1991. *Member:* State Bar of California. ***PRACTICE AREAS:*** Litigation. ***Email:*** csteele@slk-law.com

KAREN H. STILES, born Mooresville, North Carolina, February 16, 1972; admitted to bar, 2002, North Carolina. *Education:* Peace College (A.A., 1992); University of North Carolina at Chapel Hill (B.A., 1994); Meredith College (Paralegal Certification, 1994); Norman A. Wiggins, School of Law (J.D., 2002). *Member:* Mecklenburg County and North Carolina Bar Associations; North Carolina State Bar; North Carolina Association of Defense Attorneys; Defense Research Institute. (Resident, Charlotte, North Carolina Office). ***PRACTICE AREAS:*** Medical Malpractice. ***Email:*** kstiles@slk-law.com

ROBERT ERNEST SUMNER, IV, born Columbia, South Carolina, May 9, 1977; admitted to bar, 2002, North Carolina and U.S. District Court, Western District of North Carolina; 2003, South Carolina. *Education:* University of North Carolina at Chapel Hill (B.A., English, 1999); University of South Carolina (J.D., 2002). *Member:* Mecklenburg County and North Carolina Bar Associations; North Carolina State Bar; South Carolina Bar; Noarth Carolina Association of Defense Attorneys; Defense Research Institute. (Resident, Charlotte, North Carolina Office). ***PRACTICE AREAS:*** Medical Malpractice. ***Email:*** rsumner@slk-law.com

KATIE L. TOURNOUX, admitted to bar, 2002, Ohio. *Education:* Saint Mary's College (B.A., cum laude, 1999); Ohio State University Moritz College of Law (J.D., 2002). (Resident, Columbus, Ohio Office). ***PRACTICE AREAS:*** Litigation. ***Email:*** ktournoux@slk-law.com

MARK D. WAGONER, JR., born Toledo, Ohio, September 18, 1971; admitted to bar, 1997, Ohio and U.S. District Court, Northern District of Ohio; 1998, Michigan, U.S. District Court, Eastern and Western Districts of Michigan and U.S. Court of Appeals, Sixth

(This Listing Continued)

(This Listing Continued)

Circuit; 1999, U.S. District Court, Southern District of Ohio; 2001, U.S. Court of Appeals, Federal Circuit. *Education:* Georgetown University (B.A., cum laude, 1994); The Ohio State University College of Law (J.D., with honors, 1997). Member, 1995-1996 and Articles Editor, 1996-1997, Ohio State Law Journal. Author: "The Public Policy Exception to the Employment at Will Doctrine in Ohio: The Need for a Legislative Approach," The Ohio State Law Journal, 1999. President, Ohio State College of Law, Student Bar Association, 1996-1997. *Member:* Toledo, Ohio State and American Bar Associations. ***PRACTICE AREAS:*** Complex Litigation; Trial Practice; Appellate Practice; Franchise Litigation. ***Email:*** mwagoner@slk-law.com

S. FREDERICK WINIKER, III, born Charlotte, North Carolina, November 21, 1966; admitted to bar, 1995, North Carolina; 1999, U.S. District Court, Eastern District of Washington and U.S. Court Appeals, Ninth Circuit. *Education:* Wake Forest University (B.A., 1989); Gonzaga University (J.D., cum laude, 1995). *Member:* Mecklenburg and North Carolina Bar Associations. [1st Lt., U.S. Army, 1989-1992]. (Resident, Charlotte, North Carolina Office). ***LANGUAGES:*** German. ***REPORTED CASES:*** United States v. Kafka, 222 F.3d 1129, (9th Cir. 2000). ***PRACTICE AREAS:*** Commercial Litigation; Medical Malpractice. ***Email:*** rwiniker@slk-law.com

MECHELLE ZAROU, born Northville, Michigan, June 5, 1974; admitted to bar, 2000, Ohio; 2001, Michigan. *Education:* University of Michigan (B.A., 1996); Duke University (J.D. & M.A., 2000). 2000 Siegel Scholar. Author: Note, "The Good, The Bad and The Ugly: Drug Testing By Alaska Employers," Alaska Law Review, December 1999. *Member:* Toledo and Ohio State Bar Associations; Toledo Women's Bar Association; Ohio State Women's Bar Association. ***LANGUAGES:*** French. ***PRACTICE AREAS:*** Labor and Employment; Workers Compensation; Immigration and Naturalization. ***Email:*** mzarou@slk-law.com

OF COUNSEL

GREGORY G. ALEXANDER, born Cleveland, Ohio, February 12, 1929; admitted to bar, 1954, Ohio; 1983, Florida. *Education:* Culver Military Academy; Yale University (A.B., 1951); Harvard Law School (J.D., 1954). *Member:* Toledo and Ohio State (Chairman, Committee on Corporation Law, 1973) Bar Associations; The Florida Bar. ***PRACTICE AREAS:*** Estate Planning; Corporate Law. ***Email:*** galexander@slk-law.com

MARC GERTNER, born Columbus, Ohio, April 17, 1932; admitted to bar, 1957, Ohio; 1958, Rhode Island. *Education:* Harvard University (A.B., cum laude, 1954); The Ohio State University (J.D., summa cum laude, 1957). Phi Delta Phi; Order of the Coif. Director, International Foundation of Employee Benefit Plans, 1976—. *Member:* Toledo, Ohio State and American (Member, Corporation, Banking and Business Law Section) Bar Associations. ***PRACTICE AREAS:*** Labor and Employment; Employee Benefits.

JOHN F. HAYWARD, born Toledo, Ohio, November 3, 1937; admitted to bar, 1966, Ohio. *Education:* University of Notre Dame (A.B., cum laude, 1959); Georgetown University (J.D., 1965). Assistant Prosecuting Attorney, Lucas County, 1966-1971. *Member:* Toledo (President, 1992-1993), Ohio State (Member, Board of Governors, 1999-2002) and American Bar Associations; Ohio State Bar Foundation (President, 1997); American Health Lawyers Association; American Judicature Society; National Diocesan Attorneys Association. ***PRACTICE AREAS:*** Health Law; Administrative Law; Nonprofit and Charitable Organizations. ***Email:*** jhayward@slk-law.com

A. EDWARD McGINTY, born November 17, 1942; admitted to bar, 1972, Florida; 1976, U.S. Tax Court. *Education:* Loyola University and Louisiana State University (B.A., 1965); Florida State University (J.D., with honors, 1972). Phi Delta Phi. Member, Executive Council, Tax Section, The Florida Bar, 1978-1983. (Resident, Tampa, Florida Office). ***PRACTICE AREAS:*** Corporate Law.

WALTER W. RECKLESS, born Nashville, Tennessee, September 12, 1936; admitted to bar, 1969, Ohio; U.S. District Court, Southern and Northern Districts of Ohio and U.S. Court of Appeals, Sixth Circuit. *Education:* The Ohio State University (B.S., 1959; J.D., 1969). Lecturer, Personal Injury Litigation and How to Take a Case to Federal Court, Ohio Legal Center Institute. Member, Examination and Admission Committee, U.S. District Court, Southern District of Ohio, 1977—. *Member:* Columbus (Chairman, Federal District Committee, 1974-1976), Ohio State, Federal and American Bar Associations; Franklin Inns of Court. (Resident, Columbus, Ohio Office) (Also practicing Individually, Columbus Ohio). ***PRACTICE AREAS:*** Trial Practice; Personal Injury; Products Liability; Professional Negligence; Medical Negligence; Professional Malpractice; Medical Malpractice; Employment Law; White Collar Criminal Defense. ***Email:*** wreckless@slk-law.com

DARREL J. SCOTT, born Indianapolis, Indiana; admitted to bar, 1990, Indiana; 1998, Texas; 2005, Ohio. *Education:* Indiana University (B.A., 1969; M.H.A., with high honors, 1971); University of Louisville (J.D., 1990). Member, Law Review, University of Louisville. *Member:* Indiana State Bar Association; State Bar of Texas (Member, Health Law Section); American Health Lawyers Association. Fellow, American College of Healthcare Executives. ***PRACTICE AREAS:*** Health Law; Corporate Law. ***Email:*** dscott@slk-law.com

COUNSEL

ALEJANDRO J. FERNANDEZ, born Caracas, Venezuela; admitted to bar, 2001, Illinois; 2002, U.S. District Court, Northern District of Illinois; registered to practice before U.S. Patent and Trademark Office. *Education:* Palm Beach Atlantic College (B.S., 1998); Carlos III University, Madrid, Spain (European Industrial Property Prosecution Certificate, 1999); Franklin Pierce Law Center (J.D., 2001). Former Intern for Judge Randall R. Rader, U.S. Court of Appeals for the Federal Circuit, 2000. Member: Intellectual Property Owners; Minority Corporate Counsel of America. *Member:* American Intellectual Property Association. (Resident, Tampa, Florida Office). ***LANGUAGES:*** Spanish. ***PRACTICE AREAS:*** Intellectual Property; International Intellectual Property; Patent Litigation; Patent Prosecution; Mechanical Patents; Biotechnology; Drug and Medical Device Defense. ***Email:*** afernandez@slk-law.com

TAMMY N. GIROUX, born Southbridge, Massachusetts, June 7, 1969; admitted to bar, 1994, Florida; 2001, Colorado; U.S. District Court, Middle, Southern and Northern Districts of Florida (Not admitted in Ohio). *Education:* Florida State University (B.S., cum laude, 1991); Stetson University (J.D., cum laude, 1993). Phi Kappa Phi. *Member:* Hillsborough County and The Colorado Bar Associations; The Florida Bar. (Resident, Tampa, Florida Office). ***PRACTICE AREAS:*** Commercial Litigation; Fidelity and Surety. ***Email:*** tgiroux@slk-law.com

JAMES F. WHITE, JR., born Zanesville, Ohio, January 22, 1940; admitted to bar, 1965, Ohio. *Education:* Princeton University (A.B., 1962); Wharton School of Finance and Commerce (Graduate Division, 1966), University of Pennsylvania; The Ohio State University (J.D., 1965); New York University (LL.M. in Taxation, 1967). Phi Delta Phi. *Member:* Toledo, Ohio State (Member, Corporate Law Committee) and American Bar Associations. ***PRACTICE AREAS:*** Business Law; Mergers, Acquisitions and Divestitures; Taxation. ***Email:*** jwhite@slk-law.com

REPRESENTATIVE CLIENTS: AVAILABLE UPON REQUEST.

DAVID SIMKO

6620 WEST CENTRAL AVENUE
TOLEDO, OHIO 43617
Telephone: 419-517-5555
Fax: 419-517-5556
URL: http://www.lawyers.com/davidsimko

Estate Planning, Real Estate, Small Business.

DAVID SIMKO, born Toledo, Ohio, July 30, 1949; admitted to bar, 1975, Ohio and U.S. District Court, Northern and Southern Districts of Ohio. *Education:* University of Toledo (B.A., 1971); Capital University (J.D., 1975). ***PRACTICE AREAS:*** Estate Planning; Real Estate; Small Business Law.

SLOWIK & ROBINSON, LLC

TOLEDO, OHIO
(See Columbus)

Labor and Employment Law, Immigration Law, Small Business Law, Alternative Dispute Resolution, Business Formations.

THOMAS A. SOBECKI

Established in 1987

520 MADISON AVENUE, SUITE 811
TOLEDO, OHIO 43604
Telephone: 419-242-9908
Fax: 419-242-9937
Email: tsobecki@tomsobecki.com
URL: http://www.lawyers.com/tomsobecki

Civil Rights, Discrimination, Libel, Slander and Defamation, Contracts, Breach of Contract, Education Law, School Law, Labor and Employment, Americans with Disabilities Act, Family and Medical Leave Act, Sexual Harassment, Wrongful Termination, Law Enforcement, Police Misconduct, Military Law.

FIRM PROFILE: Tom Sobecki started his practice in 1987 after completing his four year military obligation serving as an attorney in the U.S. Army JAG and a one year stint with the Rudnick and Wolfe law firm in Chicago. He specializes in employment law, discrimination and other areas of civil law, and appeals.

THOMAS A. SOBECKI, born August 11, 1956; admitted to bar, 1981, Ohio; 1985, Illinois; 1988, U.S. District Court, Northern District of Ohio and U.S. Court of Appeals, 6th Circuit; 1992, U.S. Supreme Court; 1999, U.S. District Court, Southern District of Ohio. *Education:* University of Toledo (B.A., summa cum laude, 1978); Northwestern University (J.D., 1981). *Member:* Toledo, Ohio State and American Bar Associations; National Employment Lawyers Association; Ohio Employment Lawyers Association. ***REPORTED CASES:*** Hall v. ITT Automotive, 362 F. Supp.2d 952 (N.D. Ohio 2005); Kaylor v. Rankin, 356 F. Supp.2d 839 (N.D. Ohio 2005); Schroeder v. Maumee Bd. of Educ., 296 F. Supp.2d 869 (N.D. Ohio 2003); McClain v. Northwest Community Corrections Center, 95 Ohio St.3d 484 (2002); Lagunovich v. Findlay City School System, 181 F.Supp.2d 753 (N.D. Ohio 2001); Pollard v. City of Northwood, 161 F. Supp.2d 782 (N.D. Ohio 2001); Hertzfeld v. Med. College of Ohio at Toledo, 145 Ohio App.3d 616 (2001); Bourquin v. Keybank, N.A., 138 Ohio App.3d 435 (2000); Irving v. Austin, 138 Ohio App.3d 552 (2000); Griswold v. Fresenius USA, Inc., 964 F.Supp. 1166 (N.D. Ohio 1997); Simpson v. Diversitech General, Inc., 945 F.2d 156 (6th Cir. 1991); Pratt v. UAW, Local 1435, 939 F.2d 385 (6th Cir. 1991).

SPENGLER NATHANSON P.L.L.

Established in 1947

608 MADISON AVENUE, SUITE 1000
TOLEDO, OHIO 43604-1169
Telephone: 419-241-2201
FAX: 419-241-8599
Email: jsilksr@spenglernathanson.com
URL: http://www.spenglernathanson.com

General Civil and Trial Practice in all State and Federal Courts. Federal and State Civil and Criminal Practice. Corporation, Taxation, Probate and Estate Planning, Real Estate, Education, Labor and Employment, Workers' Compensation, Commercial, Securities, Bankruptcy, Health Care, Employee Benefits, Public Sector Law and Environmental Law.

FIRM PROFILE: Spengler Nathanson P.L.L., formed on February 1, 1947 by Otto Spengler, Joe Nathanson, Bert Hebenstreit and Joe Heyman, is one of the top 50 law firms in the State of Ohio. Quality and effective case management is achieved through the use of attorneys in vari-

(This Listing Continued)

SPENGLER NATHANSON P.L.L., Toledo—Continued

ous specialties and augmented with paralegal and law clerk support. The Firm utilizes state of the art computer and telecommunications systems to maintain contact with clients, research facilities and other law practitioners.

OTTO H. SPENGLER (1890-1970)
JOHN J. McCARTHY (1909-1969)
J.H. NATHANSON (1906-1992)
FRANK T. PIZZA (1925-2000)
BENJAMIN B. DURFEE (1919-2000)

MEMBERS OF FIRM

RALPH BRAGG, born Dayton, Ohio, April 15, 1934; admitted to bar, 1959, Ohio. *Education:* Otterbein College (B.A., 1956); Harvard University (J.D., 1959). *Member:* Toledo, Ohio State (Member, Board of Governors, Real Estate Section, 1994—) and American Bar Associations. ***PRACTICE AREAS:*** Real Estate Law; Business Law; Corporate Law. ***Email:*** RalphBragg@SpenglerNathanson.com

JAMES R. JEFFERY, born Toledo, Ohio, June 20, 1938; admitted to bar, 1965, Ohio; 1967, U.S. District Court, Northern District of Ohio; 1968, U.S. Court of Appeals, Sixth Circuit; 1970, U.S. Supreme Court. *Education:* The Ohio State University (B.A., 1961); University of Toledo (J.D., 1965). Delta Theta Phi. *Member:* Toledo (President, 1985-1986) and Ohio State (President, 1995-1996) Bar Associations. ***PRACTICE AREAS:*** Litigation. ***Email:*** JJeffery@SpenglerNathanson.com

NORMAN J. RUBINOFF, born Springfield, Ohio, July 8, 1941; admitted to bar, 1966, Ohio. *Education:* The Ohio State University (B.A., 1962); University of Toledo (M.B.A., 1967); Western Reserve University (J.D., 1965). Member, Board of Editors, Western Reserve Law Review, 1964-1965. *Member:* Toledo and Ohio State Bar Associations. ***PRACTICE AREAS:*** Estate Planning; Business Law; Real Estate. ***Email:*** NRubinoff@SpenglerNathanson.com

B. GARY McBRIDE, born St. Helens, Oregon, June 13, 1939; admitted to bar, 1964, Oregon; 1967, Ohio. *Education:* Willamette University (B.A., 1961; J.D., 1963); Harvard University (LL.M., 1964). Editor-in-Chief, Willamette Law Journal, 1962-1963. Special Counsel to the Attorney General of Ohio, 1971-1995. *Member:* Toledo and Ohio State Bar Associations; Oregon State Bar. ***PRACTICE AREAS:*** Special Education Law; School Law; Labor Relations Law. ***Email:*** GMcBride@SpenglerNathanson.com

DAVID G. WISE, born Dayton, Ohio, October 3, 1942; admitted to bar, 1967, Ohio; 1968, Michigan; 1980, U.S. Supreme Court; 1986, U.S. Tax Court. *Education:* Wittenberg University (B.A., 1964); University of Michigan (J.D., 1967). Member, 1980-1988 and President, 1983, Board of Education of Perrysburg, Ohio. President, Toledo Organization of Management, 1990-1991. *Member:* Toledo and Ohio State Bar Associations; State Bar of Michigan. ***PRACTICE AREAS:*** Estate Planning; Construction Law; Business Law; Real Estate. ***Email:*** DaveWise@SpenglerNathanson.com

THEODORE M. ROWEN, born Brooklyn, New York, November 7, 1945; admitted to bar, 1970, Ohio. *Education:* University of Vermont (B.A., 1967); University of Cincinnati (J.D., 1970). Order of the Coif. Member, Board of Editors, University of Cincinnati Law Review, 1969-1970. Law Clerk to Hon. Don J. Young, U.S. District Court, Northern District of Ohio, Western Division, 1970-1972. Chairman, Sixth Circuit Judicial Screening Selection Committee for Bankruptcy Judges, 1999-2000. *Member:* Toledo, Ohio State and Federal (President, 1977-1978) Bar Associations. ***PRACTICE AREAS:*** Corporate Litigation; Employment Law; School Law; Banking Law; Federal Court Litigation. ***Email:*** TedRowen@SpenglerNathanson.com

GARY D. SIKKEMA, born Grand Rapids, Michigan, July 30, 1947; admitted to bar, 1975, Ohio. *Education:* University of Michigan (B.B.A., 1970; J.D., 1975). *Member:* Toledo, Ohio State and American Bar Associations; State Bar of Michigan. ***PRACTICE AREAS:*** Real Estate; Corporate Law. ***Email:*** GarySikkema@SpenglerNathanson.com

TRUMAN A. GREENWOOD, born Columbus, Ohio, July 3, 1949; admitted to bar, 1979, Ohio. *Education:* A.F.S. Foreign Exchange Student, Goslar, Germany, 1966-1967; Denison University (B.A., 1971); University of Toledo (J.D., 1978). Associate Editor, University of Toledo Law Review, 1978-1979. Ohio General Assembly, 1989-1995. Secretary and Treasurer, Ohio Turnpike Commission, 1999—. *Member:* Toledo and Ohio State Bar Associations. [1st Lt., U.S. Army, 1972-1976]. ***LANGUAGES:*** German. ***PRACTICE AREAS:*** Litigation; Government Affairs. ***Email:*** TGreenwood@SpenglerNathanson.com

CHERYL F. WOLFF, born Dayton, Ohio, March 18, 1953; admitted to bar, 1979, Ohio. *Education:* Miami University (B.S., cum laude, 1974); The Ohio State University (J.D., with honors, 1979). Phi Beta Kappa. *Member:* Toledo and Ohio State Bar Associations. ***PRACTICE AREAS:*** School Law; Employment Discrimination Law; Labor Law. ***Email:*** CWolff@SpenglerNathanson.com

LOUISE A. JACKSON, born Bowling Green, Ohio, July 27, 1948; admitted to bar, 1977, Ohio. *Education:* Bowling Green State University (B.A., 1970); University of Colorado at Boulder (M.B.A., 1971); University of Toledo (J.D., 1976). Certified Public Accountant, Ohio, 1974. Vice Chairman, Ohio Board of Tax Appeals, 1991—. *Member:* Toledo (Treasurer, 1994-1997; Member and Past Chairman, Taxation Committee; Member, Probate Committee) and Ohio State (Member, Taxation Committee) Bar Associations; Ohio Society of Certified Public Accountants (Vice-President, 1995-1997; Past President, Toledo Chapter); Toledo Estate Planning Council. ***PRACTICE AREAS:*** Taxation Law; Corporate Law; Estate Planning; Employee Benefit Plans. ***Email:*** LJackson@SpenglerNathanson.com

RICHARD E. WOLFF, born Toledo, Ohio, March 3, 1955; admitted to bar, 1980, Ohio. *Education:* Miami University (B.A., magna cum laude, 1977); College of William and Mary (J.D., 1980). Phi Beta Kappa. Associate Editor, William and Mary Law Review, 1979-1980. *Member:* Toledo and Ohio State Bar Associations. ***PRACTICE AREAS:*** Business Law; Real Estate Law; Commercial Law; Health Care. ***Email:*** RWolff@SpenglerNathanson.com

BYRON S. CHOKA, born Fort Wayne, Indiana, June 19, 1955; admitted to bar, 1980, Ohio. *Education:* Ohio Wesleyan University (B.A., 1977); University of Toledo (J.D., 1980). Note and Comment Editor, University of Toledo Law Review, 1979-1980. Law Clerk, Lucas County Court of Common Pleas, 1980-1982. *Member:* Toledo and Ohio State Bar Associations. ***PRACTICE AREAS:*** Litigation; Federal Practice. ***Email:*** ByronChoka@SpenglerNathanson.com

JAMES C. ANDERSON, born Toledo, Ohio, January 23, 1953; admitted to bar, 1979, Ohio. *Education:* University of Toledo (B.A., magna cum laude, 1975); Ohio Northern University (J.D., 1979). Member, Toledo Estate Planning Council. *Member:* Toledo (Member, Probate, Estate Planning and Trust Law Committee) and Ohio State (Member, Probate, Estate Planning and Trust Law Sections) Bar Associations. ***PRACTICE AREAS:*** Estate Planning Law; Probate Law; Estate and Gift Taxation; Generation Skipping Tax. ***Email:*** JimAnderson@SpenglerNathanson.com

SUSAN B. NELSON, born Royal Oak, Michigan, March 13, 1953; admitted to bar, 1981, Ohio. *Education:* University of Michigan (B.A., with honors, 1975); University of Toledo (J.D., 1981). Sixth Circuit Review Editor, University of Toledo Law Review, 1980-1981. Law Clerk, Lucas County Court of Common Pleas, 1981-1983. Member, Board of Commissioners on Grievances and Discipline, 1993-1995. *Member:* Toledo and Ohio State Bar Associations; Defense Research Institute. ***PRACTICE AREAS:*** Litigation; Employment Law. ***Email:*** SusanNelson@SpenglerNathanson.com

LISA E. PIZZA, born Toledo, Ohio, December 31, 1954; admitted to bar, 1981, Ohio. *Education:* Miami University (B.A., 1976); The University of Toledo (J.D., 1980). Member, The University of Toledo Law Review, 1978-1979. Assistant Attorney General, State of Ohio, 1981-1985. *Member:* Toledo and Ohio State Bar Associations. ***SPECIAL AGENCIES:*** Ohio Chiropractic Examining Board, 1985-1987; Ohio Student Loan Commission, 1990-1993. ***PRACTICE AREAS:*** Education Law; Local Government Law; Civil Rights; Labor (Management) Law. ***Email:*** LisaPizza@SpenglerNathanson.com

JOAN C. SZUBERLA, born Memphis, Tennessee, February 3, 1942; admitted to bar, 1983, Ohio; 1985, U.S. District Court, Northern District of Ohio and U.S. Court of Appeals, Sixth Circuit; 1992, U.S. Supreme Court. *Education:* Dominican University (B.A., 1964); Johns Hopkins University (M.A.T., 1965); University of Toledo (J.D., magna cum laude, 1983). Order of the Coif. Articles Editor, The University of Toledo Law Review, 1982-1983. Law Clerk to the Honorable John W. Potter, U.S. District Court, Northern District of Ohio, Western Division, 1983-1985. *Member:* Toledo and Ohio State Bar Associations. ***PRACTICE AREAS:*** Civil Rights; Commercial Litigation; Government Liability. ***Email:*** JSzuberla@SpenglerNathanson.com

TERESA L. GRIGSBY, born Lima, Ohio, December 6, 1959; admitted to bar, 1985, Ohio. *Education:* Bowling Green State University (B.S., summa cum laude, 1982); The University of Toledo (J.D., magna cum laude, 1985). Order of the Coif. Student Articles Editor, The University of Toledo Law Review, 1984-1985. *Member:* Toledo and Ohio State Bar Associations. ***PRACTICE AREAS:*** Commercial Litigation; Governmental Liability; Insurance Defense. ***Email:*** TeresaGrigsby@SpenglarNathanson.com

MICHAEL W. BRAGG, born Toledo, Ohio, January 9, 1960; admitted to bar, 1985, Ohio. *Education:* College of Wooster (B.A., with honors, 1982); Case Western Reserve University (J.D., cum laude, 1985). Associate Editor, Case Western Reserve University Law Review, 1983-1984. *Member:* Toledo (Chairman, Real Estate Committee, 1999-2000) and Ohio State Bar Associations. ***PRACTICE AREAS:*** Corporate Law; Insolvency Law; Real Estate Law. ***Email:*** MBragg@SpenglerNathanson.com

JAMES P. SILK, JR., born April 29, 1968; admitted to bar, 1993, Ohio. *Education:* Duke University (B.A., cum laude, 1990): University of Michigan (J.D., 1993). Law Clerk, The Honorable James G. Carr, U.S. District Court, Northern District Western Division of Ohio, 1993-1995. *Member:* Toledo and Ohio State Bar Associations. ***PRACTICE AREAS:*** Civil Rights; Commercial Litigation; Governmental Liability; Insurance Defense. ***Email:*** JSilk@SpenglerNathanson.com

LAURIE J. PANGLE, born Columbus, Ohio, June 13, 1958; admitted to bar, 1983, Ohio; 1984, U.S. District Court, Northern District of Ohio; 1987, U.S. District Court, Southern District of Ohio. *Education:* University of Michigan (B.A., with honors, 1980); Valparaiso University (J.D., 1983). General Counsel, TrustCorp Company, 1986-1988. Vice President and General Counsel, 5/3 Bank, 1989-2002. Attorney, The Toledo Trust Company, 1984-1986. *Member:* Toledo and Ohio State Bar Associations. ***PRACTICE AREAS:*** Banking Law; Finance; Real Estate. ***Email:*** LPangle@SpenglerNathanson.com

PATRICIA HAYDEN KURT, born Washington, D.C., December 30, 1955; admitted to bar, 1982, Ohio and U.S. District court, Northern District of Ohio. *Education:* Michigan State University (B.A., 1979); University of Toledo College of Law (J.D., 1982). Assistant Public Defender, 1985-2001. ***PRACTICE AREAS:*** Domestic Relations (90%); Juvenile Law; Criminal Law (10%).

THOMAS A. LUPICA, born Toledo, Ohio, December 19, 1964; admitted to bar, 1990, Ohio; 1991, U.S. District Court, District of Ohio. *Education:* University of Toledo (B.A., cum laude, 1987; J.D., cum laude, 1990). Psi Chi. Technical Editor, University of Toledo Law Review, 1990. Recipient: Two American Jurisprudence Awards. *Member:* Toledo and Ohio State Bar Associations. ***PRACTICE AREAS:*** Business Law; Real Estate; Estate Planning. ***Email:*** TLupica@SpenglerNathanson.com

ANASTASIA K. HANSON, born Toledo, Ohio, October 28, 1956; admitted to bar, 2000, Ohio. *Education:* University of Toledo (B.A., 1978; MPA, 1980; J.D., magna cum laude, 2000). Underwriter, Chartered Property & Casualty, 1994. *Member, Ohio State Bar Association.* ***PRACTICE AREAS:*** Litigation; Employment Law; Insurance. ***Email:*** shanson@spenglernathanson.com

JOHN P. HAYWARD, born Toledo, Ohio, April 2, 1966; admitted to bar, 1995, Ohio; 1996, Michigan; U.S. District Court, Northern District of Ohio. *Education:* University of Notre Dame (B.A., Economics, 1988); University of Toledo (J.D., 1995). *Member:* Toledo and Ohio State Bar Associations; State Bar of Michigan. ***PRACTICE AREAS:*** Litigation; Products Liability; Employment Law; Professional Malpractice. ***Email:*** jhayward@spenglernathanson.com

(This Listing Continued)

ASSOCIATE

RANDY L. MEYER, born Defiance, Ohio, February 26, 1959; admitted to bar, 1999, Ohio. *Education:* Defiance College (B.A., 1985); University of Toledo (M.A., 1987; Ph.D., 1994; J.D., 1999). Associate Editor, University of Toledo Law Review, 1998-1999. Intern, U.S. District Court, Northern District of Ohio, 1999. Recipient, Corpus Juris Secundum Award in Contracts I, Contract II. *Member:* Toledo and Ohio State Bar Associations. [Specialist Fourth Class, U.S. Army Military Police Corps, 1977-1980]. ***PRACTICE AREAS:*** Insurance Defense; Public Sector Collective Bargaining; Probate. ***Email:*** rmeyer@spenglernathanson.com

OF COUNSEL

JOEL A. LEVINE, born Toledo, Ohio, August 30, 1938; admitted to bar, 1963, Ohio. *Education:* University of Michigan (B.A., 1960; J.D., 1963). *Member:* Toledo and Ohio State Bar Associations. ***Email:*** JoelLevine@SpenglerNathanson.com

JAMES P. SILK, SR., born Toledo, Ohio, May 22, 1931; admitted to bar, 1962, Ohio; 1975, U.S. District Court, Northern District of Ohio. *Education:* University of Notre Dame (B.A., 1953); University of Toledo (LL.B., 1962). Delta Theta Phi (President, 1960-1961); General Counsel, 1975-1996 and Head of Trust Division, 1977-1995, Fifth-Third Bank of Northwestern Ohio, N.A.; President: Trust Division, Ohio Bankers Association, 1981-1982; Toledo Bar Association, 1982-1983. *Member:* Toledo, Ohio State and American Bar Associations. ***PRACTICE AREAS:*** Estates, Trusts and Probate; Financial Institutions. ***Email:*** JSilkSr@SpenglerNathanson.com

JOSEPH S. HEYMAN, born Monroeville, Ohio, September 13, 1913; admitted to bar, 1937, Ohio. *Education:* The Ohio State University (A.B., 1935; J.D., 1937). *Member:* Toledo (President, 1963-1964), Ohio State and American Bar Associations. Fellow, American Bar Foundation. (Retired)

ANDREW E. ANDERSON, born Marquette, Michigan, July 6, 1920; admitted to bar, 1948, Michigan; 1949, Ohio. *Education:* University of Michigan (A.B., 1942; J.D., 1948). Order of the Coif; Phi Beta Kappa; Phi Kappa Phi. Editor, Michigan Law Review, 1947-1948. Lecturer on Federal Estate and Gift Taxation, University of Toledo, 1961-1966. *Member:* Toledo (President, 1971-1972), Ohio State and American (Member, Section of Corporation, Banking and Business Law) Bar Associations. Fellow, American Bar Foundation. ***Email:*** AAnderson@SpenglerNathanson.com

RICHARD A. ENTENMANN, born Toledo, Ohio, April 20, 1927; admitted to bar, 1954, Ohio. *Education:* University of Michigan (B.A., 1950; J.D., 1954). Phi Delta Phi. *Member:* Toledo, Ohio State and American Bar Associations. ***PRACTICE AREAS:*** Estate Planning Law; Probate Law; Real Estate. ***Email:*** REntenmann@SpenglerNathanson.com

LOUIS J. HATTNER, born Toledo, Ohio, October 1, 1927; admitted to bar, 1968, Ohio. *Education:* University of Toledo (B.S., 1949; J.D., 1968). *Member:* Toledo, Lucas County (President, 1976) and Ohio State Bar Associations. ***PRACTICE AREAS:*** Bankruptcy Law; Domestic Relations Law; Real Estate Law. ***Email:*** LHattner@SpenglerNathanson.com

COUNSEL FOR: Fifth-Third Bank of Northwestern Ohio, N.A.; The University of Toledo; U.S. Fidelity & Guaranty Co.; CNA Insurance Companies; Physicians Insurance Company of Ohio; Great American Insurance Companies; First Investment Co.; Midwest Elastomers, Inc.; Continental Secret Service, Inc.; Sun Refining & Marketing Co.; Tuffy Associates Corp.; Toledo Lucas County Port Authority; Toledo Board of Education; Metropolitan Park District; Washington Local Board of Education; Springfield Local Board of Education; Sylvania Board of Education; Genoa Board of Education; AVCA Corp.; Ace Hardware; The Andersons; BP Oil Company; Citizens National Bank of Norwalk; Rouse Co.; Sylvania Township, Owens Illinois, Hylant Administrative Services, Inc.
REFERENCES: Fifth-Third Bank of Northwestern Ohio, N.A.; Capital Bank, N.A.

SPITLER, HUFFMAN, YOON & NEWLOVE, LLP

TOLEDO, OHIO

(See Bowling Green)

General Civil Practice in all Courts. Corporation, Business, Personal Injury, Wrongful Death, Product Liability, Medical Malpractice, Probate and Estate Planning, Administrative and Real Estate Law, Public Utility, Trials and Appeals, Bankruptcy, Criminal Defense, Family Law, Criminal Law.

STELTENPOHL, JAMES & MENACHER CO. LPA

421 N. MICHIGAN STREET, SUITE A
TOLEDO, OHIO 43624
Telephone: 419-243-6200
Fax: 419-243-6280
Email: toledolaw@mail.com

Family Law, Divorce, Dissolution, Child Custody, Child Support, Visitation Rights, Adoption, Bankruptcy, Criminal Law, Juvenile Law, Traffic Violations, DWI, Misdemeanors, Felonies, Trusts and Estates, Wills and Probate, Corporate Law, Business Law, Business Litigation, Business Formation, Personal Injury, Slip and Fall, Automobile Accidents, Truck Accidents, Real Estate Law.

WILLIAM L. MENACHER, born 1924. (1924-2004)

DARRELL DAVID STELTENPOHL, born 1952; admitted to bar, 1999, Ohio. *Education:* University of Toledo (B.S., 1990; J.D., 1998). ***PRACTICE AREAS:*** Probate; Domestic Relations; Employment Law; Contracts; Bankruptcy; General Practice; Criminal Law; Real Estate Law. ***Email:*** dsteltenpohl@yahoo.com

MARY M. JAMES, born 1957; admitted to bar, 1999, Ohio. *Education:* University of Toledo (B.A., 1995; J.D., 1998). ***PRACTICE AREAS:*** Probate; Domestic Relations; Bankruptcy; Juvenile Law; Traffic Violations; General Practice; Real Estate Law; Criminal Law. ***Email:*** toledolaw@mail.com

STOCKWELL & COOPERMAN, A LEGAL PROFESSIONAL ASSOCIATION

Established in 1991
SUITE 1610
ONE SEAGATE
TOLEDO, OHIO 43604
Telephone: 419-247-1500
Telecopier: 419-247-1575
URL: http://www.stockwellandcooperman.com

Taxation, Wills and Probate, Trusts and Estate, Elder Law, Estate Planning, Business Law, Corporate, Partnership, Mergers and Acquisitions, Corporate Finance, Real Estate, Buying and Selling of Business, Family Business, LLC Law, Partnership Law, Small Business, Contracts, Charitable Giving, Non Profit-Organizations.

JOHN P. STOCKWELL, born Sycamore, Illinois, August 6, 1946; admitted to bar, 1973, Ohio; 1974, U.S. Tax Court and U.S. District Court, Northern District of Ohio. *Education:* The Ohio State University (B.Sc., 1968); University of Toledo (J.D., 1972). Delta Theta Phi. *Member:* Toledo (Member, Sections on: Taxation; Real Property, Probate and Trust Law), Ohio State (Member, Sections on: Taxation; Real Property, Probate and Trust Law) and American (Member, Sections on: Taxation; Real Property, Probate and Trust Law) Bar Associations. ***PRACTICE AREAS:*** Taxation Law; Corporate Law; Partnership Law; Probate and Estate Planning; Limited Liability Company Law. ***Email:*** spstockwell@sc-law.net

RONALD M. COOPERMAN, born Lynn, Massachusetts, October 27, 1943; admitted to bar, 1973, Ohio; 1974, U.S. Tax Court and U.S. District Court, Northern District of Ohio. *Education:* Miami University (B.S., 1965); University of Toledo (J.D., 1973). Beta Alpha Psi. Certified Public Accountant, Ohio, 1970. *Member:* Toledo (Member, Sections on: Taxation; Real Property, Probate and Trust Law), Ohio State (Member, Sections on: Taxation; Real Property, Probate and Trust Law) and American (Member, Sections on: Taxation; Real Property, Probate and Trust Law) Bar Associations; American Institute of Certified Public Accountants; Ohio Society of Certified Public Accountants. ***PRACTICE AREAS:*** Taxation Law; Probate and Estate Planning; Real Property Law; Corporate Law; Partnership Law; Limited Liability Company Law.

STEVEN J. POTURALSKI, born Toledo, Ohio, August 6, 1970; admitted to bar, 1997, Ohio; 1998, U.S. Tax Court and U.S. District Court, Northern District of Ohio. *Education:* University of Toledo (B.B.A., 1992; J.D., 1997). Managing Editor, University of Toledo Law Review, 1996-1997.*Member:* Toledo, Ohio State and American Bar Associations. ***PRACTICE AREAS:*** Taxation; Probate/Estate Planning; Corporate Law; Real Estate Law; Partnership Law; Limited Liability Company Law. ***Email:*** sjstockwell@sc-law.net

DREW A. NITSCHKE, born Toledo, Ohio, April 2, 1975; admitted to bar, 2000, Ohio. *Education:* University of Michigan (B.A., 1997); University of Toledo (J.D., 2000). *Member:* Toledo (Member, Sections on: Probate/Estate Planning; Business Law; Real Estate); Ohio State and American Bar Associations. ***PRACTICE AREAS:*** Taxation; Probate; Estate Planning; Corporate Law; Real Estate Law; Partnership Formation; Limited Liability Company Law. ***Email:*** danitschke@sc-law.net

OF COUNSEL

KATHERINE RAUP O'CONNELL, born Springfield, Ohio, June 1, 1957; admitted to bar, 1984, Ohio. *Education:* Wittenberg University (B.A., cum laude, 1979); Ohio State University (J.D., 1984). Member, Ohio State Law Journal, 1984. Author: Note, "Has Ohio Avoided the Wake of MITE? an Analysis of the Constitutionality of the Ohio Control Share Acquisition Act," 46 Ohio State Law Journal 203, 1985. *Member:* Toledo, Ohio State and American Bar Associations. ***PRACTICE AREAS:*** Corporate Law; Probate and Estate Planning; Real Property Law; Commercial Transactions.

REPRESENTATIVE CLIENTS: Fifth Third Bank of Northwestern Ohio, N.A.; Louisville Title Agency for N.W. Ohio, Inc.; Ringer's Drug Store; Treu House of Munch Inc.; Findley Davies, Inc.; Rimer Enterprises; Bayes, Inc.; Accountants, Inc.; Sunforest Orthopedics, Inc.
REFERENCE: Fifth Third Bank of Northwestern Ohio, N.A., Toledo, Ohio.

CHARLES M. TRABAND, JR.

608 MADISON AVENUE, SUITE 1400
TOLEDO, OHIO 43604-1121
Telephone: 419-242-1400
Fax: 419-246-5764
Email: chuck@trabandlaw.com

Labor and Employment Relations (Management Only), Corporate, Real Estate, Civil Litigation.

CHARLES M. TRABAND, JR., born Sandusky, Ohio, February 8, 1950; admitted to bar, 1978, Ohio; 1987, U.S. District Court, Northern District of Ohio. *Education:* University of Toledo (B.A., 1973; J.D., 1977). Phi Alpha Delta. Recipient: Walter Ruether Memorial Scholarship. Adjunct Professor, University of Toledo, 1992. *Member:* Toledo, Ohio State and American Bar Associations.

REPRESENTATIVE CLIENTS: Available Upon Request.

UDELL & ABRAMSON, LTD.

TOLEDO, OHIO

(See Sylvania)

Business Law, Corporate and Succession Planning, Mergers and Acquisitions, ERISA, Pension and Profit Sharing Plans, Real Estate, Taxation, Tax Litigation, Nonprofit Corporations, Estate Planning and Probate, Family Law, Employment, Litigation.

WATKINS, BATES & CAREY, LLP

Established in 1939

NATIONAL CITY BANK BUILDING
405 MADISON AVENUE, SUITE 1900
TOLEDO, OHIO 43604-1207
Telephone: 419-241-2100
Telecopier: 419-241-1960
Email: postoffice@wbc-law.com
URL: http://www.wbc-law.com

General Civil Practice. Trials and Appeals. Trust, Probate and Estate Planning, Corporation, Health and Hospital, Non-Profit Organizations, Real Estate, Taxation, Bankruptcy Law, Workers Compensation, Labor Law and Employment Law.

MEMBERS OF FIRM

HARLEY A. WATKINS (1902-1979)

WILLIAM F. BATES, born Wausau, Wisconsin, March 25, 1944; admitted to bar, 1969, Ohio; 1970, U.S. District Court, Northern District of Ohio; 1988, U.S. Supreme Court. *Education:* Bowling Green State University (B.A., 1966); University of Toledo (J.D., 1969). Pi Sigma Alpha; Delta Theta Phi. Chairman, Flower Hospital, 1990-1993. Trustee, 1979—, Vice President and Assistant Treasurer, Judson Palmer Home. Trustee, 1979— and Vice President, Zenith Foundation, Inc. Member, Board of Trustees, 1984—, President, 1988—, Goerlich Family Foundation, Inc. Trustee and Secretary/Treasurer: Towering Pines Foundation, 1997—; Flagship Foundation, 1997—; The Putman Foundation, 1998—; Toledo Bar Association Foundation, 1984—. Member, Board of Directors and President, Rotary Club of Toledo, 1998-1999; Editorial Advisory Board Ohio Probate Law Journal, 1990-1995. *Member:* Toledo, Ohio State (Member, Board of Governors, 1981—;, Vice Chair, Estate Planning, Trust and Probate Section, 2005; Member, Estate Planning, Trust and Probate Law Specialty Board) and American (Member, Sections on: Taxation; Real Property, Probate Law and Trust Law) Bar Associations. Fellow: American College of Trust and Estate Counsel; Ohio State Bar Foundation. ***PRACTICE AREAS:*** Probate and Trust Law; Health Care Law; Charitable Trusts and Foundations Law. ***Email:*** bates@wbc-law.com

JOHN M. CAREY, born Toledo, Ohio, March 4, 1951; admitted to bar, 1978, Ohio and U.S. District Court, Northern District of Ohio; U.S. District Court, Eastern District of Michigan; 1984, U.S. Court of Appeals, Sixth Circuit; 1988, U.S. Supreme Court; 2004, U.S. District Court, Southern District of Ohio. *Education:* Williams College (B.A., with honors, 1973); University of Toledo (J.D., 1977). Special Counsel, Medical College of Ohio, 1995—. *Member:* Toledo, Ohio State, Federal and American Bar Associations; American Health Lawyers Association; National Association of College and University Attorneys. ***PRACTICE AREAS:*** Civil Trial Law; Appellate Practice; Commercial Law. ***Email:*** carey@wbc-law.com

GARY O. SOMMER, born Toledo, Ohio, February 5, 1955; admitted to bar, 1984, Ohio and U.S. District Court, Northern District of Ohio; 1985, Michigan; 1988, U.S. Supreme Court. *Education:* Miami University (B.A., 1977); University of Toledo (J.D., 1983). Editor, The University of Toledo Law Review, 1983-1984. *Member:* Toledo, Ohio State and American Bar Associations; State Bar of Michigan; American Health Lawyers Association; Ohio Hospital Association; Society of Ohio Healthcare Attorneys. ***PRACTICE AREAS:*** Health Care; Corporate; Real Estate. ***Email:*** sommer@wbc-law.com

THOMAS C. GESS, born Toledo, Ohio, November 6, 1947; admitted to bar, 1982, Ohio and U.S. District Court, Northern District of Ohio. *Education:* University of Toledo (B.B.A., 1972; J.D., 1981). *Member:* Toledo, Ohio State (Member, Sections on: Estate Planning; Probate; Trust Law) and American (Member, Business Law Section) Bar Associations. ***PRACTICE AREAS:*** Business Law; Commercial Law; Estate Planning Law; Probate Law; Trust Law; Charitable Trusts and Foundations. ***Email:*** gess@wbc-law.com

KIMBERLY S. KONDALSKI, born Van Wert, Ohio, 1961; admitted to bar, 1987, Ohio and U.S. District Court, Northern District of Ohio; 1990, U.S. Court of Appeals, Sixth Circuit; 2003, U.S. Supreme Court. *Education:* Bowling Green State University (B.A., summa cum laude, 1984); University of Toledo (J.D., cum laude, 1987). Phi Beta Kappa. Adjunct Faculty Member, University of Toledo, College of Business, 1992-1995. *Member:* Toledo (Member, Committees on: Labor and Employment Law and Workers Compensation), Ohio State (Member, Labor and Employment Law Section) and American (Member, Labor and Employment Law Section) Bar Associations. ***PRACTICE AREAS:*** Employment Law; Workers' Compensation. ***Email:*** kondalski@wbc-law.com

ROBERT W. BOHMER, born Bad Axe, Michigan, June 9, 1969; admitted to bar, 1994, Ohio; 1996, U.S. District Court, Northern District of Ohio; 1997, U.S. Court of Appeals, Sixth Circuit; 2003, U.S. Supreme Court; 2004, U.S. District Court, Southern District of Ohio and Eastern District of Michigan. *Education:* Bowling Green State University (B.S.Ed., 1991); University of Toledo College of Law (J.D., cum laude, 1994). Law Clerk to the Honorable Donald R. Ford, Ohio Court of Appeals, Eleventh Appellate District, 1995-1996. *Member:* Toledo and Ohio State Bar Associations; National Association of College and University Attorneys. ***PRACTICE AREAS:*** Civil Trial Practice; Appellate Practice; Labor and Employment Law; Health Care Law; Commercial Law; Computer Law. ***Email:*** bohmer@wbc-law.com

R. KENT MURPHREE, born McAlester, Oklahoma, December 30, 1969; admitted to bar, 1995, Ohio; 1996, Michigan and U.S. District Court, Northern District of Ohio; 1997, U.S. Court of Appeals, Sixth Circuit. *Education:* University of Toledo (B.A., 1992; J.D., 1995). *Member:* Toledo and Ohio State Bar Associations. ***PRACTICE AREAS:*** Civil Trial Law; Labor and Employment Law; Real Estate Law; Commercial Law. ***Email:*** murphree@wbc-law.com

SENIOR ATTORNEY

ANN M. McCAULEY, born Alton, Illinois, January 17, 1974; admitted to bar, 1999, Ohio; 2000, Michigan; 2001, U.S. District Court, Northern District of Ohio and U.S. Court of Appeals, Sixth Circuit. *Education:* Wake Forest University (B.S., cum laude, 1996); University of Toledo (J.D., cum laude, 1999). *Member:* Toledo and Ohio State Bar Associations; State Bar of Michigan. ***PRACTICE AREAS:*** Civil Practice. ***Email:*** mccauley@wbc-law.com

ASSOCIATE

JESSICA R. HAMNER, born Sylvania, Ohio, October 3, 1978; admitted to bar, 2003, Ohio; 2004, U.S. District Court, Northern District of Ohio. *Education:* Adrian College (B.B.A., magna cum laude, 2000); University of Toledo (J.D., 2003; M.B.A., 2003). *Member:* Toledo and Ohio State Bar Associations. ***PRACTICE AREAS:*** Civil Practice. ***Email:*** hamner@wbc-law.com

COUNSEL FOR: Heidtman Steel Products, Inc.; Medical College of Ohio and Medical College Hospitals; National City Bank; Goerlich Family Foundation, Inc.; The Judson Palmer Home; Zenith Foundation, Inc.; Towering Pines Foundation; Flagship Foundation; The Putman Foundation; Bowling Green State University Foundation; Joseph L. Wolcott Scholarship Fund; Nazar Rubber Co.; Sunoco, Inc.; Put-In-Bay Boat Line Company; Morgan Specialty Graphite, Inc.; The Black Swamp Conservancy; John C. Bates Foundation.

WEBER & STERLING, LLC

TOLEDO, OHIO

(See Maumee)

Probate and Estate Planning, Trusts, Wills, Business Succession.

WESTMEYER LAW OFFICES

421 NORTH MICHIGAN STREET, SUITE C
TOLEDO, OHIO 43624-2394
Telephone: 419-244-7041
Fax: 419-244-1140
Email: joe@westmeyer.com
URL: http://www.westmeyerlaw.com

Trial Practice, Personal Injury, Automobile Accidents, Slip and Fall, Wrongful Death, Products Liability, Wills and Probate, Trusts and Estates, Estate Planning, Real Estate, Corporate Law, Business Law, Contracts, Criminal Defense, Felonies, Misdemeanors, Driving While Intoxicated, Juvenile Law, Traffic Violations, Bankruptcy, Domestic Relations, Family Law, Adoptions, Divorce, Child Custody, Child Support.

FIRM PROFILE: The father and son team of Westmeyer Law Offices have combined 40 years of trial experience. The firm handles general civil litigation and criminal law. Westmeyer Law Offices service clients in Toledo and surrounding counties.

JOSEPH W. WESTMEYER, JR., born Toledo, Ohio, February 22, 1941; admitted to bar, 1966, Ohio; 1967, U.S. District Court, Northern District of Ohio. *Education:* Xavier University (B.S.B.A., 1963); University of Toledo (J.D., 1966). *Member:* Toledo, Lucas County and Ohio State (Member, Sections on: Personal Injury; Probate; Corporate; Trust and Estates; Negligence) Bar Associations. ***PRACTICE AREAS:*** Trial Practice; Personal Injury; Probate; Estate Planning; Real Estate; Corporate Law; Criminal Defense.

ASSOCIATE

JOSEPH W. WESTMEYER, III, born Toledo, Ohio, October 23, 1973; admitted to bar, 1999, Ohio and U.S. District Court, Northern District of Ohio. *Education:* Xavier University (B.S.B.A., 1996); University of Toledo (J.D., magna cum laude, 1999). Order of the Coif. Member, University of Toledo Law Review, 1998-1999. *Member:* Toledo (Member: Grievance Investigation; Bar Admission Committee; Professionalism Committee; Young Lawyers Committee), Lucas County, Ohio State and American Bar Associations; American Inns of Court Morrison R. Waite Chapter (Barrister).

DAVID S. WILLEY

366 SPITZER BUILDING
520 MADISON AVENUE
TOLEDO, OHIO 43604
Telephone: 419-241-3310
Fax: 419-241-3312
Email: davidwilley@aol.com

Plaintiffs Personal Injury, Automobile Accidents, Dog Bites, Slip and Fall, Wrongful Death.

DAVID S. WILLEY, born Toledo, Ohio, March 5, 1954; admitted to bar, 2002, Ohio. *Education:* Dartmouth College (B.A., 1976); University of Toledo (J.D., 2002). *Member:* Toledo and Ohio State Bar Associations. ***PRACTICE AREAS:*** Plaintiffs Personal Injury.

WILLIAMS, JILEK, LAFFERTY, GALLAGHER & SCOTT CO., L.P.A.

Established in 1978

500 TOLEDO LEGAL BUILDING
416 NORTH ERIE STREET
TOLEDO, OHIO 43624-1696
Telephone: 419-241-2122
Facsimile: 419-245-3849
Email: firm@wjlgs.com
URL: http://www.WJLGS.com

Trial and Appellate Practice. Negligence, Personal Injury, Wrongful Death, Products Liability, Legal and Medical Malpractice and Railroad.

DAVID R. GOLDBERG (1932-1982)

(This Listing Continued)

MARTIN W. WILLIAMS, born Cleveland, Ohio, August 11, 1942; admitted to bar, 1969, Ohio; 1970, U.S. District Court, Northern and Western Districts of Ohio; 1971, U.S. District Court, Eastern District of Michigan. *Education:* University of Toledo (B.A., 1964; J.D., 1969). ***PRACTICE AREAS:*** Medical Malpractice; Railroad Law. ***Email:*** mwilliams@wjlgs.com

MICHAEL F. JILEK, SR., born Cleveland, Ohio, September 6, 1941; admitted to bar, 1970, Ohio; 1971, U.S. District Court, Northern District of Ohio; 1985, U.S. Court of Appeals, Sixth Circuit. *Education:* University of Dayton (B.A., 1964); University of Toledo (J.D., 1969). ***PRACTICE AREAS:*** Personal Injury Law; Legal and Medical Malpractice; Products Liability Law. ***Email:*** mjilek@wjlgs.com

JON A. LAFFERTY, born Bluffton, Ohio, August 20, 1948; admitted to bar, 1973, Ohio; 1974, U.S. District Court, Northern District of Ohio; 1985, U.S. Court of Appeals, Sixth Circuit. *Education:* Bowling Green State University (B.S., 1970); Ohio Northern University (J.D., 1973). ***PRACTICE AREAS:*** Medical Malpractice; Insurance Law; Personal Injury Law. ***Email:*** jlafferty@wjlgs.com

THOMAS W. GALLAGHER, born Chicago, Illinois, December 30, 1947; admitted to bar, 1975, Ohio; 1976, U.S. District Court, Northern District of Ohio; 1977, U.S. Court of Appeals, Sixth Circuit; 1983, U.S. Supreme Court; 1988, U.S. Court of Federal Claims. *Education:* Xavier University (B.S., 1969); Northern Kentucky University, Chase School of Law (J.D., 1974). ***PRACTICE AREAS:*** Medical Malpractice; Personal Injury Law; Products Liability Law. ***Email:*** tgallagher@wjlgs.com

ROBERT M. SCOTT, born Cleveland, Ohio, March 27, 1959; admitted to bar, 1984, Ohio; 1985, U.S. District Court, Northern District of Ohio; 1989, U.S. Court of Appeals, Sixth Circuit; 1990, U.S. Court of Federal Claims. *Education:* St. Louis University (B.A., 1981); University of Toledo College of Law (J.D., 1984). ***PRACTICE AREAS:*** Personal Injury Law; Medical Malpractice; Product Liability Law; Insurance Law. ***Email:*** rscott@wjlgs.com

---

DREW R. MASSÉ, born Columbus, Ohio, November 2, 1955; admitted to bar, 1984, Ohio; 1985, U.S. District Court, Northern District of Ohio and U.S. Court of Appeals, Sixth Circuit; 1989, Michigan; 1990, U.S. Claims Court; 1993, U.S. District Court, Eastern District of Michigan. *Education:* Ohio State University (B.A., 1980); University of Toledo (J.D., 1984). ***PRACTICE AREAS:*** Personal Injury Law; Legal and Medical Malpractice; Product Liability Law; Insurance Law. ***Email:*** dmasse@wjlgs.com

PETER O. DeCLARK, born Grand Rapids, Michigan, February 23, 1965; admitted to bar, 1990, Virginia; 1995, Ohio. *Education:* University of Iowa (B.B.A., 1987); George Mason University School of Law (J.D., 1990). ***PRACTICE AREAS:*** Personal Injury Law; Medical Malpractice; Products Liability; Insurance Law. ***Email:*** pdeclark@wjlgs.com

JENNIFER C. McCREADY, born Cincinnati, Ohio, April 18, 1972; admitted to bar, 1999, Ohio. *Education:* University of Cincinnati (B.A., 1994); University of Toledo (J.D., 1999). ***PRACTICE AREAS:*** Personal Injury; Medical Malpractice; Insurance Law. ***Email:*** jmccready@wjlgs.com

CHAD M. TUSCHMAN, born Toledo, Ohio, May 11, 1970; admitted to bar, 1995, Michigan; 1999, Illinois; 2000, U.S. Court of Appeals, Second Circuit; 2002, Ohio and U.S. District Court, Northern District of Ohio. *Education:* Indiana University (B.S., 1992); University of Toledo College of Law (J.D., 1995). ***PRACTICE AREAS:*** Medical Malpractice; Personal Injury; Products Liability. ***Email:*** CTUSCHMAN@WJLGS.COM

BIESER, GREER & LANDIS, LLP

TROY, OHIO

(See Dayton)

General Civil Practice, Trial Practice, Business Litigation, Professional Liability Defense, Personal Injury Defense, Products Liability Defense, Corporate Law, Employment Law, Commercial Law, Probate, Tax Law, White Collar Criminal Defense, Arbitration, Mediation.

KAREN DENISE BRADLEY

TROY, OHIO

(See Dayton)

Immigration Law.

CICERO & KOLLIN PLL

TROY, OHIO

(See Dayton)

Criminal Defense, Personal Injury, Family Law.

DUNGAN & LeFEVRE

A LEGAL PROFESSIONAL ASSOCIATION

Established in 1991

210 WEST MAIN STREET

TROY, OHIO 45373

Telephone: 937-339-0511

Fax: 937-335-5802

Email: mail@dungan-lefevre.com

URL: http://www.dungan-lefevre.com

Piqua, Ohio Office: 111 West Ash Street. P.O. Box 1529. Telephone: 937-773-8054. Fax: 937-773-3379.

General Civil and Criminal Trial Practice, including Medical Malpractice, Personal Injury, Wrongful Death, Products Liability, Insurance Defense, Wrongful Discharge Defense, Business Law and Commercial Litigation in all Courts, Real Estate, Condominium, Banking, Insurance, Corporate and Business, Wills and Probate, Trusts and Estates, Estate Planning, Family and Domestic Relations, Driving While Intoxicated, Tax, Bankruptcy, Municipal, Zoning and Planning and Collection Law. Appeals in all Courts.

FIRM PROFILE: This preeminent legal professional association arose from the merger of two long established law firms in 1991. One firm, Dungan, McGraw & Kappers Co., L.P.A., traces its roots in Troy, Ohio back into the early 1900's; and the second firm, LeFevre, Foster, Wannemacher, Baer & Gearhardt Co., L.P.A., traces its roots to the late 1930's. The firm name is derived from the two deceased senior partners of the two originating firms, J. Cameron Dungan and Richard H. LeFevre.

J. CAMERON DUNGAN (1903-1977)

RICHARD H. LeFEVRE (1910-1980)

WILLIAM J. McGRAW, III, born Wheeling, West Virginia, July 7, 1948; admitted to bar, 1973, Ohio; 1974, U.S. District Court, Southern District of Ohio; 1985, U.S. Tax Court. *Education:* Ohio University (B.B.A., cum laude, 1970); The Ohio State University (J.D., cum laude, 1972). Member, Editorial Board, and author, Ohio Probate Law Journal, 2003—. Selected, Ohio "Super Lawyer" in Estate Planning and Trusts, 2004, 2005. "Top 50 Lawyers in the Cincinnati/Dayton Area, 2005, Cincinnati Magazine. *Member:* Miami County (President, 1985) and Ohio State (Council Member; Treasurer, Executive Committee, Estate Planning, Probate and Trust Section, 1998—) Bar Associations. Fellow, American College of Trust and Estate Counsel. Certified Specialist in Estate Planning, Trust and Probate Law, Ohio State Bar Association. ***PRACTICE AREAS:*** Estate and Trust Planning; Probate; Estate Administration; Banking; Business; Corporate Law; Commercial Law; Real Estate; Civil Litigation. ***Email:*** bmcgraw@dungan-lefevre.com

MICHAEL A. BAER, born Celina, Ohio, May 18, 1946; admitted to bar, 1974, Ohio. *Education:* The Ohio State University (B.A., 1969; J.D., cum laude, 1974). Assistant Public Defender, Miami County, 1974-1981. Member, Million Dollar Advocates Forum (Verdict and Settlement). Selected, Ohio "Super Lawyer" in Plaintiff Medical Malpractice, 2004, 2005. Selected "Best of Bar", Greater Dayton area plaintiff's medical malpractice, 2004. *Member:* Miami County Bar Association (Ethics and Grievance Committee; Certified Bar Counsel); American Board of Trial Advocates. (Board Certified Civil Trial Advocate by The National Board of Trial Advocacy). ***PRACTICE AREAS:*** Medical Malpractice; Personal Injury; Wrongful Death; Products Liability; Civil Litigation. ***Email:*** mbaer@dungan-lefevre.com

ALAN M. KAPPERS, born Hamilton, Ohio, January 4, 1952; admitted to bar, 1977, Ohio; 1978, U.S. District Court, Southern District of Ohio; 1985, U.S. Tax Court. *Education:* Ohio Northern University (B.A., with high distinction, 1974; J.D., with distinction, 1977). ***PRACTICE AREAS:*** Real Estate; Condominium Law; Estate Planning; Probate. ***Email:*** akappers@dungan-lefevre.com

MICHELLE J. GEARHARDT, born Kaneohe Oahu, Hawaii, October 3, 1955; admitted to bar, 1980, Ohio. *Education:* Wittenberg University; The Ohio State University (B.A., 1977); University of Toledo (J.D., 1979). Certified Mediator, 1995. ***PRACTICE AREAS:*** Trial Practice; Family Law; Mediation; General Practice; Professional Malpractice; Wrongful Death; Personal Injury Litigation. ***Email:*** michelle@dungan-lefevre.com

MICHAEL L. CARGILL, born Midland, Michigan, May 6, 1947; admitted to bar, 1979, Ohio; 1981, U.S. District Court, Southern District of Ohio. *Education:* Miami University (B.S., 1969); University of Dayton (J.D., 1979). ***PRACTICE AREAS:*** Medical Malpractice; Personal Injury; Wrongful Death; General Civil Litigation. ***Email:*** mcargill@dungan-lefevre.com

JOHN E. HEMM, born Troy, Ohio, July 18, 1957; admitted to bar, 1982, Ohio; U.S. District Court, Southern District of Ohio. *Education:* Miami University (B.S., 1979); University of Dayton (J.D., 1982). Miami County Public Defender, 1991—. (Resident, Piqua, Ohio Office). ***PRACTICE AREAS:*** Criminal; Family Law; Estate Planning; General Practice. ***Email:*** jhemm@dungan-lefevre.com

DAVID L. MIKEL, born South Bend, Indiana, April 23, 1964; admitted to bar, 1989, Ohio and U.S. District Court, Southern District of Ohio. *Education:* Indiana University (B.A., 1986); University of Dayton School of Law (J.D., 1989). Member, U.S. Bankruptcy Trustee Panel, 2001—. ***PRACTICE AREAS:*** Bankruptcy; Collections; Personal Tax; Real Estate. ***Email:*** dmikel@dungan-lefevre.com

J. ANDREW WANNEMACHER, JR., born Cincinnati, Ohio, August 21, 1966; admitted to bar, 1992, New York; 1993, Ohio. *Education:* Miami University (B.A., 1989); University of Toledo (J.D., 1992). Assistant Miami County Public Defender, 1999—. (Resident, Piqua Office). ***PRACTICE AREAS:*** Domestic Relations; Criminal Law; General Practice. ***Email:*** andrew@dungan-lefevre.com

JAMES D. BROOKSHIRE, born Dayton, Ohio, May 29, 1958; admitted to bar, 1991, Ohio; 1992, U.S. District Court, Southwestern District of Ohio; 1996, U.S. Court of Appeals, Sixth Circuit; 2003, Indiana. *Education:* Eastern Kentucky University (B.A., Geology, 1983); University of Dayton (J.D., 1991). ***PRACTICE AREAS:*** Wrongful Death; Medical Malpractice; Personal Injury. ***Email:*** jamesb@dungan-lefevre.com

MATTHEW C. SORG, born Middletown, Indiana, December 16, 1967; admitted to bar, 1994, Ohio and U.S. District Court, Southern District of Ohio; 2001, U.S. Tax Court. *Education:* University of Dayton (B.A., 1989; J.D., 1993). ***PRACTICE AREAS:*** Domestic Relations; Civil Litigation; Commercial Litigation; Criminal Law. ***Email:*** msorg@dungan-lefevre.com

OF COUNSEL

WENDY JEAN GOODENOUGH, born Charlottesville, Virginia, May 30, 1970; admitted to bar, 1998, Ohio; 1999, West Virginia; 2000, Kentucky. *Education:* Ohio State University (B.A., 1993; J.D., 1998); Marshall University (M.A., 1995). ***PRACTICE AREAS:*** Trial Practice; Family Law. ***Email:*** wendyg@dungan-lefevre.com

(This Listing Continued)

DUNGAN & LEFEVRE, A LEGAL PROFESSIONAL ASSOCIATION, Troy—Continued

APPROVED ATTORNEYS FOR: The Lawyers Title Insurance Corp.; The Ohio Bar Title Insurance Co. (Agent); The First American Title Insurance Company (Agent); Old Republic Insurance Company (Agent).
REPRESENTATIVE CLIENTS: The Peoples Savings Bank of Troy; Buckeye State Mutual Insurance Co.; National City Mortgage Co.; National City Bank, Dayton, Ohio; Pax Products, Inc.; Pax Machine Works, Inc.; Kerber Sheet Metal Works, Inc.; Asepak Corp.; Mid-America Surfaces, Inc.; Stillwater Technologies, Inc.; Title Safe Agency, Inc.; Paul Sherry Chevrolet, Inc.; Atlantis Sportswear, Inc.; Brownlee Personnel Services; Hobart Corporation (PMI Food Equipment Group); Auto Acceptance Corp.; Paul Sherry Car-n-Credit; RK Hydro-Vac, Inc.; Hobart Institute of Welding Technology; F&P America Mfg. Inc.
REFERENCES: U.S. Bank N.A., Troy; National City Bank.

FAUST, HARRELSON, FULKER, McCARTHY & SCHLEMMER

12 SOUTH CHERRY STREET
P.O. BOX 8
TROY, OHIO 45373
Telephone: 937-335-8324
Fax: 937-339-7155
Email: 1fhfms@woh.rr.com

General Civil and Criminal Trial Practice. Negligence, Insurance, Probate, Workers Compensation, Family, Commercial and Corporation Law. Estate Planning and Real Estate Law, Elder Law.

MEMBERS OF FIRM

CHARLES F. FAUST (1875-1950)
WILLIAM M. HARRELSON (1921-1985)
J. ANDREW FULKER (1953-1989)
LEO H. FAUST (1899-1996)

JOHN E. FULKER, born Troy, Ohio, April 13, 1929; admitted to bar, 1953, Ohio and U.S. District Court, Southern District of Ohio; 1958, U.S. Supreme Court. *Education:* Miami University (A.B., 1950); Columbia University (J.D., 1953). Omicron Delta Kappa. Assistant County Prosecutor, Miami County, 1954-1964. General Counsel: Planning Board, 1958-1981; Zoning Board, 1958-1981, Miami County. *Member:* Miami County (President, 1970), Ohio State and American Bar Associations; Ohio Academy of Trial Lawyers; The Ohio Association of Civil Trial Attorneys; The Association of Trial Lawyers of America. Fellow, Ohio State Bar Foundation. ***PRACTICE AREAS:*** Trial Practice; Insurance Defense Law; Medical Malpractice; Estate Planning; Probate Law; General Practice. ***Email:*** 1fhfms@woh.rr.com

ROBERT A. McCARTHY, born Hartford, Connecticut, July 30, 1931; admitted to bar, 1955, Ohio; 1971, U.S. District Court, Southern District of Ohio. *Education:* University of Hartford (A.A., 1951); The Ohio State University (B.A., 1955; J.D, 1955). Phi Delta Phi. Law Director, Tipp City, Ohio, 1966-1976. City Solicitor, Troy, Ohio, 1971-1979. Member, Estate Planning Council of Miami Valley. *Member:* Miami County (President, 1975), Ohio State (Board of Governors, Probate and Trust Law Section, 1983-1985; Delegate, 2nd District, 1978—; Board of Governors, 1985-1991; President, Elect, 1988; President, 1989) and American Bar Associations. Trustee, 1989-1999 and Fellow, Ohio State Bar Foundation. [Lt., USNR, 1956-1959]. ***PRACTICE AREAS:*** Estate Planning Law; Probate Law; Taxation Law; Business Law; Elder Law. ***Email:*** 1fhfms@woh.rr.com

ROBERT N. SCHLEMMER, born Troy, Ohio, May 10, 1943; admitted to bar, 1969, Ohio and U.S. District Court, Southern District of Ohio. *Education:* Oberlin College; Wittenberg University (B.A., 1965); Case Western Reserve University (J.D., 1968). *Member:* Miami County (President, 1979), Ohio State and American Bar Associations; American Association of Hospital Attorneys. ***PRACTICE AREAS:*** General Practice; Estate Planning; Real Estate; Probate Law; Family Law; Hospital Law. ***Email:*** 1fhfms@woh.rr.com

WILLIAM J. FULKER, born Troy, Ohio, July 12, 1957; admitted to bar, 1982, Ohio; 1984, U.S. District Court, Southern District of Ohio. *Education:* The Ohio State University (B.A., 1979); Ohio Northern University (J.D., 1981). Chairman, Miami County Public Defender Commission, 1994—. *Member:* Miami County, Ohio State and American (Member, Young Lawyers Division) Bar Associations. ***PRACTICE AREAS:*** General Practice; Litigation; Real Estate Law; Medical Malpractice; Insurance Defense Law. ***Email:*** 1fhfms@woh.rr.com

ROBERT M. HARRELSON, born Troy, Ohio, June 8, 1957; admitted to bar, 1982, Ohio; 1983, Florida; 1984, U.S. District Court, Southern District of Ohio; 1996, U.S. Tax Court. *Education:* Miami University (B.S., 1979); Capital University (J.D., 1982). General Counsel: Miami County Board of Realtors, 1991—. *Member:* Miami County, Ohio State and American Bar Associations; The Florida Bar; The Association of Trial Lawyers of America; Ohio Academy of Trial Lawyers. ***PRACTICE AREAS:*** Business Law; Estate Planning Law; Probate Law; Family Law; Real Estate Law; Litigation; General Practice. ***Email:*** 1fhfms@woh.rr.com

OF COUNSEL

RICHARD J. FRAAS, born Dayton, Ohio, July 17, 1932; admitted to bar, 1959, Ohio. *Education:* Miami University (B.S., 1954); Ohio State University (J.D., 1959). Phi Alpha Delta. Trust Officer, Winters National Bank, 1960-1966. Executive Vice President and Trust Officer, Star Bank N.A., Troy, 1966-1996. *Member:* Miami County (President, 1982) and Ohio State Bar Associations; Estate Planning Council of Miami Valley and Ohio Bankers Association (Trust Division); Ohio State Bar Foundation. [U.S. Army, 1954-1956]. ***PRACTICE AREAS:*** Estate Planning; Probate Law; Taxation Law. ***Email:*** 1fhfms@woh.rr.com

COUNSEL: Miami Mutual Insurance Company; Fifth Third Bank of Western Ohio; Firstar Bank, N.A.; Upper Valley Medical Center; Summit Insurance Co.; Troy Lumber Co.; Nittsu Shosi USA, Inc.

(This Listing Continued)

APPROVED ATTORNEYS FOR: Chicago Title Insurance Company; Ohio Bar Title Insurance Co.; The Guarantee Title & Trust Co.; Fort Worth Mortgage Corp; National City Mortgage Co.; Fifth Third Bank; Firstar Bank.
REFERENCE: Fifth Third Bank.

FREUND, FREEZE & ARNOLD

A LEGAL PROFESSIONAL ASSOCIATION

TROY, OHIO

(See Dayton)

Civil Litigation including Commercial Litigation, Employment Defense, Professional Malpractice Defense, Employer Intentional Torts, Construction Litigation, Civil Rights Defense, Local Government Defense, Nursing Home Defense, Environmental Litigation and Insurance Defense.

HOCHMAN & PLUNKETT

TROY, OHIO

(See Dayton)

Personal Injury, Automobile Accidents, Workers' Compensation and Social Security Disability Law. General Civil and Criminal Practice in all Courts.

JENKS, PYPER & OXLEY CO., L.P.A.

TROY, OHIO

(See Dayton)

General Liability, Property, Workers Compensation, Bad Faith, First Party Coverage, Third Party Coverage, Construction Defect, Environmental, Toxic Tort, Employment Practices, SUI, PIP/Med Pay, Inland Marine, Intellectual Property, Sexual Harassment, Subrogation, Professional Liability, including Accountants, Real Estate, Architects & Engineers, D&O and Agents E&O, Professional Malpractice, including Dental, Attorney and Medical.

LOPEZ, SEVERT & PRATT CO., L.P.A.

Established in 1996

18 EAST WATER STREET
TROY, OHIO 45373
Telephone: 937-335-5658
Facsimile: 937-339-6446
Email: lsplaw@lsplaw.org
URL: http://www.lopezsevertpratt.com

Civil Litigation, Personal Injury, Automobile Accidents, Truck Accidents, Slip and Fall, Wrongful Death, Commercial Litigation, Criminal Law, Drug Crimes, DUI/DWI/ Juvenile Law, Traffic Violations, Family Law, Divorce, Adoptions, Child Custody, Child Support, Visitation Rights, Business Law, Business Contracts, Business Litigation, Business Enterprises, Business Formation, Buying and Selling a Business, Construction Law, Contracts, Medical Malpractice, Real Estate, Estate Planning, Trusts and Estates, Resorts and Leisure Law, Wills and Probate.

MEMBERS OF FIRM

JOSE LOPEZ, born Dayton, Ohio, December 28, 1952; admitted to bar, 1979, Ohio, U.S. District Court, Southern District of Ohio; 1993, U.S. Supreme Court; 1995, U.S. Court of Appeals, 6th Circuit. *Education:* The Ohio State University (B.A., 1975); University of Dayton (J.D., 1979). Recipient: Lewis Powell Award; Carl Weiman Award; Lawyers Lawyer Award. Winner, Midwest National Trial Competition. Assistant Prosecuting Attorney, Miami County, 1979-1981. Municipal Prosecutor, Miami County, 1981-1984. Special Prosecutor, Montgomery County, 1984-1986. Special Prosecutor, Wood County, Ohio, 1991. *Member:* Miami County (President, 1991) and Ohio State Bar Associations; Ohio Academy of Trial Lawyers; Ohio Academy of Criminal Defense Lawyers. ***PRACTICE AREAS:*** Criminal Law; Civil Litigation; Personal Injury; Medical Malpractice; Trial Practice.

TODD D. SEVERT, born Bellefontaine, Ohio, September 26, 1964; admitted to bar, 1992, Ohio and U.S. District Court, Southern District of Ohio. *Education:* University of South Carolina (B.A., 1987); University of Dayton (J.D., 1992). Troy City Council, 1995-1999. *Member:* Miami County and Ohio State Bar Associations. ***PRACTICE AREAS:*** Family Law; Corporate Law; Criminal Law.

ANDREW R. PRATT, born Troy, Ohio, July 10, 1968; admitted to bar, 1994, Ohio. *Education:* Ohio University (B.S., cum laude, 1990); Thomas M. Cooley Law School (J.D., 1994). Recipient: American Jurisprudence Award, Trial Workshop. Miami County Public Defender, 1995-2000. *Member:* Miami County Bar Association; Ohio Association of Criminal Defense Attorneys; Ohio Academy of Trial Lawyers. ***PRACTICE AREAS:*** Criminal Law; Personal Injury; Civil Litigation.

CHRISTOPHER D. CLARK, born Kettering, Ohio, December 4, 1969; admitted to bar, 1995, Ohio. *Education:* Earlham College (B.A., 1992); Ohio Northern University School of Law (J.D., 1995). Recipient, American Jurisprudence Book Award. *Member:* Miami County and Ohio State Bar Associations; Ohio Association of Trial Lawyers. ***PRACTICE AREAS:*** Personal Injury; Medical Malpractice; Civil Litigation. ***Email:*** cclark@lsplaw.org

JONATHAN S. ZWEIZIG, born Dayton, Ohio, July 18, 1973; admitted to bar, 1998, Ohio and U.S. District Court, Southern District of Ohio. *Education:* Wittenberg University (B.A., cum laude, 1995); Ohio Northern University (J.D., 1998). Editor, Ohio Northern University Law Review, 1997-1998. *Member:* Dayton, Miami County and Ohio State Bar Associations; Ohio Academy of Trial Lawyers. ***PRACTICE AREAS:*** Civil Litigation; Criminal Law.

(This Listing Continued)

ASSOCIATE

ANDREW D. LUCIA, born Washington, D.C., February 20, 1969; admitted to bar, 1996, Ohio and U.S. District Court, Southern District of Ohio. *Education:* University of Maryland, College Park (B.S., 1991); University of Dayton (J.D., 1996). *Member:* Dayton and Ohio State Bar Associations; Defense Research Institute; Ohio Academy of Trial Lawyers. ***PRACTICE AREAS:*** Medical Negligence; Personal Injury; Probate; Estate Planning; Wrongful Death; Corporate Law.

REPRESENTATIVE CLIENTS FOR JOSE LOPEZ: Crayex Corp.; Wagner Paving; Hawk Development; Independent Auto Sales; Craycon Homes, Inc.; Women Wellness Center; Milton Union Medical Center.
REPRESENTATIVE CLIENTS FOR TODD D. SEVERT: The Troy Daily News; Oxford Systems Integration; Smallenberger Lawn Care; Tipp City Custom Builders; Garden Gate Realty, Inc.
REPRESENTATIVE CLIENTS FOR ANDREW PRATT: Earhart Petroleum; Superstation, Inc.; Scott M&A; Hemm Glass; Allied Fabricators; Assembly, Inc.; Glaser Softwater, Inc.; Barhorst Realty, Inc.; National Auto Lube, Inc.
REPRESENTATIVE CLIENT FOR CHRISTOPHER CLARK: Kathy Henne Team, Inc.

McCULLOCH, FELGER, FITE & GUTMANN CO., L.P.A.

TROY, OHIO

(See Piqua)

General Civil Practice. Corporation, Insurance, Taxation, Labor and Employment, Trust and Estate Administration, Estate Planning, Commercial, Real Estate, Pension and Profit Sharing, Family and Domestic Relations, Personal Injury Law, Litigation and Civil Trials.

MILLER & LURING

Established in 1933

314 WEST MAIN STREET
TROY, OHIO 45373
Telephone: 937-339-2627
Fax: 937-339-5444
URL: http://www.millerluringlaw.com

General and Trial Practice, Collections, Estate Planning, Bankruptcy, Personal Injury, Civil, Family/Domestic Relations, Corporation, Negligence, Tax, Municipal, Probate and Real Estate.

ROGER E. LURING, admitted to bar, 1975, Ohio; 1976, U.S. District Court, Southern District of Ohio; 1980, U.S. Tax Court and U.S. Claims Court. *Education:* Miami University (A.B., 1968); University of Cincinnati (J.D., 1975). Chapter 7 Trustee, U.S. Southern District of Ohio Panel, Dayton, since 1979; Member, Bankruptcy Rules Standing Committee, Southern District of Ohio. *Member:* Miami County (President, 1993) and Ohio State Bar Associations; American Bankruptcy Law Forum; National Association of Bankruptcy Trustees; American Bankruptcy Institute. [U.S. Army, 1968-1971, First Lt.]. ***PRACTICE AREAS:*** Bankruptcy; Family Law; Personal Injury; Criminal; Real Estate. ***Email:*** rogerluring@woh.rr.com

---

NIKA R. EVANS, born Cincinnati, Ohio, March 13, 1974; admitted to bar, 2000, Ohio and U.S. District Court, Southern District of Ohio. *Education:* The Ohio State University (B.A., 1996); Ohio Northern University (J.D., 2000). Member, American Bankruptcy Law Forum. *Member:* Miami County and Ohio State Bar Associations. ***PRACTICE AREAS:*** Bankruptcy; Family Law; Personal Injury. ***Email:*** nikaevans@woh.rr.com

JASON R. FARLEY, born Cambridge, Ohio, November 21, 1976; admitted to bar, 2002, Ohio. *Education:* Otterbein College (B.A., 1999); University of Dayton (J.D., 2002). Member, American Bankruptcy Law Forum. *Member:* Miami County and Ohio State Bar Associations;. ***PRACTICE AREAS:*** Bankruptcy; Criminal; Domestic Relations; Probate. ***Email:*** jason.farle@lstcounsel.com

REPRESENTATIVE CLIENTS: St. Joseph Catholic Workers House; Miami County Recovery Services; Labpro, Inc.
REFERENCES: U.S. Bank, Troy, Ohio; Peoples Bank, Troy, Ohio.

PICKREL, SCHAEFFER & EBELING

TROY, OHIO

(See Dayton)

Banking, Civil, Corporate, General Business, Commercial Lending, Mergers and Acquisitions, Insurance, Labor and Employment, Healthcare, Municipal and Zoning, Personal Injury and Products Liability, Probate, Trust and Estate Planning, Construction, Computer, Real Estate, Environmental, Workers' Compensation Defense, Immigration, Bankruptcy and Tax Law. Trials and Appeals, School Law and Title Insurance.

SHIPMAN, DIXON & LIVINGSTON CO., L.P.A.

Established in 1899

215 WEST WATER STREET
P.O. BOX 310
TROY, OHIO 45373
Telephone: 937-339-1500
Fax: 937-339-1519
URL: http://www.sdl-law.com

West Milton, Ohio Office: 316 South Miami Street, P.O. Box 5. Telephone: 937-698-4164.

(This Listing Continued)

Civil Trials in all Courts. Personal Injury, Environmental, Corporation, Real Estate, Insurance Defense Law, Probate and Estate Planning, Social Security, Municipal and Zoning. General Practice. Civil Rights Defense Law.

FIRM PROFILE: The law firm of Shipman, Dixon & Livingston Co., L.P.A. is a full service law firm handling a broad range of civil matters. Founded in 1899 by Leonard H. Shipman, it is the successor of Shipman & Shipman. It retained its present name in 1995 when it joined with Livingston, Sell & Johnston.

The firm handles matters covering the legal needs of individuals and corporations, and handles civil cases covering collections, personal injury, defense litigation, real property, and estates. The Firm has also developed significant experience in municipal law.

Riverview Title Company is a wholly-owned subsidiary, and the Firm offers a full range of title work, closings, and real estate examinations.

The firm is devoted to providing specialized legal services to its clients. The attorneys participate in extensive continuing legal education, seminars, professional association activities and civic affairs.

LEONARD H. SHIPMAN (1874-1955)
FRANK LEONARD SHIPMAN (1906-1973)
WILLIAM M. DIXON (Retired)

JAMES R. LIVINGSTON, born Columbus, Ohio, January 17, 1943; admitted to bar, 1969, Ohio; 1975, U.S. District Court, Southern District of Ohio and U.S. Court of Appeals, 6th Circuit; 1979, U.S. Supreme Court. *Education:* The Ohio State University (B.S., 1965; J.D., 1968). Assistant City Solicitor, Troy, 1971-1976. Assistant Counsel, Planning and Zoning, Miami County, Ohio, 1972-1979. Prosecuting Attorney, Miami County, Ohio, 1981-1985. Municipal Prosecutor, West Milton, 1987-2002. *Member:* Miami County and Ohio State Bar Associations; National Organization of Social Security Claimants Representatives. [Lt., JAGC, USNR, 1968-1971]. ***PRACTICE AREAS:*** Social Security Law; Personal Injury Law; Employment Law; Probate Law. ***Email:*** jlivingston@sdl-law.com

CHARLES H. SELL, II, born Alliance, Ohio, December 5, 1947; admitted to bar, 1973, Ohio. *Education:* Western Michigan University (B.A., 1970); University of Toledo (J.D., 1973). Note and Comment Editor, University of Toledo Law Review, 1973. Author: "Workmen's Compensation—Statutory Immunity of Third Persons-Insurance Carriers," 4 University of Toledo Law Review 150, 1972. Legal Counsel, Ohio Senate Judiciary Committee, 1973-1976. Assistant Law Director, Troy, Ohio, 1976-1981. First Assistant Prosecuting Attorney, Miami County, Ohio, 1981-1985. Law Director, Village of West Milton, Ohio, 1987—. Law Director, Village of Laura, 2004—. *Member:* Miami County Bar Association. ***PRACTICE AREAS:*** Family Law; Municipal Law; Personal Injury Law; Probate; Litigation. ***Email:*** csell@sdl-law.com

W. McGREGOR DIXON, JR., born Toledo, Ohio, January 19, 1949; admitted to bar, 1975, Ohio; 1977, U.S. District Court, Southern District of Ohio; 1989, U.S. Court of Appeals, Sixth Circuit; 1991, U.S. Supreme Court; 1997, U.S. District Court, Northern District of Ohio. *Education:* Miami University (B.A., 1971); St. Mary's University (J.D., 1974); The Ohio State Bar Association College. Phi Alpha Delta. Director of Law, Troy, Ohio, 1980—. Trustee, 1983—, Miami County Law Library Association. Trustee, 1986— and President, 1991, Ohio Municipal League. Member, Editorial Advisory Board, Ohio Municipal Service, 1989. *Member:* Miami County (President, 1994), Ohio State (Member: Local Government Law Committee, 1981—; Council of Delegates, 1992-1994) and American (Member, Urban, State and Local Government Law Section, 1981—) Bar Associations; Defense Research Institute; Ohio Association of Civil Trial Attorneys; Ohio Municipal Attorneys Association (President, 1988); International Municipal Lawyers Association; National School Board Attorneys Association; Ohio Council of School Board Attorneys; Ohio State Bar Foundation. ***REPORTED CASES:*** Sell v. Price 527 F. Supp. 114 (S.D. Ohio 1981); Harshbarger v. Franks 513 F. Supp. 843 (S.D. Ohio 1987); Christopher v. Stouder Mem. Hospital 936 F.2d 870 (6th Cir. 1988); Milliron Waste Mgt., Inc. v. Crestline (1999), 135 Ohio App.3d 15; Singer v. Troy (1990), 67 Ohio App.3d 507; Wilson v. Kreusch (1996), 111 Ohio App. 3d 47; Frantz v. Village of Bradford, 245 F.3d 869 (6th Cir. 2001). ***PRACTICE AREAS:*** Municipal Law; Litigation; Civil Rights Defense; Real Estate. ***Email:*** greg.dixon@troyohio.gov

ROBERT C. JOHNSTON, born Dayton, Ohio, December 4, 1952; admitted to bar, 1978, Ohio; 1979, U.S. District Court, Southern District of Ohio. *Education:* Duke University (B.A., cum laude, 1975); Case Western Reserve University (J.D., 1978). Assistant Prosecuting Attorney, Miami County, 1981-1985. *Member:* Miami County and Ohio State (Member, Probate Law Section) Bar Associations. [With USNR, 1971-1973]. ***PRACTICE AREAS:*** Probate; Estate Planning; Business Law; Zoning Law; Insurance Law; Bankruptcy; Elder Law. ***Email:*** rjohnston@sdl-law.com

GRANT D. KERBER, born Troy, Ohio, March 22, 1972; admitted to bar, 1997, Ohio; 1998, U.S. District Court, Southern District of Ohio. *Education:* University of Dayton (B.A., 1994); University of Cincinnati (J.D., 1997). Law Director: Covington, Ohio, 1998—; City of Piqua, 2001—. West Milton Prosecutor, 2002—. *Member:* Miami County and Ohio State Bar Associations. ***PRACTICE AREAS:*** Municipal Law; Real Estate; Domestic Relations; Business Law; Civil Practice; General Practice. ***Email:*** gkerber@sdl-law.com

LENEÉ M. BROSH, born Toledo, Ohio, December 3, 1976; admitted to bar, 2002, Ohio; 2004, U.S. District Court, Southern District of Ohio. *Education:* Earlham College (B.A., 1999); University of Dayton School of Law (J.D., 2002). Assistant Miami County Municipal Prosecutor, 2003—. *Member:* Miami County and Ohio State Bar Associations. ***PRACTICE AREAS:*** Municipal Law; Domestic Relations; Juvenile Law; Civil Practice; General Practice. ***Email:*** lbrosh@sdl-law.com

JOHN A. HERNDON, born Springfield, Illinois, August 7, 1967; admitted to bar, 1996, Ohio and U.S. District Court, Southern District of Ohio. *Education:* Southern Illinois University (B.A., 1993); University of Dayton (J.D., 1996). Prosecutor, Town of Piqua, 2005—. *Member:* Dayton, Miami County and Ohio State Bar Associations. ***PRACTICE AREAS:*** Domestic Relations; Criminal Law; Municipal Prosecution; General Practice.

(This Listing Continued)

SHIPMAN, DIXON & LIVINGSTON CO., L.P.A., Troy—Continued

GENERAL COUNSEL FOR: U.S. Bank, N.A., Troy; City of Troy; Troy Board of Education; City of Piqua; Village of West Milton; Riverview Title Co.; Village of Covington; Village of Laura.
LOCAL COUNSEL FOR: Travelers Insurance Co.; Prudential Insurance Company of America; American International Group, Inc.; Nationwide Insurance Co.; Ohio Casualty Group; Kemper Insurance Group; The Buckeye Union Casualty Co.; Republic-Franklin Insurance Co.; Celina Insurance Group; Farmers Home Administration.
REPRESENTATIVE CLIENTS: Forms Express, Inc.; Miami Graphic Services, Inc.; Ohio Casualty Insurance Co.; Misato Computer Products; Piqua Granite & Marble Co., Inc.; Stanley Steamer of Miami Valley, Inc.; Miami Control Systems, Inc.; Precise Tool, Inc.; Erwin Chrysler Plymouth.
APPROVED ATTORNEYS FOR: The Ohio Bar Title Insurance Co., (Agent); Municipal League Joint Self-Insurance Pool; First American Title Insurance Co., (Agent).
REFERENCES: Fifth-Third Bank of Miami Valley, N.A.; U.S. Bank, N.A., Troy; Unizan Bank, West Milton.

THOMPSON AND DeVENY CO., L.P.A.

TROY, OHIO

(See Dayton)

Bankruptcy Law, Divorce, Child Custody, Child Support.

TOMB LAW

124 WEST MAIN STREET
TROY, OHIO 45373
Telephone: 937-689-3539
Email: jeremytomb@hotmail.com
URL: http://www.tomblaw.com

Real Estate, Business Law, Construction Law.

JEREMY TOMB, born Union, Indiana, April 1, 1968; admitted to bar, 2005, Ohio. *Education:* Wright State University (B.A., 1995); University of Toledo (J.D., 2005). ***PRACTICE AREAS:*** Real Estate; Business Law; Construction Law.

WILLIAMS, SENNETT & SCULLY CO., L.P.A.

Established in 1993
2241 PINNACLE PARKWAY
TWINSBURG, OHIO 44087-2367
Telephone: 330-405-5061
Fax: 330-405-5586
Email: attorneys@wsslaw.com
URL: http://www.wsslaw.com

Cleveland, Ohio Office: 113 St. Clair Avenue N.E., Suite 430, 44114-1214. Telephone: 216-771-8660. Fax: 216-771-8831.

General Civil Trial and Appellate Practice in all Courts. Insurance, Casualty and Surety, Life, Accident and Health, Negligence Litigation, Medical-Legal, Products Liability, Labor and Employment Law, Commercial Litigation.

FIRM PROFILE: Williams, Sennett & Scully Co., L.P.A., is a law firm that specializes in civil trial practice. The firm experience is concentrated in the areas of personal injury; property damage; life and health insurance; product liability; medical/legal malpractice; labor and employment law; commercial litigation; casualty and surety law. The firm is listed in the Bar Register of Preeminent Lawyers.

ROGER H. WILLIAMS, born Hollis, New York, November 8, 1954; admitted to bar, 1979, Ohio; 1980, U.S. District Court, Northern District of Ohio; 1987, U.S. Court of Appeals, Sixth Circuit. *Education:* Hobart College (B.A., 1976); Case Western Reserve University (J.D., 1979). *Member:* Mahoning County, Trumbull County, Cleveland, Akron, Ohio State and American (Member, Litigation Section; Law Practice Management Section) Bar Associations; Cleveland Association of Civil Trial Attorneys; Ohio Association of Civil Trial Attorneys. ***PRACTICE AREAS:*** Insurance Defense Law; Products Liability Law; Negligence Litigation. ***Email:*** rwilliams@wsslaw.com

JAMES A. SENNETT, born Cleveland, Ohio, September 11, 1952; admitted to bar, 1980, Ohio; 1981, U.S. District Court, Northern District of Ohio; 1987, U.S. Supreme Court and U.S. Court of Appeals, Sixth Circuit. *Education:* Boston College (B.A., cum laude, 1974); Case Western Reserve University (J.D., 1979). Geauga County Prosecutor Office, 1980. Geauga County Public Defender's Office, 1981-1983. *Member:* Cleveland, Akron and Ohio State (Negligence Law Committee, 1991—) Bar Associations; Cleveland Association of Civil Trial Attorneys; Ohio Association of Civil Trial Attorneys. ***PRACTICE AREAS:*** Insurance Coverage and Defense; Medical-Legal; Products Liability; Employment Law; Commercial Law. ***Email:*** jsennett@wsslaw.com

WILLIAM F. SCULLY, JR., born Bayshore, New York, July 10, 1950; admitted to bar, 1975, Ohio; 1980, U.S. District Court, Northern District of Ohio and U.S. Court of Appeals, Sixth Circuit. *Education:* University of Notre Dame (B.A., 1972); Case Western Reserve University (J.D., 1975). *Member:* Cleveland, Ohio State and American Bar Associations; Ohio Association of Civil Trial Attorneys. ***PRACTICE AREAS:*** Civil Litigation; Insurance Defense; Product Liability; Insurance Coverage; Medical-Legal; Toxic Tort; Environmental; Professional Liability Defense; Commercial Litigation; Labor and Employment Law. ***Email:*** wfs@wsslaw.com

ADAM E. CARR, born Cleveland, Ohio, September 22, 1968; admitted to bar, 1993, Ohio; 1994, U.S. District Court, Northern District of Ohio; 2002, U.S. Court of Appeals, Sixth Circuit. *Education:* Rice University (B.A., 1990); Cleveland Marshall College of Law (J.D., 1993). Delta Theta Phi, (Dean, 1996-1997). Law and Public Policy Fellowship, 1992. General Counsel, Cleveland Orthopedic and Spine Center, 1993-1995. *Member:* Cuyahoga County, Lake County, Cleveland (Young Lawyers Section) and Ohio State (General Practice, Litigation, and Young Lawyers Sections) Bar Associations. (Board Certified in Civil

(This Listing Continued)

Trial Advocacy by the National Board of Trial Advocacy). ***PRACTICE AREAS:*** Litigation; Negligence; Insurance Coverage; Bad Faith Litigation. ***Email:*** acarr@wsslaw.com

LOUIS R. MOLITERNO, born Youngstown, Ohio, June 13, 1967; admitted to bar, 1995, Ohio; 1998, U.S. District Court, Northern District of Ohio. *Education:* Kent State University (B.A., 1989); Cleveland-Marshall College of Law (J.D., 1995). Journalist for Gannett/USA Today at Chillicothe, Ohio, 1990-1992. *Member:* Cleveland and Ohio State Bar Associations. ***PRACTICE AREAS:*** Insurance Defense Litigation; Products Liability Law; Negligence Litigation. ***Email:*** lmoliterno@wsslaw.com

JOSEPH H. WANTZ, born Canton, Ohio, September 20, 1956; admitted to bar, 1982, Ohio; 1983, U.S. District Court, Northern District of Ohio; 1987, U.S. Court of Appeals, Sixth Circuit. *Education:* University of Notre Dame (B.B.A., 1979); Case Western Reserve University (J.D., 1982). *Member:* Lake County Bar Association; Cleveland Association of Civil Trial Attorneys (President, 1993-1994; Treasurer, 1992-1993; Program Chairman, 1991-1992); Ohio Association of Civil Trial Attorneys. ***PRACTICE AREAS:*** Bad Faith Litigation; Personal Injury; Insurance Coverage. ***Email:*** jwantz@wsslaw.com

KELLY N. GRIGSBY, born Oberlin, Ohio, November 20, 1969; admitted to bar, 1996, Ohio and U.S. District Court, Northern District of Ohio. *Education:* College of Wooster (B.A., 1992); Case Western Reserve University (J.D., 1995). Phi Alpha Delta. *Member:* Cleveland and Ohio Bar Associations. ***REPORTED CASES:*** State v. Henton 121 Ohio App. 3d 501. ***PRACTICE AREAS:*** Insurance Defense; Tort Defense. ***Email:*** kgrigsby@wsslaw.com

MARK S. HURA, born Cleveland, Ohio, February 16, 1960; admitted to bar, 1985, Ohio; 1986, U.S. District Court, Northern District of Ohio; 1991, California. *Education:* Purdue University (B.S., 1982); Case Western Reserve University (J.D., 1985). *Member:* Ohio State Bar Association. ***PRACTICE AREAS:*** Insurance Defense. ***Email:*** mhura@wsslaw.com

PERRIN I. SAH, born Lakewood, Ohio, July 7, 1970; admitted to bar, 1995, Ohio and U.S. District Court, Northern District of Ohio. *Education:* Bowling Green State University (B.A., 1992); Cleveland-Marshall College of Law (J.D., 1995). ***LANGUAGES:*** Mandarin Chinese. ***PRACTICE AREAS:*** Insurance Defense. ***Email:*** psah@wsslaw.com

PHILLIP C. KOSLA, born Bedford, Ohio, November 16, 1969; admitted to bar, 1997, Ohio; U.S. District Court, Northern District of Ohio. *Education:* Ohio State University (B.A., 1992; J.D., 1997). *Member:* Ohio State Bar Association. ***LANGUAGES:*** Italian. ***PRACTICE AREAS:*** Litigation. ***Email:*** pkosla@wsslaw.com

OF COUNSEL

CHARLES F. CICHOCKI, born Cleveland, Ohio, September 11, 1954; admitted to bar, 1979, Ohio and U.S. District Court, Northern District of Ohio. *Education:* Bowling Green University (B.A., 1976); Case Western Reserve University (J.D., 1979). *Member:* Lake County and Ohio State Bar Associations. ***PRACTICE AREAS:*** Civil Litigation; Criminal Law.

REPRESENTATIVE CLIENTS: Allstate Insurance Co.; American International Adjustment Co., Inc.; American States Insurance; Chesterfield Services, Inc.; Coregis Insurance Co.; Giant Eagle, Inc.; GMAC Insurance Company; Goodyear Tire & Rubber Co.; Great Oaks Insurance Company; Harleysville Insurance Company; Leader National Insurance Company; Magna Entertainment Corp.; Metropolitan Property and Casualty; Nationwide Mutual Insurance Co.; Progressive Insurance Company; Quality Resources, Inc.; Riser Foods; Royal & Sun Alliance; Russell Equipment Co., Inc.; Safeco Insurance Co.; Sentry Insurance Co.; Simon Properties Group, Inc.; State Auto Insurance Company; State Farm Insurance Cos.; The Travelers; Toys "R" Us; Universal Underwriters Insurance Co.; Unitrin Property and Casualty Insurance Group.

SEAN O. BOYLE

UPPER ARLINGTON, OHIO

(See Columbus)

State and Federal Criminal Defense, Felonies and Misdemeanors, Juvenile Law.

KINCAID, RANDALL & CRAINE

UPPER ARLINGTON, OHIO

(See Columbus)

Probate Law, Estate Planning, Wills and Trusts, Estate Administration, Will or Trust Contests, Probate Litigation, Special Needs or Medicaid Payback Trusts, Living Wills, Power of Attorneys, Estate Planning for Parents of Disabled Children, Guardianship, Conservatorship, Elder Law, Business Law, Business Formation, Business Incorporation and General Practice.

COLE ACTON HARMON DUNN

A LEGAL PROFESSIONAL ASSOCIATION

URBANA, OHIO

(See Springfield)

General Civil Practice. Business and Corporate, Insurance, Taxation, Real Estate, Probate, Criminal Law, Family Law, Banking, Labor and Employment Law, Personal Injury Law. Litigation.

CRABBE, BROWN & JAMES LLP

118 SCIOTO STREET
URBANA, OHIO 43078
Telephone: 937-652-4000
Email: info@cbjLawyers.com
URL: http://www.cbjLawyers.com

Columbus, Ohio Office: 500 South Front Street, Suite 1200. Telephone: 614-228-5511. Fax: 614-229-4559.

(This Listing Continued)

Cincinnati, Ohio Office: 30 Garfield Place, Suite 740, 45202. Telephone: 513-784-1525. Fax: 513-784-1250.
Cleveland, Ohio Office: 1280 W. Third Street. Telephone: 216-574-9312.
Lancaster, Ohio Office: 111 South Broad Street, Suite 209, 43130. Telephone: 740-689-1743. Fax: 740-689-1746.

General Insurance Defense, Product Liability, Professional Malpractice, Premises Liability, Environmental and Toxic Tort Claims, Employment and Labor Law, Tax Matters, General Business and Corporate Law and Litigation, Banking and Securities, Real Estate, Probate and Estate Planning, Criminal Law, Administrative, Regulatory and Governmental Law, Workers Compensation, Intellectual Property, Fire, Arson and Fraud, Fidelity and Surety Life, Accident and Health, Insurance Coverage Law, Construction Claims, Health and Hospital Law, Oil, Gas and Energy Law, Transportation Law, Automobile Dealer Law, Zoning, International Practice and Domestic Law, Land Use Planning, and Eminent Domain.

(For biographical data on other personnel, see Professional Biographies at Columbus, Ohio)

MARTIN, BROWNE, HULL & HARPER, P.L.L.

URBANA, OHIO

(See Springfield)

General Civil Practice. Corporate, Commercial, Insurance, Insurance Defense, Litigation, Environmental, Business, Contracts, Banking, Estate Planning, Probate, Real Estate, Taxation, Education, Labor and Employment. Trials and Appeals in State and Federal Courts.

OLIVER LAW OFFICE

URBANA, OHIO

(See Columbus)

Products Liability, Personal Injury, Wrongful Death, Latex Allergy Litigation, Medical Malpractice, Vioxx Litigation, Automobile Accidents, Insurance Law, Employment Discrimination.

PAULIG & SINGER

Established in 1953

40 MONUMENT SQUARE
SUITE 300
URBANA, OHIO 43078
Telephone: 937-653-5257
Facsimile: 937-653-3027

General Civil and Criminal Trial and Appellate Practice in all Courts. Negligence, Personal Injury, Probate and Estate Planning, Family and Domestic Relations and Insurance Law.

FIRM PROFILE: The firm of Paulig Singer & Talebi practices primarily in Champaign county with clients also in Logan, Clark, Miami, Union and Madison counties. We possess a depth of experience in all forms of litigation with extensive court background. We are also a five minute walk from all court buildings.

KARL E. PAULIG, born Urbana, Ohio, April 28, 1929; admitted to bar, 1953, Ohio; 1955, U.S. District Court, Southern District of Ohio. *Education:* Western Reserve University; The Ohio State University (B.A., 1951; J.D., 1952). Phi Alpha Delta. City Solicitor, 1955-1958 and Municipal Judge, 1958-1966, Urbana. *Member:* Champaign County (Secretary, 1955-1956; Treasurer, 1956-1958; President, 1963-1964, 1990-1991) and Ohio State Bar Associations. ***PRACTICE AREAS:*** Civil Trials; Criminal Trials; Probate; Negligence; Insurance.

BRAD C. SINGER, born Lancaster, Ohio, October 2, 1961; admitted to bar, 1989, Ohio; 1990, U.S. District Court, Southern District of Ohio. *Education:* Wright State University (B.A., 1983); Northwestern School of Law of Lewis and Clark College (J.D., 1989). *Member:* Champaign County (President, 1996) and Ohio State Bar Associations. ***PRACTICE AREAS:*** Civil Trials; Criminal Trials; Domestic Relations; Personal Injury.

REPRESENTATIVE CLIENTS: Nationwide Mutual Insurance Co.; Ohio Casualty Insurance Co.; Republic Franklin Insurance Co.; Bodey & Sons, Inc. (Building Contractor); Georgia, Inc.; Cincinnati Insurance Co.; Akins Printing, Inc.; The Stephen L. Bodey Co. (Contracting); Urbana City Board of Education; The Trinity Cos.; Waite Hill Services, Inc.; Champaign County Preservation Alliance; Maranatha Aviation, Inc.; The Cancer Association of Champaign County; Progressive Builders Incorporated.
REFERENCES: Champaign National Bank & Trust; Citizens National Bank.

MARTIN D. BURCHFIELD

124 NORTH WASHINGTON STREET
VAN WERT, OHIO 45891
Telephone: 419-238-6553
FAX: 419-238-5056
Email: burchfieldlaw@hotmail.com
URL: http://www.burchfieldlaw.com

Civil Trial Litigation in all Courts, Family/Domestic Relations, Juvenile Law, Municipal and Zoning Law.

MARTIN D. BURCHFIELD, born Sandusky, Ohio, April 14, 1961; admitted to bar, 1986, Ohio. *Education:* University of Toledo (B.A., 1983; J.D., 1986). President, Van Wert City Council, 1990-1996. Public Defender, Van Wert County, 1993-1998; Assistant Prosecutor, 1998—. *Member:* Van Wert County Bar Association (President, 1997; Chairman, Van Wert County Republican Party, 1995—). ***PRACTICE AREAS:*** General Practice; Litigation; Domestic Relations Law; Municipal Law.

REPRESENTATIVE CLIENTS: Village of Convoy, Ohio; Village of Elgin, Ohio; Village of Willshire, Ohio.

BUCKINGHAM, LUCAL, McGOOKEY & ZEIHER CO., L.P.A.

1513 STATE ROUTE 60
VERMILION, OHIO 44089
Telephone: 440-967-6136
Email: vermilion@buckinghamlaw.com
URL: http://www.buckinghamlaw.com

Sandusky, Ohio Office: 414 Wayne Street, P.O. Box 929, 44870. Telephone: 419-627-0414; 800-410-0414. Fax: 419-627-0009.

Trials in all State and Federal Courts. Wrongful Death, Personal Injury, Product Liability, Cycling Injuries, Domestic Relations, Family Law, Corporate Law, Business Law, Banking, Real Estate Law, Tax Law. Employment Law, Probate, Estate Planning, Commercial, Workers Compensation, Bankruptcy Law, Criminal Defense (Felonies and Misdemeanors); Medicaid Planning.

(For complete biographical data on all personnel, see Professional Biographies at Sandusky, Ohio)

DANIEL F. GIGIANO CO. L.P.A.

111 BROAD STREET, SUITE 206
WADSWORTH, OHIO 44281-1867
Telephone: 330-336-3330
Fax: 330-336-3331
Email: dgigiano@msn.com
URL: http://www.dangigianolaw.com

Criminal Litigation, Bankruptcy, Family Law, Civil Litigation.

DANIEL FRANK GIGIANO, born 1968; admitted to bar, 1993, Illinois; 1999, Ohio. *Education:* University of Illinois (B.A., 1990); Loyola University (J.D., 1993). ***PRACTICE AREAS:*** Criminal Litigation; Civil Litigation; Bankruptcy; Estate Planning; Real Estate. ***Email:*** gigiano@msn.com

HUNT & JOHNSON

WAPAKONETA, OHIO

(See Lima)

Family Law, Adoptions, Child Custody, Child Support, Divorce, Domestic Violence, Premarital Agreements, Spousal Support, Corporate Law, Breach of Contract, Mechanics Liens, Collections, Real Estate, Commercial Real Estate, Condominium Law, Landlord and Tenant Law, Mortgages, Taxation, Estate and Gift Taxation, Income Tax, Property Tax, Trusts and Estates, Asset Protection, Charitable Giving, Estate Litigation, Estate Planning, Guardianship and Conservatorship, Wills and Probate.

DAVIS & YOUNG

A Legal Professional Association

108 MAIN STREET, SW
SUITE 1000
WARREN, OHIO 44481
Telephone: 330-373-1717
Fax: 330-395-0610
Email: atty@davisyoung.com
URL: http://www.davisyoung.com

Cleveland, Ohio Office: 1700 Midland Building, Suite 1700, 44115. Telephone: 216-348-1700. Fax: 216-621-0602.
Akron, Ohio Office: National City Center, One Cascade Plaza, Suite 800, 44308. Telephone: 330-376-1717. Fax: 330-376-1797.
Youngstown, Ohio Office: The Commerce Building, 201 East Commerce Street, Suite 100, 44503. Telephone: 330-743-1717.

General Trial and Appellate Practice, Products Liability, General Tort, Insurance Coverage, Personal Injury, Toxic Torts, Complex Mass Tort Claims, Legal and Medical Malpractice, Municipal Liability, Civil Rights, Employment Practices Liability, and Environmental and Commercial Liability.

FIRM PROFILE: Many of Davis & Young's attorneys are members of the following organizations: Mahoning and Trumbull County and Ohio State Bar Associations, Defense Research Institute (DRI), Ohio Association of Civil Trial Attorneys (OACTA).

WILLIAM JACK MEOLA, admitted to bar, 1984, Ohio; 1986, U.S. District Court, Northern District of Ohio. *Education:* Miami University (B.A., 1981); Case Western Reserve University (J.D., 1984). *Member:* American Bar Association. ***Email:*** jmeola@dywarren.com

ASSOCIATE

ENZO C. CANTALAMESSA, admitted to bar, 2003, Ohio. *Education:* John Carroll University (B.A., Philosophy, 1995); Barry University School of Law (J.D., 2002). Assistant Public Defender, Trumbull County, Ohio, 2003-2004. ***LANGUAGES:*** Italian. ***Email:*** enzo@dywarren.com

COUNSEL FOR: Amerisure Companies; Avis Rent-A-Car System, Inc.; Central Mutual Insurance Co.; Cincinnati Insurance Co.; CNA Insurance Co.; Dana Corporation; Erie Insurance Group; The Hartford; KAISER Foundation Health Plan of Ohio; Merit Plan Insurance Co.; Motorists Mutual Insurance Cos.; Ohio Casualty Insurance Co.; Ohio Insurance Guaranty Association; Progressive Cos.; St. Paul Insurance Cos.; State Farm Mutual Automobile Insurance Co.; State Farm Fire and Casualty Insurance Co.; SYSCO Food Services of Cleveland, Inc.; T.J. Maxx Stores; Travelers Insurance Co.; Unigard Insurance Group; United

(This Listing Continued)

DAVIS & YOUNG, Warren—Continued

of Ohio Insurance Co.; University Hospitals of Cleveland; Wesfield Companies; Wolverine Mutual Insurance Co.

GUARNIERI AND SECREST

Established in 1919
GUARNIERI BLOCK
151 EAST MARKET STREET
P.O. BOX 4270
WARREN, OHIO 44482-4270
Telephone: 330-393-1584
Fax: 330-395-3831
Email: ganslaw@netdotcom.com

General Civil Practice. Corporation, Banking and Finance, Insurance, Wills, Trusts and Probate, Condemnation, Family Law, Employment Relations, Personal Injury, Workers Compensation, Administrative Law and Civil Rights, Motor Vehicle Dealerships, Estate Planning, Trials and Appeals (State and Federal).

MEMBERS OF FIRM

LEWIS L. GUARNIERI (1896-1976)

GEORGE W. SECREST (1894-1959)

PAUL A. GUARNIERI (1912-1992)

ANTHONY G. ROSSI, born Warren, Ohio, July 20, 1935; admitted to bar, 1961, Ohio. *Education:* John Carroll University (B.S.S., cum laude, 1957); Catholic University of America (J.D., 1961). Gamma Eta Gamma. Member, Mahouing Shenango Valley Estate Planning. *Member:* Trumbull County (President, 1976-1977), Ohio State and American Bar Associations; Ohio Trial Lawyers Association; Ohio Bar Foundation. [Capt., U.S. Army, T.C., Reserve Corps, Resigned]. ***PRACTICE AREAS:*** Civil Practice; Personal Injury; Probate; Family Law. ***Email:*** ganslaw@netdotcom.com

RANDIL J. RUDLOFF, born Youngstown, Ohio, July 27, 1948; admitted to bar, 1973, Ohio. *Education:* Kent State University (B.A., 1970); Ohio Northern University (J.D., 1973). Phi Alpha Delta. Member, Ohio Northern University Law Review, 1970-1973. Author: "Baseball's Anti-Trust Exemption," Ohio Northern University Law Review, 1972. *Member:* Trumbull County, Ohio State and American Bar Associations; Ohio Association of Civil Trial Attorneys. ***PRACTICE AREAS:*** Commercial Litigation; Probate; Personal Injury Law; Banking Law; Finance Law. ***Email:*** ganslaw@netdotcom.com

MICHAEL D. ROSSI, born Warren, Ohio, April 12, 1950; admitted to bar, 1975, Ohio. *Education:* University of Notre Dame (B.A., magna cum laude, 1972); Catholic University of America (J.D., 1975). Several Reported Cases. *Member:* Trumbull County (President, 1990-1991) and Ohio State Bar Associations; American Civil Liberties Union. ***PRACTICE AREAS:*** Employment Law; Federal Practice; Insurance Law; Personal Injury. ***Email:*** ganslaw@netdotcom.com

ANTHONY G. ROSSI, III, born Warren, Ohio, February 15, 1966; admitted to bar, 1991, Ohio. *Education:* Miami University (B.A., 1988); Ohio Northern University (J.D., 1991). *Member:* Trumbull County, Ohio State and American Bar Associations. ***PRACTICE AREAS:*** Family Law; Juvenile Law; Criminal Law. ***Email:*** ganslaw@netdotcom.com

ASSOCIATE

DEBORAH SMITH, born Greenville, Pennsylvania, January 20, 1970; admitted to bar, 1995, Ohio; 1996, Pennsylvania. *Education:* Indiana University of Pennsylvania (B.S., magna cum laude, 1992); Case Western Reserve University (J.D., magna cum laude, 1995). *Member:* Trumbull County, Mercer County, Ohio State, Pennsylvania and American Bar Associations. ***PRACTICE AREAS:*** Criminal Law; Family Law; Estate Planning; Appellate Practice; Civil Practice. ***Email:*** ganslaw@netdotcom.com

GENERAL COUNSEL FOR: Albert Guarnieri & Co.; Acme Music & Vending, Inc.; Service Guide, Inc.; Avalon Inn Services, Inc.; Crosby Mook Office Equipment, Inc.; Ohio Security Systems, Inc.; W.J. Service, Inc.; Nannicola, Inc.; Glunt Machine & Fabricating Co.; Seven Seventeen Credit Union Inc.; Antenucci, Inc.; Flex-Strut, Inc.
LOCAL COUNSEL FOR: Cincinnati Insurance Co.; Queens City Indemnity Co.; Ohio Motorists Association; Bonded Oil; Second National Bank of Warren; Northern Machinery, Inc; La Farge North America.

HARRINGTON, HOPPE & MITCHELL, LTD.

Established in 1834
108 MAIN AVENUE, S.W., SUITE 500
WARREN, OHIO 44481
Telephone: 330-392-1541
Fax: 330-394-6890
Email: info@hhmlaw.com
URL: http://www.hhmlaw.com

Youngstown, Ohio Office: 26 Market Street, Suite 1200, 44503-1508. Telephone: 330-744-1111. Telecopier: 330-744-2029.
Salem, Ohio Office: 2235 E. Pershing Street, Suite A, 44460. Telephone: 330-337-6586. Telecopier: 330-337-6662.

General Civil Trial and Equity Practice in all State and Federal Courts. Corporation, Banking, Creditors Rights and Bankruptcy, Labor, Probate, Estate Planning, Hospital and Health, Insurance Law, Real Estate, Commercial, Business Transactions.

FIRM PROFILE: The firm is the largest firm in Mahoning, Trumball and Columblana Counties of Ohio. The firm maintains offices in Youngstown, Warren and Salem, Ohio.

Harrington, Hoppe & Mitchell, Ltd. is a full service firm, organized into six general practice areas: Litigation; Business Services; Labor and Employment; Health Care Law; Public Sector Law; and Probate and Estate Planning.

JOHN L. POGUE, born Warren, Ohio, May 20, 1944; admitted to bar, 1969, Ohio and Indiana. *Education:* DePauw University (B.A., 1966); Indiana University (J.D., 1969). Law Clerk, Indiana Supreme Court, 1969-1970. Member, Board of Trustees, Youngstown State University, 2001—. *Member:* Trumbull County and Ohio State Bar Associations. ***PRACTICE AREAS:*** Commercial Law; Estate Planning; Corporate Law; General Practice. ***Email:*** JPogue@hhmlaw.com

NED C. GOLD, JR., born Santa Fe, New Mexico, July 23, 1941; admitted to bar, 1966, Ohio and Missouri. *Education:* St. Louis University (B.S., 1963; J.D., 1966). *Member:* Trumbull County, Ohio State and American Bar Associations; The Missouri Bar. [Judge Advocate, U.S. Air Force, 1966-1971]. (Certified Specialist in Labor & Employment Law, Ohio State Bar Association). ***PRACTICE AREAS:*** Labor and Employment Law; Commercial Law; Corporate Law. ***Email:*** NGold@hhmlaw.com

MICHAEL G. MARANDO, born Franklin, Pennsylvania, February 25, 1948; admitted to bar, 1974, Ohio. *Education:* Ohio University (B.B.A., cum laude, 1971); Villanova University (J.D., 1974). *Member:* Trumbull County and Ohio State Bar Associations. ***PRACTICE AREAS:*** Corporate Law; Labor; Real Estate; General Practice. ***Email:*** MMarando@hhmlaw.com

WILLIAM L. HAWLEY, born Cleveland, Ohio, September 15, 1954; admitted to bar, 1979, Ohio; 1989, U.S. District Court, Northern District of Ohio; 1996, U.S. Supreme Court. *Education:* Baldwin-Wallace College (B.A., 1976); The Ohio State University (J.D., 1979). *Member:* Trumbull County and Ohio State Bar Associations. ***PRACTICE AREAS:*** Litigation; Corporate Law; Employment Law; Insurance Defense; Personal Injury. ***Email:*** WHawley@hhmlaw.com

THOMAS G. CAREY, JR., born Cleveland, Ohio, December 31, 1948; admitted to bar, 1978, Ohio. *Education:* Dartmouth College (B.A., 1971); The Ohio State University (J.D., 1978). *Member:* Trumbull County and Ohio State Bar Associations. ***PRACTICE AREAS:*** Litigation; Banking Law; Probate; Bankruptcy. ***Email:*** TCarey@hhmlaw.com

KEVIN P. MURPHY, born Youngstown, Ohio, August 15, 1960; admitted to bar, 1985, Ohio; 1987, U.S. Court of Appeals, Sixth; 1991, Pennsylvania; 1999, U.S. Supreme Court. *Education:* University of Dayton (B.A., cum laude, 1982); Ohio State University (J.D., 1985). *Member:* Trumbull County (Member, Council of Delegates), Ohio State and Pennsylvania Bar Associations. ***PRACTICE AREAS:*** Litigation; Employment Law; Workers Compensation; Insurance Defense; Commercial Litigation. ***Email:*** KMurphy@hhmlaw.com

PATRICK K. WILSON, born Warren, Ohio, April 29, 1963; admitted to bar, 1988, Ohio; 1989, U.S. District Court, Northern and Southern Districts of Ohio. *Education:* Villanova University (B.A., 1985); University of Toledo (J.D., 1988). Law Director, City of Cortland, 2001—. Member, Board of Trustees, Trumbull Memorial Hospital Foundation, 2004—. *Member:* Trumbull County and Ohio State Bar Associations. ***PRACTICE AREAS:*** Litigation; Probate; Estate Planning; Labor and Employment; Municipal Law; Workers Compensation; Insurance Defense. ***Email:*** PWilson@hhmlaw.com

---

MICHAEL J. McGEE, born Bridgeport, Connecticut, February 19, 1969; admitted to bar, 1995, Illinois; 2002, Ohio, U.S. District Court, Central and Southern Districts of Illinois, U.S. District Court, Northern District of Ohio, U.S. Court of Appeals, Sixth Circuit and U.S. Supreme Court. *Education:* The Ohio State University (B.A., 1992); John Marshall Law School (J.D., 1995). *Member:* Trumbull County, Ohio State and Illinois State Bar Associations. ***PRACTICE AREAS:*** Litigation; Insurance; Personal Injury; Employment; Commercial Collections; Civil Rights; Bankruptcy; Criminal Law.

REPRESENTATIVE CLIENTS: Forum Health Hospitals and Medical Centers; Humility of Mary Healthcare; Consumers Ohio Water Company (Public Utility); City of Canfield; Beaver Township; Village of Lordstown; The City of Cortland; The Public Library of Youngstown and Mahoning County; First Energy Corp; Ohio Edison Company; ER Advanced Ceramics, Inc.; Office of Attorney General, State of Ohio; Hill, Barth & King, CPAs; Mahoning Valley Economic Development Corporation; Youngstown-Warren Regional Chamber of Commerce; A.P. O'Horo Company; Taylor Winfield Corp.; WCI Steel, Inc.; General Extrusions, Inc.; Sovereign Circuits, Inc.; Metropolitan Property & Casualty Insurance Co.; Nationwide Mutual Insurance Co.; Motorists Insurance Co.; CNA Insurance Companies; Allstate Insurance Co.; Ohio Mutual Insurance Group; American General Life and Accident Insurance Group; Coregis Insurance Company; National City Bank; Sky Bank; First Place Bank; Bank One Cleveland, N.A.; Second National Bank of Warren; V&V Real Estate Investments; Ohio Realty Company.

(For complete biographical data on all personnel at Youngstown and Lisbon, see Professional Biographies at those locations)

KEATING, KEATING & KUZMAN

Established in 1982
170 MONROE STREET, N.W.
WARREN, OHIO 44483
Telephone: 330-393-4611; 393-0121
Fax: 330-394-0101
Email: KEATINGLAW@EARTHLINK.NET
URL: http://www.lawyers.com/keatingkeating&kuzman

Litigation, Insurance Defense, Personal Injury, Automobile Accidents, Medical Malpractice, Criminal Law, Driving While Intoxicated, Hospital, Healthcare, Airport, Trust, Business, Probate and Estate Planning.

W. LEO KEATING, born Saginaw, Michigan, January 4, 1922; admitted to bar, 1950, Ohio and Wisconsin. *Education:* University of Notre Dame (B.A., 1943); Marquette University (J.D., 1950). ***PRACTICE AREAS:*** Health Care; Hospitals; Medical Malpractice; Aviation; Corporate Law. ***Email:*** wlkeatinglaw@earthlink.net

DANIEL G. KEATING, born Warren, Ohio, December 23, 1956; admitted to bar, 1982, Ohio; U.S. District Court, Northern District of Ohio. *Education:* Concordia Univer-

(This Listing Continued)

sity (B.A., 1979); University of Toledo (J.D., 1982). *Member:* Trumbull County, Ohio State and American Bar Associations; Lawyer Pilots Bar Association. ***PRACTICE AREAS:*** Medical Malpractice; Criminal Law; Civil Litigation; Employment Law; Probate; Estate Planning; Aviation Law. ***Email:*** dgkeatinglaw@earthlink.net

OF COUNSEL

JOHN J. KUZMAN, (JR.), born Girard, Ohio, September 26, 1952; admitted to bar, 1986, Ohio, and U.S. District Court - Northern District. *Education:* Youngstown State University (B.S.A.S., 1978); University of Akron (J.D., 1986). *Member:* Trumbull County and Ohio State Bar Associations. ***PRACTICE AREAS:*** Health Care; Hospital Law; Medical Malpractice; Probate; Personal Injury.

REPRESENTATIVE CLIENTS: Warren General Hospital; Continental; CIGNA; Sprint Telephone Co.; Western Reserve Port Authority; Youngstown-Warren Regional Airport; Lake Erie Mobile Homes; United Truck Parts; Aircraft Owners & Pilots Assn.; I.T.T./Hartford Insurance; CNA Insurance Co.; Great American Ins. Co.; Utica Ins.; Ohio Hospital Ins. Co.

NADER AND NADER

Established in 1953

155 SOUTH PARK AVENUE

WARREN, OHIO 44481

Telephone: 330-395-7555; 330-395-9586

FAX: 330-392-5443

Email: lawfirm@naderandnader.com

General Civil Practice in all Courts. Municipal, Corporate, Domestic, Trials, Environmental Law, Public Utility Law, Ohio Administrative Agencies and Real Estate Law.

PAUL G. NADER, born Warren, Ohio, June 3, 1925; admitted to bar, 1953, Ohio. *Education:* Centenary College; Adelbert College of Western Reserve University (B.A., 1949); Western Reserve University; Cleveland-Marshall Law School (LL.B., 1953). Assistant Prosecuting Attorney, Trumbull County, Ohio, 1961-1969. *Member:* Trumbull County (President, 1983-1984), Ohio State and American Bar Associations. ***PRACTICE AREAS:*** Real Estate; Probate.

THOMAS C. NADER, born Warren, Ohio, July 28, 1962; admitted to bar, 1987, Ohio. *Education:* The Ohio State University (B.S.B.A., 1984); Case Western Reserve University (J.D., cum laude, 1987). Assistant Ohio Attorney General, 1987-1989. *Member:* Cleveland and Ohio State Bar Associations. ***SPECIAL AGENCIES:*** Public Utilities Commission of Ohio; Industrial Commission of Ohio; Ohio Department of Liquor Control; Ohio Environmental Protection Agency. ***PRACTICE AREAS:*** Product Liability; Workers Compensation Defense; Commercial Litigation; Public Utility Law; Real Estate; Estate Planning; Environmental Litigation.

AGENTS FOR: First American Title Insurance Co.; Midland Title Security, Inc.
REFERENCES: Seven Seventeen Credit Union; First Place Bank.

NADLER NADLER & BURDMAN CO., L.P.A.

WARREN, OHIO

(See Youngstown)

General Civil Practice in all State and Federal Courts. Commercial, Creditor Rights and Collections, Bankruptcy, Reorganization, Taxation, Employment and Labor Law, Corporation, Partnership, Venture Capital, Banking, Real Estate, Shopping Center, Franchising, Environmental, Pension and Profit Sharing, Estate Planning, Probate, and Trials and Appeals.

PFAU, PFAU & MARANDO

WARREN, OHIO

(See Youngstown)

General Civil Practice in all State and Federal Courts. Insurance, Malpractice and Products Liability and Personal Injury Law, Constitutional and Real Estate Law. Trials.

LAW OFFICE OF CHARLES L. RICHARDS

159 EAST MARKET STREET, SUITE 300

WARREN, OHIO 44481-1122

Telephone: 330-373-1000

Fax: 330-394-5291

Email: CLRichards@onecom.com

Products Liability, Civil Rights Defense, Insurance Defenses, Legal Malpractice, Medical Malpractice, Litigation, Professional Liability.

CHARLES L. RICHARDS, born Youngstown, Ohio, February 5, 1942; admitted to bar, 1969, Ohio; 1970, U.S. District Court, Northern District of Ohio; 1973, U.S. Supreme Court; 1975, U.S. Court of Appeals, Sixth Circuit. *Education:* University of Notre Dame (B.B.A., 1964); University of Akron (J.D., 1969). *Member:* Trumbull County (President, 1980-1981), Ohio State and American Bar Associations; Defense Research Institute; International Association of Insurance Counsel; Ohio Association of Civil Trial Attorneys. Fellow: American College of Trial Lawyers; Ohio State Bar Foundation; American Bar Foundation. ***PRACTICE AREAS:*** Legal Malpractice Defense; Medical Malpractice Defense; Complex Business Litigation; Insurance Defense Litigation.

ASSOCIATES

ROBERT C. MAYNARD, born Cleveland, Ohio, October 10, 1936; admitted to bar, 1962, District of Columbia; 1963, Ohio. *Education:* John Carroll University (B.S.S., 1958);

(This Listing Continued)

Georgetown University (LL.B., 1962; LL.M., 1963). *Member:* American College of Trial Lawyers; Defense Research Institute. [U.S. Army Reserve, 1958-1968]. ***PRACTICE AREAS:*** Litigation; Professional Liability. ***Email:*** RMaynard@bright.net

PAULA D. MAAS, born Huntington, West Virginia; admitted to bar, 1980, West Virginia; 1987, Ohio. *Education:* Vanderbilt University (B.A., Economics, 1976); Wake Forest University School of Law (J.D., 1980). Research Editor, Law Review, 1979-1980. Member, Newton Falls Exempted Village School Board, 2000-2004. ***Email:*** PDMaas@onecom.com

JASON M. TOTH, born Warren, Ohio, October 27, 1975; admitted to bar, 2001, Ohio. *Education:* Youngstown State University (B.A., 1998); The Ohio State University (J.D., 2001). Phi Kappa Phi. Ashtabula County, Trumbull County and Ohio State Bar Associations. ***REPORTED CASES:*** State v. Root, Ohio App. LEXIS 2181, 2004; State v. Kovacici, Ohio App. LEXIS 4675, 2003; State v. Sheffey, Ohio App. LEXIS 1956, 2004; State v. Bowens, Ohio App. LEXIS 4958, 2003. ***PRACTICE AREAS:*** Litigation. ***Email:*** jmtoth@onecom.com

REPRESENTATIVE CLIENTS: County Risk Sharing Authority (CORSA); Ohio Bar Liabilty Insurance Company; Mahoning Valley Sanitary District; St. Joseph Health Center; Township of Howland, Ohio; JWF Specialty, Inc.; Trumbull County Sheriff; Portage County Board of Commissioners; Farmer's National Bank; Covelli Enterprises; VFIS Claims Management, Inc.; North American Risk Services.

DOUGLAS M. TOOT

WARREN, OHIO

(See Canfield)

Wills and Trusts, Estate Planning, Probate, Elder Law, Business Planning, Corporate and Business Law, Real Estate.

THE WERN LAW FIRM, LLC

210 SCOTT STREET, N.E.

WARREN, OHIO 44483

Telephone: 330-392-2533

Fax: 330-395-3403

Email: info@WernLegal.com

Corporate, Estate Planning, Probate, Real Estate.

CHARLES E. WERN, JR., born Coraopolis, Pennsylvania, November 11, 1932; admitted to bar, 1959, Ohio. *Education:* Duke University (B.A., 1954); Ohio Northern University (J.D., 1959). Special Counsel to Attorney General of Ohio, 1965-1969. *Member:* Trumbull County and Ohio State Bar Associations. ***PRACTICE AREAS:*** Corporate; Estate Planning; Probate; Real Estate; Mergers and Acquisitions. ***Email:*** charles@charleswern.com

---

CHARLES E. WERN III, born August 15, 1973; admitted to bar, 1999, Ohio; 2002, New York. *Education:* John Carroll University (B.A., 1995); Capital University (J.D., magna cum laude, 1999); New York University (LL.M., Tax, 2000). Order of the Curia. Member, Capital University Law Review. Associate, Reed Smith Hall Dickler LLP, New York, 2000-2004. Author: Article, "The Staple REIT on Ice: Congress' 1998 Freeze of the Grandfather Exception for Stapled REITs, 28 Capital University Law Review 717, 2000. ***PRACTICE AREAS:*** Corporate Law; Tax. ***Email:*** cwern3@wernlegal.com

MARTIN F. WHITE CO., L.P.A.

156 PARK AVENUE N.E.

WARREN, OHIO 44481

Telephone: 330-394-9692

Fax: 330-394-8589

Email: mfw850@aol.com

Litigation and Plaintiffs Practice. Wrongful Death, Medical Malpractice, Personal Injury.

MARTIN F. WHITE, born Warren, Ohio, November 12, 1952; admitted to bar, 1977, Ohio; 1993, Pennsylvania. *Education:* The Ohio State University (B.A., 1973; J.D., 1977). *Member:* Trumbull County, Ohio State, Pennsylvania and American Bar Associations; Ohio Academy of Trial Lawyers; The Association of Trial Lawyers of America; Mahoning-Trumbull County Trial Lawyers Association; Ohio Criminal Defense Lawyers Association; American Board of Trial Advocates. ***Email:*** mfw850@aol.com

MICHAEL E. BENSON

WASHINGTON C. H., OHIO

(See Columbus)

Bankruptcy Law, Foreclosures, Debtor and Creditor, Real Estate, Landlord and Tenant, Buying and Selling, Wills, Living Wills, Healthcare, Powers of Attorney.

TWYFORD & DONAHEY, P.L.L.

WASHINGTON C. H., OHIO

(See Columbus)

Personal Injury Litigation, Wrongful Death, Medical Malpractice, Products Liability, Automobile Accidents, Trucking Accidents, Head and Spinal Injuries, Motorcycle Accidents and Injuries, Uninsured Motorists, Insurance Law, Airplane Crash Litigation, Railroad Accidents, Slip and Fall, Dog Bites, Work Related Injuries, Birth Injuries, Nursing Home Abuse and Neglect.

BARBER, KAPER, STAMM & ROBINSON

124 N. FULTON STREET
WAUSEON, OHIO 43567
Telephone: 419-337-5065
Fax: 419-337-1136
URL: http://www.lawyers.com/bksr

Delta, Ohio Office: 206 Main Street. Telephone: 419-822-3211.

General Civil and Criminal Practice. Personal Injury, Insurance, Probate and Estate Planning, Real Estate, Title Examination, Collections, Commercial, Municipal and Banking Law. Trials and Appeals in all Courts.

MEMBERS OF FIRM

JOHN H. BARBER (1921-1986)

TERRY J. KAPER, born Hamilton, Michigan, August 12, 1938; admitted to bar, 1968, Ohio. *Education:* Alma College (B.S., 1961); Ohio Northern University (J.D., 1967). Village Solicitor: Delta, Ohio, 1974-2001; McClure, Ohio, 2002-2004. Law Director, Delta, Ohio, 2002-2004. Special Counsel for Attorney General, 1986-1995. *Member:* Fulton County (President, 1992) and Ohio State Bar Associations. ***PRACTICE AREAS:*** Title Examination Law; Real Estate Law; Probate Law; Banking Law; Municipal Law. ***Email:*** tkaper@bksr.org

JAN H. STAMM, born Wauseon, Ohio, June 22, 1952; admitted to bar, 1978, Ohio; 1979, Michigan and U.S. District Court, Northern District of Ohio. *Education:* Goshen College (B.A., 1974); Case Western Reserve University (J.D., 1978). Member, Moot Court Board, 1977-1978. Wauseon City Law Director, 1986-1988; Assistant Law Director, 1989—. Solicitor, Village of Lyons, 1990-1995. *Member:* Fulton County (President, 2002), Ohio State and Michigan Bar Associations; Commercial Law League; Ohio Association of Trial Lawyers. ***PRACTICE AREAS:*** Commercial Litigation and Collections; Banking Law; Real Estate Law. ***Email:*** jstamm@bksr.org

JEFFREY L. ROBINSON, born Wauseon, Ohio, April 5, 1952; admitted to bar, 1977, Ohio and U.S. District Court, Northern District of Ohio; U.S. Court of Appeals, 6th Circuit; U.S. Supreme Court. *Education:* Miami University (B.S., 1974); University of Toledo (J.D., 1976). Village Solicitor, Lyons, Ohio, 1982-1988. Law Director: City of Wauseon, 1988-2005. Special Counsel for Attorney General, 1995-2005. Fulton County Judge, Western District, 2005—. *Member:* Fulton County (President, 2004) and Ohio State Bar Associations; Ohio Association of Trial Lawyers; The Association of Trial Lawyers of America. ***PRACTICE AREAS:*** Personal Injury; General; Probate; Real Estate; Civil Litigation. ***Email:*** jrobinson@bksr.org

ASSOCIATES

STEPHEN P. BUEHRER, born Toledo, Ohio, January 1, 1967; admitted to bar, 1997, Ohio. *Education:* Bowling Green State University (B.S., summa cum laude, 1989); Capital University Law School (J.D., cum laude, 1997). Member, Order of the Curia. Contributor: The American University Journal of Gender and the Law, Vol 6., Spring 1998; Canada-United States Law Journal, Vol. 30 2004. Assistant Village Solicitor: Delta, Ohio, 1998-2004; McClure, Ohio, 2002—. Assistant Law Director, City of Wauseon, 1998—; State Representative, 1999—. *Member:* Fulton County and Ohio State Bar Associations. ***PRACTICE AREAS:*** Real Estate; Employment Law; Trust Law; Wills; Business Law. ***Email:*** sbuehrer@bksr.org

CARRIE J. NIXON, born Toledo, Ohio, March 30, 1975; admitted to bar, 2000, Ohio. *Education:* Ball State University (B.A., summa cum laude, 1997); Case Western Reserve University (J.D., cum laude, 2000). Assistant Law Director, City of Wauseon, 2001-2005. Law Director, City of Wauseon, 2005—. Assistant Village Solicitor: Delta, Ohio, 2001-2004; McClure, Ohio, 2002-2004; Village Solicitor, 2005—. *Member:* Fulton County, Ohio State and American Bar Associations. ***PRACTICE AREAS:*** General Practice; Real Estate; Collections; Civil Litigation. ***Email:*** cnixon@bksr.org

REPRESENTATIVE CLIENTS: Farmer's and Merchants State Bank; Fulton County Health Center; K & L Trucking Co.; M & K Metal Processors Inc.; Nofziger Door Sales, Inc.; Haas Door Company; City of Wauseon, Ohio; Continental Estates, Inc.
APPROVED ATTORNEYS FOR: Federal Land Bank of Louisville; Farmers Home Administration; Port Lawrence Title & Trust.
REFERENCE: Farmers and Merchants State Bank.

THE McQUADES CO., L.P.A.

WAUSEON, OHIO

(See Swanton)

General Civil Practice. Personal Injury, Wrongful Death, Products Liability, Medical Malpractice, Real Estate, Corporate and Business Law. Probate and Estate Planning, Collections, Municipal and Zoning Law. Family Law, Criminal Law. Trials and Appellate Practice in all Courts.

PLASSMAN, RUPP, SHORT & HAGANS

WAUSEON, OHIO

(See Archbold)

General Civil Practice in all Courts. Corporation, Probate and Estate Planning, Insurance Law, Personal Injury, Real Estate, Taxation, Municipal Law, Family/Domestic Relations and Trials.

MARK L. POWERS

142 NORTH FULTON STREET
P.O. BOX 393
WAUSEON, OHIO 43567-0393
Telephone: 419-335-3971
Fax: 419-335-5040
Email: mlpowers@powersupply.net
URL: http://www.mlpowers.com

General Civil Trial Practice in all State Courts. Personal Injury, Wills and Probate, Trusts and Estates, Estate Planning, Real Estate, Bankruptcy, Creditors Rights, Family Law, Divorce, Adoptions, Child Custody, Child Support, Domestic Relations, Collections, Commercial.

MARK L. POWERS, born Toledo, Ohio, January 31, 1955; admitted to bar, 1980, Ohio; 1981, U.S. District Court, Northern District of Ohio. *Education:* Ohio Northern University (B.A., 1977; J.D., 1980). Member: Wauseon Village School Board, 1984-1991; Four County Joint Vocational School Board, 1984-1987. Solicitor, Village of Fayette, 1991—. Assistant Prosecutor, Henry County, 1997-2000. Lyons Village Solicitor, 2001—. *Member:* Fulton County and Ohio State Bar Associations. ***LANGUAGES:*** German.

REFERENCE: Farmers & Merchants State Bank, Wauseon, Ohio.

RICHARD M. LEWIS

WAVERLY, OHIO

(See Jackson)

General Trial and Appellate Practice, Tort Law, Insurance Law, Medical Negligence, Employment Law, Personal Injury, Commercial Litigation, Domestic Relations, Corporation, Real Estate, Probate and Banking Law, Debtor-Creditor and Criminal Law.

ROURKE & BLUMENTHAL, LLP

WAVERLY, OHIO

(See Columbus)

Personal Injury, Negligence, Products Liability, Medical Malpractice, Nursing Home Litigation, Wrongful Death, Intentional Tort, Insurance Disputes, Automobile Accidents, Civil Trial Practice, Aviation, Professional Liability.

CHALFIE & FARLEY, CO., L.P.A.

WEST CHESTER, OHIO

(See Cincinnati)

Probate Litigation, Probate Administration, Estate Planning, Trials and Appeals, Estate and Gift Tax, Trusts, Estates, Wills, Family Law, Negligence, Wrongful Death, Will Contests, Living Trusts and Automobile Collisions.

PATRICK T. NESBITT

Established in 1986
8050 BECKETT CENTER DRIVE
SUITE 113
WEST CHESTER, OHIO 45069
Telephone: 513-755-2600
Fax: 513-874-5205
Email: pnesbitt@one.net
URL: http://www.pnesbitt.com

Business Law; Small Business Law; Business Formation; Business Planning; Business Taxation; Business Transactions; Business Transfers; Buying and Selling of Businesses; Capitol Formation; Closely Held Business Planning; Closely Held Business Law; Emerging Business Law; Emerging Growth Companies; Entrepreneurial Business Law; Family Business Law; Family Business Successions; Limited Liability Company Law; Professional Practices; Sole proprietorships; Joint Ventures; Partnerships.

FIRM PROFILE: Start-Up and Small Business focused practice with Business Formation, Business Planning, Closely Held Business, Family Business, Limited Liability Company and Tax Planning Expertise.

PATRICK T. NESBITT, born Hamilton, Ohio, July 6, 1956; admitted to bar, 1981, Ohio and U.S. District Court, Southern District of Ohio; 1982, Kentucky and U.S. Court of Appeals, 6th Circuit; 1985, U.S. District Court, Eastern District Kentucky; 1989, U.S. Supreme Court. *Education:* Ohio Wesleyan University (B.A., magna cum laude, 1978); University of Michigan (J.D., 1981). *Member:* Cincinnati, Kentucky, Ohio State Bar Associations. ***PRACTICE AREAS:*** Small Business Law; Closely Held Corporations; Business Organization; Business Formation; Limited Liability Company Law; Commercial Transactions; Business Succession Planning; Estate Planning; Trusts; Estate Administration; Probate; Wills.

Representative Clients available upon request.

BALE, BEGIN & ASSOCIATES, LTD.

140 COMMERCE PARK DRIVE
WESTERVILLE, OHIO 43082-7935
Telephone: 614-895-5600
Facsimile: 614-895-6899
Email: dgbale@aol.com
URL: http://www.lawyers.com/bb&altd

Estate Planning, Administration and Litigation, Probate, Business Succession Planning, Nonprofit Organizations, Small Business Law, Business Formation, Limited Liability Company Law, Partnership Law, Corporate Law, Contracts, Personal Injury, Automobile Accidents, Civil Litigation.

DAVID G. BALE, born Painesville, Ohio, October 27, 1952; admitted to bar, 1978, Ohio; U.S. District Court, Southern District of Ohio; U.S. Court of Appeals, Sixth Circuit. *Education:* Capital University (B.A., 1974); Wright State University (M.S., in Economics, 1975); Cleveland State University (J.D., 1978). *Member:* Columbus (Member, Common Pleas Court Committee), Ohio State (Member, Sections on: Probate; Real Property) and American Bar Associations; Ohio Association of Civil Trial Attorneys. ***PRACTICE AREAS:*** Estate Planning; Estate Administration; Trusts and Estates; Charitable Giving; Asset Protection; Nonprofit Organizations Law; Small Business Law; Business Planning. ***Email:*** dgbale@aol.com

JAMES S. BEGIN, admitted to bar, 1973, Ohio. *Education:* University of Michigan (A.B.); The Ohio State University (J.D.). ***PRACTICE AREAS:*** Personal Injury Law; Automobile Accidents and Injuries; Wills; Probate; Civil Litigation; Contested Wills. ***Email:*** jamessbegin@aol.com

BARREN & MERRY CO., L.P.A.

110 POLARIS PARKWAY, SUITE 302
WESTERVILLE, OHIO 43082
Telephone: 614-776-1000
Fax: 614-865-3396
Email: mbarren@barrenmerrylaw.com
URL: http://www.barrenandmerry.com

Creditors Rights, Workouts, Bankruptcy Law, Banking and Finance, Commercial Law, Breach of Contracts, Business Litigation.

MICHAEL J. BARREN, born Riverdale, Maryland, May 4, 1958; admitted to bar, 1983, Ohio; 1984, U.S. District Court, Southern District of Ohio; 1993, U.S. Court of Appeals, Sixth Circuit; 2000, U.S. Court of Appeals, Fourth Circuit; 2002, U.S. District Court, Northern District of Ohio. *Education:* Princeton University (B.A., Economics, 1980); Ohio State University (J.D., 1983). Past Partner: Porter, Wright, Morris & Arthur. *Member:* Columbus, Ohio State and Federal Bar Associations; Commercial Law League of America. [Major, U.S. Army Judge Advocate General Corps.]. ***PRACTICE AREAS:*** Creditors Rights; Workouts; Commercial Litigation; Bankruptcy; Commercial Law. ***Email:*** mbarren@barrenmerrylaw.com

THOMAS R. MERRY, born Erie, Pennsylvania, September 6, 1963; admitted to bar, 1989, Ohio; 1990, U.S. District Court, Southern District of Ohio; 1994, U.S. District Court, Northern District of Ohio; 1999, U.S. Court of Appeals, Sixth Circuit. *Education:* Edinboro University (B.A., Political Science, summa cum laude, 1986); University of Notre Dame (J.D., 1989). *Member:* Columbus Bar Association. ***PRACTICE AREAS:*** Commercial Bankruptcy; Workouts; Litigation. ***Email:*** tmerry@barrenmerrylaw.com

---

BETH M. MILLER, born Columbus, Ohio, February 10, 1972; admitted to bar, 2000, Ohio; 2001, U.S. District Court, Southern District of Ohio; 2003, U.S. District Court, Northern District of Ohio. *Education:* The Ohio State University (B.S., 1996); The Ohio State University College of Law (J.D., 2000). *Member:* Columbus Bar Association. ***PRACTICE AREAS:*** Collections; Bankruptcy; Real Estate; Zoning Law. ***Email:*** bmiller@barrenmerrylaw.com

LAWRENCE S. HELKOWSKI, born Greensburg, Pennsylvania, February 9, 1971; admitted to bar, 1997, Ohio and Indiana; 1998, U.S. District Court, Northern District of Ohio; 2002, U.S. District Court, Southern District of Ohio. *Education:* University of Pittsburgh (B.A., 1992); Ohio Northern University College of Law (J.D., 1997). Assistant Law Director, Wauseon, Ohio, 1998—. *Member:* Columbus, Fulton County, Ohio State and Indiana State Bar Associations. ***PRACTICE AREAS:*** Collections; Workouts; Bankruptcy; Litigation. ***Email:*** shelkowski@barrenmerrylaw.com

TAMIE I. SNYDER

299 SOUTH STATE STREET
WESTERVILLE, OHIO 03081
Telephone: 614-895-8258
Fax: 614-436-0347
URL: http://www.tamiesnyderlaw.com

Bankruptcy, Bankruptcy Chapter 7, Bankruptcy Chapter 13, Child Support, Child Custody, Visitation Rights, Divorce, Dissolution, Post Decree Modification, Spousal Support, Family Law.

TAMIE I. SNYDER, born Akron, Ohio, May 13, 1968; admitted to bar, 1999, Ohio; 2000, U.S. District Court, Southern District of Ohio. *Education:* The Ohio State University (B.S.W., 1991); Capital University Law School (J.D., 1999). Member, International Women's Insolvency and Restructuring Federation.; Credit Education Coalition. Member, Columbus Barrister Leader Program. *Member:* Columbus and Ohio State Bar Associations; 2003 Columbus Barrister Leader Program. ***PRACTICE AREAS:*** Bankruptcy; Family

(This Listing Continued)

Law; Child Support; Child Custody; Visitation Rights; Divorce; Post Divorce Modification; Spousal Support.

WILLI LAW OFFICES

Kaye P. Willi, Attorney at Law
Established in 1997
79 S. STATE STREET
SUITE D-4
WESTERVILLE, OHIO 43081
Telephone: 614-888-7090
Fax: 614-888-7064
URL: http://www.willilaw.com

Estate Planning, Business Succession Planning, Tax Planning, Small Business Law, Business Start-Ups, Real Estate, Trust Administration, Asset Protection, Charitable Giving, Guardianships, Premarital Agreements, Trusts and Estates, Probate.

KAYE P. WILLI, born Wooster, Ohio, April 9, 1955; admitted to bar, 1983, Ohio; 1986, U.S. Tax Court; 1990, U.S. District Court Southern and Northern Districts of Ohio. *Education:* Miami University (B.A., cum laude, 1976); The Ohio State University (M.A., 1980); Duke University (J.D., 1983). Phi Beta Kappa. Editorial Board, Duke Law Journal, 1982-1983. Certified Public Accountant, Ohio, 1988. *Member:* Columbus, Ohio State and American Bar Associations; Ohio Society of Certified Public Accountants; American Institute of Certified Public Accountants; Alliance Defense Fund; Christian Legal Society; Worthington Estate Planning Council. (Certified Specialist in Estate Planning, Trust and Probate Law, Ohio State Bar Association).(Also Of Counsel, The Jeffries Company, A Legal Professional Association). ***PRACTICE AREAS:*** Estate Planning; Small Business Law; Business Succession Planning; Wealth Preservation; Asset Protection; Charitable Giving; Trust Administration; Tax Planning; Estate and Gift Taxation; Fiduciary Income Tax; Guardianships; Premarital Agreements; Real Estate; Trusts and Estates; Probate.

JOSEPH D. CARNEY & ASSOCIATES, L.L.C.

WESTLAKE, OHIO
(See Cleveland)

Small, Medium and Large Business Counseling, Corporate Law, Litigation, Commercial and Residential Real Estate, Estate Planning, Employment Law Compliance, Securities Law, Capital Formation, Commercial Contracts, Mergers and Acquisitions, Financing Related Law, Employment Law, Construction, Regulatory, Liquor Law, Broker-Dealers, Insurance Law.

HAROLD L. HOM, CO., LPA

WESTLAKE, OHIO
(See Cleveland)

HUNT & COOK LLC

Established in 2001
GEMINI TOWER II, SUITE 530
2001 CROCKER ROAD
WESTLAKE, OHIO 44145
Telephone: 440-892-0400
Fax: 440-892-1966
Email: attorneys@huntcooklaw.com
URL: http://www.huntcooklaw.com

Civil Litigation and Appeals, Business and Commercial Law, Commercial Collections, Criminal Law, Divorce and Family Law, Wills and Estates, Personal Injury.

FIRM PROFILE: The law firm of Hunt & Cook LLC was established in 2001 and is located in Westlake, Ohio. Hunt & Cook's two attorneys, William Hunt and Brian Cook, collectively have over 39 years of legal experience serving individual and business clients in the areas of personal and business litigation and appeals, business and commercial law, commercial collections, suburban criminal matters, public utility matters and personal injury cases. The firm's practice is also sufficiently general to directly handle small business formation, real estate transactions and wills and trusts.

WILLIAM HARRY HUNT, born Indianapolis, Indiana, September 7, 1947; admitted to bar, 1975, Ohio; 1976, U.S. District Court, Northern District of Ohio; 1978, U.S. Supreme Court. *Education:* Purdue University (B.S., 1969; M.S.I.A., 1970); Cleveland Marshall College of Law (J.D., magna cum laude, 1975). Law Instructor, Paralegal Program, Meyers College, formerly know as Dyke College, Cleveland, Ohio, 1986-1997. Member, National Underground Utility Locating Contractors Association. *Member:* Cleveland, Cuyahoga County, Ohio State and American Bar Associations. ***SPECIAL AGENCIES:*** Public Utilities Commission of Ohio. ***PRACTICE AREAS:*** Personal Injury; Debtor and Creditor; Commercial Law; Business Law; Estate Planning. ***Email:*** whhunt@huntcooklaw.com

BRIAN ANTHONY COOK, born St. Louis, Missouri, September 24, 1966; admitted to bar, 1992, Ohio. *Education:* Fairfield University (B.A., 1988); Cleveland-Marshall College of Law (J.D., 1991). *Member:* Ohio State Bar Association. ***PRACTICE AREAS:*** Business Law; Criminal Law; Consumer Law; Contracts; Personal Injury. ***Email:*** bacook@huntcooklaw.com

KING & ASSOCIATES

28871 CENTER RIDGE ROAD
SUITE 102
WESTLAKE, OHIO 44145
Telephone: 440-899-3900
Fax: 440-892-3900
Email: jfking@kingandassociates.com
URL: http://www.kingandassociates.com

Personal Injury, Medical Malpractice, Wrongful Death, Business Litigation, Aviation Law, Litigation.

JOHN F. KING, born Pittsburgh, Pennsylvania, May 21, 1957; admitted to bar, 1983, Ohio; 1986, U.S. Court of Appeals, Sixth Circuit; 1988, District of Columbia. *Education:* Slippery Rock State College (B.S., 1980); Cleveland Marshall College of Law (J.D., 1983). Law School Liaison Committee, 1991; Law Related Education Committee, 1992. *Member:* Greater Cleveland, Ohio State and American (Member, Litigation Section) Bar Associations; The District of Columbia Bar; Ohio Academy of Trial Lawyers; The Association of Trial Lawyers of America. ***Email:*** kingassociates@law.com

STEUER, ESCOVAR, BERK & BROWN CO., L.P.A.

WESTLAKE, OHIO

(See Cleveland)

General Civil and Criminal Practice. Personal Injury, Negligence, Workers Compensation, Corporation, Mergers and Acquisitions, Taxation, Real Estate, Bankruptcy, Family, Probate and Commercial Law. Estate Planning, Trials and Medical Malpractice, Civil and Criminal Appellate Work, Insurance Defense, Business Law, Administrative Law.

PURDY & RING

WEST UNION, OHIO

(See Georgetown)

Criminal Law, DUI, Family Law, Divorce, Dissolution of Marriage, Personal Injury, Estates, Wills, Probate, Business Law, Real Estate, Appellate Practice.

SHRYOCK & MORRISON

30601 EUCLID AVENUE
WICKLIFFE, OHIO 44092
Telephone: 440-944-7020
Fax: 440-943-3096
URL: http://www.euclidavelaw.com

Family Law, Domestic Relations, Mediation, Juvenile Law, Criminal Law, Traffic Violations, Personal Injury.

MEMBERS OF FIRM

JOHN SHRYOCK, born Washington, D.C., March 28, 1951; admitted to bar, 1979, Ohio; 1980, U.S. District Court, District of Ohio. *Education:* Ohio Northern University (B.A., 1974; J.D., 1978). *Member:* Lake County and Ohio State Bar Associations. ***PRACTICE AREAS:*** Family Law; Domestic Relations; Mediation; Juvenile Law. ***Email:*** jshryock@euclidavelaw.com

RICHARD P. MORRISON, born Cleveland, Ohio, October 17, 1951; admitted to bar, 1980, Ohio; 1985, U.S. District Court, Northern District of Ohio. *Education:* Ohio State University (B.A., 1973); Capital University Law School (J.D., 1980). *Member:* Lake County and Ohio State Bar Associations. ***PRACTICE AREAS:*** Criminal Law (50%, 75); Juvenile Law (25%, 50); Traffic Violations (20%, 25); Personal Injury (5%, 10). ***Email:*** rmorrison@euclidavelaw.com

DRIGGS, HOGG & FRY CO., LPA

38500 CHARDON ROAD
WILLOUGHBY HILLS, OHIO 44094
Telephone: 440-391-5100
Fax: 440-391-5101
URL: http://www.lawyers.com/driggslaw

Corporate Law, Trusts and Estate, Business Law, Real Estate, Intellectual Property, Patents, Copyrights, Trademarks, Trade Secrets, Unfair Competition.

CHARLES M. DRIGGS, born Cleveland, Ohio, January 26, 1924; admitted to bar, 1951, Ohio. *Education:* Yale University (B.S., cum laude, 1947; J.D., 1950). Phi Delta Phi. Member: Corbey Court, 1948-1950; Dean's List, Yale University. President, Bratenahl School Board, 1958-1961. Director, Cleveland City Club, 1956-1960. Trustee, Cleveland Law Library, 1979-1991. American College of Trust and Estate Counsel, 1979. Court of Nisi Prius, 1963—. Listed Who's Who In America, 1986—; Who's Who In American Law, 1986—; Best Lawyers In America, 1989; International Who's Who, 1995. *Member:* Lake County, Cleveland, Geauga County, Ohio State and American Bar Associations. [Lt. (Senior Grade), U.S. Navy, 1942-1946]. ***PRACTICE AREAS:*** Trusts and Estates; Corporate Law; Real Estate; General Practice. ***Email:*** charles@driggslaw.com

WILLIAM N. HOGG, born Cleveland, Ohio, 1931; admitted to bar, 1959, Ohio; 1978, Colorado (inactive); 1973, U.S. Supreme Court; registered to practice before U.S. Patent and Trademark Office. *Education:* Purdue University (B.S., 1953); St. Louis University; Case Western Reserve University (LL.B., 1959). Member, Case Western Reserve University Law Review, 1958-1959. [Lt., U.S. Army, 1953-1955]. ***PRACTICE AREAS:*** Intellectual Property; Patents; Trademarks; Copyrights. ***Email:*** bill@driggslaw.com

(This Listing Continued)

JOHN J. FRY, born Cleveland, Ohio, October 29, 1961; admitted to bar, 1991, Ohio; U.S. District Court, Northern District of Ohio; U.S. Court of Appeals for the Federal Circuit; registered to practice before U.S. Patent and Trademark Office. *Education:* Case Western Reserve University (B.S. in Electrical Engineering and Applied Physics, with honors, 1983; M.S. in Electrical Engineering, with an emphasis on Digital and Intelligent Systems, 1985); Cleveland-Marshall College of Law (J.D., summa cum laude, 1990). Highest scoring applicant on the February 1991 Ohio Bar Examination. Named Inventor on ten U.S. Patents. Judicial Extern for U.S. District Court Judge George W. White. Author: "The Rejection of Executory Contracts Under the Intellectual Property Bankruptcy Proteetion Act," 37 Clev. St. L. Rev. 621, 1989. Litigation Associate, Benesch, Friedlander, Coplan & Aronoff, Cleveland, Ohio, 1990-1992. Supervisor, Monitor and Analyzer and Product Development Engineer, Bailey Controls Company, Wickliffe, Ohio, 1983-1990. Former Corporate Counsel, Reliance Electric Company. Member, Manufacturer's Alliance for Production & Innovation. *Member:* Cleveland, Lake County, and Ohio State Bar Associations; Cleveland Intellectual Property Law Association. ***PRACTICE AREAS:*** Business Law; Intellectual Property; Patents; Trademarks; Copyrights; Trade Secrets. ***Email:*** jfry@driggslaw.com

THORNBURG, BEAN & GLICK

WOODSFIELD, OHIO

(See St. Clairsville)

General Civil Practice. Corporate, Personal Injury, Probate, Insurance and Real Estate Law. Title Examinations. Trials in all Courts. Mining Law.

BAKER, DUBLIKAR, BECK, WILEY & MATHEWS

WOOSTER, OHIO

(See North Canton)

General Civil Trial and Appellate Practice in all Courts. Insurance, Products Liability, Environmental, Malpractice, Political Subdivision, Real Estate, Corporate, Commercial and Family Law.

CRITCHFIELD, CRITCHFIELD & JOHNSTON, LTD.

225 NORTH MARKET STREET
P.O. BOX 599
WOOSTER, OHIO 44691-0599
Telephone: 330-264-4444
Telecopier: 330-263-9278
URL: http://www.ccj.com

Millersburg, Ohio: 138 E. Jackson Street, 44654. Telephone: 330-674-3055.
Mt. Vernon, Ohio: 10 South Gay Street, 43050-3546. Telephone: 740-397-4040.
Medina, Ohio: 3985 Medina Road, Suite 100, 44256. Telephone: 330-723-6404.

General Practice in all Courts. Business, Corporate Law, Insurance, Estate Planning, Wills and Probate, Labor and Employment, ERISA, Health Care, Environmental Law, Workers Compensation, Banking, Taxation, Antitrust and Trade Regulation, Oil and Gas Law, Litigation, Debtor and Creditor, Municipal Law, School Law, Real Estate, Commercial Law, Construction Law.

JOHN C. JOHNSTON, III, born Wooster, Ohio, October 26, 1948; admitted to bar, 1975, Ohio. *Education:* College of Wooster (B.A., 1971); Northwestern University (J.D., 1975). Phi Beta Kappa; Phi Alpha Theta. ***PRACTICE AREAS:*** Business Law; Estate Planning; Probate; Tax Exempt Organizations. ***Email:*** johnston@ccj.com

DANIEL H. PLUMLY, born Barnesville, Ohio, May 1, 1953; admitted to bar, 1978, Ohio. *Education:* Muskingum College (B.A., summa cum laude, 1975); Case Western Reserve University (J.D., 1978). Phi Alpha Theta; Order of Coif. Member, National Moot Court Team. ***PRACTICE AREAS:*** Corporate Law; Commercial Law; Banking Law; Oil and Gas Law; Real Estate. ***Email:*** plumly@ccj.com

J. DOUGLAS DRUSHAL, born Wooster, Ohio, June 14, 1953; admitted to bar, 1977, Ohio. *Education:* Northwestern University (B.A., 1974); Ohio State University (J.D., summa cum laude, 1977). Order of the Coif. Editor, Ohio State Law Journal, 1977. Law Clerk, Judge Anthony J. Celebrezze, U.S. Court of Appeals, Sixth Circuit, 1977-1979. ***PRACTICE AREAS:*** Litigation; Real Estate Development; Commercial Law; Estate Planning. ***Email:*** ddrushal@ccj.com

PEGGY J. SCHMITZ, born Wadsworth, Ohio, January 16, 1952; admitted to bar, 1978, Ohio. *Education:* Bowling Green State University (B.A., 1973); University of Akron (J.D., 1978). ***PRACTICE AREAS:*** Labor and Employment; Higher Education; Products Liability; Business Torts Defense. ***Email:*** schmitz@ccj.com

SUSAN EILEEN BAKER, born Akron, Ohio, December 9, 1954; admitted to bar, 1992, Ohio. *Education:* Akron City Hospital School of Nursing (R.N., highest honors, 1982); Ashland College (B.S.N., magna cum laude, 1988); Case Western Reserve University (J.D., 1992). Registered Nurse, Ohio, 1983. (Certified Specialist in Workers' Compensation Law, Ohio State Bar Association). ***PRACTICE AREAS:*** Litigation; Workers' Compensation; Employment Law; Health Care. ***Email:*** baker@ccj.com

DAVID J. WIGHAM, born Cleveland, Ohio, January 3, 1959; admitted to bar, 1992, Ohio. *Education:* The College of Wooster (B.A., 1989); Cleveland-Marshall College of Law (J.D., 1992). ***PRACTICE AREAS:*** Civil Litigation; Construction Law; Creditors Rights; Oil and Gas; ERISA Litigation. ***Email:*** wigham@ccj.com

ROBERT C. GORMAN, born Elgin, Illinois, May 6, 1961; admitted to bar, 1995, Ohio. *Education:* University of Notre Dame (B.A., magna cum laude, 1983); University of Akron, School of Law (J.D., summa cum laude, 1995). Law Clerk, U.S. District Judge David D. Dowd, Jr., U.S. District Court, Northern District of Ohio, 1995-1997. ***PRACTICE AREAS:*** Labor and Employment Law; Business; ERISA Litigation; Civil Litigation. ***Email:*** gorman@ccj.com

(This Listing Continued)

ROGER D. PROPER, JR., born Millersburg, Ohio, September 27, 1971; admitted to bar, 1997, Ohio. *Education:* Miami University (B.S., 1990); University of Toledo, College of Law (J.D., 1997). ***PRACTICE AREAS:*** Estate Planning; Business Planning; Exempt Organizations; Taxation; Probate. ***Email:*** proper@ccj.com

TIMOTHY B. PETTORINI, born Columbus, Ohio, August 10, 1972; admitted to bar, 1998, Ohio. *Education:* The College of Wooster (B.A., 1995); University of Akron (J.D., cum laude, 1998). ***PRACTICE AREAS:*** Civil Litigation; Workers' Compensation; Insurance Coverage Litigation. ***Email:*** pettorini@ccj.com

---

ELIZABETH KRIEDER WRIGHT, born Oberlin, Ohio, November 16, 1971; admitted to bar, 2001, Ohio. *Education:* Denison University (B.A., magna cum laude, 1994); Case Western Reserve University School of Law (J.D., 2000). ***LANGUAGES:*** German. ***PRACTICE AREAS:*** Civil Litigation; Workers Compensation Defense; Immigration Law. ***Email:*** wright@ccj.com

JOHN H. SCHAEFFER, born Toledo, Ohio, May 12, 1964; admitted to bar, 1989, Ohio; 1993, Arizona. *Education:* The Ohio State University (B.A., 1986); University of Toledo College of Law (J.D., 1989). ***LANGUAGES:*** Sign Language. ***PRACTICE AREAS:*** Business Litigation; Labor and Employment; Banking Law. ***Email:*** schaeffer@ccj.com

TRICIA L. PLANT, born Wooster, Ohio, November 29, 1976; admitted to bar, 2002, Ohio. *Education:* Denison University (B.A., summa cum laude, 1999); Ohio State University (J.D., with honors, 2002). ***PRACTICE AREAS:*** Civil Litigation; Labor and Employment; Internet Law. **Email:** plant@ccj.com

ANDREW P. LYCANS, born Wadsworth, Ohio, July 28, 1976; admitted to bar, 2004, Ohio. *Education:* University of Akron (B.A., 1998); University of Michigan, Ann Arbor (J.D., 2003). Articles Editor, Michigan Law Review, 2002-2003. Law Clerk, Hon. Samuel H. Mays, Jr., U.S. District Court, Western District of Tennessee, 2003-2004. Author: "Cyberdemons: Regulating a Truly Worldwide Web," 101 Michigan Law Review 1925; "An Assignment by Any Other Name," 101 Michigan Law Review 1102. *Member:* Wayne County, Ohio State and American Bar Associations. ***PRACTICE AREAS:*** Commercial Litigation; Business Litigation; Trademarks; Copyrights. ***Email:*** lycans@ccj.com

KEVIN J. McALLISTER, born Orrville, Ohio, March 8, 1979; admitted to bar, 2004, Ohio. *Education:* College of Wooster (B.A., 2001); The Ohio State University (J.D., 2004). *Wayne County, Ohio State and American Bar Associations.* ***PRACTICE AREAS:*** Business Law; Real Estate; Estate Planning. ***Email:*** mcallister@ccj.com

OF COUNSEL

LINCOLN P. OVIATT, admitted to bar, 1956, Ohio. ***PRACTICE AREAS:*** Employment Law; Corporate Law; Litigation. ***Email:*** oviatt@ccj.com

BONNIE C. DRUSHAL, born Wooster, Ohio, February 12, 1953; admitted to bar, 1982, Ohio. *Education:* University of Illinois, Chicago (B.A., 1974); Ohio State University (M.A., 1977); University of Akron (J.D., 1982). *Member:* Wayne County, Ohio State and American Bar Associations. ***PRACTICE AREAS:*** Civil Litigation; Business Litigation; School Law; Labor and Employment Law. ***Email:*** bdrushal@ccj.com

REPRESENTATIVE CLIENTS: Newell Rubbermaid Inc.; The College of Wooster; Buehler Food Markets, Inc.; The Will-Burt Co.; Mobile Consultants, Inc.; Buckeye Feed Mills, Inc.; Medical Mutual of Ohio; Ohio Legacy Bank, NA; Westfield Bank, FSB; CorrChoice; Ken Miller Supply, Inc.
TITLE POLICY ISSUING AGENTS FOR: First American Title Insurance Co.

GRISI & RIEGLER

WOOSTER, OHIO

(See Akron)

Personal Injury, Medical Malpractice, Divorce, Probate and Estates, Municipal Zoning, Corporate.

LOGEE, HOSTETLER, STUTZMAN & LEHMAN, LLC

2171-B EAGLE PASS
WOOSTER, OHIO 44691
Telephone: 330-264-6115
FAX: 330-262-5729

General Practice. Insurance Law, Insurance Defense, Probate, Estate Planning, Real Estate, Corporate Law and Taxation. Trials.

MEMBERS OF FIRM

DANIEL J. HOSTETLER, born Wooster, Ohio, March 3, 1948; admitted to bar, 1973, Ohio. *Education:* Wittenberg University (B.A., 1970); Duke University (J.D., 1973). Phi Alpha Delta. Trust Officer, Huntington National Bank, 1973-1975. *Member:* Wayne County, Ohio State and American Bar Associations; American Agricultural Law Association. ***PRACTICE AREAS:*** Probate Law; Estate Planning; Taxation. ***Email:*** dhostetler@lhslaw.com

MORRIS STUTZMAN, born Arthur, Illinois, September 20, 1949; admitted to bar, 1975, Ohio. *Education:* Bluffton College (B.A., 1972); Case Western Reserve University (J.D., 1975). *Member:* Wayne County, Ohio State and American Bar Associations; Defense Research Institute, Inc.; Ohio Association of Civil Trial Attorneys; Ohio Land Title Association. ***PRACTICE AREAS:*** Business Law; Real Estate Law; Insurance Law. ***Email:*** mstutzman@lhslaw.com

RALPH E. LEHMAN, born Kidron, Ohio, December 9, 1947; admitted to bar, 1979, Ohio. *Education:* Eastern Mennonite College and Malone College (B.A., 1970); University of Akron (J.D., 1979). *Member:* Wayne County, Ohio State and American Bar Associations. Fellow, American College of Trust and Estate Counsel. (Certified Specialist in Estate Planning, Trust and Probate Law, Ohio State Bar Association). ***PRACTICE AREAS:*** Probate Law; Estate Planning. ***Email:*** rlehman@lhslaw.com

(This Listing Continued)

JERRY S. PACKARD, born Lodi, Ohio, October 28, 1950; admitted to bar, 1977, Ohio; 1979, U.S. District Court, Northern District of Ohio; 1981, U.S. Supreme Court. *Education:* University of Akron (B.A., summa cum laude, 1973); Ohio State University (J.D., 1977). Assistant Wayne County Public Defender, 1979-1989. *Member:* Wayne County, Ohio State and American Bar Associations; Ohio Association of Civil Trial Attorneys. ***PRACTICE AREAS:*** Insurance Defense; Civil Litigation; Criminal Defense. ***Email:*** jpackard@lhslaw.com

RONALD E. HOLTMAN, born McCune, Kansas, January 27, 1943; admitted to bar, 1967, Ohio. *Education:* Denison University (B.S., 1964); Case Western Reserve University (J.D., 1967). Member, Board of Editors, Case Western Reserve Law Review, 1966-1967. *Member:* Wayne County, Ohio State and American Bar Associations. [Capt., JAG, USAF, active duty, 1968-1971]. ***PRACTICE AREAS:*** Probate Law; Estate Planning; Banking Law; Commercial Law; Real Estate Law. ***Email:*** rholtman@lhslaw.com

---

CHRISTOPHER N. FINNEY, born Wooster, Ohio, July 30, 1976; admitted to bar, 2003, Ohio. *Education:* Ohio Northern University (B.S., 1998); University of Akron (J.D., 2003). Certified Public Accountant, Ohio, 2000. Member: American Institute of Certified Public Accountants; Ohio Society of Certified Public Accountants. *Member:* Wayne County, Ohio State and American Bar Associations. ***PRACTICE AREAS:*** Estate Planning; Real Estate; Probate; Corporate Law; Taxation. ***Email:*** cfinney@lhslaw.com

REPRESENTATIVE CLIENTS: Western Reserve Mutual Casualty Co.; Lightning Rod Mutual Insurance Co.; Wayne Mutual Insurance Co.; Mennonite Mutual Insurance Co.; OrrVilla Retirement Community; Lehman's Hardware, Inc.; Hartzler Lumber Co.; Gerber Poultry, Inc.; Tyler Grain & Fertilizer Co.; J. Horst Manufacturing Co.; G&S Titanium, Inc.; Sprosty Bag Co.; Pallotta Ford, Inc.; Oral-Facial Surgery Centre of Wayne and Holmes Counties, Inc.
APPROVED ATTORNEYS FOR: Commonwealth Land Title Insurance Co.

PAGANO, WILSON, THOMARIOS, GILLISSIE & LENAHAN LLC

WOOSTER, OHIO

(See Cleveland)

Criminal Law, Employment Defense, Personal Injury, Workers Compensation, Social Security Disability, Probate, Estate Planning, Family Law, Business Law, Collections.

RICHARD LAW OFFICE, LLC

127 EAST LIBERTY STREET, SUITE 100
WOOSTER, OHIO 44691
Telephone: 330-262-0034
Fax: 330-262-0080
Email: james@richardlawoffice.com
URL: http://www.richardlawoffice.com

Corporate, Business Law, Oil and Gas, Personal Injury, Wrongful Death, Estate Planning, Probate, Divorce, Dissolution, Real Estate, Litigation, Probate Avoidance.

FIRM PROFILE: Richard Law Office, LLC is a general practice law firm. The general areas of practice include: Corporation and Business Law, Oil and Gas Law, Personal Injury-Wrongful Death, Estate Planning/Probate, Divorce/Dissolution, Real Estate, Litigation, and Probate Avoidance. As a general practice law firm, we believe we are equipped to handle a wide range of legal issues to provide assistance to individuals as well as corporate and business clients.

JAMES M. RICHARD, born Lodi, Ohio, March 23, 1947; admitted to bar, 1974, Ohio; U.S. District Court, Northern District of Ohio; U.S. District Court, Western District of Texas; U.S. Tax Court. *Education:* Bluffton College (B.S., 1969); Ohio Northern University (J.D., 1974). Member, Panel of Arbitrators. *Member:* Wayne County (Member, Executive Committee, 1992-2002; President, 2002) and Ohio State Bar Associations; American Arbitration Association. [With U.S. Army, 1970-1972]. ***LANGUAGES:*** English. ***PRACTICE AREAS:*** Corporate Law; Business Law; Oil and Gas; Personal Injury; Wrongful Death; Estate Planning; Probate; Divorce; Dissolution; Real Estate; Litigation; Probate Avoidance. ***Email:*** james@richardlawoffice.com

---

ROSS LAW OFFICES P.L.L.

Established in 1903

406 NORTH MARKET STREET
WOOSTER, OHIO 44691-3598
Telephone: 330-264-1213
Fax: 330-263-6054
URL: http://www.ross-law.net

Estate Planning, Trusts and Estates, Probate, Elder Law, Guardianship, Real Estate, Taxation.

W. HOWARD ROSS (1879-1966)

FORD G. ROSS, born Wooster, Ohio, September 3, 1910; admitted to bar, 1935, Ohio. *Education:* College of Wooster (A.B., 1932); Harvard Law School (J.D., 1935). ***PRACTICE AREAS:*** Estate Planning; Trusts and Estates; Probate; Real Estate; Taxation. ***Email:*** ford@ross-law.net

WILLIAM F. ROSS, born Cleveland, Ohio, September 2, 1949; admitted to bar, 1975, Ohio. *Education:* Wittenberg University (B.A., 1971); Capital University (J.D., 1975). *Member:* National Association of Elder Law Attorneys. (Certified Specialist in Estate Plan-

(This Listing Continued)

ROSS LAW OFFICES P.L.L., Wooster—Continued

ning, Trust and Probate Law, Ohio State Bar Association). ***PRACTICE AREAS:*** Estate Planning; Trusts and Estates; Probate; Elder Law; Real Estate; Taxation. ***Email:*** bill@ross-law.net

JAMES H. ROSS, born Cleveland, Ohio, April 28, 1947; admitted to bar, 1981, Ohio. *Education:* Muskingum College (B.A., 1969); University of Toledo (J.D., 1981). Phi Kappa Phi. Member, Wayne County Veterans Service Commission, 1986—. ***PRACTICE AREAS:*** Estate Planning; Trusts and Estates; Probate; Guardianship; Elder Law; Real Estate. ***Email:*** jim@ross-law.net

REFERENCES: FirstMerit Bank, N.A. (Wooster Office); National City Bank (Wooster Office); Bank One, N.A. (Wooster Office).

LAW OFFICE OF LON VINION & PATRICIA A. RODGERS

2206 MECHANICSBURG ROAD
WOOSTER, OHIO 44691
Telephone: 330-262-2510
Fax: 330-262-2524
Email: Vinionlaw@sssnet.com
URL: http://www.vinionlaw.com

Practice limited to Matrimonial, Divorce and Family Law.

LON VINION, admitted to bar, 1979, Ohio. *Education:* Youngstown State University (B.S., 1976); University of Houston (J.D., 1978). Author: "When Custody Cases Cross the Border, a Primer on International Disputes Over Children," Vol. 4, Family Advocate, 1993; "Coming to Grips with Personal Jurisdiction Problems in Multistate Post Divorce Decree Proceedings," American Journal of Family Law, Vol. 4, Winter 1989; Child Support: Getting Tough," The Complete Lawyer, Vol. 2. No. 2, 1985; "Retroactive Modification of Accrued and Unpaid Child Support," 56 OBAR 10, 1983. Co-Author: "Ohio Domestic Relations Law," Baldwin, 1984. Author: "Child Support: Getting Tough," The Complete Lawyer, Vol. 2, No. 2, 1985; "Retroactive Modification of Accrued and Unpaid Child Support," 56 OBAR 10, 1983. Domestic Relations Referee, Wayne County, Ohio, 1981-1984. Member, American Academy of Matrimonial Lawyers. Selected as Ohio Super Lawyer, 2004, 2005, 2006. (Certified Specialist in Family Relations Law, Ohio State Bar Association). ***REPORTED CASES:*** Neville v. Neville, 99 Ohio St. 3d 275, 7-23-03; Saal v. Saal, 146 Ohio App. 3d 579, dec'd. 7-11-90; Bigley v. Bigley, 90 Ohio App. 3d 310, dec'd. 9-15-93; Hostetler v. Kennedy, 69 Ohio App. 3d 299, dec'd. 9-5-90. ***PRACTICE AREAS:*** Matrimonial Law; Interstate Child Custody Litigation; International Child Custody Litigation; Divorce. ***Email:*** vinionlaw@sssnet.com

PATRICIA A. RODGERS, admitted to bar, 1978, Ohio and Pennsylvania. *Education:* Indiana University of Pennsylvania (B.A., 1974); University of Toledo (J.D., 1977). Presenter, Pennsylvania Bar Institute. Instructor, Torts, Contracts, Domestic Relations, Real State, Westmoreland County Community College. *Member:* Westmoreland (Member, Civil Rules Committee, Chair, Family Law Committee, 1988-1990; Chair, Mandatory Continuing Legal Education Committee), Pennsylvania (Member, State Continuing Legal Education Commitee; Family Law Section) and Ohio Bar Associations; Wayne County Bar. ***PRACTICE AREAS:*** Family Practice; Matrimonial Litigation; Custody Litigation; Interstate Child Custody Litigation; International Child Custody Litigation. ***Email:*** pvlaw@sssnet.com

BARAN, PIPER, TARKOWSKY, FITZGERALD & THEIS CO., L.P.A.

6877 N. HIGH STREET, SUITE 105
WORTHINGTON, OHIO 43085-2516
Telephone: 614-436-0539
Fax: 614-436-1713
URL: http://www.baranlaw.com

General Civil Practice. Trials in all Courts. Insurance Defense, Corporate, Family Law, Estate Planning, Personal Injury, Products Liability and Construction Law. Commercial Litigation. Suretyship. Environmental and Governmental Liability. Professional Liability, Worker's Compensation.

(For Complete List of all Personnel and Biographical data, see Professional Biographies at Mansfield, Ohio)

JOHN S. JONES

867 HIGH STREET, SUITE C
WORTHINGTON, OHIO 43085
Telephone: 614-885-8118
Fax: 614-885-5559
Email: jsj@jsjlaw.com
URL: http://www.lawyers.com/jsjlaw

Estate Planning, Estate Administration, Wills, Trusts, Probate, Estates, Elder Law, Real Estate.

JOHN S. JONES, born Albany, New York, March 31, 1950; admitted to bar, 1976, Ohio; 1977, U.S. District Court, Southern District of Ohio. *Education:* Denison University (B.A., 1972); The Ohio State University (J.D., cum laude, 1976). *Member:* Columbus (Member: Probate Court Committee; Real Property Committee; Gift and Estate Tax Committee), Ohio State (Member: Real Property, Probate and Trust Committee; Elder Law Committee) and American (Member: Real Property Committee; Probate and Trust Committee; Law Practice Management) Bar Associations. ***PRACTICE AREAS:*** Estate Planning; Estate Administration; Probate Law; Elder Law; Real Estate.

KETTLEWELL & KETTLEWELL, LLC

870 HIGH STREET, SUITE 102
WORTHINGTON, OHIO 43085
Telephone: 614-436-2750
Fax: 614-436-2865
URL: http://www.kettlewells.com
URL: http://www.lawyers.com/charleskettlewelllaw

Legal Ethics and Professional Responsibility, Attorney Discipline, Preventative Consultations and Advisory Opinions, Admissions, Expert Witness in Legal Malpractice, Conflicts and Fee Disputes and Risk Management Analysis.

CHARLES W. KETTLEWELL (1941-2005)

CHARLES J. KETTLEWELL, born Columbus, Ohio; admitted to bar, 2000, Ohio. *Education:* Ohio University (B.A., cum laude, 1996) AKD International Honor Society; Capital University (J.D., 2000). *Member:* Columbus, Ohio State, and American Bar Associations; Franklin County Trial Lawyers Association; Association of Professional Responsibility Lawyers (APRL). ***PRACTICE AREAS:*** Legal Ethics (95%); General Practice (5%).

MANOS, MARTIN, PERGRAM & DIETZ CO., LPA

WORTHINGTON, OHIO

(See Delaware)

Administrative, Appellate Practice, Litigation, Business, Contracts, Corporate, Zoning, Planning and Land Use, Real Estate, Labor and Employment, Trusts and Estates, and Wills and Probate.

WILLIAM A. MORSE

A LEGAL PROFESSIONAL ASSOCIATION
SUITE 140, 933 HIGH STREET
WORTHINGTON, OHIO 43085
Telephone: 614-436-8010
Fax: 614-436-8330
Email: wmorse@wamorselaw.com
URL: http://www.lawyers.com/morsefirm

Estate Planning, Probate, Small Business and Non-Profit Corporations.

WILLIAM A. MORSE, born Cleveland, Ohio, June 30, 1944; admitted to bar, 1972, Ohio. *Education:* Miami University (B.S., 1966); The Ohio State University (J.D., cum laude, 1972). *Member:* Columbus (Member: Committee on Taxation; Estate and Gift Tax Subcommittee), Ohio State (Member, Board of Governors, Estate Planning, Trust and Probate Law Section) and American Bar Associations; Worthington Estate Planning Council (Founder and Presider, 1988—). Fellow, American College of Trust and Estate Counsel. Fellow, Columbus Bar Foundation. [1st Lt., U.S. Army Intelligence, Vietnam, 1966-1969]. ***PRACTICE AREAS:*** Estate Planning; Trusts and Estates; Wills; Probate; Charitable Giving; Non-Profit Corporations; Small Business Law; Partnerships; Limited Liability Companies; Family Business Law; Premarital Agreements. ***Email:*** wmorse@wamorselaw.com

BIESER, GREER & LANDIS, LLP

XENIA, OHIO

(See Dayton)

General Civil Practice, Trial Practice, Business Litigation, Professional Liability Defense, Personal Injury Defense, Products Liability Defense, Corporate Law, Employment Law, Commercial Law, Probate, Tax Law, White Collar Criminal Defense, Arbitration, Mediation.

FOX & ASSOCIATES CO., L.P.A.

XENIA, OHIO

(See Dayton)

Bankruptcy, Chapter 7, Chapter 13, Foreclosures, Divorce, Adoptions, Child Custody, Visitation Rights, Estate Planning, Wills and Trusts, Driving While Intoxicated and Traffic Violations.

PETERSON & PETERSON

87 S. PROGRESS DRIVE
XENIA, OHIO 45385
Telephone: 937-372-3584
Fax: 937-372-7218

Automobile and Motorcycle Accidents, Workers Compensation, Job-Related Injuries, Wrongful Death, Bus and Truck accidents, Negligence Claims, Insurance Claims, Probate, Estates, Wills, Living Trust, Guardianship, Power of Attorney, Real Estate, Contracts, Deeds, Evictions, Family Law, Divorce, Custody, Visitation, Domestic Violence, Criminal, Traffic Violations, Felonies, Misdemeanors, DUI, License Suspension, Juvenile, Bankruptcy.

PARTNERS OF FIRM

MARSHALL E. PETERSON, admitted to bar, 1955, Ohio. *Education:* Muskingum College and Ohio Northern University (LL.B., 1955). ***PRACTICE AREAS:*** Probate (40%); Real Estate (20%); Criminal Law (10%).

DAVID S. PETERSON, born Xenia, Ohio, June 4, 1959; admitted to bar, 1984, Ohio. *Education:* Wright State University (B.A., 1981); Ohio Northern University (J.D. 1984). *Member:* Greene County (Past President), Ohio State and American Bar Associations; American Trial Lawyers Association; Miami Valley Trial Lawyers Association (Past Presi-

(This Listing Continued)

dent); Ohio Trial Lawyers Association. ***PRACTICE AREAS:*** Litigation; Family Law; Criminal Law. ***Email:*** davidpeterson962@msn.com

PICKREL, SCHAEFFER & EBELING

XENIA, OHIO

(See Dayton)

Banking, Civil, Corporate, General Business, Commercial Lending, Mergers and Acquisitions, Insurance, Labor and Employment, Healthcare, Municipal and Zoning, Personal Injury and Products Liability, Probate, Trust and Estate Planning, Construction, Computer, Real Estate, Environmental, Workers' Compensation Defense, Immigration, Bankruptcy and Tax Law. Trials and Appeals, School Law and Title Insurance.

MARTIN, BROWNE, HULL & HARPER, P.L.L.

YELLOW SPRINGS, OHIO

(See Springfield)

General Civil Practice. Corporate, Commercial, Insurance, Insurance Defense, Litigation, Environmental, Business, Contracts, Banking, Estate Planning, Probate, Real Estate, Taxation, Education, Labor and Employment. Trials and Appeals in State and Federal Courts.

DAMIAN ANDREW BILLAK

103 EAST BOARDMAN STREET
YOUNGSTOWN, OHIO 44503-1828
Telephone: 330-740-0200
Fax: 330-740-0201
Email: dbillak@aol.com
URL: http://www.billakcriminaldefenselaw.com

Criminal Defense, Civil Rights, Personal Injury, Appellate Practice.

DAMIAN ANDREW BILLAK, born 1970; admitted to bar, 1995, Ohio; 1996, U.S. District Court, Northern District of Ohio; 2002, U.S Court of Appeals, Sixth Circuit and U.S. Supreme Court. *Education:* Bowling Green State University (B.A., 1992); Cleveland-Marshall College of Law (J.D., 1995). *Member:* American Bar Association; National Association of Criminal Defense Lawyers; Ohio Association of Criminal Defense Lawyers; National Organization for the Reform of Marijuana Laws (NORML); American Civil Liberties Union (ACLU). ***PRACTICE AREAS:*** Criminal Defense; Personal Injury; Appellate Practice; Civil Rights.

BRENNAN, FREDERICK, VOUROS & YARWOOD, LTD.

Established in 1964

29 EAST FRONT STREET, 2ND FLOOR
YOUNGSTOWN, OHIO 44503-1439
Telephone: 330-743-4116
Fax: 330-743-2536
Email: bfvy@sbcglobal.net
URL: http://www.bfvy.com

General Trial Practice in all Courts. Corporation and Business Law. Criminal Defense, Negligence, Family and Probate Law. Estate Planning, Personal Injury.

FIRM PROFILE: Our firm provides legal service in the areas of Corporate Law, Business Law, Real Estate Transactions, Personal Injury, Trusts and Estates, Probate Law, Estate Planning, Criminal Defense, DUI, Drug Defense, White-Collar Crime.

HARRY FREDERICK, born Youngstown, Ohio, May 5, 1926; admitted to bar, 1951, Ohio. *Education:* Ohio Northern University (J.D., 1951). Sigma Delta Kappa. Member, Canfield Charter Commission, 1968. *Member:* Mahoning County (First Chairman, Inquiry Committee, 1968-1969) and Ohio State (Member, Public Relations Committee, 1971-1972) Bar Associations. [With U.S. Navy, 1944-1946]. ***REPORTED CASES:*** Kocisko v. Charles Shutrump & Sons 488 NE 2d 171 (1986). ***PRACTICE AREAS:*** Civil Practice. ***Email:*** bfvy@sbcglobal.net

JOSEPH E. VOUROS, born Youngstown, Ohio; admitted to bar, 1950, Ohio; 1960, U.S. Supreme Court. *Education:* Youngstown State University (B.S., 1944; B.A., 1948; J.D., 1949); The Ohio State University. Special Counsel, Office of Attorney General of Ohio, 1959-1967. Assistant County Prosecutor, Mahoning County, Ohio, 1968. Assistant Law Director, City of Youngstown, Ohio, 1970-1977. *Member:* Mahoning County, Ohio State and American Bar Associations. ***LANGUAGES:*** Greek. ***REPORTED CASES:*** Alexander v. Youngstown Bd. Of Ed., 454 F. Supp. 985 (1974), State v. Prato, 206 N.E. 2d 917 (1965), Luscre v. Luscre, 340 N.E. 2d 854 (1974). ***PRACTICE AREAS:*** Corporate Law; Trusts and Estates. ***Email:*** bfvy@sbcglobal.net

RONALD D. YARWOOD, born Salem, Ohio, November 5, 1968; admitted to bar, 1997, Ohio; 1998, U.S. District Court, Northern District of Ohio; 2002, U.S. District Court, Western District of Pennsylvania. *Education:* Dyke College (B.S., magna cum laude, 1994); University of Tulsa College of Law (J.D., 1997). Phi Delta Phi. *Member:* Ohio State, Mahoning County, Stark County and American Bar Associations. [U.S. Army, 1987-1990]. ***PRACTICE AREAS:*** Criminal Defense; Personal Injury; Civil Practice; Capital Offenses; Homicide; Death Penalty; Felonies; Misdemeanors; Search and Seizure; Traffic Violations; Civil Drug Forfeiture; Drug Crimes; Wrongful Death; Automobile Negligence; Bodily Injury; White Collar Crime. ***Email:*** bfvy@sbcglobal.net

ANNE FREDERICK CRAWFORD, born 1963; admitted to bar, 1991, Ohio; 2001, U.S. Supreme Court. *Education:* Ohio Northern University (B.A.; J.D.). *Member:* Ohio State, Mahoning County (Chair, Memorial Committee) and American Bar Associations. ***PRACTICE AREAS:*** Probate; General Practice; Trusts and Estates. ***Email:*** bfvy@sbcglobal.net

DAMIAN P. DEGENOVA, born Youngstown, Ohio, January 17, 1967; admitted to bar, 1994, Ohio. *Education:* Kent State University (B.A., 1990); Capital University (J.D., 1994). Title Agent Insurance License, 2003. Poland Village Solicitor, 2001—. ***PRACTICE AREAS:*** Real Estate Title; Domestic Relations; Family Law; Business Law. ***Email:*** bfvy@sbcglobal.net

REFERENCE: The Mahoning National Bank.

CLAIR M. CARLIN, LLC

Established in 1998

62 SOUTH MAIN STREET
YOUNGSTOWN, OHIO 44514
Telephone: 330-707-0377
Fax: 330-707-0398
Email: cmc@carlin-law.com
URL: http://www.carlin-law.com
Mailing Address: P.O. Box 5369, Poland, OH 44514-0369

Practice Limited to Civil Trial Practice, including Commercial Litigation, Medical Malpractice, Personal Injury, Product Liability, Insurance Coverage Issues and Professional Liability.

FIRM PROFILE: Attorney Carlin is Certified in Civil Trial Advocacy by the National Board of Trial Advocacy. The firm's practice is civil litigation including business and commercial matters. Referral relationships are established in accordance with the Code of Professional Responsibility.

CLAIR M. CARLIN, born Sharon, Pennsylvania, April 20, 1947; admitted to bar, 1973, Ohio, Pennsylvania and U.S. District Court, Southern District of Ohio; 1975, U.S. District Court, Northern District of Ohio; 1976, U.S. Supreme Court; 1983, U.S. Court of Appeals, Sixth Circuit and U.S. Claims Court; 1985, U.S. Tax Court; 1994, U.S. Court of Appeals, Third Circuit. *Education:* The Ohio State University (B.S., 1969; J.D., 1972). Phi Alpha Delta. Member, Editorial Board, "Ohio Trial," 1991-1995. Attorney-Examiner, Ohio Department of Taxation, 1972-1973. Assistant Solicitor, City of Warren, Ohio, 1973-1975. President, Ohio Academy of Trial Lawyers Education Foundation, 1995-1996. Member, Board of Governors, 1996—, Affiliated Political Action Committee (PAC) (Chair, 1992-1992; Trustee, 1997-1999). Member, Million Dollar Advocates Forum. *Member:* Mahoning County (President, 2004-2005), Trumbull County, Ohio State (Member: Negligence Law Committee; Lawyers Assistance Committee) and American Bar Association; Ohio Academy of Trial Lawyers (Trustee, 1988-1991; Treasurer, 1992; Secretary, 1993; President Elect, 1994; President, 1995); The Association of Trial Lawyers of America. [Major, U.S. Army, Ohio National Guard, 1969-1982]. (Certified as a Civil Trial Specialist by the National Board of Trial Advocacy). ***REPORTED CASES:*** Gennaro Pavers, Inc. v. Kosydar (1975), 42 Ohio St. 2d 491; Gallimore v. Children's Hospital Medical Center (1993), 67 Ohio St. 3d 244; Gutierrez v. Police and Firemen's Disability and Pension Fund of Ohio (1994), 70 Ohio St. 3d 362; Vahila v. Hall (1997), 77 Ohio St. 3d 42; Cope v. Metropolitan Life (1998) 82 Ohio St. 3d 426; Lynch v. Yob (2002), 95 Ohio St. 3d 441; cert. denied, 123 S.Ct. 95 (2002). ***PRACTICE AREAS:*** Personal Injury; Professional Liability; Products Liability; Commercial Litigation; Civil Litigation; Medical Malpractice; Insurance Coverage. ***Email:*** cmc@carlin-law.com

---

AMY L. HIGGINS, born Sharon, Pennsylvania, September 5, 1966; admitted to bar, 2002, Ohio. *Education:* Youngstown State University (B.A., 1998); University of Akron (J.D., 2002). *Member:* Ohio State and American bar Associations; Association of Trial Lawyers of America. ***PRACTICE AREAS:*** Personal Injury; Professional Liability; Products Liability; Commercial Litigation; Civil Litigation; Medical Malpractice; Insurance Coverage. ***Email:*** alh@carlin-law.com

COMSTOCK, SPRINGER & WILSON CO., L.P.A.

Established in 1980

100 FEDERAL PLAZA EAST, SUITE 926
YOUNGSTOWN, OHIO 44503-1811
Telephone: 330-746-5643
Fax: 330-746-4925

General Civil Practice in all State and Federal Courts. Insurance Defense and Coverage, Medical Malpractice and Products Liability Law. Trials.

LAWRENCE R. SPRINGER, born East Palestine, Ohio, June 7, 1936; admitted to bar, 1961, Ohio; 1963, U.S. District Court, Northern District of Ohio; 1986, U.S. Court of Appeals, Sixth Circuit; 1996, U.S. Supreme Court. *Education:* College of Wooster (B.A., 1958); University of Michigan (J.D., 1961). *Member:* Mahoning County, Columbiana County, Ohio State (Member, Board of Governors, 1996-1999) and American Bar Associations; Ohio CLE Institute; Ohio Association of Civil Trial Attorneys; Defense Research Institute. Fellow, American College of Trial Lawyers. ***PRACTICE AREAS:*** Automobile Liability; Premises Liability; Medical Malpractice; Civil Litigation; Product Liability Law. ***Email:*** lrs@csandw.com

THOMAS J. WILSON, born Detroit, Michigan, April 5, 1950; admitted to bar, 1976, Ohio and U.S. District Court, Northern District of Ohio; U.S. Court of Appeals, Sixth Circuit. *Education:* Villanova University (B.A., 1972); University of Toledo (J.D., 1976). Associate Editor, University of Toledo Law Review, 1975-1976. *Member:* Mahoning County (President, 1988-1989), Trumbull County, Ohio State and American (Member, Section of Insurance, Negligence and Compensation Law) Bar Associations; Ohio Association of Civil Trial Attorneys; Defense Research Institute. Fellow, International Society of Barris-

(This Listing Continued)

COMSTOCK, SPRINGER & WILSON CO., L.P.A., Youngstown—Continued

ters, 1994. Fellow, American College of Trial Lawyers, 1996. ***PRACTICE AREAS:*** Automobile Liability; Premises Liability; Civil Rights Litigation; Medical Legal Malpractice; Civil Litigation; Product Liability Law. ***Email:*** tjw@csandw.com

MARSHALL D. BUCK, born Tiffin, Ohio, September 30, 1951; admitted to bar, 1981, Ohio and U.S. District Court, Northern District of Ohio; 1982, U.S. Court of Appeals, Sixth Circuit. *Education:* Ohio University (B.S., 1973); Ohio Northern University (J.D., 1980). *Member:* Mahoning County, Ohio State and American (Member, Litigation Section) Bar Associations; Ohio Association of Civil Trial Attorneys; Defense Research Institute. [Capt., U.S. Army, 1974-1977]. ***PRACTICE AREAS:*** Automobile Liability; Premises Liability; Medical Malpractice Law; Civil Litigation; Products Liability Law; Municipal Law; Civil Rights Litigation. ***Email:*** mdb@csandw.com

WM. SCOTT FOWLER, born Olmsted Falls, Ohio, December 17, 1958; admitted to bar, 1984, Ohio; 1986, U.S. District Court, Northern District of Ohio and U.S. Court of Appeals, Sixth Circuit. *Education:* Ohio Wesleyan University (B.A., 1981); Ohio State University (J.D., 1984). Phi Beta Kappa. *Member:* Mahoning County (President, 1996-1997), Ohio State and American (Member, Litigation Section) Bar Associations; Ohio Association of Civil Trial Attorneys. ***PRACTICE AREAS:*** Automobile Liability; Premises Liability; Medical Malpractice Law; Civil Litigation; Products Liability Law. ***Email:*** wsf@csandw.com

DAVID C. COMSTOCK, JR., born Youngstown, Ohio, August 7, 1962; admitted to bar, 1988, Ohio; 1989, U.S. District Court, Northern District of Ohio and U.S. Court of Appeals, Sixth Circuit; 1997, U.S. Supreme Court. *Education:* College of Wooster (B.A., 1985); Ohio State University (J.D., 1988). Omicron Delta Epsilon; Phi Delta Phi. Emergency Medical Technician, Ohio. State Certified Fire Safety Inspector. *Member:* Mahoning County, Ohio State and American (Member, Sections on: Litigation; Tort and Insurance Practice) Bar Associations; Ohio Association of Civil Trial Attorneys; Defense Research Institute; International Association of Arson Investigators (Member, Ohio Chapter); National Society of Professional Insurance Investigators (President, Ohio Chapter, 2000); National Association of Fire and Emergency Service Attorneys (President, 2004—). ***PRACTICE AREAS:*** Automobile Liability; Civil Litigation; Products Liability Law; Insurance Coverage; Insurance Defense; Political Subdivision Defense; Civil Rights. ***Email:*** dcj@csandw.com

DOUGLAS J. KRESS, born Salem, Ohio, February 6, 1969; admitted to bar, 1994, Ohio; 1995, U.S. District Court, Northern District of Ohio; 1998, U.S. Court of Appeals, Sixth Circuit. *Education:* University of Akron (B.A., cum laude, 1991); University of Toledo (J.D., cum laude, 1994). Technical Editor, University of Toledo Law Review, 1993-1994. *Member:* Mahoning County, Columbiana County, Ohio State (Member, Litigation Section) and American (Member, Litigation Section) Bar Associations. ***PRACTICE AREAS:*** Automobile Liability; Premises Liability; Medical Malpractice; Civil Litigation. ***Email:*** djk@csandw.com

MARGO S. MEOLA, born Warren, Ohio, August 28, 1969; admitted to bar, 1995, Ohio; 1998, U.S. District Court, Northern District of Ohio. *Education:* John Carroll University (B.A., 1991); Ohio Northern University (J.D., 1995). Articles Research Editor, Ohio Northern University Law Review, 1994-1995. Author: "Electromagnetic Fields and Cancer: A Legitimate Cause of Action or a Result of Media-Influenced Fear?," 21 Ohio N.U.L. Rev. 551 (1994). *Member:* Trumbull County, Mahoning County, Ohio State and American Bar Associations; Ohio Association of Civil Trial Attorneys. ***PRACTICE AREAS:*** Automobile Liability; Premises Liability; Medical Malpractice; Civil Litigation. ***Email:*** mrs@csandw.com

---

BOBBIE L. FLYNT, born Xenia, Ohio, July 27, 1967; admitted to bar, 1996, Ohio and U.S. District Court, Southern and Northern Districts of Ohio; 2003, U.S. Court of Appeals, Sixth Circuit. *Education:* Wright State University (B.S., cum laude, 1989); University of Dayton (J.D., cum laude, 1996). Executive Editor, University of Dayton Law Review, 1995-1996. *Member:* Mahoning County, Ohio State and American Bar Associations; Ohio Association of Civil Trial Attorneys; Defense Research Institute. ***PRACTICE AREAS:*** Automobile Liability; Municipal Law; Premises Liability; Civil Litigation; Medical Malpractice. ***Email:*** blf@csandw.com

KENNETH L. GOLDEN, born Houston, Texas, January 13, 1978; admitted to bar, 2004, Ohio. *Education:* The Ohio State University (B.A., 2001); Case Western Reserve University (J.D., 2004). Phi Delta Phi. ***PRACTICE AREAS:*** Civil Litigation; Insurance Defense; Medical Malpractice; Governmental Liability Defense; Arson and Insurance Fraud. ***Email:*** klg@csandw.com

OF COUNSEL

DAVID C. COMSTOCK, born Buffalo, New York, February 10, 1932; admitted to bar, 1959, Ohio; 1961, U.S. District Court, Northern District of Ohio; 1985, U.S. Court of Appeals, Sixth Circuit. *Education:* Ohio Wesleyan University (B.A., 1954); Western Reserve University (LL.B., 1959). *Member:* Mahoning County (President, 1980-1981), Ohio State (Member, Executive Committee, 1984-1987) and American Bar Associations. Fellow, American College of Trial Lawyers; Ohio Bar Foundation (Trustee, 1987-1992). ***PRACTICE AREAS:*** Medical Malpractice Law; Products Liability Law; Civil Litigation; Insurance Law; Automobile Liability. ***Email:*** dcc@csandw.com

REPRESENTATIVE CLIENTS: Allstate; Am. Nat'l. Prop. & Cas./ANPAC; American Risk Pooling Consultants Inc.; Canfield Local School District; Cardinal Joint Fire District; Catholic Health Partners; City of Warren; City of Youngstown, OH; CNA; Crawford & Co.; D&E Counseling Center; Donegal Companies; Employers Reinsurance Corp.; Encompass Ins. Co.; Federal Express; Forum Health; Giant Eagle; Grange Ins.; Great West Casualty Co.; Hastings Mutual Ins. Co.; Humility of Mary Health Partners; Leader National Ins. Co.; Mennonite Mutual Insurance Company; Meridian/State Auto; Mahoning County Bar Assoc. Grievance Committee; Nationwide Insurance; NF Joint Fire District; Northeastern Ohio Emergency Medical Services Council, Inc.; Northside Medical Center; Ohio Bar Liab. Ins. Co.; Ohio Insurance Guaranty Assoc.; Ohio Rural Fire Caucus; OTARMA; Pellin Ambulance Company; Physicians Ins. Co. of OH; Scottsdale Ins. Co; St. Paul Co.; State Farm Insurance Companies; St. Elizabeth Health Center; St. Joseph Health Center; Trumbull Memorial Hospital; Western Reserve Care System; Windsor Group; Zurich Group.

(This Listing Continued)

DAVIS & YOUNG

A Legal Professional Association

THE COMMERCE BUILDING

201 EAST COMMERCE STREET, SUITE 100

YOUNGSTOWN, OHIO 44503

Telephone: 330-743-1717

Email: atty@dyyoungstown.com

URL: http://www.davisyoung.com

Cleveland, Ohio Office: 1700 Midland Building, Suite 1700, 44115. Telephone: 216-348-1700. Fax: 216-621-0602.

Akron, Ohio Office: National City Center, One Cascade Plaza, Suite 800, 44308. Telephone 330-376-1717. Fax: 330-376-1797.

Warren, Ohio Office: 108 Main Street, SW, Suite 1000, 44481. Telephone: 330-373-1717. Fax: 330-395-0610.

General Trial and Appellate Practice, Products Liability, General Tort, Insurance Coverage, Personal Injury, Toxic Torts, Complex Mass Tort Claims, Legal and Medical Malpractice, Municipal Liability, Civil Rights, Employment Practices Liability, and Environmental and Commercial Liability.

FIRM PROFILE: Many of Davis & Young's attorneys are members of the following organizations: Mahoning and Trumbull County and Ohio State Bar Associations, Defense Research Institute (DRI), Ohio Association of Civil Trial Attorneys (OACTA).

LARRY D. WILKES, admitted to bar, 1984, Ohio. *Education:* Ohio University; Youngstown State University (A.B., 1981); Ohio Northern University (J.D., 1984). ***Email:*** lwilkes@dyyoungstown.com

ASSOCIATES

SUSAN M. WEBER, admitted to bar, 1989, Pennsylvania; 1990, U.S. District Court, Middle District of Pennsylvania; 2005, Ohio. *Education:* Youngstown State University (A.A.S., 1975); University of Maryland (B.S.N., 1986); Dickinson School of Law of the Pennsylvania State University (J.D., 1989). Member, Appellate Moot Court Board. Nursing License: Pennsylvania, 1983—. *Member:* York County (Chair, Medical-Legal Liaison Committee, 1998-1999), Pennsylvania (Chair, Interdisciplinary Committee on Medical and Health Related Issues, 1994-1995) Bar Associations. ***Email:*** sweber@dyyoungstown.com

JOHN JEFFREY LIMBIAN, born Youngstown, Ohio, August 9, 1959; admitted to bar, 1991, Ohio. *Education:* Youngstown State University (B.A., 1982); Cleveland State University (J.D., 1988); George Washington University Law School, Washing DC. (LL.M., Litigation and Dispute Resolution, 2005).

DENMEAD LAW OFFICE

YOUNGSTOWN, OHIO

(See Columbus)

Civil Trial and Appellate Practice and Personal Injury, Traumatic Brain Injury (TBI), Professional Negligence and Complex Litigation including Class Actions, Patents, Civil Rights, Civil Litigation, RICO, Employment and Political Subdivision Liability issues.

ELK & ELK CO., L.P.A.

YOUNGSTOWN, OHIO

(See Cleveland)

Automobile Accidents, Product Defects, Nursing Home Neglect, Medical Malpractice, Personal Injury.

FRIEDMAN & RUMMELL CO., L.P.A.

Established in 1911

CITY CENTRE ONE, SUITE 300

100 E. FEDERAL STREET

YOUNGSTOWN, OHIO 44503-1810

Telephone: 330-744-4137

Fax: 330-744-9962

Email: fandrlaw@fandrlaw.com

URL: http://www.fandrlaw.com

General Civil Practice in all Courts. Real Estate, Probate, Trust and Estate Planning, Taxation, Collections, Creditors Rights, Corporate, Commercial, Bankruptcy, Family Law, Business Law, Banking Law, Bankruptcy.

JOSEPH FRIEDMAN (1908-1957)

EVAN J. RUMMELL (1917-1964)

ROBERT B. WEIMER (1932-1964)

ARTHUR N. K. FRIEDMAN (1939-2003)

W. TERRY PATRICK, born Youngstown, Ohio, October 3, 1949; admitted to bar, 1977, Ohio. *Education:* University of Michigan; Youngstown State University (A.B., 1972); University of Akron (J.D., 1977). Recipient, American Jurisprudence Award in Creditors Rights, 1977. *Member:* Mahoning County and Ohio State Bar Associations; National Order of Barristers. ***PRACTICE AREAS:*** Corporate; Real Estate; Estate Planning; Commercial; Banking Law. ***Email:*** tpatrick@fandrlaw.com

(This Listing Continued)

CARL D. RAFOTH, born Youngstown, Ohio, November 27, 1940; admitted to bar, 1968, Ohio. *Education:* University of Cincinnati (B.S., Pharmacy, 1962); Youngstown State University; The Ohio State University (J.D., 1968). *Member:* Mahoning County and Ohio State Bar Associations; National Association of Bankruptcy Trustees; American Bankruptcy Law Institute. ***PRACTICE AREAS:*** Bankruptcy; Real Estate; Corporate Law; Commercial Law; Probate; Estate Planning. **Email:** crafoth@fandrlaw.com

LEONARD D. SCHIAVONE, born Youngstown, Ohio, March 25, 1952; admitted to bar, 1977, Ohio. *Education:* Purdue University (B.S., 1974); University of Cincinnati (J.D., 1977). Assistant Law Director, City of Youngstown, 1978-1980. Co-Author: "Medicare Coverage & Nursing Homes/A Broken Promise," New England Journal of Medicine, Volume 304, Page 353-355, 1981. *Member:* Mahoning County and Ohio State Bar Associations. ***PRACTICE AREAS:*** Corporate; Family Law; Real Estate; Commercial; Collections. **Email:** lschiavone@fandrlaw.com

JAMES B. DIETZ, born Youngstown, Ohio, October 25, 1964; admitted to bar, 1991, Ohio. *Education:* University of Dayton (B.S., 1987); University of Toledo (J.D., 1991). Phi Alpha Delta. *Member:* Mahoning County and Ohio State Bar Associations. (Certified Specialist in Estate Planning, Trust and Probate Law, Ohio State Bar Association). ***PRACTICE AREAS:*** Estate Planning; Probate; Corporate; Business Law; Real Estate. **Email:** jdietz@fandrlaw.com

---

ROBERT M. PALMA, born Youngstown, Ohio, July 24, 1946; admitted to bar, 1975, Ohio. *Education:* Youngstown State University (A.B., 1968); Akron University Law School (J.D., 1974). Member, Board of Directors, Youngstown Society for the Blind and Disabled, 1982-1994. Chairman, Civil Service Commission, City of Canfield, 1986-1990. Member, Board of Appeals, Canfield Joint Fire District. *Member:* Ohio Association of Civil Trial Attorneys. ***PRACTICE AREAS:*** Insurance Defense Law; Civil Practice; Trusts and Estates. **Email:** rpalma@fandrlaw.com

CHRISTOPHER J. SCHIAVONE, born Warren, Ohio, April 30, 1974; admitted to bar, 2001, Ohio. *Education:* Youngstown State University (B.S.A.S., 1997); Ohio Northern University (J.D., 2000). *Member:* Mahoning County and Ohio State Bar Associations. ***PRACTICE AREAS:*** Probate; Civil Litigation; General Practice; Estate Planning. **Email:** cschiavone@fandrlaw.com

MICHELE L. McBRIDE, born Youngstown, Ohio; admitted to bar, 2002, Ohio. *Education:* Notre Dame College (B.A., 1997); Cleveland-Marshall (J.D., 2001). Recipient: Dean's Achievement Award; Outstanding Student in the Law of Evidence; Outstanding Editor Award, Cleveland State Law Review. Articles Editor, Cleveland State Law Review. *Member:* Mahoning County and Ohio State Bar Associations; Women Law Student Association. **Email:** mlmcbride@fandrlaw.com

OF COUNSEL

C. JOHN AMSTUTZ, born Youngstown, Ohio, September 5, 1933; admitted to bar, 1958, Illinois; 1960, Ohio. *Education:* Oberlin College (A.B., 1955); University of Chicago (J.D., 1958). Phi Delta Phi. *Member:* Mahoning County and Ohio State (Member, Board of Governors, Probate and Trust Section, 1979-1983) Bar Associations. (Retired). ***PRACTICE AREAS:*** Estate Planning; Probate; Tax; Corporate; Real Estate Law. **Email:** jamstutz@fandrlaw.com

NORMAN A. RHEUBAN, born Cleveland, Ohio, February 27, 1921; admitted to bar, 1948, Ohio; 1956, U.S. Court of Military Appeals; 1971, U.S. Supreme Court. *Education:* The Ohio State University (B.A., 1942); University of Pennsylvania (L.L.B., 1948). Municipal Attorney, City of Canfield, 1970-1974. Special Counsel, Village of Columbiana, 1973-1974. Counsel: Canfield Historical Society. [U.S. Navy, 1942-1946; 1950-1954; LCDR, USNR, Ret.]. ***PRACTICE AREAS:*** Insurance Defense Law; Civil Practice; Estates and Trusts; Insurance Law.

REPRESENTATIVE CLIENTS: R.L. Lipton Distributing; Boardman Steel, Inc.; Vanderbilt Mortgage & Finance, Inc.; Tri County Wholesale Distributing, Inc.; Valley View Enterprises, Inc.; Pine Lakes Golf Club; Plaza Donuts, Inc.; AA Samuels Sheet Metal Co.; Gemco Aviation Services, Inc.; The City Asphalt & Paving Co.; Anchor Cigar & Candy Co. Inc.; The Italian Baking Co.; Schwebel Baking Co.; National City Bank, N.E.; DeNiro Cheese Co.; Meander Hospitality Group, Inc.; Butler Wick Trust Company; Mahoning Valley Economic Development Corporation; Medical Imaging Network, Inc.; The Kidney Group, Inc.; Horizon Management, Inc.; The Travelers Cos.; Canfield Historical Society; Constitution State Insurance Co.; The Tokio Marine and Fire Insurance Co., Ltd.; Topps Friendly Markets (Formerly Finest Food Stores); Zotos International Inc.; Farmer's National Bank of Canfield, Ohio; Navistar Financial Corp.; T.C. Redi-Mix, Inc.; Majestic MFG., Inc.; Anesthesiologists D.O., Inc.; Youngstown Area Jewish Federation; Regional Sparkle Markets, Inc.; Common Wealth, Inc.; The Tiffany Group, Inc.
APPROVED ATTORNEYS FOR: Ohio Bar Title Insurance Co.
REFERENCES: National City Bank, N.E.; Farmer's Nat. Bank of Canfield, Ohio; First Place Bank.

GERVELIS LAW FIRM

1045 TIFFANY SOUTH
YOUNGSTOWN, OHIO 44514
Telephone: 330-758-5899
Fax: 330-533-4822
URL: http://www.gervelislaw.com

Plaintiff Personal Injury Law, Wrongful Death Law, Products Liability Law.

MARK S. GERVELIS, born Warren, Ohio, December 3, 1946; admitted to bar, 1976, Ohio; 1977, U.S. District Court, Northern District of Ohio; 1979, U.S. Court of Appeals, Sixth Circuit; 1986, Pennsylvania; 1988, U.S. District Court, Western District of Pennsylvania; 1989, Washington. *Education:* Youngstown State University (B.A., 1972); Cleveland Marshall College of Law (J.D., 1976). Assistant County Prosecutor, Ashtabula County, Ohio, 1976-1979. *Member:* Ashtabula County, Mahoning County, Trumbull County, Ohio State, Pennsylvania, Federal and American Bar Associations; The Association of Trial Lawyers of America; Ohio Academy of Trial Lawyers; Pennsylvania Trial Lawyers Association; Mahoning/Trumbull County Academy of Trial Lawyers (President, 1989-1991). ***PRACTICE AREAS:*** Plaintiff Personal Injury Law; Wrongful Death Law; Products Liability Law.

(This Listing Continued)

HARRINGTON, HOPPE & MITCHELL, LTD.

26 MARKET STREET, SUITE 1200
YOUNGSTOWN, OHIO 44503-1508
Telephone: 330-744-1111
Telecopier: 330-744-2029
Email: info@hhmlaw.com
URL: http://www.hhmlaw.com

Warren, Ohio Office: 108 Main Avenue, S.W., Suite 500, 44481. Telephone: 330-392-1541. Telecopier: 330-394-6890.
Salem, Ohio Office: 2235 E. Pershing Street, Suite A, 44460. Telephone: 330-337-6586. Telecopier: 330-337-6662.

General Civil Trial and Equity Practice in all State and Federal Courts. Corporation, Banking, Creditors Rights and Bankruptcy, Labor, Probate, Estate Planning, Hospital and Health, Insurance Law, Real Estate, Commercial, Business Transactions.

FIRM PROFILE: The firm is the largest firm in Mahoning, Trumball and Columblana Counties of Ohio. The firm maintains offices in Youngstown, Warren and Salem, Ohio.

Harrington, Hoppe & Mitchell, Ltd. is a full service firm, organized into six general practice areas: Litigation; Business Services; Labor and Employment; Health Care Law; Public Sector Law; and Probate and Estate Planning.

PAUL M. DUTTON, born Youngstown, Ohio, January 11, 1947; admitted to bar, 1972, Ohio; 1973, U.S. District Court, Northern District of Ohio; 1976, U.S. Supreme Court; 1985, U.S. Tax Court. *Education:* Youngstown State University (B.A., 1969); Case Western Reserve University (J.D., 1972). Member, Board of Trustees, Northeast Ohio Council on High Education. Member, 1979-1987 and Chairman, 1985-1987, Board of Trustees, Youngstown State University. Member, 1987-1996 and Chairman, 1993-1995, Ohio Board of Regents. Member, Ohio Supreme Court Future Commissions, 1997-2000. Member, Board of Trustees, Central State University, 1996—. *Member:* Mahoning County and Ohio State Bar Associations. ***PRACTICE AREAS:*** Business Law; Real Estate Development; Municipal Law; Corporate Law; Estate Planning. **Email:** pdutton@hhmlaw.com

JAMES L. BLOMSTROM, born Youngstown, Ohio, September 8, 1949; admitted to bar, 1974, Ohio; 1989, Pennsylvania; U.S. District Court, Northern District of Ohio. *Education:* University of Pennsylvania (B.A., cum laude, 1971); University of Chicago (J.D., 1974). Law Clerk to Judge Paul C. Weick, U.S. Court of Appeals, Sixth Circuit, 1974-1975. *Member:* Ohio Association of Civil Trial Attorneys; Defense Research and Trial Lawyers Association; International Association of Defense Counsel. (Board Certified Civil Trial Advocacy Specialist by the National Board of Trial Advocacy). ***PRACTICE AREAS:*** Medical Malpractice Defense Law; Civil Litigation; Commercial Litigation. **Email:** JBlomstrom@hhmlaw.com

FREDERICK S. COOMBS, III, born Youngstown, Ohio, August 22, 1950; admitted to bar, 1975, Ohio; 1976, U.S. District Court, Northern District of Ohio; 1981, U.S. Court of Appeals, Sixth Circuit; 2004, U.S. District Court, Southern District of Ohio. *Education:* Denison University (B.A., with honors, 1972); The Ohio State University (J.D., cum laude, 1975). Member, Editorial Staff, Ohio State Law Journal, 1974-1975. *Member:* Mahoning County (Member, Bankruptcy Committee), Ohio State (Member, Banking, Commercial & Bankruptcy Law Committee) and American (Member, Sections of: Litigation; Corporation, Banking and Business Law) Bar Associations; Commercial Law League of America; American Bankruptcy Institute. ***PRACTICE AREAS:*** Bankruptcy Law; Creditors Rights Law; Commercial Law; Communications Law; Surety Law. **Email:** FCoombs@hhmlaw.com

RALPH A. BEARD, born Youngstown, Ohio, August 30, 1947; admitted to bar, 1975, Ohio; 1976, U.S. District Court, Northern District of Ohio. *Education:* Youngstown State University (B.A., 1971); Ohio State University (J.D., cum laude, 1975). *Member:* Mahoning County and Ohio State Bar Associations. ***PRACTICE AREAS:*** Corporation Law; Pension Law; Tax Law; Estate Planning; Trusts and Estates. **Email:** RBeard@hhmlaw.com

ALAN D. WENGER, born Salem, Ohio, February 19, 1952; admitted to bar, 1977, Ohio; 1978, U.S. District Court, Northern District of Ohio; 1985, U.S. Tax Court. *Education:* Youngstown State University; Eastern Mennonite College (B.A., 1974); Case Western Reserve University (J.D., 1977). Member, South Range Local School Board, 1985—. *Member:* Columbiana County, Mahoning County (Corporate Counsel, Labor and Employment Division), Ohio State and American Bar Associations. ***PRACTICE AREAS:*** Public Utility Law; Environmental Law; Construction Law; Labor and Employment; Corporate Law. **Email:** awenger@hhmlaw.com

JOHN T. DELLICK, born Youngstown, Ohio, August 13, 1956; admitted to bar, 1985, Ohio; U.S. District Court, Northern District of Ohio; 1988, Pennsylvania. *Education:* Youngstown State University (B.Engr., 1978); University of Akron (J.D., 1985). Member, Akron Law Review, 1983-1985. *Member:* Mahoning County, Trumbull County and Ohio State Bar Associations; Ohio Association of Civil Trial Lawyers. ***PRACTICE AREAS:*** Commercial Litigation; Civil Litigation; Personal Injury; Medical Malpractice Defense; Insurance Defense. **Email:** JDellick@hhmlaw.com

KELLY J. MORRISON, born Greenville, Pennsylvania, March 9, 1959; admitted to bar, 1985, Ohio; 1988, U.S. District Court, Northern District of Ohio. *Education:* Youngstown State University (B.A., 1982); Pepperdine University (J.D., cum laude, 1985). Member, Pepperdine Law Review. *Member:* Mahoning County (Member, Real Estate Law Section) and Ohio State Bar Associations. (Certified Specialist in Business, Commercial and Industrial Real Property Law, Ohio State Bar Association). ***PRACTICE AREAS:*** Real Estate; Corporate Law; Business Law. **Email:** KMorrison@hhmlaw.com

SHIRLEY J. CHRISTIAN, born Erie, Pennsylvania, July 13, 1954; admitted to bar, 1986, Ohio; 1987, Pennsylvania and U.S. District Court, Northern District of Ohio. *Education:* Edinboro University (B.S., 1976; MEd., 1977); Ohio Northern University (J.D., with distinction, 1986). Associate Editor, Ohio Northern University Law Review, 1986.

(This Listing Continued)

HARRINGTON, HOPPE & MITCHELL, LTD., Youngstown—Continued

Moot Court-Administrative Justice. *Member:* Mahoning County and Ohio State (Member, Board or Governors, 2002—) Bar Associations; Ohio Association of Civil Trial Attorneys; Defense Research Institute. ***PRACTICE AREAS:*** Medical Malpractice Defense; Labor and Employment. ***Email:*** SChristian@hhmlaw.com

NEIL H. MAXWELL, born Salem, Ohio, February 5, 1959; admitted to bar, 1984, Ohio. *Education:* Mount Union College (B.S., 1981); University of Akron (J.D., 1984). *Member:* Mahoning County (Member, Probate Law Section) and Ohio State Bar Associations. ***PRACTICE AREAS:*** Estate Planning; Probate. ***Email:*** NMaxwell@hhmlaw.com

MARTIN J. BOETCHER, born Zanesville, Ohio, November 7, 1961; admitted to bar, 1987, Ohio and U.S. District Court, Northern District of Ohio. *Education:* The Ohio State University (B.S.C.E., cum laude, 1984); Akron University Law School (J.D., 1987). Member, Law Review, 1985-1987. *Member:* Ohio State Bar Association (Member, Council of Delegates, 2002—; Chair, Young Lawyers Section, 1993-1994); Ohio Association of Civil Trial Attorneys; Defense Research; Trial Lawyers Association. ***PRACTICE AREAS:*** Civil Litigation; Insurance Defense; Employment Law; Workers Compensation. ***Email:*** MBoetcher@hhmlaw.com

NEIL D. SCHOR, born Cleveland, Ohio, August 28, 1963; admitted to bar, 1989, Ohio; 1990, U.S. District Court, Northern District of Ohio; 2000, U.S. Court of Appeals, Sixth Circuit; 2004, U.S. District Court, Southern District of Ohio. *Education:* University of Michigan (A.B., 1986); The Ohio State University (J.D., 1989). Member, Ohio State Journal on Dispute Resolution, 1988-1989. *Member:* Mahoning County and Ohio State Bar Associations. ***PRACTICE AREAS:*** Commercial Litigation; Public Utility Law; Municipal Law; Civil Litigation. ***Email:*** NSchor@hhmlaw.com

SHAWNA L. ERB, born Salem, Ohio, October 4, 1970; admitted to bar, 1996, Ohio. *Education:* Mount Union College (B.A., 1993); The Ohio State University (J.D., 1996). Order of the Coif. *Member:* Columbiana County, Mahoning County and Ohio State Bar Associations. ***PRACTICE AREAS:*** Corporate Law; Real Estate; Employment Law; Business Transactions; Commercial Law. ***Email:*** SErb@hhmlaw.com

LANCE A. MORRISON, born Greenville, Pennsylvania, September 23, 1966; admitted to bar, 1992, Ohio; 1998, U.S. District Court, Northern District of Ohio. *Education:* The Ohio State University (B.A., 1988; J.D., 1992). National Merit Scholar. Member, Federalist Society, 1989-1992. *Member:* Mahoning County and Ohio State Bar Associations. [Lt., U.S. Navy, JAG Corps., 1992-1997]. ***PRACTICE AREAS:*** Business Law; Corporate Law; Collections; Labor and Employment. ***Email:*** LMorrison@hhmlaw.com

---

MATTHEW D. GURBACH, born Atlanta, Georgia, November 16, 1977; admitted to bar, 2003, Ohio. *Education:* Youngstown State University (A.B., magna cum laude, 2000); Case Western Reserve University (J.D., 2003). Order of the Barristers. *Member:* Mahoning County, Ohio State and American Bar Associations; Ohio Association of Civil Trial Attorneys. ***PRACTICE AREAS:*** Litigation; Insurance Defense; Medical Malpractice. ***Email:*** maurbach@hhmlaw.com

CHRISTOPHER BARONZZI, born Salem, Ohio, May 10, 1978; admitted to bar, 2004, Ohio; 2005, U.S. District Court, Northern District of Ohio. *Education:* John Carroll University (B.S.E., 2001); Akron University Law School (J.D., cum laude, 2004). ABA Moot Court. Recipient, CALI Award, Antitrust Law. *Member:* Columbiana County, Ohio State and American Bar Associations. ***PRACTICE AREAS:*** General Practice. ***Email:*** cbaronzzi@hhmlaw.com

CARMEN V. CODJOE, born Boston, Massachusetts, August 18, 1979; admitted to bar, 2004, Ohio. *Education:* Seton Hall University (B.A., summa cum laude, 2001); The Ohio State University (J.D., 2004). Public Service Fellow. ***PRACTICE AREAS:*** General Practice. ***Email:*** ccodjoe@hhmlaw.com

REPRESENTATIVE CLIENTS: Forum Health Hospitals and Medical Centers; Humility of Mary Healthcare; Consumers Ohio Water Company (Public Utility); City of Canfield; Beaver Township; Village of Lordstown; The City of Cortland; The Public Library of Youngstown and Mahoning County; First Energy Corp; Ohio Edison Company; ER Advanced Ceramics, Inc.; Office of Attorney General, State of Ohio; Hill, Barth & King, CPAs; Mahoning Valley Economic Development Corporation; Youngstown-Warren Regional Chamber of Commerce; A.P. O'Horo Company; Taylor Winfield Corp.; WCI Steel, Inc.; General Extrusions, Inc.; Sovereign Circuits, Inc.; Metropolitan Property & Casualty Insurance Co.; Nationwide Mutual Insurance Co.; Motorists Insurance Co.; CNA Insurance Companies; Allstate Insurance Co.; Ohio Mutual Insurance Group; American General Life and Accident Insurance Group; Coregis Insurance Company; National City Bank; Sky Bank; First Place Bank; Bank One Cleveland, N.A.; Second National Bank of Warren; V&V Real Estate Investments; Ohio Realty Company.

HENDERSON, COVINGTON, MESSENGER, NEWMAN & THOMAS CO., L.P.A.

Established in 1912

SUITE 1300
6 FEDERAL PLAZA CENTRAL
YOUNGSTOWN, OHIO 44503-1473
Telephone: 330-744-1148
Telefax: 330-744-3807

Carnegie, Pennsylvania Office: 213 East Main Street, 15106. Telephone: 419-279-7025.

General Civil Trial and Appellate Practice in all Courts. Banking, Commercial, Bankruptcy, Corporate, Probate, Business, Family, Labor Relations, Public Employment Relations and School Law.

ANDREW M. HENDERSON (1904-1950)

C. A. COVINGTON, JR. (1917-1999)

JAMES L. MESSENGER, born Youngstown, Ohio, October 18, 1942; admitted to bar, 1967, Ohio; U.S. Supreme Court; U.S. Court of Appeals, Third and Sixth Circuits; U.S. District Court, Northern District of Ohio. *Education:* Ohio University (B.B.A., 1964); Syracuse University (LL.B., 1967). Member, Moot Court Board, Syracuse University, 1966-1967. Member, Youngstown Civil Service Commission. *Member:* Mahoning County (President, 1983-1984), Ohio State and American (Member, Section of Labor and Employment Law) Bar Associations; Ohio Council of School Board Attorneys (Chairman, 1983); Ohio Academy of Trial Lawyers. ***PRACTICE AREAS:*** Litigation; Employment Law; Family Law; Labor Law. ***Email:*** jmessenger@hendersoncovington.com

(This Listing Continued)

CHRISTOPHER J. NEWMAN, born Lancaster, Pennsylvania, April 2, 1948; admitted to bar, 1973, Ohio; U.S. District Court, Northern District of Ohio; 1976, U.S. Court of Appeals, Sixth Circuit; 1985, U.S. Supreme Court. *Education:* Denison University (B.A., 1970); Case Western Reserve University (J.D., 1973). *Member:* Mahoning County (Trustee, 1983-1986), Ohio State and American Bar Associations; Ohio Council of School Board Attorneys (Member, Executive Committee, 1984-1992, Chairman, 1991). ***PRACTICE AREAS:*** Real Estate Law; Family Law; Labor Law; Employment Law; School Law. ***Email:*** cnewman@hendersoncovington.com

RICHARD J. THOMAS, born Youngstown, Ohio, April 13, 1956; admitted to bar, 1985, Pennsylvania; 1987, Ohio; Pennsylvania Supreme Court; Ohio Supreme Court; U.S. District Courts, Western District of Pennsylvania, Northern District of Ohio and U.S. Court of Appeals, Third and Sixth Circuits; U.S. Supreme Court. *Education:* Youngstown State University (B.S., 1980); University of Pittsburgh (J.D., 1985). *Member:* Mahoning County, Ohio State, Pennsylvania and American Bar Associations; Association of Trial Lawyers of America. ***PRACTICE AREAS:*** Litigation; Banking Law; Commercial Law; Bankruptcy Law; Employment Law. ***Email:*** rthomas@hendersoncovington.com

DAVID K. HOLMQUIST, born Massillon, Ohio, September 29, 1936; admitted to bar, 1961, Ohio and U.S. District Court, Northern District of Ohio. *Education:* Ohio University; The Ohio State University (B.S.B.A., 1958; J.D., 1961). *Member:* Mahoning County, Trumbull County, Ohio State (Member, Corporate Counsel Section, 1971-1979; Chairman, 1975-1976) and American Bar Associations. ***PRACTICE AREAS:*** Corporate Law; Business Law; Real Estate Law; Labor Law. ***Email:*** dholmquist@hendersoncovington.com

JERRY M. BRYAN, born Youngstown, Ohio, January 5, 1966; admitted to bar, 1991, Ohio; U.S. District Court, Northern District of Ohio; U.S. Court of Appeals, Sixth Circuit and U.S. Supreme Court. *Education:* Youngstown State University (B.A., cum laude, 1988); The Ohio State University (J.D., with honors, 1991). *Member:* Mahoning County and Ohio State Bar Associations. ***PRACTICE AREAS:*** Commercial Law; Banking Law; Litigation; Bankruptcy Law. ***Email:*** jbryan@hendersoncovington.com

---

GEORGE L. WHITE, IV, born Grangeville, Idaho, September 8, 1967; admitted to bar, 1996, Ohio. *Education:* Southern Oregon State College (B.S., 1989); University of Idaho (J.D., 1995). *Member:* Mahoning County and Ohio State Bar Associations. ***PRACTICE AREAS:*** Commercial Law; Banking Law; Corporate Law; Commercial Litigation. ***Email:*** gwhite@hendersoncovington.com

SCOTT C. ESSAD, born Kansas City, Missouri, October 29, 1969; admitted to bar, 1996, Ohio; U.S. District Court, Northern District of Ohio and Western District of Pennsylvania ; U.S. Court of Appeals, Sixth, Third and Federal Circuits; 2002, Pennsylvania. *Education:* The Ohio State University (B.A., 1992); University of Toledo (J.D., 1996). *Member:* Mahoning County and Ohio State Bar Associations. ***PRACTICE AREAS:*** Commercial Litigation; Civil Litigation; Business Law; Appellate Practice. ***Email:*** sessad@hendersoncovington.com

JOHN T. HEINO, born Youngstown, Ohio, January 20, 1971; admitted to bar, 1996, Ohio; 1997, Florida; U.S. District Court, Northern District of Ohio; U.S. Court of Appeals Sixth Circuit. *Education:* Hiram College (B.A., 1993); University of Toledo (J.D., cum laude, 1996). *Member:* Lake County, Ashtabula County and Ohio State Bar Associations; The Florida Bar. ***PRACTICE AREAS:*** Litigation; Corporate Law; Banking Law; Commercial Law; Real Estate Law. ***Email:*** jheino@hendersoncovington.com

LEGAL SUPPORT PERSONNEL

DAWN E. KNISLEY, born Passaic, New Jersey, October 7, 1961. *Education:* Manatee Community College (A.S., 1986, Legal Assistant). *Member:* National Association of Legal Assistants, Inc. (Legal Assistant) (Certified Legal Assistant, Real Estate Specialist). ***PRACTICE AREAS:*** Banking and Litigation; Bankruptcy; Personal Injury; Corporate. ***Email:*** dknisley@hendersoncovington.com

LORI A. HANSON, born Hillsboro, Wisconsin, June 23, 1960. *Education:* ETI Technical College (Associate of Applied Business in Legal Assisting, 2002). ***PRACTICE AREAS:*** Banking; Civil Litigation. ***Email:*** lhanson@hendersoncovington.com

REPRESENTATIVE CLIENTS: National City Bank; Sky Bank; Bank One; First National Bank of Pennsylvania; Northside Bank; Mellon Bank; Aerolite Extrusion Co.; Aim Nationalease; Calex Corporation; Carney-McNicholas Transportation; Callos Personnel Services; Clayton Heating & Air Conditioning Co.; Edward J. DeBartolo Corp.; Ernst-Western Corp.; Falcon Transportation; Fireline, Inc.; General Extrusions; Giant Eagle; Strollo Architects, Inc.; Hynes Industries; Litco International, Inc.; Powell Systems, Inc.; Superior Beverage Group; Terreri Construction Co.; YSD Industries, Inc.; Boardman Township; Boardman Board of Education; Howland Board of Education; Liberty Board of Education; The Home Savings and Loan Company; City of Girard; City of Hubbard; Citizens Financial Services, Inc.
MR. CHRISTOPHER J. NEWMAN IS COUNSEL FOR: Better Business Bureau of Mahoning Valley, Inc.
REFERENCES: National City Bank; Sky Bank.

HENRETTA LAW OFFICES

YOUNGSTOWN, OHIO

(See Akron)

Medical Malpractice, Legal Malpractice, Nursing Home Litigation, Insurance Litigation, Automobile Accidents and Injuries and Wrongful Death.

MANCHESTER, BENNETT, POWERS & ULLMAN

A LEGAL PROFESSIONAL ASSOCIATION

Established in 1872

ATRIUM LEVEL TWO
THE COMMERCE BUILDING
201 EAST COMMERCE STREET
YOUNGSTOWN, OHIO 44503-1641
Telephone: 330-743-1171
Fax: 330-743-1190
URL: http://www.mbpu.com

General Civil Practice in all State and Federal Courts. Antitrust and Unfair Trade Practices, Commercial, Construction, Corporation, Creditor-Debtor, Bankruptcy, Employer-Employee Relations, Environmental, Estate Planning and Administration, General Business, Health Care, Insurance, Labor Relations, Litigation, Pension and Employee Benefits, Probate, Real Estate, Public Finance, Securities, School Law, Taxation, Trials, Workers Compensation.

FIRM PROFILE: Manchester, Bennett, Powers & Ullman has provided a full range of legal services to clients in Northeastern Ohio since its founding in 1872. In recent years, the firm has expanded its practice in areas such as bankruptcy and labor, to include clients in Western Pennsylvania. The firm engages in a diversified civil practice before all state and federal courts in Ohio and the federal courts in Pennsylvania. In addition, members of the firm practice before virtually all federal and state agencies and regulatory bodies. Shareholders and associates are active in professional, civic, and charitable organizations.

The firm serves businesses from Fortune 500 companies to small businesses and sole proprietorships, public employers, and nonprofit organizations. The Clients of the firm include businesses engaged in transportation, manufacturing, education, publishing, printing, health care, banking, retail merchandising, construction, government, broadcasting, real estate development, and insurance.

CURTIS A. MANCHESTER (1876-1951)

JAMES EUGENE BENNETT (1889-1964)

FRANKLIN B. POWERS (1887-1960)

MYRON E. ULLMAN (1889-1974)

STEPHEN T. BOLTON, born San Antonio, Texas, November 11, 1946; admitted to bar, 1972, Ohio and U.S. District Court, Northern District of Ohio, U.S. Tax Court, U.S. Court of Appeals, Third and Sixth Circuits, U.S. Supreme Court. *Education:* University of Virginia (B.A., 1969; LL.B., 1972). *Member:* Mahoning County, Columbiana County, Trumbull County and Ohio State (Member, Council of Delegates, Media Law Committee) Bar Associations; Ohio Council of School Board Attorneys. ***PRACTICE AREAS:*** Commercial Litigation; Employment Litigation; Insurance Defense Litigation. ***Email:*** sbolton@mbpu.com

TIMOTHY J. JACOB, born St. Marys, Pennsylvania, April 7, 1951; admitted to bar, 1977, Ohio; U.S. District Court, Northern District of Ohio; U.S. Court of Appeals, Sixth Circuit; U.S. Supreme Court. *Education:* University of Notre Dame (A.B., magna cum laude, 1973); Duke University (J.D., 1977). Phi Alpha Delta. *Member:* Mahoning County, Ohio State (Member, Labor and Employment Section) and American (Member, Labor and Employment Section) Bar Associations. ***PRACTICE AREAS:*** Employment Discrimination Law; Labor Relations (Management) Law; Federal Practice; Employment Law. ***Email:*** tjacob@mbpu.com

C. SCOTT LANZ, born Youngstown, Ohio, October 30, 1954; admitted to bar, 1980, Ohio; U.S. District Court, Northern and Southern Districts of Ohio; U.S. Court of Appeals, Sixth Circuit; U.S. Supreme Court. *Education:* Youngstown State University; Louisiana State University (B.A., 1976); The Ohio State University (J.D., 1980). *Member:* Mahoning County, Ohio State and American (Member, Litigation Section) Bar Associations. ***PRACTICE AREAS:*** Insurance Defense Law; General Civil Litigation; Employment Litigation; Workers Compensation; Personal Injury. ***Email:*** slanz@mbpu.com

MARK A. BEATRICE, born East Palestine, Ohio, March 19, 1955; admitted to bar, 1981, Ohio. *Education:* Adrian College (B.A., summa cum laude, 1977); Duke University (M.A., 1981; J.D., 1981). *Member:* Mahoning County, Columbiana County, Ohio State and American Bar Associations. ***PRACTICE AREAS:*** Commercial Law; Debtor Creditor Law; Bankruptcy Law; Pension Law; Real Estate Law. ***Email:*** mbeatrice@mbpu.com

JOSEPH R. YOUNG, JR., born Philadelphia, Pennsylvania, September 6, 1957; admitted to bar, 1982, Ohio. *Education:* Northwestern University (B.A., 1979); Duke University (J.D., 1982). *Member:* Mahoning County, Ohio State and American (Member, Labor and Employment Section) Bar Associations. ***PRACTICE AREAS:*** Workers Compensation; Labor Relations (Management) Law; General Civil Litigation. ***Email:*** jyoung@mbpu.com

JOSEPH M. HOUSER, born Indianapolis, Indiana, August 13, 1956; admitted to bar, 1981, Ohio. *Education:* Youngstown State College (B.A., magna cum laude, 1978); Cincinnati University (J.D., 1981). Phi Alpha Delta. Certified Public Accountant, Ohio, 1982. Member, Standing Panel of Chapter 7 Trustees, United States Bankruptcy Court, Northern District of Ohio, 1987-1993. Special Counsel to Ohio Attorney General, 1995—. Mahoning County Court Judge, 1997—. *Member:* Mahoning County, Ohio State and American (Member, Tax Section) Bar Associations; Ohio Society of Certified Public Accountants. ***Email:*** jhouser@mbpu.com

JEFFREY D. HEINTZ, born Sharon, Pennsylvania, June 23, 1959; admitted to bar, 1984, Ohio. *Education:* Westminster College (B.A., summa cum laude, 1981); University of Virginia (J.D., 1984). Phi Delta Phi. *Member:* Mahoning County, Trumbull County, Ohio State and American Bar Associations; Mahoning-Shenango Valley Estate Planning Council. ***PRACTICE AREAS:*** Probate Law; Corporate Law; Real Estate Law; Business Law; Trusts and Estates. ***Email:*** jheintz@mbpu.com

EDWIN ROMERO, born Youngstown, Ohio, January 22, 1949; admitted to bar, 1978, Ohio and U.S. District Court, Northern District of Ohio, U.S. Court of Appeals, Third and Sixth Circuit, U.S. Supreme Court. *Education:* Youngstown State University (A.B., 1973); Ohio State University (J.D., 1977). City Director of Law, 1985-1994. *Member:* Mahoning County Bar Association; Ohio Municipal Attorneys Association (President, 1995). ***PRACTICE AREAS:*** Labor Relations Law; Employment Law; Government Law; Civil Rights Defense Litigation; Civil Litigation. ***Email:*** eromero@mbpu.com

MARTHA L. BUSHEY, born Uniontown, Pennsylvania, February 29, 1948; admitted to bar, 1989, Ohio and U.S. District Court, Northern District of Ohio. *Education:* Youngstown State University (B.S.N., summa cum laude, 1986) University of Akron (J.D., cum laude, 1989). *Member:* Mahoning County and Ohio State Bar Associations. ***PRACTICE AREAS:*** General Practice; Business Law; Health Care; Probate Law; Annexations; Real Estate Law. ***Email:*** mbushey@mbpu.com

DAVID A. DETEC, born Youngstown, Ohio, September 26, 1953; admitted to bar, 1980, Ohio; U.S. District Court, Northern District of Ohio; U.S. Court of Appeals, Sixth Circuit; U.S. Tax Court. *Education:* Youngstown State University (A.B., cum laude, 1976); Akron University Law School (J.D., 1980). Articles Editor, Akron Law Review, 1979-1980. *Member:* Cleveland (Member, Sections on: Health Law; Commercial Law), Trumbull County, Mahoning County, Ohio State (Member: Board of Governors and Real Estate Section; Committees on Corporations and Natural Resources) and American (Member, Sections on: Corporations, Banking and Business; Construction Industry Forum) Bar Associations; Member, Ohio Division of Securities Advisory Committee. ***PRACTICE AREAS:*** Banking; Bankruptcy; Corporations; Business; Health Law; Commercial; Construction; Natural Resources; Real Estate. ***Email:*** ddetec@mbpu.com

THOMAS J. LIPKA, born Youngstown, Ohio, November 28, 1969; admitted to bar, 1996, Ohio and U.S. District Court, Northern District of Ohio; U.S. Court of Appeals, Sixth Circuit. *Education:* Oberlin College (B.A., 1992); The Ohio State University (J.D., with honors, 1996). *Member:* Mahoning County, Ohio State and American Bar Associations. ***PRACTICE AREAS:*** General Practice; Business Law; Civil Litigation; Insurance Defense Law. ***Email:*** tlipka@mbpu.com

GINA AGRESTA RICHARDSON, born Youngstown, Ohio, October 18, 1972; admitted to bar, 1999, Ohio and U.S. District Court, Northern District of Ohio; U.S. Court of Appeals, Sixth Circuit. *Education:* University of Notre Dame (B.A., 1995); University of Akron (J.D., magna cum laude, 1999). Author: "Employee Stock Ownership Plans; Uncertainties Plaguing the Duties of the ESOP Fiduciary with Respect to Voting and Defensive ESOPS," Akron Law School Tax Journal. Instructor, Basic Legal Communications, University of Akron, School of Law, 1999. *Member:* Mahoning County, Ohio State and American Bar Associations; American Bankruptcy Institute; Ohio Women's Bar Association. ***PRACTICE AREAS:*** General Practice; Business Law; Banking Law; Bankruptcy; Trademarks and Copyrights; Commercial Law; Probate Law. ***Email:*** grichardson@mbpu.com

---

JOHN T. SAVAGE, born Youngstown, Ohio, August 26, 1970; admitted to bar, 2001, Ohio. *Education:* Youngstown State University (B.A., 1993); University of Akron (J.D., 2001). *Member:* Mahoning County, Ohio State and American Bar Associations. ***PRACTICE AREAS:*** Civil Litigation; Insurance Defense; General Practice; Estate Planning. ***Email:*** jsavage@mbpu.com

GREGORY S. SMITH, born El Paso, Texas, January 8, 1978; admitted to bar, 2003, Ohio. *Education:* Ohio University (B.A., 2000); Ohio State University (J.D., 2003). *Member:* Ohio State Bar Association. ***PRACTICE AREAS:*** Civil Litigation; Business Disputes; Corporate Planning; Estate Planning. ***Email:*** gsmith@mbpu.com

LOCAL COUNSEL FOR: City of Youngstown; Ellwood Group, Inc.; Fagens, Inc.; Farmers Insurance Group; Federal Assurance Corporation; Fifth Third Bank; First National Bank of Pennsylvania; Home Savings and Loan Company; Metropolitan Life Insurance Company; Motorists Insurance Companies; Piedmont Communications Co., Inc. (WKBN TV); Salem Community Hospital; Sheetz, Inc.; Sky Bank; Speedway SuperAmerica; True North Energy, LLC; The Vindicator Printing Company; WFMJ Television, Inc.; Wilshire Credit Corporation; Youngstown State University; Youngstown Television, LLP.
GENERAL COUNSEL FOR: Briarfield of Austintown, LLC; Briarfield Manor, LLC; Builders Association of Eastern Ohio & Western Pennsylvania; Butler, Wick & Company; Century Industries Company; Cerni Motor Sales, Inc.; Compco Industries, Inc.; Diamond Steel Construction Company; Eastern Ohio Pulmonary Consultants, Inc.; Gateways to Better Living, Inc.; JADCO Limited Partnership; Maui Toys, Inc.; Mill Creek Metropolitan Park District; National Electrical Contractors Association (Pennsylvania-Ohio Chapter); Poling & Bacon Construction Company; Salem-Republic Rubber Co.; Village of New Middletown; Vista Care Center, Inc.; Western Reserve Mechanical, Inc.; Youngstown Central Area Community Improvement Corporation.
TITLE AGENTS FOR: Lawyers Title Insurance Company.

MILLSTONE & KANNENSOHN

Established in 1966

15 FEDERAL PLAZA CENTRAL
2ND FLOOR
YOUNGSTOWN, OHIO 44503
Telephone: 330-743-5181
Fax: 330-743-9704
Email: milkann@hotmail.com

General Civil Practice, Commercial Law and Collections.

MEMBER OF FIRM

FREDRIC A. KANNENSOHN, born Youngstown, Ohio, September 16, 1939; admitted to bar, 1964, Ohio; 1993, Pennsylvania. *Education:* Wharton School of Business of the University of Pennsylvania (B.S., 1961); University of Michigan (J.D., 1964). Member, National Association of Retail Collection Attorneys. President, Ohio Creditors' Attorneys Association. *Member:* Mahoning County and Ohio State (Member, Banking and Commercial Law Committee; Chairman, Subcommittee on Provisional Remedies and Execution of Judgements, 1984—) Bar Associations; Commercial Law League of America. (Managing Partner)

REPRESENTATIVE CLIENTS: Anchor Cigar and Candy; Bank One; Sky Bank; First Place Bank; Home Savings and Loan Association; First National Bank; Credit Union One, Inc.; Youngstown Federal Employees Credit Union; Youngstown, Ohio City Employees Federal

(This Listing Continued)

MILLSTONE & KANNENSOHN, Youngstown—Continued

Credit Union; Seven Seventeen Credit Union, Inc.; Seventeen Fourteen Credit Union; Ohio Edison/Penn Power Credit Union; King's Jewelry; Sherman Acquisition L.P. Assignee of Sears, Roebuck & Co.; Kaufmann's (May Department Stores); Banner Building Supply Co.; Castle Building Supply, Inc.; City Concrete; T.C. Redi-Mix; Poland Concrete; Humility of Mary Health Partners; Forum Health; Pellin Emergency Medical Services; Wilcom/Cellular One; Youngstown Television, Inc. (WKBN T.V.); City of Youngstown; City of Struthers; City of Girard; City of Campbell; State of Ohio; Rental Properties; M & S Investment Co.; P & S Equities, Inc.; Rydyl-1 LLC.; Waldon Management Corporation; Hitchcock Apartments; Simco Management Corp.

NADER AND NADER

YOUNGSTOWN, OHIO

(See Warren)

General Civil Practice in all Courts. Municipal, Corporate, Domestic, Trials, Environmental Law, Public Utility Law, Ohio Administrative Agencies and Real Estate Law.

NADLER NADLER & BURDMAN CO., L.P.A.

Established in 1917

20 FEDERAL PLAZA WEST, SUITE 600
YOUNGSTOWN, OHIO 44503-1559
Telephone: 330-744-0247; 330-747-8621
Telecopier: 330-744-8690
Email: scpatton@nnblaw.com

General Civil Practice in all State and Federal Courts. Commercial, Creditor Rights and Collections, Bankruptcy, Reorganization, Taxation, Employment and Labor Law, Corporation, Partnership, Venture Capital, Banking, Real Estate, Shopping Center, Franchising, Environmental, Pension and Profit Sharing, Estate Planning, Probate, and Trials and Appeals.

FIRM PROFILE: Established in 1917, Nadler Nadler & Burdman Co., L.P.A. is engaged in the general civil and business practice of law. Our practice embraces all civil specialties as they relate to the problems and planning concerns of business entities and their owners. The firm's clients include manufacturers, service and retail businesses, health care entities, and real estate developers. In addition, the firm represents professional practices, such as physicians and attorneys, as well as financial enterprises such as brokerages, venture capitalists, banks and insurance companies.

PETER B. GRINSTEIN, born Milwaukee, Wisconsin, November 3, 1936; admitted to bar, 1961, Wisconsin and Ohio; 1971, U.S. Supreme Court. *Education:* University of Wisconsin (B.B.A., 1958; J.D., 1961). Tau Epsilon Rho. Member, National Panel of Arbitrators, American Arbitration Association. *Member:* Mahoning County (Chairman, Grievance Committee, 1967-1976; Trustee, 1976—), Trumbull County, Ohio State and American Bar Associations; State Bar of Wisconsin; The Association of Trial Lawyers of America; The Ohio Academy of Trial Lawyers. ***PRACTICE AREAS:*** Civil Litigation; Labor Law; Employment Law. ***Email:*** pbg@nnblaw.com

MICHAEL A. GALLO, born Mt. Pleasant, Pennsylvania, July 10, 1942; admitted to bar, 1967, Ohio. *Education:* Marquette University (A.B., 1964); Catholic University of America (J.D., 1967). Standing Chapter 13 Trustee, U.S. Bankruptcy Court, Northern District, 1979—. *Member:* Mahoning County, Ohio State and American Bar Associations. ***PRACTICE AREAS:*** Bankruptcy; Reorganization; Business. ***Email:*** gallo@nnblaw.com

JAY M. SKOLNICK, born Patchogue, New York, November 8, 1941; admitted to bar, 1967, Ohio. *Education:* Emory University (A.B., 1964); University of Cincinnati (J.D., 1967). Phi Delta Phi. *Member:* Mahoning County, Ohio State and American (Member, Sections on: Taxation; Banking and Business Law) Bar Associations. ***PRACTICE AREAS:*** Tax Law; Banking; Business Law; Corporate Law. ***Email:*** jmskolnick@nnblaw.com

MARC S. STEIN, born Youngstown, Ohio, August 27, 1950; admitted to bar, 1975, Ohio. *Education:* Northwestern University (B.A., 1972); Case Western Reserve University (J.D., 1975). Member of Seminar Faculty: Ohio Sales & Use Tax, 1987; Basic Drafting of Wills and Trusts in Ohio, 1992. *Member:* Mahoning County, Ohio State (Member, Section on Probate and Trust Law) and American Bar Associations. ***PRACTICE AREAS:*** Estate Planning and Administration. ***Email:*** msstein@nnblaw.com

JOSEPH C. LUCCI, born Youngstown, Ohio, February 4, 1953; admitted to bar, 1978, Ohio; 1980, Florida and U.S. District Court, Northern District of Ohio. *Education:* Youngstown State University; University of Central Florida (B.A., cum laude, 1975); Florida State University (J.D., 1978). *Member:* Mahoning County, Ohio State and American (Member, Business Law Section) Bar Associations; The Florida Bar. ***PRACTICE AREAS:*** Bankruptcy; Creditors Rights; Commercial Litigation. ***Email:*** jclucci@nnblaw.com

ROBERT S. HARTFORD, JR., born Salem, Ohio, January 11, 1949; admitted to bar, 1974, Ohio; 1977, U.S. District Court, Northern District of Ohio; 1978, U.S. Supreme Court; 1988, U.S. Court of Appeals, Sixth Circuit. *Education:* Geneva College; Kent State University (B.B.A., with honors, 1971); University of Akron (J.D., 1974). Director of Law, City of East Palestine, Ohio, 1976-1984. Chief Assistant Prosecutor, Columbiana County, Ohio, 1977-1984. Trustee, Columbiana County Law Library Association, 1983-1984. Member, Ohio State Bar Association College, 1983. *Member:* Columbiana County, Mahoning County, Ohio State and American Bar Associations; Ohio Academy of Trial Lawyers. ***PRACTICE AREAS:*** Litigation. ***Email:*** rsh2@nnblaw.com

DONN D. ROSENBLUM, born New York, N.Y., April 30, 1954; admitted to bar, 1979, Ohio and U.S. District Court, Northern District of Ohio; 1989, U.S. Court of Appeals, Sixth Circuit; 2002, Pennsylvania. *Education:* Boston University (B.S., in Business Administration, Accounting, 1976); Capital University Law School (J.D., 1979). Delta Theta Phi. Assistant Attorney General State of Ohio, 1979-1984. Public Utilities Commission of Ohio, Assistant to the Director of Utilities, 1978-1979. *Member:* Trumbull County, Mahoning

(This Listing Continued)

County, Ohio State and American Bar Associations. ***PRACTICE AREAS:*** Civil Litigation; Workers Compensation Defense; Commercial Collections; Landlord-Tenant; Decendents Estates. ***Email:*** drosenblum@nnblaw.com

EDWARD F. SMITH, born Canandaigua, New York, August 5, 1962; admitted to bar, 1988, Ohio. *Education:* Washington University (A.B., cum laude, 1984) Phi Alpha Theta; Case Western Reserve University (J.D., cum laude, 1988). Research Editor, Case Western Reserve University Law Review, 1987-1988. *Member:* Mahoning County, Ohio State (Member, Board of Governors, Corporate Counsel Section, 1995-2001) and American Bar Associations. ***PRACTICE AREAS:*** Real Estate; Mergers and Acquisitions; Franchising; Environmental Law; Real Estate Law; Corporate Law. ***Email:*** efsmith@nnblaw.com

TIMOTHY M. REARDON, born Youngstown, Ohio September 17, 1967; admitted to bar, 1992, Ohio; 1993, U.S. District Court, Northern District of Ohio; U.S. Court of Appeals, Sixth Circuit. *Education:* Bowling Green State University (B.A., 1989); University of Toledo College of Law (J.D., cum laude, 1992). *Member:* Mahoning County (Member, Bankruptcy Committee), Ohio State (Member, Corporate Counsel Section) and American (Member, Sections on Litigation and Business Law) Bar Associations; Commercial Law League of America (Member, Bankruptcy and Insolvency Section); American Bankruptcy Institute. ***PRACTICE AREAS:*** Bankruptcy; Creditor's Rights; Commercial Litigation; Employment Law. ***Email:*** tmreardon@nnblaw.com

JOHN F. PETRONY, born Youngstown, Ohio, May 26, 1968; admitted to bar, 1993, Ohio; 1994, U.S. District Court, Northern District of Ohio. *Education:* Youngstown State University (B.A., summa cum laude, 1990); The Ohio State University (J.D., 1993). Phi Kappa Phi. Golden Key. Author: "LLC's vs. Corporations in Ohio," Ohio Lawyer, July-August 2004 at 12. Faculty Member, "Choice of Business in Ohio: How to do it Right," National Business Institute, 2001 and 2002. *Member:* Mahoning County, Ohio State (Member: Corporation Law Committee; Limited Liability Company Subcommittee; Real Estate Section) and American (Member: Sections on: Business Law; Real Property, Probate and Trust Law; Committees on: Partnerships and Unincorporated Business Organizations, Negotiated Acquisitions) Bar Associations. ***PRACTICE AREAS:*** Business Law; Mergers and Acquisitions; Limited Liability Company Law; Real Estate Law. ***Email:*** jfpetrony@nnblaw.com

FRANK J. MATUNE, born Youngstown, Ohio, January 11, 1948; admitted to bar, 1979, Pennsylvania; 1980, U.S. Tax Court; 1982, U.S. District Court, Western District of Pennsylvania; 1998, Ohio. *Education:* Notre Dame University and Illinois Benedictine University (B.A., 1970); Thomas M. Cooley Law School (J.D., 1979); Georgetown University Law School (LL.M. in Taxation, 1980). Listed in Who's Who in American Law, Sixth Edition, 1990—. Chief Tax Law Clerk, Michigan Board of Tax Appeals, Department of Revenue, Lansing, Michigan, 1978-1979. Author: "Taxation of Pennsylvania S Corporations and Shareholders," Chapter 94, Pennsylvania Tax Service, Matthew Bender Publishing Company, 1989-1994; "Reorganizations Generally," Chapter 1:12, Bender's Federal Tax Service, Matthew Bender Publishing Company, 1989—. Faculty Member: "Taxation of S Corps.," Pennsylvania Bar Association Mid-Annual Meeting, 1994; "Pennsylvania S Corporations," Professional Education Systems, Inc., 1990; "State and Local Tax Update," Pennsylvania Bar Association Annual Meeting, 1991; "Model S Corporation State Income Tax Act (Proposed)," American Bar Association Annual Meeting, 1988. Solicitor, Sharpsville School District, 1987-1995. *Member:* Allegheny County (Member, Taxation Section), Mercer County (Treasurer, 1983-1986), Mahoning County, Pennsylvania (Member: Taxation Section; Corporation, Banking and Business Law Section; Member, Tax Council, Tax Law Section, 1991-1995; Chairman, Ad Hoc Committee on Pennsylvania S Corporations and Partnerships, Tax Law Section, 1991-1998; Health Care and Hospital Law Committee), Ohio State and American (Member: Taxation Section; Committee on S Corporations) Bar Associations; Pennsylvania Society of Healthcare Attorneys. ***PRACTICE AREAS:*** Taxation Law; Mergers and Acquisitions Law; IRS Controversies; Closely Held Business Law; Health Care Law; Corporate Law. ***Email:*** fjmatune@nnblaw.com

MURRAY A. NADLER (1899-1986)

MYRON J. NADLER, born Youngstown, Ohio, July 22, 1923; admitted to bar, 1950, Ohio (Inactive); 1971, U.S. Supreme Court. *Education:* University of Pennsylvania, Wharton School of Finance (B.S. in Econ., 1947); University of Michigan (J.D., with distinction, 1950). Assistant Editor, Michigan Law Review, 1949. Co-author: "Bankruptcy Forms and Practice," Supplement, April 1964; *Nadler on Bankruptcy,* 2nd Edition, 1965; Author: Articles on Exemptions, Ohio State Law Journal, Vol. 16, 1955 and the Uniform Fraudulent Conveyance Act, Ohio State Law Journal, Vol. 22, 1961. Instructor, Youngstown University Law School, 1952-1959. Member, Mahoning County Planning Commission, 1965-1971. *Member:* Mahoning County, Ohio State (Chairman, Uniform State Laws Committee, 1962-1964; Subcommittee Chairman, Judicial Administration and Legal Reform Committee, 1965-1970) and American (Member, Section of: Business Law) Bar Associations. Fellow, Ohio State Bar Foundation. (Retired)

B. RICHARD BURDMAN, born Youngstown, Ohio, September 6, 1933; admitted to bar, 1956, Ohio; 1962, U.S. Supreme Court; 1971, U.S. Tax Court. *Education:* The Ohio State University; Youngstown University (A.B., 1954); Duke University (J.D., 1956). Phi Delta Phi. Member, Board of Visitors, Duke University School of Law; 1989-1995 Emeritus. *Member:* Mahoning County, Ohio State (Member, Unauthorized Practice of Law Committee, 1968-1969) and American (Member, Sections of: Taxation; Banking and Business Law; Real Property, Probate and Trust Law; Committee on Small Firms, 1992-1993) Bar Associations. Fellow Ohio State Bar Association. (Retired)

REPRESENTATIVE CLIENTS: Advanced Podiatry; Allied Erecting & Dismantling, Inc.; Allied Gator, Inc.; American Waste Management, Inc.; Anderson Coach & Tour; ATD Corp.; Astroshapes, Inc.; Avalon Holdings, Inc.; Baird Brothers Sawmill, Inc.; B.J. Alan Co. (fireworks wholesaler/retailer); Burdman Brothers Co. (shopping center developers); City Machine Technologies, Inc.; Classic Optical Laboratories, Inc.; Coil Slitting International LLC; Comprehensive Logistics; DAF Corporation; DAGA; D & L Energy, Inc.; District XI Area Agency on Aging (Senior Citizens); East Palestine China Co. (custom ceramic decorating); Edan Management Co., Inc. (nursing home and assisted living facility mgmt.); Edward J. Lewis, Inc. (real estate brokers); 84 Lumber Co.; Falcon Transportation, Inc.; First Place Bank; Foggy Hollow Farm (champion short horn cattle); Girard Sparkle Market, Inc.; Interstate Chemical Company, Inc.; Institutional Foods, Inc.; Liberty Industries, Inc.; MS Consultants, Inc. (engineering, surveying, environmental safety); Mayo & Associates, Inc. (real estate brokerage); MVI, Inc. (home health care); Mahoning Valley Hematology Oncology Associates, Inc.; Nannicola, Inc.; Nick Strimbu, Inc. (transportation); Phoenix Supermarkets, Inc.; Ply-Trim, Inc.; Reynolds Services, Inc.; Ross Development Corp. (real estate developer);

(This Listing Continued)

Simco Explorations (oil and gas exploration); Simco Management Corp. (real estate); Sky Bank; United Freezer & Storage Co.; United Steel Service, Inc.; Youngstown Electric Services, Inc.
REFERENCES: National City Bank; Bank One, Youngstown, N.A.; Sky Bank.

NEWMAN, OLSON & KERR

A LEGAL PROFESSIONAL CORPORATION

FIRST NATIONAL TOWER
11 FEDERAL PLAZA CENTRAL
SUITE 1200
YOUNGSTOWN, OHIO 44503-1516
Telephone: 330-747-4404
Fax: 330-747-6056

General Civil and Trial Practice in all Courts. Corporation, Banking, Commercial, Bankruptcy, Labor, Estate Planning, Probate, Insurance, Health, Personal Injury, Real Estate, Church, Non-Profit, Construction.

JOHN M. NEWMAN, born Youngstown, Ohio, 1915; admitted to bar, 1942, Ohio. *Education:* University of Pittsburgh (A.B., 1937); Youngstown University Law School (J.D., 1942). Instructor, Law School of Youngstown University, 1950-1959. Trustee, 1970-1979; Chairman, 1972-1974, Youngstown State University. Chairman of the Board of St. Elizabeth Hospital, 1977-1992. ***PRACTICE AREAS:*** Probate; Corporate; Banking; Church Law. ***Email:*** jmnnew@aol.com

E. CARROLL THORNTON, JR., born Youngstown, Ohio, 1946; admitted to bar, 1971, Ohio. *Education:* Ohio University (B.B.A., 1968); University of Cincinnati Law School (J.D., 1971). ***PRACTICE AREAS:*** Labor; Employment; Corporate. ***Email:*** tthornton@noklaw.com

DONALD P. HERRIOTT, born Rochester, Pennsylvania, 1945; admitted to bar, 1974, Ohio; 1975, Florida. *Education:* Mount Union College (B.S., 1967); Pennsylvania State University; Temple University (J.D., 1974). ***PRACTICE AREAS:*** Corporate; Estate Planning; Probate; Business Transactions; Construction. ***Email:*** dherriott@noklaw.com

ROBERT S. FULTON, born Youngstown, Ohio, 1946; admitted to bar, 1972, Ohio; 1973, U.S. District Court, Northern District of Ohio; 1975, U.S. Supreme Court. *Education:* Miami University; Youngstown State University (B.S., 1969); Case Western Reserve University (J.D., 1972). ***PRACTICE AREAS:*** Real Estate; Corporate; Commercial Litigation; Civil Litigation; Construction. ***Email:*** rfulton@noklaw.com

MARY BETH HOUSER, born Youngstown, Ohio, 1957; admitted to bar, 1982, Ohio. *Education:* Youngstown State University (B.A., magna cum laude, 1979); The Ohio State University (J.D., 1982). ***PRACTICE AREAS:*** Corporate; Banking; Church Law; Nonprofit Organizations Law. ***Email:*** mhouser@noklaw.com

JAMES G. FLOYD, born Tarentum, Pennsylvania, 1938; admitted to bar, 1971, Ohio. *Education:* Denison University (B.S.S., 1962); University of Denver (J.D., 1969). [U.S. Navy, active duty, 1963-1968; Cmdr., USNR]. ***PRACTICE AREAS:*** Bankruptcy; Commercial; Commercial Litigation; Uniform Commercial Code; Banking; Construction. ***Email:*** jfloyd@noklaw.com

LEO J. PUHALLA, born Youngstown, Ohio, 1970; admitted to bar, 1996, Ohio; 1997, U.S. District Court, Northern District of Ohio. *Education:* Youngstown State University (B.S., summa cum laude, 1993); University of Akron (J.D., cum laude, 1996). Member, Law Review, 1994-1995; Citations Editor, 1995-1996, Law Review Editorial Board, 1995-1996. ***PRACTICE AREAS:*** Bankruptcy; Collection; Commercial Law; Litigation; Church; Nonprofit Organizations Law. ***Email:*** lpuhalla@noklaw.com

BRENT E. BAKER, born Coldwater, Michigan, 1963; admitted to bar, 2000, Ohio. *Education:* Roberts Wesleyan College (B.A., 1986); Asbury Theological Seminary (M.Div., 1991); Duke University (Th.M., 1994); University of Akron (J.D., 1999). ***PRACTICE AREAS:*** Collections; Creditor Bankruptcy; Church Law. ***Email:*** bbaker@noklaw.com

OF COUNSEL

LEONARD A. OLSON, born Youngstown, Ohio, 1927; admitted to bar, 1953, Ohio. *Education:* Youngstown University (A.B., 1949); Youngstown University Law School (J.D., 1953).

PATRICK A. SEBASTIANO, born Youngstown, Ohio, October 14, 1957; admitted to bar, 1982, Ohio. *Education:* Youngstown State University (B.S.B.A., cum laude, 1979); University of Toledo (J.D., 1982). *Member:* Mahoning County, Trumbull County and Ohio State Bar Associations. ***PRACTICE AREAS:*** Estate Planning; Trust Law. ***Email:*** psebastiano@noklaw.com

GENERAL COUNSEL FOR: Catholic Diocese of Youngstown; The Youngstown Club; The Youngstown Country Club; The East Fairfield Coal Co.; Lake Park Tool & Machine, Inc.; Nemenz Supermarkets; The Winkle Electric Co.; Youngstown Arc Engraving Co.; Joe Dickey Electric, Inc.; Modern Display Plastics; Healthridge Medical Center; Valley Industrial Trucks; Health Index; Hart Products; Turning Point Counseling Center; Youngstown Area Goodwill Industries; Norman Holdings Corp.; Poma Investments, Inc.
LOCAL COUNSEL FOR: G.M.A.C.; Burlington Insurance Group; cboss Community Network; Buckeye-Industrial Mining Co.; D.W. Dickey & Sons, Inc. (Builder Supplies); City of Youngstown; Farmers National Bank; Key Bank; Second National Bank of Warren; Cantar/Polyair Corp; Sky Bank; First Financial Insurance; Forum Health; First National Bank of Pennsylvania; Orion Auto Inc.
SPECIAL COUNSEL FOR: State of Ohio; Youngstown State University Foundation; City of Warren; Home Savings and Loan Co. of Youngstown; Cortland Savings & Banking Co.

PFAU, PFAU & MARANDO

P.O. BOX 9070
YOUNGSTOWN, OHIO 44513
Telephone: 330-702-9700
Fax: 330-702-9704
Email: ppm@ppmlegal.com

General Civil Practice in all State and Federal Courts. Insurance, Malpractice and Products Liability and Personal Injury Law, Constitutional and Real Estate Law. Trials.

(This Listing Continued)

WILLIAM E. PFAU, SR. (1889-1963)

WILLIAM E. PFAU, JR. (Retired)

MEMBERS OF FIRM

WILLIAM E. PFAU III, born Youngstown, Ohio, April 19, 1951; admitted to bar, 1979, Ohio; 1989 U.S. Supreme Court. *Education:* Bowdoin College (B.A., 1973); University of Toledo (J.D., 1978). *Member:* Mahoning County, Ohio State (Member, Negligence Law Committee) and American Bar Associations; Ohio Association of Civil Trial Attorneys; American Board of Trial Advocates. ***PRACTICE AREAS:*** Products Liability; Medical Malpractice; Litigation; Insurance; Personal Injury. ***Email:*** wep@ppmlegal.com

JOHN C. PFAU, born Youngstown, Ohio, December 28, 1954; admitted to bar, 1980, Ohio. *Education:* Kenyon College (B.A., 1977); Ohio Northern University (J.D., 1979). *Member:* Mahoning County, Ohio State and American Bar Associations; Ohio Association of Civil Trial Attorneys. ***PRACTICE AREAS:*** Products Liability; Insurance; Litigation; Personal Injury; Civil Rights. ***Email:*** jcp@ppmlegal.com

MICHAEL P. MARANDO, born South Bend, Indiana, December 11, 1950; admitted to bar, 1977, Ohio and Pennsylvania. *Education:* Ohio University (B.A., 1973); Ohio Northern University (J.D., 1977). Member, Ohio Northern University Law Review, 1976-1977. Author: "Time, Inc. v. Firestone: Free Press v. Right to Reputation - Continuing Struggle to Define the Obscure," 4 Ohio Northern Law Review 91, 1976. Assistant Prosecuting Attorney, City of Youngstown, 1980. *Member:* Mahoning County, Ohio State and American (Member, Sections on: Litigation; Insurance and Tort) Bar Associations. ***PRACTICE AREAS:*** Litigation; Insurance; Personal Injury; Libel and Slander; Commercial Litigation. ***Email:*** mpm@ppmlegal.com

ASSOCIATE

JOHN A. AMS, born Akron, Ohio, March, 20 1973; admitted to bar, 2002, Ohio. *Education:* University of Akron (B.A., magna cum laude, 1995; J.D., cum laude, 2001). *Member:* Mahoning County and Ohio State Bar Associations. ***PRACTICE AREAS:*** Personal Injury; Employment Law. ***Email:*** jaa@ppmlegal.com

TRIAL COUNSEL FOR: American International Group Inc.; Grange Mutual Casualty Co.; Nationwide Cos.; Nationwide Property & Casualty Ins. Co.; Progressive Ins. Co.; The St. Paul Cos.; Victoria Ins.; Western Reserve Mutual Casualty Co.; Farmers Insurance Group; Farmland Ins. Co; Scottsdale Ins. Co.; Lowe's Home Centers, Inc.; Prison Health Services, Inc.; Team Health.

RENNER, KENNER, GREIVE, BOBAK, TAYLOR & WEBER

A LEGAL PROFESSIONAL ASSOCIATION

YOUNGSTOWN, OHIO

(See Akron)

U.S. and Foreign Patent, Trademark and Copyright Law and Licensing. Antitrust and Unfair Competition Law. Litigation.

ROTH, BLAIR, ROBERTS, STRASFELD & LODGE, L.P.A.

Established in 1969

100 FEDERAL PLAZA EAST, SUITE 600
YOUNGSTOWN, OHIO 44503-1508
Telephone: 330-744-5211
Fax: 330-744-3184
URL: http://www.roth-blair.com

General Civil Practice in all State and Federal Courts, Banking, Commercial, Corporate, Partnership, and General Business Law, Education Law, Employee Benefits and ESOP's, Estate Planning and Administration, Family Law, Employment Law, Management and Labor Relations, Insurance Defense, Mergers and Acquisitions, Pension, Profit Sharing and Retirement Plans, Personal Injury, Probate, Product Liability, Commercial, Industrial and Residential Real Estate, School Law, Securities, Trials, Venture Capital, Workers Compensation.

FIRM PROFILE: Although the firm was formed in 1969, its roots in Youngstown date back to the early 1900's to the individual practices of Benjamin F. Roth and Oscar A. Stephens. The firm handles a diversified civil practice before all State and Federal Courts in Ohio, as well as before numerous Federal and State agencies and regulatory bodies. Over the years, the firm has built a large insurance defense practice, as well as serving as general counsel for a number of local and regional corporations. The firm is well established in school law, and has a substantial probate and estate planning practice. In addition, the firm represents numerous start-up companies and deals regularly with venture capital situations.

OSCAR A. STEPHENS (1888-1975)

BENJAMIN F. ROTH (1894-1978)

DANIEL B. ROTH, born Youngstown, Ohio, September 17, 1929; admitted to bar, 1956, Ohio; 1960, U.S. Supreme Court; 1983, District of Columbia. *Education:* Miami University (B.S., 1951); Case Western Reserve University (J.D., 1956). Member, Society of Benchers (Distinguished Alumni) of Case Western Reserve University, 1986—. Omicron Delta Kappa; Phi Eta Sigma. Member, Law Review Editorial Board, 1955-1956. National Vice President, Zeta Beta Tau, 1964-1966. Vice Chairman, Executive Committee, McDonald Steel Corporation, 1981—. Director, Executive Committee, Mahoning National Bank, 1973-1999. *Member:* Mahoning County, Ohio State and American Bar Associations; The District of Columbia Bar. [Lt. Col., U.S. Air Force Reserve, active duty, 1951-1953, Retired]. ***PRACTICE AREAS:*** Corporate Law; Venture Capital Law; Family Law; Mergers and Acquisitions. ***Email:*** droth@roth-blair.com

(This Listing Continued)

ROTH, BLAIR, ROBERTS, STRASFELD & LODGE, L.P.A., Youngstown—Continued

RICHARD B. BLAIR, born Athens, Ohio, October 1, 1945; admitted to bar, 1970, Ohio. *Education:* Franklin & Marshall College (B.A., 1967); Ohio Northern University (J.D., 1970). Delta Theta Phi. Mediator, Mahoning County Common Pleas Court. Selected as Lawyer of The Year by Mahoning County Bar Association, 2004. *Member:* Mahoning County and Ohio State Bar Associations; Ohio Association of Civil Trial Attorneys; National Association of Railroad Trial Counsel; International Association of Defense Counsel; Defense Research Institute; Christian Legal Society. ***PRACTICE AREAS:*** Insurance Law; Personal Injury Law; Products Liability Law; Medical Malpractice; Mediation. ***Email:*** rbblair@roth-blair.com

JAMES E. "TED" ROBERTS, born Youngstown, Ohio, September 20, 1946; admitted to bar, 1974, Ohio; 1975, U.S. District Court, Northern District of Ohio; 1982, U.S. Tax Court; 1980, U.S. Court of Appeals, Sixth Circuit. *Education:* Youngstown State University (B.A., 1969); University of Akron School of Law (J.D., 1974). Special Counsel to Ohio Attorney General Jim Petro. Adjunct Instructor, Public Sector Collective Bargaining, Youngstown State University, 2004-2005. *Member:* Mahoning County (Past President, 2001-2002) and Ohio State (Chair, Committee for Independent Judiciary and Unjust Criticism of Judges, 2002-2005) Bar Associations; Ohio Council of School Board Attorneys; National Council of School Board Attorneys. ***REPORTED CASES:*** Mishr v. Poland Bd. of Zoning Appeals, 76 Ohio St.3d 238, 667 N.E.2d 365 (1996). ***PRACTICE AREAS:*** Labor Relations (Management) Law; School Law; Corporate Law; General Business Law; Real Estate Law; Local Government Law. ***Email:*** troberts@roth-blair.com

STUART A. STRASFELD, born Bronx, New York, January 10, 1952; admitted to bar, 1977, Ohio. *Education:* Miami University (A.B., 1974); Case Western Reserve University (J.D., 1977). Omicron Delta Kappa. Member, National Moot Court Team, 1976-1977. Trustee, Forum Health (Member, Finance Committee, Insurance Committee). *Member:* Mahoning County and Ohio State Bar Associations. ***REPORTED CASES:*** Burton Nobil & Co. v. Acme Steak Co., 115 Ohio App.3d 209 (1996). ***PRACTICE AREAS:*** Commercial Law; Corporate Law; Mergers and Acquisitions; Real Estate Law. ***Email:*** sstrasfeld@roth-blair.com

THOMAS J. LODGE, born Salem, Ohio, April 8, 1952; admitted to bar, 1977, Ohio; 1978, U.S. District Court, Northern District of Ohio. *Education:* John Carroll University (B.A., in Economics, magna cum laude, 1974); Ohio Northern University (J.D., with distinction, 1977). Phi Kappa Phi; Alpha Sigma Nu; Phi Alpha Delta. Legal Counsel, National City Bank of Cleveland, 1977-1979. *Member:* Cleveland, Mahoning County and Ohio State Bar Associations. (Certified Specialist in Estate Planning, Trust and Probate Law, Ohio State Bar Association). ***PRACTICE AREAS:*** Estate Planning Law; Probate Law; Tax Law; Business Planning Law. ***Email:*** tlodge@roth-blair.com

DAVID S. BARBEE, born Decatur, Illinois, April 8, 1962; admitted to bar, 1986, Ohio; 1987, U.S. District Court, Northern District of Ohio. *Education:* The King's College (B.A., 1983); Ohio State University College of Law (J.D., 1986). *Member:* Mahoning County and Ohio State Bar Associations. ***REPORTED CASES:*** Mowery v. Shoaf, 148 Ohio App.3d 403 (2002); Bombardier Capital, Inc. v. WW Cycles, Inc, 155 Ohio App. 3d 484 (2003). ***PRACTICE AREAS:*** Commercial Litigation; Insurance Law. ***Email:*** dbarbee@roth-blair.com

CHRISTOPHER P. LACICH, born Sharon, Pennsylvania, January 26, 1963; admitted to bar, 1992, Pennsylvania and U.S. District Court, Western District of Pennsylvania; 1993, Ohio; 1995, U.S. District Court, Northern District of Ohio; 1996, U.S. District Court, Southern District of Ohio. *Education:* Youngstown State University (B.A., 1986); University of South Dakota (J.D., 1992). Author: "Family Law Tip: The Complete Lawyer," General Practice Section, American Bar Association, Fall, 1994, Volume 11, Number 4. ***REPORTED CASES:*** Commonwealth of Pa. vs. Cummings, Volume 27, No. 23, Page 128, Mercer Co. Law Journal, 1994; In re: Beagle, 200 B.R. 595 (Bkrptcy., N.D. Ohio, 1996); State ex rel. Sanor Sawmill, Inc. vs. Industrial Comm., 101 Ohio St. 3d. 199, (Ohio Supreme Court, 2004). ***PRACTICE AREAS:*** Domestic Relations; Employer Intentional Torts; Workers' Compensation; Civil Litigation. ***Email:*** clacich@roth-blair.com

SCOTT R. DeBONIS, born Youngstown, Ohio, May 24, 1969; admitted to bar, 1995, Ohio. *Education:* The Ohio State University (B.S., 1991); Ohio Northern University (J.D., with honors, 1995). *Member:* Mahoning County, Ohio State and American Bar Associations. ***PRACTICE AREAS:*** Estate Planning; Probate; Tax Law; Medicaid Planning; Employee Benefits; Business Planning. ***Email:*** sdebonis@roth-blair.com

JOSEPH C. BISHARA, born Youngstown, Ohio, April 1, 1971; admitted to bar, 1996, Ohio; 1997, U.S. District Court, Northern District of Ohio; 2001, Florida. *Education:* University of Notre Dame (B.A., with honors, Economics, 1993); University of Cincinnati (J.D., 1996). *Member:* Mahoning County (Ohio), Collier County (Florida), The Florida Bar, and Ohio State Bar Associations. ***REPORTED CASES:*** The Promotion Co., Inc./Special Events Div. v. Sweeney, 150 Ohio App.3d 471 (2002). ***PRACTICE AREAS:*** Corporate Law; Real Estate; Construction Law; Commercial Law. ***Email:*** jbishara@roth-blair.com

---

DAVID M. MOORE, born Salem, Ohio, June 20, 1966; admitted to bar, 1993, Ohio. *Education:* Kent State University (B.A., cum laude, 1989); University of Akron (J.D., 1992). Phi Alpha Delta (KSU). Member, Kent State Honors College, 1984-1989. Student Ambassador, Kent State, 1988-1989. Legal Communications Teaching Assistant, University of Akron, 1991-1992. *Member:* Mahoning County, Columbiana County and Ohio State Bar Associations; Ohio Association of Civil Trial Attorneys. ***PRACTICE AREAS:*** Civil Litigation; Insurance Defense Litigation; Personal Injury. ***Email:*** dmoore@roth-blair.com

JOHN NICHOLAS ZOMOIDA, JR., born Youngstown, Ohio, October 26, 1974; admitted to bar, 2000, Ohio. *Education:* Youngstown State University (B.A., 1997); Cleveland-Marshall College of Law (J.D., 2000). Recipient, William K. Gardner Award for Outstanding Student. Formerly with, Ashtabula County Prosecutor's Office. *Member:* Ashtabula County, Mahoning County and Ohio State Bar Associations. ***PRACTICE AREAS:*** Business Law; Real Estate; Creditors Rights. ***Email:*** jzomoida@roth-blair.com

(This Listing Continued)

OF COUNSEL

HERBERT H. PRIDHAM, born Youngstown, Ohio, March 4, 1929; admitted to bar, 1955, Ohio. *Education:* Youngstown State University (B.A., 1951); Case Western Reserve University (LL.B., 1955). Phi Alpha Delta. ***PRACTICE AREAS:*** Probate and Trust Law.

GLENN J. SCHWARTZ, (CO., L.P.A.), born Youngstown, Ohio, June 25, 1949; admitted to bar, 1974, Ohio. *Education:* Miami University (B.A., 1971); The Ohio State University (J.D., cum laude, 1974). ***PRACTICE AREAS:*** Real Estate; Construction Law; Civil Litigation; Probate; Estate Planning.

STEFANSKI & ASSOCIATES LLC

Established in 2001

5437 MAHONING AVENUE, SUITE 22
YOUNGSTOWN, OHIO 44515
Telephone: 330-792-6220
Fax: 330-792-6250
Email: kstefanski@stefanski-law.com
URL: http://www.stefanski-law.com

Cleveland, Ohio Office: 1144 Rockefeller Building. 613 West Superior Avenue. 44113. Telephone: 216-348-2800. Fax: 216-348-1557.

Contract and Business Law, Insurance, Labor and Employment, Workers' Compensation, Civil Litigation, Trials and Appeals.

FIRM PROFILE: Stefanski & Associates LLC is a corporate defense-oriented law firm with multiple offices in northeastern Ohio. Our attorneys have extensive litigation and administrative experience, and provide legal services to our corporate clients throughout the country, as well as abroad. Our firm practice consists of administrative law, contract and business law, insurance, labor and employment, workers' compensation, civil litigation, trials and appeals.

MEMBER

D. KIM STEFANSKI, born Youngstown, Ohio, January 9, 1954; admitted to bar, 1979, Ohio and U.S. District Court, Northern District of Ohio. *Education:* University of Cincinnati (B.A., 1976; J.D., 1979). Faculty Member and Instructor, OSHA Litigation and Workers Compensation, National Business Institute. Attorney Risk Manager, Labor Relations, General Motors Corporation Lordstown Complex, 1979-1991. Member, Ohio Manufacturers' Association, Workers' Compensation Committee. Associate Member, Self-Insurers' Group of Ohio. *Member:* Mahoning County, Ohio State (Member, Workers' Compensation Committee) and American (Member, Labor Section) Bar Associations. ***PRACTICE AREAS:*** Workers Compensation; Civil Litigation; Labor and Employment; Arbitration; Negotiations; Civil Rights; Intentional Torts; Toxic Torts. ***Email:*** kstefanski@stefanski-law.com

ASSOCIATES

ERIC J. OHANIAN, born Brooklyn, New York, April 10, 1964; admitted to bar, 1990, New York, 1994, Ohio. *Education:* St. John's University (B.A., 1986); University of Akron (J.D., 1989). *Member:* New York State, Ohio State and American Bar Associations. ***PRACTICE AREAS:*** Civil Litigation; Workers Compensation; Labor and Employment. ***Email:*** eohanian@stefanskilaw.com

R. MARK GOTTFRIED, born Cleveland, Ohio, November 14, 1960; admitted to bar, 1987, Ohio and the U.S. District Court, Northern District of Ohio. *Education:* Southern Methodist University (B.A., B.S., 1983); Case Western Reserve University (J.D., 1986). (Also at Cleveland Office). ***PRACTICE AREAS:*** Civil Litigation; Trial Practice; Appellate Practice; Insurance; Torts; Labor and Employment; Workers Compensation. ***Email:*** mgottfried@stefanski-law.com

JANICE T. O'HALLORAN, born Pittsburgh, Pennsylvania, October 6, 1950; admitted to bar, 1982, Ohio. *Education:* Baldwin-Wallace College (B.A., 1970); Kent State University (M.A., 1976); Akron University Law School (J.D., 1982). *Member:* Mahoning County, Ohio State and American Bar Associations. ***PRACTICE AREAS:*** Civil Litigation; Appellate Practice; Trial Practice; Workers Compensation; Labor and Employment. ***Email:*** johalloran@stefanski-law.com

REPRESENTATIVE CLIENTS: AIM Nationalease; Austintown Local School District; ARKII Manufacturing; AVI Food Systems; Cleveland Clinic Health Systems; Ford Motor Co.; Forum Health; Omni Manor Inc.; Parker Hannifin Corp.; Schweber Baking Co.; United States Can Co./Syro Steel/Trinity Industries; Ron Carrocce Trucking; Maverick Tube Corp.; N & M Star L.P.; Commercial Metal Forming; Manpower.

TIPPING CO., L.P.A.

A LEGAL PROFESSIONAL ASSOCIATION

YOUNGSTOWN, OHIO

(See Akron)

General Civil Trial and Appellate Practice, Negligence, Personal Injury, Business, Commercial, Corporate, Probate, Workers Compensation, Administrative, Insurance, Real Estate, Bankruptcy, Estate Planning, Labor/Employment, Zoning, Municipal Law and Social Security Disability Law.

DOUGLAS M. TOOT

YOUNGSTOWN, OHIO

(See Canfield)

Wills and Trusts, Estate Planning, Probate, Elder Law, Business Planning, Corporate and Business Law, Real Estate.

KEITH D. WEINER & ASSOCIATES CO., L.P.A.

YOUNGSTOWN, OHIO

(See Cleveland)

Collections, Bankruptcy, Foreclosures, Evictions, Replevins, Mechanic Liens, Commercial Litigation, Post Judgment Collections.

MARTIN F. WHITE CO., L.P.A.

YOUNGSTOWN, OHIO

(See Warren)

Litigation and Plaintiffs Practice. Wrongful Death, Medical Malpractice, Personal Injury.

WILLIAMS, SENNETT & SCULLY CO., L.P.A.

YOUNGSTOWN, OHIO

(See Twinsburg)

General Civil Trial and Appellate Practice in all Courts. Insurance, Casualty and Surety, Life, Accident and Health, Negligence Litigation, Medical-Legal, Products Liability, Labor and Employment Law, Commercial Litigation.

CALIG & HANDELMAN, LPA

ZANESVILLE, OHIO

(See Columbus)

Bankruptcy, Personal Injury, Probate, Real Estate, Social Security, Social Security Disability, Medical Malpractice, Wrongful Death, Civil Litigation, Domestic Relations Law.

COFFMAN LAW OFFICES

604 MAIN STREET
P.O. BOX 159
ZANESVILLE, OHIO 43702-0159
Telephone: 740-454-1010
Fax: 740-454-1181
Email: info@coffmanlaw.com
URL: http://www.coffmanlaw.com

Banking, Business, Business Formations, Estate Planning, Wills, Probate, Real Estate and Title Insurance Law.

WARD D. COFFMAN, III, born Zanesville, Ohio, January 12, 1953; admitted to bar, 1978, Ohio; 1979, U.S. District Court, Southern District of Ohio; 1990, U.S. Court of Appeals, Sixth Circuit and U.S. Supreme Court; 1993, Colorado. *Education:* University of Arizona; The Ohio State University; Bowling Green State University (B.A., cum laude, 1975); Ohio Northern University (J.D., 1978). Order of the Barristers. Member, National Moot Court Team. Adjunct Professor, Real Estate Law, Central Ohio Technical College, 1979-1980. Member, Board of Directors: First Federal Bancorp, 1992—; First Federal Savings Bank, 1989—. *Member:* Muskingum County (President, 1986-1987) and Ohio State Bar Associations. ***Email:*** info@coffmanlaw.com

REPRESENTATIVE CLIENTS: First Federal Bancorp; First Federal Savings Bank of Eastern Ohio; Mattingly Foods, Inc.; Zandex Health Care Co.; Willow Haven Nursing Home; Adams Lane Care Center; Cedar Hill Care Center; Shadyside Care Center; Northview Senior Living Center; Beckett House Nursing Home; Forest Hill Care Center; ALR Insurance Services Agency, Inc.; 5B's Embroidery; Hoffer Buick-Pontiac-GMC; Stewart-Glapat Corp.; Producers Service Corp.; Formation Cementing, Inc.; Wilson Bros. Molded Plastics.

CULTICE & BROWN

Established in 1928
121 NORTH FOURTH STREET
P.O. BOX 490
ZANESVILLE, OHIO 43702-0490
Telephone: 740-453-0888
Telecopier: 740-453-0277
Email: cultice_brown@rrohio.com
URL: http://www.culticebrown.com

Business, Business Formation, Partnerships, Limited Liability Companies, Banking, Bankruptcy, Creditors Rights, Health Care, Hospital, Elder Law, Estate Planning, Probate, Estate and Trust, Administration, Taxation, Employment and Labor, Real Estate, Title Insurance, Construction Law, Employee Benefits, Discrimination, Wrongful Termination, Natural Resources, Environmental, Oil & Gas, Matrimonial and Family Law, Divorce, Child Custody, Child Support, Personal Injury, Wrongful Death, Automobile Accidents, Insurance Defense and General Civil Litigation.

C. ALFRED ZINN (1903-1977)

R. DONALD CULTICE (1922-1998)

SUSAN CULTICE BROWN, born Zanesville, Ohio, November 30, 1953; admitted to bar, 1983, Ohio; U.S. Court of Appeals, Sixth Circuit; U.S. District Court, Northern and Southern Districts of Ohio. *Education:* Miami University (B.A., 1976); Ohio Northern University (J.D., 1983). Delta Theta Phi (President, 1982-1983). *Member:* Muskingum County, Ohio State and American Bar Associations. ***PRACTICE AREAS:*** Creditors Rights; Bankruptcy; Matrimonial Law; Family Law; Divorce; Child Custody; Child Support; Visitation Rights; General Practice.

(This Listing Continued)

PETER N. CULTICE, born Zanesville, Ohio, September 1, 1958; admitted to bar, 1983, Ohio; U.S. Supreme Court; U.S. Court of Appeals, Sixth Circuit; U.S. District Court, Northern and Southern Districts of Ohio. *Education:* Emory University (B.A., 1980); Ohio Northern University (J.D., 1983). *Member:* Muskingum County, Ohio State (Chairman, Health Care Law Committee, 1996-1998; Chairman, Litigation Section, Board of Governors, 1998-2000) and American Bar Associations. ***PRACTICE AREAS:*** Health Care; Labor and Employment; Civil Litigation; Business Litigation; Business Law; Personal Injury; Insurance Defense; Mediation.

JAMES P. BROWN, born Kenton, Ohio, May 24, 1958; admitted to bar, 1984, Ohio; 1986, U.S. Tax Court; U.S. District Court, Southern District of Ohio. *Education:* Ohio Northern University (B.A., 1980; J.D., 1983). Instructor, Real Estate Law, Muskingum Area Technical College, 1989-1990. Title Insurance Agent. *Member:* Columbus, Muskingum County, Ohio State (Member, Sections on: Probate; Trust Law; Real Property) and American (Member, Sections on: Real Property; Probate; Trust Law; Business Law) Bar Associations. ***PRACTICE AREAS:*** Business; Real Estate; Estate Planning; Trust Planning; Estate Administration; Trust Administration; Probate; Banking; Taxation.

DENMEAD LAW OFFICE

ZANESVILLE, OHIO

(See Columbus)

Civil Trial and Appellate Practice and Personal Injury, Traumatic Brain Injury (TBI), Professional Negligence and Complex Litigation including Class Actions, Patents, Civil Rights, Civil Litigation, RICO, Employment and Political Subdivision Liability issues.

GOTTLIEB, JOHNSTON, BEAM & DAL PONTE, P.L.L.

Established in 1962
320 MAIN STREET
P.O. BOX 190
ZANESVILLE, OHIO 43702-0190
Telephone: 740-452-7555
Fax: 740-452-2257
Email: gjbd@zanesvillelaw.com
URL: http://www.zanesvillelaw.com

General Civil and Criminal Trial and Appellate Practice. Corporate, Taxation, Real Estate, Personal Injury, Family, Estate Planning, Probate, Insurance, Products Liability, Hospital and Bankruptcy Law.

ROSS L. JOHNSTON (Retired)

MEMBERS OF FIRM

J. ROBERT BEAM, born Morrow County, Ohio, April 13, 1936; admitted to bar, 1960, Ohio; 1962, U.S. District Court, Northern and Southern Districts of Ohio. *Education:* Ohio Northern University (B.A., with distinction, 1958; J.D., with high distinction, 1960). *Member:* Muskingum County (President, 1978) and Ohio State Bar Associations. ***PRACTICE AREAS:*** Business Law; Probate Law; Estate Planning Law. ***Email:*** beam.bob@zanesvillelaw.com

DON A. DAL PONTE, born Chicago, Illinois, August 26, 1947; admitted to bar, 1973, Ohio; 1975, U.S. District Court, Southern and Northern Districts of Ohio. *Education:* Xavier University (B.S., 1969); University of Notre Dame (J.D., 1972). Acting Judge, Zanesville Municipal Court. *Member:* Muskingum County (President, 1985) and Ohio State (Member, Family Law Committee, 1980-1986; Dispute Resolution Committee, 2001—) Bar Associations; Ohio Academy of Trial Lawyers; Ohio Society of Hospital Attorneys. ***PRACTICE AREAS:*** General Practice; Civil Litigation; Personal Injury Litigation; Business Law; Family Law; Estates; Hospital Law. ***Email:*** dalponte.don@zanesvillelaw.com

MILES D. FRIES, born Brooklyn, New York, July 24, 1953; admitted to bar, 1978, Ohio; 1979, U.S. District Court, Southern District of Ohio; 1983, U.S. District Court, Northern District of Ohio. *Education:* Brooklyn College of the City University of New York (B.A., 1975); Ohio Northern University (J.D., 1978). *Member:* Muskingum County and Ohio State Bar Associations; The Association of Trial Lawyers of America; Ohio Academy of Trial Lawyers. ***PRACTICE AREAS:*** Personal Injury Law; Insurance Defense Law; Civil Litigation; Family Law; General Practice. ***Email:*** fries.miles@zanesvillelaw.com

JAMES R. KRISCHAK, born Columbus, Ohio, September 11, 1951; admitted to bar, 1977, Ohio; 1979, U.S. District Court, Southern District of Ohio. *Education:* Oberlin College; The Ohio State University (B.Sc., 1972); Capital University (J.D., 1977). Assistant Prosecuting Attorney, 1978-1981. Title Agent for Lawyer's Title and Stewart Title. *Member:* Muskingum County (President, 2001) and Ohio State Bar Associations; Ohio Association of Criminal Defense Lawyers; Ohio Land Title Association. ***PRACTICE AREAS:*** Criminal Law; Family Law; Real Estate Law. ***Email:*** krischak.James@zanesvillelaw.com

JEFF ROBERT BEAM, born Findlay, Ohio, June 21, 1957; admitted to bar, 1982, Ohio and U.S. District Court, Northern and Southern Districts of Ohio. *Education:* Ohio Northern University (B.A., with distinction, 1979; J.D., 1982). Delta Sigma Phi; Phi Alpha Theta; Phi Alpha Kappa. *Member:* Muskingum County and Ohio State Bar Associations. ***PRACTICE AREAS:*** Creditors Rights in Bankruptcy; Real Estate; Probate; Business Law; Collections. ***Email:*** beam.jeff@zanesvillelaw.com

DONALD A. WIETMARSCHEN, born Cincinnati, Ohio, September 7, 1954; admitted to bar, 1981, Ohio and U.S. District Court, Southern District of Ohio; 1982, U.S. Tax Court. *Education:* Ohio Dominican College (B.A., 1977); Ohio Northern University (J.D., 1981); Capital University (LL.M. in Taxation, 1991). Delta Theta Phi. Author: "Planning for the Professional Athlete: Deferred Compensation Arrangements & Loans in Lieu of Compensation," 8 Ohio N.L. Review 499, 1981. *Member:* Muskingum County (President,

(This Listing Continued)

GOTTLIEB, JOHNSTON, BEAM & DAL PONTE, P.L.L., Zanesville—Continued

1996) and Ohio State Bar Associations. ***PRACTICE AREAS:*** Taxation Law; Estate Planning Law; Corporate Law; Probate Law. ***Email:*** wietmarschen.don@zanesvillelaw.com

PHILIP S. PHILLIPS, born Kenton, Ohio, September 27, 1948; admitted to bar, 1975, Ohio; 1978, U.S. District Court, Southern District of Ohio; 1990, U.S. Court of Appeals, Sixth Circuit. *Education:* Milligan College (A.B, 1970); The Ohio State University (J.D., cum laude, 1975). City Law Director, Zanesville, Ohio, 1984-1993. *Member:* Muskingum County (President, 1989) and Ohio State Bar Associations. ***PRACTICE AREAS:*** General Practice; Probate Law; Business Law. ***Email:*** phillips.phil@zanesvillelaw.com

COLE J. GERSTNER, born Lima, Ohio, February 24, 1957; admitted to bar, 1982, Ohio; 1989, Colorado; U.S. District Court, Southern District of Ohio; U.S. Court of Military Appeals. *Education:* Ohio Northern University (B.A., with high distinction, 1979); University of Toledo (J.D., 1982). Phi Alpha Theta; Omicron Delta Kappa. Law Clerk, Hon. Ralph Cole, 3rd District Court of Appeals, 1982-1983. *Member:* Muskingum County and Ohio State Bar Associations. [Captain, Judge Advocate, U.S. Air Force, 1983-1989]. ***PRACTICE AREAS:*** General Practice; Criminal Law; Family Law; Civil Litigation. ***Email:*** gerstner.cole@zanesvillelaw.com

MARK E. KAIDO, born Zanesville, Ohio, January 4, 1961; admitted to bar, 1991, Ohio. *Education:* Marietta College; Miami University (B.A., 1983); Capital University (J.D., 1990). *Member:* Muskingum County, Ohio State and American Bar Associations; Ohio Academy of Trial Lawyers. ***PRACTICE AREAS:*** General Practice; Criminal Law; Family Law. ***Email:*** kaido.mark@zanesvillelaw.com

OF COUNSEL

WAYNE W. PHILLIPS, II, born Norwalk, Ohio, September 14, 1945; admitted to bar, 1972, Ohio and U.S. District Court, Northern District of Ohio; 1973, Indiana and U.S. District Court, Southern District of Indiana; 1974, U.S. Tax Court. *Education:* Ohio Northern University (B.A., 1967; J.D., 1972). Delta Theta Phi (Clerk of Rolls, 1968-1969). Certified Public Accountant, Ohio, 1974. Personal Financial Specialist, 1989. *Member:* Muskingum County (President, 1998), Ohio State and Indiana State Bar Associations; Ohio Society of Certified Public Accountants; American Institute of Certified Public Accountants. ***PRACTICE AREAS:*** Corporate Law; Financial and Estate Planning; Retirement Plans.

ASSOCIATES

SUSAN J. MONTGOMERY McDONALD, born Zanesville, Ohio, November 17, 1973; admitted to bar, 2002, Ohio; 2003, U.S. District Court, Southern District of Ohio; 2004, U.S. District Court, Northern District of Ohio. *Education:* Muskingum College (B.A., 1996); Capital University, School of Law (J.D., 2002). ***PRACTICE AREAS:*** General Practice; Business; Estate Planning; Criminal; Family Law; Bankruptcy. ***Email:*** mcdonald.susan@zanesvillelaw.com

AARON B. PHILLIPS, born Columbus, Ohio, August 14,1975; admitted to bar, 2000, Ohio. *Education:* Messiah College (B.S.B.A., 1997); Ohio Northern University (J.D., 2000). *Member:* Muskingum County and Ohio State Bar Associations. ***PRACTICE AREAS:*** General Practice; Business; Estates. ***Email:*** phillips.aaron@zanesvillelaw.com

KINCAID, TAYLOR & GEYER

Established in 1895

50 NORTH FOURTH STREET
P.O. BOX 1030
ZANESVILLE, OHIO 43702-1030
Telephone: 740-454-2591
Telecopier: 740-454-6975
Email: ktglaw@kincaidlaw.com
URL: http://www.kincaidlaw.com

Business, Banks and Banking, Health Care, Estate Planning, Estate Administration, Real Estate, Title Insurance, Environmental, Oil and Gas, Civil Litigation, Domestic Relations, Family Law, Construction, General Civil and Criminal Trial and Appellate Practice.

J. DONALD KINCAID (1908-2001)

MEMBERS OF FIRM

R. WILLIAM GEYER, born Norwich, Ohio, April 12, 1931; admitted to bar, 1955, Ohio; U.S. District Court, Southern District of Ohio. *Education:* The Ohio State University; Muskingum College (A.B., 1952); Ohio Northern University (J.D., with distinction, 1955). Delta Theta Phi. County Court Judge, 1958-1964. *Member:* Muskingum County (President, 1962), Ohio State and American Bar Associations. ***PRACTICE AREAS:*** Business Law; Real Estate; Title Insurance; Estate Planning and Administration. ***Email:*** rwg@kincaidlaw.com

WILLIAM J. TAYLOR, born Springfield, Ohio, December 24, 1947; admitted to bar, 1973, Ohio; 1990, Montana; U.S. Supreme Court; U.S. Court of Military Appeals; U.S. Court of Appeals, Sixth Circuit; U.S. District Court, Southern and Northern Districts of Ohio, U.S. Tax Court. *Education:* The Ohio State University (B.A., 1970; J.D., 1973). Title Insurance Agent. Public Member: Ohio Oil and Gas Commission (Chairman, since 1993). *Member:* Muskingum County (President, 1988) and Ohio State (Chairman, Natural Resources Committee, 1994-1995) Bar Associations; State Bar of Montana. [Capt., JAGC, U.S. Army, 1973-1977]. ***PRACTICE AREAS:*** Business; Banks; Hospitals; Environmental Law; Oil and Gas Law; Complex and Multi-District Litigation. ***Email:*** wjt@kincaidlaw.com

SCOTT D. EICKELBERGER, born Garden Grove, California, March 13, 1966; admitted to bar, 1991, Ohio and U.S. District Court, Northern and Southern Districts of Ohio. *Education:* Miami University (B.A., 1988); University of Dayton (J.D., 1991). Delta Theta Phi. Solicitor, Village of New Concord, 1992—. *Member:* Columbus (Member, Construction Law Committee), Muskingum County, Perry County, Licking County (Member, Litigation Section), Ohio State (Member, Board of Governors, Litigation Section) and American (Forum on the Construction Industry) Bar Associations; The Association of Trial Lawyers of America. ***PRACTICE AREAS:*** Construction; Civil Litigation; Real Estate; Insurance Defense; Estate Planning; Personal Injury; Family Law. ***Email:*** scotte@kincaidlaw.com

DAVID J. TARBERT, born Zanesville, Ohio, May 7, 1968; admitted to bar, 1993, Ohio; 1994, U.S. District Court, Southern District of Ohio. *Education:* Muskingum College (B.S., summa cum laude, 1990); The Ohio State University (J.D., 1993). *Member:* Muskingum County, Ohio State and American (Member, Litigation Section) Bar Associations. ***PRACTICE AREAS:*** Personal Injury; Criminal Law; Real Estate; Title; Business; Estate Planning. ***Email:*** dtarbert@kincaidlaw.com

ASSOCIATE

GERALD J. TIBERIO, JR., born Zanesville, Ohio, November 22, 1978; admitted to bar, 2004, Ohio. *Education:* University of Dayton (B.S., 2001); University of Akron (J.D., 2004). *Member:* Muskingum County and Ohio State (Member, Sections on: Estate Planning; Trust and Probate Law) Bar Associations. ***PRACTICE AREAS:*** Real Estate; Title Insurance; Estate Planning; Business Law; Criminal Law. ***Email:*** gtiberio@kincaidlaw.com

COUNSEL FOR: All Vinyl Improvement Products; A.E.P. (American Electric Power Company); American Buildings Company; CGas, Inc.; Century National Bank; Debolt Machinery Co., Inc.; Genesis Healthcare System; Guernsey-Muskingum Electric Cooperative; Halliburton Services; Headley Construction Company; J.L. Jeffries Electric, Inc.; M.L. Transportation, Inc.; McDonalds of Zanesville; Messerschmidt Construction; Mock Woodworking Company; Muskingum College; Muskingum County Convention Facilities Authority; Zanesville-Muskingum County Port Authority; Transportation Industrial Development, Offinger Management; The Oxford Oil Company; The Times Recorder; Unizan Financial Services Group; Village of New Concord; Woodsfield Savings Bank; Zemba Bros., Ltd.

MICHELI, BALDWIN, NORTHRUP, LLP

Established in 1988

3808 JAMES COURT, SUITE 2
P.O. BOX 788
ZANESVILLE, OHIO 43702-0788
Telephone: 740-454-2545
Fax: 740-454-6372
URL: http://www.zanesvilleattorneys.com
URL: http://www.lawyers.com/mb&nc

Civil Trial Practice in State and Federal Courts. Insurance Defense, Medical Malpractice, Family and Domestic Relations, Probate and Estate Planning, Railroad, Business Law, Oil and Gas, Corporation and Commercial Law. Appellate Practice. Accident Claims, Workers Compensation, Contracts, Real Estate, Title Insurance.

FRANK J. MICHELI, born Zanesville, Ohio, March 23, 1929; admitted to bar, 1953, Ohio and U.S. District Court, Southern District of Ohio. *Education:* John Carroll University; Xavier University; Ohio Northern University (J.D., 1953). Director, Public Service, City of Zanesville, 1954. *Member:* Muskingum County, Ohio State and American Bar Associations; International Association of Defense Counsel; Ohio Association of Civil Trial Attorneys; American Board of Trial Advocates. ***PRACTICE AREAS:*** Civil Litigation; Personal Injury Law; Medical Malpractice Law.

MICHAEL J. MICHELI, born Zanesville, Ohio, May 2, 1955; admitted to bar, 1980, Ohio and U.S. District Court, Southern District of Ohio. *Education:* Bowling Green State University (B.A., 1977); Ohio Northern University (J.D., 1980). *Member:* Muskingum County, Ohio State and American Bar Associations; Ohio Association of Civil Trial Attorneys; American Society of Law & Medicine; International Association of Defense Counsel. ***PRACTICE AREAS:*** Civil Litigation; Personal Injury Law; Medical Malpractice Law. ***Email:*** mmicheli@rrohio.com

JAMES C. MICHELI (1956-1992)

STEVEN R. BALDWIN, born Zanesville, Ohio, September 14, 1958; admitted to bar, 1983, Ohio; 1984, U.S. District Court, Southern District of Ohio; 1986, U.S. Court of Appeals, Sixth Circuit; 1987, U.S. Supreme Court. *Education:* Bowling Green State University (B.S., 1980); University of Dayton (J.D., 1983). Phi Delta Phi. Solicitor, Village of Philo, 1986-1988; Village of Dresden, 1991—. *Member:* Muskingum County, Ohio State and American Bar Associations. ***PRACTICE AREAS:*** Personal Injury Law; Estate Planning Law; Corporate Law; Business Law; Health Care Administration. ***Email:*** sbaldwin@rrohio.com

MICHAEL A. NORTHRUP, born 1954; admitted to bar, 1979, Ohio. *Education:* The Ohio State University (B.A., 1976); Capital University (J.D., 1979). ***Email:*** mnorthrup@rrohio.com

---

JEREMY M. McLENDON, born Zanesville, Ohio, May 9, 1977; admitted to bar, 2002, Ohio. *Education:* Ohio Northern University (B.A., 1999; J.D., 2002). The Order of Barristers. Member, Moot Court. *Member:* Muskingum County and Ohio State Bar Associations. ***PRACTICE AREAS:*** Criminal Defense; Traffic Violations; Personal Injury; Real Estate; Title Insurance. ***Email:*** jmclendon@rrohio.com

DAVID E. MORTIMER, born Zanesville, Ohio, March 2, 1976; admitted to bar, 2002, Ohio. *Education:* Ohio Northern University (B.A., 1998; J.D., 2002). The Order of Barristers; Moot Court. *Member:* Muskingum County and Ohio State Bar Associations. ***PRACTICE AREAS:*** Criminal Defense; Traffic Violations; Domestic Relations; Landlord and Tenant Law; Bankruptcy; Personal Injury; Civil Litigation; Wrongful Death. ***Email:*** dmortimer@rrohio.com

(This Listing Continued)

OF COUNSEL

THOMAS R. BOPELEY, born 1933; admitted to bar, 1958, Ohio. *Education:* Colgate University (A.B.); The Ohio State University (LL.B.). ***PRACTICE AREAS:*** Litigation; Insurance Law; Personal Injury Law.

REPRESENTATIVE CLIENTS: CNA Insurance Co.; Medical Protective Co.; Nationwide Insurance Cos.; Continental Insurance Cos.; Motorists Mutual Insurance Co.; Kemper Group; Westfield Insurance Co.; State Auto Insurance Co.; Luburgh Construction Co.; Radiology Associates, Inc.; Blackwood Enterprises, Inc.; Baldwin Construction Co.; Royal Cleaning Co.; Ohio Oil Gathering Corp.; M & B Industrial Gas Development; Eastern Natural Gas Co.; Pike Natural Gas Co.; W. Va. Oil Gathin Corp.; Spillman Trucking, Inc.; Robert M. Neff & Sons, Inc.; Neff Machinery & Supply Co.; Village of Dresden; Texas Eastern Transmission Company; Texas Eastern Pipeline Products Company; Admiral Insurance Company; Wausau Insurance Company; Professionals Insurance Company; CNA Global Runoff Managers; Cincinnati Insurance Companies; Muskingum Emergency Physicians, Inc.; Cordial Management Co.; Genesis Healthcare Systems; Rankin & Rankin Insurance, Inc.; T & B Corners Inc.; Glen James & Sons, Inc.; Cardiology Associates of S.E.O., Inc.; Concord Mortgage Co.
REFERENCES: Bank One Cambridge, N.A., Zanesville, Ohio; Genesis Health Care Systems, Inc.

THE PLYMALE PARTNERSHIP LLP

ZANESVILLE, OHIO

(See Columbus)

Personal Injury, Products Liability, Wrongful Death, Medical Malpractice, Professional Negligence, Traumatic Brain Injury, Automobile Accidents, Nursing Home Torts, Civil Litigation.

STANDLEY LAW GROUP LLP

ZANESVILLE, OHIO

(See Dublin)

Domestic and Foreign Intellectual Property Law, including Patent, Trademark, Copyright, Unfair Competition and Trade Secret Law and related Litigation, Licensing, International Trade Matters, related Antitrust, Computer and other Technology Law.

TWYFORD & DONAHEY, P.L.L.

ZANESVILLE, OHIO

(See Columbus)

Personal Injury Litigation, Wrongful Death, Medical Malpractice, Products Liability, Automobile Accidents, Trucking Accidents, Head and Spinal Injuries, Motorcycle Accidents and Injuries, Uninsured Motorists, Insurance Law, Airplane Crash Litigation, Railroad Accidents, Slip and Fall, Dog Bites, Work Related Injuries, Birth Injuries, Nursing Home Abuse and Neglect.

ATKINS & MARKOFF

ADA, OKLAHOMA

(See Oklahoma City)

Personal Injury, Automobile Accidents, Wrongful Death, Trucking Accidents, Slip and Fall, Nursing Home Abuse, Head and Spinal Injuries, Dog Bites, Sexual Abuse, Criminal Law, Drug Crimes, DUI/DWI, Juvenile Crimes, General Practice, Family , Divorce, Adoptions, Child Custody, Child Support, Domestic Violence, Visitation Rights, Elder Law, Legal Malpractice, Medical Malpractice, Social Security, Social Security Disability, Taxation, IRS Audits, Property Tax Appeals, Tax Planning, Toxic Torts, Trust and Estate, Wills and Probate.

BOB E. BENNETT

Established in 1958

402 AMERICAN BUILDING
P.O. BOX 1631
ADA, OKLAHOMA 74821-1631
Telephone: 580-332-5311
Fax: 580-332-5351

General Civil Practice in all State and Federal Courts. Estate Planning, Trusts, Estates, Wills, Banking, Real Estates, Probate, Oil and Gas, Corporate, Health Law, Negligence, and Family Law.

BOB E. BENNETT, born Holdenville, Oklahoma, February 13, 1930; admitted to bar, 1958, Oklahoma. *Education:* East Central Oklahoma State University (B.S., 1955); University of Oklahoma (J.D., 1958). Delta Theta Phi. *Member:* Pontotoc County (President, 1960), Oklahoma (Member, Board of Governors, 1972-1975; Vice President, 1979-1980; Chair, 1977-1978, Continuing Legal Education Commission; Chair, Probate Committee, 1988-1989; Co-Chair, 1991-2003) and American Bar Associations; Oklahoma Health Lawyers Association; The American College of Trust and Estate Counsel. Fellow, American Bar Foundation (Chair, Oklahoma Fellows, 1984-1986); Oklahoma Bar Foundation; National Association of College and University Attorneys. [Veteran, Korean War]. ***PRACTICE AREAS:*** Real Estate; Health Law; Business and Corporate Law; Family Law; Civil Litigation; Wills; Trusts and Estates; Probate; Personal Injury.

REPRESENTATIVE CLIENTS: Valley View Regional Hospital; Valley View Management Group, Inc.; Kentucky Fried Chicken of Oklahoma (Ada, Pauls Valley, Locations); Allen Camper Manufacturing Co., Allen, OK.
REFERENCES: Vision Bank; Citizens Bank and Trust Co.; First United Bank & Trust Co., Ada, Okla.

BRALY & BRALY AND COYNE

A Partnership of Professional Corporations

Established in 1974

201 WEST 14TH STREET
P.O. BOX 2739
ADA, OKLAHOMA 74820
Telephone: 580-436-0871
Fax: 580-436-0889

General Civil Trial Practice in all State and Federal Courts. Personal Injury, Products Liability, Medical Malpractice, Plaintiff and Defense, Commercial, Banking, Oil and Gas, Securities, Water Rights Law, Commercial and Real Estate, Trusts and Estate Planning.

GEORGE W. BRALY, born Ada, Oklahoma, March 7, 1948; admitted to bar, 1974, Oklahoma; U.S. District Court, Eastern, Western and Northern Districts of Oklahoma; U.S. Court of Appeals, Tenth Circuit; U.S. Supreme Court. *Education:* Brown University (B.A., 1970); University of Oklahoma (J.D., 1974). Phi Delta Phi. *Member:* Oklahoma and American Bar Associations. ***PRACTICE AREAS:*** Civil Litigation; Complex Litigation; Medical Malpractice; Personal Injury; Products Liability; Aviation Accidents; Oil and Gas Law; Automobile Accidents and Injuries; Truck Accidents. ***Email:*** gwbraly@gami.com

DANIA DESCHAMPS-BRALY, born Key West, Florida, November 24, 1943; admitted to bar, 1979, Oklahoma; U.S. District Court, Western and Eastern Districts of Oklahoma; U.S. Court of Appeals, Tenth Circuit. *Education:* University of Miami (B.A., cum laude, 1976); University of Oklahoma (J.D., 1979). *Member:* Pontotoc County, Oklahoma and American Bar Associations.

H. BUCKMASTER COYNE, JR., born Danville, Virginia, October 29, 1945; admitted to bar, 1974, North Carolina; U.S. District Court, Eastern District of North Carolina; 1997, Oklahoma; U.S. District Court, Eastern, Western and Northern Districts of Oklahoma; U.S. Court of Appeals, Tenth Circuit. *Education:* Davidson College (B.A., 1971); University of North Carolina (J.D., 1974). *Member:* Carteret County, Pontotoc County, North Carolina, Oklahoma and American Bar Associations; North Carolina State Bar. [Lt. USAR, 1966-1969]. ***PRACTICE AREAS:*** Corporate Law; Condominium Law; Real Estate; Planning; Zoning Law; Commercial Law; Estate Planning; Administrative Law. ***Email:*** bcoyne@cableone.net

REFERENCES: First National Bank of Coalgate, Oklahoma; First National Bank, Ada, Oklahoma.

DEATON, DAVISON & KESSINGER

A PROFESSIONAL CORPORATION

Established in 1961

300 SOUTH RENNIE
P.O. BOX 1219
ADA, OKLAHOMA 74820
Telephone: 580-332-1752
Fax: 580-332-0827

General Civil Practice in all State and Federal Courts. Trials. Corporation, Insurance, Real Estate, Probate, Indian Affairs, Medical Legal, Oil and Gas Law and Domestic Relations.

(This Listing Continued)

AUSTIN R. DEATON, JR., born Ada, Oklahoma, March 3, 1926; admitted to bar, 1951, Oklahoma. *Education:* East Central State College; University of Oklahoma (LL.B., 1951). Phi Delta Phi. Member and Chairman, Oklahoma Judicial Nominating Commission, 1977-1983. *Member:* Pontotoc County, Oklahoma and American Bar Associations. Fellow, American College of Trial Lawyers. ***PRACTICE AREAS:*** Insurance Law; Probate; Medical-Legal Law; Oil and Gas Law. ***Email:*** austin@ddklaw.com

DENVER N. DAVISON, born Ada, Oklahoma, January 21, 1943; admitted to bar, 1968, Oklahoma. *Education:* Kemper Military School and College and University of Oklahoma (B.B.A., 1965); University of Oklahoma (J.D., 1968). Phi Delta Phi. Associate Bar Examiner, 1972-1996. Associate Editor, Oklahoma Bar Journal, 1985-1986. Member and Chairman, Oklahoma Judicial Nominating Commission, 1995-2001. *Member:* Pontotoc County, Oklahoma and American Bar Associations. [U.S. Army, Capt., 1965-1971]. ***PRACTICE AREAS:*** Commercial Law; Real Estate Law; Probate Law; Trusts and Estates. ***Email:*** denver@ddklaw.com

C. STEVEN KESSINGER, born Pauls Valley, Oklahoma, February 10, 1964; admitted to bar, 1989, Oklahoma. *Education:* East Central University (B.S., 1986); University of Oklahoma (J.D., 1989). *Member:* Pontotoc County (President, 1993-1994), Oklahoma and American Bar Associations; Oklahoma Board of Bar Examiners. ***PRACTICE AREAS:*** Criminal Law; Domestic Relations; Civil Trial Practice; Commercial Law; Probate Law. ***Email:*** steve@ddklaw.com

REPRESENTATIVE CLIENTS: Ada Shopping Center Inc.; First National Bank & Trust Company of Ada, Oklahoma; Arlington Center Ltd.
REFERENCE: First National Bank & Trust Company of Ada, Oklahoma.

KENNETH R. JOHNSON

GEORGE B. THOMPSON BUILDING
331 SOUTH RENNIE
P.O. BOX 1690
ADA, OKLAHOMA 74820
Telephone: 580-332-2558
Fax: 580-332-2777
URL: http://www.lawyers.com/kennethrjohnson

General Civil Practice in all State and Federal Courts. Corporation, Insurance, Probate, Commercial, Indian Affairs, Family, Real Estate and Oil and Gas Law.

KENNETH R. JOHNSON, born Lexington, Oklahoma, May 4, 1940; admitted to bar, 1965, Oklahoma. *Education:* University of Oklahoma (B.B.A., 1963; J.D., 1965). Phi Alpha Delta. President, Ada Cougar Booster Club, 1966-1967. Outstanding Young Attorney of Oklahoma Bar Association, 1969. *Member:* Pontotoc County (Secretary-Treasurer, 1966; Vice President, 1967; President, 1969) and Oklahoma (Associate Bar Examiner, 1967-1986) Bar Associations. ***PRACTICE AREAS:*** Corporate Law; Real Estate Law; Probate Law; Commercial Law; Family Law.

ASSOCIATE

KIRK E. JOHNSON, born Ada, Oklahoma, December 8, 1972; admitted to bar, 1998, Oklahoma. *Education:* University of Oklahoma (B.B.A., 1995; J.D., 1998). *Member:* Oklahoma Bar Association.

REPRESENTATIVE CLIENTS: Independent School District #19, Pontotoc County, Oklahoma; Town of Byng; Town of Roff; Town of Tupelo; Oklahoma; Ballard Nursing Centers; Chickasaw Nation; Pontotoc Area Vocational-Technical School District #14; Landmark Bank.
REFERENCE: First National Bank and Trust Company of Ada, Oklahoma.

WILLIAM WAYNE SPEED

314 SOUTH BROADWAY, SUITE 211
ADA, OKLAHOMA 74820
Telephone: 580-436-9090
Fax: 580-436-9066
Email: wspeed@cableone.net
URL: http://www.lawyers.com/speed

Mailing Address: P.O. Box 878, Ada, OK 74821

Insurance Defense, Personal Injury, Civil Litigation, Wills. Trusts and Estates, Family Law.

WILLIAM WAYNE SPEED, born Ada, Oklahoma, February 22, 1967; admitted to bar, 1992, Texas; 2001, Oklahoma; U.S. District Court, Northern, Southern, Eastern and Western Districts of Texas; U.S. District Court, Eastern and Western Districts of Oklahoma. *Education:* Oklahoma State University (B.S., 1988); Duke University (J.D., with honors, 1992). Recipient, Bronze Medal Award, Graduating Third in Accounting. Articles Co-Author: "Recent Developments in Property Insurance Law," Tort and Insurance Law Journal, Winter 2000; "Texas' License to Lie," International Association of Defense Counsel Newsletter, November 1995. Author and Presenter: "Payment Under Replacement Cost Insurance Policies," Property Insurance Law Committee, American Bar Association. Presenter: " Texas Change of Venue - Substance and Procedure," Vial, Hamilton, Knox & Knox Litigation Breakfast, May 1994. *Member:* Pontotoc County (Treasurer, 2002), Oklahoma and American (Member, Tort and Insurance Practice Section; Vice President, Property Insurance Law Committee, 1999) Bar Associations; State Bar of Texas.

REPRESENTATIVE CLIENTS: EMC Insurance Companies; Oklahoma Farm Bureau Mutual Insurance Company; Quad J Acoustic & Drywell, Inc.; Joe Brown Company.

TAYLOR AND MORRIS, P.C.

117 SOUTH BROADWAY
P.O. BOX 1737
ADA, OKLAHOMA 74821
Telephone: 580-332-7717
Fax: 580-332-7752
Email: tmlaw@cableone.net

Probate, Trusts and Estate Planning, Real Estate, Commercial, Corporate, Oil and Gas, Bankruptcy, Divorce, Workers' Compensation, Personal Injury and Civil Litigation in all State and Federal Courts.

GREGORY S. TAYLOR, born Oklahoma City, Oklahoma, July 24, 1948; admitted to bar, 1974, Oklahoma and U.S. District Court, Eastern and Western Districts of Oklahoma; U.S. Court of Appeals, Tenth Circuit. *Education:* Trinity University (B.A., 1970); St. Mary's University of San Antonio and University of Oklahoma (J.D., 1974). *Member:* Pontotoc County (President, 1980-1981), Oklahoma (Member, Sections on: Probate; Real Property; Chairman, Law Day Committee, 1985-1987) and American Bar Associations. Fellow, Oklahoma Bar Foundation. ***PRACTICE AREAS:*** Probate; Estate Planning; Real Estate; Oil & Gas; Commercial; Corporate; Health Law.

BRYAN W. MORRIS, born Henryetta, Oklahoma, November 16, 1965; admitted to bar, 1992, Oklahoma and U.S. District Court, Eastern and Western Districts of Oklahoma. *Education:* Oklahoma State University (B.A., Pol.Sc., 1988); University of Oklahoma (J.D., 1992). Phi Alpha Delta. *Member:* Carter County, Pontotoc County (Chairman, Law Day Committee, 2001; President, 2003); Oklahoma and American Bar Associations; American Trial Lawyers Association; Oklahoma Trial Lawyers Association. ***PRACTICE AREAS:*** Civil Litigation; Personal Injury; Family Law; Workers' Compensation; Bankruptcy; Debtor and Creditor; Criminal Law; Civil Practice. ***Email:*** morrisesq@cableone.net

REPRESENTATIVE CLIENTS: Shipes Shoes, Inc.; Service Automall, Inc.; Ada News; Buck Creek Homes, Inc.; Danielson Oil Company; Credit Bureau of Ada; Southern Oklahoma Urology, Inc.; Bolitho Media Services; Baxter & Associates Oil Operating Company; Chickasaw Housing Authority.
REFERENCES: First National Bank & Trust Co. of Ada; Citizens Bank of Ada; First United Bank & Trust of Ada, Oklahoma.

ATKINS & MARKOFF

ALTUS, OKLAHOMA

(See Oklahoma City)

Personal Injury, Automobile Accidents, Wrongful Death, Trucking Accidents, Slip and Fall, Nursing Home Abuse, Head and Spinal Injuries, Dog Bites, Sexual Abuse, Criminal Law, Drug Crimes, DUI/DWI, Juvenile Crimes, General Practice, Family , Divorce, Adoptions, Child Custody, Child Support, Domestic Violence, Visitation Rights, Elder Law, Legal Malpractice, Medical Malpractice, Social Security, Social Security Disability, Taxation, IRS Audits, Property Tax Appeals, Tax Planning, Toxic Torts, Trust and Estate, Wills and Probate.

MARK T. COKE

205 WEST CYPRESS
P.O. BOX 652
ALTUS, OKLAHOMA 73522
Telephone: 580-482-5474
Fax: 580-482-8405
Email: mtcoke@swbell.net

General Civil Practice in all State and Federal Courts. Corporation, Insurance, Probate, Estate Planning, Oil and Gas, Real Property and Municipal Law.

ROBERT B. HARBISON (1906-1983)

MARK T. COKE, born Quanah, Texas, March 23, 1950; admitted to bar, 1975, Oklahoma. *Education:* Southwestern State University (B.A., 1972); University of Oklahoma (J.D., 1975). Phi Delta Phi. *Member:* Jackson County, Oklahoma and American Bar Associations. ***PRACTICE AREAS:*** Probate; Trusts; Real Property Titles; Corporation; Banking. ***Email:*** mtcoke@swbell.net

COUNSEL FOR: NBanC of Tulsa, Altus, Kingfisher, Enid; Farm Credit Bank of Wichita; Farm Credit Services of Soutwest Oklahoma; Bädger Oil Company; American Gypsum Company.

HORTON & ASSOCIATES

Established in 1977

216 WEST COMMERCE STREET
ALTUS, OKLAHOMA 73521
Telephone: 580-482-3355
Facsimile: 580-482-0363
URL: http:www.//chorton@pacer.com
Email: chorton@pacer.com
URL: http://www.lawyers.com/altuslaw

Magnum Office: 122 North Oklahoma Ave., 73554. Telephone: 580-782-3348. Fax: 580-782-2836.

General Civil Practice, Trusts, Probate, Estate Planning, Personal Injury, Real Estate, Business, Divorce, Interstate Custody, Military, Municipal, Public Finance and Aviation Law.

CHARLES P. HORTON, born Oklahoma City, Oklahoma, February 8, 1949; admitted to bar, 1977, Oklahoma. *Education:* University of Oklahoma (B.B.A., 1972); Oklahoma City University (J.D., 1976). *Member:* Greer, Jackson County and Oklahoma Bar Associations. ***PRACTICE AREAS:*** Personal Injury; Family Law; Probate; Estate Planning; Real

(This Listing Continued)

Estate; Corporate Law; Military Law; Municipal Law; Aviation Law. ***Email:*** chorton@pacer.com

ATKINS & MARKOFF

ANADARKO, OKLAHOMA

(See Oklahoma City)

Personal Injury, Automobile Accidents, Wrongful Death, Trucking Accidents, Slip and Fall, Nursing Home Abuse, Head and Spinal Injuries, Dog Bites, Sexual Abuse, Criminal Law, Drug Crimes, DUI/DWI, Juvenile Crimes, General Practice, Family , Divorce, Adoptions, Child Custody, Child Support, Domestic Violence, Visitation Rights, Elder Law, Legal Malpractice, Medical Malpractice, Social Security, Social Security Disability, Taxation, IRS Audits, Property Tax Appeals, Tax Planning, Toxic Torts, Trust and Estate, Wills and Probate.

BUZBEE & UPCHURCH

Established in 1924

203 WEST BROADWAY
P.O. BOX 765
ANADARKO, OKLAHOMA 73005
Telephone: 405-247-2568
Fax: 405-247-2569

Hinton, Oklahoma Office: Professional Building, Suite A, 116 West Main, Hinton, Oklahoma 73047. Telephone: 405-542-3990.

General Civil and Criminal Practice. Probate, Trusts. Real Estate, Oil and Gas, Insurance, Personal Injury, Negligence, Corporation Law and Trials.

MEMBERS OF FIRM

JOHN P. BUZBEE, born Allen, Oklahoma, September 17, 1936; admitted to bar, 1960, Oklahoma. *Education:* Oklahoma Baptist University (B.A., 1958); University of Oklahoma (LL.B., 1960). Phi Alpha Delta. Assistant District Attorney, 1967-1970. Attorney, Field Solicitor's Office, U.S. Department of Interior, 1961-1963. Associate District Judge, 1971-1973. *Member:* Caddo County (President, 1973-1974), Oklahoma and American Bar Associations. ***PRACTICE AREAS:*** Trusts; Probate Law; Real Property Law; Banking Law.

VIRGIL L. UPCHURCH, born Anadarko, Oklahoma, February 14, 1930; admitted to bar, 1959, Oklahoma and U.S. District Court, Western District of Oklahoma. *Education:* University of Oklahoma (B.A., 1956; LL.B., 1959). Phi Delta Phi; Order of the Coif. Special Lecturer in Law, University of Oklahoma, 1973. County Attorney, Caddo County, Oklahoma, 1961-1965. *Member:* Caddo County (President, 1966-1968) and Oklahoma (Associate Bar Examiner, 1970-1972; Member, Trial Authority, 1977) Bar Associations; Oklahoma Criminal Defense Attorneys Association. ***PRACTICE AREAS:*** Criminal Law; Personal Injury; Probate; Trusts and Estates; Oil and Gas Law.

REPRESENTATIVE CLIENTS: Anadarko Bank & Trust Co.; Cyril State Bank, Cyril, Oklahoma; Washita Valley Bank, Fort Cobb; Shamorock Bank, Apache, Oklahoma; Town of Fort Cobb, Oklahoma; Board of Education of Binger, Oklahoma; Anadarko Publishing Co.; Caddo-Kiowa Vo Tech School District; First National Bank & Trust Co. of Weatherford, Hinton Branch.
APPROVED TITLE ATTORNEYS: First American Title Insurance Co.; Stewart Abstract & Title Co. of Oklahoma; Southwest Title & Trust Co., all of Oklahoma City; Chicago Title & Trust, Chicago, Ill.; Lacey-Pioneer Abstract Co. and Caddo County Abstract Co., Anadarko; Farm Credit Bank of Wichita, Anadarko; Legacy Bank, Hinton; Farm Service Agency, U.S. Dept. of Agriculture.

JOHNSTON & ASSOCIATES

ANADARKO, OKLAHOMA

(See Chickasha)

General Practice, Environmental Law. including Land Use, Landowners Rights Wills and Probate.

PAIN AND GARLAND

111 S.W. SECOND STREET
P.O. BOX 158
ANADARKO, OKLAHOMA 73005
Telephone: 405-247-3365
Fax: 405-247-7177
Email: jgarland@caddoelectric.net

General Civil Practice, Real Estate, Probate, Trusts, Estate Planning and Trials.

FIRM PROFILE: The firm was originally founded by Oris L. Barney in the early 1930's. Leslie Pain joined the firm as a partner in the mid 1950's. Pain and Garland continue to serve clients throughout western Oklahoma that were represented for years by Oris L. Barney.

MEMBERS OF FIRM

LESLIE PAIN (1913-2005)

JOHN W. GARLAND, born Pauls Valley, Oklahoma, August 19, 1942; admitted to bar, 1966, Oklahoma and U.S. Supreme Court. *Education:* East Central State College and University of Oklahoma (B.B.A., 1964); University of Oklahoma (LL.B., 1966). Delta Theta Phi. *Member:* Caddo County, Oklahoma and American Bar Associations. ***PRACTICE AREAS:*** Civil; Real Estate; Probate; Trials.

ASSOCIATE

RICHARD A. WILLIAMS, born Oklahoma City, Oklahoma, October 13, 1946; admitted to bar, 1976, Oklahoma. *Education:* Southwestern Oklahoma State University (B.S.,

(This Listing Continued)

1969); Oklahoma City University (J.D., 1976). Phi Delta Phi (Learned Hand Chapter, 1974-1976). *Member:* Comanche County, Grady County and Caddo County (President, 1987; Law Day Chairman, 1989) Bar Associations. ***PRACTICE AREAS:*** Civil; Real Estate; Probate; Trials.

REPRESENTATIVE CLIENTS: First State Bank, Anadarko, Okla.; Caddo Electric Cooperative, Binger, Okla.; Western Farmers Electric Cooperative, Anadarko, Okla. Town of Cement, Okla.; Town of Binger; Bank of Verden, Verden, OK; Federal Land Bank Association, Anadarko, Okla.; Arkansas-Louisiana Gas Co.; Anadarko School District; City of Anadarko, Okla.; Fort Cobb Master Conservancy District.

LAW OFFICES OF SHANNON REASOR

ANTLERS, OKLAHOMA

(See Atoka)

General Practice, Real Estate, Probate, Estate Planning, Civil Litigation.

STAMPER & PERRIN, PLLC

112 NORTH HIGH STREET
P.O. BOX 100
ANTLERS, OKLAHOMA 74523
Telephone: 580-298-3153; 580-298-3332
Fax: 580-298-3263
Email: jackieperrin@sbcglobal.net
URL: http://www.stamperperrin.com

General and Trial Practice, Personal Injury. Commercial. Probate and Real Estate Law. Banking. Family Law. Health Law, Labor, Employment and Civil Rights Law.

FIRM PROFILE: Joe Stamper began his law practice in Antlers in 1946 and he continued in partnership with various individuals until his death in 2004. Joe Stamper's dedication to the law continues through Stamper & Perrin, providing Southeastern Oklahoma effective legal representation according to specific client needs.

MEMBERS OF FIRM

JOE STAMPER (1914-2004)

JACKIE JO PERRIN, born Tulsa, Oklahoma, April 2, 1964; admitted to bar, 2002, Oklahoma. *Education:* Southeastern Oklahoma State University (B.S., 1989; M.S., 1994); Oklahoma City University School of Law (J.D., 2002). Phi Alpha Delta. *Member:* Pushmataha County, Southeastern Oklahoma and American Bar Associations. Fellow, Oklahoma Bar Foundation. ***PRACTICE AREAS:*** Trial Practice; Probate; General Practice; Real Estate; Family Law. ***Email:*** jackiejoperrin@sbcglobal.net

REPRESENTATIVE CLIENTS: Prudential Insurance Co.; Town of Antlers; U.S.F. & G. Co.; Travelers Insurance Co.; Nationwide Insurance Co.; Kiamichi Railroad Co.; Standard Title Insurance Co.; Farm Credit Services; D. Wayne Lucas; McAlester (Okla) Regional Hospital; Julian Lumber Co.; Pushmataha Hospital; Rail Operators, Inc.; Georgia-Pacific Company; Atlantic-Richfield, Los Angeles, CA; Durant Bank & Trust, Durant, OK; Clarendon Insurance Co.; Deep South Insurance Co.

ATKINS & MARKOFF

ARDMORE, OKLAHOMA

(See Oklahoma City)

Personal Injury, Automobile Accidents, Wrongful Death, Trucking Accidents, Slip and Fall, Nursing Home Abuse, Head and Spinal Injuries, Dog Bites, Sexual Abuse, Criminal Law, Drug Crimes, DUI/DWI, Juvenile Crimes, General Practice, Family , Divorce, Adoptions, Child Custody, Child Support, Domestic Violence, Visitation Rights, Elder Law, Legal Malpractice, Medical Malpractice, Social Security, Social Security Disability, Taxation, IRS Audits, Property Tax Appeals, Tax Planning, Toxic Torts, Trust and Estate, Wills and Probate.

R. BRAD BOLLES, P.C.

107 WEST MAIN
ARDMORE, OKLAHOMA 73401
Telephone: 580-226-5700
Fax: 580-226-5774
Email: rbb_atty@sbcglobal.net
URL: http://www.lawyers.com/rbradbolles

Plaintiff's Personal Injury Law and General Civil Trial Practice.

R. BRAD BOLLES, born Ardmore, Oklahoma, May 30, 1965; admitted to bar, 1990, Oklahoma and U.S. District Court, Eastern and Western Districts of Oklahoma. *Education:* University of Oklahoma (B.A., 1987; J.D., 1990). *Member:* Carter County, Oklahoma and American Bar Associations; Oklahoma Trial Lawyers Association; The Association of Trial Lawyers of America. ***PRACTICE AREAS:*** Plaintiffs Personal Injury Law; Civil Practice.

COLBERT & COLBERT

200 STANLEY
P.O. BOX 2169
ARDMORE, OKLAHOMA 73402
Telephone: 580-226-1911
Facsimile: 580-226-1907
Email: colbertlaw@aol.com
URL: http://www.lawyers.com/colbertlaw

General Practice, Civil Trial Practice, Personal Injury, Workers' Compensation.

(This Listing Continued)

MARK H. COLBERT, born Sulphur, Oklahoma, September 17, 1957; admitted to bar, 1983, Oklahoma and U.S. District Court, Northern, Eastern and Western Districts of Oklahoma and Eastern District of Texas. *Education:* University of Missouri (B.A., 1979); Oklahoma City University (J.D., 1982). Supreme Court Justice, Chickasaw Nation, 2002—. *Member:* Carter County (President, 1987), Oklahoma and American (Member, Torts and Insurance Practice Section) Bar Associations; Oklahoma Trial Lawyers Association; The Association of Trial Lawyers of America. ***PRACTICE AREAS:*** Personal Injury.

JOHN R. COLBERT, born Sulphur, Oklahoma, June 27, 1965; admitted to bar, 1990, Oklahoma and U.S. District Court, Eastern District of Oklahoma. *Education:* University of Oklahoma (B.S., 1987; J.D., 1990). *Member:* Carter County and Oklahoma Bar Associations; Oklahoma Trial Lawyers Association; The Association of Trial Lawyers of America. ***PRACTICE AREAS:*** Workers Compensation.

COLLINS & COLLINS, INC.

Established in 1950
COLLINS BUILDING
16 STANLEY
P.O. BOX 1781
ARDMORE, OKLAHOMA 73402-1781
Telephone: 580-223-8350
Fax: 580-223-0810
Email: ltcollin@swbell.net

General Civil and Trial Practice in all State and Federal Courts, Real Estate, Commercial, Municipal, Probate, Trusts and Estate Planning, Bankruptcy, Corporation, Banking and Domestic Relations Law.

T. FRED COLLINS, born El Reno, Oklahoma, October 26, 1923; admitted to bar, 1948, Oklahoma; U.S. District Court, Eastern and Western Districts of Oklahoma; U.S. Court of Appeals, Tenth Circuit; U.S. Supreme Court. *Education:* University of Oklahoma (B.S., 1945; J.D., 1948). Assistant County Attorney, 1950-1954. City Attorney, Ardmore, Oklahoma, 1958-1960. *Member:* Carter County (President, 1955, 1960) and Oklahoma Bar Associations. ***Email:*** tfcollins@prodigy.net

LORENZO T. COLLINS, born Ardmore, Oklahoma, July 7, 1957; admitted to bar, 1982, Oklahoma; U.S. District Courts, Western, Eastern and Northern Districts of Oklahoma. *Education:* University of Oklahoma (B.B.A., 1979; J.D., 1982). *Member:* Carter County (President, 1985) and Oklahoma Bar Associations. ***Email:*** ltcollin@swbell.net

DOLMAN LAW OFFICES

Established in 1905
10 W. MAIN
503 COLSTON BUILDING
P.O. BOX 1388
ARDMORE, OKLAHOMA 73402-1388
Telephone: 580-223-3619
Fax: 580-223-6415
Email: southok@prodigy.net

General Civil Practice. Trust and Estates, Taxation, Real Estate, Farm, Ranch, Corporate, Oil and Gas and Banking Law.

MEMBERS OF FIRM

JAMES L. DOLMAN (1905-1999)

JAMES B. DOLMAN, born Ardmore, Oklahoma, April 19, 1938; admitted to bar, 1962, Oklahoma; 1990, Colorado Bar. *Education:* University of Oklahoma (B.S., in Engr., 1960; J.D., 1962). Phi Alpha Delta; Omicron Delta Kappa. President: Ardmore Board of Education, 1972; United Fund of Ardmore, Inc., 1970; Arbuckle Area Council, Boy Scouts of America, 1978-1979. *Member:* Carter County, Oklahoma, Colorado and American Bar Associations; American College of Trust and Estate Counsel. ***PRACTICE AREAS:*** Estate Planning; Probate; Trust Law; Real Estate; Corporate Law. ***Email:*** southok@prodigy.net

LEGAL SUPPORT PERSONNEL

Diane Boland (Certified Legal Assistant).

FISCHL CULP McMILLIN CHAFFIN BAHNER & LONG, LLP

Established in 1952
100 E STREET, S.W.
P.O. BOX 1766
ARDMORE, OKLAHOMA 73402
Telephone: 580-223-4321
FAX: 580-226-4795
Email: fcmcb@swbell.net

General Civil Practice in all State and Federal Courts. Trials. Probate, Trusts and Estate Planning, Insurance Defense, Banking, Real Estate, Oil and Gas Law.

MEMBERS OF FIRM

LOUIS A. FISCHL (1898-1973)

JOSEPH M. CULP (1914-1997)

F. LOVELL McMILLIN (Retired)

DONALD J. CHAFFIN, born Muskogee, Oklahoma, March 4, 1952; admitted to bar, 1977, Oklahoma. *Education:* Oklahoma State University (B.A., 1974); University of Okla-

(This Listing Continued)

FISCHL CULP McMILLIN CHAFFIN BAHNER & LONG, LLP, Ardmore—Continued

homa College of Law (J.D., 1977). Member 1996-2003, Chairman 2002, and Associate Bar Examiner 1986-1996, Oklahoma Board of Bar Examiners. *Member:* Carter County (President, 1981) and Oklahoma Bar Associations. ***SPECIAL AGENCIES:*** Oklahoma Corporation Commission. ***PRACTICE AREAS:*** Oil and Gas Law; Real Estate Law; Estate Planning; Commercial Litigation; Environmental Law; Probate. ***Email:*** donchaffin@swbell.net

S. BRENT BAHNER, born Ardmore, Oklahoma, August 8, 1957; admitted to bar, 1982, Oklahoma. *Education:* Oklahoma State University and Baylor University (B.B.A., 1979); University of Oklahoma (J.D., 1982). Phi Delta Phi. *Member:* Carter County and Oklahoma Bar Associations; Oklahoma Association of Defense Counsel (Member, Board of Directors, 1988-1995); The Defense Research Institute, Inc; American Board of Trial Advocates (Advocate). ***REPORTED CASES:*** Montgomery v. City of Ardmore, 365 F.3d 926 (2004); Gillham v. Lake County Raceway, 24 P.3d 858 (2001); Alsobrook v. National Travelers Life Ins. Co., 852 P.2d 768 (1992); Economy Fire & Cas. Co. v. Faulkner, 790 F.Supp. 1082 (W.D. Okla. 1991). ***PRACTICE AREAS:*** Civil Litigation; Personal Injury Litigation; Insurance Defense Litigation. ***Email:*** bbahner@swbell.net

ROBERT D. LONG, born Ardmore, Oklahoma, November 12, 1952; admitted to bar, 1978, Oklahoma. *Education:* Southern Methodist University and University of Oklahoma (B.S., 1974; J.D., 1978). Member, Oklahoma Law Review, 1976. *Member:* Carter County, Oklahoma and American Bar Associations; Oklahoma Board of Bar Examiners (Associate Examiner, 2004 —). ***PRACTICE AREAS:*** Banking Law; Estate Planning; Oil and Gas Law; General Corporate Practice. ***Email:*** rdlong@swbell.net

ASSOCIATE

JULIE J. AUSTIN, born Ardmore, Oklahoma, 1977; admitted to bar, 2002, Oklahoma; U.S. District Court, Eastern, Northern and Western Districts of Oklahoma. *Education:* Oklahoma State University (B.S., with honors, magna cum laude, 1998); University of Oklahoma (J.D., with distinction, 2002). Phi Delta Phi. Recipient, Albert G. Hunt Practice Court Award. ; Former Member, Council Oak American Inn of Court. *Member:* Tulsa County and Oklahoma Bar Associations; Oklahoma Association of Defense Counsel. ***PRACTICE AREAS:*** Torts; Insurance Defense; Civil Litigation; Commercial Law; Family Law. ***Email:*** jaustin@swbell.net

REPRESENTATIVE CLIENTS: First National Bank and Trust Co., Ardmore, Oklahoma; Keith F. Walker Oil and Gas Co.; Oneok, Inc.; Chevron Texaco; The Quintin Little Company, Inc.; Allstate Insurance Co.; American Title Insurance Co.; Chubb Group; Cimarron Insurance Co.; Economy Fire and Casualty Co.; Employers Mutual Insurance Co.; Federated Insurance Company; Grain Dealers Mutual Insurance Co.; Lawyers Title Insurance Corp.; Oklahoma Farmers Union Mutual Insurance Co.; Shelter Insurance Co.; USAA; Homeland Stores, Inc.; Winn Dixie Texas Inc; American Agri-Business Insurance Company; Valero Energy Corporation; Charter Insurance Company; National American Insurance Company; Trinity Companies; Mercy Memorial Hospital; Citizen's Bank and Trust Co.; Patina Oil & Gas Corp.; Hewitt Minerals, Inc.

MICHAEL J. HESTER, INC.

414 SOUTH COMMERCE
P.O. BOX 2148
ARDMORE, OKLAHOMA 73402
Telephone: 580-226-6060
Fax: 580-226-6061
Email: mhesterlaw@aol.com

General Civil Trial Practice. Corporate, Commercial, Farm, Ranch and Equine Law, Probate, Real Estate, Personal Injury, Wills, Trusts and Estate Planning.

MICHAEL J. HESTER, born Portland, Oregon, September 16, 1946; admitted to bar, 1977, Oklahoma and U.S. District Court, Western, Eastern and Northern Districts of Oklahoma; 1995, South Dakota. *Education:* New Mexico Military Institute; United States Naval Academy (B.S., 1969); Oklahoma University (J.D., 1977). *Member:* Carter County (President, 1981-1982) and Oklahoma Bar Associations; State Bar of South Dakota. [Lt., U.S. Navy (Aviator), 1969-1974]. ***PRACTICE AREAS:*** General Practice; Equine Law; Real Estate Property Law; Estate Planning; Accident and Personal Injury. ***Email:*** mhesterlaw@aol.com

A List of Representative Clients will be furnished upon request.

D. MICHAEL HISEY

Established in 1984
SUITE 450 NEUSTADT PLAZA
333 WEST MAIN
P.O. BOX 66
ARDMORE, OKLAHOMA 73402
Telephone: 580-226-6270
Fax: 580-226-0571
Email: hiseylaw@cableone.net

Contracts, Adoption (In State and Inter-State), Probate, Real Estate, Trusts and Estates, Estate Planning, Guardianship, Corporate and Commercial.

D. MICHAEL HISEY, born Ardmore, Oklahoma, July 15, 1947; admitted to bar, 1972, Oklahoma; 1973, U.S. District Court, Western District of Oklahoma and U.S. Court of Military Appeals; 1979, U.S. Court of Appeals, Tenth Circuit. *Education:* Central State University; University of Oklahoma (J.D., 1972). Judge Advocate, U.S. Marines, 1973-1977. First Assistant District Attorney, 1977-1978 and Special District Judge, 1978-1984, 20th Judicial District, Oklahoma; Member, Temporary Lawyer Staffed, Panel of the Court of Appeals, 1991-1992. *Member:* Carter County (President, 1992-1993) and Oklahoma (Member: Real Property, Estate Planning and Probate Law Sections) Bar Associations.

DAVID G. MORDY P.C.

333 WEST MAIN STREET, SUITE 450
P.O. BOX 486
ARDMORE, OKLAHOMA 73402
Telephone: 508-226-3311
Fax: 508-223-1168
Email: dgmlaw@sbcglobal.net

Civil Litigation, Insurance Defense, Personal Injury, School Law, Municipal Law, Condemnation, Criminal Law.

DAVID G. MORDY, born Ardmore, Oklahoma, February 14, 1959; admitted to bar, 1985, Oklahoma and U.S. District Court, Eastern, Western and Northern Districts of Oklahoma. *Education:* University of Oklahoma (B.B.A., 1981; J.D., 1984). Graduate, National Institute of Trial Advocacy (NITA). *Member:* Carter County and Oklahoma Bar Associations. ***LANGUAGES:*** English. ***PRACTICE AREAS:*** Civil Litigation; Insurance Defense; Personal Injury; School Law; Municipal Law; Condemnation; Criminal Law.

MORDY & MORDY, P.C.

Established in 1985
110 WEST MAIN STREET
P.O. BOX 457
ARDMORE, OKLAHOMA 73402
Telephone: 580-223-4384
Facsimile: 580-226-0823
Email: mordylaw@sbcglobal.net

Civil State and Federal Practice, Corporate, Commercial Litigation, Oil and Gas, Real Estate, Ad Valorem Taxation, Probate and Employment Law.

BURKE MORDY, born El Reno, Oklahoma, April 8, 1930; admitted to bar, 1954, Oklahoma, U.S. District Court, Northern, Eastern and Western Districts of Oklahoma; U.S. Court of Appeals, Fifth and Tenth Circuits. *Education:* University of Oklahoma (B.S., 1952; LL.B., 1954). Assistant County Attorney, Carter County, Oklahoma, 1959-1962. Member, Oklahoma Legislature, 1963-1967. District Attorney, 20th Judicial District, Carter County, 1967-1971. Member, Oklahoma Crime Commission, 1967-1971. *Member:* Carter County and Oklahoma Bar Associations. [Col., U.S. Air Force Reserves, Ret.]. ***REPORTED CASES:*** United States v. Jordan, 76-1360, U.S. Court of Appeals, Fifth Circuit, 557 F.2d 1081; 1977 U.S. App. LEXIS 11990, August 15, 1977. ***PRACTICE AREAS:*** Criminal; Civil Practice; Personal Injury; Probate. ***Email:*** mordylaw@sbcglobal.net

MICHAEL C. MORDY, born Tulsa, Oklahoma, February 5, 1955; admitted to bar, 1980, Oklahoma, U.S. Court of Appeals, Tenth Circuit and U.S. District Court, Northern, Eastern and Western Districts of Oklahoma. *Education:* University of Oklahoma (B.B.A., 1977); Oklahoma City University (J.D., 1980). Recipient, American Jurisprudence Award, 1979-1980. *Member:* Carter County (Past President, 1985-1986) and Oklahoma (Member, Board of Governors, 2004—; Budget Committee, 2005) Bar Associations. Fellow, Oklahoma Bar Foundation. ***REPORTED CASES:*** Beetle Plastics v. United Ass'n of Journeymen, 96-6031, U.S. Court of Appeals, Tenth Circuit, 1996 U.S. App. LEXIS 24740, September 19, 1996. ***PRACTICE AREAS:*** Oil and Gas Law; Commercial Litigation; Civil Litigation; Federal Civil Litigation; Business Law; Employment Law; Ad Valorem Tax. ***Email:*** mordylaw@sbcglobal.net

REPRESENTATIVE CLIENTS: Thomas C. Mueller Companies; Wildhorse Oil & Gas Corporation; Cimmarron Transportation, L.L.C.; Hanover Compression Company; American Superior Feeds, Inc./Bluebonnet Feeds; Ardmore Production & Exploration, Inc.; Mark Energy Co.; Anchor Drilling Fluids U.S.A., Inc.; Keith F. Walker Oil and Gas Company, L.L.C.; Cheyenne Drilling Company; Scissortail Energy, LLC; Cantera Pipeline Company; First National Bank & Trust Co. of Ardmore; American National Bank; Landmark Bank; County Builders Supply, Inc.

THOMPSON, CAWLEY, VEAZEY & BURNS

A PROFESSIONAL CORPORATION
422 SECOND AVENUE N.W.
P.O. BOX 2460
ARDMORE, OKLAHOMA 73402
Telephone: 580-223-3020
Fax: 580-223-1942
Email: tcvb@swbell.net

Oil and Gas, Corporation, Real Estate, Estate Planning, Probate and Banking Law.

JAMES E. THOMPSON (1915-1999)

SAMUEL J. VEAZEY, born Ardmore, Oklahoma, April 30, 1946; admitted to bar, 1970, Oklahoma. *Education:* University of Oklahoma (B.A., 1967; J.D., 1970); University of Texas at Austin. Omicron Delta Kappa; Phi Alpha Delta. Member, Board of Trustees, Carter County Law Library, 1979-1991. Member, University of Oklahoma Alumni Advisory Council, 1985-1990. Member, Oklahoma Transportation Commission, (1987-1991, Vice Chairman, 1989-1991). President, Oklahoma Easter Seal Society, 1990-1992. *Member:* Carter County (President, 1978), Oklahoma (Member, Probate Code Committee, 1988-1996; Chair, Estate Planning and Probate Section, 1994) and American Bar Associations.

GLEN C. BURNS, born Frederick, Oklahoma, August 31, 1945; admitted to bar, 1974, Oklahoma. *Education:* Southwestern State College (B.A., 1967); Oklahoma City University (J.D., 1974). Phi Delta Phi. Chairman, Board of Trustees, Carter County Law Library, 1979—. Member: Ardmore Development Authority, 1980-2000. Hardy Murphy Coliseum Authority, 1980-1999. *Member:* Carter County (Secretary, 1978; Vice-President, 1979) and Oklahoma Bar Associations.

(This Listing Continued)

OF COUNSEL

MICHAEL A. CAWLEY, born Wichita, Kansas, April 15, 1947; admitted to bar, 1972, Oklahoma. *Education:* University of Oklahoma (B.A., 1969; J.D., 1972). President, The Samuel Roberts Noble Foundation, Inc., 1992—.

PAUL E. PITTS, born Minneapolis, Minnesota, November 5, 1954; admitted to bar, 1981, Oklahoma. *Education:* University of Oklahoma (B.A., 1978; J.D., 1981).

REPRESENTATIVE CLIENTS: Noble Energy, Inc.; The Samuel Roberts Noble Foundation, Inc.; First National Bank & Trust Company of Ardmore; Citizens Bank & Trust Company of Ardmore; Ardmore Development Authority.

RONALD E. WORTHEN, P.C.

Established in 1986

11 NORTH WASHINGTON
P.O. BOX 1991
ARDMORE, OKLAHOMA 73402
Telephone: 580-223-3735
Fax: 580-226-2528
Email: ronworthen@yahoo.com

Civil Practice, Criminal Law, Family Law, Divorce, including Custody, Modificating, Personal Injury, Labor Law and Probate Litigation.

RONALD E. WORTHEN, born Yuba City, California, November 12, 1943; admitted to bar, 1968, Arkansas and U.S. District Court, Eastern District of Arkansas; 1970, Oklahoma; 1971, U.S. District Court, Eastern District of Oklahoma; U.S. District Court, Western District of Oklahoma and U.S. Court of Appeals, 10th Circuit. *Education:* University of Arkansas (B.S.B.A., 1967; J.D., 1968). Recipient: Clarence E. Darrow Award, 1993; Pro Bono Award Legal Aid, Eastern Oklahoma, 1998. lst Assistant District Attorney, 1972-1974. District Attorney, 20th District, 1974-1985. Member, Oklahoma District Attorneys Training Coordination Council, 1983-1985. Vice Chairman, Pardon and Parole Board, 1999. *Member:* Carter County, Love County, Arkansas and Oklahoma Bar Associations; District Attorneys Association (Member, Board of Directors, 1976-1985); Southern Oklahoma Defense Lawyers Association (Secretary, 1987-1989; President, 1990-1994); Oklahoma Trial Lawyers Association; The Association of Trial Lawyers of America; Oklahoma Criminal Defense Lawyers Association (Member, Family Law Section). [Oklahoma National Guard, 1969-1975]. ***PRACTICE AREAS:*** Divorce; Child Custody; Criminal Law; Personal Injury; Probate; Real Estate; Labor Law. ***Email:*** ronworthen@yahoo.com

LAW OFFICES OF SHANNON REASOR

Established in 1993

209 EAST COURT
P.O. BOX 393
ATOKA, OKLAHOMA 74525
Telephone: 580-889-3343
Fax: 580-889-9334
Email: sdreasor@yahoo.com
URL: http://www.reasorlaw.com

General Practice, Real Estate, Probate, Estate Planning, Civil Litigation.

FIRM PROFILE: Reasor Law Offices began in 1994 with one attorney and one legal assistant. The firm has grown over the years to more than 7 staff members. Full service is our goal from complex litigation to probates, real estate transactions & estates, and criminal law.

SHANNON REASOR, born Ada, Oklahoma, July 20, 1968; admitted to bar, 1993, Oklahoma. *Education:* Southeastern Oklahoma State University (B.A., 1989); University of Oklahoma (J.D., 1993). City Attorney, Clayton, Oklahoma, 1995—. *Member:* Oklahoma Bar Association. (Resident). ***REPORTED CASES:*** Crocker v. Crocker, 2003 OK CIV App 50. ***PRACTICE AREAS:*** Civil Practice; Real Property; Criminal Law; Wills; Trusts and Estates.

REPRESENTATIVE CLIENTS: Weyerhaeuser Corporation; First Bank-Atoka; Ameristate-Atoka; U.S. Department of Agriculture; First American Title Insurance Company.

ATKINS & MARKOFF

BARTLESVILLE, OKLAHOMA

(See Oklahoma City)

Personal Injury, Automobile Accidents, Wrongful Death, Trucking Accidents, Slip and Fall, Nursing Home Abuse, Head and Spinal Injuries, Dog Bites, Sexual Abuse, Criminal Law, Drug Crimes, DUI/DWI, Juvenile Crimes, General Practice, Family , Divorce, Adoptions, Child Custody, Child Support, Domestic Violence, Visitation Rights, Elder Law, Legal Malpractice, Medical Malpractice, Social Security, Social Security Disability, Taxation, IRS Audits, Property Tax Appeals, Tax Planning, Toxic Torts, Trust and Estate, Wills and Probate.

BARROW & GRIMM, P.C.

BARTLESVILLE, OKLAHOMA

(See Tulsa)

Civil Trial and Appellate Practice. General Business Practice. Corporate, Commercial Litigation, Employment Law, Finance, Bankruptcy, Contract, Insurance, Real Estate, Mineral, Probate, Taxation, Estate Planning and Health Law.

BREWER, WORTEN, ROBINETT

Established in 1928

117 W. 5TH STREET
500 PROFESSIONAL BUILDING
P.O. BOX 1066
BARTLESVILLE, OKLAHOMA 74005-1066
Telephone: 918-336-4132
Fax: 918-336-9009
Email: attorney@bwrlawoffice.com

Pawhuska, Oklahoma Office: 204 First National Bank Building, 74005. Telephone: 918-287-2200.

General Civil Practice. State and Federal Litigation. Corporate, Banking, Real Estate, Oil and Gas, Probate, Trust and Estate Planning, Family and Employment Law, Personal Injury and Insurance Defense.

FIRM PROFILE: Chester A. Brewer (deceased in 2002) established his practice in Bartlesville, Oklahoma in 1928. He was joined in 1959 by Jesse J. Worten, Jr. (deceased 1983), by Bruce W. Robinett in 1967, by David B. King in 1980 and by Jesse J. Worten, III in 1983. John M. Keefer became Of Counsel to the firm in 1986 after having conducted an extensive employment and labor law practice in Tulsa, Oklahoma. James M. Elias and P. Scott Buhlinger joined the firm as associates in 1997 and as partners in 2001. Thomas J. Brown joined the firm as an associate in 2001.

The firm is a full-service law firm with its primary focus in corporate and business law, employment law, family law, estate planning, banking, oil and gas, insurance defense, real estate, personal injury and litigation.

MEMBERS OF FIRM

CHESTER A. BREWER (1901-2002)
JESSE J. WORTEN (1920-1983)

BRUCE W. ROBINETT, born Douglas, Oklahoma, February 18, 1943; admitted to bar, 1967, Oklahoma. *Education:* Oklahoma State University (B.S., 1965); Oklahoma University (LL.B., 1967). Order of the Coif; Phi Delta Phi. Member, Board of Editors, Oklahoma Law Review, 1965-1967. *Member:* Washington County, Oklahoma and American Bar Associations. Fellow, American College of Trial Lawyers. ***PRACTICE AREAS:*** Litigation; Agricultural Law; Commercial Transactions; Estate Planning; Real Estate; Oil and Gas; Banking; Probate; Corporate Law. ***Email:*** bwrobinett@bwrlawoffice.com

JESSE J. WORTEN, III, born Pawhuska, Oklahoma, May 24, 1950; admitted to bar, 1976, Oklahoma. *Education:* Oklahoma State University (B.S., 1972); Oklahoma City University (J.D., 1976). Phi Delta Phi. *Member:* Washington County, Osage County, Oklahoma and American Bar Associations; The Association of Trial Lawyers of America; American Inns of Court (Master). ***PRACTICE AREAS:*** Litigation; Litigation Defense; Insurance Defense; Professional Liability Defense; Family Law. ***Email:*** jjworten3@bwrlawoffice.com

DAVID B. KING, born Okmulgee, Oklahoma, June 7, 1955; admitted to bar, 1980, Oklahoma. *Education:* Westminster College (B.A., 1977); University of Oklahoma (J.D., 1980). Phi Delta Phi. *Member:* Washington County and Oklahoma Bar Associations. ***PRACTICE AREAS:*** Banking; Real Estate; Family Law; Insurance Defense; Litigation; Probate. ***Email:*** dking@bwrlawoffice.com

JAMES M. ELIAS, born Leavenworth, Kansas, January 29, 1963; admitted to bar, 1989, Oklahoma; 1997, Kansas. *Education:* Oklahoma State University (B.S., with distinction, 1985); University of Oklahoma (J.D., 1989). Member, Oklahoma Law Review, 1988-1989. *Member:* Washington County, Oklahoma, Kansas and American Bar Associations. ***PRACTICE AREAS:*** Litigation; Family Law; Personal Injury; Insurance Law; Commercial Litigation. ***Email:*** jim@bwrlawoffice.com

P. SCOTT BUHLINGER, born Breckinridge, Texas, May 22, 1963; admitted to bar, 1988, Missouri; 1989, Kansas; 1994, Oklahoma. *Education:* Westminster College (B.A., Economics, 1985); University of Kansas (J.D., 1988). *Member:* Washington County, Oklahoma, Kansas and Missouri Bar Associations. ***PRACTICE AREAS:*** Elder Law; Real Estate; Commercial; Banking; Probate; Estate Planning. ***Email:*** scott@bwrlawoffice.com

ASSOCIATE

THOMAS J. BROWN, born Bartlesville, Oklahoma, December 29, 1969; admitted to bar, 1998, Oklahoma. *Education:* Harding University (B.S., Biology, 1993); University of Oklahoma (J.D., 1999). *Member:* Washington County and Oklahoma Bar Associations. ***PRACTICE AREAS:*** Civil Litigation; Corporate Law; Family Law. ***Email:*** tjbrown@bwrlawoffice.com

OF COUNSEL

JOHN M. KEEFER, born Tulsa, Oklahoma, March 23, 1942; admitted to bar, 1967, Oklahoma. *Education:* Tulsa University (B.A., 1964; J.D., 1967). Phi Alpha Delta. Associate Editor, Tulsa Law Review, 1966-1967. Field Attorney, National Labor Relations Board, 14th Region, 1967-1968. *Member:* Tulsa County, Washington County, Oklahoma and American Bar Associations. ***PRACTICE AREAS:*** Employment Law; Litigation. ***Email:*** jmkeefer@bwrlawoffice.com

REPRESENTATIVE CLIENTS: Adams Investment Co.; ABB; Community State Bank, Coffeyville, Kansas; Basinger Oil Co.; Blue Ribbon Ranch, Inc.; Caney Valley National Bank of Caney, Kansas; Central States Business Forms; Chevalley-Millstead Moving and Storage; Farmland Industries, Inc.; First National Bank and Trust Company, Vinita, Oklahoma; First National Bank, Pawhuska, Oklahoma; Graham-Rogers, Inc. (Insurance General Agency); Jaytee Ranch; Kane Enterprises; Ken-Ada Ranches; Malone Motors, Inc.; Metal Goods Manufacturing, Inc.; Mullendore Cross Bell Ranch; Oilfield Pipe and Supply, Inc.; Oklahoma Bar Association Professional Liability Insurance Company; OML Municipal Assurance Group; Overlees-Woods Lumber Co.; ConocoPhillips Petroleum Company; Saddoris Companies, Inc.; Service and Technology Corp.; Smokerise Ranch, Inc.; Stotts, Barclay, Moore and Whipple PC, Certified Public Accountants; WestStar Bank; Arvest Bank; Bank of Oklahoma; Mark Roberts Motor, Inc.; Kelley Lawn & Garden, Inc.; Cylx Engineering and Construction

(This Listing Continued)

BREWER, WORTEN, ROBINETT, Bartlesville—Continued

Company; Zinc Corporation of America, a division of Horsehead Industries, Inc.; ECC Energy Corporation; Independent School District No. 2 Osage County Oklahoma; Statewide Roofing, Inc.; State Farm Mutual Industries Inc.; Hughes Ranch LLC; First Bartlesville Bank; Architectural Fabricators Company; Mark Roberts Motors; Coffeyville Resources Guide Transportation, Inc.

GARRISON, BROWN, CARLSON & BUCHANAN, PLLC

Established in 1966

530 SOUTHEAST DELAWARE
P.O. BOX 1217
BARTLESVILLE, OKLAHOMA 74003
Telephone: 918-336-2520
Fax: 918-336-7709
Email: gbcbblaw@aol.com
URL: http://www.lawyers.com/gbcbb

General Civil and Criminal Practice in all State and Federal Courts. Corporation, Taxation, Probate, Oil and Gas, Real Estate, Personal Injury, Products Liability, Negligence, Insurance, Family Law, Estate Planning, Commercial, Bankruptcy and Criminal Law. Trials.

FIRM PROFILE: The firm is dynamic and aggressive, with a record of getting exceptionally favorable results. Each of us is committed to providing quality work and effective solutions to our clients' problems. Built on successful and active legal ability, our innovation and dedication to our clients' success inspire our approach to each case and transaction.

We possess significant experience and provide dedicated personalized legal representation, and are always mindful that our clients are our first priority.

ALAN R. CARLSON, born Alva, Oklahoma, June 29, 1947; admitted to bar, 1973, Oklahoma. *Education:* Oklahoma State University (B.S., Industrial Engineering, 1970); University of Tulsa (J.D., 1973). Delta Theta Phi. Member, Moot Court Board. Listed In: "Best Lawyers in America." Author: "Damages in Oklahoma Civil Trial Practice," National Business Institute, 2003; "Proving Damages," Oklahoma Bar Association, 1998; "Effective Pleadings and Winning Motion Practice-The Answer," Oklahoma Bar Association, 1995; "Handling the Presentation of the Soft Tissue Injury Case," Texas Bar Association Seminar, Houston, Texas, 1994; "Proving the Soft Tissue Injury Case," Oklahoma Bar Association, 1989; "Opening Statement in a Personal Injury Case," Oklahoma Trial Lawyers Association, 1986; "Governmental Tort Claims Act Notice and Insurance," Oklahoma Trial Lawyers Association, 1985; "The Soft Tissue Case Using the Vocational Rehabilitation Expert," Oklahoma Trial Lawyers Association, 1985; "Recent Trends and Developments in Criminal Law," Oklahoma Trial Lawyers Association, 1983; "An Update on Federal Criminal Practice," Oklahoma Criminal Defense Lawyers Association, 1985; "Some Thoughts on Jury Voir Dire," Oklahoma Trial Lawyers Association, 1985. *Member:* Washington County Practicing Bar (Secretary, 1983-1986), Oklahoma and American Bar Associations; Oklahoma Trial Lawyers Association (Member: Board of Directors, 1981 —; Executive Committee, 1981—); The Association of Trial Lawyers of America; American Institute of Industrial Engineers; Oklahoma Criminal Defense Lawyers Association; The American Academy of Forensic Sciences. ***PRACTICE AREAS:*** Personal Injury; Products Liability; Aviation; Automobile Accidents and Injuries; Business Litigation; Insurance; Insurance Bad Faith; Premises Liability; Business Law; Probate.

KEVIN D. BUCHANAN, born Stillwater, Oklahoma, August 16, 1959; admitted to bar, 1984, Oklahoma. *Education:* Oklahoma State University (B.S., 1981); University of Tulsa College of Law (J.D., 1984). *Member:* Oklahoma Bar Association. ***PRACTICE AREAS:*** Workers Compensation; Criminal Law; Family Law; Divorce; Child Custody; Traffic Violations; Driving While Intoxicated.

REPRESENTATIVE CLIENTS: Phillips Petroleum Co.; Foster Petroleum Corp.; 66 Federal Credit Union; Tyco Oil Corp.; Viersen Drilling Co.; Midwest Pancake Houses, Inc.; Hoyt Drilling Corp.; Kaw Pancake Houses, Inc.; Major Enterprises, Inc.; Rental Transportation, Inc.; Gorman, Inc.; Plantation Apartments, Inc.; T. & R. Drilling Co.; Lucas Gas, Inc.; Utility Management Co., Inc.; Treco Sales, Inc.; Ace-Hi Energy Cos.; David Greene Operating Company; Browder & Ratcliff Oil Operators; Village Inn Pancake House, Inc.

SELBY, CONNOR, MADDUX & JANER, P.L.P.

Established in 1939

416 EAST FIFTH STREET
DRAWER Z
BARTLESVILLE, OKLAHOMA 74005
Telephone: 918-336-8114
Fax: 918-336-6441
Email: scmj@sbcglobal.net

General Civil Practice, all State and Federal Courts. Probate, Insurance, Negligence, Real Estate, Taxation, Corporate, Estate Planning, Commercial and Oil and Gas Law. Trials, Family Law.

OF COUNSEL

CHARLES W. SELBY, born Sapulpa, Oklahoma, February 22, 1911; admitted to bar, 1937, Oklahoma. *Education:* University of Oklahoma (LL.B., 1937). Assistant County Attorney, 1940-1943; 1947-1951; 1955-1956. *Member:* Washington County (President, 1940-1941), Oklahoma and American Bar Associations. [First Lieut., J.A.G.D., U.S. Army, active duty, 1943-1946]. ***PRACTICE AREAS:*** Probate Law; Contracts Law; Real Estate Law. ***Email:*** scmj@sbcglobal.net

MEMBERS OF FIRM

JAMES W. CONNOR, born Seminole, Oklahoma, August 21, 1932; admitted to bar, 1959, Oklahoma; 1960, U.S. District Court, Northern District of Oklahoma; 1965, U.S. District Court, Western District of Oklahoma; 1973, U.S. Court of Appeals, 10th Circuit. *Education:* St. Benedict's College (B.S., 1954); University of Oklahoma (LL.B., 1959). Delta Theta Phi; Order of the Coif. Assistant County Attorney, 1959-1961. County Attorney, 1961-1963. State Representative, 1963-1971. Prosecuting Officer, Court of Impeachment, Oklahoma State Senate, 1965. Minority Floor Leader, Oklahoma House of Representatives, 1965-1971. City Attorney, 1974-1975. *Member:* Washington County, Oklahoma and American Bar Associations. ***PRACTICE AREAS:*** Civil Litigation; Estate Planning; Probate Law; Corporate Law; Real Estate Law. ***Email:*** scmj@sbcglobal.net

JERRY M. MADDUX, born Bartlesville, Oklahoma, June 6, 1941; admitted to bar, 1966, Oklahoma. *Education:* Oklahoma University (B.B.A., 1963; J.D., 1966). Phi Alpha Delta. City Attorney, 1975—. *Member:* Washington County and Oklahoma Bar Associations; Oklahoma Trial Lawyers Association; National Institute of Municipal Law Officers. ***PRACTICE AREAS:*** Banking Law; Municipal Law; Real Estate Law; Probate Law; Estate Planning. ***Email:*** scmj@sbcglobal.net

THOMAS JANER, born Pompton Plains, New Jersey, March 21, 1959; admitted to bar, 1985, Oklahoma and U.S. District Court, Western, Northern and Eastern Districts of Oklahoma. *Education:* University of South Florida (B.A., cum laude, 1981); University of Oklahoma (J.D., 1984). Phi Kappa Phi; Omicron Delta Kappa; Pi Sigma Alpha. Adjunct Professor, Business law, Oklahoma Wesleyan University, 1990—. President, Washington County Youth Court Board, 1990-1991. Assistant District Attorney, 1995—. *Member:* Washington County (President, 1991-1992) and Oklahoma Bar Associations. ***PRACTICE AREAS:*** Banking Law; Family Law; Collection Law; Civil Litigation. ***Email:*** scmj@sbcglobal.net

ASSOCIATE

RUSSELL C. VACLAW, born Bartlesville, Oklahoma, April 4, 1973; admitted to bar, 2000, Oklahoma. *Education:* University of Oklahoma (B.A., 1997; J.D., 2000). Phi Delta Phi. Included, "Who's Who Among American Law Students", 1998. *Member:* Washington County (Vice President, 2004) and Oklahoma Bar Associations. ***LANGUAGES:*** Spanish. ***PRACTICE AREAS:*** Wills; Trusts; Collections; Family Law; Domestic Relations; Personal Injury; General Practice. ***Email:*** scmj@sbcglobal.net

REPRESENTATIVE CLIENTS: City of Bartlesville; The Lyon Foundation; Oakley Pontiac-Buick; Bartlesville Orthopaedic Clinic; 66 Federal Credit Union; Professional Credit Recovery, Inc.; Musselman Abstract Company.
APPROVED TITLE EXAMINERS FOR: First American Title Insurance Co.; Southwest Title & Trust Co., Inc.; Equitable Life Assurance Co.; Title Insurance Company of Minnesota; Bailey Oil Company.

DRUM & VENABLE

A PROFESSIONAL L.L.C.

Established in 1955

45 WEST 2ND STREET
P.O. BOX 340
BEAVER, OKLAHOMA 73932-0340
Telephone: 580-625-4526
Fax: 580-625-4716
Email: jerryv@ptsi.net
URL: http://www.lawyers.com/drumvenable

General Civil Practice, Probate and Estate Planning, Real Estate, Wills and Trusts; Oil and Gas, Family Law, Trials and Appeals, Commercial and Business Law.

FIRM PROFILE: The Firm was founded in 1955 by Merle Lansden and Keith Drum, both having been in the Armed Services during WW II, and in private practice in Beaver, Oklahoma, since 1945. Merle Lansden left the firm in 1967 and served as presiding District Judge of the First Judicial District of Oklahoma until he retired in 1977. The Firm continued from 1967 with various associates until the present Firm of Drum & Venable was established in 1981.

KEITH DRUM, born Beaver, Oklahoma, January 1, 1916; admitted to bar, 1940, Oklahoma; 1953, U.S. District Court, Western District of Oklahoma. *Education:* University of Oklahoma (B.A., 1938; LL.B., 1940). County Attorney, Beaver County, Oklahoma, 1941-1942. *Member:* Beaver County, Oklahoma and American Bar Associations. [1st Lt., U.S. Army, Active Duty, 1942-1946; Reserve Duty, 1938-1949]. (Retired)

JERRY L. VENABLE, born Beaver, Oklahoma, May 17, 1945; admitted to bar, 1971, Oklahoma. *Education:* University of Oklahoma (B.S., 1968; J.D., 1971). Phi Alpha Delta. *Member:* Beaver County (President), Oklahoma and American Bar Associations. ***PRACTICE AREAS:*** Family Law; Real Estate; Probate; Oil and Gas Law; Civil Litigation.

REPRESENTATIVE CLIENTS: Ralph E. Barby Estate; H.G. Adams, III Ranch; The Bank of Beaver City; Nichols Water Service, Inc.; Hardberger & Smylie, Inc.; Colorado Interstate Gas Co.
APPROVED ATTORNEYS FOR: Farmers Home Administration; First American Title Insurance Company; Federal Land Bank Association of Western Oklahoma.

TIMOTHY E. MILLS, P.C.

3910 N. COLLEGE, SUITE A
BETHANY, OKLAHOMA 73008
Telephone: 405-789-2225
Fax: 405-789-2369
Email: timmillslaw@sbcglobal.net
URL: http://www.timmillslaw.com

Labor and Employment, Collections, Family Law, Estate Planning, Real Estate.

TIMOTHY EDWARD MILLS, born 1963; admitted to bar, 2003, Oklahoma and U.S. District Court, Western District of Oklahoma. *Education:* Weber State College (B.S., 1998); Oklahoma City University School of Law (J.D., 2001). *Member:* Oklahoma County, Oklahoma and American Bar Associations; Oklahoma City Real Property Lawyers Asso-

(This Listing Continued)

ciation. ***PRACTICE AREAS:*** Labor and Employment; Collections; Family Law; Employment Law; Estate Planning; Real Estate. ***Email:*** timmillslaw@sbcglobal.net

MOYERS, MARTIN, SANTEE, IMEL & TETRICK, L.L.P.

Established in 1910

Formerly Moyers, Martin, Conway, Santee & Imel

113 WEST DAWES, SUITE 100
BIXBY, OKLAHOMA 74008
Telephone: 918-366-3935
Fax: 918-366-3936
Email: info@moyersmartin.com
URL: http://www.moyersmartin.com

Tulsa, Oklahoma Office: 1100 Mid-Continent Tower, 401 South Boston Avenue, 74103. Telephone: 918-582-5281.

Civil Practice, Banks and Banking, Bankruptcy, Business Law, Commercial Law, Construction Law, Contracts, Corporate Law, Education Law, Employee Benefits, Energy, Federal Practice, Insurance, Labor and Employment, Leases and Leasing, Litigation, Mergers, Acquisitions and Divestitures, Natural Resources, Personal Injury, Probate, Real Estate, Taxation, Trusts and Estates.

FIRM PROFILE: Listed in the Bar Register of Preeminent Lawyers, Moyers, Martin, Santee, Imel & Tetrick has been engaged in the general civil practice of law since 1910 and is one of the oldest firms in Oklahoma. The firm has an extensive history of providing clients with exceptional legal representation in a personal, timely and cost efficient manner.

(For Complete Biographical Data, see Professional Biographies at Tulsa, Oklahoma)

KIRK R. BOERSMA

111 WEST BLACKWELL
P.O. BOX 309
BLACKWELL, OKLAHOMA 74631
Telephone: 580-363-3323
888-726-4334
Fax: 580-363-3393
URL: http://www.boersmalaw.com
Email: kirk@boersmalaw.com
URL: http://www.lawyers.com/boersmalaw

Probate, Real Estate, Trusts and Estates, Wills, Natural Resources, Mortgages, Banking Law, Corporate Law, Business Law, Leases and Leasing, Nonprofit and Charitable Organizations.

KIRK R. BOERSMA, born Enid, Oklahoma, March 29, 1954; admitted to bar, 1979, Oklahoma and U.S. District Court, Northern District of Oklahoma; 1998, U.S. District Court, Western District of Oklahoma. *Education:* Northern Oklahoma College (A.A., 1974); Oklahoma State University (B.A., 1976); University of Tulsa (J.D., 1979). Phi Alpha Delta (Chapter Justice, 1978-1979). Recipient, Order of Barristers Award. Municipal Judge, City of Blackwell, 2000—. *Member:* Kay County, Oklahoma and American Bar Associations. ***PRACTICE AREAS:*** Probate; Real Estate; Trusts and Estates; Wills; Natural Resources; Mortgages; Banking Law; Corporate Law; Business Law; Leases and Leasing; Nonprofit and Chairtable Organizations.

JONATHAN C. IHRIG & ASSOCIATES

Established in 1982

107 WEST BLACKWELL
P.O. BOX 389
BLACKWELL, OKLAHOMA 74631
Telephone: 580-363-4300
Fax: 580-363-4308
Email: jcilaw@kskc.net
URL: http://www.lawyers.com/ihriglaw

General Civil Practice, Trials. Real Estate, Personal Injury, Automobile Accidents, Probate and Estate Planning, Trusts, Public Utility, Banking, Business Litigation, Insurance and Negligence Law, Wrongful Termination, Employment.

JONATHAN C. IHRIG, born Henryetta, Oklahoma, August 5, 1947; admitted to bar, 1974, Oklahoma and U.S. District Court, Western District of Oklahoma. *Education:* Oklahoma State University (B.S., 1970); Oklahoma City University (J.D., 1974). Phi Delta Phi. Assistant City Attorney, Blackwell, Oklahoma, 1977-1982. City Attorney, Braman, Oklahoma, 1979—. *Member:* Kay County (President, 1985-1986) and Oklahoma Bar Associations. ***PRACTICE AREAS:*** Public Utility Law; Insurance Defense Law; Personal Injury.

COUNSEL FOR: Kay Electric Cooperative; Town of Braman, Oklahoma; Blackwell Hospital Trust Authority; Blackwell Regional Hospital; Duck Creek Conservancy District; Shepherd Oil Co.; Shebester-Bechtel, Inc. Well Servicing; Allstate Insurance Co.; Wilkins Oklahoma Truck Supply; Blackwell Rural Water Corp.; Oklahoma Municipal Assurance Group; American Airlines Federal Credit Union; Blackwell-Tonkawa Airport Trust Authority; Emcompass Insurance; Newkirk Public Schools.

JAMES R. RODGERS

Established in 1904

105 NORTH MAIN
P.O. BOX 514
BLACKWELL, OKLAHOMA 74631
Telephone: 580-363-3684
Fax: 580-363-2434
Email: attorney@cyber-rover.com
URL: http://www.lawyers.com/rodgerslaw

General Civil Practice. Probate, Estate Planning, Real Estate, School Law, Education, Business Law, Personal Injury, Commercial and Oil and Gas Law. Trials.

FIRM PROFILE: James R. Rodgers has been practicing in the area since 1968 when the firm originally was Rodgers & Gurley. Mr. Rodgers maintains a general civil practice with an emphasis on probate, wills, trusts and estate planning. He primarily represents individuals, corporations and businesses throughout the state of Oklahoma. He has a legal assistant to help with timely attention to matters.

JAMES R. RODGERS, born Blackwell, Oklahoma, December 22, 1943; admitted to bar, 1968, Oklahoma. *Education:* University of Oklahoma (A.B., 1965); Southern Methodist University (J.D., 1968). Phi Alpha Delta. Assistant City Attorney, 1968-1975. *Member:* Kay County (President, 1978-1979), Oklahoma and American Bar Associations.

WILLIAM W. RODGERS (1907-1979)

ATTORNEYS FOR: Blackwell Board of Education; Southwest Cupid; Northern Oklahoma Disposal, Inc.; Williams Oil Company; Banc First (Blackwell Branch).

JAMES D. BRYANT

BROKEN ARROW, OKLAHOMA

(See Tulsa)

Commercial Litigation, Family Law, Divorce, Taxation, Bankruptcy.

EDGAR & PERIGO, P.C.

BROKEN ARROW, OKLAHOMA

(See Tulsa)

Family, Child Custody, Divorce, Adoptions, General Business, Guardianships, Real Estate, Probate, Estate Planning, Wills and Trusts, Civil Law, Juvenile Law.

HART LAW OFFICE

8409 EAST LANSING STREET
P.O. BOX 140206
BROKEN ARROW, OKLAHOMA 74014
Telephone: 918-271-1487
Fax: 918-296-3761
Email: amykhart@yahoo.com
URL: http://www.tulsaestatelaw.com

Estate Planning, Wills, Trusts, Probate, Living and Contested Wills, Power of Attorney, Personal Injury, Automobile and Railroad Accidents, Medical Malpractice, Property Damage, Unsafe Products, Wrongful Death.

MEMBER OF FIRM

AMY K. HART, born Oklahoma City, Oklahoma, April 25, 1974; admitted to bar, 1999, Oklahoma; 2000, Missouri. *Education:* University Center at Tulsa (B.A., 1993); University of Oklahoma (J.D., 1999). *Member:* Oklahoma and American Bar Associations; The Missouri Bar; Tulsa Estate Planning Forum. [JAG Captain, Missouri Army National Guard, 2000—; JAG Captain, U.S. Air Force Reserve, 2004—.]. ***PRACTICE AREAS:*** Estate Planning; Wills, Trusts, Probate; Living & Contested Wills; Power of Attorney; Personal Injury; Automobile & Railroad Accidents; Medical Malpractice; Property Damage; Unsafe Products; Wrongful Death. ***Email:*** amykhart@yahoo.com

SPENCE LAW OFFICE

BROKEN ARROW, OKLAHOMA

(See Tulsa)

Commercial and Civil Litigation, Construction Law, Real Property Law, General Practice Litigation, Trust and Estate Litigation, Bankruptcy.

LAW OFFICES OF SHANNON REASOR

CADDO, OKLAHOMA

(See Atoka)

General Practice, Real Estate, Probate, Estate Planning, Civil Litigation.

CYNTHIA FERRELL ASHWOOD, P.C.

814 MANVEL AVENUE
P.O. BOX 526
CHANDLER, OKLAHOMA 74834
Telephone: 405-258-0097
Fax: 405-258-1412
Email: cfaatty@brightok.net

General Civil Practice in all State and Federal Courts. Probate, Real Estate, Banking, Adoption, Commercial.

(This Listing Continued)

CYNTHIA FERRELL ASHWOOD, P.C., Chandler—Continued

CYNTHIA FERRELL ASHWOOD, born Oklahoma City, Oklahoma, May 28, 1960; admitted to bar, 1985, Oklahoma. *Education:* University of Oklahoma (B.A., 1982; J.D., 1985). Phi Alpha Delta. Editor, Oklahoma Bar Journal, 1987-1993. Assistant District Attorney, 1991-1992. *Member:* Lincoln County (Secretary/Treasurer, 1985-1986; President, 1986-1987), Oklahoma and American Bar Associations.

REPRESENTATIVE CLIENTS: Central Oklahoma Telephone Co., Inc.; First Bank of Chandler; First State Bank of Harrah; Central Oklahoma Federal Credit Union, Davenport, Okla.; City Attorney for City of Davenport, OK.; Bancfirst.
APPROVED TITLE EXAMINER FOR: American First Title & Trust Co., Oklahoma City; American Title & Insurance Co.

ATKINS & MARKOFF

CHANDLER, OKLAHOMA

(See Oklahoma City)

Personal Injury, Automobile Accidents, Wrongful Death, Trucking Accidents, Slip and Fall, Nursing Home Abuse, Head and Spinal Injuries, Dog Bites, Sexual Abuse, Criminal Law, Drug Crimes, DUI/DWI, Juvenile Crimes, General Practice, Family , Divorce, Adoptions, Child Custody, Child Support, Domestic Violence, Visitation Rights, Elder Law, Legal Malpractice, Medical Malpractice, Social Security, Social Security Disability, Taxation, IRS Audits, Property Tax Appeals, Tax Planning, Toxic Torts, Trust and Estate, Wills and Probate.

BUTTS & LENORA

Established in 1992

116 WEST EIGHTH STREET
P.O. BOX 337
CHANDLER, OKLAHOMA 74834-0337
Telephone: 405-258-1334
Fax: 405-258-0249
Email: lenoralaw@sbcglobal.net
Email: lenora@brightok.net
URL: http://www.lawyers.com/lenoralaw

Criminal Law, Civil Litigation, Family Law, Probate, Real Estate, Wills, Trusts and Estates, Personal Injury, Oil and Gas and Title Examinations.

MEMBERS OF FIRM

BENJAMIN E. BUTTS (1933-1997)

LARRY K. LENORA, born McAlester, Oklahoma, March 24, 1951; admitted to bar, 1976, Oklahoma. *Education:* University of Northern Iowa (B.A., 1973); University of Oklahoma (J.D., 1976). City Attorney, Chandler, 1980—. Supreme Court Justice, Sac and Fox Nation, 1999—. Certified Family Law Mediator. *Member:* Lincoln County (President, 1978) and Oklahoma (Member, Family Law Section) Bar Associations; National Association of Criminal Defense Lawyers; Oklahoma Criminal Defense Lawyers Association; Oklahoma Association of Municipal Attorneys. ***LANGUAGES:*** American Sign Language. ***PRACTICE AREAS:*** Criminal Law; Personal Injury Law; Family Law; Civil Litigation; Mediation. ***Email:*** lenora@brightok.net

ASSOCIATE

GREGORY A. UPTON, born Seminole, Oklahoma, August 2, 1971; admitted to bar, 1996, Oklahoma. *Education:* University of Oklahoma (B.A., 1993; J.D., 1996). *Member:* Lincoln County (President, 2001—), Oklahoma (Member, Real Property Section) and American Bar Associations. ***PRACTICE AREAS:*** Title Examinations; Real Estate; Probate; Oil and Gas Law; Wills; Trusts and Estates; Adoption Law.

REPRESENTATIVE CLIENTS: The Abstract Guaranty Company of Lincoln County; First Bank of Chandler; City of Chandler, Oklahoma; Wellston Oklahoma Public Works Authority; National American Insurance Co.; Realty Plus, Inc.; Lincoln County Sewer and Water Dist.; BancFirst, Prague, Oklahoma; Century 21.
APPROVED TITLE EXAMINERS FOR: First American Title & Trust Co., Oklahoma City; Chicago Title & Trust Co.

EAGLETON & NICHOLSON, P.C.

109 W. 9TH
CHANDLER, OKLAHOMA 74834
Telephone: 405-258-5301
Fax: 405-258-5302
Email: pordos@brightok.net

Oklahoma City Office: 3100 Bank One Center, 100 N. Broadway Avenue, 73102. Telephone: 405-236-0550. Fax: 405-236-0560. Email: eaglenk@coxinet.net

General Practice, Real Estate, Corporate Law, Commercial Law, Oil & Gas Law, Probate, Family Law, Bankruptcy, Estate Planning, Banking and Commercial Collections, Civil Litigation.

MARK J. PORDOS, born Denver, Colorado, October 30, 1958; admitted to bar, 1985, Oklahoma. *Education:* University of Oklahoma (B.A., 1980; M.B.A., 1985; J.D., 1985). Recipient, American Jurisprudence Award in Criminal Law. Member, Board of Editors, Oklahoma Law Review, 1985. Author: "Moser v. United States Steel, A New Approach to the Definition of Unspecified Minerals In An Oil and Gas Lease," Volume 37 Number Two, Oklahoma Law Review, 1984. *Member:* Lincoln County and Oklahoma Bar Associations. ***PRACTICE AREAS:*** Civil Practice; Commercial Law; Business Law; Corporate Law; Oil & Gas; Banking Law; Bankruptcy; Contracts; Real Estate; Litigation; Trusts and Estates; Probate; Personal Injury; Divorce; Child Custody.

(For Complete Biographical Data on all Personnel, see Professional Biographies at Oklahoma City)

DAN A. ERWIN

118 WEST EIGHTH STREET
CHANDLER, OKLAHOMA 74834
Telephone: 405-258-1336
Fax: 405-258-0764

General Practice. Trials. Probate, Real Estate, Corporate, Negligence, Personal Injury, Real Property, Oil and Gas Law, Wills, Trusts and Estate Planning.

DAN A. ERWIN, born Oklahoma City, Oklahoma, October 31, 1937; admitted to bar, 1963, Oklahoma. *Education:* University of Oklahoma (B.B.A., 1960); University of Arkansas and University of Oklahoma (LL.B., 1963). Phi Alpha Delta. *Member:* Lincoln County (President, 1964-1965), Oklahoma Bar Association. ***PRACTICE AREAS:*** Civil Litigation; Probate Law; Commercial Practice.

REPRESENTATIVE CLIENTS: Union Bank of Chandler, Okla.
APPROVED TITLE EXAMINER FOR: First American Title & Trust Co., Oklahoma City; Chicago Title & Trust Co.; Lawyers Title & Trust.

R. PATRICK GILMORE

P.O. BOX 9
CHANDLER, OKLAHOMA 74834
Telephone: 405-258-4262
Fax: 405-258-4520

General Civil Trial Practice, State and Federal Courts.

R. PATRICK GILMORE, born Elmore City, Oklahoma, March 24, 1951; admitted to bar, 1976, Oklahoma. *Education:* Central State University (B.A., 1973); University of Oklahoma (J.D., 1976). *Member:* Lincoln County, Oklahoma and American Bar Associations. ***PRACTICE AREAS:*** Civil Trial Practice.

COUNSEL TO: Chandler (U.S.A.), Inc.; National American Insurance Co.; Cassidy Limited Partnership; High Plains Farm and Farm Services, Inc.

THOMAS B. GOODWIN

429 BROADWAY
P.O. BOX 160
CHEYENNE, OKLAHOMA 73628
Telephone: 580-497-3378
Fax: 580-497-2297
Email: US544@aol.com

General Civil Trial Practice. Real Estate, Probate, Personal Injury, Negligence, Oil and Gas Law, Wills, Trusts.

THOMAS B. GOODWIN, born San Diego, California, May 13, 1949; admitted to bar, 1978, Oklahoma; 1981, U.S. Supreme Court. *Education:* Panhandle State University (B.S., 1975); Oklahoma University (J.D., 1978). *Member:* Roger Mills County, Oklahoma and American Bar Associations. [With U.S. Army, 1969-1971]. ***PRACTICE AREAS:*** Probate; Trusts and Estate Planning; Real Estate; Oil and Gas Law; Civil Trial; Personal Injury.

IVESTER, IVESTER & IVESTER

CHEYENNE, OKLAHOMA

(See Sayre)

Civil Litigation, Business Law, Commercial Law, Corporate Law, Partnership Law, Insurance, Real Estate, Family Law, Oil & Gas, Probate, Taxation, Trusts and Estates.

NEWELL E. WRIGHT, JR.

429 BROADWAY
P.O. BOX 160
CHEYENNE, OKLAHOMA 73628
Telephone: 580-497-3378
Fax: 580-497-2297

Practice limited to Trials and Appeals in all State and Federal Courts.

NEWELL E. WRIGHT, JR., born McAlester, Oklahoma, August 13, 1938; admitted to bar, 1970, Oklahoma; 1974, U.S. District Court, Eastern District of Oklahoma; 1977, U.S. District Court, Western District of Oklahoma; 1981, U.S. Supreme Court. *Education:* Southeastern Oklahoma State University (B.A., 1960); University of Oklahoma (J.D., 1970). Delta Theta Phi. Municipal Judge, City of McAlester, Oklahoma, 1972-1976. *Member:* Oklahoma (Member, Board of Editors; Member, Professional Responsibility Commission) and American Bar Associations; The Association of Trial Lawyers of America. ***PRACTICE AREAS:*** Trial Practice; Appellate Practice.

A List of Representative Clients will be furnished upon request.

ATKINS & MARKOFF

CHICKASHA, OKLAHOMA

(See Oklahoma City)

Personal Injury, Automobile Accidents, Wrongful Death, Trucking Accidents, Slip and Fall, Nursing Home Abuse, Head and Spinal Injuries, Dog Bites, Sexual Abuse, Criminal Law, Drug Crimes, DUI/DWI, Juvenile Crimes, General Practice, Family , Divorce, Adoptions, Child Custody, Child Support, Domestic Violence, Visitation Rights, Elder Law, Legal Malpractice, Medical Malpractice, Social Security, Social Security Disability, Taxation, IRS Audits, Property Tax Appeals, Tax Planning, Toxic Torts, Trust and Estate, Wills and Probate.

HAYS & GORDON

Established in 1947

THIRD FLOOR
MID-FIRST BANK BUILDING
228 WEST CHICKASHA AVENUE
CHICKASHA, OKLAHOMA 73018-2669
Telephone: 405-224-1950
405-224-7575
Fax: 405-222-1033
URL: http://www.haysgordon.com

General Civil Practice. Probate, Real Estate, Estate Planning, Commercial Law, Commercial Litigation, Health Law.

ROBERT J. HAYS, born Weatherford, Oklahoma, March 25, 1939; admitted to bar, 1965, Oklahoma. *Education:* Southwestern Oklahoma State University; University of Oklahoma (B.A., 1962; J.D., 1965). Phi Alpha Delta. Vice President, State Association of County Bar Presidents, 1966-1967. Regent, University of Science and Arts of Oklahoma. *Member:* Grady County (President, 1966-1967, 1973), Oklahoma (Member: Code Civil Procedure Committee, 1973; Client Security Fund Committee, 1985-1997; Bar-Media Relations Committee, 1999-2003) and American Bar Associations. Fellow, Oklahoma Bar Foundation (Trustee, 1987-1990). ***PRACTICE AREAS:*** Probate; Real Estate; Commercial Law; Estate Planning. ***Email:*** robert.hays@haysgordon.com

PHIL W. GORDON, born Duncan, Oklahoma, December 24, 1952; admitted to bar, 1978, Oklahoma, U.S. District Court, Western and Eastern Districts of Oklahoma and Court of Indian Offenses, Anadarko Oklahoma (CFR Court). *Education:* Oklahoma State University (B.S., 1975); University of Oklahoma (J.D., 1978). Phi Delta Phi. Member, Board of Directors, Chickasha Chamber of Commerce, 1995-1997. *Member:* Grady County (Treasurer, 1983-1986; President, 1987-1988) and Oklahoma (Member: Law Day Committee, 1980-1981; Board of Directors, Young Lawyers Division, 1980-1981; Bar Media Relations Committee, 1988-1993) Bar Associations; Oklahoma Health Lawyers Association; American Health Lawyers Association. ***PRACTICE AREAS:*** Real Estate; Probate Law; Estate Planning; Health Law; School Law; Commercial Law. ***Email:*** phil.gordon@haysgordon.com

REPRESENTATIVE CLIENTS: Chickasha Bank & Trust Co., Sooner State Bank; Hermetic Switch, Inc.; Bank of Union; Cochran Abstract Co.; Grady Memorial Hospital; Town of Cyril; Joe Brown Company, Inc.; Creative Metal Products, Inc.; Chickasha Dr. Pepper Bottling Co.
REFERENCE: Chickasha Bank & Trust Co.
APPROVED ATTORNEYS FOR: First American Title Insurance Co.; American Security Title Insurance Co.; Stewart Title Insurance Co.

JOHNSTON & ASSOCIATES

Established in 1994

118 NORTH FOURTH STREET
P.O. BOX F
CHICKASHA, OKLAHOMA 73023
Telephone: 405-224-4000
Fax: 405-224-0003
Email: johnstonlawfirm@sbcglobal.net

General Practice, Environmental Law. including Land Use, Landowners Rights Wills and Probate.

FIRM PROFILE: The firm also regularly practices before the Oklahoma Corporation Commission and Department of Environmental Quality. The Johnston's have achieved multi-million dollar verdicts and settlements in environmental law and are members of the Million Dollar Advocacy Forum.

KENNETH R. JOHNSTON, born Lexington, Oklahoma, November 24, 1944; admitted to bar, 1974, Oklahoma; 1976, U.S. District Court, Western District of Oklahoma; 1978, U.S. Court of Appeals, Tenth Circuit; 1980, U.S. Supreme Court. *Education:* University of Oklahoma (B.S., 1969; J.D., 1973). Member: Oklahoma Crime Commission Courts Committee, 1978-1981; Regent for University of Science and Arts of Oklahoma, 1983-1997. *Member:* Grady County (President, 1976), Oklahoma (Member, Faculties Committee, 1984) and American (Member: Agriculture Committee, 1984—; Environmental Committee, 1990—) Bar Associations; Oklahoma Trial Lawyers Association; The Association of Trial Lawyers of America. [Capt., U.S. Army Transportation Officer, 1969-1971]. ***Email:*** johnston@ionet.net

WES JOHNSTON, born Norman, Oklahoma, 1964; admitted to bar, 1989, Oklahoma; 1997, Colorado; U.S. District Court, Western District of Oklahoma; U.S. District Court, District of Colorado; U.S. Court of Appeals, Tenth Circuit; U.S. Supreme Court. *Education:* University of Oklahoma (B.A., 1986; J.D., 1989). Oxford University Law Program, 1987. Phi Delta Phi. American Inns of Court. Regent for University of Science & Arts of Oklahoma, 2003-2005. *Member:* Denver, Grady County, Colorado and Oklahoma Bar Associations; The Association of Trial Lawyers of America; Oklahoma Trial Lawyers Association. ***Email:*** johnstonlawfirm@sbcglobal.net

ASSOCIATE

JOHN H. GRAVES, born Oklahoma City, Oklahoma, December 21, 1977; admitted to bar, 2003, Oklahoma; U.S. District Court, Western District of Oklahoma; U.S. Court of Appeals, Tenth Circuit. *Education:* University of Oklahoma (B.A., magna cum laude, 2000; J.D., 2003). Order of Barristers. Recipient, American Jurisprudence Award for outstanding performance in Trial Techniques. Member: Whittier Moot Court Team, 2002; ABA Client Counseling Team, 2002; Pepperdine Entertainment Law Moot Court Team, 2003; A.T.L.A. National Student Trial Team, 2003. Member, Board of Advocates, 2001-2003. *Member:* Grady County (President, 2005), Oklahoma County, Oklahoma and American Bar Associations. ***Email:*** johnstonlawfirm@sbcglobal.net

PARK, NELSON, CAYWOOD, JONES

122 NORTH FOURTH STREET
P.O. BOX 968
CHICKASHA, OKLAHOMA 73023-0968
Telephone: 405-224-0386
Telecopier: 405-224-0907
URL: http://www.pncj.com

Civil Practice, Probate, Real Estate, Environmental Law, Commercial Law, Oil and Gas Law.

MEMBERS OF FIRM

ROBERT B. PARK (Retired)

JOHN M. NELSON, born Amber, Oklahoma, August 18, 1939; admitted to bar, 1963, Oklahoma; 1997, Texas; U.S. District Court, Western and Eastern Districts of Oklahoma; U.S. Court of Appeals, Tenth Circuit; U.S. Supreme Court. *Education:* University of Oklahoma (B.A., 1961; LL.B., 1963). Phi Delta Phi. Member, Board of Editors, Oklahoma Law Review, 1961-1963. Member, Oklahoma Crime Commission, 1971-1973. *Member:* Grady County, Oklahoma and American Bar Associations; The Association of Trial Lawyers of America. Fellow, American College of Trial Lawyers. ***PRACTICE AREAS:*** Environmental Law; General Practice; Probate; Real Estate Law; Civil Practice; Personal Injury. ***Email:*** jnelson@pncj.com

KERRY W. CAYWOOD, born Watonga, Oklahoma, February 23, 1937; admitted to bar, 1963, Oklahoma; U.S. District Court, Western and Eastern Districts of Oklahoma; U.S. Court of Appeals, Tenth Circuit; U.S. Supreme Court. *Education:* Oklahoma State University (B.S., 1959); University of Oklahoma (LL.B., 1963). Phi Delta Phi. Member, Board of Editors, Oklahoma Law Review, 1961-1963. Assistant District Attorney for District No. 6, State of Oklahoma, 1967-1970. *Member:* Grady County, Oklahoma and American Bar Associations; The Association of Trial Lawyers of America; Oklahoma Trial Lawyers Association. ***PRACTICE AREAS:*** Civil Practice; Probate; Real Estate; Commercial Law; Personal Injury; Oil and Gas Law. ***Email:*** kcaywood@pncj.com

CHARLES W. PARK, born Chickasha, Oklahoma, January 11, 1951; admitted to bar, 1976, Oklahoma; U.S. District Court, Western District of Oklahoma; U.S. Court of Appeals, Tenth Circuit; U.S. Supreme Court. *Education:* University of Oklahoma (B.A., 1973); Oxford University, Oxford, England and University of Oklahoma (J.D., 1976). Phi Alpha Delta. Member, Board of Editors, American Indian Law Review, 1975-1976. *Member:* Grady County, Oklahoma and American Bar Associations; The Association of Trial Lawyers of America. ***PRACTICE AREAS:*** Civil Practice; Probate; Real Estate; Guardianship and Conservatorship. ***Email:*** cpark@pncj.com

ANGELA CAYWOOD JONES, born Chickasha, Oklahoma, August 3, 1971; admitted to bar, 2000, Oklahoma; U.S. District Court, Western District of Oklahoma. *Education:* Oklahoma State University (B.F.A., 1993); University of Oklahoma (J.D., with highest honors, 2000). Order of the Coif. Phi Delta Phi. Note Editor, Oklahoma Law Review. Recipient: American Jurisprudence Awards in Contracts, Civil Procedure I and Land Finance. Comfort Scholar. *Member:* Grady County, Oklahoma and American Bar Associations; Oklahoma Trial Lawyers Association; The Association of Trial Lawyers of America. ***PRACTICE AREAS:*** Civil Practice; Environmental Law; Personal Injury; Real Estate; Wills; Trusts and Estates; Probate; Guardianship; Conservatorship. ***Email:*** ajones@pncj.com

REPRESENTATIVE CLIENTS: First National Bank and Trust Company, Chickasha, Oklahoma; Badgett Corporation; Chickasha Public Schools; The University of Science and Arts of Oklahoma; Gabriel Meritor Corporation; Hart Manufacturing, Inc. of Chickasha; Big Iron Transportation Company; First National Bank - Lindsay; Cyril State Bank - Cyril.
APPROVED ATTORNEYS FOR: Farm Service Agency; American First Title & Trust Co.; Southwest Title & Trust Co.
REFERENCE: The First National Bank and Trust Company, Chickasha.

B. DAVID SISSON

CHICKASHA, OKLAHOMA

(See Norman)

Bankruptcy, Domestic, Probate and Estate Planning, Family Law, Divorce, Child Custody Modifications.

LOGAN & LOWRY, LLP

CLAREMORE, OKLAHOMA

(See Vinita)

General Practice, Including Trials in all State and Federal Courts, Eminent Domain, Environmental and Coal, Banking, Commercial Transactions, Creditors' Rights and Bankruptcy, Corporation, Public Utility, Real Estate, Estate Planning and Probate, Criminal, Domestic Relations, Civil Rights, Employment, Appellate Practice and Administrative Law.

TAYLOR, BURRAGE, FOSTER, MALLETT, DOWNS & RAMSEY, P.C.

400 WEST FOURTH STREET
P.O. BOX 309
CLAREMORE, OKLAHOMA 74018-0309
Telephone: 918-343-4100
Fax: 918-343-4900
URL: http://www.soonerlaw.com
URL: http://www.lawyers.com/soonerlaw

Civil and Criminal Practice in all State and Federal Courts. Employment Law, Healthcare Law, Medical Malpractice, Professional Liability, Insurance Defense, Real Estate, Probate, Guardianships, Corporation, Commercial and Personal Injury Law.

(This Listing Continued)

TAYLOR, BURRAGE, FOSTER, MALLETT, DOWNS & RAMSEY, P.C., Claremore—Continued

MEMBERS OF FIRM

STRATTON TAYLOR, born Sallisaw, Oklahoma, 1956; admitted to bar, 1983, Oklahoma; U.S. District Court, Northern, Eastern and Western Districts of Oklahoma; U.S. Court of Appeals, Tenth Circuit and U.S. Supreme Court. *Education:* University of Tulsa (B.S.E., 1978; J.D., 1982). State Senator, 1982—. President Pro Tempore, 1995-2002, State Senate and President Pro Tempore Emeritus, 2002—, State Senate. Commissioner, National Conference of Commissioners on Uniform State Laws, 1985—. *Member:* Rogers County and Oklahoma Bar Associations; Association of Trial Lawyers of America. ***REPORTED CASES:*** Hinds v. Warren Transport, 882 P.2d 1099 (Okl. App. 1994); Morgan v. Galilean Health Ent., Inc.; 977 P.2d 357 (Okl. 1998); Southern Disposal, Inc. v. Texas Waste Management and the City of Hugo, 161 F.3d 1259 (10th Cir. 1998); B. Willis, C.P.A., Inc. v. Goodpaster and Public Service Company, 183 F.3d 1231, 1999 WL 510512 (10th Cir. 1999). ***PRACTICE AREAS:*** Civil Litigation; Insurance Defense; Condemnation; Business Representation Law; Personal Injury; Probate.

SEAN BURRAGE, born Durant, Oklahoma, 1968; admitted to bar, 1993, Oklahoma; U.S. District Court, Northern, Eastern and Western Districts of Oklahoma; U.S. Court of Appeals, Tenth Circuit and U.S. Supreme Court. *Education:* University of Oklahoma (B.B.A., 1990; J.D., 1993). Phi Delta Phi. Associate, Council Oak American Inn of Court. Legislative Counsel, U.S. Senator, David L. Boren, 1993-1994. Director of State and Federal Relations, University of Oklahoma, 1994-1996. *Member:* Rogers County (President, 2001), Oklahoma (Associate Bar Examiner) and American Bar Associations. ***REPORTED CASES:*** Magnolia Marine Transport Co. v. OK 366 F.3d 1153 (10th Cir. Okla., 2004); In re B.C. 15 P.3d 8 (Okla. Civ. App. 2000). ***PRACTICE AREAS:*** Civil Litigation; Personal Injury; Business Law; Condemnation. ***Email:*** sburrage@soonerlaw.com

TONEY D. FOSTER, born Oklahoma City, Oklahoma, 1950; admitted to bar, 1995, Oklahoma; U.S. District Court, Northern and Western Districts of Oklahoma and U.S. Supreme Court. *Education:* Oklahoma City University (B.A., 1992); University of Tulsa (J.D., 1994). *Member:* Rogers County, Oklahoma and American Bar Associations; Oklahoma Land Title Association (Former President). ***PRACTICE AREAS:*** Civil Litigation; Real Estate; Condemnation; Zoning, Planning and Land Use; Probate; Guardianship. ***Email:*** tfoster@soonerlaw.com

BRADLEY H. MALLETT, born Talihina, Oklahoma, 1968; admitted to bar, 1993, Oklahoma; U.S. District Court, Eastern, Northern and Western Districts of Oklahoma and U.S. Supreme Court. *Education:* University of Oklahoma (B.B.A., with distinction, 1990); Harvard University (J.D., 1993). *Member:* Rogers County and Oklahoma Bar Associations; Oklahoma Trial Lawyers Association; Oklahoma Criminal Defense Lawyers Association. ***PRACTICE AREAS:*** Civil Litigation; Personal Injury; Business Law; Condemnation; Family Law; Criminal Defense. ***Email:*** bmallett@soonerlaw.com

DARRELL W. DOWNS, born Pryor, Oklahoma, 1962; admitted to bar, 1987, Oklahoma; U.S. District Court, Northern, Eastern and Western Districts of Oklahoma; U.S. Court of Appeals, Tenth Circuit and U.S. Supreme Court. *Education:* University of Oklahoma (B.B.A., 1984; J.D., with distinction, 1987). Phi Alpha Delta. *Member:* Oklahoma County, Rogers County, Oklahoma and American Bar Associations; Oklahoma Association of Defense Counsel; National Health Lawyers Association; Oklahoma Health Lawyers Association; Defense Research Institute. ***PRACTICE AREAS:*** Civil Litigation; Medical Malpractice Law; Health Care Law; Employment Law; Professional Liability Law; Insurance Law. ***Email:*** ddowns@soonerlaw.com

MARK H. RAMSEY, born Oklahoma City, Oklahoma, 1958; admitted to bar, 1985, Oklahoma; 1986, U.S. District Court, Western District of Oklahoma; 1988, U.S. Court of Appeals for the Tenth Circuit; 1994, U.S. District Court, Eastern District of Oklahoma; 2000, U.S. District Court, Northern District of Oklahoma; 2001, U.S. Supreme Court. *Education:* University of Central Oklahoma (B.A., Economics, 1980); University of Oklahoma College of Law (J.D., 1984). Associate Commissioner, National Conference of Commissioners on Uniform State Laws, 1990-2000, 2002—. Former Senior Staff Attorney, Oklahoma State Senate. Author: "What is a 'Revenue Bill' within the Meaning of Our Most Recent Constitutional Amendment?" Oklahoma Bar Journal, Volume 63, No. 22, May 30, 1992, pg. 1567. Co-Author with Fred Miller and Patricia Sommer, "Uniform Laws Committee: An Update for 1993," Oklahoma Bar Journal, Volume 64, No. 12, March 27, 1993, pg. 903. Adjunct Professor, Oklahoma City University School of Law, 1993. *Member:* Rogers County, Oklahoma (Chair, Uniform Laws Committee, 1998-1999; Vice-Chair, Uniform Laws Committee, 1990-1998) and American Bar Associations. ***PRACTICE AREAS:*** Civil Litigation; Municipal Law; Condemnation; Business Law; Insurance Law. ***Email:*** mramsey@soonerlaw.com

MARK D. ANTINORO, born Wilmington, Delaware, 1969; admitted to bar, 1998, Oklahoma, U.S. District Court, Northern and Eastern Districts of Oklahoma and U.S. Court of Appeals for Tenth Circuit. *Education:* Albertus Magnus College (B.A., Political Science, 1992); University of Tulsa (J.D., 1997). *Member:* Oklahoma Bar Association (Member Board of Directors, Young Lawyers Division). ***PRACTICE AREAS:*** Personal Injury; Family Law; Criminal Defense; Municipal Law. ***Email:*** mantinoro@soonerlaw.com

CLINT RUSSELL, born Claremore, Oklahoma, 1971; admitted to bar, 2001, Oklahoma, U.S. District Court, Northern, Eastern and Western Districts of Oklahoma and U.S. Court of Appeals, Tenth Circuit. *Education:* Pennsylvania State University (B.A., with distinction, 1993); University of Oklahoma (M.A., with distinction, 1995); Oklahoma City University School of Law (J.D., magna cum laude, 2001). Phi Beta Kappa. Member, Oklahoma City Law Review. Law Clerk to Chief Judge Robin Cauthron, U.S. District Court for the Western District of Oklahoma, 2001-2002. *Member:* Oklahoma County, Rogers County, Oklahoma and American Bar Associations; Federal Bar Association. ***PRACTICE AREAS:*** Civil Litigation; Environmental Law; Business Law; Corporate Law; Admiralty and Maritime Law; Labor and Employment; Condemnation. ***Email:*** crussell@soonerlaw.com

AMY L. EVANS, born Tulsa, Oklahoma, 1968; admitted to bar, 1992, Oklahoma, U.S. District Court, Northern, Eastern and Western Districts of Oklahoma and U.S. Court of Appeals, Tenth Circuit. *Education:* University of Tulsa (B.S.B.A., 1989; J.D., 1992). Managing Editor, Tulsa Law Journal, 1991-1992. Law Clerk to the Honorable Tom R. Cornish, U.S. Bankruptcy Judge, Eastern District of Oklahoma, 1994-2003. *Member:* Oklahoma Bar Association (Director, Bankruptcy and Reorganization Section, 2003—). ***PRACTICE AREAS:*** Bankruptcy. ***Email:*** aevans@soonerlaw.com

REPRESENTATIVE CLIENTS: AIG Insurance; OMSNIC RRG; American Association of Orthodontist RRG; American Electric Power/PSO; Anchor Industries; Blue Circle; Columbia National Title Insurance; Deaconess Hospital; Engrex, Inc.; First National Bank of Antlers; First National of America; Hillcrest Hospital; Hospital Casualty Company; KAMO Power; Locke Supply Company; National American Insurance Company; National Insurance Company; Norman Regional Hospital; Oklahoma Farmers Union Insurance; Oklahoma Natural Gas Company; Samson Resources; Southwestern Electric Power Co.; Terra Nitrogen; The Chubb Group of Insurance Companies; Tulsa Stockyards; Waste Management; Western Farmers Electric Cooperative.
APPROVED ATTORNEYS FOR: Chicago Title; Commonwealth Land Title; Lawyers Title Insurance Corp.; First American Title Insurance.
REFERENCES: RCB Bank; Stillwater National Bank; Bank of Commerce, Catoosa.

PATRICK T. CORNELL, P.C.

Established in 1973

117 N. 5TH
P.O. BOX 847
CLINTON, OKLAHOMA 73601
Telephone: 580-323-6133
Fax: 580-323-7074
Email: patrickcornell@sbcglobal.net
URL: http://www.lawyers.com/cornell

General Practice in all State and Federal Courts. Probate, Personal Injury, Real Estate, Oil and Gas, Condemnation, Family, Corporation, Criminal and Banking Law.

PATRICK T. CORNELL, born Clinton, Oklahoma, October 9, 1948; admitted to bar, 1973, Oklahoma. *Education:* University of Oklahoma (B.B.A., 1970; J.D., 1973). Recipient, American Jurisprudence Award. Mayor, City of Clinton, Oklahoma, 1984-1988. *Member:* Custer County (President, 1989) and Oklahoma Bar Associations. ***PRACTICE AREAS:*** Probate Law; Corporation Law; Real Estate Law; Wills; Trusts; Banking Law.

RANDOLPH S. MEACHAM, P.C.

Established in 1998

525 SOUTH 30TH STREET
P.O. BOX 1236
CLINTON, OKLAHOMA 73601
Telephone: 580-323-4370
Fax: 580-323-4968
Email: meachamr@citlnet.net

General Practice, Civil, Trial, Family Law, Criminal Law, Personal Injury, Bankruptcy, Agricultural Law, Commercial Litigation, Banking..

RANDOLPH S. MEACHAM, born Clinton, Oklahoma, January 20, 1947; admitted to bar, 1972, Oklahoma. *Education:* University of Oklahoma (B.A., 1969; J.D., 1972). Delta Theta Phi. Attorney For: City of Duncan, Oklahoma, 1972-1976; City of Clinton, 1978—. Member, Judicial Nominating Commission, 1979-1985. Director, Oklahoma Bar Professional Liability Insurance Company, 1988-1992. *Member:* Custer County, Oklahoma and American Bar Associations; American Trial Lawyers Association; Oklahoma Trial Lawyers Association. ***PRACTICE AREAS:*** General Practice; Civil Practice; Trial Practice; Family Law; Criminal Law; Personal Injury Law; Bankruptcy; Agricultural Law; Commercial Litigation. ***Email:*** rsmeacham@sbcglobal.net

OF COUNSEL

MICHAEL G. SMITH, born Clinton, Oklahoma, September 2, 1955; admitted to bar, 1992, Texas; 2003, Oklahoma and U.S. District Court, Western District of Oklahoma. *Education:* University of Oklahoma (B.A., 1988; J.D., with honors, 1992). Phi Delta Phi; Christian Legal Society. ABI Instructor: Law and Banking. Member, Academic Hearing Tribunal, 1991. Member, Board of Advocates, 1990-1992. Teaching Assistant, Legal Research and Writing, University of Oklahoma, 1991-1992. *Member:* Amarillo Bar Association; State Bar of Texas; Panhandle Bankruptcy Bar; American Bankruptcy Institute. Life Fellow, Texas Bar Foundation. ***PRACTICE AREAS:*** Bankruptcy Law; Agricultural Law; Commercial Litigation; Banking Law; General Practice; Civil Practice; Trial Practice; Family Law; Criminal Law; Personal Injury. ***Email:*** msmith-meachamlaw@sbcglobal.net

RICHARD J. PHILLIPS

Established in 1991

5TH AND FRISCO AVENUE
P.O. BOX 1296
CLINTON, OKLAHOMA 73601
Telephone: 580-323-3044
Fax: 580-323-3059
Email: rjphill@swbell.net

Cheyenne, Oklahoma Office: Beavin Building, P.O. Box 43, 73628. Telephone: 580-497-2423.

General Civil and Criminal Practice. Probate, Real Estate, Taxation, Oil and Gas, Personal Injury, Bankruptcy and Family Law, Business Law, Wills and Estates.

RICHARD J. PHILLIPS, born Boulder, Colorado, April 9, 1961; admitted to bar, 1986, Oklahoma; 1987, U.S. District Court, Western District of Oklahoma and U.S. Court of Appeals, 10th Circuit. *Education:* Southwestern Oklahoma State University (B.S., 1983); University of Oklahoma (J.D., 1986). Phi Alpha Delta. Member, American Indian Law Review, 1984-1986. Writing Competition Co-Editor, 1985-1986. *Member:* Custer

(This Listing Continued)

County (President, 1997) Oklahoma (Member, Taxation Committee) and American Bar Associations. Fellow, Oklahoma Bar Foundation.

RODOLPH & FOSTER

Not a partnership
123 SOUTH 6TH STREET
P.O. BOX 277
CLINTON, OKLAHOMA 73601
Telephone: 580-323-6090
Fax: 580-323-6102

Taloga, Oklahoma, Office: Collier Building . Telephone: 580-328-5494.

General Civil and Criminal Practice in all State and Federal Courts. Probate, Real Estate, Oil and Gas, Personal Injury, Negligence, Banking Law, Family Law, Divorce, Custody, Wills.

DON RODOLPH, born Thomas, Oklahoma, January 14, 1943; admitted to bar, 1969, Oklahoma. *Education:* Southwestern State College (B.S., 1966); University of Oklahoma (J.D., 1969). Delta Theta Phi. *Member:* Custer County and Oklahoma Bar Associations. ***PRACTICE AREAS:*** Probate; Trusts; Estate Planning; Federal Income Tax; State Income Tax; Real Estate; Oil and Gas.

ROGER W. FOSTER, born Fairview, Oklahoma, September 3, 1945; admitted to bar, 1989, Oklahoma. *Education:* Northwestern Oklahoma State University (B.S., 1986); Oklahoma City University (J.D., 1989). Phi Delta Phi. *Member:* Custer County (President), Dewey County and Oklahoma Bar Associations. ***PRACTICE AREAS:*** Civil Trials; Criminal Defense; Divorce; Probate; Trusts; Estate Planning; Personal Injury; Social Security. ***Email:*** rogerfoster@hotmail.com

REPRESENTATIVE CLIENTS: Town of Leedey; First National Bank of Leedey; Clinton Production Credit Assn.; Town of Foss; Farmrail System, Inc.; Farmrail Corporation; Grainbelt Corp.; Town of Taloga.
APPROVED EXAMINING ATTORNEYS FOR: American First Title & Trust.

FORSYTH, CUBBAGE & ASSOCIATES, P.C.

Established in 1971
200 E. OAK STREET, SUITE 101
P.O. BOX 7
CUSHING, OKLAHOMA 74023
Telephone: 918-225-7700
Fax: 918-225-7200
URL: http://www.fca-law.com

Mediation, Business Law, Estate Planning, Trusts, Probate, Real Estate, Commercial Law, Banking Law.

JOHN E. FORSYTH, born Chicago, Illinois, November 26, 1954; admitted to bar, 1978, Oklahoma; 1982, U.S. District Court, Western District of Oklahoma; 1984, U.S. District Court, Northern District of Oklahoma; 1985, U.S. District Court, Eastern District of Oklahoma. *Education:* Regis College; Creighton University (B.S.B.A., 1976); University of Oklahoma (J.D., 1978). Phi Alpha Delta. Editor, Oklahoma Law Review, 1977-1978. Assistant District Attorney, Payne County, Oklahoma, 1979-1981. Member, 1979-1984, 1990— and Chairman, 1982-1984, Cushing City Planning Commission. Member, 1984-1987; 1993—; Chairman, 1985-1987, Cushing City Commission. Chairman, Cushing Hospital Authority, 1985-1987. *Member:* Payne County (President, 1994) and Oklahoma Bar Associations. ***PRACTICE AREAS:*** Mediation; Business Law; Estate Planning; Trusts; Probate; Real Estate; Commercial Law; Banking Law. ***Email:*** jforsyth@fca-law.com

STEPHEN B. CUBBAGE, born Oklahoma, November 27, 1941; admitted to bar, 1971, Oklahoma; U.S. District Court, Western and Northern Districts of Oklahoma. *Education:* Oklahoma University (B.A., 1964); University of Tulsa (J.D., 1971). Sigma Chi Fraternity. Municipal Judge, City of Cushing, 1972—. Chairman: Cushing Economic Development Council, 1999-2000; Cushing Education Foundation, 1995-1996. *Member:* Payne County and Oklahoma Bar Associations. Fellow, Oklahoma Bar Foundation. [Retired Captain, U.S. Marine Corp.]. ***REPORTED CASES:*** Kuykendall v. Malernee, 1973 OK Civ.App. 14, 516 P.2d 558, cited at 17 Am Jur 2d, Consumer and Borrower Protection #393. ***PRACTICE AREAS:*** Real Estate; Probate; Business Law; Commercial Law; Estate Planning; Trusts; Mediation. ***Email:*** scubbage@fca-law.com

REPRESENTATIVE CLIENTS: Dilwell Fracturing Services, Inc.; Continental Concrete, Inc.; DCA, Inc.; SST Development Group, Inc.; Spirit Bank; Pipeline Regulatory Consultants, Inc.; VMI, Inc.; Stewart Stone, Inc.; Fast Close Title & Closing Co.
LICENSED AGENT FOR: Stewart Title Guaranty; Approved examiners for all major title insurance carriers.

SZLICHTA & RAMSEY

CUSHING, OKLAHOMA

(See Stillwater)

General Practice. Trials. Family, School, Municipal, Administrative Law and Criminal Defense Law.

ATKINS & MARKOFF

DUNCAN, OKLAHOMA

(See Oklahoma City)

Personal Injury, Automobile Accidents, Wrongful Death, Trucking Accidents, Slip and Fall, Nursing Home Abuse, Head and Spinal Injuries, Dog Bites, Sexual Abuse, Criminal Law, Drug Crimes, DUI/DWI, Juvenile Crimes, General Practice, Family , Divorce, Adoptions, Child Custody, Child Support, Domestic Violence, Visitation Rights, Elder Law, Legal Malpractice,

(This Listing Continued)

Medical Malpractice, Social Security, Social Security Disability, Taxation, IRS Audits, Property Tax Appeals, Tax Planning, Toxic Torts, Trust and Estate, Wills and Probate.

BONNEY CORLEY LLP

Established in 1956
SUITE 300 BANCFIRST BUILDING
16 SOUTH 9TH STREET
DUNCAN, OKLAHOMA 73533
Telephone: 580-255-5600
Fax: 580-255-5843
Email: bcbsc@texhoma.net
URL: http://www.bonneycorley.com

General Civil Trial and Appellate Practice, State and Federal Courts. Corporation, School Law, Probate, Estate Planning, Oil and Gas, Banking, Real Property, Employment Law, Commercial Law, Domestic Relations and Personal Injury.

MEMBERS OF FIRM

HENRY C. BONNEY, born Yazoo City, Mississippi, February 16, 1936; admitted to bar, 1961, Oklahoma. *Education:* University of Oklahoma (B.S.E., 1958; LL.B., 1961). Phi Alpha Delta. *Member:* Stephens County (President, 1963), Oklahoma and American Bar Associations. [1st Lieut., U.S. Army Artillery, 1961-1963]. ***PRACTICE AREAS:*** Probate; Estate Planning; Oil and Gas Law. ***Email:*** bonney@bonneycorley.com

RONALD E. CORLEY, born Effingham, Illinois, July 24, 1942; admitted to bar, 1970, Oklahoma. *Education:* Oklahoma State University (B.A., 1965); University of Oklahoma (J.D., 1970). Order of the Coif; Phi Delta Phi. Editor, Oklahoma Law Review, 1968-1970. *Member:* Stephens County (President, 1976), Oklahoma (Associate Bar Examiner) and American Bar Associations. [Capt., U.S. Army, 1965-1967]. ***PRACTICE AREAS:*** Oil and Gas Law; Real Property. ***Email:*** corley@bonneycorley.com

DAVID L. BENEFIELD, born Paris, Texas, July 31, 1953; admitted to bar, 1978, Oklahoma. *Education:* Chipola Junior College (A.A., 1973); Florida State University (B.A., 1975); University of Oklahoma (J.D., 1977). Phi Delta Phi (Scholarship Chairman, 1976-1977). Assistant District Attorney, McCurtain County, Oklahoma, 1978. *Member:* Stephens County (President, 1985), Oklahoma and American Bar Associations. ***PRACTICE AREAS:*** School Law; Probate; Estate Planning; Employment Law. ***Email:*** benefield@bonneycorley.com

SCOTT W. STONE, born Salem, Illinois, January 30, 1959; admitted to bar, 1984, Oklahoma. *Education:* University of Oklahoma (B.A., 1981; J.D., 1984). Phi Alpha Delta. *Member:* Stephens County, Oklahoma and American Bar Associations. ***PRACTICE AREAS:*** Banking Law; Real Property; Oil and Gas Law; Commercial Law. ***Email:*** stone@bonneycorley.com

JOHN E. CAMPBELL, JR., born Duncan, Oklahoma, October 20, 1960; admitted to bar, 1985, Oklahoma. *Education:* University of Oklahoma (B.B.A., 1982); Oklahoma City University (J.D., 1985). *Member:* Stephens County, Oklahoma and American Bar Associations. ***PRACTICE AREAS:*** Probate; Estate Planning; Corporate Law. ***Email:*** campbell@bonneycorley.com

CARL O. LaMAR, born Anadarko, Oklahoma, May 23, 1961; admitted to bar, 1986, Arkansas and U.S. District Court, Eastern and Western Districts of Arkansas; 1987, U.S. Court of Appeals, 8th Circuit; 1990, Massachusetts; 1991, U.S. District Court, District of Massachusetts; 1994, Connecticut; 1998, Oklahoma. *Education:* Oklahoma State University (B.S.A., 1983); University of Arkansas (J.D., 1986). Phi Alpha Delta (Vice-President, 1984-1985). Deputy Prosecuting Attorney, 19th Judicial District of Arkansas, 1986-1987. *Member:* Stephens County, Oklahoma, Arkansas and American Bar Associations. ***PRACTICE AREAS:*** Litigation; Personal Injury; Domestic Relations. ***Email:*** lamar@bonneycorley.com

REPRESENTATIVE CLIENTS: Mack Oil Co.; Thomas Drilling Co.; M & M Supply Co.; Investors Trust Co.; Public Service Company of Oklahoma; Board of Education, Duncan Public Schools; Hazelwood Production & Exploration Company; Jones Oil Co.; Tri-J Oil and Gas Co.; First Farmers National Bank of Waurika; Cook Manufacturing Corporation; Perkins Production Co.; Consolidated Rural Water & Sewer District #1 of Jefferson County, Oklahoma.
COUNSEL FOR: BancFirst, Duncan, Oklahoma.

ELLIS, LEONARD & BUCKHOLTS

Established in 1978
PATTERSON BUILDING
929 WEST WILLOW
DUNCAN, OKLAHOMA 73533-4921
Telephone: 580-252-3240
Fax: 580-252-9596
Email: elb@texhoma.net
URL: http://www.lawyers.com/duncanok

General Civil Practice in all Courts. Banking, Commercial Law, Oil and Gas, Real Estate, Domestic Relations, Personal Injury, Probate, Estate Planning, Bankruptcy Law, Employment Law, Insurance Defense, Adoptions and Criminal Law.

FIRM PROFILE: The firm's practice is regional in scope, covering most of south-central and southwestern Oklahoma. All three partners of the firm are natives of Duncan, Oklahoma. The firm's practice is concentrated in the areas noted immediately above. Listed in Bar Register of Preeminent Lawyers.

THOMAS T. ELLIS, born Duncan, Oklahoma, September 18, 1950; admitted to bar, 1975, Oklahoma. *Education:* University of Oklahoma (B.A., 1971; J.D., 1975). Phi Delta Phi (Vice Magister, 1975). Judge, Court of Appeals, Temporary Division, 1981. *Member:* Stephens County (President, 1981), Oklahoma County, Oklahoma and American Bar Associations; Oklahoma Trial Lawyers Association; American Trial Lawyers Association. Fel-

(This Listing Continued)

ELLIS, LEONARD & BUCKHOLTS, Duncan—Continued

low, American Academy of Matrimonial Lawyers. ***PRACTICE AREAS:*** Personal Injury; Insurance Defense; Banking Law; Family Law; Criminal Law; Probate; Trusts and Estates; Wills; Guardianships; Contracts; Torts; Litigation; Mortgages; Real Estate. ***Email:*** tom@texhoma.net

PHILLIP H. LEONARD, born Duncan, Oklahoma, January 20, 1939; admitted to bar, 1963, Oklahoma. *Education:* Oklahoma University (B.A., 1961; LL.B., 1963). Member, Oklahoma University Law Review, 1962-1963. Attorney, Halliburton Services, 1964-1977. Mayor, City of Duncan, 1994-1997. *Member:* Stephens County, Oklahoma and American Bar Associations. (Retired). ***PRACTICE AREAS:*** Bankruptcy; Family Law; Probate; Guardianship; Wills; Criminal Law; Labor and Employment; Social Security; Partnership Law; Litigation; Natural Resources; Personal Injury; Commercial Law. ***Email:*** phil@texhoma.net

E. J. BUCKHOLTS, II, born Duncan, Oklahoma, November 15, 1952; admitted to bar, 1979, Oklahoma. *Education:* University of Oklahoma (B.B.A., 1975); Oklahoma City University (J.D., 1979). *Member:* Stephens County (President, 1995), Oklahoma and American Bar Associations; Oklahoma Trial Lawyers Association; National Association of Criminal Defense Lawyers. ***PRACTICE AREAS:*** Criminal Law; Family Law; Children; Banking Law; Litigation; Probate; Trusts and Estates; Wills; Guardianships; Leases and Leasing; Mortgages; Partnership Law; Real Estate; Natural Resources. ***Email:*** ej@texhoma.net

REPRESENTATIVE CLIENTS: BancFirst, Duncan, Oklahoma; First Bank & Trust Company, Duncan, Oklahoma; BancFirst, Marlow, Oklahoma; Arvest Bank, Duncan, Oklahoma; Duncan Board of Realtors; S & W Transports; C & D Trucking, Inc.; Bud Oil Co.; Grantham Funeral Home; Duncan Rent-Alls; T. H. Rogers Co.; Insurance Concept Agency, Inc.; Battison Motors, Inc., Duncan, Oklahoma; Jan L. Construction Co.; ASCOG; King Mftg.; National Rural Water Association; Halliburton Employees Federal Credit Union.
LOCAL COUNSEL FOR: Great Southwest Fire Insurance Co.; Oklahoma Farmers Union Mutual Insurance Co.; Thurston Fire and Casualty Co.; Tri-State Insurance Co.; Cimarron Insurance Co.; Silvey Companies; Gulf Insurance Co.; Scottsdale Insurance Co.; Texaco, Inc.; Union Pacific Railroad; Dotco; ASCOG and National Rural Water Association; Laze Boy; Town of Ryan, Oklahoma; BancFirst, Duncan, Oklahoma; First Bank & Trust, Duncan, Oklahoma; Republic Casualty Company; Equity Fire & Casualty Company; Texaco; Horne Properties LLC; Jones Drilling Corp.; Chisholm Trial Farm Credit.
REFERENCES: BancFirst, Duncan, Oklahoma; First Bank & Trust Co., Duncan, Oklahoma; Arvest, Duncan, Oklahoma.

WILLIAM A. GOSSETT

Established in 1995

EAST COURT CENTER
122 SOUTH 11TH, SUITE 100
DUNCAN, OKLAHOMA 73533-4704
Telephone: 580-255-3300
Fax: 580-255-3310
Email: wagatlaw@texhoma.net

General Civil Practice. Trials and Appeals in State and Federal Courts. Real Estate Law, Wills, Trusts and Estates, Corporations and Business Planning, Banking and Commercial Law, Debtor/Creditor and Bankruptcy, Insurance Claims and Disputes, Oil and Gas Law, Family Law, Personal Injury and Wrongful Death.

WILLIAM A. GOSSETT, born Ponca City, Oklahoma, November 10, 1952; admitted to bar, 1978, Oklahoma; 1985, U.S. District Court, Western District of Oklahoma. *Education:* University of Oklahoma (B.B.A., 1975; J.D., 1978). Phi Delta Phi. Author: "Notice Requirements in Foreclosure Proceedings: Due Process Considerations," Oklahoma Bar Journal, Vol. 59, No. 22 (May 28, 1988); "Applicability of Oklahoma Notice Requirements to Federal Court Foreclosure Proceedings," Oklahoma Bar Journal, Vol. 64, No. 39 (October 23, 1993); "Mortgagee's Remedies Upon Non-Receipt of Property Insurance Cancellation Notice," Consumer Financial Quarterly Report, Vol. 48, No. 3 (Summer 1994). *Member:* Stephens County (President, 1986), Oklahoma (Member, Title Examination Standard Committee; Director, 1986-1994, Chairman, 1987, Real Property Law Section) and American Bar Associations.

REPRESENTATIVE CLIENTS: BancFirst; Duncan, Oklahoma; Bank of Commerce, Duncan, Oklahoma; Mack Oil Co; Mack Energy Co.; EnerWest Trading Co.; Jenkins Energy Company; Palace Exploration Company; Patina Oil & Gas Corp.; Shields Energy, Inc.; Zinke & Trumbo, Inc.; Medical Technologies, L.L.C.
APPROVED TITLE ATTORNEY FOR: American First Title & Trust Co.; Southwest Title & Trust Co.; First American Title Insurance Co.; Lawyers Title Insurance Corp.; Farmers Home Administration; Stewart Title Guaranty Co.

JOHN R. GREEN

1106 WEST MAPLE AVENUE
P.O. BOX 700
DUNCAN, OKLAHOMA 73534-0700
Telephone: 580-255-7400
Facsimile: 580-255-0800
Email: johnrgreen@sbcglobal.net
URL: http://www.lawyers.com/johngreenlaw

General Civil Practice, Real Estate, Probate, Commercial, Insurance, Corporation, Banking, Estate Planning, Oil and Gas Law. Trials. No Small Collections.

JOHN R. GREEN, born Duncan, Oklahoma, December 27, 1942; admitted to bar, 1967, Oklahoma. *Education:* Westminster College and Oklahoma State University (B.A., 1964); University of Oklahoma (LL.B., 1967). Phi Alpha Delta. Associate Bar Examiner, 1971-1989. *Member:* Stephens County (President, 1971), Oklahoma and American Bar Associations. ***PRACTICE AREAS:*** Hospital Law; School Law; Banking Law; Trusts and Estates; Real Estate.

REPRESENTATIVE CLIENTS: Arvest Bank; Duncan Regional Hospital, Inc.; Red River Area Career Tech School District; Wetzel Production Co.; Koch Gathering Systems.

KEE LAW FIRM

Established in 1973

1102 MAPLE
P.O. BOX 1646
DUNCAN, OKLAHOMA 73534
Telephone: 580-252-2120
Telefax: 580-252-8647
Email: kanda@texhoma.net
URL: http://www.lawyers.com/kee&archer

Civil Litigation, Domestic Relations, Criminal Law, Environmental Law, International Law, Personal Injury.

FIRM PROFILE: Mr. Kee has litigated cases in State and Federal Courts. During a one year sabbatical he lived in London, England. He worked there for a Korean company and negotiated OPEC contracts in West Africa and the Middle East.

JAMES L. KEE, born Drumright, Oklahoma, October 9, 1935; admitted to bar, 1966, Oklahoma; 1978, U.S. District Court, Western District of Oklahoma; 1981, U.S. Court of Appeals, 10th Circuit. *Education:* East Central Oklahoma State University (B.S., 1961); Oklahoma City University (J.D., 1966). Phi Alpha Delta. *Member:* Stephens County (President, 2003), Oklahoma and American Bar Associations; Oklahoma Criminal Defense Lawyers Association (President, 1978); Oklahoma Trial Lawyers Association (Past Director). [U.S. Army, 101st ABN DIV, 1957-1960]. ***PRACTICE AREAS:*** Civil Litigation; Domestic Relations; Criminal Law; Environmental Law; International Law. ***Email:*** kanda@texhoma.net

JEFFERY ARCHER, born Mt. Clemens, Michigan, January 29, 1965; admitted to bar, 1995, Oklahoma; 1998, U.S. District Court, Western District of Oklahoma. *Education:* Cameron University (B.B.A., cum laude, 1992); University of Oklahoma (J.D., 1995). *Member:* Stephens County (Secretary and Treasurer, 1998) and Oklahoma Bar Associations. ***PRACTICE AREAS:*** Civil Litigation; Criminal Law; Environmental Law; Domestic Relations.

LEGAL SUPPORT PERSONNEL

BEVERLY MITCHELL
LORIE SYLVESTER

REPRESENTATIVE CLIENTS: B & B Tool Company, Inc; A.J. Paul Manufacturing Co.; Poteet Oil Ltd.; Chisolm Trail Truck & Leasing; Flanigan Developers of Oklahoma, Inc.; Sanner Pipe & Supply; Energy Services, Inc.; Century Motors, Inc.; First Bank & Trust Company.

LEACH, SULLIVAN, SULLIVAN & WATKINS

Established in 1954

921 MAIN STREET
P.O. BOX 160
DUNCAN, OKLAHOMA 73534
Telephone: 580-255-1111
Telecopier: 580-255-5587
URL: http://www.leachsullivan.com

General Civil Practice in all State and Federal Courts. Real Estate, Insurance, Probate, Commercial, Corporation, Banking, Estate Planning and Oil and Gas Law. Trials. No small collections.

FIRM PROFILE: Leach, Sullivan, Sullivan & Watkins are listed in the Bar Register of Preeminent Lawyers.

MEMBERS OF FIRM

WILLIAM O. LEACH (1919-1990)

PAUL D. SULLIVAN, born Norman, Oklahoma, January 21, 1918; admitted to bar, 1947, Oklahoma. *Education:* University of Oklahoma (B.A., 1941; LL.B., 1947). Phi Delta Phi. *Member:* Stephens County, Oklahoma and American Bar Associations. [Col., J.A.G.C., Reserve, 1946-1969, Retired]. ***PRACTICE AREAS:*** Probate; Estate Planning. ***Email:*** paul@leachsullivan.com

PATRICK D. SULLIVAN, born Duncan, Oklahoma, September 14, 1927; admitted to bar, 1951, Oklahoma. *Education:* University of Oklahoma (B.A., 1950; LL.B., 1951). Phi Delta Phi. *Member:* Stephens County (President, 1955) and Oklahoma Bar Associations. [Capt., J.A.G.D., active duty, 1952-1954; Reserve, 1954-1961]. ***PRACTICE AREAS:*** Oil and Gas; Probate; Estate Planning. ***Email:*** patrick@leachsullivan.com

MICHAEL P. SULLIVAN, born Oklahoma City, Oklahoma, October 20, 1947; admitted to bar, 1972, Oklahoma. *Education:* University of Oklahoma (B.A., 1969; J.D., 1972). Phi Delta Phi. *Member:* Stephens County (President, 1978), Oklahoma and American Bar Associations. [Capt., U.S.A.R., 1969-1980]. (Also Of Counsel, Pringle & Pringle, A Professional Corporation, Oklahoma City). ***PRACTICE AREAS:*** Banking; Corporate; Commercial; Estate Planning. ***Email:*** michael@leachsullivan.com

KENT P. SULLIVAN, born Duncan, Oklahoma, December 24, 1955; admitted to bar, 1981, Oklahoma. *Education:* University of Oklahoma (B.A., 1978; J.D., 1981). Phi Delta Phi. *Member:* Stephens County, Oklahoma and American Bar Associations; Oklahoma Trial Lawyers Association; The Association of Trial Lawyers of America. ***PRACTICE AREAS:*** Civil Litigation; Personal Injury; Insurance; Family; Environmental. ***Email:*** kent@leachsullivan.com

JAY B. WATKINS, born Woodward, Oklahoma, August 23, 1962; admitted to bar, 1987, Oklahoma. *Education:* Central State University (B.A., 1984); University of Oklahoma (J.D., 1987). Phi Alpha Theta. *Member:* Stephens County, Oklahoma and American Bar Associations. ***PRACTICE AREAS:*** Real Estate; Adoption Law; Banking; Title Examination Law. ***Email:*** jay@leachsullivan.com

(This Listing Continued)

SCOTT P. SULLIVAN, born Duncan, Oklahoma, March 29, 1968; admitted to bar, 1993, Oklahoma. *Education:* University of Oklahoma (B.B.A., 1990; J.D., 1993; M.B.A., 1998). Phi Alpha Delta. *Member:* Stephens County, Oklahoma (President, 1999; Member, Board of Directors, Young Lawyers Division; Solo and Small Firm Committee; Law Office Management Committee; Chairperson, Young Lawyers Division, Website Committee) and American Bar Associations. ***PRACTICE AREAS:*** Family Law; Real Estate. ***Email:*** scott@leachsullivan.com

REPRESENTATIVE CLIENTS: Citizens' Bank, Velma, Oklahoma; Sooner Trucking & Oil Field Services, Inc.; Leffler Construction Co.; Jack Oil Co.; Stephens County Abstract Co.; PaceCo. Financial Services, Inc.; ; Butkin Oil Co.; Raizen Oil Company; Duncan Association of Realtors, Inc.; Jackson Ranches, Inc.; Jackson Cattle Corp.; Plainsman Technology, Inc.; Legacy Bank; BancFirst of Marlow; L.A. Edwards Trusts; John E. Jackson Trust; Peoples Bank & Trust Co.; Interstate Petroleum Corporation; Southwest Title & Trust; Stewart Title & Escrow Services.

STUART, FRIEDA & HAMMOND, P.C.

Established in 1985

SUITE 100, COURT PLAZA BUILDING
1111 WEST WILLOW AVENUE
DUNCAN, OKLAHOMA 73533
Telephone: 580-252-9033
Facsimile: 580-252-6251
Email: sfhpc@texhoma.net

Litigation, Civil & Criminal and Appellate Practice. Probate, Oil and Gas, Corporate, Domestic Relations, Bankruptcy, Real Estate, Personal Injury, Municipal and Workers' Compensation Law, Trusts and Estates, Clergy Sexual Misconduct, Death Penalty, Public Sector Law.

JOHN M. STUART, born Texarkana, Arkansas, October 21, 1949; admitted to bar, 1975, Oklahoma, U.S. District Court, Northern, Eastern and Western Districts of Oklahoma, U.S. Court of Appeals, Tenth Circuit and U.S. Supreme Court; U.S. District Court, Western District of Texas. *Education:* University of Texas (B.A., 1972); Oklahoma City University (J.D., 1974). Referee, Court of Criminal Appeals, 1974-1976. Assistant Public Defender, Oklahoma County, 1977-1978. Commissioner, Oklahoma Crime Commission, 1979-1980. Director, Family Law Section, Economics Law Section and Pro Bono Panel, Legal Aid of Western Oklahoma, Inc. Associate Editor, Board of Editors, Oklahoma Bar Journal, 1992-1997. Past Member, Oklahoma Trial Lawyers Association. Director, Oklahoma Defense Lawyers Association, 1980-1984. The Association of Trial Lawyers of America; Member, American Bar Association; District 20 Representative. Young Lawyers Division, Executive Council, 1984. House of Delegates, Young Lawyers Division; Litigation Section; Family Law Section. *Member:* Stephens County (Past President) and Oklahoma (Director, Young Lawyers Division, 1979-1984; Chairman, 1985; House of Delegates; Governor, Judicial District No. 5, 1988; Committees; Long Range Planning; Budget; Vice-Chairman, Public Information Committee; Small Firm Task Force) Bar Associations. Fellow: Oklahoma Bar Foundation (Trustee, 1994-2001; President, 2000). ***PRACTICE AREAS:*** Litigation; Trial Practice; Appellate Practice; Civil Practice; Criminal Law; Oil and Gas Law; Domestic Relations; Clergy Sexual Misconduct; Death Penalty. ***Email:*** sfhpc@texhoma.net

JAMES M. FRIEDA, born St. Louis, Missouri, March 1, 1942; admitted to bar, 1981, Oklahoma, U.S. District Court, Western District of Oklahoma and U.S. Court of Appeals, Tenth Circuit. *Education:* Benedictine College (B.A., 1975); Oklahoma City University (J.D., 1980). Assistant District Attorney, Stephens County, 1979-1981. City Attorney: Duncan, 1984—; Waurika, 1993—; Ratliff City, 1993—; Terral, 1999—. Adjunct Professor, Criminal Justice, Cameron University, Lawton, Oklahoma. *Member:* Stephens County (President, 1990), Oklahoma and American Bar Associations; Oklahoma Trial Lawyers Association; The Association of Trial Lawyers of America; Oklahoma Association of Municipal Attorneys; Oklahoma Municipal League; National Institute of Municipal Law Officers. Fellow, Oklahoma Bar Foundation. [Major, F.A. USAR, 1965-1977, Resv. 1977-1988]. ***PRACTICE AREAS:*** Clergy Sexual Misconduct; Public Sector Law. ***Email:*** sfhpc@texhoma.net

DAVID W. HAMMOND, born Duncan, Oklahoma, November 4, 1960; admitted to bar, 1987, Oklahoma and U.S. District Court, Western and Eastern Districts of Oklahoma. *Education:* University of Oklahoma (B.B.A., 1983); University of Arkansas-Fayetteville (J.D., 1987). Phi Delta Delta. Assistant City Attorney, City of Duncan, 1987—. Adjunct Professor, Criminal Justice, Cameron University, Lawton, Oklahoma. *Member:* Stephens County (President, 1997; Vice-President, 2003) and Oklahoma Bar Associations. ***Email:*** sfhpc@texhoma.net

JOE K. WHITE, born Duncan, Oklahoma, November 2, 1973; admitted to bar, 2002, Oklahoma and U.S. District Court, Western District of Oklahoma. *Education:* Oklahoma State University (BS., 1998); University of Oklahoma (J.D., 2001). *Member:* Stephens County and Oklahoma Bar Associations. ***Email:*** sfhpc@texhoma.net

REPRESENTATIVE CLIENTS: First National Bank-Marlow; BancFirst; Rebel Drilling, Inc.; Thomas Acid; Perkins Insurance Co.; Whitten Insurance Co.; City of Duncan; City of Waurika; City of Ratliff City.
REFERENCES: Rebel Drilling, Inc.; First National Bank-Marlow; Jasmine, Inc.; City of Duncan; Monroe Productions, Inc.

ATKINS & MARKOFF

DURANT, OKLAHOMA

(See Oklahoma City)

Personal Injury, Automobile Accidents, Wrongful Death, Trucking Accidents, Slip and Fall, Nursing Home Abuse, Head and Spinal Injuries, Dog Bites, Sexual Abuse, Criminal Law, Drug Crimes, DUI/DWI, Juvenile Crimes, General Practice, Family , Divorce, Adoptions, Child Custody, Child Support, Domestic Violence, Visitation Rights, Elder Law, Legal Malpractice, Medical Malpractice, Social Security, Social Security Disability, Taxation, IRS Audits, Property Tax Appeals, Tax Planning, Toxic Torts, Trust and Estate, Wills and Probate.

McGEHEE & ASSOCIATES

1319 W. MAIN STREET
DURANT, OKLAHOMA 74701-4903
Telephone: 580-920-0303
Fax: 580-920-9949
Email: trgmcgehee@aol.com

Criminal Defense, Personal Injury, Family Law.

MEMBER OF FIRM

THERESA GREGO McGEHEE, born 1954; admitted to bar, 1985, Oklahoma; 1995, Texas. *Education:* Oklahoma State University (B.S., 1978); University of Oklahoma (J.D., 1985). *Member:* Oklahoma Bar Association. ***PRACTICE AREAS:*** Criminal Defense; Personal Injury; Family Law; Civil Practice; Social Security Disability; Bankruptcy.

P.L. PAT PHELPS, P.C.

Established in 1965

325 WEST EVERGREEN
P.O. BOX 882
DURANT, OKLAHOMA 74702
Telephone: 580-924-1166
Fax: 580-924-1551
Email: plphelps@netcommander.com
URL: http://www.lawyers.com/plphelps

General Trial Practice. Probate, Real Estate, Family, Personal Injury.

P.L. PAT PHELPS, born Durant, Oklahoma, February 5, 1939; admitted to bar, 1965, Oklahoma. *Education:* Southeastern Oklahoma State University (B.A., 1961); University of Oklahoma (J.D., 1965). *Member:* Oklahoma and American Bar Associations. Fellow: Oklahoma Bar Foundation; American Bar Foundation. ***PRACTICE AREAS:*** General Trial Practice. ***Email:*** plphelps@netcommander.com

REPRESENTATIVE CLIENTS: Furnished upon request.
REFERENCES: First National Bank, Durant; First United Bank and Trust Co., Durant; Landmark Bank.

TAYLOR, BURRAGE, FOSTER, MALLETT, DOWNS & RAMSEY, P.C.

DURANT, OKLAHOMA

(See Claremore)

Civil and Criminal Practice in all State and Federal Courts. Employment Law, Healthcare Law, Medical Malpractice, Professional Liability, Insurance Defense, Real Estate, Probate, Guardianships, Corporation, Commercial and Personal Injury Law.

LAW OFFICE OF STEVEN R. BOOKER, P.C.

212 E. 2ND STREET
EDMOND, OKLAHOMA 73034
Telephone: 800-842-2212

Wichita Falls, Texas Office: 705 8th Street, Suite 820, 76301. Telephone: 940-264-2108. Fax: 940-264-2106.

Elder Law, Accidents, Slip and Fall, Products Defects, Dram Shop Cases, Railroad Accidents, Dog Bites, Automobile Negligence, Wrongful Death, Breach of Warranty, Nursing Home Negligence, Civil Litigation, Plaintiff Personal Injury, Probate Litigation, Contested Wills.

(For complete biographical data on all personnel, see Professional Biographies at Wichita Falls, Texas)

BURNETT & GELNAR, PLLC

EDMOND, OKLAHOMA

(See Oklahoma City)

Business Law, Commercial Transactions, Banking, Real Estate, Taxation, Trusts and Estates, Estate Planning, Mergers and Acquisitions, Charitable and Non-Profit Organizations.

CRAIG D. CARTER

1300 E. 15TH STREET, SUITE 190
EDMOND, OKLAHOMA 73013
Telephone: 405-340-5971
Fax: 405-348-7238

Corporate Law, Securities, Taxation, Estate Planning, Health Care, Commercial Law, Bankruptcy, Business and General Practice.

CRAIG D. CARTER, born Dallas, Texas, January 25, 1966; admitted to bar, 1994, Oklahoma. *Education:* University of Oklahoma (B.B.A., 1988; J.D., 1994). Catherine Doyle Accounting Scholar; Kerr McGee Corp. Scholar. Certified Public Accountant, Oklahoma, 1989. *Member:* Oklahoma (Member: Disaster Relief Committee; Children and the Law Committee) and American Bar Associations; Healthcare Financial Management Association; Oklahoma Society of Certified Public Accountants (Member, Consulting Services Committee); Oklahoma Chamber Commerce (Member, Presidents Club). ***PRACTICE AREAS:*** Corporate Law; Securities; Taxation; Estate Planning; Health Care; Commercial Law; Bankruptcy; Business Law; General Practice.

(This Listing Continued)

CRAIG D. CARTER, Edmond—Continued

MICHELLE BROWN ROBNETT, born Oklahoma City, Oklahoma, June 30, 1958; admitted to bar, 1992, Texas; 1993, Oklahoma. *Education:* University of Kansas (B.S., Journalism, 1980); University of Oklahoma (J.D., 1992). Phi Delta Phi. Member, National Academy of Elder Law Attorneys. *Member:* Amarillo and Oklahoma Bar Associations; State Bar of Texas; College of the State Bar of Texas; Amarillo Area Estate Planning Council. ***PRACTICE AREAS:*** Probate; Estate Planning; Elder Law; Real Estate Law.

FAGIN, BROWN, BUSH, TINNEY & KISER

A PROFESSIONAL CORPORATION

EDMOND, OKLAHOMA

(See Oklahoma City)

Municipal and Public Authority Finance, Securities and Corporate Financing Law.

BENJAMIN F. HACKETT & ASSOCIATES

Established in 1980

1301 SOUTH BROADWAY
SUITE 300
EDMOND, OKLAHOMA 73034
Telephone: 405-340-8854
Fax: 405-340-8299
Email: benhackett@sbcglobal.net

Oil and Gas Law, Oil and Gas Regulation, Oil and Gas Title Examination, Real Estate, Probate, Estate Planning; Administrative Law, Corporate Law and Partnership Law, General Practice.

BENJAMIN F. HACKETT, born McAlester, Oklahoma, September 18, 1948; admitted to bar, 1976, Oklahoma. *Education:* Oklahoma State University (B.S., 1971); University of Oklahoma (J.D., 1976). *Member:* Oklahoma Bar Association; Oklahoma City Real Property Lawyers Association; Oklahoma City Mineral Lawyers Association, 1980.

REPRESENTATIVE CLIENTS: ExxonMobil Corporation; Walter Duncan, Jr.; Mewbourne Oil Company; Spring Energy Company; Phillips Petroleum Co.; Ram, Inc.

HAMMOND & ASSOCIATES

1320 E. 9TH STREET, #4
EDMOND, OKLAHOMA 73034
Telephone: 405-216-0007
Facsimile: 405-216-0671
Email: gary@hammondassociateslaw.com
URL: http://www.hammondassociateslawfirm.com

Contracts, Business Law, Commercial Litigation, Bankruptcy, Consumer Bankruptcy.

MEMBER OF THE FIRM

GARY D. HAMMOND, born Oklahoma City, Oklahoma, August 25, 1963; admitted to bar, 1990, Oklahoma, U.S. District Court, Northern, Eastern and Western Districts of Oklahoma and U.S. Court of Appeals, Tenth Circuit. *Education:* University of Oklahoma (B.B.A., 1985; J.D., 1990). Editor, ABI Circuit Update Program, Tenth Circuit. Guest Columnist, The Journal Record newspaper, Oklahoma City, Oklahoma. Author: "The Role of the Trustee," Oklahoma Bar Association Continuing Legal Education, Spring 1992, No. 454; "The Ninth Circuit Recognizes the New Value Exception to the Absolute Priority Rule," Oklahoma Bar Journal, Vol. 64, No. 44, p. 3503, November 27, 1993; "The Third Circuit Rules that Environmental Claims May Survive Chapter 11 Reorganization," Oklahoma Bar Journal, Vol. 65, No. 15, p. 1255, April 9, 1994; "The United States Supreme Court Determines That a Bank Is Allowed To Place An Administrative Freeze On A Debtor's Account," Oklahoma Bar Journal, Vol. 66, No. 46, p. 3976, December 23, 1995; "The United States Supreme Court Rules that 'Replacement Value' Is to be Used In Bankruptcies," Oklahoma Bar Journal, Vol. 68, No. 31, p. 2673, August 2, 1997; "The United States Supreme Court Determines That Reckless Conduct is Dischargeable in Bankruptcy," Oklahoma Bar Journal, Vol. 69, No. 15, p. 1268, April 11, 1998; "Advanced Real Estate Law in Oklahoma," National Business Institute, September 1997; "Impact of Bankruptcy," Real Estate Investment & Finance Law Seminar, The Conference on Consumer Finance Law, December 1997; "Update on Bankruptcy Legislation and Litigation," Commercial Law 2000, The Conference on Consumer Financial Law, December 1999; "Evolving Bankruptcy and Creditors' Rights Issues," Advanced Real Estate Law in Oklahoma, National Business Institute, September 2000; "Bankruptcy Issues and Procedures Impacting Divorce," Practical Issues Affecting the Family Law Practitioner, OBA Family Law Section, April 2001; "Bankruptcy Developments; Intersection Between Revised Article 9 and the Bankruptcy Code," Secured Transactions 2002, The Conference on Consumer Finance Law, February 2002; "Selected Bankruptcy Topics," 29th Annual Institute, National Association of Division Order Analysts, September 2002; "Current Issues in Consumer Bankruptcy," Conference on Consumer Finance Law, October 2002; "2002 Commercial Law Update," Conference on Consumer Finance Law, December 2002; "Intersections of Bankruptcy and the UCC and the Impact of Recent Developments," Bankruptcy and the UCC: Points of Intersection and Conflict, Conference on Consumer Finance Law, February 2003. *Member:* Oklahoma County (Member, Bankruptcy Section, 1991—) and Oklahoma (Member, 1991—, Director and Chairperson, 1999-2000, Bankruptcy and Reorganization Section) Bar Associations; American Bankruptcy Institute. ***PRACTICE AREAS:*** Bankruptcy; Commercial Litigation.

HAUPT BROOKS VANDRUFF, PLLC

EDMOND, OKLAHOMA

(See Oklahoma City)

Administrative/Agency, Agricultural, Bankruptcy (Chapter 7, 11, 12, 13), Civil Rights, Criminal, Domestic & Family, Employment, Estate Planning (Wills & Trusts), Finance, Debtor and Creditor Law, General Corporate and Business (Organization, Product Liability, Mergers and Acquisition, Litigation), General Trial Practice, Insurance, Medical and Nursing Home Malpractice and Probate, Personal Injury, Real Estate, Taxation (Personal and Corporate), Workers Compensation, Wrongful Death.

JACOBSON & LAASCH

Established in 1996

212 EAST SECOND STREET
EDMOND, OKLAHOMA 73034
Telephone: 405-341-3303
Fax: 405-341-6686
Email: jdj8788@aol.com

General Civil Trial Practice, Bankruptcy, Commercial Law, Telecommunications, Telephone Utility Regulation, Electric Utility Law, Public Utility Law, Administrative Law, Business Law, Corporate Law, Litigation, Appellate Practice, Insurance Defense, Debtor and Creditor, Contracts, Negligence, Oil and Gas Law.

J. DAVID JACOBSON, born Indianapolis, Indiana, February 21, 1955; admitted to bar, 1988, Oklahoma; 1992, Texas and Indiana; U.S. District Court, Western and Northern Districts of Oklahoma; U.S. Court of Appeals, Tenth Circuit; U.S. Court of Federal Claims. *Education:* Indiana University; Grace College (B.S., 1977); Oklahoma City University (J.D., 1987). Member, Staff Subcommittee on Communications, National Association of Regulatory Utility Commissioners, 1983-1988. Member, Board of Directors, Oklahoma City University Law Alumni Association. *Member:* Oklahoma and Indiana State Bar Associations; State Bar of Texas. ***PRACTICE AREAS:*** Telecommunications Law; Public Utility Law and Regulation; General Corporate Law; Commercial Law; General Litigation; Appellate Practice. ***Email:*** jdj8788@aol.com

JON W. LAASCH, born Joliet, Illinois, June 17, 1960; admitted to bar, 1985, Oklahoma, U.S. District Court, Western and Eastern Districts of Oklahoma and U.S. Court of Appeals, Fifth and Tenth Circuits. *Education:* University of Oklahoma (B.A., 1982); University of Tulsa (J.D., 1985). Delta Theta Phi. Staff, Tulsa Law Journal, 1984-1985. *Member:* Oklahoma Bar Association. ***PRACTICE AREAS:*** Oil and Gas Law; Commercial Law; Litigation; Administrative Law; Bankruptcy; Probate; Corporate Law; Insurance Defense; Appellate Practice; Contracts; Negligence.

LAW OFFICE OF MARY M. LEE, P.C.

1300 E. 9TH STREET, SUITE 4
EDMOND, OKLAHOMA 73034-5760
Telephone: 405-285-4490
Fax: 405-285-4491
Email: mml@marymlee.com
URL: http://www.marymlee.com

Patents, Trademarks, Copyrights, Trade Secrets, Unfair Competition and Related Licensing and Litigation.

MARY M. LEE, born Oklahoma City, Oklahoma, December 21, 1951; admitted to bar, 1983, Oklahoma; 1985, U.S. District Court, Western, Eastern and Northern Districts of Oklahoma; 1987, U.S. Supreme Court; 1988, U.S. Court of Appeals, Federal Circuit; registered to practice before U.S. Patent and Trademark Office. *Education:* Vanderbilt University (B.S.N., with distinction, 1974); University of Oklahoma (J.D., 1983). Member, Licensing Executives Society.*Member:* Oklahoma County, Oklahoma (Member, Patent Section) and American (Member, Patent, Trademark and Copyright Section) Bar Associations; American Intellectual Property Law Association.

LESTER, LOVING & DAVIES, P.C.

1701 SOUTH KELLY AVENUE
EDMOND, OKLAHOMA 73013
Telephone: 405-844-9900
Fax: 405-844-9958
Email: lld@lldlaw.com
URL: http://www.lldlaw.com

Civil Litigation in all State and Federal Courts. Civil Rights, Employment, Labor, Defamation, Personal Injury, Environmental, Energy, Estate Planning, Wills and Trusts, Local Government, Land Use, Corporate, Banking, Commercial, Sports, Administrative, Mediation, State Government, Equine, Non-Profit Association and Governance, Insurance, Criminal Law, Appellate Advocacy and Tax.

ANDREW W. LESTER, admitted to bar, 1981, Oklahoma; 1990, Texas; 1995, Colorado; U.S. Supreme Court. *Education:* Ludwig-Maximilians-Universitaet, Munich, Germany; Duke University (B.A., magna cum laude, 1977); Georgetown University (M.S.F.S., 1981; J.D., 1981). Phi Delta Phi. United States Magistrate Judge, Western District of Oklahoma, 1988-1996. Office of President-Elect Ronald Reagan, Transition Team, 1980-1981. Office of Governor-Elect Brad Henry, Transition Team, 2002-2003. ***LANGUAGES:*** German. ***PRACTICE AREAS:*** Civil Litigation; Civil Rights Law; Defamation Law; Employment Litigation; Local Government Law.

SUSAN BRIMER LOVING, admitted to bar, 1980, Oklahoma; U.S. Supreme Court. *Education:* University of Oklahoma (B.A., with distinction, 1972; J.D., 1979). Phi Beta

(This Listing Continued)

Kappa. Attorney General of Oklahoma, 1991-1995. Member, Oklahoma Pardon & Parole Board, 2003—. ***PRACTICE AREAS:*** Administrative Law; Mediation; Employment Law; State and Local Government; Contracts; Corporate Transactions.

SHANNON F. DAVIES, admitted to bar, 1989, Oklahoma. *Education:* University of Oklahoma (B.A., 1986); Oklahoma City University (J.D., with honors, 1989). Phi Delta Phi; Order of the Barristers. ***PRACTICE AREAS:*** Civil Litigation; Employment Law; Civil Rights Law; Commercial Litigation; Environmental Law.

SCOTT THOMPSON, admitted to bar, 1996, Maryland; 1997, Oklahoma. *Education:* Oklahoma State University (B.A., 1993); George Washington University (J.D., 1996). Phi Delta Phi. ***PRACTICE AREAS:*** Employment Law; Constitutional Law; Appellate Practice; Insurance Regulation; Banking; Commercial Law.

COURTNEY DAVIS POWELL, admitted to bar, 2002, Oklahoma. *Education:* University of Arkansas (B.A., with honors, 1999); Oklahoma City University School of Law (J.D., with honors, 2002). Phi Beta Kappa; Phi Delta Phi. *Member:* Oklahoma Bar Association. ***PRACTICE AREAS:*** Employment Litigation; Commercial Law.

OF COUNSEL

SUSAN WALTERS BIZÉ, admitted to bar, 1984, Texas; 1999, Oklahoma. *Education:* Rice University (B.A., magna cum laude, 1975; M.Acco., 1976); University of Texas (J.D., 1984). Phi Beta Kappa; Pi Delta Phi. Certified Public Accountant, Oklahoma, 1977, Texas, 1979. ***PRACTICE AREAS:*** Estate Planning; Wills; Trusts; Federal Taxation; Business Law.

GEORGE S. FREEDMAN, admitted to bar, 1993, Oklahoma. *Education:* University of Missouri (B.A., Political Science, 1990; J.D., 1993). Phi Alpha Delta. ***PRACTICE AREAS:*** Employment Law; Family Law.

JAMI J. FENNER, born Omaha, Nebraska, October 25, 1963; admitted to bar, 1989, Texas; 1990, Oklahoma. *Education:* Centenary College; Loyola University (B.B.A., magna cum laude, 1986); Tulane University (J.D., cum laude, 1989). Alpha Sigma Nu Jesuit Honor Society. ***PRACTICE AREAS:*** Government; Employment Law; Civil Rights; Torts; Litigation; Administrative Law; Health Care.

JOHNNY G. BEECH, born Chickasha, Oklahoma, September 18, 1954; admitted to bar, 1980, Oklahoma; 1991, U.S. Court of Appeals, Tenth Circuit; U.S. District Court, Northern, Eastern and Western Districts of Oklahoma; U.S. District Court, Northern District of Texas. *Education:* Southwestern Oklahoma State University (B.S., 1977); University of Arkansas at Little Rock (J.D., 1980); Tulane University School of Law (LL.M., Energy and Environment, 1985). Phi Alpha Delta. ***PRACTICE AREAS:*** Civil Litigation; Commercial Litigation; Business Litigation; Oil and Gas Law; Real Estate; Probate; Trust Law.

REPRESENTATIVE CLIENTS: SBC Communications; Voss Electric Co.; Express Meat Company; Adfitech Financial Technology Inc.; Chem-Can Services, Inc.; Oklahoma Insurance Commissioner; BancFirst Corp.; Williams Commercial Properties; Lead On, LLC; City of Ada; City of Ponca City; City of Kingfisher; City of Del City; Institute for Justice; Center for Individual Rights; Oklahoma Municipal Assurance Group; 5-Star Fabricators, Inc.; Hibdon Tire Co.; Sonic Restaurants, Inc.; City of Edmond, Oklahoma; First Financial Network; Spring Moon Enterprises; Body Works; Kerr 3 Construction Group; Barry Sanders; American State Bank; Reliance Pest Solution; The Wedel Group; NCO Financial Services, Inc.; The CCS Companies; Farmers Insurance Co.; Allstate Insurance Company; Encompass Insurance Co.; Peach Creek LLC (oil and gas chemicals); Oklahoma Oil Tactics, Inc.; United Adjustment Services, Inc.

McALISTER, McALISTER, McKINNIS & TUGGLE, P.C.

KIRKPATRICK BANK BUILDING
15 EAST 15TH STREET, SUITE 200
POST OFFICE BOX 1569
EDMOND, OKLAHOMA 73083-1569
Telephone: 405-359-0701
Fax: 405-359-0806
Email: mmmtlaw@mmmtlaw.com
URL: http://www.mmmtlaw.com

Estate and Gift Taxation, Business Law, Contracts, Commercial Law, Corporate Law, Partnership Law, Commercial Transaction, Civil Litigation, Estate Litigation, Trust Litigation, Probate, Real Estate, Mergers, Acquisitions and Divestures, Taxation, Wills, Labor and Employment Law, Estate Planning, Elder Law, Guardianship and Conservatorship, Nonprofit and Charitable Organizations.

LLOYD G. McALISTER, born Duncan, Oklahoma, January 12, 1955; admitted to bar, 1980, Texas; 1981, Oklahoma. *Education:* Oklahoma State University (B.S., 1977); University of Texas (J.D., 1980). Certified Public Accountant, Texas; Oklahoma. President, Oklahoma City Lawyer's Tax Group, 1983-1984. Fellow, and Co-Chairman, Elder Abuse Sub-Committee of Elder Law Committee, American College of Trust and Estate Counsel. Member, Director and President (1999-2000), Oklahoma City Estate Planning Council. Adjunct Professor of Law, Estate Planning and Estate Administration, Oklahoma City University School of Law, 1990-2005; University of Oklahoma School of Law, 1991-1993, 1998. *Member:* Oklahoma County and Oklahoma (Chairman, Estate Planning and Probate Section, 1991) Bar Associations; State Bar of Texas; Christian Legal Society; National Lawyers Association. ***PRACTICE AREAS:*** Estate Planning Law; Estate and Gift Taxation; Trust and Estate Law; Elder Law; Guardianship and Conservatorship; Charitable and Non-Profit Organizations; Probate; Trust Litigation; Estate Litigation. ***Email:*** lmcalister@mmmtlaw.com

KARLA McALISTER, born Durant, Oklahoma, February 23, 1955; admitted to bar, 1980, Texas; 1981, Oklahoma, U.S. Court of Appeals, Tenth Circuit and U.S. District Court, Western District of Oklahoma. *Education:* Oklahoma State University (B.S., 1977); University of Texas (J.D., 1980). Assistant District Attorney, Oklahoma County, 1980-1982. Assistant U.S. Attorney, Western District of Oklahoma, 1982-1986. *Member:* Oklahoma County and Oklahoma Bar Associations; State Bar of Texas; William J. Holloway, American Inn of Court CV (Master; Treasurer, 1999-2004; Vice President, 2004-2005; President-Elect, 2005-2006); Christian Legal Society; National Lawyers Association. ***PRACTICE AREAS:*** Estate Planning; Probate; Trusts and Estates; Estate Litigation; Trust Litigation. ***Email:*** kmcalister@mmmtlaw.com

(This Listing Continued)

TODD A. McKINNIS, born Lawton, Oklahoma, May 29, 1967; admitted to bar, 1994, Oklahoma; U.S. District Court, Western District of Oklahoma. *Education:* University of Oklahoma (B.A., 1989; J.D., with distinction, 1994). Phi Delta Phi (President, 1992-1993). Member, Federalist Society, 1993-1994. Adjunct Professor of Law, University of Oklahoma College of Law, 2000—. Participating Attorney, Rutherford Institute. *Member:* Oklahoma County and Oklahoma Bar Associations; National Lawyers Association (Vice Chairperson, Corporate Law Section, 1997-1998); Christian Legal Society (President, 1993-1994). ***REPORTED CASES:*** Swanson v. Guthrie Independent School District, et al at 135 F. 3rd 694. ***PRACTICE AREAS:*** Commercial Law; Commercial Real Estate; Business Law; Corporate Law; Partnership Law; Construction Law; Labor and Employment; Leases and Leasing; Real Estate; Estate Planning; Nonprofit and Charitable Organizations. ***Email:*** tmckinnis@mmmtlaw.com

JUDY A. TUGGLE, born Oklahoma City, Oklahoma, December 9, 1954; admitted to bar, 1992, Oklahoma. *Education:* Abilene Christian University (B.S., summa cum laude, 1973); University of Oklahoma (J.D., with honors, 1991). *Member:* Oklahoma Bar Association; Christian Legal Society; National Lawyers Association; Oklahoma Planned Giving Council; Oklahoma City Estate Planning Council. ***PRACTICE AREAS:*** Estate Planning; Trusts and Estates; Guardianship and Conservatorship; Nonprofit and Charitable Organizations; Estate and Gift Taxation; Probate; Wills; Trust Litigation; Estate Litigation. ***Email:*** jtuggle@mmmtlaw.com

JONATHAN B. AUSTIN, born Oklahoma City, Oklahoma, July 20, 1976; admitted to bar, 2003, Oklahoma. *Education:* Oklahoma State University (B.S., 1998); University of Oklahoma (J.D., 2003). *Member:* Oklahoma Bar Association. ***PRACTICE AREAS:*** Business Law; Corporate Law; Estate Planning; Real Estate; Nonprofit and Charitable Organizations. ***Email:*** jaustin@mmmtlaw.com

WENDY L. McMAHON, born Oklahoma City, Oklahoma, December 30, 1976; admitted to bar, 2004, Oklahoma and U.S. District Court, Western District of Oklahoma. *Education:* Oklahoma State University (B.S., 1999); University of Oklahoma College of Law (J.D., 2004). Comfort Scholar. Editor, American Indian Law Review. Member, Christian Legal Society, 2000—. *Member:* Oklahoma and American Bar Associations. ***PRACTICE AREAS:*** Estate Planning; Trust Administration; Trust Litigation; Elder Law; Probate. ***Email:*** wmcmahon@mmmtlaw.com

REFERENCE: Kirkpatrick Bank, Edmnd, Okla.

DAVID L. NUNN, P.C.

17 EAST FIRST STREET
EDMOND, OKLAHOMA 73034
Telephone: 405-330-4053
Fax: 405-330-8470
URL: http://www.oklahomalegal.org

Commercial Law, Corporate Law, Commercial Collections, Bankruptcy (Creditors only), Automotive Warranty and Finance Law, Consumer Finance, Creditors Rights, Contracts, Litigation.

FIRM PROFILE: The firm maintains a strong local practice in addition to representation of clients on a national basis. The firm offers a wide range of legal services while also representing clients in all areas of litigation in state and federal courts.

DAVID L. NUNN, born Sacramento, California, October 22, 1964; admitted to bar, 1991, Oklahoma, U.S. District Court, Northern, Eastern and Western Districts of Oklahoma, U.S. Court of Appeals, Tenth Circuit and U.S. Supreme Court. *Education:* East Central University (B.A., 1987); Oklahoma City University (J.D., with honors, 1990). *Member:* Commercial Law League of America; Ruth Bader Ginsburg American Inn of Court. [Capt., U.S. Army Reserve, 1986-1993]. ***PRACTICE AREAS:*** Commercial Litigation; Business Law; Commercial Collections; Consumer Collections; Automobile Fraud; Automotive Warranty Law; Creditor Bankruptcy; Finance Law; Contracts; Corporate Law; Debtor and Creditor; Litigation; Fair Debt Collection Practices Act; Creditors Rights; Consumer Law.

STRECK & ASSOCIATES

2300 SOUTH BROADWAY, SUITE 100
EDMOND, OKLAHOMA 73013
Telephone: 405-330-1303
Facsimile: 405-330-1903
URL: http://www.lawyers.com/streck&associates

Divorce, Family, Property Division, Alimony, Paternity, Child Support, Child Custody, Adoption, Guardianships, Probate, DUI.

PAUL STRECK, born Enid, Oklahoma, 1964; admitted to bar, 1989, Oklahoma and U.S. District Court, Western District of Oklahoma; U.S. Court of Appeals, Tenth Circuit. *Education:* Phillips University (B.S., Political Science, 1986); University of Oklahoma College of Law (J.D., 1988). *Member:* Oklahoma Bar Association (Family Law Section, 2002—). ***PRACTICE AREAS:*** Family Law; Divorce; Paternity; Child Custody; Bankruptcy; Probate; Criminal Law; Driving While Intoxicated.

ALBERT AND ALBERT

Established in 1982

205 WEST BROADWAY
P.O. BOX 1748
ELK CITY, OKLAHOMA 73648
Telephone: 580-225-2010
Telefax: 580-225-2011
Email: markalbert@it/net.net

General Civil Practice. Bankruptcy, Workers Compensation, Probate, Family, Real Estate, Banking, Commercial, Corporate, Insurance Bad Faith, All Personal Injury Claims, Accidental Death, Wrongful Death, Nursing home Neglect, Criminal Defense Law, Driving While Intoxicated, Drug Crimes, Felonies, Misdemeanors, Domestic Relations, Custody, Divorce. No Collections under $4,500.00.

PAUL ANTHONY ALBERT, born Elk City, Oklahoma, December 24, 1953; admitted to bar, 1979, Oklahoma; 1980, U.S. District Court, Northern District of Oklahoma; 1988, U.S. District Court, Western District of Oklahoma; 1991, Texas. *Education:* University of Oklahoma (B.A., 1975); University of Tulsa (J.D., 1979). Delta Theta Phi. *Member:* Beckham County and Oklahoma Bar Associations. ***PRACTICE AREAS:*** Family Law; Probate; Commercial; Banking; Criminal Defense. ***Email:*** palbert@intlnet.net

MARK W. ALBERT, born Elk City, Oklahoma, November 15, 1962; admitted to bar, 1988, Oklahoma and U.S. District Court, Western District of Oklahoma; 1992, Texas. *Education:* University of Oklahoma (B.A., 1985; J.D., 1988). *Member:* Beckham County and Oklahoma Bar Associations; State Bar of Texas. ***PRACTICE AREAS:*** Bankruptcy; Workers Compensation; Personal Injury; Criminal Defense; Accidental Death; Insurance Bad Faith; Nursing Home Neglect; Drug Offences; Commercial; Banking. ***Email:*** markalbert@itlnet.net

REPRESENTATIVE CLIENTS: Bank of Western Oklahoma; Great Plains Regional Hospital; Roger Mills Memorial Hospital; Great Plains National Bank; Inter Bank.
REFERENCE: Bank of Western Oklahoma.

ATKINS & MARKOFF

ELK CITY, OKLAHOMA

(See Oklahoma City)

Personal Injury, Automobile Accidents, Wrongful Death, Trucking Accidents, Slip and Fall, Nursing Home Abuse, Head and Spinal Injuries, Dog Bites, Sexual Abuse, Criminal Law, Drug Crimes, DUI/DWI, Juvenile Crimes, General Practice, Family , Divorce, Adoptions, Child Custody, Child Support, Domestic Violence, Visitation Rights, Elder Law, Legal Malpractice, Medical Malpractice, Social Security, Social Security Disability, Taxation, IRS Audits, Property Tax Appeals, Tax Planning, Toxic Torts, Trust and Estate, Wills and Probate.

IVESTER, IVESTER & IVESTER

Established in 1927

114 N. ADAMS
P.O. BOX 1950
ELK CITY, OKLAHOMA 73648-1950
Telephone: 580-225-6525
Fax: 580-225-2806
Email: ivesterlaw@itlnet.net
URL: http://www.ivesterlaw.com

Sayre Office: P.O. Box 160, 73662-0160. Telephone: 580-928-2116. Fax: 580-928-5353.

Civil Litigation, Business Law, Commercial Law, Corporate Law, Partnership Law, Insurance, Real Estate, Family Law, Oil & Gas, Probate, Taxation, Trusts and Estates.

REPRESENTATIVE CLIENT: Beckham County Rural Water District; Northfork Electric Cooperative, Inc., Sayre, Oklahoma; Sentinel Oklahoma.; Southwest State Bank, Sentinel, Oklahoma; Arrowhead Resources, Sayre, Oklahoma.
REFERENCES: Southwest State Bank; InterBank, Sayre, Oklahoma.

(For complete biographical data on all personnel, see Professional Biographies at Sayre, Oklahoma)

HENRICKSEN & HENRICKSEN LAWYERS, INC.

Established in 1978

210 NORTH CHOCTAW
EL RENO, OKLAHOMA 73036-2647
Telephone: 405-262-0983
Fax: 405-262-2049

Mailing Address: P.O. Box 1129, El Reno, OK 73036-1129

Oklahoma City, Oklahoma Office: 6440 Avondale Drive, Suite 200, 73116. Telephone: 405-848-3977.

General Civil and Criminal Trial Practice State and Federal Courts, Banking, Bankruptcy, Family, Probate and Personal Injury Law, Criminal Law, Constitutional Law.

FIRM PROFILE: Henricksen & Henricksen is listed in the Bar Register of Preeminent Lawyers.

Reported Cases: Powell v. Mullin, 343 F.3d 1215 (10th Cir. 2003); Hooper v. Mullin, 314 F.3d 1162 (10th Cir. 2002); Le v. Mullin, 2002 WL 31662748, (C.A. 10(Okla.), 2002); Camfield v. City of Oklahoma City 248 F. 3d 1214 (C.A. 10 (Okla.), 2001); Williams Raymond Mayes vs. Gary Gibson, Warden, Oklahoma State Penitentiary; 210 F.3d 1284 (10th Cir. 2000); Duane Jantzen, et al. vs. Lewis Hawkins, Individually and in his official capacity as Sheriff of Canadian County, Oklahoma and the Board of County Commissioners of The County of Canadian, 188 F.3d 1247 (10th Cir. 1999); Pindus v. Fleming Companies Inc., 146 F. 3d 1224 (C.A. 10 (Okla.), 1998); Sawatzky v. City of Oklahoma City, 906 P.2d 785 (Okla. Cr., 1995); In re Kan

(This Listing Continued)

Corp., 101 B.R. 726 (Bkrtcy. W.D. Okla., 1988); Thompson v. Andover Oil Co. 691 P.2d 77 (Okla. App., 1984); Ohio Casualty Insurance Co. vs. Phil Todd, d/b/a Todd's Tavern and Rick Robertson, 813 P.2d 508 (Okla. 1991); McIntire vs. Bethel School, Independent School District No. 3, 804 F.Supp. 1415 (W.D. Okla. 1992); Jervaughn Miller vs. State of Oklahoma 29 P.3d 1077 (2001); Shelton Jackson vs. State of Oklahoma, 41 P.3d 395 (Okla 1991); Eagon, et al v. City of Elk City, et al, 72 F.3d 1480 (10th Cir. 1996).

MARK HENRICKSEN, born Okarche, Oklahoma, August 27, 1954; admitted to bar, 1978, Oklahoma, U.S. District Court, Western District of Oklahoma, U.S. District Court, Eastern District of Oklahoma, U.S. District Court, Northern District of Oklahoma, U.S. Court of Appeals, Tenth Circuit, U.S. Tax Court and U.S. Supreme Court. *Education:* University of Oklahoma (B.S.E., 1975; J.D., 1977). Recipient: Justice Thurgood Marshall Award, Outstanding Appellate Advocacy, Oklahoma Criminal Defense Lawyers, 2001 and 2004; 2005 Angie Debo Lifetime Achievement Award, ACLU of Oklahoma. Co-Recipient, Abolitionist of the Year Award, Oklahoma Coalition to Abolish the Death Penalty, 2005. Recipient, 2005 Angie Debo Lifetime Achievement Award, ACLU of Oklahoma. Chairman, Canadian County Election Board, 1983-1987. City Attorney, City of El Reno, Oklahoma, 1986-2001. President, 1993-1998 and General Counsel, 1998-2001, American Civil Liberties Union of Oklahoma. Member: National Board of Directors, American Civil Liberties Union; Board Canadian Valley Vo-Tech Foundation; Oklahoma Human Rights Commission, 1994-1997; Canadian County Sentencing Council, 1998-2002. Member, ABA Death Penalty Moratorium Project, 2004—. *Member:* Canadian County, Oklahoma County, Oklahoma and American Bar Associations; Oklahoma Trial Lawyers Association; Oklahoma Criminal Defense Lawyers Association; National Association of Criminal Defense Lawyers. ***PRACTICE AREAS:*** Constitutional Law; Criminal; Family; Personal Injury; Probate. ***Email:*** mark.henricksen@coxinet.net

LANITA HENRICKSEN, born Sioux City, Iowa, May 5, 1948; admitted to bar, 1992, Oklahoma and U.S. District Court, Western District of Oklahoma; U.S. District Court, Eastern District of Oklahoma; U.S. District Court, Northern District of Oklahoma; 1994, U.S. Court of Appeals, Tenth Circuit and U.S. Supreme Court. *Education:* Southern Nazarene University (B.A., 1988); Oklahoma City University (J.D., 1991). Alpha Chi. Listed in Who's Who Among American Universities and Colleges. General Counsel, American Civil Liberties Union of Oklahoma. Co-Recipient, Abolitionist of the Year Award, Oklahoma Coalition to Abolish the Death Penalty, 2005. *Member:* Canadian County, Oklahoma County, Oklahoma and American Bar Associations; Oklahoma Trial Lawyers Association; Oklahoma Criminal Defense Lawyers Association; National Association of Criminal Defense Lawyers. ***PRACTICE AREAS:*** Federal; Family; Bankruptcy; Criminal Law. ***Email:*** henricksenlaw@coxinet.net

REPRESENTATIVE CLIENTS: El Reno Recreational Authority; Bank of Union.
REFERENCE: Bank of Union, Union City, Oklahoma.

RAMEY & THARP

EL RENO, OKLAHOMA

(See Yukon)

General Civil Trial and Criminal Practice in all State and Federal Courts. Real Property, Medical Malpractice, Personal Injury, Child Custody, Products Liability, Probate, Corporate, Banking and Commercial Law, Family Law.

ATKINS & MARKOFF

ENID, OKLAHOMA

(See Oklahoma City)

Personal Injury, Automobile Accidents, Wrongful Death, Trucking Accidents, Slip and Fall, Nursing Home Abuse, Head and Spinal Injuries, Dog Bites, Sexual Abuse, Criminal Law, Drug Crimes, DUI/DWI, Juvenile Crimes, General Practice, Family , Divorce, Adoptions, Child Custody, Child Support, Domestic Violence, Visitation Rights, Elder Law, Legal Malpractice, Medical Malpractice, Social Security, Social Security Disability, Taxation, IRS Audits, Property Tax Appeals, Tax Planning, Toxic Torts, Trust and Estate, Wills and Probate.

BROWN & ASSOCIATES
ATTORNEYS & COUNSELORS AT LAW, P.L.L.C.

201 NORTH GRAND, SUITE 301
ENID, OKLAHOMA 73701
Telephone: 580-234-6600
Fax: 580-234-6606
Email: mail@brownlaw-ok.com
URL: http://www.brownlaw-ok.com

Business Transactions, Estate Planning, Probate Administration, Business Association Law, Tax Law, Tax Controversies, Family Law.

G. L. (GARY) BROWN, III, admitted to bar, 1980, Oklahoma; 1981, U.S. Tax Court. *Education:* University of Oklahoma (B.B.A., 1974); University of Tulsa (J.D., 1980). Member, ACTEC-American College of Trust & Estate Counsel. Certified Public Accountant. ***PRACTICE AREAS:*** Probate; Business Transactions. ***Email:*** gary@brownlaw-ok.com

ASSOCIATE

SARAH J. LANE, born Tulsa, Oklahoma, October 27, 1976; admitted to bar, 2002, Oklahoma. *Education:* University of Tulsa (B.S.B.A., Finance, Magna Cum Laude, 1999); University of Richmond (J.D., 2002). *Member:* Garfield County, Oklahoma and American Bar Associations. ***Email:*** sarah@brownlaw-ok.com

JON R. FORD

1625 W. OWEN K. GARRIOTT, SUITE G
ENID, OKLAHOMA 73703-5653
Telephone: 580-234-0253
Fax: 580-234-0256
Email: jon@jfordlaw.com
URL: http://www.jfordlaw.com

Family Law, Divorce, Custody, Civil Litigation, Probate, Personal Injury, Wills, Trusts, Estate Planning.

FIRM PROFILE: Mr. Ford, who has achieved Martindale-Hubbell's highest rating for ethical standards and legal ability, has specialized in Family Law and Civil Litigation for over 30 years. He utilizes a paralegal to reduce costs to clients.

JON R. FORD, born Enid, Oklahoma, Oct. 30, 1943; admitted to bar, 1969, Oklahoma; 1973, U.S. District Court, Western District of Oklahoma. *Education:* Oklahoma State University (B.S., 1966); University of Oklahoma (J.D., 1969). Named Outstanding Attorney, Family Law Section, Oklahoma Bar Association, 2000. Chairman, Oklahoma Ethics Commission, 1990-1992. Commissioner of Agriculture, 1975-1976. *Member:* Garfield County (President, 1991) and Oklahoma (Chair, Family Law Section, 2002; Senior Editor, Practice Manual, Family Law Section, 2002) Bar Associations. [1st Lt. U.S. Army, Viet Nam]. ***PRACTICE AREAS:*** Family Law; Divorce; Civil Litigation.

LEGAL SUPPORT PERSONNEL

Sue Qualls (Paralegal)
Rhonda Morgan (Legal Assistant)

AMBER McLAUGHLIN GILL

Established in 1997

CONTINENTAL CENTER, SOUTH TOWER
205 WEST MAPLE, SUITE 806
P.O. BOX 3802
ENID, OKLAHOMA 73702-3802
Telephone: 580-233-3797
Fax: 580-237-2766
Email: ambergill@coxinet.net

Criminal Law, Drugs and Narcotics, Family Law, Children, White Collar Crime.

FIRM PROFILE: During her 19 years as an attorney, Amber McLaughlin Gill has been both a prosecuting attorney and criminal defense attorney, including representation of Timothy James McVeigh who was convicted of the bombing of the A.P. Murrah Federal Building in Oklahoma City, OK on April 19, 1995.

AMBER McLAUGHLIN GILL, born Houston, Texas, December 12, 1960; admitted to bar, 1986, Texas; 1987, Oklahoma and U.S. District Court, Northern District of Oklahoma; 1996, U.S. District Court, Western District of Oklahoma and U.S. Court of Appeals, Tenth Circuit; 1998, U.S. Supreme Court. *Education:* Sam Houston State University (B.S., in Law Enforcement, cum laude, 1982); Texas Tech University School of Law (J.D., 1986). Assistant County Attorney, Travis County Attorney's Office, Austin, Texas, 1989-1991. Assistant District Attorney, Travis County District Attorney's Office, Austin, Texas, 1992-1995. *Member:* Garfield County and Oklahoma (Member: Criminal Law Section; Family Law Section) Bar Associations; State Bar of Texas; Oklahoma Criminal Defense Lawyers Association (Board of Directors 2004—). ***PRACTICE AREAS:*** Criminal Law; Drugs and Narcotics; Family Law; Children; Adoption Law.

GUNGOLL, JACKSON, COLLINS, BOX & DEVOLL, P.C.

Established in 1982

323 WEST BROADWAY
P.O. BOX 1549
ENID, OKLAHOMA 73701
Telephone: 580-234-0436
Fax: 580-233-1284
Email: smith@enidlaw.com
URL: http://www.enidlaw.com

Civil Litigation, Commercial Transactions, Bankruptcy, Real Estate, Environmental Law, Family Law, Criminal Defense, Probate, Oil and Gas and Personal Injury Law, Appeals, Tax Law, Estate Planning, Products Liability.

FIRM PROFILE: Gungoll, Jackson, Collins, Box & Devoll, P.C., was founded in 1982 by Bradley A. Gungoll, Douglas L. Jackson and David M. Collins. Craig L. Box became a shareholder of the firm in 1989. Glenn A. Devoll joined the firm in 1998. While maintaining a strong local practice, the firm has rapidly grown and now represents clientele in a multi-state region of the midwest. The firm offers a wide range of legal services in its office practice, while also representing clients in all areas of litigation in state and federal courts.

BRADLEY A. GUNGOLL, born Enid, Oklahoma, January 24, 1953; admitted to bar, 1980, Oklahoma; 1981, U.S. District Court, Western and Northern and Eastern Districts of Oklahoma, U.S. Court of Appeals, Tenth Circuit and U.S. Supreme Court. *Education:* Oklahoma State University (B.S., 1975); American University, International School of Law; Oklahoma City University (J.D., 1979). Staff Member to U.S. Senator Henry Bellmon, 1978-1980. Chairman, Oklahoma Horse Racing Commission. *Member:* Garfield County (Secretary and Vice President), Oklahoma (Chairman, Mineral Law Section) and American Bar Associations. Fellow: Oklahoma Bar Foundation; Oklahoma Trial Lawyers Association; Association of Trial Lawyers of America; American College of Trial Lawyers. ***PRACTICE AREAS:*** Civil Litigation; Oil and Gas Law; Personal Injury; Environmental Law. ***Email:*** gungoll@enidlaw.com

DOUGLAS L. JACKSON, born Hobart, Oklahoma, August 20, 1951; admitted to bar, 1977, Oklahoma; 1980, District of Columbia; 1981, U.S. District Court, Western, Eastern and Northern Districts of Oklahoma; 1982, U.S. Court of Appeals, Tenth Circuit and U.S. Tax Court; U.S. Supreme Court. *Education:* Oklahoma State University (B.S., 1973); University of Oklahoma; American University (J.D., 1977). Named Outstanding Male Graduate, 1973. Chief Legislative Assistant to U.S. Senator Henry Bellmon. Legislative Officer, Office of the Secretary of Agriculture for Earl Burtz. *Member:* Garfield County and Oklahoma Bar Associations; District of Columbia Bar. ***PRACTICE AREAS:*** Civil Litigation; Debtor and Creditor Law; Commercial Law; Business Law; Bankruptcy; Banking Law. ***Email:*** jackson@enidlaw.com

DAVID M. COLLINS, born Enid, Oklahoma, November 14, 1948; admitted to bar, 1978, Oklahoma, U.S. District Court, Eastern and Western Districts of Oklahoma and U.S. District Court, Western District of Kentucky. *Education:* Phillips University (B.A., 1975); University of Oklahoma (J.D., 1978). Recipient, Phillips University Outstanding Alumnus Award. Special District Judge, 4th Judicial District, 1979-1981. *Member:* Garfield County (Secretary, 1979; President, 2003) and Oklahoma Bar Associations; Oklahoma Bar Foundation. Fellow, Oklahoma Bar Association (Member, Legislative Committee, 2004). [U.S. Navy, 1969-1973]. ***PRACTICE AREAS:*** Real Estate Law; Civil Litigation; Commercial Law; Commercial Litigation; Probate and Estates; Trust; Products Liability; Personal Injury. ***Email:*** collins@enidlaw.com

CRAIG L. BOX, born Altus, Oklahoma, August 6, 1957; admitted to bar, 1983, Oklahoma and U.S. District Court, Western and Northern Districts of Oklahoma. *Education:* Northwestern Oklahoma State University (B.S., 1979); University of Tulsa (J.D., 1983). Instructor, Economics Department, Northwestern Oklahoma State University, 1980. *Member:* Garfield County and Oklahoma Bar Associations; Oklahoma Trial Lawyers Association; The Association of Trial Lawyers of America. ***PRACTICE AREAS:*** Personal Injury; Civil Litigation; Criminal Litigation; Family Law. ***Email:*** box@enidlaw.com

GLENN A. DEVOLL, born Altus, Oklahoma, June 26, 1952; admitted to bar, 1977, Oklahoma; U.S. Court of Appeals, Fifth and Tenth Circuits; U.S. District Court, Western, Eastern and Northern Districts of Oklahoma. *Education:* Oklahoma State University; Central State University (B.S., 1974); Oklahoma City University (J.D., 1977). Delta Theta Phi (President, 1976). *Member:* Garfield County, Oklahoma (Chairman, Mineral Law Section, 1986) and American Bar Associations. Fellow, Oklahoma Bar Foundation. ***PRACTICE AREAS:*** Commercial Litigation; Banking Law; Oil and Gas Law; Real Property Law. ***Email:*** devoll@enidlaw.com

JULIA CHRISTINA RIEMAN, born Belleville, Illinois, May, 17, 1962; admitted to bar, 1992, Oklahoma; U.S. District Court, Western, Eastern and Northern Districts of Oklahoma; U.S. Court of Appeals, Tenth Circuit; U.S. Supreme Court. *Education:* Oklahoma State University (B.S., Speech, Theater, Education, 1986); University of Tulsa (J.D., with honors, 1992). Recipient: Judge W. Lee Johnson Award, 1992; Phillip Allen Porta Memorial Award, 1992; Travis I. Milsten Award, 1992; American Jurisprudence Awards in Evidence, Administrative Law, Commercial Law I, Commercial Law II, Basic Corporate Law, Decedent's Estates and Trusts and Professional Responsibility. Member, Board of Editors, Oklahoma Bar Journal, 2004-2006. *Member:* Garfield County, Oklahoma and American Bar Associations. ***PRACTICE AREAS:*** Commercial Litigation; Civil Litigation; Appeals. ***Email:*** rieman@enidlaw.com

VANCE T. NYE, born Weatherford, Oklahoma, April 25, 1968; admitted to bar, 1993, Oklahoma; U.S. District Court, Northern, Eastern and Western Districts of Oklahoma. *Education:* Southwestern Oklahoma State University (B.S., summa cum laude, 1989); University of Tulsa (J.D., with honors, 1993). Phi Delta Phi. Member, Order of the Curule (Chair). Recipient: American Jurisprudence Awards in: Contracts II, Professional Responsibility, Evidence and Family Law; Phillip Allen Porta Memorial Award; Col. Graham Kirkpatrick Award. *Member:* Garfield County and Oklahoma Bar Associations. ***PRACTICE AREAS:*** Debtor and Creditor Law; Commercial Law; Real Estate; Probate; Estate Planning. ***Email:*** nye@enidlaw.com

KARIG P. CULVER, born Tahlequah, Oklahoma, October 2, 1958; admitted to bar, 1986, Oklahoma and U.S. District Court, Northern, Eastern and Western Districts of Oklahoma. *Education:* Oklahoma State University (B.S., 1980); University of Tulsa (J.D., 1986). Delta Theta Phi. *Member:* Garfield County (Secretary, 1989-1990) and Oklahoma Bar Associations. ***PRACTICE AREAS:*** Real Estate; Probate; Estate Planning; Commercial Law; Corporate Law. ***Email:*** culver@enidlaw.com

BRADLEY E. DAVENPORT, born Duncan, Oklahoma, September 26, 1973; admitted to bar, 2000, Oklahoma; U.S. District Court, Northern District of Oklahoma. *Education:* University of Oklahoma (B.A., Letters, 1997); Vanderbilt University (J.D., 2000). *Member:* Garfield County, Oklahoma and American Bar Associations. ***PRACTICE AREAS:*** Personal Injury; Medical Malpractice; Insurance; Commercial Litigation; Business Torts. ***Email:*** davenport@enidlaw.com

BRENDON S. ATKINSON, born Sweetwater, Oklahoma, January 27, 1977; admitted to bar, 2002, Oklahoma. *Education:* Oklahoma State University (B.S., 1999); University of Oklahoma (J.D., 2002). *Member:* Garfield County and Oklahoma Bar Associations. ***PRACTICE AREAS:*** Agricultural Law; Civil Litigation; Commercial Litigation; Debtor and Creditor. ***Email:*** Atkinson@enidlaw.com

CHAD N. DAVIS, born Enid, Oklahoma, September 3, 1976; admitted to bar, 2003, Oklahoma; U.S. District Court, Northern, Eastern and Western Districts of Oklahoma. *Education:* University of Oklahoma (B.S., 1999; J.D., 2003). *Member:* Garfield County and Oklahoma Bar Associations. ***PRACTICE AREAS:*** Civil Litigation; Criminal Law; Family Law; Personal Injury; Real Estate. ***Email:*** davis@enidlaw.com

OF COUNSEL

RICHARD L. McKNIGHT, born Enid, Oklahoma, May 31, 1936; admitted to bar, 1963, Oklahoma. *Education:* University of Oklahoma (A.B., 1958; LL.B., 1963). Phi Delta

(This Listing Continued)

GUNGOLL, JACKSON, COLLINS, BOX & DEVOLL, P.C., Enid—Continued

Phi; Order of the Coif. Assistant County Attorney, 1963-1965. Member, Oklahoma Judicial Nominating Commission, 1991-1997; Chairman, 1997. *Member:* Garfield County (President, 1976), Oklahoma (Member, Board of Governors, 1977-1979) and American Bar Associations. Fellow: Oklahoma Bar Foundation (Trustee, 1985-1990; Vice-President, 1987; President Elect, 1988; President, 1989). Fellow: The American College of Trust and Estate Counsel; American Bar Foundation. ***PRACTICE AREAS:*** Probate; Trusts and Estates; Estate Planning; Real Estate. ***Email:*** mcknight@enidlaw.com

REPRESENTATIVE CLIENTS: Central National Bank & Trust; Gold Bank; Security National Bank; First Bank of Okarche; Grant County Bank; Bank of Oklahoma; National Bank of Commerce; First Capital Bank; BancOne, Texas; State Exchange Bank - Tonkawa Branch; Stockmans Bank; Chisolm Trail Farm Credit; Eastern Livestock Company; Baird, Kurtz & Dobson; Collins & Butler, CPA; Surety Abstract; Groendyke Transport, Inc.; Triangle Insurance Company; Triangle Cooperative Services; Advance Foods; Anesthesiology Management; Northwest Medical Specialties, Inc.; Northwest Pulmonary Physicians, P.C.; Chisolm Trail Broadcasting; Cummins Investment; Horne Oil Company; Enid Ford New Holland; Parrish Enterprises; Metal Roof Contractors; Oakwood Country Club; Turkey Creek Golf & Country Club; Andrew Real Estate; Century 21 Homes Plus Realty; Remax Realty; Exxon Corporation; Conoco, Inc.; Chesapeake Energy Corporation; Continental Resources Inc.; Duke Energy Field Services; Trident NGL; Concho Oil & Gas; Unity Management Systems; Louis Dreyfus Natural Gas Corporation; XTO Energy, Inc.; D & P Tank Trucks; Oxy USA, Inc.; Permian Well Service; Benson Mineral Group; Champlin Exploration; Siosi Oil & Gas; Big Buckets Rathole; B & R Construction; Northern Equipment Company; Envirotech; W.B. Johnston Grainn Company; Johnston Seed Company; Oklahoma Grain and Feed Association; Oklahoma Seed Trade Association; Oklahoma Agri-Business Association; Equity Marketing Alliance, L.L.C.; Alva Cooperative; Blackwell Cooperative; Burlington Cooperative; Carrier Cooperative; Crescent Cooperative Association; Dacoma Farmers Cooperative, Inc.; Farmers Elevator Company of Ames; Farmers Grain of Pond Creek; Nash, Jefferson & Kremlin; Garber Cooperative Association; Mid-Oklahoma Cooperative; Planters Cooperative Association; Sooner Cooperative, Inc.; State Line Grain Company.

DENNIS W. HLADIK

300 CONTINENTAL CENTER NORTH
302 NORTH INDEPENDENCE
ENID, OKLAHOMA 73701
Telephone: 580-234-6945
Fax: 580-234-6947
Email: dennishladik@coxinet.net
URL: http://www.lawyers.com/enid-law

Divorce, Family Law, Child Custody, Debtor and Creditor, Creditors Rights, Trusts and Estates, Criminal Defense, Real Estate Law, Title Opinions, Title Examinations, Business Law, Bankruptcy, Oil & Gas, Commercial Collections, Commercial Litigation, Personal Injury, Automobile Accidents, Wrongful Death, Driving While Intoxicated, Wills, Probate, Civil Litigation.

DENNIS W. HLADIK, born Hennessey, Oklahoma, December 31, 1949; admitted to bar, 1975, Oklahoma. *Education:* Oklahoma State University (B.S., 1972); Oklahoma University (J.D., 1975). Phi Delta Phi. Member and President, Kremlin-Hilldale Board of Education, 1988-2001. Public Defender for Garfield County, 1980-1995. *Member:* Garfield County (Past President) and Oklahoma Bar Associations. ***PRACTICE AREAS:*** Divorce; Family Law; Child Custody; Debtor and Creditor; Criminal Defense; Bankruptcy; Commercial Collections; Personal Injury; Wills; Civil Litigation.

JONES, OTJEN, DAVIS, NIXON & JUHL

A PROFESSIONAL ASSOCIATION OF ATTORNEYS
SUITE 1100 BROADWAY TOWER
114 EAST BROADWAY
P.O. BOX 472
ENID, OKLAHOMA 73702
Telephone: 580-242-5500
Fax: 580-242-4556
URL: http://www.stephenjoneslaw.com

Oklahoma City, Oklahoma Office: 311 North Harvey Avenue, Suite 103, 73102. Telephone: 405-604-5312. Fax: 405-604-5313.

Litigation and related matters in State and Federal Courts including: Insurance Defense, Criminal Defense and Grand Jury Practice, White Collar Crime, Complex Civil and Commercial Litigation, Business/Corporate Law, Divorce and Child Custody, School Law, Employment Law, Contested Wills and Estates, Regulation of Professionals, Professional Malpractice, and Appeals of Civil and Criminal Matters, Aviation Law.

FIRM PROFILE: The predecessor firm was established prior to statehood in Enid, Oklahoma Territory, in 1905 by Charles O. West, who became the first Attorney General of Oklahoma in 1907, and W.J. Otjen, Sr., a prominent State Senator who successfully prosecuted the removal from office of Governor Jack Walton. He later became National Commander of Veterans of the Spanish-American War. Senator Otjen's uncle, Congressman Theobald Otjen, appointed young Douglas McArthur to the United States Military Academy. Frank Carter became Senator Otjen's secretary and was the last lawyer in the county to have been admitted to the Bar on the basis of law office study. He later became Mayor of Enid.

Mr. Jones achieved national publicity when he was appointed by the United States District Court to serve as lead defense counsel for Timothy James McVeigh, charged with the bombing of the Alfred P. Murrah Federal Building in Oklahoma City on April 19, 1995. Notwithstanding that controversial case, the firm has a long history of representing clients ranging in size from Fortune 500 corporations to family-owned businesses and individuals. The firm limits itself to litigation and appellate practice involving civil, commercial, insurance, criminal, family law and matters in state and federal trial and appellate courts, and matters relating to the United States Grand Jury, the Internal Revenue Service Criminal Investigation Division, the Enforcement Division of the Oklahoma and United States Securities & Exchange Commission, and military court martial matters.

The firm maintains offices in both Enid and the capital city, Oklahoma City.

STEPHEN JONES, born Lafayette, Louisiana, July 1, 1940; admitted to bar, 1966, Oklahoma; 1969, U.S. Court of Appeals, Tenth Circuit and U.S. District Court, Western District of Oklahoma; 1970, U.S. Tax Court and U.S. Supreme Court; 1973, U.S. Court of Appeals, Eighth Circuit; 1975, U.S. Court of Appeals, Second Circuit and U.S. Court of Appeals, District of Columbia; 1979, U.S. District Court, Northern District of Oklahoma; 1980, U.S. Claims Court; 1982, U.S. Court of Appeals, Federal Circuit. *Education:* University of Texas; University of Oklahoma (LL.B., 1966). Phi Alpha Delta. Associate Editor, Oklahoma Bar Journal, 1979-1986. Author: "John W. Davis," Oklahoma Law Review Vol. 27 No. 1, Winter, 1974; "The Case Against Presidential Impeachment," Oklahoma Bar Association Journal, Oklahoma Criminal Defense Form Book, 1974; "Oklahoma Politics," Vol. I, 1907-1962; "Was President Nixon Guilty: The Case For The Defense," Oklahoma Bar Association Journal, Winter 1978; "Vernon's Oklahoma Forms, 2d: Criminal Law, Practice & Procedure," West Group, 1999; "U.S. v. McVeigh: Defending the 'Most Hated Man in America,'" Oklahoma Law Review Vol. 51 No. 4, Winter, 1998; "Others Unknown: The Oklahoma City Bombing Case and Conspiracy," Public Affairs, 1998; "A Lawyer's Ethical Duty to Represent the Unpopular Client," Chapman Law Review Vol. 1 No. 1. Spring, 1998; "Representing Timothy McVeigh", Litigation, Spring, 2002, Vol. 28, Number 3. Listed in, Who's Who in America. Chester Bedell Memorial Lecturer, "The Independence of American Lawyers," Florida Bar Association, 1999. Assistant Professor, University of Oklahoma, 1973-1976; Adjunct Professor, Phillips University, 1983-1990. Secretary, Minority Conference, Texas Legislature, 1960-1961. Assistant to Honorable Richard Nixon, New York, 1964. Administrative Assistant, Congressman Paul Findley, Washington, D.C., 1966-1969. Legal Assistant to Governor of Oklahoma, 1967. Member, U.S. Delegation to NATO (North Atlantic Assembly), 1968. Special Assistant District Attorney, 1977. Member, State Supreme Court Committee on Civil Jury Instructions, 1979-1981. Special United States Attorney, Northern District of Oklahoma, 1979. Special Counsel to the Governor of Oklahoma, 1995. Member, Oklahoma Court of Criminal Appeals Advisory Committee on Court Rules, 1980. Judge of Temporary Division, Oklahoma Court of Appeals, 1982. Republican Nominee, United States Senate, 1990. *Member:* Garfield County, Oklahoma and American (Member, Section of: Criminal Justice; Taxation) Bar Associations; National Association of Criminal Defense Lawyers; Oklahoma Criminal Defense Lawyers Association (Board of Directors; Recipient, "Lord Erskine Award", 1989). ***REPORTED CASES:*** Vinyard v. King, 728 F.2d 428 (10th Cir. 1984); Perrin v. Anderson, 784 F.2d 1040 (10th Cir. 1986); U.S. v. Laughlin, 26 F.3d 1523 (10th Cir. 1994); Nesbitt v. Apple, 891 P.2d 1235 (Okla. 1995); Burkhardt v. City of Enid, 771 P.2d 608 (Okla. 1989); State ex. rel. Oklahoma Bar Association v. Schaffer, 648 P.2d 355 (Okla. 1982); In re Initiative Petition No. 317, State Question No. 556, 648 P.2d 1207 (Okla. 1982); Collins v. State, 561 P.2d 1373 (Okla. Crim. App. 1977); United States of America v. Timothy James McVeigh, et al., 918 F.Supp. 1467 (W.D. Okla. 1996); United States of America v. Timothy James McVeigh, et al., 169 F.R.D. 362 (D. Colo. 1996); Democratic Party of Oklahoma v. Republican State Committee 652 Pacific 2nd 271. ***PRACTICE AREAS:*** Civil; Trial Practice; Civil Appeals; Insurance Defense; White Collar Criminal Defense; Personal Injury; Appellate Practice; Criminal Law; Federal Criminal Law; Capital Offenses; Military Courts Martial; Grand Jury Practice; Aviation Law. ***Email:*** sjones@steohenjoneslaw.com

APRIL McCURDY DAVIS, born Norman, Oklahoma, April 1, 1972; admitted to bar, 1998, Oklahoma; 2003, U.S. Court of Appeals, Tenth Circuit and U.S. District Court, Western District of Oklahoma. *Education:* University of Oklahoma (B.S., with honors, 1994); University of North Dakota College of Law (J.D., with distinction, 1997). Law Women's Caucus. Staff Writer, North Dakota Law Review, 1996-1997. *Member:* Oklahoma Bar Association (Member, Young Lawyers Division, 1998). ***PRACTICE AREAS:*** Civil Practice; Family Law; Trust and Estates; Child Custody; Employment; Labor Law; Insurance. ***Email:*** adavis@enid.com

RODNEY A. NIXON, born Tulsa, Oklahoma, December 18, 1969; admitted to bar, 2003, Oklahoma and U.S. District Court, Western District of Oklahoma; 2005, U.S. District Court, Northern District of Oklahoma. *Education:* Oklahoma State University (B.B.A., Hotel and Restaurant Administration, 1992); University of Tulsa (J.D., 2003). Chair, Order of the Curule. Recipient, William H. Bell Award. Articles Editor, Energy Law Journal, 2002. *Member:* Oklahoma Bar Association. ***PRACTICE AREAS:*** Civil Litigation. ***Email:*** rnixon@stephenjoneslaw.com

DEANNA JUHL, born Park Ridge, Illinois, November 13, 1976; admitted to bar, 2002, Connecticut; 2004, Oklahoma. *Education:* St. Louis University (B.A., English, magna cum laude, 1999); Western New England College School of Law (J.D., 2002). *Member:* Oklahoma Bar Association. ***PRACTICE AREAS:*** Family Law; Criminal Law; Civil Litigation; Criminal Defense; Insurance Defense; Secured Transactions.

ASSOCIATES

JENNIFER J. GIDEON, born Albuquerque, New Mexico, August 18, 1969; admitted to bar, 1998, Oklahoma and U.S. District Court, Western District of Oklahoma. *Education:* University of Oklahoma (B.A., 1995; J.D., with Distinction, 1998); University of Texas, Austin (LL.M., 2003). Order of the Barristers. Member, 1996-1998 and Note Editor, 1997-1998, Oklahoma Law Review. Recipient: American Jurisprudence Award for Property, Fall 1995; First Year Moot Court Competition, Winner, 1996; Student Bar Association Award, 1998; Rayburn L. Foster Scholarship; Marshall Huser Scholarship; Leon J. York Scholarship. Member: Student Bar Association (Representative, 1996-1997; President, 1997-1998); American Inns of Court, Luther Bohanon Inn, (Student Pupil, 1997-1998); American Trial Lawyers Association (Trial Team Member, 1998). Teaching Assistant, Legal Research and Writing, 1996-1998; National Moot Court Team, 1997-1998. Co-Author: "United States v. McVeigh: Defending the Most Hated Man in America," Oklahoma Law Review, Vol. 51, No. 4, Winter 1998. Co-Author and Editor: *Oklahoma Criminal Law, Practice and Procedure,* published by West Publishing Company, May 2000. Staff Attorney, Clinton Law Center, Legal Aid of Western Oklahoma, Inc., 1999-2000. Staff Attorney, Supportkids, Inc. Assistant City Attorney, City of Enid, 2003-2005. Formerly With, Mitchel, Gaston, Riffel & Riffel, Enid. *Member:* Garfield County and Oklahoma Bar As-

(This Listing Continued)

sociations. ***LANGUAGES:*** Spanish. ***SPECIAL AGENCIES:*** Board Member, Youth and Family Services, Enid OK. ***PRACTICE AREAS:*** Criminal; Family; Workers Compensation; Civil. ***Email:*** jgideon@stephenjoneslaw.com

JILL J. GRAHAM, born December 18, 1979; admitted to bar, 2005, Oklahoma. *Education:* Oklahoma State University (B.S. cum laude); University of Tulsa (J.D., 2004). Phi Delta Phi. Author: Jill Parker, Comment, "West meets East: A Discussion of European Union Enlargement and Human Rights," 11 Tulsa J. Comp. & Int'/L. 603. *Member:* Oklahoma Bar Association (Member, Young Lawyers Division, 2005). ***PRACTICE AREAS:*** Criminal Defense; Family Law. ***Email:*** jgraham@stephenjoneslaw.com

REPRESENTATIVE CLIENTS: Minolta; Shell Oil Co.; Mesa Limited Partnership; Wells Fargo; Sotheby Park-Benet; Crawford & Co.; Firestone Tire & Rubber Co.; U.S. Insurance Group; City of Enid; Enid Publishing Co.; Emerson Electric Co.; Mid-Continent Casualty Insurance Co.; Dresser Industries; Republican National Committee; NAACP Legal Defense Fund; Sears & Roebuck, Co.; Associates Financial Services, Inc.; Excel Corp. (Cargill, Inc.); Melvin Simon & Associates; St. Paul Property and Liability; Associated Aviation Underwriters; Gulf Insurance Group; Independent Petroleum Association of America; State Farm Insurance Co.; Home Insurance Co.; Aetna; Ranger Insurance; Employer's Casualty Corporation; Kawasaki Motor Corporation; Amwest Insurance; Transport Life Insurance Company; National American Insurance Company; Old Surety Life Insurance Company; Mead Reinsurance Corporation; E & O Professionals; Enid Police Department; State Treasurer of Oklahoma; Governor of Oklahoma; Tandy Corp.; Enid Motor Speedway; Garfield County Fairgrounds Trust Authority; Garfield County Commissioners; BCS Insurance Company; Naughton Insurance, Inc.; Claims Professionals Associated, Inc.; Lloyds of London; American Reserve Life Insurance Co.
REFERENCES: First State Bank of Pond Creek, Enid, Oklahoma; Security National Bank.

CLARK McKEEVER

3RD FLOOR, CONTINENTAL TOWER
P.O. BOX 1026
ENID, OKLAHOMA 73702
Telephone: 580-234-4133
Fax: 580-234-4137

Probate, Guardianship, Real Estate, Commercial Law, Estate Planning.

CLARK McKEEVER, born Enid, Oklahoma, August 15, 1954; admitted to bar, 1979, Oklahoma; 1980, U.S. District Court, Western District of Oklahoma; 1985, U.S. Court of Appeals, 10th Circuit. *Education:* Texas Christian University (B.B.A., 1976); Oklahoma University (J.D., 1979). *Member:* Garfield County, Oklahoma and American Bar Associations. ***PRACTICE AREAS:*** Real Estate Law; Commercial Law; Probate Law; Guardianship Law; Estate Planning.

H.G. McKEEVER (1872-1940)

H. H. McKEEVER (1906-1975)

DOUGLAS C. McKEEVER (1918-1985)

APPROVED TITLE EXAMINERS FOR: First American Title Insurance Co.; Lawyers Title Insurance Co.

MITCHELL & DeCLERCK, P.L.L.C.

Established in 1907

202 WEST BROADWAY
ENID, OKLAHOMA 73701-4018
Telephone: 580-234-5144
Facsimile: 580-234-8890

General Civil Practice Litigation. Banking, Commercial, Corporate, Personal Injury, Insurance, Real Estate, Estate Planning, Collections (Professionals) Debtor Creditor, Probate, Bankruptcy, Trusts, Family Law, Wills, Estates.

FIRM PROFILE: The firm has been in continuous existence since statehood, and was founded by P.C. Simons, former Attorney General of Oklahoma Territory.

The lawyers are active in civic affairs in northwest Oklahoma, and serve clients throughout Oklahoma and the southwest United States with a combined legal experience of 190 years.

P.C. SIMONS (1870-1962)

E. B. MITCHELL (1895-1976)

EARL B. MITCHELL, JR. (1924-2003)

EDWARD A. DeCLERCK (1916-2002)

LARRY D. LAHMAN, born Carmen, Oklahoma, October 24, 1943; admitted to bar, 1973, Oklahoma; 1979, U.S. Supreme Court, U.S. Court of Appeals, Tenth Circuit and U.S. District Court, Northern and Western Districts of Oklahoma. *Education:* Northwestern Oklahoma State University (B.S., 1965); Oklahoma State University; North Carolina State University; University of Maryland; Central State University; Phillips University; University of Oklahoma (J.D., 1973). Phi Alpha Delta; Blue Key. *Member:* Garfield County, Oklahoma and American Bar Associations. [Lieut. Col., U.S. Army Special Forces, 1966-1970; U.S. Army Reserve Special Forces, 1970-1996]. ***PRACTICE AREAS:*** Bankruptcy Law; Banking; Commercial Collection Law. ***Email:*** ldl@mdpllc.com

E. W. (BILL) SHAW, born Carbondale, Illinois, August 23, 1942; admitted to bar, 1974, Oklahoma; 1979, U.S. Supreme Court, U.S. Court of Appeals, 10th Circuit and U.S. District Court, Northern and Western Districts of Oklahoma. *Education:* Olivet Nazarene College (B.S., 1966); University of Tulsa (J.D., 1973). Delta Theta Phi. Certified Mediator for District Courts. *Member:* Garfield County and Oklahoma Bar Associations. [Capt., USAF, 1966-1971; Oklahoma Air National Guard, 1971-1973]. ***PRACTICE AREAS:*** Personal Injury Litigation; Commercial Litigation; Insurance Law; Municipal Law. ***Email:*** ews@mdpllc.com

DAVID C. BUTLER, born Enid, Oklahoma, 1945; admitted to bar, 1976, Oklahoma and U.S. District Court, Western District of Oklahoma; 1978, U.S. Court of Appeals, 10th Circuit; 1979, U.S. Supreme Court. *Education:* University of Oklahoma (B.A., 1967; J.D., 1976). Phi Delta Phi. Member, Board of Editors, Oklahoma Bar Journal, 1988-1991. Editor, Title Examination Standards Handbook, 1994; 1998. Member, Garfield County Excise Board, 1993-1996. *Member:* Garfield County, Oklahoma (Member, Board of Governors, 2001—; Member, Title Examination Standards Committee; Chair, Real Property Section, 1992; Member, Advisory Committee to Supreme Court on Rules Revisions) Bar Associations. [1st Lt., USAF, 1970-1972]. ***PRACTICE AREAS:*** Real Estate; Probate; Trusts and Estates; Litigation; Appellate Practice; Bankruptcy. ***Email:*** dcb@mdpllc.com

MICHAEL C. BIGHEART, born Ponca City, Oklahoma, February 16, 1950; admitted to bar, 1983, Oklahoma; 1984, U.S. District Court, Western District of Oklahoma; 2004, U.S. Supreme Court. *Education:* Wichita State University (B.B.A., 1972); University of Tulsa (J.D., 1981). *Member:* Garfield County, Oklahoma and American Bar Associations; Oklahoma Trial Lawyers Association; The Association of Trial Lawyers of America. Fellow, Oklahoma Bar Foundation. ***PRACTICE AREAS:*** Litigation; Banks and Banking; Natural Resources; Labor and Employment. ***Email:*** mcb@mdpllc.com

TIM E. DeCLERCK, born Enid, Oklahoma, November 15, 1956; admitted to bar, 1983, Oklahoma; 1984, U.S. District Court, Western District of Oklahoma; 1991, U.S. Supreme Court. *Education:* University of Oklahoma (B.A., 1980; J.D., 1983). Phi Alpha Delta. *Member:* Garfield County, Oklahoma and American Bar Associations. ***PRACTICE AREAS:*** Trusts and Estates; Contested Trusts and Estates; Estate Planning; Banking Law; Divorce; General Practice. ***Email:*** ted@mdpllc.com

OF COUNSEL

P. JOHN HODGDEN, born Enid, Oklahoma, May 27, 1964; admitted to bar, 1991, Oklahoma; 1993, Texas; 1996, Colorado. *Education:* University of Oklahoma (B.A., Finance, 1986; J.D., 1990). ***PRACTICE AREAS:*** Civil Litigation; Family Law; Personal Injury. ***Email:*** pjh@mdpllc.com

FORREST L. PEPPER DeVAUGHN, born Enid, Oklahoma, November 8, 1974; admitted to bar, 2000, Oklahoma and U.S. District Court, Northern, Eastern and Western Districts of Oklahoma; U.S. Supreme Court. *Education:* Oklahoma State University (B.S., Economics, 1993); University of Tulsa (J.D., 2000). Phi Delta Phi. *Member:* Garfield County and Oklahoma Bar Associations. ***REPORTED CASES:*** Gonzales ex rel Gonzalez v. Combined Insurance Co. of America, 57 P.3d 109; 2002 OK CIV APP 101, OKLA. CIV. APP. DIV 1, Apr. 12, 2002. ***PRACTICE AREAS:*** Products Liability; Qui Tam Litigation; Class Actions. ***Email:*** fld@mdpllc.com

ROGER L. EDIGER, born Enid, Oklahoma, November 17, 1954; admitted to bar, 2002, Oklahoma; U.S. District Court, Western District of Oklahoma. *Education:* Tabor College (B.A., 1977); University of Oklahoma (J.D., 2002). *Member:* Garfield County and Oklahoma Bar Associations; Christian Legal Society. ***PRACTICE AREAS:*** Bankruptcy; Banks and Banking; Personal Injury; General Practice. ***Email:*** rle@mdpllc.com

ATTORNEYS FOR: Cleo State Bank; Meno Guaranty Bank; First State Bank, Waynoka, Oklahoma; Helena Cities and Towns of Carmen, Aline, Drummond, and Nash; NBank; Ward Petroleum Corporation; D.C. Bass and Sons Construction; Faulkner Corporation; Brittany Petroleum Ltd.; Superior Oil and Gas, L.L.C.; Pope Distributing Company; Mid America Wholesale; First State Bank, Yukon, Oklahoma; Bank of Beaver City; Dillingham Insurance; Geronimo Trucking; Spess Oil Company; St. Mary's Regional Medical Center; Birthwise; F&F Tool Company; Enid Hospital Authority; Central National Bank & Trust Co. of Enid; State Exchange Bank of Lamont; Farm Credit of Enid, ACA.
LOCAL COUNSEL FOR: American Mercury Group; Great West Casualty Company; Harbor Insurance Co.; Oklahoma Farmer Union Mutual Ins. Co.; U.S. Agbank; F.C.B. Boy Scouts of America; Oklahoma Farmer's Union Mutual Insurance Co.; Enid P.T. Professionals, Inc.

TRAYNOR, LONG, WYNNE & WOODWARD, P.C.

A PROFESSIONAL CORPORATION

Established in 1950
1010 WEST MAPLE
P.O. BOX 3247
ENID, OKLAHOMA 73702
Telephone: 580-233-4455
Toll Free: 1-877-439-4455
Fax: 580-233-4502
Email: tlww@coxinet.net

Okeene, Oklahoma Office: 214 South Main Street. 73763. Telephone 580-822-4458. Fax: 580-822-4473.

General Civil and Criminal Practice in all State and Federal Courts, Personal Injury, Insurance Law, Family Law, Wills and Trusts, Probate and Estate Planning, Business Organizations, Sales, Mergers and Acquisitions, Reorganizations, Real Estate, Commercial, Business Law, Criminal, Municipal Law, Education Law.

WILL T. WRIGHT (1908-1986)

TIMOTHY R. TRAYNOR, born Enid, Oklahoma, October 31, 1943; admitted to bar, 1968, Oklahoma; 1973, U.S. District Court, Western District of Oklahoma; 1979, U.S. Tax Court. *Education:* University of Oklahoma (B.B.A., 1965; J.D., 1968). Phi Eta Sigma; Phi Alpha Delta. Associate Examiner, Oklahoma Board of Bar Examiners, 1973-1975. *Member:* Garfield County (President, 1986) and Oklahoma (Chairman, Taxation Section, 1978) Bar Associations. Fellow, Oklahoma Bar Foundation. [U.S. Army, 1968-1970]. ***PRACTICE AREAS:*** Estate Planning; Trusts and Estates; Taxation; Commercial Contracts; Business Planning; Business Organizations. ***Email:*** trt.tlww@coxinet.net

JAMES F. LONG, born Kansas City, Missouri, May 24, 1948; admitted to bar, 1974, Oklahoma and Kansas. *Education:* Phillips University (B.A., 1970); Washburn University of Topeka (J.D., 1974). Municipal Judge, Enid, 1983—. *Member:* Garfield County (President, 2000) and Oklahoma Bar Associations; Fellow, Oklahoma Bar Foundation. ***PRACTICE AREAS:*** Personal Injury Law; Probate Law; Insurance Law; Family Law. ***Email:*** jfl.tlww@coxinet.net

JOHN H. WYNNE, born Oklahoma City, Oklahoma, November 3, 1949; admitted to bar, 1974, Oklahoma and U.S. District Court, Western District of Oklahoma. *Education:* Oklahoma State University (B.S., 1971); University of Tulsa (J.D., 1974). City Commissioner, Enid Oklahoma, 1979-1983. Temporary Court of Appeals, 1982. Oklahoma Attor-

(This Listing Continued)

TRAYNOR, LONG, WYNNE & WOODWARD, P.C., A PROFESSIONAL CORPORATION, Enid—Continued

neys Mutual Insurance Company (Director, 1994—). *Member:* Garfield County (President, 1994) and Oklahoma Bar Associations; Oklahoma Association of Municipal Attorneys. Fellow, Oklahoma Bar Foundation. ***PRACTICE AREAS:*** Municipal Law; Real Estate; Probate; Trusts and Estates; Business Organization; Contracts. ***Email:*** jhw.tlww@coxinet.net

PAUL K. WOODWARD, born Liberal, Kansas, December 20, 1959; admitted to bar, 1985, Oklahoma, U.S. District Court, Western and Northern Districts of Oklahoma. *Education:* Oklahoma Christian College (B.S., 1982); Oklahoma City University (J.D., 1984). *Member:* Garfield County and Oklahoma Bar Associations. ***PRACTICE AREAS:*** Criminal Law; Real Estate; Litigation; Probate. ***Email:*** pkw.tlww@coxinet.net

ELISE D. EVANS, born Fort Smith, Arkansas, November 4, 1979; admitted to bar, 2005, Oklahoma. *Education:* University of Oklahoma (B.B.A., 2002; J.D., 2005). *Member:* Garfield County and Oklahoma Bar Associations. ***PRACTICE AREAS:*** Family Law; School Law; Criminal Law; Bankruptcy; Litigation. ***Email:*** ede.tlww@coxinet.net

REPRESENTATIVE CLIENTS: U.S. Gypsum; Champlin Family Trusts; Geo.Wilson Charitable Trust; Enid Community Foundation; State Guaranty Bank of Okeene; Oklahoma Municipal Assurance Group; Advance Food Co.; Guarantee Abstract Co.; Scheffe Prescription Shops; Cummins Construction Co.; K-M Properties; Janzen Oldsmobile; U.I. Smith Oil & Gas; K.C. Imports; Oklahoma West Physicians Group; Emrick's Van & Storage; Integris Bass Baptist Health Center; Radiology Associates of Enid; Maxey Family Trusts; Mayer Charitable Remainder Trust; Pumpstar, Inc.; City of Enid, OK; First Bank & Trust of Perry, OK; Evans Drug Co.
REFERENCES: Central National Bank & Trust Company of Enid; Liberty Federal Savings Bank.

MITCHELL A. HALLREN

116 EAST ELM
P.O. BOX 428
FAIRVIEW, OKLAHOMA 73737
Telephone: 580-227-4449
Fax: 580-227-4448
Email: hallrenlaw@sbcglobal.net

Trial Practice, Probate, Real Property, Oil and Gas Law, Real Estate Title Law, Commercial and Family Law.

MITCHELL A. HALLREN, born Norman, Oklahoma, August 25, 1952; admitted to bar, 1978, Oklahoma; 1983, U.S. District Court, Western District of Oklahoma. *Education:* University of Oklahoma (B.A., 1975; J.D., 1978). Past-President, Fairview Chamber of Commerce. *Member:* Major County (President) and Oklahoma (Member, Sections on: Mineral Law; Family Law) Bar Associations. ***PRACTICE AREAS:*** Real Estate; Oil and Gas Law; Commercial Law; Probate; Family Law; Trial Practice.

REPRESENTATIVE CLIENTS: Chesapeake Exploration, Ford Motor Credit; PGS Onshore, Inc.; Jebco Seismic, L.P.; Town of Canton; Wells Fargo Bank.

JOHN W. McCUE, II

118 EAST BROADWAY
P.O. BOX 503
FAIRVIEW, OKLAHOMA 73737
Telephone: 580-227-3939
Fax: 580-227-3607
Email: mccuelaw@io2online.com

General, Real Estate, Probate, Oil and Gas Law and Banking Law.

FIRM PROFILE: Since Mr. McCue, II started his solo practice, he has focused on Real Estate, Oil and Gas Law, Probate, Banking and General Law. He primarily represents a variety of clients throughout Northwest Oklahoma.

JOHN W. McCUE, II, born Fairview, Oklahoma, April 6, 1943; admitted to bar, 1968, Oklahoma; 1978, U.S. Supreme Court; 1979, U.S. District Court, Western District of Oklahoma; 1982, U.S. Court of Appeals, Tenth Circuit; 1984, U.S. District Court, Northern District of Texas; 1989, U.S. Court of Appeals, Fifth Circuit. *Education:* Oklahoma State University (B.S., 1965); University of Oklahoma (J.D., 1968). Phi Alpha Delta. Municipal Judge, City of Fairview, 1991-2001. Pro Bono Service Award, Oklahoma Bar Association, 2002. *Member:* Major County (Secretary, 1972—), Oklahoma (Associate Bar Examiners, 1973-1975; Secretary-Treasurer, 1982; Chairman-Elect, 1984 and Chairman, 1985, Mineral Law Section) and American Bar Associations. ***PRACTICE AREAS:*** General Practice; Probate; Oil and Gas Law; Real Estate; Banking Law.

COUNSEL FOR: Farmers & Merchants National Bank, Fairview; Fairview Savings & Loan Association, Fairview; Major County Trust Authority; Fairview Industrial Development Authority; Major County Economic Development Corporation; Fairview Abstract Company.
REPRESENTATIVE CLIENTS: Cleo State Bank, Cleo Springs; Meno Guaranty Bank, Meno.
APPROVED EXAMINING ATTORNEY FOR: First American Title Insurance Company.

BENSON & BENSON, INC.

A PROFESSIONAL CORPORATION
Established in 1950
124 NORTH 9TH STREET
P.O. BOX 486
FREDERICK, OKLAHOMA 73542-0486
Telephone: 580-335-7541
Fax: 580-335-7543
Email: Bensonlawfirm@pldi.net
URL: http://www.bensonlawfirm.net

General Civil Practice. Banking, Corporation, Insurance, Oil and Gas, Probate and Real Estate Law. Civil Trials, Trusts and Estates, Estate Planning, Family Law, Criminal Law.

LOYD L. BENSON, born Comanche, Oklahoma, April 2, 1940; admitted to bar, 1965, Oklahoma. *Education:* University of Oklahoma (B.A., 1962; J.D., 1965). Author: "Survey of Juvenile and Family Courts," Oklahoma and the Law, 1979; "Requirements for Ordinances and Resolutions," 48 OBAJ 131, 1983. City Attorney, City of Grandfield, Oklahoma, 1970—. Assistant District Attorney, 1970. President, Oklahoma Municipal Attorneys Association, 1979. Speaker of the Oklahoma House of Representatives, 1996-2000, and Member, 1984-2002, Oklahoma House of Representatives. *Member:* Tillman County (President, 1972-1975), Oklahoma (Member: Oklahoma Professional Responsibility Tribunal, 1981-1985) and American Bar Associations. [Capt., U.S. Army, 1965-1967]. ***PRACTICE AREAS:*** Banking; Corporation; Insurance; Oil and Gas; Probate; Real Estate; Family; Personal Injury.

BRADFORD L. BENSON, born Norman, Oklahoma, November 17, 1964; admitted to bar, 1992, Oklahoma and Texas; 1993, U.S. District Court, Western District of Oklahoma. *Education:* University of Oklahoma (B.B.A., 1988); Southern Methodist University (J.D., 1991). Clerk to Presiding Judge, Oklahoma Court of Criminal Appeals, 1994-1995. City Attorney, Town of Tipton, Oklahoma, 1995—. *Member:* Tillman County (President, 1995—), Oklahoma and American Bar Associations; State Bar of Texas. ***PRACTICE AREAS:*** Banking; Corporation; Probate; Real Estate; Criminal; Family; Personal Injury. ***Email:*** Bensonlawfirm@pldi.net

REPRESENTATIVE CLIENTS: BancFirst, Frederick; Tipton Children's Home; Southwest Rural Electric Assn. Inc.; First State Bank in Grandfield; Farmers Home Administration; Tillman Co. Industrial Trust Authority; Memorial Hospital and Physicians Group; Southwest Rural Development Authority.
APPROVED ATTORNEYS FOR: First American Title Insurance Co.; Southwest Title & Trust; American Guaranty Co.

MASSAD, EVANS & KENT, INC.

A PROFESSIONAL CORPORATION
120 NORTH NINTH STREET
DRAWER 606
FREDERICK, OKLAHOMA 73542
Telephone: 580-335-5531
Fax: 508-335-5532
Email: meklaw@pldi.net
URL: http://www.lawyers.com/meklaw

General Civil and Criminal Practice in Oklahoma state courts, Agricultural Law, Bank and Banking, Bankruptcy, Business Law, Children, Collections, Contracts, Education Law, Eminent Domain, Family Law, Guardianship and Conservatorship, Insurance, Legal Ethics and Professional Responsibility, Mortgages, Municipal Law, Personal Injury, Real Estate, Trusts and Estates, Wills.

ANTHONY M. MASSAD, born Shidler, Oklahoma, June 15, 1928; admitted to bar, 1955, Oklahoma. *Education:* University of Oklahoma (B.A., 1949; J.D., 1955). Delta Theta Phi. Assistant County Attorney, Tillman County, 1959-1964. State Senator, 1965-1968. *Member:* Tillman County (President, 1960-1961), Oklahoma (President, 1989) and American Bar Associations; Oklahoma Trial Lawyers Association. Fellow, American Bar Foundation; Oklahoma Bar Foundation (Life Fellow). [Major, Infantry, U.S.A.R., Retired]. ***PRACTICE AREAS:*** Contracts; Eminent Domain; Personal Injury; Real Estate; Trusts and Estates; Wills.

MICHAEL D. EVANS, born Columbia, Missouri, October 23, 1946; admitted to bar, 1973, Oklahoma. *Education:* Oklahoma State University (B.A., 1969); University of Oklahoma (J.D., 1973). Phi Alpha Delta. Assistant District Attorney, Third Judicial District of Oklahoma, Tillman County, 1975-1982, 1998. City Attorney, Frederick, 1982—. *Member:* Tillman County (Past President), Oklahoma (President, 2005; President Elect, 2004; Vice President, 2001; Board of Governors, 1996-1998; Chairman, Professional Responsibility Commission, 1992; 1995) and American Bar Associations. Fellow, Oklahoma Bar Foundation; Life Fellow, American Bar Foundation. ***PRACTICE AREAS:*** Agricultural Law; Bankruptcy; Family Law; Mortgages; Municipal Law. ***Email:*** mike@meklaw.com

JOHN P. (PAT) KENT, born Frederick, Oklahoma, January 27, 1950; admitted to bar, 1976, Oklahoma and U.S. District Court, Western District of Oklahoma. *Education:* Oklahoma State University (B.S., 1972); University of Oklahoma (M.B.A., 1974; J.D., 1976). City Attorney, Tipton, 1979-1991. Municipal Judge, Frederick, 1985-1991. *Member:* Tillman County (Past President), Oklahoma (Chairman, Mandatory Continuing Legal Education Commission, 1995-2000; Member, Professional Responsibility Tribunal, 2001—) and American Bar Associations. Fellow: Oklahoma Bar Association; American Bar Association. ***PRACTICE AREAS:*** Banking Law; Domestic Relations; Real Estate; Education Law; Insurance; Wills; Trusts and Estates. ***Email:*** pat@meklaw.com

JOHN B. WILSON, JR. (1912-1971)

TY JOHNSON, born Hobart, Oklahoma, February 10, 1975; admitted to bar, 2002, Texas; 2004, Oklahoma; 2005, U.S. District Court, Western District of Oklahoma. *Educa-*

(This Listing Continued)

tion: Vanderbilt University (B.S., magna cum laude, 1997; J.D., 2002). Phi Beta Kappa; Order of the Coif. Assistant City Attorney, Frederick, Oklahoma, 2004—. *Member:* Tillman County and Oklahoma Bar Associations; State Bar of Texas; Oklahoma Bar Foundation. ***PRACTICE AREAS:*** Agricultural Law; Corporate Law; Bankruptcy; Civil Litigation; Criminal Law; Family Law. **Email:** ty@meklaw.com

REPRESENTATIVE CLIENTS: American Cattle Services, Inc.; Tillman Producers Cooperative; Oklahoma Cotton Compress Association; Oklahoma Boll Weevil Eradication Organization, a state agency; Bank of the Wichitas; First National Bank in Altus; BankFirst, Frederick; Guarantee State Bank, Mangum; Frederick Public Schools; City of Frederick; Frederick Public Works Authority; Gold Bank, Hobart; Tillman County-City of Frederick Memorial Hospital.
APPROVED ATTORNEYS FOR: Southwest Title & Trust Co., Oklahoma City, Oklahoma; American First Title & Trust, Oklahoma City; U.S.A., Farm Service Agency; Ag Preference Credit Associaton; First American Title Insurance Co.

McBEE, BENSON & BENSON

FREDERICK, OKLAHOMA

(See Benson & Benson)

LOGAN & LOWRY, LLP

19 EAST 3RD STREET
P.O. BOX 452469
GROVE, OKLAHOMA 74345-2469
Telephone: 918-786-7511
Fax: 918-786-5687
Email: loglow@galstar.com

Vinita, Oklahoma Office: 101 South Wilson Street. P.O. Box 558. 74301-0558. Telephone: 918-256-7511. Fax: 918-256-3187.

General Practice, Including Trials in all State and Federal Courts, Eminent Domain, Environmental and Coal, Banking, Commercial Transactions, Creditors' Rights and Bankruptcy, Corporation, Public Utility, Real Estate, Estate Planning and Probate, Criminal, Domestic Relations, Appellate Practice and Administrative Law.

FIRM PROFILE: J. Duke Logan and Richard W. Lowry founded the law firm in 1963. The firm has grown during the last 39 years through lateral recruitment and in-house training of new associates. The firm's practice is regional in scope, covering all of northeast Oklahoma. The firm regularly tries commercial and tort cases in both federal and state courts throughout the Midwest, and has tried eminent domain cases throughout Oklahoma.

REPRESENTATIVE CLIENTS: Northeast Oklahoma Electric Cooperative, Inc.; IBC Bank; Bank of Gravett, Arkansas; Grand Lake Bank; First National Bank & Trust Company of Grove; American Cancer Society, Heartland Division, Inc.; C & L Supply, Inc.; Garland Coal and Mining Inc.; Anchor Industries, Inc.; Tower Components, Inc.; Farrell-Cooper Mining Co.; Northeast Area Vo-Tech Schools; Oklahoma Wildlife Federation; Craig General Hospital; Alternate Fuels, Inc.; Advanced Medical Instruments Inc.; Doctor's Optical Supply, Inc.; Inter Tribal Council, Inc.; Nautilus Insurance Co.; Hanover Insurance Cos.; Lend Lease Agri-Business, Inc.; The Equitable Life Assurance Society of the United States; Har-Ber Village Foundation; Triangle Insurance Company; Blitz, USA; ROCMND Area Youth Services, Inc.
GENERAL COUNSEL: First National Bank & Trust Company of Vinita; Northeast Oklahoma Electric Cooperative, Inc.; C & L Supply, Inc.; Franks and Son, Inc.; Franks Operating Company; OK Freight Brokers, Inc.; Northeast Holding Company, Inc.; Diesel Services, Inc.; Granite Investments, Inc.
REFERENCE: First National Bank and Trust Company of Vinita, Oklahoma.
APPROVED ATTORNEYS FOR: Lawyer's Title Insurance Co.; Chicago Title Insurance Co.; First American Title Insurance Co.; Farmers Home Administration.

(For complete biographical data on all personnel, see Professional Biographies at Vinita, Oklahoma)

ATKINS & MARKOFF

GUTHRIE, OKLAHOMA

(See Oklahoma City)

Personal Injury, Automobile Accidents, Wrongful Death, Trucking Accidents, Slip and Fall, Nursing Home Abuse, Head and Spinal Injuries, Dog Bites, Sexual Abuse, Criminal Law, Drug Crimes, DUI/DWI, Juvenile Crimes, General Practice, Family , Divorce, Adoptions, Child Custody, Child Support, Domestic Violence, Visitation Rights, Elder Law, Legal Malpractice, Medical Malpractice, Social Security, Social Security Disability, Taxation, IRS Audits, Property Tax Appeals, Tax Planning, Toxic Torts, Trust and Estate, Wills and Probate.

FRANK W. DAVIS

Established in 1965

115 NORTH DIVISION
GUTHRIE, OKLAHOMA 73044
Telephone: 405-282-1420
Fax: 405-282-4423

General Civil and Criminal Practice. Probate, Real Estate and Oil and Gas Law.

FRANK W. DAVIS, born Ada, Oklahoma, August 24, 1936; admitted to bar, 1959, Oklahoma; 1965, U.S. District Court, Western District of Oklahoma. *Education:* East Central University, Oklahoma (B.A., 1958); University of Illinois and University of Oklahoma (LL.B., 1959). County Attorney, Logan County, Oklahoma, 1961-1965. Municipal Judge, 1974-1978. Member, Oklahoma House of Representatives, 1978-2004; Vice-Chairman, Judiciary Committee, 1981-1982, 1989, 1991-2004; Minority Leader, 1982-1986. *Member:* Logan County (Vice President, 1971-1973; President, 1974-1975) and Oklahoma (Member, Sections on: Real Property; Mineral Law) Bar Associations. ***REPORTED CASES:*** Lingerfelt V. Winn-Dixie Texas, Inc., Okla. 645 P. 2d 485; Allison V. Heckler, (10th Cir) 711 F. 2d 145; Estate of Katschor, Okla., 543 P. 2d 560; Lawrance V. Patton, Okla., 710 P. 2d 108; Campbell v. White, Okla., 856 P. 2d 255. ***PRACTICE AREAS:*** Probate; Civil Litigation; Contested Trusts and Estates; Real Estate; Water Utilities.

(This Listing Continued)

REPRESENTATIVE CLIENTS: Masonic Charity Foundation of Oklahoma; Logan County Industrial Development Authority; Rural Water District #1, Logan County; Rural Water District #3, Logan County; Rural Water District #5, Garfield County.

TIM W. GREEN, P.C.

213 EAST OKLAHOMA AVENUE
GUTHRIE, OKLAHOMA 73044
Telephone: 405-282-1919
Fax: 405-282-1930
Email: greentiml@aol.com

General Civil Practice, Oil and Gas, Real Property, Election Law, Wills, Trusts, Probate, Estate Planning, Corporate Law, Articles of Incorporation, Mineral Law, Oil and Gas Conservation Law, Farm and Ranch Law, Civil Litigation.

TIM W. GREEN, born Carney, Oklahoma, October 23, 1952; admitted to bar, 1978, Oklahoma; 1979, U.S. District Court, Western District of Oklahoma; 1986, U.S. Supreme Court. *Education:* Central State University (B.A., 1975); Oklahoma City University (J.D., with honors, 1978). Phi Delta Phi. *Member:* Logan County (Vice President, 1997—) and Oklahoma (Member, Section on Mineral Law) Bar Associations; The Federalist Society For Law & Public Policy Studies. ***SPECIAL AGENCIES:*** Oklahoma Corporation Commission. ***REPORTED CASES:*** Abstracts of Oklahoma, Inc. vs. Payne County Title Company, et al, 825 P.2d 1334 (Okla. 1992).

REPRESENTATIVE CLIENTS: Governor Frank Keating; Congressman J.C. Watts; Congressman Ernest Istook; Congressman Tom Coburn; Congressman Frank Lucas; Guthrie First Capital Bank; Guthrie Savings, Inc.; Abstracts of Oklahoma, Inc.; Britz, Inc.; P.T. Murino Jaya of Indonesia; Ward Petroleum Corporation.

FIELD & HICKS, P.C.

Established in 1919

400 NORTHEAST 12TH STREET
P.O. BOX 1347
GUYMON, OKLAHOMA 73942
Telephone: 580-338-6503
Fax: 580-338-6505
Email: llfpc@ptsi.net
URL: http://www.lawyers.com/larryfield-law

Real Estate, Trusts and Estates, Business Law, Litigation, Commercial Law, Banking Law, Construction, Contracts, Wills and Probate, Government and Insurance.

LARRY L. FIELD, born Liberal, Kansas, August 20, 1937; admitted to bar, 1964, Oklahoma; 1971, U.S. Supreme Court. *Education:* Oklahoma State University (B.S., 1960); University of Oklahoma (J.D., 1964). Phi Delta Phi. *Member:* Texas County and Oklahoma Bar Associations. **Email:** llf2148@aol.com

CORY BRANDON HICKS, born Guymon, Oklahoma; admitted to bar, 2002, Oklahoma. *Education:* Oklahoma Baptist University (B.A., 1997); University of Oklahoma (J.D., 2002). Phi Delta Phi. Member: Oklahoma Law Review; ATLA National Student Trial Team. Author: "Nealis v. Baird: The Oklahoma Supreme Court Extends Fetal Rights in Wrongful Death Suits but Leaves Important Questions Unanswered," 54 Okla. L. Rev. 859 (2001). *Member:* Texas County and Oklahoma Bar Associations. **Email:** cbhicks@ptsi.net

REPRESENTATIVE CLIENTS: City National Bank & Trust Co., Guymon, Oklahoma; Grounds Land & Cattle Co.; Pride Feeders, Inc.; Northwest Line Construction, Inc.; Pony Creek Farms, Inc.; Long Farms, Inc.; Guaranty Abstract & Title Co.; Wiebe Farms, Inc.
APPROVED TITLE EXAMINERS FOR: First American Title Insurance Co.; Chicago Title Insurance Co.

DAVID K. PETTY

A PROFESSIONAL CORPORATION

301 WEST FIFTH
P.O. BOX 1187
GUYMON, OKLAHOMA 73942
Telephone: 580-338-5484
Fax: 580-338-0066
Email: pettyd@ptsi.net

General, Civil Trial Practice, Personal Injury, Probate, Real Estate, Oil and Gas, Municipal and Banking Law.

DAVID K. PETTY, born Muskogee, Oklahoma, October 6, 1939; admitted to bar, 1964, Oklahoma; 1971, U.S. Supreme Court. *Education:* Oklahoma State University (B.S., 1961); University of Oklahoma (J.D., 1964). Phi Delta Phi. City Attorney, Guymon, Oklahoma, 1978—. Director, Professional Liability Insurance Corporation, Oklahoma Bar Association, 1983-1984; 1985-1990. *Member:* Texas County, Oklahoma (Member, Commission on Continuing Legal Education, 1978-1984; Chairman, Mandatory Continuing Legal Education Commission, 1986; Member, Board of Governors, 1980-1983; President, 1987) and American Bar Associations. Fellow: Oklahoma Bar Foundation; American Bar Foundation; American College of Trust and Estate Counsel; American College of Trial Lawyers.; Oklahoma Trial Lawyers Association; The Association of Trial Lawyers of America. ***PRACTICE AREAS:*** Trusts and Estates; Probate; Litigation; Oil and Gas Law; Personal Injury; Real Estate; Banks and Banking; General Practice. **Email:** pettypc@ptsi.net

ATTORNEY FOR: First National Bank, Texhoma, Oklahoma; Town of Hardesty; City of Guymon; Dorchester Minerals Operating LP; Town of Goodwell; CJ NutraCon, Inc.; Seaboard Corporation.
APPROVED EXAMINING ATTORNEY FOR: American First Title & Trust Co.; Southwest Title & Trust Co.; Lawyers Title Insurance Corp.; Chicago Title Insurance Co.
REPRESENTATIVE CLIENT: First National Bank, Texhoma, Oklahoma.

WRIGHT, DALE, JETT & CARTER

Established in 1907

DALE BUILDING
114 EAST 4TH STREET
P.O. BOX 591
GUYMON, OKLAHOMA 73942
Telephone: 580-338-6591
Fax: 580-338-8244
Email: blwlaw@ptsi.net

General Practice. Corporation, Real Estate, Oil and Gas, Estate Planning, Wills, Probate and Tax Law. Trials.

FIRM PROFILE: The law firm of Wright, Dale, Jett & Carter was founded by the late Judge F. Hiner Dale in January of 1907. Judge Dale had received his law degree from the University of Missouri in 1906, and settled at Guymon in the new state of Oklahoma, where he was to make his home for the rest of his life. He began practicing law in the same spot where the firm's present office building is located.

MEMBERS OF FIRM

F. HINER DALE (1881-1969)

VINCENT DALE (1912-1977)

BRYAN L. WRIGHT, born Optima, Oklahoma; admitted to bar, 1966, Kansas and Oklahoma. *Education:* Oklahoma State University (B.S. and M.S., 1962); Washburn University (J.D., 1966). Certified Public Accountant, Oklahoma, 1965. City Attorney, Guymon, OK, 1966-1974. *Member:* National Telephone Cooperative Association Legal Committee.

DOUGLAS DON DALE, born Guymon, Oklahoma; admitted to bar, 1977, Oklahoma. *Education:* University of Oklahoma (B.B.A., 1972); University of Tulsa (J.D., 1977). Municipal Judge, Guymon, Oklahoma, 1978—. *Member:* Oklahoma Bar Association (Member, Mineral Law Section).

A. CLARK JETT, born St. Joseph, Missouri; admitted to bar, 1977, Oklahoma. *Education:* University of Oklahoma (B.B.A., 1974; J.D., 1977). *Member:* Oklahoma Bar Association (Member, Real Property Section).

PEGGY L. CARTER, born Guymon, Oklahoma, April 24, 1969; admitted to bar, 1994, Oklahoma. *Education:* Oklahoma State University (B.A., 1991); University of Oklahoma (J.D., 1994). *Member:* Oklahoma Bar Association (Member, Family Law Section).

OF COUNSEL

Don Dale

TRAYNOR, LONG, WYNNE & WOODWARD, P.C.

A PROFESSIONAL CORPORATION
HENNESSEY, OKLAHOMA
(See Enid)

HAROLD E. HEATH LAW OFFICES

103 WEST MAIN - P.O. BOX 472
HOLDENVILLE, OKLAHOMA 74848
Telephone: 405-379-5445
Fax: 405-379-5446
Email: harold@heathlawoffice.com

Banking, Real Estate, Bankruptcy, Probate, Oil and Gas and Corporation Law. General and Criminal Trial Practice.

HAROLD E. HEATH, born Lawton, Oklahoma, June 23, 1947; admitted to bar, 1974, Oklahoma. *Education:* Central State University (B.A., 1969); University of Oklahoma (J.D., 1973). *Member:* Hughes County (President, 1978-1980; 2002-2004), Oklahoma and American Bar Associations. ***PRACTICE AREAS:*** Real Estate; Banking; Probate; Trusts and Estates. **Email:** harold@heathlawoffice.com

ASSOCIATE

CHRISTOPHER BLOCKCOLSKI, born Pryor, Oklahoma, June 3, 1979; admitted to bar, 2004, Oklahoma. *Education:* Northeastern Oklahoma State University (B.B.A., 2001); University of Oklahoma (J.D., 2004). Municipal Judge, City of Holdenville, 2005—. *Member:* Hughes County (President, 2004—), Oklahoma and American Bar Associations. ***PRACTICE AREAS:*** Real Estate; Probate; Trusts and Estates; Bankruptcy; Civil Practice. ***Email:*** chris@heathlawoffice.com

REPRESENTATIVE CLIENTS: First United Bank & Trust Company; Bank of Commerce, Wetumka, Oklahoma; The Bank, N.A., Holdenville, OK.
APPROVED ATTORNEYS FOR: Southwest Title & Trust Co.; First American Title & Trust Co.
REFERENCES: First United Bank & Trust Company, Holdenville, Oklahoma; The Bank, N.A., Holdenville, OK.

THOMAS J. HADLEY

115 S. BROADWAY
HUGO, OKLAHOMA 74743
Telephone: 580-326-3108
Fax: 580-326-3182

General Practice, Trial Practice, Personal Injury, Labor and Employment.

(This Listing Continued)

THOMAS J. HADLEY, born Lockport, New York, October 12, 1951; admitted to bar, 1988, Pennsylvania and U.S. District Court, Western District of Pennsylvania; 1989, Oklahoma; 1990, U.S. District Court, Eastern and Western Districts of Oklahoma; U.S. Court of Appeals, Third and Tenth Circuits. *Education:* United States Coast Guard Academy (B.S., 1973); University of Pittsburgh (J.D., 1988). Phi Alpha Delta. Member, North Eastern Esturine Research Society (NEERS), 1972-1974. *Member:* Choctaw County, Pushmataha County, Oklahoma, Pennsylvania and American (Member, Sections on: Tort and Insurance Practice; Labor and Employment Law; Real Property, Probate and Trust Law) Bar Associations. [Lieut., Coast Guard, 1973-1982]. ***PRACTICE AREAS:*** General Practice; Trial Practice; Personal Injury; Labor and Employment Law.

RABON, WOLF & RABON

Established in 1946

402 EAST JACKSON
P.O. BOX 726
HUGO, OKLAHOMA 74743
Telephone: 580-326-6427
Fax: 580-326-6032
Email: rawol@sbcglobal.net

General Civil Practice in all State and Federal Courts. Indian, Negligence, Insurance, Commercial, Real Estate and Probate Law. Trials. No Collections under $5000.00.

MEMBERS OF FIRM

BOB RABON, born Hugo, Oklahoma, December 19, 1939; admitted to bar, 1968, Oklahoma. *Education:* Southeastern State College (B.S., 1963); University of Oklahoma (J.D., 1968). Fellow, American College of Trial Lawyers. *Member:* Oklahoma Bar Association (Member: President, 1993; Chairman, Judicial Nominating Commission, 1995; Oklahoma Council on Judicial Complaints, 2000-2002). ***PRACTICE AREAS:*** Commercial; Indian; Negligence; Probate; Real Property.

J. FRANK WOLF, III, born Demopolis, Alabama, March 20, 1959; admitted to bar, 1985, Oklahoma. *Education:* East Central State University (B.S., 1982); University of Tulsa (J.D., 1985). ***PRACTICE AREAS:*** Probate; Personal Injury; Family Law; Collections; Real Property.

ROBERT L. RABON, born Hugo, Oklahoma, January 1, 1961; admitted to bar, 1989, Oklahoma. *Education:* Oklahoma State University (B.A., 1984); Oklahoma City University (J.D., 1988). ***PRACTICE AREAS:*** Negligence; Real Property; Family Law.

REPRESENTATIVE CLIENTS: Lone Star Gas Co.; Western Farmers Electric Cooperative, Inc., Oklahoma; Midcontinent Casualty; Virginia Surety Co.; General Accident Group; Western Casualty Co.; Lawyers Surety Corp.
GENERAL COUNSEL FOR: Security First National Bank, Hugo; Choctaw Nation; Chickasaw Nation; Housing Authority of Choctaw Nation of Oklahoma; Hugo Municipal Authority; Hugo Airport Authority; Hugo Industrial Authority; Red River Farmers Cooperative; Hugo Public Schools; Choctaw Electric Cooperative.
APPROVED TITLE ATTORNEYS FOR: American Land and Aircraft Title Co.; Farmers Home Administration.
REFERENCES: Security First National Bank, Hugo, Okla.; First United, Hugo, Okla.; Liberty National Bank, Paris, Texas.

DAVIS & THOMPSON

Established in 1943

DAVIS-THOMPSON-UNDERWOOD BUILDING
DRAWER 487
JAY, OKLAHOMA 74346
Telephone: 918-253-4298
FAX: 918-253-8110
URL: http://www.lawyers.com/davisandthompson

Residential and Commercial Real Estate, Family Law, Divorce, Criminal Law, Personal Injury, Banking Law.

GENE A. DAVIS (1930-1987)

PHIL K. THOMPSON, born Southwest City, Missouri, October 5, 1947; admitted to bar, 1972, Oklahoma. *Education:* University of Tulsa (J.D., 1972). City Attorney, Jay, Oklahoma, 1977—. Temporary Judge, State Supreme Court of Appeals, 1981—. Member, Title Standards Committee and Professional Responsibility Trial Panel. ***PRACTICE AREAS:*** Title Examinations; Real Estate; Banking Law; Foreclosures.

BOBBY C. RAMSEY, born Mt. Shasta, California, December 10, 1956; admitted to bar, 1983, Oklahoma. *Education:* University of Tulsa (J.D., 1983). Assistant District Attorney. Certified Mediator for Family and Divorce. ***PRACTICE AREAS:*** Divorce; Personal Injury; Criminal Law.

TOMMY R. DYER, JR., born Claremore, Oklahoma, March 27, 1965; admitted to bar, 1990, Oklahoma. *Education:* University of Tulsa (J.D. with honors, 1990). Member, Energy Law Journal, 1989-1990. American Jurisprudence Award for: Contracts, Appellate Advocacy, Civil Procedure, Real Estate Finance, Commercial Law and Taxation of Corporations and Shareholders. ***PRACTICE AREAS:*** Civil Litigation; Appellate Practice; Probate; Debtor and Creditor.

BRANDON A. JOHNSON, born Oklahoma City, Oklahoma, October 28, 1960; admitted to bar, 1988, Oklahoma. *Education:* Oklahoma City University (J.D., 1988). ***PRACTICE AREAS:*** Divorce; Civil Litigation.

REPRESENTATIVE CLIENTS: Available on Request.

LOGAN & LOWRY, LLP

JAY, OKLAHOMA

(See Vinita)

General Practice, Including Trials in all State and Federal Courts, Eminent Domain, Environmental and Coal, Banking, Commercial Transactions, Creditors' Rights and Bankruptcy, Corporation, Public Utility, Real Estate, Estate Planning and Probate, Criminal, Domestic Relations, Civil Rights, Employment, Appellate Practice and Administrative Law.

TAYLOR, BURRAGE, FOSTER, MALLETT, DOWNS & RAMSEY, P.C.

JAY, OKLAHOMA

(See Claremore)

Civil and Criminal Practice in all State and Federal Courts. Employment Law, Healthcare Law, Medical Malpractice, Professional Liability, Insurance Defense, Real Estate, Probate, Guardianships, Corporation, Commercial and Personal Injury Law.

LANDRETH LAW FIRM PLC

801 E. B STREET
JENKS, OKLAHOMA 74037
Telephone: 918-296-0460
Fax: 918-296-0404
Email: llandreth@landrethlaw.com
URL: http://www.landrethlaw.com

Environmental Law, Natural Resources, Administrative Law.

LLOYD W. LANDRETH, born Midwest City, Oklahoma, May 29, 1959; admitted to bar, 1987, Colorado; 1994, Oklahoma. *Education:* Oklahoma State University (B.S., 1981); University of Colorado (J.D., 1986). *Member:* Tulsa County, Oklahoma, Colorado and American Bar Associations. ***PRACTICE AREAS:*** Environmental Law; Natural Resources; Administrative Law. ***Email:*** llandreth@landrethlaw.com

LAURA C. HILL, born Midwest City, Oklahoma, June 15, 1977; admitted to bar, 2002, Oklahoma and U.S. District Court, Northern District of Oklahoma. *Education:* University of Oklahoma (B.A., with distinction, 1999); Tulsa University (J.D., with highest honors, 2002). Valedictorian. Order of the Curule Chair; Phi Delta Phi; Phi Kappa Phi. Women's Law Caucus. Notes and Comments Editor, Tulsa Law Review, 2001-2002. Law Clerk to the Hon. Sam A. Joyner, U.S. Magistrate Judge, Northern District of Oklahoma, 2002-2003. Author: Note, "To Squeeze or Not to Squeeze? A Different Perspective," 37 Tulsa L. Rev. 425 (2001). American Inns of Court, Hudson Hall Wheaton Chapter. ***PRACTICE AREAS:*** Environmental Law; General Civil Litigation; Indian Law. ***Email:*** lhill@landrethlaw.com

SCOTT WILLIAM MCEACHIN

117 NORTH BIRCH STREET
JENKS, OKLAHOMA 74037
Telephone: 918-296-0405
Facsimile: 918-296-3628
Email: scott@mceachinlaw.com

Oil and Gas Law, Corporate Law, Small Business Law, Business Law.

SCOTT WILLIAM MCEACHIN, born Tulsa, Oklahoma, December 12, 1951; admitted to bar, 1976, Oklahoma and U.S. District Court, Northern and Western Districts of Oklahoma. *Education:* University of California at Santa Barbara (B.A., History/Political Science, 1973); University of Oklahoma (J.D., 1976). *Member:* Oklahoma Bar Association. ***PRACTICE AREAS:*** Oil and Gas Law; Corporate Law; Small Business Law; Business Law.

ATKINS & MARKOFF

KINGFISHER, OKLAHOMA

(See Oklahoma City)

Personal Injury, Automobile Accidents, Wrongful Death, Trucking Accidents, Slip and Fall, Nursing Home Abuse, Head and Spinal Injuries, Dog Bites, Sexual Abuse, Criminal Law, Drug Crimes, DUI/DWI, Juvenile Crimes, General Practice, Family , Divorce, Adoptions, Child Custody, Child Support, Domestic Violence, Visitation Rights, Elder Law, Legal Malpractice, Medical Malpractice, Social Security, Social Security Disability, Taxation, IRS Audits, Property Tax Appeals, Tax Planning, Toxic Torts, Trust and Estate, Wills and Probate.

ATKINS & MARKOFF

LAWTON, OKLAHOMA

(See Oklahoma City)

Personal Injury, Automobile Accidents, Wrongful Death, Trucking Accidents, Slip and Fall, Nursing Home Abuse, Head and Spinal Injuries, Dog Bites, Sexual Abuse, Criminal Law, Drug Crimes, DUI/DWI, Juvenile Crimes, General Practice, Family , Divorce, Adoptions, Child Custody, Child Support, Domestic Violence, Visitation Rights, Elder Law, Legal Malpractice, Medical Malpractice, Social Security, Social Security Disability, Taxation, IRS Audits, Property Tax Appeals, Tax Planning, Toxic Torts, Trust and Estate, Wills and Probate.

LAW OFFICE OF STEVEN R. BOOKER, P.C.

LAWTON, OKLAHOMA

(See Wichita Falls, Texas)

Elder Law, Accidents, Slip and Fall, Products Defects, Dram Shop Cases, Railroad Accidents, Dog Bites, Automobile Negligence, Wrongful Death, Breach of Warranty, Nursing Home Negligence, Civil Litigation, Plaintiff Personal Injury, Probate Litigation, Contested Wills.

BURGESS, BURGESS, BURGESS & HIGHTOWER

A Partnership of Professional Corporations

Established in 1982
21 N.W. 44TH STREET, SUITE 201
LAWTON, OKLAHOMA 73505
Telephone: 580-355-8920
Fax: 580-355-8999
Email: legal@burgess-hightower.com

FIRM PROFILE: Burgess, Burgess, Burgess & Hightower principally concentrates in the areas of General Civil Practice, Federal and State Trial Practice, Creditors Rights, Banking and Lending, Real Estate, Contract, Commercial, Corporation, Personal Injury, Creditor Bankruptcy, Probate, Wills and Estate Planning.

We are a debt relief agency. We help people file for bankruptcy relief under the Bankruptcy Code.

BILL W. BURGESS, JR., born Stuttgart, Germany, June 1, 1956; admitted to bar, 1981, Oklahoma, U.S. District Court, Western District of Oklahoma and U.S. Court of Appeals, Tenth Circuit. *Education:* Cameron University (B.A., magna cum laude, 1978); University of Oklahoma (J.D., 1980). Phi Kappa Phi; Phi Delta Phi; Order of the Barristers. Regent, Oklahoma State Regents for Higher Education. Past Chairman, Lawton Chamber of Commerce and Industry, Inc. Past President, Boy Scouts of America for Southwest Oklahoma; Cameron Foundation, Inc. Past President, Crime Stoppers, Lawton, Oklahoma. ***PRACTICE AREAS:*** Real Estate; Banking Law; Lending Law; Commercial Litigation; Creditors Rights.

BRAD W. BURGESS, born Stuttgart, Germany, November 8, 1957; admitted to bar, 1983, Oklahoma, U.S. District Court, Western, Northern and Eastern Districts of Oklahoma and U.S. Court of Appeals, Tenth Circuit. *Education:* Texas Tech University; Cameron University (B.A., magna cum laude, 1980); University of Oklahoma (J.D., 1983). Phi Kappa Phi. Member, State Banking Board, 1994-2003; Commissioner, Oklahoma Dept. of Transportation, 2003—. Vice President, Board of Directors, Crimestoppers, 1999—. Chairman of Finance, Boy Scouts of America, Black Beaver District. *Member:* Comanche County Bar Association; Oklahoma Bar Association (Member, Business and Corporate Law Section); American Bar Association. ***PRACTICE AREAS:*** Trial Practice; Banking Law; Lending Law; Creditor Bankruptcy; Real Estate. ***Email:*** brad@burgess-hightower.com

SYLVIA M. BURGESS, born Stuttgart, Germany, February 12, 1957; admitted to bar, 1982, Oklahoma, U.S. District Court, Western District of Oklahoma and U.S. Court of Appeals, Tenth Circuit; 1983, U.S. Tax Court and U.S. Court of Federal Claims. *Education:* Cameron University (B.A., magna cum laude, 1979); University of Oklahoma (J.D., 1982); Southern Methodist University (LL.M., Taxation, 1984). Phi Kappa Phi; Phi Delta Phi. Editor, 1981-1982 and Editorial Advisor, 1982, Oklahoma Law Review. Author: "Special Powers of Appointment: It's the Courts' Move," Vol. 34, No. 4. University of Oklahoma Law Review, Fall 1981; "Cafeteria Plans and Alternative Methods for Providing Nontaxable Benefits to Employees," Vol. 13, No.'s 6 & 7, Tax Management Compensation Planning Journal, June and July, 1985. Member: Oklahoma Employee Benefits Council (Governor Bellmon's appointee), 1987-1990; Board of Directors, Teen Court; Marie Detty Youth Services, Inc.; Real Property, Probate and Trust Law Section and Taxation Section, American Bar Association. President: Junior League Lawton, Oklahoma, Inc., 1989-1990; Comanche County Bar Association, 1992. Chairman, Taxation Section, Oklahoma Bar Association, 1991. ***PRACTICE AREAS:*** Estate Planning; Employee Benefits; Corporate Law; Taxation; Wills; Trust Law.

M. MONTY HIGHTOWER, born Duncan, Oklahoma, November 24, 1955; admitted to bar, 1990, Oklahoma and U.S. District Court, Western District of Oklahoma. *Education:* University of Oklahoma (B.B.A., Finance, 1978; J.D., 1990). Phi Alpha Delta; Phi Delta Phi. Recipient, American Jurisprudence Award. Member, Oklahoma Trial Lawyers Association. *Member:* Comanche County Bar Association; Oklahoma Bar Association (Member, Sections on: Bankruptcy, Estate Planning and Probate, Family Law, Financial Institutions and Commercial Law, and Real Property Law). ***PRACTICE AREAS:*** Real Estate; Probate; Domestic Relations; Commercial Litigation; Banking Law; Bankruptcy. ***Email:*** monty@burgess-hightower.com

All attorneys of the firm are members of the Comanche County, Oklahoma and American Bar Associations.

REPRESENTATIVE CLIENTS: Banc First; Arvest Bank; Telos OK, LLC; American Electric Power; CenterPoint Energy; Republic Paperboard; Wackenhut Corp.; BAR S Foods; Lawton Chamber of Commerce and Industry, Inc.; Security National Auto Acceptance Corp.; KSWO Television (ABC television affiliated of Lawton); KFDA-TV (CBS television affiliate of Amarillo, Texas); KXXV-TV (ABC television affiliate of Waco, Texas); KWES-TV (NBC television affiliate of Midland/Odessa, Texas); Century Life Insurance Company; Billingsley Ford of Lawton, Inc.; H G Jenkins Construction, Inc.; Surgery Center of Lawton; American Gypsum Company; Bank of Hawaii; Travelers Group; Inland Services; St. Paul Insurance Company; Continental General Insurance Company; Waurika Project Master Conservancy District; Lawton Public Schools; Northrop Grumman, Inc.; Southwest Coca-Cola Bottling Co., Inc.; Beneficial of Oklahoma; FMC Financial Corp.; Texaco Distributorship of Lawton, Oklahoma; Lawton Publishing Co.; Affiliated Transportation Systems, Inc.; Brox Industries, Inc.; The Burkburnett Bank, Burkburnett, Texas; Great Plains Area Vo-Tech School.

ELLIS, LEONARD & BUCKHOLTS

LAWTON, OKLAHOMA

(See Duncan)

General Civil Practice in all Courts. Banking, Commercial Law, Oil and Gas, Real Estate, Domestic Relations, Personal Injury, Probate, Estate Planning, Bankruptcy Law, Employment Law, Insurance Defense, Adoptions and Criminal Law.

MICHAEL C. FLANAGAN

ATTORNEY AT LAW

LAWTON, OKLAHOMA

(See Walters)

General Practice in all Federal and State Courts. Trials. Probate, Real Estate, Taxation, Bankruptcy, Estate Planning, Family Law, Education Law, Oil and Gas Law, Commercial Law.

GODLOVE, MAYHALL, DZIALO, DUTCHER & ERWIN

A PROFESSIONAL CORPORATION

Established in 1939

802 "C" AVENUE

P.O. BOX 29

LAWTON, OKLAHOMA 73502

Telephone: 580-353-6700

Fax: 580-353-2900

Email: gmdde@sirinet.net

Litigation, Collections, Corporate, Banking, Real Estate, Estate Planning, Probate, Personal Injury, Workers Compensation, Taxation, Bankruptcy and Domestic Relations, Courts-Martial and Military Administrative Law. General Civil, Trial and Appellate Practice in all State and Federal Courts.

FIRM PROFILE: Godlove, Mayhall, Dzialo, Dutcher & Erwin, P.C. is Lawton/Ft. Sill's oldest law firm, having been established in 1939. A majority of its members are 3rd or 4th generation Lawtonians. Its members are active in the community - all serving or having served in key leadership positions for local civic and charitable organizations. Members of the firm also hold or have held leadership positions in the Comanche County and Oklahoma Bar Associations. The firm serves its individual and business clients statewide.

W. W. GODLOVE (1908-1982)

ERNEST F. GODLOVE, born Lawton, Oklahoma, 1941; admitted to bar, 1966, Oklahoma. *Education:* Duke University (B.A., 1963); University of Oklahoma (J.D., 1966). Order of the Coif; Phi Delta Phi. Member of Staff, 1964-1966 and Editor-in-Chief, 1965-1966, Oklahoma Law Review. *Member:* Comanche County, Oklahoma (Member: Board of Editors, Oklahoma Bar Journal, 1977-1981; Board of Governors, 1984-1986) and American Bar Associations. Fellow, Oklahoma and American Bar Foundations. **PRACTICE AREAS:** Real Estate; Probate; Corporate Law; Trusts and Estates; Banks and Banking. **Email:** efg@sirinet.net

MICHAEL C. MAYHALL, born Lawton, Oklahoma, 1948; admitted to bar, 1975, Oklahoma; 1977, U.S. Court of Appeals, Tenth Circuit; U.S. Tax Court and U.S. Claims Court. *Education:* University of Oklahoma (B.B.A., 1970; J.D., 1975). Phi Delta Phi. Certified Public Accountant, Oklahoma, 1975. Member, Board of Directors, Oklahoma Attorneys Mutual Insurance Company, 1996—. Trustee, Oklahoma Bar Foundation, 1996-2003, President, 2002. *Member:* Comanche County (President, 1988), Oklahoma (Vice-President, 1998; Member, Section on Taxation; Chairman, Section on Taxation, 1980-1981; Member, Board of Governors, 1990-1992) and American (Member, Section on Taxation) Bar Associations; Oklahoma Society of Certified Public Accountants. Fellow: Oklahoma Bar Foundation; American Bar Association. **PRACTICE AREAS:** Taxation; Probate; Trusts and Estates; Corporate. **Email:** mmayhall@sirinet.net

EDWARD W. DZIALO, JR., born Monterey, California, 1948; admitted to bar, 1978, Oklahoma and U.S. Court of Appeals, Tenth Circuit; 1983, U.S. Supreme Court, U.S. Claims Court and U.S. Court of Appeals for the Federal and Fifth Circuits. *Education:* University of Dayton and Cameron University (B.S., 1974); Oklahoma City University (J.D., 1978). *Member:* Comanche County (President, 1990), Oklahoma and American (Member, Section on Corporation, Banking and Business Law) Bar Associations; The Association of Trial Lawyers of America; Oklahoma Trial Lawyers Association. Fellow, Oklahoma Bar Foundation. [Capt., U.S. Army, Aviation-Field Artillery, 1968-1973]. **PRACTICE AREAS:** Personal Injury; Business Law; Labor and Employment; Bankruptcy; Workers Compensation. **Email:** ewd@sirinet.net

J. BLAKE DUTCHER, JR., born Lawton, Oklahoma, 1957; admitted to bar, 1982, Oklahoma; 1983, U.S. Army Court of Military Review; 1986, U.S. District Court, Western District of Oklahoma and U.S. Court of Appeals, 10th Circuit. *Education:* Westminster College (B.A., cum laude, 1979); University of Oklahoma (J.D., 1982). Special Assistant U.S. Attorney, Western District of Oklahoma, 1986. *Member:* Comanche County (President, 1994) and Oklahoma Bar Associations. [Major, JAGC, USAR, Ret.]. **PRACTICE AREAS:** Personal Injury; Military Law; Criminal Law; Family Law; Collections. **Email:** jbd@sirinet.net

SHON T. ERWIN, born Lawton, Oklahoma, 1961; admitted to bar, 1986, Oklahoma; 1988, U.S. District Court, Western District of Oklahoma. *Education:* Oral Roberts University (B.A., magna cum laude, 1983); University of Oklahoma (J.D., 1986). U.S. Magistrate Judge, (part-time) U.S. District Court, Western District of Oklahoma, 1995—. Trustee, Oklahoma Bar Foundation, 2004—. *Member:* Comanche County (President, 1993), Oklahoma (Member: Young Lawyer's Division Board of Directors 1991-1996; Real Property, Probate and Trust Law Section) and American (Member, Section on Real Property Law) Bar Associations. Fellow, Oklahoma Bar Foundation. **PRACTICE AREAS:** Real Estate; Probate; Trusts and Estates; Banks and Banking; Children; Wills; Mortgages; Commercial Real Estate. **Email:** shonlaw@sirinet.net

(This Listing Continued)

REPRESENTATIVE CLIENTS: International Bank of Commerce; Arvest Bank; Liberty National Bank; Guarantee State Bank; Great Plains National Bank; Wells-Fargo Bank; Bank of America; General Motors Acceptance Corporation; Affiliated Van Lines; Bombardier Inc. (Group Canadair); Clover Realty, Inc.; Comanche County Industrial Development Authority; EZ Go Foods, Inc,; Glenn Oil Company, Inc.; Goodyear Tire & Rubber Company; Jan-L Construction, Inc.; Johnson Oil Company; Independent Insurance Agents of Lawton, Inc.; Lawton Chamber of Commerce and Industry, Ind.; Lawton Industrial Development Authority; Lawton Industrial Foundation, Inc.; Sears Roebuck and Co.; Community Escrow & Title Co.; T & G Construction Co., Inc.; U.S. Cellular Corp.; Midwest Equity Group; C & C Distributors, Inc.; Braums Ice Cream Co.; Regional Air, Inc.

HAUPT BROOKS VANDRUFF, PLLC

LAWTON, OKLAHOMA

(See Oklahoma City)

Administrative/Agency, Agricultural, Bankruptcy (Chapter 7, 11, 12, 13), Civil Rights, Criminal, Domestic & Family, Employment, Estate Planning (Wills & Trusts), Finance, Debtor and Creditor Law, General Corporate and Business (Organization, Product Liability, Mergers and Acquisition, Litigation), General Trial Practice, Insurance, Medical and Nursing Home Malpractice and Probate, Personal Injury, Real Estate, Taxation (Personal and Corporate), Workers Compensation, Wrongful Death.

ROBERT HIGHSAW

LAWTON, OKLAHOMA

(See Oklahoma City)

Workers Compensation, Federal Workers Compensation, Workers Compensation Appeals, Workers Compensation Defense, Workers Compensation Self-Insurance, Workers Compensation Subrogation, Immigration and Naturalization, Business Immigration, Citizenship, Consular Law, Deportation, Diplomatic Immunity, Employment Authorization, Employment Immigration, Employment Visas, Family Immigration Law, Immigration Discrimination, Immigration Law, Investor Visas, Labor Certifications, Permanent Visas, Political Asylum, Refugee Law, Religious Visas, Visas, Social Security, Social Security Appeals, Social Security Disability, Social Security Disability Insurance, Supplemental Security Income, Administrative Law, Longshore and Harbor Workers Compensation.

JOHNSTON & ASSOCIATES

LAWTON, OKLAHOMA

(See Chickasha)

General Practice, Environmental Law. including Land Use, Landowners Rights Wills and Probate.

LEACH, SULLIVAN, SULLIVAN & WATKINS

LAWTON, OKLAHOMA

(See Duncan)

General Civil Practice in all State and Federal Courts. Real Estate, Insurance, Probate, Commercial, Corporation, Banking, Estate Planning and Oil and Gas Law. Trials. No small collections.

O. CHRISTOPHER MEYERS, INC.

Established in 1970

15 N.W. 44TH STREET

LAWTON, OKLAHOMA 73505

Telephone: 580-355-0341

Fax: 580-355-0359

Email: cmeyers@sirinet.net

URL: http://www.lawyers.com/cmeyerslaw

Tax Planning, Tax Litigation, Living Trusts, Estate Planning, Probate Administration, Real Estate Exchanges, Pension & Profit Sharing Plans, Buying and Selling Businesses.

O. CHRISTOPHER MEYERS, born Shawnee, Oklahoma, May 6, 1944; admitted to bar, 1969, Oklahoma; 1972, U.S. Tax Court and U.S. Claims Court; U.S. Court of Appeals, Tenth Circuit, U.S. Supreme Court and U.S. District Court, Western District of Oklahoma. *Education:* Oklahoma University (B.B.A., 1966; J.D., 1969); Georgetown University (LL.M., in Taxation, 1972). Phi Alpha Delta. *Member:* Comanche County (President, 1980), Oklahoma Bar Association (Member and President, Taxation Section, 1988); Oklahoma Society of Certified Public Accountants. **REPORTED CASES:** Schlesinger v. Councilman, 43 L. Ed.2nd 591. **PRACTICE AREAS:** Taxation; Trusts and Estates; Elder Law; Business Law; Real Estate; Probate; Litigation. **Email:** cmeyers@sirinet.net

REPRESENTATIVE CLIENTS: Sirius Systems, Inc.; Lawton Family Practice, Clinic, Inc.; Cameron University Foundation, Inc.; Medicine Park Telephone Co.
REFERENCE: Banc First Bank.

NEWCOMBE, REDMAN, ROSS & NEWCOMBE, P.C.

A PROFESSIONAL CORPORATION

513 C AVENUE

LAWTON, OKLAHOMA 73501

Telephone: 580-355-8000

FAX: 580-355-8007

General Civil Practice. Trials. Insurance Defense, Probate, Criminal, Domestic Relations, Real Estate and Oil and Gas Law.

(This Listing Continued)

FIRM PROFILE: Newcombe, Redman, Ross & Newcombe, P.C. has emphasized diversification and specialization in all fields. Its General Civil Practice includes: Insurance Defense, Criminal, Real Estate and Probate Law. The firm encourages continuing professional development and participation in legal education, seminars, professional association activities and civic affairs. The firm is devoted to maintaining excellent standards in client guidance, relationships and growth. Within the broad practice sections, attorneys handle a wide variety of complex legal matters.

RALPH W. NEWCOMBE, born Blanchard, Oklahoma, August 30, 1931; admitted to bar, 1960, Oklahoma and U.S. District Court, Western District of Oklahoma; 1961, U.S. District Court, Northern District of Oklahoma. *Education:* Midwestern University (B.S., 1953); University of Oklahoma (LL.B., 1960). Delta Theta Phi. *Member:* Comanche County, Oklahoma and American Bar Associations. ***PRACTICE AREAS:*** Insurance Defense; Oil and Gas; Complex Litigation. ***Email:*** RNewcombe@newcombeandredmanpc.com

MANVILLE REDMAN, born Oklahoma City, Oklahoma, August 17, 1925; admitted to bar, 1949, Oklahoma; 1950, U.S. District Court, Western District of Oklahoma and U.S. Court of Appeals, Tenth Circuit. *Education:* University of Oklahoma (B.A., 1948; LL.B., 1949). Phi Alpha Delta. County Attorney, Comanche County, 1953-1957. Member, Oklahoma House of Representatives, 1960-1962. City Attorney, Lawton, Oklahoma, 1961-1973. Special Justice, Oklahoma Supreme Court, 1972. *Member:* Comanche County (President, 1977) and Oklahoma Bar Associations. ***PRACTICE AREAS:*** Insurance Defense; Probate; Oil and Gas; Real Estate. ***Email:*** mredman@newcombeandredmanpc.com

EDDIE Y. NEWCOMBE (1940-1992)

ROBERT L. ROSS, born Lawton, Oklahoma, August 22, 1952; admitted to bar, 1977, Oklahoma. *Education:* University of Oklahoma (B.A., 1974; J.D., 1977). Instructor, Business and Banking Law, Cameron University, Lawton, Oklahoma, 1983. Assistant District Attorney: Seminole County, 1977-1978; Comanche County, 1978-1980. *Member:* Comanche County and Oklahoma Bar Associations. ***PRACTICE AREAS:*** Insurance Defense; Environmental Litigation; General Litigation. ***Email:*** RRoss@newcombeandredmanpc.com

STEPHEN K. NEWCOMBE, born Pensacola, Florida, November 13, 1956; admitted to bar, 1983, Oklahoma and U.S. District Court, Western District of Oklahoma. *Education:* University of Oklahoma (B.B.A., 1979; J.D., 1982). *Member:* Oklahoma Bar Association. ***PRACTICE AREAS:*** Insurance Defense; Oil and Gas; Domestic; Criminal. ***Email:*** SNewcombe@newcombeandredmanpc.com

JOEL A. PERLMUTTER, born Cleveland, Ohio, September 18, 1956; admitted to bar, 1987, Ohio; 2003, Oklahoma. *Education:* Cleveland State University (B.B.A., 1979); Cleveland Marshall College of Law (J.D., 1987). ***PRACTICE AREAS:*** Immigration Law; Domestic Relations; Criminal Law; Civil Litigation; Probate. ***Email:*** Joel@newcombeandredmanpc.com

REPRESENTATIVE CLIENTS: Caddell Transit Corp., Lawton, Oklahoma; Vernon Klein Truck & Equipment Co.; Kennedy & Company, Lawton, Oklahoma; American States Insurance Co.; Independent Fire & Casualty Co.; Southwest Insurance Group; State Farm Insurance Co.; Dairyland Insurance Co.; Travelers Insurance Co.; Warhess Investment Co.; Carey Johnson Oil Co.; Automobile Club Inter-Insurance Exchange; Employers Mutual Co.; MFA Insurance Co.; Criterion Insurance Co.; Harbor Insurance Co.; Great West Casualty Co.; Home Insurance Co.; Great American Insurance Co.; Providence Washington Insurance Group; Cimarron Insurance Co., Inc.; Maryland Casualty Co.; Mesquite Oil & Gas Co.; T & R Drilling and Production Co.; Ewing Oil Co.; Red River Royalty Development Co.; Red-Winn Corp.; Scoggins Century 21 Realty; Sentry Insurance; Republic Insurance; American First Title and Trust Co.; Southwest Title and Trust Co.; Lawyers Title Insurance Corp.; Stewart Title and Escrow Service; Community Escrow & Title Co.
REFERENCE: City National Bank, Lawton, Oklahoma.

THE PARRISH LAW FIRM

A PROFESSIONAL CORPORATION

LAWTON, OKLAHOMA

(See Oklahoma City)

Personal Injury, Slip and Fall, Automobile Accidents, Trucking Accidents, Wrongful Death, Workers Compensation, Nursing Home Abuse.

SCOTT RAY LAW FIRM

P.O. BOX 1676
LAWTON, OKLAHOMA 73502
Telephone: 580-248-5557
Fax: 580-248-5556
URL: http://www.lawtonlawyer.com

General Civil Litigation, Medical Malpractice, Family Law, Children, Federal Practice, Civil Practice, Traffic Violations, Wrongful Death, Negligence, Trial Practice, Products Liability, Premises Liability, Torts, Criminal Law.

G. SCOTT RAY, born Altus, Oklahoma, September 4, 1955; admitted to bar, 1982, Oklahoma; 2002, Utah. *Education:* University of Oklahoma (B.A., 1977; M.A., 1978); Oklahoma City University School of Law (J.D., 1981). Phi Delta Phi. Member, Moot Court Board. Editor-in-Chief, Oklahoma City University Law Review, 1980-1981. ***PRACTICE AREAS:*** Civil Litigation; Medical Malpractice; Family Law; Children; Federal Practice; Civil Practice; Traffic Violations; Wrongful Death; Negligence; Trial Practice; Products Liability; Premises Liability; Torts; Criminal Law. ***Email:*** scott@lawtonlawyer.com

DON L. SMITH

Established in 1972

612 SW "D" AVENUE
LAWTON, OKLAHOMA 73501-4570
Telephone: 580-248-7525
Telefax: 580-248-7557
Email: dlsatty@sirinet.net

General Civil Practice. Real Estate, Banking, Probate, Commercial Law, Corporate, Litigation.

DON L. SMITH, born Muskogee, Oklahoma, January 13, 1947; admitted to bar, 1972, Oklahoma; 1973, U.S. District Court, Western District of Oklahoma; 1975, U.S. Supreme Court; 1976, U.S. District Court, Northern District of Oklahoma. *Education:* Oklahoma State University (B.S., 1970); University of Oklahoma (J.D., 1972). *Member:* Comanche County (Secretary-Treasurer, 1972-1973) and Oklahoma (Member, Real Property Law Section) Bar Associations. ***PRACTICE AREAS:*** Real Property; Banking Law; Decedents Estates; Commercial Transactions; Civil Litigation.

REPRESENTATIVE CLIENTS: Arvest/Oklahoma National Bank; Liberty National Bank; IBC Bank; City National Bank & Trust Co.; BancFirst; People's State Bank; Guarantee State Bank; First Southwest Bank of Frederick, Oklahoma; Shamrock Bank, Apache, Oklahoma; Comanche County Home Finance Authority; Lawton Publishing Co., Inc.; Gore East, Inc.; Southwestern Medical Center, Inc.; Becker Funeral Home, Inc.; Wyatt Acres Realty Co.; Cecil Lawson Buick-Cadillac-Mitsubishi; Milo Gordon Chrysler-Plymouth-Honda; Landmark Engineering; Re/Max Professional Realtors of Lawton; Elgin Realty, Elgin, Oklahoma; Billingslea Lumber Co., L.L.C.

WADE AND MACKEY

A PROFESSIONAL CORPORATION

431 "C" AVENUE
P.O. BOX 2515
LAWTON, OKLAHOMA 73502
Telephone: 580-357-7700
Fax: 580-357-7706
URL: http://www.wademackey.com
URL: http://www.lawyers.com/wademackey

General Civil and Trial Practice in State and Federal Courts. Banking, Estate Planning, Probate, Real Estate, School, Health Care, Corporate and Business Law.

CHARLES E. WADE, JR., born Oklahoma City, Oklahoma, September 14, 1940; admitted to bar, 1965, Oklahoma and U.S. District Court, Western District of Oklahoma; 1969, U.S. Supreme Court. *Education:* St. Louis University (B.S., 1962); University of Oklahoma (J.D., 1965). Order of the Coif. Member, Board of Editors, Oklahoma Law Review, 1963-1965. National Council of School Attorneys, Board of Directors, 1979-1983; President, Oklahoma School Board Attorneys Association, 1981-1983; 2002-2003. Chairman, Great Plains Technology Foundation, 1980—. President, Lawton Chamber of Commerce, 1980-1981. President, Association of U.S. Army Southwest Oklahoma Chapter, 1984-1986. *Member:* Comanche County and Oklahoma (Member, Board of Governors, 1987-1990; Vice-President, 1991) Bar Associations. Oklahoma Bar Foundation. [Capt., JAGC, USAF, 1966-1969]. ***PRACTICE AREAS:*** Probate Law; School Law; Real Estate Law; Banking Law; Health Care Law. ***Email:*** wade@wademackey.com

JOHN C. MACKEY, born Austin, Texas, October 23, 1944; admitted to bar, 1969, Oklahoma. *Education:* Cameron University (A.A., 1964); University of Oklahoma (B.A., 1966; J.D., 1969). Assistant Public Defender, Oklahoma County, 1971-1972. Assistant District Attorney, 1972 and Special District Judge, 1973-1974, Comanche County. Trustee, Comanche County Industrial Development Authority. Board Member, Waurika Lake Master Conservancy District. *Member:* Comanche County (President, 1987-1988) and Oklahoma Bar Associations. ***PRACTICE AREAS:*** Estate Planning; Real Estate Law; Probate Law; Banking Law; Health Care Law. ***Email:*** mackey@wademackey.com

REPRESENTATIVE CLIENTS: City National Bank and Trust Co.; Liberty National Bank; Fort Sill Sill National Bank; Lawton Public Schools; Altus Public Schools; Great Plains Technology Center; Comanche County Hospital Authority; Lawton Metropolitan Area Airport Authority; Stewart Escrow & Title Service, Inc.; P-A Chevrolet, Inc.; Milo Gordon Auto Mall; Oklahoma Attorneys Mutual Insurance Company; Co-Op Services, Inc.; National American Insurance Company; Farm Credit of Central Oklahoma; Percussive Arts Society; Southwest Oklahoma Federal Credit Union; Marie Detty Youth and Family Services Center, Inc.; Goodyear Tire & Rubber Co.
APPROVED COUNSEL FOR: American Guaranty Title and Trust Co.; Chicago Title Insurance Co.; Southwest Title & Trust Co.; Lawyers' Title Insurance Co.; First American Title Insurance Co.; Stewart Title Co.; American Eagle Title Insurance Company; Old Republic National Insurance Co.

WALKER, FERGUSON & FERGUSON

LAWTON, OKLAHOMA

(See Oklahoma City)

General Civil Practice. Insurance Defense, Banking and Commercial Law, Federal, State and Local Taxes, Real Estate, Oil and Gas, Probate, Administrative and Legislative Law. Transportation, Communications, Cable TV, Workers Compensation Law, Employer Liability Law, Employment (Management), Telecommunications, Commercial Litigation, Taxation, Subrogation, Trials in State and Federal Courts.

JOHN P. ZELBST LAW FIRM

Established in 1980

411 S.W. 6TH
P.O. BOX 365
LAWTON, OKLAHOMA 73502-0365
Telephone: 580-248-4844
Fax: 580-248-6916
Email: ZelbstLawFirm@cs.com

Personal Injury Trial Practice and General Civil Trial Practice. Medical Malpractice. Criminal Trial Practice.

JOHN P. ZELBST, born Lawton, Oklahoma, April 6, 1954; admitted to bar, 1980, Oklahoma and U.S. District Court, Western, Eastern and Northern Districts of Oklahoma; U.S. Court of Appeals, Tenth Circuit; U.S. Supreme Court; U.S. Court of Appeals, Fifth Circuit; U.S. District Court, Eastern and Western Districts of Arkansas; U.S. District Court, Northern District of Texas; U.S. District Court, District of Colorado; U.S. District Court, Eastern District of Texas. *Education:* Cameron University (B.A., 1976); University of Tulsa (J.D., 1980). Member, Board of Trustees of Comanche County Memorial Hospital, Lawton, Oklahoma. Faculty Member for Gerry Spence Trial Lawyers College, DuBois, Wyoming. *Member:* Oklahoma and American Bar Associations; Oklahoma Trial Lawyers Association (President, 2001); The Association of Trial Lawyers of America; Oklahoma Criminal Defense Association; National Association of Criminal Defense Lawyers. **REPORTED CASES:** Mr. Zelbst and his associates have obtained many large settlements and verdicts on behalf of their injured clients. Including the largest known personal injury verdict in the state of Oklahoma-24 million dollars, Henderson v. Petro Energy Transport Co. et al., DC Jackson County CJ-95-64. **PRACTICE AREAS:** Personal Injury; Medical Malpractice; Federal Practice; Civil Trial; Criminal Law; Trial Practice; Wrongful Termination; Products Liability; Premises Liability; Torts. **Email:** ZelbstLawFirm@cs.com

ASSOCIATES

TOMMY L. SIMS, born Lawton, Oklahoma, December 15, 1954; admitted to bar, 1988, Oklahoma. *Education:* Cameron University (B.S., 1979); University of Oklahoma Law School (J.D., 1988). *Member:* Oklahoma Bar Association; Oklahoma Trial Lawyers Association. **PRACTICE AREAS:** Personal Injury; Medical Malpractice; Premises Liability; Contracts; Criminal Law; Traffic Violations; Equine Law. **Email:** tlsims_jpzlaw@sbcglobal.net

CHANDRA L. HOLMES RAY, born San Antonio, Texas, September 11, 1965; admitted to bar, 1990, Oklahoma and U.S. District Court, Northern, Western and Eastern Districts of Oklahoma; U.S. Court of Appeals, Tenth Circuit. *Education:* University of Tulsa (B.S., 1987; J.D., 1990). Phi Alpha Delta. Member, University of Tulsa Law Journal, 1988-1990. Author: "Child Sexual Abuse Accommodation Syndrome: Curing the Effects of a Misdiagnosis in the law of Evidence," Vol. 25 Issue 1 Tulsa Law Journal, 1989. *Member:* Oklahoma Bar Association; Oklahoma Trial Lawyers Association. **PRACTICE AREAS:** General Civil Litigation; Medical Malpractice; Family Law; Children; Adoption; Federal Practice; Civil Practice; Traffic Violations; Wrongful Termination; Trial Practice; Products Liability; Premises Liability; Torts. **Email:** chandra_jpzlaw@sbcglobal.net

REFERENCE: City National Bank.

HORTON & ASSOCIATES

Established in 1977

122 NORTH OKLAHOMA AVENUE
MANGUM, OKLAHOMA 73554
Telephone: 580-782-3348
Facsimile: 580-782-2836
Email: chorton@pacer.com

Altus Office: 216 West Commerce Street. Telephone: 580-482-3355. Fax: 580-482-0363

General Civil Practice, Trusts, Probate, Estate Planning, Personal Injury, Real Estate, Business, Divorce, Interstate Custody, Military, Municipal, Public Finance and Aviation Law.

(See Altus)

MERCER LAW FIRM, P.C.

Established in 2004

2626 S. 14TH STREET, SUITE C-20
McALESTER, OKLAHOMA 74501
Telephone: 918-420-5850
Fax: 918-420-5855
Email: tod@todmercerlaw.com
URL: http://www.lawyers.com/mercerlawfirm

Insurance Bad Faith, Personal Injury, Insurance, Extra Contractual Insurance Claims, Accident Insurance, Catastrophic Injury, Mediation.

FIRM PROFILE: The firm handles all types of insurance related cases. The majority of the firm's clients are policy holders that need assistance in dealing with their insurance company in regard to a claim for benefits.

TOD S. MERCER, born Oklahoma City, Oklahoma, December 22, 1958; admitted to bar, 1991, Oklahoma. *Education:* University of Oklahoma (B.A., Political Science, 1984); Oklahoma City University (J.D., 1990). Phi Delta Phi. Member, Bad Faith Litigation Insurance Group. *Member:* Oklahoma Bar Association; Oklahoma Trial Lawyers Association; The Association of Trial Lawyers of America. **LANGUAGES:** English. **PRACTICE**

(This Listing Continued)

AREAS: Insurance Bad Faith; Personal Injury; Insurance; Extra Contractual Insurance Claims; Accident Insurance; Catastrophic Injury; Mediation. **Email:** tod@todmercerlaw.com

REPRESENTATIVE CLIENT: Southeast Oklahoma Box Company, Inc.

STEIDLEY & NEAL

100 EAST CARL ALBERT PARKWAY
P.O. BOX 1165
McALESTER, OKLAHOMA 74502
Telephone: 918-423-4611
Fax: 918-423-4620

Tulsa, Oklahoma Office: Exchange Tower, Suite 800. 4500 South Garnett Road. 74146. Telephone: 918-664-4612. Fax: 918-664-4133.

Insurance Defense and Personal Injury Law, Medical and Legal Malpractice, Municipal Law, Insurance Law, Civil Rights and Employment Law.

SENIOR MEMBERS OF FIRM

W. G. "GIL" STEIDLEY, JR., born Amarillo, Texas, September 30, 1944; admitted to bar, 1969, Oklahoma, U.S. District Court, Eastern, Northern and Western Districts of Oklahoma and Eastern and Western Districts of Arkansas, U.S. Court of Appeals, Tenth, Eighth and Fifth Circuits and U.S. Supreme Court. *Education:* University of Oklahoma (B.B.A., 1966; J.D., 1969). Adjunct Settlement Judge, United States District Court, Eastern District of Oklahoma, 1999—. *Member:* Oklahoma (Associate Bar Examiner, 1974-1989; Member, President's Task Force on Advertising & Solicitation, 1994-1995; Chairman, 2003 and Member, 2001-2004, Professional Responsibility Commission); Defense Research Institute. Fellow: American College of Trial Lawyers. **PRACTICE AREAS:** Insurance; Personal Injury; Insurance Bad Faith; Litigation. **Email:** wgs@steidley-neal.com

CHARLES D. "BUDDY" NEAL, JR., born McAlester, Oklahoma, January 4, 1949; admitted to bar, 1975, Oklahoma, U.S. District Court, Eastern, Western and Northern Districts of Oklahoma and Eastern and Western Districts of Arkansas, U.S. Court of Appeals, Tenth, Eighth and Fifth Circuits and U.S. Supreme Court. *Education:* Oklahoma State University (B.S., 1972); Oklahoma City University (J.D., 1975). Phi Alpha Delta. *Member:* Pittsburg County (House of Delegates, President, 1980-1981), Oklahoma (President, 2001; Board of Governors, 1995-1997) and American Bar Associations; Defense Research Institute; Oklahoma Association of Defense Counsel. Fellow: American Bar Foundation; Oklahoma Bar Foundation (Board of Trustees, 1998-2001). Fellow, American College of Trial Lawyers. **PRACTICE AREAS:** Insurance; Government; Personal Injury. **Email:** cdn@steidley-neal.com

MEMBERS OF FIRM

MARK A. CLAYTON, born Oklahoma City, Oklahoma, July 10, 1965; admitted to bar, 1991, Oklahoma, U.S. District Court, Eastern District of Oklahoma and Eastern District of Texas and U.S. Court of Appeals, Tenth Circuit. *Education:* University of Oklahoma (B.B.A., 1988; J.D., 1991). Municipal Judge, Clayton, OK, 1994—. Member, 2001 Youth Emergency Shelter, McAlester, OK. Former Board of Directors, Young Lawyers Division, Oklahoma Bar Association, 1992-1994. *Member:* Pittsburg County (Vice President, 1996, President, 1997), Oklahoma (Member, Client Security Fund) Bar Associations; Oklahoma Association of Defense Counsel (Board of Directors); Oklahoma Association of Defense Counsel;. **PRACTICE AREAS:** Insurance Defense; Personal Injury. **Email:** mac@steidley-neal.com

MICHAEL W. HOGAN, born Muskogee, Oklahoma, March 26, 1958; admitted to bar, 1986, Oklahoma; 1987, U.S. District Court, Eastern District of Oklahoma; 1988, U.S. Court of Appeals, Tenth Circuit. *Education:* Northeastern Oklahoma State University (B.S., 1980); Oklahoma City University (J.D., 1986). Private Pilots License, Single Engine, 1980 and Instrument Rating, 1983. Commercial Pilots License, 1985. Multi-Engine Aircraft License, 1986. Municipal Judge, Haileyville, Oklahoma, 1986-1994, Checotah, Oklahoma, 1999— and Kiebs, Oklahoma, 2004—. *Member:* Pittsburg County (President, 1992; Secretary/Treasurer, 1990) and Oklahoma Bar Associations (Associate Bar Examiner, 1995-2004; Member, Board of Governors, 2005—); Oklahoma Association of Defense Counsel. **PRACTICE AREAS:** Trucking Liability; Products Liability; Insurance Defense. **Email:** mwh@steidley-neal.com

ERIC D. JANZEN, born Ardmore, Oklahoma, September 28, 1964; admitted to bar, 1990, Oklahoma, U.S. District Court, Eastern, Northern and Western Districts of Oklahoma and Eastern and Western Districts of Arkansas, U.S. Court of Appeals, Tenth and Eighth Circuits and U.S. Supreme Court. *Education:* University of Oklahoma (B.A., 1987; J.D., 1990). Member, Oklahoma Law Review, 1989-1990. *Member:* Pittsburgh County Bar Association (Vice President, 1995); National School Counsel of School Attorneys. **PRACTICE AREAS:** Insurance Defense; Personal Injury. **Email:** edj@steidley-neal.com

F. NILS RAUNIKAR, born Muskogee, Oklahoma, November 18, 1961; admitted to bar, 1991, Oklahoma; U.S. District Court, Eastern and Western Districts of Oklahoma and U.S. Court of Appeals, 10th Circuit. *Education:* Eastern Oklahoma State College (A.D., Nursing, 1982); Oklahoma East Central University (B.S., 1985); University of Oklahoma (J.D., 1991). Registered Nurse, Oklahoma, 1982. Municipal Judge, Wilburton, Oklahoma, 1994—. *Member:* Pittsburg County (President 1999), Oklahoma (Mentor Committee, 1999-2000; Mento Committee Chair, 201) and American Bar Association; Association of Trial Lawyers of America. Bar Association. **PRACTICE AREAS:** Insurance Defense; Personal Injury; Medical Malpractice. **Email:** fnr@steidley-neal.com

WHITNEY M. ESCHENHEIMER, born Oklahoma City, Oklahoma, July 9, 1970; admitted to bar, 1996, Oklahoma and U.S. District Court, Eastern, Western and Northern Districts of Oklahoma. *Education:* University of Kansas (B.A., with distinction, 1992); University of Oklahoma (J.D., with distinction, 1996). In-house Counsel, Mid-Continent Casualty Company, Tulsa Oklahoma (2000-2001) *Member:* Oklahoma and American Bar Associations. **PRACTICE AREAS:** Insurance Law; Negligence; Workers' Compensation; Employment Law; Medical Malpractice Defense; Products Liability; Bad Faith Litigation; Litigation. **Email:** wme@steidley-neal.com

(This Listing Continued)

SEAN M. McKELVEY, born Fort Hood, Texas, May 9, 1970; admitted to bar, 1996, Oklahoma; U.S. District Court, Northern, Eastern and Western District of Oklahoma and U.S. Court of Appeals, 10th Circuit. *Education:* University of Texas at Arlington (B.A., 1993); Oklahoma City University (J.D., 1996). Phi Delta Phi. Order of the Barristers. Member Moot Court Board, 1994-1995. Member, Oklahoma City University Law Review, 1994-1996. Member, National Moot Court Competition Team, American Bar Association, 1996. Attorney, Town of Talihina. *Member:* Pittsburg County and Oklahoma Bar Associations. ***PRACTICE AREAS:*** Insurance Defense; Municipal Law; Civil Rights Litigation; Insurance Bad Faith Litigation; Employment Law; Federal Practice. ***Email:*** smm@steidley-neal.com

ASSOCIATES

MARK E. FIELDS, born McAlester, Oklahoma, September 22, 1974; admitted to bar, 2001, Oklahoma; U.S. District Court, Northern, Eastern and Western District of Oklahoma and U.S. Court of Appeals, 10th Circuit. *Education:* University of Oklahoma (B.A., 1997; J.D., 2001). *Member:* Pittsburg County and Oklahoma Bar Associations. ***PRACTICE AREAS:*** Insurance Defense; Litigation; Municipal Law; Federal Practice. ***Email:*** mef@steidley-neal.com

MICHELLE HARRIS, born January 2, 1971; admitted to bar, 2000, Oklahoma, U.S. District Court, Northern, Eastern and Western Districts of Oklahoma and U.S. Court of Appeals, Tenth Circuit. *Education:* Midwestern State University (B.A., 1995); University of Tulsa (J.D., 2000). Phi Delta Phi. *Member:* Tulsa County and Oklahoma (Young Lawyers Division Liaison, 2005; Member, Evidence Code Committee) Bar Associations; Defense Research Institute. ***PRACTICE AREAS:*** Civil Litigation; Legal Malpractice; Federal Practice; Employment Law; Civil Rights Law; Insurance Bad Faith Litigation. ***Email:*** mbh@steidley-neal.com

BRETT D. CABLE, born McAlester, Oklahoma, February 3, 1971; admitted to bar, 2002, Oklahoma; U.S. District Court, Eastern District of Oklahoma and U.S. Court of Appeals, 10th Circuit. *Education:* Southern Methodist University (B.B.A., Edwin L. Cox School of Business, 1993); University of Tulsa (J.D., 2002). Law Clerk, Richards and Connor, 2001-2002. *Member:* Pittsburg County and Oklahoma (Director, 2002— and Liaison, Law Related Education Committee, Young Lawyers Division; Member, Law Day Committee, 2005—) Bar Associations. ***PRACTICE AREAS:*** Civil Litigation; Business Law; Wills; Probate.

GUY A. GAYLOR, born Muskogee, Oklahoma; admitted to bar, 2002, Oklahoma; 2004, U.S. District Court, Northern and Eastern Districts of Oklahoma; U.S. Court of Appeals, Tenth Circuit. *Education:* University of Tulsa (B.A., 1993; J.D., 2002). ***PRACTICE AREAS:*** Civil Rights; Employment Law; Federal Practice. ***Email:*** guy@steidley-neal.com

AMY BETH DOBBINS, born Wagoner, Oklahoma; admitted to bar, 2001, Oklahoma. *Education:* University of Central Oklahoma (B.A.Ed., 1996); University of Oklahoma (J.D., 2001). Dean's List; Kappa Delta Pi. Recipient: Wal-Mart Foundation Scholarship; American Jurisprudence Award in State Securities Regulation. Senator, Student Government Association. Certified English Teacher, 1997. Member: Christian Legal Society, 1998-2001; Alternative Dispute Resolution Society, 1998-2001. Member, Board of Directors, Chamber of Commerce, Coweta, Oklahoma, 2003. Volunteer Mediator, Northeastern Oklahoma, Certified Civil/Commercial Mediator and Family & Divorce Mediator, Early Settlement Program. *Member:* Tulsa County, Wagoner County, Oklahoma (Liaison, Professionalism Committee, Young Lawyers Division) and American Bar Associations. (Also at Tulsa Office). ***PRACTICE AREAS:*** Insurance Defense. ***Email:*** abd@steidley-neal.com

OF COUNSEL

SCOTT D. McDONALD, born Fort Worth, Texas; admitted to bar, 1991, Texas; 1992, U.S. District Court, Northern District of Texas; 1993, U.S. District Court, Eastern and Western Districts of Texas; U.S. Court of Appeals, Fifth Circuit; 2004, Oklahoma; U.S. District Court, Eastern and Western Districts of Oklahoma and U.S. Court of Appeals, Tenth Circuit. *Education:* University of Texas at Austin (B.A., with honors, 1989); University of Texas School of Law (J.D., 1991). *Member:* Pittsburg County and Oklahoma Bar Associations; State Bar of Texas. ***LANGUAGES:*** Spanish. ***PRACTICE AREAS:*** Litigation; Business Law; Bankruptcy. ***Email:*** sdm@steidley-neal.com

JERRY E. TRUSTER, born Columbus, Ohio, February 16, 1943; admitted to bar, 1970, Oklahoma, U.S. District Court, Northern, Eastern and Western Districts of Oklahoma, U.S. Court of Appeals, Tenth Circuit and U.S. Supreme Court. *Education:* Ohio State University (B.S., 1966); University of Tulsa (J.D., 1969). Phi Alpha Delta. Assistant District Attorney, Tulsa, Oklahoma, 1972-1981. First Assistant District Attorney, 1981. Assistant District Attorney, Tulsa County, 1998-1999. Chief of Criminal Division, 1998. *Member:* Tulsa County and Oklahoma Bar Associations; Oklahoma District Attorneys Association; Tulsa County Criminal Defense Lawyers Association; Oklahoma Criminal Defense Lawyers Association; National Association of Criminal Defense Lawyers. Fellow, Oklahoma Bar Foundation. [Captain, U.S. Army, 1970-1972]. (Resident Tulsa Office). ***PRACTICE AREAS:*** Insurance Defense; Criminal Defense. ***Email:*** jet@steidley-neal.com

REPRESENTATIVE CLIENTS: AAA Inter-Insurance Exchange; AIG; AI Transport; Acceptance Insurance Co.; BP-Amoco Production Co.; Baker-Hughes Oilfield Operations, Inc.; Brotherhood Mutual Insurance Co.; Choctaw Nation of Oklahoma; City of Caddo, Oklahoma; COREGIS Insurance Company; Crawford & Company; Enogex, Incorporated; Equity Insurance Co.; ESIS/CIGNA; Farmers Alliance Mutual Insurance Co.; Farrell-Cooper Mining; Federated Rural Electric Insurance Corp.; Gallagher Bassett Services; General Motors Corporation; Genesis Insurance Co.; Gibraltar National Insurance Co.; Housing Authority of Creek Nation of OK; James Hodge Ford, Inc.; Kansas City Southern Railway; Marathon Oil Company; Maryland Insurance Company; McAlester Public Schools; Mid-Continent Group; Mustang Fuel Corporation; National American Insurance Co.; Oklahoma Attorneys Mutual Insurance Co.; Oklahoma Municipal Assurance Group; Oklahoma Farm Bureau Mutual Insurance Co.; Oklahoma Farmers Union Mutual Insurance Co.; Oklahoma Rural Water Association; Shelter Insurance Company; Transportation Claims, Inc.; Tri-County Autoplex; Tri-State Insurance; Vanliner Insurance Co.; Warren Foundation-McAlester Clinic.

STIPE, HARPER, LAIZURE, USELTON, EDWARDS & BELOTE, LLP

Established in 1954

343 EAST CARL ALBERT PARKWAY
P.O. BOX 1369
McALESTER, OKLAHOMA 74502
Telephone: 918-423-0421
Fax: 918-423-0266
URL: http://www.stipelaw.com

Muskogee, Oklahoma Office: 384 South 33rd Street. Telephone: 918-683-5050. Telefax: 918-682-5700

Oklahoma City, Oklahoma Office: 4111 North Lincoln Boulevard. Telephone: 405-524-2268.

Tulsa, Oklahoma Office: 2417 E. Skelly Drive. Telephone: 918-749-0749.

General Civil and Criminal Trial Practice. Personal Injury, Workers Compensation, Probate, Federal Employers Liability, Medical Malpractice, Products Liability Law, Mass Torts, Class Actions.

MEMBERS OF FIRM

EDDIE HARPER, born McAlester, Oklahoma, March 9, 1938; admitted to bar, 1963, Oklahoma; 1973, U.S. Supreme Court. *Education:* University of Oklahoma (B.S., 1960; LL.B., 1963). Phi Alpha Delta. Attorney, U.S. Attorney's Office, Muskogee, Oklahoma, 1966-1967. Assistant District Attorney, McAlester, Oklahoma, 1967-1969. *Member:* Oklahoma Bar Association (Co-Chairman, Workmen's Compensation Section, 1975). ***PRACTICE AREAS:*** Personal Injury; Products Liability; Workers Compensation; Oil and Gas; Criminal Law. ***Email:*** eharper@stipelaw.com

RUSSELL G. USELTON, born McAlester, Oklahoma, January 6, 1955; admitted to bar, 1983, Oklahoma, and U.S. District Court, Eastern District of Oklahoma and U.S. Court of Appeals, Tenth Circuit. *Education:* Southeastern Oklahoma State University (B.S., 1979); University of Arkansas School of Law (J.D., 1982). *Member:* Pittsburg County and Oklahoma Bar Associations; Oklahoma Trial Lawyers Association; The Association of Trial Lawyers of America. ***PRACTICE AREAS:*** Products Liability; Personal Injury; Medical Malpractice; Federal Employer's Liability Act; Insurance Law; Wrongful Death. ***Email:*** ruselton@stipelaw.com

TONY W. EDWARDS, born McAlester, Oklahoma, September 28, 1956; admitted to bar, 1982, Oklahoma; 1984, U.S. District Court, Eastern District of Oklahoma; 1985, U.S. District Court, Western District of Oklahoma; 1987, U.S. District Court, Eastern District of Arkansas. *Education:* East Central University (B.A., 1979); University of Oklahoma (J.D., 1982). Phi Alpha Delta. *Member:* Pontotoc County (Vice-President, 1983; Secretary Treasurer, 1984) and Oklahoma Bar Associations; Oklahoma Trial Lawyers Association. ***PRACTICE AREAS:*** Products Liability; Personal Injury; Medical Malpractice; Criminal; Bankruptcy. ***Email:*** tedwards@stipelaw.com

ANTHONY M. LAIZURE, born Oklahoma City, Oklahoma, August 27, 1955; admitted to bar, 1980, Oklahoma. *Education:* University of Oklahoma (B.S., 1977; J.D., 1980). *Member:* Oklahoma Bar Association. (Resident, Tulsa Office). ***REPORTED CASES:*** Donald Craig Brown v. St. John Medical Center, 1996 WL 414047 (Okla.App., June 7, 1996) (NO. 85, 541); Benning v. Pennwell Pub Co., 885 P.2d 652 (Okla., Oct. 18, 1994) (NO. 79,980); Anderson v. Spiro Nursing Home, 853 P.2d 246 (Okla.App., March 30, 1993) (NO. 80230); Hinds v. General Motors Corp., 988 F.2d 1039, 38 Fed. R. Evid. Serv. 516, Prod. Liab. Rep. (CCH) P 13,445 (10th Cir. Okla., March 16, 1993) (NO. 91-7006); Pearson v. Hope Lumber & Supply Co., Inc., 820 P. 2d 443, 122 Lab. Cas. P 57,013, 6 IER Cases 1580 (Okla. Nov. 5, 1991) (NO. 72, 017); Frank By and Through Gray v. Merciez, 806 P. 2d 1147 (Okla.App., Feb. 19, 1991) (NO. 72, 161, 72,175); U.S. v. McNutt, 908 F.2d 561 (10th Cir. Okla. July 3, 1990) (NO. 89-5153, 89-5167); Fields v. A & B Electronics, 788 P.2d 940 (Okla., Jan. 30, 1990) (NO. 70,029); Ellis v. Consolidated Diesel Elec. Corp., 894 F.2d 371, 20 Bkrptcy. Ct. Dec. 56, Bkrptcy. L. Rep. P 73, 214 (10th Cir. Okla. Jan. 18, 1990) (NO. 88-2424); Pearson v. Niagra Mach. & Tool Works, 701 F.Supp. 195 (N.D.Okla. Dec. 19, 1988) (NO. 88-C-71-B); Durant v. State, 717 P.2d 1161 (Okla. Crim. App., April 25, 1986) (NO. F-84-364); U.S. v. Draper, 762 F.2d 81 (10th Cir. Okla., May 9, 1985) (NO. 84-2544, 84-2545); U.S. v. Worley, 751 F.2d 348 (10th Cir. Okla., Dec. 28, 1984) (NO. 84-1112); U.S. v. Draper, 746 F.2d 662 (10th Cir. Okla., Oct. 17, 1984) (NO. 83-2346, 83-2347); U.S. v. Warhop, 732 F.2d 775 (10th Cir. Okla., April 18, 1984) (NO. 83-1569); U.S. v. James, 728 F.2d 465 (10th Cir. Okla., Feb. 29, 1984) (NO. 82-2607); U.S. v. Whitt, 718 F.2d 1494, 14 Fed. R. Evid. Serv. 944 (10th Cir., Okla., Sept. 30, 1983) (NO. 82-2213); U.S. v. Primrose, 718 F.2d 1484, 14 Fed. R. Evid. Serv. 282 (10th Cir., Okla., Sept. 30,1983) (NO. 82-1842). ***PRACTICE AREAS:*** Personal Injury; Products Liability; Medical Negligence. ***Email:*** tlaizure@stipelawtulsa.com

JAMES A. BELOTE, born McAlester, Oklahoma, November 9, 1962; admitted to bar, 1988, Oklahoma and U.S. District Court, Western District of Oklahoma; 1990, Texas. *Education:* University of Oklahoma (B.B.A. in Finance, 1985; J.D., 1988). Phi Alpha Delta. *Member:* Oklahoma County, Oklahoma and American Bar Associations; State Bar of Texas. (Resident, Oklahoma City Office). ***PRACTICE AREAS:*** Personal Injury; Products Liability; Employment Law; Criminal Defense; Civil Rights. ***Email:*** jbelote@stipelawokc.com

---

TIMOTHY D. MAXCEY, born Clovis, New Mexico, December 31, 1963; admitted to bar, 1989, Oklahoma; U.S. District Court, Eastern, Northern and Western Districts of Oklahoma and U.S. Court of Appeals, Tenth Circuit. *Education:* Oklahoma Christian College (B.S., 1986); Texas Technical University (J.D., 1989). Phi Beta Lambda; Alpha Chi; Phi Alpha Delta. Board of Barristers. *Member:* Pittsburg County and Oklahoma Bar Associations; The Association of Trial Lawyers of America; Oklahoma Trial Lawyers Association. ***PRACTICE AREAS:*** Personal Injury; Nursing Home Negligence; Probate; Insurance Law; Wrongful Death. ***Email:*** tmaxcey@stipelaw.com

(This Listing Continued)

STIPE, HARPER, LAIZURE, USELTON, EDWARDS & BELOTE, LLP, McAlester—Continued

MARK L. EDWARDS, born Oklahoma City, Oklahoma, November 11, 1969; admitted to bar, 1996, Oklahoma, U.S. District Court, Eastern, Northern and Western Districts of Oklahoma and U.S. Court of Appeals, Tenth Circuit and Fifth Circuit. *Education:* Oklahoma Christian College (B.S., cum laude, 1992); University of Oklahoma (J.D., 1996). Recipient: Academic Achievement Award, Trial Techniques; Albert C. Hunt Practice Court Award. *Member:* Oklahoma County, Oklahoma and American (Member, Tort and Insurance Practice Section; Member, Committees on: Medicine and Law; Trial Techniques) Bar Associations; Million Dollar Advocates Forum. ***PRACTICE AREAS:*** Trucking Litigation; Wrongful Death; Personal Injury; Class Actions. ***Email:*** medwards@stipelaw.com

TREVOR J. FURLONG, born Vicksburg, Michigan, December 31, 1973; admitted to bar, 2005, Oklahoma; U.S. District Court, Eastern, Northern and Western Districts of Oklahoma. *Education:* Davenport University (B.S., magna cum laude, 2001); University of Oklahoma (J.D. with distinction, 2004). Order of Barristers, Luther Bohanan Inn of Court. Recipient, Academic Achievement Awards, Administrative Law. Editor-in-Chief, American Indian Law Review. *Member:* Oklahoma and American Bar Associations. [ES, U.S. Navy, 1992-1999.]. ***PRACTICE AREAS:*** Personal Injury; Family Law; Criminal Defense; Trucking Litigation; Wrongful Death. ***Email:*** tfurlong@stipelaw.com

OF COUNSEL

CLYDE STIPE, born Blanco, Oklahoma, January 13, 1929; admitted to bar, 1957, Oklahoma. *Education:* University of Oklahoma; Eastern Oklahoma A. & M. College; Oklahoma City University (LL.B., 1957). U.S. Assistant District Attorney, Muskogee, Oklahoma, 1961-1962. *Member:* Pittsburg County (Secretary-Treasurer, 1958-1959; Vice President, 1959-1960) and Oklahoma Bar Associations; Oklahoma Trial Lawyers Association. [With U.S. Navy, 1945-1952]. ***PRACTICE AREAS:*** Products Liability; Personal Injury; Social Security; Probate; Medical Malpractice. ***Email:*** cstipe@stipelaw.com

REPRESENTATIVE CLIENTS: Sooner Federal Savings & Loan Assn.; Safeway Stores, Inc.; U.M.W.A. (State); AFL-CIO (State); Kiamichi Electric Cooperative.

(For personnel at Muskogee, Oklahoma City and Tulsa, see Professional Biographies at those locations)

WAGNER & WAGNER, P.C.

McALESTER, OKLAHOMA

(See Oklahoma City)

Family Law, Personal Injury, Automobile Accidents, Truck Accidents, Wrongful Death, Divorce, Alimony, Child Support, Workers Compensation, Social Security Disability, Employment, Employment Discrimination, Wrongful Termination, Adoptions.

BEAUCHAMP AND BEAUCHAMP

Not a Partnership
201 EAST CENTRAL
MIAMI, OKLAHOMA 74355
Telephone: 918-542-2860
Fax: 918-542-7100

General Civil Practice and State Courts. Trials. Real Estate, Probate, Social Security and Workers Compensation Law, Personal Injury, Family, Divorce, General Negligence and Products Liability Law, Criminal Defense, Driving While Intoxicated.

FIRM PROFILE: General practice of law.

HERSCHEL G. E. BEAUCHAMP (1910-1998)

GLENN BEAUCHAMP, born Miami, Oklahoma, February 21, 1947; admitted to bar, 1984, Oklahoma. *Education:* Northeastern A & M Junior College (A.A., 1967); Oklahoma University (B.A., 1969); Oklahoma City University (J.D., 1983). Phi Theta Kappa; Phi Alpha Delta. Member, Moot Court Board, 1982-1983. Municipal Court Judge, Fairland, North Miami and Wyandotte, 1991—. City Prosecutor, City of Miami, Oklahoma. Member, Oklahoma Municipal Judges Association. *Member:* Oklahoma and American Bar Associations; Oklahoma Trial Lawyers Association; The Association of Trial Lawyers of America; Oklahoma Criminal Defense Lawyers; National Association of Criminal Defense Lawyers. [1st Lieut., U.S. Army, 1972-1976]. ***PRACTICE AREAS:*** Adoptions; Personal Injury; Social Security; General Practice.

APPROVED ATTORNEYS FOR: American First Title & Trust Co.
REFERENCES: First National Bank of Miami, Oklahoma; Security Bank & Trust Co., Miami, Oklahoma; Bank of Miami; Green County Federal Savings and Loans, Miami, OK.

LOGAN & LOWRY, LLP

MIAMI, OKLAHOMA

(See Vinita)

General Practice, Including Trials in all State and Federal Courts, Eminent Domain, Environmental and Coal, Banking, Commercial Transactions, Creditors' Rights and Bankruptcy, Corporation, Public Utility, Real Estate, Estate Planning and Probate, Criminal, Domestic Relations, Civil Rights, Employment, Appellate Practice and Administrative Law.

THE CROSTHWAIT LAW FIRM

A PROFESSIONAL CORPORATION
Attorneys and Counselors at Law
Established in 1974
THE TIMBERS OFFICE PARK
1384 SOUTH DOUGLAS BOULEVARD
MIDWEST CITY, OKLAHOMA 73130
Telephone: 405-733-1683
Fax: 405-741-1688
Email: joe.crosthwait@lawoklahoma.com
URL: http://www.crosthwaitlaw.com

Estate Planning, Wills, Trust Law, Elder Law, Probate, Estate Litigation, Serious or Complex Personal Injury, Automobile Accidents, Motorcycle Accidents, Slip and Fall, Wrongful Death, Real Estate, Family Law, Divorce, Child Custody, Child Support.

M. JOE CROSTHWAIT, JR., born Oklahoma City, Oklahoma, September 7, 1948; admitted to bar, 1974, Oklahoma, U.S. District Court, Eastern, Western and Northern Districts of Oklahoma and U.S. Court of Appeals, Tenth Circuit. *Education:* University of Oklahoma (B.A., 1971); Oklahoma City University (J.D., 1974). Phi Alpha Delta. Certified Financial Planner; Assistant Municipal Judge, City of Midwest City, 1985-1996. Judge, Temporary Court of Appeals, State of Oklahoma, 1994-1995. Member: Board of Directors, Oklahoma Congregate Housing for the Elderly and Disabled, 1982—; Midwest City Regional Hospital Ethics Committee, 1986—. Chair, ABA Standing Committee on Solo and Small Firms. Member: ABA Task Force on Personal Legal Services; ABA Committee on Research on the Future of the Profession, 1999-2003. President, OCU School of Law Alumni Association, 2002-2004. Member, Oklahoma Adoption Law Reform Committee, 1995-1998. Member and Chair, Midwest City Economic Development Commission, 1986-1994. Master, Ruth Bader Ginsburg American Inn of Court. Member, Executive Council, National Conference of Bar Presidents. *Member:* Oklahoma County (President, 1994-1995), Oklahoma (President, 2000; Fellow, Young Lawyers Division) and American (House of Delegates) Bar Associations; The Association of Trial Lawyers of America; Oklahoma Trial Lawyers Association. Fellow: Oklahoma Bar Foundation (Trustee, 1995-2000). Fellow, American Bar Foundation. Sustaining Fellow: College of Law Practice Management. ***REPORTED CASES:*** Pulliam v. Pulliam, 796 P.2d 623, 59 USLW 2119, 1990 OK71; Kerby v. Kerby, 60 P.3d 1038, 2002 OK 91; Swick v. Swick, 864 P.2d 819, 1993 OK 151. ***PRACTICE AREAS:*** Estate Planning; Estate Litigation; Personal Injury. ***Email:*** joe.crosthwait@lawoklahoma.com

TRACI L. SODERSTROM, born Fort Hood, Texas, April 20, 1973; admitted to bar, 2003, Oklahoma. *Education:* East Central University (B.S., 1996); Oklahoma City University (J.D., cum laude, 2003). Phi Alpha Delta. Recipient: Judge Dwain Box Award for Outstanding Appellate Advocacy, 2003; CALI Excellence in the Future Award for Domestic Violence, 2001 and Trial Practice, 2003. Associate, Ruth Bader Ginsburg American Inn of Court. Volunteer, Oklahoma Lawyers for Children. ***LANGUAGES:*** American Sign Language. ***PRACTICE AREAS:*** Family Law; Appellate Practice. ***Email:*** tracisoderstrom@coxinet.net

REPRESENTATIVE CLIENTS: Rueb Group, Ltd.; Amtel Service Corporation; Park State Bank; Air Quality Laboratories, Inc.

ATKINS & MARKOFF

MUSKOGEE, OKLAHOMA

(See Oklahoma City)

Personal Injury, Automobile Accidents, Wrongful Death, Trucking Accidents, Slip and Fall, Nursing Home Abuse, Head and Spinal Injuries, Dog Bites, Sexual Abuse, Criminal Law, Drug Crimes, DUI/DWI, Juvenile Crimes, General Practice, Family , Divorce, Adoptions, Child Custody, Child Support, Domestic Violence, Visitation Rights, Elder Law, Legal Malpractice, Medical Malpractice, Social Security, Social Security Disability, Taxation, IRS Audits, Property Tax Appeals, Tax Planning, Toxic Torts, Trust and Estate, Wills and Probate.

BONDS & MATTHEWS LAW FIRM, P.L.L.C.

Established in 1940
444 COURT STREET
P.O. BOX 1906
MUSKOGEE, OKLAHOMA 74402-1906
Telephone: 918-683-2911
Fax: 918-687-0846

General Practice in all Oklahoma State and Federal Courts, Trial and Appellate Practice, Personal Injury and Wrongful Death actions, Products Liability claims, Civil Rights Litigation, including Wrongful Discharge, Discrimination and Excessive Force, Governmental and Municipal Law, Railroad Defense, Insurance Defense, School Law, Business Litigation, Banking, Administrative Law, Real Estate, Probate and Estates, Domestic Relations, Bankruptcy, Criminal Defense, Equine (including Racing Commission), OSHA Related Injury and Death, Franchise Law, Nursing Home Negligence, Employment.

MEMBERS OF FIRM

ALBERT R. MATTHEWS, born Checotah, Oklahoma, December 15, 1930; admitted to bar, 1960, Oklahoma. *Education:* Oklahoma State University (B.S., 1957); University of Oklahoma (LL.B., 1960). Phi Alpha Delta (Vice President, 1959-1960); Omicron Delta Chi; Order of the Coif. Editor-in-Chief, Oklahoma Law Review, 1960. *Member:* Muskogee County, Oklahoma and American Bar Associations. ***PRACTICE AREAS:*** Personal Injury; Truck Accidents; Employment Law; Equine Law; Nursing Home Negligence; Real Estate.

(This Listing Continued)

A. CAMP BONDS, JR., born Muskogee, Oklahoma, April 2, 1942; admitted to bar, 1968, Oklahoma. *Education:* University of Oklahoma (B.S., 1965; J.D., 1968). *Member:* Muskogee County and Oklahoma (Member: Board of Editors, 1993-1996; Board of Governors, 2003—) Bar Associations. ***PRACTICE AREAS:*** Railroad Defense; Personal Injury; Bankruptcy.

ASSOCIATES

JULIET N. BRENNAN, born Charleston, West Virginia, July 4, 1960; admitted to bar, 1987, Oklahoma, U.S. District Court, Eastern and Northern Districts of Oklahoma, U.S. Court of Appeals, Tenth Circuit and U.S. Supreme Court. *Education:* University of Kentucky (B.A., 1982); University of Mississippi (J.D., 1986). Phi Alpha Delta. *Member:* Muskogee County (President, 1997-1998) and Oklahoma Bar Associations. ***PRACTICE AREAS:*** Railroad Defense; Family; Appellate; Probate; General Civil; Insurance Defense; School Law; Civil Rights. ***Email:*** jbrennan@azalea.net

JEFF M. BONDS, born Muskogee, Oklahoma, February 19, 1969; admitted to bar, 1994, Oklahoma. *Education:* Westminster College (B.S., 1991); Oklahoma City University School of Law (J.D., 1994). *Member:* Muskogee and Oklahoma Bar Associations. ***PRACTICE AREAS:*** General Civil; Family; Railroad Defense.

MARTHA J. CHERBINI, born Fort Dix, New Jersey, November 15, 1948; admitted to bar, 1989, Virginia, U.S. District Court, Eastern District of Virginia and U.S. Court of Appeals, Fourth Circuit; 1997, Oklahoma; U.S. District Court, Eastern and Northern Districts of Oklahoma. *Education:* George Mason University (B.A., 1986); George Mason University School of Law (J.D., 1989). Phi Delta Phi. Chief Justice, Moot Court Board, 1988-1989. *Member:* Muskogee County and Oklahoma Bar Associations. ***PRACTICE AREAS:*** Family Law; Personal Injury; General Civil; Employment Law. ***Email:*** mcherbin@azalea.net

REPRESENTATIVE CLIENTS: Some of the firms corporate clients include: BNSF Railway Company; Muskogee Regional Medical Center; Western Surety Company; Territory National Bank; Maternal and Family Practices, Inc.; Mobility Plus; Muskogee Golf; C and L Mobile Homes; Eaglecrest Estates; Advance Computers, Inc.; International Sports Management; Town of Warner; Town of Gore; Hopes and Dreams Futurity.

FREDERIC DORWART

MUSKOGEE, OKLAHOMA

(See Tulsa)

General Civil Practice including Oil and Gas, Banking and Business Planning, Securities Regulation, Technology Sales and Licensing, Mergers and Acquisitions, Corporation, White Collar Crime, Environmental, Employment Law, Health Care Law, Securities fraud, Securities Arbitration, Commercial Litigation, Business Litigation.

GAGE & WILLIAMS LAW FIRM

530 COURT STREET
P.O. BOX 87
MUSKOGEE, OKLAHOMA 74401
Telephone: 918-687-5424
Fax: 918-687-0761

General Civil Practice before State and Federal Courts. Insurance, Negligence, Corporation, Real Estate and Probate Law.

MEMBERS OF FIRM

EDWIN L. GAGE, born Enid, Oklahoma, January 5, 1940; admitted to bar, 1966, Oklahoma and U.S. Court of Military Appeals; 1969, U.S. District Court, Eastern, Northern and Western Districts of Oklahoma; U.S. Supreme Court. *Education:* University of Oklahoma (B.A., 1963; J.D., 1966). Phi Alpha Delta. Assistant U.S. Attorney, 1970-1976 and U.S. Land Commissioner, 1981—, Eastern District of Oklahoma. *Member:* Muskogee County and Oklahoma Bar Associations; National Health Lawyers Association. [Capt., JAGC, U.S. Army, 1966-1970; USAR, 1970-1987]. ***REPORTED CASES:*** Bartmann vs. Maverick Tube Corp., 853 F.2d 1540 (10th Cir. 1988); Morgan Pipe and Supply Co., Inc. vs. Schwartz, 680 F.Supp. 1499 (E.D. OK. 1988). ***PRACTICE AREAS:*** Real Property Law; Probate Law. ***Email:*** egage@azalea.net

BETTY OUTHIER WILLIAMS, born Woodward, Oklahoma, September 11, 1947; admitted to bar, 1972, Oklahoma, U.S. District Court, Northern District of Oklahoma and U.S. Court of Appeals, Tenth Circuit; 1973, U.S. District Court, Eastern District of Oklahoma; 1980, U.S. Supreme Court; 1988, U.S. District Court, Western District of Oklahoma. *Education:* Oklahoma City University (B.A., 1969); Vanderbilt University (J.D., 1972). Member, Board of Editors: "Oklahoma Law Enforcement & Operations Bulletin"; Oklahoma Bar Journal, 1997—. Chairman: Local Rules Committee; U.S. District Court for the Eastern District of Oklahoma, 1995; Chairman, Rules Committee, U.S. Bankruptcy Court for the Eastern District of Oklahoma, 1994. Adjunct Settlement Judge, U.S. District Court, Eastern District of Oklahoma. Assistant U.S. Attorney 1973-1981. U.S. Attorney 1981-1982. Appellate Judge, Oklahoma Court on the Judiciary, 2003-2005. *Member:* Muskogee County, Oklahoma (Member, Board of Governors, 2000-2002) and American Bar Associations; Oklahoma Bar Foundation (President, 1996; Member, Board of Editors, 1997—); Oklahoma Association of Defense Counsel; Defense Research Institute. ***REPORTED CASES:*** Young v. Vermillion, 1999 992 P2d 917 (OK. Civ App 1999); Johnson v. Martin, 195 73d 1208 (10th Cir 1999); Beck v. Muskogee, 195 F3d 553 (10th Cir. 1999). ***PRACTICE AREAS:*** Bankruptcy Law; Federal Civil Litigation; State Civil Litigation. ***Email:*** bowlaw@sbcglobal.net

---

EDITH M. GREGORY, born St. Louis, Missouri, June 25, 1945; admitted to bar, 1987, Oklahoma. *Education:* Oklahoma State University (B.S., 1968); University of Tulsa (J.D., 1986). Phi Delta Phi. *Member:* Muskogee County and Oklahoma Bar Associations. ***PRACTICE AREAS:*** General Civil Practice. ***Email:*** egregory@intellex.com

(This Listing Continued)

REPRESENTATIVE CLIENTS: Nationwide Insurance Co.; Oklahoma Municipal Assurance Group; Golden Rule Ins. Co.; Tastee Freeze International, Inc.; Security Alarms Co., Inc.

MARK GREEN

706 WEST OKMULGEE
P.O. BOX 2362
MUSKOGEE, OKLAHOMA 74402
Telephone: 918-683-0309
Fax: 918-687-5964
Email: green@azalea.net

General Civil and Criminal Trial and Appellate Practice in all State and Federal Courts. Negligence, Personal Injury, Products Liability, Bankruptcy Law.

MARK GREEN, born Fort Smith, Arkansas, November 6, 1953; admitted to bar, 1978, Oklahoma and U.S. District Court, Eastern District of Oklahoma; 1979, U.S. Court of Appeals, Tenth Circuit; 1980, U.S. District Court, Northern District of Oklahoma. *Education:* Oklahoma University (B.B.A., 1975; J.D., 1977). Phi Delta Phi. Assistant District Attorney and Assistant U.S. Attorney, Eastern District of Oklahoma, 1978-1983. *Member:* Muskogee County and Oklahoma Bar Associations. ***PRACTICE AREAS:*** Federal Criminal Law; Criminal Defense; Personal Injury Law; Federal Civil Practice; Civil Practice.

LOCKE & MOORE

314 WEST BROADWAY
P.O. BOX 1468
MUSKOGEE, OKLAHOMA 74402
Telephone: 918-687-4900
Fax: 918-687-5969
Email: lockenmoore@yahoo.com

General Practice including Family Law, Criminal Law, Business Law, Bankruptcy, Personal Injury, Wills, Trusts and Estates, Probate.

MEMBERS OF FIRM

ROBERT LOCKE, born Corpus Christi, Texas, September 3, 1943; admitted to bar, 1970, Oklahoma. *Education:* Oklahoma State University (B.S., 1966); Tulsa University (J.D., 1969). Delta Theta Phi. Municipal Judge, 1972-1973. *Member:* Muskogee County and Oklahoma Bar Associations; Oklahoma Trial Lawyers Association. ***PRACTICE AREAS:*** Personal Injury Law; Worker's Compensation; Bankruptcy; Civil Litigation; Product Liability; Criminal; Family Law; Divorce; Child Custody. ***Email:*** lockenmoore@yahoo.com

LARRY DEAN MOORE, born Muskogee, Oklahoma, June 19, 1959; admitted to bar, 1988, Oklahoma. *Education:* Northeastern Oklahoma State University (B.A., 1983); University of Tulsa (J.D., 1988). First Assistant District Attorney, Oklahoma, 1987-1997. *Member:* Muskogee County and Oklahoma Bar Associations. ***PRACTICE AREAS:*** Criminal Law; Divorce; Personal Injury; Bankruptcy; Workers Compensation; Driving While Intoxicated; Traffic Violations. ***Email:*** lockenmoore@yahoo.com

OF COUNSEL

CORRINE O'DAY, born Norwich, New York, November 2, 1962; admitted to bar, 2003, Oklahoma. *Education:* University of Tulsa (B.S.B.A., 1991; J.D., with honors, 2003). Phi Delta Phi; Order of Barristers. Recipient, Elaine Osborne Jacobson Award for Women in Health Law, 2003. *Member:* Oklahoma Bar Association; American Trial Lawyers Association; American Health Lawyers Association. ***PRACTICE AREAS:*** Health Law; Civil Rights; Employment Law; Indian Law; Appellate Practice. ***Email:*** attorney@coroday.com

---

YASODHARA "MITTY" MOHANTY MEANS P.C.

Established in 2001
SERES BUILDING
215 STATE STREET, SUITE 503
MUSKOGEE, OKLAHOMA 74401
Telephone: 918-686-6255
Fax: 918-686-5503
URL: http://www.meanslawoffice.com
Email: mittymohanty0186@sbcglobal.net
URL: http://www.mittymohantylaw.com

Mediation, Federal Litigation, Civil Litigation, Representation of Nurses and other Health Care Professionals, Administration Law, Corporate Law, Business Litigation, Estate Plan, Probate, Insurance and Surety Law.

YASODHARA M. MOHANTY MEANS, born Cuttack, India, March 2, 1952; admitted to bar, 1981, Oklahoma; 2000, U.S. District Court, Western District of Arkansas. *Education:* University of Oklahoma (B.A., 1972; J.D., 1981); Oxford University, Oxford, England (B.A., with honors, Philosophy, Politics, Economics, 1974; M.A., 1979); University of Wisconsin-Madison (M.A., Philosophy of Law, 1975). Phi Beta Kappa; Phi Alpha Delta. Assistant Attorney General, 1990-2000. Judge, Temporary Court of Appeals, Panel XLVII, January-July 1992. Barrister, American Inns of Court, Halloway Chapter, 1996-1997. Assistant Attorney General, State of Oklahoma, 1990-2000. *Member:* Oklahoma County, Cleveland County, Muskogee County, Oklahoma (Member: Ethics Committee; Administrative Law Section; ADR Committee) and American Bar Associations; Oklahoma Association of Defense Counsel; Association of Attorney Mediators; Women Lawyers of Oklahoma; Defense Research Institute; National Institute of Trial Advocacy; South Asian Bar Association. (Of Counsel to Locke & Moore). ***LANGUAGES:*** Hindi, Oriya, Bengali, Spanish and English. ***REPORTED CASES:*** Anderson v. CNA; Hughes v. Fidelity; Col-

(This Listing Continued)

YASODHARA "MITTY" MOHANTY MEANS P.C., Muskogee—Continued

clazier v. Oklahoma Indigent Defense System; State of Oklahoma ex. rel. Oklahoma Health Care Authority vs. R. J. Reynolds; Monnet v. Freeman, United States District Court for the Western District of Oklahoma. ***PRACTICE AREAS:*** Mediation; Administrative Law; Health Law; Nursing Law; Health Care; Corporate Law; Civil Litigation; Estate Planning; Probate; Adoption Law.

REPRESENTATIVE CLIENTS: Nurses Services Organizations; Healthcare Innovation.

RIGGS, ABNEY, NEAL, TURPEN, ORBISON & LEWIS

A PROFESSIONAL CORPORATION

Established in 1972

FIRST NATIONAL SEVERS BUILDING, SUITE 508

215 STATE STREET

MUSKOGEE, OKLAHOMA 74402

Telephone: 918-687-5404; Toll Free: 800-722-1332

Fax: 918-687-1128

URL: http://www.riggsabney.com

Tulsa, Oklahoma Office: Frisco Building, 502 West Sixth Street, 74119. Telephone: 918-587-3161. Fax: 918-587-9708.

Oklahoma City, Oklahoma Office: Paragon Building, Suite 101. Telephone: 405-843-9909. Facsimile: 405-842-2913.

Denver, Colorado Office: 621 17th St., Ste. 1900. Telephone: 303-298-7392. Facsimile: 303-398-7398.

General Civil, Trial and Appellate Practice before all State and Federal Courts and Agencies, Alternative Dispute Resolution, Banking, Corporate, Securities, Anti-trust, Administrative, Government Relations, Real Estate, Commercial Transactions, Oil and Gas, Estate Planning, Probate, Taxation, Employment and Discrimination, Employee Benefits, Social Security, Bankruptcy and Reorganization, Family Law, Healthcare, Negligence, Personal Injury, Products Liability, Medical Malpractice, Transportation, and Indian Law.

ASSOCIATES

John D. Luton
Victoria L. Rackley

SANDERS & ASSOCIATES, P.C.

MUSKOGEE, OKLAHOMA

(See Tulsa)

Personal Injury, Workers Compensation, Social Security, Automobile Insurance Coverage.

WRIGHT, STOUT, FITE & WILBURN

Established in 1929

300 WEST BROADWAY

P.O. BOX 707

MUSKOGEE, OKLAHOMA 74402-0707

Telephone: 918-682-0091

Fax: 918-683-6340

Email: weldon@wsfw-ok.com

General Civil Practice in all State and Federal Courts. Trials, Insurance, Real Estate, Corporate, Banking, Bankruptcy, Civil Rights, Family and Probate Law, Eminent Domain, Employment Law and Mediation Services.

FIRM PROFILE: The firm was founded in 1929 by Joe H. Kennedy who died in 1984 at the age of 79. Mr. Kennedy was joined in the practice by his son, Joe R. Kennedy, in 1964. Since that time, the firm's practice has steadily grown. Ron Wright joined the firm in 1971, with Weldon Stout joining in 1980. Upon the retirement of Joe R. Kennedy in January, 1992, Bart Fite joined the successor partnership of Wright, Stout & Fite and upon Paula Wilburn joining the firm in 1999 the successor partnership of Wright, Stout, Fite & Wilburn was formed.

The firm's practice initially was concentrated in the areas of banking and the defense of a wide range of personal injury/property damage and related insurance matters. Since that time, the firm's practice has steadily expanded in order to meet the litigation and other needs of many of its regional and national clients. Its areas of practice have also now expanded to include specialties in estate and probate, commercial law, bankruptcy law, insurance defense, governmental and municipal law and eminent domain. All of the firm's lawyers are involved in the trial of cases in state and federal courts, representing clients locally, regionally and nationally.

MEMBERS OF FIRM

J. RON WRIGHT, born Durant, Oklahoma, May 12, 1944; admitted to bar, 1969, Oklahoma. *Education:* University of Oklahoma (B.A., 1966; J.D., 1969). Associate Member, Board of Bar Examiners, 1985-1994. Member, 1994— and Chair, 2000, Board of Bar Examiners. Member, 1987-1990 and Chair, 1990, Rules Committee, U.S. Bankruptcy Court, Eastern District of Oklahoma. Member, Committee for Admissions and Grievances, 1995—and Chair, 1995-1997 and 2002—, U.S. District Court, Eastern District of Oklahoma. Trustee, Oklahoma Humanities Council. *Member:* Muskogee County, Oklahoma and American Bar Associations. ***PRACTICE AREAS:*** Civil Litigation; Commercial Law; Banking Law; Bankruptcy Law; Trusts; Estate Planning. ***Email:*** ron@wsfw-ok.com

WELDON W. STOUT, born Conway, Arkansas, July 20, 1949; admitted to bar, 1974, Oklahoma; U.S. District Court, Eastern, Northern and Western Districts of Oklahoma and U.S. Court of Appeals, 10th Circuit. *Education:* University of Oklahoma (B.A., 1971); Oklahoma City University (J.D., 1974). Assistant District Attorney, Stephens County, 1974-1978. Chief Prosecutor of Muskogee County, 1978-1980. *Member:* Muskogee County (President, 1980) and Oklahoma (Member, Board of Governors, 1989-1991) Bar Associations. ***PRACTICE AREAS:*** Civil Litigation; Personal Injury Law; Insurance Law; Federal Court Litigation; Mediation; Arbitration. ***Email:*** weldon@wsfw-ok.com

C. BART FITE, born Denver, Colorado, August 21, 1959; admitted to bar, 1984, Oklahoma. *Education:* Oklahoma State University (B.S., 1981); University of Oklahoma (J.D., 1984). Recipient, American Jurisprudence Award for Excellence in Commercial Law I, 1984. Assistant Municipal Judge, 1985-1998 and Municipal Judge, 1998—, City of Muskogee, Oklahoma. Municipal Judge, Town of Okay, Oklahoma, 1985—. Tribal Prosecutor for Cherokee Nation, 1995-1997. District Judge, Cherokee Nation, 2001—. *Member:* Muskogee County, Oklahoma and American Bar Associations. ***REPORTED CASES:*** Taff vs. City of Muskogee, 782 P.2d 155; Dept. of Transportation v. Eldee Panell, 853 P.2d 244 (Okla. App. 1993); Patterson v. Town of Muldrow, 865 P.2d 1269 (Okla. App., 1993); Simpson v. City of Muskogee, 879 P.2d 1269 (Okla. App. 1994); Minie v. Hudson, City of Okmulgee, 934 P.2d 1082 (Okl. App. 1997); Eriksson v. Jones, 37 P.3d 823 (Okl. App. 2001). ***PRACTICE AREAS:*** Civil Law; Municipal Law; Employment Law; Eminent Domain; Workers' Compensation Law. ***Email:*** bart@wsfw-ok.com

PAULA A. RANALLO WILBURN, born Tahlequah, Oklahoma, January 5, 1962; admitted to bar, 1987, Oklahoma. *Education:* University of Oklahoma (B.A., 1984); University of Tulsa (J.D., 1987). Pi Sigma Alpha, Delta Theta Phi, Golden Key. Recipient, American Jurisprudence Award for Excellence in Commercial Law II, 1986. Adjunct Professor, Northeastern State University. *Member:* Muskogee County, Oklahoma and American Bar Associations. ***PRACTICE AREAS:*** Family Law; Real Estate; Civil Trial; Domestic Law; Real Property Law. ***Email:*** paula@wsfw-ok.com

ASSOCIATE

JUSTIN C. STOUT, born Duncan, Oklahoma, December 19, 1976; admitted to bar, 2002, Oklahoma. *Education:* University of Oklahoma (B.A., 1999; J.D., 2002). ***PRACTICE AREAS:*** Family Law; Personal Injury; Bankruptcy; Products Liability. ***Email:*** justin@wsfw-ok.com

REPRESENTATIVE CLIENTS: Ft. James Paper Co.; Arkhola Sand & Gravel Co.; Equity Mutual Insurance Co.; United Services Auto Assn.; Equitable Life & Casualty; Universal Underwriters Insurance Co.; Union Mutual Insurance Co.; Oklahoma Department of Transportation; Oklahoma Turnpike Authority; Highlands Insurance Co.; Muskogee Daily Phoenix; BancFirst Muskogee; Municipal Assurance Group; North America Livestock, Inc.; City of Muskogee; Advanced Warnings, Inc.; Bank of America (Muskogee); Republic Casualty; Hometown Hospice, L.L.C.; Muskogee Regional Medical Center; Armstrong Bank; First State Bank.

ATKINS & MARKOFF

NORMAN, OKLAHOMA

(See Oklahoma City)

Personal Injury, Automobile Accidents, Wrongful Death, Trucking Accidents, Slip and Fall, Nursing Home Abuse, Head and Spinal Injuries, Dog Bites, Sexual Abuse, Criminal Law, Drug Crimes, DUI/DWI, Juvenile Crimes, General Practice, Family, Divorce, Adoptions, Child Custody, Child Support, Domestic Violence, Visitation Rights, Elder Law, Legal Malpractice, Medical Malpractice, Social Security, Social Security Disability, Taxation, IRS Audits, Property Tax Appeals, Tax Planning, Toxic Torts, Trust and Estate, Wills and Probate.

BENEDUM & BENEDUM, INC.

Established in 1899

131 E. MAIN STREET, SUITE 200

NORMAN, OKLAHOMA 73069

Telephone: 405-321-2212

Fax: 405-321-5438

Email: benbenedum@hotmail.com

General Practice. Business Law, Commercial Litigation, Insurance, Probate, Oil and Gas, Personal Injury and Real Estate Law. Trials. Collections over $10,000.00.

T. R. BENEDUM (1905-1991)

BEN T. BENEDUM, born Norman, Oklahoma, August 12, 1936; admitted to bar, 1965, Oklahoma. *Education:* University of Oklahoma (B.B.A., 1959; J.D., 1965); Indiana University (M.B.A., 1961). Phi Alpha Delta. *Member:* Cleveland County and Oklahoma Bar Associations. [Capt., Military Police Corps, U.S. Army, active duty, 1959-1961; USAR, 1962-1968]. ***PRACTICE AREAS:*** Probate; Real Estate Law; Commercial Law. ***Email:*** benbenedum@hotmail.com

REPRESENTATIVE CLIENTS: Oklahoma Gas & Electric Co.; First Fidelity Bank, N.A.; Cleveland County Abstract Co.; Thompson Pool and Patio; Psychtest Corporation; Energytech.com, Inc.; Housing Systems, LLC; Elephant Trunk Storage, LLC; Best Western Greentree Hotel and Suites, LLC; Preferred Realty, Inc.

DAVID BERNSTEIN

BERNSTEIN LAW BUILDING

104 WEST GRAY STREET

P.O. BOX 1692

NORMAN, OKLAHOMA 73070-1692

Telephone: 405-329-1484

Toll Free: 1-800-235-0529

Facsimile: 405-329-5949

URL: http://www.lawyers.com/dblaw

Email: dbnormanok@aol.com

URL: http://www.dblaw.net

Complex Personal Injury, Airplane Crashes, Product Liability, Medical Malpractice, Unsafe Products, Workers Compensation, Nursing Home Abuse, Insurance, Automobile Accidents, Dog Bites, Slip and Fall, Wrongful Death.

(This Listing Continued)

FIRM PROFILE: Mr. Bernstein is a featured speaker at Personal Injury Seminars, which teach and advise other attorneys on Personal Injury claims. In addition, Mr. Bernstein was co-counsel on a wrongful death case where the jury brought back a verdict of over $9,000,000, which is one of the largest wrongful death verdicts in Oklahoma history.

DAVID BERNSTEIN, born Norman, Oklahoma, August 17, 1958; admitted to bar, 1983, Oklahoma, U.S. Court of Appeals, Tenth Circuit and U.S. District Court, Eastern and Western Districts of Oklahoma. *Education:* University of Kansas (B.A., 1980); University of Oklahoma (J.D., 1983). Phi Alpha Delta. *Member:* Cleveland County Bar Association; Oklahoma Bar Association; The Association of Trial Lawyers of America; Oklahoma Trial Lawyers Association. ***PRACTICE AREAS:*** Personal Injury; Products Liability; Medical Malpractice; Airplane Crash Litigation; Unsafe Products; Workers Compensation; Nursing Home Abuse; Insurance; Automobile Accidents and Injuries; Dog Bites; Slip and Fall; Wrongful Death.

CROWE & DUNLEVY
A PROFESSIONAL CORPORATION

Established in 1902

2500 SOUTH MCGEE, SUITE 140
NORMAN, OKLAHOMA 73072-6705
Telephone: 405-321-7317
Fax: 405-360-4002
Email: bryantd@crowedunlevy.com
URL: http://www.crowedunlevy.com

Oklahoma City, Oklahoma Office: 20 North Broadway, Suite 1800, 73102-8273. Telephone: 405-235-7700. Fax: 405-239-6651.
Tulsa, Oklahoma Office: 500 Kennedy Building, 321 South Boston Avenue, 74103-3313. Telephone: 918-592-9800. Fax: 918-592-9801.

General Practice. Litigation of all types in both state and federal court. All types of alternative dispute resolution methodologies. Administrative Law, Antitrust, Appellate, Aviation, Bankruptcy and Creditors' Rights, Business Organizations, Commercial Real Estate, Commercial Transactions, Consumer Credit, Corporate and Securities Finance, Environmental, ERISA, Estates and Trusts, Family Law, Financial Institutions and Finance, Franchising and Distribution, Healthcare, Initiative Petition, Insurance Litigation and Regulation, Intellectual Property and Technology, International Business, Labor and Employment, Medicare/Medicaid Fraud and Abuse, Medical Malpractice Defense, Mergers and Acquisitions, Oil and Gas, Oklahoma Corporation Commission, Patent, Trademark, Copyright and Related Matters, Products Liability, Public Finance, School Law, Small Business and Venture Capital, Taxation, White Collar Crime.

FIRM PROFILE: Crowe & Dunlevy, founded in 1902, is the largest and one of the oldest law firms in Oklahoma. The Firm was founded in Oklahoma City and has enjoyed steady and consistent growth, expanding in October of 1989 to include an office in Tulsa and September of 1991 to include an office in Norman. Crowe & Dunlevy is the Oklahoma member of Lex Mundi, an international association of 146 independent law firms, which provides contacts and relationships with leading law firms throughout the world.

Crowe & Dunlevy is organized as a professional corporation and is engaged in most areas of the practice of law. The Firm serves clients ranging from individuals to small businesses to large national and multi-national corporations. The diversity of legal representations within the Firm is underscored by the fact that the Firm's largest client represents less than five percent of its annual fee income.

The Firm is committed to a philosophy of providing on a timely basis high quality legal services to its clients at a reasonable cost. The Firm strives to maintain state of the art library, administrative and other services conducive to the realization of this objective. The Firm has consistently avoided the practice of staffing its cases in a manner in which lawyers provide unnecessary services at unnecessary expense to its clients.

Due to the wide range of experience, the Firm is able to respond to clients with its ability to assemble a legal team with the availability of knowledge and expertise necessary to maximize effective representation. This philosophy encourages timely solutions to client needs in a practical problem-solving environment and at a reasonable cost.

Crowe & Dunlevy is proud to recognize the leadership achievements of its members, both past and present, including: Presidents of the American, Oklahoma, Oklahoma County, Tulsa County and Cleveland County Bar Associations; President of the National Health Lawyers Association; President of the American College of Trial Lawyers; President of the American College of Mortgage Attorneys; Trustee of the United States Supreme Court Historical Society; Chief Judge, United States Court of Appeals, for the 10th Circuit; United States District Judge; Oklahoma Court of Appeals Judge; United States Tax Court Judge; United States Magistrate Judge; United States Attorneys; District Attorneys; United States Ambassador; Deputy Attorney General of the United States; Former Lead and Associate Counsels of the Office of Independent Counsel; Chair of the Murrah Federal Building Memorial Task Force, the Oklahoma City National Memorial Foundation and the Board of Trustees of the Oklahoma City National Memorial Trust; White House Fellow; Deans of the University of Oklahoma College of Law; Mayors; State Representative; Oklahoma Corporation Commissioner; Members of the Boards of Regents for major state universities, and numerous listings in Who's Who in America, Who's Who in American Law, Who's Who in the World and The Best Lawyers in America.

ROBERT L. PENDARVIS, born Barnsdall, Oklahoma, 1929; admitted to bar, 1957, Oklahoma. *Education:* University of Oklahoma (B.A., 1951; LL.B., 1957). Phi Alpha Delta. County Attorney, Cleveland County, Oklahoma, 1960-1961. Adjunct Professor, Political Science, University of Oklahoma, 1971-1973. Recipient: Outstanding Service to Public Award, 1993, Oklahoma Bar Association. Chairman of Family Law Section and Administration of Justice Committee, 1986 and 1990, Board of Governors, 1995, Oklahoma Bar Association. Attorney for Norman Public Schools. Bond Attorney for Norman Public Schools. ***PRACTICE AREAS:*** Civil Litigation; Criminal Litigation; Estate Planning; Probate Administration; School Law. ***Email:*** pendarvr@crowedunlevy.com

GARY C. RAWLINSON, born Champaign, Illinois, 1941; admitted to bar, 1966, Oklahoma. *Education:* University of Oklahoma (B.A., 1963); Cornell University (LL.B., 1966). Adjunct Professor of Law, Business Enterprises, University of Oklahoma College of Law, 1976. Special Lecturer in Law, Corporations and Secured Transactions, University of Oklahoma College of Law, 1978-1981. Past President, Cleveland County Bar Association. Oklahoma Bar Association Award for Outstanding Young Lawyer (1970). *Member:* American College of Real Estate Lawyers. ***PRACTICE AREAS:*** Commercial Law; Real Estate; Estate Planning; Estate Administration. ***Email:*** rawlinsg@crowedunlevy.com

MARY ROBERTSON, born Oklahoma City, Oklahoma, 1958; admitted to bar, 1983, Oklahoma. *Education:* Southern Methodist University (B.S., 1979); University of Oklahoma (J.D., 1983). Phi Delta Phi. Order of the Coif. Member, Oklahoma Law Review, 1982-1983. Lecturer: Current Issues in Debtor/Creditor Law (1997); Consumer Financial Services Law, Regulations and Compliance in the 1990s (1994); Creditor/Debtor Rights (1992-1994); Real Estate Mortgage Law and Finance (1992); Institute on Consumer Financial Services Law (1992); Banking Law Update (1991); Update on Consumer Financial Services (1989). Author: "The 'New and Improved' Real Estate Settlement Procedures Act and Regulation X," Consumer Finance Law Quarterly Report 273 (1993); "Update on the Real Estate Settlement Procedures Act," 45 Consumer Finance Law Quarterly Report 382 (1991). Member, Conference on Consumer Finance Laws. Associate Bar Examiner, Oklahoma Bar Association, 1988—. ***PRACTICE AREAS:*** Business Law; Labor and Employment; Insurance; Commercial Contracts; Business Tort Litigation. ***Email:*** robertsm@crowedunlevy.com

CHRISTOPHER R. GRAVES, born Blackwell, Oklahoma, 1955; admitted to bar, 1992, Oklahoma; 1994, Colorado; U.S. District Court, Northern, Eastern and Western Districts of Oklahoma; U.S. District Court, Northern District of Texas; U.S. Court of Appeals, Fifth and Tenth Circuits. *Education:* University of Oklahoma (B.B.A., 1978; J.D., with highest honors, 1992). Order of the Coif. Phi Delta Phi. *Member:* Oklahoma and Colorado Bar Associations. ***PRACTICE AREAS:*** Litigation; Commercial Real Estate; Commercial Transactions; Probate. ***Email:*** gravesc@crowedunlevy.com

JOHN H. SPARKS, born Dallas, Texas, 1969; admitted to bar, 1994, Oklahoma; 1997, District of Columbia. *Education:* Harvard College (A.B., 1991); University of Oklahoma (J.D., 1994). Phi Delta Phi. Legislative Assistant for Congressman Bill K. Brewster, 1994-1996. *Member:* Cleveland County, Tulsa County, Federal and Oklahoma Bar Associations; The District of Columbia Bar; Oklahoma Association of Defense Counsel (Member, Board of Directors); Defense Research Institute; American Trial Lawyers Association; American Health Lawyers Association. ***PRACTICE AREAS:*** Litigation; Medical Malpractice; Health Care; Insurance; Products Liability. ***Email:*** sparksj@crowedunlevy.com

All lawyers are members of the Cleveland County, Oklahoma and American Bar Associations.

REPRESENTATIVE CLIENTS: Arvest Trust Co., N.A.; Big Red Sports/Imports, Inc.; Bio Cide International, Inc.; Don Cies Real Estate, Inc.; First State Bank, Noble; Harold's Stores, Inc.; Hitachi Computer Products (America), Inc.; Household Automotive Finance Corporation; McSha Properties, Inc.; Monumental Life Insurance Company; Norman Board of Education; Norman Clinic, Inc.; Norman Regional Hospital; Peoples Benefit Life Insurance Company; Saxon Publishers, Inc.

(For complete Client listing and Biographical Data on other Personnel, see Professional Biographies for Crowe & Dunlevy, A Professional Corporation, Oklahoma City and Tulsa)

FLOYD LAW FIRM, P.C.

Established in 1970

118 EAST MAIN STREET
P.O. BOX 396
NORMAN, OKLAHOMA 73070
Telephone: 405-364-6660
Fax: 405-360-5076
Email: floydpc@swbell.net

Municipal and Public Authority Financing. Securities and Corporate Financing Law. Banking Law. Municipal and Local Government Law.

FIRM PROFILE: Floyd Law Firm was founded in 1970 by Glenn Floyd and joined by Lynne Driver and Philip R. Russ in 1994, J. Brent Clark in 1995 and Charles Rainholt in 2002. The firm specializes in municipal finance and works throughout the Southwest in public finance.

GLENN E. FLOYD, born Bakersfield, Missouri, August 16, 1937; admitted to bar, 1967, Oklahoma. *Education:* East Central State College (B.S., 1958); University of Arkansas (M.A., 1961); University of Texas, University of Oklahoma (J.D., 1967); Harvard Law School (LL.M., 1968). Phi Delta Phi; Order of the Coif; Pi Mu Epsilon. Author: Tax-Exempt Municipal Bonds In Oklahoma, 1st Edition, 1972; Tax-Exempt Municipal Bonds—Oklahoma's Use in Industrial Development, Tax-Exempt Municipal Bonds in Oklahoma, 2d Edition, 1978; Tax-Exempt Municipal Bonds in Oklahoma, 4th Edition, 1993. Special Lecturer, University of Oklahoma College of Law, 1969-1971. Member, Oklahoma House of Representatives, 1975-1978. *Member:* Cleveland County, Oklahoma and American Bar Associations; National Association of Bond Lawyers (Charter Member). Fellow, American College of Bond Counsel. ***PRACTICE AREAS:*** Municipal/Public Authority Financing; Corporate; Banking.

B. LYNNE DRIVER, born Wynnewood, Oklahoma, February 23, 1958; admitted to bar, 1994, Oklahoma. *Education:* University of Oklahoma (B.S., 1980); Oxford University, England (Law Study, 1992); University of Oklahoma (J.D., 1993); Southern Methodist University (LL.M., Taxation, 1995). Phi Delta Phi; Distinguished Graduate. Recipient: American Jurisprudence Awards; Hardin Ballard Outstanding Appellate Advocacy Student. Teaching Assistant, 1992-1993, and Research and Writing Assistant, 1993, University of

(This Listing Continued)

FLOYD LAW FIRM, P.C., Norman—Continued

Oklahoma College of Law. *Member:* Cleveland County, Oklahoma and American Bar Associations; State Bar of Texas; National Association of Bond Lawyers. ***PRACTICE AREAS:*** Municipal/Public Authority Financing; Taxation Law.

J. BRENT CLARK, born Holdenville, Oklahoma, November 25, 1948; admitted to bar, 1975, Oklahoma; 1983, New York, U.S. Supreme Court, U.S. Court of Appeals, 10th Circuit and U.S. District Court, Western, Eastern and Northern Districts of Oklahoma; 1993, Missouri. *Education:* University of Oklahoma (B.A., with honors, 1971; J.D., 1975); Oxford University (1971). Phi Beta Kappa. Author: 3rd Down & Forever (St. Martin's Press) and Sooner Century (Quality Sports Publications). *Member:* Oklahoma, New York State and American Bar Associations; The Missouri Bar; National Association of Bond Lawyers. ***PRACTICE AREAS:*** Public Finance; Taxation; Business Law.

JEFF F. RALEY, born Ancon, Panama, May 3, 1947; admitted to bar, 1972, Oklahoma; U.S. District Court, Western District of Oklahoma; U.S. Court of Appeals, Tenth Circuit. *Education:* University of Oklahoma (B.S., 1969; J.D., 1972). Kay County Assistant District Attorney, 1972-1974. Blackwell City Attorney, 1975-1987. Norman City Attorney, 1987-2004. Appointed Judge, Court of Appeals, Temporary Division No. 74. Served on: Board of Trustees, Oklahoma Bar Foundation; Board of Directors, Oklahoma Municipal Power Authority and Oklahoma Municipal Attorney's Association. *Member:* Cleveland County, Oklahoma and American Bar Associations. ***PRACTICE AREAS:*** Public Finance; Municipal Law; Civil. **Email:** floydpc@swbell.net

OF COUNSEL

CHARLES P. RAINBOLT, born Cordell, Oklahoma, June 27, 1948; admitted to bar, 1974, Oklahoma; 1977, U.S. District Court, Western District of Oklahoma; 1990, U.S. Supreme Court. *Education:* University of Oklahoma (B.A., 1970; J.D., 1973). Member, Board of Bar Examiners, 1989—. State Director, USDA Rural Development (formerly Farmers Home Administration), 1993-2001). ***PRACTICE AREAS:*** Municipal Law; Public Finance. **Email:** floydpc@swbell.net

PHILIP R. RUSS, born Wheeler, Texas, June 2, 1943; admitted to bar, 1967, Oklahoma and Texas; 1968, U.S. Supreme Court; 1974, U.S. Court of Appeals, Third, Fifth, Sixth, Tenth and Eleventh Circuits; U.S. District Court, Northern and Southern Districts of Texas and U.S. District Court, Western District of Oklahoma. *Education:* Texas Technological College (B.A., 1964); University of Oklahoma (J.D., 1967). Phi Alpha Delta. *Member:* Amarillo and Oklahoma Bar Associations; State Bar of Texas; Texas Trial Lawyers Association. (Also Practicing Individually, Amarillo, Texas). ***PRACTICE AREAS:*** Municipal Law; Public Finance; Business Law.

REPRESENTATIVE CLIENTS: Bank of Oklahoma; Bank One Capital Markets, Inc.; George K. Baum & Company, Inc.; Crews & Associates, Inc.; Kirkpatrick Pettis; J.C. Bradford & Co.; A.G. Edwards & Sons, Inc.; Fahnestock & Co., Inc.; Kirchner, Moore & Co.; Lawson Financial Corporation; Morgan Keegan & Co.; Leo Oppenheim & Co.; Rauscher Pierce Refsnes, Inc.; Stephens, Inc.; Canadian County Home Finance Authority; Cleveland County Home Loan Authority; Oklahoma Capitol Improvement Authority; Oklahoma Department of Human Services; Oklahoma Housing Finance Agency; Oklahoma Development Finance Authority; Oklahoma Industrial Finance Authority; Oklahoma State University; Rural Enterprises of Oklahoma, Inc.; University of Central Oklahoma; University of Oklahoma.
REFERENCES: BancFirst Oklahoma City, Oklahoma; University of Oklahoma, Norman.

HENRICKSEN & HENRICKSEN LAWYERS, INC.

NORMAN, OKLAHOMA

(See El Reno)

General Civil and Criminal Trial Practice State and Federal Courts, Banking, Bankruptcy, Family, Probate and Personal Injury Law, Criminal Law, Constitutional Law.

ROBERT HIGHSAW

NORMAN, OKLAHOMA

(See Oklahoma City)

Workers Compensation, Federal Workers Compensation, Workers Compensation Appeals, Workers Compensation Defense, Workers Compensation Self-Insurance, Workers Compensation Subrogation, Immigration and Naturalization, Business Immigration, Citizenship, Consular Law, Deportation, Diplomatic Immunity, Employment Authorization, Employment Immigration, Employment Visas, Family Immigration Law, Immigration Discrimination, Immigration Law, Investor Visas, Labor Certifications, Permanent Visas, Political Asylum, Refugee Law, Religious Visas, Visas, Social Security, Social Security Appeals, Social Security Disability, Social Security Disability Insurance, Supplemental Security Income, Administrative Law, Longshore and Harbor Workers Compensation.

JOHNSTON & ASSOCIATES

NORMAN, OKLAHOMA

(See Chickasha)

General Practice, Environmental Law. including Land Use, Landowners Rights Wills and Probate.

KOOP & MEDLEY

NORMAN, OKLAHOMA

(See Oklahoma City)

Litigation, Negligence, Products Liability.

JIM LOFTIS P.C.

225 NORTH PETERS
NORMAN, OKLAHOMA 73069
Telephone: 405-366-1400
Fax: 405-366-0041
Email: jimloftis@coxinet.net
URL: http://www.lawyers.com/loftislaw

Personal Injury, Medical Malpractice, Products Liability, Workers Compensation.

JIM D. LOFTIS, born Ardmore, Oklahoma, November 30, 1958; admitted to bar, 1988, Missouri; 1990, Oklahoma; U.S. District of Court, Western, Eastern and Northern Districts of Oklahoma; U.S. Court of Appeals, Tenth Circuit. *Education:* Southeastern Oklahoma State University (B.S., 1984); University of Oklahoma (J.D., 1988). Adjunct Professor, Civil Pretrial Litigation, University of Oklahoma College of Law. *Member:* Cleveland County (Past President) and Oklahoma Bar Associations; The Missouri Bar; Oklahoma Trial Lawyers Association (President, 2003); The Association of Trial Lawyers of America. ***PRACTICE AREAS:*** Personal Injury; Medical Malpractice; Products Liability; Workers Compensation.

McBRIDE LAW FIRM

NORMAN, OKLAHOMA

(See Oklahoma City)

Criminal Law, DUI, Drug Crimes, Felonies, Misdemeanors, Personal Injury, Automobile Accidents, Trucking Accidents, Wrongful Death, Family Law, Divorce, Child Custody.

McCOY LAW FIRM

NORMAN, OKLAHOMA

(See Oklahoma City)

Criminal Trials and Appeals, Civil Rights Litigation and Appeals, Civil Litigation and Appeals, Habeas Corpus Litigation, Stock Market Arbitration.

NASH, COHENOUR & KELLEY, P.C.

NORMAN, OKLAHOMA

(See Oklahoma City)

Commercial and Bankruptcy Law (Creditors only). Civil Litigation, Insurance Defense, Real Property, Foreclosures, Corporations, Partnerships, Fiduciary and Trust Litigation, Collections, Estate Planning and Probate, Trusts, Federal and State Taxation Law.

PARSONS & ASSOCIATES LAW FIRM

A CORPORATION

227 EAST GRAY STREET
P.O. BOX 1265
NORMAN, OKLAHOMA 73070-1265
Telephone: 405-321-7887
Fax: 405-321-7715
URL: http://www.lawyers.com/parsonsassociates

Banking Litigation, Business Litigation, Business Torts, Commercial Collections, Commercial Litigation, Corporate Contracts, Creditors Rights, Lawsuits, Lender Liability, Internet Violations, Oklahoma Lottery, Employer Defense and Trial Practice in All Courts.

RANDY A. PARSONS, born Fulton, New York, July 10, 1953; admitted to bar, 1988, Oklahoma. *Education:* New York University (B.A., 1975); Oklahoma City University (J.D., 1988). Phi Delta Phi. *Member:* Cleveland County, Oklahoma County, Oklahoma and American (Member, Sections on: Business Law and Litigation) Bar Associations. ***PRACTICE AREAS:*** Banking Litigation; Business Torts; Commercial Collections; Commercial Litigation; Corporate Contracts; Creditors Rights.

REPRESENTATIVE CLIENTS: Coppermark Bank; Hill & Company; Republic Bank of Norman; First Fidelity Bank; Service Experts Corporation; Arvest Bank; Redbud Glass Company.

PITCHLYNN & ASSOCIATES, P.A.

124 EAST MAIN STREET
P.O. BOX 427
NORMAN, OKLAHOMA 73070
Telephone: 405-360-9600
Fax: 405-447-4219
URL: http://www.pitchlynnlaw.com

Indian Gaming Law, Business and Corporate Law, Insurance Litigation, Criminal Defense, General Litigation.

PATRICK A. MORSE (1956-2004)

GARY S. PITCHLYNN, born Wewoka, Oklahoma, November 16, 1947; admitted to bar, 1977, Oklahoma; U.S. District Court, Eastern, Northern and Western Districts of Oklahoma; U.S. Court of Appeals, Tenth Circuit and U.S. Supreme Court. *Education:* University of Oklahoma (B.A., Journalism, 1972); Oklahoma City University School of Law (J.D., 1977). Member, American Indian Chamber of Commerce. *Member:* Cleveland County and Oklahoma Bar Associations; Muscogee (Creek) Nation Bar Association. Fellow, Oklahoma Bar Foundation. ***PRACTICE AREAS:*** Indian Gaming Law; Business Law; Corporate Law; Insurance Litigation; Criminal Defense; Litigation. **Email:** gpitchlynn@pitchlynnlaw.com

(This Listing Continued)

O. JOSEPH WILLIAMS, born Claremore, Oklahoma, February 27, 1975; admitted to bar, 2001, Oklahoma; U.S. District Court, Eastern, Northern and Western Districts of Oklahoma; U.S Court of Appeals, Tenth Circuit and U.S. Supreme Court. *Education:* Murray State College (A.A.S., 1994); Southeastern Oklahoma State University (B.S., 1995); Oklahoma City University (M.B.A., 1998; J.D., 2001). Delta Mu Delta-Theta Mu Chapter; Phi Delta Phi. Member, American Indian Chamber of Commerce of Oklahoma. *Member:* Cleveland County, Oklahoma and Federal Bar Associations; Muscogee (Creek) Nation Bar Association; Oklahoma Indian Bar Association; Lutheran Bannon Inn of Court. ***PRACTICE AREAS:*** Indian Gaming Law; Business Law; Corporate Law; Insurance Litigation; Criminal Defense; Litigation. ***Email:*** jwilliams@pitchlynnlaw.com

DAVID MORSE, born Sallisaw, Oklahoma, January 15, 1952; admitted to bar, 1979, Oklahoma; U.S. District Court, Eastern and Western Districts of Oklahoma; U.S Court of Appeals, Tenth Circuit and U.S. Supreme Court. *Education:* University of Oklahoma (B.A., 1976; J.D., 1979). *Member:* Cleveland County and Oklahoma Bar Associations. Fellow, Oklahoma Bar Foundation. ***PRACTICE AREAS:*** Real Estate; Labor and Employment; Personal Injury; Criminal Law; Litigation; Oil and Gas Law. ***Email:*** dmorse@pitchlynnlaw.com

RESIDES & RESIDES, PLLC

NORMAN, OKLAHOMA

(See Oklahoma City)

General Practice.

SALEM LAW OFFICES

111 NORTH PETERS, SUITE 100
NORMAN, OKLAHOMA 73069-7235
Telephone: 405-366-1234
Fax: 405-366-8329; 405-"FON-UFAX"
Email: mcsalem@swbell.net

Constitutional Law and Civil Rights, General Civil, Criminal Trial and Appellate Practice. State and Federal Courts. Personal Injury, Product Safety, Domestic Relations, Guardianship, Probate Law.

MICHEAL C. SALEM, born Cushing, Oklahoma, June 29, 1949; admitted to bar, 1975, Oklahoma; U.S. Supreme Court; U.S. Court of Appeals, Tenth Circuit; U.S. District Court, Western District of Oklahoma; Tribal Court of Indian Offenses, Anadarko Area Office. *Education:* University of Oklahoma (B.S., Electrical Engineering, 1971; M. Public Administration, 1975; J.D., 1975). Recipient: Solo Practitioner of the Year Award, General Practice, Solo, and Small Firm Section, American Bar Association, 2001-2002; Oklahoma Courageous Advocacy Award, Oklahoma Bar Association, 1984; Angie Debo Civil Liberties Award, ACLU Oklahoma, 1983; Angie Debo Civil Liberties Award, ACLU Oklahoma, 1996; Meritorious Volunteer Services, ACLU, 1982; Nominee, Community Interest Award, The Law and You Foundation, 1994; Golden Gavel Award, Oklahoma Bar Association, 1996. Listed in: Fifth and Ninth Edition, Marquis, Who's Who in American Law. Member, Judicial Conference of the Tenth Circuit of the United States. *Member:* Cleveland County (President, 1988-1989; Editor, Cleveland County Bar Flyer Newsletter, 1987-1991), Oklahoma (Member, House of Delegates, 1988—; Committee Member, Client Security Fund, 1990—; Chairman, 1996-1997 and 1999-2000; Vice-Chair, 1997-1998) and American Bar Associations; Oklahoma Trial Lawyers Association; The Association of Trial Lawyers of America; Oklahoma Criminal Defense Lawyers Association. Sustaining Fellow, Oklahoma Bar Foundation. ***PRACTICE AREAS:*** Constitutional Law; Civil Rights; General Practice; Criminal Law; Appellate Practice; Personal Injury; Product Safety; Domestic Relations; Guardianship; Probate.

B. DAVID SISSON

Established in 1990
OLD TOWNE SQUARE
224 WEST GRAY, SUITE 202
P.O. BOX 534
NORMAN, OKLAHOMA 73070-0534
Telephone: 405-447-2521
Fax: 405-447-2552
URL: http://www.lawyers.com/sissonlawoffice
Email: sisson@sissonlawoffice.com
URL: http://www.sissonlawoffice.com

Bankruptcy, Domestic, Probate and Estate Planning, Family Law, Divorce, Child Custody Modifications.

B. DAVID SISSON, born Oklahoma City, Oklahoma, February 25, 1951; admitted to bar, 1990, Oklahoma, U.S. District Court, Western and Eastern Districts of Oklahoma and U.S. Tax Court; 2000, U.S. Court of Appeals, Tenth Circuit. *Education:* Central State University (B.M., summa cum laude, 1973); University of Oklahoma (J.D.,1990). Phi Delta Phi. National Registry of Who's Who. *Member:* Cleveland County, Oklahoma (Member, Sections on Family Law, Probate, Bankruptcy & Reorganization, Tax) and American Bar Associations; American Bankruptcy Institute; National Association of Consumer Bankruptcy Attorneys. ***REPORTED CASES:*** Baptist Medical Center of Oklahoma v. Aguirre, 930 P.2d 213 (1996); 1999 WL 259619 (Okla.) In re Alexander 1999 OK 31. ***PRACTICE AREAS:*** Bankruptcy; Family Law; Probate & Estate Planning.

SMITH LAW OFFICE, P.C.

104 EAST EUFAULA
NORMAN, OKLAHOMA 73069
Telephone: 405-360-2660
Fax: 405-360-6702
Email: djsmithlaw@aol.com
URL: http://www.dougsmithlaw.com

Criminal, Personal Injury, Family Law, Driving While Intoxicated, Traffic Violations, Automobile Accidents, Divorce, Child Custody.

DOUGLAS J. SMITH, born North Platte, Nebraska, June 27, 1961; admitted to bar, 1990, Oklahoma and U.S. District Court, Western District of Oklahoma. *Education:* Oklahoma Wesleyan University (B.S., 1985); University of Oklahoma (J.D., 1990). *Member:* Oklahoma Bar Association. ***PRACTICE AREAS:*** Criminal Law; Personal Injury; Family Law; Drugs and Narcotics; White Collar Crime.

STOCKWELL LAW OFFICES

A PROFESSIONAL CORPORATION

Established in 1963
119 EAST MAIN STREET
P.O. BOX 519
NORMAN, OKLAHOMA 73070
Telephone: 405-321-9414
Fax: 405-321-9416
Toll Free: 800-360-9414
Email: stockwelllaw@stockwelllaw.com
URL: http://www.stockwelllaw.com

Personal Injury, Family Law, Criminal, Wills and Probate, Expungement Law, DUI Defense, Drivers License Revocation, Elder Law.

BENJAMIN E. STOCKWELL (1931-1990)

PEGGY STOCKWELL, born Oklahoma City, Oklahoma, October 13, 1954; admitted to bar, 1983, Oklahoma; 1985, Florida; U.S. Court of Appeals, Tenth Circuit; U.S. District Court, Northern, Eastern and Western Districts of Oklahoma. *Education:* University of Oklahoma (B.A., English, 1978; J.D., 1983). Phi Delta Phi; Order of the Coif. *Member:* Cleveland County (Vice President, 1998-1999; President Elect, 1999-2000; President, 2000-2001), Oklahoma (Member: Family Law Section; Professional Tribunal; Co-Chair, Disaster Relief Committee, 2003) and American (Member, Family Law Section) Bar Associations; The Florida Bar. ***Email:*** peggy@stockwelllaw.com

DAVE STOCKWELL, born Oklahoma City, Oklahoma, June 3, 1956; admitted to bar, 1989, Oklahoma and U.S. District Court, Western District of Oklahoma. *Education:* University of Oklahoma (B.S., 1979; J.D., 1989). Phi Delta Phi. Recipient, American Jurisprudence Award, Torts II, 1987. Listed, Who's Who Among American Law Students, 1988-1989. *Member:* Cleveland County (Team Member, Drug Court; Chairman: Community Sentencing Planning Council, 1998-2003; Law Day, 1991; Secretary/Treasurer, 1991-1992; Vice President, 1992-1993; President-Elect, 1993-1994; President, 1994-1995), Oklahoma (Member, Board of Directors, Young Lawyers Division, 1991; Vice-Chair, Community Law Week Committee, 1990; Disaster Legal Assistance Committee, 1990; Issues Affecting the Legal Profession Committee, 1990; Task Force: Law Practice Management; Vice-Chairperson, Law Office Management Assistance Committee, 1997, 1998 Chairman, Management Assistance Program, 1999-2000; Co-Chair, Disaster Relief Committee, 2003) and American Bar Associations; ATLA; Oklahoma Trial Lawyers Association (Member, Advisory Board); Oklahoma Criminal Defense Lawyers Association; The National College for DUI Defense. ***Email:*** dave@stockwelllaw.com

REFERENCES: City National Bank and Trust Co., Norman; Interactive Communications, Norman.

TAWWATER & SLAMA, LLP

NORMAN, OKLAHOMA

(See Oklahoma City)

Civil Trial Practice. Negligence, Products Liability, Medical Malpractice, Insurance Bad Faith, Personal Injury, Wrongful Death, HMO Law, Nursing Home Negligence, Automobile Accidents, Construction Injuries, Pharmaceutical Litigation, Mass Torts, Class Action Torts.

MARY A. TRAVIS
ATTORNEY AT LAW

NORMAN, OKLAHOMA

(See Oklahoma City)

Bankruptcy, Family Law, Criminal Law and Insurance.

KEVIN "D" WATLEY

SUITE 202-A, 224 WEST GRAY STREET
P.O. BOX 1304
NORMAN, OKLAHOMA 73070-1304
Telephone: 405-321-5858

Federal Income, Estate and Gift Taxation, Federal and State Tax Representation and Litigation, Estate Planning, Probate and Trusts Law.

FIRM PROFILE: Mr. Watley is listed in the Bar Register of Preeminent Lawyers.

(This Listing Continued)

KEVIN "D" WATLEY, Norman—Continued

KEVIN "D" WATLEY, born Lincoln, Nebraska, 1955; admitted to bar, 1981, Oklahoma, U.S. Tax Court and U.S. Claims Court; 1982, Nebraska, U.S. District Court, Western District of Oklahoma and U.S. Court of Appeals, Tenth Circuit; 1985, U.S. Supreme Court; 1989, U.S. District Court, Eastern District of Oklahoma. *Education:* University of Oklahoma (B.Ac., 1977; M.B.A., 1981; J.D., 1981). Beta Gamma Sigma. Certified Public Accountant, Oklahoma, 1978. Author: "The Tax Man Cometh," Oklahoma Bar Journal, 1982. Visiting Lecturer of Accounting, University of Oklahoma, 1983-1989, 1992-1995. Municipal Judge, Hall Park, Cleveland County, 1985-1987, 1990-1993. *Member:* Oklahoma and Nebraska State and American Bar Associations; American Institute of Certified Public Accountants; Oklahoma Society of Certified Public Accountants; Oklahoma Criminal Defense Lawyers Association (Treasurer, 1985-1999). ***SPECIAL AGENCIES:*** Internal Revenue Service; Oklahoma Tax Commission.

RODNEY D. WATSON & ASSOCIATES, P.C.

THE REPUBLIC BUILDING
401 WEST MAIN, SUITE 310
NORMAN, OKLAHOMA 73069
Telephone: 405-364-9480
Facsimile: 405-364-0425
Email: rwatson@rodneywatsonassociates.com
URL: http://www.rodneywatsonassociates.com

Slip and Fall, Sex Crimes, Discrimination, Personal Injury, Family Law, Civil Litigation, Criminal Litigation, Automobile Accidents, DUI, Trucking Accidents, Medical Malpractice, Family, Divorce, Child Custody, Visitation Rights, Dog Bites, Adoption Law, Wills, Trust Law, Estate Planning.

RODNEY D. WATSON, born Altus, Oklahoma, August 20, 1953; admitted to bar, 1983, Oklahoma; U.S. District Court, Western District of Oklahoma; U.S. Bankruptcy Court for the Western District of Oklahoma and U.S. Supreme Court. *Education:* United States Air Force Academy; University of Oklahoma (B.A., Political Science, 1975; J.D., 1983). Phi Alpha Delta. *Member:* Cleveland County, Oklahoma and American Bar Associations. [U.S. Navy, 1980-1981]

ALISON A. PETRONE, born Henryetta, Oklahoma, march 26, 1978; admitted to bar, 2003, Oklahoma and U.S. District Court, Western District of Oklahoma. *Education:* University of Oklahoma (B.A., 2000; J.D., 2003).

WILLIAM E. WOODSON, PLLC

307 EAST EUFAULA STREET
NORMAN, OKLAHOMA 73069
Telephone: 405-360-1222
Fax: 405-360-1269

Practice includes Personal Injury, Medical Malpractice, Products Liability, Workers Compensation, Litigation State and Federal Courts.

WILLIAM E. WOODSON, born Oklahoma City, Oklahoma, May 3, 1945; admitted to bar, 1971, Oklahoma and U.S. District Court, Northern District of Oklahoma; 1973, U.S. District Court, Western District of Oklahoma; 1982, U.S. Court of Appeals, Tenth Circuit. *Education:* Central State University (B.A., 1968); University of Tulsa (J.D., 1970). Delta Theta Phi. Member, City Council, Norman, Oklahoma, 1974-1976. *Member:* Cleveland County (President, 1979-1980), Oklahoma and American Bar Associations; Oklahoma Trial Lawyers Association (Member, Board of Directors; Ex-Officio Area Council Representative, District 4, 1989—; Chairman, Judicial Nominating Commission); The Association of Trial Lawyers of America (Sustaining Member). ***PRACTICE AREAS:*** Personal Injury; Medical Malpractice; Products Liability; Workers Compensation. ***Email:*** wwoodson@sbcglobal.net

LOGAN & LOWRY, LLP

NOWATA, OKLAHOMA

(See Vinita)

General Practice, Including Trials in all State and Federal Courts, Eminent Domain, Environmental and Coal, Banking, Commercial Transactions, Creditors' Rights and Bankruptcy, Corporation, Public Utility, Real Estate, Estate Planning and Probate, Criminal, Domestic Relations, Civil Rights, Employment, Appellate Practice and Administrative Law.

ABEL, MUSSER, SOKOLOSKY, MARES & KOURI

Established in 1976

ONE LEADERSHIP SQUARE, SUITE 600
211 NORTH ROBINSON
OKLAHOMA CITY, OKLAHOMA 73102
Telephone: 405-239-7046
Fax: 405-272-1090
Email: contactus@abelmusser.com
URL: http://www.abellawfirm.com

General Civil and Criminal Practice in all Courts. Personal Injury. Family. Workers Compensation. Products Liability Law. Trials. Medical Malpractice, Insurance Litigation, Automobile Accidents, Insurance Bad Faith.

(This Listing Continued)

ED ABEL, born Okemah, Oklahoma, February 1, 1942; admitted to bar, 1966, Oklahoma. *Education:* University of Oklahoma (B.A., 1963; J.D., 1966). Delta Sigma Rho; Phi Delta Phi; Order of the Coif; Order of the Barristers. Member: Oklahoma Law Review, 1966. Recipient: Earl Sneed Award, 1985 and 2001; Outstanding Continuing Legal Education Contribution; Leo H. Whinery Distinguished Service Award for Outstanding Contributions to the Oklahoma Law of Evidence, 2000. Co-Author: Oklahoma Evidence Code; Oklahoma Pleading Code. *Member:* Oklahoma County (Member, Civil Justice Reform Act (1990) Advisory Group of the United States District Court, Western District of Oklahoma; Chairman, Early Intervention Subcommittee; Leader and Promoter in Development of the Early Neutral Evaluation Program), Oklahoma (Chairman, Civil Code Procedure Committee; Member, Civil Code Procedure Committee) and American (Member, Negligence and Insurance Sections) Bar Associations; Oklahoma Trial Lawyers Association (Member, Board of Governors; Past President; Chairman, Key Man Committee; Member, Legislative and Executive Committees; Active in Speakers' Bureau); The Association of Trial Lawyers of America (Member, Former State Committeeman; Former Second National Vice-Chairman State Committeemen; Former First National Vice-Chairman State Committeemen; Former National Chairman State Committeemen; Former Member, Executive Committee; Former Mid-West Regional Task Force Coordinator; Former Member, Board of Governors); American Board of Trial Advocates; Texas Trial Lawyers Association. ***REPORTED CASES:*** Messler v. Simmons, Gun Specialties Inc. (Okla.); Townsend v. State Farm (Okla.); Phillips v. State Farm (10th Cir.); Riley v. Brown & Root (Okla.); Anderson v. Eichner (Okla.); Brown v. Alliance Real Estate Group (Okla). ***PRACTICE AREAS:*** Personal Injury Litigation; Product Liability Litigation; Negligence Litigation; Medical Negligence Litigation. ***Email:*** edabel@abelmusser.com

SIDNEY A. MUSSER, JR., born Oklahoma City, Oklahoma, August 7, 1940; admitted to bar, 1969, Oklahoma. *Education:* University of Oklahoma (B.A., 1966; J.D., 1969). Phi Alpha Delta. *Member:* Oklahoma County and Oklahoma Bar Associations; Oklahoma Trial Lawyers Association (Member, Board of Directors, 1976-1983); The Association of Trial Lawyers of America. ***PRACTICE AREAS:*** Workers Compensation Law; Personal Injury Law. ***Email:*** sid@musserandkourilaw.com

JERRY D. SOKOLOSKY, born Oklahoma City, Oklahoma, April 12, 1937; admitted to bar, 1962, Oklahoma. *Education:* Oklahoma University (B.B.A., 1959; LL.B., 1962). Co-author: "An Overview of Libel in Oklahoma," Oklahoma Bar Journal, Vol. 50-No. 38, 1979. Member, Oklahoma House of Representatives, 1964-1968. General Counsel: Oklahoma Press Association, 1972—; Oklahoma Real Estate Commission, 1976—. *Member:* Oklahoma Bar Association.

LYNN BRUSIN MARES, born Stockton, California, March 27, 1945; admitted to bar, 1985, Oklahoma; U.S. District Court, Western, Eastern and Northern Districts of Oklahoma; U.S. Court of Appeals, Tenth Circuit; U.S. Supreme Court. *Education:* University of Albuquerque (B.S., summa cum laude, 1967); University of Oklahoma (J.D., 1985). Recipient: 1993 Outstanding Service Award, Law & You Foundation; Mona Lambird Service to Children Award, Oklahoma Lawyers for Children. Adjunct Professor of Law, University of Oklahoma Legal Assistant Program. Member, Board of Directors, Oklahoma Lawyers for Children. Trustee and Editor, Law & You Foundation, 1990-1996. *Member:* Oklahoma (Member, Legal Assistant Services Committee) and Federal Bar Associations; Oklahoma Trial Lawyers Association; The Association of Trial Lawyers of America. ***LANGUAGES:*** Spanish. ***REPORTED CASES:*** Riley v. Brown & Root (Okla. & 10th Cir.); Townsend v. State Farm (Okla.); Anderson v. Eichner (Okla.); Phillips v. State Farm (10th. Cir.); Brown v. Alliance Real Estate Group (Okla.); Abel v. Madden (Okla.); Ross v. Peters (Okla.); Simpson v. City of Muskogee (Okla. App.); Walden v. Sparkman Bros. Corp (Okla. App.); Reynolds v. Union Public Schools (Okla. App.); Allen v. Lynn Hickey Dodge (Okla.); Herren v. Farm Bureau Mutual Ins. Co. (Okla. App.); Allenberg v. Bentley Hedges Travel Services Inc. (Okla.); Watford v. West (Okla.). ***PRACTICE AREAS:*** Personal Injury Law; Insurance Litigation; Products Liability. ***Email:*** lynnbmares@abelmusser.com

HARRY J. (TREY) KOURI, III, born Wichita, Kansas, May 4, 1965; admitted to bar, 1990, Oklahoma and U. S. District Court, Western, Northern and Eastern Districts of Oklahoma. *Education:* Kansas University (B.S.B., 1987); Oklahoma City University (J.D., 1989). Recipient, American Jurisprudence Award in Trial Practice. *Member:* Oklahoma County, Oklahoma and American Bar Associations; Oklahoma Trial Lawyers Association; The Trial Lawyers for Public Justice; American Trial Lawyers Association. ***PRACTICE AREAS:*** Workers Compensation; Personal Injury. ***Email:*** trey@musserandkourilaw.com

ASSOCIATES

KELLY S. BISHOP, born Oklahoma City, Oklahoma, September 8, 1965; admitted to bar, 1993, Oklahoma; U.S. District Court, Western, Eastern and Northern Districts of Oklahoma; U.S. Supreme Court. *Education:* Oklahoma State University (B.S., 1987); University of Oklahoma (J.D., 1993). Phi Kappa Phi; Phi Delta Phi. *Member:* Oklahoma County, Oklahoma and American Bar Associations; The Association of Trial Lawyers of America; Oklahoma Trial Lawyers Association (Member, Advisory Board, 1999—); American Inns of Court. ***PRACTICE AREAS:*** Personal Injury Law; Medical Negligence; Products Liability; Insurance Litigation. ***Email:*** kbishop@abelmusser.com

BARRY R. DAVIS, born Havre De Grace, Maryland, April 5, 1949; admitted to bar, 1975, Oklahoma; 1977, U.S. District Court, Western District of Oklahoma; 1979, U.S. Court of Appeals, Tenth Circuit. *Education:* University of Oklahoma (B.A., 1971); Oklahoma City University (J.D., 1975). Phi Delta Phi. Arbitrator, U.S. District Court, Western District of Oklahoma, 1985—. *Member:* Oklahoma County and Oklahoma Bar Associations. ***PRACTICE AREAS:*** Insurance Litigation; Commercial Litigation; Mediation; Arbitration. ***Email:*** barrydavis@brdavis.com

STEVEN T. HORTON, born Shawnee, Oklahoma, September 14, 1966; admitted to bar, 1992, Oklahoma and U.S. District Court, Western, Northern and Eastern Districts of Oklahoma; U.S. Supreme Court. *Education:* Oklahoma State University (B.S., 1989); University of Oklahoma (J.D., 1992). Phi Delta Phi. Member, Luther Bohanon American Inns of Court, 1997—; Oklahoma Association of Defense Counsel, 1992-1998. *Member:* Oklahoma County, Oklahoma and American Bar Associations; Oklahoma Trial Lawyers Association. ***PRACTICE AREAS:*** Personal Injury; Medical Negligence; Products Liability; Insurance Law. ***Email:*** shorton@abelmusser.com

(This Listing Continued)

BRENT L. NEIGHBORS, born Whiteman Air Force Base, Missouri, April 26, 1968; admitted to bar, 1994, Oklahoma and U.S. District Court, Western and Eastern Districts of Oklahoma. *Education:* Baylor University (B.A., 1990); Oklahoma City University (J.D., 1994). Member, Moot Court Board (Vice-President, 1993). *Member:* Oklahoma County, Oklahoma and American Bar Associations; Association of Trial Lawyers of America; Oklahoma Trial Lawyers Association. ***PRACTICE AREAS:*** Personal Injury; Medical Negligence; Products Liability; Insurance Law. ***Email:*** bneighbors@abelmusser.com

LYNNE C. ZACCARIA, born Bryn Mawr, Pennsylvania, November 18, 1958; admitted to bar, 2000, Oklahoma and U.S. District Court, Western, Eastern and Northern Districts of Oklahoma; U.S. Supreme Court. *Education:* Villanova University (B.S.N., 1980; M.S.N., 1991); University of Oklahoma (J.D., with distinction, 2000). Phi Delta Phi. Recipient: Graduate Achievement Award for Academic Excellence and Leadership in Nursing, 1990; Bausch and Lomb Science Award, 1976; American Jurisprudence Awards in Managed Health care, 1999, and Law and Cyberspace, 2000. Registered Nurse, Pennsylvania, 1980 and Oklahoma, 1991—. Member, Pennsylvania State Nurses Association, 1980-1991. *Member:* Oklahoma Bar Association (Member, Health Law Section); American Bar Association; The Association of Trial Lawyers of America; Oklahoma Trial Lawyers Association; American Society of Law, Medicine and Ethics; American Health Lawyers Association; Oklahoma Nurses Association; Oklahoma Lawyers for Children; Oklahoma Association of Mediators and Arbitrators. ***PRACTICE AREAS:*** Medical Negligence Litigation; Health Law; Personal Injury; Insurance Law; Products Liability; Civil Family Law Mediation. ***Email:*** lzaccaria@abelmusser.com

OF COUNSEL

JOHN A. ALBERTS, born Oklahoma City, Oklahoma, November 3, 1964; admitted to bar, 1990, Oklahoma. *Education:* Oklahoma State University (B.S., 1987); Oklahoma City University (J.D., 1990). Mock Trial Judge, 1997-1998. Kay County District Attorneys Office, 1990-1994. Secretary, Kay County Bar Association, 1994. *Member:* Canadian County and Oklahoma County (Member, Young Lawyers Division, Liaison for Law Related Services for the Underprivileged Committee, 1992; Young Lawyer Liaison Criminal Law Committee, 1994; Director-at-Large, 1992-1994) Bar Associations. ***PRACTICE AREAS:*** Criminal Law; Family Law; Driving While Intoxicated; Personal Injury; General Practice. ***Email:*** alberts239704@msn.com

WARNER E. LOVELL, JR., born Fort Worth, Texas, April 12, 1944; admitted to bar, 1970, Oklahoma. *Education:* University of Oklahoma (B.A., 1966; J.D., 1970). Phi Alpha Delta. *Member:* Oklahoma County, Oklahoma (Member, Family Law Section) and American Bar Associations; Oklahoma Trial Lawyers Association. ***PRACTICE AREAS:*** Family Law; Insurance Bad Faith; Personal Injury Law.

LEO H. WHINERY, born Kansas City, Kansas, September 20, 1926; admitted to bar, 1951, Missouri; 1962, Oklahoma; 1979, U.S. Supreme Court; 1980, U.S. District Court, Western District of Oklahoma and U.S. Court of Appeals, Tenth Circuit. *Education:* University of Missouri (A.B., 1949; LL.B., 1951); Columbia University (LL.M., 1955). Phi Alpha Delta (Justice, Benton Chapter, 1950-1951); Order of the Coif. Editor-in-Chief, University of Missouri, Kansas City Law Review, 1950-1951. Edwin H. Armstrong Fellow, Columbia University Law School, 1954-1955. Author: "Manual of Evidence," Oklahoma Highway Safety Program, 1973; "Predictive Sentencing; An Empirical Evaluation," Lexington Books, D.C. Heath & Co., 1976; "Commentary to Oklahoma Evidence Code," West Publishing Co., 12 Oklahoma Statutes Annotated §§2101 et seq., 1978; "Readings on Evidence: A Federal Approach," University of Oklahoma Continuing Legal Education, 1982; "Whinery, Oklahoma Evidence, V.I. Guide to Oklahoma Evidence Code," West Publishing Co., 1985. Professor of Law, University of Oklahoma, 1959—. Member of Faculty, National Judicial College, 1972—; Chairman, Faculty Council, 1987. Lecturer, American Academy of Judicial Education, 1974—. Judge, 1961-1978 and Presiding Judge, 1964-1978, Municipal Criminal Court, Norman, Oklahoma. *Member:* Cleveland County, Oklahoma and American Bar Associations. [Corp. USAF, 1944-1946]. ***PRACTICE AREAS:*** Evidence Law; Probate Law; Juvenile Offender Law.

ROBERT S. ABERNATHY

3555 N.W. 58TH STREET, SUITE 510

OKLAHOMA CITY, OKLAHOMA 73112

Telephone: 405-946-8022

Fax: 405-942-8362

URL: http://www.lawyers.com/abernathy

Real Property, Oil and Gas Law, Corporate Law, Probate, General Practice.

ROBERT S. ABERNATHY, born Oklahoma City, July 21, 1965; admitted to bar, 1992, Oklahoma; 1993, U.S. District Court, Western District of Oklahoma; 1995, U.S. District Court, Eastern District of Oklahoma. *Education:* University of Oklahoma (B.A., 1989); Oklahoma City University (J.D., 1992). *Member:* Oklahoma County, Oklahoma (Member, Education Committee, 1997; Director, Young Lawyers Division, 1993-1994) and American Bar Associations. ***PRACTICE AREAS:*** Real Property; Oil and Gas Law; Corporate Law; Probate; General Practice.

ABOWITZ, TIMBERLAKE & DAHNKE, P.C.

Established in 1978

10TH FLOOR HIGHTOWER BUILDING

105 NORTH HUDSON

OKLAHOMA CITY, OKLAHOMA 73102

Telephone: 405-236-4645

Facsimile: 405-239-2843

Email: mainmail@abowitzlaw.com

URL: http://www.abowitzlaw.com

Mailing Address: P.O. Box 1937, Oklahoma City, OK 73101

(This Listing Continued)

Civil Trial and Appellate Practice in all State and Federal Courts, including General Tort, Business and Securities Litigation, Products Liability, Insurance, Professional Liability, Workers Compensation and Antitrust Law, Employment and Civil Rights Law.

FIRM PROFILE: Since its establishment in 1978, the firm has maintained a national Civil Trial and Appellate practice. The firm is listed in the Bar Register of Preeminent Lawyers.

LAW FIRM ALLIANCES/ASSOCIATIONS: ***INTERNATIONAL NETWORK OF BOUTIQUE LAW FIRMS***

MURRAY E. ABOWITZ, born Philadelphia, Pennsylvania, April 5, 1941; admitted to bar, 1971, Oklahoma and U.S. District Court, Western District of Oklahoma; 1972, U.S. Court of Appeals, 10th Circuit, U.S. District Court, Eastern District of Oklahoma and U.S. District Court, Eastern District of Texas; 1977, U.S. Supreme Court; 1978, U.S. District Court, Northern District of Oklahoma; U.S. District Court, Southern and Eastern Districts of New York; U.S. District Court, Eastern District of Louisiana; U.S. District Court, Eastern District of Missouri; U.S. District Court, Northern District of Ohio. *Education:* University of Pennsylvania (B.S., 1965); Seton Hall University School of Law (J.D., 1971). Member, Oklahoma State Board of Mental Health and Substance Abuse, 1989-1991. *Member:* Oklahoma County (Member, Board of Directors, 1989-1992) and Oklahoma (Chairman, Legal Assistants Committee, 1980-1981; Chairman, Legal Intern Committee, 1985-1986; 1991; 1993; Delegate, 1990-1991) Bar Associations; Oklahoma Association of Defense Counsel (Vice President, 1980-1981); Federation of Insurance and Corporate Counsel (Chair, Professional Liability Section, 1992-1993; Chair, Excess, Surplus Lines and Reinsurance Section, 1984-1985); Trial Attorneys of America; American Board of Trial Advocates (Past President, Oklahoma Chapter); Luther Bohanon American Inn of Court XXIII (Master of the Bench Emeritus; Former Counsel of the Inn; Member, Executive Committee). Fellow, American College of Trial Lawyers (Past Chairperson, Legal Ethics Committee). ***REPORTED CASES:*** Anderson vs. Northwestern Electric Co-op, 760 P.2d 188 (Okla. 1988); Angelo vs. Armstrong World Industries, 11 F.3d 957 (10th Cir. 1993); Beeman vs. Manville Corp. Asbestos Disease Compensation Fund, 496 N.W.2d 247 (Iowa 1993); Bristol vs. Fireboard Corp., 789 F.2d 846 (10th Cir. 1986); Case vs. Fibreboard Corp., 743 P.2d 1062 (Okla. 1987); Coleman vs. Turpen, 697 F.2d 1341 (10 Cir. 1982), app. after remand 827 F.2d 667 (10th Cir. 1987); Esther vs. Wiemer, 859 P.2d 1140 (Okla. App. 1993); F.D.I.C. vs. Ferguson, 982 F.2d 404 (10th Cir. 1991); Fisher vs. Owens Corning Fiberglass Corp., 868 F.2d 1175 (10th Cir. 1989); Fox vs. Mazda Corp. of America, 806 F.2d 953 (10th Cir. 1986), app. after remand 868 F.2d 1190 (10th Cir. 1989); Frielling vs. Malowest, Inc., 814 F. Supp. 75 (W.D. Okla 1993); Garner vs. Haliburton Co., 474 F.2d 290 (10th Cir. 1973); Huff vs. Fibreboard Corp., 836 F.2d 473 (10th Cir. 1987); In re: Longhorn 1979-II Drilling Program, 32 B.R. 923 (Bankr. W.D. Okla. 1983); In re: Longhorn Securities Litigation, 573 F. Supp. 255; 573 F.Supp. 274: 573 F. Supp. 278 (W.D. Okla. 1983); Jorgensen vs. Meade Johnson Labs, Inc., 483 F.2. 237 (10th Cir. 1973); Matter of Death of Takagi, 662 P.2d 308 (Okla. 1983); Mitchell vs. Lepak Trucking Co., 561 P.2d 967 (Okla 1977); Professional Assets Management, Inc. vs. Penn Square Bank, N.A., 607 F. Supp. 1290 (1985); 616 F.Supp. 1418 (W.D. Okla. 1985); Shebester vs. Triple Crown Insurers, 826 P.2d 603 (Okla. 1992); 974 F.2d 135 (10th Cir. 1992); Strickland vs. American Bakery & Confectionery Workers Union and Industry National Welfare Fund, 525 P.2d 10 (Okla. 1974); Shaffer v. Jeffery, 915 P.2d 910 (Okla. 1996); Post Oak Oil Co. v. Stack and Barnes, P.C., 913 P.2d 1311 (Okla. 1996); Huffman v. Altec Int'l, Inc., 546 N.W.2d 162 (Wisc. Ct.App. 1996); Warner v. Hillcrest Medical Center, 914 P.2d 1060 (Okla. Ct.App. 1995); Marshall v. Fenton, Fenton, Smith, Reneau and Moon, P.C., 899 P.2d 621 (Okla. 1995); Parrish v. Lilly, 883 P.2d 158 (Okla. 1993), In Re Keene Corporation, 208 B.R. 112 (S.D.N.Y. 1997); Lippe v. Bairnco Corp., 230 B.R. 906, 1999 WL 13673 (S.D.N.Y.); Timberlake Const. Co. v. U.S. Fidelity and Guar. Co., 71 F.3d 335 (10th Cir. 1995); Lippe, et al. v. Bairnco Corp., et al., 249 F.Supp.2d 357 (S.D.N.Y. 2003); Michael Foundation v. Urantia Foundation, 61 Fed. Appx. 538 (10th Cir. 2003), 72 USLW 3093 (No. 03-77). ***PRACTICE AREAS:*** Litigation; Professional Liability; Toxic Torts; Insurance; Personal Injury; Products Liability; Commercial Litigation; Complex Litigation; Attorney Discipline. ***Email:*** mea@abowitzlaw.com

SARAH JACKSON TIMBERLAKE, born Houston, Texas, March 24, 1954; admitted to bar, 1980, Oklahoma; U.S. District Court, Northern, Western and Eastern Districts of Oklahoma; U. S. Court of Appeals, Tenth Circuit; U.S. Supreme Court. *Education:* University of Oklahoma (B.A., 1976; J.D., 1980). Phi Beta Kappa; Phi Delta Phi. *Member:* Oklahoma County (Member, Bench and Bar Committee, Judicial Evaluation Panel) and Oklahoma (Chair, Insurance Law Section, 1993-1995; Managing Trustee, Group Insurance Trust) Bar Associations; Oklahoma Association of Defense Counsel (Secretary-Treasurer, 1988; President, 1990; Member, Board of Directors); Defense Research Institute; American Inn of Court XXIII (Barrister); Federation of Insurance and Corporate Counsel (Vice-President; Past Chair, External Projects Committee and Transportation Section). ***REPORTED CASES:*** Horinek vs. Board of County Comrs. of Kay County, 667 P.2d 479 (Okla. App. 1983); Snethen vs. Oklahoma State Union of Farmers Education & Co-op. Union of America, 664 P.2d 377, 38 A.L.R.4th 531 (Okla. 1983); Timberlake Construction Co. v. U.S. Fidelity and Guar. Co., 71 F.3d 335 (10th Cir. 1995); First Financial Ins. Co. v. Roach, 80 F.3d 426 (10th Cir. 1996); Progressive Cas. Inc. Co. v. Engemann, 268 F.3d 985 (10th Cir. 2001); Strader-Faiazi v. Edmond Fourth of July Festivals, 28 P.3d 1161 (Okla.Civ. App. 2001). ***PRACTICE AREAS:*** Insurance; Personal Injury; Products Liability; Premises Liability; Transportation; Labor and Employment; Litigation. ***Email:*** sjt@abowitzlaw.com

GEORGE W. DAHNKE, born Union City, Tennessee, October 9, 1940; admitted to bar, 1965, Oklahoma; U.S. District Court, Western District of Oklahoma; 1968, U.S. District Court, Northern and Eastern Districts of Oklahoma; 1969, U.S. Court of Appeals, Tenth Circuit; 1981, U.S. Supreme Court; 1998, Muscogee (Creek) Nation Supreme Court. *Education:* Westminster College (B.A., 1962); Northwestern University (J.D., 1965). *Member:* Oklahoma County, Oklahoma and American Bar Associations. [U.S. Army (Artillery), 1965-1967, Capt.]. ***REPORTED CASES:*** Allied Steel Const. Co. v. Employers Cas. Co., 422 F.2d 1369 (10th Cir. 1970); Arbest Const. Co., Inc. v. First Nat. Bank & Trust Co. of Oklahoma City, 777 F.2d 581 (10th Cir. 1985); W.P. Atkinson Enterprises, Inc. v. District Court of Oklahoma County, 516 P.2d 541 (Okla. 1973); Barnett v. Life Ins. Co. of the Southwest, 562 F.2d 15 (10th Cir. 1977); Brown v. U.S. Nat. Bank of Omaha, 220 Neb. 684, 371 N.W.2d 692 (1985); Brownlee v. Lear Siegler Management Services Corp., 15 F.3d 976 (10th Cir. 1994); Bruce v. Martin-Marietta Corp., 418 F.Supp. 837 (W.D. Okla. 1975); Bruce v. Martin-Marietta Corp. 544 F.2d 442 (10th Cir. 1976); Carlton v. Bello, 390 F.Supp.

(This Listing Continued)

ABOWITZ, TIMBERLAKE & DAHNKE, P.C., Oklahoma City—Continued

1321 (W.D. Okla. 1975); Coble v. Bowers, 809 P.2d 69 (Okla. App. 1990); Cox v. Kelsey-Hayes Co., 594 P.2d 354 (Okla. 1978); Erwin v. U.S., 302 F.Supp. 693 (W.D. Okla. 1969); Federal Deposit Ins. Corp. v. Geldermann, Inc., 763 F. Supp. 524 (W.D. Okla. 1990); Federal Deposit Ins. Corp. v. McKnight, 769 F.2d 658 (10th Cir. 1985); Federal Deposit Ins. Corp. v. UMIC., Inc., 136 F.3d 1375 (10th Cir. 1998); First Bank of Okarche v. Lepak, 961 P.2d 194 (Okla. 1998); First Nat. Bank and Trust Co. of Oklahoma City v. Iowa Beef Processors, Inc. 626 F.2d 764 (10th Cir. 1980); Freeman v. Alex Brown & Sons, Inc., 73 F.2d 279 (10th Cir. 1996); Freeman v. Prudential Securities, Inc., 856 P.2d 592 (Okla. App. 1993); Geller v. Prudential-Bache Securities, Inc., 591 F.Supp 27 (W.D. Okla. 1983); Gilchrist v. Strong, 299 F.Supp. 807 (W.D. Okla. 1969); Gulf Ins. Co. v. Gold Cross Ambulance Service Co., 327 F. Supp. 149 (W.D. Okla. 1971); Gulf Ins. Co. v. Lane, 53 F.R.D. 107 (W.D. Okla. 1971); Gumerson v. Farha, 538 P.2d 617 (Okla. App. 1975); Hamper v. Transcon Lines Corp., 425 F.2d 1178 (10th Cir. 1970); Haas v. Firestone Tire & Rubber Co., 563 P.2d 620 (Okla. 1976); Hise v. Philip Morris, Inc., 46 F.Supp. 1201 (N.D.,Okla. 1999); Holland v. Dolese Co., 643 P.2d 317 (Okla. 1982); Hotel Riviera, Inc. v. First Nat. Bank and Trust Co. of Oklahoma City, 580 F.Supp. 122 (W.D. Okla. 1983); Hotel Riviera, Inc. v. First Nat. Bank and Trust Co. of Oklahoma City, 768 F.2d 1201 (10th Cir. 1985); Hudgens v. Cook Industries, Inc., 521 P.2d 813, 78 A.L.R.3d 902 (Okla. 1973); Jesko v. American-First Title and Trust Co., 603 F.2d 815 (10th Cir. 1979); Key v. Rutherford, 645 F.2d 880 (10th Cir. 1981); Manley v. Fong, 734 F.2d 1415 (10th Cir. 1984); National Indem. Co. v. U.S. Pollution Control, Inc., 717 F.Supp. 765 (W.D. Okla. 1989); Robinson v. State Stove & Mfg. Co., Inc., 518 P.2d 902 (Okla. App. 1973); Seattle-First Nat. Bank v. Federal Deposit Ins. Corp., 619 F. Supp. 1351, 84 A.L.R. Fed. 305 (W.D. Okla. 1985); Unigard Mut. Ins. Co. v. State Farm Mut. Auto Ins. Co., 466 F.2d 865 (10th Cir. 1972); Wagnon v. Carter, 539 P.2d 735 (Okla. 1975); Williams Petroleum Co. v. Midland Cooperatives, Inc., 679 F.2d 815 (10th Cir. 1982); Woods Development Co. v. Meurer Abstract & Title Co., 712 P.2d 30 (Okla. 1985); Young v. First State Bank, Watonga, 628 P.2d 707 (Okla. 1981). ***PRACTICE AREAS:*** Insurance; Commercial Law; Products Liability; Professional Liability; Securities. ***Email:*** gwd@abowitzlaw.com

KAYCE L. GISINGER, born Oklahoma City, Oklahoma, May 22, 1962; admitted to bar, 1988, Oklahoma and U.S. District Court, Western District of Oklahoma; U.S. District Court, Eastern District of Oklahoma and U.S. district Court, Northern District of Oklahoma; U.S. Supreme Court. *Education:* Cameron University (B.A., in English, 1985); Oklahoma City University (J.D., 1988). Phi Delta Phi. Moot Court Board. Recipient: American Jurisprudence Award for Contracts. *Member:* Oklahoma Bar Association; Oklahoma Association of Defense Counsel; Defense Research Institute. ***PRACTICE AREAS:*** Insurance; Litigation; Personal Injury; Toxic Torts; Premises Liability; Negligence; Torts. ***Email:*** klg@abowitzlaw.com

---

LISA LUSCHEN DIETRICH, born Kansas City, Missouri, October 5, 1960; admitted to bar, 1985, Oklahoma; 1986, U.S. District Court, Western, Northern and Eastern Districts of Oklahoma; 1992, U.S. Court of Appeals, 10th Circuit; 2004, U.S. Supreme Court. *Education:* Stephens College (B.A., 1982); University of Oklahoma (J.D., 1985). Phi Delta Phi. Recipient: American Jurisprudence Award, Commercial Transactions. Co-Author: "Taking Depositions - Why, Who, Where, When and How," For the Defense (Jan, 1995); "Insurance Agents & Brokers," Federation of Insurance and Corporate Counsel, Update (Aug. 1990). *Member:* Oklahoma County, Oklahoma and American Bar Associations; Defense Research Institute. ***REPORTED CASES:*** Creek Nation Indian Housing vs. U.S., 677 F. Supp. 1120 (E.D. Okla. 1988); Harbour vs. Mid-Continent Cas. Co., 752 P.2d 258 (Okla 1987). ***PRACTICE AREAS:*** Insurance; Personal Injury; Products Liability; Workers Compensation; Professional Liability. ***Email:*** lld@abowitzlaw.com

BLAKE A. BITTEL, born Wakeeney, Kansas, August 8, 1971; admitted to bar, 1997, Oklahoma and U.S. District Court, Western District of Oklahoma; 2000, U.S. District Court, Northern, Western and Eastern Districts of Oklahoma; U.S. Supreme Court. *Education:* Ft. Hays State University (B.A., 1994); Oklahoma City University School of Law (J.D., 1997). Phi Delta Phi. Recipient, CALI Awards, Pretrial Litigation, 1997. Staff Editor, Oklahoma City University Law Review, 1995-1997. *Member:* Oklahoma Bar Association; Oklahoma Young Lawyers Association (Member, CLE Committee); Defense Research Institute; Oklahoma Association of Defense Counsel. ***REPORTED CASES:*** American Medical Security v. Josephson 15 P3d 976 (Okla. liv. App. 2000). ***PRACTICE AREAS:*** Insurance; Personal Injury; Products Liability; Professional Liability Defense; Contracts. ***Email:*** bab@abowitzlaw.com

MARY B. SCOTT, born Oklahoma City, Oklahoma, April 30, 1960; admitted to bar, 1988, Oklahoma and U.S. District Court, Western District of Oklahoma; 2000, U.S. Court of Appeals, Tenth Circuit. *Education:* Oklahoma State University (B.S.B.A., 1982); Oklahoma City University School of Law (J.D., 1988). Recipient, Two West's Publishing Awards, 1986-1987. *Member:* Oklahoma Bar Association; Oklahoma Association of Defense Counsel. ***PRACTICE AREAS:*** Insurance; Litigation. ***Email:*** mbs@abowitzlaw.com

HENRY A. MEYER, III, born Springfield, Missouri, January 4, 1948; admitted to bar, 1977, Oklahoma; U.S. Supreme Court; U.S. Court of Appeals, Tenth Circuit; 1981, U.S. District Court, Northern, Eastern and Western Districts of Oklahoma. *Education:* University of Oklahoma (B.A., 1971); Georgetown University (J.D., 1977). Recipient: Distinguished Alumni Award from Dean of Georgetown Law Center, 2002. Legislative Assistant to the Honorable James R. Jones, U.S. House of Representatives, Ways and Means Committee, 1973-1977. City Attorney, Woodward, Oklahoma, 1981-1987. Judge, Temporary Court of Appeals, State of Oklahoma, 1991. Commissioner, Tourism and Recreation, Oklahoma, 1991-1992. Chairman, Oklahoma Indigent Defense System, 1992-1993. Member, Oklahoma City Regional Board of Directors, National Conference of Christians and Jews, 1994-2001. *Member:* Oklahoma (Member, Board of Governors, 1986-1989) and American Bar Associations; Oklahoma Trial Lawyers Association; The Association of Trial Lawyers of America. Robert J. Turner American Inn of Court (President, 2003-2004). Fellow: American Bar Foundation; Oklahoma Bar Association. ***REPORTED CASES:*** State of Oklahoma v. RJ Reynolds, et al., District Court of Cleveland County, Okla, CJ-96-1499; Special Indemnity Fund v. Estill, Supreme Court of the State of Oklahoma, WC-87695; Johnson v. The Oklahoma Corporation Commission, Supreme Court of the State of Oklahoma, PR-87827; Special Indemnity Fund v. White, Supreme Court of the State of Oklahoma, WC-88272; Stidham v. Special Indemnity Fund, Supreme Court of the State of Oklahoma, WC-86902; Special Indemnity Fund v. Payton, Supreme Court of the State of Oklahoma, WC-90173; Special Indemnity Fund v. Cunningham, Supreme Court of the State of Oklahoma, WC-90897; Special Indemnity Fund v. Taylor, Supreme Court of the State of Oklahoma, WC-92825; Glover Construction Co. v. Oklahoma Dept. of Transportation, Supreme Court of the State of Oklahoma, SD-95132; Department of Transportation v. Fulsom Construction Company, Supreme Court of the State of Oklahoma, DF-95732; Glover Construction Company v. Department of Transportation, Supreme Court of the State of Oklahoma, WC-DF96630; Rittenhouse v. State Election Boare et al, Supreme Court of the State of Oklahoma, MA-98032; HCA Health Services et al. v. Coats, Supreme Court of the State of Oklahoma, MA-98733; Womack v. HCA Health Services, et al., Supreme Court of the State of Oklahoma, DF-99430; Ford et al. v. General Motors, Supreme Court of the State of Oklahoma, IN-100474; Johnson Farms v. Iochem Corp., Supreme Court of the State of Oklahoma, DF-87817. ***PRACTICE AREAS:*** Civil Litigation; Products Liability; Appellate Practice; Criminal. ***Email:*** ham@abowitzlaw.com

(This Listing Continued)

JONATHAN C. HORTON, born Fort Worth, Texas, April 13, 1974; admitted to bar, 2002, Oklahoma and U.S. District Court, Western District of Oklahoma. *Education:* Lubbock Christian University (B.S., 1996); Oklahoma City University School of Law (J.D., 2001). Phi Delta Phi. *Member:* Oklahoma County and Oklahoma Bar Associations; Oklahoma Trial Lawyers Association; The Association of Trial Lawyers of America. ***PRACTICE AREAS:*** Personal Injury; Products Liability; Professional Liability; Civil Litigation; Appellate Practice. ***Email:*** jch@abowitzlaw.com

MS. CHRISTINE M. CAVE, born Ketchikan, Alaska, 1972; admitted to bar, 2003, Oklahoma and U.S. District Court, Western District of Oklahoma; 2005, U.S. District Court, Northern District of Oklahoma. *Education:* Eastern Washington University (B.A., cum laude, 1994); University of Oklahoma (J.D., summa cum laude, 2003). Order of the Coif. Chief Articles Editor, Oklahoma Law Review. Recipient, American Jurisprudence awards for academic excellence in the areas of Administrative Law, Civil Procedure I, Evidence, Legislation and the Courts, Property, Public International Law, Torts II and Trial Techniques. Law Clerk to the Honorable Robin J. Cauthron, U.S. District Court for the Western District of Oklahoma. Adjunct Professor, University of Oklahoma College of Law. Author, Article, "Comment, Trusts: Monkeying Around With Our Pets Futures: Why Oklahoma Should Adopt a Pet Trust Statute," 55 Okla. L. Rev. 627 (2002). Contributing Author with Steven Gensler and Carol Posegate, "Federal Rules of Civil Procedure," (Thomson West forthcoming 2006). *Member:* Oklahoma Bar Association (Chair, YLD Mock Trial Committee, 2003—); Oklahoma County Bar Association (2003, Director, YLD 2004-2005); Federal and American Bar Associations.

OF COUNSEL

WILLIAM C. McALISTER, born Oklahoma City, Oklahoma, June 14, 1938; admitted to bar, 1969, Oklahoma; 1970, U.S. District Court, Western District of Oklahoma and U.S. Court of Appeals, Tenth Circuit; 1973, U.S. District Court, Northern and Eastern Districts of Oklahoma; 1977, U.S. Court of Appeals, Fifth Circuit; 1981, U.S. Court of Appeals, Eleventh Circuit; 1992, U.S. District Court, Northern District of Texas; 2004, U.S. Supreme Court. *Education:* University of Oklahoma (B.S., in Mech. Engr., 1961); Oklahoma City University (J.D., 1969). Sigma Tau; Omicron Delta Kappa; Phi Delta Phi. Law Clerk for the Hon. Fred Daugherty, Chief Judge, U.S. District Court, Western District of Oklahoma and Judge, U.S. District Court, Eastern and Northern Districts of Oklahoma, 1973-1977. Judge, Oklahoma Court of Appeals, Temporary Division, 1981-1983. *Member:* Oklahoma County (Director, 1999-2002) and Oklahoma (Member, Civil Procedure Committee) Bar Associations; Oklahoma Association of Defense Counsel; Defense Research Institute; American Arbitration Association. [Col. Ret., U.S. Army, 1961-1964; USAR, 1964-1988]. ***REPORTED CASES:*** Amoco Pipe Line Co. v. Montgomery, 487 F.Supp.1268 (W.D. Okla. 1980); Baptist Medical Center of Oklahoma v. Willis, 943 P.2d 155 (Okla. App. 1997); Farmers & Merchants Nat. Bank v. Bryan, 902 F.2d 1520 (10th Cir. 1990); Halliburton Oil Co. v. Aetna Insurance Co., 491 F.Supp. 595 (W.D. Okla. 1978); Hartford Acc. & Indemnity Co. v. Pacific Mutual Life Ins. Co., 861 F.2d 250 (10th Cir. 1988); Hatley v. Mobil Pipe Line Co., 512 P.2d 182 (Okla. 1973); Haws v. Luethje, 503 P.2d 871 (Okla. 1972); Johnson v. Wade, 642 P.2d 255 (Okla. 1982); Jorgensen v. Meade Johnson Laboratories, Inc., 336 F.Supp. 961 (W.D.Okla. 1972); Jorgensen v. Meade Johnson Laboratories, Inc., 483 F.2d 237 (10th Cir. 1973); Keen v. Detroit Diesel Allison, 569 F.2d 547 (10th Cir. 1978); King v. Woodward, 496 P.2d 801 (Okla. 1972); Lambert, Roberts, Jaques & Scrivner v. Crabtree, 615 P.2d 1027 (Okla. App. 1979); In re Magic Circle Energy Corp., 64 B.R. 269 (Bk. W.D. Okla. 1986); Markel Services, Inc. v. National Farm Lines, 426 F.2d 1123 (10th Cir. 1970); Sandia Federal Sav. & Loan v. Vernon Sav. & Loan, 860 F.2d 608 (5th Cir. 1988); Sandia Federal Sav. & Loan v. Vernon Sav. & Loan, 877 F.2d 345 (5th Cir. 1989); Squyres v. Hilliary, 599 F.2d 918 (10th Cir. 1979); Stuckey v. Young Exploration Co., 586 P.2d 726 (Okla. 1978); Texas Eastern Transmissions Corp. v. Marine Office-Appleton & Cox, 579 F.2d 561 (10th Cir. 1978); U.C. Leasing, Inc. v. State of Oklahoma ex rel State Bd. of Public Affairs, 737 P.2d 1191 (Okla. 1987); YWCA of Oklahoma City v. Melson, 944 P.2d 304 (Okla. 1997); Progressive Cas. Inc. Co. v. Engemann, 268 F.3d 985 (10th Cir. 2001); Winston v. Stewart & Elder, P.C. 55 P3d 1063 (Okla. 2002). ***PRACTICE AREAS:*** Appellate Practice; Insurance Law; Arbitration. ***Email:*** wcm@abowitzlaw.com

REPRESENTATIVE CLIENTS: Admiral Insurance Co.; Airgas, Inc.; Altec International, Inc.; American Founders Life Insurance Co.; American Medical Security; Auto-Owners Insurance Co.; Carolina Casualty Insurance Co.; Case Corporation; Certain Underwriters at Lloyds of London; Chesapeake Operating, Inc.; Cummins Construction Co.; Cummins Engine Co., Inc.; Evanston Insurance Co.; Fireman's Fund Insurance Co.; Foundation Reserve Insurance Co.; Integris Health, Inc.; Investors Underwriting Managers, Inc.; Liberty Mutual Insurance Co.; Lorillard Tobacco Co.; Meadowbrook Insurance Group; Medtronic Sofamor Danek, Inc.; Mutual Service Insurance Cos.; National Farmers Union Mutual Insurance Co.; Oklahoma Attorneys Mutual Insurance Co.; Oklahoma Farmers Union Mutual Insurance Co.; Oklahoma Goodwill Industries, Inc.; Philip Morris, Inc.; Physicians Liability Insurance Co.; Progressive Companies; D.B. Riley, Inc.; Royal and Sun Alliance; Shand Morahan & Co., Inc.; The May Department Stores Co., Inc.; Timberlake Construction Co., Inc.; The UNITRIN Companies; United Wisconsin Life Insurance Company; VIACOM.
REFERENCE: Arvest Bank, Oklahoma City, Oklahoma.

ADAMS & ASSOCIATES, P.C.

CITY PLACE BUILDING
204 NORTH ROBINSON
TWENTY-FIFTH FLOOR
OKLAHOMA CITY, OKLAHOMA 73102
Telephone: 405-232-9100
Fax: 405-232-9114
Email: Adams44@swbell.net
URL: http://www.lawyers.com/adams-associates

General Civil and Criminal Trial and Appellate Practice in State and Federal Courts, Administrative, Automobile, Banking, Bankruptcy, Commercial, Corporate, Estate Planning, Equine, Health Care, Insurance Defense and Regulatory, International Law, Oil & Gas, Probate, Personal Injury, Real Estate, Taxation, Telecommunications and Transportation.

FIRM PROFILE: Adams & Associates, P.C. was founded by R. Scott Adams, who has practiced law in Oklahoma City since 1989. Mr. Adams is best known for the great success he has achieved trying high profile and controversial criminal cases. In addition to trying cases in all state and federal courts, Adams & Associates, P.C. has a well established corporate and general civil practice. The firm is listed in the Bar Register of Preeminent Lawyers under Civil Trial, Personal Injury and Criminal Trial Practice.

R. SCOTT ADAMS, born Altus, Oklahoma, August 17, 1963; admitted to bar, 1989, Oklahoma and U.S. District Court, Western District of Oklahoma; 1990, U.S. District Court, Eastern District of Oklahoma. *Education:* University of Central Oklahoma (B.B.A., 1986); Oklahoma City University (J.D., 1989). Alpha Chi. Who's Who Among Marketing Students. President of Law Class, Oklahoma City University, 1988-1989. Member, Board of Governors, 1987-1989. *Member:* Oklahoma Bar Association; National Association of Criminal Defense Lawyers (Lifetime Member). ***PRACTICE AREAS:*** Criminal Trial Practice; Corporate; General Trial Practice.

REPRESENTATIVE CLIENTS: Deere Credit Services, Inc.; Deere & Co.; John Deere Insurance Co.; BancInsure, Inc.; Farmers Insurance Group; Oklahoma Farm Bureau Insurance Co.; Oklahoma Farmers Union Mutual Insurance Co.; Argonaut Southwest Insurance Company; Sentry Diaryland Insurance Group; The Hartford Insurance Company; St. Paul Fire and Marien Insurance Companies; State Farm Fire and Casualty Co.; State Farm Mutual Automobile Insurance Co.; National American Insurance Co.; Montgomery Ward Credit Corporation; Monogram Bank, U.S.A.; General Electric Capital Corporation; Transamerica Commercial Finance; Guaranty Bank & Trust Co.; Resolution Trust Corporation; J.I. Chase Credit Corp.; J.I. Chase Co.; First National Bank of Oklahoma; Bank of Hydro; Citizens State Bank; Nations Bank; First Capital Bank of Guthrie; Mobile Mining & Minerals, Inc.; Empire Bank, N.A.; Pacific States Transport; Independent Freightways; Dixie Liquor Co.; Con Agra Fertilizer Co.; Long Distance Savers, Inc.; Powers Autoplex; Powers Mitsubishi; Powers Toyota; Powers Honda; Bob Howard Auto Mall; Jim Glover Dodge; Christie's Toy Box, Inc; The Adams Course.

JOHN B. ALBERT

204 NORTH ROBINSON, SUITE 3030
OKLAHOMA CITY, OKLAHOMA 73102
Telephone: 405-232-3906; Mobile: 405-834-2409
Fax: 405-928-2889
URL: http://www.johnalbertlaw.com

Criminal Defense, Civil Practice, Driving While Intoxicated, Traffic Violations, Driving Under the Influence, Drug Trafficking, Homicide, Felonies and White Collar Crime.

FIRM PROFILE: John B. Albert is listed in the Bar Register of Preeminent Lawyers under Criminal Law.

JOHN B. ALBERT, born Oklahoma City, Oklahoma, September 15, 1967; admitted to bar, 1992, Oklahoma and U.S. District Court, Western District of Oklahoma. *Education:* University of Oklahoma (B.A., 1989; J.D., 1992). Recipient, Clarence Darrow Award, 1994. *Member:* Oklahoma County and Oklahoma Bar Associations; Oklahoma Criminal Defense Lawyers Association. ***PRACTICE AREAS:*** Criminal Defense; Civil Practice; Driving While Intoxicated; Traffic Violations; Driving Under the Influence; Drug Trafficking; Homicide; Felonies; White Collar Crime.

ASSOCIATE

JOSHUA A.L. LEE, born Denver, Colorado, November 12, 1976; admitted to bar, 2003, Oklahoma. *Education:* Oklahoma State University (B.S., 2000); University of Oklahoma. *Member:* Oklahoma County and Oklahoma Bar Associations.

THE LAW OFFICE OF ROBERT H. ALEXANDER, JR.

ATTORNEYS AND COUNSELORS AT LAW, P.C.

Established in 1988

FIRST NATIONAL CENTER, 24TH FLOOR
120 NORTH ROBINSON
P.O. BOX 868
OKLAHOMA CITY, OKLAHOMA 73101-0868
Telephone: 405-232-0803
Facsimile: 405-232-0519
Email: alexattys@productlaw.com
URL: http://www.productlaw.com

Pharmaceutical, Automotive, Mechanical and General Products Liability Defense, General Civil Trial and Appellate Practice.

(This Listing Continued)

FIRM PROFILE: The firm has gained a national reputation defending manufacturers against product liability claims, and defends its many Fortune 500 clients nationally, regionally, and throughout Oklahoma (Visit our website, www.productlaw.com, for more detailed information about the firm, its principal, and its attorneys).

Representative Clients: The firm clients include pharmaceutical companies, oil companies, automobile manufacturers, and manufacturers of various power tools, appliances and products containing asbestos, including Wal-Mart, Purdue Pharmaceuticals, Wyeth Pharmaceuticals, GlaxoSmithKline, Electrolux, Anheuser Bush, ConocoPhillips, BP Amoco, Land Rover, DuPont, Motorola and Bank of America to name a few.

ROBERT H. ALEXANDER, JR., born Little Rock, Arkansas, 1951; admitted to bar, 1977, Oklahoma; 1980, District of Columbia. *Education:* Howard University (B.A., magna cum laude, 1973); Harvard Law School (J.D., 1976). Phi Beta Kappa. *Member:* Oklahoma, American (Co-Chair, Product Liability Litigation Committee, Litigation Section; Chair, Mock Trial of the Century at the 1998 ABA meeting) and National Bar Associations; International Association of Defense Counsel; Product Liability Advisory Council; William J. Holloway, Jr. American Inn of Court CV (Master). ***PRACTICE AREAS:*** Products Liability Defense; Civil Trial Practice; Appellate Practice.

ANNITA M. BRIDGES, born Columbia, South Carolina, 1951; admitted to bar, 1976, Colorado; 1979, Oklahoma. *Education:* Howard University (B.A., cum laude, 1973); Georgetown University Law Center (J.D., 1976); National Judicial College, University of Nevada, Reno (Administrative Law Judge Certification, 1998). Member, Alternative Dispute Resolution Advisory Committee, U.S. District Court, Western Districts of Oklahoma. *Member:* Oklahoma Bar Association (Chairman, Alternative Dispute Resolution Section, 1998-2000); William J. Holloway, Jr. American Inn of Court (Master). ***PRACTICE AREAS:*** Alternative Dispute Resolution.

ASSOCIATES

ROBERT W. IVY, born Chicago, Illinois, 1964; admitted to bar, 1990, Illinois (Not admitted in Oklahoma). *Education:* Northwestern University (B.S., 1986); Notre Dame Law School (J.D., 1990). *Member:* Chicago and Illinois State Bar Associations; American Trial Lawyers Association; Illinois Trial Lawyers Association. ***PRACTICE AREAS:*** Products Liability; Commercial Litigation.

CARMEN M. PALOMO, born San Francisco, 1969; admitted to bar, 1997, California; 2004, Texas; 2005, Oklahoma. *Education:* California State University, Hayward (B.S., summa cum laude, 1993); University of California, Davis School of Law (J.D., 1997). *Member:* Butte County, Glenn County and Oklahoma Bar Associations; State Bar of California; State Bar of Texas. ***PRACTICE AREAS:*** Commercial Litigation; Products Liability.

MARILYN S. MORPHIS, born Elk City, Oklahoma, 1963; admitted to bar, 1988, Oklahoma; 1990, Texas. *Education:* Oklahoma State University (B.S., 1985); University of Tulsa College of Law (J.D., 1988). Order of the Curule Chair. Editor-in-Chief, Tulsa Law Journal, 1987-1988. *Member:* Dallas and American Bar Associations; State Bar of Texas; Texas Association of Defense Counsel; Defense Research Institute. ***PRACTICE AREAS:*** Products Liability; Commercial Litigation.

OF COUNSEL

JOHN J. LOVE, born Oklahoma City, Oklahoma, 1950; admitted to bar, 1976, Oklahoma. *Education:* Georgetown University (B.S.F.S., 1972); University of Oklahoma (J.D., 1976). Editor, Oklahoma Law Review, 1974-1976. *Member:* Oklahoma County, Oklahoma and American Bar Associations. ***PRACTICE AREAS:*** Products Liability.

REPRESENTATIVE CLIENTS: Wal-Mart; Purdue Pharmaceuticals; Wyeth Pharmaceuticals; GlaxoSmithKline; Electrolux; Anheuser Busch Companies; Vermeer Manufacturing Companies; ConocoPhillips; BP Amoco; Bank of America; Vulcan Materials Company; General Mills; Ford Motor Company; Toyota Motor Sales, U.S.A., Inc.; Volvo GM Heavy Truck Corporation; Land Rover, Inc.; E.I. DuPont de Nemours & Company; Motorola Communications and Electronics, Inc.; Ford Motor Credit Company; Hughes Aircraft Company; Nissan North America, Inc.; Anchor Hocking; Snapper, Inc.; Shoney's Inc.; Raytheon Corporation; Ful-Fab, Inc.

ANDERSON, McCOY & ORTA

A PROFESSIONAL CORPORATION

Established in 1992

2600 BANK ONE CENTER
100 NORTH BROADWAY
OKLAHOMA CITY, OKLAHOMA 73102
Telephone: 405-236-0003
Facsimile: 405-236-1448
Email: amo@amopc.com
URL: http://www.amopc.com

Commercial Mortgage Backed Securities Transactions, Real Estate Finance, Securitization Document Management, Loan Servicing Transactions, Commercial and Residential Real Estate Litigation, Real Estate Foreclosures and Bankruptcy.

MICHAEL A. ANDERSON, born Oklahoma City, Oklahoma, March 22, 1959; admitted to bar, 1985, Oklahoma; 1992, Texas; U.S. District Court, Western, Northern and Eastern Districts of Oklahoma. *Education:* Central State University (B.A., 1982); Oklahoma City University (J.D., 1985). Co-Author: Oklahoma Comments to Revised Article 9, 12A Oklahoma Statutes Annotated 1-9-101 to 1-9-710 nn," West Group, 2002. Co-Author: "Purchase and Sale of Hazardous Waste Transportation Service: Federal Legal Considerations," 31 Transportation Journal. Adjunct Professor, Commercial Transactions and Environmental Law, Oklahoma City University, 1991-1995. Barrister, American Inn of Court XXIII. *Member:* Oklahoma Bar Association (Member, Executive Committee, Financial Institutions Section; Committee Chair, U.C.C. Article 9 Legislative Review Subcommittee);

(This Listing Continued)

ANDERSON, McCOY & ORTA, A PROFESSIONAL CORPORATION, Oklahoma City—Continued

State Bar of Texas; Commercial Mortgage Securities Association. ***PRACTICE AREAS:*** Commercial Mortgages; Mortgage Backed Securities; Real Estate Finance; Loans; Real Estate Litigation; Secured Transactions. ***Email:*** manderson@amopc.com

J. MICHAEL McCOY, born Duncan, Oklahoma, February 21, 1958; admitted to bar, 1986, Oklahoma; U.S. District Court, Western and Northern Districts of Oklahoma and U.S. Court of Appeals, Tenth Circuit. *Education:* University of Oklahoma (B.B.A., 1980); Oklahoma City University (J.D., 1986). Recipient, Nesbitt Energy Prize. Faculty: Oklahoma Bar Association Department of Continuing Legal Education; Oklahoma City University Department of Continuing Legal Education. *Member:* Oklahoma and American Bar Associations; Commercial Mortgage Securities Association. ***REPORTED CASES:*** FDIC v. Grady Properties Company, 927 F.2d 528 (10th Cir 1991). ***PRACTICE AREAS:*** Commercial Transactions; Mortgage Backed Securities; Commercial Mortgages; Real Estate Finance; Loans. ***Email:*** mmccoy@amopc.com

VANESSA A. ORTA, born Mathis, Texas, September 18, 1963; admitted to bar, 1989, Oklahoma; U.S. District Court, Western District of Oklahoma. *Education:* Texas Christian University (B.A., 1986); University of Oklahoma (J.D., 1989). *Member:* Oklahoma Bar Association; Commercial Mortgage Securities Association (Member, Loan Document Integrity Committee). ***PRACTICE AREAS:*** Commercial Transactions; Real Estate; Mortgage Foreclosure. ***Email:*** vorta@amopc.com

---

KIMBERLEE TAGGART SPADY, born Oklahoma City, Oklahoma, January 23, 1968; admitted to bar, 1993, Oklahoma; U.S. District Court, Western and Eastern Districts of Oklahoma; U.S. Court of Appeals, Tenth Circuit. *Education:* Oklahoma State University (B.S., Agriculture, 1990); Oklahoma City University School of Law (J.D., summa cum laude, 1993). Vice Magister, Phi Delta Phi, 1992-1993; Order of the Barristers. Hatton W. Sumners Scholar. Recipient: Outstanding Graduate, Oklahoma Bar Association; Judge Tom Brett Award for Excellence in Criminal Law; Oklahoma City University Award for Service to the Law School; American Bar Association Award for Excellence in Land Use Law; RIA Award for Excellence in Tax Law. Former Administrative Law Judge, Merit Protection Commission, State of Oklahoma. Former Member, William J. Holloway American Inn of Court. *Member:* Caddo County, Oklahoma (Director, Young Lawyers Division; Chairperson, New Lawyer Orientation) Bar Associations. ***REPORTED CASES:*** Lee v. Griffith, 1999 OK 32, 990 P.2d 232. ***PRACTICE AREAS:*** Real Estate Litigation; Commercial Law. ***Email:*** kspady@amopc.com

MARK J. PEREGRIN, born Oklahoma City, Oklahoma, March 2, 1961; admitted to bar, 1987, Oklahoma; U.S. District Court, Western, Northern and Eastern Districts of Oklahoma. *Education:* Sam Houston State University (B.S., magna cum laude, 1983); University of Oklahoma (J.D., 1987). Recipient: Golden Kay National Honor Society; President's Honor Roll; American Jurisprudence Award (Torts). *Member:* Oklahoma County and Oklahoma Bar Associations. ***REPORTED CASES:*** Bank One, Oklahoma, N.A. v. Tanner, 23 P.3rd 977 (2001 OK CIV APP 57 certiorari denied); Terrell v. MRM Properties, 812 P.2d 418 (1991 OK CIV APP 51). ***PRACTICE AREAS:*** Real Estate Litigation; Foreclosures; Bankruptcy. ***Email:*** mperegrin@amopc.com

JEANETTE A. OATES, born Oklahoma City, Oklahoma, November 11, 1967; admitted to bar, 2002, Oklahoma. *Education:* University of Central Oklahoma (B.A., Accounting, 1991); University of Oklahoma (J.D., 2002). Recipient: Comfort Scholar; President's Honor Roll; American Jurisprudence Award (Torts). *Member:* Oklahoma Bar Association; Commercial Mortgage Securities Association; Oklahoma Bar Foundation; Christian Legal Society. ***PRACTICE AREAS:*** Commercial Mortgages; Mortgage Backed Securities; Real Estate Finance. ***Email:*** joates@amopc.com

HILARY M. NOLAN, born Ballinasloe, Ireland, December 24, 1970; admitted to bar, 2002, Oklahoma. *Education:* Waterford Institute of Technology (B.S., Business Studies, 1993); California State University (M.B.A., Finance, 1996); Oklahoma City University School of Law (J.D., 2002). Certified Public Accountant (1999). Publications: "Poverty Levels and Federal Tax Thresholds: 2001," J. of Tax Practice and Proc., Aug-Sept 2001; "Does Real Estate Have a Place in the Investment Portfolio of Tomorrow?" 18 Rev. of Bus., 1997. Member: Oklahoma Bar Association; Commercial Mortgage Securities Association. ***PRACTICE AREAS:*** Commercial Mortgages; Mortgage Backed Securities; Real Estate Finance; Securitization. ***Email:*** hnolan@amopc.com

BEN F. MEEK, III, born Kermit, Texas, January 24, 1958; admitted to bar, 1986, Oklahoma; 1987, U.S. District Court, Western, Northern and Eastern Districts of Oklahoma and U.S. Court of Appeals, 10th Circuit. *Education:* Baylor University (B.A., 1981); Pittsburg State University (M.A., English, 1986); Oklahoma City University (J.D., 1985). Sigma Tau Delta. Former Member, William J. Holloway American Inn of Court. *Member:* Oklahoma and American Bar Associations; The Association of Trial Lawyers of America. ***Email:*** bmeek@amopc.com

REPRESENTATIVE CLIENTS: ABN Amro/LaSalle Bank; N.A. Trust Services; Arcap Reit, Inc; Bear Stearns & Co., Inc.; Countrywide Commercial Real Estate Finance, Inc.; Criimi Mae Services Limited Partnership; Credit Suisse First Boston; Deutsche Bank; J.P. Morgan Chase Bank; LaSalle Bank N.A. Commercial Conduit Group; Merill Lynch & Co.; Midland Loan Services, Inc.; Morgan Stanley; ORIX Capital Markets, L.L.C.; Washington Mutual Bank; Bank One N.A.; Countrywide Home Loans, Inc.; Foreclosure Management Company.

ANDREWS DAVIS

A PROFESSIONAL CORPORATION

Established in 1941

CHASE TOWER
100 N. BROADWAY AVENUE, SUITE 3300
OKLAHOMA CITY, OKLAHOMA 73102-8812
Telephone: 405-272-9241
Fax: 405-235-8786
Email: andrewsdavis@andrewsdavis.com
URL: http://www.andrewsdavis.com

Administrative, Aircraft Finance and Leasing, Alternative Dispute Resolution, Antitrust, Appellate Practice, Banking, Bankruptcy, Blue Sky, Broker-Dealer Registration, Business, Casinos and Gambling, Commercial, Commercial Real Estate, Computers and Software, Construction Contracts, Corporate, Corrections, Creditors Rights, Debt and Equity Finance, E-Commerce, Employee Benefits, Employment Law, Environmental, Equipment Leasing, ERISA, Estate Planning, Finance, Gaming, Health Care, Historic Preservation, Indian Gaming, Insurance, Initial Public Offerings, Intellectual Property, International Business, Investment Banking, Landlord and Tenant, Limited Liability Company Law, Limited Partnerships, Litigation, Local Government Contracts, Media, Mergers and Acquisitions, Mortgages, Municipal Bonds, Native American, Oil and Gas, Partnership, Private Placement, Probate, Professional Liability, Public Corporations, Real Estate Title Insurance, Real Property, Regulatory, Securities, Shareholder Agreements, Surety, Taxation, Technology, Trade Association, Trade Mark Registration, Trial Practice, Trusts and Estates, Venture Capital.

LAW FIRM ALLIANCES/ASSOCIATIONS: ***MERITAS:*** *Andrews Davis is the Oklahoma City member of MERITAS, a worldwide association of more than 200 independent litigation and business law firms in more than 70 countries.*

L. KARLTON MOSTELLER (1895-1966)

JOHN C. ANDREWS (1926-2001)

MONA S. LAMBIRD (1938-1999)

J. EDWARD BARTH, born Oklahoma City, Oklahoma, October 24, 1937; admitted to bar, 1962, Oklahoma. *Education:* Yale University (B.A., 1959); University of Michigan (J.D., 1962). Phi Delta Phi. Law Clerk to Chief Judge, U.S. Court of Appeals, Tenth Circuit, 1963-1964. Chairman, Committee on Admissions and Grievances, U.S. District Court, Western District of Oklahoma. Chairman, Oklahoma City Metropolitan Area Projects Citizens Oversight Board. Past President and Trustee, Oklahoma City Community Foundation. *Member:* Oklahoma County (Member, Board of Directors, 1975-1977) and Oklahoma Bar Associations. ***PRACTICE AREAS:*** Business Transactions; Corporate Law; Mergers and Acquisitions; International Business Law; Commercial Real Estate Acquisitions; Administrative Law; Alternative Dispute Resolution; Asset Protection; Civil Litigation; Commercial Law; Construction Contracts; Estate Planning; Finance; Landlord and Tenant Law; Partnership Law; Probate; Real Estate Brokerage Law; Trade Association Law; Trusts and Estates. ***Email:*** jebarth@andrewsdavis.com

KENNIS M. BELLMARD II, born Ponca City, Oklahoma, June 6, 1958; admitted to bar, 1990, Oklahoma and U.S. District Court, Northern and Western Districts of Oklahoma. *Education:* Northern Oklahoma College (A.A., 1978); Oklahoma State University (B.S., 1981); University of Oklahoma (J.D., 1989). Phi Delta Phi. Editor-in-Chief, 1988-1989, Writing Competition Editor, 1987-1988 and Staff Member, 1986-1987, American Indian Law Review, University of Oklahoma. Negotiated the first three federally approved Tribal-State of Oklahoma Class III gaming compacts on behalf of the Tonkawa and Miami Tribes and for the Miami-Modoc tribal joint venture and subsequently negotiated a Class III Compact for the Otoe-Missouria Tribe and was involved in the federal approval of the Comanche-State of Oklahoma Class III Compact. Author: "Endeavoring to Preserve: Becoming and Being a Tribal Attorney," Kansas Journal of Law and Public Policy, 9 Kan. J.L. & Pub. Pol'y 752 (2000). Enrolled member of the Kaw Tribe. *Member:* Oklahoma Bar Association (Member, Indian Law Section). ***PRACTICE AREAS:*** Casino Law; Federal Indian Law; Gaming Law; Indian Economic Development; Indian Gaming Law; Legislative Practice; Native American Law; State-Tribal Relations; Tribal Government; Tribal Law. ***Email:*** kbellmard@andrewdavis.com

C. TEMPLE BIXLER, born Watonga, Oklahoma, June 5, 1930; admitted to bar, 1956, Oklahoma. *Education:* University of Oklahoma (A.B., 1954; LL.B., 1956). Dean's Honor Roll. Phi Alpha Delta. Member, Board of Editors, Article and Book Review Editor, Oklahoma Law Review, 1955-1956. Special Lecturer in Law, Real Property, University of Oklahoma, 1976-1977. Adjunct Professor of Law, Oklahoma Land Titles, Oklahoma City University, 1978. Instructor, Legal Aspects of Real Estate, Graduate Realtors Institute, Oklahoma Association of Realtors, 1981-1986. *Member:* Oklahoma Bar Association. ***PRACTICE AREAS:*** Real Estate; Real Property; Real Estate Finance; Oil and Gas Finance; Oil and Gas Law; Probate. ***Email:*** ctbixler@andrewsdavis.com

JAMES F. DAVIS, born Muskogee, Oklahoma, March 7, 1933; admitted to bar, 1957, Oklahoma. *Education:* University of Oklahoma (B.B.A., 1955; LL.B., 1957). Phi Alpha Delta. Managing Editor, Oklahoma Law Review, 1956-1957. Special Lecturer in Law, Trusts and Advanced Estate Planning, Oklahoma City University, 1973-1980. *Member:* Oklahoma Bar Association. ***PRACTICE AREAS:*** Business Law; Civil Practice; ERISA; Taxation Law; Trusts and Estates. ***Email:*** jfdavis@andrewsdavis.com

ALAN C. DURBIN, born Bartlesville, Oklahoma, July 29, 1942; admitted to bar, 1972, Oklahoma. *Education:* University of Oklahoma (B.A., 1965; M.A., 1966; J.D., 1972). Phi Delta Phi; Pi Sigma Alpha. Contributing Author: "Fifty State Construction Lien and Bond Law," John Wiley & Sons, Inc., New York, 1992. Co-Author: "Oklahoma Real Estate Forms-Practice," Aspen Publishers, Inc., Baltimore, Md., 1987. Author: "Statutory Formalities Governing Conveyances," Oklahoma Bar Association and Continuing Legal Education Publication No. 205, Spring, 1985; "Alternatives to Foreclosure," Oklahoma Bar Association and Continuing Legal Education Publication No. 208, Fall, 1985. Author: "The Oklahoma Power of Sale Mortgage Foreclosure Act: Issues and Considerations Affecting Title to Property," Publication No. 258, Spring, 1987; Author: "Real Estate Financing: Sources and Techniques for Improved Properties," "Basic Real Estate Law in Oklahoma," National Business Institute, Inc., Eau Claire, Wisconsin, 1988. Author: "Express Trusts and

(This Listing Continued)

Title to Real Property: Reflections on an Entity Theory in the Context of Business Trusts," Oklahoma Bar Association and Continuing Legal Education Publication No. 417, Spring 1991. Member, Legislative Liaison Committee, (Co-Chairman, 1992-1995). Member, Title Examinations Committee, Member, Board of Directors and Chair, 2002, Real Property Section, Member, Continuing Legal Education Commission, 1996-2001, Oklahoma Bar Association. *Member:* Oklahoma Bar Association (Member, Title Examinations Committee; Member, Board of Directors and Chair, 2002, Real Property Law Section; Member, Continuing Legal Education Commission, 1996-2001); Oklahoma Land Title Association. ***PRACTICE AREAS:*** Real Estate; Commercial Real Estate; Commercial Real Estate Finance; Commercial Real Estate Foreclosure; Landlord and Tenant Law; Real Estate Title Insurance; Condominium Law; Aircraft Finance and Leasing; Aircraft Sales; Aircraft Title; Banking Law; Business Law; Equipment Leasing; Finance; Financial Institutions Law. ***Email:*** acdurbin@andrewsdavis.com

JOHN F. FISCHER, II, born Stillwater, Oklahoma, September 23, 1948; admitted to bar, 1976, Oklahoma; 1979, U.S. Supreme Court, U.S. Court of Appeals, Tenth Circuit, U.S. District Court, Western, Eastern and Northern Districts of Oklahoma and U.S. Court of Federal Claims. *Education:* University of Oklahoma (B.A., 1971; M.A., 1972; J.D., 1975). Author: "Antitrust Law in Oklahoma," 48 Oklahoma Bar Journal 413, 1977; "Regulated Industries and the Antitrust Laws," 53 Oklahoma Bar Journal 1831, 1982; "Antitrust Impact on Managed Care," Conference on Consumer Finance Law, May 1996; "Confidentiality of Medical Records," Computerized Health Information, Lorman Education Services, Oklahoma City, OK, September 1998; "Physician Practice Mergers: Defining Relevant Markets," American Health Lawyers Association Annual Antitrust in the Healthcare Field, Washington, D.C., February 1999. Assistant Attorney General, Oklahoma, 1976-1980. President, William J. Holloway Jr., American Inn of Court CV, 2001-2002. Oklahoma representative to Tenth Circuit Advisory Committee. *Member:* Oklahoma, Federal and American Bar Associations; American Health Lawyers Association. ***PRACTICE AREAS:*** Antitrust; Health Care; Appellate Practice; Complex Litigation; Business Transactions; Federal Civil Practice; Covenants Not To Compete; Media Law; Trial Practice; Real Estate; Administrative Law; Alternative Dispute Resolution; Professional Liability; Regulatory Law; Insurance; Surety Law; Corrections Law. ***Email:*** jffischer@andrewsdavis.com

MATTHEW H. GRIFFITH, born Shawnee, Oklahoma, January 31, 1970; admitted to bar, 2000, Oklahoma. *Education:* University of Central Oklahoma (B.A., 1992); University of Oklahoma (J.D., 2000). Phi Delta Phi; Carl Albert Executive Fellowship; Dean's Honor Roll. *Member:* Oklahoma County (YLD Board of Directors, 2001—; YLD Chair, 2003), Oklahoma (YLD Board of Directors, 2002—) and American Bar Associations. ***PRACTICE AREAS:*** Business Law; Business Transactions; Corporate Law; Securities; Mergers and Acquisitions; Venture Capital; Corporate Finance; Partnership Law; Commercial Transactions; Shareholder Agreements; Private Placement; Limited Liability Company Law; Blue Sky Law; Broker-Dealer Registration; Initial Public Offerings; Debt and Equity Finance; Investment Banking Law. ***Email:*** mhgriffith@andrewsdavis.com

TIMOTHY M. LARASON, born Shattuck, Oklahoma, November 28, 1939; admitted to bar, 1969, Oklahoma. *Education:* University of Oklahoma (B.B.A., 1962); Northwestern University; Oklahoma City University (J.D., 1968). Phi Alpha Delta. Listed in: Best Lawyers in America. Author: "Tax Partnerships for Oil and Gas Operations," Journal of Taxation, Vol. 60, No. 1, January, 1984. Lecturer: "Sales Tax On Out of State Shipments" and "Hot Button Oklahoma Tax Issues," Oklahoma Tax Institute, 1994 and 2004. Member: Editorial Board, Tax Ideas, 1992-2003; Committee on Partnerships, Section of Taxation, American Bar Association, 1973—. Editor, Oklahoma Tax Journal, 1998-2003. *Member:* Oklahoma Bar Association. ***REPORTED CASES:*** Dillingham v. U.S., 81-2 USTC ¶9601, 48 AFTR2d 81-5815 (W.D. Okla 1981); Fort Howard Paper Co. v. Oklahoma Tax Commission, 1989 OK Civ.App 101, 792 P.2d 87 and Samson v. Oklahoma Tax Commission, 1998 OK 82, 976 P.2d 532. ***PRACTICE AREAS:*** Federal Taxation; State Taxation; Partnership Law; Limited Liability Company Law; Oil and Gas Taxation; Estate and Gift Taxation. ***Email:*** larason@andrewsdavis.com

MARK H. PRICE, born Miami, Oklahoma, September 6, 1941; admitted to bar, 1966, Oklahoma. *Education:* Northwestern University (B.S., 1963); University of Oklahoma (J.D., 1966). Phi Alpha Delta. *Member:* Oklahoma Bar Association. ***PRACTICE AREAS:*** Health Care; Physician Practices; Managed Care Contracts; Trusts and Estates; Estate Planning; Wills; Probate Administration; Business Law; Business Planning; Pension and Profit Sharing Plans; Charitable Trusts and Foundations; Nonprofit Organizations Law; Employment Contracts; Guardianship and Conservatorship; Leases and Leasing; Partnership Law; Country Club Law. ***Email:*** mhprice@andrewsdavis.com

D. JOE ROCKETT, born Drumright, Oklahoma, May 3, 1942; admitted to bar, 1967, Oklahoma. *Education:* University of Oklahoma (B.A., 1964; J.D., 1967). Phi Delta Phi. *Member:* Oklahoma (Chairman, Business Associations Section, 1985; Member, Securities Liaison Standing Committee, Business Law Section, 1983) and American (Member, Subcommittee on Partnerships, Trusts and Unincorporated Associations, Federal Regulation of Securities Committee, Section on Corporation, Banking and Business Law, 1984) Bar Associations. ***PRACTICE AREAS:*** Business Law; Business Transactions; Corporate Law; Securities Offerings; Mergers and Acquisitions; Venture Capital; Corporate Finance; Partnership Law; Commercial Transactions; Shareholder Agreements; Private Placement; Limited Liability Company Law; Blue Sky Law; Broker-Dealer Registration; Initial Public Offerings; Debt and Equity Finance; Investment Banking Law. ***Email:*** djrockett@andrewsdavis.com

ANNE E. ZACHRITZ, born Oklahoma City, Oklahoma, September 21, 1963; admitted to bar, 1991, Minnesota; 1993, Oklahoma; 1994, Texas; U.S. Supreme Court; U.S. Court of Appeals, Tenth Circuit; U.S. District Court, District of Minnesota; U.S. District Court, Eastern, Northern and Western Districts of Oklahoma; Muscogee (Creek) Nation Supreme Court. *Education:* Colorado State University (B.A., 1985); William Mitchell College of Law (J.D., 1991). Phi Delta Phi. Director, Mesta Park Neighborhood Association Historic Preservation Committee. *Member:* State Bar Texas; Oklahoma County, Oklahoma, Minnesota State, Federal (Director, Oklahoma City Chapter) and American Bar Associations; William J. Holloway, Jr. American Inn of Court (Master). ***PRACTICE AREAS:*** Employment Defense; Employment Litigation; Federal Employment Law; Employment Law; Federal Civil Practice; Commercial Litigation; Civil Litigation; Complex Litigation; Alternative Dispute Resolution; Historic Preservation; Confidentiality Agreements; Covenants Not To Compete; Employee Discipline; Employee Drug Testing; Employer Rights; Personnel Policies; Insurance; Surety Law. ***Email:*** aezachritz@andrewsdavis.com

---

VALERIE R. DEVOL, born Muskogee, Oklahoma, March 7, 1966; admitted to bar, 1997, Missouri; 1998, Kansas; 2003, Oklahoma. *Education:* University of Oklahoma (B.B.A., 1988); University of Missouri at Kansas City (M.B.A., 1991; J.D., 1997; LLM., 1998). *Member:* The Missouri Bar; Kansas and Oklahoma Bar Associations. ***PRACTICE AREAS:*** Taxation; Banking Law; Business Law; Buy-Sell Agreements; Corporate Law; Deferred Compensation; Employee Benefits; ERISA; Finance; Incorporation; Limited Liability Company Law; Mergers and Acquisitions; Nonprofit and Charitable Organizations; Partnership Law; Probate; Public Finance; Tribal Taxation; Trusts and Estates; Wills. ***Email:*** vrdevol@andrewsdavis.com

L. MATTHEW DOBSON, born Tulsa, Oklahoma, June 13, 1975; admitted to bar, 2005, Oklahoma; U.S. District Court, Eastern, Northern and Western Districts of Oklahoma; U.S. Court of Appeals, Tenth Circuit; Pawnee Nation Tribal Court; Ponca Tribal Court; Muscogee Creek Nation Tribal Court; Cherokee Nation Tribal Court. *Education:* Wichita State University (B.G.S., 1998; M.Ed., 2002); Oklahoma City University (J.D., 2005). The Order of Barristers. Oklahoma City University Outstanding Trial Court Advocate. Outstanding Association of Trial Lawyers of America (ATLA) Advocator. *Member:* Oklahoma County and Oklahoma Bar Associations; William J. Holloway, Jr. American Inn of Court. ***PRACTICE AREAS:*** Alternative Dispute Resolution; Corporate Law; Litigation; Trial Practice; Native American Law; Sports Law; Entertainment Law; Securities; Appellate Practice; Partnership Law; Venture Capital; Business Law; Limited Liability Company Law. ***Email:*** lmdobson@andrewsdavis.com

SANDRA BENISCHEK HARRISON, born Oxnard, California; admitted to bar, 2000, Oklahoma and U.S. District Court, Western District of Oklahoma; 2005, U.S. Supreme Court, U.S. District Court, Eastern and Northern Districts of Oklahoma, U.S. Court of Appeals, Tenth Circuit, Supreme Court for the Pawnee Nation of Oklahoma, Cheyenne-Arapaho District Court and U.S. Court of Appeals for the District of Columbia Circuit. *Education:* University of New Mexico (B.A., 1991); University of Oklahoma (Master of Public Administration, 1993; J.D., 2000). Phi Delta Phi. Member, National NALSA Moot Court Team, University of Oklahoma, Indian Law, 2000. Recipient, Pi Alpha Alpha National Student Manuscript Award for "Reforming Medicaid in Oklahoma." Editor-in-Chief, American Indian Law Review, University of Oklahoma, 2000. Listed in: Who's Who Among American Law Students, 2000. Author: "Clean Air in Indian Country: Regulation and Environmental Justice," VILLANOVA ENVTL LAW JOURNAL, Vol XII, Issue 2, pp. 211-233. President, Edgemere Park Preservation, Inc., 2002-2004. Ginsburg Inn of Court (1999-2004). *Member:* Oklahoma County Bar Association (Chairman, State Mock Trial Committee, 2004-2005; Executive-Vice-Chair, 2003-2004; Vice-Chair, Case Development, 2002-2003); Oklahoma Indian Bar Association; Cherokee Nation Bar Association; Federal Bar Association. ***PRACTICE AREAS:*** Native American Law; Indian Gaming Law; Federal Indian Law; Litigation; Legislative Practice; Historic Preservation; Environmental Law; Local Government Contracts; State Legislative Practice; State-Tribal Relations; Administrative Law; Appellate Practice; Indian Child Welfare Act; Indian Economic Development; Indian Land Law; Native American Civil Rights; Tribal Government; Civil Litigation; Complex Litigation; Federal Civil Litigation; Trial Practice. ***Email:*** sbharrison@andrewsdavis.com

JENNIFER HENSHAW McBEE, born Muskogee, Oklahoma, February 22, 1976; admitted to bar, 2001, Oklahoma, U.S. District Court, Eastern, Northern and Western Districts of Oklahoma, U.S. Court of Appeals, Tenth Circuit, U.S. Court of Appeals for the District of Columbia Circuit, Pawnee Nation Tribal Court, Kaw Nation Tribal Court, Cheyenne and Arapaho Tribal Court, Tonkawa Tribal Court, Courts of Indian Offenses (CFR), Anadarko and Seminole District Courts and Ponca Tribal Court. *Education:* Oklahoma State University (B.A. 1998); University of Oklahoma (J.D. 2001). Order of the Barristers. Editor, American Indian Law Review, 1999-2001. Attorney General, Seminole Nation of Oklahoma. Tribal Prosecutor, Kaw Nation and Tonkawa Tribe. Public Defender, Pawnee Nation. Designee of Governor Brad Henry, Oklahoma Indian Affairs Commission. *Member:* Oklahoma Bar Association; Oklahoma Indian Bar Association; Muscogee Creek Bar Association; Cherokee Bar Association; William H. Holloway, Jr. American Inn of Court. ***PRACTICE AREAS:*** Casino Law; Civil Litigation; Federal Indian Law; Gaming Law; Indian Child Welfare Act; Indian Economic Development; Indian Gaming Law; Indian Land Law; Indian Water Claims; Native American Civil Rights; Native American Law; State-Tribal Relations; Tribal Government; Tribal Law. ***Email:*** jhmcbee@andrewsdavis.com

JENNIFER B. SCOTT, born Norman, Oklahoma, October 9, 1977; admitted to bar, 2003, Oklahoma, U.S. District Court, Northern, Eastern and Western Districts of Oklahoma and U.S. Court of Appeals, Tenth Circuit. *Education:* University of Oklahoma (B.A., 2000; J.D., 2003). Phi Beta Kappa. Assistant Editor, Oklahoma Law Review. *Member:* Oklahoma County, Oklahoma and American Bar Associations. ***PRACTICE AREAS:*** Real Estate; Real Property; Commercial Real Estate; Commercial Real Estate Finance; Mortgages; Litigation; Civil Practice; Civil Rights; Construction Law; Landlord and Tenant Law; Foreclosures; Banking Law; Loans; Antitrust; Corrections Law. ***Email:*** jbscott@andrewsdavis.com

LEIF E. SWEDLOW, born New York City, N.Y., July 17, 1970; admitted to bar, 1997, Oklahoma; 2003, Texas, U.S. District Court, Northern and Western Districts of Oklahoma, U.S. District Court, Northern District of Texas and U.S. Court of Appeals, Tenth Circuit. *Education:* Oklahoma City University (B.A., 1991; J.D., 1997). Team Member: John Marshall Law School Information Technology and Privacy Law Moot Court Competition, 1995-1996; Jessup International Moot Court Competition, achieving a top five ranking worldwide for written briefs, 1996-1997. Editor, O.C.U. Law Review. *Member:* Oklahoma Bar Association; State Bar of Texas. [Oklahoma National Guard, 1992-1997]. ***PRACTICE AREAS:*** Business Law; Civil Appeals; Commercial Law; Commercial Leasing; Complex Litigation; Computers and Software; Corporate Law; Debtor and Creditor; E-Commerce; Employment Law; Federal Civil Practice; Information Technology; Intellectual Property; Internet Law; Litigation; Technology and Science; Trade Secrets; Trademarks. ***Email:*** lswedlow@andrewsdavis.com

(This Listing Continued)

ANDREWS DAVIS, A PROFESSIONAL CORPORATION, Oklahoma City—Continued

OF COUNSEL

LYNN O. HOLLOMAN, born Covington, Oklahoma, January 28, 1944; admitted to bar, 1969, Oklahoma. *Education:* Oklahoma State University (B.A., 1966); University of Oklahoma (J.D., 1969). Kappa Beta Pi; Phi Beta Kappa. *Member:* Oklahoma Bar Association. ***REPORTED CASES:*** Baker v. Massey 569 P.2d 987 (Okla. 1978), Matter of Kelsey's Estate, 579 P.2d 838 (Okla. 1978). ***PRACTICE AREAS:*** Probate Law; Estate Planning Law; Asset Protection; Trusts and Estates. ***Email:*** loholloman@andrewsdavis.com

ROBERT B. MILSTEN, born Tulsa, Oklahoma, November 6, 1932; admitted to bar, 1956, Oklahoma. *Education:* Indiana University (B.S., 1954); University of Oklahoma (LL.B., 1956); Southern Methodist University. Phi Delta Phi. Attorney, Office of Chief Counsel, Internal Revenue Service, Dallas, Texas and Nashville, Tennessee, 1958-1962. *Member:* Oklahoma County, Oklahoma and American (Member, Committee on Civil and Criminal Tax Penalties, Section of Taxation, 1962-1998; Southwest Region, IRS/Bar Liaison Committee, 1994—) Bar Associations. ***PRACTICE AREAS:*** Taxation Law; Commercial Law; Estate and Gift Taxation. ***Email:*** rbmilsten@andrewsdavis.com

STEPHEN J. MORIARTY, born New York, N.Y., September 16, 1957; admitted to bar, 1982, Oklahoma; 1983, U.S. District Court, Western District of Oklahoma; 1984, U.S. Court of Appeals, Tenth Circuit. *Education:* State University of New York at Stony Brook (B.A., 1979); University of Tulsa (J.D., 1982). Co-Author: "Mortgage Foreclosure Sales as Fraudulent Conveyances: The Durrett Issue," 10 Oklahoma City Law Review, 1985; "Advanced Collections and the Bankruptcy Process in Oklahoma," National Business Institute, 1994; "Oklahoma Foreclosure and Repossession," National Business Institute, 1995; "Fundamentals of Bankruptcy Law and Procedure in Oklahoma," National Business Institute, 1996- 2002; "Discharge and Dischargeability" and "Technology and ECF in the Bankruptcy Courts," Sterling Educational Seminars, 2002; "Aligning Your Practice With the Bankruptcy Abuse Protection Act of 2005," National Business Institute, 2005. *Member:* Oklahoma County (Member, Bankruptcy Law Section) and Oklahoma (Member, Bankruptcy Law Section) Bar Associations. ***REPORTED CASES:*** In re Western Real Estate Fund, Inc., 75 B.R. 580 (Bankr. W.D. Okla. 1987); In re Continental Resources Corp., 799 F. 2d 622 (10th Cir. 1986); In re Volador Equity/Income Fund '86-'87, 131 B.R. 739 (Bankr. W.D. Okla. 1991); F.D.I.C. v. Casey, 741 P.2d 463 (Okla. 1987). ***PRACTICE AREAS:*** Bankruptcy; Real Estate Bankruptcy; Mortgage Bankruptcy; Commercial Litigation; Creditors Rights. ***Email:*** sjmoriarty@andrewsdavis.com

REPRESENTATIVE CLIENTS: Bank of America, N.A.; Burgess Services, L.L.C.; Chickasaw Telecom, Inc.; Clements Foods Company; Comanche Nation Housing Authority; Cornell Corrections, Inc.; Countrywide Home Loans, Inc.; Dovenmuehle Mortgage, Inc.; Enterprise Oklahoma Venture Fund, L.L.C.; Federal National Mortgage Association; First State Bank of Altus; Global Industrial Leasing, L.L.C.; Healthcare Partners Investments, L.L.C.; Huntington Mortgage Company; Kaw Nation Enterprise Development Authority; Miami Tribe of Oklahoma; MetaFund Corporation; Neuroscience Specialists, Inc.; North OKC Endoscopy, L.L.C.; Oklahoma City Metropolitan Association of Realtors; Oklahoma Industrial Venture Management Company; Oklahoma Lottery Commission; QVC, Inc.; Seminole Nation of Oklahoma; Shand Morahan & Company; Smith Cogeneration, Inc.; Southwest Hotel & Casino Corporation; Stewart Title Guaranty Company; TDP Energy Company; The Physician Group, P.L.L.C.; Tonkawa Tribal Gaming Commission; UMB Bank, N.A.; Waste Control, Inc.; Waterfield Mortgage Company, Inc.; Wachovia Bank, N.A.

ATKINS & MARKOFF

9211 LAKE HEFNER PARKWAY
SUITE 104
OKLAHOMA CITY, OKLAHOMA 73120
Telephone: 405-607-8757
Fax: 405-607-8749
URL: http://oklalawyer.com
URL: http://www.lawyers.com/atkinsandmarkoff

Personal Injury, Automobile Accidents, Wrongful Death, Trucking Accidents, Slip and Fall, Nursing Home Abuse, Head and Spinal Injuries, Dog Bites, Sexual Abuse, Criminal Law, Drug Crimes, DUI/DWI, Juvenile Crimes, General Practice, Family , Divorce, Adoptions, Child Custody, Child Support, Domestic Violence, Visitation Rights, Elder Law, Legal Malpractice, Medical Malpractice, Social Security, Social Security Disability, Taxation, IRS Audits, Property Tax Appeals, Tax Planning, Toxic Torts, Trust and Estate, Wills and Probate.

MEMBER OF FIRM

JEFFREY R. ATKINS, born Tulsa, Oklahoma, October 23, 1968; admitted to bar, 1993, Oklahoma. *Education:* University of Central Oklahoma (B.B.A., 1990); University of Oklahoma (J.D., 1993). ***PRACTICE AREAS:*** Personal Injury; Automobile Accidents; Wrongful Death. ***Email:*** jatkins@oklalawyer.com

ATKINSON, HASKINS, NELLIS, BRITTINGHAM, GLADD & CARWILE

OKLAHOMA CITY, OKLAHOMA

(See Tulsa)

Medical and Legal Malpractice, Negligence, Insurance, General Civil Practice, Trials and Appeals, Product Liability, Environmental, Oil and Gas, Aviation, Corporation and Antitrust, Securities, Broker-Dealer Disputes, Workers' Compensation, Civil Rights, Employment Law, Pharmaceutical Defense, Commercial Litigation, Construction Litigation, Bankruptcy, Antitrust.

BAER, TIMBERLAKE, COULSON & CATES, P.C.

SUITE 300, 5901 NORTH WESTERN
OKLAHOMA CITY, OKLAHOMA 73118-1237
Telephone: 405-842-7722
Fax: 405-848-9349
Email: james@baer-timerlake.com

Tulsa, Oklahoma Office: 6846 South Canton, Suite 100, 74136. Telephone: 918-491-3100. Fax: 918-497-5927.

General Civil Practice. Real Estate, Mortgage, Corporate Law and Creditor Bankruptcy Practice.

FIRM PROFILE: Baer, Timberlake, Coulson & Cates, P.C. is a member of the United States Foreclosure Network.

GARY D. BAER, born Hays, Kansas, January 28, 1938; admitted to bar, 1962, Oklahoma. *Education:* University of Oklahoma (B.B.A., 1959; LL.B., 1962). President, Oklahoma County Legal Aid Society, 1970. *Member:* Oklahoma County and Oklahoma Bar Associations. ***Email:*** gary@baer-timberlake.com

DONALD J. TIMBERLAKE, born Ponca City, Oklahoma, July 5, 1941; admitted to bar, 1966, Oklahoma. *Education:* Oklahoma State University (B.S., 1963); University of Oklahoma (J.D., 1966). Phi Alpha Delta. Assistant Attorney General, State of Oklahoma, 1968. *Member:* Oklahoma County and Oklahoma Bar Associations; Oklahoma Trial Lawyers Association. [J.A.G.C., U.S. Army, 1966-1968]. ***Email:*** don@baer-timberlake.com

JAMES P. CATES, born Checotah, Oklahoma, August 14, 1964; admitted to bar, 1989, Oklahoma and U.S. District Court, Western District of Oklahoma. *Education:* University of Oklahoma (B.A., 1986; J.D., 1989). Omicron Delta Kappa. Board of Advocates (President, 1988-1989). Charter Member, Oklahoma City Commercial Law Attorneys Association. *Member:* Oklahoma County, Cleveland County and Oklahoma Bar Associations. ***Email:*** james@baer-timberlake.com

DONALD J. TIMBERLAKE, JR., born Fort Hood, Texas, August 13, 1967; admitted to bar, 1993, Oklahoma and U.S. District Court, Northern District of Oklahoma. *Education:* Southern Methodist University (B.B.A., 1990); Oklahoma City University (J.D., 1993). *Member:* Oklahoma Bar Association. ***Email:*** jim@baer-timberlake.com

SCOTT E. COULSON, born Tulsa, Oklahoma, March 23, 1963; admitted to bar, 1988, Oklahoma and U.S. District Court, Northern District of Oklahoma. *Education:* University of Oklahoma (B.B.A., 1985); University of Tulsa (J.D., 1988). Delta Theta Phi. *Member:* Tulsa County, Oklahoma and American Bar Associations. (Resident, Tulsa Office). ***PRACTICE AREAS:*** Real Estate Law; Commercial Law; Government Law.

STEVEN A. HEATH, born Fort Leonard Wood, Missouri, March 7, 1951; admitted to bar, 1982, Oklahoma. *Education:* University of Iowa (B.A., 1974); University of Tulsa (J.D., 1982). *Member:* Tulsa County and Oklahoma Bar Associations. (Resident, Tulsa Office). ***PRACTICE AREAS:*** Business Litigation; Creditors Rights Law; Secured Transactions Law; Real Estate Transactions; Employment Law.

MATTHEW J. HUDSPETH, born Tulsa, Oklahoma, June 9, 1966; admitted to bar, 1992, Oklahoma and U.S. District Court, Eastern and Western Districts of Oklahoma; 1998, U.S. District Court, Northern District of Oklahoma. *Education:* Southern Methodist University (B.A., 1989); University of Tulsa (J.D., 1992). Criminal Indigent Defense Attorney, Okmulgee County, 1995-1996. Previous Employment, Associate, Tolle & Parish, Okemah, OK. *Member:* Okfuskee County, Okmulgee County, Oklahoma and American Bar Associations; Muskogee (Creek) Nation Bar Association. (Resident, Tulsa Office). ***PRACTICE AREAS:*** Title Examination; Collections; Foreclosure; Civil Litigation.

RICHARD A. CHAPMAN, born Sterling, Illinois, April 11, 1965; admitted to bar, 1998, Oklahoma. *Education:* Southern Illinois University, Carbondale (B.A., 1992); University of Tulsa (J.D., 1997). [U.S. Army, 1985-1988; U.S. Army Reserve, 1982-1985]. ***PRACTICE AREAS:*** Creditors Rights. ***Email:*** rchapman@baer-timberlake.com

SPENCER B. HOUSLEY, born McAlester, Oklahoma, August 2, 1977; admitted to bar, 2004, Oklahoma. *Education:* University of Oklahoma (B.A., 2000; J.D., 2004). Top Five Speaker, University of Oklahoma Moot Court Competition. Member, International Legal Society, Oklahoma University, 2001-2004. ***PRACTICE AREAS:*** Foreclosures. ***Email:*** shousley@baer-timberlake.com

ROSEMARY CLINTON, born Talhina, Oklahoma, August 25, 1948; admitted to bar, 1989, Oklahoma. *Education:* University of Tulsa (B.F.A., 1980; J.D., 1988). Author: "Indian Title in Oklahoma" ; "Indian Title Revisited," First American Seminar. *Member:* Tulsa County and Oklahoma Bar Associations; Native American Bar Association. ***PRACTICE AREAS:*** Real Estate; Commercial Real Estate; Residential Real Estate; Foreclosures. ***Email:*** rclinton@baer-timberlake.com

JAMES H. THIESSEN, born Charleston, West Virginia, August 8, 1973; admitted to bar, 2004, Oklahoma. *Education:* University of Oklahoma (B.S., 1997); University of Oklahoma College of Law (J.D., 2004). Member, Luther Bohanon American Inn of Court, 2003-2004. Presenter, VA Regional Loan Center, Houston, Texas. ***PRACTICE AREAS:*** Real Property. ***Email:*** jht@baer-timberlake.com

REPRESENTATIVE CLIENTS: Accredited Home Lenders; Bank of America; Centex Home Equity Company, LLC; JP Morgan Chase Bank; Commercial Federal Bank; Countrywide Home Loans; Eastern Savings Bank; EMC Mortgage Corporation; Fairbanks Capital Corp.; FBS Mortgage Corporation; FCI National Lender Services; Federal National Mortgage Association; Fidelity National Foreclosure Services; Fremont Investment & Loan; Green Tree Servicing LLC; HomeEq Servicing Corporation; Household Finance Corporation; IndyMac Bank; Litton Loan Servicing; Midland Mortgage Company; MidFirst Bank; New Century Mortgage Corporation; Novastar Mortgage; Ocwen Federal Bank; Principal Residential Mortgage, Inc.; Symetrics; Wendover Financial Services Corp.

F. SMITH BARNES, P.C.

Established in 1960

1012 NORTHWEST GRAND BOULEVARD

OKLAHOMA CITY, OKLAHOMA 73118

Telephone: 405-848-1776

Fax: 405-840-1164

URL: http://www.fsmithbarnes.com

Practice including Corporate, Real Estate, Estate Planning and Probate Law, Commercial and Residential Real Estate, Contracts.

FIRM PROFILE: Mr. Barnes is listed in the Bar Register of Preeminent Lawyers in Trusts and Estates, Wills and Probate and Business Law.

F. SMITH BARNES, born Fletcher, Oklahoma, December 11, 1938; admitted to bar, 1968, Oklahoma; U.S. Court of Appeals, Tenth Circuit; U.S. District Court, Northern, Eastern and Western Districts of Oklahoma. *Education:* University of Oklahoma (B.A., 1962; J.D., 1968). Phi Alpha Delta. *Member:* Oklahoma County, Oklahoma and American Bar Associations. [U.S. Army, 1st Lt., 1963-1965]

RAY BAYS & ASSOCIATES

Established in 1979

6444 SOUTH WESTERN AVENUE

OKLAHOMA CITY, OKLAHOMA 73139-1710

Telephone: 405-632-4494

Fax: 405-632-0273

Email: raybays@aol.com

URL: http://www.lawyers.com/raybays

General Civil Trial Practice in State and Federal Courts. Mediation, Personal Injury, Probate, Commercial, Criminal, Insurance Plaintiff/Defense, Wrongful Death, Nursing Injury, Products Liability, Social Security and Workers Compensation Law. Divorce/Custody, Construction Injury, Agricultural Injury, Medical Malpractice.

FIRM PROFILE: Ray Bays started his own practice in Oklahoma City in 1979. His firm serves central Oklahoma in a variety of legal areas for both plaintiff and defense. Mr. Bays focuses on litigation and mediation in most civil as well as criminal areas. One of the strengths of the firm is the diversity and experience of the associates, who handle an assortment of practice areas in state and federal courts.

RAY BAYS, born Stillwater, Oklahoma, July 29, 1944; admitted to bar, 1979, Oklahoma, U.S. District Court, Western District of Oklahoma and U.S. Tax Court. *Education:* Oklahoma State University (B.S., 1970); Oklahoma City University (J.D., 1978). Phi Delta Phi. *Member:* Oklahoma County, Oklahoma and American Bar Associations; Oklahoma Trial Lawyers Association; The Association of Trial Lawyers of America. [United States Navy, 1963-1969]. ***PRACTICE AREAS:*** Personal Injury; Insurance; Mediation; Criminal; Wrongful Death; Nursing Injury; Construction Injury; Agricultural Injury; Probate; Family Law; Social Security.

ASSOCIATE

CHRIS D. CALDWELL, born Wellington, Texas, February 3, 1953; admitted to bar, 1977, Oklahoma; 1985, U.S. Court of Appeals, 10th Circuit; 1986, U.S. District Court, Western District of Oklahoma. *Education:* Southwestern Oklahoma State University (B.A., 1974); Oklahoma City University (J.D., 1976). Phi Alpha Delta. Licensed Insurance Agent, 1988. *Member:* Oklahoma Bar Association. ***REPORTED CASES:*** Jordan v. Shattuck Nat. Bank, 868 F.2d. 383 (10th Cir. 1989). ***PRACTICE AREAS:*** Family Law; Personal Injury; Worker's Compensation; Criminal Law; Probate.

BEELER, WALSH & WALSH P.L.L.C.

4508 N. CLASSEN BOULEVARD

OKLAHOMA CITY, OKLAHOMA 73118

Telephone: 405-843-7600; 405-810-9339

Facsimile: 405-606-7050

URL: http://www.beelerwalsh.com

Insurance Defense, Automobile Accidents, Personal Injury, Medical Malpractice, Products Liability, Nursing Home Negligence.

FIRM PROFILE: The firm maintains a general civil trial practice with an emphasis on Federal and State court litigation in the areas of personal injury defense, products liability defense, insurance and general tort litigation. The firm also handles toxic tort litigation, motorcycle accidents, trucking accidents, railroad accidents, professional liability matters and Fen-Phen Litigation.

JEFF R. BEELER, admitted to bar, 1975, Oklahoma, U.S. District Court, Western, Eastern and Northern Districts of Oklahoma, U.S. District Court, Northern District of Texas and U.S. Court of Appeals, 10th Circuit. *Education:* University of Oklahoma (B.A., 1972; J.D, 1975). *Member:* Oklahoma and American Bar Associations; Oklahoma Association of Defense Counsel; International Association of Defense Counsel; American Inn of Court CV (Master, 1990-1993); Defense Research Institute. ***PRACTICE AREAS:*** Insurance Negligence; Products Liability; Workers Compensation. ***Email:*** jbeeler@beelerwalsh.com

MICHAEL ALLEN WALSH, born Wheeling, West Virginia, April 8, 1954; admitted to bar, 1980, Oklahoma; U.S. District Court, Western, Eastern and Northern Districts of Oklahoma; U.S. Court of Appeals, Tenth Circuit. *Education:* University of Oklahoma (B.A., 1977); Oklahoma City University (J.D., 1980). *Member:* Oklahoma County, Oklahoma and American Bar Associations. ***PRACTICE AREAS:*** Litigation; Personal Injury; Insurance; Fire Loss; Products Liability. ***Email:*** mwalsh@beelerwalsh.com

(This Listing Continued)

REGENA McNEILL WALSH, born Woodward, Oklahoma, May 13, 1964; admitted to bar, 1990, Oklahoma; U.S. District Court, Western and Eastern Districts of Oklahoma; U.S. Court of Appeals, Tenth Circuit. *Education:* Oklahoma State University (B.S., 1987); University of Oklahoma (J.D., 1990). *Member:* Oklahoma County, Oklahoma and American Bar Associations. ***PRACTICE AREAS:*** Insurance Defense. ***Email:*** rwalsh@beelerwalsh.com

JAMES B. BUXTON, born Duncan, Oklahoma, January 6, 1975; admitted to bar, 2001, Oklahoma; U.S. District Court, Western, Eastern and Northern Districts of Oklahoma. *Education:* University of Mississippi (B.A., 1998); Oklahoma City University (J.D., 2001). *Member:* Oklahoma and American Bar Associations. ***PRACTICE AREAS:*** Litigation; Personal Injury; Insurance; Negligence; Products Liability. ***Email:*** jbuxton@beelerwalsh.com

OF COUNSEL

BEN BARNES, admitted to bar, 1994, Oklahoma. *Education:* University of Texas at Dallas (B.A., Government and Politics, 1990); Oklahoma City University (J.D., 1994).

REPRESENTATIVE CLIENTS: AIG/American International Companies; Arkansas Farm Bureau Mutual Insurance Co.; Asplundh Tree Expert Co.; Bituminous Insurance Company; Central Insurance Company; Circle K; Commonwealth Insurance; Crawford & Company; Department of Public Safety Federal Credit Union; Direct Staffing Solutions; Employers General Insurance Company; Equity Insurance Company; Essex Insurance; First State Bank of Austin; Frontier Insurance Company; GAB-Robboms Business Services; Golden Corral Corporation; Granite State Insurance Co.; GuideOne Insurance Company; Harbor Insurance Company; Hardee's; Home Depot; ITT Reznor; JBL Trinity Group, Ltd.; Jefferson Insurance Co.; Ladder Management Service; LeMars Insurance Company; Lexington Insurance Company; Maryland Casualty Insurance Company; McDonald's Corporation; Minnesota Mutual Insurance Company; Mutual Services Insurance Company; National Auto Insurance Company; National Farmers Union Insurance Co.; National Union Insurance Company; Northstar Companies; Oklahoma General Agency; Oklahoma Farmers Union Mutual Ins. Co.; Oklahoma Property & Casualty; Oxford First Corporation; Oxford Finance Companies; Provident American Insurance Company; Republic Casualty Co.; Service Management Systems; Silver Dollar City; The Kemper Group; The Silvey Companies; Transamerica Insurance Co.; Trinity Universal; USAA Casualty Insurance Company; Utita Mutual Insurance Company; Ward North America, Inc.; Willis Corroon.

BEHRENS, TAYLOR, WHEELER & CHAMBERLAIN

Established in 1979

SUITE 400

6 NORTHEAST 63RD

OKLAHOMA CITY, OKLAHOMA 73105-1014

Telephone: 405-848-1014

Fax: 405-848-3155

Civil Practice including Trials in all State and Federal Courts. Appellate, Oil and Gas, Environmental, Corporation Commission, Energy, Telecommunications, Public Utility, Corporate, Bankruptcy and Reorganization, Banking, Real Estate, Title Examination, Commercial, Administrative, Federal and State Taxation, Financing, Estate Planning and Probate, Arbitration, Employment, Securities, Personal Injury and Family Law.

VERLAND E. (BUDDY) BEHRENS, born Pawnee, Oklahoma, May 29, 1950; admitted to bar, 1975, Oklahoma and U.S. District Court, Western, Eastern and Northern Districts of Oklahoma. *Education:* Oklahoma State University (B.A., 1972); Oklahoma City University (J.D., 1975). Phi Alpha Delta. Member, Oklahoma City Association of Petroleum Landmen. *Member:* Oklahoma (Member, Mineral Law Section), Oklahoma County and American (Member, Energy Litigation Section) Bar Associations. ***PRACTICE AREAS:*** Oil and Gas; Energy; Commercial Litigation; Environmental Litigation; Municipal; Regulatory Law; Telecommunications. ***Email:*** veb_law@swbell.net

K. DAVID TAYLOR, born Perry, Oklahoma, November 19, 1950; admitted to bar, 1980, Oklahoma and U.S. District Court, Western District of Oklahoma. *Education:* Oklahoma State University (B.S., 1972); Oklahoma City University (J.D., 1979). Member, Oklahoma City Association of Petroleum Landmen. *Member:* Oklahoma, Oklahoma County and American Bar Associations. ***PRACTICE AREAS:*** Oil and Gas.

CHERI MARIE WHEELER, born La Porte, Indiana, January 22, 1952; admitted to bar, 1981, Oklahoma. *Education:* University of Oklahoma (B.S., cum laude, 1977); Oklahoma City University (J.D., 1981). *Member:* Oklahoma (Member: Mineral and International Law Sections) and American (Member: Energy, Environmental and International Law Sections); Oklahoma City Mineral Lawyers Association; American Society of International Law; Society of Petroleum Engineers, Women in Energy; Organization of Women in International Trade. ***PRACTICE AREAS:*** Civil; Administrative; Environmental; Oil and Gas; Public Utility. ***Email:*** cmw_law@swbell.net

RICK D. CHAMBERLAIN, born Tulsa, Oklahoma, June 2, 1954; admitted to bar, 1985, Oklahoma. *Education:* University of Tulsa (B.S.B.A., with honors, accounting, 1982; J.D., 1985). Phi Delta Phi. University of Tulsa Law Journal, 1984-1985. Author: "A New Dimension in the Ratable Taking of Natural Gas in Oklahoma: Enrolled House Bill 1221," 20 Tulsa Law Journal 77, 1984. Certified Public Accountant, 1989, Oklahoma. Assistant Attorney General, Lead Attorney-Public Utilities Unit, State of Oklahoma, 1991-1997; Assistant General Counsel, Public Utilities, Oklahoma Corporation Commission, 1989-1991. Assistant General Counsel, Federal Energy Regulatory Commission, 1985-1986. *Member:* Oklahoma and American Bar Associations. ***PRACTICE AREAS:*** Telecommunications; Energy; Taxation; Estate Planning; Probate; Corporate; Commercial; Administrative; Litigation. ***Email:*** rdc_law@swbell.net

A List of Representative Clients will be furnished upon request.

DAVID BERNSTEIN

OKLAHOMA CITY, OKLAHOMA

(See Norman)

Complex Personal Injury, Airplane Crashes, Product Liability, Medical Malpractice, Unsafe Products, Workers Compensation, Nursing Home Abuse, Insurance, Automobile Accidents, Dog Bites, Slip and Fall, Wrongful Death.

BIRDWELL LAW OFFICE

Established in 1980

SUITE 200 INVESTORS CAPITAL BUILDING
217 NORTH HARVEY
OKLAHOMA CITY, OKLAHOMA 73102
Telephone: 405-236-4675
Fax: 405-235-1209
Email: dwbirdwell@aol.com

Indian Law, Oil and Gas, Probate, Real Estate Law, Personal Injury and Commercial Litigation.

DWIGHT W. BIRDWELL, born Amarillo, Texas, January 19, 1948; admitted to bar, 1976, Oklahoma and U.S. District Court, Western District of Oklahoma. *Education:* Northeastern Oklahoma State University (B.A., 1972); University of Oklahoma (J.D., 1976). Alpha Chi; Order of the Coif; Phi Delta Phi. Recipient, American Jurisprudence Awards in Real Property, Trusts and Criminal Procedure. Author: "A Hundred Miles of Bad Road"; "An Armored Cavalryman in Vietnam," 1967-1968, Presidio Press, 1997. Member, Judicial Appeals Tribunal (Supreme Court) of the Cherokee Nation, 1987-1999. *Member:* Oklahoma County, Oklahoma and American Bar Associations; Oklahoma City Title Attorneys Association. [With U.S. Army, 1966-1968]. ***PRACTICE AREAS:*** Oil and Gas Law; Probate Law; Real Estate Law; Indian Law; Personal Injury; Commercial Litigation.

REPRESENTATIVE CLIENTS: The GHK Companies; ExxonMobil Corporation; BP Amoco Corporation; The Anschutz Corporation; Cabot Exploration Co.; Marathon Oil Company; Sonat Exploration Company; Plains Resources, Inc.; Central New Holland, Inc.
REFERENCES: Available upon request.

J. KEVIN BLANEY, P.C.

2601 CITY PLACE
204 NORTH ROBINSON
P.O. BOX 657
OKLAHOMA CITY, OKLAHOMA 73102
Telephone: 405-235-8445
Fax: 405-236-3410
Email: kblaney@kevinblaney.com
URL: http://www.lawyers.com/jkevinblaney

Commercial Litigation, Banking Law, Real Estate.

J. KEVIN BLANEY, born Wheeling, West Virginia, February 11, 1952; admitted to bar, 1977, Oklahoma; U.S. District Court, Western, Eastern and Northern Districts of Oklahoma; U.S. Court of Appeals, Tenth Circuit and U.S. Supreme Court. *Education:* Muskingum College (B.A., 1974); Oklahoma City University (J.D., 1977). Phi Delta Phi. Oklahoma City University Law Review, 1976. *Member:* Oklahoma County (Member, Fee Grievance and Ethics Committee, 1981), Oklahoma (Member: Banking Law Section; Bankruptcy and Reorganization Section) and American Bar Associations; Commercial Law League of America. ***PRACTICE AREAS:*** Bank Collections; Bank Foreclosures; Banking Law; Loan Workouts; Secured Lending; Business Transactions; Commercial Litigation; Commercial Collections; Secured Collections; Commercial Real Estate Foreclosure; Commercial Real Estate Workouts; Construction Claims; Construction Litigation; Mechanics Liens; Creditors Rights; Secured Creditors Rights; Secured Finance; Commercial Leasing; Commercial Landlord and Tenant Law; Civil Litigation; Commercial Mortgages; Mortgage Bankruptcy; Mortgage Foreclosure; Mortgage Tax; Mortgage Workouts; Land Acquisitions; Land Sales; Real Estate Bankruptcy; Real Estate Contracts; Real Estate Foreclosure; Real Estate Workouts.

MICHAEL J. BLASCHKE, P.C.

825 ROBINSON RENAISSANCE, 119 N. ROBINSON
OKLAHOMA CITY, OKLAHOMA 73102
Telephone: 405-319-0400
Fax: 405-319-0404
Email: mjblaschke@aol.com

Oil and Gas Litigation, Commercial Litigation, Oil and Gas Law.

MICHAEL J. BLASCHKE, born Oklahoma City, Oklahoma, April 18, 1949; admitted to bar, 1978, Oklahoma; U.S. Supreme Court; U.S. Court of Appeals, Tenth Circuit and U.S. District Court, Northern and Western Districts of Oklahoma. *Education:* University of Oklahoma (B.A., 1975; J.D., 1978). Member, Oklahoma Law Review. *Member:* Oklahoma County, Oklahoma and American Bar Associations; Mineral Lawyers Group. [With U.S. Army, 1971-1973]. ***REPORTED CASES:*** Vinson v. Medley, 737 P.2d 932, 96 O.G.R. 344 (Okla. 1988); Ladder Energy Company v. Intrust Bank, N.A., 931 P.2d 83 (Okla.App. 1996); Davis Oil Company v. Cloud, 766 P.2d 1347, 106 O.G.R. 318 (Okla. 1989). ***PRACTICE AREAS:*** Oil and Gas Litigation; Commercial Litigation; Oil and Gas Law. ***Email:*** mjblaschke@aol.com

WILLIAM H. BOCK, INC.

6402 N. SANTA FE AVENUE, SUITE A
OKLAHOMA CITY, OKLAHOMA 73116
Telephone: 405-848-5400
Fax: 405-848-5479
Email: bocklaw@sbcglobal.net
URL: http://www.lawyers.com/bocklaw

Criminal Defense in State and Federal Court, Personal Injury, Trial Practice, Driving While Intoxicated, Drug Crimes, Juvenile Law, Military Court Marshal.

WILLIAM H. BOCK, born Oklahoma City, Oklahoma, June 30, 1964; admitted to bar, 1990, Oklahoma and U.S. District Court, Western and Northern Districts of Oklahoma; U.S. Court of Appeals, Tenth Circuit. *Education:* Central State University (B.S., Finance, 1987); Oklahoma City University (J.D., 1990). *Member:* Oklahoma County and Oklahoma Bar Associations; Oklahoma Criminal Defense Lawyers. ***PRACTICE AREAS:*** Criminal Defense; Trial Practice; Criminal Forfeiture; Juvenile Law; Personal Injury. ***Email:*** bocklaw@sbcglobal.net

ASSOCIATE

MICHELLE GREENE, born Lawton, Oklahoma, December 27, 1971; admitted to bar, 1997, Oklahoma and U.S. District Court, Western and Northern Districts of Oklahoma. *Education:* University of Oklahoma (B.A., 1994); Oklahoma City University School of Law (J.D., 1997). *Member:* Oklahoma Bar Association; William J. Holloway Inn of Court; American Inns of Court. ***PRACTICE AREAS:*** Criminal Defense; Trial Practice; Criminal Forfeiture; Juvenile Law; Personal Injury. ***Email:*** rodgerslaw@sbcglobal.net

---

BONHAM & HOWARD

An Association of Professional Associates
Not A Partnership

LAND MARK TOWERS WEST, SUITE 200
3555 NW 58TH STREET
OKLAHOMA CITY, OKLAHOMA 73112
Telephone: 405-943-6650
Facsimile: 405-943-6655
URL: http://www.bonhamandhoward.com

Tulsa, Oklahoma Office: 15 W. 6th Street, 74119. Telephone: 918-744-7440. Fax: 918-744-9358.

General, Civil and Trial Practice in Federal Courts and all State Courts, Insurance Defense, Property and Casualty, Workers' Compensation, Products Liability, Surety, Civil Rights Defense, Regulatory and Administrative Law, Corporate, Estate Planning, Probate.

J. TED BONHAM, born Cordell, Oklahoma, January 29, 1936; admitted to bar, 1967, Oklahoma; U.S. District Court, Western District of Oklahoma. *Education:* Oklahoma State University (B.S., 1957); University of Oklahoma (J.D., 1967). ***Email:*** jtedbonham@sbcglobal.net

JAMES W. SWANK, JR., born Norman, Oklahoma, October 21, 1943; admitted to bar, 1972, Oklahoma; U.S. District Court, Northern, Eastern and Western Districts of Oklahoma and U.S. Court of Appeals, Tenth Circuit. *Education:* University of Oklahoma (B.B.A., 1965); Southern Methodist University (J.D., 1972). Assistant Insurance Commissioner, Oklahoma Insurance Department, 1974. ***Email:*** jamesswank@sbcglobal.net

JEFFREY D. BLACK, born Adel, Iowa, June 29, 1964; admitted to bar, 1990, Oklahoma; U.S. Court of Appeals, Tenth Circuit and U.S. District Court, Northern, Eastern and Western Districts of Oklahoma. *Education:* University of Oklahoma (B.B.A., Finance-Management, 1987); Oklahoma City University (J.D., 1989). *Member:* Oklahoma County and American (Member, Sections on: Defense Litigation; Workers' Compensation) Bar Associations. ***PRACTICE AREAS:*** Workers Compensation; Defense Litigation. ***Email:*** jeffreydblack@sbcglobal.net

WESLEY E. COMBS, born Marysville, California, August 14, 1954; admitted to bar, 1988, Oklahoma; U.S. District Court, Northern, Eastern and Western Districts of Oklahoma. *Education:* Northeastern Oklahoma State University (B.A., 1985); University of Arkansas (J.D., 1987). ***Email:*** wescombs@sbcglobal.net

OF COUNSEL

DAVID L. THOMAS, born Ft. Smith, Arkansas, September 26, 1954; admitted to bar, 1978, Oklahoma; U.S. District Court, Western, Northern and Eastern Districts of Oklahoma and U.S. Court of Appeals, Tenth Circuit. *Education:* Southeastern Oklahoma State University (B.A., 1975); University of Oklahoma College of Law (J.D., with honors, 1978). Order of the Coif. Recipient: Corpus Juris Secundum Award, 1976. Editor, 1976-1978 and Article and Book Review Editor, 1977-1978, Oklahoma Law Review. *Member:* Oklahoma County and Oklahoma Bar Associations. ***REPORTED CASES:*** Davis v. CMS Continental Natural Gas, Inc., 23 P.3d 288, 2001 OK 33; F.D.I.C. v. Grant, 8 F.Supp.2d 1275, N.D.Okla.1998; Liddington v. Burns, 916 F.Supp 1140, W.D.Okla. 1996; Liddington v. Burns, 916 F.Supp. 1127, W.D.Okla. 1995; Resolution Trust Corp. v. Grant, 901 P.2d 807, 64 USLW 2078 1995 OK 68 1995; Burghart v. Frisch's Restaurants, Inc., 865 F.2d 1162 10th Cir. (Okla.) 1989; Malik v. Apex Intern. Alloys, Inc., 762 F.2d 77 10th Cir. (Okla.) 1985; Heinold Hog Market, Inc. v. McCoy, 700 F.2d 611, 12 Fed.R.Evid.Serv. 1276 10th Cir. (Colo.) 1983; Bingham v. Hollingsworth Mfg. Co., Inc., 695 F.2d 445 10th Cir. (Okla.) 1982; State v. County Beverage License No. ABL-78-145 of McMar General Stores, 652 P.2d 292 1982 Okla. 114; Pate v. MFA Mut. Ins. Co., 649 P.2d 809 1982 OK CIV APP 36 Okla.App.Div.2; Jacobs v. Lancaster, 526 F.Supp. 767, W.D.Okla. 1981. ***PRACTICE AREAS:*** Personal Injury; Toxic Tort Defense; Medical Malpractice.

REPRESENTATIVE CLIENTS: Oklahoma Safety Association; Claims Indemnity Services, Inc.; The Travelers Group; State Insurance Fund/CompSource Oklahoma; Texas County Mutual Insurance Co.; Dot-Line Transportation; Oklahoma Property & Casualty Insurance; Guaranty Assn.; The Chubb Group of Insurance Co.; Federal Insurance Group; Ranger

(This Listing Continued)

Insurance Co.; D & M Surety, Inc.; MGI-Mechanical Breakdown Insurers; The Heritage Group, Inc.; Oklahoma County Sheriff, John Whetsel; Ensuro Holdings, Inc.; General Thomas P. Stafford and related Companies; Providence Property and Casualty Insurance Co.; Imperial Casualty and Indemnity Co.; Dallas General Insurance Co.; The Hartford Insurance Group; Oklahoma Manufactured Housing Association; Midlands Management Corp.; Dallas Fire and Safety Insurance Co.; AMS Staff Leasing; Claims and Risk Services; BancInsure Insurance Co.; International Fidelity Insurance Co.; American Surety Co.

LAW OFFICE OF STEVEN R. BOOKER, P.C.

OKLAHOMA CITY, OKLAHOMA

(See Wichita Falls, Texas)

Elder Law, Accidents, Slip and Fall, Products Defects, Dram Shop Cases, Railroad Accidents, Dog Bites, Automobile Negligence, Wrongful Death, Breach of Warranty, Nursing Home Negligence, Civil Litigation, Plaintiff Personal Injury, Probate Litigation, Contested Wills.

WILLIAM C. BOWLBY

A PROFESSIONAL CORPORATION

SUITE 105, ATRIUM BUILDING
3601 NORTH CLASSEN BOULEVARD
OKLAHOMA CITY, OKLAHOMA 73118
Telephone: 405-528-8783
Fax: 405-528-1625
Email: bowlbylaw@aol.com
URL: http://www.bowlbylaw.com

General Civil Litigation in State and Federal Courts, Divorce, Custody, Bankruptcy, Mechanics Liens, Debtor and Creditor, Landlord and Tenant, Personal Injury.

WILLIAM C. BOWLBY, born Washington, D.C., October 26, 1941; admitted to bar, 1972, Oklahoma, U.S. District Court, Western and Northern Districts of Oklahoma and U.S. Court of Appeals, Tenth Circuit. *Education:* Central State University (B.S., 1966); University of Oklahoma (J.D., 1971). Recipient: Leadership Award; Golden Gavel Award of Merit; Pro-bono Appreciation and Award of Merit. *Member:* Oklahoma County and Oklahoma Bar Associations (Member, Committee on Continuing Education, Chairman; Law Day Committee; Directory Committee). [Lt., U.S. Army, Armor, 1966-1969]. ***REPORTED CASES:*** Schuminsky v. Field, 606 p 2d 1133 (Okla. 1980); Mitchell Manor Convalescent Home, Inc. v. Oklahoma Health Planning Comm., 808 p 2d 998 (Okla. 1991); Prime Electric Co., Inc. v. Oklahoma State Dept. of Labor 921 p2d 363 (Okla. 1996).

REPRESENTATIVE CLIENTS: Emsco Electric Supply Co., Inc.; LSB Industries, Inc.; El Dorado Chemical Co.; International Environmental Corp.; Prime Electric Co., Inc.; Hisway Transportation, Inc.; Park Harvey Center; Goodwill Industries of Oklahoma, Inc.; Malco, Inc.
REFERENCE: Bank of America.

BRIGHT LAW FIRM

204 N. ROBINSON, SUITE 2625
OKLAHOMA CITY, OKLAHOMA 73102
Telephone: 405-232-8001: 405-210-7483
Fax: 405-232-3641
Email: mbright@earthlink.net
URL: http://www.brightlawfirm.com

Criminal Defense, Drug Crimes, DUI, DWI, Domestic Violence, White Collar Crime, Larseny, Traffic Violations, Misdemeanors, Felonies, Assault, Assault and Battery, Family Law, Personal Injury, Bankruptcy, Environmental Law.

MARK EDWARD BRIGHT, born Silver Spring, Maryland, October 27, 1969; admitted to bar, 1997, Oklahoma. *Education:* University of South Florida (B.A., 1992); University of Oklahoma (J.D., 1997). Member, Robert J. Turner American Inn of Court. Member, Bricktown Rotary Club. *Member:* Oklahoma County, Oklahoma (Fellow) and American Bar Associations; Association of Trial Lawyers of America; Oklahoma Criminal Defense Lawyers; Oklahoma County Criminal Defense Lawyers Association. ***PRACTICE AREAS:*** Criminal Defense; Family Law; Personal Injury; Bankruptcy; Environmental Law; Drug Crimes; DUI; DWI; Domestic Violence; White Collar Crime; Traffic Violations; Misdemeanors; Felonies; Assault and Battery. ***Email:*** mbright@earthlink.net

BRITTON, RAMSEY AND GRAY, P.C.

700 CORPORATE TOWER
101 NORTH ROBINSON STREET
OKLAHOMA CITY, OKLAHOMA 73102
Telephone: 405-239-2393
Fax: 405-232-5135
Email: firm@lawbrg.com
URL: http://www.lawbrg.com

General Civil Litigation in State and Federal Courts. Corporate, Insurance Law, Commercial Law, Bankruptcy, Banking, Real Estate, Corporate and Business Law, Estate Planning, Trusts and Probate, Copyrights and Trademarks, Business Litigation, Employment and Health Care.

FIRM PROFILE: This firm is listed in the Bar Register of Preeminent Lawyers in the areas of Banking Law, Business Law, and Civil Trial Practice.

JAMES E. BRITTON, born Roswell, New Mexico, 1946; admitted to bar, 1974, Oklahoma, U.S. District Court, Western, Eastern and Northern Districts of Oklahoma and U.S. Court of Appeals, Tenth Circuit. *Education:* Iowa State University; Oklahoma State University (B.S., 1968); University of Oklahoma (J.D., 1974). Phi Delta Phi; Order of the Coif. Research Editor, Oklahoma Law Review, 1973-1974. *Member:* Oklahoma County (Ethics Committee; Law Day Chairman) and Oklahoma (Uniform Laws Committee (Chairman, 1993-1997); Legislative Review Committee) Bar Associations. ***PRACTICE AREAS:*** Banking Law; Real Estate; Corporate; Business Law. ***Email:*** james.britton@lawbrg.com

RODNEY C. RAMSEY, born Elk City, Oklahoma, December 20, 1956; admitted to bar, 1982, Oklahoma; 1985, U.S. District Court, Western District of Oklahoma; U.S. District Court, Northern District of Oklahoma; U.S. District Court, Eastern District of Oklahoma, U.S. Court of Appeals, 10th Circuit and U.S. Supreme Court. *Education:* Oklahoma State University (B.A., 1979); University of Oklahoma (J.D., 1982). Phi Delta Phi. Editor, Oklahoma Law Review, 1981-1982. Recipient: George J. Fagin Municipal Law Endowment Award, 1981-1982. Municipal Judge, Town of Butler, Oklahoma, 1982-1984. *Member:* Oklahoma County, Oklahoma and American Bar Associations; International Association of Defense Counsel; Oklahoma Association of Defense Counsel. ***PRACTICE AREAS:*** Insurance Law; Business Litigation. ***Email:*** rodney.ramsey@lawbrg.com

MICHAEL D. GRAY, born Duncan, Oklahoma, September 10, 1960; admitted to bar, 1985, Oklahoma, U.S. District Court, Western, Eastern and Northern Districts of Oklahoma and U.S. Court of Appeals, Tenth Circuit. *Education:* Cameron University (B.A., 1982); University of Oklahoma (J.D., with honors, 1985). Phi Delta Phi; Order of the Coif. Note Editor, 1984-1985, Oklahoma Law Review. *Member:* Oklahoma County, Oklahoma and American Bar Associations; Magister Holmes Inn of Court. ***PRACTICE AREAS:*** Business Litigation; Employment Law; Bankruptcy. ***Email:*** michael.gray@lawbrg.com

ANDREW D. SCHWARTZ, born Denville, New Jersey, October 29, 1968; admitted to bar, 1994, Texas and U.S. District Court, Northern District of Texas; 1997, Oklahoma and U.S. District Court, Northern, Western and Eastern Districts of Oklahoma. *Education:* University of Texas at Austin (B.S., 1990); University of Tulsa (J.D., 1994). Member, Tulsa Journal of Comparative & International Law. *Member:* State Bar of Texas; Oklahoma Bar Association. ***PRACTICE AREAS:*** Civil Litigation; Business Litigation. ***Email:*** andrew.schwartz@lawbrg.com

OF COUNSEL

W. SAMUEL DYKEMAN, born Pittsburgh, Pennsylvania, August 30, 1928; admitted to bar, 1953, Oklahoma, U.S. District Court, Western District of Oklahoma and U.S. Court of Appeals, Tenth Circuit. *Education:* Oklahoma State University (B.S., 1950); University of Oklahoma (LL.B., 1953). Phi Alpha Delta. *Member:* Oklahoma County, Oklahoma and American Bar Associations. ***PRACTICE AREAS:*** Litigation; Probate; Wills; Trusts; Corporate Law; Commercial Law; Real Property; Partnerships. ***Email:*** sam.dykeman@lawbrg.com

CHRISTA B. RICHARDSON, born Ames, Iowa, 1971; admitted to bar, 1997, Missouri; 2001, Oklahoma. *Education:* Southern Methodist University (B.A., 1993); University of Oklahoma (J.D., with honors, 1997). Chief Notes Editor, Oklahoma Law Review (1996-1997). *Member:* Kansas City Metropolitan and Oklahoma Bar Associations; The Missouri Bar. ***PRACTICE AREAS:*** Real Estate; Banking Law; Business Law. ***Email:*** christa.richardson@lawbrg.com

REPRESENTATIVE CLIENTS: Allison's Fun Company, Inc.; Absentee Shawnee Tribe of Indians of Oklahoma; Association of County Commissioners; Allied Insurance Group; American Fidelity Insurance; Barrett Trailers, Inc; Bank of America, N.A.; AllNations Bank; Community Action Agency of Oklahoma City and Oklahoma/Canadian Counties, Inc.; BankFirst; Union Bank, N.A.; Coregis Insurance Carriers; Erie Insurance Companies; Capitol Indomnity Co.; Community State Bank, Poteau, Oklahoma; Farmers State Bank, Quinton, Oklahoma; GMAC Commercial Mortgage Corporation; Sunset Mortgage Company, L.P.; Integrated Health Services, Inc.; Nurse's Home Care, Inc.; Madill Care Facility, Inc.; Marietta Facility Care, Inc.; JM Huber Corporation; Huber Engineered Woods LLC; Tishamingo Care Facility Inc.; Four Seasons Nursing Care Center of Durant, Inc.; Manor Care Health Services, Inc.; Pinnacle Healthcare Group; Old American Insurance Company; Kemper Surety; Yellow Freight Systems, Inc.; Zurich North America; Kansas City Life Insurance Company; IESI Corporation; Center Point Disposal, Inc.; Total Waste Systems, Inc.; Lifestyles Manufactured Homes, Inc.; Davis Corporation; Sooner Energy Services, Inc.; Red Rock Petroleum Company; Red Rock Distributing Company; Driver Pipeline Co., Inc.; R.F.D. Exploration, Inc.; Mercedes-Benz Credit Corporation; Manor Care Health Services, Inc.; Carter Health Care Management, Inc.; McCaleb Homes, Inc.; Home Creations; MERCO Consultants; Native American Culture Center; Weldon Parts, Inc.; Werner Enterprises.

GARY L. BROOKS AND ASSOCIATES, P.L.L.C.

7100 NORTH CLASSEN BOULEVARD, SUITE 300
OKLAHOMA CITY, OKLAHOMA 73116-7101
Telephone: 405-840-1066
Fax: 405-843-8446
Email: GLB@medlaws.com
URL: http://www.medlaws.com

Plaintiffs Medical Malpractice, Products Liability, Personal Injury, Catastrophic Injury, Automobile Accidents, Brain Injuries, State and Federal Courts.

FIRM PROFILE: Gary L. Brooks & Associates, P.L.L.C. is a personal injury litigation firm concentrating on representing people who have been injured due to medical malpractice. We particularly focus on birth trauma and cerebral palsy cases.

Gary L. Brooks & Associates, P.L.L.C. are listed in the Bar Register of Preeminent Lawyers.

GARY L. BROOKS, born Albuquerque, New Mexico, November 8, 1950; admitted to bar, 1975, Oklahoma; 1976, U.S. District Court, Western District of Oklahoma; 1985, U.S. District Court, Northern District of Oklahoma; 1986, U.S. Supreme Court and U.S. Court of Appeals, Tenth Circuit; 1989, U.S. District Court, Northern District of Texas; 1990, U.S. Claims Court; 1993, U.S. District Court, Eastern and Western Districts of Arkansas; 1994, District of Columbia and Texas. *Education:* Reed College; University of Oklahoma (B.A., with high honors, 1972; J.D., 1975). *Member:* Oklahoma Bar Association; District of Columbia Bar; State Bar of Texas; Oklahoma Trial Lawyers Association (President, 1999); The Association of Trial Lawyers of America; Birth Trauma Litigation Group; Mensa; American Board of Trial Advocates. (Board Certified in Civil Trial Advocacy by the National Board of Trial Advocacy) (Board Certified in Medical Professional Liability by the

(This Listing Continued)

GARY L. BROOKS AND ASSOCIATES, P.L.L.C., Oklahoma City—Continued

American Board of Professional Liability Attorneys). ***PRACTICE AREAS:*** Medical Malpractice Law; Products Liability Law; Personal Injury Law. ***Email:*** glb@medlaws.com

ANN BROOKS, born Fort Smith, Arkansas, August 1, 1962; admitted to bar, 1994, Oklahoma, U.S. Court of Appeals, Tenth Circuit, U.S. District Court, Western and Northern Districts of Oklahoma and U.S. District Court, Eastern and Western Districts of Arkansas. *Education:* University of Arkansas, 1982-1984; Central State University (B.A., 1990); University of Oklahoma (J.D., 1993). *Member:* Oklahoma and American Bar Associations; Oklahoma Trial Lawyers Association (Board of Directors, 1997-2003); The Association of Trial Lawyers of America. ***PRACTICE AREAS:*** Personal Injury. ***Email:*** dab@medlaws.com

BULLARD & HOEHNER, P.C.

Established in 1992

312 N.W. 13TH STREET
P.O. BOX 780
OKLAHOMA CITY, OKLAHOMA 73101-0780
Telephone: 405-604-5000
Facsimile: 405-604-5005
Email: mail@bullard-hoehner.com
URL: http://www.lawyers.com/bullard-hoehner

Workers Compensation Defense, Litigation, Insurance Coverage, Environmental, Products Liability.

DONALD A. BULLARD, born Chickasha, Oklahoma, April 17, 1959; admitted to bar, 1984, Oklahoma and U.S. District Court, Western District of Oklahoma. *Education:* Southwestern Oklahoma State University (B.S., 1981); University of Oklahoma (J.D., 1984). *Member:* Oklahoma County, Oklahoma and American (Member, Sections on: Labor and Employment; Litigation; Tort and Insurance Practice) Bar Associations; Defense Research Institute. ***PRACTICE AREAS:*** Workers Compensation Defense; Insurance Coverage; Tort Defense. ***Email:*** don@bullard-hoehner.com

DANIEL J. HOEHNER, born Okarche, Oklahoma, December 23, 1958; admitted to bar, 1984, Oklahoma; 1985, U.S. District Court, Western District of Oklahoma. *Education:* Oklahoma State University (B.S., 1981); University of Oklahoma (J.D., 1984). Member, American Inns of Court XXIII. *Member:* Oklahoma County, Oklahoma and American (Member, Torts and Insurance Section) Bar Associations. ***PRACTICE AREAS:*** Insurance Coverage; Tort Defense; Environmental. ***Email:*** dan@bullard-hoehner.com

ROBERT C. SIMPSON, JR., born July 17, 1972; admitted to bar, 2001, Oklahoma. *Education:* University of San Francisco (B.A., 1995); University of Oklahoma (J.D., 2001). ***PRACTICE AREAS:*** Workers Compensation. ***Email:*** robbie@bullard-hoehner.com

ELIZABETH HONEYWELL GRAY, born Tyler, Texas, March 27, 1957; admitted to bar, 1982, Oklahoma and U.S. District Court, Western District of Oklahoma. *Education:* Southeastern Oklahoma State University (B.A., 1979); Oklahoma City University (J.D., 1982). ***PRACTICE AREAS:*** Workers Compensation; Bankruptcy; Real Estate; Contracts; Domestic Relations.

MICHAEL T. EGAN, born Edmond, Oklahoma, October 6, 1958; admitted to bar, 1984, Oklahoma. *Education:* University of Oklahoma (B.A., 1980); Oklahoma City University (J.D., 1984). Phi Alpha Delta. *Member:* Oklahoma Bar Association. ***PRACTICE AREAS:*** Workers Compensation Law.

OF COUNSEL

LEE ENDICOTT, born Oklahoma City, Oklahoma, January 15, 1959; admitted to bar, 1984, Oklahoma. *Education:* Oklahoma State University (B.S., 1981); University of Oklahoma (J.D., 1984). Phi Delta Phi. Recipient: Oklahoma County Outstanding Young Lawyer Award, 1990-1991. *Member:* Oklahoma County (Member, Board of Directors, 1990-1991; Social Committee, 1986-1988; Young Lawyers Division, 1986-1993, Chairman, 1990-1991), Oklahoma (Member, Young Lawyers Division, Board of Directors, 1990-1991) and American Bar Associations. ***PRACTICE AREAS:*** Civil Trials; Property Insurance; Personal Injury; Products Liability; Probate. ***Email:*** lee@bullard-hoehner.com

REPRESENTATIVE CLIENTS: Albertson's; American Agency System, Inc.; Alexsis; Asplundh Tree Expert Co.; Ace-USA, Inc.; Claims and Risk Services; RSKCo. Claims Service, Inc.; Commercial Union Insurance Company; CompSource Oklahoma, Inc.; Consolidated Benefits Resources; Continental Loss Adjusting; Crawford and Company; Electric Insurance; Farmers Insurance Company; Fireman's Fund Insurance; GAB Robins North America; Gallagher Basset; Gates McDonald; Grace Living Centers; The Hartford; Kwikset; Mercury Marine; National Union Fire Insurance; Oklahoma Food Services; Pinkerton Security, Inc.; Remington Park; Rollins Risk Management; Sentry Insurance; Smith Environmental Technology Corp.; Sooner Trailer Manufacturing; Wrangler Jeans/VF Workwear.

BURCH & GEORGE

A PROFESSIONAL CORPORATION

1500 CITY PLACE BUILDING
204 NORTH ROBINSON
OKLAHOMA CITY, OKLAHOMA 73102
Telephone: 405-239-7711
Toll Free: 1-877-239-7711
Fax: 405-239-7795
Email: derekburch@burch-george.com
URL: http://www.lawyers.com/burchgeorge

General Civil Trial Practice in all State and Federal Courts, Personal Injury, Products Liability, Medical Malpractice and Insurance Litigation.

(This Listing Continued)

DEREK K. BURCH, born Dallas, Texas, October 22, 1961; admitted to bar, 1989, Oklahoma and U.S. District Court, Northern, Eastern and Western Districts of Oklahoma; U.S. Court of Appeals, Tenth Circuit. *Education:* Oklahoma State University (B.S., 1984); Oklahoma City University School of Law (J.D., 1988). *Member:* Oklahoma County, Oklahoma and American Bar Associations; The Association of Trial Lawyers of America (Member, President's Club); Oklahoma Trial Lawyers Association (Member: Advisory Board, 1994-1995, 1999-2003; Board of Directors, 2003—). ***PRACTICE AREAS:*** Civil Practice; Personal Injury; Products Liability; Medical Malpractice; Insurance Litigation. ***Email:*** derekburch@burch-george.com

KELLY A. GEORGE, born Snyder, Oklahoma, November 1, 1962; admitted to bar, 1989, Oklahoma, U.S. District Court, Eastern and Western Districts of Oklahoma and U.S. Court of Appeals, Tenth Circuit. *Education:* Oklahoma Christian College (B.S., 1985); Oklahoma City University; University of Oklahoma (J.D., 1989). Phi Delta Phi. Past Member, Wm. I Hollaway Jr. American Inns of Court, American Inn of Court CV. *Member:* Oklahoma County (Past Member, Board of Directors, Young Lawyers Division, 1993-1994), Oklahoma (Past Member, Board of Directors, Young Lawyers Division, 1993-1994) and American Bar Associations; The Association of Trial Lawyers of America (Member, President's Club); Oklahoma Trial Lawyers Association (Member: Advisory Board, 1999-2002; Board of Directors, 2003-2005); American Agriculture Lawyers Association. ***PRACTICE AREAS:*** Civil Practice; Personal Injury; Products Liability; Medical Malpractice; Insurance Litigation. ***Email:*** kellygeorge@burch-george.com

OF COUNSEL

KENNETH G. COLE, born Van Nuys, California, May 31, 1961; admitted to bar, 1986, Oklahoma and U.S. District Court, Northern, Eastern and Western Districts of Oklahoma and U.S. Court of Appeals, Tenth Circuit. *Education:* Southwestern Oklahoma State University (B.A., cum laude, 1983); University of Oklahoma (J.D., 1986). Phi Alpha Delta. *Member:* Oklahoma Bar Association; Oklahoma Trial Lawyers Association (Chairman: Legislation Committee, 199601997; Amicus Curie Committee, 2004-2005; Board of Directors, 1997-1998; Advisory Board, 1998-1999). ***PRACTICE AREAS:*** Civil Practice; Personal Injury; Products Liability; Medical Malpractice; Insurance Litigation. ***Email:*** kennycole@burch-george.com

ASSOCIATE

DEEANN L. GERMANY, born Oklahoma City, Oklahoma, September 30, 1971; admitted to bar, 1999, Oklahoma, U.S. District Court, Eastern and Western Districts of Oklahoma. *Education:* Oklahoma State University (B.S., 1993); University of Oklahoma (J.D., 1998). Phi Delta Phi. *Member:* Oklahoma County, Oklahoma and American Bar Associations; The Association of Trial Lawyers of America; Oklahoma Trial Lawyers Association. ***PRACTICE AREAS:*** Civil Practice; Personal Injury; Products Liability; Medical Malpractice; Insurance Litigation. ***Email:*** deeanngermany@burch-george.com

BURNETT & GELNAR, PLLC

Established in 2003

13838 QUAIL POINTE DRIVE, SUITE C
OKLAHOMA CITY, OKLAHOMA 73134-1020
Telephone: 405-302-0400
Fax: 405-302-0411
Email: info@burnettgelnar.com
URL: http://www.burnettgelnar.com

Mailing Address: P.O. Box 21387, Oklahoma City, OK 73156-1387

Business Law, Commercial Transactions, Banking, Real Estate, Taxation, Trusts and Estates, Estate Planning, Mergers and Acquisitions, Charitable and Non-Profit Organizations.

FIRM PROFILE: Legal and tax services for businesses and individuals since 1985. We focus our practice on Business Law, Estate Planning and Taxation.

KEVIN W. BURNETT, born Tulsa, Oklahoma, April 1, 1960; admitted to bar, 1985, Oklahoma, U.S. District Court, Northern and Western District of Oklahoma and U.S. Tax Court. *Education:* Oklahoma State University (B.S., 1982); University of Tulsa (J.D., 1985). Delta Theta Phi. Certified Public Accountant, Oklahoma, 1988. *Member:* American, Oklahoma County and Oklahoma Bar Associations; American Institute of Certified Public Accountants; Oklahoma Society of Certified Public Accountants. ***PRACTICE AREAS:*** Business Law; Commercial Law; Contracts; Corporate Law; Intellectual Property Licensing; Civil Litigation; Mergers, Acquisitions and Divestitures; Estate Planning; Nonprofit and Charitable Organizations; Partnership Law; Real Estate. ***Email:*** kevin@burnettgelnar.com

STEPHEN C. GELNAR, born Oklahoma City, Oklahoma, July 9, 1966; admitted to bar, 1999, Oklahoma and U.S. District Court, Western District of Oklahoma. *Education:* Oklahoma State University (B.S., 1988); Oklahoma City University (J.D., magna cum laude, 1999). Phi Delta Phi. Member, Moot Court Honors Board, 1997-1999. Recipient: Oklahoma City University R. Merit Scholar Award; Cali (Formerly amjur) Awards. Law Review Staff, 1997-1999. *Member:* Oklahoma County, Oklahoma and American Bar Associations. ***PRACTICE AREAS:*** Corporate Law; Banking Law; Real Estate Law; Mergers and Acquisitions. ***Email:*** steve@burnettgelnar.com

RONALD L. BROWN, born Norman, Oklahoma, November 12, 1958; admitted to bar, 1983, Oklahoma; U.S. District Court, Western District of Oklahoma. *Education:* University of Oklahoma (B.A., 1980; J.D., 1983). *Member:* Oklahoma County, Oklahoma and American Bar Associations. ***PRACTICE AREAS:*** Trusts and Estates; Civil Litigation; Real Estate; Business Law. ***Email:*** ron@burnettgelnar.com

DAWN M. KISSINGER-CHRISTEL, born Fond du Lac, Wisconsin, April 15, 1973; admitted to bar, 2001, Oklahoma. *Education:* St. Norbert College (B.A., cum laude, 1995); Oklahoma City University School of Law (J.D., 2001). Phi Delta Phi. Faculty Honor Roll; Merit Scholar; Vice-President, Merit Scholars Association; White House Intern. *Member:*

(This Listing Continued)

Oklahoma County, Oklahoma and American Bar Associations. **PRACTICE AREAS:** Labor and Employment; Civil Litigation; Commercial Law; Corporate Law. **Email:** dawn@burnettgelnar.com

BURTON & ASSOCIATES, P.C.

Established in 1992
308 NW 13TH, SUITE 100
P.O. BOX 2666
OKLAHOMA CITY, OKLAHOMA 73103
Telephone: 405-232-0555; 800-257-5533
Fax: 405-232-1849
Email: okc@burtonlaw.com
URL: http://www.burtonlaw.com

Tulsa Office: 1861 East 15th Street, 74104. Telephone: 918-747-4600. Fax: 918-744-6300. Email: Tulsa@burtonlaw.com.
Walters, Office: 122 North Broadway, 73572. Telephone: 580-875-2200. Fax: 580-875-2202. Email: Walters@burtonlaw.com.

Workers Compensation, Wrongful Termination, Personal Injury, Automobile Accidents, Bankruptcy, Social Security.

FIRM PROFILE: Firm established in 1992 by Lew Gravitt as solo practitioner. Brandon Burton joined the firm in 1995 and continued the practice following Mr. Gravitt's death in 1997. Practice areas include Workers' Compensation, Personal Injury, Social Security Disability, Employment Law and Bankruptcy.

LEW GRAVITT (1954-2005)

BRANDON J. BURTON, born Wichita Falls, Texas, December 11, 1968; admitted to bar, 1997, Oklahoma; U.S. District Court, Western, Eastern and Northern Districts of Oklahoma. *Education:* Oklahoma State University (B.S., 1991; M.S., 1993); Oklahoma City University (J.D., 1996). Member, Governor Henry's Workers' Compensation Task Force, 2004-2005. *Member:* Oklahoma County (Member, Workers Compensation Section) and Oklahoma (Member, Workers Compensation Section; Young Lawyers CLE Committee) Bar Associations; Oklahoma Trial Lawyers Association; The Association of Trial Lawyers of America; Lawyers for Working Oklahomans (Board Member and President, 2002-2003); National Workplace Injury Litigation Group; Luther Bohannon American Inns of Court. **REPORTED CASES:** B.E.&K. Const. v. Abbott; Ibarra v. Hitch; M.I.T.F. v. Pullum. **PRACTICE AREAS:** Workers Compensation (75%); Social Security Disability (15%); Employment Law (1%); Personal Injury (9%). **Email:** brandon@burtonlaw.com

---

T.R. BANKS, born Clinton, Oklahoma, 1972; admitted to bar, 2000, Oklahoma; U.S. District Court, Western, Eastern and Northern Districts of Oklahoma. *Education:* Oklahoma State University (B.S., 1996); Oklahoma City University (J.D., 1999). *Member:* Oklahoma Bar Association; Oklahoma Trial Lawyers Association; The Association of Trial Lawyers of America; Lawyers for Working Oklahomans. **REPORTED CASES:** Bryan v. Bryan; Thompson v. J.W. Buek. **PRACTICE AREAS:** Workers Compensation (80%); Personal Injury (5%); Social Security Disability (5%); Bankruptcy (10%). **Email:** tr@burtonlaw.com

OF COUNSEL

GREGORY R. RASNAKE
STEVE DAVIS
WILLIAM A. ROBINSON

CALDWELL & RUSSELL, P.C.

Established in 1998
201 ROBERT S. KERR, SUITE 800
OKLAHOMA CITY, OKLAHOMA 73102
Telephone: 405-232-1456
Fax: 405-232-1450

Workers Compensation Defense.

M. DAN CALDWELL, born Ardmore, Oklahoma, July 21, 1949; admitted to bar, 1977, Oklahoma. *Education:* University of Oklahoma (B.B.A., 1971; J.D., 1977). Phi Delta Phi. *Member:* Oklahoma County, Cleveland County, Oklahoma and American Bar Associations; International Association of Defense Counsel; Oklahoma Association of Defense Counsel; (Board of Governors, 1986-1990; President, 1992); Workers' Compensation Defense Council; Worker's Compensation Advisory Counsel (1998—); Defense Research Institute. **PRACTICE AREAS:** Workers Compensation. **Email:** dcaldwel@complawcaldwell.com

KRISTI BYNUM RUSSELL, born El Reno, Oklahoma, May 23, 1970; admitted to bar, 1996, Oklahoma. *Education:* Oklahoma City University (B.A., summa cum laude, 1992); University of Oklahoma (J.D., 1996). Phi Alpha Delta (Justice, 1995). Recipient: Academic Achievement Awards, Counseling and Interviewing and Mass Media Law. *Member:* Oklahoma County, Oklahoma (Board of Directors, Workers Compensation Section, 2004—) and American Bar Associations; Oklahoma Association of Defense Counsel; Defense Research Institute. **PRACTICE AREAS:** Workers Compensation. **Email:** krussell@complawcaldwell.com

---

ANGELA D. THOMPSON, born Alva, Oklahoma, May 30, 1971; admitted to bar, 1996, Oklahoma and U.S. District Court, Western District of Oklahoma. *Education:* University of Oklahoma (B.A., 1993; J.D., 1996). *Member:* Oklahoma Bar Association; Oklahoma Association of Defense Counsel; Defense Research Institute. **PRACTICE AREAS:** Workers Compensation. **Email:** athompson@complawcaldwell.com

CALVERT LAW FIRM

Established in 1990
1041 N.W. GRAND BOULEVARD
OKLAHOMA CITY, OKLAHOMA 73118
Telephone: 405-848-5000
Fax: 405-848-5052
URL: http://www.calvertlaw.com

Business & Complex Litigation, Mergers & Acquisitions, Taxation, Real Estate, Debtor, Creditor & Insolvency; Securities Arbitration.

RANDALL K. CALVERT, born Stillwater, Oklahoma, February 5, 1958; admitted to bar, 1990, Oklahoma, 2000, Texas, U.S. District Court, Western, Northern and Eastern Districts of Oklahoma, U.S. Court of Appeals, Tenth Circuit and U.S. Tax Court. *Education:* Oklahoma State University (B.S., Accounting); Oklahoma City University (J.D., with distinction). Phi Delta Phi. Beta Gamma Sigma. Moot Court Board; Order of Barristers. Research Editor, Oklahoma City University Law Review. Certified Public Accountant, 1980. Commissioner, Oklahoma Racing Commission. *Member:* Oklahoma County, Oklahoma and American Bar Associations; American Inns of Court (Master, William J. Holloway, Jr. Inn); Public Investors Arbitration Bar Association; Oklahoma Trial Lawyers Association; The Association of Trial Lawyers of America; National Association of Dealer Counsel. **LANGUAGES:** Spanish. **PRACTICE AREAS:** Business Litigation; Mergers and Acquisitions. **Email:** rcalvert@calvertlaw.com

W. BRETT WILLIS, born Oklahoma City, Oklahoma, January 9, 1968; admitted to bar, 1993, Oklahoma, U.S. District Court, Western, Northern and Eastern Districts of Oklahoma and U.S. Court of Appeals, Tenth Circuit. *Education:* University of Oklahoma (B.B.A., Finance, 1990; J.D., 1993). Member, Luther Bohanon American Inns of Court. *Member:* Oklahoma County (Social Committee Chair, 1997-1998; Member, Young Lawyers Division; Vice-Chair, 1996-1998; Board of Directors, 1994-1998; Member, Community Outreach Committee, 1993-1996 and Chair, 1994-1995); Oklahoma (Member: Young Lawyers Division; Board of Directors, 1995-1999; Children and The Law Committee, 1993-1995; New Attorney Orientation Committee, 1994; Chair, Mock Trial Committee, 1995-1996 and Vice Chair, 1994-1995) and American (Member: Planning Board, 1995-1996; Litigation Section). **REPORTED CASES:** King v. Modern Music, 33 P.3d 947; Kimble v. Arney, 90 P.3d 598. **PRACTICE AREAS:** Litigation. **Email:** bwillis@calvertlaw.com

MONICA J. HOENSHELL, born Enid, Oklahoma, March 10, 1978; admitted to bar, 2003, Oklahoma. *Education:* Oklahoma State University (B.A., Psychology, 2003); University of Oklahoma (J.D., with distinction, 2003); New York University (LL.M., Taxation, 2004). Recipient, American Jurisprudence Awards, Torts, and Income Taxation of Trusts and Estates. *Member:* Oklahoma and American Bar Associations; National Association of Dealer Counsel. **PRACTICE AREAS:** Taxation; Trusts and Estates; Business Law. **Email:** mhoenshell@calvertlaw.com

JOHN W. SWINFORD, JR., born Oklahoma City, Oklahoma, February 7, 1944; admitted to bar, 1969, Oklahoma; 1970, U.S. District Court, Western District of Oklahoma. *Education:* Wesleyan University (B.A., 1966); University of Oklahoma (J.D., 1969). Attorney, Oklahoma City Urban Renewal Authority, 1969-1973. *Member:* Oklahoma County Bar Association (President, Bankruptcy Section, 1998); Oklahoma and American Bar Associations; Oklahoma City Real Property Attorneys Association (President, 1977). **PRACTICE AREAS:** Real Estate Litigation; Bankruptcy. **Email:** jswinford@calvertlaw.com

STANLEY F. CARROLL, P.C.

Established in 1995
1900 N.W. EXPRESSWAY, SUITE 1300
OKLAHOMA CITY, OKLAHOMA 73118
Telephone: 405-848-2255
Fax: 405-840-4701
Email: stan4law@aol.com
URL: http://www.stan4law.com

General Civil Litigation in State and Federal Courts, Contracts, Commercial Real Estate, Landlord and Tenant, Real Estate Law, Construction Law, Business Law, Family Law, Divorce, Child Custody, Wills, Probate, Trusts and Estates.

STANLEY F. CARROLL, born Miami, Oklahoma, March 3, 1954; admitted to bar, 1983, Oklahoma and U.S. District Court, Western District of Oklahoma. *Education:* Northeastern Oklahoma A & M College (A.A., 1977); University of Oklahoma (B.A., 1979; J.D., 1982). Board Member, Cleveland County Family YMCA (1999—). *Member:* Oklahoma County and Oklahoma (Member, Section on Family Law) Bar Associations; Oklahoma City Real Property Lawyers Association. **PRACTICE AREAS:** Contracts; Family Law; General Civil Litigation; Real Estate Law; Landlord and Tenant Law. **Email:** stan4law@aol.com

CATHCART & DOOLEY

A PROFESSIONAL CORPORATION
CORNETT BUILDING
2807 CLASSEN BOULEVARD
OKLAHOMA CITY, OKLAHOMA 73106
Telephone: 405-524-1110
Fax: 405-524-4143

Insurance Defense, Insurance and Subrogation, Property Insurance, Fire and Casualty and Insurance Law. Negligence Trial Practice.

(This Listing Continued)

CATHCART & DOOLEY, A PROFESSIONAL CORPORATION, Oklahoma City—Continued

WILLIAM R. CATHCART, born New York, N.Y., September 20, 1945; admitted to bar, 1971, Oklahoma; U.S. Supreme Court; U.S. Court of Appeals, Tenth Circuit; U.S. District Court, Northern, Eastern and Western Districts of Oklahoma. *Education:* Roanoke College (B.A., 1967); Oklahoma City University (J.D., 1971). Phi Alpha Delta. *Member:* Oklahoma County, Oklahoma and American Bar Associations; Oklahoma Association of Defense Counsel; Defense Research Institute; International Association of Defense Counsel. **PRACTICE AREAS:** Fire Insurance Law; Fire Loss Litigation; Arson and Insurance Fraud Defense Law; Insurance Defense Law; Products Liability Law. **Email:** bcathcart@cgdlawfirm.com

CARY D. DOOLEY, born Tulsa, Oklahoma, October 17, 1963; admitted to bar, 1988, Oklahoma and U.S. District Court, Eastern and Western Districts of Oklahoma. *Education:* Baylor University (B.A., 1985); University of Oklahoma (J.D., 1988). Recipient, American Jurisprudence Award, International Law. *Member:* Oklahoma County (Board of Directors, Young Lawyers Division, 1991-1995; Vice-Chairperson, 1992-1993; Chairperson, 1993; Outstanding Director, 1993) and Oklahoma (Member, Board of Directors, Young Lawyers Division, 1988-1990; 1993-1996; Treasurer, 1995) Bar Associations. **PRACTICE AREAS:** Insurance Subrogation; Products Liability Law; Arson and Insurance Fraud Defense Law; Personal Injury Law; Insurance Defense Law. **Email:** cdooley@cgdlawfirm.com

VIRGINIA CATHCART HOLLEMAN, born Salem, Virginia, December 25, 1966; admitted to bar, 1993, Oklahoma, U.S. Court of Appeals, Tenth Circuit, U.S. District Court, Eastern, Northern and Western Districts of Oklahoma and U.S. Supreme Court. *Education:* University of Oklahoma (B.B.A., 1989; J.D., 1993). Iota Tau Tau. *Member:* Oklahoma County and Oklahoma Bar Associations. **PRACTICE AREAS:** Arson and Insurance Fraud Defense; Insurance Defense; Insurance Subrogation; Products Liability; Automobile Negligence; Appeals. **Email:** vholleman@cgdlawfirm.com

SCOTT CALDWELL, born Oklahoma City, Oklahoma, October 13, 1972; admitted to bar, 2000, Oklahoma, U.S. District Court, Northern, Eastern and Western Districts of Oklahoma. *Education:* Southwestern Oklahoma State University (B.M.E., 1996); University of Oklahoma (J.D., 2000). *Member:* Oklahoma Bar Association. **LANGUAGES:** French. **PRACTICE AREAS:** Insurance; Subrogation; Products Liability; Insurance Defense; Probate; Estate Planning. **Email:** scaldwell@cgdlawfirm.com

LAURIE J. MILLER, born Dallas, Texas, January 12, 1965; admitted to bar, 2003, Oklahoma, U.S. District Court, Eastern, Northern and Western Districts of Oklahoma. *Education:* Oklahoma City University (B.A., 1993; J.D., 2002). *Member:* Cleveland County, Oklahoma County, Oklahoma and American Bar Associations. **PRACTICE AREAS:** Insurance Defense; Subrogation; Products Liability; Personal Injury. **Email:** lmiller@cgdlawfirm.com

JAMES S. DILBECK, born Pauls Valley, Oklahoma, July 27, 1979; admitted to bar, 2004, Oklahoma. *Education:* Southeastern Oklahoma State University (B.A., 2001); University of Oklahoma (J.D., 2004). **PRACTICE AREAS:** Insurance; Subrogation; Products Liability; Insurance Defense. **Email:** sdilbeck@cgdlawfirm.com

REPRESENTATIVE CLIENTS: Allstate Insurance Company; American Modern Home Insurance Co.; American National Property & Casualty Co.; Atlanta Casualty Companies; Chubb Group of Insurance Companies; Farmers Insurance Co.; Foremost Insurance Co.; Grain Dealers Mutual Insurance Company; Guaranty National Insurance Co.; Guide One Mutual Insurance Company; Hanover Insurance Co.; Indiana Lumbermans Mutual Insurance Co.; Meridian Resource Co.; National Lloyds Insurance Company; North Star Mutual Insurance Company; Oklahoma Farm Bureau Mutual Insurance Company; Oklahoma Farmers Union Mutual Insurance Company; Preferred Risk Mutual Insurance Company; Prudential Property and Casualty Company; Republic Insurance Co.; State and County Mutual Fire Insurance Company; Shelter Mutual Insurance Co.; State Farm Fire and Casualty Company; State Farm Mutual Auto Insurance Company; Tennessee Farm Bureau Mutual Insurance Co.; Thomas Jefferson Insurance Co.; United Casualty Insurance; United Services Auto Assoc.; Wellington Insurance Company; Westfield Insurance Co.

THE CHEEK LAW FIRM

Established in 1943

(Formerly Cheek, Cheek & Cheek)

LAW CENTER BUILDING
311 NORTH HARVEY
OKLAHOMA CITY, OKLAHOMA 73102
Telephone: 405-272-0621
Fax: 405-232-1707
Email: triddles@cheeklaw.com
Email: tcheek@cheeklaw.com

General Civil Practice in all State and Federal Courts. Personal Injury Defense, Insurance Defense, Products Liability Defense, Automobile Injury Defense, Motor Carrier Liability, Medical Malpractice Defense, Corporation, Aircraft Titles, Insurance and Probate Law, Labor and Employment Law (Management), Commercial Litigation. Trials in all Courts.

FIRM PROFILE: The Cheek Law Firm is Listed in the Bar Register of Preeminent Lawyers under Insurance Defense.

JAMES C. CHEEK (1885-1960)
ALEX CHEEK (1916-1996)
WILLIAM C. CHEEK (1923-1997)

TIM N. CHEEK, born Oklahoma City, Oklahoma, October 28, 1958; admitted to bar, 1985, Oklahoma and U.S. District Court, Western District of Oklahoma. *Education:* Whitworth College (B.A., cum laude, 1981); University of Oklahoma (M.B.A., 1985; J.D., 1985). Phi Alpha Delta. Recipient, American Jurisprudence Award in Torts I. Adjunct Professor, University of Central Oklahoma, Business Law, 1992-1999. *Member:* Oklahoma Bar Association; Oklahoma Association of Defense Counsel. **REPORTED CASES:** Miller V. American Trust Insurance Co., Ltd. 931 F.2d 703 (10th Cir. 1991); MIC Property and Casualty Insurance Corp. V. International Insurance Corp., 990 F2d 573 (10th Cir. 1993). **PRACTICE AREAS:** Product Liability; Insurance Defense; Medical Malpractice Defense; Litigation; Insurance Coverage Opinions; Insurance Bad Faith; Federal Civil Litigation; State Civil Litigation; Appeals; Motor Carrier Liability. **Email:** tcheek@cheeklaw.com

JOHN D. CHEEK, born Oklahoma City, Oklahoma, August 7, 1920; admitted to bar, 1943, Oklahoma. *Education:* University of Oklahoma (B.A., 1943; LL.B., 1947). *Member:* Oklahoma County, Oklahoma and American Bar Associations; Federation of Insurance and Corporate Counsel (Vice President, 1957). **REPORTED CASES:** Allstate Insurance Co. v. Daniels, 87 F.R.D. 1 (D.C. Okl. 1978); Maws v. Luethue, 503 P.2d 871 (Okl. 1972). **PRACTICE AREAS:** Trucking Law; Auto Law; Negligence Law.

ASSOCIATES

DARIN TODD RIDDLES, born Oklahoma City, Oklahoma, February 28, 1967; admitted to bar, 1994, Oklahoma. *Education:* University of Oklahoma (M.B.A., J.D., 1994). **REPORTED CASES:** Woolard v. JLG Industries, Inc., 210 F.3d 1158 (10th Cir. 2000); Mares v. Lockard 2 P.3d 384 (Ok.Civ.App.2000); Wooten v. Hudson 71 F.Supp.2d 1149, ED, Okla. Sep 30, 1999. **PRACTICE AREAS:** Insurance Defense; Personal Injury; Business Litigation; International Business Transactions; Insurance Coverage Opinions; Insurance Bad Faith; Federal Civil Litigation; State Civil Litigation; Appeals; Medical Malpractice; Products Liability; Motor Carrier Liability; Trucking Law. **Email:** triddles@cheeklaw.com

SCOTT M. INMAN, born Midwest City, Oklahoma, October 2, 1978; admitted to bar, 2004, Oklahoma. *Education:* University of Oklahoma (B.A., 2001; J.D., 2004). **PRACTICE AREAS:** Insurance Defense. **Email:** sunman@cheeklaw.com

REPRESENTATIVE GENERAL CLIENTS: Armour Swift-Ekrich, Inc.; Big Three Industries; Corporation Guaranty & Trust; Culligan International, Inc.; Federal Aviation Title Co.; Government Employees Finance Co.; Refrigerated Transport, Inc.; Security Devices, Inc.; Vorderlandwehr, Inc.
REPRESENTATIVE INSURANCE CLIENTS: Administrative Claim Service, Inc.; Aegis Security Insurance Company; Allied Insurance Group; American Continental Insurance Company; American Fidelity Insurance Co.; American Re-Ins. Co.; American Southern Insurance Company; Balboa Insurance Company; California State Automobile Insurance Company; Carolina Casualty Co.; Carl Warren & Co.; 21st Century Insurance Group; Cincinnati Insurance Company; Essex Insurance Company; Evanston Insurance Company; First Security Insurance Co.; First State Insurance; G.A.B. Business Service; Government Employees Insurance Co.; Graham-Rogers Insurance; Grange Insurance Company; Great West Casualty Co.; Harbor Insurance Co.; Highlands Insurance Co.; Johnson Claim Service; K&K Insurance; Lloyds of London; Markel Insurance Company; Millers National Insurance Co.; Nationwide Insurance Company; Protective Insurance Company; R&R Select, Inc.; Redland Insurance Company; Seaboard Underwriters, Inc.; Terra Nova Insurance Company; TransAmerica Insurance Co.; Voyager Indemnity Insurance Company; Chef's Requested Foods, Inc.; Warren Properties, Inc.

CLARK & MITCHELL, P.C.

Established in 1991

101 PARK AVENUE, SUITE 210
OKLAHOMA CITY, OKLAHOMA 73102
Telephone: 405-235-8488
Fax: 405-235-7979
Email: clark@clarkmitchell.com
URL: http://www.lawyers.com/clarkmitchell

Trials State and Federal Courts. Medical Malpractice, Nursing Home Malpractice, Legal Malpractice, Automobile Accidents, Personal Injury, Professional Liability.

FIRM PROFILE: The firm is a "boutique" specializing in medical and professional negligence.

STEVEN E. CLARK, born Norman, Oklahoma, September 15, 1950; admitted to bar, 1975, Oklahoma. *Education:* University of Oklahoma (B.A., 1972; J.D., 1975). Phi Alpha Theta; Phi Delta Phi. Adjunct Professor, Oklahoma City University College of Law, 1987. Vice Chairman, Oklahoma County Election Board, 1982. *Member:* Oklahoma County, Oklahoma and American (Member: Section on Tort and Insurance Practice; Law and Medicine Committee) Bar Associations; Oklahoma Trial Lawyers Association (Member, Board of Directors, 1981-1982; 1993-1994; Treasurer, 1981); The Association of Trial Lawyers of America (Member, Birth Trauma Committee); American Board of Trial Advocates. Fellow, American College of American Trial Lawyers. **PRACTICE AREAS:** Medical Malpractice; Personal Injury; Professional Liability; Legal Malpractice; Automobile Accidents. **Email:** clark@clarkmitchell.com

HEATHER JOHNSON MITCHELL, born Osmond, Nebraska, October 16, 1965; admitted to bar, 1990, Oklahoma. *Education:* University of Oklahoma (B.A., Nursing, 1987); Oklahoma City University (J.D., 1990). Phi Delta Phi. Recipient, Member of the Year Award, Oklahoma Trial Lawyers Association, 1999. Registered Nurse, Oklahoma, 1987—. *Member:* Oklahoma Bar Association; Oklahoma Trial Lawyers Association (Member of the Year, 1999). **PRACTICE AREAS:** Medical Malpractice; Nursing Malpractice. **Email:** heather@clarkmitchell.com

CLARK, STAKEM, WOOD & PATTEN, P.C.

Established in 1987

SUITE 400
101 PARK AVENUE
OKLAHOMA CITY, OKLAHOMA 73102
Telephone: 405-232-4271
Fax: 405-232-4275
URL: http://www.cswp-law.com

Norman, Oklahoma Office: 103 West Boyd, Suite K, 73069. Telephone: 405-321-0610. Fax: 405-321-7571.

(This Listing Continued)

Business Planning, Commercial, Corporate, Federal and State Taxation, School Law, Real Estate Administration, Telecommunications Regulation, Civil Rights, Domestic Relations, Employment, Officers and Directors Liability, Securities Litigation, Torts, Estate Planning, Probate, Elder Law, Arbitration and Mediation, Trials and Appeals in all State and Federal Courts.

JACK G. (CHIP) CLARK, JR., born Oklahoma City, Oklahoma, January 6, 1945; admitted to bar, 1969, Oklahoma, U.S. District Court, Western District of Oklahoma, U.S. Court of Appeals, Tenth Circuit and U.S. Tax Court. *Education:* Westminster College and University of Oklahoma (B.A., 1966); University of Oklahoma (J.D., 1969). Phi Alpha Delta. Member, Board of Directors, Oklahoma City Beautiful, 1994— (Recipient, Leadership Award, 1998). Member, Taxation Section and Real Property, Probate and Trust Law Section, American Bar Association. Member, Probate Code Committee, 1988—, Member, 2003— and Chairman, 2004, Law Related Education Committee, Oklahoma Bar Association. Member, 1988-1993 and Chairman, 1991-1993, Lawyer Referral Service Committee (Recipient: Service Award, 1993), Member, 1993— and Chairman, 1999-2003, Law Related Education Committee (Recipient: Outstanding Committee Award, 2003), Member, Community Service Committee, 1994-1995 and Member, Board of Directors, 1999-2002, Oklahoma County Bar Association. [Capt., U.S. Army, Adjutant General's Corps, 1969-1971]. ***PRACTICE AREAS:*** Business Planning Law; Taxation Law; Estate Planning Law; Telecommunications. ***Email:*** cclark@cswp-law.com

RONALD E. STAKEM, born Cumberland, Maryland, April 27, 1947; admitted to bar, 1975, Oklahoma, U.S. District Court, Western, Northern and Eastern Districts of Oklahoma; U.S. Court of Appeals, Ninth and Tenth Circuits and U.S. Supreme Court. *Education:* Harvard College (B.A., 1969); University of Oklahoma (J.D., 1975). Member, Community Council of Central Oklahoma, 1980-1989. Member, Committee on Pre-Paid Legal Services, Oklahoma Bar Association, 1981-1982. Member: Oklahoma County Bar Association, Board of Directors, 1996-1999; Committee on Fee Grievance and Ethics, 1985-1998; Bench and Bar Committee, 1994-1999; Chairman: Subcommittee on Judicial Candidate Evaluation Project, 1995; Subcommittee on Judicial Performance Evaluation, 1995, Oklahoma County Bar Association. Member, Litigation Section, American Bar Association. ***PRACTICE AREAS:*** Litigation; School Law; Commercial Law; Telecommunications Regulation; Public Utility Regulation; Mediation. ***Email:*** rstakem@cswp-law.com

BETTY GARRETT WOOD, born Oklahoma City, Oklahoma, March 14, 1951; admitted to bar, 1980, Oklahoma. *Education:* University of Oklahoma (B.A., 1973; J.D., 1980). Member, Board of Editors, Oklahoma Law Review, 1979-1980. Author: "Estate Planning: Validity of Inter Vivos Transfers Which Reduce or Defeat the Surviving Spouse's Statutory Share in Decedent's Estate," 32 Oklahoma Law Review 837, 1979. Chairperson, Board of Directors, Alzheimer's Association, Oklahoma and Arkansas Chapter, 2003-2005. Member, Board of Directors, Alzheimer's Association, Oklahoma Chapter, 1990-1996 and 1999—; President, 1995; Chairman, Central Oklahoma Branch Leadership Council, 1999—. Member, Oklahoma Attorney General's Task Force to Improve End-of-Life Line in Oklahoma, 2004-2005. Member, Senior Advisory Council, Oklahoma Publishing Company. *Member:* National Academy of Elder Law Attorneys; Oklahoma City Estate Planning Council. ***PRACTICE AREAS:*** Estate Planning Law; Probate Law; Elder Law. ***Email:*** bgwood@cswp-law.com

REBECCA J. PATTEN, born Norman, Oklahoma, April 28, 1952; admitted to bar, 1977, Oklahoma; U.S. District Court, Western, Northern and Eastern Districts of Oklahoma; 1984, U.S. Court of Appeals, Tenth Circuit and U.S. Supreme Court. *Education:* University of Oklahoma (B.A., with highest honors, 1974); University of Chicago (J.D., 1977). Phi Beta Kappa. Assistant District Attorney, Cleveland County, Oklahoma, 1980-1982. *Member:* American Bar Association (Member, Real Property, Probate and Trust Section). (Resident, Norman Office). ***PRACTICE AREAS:*** Fiduciary Law; Governmental Law; Trusts and Estates. ***Email:*** rjpatten@cswp-law.com

All Attorneys are Members of the Oklahoma or Cleveland County and Oklahoma Bar Associations.

REPRESENTATIVE CLIENTS: MCI; Cooperative Counsel of Oklahoma School Administrators; Ground Water Protection Council; Oil Field Ignition Parts Co.; Flex-Ability Concepts, LLC; Progressive Stamping, LLC; Mistletoe Wholesale Florists Co.; Central Oklahoma Master Conservancy District; Victory Glass Co., Inc.; Holiday International, Inc.; E.H. Properties, L.L.C.; Oklahoma Malt Beverage Association; Air & Sea Travel, Inc.; Keystaff Staffing Services.
REFERENCE: Bank One Oklahoma, N.A.

C. CRAIG COLE & ASSOCIATES

Established in 1972

317 NORTHWEST TWELFTH STREET
OKLAHOMA CITY, OKLAHOMA 73103-3704
Telephone: 405-232-8700
Fax: 405-232-1655
URL: http://www.lawyers.com/colelaw
Email: thefirm@ccc-a.com
URL: http://www.ccc-a.com

Antitrust, Arbitration, Aviation, Banking Law, Bankruptcy, Civil Liability, Commercial Law, Commercial Collections and Litigation, Commercial Insurance Defense, Consumer Finance, Corporate Law, Covenants Not to Compete, Creditors Rights, Dealership Law, Debtor and Creditor, Defense Litigation, Ecclesiastical Law, Employment Law, Environmental Law, Federal Civil, Franchise Law, Health Care Law, Land Use Litigation, Mediation, Oil and Gas, Partnerships, Personal Injury Defense, Personal Property, Probate, Products Liability Defense, Real Estate, Subrogation, Wage and Hour Law, Workers Compensation Defense, Wrongful Termination Defense.

FIRM PROFILE: Our Firm is dedicated to furnishing our clients specialized assistance for their global business and personal legal needs. This assistance is tailored to safeguard our clients' time and money and to prevent future legal pitfalls by implementing cost-effective measures now to avoid costly mistakes in the future. Our Firm has experience in numerous areas of corporate and business representation and litigation so that the client does not require multiple law firms to provide preventive measures in its day-to-day operations. If our firm is not able to take a particular case due to a conflict or some other reason, we can refer you to other firms that can handle your case in a competent and aggressive manner.

We invite our clients to tell us what they want in an attorney-client relationship and what they like or dislike about our services. This open communication improves our services to each client and builds a trusting, secure and long-lasting relationship with all clients of the Firm. If we are not a part of your team, we need to be. C. Craig Cole & Associates gives you an edge in your business.

C. CRAIG COLE, born Oakland, California, February 25, 1944; admitted to bar, 1972, Oklahoma, U.S. Court of Appeals, Tenth Circuit, U.S. District Court, Western District of Oklahoma and U.S. Bankruptcy Court, Western District of Oklahoma; 1993, U.S. District Court, Eastern and Northern Districts of Oklahoma. *Education:* Central State University (B.A., 1968); Oklahoma City University (J.D., 1972). Instructor: Law and Banking, South Oklahoma City Junior College, 1975-1976; Moore Norman Technical Institute, 1977-1978. *Member:* Oklahoma County and Oklahoma Bar Associations. ***PRACTICE AREAS:*** Commercial Law; Labor and Employment; Real Estate; Corporate Law; Personal Injury; Alternative Dispute Resolution; Health Care Law.

REPRESENTATIVE CLIENTS: Automobile Dealerships, Trucking, Aviation, Banking, Nursing Homes.

COLLINS, ZORN & WAGNER, P.C.

429 N.E. 50TH, SECOND FLOOR
OKLAHOMA CITY, OKLAHOMA 73105-1815
Telephone: 405-524-2070
1-800-916-0676
Facsimile: 405-524-2078
Email: czwg@czwglaw.com

Trial Practice State and Federal Courts. Appellate Practice. Civil Rights, Employment Law. Insurance Defense, Manufacturers' Products Liability, Workers Compensation.

CHRISTOPHER J. COLLINS, born Enid, Oklahoma, January 26, 1953; admitted to bar, 1980, Oklahoma, U.S. District Court, Western, Eastern and Northern Districts of Oklahoma and U.S. Court of Appeals, Tenth Circuit. *Education:* Central State University (B.A., cum laude, 1976); University of Oklahoma (J.D., 1980). Phi Delta Phi. *Member:* Oklahoma County, Oklahoma and American Bar Associations; Oklahoma Association of Defense Counsel (Past Secretary/Treasurer, 1983-1985 and Vice President, 1985-1986); Defense Research Institute; International Association of Defense Counsel. ***REPORTED CASES:*** Parker v. Strong, 717 F.Supp. 767 (WD Okla, 1989); McEwen v. City of Norman, 926 F.2d. 1539 (10th Cir. 1991). ***PRACTICE AREAS:*** Civil Rights; Employment Law; Products Liability; Civil Litigation; Insurance Defense. ***Email:*** cjc@czwglaw.com

DANIEL K. ZORN, born Phillips, Wisconsin, January 15, 1952; admitted to bar, 1977, Oklahoma, U.S. District Court, Western, Eastern and Northern Districts of Oklahoma, U.S. District Court, Northern District of Texas an d U.S. Court of Appeals, Tenth Circuit. *Education:* University of Wisconsin at Stevens Point (B.S., Political Science and History, 1973); Oklahoma City University (J.D., 1976). Phi Delta Phi. Member, Oklahoma City University Law Review. *Member:* Oklahoma County, Oklahoma and American Bar Associations; Oklahoma Association of Defense Counsel; Defense Research Institute. ***PRACTICE AREAS:*** Insurance Defense; Products Liability; Workers Compensation. ***Email:*** dkz@czwglaw.com

JASON C. WAGNER, born Marion, Kansas, July 21, 1965; admitted to bar, 1991, Oklahoma, U.S. District Court, Northern, Western and Eastern Districts of Oklahoma and U.S. Court of Appeals, 10th Circuit; 1998, U.S. Supreme Court. *Education:* University of Oklahoma (B.A., 1987; J.D., 1991). *Member:* Oklahoma County, Oklahoma and American Bar Associations. ***REPORTED CASES:*** Hollingsworth v. Hill, 110 F.3d 733 (10th Cir. 1997). ***PRACTICE AREAS:*** Civil Rights; Civil Litigation; Employment Law; Products Liability. ***Email:*** jcw@czwglaw.com

ROBERT RAY JONES, JR., born Hammond, Louisiana, October 31, 1970; admitted to bar, 2004, Oklahoma and U.S. District Court, Western District of Oklahoma. *Education:* Louisiana Tech University (B.S., History, 1994); Oklahoma City University School of Law (J.D., cum laude, 2004). Phi Delta Phi. Member, Oklahoma City University of Law Review. *Member:* American Bar Association. ***PRACTICE AREAS:*** Insurance Defense; Civil Rights; Employment Law.

ANDREW A. ARTUS, born Corpus Christi, Texas, April 7, 1965; admitted to bar, 1994, Oklahoma. *Education:* Southwest Texas State University (B.B.A., Management, 1987); University of Oklahoma (J.D., 1994). Assistant Attorney General, Oklahoma, 1994. *Member:* Oklahoma County and Oklahoma Bar Associations. ***PRACTICE AREAS:*** Civil Rights Defense; Insurance Defense; Personal Injury; Family Law; Workers Compensation. ***Email:*** aaa@czwglaw.com

STEPHEN L. GERIES, born Clovis, New Mexico, June 26, 1970; admitted to bar, 2001, Oklahoma. *Education:* West Texas State University (B.S., 1993); Oklahoma City University School of Law(J.D., 2001). Phi Delta Phi; Delta Mu Delta. Member: Moot Court Honor Board; Federalist Society. Assistant District Attorney, Lincoln County District Attorney's Office, Oklahoma, 2002-2003. *Member:* Oklahoma County Bar Association. ***PRACTICE AREAS:*** Insurance Defense; Civil Rights; Civil Litigation; Employment Law; Constitutional Law. ***Email:*** steve@czwglaw.com

STEPHEN R. PALMER, born Stuttgart, Germany, May 7, 1971; admitted to bar, 1996, Oklahoma; 1997, U.S. District Court, Northern, Eastern and Western Districts of Oklahoma and U.S. Court of Appeals, Tenth Circuit. *Education:* Oklahoma Baptist University (B.A., 1993); Oklahoma City University (J.D., 1996). *Member:* Oklahoma County and Oklahoma Bar Associations; Defense Research Institute. ***PRACTICE AREAS:*** Products Liability; Civil Litigation; Insurance Defense. ***Email:*** srp@czwglaw.com

(This Listing Continued)

COLLINS, ZORN & WAGNER, P.C., Oklahoma City—Continued

JODI SUE CASEY, born Concordia, Kansas; admitted to bar, 1997, Oklahoma; 2003, U.S. District Court, Northern, Eastern and Western Districts of Oklahoma and U.S. Court of Appeals, Tenth Circuit. *Education:* Oklahoma City University (B.A., 1994); Oklahoma City University School of Law (J.D., 1997). Recipient, CALI Award for Excellence in Commercial Paper. Assistant District Attorney, Oklahoma County, 1997-2003. *Member:* Oklahoma County and Oklahoma Bar Associations. ***PRACTICE AREAS:*** Civil Litigation; Civil Rights; Insurance Defense; Employment Law. ***Email:*** jodi@czwglaw.com

TIMOTHY E. LURTZ, born Garden City, Kansas, 1964; admitted to bar, 1991, Oklahoma, U.S. District Court, Western, Northern and Eastern Districts of Oklahoma and U.S. Court of Appeals, Tenth Circuit. *Education:* University of Oklahoma (B.A., 1988; J.D., 1991). Phi Delta Phi. *Member:* Oklahoma County and Oklahoma Bar Associations; Oklahoma Association of Defense Counsel; Defense Research Institute. ***PRACTICE AREAS:*** Insurance Defense; Personal Injury; Civil Litigation. ***Email:*** tel@czwglaw.com

REPRESENTATIVE CLIENTS: Association of County Commissioners of Oklahoma (ACCO); Bell Sports, Inc.; Sweetwater International Corp.; Alpha Therapeutic Corporation; Crawford & Company; First Mercury Syndicate Inc.; Food Lion, Inc.; LeMars Mutual Insurance Co.; Maryland Insurance Group; Oklahoma Restaurant Group Self Insurance Association; National Interstate Transportation Specialists; Oklahoma Transit Insurance Company; United Southern Assurance Company; Petrosurance Casualty Insurance Co.; Zurich-American Insurance Group; Credit General Insurance Co.; Alexsis Risk Management Services, Inc.; Professional Claim Managers; Colony Insurance Co.; Credit Insurance Co.; Autocraft Industries; Harper County, Okmulgee County and LeFlore County; Reliant American Insurance Group.

COMMERCIAL LAW GROUP, P.C.

Established in 1991

2725 OKLAHOMA TOWER
210 PARK AVENUE
OKLAHOMA CITY, OKLAHOMA 73102-5643
Telephone: 405-232-3001
Fax: 405-232-5553
Email: postmaster@clgroup.org

Banking, Bankruptcy, Complex Commercial Transactions, Corporate Law, Energy, Entrepreneur Representation, Equine Law, Mergers and Acquisitions, Oil and Gas, Real Estate, Venture Capital, Complex Commercial Credit Workouts and Reorganization.

FIRM PROFILE: The Commercial Law Group is a successor to Self, Giddens & Lees, Inc. established in 1991. The firm specializes in handling complex commercial matters which require the direct involvement of experienced senior lawyers. The focus of our firm is to be both businessmen and first class lawyers. We pride ourselves in finding the best team for a matter even if a lawyer is located in another firm. Accordingly, the firm maintains formal ongoing referral arrangements with multiple firms in Oklahoma and other states, including large full service firms and small firms with specialized expertise.

THOMAS J. BLALOCK, born Oklahoma City, Oklahoma, 1961; admitted to bar, 1986, Oklahoma; U.S. District Court, Western District of Oklahoma. *Education:* Oklahoma State University (B.S., 1983); University of Oklahoma (J.D., 1986). Author: "The Oklahoma Surface Damages Act: Constitutional Inquiries, 1985," Student Monograph Series, Urban, State and Local Law Newsletter, Volume 9, No. l, Fall, 1985. Barrister, William J. Holloway, Jr., American Inn of Court, 1997-2000. *Member:* Oklahoma County, Oklahoma (Co-chair, State High School Mock Trial Competition, 1990-1991) and American Bar Associations. ***PRACTICE AREAS:*** Commercial Transactions; Real Estate; Venture Capital; Equine Law; Workouts; Litigation. ***Email:*** tblalock@clgroup.org

C. RAY LEES, born Guymon, Oklahoma, 1954; admitted to bar, 1979, Oklahoma. *Education:* Southwestern Oklahoma State University (B.A., cum laude, 1976); University of Oklahoma (J.D., 1979). Order of the Coif. Editor, Oklahoma Law Review, 1977-1979. *Member:* Oklahoma County, Oklahoma (Law Schools Committee, 1987-1991) and American Bar Associations. ***PRACTICE AREAS:*** Banking; Commercial Transactions; Energy; Mergers and Acquisitions. ***Email:*** rlees@clgroup.org

SHANNON T. SELF, born Thomas, Oklahoma, 1956; admitted to bar, 1984, Oklahoma. *Education:* University of Oklahoma (B. Accty., B.B.A., highest honors, 1979); Northwestern University (J.D., magna cum laude, 1984). Order of the Coif. Member, Northwestern University Law Review, 1983-1984. Northwestern University Law Board, 1999—. Certified Public Accountant, Oklahoma, 1980. Adjunct Professor, University of Oklahoma, College of Law, 1987-1989. *Member:* Oklahoma County, Oklahoma and American Bar Associations. ***PRACTICE AREAS:*** Commercial Transactions; Oil and Gas; Real Estate; Corporate Law; Workouts; Venture Capital; Equine Law. ***Email:*** SSelf@clgroup.org

MICHAEL D. MELEEN, born Tulsa, Oklahoma, 1971; admitted to bar, 1998, Oklahoma. *Education:* Oral Roberts University (B.S., magna cum laude, 1993); University of Oklahoma (J.D. with honors, 1998). *Member:* Oklahoma County, Oklahoma and American Bar Associations. ***PRACTICE AREAS:*** Commercial Transactions; Real Estate; Workouts. ***Email:*** mmeleen@clgroup.org

KENDRA D. PARSONS, born East Pennsboro, Pennsylvania, September 11, 1978; admitted to bar, 2003, Oklahoma. *Education:* University of Central Oklahoma (B.A., 2000); University of Oklahoma (J.D., 2003). *Member:* Oklahoma County and Oklahoma Bar Associations. ***PRACTICE AREAS:*** Commercial Transactions; Real Estate; Workouts. ***Email:*** kparsons@clgroup.org

OF COUNSEL

THERESA B. LEWIS, born Enid, Oklahoma, July 10, 1962; admitted to bar, 1997, Texas; 2004, Oklahoma. *Education:* Oklahoma State University (B.S.M.E., 1985); Southern Methodist University (J.D., cum laude, 1997). Phi Delta Phi. Author: "Patent Protection for the Pharmaceutical Industry: A Survey of the Patent Laws of Various Countries," 30 International Lawyer 835, 1996. *Member:* Oklahoma County, Oklahoma and American Bar Associations; Texas Bar Association. ***PRACTICE AREAS:*** Corporate Law; Business Transactions; Partnership Transactions; Private Investment Funds. ***Email:*** tlewis@clgroup.org

REPRESENTATIVE CLIENTS: Chesapeake Energy Corporation; Arvest Bank; Carter Chevrolet Agency, Inc.; The Oklahoma Grocers Association; Chisholm Private Capital Partners; Stillwater National Bank & Trust Co.; First Bank of Medicine Lodge.

CONNER & WINTERS, LLP

Established in 1933

ONE LEADERSHIP SQUARE
211 NORTH ROBINSON, SUITE 1700
OKLAHOMA CITY, OKLAHOMA 73102-7101
Telephone: 405-272-5711
Facsimile: 405-232-2695
Email: postmaster@cwlaw.com
URL: http://www.cwlaw.com

Tulsa, Oklahoma Office: 3700 First Place Tower, 15 East 5th Street, 74103-4344. Telephone: 918-586-5711. Facsimile: 918-586-8982.
Fayetteville, Arkansas Office: 100 West Center Street, Suite 200, 72701-6081. Telephone: 479-582-5711. Facsimile: 479-587-1426.
Santa Fe, New Mexico Office: 303 Paseo De Peralta, 87501. Telephone: 505-983-6497. Facsimile: 505-983-6478.
Jackson, Wyoming Office: 155 East Pearl Street, Suite 200, P.O. Box 4099, 83001-4099. Telephone: 307-733-2547. Fax: 307-733-3947.
Washington, DC Office: 1627 I Street, N.W., Suite 900, 20006. Telephone: 202-887-5711. Fax: 202-887-6999.
Houston, Texas Office: 1000 Louisiana, Suite 1301, 77002-5005. Telephone: 713-355-5711. Fax: 713-651-3929.

General Civil Practice. Trial and Appeals of Civil Cases in all State and Federal Courts. Administrative Proceedings, Alternative Dispute Resolution, Bankruptcy and Reorganization, Construction, Corporate and Securities, Employee Benefits, Employment and Labor Relations, Energy, Environmental, Estate Planning, Trust and Probate, Federal and State Taxation, Federal White Collar Criminal Defense, Financial Services and Banking, Governmental Affairs, Insurance and Risk Management, International, Litigation and Antitrust, Products Liability, Propane, Real Estate, Tax Exempt Organizations and Charitable Foundations and Workers' Compensation.

FIRM PROFILE: Founded in 1933, Conner & Winters, LLP has become one of the largest and most diverse law firms in the South Central Region of the United States.

The Firm serves a broad range of clients in local, state, regional, national, and international arenas. Its clients include businesses of all sizes and types-locally-owned companies to multinational corporations, individuals, estates and trusts, municipalities and other public-sector organizations, institutions, and charitable foundations.

Conner & Winters, LLP is a full-service firm with numerous specialty groups. Many of its lawyers have experience in several practice areas and that diversity allows the Firm to provide a broad array of legal services to numerous and varied clients. The Firm's lawyers work together to perform legal services with expertise, consistent quality and in a cost-effective manner.

IRWIN H. STEINHORN, born Dallas, Texas, August 13, 1940; admitted to bar, 1964, Texas; 1965, U.S. District Court, Northern District of Texas; 1970, Oklahoma and U.S. District Court, Western District of Oklahoma. *Education:* University of Texas at Austin (B.B.A., 1961; LL.B., 1964). Phi Alpha Delta. Adjunct Professor of Law, Oklahoma City University School of Law, 1979—. Chairman, Business Law Section, Oklahoma Bar Association, 1988-1989. Sr. Vice President and General Counsel, LSB Industries, Inc. (NYSE), 1970-1986. Vice President and General Counsel, USPCI, Inc. (NYSE), 1986-1988. Listed in The Best Lawyers in America (Corporate, Mergers and Acquisitions and Securities Law). ***PRACTICE AREAS:*** Corporate Law; Securities Law; Environmental Law. ***Email:*** isteinhorn@cwlaw.com

JOHN W. FUNK, born Oklahoma City, Oklahoma, 1953; admitted to bar, 1978, Oklahoma. *Education:* University of Oklahoma (B.B.A., 1975; J.D., 1978). Phi Delta Phi. Editor, Oklahoma Law Review. ***PRACTICE AREAS:*** Banking; Corporate; Commercial Transactions; Real Estate. ***Email:*** jfunk@cwlaw.com

JARED D. GIDDENS, born Ponca City, Oklahoma, 1956; admitted to bar, 1981, Oklahoma. *Education:* Central State University (B.S., cum laude, 1978); University of Oklahoma (J.D., 1981). Editor, 1979-1981 and Note Editor, 1981, Oklahoma Law Review. Certified Public Accountant, Oklahoma, 1980. ***REPORTED CASES:*** May-Li Barki, M.D., Inc. v. Liberty Bank and Trust Co., 1999 OK 87, 20 P.3d 135; Dunlap v. Sentry Group Services, Inc., 217 F.3d 311 (5th Cir. 2000); FDIC v. Hastie, 2 F.3d 1042 (10th Cir. 1993); Brooks v. Interfirst Bank, 844 F.2d 258 (5th Cir. 1988). ***PRACTICE AREAS:*** Litigation; Reorganization; Bankruptcy. ***Email:*** jgiddens@cwlaw.com

KIRAN A. PHANSALKAR, born Ponca City, Oklahoma, May 25, 1960; admitted to bar, 1985, Oklahoma; 1990, Texas, U.S. District Court, Western and Northern Districts of Oklahoma, U.S. District Court, Northern District of Texas and U.S. Court of Appeals, Fifth and Tenth Circuits. *Education:* Oklahoma State University (B.S., 1982); University of Oklahoma (J.D., with distinction, 1985). Phi Delta Phi. Research Editor, Oklahoma Law Review. Adjunct Professor, Oklahoma City University School of Law. ***PRACTICE AREAS:*** Bankruptcy Law; Real Estate; Commercial Litigation. ***Email:*** kphansalkar@cwlaw.com

VICTOR F. ALBERT, born Oklahoma City, Oklahoma, 1960; admitted to bar, 1987, Oklahoma. *Education:* University of Oklahoma (B.B.A., 1984); Oklahoma City University (J.D., 1986). *Member:* Oklahoma County, Oklahoma and American Bar Associations. ***PRACTICE AREAS:*** Insurance Defense; ERISA Litigation; Personal Injury; Employment Law. ***Email:*** valbert@cwlaw.com

(This Listing Continued)

MITCHELL D. BLACKBURN, born Ada, Oklahoma, October 30, 1961; admitted to bar, 1987, Oklahoma and U.S. District Court, Western District of Oklahoma. *Education:* Central State University (B.S., 1984); University of Oklahoma (J.D., with distinction, 1987). Member, Oklahoma Law Review. ***PRACTICE AREAS:*** Civil Litigation; Environmental Litigation; Environmental Regulation. ***Email:*** mblackburn@cwlaw.com

MARK H. BENNETT, born Oklahoma City, Oklahoma, May 20, 1964; admitted to bar, 1990, Oklahoma, U.S. District Court, Western District of Oklahoma and U.S. Tax Court. *Education:* DePauw University (B.A., 1987); Oklahoma City University (J.D., 1990); Southern Methodist University (LL.M., Taxation, 1991). Phi Delta Phi; Order of the Barristers. ***PRACTICE AREAS:*** Corporate Law; Taxation; Estate Planning. ***Email:*** mbennett@cwlaw.com

BRYAN J. WELLS, born Tulsa, Oklahoma, 1963; admitted to bar, 1988, Oklahoma, U.S. Court of Appeals, Fifth and Tenth Circuits and U.S. District Court, Eastern, Western and Northern Districts of Oklahoma. *Education:* University of Oklahoma (B.B.A., Finance, 1984; J.D., 1988). ***LANGUAGES:*** French. ***REPORTED CASES:*** May-Li Barki, M.D., Inc. v. Liberty Bank and Trust Co., 1999 OK 87, 20 P.2d 135; Dunlap v. Sentry Group Services, Inc., 217 F.3d 311 (5th Cir. 2000); FDIC v. Hastie, 2 F.3d 1042 (10th Cir. 1993); Brooks v. Interfirst Bank, 844 F.2d 258 (5th Cir. 1988). ***PRACTICE AREAS:*** Commercial Litigation; Bankruptcy. ***Email:*** bwells@cwlaw.com

LAURA L. McCASLAND HOLBROOK, born Oklahoma City, Oklahoma, October 27, 1971; admitted to bar, 1997, Oklahoma and U.S. District Court, Western and Northern Districts of Oklahoma. *Education:* Oklahoma State University (B.A., with highest honors, 1990); Oklahoma City University (J.D., 1997). Hatton Summers Scholar. Note Editor, 1996-1997 and Staff Member, 1995-1997, Oklahoma City University Law Review. ***PRACTICE AREAS:*** Litigation; Bankruptcy. ***Email:*** lmccasland@cwlaw.com

ASSOCIATES

JOHN E. GATLIFF II, born Oklahoma City, Oklahoma, September 1, 1960; admitted to bar, 1998, Oklahoma, U.S. District Court, Western District of Oklahoma, U.S. District Court, Northern District of Texas and U.S. Court of Appeals, Fifth Circuit. *Education:* University of Oklahoma (B.A., 1982; J.D., with honors, 1998); Southwestern Baptist Theological Seminary (M.A.R.E., 1987). Member, American Indian Law Review, 1998. ***PRACTICE AREAS:*** Litigation; Bankruptcy. ***Email:*** jgatliff@cwlaw.com

J. DILLON CURRAN, born Enid, Oklahoma, January 19, 1977; admitted to bar, 2002, Oklahoma. *Education:* Oklahoma State University (B.S., magna cum laude, 1999); University of Oklahoma (J.D., with highest honors, 2002). Phi Kappa Phi; Order of the Coif. Assistant Articles Editor, Oklahoma Law Review, 2001-2002. President of the Class of 2002, 1999-2000, 2001-2002. ***PRACTICE AREAS:*** Civil Litigation; Bankruptcy; Commercial Litigation. ***Email:*** dcurran@cwlaw.com

WILLIAM M. ("BILLY") LEWIS, born Pratt, Kansas, July 1, 1976; admitted to bar, 2003, Oklahoma and U.S. District Court, Western District of Oklahoma. *Education:* Oklahoma City University (B.B.A., 2000; J.D., 2003). Phi Delta Phi; Hatton W. Sumners Scholar. ***PRACTICE AREAS:*** Corporate; Litigation; Bankruptcy; Securities. ***Email:*** blewis@cwlaw.com

OF COUNSEL

PETER B. BRADFORD, born Chicago, Illinois, January 23, 1936; admitted to bar, 1961, Oklahoma, U.S. District Court, Northern, Western and Eastern Districts of Oklahoma and U.S., Court of Appeals, Eighth and Tenth Circuits. *Education:* Grinnell College (B.A., 1959); University of Tulsa (J.D., 1961). Listed in The Best Lawyers in America (Business Litigation). *Member:* American Arbitration Association; Association of Attorney Mediators (President, Oklahoma Chapter); American College of Trial Lawyers. ***PRACTICE AREAS:*** Arbitration/Mediation; Civil Litigation; Criminal Litigation. ***Email:*** pbradford@cwlaw.com

SHELIA M. DARLING, born Shreveport, Louisiana, May 8, 1959; admitted to bar, 1988, Oklahoma; U.S. Supreme Court. *Education:* University of Oklahoma (B.A., 1984; J.D., 1988). Order of the Coif. Member, Oklahoma Law Review, 1986-1988. ***PRACTICE AREAS:*** Litigation. ***Email:*** sdarling@cwlaw.com

(For Biographical Data of other Firm Personnel, See Professional Biographies in Tulsa, Oklahoma, Jackson, Wyoming, Fayetteville, Arkansas, Washington, D.C., Santa Fe, New Mexico and Houston, Texas)

WILLIAM R. COOK II, PLLC

1900 N.W. EXPRESSWAY
SUITE 1350
OKLAHOMA CITY, OKLAHOMA 73118-1805
Telephone: 405-858-1920
Facsimile: 405-858-1921
Email: williamcook@wrciilaw.com
URL: http://www.wrcooklaw.com

Federal and State Income Taxation, Estate and Gift Taxation Law, Tax Controversies and Tax Litigation. Probate, Estate Planning, Trust Law, Wills.

WILLIAM R. COOK II, born Wichita Falls, Texas, January 18, 1952; admitted to bar, 1978, Texas and Oklahoma; 1981, U.S. Claims Court; 1982, U.S. Tax Court and U.S. Supreme Court. *Education:* University of Oklahoma (B.B.A., 1974); University of Texas (J.D., 1977); Southern Methodist University (LL.M. in Taxation, 1981). Beta Gamma Sigma; Phi Delta Phi. Law Clerk to Judge William A. Goffe, U.S. Tax Court, 1981-1983. *Member:* Oklahoma and American Bar Associations; State Bar of Texas; Oklahoma State Society of Certified Public Accountants. ***PRACTICE AREAS:*** Federal Income Tax; Estate and Gift Taxation; Tax Controversies; Trusts and Estates; Probate.

COOPER, McKINNEY & WOOSLEY, PLLP

OKLAHOMA CITY, OKLAHOMA

(See Tulsa)

General Civil Practice, Civil Litigation, Major Transactions, Business Organization, Employment Law, Health Care, Employee Benefits, Banking, Estate Planning, Education Law, Construction, Oil and Gas, Real Estate and Environmental Law.

CORBYN LAW FIRM

Established in 2000

TWO LEADERSHIP SQUARE
211 NORTH ROBINSON, SUITE 1120
OKLAHOMA CITY, OKLAHOMA 73102
Telephone: 405-239-7055
Telefax: 405-239-2436
Email: gcorbyn@corbynlaw.com
URL: http://www.lawyers.com/georgecorbyn

Civil Trial and Appellate Practice, State and Federal Courts.

GEORGE S. CORBYN, JR., born Oklahoma City, Oklahoma, December 4, 1947; admitted to bar, 1973, Oklahoma and U.S. District Court, Eastern, Northern and Western Districts of Oklahoma; 1974, U.S. Court of Appeals, Tenth Circuit and U.S. Supreme Court. *Education:* Stanford University (B.A., 1970); University of Oklahoma (J.D., 1973). Phi Delta Phi. Listed in: The Best Lawyers in America (Business Litigation); Chambers USA America's Leading Business Lawyers. *Member:* Oklahoma County (Director, 1978-1981, 1989-1991), Oklahoma and American (Member, Litigation Section) Bar Associations; American Inn of Court CV (Master); Fellow, American College of Trial Lawyers. ***REPORTED CASES:*** In re: CFS Related Securities Fraud Litigation, 256 F.Supp. 2d 1227 (ND Okla. 2003); Marlin Oil Co. v. Barby Energy Corp., 55 P.3d 446 (Okla. App.2002); State of Oklahoma v. Dudman, 981 P.2d 314 (Okla. 1999); Dyco Petroleum Corp. v. Mesa Operating Co., 935 F.Supp. 1193 (W.D. Okla 1996); Cantrell v. United States Soccer Federation, 924 P.2d 789 (Okla. App. 1996); Scales v. Sonic Industries Inc., 887 F.Supp. 1435 (E.D., Okla. 1995); Box v. Cornish 889 P.2d 1282 (Okla.App.1994); Pack v. Santa Fe Minerals, 869 P.2d 323 (Okla.1994); Federal Deposit Insurance Corporation v. Regier, Carr & Monroe, 996 F.2d 222 (10th Cir.1993); Powell v. American Casualty Company, 772 F.Supp. 1188 (W.D. Okla 1991); Big Four Petroleum Co. v. Quirk, 755 P.2d 632 (Okla.1988); McKinnon v. Cairns, 698 F. Supp. 852 (W.D. Okla.1988); Ellison v. An-Son Corp., 751 P.2d 1102 (Okla.App.1988); Ellison v. Gray, 702 P.2d 360 (Okla.1985); Hoyt v. Continental Oil Company, 606 P.2d 560 (Okla.1980); R.J. Enstrom Corporation v. Interceptor Corporation, 555 F.2d 277 (10th Cir.1977); U.S. v. Haala, 532 F.2d 1324 (10th Cir. 1976). ***PRACTICE AREAS:*** Business Litigation. ***Email:*** gcorbyn@corbynlaw.com

KATHRYN M. ZYNDA, born Oklahoma City, Oklahoma, September 19, 1966; admitted to bar, 1993, Oklahoma, U.S. District Court, Eastern, Northern and Western Districts of Oklahoma and U.S. Court of Appeals, Tenth Circuit. *Education:* University of Oklahoma (B.A., 1989; J.D., 1993). Phi Beta Kappa. *Member:* Oklahoma County Bar Association; American Inn of Court (Barrister). ***REPORTED CASES:*** EEOC v. Voss Elec. Co. d/b/a Voss Lighting, 257 F.Supp. 2d 1354 (W.D. Okla. 2003); Keirsey v. Banner Life Ins. Co., 2004 WL 1814186 (10th Cir. August 16, 2004). ***PRACTICE AREAS:*** Civil Litigation. ***Email:*** kzynda@corbynlaw.com

REPRESENTATIVE CLIENTS: Big D Industries, Inc.; Chubb Group of Insurance Companies; City of Enid; Crawley Petroleum Corporation; Dowley, Inc.; Executive Risk Indemnity; Irish Realty, Inc.; Marlin Oil Corporation; Midlands Claims Administrators, Inc.; Oklahoma Attorneys Mutual Insurance Company; Okland Oil Company; U.S. Food Service, Inc.; Warren Drilling Company; Westport Insurance Company; TIG Insurance; General Growth Management Inc.; Archer Daniels Midland Co., Inc.; Rent-A-Center; Key Energy Corporation; Oklahoma City Public Schools; Compass Bank; Newfield Exploration Inc.; Jana Partners LLC; Sonic Development of Central Texas; MTV Capital Limited Partnership.

COYLE LAW FIRM

Established in 1988

119 NORTH ROBINSON, SUITE 320
OKLAHOMA CITY, OKLAHOMA 73102
Telephone: 405-232-1988
Fax: 405-272-9859
Email: email@coylelaw.com

Criminal Trial and Appellate Practice in all State and Federal Courts. Grand Jury Investigations, White Collar and Complex Crimes, Drugs, DUI, Murder, Sex Crimes, Obscenities, Securities Fraud, Personal Injury, Condemnation, Driving While Intoxicated, Criminal Records Expungements, Civil Rights.

FIRM PROFILE: The firm practices criminal and civil trial law. We have defended cases in State and Federal courts throughout the nation. Each client's case is handled through a team approach that involves experienced defense lawyers, paralegals and investigators. We stick up for people. Coyle Law Firm is listed in the Bar Register of Preeminent Lawyers under Criminal Trial Practice.

JOHN W. COYLE, III, born Oklahoma City, Oklahoma, March 7, 1948; admitted to bar, 1974, Oklahoma, U.S. District Court, Northern, Eastern and Western Districts of Oklahoma, U.S. District Court, Northern District of Texas and U.S Court of Appeals, Second, Fifth, Ninth and Tenth Circuits. *Education:* Oklahoma City University (B.A., 1971; J.D., 1974). Phi Alpha Delta. Recipient: Clarence Darrow Award, Oklahoma's Outstanding Criminal Defense Lawyer, Oklahoma Criminal Defense Lawyers Association, 1995. Listed in: Best Lawyers in America, 1999- 2004; Bar Register of Preeminent Lawyers. Instructor, Criminal Law and Procedure: Oklahoma Bar Review, 1988-1997. Frequent Speaker and Lecturer, Oklahoma Continuing Legal Education, The University of Oklahoma School of

(This Listing Continued)

COYLE LAW FIRM, Oklahoma City—Continued

Law and Oklahoma City University. Legal Analyst, ABC Television News and Local Affiliates and Commentator, Court TV. *Member:* Oklahoma Bar Association (Chairman: Criminal Law Committee, 1999-2000; Evidence Committee, 2000-2002); Oklahoma Trial Lawyers Association (Member: Board of Directors, 1991, 1993; Advisory Board, 1998-2002); Oklahoma Criminal Defense Lawyers Association (Member, Board of Directors, 1996-1997; National Association of Criminal Defense Lawyers (Legislative Coordinator, 1994-2002); First Amendment Lawyers Association; Master, American Inns of Court. ***PRACTICE AREAS:*** Criminal Defense; Securities Litigation. ***Email:*** jc@coylelaw.com

---

JAMES L. HANKINS, born Enid, Oklahoma, October 7, 1968; admitted to bar, 1993, Oklahoma and U.S. District Court, Western District of Oklahoma; 1994, U.S. Court of Appeals, Tenth Circuit. *Education:* Northwestern Oklahoma State University (B.S., 1990); University of Oklahoma College of Law (J.D., 1993). Oklahoma Law Review, 1993. Author: Comment, "Criminal Law: Criminal "Anti-Stalking" Laws: Oklahoma Hops on the Legislative Bandwagon," 46 Okla. L. Rev. 109, 1993. Adjunct Professor, Northwestern Oklahoma State University, 1994, 1995. *Member:* Garfield County and Oklahoma Bar Associations; National Association of Criminal Defense Lawyers. ***REPORTED CASES:*** Revilla v. Gibson, 283 F.3d 1203 (10th Cir. 2002); Neill v. Gibson, 278 F.3d 1044 (10th Cir. 2001); Toles v. Gibson, 269 F.3d 1167 (10th Cir. 2001); Neill v. Gibson, 263 F.3d 1184 (10th Cir. 2001); Clayton v. Gibson, 199 F.3d 1163 (10th Cir. 1999); Clayton v. Gibson, 196 F.3d 1119 (10th Cir. 1999); Stafford v. Ward, 59 F.3d 1025 (10th Cir. 1995); Stafford v. Ward, 60 F.3d 668 (10th Cir. 1995); Stafford v. Saffle, 34 F.3d 1557 (10th Cir. 1994); United States v. McVeigh, 896 F. Supp. 1549 (W.D. Okla. 1995); Stafford v. State, 1995 OK CR 35, 899 P.2d 657. ***PRACTICE AREAS:*** Criminal Law; Habeas Corpus. ***Email:*** jh@coylelaw.com

ASHLEY L. ALTSHULER, born Hanover, New Hampshire, December 6, 1969; admitted to bar, 1999, Oklahoma. *Education:* University of Oklahoma (B.A., 1994); Oklahoma City University School of Law (J.D., 1998). Phi Alpha Delta. Moot Court Honors Board, Oklahoma City University Law School. ***PRACTICE AREAS:*** Criminal Law. ***Email:*** aa@coylelaw.com

JOHN W. "BILLY" COYLE, IV, born Oklahoma City, Oklahoma, October 10, 1974; admitted to bar, 2004, Oklahoma and U.S. District Court, Western District of Oklahoma. *Education:* Florida State University (B.S., 1998); University of Oklahoma (J.D., 2003). *Member:* Oklahoma County Bar Association; Oklahoma Criminal Defense Lawyers Association; Oklahoma County Criminal Defense Lawyers Association; Luther Bohanon American Inn of Court (2002-2003, Student Pupil). [Sergeant, U.S. Marine Corps Reserve, 1993-2000]. ***PRACTICE AREAS:*** Criminal Defense. ***Email:*** bc@coylelaw.com

OF COUNSEL

ROBERT D. BARON, born Moline, Illinois, June 11, 1943; admitted to bar, 1968, Oklahoma; 1975, U.S. Supreme Court; U.S. District Court, Western, Eastern and Northern Districts of Oklahoma and U.S. District Court, District of Colorado; U.S. Court of Appeals, Ninth and Tenth Circuits. *Education:* University of Iowa (B.A., 1965); University of Oklahoma (J.D., 1968). Phi Alpha Delta. Staff Attorney, Department of Highways, 1969-1971. Chairman, Ad Hoc Committee, State Legislative Council on Uniform Eminent Domain Code, 1971-1973. Member, State Human Rights Commission, 1976-1980. Past Member, Faculty, National Institute for Trial Advocacy; Oklahoma College of Advocacy. Chairman: Judicial Selection Sub-Committee, 1977-1978; Legislation Committee, 1980-1981; Member, Board of Directors, 1982-1985, 1993-1995, 1999-2001, Oklahoma County Bar Association. Member, Real Property Committee, 1972-1973; Chairman, Awards Committee, 1984, 1990, Oklahoma Bar Association. Past Member and Member, Board of Directors, 1978-1982, Oklahoma Trial Lawyers Association. Editor, Torts Section, The Advocate, 1980; Treasurer, 1982). *Member:* American Bar Association; The Association of Trial Lawyers of America. Lifetime Fellow, Oklahoma Bar Foundation. ***PRACTICE AREAS:*** Civil Litigation; Products Liability; Medical Malpractice; Personal Injury; Condemnation. ***Email:*** rbaron@concentric.net

A list of Representative Clients will be furnished upon request.

THE CROSTHWAIT LAW FIRM

A PROFESSIONAL CORPORATION

OKLAHOMA CITY, OKLAHOMA

(See Midwest City)

Estate Planning, Wills, Trust Law, Elder Law, Probate, Estate Litigation, Serious or Complex Personal Injury, Automobile Accidents, Motorcycle Accidents, Slip and Fall, Wrongful Death, Real Estate, Family Law, Divorce, Child Custody, Child Support.

CROWE & DUNLEVY

A PROFESSIONAL CORPORATION

Established in 1902

20 NORTH BROADWAY, SUITE 1800
OKLAHOMA CITY, OKLAHOMA 73102-8273
Telephone: 405-235-7700
Fax: 405-239-6651
Email: bryantd@crowedunlevy.com
URL: http://www.crowedunlevy.com

Tulsa, Oklahoma Office: 500 Kennedy Building, 321 South Boston Avenue, 74103-3313. Telephone: 918-592-9800. Fax: 918-592-9801.

Norman, Oklahoma Office: 2500 South McGee, Suite 140, 73072-6705. Telephone: 405-321-7317. Fax: 405-360-4002.

(This Listing Continued)

General Practice. Litigation of all types in both state and federal court. All types of alternative dispute resolution methodologies. Administrative Law, Antitrust, Appellate, Aviation, Bankruptcy and Creditors' Rights, Business Organizations, Commercial Real Estate, Commercial Transactions, Consumer Credit, Corporate and Securities Finance, Environmental, ERISA, Estates and Trusts, Family Law, Financial Institutions and Finance, Franchising and Distribution, Healthcare, Initiative Petition, Insurance Litigation and Regulation, Intellectual Property and Technology, International Business, Labor and Employment, Medicare/Medicaid Fraud and Abuse, Medical Malpractice Defense, Mergers and Acquisitions, Oil and Gas, Oklahoma Corporation Commission, Patent, Trademark, Copyright and Related Matters, Products Liability, Public Finance, School Law, Small Business and Venture Capital, Taxation, White Collar Crime.

FIRM PROFILE: Crowe & Dunlevy, founded in 1902, is the largest and one of the oldest law firms in Oklahoma. The Firm was founded in Oklahoma City and has enjoyed steady and consistent growth, expanding in October of 1989 to include an office in Tulsa and September of 1991 to include an office in Norman. Crowe & Dunlevy is the Oklahoma member of Lex Mundi, an international association of 146 independent law firms, which provides contacts and relationships with leading law firms throughout the world.

Crowe & Dunlevy is organized as a professional corporation and is engaged in most areas of the practice of law. The Firm serves clients ranging from individuals to small businesses to large national and multi-national corporations. The diversity of legal representations within the Firm is underscored by the fact that the Firm's largest client represents less than five percent of its annual fee income.

The Firm is committed to a philosophy of providing on a timely basis high quality legal services to its clients at a reasonable cost. The Firm strives to maintain state of the art library, administrative and other services conducive to the realization of this objective. The Firm has consistently avoided the practice of staffing its cases in a manner in which lawyers provide unnecessary services at unnecessary expense to its clients.

Due to the wide range of experience, the Firm is able to respond to clients with its ability to assemble a legal team with the availability of knowledge and expertise necessary to maximize effective representation. This philosophy encourages timely solutions to client needs in a practical problem-solving environment and at a reasonable cost.

Crowe & Dunlevy is proud to recognize the leadership achievements of its members, both past and present, including: Presidents of the American, Oklahoma, Oklahoma County, Tulsa County and Cleveland County Bar Associations; President of the National Health Lawyers Association; President of the American College of Trial Lawyers; President of the American College of Mortgage Attorneys; Trustee of the United States Supreme Court Historical Society; Chief Judge, United States Court of Appeals, for the 10th Circuit; United States District Judge; Oklahoma Court of Appeals Judge; United States Tax Court Judge; United States Magistrate Judge; United States Attorneys; District Attorneys; United States Ambassador; Deputy Attorney General of the United States; Former Lead and Associate Counsels of the Office of Independent Counsel; Chair of the Murrah Federal Building Memorial Task Force, the Oklahoma City National Memorial Foundation and the Board of Trustees of the Oklahoma City National Memorial Trust; White House Fellow; Deans of the University of Oklahoma College of Law; Mayors; State Representative; Oklahoma Corporation Commissioner; Members of the Boards of Regents for major state universities, and numerous listings in Who's Who in America, Who's Who in American Law, Who's Who in the World and The Best Lawyers in America.

V. P. CROWE (1897-1974)

FRED W. DUNLEVY (1914-1994)

GARY W. DAVIS, born Iola, Kansas, 1931; admitted to bar, 1957, Kansas and Oklahoma. *Education:* University of Kansas (B.A., 1954; J.D., 1957). Phi Delta Phi; Order of the Coif. Member, Board of Editors, Kansas Law Review, 1954-1957. Author: "Business and Commercial Litigation in Federal Courts" and "Federal Regulation of the Natural Gas Industry," The Oil Daily, Special Report, 1983; "Legal Consideration in The Purchase and Sale of Oil and Gas Properties," Oil and Gas Analyst, November-December, 1983. Director: American Petroleum Institute, 1977-1979; National Petroleum Refiners Association, 1976-1978. Board of Governors, University of Kansas, School of Law, 1982-1985; Oklahoma City Mineral Lawyers Society. Guest Lecturer, Trial Tactics, University of Oklahoma School of Law, 1990-1991. Listed in *The Best Lawyers in America* (Business Litigation and Natural Resources Law). Listed as the Oklahoma lawyer in *The International Who's Who of Oil & Gas Lawyers 2004*. Listed in *Chambers USA America's Leading Lawyers in Business*, 2003 and 2004. Oil & Gas Litigation Department Head. Oil and Gas Department Head. ***PRACTICE AREAS:*** Oil and Gas Litigation; Environmental Litigation; Commercial Litigation. ***Email:*** davisg@crowedunlevy.com

ANDREW M. COATS, born Oklahoma City, Oklahoma, 1935; admitted to bar, 1963, Oklahoma. *Education:* University of Oklahoma (B.A., 1957; J.D., 1963). Phi Beta Kappa; Order of the Coif; Phi Delta Phi. Outstanding Law Graduate, 1963. Special Lecturer in Law, University of Oklahoma Law School, 1971-1972. District Attorney, Oklahoma County, Oklahoma, 1976-1980. Outstanding Lawyer in Oklahoma, 1977. Mayor, Oklahoma City, Oklahoma, 1983-1987. Chairman, Oklahoma Young Lawyers Conference, 1968-1969. President: Oklahoma County Bar Association, 1975-1976; President: Oklahoma Bar Association, 1992-1993. Charter Oklahoma President, American Board of Trial Advocates. President, American College of Trial Lawyers, 1996-1997. Fellow, International Academy of Trial Lawyers. Dean, University of Oklahoma College of Law, 1996—. Listed in *The Best Lawyers of America* (Business Litigation). Trustee, United States Supreme Court Historical Society, 1995—. ***PRACTICE AREAS:*** Trial Practice; Appellate Practice; Products Liability; Criminal Law. ***Email:*** coatsa@crowedunlevy.com

ALLEN D. EVANS, born Oklahoma City, Oklahoma, 1938; admitted to bar, 1963, Oklahoma. *Education:* University of Oklahoma (B.A., 1960); University of Michigan (J.D., 1963). Chairman, Estates and Trusts Practice Section of Crowe & Dunlevy. Fellow, American College of Trust and Estate Council. Fellow, The International Academy of Estate and Trust Law. Fellow, American Bar Foundation. Fellow, Oklahoma Bar Foundation. Former Regent and Oklahoma State Chairman, American College of Trust and Estate Counsel.

(This Listing Continued)

Member, Oklahoma Bar Association Committee on Probate Code Reform. Former Chairman, Section of Probate and Trust Law, Oklahoma Bar Association. Former Chairman, Lawyer's Tax Group, Oklahoma City, Oklahoma. Former President, Oklahoma City Estate Planning Council. Member, Section of Real Estate, Probate and Trust Law, American Bar Association. Listed in *The Best Lawyers in America* (Trusts and Estates). ***PRACTICE AREAS:*** Estate Planning; Estate Administration; Estate and Gift Taxation; Trusts and Estates Taxation; Charitable Trusts and Foundations. ***Email:*** evansa@crowedunlevy.com

D. KENT MEYERS, born Oklahoma City, Oklahoma, 1938; admitted to bar, 1964, Oklahoma. *Education:* University of Oklahoma (B.B.A., 1960; J.D., 1964); Harvard Law School (LL.M ., with emphasis in Antitrust and Commercial Law, 1976). Co-Author: "Private Enforcement of the Antitrust Laws Works Occasionally: The Board of Regents of the Univ. Of Okla. v. NCAA, a Case in Point," 48 *Oklahoma Law Review* 669 (1995). Adjunct Professor in Law, Antitrust, Bankruptcy, Professional Responsibility, Trial Techniques, University of Oklahoma College of Law, 1974—. President, Oklahoma County Bar Association, 1983. Fellow, American College of Trial Lawyers. Member, Oklahoma Judicial Nominating Commission, 1985-1991, Chairman, 1990-1991. Chairman, Commercial Law Committee, Oklahoma Bar Association, 1978-1982; Professionalism Committee, Oklahoma Bar Association, 1988 (Member, 1986-1988, Chairman, 1988). Listed in *The Best Lawyers in America* (Bankruptcy Law and Business Litigation). ***PRACTICE AREAS:*** Antitrust Litigation; Intellectual Property Litigation; Business Litigation; Bankruptcy Litigation; Sports Antitrust. ***Email:*** meyersd@crowedunlevy.com

PRESTON G. GADDIS II, born Tulsa, Oklahoma, 1938; admitted to bar, 1962, Oklahoma. *Education:* University of Oklahoma (A.B., 1960; LL.B., 1962); Georgetown University (LL.M., 1965). Phi Alpha Delta; Order of the Coif. Editor, Federal Bar Journal, 1963-1965. Author: "Registration of Aircraft and Recording of Conveyances under the Federal Aviation Act of 1958," PLI Handbook No. 195, 1978; "Registering Leased Aircraft in the U.S.," Airfinance Journal, No. 90, page 48, May 1988; Aircraft Financing Chapter, Matthew Bender's *Commercial Financing Guide;* "US Registration of Non-US Owned Aircraft: Is The US a Flag of Convenience for Aircraft?" *Essays in Airfinance Law and Taxation,* 1993-1994. Chairman, Section on Corporation, Banking and Business Law, Oklahoma Bar Association, 1978. [U.S. Army Judge Advocate Generals Corp., 1962-1965]. ***PRACTICE AREAS:*** Aircraft Financing and Leasing; Aircraft Title; Aircraft Sales. ***Email:*** gaddisp@crowedunlevy.com

CLYDE A. MUCHMORE, born Los Angeles, California, 1942; admitted to bar, 1967, Oklahoma; U.S. Court of Appeals, Tenth, Fifth and Ninth Circuits, Temporary Emergency Court of Appeals and U.S. Supreme Court. *Education:* Rice University (B.A., magna cum laude, 1964); University of Oklahoma (J.D., with honors, 1967). Phi Beta Kappa; Order of the Coif; Phi Delta Phi. Editor, Oklahoma Law Review, 1965-1967. Recipient, Nathan Scarritt Prize, 1967. Special Lecturer in Law, Appellate Advocacy and Constitutional Law, Federal Courts, University of Oklahoma College of Law. Co-Author: *Oklahoma Civil Procedure Forms and Practice* (Lexis Law Publishing, 1987—); *Oklahoma Appellate Practice* (Thomson West Publishing, 1999—). Adjunct Professor, Constitutional Law and Evidence, Oklahoma City University School of Law. Appointed by Chief Justice of Oklahoma Supreme Court as Chairman of Committee to Assist in Revising Rules of Appellate Procedure in Civil Cases, which submitted proposal that culminated in new rules adopted in 1996. Fellow, American College of Trial Lawyers, 1984—. Member, American Academy of Appellate Lawyers, 1993—. Listed in *The Best Lawyers in America* (First, Amendment Law and Business Litigation). ***PRACTICE AREAS:*** Civil Litigation; Appellate Practice; Communications and Media; Constitutional Law. ***Email:*** muchmore@crowedunlevy.com

WILLIAM G. PAUL, born Pauls Valley, Oklahoma, 1930; admitted to bar, 1956, Oklahoma; 1957, U.S. District Court, Western, Northern and Eastern Districts of Oklahoma; 1958, U.S. Court of Appeals, Tenth Circuit; 1970, U.S. Supreme Court; 1985, U.S. Court of Appeals, Fifth Circuit. *Education:* University of Oklahoma (B.A., 1952; J.D., 1956). Phi Delta Phi; Order of the Coif; Phi Beta Kappa; Order of Barristers. Article and Book Editor, Oklahoma Law Review, 1954-1956. Senior Vice President and General Counsel, Phillips Petroleum Company, 1985-1995. Recipient, Distinguished Service Citation, University of Oklahoma, 1985. Distinguished Alumni Award, University of Oklahoma, 1999; Doctor of Laws degree, Oklahoma City, 1999. Director, 1986—, Secretary, 1991-1992, Treasurer, 1993-1994, Vice President, 1995-1996, and President, 1997-1998, American Bar Endowment. Chair, Law Center Advisory Board, College of Law, University of Oklahoma, 1977-1978. Director: National Center for State Courts, 1993—; American Judicature Society, 1982-1988. Member, Executive Committee, CPR Institute for Dispute Resolution, 1992—; General Committee on Law, American Petroleum Institute, 1985-1995 (Chair, 1994-1995). Fellow: American Bar Foundation (Chair, 1990-1991); American College of Trial Lawyers. Life Benefactor Fellow: American Bar Foundation (Director, 1988-1991 and 1997—). Member: Oklahoma County (President, 1971), Oklahoma (President, 1976) and American (President, 1999-2000; President-Elect, 1998-1999, Board of Governors, 1995—) Bar Associations; Chair, Committee on Research about the Future of the Legal Profession, 1995-1997. Member, Commission to Review Process of ABA Accreditation of American Law Schools, 1994-1995; Long Range Program and Financial Committee, 1988-1990; Coordinating Committee on Professionalism, 1986-1992; House of Delegates, 1975-1977 and 1979—; State Delegate from Oklahoma, 1986-1995; Council, Section of Litigation, 1989-1993; Commission on Women in the Profession, 1993-1995, Vice-Chair, 1994-1995; Committee on Corporate Law Departments, Section of Business Law, 1986-1995; Association of General Counsel, 1989—; National Conference of Bar Presidents (President, 1985-1986); American Law Institute; Martindale-Hubbell Legal Advisory Board, 1990—; The Southwestern Legal Foundation (Trustee, 1982—), Vice-Chair, 1996—, Chair, Research Fellows, 1992-1993. Recipient, President's Award, Oklahoma Bar Association, 1994; University of Oklahoma Regents' Alumni Award, 1997. Chair, Board of Visitors, University of Oklahoma College of Arts and Sciences, 1997-1998. Member, Board of Directors, Gilcrease Museum, Tulsa, 1992-1995. [With USMC, active duty, 1952-1954; Col., USMCR]. ***PRACTICE AREAS:*** Alternate Dispute Resolution; Corporate Law; Appellate Practice; Litigation; Natural Resources. ***Email:*** paulw@crowedunlevy.com

ARLEN E. FIELDEN, born Jay, Oklahoma, 1941; admitted to bar, 1965, Oklahoma; 1968, Florida; 1971, U.S. Supreme Court. *Education:* Oklahoma State University (B.S., 1962); University of Oklahoma (J.D., 1965). Order of the Coif; Phi Delta Phi. Editor, Oklahoma Law Review, 1963-1964. Member: Oklahoma Association of Defense Counsel; International Association of Defense Counsel; Defense Research Institute; Pittsburgh Institute of Legal Medicine. Frequent speaker on issues relating to his areas of practice. In 1995 was Invited to Testify before Texas Senate concerning Tort Reform Litigation. ***PRACTICE AREAS:*** Insurance Defense; Workers Compensation; Labor and Employment; International Law; Litigation. ***Email:*** fieldena@crowedunlevy.com

HARRY A. WOODS, JR., born Hartford, Arkansas, 1941; admitted to bar, 1970, Oklahoma; 1971, U.S. Supreme Court. *Education:* Oklahoma State University (B.A., 1963); New York University (J.D., 1966). Member: American Law Institute; International Association of Defense Counsel; Board of Governors (2001-2003), Legal Ethics Committee (Chairperson, 1997-1998) and Professional Responsibility Tribunal (1999-2005), Oklahoma Bar Association (President, 2004); Board of Directors (2001-2005) and Professionalism Committee (Co-Chair, 1999), Oklahoma County Bar Association; President, Ruth Bader Ginsburg American Inn of Court (1998-2000). Councilman, City of Edmond, Oklahoma, 1975-1979. Recipient: Oklahoma Bar Association Neil Bogan Professionalism Award (1998) and Golden Gavel Award (1993 and 1998); Benjamin F. Butler Award, New York University College of Law, 1966. Root-Tilden Scholar, 1963-1966. Listed in *The Best Lawyers in America* (Business Litigation); *Who's Who of Product Liability Defense Lawyers* (Law Business Research). ***PRACTICE AREAS:*** Litigation; Products Liability; Securities; Business Litigation; Torts; Contracts. ***Email:*** woodsh@crowedunlevy.com

JIMMY GOODMAN, born Tulsa, Oklahoma, 1945; admitted to bar, 1971, Oklahoma. *Education:* University of Oklahoma (B.A., 1968); Stanford Law School (J.D., 1971). Editor, Stanford Law Review, 1970-1971. ABA Council on Racial and Ethnic Justice, 2003-2005; ABA Commission on Racial and Ethnic Diversity, 1999-2002; ABA Section of Litigation (Council, 1994-1997); Co-Chair, Diversity Plan Implementation Working Group, 2004-2005; Co-Director, Division 7, 2002-2004; Co-Chair, Task Force for the Minority Trial Lawyer, 1993-1997; Chair (1988-1991) and Member (1991-1993), Task Force on Trial by Jury. Oklahoma County Bar Association (President, 1995-1996; OCBA Delegate to the ABA House of Delegates, August 1996-2004; Board of Directors, 1990-2004; Chair, Lawyer Referral Service Committee and Member, Bench and Bar, Membership, and Fee Grievance and Ethics Committees). Oklahoma Bar Foundation (Fellow, President, 2001; Trustee, 1996-2002). American Bar Association (House of Delegates, 1996-2004); Legal Aid of Western Oklahoma (Board of Directors, 1989-1995). Oklahoma Bar Association (Oklahoma Bar Association Public Service Award, 1986). ***PRACTICE AREAS:*** Commercial and Business Torts; Life and Health Insurance Litigation; Banking Litigation; Real Estate Litigation; Products Liability Defense. ***Email:*** goodmanj@crowedunlevy.com

EARL A. SKARKY, born Enid, Oklahoma, 1944; admitted to bar, 1972, Oklahoma. *Education:* University of Oklahoma (B.B.A., with distinction, 1966; J.D., 1972); Harvard University (LL.M., 1973). Beta Gamma Sigma; Phi Delta Phi; Order of the Coif. Editor-in-Chief, Oklahoma Law Review, 1971-1972. *Member:* National Association of Bond Lawyers. ***PRACTICE AREAS:*** Public Finance; Real Estate; Corporate Law; Securities. ***Email:*** skarkye@crowedunlevy.com

JAMES H. HOLLOMAN, JR., born Wichita Falls, Texas, 1946; admitted to bar, 1969, Oklahoma and U.S. District Court, Western District of Oklahoma; 1973, U.S. Tax Court. *Education:* University of Oklahoma (B.B.A., 1967; J.D., 1969); New York University (LL.M. in Taxation, 1973). Beta Gamma Sigma; Phi Delta Phi; Order of the Coif. Editor, Oklahoma Law Review, 1967-1969. Author: "Income Taxation of Estates in Bankruptcy," 60 *American Bar Association Journal 1124,*1974; "Are Overriding Royalties Unrelated Business Income?" 24 *Oil and Gas Tax Quarterly* 1, 1975; "Comparison of Oklahoma and Federal Estate Tax," 22 Oklahoma Law Review 302, 1969; "A Ranch's Tax Advantages," 22 Oklahoma Law Review 451, 1969. Co-Author: "Oklahoma Corporate Forms," Treatise, LexisNexis (1988—). Chair, Section of Taxation, Oklahoma Bar Association, 1976. Certified Public Accountant, Oklahoma, 1968. Member, (President, 1993 and 1997), Board of Education, Deer Creek Public Schools, 1988-1998. Trustee, Oklahoma City Community Foundation, 1996— (Chair, Investment Committee, 1999—). National Board of Advisors to the Graduate Tax Program, New York University School of Law (1998—). Listed in *The Best Lawyers in America* (Tax Law, Trusts and Estates, and Employee Benefits Law). [Capt., U.S. Marine Corps., Judge Advocate, 1969-1972]. ***PRACTICE AREAS:*** Taxation; Business Law; Employee Benefits; Trusts and Estates; Mergers, Acquisitions and Divestitures. ***Email:*** hollomaj@crowedunlevy.com

RICHARD C. FORD, born Baltimore, Maryland, 1946; admitted to bar, 1975, Oklahoma. *Education:* Princeton University (A.B., 1968); University of Oklahoma (J.D., 1974). Phi Delta Phi; Order of the Coif. Editor, Oklahoma Law Review, 1973-1974. Special Lecturer in Law, Legal Research and Writing, 1978 and Appellate Advocacy, 1979, University of Oklahoma College of Law. Associate Counsel, Office of Independent Counsel, Iran/Contra, 1986-1993. ***PRACTICE AREAS:*** Products Liability; Appellate Practice; Environmental Law; Insurance; Toxic Torts; Telecommunications; Class Actions. ***Email:*** fordr@crowedunlevy.com

JOHN J. GRIFFIN, JR., born Oklahoma City, Oklahoma, 1950; admitted to bar, 1975, Oklahoma. *Education:* University of Oklahoma (B.A., with special distinction, 1972); New York University (J.D., 1975). Phi Beta Kappa. Root Tilden Scholar; Berg Award. Chairman, Young Lawyers' Division, Oklahoma Bar Association, 1979. Outstanding Young Lawyer, Oklahoma Bar Association, 1980. ***PRACTICE AREAS:*** Oil and Gas Litigation; Environmental Litigation; Complex Litigation; Class Action Defense. ***Email:*** griffinj@crowedunlevy.com

BROOKE SMITH MURPHY, born Oklahoma City, Oklahoma, 1945; admitted to bar, 1975, Oklahoma. *Education:* University of Oklahoma (B.A., with special distinction, 1967); University of Wisconsin (J.D., magna cum laude, 1975). Phi Beta Kappa; Order of the Coif. Editor, Wisconsin Law Review, 1974-1975. Recipient: Wisconsin Law Alumni Association Award, 1974; Joseph Davies Award, 1974. Master of the Bench, American Inns of Court. Served as member, United States Magistrate Selection Panel, Federal District Court, Western District of Oklahoma; Member: Intellectual Property Section, Oklahoma Bar Association; and American Health Lawyers Association. Past Vice-President, Oklahoma County Bar Association. Commissioner: Oklahoma Bar Association Mandatory Continuing Legal Education Commission. Fellow, Oklahoma Bar Foundation. ***PRACTICE AREAS:*** Civil Litigation; Federal Civil Litigation; Intellectual Property Litigation; Health Care. ***Email:*** murphyb@crowedunlevy.com

MICHAEL M. STEWART, born Oklahoma City, Oklahoma, 1947; admitted to bar, 1977, Oklahoma. *Education:* Yale University (B.A., 1970); University of Oklahoma (J.D.,

(This Listing Continued)

CROWE & DUNLEVY, A PROFESSIONAL CORPORATION, Oklahoma City—Continued

with honors, 1976). Phi Delta Phi; Order of the Coif. Managing Editor, Oklahoma Law Review, 1976. Recipient, Nathan Scarritt Prize, 1976. Vice Chairman, Section of Business Associations, Oklahoma Bar Association, 1979-1980. Listed in *The Best Lawyers in America* (Banking Law and Corporate Law). Author: "Potential Immortality of the Old Oklahoma Business Corporation Act," 65 OBAJ 4269 (1994). ***PRACTICE AREAS:*** Business Law; Corporate Law; Securities; Banks and Banking; Natural Resources. ***Email:*** stewartm@crowedunlevy.com

LEONARD COURT, born Ardmore, Oklahoma, 1947; admitted to bar, 1973, Oklahoma. *Education:* Oklahoma State University (B.A., 1969); Harvard Law School (J.D., 1972). Phi Kappa Phi. First Place Team, Outstanding Oralist, Ames Moot Court Competition, 1972. Listed in: *Who's Who in American Law,* 1991—; *Who's Who in the Southwest,* 20th and 22nd Editions; *The Best Lawyers in America (Labor and Employment Law); Who's Who in America,* 1990—; *Guide to Leading U.S. Labor and Employment Lawyers.* Author: "Effective and Ethical Use of Expert Witnesses," Labor Law Developments, 1993 (Matthew Bender). Co-Author: "Selecting A Union Representative: Management's Role," 26 Oklahoma Law Review 28, 1973. Council Member, Labor Law Section, Oklahoma Bar Association, 1978-1981, 1984-1986, (Chairman, 1986). Adjunct Professor, University of Oklahoma College of Law, 1983-1984, 1988 and 1999—; Oklahoma City University School of Law, 1998—. Guest Lecturer, Oklahoma State University, College of Business, 1996 and 1998. . Fellow: American College of Labor and Employment Lawyers. Member: Equal Employment Opportunity Committee, Section on Labor and Employment Law, American Bar Association, 1979—, Employment and Labor Relations Law Committee, Litigation Section, 1983—; Southwest Legal Foundation (Planning Committee, Annual Institute on Labor Law, 1983—); Labor Relations Committee, United States Chamber of Commerce (Chairman, F.L.S.A. Steering Committee). President, Oklahoma State University Alumni Association, 1995-1996. Oklahoma State University Alumni Association Distinguished Alumni Award, 1998. [U.S. Air Force]. ***PRACTICE AREAS:*** Employment Discrimination; Labor and Employment Law; Wage and Hour Law. ***Email:*** courtl@crowedunlevy.com

CYNDA C. OTTAWAY, born Altus, Oklahoma, 1953; admitted to bar, 1978, Oklahoma. *Education:* University of Oklahoma (B.A., 1975; J.D., with honors, 1978). Phi Beta Kappa; Order of the Coif. Editor, Oklahoma Law Review. Regent, American College of Trust and Estate Counsel. Past Chair, Estate Planning Section, Oklahoma Bar Association. Past President and Board Member, Oklahoma City Estate Planning Council. Listed in *The Best Lawyers in America* (Trusts and Estates). ***PRACTICE AREAS:*** Estate Planning; Trusts and Estates; Federal Taxation; State Taxation. ***Email:*** ottawayc@crowedunlevy.com

JUDY HAMILTON MORSE, born McAlester, Oklahoma, 1946; admitted to bar, 1979, Oklahoma. *Education:* University of Oklahoma (B.A., 1968; J.D., 1979). Order of the Coif; Phi Beta Kappa; Phi Delta Phi. Editor-in-Chief, Oklahoma Law Review, 1978-1979. Recipient, Nathan Scarritt Prize, 1979. Master, William J. Holloway, Jr. American Inn Court, CV. Member: Committee on Admissions and Grievances, Western District of Oklahoma (1992—); Oklahoma Bar Association (Bankruptcy Section, Awards Committee, Chair, 2003-2004). Trustee and President Elect: Oklahoma Bar Foundation; At Large Trustee (American Inns of Court Foundation, 2002—). American Bar Association Standing Committee on Federal Judiciary (1999-2003). Director, Oklahoma Appleseed Center for Law and Justice. Listed in *The Best Lawyers in America.*. ***PRACTICE AREAS:*** Business Litigation; Commercial Litigation; Bankruptcy. ***Email:*** morsej@crowedunlevy.com

MARK D. CHRISTIANSEN, born Olney, Texas, 1955; admitted to bar, 1980, Oklahoma. *Education:* University of Oklahoma (B.A., with highest honors, 1977; J.D., 1980). Order of the Coif. Editor, Oklahoma Law Review, 1979-1980. Member of Board of Editors, Oil and Gas Reporter, published by LexisNexis Matthew Bender (1996—). Author: "Class Actions Pushed to the Extreme: Will Class Action Plaintiff Lawyers Be Permitted to Re-Zone Our Courts for Tract Housing?" 24 Journal of Land, Resources and Environmental Law 77 (2004)(Rocky Mountain Mineral Law Institute 50th Anniversary Issue); "The Confused State of Oil and Gas Royalty Check Stub Law," 17 Texas Oil & Gas Law Journal 13 (2003)(LexisNexis Matthew Bender); "A Landman's Guide to Drafting Provisions for the Allocation of Gas Marketing Related Costs Under the Oil and Gas Leas," 45 Rocky Mountain Mineral Law Institute 21 -1 (1999); "Preferential Right of Purchase Issues in Oil and Gas Property Sales," ABA Natural Resources & Environment, Vol. 10, No. 4 (Spring 1996); "A Comparison of the Model Form Gas Balancing Agreements," 40 Rocky Mountain Mineral Law Institute, 15-1 (1994); Co-Author, "COPAS for Landmen and Lawyers," 48 Rocky Mountain Mineral Law Institute (2002); Lead Editor and Co-Author of annual reports of case law and legal developments in energy law in the United States for the "Year in Review" publication of the American Bar Association (1985—). Co-Chair, 50th and 51st Annual Institutes on Oil and Gas Law and Taxation, Center for American and International Law (1999-2000). Chair, Energy and Natural Resources Litigation Committee (2001-2003), and Chair, Oil and Natural Gas Exploration and Production Committee (1999-2001), American Bar Association Section of Environment, Energy, and Resources. President, Oklahoma City Mineral Lawyers Society (1989-1990). Trustee-at-Large for the Rocky Mountain Mineral Law Foundation (2003—). Chair of the Legal Committee for the Oklahoma Independent Petroleum Association (2001-2003). Chair of the Legal Committee for the Mid-Continent Oil and Gas Association of Oklahoma (2004—). Member of Executive Committee for the Institute for Energy Law of the Center for American and International Law (2000—). Co-recipient, 1999 John Rogers Award, presented by the Center for American and International Law to the Editors of the Oil and Gas Reporter. Listed in The Best Lawyers in America (Natural Resources Law)(1997—). ***PRACTICE AREAS:*** Oil and Gas Litigation; Oil and Gas Transactions; Oil and Gas Contracts. ***Email:*** christim@crowedunlevy.com

MICHAEL S. LAIRD, born Great Lakes, Illinois, 1951; admitted to bar, 1979, Oklahoma. *Education:* Harvard University (B.A., cum laude, 1973); University of Oklahoma (J.D., 1979). Phi Delta Phi. Article and Book Review Editor, Oklahoma Law Review, 1978-1979. Author: "Water Rights: The Winters Cloud Over the Rockies: Indian Water Rights and the Development of Western Energy Resources," 7 American Indian Law Review 155 (1979). Adjunct Professor of Law, Oklahoma City University, 1982. Fellow, American College of Mortgage Attorneys. ***PRACTICE AREAS:*** Commercial Real Estate; Real Estate Finance; Real Estate Leasing; Construction Contracts; Hotel and Resort Law; Land Development; Zoning Law. ***Email:*** lairdm@crowedunlevy.com

MACK J. MORGAN III, born Fort Knox, Kentucky, 1955; admitted to bar, 1980, Kentucky; 1982, Oklahoma. *Education:* Vanderbilt University (B.A., cum laude, 1977); University of Kentucky (J.D., 1980). Research Editor, Kentucky Law Journal, 1979-1980. ***PRACTICE AREAS:*** Antitrust; Business Litigation; Commercial Litigation; Intellectual Property Litigation; Securities Litigation. ***Email:*** morganm@crowedunlevy.com

ANTON J. RUPERT, born Oklahoma City, Oklahoma, 1955; admitted to bar, 1981, New York; 1982, Oklahoma. *Education:* Harvard University (A.B., magna cum laude, 1977); Stanford University (J.D., 1980). Adjunct Professor of Law, University of Oklahoma School of Law. ***PRACTICE AREAS:*** Products Liability; Toxic Torts; Construction Law; Trial Practice. ***Email:*** ruperta@crowedunlevy.com

KAREN S. RIEGER, born Baltimore, Maryland, 1956; admitted to bar, 1981, Oklahoma. *Education:* University of Oklahoma (B.A., with distinction, 1978; J.D., with honors, 1981). Phi Beta Kappa; Phi Delta Phi; Order of the Coif. Adjunct Professor of Health Care Law, University of Oklahoma College of Law. Member: American Bar Association Health Law Section; American Health Lawyers Association (Vice Chair, Long Term Care Committee, 1997-2001; Member, Credentialing and Peer Review Committee). Articles and Note Editor, Oklahoma Law Review, 1980-1981. Former Chairperson, Health Law Section, Oklahoma Bar Association. Board of Editors, Oklahoma Bar Journal, 1996-2001. Member: Oklahoma Health Lawyers Association (Director, 1997—), President (2000-2001). Listed in: *The Best Lawyers in America* (Health Care Law). Chairperson, American Health Lawyers Association Committee which wrote *The Hearing Officer Guidebook,* 1998. Co-Author: (with Eric S. Fisher) AHLA Practice Guide, "Healthcare Entity Bylaws and Related Documents: Navigating the Medical Staff/Healthcare Entity Relationship," 2000. ***PRACTICE AREAS:*** Health Care; Hospital Law; Medicare and Medicaid; Business Law; Corporate Law. ***Email:*** riegerk@crowedunlevy.com

HARVEY D. ELLIS, JR., born Kansas City, Missouri, 1954; admitted to bar, 1982, Oklahoma, Oklahoma Supreme Court and U.S. District Court, Western District of Oklahoma; 1983, U.S. Court of Appeals, Tenth Circuit; 1984, U.S. Court of Appeals, Ninth Circuit; 1986, U.S. Court of Appeals, Fifth Circuit; 1992, U.S. Supreme Court; 1996, U.S. District Court, Eastern District of Oklahoma; 1997, U.S. District Court, Northern District of Oklahoma; 2003, U.S. Court of Appeals for the Federal Circuit. *Education:* University of Oklahoma (B.A., 1979; J.D., secundum cum laude and with honors, 1982). Order of the Coif. Member, Oklahoma Law Review Judiciary Committee, 1981, and Editorial Advisor, 1981-1982. Appointed by Oklahoma Supreme Court Chief Justice Ralph Hodges in 1994 to serve on the Oklahoma Supreme Court Committee to Assist in Revising Rules of Appellate Procedure in Civil Cases, Rules of the Supreme Court and Rules on Practice and Procedure in the Court of Appeals and on Certiorari to the Court. Member, Civil Procedure Committee, Oklahoma Bar Association (1999-2004). Chair of Crow & Dunlevy's Ethics Committee. Author: *Constitutional Law: The Death Penalty: A Critique ofThe Philosophical Bases Held to Satisfy the Eighth Amendment Requirements for Its Justification,* 34 Oklahoma Law Review 567 (1981); *The 1991 Repeal of the 1990 Judgments and Appeals Act,* 62 O.B.J. 2793 (1991); *The New Oklahoma Supreme Court Rules,* 67 O.B.J. 3991 (1996). Co-Author: Ellis and Muchmore, *Oklahoma Appellate Practice,* Thomson West Publishing, 1999—; Muchmore and Ellis, *Civil Procedure Forms and Practice* (2nd Ed. Lexis Law Pub.); H. Ellis and A. Howard, *Oklahoma's Collateral Order Doctrine? Appealability of Prejudgment Order After Hammonds,* 75 O.B.J. 759 (2004). ***REPORTED CASES:*** Board of Regents of University of Oklahoma v. N.C.A.A., 546 F.Supp 1276 (W.D. Okla. 1982), Aff'd, 707 F.2d 1147 (10th Cir. 1983), Aff'd, 468 U.S. 85, 82 L.Ed. 2d 70 (1984), On Remand, 601 F.Supp. 307 (W.D. Okla. 1984); In Matter of College Football Association and Capital Cities/ABC, Inc., No. 9242, 5 CCH Trade Reg. Rptr. §23,631 (June 16, 1994); Silkwood v. Kerr McGee Corp., 485 F.Supp. 566 (W.D. Okla. 1979), Aff'd in Part, Rev'd in Part, 667 F.2d 908 (10th Cir. 1981), Rev'd, 464 U.S. 238, 78 L.Ed.2d 443 (1984), Rehearing Denied, 465 U.S. 1074, 79 L.Ed.2d 754 (1984), On Remand, 769 F.2d 1451 (10th Cir. 1985), Cert. Denied, 476 U.S. 1104, 90 L.Ed. 356 (1986); Ethics Comm'n of State of Oklahoma v. Cullison, 850 P.2d 1069 (Okla. 1993); Prudential Property & Casualty Co. v. Grimes, 725 P.2d 1246 (Okla. 1986); Homeland Stores, Inc. v. Resolution Trust Corporation, 17 F.3d 1269, Cert. Denied, 130 L.Ed.2d 279 (1994); Hayes v. Central State Orthopedic Specialist, Inc., 2002 OK 30, 51 P.3d 562. ***PRACTICE AREAS:*** Appellate Practice; Constitutional Law; Business Associations Disputes. ***Email:*** ellish@crowedunlevy.com

GAYLE L. BARRETT, born Oklahoma City, Oklahoma, 1947; admitted to bar, 1983, Oklahoma. *Education:* University of Oklahoma (B.S., 1969); Oklahoma City University (J.D., with high distinction, 1982). Staff Editor, Oklahoma City University Law Review, 1981-1982. Board of Directors: Oklahoma County Bar Association, 1994-1997. Member: Labor and Employment Law Section, American Bar Association; Labor and Employment Law Section, Oklahoma Bar Association, Labor and Employment Law Section (Chairperson, 1992 and Past Secretary); Defense Research Institute. Master in the Ruth Bader Ginsburg Inn of Court. Author: "Buffalo Chips to Senate Seats: Women at Work in Oklahoma," *University Printing Services (1979); contributing author, "Annual Survey of Oklahoma Law, Family Law," Oklahoma City University Law Review,* Volume 6, Spring 1981; "Annual Survey of Oklahoma Law, Constitutional Law," *Oklahoma City University Law Review,* Volume 6, Fall 1981; "Employer's Obligations Under Recent Amendments to the Federal Fair Credit Reporting Act," *The World Reports,* Vol. X, No. 1, Spring 1998; "Workplace Sexual Harassment —What Next," *The Briefcase,* November 1997; "Who is Responsible: EEOC Guidance on Liability for Discrimination Against Temporary Workers," *The Briefcase,"* January 1998; "Navigating Through the 'Icebergs ' of Employment Law —Pre-Employment Inquiries, Part II" *The Briefcase,* August 1998; "Current Status of Employer Liability for Supervisor-Created Sexual Hostile Environment," *The Briefcase,* September 1998. Listed in *The Best Lawyers in America* (Labor and Employment Law) and as one of the leading attorneys in Oklahoma in Employment Law by Chambers & Partners, Legal Publishers in *Chambers USA America's Leading Business Lawyers,* 2003-2004. General Counsel, Oklahoma City Human Resources Society. ***PRACTICE AREAS:*** Litigation; Labor and Employment. ***Email:*** barrettg@crowedunlevy.com

L. MARK WALKER, born Ada, Oklahoma, 1957; admitted to bar, 1983, Oklahoma. *Education:* University of Oklahoma (B.B.A., with special distinction, 1980; J.D., 1983). Phi Eta Sigma; Beta Gamma Sigma; Delta Theta Phi; Order of the Coif. Note Editor, Okla-

(This Listing Continued)

homa Law Review, 1982-1983. Author: "Surface Damages, Operators, and the Oil and Gas Attorney," 36 Oklahoma Law Review 414, 1983; "The Oil and Gas Operator's Duty to Protect Nonoperators from Drainage," 59 Okla. B.J. 3675, 1988. Co-Author: "Injuries to Land Resulting from Oil and Gas Operations: Measure of Damages," 60 Okla. B.J. 3245, 1989; "An Abridged Primer on the Law of Public Nuisance," 30 U. Tulsa Law Journal 355, 1994; "Money Damages Versus Cleanup in Pollution Cases," 48 Oklahoma Law Review 79, 1995. Lecturer, various American Bar Association and Oklahoma Bar Association seminars relating to oil and gas and environmental issues. Member: Oklahoma City Mineral Lawyers' Society; Environmental Law Section, CLE Committee, Oklahoma Bar Association, 1992. ***PRACTICE AREAS:*** Oil and Gas Law; Oil and Gas Litigation; Environmental Litigation; Pollution. ***Email:*** walkerm@crowedunlevy.com

STEPHEN L. DEGIUSTI, born Oklahoma City, Oklahoma, 1958; admitted to bar, 1983, Oklahoma; U.S. Supreme Court; U.S. Court of Appeals, Tenth Circuit; U.S. District Court, Northern, Western and Eastern Districts of Oklahoma. *Education:* Central State University (B.A., summa cum laude, 1980); University of Oklahoma (J.D., with honors, 1983). Order of the Coif. Note Editor, Oklahoma Law Review, 1982-1983. Author: Constitutional Law: "*Widmar v. Vincent:* A Departure from the Traditional Approach to Cases Involving Religion and Education," 35 Oklahoma Law Review 604, 1983. ***PRACTICE AREAS:*** Civil Litigation; Commercial Law; Environmental Law; Oil and Gas Pollution; Debtor and Creditor; Post Judgment Collections; Motor Vehicle Accidents; Nursing Home Liability. ***Email:*** degiusts@crowedunlevy.com

MARK S. GROSSMAN, born Oklahoma City, Oklahoma, 1957; admitted to bar, 1983, Oklahoma. *Education:* Yale University (B.A., cum laude 1979); University of Southern California (J.D., 1983). Author: "Oklahoma School Finance Litigation: Shifting From Equity to Adequacy," 28 Univ. of Michigan J. of Law Reform 521, 1995. ***PRACTICE AREAS:*** Complex Commercial Litigation; Appellate Practice; Real Estate Litigation; Tort Liability; Antitrust. ***Email:*** grossman@crowedunlevy.com

KEVIN D. GORDON, born Oklahoma City, Oklahoma, 1958; admitted to bar, 1984, Oklahoma and U.S. District Court, Western, Northern and Eastern Districts of Oklahoma; U.S. Court of Appeals, 10th Circuit; U.S. Supreme Court. *Education:* Westminster College (B.A., cum laude, 1981); Washington University, St. Louis (J.D., 1984). Order of the Coif. Editor, Washington University Law Quarterly, 1982-1984. Listed in Best Lawyers in America (Health Care Law). Adjunct Professor of Law, Managed Care Law, University of Oklahoma (1997—). Frequent Lecturer at National and Local Seminars on Healthcare and Insurance Litigation Topics. American Health Lawyers Association, (2002 Leadership Team / ListServe Moderator for HMO & Health Plans Practice Group); American Bar Association-Insurance Coverage Litigation Committee, Health Law Litigation Committee Business Torts Litigation Committee; Oklahoma Association Defense Counsel; Professionalism Committee, Program Planner and Moderator, OBA Insurance Law Update (1999-2003) and Advanced Litigation Seminar (2000). Recipient, 1999 Oklahoma Bar Association Earl Sneed Award (Outstanding CLE Contribution). President, Ruth Bader Ginsberg American Inn of Court (Recipient of the 1998 Master of the Year Award); Oklahoma Bar Foundation. ***PRACTICE AREAS:*** Health Care; Insurance and Commercial Litigation. ***Email:*** gordonk@crowedunlevy.com

REEDER E. RATLIFF, born Sioux City, Iowa, 1960; admitted to bar, 1985, Oklahoma. *Education:* University of Oklahoma (B.B.A., with honors, 1982; J.D., with highest honors, 1985); New York University (LL.M., in Taxation, 1986). Order of the Coif. Chief Note Editor, Oklahoma Law Review, 1984-1985. Graduate Editor, Tax Law Review, 1985-1986. Adjunct Professor of Law, Corporate Tax and Accounting for Lawyers, Oklahoma City University School of Law, 1987-1991. Oklahoma Reporter, State Limited Partnership Laws (Aspen Law and Business), and Oklahoma Report on State Limited Liability Company and Partnership Laws (Aspen Law and Business). Past Chairman, Business and Corporate Law Section, Oklahoma Bar Association. Member: Oklahoma Society of Certified Public Accountants; American Institute of Certified Public Accountants. Listed in *The Best Lawyers in America* (Tax Law), and *Chambers USA,* America's Leading Lawyers for Business (Tax). ***PRACTICE AREAS:*** Taxation; Business Law. ***Email:*** ratliffr@crowedunlevy.com

TODD TAYLOR, born Altus, Oklahoma, 1961; admitted to bar, 1986, Oklahoma. *Education:* Southwestern State University (B.S., summa cum laude, 1982); University of Oklahoma (J.D., with highest honors, 1986). Order of the Coif. Recipient, Welcome D. Pierson Memorial Award; West Publishing Company Tax Award. Former Chairman for Tenth Circuit, Litigation Section-State Legislation Committee, American Bar Association. Author: "The New Real Estate Appraisal Rules Under FIRREA," OBA Journal, Vol. 63 at pg. 2495, September 12, 1992; "Recent Amendments to UCC Articles 2A, 3 and 4," OBA/CLE Commercial Law, Publication No. 422, 1991; "Recent Development Under Article 9," OBA/CLE Commercial Law, Publication No. 412, 1991; "Creating and Perfecting Security Interest under Oklahoma UCC," OBA/CLE Secured Lending Transactions, Publication No. 344, 1989; "Handling a Lender Liability Case," PES Lender Liability in Oklahoma, 1987. ***REPORTED CASES:*** McCurdy Group v. American Biomedical Group, Inc., 9 Fed. Appx. 882, 2001 WL 5369 (10th Cir. 2001); Garrett v. Bryan Cave LLP, 211 F.3d 1278 (10th Cir. 2000); Laxmi Investments, LLC v. Golf USA, 193 F.3d 1095 (9th Cir. 1999); Barker v. Golf USA, 154 F.3d 788 (8th Cir. 1998); United States ex rel. Trim v. McKean, 31 F. Supp.2d 1308 (W.D. Okla. 1998); United States ex rel. Semptner v. Medical Consultants, Inc., 170 F.R.D. 490 (W.D. Okla. 1997); United States v. Mitchell, 15 F.3d 953 (10th Cir. 1994); Cassity v. Pitts, 995 F.2d 1009 (10th Cir. 1993); Woolf v. Universal Fidelity Life Ins. Co., 849 P.2d 1093 (Okla. App. 1992); Cassity v. Pitts, 839 P.2d 192 (Okla. 1992); Big Chief Drilling Co. v. United States, 26 Cl. Ct. 1276 (1992); Continental Casualty Co. v. Southwestern Bell Telephone Co., 860 F.2d 970 (10th Cir. 1988). ***PRACTICE AREAS:*** Business Litigation; Corporate Litigation; Banking Litigation; Health Care Litigation; Trust Litigation; Estate Litigation; Arbitration. ***Email:*** taylort@crowedunlevy.com

ROGER A. STONG, born Chicago, Illinois, 1962; admitted to bar, 1986, Oklahoma. *Education:* University of Virginia (B.A., 1983); Indiana University (J.D., cum laude, 1985); University of Oklahoma (M.B.A., 1986). Past Chairman, Business and Corporate Law Section, Oklahoma Bar Association. Listed in *Best Lawyers in America* (Corporate Law). ***PRACTICE AREAS:*** Intellectual Property; Securities; Bankruptcy; Corporate Law. ***Email:*** stongr@crowedunlevy.com

LEANNE BURNETT, born Nashville, Tennessee, 1949; admitted to bar, 1989, Oklahoma. *Education:* Southern Methodist University (B.A., 1971); University of Oklahoma (J.D., with honors, 1989). Phi Beta Kappa; Phi Delta Phi; Order of the Coif; Order of the Barristers. American Inns of Court. Managing Editor, Oklahoma Environmental Law Handbook, 1995-1997; Co-Author: "Common Law Pollution," Chapter 1993-1996, Environmental Law Section, Oklahoma Bar Association; "Oklahoma Environmental Update," State Environmental Law Annual Report, 1990-1993 Editions. Government Institutes, Inc.; "Environmental Risk Avoidance in Property Transactions," Seminar: Effectively Assisting Your Client With Basic Environmental Issues, 1993, Oklahoma Bar Association; "Liability for Dissolved Corporations," War Stories from the Environmental Front, 1996. (Oklahoma Case Studies in Environmental Law), Oklahoma Bar Association. Secretary, Environmental Law Section (1993-1994), CLE Committee Chairperson (1994-1995) and Section Chairperson, (1999), Cleveland County Bar Association. ***PRACTICE AREAS:*** Complex Litigation; Class Action Defense; Environmental Litigation; Toxic Tort Defense; Tobacco Litigation; Child Advocacy. ***Email:*** burnettl@crowedunlevy.com

PAUL D. TRIMBLE, born Oklahoma City, Oklahoma, 1962; admitted to bar, 1989, Oklahoma. *Education:* University of Oklahoma (B.B.A., 1984); Oklahoma City University (1986-1988) and University of Oklahoma (J.D., 1989). Phi Delta Phi. Certified Public Accountant, Oklahoma, 1986. Member, Mineral Lawyers' Society of Oklahoma County. ***PRACTICE AREAS:*** Oil and Gas Litigation. ***Email:*** trimblep@crowedunlevy.com

TIMILA S. ROTHER, born Oklahoma City, Oklahoma, 1964; admitted to bar, 1990, Oklahoma. *Education:* University of Oklahoma (B.A., 1987; J.D., with honors, 1990). Member, National Mock Trial Team. Assistant Legal Research and Writing Instructor. Recipient, Maurice H. Merrel Public Law Scholarship. Member: Ethics Committee, Litigation Section and Health Care Section, Oklahoma Bar Association. ***PRACTICE AREAS:*** Litigation; Insurance; Health Care Contracts; Civil Appeals; Legal Ethics. ***Email:*** rothert@crowedunlevy.com

TAMELA R. HUGHLETT, born Oklahoma City, Oklahoma, 1965; admitted to bar, 1992, Oklahoma. *Education:* Central State University (B.A., cum laude, 1988); University of Oklahoma (J.D., with highest honors, 1992). Order of the Coif. Member, Oklahoma Law Review, 1990-1992. Managing Editor, American Indian Law Review, 1991-1992. Recipient: American Jurisprudence Awards in Torts I, Property II and Labor-Management Relations; Salem Civil rights Award; Rayburn L. Foster Memorial Scholarship, 1990-1991 and 1991-1992; Charles B. Memminger Memorial Scholarship; Ray Teague Memorial Scholarship; Oklahoma City Title Attorneys Association Scholarship. Author: Oklahoma Law Review, Comment, "International Law: The Use of International Law as A Guide to interpretation of the United States Constitution," 45 Okla. L. R. 169, 1992. Adjunct Professor, University of Oklahoma College of Law, Civil Pretrial Litigation (1996—). President, Central Oklahoma Federalist Society. Chair, Mentorship/Leadership Committee, Ruth Bader Ginsburg American Inn of Court. ***PRACTICE AREAS:*** Litigation; Business Litigation; Commercial Litigation; Insurance Litigation. ***Email:*** hughlett@crowedunlevy.com

RUSTIN J. STRUBHAR, born Oklahoma City, Oklahoma, 1967; admitted to bar, 1993, Oklahoma. *Education:* Oklahoma Baptist University (B.S., cum laude, 1990); University of Oklahoma (J.D., with honors, 1993). Order of the Coif; Phi Kappa Phi. Member, Oklahoma Law Review, 1991-1993. Recipient: Kerr McGee Environmental Scholarship. ***PRACTICE AREAS:*** Complex Litigation; Civil Litigation; Products Liability; Health Care. ***Email:*** strubhar@crowedunlevy.com

PHILLIP L. FREE, JR., born Altus, Oklahoma, 1966; admitted to bar, 1993, Oklahoma; U.S. Court of Appeals for the Federal and Tenth Circuits; registered to practice before U.S. Patent and Trademark Office. *Education:* Southwestern Oklahoma State University (B.S., Chemistry, cum laude, 1988); University of Oklahoma (J.D., 1993). Phi Delta Phi; Sigma Pi Sigma; Alpha Pi Omega. Co-Author, "Intellectual Property Litigation: Are Oklahoma Courts Missing the Mark(man)?" 69 Okl. B.J. 792 (1998). ***PRACTICE AREAS:*** Intellectual Property Litigation; Patents; Trademarks; Unfair Competition; Copyrights; Trade Secrets. ***Email:*** freephil@crowedunlevy.com

CYNTHIA L. ANDREWS, born 1965; admitted to bar, 1994, Oklahoma. *Education:* University of Oklahoma (B.B.A., with special distinction, 1989); Oklahoma City University (J.D., summa cum laude, 1994); New York University (LL.M., Taxation, 1996). Phi Delta Phi. Editor in Chief, Oklahoma City University Law Review. Graduate Editor, Tax Law Review, 1995-1996. Recipient: Harry J. Rudick Memorial Award, New York University (outstanding graduate); New York University 1996 Tax Society Prize; Outstanding Graduate Award for Academic Excellence and Outstanding Service; RIA Publishing Company Award for Excellence in Tax Law; Phi Delta Phi Berry-Opala Award; Hatton W. Summers Scholar; Law Review Board of Editors Award for Outstanding Note; Judge Tom Brett Award for Excellence in Criminal Law; American Jurisprudence Awards: Contracts I and II, Torts I, Property I and II, Criminal Law, Constitutional Law II and Business Planning. Certified Public Accountant, Oklahoma, 1990. ***PRACTICE AREAS:*** Taxation; Trusts and Estates; Mergers, Acquisitions and Divestitures; Partnership Law. ***Email:*** andrewsc@crowedunlevy.com

C. ROBERT STELL, born Midwest City, Oklahoma, 1968; admitted to bar, 1994, Oklahoma. *Education:* Oklahoma State University (B.S., 1991); University of Oklahoma (J.D., with highest honors, 1994). Order of the Coif. Member, Oklahoma Law Review. Member, Mineral Lawyers Society of Oklahoma City. Contributing Author: *Business & Commercial Litigation in Federal Courts,* Ch. 79 on Energy Law (West 1998). [Oklahoma Army National Guard, 1989-1999]. ***REPORTED CASES:*** Duncan Oil Prop., Inc. v. Vastar Resources, Inc., 16 P.3d 465 (Okla. 2000); Burns v. Great Lakes Higher Ed. Corp., 246 B.R. 694 (W.D. Okla. 1999). ***PRACTICE AREAS:*** Civil Litigation; Oil and Gas Litigation; Environmental Litigation; Student Loan Discharge on Bankruptcy. ***Email:*** stellc@crowedunlevy.com

WILLIAM H. HOCH, III, born Oklahoma City, Oklahoma, 1966; admitted to bar, 1993, Oklahoma and U.S. District Court, Northern, Western and Eastern Districts of Oklahoma, U.S. Court of Appeals, Tenth Circuit. *Education:* The Catholic University of America (B.A., 1988); The Columbus School of Law of The Catholic University of America (J.D., 1993). Legislative Assistant and Legislative Director to U.S. Representative Glenn English, 1988-1993. Law Clerk to The Honorable Richard L. Bohanon, U.S. Bankruptcy Court, Western District of Oklahoma, 1993-1995. Adjunct Professor, Pre-Trial Practice, University of Oklahoma College of Law. Chair, Commission on Homelessness and Poverty, American Bar Association (2001—). Assistant to President of American Bar As-

(This Listing Continued)

CROWE & DUNLEVY, A PROFESSIONAL CORPORATION, Oklahoma City—Continued

sociation (2000-2001). Member, Luther Bohanon Inn of Court. ***PRACTICE AREAS:*** Bankruptcy; Commercial Law; Antitrust and Trade Regulation; Trademark Infringement; Counterfeiting. ***Email:*** hochw@crowedunlevy.com

JEREMY TUBB, born Oklahoma City, Oklahoma, 1969; admitted to bar, 1995, Oklahoma. *Education:* Connecticut College (B.A., cum laude, 1991); University of Oklahoma (J.D., with honors, 1995). Order of the Coif; Phi Kappa Phi. Member, Oklahoma Law Review, 1993-1995. Recipient: American Jurisprudence Awards for Torts I and Mass Media Law. ***PRACTICE AREAS:*** Litigation; Labor and Employment. ***Email:*** tubbj@crowedunlevy.com

J. ROBERT KALSU, born Oklahoma City, Oklahoma, 1970; admitted to bar, 1995, Texas; 1996, Oklahoma and U.S. District Court, Western District of Oklahoma. *Education:* University of Oklahoma (B.B.A., with special distinction, 1992); Southern Methodist University School of Law (J.D., 1995). Phi Alpha Delta. Associate Managing Editor, SMU Law Review Association. Chief Justice in Jackson Walker Moot Court Competition. Member: American Bar Association; State Bar of Texas; Oklahoma Bar Association; Oklahoma County Bar Association Young Lawyers Division, Treasurer (1996-1999), Board of Directors (1996-1999); Christian Legal Society. ***PRACTICE AREAS:*** Aviation Law; Corporate Law. ***Email:*** kalsub@crowedunlevy.com

WILLIAM L. TEAGUE, born Cecil County, Maryland, 1963; admitted to bar, 1994, Oklahoma. *Education:* Southern Nazarene University (A.B., cum laude, 1990); Oklahoma City University (J.D., summa cum laude, 1993). Phi Delta Phi. Member, Moot Court Board, Oklahoma City University Law Review. Author: " Pre-Election Constitutional Review of Initiative Petitions: A Pox on Vox Populi? In re Initiative Petition No. 347, State Question No. 639," 17 Oklahoma City University L. Rev. 201 (Spring, 1992); "A Security Interest by Any Other Name: Resolving the True Lease Versus Lease Intended as Security Question Under the Amended Version of Uniform Commercial Code Section 1-201(37)," 49 Consumer Finance Law Quarterly Report 270 (1995). Adjunct Professor of Law, Oklahoma City University School of Law. Member: Forums on Air and Space Law, Business Law, Oklahoma County, Oklahoma and American (Forum on Air and Space Law, Business Law) Bar Associations. ***PRACTICE AREAS:*** Aircraft Title; Aircraft Sales; Aircraft Finance and Leasing; Aircraft Tax Free Exchanges. ***Email:*** teaguew@crowedunlevy.com

ERIC S. FISHER, born Baltimore, Maryland, 1965; admitted to bar, 1996, Oklahoma. *Education:* University of Kansas (B.S., 1988); Northwestern University (M.S., 1989); University of Oklahoma (J.D., with honors, 1996). Editor-in-Chief, *Oklahoma Law Review,* 1995-1996. Recipient: Baker & Hoster Scholarship for Most Outstanding Law Review Note, 1994; Frank C. Love Memorial Scholarship, 1995; American Jurisprudence Award in Legal Research and Writing and Transactions in Goods (Art. 2). Author: "Healthcare Entity Bylaws and Related Documents: Navigating the Medical Staff/Healthcare Entity Relationship," American Health Lawyers Association Practice Guidebook, December 2000; "Maneuvering the Mundane Minefield: A Practical Guide to Legal Opinions in Healthcare Merger and Acquisitions Transactions," *Journal of Health Law,* Spring 1999; "Healthcare Joint Ventures: Drafting to Meet Objectives," BNA Health Law & Business Series Portfolio No. 2200, May 1999; "AIDSPHOBIA: A National Survey of Emotional Distress Claims for the Fear of Contracting AIDS," *Tort & Insurance Law Journal,* Fall 1997; "Informed Consent in Oklahoma: A Search for Reasonableness and Predictability in the Aftermath of *Scott v. Bradford,"* 49 Okla. L. Rev. (1997); "Potter v. Firestone: Setting the Standard of Recovery for Fear of Cancer or Shall Plaintiffs Forever Be Waiting on a Miracle?" *Tort & Insurance Law Journal,* Summer, 1995; "Antitrust Safety Zones for Physician Network Joint Ventures: Physician, heal thyself," 48 Okla. L. Rev. 89 (1995). Member, Luther Bohanon American Inns of Court, American Health Lawyers Association, American Bar Association Health Law and Business Law Sections, Oklahoma Health Lawyers Association, Oklahoma Association of Healthcare Ethics, Oklahoma Society of Healthcare Risk Management. ***PRACTICE AREAS:*** Business Law; Corporate Law; Health Care; Mergers, Acquisitions and Divestitures; Administrative Law. ***Email:*** fishere@crowedunlevy.com

JOHN M. THOMPSON, born Muskogee, Oklahoma, 1972; admitted to bar, 1998, Oklahoma. *Education:* University of Oklahoma (B.A., 1994; M.B.A., 1998; J.D., 1998). Phi Delta Phi. Recipient, American Jurisprudence Award, Partnership Taxation. Certified Public Accountant, Oklahoma, 1994. *Member:* Oklahoma County and Oklahoma Bar Associations; Oklahoma Society of Certified Public Accountants. ***PRACTICE AREAS:*** Business and Commercial Litigation; Securities Litigation; Financial Institutions and Finance; Real Estate Litigation; Bankruptcy and Creditor's Rights. ***Email:*** thompsoj@crowedunlevy.com

---

MARY HIRTH TOLBERT, born New Haven, Connecticut; admitted to bar, 1994, Massachusetts and District of Columbia; 1997, Oklahoma. *Education:* University of Michigan (B.A., 1989); Yale University (J.D., 1993). Senior Editor, *Yale Law Journal,* 1991-1993. Editor, *Yale Journal on Regulation,* 1990-1991. Member: Yale Legal History Forum, 1992-1993; Litigation and Antitrust Section, American Bar Association. ***PRACTICE AREAS:*** Litigation; Antitrust. ***Email:*** tolbertm@crowedunlevy.com

CHARLES B. GOODWIN, born Clinton, Oklahoma, 1970; admitted to bar, 1997, Oklahoma; U.S. District Court, Western and Northern Districts of Oklahoma. *Education:* University of Oklahoma (B.A. in Letters, 1994; B.A. in Economics, 1994; J.D., 1997). Note Editor, *Oklahoma Law Review,* 1996-1997. Law Clerk to the Honorable Claire V. Eagan, Northern District of Oklahoma, 1998; Law Clerk to the Honorable Lee R. West, Western District of Oklahoma, 1998-2000; Law Clerk to the Honorable Vicki Miles-LaGrange, Western District of Oklahoma, 2000. Author: *The Progeny of United States v. Lopez and the Future of Judicial Review of Federal Power Under the Commerce Clause,* 49 Okla. L. Rev. 159 (1996). Harry Alley - Leroy Allen Memorial Prize for Best Case Note of 1996. ***PRACTICE AREAS:*** Appellate Practice; Civil Litigation; Constitutional Law. ***Email:*** goodwinc@crowedunlevy.com

STACEY D. SPIVEY, born Ardmore, Oklahoma, 1970; admitted to bar, 1997, Oklahoma. *Education:* University of Oklahoma (B.A., Psychology, with special distinction, 1992; J.D., with highest honors, 1997). Phi Kappa Phi; Phi Alpha Delta; Order of the Coif. Graduated first academically in her law class. Outstanding University of Oklahoma 1997 Senior Law Student, Oklahoma Bar Association. Teaching Assistant, Legal Research and Writing, University of Oklahoma, College of Law, 1995-1997. Chief Article and Book Review Editor, Oklahoma Law Review, 1996-1997. Recipient: Academic Achievement Awards for Torts I, Legal Research and Writing I and II, Civil Procedure I and II, Contracts II, Evidence, Constitutional Law II, Equal Employment Opportunity, Wills and Trusts, and Trial Techniques; West Publishing Company Award. Ruth Bader Ginsburg American Inn of Court, Associate Member, 1997-1999 and 2001-2004. Contributing writer for Oklahoma County Bar Association publication, *The Briefcase,* 1997-1998. *Member:* Oklahoma County, Oklahoma and American Bar Associations (Member, Estate Planning, Trusts and Estates). ***PRACTICE AREAS:*** Estate Planning and Taxation; Trusts; Probate; Guardianship. ***Email:*** spiveys@crowedunlevy.com

COURTNEY K. WARMINGTON, born Ponca City, Oklahoma, 1974; admitted to bar, 1999, Oklahoma. *Education:* Oklahoma State University (B.A., Public Relations, 1995); Oklahoma City University School of Law (J.D., 1999). Phi Delta Phi. Articles Editor, *Oklahoma City University Law Review.* Oklahoma City University Moot Court Competition Best Oralist, 1998. Recipient: CALI Award for Legal Research and Writing I; Hatton Sumners Foundation Academic Scholarship. Member, Moot Court Honors Board. Merit Scholars Organization President, 1998-1999. Member, Board of Directors, Young Lawyers Division, Oklahoma County Bar Association. Member, Ethics Committee, Oklahoma Bar Association. ***PRACTICE AREAS:*** Labor and Employment Law. ***Email:*** warmingc@crowedunlevy.com

DAVID W. CARLSON, born San Diego, California, 1970; admitted to bar, 2000, Oklahoma. *Education:* University of Oklahoma (B.B.A., 1993; J.D., with honors, 2000). Order of the Coif. Phi Delta Phi. Member, *Oklahoma Law Review. Member, Ruth Bader Ginsburg American Inn of Court. Recipient:* American Jurisprudence Awards in Contracts, Income Tax of Corporations, Wealth Transfer Tax. Comfort Scholarship. ***PRACTICE AREAS:*** Energy, Environment, Litigation and Trial, Oil and Gas; Commercial Real Estate; Commercial Transactions. ***Email:*** carlsond@crowedunlevy.com

ADAM W. CHILDERS, born Urbana, Illinois, 1973; admitted to bar, 2000, Oklahoma. *Education:* University of Oklahoma (B.A., Political Science, 1997; J.D., with honors, 2000). Phi Beta Kappa; Phi Delta Phi; The Order of the Barristers. Luther Bohanon American Inn of Court. Recipient: American Jurisprudence Awards in Torts I and Intellectual Property; J. Marshall Huser Scholarship; Oklahoma Bar Foundation Chapman Rogers Scholarship. ***PRACTICE AREAS:*** Labor and Employment Law. ***Email:*** childera@crowedunlevy.com

DAVID M. SULLIVAN, born Oklahoma City, Oklahoma, 1974; admitted to bar, 2000, Oklahoma; U.S. District Court, Western District of Oklahoma; registered to practice before U.S. Patent and Trademark Office. *Education:* Oklahoma State University (B.S., Chemical Engineering, 1997); University of Oklahoma (J.D., 2000). Phi Delta Phi. Recipient: Academic Achievement Award in Advanced Intellectual Property Law. ***PRACTICE AREAS:*** Patents; Trademarks; Copyrights; Trade Secrets. ***Email:*** sullivad@crowedunlevy.com

DAVID V. STEWART, born Oklahoma City, Oklahoma, 1969; admitted to bar, 2001, Oklahoma. *Education:* University of Oklahoma (B.A., 1992; M.Ed., 1996; J.D., 2001). Recipient: Charles B. Memminger Memorial Scholarship; Academic Achievement Awards. Member, Oklahoma Law Review. ***Email:*** stewartd@crowedunlevy.com

WILLIAM E. VAN EGMOND, born Oklahoma City, Oklahoma, 1973; admitted to bar, 2001, Oklahoma. *Education:* University of Richmond (B.A., 1995); University of Oklahoma (M.A., 1998); University of Texas at Austin (J.D., 2001). Member, Graduate Student Senate, University of Oklahoma. Recipient, Lois A. Donaldson Scholarship, University of Texas. Graduate Teaching Assistant, University of Oklahoma. ***Email:*** vanegmow@crowedunlevy.com

JAMES W. LARIMORE, born San Angelo, Texas, 1975; admitted to bar, 2001, Oklahoma. *Education:* University of Oklahoma (B.B.A., with special distinction, 1997); University of Texas at Austin (J.D., with honors, 2001). Recipient: Townes Hall Society Scholarship; National Merit Scholarship; David A. Burr Scholarship; Oklahoma State Board of Regents Scholarship; Consul Award, 2001. Named Teaching Assistant of the Year, 2000-2001. Member, Texas Law Review. ***PRACTICE AREAS:*** Corporate Law; Securities; Taxation. ***Email:*** larimorj@crowedunlevy.com

R. REAGAN D. ALLEN, admitted to bar, 2002, Oklahoma. *Education:* University of Missouri (B.S., 1996); Franklin Pierce Law Center (J.D., 2003). ***PRACTICE AREAS:*** Bankruptcy. ***Email:*** allenr@crowedunlevy.com

JENNIFER L. BERRY, admitted to bar, 2003, Oklahoma. *Education:* University of Tulsa (B.S.B.A., 1998); Oklahoma City University School of Law (J.D., 2003).

MICHAEL W. BOWLING, admitted to bar, 2003, Oklahoma. *Education:* Duke University (B.A., 1998); University of Michigan (J.D., 2003). ***LANGUAGES:*** Russian.

JENNIFER A. DUTTON, admitted to bar, 2003, Oklahoma. *Education:* Olahoma City University (B.A., 2000); Oklahoma City University School of Law (J.D., 2003).

ALISON HOWARD, admitted to bar, 2003, Oklahoma. *Education:* University of Notre Dame (B.A., 1997; J.D., 2003).

MARIE JOHNSTON, admitted to bar, 2003, Oklahoma. *Education:* Oklahoma State University (B.S., 2000); University of Oklahoma (J.D., 2003).

JUSTIN C. SULLIVAN, born 1973; admitted to bar, 2000, Texas; 2003, Oklahoma. *Education:* University of Virginia (B.S., 1995); Duke University (J.D., 2000). ***PRACTICE AREAS:*** Bankruptcy.

JOHN W. GARRETT, born Oklahoma City, Oklahoma, 1978; admitted to bar, 2004, Oklahoma. *Education:* Southern Methodist University (B.B.A., in Finance, 2000); Oklahoma City University School of Law (J.D., magna cum laude, 2004); New York University School of Law (LL.M., in Taxation, 2005). Phi Kappa Phi. Recipient, Oklahoma Bar Association, Business and Corporate Law Section Award. Faculty Honor Roll. ***PRACTICE AREAS:*** Taxation. ***Email:*** garrettj@crowedunlevy.com

DANIEL P. JOHNSON, born Oklahoma City, Oklahoma, 1979; admitted to bar, 2005, Oklahoma. *Education:* University of Central Oklahoma (B.A., 2002); University of Oklahoma College of Law (J.D., with honors, 2005). Order of the Coif; Phi Alpha Theta; Pi Sigma Alpha. Law Review, Note Editor. William T. Comfort Scholar.Salem Recipient, Civil

(This Listing Continued)

Rights Award. Author: "Desert Palace Inc. v. Costa: Returning to Title VII's Core Principles by Eliminating the Direct Evidence Requirement in Mixed Motive Cases," 57 Okla. L.Rev. 403, Issue 2, 2004. *Member:* Oklahoma County, Oklahoma and American Bar Associations. ***PRACTICE AREAS:*** Litigation. ***Email:*** johnsond@crowedunlevy.com

JONATHAN D. ECHOLS, born Oklahoma City, Oklahoma, 1979; admitted to bar, 2005, Oklahoma. *Education:* University of Oklahoma (B.A., 2002); Oklahoma City University (J.D., summa cum laude, 2005). ***PRACTICE AREAS:*** Litigation. ***Email:*** echolsj@crowedunlevy.com

OF COUNSEL

BRUCE H. JOHNSON, born Greencastle, Indiana, 1913; admitted to bar, 1936, Indiana; 1948, U.S. Supreme Court; 1951, Oklahoma. *Education:* Butler University (A.B., 1933); University of Indiana (J.D., 1936). Phi Delta Phi. Attorney, Office of Chief Counsel, Bureau of Internal Revenue, Washington, D.C., 1947-1951. Assistant Head of Interpretative Division, Office of Chief Counsel, Bureau of Internal Revenue, Washington, D.C., 1950-1951. Member of Council, Section of Taxation, American Bar Association, 1964-1966. Life Member, American Law Institute. ***PRACTICE AREAS:*** Tax Law.

LAWRENCE E. WALSH, born Port Maitland, Nova Scotia, 1912; admitted to bar, 1936, New York; 1981, Oklahoma. *Education:* Columbia University (A.B., 1932; LL.B., 1935). Awarded LL.D. by: Union University, 1959; St. John's University, 1976; Vermont Law School, 1976. Counsel to the Governor of New York, 1950-1951. Counsel to the New York Public Service Commission, 1951-1953. U.S. District Judge, Southern District of New York, 1954-1957. Deputy Attorney General of the United States, 1957-1960. Partner, Davis Polk & Wardwell, 1961-1981. Independent Counsel, Iran/Contra, 1986-1994. President: New York State Bar Association, 1966-1967; American Bar Association, 1975-1976. Trustee Emeritus, Columbia University. Fellow: American College of Trial Lawyers; American Bar Foundation. *Member:* The Association of the Bar of the City of New York; New York State Bar Association; New York County Lawyers Association; American Judicature Society; American Law Institute. ***PRACTICE AREAS:*** Alternative Dispute Resolution; Federal Practice; Litigation; Administrative Law.

VAL R. MILLER, born Duncan, Oklahoma, 1922; admitted to bar, 1949, Oklahoma. *Education:* University of Oklahoma (LL.B., 1949). Delta Theta Phi. State Representative, 1950-1954. ***PRACTICE AREAS:*** Commercial Law; Oil and Gas Law; Civil Practice.

JAMES C. GIBBENS, born Oklahoma City, Oklahoma, 1923; admitted to bar, 1950, Oklahoma. *Education:* Yale University (B.A., 1947); Harvard Law School (LL.B., 1950). Author: "The Effect of Conservation Legislation on Implied Covenants in Oil and Gas Leases," 4 Okla. L. Rev. 337 (1951); "Suggested Amendments to the Oklahoma Business Corporation Act," 30 Okla. L. Rev. 549 (1977). Co-Author: "The Proposed New Oklahoma Business Corporation Act," 57 Okl. B.J. 508 (1986). Former Chairman, Business Associations Section and Taxation Section, Oklahoma Bar Association. Member: Partnerships and Unincorporated Business Organizations and Banking Law Committees, Business Law Section, American Bar Association; Federal Bar Association; National Association of Bond Lawyers. Listed in, The Bond Buyer's Directory of Municipal Bond Dealers of the United States; The Best Lawyers in America (Corporate Law). ***PRACTICE AREAS:*** Corporate Law; Government Securities; Blue Sky Law; Tax Exempt Bonds; Aircraft Finance.

JAMES A. PEABODY, born Oklahoma City, Oklahoma, 1929; admitted to bar, 1953, Oklahoma; 1954, Illinois. *Education:* University of Oklahoma (A.B., 1951; LL.B., 1953; J.D., 1970). Phi Beta Kappa; Order of the Coif; Phi Alpha Delta. Note Editor, Oklahoma Law Review, 1952-1953. Retired 1991, Of Counsel to the Firm. (Retired). ***PRACTICE AREAS:*** Oil and Gas Property Sales; Real Estate Title Examination; Finance. ***Email:*** peabodyj@crowedunlevy.com

JAMES W. GEORGE, born Okmulgee, Oklahoma, 1930; admitted to bar, 1957, Oklahoma. *Education:* Bradley University and University of Oklahoma (B.A., 1956; LL.B., 1957). Phi Alpha Delta. Lecturer in Oil and Gas Law, Oklahoma City University School of Law, 1967. Chairman, Administrative Law Section, Oklahoma Bar Association, 1967. Author, "*The Preclusive Effect of Oil and Gas Regulatory Orders in Subsequent Litigation ('If at First You Don't Succeed...').*" 49th Oil and Gas Inst.- (Matthew Bender, 1998). Listed in The Best Lawyers in America (Natural Resources Law). ***PRACTICE AREAS:*** Oil and Gas Law; Oil and Gas Regulation; Oil and Gas Litigation; Oil and Gas Contracts; Oil and Gas Exploration; Oil and Gas Title Examination. ***Email:*** georgej@crowedunlevy.com

ROBERT A. REECE, born Oklahoma City, Oklahoma, 1944; admitted to bar, 1969, Oklahoma. *Education:* Westminster College, University of Oklahoma (B.B.A., 1966; J.D., 1969); University of Texas (M.B.A., 1970). Beta Gamma Sigma; Order of the Coif; Phi Delta Phi. Editor, Oklahoma Law Review, 1968-1969. Chairman, Section of Probate and Estate Planning, Oklahoma Bar Association, 1979. ***PRACTICE AREAS:*** Probate; Estate Planning.

KENNI B. MERRITT, born Houston, Texas, 1950; admitted to bar, 1980, Oklahoma; 2001, Washington. *Education:* University of Oklahoma (B.A., 1972; M.Ed., 1973; J.D., 1979). Order of the Coif; Phi Delta Phi. Note Editor, Oklahoma Law Review, 1979. Chairman, Business Law Section, Oklahoma Bar Association, 1993. Adjunct Professor of Law, Oklahoma City University School of Law, 1999. Member, Washington State Bar Association. Author: "Voluntary Governmental Compliance Programs - Chicken Soup for the Employee Benefit Plan," 25 Oklahoma City University Law Review 351 (Spring/Summer 2000). Listed in *The Best Lawyers in America* (Corporate Law and Employee Benefits). ***PRACTICE AREAS:*** Employee Benefits; Business Law. ***Email:*** merrittk@crowedunlevy.com

TERRY R. HANNA, born Wadsworth, Ohio, 1947; admitted to bar, 1972, Oklahoma; 1973, U.S. Tax Court; 1989, U.S. Supreme Court. *Education:* University of Oklahoma (B.B.A., 1968; J.D., 1972); New York University (LL.M. in Taxation, 1973); Dallas Theological Seminary (M.A.B.S., 1988). Phi Delta Phi. Certified Public Accountant, Oklahoma, 1970. Member, Board of Editors, Oklahoma Law Review, 1971-1972. Special Lecturer in Law, University of Oklahoma College of Law, 1978-1980. Listed in The Best Lawyers in America (Tax Law), 1997—. President, Taxation Section, Oklahoma Bar Association, 1977. *Member:* Christian Legal Society; Sports Lawyers Association. ***PRACTICE AREAS:*** Federal Taxation; State Taxation; Nonprofit Tax Law; Estate Planning; Professional Sports Law. ***Email:*** hannat@crowedunlevy.com

(This Listing Continued)

JERRY L. BRUST, born Oklahoma City, Oklahoma, 1941; admitted to bar, 2001, Oklahoma and U.S. District Court, Western and Eastern Districts of Oklahoma. *Education:* University of Oklahoma (B.A., 1963; J.D., with honors, 2000). Adjunct Professor, University of Oklahoma, 2000-2001. Human Resource and Labor Relations positions with Caterpillar, Inc., 1967-1998, including Corporate Director of Human Resources and Corporate Director of Labor Relations. [Captain, Adjutant Gen. Corps, U.S. Army, 1963-1967]. ***PRACTICE AREAS:*** Labor and Employment. ***Email:*** brustj@crowedunlevy.com

HENRY RHEINBERGER, born Tulsa, Oklahoma, 1933; admitted to bar, 1961, Oklahoma. *Education:* University of Notre Dame (B.S., 1958); University of Oklahoma (J.D., 1961). Phi Delta Phi. Editor, Oklahoma Law Review, 1959-1961. Member, Real Property Section, Oklahoma Bar Association (Board of Directors, 1980-1982; Chairman, 1982). Lifetime Achievement Award from Real Property Law Section, Oklahoma Bar Association, 1993. Listed in The Best Lawyers of America (Real Estate Law). ***PRACTICE AREAS:*** Real Estate; Mortgage Foreclosure. ***Email:*** rheinbeh@crowedunlevy.com

ROBERT M. JOHNSON, born Thomas, Oklahoma, 1942; admitted to bar, 1967, Oklahoma. *Education:* Oklahoma State University (B.S., 1964); University of Oklahoma (J.D., 1967); Oklahoma City University (Honorary Doctor of Laws, 2001). Order of the Coif; Phi Delta Phi (Magister of Holmes Inn, 1966); Lambda Alpha. Editor, Oklahoma Law Review, 1965-1967 (Case Editor, 1996). Special Lecturer in Law: Real Estate Financing, 1972-1973; Real Estate Contracts, 1984, University of Oklahoma College of Law. Fellow: Board of Regents (President, 1994-1995), Chair of Executive Committee (1995-1996), American College of Mortgage Attorneys; Fellow, Oklahoma Bar Foundation. First Managing Editor, *Oklahoma Environmental Law Handbook,* 1992-1996. Chairman, Environmental Law Handbook Committee, Oklahoma Bar Association (1992-1996). Oklahoma Contributing Editor, The Law of Distressed Real Estate. Oklahoma Contributing Editor, National Mortgage Law Summary. Member: American College of Real Estate Lawyers (1984 —); City of Nichols Hills Planning Commission (1994-1996); Oklahoma City Commercial Real Estate Council; Oklahoma City Committee of One Hundred; Board of Greater Oklahoma City Chamber of Commerce. Appointed by Mayor of Oklahoma City as Chair, Murrah Federal Building Memorial Task Force (1995 —); Chair, Oklahoma City National Memorial Foundation (1996-1998). Appointed by the President of the United States as a Member of the Board of Trustees, Oklahoma City National Memorial Trust (Chairman, 1998 —). Recipient: 1996 Goodness of the Community Award from Murrah Building Survivors Association; 1998; Dean A. McGee Award from Oklahoma City Downtown Now; 1998 Ellen Hardin Walworth Medal for Patriotism; 1998 Outstanding Service to the Public Award from Oklahoma Bar Association; 2000 Community Service Award from Oklahoma County Bar Association; 2000 Distinguished Service Award, Oklahoma County/City Historical Society. Listed in: *The Best Lawyers in America* (Real Estate Law); *Who's Who in Real Estate; Who's Who in American Law* and *Who's Who in the World.* ***PRACTICE AREAS:*** Real Estate; Finance; Business Law; Lender Liability; Environmental Liability. ***Email:*** johnsonr@crowedunlevy.com

JAMES F. HARTMANN, JR., born Albany, New York, 1944; admitted to bar, 1969, Oklahoma. *Education:* University of Minnesota (B.A., 1966); University of Michigan (J.D., 1969). Member, American College of Real Estate Lawyers. Listed in *The Best Lawyers in America* (Real Estate Law). ***PRACTICE AREAS:*** Commercial Real Estate; Uniform Commercial Code; Commercial Leasing; Asset Based Finance; Aircraft Title. ***Email:*** hartmanj@crowedunlevy.com

Unless otherwise indicated all Lawyers listed are Members of the Oklahoma County, Oklahoma and American Bar Associations.

REPRESENTATIVE CLIENTS: Atlantic Richfield Co.; Aetna Life Insurance Co.; AmCare; American National Insurance Co.; American Airlines, Inc.; Anadarko Petroleum Corp.; Armstrong World Industries; ASC Machine Tools, Inc.; BancFirst; Bank of America, N.A.; Bank of Oklahoma, N.A.; Bank One, Oklahoma, N.A.; Bechtel Group, Inc.; Blue Cross/Blue Shield of Oklahoma; The Boeing Company; Boston Mutual Life Insurance Company; BP/Amoco Corporation; Buford Properties, Inc.; Capital Cities/ABC, Inc.; Chevron Texaco U.S.A., Inc.; CHUBB Executive Risk Insurance; Commonwealth Life Insurance Company; Concentra; Connecticut Mutual Life Ins. Co.; Conoco, Inc.; Dollar Systems, Inc.; Dow Corning Corporation; Equitable Life Assurance Co. (N.Y.); Exxon Mobil Corporation; Flint Industries, Inc.; Ford Motor Co.; Fortis Insurance Co.; GMX Resources; Goodyear Tire & Rubber Company; Harold's Stores, Inc.; Helmerich & Payne, Inc.; Hillcrest Healthcare System; Homeland Stores, Inc.; Hunzicker Brothers, Inc.; Ins. Co. of North America, INAPRO/CIGNA; INTEGRIS Health, Inc.; J.C. Penney Life Ins. Co.; John Alden Life Ins. Co.; John Hancock Life Insurance Co.; Lawyers Title Insurance Corp.; Liberty Nat. Life. Ins. Co.; Life Insurance Company of Georgia; Lincoln National Life Insurance Co.; Lloyd's of London; Marathon Oil Company; Massachusetts Mutual Life Insurance Co.; Mercy Hospital; Metropolitan Life Insurance Co.; MONY Life Insurance Co.; New England Mutual Life; New York Life Insurance Co.; Norman Regional Hospital; Oklahoma Association of Health Plans; Oklahoma Foundation for Medical Quality; Phoenix Life Insurance Co.; Pre-Paid Legal Services; Protective Life Ins. Company; Sheffield Steel Corporation; Southwestern Bell Telephone Co.; St. Anthony Hospital; Thrifty Rent-A-Car System, Inc.; Trammell Crow Company; Transamerica Occidental Life; USAirways, Inc.; VHA of Oklahoma/Arkansas, Inc.; The Williams Companies; Williams Communications Group, Inc.

(For Biographical Data on other Personnel, see Professional Biographies at Tulsa and at Norman for Crowe & Dunlevy)

DAUGHERTY, FOWLER, PEREGRIN & HAUGHT

A PROFESSIONAL CORPORATION

Established in 1986

204 NORTH ROBINSON
900 CITY PLACE
OKLAHOMA CITY, OKLAHOMA 73102-6800
Telephone: 405-232-0003
Facsimile: 405-232-0865
Email: dfph@dfph.com
URL: http://www.dfph.com

Aircraft Title, Aircraft Finance and Leasing, Civil Litigation and Arbitration.

FIRM PROFILE: The firm's practice is concentrated in the area of aviation title and finance law. The Federal Aviation Act of 1958, as amended and recodified in Title 49 of the United States Code, provides that all instruments affecting title to or an interest in aircraft, or which pertain to the registration of aircraft in the United States must be filed with the Aircraft Reg-

(This Listing Continued)

DAUGHERTY, FOWLER, PEREGRIN & HAUGHT, A PROFESSIONAL CORPORATION, Oklahoma City—Continued

istry, a branch of the Federal Aviation Administration, which is located in Oklahoma City, Oklahoma. Acting as special FAA counsel, the firm represents clients throughout the world in major transactions involving the sale, leasing and financing of private and commercial aircraft. The Firm also provides services in the areas of General Civil Practice in all State and Federal Courts, Commercial Law, Products Liability, Negligence, Civil Rights, Construction Law, Employment Law, Arbitration and Mediation.

DANIEL J. FOWLER (Retired)

ROBERT M. PEREGRIN, born Plainfield, New Jersey, July 3, 1957; admitted to bar, 1982, Oklahoma, U.S. Supreme Court, U.S. Court of Appeals, Tenth Circuit and U.S. District Court, Western District of Oklahoma. *Education:* Central State University (B.A., 1979); University of Oklahoma (J.D., 1982). Phi Alpha Delta. *Member:* Oklahoma County and Oklahoma Bar Associations; American Inns of Court XXIII (Barrister, 1989-1990). ***PRACTICE AREAS:*** Aviation Title Law; Aircraft Law; Finance Law. ***Email:*** rperegrin@dfph.com

SUSAN H. HAUGHT, born Muskogee, Oklahoma, August 31, 1955; admitted to bar, 1985, Oklahoma; U.S. District Court, Western District of Oklahoma; U.S. Court of Appeals, Tenth Circuit. *Education:* Oklahoma State University; University of Oklahoma (B.S., 1977); Oklahoma City University (J.D., 1984). Alpha Lambda Delta; Phi Delta Phi. *Member:* Oklahoma County, Oklahoma and American (Aircraft Financing Subcommittee, Business Law Section; Forum Committee on Air and Space Law) Bar Associations. American Inn of Court XXIII (Barrister, 1990-1992). ***PRACTICE AREAS:*** Aviation Title Law; Aircraft Law; Finance Law. ***Email:*** shaught@dfph.com

ROBIN D. JENSON, born San Antonio, Texas, 1957; admitted to bar, 1987, Oklahoma. *Education:* Oklahoma State University (B.S., 1979); Oklahoma City University (J.D., 1986). Phi Delta Phi. Recipient, American Jurisprudence Award, Criminal Procedure. Author: "Who Has The Capacity to Grant an Oil and Gas Lease in Oklahoma?" 13 Oklahoma City University Law Review 82, 1988. ***PRACTICE AREAS:*** Aircraft Financing and Leasing; Aircraft Title; Aircraft Sales; Aviation Regulation; Aviation and Aerospace. ***Email:*** rjenson@dfph.com

OF COUNSEL

R. STEVEN HAUGHT, born Norman, Oklahoma, March 20, 1953; admitted to bar, 1978, Oklahoma, U.S. District Court, Western District of Oklahoma and U.S. Court of Appeals, Tenth Circuit; 1980, U.S. District Court, Eastern District of Oklahoma; 1981, U.S. District Court, Northern District of Oklahoma; 1983, U.S. Supreme Court; 1990, U.S. Court of International Trade; 1993, U.S. Court of Federal Claims. *Education:* Georgetown University (A.B., 1974); University of Oklahoma (J.D., 1978). Member, Order of Barristers. Contributing Author, Oklahoma Environmental Law Handbook, 1992—. Author: "Responding to a Rule 34 Request for Entry and Inspection", For the Defense, January 1987; "Immunity of State Activities from Municipal Zoning," Oklahoma Bar Journal, Vol. 49, No. 31, p. 1491. Member: Panel of Arbitrators, American Arbitration Association; NASD; NYSE and National Arbitration Forum. *Member:* Tenth Circuit Judicial Conference, Oklahoma Bar Association; Federal Bar Association. ***PRACTICE AREAS:*** Aviation Law; Finance Law; Civil Litigation. ***Email:*** rsh@dfph.com

DAY, EDWARDS, PROPESTER & CHRISTENSEN, P.C.

Established in 1982

SUITE 2900 OKLAHOMA TOWER
210 PARK AVENUE
OKLAHOMA CITY, OKLAHOMA 73102-5605
Telephone: 405-239-2121
Telecopier: 405-236-1012
URL: http://www.dayedwards.com

Tulsa, Oklahoma Office: 320 South Boston Avenue, Suite 805, 74103. Telephone: 918-592-2121. Facsimile: 918-388-6601.

General Civil Trial. Trial of Civil Cases in all State and Federal Courts. Administrative Law, Agribusiness, Anti-Trust Law, Arbitration and Mediation of disputes, Banking Regulation and Transactions, Bankruptcy and Insolvency Law, Commercial Law, Corporate Law, Employment Law, Energy Law, Environmental Law, Franchising Regulation and Transactions, Health Care Law, Insurance Law, International Law, Labor Relations, Litigation, Mergers and Acquisitions, Natural Resources, Products Liability, Professional Malpractice, Real Estate Law, Securities Regulation and Transactions and Workers Compensation.

FIRM PROFILE: The firm offers diverse legal services to local, national and international clients which include some of the most prestigious banking, brokerage, financial, insurance and industrial businesses in the United States and the global economy. Our clients include a large number of major, publicly owned domestic and international corporations, as well as closely held domestic and international corporations, banks, financial institutions, partnerships and individuals, which have been represented by us as general, regional or special counsel. The firm is frequently retained by other law firms to act as lead, special or local counsel in connection with major transactions or complex litigation. The firm's litigation practice extends to all areas of the United States. Primary areas of expertise are: Employment Law (including discharge, EEOC and discrimination, hiring and unions); Financial and Securities Transactions (including agribusiness, asset based finance, banking regulation and transactions, business associations, energy and co-generation regulation and transactions, franchising, insurance coverage, leveraged leasing, liability management, mergers and acquisitions, regulatory compliance, all forms of securities and all forms of public and private securities offerings); Health and Hospital Law (including licensure, regulatory compliance, acquisitions, strategic joint ventures, managed health care malpractice, preferred provider organizations, telemedicine, fraud and abuse); Insolvency Law (including director and officer liability, bankruptcy, reorganization and restructuring); Litigation (including litigation before state and federal trial and appellate courts; representation in regulatory and arbitration proceedings; and, litigation in securities cases, "white collar" criminal cases, anti-trust cases, lender liability cases, commercial torts, bodily injury, employment and EEOC claims, environmental claims, health law, and professional malpractice); Real Estate and Environmental Law (including construction, development, leasing, sales, environmental compliance and mortgage banking); Natural Resources (including agriculture, energy, oil and gas pollution); International Law (including international commercial transactions, customs, export controls, and immigration); Insurance (including insurance coverage, insurance defense, uninsured motorist, casualty, products liability, and wrongful termination); Workers' Compensation (including workers' compensation, insurance defense, Own Risk Defense, and Group Self-Insured Defense). Complex Litigation and White Collar Crime have become fast growing and successful sectors of the firm's practice. The firm has been engaged to both prosecute and defend Litigation matters in several distant areas of the United States. While the scope of the firm's expertise has substantially expanded, a significant sector of the firm's practice remains focused on banking clients.

BRUCE W. DAY, born Wichita, Kansas, September 1, 1945; admitted to bar, 1972, Oklahoma and U.S. District Court, Western District of Oklahoma; 1975, U.S. District Court, Northern District of Oklahoma; 1977, U.S. Court of Appeals, Tenth Circuit. *Education:* University of Oklahoma (B.A., 1969; J.D., 1972). Phi Delta Phi. Author: "A Timely Review of the Fiduciary Obligations of Bank Officers and Directors," 59 OBJ 35, 1990; "Impact of Oklahoma Securities Act on Formation of Closely Held Corporations," 50 OBJ 1154, 1979; "What Do You Mean My Client Violated the Securities Law?" 51 OBJ 453, 1980. Lecturer: Oklahoma Bankers Association Continuing Education Seminars sponsored by the University of Oklahoma College of Law, Oklahoma City University School of Law, University of Tulsa College of Law and The Oklahoma Bar Association on the following topics: Venture Capital, Securities, Stockbroker Litigation and Arbitration, Regulation D, Banking and Banking Regulations, Banking Regulators' Current Perspective, Syndications: Private and Public Offerings, and "Dark Clouds Over the Oil Patch: Current Problems/Current Perspective"; Securities Arbitration Institute, series on Securities Arbitration, 1993-1994; Brigham Young University, "International Energy Development Conference/Canada, United States". Administrator, Oklahoma Department of Securities, 1975-1978. *Member:* Oklahoma County, Oklahoma (Member: Chairman, Business Association Section, 1980; Securities Liaison Committee, 1983—) and American (Member, Sections on Corporation, Banking and Business Law) Bar Associations; Oklahoma Bar Corporation, Board of Directors, 1979-1983. ***REPORTED CASES:*** Keith Schooley v. Merrill Lynch, Case No. 95-6465 (10th cir., April 1, 1997); Merrill Lynch, Pierce, Fenner & Smith, Inc., et al. v. Gravitt (U.S.D.C., W.D., Okla., Civ-94-1949, September 15, 1995); Freeman v. Alex Brown & Sons, Inc., 860 F. supp. 780 (E.D. Okla. 1994); Mustang Partners v. Merrill, Lynch, Pierce, Fenner & Smith, Inc. (U.S.D.C., W.D. Missouri, 91-0614-CV-W-9, 1993); ARW Exploration Corporation v. Aguirre (1992 Transfer Binder) Fed. Sec. L. Rep. (CCH) ¶96, 473 (W.D. Okla. 1991); Adams v. Merrill Lynch Pierce Fenner & Smith, Inc., 888 F.2d 696 (10th Cir. 1989); Nikkel v. Stifel Nicolous & Co., Inc., 542 P.2d 1305 (Okla. 1975); State ex rel. Day v. Petco Oil & Gas, Inc., 558 P.2d 1163 (Okla. 1977). ***TRANSACTIONS:*** Formation of the first state specific venture capital fund; Private and public securities offerings; Organization of self insurance group(s); Structure and initiation of consultancy and network; Securities retail brokerage defense for national securities firms; Due diligence for venture capital investments and underwriting syndications; Reorganization and general corporate representation. ***PRACTICE AREAS:*** General Corporate Law; Federal and State Securities Law and Litigation; Retail Securities; Sales Practice; Employment; Regulatory Proceedings. ***Email:*** bruceday@dayedwards.com

JOE E. EDWARDS, born Tulsa, Oklahoma, January 10, 1949; admitted to bar, 1974, Oklahoma and U.S. District Court, Western District of Oklahoma; 1977, U.S. District Court, Northern District of Oklahoma, U.S. Supreme Court and U.S. Court of Appeals, Tenth Circuit; 1991, U.S. District Court, Eastern District of Wisconsin; 1998, Texas. *Education:* University of Oklahoma (B.B.A., 1971; M.A.P.A., 1972); Oklahoma City University (J.D., 1974). Phi Delta Phi. Author: "*Participate in the Conduct of an Enterprise: Rx for RICO Liability*," 64 Oklahoma Bar Journal 2142, 1993. Lecturer for Continuing Legal Education Seminars sponsored by the University of Oklahoma College of Law, Oklahoma City University School of Law, the Oklahoma Bar Association and the Texas Association of Bank Counsel on the following topics: Banking, Bankruptcy, Creditor's Remedies and Debtor's Rights, Energy, Failed and Failing Banks, Lending to the Troubled Venture, Loan Participations, Mortgage Foreclosure, Officers and Directors Liability, and Real Estate Problem Loans, 1980-1993. Arbitrator, Federal Court annexed arbitration program, 1985—. *Member:* Oklahoma County (Member, Bankruptcy Law Section), Oklahoma (Member, Sections on: Banking and Commercial Law; Bankruptcy; Litigation), Federal and American (Member, Sections on: Business Law; Litigation; Real Property; Probate and Trust; Economics of Law Practice) Bar Associations. ***REPORTED CASES:*** Bank of America v. Johnson, 186 F.Supp.2d 1182; Cherokee Nation v. NationsBank, N.A. 67 F.Supp.2d. 1303 (E.D. Okla. 1999); Brannon v. Boatmen's National Bank of Oklahoma, 976 P.2d 1077 (OK Ct. App. 1999); Barrett Refining Corp., 221 B.R. 795 (Bankr. W.D. Okla. 1998); Brannon v. Boatmen's First Nat'l Bank of Oklahoma, 153 F.3d 1144 (10th Cir. 1998); Brannon v. Boatmen's Bancshares, Inc., 952 F. Supp. 1478 (W.D. Okla. 1997); Marshall v. AFGE, F. Supp. 1319 (W.D. Okla. 1997); Octagon Gas Systems, Inc. v. Rimmer, 995 F.2d 948 (10th Cir. 1993); Grove Holding Corp. v. First Wisconsin Natl. Bank of Sheboygan, 803 F.Supp. 1486 (E.D. Wisc. 1992); In Re Schick Oil & Gas, Inc., 35 B.R. 282 (W.D. Okla. 1983); Heritage Land Co. v. FDIC, 572 F.Supp. 1265 (W.D. Okla. 1983); Chase Manhattan Bank, N.A. v. FDIC, 554 F.Supp. 251 (W.D. Okla. 1983); Earthmovers, Inc. v. Clarence L. Boyd Company, Inc., 554 P.2d 877 (Okl. App. 1976). ***TRANSACTIONS:*** Bank charter application and protest; Restructure financing for bank holding company with regulatory approval; Obtain regulatory approval for organization and operation of bank subsidiaries; Obtain regulatory approval for organization and operation of bank holding company subsidiaries; Negotiate reversal of one billion dollars in loan participations for FDIC with multiple lenders; Hostile tender offer for publicly traded company by publicly traded company; Acquisition and Development of Founders Plaza, a 20 acre commercial development; Redevelopment and construction of Timber Ridge, a residential community;

(This Listing Continued)

(This Listing Continued)

Redevelopment and construction of The Trails, a residential community; Development and Construction of Robinson Plaza, a central business district office building; Senior Notes and Credit Agreement for interstate trucking company; Credit Facility with interest rate swaps for publicly traded energy company; Credit Agreement for road machinery manufacturer; Credit Agreement for integrated dairy and retail sales business; Credit Agreement for retail furniture business; Oklahoma Development Finance Authority 1990 Pooled Business Financing Program; Complete Debt Restructure for publicly traded conglomerate including issuance of new securities; Acquisition and Refinance of two recreational theme parks; Senior Secured Term Debt and Credit Agreement for large gathering and pipeline transmission company; Debtor in possession financing for petro-chemical equipment manufacturing company; Debtor in possession financing for nursing homes; Finance distribution of feature length commercial movie; Contract and export licensing of engineering technology into European Common Market; International Letters of Credit to finance export and import of goods and technology. ***PRACTICE AREAS:*** Banking; Energy; International; Litigation; White Collar Crime; Real Estate Law. ***Email:*** edwards@dayedwards.com

RICHARD P. PROPESTER, born Elmira, New York, December 20, 1952; admitted to bar, 1978, Oklahoma. *Education:* University of Rochester (B.A., 1975); Oklahoma City University (J.D., with distinction, 1978). Author: Comment, *State Board of Public Affairs v. Principal Funding Corporation: Abrogation of Contractual Sovereign Immunity in Oklahoma*, 2 Oklahoma City University Law Review 726-739, 1977; *Survey of Oklahoma Law: Insurance*, 1 Oklahoma City University Law Review, 1976. ***PRACTICE AREAS:*** Commercial Litigation; Bankruptcy; Banking Law; Consumer Finance. ***Email:*** rpropester@dayedwards.com

D. WADE CHRISTENSEN, born El Reno, Oklahoma, December 14, 1954; admitted to bar, 1983, Oklahoma and U.S. District Court, Northern and Western Districts of Oklahoma; 1985, U.S. District Court, Eastern District of Oklahoma; 1987, U.S. Court of Appeals, 10th Circuit and U.S. Supreme Court. *Education:* George Washington University, Washington, D.C.; Oklahoma State University (B.S. in Business Administration, 1977); University of Tulsa (J.D., 1983). Phi Delta Phi. Lecturer at Adult Education seminars on the following topics: Workers' Compensation Law; Claims Handling and Case Management. *Member:* Oklahoma County (Member, Workers' Compensation Committee), Oklahoma and American Bar Associations; Oklahoma Association of Defense Counsel; Defense Research Institute. ***PRACTICE AREAS:*** Workers; Employment Law; Health Care; Insurance Defense; Personal Injury; General Corporate; Civil Litigation. ***Email:*** dwade@dayedwards.com

J. CLAY CHRISTENSEN, born El Reno, Oklahoma, October 26, 1961; admitted to bar, 1986, Oklahoma; U.S. District Court, Western, Eastern and Northern Districts of Oklahoma; U.S. Court of Appeals, Tenth and Eighth Circuits; U.S. Supreme Court. *Education:* Oklahoma State University (B.S., 1983); University of Oklahoma (J.D., with highest honors, 1986). Order of the Coif. Recipient: American Jurisprudence Awards in Torts II, Remedies, Estate and Gift Taxation; Dean Earl Brown Award. *Member:* Oklahoma County (Member, Church, State and School Committee), Oklahoma and American Bar Associations; Oklahoma City Mineral Law Society. ***REPORTED CASES:*** Blaser Farms v. Anadarko Petroleum Corp., 893 F.2d 259 (10th Cir. 1990). ***TRANSACTIONS:*** $100,000,000 Credit Agreement for integrated dairy and retail sales business; $7,500,000 Credit Facility for large independent oil and gas producer; Negotiated sale of many businesses; Establishment of franchises; Multi-state litigation on dealer/distribution issues; Debtor in possession financing for nursing home; Medicare Fraud and Abuse; Home Health business litigation and transactions; Hospice Representation; Assisted Living center litigation and transactions; Large and small bank representation and consultation. ***PRACTICE AREAS:*** Litigation; Health Law; Agriculture; Commercial; Banking; Bankruptcy; Oil and Gas. ***Email:*** jclay@dayedwards.com

JEANETTE C. TIMMONS, born Tokyo, Japan; admitted to bar, 1979, Oklahoma. *Education:* University of Oklahoma (B.B.A., with distinction, 1975; J.D., 1978). Author: "Regulation D in Oklahoma - A General Practitioner's Guide," Oklahoma City University Law Review, Fall, 1983. Associate General Counsel, Oklahoma Department of Securities (1979-1981). Corporate Secretary and Counsel, NYSE-listed Delaware corporation involved in energy products and services (1990-1993). Corporate Secretary and General Counsel, Nasdaq-listed Delaware corporation engaged in domestic and international oil and gas exploration and production (1990-1993). Public Member, Oklahoma Accountancy Board (1995-1999 and 2001-2003), transactions include representation of companies in numerous public and private securities offerings, including initial public offerings, merger and acquisition transactions, going private transactions, tender offers, board of directors' representation; representation of broker-dealers in compliance matters and in arbitration. *Member:* Oklahoma County, Oklahoma and American (Member, Section on Business Law) Bar Associations. ***PRACTICE AREAS:*** Corporate Law; Securities; Banks and Banking; Securities Litigation. ***Email:*** jtimmons@dayedwards.com

JOEL WARREN HARMON, born Duncan, Oklahoma, May 26, 1960; admitted to bar, 1985, Oklahoma, U.S. District Court, Western, Eastern and Northern Districts of Oklahoma; 1986, U.S. Court of Appeals, Tenth Circuit; 1993, U.S. Supreme Court; 1998, Texas, U.S. District Court, Northern and Southern Districts of Texas. *Education:* Oklahoma Christian University (B.S., magna cum laude, Accounting, 1982); University of Oklahoma (J.D., 1985). *Member:* Oklahoma County, Oklahoma (Bankruptcy and Reorganization Section) and American (Committee on Banking Law and Subcommittee on Loan Workouts and Bankruptcy; Business and Corporate Litigation Committee and Subcommittees on Bankruptcy Litigation and Environmental Litigation) Bar Associations. ***REPORTED CASES:*** Farha v. FDIC, 963 F.2d 283 (10th Cir. 1992); Octagon Gas Systems, Inc. v. Rimmer, 995 F.2d 948 (10th Cir. 1993); In re: Barrett Refining Corp., 221 B.R. 795 (Bankr.W.D.Okla. 1998); Bank of America N.A. v. Johnson, 186 F.Supp.2d 1182 (W.D. Okla. 2001). ***PRACTICE AREAS:*** Commercial Law; Banking Law; Financial Law; Bankruptcy Litigation; Creditors Rights Law. ***Email:*** jharmon@dayedwards.com

BILL POWELL GUEST, born Oklahoma City, Oklahoma, July 20, 1963; admitted to bar, 1994, Oklahoma, U.S. District Court, Western and Northern Districts of Oklahoma, U.S. District Court, Northern and Southern Districts of Texas, U.S. District Court, District of Colorado and U.S. Court of Appeals, Tenth and Federal Circuits. *Education:* University of Oklahoma (B.B.A., with distinction, mgmt., 1985); University of Oklahoma (J.D., honors, 1994). Phi Eta Sigma; Order of the Coif. Research Editor, Oklahoma Law Review. Recipient, Scholastic Achievement Awards in State Securities and Land Use Controls, 1993-1994. Author: "Oklahoma's Limited Liability Company Act: Concerns, Considerations and Conclusions," 46 Okla. L. Rev. 349, 1993; "Litigation and Arbitration Under Rule 506 After Pre-Emption and Gustafson," Advanced Securities Litigation and Arbitration, September, 2000; "Conflicts of Law Issues in Securities Litigation and Arbitration," Advanced Securities Litigation and Arbitration, September, 2000; "Theories of Common Law Liability in Broker-Dealer Cases," Advanced Securities Litigation and Arbitration, October, 2000; "Theories of Determining the Amount of Recovery Under the Securities Laws in Broker-Dealer Cases," Advanced Securities Litigation and Arbitration, October, 2000. Co-Author: Recent Developments in Civil Securities Litigation, 1994 and 1995, CLE Materials. Adjunct Professor of Law: Corporations, Agency and Partnership Law, 1999— and Legal Research and Writing and Appellate Advocacy, 1995-2001, University of Oklahoma College of Law. Adjunct Professor of Law, Legal Research and Advanced Legal Research, Department of Legal Assistant Education, 1998—. Lecturer: Corporations and Agency and Partnership Law, Oklahoma Bar Review, 1999—. *Member:* Oklahoma County, Oklahoma and American Bar Associations. ***PRACTICE AREAS:*** Litigation and Arbitration; Banking Law; Federal and State Securities Law; Commercial and Business Law. ***Email:*** bguest@dayedwards.com

(This Listing Continued)

D. MICHAEL O'NEIL, JR., born Oklahoma City, Oklahoma, December 7, 1947; admitted to bar, 1972, Oklahoma. *Education:* Santa Clara University (B.A., 1969); University of Oklahoma (J.D., 1972). Phi Delta Phi. *Member:* Oklahoma County, Oklahoma and American Bar Associations. ***REPORTED CASES:*** Thomas v. Vertigo, Inc., 1995 OK CIV APP 45, 900 P.2d 458, 66 OBJ 2587, Case No. 82308, Decided 3/7/95. ***PRACTICE AREAS:*** Broker-Dealer Arbitration; Securities; Business Transactions; Civil Litigation; Business Litigation. ***Email:*** dmoneil@dayedwards.com

P. DAVID NEWSOME, JR., born Stuttgart, Arkansas, August 15, 1947; admitted to bar, 1976, Oklahoma. *Education:* Central State College (B.A., 1970); University of Oklahoma (J.D., 1976). Managing Editor, Oklahoma Law Review, 1974-1975. Adjunct Professor of Law, University of Tulsa, 1986, 1998 and 2004. Staff Attorney, U.S. Securities and Exchange Commission, 1977-1979. Administrator, Oklahoma Department of Securities, 1983-1984. General Counsel, Williams Communications Group, Inc. 2000-2002. Senior Adjunct Settlement Judge, U.S. District Court, Northern District of Oklahoma. ***PRACTICE AREAS:*** Securities Regulation Law; Corporate Law; Arbitration and Mediation. ***Email:*** dnewsome@dayedwards.com

KELLEY C. CALLAHAN, born Oklahoma City, Oklahoma, August 22, 1952; admitted to bar, 1980, Oklahoma and U.S. District Court, Western District of Oklahoma; 1993, Colorado. *Education:* Colgate University (B.A., cum laude, 1974); University of Oklahoma (J.D., with honors, 1980). Phi Beta Kappa; Phi Delta Phi. Order of the Coif. Editor, Oklahoma Law Review, 1979-1980. Past-Director, Crowe & Dunlevy, Oklahoma City, Oklahoma. *Member:* Oklahoma County, Oklahoma (Chair, Appellate Practice Law Section, 1999) and American Bar Associations; Defense Research Institute. ***REPORTED CASES:*** Gross v. PruCare, Oklahoma County, Oklahoma, September, 1966 (case was tried to a successful jury verdict). ***PRACTICE AREAS:*** Securities Arbitration; Commercial Litigation; Complex Litigation; Mass Torts; Health Insurance; Health Care; Drug and Medical Device Defense. ***Email:*** kcallahan@dayedwards.com

THOMAS PITCHLYNN HOWELL, IV, born Sulphur, Oklahoma, April 22, 1951; admitted to bar, 1983, Oklahoma and U.S. District Court, Western District of Oklahoma; 1984, U.S. District Court, Eastern and Northern Districts of Oklahoma and U.S. Court of Appeals, Tenth Circuit; 1991, U.S. District Court, Eastern District of Wisconsin. *Education:* Harvard University (A.B., cum laude, 1973; A.M., 1976); University of Oklahoma (J.D., 1983). Order of Barristers; Order of the Coif. Captain, Jessup International Law Moot Court Team, 1981-1982. Recipient, Albert C. Hunt Practice Court Award, 1982-1983. Note Editor, Oklahoma Law Review, 1982-1983. Author: "Medical Leases and Patient Referrals Under Oklahoma Law: Are They Mutually Exclusive?" 87 J. Okla. St. Med. Ass'n, 1994. *Member:* Oklahoma County, Oklahoma State and American (Member, Commercial, Banking and Financial Transactions Committee) Bar Associations. ***REPORTED CASES:*** Diamond v. Union Bank & Trust of Bartlesville, 776 F.Supp. 542 (N.D. Okla. 1991); Grove Holding Corp. v. First Wisconsin Natl. Bank of Sheboygan, 803 F.Supp. 1486 (E.D. Wisc. 1992); City Savings, F.S.B. v. Welsh, 793 F.Supp. 1046 (W.D. Okla. 1992); Cimarron Federal Sav. & Loan Assn. v. McKnight, 840 P. 2d. (Okla. Ct. App. 1992); Prudential Ins. Co. of America v. Allied Tower, Ltd., 874 P. 2d 36 (Okla. 1993); Brannon v. Boatmen's Bancshares, Inc., 952 F. Supp. 1478 (W.D. Okla. 1997). ***PRACTICE AREAS:*** Commercial Law; Litigation; Arbitration; Bankruptcy; Lender Liability; Employment Law. ***Email:*** thowell@dayedwards.com

NICK C. LINHOLM, born Oklahoma City, Oklahoma, January 30, 1962; admitted to bar, 1990, Oklahoma; 1993, U.S. District Court, Western District of Oklahoma; 1994, U.S. District Court, Eastern District of Oklahoma; 1996, U.S. District Court, Northern District of Oklahoma, U.S. Court of Appeals, Tenth Circuit and U.S. Supreme Court. *Education:* Oklahoma State University (B.S., Accounting, minors in Finance and Management, 1987); Oklahoma City University School of Law (J.D., 1990). *Member:* Oklahoma County (Mock Trial Committee, 1995—), Oklahoma (Legal Services Committee, 1996—; Children in Law Committee, 1996—) and American Bar Associations; Oklahoma Association of Defense Counsel; Defense Research Institute. ***PRACTICE AREAS:*** Workers Compensation; Insurance Defense; Personal Injury; Civil Litigation; Aircraft Title; Commercial Aircraft Leasing; Aircraft Finance. ***Email:*** nlinholm@dayedwards.com

MYRA PALEVSKY KAUFMAN, born Miami, Florida, April 11, 1971; admitted to bar, 1995, Maryland; 1996, U.S. District Court, District of Maryland and U.S. Court of Federal Claims; 1997, District of Columbia; 1999, Oklahoma and U.S. District Court, Western District of Oklahoma; 2004, U.S. Supreme Court. *Education:* American University (B.A., 1991); University of Miami (J.D., 1995); Georgetown University (1995). Recipient, American Jurisprudence Award for Excellence in Evidence. Editor, Oklahoma Senior Citizens Handbook, Third Edition, 1991. Outstanding Committee Chairperson, Oklahoma Bar Association, Young Lawyers Division, 2004—. *Member:* Oklahoma County (Outstanding Director, 2002 and 2004 and Vice-President, 2003—, Young Lawyers Division) and Okla-

(This Listing Continued)

DAY, EDWARDS, PROPESTER & CHRISTENSEN, P.C., Oklahoma City—Continued

homa (Vice-Chair, 2006 National Mock Trial Task Force, 2004—) Bar Associations. ***PRACTICE AREAS:*** Securities; Intellectual Property; Litigation; Class Actions; Complex Litigation; Transportation; Trucking Law. ***Email:*** mkaufman@dayedwards.com

GARY L. FARNUM, born Tulsa, Oklahoma, August 31, 1954; admitted to bar, 1996, Oklahoma, U.S. District Court, Western, Nothern and Eastern Districts of Oklahoma. *Education:* East Central Oklahoma State University (B.A., 1975); Oklahoma City University School of Law (J.D., 1996). Phi Delta Phi. Member, Merit Scholar Organization. Member, Moot Court Board. Listed in Who's Who American Law Students, 1994-1995, 1995-1996. Licensed Oklahoma Nursing Home Administrator, 1990—. Executive Resource Editor of OCU Law Review. Recipient, OCU Law Scholarship and Kerr Foundation Scholarship; American Jurisprudence Award, Legal Research and Writing II-Appellate Advocacy. First place brief and second place Team, Intramural Moot Court Competition, 1994-1995. Graduate, Nursing Home Administrator Program, University of Oklahoma Continuing Education Center, 1989-1990. *Member:* Oklahoma County, Oklahoma and American Bar Associations. ***PRACTICE AREAS:*** Commercial Law; Insurance Defense Law; Health Law; Employment Law. ***Email:*** gfarnum@dayedwards.com

JEFFREY E. TATE, born Midwest City, Oklahoma, November 30, 1970; admitted to bar, 1996, Oklahoma, U.S. District Court, Western, Northern and Eastern Districts of Oklahoma and U.S. Court of Appeals, Tenth Circuit. *Education:* Oklahoma State University (B.A., 1993); University of Oklahoma (J.D., 1996). Editor, ABI Circuit Update Program, Tenth Circuit. Author: "Lien Stripping of Wholly Unsecured Second Mortgages is Becoming the Norm ¿ and a Trap for the Unwary," Oklahoma Banker, Oklahoma Banker's Association, November, 2000 Edition; "Bankruptcy Update ¿ Developing Issues," May 2003, Vol. 58, No. 3, P. 1323, The Business Lawyer; "Conference on Consumer Finance Law," (new federal rules of bankruptcy procedure), Winter 2003, Vol. 57, No. 1, P. 48; "Selected Issues in Bankruptcy Reform," Winter 2003, Vol. 57, No. 1, P. 53, The Quarterly Report. *Member:* Oklahoma County Bar Association (Member, Sections on: Bankruptcy Law; Litigation, 1998—; Chair, Young Lawyers Division, 2002-2003); American Bankruptcy Institute (Member, Conference on Consumer Finance Law, 2004—). ***REPORTED CASES:*** In re Alexander, 980 P.2d 659 (Okla. 1999); Corman v. H-30 Drilling, Inc., 40 P.3d 1051 (Okla. 2001). ***PRACTICE AREAS:*** Insolvency; Bankruptcy Litigation; Business Law; Commercial Law; Banking Law; Financial Law; Collection Law; Employment Litigation. ***Email:*** jtate@dayedwards.com

GREGORY J. CRAWFORD, born Oklahoma City, Oklahoma, October 3, 1963; admitted to bar, 1997, Oklahoma and U.S. District Court, Western District of Oklahoma; 2000, U.S. District Court, Northern and Eastern Districts of Oklahoma. *Education:* Stanford University (A.B., 1985); University of Oklahoma (J.D., 1997). Certified Public Accountant, California, 1989. Lecturer: University of Oklahoma's Graduate School of Trial Advocacy, 2000 and 2004. *Member:* Tulsa County, Oklahoma County and Oklahoma Bar Associations. ***PRACTICE AREAS:*** Securities Law. ***Email:*** gcrawford@dayedwards.com

L. NAZETTE ZUHDI, born Oklahoma City, Oklahoma, April 2, 1972; admitted to bar, 1997, Oklahoma and U.S. District Court, Western District of Oklahoma; 2000, Texas. *Education:* University of Oklahoma (B.A., 1994; J.D., with distinction, 1997); Oxford University, England (Summer Law Program, 1995); Pepperdine University (Visiting Student, 1996); DePaul University (Masters in Health Law, 1998). Dean's List; President's List, 1994. *Member:* Oklahoma County, Oklahoma and American (Member, Litigation Section) Bar Associations; State Bar of Texas; Oklahoma Health Lawyers Association. ***PRACTICE AREAS:*** Banking Law; Finance; Health Law; Health Care Law. ***Email:*** nzuhdi@dayedwards.com

TARA A. LaCLAIR, born West Branch, Michigan; admitted to bar, 1999, California, U.S. District Court, Central District of California and Supreme Court of California; 2001, Michigan; 2003, U.S. District Court, District of Colorado; 2004, U.S. District Court, Western District of Oklahoma, U.S. District Court, Eastern District of Michigan and U.S. Court of Appeals, Tenth Circuit (Not admitted in Oklahoma). *Education:* Eastern Michigan University (B.B.A., 1994); Pepperdine University School of Law (J.D., cum laude, 1999); Georgetown University Law Center (LL.M., Securities and Financial Regulation, 2000). Phi Alpha Delta; Beta Gamma Sigma; Golden Key Honor Society. Recipient: American Jurisprudence Award in Remedies; Nathan Burkan Memorial Competition for Copyright Law (Pepperdine University); Certificate of Special Tribute, State of Michigan. *Member:* Washtenaw County, Los Angeles County, Federal and American Bar Associations. ***PRACTICE AREAS:*** State Legislative Practice; Federal Litigation; Securities Litigation; Securities Arbitration; Commercial Litigation. ***Email:*** tlaclair@dayedwards.com

A. AINSLIE STANFORD, II, born Tulsa, Oklahoma, February 19, 1975; admitted to bar, 2000, Oklahoma. *Education:* University of Oklahoma (B.A., Finance, 1997; J.D., 2000); Oxford University, England (Summer Law Program, 1998). *Member:* Oklahoma, Oklahoma County and Tulsa County Bar Associations; Luther Bohanon American Inn of Court (1997-2002; 2004—). ***PRACTICE AREAS:*** Securities Law. ***Email:*** astanford@dayedwards.com

LISA MICHELE MOLSBEE, born Lufkin, Texas, October 29, 1974; admitted to bar, 2002, Oklahoma and U.S. District Court, Western and Northern Districts of Oklahoma; 2004, U.S. Court of Appeals, Tenth Circuit. *Education:* Stephen F. Austin State University (B.A., Journalism, 1995); Oklahoma City University School of Law (M.L.A., Mass Communications, with honors, 1997; J.D., summa cum laude, 2002). Recipient, CALI Excellence for the Future Awards for Oil and Gas, Legal Profession and Wills. *Member:* Oklahoma County, Oklahoma and American Bar Associations. ***PRACTICE AREAS:*** Bank Law; Bankruptcy; Creditors Rights. ***Email:*** lmolsbee@dayedwards.com

ROBERT J. CARLSON, born Suffern, New York, November 27, 1969; admitted to bar, 2002, Oklahoma, U.S. District Court, Northern District of Oklahoma and U.S. Court of Appeals, Tenth Circuit. *Education:* University of Tulsa (B.S.B.A., Economics, 1992; J.D., 2001); Oklahoma State University (M.S., Economics, 1994). Recipient: Scholastic Achievement Awards in, Legal Research and Writing, Corporate Law, Unfair Trade Practices and Federal Securities Regulation. Member, National Association for Business Economics, 1998-2002. *Member:* Tulsa County, Oklahoma and American Bar Associations. ***PRACTICE AREAS:*** Arbitration; Securities Law; Deceptive Trade Practices; Unfair Competition; Civil Litigation; Business Law; Commercial Law; Civil Appeals; Litigation. ***Email:*** rcarlson@dayedwards.com

OF COUNSEL

ROBERT S. BAKER, born Oklahoma City, Oklahoma, June 5, 1937; admitted to bar, 1961, Oklahoma and U.S. District Court, Western District of Oklahoma; 1969, U.S. District Court, Eastern District of Oklahoma; 1970, U.S. Court of Appeals, Tenth Circuit and U.S. Supreme Court; 1993 U.S. District Court, Northern District of Oklahoma. *Education:* University of Oklahoma (LL.B., 1961); George Washington University. Phi Delta Phi (Vice-President, 1961). Case Editor, Oklahoma Law Review, 1961. President, Oklahoma Junior Bar Conference, 1964. Trustee, Oklahoma Bar Foundation, 1964-1970. Associate Municipal Judge, 1964-1973. Director, National Young Lawyer's Conference, 1967. General Counsel: Oklahoma Sheriff's and Peace Officers Association, 1969-1974; Oklahoma Highway Patrol Troopers Association, 1976—. Member, Oklahoma Highway Patrol Legal Advisory Committee, 1971-1974. Chairman, Oklahoma Board of Medicolegal Investigations, Office of the Chief Medical Examiner, 1974-1984 and 1987—. *Member:* Oklahoma and American (Member, 1970-1974 and Vice-Chairman, 1973, Automobile Law Committee) Bar Associations; Oklahoma Association of Defense Counsel; Federation of Insurance and Corporate Counsel; International Association of Insurance and Corporate Counsel. ***PRACTICE AREAS:*** Products Liability; Insurance; Trial Practice; Corporate Litigation; Securities Litigation; Arbitration.

HERBERT F. (JACK) HEWETT, born Durant, Oklahoma, April 29, 1926; admitted to bar, 1950, Oklahoma; 1961, U.S. Supreme Court; 1963, U.S. District Court, Western District of Oklahoma and U.S. Court of Appeals, Tenth Circuit. *Education:* Louisiana Polytechnic Institute, Duke University and University of Oklahoma (B.A., 1947); Yale Law School (LL.B., 1950). Law Clerk, U.S. District Court, Western District of Oklahoma, 1950-1951. Member, State Election Board, 1961-1963. Member and Vice-Chairman, Oklahoma Securities Commission, 1966-1969. *Member:* Oklahoma County, Oklahoma and American Bar Associations. ***PRACTICE AREAS:*** Business Law; Corporate Law; Securities Regulation Law.

KENNETH A. BROKAW, born Anadarko, Oklahoma, November 14, 1951; admitted to bar, 1983, Oklahoma, U.S. District Court, Eastern, Western and Northern Districts of Oklahoma, U.S. District Court, District of Colorado and U.S. Court of Appeals, Tenth Circuit. *Education:* University of Oklahoma (B.A., History, with distinction, 1978; J.D., 1983). Phi Beta Kappa; Phi Alpha Theta. Member, American Inn of Court XXIII, 1991-1994. Author/Lecturer for Continuing Legal Education Seminars: sponsored by the Oklahoma Bar Association: "Insurance Law in Oklahoma Premises and Commercial Liability" (1994); "Identifying and Using Insurance Coverage: Uninsured/Underinsured Motorist" (1990); "Insurance Coverage Law in Oklahoma" (National Business Institute, 1997). *Member:* Oklahoma County, Oklahoma and American Bar Associations; Oklahoma Association of Defense Counsel. ***REPORTED CASES:*** Breakfield v. Oklahoma Farmers Union Mutual Insurance Company, 910 P.2d 991 (Okla. 1995); Withrow v. Pickard, 905 P.2d 800 (Okla. 1995); Phillips v. Oklahoma Farmers Union Mutual Insurance Company, 867 P.2d 1361 (Okla.App. 1993); Starrett v. Oklahoma Farmers Union Mutual Insurance Company, 849 P.2d 397 (Okla. 1993); Shelter Mutual Insurance Company v. Littlejim, 927 F.2d 1132 (10th Cir. 1991); Nunn v. Stewart, 756 P.2d 6 (Okla. 1988). ***PRACTICE AREAS:*** Insurance Defense Law; Insurance Coverage Litigation; Insurance Bad Faith. ***Email:*** kbrokaw@dayedwards.com

REPRESENTATIVE CLIENTS: Accord Human Resources; AIG Aviation, Inc.; Aig Insurance; Arch Insurance Company; Banc of America Securities LLC; BancFirst; BancFirst Corporation; Bank of America Corporation; Bank of America, N.A.; Barlett Collins; Barnett & Associates; BASF; Cambridge Intergrated Services; Casualty Reciprocal Exchange (Dodson Insurance Group); Claims and Risk Services, Inc.; Claims Control, Inc.; CNA Insurance Company; COMAV Managers, Inc.; Comerio Ercole, SPA; Community Rehabilitation Corporation; CompSource Oklahoma; Conair Corporation; Condea Vista Chemical Company; Crawford & Company; Cystodiagnostics, Inc.; Danny Wright Dozer & Pipeline, Inc.; DeLonghi America, Inc.; DeLonghi Spa; Dor-O-Matic; Employers Mutual Companies; Equitable Plan Services, Inc.; ESIS; Eurich Specialties London, Ltd.; Fidelity Brokerage Services, Inc.; Fire & Casualty Insurance Company; Fireman's Fund Insurance; First American Insurance; First National Bank of Fletcher; First National Bank of Seiling; First State Bank of Elmore City; Fluid Technologies, Inc.; Foremost Insurance Co.; Frontier Insurance Co.; General Insurance Co. of America; General Security Insurance Company; Gold Bank; Healthback Holdings LLC; Indiana Lumbermen's Mutual Insurance Co.; Ingersoll-Rand Corporation; Jaeqer & Haines, Inc.; Jetta Corporation; JPMorgan Chase Bank, N.A.; Kawasaki Motors Corp.; Legion Insurance Co.; LSB Industries, Inc.; Legacy Bank; Lumbermen's Underwriting Alliance (Lynn Insurance Group); Merrill Lynch, Pierce, Fenner & Smith, Incorporated; Metropolitan Health Care; Mills Biopharmaceuticals, Inc.; North American Specialty; Old Republic Insurance; Oklahoma Business Owners Association; Oklahoma Department of Wildlife Conservation; Oklahoma Farmers Union Mutual Insurance Company; Oklahoma Lumbermen's Association; Oklahoma Property and Casualty Insurance Guaranty Association; Oklahoma Restaurant Group; QBE Insurance Corporation; RSA Surplus Lines Insurance Services, Inc.; St. John's Hospital; Safety National Casualty Corp.; Sagamore Insurance Company; South Carolina Insurance Company; The Fire & Casualty Insurance Company of Connecticut; TMS, Inc.; Transamerica Commercial Finance Corp.; Triangle Insurance Company; T.S. Phillips Investments, Inc.; Universal Underwriters Group; U.S. Fidelity & Guaranty; Waukesha-Pearce Industries, Inc.; Webco; Western National Insurance Company; Zurich American Insurance.

(This Listing Continued)

DeBEE GILCHRIST

A PROFESSIONAL CORPORATION

100 NORTH BROADWAY AVENUE

SUITE 1500

OKLAHOMA CITY, OKLAHOMA 73102

Telephone: 405-232-7777

Facsimile: 405-232-9898

Email: firm@debeegilchrist.com

URL: http://www.debeegilchrist.com

Acquisitions and Divestitures, Administrative Law; Aircraft Title Law; Aircraft Financing Law; Aviation Law; Banking Law, Commercial Transactions; Commercial Aircraft Leasing; Charitable and Exempt Organizations, Corporation, Estate Planning, Federal and State Taxation Law, General Civil Law, Municipal Law; Partnership Law, Privatization Law; Probate and Estate Administration, Real Property Transactions, Public Private Partnerships, and Commercial Litigation.

(This Listing Continued)

H. EDWARD DeBEE, III, born Oklahoma City, Oklahoma, October 14, 1952; admitted to bar, 1978, Oklahoma and U.S. Tax Court; 1979, U.S. Claims Court; 1980, U.S. District Court, Western District of Oklahoma; 1985, U.S. Supreme Court. *Education:* Oklahoma State University (B.S., 1974); University of Oklahoma (J.D., 1977); New York University (LL.M., in Taxation, 1979). Certified Public Accountant, Oklahoma, 1978. Member: Academy Selection Board, 1994; Tax Policy Committee, appointed by Senator Don Nickles, 1994-2004; Governor's Small Business Summit, 1995. Member, Board of Directors, Integris Baptist Medical Center, 2002—. *Member:* Oklahoma County, Oklahoma (Member, Taxation Section) and American Bar Associations; National Council for Public-Private Partnerships. ***PRACTICE AREAS:*** Mergers and Acquisitions; Federal Taxation; Corporate Reorganizations; Tax Controversies; Healthcare Contracts; Administrative Agency Practice; Broadcast Station Transfers; Municipal Contracts and Finance; Lease Finance; State Taxation; Estate and Gift Taxation; Tax Exempt Organizations; Real Estate Finance. ***Email:*** edebee@debeegilchrist.com

JACK P. GILCHRIST, born Dallas, Texas, September 9, 1961; admitted to bar, 1989, Oklahoma. *Education:* University of Oklahoma (B.A., 1984; J.D., 1989); Dallas Theological Seminary (M.A., 1986). Chief Note Editor, Oklahoma Law Review, 1988-1989. Author: "US Registration of Aircraft Under Foreign Ownership," Studies in Leasing Law and Tax, 1995; "US Law: Protecting Lenders' Interests in Aircraft, Engines, Propellers and Spare Parts," Studies in Leasing Law and Tax, 1996. Delegate, American Convention of Law Reviews, 1988. Executive Assistant to the Director, Oklahoma Department of Corrections, 1983. *Member:* Oklahoma County, Oklahoma, Federal (Member, Executive Committee, Oklahoma City Chapter), American (Member: Business Law Section; Aircraft Finance and Contracts Division of the Forum on Air And Space Law; Aircraft Finance Subcommittee; Committee on Uniform Commercial Code; Subcommittee on International Commercial Law; Subcommittee on Leasing; Subcommittee on Secured Transactions) and International Bar Associations; Transportation Lawyers Association. ***PRACTICE AREAS:*** Aircraft Finance and Leasing; Aircraft Sales; Aircraft Title; Aviation Law; International Aviation Law; Aeronautical Regulation; Aviation Regulation; Commercial Law; Commercial Transactions; Business Law; Corporate Commercial Law; Administrative Agency Practice; Civil Practice. ***Email:*** jgilchrist@debeegilchrist.com

---

BRIAN THOMAS FAGAN, born Monticello, Mississippi, January 21, 1970; admitted to bar, 1997, Oklahoma. *Education:* University of Tulsa (B.S.B.A., 1992; J.D., 1996). *Member:* Oklahoma County, Oklahoma and American Bar Associations. ***PRACTICE AREAS:*** Estate and Gift Taxation; Health Care Law; Commercial Contracts; Closely Held Corporations; Partnership Organization; Real Property; Individual Taxation; Corporate Taxation; Tax Controversies; Mergers and Acquisitions. ***Email:*** bfagan@debeegilchrist.com

BARRETT J. KNUDSEN, born Breckenridge, Minnesota, December 23, 1971; admitted to bar, 1998, Oklahoma and U.S. District Court, Western District of Oklahoma. *Education:* Oral Roberts University (B.S., 1994); University of Oklahoma (J.D., 1998). *Member:* Oklahoma and Federal (Oklahoma City Chapter) Bar Associations. ***PRACTICE AREAS:*** Aircraft Finance and Leasing; Aircraft Sales; Aviation Law; Aircraft Title; Aviation Regulation; Commercial Transactions; Closely Held Corporations; Nonprofit Organizations. ***Email:*** bknudsen@debeegilchrist.com

LAWN B. GARDNER, born Oklahoma City, Oklahoma, August 12, 1962; admitted to bar, 1994, Oklahoma. *Education:* University of Central Oklahoma (B.S., cum laude, 1987); University of Oklahoma College of Law (J.D., Order of the Coif, 1994). Recipient, Academic Achievement Award, 1993. Certified Public Accountant, Oklahoma, 1989. *Member:* Oklahoma and American Bar Associations. ***PRACTICE AREAS:*** Business Law; Commercial Transactions; Corporate Law; Mergers and Acquisitions; Commercial Lending; Securities Law. ***Email:*** lgardner@debeegilchrist.com

BLAINE M. PETERSON, born Midwest City, Oklahoma, June 9, 1971; admitted to bar, 1999, Oklahoma. *Education:* University of Oklahoma (B.B.A., Accounting, 1994; J.D., with distinction, 1999). Phi Delta Phi. Recipient, American Jurisprudence Award, Civil Procedure. Certified Public Accountant, Oklahoma, 1995. *Member:* Oklahoma County, Oklahoma and American Bar Associations; Oklahoma Society of Certified Public Accountants. ***PRACTICE AREAS:*** Estate and Gift Taxation; Individual Taxation; Corporate Taxation; Tax Controversies; Business Valuation; Business Law; Probate; Guardianships; Tax Exempt Organizations. ***Email:*** bpeterson@debeegilchrist.com

CAROLE L. HOUGHTON, born Modesto, California, July 7, 1970; admitted to bar, 1998, Oklahoma and U.S. District Court, Western, Eastern and Northern Districts of Oklahoma; 2001, Texas and U.S. District Court, Northern, Eastern, Southern and Western Districts of Texas. *Education:* California State University, Northridge (B.A., Psychology, 1993); Oklahoma City University School of Law (J.D., cum laude, 1998). *Member:* Oklahoma Bar Association; State Bar of Texas. ***PRACTICE AREAS:*** Aircraft Finance and Leasing; Aircraft Sales; Aircraft Title; Aviation Law; Commercial Transactions; Real Property; Commercial Litigation; Banking Litigation. ***Email:*** choughton@debeegilchrist.com

STEVEN R. McCONNELL, born Irving, Texas, April 5, 1967; admitted to bar, 1994, Oklahoma and U.S. District Court, Western District of Oklahoma; U.S. Court of Appeals, Tenth Circuit. *Education:* University of Oklahoma (B.A., 1989; B.F.A., 1990); Oklahoma City University School of Law (J.D., 1993). *Member:* Oklahoma and American Bar Associations. ***PRACTICE AREAS:*** Estate Planning; Trust Administration; Banking. ***Email:*** smcconnell@debeegilchrist.com

OF COUNSEL

DON HAGER, born McAlester, Oklahoma, November 28, 1940; admitted to bar, 1968, Oklahoma. *Education:* Oklahoma State University (B.S., Accounting, 1964); University of Tulsa (J.D., 1968). Phi Delta Phi. Member, American Society of Corporate Secretaries, 1985—. *Member:* Oklahoma County, Oklahoma and American Bar Associations. ***PRACTICE AREAS:*** Corporate Law; Tax Law; Estate Planning; Trust Administration. ***Email:*** dhager@debeegilchrist.com

DERRICK & BRIGGS, LLP

A Professional Partnership

CHASE TOWER, 28TH FLOOR
100 NORTH BROADWAY AVENUE
OKLAHOMA CITY, OKLAHOMA 73102-8831
Telephone: 405-235-1900
Facsimile: 405-235-1995
URL: http://www.derrickandbriggs.com

Business Law, including Corporations, Limited Liability Companies and Partnerships, Mergers and Acquisitions, Securities Regulation, Business and Oil and Gas Financing, Publishing Law, Probate and Estate Planning, Entertainment Law; No Trial Work.

GARY W. DERRICK, born Enid, Oklahoma, November 3, 1953; admitted to bar, 1979, Oklahoma. *Education:* Oklahoma State University (B.A., 1976); University of Oklahoma (J.D., 1979). Omicron Delta Kappa; Blue Key; Phi Delta Phi. Recipient: American Jurisprudence Award; Earl Sneed Continuing Legal Education Award, Oklahoma Bar Association. Listed in Best Lawyers in America, 2001-2002, 2003-2004, 2005-2006; Chambers USA, 2002-2003, 2003-2004, 2005-2006. Author: "Rights, Duties, and Liabilities of Directors, Officers and Shareholders," and with Faught, Irving, "Introduction: History of the General Corporation Act: Variances From Delaware Law and Limited Liability Companies in Oklahoma Business Organizations," (I Faught ed. 2003); "New Developments in Oklahoma Business Entity Law," 56 Oklahoma Law Review 259, 2003; "Oklahoma Limited Liability Companies and Limited Liability Partnerships," 22 Oklahoma City University Law Review, 643, 1997. Chairman, General Corporation Act Committee, 1986—. Chairman, Business Associations Section, Oklahoma Bar Association, 1986-1987, 2004—. Member, Section on Business Law, American Bar Association. *Member:* American Society of Corporate Secretaries (President, Oklahoma/Arkansas Chapter, 1994-1995). ***PRACTICE AREAS:*** Business Law; Corporate Law; Limited Liability Company Law; Partnership Law; Mergers and Acquisitions; Securities Regulation; Oil and Gas Finance. ***Email:*** derrick@derrickandbriggs.com

M. COURTNEY BRIGGS, born Philadelphia, Pennsylvania, March 28, 1960; admitted to bar, 1991, Oklahoma and U.S. District Court, Western District of Oklahoma. *Education:* Wesleyan University (B.A., 1982); University of Oklahoma (J.D., with distinction, 1991). Recipient: Hardin Ballard Memorial Award for Outstanding Student in Appellate Advocacy; American Jurisprudence Awards; Academic Achievement Award; Oklahoma Bar Association Award for Outstanding Service to the Young Lawyers Division (1995 and 1996); Outstanding Young Lawyer Award, Oklahoma Bar Association, 1998; Golden Gavel Award, Oklahoma Bar Association, 1999; Mona Salyer Lambird Spotlight Award, Oklahoma Bar Association, 2001. Managing Editor, 1990-1991, Assistant Managing Editor, 1989-1990, Oklahoma Law Review. Author: Note, "Securities: Statute of Limitation for 10b-5 Actions," 43 Okla. L. Rev. 391, 1990. Member, Board of Advocates, 1989—. *Member:* Oklahoma County (Chairperson: New Attorney Orientation Committee, 1994; Awards Committee, 2000-2005); Oklahoma (Member, Board of Governors, 1997; Mandatory Legal Education Commission, 2005; Chairperson: Young Lawyers Division, 1997; Oklahoma High School Mock Trial Program, 1994-1995; Disaster Legal Services Committee, 1999; Law-Related Education Committee, 2002-2003. Director, Young Lawyers Division, 1995-1998; Vice-Chairperson, Women in the Law Committee, 1998-2000) and American (Liaison, Commission on Legal Problems of the Elderly, 1996-1998; Member, Publications Committee, Young Lawyers Division, 1996; Assembly Delegate, Young Lawyers Division, 1995-1998) Bar Associations; International Young Lawyers Association, 1995-2004; Society of Children's Book Writers and Illustrators. ***LANGUAGES:*** French and Italian. ***PRACTICE AREAS:*** Publishing Law; Business Law; Estate Planning; Probate; Entertainment Law. ***Email:*** briggs@derrickandbriggs.com

REPRESENTATIVE CLIENTS: Furnished Upon Request.

DERRYBERRY, QUIGLEY, SOLOMON & NAIFEH, P.A.

Established in 1979

4800 NORTH LINCOLN BOULEVARD
OKLAHOMA CITY, OKLAHOMA 73105
Telephone: 405-528-6569
Fax: 405-528-6462
URL: http://www.Derryberrylaw.com
URL: http://www.lawyers.com/derryberrylaw
Email: Derryberry@Derryberrylaw.com
URL: http://www.statecapitallaw.org

Civil Trial Practice, Administrative and Governmental, Commercial, Insurance Regulatory and Defense. Workers' Compensation, Construction, Probate, Estates and Trusts, Real Estate, Bankruptcy, Public Utility, Personal Injury, Corporation, Taxation, Banking, Health and Hospital, Professional Licensing, Oil and Gas, Municipal and Public Authority Finance, Transportation, Common Carrier, Educational Law, Employment Law, Environmental Law, Arbitration and Mediation.

FIRM PROFILE: The Firm was Established in 1979 by Larry Derryberry, following his service as Attorney General of the State of Oklahoma from 1971 to 1979. The firm provides representation in both private and public sectors.

LARRY DERRYBERRY, born Altus, Oklahoma, April 22, 1939; admitted to bar, 1963, Oklahoma; 1971, U.S. Supreme Court; U.S. Court of Appeals, Tenth Circuit; U.S. District Court, Western, Northern and Eastern Districts of Oklahoma. *Education:* Oklahoma University (B.A., 1961; LL.B., 1963). Phi Delta Phi. Editor, Oklahoma Law Review, 1962-1963. Member, 1963-1971, Speaker Pro Tempore, 1969-1971, House of Representatives, State of Oklahoma. Attorney General, State of Oklahoma, 1971-1979. *Member:* Jackson County (President, 1964), Oklahoma County, Oklahoma and American Bar Associations. ***SPECIAL AGENCIES:*** Oklahoma Insurance Department; Oklahoma State Board for Property and Casualty Rates; Oklahoma Corporation Commission; Oklahoma Tax

(This Listing Continued)

DERRYBERRY, QUIGLEY, SOLOMON & NAIFEH, P.A., Oklahoma City—Continued

Commission; Oklahoma Department of Health. ***PRACTICE AREAS:*** Administrative Law; Election, Campaign and Political Law; Government; Insurance; Utility Law; Health Care. ***Email:*** lderryberry@derryberrylaw.com

STEPHEN G. SOLOMON, born Oklahoma City, Oklahoma, August 29, 1948; admitted to bar, 1977, Oklahoma, U.S. District Court, Eastern, Northern and Western Districts of Oklahoma; U.S. Court of Appeals, Fifth and Tenth Circuits; U.S. Claims Court; U.S. Supreme Court. *Education:* University of Oklahoma (B.B.A., 1971); Oklahoma City University (J.D., 1977). Executive Assistant Attorney General, 1971-1972. Director, Charter National Bank. *Member:* Oklahoma County, Oklahoma and American Bar Associations. ***PRACTICE AREAS:*** Commercial Litigation; Arbitration; Construction Law; Real Estate; Banks and Banking; Bankruptcy Law. ***Email:*** ssolomon@derryberrylaw.com

ROBERT N. NAIFEH, JR., born Norman, Oklahoma, October 3, 1957; admitted to bar, 1983, Oklahoma and U.S. District Court, Western, Northern and Eastern Districts of Oklahoma; U.S. Court of Appeals, 10th Circuit. *Education:* University of Oklahoma (B.A., 1979); Oklahoma City University (J.D., 1983). Phi Delta Phi. Recipient: Phi Delta Phi Graduate of the Year, Hand Inn, 1983. Lecturer: "Insurance Coverage Law in Oklahoma," National Business Institute, 1996-1997; "Advanced Insurance Coverage Conference Top 10 Issues for Practitioners," Mealey's 2003. Recipient, Outstanding Achievement Award, Oklahoma State Chamber of Commerce, 1995. President, Oklahoma City University School of Law Alumni Association, 1988. *Member:* Oklahoma County and Oklahoma Bar Associations. ***SPECIAL AGENCIES:*** Oklahoma Insurance Department; Oklahoma Association of Defense Counsel. ***PRACTICE AREAS:*** Insurance; Insurance Defense; Insurance Coverage; Insurance Regulation; Commercial Insurance; Uninsured and Underinsured Motorists; Insurance Bad Faith Defense. ***Email:*** rnaifeh@derryberrylaw.com

PATRICK D. SHORE, born Oklahoma City, Oklahoma, December 16, 1954; admitted to bar, 1981, Oklahoma and U.S. District Court, Western and Eastern Districts of Oklahoma; U.S. Court of Appeals, Tenth Circuit. *Education:* University of Oklahoma (B.A., Journalism, 1977); Oklahoma City University (J.D., 1981). Deputy General Counsel, Oklahoma Corporation Commission, 1985-1986. *Member:* Oklahoma Bar Association. ***SPECIAL AGENCIES:*** Oklahoma Corporation Commission; Oklahoma State Department of Health. ***REPORTED CASES:*** Branch Trucking Co. et al v. Oklahoma Tax Commission 801 P.2d 686 (Okl. 1990); Hargrave v. Canadian Valley Electric Cooperative 792 P.2d 50 (Okla. 1990). ***PRACTICE AREAS:*** Utility Law; Electric Cooperatives Law; Public Utility Regulation; Administrative Law; Appellate Practice; Certificates of Need; Regulatory Agency Practice. ***Email:*** pshore@derryberrylaw.com

JEROME S. SEPKOWITZ, born Amarillo, Texas, May 14, 1947; admitted to bar, 1973, Oklahoma; U.S. District Court, Western District of Oklahoma; U.S. District Court, Eastern District of Oklahoma; U.S. Court of Appeals, Tenth Circuit. *Education:* Oklahoma University (B.A., 1969; J.D., 1973). Member, Mediation Panel, Oklahoma County and Western District of Oklahoma. *Member:* Oklahoma County and Oklahoma Bar Associations. ***PRACTICE AREAS:*** Bankruptcy; Commercial Law; Debtor and Creditor; Civil Litigation; Collections. ***Email:*** jsepkowitz@derryberrylaw.com

DONALD B. NEVARD, born Chicago, Illinois, June 13, 1947; admitted to bar, 1973, Oklahoma; 1976, U.S. Supreme Court. *Education:* Ohio University (B.B.A., 1969); The Ohio State University (J.D., 1973). Member, Blue Key. Assistant Attorney General, State of Oklahoma, 1973-1975. General Counsel, Oklahoma Tax Commission, 1975-1976. *Member:* Oklahoma County (Chairman, Public Service Committee, 1976-1977) and Oklahoma Bar Associations. ***LANGUAGES:*** Spanish. ***SPECIAL AGENCIES:*** Oklahoma Tax Commission. ***PRACTICE AREAS:*** Trusts and Estates; Taxation; Real Estate; Corporate Law; Probate; Commercial Real Estate; Business Law; Wills. ***Email:*** dnevard@derryberrylaw.com

GEORGE W. VELOTTA II, born Evansville, Indiana, October 1, 1953; admitted to bar, 1978, Oklahoma; 1981, U.S. District Court, Western District of Oklahoma; 2003, U.S. District Court, Eastern District of Oklahoma and U.S. Court of Appeals, Tenth Circuit. *Education:* Oklahoma State University (B.S. Political Science, 1975); University of Oklahoma (J.D., 1978). Recipient, American Jurisprudence Award for Trusts. Member, Oklahoma Liquefied Petroleum Gas Board. *Member:* Oklahoma (Member, Law Related Education Committee) and American Bar Associations. ***SPECIAL AGENCIES:*** Oklahoma Insurance Department; Oklahoma Corporation Commission. ***REPORTED CASES:*** American Biomedical Group, Inc. v. Norman Regional Hospital Authority 855 P.2d 1074 (Okl. App., 1993); Larry Jones International Ministries, Inc. v. Means, et. al., 946 P.2d 699 (Okla., 1997); Weatherford v. Senior Security Life Ins. Co., 916 P.2d 288 (Okla. App. 1996); Oklahoma Property and Cas. Ins. Guaranty Ass'n v. Classic Fire and Marine Ins. Co., 1998 Ok. Civ. App. 133. ***PRACTICE AREAS:*** Litigation; Commercial Law; Commercial Real Estate; Insurance Regulation; Oil and Gas Law. ***Email:*** bvelotta@derryberrylaw.com

DOUGLAS A. RICE, born Phoenix, Arizona, January 15, 1969; admitted to bar, 1994, Oklahoma, U.S. District Court, Western District of Oklahoma and U.S. Court of Appeals, Tenth Circuit. *Education:* Oklahoma State University (B.S., 1991); University of Oklahoma (J.D., 1994). Phi Delta Phi. Recipient, American Jurisprudence Award in Criminal Law. Member, National Trial Team, 1994. *Member:* Oklahoma County, Oklahoma (Member, Labor and Employment Law Section; Government and Administrative Law Section) and American (Member, Labor and Employment Law Section) Bar Associations; Oklahoma Association of Defense Counsel. ***REPORTED CASES:*** Roberts v. Progressive Independence, Inc., 183 F.3d 1215 (10th Cir 1999). ***PRACTICE AREAS:*** Labor and Employment; Litigation; Civil Rights; Administrative Law; Insurance; Personal Injury. ***Email:*** drice@derryberrylaw.com

STEPHEN L. McCALEB, born Arlington, Texas, April 12, 1968; admitted to bar, 1994, Oklahoma. *Education:* University of Oklahoma (B.A., 1990; J.D., 1994). Phi Delta Phi. Member, National Trial Team, 1994. Lecturer, Oklahoma Bar Association CLE: "How Workers' Compensation Insurance Rates Are Calculated," Workers Compensation Law Update, April 1997; "How to Deal Effectively with the Oklahoma Insurance Department," Insurance Law Update, April 1999; "The Duties of the Oklahoma Insurance Department," Administrative Law, May 1999; "Insolvent Insurers," Insurance Law Update, 2002. *Member:* Oklahoma Bar Association. ***SPECIAL AGENCIES:*** Oklahoma Insurance Department. ***REPORTED CASES:*** Oklahoma State Senate, Intervenor/Appellant v. State Board for Property & Casualty Rates, 11 P.3d 1242 (Okla., 2000). ***Email:*** smccaleb@derryberrylaw.com

CALEB J. MUCKALA, admitted to bar, 2004, Oklahoma and U.S. District Court, Western District of Oklahoma. *Education:* University of Oklahoma (B.A., 2001); Oklahoma City University School of Law (J.D., 2004). Phi Delta Phi, Historian. Member, American Bar Association Appellate Advocacy Moot Court Team, 2003-2004. Recipient, CALI Award, Constitutional Law I. Formerly with, Oklahoma Property and Casualty Insurance Guaranty Association. *Member:* Oklahoma County and Oklahoma Bar Associations. ***PRACTICE AREAS:*** Insurance; Insurance Defense; Insurance Coverage; Litigation; Government. ***Email:*** Cmuckala@derryberrylaw.com

SHERRI T. FLEMING, born Chicago, Illinois, November 30, 1971; admitted to bar, 2002, Michigan; 2005, Oklahoma; U.S. District Court, Western and Eastern Districts of Michigan. *Education:* Northeastern Illinois University (B.A., 1990); Thomas M. Cooley Law School (J.D., 2001); Wayne State University Law School (LL.M., Taxation, 2005). Senior Articles Editor, Journal of Practical and Clinical Law. Moot Court and Mock Trial Competition. Assistant Attorney General, Michigan, 2002-2004. *Member:* Oklahoma and American Bar Associations; State Bar of Michigan; National Association of Bond Lawyers. ***PRACTICE AREAS:*** Taxation; Probate; Trusts and Estates; Real Estate; Wills. ***Email:*** sfleming@derryberrylaw.com

OF COUNSEL

PAUL E. QUIGLEY, born Galesburg, Illinois, December 10, 1951; admitted to bar, 1978, Oklahoma; U.S. Court of Appeals Tenth Circuit. *Education:* Oklahoma State University (B.S., 1974); Oklahoma University (J.D., 1978). Phi Beta Kappa; Phi Delta Phi. Recipient, American Jurisprudence Award in Commercial Law, Certified Master in Trial Advocacy. Graduate, National Institute of Trial Advocacy. Lecturer: "Ethics and Professionalism in the Law," National Business Institute, 1997-1998. *Member:* Oklahoma County (Chairman, Fee Grievance & Ethics Committees, 1996-1999), Oklahoma and American Bar Associations; Oklahoma Trial Lawyers Association; The Association of Trial Lawyers of America. ***PRACTICE AREAS:*** Torts; Commercial Litigation; Insurance Litigation; Trial Practice; Civil Liability.

J. ERIC TURNER, born Fort Worth, Texas, January 26, 1958; admitted to bar, 1983, Oklahoma and U.S. District Court, Western and Northern Districts of Oklahoma; U.S. Court of Appeals Tenth Circuit. *Education:* Austin College (B.A., 1980); University of Oklahoma (J.D., 1983). Pi Gamma Mu. Municipal Judge, City of McLoud 1987-1989. *Member:* Oklahoma (Member, Insurance Section) Bar Association; Defense Research Institute.

JUSTIN A. WHITEFIELD, born Pauls Valley, Oklahoma, February 3, 1973; admitted to bar, 1997, Oklahoma. *Education:* Oklahoma State University (B.A., 1993); University of Oklahoma (J.D., 1997). Phi Delta Phi; Inns of the Court. Member, National Moot Court Team, 1996. Recipient, American Jurisprudence Award, Consumer Law, 1996. *Member:* Oklahoma and American Bar Associations. ***PRACTICE AREAS:*** Governmental Relations; Administrative Law; Civil Litigation; Probate; Bankruptcy.

REPRESENTATIVE CLIENTS: American International Group (AIG); American Honda Finance Co.; American Insurance Association (AIA); American Premium Brands, Ltd.; American Resource Mortgage, Inc.; Aramark Corporation, Inc.; Association of County Commissioners; BancFirst Corporation; Bank One Credit Company; Bituminous Insurance Companies; Blackledge & Associates; Caterpillar Financial Services; CompSource Oklahoma; Dodge Town, U.S.A.; DRC, Inc.; First National Center, L.L.C.; Home Creations; Hooters of America, Inc.; Humana, Inc.; Hyundai Motor Finance, Co.; Hyatt Legal Plan; Ideal Homes; International Fidelity Insurance Company; Interstate Hotels; J.C. Potter Company; National Association of Sonic Drive-Inn's; National Council on Compensation Insurance (NCCI); Nissan Motor Acceptance Corp.; Oklahoma Association of Electric Cooperatives; Oklahoma Employers Safety Group; Oklahoma Farm Bureau Mutual Insurance Company; Oklahoma Management Group; Oklahoma Property and Casualty Insurance Guaranty Association; Oklahoma R.E.&T. Credit Union; Oklahoma State Bank; ONYX Acceptance Corp.; Pharmcare OK, Inc.; Plantation Village Assisted Living Center; Plantation Village Nursing Center; Progressive Insurance Company; Rexair, Inc.; Southwest Health Care; Spear & McCaleb Engineering Co.; State of Oklahoma Insurance Department; Summit Life Corporation; Sunray Oil Company; Teachers Insurance & Annuity Association (TIAA-CREF); The Oklahoma Petroleum Workers Compensation Association (TOPWCA); The Oklahoma State Chamber of Commerce; Trustmark Title Corporation; UMB Bank; Vantage Open MRI, L.L.C.; Walgreen Drug Stores; Wal-Mart Stores, Inc.; Western Farmers Electric Cooperative.

THE DeVORE LAW FIRM

A PROFESSIONAL CORPORATION

Established in 1982

1318 NORTH ROBINSON

OKLAHOMA CITY, OKLAHOMA 73103-4822

Telephone: 405-232-4997

Fax: 405-236-3940

Email: devorelaw@devorelawfirm.com

Oil and Gas, Commercial Litigation, Class Actions, Aircraft Litigation, Environmental/Pollution, Real Property, Contracts, Personal Injury, Products Liability.

ALLAN DeVORE, born Columbus, Ohio, September 11, 1952; admitted to bar, 1978, Oklahoma, U.S. Court of Appeals, 10th Circuit and U.S. District Court, Western District of Oklahoma; 1980, U.S. District Court, Eastern District of Oklahoma; 1981, U.S. District Court, Northern District of Oklahoma; 1990, U.S. Supreme Court. *Education:* Southern Methodist University, Oklahoma State University (B.A., 1973); University of Oklahoma (M.B.A., 1977; J.D., 1977). *Member:* Oklahoma County and Oklahoma Bar Associations; The Association of Trial Lawyers of America. ***PRACTICE AREAS:*** Oil and Gas Litigation; Commercial Litigation; Environmental Litigation.

JANE G. ROWE, born Wichita Falls, Texas, August 18, 1959; admitted to bar, 1985, Oklahoma; 1986, U.S. District Court, Western District of Oklahoma; 2000, U.S. Supreme Court; U.S. Court of Appeals, Tenth Circuit. *Education:* University of Oklahoma (B.A.,

(This Listing Continued)

1982; J.D., 1985). Phi Delta Phi. Recipient, American Jurisprudence Award in Conflicts of Law. *Member:* Oklahoma County and Oklahoma Bar Associations. ***PRACTICE AREAS:*** Oil and Gas Litigation; Commercial Litigation; Environmental Litigation.

JACQUELYN L. THOMPSON, born Chickasha, Oklahoma, June 15, 1978; admitted to bar, 2003, Oklahoma and U.S. District Court, Western District of Oklahoma. *Education:* Southwestern Oklahoma State University (B.B.A., 2000); University of Oklahoma College of Law (J.D., with honors, 2003). Order of Barristers. Certified Public Accountant, 2003. *Member:* Oklahoma and American Bar Associations. ***PRACTICE AREAS:*** Oil and Gas Litigation; Commercial Litigation; Environmental Litigation. ***Email:*** jackie@devorelawfirm.com

REPRESENTATIVE CLIENTS: Association of Land and Mineral Owners; Continental Resources, Inc.; Continental Gas, Inc.; Invoil, Inc.; Norexco Petroleum Co.; Miller Cattle Company; Sloan Oil Corporation; Alta Mesa Resources, Inc.; American Land Company; Lobo Exploration Company; Galveston Bay Resources, Inc.

DOERNER, SAUNDERS, DANIEL & ANDERSON, L.L.P.

Established in 1896

ONE LEADERSHIP SQUARE, SUITE 501
OKLAHOMA CITY, OKLAHOMA 73102
Telephone: 405-319-3500
Fax: 405-319-3509
URL: http://www.dsda.com

Tulsa, Oklahoma Office: Suite 500, 320 South Boston Avenue. Telephone: 918-582-1211. Fax: 918-591-5360. URL: http://www.dsda.com.

Federal Civil Practice, State Civil Practice, Administrative Law, Appellate Practice, Antitrust, Bankruptcy, Creditors' Rights and Loan Workouts, Construction Law, Consumer Credit, Corporate, Commercial and Securities, Employment and Labor, Environmental, ERISA and Employee Benefits, Estates, Trusts and Probate, Family Law, General Litigation, Health Care, Indian Law, Intellectual Property, Patents, Trademarks, Copyrights, International Business, Mediation and Arbitration, Media and First Amendment Law, Medicare/Medicaid Fraud and Abuse, Mergers and Acquisitions Law, Oil and Gas, Oklahoma Corporation Commission, Products Liability, Public Trust and Tax Exempt Financing, Real Estate, Rural Water District Competition, Securities Litigation, Small Business and Venture Capital, Taxation, Telecommunications, Toxic Tort Litigation and Workers' Compensation.

PARTNERS IN TULSA, OKLAHOMA

Sam P. Daniel	***Richard H. Foster***
William C. Anderson	***Charles S. Plumb***
G. Michael Lewis	***Leonard I. Pataki***
Lawrence T. Chambers, Jr.	***S. Douglas Dodd***
Dallas E. Ferguson	***Elise Dunitz Brennan***
Sam G. Bratton II	***Jon E. Brightmire***
Gary M. McDonald	***Tom Q. Ferguson***
H. Wayne Cooper	***Richard J. Eagleton***
Kevin C. Coutant	***Rebecca McCarthy Fowler***
Richard P. Hix	***Michael C. Redman***
William F. Riggs	***Steven K. Metcalf***
Lewis N. Carter	***Russell W. Kroll***
Linda Crook Martin	***Rachel Blue***
James Patrick McCann	***James C. Milton***

ASSOCIATES

Audra K. Hamilton	***David L. Iandiorio***
William H. Spitler	***N. Lance Bryan***
Young Pei	***Chad J. Kutmas***
Chad M. Hinrichs	***Heather D. Flynn***
Johnathan D. Horton	***Elizabeth W. Carroll***
Robert Spoo	***E. McLaine DeWitt Herndon***
Lesley Ford Richer	***Steven P. Tepera***

Raymond H. Tipton III

OF COUNSEL

MICHAEL MINNIS, born Wichita, Kansas, February 22, 1944; admitted to bar, 1969, Oklahoma; 1972, California; 1976, U.S. Supreme Court; 1981, District of Columbia. *Education:* University of Oklahoma (B.A., Journalism, 1966; J.D., 1969). Appointed, Judge, Court of Appeals Temporary Division No. 174, 1982. Chief Judge, Town of Valleybrook, 1982-1983. *Member:* Oklahoma and Federal (President, 1982-1983, Oklahoma City Chapter) Bar Associations; State Bar of California; The District of Columbia Bar. [Trial/Defense Counsel United States Marine Corp (1969-1972), Lieutenant Colonel (Retired), USAFR]. ***REPORTED CASES:*** Citizen Band Pottawatomie Indian Tribe of Okla. v. Okla. Tax Comm'n, 111 S.Ct. 905 (1991); Continental Casualty Co. v. Southwestern Bell Telephone Co., 860 F.2d 970 (10th Cir. Okl. 1988); McCain v. KTVY, Inc., 738 P.2d 960 (Okl. App.Ct. 1987); Miskovsky v. Okla. Pub. Co., 654 P.2d 587 (Okl. 1982), cert. denied, 459 U.S. 923 (1982); Okl. Pub. Co. v. Dist. Court of Okl. County, 430 U.S. 308 (1977). ***PRACTICE AREAS:*** Media Law; Indian Law. ***Email:*** mminnis@dsda.com

DAVID McCULLOUGH, born Anadarko, Oklahoma, January 6, 1953; admitted to bar, 1984, Oklahoma, U.S. Supreme Court, U.S. Court of Appeals, Tenth Circuit and U.S. District Court, Western District of Oklahoma; 1992, Texas. *Education:* Oxford University, Queens College, Oxford, England (1982); University of Oklahoma (B.A., Journalism, 1977; J.D., 1984). Advisory Board Member, Native American Alliance Foundation. Member, Board of Directors and Founding Member, FOI Oklahoma, Inc. *Member:* Oklahoma, Federal and American Bar Associations. ***PRACTICE AREAS:*** Media Law; Indian Law. ***Email:*** dmccullough@dsda.com

(For complete biographical data on Tulsa Personnel, see Professional Biographies at Tulsa, Oklahoma)

FREDERIC DORWART

OKLAHOMA CITY, OKLAHOMA

(See Tulsa)

General Civil Practice including Oil and Gas, Banking and Business Planning, Securities Regulation, Technology Sales and Licensing, Mergers and Acquisitions, Corporation, White Collar Crime, Environmental, Employment Law, Health Care Law, Securities fraud, Securities Arbitration, Commercial Litigation, Business Litigation.

DOUGHERTY & HESSIN

OKLAHOMA CITY, OKLAHOMA

(See McAfee & Taft, A Professional Corporation)

DUBBERSTEIN HEINEN & MORRIS PC

777 N.W. GRAND BOULEVARD
SUITE 150
OKLAHOMA CITY, OKLAHOMA 73118
Telephone: 405-942-8700
Facsimile: 405-608-0447
Email: dhm@dhmlaw.net

Civil Litigation, Business Transactions, Oil and Gas Litigation, Oil and Gas Acquisitions, Oil and Gas Contracts, Oil and Gas Title Examination.

FIRM PROFILE: General Civil Practice with emphasis on oil and gas transactions and disputes. Partners have combined sixty-two years of experience. Diverse clientele ranging from start ups to publicly-traded entities. Exhaustive client listing available upon request.

MARK J. DUBBERSTEIN, born Enid, Oklahoma, July 23, 1953; admitted to bar, 1978, Oklahoma; 1979, U.S. District Court, Eastern and Western Districts of Oklahoma; 1998, U.S. Court of Appeals, Tenth Circuit. *Education:* Oklahoma State University (B.A., 1975); University of Oklahoma (J.D., 1978). Phi Delta Phi. Editor, Oklahoma Law Review, 1976-1978. Visiting Assistant Professor, University of Oklahoma, 1980-1981. Associate, Oklahoma Board of Bar Examiners, 1984-1986. *Member:* Oklahoma Bar Association. ***PRACTICE AREAS:*** Civil Litigation; Business Transactions; Oil and Gas Acquisitions; Oil and Gas Contracts; Oil and Gas Title Examination.

GARY J. HEINEN, born Oklahoma City, Oklahoma, July 11, 1958; admitted to bar, 1987, Oklahoma and U.S. District Court, Western District of Oklahoma; 2004, U.S. Supreme Court. *Education:* Central State University (B.B.A., 1980); University of Oklahoma (J.D., 1987). *Member:* Oklahoma County, Oklahoma and American Bar Associations. ***PRACTICE AREAS:*** Civil Litigation; Oil and Gas Litigation; Oil and Gas Title Examination.

STEPHEN M. MORRIS, born Wichita, Kansas, May 17, 1959; admitted to bar, 1984, Oklahoma and U.S. District Court, Western District of Oklahoma; 1988, U.S. District Court, Northern District of Oklahoma; 2000, U.S. Court of Appeals, Tenth Circuit; 2004, U.S. Supreme Court. *Education:* University of Oklahoma (B.B.A., with honors, 1981; J.D., with distinction, 1984). Phi Delta Phi (1982-1984). Note Editor, Oklahoma Law Review, 1982-1984. *Member:* Oklahoma, Oklahoma County and American Bar Associations. ***PRACTICE AREAS:*** Oil and Gas Law; Title Examination; Contracts; Real Estate; Civil Litigation.

DUNLAP, CODDING & ROGERS, P.C.

1601 NORTHWEST EXPRESSWAY, SUITE 1000
OKLAHOMA CITY, OKLAHOMA 73118
Telephone: 405-607-8600
Fax: 405-607-8686
URL: http://www.okpatents.com

Patent, Trademark, Unfair Competition, Trade Secret, Antitrust and Copyright Practice and related trial practice, Complex Civil Litigation.

JERRY J. DUNLAP, born Chelsea, Oklahoma, February 12, 1925; admitted to bar, 1952, Oklahoma; 1969, U.S. Supreme Court; registered to practice before U.S. Patent and Trademark Office. *Education:* University of Oklahoma (B.S.M.E., 1948); University of Tulsa (J.D., 1952). Delta Theta Phi. Avatar Master, Oklahoma. Registered Professional Engineer Oklahoma, 1955. Assistant Professor, Patent Trademark and Copyright Law, Oklahoma City University, 1962-1967. *Member:* Oklahoma County, Oklahoma (President, Section on Patent Law, 1974-1975) and American (Member, Sections on: Patent, Trademark and Copyright Law; Economics of Law Practice Law and Law Practice Management Section) Bar Associations; American Intellectual Property Law Association. [Lt., JG, U.S. Navy, 1943-1946; 1952-1953]. ***PRACTICE AREAS:*** Patent Law; Trademark Law; Unfair Competition Law; Trade Secrets Law; Antitrust Law; Copyright Law; Mediation. ***Email:*** jerry_dunlap@okpatents.com

CHARLES A. CODDING, born Oklahoma City, Oklahoma, May 26, 1939; admitted to bar, 1970, Oklahoma; registered to practice before U.S. Patent and Trademark Office. *Education:* Oklahoma State University (B.S.E.E., 1962); Oklahoma City University (J.D., 1970). Phi Delta Phi. *Member:* Oklahoma and American Bar Associations. ***PRACTICE AREAS:*** Patent Law; Trademark Law; Unfair Competition Law; Trade Secrets Law; Antitrust Law; Copyright Law. ***Email:*** charles_codding@okpatents.com

(This Listing Continued)

DUNLAP, CODDING & ROGERS, P.C., Oklahoma City—Continued

G. NEAL ROGERS, born Elk City, Oklahoma, August 21, 1949; admitted to bar, 1981, Oklahoma and U.S. Supreme Court. *Education:* University of Central Oklahoma (B.A., 1976); Oklahoma City University (J.D., 1980). Wagner Labor Law finalist, 1979. Member, 1979-1980 and Chairman, 1980, Moot Court Board. Author: "Licensing Technology with a Public University: The Basics," July 2000; "Patented Business Methods," February 2000; "A Trademark and Copyright Primer," February 1999. Adjunct Professor, Intellectual Property Law, Oklahoma City University School of Law. Researcher, Oklahoma Supreme Court Committee on Uniform Jury Instructions. Member, Executive Board, Oklahoma City University School of Law. *Member:* Oklahoma County, Oklahoma and American Bar Associations. ***PRACTICE AREAS:*** Intellectual Property; Litigation; Employment; Insurance Law. ***Email:*** neal_rogers@okpatents.com

MARC A. BROCKHAUS, born Norman, Oklahoma, October 12, 1968; admitted to bar, 1998, Oklahoma; registered to practice before the U.S. Patent and Trademark Office. *Education:* University of Oklahoma (B.S.E.E., 1993; M.B.A., 1997; J.D., 1997). Beta Gamma Sigma. *Member:* Oklahoma County and Oklahoma Bar Associations. ***PRACTICE AREAS:*** Patent Law; Trademark Law; Copyright Law. ***Email:*** marc_brockhaus@okpatents.com

NICHOLAS D. ROUSE, born Oklahoma City, Oklahoma, March 6, 1964; admitted to bar, 1990, Oklahoma; registered to practice before U.S. Patent and Trademark Office. *Education:* University of Oklahoma (B.S., P.E., 1987; J.D., 1990). *Member:* Oklahoma Bar Association (Member, Intellectual Property Law Section). ***PRACTICE AREAS:*** Patent Law; Trademark Law; Unfair Competition Law; Trade Secrets Law; Copyright Law. ***Email:*** nick_rouse@okpatents.com

DOUGLAS J. SOROCCO, born South Bend, Indiana, September 21, 1970; admitted to bar, 1996, Illinois; 1997, Oklahoma; registered to practice before U.S. Patent and Trademark Office. *Education:* Butler University (B.S., Chem/Biochem., 1993); University of Dayton/Northwestern University (J.D., 1996). Staff Member, University of Dayton Law Review, 1994-1995. Recipient: Mugul Moot Court Competition-Oralist Award, 1995. Author: "Do The Courts Know Best?: Best Mode," University of Dayton, Intellectual Property Law Journal, Vol.1, Iss.1, 1995. Lecturer, Technical and Healthcare/Biotechnical issues for National Business Institute and American Academy of Developmental Medicine, among others. Adjunct Professor, Oklahoma City University School of Law, 2000—. Adjunct Faculty Appointment, University of Oklahoma, Health Sciences Center, 2002—. Member, Board of Directors, Spina Bifida Association of America. *Member:* Chicago, Illinois State, Oklahoma and American Bar Associations; American Intellectual Property Association; Licensing Executive Society (Chair, Oklahoma Chapter). ***LANGUAGES:*** Spanish. ***PRACTICE AREAS:*** Patent; Copyright; Trademark; Antitrust; Intellectual Property Licensing and Litigation. ***Email:*** doug_sorocco@okpatents.com

JOSEPH P. TITTERINGTON, born Tulsa, Oklahoma, October 3, 1954; admitted to bar, 1980, Oklahoma; 1981, U.S. District Court, Western, Eastern and Northern Districts of Oklahoma and U.S. Court of Appeals, Tenth and Federal Circuits. *Education:* Oklahoma State University (B.S., 1976); University of Oklahoma (J.D., 1980). *Member:* Oklahoma County, Oklahoma, Federal and American Bar Associations. ***PRACTICE AREAS:*** Intellectual Property Litigation; Antitrust Law; Commercial Litigation. ***Email:*** joe_titterington@okpatents.com

R. TRENT PIPES, born Long Beach, California, July 10, 1957; admitted to bar, 1985, Oklahoma and U.S. District Court, Western District of Oklahoma; 2000, U.S. District Court, Northern District of Oklahoma, U.S. District Court, Southern District of Illinois and U.S. Supreme Court. *Education:* Oklahoma City University (B.M., 1979; J.D., with distinction, 1985). Phi Delta Phi. Member: Order of the Barristers; Board of Editors, Oklahoma City University Law Review, 1984-1985. Recipient: Corpus Juris Secundum Award; Hornbook Award; American Jurisprudence Awards in Contracts, Civil Procedure, Wills and Estates and Remedies. Instructor: Legal Research and Writing, Oklahoma City University School of Law, Fall, 1987-1988; Trademark, 2002; Trademark and Unfair Competition, 2002. *Member:* Oklahoma County (Member, Intellectual Property Section) and Oklahoma Bar Associations. ***PRACTICE AREAS:*** Commercial Law; Trademarks; Litigation. ***Email:*** trent_pipes@okpatents.com

---

GLEN M. BURDICK, born Ponca City, Oklahoma, January 10, 1937; admitted to bar, 1966, Oklahoma; registered to practice before U.S. Patent and Trademark Office. *Education:* University of Oklahoma (B.S., 1959; J.D., 1966). Order of the Coif. Editor-in-Chief, Oklahoma Law Review, 1965-1966. *Member:* Oklahoma Bar Association (Member, Patent, Trademark and Copyright Section). ***PRACTICE AREAS:*** Patents; Trademarks; Copyrights; Unfair Competition Law; Trade Secret Law. ***Email:*** mike_burdick@okpatents.com

RICHARD NELSON, born Peoria, Illinois, August 12, 1953; admitted to bar, 1981, Oklahoma; 1982, U.S. District Court, Western District of Oklahoma; 1984, U.S Court of Appeals, 10th Circuit; registered to practice before U.S. Patent and Trademark Office. *Education:* Bradley University (B.S., 1975); Oklahoma City University (J.D., 1981). *Member:* Oklahoma County and Oklahoma Bar Associations. ***PRACTICE AREAS:*** Electronic Technology. ***Email:*** richard_nelson@okpatents.com

MICHAEL HOYT SMITH, born Oklahoma City, Oklahoma, October 4, 1968; admitted to bar, 2001, Oklahoma and U.S. District Court, Western District of Oklahoma; registered to practice before U.S. Patent and Trademark Office. *Education:* Oklahoma Baptist University (B.S., 1991); University of Oklahoma (J.D., 2001). *Member:* Oklahoma Bar Association; American Intellectual Property Association. ***PRACTICE AREAS:*** Patents; Trademarks; Copyrights; Trade Secrets. ***Email:*** mike_smith@okpatents.com

JULIANNA G. DELIGANS, born Tulsa, Oklahoma, 1977; admitted to bar, 2003, Oklahoma and U.S. District Court, Western District of Oklahoma. *Education:* Oklahoma State University (B.S., Cell and Molecular Biology, with honors, 2000); University of Oklahoma (J.D., 2003). *Member:* Oklahoma (Member, Intellectual Property Section) and American Bar Associations. ***PRACTICE AREAS:*** Patents; Trademarks; Copyrights; Contracts. ***Email:*** julianna_deligans@okpatents.com

PATENT AGENTS

CHRISTOPHER W. CORBETT, born Oklahoma City, Oklahoma, April 28, 1953. *Education:* Oklahoma State University (B.S., 1974; M.S., 1977); University of California at Davis (Ph.D., 1985). Registered to practice before U.S. Patent and Trademark Office, 1992. Member, American Association for the Advancement of Science, 1979—. ***PRACTICE AREAS:*** Biotechnology; Chemistry; Pharmaceuticals. ***Email:*** chris_corbett@okpatents.com

KATHRYN HESTER, born Little Rock, Arkansas, May 17, 1971. *Education:* Southern Nazarene University (B.S., summa cum laude, 1993); University of Oklahoma (Ph.D., with honors, 1999). Registered to practice before the U.S. Patent and Trademark Office, 2000. Recipient, U.S. Environmental Protection Agency STAR Graduate Fellowship. Member: American Society for Microbiology; American Society for Biochemistry and Molecular Biology; American Association for the Advancement of Science. *Member:* Oklahoma Bar Association (Associate Member, Intellectual Property Section). ***PRACTICE AREAS:*** Biotechnology; Chemical; Pharmaceutical; Mechanical; Patent Preparation and Prosecution. ***Email:*** kathryn_hester@okpatents.com

REFERENCE: Local Oklahoma Bank, Oklahoma City.

DUNN, SWAN & CUNNINGHAM, P.C.

2800 OKLAHOMA TOWER
210 PARK AVENUE
OKLAHOMA CITY, OKLAHOMA 73102-5604
Telephone: 405-235-8318
Fax: 405-235-9605

Corporate, Securities, State and Federal Tax, Commercial, Construction, Banking, Real Estate, Oil and Gas, Trusts, Wills and Probate Law. General Civil Practice in State and Federal Courts, and Administrative Agencies.

FIRM PROFILE: Dunn, Swan & Cunningham, P.C. is listed under Securities Law in the Bar Register of Preeminent Lawyers.

MICHAEL E. DUNN, born Oklahoma City, Oklahoma, May 7, 1946; admitted to bar, 1972, Oklahoma. *Education:* Central State University (B.S., Accounting, 1968); University of Oklahoma (J.D., 1972). President, Oklahoma City Tax Lawyers Group, 1979. President, Oklahoma City Estate Planning Council, 1981-1982. Oklahoma City Board of Adjustment. *Member:* Oklahoma County, Oklahoma and American (Member, Sections on: Natural Resources and Taxation) Bar Associations. ***PRACTICE AREAS:*** Securities; Public Offerings; Corporate Law; Business Law; Taxation.

SHELDON B. SWAN, born Oklahoma City, Oklahoma, March 14, 1960; admitted to bar, 1985, Oklahoma; 1986, U.S. District Court, Western and Northern Districts of Oklahoma; 1992, U.S. Court of Appeals, Tenth Circuit; 1999, U.S. Court of Appeals, Fifth Circuit. *Education:* Oklahoma State University (B.S., Accounting, 1982); University of Oklahoma (J.D., with distinction, 1985). Phi Delta Phi; Beta Alpha Psi. *Member:* Oklahoma County, Oklahoma and American Bar Associations; The Association of Trial Lawyers of America. ***REPORTED CASES:*** Curtis v. AmQuest Bank, N.A., 966 P.2d 810 (Okla. Civ. App. Div. 3 1998); Century Investment Group, Inc. v. Bake Rite Foods, Inc., 7 P.3d 510 (OK App. 2000); Germino v. Hillyer (2003) 107 Cal. App. 4th 951, 132 Cal. Rptr. 2d 478; Oaks Owners' Ass'n v, Keim, 96 P.3d 1200 (Okla. Civ. App. Div. 3 2004); W. Oil & Gas J.V., Inc. V. Griffiths, 2003 U.S. App. Lexis 25014 (5th Cir. Tex. 2003); Intercon, Inc. v. Bell Atl. Internet Solutions, 41 F. Supp. 2d 1245 (W.D. Okla. 1993). ***PRACTICE AREAS:*** Business Litigation; Commercial Litigation; Securities Litigation; Construction Law; Probate; Trust Litigation. ***Email:*** sswan3435@aol.com

CLELL I. CUNNINGHAM III, born Oklahoma City, Oklahoma, November 17, 1953; admitted to bar, 1980, Oklahoma; 1983, U.S. District Court, Western and Northern Districts of Oklahoma; 1987, U.S. Court of Appeals, Tenth Circuit; 2003, U.S. Court of Appeals, Second Circuit. *Education:* University of Northern Colorado (B.A., 1977); University of Arizona (J.D., with distinction, 1980). Phi Alpha Delta. General Counsel, Oklahoma Department of Securities, 1993-1995. *Member:* Oklahoma County (Member, Fee Grievance and Ethics Committee, 1993-2002) and Oklahoma Bar Associations. ***SPECIAL AGENCIES:*** Oklahoma Department of Securities. ***REPORTED CASES:*** Dabit v Merrill Lynch, Pierce, Fenner & Smith, Inc., 395 F.3d 25 (2005); Century Investment Group, Inc. v. Bake Rite Foods, Inc., 7 P.3d 510 (OK App. 2000); In the matter of Edwards Irrevocable Trust, 966 P.2d 810 (OK 1998); Groce v. Foster, 880 P.2d 902 (OK 1994); Baptist Building Corp. v. Barnes, 874 P.2d 68 (OK App. 1994); Borst v. Bright Mortg. Co., 824 P.2d 1102 (OK 1992); Metro Oil Company, Inc. v. Sun Refining and Marketing Company, 936 F.2d 401 (10th Cir. 1991); Johnson v. Beatrice Foods Co., 921 F.2d 1015 (10th Cir. 1990); Krause v. Dresser Industries, Inc., 910 F.2d 674 (10th Cir. 1990); Goss v. Trinity Savings & Loan Assoc., 813 P.2d 492 (Okla. 1991); Robinson v. Kirby, 793 P.2d 315 (Okla. App. 1990); Musson v. Rice, 739 P.2d 1004 (Okla. 1987). ***PRACTICE AREAS:*** Securities Regulation; Broker-Dealer Regulation; Securities Fraud; Real Estate; Commercial Litigation. ***Email:*** skip@dscpc.com

OF COUNSEL

JACKIE L. HILL, JR., born Oklahoma City, Oklahoma, March 21, 1961; admitted to bar, 1986, Oklahoma and U.S. District Court, Western and Eastern Districts of Oklahoma; 1987, U.S. District Court, Northern District of Oklahoma and U.S. Court of Appeals, Tenth Circuit. *Education:* Oklahoma State University (B.S., 1983); University of Oklahoma (J.D., with distinction, 1986). Phi Alpha Delta. *Member:* Oklahoma County, Oklahoma and American (Member, Section on Bankruptcy) Bar Associations. (Also practicing individually at the same address). ***PRACTICE AREAS:*** Bankruptcy; Banking; Real Estate; Corporate Law; Business Litigation. ***Email:*** jackie@jhilllaw.com

(This Listing Continued)

DURBIN, LARIMORE & BIALICK, P.C.

Established in 1983

920 NORTH HARVEY
OKLAHOMA CITY, OKLAHOMA 73102-2610
Telephone: 405-235-9584
Fax: 405-235-0551
Email: dlb@dlb.net
URL: http://www.dlb.net

Casualty and Insurance, Fire, Product Liability, Personal Injury, Litigation, Federal and State, Corporate, Real Estate, Banking and Commercial Law.

GERALD E. DURBIN, II, born Oklahoma City, Oklahoma, October 25, 1944; admitted to bar, 1971, Oklahoma. *Education:* University of Oklahoma (B.B.A., 1968; J.D., 1971). Phi Alpha Delta. *Member:* Oklahoma County and Oklahoma (Member, Sections on: Litigation; Evidence; Torts) Bar Associations; Oklahoma Association of Defense Counsel. ***PRACTICE AREAS:*** Litigation; Personal Injury Law; Insurance Law; Environmental Law; Product Liability Law; Medical Malpractice. ***Email:*** gdurbin@dlb.net

JAMES K. LARIMORE, born Oklahoma City, Oklahoma, September 15, 1949; admitted to bar, 1974, Oklahoma. *Education:* University of Oklahoma (B.A., with distinction, 1971; J.D., with special distinction, 1974). Phi Delta Phi; Order of the Coif. Editor, Oklahoma Law Review, 1973-1974. *Member:* Oklahoma County, Oklahoma and American (Member, Sections on: Business Law; Real Property and Probate) Bar Associations; The Association of Trial Lawyers of America. ***PRACTICE AREAS:*** Commercial Transactions; Real Estate Law; Banking Law; Commercial Litigation. ***Email:*** jlarimore@dlb.net

MARK E. BIALICK, born New York, New York, March 1, 1956; admitted to bar, 1981, Oklahoma, U.S. District Court, Northern and Western Districts of Oklahoma, U.S. Court of Appeals, Tenth Circuit and U.S. Supreme Court. *Education:* University of Oklahoma (B.A., 1978; J.D., 1981). Editor, Oklahoma Law Review, 1979-1981. Listed in Best Lawyers in America. *Member:* Oklahoma Bar Association; Oklahoma Association of Defense Counsel; Defense Research Institute. ***PRACTICE AREAS:*** Litigation; Personal Injury Law; Insurance Law; Fire; Products Liability Law. ***Email:*** mbialick@dlb.net

DAVID B. DONCHIN, born Oklahoma City, Oklahoma, September 15, 1959; admitted to bar, 1984, Oklahoma and U.S. District Court, Western District of Oklahoma; 1987, U.S. Court of Appeals, Tenth Circuit. *Education:* University of Oklahoma (B.A., in Journalism, 1981; J.D., 1984). President, University of Oklahoma College of Law Alumni Association, 1987-1988. Former Adjunct Professor, University of Oklahoma College of Law, 1996. *Member:* Oklahoma County (Chairman, 1987-1988, Young Lawyers Division) and Oklahoma (Member, Board of Directors, 1987) Bar Associations; Oklahoma Association of Defense Counsel; American Inns of Court. ***PRACTICE AREAS:*** Litigation; Personal Injury Law; Insurance Law; Products Liability Law; Environmental Law; Employment Law; Medical Malpractice Law. ***Email:*** ddonchin@dlb.net

MICHEAL L. DARRAH, born Oklahoma City, Oklahoma, July 25, 1951; admitted to bar, 1977, Oklahoma, U.S. Court of Appeals, 10th Circuit and U.S. District Court, Western, Northern and Eastern Districts of Oklahoma. *Education:* Central State University (B.A., 1974); Oklahoma City University (J.D., 1977). Delta Theta Phi. Assistant District Attorney, Oklahoma County, 1977-1979. *Member:* Oklahoma County and Oklahoma Bar Associations; Oklahoma Trial Lawyers Association; Oklahoma Association of Defense Counsel; Defense Research Institute. ***PRACTICE AREAS:*** State and Federal Civil Litigation; Insurance Defense Law; Subrogation; Products Liability; Environmental; Oil and Gas Law. ***Email:*** mdarrah@dlb.net

J. LOGAN JOHNSON, born Norman, Oklahoma, June 1, 1963; admitted to bar, 1988, Oklahoma, U.S. District Court, Eastern, Northern and Western Districts of Oklahoma and U.S. Supreme Court. *Education:* University of Oklahoma (B.B.A., 1985; J.D., 1988). *Member:* Oklahoma County, Oklahoma and American Bar Associations. ***PRACTICE AREAS:*** Litigation; Personal Injury; Insurance Law; Products Liability. ***Email:*** ljohnson@dlb.net

RODNEY D. STEWART, born Wylie, Texas, August 23, 1968; admitted to bar, 1993, Oklahoma; 1994, U.S. District Court, Western, Eastern and Northern Districts of Oklahoma. *Education:* Cameron University (B.B.A., 1990); University of Oklahoma (J.D., with distinction, 1993). Member, Order of Barristers. *Member:* Oklahoma County, Oklahoma and American Bar Associations. ***PRACTICE AREAS:*** Litigation; Personal Injury Law; Insurance Law; Products Liability Law. ***Email:*** rstewart@dlb.net

R. BRAD MILLER, born Oklahoma City, Oklahoma, November 26, 1960; admitted to bar, 1985, Oklahoma. *Education:* East Central Oklahoma State University (B.A., with honors, 1982); University of Oklahoma College of Law (J.D., with distinction, 1985). Recipient, American Jurisprudence Award, Criminal Procedure; Oklahoma's Outstanding Prosecutor, 1997-1998.*Member:* Oklahoma County and Oklahoma Bar Associations; Oklahoma District Attorneys Counsel. ***PRACTICE AREAS:*** Litigation; Insurance Defense; Personal Injury; Medical Malpractice. ***Email:*** bmiller@dlb.net

KATHERINE TAYLOR LOY, born Oklahoma City, Oklahoma, January 26, 1967; admitted to bar, 1992, Oklahoma, U.S. District Court, Northern, Eastern and Western Districts of Oklahoma, U.S. Court of Appeals, Tenth Circuit and U.S. Supreme Court. *Education:* University of Oklahoma (B.B.A., with academic distinction, 1989; J.D., with honors, 1992). Order of the Coif. *Member:* Oklahoma County and Oklahoma Bar Associations. ***PRACTICE AREAS:*** Insurance Law; Litigation; Personal Injury; Products Liability. ***Email:*** kloy@dlb.net

---

HILARY S. ALLEN, born Raleigh, North Carolina, December 23, 1970; admitted to bar, 1996, Oklahoma, U.S. District Court, Western, Northern and Eastern Districts of Oklahoma and U.S. Court of Appeals, Tenth Circuit. *Education:* University of Oklahoma (B.A., 1993; J.D., 1996). *Member:* Oklahoma County bar Association; Luther Bohanon America Inns of Court (Past Member). ***PRACTICE AREAS:*** Litigation; Personal Injury; Insurance Law; Products Liability; Medical Malpractice; Employment Law. ***Email:*** hallen@dlb.net

E. EDD PRITCHETT, JR., born Oklahoma City, Oklahoma, October 1, 1969; admitted to bar, 1995, Oklahoma; 1996, U.S. District Court, Northern, Eastern and Western Districts of Oklahoma. *Education:* Oklahoma State University (B.A., 1992); University of Oklahoma (J.D., 1995). Phi Delta Phi. Order of the Coif. Who's Who: American Law Students, Edition 15, 1995. Member, Ruth Bader Ginsburg Inn of Court, 1996-1998. *Member:* Oklahoma County Bar Association (Member, Young Lawyer's Division, Board of Directors, 1998-1999); Oklahoma Bar Association (Chairman of the New Member Orientation Committee of the Young Lawyer's Division, 1998). ***PRACTICE AREAS:*** Litigation; Insurance Law; Personal Injury. ***Email:*** epritchett@dlb.net

GLEN MULLINS, born Fort Ord, California, October 1, 1948; admitted to bar, 1976, Oklahoma and U.S. District Court, Eastern, Northern and Western Districts of Oklahoma; 1980, U.S. Court of Appeals, Tenth Circuit. *Education:* University of Oklahoma (B.A., 1970; J.D., 1976). Law Clerk for the Hon. Fred Daugherty, Chief Judge, U.S. District Court, Western District of Oklahoma, 1976-1979. *Member:* Oklahoma County, Oklahoma and American Bar Associations; Oklahoma Trial Lawyers Association (Member, Board of Directors, 1993); The Association of Trial Lawyers of America. [Lt., U.S. Army, 1970-1972]. ***PRACTICE AREAS:*** Litigation; Insurance Law; Personal Injury Law.

AMY L. ALDEN, born Oklahoma City, Oklahoma, January 8, 1971; admitted to bar, 1996, Oklahoma, U.S. District Court, Northern and Western Districts of Oklahoma, U.S. Court of Appeals, Tenth Circuit and U.S. Supreme Court. *Education:* Oklahoma State University (B.A., 1993); University of Oklahoma (J.D., 1996). President, Phi Delta Phi. Pupil, Luther Bohannon American Inn of Court XXIII, 1995-1996; Associate, 2000-2002; Member, 1994-1996, Vice President, 1995-1996, Board of Advocates. *Member:* Oklahoma County (Member, Board of Directors, Young Lawyers Division, 1997-1999) and Oklahoma (Member, Young Lawyers Division, 1996) Bar Associations.

RYAN DELIGANS, born Oklahoma City, Oklahoma, February 25, 1977; admitted to bar, 2003, Oklahoma and U.S. District Court, Western District of Oklahoma. *Education:* New Mexico State University (B.A., 1999); University of Oklahoma (J.D., 2003). Outstanding Graduate, Trial Practice, 2003. Vice President, 2001-2002 and President, 2002-2003, Student Bar Association. *Member:* Oklahoma County and Oklahoma Bar Associations. ***PRACTICE AREAS:*** Litigation; Personal Injury; Insurance; Products Liability. ***Email:*** rdeligans@dlb.net

CHARLES B. WILLIAMS, born Portsmouth, Virginia, December 29, 1976; admitted to bar, 2003, Oklahoma. *Education:* University of Oklahoma (B.B.A., 2000; J.D., 2003). ***PRACTICE AREAS:*** Civil Litigation; Corporate Law. ***Email:*** bwilliams@dlb.net

JAMES M. SIDERIAS, born October 10, 1973; admitted to bar, 1999, Oklahoma. *Education:* Oklahoma Baptist University (B.A., magna cum laude, 1996); University of Oklahoma College of Law (J.D., 1999). Phi Delta Phi. District Attorney's Office Oklahoma County, Oklahoma, 1998-2005. *Member:* Oklahoma County and Oklahoma Bar Associations.

REPRESENTATIVE CLIENTS: Aetna Insurance Co.; Air Cargo; Alamo Car Rental; Allied Bankers Life Insurance Co.; Allstate Insurance Co.; American Building Maintenance Co.; American Economy; American Financial Corp., Moore Group; American States Insurance Co.; Amica Insurance Co.; Argonaut Great Central Insurance Co.; Atlas Insurance Co.; Bank One Oklahoma, N.A.; Braum's Dairy; Brotherhood Mutual Insurance Co.; Charleston's Restaurant Group, Inc. (fka Hal Smith Restaurant Group, Inc.); CNA; CRST International, Inc.; Colt Industries, Inc.; Commercial Union Ins. Co.; Continental Insurance Co.; F.A. Highley Co., Inc.; Federal Express Corp.; Federal Home Loan Mortgage Corporation; First National Bank of Chandler; Fleming Guardian; GAB Business Services, Inc.; Great Central Insurance Co.; Hanover Insurance Co.; J.B. Hunt Trucking Co.; Insurer's Nationwide Insurance Co.; Jasco Products Company, L.L.C.; Kansas City Fire & Marine; Kemper Insurance Co.; Lloyd's of London; Lumbermens Insurance Co.; Lumbermens Mutual Casualty Co.; Mid-Continent Casualty Co.; MidFirst Bank, F.S.B.; National American Insurance Co.; National Foundation Life Insurance Co.; Nationwide Insurance Co.; Northbrook Insurance Co.; Oklahoma Property and Casualty Co.; Omega Insurance Group; One Beacon Insurance Group; Safeco Ins. Co.; Shelter Insurance Companies; Stanley Tool Company; Union Mutual Insurance Co.; United Capital Insurance Co.; Watkins Freight Lines; Zurich-American Ins. Co.

(This Listing Continued)

EAGLETON & NICHOLSON, P.C.

Established in 1925

3100 BANK ONE CENTER
100 N. BROADWAY AVENUE
OKLAHOMA CITY, OKLAHOMA 73102
Telephone: 405-236-0550
Fax: 405-236-0560
Email: eaglenk@coxinet.net

Chandler, Oklahoma Office: 109 W. 9th, 74834. Telephone: 405-258-5301. Fax: 405-258-5302. Email: pordos@brightok.net

Litigation, Civil Practice, Commercial Law, Business Law, Bankruptcy, Contracts, Real Estate, Commercial Collections, Business Entities, Oil and Gas, Banks and Banking, Trusts and Estates, Construction Litigation, Children, Family Law.

JAMES R. EAGLETON (1903-1990)

DON R. NICHOLSON II, born Oklahoma City, Oklahoma, April 2, 1935; admitted to bar, 1965, Oklahoma, U.S. Court of Appeals, 10th Circuit and U.S. Supreme Court. *Education:* University of Oklahoma (B.B.A., 1962; J.D., 1965). Beta Gamma Sigma; Phi Alpha Delta. Certified Public Accountant, Oklahoma, 1964. Co-Founder, Oklahoma Lawyers for Children. *Member:* American Bar Association; Oklahoma Trial Lawyers Association.

W. DAVIDSON PARDUE, born Bristol, Virginia, June 30, 1947; admitted to bar, 1972, Oklahoma; 1973, U.S. District Court, Western and Northern Districts of Oklahoma; U.S. Court of Appeals, Tenth Circuit; U.S. Court of Appeals, Federal Circuit; U.S. Court of Federal Claims. *Education:* University of Oklahoma (B.A., 1969; J.D., 1972). *Member:* Oklahoma County, Oklahoma and American Bar Associations. ***REPORTED CASES:*** Jerry Chambers Exploration Co. v. Headington Penn Corp., et al., Published Opinion Court of Appeals of Oklahoma, July, 1994, interpretation of gas balancing clause of Joint Operating Agreement. ***PRACTICE AREAS:*** Oil and Gas Law; Construction Litigation; Commercial Transactions; Commercial Litigation; Bankruptcy; Real Estate.

(This Listing Continued)

EAGLETON & NICHOLSON, P.C., Oklahoma City—Continued

JEFFREY M. LOVE, born Oklahoma City, Oklahoma, August 8, 1970; admitted to bar, 1995, Oklahoma and U.S. District Court, Western and Eastern Districts of Oklahoma. *Education:* University of Oklahoma (B.A., 1992; J.D., 1995). Member, University of Oklahoma Law Review. *Member:* Oklahoma Bar Association.

RONALD R. TRACY, born Los Angeles, California, October 17, 1968; admitted to bar, 1995, California; 1997, Oklahoma; U.S. District Court, Western, Eastern and Northern Districts of Oklahoma. *Education:* University of California, Los Angeles (B.A., 1991); Loyola Marymount University (J.D., 1995). Phi Delta Phi. Recipient, American Jurisprudence Award in Family Law and Marital Property. *Member:* Oklahoma Bar Association.

OF COUNSEL

ROBERT V. VARNUM, born Shawnee, Oklahoma, December 22, 1946; admitted to bar, 1973, District of Columbia; 1976, U.S. Supreme Court; 1983, Maryland; 1989, Oklahoma. *Education:* Oklahoma Baptist University (B.A., 1969); Georgetown University (J.D., 1973). *Member:* Oklahoma and American Bar Associations; National Network of Estate Planning Attorneys.

REPRESENTATIVE CLIENTS: Allstate Electrical Contractors, Inc.; Baker Hughes, Inc.; Baker Oil Tools, Inc.; Cheyenne Oil Properties; City National Bank of Fort Smith; Consolidated Pipeline Co.; Dallas-Fort. Worth Roofing Supply, Inc.; Eakin Exploration, Inc.; Hodges Trucking Co.; Hughes Christensen, Inc.; Hurst Oil Investments, Inc.; J & R International Power, Inc.; Mineral Investment Corp.; Ramsey Property Management; Shriners Hospital for Children, Inc.; Union National Bank, Chandler; Veenker Resources, Inc., Traffic & Lighting Systems, Inc.; First City Servicing Corp.; MidFirst Bank, Central Oklahoma Federal Credit Union; Layton Energy Inc.

EDDY & JONES, P.C.

COURT PLAZA BUILDING
228 ROBERT S. KERR, SUITE 220
OKLAHOMA CITY, OKLAHOMA 73102
Telephone: 405-239-2524
Fax: 405-239-2665
Email: ejlaw@eddyjoneslaw.com
URL: http://www.eddyjoneslaw.com

Employment Discrimination, Criminal Law, Civil Rights, Employment Law, Disability Rights, Guardianships, Children's Rights, Education Law, General Practice, Contract Law.

RAND C. EDDY, born New York, New York, August 5, 1961; admitted to bar, 1986, Oklahoma; U.S. District Court, Western, Northern and Eastern Districts of Oklahoma; U.S. Court of Appeals, Tenth Circuit; U.S. Supreme Court. *Education:* Franklin & Marshall College (B.A., 1983); Oklahoma City University (J.D., 1986). Notes and Comments Editor, Oklahoma City University Law Review, 1985-1986. Listed in: The Best Lawyers in America, America's Registry of Outstanding Professionals. *Member:* Oklahoma County, Oklahoma and American Bar Associations; Oklahoma Employment Lawyers Association; National Employment Lawyers Association; Oklahoma Trial Lawyers Association; Outstanding Lawyers of America. ***PRACTICE AREAS:*** Employment Discrimination; Criminal Defense Law; Civil Rights; Contract Law; Litigation; Trial Practice. ***Email:*** rand@eddyjoneslaw.com

KINDANNE C. JONES, born New Haven, Connecticut, November 1, 1960; admitted to bar, 1985, Oklahoma; U.S. District Court, Western, Northern and Eastern Districts of Oklahoma; U.S. Court of Appeals, Tenth Circuit; U.S. Supreme Court. *Education:* University of Oklahoma (B.A., with highest honors, 1982); Boston College (J.D., with honors, 1985). Phi Beta Kappa. *Member:* Oklahoma County and Oklahoma Bar Associations; Oklahoma Employment Lawyers Association; National Employment Lawyers Association. ***PRACTICE AREAS:*** Employment Law; Criminal Law; Civil Rights; Disability Rights; Education Law; Children's Rights. ***Email:*** kindy@eddyjoneslaw.com

LINDA SAMUEL-JAHA, born Oklahoma City, Oklahoma; admitted to bar, 1992, Oklahoma; 1993, U.S. District Court, Western, Eastern and Northern Districts of Oklahoma; 1994, U.S. Court of Appeals, Tenth Circuit. *Education:* Central State University (B.S., 1988); Oklahoma City University School of Law (J.D., 1992). Recipient: Outstanding Young Alumni, Oklahoma City University School of Law, 2001; Mona Salyer Lambiad Spotlight Award, 2002; Ada Lois Sipuel Diversity Award. Member: Public Employees Relation Board; Board of Directors, Legal Services of Oklahoma; Ruth Bader Gensburg American Inn of Court). *Member:* Oklahoma County (Member, Board of Directors, 2003—; Co-Chair, Diversity Committee) and Oklahoma (Member, Lawyers for Children) Bar Associations. ***PRACTICE AREAS:*** Labor and Employment. ***Email:*** linda@eddyjoneslaw.com

SHERRI ANN CARVER, born Shawnee, Oklahoma, June 11, 1965; admitted to bar, 1991, Oklahoma; U.S. District Court, Western District of Oklahoma and U.S. Court of Appeals, Ninth Circuit; 2003, Washington. *Education:* Oklahoma City University (B.A., 1988); Oklahoma City University School of Law (J.D., 1991). Staff Editor, Oklahoma City University Law Review, 1990-1991. *Member:* Oklahoma and Washington State Bar Associations; Oklahoma Employment Lawyers Association. ***PRACTICE AREAS:*** Employment Discrimination; Contracts; Litigation; Government Contracts; Municipal Law. ***Email:*** sherri@eddyjoneslaw.com

EDINGER & BLAKLEY, P.C.

POSSUM CREEK PLACE
6301 N. WESTERN, SUITE 150
OKLAHOMA CITY, OKLAHOMA 73118-1058
Telephone: 405-286-0251
Facsimile: 405-286-0893

Civil Litigation and Regulatory Proceedings in the areas of Telecommunications, Antitrust, Energy and Environmental Law.

ROBERT D. EDINGER, born Oklahoma City, Oklahoma, September 20, 1952; admitted to bar, 1979, Oklahoma, U.S. District Court, Northern and Western Districts of Oklahoma; U.S. Court of Appeals, Tenth Circuit and U.S. District Court, Southern and Northern Districts of Texas; U.S. Supreme Court. *Education:* University of Oklahoma; Oklahoma City University (B.A., 1974); University of Oklahoma (J.D., 1979). Author: Gas Transportation Opportunities In The Current Regulatory Environment, Landman (Oct. 1989). *Member:* Oklahoma Bar Association. ***REPORTED CASES:*** Telecor Communications, Inc., et al. v. Southwestern Bell Telephone Co., 305 F.3d 1124 (10th Cir. 2002); Eastwood vs. National Bank of Commerce, Altus, Okla., 673 F.Supp. 1068 (W.D. Okla. 1987). ***PRACTICE AREAS:*** Civil Litigation; Regulatory Proceedings; Telecommunications; Antitrust; Energy; Environmental Law. ***Email:*** redinger@edinger-blakley.com

KENNETH H. BLAKLEY, born Oklahoma City, Oklahoma, January 28, 1959; admitted to bar, 1985, Oklahoma, U.S. District Court, Eastern, Northern and Western Districts of Oklahoma and U.S. Supreme Court; 1993, Texas. *Education:* University of Oklahoma (B.B.A., 1981; J.D., with Distinction, 1985). Phi Delta Phi. Member, Oklahoma Law Review, 1983-1985. Recipient, Maurice Merrill Award, 1983. Adjunct Professor of Oil, Gas and Environmental Law, University of Oklahoma, 1999-2002. *Member:* Oklahoma Bar Association; State Bar of Texas. ***REPORTED CASES:*** Union Texas Petroleum Corp. vs. Jackson, 909 P.2d 131 (Okla. App. 1995). ***PRACTICE AREAS:*** Civil Litigation; Regulatory Proceedings; Telecommunications; Antitrust; Energy; Environmental Law. ***Email:*** kblakley@edinger-blakley.com

EDMONDS, COLE, HARGRAVE, GIVENS, RYAN & WOODSON, P.C.

Established in 1985

ONE NORTH HUDSON, SUITE 200
OKLAHOMA CITY, OKLAHOMA 73102
Telephone: 405-272-0322
Fax: 405-235-4654
Email: echgwrw@edmonds-cole.com

Southeast Oklahoma Office: 117 1/2 S. Wewoka, P.O. Box 1342, Wewoka, Oklahoma 74884. Telephone: 405-257-5550.

General Civil Practice. Insurance, Casualty and Surety Law, Negligence Trial Practice, Environmental Law, Employment Law, Civil Rights Law, Lender Liability Law.

DAVID W. EDMONDS, born Washington, D.C., December 10, 1938; admitted to bar, 1965, Oklahoma, U.S. District Court, Eastern, Western and Northern Districts of Oklahoma and U.S. Court of Appeals, Tenth Circuit. *Education:* University of Maryland; University of Oklahoma (LL.B., 1965). Phi Delta Phi. *Member:* Oklahoma County and Oklahoma Bar Associations; Association of Trial Lawyers of America; Oklahoma Trial Lawyers Association. ***PRACTICE AREAS:*** Insurance Trial Practice; Negligence Trial Practice; General Civil Practice; Medical Malpractice; Products Liability. ***Email:*** dedmonds@edmonds-cole.com

DAVID H. COLE, born Oklahoma City, Oklahoma, February 27, 1947; admitted to bar, 1973, Oklahoma, and U.S. District Court, Eastern, Northern and Western Districts of Oklahoma. *Education:* University of Oklahoma (B.B.A., 1970; J.D., 1973). *Member:* Oklahoma County, Oklahoma and American Bar Associations; Oklahoma Association of Defense Counsel. ***PRACTICE AREAS:*** Insurance Trial Practice; Negligence Trial Practice. ***Email:*** dcole@edmonds-cole.com

JOHN R. HARGRAVE, born Wewoka, Oklahoma, February 26, 1955; admitted to bar, 1980, Oklahoma, U.S. District Court, Eastern, Northern and Western Districts of Oklahoma, U.S. Court of Appeals, Tenth and Fifth Circuits; U.S. Supreme Court. *Education:* East Central Oklahoma State University (B.A., 1977); University of Oklahoma (J.D., 1980). Member, The Order of Barristers. *Member:* Oklahoma County, Seminole County, Oklahoma (Member, Board of Directors, Young Lawyers Division, 1986-1987) and American Bar Associations; The Association of Trial Lawyers of America; Oklahoma Trial Lawyers Association. ***PRACTICE AREAS:*** General Civil Practice. ***Email:*** jhargrave@edmonds-cole.com

GREG D. GIVENS, born Seminole, Oklahoma, September 25, 1958; admitted to bar, 1983, Oklahoma and U.S. District Court, Western District of Oklahoma. *Education:* University of Oklahoma (B.A., 1980; J.D., 1983). Phi Beta Kappa; Omicron Delta Kappa. *Member:* Oklahoma County, Oklahoma and American (Member, Tort and Insurance Practice Section) Bar Associations; Oklahoma Association of Defense Counsel. ***PRACTICE AREAS:*** General Civil Practice; Insurance Trial Practice. ***Email:*** ggivens@edmonds-cole.com

MICHAEL S. RYAN, born Winfield, Kansas, August 7, 1957; admitted to bar, 1990, Oklahoma. *Education:* Central State University (B.A., 1979); Oklahoma City University School of Law (J.D., with distinction, 1990). Phi Delta Phi; Order of the Barristers. Member: Jessup Int'l Law Moot Court Team, 1989-1990.*Member:* Oklahoma County and Oklahoma Bar Associations; The Association of Trial Lawyers of America. ***PRACTICE AREAS:*** Insurance Trial Practice; Personal Injury; Medical Negligence; Product Liability; Employment Law; General Civil Practice. ***Email:*** mryan@edmonds-cole.com

MICHAEL WOODSON, born Enid, Oklahoma, April 30, 1968; admitted to bar, 1994, Oklahoma and U.S. District Court, Eastern, Western and Northern Districts of Oklahoma; U.S. Court of Appeals, Tenth Circuit. *Education:* Northwestern Oklahoma State University

(This Listing Continued)

(B.S., 1991); University of Oklahoma (J.D., 1994). *Member:* Oklahoma County and Oklahoma Bar Associations; Oklahoma Association of Defense Counsel. ***PRACTICE AREAS:*** Insurance Trial Practice; Products Liability; General Civil Practice. ***Email:*** mwoodson@edmonds-cole.com

---

CLINTON D. WHITWORTH, born Frederick, Oklahoma, September 11, 1971; admitted to bar, 2000, Oklahoma and U.S. District Court, Western District of Oklahoma. *Education:* Oklahoma City University (B.S., 1995); University of Tulsa (J.D., 2000). Phi Delta Phi. Recipient, CALI Award. Article Editor, University of Tulsa Journal of Comparative and International Law, 1999-2000. *Member:* Oklahoma County, Oklahoma and American Bar Associations; Oklahoma Association of Defense Counsel; The Association of Trial Lawyers of America. ***PRACTICE AREAS:*** Personal Injury; Civil Practice; Products Liability; Construction Law; Insurance Defense; Agricultural Law. ***Email:*** cwhitworth@edmonds-cole.com

SCOTT R. FARRIS, born Oklahoma City, Oklahoma, November 13, 1970; admitted to bar, 1997, Oklahoma and U.S. District Court, Western, Eastern and Northern Districts of Oklahoma; U.S. Court of Appeals, 10th Circuit. *Education:* Texas Christian University (B.S., 1993); Oklahoma City University School of Law (J.D., 1996). Member Oklahoma Board of Realtors, 1998. *Member:* Oklahoma County, Oklahoma and American Bar Associations. ***PRACTICE AREAS:*** Civil Practice; Trial Practice; Business Litigation; Commercial Transactions; Real Estate; Natural Resources. ***Email:*** sfarris@edmonds-cole.com

SHEILA R. BENSON, born Hartford, Connecticut, July 4, 1976; admitted to bar, 2001, Oklahoma, U.S. District Court, Eastern, Western and Northern Districts of Oklahoma and U.S. Court of Appeals, Tenth Circuit. *Education:* Colorado State University (B.A., 1997); University of Oklahoma, Norman (J.D., 2001). Phi Delta Phi. Oklahoma City, Oklahoma and American Bar Associations. ***PRACTICE AREAS:*** Civil Practice. ***Email:*** sbenson@edmonds-cole.com

SUSAN LYNN EADS, born Alton, Illinois, June 17, 1973; admitted to bar, 1998, Oklahoma. *Education:* University of Illinois (B.A., 1995); University of Oklahoma (J.D., 1998). *Member:* Oklahoma County, Oklahoma and American Bar Associations. ***PRACTICE AREAS:*** Civil Practice; Personal Injury. ***Email:*** seads@edmonds-cole.com

BRANDON P. WILSON, born Oklahoma City, Oklahoma, June 9, 1976; admitted to bar, 2002, Oklahoma and U.S. District Court, Western, Eastern and Northern Districts of Oklahoma; U.S. Court of Appeals, Tenth Circuit. *Education:* University of Central Oklahoma, Edmond (B.A., 1998); University of Oklahoma (J.D., 2002). *Member:* Oklahoma County, Oklahoma, American and Federal Bar Associations. ***PRACTICE AREAS:*** Civil Practice. ***Email:*** bwilson@edmonds-cole.com

NEVIN R. KIRKLAND, born National City, California, January 21, 1972; admitted to bar, 2003, Oklahoma; U.S. District Court, Western District of Oklahoma. *Education:* University of Central Oklahoma (B.A., 1999); Oklahoma City University School of Law (J.D., 2003). Phi Delta Phi. Research Editor, Oklahoma City University Law Review, 2002-2003. *Member:* Oklahoma Bar Association. ***PRACTICE AREAS:*** Civil Practice (100%); Personal Injury. ***Email:*** nkirkland@edmonds-cole.com

KELSIE M. SULLIVAN, born Denison, Texas, July 5, 1979; admitted to bar, 2004, Oklahoma. *Education:* University of Oklahoma (B.A., 2001; J.D., 2004). Amjur Gender Based Discrimination. *Member:* Oklahoma County, Oklahoma and American Bar Associations. ***PRACTICE AREAS:*** Civil Practice. ***Email:*** ksullivan@edmonds-cole.com

REPRESENTATIVE CLIENTS: American National Property & Casualty Co.; American States Insurance Co.; Brunswick Corporation; Clarendon National Insurance Co.; Coates Roofing Company; Coors Technical Ceramics Co.; Corporate Claims Management, Inc.; Credit Collections, Inc.; Easy Rider, Inc.; Elliott Homes, Inc.; Farmers Insurance Group of Companies; First National Bank in Wewoka; Fry Land & Cattle Co., Inc.; GAB Business Services, Inc.; G.E.M. Transportation; Great West Casualty Co.; Independent Occupational Health Centers; Koch Industries, Inc.; Kraft, Inc.; McKesson Corp.; Mercury Marine, Division of Brunswick Corp.; Montgomery Ward; National American Insurance Cos.; North American Risk; Ohio Casualty Group; Oklahoma Farm Bureau Mutual Insurance Company; Pioneer Standard Electronics, Inc.; Pool Company; Safeco Insurance Co.; Sentry Insurance Co.; Sooner Directional Drilling, Inc.; St. Paul Fire and Marine Ins. Co.; Sunbeam Corporation; Swift Transportation Co., Inc.; TXO Production Corp.; Underwriters of Lloyds; Union Standard Ins. Co.; U.S. Liability Insurance Co.; U.S. Risk, Inc.; West American Insurance; Wilkie Mfg.

KENT ELDRIDGE, P.C.

Established in 1981

1100 NORTH SHARTEL

OKLAHOMA CITY, OKLAHOMA 73103-2618

Telephone: 405-235-6565

Fax: 405-236-1814

Email: kent@kenteldridge.com

URL: http://www.kenteldridge.com

Criminal Law, Federal Criminal Law, White-Collar Crime, Drug Defense, Felonies, Insanity Defense, DUI, Juvenile, Divorce, Personal Injury, Workers Compensation, Administrative Adjudications.

KENT ELDRIDGE, born Oklahoma City, Oklahoma, January 22, 1949; admitted to bar, 1976, Oklahoma and U.S. District Court, Western District of Oklahoma; 1980, U.S. Supreme Court; 1981, U.S. Court of Appeals, 10th Circuit; 1986, U.S. District Court, Northern District of Oklahoma. *Education:* University of Oklahoma (B.A., 1973; J.D., 1976). *Member:* Oklahoma Bar Association; Federal Bar Association; Oklahoma Criminal Defense Lawyers Association (Charter Member); Oklahoma County Criminal Defense Lawyers Association (Charter Member, Board of Directors); National Association of Criminal Defense Lawyers; Oklahoma Trial Lawyers Association; The Association of Trial Lawyers of America. ***REPORTED CASES:*** Hays vs Murphy, 663 F.2d 1004 (10th Cir. 1981); Murrah v. City of Oklahoma City, 620 P.2d 1335, 1980 OK CR 110 (Okla. Crim.App. 1908); State, ex. rel. Coates v. Rakeshaw, 610 P.2d 256, 1980 OK CR 24 (Okla. Crim. App. 1980); Paulson v. Sternlof, 2000 OK CIV APP 128, 15 P.3d 981 (Okla. Civ. App. Div. 1) 2000. ***PRACTICE AREAS:*** Criminal Law; Personal Injury Law; Workers Compensation Law; Administrative Adjudications; Civil Litigation; Divorce. ***Email:*** kent@kenteldridge.com

(This Listing Continued)

REPRESENTATIVE CLIENT: American Federation of Teachers AFL-CIO-Local #2309.

ELIAS, BOOKS, BROWN & NELSON, P.C.

TWO LEADERSHIP SQUARE

211 NORTH ROBINSON, SUITE 1300

OKLAHOMA CITY, OKLAHOMA 73102-7114

Telephone: 405-232-3722

Fax: 405-232-3746

URL: http://www.eliasbooksbrown.com

Civil Practice including Trials in all State and Federal Courts, Appellate, Oil and Gas, Ad Valorem Taxation, Administrative, Corporation Commission, Environmental, Corporate, Bankruptcy and Reorganization, Commercial, State and Local Taxation, Financing, Real Estate, Title Examination, Banking Law, Commercial Litigation.

LAW FIRM ALLIANCES/ASSOCIATIONS: **AMERICAN PROPERTY TAX COUNSEL**

WILLIAM K. ELIAS, born Atchison, Kansas, February 21, 1955; admitted to bar, 1981, Oklahoma and U.S. District Court, Western, Northern and Eastern Districts of Oklahoma, U.S. Court of Appeals, Tenth Circuit and U.S. Supreme Court. *Education:* Oklahoma State University (B.A., 1977); University of Tulsa (J.D., with honors, 1981). Phi Kappa Phi; Phi Alpha Delta. *Member:* Oklahoma County and Oklahoma (Member, Mineral Law and Taxation Sections) Bar Associations; American Property Tax Counsel; Oklahoma City Mineral Lawyers Society. ***PRACTICE AREAS:*** Ad Valorem Taxation; Oil and Gas; Litigation. ***Email:*** wkelias@eliasbooksbrown.com

RICHARD K. BOOKS, born Monte Vista, Colorado, September 25, 1952; admitted to bar, 1977, Oklahoma; U.S. District Court, Western District of Oklahoma; U.S. Court of Appeals, Tenth Circuit; 1985, U.S. Supreme Court. *Education:* Phillips University (B.A., 1974); University of Oklahoma (J.D., 1977). Phi Delta Phi; Order of the Coif. Editor, University of Oklahoma Law Review, 1975-1977. President, Oklahoma City Mineral Lawyers Society, 1980-1981. *Member:* Oklahoma and American Bar Associations. ***SPECIAL AGENCIES:*** Oklahoma Corporation Commission. ***PRACTICE AREAS:*** Oil and Gas; Litigation; Administrative Law. ***Email:*** rkbooks@eliasbooksbrown.com

L. VANCE BROWN, born Oklahoma City, Oklahoma, June 25, 1959; admitted to bar, 1984, Oklahoma and U.S. District Court, Western and Northern Districts of Oklahoma. *Education:* University of Oklahoma (B.S., Geology, 1981; J.D., 1984). Phi Delta Phi. *Member:* Oklahoma County, Oklahoma and American (Member, Litigation Section) Bar Associations; Oklahoma City Mineral Lawyers Association. ***PRACTICE AREAS:*** Civil Litigation; Oil and Gas; Corporate; Real Property. ***Email:*** lvbrown@eliasbooksbrown.com

LYLE R. NELSON, born Muskogee, Oklahoma, April 6, 1959; admitted to bar, 1984, Oklahoma and U.S. District Court, Western, Northern and Eastern Districts of Oklahoma. *Education:* Northeastern Oklahoma State University (B.S., 1981); University of Oklahoma (J.D., 1984). Chapter 7 Panel Trustee, Western District of Oklahoma.*Member:* Oklahoma Bar Association. ***PRACTICE AREAS:*** Bankruptcy; Creditors Rights; Commercial Litigation; Collections. ***Email:*** lyle@lylenelsonlaw.com

---

AMY E. WELLINGTON, (admission pending). *Education:* Stanford University (B.A., 2002); University of Oklahoma (J.D., 2005). ***PRACTICE AREAS:*** Business Litigation; Ad Valorem Tax.

MARJORIE CREASEY, born Butler, Missouri, March 5, 1974; admitted to bar, 1999, Oklahoma and U.S. District Court, Western District of Oklahoma. *Education:* University of Central Oklahoma (B.S., 1996); University of Oklahoma (J.D., 1999). *Member:* Oklahoma Bar Association. ***PRACTICE AREAS:*** Bankruptcy; Creditors Rights; Collections; Commercial Litigation. ***Email:*** maarjie@lylenelsonlaw.com

RICHARD J. DENNY, III, born Fresno, California, March 28, 1970; admitted to bar, 2003, Oklahoma and U.S. District Court, Western District of Oklahoma. *Education:* East Central Oklahoma State University (B.S., Legal Studies, 1999); University of Oklahoma (J.D., 2002). Alpha Chi; Lambda Epsilon Chi. *Member:* Oklahoma County, Oklahoma (Member, Mineral Law Section) and American (Member, Environmental, Energy and Resources Section) Bar Associations. [Petty Officer, U.S. Navy, 1991-1995.]. ***PRACTICE AREAS:*** Oil and Gas Law; Property Tax; Litigation; Commercial Law. ***Email:*** rdenny@eliasbooksbrown.com

LINDA J. BLAN-BYFORD, born Claremore, Oklahoma, August 12, 1970; admitted to bar, 2003, Oklahoma and U.S. District Court, Western District of Oklahoma. *Education:* Oklahoma State University (B.S., 1992; M.S., 1994); Oklahoma City University (J.D., 2003). Phi Delta Phi. Order of Barristers. Recipient: Outstanding Female Graduate Award, 2003; Cali Awards in Contracts, Oil & Gas Law and Land Use. *Member:* Oklahoma and American Bar Associations; Mineral Lawyers Society; The Association of Trial Lawyers of America. ***PRACTICE AREAS:*** Civil Litigation; Oil and Gas Law; State Taxation; Local Taxation. ***Email:*** lbyford@eliasbooksbrown.com

OF COUNSEL

TIMOTHY C. DOWD, born Tulsa, Oklahoma, July 22, 1953; admitted to bar, 1979, Oklahoma, U.S. District Court, Northern, Eastern and Western Districts of Oklahoma and Northern District of Texas; U.S. Court of Appeals, Eighth and Tenth Circuits. *Education:* University of Oklahoma (B.A., 1975); University of Tulsa (J.D., 1979). Author: "Preferential Rights to Purchase in Oil and Gas Transactions," 49 Rocky Mtn. Min. L. Inst. 55 (2003); "Oil and Gas Liens in Oklahoma," 51 Okla.L.Rev. 309 (1998); "Uniform Fraudulent Transfer Act," 68 Oklahoma Bar Journal 1915 (1997); "The Doctrine of Merger Of Title When The Mortgagee Acquires the Mortgagor's Land," 58 Oklahoma Bar Journal 823 (1987). Member, Legal Committee of Interstate Oil and Gas Compact Commission. Advisory Council to the Management Well Commission of Oklahoma. *Member:* Oklahoma County, Oklahoma (Member, Mineral Law Section) and American (Member, Natural Resources

(This Listing Continued)

ELIAS, BOOKS, BROWN & NELSON, P.C., Oklahoma City—Continued

Law Section) Bar Associations; Oklahoma City Mineral Lawyers Society (President, 1997-1998); Oklahoma City Real Property Lawyers Association. ***PRACTICE AREAS:*** Oil and Gas Law; Oil and Gas Litigation; Oil and Gas Title Examination; Bankruptcy; Reorganization; Real Property; Civil Litigation. ***Email:*** timdowd@eliasbooksbrown.com

REPRESENTATIVE CLIENTS: Barbour Energy Corp.; BP Amoco Production Co.; Bancfirst; Bituminous Insurance Co.; Bravo Natural Resources, Inc.; Cago, Inc.; Chesapeake Exploration Limited Partnership; CIS Oil & Gas, Inc.; Crimson Energy, LC; DNR Oil & Gas, Inc.; Enbridge Inc.; Enogex, Inc.; EOG Resources, Inc.; Iochem Corporation; CMS Energy; ONEOK, Inc.; J.M. Huber Corp.; The Kansas City Southern Railway Company; Newfield Exploration, Inc.; Range Resources Corp.; RKK Production Co.; Southern Union Co.; SBC Communications, Inc.; Technical Energy Services, Inc.; TekEnergy, Inc.; Trinity Hospice, LLC; Wachovia Bank, NA; Western Gas Resources, Inc.; Western Heritage Insurance Co.; XTO Energy Co.

ELLIOTT & PEDERSON

Established in 1988
CITY PLACE BUILDING
TWENTY-SECOND FLOOR
204 NORTH ROBINSON AVENUE
OKLAHOMA CITY, OKLAHOMA 73102
Telephone: 405-236-3600
Fax: 405-239-2265
Email: firm@kwelliott.com
URL: http://www.kwelliott.com

ERISA, Premises Liability, Insurance Bad Faith, Insurance Subrogation, Fire Insurance Law, Inland Marine and Casualty Law, Medical Malpractice, Nursing Home Litigation, Toxic Substances, Environmental Law, Fidelity and Surety, Products Liability, Construction Law, Defense Law, Civil Trials in all Courts.

MEMBERS OF FIRM

KENNETH W. ELLIOTT, born Houston, Texas, 1953; admitted to bar, 1979, Oklahoma and U.S. District Court, Western, Eastern and Northern Districts of Oklahoma. *Education:* University of Oklahoma (B.S., with honors, 1976; J.D., with honors, 1979). Member, Board of Directors, Oklahoma State Insurance Fund, 1987-1990. Commissioner, National Conference of Commissioners on Uniform State Laws, 1995—. Member, Drafting Committee on Apportionment of Tort Liability, 1999—. Member, Drafting Committee, Electronic Transactions Act, 1997—. Member, Drafting Committee Uniform Power of Attorney. Commissioner, Oklahoma Ethics Commission, 1997—. *Member:* Oklahoma and American Bar Associations; Oklahoma Association of Defense Counsel. ***REPORTED CASES:*** Estate of Glen Williams v. Preferred Risk Ins. Co., 867 P.2d 485 (Okla.Civ.App. 1993); Lewis v. Farmers Ins. Co., 681 P.2d 67 (Okla. 1983); Shinault v. Mid-Century, 654 P.2d 618 (Okla. 1982). ***PRACTICE AREAS:*** Fire Litigation; Arson and Fraud Litigation; Products Liability; Personal Injury Defense; Commercial Litigation; Automobile Negligence; Premises Liability; Medical Malpractice; Nursing Home Litigation; Insurance Bad Faith; Construction Law; Surety and Fidelity Law; Coverage Opinions; Subrogation. ***Email:*** kelliott@kwelliott.com

DEVAN A. PEDERSON, born Ponca City, Oklahoma, 1969; admitted to bar, 1996, Oklahoma, U.S. District Court, Western and Northern Districts of Oklahoma, U.S. Court of Appeals, Tenth Circuit and U.S. Supreme Court. *Education:* Oklahoma State University (B.A., 1992); University of Oklahoma (J.D., with distinction, 1996). Recipient, American Jurisprudence Award in Constitutional Law. *Member:* Oklahoma County Bar Association; Oklahoma Association of Defense Counsel. ***REPORTED CASES:*** Paulson v. Sternlof, 15 P.3d 981 (Okla.Civ.App. 2000). ***PRACTICE AREAS:*** Fire Litigation; Arson and Fraud Litigation; Products Liability; Personal Injury Defense; Commercial Litigation; Automobile Negligence; Premises Liability; Medical Malpractice; Nursing Home Litigation; Insurance Bad Faith; Construction Law; Toxic Torts; Examinations Under Oath; Coverage Opinions; Subrogation. ***Email:*** dpederson@kwelliott.com

LEGAL SUPPORT PERSONNEL

JENNY ALLEN, (Legal Assistant)

REPRESENTATIVE CLIENTS: Sentry Insurance Companies; Farmers Insurance Group; Oklahoma Farm Bureau Mutual Insurance Co.; Interstate Insurance Group; Velsicol Chemical Corp.; Travelers Insurance Co.; State Farm Insurance Co.; Gilbertson Construction, Co.; St. Paul Fire and Marine Casualty Co.; Wausau Insurance Co.; Penn-America Insurance Co.; Koppers Company, Inc.; BancInsure; Oklahoma Department of Transportation; Healthcare Recoveries, Inc.; Vesta Insurance Co.; Benchmark Insurance Co.; Orion Insurance Co.; Providian Financial Corp.; EMG Insurance Co.; GHS Insurance Co.; TransPaC Solutions; Ingenix; Xerox Corp.

REES T. EVANS

501 NORTHWEST 13TH STREET
OKLAHOMA CITY, OKLAHOMA 73103
Telephone: 405-232-4311
Fax: 405-232-4315
Email: r.t.evans@att.net
URL: http://www.lawyers.com/reestevanslaw

Practice Limited to Family Law including Trials, Appeals, and Mediations in Divorce, Alimony, Child Support and Child Custody Matters.

REES T. EVANS, born Oklahoma City, Oklahoma, November 10, 1945; admitted to bar, 1971, Oklahoma. *Education:* University of Virginia (B.A., 1968); University of Oklahoma (J.D., 1971). Phi Delta Phi. Municipal Judge, Municipal Courts of the City of Oklahoma City, 1975-1982. Member, 1976-1982 and President, 1980-1981, Oklahoma Municipal Judges Conference. Author: "Communicating with the Adverse Party: Ethical Limitations," Fairshare, Aug. 1990; "Support Alimony: How to get it, keep it, collect it and defend it," Oklahoma Family Law Journal, Dec. 1996; "Child Support Guidelines: The 1999 Amendments," Oklahoma Family Law Journal, June 1999; "Emergency Jurisdiction Under the UCCJEA: An Update," Oklahoma Family Law Journal, Dec. 2000. Contributing Editor and Section Editor, Oklahoma Family Law Practice Manual, 2002. *Member:* Oklahoma County (Chairman, Family Law Section, 1985-1988), Oklahoma (Chairman, Family Law Section, 1988-1989) and American (Member, Sections on: Litigation; Family Law; Executive Member, Family Law Section Continuing Legal Education Committee, 1987-1991; Executive Member, Marital Torts and Domestic Violence Committee, 1993-1994) Bar Associations.

FABIAN & ASSOCIATES, INC., P.C.

228 ROBERT S. KERR, SUITE 700
OKLAHOMA CITY, OKLAHOMA 73102
Telephone: 405-232-4384
Fax: 405-232-5334
Toll Free: 1-877-435-7384
Email: sfabian@sbcglobal.net
URL: http://www.lawyers.com/okc-dui

Driving Under The Influence, Traffic Violations, Criminal Defense.

STEPHEN G. FABIAN, JR., admitted to bar, 1973, Oklahoma. *Education:* Wichita State University (B.M.E., 1968); Oklahoma City University (J.D., 1973). ***PRACTICE AREAS:*** Driving While Intoxicated; Traffic Violations. ***Email:*** sfabian@sbcglobal.net

FAGIN, BROWN, BUSH, TINNEY & KISER

A PROFESSIONAL CORPORATION
Established in 1935
120 N. ROBINSON
1900 FIRST NATIONAL CENTER WEST
OKLAHOMA CITY, OKLAHOMA 73102
Telephone: 405-235-3413
Fax: 405-235-7436; 405-235-2807
Email: fbbtk@faginfirm.com

Municipal and Public Authority Finance, Securities and Corporate Financing Law.

GARY M. BUSH, born Orange, California, March 7, 1943; admitted to bar, 1968, Oklahoma. *Education:* Altus Junior College (A.A., 1963); University of Oklahoma (B.S., 1965; J.D., 1968). Order of the Coif; Phi Delta Phi. Assistant Attorney General, Oklahoma, 1971. *Member:* Oklahoma County, Oklahoma and American Bar Associations; National Association of Bond Lawyers. ***PRACTICE AREAS:*** Municipal; Public Authority Finance; Securities; Corporate Finance Law. ***Email:*** gbush@faginfirm.com

WM. DON KISER, born Okmulgee, Oklahoma, January 13, 1943; admitted to bar, 1971, Oklahoma; 1975, U.S. Supreme Court. *Education:* Oklahoma State University (B.S., 1965); University of Oklahoma (J.D., 1971). Phi Alpha Delta. Special Lecturer, University of Oklahoma College of Law, 1973. Assistant Attorney General, Oklahoma, 1974-1978. *Member:* Oklahoma County, Oklahoma and American Bar Associations; National Association of Bond Lawyers. ***PRACTICE AREAS:*** Municipal; Public Authority Finance; Securities; Corporate Financing Law. ***Email:*** dkiser@faginfirm.com

ALLAN ARTHUR BROOKS, III, born Oklahoma City, Oklahoma, January 21, 1960; admitted to bar, 1985, Oklahoma. *Education:* Oklahoma State University (B.S., 1982); University of Oklahoma (J.D., 1985). Phi Delta Phi. *Member:* Oklahoma County, Oklahoma and American Bar Associations; National Association of Bond Lawyers. ***PRACTICE AREAS:*** Municipal; Public Authority Finance; Securities; Corporate Financing Law. ***Email:*** abrooks@faginfirm.com

NATHAN D. ELLIS, born Grand Rapids, Michigan, June 18, 1973; admitted to bar, 2000, Oklahoma. *Education:* University of Oklahoma (B.S., 1996; M.B.A., 1999; J.D., 1999). *Member:* Oklahoma County, Cleveland County, Oklahoma, and American Bar Associations; National Association of Bond Lawyers. ***PRACTICE AREAS:*** Municipal; Public Authority Finance; Securities; Corporate Finance Law. ***Email:*** nellis@faginfirm.com

GEORGE J. FAGIN (1908-1994)

MICHAEL D. TINNEY (1944-1989)

J. SCOTT BROWN (Retired)

FEDERMAN & SHERWOOD

120 NORTH ROBINSON, SUITE 2720
OKLAHOMA CITY, OKLAHOMA 73102
Telephone: 405-235-1560
Fax: 405-239-2112
URL: http://www.federmanlaw.com

Mailing Address: Attn: Nancy Beatty, 120 North Robinson, Suite 2720, Oklahoma City, OK 73102

Dallas, Texas Office: 2926 Maple Avenue, Suite 200, 75201. Telephone: 214-696-1100. Facsimile: 214-740-0112.

Litigation, Arbitration, Securities Litigation, Products Liability, Class Actions.

WILLIAM B. FEDERMAN, born New York, New York, January 31, 1958; admitted to bar, 1982, Oklahoma and U.S. District Court, Western District of Oklahoma; 1983, U.S. District Court, Northern District of Oklahoma and U.S. Court of Appeals, Tenth Circuit; 1985, District of Columbia; 1988, New York; 1995, Texas, U.S. District Court, Eastern District of Oklahoma and U.S. District Court, Northern and Southern Districts of Texas; 1999, U.S. Court of Appeals, Federal Circuit; 2002, U.S. District Court, Eastern District of Texas and U.S. District Court, District of Colorado; 2003, U.S. Court of Appeals, Second and

(This Listing Continued)

Fourth Circuits; 2004, U.S. Court of Appeals, Fifth Circuit. *Education:* Boston University (B.A., cum laude, 1979); University of Tulsa (J.D., 1982). Phi Alpha Delta (Treasurer, 1980-1982).

JOHN CHARLES SHERWOOD, born Dallas, Texas, December 18, 1958; admitted to bar, 1984, Texas, U.S. District Court, Northern District of Texas, U.S. Court of Appeals, Fifth Circuit, U.S. Supreme Court and U.S. Tax Court (Not admitted in Oklahoma). *Education:* Texas Christian University (B.B.A., Accounting, magna cum laude, 1981); Baylor University (J.D., 1984). Certified Public Accountant, Texas, 1985. Lecturer, "Other People's Money," Dallas Bar Association, Solo and Small Firm Section, 1996 and 1998. *Member:* Dallas Bar Association (Chairperson, Solo and Small Firm Section); The Association of Trial Lawyers of America; Texas Trial Lawyers Association; The College of the State Bar of Texas. (Board Certified, Civil Trial Law; Personal Injury Trial Law, Texas Board of Legal Specialization). ***PRACTICE AREAS:*** Litigation.

STUART W. EMMONS, born Stillwater, Oklahoma, August 9, 1961; admitted to bar, 1987, Oklahoma and U.S. District Court, Western District of Oklahoma; 1990, U.S. District Court, Northern District of Oklahoma; 1992, U.S. Court of Appeals, Tenth Circuit; 1994, U.S. Court of Appeals, Eighth Circuit; 2003, U.S. District Court, Southern District of Texas and U.S. Court of Appeals, Second and Fourth Circuits; 2004, U.S. District Court, Northern District of Texas and U.S. Court of Appeals, Fourth Circuit; 2005, U.S. Supreme Court; registered to practice before U.S. Patent and Trademark Office. *Education:* University of Oklahoma (B.B.A., Accounting, with distinction, 1984; J.D., with distinction, 1987). Law Clerk to the Hon. Layn R. Phillips, U.S. District Court, Western District of Oklahoma, 1988-1989. *Member:* Oklahoma County and Oklahoma Bar Associations.

W. TODD VER WEIRE, born Los Angeles, California, May 28, 1966; admitted to bar, 1993, Arkansas and U.S. District Court, Eastern and Western Districts of Arkansas; 2003, Mississippi, Texas, U.S. District Court, Northern and Southern Districts of Mississippi and U.S. Court of Appeals, Fifth Circuit; 2004, Arizona; 2005, Oklahoma, U.S. District Court, Southern, Eastern and Northern Districts of Texas and U.S. District Court, Eastern District of Oklahoma. *Education:* Texas Christian University (B.B.A., 1989); University of Richmond (J.D., 1992); University of Arkansas (LL.M., 2000). Recognized, Outstanding Young Trial Attorney, Arkansas Trial Lawyer's Association, 2000. Named and Honored, Professional in the National Director of Who's Who in Executives and Professionals, 1997-1998. *Member:* Arkansas Bar Association; The Mississippi Bar; State Bar of Texas; State Bar of Arizona. Melvin Belli Association (Fellow).

JENNY L. EVANS, born McAlester, Oklahoma, October 5, 1972; admitted to bar, 1999, Oklahoma; U.S. District Court, Western District of Oklahoma; U.S. Court of Appeals, Tenth Circuit. *Education:* Southeastern Oklahoma State University (B.A., 1996); University of Oklahoma (J.D., with distinction, 1999). Dean's List; Phi Delta Phi (1996-1999); Kappa Alpha Theta. Law Clerk to the Hon. Doyle W. Argo, U.S. District Court, Western District of Oklahoma, 2002-2004. *Member:* Oklahoma County, Oklahoma and American Bar Associations. ***REPORTED CASES:*** Wallace v. Mental Health Services of Southern Oklahoma, 33 P.3d 966 (OKLA CT APP 2001). ***PRACTICE AREAS:*** Commercial Litigation; Bankruptcy.

JENNIFER F. SHERRILL, born Fort Smith, Arkansas, August 22, 1974; admitted to bar, 2003, Oklahoma, U.S. District court, Western, Northern and Eastern Districts of Oklahoma and U.S. District court, Northern, Southern and Eastern Districts of Texas. *Education:* Hendrix College (B.A., 1996); University of Arkansas (M.S., Plant Pathology, 1998); University of Tulsa, College of Law (J.D., with highest honors, 2002). Chair, Order of the Curule. Recipient: Outstanding Law Student Award. Author, "An Inter- and Intra-species variation in Colletotrichum and Mechanisms Which Affect Population Structure, In Collectotrichum: Host Specificity, Pathology, and Host-Pathogen Interaction". *Member:* Oklahoma and American Bar Associations.

OF COUNSEL

A. DANIEL WOSKA, born Dallas, Texas, November 1, 1952; admitted to bar, 1978, Oklahoma, U.S. District Court, Northern, Eastern and Western Districts of Oklahoma, U.S. District Court, Northern and Western Districts of Texas, U.S. Court of Appeals, Tenth and Fifth Circuits, U.S. Tax Court and U.S. Supreme Court. *Education:* University of Oklahoma (B.A., 1974); Oklahoma City University (J.D., 1977). Phi Alpha Delta. Recipient, Outstanding Committee Chairman, Young Lawyers Division, Oklahoma Bar Association, 1986. Lecturer: "Dysfunction in the Workplace," 1990; "Juggling the Roles in Your Life," Oklahoma County Bar Association, 1990; Operation Handshake, Oklahoma City University; Oklahoma Bar Association: "Arbitration Between Individuals in Different States," 1990; "The Evolution of Arbitration: 1953—; Is Arbitration in Oklahoma Between Oklahoma Residents Constitutionally Unenforceable?"' "Confirming and Vacating the Arbitration Award". *Member:* Oklahoma County (Member: Young Lawyer's Division; Bar Counsel, 1987-1990; Alternative Dispute Resolution Committee, 1990—; Director, 1990-1993; Oklahoma Young Lawyers Division, 1982-1987; Alternate Dispute Resolution Committee, 1992—; Legal Ethics Committee, 1993-1998) and American (Member, Sections on: Litigation, 1983—; General Practice, 1985—; Chairman, Alternate Dispute Resolution Committee, 1996) Bar Associations; Oklahoma Trial Lawyers Association; The Association of Trial Lawyers of America; The Christian Legal Society; The Rutherford Institute; PIABA.

RODNEY J. HEGGY, born St. Louis, Illinois, August 26, 1955; admitted to bar, 1981, Texas and U.S. District Court, Northern and Southern Districts of Texas; 1982, Oklahoma, U.S. District Court, Western, Northern and Eastern Districts of Oklahoma and U.S. Court of Appeals, Tenth and Eighth Circuits. *Education:* Southeastern Oklahoma State University (B.A., 1977); University of Louisiana (Master of Science, 1978); University of Houston (J.D., 1981). Author: "The Trial Lawyer's Purgatory: the Document Depository in Complex Litigation," (BRS, 1990); "Oklahoma Toxic Torts Law: Elements, Standards for Evaluating Proof, and Suggestions for Practitioners," (NBI, 1992); "Environmental Law for Business and Lenders: Litigation Prevention and Avoidance, Insurance Coverage and Evaluation of Proof," (Oklahoma City University, 1992); "Using, Drafting and Enforcing Arbitration Clauses," (Oklahoma Bar Association, 1992); "Ethical Considerations in Insurance Coverage Claims," (NBI, 1997); "Extra-Contractual Insurance Claims Liability-Bad Faith, Insurance Coverage Law in Oklahoma," (NBI, 1997); "Mandatory Arbitration of Employment Law Claims," and "Employee Misconduct and Workplace Torts," (SES, 2003). Member, 2000 and President, 2002—, Board of Education, 1-31, Banner Public Schools. Arbitrator/Neutral: American Arbitration Association; New York Stock Exchange, Inc.; NASD Dispute Resolution, Inc. *Member:* Oklahoma Bar Association; State Bar of Texas; International Association of Defense Counsel; Defense Research Institute; Oklahoma Association of Defense Counsel. (Also practicing individually). ***PRACTICE AREAS:*** Commercial Arbitration; Commercial Litigation; Employment Law; Insurance; Fraud. ***Email:*** rheggy@cox.net

WILLIAM P. WASSON, born College Station, Texas, August 5, 1971; admitted to bar, 2001, Oklahoma; U.S. District Court, Western District of Oklahoma; 2003, U.S. Court of Appeals, Tenth Circuit; 2004, U.S. Court of Appeals, Ninth Circuit. *Education:* University of Houston (B.A., summa cum laude, 1996); University of Oklahoma (J.D. with honors, 2000). Dean's List; Order of the Coif. Recipient, American Jurisprudence Award in Statutory Interpretation, 1999. Author, "Does the Collateral Source Rule Apply to Write-Offs Under either Medicare or Medicaid?, Defense Counsel Journal, April, 2004. Chief of Staff for Chairman of Appropriations, Oklahoma State Senate, January-December, 2001. Research Assistant, University of Oklahoma College of Law, 1998-1999. ***LANGUAGES:*** Spanish.

FELLERS, SNIDER, BLANKENSHIP, BAILEY & TIPPENS

A PROFESSIONAL CORPORATION

Established in 1964

BANK ONE TOWER
100 NORTH BROADWAY, SUITE 1700
OKLAHOMA CITY, OKLAHOMA 73102-8820
Telephone: 405-232-0621
Fax: 405-232-9659
Email: fsbb&t@icnet.net
URL: http://www.fellerssnider.com

Tulsa, Oklahoma Office: The Kennedy Building, 321 South Boston, Suite 800. Telephone: 918-599-0621. Fax: 918-583-9659.

General Practice. Trial of all Cases in State and Federal Courts. Commercial, Corporate, Oil and Gas, Banking and Banking Regulation, Administrative, Probate, Estate Planning, Transportation, Bankruptcy, Securities, Insurance, Federal and State Taxation, Unfair Competition, Aircraft Finance and Leasing, Aircraft Sales, Aircraft Title, Real Property, Employment, Workers' Compensation, Intellectual Property, and Antitrust Law.

FIRM PROFILE: The law firm of Fellers, Snider, Blankenship, Bailey & Tippens was founded in Oklahoma City in 1963. In four decades, the Firm has grown in size, scope and reputation, attracting attorneys with a wide array of skills and experience. Our attorneys have held numerous leadership positions, including President of the American Bar Association, President of the Oklahoma Bar Association, President of the Oklahoma County Bar Association, President of the Oklahoma Bar Foundation, Professor of Law and Associate Dean of the University of Oklahoma College of Law, Professor of Law of the Oklahoma City University College of Law and others. Our common bond is our dedication to delivering the highest quality of legal service available. Fellers, Snider is listed in the Bar Register of Preeminent Lawyers.

JAMES D. FELLERS (1913-1997)

JOHN JOSEPH SNIDER (1928-1997)

TERRY W. TIPPENS, born Elk City, Oklahoma, November 15, 1945; admitted to bar, 1971, Oklahoma; 1989, U.S. Supreme Court; 1994, U.S. Court of Federal Claims; 1995, U.S. Tax Court. *Education:* Oklahoma State University (B.S., 1968); University of Oklahoma (J.D., 1971). Omicron Delta Kappa; Phi Kappa Phi; Phi Delta Phi. Director, 1988-1991, Vice President, 1989-1990, Oklahoma County Bar Association. *Member:* International Society of Barristers; American Inns of Court. ***PRACTICE AREAS:*** Civil Litigation; Banking Law; Oil and Gas Contracts; Water Law; Commercial Arbitration; Environmental Liability. ***Email:*** ttippens@fellerssnider.com

K. NICHOLAS WILSON, born Carlisle, Pennsylvania, February 13, 1943; admitted to bar, 1968, Oklahoma. *Education:* Princeton University and Oklahoma City University (B.A., 1965); University of Oklahoma (J.D., 1968). Phi Delta Phi. Editor, Oklahoma Law Review, 1966-1968. Instructor, Oklahoma City University School of Law, 1973-1977. *Member:* International Association of Defense Counsel. ***PRACTICE AREAS:*** Civil Litigation; Aircraft Title; Aircraft Finance and Leasing. ***Email:*** nwilson@fellerssnider.com

HARRY H. SELPH, II, born Stillwater, Oklahoma, October 23, 1942; admitted to bar, 1970, Oklahoma. *Education:* Oklahoma State University (B.S., 1965); University of Oklahoma (J.D., 1970). Phi Delta Phi. Editor-In-Chief, Oklahoma Law Review, 1969-1970. Fellow: Oklahoma Bar Foundation; Oklahoma State University Foundation (Member, Board of Trustees). ***PRACTICE AREAS:*** Natural Resources; Utility Law; Commercial Law; Mergers and Acquisitions; Real Estate; Arbitration. ***Email:*** hselph@fellerssnider.com

WARREN F. BICKFORD, IV, born Blackwell, Oklahoma, September 11, 1949; admitted to bar, 1974, Oklahoma. *Education:* University of Oklahoma (B.B.A., 1971; J.D., 1974). Phi Delta Phi. Associate General Counsel, Oklahoma Department of Securities, 1975-1977. Member, Oklahoma Criminal Defense Lawyers Association. ***PRACTICE AREAS:*** Business Law; Litigation; Criminal Defense. ***Email:*** wbickford@fellerssnider.com

JOHN B. HEATLY, born Vinita, Oklahoma, October 4, 1950; admitted to bar, 1976, Oklahoma. *Education:* Oklahoma State University (B.S., 1972); University of Oklahoma (J.D., 1976). Member, Board of Directors, 1996-1998, Fee Grievance and Ethics Committee, 1989-1999, Oklahoma County Bar Association. Member, Title Standards Committee, Oklahoma Bar Association, 1980-1981. ***PRACTICE AREAS:*** Commercial Litigation; Civil Appeals; Bankruptcy; Real Estate. ***Email:*** jheatly@fellerssnider.com

(This Listing Continued)

FELLERS, SNIDER, BLANKENSHIP, BAILEY & TIPPENS,
A PROFESSIONAL CORPORATION, Oklahoma City—Continued

MICHAEL R. FORD, born Blackwell, Oklahoma, September 1, 1945; admitted to bar, 1970, Oklahoma. *Education:* Northwestern University and University of Oklahoma (B.A., 1967); University of Oklahoma (J.D., 1970); George Washington University National Law Center (LL.M., in Taxation, 1974). Order of the Coif; Phi Delta Phi. Editor, Oklahoma Law Review, 1969-1970. Author: "Estate Planning for Oil and Gas Interests," Prentice-Hall, Oil and Gas Taxes Natural Resources, 1982; "The Whys and Wherefores of Revocable Trusts," Prentice-Hall, Successful Estate Planning Ideas and Methods Service, October/November, 1983; "Choice of Entity for Oil and Gas Activities Under the Tax Reform Act of 1986," Prentice-Hall Oil and Gas Taxes Natural Resources, 1988. *Member:* American Law Institute. Fellow, Oklahoma Bar Foundation. ***PRACTICE AREAS:*** Real Estate; Taxation Law; Banking Law; Commercial Law; Mergers and Acquisitions. ***Email:*** mford@fellerssnider.com

ERIC S. EISSENSTAT, born Iowa City, Iowa, January 15, 1958; admitted to bar, 1983, Oklahoma; 1988, U.S. Supreme Court. *Education:* Oklahoma State University (B.S., with honors, 1980); University of Oklahoma (J.D., with honors, 1983). Phi Kappa Phi; Order of the Coif. Note Editor, Oklahoma Law Review, 1982-1983. Chair, Young Lawyers Division, 1991; Oklahoma Bar Association, Outstanding Young Lawyer, 1992. Member, Board of Governors, Oklahoma Bar Association, 1991. Chair, Young Lawyers Division of Litigation Section, America Bar Association, 1991. Vice-Chair, Membership Committee ABA Section of Antitrust, 1993-1997; Council, Liaison ABA Section of Antitrust, 1991-1993. Membership Chair, Computer Litigation Committee, ABA Section of Litigation, 1998. Speaker and Moderator, OBA Seminars on Business Torts, Computer Law and Antitrust Issues; Speaker, American Legal Seminars Business Torts Forum, Chicago, IL; Speaker, ABA Annual Meeting on Punitive Damages; Workshop Leader, Oklahoma Trial Lawyers Association/University of Oklahoma College of Advocacy. Fellow, Oklahoma Bar Foundation. ***PRACTICE AREAS:*** Civil Litigation; Business Torts; Computer Law; Antitrust; Securities. ***Email:*** eeissenstat@fellerssnider.com

STEPHEN R. STEPHENS, born Purcell, Oklahoma, September 11, 1958; admitted to bar, 1983, Oklahoma. *Education:* Tulane University of Louisiana; Oklahoma State University (B.S., 1980); University of Oklahoma (J.D., 1983). Phi Alpha Delta. ***PRACTICE AREAS:*** Civil Litigation; Business and Commercial Law. ***Email:*** sstephens@fellerssnider.com

DONEEN DOUGLAS JONES, born Oklahoma City, Oklahoma, November 8, 1951; admitted to bar, 1981, Oklahoma. *Education:* University of Oklahoma (B.S., 1972; J.D., 1981). ***PRACTICE AREAS:*** Bankruptcy Law; Litigation; Commercial Law; Oil and Gas Law. ***Email:*** djones@fellerssnider.com

THOMAS J. ENIS, born Maryville, Missouri, 1937; admitted to bar, 1966, Missouri; 1973, Oklahoma. *Education:* Rockhurst College (B.S., in Chemistry, 1958); University of Missouri at Columbia (J.D., 1966). Phi Delta Phi; Order of the Coif. Editor-in-Chief, Missouri Law Review, 1965-1966. Professor of Law, 1967-1974 and Associate Dean, 1970-1974, University of Oklahoma College of Law. *Member:* Oklahoma County, Oklahoma and American Bar Associations; The Missouri Bar. Fellow, Oklahoma Bar Foundation. ***PRACTICE AREAS:*** Oil and Gas Law; Environmental Law; Litigation; Business Law. ***Email:*** tenis@fellerssnider.com

JOE C. LEWALLEN, JR., born Tulsa, Oklahoma, July 17, 1960; admitted to bar, 1985, Oklahoma. *Education:* Oklahoma State University (B.S., 1982); University of Oklahoma (J.D., 1985). Phi Delta Phi; Pi Sigma Alpha. ***PRACTICE AREAS:*** Commercial Real Estate; Commercial Law; Contracts; Finance; Business Law; Leases and Leasing. ***Email:*** jlewallen@fellerssnider.com

GREGORY A. CASTRO, born Wichita, Kansas, February 7, 1961; admitted to bar, 1986, Oklahoma. *Education:* Oklahoma State University (B.S., 1983); University of Oklahoma (J.D., 1986). Phi Delta Phi. ***PRACTICE AREAS:*** Civil Litigation; Business Law; Patent and Antitrust Litigation; Employment Law. ***Email:*** gcastro@fellerssnider.com

KEVIN R. DONELSON, born Dumas, Texas, November 15, 1961; admitted to bar, 1988, Oklahoma. *Education:* Southwestern Oklahoma State University (B.A., 1984); University of Oklahoma (J.D., with highest honors, 1988). Phi Delta Phi; Order of the Coif. Member, Oklahoma Law Review, 1986-1988. Administrative Law Judge, Oklahoma Department of Labor. Barrister, Ruth Bader Ginsburg Inn of Court; Robert J. Turner Inn of Court. ***PRACTICE AREAS:*** General Civil Litigation; Labor and Employment Law. ***Email:*** kdonelson@fellerssnider.com

MARK K. STONECIPHER, born Oklahoma City, Oklahoma, June 6, 1957; admitted to bar, 1983, Oklahoma; U.S. Court of Appeals, Tenth Circuit. *Education:* Oklahoma City University (B.S., magna cum laude, 1980); University of Oklahoma (J.D., 1983). Editor, 1982-1983 and Note Editor, 1983, Oklahoma Law Review. Recipient: Presidents Award, Oklahoma Bar Association, 1989; Oklahoma Outstanding Young Lawyers Award, 1990. Chair, Young Lawyers Division, Oklahoma Bar Association, 1989. Member, Board of Directors, Oklahoma Attorneys Mutual Insurance Company; Board of Trustees, Oklahoma Bar Foundation. Member, American Inns of Court XXIII, 1987-1989. ***PRACTICE AREAS:*** Litigation; Oil and Gas; Environmental; Commercial Law; Corporate Law. ***Email:*** mstonecipher@fellerssnider.com

ANDREW L. WALDING, born Shawnee, Oklahoma, October 21, 1953; admitted to bar, 1990, Oklahoma; U.S. Court of Appeals, Tenth Circuit; U.S. Tax Court. *Education:* University of Arkansas; University of Oklahoma (B.B.A., 1976; J.D., 1990); Georgetown University (LL.M., 1991). Certified Public Accountant, Oklahoma, 1978. ***PRACTICE AREAS:*** Complex Civil Litigation; Oil & Gas; Tax Controversies. ***Email:*** awalding@fellerssnider.com

BRYAN N.B. KING, born Ft. Rucker, Alabama, January 25, 1970; admitted to bar, 1995, Oklahoma; U.S. District Court, Western, Eastern and Northern Districts of Oklahoma. *Education:* Pepperdine University (B.A., Humanities, 1991); University of Oklahoma (J.D., 1995). Member, Board of Advocates. Member, Oklahoma Lawyers for Children. *Member:* William J. Holloway American Inns of Court. ***PRACTICE AREAS:*** Workers Compensation; Commercial Litigation; Employment Law; Insurance Defense; Personal Injury. ***Email:*** bking@fellerssnider.com

(This Listing Continued)

BRENT M. JOHNSON, born Tacoma, Washington, October 3, 1969; admitted to bar, 1996, Oklahoma; U.S. District Court, Western and Northern Districts of Oklahoma. *Education:* Stanford University (B.A., 1992); University of Oklahoma (J.D., 1996). Note Editor, Oklahoma Law Review, 1995-1996. ***PRACTICE AREAS:*** Commercial Litigation; Probate; Commercial Transactions. ***Email:*** bjohnson@fellerssnider.com

CHARLES C. CALLAWAY, JR., born Washington, D.C., July 15, 1956; admitted to bar, 1981, Oklahoma. *Education:* University of Oklahoma (B.A., with honors, 1978; J.D., 1981). Article Editor, 1980 and Symposium Editor, 1981, Oklahoma Law Review. *Member:* Oklahoma County, Oklahoma and American (Member, Sections on: Business Law; Real Property) Bar Associations. ***PRACTICE AREAS:*** Commercial Law; Commercial Real Estate; Finance; Leases and Leasing; Mortgages. ***Email:*** ccallaway@fellerssnider.com

WILLIAM H. WHITEHILL, JR., born Bellefonte, Pennsylvania, April 10, 1960; admitted to bar, 1986, Oklahoma. *Education:* Cameron University (B.S., 1983); University of Oklahoma (J.D., 1986). Recipient, American Jurisprudence Award, Remedies. Certified Public Accountant, Oklahoma, 1983. Co-Author: "The Money Laundering Control Act: An Attack On The Business Side of Organized Crime," The Oklahoma Bar Journal, 1988; "New Federal Legislation May Be A Trap For The Unwary," Oklahoma Business Magazine, 1988; "Attorney, Accountant and Clients: Roles In A Criminal Tax Fraud Investigation," The Oklahoma Bar Journal, 1991; "Property Tax Law in Oklahoma," NBI, 1996, 1999, 2000, 2001; "Likekind Real Estate Exchanges," 2001. ***PRACTICE AREAS:*** Taxation; Commercial Real Estate; Aircraft Finance and Leasing; Commercial Law; Public Finance; Business Law. ***Email:*** bwhitehill@fellerssnider.com

RANDALL K. McCARTHY, born Oklahoma City, Oklahoma, 1965; admitted to bar, 1995, Oklahoma; U.S. District Court, Western District of Oklahoma and U.S. Court of Appeals for the Federal Circuit; registered to practice before U.S. Patent and Trademark Office. *Education:* University of Oklahoma (B.S.E.E., 1987); Oklahoma City University (J.D., summa cum laude, 1995). Phi Delta Phi. President, Intellectual Property Section, Oklahoma Bar Association, 1999. *Member:* Institute of Electrical and Electronics Engineers; American Intellectual Property Law Association. ***PRACTICE AREAS:*** Intellectual Property; Computer and Software Patents; Patent Licensing; Patent Litigation; Trademarks. ***Email:*** rmccarthy@fellerssnider.com

JAY P. WALTERS, born Tulsa, Oklahoma, October 18, 1968; admitted to bar, 1996, Virginia; 1997, Oklahoma, District of Columbia, U.S. District Court, Western District of Oklahoma, U.S. District Court for the District of Columbia and U.S. District Court, Eastern District of Virginia. *Education:* Austin College (B.A., 1991); George Washington University Law School (J.D., with honors, 1996). Environmental Lawyer. Moot Court Board. Judicial Law Clerk, Hon. Robin J. Cauthron, U.S. District Court, Western District of Oklahoma, 1996-1997. Associate, Dow, Lohnes & Albertson, Washington, D.C., 1997-2000. *Member:* Virginia State Bar; District of Columbia Bar. ***Email:*** jwalters@fellerssnider.com

MARGARET A. BOMHOFF, born Kansas City, Missouri, January 26, 1962; admitted to bar, 1987, Oklahoma and U.S. District Court, Northern and Western Districts of Oklahoma. *Education:* University of Oklahoma (B.A., with distinction, 1984; J.D., 1987). Phi Beta Kappa. ***PRACTICE AREAS:*** Workers Compensation. ***Email:*** mbomhoff@fellerssnider.com

BROOKS A. RICHARDSON, born Tuscaloosa, Alabama, June 10, 1970; admitted to bar, 1998, Oklahoma and Missouri; 1999, Kansas. *Education:* Duke University (B.A., 1993); University of Oklahoma (J.D., 1998). Order of the Coif. Chief Articles Editor, Oklahoma Law Review, 1997-1998. Law Clerk to the Honorable Dean Whipple, U.S. District Court for the Western District of Missouri, 1998-2000. Former Legislative Assistant to U.S. Senator David L. Boren. *Member:* Oklahoma and American Bar Associations. ***PRACTICE AREAS:*** Commercial Litigation; ERISA Litigation; Business Torts. ***Email:*** brichardson@fellerssnider.com

DANIEL P. DOOLEY, born Austin, Minnesota, 1948; admitted to bar, 2000, Oklahoma; registered to practice before U.S. Patent and Trademark Office. *Education:* University of Minnesota (B.M.E., 1972); University of St. Thomas (M.B.A., summa cum laude, 1976); Oklahoma City University (J.D., 1999); Franklin Pierce Law Center (LL.M., 2000). Phi Delta Phi. Merit Scholar. ***PRACTICE AREAS:*** Patents; Trademarks; Trade Secrets; Technology and Science; Corporate Law. ***Email:*** ddooley@fellerssnider.com

---

KELLI M. MASTERS, born Oklahoma City, Oklahoma, July 5, 1973; admitted to bar, 2000, Oklahoma. *Education:* University of Oklahoma (B.A., Journalism, 1995; J.D., with honors, 1999). Phi Delta Phi. ***PRACTICE AREAS:*** Civil Litigation; Nonprofit Organizations Law; Tax Exempt Organizations. ***Email:*** kmasters@fellerssnider.com

N. JANINE WHEELER, born Oklahoma City, Oklahoma, March 20, 1966; admitted to bar, 1991, Oklahoma; U.S. District Court, Western and Northern Districts of Oklahoma. *Education:* University of Oklahoma (B.B.A., with distinction, 1988; J.D., with honors, 1991). Phi Eta Sigma. Member, Mortar Board. Recipient, Woman's Letzeiser Award. Note Editor, Oklahoma Law Review. Author: "The Absolute Priority Rule: Necessity as a Recently Emphasized Element," 46 Consumer Fin. L. Q. Rep. 42, 1992. ***PRACTICE AREAS:*** Bankruptcy Law; Commercial Litigation; Real Estate Law. ***Email:*** jwheeler@fellerssnider.com

LANCE E. LEFFEL, born Bossier City, Louisiana, October 21, 1975; admitted to bar, 2002, Oklahoma and U.S. District Court, Western, Eastern and Northern Districts of Oklahoma. *Education:* University of Oklahoma (B.A., 1998; J.D., with distinction, 2002). *Member:* Oklahoma and National Bar Associations; Robert J. Turner American Inn of Court (Associate). ***PRACTICE AREAS:*** Insurance Law; Product Liability Law; Commercial Litigation; Contracts; Transportation Law. ***Email:*** lleffel@fellerssnider.com

NICHOLAS V. MERKLEY, born Vernal, Utah, May 31, 1979; admitted to bar, 2004, Oklahoma. *Education:* University of Oklahoma (B.B.A., 2001; J.D., 2004). *Member:* Oklahoma County and Oklahoma Bar Associations; Luther Bohanan American Inn of Court. ***PRACTICE AREAS:*** Civil Litigation; Insurance. ***Email:*** nmerkley@fellerssnider.com

MICHAEL H. BROWN, born Birmingham, Alabama, October 11, 1979; admitted to bar, 2005, Oklahoma. *Education:* Southern Methodist University (B.A., summa cum laude,

(This Listing Continued)

2002); University of Texas School of Law (J.D., with honors, 2005). *Member:* Oklahoma County, Oklahoma and American Bar Associations. ***PRACTICE AREAS:*** Real Estate; Commercial Litigation; Corporate Law. ***Email:*** mbrown@fellerssnider.com

CASEY TIPPENS DELANEY, born Weatherford, Oklahoma, May 16, 1980; admitted to bar, 2005, Oklahoma. *Education:* Oklahoma State University (B.A., with honors, 2002); University of Oklahoma (J.D., 2005). Finalist, Moot Court Competition, 2003. Top Ten Oralist, Moot Court Competition 2003. Articles Editor, American Indian Law Review, 2004-2005. Author: "Everglades, Dirty Water and the Miccosukee Indian Tribe: Will the Supreme Court say Enough is Enough?" American Indian Law Review, Spring 2004. *Member:* American Bar Association; Luther Bohanan Inn of Courts (Student Member). ***PRACTICE AREAS:*** Civil Litigation. ***Email:*** cdelaney@fellerssnider.com

OF COUNSEL

JAP W. BLANKENSHIP, born Lawton, Oklahoma, February 10, 1935; admitted to bar, 1963, Oklahoma. *Education:* University of Oklahoma (B.A., 1957; LL.B., 1963). Omicron Delta Kappa; Phi Alpha Delta. Editor, Oklahoma Law Review, 1963. Fellow: American Bar Foundation; Oklahoma Bar Foundation (President, 1994). ***PRACTICE AREAS:*** Real Property; Aircraft Finance and Leasing; Aircraft Sales; Aircraft Title. ***Email:*** jblankenship@fellerssnider.com

BURCK BAILEY, born Vinita, Oklahoma, August 22, 1934; admitted to bar, 1961, Missouri; 1963, Oklahoma; 1969, U.S. Supreme Court; 1982, U.S. District Court, Northern District of Texas. *Education:* Westminster College (B.A. cum laude, 1958); New York University (LL.B., 1961). Omicron Delta Kappa. President, Oklahoma County Bar Association, 1983-1984. President, Oklahoma Bar Association, 1988. Member, Oklahoma Judicial Nominating Commission, 1997-2003; Chairman, 2002-2003. Fellow: American College of Trial Lawyers (State Chairman, 1993-1994); American Academy of Appellate Lawyers; International Academy of Trial Lawyers; American Bar Foundation. ***PRACTICE AREAS:*** Civil Litigation; Criminal Defense. ***Email:*** bbailey@fellerssnider.com

PAUL W. DUDMAN, born Bishop's Stortford, England, January 19, 1949; admitted to bar, 1974, Solicitor of Supreme Court of England and Wales; 1975, Oklahoma. *Education:* Exeter University, Exeter, Devon, England (LL.B., with honors, 1970). *Member:* International Bar Association; The Law Society (England). ***PRACTICE AREAS:*** Trusts and Estates; Probate; Wills; Nonprofit and Charitable Organizations; Business Law. ***Email:*** pdudman@fellerssnider.com

BILL D. McCARTHY, born El Reno, Oklahoma, 1934; admitted to bar, 1972, Oklahoma; U.S. Court of Appeals for the Federal and Tenth Circuits; registered to practice before U.S. Patent and Trademark Office. *Education:* University of Oklahoma (B.S., Chemical Engineering, 1957; M.S., Chemical Engineering, 1963); Oklahoma City University (J.D., 1972). Phi Delta Phi. Registered Professional Engineer, Oklahoma, 1965. Adjunct Professor, Oklahoma City University School of Law. President, 1978-1949 and Member, Patent, Trademark and Copyright Section, Oklahoma Bar Association. *Member:* American Bar Association; American Intellectual Property Law Association; Oklahoma Society of Professional Engineers (State President, 1971); National Society of Professional Engineers (Director, 1969-1971). ***PRACTICE AREAS:*** Intellectual Property Infringement; Intellectual Property Licensing; Intellectual Property Litigation; Intellectual Property Procurement; Intellectual Property Rights. ***Email:*** bmccarthy@fellerssnider.com

MITCHELL K. McCARTHY, born Oklahoma City, Oklahoma, 1960; admitted to bar, 1999, Oklahoma, U.S. District Court, Western District of Oklahoma and U.S. Court of Appeals for the Federal Circuit; registered to practice before U.S. Patent and Trademark Office. *Education:* University of Oklahoma (B.S.M.E., 1985); Oklahoma City University (J.D., 1999). Phi Delta Phi. *Member:* Oklahoma Bar Association (Director/Secretary, Intellectual Property Section, 2003); American Society of Mechanical Engineers; American Intellectual Property Law Association. ***PRACTICE AREAS:*** Intellectual Property; Patent Preparation and Prosecution; Patent Licensing; Patent Litigation; Trademarks; Copyrights. ***Email:*** mmccarthy@fellerssnider.com

All Attorneys are Members of the Oklahoma County, Oklahoma and American Bar Associations.

REPRESENTATIVE CLIENTS: Aetna Life Insurance Co.; Adams Investment Company, Inc.; A.G. Edwards & Sons, Inc.; American Agency Systems; American Express Co.; Amoco Corporation; Archon Group L.P.; A.S.C. Incorporated; ATÆ Corp.; BancFirst; Bank One; Bank of America, N.A.; Bayliner Marine Corporation; BellSouth Communication Systems, Inc.; Bogo Energy Corp; BP America, Inc.; Brunswick Corporation; CenterPoint Energy Arkla, a division of CenterPoint Resources Group; Century Martial Arts Supply Inc.; Charter Communications Corporation; Chevron U.S.A., Inc.; Chrysler Financial Corp.; Chubb Group Insurance; Cingular Wireless, LLC; City of Tulsa-Rogers County Port Authority; Connecticut General Life Insurance Co.; Conoco Inc.; Continental Resources, Inc.; Corken, Inc.; Cunningham Lindsey Claims Management; Dillon, Read & Co., Inc.; Doug Carson & Associates, Inc.; Ellsworth Motor Freight Lines, Inc.; Enogex Inc.; Exxon Mobil Corporation; Farmers Insurance; Farmland Industries; Filtrex, Inc.; Fleet National Bank; Follett Corporation; Frank's Tong Service, Inc.; Gallagher Bassett Claims Services; GatesMcDonald; General Electric Capital Corp.; Guaranty Bank and Trust Co.; Halliburton Co.; Harold Simpson, Inc.; Hertz Corp.; Hormel Foods Corporation; IBC Securities Corp.; Igloo Corporation; International Bank of Commerce; Jennie-O Turkey Store, Inc.; Johnson Controls World Services, Inc.; Kawasaki Motors Corp. USA; Life Insurance Company of North America; Kerr-McGee Corp.; LG&E Energy Marketing Inc.; Little Giant Pump Company; Magellan Midstream Partners, L.P.; Marathon Oil Co.; McKinley Properties, Inc.; Mercedes-Benz Credit Corporation; MetalFab, Inc.; Mosher-Adams Inc.; Motion Picture Association of America; Murphy Farms, Inc.; Northstar Presidio Management Companies, LLC; Oklahoma City Water Utilities Trust; Oklahoma Gas & Electric Corp.; Oklahoma State University; Outboard Marine Corporation; Panhandle Royalty Company; Phelps Dodge; Professional Cattle Consultants; Progress Energy, Inc.; Raptor Properties; Republic Insurance Group; Ritchie Capital Management, LLC; Richie Capital Management; RLI Insurance; Rupture Pin Technology, Inc.; Seagate Technology LLC; Service Corporation Intl.; Sharp Personnel; Sonic Corp.; Sonic Industries, Inc.; Sonic Restaurants, Inc.; Southwest Risk Management; Southwestern Bell Communications Services, Inc.; Southwestern Bell Telephone, L.P.; Stars Restaurants Corp.; Sykes Enterprises, Inc.; Taylor Valve Technology, Inc.; Tierra Vista; Torchmark Development Corp.; Tyson Foods, Inc.; United Parcel Service; UroCor, Inc.; USAA; USLife Corp.; VIP Foods, Inc.; Volvo Commercial Finance LLC The Americas; Wal-Mart Corporation; Wexford Capital, LLC; Wexford Management, LLC; The Williams Companies; Williams Power Company, Inc.; WilTel Communications Group, Inc.;Yamaha Motor Corporation USA; Zebco Corporation; ZEECO, Inc.

(For biographical data on other personnel, see Professional Biographies at Tulsa, Oklahoma)

FENTON, FENTON, SMITH, RENEAU & MOON

Established in 1947

211 NORTH ROBINSON
SUITE 800 N
OKLAHOMA CITY, OKLAHOMA 73102
Telephone: 405-235-4671
Telecopier: 405-235-5247
Email: mail@fentonlaw.com

General Civil Practice. Casualty, Surety and Insurance Law, Workers Compensation, Employers Liability, Medical and Hospital Malpractice, Products Liability, Toxic Tort and Environmental Law, School Law, Real Property, Title Examination, Title Insurance, Probate, Mortgage Foreclosure, Corporate, Commercial, Zoning, Planning and Subdivision, Real Estate Development, Municipal Law. Trials in all State and Federal Courts.

FIRM PROFILE: The firm was founded in 1947 by Edgar R. Fenton (1890-1977) and Elliott C. Fenton. They were joined in the practice by William G. Smith in 1956. The firm became Fenton, Fenton, Smith, Reneau & Moon in 1965.

The firm has steadily grown to its present size of 26 lawyers in order to meet the litigation and other needs of its many regional and national clients. Its areas of practice have also expanded to include personal injury, property damage, toxic tort, environmental law, constitutional and school law, first party insurance matters, employers liability, real property, corporate and commercial law, probate and business related litigation, in addition to the firm's traditional involvement in defense of suretyship, medical and hospital malpractice, product liability, workers' compensation, casualty insurance, and general liability matters. All of the firm's members are trial lawyers and admitted to practice before all Oklahoma state and federal courts. All members of the firm are members of the Oklahoma County, State and American Bar Associations and the Oklahoma Association of Defense Counsel. Several members of the firm are members of the Defense Research Institute, American Board of Trial Advocates, the International Association of Defense Counsel, Association of Trial Attorneys, American Association of Hospital Attorneys and the American College of Trial Lawyers.

Complete firm resumes are available upon request.

EDGAR FENTON (1890-1977)
MILTON R. MOON (1921-1988)
WM. G. SMITH (1919-1993)

DALE RENEAU, born Hobart, Oklahoma, April 15, 1931; admitted to bar, 1956, Oklahoma. *Education:* University of Oklahoma (B.A., 1953; LL.B., 1956). Delta Theta Phi. ***PRACTICE AREAS:*** Hospital Liability Defense; Medical Malpractice Defense; Wrongful Termination Defense; Products Liability Defense; Mediation. ***Email:*** dreneau@fentonlaw.com

DONALD R. WILSON, born Yale, Oklahoma, December 31, 1942; admitted to bar, 1967, Oklahoma. *Education:* University of Oklahoma (B.A., 1965; J.D., 1967). Omicron Delta Kappa; Phi Alpha Delta. Judge, Special Courts-Martial, U.S. Army, 1969-1971. ***PRACTICE AREAS:*** Insurance Litigation; Insurance Coverage; Products Liability Defense; Gas Explosions; Automobile Negligence; Tort Defense; Insurance Agents and Broker Defense; Truck Accidents. ***Email:*** drwilson@fentonlaw.com

STEPHEN PETERSON, born Flora, Illinois, June 7, 1950; admitted to bar, 1975, Oklahoma. *Education:* University of Oklahoma (B.A., 1972; J.D., 1975). Phi Delta Phi. ***PRACTICE AREAS:*** Product Liability Defense; Medical Malpractice Defense; Dental Malpractice Defense; Hospital Liability Defense; Nursing Home Negligence; Environmental Law. ***Email:*** sbpeterson@fentonlaw.com

JOHN A. McCALEB, born Oklahoma City, Oklahoma, May 5, 1951; admitted to bar, 1976, Oklahoma. *Education:* University of Oklahoma (B.A., 1973; J.D., 1976). Phi Beta Kappa; Phi Delta Phi; Order of the Coif. Member, Oklahoma Law Review, 1975-1976. ***PRACTICE AREAS:*** Workers Compensation Defense; Workers Compensation Appeals; Employer Liability. ***Email:*** jamccaleb@fentonlaw.com

C. WILLIAM THRELKELD, born Ponca City, Oklahoma, December 8, 1950; admitted to bar, 1976, Oklahoma. *Education:* University of Oklahoma (B.S., 1974; J.D., 1976). Phi Delta Phi. *Member:* Federation of Defense and Corporate Counsel. ***PRACTICE AREAS:*** Insurance; Insurance Bad Faith; Title Insurance Litigation; Construction Law; Surety; Products Liability; Drug and Medical Product Liability; Toxic Tort; Antitrust; Environmental Law; Libel, Slander and Defamation; Commercial Law. ***Email:*** cwthrelkeld@fentonlaw.com

TOM E. MULLEN, born Tulsa, Oklahoma, August 19, 1954; admitted to bar, 1979, Oklahoma. *Education:* University of Oklahoma (B.A., 1976; J.D., 1979). Phi Alpha Delta (Vice Justice, 1978). Member, Moot Court Board. ***PRACTICE AREAS:*** Insurance Bad Faith; Property Loss; Property Insurance Coverage; Fire Loss; Construction Defects; Automobile Liability; Manufacturers Liability; Breach of Contract. ***Email:*** temullen@fentonlaw.com

BRENDA K. PETERSON, born Oklahoma City, Oklahoma, April 5, 1957; admitted to bar, 1983, Oklahoma. *Education:* Oklahoma State University (B.S., 1979); Oklahoma City University (J.D., 1983). Phi Delta Phi. ***PRACTICE AREAS:*** Insurance Defense; Automobile Liability Defense; Personal Injury Defense; Construction Defects; Workers Compensation. ***Email:*** bpeterson@fentonlaw.com

BEVERLY S. PEARSON, born Waurika, Oklahoma, November 7, 1950; admitted to bar, 1983, California; 1985, Oklahoma. *Education:* East Central Oklahoma State University (B.A., 1972); Oklahoma State University (M.S., 1973); University of San Diego School of Law (J.D., 1983). ***PRACTICE AREAS:*** Insurance Defense; Medical Malpractice Defense; Insurance Coverage; Products Liability; Personal Injury; Premises Liability Defense; Labor and Employment Law Defense. ***Email:*** bspearson@fentonlaw.com

MICHAEL D. DUNCAN, born Durant, Oklahoma, September 14, 1958; admitted to bar, 1985, Oklahoma. *Education:* Eastern Oklahoma State College; University of Oklahoma (B.A., Journalism, 1980; J.D., 1985). Recipient, American Jurisprudence Award,

(This Listing Continued)

FENTON, FENTON, SMITH, RENEAU & MOON, Oklahoma City—Continued

Constitutional Law. ***PRACTICE AREAS:*** Insurance Defense; Automobile Insurance; Insurance Bad Faith; General Liability Defense; Defamation; Nursing Liability; Products Liability; Personal Injury. ***Email:*** mdduncan@fentonlaw.com

MICHAEL S. McMILLIN, born Ardmore, Oklahoma, June 25, 1962; admitted to bar, 1987, Oklahoma. *Education:* University of Oklahoma (B.B.A., 1984; J.D., 1987). Alpha Lamda Delta. ***PRACTICE AREAS:*** Medical Malpractice Defense; Products Liability Defense; Insurance Defense; Personal Injury Defense; Automobile Litigation; Trucking Litigation. ***Email:*** msmcmillin@fentonlaw.com

GREG K. BALLARD, born Pauls Valley, Oklahoma, February 10, 1961; admitted to bar, 1990, Oklahoma. *Education:* East Central University (B.S., 1986); University of Oklahoma, College of Law (J.D., 1990). Member, Oklahoma Law Review, 1988-1990. ***PRACTICE AREAS:*** Workers Compensation Defense; Employer Liability. ***Email:*** gkballard@fentonlaw.com

C. TODD WARD, born Fairfax, Oklahoma, August 25, 1963; admitted to bar, 1990, Oklahoma. *Education:* University of Oklahoma (B.S., 1986; J.D., 1990). Phi Delta Phi. ***PRACTICE AREAS:*** General Liability Defense; Civil Liability; Products Liability Defense; Construction Liability; First and Third Party Insurance Defense; Insurance Bad Faith; Trucking Liability; Environmental Insurance Defense; Toxic Tort Defense. ***Email:*** ctward@fentonlaw.com

JOHN B. VERA, born Oklahoma City, Oklahoma, May 16, 1963; admitted to bar, 1991, Oklahoma. *Education:* University of Oklahoma (B.B.A., 1986; J.D., with distinction, 1991). ***LANGUAGES:*** Dutch. ***PRACTICE AREAS:*** Workers Compensation Defense; Employer Liability. ***Email:*** jbvera@fentonlaw.com

ALBERT LEWIS TAIT, JR., born Fort Campbell, Kentucky, April 2, 1950; admitted to bar, 1980, Oklahoma. *Education:* University of Oklahoma (B.B.A., 1975; J.D., 1980). Phi Delta Phi. Barrister, 1992-1995 and Master, 1998—, American Inns of Court, Luther Bohanon Inn. [U.S. Army, 1969-1973; Capt., Active Reserve, 1981-1986]. ***PRACTICE AREAS:*** Construction Defects; Employment Law; Environmental Law; Insurance; Insurance Bad Faith; Litigation; Personal Injury; Products Liability; Toxic Torts. ***Email:*** altait@fentonlaw.com

---

JOHN MARK MCALESTER, born Muskogee, Oklahoma, June 18, 1973; admitted to bar, 1998, Oklahoma. *Education:* University of Central Oklahoma (B.B.A., 1995); University of Oklahoma (J.D., 1998). *Member:* Defense Research Institute. ***Email:*** jmmcalester@fentonlaw.com

BRION HITT, born Lawton, Oklahoma, October 3, 1974; admitted to bar, 2001, Oklahoma. *Education:* Cameron University (B.S., 1998); University of Oklahoma (J.D., 2001). *Member:* Defense Research Institute. ***PRACTICE AREAS:*** Civil Practice. ***Email:*** bbhitt@fentonlaw.com

RYAN R. CHAFFIN, born Chickasha, Oklahoma, November 22, 1974; admitted to bar, 2002, Oklahoma. *Education:* University of Oklahoma (B.A., 1998; J.D., 2002). Phi Delta Phi, 2001-2002. Recipient, Academic Achievement Award in Evidence, 2001. *Member:* Oklahoma and American Bar Associations; Association of Defense Counsel; Defense Research Institute. ***PRACTICE AREAS:*** Insurance Defense. ***Email:*** rrchaffin@fentonlaw.com

JOHN C. KMETZ, born New Haven, Connecticut, December 30, 1966; admitted to bar, 2004, Oklahoma. *Education:* Trinity College (B.A., 1989); University of Oklahoma (J.D., 2004). Phi Delta Phi. ***PRACTICE AREAS:*** Civil Practice; Insurance Defense. ***Email:*** jckmetz@fentonlaw.com

OF COUNSEL

STACEY HAWS FELKNER, born Grafton, North Dakota, February 20, 1966; admitted to bar, 1991, Oklahoma; 1992, U.S. District Court, Western, Northern and Eastern Districts of Oklahoma; U.S. Court of Appeals, Tenth Circuit. *Education:* University of Oklahoma (B.A., Journalism, 1988; B.A., Political Science, with distinction, 1988; J.D., with honors, 1991). Phi Beta Kappa; Phi Delta Phi. Order of the Coif. Member, Oklahoma Law Review. Author: "Qualified Immunity Defense in Civil Rights Actions," 59 Am Jur Proof of Facts 3d (2000); "1993 Changes to Rule 11 and Rule 2011," 65 Oklahoma Bar Journal 1119 (1994). *Member:* Oklahoma Bar Association. ***PRACTICE AREAS:*** Civil Rights Defense; Police Liability; Insurance Defense; Appellate Practice.

ELLIOTT C. FENTON

JAMES P. KELLEY, born Oklahoma City, Oklahoma, February 12, 1944; admitted to bar, 1970, Oklahoma. *Education:* Notre Dame University; St. Louis University; University of Oklahoma (B.A., 1969); Oklahoma City University (J.D., 1970). *Member:* Oklahoma Bar Association. (Member of Kelley, Kelley & Gregory). ***PRACTICE AREAS:*** Commercial Real Estate; Real Estate; Title Insurance; Corporate Law; Probate.

GERALD E. KELLEY, born Oklahoma City, Oklahoma, April 20, 1952; admitted to bar, 1978, Oklahoma. *Education:* University of Oklahoma (B.A., 1974; J.D., 1977). Phi Beta Kappa; Phi Delta Phi; Order of the Coif. Editor, Oklahoma Law Review, 1975-1978. Staff Attorney, Department of Human Services, 1979-1981. *Member:* Oklahoma Bar Association. (Member of Kelley, Kelley & Gregory). ***PRACTICE AREAS:*** Adoption Law; Collections; Guardianship and Conservatorship; Trusts and Estates; Mortgages.

J. MITCHELL GREGORY, JR., born San Antonio, Texas, November 18, 1944; admitted to bar, 1974, Oklahoma. *Education:* Oklahoma Baptist University (B.A., cum laude, 1966); University of Oklahoma (J.D., 1974). Omicron Delta Kappa. *Member:* Oklahoma County, Oklahoma and American Bar Associations. [Capt., USAF, 1966-1970]. ***PRACTICE AREAS:*** Commercial Real Estate; Debtor and Creditor; Mortgages; Real Estate; Probate. ***Email:*** mgregory@ionet.net

ROSS L. GREGORY, born Minot, North Dakota, June 5, 1968; admitted to bar, 1996, Texas; 1999, Oklahoma, U.S. District Court, Western, Northern and Eastern Districts of Oklahoma. *Education:* Dartmouth College (A.B., 1990); Brooklyn Law School (J.D., 1996). Associate General Counsel, Midfirst Bank. *Member:* Oklahoma Bar Association; State Bar of Texas; Oklahoma City Real Property Lawyers Association. (Member of Kelley, Kelley & Gregory). ***PRACTICE AREAS:*** Commercial Transactions; Real Estate Law; Bankruptcy Law; Mortgage Foreclosure. ***Email:*** Ross@gregorylawfirm.com

SUSAN ANN KNIGHT, born Dayton, Ohio, July 12, 1957; admitted to bar, 1992, Oklahoma; U.S. District Court, Western and Eastern Districts of Oklahoma; U.S. Court of Appeals, Tenth Circuit. *Education:* University of Oklahoma (B.A., 1986; M.Ed., 1988; J.D., 1991). *Member:* Cleveland County, Oklahoma County and American Bar Associations; Oklahoma Bar Association; Oklahoma Association of Defense Counsel; Defense Research Institute. ***PRACTICE AREAS:*** Civil Rights Defense; Police Liability; Trucking Law; Insurance Defense; Employment Law; Civil Litigation; Workers' Compensation.

ROBERT EDWARD MANCHESTER, born Springfield, Massachusetts, June 14, 1936; admitted to bar, 1967, Oklahoma, U.S. District Court, Western, Eastern and Northern Districts of Oklahoma and U.S. Court of Appeals, Tenth Circuit; 1990, U.S. Supreme Court. *Education:* Central State College (B.A., 1962); Oklahoma City University (J.D., 1967). Phi Alpha Delta. Author: "Indemnity Agreements in a Products Liability Action," The Advocate, July/August, 1981. *Member:* Oklahoma County and American Bar Associations; Oklahoma Bar Association; Oklahoma Association of Defense Counsel; Defense Research Institute; International Association of Defense Counsel. ***PRACTICE AREAS:*** Civil Rights Defense; Police Civil Liability; Insurance Defense; Products Liability.

REPRESENTATIVE CLIENTS: AIG Risk Management, Inc.; The Alliance Insurance Cos.; American Association of Oral and Maxillofacial Surgeons Insurance Co.; American Fidelity Insurance Co.; American Guaranty Title Insurance Co.; Avis Car Rentals, Inc.; Black & Decker Corp.; Cabot Corp.; Capital Abstract & Title Co.; Carrier Corportion; Catholic Social Ministries; Chrysler Corp.; Chubb Group of Insurance Companies; CIGNA; City of Oklahoma City; Commercial Union Insurance Co.; Connelly Paving Co.; Conoco, Inc.; CNA Insurance Cos.; Convalescent Services, Inc.; Crawford & Co.; Employers Insurance of Wausau; Fireman's Fund; First American Title & Trust Co.; First National Bank of Midwest City (Real Estate); Florists' Mutual Insurance Co.; Foremost Insurance Company; Fraternal Order of Police, Lodge 123; Gulf Insurance Co.; Halliburton Services; Horace Mann Insurance Cos.; Hospital Casualty Co.; Insurance Company of North America; IRI International, Inc.; Kemper National Insurance Co.; Lawyers Title Insurance Corp.; Liberty Mutual Insurance Company; The Maryland Casualty Co.; McCorkle Truck Lines, Inc.; The National Fraternal Order of Police Defense Fund; National Indemnity Co.; Neighborhood Services Organization Project Adopt; NorAm Energy Corporation; Oklahoma City Abstract & Title Co.; The Oklahoma Publishing Co.; Otis Elevator Company; Payless Cashways, Inc.; Physicians Liability Insurance Company; Podiatry Insurance Co.; Pratt Whitney; Ranger/Pan American Cos.; Riscorp; Roadway Express, Inc.; SAIA; The St. Paul Insurance Cos.; Seaboard Farms, Inc.; Seikel Enterprises, Inc.; Silvey Companies; State Farm Mutual Automobile Insurance Company; Stewart Abstract & Title of Oklahoma; Stoeger Industries Inc.; Texaco Inc.; ThyssenKrupp Elevator Corporation; Travelers Insurance Companies; Union Standard Insurance Company; United Technologies; Vantage Paving, Inc.; United States Fidelity & Guaranty Co.; Westinghouse Electric Corp.; XL Specialty Insurance Company.

MARK K. FITCH

1900 N.W. EXPRESSWAY, SUITE 1300

OKLAHOMA CITY, OKLAHOMA 73118-1822

Telephone: 405-848-7100

Fax: 405-848-8241

Email: mfitch@ilinkusa.net

Estate Planning, Wills and Probate, Trusts, Elder Law, Real Property, Federal and State Taxation Law, including Individual, Estate and Gift, Corporations, Partnerships, Fiduciary and Trust Litigation.

FIRM PROFILE: Mark K. Fitch began practicing law in Oklahoma City in 1983 at a midsize firm. After two years, he started his own practice where the majority of his effort has been spent on estate planning, wills and trusts. Mr. Fitch represents clients from "all walks of life" with various socioeconomic backgrounds. His philosophy is to provide quality legal services at reasonable fees.

MARK K. FITCH, born Ardmore, Oklahoma, November 8, 1957; admitted to bar, 1983, Oklahoma, U.S. Tax Court and U.S. District Court, Western District of Oklahoma. *Education:* University of Oklahoma (B.Ac., 1980; J.D., 1983). Delta Theta Phi. Member, American Indian Law Review, 1981-1983. *Member:* Oklahoma County, Oklahoma and American Bar Associations. ***PRACTICE AREAS:*** Estate Planning Law; Probate Law; Real Property Law; Federal and State Income Tax; Estate and Gift Tax Law.

A List of Representative Clients will be furnished upon request.

FOLIART, HUFF, OTTAWAY & BOTTOM

A PROFESSIONAL CORPORATION

Established in 1949

THE BANK OF OKLAHOMA PLAZA

201 ROBERT S. KERR AVENUE, 12TH FLOOR

OKLAHOMA CITY, OKLAHOMA 73102

Telephone: 405-232-4633

FAX: 405-232-3462

Email: foliartfirm@oklahomacounsel.com

General Civil, Trial and Appellate Practice in State and Federal Courts. Insurance Defense, Medical Malpractice, Professional Liability, Products Liability, Personal Injury, Health Care, Employment, Intellectual Property and Negligence Law. Complex Litigation, including Class Actions and Environmental Law.

FIRM PROFILE: The firm was founded in 1949 by Draper Grigsby (1896-1954) and James D. Foliart. It was known then and now as a trial firm, with outstanding success in the courtroom.

During its history the firm has specialized in civil litigation, with emphasis on trial advocacy. The trial lawyers of the firm have successfully tried hundreds of jury cases.

(This Listing Continued)

The firm's growth and diversity of expertise have kept pace with the expansion and complexity of the modern civil litigation system. It is recognized as an established premier law firm dedicated to professional excellence and client results.

JAMES D. FOLIART, born McAlester, Oklahoma; admitted to bar, 1948, Oklahoma; U.S. District Court, Northern, Eastern and Western Districts of Oklahoma; U.S. Court of Appeals, Tenth Circuit. *Education:* Northwestern Oklahoma State University (A.B., 1940); University of Oklahoma (LL.B, 1948). Recipient, Outstanding Alumni Professional Award, Northwestern Oklahoma State University. Listed in *The Best Lawyers in America,* all Editions, 1977-2000. Member, United States Air University Board of Visitors, 1969-1971. Visiting Faculty Member, Hastings College of Advocacy, San Francisco. Member: University of Oklahoma Foundation; University of Oklahoma College of Law Foundation; Northwestern Oklahoma State University Foundation. *Member:* Oklahoma County (Past Member, Board of Directors), Oklahoma (Past Member, Board of Governors) and American Bar Associations; American Board of Trial Advocates; Federation of Insurance and Corporate Counsel; International Association of Defense Counsel; Defense Research Institute; Trial Attorneys of America; Oklahoma Association of Defense Counsel (Lifetime Achievement Award). Fellow: American College of Trial Lawyers; International Academy of Trial Lawyers; International Society of Barristers; Oklahoma Bar Foundation. ***PRACTICE AREAS:*** Personal Injury Law; Medical Malpractice Law; Professional Liability Law; Products Liability Law; Insurance Law.

GLEN D. HUFF, born Altus, Oklahoma, October 16, 1949; admitted to bar, 1975, Oklahoma. *Education:* University of Oklahoma (B.A., 1970; J.D., 1975). Phi Delta Phi. Associate Editor, Oklahoma Law Review, 1973-1974. *Member:* Oklahoma County, Oklahoma and American Bar Associations; Federation of Insurance and Corporate Counsel; Oklahoma Association of Defense Counsel (President, 1986-1987; Past Member, Board of Governors); American Academy of Healthcare Attorneys; American Board of Trial Advocates (President, Oklahoma Chapter, 1999); National Health Lawyers Association; Oklahoma Health Lawyers Association; Oklahoma Hospital Association; Defense Research Institute; American Society of Law & Medicine; American College of Forensic Examiners; American Inns of Court (Master). ***PRACTICE AREAS:*** Medical Malpractice Law; Health Care Law; Professional Liability Law; Class Actions; Insurance Law. ***Email:*** glenhuff@oklahomacounsel.com

LARRY D. OTTAWAY, born Stillwater, Oklahoma, November 1, 1948; admitted to bar, 1974, Oklahoma. *Education:* University of Oklahoma (B.A., 1971; J.D., 1974). Phi Eta Sigma; Phi Beta Kappa. *Member:* Oklahoma County, Oklahoma and American (Co-Chairman, Sub-Committee on Products Liability, 1979-1983; Member, Sub-Committee on Medical Devices, 1985-1986) Bar Associations; International Bar Association; Oklahoma Association of Defense Counsel; The Association of Trial Lawyers of America; International Association of Defense Counsel; International Association of Defense Counsel Trial Academy Faculty; American Academy of Healthcare Attorneys; American Board of Trial Advocates (Member, National Board, 1986. Chairman, Region 6, 1991); American Inns of Court (Master Emeritus); Defense Research Institute. Fellow: Oklahoma Bar Foundation; American College of Trial Lawyers. ***PRACTICE AREAS:*** Personal Injury Law; Products Liability Law; Medical Malpractice Law; Professional Liability Law; Insurance Law. ***Email:*** larryottaway@oklahomacounsel.com

MONTY B. BOTTOM, born Sentinel, Oklahoma, January 30, 1957; admitted to bar, 1982, Oklahoma; 2000, Texas. *Education:* Southwestern Oklahoma State University (B.S., 1979); University of Notre Dame (J.D., 1982). *Member:* Oklahoma County, Oklahoma and American Bar Associations; American Board of Trial Advocates; Oklahoma Association of Defense Counsel; Defense Research Institute. ***PRACTICE AREAS:*** Personal Injury Law; Medical Malpractice Law; Professional Liability Law; Products Liability Law; Insurance Law. ***Email:*** montybottom@oklahomacounsel.com

MICHAEL C. FELTY, born Dayton, Ohio, August 16, 1954; admitted to bar, 1984, Oklahoma; 1995, Texas; registered to practice before U.S. Patent and Trademark Office. *Education:* Cameron University (B.S., 1981); University of Oklahoma (J.D., 1984). *Member:* Oklahoma County, Oklahoma and American Bar Associations; State Bar of Texas; International Association of Defense Counsel; Defense Research Institute; Oklahoma Association of Defense Counsel (President, 1997; Member, Board of Directors, 1994-1998). ***PRACTICE AREAS:*** Litigation; Product Liability; Transportation; Insurance; Intellectual Property; Commercial Litigation. ***Email:*** michaelfelty@oklahomacounsel.com

SUSAN A. SHORT, born Oklahoma City, Oklahoma, July 16, 1953; admitted to bar, 1985, Oklahoma. *Education:* University of Oklahoma (B.S.N., 1976; J.D., 1985). American Inns of Court (Barrister). *Member:* Oklahoma County, Oklahoma and American Bar Associations; Oklahoma Association of Defense Counsel; Oklahoma Health Lawyers Association; Defense Research Institute. ***PRACTICE AREAS:*** Medical Malpractice Law; Health Care Law; Professional Liability Law; Antitrust Law. ***Email:*** susanshort@oklahomacounsel.com

DAVID A. BRANSCUM, born Galveston, Texas, December 31, 1960; admitted to bar, 1986, Oklahoma; 1990, Minnesota. *Education:* St. Olaf College (B.A., 1983); University of Oklahoma (J.D., 1986). Author, "Duty of Hospitals in Oklahoma: How will Oklahoma's New Uniform Jury Instruction 14.6 Be Applied?" 65 Oklahoma Bar Association J.31, P. 2644, July 30, 1994. *Member:* Oklahoma County, Oklahoma and American Bar Associations; Oklahoma Association of Defense Counsel; National Health Lawyers Association; Oklahoma Health Lawyers Association; Defense Research Institute. ***PRACTICE AREAS:*** Medical Malpractice Law; Health Care Law; Professional Liability Law; Insurance Law; Personal Injury Law. ***Email:*** davidbranscum@oklahomacounsel.com

DAVID K. McPHAIL, born Oklahoma City, Oklahoma, August 3, 1964; admitted to bar, 1989, Oklahoma. *Education:* University of Oklahoma (B.B.A., 1986; J.D., 1989). Phi Delta Phi; Phi Alpha Delta. Note Editor, Oklahoma Law Review, 1988-1989. Author: "Bankruptcy: Determination of an Appropriate Cram-down Interest Rate for the Family Farmer," Oklahoma Law Review, Vol. 41, No. 3, p. 489. Barrister, Robert J. Turner American Inn of Court. *Member:* Oklahoma County, Oklahoma and American Bar Associations; The Association of Trial Lawyers of America; Oklahoma Association of Defense Counsel; Oklahoma Health Lawyers Association; Defense Research Institute. ***PRACTICE AREAS:*** Medical Malpractice Law; Nursing Home Litigation; Nursing Home Abuse and Neglect; Health Care Law; Professional Liability Law; Insurance Law; Products Liability Law; Personal Injury Law. ***Email:*** davidmcphail@oklahomacounsel.com

MICHAEL T. MALOAN, born Corpus Christi, Texas, February 8, 1967; admitted to bar, 1993, Oklahoma. *Education:* Trinity University (B.A., 1989); University of Oklahoma (J.D., with honors, 1993). Associate, Robert J Turner American Inn of Court, 1999-2001. Note Editor, Oklahoma Law Review, 1992-1993; Alley-Allen Memorial Prize for Best Case Note, 1992. Author: "Federal Jurisdiction and Practice: The American National Red Cross and the Interpretation of 'Sue and Be Sued' Clauses", 45 Okla. L.R. 739 (1993). *Member:* Oklahoma County, Oklahoma and American Bar Associations; Oklahoma Association of Defense Counsel; Defense Research Institute. ***PRACTICE AREAS:*** Medical Malpractice Law; Professional Liability Law; Insurance Law; Personal Injury Law; Products Liability Law; Environmental Law. ***Email:*** michaelmaloan@oklahomacounsel.com

ROBERT D. HOISINGTON, born Enid, Oklahoma, January 8, 1968; admitted to bar, 1993, Oklahoma. *Education:* Oklahoma State University (B.A., 1990); University of Oklahoma (J.D., with distinction, 1993). Order of Barristers. N.T.L.A. Trial Team, University of Oklahoma, 1993. Recipient: Albert C. Hurt Practice Court Award; American Jurisprudence Award, Secured Transactions; Academic Achievement, Water Law. *Member:* Oklahoma Bar Association; Defense Research Institute; American Trial Lawyers Association; Luther Bohanon American Inn of Court. ***PRACTICE AREAS:*** Medical Malpractice Law; Insurance Law; Civil Practice. ***Email:*** roberthoisington@oklahomacounsel.com

AMY SHERRY FISCHER, born Lawton, Oklahoma, August 13, 1970; admitted to bar, 1995, Oklahoma. *Education:* University of Tulsa (B.A., 1992); University of Oklahoma (J.D., with distinction, 1995). Phi Delta Phi. Recipient: Academic Achievement Award, Secured Transactions. *Member:* Oklahoma County, Oklahoma and American Bar Associations; Oklahoma Association of Defense Counsel; Defense Research Institute. ***PRACTICE AREAS:*** Insurance Law; Medical Malpractice Law; Products Liability; Professional Liability Law; Personal Injury Law. ***Email:*** amyfischer@oklahomacounsel.com

DENISE D. CANADA, born El Dorado, Arkansas, May 6, 1956; admitted to bar, 1996, Oklahoma. *Education:* Oklahoma City University; University of Oklahoma (B.A., 1979; J.D., with distinction, 1996). Phi Delta Phi. Associate Editor, American Indian Law Review. Member, Moot Court Board. Recipient: American Jurisprudence Award, Legal Research and Writing II; Academic Achievement Award, Insurance Law; Oklahoma City University School of Law Merit Scholar; ATLA Student Trial Advocacy Competition. *Member:* Oklahoma County, Oklahoma and American Bar Associations; Oklahoma Association of Defense Counsel; Defense Research Institute. ***PRACTICE AREAS:*** Medical Malpractice Law; Health Care Law; Employment Law. ***Email:*** denisedcanada@oklahomacounsel.com

---

STEVEN JAMES JOHNSON, born Shattuck, Oklahoma, January 13, 1970; admitted to bar, 1995, Oklahoma. *Education:* Oklahoma State University (B.B.A., 1992); University of Oklahoma (J.D., 1995). Recipient, Academic Achievement Award, Employment Law. *Member:* Oklahoma County, Oklahoma and American Bar Associations; Oklahoma Association of Defense Counsel; Defense Research Institute; Ruth Bader Ginsburg American Inn of Court. ***PRACTICE AREAS:*** Medical Malpractice Law; Health Care Law; Nursing Home Negligence; Personal Injury. ***Email:*** stevenjohnson@oklahomacounsel.com

WHITNEY E. BUERGLER, born Richmond, Virginia, June 10, 1976; admitted to bar, 2001, Oklahoma. *Education:* Oklahoma State University (B.A., 1998); University of Oklahoma (J.D., 2001). *Member:* Oklahoma Bar Association; Oklahoma Association of Defense Counsel. ***PRACTICE AREAS:*** Medical Malpractice; Health Care; Insurance. ***Email:*** whitneybuergler@oklahomacounsel.com

AMANDA F. MILLER, born Clearwater, Florida, February 1, 1975; admitted to bar, 2001, Oklahoma. *Education:* University of Oklahoma (B.A., 1998; J.D., with Distinction, 2001). Recipient: American Jurisprudence Award, Legislation and the Courts; Moot Court Finalist. *Member:* Oklahoma County and Oklahoma Bar Associations; Defense Research Institute; Oklahoma Association of Defense Counsel. ***PRACTICE AREAS:*** Medical Malpractice; Health Care; Insurance. ***Email:*** amandamiller@oklahomacounsel.com

JASON T. ROGERS, born Fort Smith, Arkansas, October 4, 1974; admitted to bar, 1999, Oklahoma and U.S. District Court, Eastern District of Oklahoma; U.S. District Court, Western District of Oklahoma. *Education:* Oklahoma State University (B.S., 1996); University of Oklahoma (J.D., with Distinction, 1999). Phi Delta Phi. *Member:* Oklahoma Bar Association. ***PRACTICE AREAS:*** Insurance; Products Liability; Medical Malpractice; Personal Injury. ***Email:*** jasonrogers@oklahomacounsel.com

LARRY H. HARDEN, born Ada, Oklahoma, April 5,1972; admitted to bar, 2000, Oklahoma; U.S. District Court, Western District of Oklahoma. *Education:* Oklahoma State University (B.S., Agricultural Economics, 1997); Oklahoma City University School of Law (J.D., 2000). Assistant District Attorney, 23rd District Attorney's Office, State of Oklahoma, 2000-2003. Member, Oklahoma Bar Association, House of Delegates, 2000, 2001 and 2002. *Member:* Oklahoma County Bar Association; Oklahoma Bar Association; American Bar Association; Defense Research Institute; Oklahoma Association of Defense Counsel. Fellow, Oklahoma Bar Foundation. ***PRACTICE AREAS:*** Medical Malpractice; Health Care; Insurance. ***Email:*** larryharden@oklahomacounsel.com

BLAKE D. BEELER, born Oklahoma City, Oklahoma, December 16, 1975; admitted to bar, 2003, Oklahoma. *Education:* University of Oklahoma (B.A., 1998; J.D., 2002). *Member:* Oklahoma Bar Association; Defense Research Institute. ***PRACTICE AREAS:*** Insurance; Products Liability; Medical Malpractice; Personal Injury. ***Email:*** blakebeeler@oklahomacounsel.com

REPRESENTATIVE CLIENTS: Agora Syndicate, Inc.; Alpha Care Properties, it's nursing homes; Aluminum Company of America; Amberwood Nursing Center, Oklahoma City; American International Companies; American International Group; Amsted Industries; Bayer Corporation; Blue Cross/Blue Shield of Oklahoma; Boise Cascado; Century American Insurance Co.; Chrysler Corp.; CNA HealthPro; The Coleman Company, Inc.; Columbia/HCA Healthcare Corporation; Community Health Systems, Inc.; Consolidated Freightways, Inc.; Ethicon, Inc.; GAN North American Insurance; Grace Living Centers, it's nursing homes; Gulf Insurance Co.; Highland Park manor, Enid, Oklahoma; Homeland Stores, Inc.; Honda North America, Inc.; Integris Baptist Medical Center; Integris Health, Oklahoma City; Janssen Pharmaceuticals; Johnson & Johnson ; Maryland Casualty Company; Medical Protective Ins.; Nissan North America, Inc.; Pfizer, Inc.; Oklahoma Blood Institute; Physicians Liability Insurance Co.; Platte River Insurance Company; Primerica Financial Services; Reliance In-

(This Listing Continued)

FOLIART, HUFF, OTTAWAY & BOTTOM, A PROFESSIONAL CORPORATION, Oklahoma City—Continued

surance Co.; Republic Insurance Group; The St. Paul Insurance Cos.; G. D. Searle & Co.; Sentry Insurance Co.; SSM Healthcare; Southwest Health Care Management, Inc.; Spectrum Emergency Care, Inc.; Syntex (U.S.A.) Inc.; Tamarack American; Tenet Health System; Zurich; Travelers Insurance Company; Western Heritage Insurance Company, it's insured nursing homes; Zurich Insurance Company.

FULLER, TUBB, POMEROY & STOKES

A PROFESSIONAL CORPORATION

Established in 1964

1000 BANK OF OKLAHOMA PLAZA
201 ROBERT S. KERR AVENUE
OKLAHOMA CITY, OKLAHOMA 73102
Telephone: 405-235-2575
Fax: 405-232-8384
Email: ftps@ftpslaw.com
URL: http://www.ftpslaw.com

General Practice, Litigation, Bankruptcy, Bankruptcy Reorganization, Commercial Workouts, Corporate, Corporate Finance, Real Estate, Probate, Estate Planning, Administrative Law, Commercial Law, Alternative Dispute Resolution, Arbitration, Mediation, Securities, Appellate Practice, Employment Law, Insolvency, Debtor/Creditor Rights.

G. M. FULLER (1920-1999)

JERRY TUBB, born Oklahoma City, Oklahoma, July 3, 1939; admitted to bar, 1964, Oklahoma. *Education:* University of Oklahoma (B.A., 1961; LL.B., 1964). Phi Alpha Delta; Order of the Coif. *Member:* Oklahoma County (Member, Board of Directors, 1967-1969; President, 1981-1982), Oklahoma (Member, Board of Governors, 1988-1990; Member, 1972-1983 and Chairman, 1978, Oklahoma Board of Bar Examiners; Vice-Chairman, 1986 and Chairman, 1987, Professional Responsibility Commission) and American Bar Associations. Fellow: American Bar Foundation; Oklahoma Bar Foundation (Trustee, 1992, 1993; Vice-President, 1995-1996; President, 1996-1997); American Arbitration Association. ***PRACTICE AREAS:*** Commercial Law; Bankruptcy Law; Commercial Workouts; Mediation. ***Email:*** jtubb@ftpslaw.com

L. DAVID POMEROY, born Bartlesville, Oklahoma, March 23, 1941; admitted to bar, 1966, Oklahoma. *Education:* University of Oklahoma (B.B.A., 1964; LL.B., 1966). Phi Alpha Delta. Member, Board of Editors, Oklahoma Law Review, 1964-1966. *Member:* Oklahoma County (Member, Board of Directors, 1983-1996; President, 1992-1993; President, Board of Trustees, Oklahoma County Law Library, 1987-1990), Oklahoma (Member: Board of Governors, 1998-2000; Professional Responsibility Tribunal) and American (Delegate, 1995-1996) Bar Associations; American Inn of Court CV (Master Emeritus). Fellow: American Bar Foundation; Oklahoma Bar Foundation (Trustee, 2001—). ***REPORTED CASES:*** Marine Midland Business Loans, Inc. vs. Patricia G. Carey 938 F.2d 1073 (10th Cir. 1991); Teachers Ins. and Annuity Ass'n of America vs. Oklahoma Tower Associates Ltd. Partnership, 798 P.2d 618 (Okla. 1990); Commodore Home Systems v. Citicorp Acceptance Co., 780 P.2d 674 (Okla. 1989); State v. Guardian Life Ins. Co., 1997 Ok 10, P. 2d. ***PRACTICE AREAS:*** General Practice; Commercial Law; Bankruptcy; Litigation; Mediation. ***Email:*** dpomeroy@ftpslaw.com

TERRY STOKES, born Fort Worth, Texas, November 29, 1959; admitted to bar, 1985, Oklahoma, U.S. District Court, Northern, Eastern and Western Districts of Oklahoma and U.S. Court of Appeals, Tenth Circuit. *Education:* Oklahoma Christian University of Science and Arts (B.S., Accounting, 1982); Oklahoma City University (J.D., 1984). Phi Delta Phi. *Member:* Oklahoma County, Oklahoma and American Bar Associations; American Inn of Court CV (Barrister). ***REPORTED CASES:*** Marine Midland Business Loans, Inc. vs. Patricia G. Carey 938 F.2d 1073 (10th Cir. 1991); Teachers Insurance and Annuity Association of America vs. Oklahoma Tower Associates Ltd. Partnership, 798 P.2d 618 (Okla. 1990); Norwest Colorado, Inc. v. Partridge Capitol Corp. and Joe R. Love, 891 P.2d 624 (Okla. App. 1995). ***PRACTICE AREAS:*** General Civil Practice; Commercial Law; Labor and Employment; Litigation; Appellate Practice. ***Email:*** tstokes@ftpslaw.com

OF COUNSEL

MICHAEL A. BICKFORD, born Blackwell, Oklahoma, August 16, 1958; admitted to bar, 1983, Oklahoma; 1986, U.S. Tax Court; 1999, Alaska. *Education:* University of Oklahoma (B.B.A., 1979; J.D., 1983). Order of the Coif. Member, Board of Editors, Oklahoma Law Review, 1982-1983. *Member:* Oklahoma County, Oklahoma, Alaska and American Bar Associations; American Institute of Certified Public Accountants. ***PRACTICE AREAS:*** Commercial Law; Bankruptcy; Litigation; Tax Controversies; Tax Planning; Estate Planning. ***Email:*** mabick@abanet.org

THOMAS J. KENAN, born January 12, 1932; admitted to bar, 1958, Oklahoma; 1965, U.S. Supreme Court; 1966, U.S. District Court, Western District of Oklahoma; 1968, U.S. Court of Appeals, Tenth Circuit. *Education:* University of Oklahoma (B.A., 1953; LL.B., 1958); New York University (LL.M., 1959); University of Paris, Paris, France. Order of the Coif; Phi Beta Kappa. Member, Board of Editors, Oklahoma Law Review, 1956-1958. Lecturer in Law, New York University Law School, 1961 and Oklahoma City University, College of Law, 1971. Legislative Assistant to Rep. Carl Albert, Majority Leader, U.S. House of Representatives, 1962-1966. *Member:* Oklahoma Bar Association (Associate Bar Examiner, Oklahoma Board of Bar Examiners, 1968-1980). ***PRACTICE AREAS:*** Securities; Bankruptcy; Corporate. ***Email:*** kenan@ftpslaw.com

ROLAND TAGUE, born Oklahoma City, Oklahoma, April 28, 1940; admitted to bar, 1965, Oklahoma; 1969, U.S. Supreme Court. *Education:* University of Oklahoma (B.B.A., 1962; J.D., 1965). Phi Alpha Delta (Secretary, 1963-1965). Assistant Municipal Counselor, Oklahoma City, 1965-1972. *Member:* Oklahoma County Bar Association (Outstanding Young Lawyer, 1972; Director, 1975-1977; 1994-1996; Chairman, Alternative Dispute Resolution Committee, 1996-1999); Oklahoma Bar Association; Oklahoma City Real

(This Listing Continued)

Property Lawyers Association (President, 1996). ***PRACTICE AREAS:*** Real Property; Commercial; Land Use; Probate; Civil Litigation; Mediation. ***Email:*** tague@ftpslaw.com

DAN M. PETERS, born Oklahoma City, Oklahoma, January 23, 1957; admitted to bar, 1982, Oklahoma; U.S. Supreme Court, U.S. Court of Appeals, Tenth Circuit and U.S. District Court, Northern, Eastern and Western Districts of Oklahoma. *Education:* Oklahoma State University (B.S., 1979); University of Oklahoma (J.D., 1982). Assistant Attorney General, Oklahoma, 1990-1995. General Counsel, Oklahoma Department of Labor, 1995-1996. *Member:* Oklahoma County, Oklahoma Bar Associations. ***PRACTICE AREAS:*** Business Litigation; Consumer Litigation; Commercial Litigation; Labor and Employment; Civil Rights Litigation; Administrative Law. ***Email:*** dpeters@ftpslaw.com

LEGAL SUPPORT PERSONNEL

SHERIE S. ADAMS, born Fort Worth, Texas, March 24, 1944. *Education:* Midwestern State University; University of Oklahoma Law Center (Legal Asst. Certificate, 1987). Certified Legal Assistant (CLA), 1988; Civil Litigation Specialist (CLAS), 1989. *Member:* National Association of Legal Assistants. (Legal Assistant). ***PRACTICE AREAS:*** General Practice; Securities. ***Email:*** adams@ftpslaw.com

REPRESENTATIVE CLIENTS: Key Bank; DVI Financial Services, Inc.; Ellis Construction Specialties; Fidelity Union Life Insurance Co.; First Mortgage Company, L.L.C.; Driftwood Hospitality Management, Inc.; ITT Hartford; Oklahoma Association of Insurance Agents; Pitney Bowes, Inc.; Steve Owens & Associates; Taber Brokerage Services; Taco Cabana; Weokie Credit Union.; Peachtree Settlement Funding LLC; Southern Hospitality, Inc.; Boynton Williams & Associates; C-P Integrated Services, Inc.; Earlsboro Energies Corporation; First Bank and Trust Company, Perry, OK; Harcourt, Inc.; HSBC North America; Household Finance Corp.

GABLE & GOTWALS

A PROFESSIONAL CORPORATION

FIFTEENTH FLOOR, ONE LEADERSHIP SQUARE
211 NORTH ROBINSON AVENUE
OKLAHOMA CITY, OKLAHOMA 73102-7101
Telephone: 405-235-5500
Fax: 405-235-2875
Email: info@gablelaw.com
URL: http://www.gablelaw.com

Tulsa, Oklahoma Offices: 1100 Oneok Plaza, 100 West Fifth Street 74103-4217. Telephone: 918-595-4800. Fax: 918-595-4990.

Administrative Law, Alternative Dispute Resolution, Antitrust, Bankruptcy, Banks and Banking, Class Actions, Commercial Law, Communications and Media, Copyright, Corporate Law, Employee Benefits, Energy, Environmental Law, Family Law, Finance, Franchises and Franchising, General Practice, Guardianship and Conservatorship, Insurance, Intellectual Property, Labor and Employment, Litigation, Mergers, Acquisitions and Divestitures, Natural Resources, Patents, Personal Injury, Probate, Property Law, Real Estate, RICO, Regulatory Law, Securities, Software Licensing, Taxation, Trademarks, Torts, Utility Law, Workers Compensation.

FIRM PROFILE: Gable & Gotwals is a full-service law firm representing a diversified client base in Oklahoma, the Southwest and across the nation. The firm provides efficient, professional and ethical representation for all clients at competitive rates. With expertise ranging from energy litigation and labor law to the rapidly evolving specialties of ADR, technology and intellectual property -- ensure Gable & Gotwals has the depth to serve both small and large clients. Though Oklahoma-based, our connections and reach are global. Fortune 500 corporations, entrepreneurs, privately owned companies, foundations and individuals entrust us every day with the stewardship and strategic management of their legal challenges.

LEADERSHIP SQUARE OFFICE PERSONNEL

STEVEN L. BARGHOLS, born Cherokee, Iowa, 1951; admitted to bar, 1976, Oklahoma. *Education:* Drake University; University of Oklahoma (B.A., 1973); University of Texas (J.D., 1976). Phi Beta Kappa. President, 1996-1997, Vice President, 1995-1996 and Member, Board of Directors, 1991-1998, Oklahoma County Bar Association. Member, mediation and arbitration panels certified by U.S.D.C., Western District of Oklahoma. President, Oklahoma County Bar Foundation, 1995—. Fellow: American Bar Foundation. ***PRACTICE AREAS:*** Oil and Gas Law; Mediation and Arbitration; Litigation. ***Email:*** sbarghols@gablelaw.com

SIDNEY G. DUNAGAN, born McLeansboro, Illinois, 1943; admitted to bar, 1968, Oklahoma. *Education:* University of Tulsa (B.A., 1965; J.D., 1967). Editor-in-Chief, Tulsa Law Journal, 1967. Judge, Temporary Court of Appeals, 1981 and 1991. Member, Board of Governors, 1984-1986, Vice President, 1987 and President, 1994, Oklahoma Bar Association. Trustee, Oklahoma Bar Foundation, 1992-1993. President, Tulsa County Bar Association, 1990-1991. Member, House of Delegates, American Bar Association, 1993-1994. Fellow: American Bar Foundation (State Chairman, Oklahoma Fellows, 1989-1991); American College of Trial Lawyers. ***PRACTICE AREAS:*** Oil and Gas Litigation; Professional Liability; Products Liability; Complex Litigation; Construction Law. ***Email:*** sdunagan@gablelaw.com

DAVID L. KEARNEY, born Piqua, Ohio, 1960; admitted to bar, 1985, Oklahoma. *Education:* University of Oklahoma (B.B.A., 1982; J.D., with distinction, 1985). ***PRACTICE AREAS:*** Oil and Gas Law; Commercial Litigation; Insurance Law. ***Email:*** dkearney@gablelaw.com

ERIC R. KING, born Wembley, England, 1946; admitted to bar, 1976, Oklahoma. *Education:* Oklahoma Christian College (B.S.E., 1970); University of Oklahoma (J.D., 1976). President, Mineral Lawyers Society of Oklahoma City, 1992-1993. ***PRACTICE AREAS:*** Oil and Gas Law; Energy Law; Public Utility Law; Environmental Litigation; Administrative Law; Title Examination; Condemnation Litigation; Real Estate. ***Email:*** eking@gablelaw.com

ROB F.M. ROBERTSON, born Oklahoma City, Oklahoma, 1961; admitted to bar, 1987, Oklahoma. *Education:* University of Oklahoma (B.B.A., with special distinction,

(This Listing Continued)

1984; J.D., with highest honors, 1987). Order of the Coif. Oklahoma Law Review. ***PRACTICE AREAS:*** Energy; Natural Resources; Civil Business Litigation; Public Utilities; Environmental Litigation; Real Estate Litigation; Oil and Gas Law; Administrative Law. ***Email:*** rrobertson@gablelaw.com

LEASA M. STEWART, born Guthrie, Oklahoma, 1966; admitted to bar, 1991, Texas; 1999, Oklahoma. *Education:* University of Oklahoma (B.S., with special distinction, 1988); Georgetown University (J.D., cum laude, 1991). Phi Beta Kappa. Administrative Editor, Georgetown International Environmental Law Review, 1990-1991. *Member:* Federal Bar Association; Defense Research Institute. ***PRACTICE AREAS:*** Oil and Gas Litigation; Civil Business Litigation; Insurance Litigation; Public Utilities; Appellate Practice. ***Email:*** lstewart@gablelaw.com

ASSOCIATES

JOHN MARTIN BENSON, born Duncan, Oklahoma, 1976; admitted to bar, 2001, Oklahoma. *Education:* University of Oklahoma (B.A., Political Science, with distinction, 1998; J.D., with highest honors, 2001). Order of the Coif. ***PRACTICE AREAS:*** Civil Litigation; Energy Law; Business Organization. ***Email:*** jbenson@gablelaw.com

DANIEL A. NICKEL, born Wichita, Kansas, 1979; admitted to bar, 2004, Oklahoma. *Education:* Wichita State University (B.B.A., 2000); University of Oklahoma (J.D., 2004). Member, University of Oklahoma Law Review, 2002-2003. ***PRACTICE AREAS:*** Civil Litigation; Oil and Gas Law; Business Organization. ***Email:*** dnickel@gablelaw.com

AMY M. STIPE, born Tacoma, Washington, 1973; admitted to bar, 1999, Oklahoma. *Education:* University of Oklahoma (B.A., 1995; J.D., with honors, 1999). Phi Delta Phi. Order of the Coif. Member, William J. Holloway, Jr., American Inns of Court. President, Mineral Lawyers Society of Oklahoma City. Judge's Committee Officer, Oklahoma Board of Advocates, 1997-1998. ***PRACTICE AREAS:*** Civil Litigation; Oil and Gas Law; Insurance Litigation; Business Litigation. ***Email:*** astipe@gablelaw.com

JEREMY K. WEBB, born 1976; admitted to bar, 2002, Texas (Not admitted in Oklahoma). *Education:* University of Oklahoma (B.A., summa cum laude, 1999); University of Virginia (J.D., 2002). Article/Notes Editor, Virginia Journal of Law and Politics. ***PRACTICE AREAS:*** Litigation; Labor and Employment. ***Email:*** jwebb@gablelaw.com

OF COUNSEL

LINDA A. KING, born Temple, Texas, 1947; admitted to bar, 1977, Oklahoma. *Education:* Oklahoma Christian College (B.A., 1969); University of Oklahoma (J.D., 1977). President, Mineral Lawyers Society of Oklahoma City, 1999-2000. ***PRACTICE AREAS:*** Oil and Gas Law; Title Examination; Real Estate. ***Email:*** lking@gablelaw.com

JOSEPH T. THAI, admitted to bar, 1998, Illinois; 1999, Massachusetts; 2001, U.S. Court of Appeals, Tenth Circuit and U.S. District Court, District of Massachusetts; 2002, Oklahoma. *Education:* Harvard University (A.B., English, summa cum laude, 1995; J.D., cum laude, 1998). Phi Beta Kappa. Executive Editor, Harvard Journal of Law and Public Policy, 1998. Recipient, John Harvard Scholarship; Stride-Rite Scholarship. Law Clerk to: Judge David M. Ebel, U.S. Court of Appeals, Tenth Circuit, Denver, Colorado, 1998-1999; Justice John Paul Stevens and Justice Byron R. White (retired), U.S. Supreme Court, 2000-2001. Assistant Attorney General, Criminal Appellate Division, Office of the Attorney General, Boston, MA., 1999-2000. *Member:* Massachusetts and Illinois State Bar Associations. ***LANGUAGES:*** Vietnamese. ***PRACTICE AREAS:*** Appellate Practice; Litigation; Criminal Law; Civil Rights. ***Email:*** jthai@gablelaw.com

(For complete biographical data on other personnel, see Professional Biographies at Tulsa, Oklahoma)

GARVIN, AGEE, CARLTON & MASHBURN, L.L.P.

2100 CITY PLACE TOWER
204 NORTH ROBINSON AVENUE
OKLAHOMA CITY, OKLAHOMA 73102
Telephone: 405-232-9996
Fax: 405-232-9979
URL: http://www.attysatlaw.com

Pauls Valley Office: 101 E. Grant Avenue, P.O. Box 10, 73075. Telephone: 405-238-5559. Fax: 405-238-5666.

General Civil Practice. Personal Injury, Property Damage, Products Liability, Insurance and Commercial Litigation. Real Estate, Probate, Estate Planning and Trusts. Oil and Gas, Business, Commercial, Banking, Bankruptcy, Collections, Employment, School and Municipal Law.

(For Complete Biographical Data on all Personnel see Professional Biographies at Pauls Valley)

THE GOODING LAW FIRM

A PROFESSIONAL CORPORATION
Established in 1989
1200 CITY PLACE BUILDING
204 N. ROBINSON
OKLAHOMA CITY, OKLAHOMA 73102
Telephone: 405-948-1978
Telecopier: 405-948-0864
Email: cgooding@goodingfirm.com
URL: http://www.goodingfirm.com

General, Civil, Criminal, Commercial, Bankruptcy, Personal Injury and Insurance Litigation.

FIRM PROFILE: The Gooding Law firm prides itself on being able to offer the same services as larger law firms, but with all the qualities and advantages of a small law firm. The firm's clients range in size from fortune 500 companies to the family owned business to individuals. The Gooding Law Firm, P.C. is listed in the Bar Register of Preeminent Lawyers.

(This Listing Continued)

O. CLIFTON GOODING, born Paris, Texas, October 8, 1959; admitted to bar, 1983, Oklahoma, U.S. Supreme Court, U.S. Court of Appeals, Tenth Circuit, U.S. District Court, Western, Eastern and Northern Districts of Oklahoma and U.S. District Court, Northern and Western Districts of Texas. *Education:* Oklahoma State University (B.S., 1980); University of Oklahoma (J.D., 1983). Phi Kappa Phi; Phi Alpha Delta; Order of the Coif. Recipient, American Jurisprudence Award in Torts and Property, 1980. Editor and Chairman, Judiciary Committee, Oklahoma Law Review, 1982-1983. Lecturer, Business Law, University of Oklahoma, 1982-1983. State Secretary, Oklahoma Democratic Party, 1989-1991. *Member:* Oklahoma County, Oklahoma and American Bar Associations. ***PRACTICE AREAS:*** Trial Practice; Civil Litigation; Criminal Law. ***Email:*** cgooding@goodingfirm.com

REPRESENTATIVE CLIENTS: General Electric Capital Corp.; Bank of Hydro; Citizens State Bank; First National Bank & Trust Co.; Guarantee State Bank; First Capital Bank of Guthrie; Mobil Mining & Minerals, Inc.; Emprise Bank, NA; Pacific States Transport; Independent Freightways; Dixie Liquor Co.; Con Agra Fertilizer Co.; Health Care Property Investors, Inc.; Capps Insurance Agency, Inc.; First National Bank & Trust Co. of Shawnee; BancFirst; PHI Financial Services, Inc.; Pioneer Seed, Inc.; H&R Accounts; Nebraska Farm Bureau Insurance Co.; Deutsche Financial Services Corp.; Armed Forces Insurance; Countrywide Home Loans, Inc.; Hibernia National Bank; BOK Mortgage; Superior Bank; Citi Mortgage; Extraco Mortgage; Washington Mutual; VW Credit, Inc.; Wells Fargo Home Mortgage Inc.; Union Acceptance Corp.; Commercial Federal Bank, FSB; Union Federal Bank of Indianapolis; State Farm, FSB; Kansas Bankers Security; Wexford & James, Inc.; H&R Accounts; D&S Limited; Naeda Financial, Ltd., L.P.; Capital Abstracr & Title Company; McClain Bank, N.A.

LOUIS MITCHELL GREEN

3555 N.W. 58TH STREET, SUITE 510
OKLAHOMA CITY, OKLAHOMA 73112
Telephone: 405-942-8292
Fax: 405-942-8362
Email: lmitchgreen@netscape.net
URL: http://www.okclemonlaw.com

Lemon Law, Consumer Fraud, Consumer Protection, Warranties, Mobile Homes, Odometer Fraud, Fair Debt Collection, Fair Credit Reporting, Equal Credit Opportunity Act.

LOUIS MITCHELL GREEN, born New York City, New York, 1962; admitted to bar, 1988, Oklahoma; U.S. Court of Appeals, Tenth Circuit. *Education:* University of Texas at Austin (B.A., 1984); Oklahoma City University School of Law (J.D., 1987). Phi Alpha Delta. *Member:* Oklahoma Bar Association; National Association of Consumer Advocates. ***PRACTICE AREAS:*** Lemon Law; Consumer Fraud; Consumer Protection; Warranty Law; Fair Debt Collection Practices Act; Fair Credit Reporting Act.

GREEN, JAMES & WILLIAMS

Established in 1966
601 N.W. 13TH STREET
P.O. BOX 2248
OKLAHOMA CITY, OKLAHOMA 73101-2248
Telephone: 405-525-0033
Fax: 405-525-0528
Email: gjw@flash.net

Fire, Inland Marine, Casualty and Insurance Law. Toxic Substances and Structural Failures, including Toxic Mold, Defense Law. Products Liability, Personal Injury, Probate, Family Law, Civil Trials in all Courts and Adoption.

CLARENCE P. GREEN (1921-1999)

EARL G. WILLIAMS (1926-2003)

MICKEY JAMES, born Norman, Oklahoma, February, 1940; admitted to bar, 1966, Oklahoma. *Education:* Oklahoma City University (B.A., 1963; J.D., 1966). Phi Alpha Delta. *Member:* Oklahoma County (Member, Grievance and Ethics Committee, 1977-1982), Oklahoma (Member, Grievance and Ethics Committee, 1978-1982) and American Bar Associations. ***REPORTED CASES:*** Clark v. Brien, et al (Underwriters at Lloyd's London), 59 F.3d 1082 (10th Cir. 1995), cert. den. 116 S.Ct. 800; London v. Trinity Cos., Trinity Universal Ins. Co. of Kansas, Inc. 877 P.2d 620 (Okl.App. 1994); Rogers v. Kansas City Fire & Marine, 871 P.2d 443 (Okl.App. 1994); Williamson v. EMASCO Ins. Co., 696 F.Supp. 1583 (W.D. Okla. 1988); Vaughn v. Chrysler Corp., 442 F.2d 619, cert. den., 92 S.Ct. 106 (10th Cir. 1971); DeMik v. Cargill, 485 P.2d 229 (Okl. 1971), 58 ALR3d 1042.

MARCIE JAMES, born Norman, Oklahoma, November, 1940; admitted to bar, 1982, Oklahoma. *Education:* University of Oklahoma (B.B.A., 1962; J.D., 1982). Phi Alpha Delta. *Member:* Oklahoma County, Oklahoma (Member, Family Law Section) and American Bar Associations.

LEGAL SUPPORT PERSONNEL

PATRICIA FRAKES, born Oklahoma City, Oklahoma, July, 1954. *Education:* Rose State College (A.A.S. Legal Assistant, 1989). Phi Theta Kappa. *Member:* National Association of Legal Assistants; Oklahoma Paralegal Association. *Associate Member:* American Bar Association. (CLA)

REPRESENTATIVE CLIENTS: Employers Mutual Cos.; Farmers Alliance Mutual Insurance Co.; Interstate Insurance Group; Jewelers Mutual Insurance Co.; The Silvey Companies; Starr Technical Risks Agency, Inc.; The Trinity Cos.; Ohio Casualty Group; Daimler Chrysler Ins. Co.; Underwriters at Lloyd's London; Utica National Insurance Group; Nautilus Insurance Co.; Northland Insurance Co.; Horace Mann Cos.; Unum Life Insurance Co; Allianz Insurance Company; Zunch U.S.; Caliber One Indemnity Co.

GRIFFIN, REYNOLDS & ASSOCIATES

416 S.W. 79TH STREET
SUITE 200
OKLAHOMA CITY, OKLAHOMA 73139-8121
Telephone: 405-721-9500
Fax: 405-721-9503

Personal Injury, Insurance Bad Faith, Family Law, Wills, Trust Law, Probate, Bankruptcy, Auto Accidents, Trucking Accidents, Motorcycle Accidents, Wrongful Death, Products Liability, Nursing Home Abuse, Medical Malpractice, Divorce, Child Custody, Adoptions, Child Support and Workers Compensation Law.

BILLY D. GRIFFIN, born Muskogee, Oklahoma, November 24, 1972; admitted to bar, 1999, Oklahoma and U.S. District Court, Western District of Oklahoma, U.S. District Court, Northern District of Oklahoma and U.S. Court of Appeals, Tenth Circuit. *Education:* Northeastern Oklahoma State University (B.S., 1995); Oklahoma City University School of Law (J.D., 1998). *Member:* Oklahoma, Oklahoma County and American Bar Associations; Oklahoma Trial Lawyers Association; The Association of Trial Lawyers of America. ***PRACTICE AREAS:*** Personal Injury; Medical Malpractice; Products Liability.

JASON B. REYNOLDS, born Springfield, Missouri, February 7, 1973; admitted to bar, 1998, Oklahoma; 1999, U.S. District Court, Western District of Oklahoma, U.S. District Court, Northern District of Oklahoma and U.S. Court of Appeals, Tenth Circuit. *Education:* University of Arkansas (B.A., 1995); University of Oklahoma (J.D., 1998). *Member:* Oklahoma Bar Association; Oklahoma Trial Lawyers Association; The Association of Trial Lawyers of America. ***PRACTICE AREAS:*** Personal Injury; Medical Malpractice; Products Liability; Family Law; Probate.

THE GROOM LAW FIRM, P.C.

100 NORTH BROADWAY, SUITE 3000
OKLAHOMA CITY, OKLAHOMA 73102
Telephone: 405-235-1440
Fax: 405-235-1708

Insurance Defense, Workers' Compensation Defense, Bankruptcy, Employment and Labor Law, Commercial and Business Litigation, Personal Injury Litigation.

M. THAD GROOM, born Oklahoma City, Oklahoma, September 16, 1960; admitted to bar, 1985, Oklahoma, U.S. District Court, Western and Northern Districts of Oklahoma and U.S. Court of Appeals, Tenth Circuit. *Education:* Oklahoma State University (B.S., 1982); Oklahoma City University (J.D., 1985). Phi Delta Phi. *Member:* Oklahoma County and Oklahoma Bar Associations; The Association of Trial Lawyers Of America. ***PRACTICE AREAS:*** Workers' Compensation Defense Litigation; Employment Law; Insurance Defense Law; Personal Injury Law. ***Email:*** thad@groomlawfirm.com

TAVA SEIFERT JONES, born Altus, Oklahoma, February 3, 1969; admitted to bar, 1996, Oklahoma and U.S. District Court, Northern, Eastern and Western Districts of Oklahoma. *Education:* Oklahoma State University (B.S., Bus. Adm., 1990); University of Oklahoma (J.D., 1995). *Member:* Oklahoma County, Oklahoma (Member, Workers' Compensation Section) and American Bar Associations; Oklahoma Association of Defense Counsel. ***PRACTICE AREAS:*** Employment Litigation; Workers Compensation Defense; Insurance Defense. ***Email:*** tava@groomlawfirm.com

OF COUNSEL

SID M. GROOM, JR., born Oklahoma City, Oklahoma, January 27, 1925; admitted to bar, 1951, Oklahoma. *Education:* Syracuse University and University of Oklahoma (B.S., 1949); University of Oklahoma (J.D., 1951). Sigma Pi Sigma. *Member:* Oklahoma Bar Association. ***PRACTICE AREAS:*** Oil and Gas; Title Examination; Probate; Estate Planning.

JAMES M. KAUFMAN, born Oklahoma City, Oklahoma, February 28, 1951; admitted to bar, 1976, Oklahoma and U.S. District Court, Western District of Oklahoma; 1977, U.S. Court of Appeals, Tenth Circuit; 1983, U.S. Supreme Court. *Education:* University of Oklahoma (B.B.A., 1973; J.D., 1976). Managing Trial Attorney, The Continental Insurance Company, 1984-1994. Arbitrator, Civil Arbitration Panel, U.S. District Court, Western District of Oklahoma, 1985—. *Member:* Oklahoma County, Oklahoma and American Bar Associations. ***REPORTED CASES:*** Moore v. Delivery Services, Inc., 618 P.2d 408, 1980 OK Civ App 38; Kansas City Fire and Marine Ins. Co. v. Rogers, 871 P.2d 443, 1994 OK Civ App; Harder v. F.C. Clinton, Inc., 948 P.2d 298, 1997 OK 137; Atchley v. Hewes, 965 P.2d 1012, 1998 OK Civ App 143; Wooten v. Hudson, 71 F.Supp. 2d 1149 (USDC Ed Okl. 1999). ***PRACTICE AREAS:*** Civil Practice; Trial Practice; Commercial Litigation; Insurance; Personal Injury. ***Email:*** jim@groomlawfirm.com

ERIC J. GROVES & ASSOCIATES

THE ROBINSON RENAISSANCE BUILDING
119 NORTH ROBINSON, SUITE 777
OKLAHOMA CITY, OKLAHOMA 73102
Telephone: 405-236-5303
Fax: 405-236-5309
Email: ejg777@aol.com
URL: http://www.lawyers.com/groves&associates

General Civil and Criminal Trial Practice. Municipal, Zoning and Land Use, Commercial Litigation, White Collar Crime, Family Law, Development Real Estate.

ERIC J. GROVES, born Philadelphia, Pennsylvania, December 8, 1942; admitted to bar, 1970, Oklahoma, U.S. District Court, Western District of Oklahoma and U.S. Court of Appeals, Tenth Circuit; 1976, U.S. Supreme Court. *Education:* Dickinson College (B.A., 1964); University of Oklahoma (J.D., 1970). Associate General Counsel, Oklahoma Securities Commission, 1971-1972. Vice Mayor, Oklahoma City, 1976. Member, City Council of Oklahoma City, 1974-1979; 1999. Judge, Temporary Division, Court of Appeals of the State of Oklahoma, 1983. Chairman, Oklahoma City Bond Advisory Committee, 1992-2000. Member, MAPS Citizens Oversight Board, 1994—. *Member:* Oklahoma County and Oklahoma Bar Associations. [1st Lt., U.S. Army, 1964-1966]. ***SPECIAL AGENCIES:*** Practice before Municipal, County and State Agencies. ***PRACTICE AREAS:*** Architectural and Engineering Malpractice; Construction; Zoning; Planning and Land Use; Civil Rights Law; Commercial Litigation; White Collar Crime.

(This Listing Continued)

REPRESENTATIVE CLIENTS: Best Western Saddleback Inn; Security Designers, Inc.; Raindance Sprinklers, Inc.; Yellow Cab Co.

GUM, PUCKETT & MACKECHNIE, L.L.P.

105 NORTH HUDSON, SUITE 900
OKLAHOMA CITY, OKLAHOMA 73102
Telephone: 405-488-1212
Fax: 405-488-1216

Oil and Gas, Insurance Defense, Personal Injury, General Civil Practice in all State and Federal Courts, Oklahoma Corporation Commission.

MEMBERS OF FIRM

ROBERT G. GUM, born Tulsa, Oklahoma, February 15, 1952; admitted to bar, 1977, Oklahoma; 1982, U.S. District Court, Western, Eastern and Northern Districts of Oklahoma and U.S. Court of Appeals, Tenth Circuit. *Education:* Oklahoma State University (B.A., 1974); University of Oklahoma (J.D., 1977). Phi Delta Phi. Listed, Best Lawyers in America, Natural Resources Law. *Member:* Oklahoma County, Oklahoma and American Bar Associations; Mineral Lawyers Society of Oklahoma City. ***PRACTICE AREAS:*** Oil and Gas Law; Litigation; Insurance. ***Email:*** rggum@gpmlegal.net

CHARLES L. PUCKETT, JR., born McAlester, Oklahoma, September 7, 1949; admitted to bar, 1977, Oklahoma; 1978, Texas and U.S. District Court, Western District of Oklahoma. *Education:* University of Oklahoma (B.B.A., 1971; J.D., 1977). Phi Delta Phi. Recipient, Maurice Merrill Oil and Gas Award, 1976. Member, Oklahoma Law Review, 1975-1977. *Member:* Oklahoma County, Oklahoma and American Bar Associations; State Bar of Texas; Mineral Lawyers Society of Oklahoma City. ***PRACTICE AREAS:*** Oil & Gas Law; Commercial Litigation. ***Email:*** clpuckett@gpmlegal.net

JOHN A. MACKECHNIE, born Kansas City, Missouri, December 24, 1950; admitted to bar, 1978, Oklahoma, U.S. District Court, Western, Eastern and Northern Districts of Oklahoma and U.S. Court of Appeals, Tenth Circuit. *Education:* Oklahoma City University (B.S., 1973; J.D., 1978). Delta Theta Phi. Author, Papers and Speeches: "So. Ute Indian Tribe v. Amoco Production: Title to Coal Bed Methane"; "Review of the Accommodation Doctrine Case Law of Oil and Gas Law"; "The Mineral Interests Use of Surface." *Member:* Oklahoma (Member, Mineral Law Section) and American (Member, Environment, Energy and Resources Law Section) Bar Associations; Oklahoma City Real Property Lawyers Association; Oklahoma City Mineral Lawyers Society (President, 2002-2003); National Association of Railroad Trial Counsel; Rocky Mountain Mineral Foundation. ***PRACTICE AREAS:*** Oil and Gas Law; Real Property; Contracts; Torts; Insurance; Railroad; Trial Practice; Appellate Practice. ***Email:*** mackechnie@gpmlegal.net

ASSOCIATES

JIM D. DOWELL, born Oklahoma City, Oklahoma, 1971; admitted to bar, 2002, Oklahoma and U.S. District Court, Western District of Oklahoma. *Education:* Abilene Christian University (B.A., summa cum laude, 1994); University of Oklahoma (J.D., with highest honors, 2002). Order of the Coif. Recipient: Comfort Scholarship, 1999-2002; American Jurisprudence Awards in Contracts, Civil Procedure, Agricultural Biotechnology, Criminal Procedure and Water Law. Note Editor, Oklahoma Law Review, 2001-2002. Author: Note, "Criminal Procedure: Tenth Circuit Erroneously Allows Officer's Intentions to Define Reasonable Searches; United States v. Carey," Oklahoma Law Review, Volume 54-3, Fall, 2001. *Member:* Oklahoma County, Oklahoma and American Bar Associations. ***PRACTICE AREAS:*** Civil Litigation; Insurance; Oil and Gas Law; Business Law; Personal Injury. ***Email:*** jddowell@gpmlegal.net

MEREDITH A. WEGENER, born Oklahoma City, Oklahoma, 1977; admitted to bar, 2003, Oklahoma and U.S. District Court, Western District of Oklahoma. *Education:* Trinity University (B.A., English, 1999); University of Oklahoma (J.D., with honors, 2003). Order of the Coif. Managing Editor and Founding Board Member, Oklahoma Journal of Law and Technology, 2002-2003. Recipient: Natalie Pierpont and the Oklahoma Bar Foundation Scholarships; American Jurisprudence Awards in Contracts, Legal Research and Writing, Criminal Procedure, International Business Transactions, Family Law and Trial Techniques. Winner, Calvert Law and Liberty Upper-class Moot Court Competition. President, Board of Advocates, 2001-2002. Former Member, Luther Bohannon and the Ruth Bader Ginsburg American Inns of Court. *Member:* Oklahoma County, Oklahoma and American Bar Associations. ***PRACTICE AREAS:*** Civil Litigation; Insurance Defense; Personal Injury; Business Law. ***Email:*** mawegener@gpmlegal.net

REPRESENTATIVE CLIENTS: Bituminous Insurance companies; Blue Dolphin Production, LLC; Cleary Petroleum; Combined Resources, Inc.; Duncan Oil Properties, Inc.; Earlsboro Energies Corporation, Enogex, Inc.; Environmental Management, Inc.; GHK Company; Jordan Drilling Services, Inc.; Pence Brothers Drilling Co., Inc.; Pride Energy Company, Range Resources Corporation; Southern International, Incorporated; Spartan Resources, LLC; Stesco Operating Company; Triad Energy Corporation of Texas; Lobar Oil Company, Inc.

BENJAMIN F. HACKETT & ASSOCIATES

OKLAHOMA CITY, OKLAHOMA

(See Edmond)

Oil and Gas Law, Oil and Gas Regulation, Oil and Gas Title Examination, Real Estate, Probate, Estate Planning; Administrative Law, Corporate Law and Partnership Law, General Practice.

LAW OFFICE OF BARRY L. HAFAR

ONE NORTH HUDSON AVENUE, SUITE 700
OKLAHOMA CITY, OKLAHOMA 73102-5011
Telephone: 405-236-1994
Fax: 405-236-1861
Email: blhafar@swbell.net

Family Law, Adoptions, Step Parent Adoptions, Child Custody, Children, Post-Decree Modifications, Guardianships, Probate, Bankruptcy, General Practice.

BARRY L. HAFAR, born Blair, Nebraska, September 22, 1956; admitted to bar, 1993, Oklahoma and U.S. District Court, Western District of Oklahoma. *Education:* University of Central Oklahoma (B.B.A., 1990); University of Oklahoma (J.D., 1993). Phi Delta Phi. Recipient, Certificate of Recognition, Phi Delta Phi, 1997. *Member:* Oklahoma County, Oklahoma (Member, Family Law Section) and American (Member, Sections on: Family Law) Bar Associations. ***PRACTICE AREAS:*** Family Law; Adoption Law; Step Parent Adoptions; Child Custody; Children; Post-Decree Modifications; Guardianships; Probate; Bankruptcy; General Practice.

HALL, ESTILL, HARDWICK, GABLE, GOLDEN & NELSON

A PROFESSIONAL CORPORATION
BANK ONE CENTER
SUITE 2900
100 NORTH BROADWAY
OKLAHOMA CITY, OKLAHOMA 73102-8827
Telephone: 405-553-2828
Facsimile: 405-553-2855
URL: http://www.HallEstill.com

Tulsa, Oklahoma Office: 320 South Boston Avenue, Suite 400, 74103. Telephone: 918-594-0400. Facsimile: 918-294-0505.

Washington, D.C. Office: Suite 700, North Building, 1120 20th Street N.W., 20036-3406. Telephone: 202-973-1200. Facsimile: 202-973-1212.

Fayetteville, Arkansas Office: One East Center Street, Suite 315, 72701. Telephone: 479-973-5200. Facsimile: 479-973-0520.

General Civil Practice. Trials and proceedings before all State and Federal Courts and Agencies. Antitrust, Bankruptcy, Banking, Construction, Corporate, Commercial, Securities, Employee Benefits, Executive Compensation, Energy, Natural Resources, Energy Regulatory, Environmental, Estate Planning, Probate, Family Law, Domestic, Healthcare, Medical Malpractice, Indian Law, Intellectual Property, International Law and Trade, Labor, Employment, Legislative, Administrative Law, Litigation, Media, Real Estate, Taxation, Telecommunications, Tort, Insurance Defense, Utility Law.

FIRM PROFILE: Hall, Estill, Hardwick, Gable, Golden & Nelson, P.C. is listed in Martindale Hubbell's Bar Register of Preeminent Lawyers.

ROBERT D. NELON, born Shawnee, Oklahoma, August 8, 1946; admitted to bar, 1971, Oklahoma and U.S. Court of Appeals, Tenth Circuit; 1972, U.S. Court of Military Appeals; 1989, U.S. Supreme Court; 1992, U.S. Court of Appeals, Eighth Circuit; 1993, U.S. Court of Appeals, Second Circuit. *Education:* Northwestern University (B.A., 1968); University of Oklahoma (J.D., 1971). Phi Delta Phi. Listed in *The Best Lawyers in America.* Editor, Oklahoma Law Review, 1969-1971. Author: "The Media and Private Figure Defamation Actions in Oklahoma: A Critique," Oklahoma Bar Journal, Vol. 51, November, 1980; "Media Defamation in Oklahoma: A Modest Proposal and New Perspectives - Part I," 34 Oklahoma Law Review 478, Part II, 34 Oklahoma Law Review 737, 1981; "The Peculiar Case of State v. Terry Lynn Nichols: Are Television Cameras Really Banned from Oklahoma Criminal Proceedings?" 3 Vanderbilt J.E.L.P. 4 (2001). *Member:* Oklahoma and American (Section of Antitrust Law, Forum Committee on Communications Law) Bar Associations; American Judicature Society. ***PRACTICE AREAS:*** Litigation; Communications Law; Antitrust Law; Media. ***Email:*** BNELON@HallEstill.com

J. FRED GIST, born Oklahoma City, Oklahoma, February 2, 1951; admitted to bar, 1976, Texas; 1977, Oklahoma. *Education:* University of Oklahoma (B.A., 1973); University of Texas (J.D., 1976). *Member:* Oklahoma County and Oklahoma Bar Associations; State Bar of Texas; Oklahoma City Mineral Lawyers Society. ***PRACTICE AREAS:*** Oil and Gas Law; State Energy Regulatory Law; Public Utility Regulatory Law; Natural Resources Law; Legislative; Telecommunications. ***Email:*** FGIST@HallEstill.com

MICHAEL E. SMITH, born Hobart, Oklahoma, June 30, 1946; admitted to bar, 1975, Oklahoma and U.S. Court of Military Appeals; 1976, Hawaii 1979, U.S. Supreme Court; 1982, U.S. District Court, Western District of Oklahoma; 1984, U.S. Court of Appeals, Tenth Circuit; 1993, U.S. District Court, Northern District of Oklahoma; 1996, U.S. District Court, Eastern District of Oklahoma. *Education:* U.S. Military Academy, West Point, N.Y. (B.S., 1969); University of Oklahoma (J.D., 1975). Author: "Survey on State Class Action Law-Oklahoma," published by The American Bar Association, Litigation Section, Class Action Committee, yearly supplement to Newberg on Class Actions. Co-Author: "Joint Operating Agreement Exhibits: A Survey," 47 Rocky Mt.Min.L.Inst.14 (2001). *Member:* Oklahoma and American Bar Associations; The Association of Trial Lawyers of America. ***PRACTICE AREAS:*** Civil Litigation (Federal and State); Oil and Gas Law; Commercial Litigation; Environmental Law; Labor. ***Email:*** MESMITH@HallEstill.com

RALPH E. SEALS, JR., born Hobart, Oklahoma, May 16, 1949; admitted to bar, 1975, Oklahoma; 1979, U.S. District Court, Western and Northern Districts of Oklahoma; 1993, U.S. Court of Appeals, 10th Circuit. *Education:* Oklahoma State University (B.S., 1971); University of Oklahoma (J.D., 1975). *Member:* Garfield County, Oklahoma and American Bar Associations. ***PRACTICE AREAS:*** Oil and Gas Law; Civil Litigation; Real Property; Oil Pollution; Appellate Practice; Environmental. ***Email:*** RSeals@HallEstill.com

ROBERT D. LOONEY, JR., born Oklahoma City, Oklahoma, February 4, 1946; admitted to bar, 1970, Oklahoma; 1975, U.S. District Court, Western, Northern and Eastern

(This Listing Continued)

Districts of Oklahoma; 1979, U.S. Court of Appeals, Tenth Circuit. *Education:* University of Oklahoma (B.A., 1967); Georgetown Law Center; University of Oklahoma (J.D., 1970). Phi Delta Phi. Editor, Oklahoma Law Review, 1969-1970. *Member:* Oklahoma (Vice Chairman of Tort Laws Committee, 1991-1992), American (Sections on Litigation, Tort and Insurance Practice) and Federal Bar Associations; Oklahoma Association of Defense Counsel; Defense Research Institute; International Association of Defense Counsel; Advocate, American Board of Trial Advocates. [Capt., U.S. Army, 1970-1972]. ***PRACTICE AREAS:*** Drug and Medical Device Defense; Products Liability Defense; Civil Litigation (Federal and State); Bad Faith Law; Insurance Defense; Insurance Law. ***Email:*** rlooney@hallestill.com

SHARON T. THOMAS, born Covina, California, July 28, 1954; admitted to bar, 1981, Oklahoma and U.S. District Court, Western District of Oklahoma; 1985, U.S. Court of Appeals, Tenth Circuit and U.S. Supreme Court. *Education:* University of Oklahoma (B.A., 1978; J.D., 1981). Note Editor, University of Oklahoma Law Review, 1980-1981. Recipient, American Jurisprudence Award in Labor Law. *Member:* Oklahoma and American Bar Associations. ***PRACTICE AREAS:*** Appeals; Oil and Gas Law; Civil Litigation. ***Email:*** STHOMAS@HallEstill.com

MICHAEL J. MASSAD, born Frederick, Oklahoma, March 21, 1960; admitted to bar, 1985, Oklahoma, U.S. District Court, Eastern, Northern and Western Districts of Oklahoma and U.S. Court of Appeals, Tenth Circuit. *Education:* University of Oklahoma (B.B.A. in Finance, with distinction, 1982; J.D., 1985). Beta Gamma Sigma; Phi Delta Phi. Recipient, American Jurisprudence Award in Business Association I. *Member:* Oklahoma County and Oklahoma Bar Associations (Member, Mineral Law Section; Budget Director, 2000; Secretary, 2001; Vice-Chairman, 2002, Chairman, 2003). ***PRACTICE AREAS:*** Oil and Gas; Civil Litigation. ***Email:*** MMASSAD@HallEstill.com

DANIEL J. GLOVER, born Okmulgee, Oklahoma, December 11, 1961; admitted to bar, 1987, Oklahoma; U.S. District Court, Western District of Oklahoma. *Education:* Oklahoma State University (B.S., 1984); University of Oklahoma (J.D., with distinction, 1987). Phi Delta Phi. *Member:* Oklahoma and American Bar Associations. ***PRACTICE AREAS:*** Commercial Transactions; General Corporate; General and Civil Trial Practice; Commercial Litigation; Real Estate. ***Email:*** DGLOVER@HallEstill.com

KENT A. GILLILAND, born Frederick, Oklahoma, May 30, 1959; admitted to bar, 1987, Oklahoma and U.S. District Court, Western District of Oklahoma. *Education:* University of Oklahoma; Oklahoma State University (B.S., 1982); Oklahoma City University (J.D., with honors, 1988). Phi Delta Phi (Magister, 1985-1987). Recipient: Berry-Opala Academic Excellence Award, 1987; American Jurisprudence Awards for Banking Law, Commercial Paper, Corporations, Securities Regulations, Civil Procedure I, Conflicts of Law, Constitutional Law and Professional Responsibility. Co-Author: "Possessions, Receivers, Rents: Oklahoma," Dunaway, Baxter, The Law of Distressed Real Estate, Volume I, Clark Boardman, New York, 1985 and 1988. *Member:* Oklahoma County, Oklahoma and American (Member, Sections on: Real Property; Probate and Trust; Environmental Law; Business Law) Bar Association. ***PRACTICE AREAS:*** Real Estate; Commercial Law; Corporate Law; Banking Law; Finance. ***Email:*** KGILLILAND@HallEstill.com

JON A. EPSTEIN, born Boston, Massachusetts, June 17, 1963; admitted to bar, 1988, Oklahoma, U.S. District Court, Northern, Eastern and Western Districts of Oklahoma; U.S. Claims Court; U.S. Court of Appeals, Tenth Circuit; U.S. Supreme Court. *Education:* University of Texas (B.A., 1985); University of Oklahoma (J.D., with distinction, 1988). Phi Delta Phi (President, 1987-1988). Libel Defense Resource Center ("LDRC") Media Law Letter Committee. Certified Mediator. Approved securities arbitrator for the New York Stock Exchange. *Member:* Oklahoma County, Oklahoma and American Bar Associations. ***PRACTICE AREAS:*** Civil Litigation; Media; Banking; Securities; Labor; Insurance. ***Email:*** JEPSTEIN@HallEstill.com

ELAINE R. TURNER, born Fort Dix U.S.A.B., New Jersey; admitted to bar, 1989, Oklahoma; U.S. District Court, Western, Northern and Eastern Districts of Oklahoma, U.S. Court of Appeals, Tenth Circuit and U.S. Supreme Court. *Education:* University of Oklahoma (B.B.A., 1985); Oklahoma City University (J.D., 1989). Beta Gamma Sigma; Phi Delta Phi. Hatton W. Sumners Scholar. Member: Jessup International Law Moot Court Team; Order of Barristers; Moot Court Board. Staff Editor, Oklahoma City University Law Review, 1988-1989. Recipient, American Jurisprudence Awards for: Contracts I; Civil Procedure I. *Member:* Oklahoma County, Oklahoma and American Bar Associations. (Resident). ***PRACTICE AREAS:*** Labor and Employment; Commercial Litigation; Civil Litigation. ***Email:*** ETURNER@HallEstill.com

LARRY G. BALL, born Oklahoma City, Oklahoma, April 11, 1962; admitted to bar, 1987, Oklahoma and U.S. District Court, Eastern and Western Districts of Oklahoma. *Education:* University of Oklahoma (B.B.A., Finance, 1984; J.D., with distinction, 1987). *Member:* Oklahoma County (Member, Bankruptcy Section), Oklahoma and American Bar Associations; Commercial Law League of America; American Bankruptcy Institute. Fellow, American Bar Foundation. ***PRACTICE AREAS:*** Bankruptcy; Commercial Law; Litigation; Intellectual Property. ***Email:*** LBALL@HallEstill.com

STEPHEN R. PITCOCK, born Los Angeles, California, December 8, 1957; admitted to bar, 1983, Oklahoma and U.S. District Court, Western District of Oklahoma; 1990, Texas; U.S. Court of Appeals, Tenth Circuit. *Education:* University of Tulsa (B.S., History and Economics, with honors, 1980); Southern Methodist University (J.D., 1983). Phi Alpha Theta. *Member:* Oklahoma County, Oklahoma and American Bar Associations; State Bar of Texas; National Academy of Elder Law Attorneys; WealthCounsel, LLC. ***PRACTICE AREAS:*** Estate Planning; Probate Administration; Trusts and Estates; Asset Protection. ***Email:*** srpitcock@hallestill.com

CHRISTIAN S. HUCKABY, born Oklahoma City, Oklahoma, August 10, 1970; admitted to bar, 1995, Oklahoma and U.S. District Court, Western District of Oklahoma. *Education:* University of Oklahoma (B.A., Political Science, 1992; J.D., 1995). Phi Delta Phi. Recipient, American Jurisprudence Award for Civil Procedure. *Member:* Grady County and Oklahoma Bar Associations. ***PRACTICE AREAS:*** Insurance Defense; Tort Litigation; Products Liability; Environmental Law; Civil Law; Appellate Practice. ***Email:*** CHUCKABY@HallEstill.com

SUSANNA GATTONI VOEGELI, born Oklahoma City, Oklahoma, May 8, 1972; admitted to bar, 1997, Oklahoma and U.S. District Court, Northern, Eastern and Western Districts of Oklahoma. *Education:* University of Oklahoma (B.A., 1994; J.D., with honors,

(This Listing Continued)

HALL, ESTILL, HARDWICK, GABLE, GOLDEN & NELSON, A PROFESSIONAL CORPORATION, Oklahoma City—Continued

1997). Phi Delta Phi. Member: Order of the Coif; Order of the Barristers. Recipient: Trial Handbook Award; American Jurisprudence Awards in Civil Procedure, Contracts, Trial Techniques, International Commercial Transactions, Family Law and Advanced Legal Research. *Member:* Oklahoma Bar Association. ***PRACTICE AREAS:*** Civil Litigation; Labor and Employment; Media. ***Email:*** SVOEGELI@HallEstill.com

J. TODD WOOLERY, born Oklahoma City, Oklahoma, February 21, 1974; admitted to bar, 2000, Oklahoma, U.S District Court, Western District of Oklahoma and U.S. Court of Appeals, Tenth and Seventh Circuits. *Education:* University of Oklahoma (B.A., 1997; J.D., 2000). Order of the Barristers. Member: 2000 NTC Trial Team; 1999 ATLA Trial Team; 1999 ABA Negotiation Team. Recipient, Academic Achievement in Oil and Gas Law Award. *Member:* Oklahoma County, Oklahoma (Member, Committees on: Evidence Code; Civil Procedure) and American Bar Associations. ***PRACTICE AREAS:*** Litigation; Energy; Environmental; Tort Defense; Insurance Defense. ***Email:*** TWOOLERY@HallEstill.com

SARAH K. OBERNDORFER, born July 21, 1978; admitted to bar, 2002, Oklahoma; U.S. District Court, Western District of Oklahoma. *Education:* Southern Nazarene University (B.S., 1999); University of Oklahoma College of Law (J.D., with honors, 2002). Order of the Barristers. Member, National Moot Court Teams. 2001 and 2002. Member, National Trial Team, 2002. Recipient of Academic Achievement Awards in Trial and Legal Research and Writing. *Member:* Oklahoma and American Bar Associations. ***PRACTICE AREAS:*** Litigation; Labor and Employment; Media; Environmental; Probate; Estate Planning. ***Email:*** SOBERNDORFER@HallEstill.com

DESSA J. BAKER, born Dallas, Texas, May 28, 1980; admitted to bar, 2005, Oklahoma. *Education:* University of Oklahoma (B.B.A., International Business, with distinction, minors in Spanish and Legal Studies, 2002); Duke University (J.D., cum laude, 2005; LL.M., International and Comparitive Law, 2005). *Member:* Oklahoma County, Oklahoma (Board Member, Oklahoma State High School Mock Trial Program, Young Lawyers Division) and American Bar Associations. ***PRACTICE AREAS:*** Litigation. ***Email:*** dbaker@hallestill.com

ASHLEY A. BOWEN, born Hattiesburg, Mississippi, July 14, 1980; admitted to bar, 2005, Oklahoma. *Education:* Oklahoma City University (B.S., Finance, summa cum laude with honors, 2002); Oklahoma City University School of Law (J.D., 2005). *Member:* Oklahoma County, Oklahoma (Young Lawyers Division) and American Bar Associations. ***PRACTICE AREAS:*** Business Litigation; Media Law; Commercial Law; Corporate Law. ***Email:*** ABOWEN@HallEstill.com

(For Complete Biographical Data on all Personnel, see Professional Biographies at Tulsa, Oklahoma)

HAMPTON AND MILLIGAN

Established in 1980
119 NORTH ROBINSON AVENUE
SUITE 225
OKLAHOMA CITY, OKLAHOMA 73102-4613
Telephone: 405-235-5620
Fax: 405-232-4901
Email: AttysHandM@aol.com

Oil and Gas Title Examination, Oil and Gas Litigation, Riparian Rights, Real Estate Title, Probate Administration, Condemnation.

FIRM PROFILE: From its inception in 1980, the law firm of Hampton and Milligan has been guided by the following principles: strict adherence to the highest professional standards of performance, accountability, and accessibility. The firm offers the highest level of amenities found in the largest law firms, but with the accountability and accessibility of a small law firm. It's the discipline to stay committed to these principles that has enabled the firm to boast a client list comprised of clients ranging from family owned businesses to Fortune 500 corporations.

J. DAVID HAMPTON, born Siloam Springs, Arkansas, September 21, 1955; admitted to bar, 1980, Oklahoma. *Education:* University of Oklahoma (B.A., 1977; J.D., 1980). *Member:* Oklahoma Bar Association; Oklahoma City Association of Petroleum Landmen; Southern Oklahoma Association of Petroleum Landmen. ***PRACTICE AREAS:*** Oil and Gas Title Examination; Oil and Gas Litigation; Riparian Rights; Real Estate Title Examination; Environmental Law. ***Email:*** attyshandm@aol.com

DANIEL A. MILLIGAN, born Los Angeles, California, March 8, 1960; admitted to bar, 1987, Oklahoma; 1995, Texas. *Education:* University of Oklahoma (B.A., 1984; J.D., 1987). *Member:* Oklahoma Bar Association; State Bar of Texas. ***PRACTICE AREAS:*** Oil and Gas Title Examination; Oil and Gas Litigation; Oil and Gas Acquisitions; Real Estate Title; Probate Administration; Ancillary Probate. ***Email:*** attyshandm@aol.com

ASSOCIATE

DIANE DeFILIPPO, born Lincoln, Nebraska, November 24, 1952; admitted to bar, 1978, Oklahoma. *Education:* University of Oklahoma (B.A., 1974; J.D., 1978). *Member:* Oklahoma Bar Association. ***PRACTICE AREAS:*** Oil and Gas Title Examination; Oil and Gas Leasing; Real Estate Title Examination; Real Estate Litigation. ***Email:*** didefil@aol.com

REPRESENTATIVE CLIENTS: BP Amoco; Anadarko Petroleum Corporation; Chesapeake Energy Corporation; Devon Energy Corporation; Dominion Exploration & Production, Inc.; El Paso Production Company; EOG Resources, Inc.; J-Brex Company; Noble Materials, Inc.; Questar Exploration & Production Company; Range Resources Corp.; Unit Petroleum Company; Williams Energy Services.

HARTZOG CONGER CASON & NEVILLE

A PROFESSIONAL CORPORATION
Established in 1979
1600 BANK OF OKLAHOMA PLAZA
201 ROBERT S. KERR
OKLAHOMA CITY, OKLAHOMA 73102
Telephone: 405-235-7000
Facsimile: 405-996-3403
URL: http://www.hartzoglaw.com

Administrative Law, Appellate Practice, Business Transactions, Civil Litigation, Commercial Lending, Commercial Real Estate, Corporate and Securities, Employee Benefits/ERISA, Employment Law, Family Law, Federal and State Taxation, Healthcare Law, Insurance, Intellectual Property, Products Liability, Tax-Exempt Organizations, Trusts and Estates, Wealth Transfer Planning, Oil and Gas.

FIRM PROFILE: The Firm is highly specialized in those practice areas in which it engages. The Firm's clientele is generally comprised of publicly and privately held businesses, high networth individuals and families, trusts and estates, and charitable organizations. Great emphasis is placed upon quality and service. The firm is listed in the Bar Register of Preeminent Lawyers.

LARRY D. HARTZOG, born Clinton, Oklahoma, May 4, 1934; admitted to bar, 1959, Oklahoma. *Education:* University of Arizona and University of Oklahoma (B.B.A., 1956); University of Oklahoma (LL.B., 1959). Law Clerk, Honorable Ross Rizley, U.S. District Judge for the Western District of Oklahoma, 1959-1960. *Member:* Oklahoma and American Bar Associations. ***PRACTICE AREAS:*** Corporate; Securities; Business Law. ***Email:*** lhartzog@hartzoglaw.com

LEN CASON, born Oklahoma City, Oklahoma, September 24, 1947; admitted to bar, 1972, Oklahoma; 1975, California; 1976, Texas. *Education:* University of Oklahoma (B.A., 1969; J.D., 1972); Southern Methodist University (LL.M. in Taxation, 1979). Order of the Coif; Phi Delta Phi. Oklahoma Law Review, 1971-1972. Adjunct Professor of Law in Tax, University of Oklahoma, 1981—. Listed in Best Lawyers in America, Tax Law and Corporate Law. *Member:* Oklahoma (Chairman, Tax Section, 1983) and American Bar Associations; State Bar of Texas; State Bar of California. Fellow, American College of Tax Counsel. Fellow, American College of Trust and Estate Counsel. [Capt., JAGC, USAF 1972-1976]. ***PRACTICE AREAS:*** Corporate; Business Law; Trusts; Estate Planning; Tax Law; Tax Controversies. ***Email:*** lcason@hartzoglaw.com

JACK L. (DREW) NEVILLE, JR., born Oklahoma City, Oklahoma, July 29, 1947; admitted to bar, 1972, Oklahoma; 1977, U.S. Supreme Court. *Education:* Oklahoma University (B.B.A., 1969; J.D., 1972). Assistant U.S. Attorney, Western District of Oklahoma, 1975-1976. Legislative Assistant, U.S. Senate, Washington, D.C., 1974-1975. Director, Oklahoma County Bar Association, 1989-1991. Past President, Federal Bar Association. Oklahoma City Chapter. Past President, Luther Bohanon American Inn of Court, Oklahoma City Chapter. Listed in Best Lawyers in America, Criminal and Civil. *Member:* Oklahoma and American Bar Associations. Fellow, American College of Trial Lawyers. ***PRACTICE AREAS:*** Federal Criminal Practice; Federal Securities Litigation; General Corporate Litigation; Business Litigation. ***Email:*** dneville@hartzoglaw.com

DAVID E. PEPPER, born Bartlesville, Oklahoma, September 13, 1950; admitted to bar, 1975, Oklahoma; 1976, U.S. District Court, Western and Northern Districts of Oklahoma and U.S. Court of Appeals, Tenth Circuit. *Education:* University of Oklahoma (B.B.A., 1972); Oklahoma City University (J.D., 1975). Phi Delta Phi. *Member:* Oklahoma and American Bar Associations. ***PRACTICE AREAS:*** Oil and Gas Law; General Civil Litigation; Property Law. ***Email:*** dpepper@hartzoglaw.com

STEVEN C. DAVIS, born Guthrie, Oklahoma, August 27, 1958; admitted to bar, 1983, Oklahoma. *Education:* Oklahoma State University (B.S., 1980); University of Oklahoma (J.D. with honors, 1983). Phi Kappa Phi; Phi Delta Phi; Order of the Coif. Recipient, Nathan Scarritt Prize, 1983. Note Editor, Oklahoma Law Review, 1982-1983. Certified Public Accountant, Oklahoma, 1980. *Member:* Oklahoma (Treasurer, 1987, Secretary, 1988, Chairman Elect, 1989 and Chairman, 1990, Section of Taxation) and American Bar Associations; Oklahoma Society of Certified Public Accountants; American Institute of Certified Public Accountants; American Heart Association, Oklahoma Affiliate (Past Chairman). ***PRACTICE AREAS:*** Federal Income Tax; State Income Tax; Estate and Gift Taxation; Tax Controversies; Corporate Law; Estate Planning; Trusts. ***Email:*** sdavis@hartzoglaw.com

RUSSELL COOK, born Oklahoma City, Oklahoma, May 12, 1952; admitted to bar, 1982, Oklahoma. *Education:* University of Oklahoma (B.A., 1979); Oklahoma City University (J.D. with distinction, 1982). Member, Oklahoma City University Law Review. *Member:* Oklahoma and American Bar Associations; The Association of Trial Lawyers of America. ***PRACTICE AREAS:*** Civil Litigation. ***Email:*** rcook@hartzoglaw.com

JOSEPH P. HOGSETT, born Bartlesville, Oklahoma, November 25, 1960; admitted to bar, 1986, Oklahoma. *Education:* Trinity University (B.S., cum laude, 1983); University of Texas (J.D. with honors, 1986). Phi Delta Phi. *Member:* Oklahoma County and Oklahoma Bar Associations. ***PRACTICE AREAS:*** Real Estate; Commercial Law; Financial Law; Business; Corporate Law. ***Email:*** jhogsett@hartzoglaw.com

JOHN D. ROBERTSON, born Lawrence, Kansas, October 25, 1961; admitted to bar, 1986, Oklahoma. *Education:* Oklahoma State University (B.S., 1983); University of Oklahoma (J.D., 1986). Order of the Coif. Note Editor, Oklahoma Law Review, 1985-1986. Recipient, Nathan Scarritt Prize, 1986. *Member:* Oklahoma and American Bar Associations. ***PRACTICE AREAS:*** Corporate Law; Securities; Business Law. ***Email:*** jrobertson@hartzoglaw.com

LAURA HAAG McCONNELL, born Abilene, Texas, April 28, 1961; admitted to bar, 1987, Oklahoma, U.S. District Court, Western, Eastern and Northern Districts of Oklahoma, U.S. Court of Appeals, Tenth Circuit and U.S. Supreme Court. *Education:* Oklahoma Baptist University (B.S., magna cum laude, 1983); University of Oklahoma (J.D. with highest honors, 1987). Order of the Coif. Member, Oklahoma Law Review. Instructor, Legal Research and Writing, University of Oklahoma, 1985-1987. *Member:* Oklahoma County, Oklahoma and American Bar Associations. ***REPORTED CASES:*** Robinson v. City of Ed-

(This Listing Continued)

mond, 160 F.3d 1275 (10th cir. 1998); Robinson v. City of Edmond, 68 F.3d 1226 (10th Cir. 1995); Crysco Oilfield Services Inc. v. Hutchison-Hayes International, Inc. 913F.2d 850 (10th Cir. 1990); Smith v. Speligene, 990 P.2d 312 (OK App. 1999); Horton v. State of Oklahoma, 915P.2d 352 (Okla 1996); Dorn v. Dorn, 24 P.3d 886 (OK App. 2001) In the Matter of the adoption of CDM, _P.3d_, 2001 OK 103; Myers v. Lashley, _P.3d_, 2002 OK 14. ***PRACTICE AREAS:*** Civil Litigation; Employment Law; Family Law; Appellate Practice. ***Email:*** lmcconnell@hartzoglaw.com

WILLIAM A. JOHNSON, born Oklahoma City, Oklahoma, August 25, 1951; admitted to bar, 1977, Oklahoma; 1978, U.S. District Court, Western District of Oklahoma; 1981, U.S. Court of Appeals, Tenth Circuit; 1984, U.S. District Court, Eastern District of Oklahoma. *Education:* University of Oklahoma (B.A., 1973); Oklahoma City University (J.D., 1977). *Member:* Oklahoma County, Oklahoma and American Bar Associations; Association of Trial Lawyers of America. ***PRACTICE AREAS:*** Business; Federal Criminal Practice; Litigation; Oil and Gas Law. ***Email:*** bjohnson@hartzoglaw.com

SUSAN B. SHIELDS, born Bartlesville, Oklahoma, December 13, 1963; admitted to bar, 1989, California; 1992, Oklahoma. *Education:* Stanford University (B.A. departmental honors, Public Policy, 1986); University of California School of Law at Los Angeles (J.D., 1989). *Member:* Oklahoma County, Oklahoma and American Bar Associations; State Bar of California. ***PRACTICE AREAS:*** Estate Planning; Trust Law; Probate; Tax Controversies; Tax Exempt Organizations. ***Email:*** sshields@hartzoglaw.com

BILLY M. CROLL, born Houston, Texas, January 24, 1954; admitted to bar, 1979, Oklahoma; 1987, U.S. District Court, Western District of Oklahoma and U.S. Court of Appeals, Fifth Circuit. *Education:* Oklahoma State University (B.S., 1976); University of Oklahoma (J.D., 1979). *Member:* Oklahoma County, Oklahoma (Member, Mineral Law Section) and American Bar Associations. ***REPORTED CASES:*** Munich American Reinsurance Company; NAC Reinsurance Corporation vs. John P. Crawford Insurance Commissioner of the State of Oklahoma, as Receiver of Employers National Insurance Corporation 141 F.3d 585 (5th Cir. 1998). ***PRACTICE AREAS:*** Civil Litigation; Oil and Gas Law; Real Property Law; Insurance Law. ***Email:*** bcroll@hartzoglaw.com

RYAN S. WILSON, born Stillwater, Oklahoma, August 28, 1965; admitted to bar, 1990, Oklahoma, U.S. District Court, Western, Northern and Eastern Districts of Oklahoma, U.S. Court of Appeals, Tenth Circuit and U.S. Supreme Court. *Education:* Oklahoma State University (B.S., 1987); University of Oklahoma (J.D., 1990). Order of the Coif. Note Editor, Oklahoma Law Review, 1989-1990, and Outstanding Note Editor, 1990. *Member:* Oklahoma County, Oklahoma and American Bar Associations. ***PRACTICE AREAS:*** Civil Litigation; Employment Law; Products Liability; Business Litigation; Unfair Trade Practices; Administrative Law; Appellate Practice. ***Email:*** rwilson@hartzoglaw.com

AMY J. SINE, born Pittsburgh, Pennsylvania, December 16, 1962; admitted to bar, 1988, Texas; 1989, Oklahoma. *Education:* University of Oklahoma (B.A. with highest honors, 1985; B.B.A. with special distinction, 1985); Vanderbilt University (J.D., 1988). Phi Beta Kappa; Beta Gamma Sigma. Member, Order of the Coif. Editor, Vanderbilt Law Review, 1987-1988. Law Clerk to Judge Jerry Bachmeyer, U.S. District Court, Northern District of Texas. Board of Directors, Oklahoma City Estate Planning Council. *Member:* Oklahoma County, Oklahoma (Member, Estate Planning, Probate and Trust Section; Chair-Elect, 2002; Treasurer, 2001) and American Bar Associations; State Bar of Texas. ***PRACTICE AREAS:*** Estate Planning; Trusts; Probate; Tax Exempt Organizations. ***Email:*** asine@hartzoglaw.com

JON H. TRUDGEON, born Miami, Oklahoma, May 13, 1939; admitted to bar, 1964, Oklahoma; 1968, U.S. Tax Court; 1970, U.S. District Court, Western District of Oklahoma and U.S. Court of Appeals, Tenth Circuit; 1976, U.S. Claims Court. *Education:* University of Oklahoma (B.B.A., 1961; LL.B., 1964). Phi Alpha Delta. Listed, Best Lawyers in America. *Member:* Oklahoma County (Treasurer, 1981-1983; Director, 1986-1988; Vice President, 1988-1989), Oklahoma (Member, Board of Governors, 1994-1996; Board of Editors, 1989-1995) and American (Member, Sections on: Real Property, Trusts and Probate) Bar Associations; Oklahoma City Estate Planning Council (Director, 1984-1987; President, 1991; President, Oklahoma City Lawyers Tax Group, 1972-1973). Fellow: Oklahoma Bar Foundation (Trustee, 1989—; President, 1989-1990); The American College of Trust and Estate Counsel; American Bar Foundation; Oklahoma County Bar Foundation (Trustee, 1989—). [USAF, JAG, 1964-1968]. ***PRACTICE AREAS:*** Employment Benefits Law; Nonprofit and Tax Exempt Organizations; Trusts and Estates; Wills and Probate; Tax Law; Estate Planning Law. ***Email:*** jtrudgeon@hartzoglaw.com

CHARLES E. GEISTER, III, born Cleveland, Ohio, May 7, 1955; admitted to bar, 1980, Oklahoma and U.S. District Court, Western, Eastern and Northern Districts of Oklahoma; 1981, U.S. Court of Appeals, Tenth Circuit. *Education:* University of Oklahoma (B.A., 1977; J.D. with honors, 1980). Phi Delta Phi; Order of the Coif. Editor-in-Chief, Oklahoma Law Review, 1979-1980. Recipient: CJS Award, 1980; Paul K. Frost Award, 1979. Lecturer and Faculty Member, "Insurance Law," Oklahoma Bar Seminar, 1986; Member, Lawyer Panel LXVIII of Court of Appeals assisting Oklahoma Supreme Court Caseload. *Member:* Oklahoma County (Board of Directors, 1991-1993; Bench and Bar Committee, 1989 and 2000-2001), Oklahoma (Member, Civil Procedure Committee, 1995-1999) and American Bar Associations; Luther Bohanon American Inn of Court (Barrister). ***REPORTED CASES:*** Evans v. McDonald's Corp., 936 F.2d 1087 (10th Cir., 1991); Wood v. Eli Lilly & Co., 38 F.3d 510 (10th Cir., 1994); Crabtree v. Muchmore, 904 F.2d 1475 (10th Cir., 1990). ***PRACTICE AREAS:*** Civil Litigation; Employment Law; Life Insurance; ERISA Litigation; Products Liability; Health and Disability Insurance. ***Email:*** cgeister@hartzoglaw.com

ARMAND PALIOTTA, born New York City, N.Y., March 17, 1967; admitted to bar, 1992, Oklahoma. *Education:* University of Oklahoma (B.A., 1989; J.D. with highest honors, 1992). Order of the Coif. Recipient: Judicature Society Award; Frank C. Love Memorial Scholarship; Charles B. Memminger Memorial Scholarship. Assistant Article Editor, Oklahoma Law Review, 1990-1992. *Member:* Oklahoma Bar Association. ***PRACTICE AREAS:*** Corporate Law; Securities; Business Law; Tax Law; Tax Controversies. ***Email:*** apaliotta@hartzoglaw.com

RICHARD B. KELLS, born Providence, Rhode Island, September 10, 1953; admitted to bar, 1978, Oklahoma and U.S. Tax Court. *Education:* Central Connecticut State University (B.S. in Accounting, 1975); Oklahoma City University (J.D., 1977); New York University (LL.M. in Taxation, 1979). Editor, Oklahoma City Law Review, 1976-1977. Certified Public Accountant, Oklahoma, 1979. Author: "Planning Techniques for Avoiding Sublease Treatment on Assigning Oil and Gas Leases," Vol. 31, No. 4, Oil and Gas Tax Quarterly, 1983; "Tax Aspects of State and Municipal Bonds Issued in Oklahoma," 52 Oklahoma Bar Journal 1329, 1981; "Multistate Business Tax Reporting," CLA Advantage, September 1997. Director and Officer, Oklahoma City Estate Planning Council, 1996—. Adjunct Professor of Law, Oklahoma City University, 1981-1985. President, Oklahoma City Lawyers Tax Group, 1983. Listed in Best Lawyers in America, Tax Law and Trusts and Estates Law, 1987—. Fellow, American College of Trust and Estate Counsel. ***PRACTICE AREAS:*** Federal Taxation; State Taxation; Estate Planning; Trust Law; Probate. ***Email:*** rkells@hartzoglaw.com

J. CHRISTIAN GUZZY, born Greensburg, Pennsylvania, March 14, 1970; admitted to bar, 1996, Oklahoma. *Education:* Harvard University (A.B., cum laude, 1992); University of Oklahoma (J.D. with highest honors, 1996). Order of the Coif. *Member:* Oklahoma and American Bar Associations. William J. Holloway, Jr. American Inn of Court (Associate). ***PRACTICE AREAS:*** Corporate Law; Business Law; Environmental Law. ***Email:*** cguzzy@hartzoglaw.com

BERNARD J. ROTHBAUM, born Oklahoma City, Oklahoma, July 11, 1945; admitted to bar, 1970, Oklahoma; 1974, U.S. Supreme Court. *Education:* University of Oklahoma (B.A., 1967; J.D., 1970). Phi Delta Phi. Member, University of Oklahoma Law Review, 1969-1970. Temporary Judge, Court of Appeals, Oklahoma, 1982. *Member:* Oklahoma, Federal (Member, Board of Directors, 1973-1974; National Governor, Council of Younger Lawyers, 1974) and American (Member, Sections on: Corporation, Banking and Business Law; Antitrust Law; Litigation) Bar Associations. ***PRACTICE AREAS:*** Securities Regulation Law; Banking Law; Antitrust Law; Federal Criminal Practice. ***Email:*** bjrothbaum@hartzoglaw.com

---

MICHAEL J. NOVOTNY, born Denver, Colorado, July 23, 1959; admitted to bar, 1992, Oklahoma and U.S. District Court, Western District of Oklahoma. *Education:* University of Colorado (B.S., cum laude, 1982); University of Oklahoma (J. D. with honors, 1992). *Member:* Oklahoma and American Bar Associations. ***PRACTICE AREAS:*** Oil and Gas Law; Civil Litigation; Title Examination; Business Law. ***Email:*** mnovotny@hartzoglaw.com

BYRON K. LINKOUS, born Perry, Florida, October 15, 1969; admitted to bar, 1999, Oklahoma. *Education:* University of Oklahoma (B.A. with distinction, 1992; M.B.A., J.D. with highest honors, 1998). Phi Delta Phi; Order of the Coif; Paul K. Frost Award, 1998. ***PRACTICE AREAS:*** Civil Litigation; Business Litigation; Real Property; Business Transactions. ***Email:*** blinkous@hartzoglaw.com

KEVIN B. RATLIFF, born Tulsa, Oklahoma, July 11, 1971; admitted to bar, 1998, Oklahoma. *Education:* University of Oklahoma (B.B.A., Economics, 1994); Oklahoma City University (J.D. with honors, 1998). Phi Delta Phi. Recipient, CALI Awards in: Estate and Gift Taxation; Oil and Gas Law. *Member:* Oklahoma County and Oklahoma Bar Associations; Oklahoma City Estate Planning Council; Oklahoma City Tax Lawyers Group. ***PRACTICE AREAS:*** Trusts and Estates; State Taxation; Local Taxation; Tax Planning; Tax Controversies. ***Email:*** kratliff@hartzglaw.com

J. LESLIE LaREAU, born Shawnee, Oklahoma, September 28, 1964; admitted to bar, 1994, Oklahoma. *Education:* University of Oklahoma (B.B.A., 1986; J.D., with highest honors, 1994). Phi Delta Phi; Order of the Coif. Recipient: Nathan Scarritt Prize, 1994; American Judicature Awards. Member, Oklahoma Law Review, 1993-1994. Certified Public Accountant, Oklahoma, 1986. *Member:* Oklahoma and American Bar Associations; Oklahoma Society of Certified Public Accountants. ***PRACTICE AREAS:*** Wealth Transfer Planning; Trusts and Estates; Tax Planning; Tax Controversies. ***Email:*** llareau@hartzoglaw.com

ALIX LORMAND SAMARA, born Weisbaden, Germany, 1977; admitted to bar, 2002, Texas (Not admitted in Oklahoma). *Education:* Southern Methodist University (B.A., magna cum laude, 1999); George Washington University Law School (J.D., 2002). Tau Kappa Alpha; Golden Key; Alpha Lambda Delta. Member, American Intellectual Property Law Review 2000-2002. Vice-President, Trial Court Board. Regional Champion ATLA Student Trial Advocacy Competition, 2001. Outstanding Trial Court Board Member, 2002. Student Bar Association 3L Class Representative. *Member:* Dallas Bar Association; State Bar of Texas. ***LANGUAGES:*** German and French. ***PRACTICE AREAS:*** Litigation.

KURT M. RUPERT, born Oklahoma City, Oklahoma, April 23, 1960; admitted to bar, 1986, Oklahoma; U.S. District Court, Western, Northern and Eastern Districts of Oklahoma; U.S. Court of Appeals, Tenth Circuit; U.S. Supreme Court. *Education:* University of Oklahoma (B.A., Economics, 1982; J.D., highest honor, 1986). Phi Beta Kappa; Order of the Coif. Managing Editor, Oklahoma Law Review, 1985-1986. *Member:* Oklahoma County, Oklahoma and American Bar Associations. ***REPORTED CASES:*** United States ex rel. B & D Mechanical Contractors vs. St. Paul Mercury Ins. Co., 70 F.3d 1115 (10th Cir. 1995), cert. denied, 517 U.S. 1167, 116 S.Ct. 1568, 134 L. Ed. 2d 667 (1996); Neil Acquisition, L.L.C. vs. Wingrod Investment Corp., 1996 OK 125, 932 P.2d 1100 (Okla. 1996). ***PRACTICE AREAS:*** Litigation.

KENT W. GARDNER, born Woodward County, Oklahoma, September 29, 1978; admitted to bar, 2004, Oklahoma. *Education:* Oklahoma State University (B.S., summa cum laude, 2001); University of Oklahoma (J.D., with honors, 2004). Harry S. Truman Scholar. Kailas and Becky Rao Scholar. Recipient, American Jurisprudence Award in Family Law, 2003 and Partnership Tax, 2004. ***PRACTICE AREAS:*** Business Transactions; Corporate Law; Estate Planning; Trusts; Tax Controversies. ***Email:*** kgardner@hartzoglaw.com

LINCOLN C. McELROY, born Stillwater, Oklahoma, February 4, 1979; (admission pending). *Education:* Oklahoma Baptist University (B.A., magna cum laude, 2001); University of Oklahoma (J.D., with highest honors, 2004). Recipient, American Jurisprudence Award in Civil Procedure I and Tribal Courts. Assistant Articles Editor, Oklahoma Law Review, 2003-2004. ***PRACTICE AREAS:*** General Litigation. ***Email:*** lmcelroy@hartzoglaw.com

ROBERT S. DURAN, JR., born McAlester, Oklahoma, April 1, 1976; admitted to bar, 2001, Texas (Not admitted in Oklahoma). *Education:* Oklahoma Baptist University

(This Listing Continued)

HARTZOG CONGER CASON & NEVILLE, A PROFESSIONAL CORPORATION, Oklahoma City—Continued

(B.B.A., summa cum laude, with honors, 1998); Vanderbilt University (J.D., 2001). John Wesley Raley Scholar. *Member:* State Bar of Texas; American Bar Association. ***PRACTICE AREAS:*** Litigation. ***Email:*** rduran@hartzoglaw.com

DAVID ALLEN ELDER, born Durham, North Carolina, 1976; admitted to bar, 2002, Texas; 2003, District of Columbia; 2005, Oklahoma. *Education:* Rhodes College (B.A., magna cum laude, 1999) Phi Beta Kappa; Harvard Law School (J.D., 2002). *Member:* Oklahoma and American Bar Associations; District of Columbia Bar; State Bar of Texas. ***PRACTICE AREAS:*** Litigation; Energy and Natural Resources; Administrative Law; Corporate Law. ***Email:*** delder@hartzoglaw.com

OF COUNSEL

J. WILLIAM CONGER, born Shreveport, Louisiana, March 6, 1945; admitted to bar, 1971, Oklahoma. *Education:* University of Oklahoma (B.A., 1967); Louisiana State University; University of Oklahoma (J.D., 1971). Phi Alpha Delta. Recipient, Commendation Award 1970-1971 by the International Academy of Trial Lawyers. Adjunct Professor of Law, Oklahoma City University School of Law. Fellow: American Bar Foundation; Oklahoma Bar Foundation. Listed, Best Lawyers in America. *Member:* Oklahoma County (President, 2000-2001; Director, 1989-1992), Oklahoma and American Bar Associations; Master Emeritus, Past President, William J. Holloway, Jr. American Inn of Court. ***PRACTICE AREAS:*** Litigation.

KENT F. FRATES, born Oklahoma City, Oklahoma, September 27, 1938; admitted to bar, 1964, Oklahoma; 1965, Arizona. *Education:* Stanford University (B.A., 1960); Oklahoma City University; University of Arizona (J.D., 1964). Phi Alpha Delta. Oklahoma House of Representatives, Member, 1970-1978 and Minority Leader, 1976-1978. *Member:* Oklahoma Bar Association; State Bar of Arizona. ***PRACTICE AREAS:*** Real Estate; Water Law; Insurance Law; Health Care Law; Personal Injury Law. ***Email:*** KFfrates@nsis.nci

KENNETH R. DAVIS, born Guthrie, Oklahoma, October 16, 1964; admitted to bar, 1990, Oklahoma. *Education:* Oklahoma State University (B.S., Agriculture Economics, 1986); University of Oklahoma (J.D., 1990). Order of the Coif. Note Editor, Oklahoma Law Review, 1989-1990. Recipient, Nathan S. Scarritt Prize, 1990. *Member:* Oklahoma County and Oklahoma Bar Associations. ***PRACTICE AREAS:*** Commercial Law; Banking Law; Bankruptcy Law. ***Email:*** kdavis@hartzoglaw.com

JAMES D. KALLSTROM, born Akron, Ohio, September 20, 1950; admitted to bar, 1976, Ohio; 1982, Oklahoma. *Education:* Kenyon College (B.A., 1973); Case Western Reserve University (J.D., 1976). *Member:* Oklahoma Bar Association; Oklahoma City Real Property Lawyers Association; The Federalist Society. ***PRACTICE AREAS:*** Real Estate Law; Oil and Gas Law. ***Email:*** jkallstrom@hartzoglaw.com

A List of Representative Clients will be furnished upon request.

HAUPT BROOKS VANDRUFF, PLLC

ONE NORTH HUDSON, NINTH FLOOR
OKLAHOMA CITY, OKLAHOMA 73102
Telephone: 405-231-4600
Facsimile: 405-231-4601
Email: info@hauptbrooks.com
URL: http://www.hbvlawyers.com

Edmond, Oklahoma Office: 200 East 10th Street Plaza, Suite A, 73034. Telephone: 405-348-2529. Facsimile: 405-330-4872.

Lawton, Oklahoma Office: 5 N.W. 16th Street, 73507. Telephone: 580-355-4000. Facsimile: 405-231-4600.

Administrative/Agency, Agricultural, Bankruptcy (Chapter 7, 11, 12, 13), Civil Rights, Criminal, Domestic & Family, Employment, Estate Planning (Wills & Trusts), Finance, Debtor and Creditor Law, General Corporate and Business (Organization, Product Liability, Mergers and Acquisition, Litigation), General Trial Practice, Insurance, Medical and Nursing Home Malpractice and Probate, Personal Injury, Real Estate, Taxation (Personal and Corporate), Workers Compensation, Wrongful Death.

ROBERT J. HAUPT, born St. Louis, Missouri, July 1, 1961; admitted to bar, 2001, Oklahoma; 2003, District of Columbia; U.S. Court of Federal Claims; U.S. Court of Appeals, Tenth Circuit; U.S. District Court, Eastern and Western Districts of Oklahoma; U.S. District Court, Eastern District of Texas. *Education:* Oklahoma Baptist University (B.A., Psychology and Sociology, magna cum laude, 1981); Seinan Gakuin University, Fukuoka, Japan (Diploma, 1981); University of Chicago (M.A., Social Sciences, 1982-1983); Oklahoma City University (J.D., with high honors, 2000). Phi Eta Sigma; Psi Chi; Phi Delta Phi. Recipient, Oklahoma City University: Merit Scholar; 2nd in graduating class. Certified Hotel Administrator, University of Michigan, 1987. Certified Association Manager, Florida State University, 1996. Licensed Real Estate Broker: Arkansas, 1988; Florida, 1995; Oklahoma, 1995. Real Estate Developer, Commercial and Residential Properties, 1983-2000. Author, "Never Lay a Salmon on the Ground with his Head Toward the River-State of Washington Sues Yakamas Over Alcohol Ban," American Indian Law Review, University of Oklahoma, Vol. 26, No 1., September, 2002; "Thoughts on Long Term Rentals," Hotel Business, January 2003; "A Question on Wine," Oklahoma County Bar Briefcase, April 2003; "Critics Miss the Court's Point," Daily Oklahoman, July 9, 2003; "Did you Hear the One About the Lawyer...," Oklahoma County Bar Briefcase, December 2003; "When is a Farmer a 'Family Farmer'-An Analysis of Chapter 12 Qualification," Oklahoma City University Law Review, Oklahoma City University, Fall 2004; "When is a Farmer a Family Farmer?" Okla. City Univ. Law Review, Fall 2005; "Founders Sought Real Separation," Daily Oklahoma, March 25, 2003. Co-Author: "Negotiating and Drafting Acquisition Agreements in Oklahoma," National Business Institute, June 20, 2003. Member, Executive Board, 2002—, Member, Alumni Association, 2001— and Co-Chair, Annual Gala Committee, 2002—, Oklahoma City University Law School. *Member:* Oklahoma (Member, Committees on: Professionalism, 2004-2006; Law Schools, 2004-2006), Minnesota State, Federal and American Bar Associations; Washington D.C. Bar Association; The American Trial Lawyers Association; Federal Court of Claims Bar Association; American Bankruptcy Institute; Agricultural Bar Association. ***PRACTICE AREAS:*** Administrative Law; Agency Law; Agricultural Law; Bankruptcy; Civil Rights; Employment; Finance; General Corporate; Business Law; General Trial Practice; Insurance; Real Estate; Products Liability. ***Email:*** rhaupt@hauptbrooks.com

CARSON M. BROOKS, born Ardmore, Oklahoma, March 12, 1976; admitted to bar, 2001, Oklahoma. *Education:* Oklahoma State University (B.S., Agricultural Sciences and Natural Resources, 1998); Oklahoma City University School of Law (J.D., 2001). Phi Delta Phi. Merit Scholar. Recipient, CALI Excellence for the Future Award in Legal Research and Writing. Representative, Oklahoma City University Board of Student Governors. *Member:* Oklahoma County and Oklahoma Bar Associations. (Also at Lawton Office). ***PRACTICE AREAS:*** Administrative Law; Agency Law; Estate Planning; Finance; General Corporate; Business Law; General Trial Practice; Insurance; Personal Injury; Natural Resources; Environmental Law; Consumer Bankruptcy. ***Email:*** cbrooks@hauptbrooks.com

JOEL WAYNE VANDRUFF, born Stillwater, Oklahoma, June 25, 1969; admitted to bar, 2001, Oklahoma. *Education:* Oklahoma State University (B.S., Political Science, 1994); Oklahoma City University (J.D., 2000). Formerly with Federal Bureau of Prisons. *Member:* Oklahoma County and Oklahoma Bar Associations; Oklahoma Criminal Defense League Association. [Sergeant, Oklahoma National Guard, 1/179th Infantry Brigade, 1989-1997]. ***PRACTICE AREAS:*** Criminal Defense; Personal Injury; Workers Compensation; Products Liability; Automobile Accidents and Injuries; Severe Burns. ***Email:*** jvandruff@hauptbrooks.com

JAMES M. BARBER, born East Saint Louis, Illinois, March 31, 1961; admitted to bar, 2002, Oklahoma and U.S. District Court, Eastern District of Oklahoma; 2003, U.S. District Court, Western District of Oklahoma. *Education:* University of Central Oklahoma (B.S., 1997); Oklahoma City University School of Law (J.D., 2002). Member: Moot Court Honors Board, Oklahoma City University, 1999; Ruth Bader Ginsburg Inns of the Court, 2002-2003. Registered Nurse, Oklahoma, 1982—. *Member:* Oklahoma Bar Association; Oklahoma Trial Lawyers Association. [With U.S. Air Force, 1978-1980; Major, Air Force Reserve, 1982-1992]. ***PRACTICE AREAS:*** Medical Malpractice; Nursing Negligence; Nursing Home Litigation; Products Liability; Criminal Defense. ***Email:*** mbarber@hauptbrooks.com

TONI HIMES CAPRA, born Chickasha, Oklahoma, May 1, 1956; admitted to bar, 1996, Oklahoma; U.S. District Court, Eastern and Western Districts of Oklahoma; U.S. District Court, Northern District of Texas. *Education:* Central State University (B.S., Liberal Arts, 1992); Oklahoma City University School of Law (J.D., 1995). *Member:* Oklahoma County and Oklahoma Bar Associations; Oklahoma Trial Lawyers Association; Oklahoma Criminal Defense Lawyers Association. ***PRACTICE AREAS:*** Family Law; Criminal Law; Workers Compensation; Personal Injury. ***Email:*** tcapra@hauptbrooks.com

BRADFORD A. MAZO, born Providence, Rhode Island, July 22, 1949; admitted to bar, 1981, California; 2001, Oklahoma. *Education:* Wayne State University (B.A., 1976); McGeorge School of Law, University of the Pacific (J.D., 1981; LL.M., Taxation, 1983). ***PRACTICE AREAS:*** Business Law (50%); Estate Planning (10%); Taxation (10%); Bankruptcy (20%); Real Estate (10%). ***Email:*** bmazo@hauptbrooks.com

RUTH LAWRENCE MOR, born October 7, 1954; admitted to bar, 1985, Oklahoma; 1986, U.S. District Court, Western District of Oklahoma. *Education:* Central State University (B.A., 1977); Oklahoma City University (J.D., 1985). Administrative Law Judge: Oklahoma Department of Agriculture, 2004-2005; Oklahoma Department of Labor, 1995-1996. Associate General Counsel, Oklahoma Corporation Commission, 1996-2003. Assistant Attorney General, State of Oklahoma, 1987-1995. *Member:* Oklahoma Bar Association. ***PRACTICE AREAS:*** Civil Rights; Administrative Law; Commercial Litigation; Civil Litigation; Agricultural Law; Employment Law. ***Email:*** rmor@hauptbrooks.com

CHARLES W. WRIGHT, born November 12, 1943; admitted to bar, 1983, Oklahoma. *Education:* Central State University (B.A., Education, 1966); University of Oklahoma (M.A., Sociology, 1972); Notre Dame University (Ph.D., Sociology, 1976); Oklahoma City University (J.D., 1983). Assistant Professor, University of Oklahoma, 1974-1983. Assistant General Counsel, Oklahoma Corporation Commission, 1997-2004. *Member:* Oklahoma Bar Association. ***PRACTICE AREAS:*** Environmental Law; Commercial Litigation; Civil Litigation; Family Law; Civil Rights; Consumer Law. ***Email:*** cwright@hauptbrooks.com

ADAM C. BRANDENBURG, born November 12, 1972; admitted to bar, 2004, Oklahoma; U.S. District Court, Western District of Oklahoma. *Education:* University of Oklahoma (B.B.A., International Business Studies, 2000); Oklahoma City University (J.D., 2004). *Member:* Oklahoma Bar Association. [Operational Specialist, U.S. Navy, 1994-1998]. ***PRACTICE AREAS:*** Oil and Gas Law; Commercial Transactions; Commercial Litigation; Civil Litigation; Family Law; Civil Rights; Consumer Law. ***Email:*** abrandenburg@hauptbrooks.com

OF COUNSEL

LAWRENCE R. SCOTT, born May 24, 1956; admitted to bar, 1981, Oklahoma. *Education:* Phillips University (B.A., summa cum laude, 1978); University of Oklahoma (J.D., 1981). *Member:* Oklahoma Bar Association; Oklahoma Criminal Defense Lawyers Association; National Association of Criminal Defense Lawyers; American Collectors Association. ***Email:*** lrscott@mbo.net

RICHARD D. MORRISSETTE, born Rochester, New Hampshire, April 28, 1956; admitted to bar, 1985, Oklahoma. *Education:* University of New Hampshire (B.A., Economics & Political Science); University of Tulsa (J.D., 1984). New Hampshire House of Representatives (1976-1981); Staff Member of U.S. Senator John Durkin (1978); Registered Lobbyist, State of Oklahoma. *Member:* Oklahoma Bar Association; Oklahoma Criminal Defense Association; Oklahoma Trial Lawyers Association; Oklahoma County Criminal Trial Lawyers Association. ***Email:*** RMorri4340@aol.com

REPRESENTATIVE CLIENTS: HG CORP (Salt Lake City, Utah); World Airport Inns (Oklahoma City); PC-KH Corporation (Hot Springs Vacation Rentals and Property Management Co., Destin, Florida); SLC Motels (Minneapolis, Minnesota); Team Realty (Oklahoma City);

(This Listing Continued)

Diamondhead Realty and Development Co. (Hot Springs, Arkansas); LJK Companies, Inc. (Eden Prairie, Minnesota); Wells Fargo Bank (Minneapolis, Minnesota); Frontier State Bank; C.I.T. Lending Services Corp.; Amcon Resources, Inc.; Trinity Finance Co., Inc.; Claypool Cattle Company; Smith Bros. Farms; Diamond Graphics, Inc.; Frontier State Bank (Oklahoma City, Oklahoma), Stream Line Logistics; Howard Brothers Florist; Western American Auctions; Southern Production Program, Inc.; Future Healthcare Services, Inc.; Prudential/Wachovia Securities; Farmers Insurance Group of Companies; GMAC Commercial Mortage.

HEGGY & ASSOCIATES, LLC

2716W FIRST NATIONAL CENTER
120 NORTH ROBINSON
OKLAHOMA CITY, OKLAHOMA 73102
Telephone: 405-235-1551
Fax: 866-858-0358

Commercial Litigation and Arbitration, Securities Litigation, Employment Law, Insurance Law, Fraud Investigations, Broker-Dealer Arbitration.

RODNEY J. HEGGY, born St. Louis, Illinois, 1955; admitted to bar, 1981, Texas and U.S. District Court, Northern and Southern Districts of Texas; 1982, Oklahoma, U.S. District Court, Western, Northern and Eastern Districts of Oklahoma and U.S. Court of Appeals, Tenth and Eighth Circuits. *Education:* Southeastern Oklahoma State University (B.A., 1977); University of Louisiana (M.S., 1978); University of Houston (J.D., 1981). Author: "The Trial Lawyer's Purgatory: the Document Depository in Complex Litigation," BRS, 1990; "Oklahoma Toxic Torts Law: Elements, Standards for Evaluating Proof, and Suggestions for Practitioners," NBI, 1992; "Environmental Law for Business and Lenders: Litigation Prevention and Avoidance, Insurance Coverage and Evaluation of Proof," Oklahoma City University, 1992; "Using, Drafting and Enforcing Arbitration Clauses," Oklahoma Bar Association, 1992; "Ethical Considerations in Insurance Coverage Claims," NBI, 1997; "Extra-Contractual Insurance Claims Liability-Bad Faith, Insurance Coverage Law in Oklahoma," NBI, 1997; "Mandatory Arbitration of Employment Law Claims," and "Employee Misconduct and Workplace Torts," SES, 2003. (Also of Counsel to Federman & Sherwood). ***REPORTED CASES:*** Anderson v. Citigroup, NASD 03-07920 (2004); Hobi v. Goldman Sacks, NASD 04-01816 (2005); Park v. A.G. Edwards, NASD 04-04583 (2005); Schooley v. Merrill Lynch, Pierce, Fenner & Smith Inc., 867 F. Supp. 989 10 D. OK (1994). ***PRACTICE AREAS:*** Commercial Arbitration; Commercial Litigation; Employment Law; Insurance; Fraud. ***Email:*** rheggy@cox.net

HELMS & UNDERWOOD

2500 FIRST NATIONAL CENTER
120 NORTH ROBINSON AVENUE
OKLAHOMA CITY, OKLAHOMA 73102
Telephone: 405-319-0700
Fax: 405-319-9292
Email: conner@helmsunderwood.com

Litigation, Commercial Law, Oil and Gas Law, Corporate Law, Mergers and Acquisitions, Intellectual Property, Copyright and Trademarks, Internet Law, Entertainment Law, Employment Law, Family Law, Probate, Trusts, Estate Planning, Immigration Law, Intellectual Property.

CONNER L. HELMS, born Spearman, Texas, October 18, 1961; admitted to bar, 1987, Oklahoma; 1991, Texas; U.S. District Court, Western, Eastern and Northern Districts of Oklahoma and Northern, Southern, Eastern and Western Districts of Texas; U.S. Court of Appeals, Fifth, Ninth and Tenth Circuits; U.S. Supreme Court. *Education:* University of Oklahoma (B.B.A., 1984); Oklahoma City University (J.D., 1986). *Member:* Oklahoma County, Oklahoma and American Bar Associations; State Bar of Texas; American Trial Lawyers Association. ***PRACTICE AREAS:*** Federal and State Court Litigation; Commercial Law; Oil and Gas Law; Corporate Law; Employment Law; Estate Planning; Immigration Law. ***Email:*** conner@helmsunderwood.com

GARY R. UNDERWOOD, born Chickasha, Oklahoma, May 18, 1945; admitted to bar, 1975, Oklahoma; U.S. District Court, Western, Eastern and Northern Districts of Oklahoma; U.S. Court of Appeals, Tenth Circuit. *Education:* University of Oklahoma (B.B.A., 1970); Oklahoma City University (J.D., 1975). *Member:* Oklahoma County, Oklahoma and American Bar Associations; The Association of Trial Lawyers of America. ***PRACTICE AREAS:*** Litigation; Federal Practice; Probate; Estate Litigation; Trust Litigation. ***Email:*** gary@helmsunderwood.com

DARREN R. COOK, born Irving, Texas, January 30, 1971; admitted to bar, 1997, Oklahoma and Texas; U.S. District Court, Western and Eastern Districts of Oklahoma and Northern District of Texas and U.S. Court of Appeals, Tenth Circuit. *Education:* University of Oklahoma (B.A., 1993; J.D., 1996). Member, American Indian Law Review. Outstanding Special Features Editor. *Member:* Oklahoma County, Oklahoma and American (Member, Litigation Section) Bar Associations; State Bar of Texas. ***PRACTICE AREAS:*** Litigation; Copyright; Trademark; Entertainment Law; Business Law; Federal Practice. ***Email:*** darren@helmsunderwood.com

ASSOCIATES

REBECCA A. FARRIS, born Oklahoma City, Oklahoma, October 22, 1972; admitted to bar, 1999, Oklahoma and U.S. District Court, Western District of Oklahoma. *Education:* Oklahoma State University (B.A., 1995); University of Oklahoma (J.D., 1999). Phi Delta Phi. *Member:* Oklahoma County, Oklahoma and American Bar Associations; American Immigration Lawyers Association. ***PRACTICE AREAS:*** Civil Litigation; Immigration Law; Employment Law; Probate. ***Email:*** rfarris@helmsunderwood.com

RACHEL K. McCOMBS, born Ft. Leavenworth, Kansas, March 5, 1975; admitted to bar, 2001, Oklahoma; 2003, U.S. Court of Appeals, Federal Circuit and U.S. Court of International Trade; U.S. District Court, Western District of Oklahoma; U.S. Court of Appeals, 10th Circuit. *Education:* University of Oklahoma (B.A. cum laude, 1998); University of Oklahoma (J.D. with dist., 2001); University of London (LL.M. with merit, 2002). Phi

(This Listing Continued)

Delta Phi. *Member:* Oklahoma and American Bar Associations; Organization of Women in International Trade. ***PRACTICE AREAS:*** Civil Litigation; International Law; Medical Malpractice; Employment Law. ***Email:*** rmccombs@helmsunderwood.com

ERIN M. MOORE, born Oklahoma City, Oklahoma, June 2, 1979; (admission pending). *Education:* Haverford College (B.S., 2001), University of Oklahoma (J.D., 2005). *Member:* Oklahoma Bar Association. ***PRACTICE AREAS:*** Civil Litigation. ***Email:*** emoore@helmsunderwood.com

OF COUNSEL

JULIAN D. HELMS, born Arkadelphia, Arkansas, February 22, 1932; admitted to bar, 1956, Texas; 1970, Oklahoma; 1971, U.S. Supreme Court. *Education:* West Texas State University, Trinity University and Texas Technological University (B.B.A., 1954); University of Texas (J.D., 1957). *Member:* Dallas, Oklahoma and American Bar Associations; State Bar of Texas. ***PRACTICE AREAS:*** Oil and Gas Law; Banking Law; Commercial Law; Mergers and Acquisitions Law; Trust Law; Estate Planning Law.

BRIAN T. HERMANSON

OKLAHOMA CITY, OKLAHOMA

(See Ponca City)

Litigation, Criminal Law, Family Law, Divorce, Personal Injury.

HESTER, SCHEM, HESTER & BATSON

5400 NORTH GRAND BOULEVARD, SUITE 265
OKLAHOMA CITY, OKLAHOMA 73112
Telephone: 405-947-8866
Fax: 405-947-1140
URL: http://www.hesterlaw.net
URL: http://www.okcfamilylaw.com

Family Law including: Divorce, Child Custody, Adoptions, Spousal Support, Premarital Agreements, Child Support and Post Decree Modifications.

JON L. HESTER, born Eschwege, Germany, April 30, 1948; admitted to bar, 1973, Oklahoma. *Education:* Alaska Methodist University (B.A., 1970); University of Oklahoma (J.D., 1972). Adjunct Faculty Member: University of Oklahoma, 1979; Rose State College, 1978-1983. Judge, Family Relations Division, 1976-1982. *Member:* Oklahoma Bar Association (Chairman, Section on Family Law, 1982-1983; 1986). Fellow, American Academy of Matrimonial Lawyers (President, Oklahoma Chapter, 1988-1989, 2004-2005; Member, National Board of Governors, 1989-1992). ***REPORTED CASES:*** Representative: Rogers v. Rogers, 1999 OK CIV APP 123, 994 P.2d 102; Carpenter v. Carpenter, 1983 OK 2, 657 P.2d 646. ***Email:*** jhester@hesterlaw.net

CHARLES O. SCHEM, born Oklahoma City, Oklahoma, March 14, 1954; admitted to bar, 1980, Oklahoma and U.S. District Court, Western District of Oklahoma. *Education:* University of Oklahoma (B.A., 1976; J.D., 1979). *Member:* Oklahoma County and Oklahoma Bar Associations. ***PRACTICE AREAS:*** Family Law. ***Email:*** cschem@hesterlaw.net

SCOTT A. HESTER, born Oklahoma City, Oklahoma, December 17, 1973; admitted to bar, 2000, Oklahoma. *Education:* University of Oklahoma (B.A., Letters, 1997; J.D., 2000). *Member:* Oklahoma Bar Association. ***PRACTICE AREAS:*** Divorce; Child Custody; Family Law; Adoption Law; Paternity. ***Email:*** shester@hesterlaw.net

CHRISTINE A. BATSON, born Torrejón De Ardoz, Spain, November 9, 1967; admitted to bar, 2000, Oklahoma and U.S. District Court; Western District of Oklahoma. *Education:* University of Oklahoma (B.S., 1997; J.D., 2000). *Member:* Oklahoma County and Oklahoma Bar Associations; Ruth Bader Inns of Court. ***PRACTICE AREAS:*** Divorce; Child Custody; Family Law. ***Email:*** cbatson@hesterlaw.net

ROBERT HIGHSAW

3801 N. CLASSEN BOULEVARD
OKLAHOMA CITY, OKLAHOMA 73118
Telephone: 405-525-7680
Fax: 405-525-8038
Email: highsaw@sbcglobal.net
URL: http://www.roberthighsaw.com

Workers Compensation, Federal Workers Compensation, Workers Compensation Appeals, Workers Compensation Defense, Workers Compensation Self-Insurance, Workers Compensation Subrogation, Immigration and Naturalization, Business Immigration, Citizenship, Consular Law, Deportation, Diplomatic Immunity, Employment Authorization, Employment Immigration, Employment Visas, Family Immigration Law, Immigration Discrimination, Immigration Law, Investor Visas, Labor Certifications, Permanent Visas, Political Asylum, Refugee Law, Religious Visas, Visas, Social Security, Social Security Appeals, Social Security Disability, Social Security Disability Insurance, Supplemental Security Income, Administrative Law, Longshore and Harbor Workers Compensation.

ROBERT HIGHSAW, born Oxford, Mississippi, October 23, 1953; admitted to bar, 1979, Oklahoma. *Education:* Lawrence University (B.A., 1976); University of Tulsa (J.D., 1979). Phi Delta Phi. *Member:* Oklahoma County, Oklahoma (Member, Board of Directors, Workers Compensation Section, 1990-1994; Chairman, Board of Directors, Workers Compensation Section, 1993) and American Bar Associations.

JACKIE L. HILL, JR.

2800 OKLAHOMA TOWER
210 PARK AVENUE
OKLAHOMA CITY, OKLAHOMA 73102-5604
Telephone: 405-232-4456
Fax: 405-232-4457
Email: jackie@jhilllaw.com

Bankruptcy, Banking Law, Real Estate, Business Litigation, Corporate Law.

JACKIE L. HILL, JR., born Oklahoma City, Oklahoma, March 21, 1961; admitted to bar, 1986, Oklahoma and U.S. District Court, Western and Eastern Districts of Oklahoma; 1987, U.S. District Court, Northern District of Oklahoma and U.S. Court of Appeals, Tenth Circuit. *Education:* Oklahoma State University (B.S., 1983); University of Oklahoma (J.D., with distinction, 1986). Phi Alpha Delta. *Member:* Oklahoma County, Oklahoma and American Bar Associations. ***PRACTICE AREAS:*** Bankruptcy; Banking; Real Estate; Business Litigation; Corporate Law.

OF COUNSEL TO

DUNN, SWAN & CUNNINGHAM, Oklahoma City, Oklahoma.

HILTGEN & BREWER, P.C.

Established in 1996

ONE BENHAM PLACE, SUITE 800
9400 N. BROADWAY EXTENSION
OKLAHOMA CITY, OKLAHOMA 73114-7401
Telephone: 405-605-9000
Facsimile: 405-605-9010
Email: administrator@hiltgenbrewer.com
URL: http://www.hiltgenbrewer.com

Civil Litigation, Insurance Defense, Manufacturers' Products Liability, Negligence, Premises Liability, Environmental Law, Construction and Complex Commercial Litigation, Trucking Law, Employment and Labor Law, Insurance and Workers' Compensation.

FIRM PROFILE: Hiltgen & Brewer, P.C., is listed in the Bar Register of Pre-Eminent Lawyers under Insurance Defense.

CARY E. HILTGEN, born Manhattan, Kansas, May 17, 1954; admitted to bar, 1981, Oklahoma; U.S. District Court, Nothern, Eastern and Western Districts of Oklahoma; U.S. District Court, District of Arizona; U.S. District Court, Central District of Illinois; U.S. District Court, Western District of New York; U.S. District Court, District of Nebraska; U.S. District Court, District of Utah; U.S. Court of Appeals, Third, Seventh, Eighth, Ninth and Tenth Circuits. *Education:* Hutchinson Community Junior College (A.A., 1974); Northwest Missouri State University (B.S., 1976); Oklahoma City University (J.D., 1980). *Member:* Oklahoma County and Oklahoma Bar Associations; International Association of Defense Counsel; Defense Research Institute (Chair, Product Liability Committee; Member, Law Institutes Committee); Trucking Industry Defense Association; Oklahoma Association of Defense Counsel. ***REPORTED CASES:*** Midwest Grain Products of Illinois, Inc. v. Productization, Inc. 228 F.3d 784 (7th Cir., Ill., Oct 3, 2000); Kinserlow v. CMI Corp., 217 F.3d 1021, Prod. Liab. Rep. (CCH) P 15, 862 (8th Cir., Mo., Jul 5, 2000)(No. 99-3668); Surace v. Caterpillar, Inc., 111 F.3d 1039, 46 Fed. R. Evid. Serv. 1487, Prod. Liab. Rep. (CCH P 14,917 (3rd Cir., Pa., Apr. 22, 1997) (No. 95-1805); Rambo v. American Southern Ins. Co., 839 F.2d 1415 (10th Cir., Okla., Feb 26, 1988) (No. 85-2417); Shore Slurry Seal, Inc. v. CMI Crop., 964 F.Supp. 152 (D.N.J., May 12, 1997) (No. CIV. A. 97-168, JEI). ***PRACTICE AREAS:*** Products Liability; Insurance Defense; Environmental Law; Commercial Litigation; Trucking Law. ***Email:*** cehiltgen@hiltgenbrewer.com

MICHAEL W. BREWER, born Pryor, Oklahoma, October 20, 1960; admitted to bar, 1986, Oklahoma. *Education:* University of Oklahoma (B.S.M.E., 1982; J.D., 1986). Phi Delta Phi. Recipient, American Jurisprudence Award in Anti-Trust, Fall 1985. Author: Note, "Workers' Compensation: Erosion of the Exclusive Remedy Provision," Vol. 38-3, Oklahoma L. Rev., Fall 1985. *Member:* Oklahoma County (Director, 1995-1999; Member: Board of Directors, 1995-1998; Committees on: Bench and Bar, 1994; Continuing Legal Education, 1992-1995; Fee Grievance, 1996—; Young Lawyers Division Board of Directors, 1992-1993; Oklahoma (Chair, Publications Committee, Young Lawyers Division, 1988-1989; Editor, Young Lawyers Division Newsletter, 1988-1989. Member: Continuing Legal Education Committee, 1991-1995; Board of Directors, Young Lawyers Division, 1990-1993) Bar Associations; Western District of Oklahoma ENE Panel; Oklahoma Association of Defense Counsel (Member, Board of Directors, State DRI Representative, 2000-2003); Defense Research Institute (Oklahoma State DRI Representative; Vice-Chairman, Technology Committee; Co-Chairman, Technology SLG Products Liability Committee; E-Discovery Task Force; Employment Law Steering Committee); Transportation Lawyers Association; Federation of Defense and Corporate Counsel; The Arbitration Forum. Barrister, William J. Holloway, Jr., American Inns of Court CV, 1993-1996. ***REPORTED CASES:*** Allstate v. Brown, 920 F.2d 664 (C.A.10th Cir. 1990); English v. Wal-Mart, 16 P.3d 1136 (OK Cir App 5 2001); Meadows v. Wal Mart, 2001 WL 246355 (OK 25 2001). ***PRACTICE AREAS:*** Business Litigation; Products Liability Law; Insurance Defense Law; Premises Liability; Personal Injury Law; Employment Law. ***Email:*** mwbrewer@hiltgenbrewer.com

---

BROCK C. BOWERS, born Shawnee, Oklahoma, October 15, 1969; admitted to bar, 1994, Oklahoma; U.S. District Court, Western and Eastern District of Oklahoma; U.S. Court of Appeals, Tenth Circuit. *Education:* University of Oklahoma (B.A., 1991; J.D., 1994). Phi Beta Kappa. *Member:* Oklahoma and American Bar Associations; Defense Research Institute; Oklahoma Association of Defense Counsel. ***PRACTICE AREAS:*** Insurance Defense; Products Liability; Subrogation; Premises Liability; Employment Law; Trucking Law. ***Email:*** bcbowers@hiltgenbrewer.com

(This Listing Continued)

T. SHANE CURTIN, born Midwest City, Oklahoma, May 11, 1966; admitted to bar, 1991, Oklahoma; U.S. District Court, Western District of Oklahoma. *Education:* University of Central Oklahoma (B.B.A., Human Resource Management, 1988); University of Oklahoma (J.D., 1991). Phi Delta Phi. *Member:* Oklahoma and American Bar Associations; Oklahoma Association of Defense Counsel. ***PRACTICE AREAS:*** Workers Compensation. ***Email:*** tscurtin@hiltgenbrewer.com

JENNIFER E. JACKSON, born Denver, Colorado, January 30, 1977; admitted to bar, 2002, Oklahoma. *Education:* Oklahoma Baptist University (B.A., 1999); University of Oklahoma (J.D., 2002). *Member:* Oklahoma County and American Bar Associations; Defense Research Institute. ***PRACTICE AREAS:*** Products Liability Defense; Employment Defense; Insurance Defense. ***Email:*** jjackson@hiltgenbrewer.com

NORMAN LEMONIK, born New York, N.Y., March 6, 1954; admitted to bar, 1980, Michigan; U.S. District Court, Eastern District of Michigan; 1990, Oklahoma; U.S. District Court, Northern, Eastern and Western; U.S. Court of Appeals, Tenth Circuit. *Education:* Syracuse University (B.S., 1976); New York Law School (J.D., 1980). *Member:* State Bar of Michigan; Oklahoma Bar Association; Oklahoma Association of Defense Counsel; Defense Research Institute. ***REPORTED CASES:*** Frieling v. Malowest, Inc., 814 F. Supp. 75 (W.D. Okla. 1993); Horace Mann Ins. Co. v. Johnson, 953 F.2d 575 (10th Cir. 1991); Hormel Food Corp. v. Hale, 918 R.2 91 (Okla. App. 1996); Shaffer v. Jeffery, 915 P.2d 910 (Okla. 1996); Post Oak Oil Co. v. Stack and Barnes, P.C., 913 P.2d 1311 (Okla. 1996); Huffman v. Altec Int'l, Inc., 546 N.W.2d 162 (Wisc. Ct. App. 1996); Trinity Universal Ins. Co. v. Broussard, 932 F. Supp. 1307 (ND Okla 1996). ***PRACTICE AREAS:*** Workers Compensation; Insurance Defense; Insurance Coverage. ***Email:*** nlemonik@hiltgenbrewer.com

SCOTT C. SUBLETT, born Sterling, Colorado, July 12, 1952; admitted to bar, 1979, Oklahoma; U.S. District Court, Northern and Western Districts of Oklahoma. *Education:* University of Colorado (B.S., 1975); University of Tulsa (J.D. with honors, 1979). Phi Delta Phi. Recipient, American Jurisprudence Award in Commercial Law, 1978. *Member:* Oklahoma Bar Association. ***PRACTICE AREAS:*** Litigation; Corporate Law; Banking Law. ***Email:*** scsublett@hiltgenbrewer.com

JEREMY Z. CARTER, born Shawnee, Oklahoma, September 14, 1977; admitted to bar, 2003, Oklahoma. *Education:* Oklahoma State University (B.S., Political Science, 2000); University of Oklahoma (J.D., 2003). Sigma Chi. *Member:* Cleveland County, Oklahoma and American Bar Associations. ***Email:*** jzcarter@hiltgenbrewer.com

JEFF C. GROTTA, born Watertown, South Dakota, November 10, 1961; admitted to bar, 1993, Oklahoma; 1994, U.S. District Court, Northern, Eastern and Western Districts of Oklahoma. *Education:* University of Oklahoma (B.A., 1987; J.D., with honors, 1993). Phi Delta Phi. Technical Editor, American Indian Law Review, 1992-1993. Student Clerk to the Hon. Marian Opala, Oklahoma Supreme Court. Law Clerk to the Hon. Bana Blasdel, U.S. Magistrate Judge, Western District of Oklahoma. Staff Attorney to the Hon. Reta M. Strubhar, Oklahoma Court of Criminal Appeals. *Member:* Oklahoma County (Member, Continuing Legal Education Committee), Oklahoma (Member: YLD Mock Trial Committee; Community Law Week Committee) and American Bar Associations; Oklahoma Association of Defense Counsel; Defense Research Institute. ***LANGUAGES:*** Russian. ***PRACTICE AREAS:*** Business Law; Commercial Law; Insurance; Personal Injury Defense; Products Liability; Debtor and Creditor. ***Email:*** jcgrotta@hiltgenbrewer.com

J. RANDY BAKER, born Oklahoma City, Oklahoma, September 28, 1955; admitted to bar, 1980, Oklahoma. *Education:* Oklahoma State University (B.S., 1977); Oklahoma City University (J.D. with honors, 1980). Phi Alpha Delta (Treasurer, 1978-1979). Member and Notes Editor, Oklahoma City University Law Review, 1978-1979. Law Clerk to Hon. Luther B. Eubanks, Chief Judge, U.S. District Court, Western District of Oklahoma, 1982-1984. Author: "Survey of Oklahoma Law: Defamation," 4 Oklahoma City University L. Rev., 310-325, 1979. Contributing Author: "Employee Benefits Law," (2000 Supplement). Adjunct Professor, Appellate Advocacy, Legal Research and Writing, Oklahoma City University, School of Law, 1980-1981.*Member:* Oklahoma County, Oklahoma and American Bar Associations. ***PRACTICE AREAS:*** Insurance Defense; Products Liability; Personal Injury; ERISA; Employment Law; Civil Rights; Toxic Torts; Commercial Litigation; Administrative Law; Complex and Multi-District Litigation.

LYNNE F. SAUNDERS, born New Orleans, Louisiana, 1956; admitted to bar, 1994, Oklahoma; U.S. District Court, Western District of Oklahoma. *Education:* University of Maryland (B.S., 1978); Oklahoma City University School of Business (M.B.A., with high honors, 1982); Oklahoma City University School of Law (J.D., summa cum laude, 1993). Moot Court. Member, Oklahoma City University Law Review. Law Clerk to the Hon. Vicki Miles-LaGrange, U.S. District Court, Western District of Oklahoma, 1994-1998. Consumer and Housing Attorney, Legal Aid of Western Oklahoma, 1994. Member: Oklahoma City University Law School Alumni Board; League of Women Voters of Oklahoma County; Leadership Midwest City; Midwest City Chamber of Commerce; Rose State College Foundation. Chair, Board of Regents of Rose State College. *Member:* Oklahoma County (Member: Law Related Education Committee; Legal Aid Committee), Oklahoma (Member, Diversity Committee), American (Member, Sections on: Business Litigation; Intellectual Property) and National Bar Associations; Oklahoma Lawyers for Children; Diversity Committee and Law Schools Committee, Ruth Bader Ginsburg American Inn of Court; Oklahoma Association of Black Lawyers; American Association of University Women. [Capt., U.S. Air Force, 1979-1983]. ***PRACTICE AREAS:*** Litigation. ***Email:*** lfsaunders@hiltgenbrewer.com

REPRESENTATIVE CLIENTS: Allstate Insurance Co.; American Agency System, Inc.; Arkansas Best Corp.; Associated Underwriters; Aventis Behring; Bid-Well Corp.; Burlington Motor Carriers, Inc.; California Casualty Indemnity Exchange; California Casualty Insurance Co.; California Casualty Management Co.; Cannon Express Corp.; Cardinal Logistics; ACE-INA; Claims Management, Inc.; Clarendon National Insurance Co.; CMI Corp.; CNA E&S; Colonial Freight Systems, Inc.; Continental National Indemnity Co.; Deere & Co.; E&O Professionals; ESIS; Essex Insurance Co.; Farmland Mutual Insurance Co.; Fireman's Fund; First American Insurance Co.; Fleming Foods, Inc.; Fulcrum Insurance Co.; Gryphon Insurance Group; HCR-Manorcare; Harco National Insurance Co.; Haskell Lemon Construction Company; Home Depot U.S.A., Inc.; Hormel Foods; IBP, Inc.; Inca Metal Products Corp.; Johnson Ross Corp.; Kemper Insurance Co.; Lexington Insurance Co.; Load King Trailers; Markel West, Inc.; Metro Pave, Inc.; Midlands Claim Administrators, Inc.; Midlands Management Corp.; Millers Mutual Fire Insurance Co.; M.S. Carriers, Inc.; National Food Processors Association; Nestle USA, Inc.; Campbell Soup Co.; National Transportation Adjusters; PBX, Inc.; Perry Enterprises, Inc.; Phillips Petroleum Co.; Prime Inc.; Starkist Tuna; Reliance Insurance Co.; Rhone Poulenc Co.; Robertson Transportation Services; St. Paul Fire & Marine Insurance Co.; Terex Corp.; Titan Indemnity Co. (St.Paul); Tracker Marine; Tri-Star

(This Listing Continued)

Risk Management; Tyson Foods Inc.; Underwriters at Lloyds; United Safety & Claims; Westport Insurance Corp.; Willis Administrative Services; W. E. Love & Associates; Workmed Benefit Services Corp.

HOLBROOK & TOFFOLI

An Association of Attorneys
2205 FIRST NATIONAL CENTER
120 NORTH ROBINSON
OKLAHOMA CITY, OKLAHOMA 73102
Telephone: 405-232-3664
Telefacsimile: 405-236-1286

Creditor Bankruptcy, Creditors Rights in Bankruptcy, Debtor and Creditor Bankruptcy, Debtor and Creditor Reorganization, Debtor and Creditor Workouts, Debtor Bankruptcy, Secured Creditors Rights, Unsecured Creditors Rights and General Business Transactions.

MEMBERS OF FIRM

L. WIN HOLBROOK, born Oklahoma City, Oklahoma, November 21, 1942; admitted to bar, 1971, Oklahoma; 1984, U.S. District Court, Western District of Oklahoma; 1990, U.S. Court of Appeals, Tenth Circuit. *Education:* Oklahoma City University (B.S., 1966; J.D., 1971). Phi Alpha Delta. Panel Trustee, U.S. Bankruptcy Court, Western District of Oklahoma, 1985—. *Member:* Oklahoma (Member, Bankruptcy and Reorganization Section) and American (Member, Sections on: Real Property, Probate and Trust Law; Business) Bar Associations. ***PRACTICE AREAS:*** Debtor and Creditor Reorganization; Debtor and Creditor Bankruptcy; Creditors Rights in Bankruptcy; Debtor Bankruptcy. ***Email:*** wholbrook@htlaw.org

MARK B. TOFFOLI, born New York, New York, August 25, 1954; admitted to bar, 1982, Oklahoma; 1983, U.S. District Court, Western District of Oklahoma; 1984, U.S. Court of Appeals, Tenth Circuit. *Education:* Montana State University (B.S., 1976); Oklahoma City University School of Law (J.D., 1982). Lecturer, Bankruptcy, Department of Legal Assistance Education, Oklahoma University Law Center, 1986. Attorney, 1987-1991 and Senior Attorney, 1991-1997, Office of United States Trustee, Department of Justice. *Member:* Oklahoma Bar Association (Member, Public Information Committee, 1990—). ***PRACTICE AREAS:*** Creditor Bankruptcy; Creditors Rights in Bankruptcy; Debtor and Creditor Bankruptcy; Debtor and Creditor Reorganization; Debtor Bankruptcy. ***Email:*** mtoffoli@htlaw.org

MARK E. MONFORT, born Rapid City, South Dakota, August 6, 1948; admitted to bar, 1973, Oklahoma; 1980, U.S. District Court, Western District of Oklahoma. *Education:* University of Oklahoma (B.A., 1970; J.D., 1973); University of Washington (LL.M., 1996). Assistant Municipal Counselor, City of Oklahoma City, 1973-1980. Director of Registration, Oklahoma Department of Securities, 1978-1980. *Member:* Oklahoma County, Oklahoma and American Bar Associations. ***PRACTICE AREAS:*** Bankruptcy; Corporate Law; Civil Practice.

REPRESENTATIVE CLIENTS: Furnished Upon Request.

HOLDEN & CARR

OKLAHOMA CITY, OKLAHOMA

(See Tulsa)

Insurance Defense, Medical Malpractice Defense, Nursing Home Defense, Toxic Mold Defense, Casualty Insurance, Commercial Litigation, Banking, Appeals, Coverage Opinions, Labor and Employment Litigation, Contracts.

HOLLADAY, CHILTON & DEGIUSTI, PLLC

CITY PLACE, SUITE 1550
204 NORTH ROBINSON
OKLAHOMA CITY, OKLAHOMA 73102
Telephone: 405-236-2343
Facsimile: 405-236-2349
URL: http://www.hcdattorneys.com

Complex Commercial and Business Litigation, Insurance Coverage, Securities Fraud, Class Action Suits, Banking, Real Estate, Business Torts, Bankruptcy, Environmental and General Business Contract Litigation in State and Federal Courts.

DON G. HOLLADAY, born Duncan, Oklahoma, August 27, 1944; admitted to bar, 1969, Oklahoma. *Education:* Oklahoma Baptist University; University of Oklahoma (B.A., 1966); University of Oklahoma College of Law (J.D., 1969). Phi Delta Phi (Clerk, 1967-1968). Listed, The Best Lawyers in America, Business Litigation. Author: "Evidence: Mental Defects and Witness Competency," Oklahoma Bar Journal, Volume 40, Number 44, November 1969; "The Boundaries of the Warrantless Search," 13 Air Force JAG Law Review 44, Winter, 1971; "Pretrial Mental Examinations Under Military Law: A Reexamination," 16 Air Force JAG Law Review 14, Fall 1974; "Appellate Jurisdiction in Cases Involving Multiple Claims," Oklahoma Bar Journal, Volume 60, Number 48, December 1989. Visiting Professor of Law, University of Oklahoma Law Center, 1987-1988. Faculty Member, Southern Regional National Institute for Trial Advocacy, 1988—. Adjunct Professor of Law, Trial Techniques and Complex Litigation, University of Oklahoma Law Center, 1989—. Bar Review Lecturer, Federal Jurisdiction. [Capt., Judge Advocate, USAF, 1969-1975]. ***PRACTICE AREAS:*** Civil Litigation; Federal Litigation; Environmental Insurance Coverage. ***Email:*** dholladay@hcdattorneys.com

GARY S. CHILTON, born Wichita, Kansas, December 18, 1954; admitted to bar, 1981, Oklahoma; 1985, U.S. Supreme Court; 1990, Missouri; U.S. District Court, Western, Eastern and Northern Districts of Oklahoma; 1996, U.S. Court of Appeals, Tenth Circuit. *Education:* University of Kansas (B.S., 1977); University of Kansas School of Law (J.D., 1981). Listed, The Best Lawyers in America, Business Litigation. Author: "The Implied Covenant of Good Faith and Fair Dealing in Oklahoma: Ex Contractu or Ex Delicto?" 69 Oklahoma Bar Journal 3167, 1998. ***PRACTICE AREAS:*** Civil Litigation; Business Litigation; Federal Civil Litigation; Real Estate Litigation; Oil and Gas Litigation; Bankruptcy Litigation. ***Email:*** gchilton@hcdattorneys.com

TIMOTHY D. DEGIUSTI, born Oklahoma City, Oklahoma, December 11, 1962; admitted to bar, 1988, Oklahoma, U.S. District Court, Western District of Oklahoma and U.S. Court of Appeals, Tenth Circuit; 1989, U.S. District Court, Northern District of Oklahoma; 1990, U.S. Army Court of Military Review; 1998, U.S. Court of Appeals for the Armed Forces. *Education:* University of Oklahoma (B.A., with distinction, 1985); University of Oklahoma College of Law (J.D., 1988). Member, Order of Barristers. Master of the Bench, Luther Bohanon American Inn of Court. Author: "Unlawful Command Influence, Raising and Litigating the Issue," The Army Lawyer, September 1993. Adjunct Professor of Law, University of Oklahoma College of Law, 1998-2003. [Judge Advocate, Reserve Components, 1993-2003; Capt., U.S. Army JAG Corps, 1990-1993]. ***PRACTICE AREAS:*** Civil Litigation; Federal Litigation; Insurance; Military Law. ***Email:*** tdegiusti@hcdattorneys.com

HEIDI J. LONG, born Marshall, Minnesota, May 7, 1972; admitted to bar, 1997, Oklahoma and U.S. District Court, Western District of Oklahoma; 1999, U.S. District Court, Northern District of Oklahoma. *Education:* Southwestern Oklahoma State University (B.A., 1993); University of Oklahoma College of Law (J.D., with distinction, 1997). Phi Delta Phi. Recipient: Pro Bono Award, Oklahoma County Bar Association, 2002; Outstanding Young Lawyer, Oklahoma County Bar Association, 2001-2002. Trustee, Oklahoma County Law Library, 2002-2004. *Member:* Oklahoma County Bar Association (Chairperson, Young Lawyers Division, 2001-2002; Co-Chairperson, Voices for Children Committee, 2000-2003; Chairperson, Law Day Committee, 2005; Member Board of Directors, 2005—); Oklahoma Bar Association (Member, Access to Justice Committee, 2003—); William J. Holloway Jr. American Inn of Court, 2002. ***PRACTICE AREAS:*** Civil Litigation. ***Email:*** hlong@hcdattorneys.com

---

GIDEON A. LINCECUM, born Shreveport, Louisiana, August 7, 1972; admitted to bar, 2003, Oklahoma. *Education:* Louisiana State University at Shreveport (B.G.S., 1997); Oklahoma City University School of Law (J.D., 2002). Phi Alpha Delta. Recipient: Scholarship Award, William J. Holloway, Jr. American Inn of Court, 2001-2002; Oklahoma City University Law Review, Research Editor; Author: Note, "Electronic Surveillance: Protecting the Privacy Ecosystem from the FBI's Carnivore," 28 Okla. City U.L. Rev. 29, 2003. *Member:* Oklahoma County, Oklahoma and American Bar Associations. ***PRACTICE AREAS:*** Civil Litigation. ***Email:*** glincecum@hcdattorneys.com

JAMES E. WARNER, III, born Claremore, Oklahoma, May 11, 1976; admitted to bar, 2002, Oklahoma and U.S. District Court, Western District of Oklahoma. *Education:* Northeastern Oklahoma State University (B.S., cum laude, 1998); University of Oklahoma (J.D., 2002). Member: Black Law Students Association; Oklahoma International Law Society. Associate, Luther Buhanon American Inn of Court, 2002—. Executive Editor, American Indian Law Review, 2001-2002. *Member:* Oklahoma County, Oklahoma and American Bar Associations. ***PRACTICE AREAS:*** Civil Litigation; Federal Civil Litigation; Business Litigation; Insurance Coverage. ***Email:*** jwarner@hcdattorneys.com

HOLLOWAY, DOBSON & BACHMAN

A PROFESSIONAL CORPORATION
Established in 1947
SUITE 900
ONE LEADERSHIP SQUARE
211 NORTH ROBINSON
OKLAHOMA CITY, OKLAHOMA 73102-7102
Telephone: 405-235-8593
Fax: 405-235-1707
URL: http://www.hollowaydobson.com

Litigation, Appellate Practice, Alternate Dispute Resolution, Mediation, Aviation Law, Bankruptcy, Banks and Banking, Lender Liability, Business Law, Anti-trust and Unfair Competition, Mergers and Acquisitions, Civil Rights, Commercial Law, Construction Law, Corporate Law, Oil and Gas Law, Personal Injury, Products Liability, Labor and Employment Law, Municipal and other Governmental Subdivisions, Workers' Compensation, Professional Malpractice, Medical Malpractice, Toxic Torts, Health Law, Trusts and Estates, Probate, Wills, Negligence, Casualty and Surety Insurance, Real Estate and Environmental Law.

FIRM PROFILE: Holloway, Dobson & Bachman, founded in 1947 by Russell Holloway, is organized as a professional corporation and is engaged in numerous areas of the practice of law. The Firm's attorneys have been practicing law for an average of 20 years in a variety of specialized areas. The attorneys of Holloway, Dobson & Bachman have a solid reputation of caring for and aggressively representing their clients. Moreover, the Firm is committed to diversity and was a recent recipient of the Ada Louis Fisher Diversity Award awarded by the Oklahoma Black Lawyers Association. For more than the past four decades our Firm has been active in tort litigation of all forms and currently includes, but is not limited to claims of negligence, personal injury, manufacturers products liability, hospital and medical malpractice, legal malpractice, aviation law, drug litigation, bad faith, toxic tort, employment discrimination, wrongful discharge, breach of contract and workers' compensation. The mission of the Firm is to represent its clients with the goal of achieving, promptly and efficiently, the outcome established by the client with the counsel of an able, experienced and dedicated attorney. Holloway, Dobson & Bachman is listed in the Bar Register of Preeminent Lawyers.

PAGE DOBSON, born Oklahoma City, Oklahoma, July 26, 1935; admitted to bar, 1959, Oklahoma. *Education:* University of Oklahoma (B.A., 1957; LL.B., 1959). Phi Alpha Delta; Omicron Delta Kappa. Member, Arbitration Panel, U.S. District Court, Western District of Oklahoma. *Member:* Oklahoma County (Former Director and Officer), Oklahoma (Former Delegate) and American Bar Associations; Oklahoma Association of De-

(This Listing Continued)

HOLLOWAY, DOBSON & BACHMAN, A PROFESSIONAL CORPORATION, Oklahoma City—Continued

fense Counsel. Fellow: Oklahoma Bar Foundation; American Bar Foundation. ***PRACTICE AREAS:*** Products Liability; Torts; Civil Practice; Insurance Defense; Employment Law; Drug Litigation. ***Email:*** pdobson@hollowaydobson.com

GARY C. BACHMAN, born Louisville, Kentucky, December 9, 1943; admitted to bar, 1970, Oklahoma. *Education:* Oklahoma Central State College (B.S., 1966); Oklahoma City University (J.D., 1970). Alpha Chi; Phi Delta Phi. Municipal Judge, Midwest City. Seminar Moderator and Instructor, "Insurance," Oklahoma Bar Association. *Member:* Oklahoma County, Oklahoma and American Bar Associations. ***PRACTICE AREAS:*** Personal Injury; Insurance Law; Environmental Law; Employment Law; Products Liability; Medical Malpractice. ***Email:*** gbachman@hollowaydobson.com

DAN L. HOLLOWAY, born Oklahoma City, Oklahoma, March 14, 1949; admitted to bar, 1983, Oklahoma. *Education:* University of Oklahoma (B.S., 1979; J.D., 1983). Phi Delta Phi; Order of the Coif. *Member:* Oklahoma County, Oklahoma and American Bar Associations; Christian Legal Society; Christian Conciliation Service; Oklahoma Trial Lawyers Association; The American Trial Lawyers Association. ***PRACTICE AREAS:*** Medical Malpractice; Church Law; Products Liability; Pharmaceutical Litigation; Nursing Home Litigation; Personal Injury. ***Email:*** dholloway@hollowaydobson.com

MARK E. DUVALL, born San Mateo, California, June 3, 1961; admitted to bar, 1986, Oklahoma. *Education:* Central Michigan University (B.S., 1983); University of Oklahoma (J.D., 1986). Phi Alpha Delta. President's Honor Roll, Central Michigan University.*Member:* Oklahoma County (Member, Young Lawyers Board of Directors, 1987-1989) Oklahoma and American Bar Associations. ***PRACTICE AREAS:*** Workers' Compensation; Labor and Employment; Insurance Defense; Civil Litigation. ***Email:*** mduvall@hollowaydobson.com

J. WILLIAM ARCHIBALD, born Ainsworth, Nebraska, August 27, 1954; admitted to bar, 1981, Oklahoma. *Education:* University of Tulsa; Oklahoma State University (B.S., 1977); University of Oklahoma (J.D., 1981). *Member:* Kingfisher County (President, 1985), Oklahoma County and Oklahoma Bar Associations. ***PRACTICE AREAS:*** Workers' Compensation; Employment Law; Insurance Defense; Products Liability; Personal Injury. ***Email:*** barchibald@hollowaydobson.com

STEPHEN D. BACHMAN, born Oklahoma City, Oklahoma, July 19, 1964; admitted to bar, 1990, Oklahoma. *Education:* Central State University (B.A., 1987); Oklahoma City University (J.D., with honors, 1990). *Member:* Oklahoma County, Oklahoma and American Bar Associations. ***PRACTICE AREAS:*** Products Liability; Personal Injury; Trucking Litigation; Nursing Home Negligence; Medical Malpractice; Pharmaceutical Litigation. ***Email:*** sbachman@hollowaydobson.com

MICHAEL E. SMITH, born Waynesboro, Pennsylvania, October 17, 1950; admitted to bar, 1978, Oklahoma. *Education:* University of Oklahoma (B.B.A., 1972); Oklahoma City University (J.D., 1978). Phi Delta Phi. *Member:* Oklahoma County, Oklahoma and American Bar Associations; Oklahoma Trial Lawyers Association. ***PRACTICE AREAS:*** Civil Rights Law; Insurance Law; Aviation Law; Employment Law; Medical Malpractice; Products Liability; Nursing Home Liability. ***Email:*** msmith@hollowaydobson.com

BRYAN G. GARRETT, born Oklahoma City, Oklahoma, May 7, 1972; admitted to bar, 1998, Oklahoma. *Education:* Southern Methodist University (B.A., 1994); University of Oklahoma (J.D., 1997). *Member:* Oklahoma Bar Association; Oklahoma Trial Lawyers Association; The American Trial Lawyers Association. ***PRACTICE AREAS:*** Civil Litigation; Products Liability; Insurance Defense; Personal Injury; Employment Law; Premises Liability; Insurance; ERISA; Trucking Law; Nursing Home Negligence. ***Email:*** bgarrett@hollowaydobson.com

---

LU ANN STOUT, born Elk City, Oklahoma, August 25, 1957; admitted to bar, 1987, Oklahoma. *Education:* University of Oklahoma (B.B.A., 1978) Oklahoma City University (J.D., 1987). *Member:* American Bar Association; Oklahoma County and Oklahoma Bar Associations; Defense Research Institute. ***PRACTICE AREAS:*** Complex and Multi-District Litigation; Insurance; Products Liability; Personal Injury; Toxic Torts; ERISA; Employment Law. ***Email:*** lstout@hollowaydobson.com

KENYATTA R. BETHEA, born November, 27, 1974; admitted to bar, 2000, Oklahoma. *Education:* Oklahoma University (B.A., 1997; J.D., 2000). Officer, Black Law Student Association. Semifinalist, Frederick Douglass Moot Court Competition. Recipient, Best Respondent's Brief Award, National Black Law Student Association. *Member:* Oklahoma and American Bar Associations; Oklahoma Trial Lawyers Association; American Trial Lawyers Association. ***PRACTICE AREAS:*** Insurance Defense; Products Liability; Personal Injury; Medical Malpractice; Labor and Employment; Workers Compensation; General Civil Litigation; Nursing Home Litigation. ***Email:*** kbethea@hollowaydobson.com

MARISSA T. OSENBAUGH, born Olathe, Kansas, July 8, 1978; admitted to bar, 2003, Oklahoma. *Education:* Friends University (B.S., 2000); University of Oklahoma (J.D., 2003). *Member:* Oklahoma and American Bar Associations. ***PRACTICE AREAS:*** Insurance Defense; Employment Law; Workers Compensation; Civil Litigation; Personal Injury; Medical Malpractice; Nursing Home Litigation. ***Email:*** mosenbaugh@hollowaydobson.com

OF COUNSEL

RUSSELL B. HOLLOWAY (1920-2004)

DAVID H. DOBSON, born Lawton, Oklahoma, January 2, 1960; admitted to bar, 1987, Oklahoma. *Education:* University of Oklahoma (B.A., 1983); Oklahoma City University (J.D., 1987). *Member:* Oklahoma County, Oklahoma and American Bar Associations. ***PRACTICE AREAS:*** ERISA Litigation; Insurance Defense; Health Law; Civil Rights; Personal Injury. ***Email:*** ddobson@hollowaydobson.com

GREG HAUBRICH, born Hallock, Minnesota, June 29, 1952; admitted to bar, 1986, Oklahoma and U.S. District Court, Northern, Eastern and Western Districts of Oklahoma; 1987, U.S. Court of Appeals, Tenth Circuit; 2002, U.S. Supreme Court. *Education:* Southwest Missouri State University (B.S., summa cum laude, 1982); University of Oklahoma (J.D. with distinction, 1986). *Member:* Oklahoma Bar Association; Oklahoma Trial Lawyers Association (Board of Directors). ***PRACTICE AREAS:*** Toxic Exposure; Personal Injury; Products Liability; Insurance. ***Email:*** ghaubrich@hollowaydobson.com

REPRESENTATIVE CLIENTS: Action Safety Supply Co.; AIG Aviation, Inc.; American Express Financial Advisors Inc.; American International Group; Benchmark Insurance Co.; Beneficial Insurance Group; Blue Cross Blue Shield of Oklahoma; Cambridge Integrated Services Group, Inc.; Capital Aviation, Inc.; Capitol Cardiovascular, Inc.; Chubb Group of Insurance Cos.; Church Mutual Insurance Co; City of Midwest City; CompSource Oklahoma; Cooper Tire & Rubber Co.; Danaher Corporation; Dolese Co.; Dresser Industries, Inc.; ESIS; Ford Motor Credit Co.; General Council of the Assemblies of God; General Motors Corp.; Gerling American Insurance, Co.; GMAC Mortgage; Halliburton Energy Services, Inc.; Hertz Claim Management; Hobby Lobby Stores, Inc.; Horace Mann Insurance; International Pentecostal Holiness Church; International Truck & Engine Corp.; Kohler Company; KONE Inc.; Lancer Claims; Kraft Foods North America Inc.; Legion Insurance; Liberty Mutual Insurance Company; Lone Star Industries, Inc.; Mercy Health Centers; MetLife; Mid-Del Schools; National American Insurance; Nissan Motor Acceptance Corp.; Nissan North America; Oklahoma County-State of Okalahoma; Oklahoma District Council of the Assemblies of God; OK Property & Casualty Association; Rental Adjusting Services; Royal Indemnity Company; Royal Insurance Company of America; Royal Sun Alliance; St. Paul Insurance; Sentry Insurance Company; TDK U.S.A.; Texas Property and Casualty Guaranty Association; TIG Insurance; Tokio Marine & Fire Insurance; Uniroyal Holding, Inc.; Volvo Finance North America, Inc.; Volvo North America; Winn Dixie, Inc.; XL Capitol, Ltd.; XL Environmental.

GARY B. HOMSEY

Established in 1974

HOMSEY LAW CENTER
4816 CLASSEN BOULEVARD
OKLAHOMA CITY, OKLAHOMA 73118
Telephone: 405-843-9923
Telecopier: 405-848-4223; Toll Free 1-800-845-9923
Email: gbh@homseylawcenter.com
URL: http://www.homseylawcenter.com

Trial Practice and Civil Litigation in Negligence Actions, Insurance Litigation, Personal Injury, Automobile/Trucking Litigation (18-Wheeler), Trucking Accidents, Motorcycle Accidents, Railroad Accidents, Dog Bites, Dog Attacks, Consumer Fraud, Deceptive Trade Practices, Product Liability, Workers' Compensation, Environmental Law, Nursing Home Negligence, Dram Shop and Liquor Liability and Wrongful Death.

FIRM PROFILE: Since being licensed to practice law in 1974, Gary B. Homsey has strived to bring excellence to the representation of injured persons and families of loved ones who have been injured or killed due to the wrongful conduct of another. As past president of the Oklahoma Trial Lawyers Association, Gary B. Homsey vigilantly oversees and protects the rights of injured victims. Mr. Homsey is a frequent lecturer for the Oklahoma Trial Lawyers Association, Oklahoma Bar Association, National Business Institute, Oklahoma University School of Business, Oklahoma University School of Law, University of Houston Law Foundation, Oklahoma University College of Trial Advocacy, Oklahoma City University, American Board of Trial Advocates, Lorman Education Services, National Institute of Trial Advocacy, American Inn of Court, and various universities.

GARY B. HOMSEY, born Oklahoma City, Oklahoma, April 29, 1949; admitted to bar, 1974, Oklahoma and U.S. District Court, Western District of Oklahoma; 1978, U.S. Supreme Court; 1979, U.S. Court of Appeals, 10th Circuit. *Education:* Oklahoma State University (B.S., 1971); Oklahoma City University (J.D., 1974). Phi Alpha Delta. Recipient: Oklahoma Trial Lawyers Association President's Award, Outstanding Service in Tort Reform Legislation, 1995; Mark of Distinction Award, Oklahoma City University School of Law, 2001. Delegate, Oklahoma County Bar Association to Oklahoma State Bar Association, 1979-1980. Member: Arbitration Panel for the Western District of Oklahoma of U.S. District Court, 1985—; Kerr Support Committee, Oklahoma City University Law School, 1987—; Dean's Advisory Counsel, Oklahoma City University Law School, 1987—. Lecturer: Oklahoma Trial Lawyers; Oklahoma Bar; National Business Institute; Oklahoma University School of Business; Oklahoma University School of Law; University of Houston Law Foundation; Oklahoma University College of Trial Advocacy; American Board of Trial Advocates, Lorman Education Services, Oklahoma City University; National Institute of Trial Advocacy. Member: Bishop's Council; Law Dean's Development Council, Oklahoma City University, 1992—. Dedicated, Homsey Moot Court Auditorium, New Law School Building, Oklahoma City University, 1995. Board of Directors, OCU Law Alumni Association, 2000—; Executive Board, OCU School of Law, 2000—. Member, Million Dollar Advocates Forum, 1997. Board Member, Oklahoma Appleseed Center of the National Appleseed Foundation. Vice President of Oklahoma Chapter, 2003. Member of the College of Master Advocates and Barristers (an International Legal Honor Society), 2001. *Member:* Oklahoma County (Member: Fee Grievance and Ethics Committee, 1987—; Panel to Evaluate Judicial Candidates in Contested Races, 1994, OCBA Bench and Bar, 1995—; Board of Directors, 2000—), Oklahoma (Member, Bench and Bar Committee, 1988—, Administration of Justice Committee, 1994—; OBA Task Force on Advertising and Solicitation, 1994) and American Bar Associations; Oklahoma Trial Lawyers Association (Secretary and Treasurer, 1989-1990; Vice-President, 1991, President-Elect, 1992; President, 1993); The Association of Trial Lawyers of America (President's Council, 1993); National Academy of Trial Barristers (Senior Counsel, 2001); American Judicature Society; American Society of Law and Medicine, Inc.; American Inn of Court (Master); Trial Lawyers for Public Justice Foundation; American Board of Trial Advocates. Fellow, Oklahoma Bar Foundation; National Institute of Trial Advocacy. (Member, Homsey, Cooper, Hill & Associates). ***PRACTICE AREAS:*** Personal Injury; Litigation; Insurance Litigation; Automobile Negligence; Product Liability Law; Workers' Compensation Law; Environmental Law; Nursing Home Negligence; Labor and Employment Law; Dram Shop; Liquor Liability; Wrongful Death.

REPRESENTATIVE CLIENTS: International Brotherhood of Teamsters Local 886; American Federation of Teachers (locally and nationally); American Federation of Government Employees; United Rubber and Steel Workers; Oklahoma City Firefighters Local 157.
REFERENCES: Bank One, Oklahoma, N.A.; Nichols Hills Bank & Trust; Central National Bank.

(This Listing Continued)

MICHAEL S. "MICKEY" HOMSEY & ASSOCIATES, INC.

719 NORTH SHARTEL
OKLAHOMA CITY, OKLAHOMA 73101-0718
Telephone: 405-235-6622
Fax: 405-236-0096
Email: mhomsey@swbell.net

Criminal Law, Personal Injury, Family Law, Workers Compensation, Automobile Accidents and Injuries, Wrongful Death, Child Custody, Divorce, Child Support.

MICHAEL S. HOMSEY, born Oklahoma City, Oklahoma, October 11, 1951; admitted to bar, 1976, Oklahoma and U.S. District Court, Western District of Oklahoma; 1984, U.S. Supreme Court. *Education:* Oklahoma State University (B.A., 1973); Oklahoma City University (J.D., 1976). Assistant District Attorney, Oklahoma County, 1977-1979. Municipal Judge: Harrah, Oklahoma, 1979-1983; Choctaw, Oklahoma, 1981-1984. Member, Board of Adjustments, Oklahoma City, 1991-2002. *Member:* Oklahoma County and Oklahoma Bar Associations; Federal Bar Association of the Western District of Oklahoma; Oklahoma Trial Lawyers Association. ***REPORTED CASES:*** Rader v. Farmers Insurance Co., Inc., 68 O.B.J. 654 (1997). ***PRACTICE AREAS:*** Criminal; Personal Injury; Automobile Accidents and Injuries; Wrongful Death; Child Custody; Divorce; Family Law; Child Support. ***Email:*** mhomsey@swbell.net

TERRY R. McMILLAN, born Kingfisher, Oklahoma, September 21, 1964; admitted to bar, 1990, Oklahoma; 1991, Kansas. *Education:* Oklahoma State University (B.S., 1986); Oklahoma City University (J.D., 1990). Golden Key Honor Society. Member, Oklahoma Agricultural Economics Association. *Member:* Oklahoma County, Oklahoma and Kansas Bar Associations. ***PRACTICE AREAS:*** Workers Compensation; Personal Injury; Criminal Law; Family Law. ***Email:*** mhmomsey@swbell.net

A list of Representative Clients will be furnished upon request.

THOMAS W. HOSTY, P.C.

204 N. ROBINSON, SUITE 1717
P.O. BOX 20685
OKLAHOMA CITY, OKLAHOMA 73156-0685
Telephone: 405-235-4040
Fax: 405-553-9925
Cell: 405-210-3462
Email: twhoklaw@aol.com
URL: http://www.hostylaw.com
Mailing Address: P.O. Box 20685, Oklahoma City, OK 73156-0685

Criminal Defense, Driving While Intoxicated, DPS, City Tickets, Traffic Violations, Felonies, Misdemeanors, Drug Charges.

THOMAS W. HOSTY, born Birmingham, Alabama, 1967; admitted to bar, 1992, Oklahoma and U.S. District Court, Western District of Oklahoma; U.S. Court of Appeals, Tenth Circuit. *Education:* University of Central Oklahoma (B.B.A., 1989); Loyola University (J.D., 1992). Practitioner and Instructor, NHTSA Certified SFST. Certified, Independent Operator, Intoxllyzer 5000-D, Oklahoma Board of Chemical Tests. Vice President, Uptown Kiwanis Club, 1998-2000. Member, Oklahoma City Downtown Exchange Club. *Member:* Oklahoma County and American Bar Associations; The Association of Trial Lawyers of America; National Association of Criminal Defense Lawyers. ***PRACTICE AREAS:*** Driving While Intoxicated; Criminal Defense. ***Email:*** twhoklaw@aol.com

KATHERINE L. CASEY, born 1968; admitted to bar, 1994, Oklahoma. *Education:* Oklahoma City University (B.S., 1989); University of Oklahoma (J.D., 1994). ***PRACTICE AREAS:*** Driving While Intoxicated; Criminal Defense; General Practice. ***Email:*** twhoklaw@aol.com

HUCKABY, FLEMING, GREENWOOD & OLSSON, LLP

1215 CLASSEN DRIVE
P.O. BOX 60130
OKLAHOMA CITY, OKLAHOMA 73103
Telephone: 405-235-6648
Fax: 405-235-1533
URL: http://www.hfgolaw.com

State and Federal Civil Litigation and Appellate Practice. Insurance Defense, Subrogation, Arbitration, Mediation, Tort Law, Product Liability, Vehicular Negligence, Premises Liability.

MEMBERS OF THE FIRM

ROBERT L. HUCKABY, born Effingham, Illinois, May 6, 1940; admitted to bar, 1964, Oklahoma. *Education:* University of Oklahoma (B.A., 1962; LL.B., 1964).

KENT FLEMING, born Oklahoma City, Oklahoma, October 9, 1937; admitted to bar, 1965, Oklahoma. *Education:* University of Oklahoma (B.S., 1960; J.D., 1965). ***Email:*** fleming@huckabyfleming.com

WILLIAM D. GREENWOOD, born Oklahoma City, Oklahoma, March 11, 1951; admitted to bar, 1982, Oklahoma. *Education:* Central State University (B.S., 1975); University of Oklahoma (J.D., 1982). ***Email:*** greenwood@huckabyfleming.com

(This Listing Continued)

BRENTLY C. OLSSON, born Tulsa, Oklahoma, September 20, 1963; admitted to bar, 1988, Oklahoma. *Education:* Oral Roberts University (B.A., 1985); University of Tulsa (J.D., 1988). ***Email:*** olsson@huckabyfleming.com

ASSOCIATE

CHRISTOPHER M. MURPHY, born Bremerton, Washington, August 06, 1974; admitted to bar, 2000, Oklahoma. *Education:* University of Oklahoma (B.B.A., 1997); University of Tulsa College of Law (J.D., 2000). ***Email:*** murphy@huckabyfleming.com

REPRESENTATIVE CLIENTS: Hartford Insurance; Travelers Insurance Company; Scottsdale Insurance Co.; National Casualty Insurance Co.; American Equity Insurance Co.; American Indemnity Group; National Alliance Insurance Co.; National American Insurance Co.; RSA Surplus Lines Insurance Co.; Baker Hughes; Yellow Cab.

DAVID D. HUNT, II

A PROFESSIONAL CORPORATION
1428 NORTHWEST 35TH STREET
P.O. BOX 18896
OKLAHOMA CITY, OKLAHOMA 73154-0896
Telephone: 405-528-0168
Fax: 405-528-3508
URL: http://www.hunt-law.com

Oil and Gas, Oil and Gas Title Examination, Commercial Real Estate Finance.

DAVID D. HUNT, II, born Oklahoma City, Oklahoma, 1957; admitted to bar, 1982, Oklahoma and U.S. District Court, Western District of Oklahoma. *Education:* University of Oklahoma (B.A., 1979; J.D., 1982). Lecturer: Oil and Gas Law, Title Examination, Indian Land Titles, SBA Lending. *Member:* Oklahoma County and Oklahoma Bar Associations; Mineral Lawyers Society of Oklahoma City. ***REPORTED CASES:*** W.L. Kirkman, Inc. v. Okla. Corp. Comm., 676 P.2d 283 (Okla. App. 1983); Barbour Energy Corp. v. Bell, 928 P.2d. 968 (Okla. App. 1996). ***PRACTICE AREAS:*** Oil and Gas Law; Oil and Gas Title Examination; Commercial Real Estate Finance.

REPRESENTATIVE CLIENTS: BancFirst; Barbour Energy Corporation; Chesapeake Energy Corporation; El Paso Energy Corporation; Oil-Law Records Corporation and Rural Enterprises of Oklahoma, Inc.

GARVIN A. ISAACS, INC.

RAINY MOUNTAIN BUILDING
123 N.W. EIGHTH STREET
OKLAHOMA CITY, OKLAHOMA 73102-5804
Telephone: 405-232-2060
Fax: 405-232-9035

Medical Malpractice, Nursing Home Negligence, Products Liability, Bad Faith Insurance, Toxic Torts, Oil and Gas Fraud, Murder Cases and White Collar Crime.

FIRM PROFILE: Garvin A. Isaacs, Inc., is engaged in trial practice which focus on personal injury litigation including medical malpractice, nursing home negligence, products liability cases against automobile manufacturers, products liability against drug manufacturers, toxic torts, bad faith refusal of insurance company to pay valid claims, fraud by oil and gas producers and pipelines perpetrated by mineral owners. The firm has successfully defended persons accused of crimes in both state and federal courts, with heavy emphasis upon defending persons charged with murder and white collar crimes. The firm has also successfully defended persons accused of crimes involving income tax.

GARVIN A. ISAACS, born Carnegie, Oklahoma, April 3, 1945; admitted to bar, 1974, Oklahoma; 1987, New Mexico, U.S. District Court, Northern, Eastern and Western Districts of Oklahoma, U.S. District Court, District of New Mexico and U.S. Court of Appeals, Tenth Circuit; 1994, U.S. Supreme Court. *Education:* Texas Christian University (B.A., 1967); Oklahoma City University (J.D., 1974). Phi Delta Phi. Recipient: American Jurisprudence Awards for Criminal Law and Administrative Law; The Judge Tom Brett Criminal Law Award; 1998, Angie Debo Civil Libertarian Award; 2004 Lord Erskine Award of the Oklahoma Criminal Defense Lawyers Association. Assistant District Attorney, Oklahoma County, 1974-1975. First Assistant Public Defender, Oklahoma County, 1976-1978. Special Prosecutor, State of Oklahoma Ethics Commission vs. Frank Keating, Governor of Oklahoma, 1997-1998. Instructor: Trial Lawyers College, 1994-2003; National College for Criminal Defense, 1979-1992; Western Trial Advocacy Institute, University of Wyoming, School of Law, 1981-2005; Kentucky Department of Public Advocacy, 1985. Guest Lecturer, University of Oklahoma School of Law, "Fundamentals of Criminal Trial Practice" and Voir Dire," 2003-2005. Lecturer: Florida Public Defenders Association, 1981, 1985, 1999; New Mexico Public Defenders, 1981, 2004; Montana Criminal Defense Lawyers, 2005; Colorado Public Defenders, 1983, 1985; Texas Criminal Defense Lawyers, 1983; Nebraska Trial Lawyers, 1985; Kansas Public Defenders, 1985, 1990, 1998; Vermont Public Defenders, 1987; Canadian Criminal Trial Lawyers, 1987; Trial Advocacy Workshop, Harvard Law School, 1991; New Hampshire Public Defenders, 1993, 1999; Wisconsin Federal Defenders, 2005. *Member:* The Association of Trial Lawyers of America; National Association of Criminal Defense Lawyers (Life Member); Oklahoma Criminal Defense Lawyers Association; Oklahoma Trial Lawyers Association. ***REPORTED CASES:*** Isaacs v. District Court of Oklahoma County, 818 P.2d 1247 (Okla. Crim. 1991); Bechtel v. State, 840 P.2d 1 (Okla. Crim. 1992); Bryant v. Independent School District. No. I-38 of Garvin County, OK, 334 F.3d 928 (10th Cir. 2003). ***PRACTICE AREAS:*** Murder Cases; White Collar Crime; Income Tax; Personal Injury; Nursing Home Negligence; Medical Malpractice; Products Liability; Insurance Bad Faith; Environmental Law; Automobile Litigation; Oil and Gas Fraud.

NANCY A. ZERR, born Kansas City, Missouri, November 11, 1955; admitted to bar, 1994, Wyoming; 1998, Oklahoma. *Education:* Arkansas Tech University (B.S., summa

(This Listing Continued)

GARVIN A. ISAACS, INC., Oklahoma City—Continued

cum laude, 1977); Memphis State University (Nuclear Reactor Engineering, 1981-1982); University of Wyoming (J.D., 1994). President, Johnson County Bar Association, 1995-1997. Assistant City Attorney, Buffalo, Wyoming, 1995-1997. Assistant Wyoming Public Defender, Fourth Judicial District, Johnson and Sheridan Counties, 1996-1997. Member, Drug Court Planning Team, Sheridan County, Wyoming, 1997. *Member:* Wyoming State Bar; Oklahoma Bar Association. ***REPORTED CASES:*** Goodrich v. Stobbe, 908 P.2d 416 (Wyo. 1995). ***PRACTICE AREAS:*** Criminal Defense; Personal Injury; Medical Malpractice; Civil Rights.

JENNINGS COOK HOISINGTON & TEAGUE, P.C.

Established in 2000

204 NORTH ROBINSON, SUITE 1000
OKLAHOMA CITY, OKLAHOMA 73102
Telephone: 405-609-6000
Facsimile: 405-609-6501
Email: JCH@JCHLaw.com
URL: http://www.jchlaw.com

Product Liability Defense, Insurance Defense, Personal Injury Defense, Employment Law, Civil Rights Law, Personal Injury, General Civil Litigation, Transportation..

JAMES A. JENNINGS, III, born Wynnewood, Oklahoma, 1949; admitted to bar, 1974, Oklahoma. *Education:* Oklahoma State University (B.A., 1971); Oklahoma University (J.D., 1974). Phi Delta Phi. Assistant District Attorney, Oklahoma County, 1974-1977. *Member:* Oklahoma County, Oklahoma and American Bar Associations; Defense Research Institute; International Association of Defense Counsel; Product Liability Advisory Council. ***PRACTICE AREAS:*** Products Liability; Insurance Defense; Insurance Bad Faith. **Email:** JAJ@JCHLaw.com

RODNEY L. COOK, born Oklahoma City, Oklahoma, 1957; admitted to bar, 1983, Oklahoma; U.S. District Court, Western, Eastern and Northern Districts of Oklahoma; U.S. Court of Appeals, Tenth Circuit. *Education:* University of Oklahoma (B.S., 1980; J.D., 1983). Phi Delta Phi. Member, National Mock Trial Team, 1983. Clerk, Oklahoma Court of Criminal Appeals, 1981. Publication: "Hedonic Damages," 62 Oklahoma Bar Journal 2353, 1991. Recognized in the National Law Journal for Top Ten Defense Verdicts, 2002. *Member:* Oklahoma County, Oklahoma and American Bar Associations; Defense Research Institute. ***PRACTICE AREAS:*** Product Liability; Insurance Defense; Warranty Law; Fraternity Law. **Email:** RLC@JCHLaw.com

CARRIE PALMER HOISINGTON, born Manhattan, Kansas, 1968; admitted to bar, 1993, Oklahoma; U.S. District Court, Western, Eastern and Northern Districts of Oklahoma; U.S. Court of Appeals, Tenth Circuit. *Education:* Kansas State University (B.S., 1990); University of Oklahoma (J.D., 1993). Phi Alpha Delta (Justice, 1992); Board of Advocates; Order of Barristers. Recipient, Scholastic Achievement Award in Complex Litigation. Member, University of Oklahoma Law Review. Publications: "The Effect of Standards Compliance on Punitive Damages Claims In Automobile Cases," For The Defense, October, 1998; Seminars: Trucking Law in Oklahoma; August 2005. *Member:* Oklahoma County and Oklahoma Bar Associations; Defense Research Institute; National Trial Lawyers Association (NTLA) Trial Team (1993); American Trial Lawyers Association (ATLA) Trial Team (1992); Trial Attorneys of America (TAA). ***PRACTICE AREAS:*** Product Liability; Warranty; Insurance Defense; Insurance Bad Faith; Transportation. **Email:** CPH@JCHLaw.com

J. DERRICK TEAGUE, born Oklahoma City, Oklahoma, 1967; admitted to bar, 1993, Oklahoma; U.S. District Court, Northern, Eastern and Western Districts of Oklahoma; U.S. Court of Appeals, Tenth Circuit. *Education:* Oklahoma State University (B.S., 1990); Oklahoma City University (J.D., 1993). *Member:* Oklahoma County, Oklahoma and American Bar Associations. ***PRACTICE AREAS:*** Product Liability; Insurance Defense; Insurance Bad Faith; Civil Litigation; Transportation; Warranty Law. **Email:** JDT@JCHLaw.com

ASSOCIATES

JEFFREY W. MILLER, born Enid, Oklahoma, 1966; admitted to bar, 1994, Oklahoma; U.S. District Court, Western, Eastern and Northern Districts of Oklahoma. *Education:* Oklahoma State University (B.S., Manufacturing Engineering Technology, 1990); University of Oklahoma College of Law (J.D., 1994). *Member:* Oklahoma and American Bar Associations. ***PRACTICE AREAS:*** Insurance Defense; Product Liability; Construction; Civil Litigation. **Email:** JWM@JCHLaw.com

LINDA G. KAUFMANN, born Enid, Oklahoma, January 8, 1964; admitted to bar, 1991, Oklahoma and U.S. District Court, Western District of Oklahoma and U.S. Court of Appeals, Tenth Circuit. *Education:* University of Oklahoma (B.S., 1988); Oklahoma City University (J.D., 1991). Phi Delta Phi. Editor-in-Chief, Oklahoma City University Law Review, 1990-1991. Recipient, American Jurisprudence Awards: Legal Research and Writing II, Trial Practice, Federal Jurisdiction and Complex Litigation. *Member:* Oklahoma Bar Association. ***REPORTED CASES:*** Telecor Communications, Inc., et al. v. Southwestern Bell Telephone Co., 305 F.3d 1124 (10th Cir. 2002). ***PRACTICE AREAS:*** Civil Litigation; Products Liability. **Email:** LGK@JCHLaw.com

REPRESENTATIVE CLIENTS: AlliedSignal Corporation; American Isuzu Motors, Inc.; Apollo Pools, Inc.; Associated Wholesale Grocers, Inc.; BMW A.G.; BMW, N.A.; Baldwin Acoustic & Drywall, Inc.; Bituminous Insurance Cos.; Bristol-Myers Squibb Co.; Cambridge Integrated Services Group, Inc.; Cardiac Pacemakers, Inc.; Caterpillar Inc.; Caterpillar Paving Products Inc.; Cherokee Insurance Co.; City of Midwest City; Clarendon National Insurance Co.; Columbia Machines, Inc.; Countrywide Services, Inc.; Crawford and Co.; Cunningham-Lindsey; Daewoo Motor America, Inc.; DaimlerChrysler, Inc.; Deep South Surplus, Inc.; Durabla Manufacturing Co.; Dutchmen Manufacturing, Inc.; E.I. DuPont de Numours & Co.; Fecken-Kirfel GmbH & Co. Maschinenfabrik de Freightliner, Inc.; GuideOne Insurance Co.; Harley-Davidson Corporation; Herbert Olbrich GmbH & Co. KG; Honeywell; Hyundai Motor America, Inc.; Hyundai Motor Corporation; Ignition Systems & Controls, LP; International Truck and Engine Corporation; International Managers, Inc.; Isuzu Motors America; Isuzu Motors Limited; Key Safety Systems; Kia Motors America, Inc.; Kia Motors Corporation; KONE Elevators/Escalators; Liberty Bell Agency; LMS Claims Services; Long Manufacturing; Mack Trucks, Inc.; Master Protection Corporation; Mitsubishi Motors North America, Inc.; Mitsubishi Motors R&D of America; New United Motor Manufacturing, Inc.; North America Honda, Inc.; Oklahoma Department of Transportation; PACCAR Inc.; Porsche Cars North America, Inc.; Purina Mills, Inc.; Ralston Purina Corporation; Royal & SunAlliance; Shelter General Insurance Co.; Shelter Mutual Insurance Co.; Solar Turbines, Inc.; St. Paul Travelers; State Auto Insurance Co.; Tokio Marine & Fire Insurance Group; Toyota Motor Corporation; Toyota Motor Sales U.S.A., Inc.; TRW Vehicle Safety Systems, Inc.; Tyco International, Inc.; Underwriters Laboratory; Underwriters at Lloyds London; Valu Merchandisere Co.; Van Dorn Demag Corporation; Ward North America, Inc.; Winnebago Industries, Inc.; Zurich American Insurance Co.

(This Listing Continued)

JOHNSON AND HANAN, P.C.

BANK ONE CENTER, SUITE 2750
100 NORTH BROADWAY AVENUE
OKLAHOMA CITY, OKLAHOMA 73102
Telephone: 405-232-6100
Fax: 405-232-6105
Email: jhht@johnsonhanan.com

General Civil, Trial and Appellate Practice in all State and Federal Courts. Insurance and Casualty, Medical, Legal and Professional Malpractice, Negligence, and Personal Injury Law. Health Law in State and Federal Agencies.

A. SCOTT JOHNSON, born Oklahoma City, Oklahoma, April 26, 1950; admitted to bar, 1979, Oklahoma, U.S. District Court, Western, Eastern, and Northern Districts of Oklahoma and U.S. Court of Appeals, Tenth Circuit. *Education:* Arizona State University (B.S., 1974; M.A., 1976); Oklahoma City University (J.D., 1978). Research Editor, Oklahoma City University Law Review, 1978. *Member:* Oklahoma County, Oklahoma and American Bar Associations; The American Board of Trial Advocates; Defense Research Institute; International Association of Defense Counsel; Oklahoma Association of Defense Counsel. ***PRACTICE AREAS:*** Medical Malpractice; Health Law; Personal Injury Defense. **Email:** scottjohnson@johnsonhanan.com

MARY B. HANAN, born Shattuck, Oklahoma, January 30, 1954; admitted to bar, 1983, Oklahoma and U.S. District Court, Western, Eastern and Northern Districts of Oklahoma; 1991, U.S. Court of Appeals, Tenth Circuit. *Education:* Oklahoma State University (B.S., 1976); University of Oklahoma (J.D., 1983). Recipient, American Jurisprudence Award. *Member:* Oklahoma County, Oklahoma and American Bar Associations; American Society of Law and Medicine; Oklahoma Health Lawyers Association; Oklahoma Association of Defense Counsel; Defense Research Institute. ***PRACTICE AREAS:*** Medical Malpractice; Health Law; Personal Injury Defense. **Email:** maryhanan@johnsonhanan.com

ALEXANDER C. VOSLER, born Oklahoma City, Oklahoma, August 3, 1974; admitted to bar, 2002, Oklahoma and U.S. District Court, Northern, Eastern and Western Districts of Oklahoma. *Education:* University of Kentucky (1992-1994); Eastern Kentucky University (B.S., 1996); Thomas M. Cooley Law School (J.D., 2001). *Member:* Oklahoma County, Oklahoma and American Bar Associations. ***PRACTICE AREAS:*** Medical Malpractice Defense; Dental Malpractice Defense. **Email:** avosler@johnsonhanan.com

JON M. WILLIFORD, born Little Rock, Arkansas, January 22, 1976; admitted to bar, 2002, Oklahoma; U.S. District Court, Western District of Oklahoma. *Education:* University of Oklahoma (B.B.A., 1999; J.D., 2002). Associate Member, American Inns of Court, Luther Bohanon Chapter, 2001-2002. *Member:* Oklahoma (Member, Board of Directors, Young Lawyers Division) and American (Member, Litigation Section; Health Law and Trial Practice Committees) Bar Associations. ***PRACTICE AREAS:*** Medical Malpractice; Health Law. **Email:** jwilliford@johnsonhanan.com

BRYAN E. STANTON, born San Antonio, Texas, November 25, 1975; admitted to bar, 2001, Oklahoma and U.S. District Court, Eastern, Northern and Western Districts of Oklahoma. *Education:* University of Oklahoma (B.A., 1998); University of Tulsa College of Law (J.D., 2001). Senior Staff, Tulsa Law Journal, 2000-2001. *Member:* Oklahoma County, Oklahoma and American Bar Associations. ***PRACTICE AREAS:*** Medical Malpractice; Health Law; Dental Malpractice Defense. **Email:** bstanton@johnsonhanan.com

JUSTIN P. EILERS, born Shattuck, Oklahoma, February 14, 1978; admitted to bar, 2004, Oklahoma and U.S. District Court, Eastern and Northern Districts of Oklahoma. *Education:* Oklahoma State University (B.S., 2000); University of Oklahoma (J.D., 2004). *Member:* Oklahoma County and Oklahoma Bar Associations. ***PRACTICE AREAS:*** Medical Malpractice; Health Law; Personal Injury Defense. **Email:** jeilers@johnsonhanan.com

JAMES D. GRAVES, born Columbus, Georgia, October 3, 1975; admitted to bar, 2004, Oklahoma and U.S. District Court, Eastern and Western Districts of Oklahoma. *Education:* University of Oklahoma (B.A., 2001); University of Oklahoma College of Law (J.D., 2004). Magister, Phi Delta Phi. Topic Editor, Oklahoma Journal of Law and Technology. Professor, Legal Studies, Metropolitan College. *Member:* Oklahoma and American Bar Associations. ***PRACTICE AREAS:*** Medical Malpractice; Health Law; Personal Injury Defense; Contract Litigation. **Email:** jgraves@johnsonhanan.com

NIKI S. BATT, born Ponca City, Oklahoma, August 2, 1978; admitted to bar, 2004, Oklahoma and U.S. District Court, Western District of Oklahoma. *Education:* Oklahoma State University (B.A., 2001); University of Oklahoma (J.D., 2004). Phi Delta Phi. Member: American Indian Law Review, 2003-2004; University of Oklahoma College of Law Board of Advocates, 2002-2004; Pepperdine National Moot Court Competition. *Member:* Oklahoma County and Oklahoma Bar Associations. ***PRACTICE AREAS:*** Medical Malpractice; Health Law; Personal Injury Defense. **Email:** nbatt@johnsonhanan.com

JOHN B. HILL, born Guthrie, Oklahoma, May 31, 1972; admitted to bar, 2003, Oklahoma and U.S. District Court, Eastern, Western and Northern Districts of Oklahoma. *Education:* Southeastern Oklahoma State University (B.A., 1999); Oklahoma City University School of Law (J.D., 2002). *Member:* Oklahoma County and Oklahoma Bar Associations. ***PRACTICE AREAS:*** Medical Malpractice; Health Law; Personal Injury Defense. **Email:** jhill@johnsonhanan.com

JONES, ANDREWS & ORTIZ

21 E. MAIN STREET, SUITE 101
OKLAHOMA CITY, OKLAHOMA 73104
Telephone: 405-601-8713
Fax: 405-232-8330
URL: http://www.jao-law.com

San Antonio, Texas Office: 10100 Reunion Place, Suite 600, 78216. Telephone: 210-344-3900. Telecopier: 210-366-4301.

Civil Trial Law and Insurance Defense.

FIRM PROFILE: Jones, Andrews & Ortiz, A Professional Corporation, was founded in 1990 by David Jones. Prior to the forming of Jones, Andrews & Ortiz, David Jones was a partner in the San Antonio, Texas office of Fulbright & Jaworski, and Dan Andrews was an associate there. Both had considerable experience in the area of insurance defense and enjoyed a strong reputation among insurance companies and major corporations for effective representation. In order to maintain the level of personalized service their clients desired, they felt it necessary to establish their own practice to directly address their clients' needs. The firm name was changed in November 2000 to recognize the contributions of Ray Ortiz.

Two of the shareholders are board certified by the Texas Board of Legal Specialization. The firm's attorneys possess superior litigation skills and exhibit unquestionable integrity. This has led to rapid growth and the expansion of areas of specialization to meet the needs of its ever-widening client base. Jones, Andrews & Ortiz has earned the highest rating in legal ability and ethical standards from Martindale-Hubbell.

ASSOCIATE

BRUCE A. ROBERTSON, born Oklahoma City, Oklahoma, July 2, 1960; admitted to bar, 1989, Oklahoma. *Education:* University of Oklahoma (B.B.A., 1986; J.D., 1989). *Member:* Oklahoma County, Oklahoma and American Bar Associations. ***PRACTICE AREAS:*** Insurance Defense; Insurance Coverage; Products Liability; Fire Insurance; Casualty Insurance; Insurance Bad Faith.

(For complete biographical data on all personnel, see Professional Biographies at San Antonio, Texas)

KERR, IRVINE, RHODES & ABLES

A PROFESSIONAL CORPORATION
Established in 1945
201 ROBERT S. KERR AVENUE, SUITE 600
OKLAHOMA CITY, OKLAHOMA 73102-4267
Telephone: 405-272-9221
Fax: 405-236-3121
URL: http://www.kiralaw.com

General Civil Practice in all State and Federal Courts. Corporation, Probate, Insurance, Banking, Administrative, Employment, Water, Environmental, Oil and Gas, Agricultural Law, Commercial Litigation, and Insurance Law.

FIRM PROFILE: History: The firm was founded in 1955 as Kerr, Conn & Davis by Aubrey Kerr, Jack Conn and Jack Davis. Initially its practice was general with emphasis in the fields of oil and gas, banking, and business organizations and transactions. During its early years, the lawyers who joined the firm were for the most part experienced in their respective fields. In 1955, Robert S. Kerr, Jr., joined the firm. In 1981, Robert S. Kerr, Jr., Francis S. Irvine, who had been with the firm since 1957, and Horace G. Rhodes, who joined the firm in 1972, joined together to form the current firm. Since then the firm has expanded primarily through employment of laterally experienced lawyers with talents and specialties. The firm has added attorneys with significant experience in insurance transactions and regulatory matters, insurance litigation, administrative law and employment law. Most recently, the firm has employed lawyers with exceptional skills and experience in the areas of agricultural, environmental and water law.

Areas of Practice: For many years Kerr, Irvine, Rhodes & Ables has provided a full range of legal services to its clients. Primary areas of expertise are still considered to be insurance regulatory, administrative, real estate and litigation, along with business organizations and transactions. While litigation spans virtually every field of law, the focus continues to be in the insurance, environmental and water law areas.

Client Base: The firm is general counsel for numerous public companies in insurance and insurance related industries. The firm also administers, and serves as counsel to, the Oklahoma Life & Health Insurance Guaranty Association, the Oklahoma Association of Life Insurance Companies and the Environmental Federation of Oklahoma. In addition, the firm represents many individuals and entities in connection with general litigation, mergers, acquisitions and various regulatory matters. The firm also offers many services to its individual clients in the areas of trust and estate law, oil and gas, real estate, environmental law, and negligence.

Kerr, Irvine, Rhodes & Ables is listed in the Bar Register of Preeminent Lawyers in the areas of Corporate Law, Administrative Law, Insurance Defense, Civil Trial Practice, Environmental Law, Labor and Employment Law and General Practice.

ROBERT S. KERR, JR. (1926-2004)

HORACE G. RHODES, born Oklahoma City, Oklahoma, November 24, 1927; admitted to bar, 1955, Oklahoma, U.S. District Court, Western District of Oklahoma, U.S. Court of Appeals, Tenth Circuit, U.S. Supreme Court. *Education:* University of Oklahoma (B.S., 1950; J.D., 1955). Phi Delta Phi. Deputy Insurance Commissioner and General Counsel to the Insurance Commissioner, State of Oklahoma, 1955-1958. Counsel to Special Joint Legislative Committee to Recodify Oklahoma Insurance Code, 1955-1957. Senior Counsel Oklahoma Life Insurance Guaranty Association. *Member:* Interamerican Federation of Lawyers; Federation of Regulatory Counsel. ***LANGUAGES:*** Spanish. ***PRACTICE AREAS:*** Insurance Law; Corporate Law; International Law. **Email:** kira201@aol.com

J. ANGELA ABLES, born Ada, Oklahoma, January 23, 1950; admitted to bar, 1976, Oklahoma and U.S. District Court, Northern District of Oklahoma; 1978, U.S. Court of Appeals, Tenth Circuit; 1981, U.S. District Court, Western District of Oklahoma; 1984, U.S. Supreme Court; 1998, U.S. District Court, Eastern District of Oklahoma. *Education:* East Central Oklahoma State University (B.A., with honors, 1972); Oklahoma City University (J.D., 1975). Recipient, Distinguished Alumnus Award, East Central University 1983. Assistant Attorney General, Oklahoma, 1976-1978. Deputy Insurance Commissioner, Oklahoma, 1980-1985. Member, Director, 1987-1999 and Chairman of the Board, 1999, Federation of Regulatory Counsel, 1987-2000. Vice-Chairman, State of Oklahoma Election Board, 1985-1989. Arbitrator, U.S. District Court, Western District of Oklahoma. Early Neutral Evaluator, U.S. District Court, Western District of Oklahoma. General Counsel and Executive Vice-President, Association of Oklahoma Life Insurance Companies, 2001—. Board of Directors, Oklahoma Attorneys Mutual Insurance Company. *Member:* Oklahoma County (Co-Chairman, Legislative Committee, 1990-1991; Member, Community Services Committee, 2001—), Oklahoma (Chairman, 1999-2001 and Vice Chair, 2001-2002, Insurance Committee; Chairman, 2002—) and American (Member, Torts and Insurance Practice Section) Bar Associations; Oklahoma Association of Defense Counsel. ***REPORTED CASES:*** Turpen, State exrel. v. Oklahoma State Bd. for Property and Cas. Rates, 731 P.2d 394 (Okl. 1986); Pacificare of Oklahoma, Health Maintenance Organization, & Community Care Organization, Inc. v. Oklahoma Health Care Authority Board et al., 2001 OK Civ. App. 73. ***PRACTICE AREAS:*** Insurance Law; Corporate Law; Appellate Practice; Administrative Law. **Email:** aables@kiralaw.com

JAMES W. RHODES, born Oklahoma City, Oklahoma, June 11, 1958; admitted to bar, 1984, Oklahoma, U.S. District Court, Western and Northern Districts of Oklahoma, U.S. Court of Appeals, Tenth Circuit and U.S. Supreme Court. *Education:* Wesleyan University (B.A., 1980); University of Oklahoma (J.D., 1984). Chairman, National Organization of Life and Health Insurance Guaranty Association Legal Seminar, 1993-1996. General Counsel, Oklahoma Life and Health Guaranty Association, 1988—. Associate General Counsel, Association of Oklahoma Life Insurance Companies, 1987-1988. Chairman: National Organization of Life and Health Insurance Guaranty Associations Task Force for Summit National Life Insurance Company, 1994—; National American Insurance Co., 1995—. Member: Universe Life & Trust Insurance Company, 1998—; National Organization of Life and Health Insurance Guaranty Association Legal and Assessment Data Base Committees, 1993—. Editor in Chief, Annotated Life and Health Insurance Guaranty Association Model Act, 1995—. ***REPORTED CASES:*** Grimes v. Crown Life Ins. W., 857 F2 699; Cockrell v. Grimes, 740 P. 2d 746; Oklahoma Life & Health Insurance Guar. Ass'n v. Hilti Retirement Sav. Plan, 939 P. 2d 1110 (Okla., Mar 11, 1997) (NO. 82,447); State ex rel. John P. Crawford, Insurance Commissioner as receiver for American Standard Life and Accident Insurance Company, Oklahoma Life and Health Insurance Guaranty Association v. Guardian Life Insurance Company of America, 954 P. 2d 1235 (Ok. 1998) (NO. 84,563); Claborn v. Washington National Ins. Co., 910 P. 2d 1046 (Okla., Jan 23, 1996) (NO. 78,682); Bank of Oklahoma, N.A. v. Continental Cas. Co., 849 P. 2d 1091 (Okla. App., Oct 13, 1992) (NO. 78,103); Testerman v. First Family Life Ins. Co., 808 P. 2d 703 (Okla. App., Dec 04, 1990) (NO. 70,798); Bane v. Anderson, Bryant & Co., 786 P. 2d 1230, Blue Sky L. Rep. P 73,036 (Okla., Oct 24, 1989) (NO. 68,048); Cockrell v. Grimes, 740 P. 2d 746 (Okla. App., Apr 07, 1987) (NO. 65,046); Grimes v. Crown Life Ins. Co., 857 F. 2d 699 (10th Cir. (Okla.), Sep 16, 1988) (NO. 86,1905); Unisys Corp v. Cal. Life & Health Insurance Guaranty Association, 74 Cal Rptr 2d 106 (Cal. App 1998). ***PRACTICE AREAS:*** Insurance Insolvency Law; Insurance Administrative Law; Appellate Law. **Email:** buhohgr@aol.com

JAMES R. BARNETT, born Ada, Oklahoma, September 6, 1942; admitted to bar, 1967, Oklahoma; 1971, U.S. District, Western District of Oklahoma; 1973, U.S. Court of Appeals, Tenth Circuit; 1975, U.S. Supreme Court. *Education:* University of Oklahoma (B.A., 1964; J.D., 1967). Phi Alpha Delta. Member and Chairman, 1987-1988, Interstate Council on Water Policy. Member, National Water Resources Association and American Water Resources Association. Assistant Attorney General, 1972-1977. Executive Director, Oklahoma Water Resources Board, 1977-1991. Chief of Law Reform, Legal Aid Society, 1970-1972. President and General Counsel, Environmental Federation of Oklahoma, 1991—. *Member:* Oklahoma County, Oklahoma (Member, Sections on: Environmental Law, Government, Administrative Law Practice) and American (Member, Natural Resources, Energy and Environmental Law Section) Bar Associations. [U.S. Army, 1st Lieutenant M.I., 1967-1970]. ***REPORTED CASES:*** City of Nicols Hills v. Peggy Richardson, Okl. CCA, 939 P 2d. 17 (1997); State ex rel. Pollution Control Coordinating Board v. Kerr-McGee Corp., et al, Okl. S.C., 619 P. 2d 858 (1980); Hodges v. Oklahoma Water Resources Board, Okl. S.C., 580 P. 2d 980 (1978); Lowery v. Hodges, Okl. S.C., 555 P. 2d 1016 (1976). ***PRACTICE AREAS:*** Water Law; Environmental Law; Administrative Law; Natural Resources Law. **Email:** jrb@kiralaw.com

R. THOMAS LAY, born Nowata, Oklahoma, November 4, 1948; admitted to bar, 1973, Oklahoma and U.S. District Court, Western District of Oklahoma; 1985, U.S. Supreme Court. *Education:* Oklahoma State University (B.S., 1970); Oklahoma City University School of Law (J.D., 1973). Phi Delta Phi. Recipient, American Jurisprudence Award. Author: "Beneficial Use Requirements of Appropriative Water Right and Loss of Rights due to Nonuse," 37 Okla. L. Rev. 67 (1984); "Dam Failures, Common and Emerging Theories of Liability," 43 Okla. L. Rev. 103 (1990). Adjunct Professor, Oklahoma State University, Environmental Law, Oklahoma City, Oklahoma, 1991—. Assistant Municipal Counselor, Oklahoma City, 1973-1976. Assistant Attorney General, Oklahoma, 1976-1979. General Counsel, Oklahoma Water Resources Board, 1979-1985. *Member:* Oklahoma County, Oklahoma and American Bar Associations. ***REPORTED CASES:*** Ricks Exploration v. Oklahoma Water Resources Board, 695 P. 2d 498, Oklahoma Supreme Court, 1984; Oklahoma Water Resources Board v. Texas County Irr. and Water Resources Assn. Inc., 711 P. 2d 38, Oklahoma Supreme Court, 1984; Reherman v. Oklahoma Water Resources Board, 679 P. 2d 1296, Oklahoma Supreme Court, 1984; Field v. Oklahoma Water Resources Board, 645 P. 2d 511, Oklahoma Supreme Court, 1982; Oklahoma and Texas v. New Mexico, 107 S.Ct. 2279, 482 U.S. 124, 96 L. Ed. 2d 105 (1987). ***PRACTICE AREAS:*** Environmental Law; Water Law; Administrative Law; Agricultural Law. **Email:** rtl@kiralaw.com

(This Listing Continued)

KERR, IRVINE, RHODES & ABLES, A PROFESSIONAL CORPORATION, Oklahoma City—Continued

JEFF L. HARTMANN, born Chicago, Illinois, July 6, 1942; admitted to bar, 1966, Oklahoma. *Education:* Oklahoma State University (1963); Oklahoma City University (1964); Oklahoma University (LL.B., 1966). *Member:* Oklahoma County and Oklahoma Bar Associations.

OF COUNSEL

ROBERT A. MILLER, born Shawnee, Oklahoma, March 10, 1943; admitted to bar, 1968, Oklahoma and U.S. District Court, Eastern, Western and Northern Districts of Oklahoma; U.S. Court of Appeals, Tenth Circuit. *Education:* University of Oklahoma (B.B.A., 1965; J.D., 1968). Administrative Law Judge, Oklahoma Corporation Commission, 1968-1972. Assistant General Counsel, 1969, Assistant Conservation Attorney, 1970 and Trial Examiner, 1970-1973, Corporation Commission of Oklahoma. Member, Rocky Mountain Mineral Law Institute. *Member:* Oklahoma County, Oklahoma (Member, Sections on: Mineral Law; Administrative Law) and American (Member, Sections on: Energy; Criminal Law; Litigation) Bar Associations; The Association of Trial Lawyers of America. ***Email:*** ram@kiralaw.com

All Attorneys are Members of the Oklahoma County, Oklahoma and American Bar Associations.

REPRESENTATIVE CLIENTS: Allstate Insurance Company; Association of Oklahoma Life Insurance Companies.; Oklahoma Life and Health Guaranty Assn.; American Fidelity Corp.; American Fidelity Assurance Co.; Occidental Life Insurance Company of North Carolina; Service Master Industries Inc.; Midland Mortgage Co.; Delta Dental Plan of Oklahoma; Oklahoma National Life Insurance Co.; Bankers Preferred Life Insurance Co.; Mission Life Insurance Co.; Protective Life Insurance Co.; Pre-Paid Legal, Inc.; Services, Inc.; Savings Life Group; Financial Security Assurance, Inc. (New York); Property and Casualty Insurance Association of America; Fansteel, Inc.; Anthem, Inc.; Alleghany Corporation; ANR Pipeline Co.; Colorado Interstate Gas Co.; Washington National Insurance Co.; Great West Life Assurance; Kerr-McGee Corp.; Monumental General Life Insurance Co.; Jordan-Delaurenti, Inc.; J.D.B. Construction Co.; Mega Life & Health Insurance Company; Mid-West Life Insurance Company; Groundwater Technology; Okla. Gas & Electric Co.; Pig Improvement Co.; Seaboard Farms; Sequoyah Fuels; City of Ada; City of Ponca City; City of Kingfisher; City of Perry; City of Crescent; City of Chickasha; City of El Reno; Conseco, Inc.; National Organization of Life & Health Insurance Guaranty Association; Variable Annuity Life Insurance Co.; USG Annuity Life Co.; The Franklin Insurance Co.; Midlands Management Corporation; Bethany-Warr Acres Public Works Authority; United Teacher Association Insurance Company; Medical Research of Mid-Oklahoma, L.L.C.; Home Depot USA, Inc.; Lugert Altos Irrigation District; Vall Inc.; Land O Lakes; Fort James Corp.; Hanor Co., Inc.; Directers Life Assurance; Homeshield Insurance Co.; Community Care HMO; Republic Insurance Companies; Leaders Life Insurance Company; New York Life; Farmers Insurance Company; Oklahoma Society of Certified Public Accountants; Public Service of Oklahoma, Inc.; Universal Fidelity Life Ins. Co.; Top Flight Insurance Company; HCC Insurance Holdings, Inc.; Life Assurance Company, Inc.; Harbor Insurance Company.

KING LAW FIRM

Established in 1972

15 NORTH ROBINSON, SUITE 1100
OKLAHOMA CITY, OKLAHOMA 73102
Telephone: 405-239-6143
Fax: 405-236-3934
Email: King@King-Lawfirm.com
Email: king@king-lawfirm.com

General Civil and Trial Practice in all State and Federal Courts, Insurance Defense, Bad Faith, Negligence, Products Liability, Workers' Compensation, Labor and Employment, and Business Law. Litigation in all State and Federal Courts.

FIRM PROFILE: King Law Firm is listed in the Bar Register of Preeminent Lawyers and Best's Directory of Recommended Insurance Attorneys and Adjusters.

TOM L. KING, born Tulsa, Oklahoma; admitted to bar, 1970, Oklahoma, U.S, District Court, Western, Eastern and Northern Districts of Oklahoma, U.S. District Court, Northern District of Texas, U.S. Court of Appeals, Fifth and Tenth Circuits, U.S. Court of Federal Claims and U.S. Court of Appeals for the Federal Circuit. *Education:* University of Oklahoma (B.A., 1966; J.D., 1970). Administrative Assistant to Commissioner of Public Safety, 1967-1970. Assistant General Counsel of Oklahoma Department of Public Safety, 1970. Seminars: Defending Products Liability Cases After Tort Reform, Oklahoma Bar Association, 1996; Federal Rules of Civil Procedure - Oklahoma Association of Defense Counsel 1995; Revisions to Federal Rules of Civil procedure/Rule 26, FICC - 1994; Trying a Personal Injury Case: Preparation of Witnesses and Voir Dire for the Defendant, Oklahoma City University, 1993; Trial Preparation and Techniques for Personal Injury/Wrongful Death Actions: Discovery, 1991; Preparing Witnesses and Exhibits for Trial, 1985. Member, Board of Directors: City Bank & Trust Co.; All-American Bottling Co.; Special CARE, Inc. Member, National Claims Advisory Board, 1982. *Member:* Oklahoma County (Chairman, Bench and Bar Committee, 1986-1988; Oklahoma County Bar President's Award, 1987), Oklahoma and American Bar Associations; Oklahoma Trial Lawyers Association; Oklahoma Association of Defense Counsel; Federation of Insurance and Corporate Counsel; Defense Research Institute. ***Email:*** king@king-lawfirm.com

ASSOCIATES

RICHARD M. GLASGOW, born Oklahoma City, Oklahoma; admitted to bar, 1990, Oklahoma, U.S. District Court, Western, Eastern and Northern Districts of Oklahoma, U.S. Tax Court and U.S. Court of Appeals, Tenth Circuit. *Education:* University of Central Oklahoma (B.S., 1973); Oklahoma City University (J.D., 1989). Certified Public Accountant, Oklahoma, 1978. *Member:* Oklahoma County, Oklahoma and American Bar Associations; Oklahoma Trial Lawyers Association; The Association of Trial Lawyers of America. ***Email:*** king@king-lawfirm.com

(This Listing Continued)

JUSTIN T. KING, born Oklahoma City, Oklahoma, 1972; admitted to bar, 2000, Oklahoma; U.S. District Court, Western and Northern Districts of Oklahoma. *Education:* Washington & Lee University (B.A., 1995); University of Oklahoma (J.D., 2000). Outstanding Comment Author, Oklahoma Law Review, 1999. Chief Article and Book Review Editor, Oklahoma Law Review, 1999-2000. Law Clerk to, Chief Judge Terry C. Kern, U.S. District Court, Northern District of Oklahoma, 2000-2001. Author: "Am I My Brother's Keeper?' Sherrice's Law: A Balance of American Notions of Duty and Liberty," 52 Okla. L. Rev. 613 (2000). *Member:* Oklahoma County, Oklahoma and American Bar Associations. ***PRACTICE AREAS:*** Litigation; Commercial Transactions. ***Email:*** king@king-lawfirm.com

REPRESENTATIVE CLIENTS: All American Bottling Company; American Fidelity Insurance Co.; American International Group, Inc.; BancInsure; C.L. Frates and Company; Church Mutual Insurance Company; Commerce and Industry Insurance Co.; Crawford & Co.; Cunningham Lindsey U.S. Inc.; GAB Robbins North America, Inc.; Gainsco Companies; Gallagher Bassett Services, Inc.; Insurance Company of the State of Pennsylvania; Jefferson Insurance Company of New York; Lexington Insurance Company; Lowe's Home Centers, Inc.; MGA Insurance Company, Inc.; Montgomery KONE, Inc.; Murray Biscuit Company, L.L.C.; NAS Insurance Group; National Union Fire Insurance Company; Oklahoma Farmers Union Mutual Insurance Company; Philadelphia Insurance Company; Reliant American Group; Republic Insurance Company; Travelers Property Casualty Co.; York Claims Service, Inc.

KIRK & CHANEY

101 PARK AVENUE, SUITE 800
OKLAHOMA CITY, OKLAHOMA 73102-7202
Telephone: 405-235-1333
Fax: 405-235-5914

Civil Trial Practice in all State and Federal Courts. Oil and Gas, Real Estate, Securities, Administrative, Commercial Law and Family Law.

MEMBERS OF FIRM

JAMES A. KIRK, born Oklahoma City, Oklahoma; admitted to bar, 1968, Oklahoma; 1970, U.S. Tax Court; 1971, U.S. Supreme Court and U.S. Court of Appeals, Tenth, Fifth and Fourth Circuits. *Education:* Central State College; University of Oklahoma (B.B.A., 1964; J.D., 1968). Phi Alpha Delta. Listed in: The Best Lawyers in America (Business Litigation and Family Law). Member, 1977-1984 and President, 1980-1982, Oklahoma Board of Corrections. Member, Governor's Criminal Justice Advisory Committee, 1981-1984 and Chairman, Corrections Subcommittee, 1981-1984. Member, 1985-1991 and President, 1988-1989, Oklahoma Horse Racing Commission; Oklahoma State Bureau of Investigation Commission, 1992-1999. Luther Bohanon American Inn of Court XXII, 1987—. *Member:* Oklahoma County, Oklahoma and American (Member, Sections on: Corporation, Banking and Business Law; Litigation; Family Law) Bar Associations. Fellow, American College of Trial Lawyers. ***PRACTICE AREAS:*** Commercial Law; Complex Litigation; Oil and Gas Law; Family Law. ***Email:*** kirk@kirkandchaney.com

JAMES M. CHANEY, born Elk City, Oklahoma; admitted to bar, 1980, Oklahoma; 1981, U.S. District Court, Northern District of Texas, U.S. District Court, Western District of Oklahoma and U.S. Court of Appeals, Tenth Circuit; 1983, U.S. Court of Appeals, Fourth Circuit; 1984, U.S. Court of Appeals, Fifth Circuit; 1991, U.S. Court of Appeals, Eighth Circuit. *Education:* Oklahoma City University (B.A., 1977); Cornell University; University of Oklahoma (J.D., 1980). Assistant District Attorney, Oklahoma County, 1980. *Member:* Oklahoma County, Oklahoma and American Bar Associations. ***PRACTICE AREAS:*** Commercial Law; Oil and Gas Law; Complex Litigation. ***Email:*** chaney@kirkandchaney.com

ALLEN CAMPBELL, born Oklahoma City, Oklahoma; admitted to bar, 1983, Oklahoma; 1984, U.S. District Court, Western District of Oklahoma; U.S. Tax Court; U.S. Claims Court; 1987, U.S. Court of Appeals, Tenth Circuit. *Education:* University of Oklahoma (B.B.A., 1979); Oklahoma City University (J.D., with honors, 1983); New York University (LL.M., in Taxation, 1984). *Member:* Oklahoma County, Oklahoma and American Bar Association. ***PRACTICE AREAS:*** Commercial Law; Complex Litigation; Oil and Gas Law; Family Law; General Practice. ***Email:*** campbell@kirkandchaney.com

MATTHEW L. STANDARD, born Oklahoma City, Oklahoma; admitted to bar, 1986, Oklahoma; U.S. District Court, Western District of Oklahoma; U.S. Court of Appeals, Eighth and Tenth Circuit. *Education:* University of Oklahoma (B.B.A., 1983; J.D., 1986). Certified Public Accountant, Oklahoma, 1984. *Member:* Oklahoma and American Bar Associations. ***PRACTICE AREAS:*** Civil Litigation; Class Actions; Oil and Gas Law; Employment Law; Appellate Practice. ***Email:*** standard@kirkandchaney.com

THOMAS J. DANIEL IV, born Tulsa, Oklahoma; admitted to bar, 1986, Oklahoma and U.S. District Court, Western District of Oklahoma; U.S. Court of Appeals, Tenth Circuit. *Education:* University of Oklahoma (B.B.A., with distinction, 1983; J.D., 1986). Phi Delta Phi. *Member:* Oklahoma County (Member, Young Lawyers Division, Board of Directors, 1988-1990; Chairperson, Ask a Lawyer Committee, 1989-1991; Speakers Bureau/Media Relations Committee, 1989-1990) Oklahoma and American (Member, Litigation Section) Bar Associations; Oklahoma Trial Lawyers Association. ***PRACTICE AREAS:*** Litigation; Oil and Gas; Domestic Law. ***Email:*** daniel@kirkandchaney.com

CHERYL P. HUNTER, born Stillwater, Oklahoma; admitted to bar, 1982, Oklahoma; 1991, Texas, U.S. District Court, Western, Eastern and Northern Districts of Oklahoma; U.S. Supreme Court; U.S. Court of Appeals, Fifth and Tenth Circuits. *Education:* Oklahoma State University (B.S., 1979); University of Oklahoma (J.D., 1982). Phi Delta Phi (President). Recipient, University of Oklahoma College of Law, Student Bar Association Service Award; Governors Commission on Government Performance, 1994-1995. Member, University of Oklahoma Law Review, 1981-1982. Commissioner, Oklahoma Commission on Teacher Preparation, 2000-2004. Chairman, Oklahoma Indigent Defense System Board, 1997-2000. Member, Oklahoma State Regents for Higher Education, 2000—. Member, Governors Commission on Government Performance, 1994-1995. *Member:* Oklahoma County (Vice President, 1993-1994), Oklahoma (Chairman, Chairman-Elect, Treasurer, Secretary, Financial Institutions Section; Member, Board of Directors, Young Lawyers Division, 1987-1990) Bar Associations; State Bar of Texas. Luther Bohanon American Inns of

(This Listing Continued)

Court XXII, Master. **PRACTICE AREAS:** Real Estate Law; Employment Law; Commercial Transactions; Insurance Receivership; Litigation in State and Federal Courts. **Email:** chunter@kirkandchaney.com

JOSEPH P. BALKENBUSH, born Oklahoma City, Oklahoma, August 19, 1954; admitted to bar, 1987, Oklahoma; U.S. District Court, Eastern, Western and Northern Districts of Oklahoma. *Education:* National University (B.B.A., 1979); Oklahoma City University (J.D., 1986). Judge, Domestic Relations Docket, District Court, Oklahoma County, Oklahoma, 1996-2001. *Member:* Oklahoma County (Director, 2003—) and Oklahoma Bar Associations; Oklahoma Association of Mediators and Arbitrators (2004—); International Association of Collaborative Practitioners (2004—). [Sgt., USMC, 1976-1980]. **PRACTICE AREAS:** Family Law; Probate; Mediation. **Email:** jbalkenbush@kirkandchaney.com

ASSOCIATE

KATHERINE H. PENCE, born Barksdale AFB, Louisiana; admitted to bar, 1998, Oklahoma and U.S. District Court, Western District of Oklahoma. *Education:* University of Oklahoma (B.A., 1995; J.D., 1998). **PRACTICE AREAS:** Family Law; Civil Litigation. **Email:** kpence@kirkandchaney.com

OF COUNSEL

JACK G. BUSH, born Oklahoma City, Oklahoma; admitted to bar, 1959, Oklahoma; U.S. District Court, Western, Eastern and Northern Districts of Oklahoma; U.S. Court of Appeals, 4th, 5th and 10th Circuits. *Education:* University of Central Oklahoma (B.A., 1956); Oklahoma City University (J.D., 1959). Phi Alpha Delta. *Member:* Oklahoma County, Oklahoma and American Bar Associations; Oklahoma Trial Lawyers Association. **PRACTICE AREAS:** Business Law; Civil Litigation; Corporate Law; Municipal Law; Probate; Real Estate; Wills.

REPRESENTATIVE CLIENTS: Samson Resources Co.; Trigen Energy Corp.; Cingular Wireless; National American Insurance Company; Love's Travel Stops & Country Stores, Inc.

KIRSCHNER KISNER LEE, P.L.L.C.

Established in 1999

CHASE CENTER
100 NORTH BROADWAY AVENUE, SUITE 3030
OKLAHOMA CITY, OKLAHOMA 73102-8838
Telephone: 405-239-3300; Toll Free: 888-978-3300
Facsimile: 405-235-3352
URL: http://www.kirschnerlaw.com

Commercial Law, General Civil and Appellate Practice in State and Federal Courts. Bankruptcy and Commercial Transactions, Business Law, Contracts, Corporate Law, Banks and Banking, Insurance Defense, Workers' Compensation, Alternative Dispute Resolution, Labor and Employment, Health Care, International Law, Arbitration, Mediation, Mergers, Acquisitions and Divestitures, Personal Injury, Product Liability, Malpractice, Family Law, Partnership Law, Finance, Real Estate, Wills, Trusts and Estates, and Construction Law.

FIRM PROFILE: The Kirschner Law Firm is listed in the Bar Register of Preeminent Lawyers under Commercial Law.

MICHAEL PAUL KIRSCHNER, born Enid, Oklahoma, April 10, 1943; admitted to bar, 1968, Oklahoma, U.S. District Court, Western, Northern and Eastern Districts of Oklahoma, U.S. Court of Appeals, Tenth, Fifth and Fourth Circuits and U.S. Supreme Court. *Education:* Westminster College for Men; Oklahoma City University School of Law (B.A., 1966; J.D., 1968). *Member:* Oklahoma County, Oklahoma and American Bar Associations; American Inn of Court No. XXIII (Master of the Bench and Inn Counselor). **PRACTICE AREAS:** Bankruptcy Law; Banking Law; Commercial Law; Civil Practice; Business Law; Arbitration; Appellate Practice; Debtor and Creditor; Insurance Law. **Email:** mike@tklf.com

DAVID W. KISNER, born Muskogee, Oklahoma, July 2, 1940; admitted to bar, 1968, Oklahoma and U.S. District Court, Western District of Oklahoma. *Education:* Northeastern Oklahoma State University (B.S., 1962); University of Tulsa College of Law (J.D., 1967). Phi Delta Phi. Hearing Examiner, Oklahoma Real Estate Commission, 1974. Mediator, Oklahoma Mediation/Arbitration Service. *Member:* Oklahoma County and Oklahoma Bar Associations; Oklahoma Trial Lawyers Association. **PRACTICE AREAS:** Mediation; Arbitration; Family Law; Probate; Commercial Law. **Email:** dkisner@legealassociatesllc.net

JIM W. LEE, born Alexandria, Louisiana, July 5, 1939; admitted to bar, 1968, Oklahoma; 1972, U.S. District Court, Western, Eastern and Northern Districts of Oklahoma and U.S. Court of Appeals, 10th Circuit; 1979, U.S. Supreme Court. *Education:* Oklahoma State University and Baylor University (B.B.A., 1961); Oklahoma City University (J.D., 1968). Phi Delta Phi. Member, Advisory Committee, Oklahoma City University Law School, 1975—. Arbitrator, U.S. District Court, Western District of Oklahoma, 1985—. Board of Review, Oklahoma Employment Security Commission. *Member:* Oklahoma and American Bar Associations. **PRACTICE AREAS:** Insurance Law; Civil Jury Trials; Workers Compensation; Personal Injury; Products Liability; Professional Liability; Medical Malpractice. **Email:** jim.lee@legalassociatesllc.net

---

LORRIE A. CORBIN, born Dallas, Texas, February 17, 1970; admitted to bar, 1995, Oklahoma, U.S. District Court, Northern and Western Districts of Oklahoma, and U.S. Court of Appeals, Tenth Circuit. *Education:* Midwestern State University (B.A., cum laude, 1992); Oklahoma City University School of Law (J.D., cum laude, 1995). *Member:* Oklahoma Bar Association; American Inn of Court No. XXIII (Barrister). **PRACTICE AREAS:** Bankruptcy; Commercial Litigation; Construction Law; Civil Practice; Labor and Employment Law. **Email:** lorrie@tklf.com

REPRESENTATIVE CLIENTS: Available Upon Request.

KLINE, KLINE, ELLIOTT & BRYANT, P.C.

Established in 1983

KLINE LAW BUILDING
720 N.E. 63RD STREET
OKLAHOMA CITY, OKLAHOMA 73105
Telephone: 405-848-4448
Fax: 405-842-4539
Email: kline@klinefirm.org
URL: http://www.klinefirm.org

General Trial and Appellate Practice in all State and Federal Courts. Civil and Criminal, Bankruptcy and Commercial Law. Employment and Civil Rights Litigation.

FIRM PROFILE: The firm was founded in February 1983, at the time of David Kline's retirement as Chief Bankruptcy Judge of the Western District of Oklahoma; and his son Timothy Kline's leaving a local law firm in which he was the bankruptcy section coordinator. Starting with this outstanding base in bankruptcy law, the firm began expanding into other areas of the law by associating itself with outstanding attorneys in the fields of Tax, Commercial Law, Wills and Probate, Insurance Defense Law, Labor Law and Oil and Gas.

DAVID A. KLINE, born Keota, Oklahoma, September 27, 1923; admitted to bar, 1949, Oklahoma. *Education:* Oklahoma City University; University of Oklahoma (J.D., 1950). Phi Delta Phi; Order of the Coif. Member, Oklahoma Law Review. 1949-1950. Law Clerk, U.S. District Judges and Federal Court Special Master, Oklahoma, 1952-1961. Adjunct Professor of Law, Oklahoma City University, 1980-1984. Contributing Author: *Cowans Bankruptcy Law and Practice,* Third Edition, West Publishing Company. First Assistant U.S. Attorney, Oklahoma, 1961-1969. President, 1977-1978 and Member, Board of Governors, 1972-1982, National Conference of Bankruptcy Judges. Faculty Member, Federal Judicial Center, Washington, D.C., National Seminar for Bankruptcy Judges, 1972-1986. Board of Directors, 1972—and Chairman, 1993, Consumer Credit Counseling Service of Central Oklahoma. Board of Directors, 1972-1974 and President, 1974, Oklahoma County Legal Aid Society. Consultant, Norton Bankruptcy Law and Practice, Callaghan & Company, Board of Advisors, Annual Survey of Bankruptcy Law, 1979. Digest Editor, American Bankruptcy Law Journal, 1974-1977. *Member:* Oklahoma County and Oklahoma Bar Associations; National Conference of Bankruptcy Judges (Associate). Fellow, American College of Bankruptcy. **PRACTICE AREAS:** Federal Practice; Civil Law; Criminal Law; Bankruptcy Law. **Email:** dkline@klinefirm.org

TIMOTHY D. KLINE, born Oklahoma City, Oklahoma, July 16, 1949; admitted to bar, 1976, Oklahoma and U.S. District Court, Western and Eastern Districts of Oklahoma. *Education:* Central State University and University of Oklahoma (B.A., 1971); University of Oklahoma (J.D., 1976). Phi Delta Phi. Law Clerk to U.S. District Judge, 1976-1979. Adjunct Professor, Bankruptcy, Oklahoma City University Law School, Spring, 1980-1984. *Member:* Oklahoma County (President, 1998-1999), Oklahoma, American and Federal Bar Associations. Fellow, American College of Bankruptcy. (Certified Specialist, Business Bankruptcy Law, American Bankruptcy Board of Certification) (Certified Specialist, Consumer Bankruptcy Law, American Bankruptcy Board of Certification). **PRACTICE AREAS:** Federal Practice; Commercial Law; Bankruptcy Law. **Email:** tkline@klinefirm.org

G. DAVID BRYANT, born Norman, Oklahoma, April 23, 1949; admitted to bar, 1975, Oklahoma, U.S. District Court, Western, Northern and Eastern Districts of Oklahoma and U.S. Court of Appeals, Tenth Circuit; 1981, U.S. Court of Appeals, Seventh Circuit. *Education:* University of Oklahoma (B.A., 1973); Oklahoma City University (J.D., 1975). Phi Delta Phi. Recipient, American Jurisprudence Award, Commercial Paper, Bank Deposits and Collections. Co-Author, "Oklahoma Comments," Uniform Commercial Code Article 8, Investment Securities, 1995. Chapter 7 Panel Trustee, U.S. Bankruptcy Court, Western District of Oklahoma. *Member:* Oklahoma County (Member, Committees on: Grievance, 1977; Public Service, 1977; Alternative Dispute Resolution, 1998), Oklahoma (Member, Committee on Alternative Dispute Resolution) and American (Member, Sections of: Litigation; Alternative Dispute Resolution; Human Rights) Bar Associations; The Association of Trial Lawyers of America (Member, Sections on Commercial and Criminal). **PRACTICE AREAS:** Civil Litigation (State and Federal); Insurance Defense Litigation; Civil Mediation; Commercial Mediation; Bankruptcy Litigation. **Email:** dbryant@klinefirm.org

STEPHEN W. ELLIOTT, born Portland, Oregon, December 20, 1954; admitted to bar, 1981, Oklahoma, U.S. District Court, Western and Northern Districts of Oklahoma, U.S. District Court, Northern District of Texas, U.S. Court of Appeals, Fifth and Tenth Circuits and U.S. Supreme Court. *Education:* University of Tulsa (B.S., with honors, 1977; J.D., 1981). *Member:* Oklahoma County, Oklahoma and American Bar Associations. **REPORTED CASES:** Hoover, In re, 32 B.R. 842 (Bkrptcy.Okla. 1983); Ramco Wells Service, Inc., In re, 32 B.R. 525 (Bkrptcy.Okla. 1983); Amarex, Inc. v. El Paso Natural Gas Co., 772 P.2d 905 (Okla. 1987); Danks, In re, 123 B.R. 652 (Bkrptcy.W.D.Okla. 1991); MIF Realty L.P. v. Duncan Development Co., 892 P.2d 664 (Okla.App. 1995). **PRACTICE AREAS:** Civil Litigation; Bankruptcy Law; Commercial Law. **Email:** selliott@klinefirm.org

---

CLAY P. BOOTH, born Oklahoma City, Oklahoma, August 10, 1959; admitted to bar, 1986, Oklahoma; 1987, U.S. District Court, Western District of Oklahoma; 1991, U.S. Court of Appeals, 10th Circuit. *Education:* Oklahoma State University (B.S., 1982); Oklahoma City University (J.D., 1986). Recipient, American Jurisprudence Award, Constitutional Law, 1984. *Member:* Oklahoma and American Bar Associations. **PRACTICE AREAS:** Commercial Law; Creditors Rights; Collections; Mortgage Foreclosure; Bankruptcy. **Email:** cbooth@klinefirm.org

LISA M. MUEGGENBORG, born Kingfisher, Oklahoma, June 23, 1969; admitted to bar, 2000, Oklahoma. *Education:* University of Central Oklahoma (B.B.A., 1992); Oklahoma City University School of Law (J.D., 1999). *Member:* Oklahoma and American Bar Associations. **PRACTICE AREAS:** Civil Practice; Administrative Law. **Email:** lmueggenborg@klinefirm.org

(This Listing Continued)

KLINE, KLINE, ELLIOTT & BRYANT, P.C., Oklahoma City—Continued

CHRISTOPHER T. STEIN, born Berea, Ohio, December 24, 1964; admitted to bar, 2000, Oklahoma; U.S. District Court, Western and Eastern Districts of Oklahoma; 2002, U.S. District Court, Northern District of Oklahoma. *Education:* Indiana University of Pennsylvania (B.S., 1987); Oklahoma City University School of Law (J.D., 2000). Recipient: CALI Award for Academic Excellence; Burbridge Award. Airline Transport Pilot, 1990. President, Experimental Aircraft Association, 1984. *Member:* Oklahoma County and Oklahoma Bar Associations. ***PRACTICE AREAS:*** Bankruptcy; Commercial Law; Litigation; Mediation. ***Email:*** cstein@klinefirm.org

SUSAN CAREY, born Denver, Colorado, September 4, 1977; admitted to bar, 2003, Oklahoma. *Education:* Oklahoma State University (B.A., 2000); University of Oklahoma (J.D., 2003). ***Email:*** scarey@klinefirm.org

LYNNELL A. HARKINS, born Houston, Texas, September 26, 1939; admitted to bar, 1982, Oklahoma; 1983, U.S. District Court, Western District of Oklahoma. *Education:* University of Colorado (B.S., 1970); Oklahoma City University (M.C.J.A., 1978; J.D., 1982). Bench and Bar. Special District Judge, 1985-1988. Member, Oklahoma State Pardon and Parole Board, 2004-2006. Member, Disaster Response and Relief, 1998-2006. Associate Member, ASCP, 1970—. *Member:* Oklahoma Bar Association. ***PRACTICE AREAS:*** Bankruptcy; Labor; Probate; Family. ***Email:*** lharkins@klinefirm.org

OF COUNSEL

RICHARD M. HEALY, III, born Boston, Massachusetts, May 15, 1950; admitted to bar, 1979, Oklahoma; 1980, U.S. District Court, Western District of Oklahoma; 1983, U.S. District Court, Northern and Eastern Districts of Oklahoma and U.S. Court of Appeals, Tenth Circuit. *Education:* Oklahoma State University; University of Oklahoma (B.A., 1976); Oklahoma City University (J.D., 1979). Phi Delta Phi. *Member:* Oklahoma County, Oklahoma and American Bar Associations; Defense Research Institute; Oklahoma Association of Defense Counsel. ***PRACTICE AREAS:*** Insurance Defense; Products Liability; Professional Liability Defense. ***Email:*** rhealy@klinefirm.org

PATRICK M. CASTLEBERRY

S. THOMAS ADLER

STEVEN J. GOETZINGER

REPRESENTATIVE CLIENTS: BancFirst; Essex Insurance Co; Nautilus Insurance Co.; Private Database Systems Inc.; Scottsdale Insurance Co.; General Finance Inc.; American Equity Insurance; Barrett Refining Corp.; Realty Management; AXA Global U.S. Risks; Carrier Corp.; Oklahoma City and County Health Department; BBB of Oklahoma; First Bethany Bank & Trust; Southwestern Wire, Inc.; Associated Communications & Research; Phillips University; Farm Fresh; Camrose Technologies; First Fidelity Bank; American Reliable Insurance Co.; Kempes Insurance Co.; Rural Community Insurance Services; Wells Fargo Bank, N.A.; City of Ponca City; Jeld-Wen, Inc.; OG&E.

RICHARD M. KLINGE & ASSOCIATES, P.C.

Established in 1993

3555 NORTHWEST 58TH STREET
SUITE 1000
OKLAHOMA CITY, OKLAHOMA 73112
Telephone: 405-917-0398
Fax: 405-917-0323
Email: rklinge@klingelaw.com

Transactional Practice including Health Law, Computer Law, Electronic Commerce, Intellectual Property, Information Law, Contracts, Commercial, Internet Law, and Corporate Law.

FIRM PROFILE: The law firm of Richard M. Klinge & Associates is listed in the Bar Register of Preeminent Lawyers in the areas of Business Law, Health Law, Computer Law, Intellectual Property Law.

RICHARD M. KLINGE, born Omaha, Nebraska, April 20, 1949; admitted to bar, 1974, Kansas; 1980, Oklahoma. *Education:* Kansas Newman College (B.S., 1971); Washburn University (J.D., 1974). Member, Board of Editors, Washburn Law Journal, 1972-1974. Author: "Civil Procedure: The Effect of Long Arm Statutes Upon Venue Standards," 12 Washburn L.J. 107, 1972; "Equipment of Criminal Convictions in Kansas; A Necessary Rehabilitation Tool," 13 Washburn L.J. 93, 1974. Instructor in Business Law, Kansas Newman College, 1978-1980. *Member:* Oklahoma and American Bar Associations; Computer Law Association. ***REPORTED CASES:*** Rainbow Travel Service v. Hilton Hotels Corporation, 896 F.2d 1233. ***PRACTICE AREAS:*** Health Law; Computer Law; Electronic Commerce; Intellectual Property; Information Law; Contracts; Commercial Law; Corporate Law. ***Email:*** rklinge@tsgincorporated.com

KOOP & MEDLEY

THE MANEY HISTORIC DISTRICT
725 NORTHWEST ELEVENTH
OKLAHOMA CITY, OKLAHOMA 73103
Telephone: 405604-5953
Fax: 405-604-9775
Email: billmedley@coxinet.net

Litigation, Negligence, Products Liability.

STANLEY KOOP, born Oklahoma City, Oklahoma, September 18, 1969; admitted to bar, 1997, Oklahoma and U.S. District Court, Western District of Oklahoma. *Education:* University of Oklahoma (B.B.A., 1991; J.D., 1996). *Member:* Oklahoma County and Oklahoma Bar Associations; The Association of Trial Lawyers of America; Oklahoma Association of Defense Counsel; Defense Research Institute. ***PRACTICE AREAS:*** Personal Injury; Automobile Accidents and Injuries; Nursing Home Abuse and Neglect; Products Liability. ***Email:*** stankoop@coxinet.net

WILLIAM C. MEDLEY, IV, born Bartlesville, Oklahoma, March 26, 1970; admitted to bar, 1997, Oklahoma and U.S. District Court, Eastern, Western and Northern Districts of Oklahoma. *Education:* University of Oklahoma (B.B.A., 1992; J.D., 1997). Phi Delta Phi. *Member:* Oklahoma County, Oklahoma and American Bar Associations; Oklahoma Association of Defense Counsel; American Inn of Court XXIII. ***PRACTICE AREAS:*** Personal Injury; Products Liability; Medical Malpractice. ***Email:*** billmedley@coxinet.net

KORNFELD FRANKLIN RENEGAR & RANDALL

A PROFESSIONAL CORPORATION

Established in 1973

4100 PERIMETER CENTER DRIVE, SUITE 150
OKLAHOMA CITY, OKLAHOMA 73112
Telephone: 405-840-2731
Fax: 405-946-0376
Email: kfrr@swbell.net

Edmond, Oklahoma Office: 2964 Via Esperanza, 73013. Telephone: 405-285-8118. Facsimile: 405-285-8119. Email: grenegar@lawyer.com

General Civil Practice. Class Action Litigation, Federal and State Taxation, Oil and Gas, Corporate, Estate Planning, Banking, Employment Law, Bankruptcy, Communications, Real Estate, Pollution Litigation, Railroad and Insurance Law. Trials and Appellate Practice in all State and Federal Courts before Mediation and Arbitration Panels and Administrative Agencies.

FIRM PROFILE: The firm is a full-service law firm whose history can be traced back to the early 1920's. The firm possesses strength in all areas and is regarded nationally as having superior expertise in the areas of taxation, oil and gas and employment law.

HARVEY L. HARMON (1920-1990)

BEN FRANKLIN (1912-2002)

JULIAN P. KORNFELD, born Dallas, Texas, May 1, 1934; admitted to bar, 1958, Texas; 1963, Oklahoma. *Education:* University of Texas (B.B.A., 1955; LL.B., 1957); New York University (LL.M., in Taxation, 1962). Chairman, Taxation Section Oklahoma Bar Association, 1969. *Member:* State Bar of Texas. ***PRACTICE AREAS:*** Taxation Law; Federal Income, Estate and Gift Taxation Law. ***Email:*** kfrr@swbell.net

CLARKE L. RANDALL, born Washington, D.C.; admitted to bar, 1976, Oklahoma. *Education:* Indiana University (A.B., 1971); University of Oklahoma (J.D., 1976); Southern Methodist University (LL.M., in Taxation, 1978). Author: "Fiduciary Duties of Investment Company Directors and Management Companies Under the Investment Company Act of 1940," 31 Oklahoma Law Review, 635, 1978. Assistant Public Defender, Tulsa County, 1976-1977. ***PRACTICE AREAS:*** Federal Taxation; Tax Planning; Tax Controversies; Estate Planning and Probate; State and Local Taxation; General Business; Corporations. ***Email:*** kfrr@swbell.net

GREGG R. RENEGAR, born Oklahoma City, Oklahoma, January 1, 1949; admitted to bar, 1975, Oklahoma; U.S. District Court, Western, Northern and Eastern Districts of Oklahoma; U.S. Court of Appeals, Tenth Circuit; U.S. Court of Federal Claims; U.S. Supreme Court. *Education:* Oklahoma State University (B.S., 1971); Oklahoma City University (J.D., with honors, 1975). Phi Alpha Delta. Listed in Who's Who in American Law, 13th Ed., 1996. Author: "Notice and Demand Upon Lessee for Breach of an Implied Covenant in Oklahoma—Is It a Necessity?" Oklahoma Bar Association Journal, 1979; "The Tax Treatment of Gain on Sale of Principal Residence," Oklahoma Bar Association Journal, 1980; "Notice and Demand Upon Lessee for Breach of an Implied Covenant in Oklahoma and Arkansas," The Landman, 1980; "Slander of Title in the State of Oklahoma", Oklahoma Bar Association Journal, 1994. Lecturer: "Oil and Gas Law", 19th Arkansas Natural Resources Law Institute, 1980; "Basic Oil and Gas in Oklahoma", Oklahoma City University School of Law, 1982; "Financial Survival in the Oil Patch," Oklahoma City University School of Law, 1983; "Oil and Gas Leases and Title Examination," Oklahoma City University School of Law," 1984; "Debtor-Creditor Law in the Oil Patch, "Oklahoma City University School of Law, 1984; "Royalties on Take-or-Pay Settlements", Tax Section of Oklahoma City Chapter of COPAS, 1994. Director, North Oklahoma City Rotary Club. Advisory Council and Chairman, Salvation Army and Salvation Army Adult Rehabilitation Center. *Member:* Oklahoma City Mineral Lawyers Society; Oklahoma City Real Estate Attorneys Association (President, 1987-1988); American Trial Lawyers Association; Rocky Mountain Mineral Law Foundation. ***REPORTED CASES:*** Starke v. H.U.D., 454 F.Supp. 477 (W.D.Okl. 1977); Perrin v. Tenneco Oil Company, 505 F.Supp. 23 (W.D. Okl. 1980); Lamb v. Griffin Television, Inc., 804 F.Supp. 1430 (W.D. Okl. 1992); Roye Realty & Developing, Inc. v. Watson v. Arkansas Louisiana Gas Company, 949 P.2d 1208 (Okl. 1996); Tenneco Oil Company v. Joiner, 696 F.2d 768 (10th Cir. 1982); Armbruster v. Thetis Energy Corp., 675 P.2d 476 (Ct. App. Okl. 1984); Marshall v. El Paso Natural Gas Company, 874 F.2d 1373 (10th Cir. 1989); Goodall v. Trigg Drilling Company, Inc., 944 P.2d 292 (Okl. 1997); Oneok, Inc. v. Ming, 962 P.2d 1286 (Okl. 1998); Estate of Goodwin, 18 P.3d 373 (Okl. Civ. App. 2000); Howard v. Crawford, 16 P.3d 473 (Okl. Civ. App. 2000); Goss v. Wood, 15 P.3d 517 (Okl. Civ. App. 2000); Sias v. Edge Communications, 8 P.3d 182 (Okl. Civ. App. 2000); Mare Oil Company v. Deep Blue Royalties, L.L.C. 2003 OK. Civ. App. 21; Clark v. Clark 57 P.3d 95 (OK. 2002). ***PRACTICE AREAS:*** Federal Civil Litigation; Trial Practice; Energy Law; Oil and Gas Law; Business Law; Administrative Agency Practice; Environmental Law; Eminent Domain; Commercial Real Estate Development; Probate; Class Actions; Trust Litigation. ***Email:*** grenegar@lawyer.com

JOAN A. RENEGAR, born Fairfield, California, August 7, 1950; admitted to bar, 1979, Oklahoma, U.S. District Court, Western District of Oklahoma and U.S. Tax Court. *Education:* University of Oklahoma (B.A., 1972); Oklahoma City University (M.A.T., 1973; J.D., 1979). Phi Alpha Delta. Member, Oklahoma City University Law Review. Robert J. Turner, American Inn of Court. ***REPORTED CASES:*** Estate of Goodwin, 18 P.3e 373 (Okl. Civ. App. 2000); Howard v. Crawford, 16 P. 3d 473 (Okl. Civ. App. 2000); Sias v.

(This Listing Continued)

Edge Communications, 8 P. 3d 182 (Okl. Civ. App. 2000); Goss Family Ltd. Partnership v. Wood, 15 P.3d 517 (Okl. 2000); Mare Oil Company v. Deep Blue Royalties, L.L.C. 2003 OK. Civ. App. 21; Clark v. Clark 57 P.3d 95 (OKL. 2002). ***PRACTICE AREAS:*** Business Litigation; Employment Law; Environmental Law; Energy Law; Class Actions; Qui Tam. ***Email:*** jrenegar@lawyer.com

OF COUNSEL

MARCELO M. PUIGGARI, born New York, N.Y., June 27, 1958; admitted to bar, 1984, Oklahoma; 1985, Texas; 1988, U.S. Tax Court; U.S. District Court, Western District of Oklahoma. *Education:* Washington University (A.B., 1981); Oklahoma City University (J.D., 1984); Southern Methodist University (LL.M. in Taxation, 1986). ***LANGUAGES:*** Spanish. ***PRACTICE AREAS:*** Federal Taxation; Tax Planning; Tax Controversies; Estate Planning and Probate; State and Local Taxation; General Business; Corporations. ***Email:*** kfrr@swbell.net

All Members of this Firm Belong to the Oklahoma County and Oklahoma Bar Associations.

REPRESENTATIVE CLIENTS: Ackerman McQueen, Inc.; Action Wholesale Liquor; Aztec Exploration, Inc.; Aztec Specialty Co.; B.R.I. Imports, Inc.; Bowlware Construction, Inc.; Century Incorporated; Clements Exploration Co.; Cummins Investment Corporation; D.E. Davis, Inc.; Dillingham Ranch, L.C.; EDS Corp.; Eateries, Inc.; Farm Service Co.; Faulkner Corporation; Fremont Energy Corp.; Frontier Terminal & Trading Co.; General Motors Corp.; General Motors Acceptance Corp.; Goldman Enterprises; Griffin Television, LL.C.; Harris Development; Merco of Oklahoma, Inc.; Mewbourne Oil Co.; Oklahoma Medical Research Foundation; Raptor Properties, LLC; Roxana Oil Company; Rozel Ranch, Inc.; The Salvation Army; Standard Iron & Metal Co.; The Womble Company.

KUNZMAN & BOLLINGER, INC.

SUITE 600
5100 NORTH BROOKLINE
OKLAHOMA CITY, OKLAHOMA 73112
Telephone: 405-942-3501
Fax: 405-942-3527
Email: Kunzboll@sbcglobal.net

Business and Corporation Law. Securities, Oil and Gas, Federal Taxation.

WALLACE W. KUNZMAN, JR., born Fairfield, Iowa, June 26, 1949; admitted to bar, 1976, Oklahoma and U.S. District Court, Western District of Oklahoma; 1977, New Mexico; 1981, U.S. District Court, District of New Mexico. *Education:* University of New Mexico (B.B.A., 1972); Oklahoma City University (J.D., with distinction, 1976). Phi Delta Phi. Recipient: Oklahoma City Society of Title Attorneys Award, 1976; American Jurisprudence Awards in Property I and II, and Wills and Estates; Phi Delta Phi Outstanding Graduate Award, 1976. Who's Who in American Law, 1990. Member, NASD Board of Arbitrators; Select Committee to the Oklahoma Securities Administrator, 1986-1990. Special Lecturer: Tulsa University Law School Continuing Education Division, 1990—; Oklahoma City University Continuing Legal Education, 1986; Lecturer: Oklahoma Society of Certified Public Accountants, 1990; Investment Program Association, 2002—. Member, Adjunct Professor, Oklahoma City University, 1982. Alumni Board Oklahoma City University, 1990—. Member: Investment Program Association, 2001; Legal Affairs Committee to Investment Program Association, 2001—. *Member:* Oklahoma County, Oklahoma and American Bar Associations; State Bar of New Mexico; State Bar of Texas (inactive). ***PRACTICE AREAS:*** Business/Corporate Securities; Oil and Gas. ***Email:*** wkunzman@sbcglobal.net

GERALD A. BOLLINGER, born Glasgow, Montana, April 11, 1950; admitted to bar, 1976, Montana and U.S. District Court, District of Montana; 1982, Oklahoma and U.S. District Court, Western District of Oklahoma. *Education:* Macalester College; University of Montana (B.A., 1972; J.D., 1976); Boston University (LL.M. in Taxation, 1981). Law Clerk, Montana Supreme Court, 1976-1977. Special Lecturer, Tulsa University Law School Continuing Education Division, 1990—. Lecturer, National Business Institute, Inc., 1995. *Member:* State Bar of Montana; Oklahoma and American Bar Associations; State Bar of Texas (inactive). ***PRACTICE AREAS:*** Federal Taxation; Business/Corporate Securities; Oil and Gas; Estate Planning. ***Email:*** gbollinger@sbcglobal.net

REPRESENTATIVE CLIENTS: Atlas America, Inc.; Atlas Resources, Inc.; Anthem Securities, Inc., Bryan Funding, Inc., Pittsburgh, Pennsylvania; Eneric Financial Services, Fairfield, Iowa; Marlin Exploration, Inc., Shreveport, Louisiana; Heritage Benefits Financial Services, Inc., Seattle, Washington; Eagle Energy, Inc. Indian Harbour Beach, Florida; Resource America, Inc.; LEAF Financial Corp.; Resource Capital Partners, Inc.; Chadwick Securities, Inc., Philadelphia, Pennsylvania; Couch Financial Services, Inc, Dallas, Texas; Leasehold Management Corp.; F.D. Thompson & Co., PLC; Black Gold Trading, L.L.C.; Surgery Centers of America II; BOGO Energy Corporation; Pro-Vision, L.L.C., Oklahoma City, Oklahoma; Carey Financial Corp., New York, New York.

KUTAK ROCK LLP

Established in 1965

SUITE 475
6305 WATERFORD BOULEVARD
OKLAHOMA CITY, OKLAHOMA 73118-1116
Telephone: 405-848-2475
FAX: 405-842-5748
URL: http://www.kutakrock.com

Atlanta, Georgia Office: Suite 2100, 225 Peachtree Street, NE, 30303-1731. Telephone: 404-222-4600. Facsimile: 404-222-4654.
Denver, Colorado Office: Suite 3100, 1801 California Street, 80202-2658. Telephone: 303-297-2400. Facsimile: 303-292-7799.
Des Moines, Iowa Office: Suite 124, Highland Building, 4201 Westown Parkway, Des Moines, 50266-6720. Telephone: 515-224-1266. Facsimile: 515-457-7669.
Kansas City, Missouri Office: Valencia Place, Suite 200, 444 West 47th Street, 64112-1914. Telephone: 816-960-0090. Telefax: 816-960-0041.

(This Listing Continued)

Fayetteville, Arkansas Office: The Three Sisters Building, 214 West Dickson Street, 72701-5221. Telephone: 501-973-4200. Facsimile: 501-973-0007.
Little Rock, Arkansas Office: Suite 1100, 425 West Capitol Avenue, 72201-3409. Telephone: 501-975-3000. Facsimile: 501-975-3001.
Los Angeles, California Office: Suite 3000, 555 West Fifth Street, 90013-1010. Telephone: 213-996-8478. Facsimile: 213-996-8479.
Lincoln, Nebraska Office: Suite 314, Meridian Park Office Building, 6940 O Street, 68510-2499. Telephone: 402-464-8200. Facsimile: 402-464-8204.
Omaha, Nebraska Office: The Omaha Building, 1650 Farnam Street, 68102-2186. Telephone: 402-346-6000. Facsimile: 402-346-1148.
Scottsdale, Arizona Office: Suite 300, 8601 N. Scottsdale Road, 85253-2742. Telephone: 480-429-5000. Facsimile: 480-429-5001.
Washington, D.C. Office: Suite 1000, 1101 Connecticut Avenue, NW, 20036-4374. Telephone: 202-828-2400. Facsimile: 202-828-2488.
Irvine, California Office: Suite 1100, 18201 Von Karman Avenue, 92612-1077. Telephone: 949-417-0999. Facsimile: 949-417-5394.
Pasadena, California Office: Suite 308, 201 South Lake Avenue, 91101-3004. Telephone: 626-432-1630. Facsimile: 626-432-1614.
Richmond, Virginia Office: Bank of America Center, Suite 800, 1111 East Main Street, 23219-3103. Telephone: 804-644-0313. Facsimile: 804-644-0313.
Chicago, Illinois Office: One South Wacker Drive, 60606-4614. Telephone: 312-602-4100. Facsimile: 312-602-4101.
Wichita, Kansas Office: Suite 370, 8301 East 21st Street North, 67206-2935. Telephone: 316-609-7900. Facsimile: 316-630-8021.

Civil Litigation and Bankruptcy, Public Finance, Corporate and Structured Finance, Banking and Commercial Lending, Real Estate Law, Taxation Law, Health Care and Hospital Law.

FIRM PROFILE: Founded in Omaha in 1965, Kutak Rock conducts a full-service, multidisciplinary practice. While the firm has long had a nationally recognized public and corporate finance practice, we have also developed a sophisticated business and litigation practice representing clients across the country in complex transactions and major litigation. Kutak Rock has represented every major investment banking firm in the United States; major European, Asian and domestic money-center banks; savings and loan associations; insurance companies; national real estate syndicators and developers; major national franchising enterprises; and numerous other financial institutions, businesses and state and local governmental units. The firm's litigation practice group represents corporate and individual clients in federal and state courts nationwide in complex civil litigation matters and represents clients in arbitration and mediation proceedings. The Firm's Healthcare/hospital law group represents hospitals and physician organizations in numerous states.

PARTNER

MARK F. SELVIDGE, born Ardmore, Oklahoma, January 21, 1947; admitted to bar, 1973, Oklahoma. *Education:* University of Oklahoma (B.A., 1968; J.D., 1972). ***Email:*** mark.selvidge@kutakrock.com

(For biographical data of Atlanta Lawyers, see Professional Biographies at Atlanta, Georgia).
(For biographical data of Chicago Lawyers, see Professional Biographies at Chicago, Illinois).
(For biographical data of Denver Lawyers, see Professional Biographies at Denver, Colorado).
(For biographical data of Des Moines Lawyers, see Professional Biographies at West Des Moines, Iowa).
(For biographical data of Fayetteville Lawyers, see Professional Biographies at Fayetteville, Arkansas).
(For biographical data of Kansas City Lawyers, see Professional Biographies at Kansas City, Missouri)
(For biographical data of Little Rock Lawyers, see Professional Biographies at Little Rock, Arkansas).
(For biographical data of Irvine Lawyers, see Professional Biographies at Irvine, California).
(For biographical data of New York Lawyers, see Professional Biographies at New York, N.Y.).
(For biographical data of Omaha Lawyers, see Professional Biographies at Omaha, Nebraska).
(For biographical data of Pasadena Lawyers, see Professional Biographies at Pasadena, California).
(For biographical data of Pittsburgh Lawyers, see Professional Biographies at Pittsburgh, Pennsylvania).
(For biographical data of Richmond Lawyers, see Professional Biographies at Richmond, Virginia).
(For biographical data of Scottsdale Lawyers, see Professional Biographies at Scottsdale, Arizona).
(For biographical data of Washington Lawyers, see Professional Biographies at Washington D.C.).

LAWSON, KING & SHELTON, PLLC

Established in 1999

2501 NORTH STILES
OKLAHOMA CITY, OKLAHOMA 73105
Telephone: 405-523-2501
Fax: 405-523-2324

Tulsa, Oklahoma Office: 10777 S. Memorial Drive, Suite C, 74133-7351. Telephone: 918-369-9980. Fax: 918-369-9981.

General Civil Practice before all State and Federal Courts, Trials, Insurance Defense, Personal Injury, Negligence, Workers' Compensation and Products Liability.

MEMBERS OF FIRM

STEVE L. LAWSON, born Oklahoma City, Oklahoma, February 2, 1962; admitted to bar, 1987, Oklahoma. *Education:* University of Oklahoma (B.S., Petroleum Engineering,

(This Listing Continued)

LAWSON, KING & SHELTON, PLLC, Oklahoma City—Continued

1984); Oklahoma City University (J.D., 1987). *Member:* Oklahoma County and Oklahoma Bar Associations. ***PRACTICE AREAS:*** Litigation; Insurance Defense Law; Civil Practice; Appellate Practice. ***Email:*** steve.lawson@okfb.com

JEFFREY A. KING, born Washington, D.C., December 18, 1946; admitted to bar, 1972, Oklahoma; 1973, U.S. District Court, Northern and Eastern Districts of Oklahoma; 1986, U.S. Court of Appeals, Tenth Circuit. *Education:* Westminster College (B.A., 1969); University of Oklahoma (J.D., 1972). Phi Delta Phi. *Member:* Tulsa County and Oklahoma and American Bar Associations. (Resident, Tulsa Office). ***PRACTICE AREAS:*** Insurance Defense Law; Personal Injury; Litigation; Civil Practice; Workers Compensation. ***Email:*** jeff.king@okfb.com

TAMI J. SHELTON, born Purcell, Oklahoma, November 16, 1968; admitted to bar, 1994, Oklahoma; U.S. District Court, Eastern and Western Districts of Oklahoma. *Education:* East Central Oklahoma State University (B.S., 1991); University of Oklahoma (J.D., 1994). *Member:* Oklahoma County and Oklahoma Bar Associations; Oklahoma Association of Defense Counsel. ***PRACTICE AREAS:*** Insurance Law; Litigation; Civil Practice; Appellate Practice. ***Email:*** tj.shelton@okfb.com

---

HEATHER DAWN LAKE, born Lincoln, Nebraska, April 26, 1971; admitted to bar, 1996, Oklahoma and U.S. District Court, Eastern and Western Districts of Oklahoma. *Education:* Oklahoma State University (B.A., Psychology, 1993); University of Oklahoma (J.D., 1996). *Member:* Oklahoma Bar Association. ***PRACTICE AREAS:*** Insurance Law; Employment Law; Civil Practice; Insurance Defense; Personal Injury. ***Email:*** heather.lake@okfb.com

M. CHRISTIAN TOLEN, born Kansas City, Missouri, March 16, 1975; admitted to bar, 2001, Oklahoma. *Education:* Truman State University (B.S. Biology, 1997);University of Missouri (J.D., 2000). Phi Alpha Delta. *Member:* Oklahoma Bar Association. (Resident, Tulsa Office). ***PRACTICE AREAS:*** Insurance Law; Civil Practice. ***Email:*** christian.tolen@okfb.com

RICHARD B. SELMAN, born Tulsa, Oklahoma, February 12, 1975; admitted to bar, 2000, Oklahoma and U.S. District Court, Northern, Eastern and Western Districts of Oklahoma. *Education:* University of Oklahoma (B.B.A., 1997; J.D., 2000). Recipient, American Jurisprudence Award, Insurance Law. *Member:* Tulsa and Oklahoma Bar Associations. (Resident, Tulsa Office). ***PRACTICE AREAS:*** Insurance Defense; Personal Injury; Civil Practice; Wills; Trusts and Estates. ***Email:*** richard.selman@okfb.com

STEVEN W. DANIELS, born Enid, Oklahoma, January 23, 1962; admitted to bar, 1987, Oklahoma; 1989, California and U.S. District Court, Western, Eastern and Northern Districts of Oklahoma. *Education:* University of Oklahoma (B.A., 1984; J.D., 1987). Phi Delta Phi. *Member:* Oklahoma County, Tulsa County and Oklahoma Bar Associations; Oklahoma Association of Defense Counsel. ***PRACTICE AREAS:*** Insurance Law; Insurance Defense; Products Liability; Premises Liability; Environmental Liability; Nursing Home Litigation; Insurance Fraud Litigation; Uninsured Motorist Coverage; Personal Injury; Mediation; Arbitration. ***Email:*** steven.daniels@okfb.com

JOHN R. DENNENY, born Kirkwood, Missouri, 1956; admitted to bar, 1981, Oklahoma; U.S. District Court, Northern, Eastern and Western Districts of Oklahoma; U.S. Court of Appeals, Tenth Circuit; U.S. Supreme Court. *Education:* Oklahoma State University (B.S., 1978); University of Oklahoma (J.D., 1981). Phi Kappa Phi; Beta Gamma Sigma; Phi Eta Sigma; Phi Delta Phi. Law Clerk to Honorable Luther B. Eubanks, Chief Judge for the U.S. District Court, Western District of Oklahoma, 1981-1982. *Member:* Oklahoma County and Oklahoma Bar Associations. ***PRACTICE AREAS:*** Insurance Defense; Products Liability; Civil Litigation; Personal Injury. ***Email:*** john.denneny@okfb.com

---

LEE & GOOCH, P.C.

6011 NORTH ROBINSON
OKLAHOMA CITY, OKLAHOMA 73118-7425
Telephone: 405-848-1983
Fax: 405-848-4978
Toll Free: 800-717-1983
Email: leelawok@swbell.net
URL: http://www.lawyers.com/leegoochpc

Trial Practice State and Federal Courts. Civil Rights, Employment Law. Discrimination. Appellate Practice and Insurance Defense.

DAVID W. LEE, born Lubbock, Texas, December 2, 1947; admitted to bar, 1973, Oklahoma and U.S. District Court, Western District of Oklahoma; 1980, U.S. District Court, Northern District of Oklahoma; U.S. Court of Appeals, Tenth Circuit; U.S. Supreme Court. *Education:* University of Oklahoma (B.S., 1970; J.D., 1973). Phi Delta Phi. Author: "Handbook of Section 1983 Litigation," Aspen Publishers, Inc. (2005); "Defending 42 U.S.C. § 1983 Actions", 6th Ed.; "Grand Juries in Oklahoma: Where Are We Now?" 68 Oklahoma Bar Journal, July 26, 1997; "Burden Shifting and Summary Judgement in Federal Employment Discrimination Cases," 67 Oklahoma Bar Journal 2861 (1966); "Qualified Immunity Under 42 U.S.C., 1983 for Public Officials, 25 The Urban Lawyer 97, 1993. Adjunct Professor: Oklahoma City University School of Law, 1985-2004; University of Oklahoma College of Law, 2002-2003. *Member:* Oklahoma County and Oklahoma Bar Associations. ***REPORTED CASES:*** Thompson v. Oklahoma, 487 U.S. 815 (1988). ***PRACTICE AREAS:*** Employment Law; Civil Rights Law; Discrimination; Insurance Defense; Appellate Practice.

AMBRE CAMILLE GOOCH, born Ft. Benning, Georgia, November 21, 1970; admitted to bar, 1996, Oklahoma, U.S. District Court, Eastern, Western and Northern Districts of Oklahoma and U.S. Court of Appeals, Tenth Circuit. *Education:* University of Oklahoma (B.B.A., 1993; J.D., 1996). *Member:* Oklahoma County, Oklahoma and American Bar Associations. ***PRACTICE AREAS:*** Civil Rights Defense; Employment Law.

(This Listing Continued)

REPRESENTATIVE CLIENTS: Oklahoma State University; Oklahoma State Insurance Fund; Association of County Commissioners of Oklahoma; Oklahoma Municipal Assurance Group (OMAG); City of Midwest City; Oklahoma Department of Transportation; Oklahoma Bureau of Narcotics and Dangerous Drugs; Oklahoma AÆ Board of Regents; Board of Commissioners of Cleveland County; Board of Commissioners of Garvin County; Deer Creek Rural Water Corp.; Monte R. Lee and Company; City of Enid, Oklahoma.

JOHN T. LILLY

1900 N.W. EXPRESSWAY, SUITE 1300
OKLAHOMA CITY, OKLAHOMA 73118
Telephone: 405-286-2110
Fax: 405-840-4701
Email: jtlilly10@aol.com

Business and Corporate Law, Oil and Gas, Venture Capital, Business Litigation, Oil and Gas Litigation, Tax Law, Real Estate Planning, Estate, Probate and Trust Litigation, Property Tax Litigation.

JOHN T. LILLY, born Oklahoma City, December, 1960; admitted to bar, 1986, Texas and U.S. Tax Court; 1992, Oklahoma; 1998, U.S. Court of Appeals, Tenth Circuit. *Education:* University of Oklahoma (B.B.A., with honors, 1983; J.D., with honors, 1986). Order of the Coif; Beta Gamma Sigma; Phi Delta Phi. Certified Public Accountant, Texas, 1987. Presentations: Current Issues in Oil and Gas Operating Agreements, Mineral Lawyers Society of Oklahoma City, May 2004; Considerations to Selecting a Business Entity, Oklahoma Society of CPA's, August 2004; Structuring Limited Partnerships for the Family Business, Dallas Chapter, Texas Society of CPA's, 1993; *Member:* Oklahoma and American Bar Associations.

JAMES P. LINN LAW FIRM, P.L.L.C.

THE TOWER
1601 NW EXPRESSWAY
SUITE 1710
OKLAHOMA CITY, OKLAHOMA 73118
Telephone: 405-239-6781
Facsimile: 405-516-5525

Civil Trial Practice in all State and Federal Courts, White Collar Criminal Defense, Commercial and Business Litigation, Business Law, Estate Planning, Taxation, Corporate and Real Property.

JAMES P. LINN, born Spearman, Texas, April 21, 1926; admitted to bar, 1950, Texas; 1970, Oklahoma; 1971, U.S. Supreme Court; 1990, New York and U.S. District Court, Southern and Eastern Districts of New York. *Education:* Texas A. & M. University; West Texas State College; University of Texas (LL.B., 1950). Delta Theta Phi. *Member:* Oklahoma, New York State and American Bar Associations; State Bar of Texas. ***PRACTICE AREAS:*** Litigation. ***Email:*** jlinn@linnlaw.net

STEPHEN R. JOHNSON, born Cleveland, Ohio, December 11, 1956; admitted to bar, 1982, Oklahoma and U.S. District Court, Western District of Oklahoma; 1985, U.S. Court of Appeals, Tenth Circuit; 1986, U.S. Court of Appeals, Fourth Circuit; 1999, U.S. Court of Appeals, District of Columbia Circuit; 2000, U.S. Supreme Court. *Education:* University of Arizona (B.A., 1979); University of Tulsa (J.D., 1982). Phi Alpha Delta. *Member:* Oklahoma and American Bar Associations. ***PRACTICE AREAS:*** Litigation. ***Email:*** sjohnson@linnlaw.net

OF COUNSEL

JOHN D. SINGLETON, born Shreveport, Louisiana, April 16, 1952; admitted to bar, 1977, Oklahoma; 1978, U.S. Tax Court; 1979, U.S. District Court, Western District of Oklahoma and U.S. Court of Appeals, 10th Circuit. *Education:* Oklahoma State University (B.S., 1974); Oklahoma City University (J.D., 1976); Boston University (LL.M. in Taxation, 1977). *Member:* Oklahoma and American Bar Associations. ***PRACTICE AREAS:*** Business Law; Business Transactions; Taxation and Estate Planning. ***Email:*** jsingleton@linnlaw.net

Names of Representative Clients available upon request.

LOONEY, NICHOLS & JOHNSON, PLLC

Established in 1931

528 NORTHWEST 12TH
OKLAHOMA CITY, OKLAHOMA 73103
Telephone: 405-235-7641
Fax: 405-239-2050; 239-2052
Email: firm@lnjlaw.com

General Civil Practice in all State and Federal Courts, Workers Compensation. Insurance, Aircraft, Trials. Drug and Medical Device Claims, Products Liability, Environmental Law, Bad Faith Litigation, Appellate Practice.

NED LOONEY (1886-1965)

CLYDE J. WATTS (1907-1975)

WILLARD R. BERGSTRASSER (1922-1993)

HENRY W. NICHOLS (1923-2002)

ROBERT DUDLEY LOONEY, born Tishomingo, Oklahoma, 1919; admitted to bar, 1942, Oklahoma. *Education:* Oklahoma University (B.A., 1941). *Member:* Oklahoma County, Oklahoma and American Bar Associations; Oklahoma Association of Defense Counsel; Law Science Academy of America; International Association of Defense Counsel; Defense Research Institute. Fellow: American College of Trial Lawyers; International

(This Listing Continued)

Academy of Trial Lawyers. ***PRACTICE AREAS:*** Insurance Law; Civil Litigation; Personal Injury Defense Law; Products Liability Law; Probate Law. ***Email:*** firm@lnjlaw.com

BURTON J. JOHNSON, born Providence, Rhode Island, May 16, 1920; admitted to bar, 1950, Oklahoma. *Education:* Oklahoma City University. Trustee, Fisher Jr. College, Boston, Mass., 1957-1964. State Chairman, Defense Research Institute, 1965—; Regional Vice President and Board Member, 1965-1978; President and Chairman of the Board, 1979-1981 (DRI). *Member:* Oklahoma County, Oklahoma and American Bar Associations; Oklahoma Association of Defense Counsel (Director, 1966—); International Association of Defense Counsel; Federation of Insurance Counsel; Law-Science Academy of America. ***PRACTICE AREAS:*** Products Liability Law; Civil Rights Defense Law; Insurance Coverage Law; First Party Litigation; Aviation Law; Automobile Law; General Liability Law. ***Email:*** bjohnson@lnjlaw.com

EDWIN F. GARRISON, born Bridgeport, Oklahoma, October 30, 1939; admitted to bar, 1967, Oklahoma. *Education:* Texas Tech University and Southwestern State College (B.S., 1963); Oklahoma City University and University of Tulsa (J.D., 1967). *Member:* Oklahoma County, Oklahoma and American Bar Associations; Defense Research Institute; American Board of Trial Advocates; Oklahoma Association of Defense Counsel. ***PRACTICE AREAS:*** Insurance Law; Tort Defense Law; Civil Rights; Products Liability. ***Email:*** egarrison@lnjlaw.com

TENAL S. COOLEY, III, born Stillwater, Oklahoma, November 6, 1950; admitted to bar, 1977, Oklahoma. *Education:* Centenary College (B.A., 1973); Oklahoma City University (J.D., 1977). *Member:* Oklahoma County, Oklahoma and American Bar Associations; Oklahoma Association of Defense Counsel. ***PRACTICE AREAS:*** Workers Compensation Defense Law; General Liability Defense Law; Wrongful Termination Defense Law; Bad Faith Defense Law; Products Liability Defense Law; Americans with Disabilities Act. ***Email:*** tcooley@lnjlaw.com

TIMOTHY L. MARTIN, born Oklahoma City, Oklahoma, March 29, 1947; admitted to bar, 1983, Oklahoma. *Education:* University of Oklahoma (B.B.A., 1971); Oklahoma City University (J.D., 1983). *Member:* Oklahoma County, Oklahoma and American Bar Associations; Defense Research Institute. ***PRACTICE AREAS:*** Products Liability Law; Civil Rights Defense Law; Aviation Law; Automobile Law; General Liability Law; Environmental Law; Insurance Law. ***Email:*** tmartin@lnjlaw.com

H. GRADY PARKER, JR., born Casper, Wyoming, December 31, 1961; admitted to bar, 1991, Oklahoma and U.S. Federal Court, Western District of Oklahoma. *Education:* University of Oklahoma (B.B.A., 1985); Oklahoma City University (J.D., 1991). *Member:* Oklahoma County, Oklahoma and American (Tort & Insurance Section, 1992) Bar Associations; Oklahoma Association of Defense Counsel. ***PRACTICE AREAS:*** Workers Compensation Law; Employer Liability Law; Wrongful Termination Defense Law; General Liability Defense; Bad Faith Defense Law; Products Liability Defense; Americans with Disabilities Act. ***Email:*** gparker@lnjlaw.com

BRANDON S. NICHOLS, born Oklahoma City, Oklahoma, September 9, 1975; admitted to bar, 2001, Oklahoma; U.S. District Court, Western, Eastern and northern Districts of Oklahoma. *Education:* Northeastern Oklahoma State University (B.A., English, 1998); Oklahoma City University School of Law (J.D., 2000). Listed in, Strathmore's Who's Who of Attorneys. *Member:* Oklahoma County, Oklahoma and American (Member, Sections on: Environment; Insurance; Product Liability; Tort, 2001) Bar Associations; Oklahoma Association of Defense Council; Defense Research Institute. ***PRACTICE AREAS:*** Insurance Defense; Automobile Accidents and Injuries; Truck Accidents; Premises Liability; Insurance Bad Faith; Employment Law; Oilfield Drilling; Professional Liability; Construction Defects; Products Liability; Warranty Law; Aviation Law. ***Email:*** bnichols@lnjlaw.com

---

THOMAS ROWE KENDRICK, born Russell, Kansas, November 16, 1971; admitted to bar, 1998, Oklahoma. *Education:* University of Central Oklahoma (B.A., 1995); Oklahoma City University School of Law (J.D., 1998). *Member:* Oklahoma County and Oklahoma Bar Associations; Defense Research Institute; Oklahoma Association of Defense Counsel. ***PRACTICE AREAS:*** Insurance Defense; Tort Litigation; Products Liability; Insurance Bad Faith Litigation. ***Email:*** tkendrick@lnjlaw.com

KENNETH L. WOOD, born Oklahoma City, Oklahoma, December 20, 1964; admitted to bar, 1993, Oklahoma; U.S. District Court, Western District of Oklahoma. *Education:* University of Oklahoma (B.A., Political Science, 1989); Oklahoma City University School of Law (J.D., 1993). Phi Delta Phi. Member: Moot Court Board; National Organization of Social Security Claimants Representatives. Former Staff Attorney, Oklahoma Workers' Compensation Court. *Member:* Oklahoma Bar Association; Lawyers for Working Oklahomans. ***PRACTICE AREAS:*** Workers Compensation; Social Security Disability.

CHARLES F. MOSER, born Tribune, Kansas, June 25, 1964; admitted to bar, 1990, Oklahoma and U.S. District Court Western and Eastern Districts of Oklahoma; 1991, Kansas, U.S. District Court, District of Kansas, U.S . District Court, Northern District of Texas, U.S. Court of Appeals, Tenth Circuit and U.S. Supreme Court. *Education:* Barton County Community College (A.S., 1984); Fort Hays State University (B.B.A., magna cum laude, 1987); Oklahoma City University (J.D., with high distinction, 1990). Phi Delta Phi. Order of the Barristers. Hatton W. Sumners Scholar. Member, National Moot Court Team, 1989-1990. Outstanding Graduate, 1990. Recipient, Dean's Service Award. Member, Oklahoma City University Law Review, 1988-1990. Co-Author, "Saying It Well Without Language: Computer Assisted Videos in Railroad Cases," Trial, p.46, September 1995. *Member:* Oklahoma County, Oklahoma, Kansas and American (Member, Litigation Section) Bar Associations; Oklahoma Trial Lawyers Association; The Association of Trial Lawyers of America; American Inn of Court CV; Ruth Bader Ginsburg (Barrister; Senior Counsel) and William J. Holloway American Inns of Court. Fellow, Oklahoma Bar Foundation. ***REPORTED CASES:*** Williams v. Harrop Industries, Inc., 73 P.2d 902 (Okla. App. 2003); Farrimond v. Fisher, 8 P.3d 872 (Okla. 2000). ***PRACTICE AREAS:*** Personal Injury; Products Liability; Professional Liability; Railroad Law; Motor Vehicle Accidents; Truck Accidents.

REPRESENTATIVE CLIENTS: Allied Dealer Insurance Company; American Home Assurance Company; American Insurance Group; Avemco Insurance Company; Aviation Adjustment Bureau; Aviation Insurance Managers, Inc.; Bituminous Insurance Company; Capital Indemnity Co.; CIGNA; City of Shawnee, Oklahoma; CNA Insurance Company; Colonial Insurance Company of California; Commercial Union Insurance Company; Continental Insurance Group; Cravens, Dargen & Co; Crawford & Company; Cumis Insurance Company; CUNA Mutual Insurance Company; Dayton Tire & Rubber Co.; Employees Mutual Insurance Company; Employees Reinsurance Corp.; Federal Insurance Company; General Casualty Company; General Insurance Company of America; Great American Insurance Company; Industrial Underwriters Insurance Company; Jefferson Insurance Group; John Deere Insurance Co.; Kansas City Fire & Marine Insurance Company; Little Giant Pump Company; Lloyd's London; Maryland Casualty Company; Michelin North America, Inc.; National Union Fire Insurance Company; Newell Coach Co.; Northwestern National Insurance Company; Phoenix Aviation Managers, Inc.; Providence Washington Insurance Group; Reliance Insurance Company; Safeco Insurance Company of America; Security Insurance Company of Hartford; St. Paul Fire & Marine Insurance Company; Talent Tree Personnel Service; Travelers Group; U.S. Aviation Underwriters; Utility Equipment Co.; Uniroyal Tire Co., Inc.; United Pacific Insurance Company; Universal Underwriters; Zurich America.

BRIAN T. LOUGHRIN

115 S.W. 89TH STREET
OKLAHOMA CITY, OKLAHOMA 73139
Telephone: 405-634-2100
Fax: 405-634-6870
Email: donatio@aol.com

Criminal Defense, Bankruptcy Chapter 7, Driving While Intoxicated, Felonies, Sexual Assault, Federal Criminal Law, Personal Bankruptcy, Criminal Law, Sex Crimes.

BRIAN T. LOUGHRIN, born Grand Rapids, Michigan, January 25, 1962; admitted to bar, 1998, Oklahoma, U.S. District Court, Western District of Oklahoma and U.S. Court of Appeals, Tenth Circuit. *Education:* Michigan State University (B.A., 1985); Detroit College of Law at Michigan State University (J.D., 1998). *Member:* Oklahoma County and American (Member, Sections on: Young Lawyers and Criminal Justice) Bar Associations; Oklahoma Bar Association; The Incorporated Society of Irish American Lawyers.

ROBERT T. LUTTRELL, III P.C.

100 PARK AVENUE, SECOND FLOOR
OKLAHOMA CITY, OKLAHOMA 73102-8099
Telephone: 405-235-1946
Fax: 405-235-2046
URL: http://www.luttrell-lawfirm.com
Email: robert.luttrell@luttrell-law.com
URL: http://www.luttrell-law.com

Commercial Law, Contracts, Real Estate, Consumer Finance Law, Banking Law.

ROBERT T. LUTTRELL, III, born Oklahoma City, Oklahoma, June 12, 1946; admitted to bar, 1973, Oklahoma; 1979, U.S. Supreme Court. *Education:* University of Oklahoma (B.A., 1968; J.D., 1973); University of San Diego. Phi Delta Phi. Co-Author: Oklahoma Comments to UCC Articles 3, 4, 4A, 5, 6 and 8 (West Publishing Company). Author: "Update on the Fair Credit Reporting Act," 43 Consumer Finance Law Quarterly Report; "Regulatory Enforcement Authority and Criminal Enhancements," 44 Consumer Finance Law Quarterly Report. Adjunct Professor: Financial Institutions Law and Transactions in Goods. University of Oklahoma Law Center; Commercial Paper, Oklahoma City University Law School. Member, Conference on Consumer Finance Law. *Member:* Oklahoma County, Oklahoma (Chairman, Banking and Commercial Law Section, 1982-1983) and American Bar Associations. [Captain, USNR]. ***REPORTED CASES:*** Baptist Medical Center of Oklahoma, Inc. v. Trans Con Lines, 1993 OK 38, 852 P.2d 139; First Bank of Okarche v. Lepak, 1998 OK 46, 961 P2d 194. ***PRACTICE AREAS:*** Commercial Law; Contracts; Real Estate; Consumer Finance Law; Commercial Real Estate; Commercial Finance; Banking Law; Litigation.

REPRESENTATIVE CLIENTS: MidFirst Bank; Tinker Federal Credit Union; Midland Mortgage Corp.; First Security Bank and Trust Co.; City Bank & Trust; UMB Bank, N.A.; Centex Home Equity Corp.; Member's Trust Federal Credit Union; CBN Steel Construction, Inc.

LYTLE SOULÉ & CURLEE, P.C.

Established in 1902
1200 ROBINSON RENAISSANCE
119 NORTH ROBINSON
OKLAHOMA CITY, OKLAHOMA 73102
Telephone: 405-235-7471
Telecopy: 405-232-3852
Email: info@lytlesoule.com
URL: http://www.lytlesoule.net

General Civil Practice. Employment Law, Labor Relations, Civil Litigation, Business Organization, Taxation, Oil and Gas, Civil Rights, ERISA Litigation, Probate, Trust Law, Banking, Real Estate, Construction, Insurance Defense, Aircraft Title and Financing Law and Environmental Law.

FIRM PROFILE: Founded as Shartel & Wells on January 1, 1902, Lytle Soulé & Curlee, a Professional Corporation is the oldest firm in Oklahoma City and one of the oldest firms in the state.

The firm represents business entities and individuals in all aspects of a general, civil business practice. Predominate areas of concentration include management representation in labor and employment law, ERISA litigation, real estate, construction, commercial transactions, Corporation Commission, aircraft finance, insurance defense, environmental law, oil and gas and bankruptcy law, as well as creditors' rights, probate, trusts and estate planning. The firm engages in litigation in all state and federal courts.

Lytle Soulé & Curlee emphasizes accessibility, quality and cost control. The firm does not assign more lawyers or staff to a project than it warrants. Assignment of each matter to a specific attorney allows consistent communication and personal service. We are proud of our national

(This Listing Continued)

LYTLE SOULÉ & CURLEE, P.C., Oklahoma City—Continued

and local clients, our reputation for professionalism and the ability to provide large firm capabilities with the benefits and personal attention of a smaller organization. Our reputation has been earned with a century of excellent service to our clients.

ROY COBB LYTLE (1902-1982)

EDWARD E. SOULÉ (1924-1984)

WILLIAM D. CURLEE (1929-1992)

JAMES C. CHANDLER, born Cambridge, Missouri, June 14, 1936; admitted to bar, 1963, Oklahoma; 1980, U.S. Supreme Court. *Education:* Oklahoma State University (B.S., 1958); University of Oklahoma (LL.B., 1963). Phi Alpha Delta; Phi Kappa Phi; Order of the Coif. Recipient, American Jurisprudence Award in Evidence, Bills and Notes. Article and Book Review Editor, Oklahoma Law Review, 1963. Outstanding Young Lawyer, Oklahoma Bar Association, 1968. Associate Bar Examiner, Oklahoma Board of Bar Examiners, 1970-1973. Member, United States Magistrate Judge Merit Selection Panel, U.S. District Court, Western District of Oklahoma, 1984—. Adjunct Professor, Property Law, University of Oklahoma Law School, 1987; Best Lawyers Consumer Guide. *Member:* Oklahoma County, Oklahoma and American Bar Associations. [1st Lt., CIC, U.S. Army, 1959-1962]. ***REPORTED CASES:*** Steiger v. Commerce Acceptance of Oklahoma City, Inc., 455 P.2d 81 (Okl. 1969); Firestone Tire & Rubber Co. v. Barnett, 475 P.2d 164 (Okl. 1970); Atlan Industries, Inc. v. O.E.M., Inc. 555 F.Supp. 184 (W.D. Okl. 1983); Gilbert Central Corp. v. State of Oklahoma, 716 P.2d 654 (Okl. 1986); Bolton v. Scrivner, Inc., 36 F.3d 939 (10th Cir. 1994); Massey v. Scrivner, Inc., 901 F.Supp. 1546 (W.D. Okl. 1994); Milton v. Scrivner, Inc., 53 F.3d 1118 (10th Cir. 1995). ***PRACTICE AREAS:*** Employment Law; Probate Law; Real Estate Law; Civil Rights Defense Law; Aircraft Title and Financing Law. ***Email:*** chandler@lytlesoule.com

DONALD K. FUNNELL, born Oklahoma City, Oklahoma, December 19, 1955; admitted to bar, 1984, Oklahoma. *Education:* Oklahoma City University; Central State University (B.B.A., 1980); University of Oklahoma (J.D., with honors, 1984). Phi Delta Phi. Editor, Oklahoma Law Review, 1982-1984. Author: "Secured Transactions: Certificates of Title Delivery or Notation? The Lender's Dilemma," 37 Oklahoma Law Review 618, 1984. *Member:* Oklahoma County, Oklahoma and American Bar Associations. ***PRACTICE AREAS:*** Real Estate Law; Construction; Environmental; Commercial Transactions; Litigation; Labor and Employment Law. ***Email:*** funnell@lytlesoule.com

G. DAVID ROSS, born Tulsa, Oklahoma, January 16, 1954; admitted to bar, 1979, Oklahoma. *Education:* Oklahoma State University (B.S., 1976); University of Oklahoma (J.D., 1979). Phi Delta Phi. *Member:* Oklahoma County, Oklahoma and American Bar Associations; Oklahoma Association of Defense Counsel; The Association of Trial Lawyers of America. [Capt., JAGC, U.S. Army, 1979-1983]. ***PRACTICE AREAS:*** Civil Litigation; Employment Law; Civil Rights Defense Law; Products Liability; Insurance Law; Internet Law; Piracy Law. ***Email:*** ross@lytlesoule.com

GORDON D. RYAN, born Lyons, Kansas, March 15, 1936; admitted to bar, 1961, Kansas; 1969, Texas; 1972, Colorado; 1981, Oklahoma. *Education:* University of Kansas (B.A., 1958; LL.B., 1961). Author: "Force Pooling in Oklahoma: The Joys and Trauma of the Oklahoma Law," 42nd Annual Institute Southwestern Legal Foundation (1991). *Member:* Oklahoma, Kansas and Colorado Bar Associations; State Bar of Texas; Rocky Mountain Mineral Law Foundation; Mineral Lawyers Society; IOCC Legal Committee. ***PRACTICE AREAS:*** Oil and Gas Law; Corporate Commission Practice; Regulatory Law. ***Email:*** ryan@lytlesoule.com

PATRICIA J. HANSON, born Spokane, Washington, November 21, 1955; admitted to bar, 1981, Oklahoma. *Education:* University of Oklahoma (B.A., with high honors, 1977; J.D., with honors, 1981). Order of the Coif; Phi Beta Kappa; Phi Delta Phi. Note Editor, Oklahoma Law Review, 1979-1981. Recipient, Nathan Scarritt Prize, 1980-1981 (awarded to senior ranked first academically in graduation class); American Jurisprudence Awards in Contracts I & II, Criminal Law, Torts I & II, Criminal Procedure, Evidence, Workers Compensation, Professional Responsibility. *Member:* Oklahoma County and Oklahoma Bar Associations. ***PRACTICE AREAS:*** Aircraft Title and Financing Law. ***Email:*** hanson@lytlesoule.com

DAVID W. KIRK, born Okmulgee, Oklahoma, January 19, 1957; admitted to bar, 1985, Oklahoma, U.S. District Court, Northern, Eastern and Western Districts of Oklahoma, U.S. Court of Appeals, Tenth Circuit and U.S. Supreme Court. *Education:* College of William & Mary (B.A., 1979); University of Oklahoma (J.D., 1985). *Member:* Oklahoma County, Oklahoma and American Bar Associations; Oklahoma Association of Defense Counsel; Defense Research Institute, Inc. ***PRACTICE AREAS:*** Employment Litigation; Civil Rights; Discrimination; Business Litigation; Insurance Litigation. ***Email:*** kirk@lytlesoule.com

B. GORE GAINES, born Pryor, Oklahoma, January 6, 1969; admitted to bar, 1995, Oklahoma, U.S. District Court, Northern, Eastern and Western Districts of Oklahoma and U.S. Court of Appeals, Tenth Circuit. *Education:* University of Oklahoma (B.B.A., 1991); Oklahoma City University (J.D., cum laude, 1994). Phi Delta Phi. OCU Board of Governors Representative, 1990-1991. Jessup Moot Court Team. Associate, Ruth Bader Ginsburg American Inn of Court. Assistant Attorney General, Oklahoma, 1995-1996. *Member:* Oklahoma Bar Association. ***REPORTED CASES:*** Schmidt v. Grady County, 1997 OK 92, 943 P.2d 595; Clanton v. Cooper, 129 F.3d 1147 (10th Cir. 1997); Bittle v. Okla. City Univ., 2000 OK Civ.App. 66, 6 P3rd 509; DeGarza v. Okla. City Univ., 2001 OK Civ App 28, 20 P.3d 152. ***PRACTICE AREAS:*** Employment Law; Insurance; Products Liability; General Practice; Water Law; Education Law. ***Email:*** gaines@lytlesoule.com

---

JASON C. HASTY, born Weatherford, Oklahoma, October 10, 1969; admitted to bar, 1994, Oklahoma and U.S. District Court, Western District of Oklahoma. *Education:* Southwestern Oklahoma State University (B.A., 1991); University of Oklahoma (J.D., 1994). *Member:* Major County and Oklahoma Bar Associations. ***PRACTICE AREAS:*** Aircraft Title; Finance Law. ***Email:*** hasty@lytlesoule.com

(This Listing Continued)

GRANT M. LUCKY, born Riverside, California, April 24, 1971; admitted to bar, 1997, Oklahoma. *Education:* University of Tulsa (B.A., History, 1993); Oklahoma City University (J.D., 1997). Phi Alpha Theta Honor Society. CALI Award, Mergers and Acquisitions, Constitutional Law, Property and Slavery. *Member:* Oklahoma and Federal Bar Associations; Ruth Bader Ginsburg American Inn of Court. ***PRACTICE AREAS:*** Family Law; Criminal Law; Civil Litigation; Criminal Defense.

REPRESENTATIVE CLIENTS: Aetna U.S. Health Care, Inc.; Aetna Life Insurance Company; AIG; Amoco Production Company; Asset Management Advisors, L.L.C.; Association of Plumbing, Heating & Cooling Contractors of Oklahoma; BP America Production Company; Bricktown Wire Company, L.L.C.; Chromalloy Division-Oklahoma; Chromalloy Gas Turbine Corp.; CMH Manufacturing, Inc.; CMH Parks, Inc.; Conoco Inc.; Continental Resources, Inc.; CUNA Mutual Insurance; Del Rancho, Inc.; Del Rancho USA, Inc.; Dewberry & Davis; Dewberry Design Group Incorporated; Dulaney Bros. Investments; Elson Oil Co.; Environmental Management, Inc.; Farmers Insurance Group of Companies; Great American Insurance Company; Hanna Oil and Gas Company; Harco National Insurance Company; Heritage Communications, Inc.; The Heritage Group; Honeywell Information Systems, Inc.; Household Finance Corp.; Ingram Industries, Inc.; Municipal Employees Credit Union of Oklahoma City; Oklahoma City University; Oklahoma Industries Authority; Oklahoma Housing Finance Agency; Oklahoma Medical Research Foundation, Inc.; Oklahoma Municipal Assurance Group; Photographic Society of America, Inc.; Pratt Discount Foods, Inc.; Rife Oil Properties, Inc.; Roberts Truck Center, Inc.; Shawver & Son, Inc.; Shawver Electric, Inc.; State of Oklahoma; Stevens Trucking, Co.; St. Gregory's College; Tex-Ok Energy, L.L.C.; Vanderbilt Mortgage & Finance; Waste Management of Oklahoma, Inc.; Weyerhaeuser Company; Wynn Construction Company, Inc.

MAHAFFEY & GORE

A PROFESSIONAL CORPORATION

Established in 1980

SUITE 1100 TWO LEADERSHIP SQUARE
211 NORTH ROBINSON
OKLAHOMA CITY, OKLAHOMA 73102-7107
Telephone: 405-236-0478
FAX: 405-236-1520
Email: lawfirm@mahaffeygore.com

General Civil Trial and Appellate Practice. Oil and Gas, Real Property, Land Titles, Environmental, Employment, Trust and Business Law.

FIRM PROFILE: Mahaffey & Gore is listed in the Bar Register of Preeminent Lawyers under Oil & Gas Law.

GREGORY L. MAHAFFEY, born Fort Worth, Texas, August 22, 1950; admitted to bar, 1975, Oklahoma and U.S. District Court, Northern and Western Districts of Oklahoma; 1978, U.S. District Court, Eastern District of Oklahoma and U.S. Court of Appeals, Tenth Circuit; 1985, U.S. Supreme Court. *Education:* Oklahoma State University and Texas Tech University (B.S.I.E., 1972); University of Oklahoma (J.D., 1975). Tau Beta Pi; Alpha Pi Mu; Phi Delta Phi. *Member:* Oklahoma County, Oklahoma and American Bar Associations; Mineral Lawyers Group (Member, President, 1990-1991). ***REPORTED CASES:*** Stolz Wagner & Brown vs. J. Walter Duncan, 417 F. Supp. 552 (W.D. Okla. 1976); PCX Corporation vs. Oklahoma Corporation Commission, 699 P. 2d 1103 (Okla. App. 1984); LPCX Corp. vs. Faulkner, 818 P.2d 431 (Okla. 1991): Withrow vs. Red Eagle Oil Co., 755 P.2d 622 (Okla. 1988); French Petroleum vs. Oklahoma Corporation, Commission, 805 P.2d 650 (Okla. 1991); Nilsen vs. Ports of Call Oil Company, 711 P.2d 98 (Okla. 1985); Arrowhead Energy Company v. Baron Exploration Company 930 P.2d 181 (Okla. 1997). ***PRACTICE AREAS:*** Administrative Law; Oklahoma Corporation Commission Law; Civil Litigation; Appellate Practice. ***Email:*** gmahaffey@mahaffeygore.com

RICHARD J. GORE, born Oklahoma City, Oklahoma, November 20, 1944; admitted to bar, 1975, Oklahoma; 1977, U.S. District Court, Western, Northern and Eastern Districts of Oklahoma and U.S. Court of Appeals, Tenth Circuit. *Education:* University of Oklahoma (B.A., 1967; J.D., 1975). Phi Delta Phi. Magister, Oklahoma Law Review, 1974-1975. Clerk, Hon. Judge Murrah, Tenth Circuit, 1975-1976. *Member:* Oklahoma County and American Bar Associations; Mineral Lawyers Group. [Capt., U.S. Marine Corps, 1967-1972]. ***LANGUAGES:*** French. ***REPORTED CASES:*** Nilsen vs. Tenneco 614 P2d 36 (Okl. 1980); Amoco Prod. Co. vs. Okl. Corp. Comm. 151 P2d 203 (Okl. 1986); Nilsen v. Ports of Call Oil Company, 711 P.2d 98 (Okl. 1985). ***PRACTICE AREAS:*** Administrative Law; Oklahoma Corporation Commission Law; Civil Litigation.

ARTHUR W. SCHMIDT, born Hallettsville, Texas, November 11, 1952; admitted to bar, 1979, Oklahoma; 1982, U.S. District Court, Northern and Western Districts of Oklahoma, U.S. Court of Appeals, Tenth Circuit and U.S. Court of Federal Claims. *Education:* Phillips University (B.S., cum laude, 1976); University of Oklahoma (J.D., 1979). Phi Delta Phi. *Member:* Oklahoma County, Oklahoma and American Bar Associations; Mineral Lawyers Group; Oklahoma City Association of Petroleum Landmen. ***REPORTED CASES:*** Fisher v. Grace Petroleum Corp., 830 P.2d 1380 (Okla. App. 1991); LPCX Corporation v. Faulkner, et al., 818 P.2d 431 (Okla. 1991). ***PRACTICE AREAS:*** Civil Litigation; Contracts Law; Employment Law; Commercial Law. ***Email:*** aws1812@cs.com

BRUCE R. ROOKER, born Miami, Florida, June 8, 1954; admitted to bar, 1979, Oklahoma and U.S. District Court, Western District of Oklahoma. *Education:* East Central Oklahoma State University (B.A., 1976); University of Oklahoma (J.D., 1979). Order of the Coif; Phi Delta Phi (Magister, 1979). Member, Board of Editors, Oklahoma Law Review, 1977-1979. *Member:* Oklahoma County, Oklahoma and American Bar Associations; Mineral Lawyers Group. ***PRACTICE AREAS:*** Title Examination; Oil and Gas Law; Oil and Gas Acquisitions; Contracts Law; Real Estate Law.

LEE D. GROENEVELD, born Sioux City, Iowa, January 5, 1969; admitted to bar, 1994, Texas; 1997, U.S. District Court, Northern and Western Districts of Oklahoma and U.S. District Court, Eastern, Northern and Western Districts of Texas, U.S. Court of Appeals, Fifth Circuit; 1998, Oklahoma. *Education:* Southern Methodist University (B.S. cum laude, 1991); University of Texas at Austin (J.D., 1994). *Member:* Oklahoma and American Bar Associations; State Bar of Texas. ***PRACTICE AREAS:*** Civil Litigation; Oil and Gas Litigation; Employment Law.

(This Listing Continued)

DEENA TYLER, born Mobile, Alabama, August, 1972; admitted to bar, 2000, Oklahoma. *Education:* University of Oklahoma (B.B.A., 1994; J.D., 2000). *Member:* Oklahoma and American Bar Associations. ***PRACTICE AREAS:*** Civil Litigation; Oil and Gas Litigation; Employment Law. ***Email:*** dtyler@mahaffeygore.com

RYAN W. SEARS, born Bartlesville, Oklahoma, October 22, 1978; admitted to bar, 2004, Oklahoma. *Education:* University of Oklahoma (B.A., with honors, Political Science and Economics, 2001); University of Oklahoma College of Law (J.D., with honors, 2004). *Member:* Oklahoma County, Oklahoma and American Bar Associations. ***PRACTICE AREAS:*** Oil and Gas Law; Civil Litigation; Appellate Practice. ***Email:*** rsears@mahaffeygore.com

REPRESENTATIVE CLIENTS: Anadarko Petroleum Corp.; Baron Exploration Company; Barrett Resources Corp.; Brigham Oil & Gas, LP; Chaparral Energy, LLC; Cheyenne Petroleum Company; Cimarex Energy Co.; Craig Elder Oil & Gas, LLC; Finley Resources, Inc.; First United Bank of Sapulpa; The GHK Company; HCM, A Partnership; Oxley Petroleum Company; Southeast Area Health Center, Inc.; Stephens Production Company; Victory Financial Group, Inc.; Wagner & Brown; Washita Oil & Gas, LLC.

MARTIN LAW OFFICE

SUITE 360
119 NORTH ROBINSON AVENUE
OKLAHOMA CITY, OKLAHOMA 73102
Telephone: 405-236-8888
Fax: 405-236-8844
Email: mack@martinlawoffice.net
URL: http://www.martinlawoffice.net

Criminal Defense. White Collar Fraud, Homicide, Grand Jury Practice, Trial and Appellate Practice in all Courts.

FIRM PROFILE: For over twenty-five years this firm has specialized in criminal defense with emphasis on grand jury, trial and appellate practice. The firm practices throughout the State of Oklahoma in State and Federal Court matters. The firm also practices in numerous other States, both in State and Federal Courts. These have included California, Nevada, Colorado, New Mexico, Nebraska, Texas, Mississippi, Illinois, Michigan, Florida, Iowa and North Carolina. Mr. Martin is an active lecturer in continuing legal education seminars throughout the State of Oklahoma for various different groups and bar associations. For over 10 years years Mr. Martin has been listed in the Bar Registry of Preeminent Lawyers and The Best Lawyers in America.

Firms Reported Cases: United States v. Soderstrand, 412 F.3d 1146 (10th Cir. 2005); United States v. Van Meter, 278 F.3d 1156 (10th Cir. 2002); United States v. Day, 223 F. 3d 1225 (10th Cir. 2000); United States v. Dickerson, 195 F 3d 1183 (10th Cir. 1999); United States v. Gonzales, 58 F 3d 506 (10th Cir. 1995); United States v. Migliaccio, 34 F 3d 1517 (10th Cir. 1994); United States v. Hollis, 971 F 2d 1441 (10th Cir. 1992) cert denied, 507 U.S. 985 (1993); United States v. Cooper, 956 F 2d 960 (10th Cir. 1992); United States v. Edgmon, 952 F 2d 1206 (10th Cir. 1991); State v. McElwee, District Judge, 972 P 2d 876 (Ok). Cir 1999); State ex rel, Oklahoma State Board of Medical Licensee and Supervision v. Migliaccio, 917 P 2d 483 (Okl App 1996); In the Matter of M.A.H., 855 P. 2d 1066 (Okl. 1993); State ex rel. Macy v. 1983 Cadillac Eldorado 852 P. 2d 810 (Okl App. 1993); Allison v. State, 675 P. 2d 142 (Ok). cr. 1983); J.M.R. v. Moore 610 P 2d 811 (Okl Cr. 1980).

MACK K. MARTIN, born Chattanooga, Oklahoma, November 27, 1953; admitted to bar, 1979, Oklahoma and U.S. District Court, Western, Eastern and Northern Districts of Oklahoma; U.S. District Court, District of Colorado, U.S. District Court, Eastern District of Michigan, U.S. District Court, Northern District of Illinois, U.S. Court of Appeals, Fourth and Tenth Circuits and U.S. Supreme Court. *Education:* Cameron University (B.A., 1976); Oklahoma City University (J.D., 1978). Board Member, Moot Court. Recipient, Outstanding Law Review Alumni Award, Oklahoma City University School of Law, 2003. Research Editor, Oklahoma City University Law Review. Lecturer, Continuing Legal Education Seminars: Oklahoma Bar Association; Oklahoma Criminal Defense Lawyers Association; University of Oklahoma; Oklahoma City University; Oklahoma County Bar Association; Cleveland County Bar Association; McClain County Bar Association; Comanche County Bar Association; Beckham County Bar Association. Member, Criminal Justice Act Panel Selection Committee, Western District of Oklahoma, 1988-2003. Listed in Best Lawyers in America, 1993—. *Member:* Oklahoma County (Member: Board of Directors, 1994-1996; Former Chairman: Criminal Law Committee; Fee Grievance and Ethics Committee; Bench and Bar Committee), Oklahoma (Former Chairman, Criminal Law Section) and Federal (President, Oklahoma City Chapter, 1992-1993) Bar Associations; Oklahoma Trial Lawyers Association (Member, Advisory Board, 1992-1995); Oklahoma Criminal Defense Lawyer's Association (Member, Board of Directors; President, 1988; Recipient, Lord Erskine Lifetime Achievement Award in Criminal Defense, 2000); National Association of Criminal Defense Lawyers (Lifetime Member); William J. Holloway, Jr. American Inns of Court (Master). Fellow: American Board of Criminal Lawyers; American College of Trial Lawyers. ***PRACTICE AREAS:*** Criminal Law.

LAUREL SUSAN DARROW, born Moore, Oklahoma, January 27, 1965; admitted to bar, 1990, Oklahoma and U.S. District Court, Western District of Oklahoma; 1992, U.S. Court of Appeals, Tenth Circuit. *Education:* University of Oklahoma (B.A., Finance, 1987; J.D., 1990). Phi Delta Phi. *Member:* Oklahoma County, Oklahoma, Federal (Member, City Chapter) and American Bar Associations; Women Lawyers of Oklahoma City; Oklahoma Criminal Defense Lawyers Association; National Association of Criminal Defense Lawyers; Luther Bohanan American Inns of Court.

McAFEE & TAFT

A PROFESSIONAL CORPORATION
Established in 1952
211 NORTH ROBINSON
OKLAHOMA CITY, OKLAHOMA 73102-7103
Telephone: 405-235-9621
Facsimile: 405-235-0439
URL: http://www.mcafeetaft.com

REVISER OF THE OKLAHOMA LAW DIGEST FOR THIS DIRECTORY.

General Civil Practice. Administrative Law, Aircraft Financing and Leasing, Antitrust Law, Banking and Financial Institutions, Bankruptcy Law, Business Organizations and Transactions, Construction Law, Corporate and Securities Law, Creditors Rights, Employee Benefits, Energy Law, Entertainment Law, Environmental Law, Federal Aviation Administration and Aviation Title Law, Franchising, Health Care, Insurance, Intellectual Property, International Law, Labor and Employment Law, Mergers and Acquisitions, Nonprofit and Tax Exempt Organizations, Oil and Gas Coverage, Products Liability, Real Estate, Tax Law, Trust, Estate Planning and Probate, Workers' Compensation Defense. General Civil Trial Practice and Appellate Practice, including trials and proceedings in all federal and state courts, before mediation and arbitration panels and administrative agencies.

FIRM PROFILE: The firm was founded in 1952 by Kenneth E. McAfee and Richard G. Taft and has enjoyed continued and balanced growth to its present size. The firm is a full-service civil practice law firm, which possesses strength and depth in all phases of its practice. In the business and legal community, the firm is regarded as one of the most prominent and respected firms in the state. The firm and its lawyers are listed in the Bar Register of Preeminent Lawyers.

LAW FIRM ALLIANCES/ASSOCIATIONS: ***TERRALEX, THE WORLDWIDE NETWORK OF INDEPENDENT LAW FIRMS***

KENNETH E. McAFEE (1903-1986)
RICHARD G. TAFT (1913-1999)
JOSEPH G. RUCKS (1913-1988)
REFORD BOND (1930-1989)
STEWART W. MARK (1915-1993)
JUDSON S. WOODRUFF (1925-1997)

TERRY R. BARRETT, born Ardmore, Oklahoma, November 5, 1944; admitted to bar, 1973, Oklahoma. *Education:* University of Oklahoma (B.B.A., 1967; J.D., 1973). Order of the Coif; Phi Delta Phi. Member, Board of Editors, Oklahoma Law Review, 1972-1973. *Member:* Oklahoma County, Oklahoma, Federal Energy and American Bar Associations. ***PRACTICE AREAS:*** Oil and Gas Acquisitions; Oil and Gas Law; Natural Gas Contracts; Litigation. ***Email:*** terry.barrett@mcafeetaft.com

T. MICHAEL BLAKE, admitted to bar, 1996, Oklahoma. *Education:* Duke University (A.B., 1993); University of Oklahoma College of Law (J.D., with highest honors, 1996) Order of the Coif; New York University (LL.M., Taxation, 1997). Chief Articles and Book Review Editor, Oklahoma Law Review. Author: Water: PUD No. 1 of Jefferson County v. Washington Department of Ecology: State Water Quality Certification of Federal Licensed Hydropower Projects, Oklahoma Law Review, Vol. 48 No. 4, Winter 1995; "Reservoir Management and Recreation," Oklahoma Water Law Project Monograph: The Impact of Franco-American Charolaise, Ltd. v. Oklahoma Water Resources Board, Project Report #A-130, Oct. 1995. ***PRACTICE AREAS:*** Taxation; Mergers, Acquisitions and Divestitures; Corporate Law; Partnership Law; Business Law. ***Email:*** mike.blake@mcafeetaft.com

JOSEPH H. BOCOCK, born Oklahoma City, Oklahoma, April 29, 1954; admitted to bar, 1978, Oklahoma; U.S. District Court, Northern, Eastern and Western Districts of Oklahoma; U.S. Court of Appeals, Tenth Circuit. *Education:* Dartmouth College (A.B., magna cum laude, 1975); University of Oklahoma (J.D., 1978). Order of the Coif. Member, Oklahoma Law Review. Listed in Best Lawyers in America, Commercial Litigation. Listed in Chambers USA as a Leading Individual in Commercial Litigation. Firm Practice Group Leader in the area of Litigation, 2001-2004. Master, William Holloway American Inn of Court. Board Member, Oklahoma Advisory Council, American Arbitration Association. *Member:* Oklahoma County, Oklahoma and American Bar Associations; Oklahoma Bar Foundation. ***PRACTICE AREAS:*** Civil Litigation (70%); Arbitration (30%). ***Email:*** joseph.bocock@mcafeetaft.com

STEVEN W. BUGG, born Enid, Oklahoma, June 9, 1956; admitted to bar, 1982, Oklahoma; U.S. Court of Appeals, Tenth Circuit; 1994, U.S. Court of Appeals, Federal Circuit; 1996, U.S. Supreme Court. *Education:* University of Oklahoma (B.B.A., 1978; M.B.A., 1982; J.D., 1982). Order of the Coif. Editor, Oklahoma Law Review, 1981-1982. Barrister, American Inn of Court XXIII, 1987-1989. *Member:* Oklahoma County, Oklahoma and American Bar Associations. ***PRACTICE AREAS:*** Commercial Law; Bankruptcy; Civil Litigation; Indian Law. ***Email:*** steven.bugg@mcafeetaft.com

JENNIFER H. CALLAHAN, born Grass Valley, California, July 30, 1968; admitted to bar, 1996, Oklahoma. *Education:* California Polytechnic State University (B.S., summa cum laude, 1991); Oklahoma City University (M.S., Accounting, 1993); University of Oklahoma (J.D., with highest honors, 1996). Order of the Coif. Member, Oklahoma Law Review, 1995-1996. *Member:* Oklahoma and American Bar Associations. ***PRACTICE AREAS:*** Tax Law; Employee Benefits; Tax Exempt Organizations; State Taxation; Energy Project Development. ***Email:*** jennifer.callahan@mcafeetaft.com

STEVEN P. COLE, born Oklahoma City, Oklahoma, 1960; admitted to bar, 1985, Oklahoma; 1986, U.S. Tax Court and U.S. Court of Appeals, Tenth Circuit; 2002, Texas. *Education:* University of Oklahoma (B.B.A., with distinction, 1982; J.D., with honors, 1985); New York University (LL.M. Taxation, 1988). Beta Gamma Sigma; Order of the Coif. Member, American Inn of Court XXIII, 1988-1990. Note Editor, Oklahoma Law Review, 1984-1985. *Member:* Oklahoma County, Oklahoma and American Bar Associations; State Bar of Texas. ***REPORTED CASES:*** Estate of Leder, 893 F.2d 237 (10th Cir. 1989),

(This Listing Continued)

McAFEE & TAFT, A PROFESSIONAL CORPORATION, Oklahoma City—Continued

aff'g 89 T.C. 235 (1987); Estate of Flowers, 848 P.2d 1146 (Okla. 1993). ***PRACTICE AREAS:*** Taxation; Partnership Law; Corporate Law; Nonprofit and Charitable Organizations; Strategic Alliances. ***Email:*** steven.cole@mcafeetaft.com

W. CHRIS COLEMAN, born Idabel, Oklahoma, December 7, 1956; admitted to bar, 1982, Oklahoma. *Education:* Midwestern State University; University of Oklahoma (B.A., with distinction, 1979; J.D., 1982). Phi Eta Sigma; Phi Beta Kappa; Order of the Coif. Member, Oklahoma Law Review, 1981-1982. *Member:* Oklahoma and American Bar Associations. ***PRACTICE AREAS:*** Corporate Law; Financing Law; Securities. ***Email:*** chris.coleman@mcafeetaft.com

RICHARD D. CRAIG, born Borger, Texas, January 29, 1957; admitted to bar, 1984, Oklahoma, U.S. Tax Court, U.S. Claims Court, U.S. District Court, Western District of Oklahoma and U.S. Supreme Court. *Education:* East Central University (B.S., Accounting, with highest honors, 1979); University of Oklahoma (J.D., with highest honors, 1984); New York University (LL.M., Taxation, 1985). Member, Order of the Coif. Editor-in-Chief, Oklahoma Law Review, 1983-1984. Graduate Editor, Tax Law Review, 1984-1985. Certified Public Accountant, Oklahoma, 1981. Listed in: The Best Lawyers in America. Adjunct Professor, Oklahoma City University and University of Oklahoma, 1988-1990. Board Member: Norman Community Foundation; Norman Chamber of Commerce. *Member:* Cleveland County, Oklahoma County, Oklahoma (Chairman, Taxation Law Section, 1994) and American (Member, Limited Liability Company Subcommittee, Business Law Section) Bar Associations; Oklahoma Society of Certified Public Accountants. Fellow: American College of Trust and Estate Counsel. ***PRACTICE AREAS:*** Trusts and Estates; Taxation; Litigation. ***Email:*** richard.craig@mcafeetaft.com

C. BRUCE CRUM, born Oklahoma City, Oklahoma, December 3, 1950; admitted to bar, 1977, Oklahoma. *Education:* Colgate University (A.B., 1972); Columbia University (M.B.A., 1974); University of Oklahoma (J.D., 1977). Order of the Coif; Phi Delta Phi. Member, Board of Editors, Oklahoma Law Review, 1975-1977. *Member:* Oklahoma and American Bar Associations. ***PRACTICE AREAS:*** Banking Law; Corporate Law; Securities. ***Email:*** bruce.crum@mcafeetaft.com

ROBERT W. DACE, born Guymon, Oklahoma, August 24, 1953; admitted to bar, 1983, Oklahoma. *Education:* United States Military Academy (B.S., 1975); University of Oklahoma (J.D., 1983). Editor-in-Chief, Oklahoma Law Review. 1982-1983. Author: "A General Practitioner's Guide to Intellectual Property — Patents, Trademarks, Copyrights and Trade Secrets," 70 Okla. Bar Journal 1703 (1999). President, Robert J. Turner Inn of Court, 2004-2005. [Captain, U.S. Army, 1975-1980]. ***REPORTED CASES:*** Wilson v. Massachusetts Indemnity and Life Insurance Co., 920 F.2d 1548 (10th Cir. 1990); Federal Deposit Ins. Corp., v. Oaklawn Apartments, 959 F.2d 170 (10th Cir. 1992); Tatum v. Philip Morris Inc., 809 F. Supp. 1452 (W.D. Okla. 1992); So-Lo Oil Co. v. Total Petroleum, 832 P.2d 14 (Okla. 1992); Nichols v. Midcontinent Pipe Line Co., 933 P.2d 272 (Okla. 1996); Scottsdale Ins. Co v. Subscription Plus, Inc., 2002 WL 1496366,299F.3d 618 (7th Cir. 2002). ***PRACTICE AREAS:*** Complex Business Litigation; Intellectual Property Litigation; Products Liability Litigation. ***Email:*** bob.dace@mcafeetaft.com

BRADLEY K. DONNELL, born Enid, Oklahoma, January 30, 1968; admitted to bar, 1994, Oklahoma; U.S. District Court, Northern, Western and Eastern Districts of Oklahoma; U.S. Court of Appeals, Tenth Circuit. *Education:* University of Oklahoma (B.B.A., 1990); Oklahoma City University (J.D., summa cum laude, 1994). Phi Delta Phi. Hatton Summers Scholar. Merit Scholar. Law Review. Recipient: American Jurisprudence Awards. *Member:* Oklahoma County, Oklahoma and American Bar Associations; Oklahoma Association of Defense Counsel; Defense Research Institute; Luther Bohanon Inn of Court. [1st Lt., A.F. Reserve, 1988-1993]. ***REPORTED CASES:*** Tucker v ADG, Inc. 102 P.3d 660 (Okla. 2004). ***PRACTICE AREAS:*** Employment Law; Products Liability Law; Civil and General Litigation; Tort Defense Law; Contract Law; Insurance Coverage Law; Aviation Law; Bad Faith Defense Law; Construction Law; Construction Insurance Defense; Construction Litigation. ***Email:*** brad.donnell@mcafeetaft.com

CLIFFORD CLARK DOUGHERTY, III, born Attica, Kansas, January 23, 1960; admitted to bar, 1985, Oklahoma; registered to practice before U.S. Patent and Trademark Office. *Education:* University of Oklahoma (B.S., Chemistry, 1982; J.D., with distinction, 1985). Phi Delta Phi. Member, Oklahoma Law Review, 1984-1985. Author: "The Oklahoma Deceptive Trade Practices Act-The Requirement of Competition Between the Parties," Oklahoma Law Review, Vol. 37, No. 4, 1984; "Intellectual Property, The Trademark Law Revision Act of 1988," The Oklahoma Bar Journal, Vol. 60, No. 35, 1989. Listed in The Best Lawyers in America. *Member:* Oklahoma County, Oklahoma (Past President, Intellectual Property Section) and American (Member, Section on Patent, Trademark and Copyright Law) Bar Associations; International Trademark Association; Oklahoma Venture Forum. ***PRACTICE AREAS:*** Intellectual Property; Intellectual Property Litigation. ***Email:*** cliff.dougherty@mcafeetaft.com

GREGG B. EICHNER, born Seattle, Washington; admitted to bar, 1994, Oklahoma. *Education:* University of North Carolina at Chapel Hill (B.S., 1991); Washington University (J.D., 1994). *Member:* Oklahoma and American Bar Associations. ***PRACTICE AREAS:*** Franchise Law; Corporate Law; Banks and Banking; Bank Holding Company Law; Bank Holding Company Regulation; Bank Mergers and Acquisitions; Banking Regulation; Savings and Loan Regulation; Contracts; Commercial Contracts; Business Law. ***Email:*** gregg.eichner@mcafeetaft.com

SAM R. FULKERSON, born Sapulpa, Oklahoma, December 6, 1959; admitted to bar, 1991, Oklahoma and U.S. District Court, Western, Northern and Eastern Districts of Oklahoma; 1993, U.S. District Court, Northern District of Texas and U.S. Court of Appeals, Tenth Circuit; 1996, U.S. Supreme Court. *Education:* University of Oklahoma (B.A., with distinction, 1982; J.D., with honors, 1991); University of North Carolina, Chapel Hill (M.A., with honors, 1985). Phi Beta Kappa. Member, Oklahoma Law Review, 1990-1991. Author: "National Indemnity Company v. United States Pollution Control: Environmental Clean-Up Costs are 'Damages' Under Oklahoma Insurance Law," 43 Okl. L. Rev. 705 (1990); "Age Discrimination in the Workplace," Society for Human Resource Management Foundation (1999). Listed in: Best Lawyers in America, Managment/Employment; Chambers USA, Leader in the Field of Labor and Employment Law. *Member:* Oklahoma (Chair, Labor and Employment Law Section, 2001) and American (Member, Labor and Employment Law Section) Bar Associations. (Practice Group Leader, Labor and Employment). ***REPORTED CASES:*** Bolton v. Scrivner, Inc., 836 F.Supp. 783 (W.D. Okl. 1993), aff'd, 36 F.3d 939 (10th Cir. 1994), cert. denied 115 S.Ct. 1104 (1995); Milton v. Scrivner, Inc. 901 F.Supp. 1541 (W.D. Okl. 1994), aff'd, 53 F. 3d 1118 (10th Cir. 1995); Massey v. Scrivner, Inc., 901 F.Supp. 1546 (W.D. Okl. 1994), aff'd, 53 F.3d 1118 (10th Cir. 1995); Sarsycki v. United Parcel Service, 862 F.Supp. 336 (W.D. Okl. 1994); Atkinson v. Halliburton Company, 905 P.2d 772 (Okl. 1995); Dodoo v. Seagate Tech., Inc., 235 F.3d 522 (10th Cir. 2000); Cole v. Halliburton Co., 6 Wage & Hour Cases 2d 990 (W.D. Okl. 2000); Walker v. United Parcel Service, Inc., 240 F.3d 1268 (10th Cir. 2001); Pierce, et al v. Kellogg, Brown & Root, Inc., 245 F.Supp.2d 1212 (E.D. Okl. 2003). ***PRACTICE AREAS:*** Labor and Employment Law. ***Email:*** sam.fulkerson@mcafeetaft.com

GARY F. FULLER, born Durant, Oklahoma, October 12, 1936; admitted to bar, 1959, Oklahoma; 1963, Texas. *Education:* University of Oklahoma (B.B.A., 1957); Academy of International Law, The Hague, Netherlands, University of Oklahoma (LL.B., 1959); Yale Law School (LL.M., 1963). Phi Alpha Delta. Member, Board of Editors, 1957-1959; Article and Book Review Editor, 1959, Oklahoma Law Review. Listed in The Best Lawyers of America, Corporate Law and Tax Law. Listed in Chambers USA, Corporate, M&A and Tax. Instructor, University of Oklahoma College of Law, 1977. *Member:* Oklahoma and American Bar Associations; State Bar of Texas. [First Lieut., U.S.A.F., Judge Advocate, 1959-1962]. ***PRACTICE AREAS:*** Corporate Law; Tax Law; Estate Planning. ***Email:*** gary.fuller@mcafeetaft.com

ROBERT L. GARBRECHT, born Midland, Texas, August 13, 1964; admitted to bar, 1990, Oklahoma. *Education:* University of Oklahoma (B.B.A., with distinction, 1986; J.D., with highest honors, 1990). Beta Gamma Sigma. Order of the Coif. Certified Public Accountant, Oklahoma, 1987. Adjunct Faculty Member (Corporations) University of Oklahoma College of Law. *Member:* Oklahoma County, Oklahoma and American Bar Associations. ***REPORTED CASES:*** In re Assessment of Real Property of Integris Realty Corp., 2002 OK 85, 58 P.3d 200. ***PRACTICE AREAS:*** Corporate Law; Business Organizations; Commercial Real Estate; Mergers, Acquisitions and Divestitures; Computers and Software; State and Local Taxation; Ad Valorem Taxation; Energy Project Development. ***Email:*** rob.garbrecht@mcafeetaft.com

ROBERT H. GILLILAND, JR., born Ponca City, Oklahoma, May 12, 1941; admitted to bar, 1966, Oklahoma. *Education:* Texas Christian University (B.A., 1963); University of Oklahoma (J.D., 1966). Phi Alpha Delta. Member, Board of Editors, Oklahoma Law Review, 1964-1966. Listed in: The Best Lawyers in America; The National Registry of Who's Who, Life Member. *Member:* Oklahoma County (Member, Board of Directors, 1981-1983), Oklahoma and American Bar Associations; American Inn of Court CV (Master). [Captain, U.S. Army, Judge Advocate, 1966-1970]. ***PRACTICE AREAS:*** Civil Litigation; Federal Civil Litigation; Trial Practice. ***Email:*** robert.gilliland@mcafeetaft.com

SHAWN E. HARRELL, born Oklahoma City, Oklahoma, June 24, 1970; admitted to bar, 1995, Oklahoma; U.S. District Court, Northern, Western and Eastern Districts of Oklahoma; U.S. Court of Appeals, Tenth Circuit. *Education:* Southern Methodist University (B.A., cum laude, 1992); University of Oklahoma (J.D., 1995). Board of Advocates. Phi Delta Phi. Recipient, American Jurisprudence Award in Professional Responsibility, 1993. *Member:* Oklahoma County, Oklahoma and American Bar Associations; Defense Research Institute; Oklahoma Association of Defense Counsel. ***REPORTED CASES:*** Gripe v. City of Enid, 312 F.3d 1184 (10th Cir. 2002); Christian v. Gray, 65 P.3d 591 (Okla. 2003); Kuykendall v. Gulfstream Aerospace Technologies, 66 P.3d 37 (Okla. 2002). ***PRACTICE AREAS:*** Commercial Litigation; Employment Litigation; Products Liability; Bad Faith Litigation. ***Email:*** shawn.harrell@mcafeetaft.com

PHILIP D. HART, born Holdenville, Oklahoma, September 16, 1936; admitted to bar, 1960, Oklahoma and District of Columbia. *Education:* University of Oklahoma (B.A., with distinction, 1958; LL.B., 1960). Phi Beta Kappa; Order of the Coif. Listed in: The Best Lawyers in America, 1989—. Recipient, Eugene Kuntz Award, for Contributions to Natural Resources Law and Policy, 2000. Adjunct Faculty Member: Oil and Gas, Oklahoma City University School of Law, 1976-2004; University of Oklahoma College of Law, 2000-2001; Energy Law, University of Oklahoma College of Law, 2002-2004. *Member:* Oklahoma and American Bar Associations. ***PRACTICE AREAS:*** Oil and Gas Litigation; Civil Litigation; Appellate Practice; Administrative Law. ***Email:*** philip.hart@mcafeetaft.com

JOHN N. HERMES, born New York, New York, May 7, 1946; admitted to bar, 1975, Oklahoma, U.S. District Court, Eastern, Western and Northern Districts of Oklahoma, U.S. Tax Court, U.S. Claims Court, U.S. Court of Appeals, Fifth, Tenth and Federal Circuits and U.S. Supreme Court. *Education:* Ripon College (A.B., 1968); University of Oklahoma (J.D., 1975). Phi Delta Phi. Member, 1973-1975 and Editor-in-Chief, 1974-1975, Oklahoma Law Review. Member, Committee on Admissions and Grievances, U.S. District Court, Western District of Oklahoma, 1984—. Listed in The Best Lawyers in America. Director, Legal Aid Services of Oklahoma. Director, Oklahoma Lawyers for Children. *Member:* Oklahoma County (Former Member, Board of Directors), Oklahoma and American Bar Associations; American Inn of Court CV (Master). Fellow: American College of Trial Lawyers; American Bar Foundation; Oklahoma Bar Foundation (Trustee, 1990-1995). [Captain, U.S. Army, 1968-1972]. ***PRACTICE AREAS:*** Banking Litigation; Business Litigation; Civil Litigation; Securities Litigation; Trial Practice. ***Email:*** john.hermes@mcafeetaft.com

FRANK D. HILL, born Ardmore, Oklahoma, December 30, 1940; admitted to bar, 1966, Texas; 1971, Oklahoma. *Education:* University of Oklahoma (B.B.A., 1963); University of Texas at Austin (LL.B., 1966); The George Washington University (LL.M. in Taxation, 1969). Phi Delta Phi. Listed in The Best Lawyers in America. Listed in Chambers USA Leading Business Lawyers. Chairman of the Board of Trustees of Oklahoma City National Memorial Foundation. Vice-President and Director of Oklahoma City Museum of Art. *Member:* Oklahoma County, Oklahoma and American Bar Associations; State Bar of Texas; American College of Real Estate Lawyers. Oklahoma Bar Foundation (Trustee, 1996-2002). [Capt., Judge Advocate General's Corps, U.S. Army, 1967-1970]. ***PRACTICE AREAS:*** Commercial Real Estate Acquisitions; Commercial Real Estate Sales; Commercial Real Estate Finance; Commercial Real Estate Development; Business Taxation; Tax Deferred Exchanges; Tax Exempt Organizations; Private Equity; Energy Project Development; Health Care Mergers and Acquisitions. ***Email:*** frank.hill@mcafeetaft.com

(This Listing Continued)

HENRY D. HOSS, born Houston, Texas, February 11, 1960; admitted to bar, 1985, Oklahoma. *Education:* University of Oklahoma (B.S., in Mech. Engr. 1982); University of Tulsa (J.D., 1985). Phi Delta Phi (President, 1984-1985; Recipient, Outstanding Service Award, 1985). Member, Order of the Barristers. *Member:* Oklahoma County, Oklahoma and American Bar Associations. ***PRACTICE AREAS:*** Civil Litigation; Construction Law; Construction Litigation; Construction Arbitration; Aircraft Litigation; Products Liability. ***Email:*** henry.hoss@mcafeetaft.com

LAURENCE M. HUFFMAN, born Norman, Oklahoma, March 9, 1949; admitted to bar, 1974, Oklahoma; 1978, U.S. Supreme Court. *Education:* University of Oklahoma (B.A., with high honors, 1971; J.D., 1974); The George Washington University (LL.M., 1977). Phi Beta Kappa; Order of the Coif; Phi Delta Phi (Exchequer, 1973). Member, Board of Editors, 1972-1974 and Article and Book Review Editor, 1973, Oklahoma Law Review. *Member:* Oklahoma, Oklahoma County and American Bar Associations. Fellow, Oklahoma Bar Foundation. [Capt., Judge Advocate General Corps, U.S. Army, 1974-1978]. ***PRACTICE AREAS:*** Antitrust and Trade Regulation; Natural Resources; Litigation. ***Email:*** larry.huffman@mcafeetaft.com

JAMES DUDLEY HYDE, born Oklahoma City, Oklahoma, May 20, 1944; admitted to bar, 1969, Texas and U.S. Court of Military Appeals; 1974, Oklahoma. *Education:* University of Oklahoma (B.A., 1966); Southern Methodist University (J.D., 1969); George Washington University (L.L.M., 1974). Phi Delta Phi (Magister, 1968-1969). Listed in Best Lawyers in America (Employee Benefits). Associate Editor, Journal of Air Law and Commerce, 1968-1969. Chairman, 1992-1998 and Member, EP/EO Council, Dallas Key District, Internal Revenue Service. President, 2000-2001 and Member, Southwest Employee Benefits Association. Member: Oklahoma City Employee Benefits Conference; Oklahoma City Tuesday Tax Group. *Member:* Oklahoma County, Oklahoma and American Bar Associations. Charter Fellow, American College of Employee Benefits Counsel. [Captain, Judge Advocate General Corps, 1969-1974]. ***PRACTICE AREAS:*** Employee Benefits; ERISA; State Taxation. ***Email:*** dudley.hyde@mcafeetaft.com

MICHAEL E. JOSEPH, born Tulsa, Oklahoma, August 8, 1951; admitted to bar, 1976, Oklahoma. *Education:* University of Oklahoma (B.A., 1973; J.D., 1975). Phi Delta Phi. Member, Board of Editors, Oklahoma Law Review, 1974-1975. *Member:* Oklahoma and American Bar Associations. ***PRACTICE AREAS:*** Business Law; Corporate Law; Health Care; Franchises and Franchising; Nonprofit and Charitable Organizations; Real Estate.

JOHN A. KENNEY, born Oklahoma City, Oklahoma, August 3, 1948; admitted to bar, 1975, Texas (inactive); 1981, Oklahoma. *Education:* University of Oklahoma (B.S.I.E. with distinction, 1971; J.D., 1975). Tau Beta Pi; Order of the Coif; Phi Delta Phi. Listed in The Best Lawyers in America. Member Board of Editors, Oklahoma Law Review, 1973-1975. Member, Civil Justice Advisory Committee, U.S. District Court, Western District of Oklahoma, 1994-1997. Magistrate Judge Selection Committee, 1998-2001. *Member:* Oklahoma County (Recipient, Outstanding Member Award, 1988-1989; Bar Counsel, 1991-1996; Board of Directors, 1996—, President, 1999-2000), Oklahoma (Administration of Justice Committee, 1990-2000; Specialization Task Force and Professionalism and Civility Task Force, Patent, Trademark and Copyright Section) and American (Member, Patent, Trademark and Copyright Section) Bar Associations. ***PRACTICE AREAS:*** Intellectual Property Litigation; Technical Litigation; Products Liability; Complex Litigation. ***Email:*** john.kenney@mcafeetaft.com

DAVID J. KETELSLEGER, born Moorhead, Minnesota, May 15, 1964; admitted to bar, 1990, Oklahoma. *Education:* University of Montana (B.A., summa cum laude, 1986); University of Oklahoma (J.D., with highest honors, 1990). Order of the Coif. Certified Public Accountant, Oklahoma, 1987—. *Member:* Oklahoma County and American Bar Associations. ***PRACTICE AREAS:*** Securities; Business Law; Corporate Law; Tax Law. ***Email:*** david.ketelsleger@mcafeetaft.com

MICHAEL J. LABRIE, born San Bernardino, California, January 25, 1968; admitted to bar, 1994, Oklahoma; registered to practice before U.S. Patent and Trademark Office. *Education:* University of Oklahoma (B.S., Mechanical Engineering, 1991); Oklahoma City University (J.D., magna cum laude, 1994). Phi Delta Phi. Editor, OCU Law Review. Moot Court Board. Faculty Honor Roll; Merit Scholar. Director, Oklahoma Venture Forum. Chairman, Norman Planning Commission. Director, Christmas In April of Cleveland County. *Member:* Oklahoma County, Oklahoma and American (Member, Intellectual Property Section) Bar Associations; National Society of Professional Engineers; Oklahoma Society of Professional Engineers; American Intellectual Property Law Association. ***PRACTICE AREAS:*** Intellectual Property; Patents; Trademarks; Copyright; Computer and Software; High Technology. ***Email:*** michael.labrie@mcafeetaft.com

MYRNA SCHACK LATHAM, born La Junta, Colorado, July 25, 1956; admitted to bar, 1985, Oklahoma, U.S. Court of Appeals, Tenth Circuit and U.S. District Court, Western and Northern Districts of Oklahoma. *Education:* Bethany Nazarene College (B.A., 1978); University of Oklahoma (J.D., with honors, 1985). Phi Delta Phi; Order of the Coif. Coauthor: "Specialized Approaches to Outsourcing Legal Work," Ch. 26, "Successful Partnering Between Inside and Outside Counsel," West Group/American Association of Corporate Counsel, 2000. Co-Author: "The Role of Lawyers in 'Corporate Responsibility,'" Oklahoma Bar Journal, Dec. 11, 2004. Director and General Counsel, Oklahoma Business Ethics Consortium and Oklahoma Business Ethics Foundation. Member, Oklahoma City Commercial Real Estate Council. *Member:* Oklahoma County (Member, Editorial Committee), Oklahoma, and American (Member, Health Law and Real Estate Sections) Bar Associations; American Health Lawyers Association. Oklahoma Bar Foundation. ***PRACTICE AREAS:*** Real Estate; Business Law; Health Care Law. ***Email:*** myrna.latham@mcafeetaft.com

MICHAEL F. LAUDERDALE, born Muskogee, Oklahoma, January 2, 1965; admitted to bar, 1990, Oklahoma, U.S. Supreme Court, U.S. Court of Appeals, Tenth Circuit and U.S. District Court, Western, Eastern and Northern Districts of Oklahoma. *Education:* University of Oklahoma (B.B.A., with special distinction, 1987; J.D., with honors, 1990). Beta Gamma Sigma; Order of the Coif. Administrative Law Judge, Oklahoma Department of Labor, 2002-2004. *Member:* Oklahoma County, Oklahoma and American Bar Associations. ***PRACTICE AREAS:*** Employment Law; Non-Competition Agreements; Non-Solicitation Agreements; Confidentiality Agreements; Corporate Health Care Law; Employment Arbitration; Fair Labor Standards; Wage and Hour Law; Civil Litigation; Franchise Litigation. ***Email:*** michael.lauderdale@mcafeetaft.com

(This Listing Continued)

STEVEN T. LEDGERWOOD, born Okmulgee, Oklahoma, November 2, 1966; admitted to bar, 1992, Oklahoma. *Education:* University of Oklahoma (B.A., 1989; J.D., with highest honors, 1992); New York University (LL.M. in Taxation, 1993). Order of the Coif. Recipient, Nathan Scarritt Award for the highest academic standing. Editor-in-Chief, Oklahoma Law Review, 1991-1992. Graduate Editor, Tax Law Review, 1992-1993. Author: *Oklahoma LLCs v. Limited Partnerships:* Choice of Entity for Valuation Discounts after 1997, 22 Okla. City U. L. Rev. 611 (1997). Co-Author: Oklahoma Limited Liability Company Forms and Practice Manual, Data Trace Legal Publishers. Guest Lecturer on International Taxation at O.U. College of Business. Guest Lecturer on Choice of Entity Planning, Limited Liability Companies and Federal Tax Litigation at O.U. College of Law. *Member:* Oklahoma (Section of Taxation) and American (Sections of Taxation; Tax Litigation Committee, Litigation Section) Bar Associations. ***PRACTICE AREAS:*** Taxation; Partnership; Limited Liability Company Law; Estate Planning; Federal Tax Litigation. ***Email:*** steven.ledgerwood@mcafeetaft.com

SCOTT D. McCREARY, born Vinita, Oklahoma, June 8, 1965; admitted to bar, 1992, Oklahoma. *Education:* Oklahoma State University (B.S., 1988); University of Oklahoma (J.D., with distinction, 1992). Phi Delta Phi. Recipient: American Jurisprudence Award, Federal Securities. *Member:* Oklahoma County, Oklahoma, Federal and American (Member: Business Law Section; Aircraft Finance and Contracts Division of the Forum on Air and Space Law; Aircraft Financing Subcommittee) Bar Associations. ***SPECIAL AGENCIES:*** Federal Aviation Administration. ***PRACTICE AREAS:*** Aircraft Title Law; Aviation Law; Aircraft Finance; Commercial Aircraft Leasing. ***Email:*** scott.mccreary@mcafeetaft.com

JAMES C. McMILLIN, born Oklahoma City, Oklahoma, June 27, 1949; admitted to bar, 1977, New York; 1979, District of Columbia; 1980, U.S. Supreme Court; 1997, Oklahoma. *Education:* University of Oklahoma (B.A., 1971); New York University (J.D., 1976). Root-Tilden Scholar. Contributing Editor, Oil and Gas Price Regulation Analyst, 1980-1984. Author: "Recent Developments in Litigation under the Securities Act of 1933," The Review of Securities & Commodities Regulation, Vol. 33, No. 1, 2000; "Principled Fairness in the Regulation of Petroleum Prices," 57 Texas Law Review 573, 1979; "Military Law," Annual Survey of American Law 97, 1974-1975. Arbitrator, Arbitration Panel for the U.S. District Court, Eastern District of New York, 1986-1996. *Member:* The Association of the Bar of the City of New York; Oklahoma, New York State and American Bar Associations; The District of Columbia Bar; Federal Bar Council. Fellow, Oklahoma Bar Foundation. [With U.S. Army, 1971-1973]. ***PRACTICE AREAS:*** Securities Litigation; Intellectual Property Litigation; Complex Litigation; Business Litigation; Mass Tort Litigation; Antitrust and Trade Regulation; Arbitration. ***Email:*** james.mcmillin@mcafeetaft.com

SALLY MOCK, born Wichita Falls, Texas, February 28, 1943; admitted to bar, 1973, Oklahoma. *Education:* University of Oklahoma (B.S., 1965; M.N.S., 1969; J.D., 1973). Phi Beta Kappa; Order of the Coif; Phi Delta Phi. Editor, Oklahoma Law Review, 1971-1973. Law Clerk to Judge William J. Holloway, U.S. Court of Appeals, Tenth Circuit, 1973-1974. Member, 1984-2005 and Chair, 1997 and 2004, Oklahoma Board of Bar Examiners. *Member:* Oklahoma and American Bar Associations. ***PRACTICE AREAS:*** Commercial Real Estate; Finance; Mortgages; Secured Transactions. ***Email:*** sally.mock@mcafeetaft.com

MARK RICHARD MULLINS, born Lima, Peru, February 13, 1963; admitted to bar, 1988, Oklahoma and U.S. District Court, Western District of Oklahoma; 1989, U.S. Court of Appeals, Tenth Circuit; 1994, U.S. Supreme Court; 1998, U.S. District Court, Eastern District of Oklahoma; 2001, U.S. District Court, Northern District of Oklahoma. *Education:* University of Oklahoma (B.A., with high honors, 1985; J.D., with honors, 1988). Phi Beta Kappa; Alpha Lambda Delta; Golden Key. *Member:* Oklahoma County and Oklahoma Bar Associations. ***PRACTICE AREAS:*** Civil Litigation. ***Email:*** richard.mullins@mcafeetaft.com

RICHARD D. NIX, born Duncan, Oklahoma, October 3, 1960; admitted to bar, 1985, Oklahoma. *Education:* University of Oklahoma (B.B.A., 1982; J.D., 1985). Phi Delta Phi. Member, Oklahoma Law Review, 1985. *Member:* Oklahoma County, Oklahoma and American Bar Associations. ***PRACTICE AREAS:*** Employee Benefits; Corporate Law. ***Email:*** richard.nix@mcafeetaft.com

J. MICHAEL NORDIN, born Oklahoma City, Oklahoma, February 21, 1957; admitted to bar, 1982, Oklahoma. *Education:* University of Oklahoma (B.A., 1979; J.D., 1982). Editor-in-Chief, Oklahoma Law Review, 1981-1982. *Member:* Oklahoma County, Oklahoma and American Bar Associations; Oklahoma Health Lawyers Association; American Health Lawyers Association. ***PRACTICE AREAS:*** Commercial Law; Commercial Real Estate; Corporate Law; Mergers, Acquisitions and Divestitures; Leases and Leasing; Health Care Business. ***Email:*** michael.nordin@mcafeetaft.com

JOHN A. PAPAHRONIS, born Oklahoma City, Oklahoma, July 21, 1958; admitted to bar, 1983, Oklahoma. *Education:* University of Oklahoma (B.A., with highest honors, 1980); Northwestern University (J.D., 1983). Beta Gamma Sigma. Member, Editorial Board, Northwestern Journal of International Law and Business, 1982-1983. Author: "Taxation of Americans Abroad under the ERTA - An Unnecessary Windfall," Northwestern Journal of International Law and Business, Vol. 4, 1982. *Member:* Oklahoma and American Bar Associations. ***PRACTICE AREAS:*** Employee Benefits. ***Email:*** john.papahronis@mcafeetaft.com

ROSS A. PLOURDE, born Millinocket, Maine, April 30, 1956; admitted to bar, 1982, Oklahoma. *Education:* University of Maine (B.A., 1979); Oklahoma City University (J.D., with distinction, 1982). Notes Editor, Oklahoma City University Law Review, 1981-1982. Research Assistant, Oklahoma Court of Criminal Appeals, 1981. Assistant Attorney General, State of Oklahoma, 1982. Listed in The Best Lawyers In America. Member, Mayor's Judicial Advisory Council, 2002-2005. *Member:* Oklahoma County, Oklahoma (Chair, Financial Institutions and Commercial Law Section, 2003-2004), Federal (President, Oklahoma City Chapter, 1997-1998) and American Bar Associations. ***PRACTICE AREAS:*** Business Litigation; Bankruptcy. ***Email:*** ross.plourde@mcafeetaft.com

FRANK L. POLK, born Oklahoma City, Oklahoma, June 16, 1954; admitted to bar, 1981, Oklahoma. *Education:* University of Oklahoma (B.A., with distinction, 1976); Duke University (J.D., 1980). Phi Beta Kappa; Omicron Delta Kappa. Co-Chairperson, Seminar on FAA Aircraft Registration, Lien and Security Issues, Strategic Research Institute, 1994-2005. Seminar Lecturer: "Aircraft Ownership and Registration," 5th-13th Annual NBAA Tax Conferences on Business Aviation and Taxes; "Advanced Corporate Aircraft Cost Shar-

(This Listing Continued)

MCAFEE & TAFT, *A PROFESSIONAL CORPORATION, Oklahoma City—Continued*

ing Programs" and "FAA Registration Issues in Corporate Aircraft Transactions," "Non-consensual Liens Under The Federal Aviation Act of 1958," Symposium on Aircraft Registration and Lien Recordation, Federal Bar Association and Oklahoma City University, 1991. Frequent speaker on FAA registration issues and the Cape Town Convention on International Intersts In Mobile Equipment at additional seminars, including National Business Aviation Association Regional Tax Forums and The SRI Corporate Jet Transactions Seminar. *Member:* Oklahoma and American (Member: Aircraft Finance and Contracts Division of the Forum on Air and Space Law; Aircraft Financing Subcommittee) Bar Associations; National Business Aviation Association (Member, Tax Committee). ***SPECIAL AGENCIES:*** Federal Aviation Administration. ***PRACTICE AREAS:*** Aircraft Title; Aircraft Finance and Leasing; International Aviation Law; Aviation Regulation; Aircraft Sales. ***Email:*** frank.polk@mcafeetaft.com

LOUIS J. PRICE, born Miami, Oklahoma, February 23, 1953; admitted to bar, 1978, Oklahoma. *Education:* Northwestern University (B.S., 1975); University of Oklahoma (J.D., 1978). Phi Delta Phi. Member, Board of Editors, Oklahoma Law Review, 1977-1978. *Member:* Oklahoma County, Oklahoma and American Bar Associations. ***PRACTICE AREAS:*** Bankruptcy; Commercial Law; Debtor and Creditor; Finance. ***Email:*** louis.price@mcafeetaft.com

TONY G. PUCKETT, born Oklahoma City, Oklahoma, March 28, 1961; admitted to bar, 1988, Oklahoma and U.S. District Court, Western District of Oklahoma; 1991, U.S. Court of Appeals, Eighth Circuit; 1992, U.S. District Court, Eastern District of Oklahoma; 1994, U.S. Court of Appeals, Tenth Circuit; 1995, U.S. District Court, Northern District of Oklahoma; 1997, U.S. Supreme Court. *Education:* Colorado College (B.A., 1983); University of Oklahoma (J.D., with distinction, 1988). Recipient, American Jurisprudence Award, Contracts II. Listed in Best Lawyers in America. Author: "Supreme Court Broadens Liability for Sexual Harassment?" V. 69, No. 31, Okla. Bar Journal 2784 (8/1/98); "Supreme Court Decides Same-Sex Sexual Harassment Issue," V. 69, No. 17, Okla. Bar Journal 1465 (4/25/98); "Reviewing the State's Drug and Alcohol Testing Act," V. 29, No. 3, Oklahoma Cities and Towns (2/29/99). Contributing author, How Arbitration Works (6th Ed., BNA). Co-author, Age Discrimination in the Workplace: A Primer for Human Resource Professionals, published by the Society for Human Resource Management Foundation. Speaker: Annual Labor Management Conference sponsored by the National Academy of Arbitrators, Southwest Region, 2000 and 2001; International Personnel Management Association, Southern Region Conference, 2001. *Member:* Oklahoma County, Oklahoma (Past-Chair, Labor and Employment Law Section) and American (Member, Labor and Employment Law Section) Bar Associations; Society for Human Resources Management; Oklahoma Municipal Attorneys Association. Fellow, Oklahoma Bar Foundation. ***REPORTED CASES:*** Beaird v. Seagate Technology, 76 FEP Cases 1865 (CA 10 1998); Seymore v. Shawver & Sons, 73 FEP Cases 1133 (CA 10 1997); Doan v. Seagate Technology, 70 FEP Cases 1202 (CA 10 1996); Furr v. Seagate Technology, 70 FEP Cases 1325 (CA 10 1996); City of Anadarko v. Fraternal Order of Police, Lodge 118, 1997 OK 14, 934 P.2d 328; Midwest City v. Jarrell, 2001 OK CIV APP 125, 33 P.3d 962; Hollytex Carpet Mills, Inc. v. Hinkle,1991 OK CIV APP 43, 819 P.2d 289; City of Broken Arrow, 117 LA 1454 (Goodman 2002); City of Del City, 117 LA 393 (McReynolds 2002); City of Norman, 115 LA 827 (McReynolds 2001); City of Broken Arrow, 114 LA 881 (Goodman 2000); Eemond Police Dept., 113 LA 929 (Bumpass 2000); City of Anadarko, 113 LA 559 (Baroni 1999); Earthgrains Co., 113 LA 306 (Wang 1999); City of Ada, 113 LA 422 (Goodman 1999); City of Ada, 112 LA 530 (Eisenmenger 1999). ***PRACTICE AREAS:*** Labor and Employment Law (90%); Civil Litigation (10%). ***Email:*** tony.puckett@mcafeetaft.com

ANTHONY L. RAHHAL, born Okemah, Oklahoma, September 6, 1960; admitted to bar, 1991, Oklahoma and U.S. District Court, Western District of Oklahoma; registered to practice before U.S. Patent and Trademark Office. *Education:* Oklahoma State University (B.S., 1983); University of Oklahoma (J.D., with highest honors, 1991). Order of the Coif. Adjunct Professor, Patent Law, University of Oklahoma College of Law. *Member:* Oklahoma County, Oklahoma and American (Member and Past President, Section on: Patent, Trademark and Copyright Law) Bar Associations. ***PRACTICE AREAS:*** Patent Law; Trademark Law; Copyright Law; Unfair Competition Law; Antitrust Law; Commercial Litigation. ***Email:*** anthony.rahhal@mcafeetaft.com

DEE A. REPLOGLE, JR., born Oklahoma City, Oklahoma, October 1, 1943; admitted to bar, 1968, Oklahoma. *Education:* Stanford University (B.A., 1965); University of Oklahoma (J.D., 1968); New York University (LL.M. in Taxation, 1970). Law Clerk for Judge William J. Holloway, Jr., U.S. 10th Circuit Court of Appeals, 1968-1969. Instructor, School of Law, Oklahoma City University, 1971-1975. Member, Board of Regents, University of Oklahoma, 1975-1982. *Member:* Oklahoma County, Oklahoma and American Bar Associations. ***PRACTICE AREAS:*** Corporate Law; Tax Law. ***Email:*** dee.replogle@mcafeetaft.com

RICHARD A. RIGGS, born Oklahoma City, Oklahoma, May 10, 1949; admitted to bar, 1974, Oklahoma. *Education:* Westminster College and University of Oklahoma (B.A., 1971); University of Michigan (J.D., 1974). Phi Beta Kappa; Phi Delta Phi. Member, Board of Editors, University of Michigan Journal of Law Reform, 1973-1974. *Member:* Oklahoma County, Oklahoma and American Bar Associations; American College of Real Estate Lawyers. ***PRACTICE AREAS:*** Commercial Real Estate; Leases and Leasing; Secured and Unsecured Lending Transactions. ***Email:*** richard.riggs@mcafeetaft.com

REID E. ROBISON, born San Francisco, California, December 7, 1944; admitted to bar, 1968, Oklahoma; 1971, Colorado. *Education:* University of Oklahoma (B.A., 1966; J.D., 1968). Order of the Coif; Phi Alpha Delta. Member, Board of Editors, Oklahoma Law Review, 1966-1968. Assistant Attorney General, Oklahoma, 1968. Listed in Best Lawyers in America and Chambers USA, America's Leading Business Lawyers. *Member:* Oklahoma County, Oklahoma and American Bar Associations; American Inns of Court (Master). Fellow: Oklahoma Bar Foundation; International Academy of Trial Lawyers. [Capt., USAF, Judge Advocate, 1968-1972]. ***PRACTICE AREAS:*** Litigation; Complex Litigation; Antitrust; Class Actions; Criminal Defense; Manufacturers Liability; Securities Litigation; Tax Litigation; Professional Liability Defense. ***Email:*** reid.robison@mcafeetaft.com

(This Listing Continued)

JOHN E. SARGENT, JR., born Bell, California, May 27, 1943; admitted to bar, 1970, Oklahoma. *Education:* Villanova University (B.S., 1965); University of Oklahoma (J.D., 1970). Delta Theta Phi. *Member:* Oklahoma County and Oklahoma Bar Associations. ***PRACTICE AREAS:*** Real Estate Development; Real Estate Finance; Condominium Law; Zoning Law. ***Email:*** john.sargent@mcafeetaft.com

JOHN N. SCHAEFER, born Des Moines, Iowa, June 9, 1940; admitted to bar, 1966, Texas; 1973, Oklahoma. *Education:* University of Oklahoma (B.B.A., 1963); University of Texas (LL.B., 1966); The George Washington University (LL.M. in Taxation, 1969). Phi Alpha Delta. *Member:* State Bar of Oklahoma; Oklahoma County Bar; American Bar Associations. [Capt., JAGC, U.S. Army, 1966-1970]. ***LANGUAGES:*** Spanish. ***PRACTICE AREAS:*** Probate Administration; Estate and Gift Taxation; Tax Planning; Trust and Estates Taxation; Deferred Compensation. ***Email:*** john.schaefer@mcafeetaft.com

SCOTT W. SEWELL, born Ponca City, Oklahoma, December 23, 1956; admitted to bar, 1982, Oklahoma. *Education:* Oklahoma State University (B.S., 1979); University of Oklahoma (J.D., 1982). Certified Public Accountant, Oklahoma, 1982. *Member:* Oklahoma County, Oklahoma and American Bar Associations; Oklahoma Society of Certified Public Accountants. ***PRACTICE AREAS:*** Probate; Estate Planning; Employee Benefits. ***Email:*** scott.sewell@mcafeetaft.com

JAMES W. SHARROCK, born Stillwater, Oklahoma, December 5, 1947; admitted to bar, 1973, Oklahoma and Texas. *Education:* University of Oklahoma (B.A., 1970; J.D., 1973). Omicron Delta Kappa; Phi Delta Phi; Omicron Delta Epsilon. President-Elect Rotary Club of Oklahoma City. Vice-President Leadership Oklahoma City. *Member:* Oklahoma County, Oklahoma and American Bar Associations; State Bar of Texas. ***PRACTICE AREAS:*** Banking Regulation; Real Estate; Banks and Banking; Corporate Law; Asset Based Finance; Real Estate Finance; Health Care Corporate Law. ***Email:*** jim.sharrock@mcafeetaft.com

MARK D. SPENCER, born Tampa, Florida, 1959; admitted to bar, 1987, Oklahoma, U.S. Supreme Court, U.S. Court of Appeals, Fifth, Eighth, Ninth and Tenth Circuits, U.S. District Court, Northern, Eastern and Western Districts of Oklahoma. *Education:* Tulane University (B.A., 1981); The John Marshall Law School (J.D., with distinction, 1987). Order of John Marshall. Associate Justice, Moot Court Executive Board, 1986-1987. Third Place, William Starr Insurance Law Moot Court Competition, Hartford, Connecticut, 1986. Second Place, Illinois State Bar Association Moot Court Competition, Springfield, Illinois,1986. Barrister, Luther Bohanon American Inn of Court, 1994-1997. Barrister, 1998-2002 and Master, 2003—, Ruth Bader Ginsburg American Inn of Court. . Law Clerk to the Hon. William J. Holloway, Jr., Chief Judge, U.S. Court of Appeals, Tenth Circuit, 1987-1988. Hearing Officer, Oklahoma State Board of Examiners of Psychologists, 1995-1996. ***REPORTED CASES:*** Great West Life & Annuity Ins. Co. v. Knudson, 534 U.S. 204 (2002) (amicus curiae); Gaither v. Aetna Life Ins. Co., 394 F.3d 792 (10th Cir. 2004); Conover v. Aetna US Healthcare, 320 F.3d 1076 (10th Cir. 2003), cert. denied, 129 S. Ct. 2902 (2004); Beaird v. Seagate Technology, 145 F.3d 1159 (10th Cir.), cert. denied, 525 U.S. 1054 (1998); Gaylor v. John Hancock Mut. Life Ins. Co., 112 F.3d 460 (10th Cir. 1997); Shamrock Drilling Fluids, Inc. v. Miller, 32 F.3d 455 (10th Cir. 1994); Warner v. Aetna Health Inc., 333, F.Supp. 2d 1149 (W.D. Okla. 2004); Conover v. Aetna US Healthcare, Inc., 167 F. Supp. 2d 1317 (N.D. Okla. 2001); Great West Life & Annuity Ins. Co. v. Clingenpeel, 996 F. Supp. 1348 & 1353 (W.D. Okla. 1998); Melton v. White, 848 F. Supp. 1511 & 1513 (W.D. Okla. 1994); Metro. Life Ins. Co. v. Browning, 839 F. Supp. 1508 (W.D. Okla. 1993); Ferguson v. The Prudential Ins. Co. of Am., 777 F. Supp. 15 (W.D. Okla. 1991); Cranfill v. Aetna Life Ins. Co., 2002 OK 26, 49 P.3d 703 (Okla. 2002). ***PRACTICE AREAS:*** ERISA Litigation; Insurance Defense; Labor and Employment Law; Appellate Practice; Employee Benefits. ***Email:*** mark.spencer@mcafeetaft.com

C. DAVID STINSON, born Johnstown, Pennsylvania, December 27, 1946; admitted to bar, 1976, Oklahoma. *Education:* Oklahoma State University (B.A., 1969); University of Oklahoma (J.D., 1976). Order of the Coif. Member, Board of Editors, Oklahoma Law Review, 1974-1976. *Member:* Oklahoma County, Oklahoma and American Bar Associations. ***PRACTICE AREAS:*** Oil and Gas Law; Corporate Law. ***Email:*** david.stinson@mcafeetaft.com

JEFF L. TODD, born Colby, Kansas, June 4, 1972; admitted to bar, 1997, Oklahoma and U.S. District Court, Western and Northern Districts of Oklahoma; 2003, U.S. Tax Court. *Education:* Northwestern Oklahoma State University (B.A., 1994); Oklahoma College of Law (J.D., with highest honors, 1997). Order of the Coif. Recipient: Frank C. Love Memorial Scholarship; Cecil L. Hunt Memorial Scholarship; Rocky Mountain Mineral Law Foundation Scholarship for Scholastic Excellence. Note Editor, Oklahoma Law Review, 1996-1997. Author: "Oklahoma Law Review - Understanding When to Obtain an NPDES Permit." Teaching Assistant, Legal Writing, Oklahoma College of Law. ***PRACTICE AREAS:*** Agriculture Law; Civil Litigation; Business Litigation; Health Care Litigation; Real Estate Litigation; Oil and Gas Litigation. ***Email:*** jeff.todd@mcafeetaft.com

ELIZABETH DALTON TYRRELL, born Richmond, Virginia, September 19, 1959; admitted to bar, 1985, Oklahoma. *Education:* University of Virginia (B.A., 1981); Southern Methodist University (J.D., 1985). Phi Delta Phi. Member, Order of the Coif. Editor, Journal of Air Law and Commerce, 1984-1985. *Member:* Oklahoma County, Oklahoma (Former Chair, Health Law Section) and American Bar Associations; Oklahoma Health Lawyers Association (Director); American Health Lawyers Association. ***PRACTICE AREAS:*** Corporate Law; Health Care; Franchise Law. ***Email:*** elizabeth.tyrrell@mcafeetaft.com

PETER T. VAN DYKE, born Glens Falls, New York, March 3, 1942; admitted to bar, 1969, New York and U.S. Court of Military Appeals; 1973, Oklahoma; 1989, U.S. Supreme Court; U.S. Court of Appeals, Fifth and Tenth Circuits; U.S. District Court, District of Oklahoma and Texas. *Education:* University of Rhode Island (B.S., 1964); Albany Law School of Union University (J.D., cum laude, 1968); George Washington University (LL.M., in Labor Law, 1973). Member, Justinian Society. Editor, Albany Law Review Board-Recent Decision, 1967-1968. Listed in Best Lawyers in America (Labor & Employment Law, Management). *Member:* Oklahoma County and Oklahoma (Past Chairman, Labor and Employment Law Section) Bar Associations. [Capt., JAGC, U.S. Army, 1969-1973]. ***REPORTED CASES:*** Walker v. United Postal Service, Inc., 240 F.3d 1268 (10th Cir. 2001); Bolton v. Scrivner, Inc., 836 F. Supp. 783 (W.D. Okl. 1993), aff'd, 36 F.3d 939 (10th Cir. 1994); Brock v. Ing. 827 F.2d 1426 (10th Cir. 1987); Morris v. Adams-Millis corp., 758 F.2d 1352 (10th

(This Listing Continued)

Cir. 1985); N.L.R.B. v. Dixon Industries, Inc., 700 F.2d 595 (10th Cir. 1980); N.C.R.B. v. Northeast Oklahoma City Mfg. Co., 631 F.2d 669 (10th Cir. 1980); Sarsycki v. United Parcel Service, 862 F.Supp. 336 (W.D. Okl. 1994); Atkinson v. Halliburton Company, 905 P.2d 772 (Okl. 1995); Allen v. Transok Pipe Line Company, 552 P.2d 375 (Okl. 1976). **PRACTICE AREAS:** Labor and Employment Law; Civil Litigation. **Email:** peter.vandyke@mcafeetaft.com

ERIN M. VAN LAANEN, born La Jolla, California, September 9, 1960; admitted to bar, 1991, Oklahoma and U.S. District Court, Western District of Oklahoma. *Education:* Central State University (B.B.A., magna cum laude, 1988); University of Oklahoma (J.D., 1991). Order of the Coif; Phi Kappa Phi. Inclusion in exclusive Guide to the World's Aviation Lawyers, Legal Media Group, 2004. Assistant Articles Editor, Oklahoma Law Review, 1990-1991. Instructor, Legal Research & Writing and Appellate Advocacy, University of Oklahoma College of Law, 1989-1991. President, Organization for the Advancement of Women in Law, University of Oklahoma College of Law, 1989-1990. *Member:* Oklahoma County, Oklahoma and American Bar Associations. **SPECIAL AGENCIES:** Federal Aviation Administration. **PRACTICE AREAS:** Aircraft Title; Aircraft Finance and Leasing; International Aviation Law; Aviation and Aerospace; Aircraft Sales; Capetown/Unidroit International Registration. **Email:** erin.vanlaanen@mcafeetaft.com

JOSEPH WALTERS, born New York, N.Y., October 10, 1950; admitted to bar, 1986, Oklahoma and U.S. District Court, Western District of Oklahoma; 1988, U.S. Court of Appeals, Tenth Circuit; 1995, U.S. District Court, Northern District of Oklahoma. *Education:* LeMoyne College; State University of New York at Binghamton (B.A., 1973); University of Oklahoma (J.D., with honors, 1986). Phi Alpha Delta; Order of the Coif. Recipient, American Jurisprudence Awards in Torts and Water Law. Instructor, Legal Research and Writing and Appellate Advocacy, University of Oklahoma, College of Law, 1984-1986. *Member:* Oklahoma County, Oklahoma and American (Member, Section on Litigation) Bar Associations; American Inns of Court, Luther Bohanon Chapter, 1990-1992. **PRACTICE AREAS:** Litigation; Administrative Law; Products Liability; Government Contracts; Family Law; Criminal Defense Law. **Email:** joe.walters@mcafeetaft.com

JERRY A. WARREN, born Bartlesville, Oklahoma, January 9, 1943; admitted to bar, 1968, Oklahoma. *Education:* University of Oklahoma (B.A., 1965; J.D., 1968). Phi Delta Phi; Order of the Coif. Member, Board of Editors, Oklahoma Law Review, 1966-1968. Instructor, Securities Regulation, School of Law, Oklahoma City University, 1973. Listed in the Chambers USA Guide to America's Leading Lawyers for Business (Corporate/M&A). *Member:* Oklahoma County, Oklahoma and American Bar Associations. **PRACTICE AREAS:** Corporate Law; Securities. **Email:** jerry.warren@mcafeetaft.com

DREW D. WEBB, born Guthrie, Oklahoma, April 27, 1960; admitted to bar, 1985, Oklahoma; 1986, U.S. District Court, Western District of Oklahoma; 1987, U.S. District Court, Northern District of Oklahoma, U.S. Court of Appeals, Tenth Circuit and U.S. Supreme Court; 2001, U.S. District Court, Eastern District of Oklahoma. *Education:* University of Oklahoma (B.A., special distinction, 1982); Harvard University (J.D., cum laude, 1985). Certified Mediator. Certified BBB Auto Line Arbitrator. *Member:* Oklahoma County and Oklahoma Bar Associations. **PRACTICE AREAS:** Business Litigation; Trust and Estate Litigation; Construction Litigation; Insurance Litigation; Real Estate Litigation; Products Liability Litigation. **Email:** drew.webb@mcafeetaft.com

JAMES R. WEBB, born Oklahoma City, Oklahoma, September 18, 1967; admitted to bar, 1993, Colorado; 1995, Oklahoma. *Education:* Austin College (B.A., 1989); Washington University at St. Louis (J.D., 1993). Order of the Coif. Amandus Brackman Moot Court Award; American Jurisprudence Awards, Evidence and Trial Practice. Associate Editor, Washington University Law Quarterly, 1991-1993. First Place, Wiley Rutledge Moot Court, 1992. *Member:* Oklahoma, Colorado and American Bar Associations. **PRACTICE AREAS:** Civil Litigation; Labor and Employment Law; Products Liability; Class Actions; Complex and Multi-District Litigation. **Email:** jim.webb@mcafeetaft.com

STEVEN R. WELCH, born Rochelle, Illinois, September 23, 1950; admitted to bar, 1979, Oklahoma. *Education:* University of Oklahoma (B.A., 1976; J.D., 1979). Order of the Coif; Phi Delta Phi. Member, Board of Editors, Oklahoma Law Review, 1977-1979. *Member:* Oklahoma and American Bar Associations. **PRACTICE AREAS:** Commercial Law; Acquisitions; Environmental Law; Oil and Gas Law; Mining and Minerals. **Email:** steven.welch@mcafeetaft.com

NATHAN L. WHATLEY, born Lubbock, Texas, April 14, 1967; admitted to bar, 1992, Oklahoma; U.S. District Court, Western, Eastern and Northern Districts of Oklahoma; U.S. District Court, Northern District of Texas; U.S. Court of Appeals, Tenth Circuit; U.S. Supreme Court. *Education:* University of Oklahoma (B.A., with highest honors, 1989; J.D., with highest honors, 1992). Phi Beta Kappa; Order of the Coif. Recipient, American Jurisprudence Award, Contracts, Torts, Civil Procedure and Criminal Law. Member, Oklahoma Law Review, 1990-1992. Author: "United States v. Noriega: Criminal Forfeiture of Attorney Fees and Due Process Requirements," 44 Oklahoma Law Review 729, 1992. Legal Counsel to: Oklahoma City Metro Employer Council; Society for Human Resource Management; Sooner Human Resources Society. *Member:* Oklahoma County, Oklahoma (Past Chair, Labor and Employment Law Section) and American Bar Associations. **REPORTED CASES:** Burks v. Oklahoma Publishing Co., 81 F.3d 975 (10th Cir. 1996); Bell v. Dillard Dept. Stores, Inc., (10th Cir. 1996); Danner v. Dillard Dept. Stores, Inc., 949 P.2d 680 (Okla. 1997); Gripe v. City of Enid, 312 F.3d 1184 (10th Cir. 2002); Kuykendall v. Gulfstream Aerospace Technologies,66 P.3d 374 (Okla. 2002). **PRACTICE AREAS:** Labor and Employment Law; Civil Litigation. **Email:** nathan.whatley@mcafeetaft.com

JENNIFER WHEELER, born Tulsa, Oklahoma, June 14, 1972; admitted to bar, 1997, Oklahoma. *Education:* University of Tulsa (B.A., English, 1994); University of Oklahoma (J.D., with honors, 1997). Recipient: American Jurisprudence Award - Jurisprudence; Albert C. Hunt Practice Court Award; Mineral Lawyers' Society of Oklahoma City Scholarship. Author, "Section 307 of the Sarbanes-Oxley Act: Irreconcilable with the ABA's Model Rules and the Oklahoma Rules of Professional Conduct?" (2003). Member, National Trial Team. Student Member, Luther Bohanon American Inn of Court. *Member:* Oklahoma County Bar Association; Oklahoma Bar Association; American Bar Association. **PRACTICE AREAS:** Corporate Law; Securities Law. **Email:** jennifer.wheeler@mcafeetaft.com

ELIZABETH SCOTT WOOD, born Ada, Oklahoma, August 7, 1950; admitted to bar, 1980, Oklahoma, U.S. Supreme Court, U.S. Court of Appeals, Tenth Circuit and U.S.

(This Listing Continued)

District Court, Western Northern and Eastern Districts of Oklahoma. *Education:* University of Oklahoma (B.A., 1971; J.D., 1980). Phi Beta Kappa; Phi Delta Phi; Order of the Coif. Member and Note Editor, Oklahoma Law Review, 1979-1980. *Member:* Oklahoma County, Oklahoma and American (Member, Labor and Employment Law and Dispute Resolution Sections) Bar Associations. **PRACTICE AREAS:** Labor and Employment Law; Civil Litigation; Arbitration; Alternative Dispute Resolution. **Email:** elizabeth.wood@mcafeetaft.com

SHERYL N. YOUNG, born Aransas Pass, Texas, August 1, 1950; admitted to bar, 1990, Oklahoma, U.S. Court of Appeals, Seventh, Tenth and Eleventh Circuits, U.S. District Court, Western District of Oklahoma and U.S. Supreme Court. *Education:* University of Central Oklahoma (B.S., magna cum laude, 1972, Alpha Chi); Oklahoma City University (J.D., with distinction, 1990). Phi Delta Phi; Order of Barristers. Hatton Summer Scholar. Recipient, Archibald Cox Award in Appellate Advocacy; Judge Dwain Box Award for Outstanding Advocate. *Member:* Oklahoma, Oklahoma County and American Bar Associations. **REPORTED CASES:** Biswell Stores Inc. v. Indian Nations Communications of Cushing, Inc., 98 F.3d 1349 (Table) 1996 WL 560798, 1996-2 Trade Cases P 71,578 (10th Cir.1996), Gamble v. Jeld-Wen, Inc., 501 S.E.2d 393 (Va.1998). Fleming, Inc. v. Super Center, 1999 OK CIV APP 18, 977 P.2d 367. Scottsdale Ins. Co. v. Subscriptions Plus, Inc., 299 F.3d 618 (7th Cir., 2002). United States v. Botefuhr, 309 F.3d 1263 (10th Cir. 2002), Forgues ex rel. Martine v. Heart of Texas Dodge, Inc. 266 Wis.2d 1060, 668 N.W.2d 562 (Table), 2003 WL 21801424 (Wis.App.), 2003 WI App 188. Griffin v. Griffin, 2004 WL 1506158 (Okla.Civ.App. Div. 3), 2004 OK CIV APP 58, _P.3d _, cert denied (2004); Conoco, Inc. v. Agrico Chemical Co., 2004 OK 83, 115 P.3d 829. **PRACTICE AREAS:** Civil Litigation; Intellectual Property; Mediation; Family Law. **Email:** sheryl.young@mcafeetaft.com

ASSOCIATES

M. CRAIG ADKINS, born Norman, Oklahoma, December 17, 1968; admitted to bar, 1996, Oklahoma. *Education:* University of Oklahoma (B.A., magna cum laude, 1991; M.B.A./J.D., with honors, 1996). Phi Beta Kappa; Order of the Coif. Note Editor, Oklahoma Law Review. Member, American Indian Law Review. *Member:* Oklahoma County, Oklahoma and American Bar Associations. **PRACTICE AREAS:** Commercial Law; Business Law; Commercial Real Estate; Leases and Leasing. **Email:** craig.adkins@mcafeetaft.com

MELINDA S. BLACKMAN, born Oklahoma City, Oklahoma, June 15, 1971; admitted to bar, 2000, California, U.S. District Court, Northern District of California and U.S. Court of Appeals, Ninth Circuit; 2004, Oklahoma. *Education:* Vanderbilt University (B.A., 1993); University of Oklahoma College of Law (J.D., highest honors, 2000). Phi Kappa Phi; Order of the Coif. Recipient: William T. and James T. Comfort Scholar, 1998-2000. Chief Note Editor, 1999-2000 and Member, 1998-1999, Oklahoma Law Review. Judicial Extern for the Hon. Lee R. West, U.S. District Court Judge, Western District of Oklahoma, 2000. Teaching Assistant for Legal Writing and Appellate Advocacy, 1998-1999. Author: "United States v. Balsys: Setting a Boundary for the Self-Incrimination Clause," 53 Oklahoma Law Review 127 (2000). Securities Litigation Associate, Morrison & Foerster, San Francisco, 2000-2002. Interim Assistant General Counsel, Board of Regents of Oklahoma Colleges, 2004. *Member:* Oklahoma County Bar Association; American Bar Association. **PRACTICE AREAS:** Aviation Law. **Email:** mindy.blackman@mcafeetaft.com

BRANDON L. BUCHANAN, born Norman, Oklahoma, April 8, 1974; admitted to bar, 2000, Oklahoma; U.S. District Court, Western Northern and Eastern Districts of Oklahoma. *Education:* University of Oklahoma (B.A., cum laude, 1996; J.D., 2000). Phi Beta Kappa, 1996. Law Clerk to Oklahoma Supreme Court Justice Marian P. Opala, 1999. Legislative Director, University of Oklahoma, 1996-2000. Legal Advisor: Oklahoma State Senate Judiciary, 2001; Luther Bohanon American Inn of Court. *Member:* Oklahoma County, Oklahoma and American Bar Associations; Oklahoma Association of Defense Counsel; International Association of Defense Counsel; Defense Research Institute. **PRACTICE AREAS:** Litigation; Commercial Law; Commercial Litigation; Construction Law; Contracts; Civil Rights Defense; Labor and Employment; Medical Malpractice; Products Liability; Torts. **Email:** brandon.buchanan@mcafeetaft.com

KYMALA B. CARRIER, born Oklahoma City, Oklahoma, July 22, 1957; admitted to bar, 1998, Oklahoma. *Education:* University of Oklahoma (B.A., 1995; J.D., with highest honors, 1998). Phi Delta Phi; Order of the Coif. *Member:* Oklahoma Bar Association. **PRACTICE AREAS:** Civil Litigation. **Email:** kym.carrier@mcafeetaft.com

STEPHANIE P. CHAPMAN, born Tulsa, Oklahoma, November 30, 1976; admitted to bar, 2002, Oklahoma. *Education:* University of Oklahoma (B.A., magna cum laude, 1998; J.D., with highest honors, 2002). Order of the Coif. Managing Editor, Oklahoma Law Review, 2001-2002. Author, "MCI Telecommunications Corp. v. Public Service Commission: The Tenth Circuit Rebuffs the Supreme Court Trend Supporting State Immunity," 55 Okla. L. Rev. 175 (2002). *Member:* Oklahoma Bar Association. **PRACTICE AREAS:** Tax Law; Commercial Transactions; Securities. **Email:** stephanie.chapman@mcafeetaft.com

TODD COURT, born February 20, 1974; admitted to bar, 2002, Oklahoma. *Education:* Oklahoma State University (B.S., Business Administration); Oklahoma City University (J.D., summa cum laude, 2002). Phi Delta Phi. Member, ABA National Appellate Advocacy Team, 2001. Recipient: T. Harley Jordan Award for Excellence in Criminal Procedure; CALI Awards in: Contracts II; Criminal Procedure; Evidence; Property II; Secured Transactions; Employment Law. *Member:* Oklahoma Bar Association. **PRACTICE AREAS:** Litigation; Corporate Law; Employment Law. **Email:** todd.court@mcafeetaft.com

TEENA P. DUNN, born Oklahoma City, Oklahoma, January 29, 1959; admitted to bar, 1994, Oklahoma. *Education:* University of Central Oklahoma (B.A., 1980); Oklahoma City University (J.D., cum laude, 1994). Phi Delta Phi. Order of the Barristers. Member: Jessup International Moot Court Team; National Moot Court Team; Moot Court Board, 1993-1994; Oklahoma City University Law Review. Recipient: Kerr Foundation Scholarship; American Jurisprudence Awards for Administrative Law. *Member:* Oklahoma and American Bar Associations. **SPECIAL AGENCIES:** Federal Aviation Administration. **Email:** teena.dunn@mcafeetaft.com

MARK D. FOLGER, born Oklahoma City, Oklahoma, November 16, 1976; admitted to bar, 2005, Oklahoma. *Education:* DePauw University (B.A., 1999); Oklahoma City University (J.D., magna cum laude, 2005). Phi Delta Phi. Recipient, Phillips Allen Porta Me-

(This Listing Continued)

McAFEE & TAFT, A PROFESSIONAL CORPORATION, Oklahoma City—Continued

morial Legal Ethics Award; CALI awards in Legal Analysis, Legal Profession, Complex Litigation and Trial Practice. Student Member of William J. Holloway, Jr. American Inn of Court. ***PRACTICE AREAS:*** Litigation. ***Email:*** mark.folger@mcafeetaft.com

SPENCER W. HAINES, born Oklahoma City, Oklahoma, December 4, 1975; admitted to bar, 2004, Oklahoma. *Education:* Oklahoma State University (B.S., Accounting, 1998); University of Oklahoma College of Law (J.D., with highest honors, 2004). Order of the Coif. William T. Comfort Scholar; John McHenry Mee Scholar. Recipient: Nathan Scarritt Prize; American Jurisprudence Awards. Certified Public Accountant, Oklahoma, 1998—. Assistant Editor, University of Oklahoma Law Review. Senior Accountant, Arthur Andersen, 1998-2001. ***PRACTICE AREAS:*** Corporate Law; Securities Law; Taxation. ***Email:*** spencer.haines@mcafeetaft.com

STEPHEN M. HETRICK, born Oklahoma City, Oklahoma, August 4, 1978; admitted to bar, 2003, Oklahoma and U.S. District Court, Western District of Oklahoma. *Education:* University of Central Oklahoma (B.S., Accounting, summa cum laude, 2000); University of Oklahoma (J.D., with highest honors, 2003). Order of the Coif. Recipient, American Jurisprudence Awards in: Individual Income Tax, Income Taxation of Trusts and Estates, Wealth Transfer Tax, Wills and Trusts, Pensions and Benefits, Health Law, Criminal Law and Torts. *Member:* Okalhoma County, Oklahoma and American Bar Associations. ***PRACTICE AREAS:*** Corporate Law; Commercial Law; Real Estate Law. ***Email:*** stephen.hetrick@mcafeetaft.com

ALAN G. HOLLOWAY, born McAlester, Oklahoma; admitted to bar, 1996, Oklahoma and U.S. District Court, Western District of Oklahoma; 1997, U.S. Tax Court. *Education:* East Central University (B.S., Accounting, 1991; B.S., Computer Science, 1991); University of Oklahoma (J.D., 1996). Recipient, Albert G. Kulp Award. Carl Albert Executive Fellow. Editor, Oklahoma Law Review. Listed in Who's Who Among American Law Students. Member, Christian Legal Society, 1994—. Certified Public Accountant, Oklahoma, 1992. *Member:* Oklahoma County, Oklahoma and American (Section of Taxation) Bar Associations; Oklahoma Society of Certified Public Accountants (Tax Committee); American Institute of Certified Public Accountants. ***PRACTICE AREAS:*** Tax Law. ***Email:*** alan.holloway@mcafeetaft.com

JUSTIN L. JACKSON, born Claremore, Oklahoma, February 20, 1975; admitted to bar, 2000, Oklahoma. *Education:* University of Oklahoma (B.B.A., with special distinction, 1997; J.D., with highest honors, 2000). Phi Delta Phi; Order of the Coif; Comfort Scholar. Recipient, American Jurisprudence Awards: Property, Corporate Income Tax, Criminal Law and Criminal Procedure. Associate Note Editor of Oklahoma Law Review-.*Member:* Oklahoma County, Oklahoma and American Bar Associations. ***PRACTICE AREAS:*** Securities; Corporate Law; Mergers and Acquisitions; Franchise; Business Law; Buying and Selling of Businesses; Buy-Sell Agreements; Business Transactions; Corporate Contracts; Corporate Finance; Public Corporations; S Corporations; Tender Offers; Corporate Formation; Blue Sky Law; Insider Trading; Public Offerings; Securities Disclosure; Securities Finance; Securities Offerings; Shareholder Agreements. ***Email:*** justin.jackson@mcafeetaft.com

JAMES BRADLEY KLEPPER, born Mangum, Oklahoma, March 19, 1967; admitted to bar, 2001, Oklahoma. *Education:* University of Oklahoma (B.Arch., 1992); Oklahoma City University School of Law (J.D., 2000). Phi Delta Phi. Recipient, Cali Awards in Law & Medicine, Criminal Procedure II, Professional Responsibility. Licensed Architect. *Member:* American Institute of Architects; Oklahoma Municipal Contractors Association. ***PRACTICE AREAS:*** Intellectual Property. ***Email:*** brad.klepper@mcafeetaft.com

MARK W. MALONE, born Fort Worth, Texas, October 5, 1967; admitted to bar, 2002, Oklahoma. *Education:* Texas Christian University (B.S., 1990); Oklahoma City University School of Law (J.D., magna cum laude, 2002). Phi Delta Phi. Member, Merit Scholars. Recipient, CALI Awards. Listed in Who's Who Among American Law Students. Member, Oklahoma City University Law Review. *Member:* Oklahoma and American Bar Associations. ***PRACTICE AREAS:*** Wills; Trusts and Estates; Probate; Guardianship and Conservatorship. ***Email:*** mark.malone@mcafeetaft.com

MICHAEL D. McCLINTOCK, born Billings, Montana, June 19, 1970; admitted to bar, 1998, Oklahoma and U.S. District Court, Western District of Oklahoma; 1999, U.S. Court of Appeals, Tenth Circuit; 2000, U.S. District Court, Eastern District of Oklahoma; 2000, U.S. District Court, Northern District of Oklahoma; 2000, U.S. District Court, Northern District Texas; 2003, U.S. Supreme Court. *Education:* U.S. Merchant Marine Academy, Kings Point (B.S., 1992); Oklahoma City University School of Law (J.D., summa cum laude, 1998). Phi Delta Phi. Comment Editor, Law Review. Law Clerk, Honorable Robert H. Henry, U.S. Court of Appeals, Tenth Circuit, 1998-1999. *Member:* Oklahoma County, Oklahoma and American Bar Associations. [Lt., U.S. Navy, 1992-1995; Active Duty, 1995-2000 Reserves]. ***REPORTED CASES:*** Accuweather, Inc. v. Total Weather, Inc., 223 F.Supp.2d 612 (M.D.Pa. 2002); First United Bank & Trust Co. v. Jinseok Yang; Claim Number: FA0206000114649 Q-Trade Canada, Inc. v. Bank of Hydro Oklahoma, Case No. AF-0169. ***PRACTICE AREAS:*** Intellectual Property Litigation (50%); Business Litigation (50%). ***Email:*** michael.mcclintock@mcafeetaft.com

CHARLES L. McLAWHORN, III, born Greenville, North Carolina, December 27, 1976; admitted to bar, 2002, Oklahoma. *Education:* University of Oklahoma (B.S., Zoology, 1999; J.D., with honors, 2002). Order of the Barristers. Recipient, American Jurisprudence Award in Trademarks. *Member:* Oklahoma Bar Association. ***PRACTICE AREAS:*** Intellectual Property; Litigation. ***Email:*** chad.mclawhorn@mcafeetaft.com

M. BRANDON MEYER, born Guymon, Oklahoma, February 10, 1969; admitted to bar, 2001, Oklahoma. *Education:* Oklahoma State University (B.B.S., 1991); Oklahoma City University School of Law (J.D., 2001). Phi Delta Phi. Merit Scholar, Oklahoma City University School of Law. Articles Editor, Law Review. Certified Public Accountant. *Member:* Oklahoma Bar Association; American Institute of Certified Public Accountants; Oklahoma Society of Certified Public Accountants. ***PRACTICE AREAS:*** ERISA; Employee Benefits; Tax Law. ***Email:*** brandon.meyer@mcafeetaft.com

BEAUCHAMP M. PATTERSON, admitted to bar, 2001, Oklahoma. *Education:* University of New Mexico (B.A., 1994); Oklahoma City University School of Law (J.D., 2001). Phi Delta Phi. *Member:* Oklahoma County, Oklahoma and American (Member, Litigation Section) Bar Associations. ***PRACTICE AREAS:*** Civil Litigation. ***Email:*** beau.patterson@mcafeetaft.com

JEAN L. PINKSTON, born Austin, Texas, July 26, 1966; admitted to bar, 1997, Oklahoma; registered to practice before U.S. Patent and Trademark Office. *Education:* University of Oklahoma (B.S., with high honors, 1988; J.D., with highest honors, 1997). Order of the Coif; Phi Kappa Phi; Phi Alpha Delta. Note Editor, Oklahoma Law Review. Recipient, Academic Achievement Awards. Harrison W. Ewing Fellowship. Member, Oklahoma University Law Review. Author: Oklahoma Law Review Vol. 48-4; Oklahoma Law Review Vol. 49-3. *Member:* Oklahoma County, Oklahoma and American (Member, Patent, Trademark and Copyright Section) Bar Associations; Oklahoma City International Trade Association; Ruth Bader Ginsberg American Inn of Court; Oklahoma Lawyers for Children. ***PRACTICE AREAS:*** Business Litigation; Patent Law; Trademark Law; Copyright Law. ***Email:*** jean.pinkston@mcafeetaft.com

JENNIFER BETH RADER, born Jonesboro, Arkansas, August 10, 1972; admitted to bar, 2001, Oklahoma. *Education:* Southern Nazarene University (B.S., 1996); University of Oklahoma (J.D., with highest honors, 2001). Order of the Coif. Member, Board of Editors, Oklahoma Law Review. Recipient: American Jurisprudence Awards: Torts, Civil Procedure, Criminal Procedure and Real Property; Comfort Scholarship and Oklahoma Real Property Award. Oklahoma Teaching License issued in 1992. ***PRACTICE AREAS:*** Intellectual Property; Litigation. ***Email:*** jenna.rader@mcafeetaft.com

NATALIE K. RAMSEY, born Chickasha, Oklahoma, September 27, 1976; admitted to bar, 2002, Oklahoma. *Education:* Oklahoma State University (B.S., summa cum laude, 1999); University of Oklahoma (J.D., with honors, 2002). Phi Delta Phi. Recipient: Comfort Scholarship Award; American Jurisprudence Awards in: Constitutional Law; Contracts. *Member:* Oklahoma County, Oklahoma and American Bar Associations. ***PRACTICE AREAS:*** Civil Litigation; Employment Law. ***Email:*** natalie.ramsey@mcafeetaft.com

DAVID RIDGWAY, born El Paso, Texas, October 30, 1973; admitted to bar, 2003, Oklahoma. *Education:* University of Oklahoma (B.B.A., Finance, 1996); University of Oklahoma (J.D., honors, 2003). Recipient, American Jurisprudence Awards in Oil and Gas and Land Use Control. ***PRACTICE AREAS:*** Corporate Law; Commercial Law; Health Care; Real Estate. ***Email:*** david.ridgway@mcafeetaft.com

PATRICIA A. ROGERS, born Chelsea, Massachusetts, December 22, 1960; admitted to bar, 1999, Oklahoma. *Education:* University of Pittsburgh (B.A., magna cum laude, 1983); Johns Hopkins University School of Hygiene and Public Health (M.H.S., 1985); Oklahoma City University (J.D., summa cum laude, 1999). Managing Editor, Oklahoma City University Law Review, 1998-1999. Member, Board of Directors, Infant Crisis Services, Inc., 2005. *Member:* Oklahoma Bar Association; American Health Lawyers Association (Treaurer, 2005). [USAF Medical Service Corps, 1985-1989 (AD); 1989-1999 (Reserve)]. ***PRACTICE AREAS:*** Health Care; Corporate Law.

PAUL A. ROSS, born Oklahoma City, Oklahoma, May 15, 1975; admitted to bar, 2002, Oklahoma; U.S. District Court, Northern, Eastern and Western Districts of Oklahoma. *Education:* Oklahoma State University (B.S., 1997); Oklahoma City University (J.D., summa cum laude, 2002). Top Ten Student, Oklahoma State University College of Education, 1997. Recipient: Oklahoma City University Law Merit Scholarship; 13 CALI Awards; West Publishing Outstanding Scholastic Achievement Award; Judge Tom Brett Award for Excellence in Criminal Law Studies; Ernest L. Wilkinson Award for Excellence in Native American Law. *Member:* Oklahoma County, Oklahoma and American Bar Associations. ***PRACTICE AREAS:*** Labor and Employment; Litigation. ***Email:*** paul.ross@mcafeetaft.com

RICHARD J. SALAMY, born Oklahoma City, Oklahoma, November 15, 1966; admitted to bar, 1992, Texas; 1998, Oklahoma. *Education:* Baylor University (B.A., cum laude, 1989); Baylor Law School (J.D., 1992). Phi Beta Kappa; Omicron Delta Kappa. Assistant District Attorney, Tarrant County District Attorney's Office, Fort Worth, Texas, 1993-1997. *Member:* Oklahoma and American Bar Associations; State Bar of Texas; American Immigration Lawyers Association. ***PRACTICE AREAS:*** Business Law; Commercial Real Estate; Secured Lending; Business Immigration. ***Email:*** richard.salamy@mcafeetaft.com

RONALD T. SHINN, JR., born Ravenna, Ohio, December 29, 1974; admitted to bar, 2002, Oklahoma; U.S. District Court, Western, Eastern and Northern Districts of Oklahoma; U.S. Court of Appeals, Federal Circuit; U.S. Court of Appeals, Tenth Circuit. *Education:* Miami University (B.A., Political Science, 1996); University of Oklahoma (J.D., 2002). Recipient, American Jurisprudence Awards in: Constitutional Law; First Amendment; Legal Research & Writing I and II; Antitrust I and II; Equal Employment Opportunities; Alternative Dispute Resolution; Criminal Law. Note Editor, Oklahoma Law Review, 2001-2002. Author, Note, "Establishment Clause v. Free Expression: Adler v. Duval County School Board," 54 Okla. L. Rev. 775 (2002). Legislative Assistant, 1996-1997 and Press Secretary, 1997-1999, Representative Wally Herger (Calif.), Washington, D.C. *Member:* Oklahoma Bar Association. ***PRACTICE AREAS:*** Commercial Litigation; Labor and Employment; Antitrust. ***Email:*** ron.shinn@mcafeetaft.com

JOSHUA D. SMITH, born Bartlesville, Oklahoma, January 19, 1980; admitted to bar, 2005, Oklahoma. *Education:* University of Oklahoma (B.A., 2002; J.D., with highest honors, 2005). Order of the Coif. Member, Judiciary Committee, Oklahoma Law Review. Recipient, Paul and Jo Ann Sharp Law Review Award; American Jurisprudence Awards in Property, Securities Regulation, Commercial Law and Professional Responsibility; Oklahoma Bar Association's Corporate Law Section Award, 2003. ***PRACTICE AREAS:*** Business Law; Corporate Law. ***Email:*** josh.smith@mcafeetaft.com

SPENCER F. SMITH, born Oklahoma City, Oklahoma, December 17, 1971; admitted to bar, 1998, Texas; 2005, Oklahoma; U.S. District Court, Western and Southern Districts of Texas and Western and Northern Districts of Oklahoma; U.S. Court of Appeals, Fifth and Ninth Circuits. *Education:* University of Oklahoma (B.A., cum laude, 1994); University of Texas (J.D., with honors, 1998). *Member:* Travis County, Oklahoma and American Bar Associations; State Bar of Texas; Austin Young Lawyers Association. ***PRACTICE AREAS:*** Litigation; Products Liability; Torts; Complex and Multi-District Litigation; Appellate Practice; Class Actions; Construction Litigation; Contract Litigation; Civil Fraud; Insurance Litigation; Securities Arbitration; Securities Litigation. ***Email:*** spencer.smith@mcafeetaft.com

(This Listing Continued)

(This Listing Continued)

W. BLAKE SONNE, JR., born St. Louis Park, Minnesota, August 5, 1977; admitted to bar, 2004, Oklahoma; U.S. District Court, Western District of Oklahoma. *Education:* Marist College (B.S. in Business Management, summa cum laude, 2001); University of Oklahoma College of Law (J.D., with highest honors, 2004). Order of the Coif; William T. Comfort Scholar. Member, Whittier Juvenile Law Moot Court Team. Recipient, American Jurisprudence Awards. Note Editor and Member, Editorial Board, University of Oklahoma Law Review. ***PRACTICE AREAS:*** Labor and Employment; Litigation. ***Email:*** blake.sonne@mcafeetaft.com

ABBEY B. STALLINGS, born Enid, Oklahoma, September 19, 1977; admitted to bar, 2004, Oklahoma and U.S. District Court, Western District of Oklahoma. *Education:* University of Oklahoma (B.A. in Letters, magna cum laude, 2000); University of Oklahoma College of Law (J.D., with highest honors, 2004). Phi Beta Kappa; Order of the Coif. William T. Comfort Scholar; McKinney& Stringer Scholar. Assistant Editor, University of Oklahoma Law Review. Intern, Department of Justice. ***PRACTICE AREAS:*** Litigation. ***Email:*** abbey.stallings@mcafeetaft.com

JOHN D. STINER, born Oklahoma City, Oklahoma, December 14, 1971; admitted to bar, 1998, Oklahoma, U.S. District Court, Western District of Oklahoma, U.S. Court of Appeals, Third and Tenth Circuits. *Education:* Georgetown University (B.S.F.S., 1993); University of Oklahoma (J.D., 1998). Order of the Coif. Note Editor, Oklahoma Law Review. Kerr-McGee Scholar. Recipient: Frank Love Memorial Scholarship; Harry Alley-Leroy Allen Memorial Prize for Outstanding Case Note, 1997. Author: Shaffer v. Jeffery: The Oklahoma Supreme Court Rejects The Separability Doctrine and Takes A Step Back in The Enforcement of Arbitration Clauses Under Oklahoma Law, 50 Okla. L. Rev. 243 (1997). *Member:* Oklahoma and American Bar Associations. ***PRACTICE AREAS:*** Business Litigation; Bankruptcy. ***Email:*** john.stiner@mcafeetaft.com

CHERYL VINALL, born Fort Worth, Texas, April 9, 1974; admitted to bar, 2000, New York; 2004, Oklahoma. *Education:* Oklahoma Baptist University (B.A., 1995); Georgetown University (J.D., 1998). *Member:* Oklahoma and American Bar Associations. ***PRACTICE AREAS:*** Business Law; Commercial Law; Contracts; Corporate Law; Mergers, Acquisitions and Divestitures. ***Email:*** cheryl.vinall@mcafeetaft.com

AMY D. WHITE, born Sweetwater, Tennessee, April 13, 1975; admitted to bar, 2001, Oklahoma U.S. District Court, Western and Northern Districts of Oklahoma; U.S. Court of Appeals, Tenth Circuit. *Education:* University of Tennessee (B.A., 1997); Oklahoma City University (J.D., 2001). Phi Delta Phi. Editor in Chief, Oklahoma City University Law Review. Merit Scholar. Moot Court Honors Board. *Member:* Oklahoma Bar Association. ***REPORTED CASES:*** Christian v. Gray, 65 P.3d 591 (Okla. 2003). ***PRACTICE AREAS:*** Litigation. ***Email:*** amy.white@mcafeetaft.com

OF COUNSEL

JACQUE J. BRAWNER, born Watonga, Oklahoma, January 2, 1953; admitted to bar, 1977, Oklahoma; 1978, U.S. District Court, Western District of Oklahoma; 1979, U.S. Court of Appeals, Tenth Circuit; 1992, U.S. District Court, Eastern District of Oklahoma. *Education:* Oklahoma State University (B.S., 1975); Oklahoma City University (J.D., 1977); National Judicial College; Workers' Compensation College. Phi Alpha Delta; Iota Tau Tau; Delta Delta Delta. Recipient, The Outstanding Young Lawyer of Oklahoma, Oklahoma Bar Association, 1985. Author: "Workers' Compensation in Oklahoma," Women's Law Resource Manual, 1988. Administrator, Workers' Compensation Court, 1982-1984. Workers' Compensation Judge, 1984-1988. Sustaining Member, Oklahoma City Junior League. Graduate, Leadership Oklahoma City. *Member:* Oklahoma County, Oklahoma and American Bar Associations; Oklahoma Association of Defense Counsel. ***PRACTICE AREAS:*** Workers Compensation (100%). ***Email:*** jacque.brawner@mcafeetaft.com

MARK E. BURGET, born Wiesbaden, Germany, February 11, 1954; admitted to bar, 1979, Oklahoma. *Education:* University of Oklahoma (B.B.A., 1976; J.D., 1979); New York University (LL.M. in Taxation, 1982). Order of the Coif; Beta Gamma Sigma; Phi Delta Phi. Editor, 1977-1979 and Managing Editor, 1978, Oklahoma Law Review. Certified Public Accountant, Oklahoma, 1978. *Member:* Oklahoma County, Oklahoma and American Bar Associations; American Institute of Certified Public Accountants; Oklahoma Society of Certified Public Accountants. ***PRACTICE AREAS:*** Corporate Law; Partnership Law; Tax Law.

GARY W. CATRON, born Hamilton, Ohio, September 19, 1944; admitted to bar, 1976, Texas; 1980, U.S. Court of Appeals, 10th Circuit; 1981, Oklahoma. *Education:* Miami University (B.A., 1965); Harvard University (Ph.D., 1971); University of Texas (J.D., 1976). Phi Beta Kappa. *Member:* Oklahoma Bar Association. ***PRACTICE AREAS:*** Civil Litigation; Oil and Gas Law. ***Email:*** gary.catron@mcafeetaft.com

STANLEY L. CUNNINGHAM, born Durant, Oklahoma, February 7, 1938; admitted to bar, 1963, Oklahoma. *Education:* University of Oklahoma (B.S., 1960; LL.B., 1963). Order of the Coif; Phi Alpha Delta. Listed in *Best Lawyers in America* and *Who's Who in American Law.* Article and Book Review Editor, Oklahoma Law Review, 1963. Recipient, Rocky Mountain Mineral Law Award. Special Lecturer, Oil and Gas Contracts, University of Oklahoma College of Law, 1979 and 1982, Litigation, 1996. Lecturer, Southwestern Legal Foundation, 1986, 1989. Lecturer, Federal Energy Bar Association, 1986. *Member:* Oklahoma County, Oklahoma (Chairman, Administrative Law Section, 1966), Federal Energy and American Bar Associations; American Society of International Law. ***PRACTICE AREAS:*** Litigation; Oil and Gas Law; International Law. ***Email:*** stanley.cunningham@mcafeetaft.com

C. CLARK DOUGHERTY, JR., born New Eagle, Pennsylvania, February 9, 1935; admitted to bar, 1966, Oklahoma; 1967, Missouri; 1970, U.S. District Court, Western and Northern Districts of Oklahoma; 1971, U.S. Court of Appeals, 10th Circuit; 1983, U.S. Court of Appeals for the Federal Circuit; 1988, U.S. Supreme Court; registered to practice before U.S. Patent and Trademark Office. *Education:* University of Oklahoma (B.S., Ch.E., 1958); University of Oklahoma and Oklahoma City University (J.D., 1966). Listed in Best Lawyers in America. Registered Professional Engineer, Oklahoma, 1963. *Member:* Oklahoma County, Oklahoma and American (Member, Patent, Trademark and Copyright Section) Bar Associations; American Intellectual Property Law Association. ***PRACTICE AREAS:*** Patent Law; Trademark Law; Copyright Law; Unfair Competition Law; Antitrust Law; Commercial Litigation. ***Email:*** clark.dougherty@mcafeetaft.com

(This Listing Continued)

THEODORE M. ELAM, born Enid, Oklahoma, December 18, 1934; admitted to bar, 1959, Oklahoma. *Education:* University of Colorado and University of Oklahoma (B.B.A., 1957); University of Oklahoma (LL.B., 1959). Order of the Coif; Omicron Delta Kappa; Phi Alpha Delta. Listed in "Best Lawyers in America" and "Who's Who". Member, Board of Editors, 1958-1959 and Note Editor, 1959, Oklahoma Law Review. Assistant Professor of Business Law, 1959; Adjunct Faculty Member, Business Planning, Corporate Finance Law and Securities Regulation, University of Oklahoma College of Law. *Member:* Oklahoma County, Oklahoma and American Bar Associations. ***PRACTICE AREAS:*** Securities; Corporate Law; Finance; Real Estate. ***Email:*** ted.elam@mcafeetaft.com

GREGORY FROGGE, born Oklahoma City, Oklahoma, October 29, 1964; admitted to bar, 1989, Missouri; 1990, Kansas; 1995, Oklahoma. *Education:* University of Missouri at Columbia (B.A., 1986); University of Oklahoma (J. D., 1989); Loyola University of Chicago (LL.M., Health Law, 1990). Author: "Advancing Medical Technology: Can the Hospital Board Keep Pace?" Kansas Journal of Law & Public Policy, Spring, 1993. Adjunct Faculty Member, MBA Health Administration, Oklahoma City University, Spring, 1996. Listed in The Best Lawyers in America. *Member:* The Missouri Bar; Oklahoma County, Oklahoma (Chair, Health Law Section, 1997-1998) and American Bar Associations; Oklahoma Health Lawyers Association (President, 1997); American Health Lawyers Association. ***PRACTICE AREAS:*** Health Care; Corporate Law; Commercial Law; Nonprofit Corporations; Administrative Law; Mergers and Acquisitions. ***Email:*** greg.frogge@mcafeetaft.com

E. HARRY GILBERT, III, born Oklahoma City, Oklahoma, January 16, 1952; admitted to bar, 1979, Oklahoma; 1980, U.S. District Court, Western District of Oklahoma and U.S. Court of Appeals, Tenth Circuit; 1983, U.S. Court of Appeals for the Federal Circuit; 1989, U.S. District Court, Northern District of Oklahoma; registered to practice before U.S. Patent and Trademark Office. *Education:* University of Oklahoma (B.S.E.E., with special distinction, 1975; J.D., 1979). Tau Beta Pi; Eta Kappa Nu; Phi Eta Sigma; Order of the Coif. Member, Oklahoma Law Review, 1977-1979. Adjunct Professor of Law, University of Oklahoma, 1996. *Member:* Oklahoma Bar Association (Member, Intellectual Property Section); Institute of Electrical and Electronic Engineers. ***PRACTICE AREAS:*** Patent Law; Trademark Law; Copyright Law; Unfair Competition Law. ***Email:*** harry.gilbert@mcafeetaft.com

WILLIAM D. HALL, born Canton, Ohio, December 13, 1962; admitted to bar, 1990, Ohio; 1993, Oklahoma; registered to practice before the U.S. Patent & Trademark Office. *Education:* Grove City College (B.S., Chem., 1985); University of Akron School of Law (J.D., 1990). ***PRACTICE AREAS:*** Intellectual Property; Software Licensing. ***Email:*** bill.hall@mcafeetaft.com

NEAL R. KENNEDY, born Oklahoma City, Oklahoma, August 31, 1945; admitted to bar, 1983, Oklahoma; 1986, U.S. District Court, Western District of Oklahoma; registered to practice before U.S. Patent and Trademark Office. *Education:* University of Oklahoma (B.S.M.E., 1968); University of Arizona (M.S. M.E., 1970); Oklahoma City University (J.D., with honors, 1982). Phi Delta Phi; Sigma Tau; Pi Tau Sigma. Registered Professional Engineer, Oklahoma, 1973. Author: "A Look at Computer Crime - Oklahoma and Federal Law," 54 Okla. Bar J. 3263, 1983. Adjunct Professor of Law, Oklahoma City University, 1996-1998. Instructor Legal Assistant Education, University of Oklahoma, 2001-2003. *Member:* Oklahoma County, Oklahoma and American (Member Intellectual Property Law Section) Bar Associations; National Society of Professional Engineers; American Society of Mechanical Engineers; Oklahoma Society of Professional Engineers. ***PRACTICE AREAS:*** Patent Law; Trademark Law; Copyright Law. ***Email:*** nick.kennedy@mcafeetaft.com

JOHN M. MEE, born Oklahoma City, Oklahoma, March 19, 1930; admitted to bar, 1954, Oklahoma. *Education:* Pomona College (A.B., 1951); University of Oklahoma (LL.B., 1954). Phi Alpha Delta. Member, Oklahoma Law Review, 1952-1954. Co-Author, "Successful Partnering Between Inside and Outside Counsel," published by The West Group and the American Corporate Counsel Association. Trial Attorney, U.S. Dept. of Justice, 1954-55. *Member:* Oklahoma County (Director, 1966-1968), Oklahoma and American Bar Associations. [First Lieut., USAF, Judge Advocate, 1955-1957]. ***PRACTICE AREAS:*** Mergers, Acquisitions and Divestitures; Business Law; Corporate Law; Securities; Finance. ***Email:*** john.mee@mcafeetaft.com

JAMES C. PRINCE, born Canandaigua, New York, December 18, 1952; admitted to bar, 1981, Oklahoma. *Education:* Oklahoma State University (B.S., 1974); University of Oklahoma (J.D., 1981). Phi Eta Sigma; Beta Alpha Psi; Order of the Coif. Member, 1980-1981 and Research Editor, 1980, University of Oklahoma Law Review. Certified Public Accountant, Oklahoma, 1974. Listed in the Best Lawyers in America. *Member:* Oklahoma and American Bar Associations. ***PRACTICE AREAS:*** Employee Benefits Law; Health Care Law; Business Law. ***Email:*** jim.prince@mcafeetaft.com

WILLIAM W. RODGERS, born Oklahoma City, Oklahoma, October 27, 1937; admitted to bar, 1964, Texas; 1965, Oklahoma. *Education:* University of Oklahoma (B.A., 1959); Southern Methodist University (LL.B., 1964); Southwestern Graduate School of Banking. Law Clerk to Hon. Alfred P. Murrah, U.S. Court of Appeals, Tenth Circuit, 1964-1965. Former Instructor, Southwestern Graduate School of Banking. Dean of Bankers, 1995. Former President, Oklahoma Bankers Association, 1979. Recipient, Outstanding Banker Award, Oklahoma Bankers Association. *Member:* Oklahoma Bar Association; State Bar of Texas. [Officer, U.S. Navy, 1959-1961]. ***Email:*** william.rodgers@mcafeetaft.com

JAY SHANKER, born Oklahoma City, Oklahoma, 1953; admitted to bar, 1981, California (Not admitted in Oklahoma). *Education:* Yale University (B.A., 1976); New York University School of Law (J.D., 1981). Co-Author, "Entertainment Law & Business: 2nd Edition" (Juris 2005). Contributing Editor, Entertainment Industry Contracts (Matthew Bender 1986). Adjunct Professor, Entertainment Law, University of Oklahoma and Oklahoma City University Law Schools, 2005. *Member:* Los Angeles County Bar Association; State Bar of California. ***PRACTICE AREAS:*** Entertainment Law. ***Email:*** jay.shanker@mcafeetaft.com

MARY ELLEN TERNES, born Charlottesville, Virginia, October 24, 1962; admitted to bar, 1995, Arkansas; 2002, South Carolina; 2003, District of Columbia and Oklahoma. *Education:* Vanderbilt University (B.E.Ch.E., 1984); University of Arkansas at Little Rock (J.D., high honors, 1995). Managing Editor, UALR Law Journal, 1993-1995. Clerk, Air and Radiation Division, USEPA Office of General Counsel's Summer Honors Program, 1994.

(This Listing Continued)

McAFEE & TAFT, A PROFESSIONAL CORPORATION, Oklahoma City—Continued

Formerly, Chemical Engineer and on-scene coordinator and permit engineer in Environmental Remediation and Permitting for EPA Region 6 and industry. Specialist in emergency response, site remediation and hazardous waste combustor permitting under CAA, RCRA, TSCA. Technical Chair, HWC Combuster Specialty Conference, Air and Waste Management Association, 1999. Member, Air and Hazardous Waste Committees, Arkansas Environmental Federation, 1995-2001. Member, Technical Committee, South Carolina Chamber of Commerce, 2002. Member, Air and Hazardous Waste, Environmental Federation of Oklahoma, 2003 —. *Member:* Arkansas, Oklahoma and American (Member, Section on Environment, Energy and Resources; Vice Chair, Air Quality Committee, 1996-1999, 2001—; Vice Chair, Ethics Committee, 2003—; Chair, Air Quality Committee, 1999-2001; Chair, 33rd Annual Conference on Environmental Law; Council, term ending 2007) Bar Associations; South Carolina Bar; District of Columbia Bar; American Institute of Chemical Engineers. ***PRACTICE AREAS:*** Environmental Law; Environmental Real Estate; Hazardous Materials; Wetlands; Underground Storage Tanks; Superfund; Citizen Suit Practice; Indoor Air Quality and Mold. ***Email:*** maryellen.ternes@mcafeetaft.com

A list of representative clients will be furnished upon request.

REVISER OF THE OKLAHOMA LAW DIGEST FOR THIS DIRECTORY.

McALISTER, McALISTER, McKINNIS & TUGGLE, P.C.

OKLAHOMA CITY, OKLAHOMA

(See Edmond)

Estate and Gift Taxation, Business Law, Contracts, Commercial Law, Corporate Law, Partnership Law, Commercial Transaction, Civil Litigation, Estate Litigation, Trust Litigation, Probate, Real Estate, Mergers, Acquisitions and Divestures, Taxation, Wills, Labor and Employment Law, Estate Planning, Elder Law, Guardianship and Conservatorship, Nonprofit and Charitable Organizations.

McBRIDE LAW FIRM

204 NORTH ROBINSON, SUITE 3030
OKLAHOMA CITY, OKLAHOMA 73102
Telephone: 405-232-3906
Fax: 405-232-3641
Email: mcblaw@cox.net
URL: http://www.mcbridelawyers.com

Criminal Law, DUI, Drug Crimes, Felonies, Misdemeanors, Personal Injury, Automobile Accidents, Trucking Accidents, Wrongful Death, Family Law, Divorce, Child Custody.

MICHAEL DAVID McBRIDE, born Oklahoma City, Oklahoma, November 22, 1967; admitted to bar, 1994, Oklahoma. *Education:* University of Oklahoma, Norman (B.B.A., 1991; J.D., 1994). Recipient: American Juris Prudence Award, Corpus Juris Secondum, Criminal 1992. *Member:* Oklahoma and Oklahoma County Bar Associations; Oklahoma County Criminal Defense Lawyers Association. ***PRACTICE AREAS:*** Criminal Law; DUI; Drug Crimes; Felonies; Misdemeanors; Personal Injury; Automobile Accidents; Truck Accidents; Wrongful Death; Family Law; Divorce; Child Custody. ***Email:*** mcblaw@cox.net

McCOY LAW FIRM

120 N. ROBINSON, SUITE 1816
OKLAHOMA CITY, OKLAHOMA 73102
Telephone: 405-602-5405
Email: GloydMcCoy@coxinet.net

Criminal Trials and Appeals, Civil Rights Litigation and Appeals, Civil Litigation and Appeals, Habeas Corpus Litigation, Stock Market Arbitration.

GLOYD L. McCOY, born Lindsay, Oklahoma, July 4, 1956; admitted to bar, 1982, Oklahoma, U.S. District Court, Western, Eastern and Northern Districts of Oklahoma; U.S. Court of Appeals, Fifth and Tenth Circuits. *Education:* Central State University (B.A., 1978); University of Oklahoma (J.D., 1981). Instructor, Criminal Law and Appellate Procedure, Oklahoma Continuing Legal Education. Assistant Attorney General, Oklahoma, 1982-1983; Assistant Appellate Public Defender, 1985-1992; Appellate Indigent Defender, 1992-1993. *Member:* Oklahoma and American Bar Associations; Oklahoma Criminal Defense Lawyers Association; National Association of Criminal Defense Lawyers; Oklahoma Trial Lawyers Association. ***PRACTICE AREAS:*** Criminal Trials and Appeals; Civil Rights Litigation and Appeals; Civil Litigation and Appeals; Habeas Corpus Litigation.

McKINNEY & STRINGER

A PROFESSIONAL CORPORATION
Established in 1971
CORPORATE TOWER
101 NORTH ROBINSON
SUITE 1300
OKLAHOMA CITY, OKLAHOMA 73102-5510
Telephone: 405-239-6444
Telecopier: 405-239-7902
URL: http://www.McKinneyStringer.com

Tulsa, Oklahoma Office: Mid Continent Tower, 401 S. Boston, Suite 600. Telephone: 918-582-3176. Fax: 918-582-1403.

(This Listing Continued)

Litigation; Appellate Practice; Alternate Dispute Resolution; Administrative Law; Antitrust and Trade Regulation; Aviation Law; Bankruptcy; Banks and Banking; Business Law; Civil Rights; Commercial Law; Computer and Technology Issues; Corporate Law; Mergers and Acquisitions; Energy; Oil and Gas Law; Environmental Law; Government Agency Practice; Health Care; Immigration Law; Insurance; Intellectual Property; Trademarks; Patent Litigation; Labor and Employment; Workers Compensation; Medical Malpractice; Personal Injury; Toxic Torts; Products Liability; Probate; Real Estate; Securities Law; Taxation; Trusts and Estates; Wills.

FIRM PROFILE: Since its founding in 1971, McKinney & Stringer has grown into a multi-specialty firm serving clients in a wide range of business, industries and interest on both a local and national scale. Now one of Oklahoma's largest firms, McKinney and Stringer has continued to steadily expand not only the number of attorneys and professional support staff, but also the diversity of its practice areas, breadth of its client base, and the geographical location of its resources.

McKinney & Stringer maintains offices in both Oklahoma City and Tulsa. Its major practice areas focus on all aspects of corporate law and business transactions; intellectual property law; complex business litigation; insurance defense, product liability and personal injury law; environmental law; energy law and employment law. McKinney & Stringer provides clients, from individuals to large national corporations, with a full service law firm - a firm that combines up-to-date technological resources and a professional support staff with dedicated attorneys who are experienced in virtually every dimension of the legal profession. The firm has built its reputation on the pursuit of innovative, practical and cost-effective solutions for its clients' legal and business problems, and remains committed to this goal.

DIRECTORS

KENNETH N. McKINNEY, born Enid, Oklahoma, February 13, 1936; admitted to bar, 1962, Oklahoma. *Education:* University of Oklahoma (B.S., 1959; LL.B., 1962). ***PRACTICE AREAS:*** Civil Litigation; Environmental Law; Securities Law; Complex Business Law. ***Email:*** McKinneyK@McKinneyStringer.com

N. MARTIN STRINGER, born Hagley, England, June 6, 1940; admitted to bar, 1964, Oklahoma. *Education:* University of Oklahoma (B.S., 1961; LL.B., 1964). ***PRACTICE AREAS:*** Securities Law; Corporate Law; Banking Law; Complex Business Law. ***Email:*** StringerM@McKinneyStringer.com

GEORGE D. DAVIS, born Oklahoma City, Oklahoma, August 15, 1944; admitted to bar, 1971, Oklahoma. *Education:* Oklahoma State University (B.A., 1966); University of Oklahoma (J.D., 1971). ***PRACTICE AREAS:*** Insurance Defense Law; Natural Resources Litigation; Architectural and Engineering Malpractice Law. ***Email:*** DavisG@McKinneyStringer.com

DAVID A. CHEEK, born Oklahoma City, Oklahoma, June 22, 1948; admitted to bar, 1974, Oklahoma. *Education:* Trinity University (B.A., 1970); University of Oklahoma (J.D., 1974). ***PRACTICE AREAS:*** Commercial Law; Business Litigation; Bankruptcy; Oil and Gas Litigation; Contracts; Debtor and Creditor. ***Email:*** CheekD@McKinneyStringer.com

RONALD L. WALKER, born Enid, Oklahoma, December 10, 1953; admitted to bar, 1979, Oklahoma. *Education:* Phillips University (B.A., 1976); University of Oklahoma (J.D., 1979). ***PRACTICE AREAS:*** Personal Injury Law; Bad Faith Law; Environmental Litigation; Insurance Litigation; Class Action Litigation; Products Liability; Torts; Federal Civil Litigation; Antitrust. ***Email:*** WalkerR@McKinneyStringer.com

ROBERT D. TOMLINSON, born Anadarko, Oklahoma, September 27, 1946; admitted to bar, 1975, Oklahoma. *Education:* Oklahoma State University (B.S., 1969; M.S., 1969); Oklahoma City University (J.D., 1975). General Counsel, The Charles Machine Works, 1975-1982. ***PRACTICE AREAS:*** Products Liability; Environmental Litigation; Business Litigation; Intellectual Property Litigation; Antitrust; Professional Liability. ***Email:*** TomlinsonR@McKinneyStringer.com

ROBERT L. ROARK, born Austin, Texas, November 20, 1945; admitted to bar, 1975, Oklahoma. *Education:* Oklahoma State University (B.S., 1968); University of Oklahoma (J.D., 1975). Assistant City Attorney, Tulsa, Oklahoma, 1978-1980. ***PRACTICE AREAS:*** Environmental Litigation; Business Litigation; Corporate Litigation; Contract Litigation. ***Email:*** RoarkR@McKinneyStringer.com

MARY E. NELSON, born Arkansas City, Kansas, November 10, 1960; admitted to bar, 1986, Oklahoma. *Education:* University of Oklahoma (B.A., with highest honors, 1983; J.D., with distinction, 1986). ***PRACTICE AREAS:*** Complex Business Litigation; Environmental Law; Anti-Trust, Oil and Gas. ***Email:*** NelsonM@McKinneyStringer.com

DAVID A. WALLS, born Amarillo, Texas, October 13, 1958; admitted to bar, 1988, Oklahoma. *Education:* Baylor University; University of Texas (B.B.A., 1981); Oklahoma City University (J.D., 1987). ***PRACTICE AREAS:*** Business Litigation; Insurance Litigation; Environmental Litigation; Products Liability; Personal Injury. ***Email:*** WallsD@McKinneyStringer.com

PHILIP B. SEARS, born Rockville Center, New York, August 21, 1948; admitted to bar, 1977, Oklahoma. *Education:* Pennsylvania State University (B.S., 1970); Oklahoma City University (J.D., 1976). [1st Lt., U.S. Army, 1970-1972]. ***PRACTICE AREAS:*** Corporate Law; Securities Law. ***Email:*** SearsP@McKinneyStringer.com

CONNIE M. WOLFE, born Seattle, Washington, October 2, 1965; admitted to bar, 1991, Oklahoma. *Education:* Central State University (B.S., 1987); University of Oklahoma (J.D., 1991). ***PRACTICE AREAS:*** Personal Injury; Insurance Defense; Workers Compensation. ***Email:*** WolfeC@McKinneyStringer.com

RICHARD J. HARRIS, born Oklahoma City, Oklahoma, October 6, 1965; admitted to bar, 1995, Oklahoma. *Education:* Oklahoma State University (B.S., with honors, 1987); Cornell University (J.D., magna cum laude, 1994). ***PRACTICE AREAS:*** Insurance Defense; Commercial Litigation; Employment Law; General Civil Litigation. ***Email:*** HarrisR@McKinneyStringer.com

(This Listing Continued)

JEFFERSON I. RUST, born Miami, Florida, November 18, 1957; admitted to bar, 1995, Oklahoma. *Education:* Winthrop University (B.S., 1981); Oklahoma City University (J.D., summa cum laude, 1995). ***PRACTICE AREAS:*** Employment Law; Civil Rights; Business Litigation. ***Email:*** RustJ@McKinneyStringer.com

JAMES L. CRUMPLEY, born Norwalk, California, November 4, 1964; admitted to bar, 1995, Oklahoma. *Education:* Oklahoma Christian College (B.S., Accounting, 1986); Oklahoma City University (J.D., summa cum laude, 1995). Certified Public Accountant, 1989. ***PRACTICE AREAS:*** Corporate Law; Taxation; Estate Planning; Mergers and Acquisitions; Employee Benefit Taxation; Nonprofit Organizations. ***Email:*** CrumpleyJ@McKinneyStringer.com

SEAN V. O'CONNELL, born Bridgeport, Connecticut, August 27, 1966; admitted to bar, 1997, Oklahoma; registered to practice before U.S. Patent and Trademark Office. *Education:* University of Notre Dame (B.S.E.E., 1988); University of Nebraska (M.S.C.S., 1993); Creighton University (J.D., cum laude, 1997). [Captain, USAF, 1989-1994]. ***PRACTICE AREAS:*** Patents; Trademark; Copyright; Intellectual Property Litigation; Patent Litigation. ***Email:*** OConnellS@McKinneyStringer.com

TOBY M. McKINSTRY, born Lubbock, Texas, June 10, 1972; admitted to bar, 1998, Oklahoma. *Education:* Texas Tech University (B.S., 1994); Oklahoma City University (J.D., 1997). ***PRACTICE AREAS:*** Insurance Defense; Business Litigation; Products Liability; Business Torts; Insurance Bad Faith; Environmental Litigation; Personal Injury. ***Email:*** McKinstryT@McKinneyStringer.com

J. DEREK HARDBERGER, born Oklahoma City, Oklahoma, July 25, 1968; admitted to bar, 1994, Oklahoma. *Education:* University of Oklahoma (B.B.A., 1991); University of Tulsa (J.D., 1994); George Washington University National Law Center (LL.M., 1995). ***PRACTICE AREAS:*** Environmental; Regulatory; Administrative; Corporate Litigation. ***Email:*** HardbergerJ@McKinneyStringer.com

OF COUNSEL

J. DERRILL CODY, born Ada, Oklahoma, July 5, 1938; admitted to bar, 1964, Oklahoma. *Education:* East Central State College (B.A., 1960); University of Oklahoma (LL.B., 1964). Phi Delta Phi. Member, Board of Directors: Texas Eastern Products Pipeline Co., 1990—; Plains Petroleum Company, 1990-1995; Barnett Resources Corporation, 1995—. ***PRACTICE AREAS:*** Natural Resources Law; Oil and Gas Law. ***Email:*** CodyD@McKinneyStringer.com

CHARLES C. GREEN, born Ada, Oklahoma, July 4, 1934; admitted to bar, 1958, Oklahoma. *Education:* University of Oklahoma (B.A., 1956; LL.B., 1958). ***PRACTICE AREAS:*** Business Litigation; Administrative Law; Regulatory Law; Real Estate Law. ***Email:*** GreenC@McKinneyStringer.com

JAY L. JONES, born Ada, Oklahoma, 1966; admitted to bar, 1994, Oklahoma. *Education:* University of Oklahoma (B.F.A., 1990); University of Oklahoma (J.D., 1993). ***PRACTICE AREAS:*** Labor and Employment; Workers Compensation. ***Email:*** JonesJ@Mckinneystringer.com

PHILIP L. (LARRY) SAVAGE, born Oklahoma City, Oklahoma, April 6, 1938; admitted to bar, 1964, Oklahoma. *Education:* Dartmouth College (B.A., 1960; M.B.A., 1961); University of Oklahoma (LL.B., 1964). ***PRACTICE AREAS:*** Securities Law; Oil and Gas Law; Real Estate Law; Corporations Law. ***Email:*** SavageL@McKinneyStringer.com

ROBERT C. THOMPSON, born Oklahoma City, Oklahoma, December 13, 1947; admitted to bar, 1975, Oklahoma. *Education:* Southwestern Oklahoma State University (B.S., 1970); University of Oklahoma (J.D., 1975). City Attorney: City of Harrah, 1978; Nicoma Park, 1980. [U.S. Army, 1970-1972]. ***PRACTICE AREAS:*** Commercial Law; Banking Law; Real Estate Law; Municipal Law; Business Litigation. ***Email:*** ThompsonR@McKinneyStringer.com

A. MICHELLE CAMPNEY, born Tahlequah, Oklahoma, January 5, 1963; admitted to bar, 1988, Oklahoma. *Education:* University of Oklahoma (B.B.A., 1984); University of Oklahoma (J.D., 1988). ***PRACTICE AREAS:*** Business Litigation; Insurance Defense; Constitutional Law; Intellectual Property Litigation; Antitrust Litigation. ***Email:*** CampneyM@McKinneyStringer.com

AMIR M. FARZANEH, born Tehran, Iran, June 6, 1963; admitted to bar, 1996, Oklahoma 2002, Texas. *Education:* University of Oklahoma (B.S., Nuclear Medicine, 1988; M.S., Health Administration, 1990); Oklahoma City University Law School (J.D., 1995). ***PRACTICE AREAS:*** Immigration Law. ***Email:*** FarzanehA@Mckinneystringer.com

ASSOCIATES

KEITH D. TRACY, born Sayre, Oklahoma, January 10, 1971; admitted to bar, 1996, Oklahoma. *Education:* Oklahoma State University (B.A., 1993); Oklahoma City University (J.D., with honors, 1996). Intern Judge Tim Leonard, U.S. District Court, Western District of Oklahoma, 1995; Justice Marian P. Opala, Oklahoma Supreme Court, 1995. Adjunct Professor, Evidence, Oklahoma City University School of Law. ***PRACTICE AREAS:*** Antitrust; Aviation Litigation; Business Litigation; Business Torts; Class Action Litigation; Complex and Multi-District Litigation; Energy Litigation; False Claims Act; Intellectual Property Litigation; Federal Civil Litigation; Oil and Gas Litigation; Nonprofit Organizations Law; Patent Infringement; Patent Litigation; Product Liability Litigation; Amateur Sports Law. ***Email:*** TracyK@McKinneyStringer.com

CODY J. McPHERSON, born Purcell, Oklahoma, August 23, 1977; admitted to bar, 2004, Oklahoma. *Education:* University of Oklahoma (B.A., with distinction, 2001); Oklahoma City University School of Law (J.D., magna cum laude, 2004). Phi Delta Phi, Phi Kappa Phi, Merit Scholar. The Honorable Phil E. Daugherty Memorial Scholarship. ***PRACTICE AREAS:*** Business Litigation; Commercial Litigation. ***Email:*** McPhersonC@Mckinneystringer.com

JOHN P. FALCONE, born Bellerose, New York, November 14, 1971; admitted to bar, 1996, New Jersey; 1997, New York; 1999, Oklahoma. *Education:* State University of New York at Albany (B.A., 1993); Fordham University (J.D., 1996). ***PRACTICE AREAS:*** Business Litigation. ***Email:*** FalconeJ@McKinneyStringer.com

(This Listing Continued)

LAWRENCE F. GRABLE, born Fort Bragg, North Carolina, July 19, 1974; admitted to bar, 2001, Oklahoma; registered to practice before U.S. Patent and Trademark Office. *Education:* Northeastern Oklahoma State University (B.S., 1997); University of Tulsa College of Law (J.D., 2001). ***PRACTICE AREAS:*** Patent; Trademark; Copyright. ***Email:*** grablel@mckinneystringer.com

RANDY J. GRAU, born Aurora, Colorado, December 3, 1975; admitted to bar, 2001, Oklahoma. *Education:* Pepperdine University School of Law (B.A., 1998); University of Oklahoma at Norman (J.D., 2001). ***PRACTICE AREAS:*** General Business Litigation; Labor and Employment; Commercial Law. ***Email:*** graur@mckinneystringer.com

LANCE E. SCHNEITER, born Shawnee, Oklahoma; admitted to bar, 2002, Oklahoma. *Education:* University of Central Oklahoma (B.A., Psychology, 1999); University of Oklahoma (J.D., 2002). ***PRACTICE AREAS:*** Business Litigation. ***Email:*** SchneiterL@Mckinneystringer.com

SHANNON L. FERRELL, born Stillwater, Oklahoma, November 4, 1975; admitted to bar, 2003, Oklahoma. *Education:* Oklahoma State University (B.A., 1998; M.A., 2001); Oklahoma City University School of Law (Certificate in Business Law and Financial Services; J.D., summa cum laude, 2003). ***PRACTICE AREAS:*** Environmental Law. ***Email:*** FerrellS@Mckinneystringer.com

BENJAMIN E. RUSS, born Dallas, Texas, May 7, 1974; admitted to bar, 2004, Oklahoma. *Education:* Oklahoma State University (B.S., Finance, 1996); Oklahoma City University School of Law (J.D., 2004). Phi Delta Phi. ***PRACTICE AREAS:*** Insurance Litigation; Personal Injury; Insurance Defense; Commercial Litigation; Insurance Coverage. ***Email:*** RussB@Mckinneystringer.com

REGINA M. MARSH, born Lawton, Oklahoma, 1970; admitted to bar, 2004, Oklahoma. *Education:* Oklahoma City University (B.S., magna cum laude, 1994); University of Oklahoma (J.D., with honors, 2004). Intern to Vice-Chief Justice Marion P. Opala. ***PRACTICE AREAS:*** Labor and Employment; Employment Law; Litigation; Business Law; Labor Law. ***Email:*** MarshR@Mckinneystringer.com

MELISSA M. CHASE, born Rochester, New York, November 10, 1969; admitted to bar, 2000, Oklahoma. *Education:* University of Central Florida (B.A., 1995); Regent University School of Law (J.D., 2000). ***PRACTICE AREAS:*** Immigration Law. ***Email:*** ChaseM@Mckinneystringer.com

REPRESENTATIVE CLIENTS: Allstate Insurance Company; American Airlines; Amateur Softball Association; AT&T/Lucent Technologies; Allied Waste Systems, Inc.; Bank of Oklahoma, N.A.; Bank One, Oklahoma, N.A.; Black & Decker, Inc.; Calpine; Duke Energy Corp.; Emerson Electric Co.; Express Personnel Services; Financial Network Investment Corp.; First Fidelity Bank, N.A.; Foundation Health System, Inc.; Frankfurt-Short-Bruza Assoc.; Holcim, Inc.; Kerr-McGee Corporation; M-D Building Products, Inc.; Mercy Health Center, Inc.; Michelin North America, Inc.; Microsoft Corporation, MidFirst Bank; Nanobiomagnetics, Inc.; National Bank of Commerce; National Cowboy & Western Heritage Museum; Northland Insurance Co.; Oklahoma Cardiovascular Associates; Mutual of Omaha Insurance Co.; Oklahoma Farmers Union; Oklahoma Foundation for Digestive Research; Oklahoma Foundation for Cardiovascular Research; Oklahoma Heart Hospital; Philip Morris Inc.; Ridley Motorcycle Company; Robert S. & Grayce B. Kerr Foundation; Safeco Insurance Company; Stage Stores, Inc.; State Auto Insurance Companies; Terra Nitrogen Corporation; Teneska, Inc.; The Charles Machine Works, Inc.; The Goodyear Tire & Rubber Company; The Samuel Roberts Noble Foundation, Inc.; W. H. Braum, Inc.; Weather-Tite, Inc.; York International Corp.

MARGARET McMORROW-LOVE

228 ROBERT S. KERR AVENUE
SUITE 540
OKLAHOMA CITY, OKLAHOMA 73102
Telephone: 405-235-3848
Facsimile: 405-235-3863
Email: mcmorrowlove@sbcglobal.net

Civil Rights Law, Employment Law, Litigation, Municipal Law, Products Liability and General Civil Practice.

MARGARET McMORROW-LOVE, born Weymouth, Massachusetts, June 6, 1951; admitted to bar, 1977, Oklahoma. *Education:* Trinity College (B.A., magna cum laude, 1973) Phi Beta Kappa; University of Oklahoma (J.D., 1977). Order of the Coif. Editor, Oklahoma Law Review, 1975-1977. *Member:* Oklahoma and American Bar Associations.

REPRESENTATIVE CLIENTS: Oklahoma Municipal League; Oklahoma Municipal Assurance Group; Advance Food Company; Oklahoma Farmers Union Mutual Insurance Company; National American Insurance Company; City of Shawnee; City of Warr Acres; City of Altus; City of Prague; City of Oklahoma City; Southern Oklahoma Development Authority; Independent School District No. 89; City of Crescent.

JOHN C. McMURRY, P.C.

SUITE 215, 301 NORTH HARVEY
OKLAHOMA CITY, OKLAHOMA 73102
Telephone: 405-236-0038
Fax: 405-232-5010
Email: jcmcmurry@sbcglobal.net

Civil Trials and Appeals. Trials in all State and Federal Courts.

JOHN C. McMURRY, born Sentinel, Oklahoma, June 18, 1944; admitted to bar, 1971, Oklahoma and Kansas. *Education:* Washington & Lee University (B.A., 1966); University of Oklahoma (J.D., 1971). Phi Delta Phi. Editor, Oklahoma Law Review, 1969-1971. *Member:* Oklahoma County, Kansas, Oklahoma and American Bar Associations; Oklahoma Trial Lawyers Association; The Association of Trial Lawyers of America. ***REPORTED CASES:*** United States ex rel. King v. Hillcrest Health Center, Inc., 264 F.3d 1271 (10th Cir. 2001); Oklahoma Radio Associates v. FDIC, 987 F.2d 685 (10th Cir. 1993); Heggy v. Heggy, 944 F.2d 1537 (10th Cir. 1991); Taylor v. Gilmartin, 686 F.2d 1346 (10th Cir. 1982); Hackney v. Newman Memorial Hospital, Inc., 621 F.2d 1069 (10th Cir. 1980); In re Longhorn Securities Litigation, 573 F.Supp. 255 (W.D. Okla. 1983); In re Longhorn Securities Litigation, 573 F.Supp. 274 (W.D. Okla. 1983); In re Longhorn Securities Liti-

(This Listing Continued)

JOHN C. McMURRY, P.C., Oklahoma City—Continued

gation, 573 F.Supp. 278 (W.D. Okla. 1983); Hutson v. Sureddi, 2002 OK CIV APP 28, 41 P.3d 993. ***Email:*** jcmcmurry@sbcglobal.net

MEE, MEE & HOGE

A Professional Limited Liability Partnership
50 PENN PLACE, SUITE 1400
1900 NORTHWEST EXPRESSWAY
OKLAHOMA CITY, OKLAHOMA 73118
Telephone: 405-848-9100
Fax: 405-848-9101
Email: E-mail@meehoge.com
URL: http://www.lawyers.com/meehoge

Civil Litigation, Creditor Collections and Bankruptcy, Financial Institution Defense, Real Estate, Contracts, Commercial Law, Business Organizations and Transactions, Estate and Charitable Planning, Tax Law, Wills, Trusts and Probate.

JOHN W. MEE, JR., born Oklahoma City, Oklahoma, September 11, 1939; admitted to bar, 1964, Oklahoma. *Education:* University of Oklahoma (B.A., 1961; LL.B., 1964); New York University (LL.M., in Taxation, 1967). Phi Alpha Delta. Editor, Oklahoma Law Review, 1963-1964. Fellow, Kenneson Foundation, New York University; Fellow, American College of Trust and Estate Counsel. Faculty, Oklahoma Bar Review (Wills and Estates). Past President, Oklahoma Planning Giving Council. Director and Past Chairman, Advisory Board, Salvation Army. Director, Christian Leadership Foundation of Oklahoma City. Elder, First Presbyterian Church of Edmond. *Member:* Oklahoma County, Oklahoma and American Bar Associations; National Academy of Elder Law Attorneys. [1st Lt., U.S. Army, 1964-1966]. ***PRACTICE AREAS:*** Estate and Gift Taxation; Estate and Trust Administration; Tax Planning; Probate; Charitable Tax Planning; Tax Exempt Organizations; Business Organizations and Transactions; Real Estate Transactions. ***Email:*** jwmjr@meehoge.com

JOHN W. MEE, III, born Pittsburgh, Pennsylvania, August 10, 1965; admitted to bar, 1990, Oklahoma and U.S. District Court, Eastern, Western and Northern Districts of Oklahoma. *Education:* University of Oklahoma (B.B.A., with distinction, 1987; J.D., 1990). Beta Gamma Sigma; Phi Delta Phi. *Member:* Oklahoma and American Bar Associations. ***PRACTICE AREAS:*** Business Litigation; Creditor Representation; Secured Transactions; Bankruptcy; Corporate Law; Real Estate. ***Email:*** jwm3@meehoge.com

ARTHUR F. HOGE III, born Ft. Smith, Arkansas, 1953; admitted to bar, 1981, Oklahoma. *Education:* Westminster College (B.A., 1975); Southern Methodist University (J.D., cum laude, 1981). Omicron Delta Kappa; Phi Mu Epsilon; Phi Delta Phi; Order of the Coif. Exxon Scholar. Executive Editor, Southwestern Law Journal, 1980-1981. Board Member and Executive Committee Member, Integris Baptist Medical Center Foundation. Chairman, Integris Planned Giving Council. President and Chairman, International Board of Directors, Phi Delta Theta Fraternity, 2000-2002. Past President, Kiwanis Club of Oklahoma City. General Counsel: Sigma Nu Fraternity, Inc.; Fraternity Information and Programming Group, Inc. (FIPG); Delta Delta Delta National House Corporation. *Member:* Oklahoma County, Oklahoma and American Bar Associations; Oklahoma City Estate Planning Council. ***PRACTICE AREAS:*** Civil Litigation; Employment Litigation; Trust Litigation; Estate Litigation; Probate; Fraternity Liability; Estate Planning; Charitable Giving; Trust Administration; Tax Planning; Creditors Rights; Ad Valorem Tax. ***Email:*** ahoge@meehoge.com

---

BRINDA K. WHITE, born Shattuck, Oklahoma, September 18, 1951; admitted to bar, 1982, Oklahoma and U.S. District Court, Western District of Oklahoma; 1984, U.S. Court of Appeals, Tenth Circuit; 1994, U.S. District Court, Northern District of Oklahoma. *Education:* Northwestern State College (B.A. Ed., with high honors, 1973); University of Oklahoma (M.Ed., 1974; Ph.D., 1978; J.D., 1982). Order of the Coif. Law Clerk, U.S. District Judge, Lee R. West, 1982-1983. Chief Judge, William J. Holloway, Jr., Tenth Circuit Court of Appeals, 1983-1985. *Member:* Oklahoma and American Bar Associations; Ruth Bader Ginsburg American Inn of Court (Master). ***PRACTICE AREAS:*** Civil Litigation; Appellate Practice; Probate; Estate Planning; Business Transactions. ***Email:*** bkw@meehoge.com

JOSHUA CLARK GREENHAW, born Chattanooga, Tennessee, October 21, 1973; admitted to bar, 2001, Oklahoma. *Education:* University of Oklahoma (B., Architecture, 1997; J.D., 2001). *Member:* Tulsa County, Oklahoma and American Bar Associations; American Trial Lawyers Association. ***PRACTICE AREAS:*** Commercial Litigation; Real Estate; Bankruptcy. ***Email:*** jcg@meehoge.com

MENDROS LAW OFFICE, PLLC

d/b/a Mendros & Stout
THE HIGHTOWER BUILDING
105 N. HUDSON, SUITE 540
OKLAHOMA CITY, OKLAHOMA 73102
Telephone: 405-605-8639; 405-408-1561
Fax: 405-605-8640
URL: http://www.jayemendros.com
Email: jayemendros@cox.net
URL: http://www.mendroslawoffice.com

Mailing Address: PO Box 1725, Oklahoma City, OK 73101-1725

Criminal Defense, DUI/DWI, Drug Crimes, Homicide, Juvenile Crimes, Appeals.

FIRM PROFILE: With over a decade's worth of experience in Criminal Law, this office provides quality, experienced representation on all State felony and misdemeanor charges, from homicide to DUI. Our practice is focused on criminal defense. We are dedicated to finding the best possible resolution to our clients' legal difficulties.

(This Listing Continued)

JAYE MENDROS, born Portland, Maine, November 1, 1970; admitted to bar, 1994, Oklahoma. *Education:* University of Oklahoma (B.A., 1991; J.D., 1994). Order of the Coif. Order of the Barristers. Note Editor, Oklahoma Law Review, 1993-1994. Recipient: Civil Libertarian Award, 1994; Salem Civil Rights Award, 1994. Member, American Inns of Court, 1993-1994. Author: Note, "Morgan v Illinois Takes a Step Toward Eliminating Hanging Juries in Capital Cases," Oklahoma Law Review, 1994. Oklahoma County Public Defender's Office, general felony division, 1995-1997. Oklahoma Court of Criminal Appeals, Judicial Assistant to Charles S. Chapel, 1994-1995, 1997-2000. Oklahoma Indigent Defense System DNA and Capital Trial Divisions 2000-2002, Private Practice 2002—. *Member:* Oklahoma Bar Association (Member, Criminal Defense Section; Appellate Section); Oklahoma Criminal Defense Lawyers Association; Oklahoma County Criminal Defense Lawyers Association; National Criminal Defense Lawyer's Association. ***LANGUAGES:*** Greek, French. ***REPORTED CASES:*** US v. Rice; State v. Childress. ***PRACTICE AREAS:*** Criminal Defense. ***Email:*** jayemendros@cox.net

Languages: Greek and French.

MERRITT & ASSOCIATES, P.C.

917 NORTH ROBINSON
P.O. BOX 1377
OKLAHOMA CITY, OKLAHOMA 73101
Telephone: 405-236-2222
Nationwide Toll Free: 1-800-690-2277
Fax: 405-232-8630
URL: http://www.merrittfirm.com
Email: referralattorney@merrittfirm.com
URL: http://www.lawyers.com/merritt&associatespc

Houston, Texas Office: 10101 Southwest Freeway, Suite 400. Telephone: 713-690-77074; 1-800-690-2277.

Practice Limited to Personal Injury Law, including Products Liability, Medical Malpractice, Aviation Litigation, Truck Accidents, Fires and Explosions.

JOHN M. MERRITT, born Fletcher, Oklahoma, June 25, 1938; admitted to bar, 1968, Oklahoma; 1972, U.S. District Court, Western District of Oklahoma; 1975, U.S. Court of Appeals, 5th and 10th Circuits; 1984, U.S. Supreme Court; 1987, Michigan, Pennsylvania and Texas. *Education:* Oklahoma City University (LL.B., 1968). Editor, Product Liability Column of The Advocate, 1982—. *Member:* Oklahoma, Pennsylvania and American Bar Associations; State Bar of Michigan; State Bar of Texas; Oklahoma Trial Lawyers Association (Director, 1984—); The Association of Trial Lawyers of America; American Board of Trial Advocates. (Certified as a Civil Trial Advocate by the National Board of Trial Advocacy). ***PRACTICE AREAS:*** Personal Injury; Products Liability; Medical Malpractice; Aviation; Toxic Torts. ***Email:*** john.merritt@merrittfirm.com

---

MICHAEL M. BLUE, born Denver, Colorado, December 29, 1962; admitted to bar, 1989, Oklahoma, U.S. District Court, Northern, Eastern and Western Districts of Oklahoma, District of Colorado, Northern, Southern and Eastern Districts of Texas and Eastern District of Michigan, U.S. Court of Appeals, Third, Eighth and Tenth Circuits and U.S. Supreme Court. *Education:* University of Oklahoma (B.A., 1985); Oklahoma City University (J.D., 1989). Author: The Advocate Journal, Evidence Section, Oklahoma Trial Lawyer's Association. *Member:* Oklahoma and American Bar Associations; Oklahoma Trial Lawyers Association (Vice Chair, Amicus Curiae Committee, 1998; Member, Advisory Board, 1998—); The Association of Trial Lawyers of America.

ANTHONY D. PHELPS, born Oklahoma City, Oklahoma, June 5, 1963; admitted to bar, 1994, Oklahoma and U.S. District Court, Western, Eastern and Southern Districts of Oklahoma. *Education:* University of Oklahoma (B.A., English, 1991; J.D., 1994). Phi Delta Phi, Phi Alpha Delta. Member, 1992 and Chief Article Editor, 1993-1994, Oklahoma Law Review. Member, Historian Golden Key Honor Society, 1989-1991. *Member:* Oklahoma County and Oklahoma Bar Associations; Association of Trial Lawyers of America; Oklahoma Trial Lawyers Association; Defense Research Institute. ***PRACTICE AREAS:*** Personal Injury; Products Liability; Medical Malpractice.

BARBARA ANNE MERRITT, born Oklahoma City, Oklahoma, October 1, 1952; admitted to bar, 1990, Oklahoma and U.S. District Court, Northern, Eastern and Western Districts of Oklahoma. *Education:* University of Oklahoma (B.S.,1974; M.Ed., 1975); Oklahoma City University School of Law (J.D., 1990). Asssistant Dean, School of Law, Oklahoma City University, 1993-1996. Associate Director, Law Alumni Relations and Law Development, Oklahoma City University, 1992-1993. *Member:* Oklahoma Bar Association.

KATHLEEN J. ADLER, born Seattle, Washington, December 9, 1947; admitted to bar, 1983, Oklahoma and U.S. District Court, Western, Eastern and Northern Districts of Oklahoma. *Education:* University of Oklahoma (B.A., with distinction, 1980; J.D., 1983). Phi Beta Kappa; Kappa Tau Alpha; Delta Theta Phi. Member, National Moot Court Team, 1982. *Member:* Oklahoma County, Canadian County and Oklahoma Bar Associations; Oklahoma Association of Defense Counsel; International Aviation Womens Association. ***PRACTICE AREAS:*** Aviation Law; Products Liability Law; Insurance Defense Law.

M.R. MEYERS & ASSOCIATES, P.C.

Established in 1993
3421 N.W. 50TH STREET
OKLAHOMA CITY, OKLAHOMA 73112
Telephone: 405-843-6000
1-800-293-7472
Fax: 405-604-0329
Email: mrobles-kropp@coxinet.net

Employee Benefits, Retirement Plans, ERISA.

(This Listing Continued)

MARIA ROBLES MEYERS, admitted to bar, 1988, Oklahoma, U.S. District Court, Northern and Western Districts of Oklahoma and U.S. Court of Appeals, Tenth Circuit. *Education:* University of San Francisco (B.S., with honors, 1976); University of Oklahoma School of Law (J.D., with honors, 1988). Order of the Coif. Certified Public Accountant: California, 1980; Oklahoma, 1990. Adjunct Professor, Oklahoma City University. *Member:* Oklahoma County, Oklahoma and American Bar Associations; Oklahoma Society of Certified Public Accountants; American Institute of Certified Public Accountants. ***LANGUAGES:*** Spanish. ***PRACTICE AREAS:*** Employee Benefits; Retirement Planning; ERISA.

MILLER DOLLARHIDE

A PROFESSIONAL CORPORATION

100 PARK AVENUE, SECOND FLOOR

OKLAHOMA CITY, OKLAHOMA 73102-8099

Telephone: 405-236-8541

Facsimile: 405-235-8130

URL: http://www.millerdollarhide.com

General Civil, Trial and Appellate Practice in all State and Federal Courts. Banking, Estate Planning, Negligence, Personal Injury, Probate, Real Estate, Corporation, Trusts, Business Entity, Employment Law, Insurance Defense.

FIRM PROFILE: Miller Dollarhide is a full-service law firm and has an active civil litigation practice representing both plaintiffs and defendants. The majority of the Firm's litigation involves commercial/business litigation, employment matters, insurance defense, healthcare issues (including medical malpractice defense), insurance coverage and bad faith, personal injury and probate disputes. We also have a successful appellate practice.

ELIZABETH RILEY CASTLEBERRY, born Oklahoma City, Oklahoma, June 25, 1958; admitted to bar, 1983, Oklahoma, U.S. District Court, Northern, Eastern and Western Districts of Oklahoma and U.S. Court of Appeals, Tenth Circuit. *Education:* Oklahoma State University (B.S., 1980); University of Oklahoma (J.D., 1983). Recipient: Eugene E. Koontz Oxford Scholarship, 1982. Barrister, Luther Bohanon American Inn of Court, 1992-1994. *Member:* American Bar Associations. ***REPORTED CASES:*** Woolard v. JLG Industries, Inc., 210 F.3d 1158 (10th Cir. 2000); F.D.I.C. v. Appling, 992 F.2d 1109 (10th Cir. 1993); Smith v. Phillips, 881 F.2d 902 (10th Cir. 1989); Corder v. Oklahoma Medical Research Foundation, 1999 OK CIV APP 33, 980 P.2d 1122. ***PRACTICE AREAS:*** Employment Law; Civil Rights; Civil and Business Litigation. ***Email:*** ecastleberry@millerdollarhide.com

JACK S. DAWSON, born Bethany, Oklahoma, December 24, 1940; admitted to bar, 1972, Oklahoma. *Education:* Oklahoma University; Central State University; Oklahoma City University (J.D., 1972). Recipient, Oklahoma Bar Association Outstanding Law Student Award, Oklahoma City University, 1972. Certified: Arbitrator; Mediator; Advocate. *Member:* Oklahoma County (President, 1986-1987); Oklahoma (Member, Board of Governors, 1995-1997) and Federal (President, City Chapter, 1995) Bar Associations; Chief Master, Professional Responsibility Tribunal, 1993-1994. Founder, The Arbitration Forum. Master, American Inns of Court. [USNR, Capt., Ret.]. ***REPORTED CASES:*** First Tier Manufacturing Co. v. Investors Mortgage Insurance Co. 498 U.S. 269 (1991); Woolard v. JLG Industries, Inc. 210 F.3d 1158 (10th Cir. 2000); State ex rel. Oklahoma Bar Ass'n v. Harper, 2000 OK 6, 995 P.2d 1143; State ex rel. Oklahoma Bar Ass'n v. Upton, 1999 OK 92, 991 P.2d 544; Comer v. Preferred Risk Mut. Ins. Co., 1999 OK 86, 991 P.2d 1006. ***PRACTICE AREAS:*** Litigation. ***Email:*** jdawson@millerdollarhide.com

KIERAN D. MAYE, JR., born Brooklyn, New York, September 17, 1958; admitted to bar, 1985, Oklahoma; 1990, Texas. *Education:* Oklahoma State University (B.S., 1982); University of Oklahoma (J.D. with honors, 1985). Author: "Expert Testimony in Oklahoma after Kuhrno Tire Co. v. Carmichael," 70 OBAJ 3857, December 25, 1999; "Christian v. Gray, The Evolution of the Law of Expert Testimony in Oklahoma," 74 O.B.A.J. 2367, September 6, 2003. Adjunct Professor of Law, Oklahoma City University. Member, U.S. Judicial Conference for the Tenth Circuit. *Member:* American Bar Associations; State Bar of Texas. ***REPORTED CASES:*** Shadid v. Northern Automotive Co., 951 P.2d 1094 (OK. Civ. App. 1997); Cudd Pressure Control, Inc. v. Cornelius, 1996 WL122018 (10th Cir. 1996); State ex rel. Moshe Tal v. City of Oklahoma City, 2000 OK 70 —P.3d—. ***PRACTICE AREAS:*** Commercial Litigation; Federal Civil Litigation; Civil Litigation; Complex Litigation; Civil Appeals. ***Email:*** kdmaye@millerdollarhide.com

JAMES A. SCIMECA, born Tulsa, Oklahoma, February 5, 1960; admitted to bar, 1984, Oklahoma. *Education:* University of Oklahoma (B.A., 1981; J.D., 1984). *Member:* The Association of Trial Lawyers of America. ***REPORTED CASES:*** Barnes v. Oklahoma Farm Bureau Mutual Ins. Co., 2000 OK 55, 11 P. 3d 162; Smith v. Baptist Foundation of Oklahoma, 2002 OK 57, 50 P.3d 1132; Hall v. Globe Life & Accident Ins., 1999 OK 89, 998 P2d 603; Mutual Assurance Administrators v. U.S. Risk Underwriters, 1999 OK CIV APP 129, 983 P2d 795; Clements v. ITT Hartford Insurance, 1999 OK CIV APP 6, 973 P2d 902; Withiam v. Baptist Health Care of Oklahoma, 98 F.3d 581 (10th Cir. 1996); Berkeley Federal Bank & Trust v. Selby, 1998 OK CIV APP 102, 969 P.2d 369. ***PRACTICE AREAS:*** Appellate Practice; Civil Litigation; Employment Litigation; Insurance Coverage; Uninsured Motorist Insurance Coverage. ***Email:*** jscim@millerdollarhide.com

JAMES C. SHAW, born Sumter, South Carolina, January 25, 1949; admitted to bar, 1978, Oklahoma. *Education:* Presbyterian College (B.S., 1971); Georgia State University (M.P.A., 1974); University of South Carolina (J.D., 1978). Certified Public Accountant, Oklahoma, 1978. Author: "Mortgage Foreclosure Proceedings," Oklahoma Bar Association, Spring 1990; "Business Valuations Appellate Decisions in Oklahoma," Oklahoma Bar Journal, October 31, 1998. Chair, Savings and Loan Counsel Section, Oklahoma Bar Association, 1985. Commercial Arbitrator, American Arbitration Association. Member and Accredited in Business Valuations, American Institute of Certified Public Accountants. General Counsel: Baptist General Convention, Oklahoma; Oklahoma United Methodist Foundation, Inc. President, Oklahoma City Real Property Lawyers Association, 1994. ***REPORTED CASES:*** Sooner Federal Savings & Loan Asso. v. Smoot, 735 P.2d 555 (Okl. 1987). ***PRACTICE AREAS:*** Commercial Transactions; Real Estate; Estate Planning; Probate; Tax Exempt Organizations. ***Email:*** jcshaw@millerdollarhide.com

(This Listing Continued)

TSINENA BRUNO, born Oklahoma City, Oklahoma, October 12, 1960; admitted to bar, 1997, Oklahoma; U.S District Court, Northern, Eastern and Western Districts of Oklahoma; U.S. Court of Appeals, Tenth Circuit; U.S. Supreme Court. *Education:* Oklahoma City University (B.S., 1991; J.D., 1994). Phi Alpha Delta. Member, Moot Court Board. Co-Author: with David A. Kline, "Ethical Considerations in a Business Bankruptcy," Oklahoma Bar Association Ninth Annual Bankruptcy Seminar, December 9, 1994. Adjunct Professor, Bankruptcy and Federal Labor Law, Oklahoma City University, 1996-1997. ***PRACTICE AREAS:*** Bankruptcy; Family Law; Federal Employment Law. ***Email:*** tbruno@millerdollarhide.com

HOLLY M. HILLERMAN, born Oklahoma City, Oklahoma, December 14, 1970; admitted to bar, 1996, Oklahoma, U.S. District Court, Western District of Oklahoma and U.S. Court of Appeals, Tenth Circuit. *Education:* Oklahoma State University (B.A., 1993); University of Oklahoma College of Law (J.D., 1996). Phi Delta Phi. Co-Author: "Vernon's Oklahoma Forms, 2d: Criminal Law, Practice and Procedure," West Publishing, 1999; "McVeigh, McJustice, McMedia," U. Chi. Legal F.53, 1998. *Member:* Oklahoma Bar Association. ***PRACTICE AREAS:*** Civil Litigation. ***Email:*** hhillerman@millerdollarhide.com

RICHARD L. ROSE, born Oklahoma City, Oklahoma, July 20, 1969; admitted to bar, 2004, Oklahoma. *Education:* Southern Nazarene University (B.S., 2000); Oklahoma City University (J.D., magna cum laude, 2003). Phi Delta Phi; Order of the Barristers. *Member:* Oklahoma Bar Association; American Bar Association. ***PRACTICE AREAS:*** Litigation. ***Email:*** rrose@millerdollarhide.com

OF COUNSEL

CHARLES L. DOLLARHIDE, II, born Oklahoma City, Oklahoma, March 4, 1943; admitted to bar, 1974, Oklahoma, *Education:* Oklahoma State University (B.S., 1965); Oklahoma City University (J.D., 1974); Phillips Theological Seminary (M.Div., 1996). Recipient, Board of Governors Scholastic Award, Oklahoma City University, 1974. Continuing Legal Education Instructor and Author: "Administering The Estate of The Small Business Owner," Oklahoma Bar Association, 1995; "Conflicts of Interests for the Estate Planning Lawyer," Oklahoma City University, 1987-1989; "Revocable Trusts," Oklahoma City University, 1985-1986. ***PRACTICE AREAS:*** Probate; Trust Planning; Wills. ***Email:*** mdds@millerdollarhide.com

GEORGE MILLER, born Eufaula, Oklahoma, July 23, 1912; admitted to bar, 1938, Oklahoma. *Education:* Davidson College; University of Oklahoma (A.B., 1936; LL.B., 1938). Order of the Coif. Attorney, State School Land Commission, 1940-1942. Judge, Military Government Courts, Germany, 1946-1948. Special Attorney, Securities Commission of Oklahoma, 1958-1959. Appointed Special Justice, Oklahoma Supreme Court, November 19, 1956. *Member:* Oklahoma and American Bar Associations. [Captain of Field Artillery, U.S. Army, World War II]. ***PRACTICE AREAS:*** Probate.

ROBERT E. NORMAN, born Daytona Beach, Florida, August 10, 1965; admitted to bar, 1991, Oklahoma. *Education:* University of Oklahoma (B.A., 1987; J.D., 1991). Order of the Barristers. National Trial Team; National Appellate Advocacy Team. President, College of Law Board of Advocates, 1990-1991. *Member:* Oklahoma County, Oklahoma (Member, Young Lawyers Division Board of Directors, 1999-2002; Chair, High School Mock Trial Program, 1999) and American (Member, Employment Law and Litigation Sections) Bar Associations. ***REPORTED CASES:*** Flowers v. EZCorp., Inc., 307 F. Supp.2d 1191 (N.D. Okla. 2004); EEOC v. W.H. Braum Inc., 347 F.3d 1192 (10th Cir. 2003); Duffy v. Cope, 2000 OK CIV APP 140, 18 P.3d 366; K & K Food Services, Inc. v. S & H, Inc., 2000 OK 31, 3 P.3d 705; Fugate v. Mooney, 1998 OK CIV APP 48, 958 P.2d 818. ***PRACTICE AREAS:*** Employment Law (40%); Civil Litigation (40%); Consumer Credit (10%); Corporate Law (10%). ***Email:*** rnorman@millerdollarhide.com

All Directors and Associates of the Firm are Members of the Oklahoma County and Oklahoma Bar Associations.

REPRESENTATIVE CLIENTS: Baptist Foundation of Oklahoma; Baptist General Convention of Oklahoma; Baptist Retirement Centers of Oklahoma, Inc.; Chicago Title Insurance Co.; Chicksaw Holding Co., Inc. and its subsidiaries; Chicksaw Technolgy, Inc.; Country Companies Insurance; Ecology Management, Inc.; Executive Risk Insurance Co.; Finova Captial Corp.; Golden Eagle Golf and Country Club, Inc.; INTEGRIS Rural Health; Landmark Construction Group, Inc.; Oklahoma Medical Research Foundation; Oklahoma United Methodist Foundation; Red Rock Distributing Co.; Sabolich, Inc.; Stoldt-Stotts, Inc.

THE MILLS LAW FIRM, P.C.

Established in 1984

ROBINSON RENAISSANCE, SUITE 500

119 NORTH ROBINSON

OKLAHOMA CITY, OKLAHOMA 73102

Telephone: 405-239-2501

Fax: 405-239-2575

Email: attymail@millsfirm.com

General Civil Practice. Trials in all State and Federal Courts. Insurance Defense, Products Liability, Bad Faith, Civil Rights, Commercial Litigation, Uninsured Motorist Coverage, Employment Law, Professional Liability, Personal Injury, Insurance Coverage, Nursing Home Defense.

EARL D. MILLS, born Chalk, Texas, February 18, 1931; admitted to bar, 1959, Oklahoma; U.S. Supreme Court. *Education:* Central State University (B.S., 1951); University of Tulsa and Oklahoma City University (J.D., 1959). Listed in Best Lawyers in America. Master, American Inn of Court CV. Assistant County Attorney, Oklahoma County, 1961-1962. *Member:* Oklahoma County and Oklahoma Bar Associations; Federation of Insurance and Corporate Counsel; Oklahoma Association of Defense Counsel; American Board of Trial Advocates. Fellow: American College of Trial Lawyers; International Academy of Trial Lawyers; Trial Attorneys of America; Trucking Industry Defense Association. ***PRACTICE AREAS:*** Accidents; Personal Injury Law; Litigation; Products Liability Law; Insurance Defense; Trucking Defense.

(This Listing Continued)

THE MILLS LAW FIRM, P.C., Oklahoma City—Continued

ROBERT B. MILLS, born Oklahoma City, Oklahoma, June 19, 1957; admitted to bar, 1982, Oklahoma; 1998, Texas. *Education:* University of Oklahoma (B.A., 1979; J.D., 1982). *Member:* Oklahoma County and Oklahoma Bar Associations; Oklahoma Association of Defense Counsel; Defense Research Institute. ***PRACTICE AREAS:*** Insurance Coverage Law; Insurance Defense; Civil Trial Practice; Personal Injury Law; Uninsured Motorist Law; Product Liability Law; Employment Law; Insurance Bad Faith; Civil Rights; Trucking Defense. ***Email:*** bob@millsfirm.com

W. WAYNE MILLS, born Stillwater, Oklahoma, August 3, 1954; admitted to bar, 1983, Oklahoma; 1997, Texas. *Education:* Central State University (B.A., 1980); Oklahoma State University; Oklahoma City University (J.D., 1983). *Member:* Oklahoma County and Oklahoma Bar Associations; Oklahoma Association of Defense Counsel; Trucking Industry Defense Association; Federation of Insurance and Corporate Counsel. (Also with W. Wayne Mills & Associates, P.C.). ***PRACTICE AREAS:*** Accidents; Personal Injury Law; Products Liability Law; Environmental Law; Insurance Bad Faith; Nursing Home Defense; Civil Rights; Insurance Defense; Civil Trial Practice; Trucking Defense. ***Email:*** wayne@millsfirm.com

---

MARGARET K. MYERS, born Dallas, Texas, July 13, 1966; admitted to bar, 1995, Oklahoma, U.S. District Court, Western and Northern Districts of Oklahoma, U.S. Court of Appeals, Tenth Circuit and U.S. Supreme Court. *Education:* University of Central Oklahoma (B.A., 1991); Oklahoma City University (J.D., 1994). *Member:* Oklahoma County and Oklahoma Bar Associations. ***PRACTICE AREAS:*** Insurance Defense; Insurance Coverage Law; Personal Injury; Products Liability; Appellate Practice; Civil Practice; Trucking Defense; Commercial Litigation; Employment Law; Insurance Bad Faith; Environmental Law. ***Email:*** margaret@millsfirm.com

DANIEL K. JONES, born Oklahoma City, Oklahoma, April 5, 1970; admitted to bar, 1997, Oklahoma and U.S. District Court, Western and Eastern Districts of Oklahoma. *Education:* University of Oklahoma (B.A., 1993; J.D., 1997). Phi Delta Phi. *Member:* Oklahoma County and Oklahoma Bar Associations. ***LANGUAGES:*** Spanish. ***PRACTICE AREAS:*** Insurance Defense; Civil Practice; Products Liability; Personal Injury; Medical Malpractice; Uninsured Motorists Law; Trucking Defense. ***Email:*** danny@millsfirm.com

REPRESENTATIVE CLIENTS: AABF Freight System, Inc.; American Reliable Ins. Co.; Arkansas Farm Bureau; Atlantic Projects; Crawford & Company; Cunningham & Lindsey; Dow Chemical Company; Empire Fire & Marine; Great West Casualty Company; Gruma Corporation; Horizon Healthcare Corporation; Lincoln General Insurance Co.; National American Insurance Co.; National Lloyds Insurance Company; Nebraska Farm Bureau Mutual Insurance Company; Nobel Insurance Co.; Oklahoma Farm Bureau Mutual Ins. Co.; Oklahoma Property & Casualty Insurance Guaranty Association; Rocor International, Inc.; Scott Technologies; Scottsdale Insurance Company; Texas Farm Bureau Mutual Ins. Co.; Traffic & Lightning Systems, Inc.; Transportation Claims, Inc.; Unicco Service Company; US Aviation Underwriters; Zurich Insurance Company.

MOCK, SCHWABE, WALDO, ELDER, REEVES & BRYANT

A Professional Limited Liability Company

Established in 1982

FOURTEENTH FLOOR, TWO LEADERSHIP SQUARE
211 NORTH ROBINSON AVENUE
OKLAHOMA CITY, OKLAHOMA 73102
Telephone: 405-235-1110
Fax: 405-235-0333
URL: http://www.mswerb.com

General Civil, Trial Practice and Appellate Practice in all State and Federal Courts. Business Entities, Construction Law, Commercial Law and Transactions, Bankruptcy, Debtor and Creditor, Banking, Real Property, Eminent Domain, Oil and Gas, Energy, Products Liability, Employment Law, Insurance, Estate Planning, Probate, Administrative, Federal and State Taxation Law, Telecommunications and Environmental Law.

RANDALL D. MOCK, born Oklahoma City, Oklahoma, 1943; admitted to bar, 1968, Oklahoma; 1970, U.S. Tax Court. *Education:* University of Oklahoma (B.B.A., 1965; J.D., 1968); New York University (LL.M. in Taxation, 1970). Beta Gamma Sigma; Phi Delta Phi. Order of the Coif. Editor, Oklahoma Law Review, 1966-1968. Graduate Editor, Tax Law Review, 1969-1970. Kenneson Fellow, New York University, 1969-1970. Certified Public Accountant, Oklahoma, 1966. Co-Author, *Oklahoma Corporate Forms*, Lexis Publishing, Inc., 1989. *Member:* Oklahoma County, Oklahoma (Chairman, Taxation Section, 1974) and American Bar Associations; Oklahoma City Estate Planning Council (President, 1987-1988; Director, 1980-1988); Oklahoma City Tax Lawyers Group (President, 1973). Fellow, American College of Tax Counsel. ***PRACTICE AREAS:*** Estate Planning; Taxation; Business Entities; Commercial Transactions. ***Email:*** rmock@mswerb.com

G. BLAINE SCHWABE, III, born Tulsa, Oklahoma, 1947; admitted to bar, 1974, Oklahoma; 2001, Maine. *Education:* University of Oklahoma (B.B.A., 1970; J.D., 1974). Order of the Coif; Phi Delta Phi (Magister); Oklahoma Law Review. Adjunct Professor of Law, Oklahoma City University School of Law, Bankruptcy, 2001-2004, Debtor-Creditor Relations, 1978-1983. Special Lecturer in Law, Bankruptcy and Commercial Litigation, University of Oklahoma Law School, 1976-1982. *Member:* Oklahoma County, Oklahoma (Chairman, Past Chairman and Director, Bankruptcy and Reorganization Section, 1985—; Member, Farm Crisis Task Force, 1991-2000), Maine State and American Bar Associations. American College of Bankruptcy (3rd Class; 10th Circuit Regent). ***PRACTICE AREAS:*** Business Litigation; Commercial Law; Insolvency Law; Bankruptcy Law; Telecommunications Law; Insurance Rehabilitation and Liquidation. ***Email:*** gschwabe@mswerb.com

JAMES R. WALDO, born Oklahoma City, Oklahoma, 1946; admitted to bar, 1974, Oklahoma. *Education:* Duke University (A.B., 1968); University of Oklahoma (J.D., 1974). Phi Delta Phi. Order of the Coif. Managing Editor, Oklahoma Law Review, 1973-1974. Contributing Editor: Oklahoma Environmental Law Handbook; Vernon's Oklahoma,

(This Listing Continued)

Forms 2d Real Estate (Eminent Domain). *Member:* Oklahoma County, Oklahoma and American Bar Associations; Mineral Lawyers Society of Oklahoma City; Oklahoma City Real Property Lawyers Association (President, 2004). ***PRACTICE AREAS:*** Real Estate; Foreclosure; Eminent Domain; Civil Litigation. ***Email:*** jwaldo@mswerb.com

JAMES C. ELDER, born Detroit, Michigan, 1947; admitted to bar, 1972, Oklahoma. *Education:* University of Oklahoma (B.A., 1969; J.D., 1972). Phi Delta Phi. Order of the Coif. Article and Book Review Editor, Oklahoma Law Review, 1971-1972. Special Lecturer in Law, Real Estate Mortgages, Oklahoma City University School of Law, 1983. Director, United Way of Central Oklahoma. Member, Oklahoma City Real Property Lawyers Association. Member: Oklahoma County, Oklahoma and American (Member, Real Property, Probate and Trust Law Section; Chair, Closing Issues Subcommittee of Title Insurance Committee, 1996-2002; and Business Law Section) Bar Associations. Life Fellow, Oklahoma Bar Foundation. [Captain, USAR, 1972-1978]. ***PRACTICE AREAS:*** Real Estate Finance; Mortgage; Real Estate Development; Real Estate Sales; Real Estate Leasing. ***Email:*** jelder@mswerb.com

JOHN R. REEVES, born Oklahoma City, Oklahoma, 1949; admitted to bar, 1974, Oklahoma. *Education:* University of Oklahoma (B.B.A., 1971); Florida State University (M.B.A., 1974; J.D., with highest honors, 1974). Beta Gamma Sigma; Phi Kappa Phi; Phi Delta Phi. *Member:* Oklahoma County, Oklahoma and American Bar Associations; Mineral Lawyers Society of Oklahoma City (President, 1985-1986); Oklahoma City Real Property Lawyers Association (President, 1986). ***PRACTICE AREAS:*** Energy Law; Oil and Gas Law; Administrative Law. ***Email:*** jreeves@mswerb.com

GARY A. BRYANT, born Oklahoma City, Oklahoma, 1951; admitted to bar, 1977, Oklahoma. *Education:* University of Oklahoma (B.B.A., with special distinction, 1972); University of Texas (J.D., with honors, 1977). Beta Gamma Sigma; Phi Delta Phi. Order of the Coif. Special Lecturer in Law, Consumer Credit, Consumer Sales, Truth in Lending Simplification and Reform Act, Debtor-Creditor and Bankruptcy Law, Oklahoma City University School of Law, 1981-1983. Master Emeritus, William J. Holloway, Jr. American Inn of Court CV. Frequent author and special lecturer on bankruptcy. *Member:* Oklahoma County, Oklahoma (Director, Young Lawyers Division, 1977-1981; Associate Bar Examiner, 1983-1987) and American Bar Associations. ***PRACTICE AREAS:*** Banks and Banking; Secured Lending; Bankruptcy; Insolvency; Business Litigation. ***Email:*** gbryant@mswerb.com

SARAH ALEXANDER HALL, born New Orleans, Louisiana, 1964; admitted to bar, 1989, Oklahoma. *Education:* University of Oklahoma (B.B.A., with special distinction, 1986; J.D., with highest honors, 1989). Beta Gamma Sigma; Phi Delta Phi. Recipient, Bess Zeldrich Ungerman Scholarship. Frequent author and special lecturer on bankruptcy. *Member:* Oklahoma County (President, Bankruptcy Section, 1997-1998), Oklahoma (Associate Bar Examiner, 1996—; Member, Bankruptcy Section) and American Bar Associations (Member, Business Law and Labor Law Sections); American Bankruptcy Institute. ***PRACTICE AREAS:*** Bankruptcy; Insolvency; Business Litigation; Commercial Law; Insurance Rehabilitation and Liquidation. ***Email:*** shall@mswerb.com

ZACHARY W. ALLEN, born Norman, Oklahoma, 1963; admitted to bar, 1988, Texas; 1995, Oklahoma. *Education:* University of Oklahoma (B.B.A., with special distinction, 1985); Southern Methodist University (J.D., 1988). Beta Gamma Sigma. Notes and Comments Editor, Journal of Air Law and Commerce, 1987-1988. Recipient, Best Casenote Award, Journal of Air Law and Commerce. *Member:* Dallas, Oklahoma County, Oklahoma and American Bar Associations; State Bar of Texas. (Board Certified, Real Estate Law, Texas Board of Legal Specialization). ***PRACTICE AREAS:*** Real Estate Law; Business Law. ***Email:*** zallen@mswerb.com

J. MATTHEW THOMPSON, born Oklahoma City, Oklahoma, 1969; admitted to bar, 1995, Oklahoma. *Education:* Dartmouth College (A.B., cum laude, 1992); University of Oklahoma College of Law (J.D., with honors, 1995); Harvard Law School (LL.M., 2003). Phi Delta Phi; Phi Kappa Phi. Member, Oklahoma Law Review, 1993-1995; Editor-in-Chief, 1994-1995. Recipient: Harry Alley-Leroy Allen Prize for Best Case Note, 1994; Maurice H. Merrill Scholarship, 1994. Member, The Luther L. Bohanon American Inn of Court XXII, 1994-1995; 2003—. Author of various articles on products liability, oil and gas law and Oklahoma water law. *Member:* Oklahoma County, Oklahoma and American Bar Associations; American Law and Economics Association; American Psychology- Law Society; Dartmouth Lawyers Associations. Fellow, Oklahoma Bar Foundation. ***PRACTICE AREAS:*** Civil Litigation; Products Liability; Oil and Gas Law. ***Email:*** jthompson@mswerb.com

ASSOCIATE

WHITNEY ALVIS, born Carthage, Missouri, 1977; admitted to bar, 2005, Oklahoma. *Education:* University of Oklahoma (B.S., 2000; M.B.A., 2002; J.D., 2005). Betta Gamma Sigma; Order of the Coif. Recipient, Allie M. and Robert E. Stephenson Scholarship. *Member:* Oklahoma County, Oklahoma and American Bar Associations; Oklahoma City Estate Planning Council; Oklahoma City Tax Lawyer Group. ***PRACTICE AREAS:*** Estate Planning; Taxation; Business Entities; Commercial Transactions.

REPRESENTATIVE CLIENTS: AnSon Partners, LLC; Apache Corp.; Arcon Group; ARC Pipe Line Co.; BancFirst; Bank of America, N.A.; Bank of Union; Baskin Robbins USA, Co.; Big Mac Trucking Cos.; BP America Production Company; Cabot Oil & Gas Corp.; Chaparral, LLC; Chesapeake Operating Inc.; Conoco Phillips Company; Farm Credit Bank of Wichita; Federal Deposit Insurance Corp.; Fidelity Bank, Wichita; First Oklahoma Corp.; Hadson Petroleum (USA), Inc.; J.M. Huber Corporation; J.P. Morgan Chase Bank, N.A.; Last Frontier Council, Boy Scouts of America; The Lincoln National Life Insurance Co.; International Bank of Commerce; LSB Industries, Inc.; Massachusetts Mutual Life Insurance Co.; Mesa Operations Limited Partnership; Metropolitan Life Insurance Co.; New Holland, North America, Inc.; Oklahoma Capitol Improvement Authority; Oklahoma Turnpike Authority; Pan-American Life Insurance Co.; Southwestern Life Insurance Co.; Sunflower Bank, N.A.; Teppco Crude Pipeline, L.P.; Texaco Inc.; Tex/Con Oil & Gas Co.; Textron Financial Corporation; The CIT Group; Trammel Crow Company.

MONNET, HAYES, BULLIS, THOMPSON & EDWARDS

Established in 1946

SUITE 1719 FIRST NATIONAL CENTER WEST
120 NORTH ROBINSON
OKLAHOMA CITY, OKLAHOMA 73102
Telephone: 405-232-5481
Fax: 405-235-9159
Email: office@monnethayes.com

General Civil Practice in all State and Federal Courts, Appellate Practice, Insurance, Banking, Bankruptcy, Business Law, Class Action Defense, Corporation, Partnership Law, Oil and Gas, Commercial Planning, Personal Injury, Real Estate, Oil and Gas Title Examination, Real Estate Title Examination, Tax Planning and Litigation, Environmental, Estate Planning, Trusts, Wills, Probate Law, Guardianship and Family Law.

MEMBERS OF FIRM

CLAUDE MONNET (1899-1980)

LYNN J. BULLIS, JR. (1910-1984)

COLEMAN H. HAYES (1903-1985)

RUSSELL F. THOMPSON (1920-1985)

JOHN T. EDWARDS, born Pawhuska, Oklahoma, February 22, 1927; admitted to bar, 1951, Oklahoma, U.S. District Court, Western, Northern and Eastern Districts of Oklahoma, U.S. District Court, Eastern District of Arkansas, U.S. Supreme Court and U.S. Court of Appeals, Tenth Circuit. *Education:* University of Oklahoma (B.A., 1949; LL.B., 1951). Phi Alpha Delta. *Member:* Oklahoma and American Bar Associations; Fellow: American College of Trial Lawyers; American Board of Trial Advocates; International Association of Defense Counsel; Robert J. Turner American Inn of Court (President, 1999-2000). ***PRACTICE AREAS:*** Products Liability Law; Tort Law; Business Litigation; Trial Practice; Appellate Practice; Insurance Litigation. ***Email:*** jedwards@monnethayes.com

JAMES M. PETERS, born Tishomingo, Oklahoma, May 16, 1939; admitted to bar, 1965, Oklahoma; 1969, U.S. District Court, Western, Northern and Eastern Districts of Oklahoma, U.S. Court of Appeals, Tenth Circuit and U.S. Court of Federal Claims. *Education:* Oklahoma State University (B.A., 1962); University of Oklahoma (J.D., 1965). Phi Alpha Delta. Member, Board of Editors, University of Oklahoma Law Review, 1964-1965. Assistant U.S. Attorney, Western District of Oklahoma, 1969-1975. *Member:* Oklahoma Bar Association; Rocky Mountain Mineral Law Foundation. ***SPECIAL AGENCIES:*** Oklahoma Corporation Commission. ***PRACTICE AREAS:*** Trial Practice; Appellate Practice; Class Actions; Condemnation Law; Litigation; Oil and Gas Law; Environmental Law; White Collar Crime. ***Email:*** jpeters@monnethayes.com

JAMES S. DRENNAN, born Enid, Oklahoma, June 24, 1950; admitted to bar, 1977, Oklahoma. *Education:* Oklahoma State University (B.S., 1972; M.S., 1974); University of Oklahoma (J.D., 1977). Phi Kappa Phi; Phi Delta Phi. Member, Oklahoma City Mineral Lawyers Society. Editor, Oklahoma Law Review, 1975-1977. *Member:* Oklahoma and American Bar Associations. ***SPECIAL AGENCIES:*** Oklahoma Corporation Commission. ***PRACTICE AREAS:*** Oil and Gas Law; Estate Planning; Real Estate (Property) Law; Corporate Law; Business Law. ***Email:*** jdrennan@monnethayes.com

RANDALL A. BRESHEARS, born Oklahoma City, Oklahoma, July 12, 1954; admitted to bar, 1979, Oklahoma; U.S. Supreme Court; U.S. District Court, Western, Northern and Eastern Districts of Oklahoma; U.S. Court of Appeals, 10th Circuit; U.S. District Court, Eastern District of Arkansas. *Education:* Oklahoma State University (B.A., 1976); Tulsa University (J.D., 1979). *Member:* Oklahoma and American Bar Associations; American Board of Trial Advocates. ***PRACTICE AREAS:*** Insurance Defense Law; Personal Injury Law; Trial Practice; Employment Law. ***Email:*** rbreshears@monnethayes.com

SARAH H. STUHR, born Oklahoma City, Oklahoma, December 31, 1956; admitted to bar, 1981, Oklahoma. *Education:* University of Tulsa (B.A., 1978); University of Oklahoma (J.D., 1981). Phi Delta Phi. Member, Oklahoma City Mineral Lawyers Society. *Member:* Oklahoma Bar Association. ***PRACTICE AREAS:*** Oil and Gas Law; Title Examinations Law; Appellate Practice; Civil Litigation; Contracts. ***Email:*** sstuhr@monnethayes.com

GAYLE FREEMAN COOK, born Oklahoma City, Oklahoma, January 13, 1949; admitted to bar, 1975, Oklahoma; 1977, U.S. District Court, Western District of Oklahoma; 1980, U.S. Court of Appeals, Tenth Circuit and U.S. Supreme Court; 1981, U.S. District Court, Northern District of Oklahoma. *Education:* University of Oklahoma (B.S., 1971; M.Ed., 1972); Oklahoma City University (J.D., 1974). Phi Delta Phi; Iota Tau Tau (Secretary, 1977-1979). Member, Mortar Board. Recipient: Bronze Letzeiser Medal; American Jurisprudence Prize Award for Administrative Law. Law clerk to Oklahoma Supreme Court Justice Don Barnes, 1975-1978. Law Clerk to Oklahoma Court of Criminal Appeals Judge Tom R. Cornish, 1978-1981. *Member:* Oklahoma County (Member: Law Day Committee, 1977-1978; Social Committee, 1979-1981; Fee Grievance and Ethics Committee, 1985—) and Oklahoma (Member, Public Information Committee, 1978—; Chairman, 1990) Bar Associations; Robert J. Turner American Inn of Court (Administrator 1999-2004). ***PRACTICE AREAS:*** Appellate Practice; Oil and Gas Law; Estate Planning; Wills; Trusts; Real Estate; Probate; Guardianship; Conservatorship. ***Email:*** gcook@monnethayes.com

ROBERT C. SMITH, JR., born Leaksville, North Carolina, December 6, 1950; admitted to bar, 1980, Oklahoma; 1981, U.S. District Court, Northern, Eastern and Western Districts of Oklahoma; 1985, U.S. Court of Appeals, Tenth Circuit; 1995, U.S. Court of Federal Claims; 2001, U.S. Supreme Court. *Education:* University of North Carolina, Greensboro (B.S., 1976); Oklahoma City University (J.D., 1980). Phi Delta Phi. Editor-in-Chief, Oklahoma City University Law Review, 1979-1980. Legal Writing Instructor, Oklahoma City University Law School, 1984—. Assistant Attorney General for the State of Oklahoma, 1981-1983. Law Clerk for the Honorable Stewart M. Hunter, Oklahoma Court of Appeals, 1983-1984. *Member:* Oklahoma County, Oklahoma, Federal and American Bar Associations; Ginsburg American Inn of Court. ***PRACTICE AREAS:*** Trial Practice; Appellate Practice; Oil and Gas Law; Bankruptcy; Business Law; Municipal Law; Employment Law; Torts; Insurance; Real Estate; Intellectual Property; Trademarks; Patents; Unfair Competition. ***Email:*** rsmith@monnethayes.com

SHANNON L. EDWARDS, born Oklahoma City, Oklahoma, November 13, 1960; admitted to bar, 1987, Oklahoma and U.S. District Court, Western, Northern and Eastern Districts of Oklahoma; 1990, U.S. Court of Appeals, Tenth Circuit. *Education:* University of California at Berkeley (A.B., 1983); Georgetown University (J.D., 1986). Law Clerk to Honorable Luther Eubanks, U.S. District Judge for Western District of Oklahoma, 1986-1987. Attorney, Office of the United States Trustee, U.S. Department of Justice, 1987-1989. Supreme Court Judge, Osage Nation, 1994-1997. *Member:* Oklahoma Bar Association; Robert J. Turner American Inn of Court (1999—; President, 2005). ***PRACTICE AREAS:*** Civil Litigation; Insurance Litigation; Trial Practice; Torts; Appellate Practice. ***Email:*** sedwards@monnethayes.com

---

CHRISTOPHER J. PERRY, born Lynn, Massachusetts, December 17, 1966; admitted to bar, 1991, Oklahoma and U.S. District Court, Western District of Oklahoma. *Education:* University of Oklahoma (B.B.A., 1988; J.D., 1991). *Member:* Oklahoma Bar Association. ***PRACTICE AREAS:*** Civil Litigation; Oil and Gas Litigation; Real Estate Law; Internet Law; Internet Technology. ***Email:*** cperry@monnethayes.com

MICHAEL S. PETERS, born Oklahoma City, Oklahoma, December 27, 1966; admitted to bar, 1992, Oklahoma; U.S. District Court, Western District of Oklahoma; 1993, U.S. District Court, Eastern and Northern Districts of Oklahoma and U.S. Court of Appeals, Tenth Circuit. *Education:* Westminster College (B.A., 1989); Oklahoma City University (J.D., 1992). *Member:* Oklahoma and American Bar Associations. ***PRACTICE AREAS:*** Oil and Gas Law; Civil Litigation; Environmental Law; Wills; Estate Planning. ***Email:*** mpeters@monnethayes.com

ROBERT A. FRENCH, born New York, New York, October 16, 1959; admitted to bar, 1993, Oklahoma; U.S. District Court, Western and Northern Districts of Oklahoma; U.S. Court of Appeals, Tenth Circuit. *Education:* University of Oklahoma (B.A., 1984; M.A., 1988; J.D., 1993). Phi Kappa Phi Honor Society. Order of the Coif. Recipient: American Jurisprudence Awards: Torts I, Torts II; Academic Achievement Awards: Intellectual Property, Criminal Procedure. Winner, N. H. Burkan Memorial Copyright Law Writing Competition, 1993. Member, Oklahoma Law Review, 1991-1993. *Member:* Oklahoma Bar Association. ***PRACTICE AREAS:*** Civil Litigation; Environmental Law; Copyright Law. ***Email:*** bfrench@monnethayes.com

REPRESENTATIVE CLIENTS: American International Group; Arbuckle Enterprises, Inc.; Chase Manhattan Bank; Chevron Chemical Co.; Chevron U.S.A., Inc.; Citation Oil & Gas Corporation; Fireman's Fund Insurance Company; First Colony Life Insurance Company; The First National Bank of Thomas; Globe Life & Accident Insurance Co.; H & L Operating Company; JP Morgan/Chase Bank, N.A.; Kerr McGee Corp.; The Life Insurance Company of Virginia; Magnum Hunter Resources, Inc.; Marketing Information Network, Inc.; Midwest Mortgage Co.; Natural Gas Pipeline Company of America; Oak Tree Partners, L.L.C.; Oklahoma National Stock Yards Co.; OXY USA, Inc.; Questar Exploration and Production Co.; Rockwell International; Santa Fe Minerals, Inc.; Singer-Fleischaker Operating Co.; Southwest National Bank of Weatherford; Torchmark Corporation; Townsco Contracting Co.; Toys R Us; Travelers Insurance Co.; United American Insurance; Wausau Insurance Company; XTO Energy, Inc.

STANLEY D. MONROE & ASSOCIATES

OKLAHOMA CITY, OKLAHOMA

(See Tulsa)

General Trial Practice in State and Federal Courts, Criminal Appellant Practice-10th Circuit; Criminal Law, Family Law, Juvenile Law, Personal Injury, Medical Malpractice.

SUSAN P. MORAN

4200 PERIMETER CENTER DRIVE
SUITE 120
OKLAHOMA CITY, OKLAHOMA 73112
Telephone: 405-947-2024
Fax: 405-947-2252

Estate Planning, Probate, Trusts and Estates and Real Estate, Asset Protection, State and Federal Taxation, Corporate and Business Law.

SUSAN P. MORAN, born Oklahoma City, Oklahoma, February 27, 1953; admitted to bar, 1978, Oklahoma and U.S. District Court, Western District of Oklahoma; 1979, U.S. Tax Court; 1991, U.S. Supreme Court. *Education:* University of Oklahoma (B.B.A., 1975; J.D., 1978); New York University (LL.M., in Taxation, 1981). Member, Board of Editors, Oklahoma Law Review, 1977-1978. Certified Public Accountant, Oklahoma, 1976. Author: "Effect of 1976 Tax Reform on the Uses of Trusts in Estate Planning," 30 Oklahoma Law Review 644, 1977. *Member:* Oklahoma County and Oklahoma Bar Associations; American Institute of Certified Public Accountants; The William J. Holloway, Jr. American Inn of Court; Oklahoma City Estate Planning Council; Oklahoma City Tax Lawyers Breakfast Group.

MORGAN & ASSOCIATES, P.C.

Established in 1987

THE OIL CENTER, SUITE 205E
2601 NORTHWEST EXPRESSWAY
OKLAHOMA CITY, OKLAHOMA 73112
Telephone: 405-425-0700
Fax: 405-425-0739
Email: maa@ionet.net

Litigation Practice, includes Collections, Commercial and Creditor Rights Law. State and Federal Courts.

(This Listing Continued)

MORGAN & ASSOCIATES, P.C., Oklahoma City—Continued

PORTER H. MORGAN, III, born Oklahoma City, Oklahoma, January 11, 1945; admitted to bar, 1971, Oklahoma, U.S. District Court, Western District of Oklahoma. *Education:* Westminster College (1963-1965); University of Oklahoma (B.A., 1967; J.D., 1971). Phi Delta Phi. Editor, Oklahoma Law Review, 1971. President, Board of Directors, Mental Health Association of Oklahoma County, 1982-1983, 2000-2001. Legal Counsel, Mental Health Association of Oklahoma County, 1983-1984. Commercial Law League. Author: "Oil and Gas-Understanding the Division Order Title Opinion," Oklahoma Bar Journal, Vol. 56, No. 13, March 30, 1985. *Member:* Oklahoma County, Oklahoma and American Bar Associations. [Capt., U.S. Army, 1972]. ***PRACTICE AREAS:*** Collection & Creditor's Rights; Commercial Law. ***Email:*** maa@ionet.net

---

BOBBY G. IRBY, born Plano, Texas, January 5, 1977; admitted to bar, 2003, Oklahoma and U.S. District Court, Western District of Oklahoma; 2004, U.S. District Court, Northern District of Oklahoma. *Education:* University of Texas at Arlington (B.S., 1999); Oklahoma City University (J.D., 2003). Alpha Chi. Phi Delta Phi. Member: National Association of Business Economists, 1997-1999; American Collectors Association, 2005. ***PRACTICE AREAS:*** Creditors Rights; Collections; Commercial Law. ***Email:*** birby@morganandassoc.com

MATTHEW S. MOGAN, born Mesa, Arizona, October 9, 1978; admitted to bar, 2004, Oklahoma. *Education:* University of Oklahoma (B.B.A., 2001; J.D., 2004). ***PRACTICE AREAS:*** Creditors Rights; Collections; Commercial Law. ***Email:*** smogan@morganandassoc.com

KEITH A. DANIELS, born Oklahoma City, Oklahoma, June 15, 1972; admitted to bar, 2003, Oklahoma; 2004, U.S. District Court, Western and Northern Districts of Oklahoma. *Education:* University of Central Oklahoma (B.A., 1995); University of Oklahoma (J.D., 2003). Recipient, American Jurisprudence Award in Real Estate Finance. ***PRACTICE AREAS:*** Creditors Rights; Collections; Bankruptcy; Commercial Law. ***Email:*** kdaniels@morganandassoc.com

OF COUNSEL

SIDNEY D. BROWN, born Glover, Oklahoma, November 17, 1947; admitted to bar, 1979, Oklahoma; 1983, U.S. District Court, Western and Northern Districts of Oklahoma and U.S. Supreme Court. *Education:* Central State University (B.A., 1971; M.A., 1975); Oklahoma City University (J.D., 1979). Phi Alpha Theta Honor Society, History. Referee, Oklahoma County District Court, Juvenile Division, 1980-1986. Adjunct Professor: Oklahoma City University Law School, 1988; University of Central Oklahoma, Criminal Justice, 1987-2000. Assistant Attorney General, January 1991—. Presiding Judge of Juvenile Division, District Court, 1987-1991. *Member:* Cleveland County, Oklahoma County, Oklahoma and American (Member, Family Law Section) Bar Associations.

REPRESENTATIVE CLIENTS: American Airlines; American Frieghtways, Inc.; Americrest Bank; Apple Computers, Inc.; Bank of Oklahoma; Citgo Petroleum Corporation; Citibank; Citizens Communications; Conoco, Inc.; Deaconess Hospital; Guaranty Bank & Trust; Locke Supply; Mapco Products, Inc.; Oklahoma Gas & Electric; Phillips Petroleum Company; Pier One; Sinclair Oil; St. Anthony Hospital; Sunoco Inc.

MORICOLI, HARRIS & COTTINGHAM

A PROFESSIONAL CORPORATION

Established in 1983

TWO LEADERSHIP SQUARE, SUITE 1200
211 NORTH ROBINSON
OKLAHOMA CITY, OKLAHOMA 73102-7114
Telephone: 405-235-3357
Fax: 405-232-6515
Email: mhcok@mhcok.com

Mineral Law, Oil and Gas Law, Civil Litigation, Complex Litigation, Federal Civil Litigation, Regulatory Agency Practice.

FIRM PROFILE: Moricoli, Harris & Cottingham is a full service law firm which concentrates its practice in oil and gas law, telecommunications, commercial and general litigation. The firm's litigation practice focus has been primarily involved in oil and gas and property law. However, the firm also defends personal injury and environmental damage cases, is involved in telecommunications cases, advertising and communications cases, and is involved in matters governed by the Bankruptcy Code and Uniform Commercial Code. Much of the firm's litigation involves technical and engineering matters requiring the assistance of experts as witnesses and/or trial consultants.

The firm represents its clients in litigation in all state and federal courts. The firm also practices before the Oklahoma Corporation Commission, the Oklahoma Department of Transportation and other state and local regulatory and administrative bodies.

The firm offers title examination services, as well as legal services related to commercial property transactions, loan workouts, and bankruptcy. In addition, a substantial portion of the firm's practice involves legal counsel pertaining to oil and gas operations and compliance with federal, state and local law.

JOHN C. MORICOLI, JR., born Fort Worth, Texas, July 2, 1945; admitted to bar, 1974, Oklahoma; U.S. Court of Appeals, Tenth Circuit and U.S. District Court, Northern, Eastern and Western Districts of Oklahoma. *Education:* University of Oklahoma (B.S.M.E., 1968; J.D., 1974). Phi Delta Phi. *Member:* Oklahoma and American Bar Associations. [Capt., U.S. Army, Active Duty, 1968-1971]. ***SPECIAL AGENCIES:*** Oklahoma Corporation Commission. ***PRACTICE AREAS:*** Mineral Law; Oil and Gas Law; Civil Litigation; Complex Litigation; Federal Civil Litigation; Regulatory Agency Practice. ***Email:*** jmoricoli@mhcok.com

(This Listing Continued)

MICHAEL G. HARRIS, born Sterling, Colorado, November, 27, 1951; admitted to bar, 1978, Oklahoma; 1982, California; U.S. Court of Appeals, Tenth Circuit and U.S. District Court, Northern and Western Districts of Oklahoma. *Education:* University of Oklahoma (B.A., 1974; J.D., 1978). Phi Beta Kappa; Order of the Coif. Member, Oklahoma Law Review, 1976-1978. *Member:* Oklahoma and American Bar Associations; State Bar of California. ***PRACTICE AREAS:*** Civil Litigation; Oil and Gas Law; Telecommunications Law. ***Email:*** mharris@mhcok.com

DALE E. COTTINGHAM, born Oklahoma City, Oklahoma, December 26, 1956; admitted to bar, 1982, Oklahoma; U.S. Supreme Court; U.S. Court of Appeals, Tenth Circuit and U.S. District Court, Northern, Eastern and Western Districts of Oklahoma. *Education:* Oklahoma Baptist University (B.A., with honors, 1979); Southern Methodist University (J.D., 1982). Omicron Delta Kappa. Adjunct Professor of Law, Oklahoma City University in Environmental Law, Water Law and Natural Resources Law. Co-Author: "Injuries to Land Resulting From Oil and Gas Operations: Measure of Damages," 60 Oklahoma Bar Association Journal 3245, December 1989. Author: "An Abridged Primer on the Law of Public Nuisance," 30 University of Tulsa Law Review 355, Winter, 1994; "Advancement of Litigation Costs by Attorneys: The Slow Death of the Champerty Doctrine," 66 Oklahoma Bar Association Journal 1765, May 1995. *Member:* Oklahoma and American Bar Associations. ***PRACTICE AREAS:*** Civil Litigation; Complex Litigation; Federal Civil Litigation; Environmental Law; Mineral Law; Oil and Gas Law; Water Law. ***Email:*** dcottingham@mhcok.com

BRIAN R. MATULA, born Oklahoma City, Oklahoma, March 27, 1967; admitted to bar, 1991, Oklahoma and U.S. District Court, Western District of Oklahoma; 1995, U.S. Court of Appeals, Tenth Circuit; 1996, U.S. District Court, Northern District of Oklahoma. *Education:* Oklahoma State University (B.A., 1988); University of Kansas (J.D., 1991). Phi Kappa Phi; Phi Delta Phi. *Member:* Oklahoma and American Bar Associations. ***PRACTICE AREAS:*** Mineral Law; Oil and Gas Law; Civil Litigation; Federal Civil Litigation. ***Email:*** bmatula@mhcok.com

PHILIP A. SCHOVANEC, born Enid, Oklahoma, June 21, 1968; admitted to bar, 1994, Oklahoma and U.S. District Court, Western and Northern Districts of Oklahoma; 1996, U.S. Court of Appeals, Tenth Circuit. *Education:* Oklahoma State University (B.S., 1991); University of Oklahoma (J.D., 1994). Editor-in-Chief, Oklahoma Law Review, 1993-1994. Author: "The Sale of Property Under Section 363: The Validity of Sales Conducted Without Proper Notice," 46 Okla. L. Rev. 489 (1994). *Member:* Oklahoma County, Oklahoma and American Bar Associations. ***PRACTICE AREAS:*** Civil Litigation; Complex Litigation; Federal Civil Litigation; Telecommunications; Oil and Gas Law; Business Law; Trusts and Estates. ***Email:*** pschovanec@mhcok.com

WILLIAM H. HICKMAN, born Dallas, Texas, November 24, 1968; admitted to bar, 1999, Oklahoma, U.S. District Court, Western District of Oklahoma and U.S. Court of Appeals, Tenth Circuit; 2000, Northern and Eastern Districts of Oklahoma. *Education:* U.S. Air Force Academy (B.S., 1991); Auburn University (M.B.A., 1993); University of Oklahoma (J.D., with highest honors, 1999). Phi Delta Phi. Native American National Moot Court Team. *Member:* Oklahoma and American Bar Associations; National Contract Management Association (NCMA). [Captain, USAF, Active Duty, 1991-1996]. ***PRACTICE AREAS:*** Civil Litigation; Complex Litigation; Federal Civil Litigation; Oil and Gas Law; Business Law; Government Contracts; Outdoor Advertising; Telecommunications Law. ***Email:*** whickman@mhcok.com

---

LISA A. GARRETT, born Fort Campbell, Kentucky, February 5, 1977; admitted to bar, 2002, Oklahoma and U.S. District Court, Western District of Oklahoma. *Education:* Cameron University (B.A., 1999); University of Oklahoma (J.D., 2002). Order of the Barristers. Member, Thomas Tang Moot Court Team. *Member:* Oklahoma and American Bar Associations. ***PRACTICE AREAS:*** Civil Litigation; Complex Litigation; Federal Civil Litigation; Oil and Gas Law; Telecommunications Law; Employment Law. ***Email:*** lgarrett@mhcok.com

JEREMY R. FITZPATRICK, born Chickasha, Oklahoma, November 17, 1977; admitted to bar, 2004, Oklahoma. *Education:* University of Oklahoma (B.B.A., 2001; J.D., 2004). Author: "The Competent Ward," 28 AM Indian L. Rev. 189, 2004. *Member:* Oklahoma and American Bar Associations; American Association of Professional Landmen; Association of International Petroleum Negotiators. ***PRACTICE AREAS:*** Natural Resources; Oil and Gas Law; Real Estate Law; Civil Litigation; Complex Litigation; Federal Civil Litigation. ***Email:*** jfitzpatrick@mhcok.com

REPRESENTATIVE CLIENTS: Amerac Energy Corporation; Amoco Production Company; B.P. America, Inc.; B.P. America Production company; B.P. Exploration, Inc.; BTA Oil Producers; CNG Producing Company; Chesapeake Energy Corporation; Chesapeake Exploration Limited Partnership; Chesapeake Operating, Inc.; Cimarex Energy Company; Clear Channel Communications, Inc.; Clear Channel Outdoor, Inc.; Colony Petroleum, L.L.C.; Conoco Inc; Cox Oklahoma Telcom, L.L.C.; Davis Oil Co.; Dynergy, Inc.; Enron Oil & Gas Company; Fina Oil & Chemical Company; Forest Oil Corporation; Green Operating Company, Inc.; Carl E. Gungoll Exploration, Inc.; Halliburton Oil Producing Company; Hallwood Petroleum, Inc.; Henry Holding Corporation; Hillin-Simon Oil Co.; Gary Kading; K & Y Investments, L.L.C.; Key Production Co., Inc.; Kidd Oil & Gas Company; Lamar Outdoor Advertising; Lario Oil & Gas Co.; Ocean Energy; Pioneer Natural Resources USA, Inc.; Plains Resources, Inc.; Redstone Oil & Gas Company; Rosewood Resources;St. Mary Land & Exploration Co.; St. Mary Operating Co.; Sanguine, Ltd.; Seagull Energy E&P, Inc.; Snyder Oil Company; Texinia Oil and Gas, Inc.; Truckstops Corporation of America; Unit Petroleum Co.; Vastar Resources, Inc.; Wagner Brown.

MULINIX OGDEN HALL ANDREWS & LUDLAM A PROFESSIONAL LIMITED LIABILITY COMPANY

3030 OKLAHOMA TOWER
210 WEST PARK AVENUE
OKLAHOMA CITY, OKLAHOMA 73102
Telephone: 405-232-3800
Telecopier: 405-232-8999
URL: http://www.lawokc.com

Norman, Oklahoma Office: 905 24th Avenue, NW, Suite B-1. Telephone: 405-329-0003.

(This Listing Continued)

General Civil and Criminal Trial and Appellate Practice in State and Federal Courts. Business and Commercial Litigation, Appellate Litigation, Eminent Domain, Administrative, Banking, Bankruptcy, Business Transactions, Corporate, Trust and Estate Planning, Probate, Health Care, Insurance Defense and Regulatory, Construction Law, Environmental Law, Oil and Gas, Real Estate, Taxation, Telecommunications and Transportation, Aviation Law.

RUSSELL L. MULINIX, born Muskogee, Oklahoma, 1955; admitted to bar, 1980, Oklahoma; U.S. Supreme Court, U.S. Court of Appeals, Tenth and Eleventh Circuits, U.S. District Court, Western, Northern and Eastern Districts of Oklahoma and U.S. District Court, Northern District of Texas. *Education:* Oklahoma State University (B.S., 1977); University of Oklahoma (J.D., 1980). Editor, Oklahoma Law Review, 1978-1980. Member: Pro Bono Panel, Legal Aid of Western Oklahoma, Inc., 1984—; Board of Trustees, Oklahoma Housing Finance Agency, 1993-1994. *Member:* Oklahoma County, Oklahoma and American Bar Associations; Judicial Conference for the Tenth Circuit; Oklahoma Lawyers for Children. ***PRACTICE AREAS:*** Litigation; Banking; Commercial; Real Estate. ***Email:*** rusty@lawokc.com

RICHARD C. OGDEN, born Guymon, Oklahoma, July 10, 1963; admitted to bar, 1989, Oklahoma; U.S. Supreme Court, Tenth Circuit, U.S. District Court, Western, Northern and Eastern Districts of Oklahoma. *Education:* Oklahoma State University (B.S., 1986); University of Oklahoma (J.D., 1989); Oxford University, Queens College, Oxford England. 1994 Outstanding Young Lawyer for Oklahoma County. 1997 Outstanding Young Lawyer for Oklahoma. *Member:* Oklahoma County (Member, Board of Directors, 1993-1994, 1996; Young Lawyers Division; Chairperson, 1993-1994), Oklahoma (Member: Board of Governors, 1996; Young Lawyers Division; Chairperson, 1996) and American (Member, House of Delegates, 1995-1997) Bar Associations. ***PRACTICE AREAS:*** Commercial Litigation; Creditor Bankruptcy; Appellate Practice; Civil Litigation; Commercial Collections. ***Email:*** rco@lawokc.com

JOEL C. HALL, born Kansas City, Missouri, November 18, 1963; admitted to bar, 1989, Oklahoma, U.S. District Court, Western, Northern and Eastern Districts of Oklahoma and U.S. Court of Appeals, Tenth Circuit. *Education:* University of Oklahoma (B.B.A., 1986; J.D., with honors, 1989). Phi Delta Phi. Lawyer/Pupil, Luther Bohanon American Inns of Court, 1990-1991. Member, Chapter 7 Trustee Bankruptcy Panel, U.S. Western District of Oklahoma. *Member:* Oklahoma and American Bar Associations. ***PRACTICE AREAS:*** Civil Litigation; Commercial Litigation; Debtor/Creditor Rights. ***Email:*** joel@lawokc.com

J. DON ANDREWS, born Oklahoma City, Oklahoma, May 28, 1964; admitted to bar, 1989, Oklahoma and U.S. District Court, Western, Northern and Eastern Districts of Oklahoma. *Education:* University of Oklahoma (B.F.A., 1986); Oklahoma City University (J.D., 1989). *Member:* Oklahoma County, Oklahoma and American Bar Associations. ***PRACTICE AREAS:*** Civil Litigation; Commercial Litigation; Bankruptcy; Repossessions; Collections; Probate; Estate Planning; Corporate Law; Landlord/Tenant Law; Foreign Judgments. ***Email:*** jdon@lawokc.com

JEFFERY S. LUDLAM, born Oklahoma City, Oklahoma, November 28, 1973; admitted to bar, 1999, Oklahoma and U.S. District Court, Western, Northern and Eastern Districts of Oklahoma. *Education:* University of Oklahoma (B.B.A., 1996; J.D., 1998). *Member:* Oklahoma County Bar Association (Member, Board of Directors, 2000-2003; Young Lawyers Division). ***PRACTICE AREAS:*** Franchise Law; Commercial Litigation; Commercial Transactions; Aviation Litigation; Construction Litigation; Environmental Litigation; Bankruptcy; Estate Planning. ***Email:*** jeff@lawokc.com

ASSOCIATES

JAMES W. SHEPHERD, born San Diego, California, November 25, 1975; admitted to bar, 2003, Oklahoma and U.S. District Court, Western and Northern Districts of Oklahoma. *Education:* University of Oklahoma (B.A., 1998; M.B.A., 2000); Oklahoma City University School of Law (J.D., 2003). Phi Delta Phi. *Member:* Oklahoma and American Bar Associations. ***PRACTICE AREAS:*** Civil Litigation. ***Email:*** jamey@lawokc.com

RUSSELL A. WANTLAND, born Oklahoma City, Oklahoma, 1976; admitted to bar, 2003, Oklahoma and U.S. District Court, Western, Northern and Eastern Districts of Oklahoma. *Education:* University of Oklahoma (B.B.A., 1999; M.B.A., 2003; J.D., 2003). Phi Delta Phi (Vice President). Founding Editor, Oklahoma Journal of Law and Technology. Recipient: American Jurisprudence Awards (Torts, Contracts II and Bankruptcy); Top Brief Award, Pepperdine Entertainment Law Moot Court Competition. *Member:* Oklahoma County and Oklahoma Bar Associations. ***PRACTICE AREAS:*** Commercial Litigation; Creditor Bankruptcy; Civil Litigation; Commercial Transactions; Intellectual Property Litigation. ***Email:*** russell@lawokc.com

T. MATTHEW SMITH, born Weatherford, Oklahoma, July 10, 1978; admitted to bar, 2005, Oklahoma. *Education:* University of Oklahoma (B.A., 2001, with high honors; M.B.A., 2005; J.D., 2005). *Member:* Oklahoma and American Bar Associations; Robert J. Turner Inn of the Court. ***PRACTICE AREAS:*** Creditor Bankruptcy; Civil Litigation; Commercial Transactions. ***Email:*** matt@lawokc.com

OF COUNSEL

JOHN S. GARDNER, born Oklahoma City, Oklahoma, August 20, 1955; admitted to bar, 1993, Oklahoma, U.S. District Court, Western, Eastern and Northern Districts of Oklahoma, U.S. Court of Appeals, Tenth Circuit. *Education:* United States Naval Academy (B.S., 1977); Georgetown University (M.A., 1990); University of Oklahoma (J.D., with highest honors, 1992). Order of the Coif. Recipient, American Jurisprudence Award. *Member:* Oklahoma County, Oklahoma, Federal and American (Member, Sections on: Litigation; Environment, Energy and Resources) Bar Associations. [U.S. Navy, 1977-1990, Commander]. ***PRACTICE AREAS:*** Products Liability; Construction Litigation; Environmental Litigation; Personal Injury Litigation. ***Email:*** gardner@lawokc.com

SALLY KETCHUM EDWARDS, born Duncan, Oklahoma, April 26, 1953; admitted to bar, 1979, Oklahoma; U.S. District Court, Western District of Oklahoma; U.S. Tax Court. *Education:* University of Central Oklahoma (B.A., 1975); University of Oklahoma (J.D., 1979); Oxford University, Queens College, Oxford, England. Phi Delta Phi. Recipient: Alfred P. Murrah Award; Jessup Moot Court Award; American Jurisprudence Award; Outstanding Young Women of America. *Member:* Oklahoma County, Oklahoma and American Bar Associations. ***PRACTICE AREAS:*** Wills; Trust Law; Estate Planning; Probate; Taxation. ***Email:*** sally@lawokc.com

ARMANDO J. ROSELL, born Lawton, Oklahoma, May 4, 1972; admitted to bar, 2000, Oklahoma. *Education:* Southern Methodist University (B.B.A., Finance, 1995); Oklahoma City University (J.D., 2000). Phi Delta Phi. Managing Editor, Oklahoma City University Law Review, 1999-2000. *Member:* Oklahoma County, Oklahoma and American Bar Associations. ***PRACTICE AREAS:*** Business Litigation; Banking; Bankruptcy; Real Estate; Transportation; Corporate Law; Entity Formation; Sports and Entertainment Law; Creditors Rights. ***Email:*** rosell@lawokc.com

TRAVIS W. WATKINS, born Norfolk, Virginia, September 28, 1973; admitted to bar, 1999, Oklahoma; U.S. District Court, Northern, Eastern and Western Districts of Oklahoma; U.S. Court of Appeals, Tenth Circuit. *Education:* William Jewell College (B.A., 1995); Oklahoma City University (J.D., 1999). Member, Moot Court Honors Board, 1998-1999. Recipient, CALI Award for Legal Research and Writing. *Member:* Oklahoma County, Oklahoma and American (Member, Litigation Section) Bar Associations. ***REPORTED CASES:*** Meadows v. Wal-Mart 21 P.3d 48 (Okla. 2001); English v. Wal-Mart 16 P.3d 1136 (Okla Ct. App. 2001). ***PRACTICE AREAS:*** Personal Injury; Employment Law; Criminal Law; Litigation. ***Email:*** travis@lawokc.com

HARLAN G. HENTGES, born Perry, Oklahoma, July 14, 1965; admitted to bar, 1992, Texas; 1998, Oklahoma and U.S. District Court, Western District of Oklahoma. *Education:* Oklahoma State University (B.S., Agricultural Economics, 1987); University of Texas (M.P.Aff., 1992; J.D., 1992). *Member:* Oklahoma Bar Association; American Agricultural Law Association. ***PRACTICE AREAS:*** Agricultural Law; Estate Planning; Insurance Defense; Business Litigation; Business Planning; Appellate Practice; Eminent Domain; Oil and Gas Litigation.

DONALD E. DESPAIN, born Ponca City, Oklahoma, August, 1945; admitted to bar, 1973, Oklahoma. *Education:* University of Oklahoma (B.B.A., 1967; J.D., 1973). Phi Delta Phi; Order of the Coif. Editor, 1971-1973 and Topic Editor, 1972, Oklahoma Law Review. *Member:* Oklahoma Bar Association. ***PRACTICE AREAS:*** Commercial Real Estate; Corporate Law; Commercial Transactions; Banking Law. ***Email:*** ddespain@lawokc.com

JOSEPH K. GOERKE, born Oklahoma City, Oklahoma, August 31, 1964; admitted to bar, 1989, Oklahoma; U.S. Court of Appeals, Tenth Circuit, U.S. District Court, Eastern and Western Districts of Oklahoma. *Education:* Oklahoma State University (B.S., 1986); University of Oklahoma (J.D., 1989). ***PRACTICE AREAS:*** Insurance Defense; Civil Litigation; Business Litigation; Personal Injury; Subrogation; Insurance Coverage. ***Email:*** jgoerke@lawokc.com

KYLE EDWARD GOERKE, born Watonga, Oklahoma, June 5, 1959; admitted to bar, 1987, Oklahoma; U.S. District Court, Western District of Oklahoma, U.S. Court of Military Appeals, U.S. Army Court of Military Review and District Court of Cheyenne-Arapaho Tribes. *Education:* United States Air Force Academy, Oklahoma State University (B.S., 1983); University of Oklahoma (J.D., 1986). *Member:* Blaine County, Oklahoma and American Bar Associations; Oklahoma Army National Guard (LTC - JAGC). ***PRACTICE AREAS:*** Real Estate; Probate; Banking; Personal Injury; Commercial Law; Oil and Gas Law; Workers Compensation. ***Email:*** kylegoerke@lawokc.com

REPRESENTATIVE CLIENTS: List Available Upon Request.

MULLINS, HIRSCH & JONES, P.C.

100 PARK AVENUE
SUITE 400
OKLAHOMA CITY, OKLAHOMA 73102
Telephone: 405-235-2335
Fax: 405-232-7930
Email: lawyers@mhj-law.com
URL: http://www.oklahomafamilylaw.com

Civil Litigation, Oil and Gas, Corporation Commission, Title Examinations, Employment, Banks and Banking Law, Products Liability, Family Law, Adoption, Child Custody, Child Support, Wills and Probate, Guardianships, Trusts and Estates Law.

MICHAEL L. MULLINS, born Memphis, Tennessee, March 18, 1964; admitted to bar, 1990, Oklahoma and U.S. District Court, Western District of Oklahoma. *Education:* University of Oklahoma (B.B.A., in Finance, 1987; J.D., 1990). Author: "Civility in the Legal Profession," Oklahoma Bar Association, Continuing Legal Education, Summer 1996; "Private Investigators," Oklahoma Bar Association, Family Law Section, Continuing Legal Education, July 1996; "Visitation & Alimony/Property Division Enforcement 'Rights, Remedies & Differences'," Oklahoma Bar Association, Family Law Section, Continuing Legal Education, September 1996; "Child Custody/Visitation", Oklahoma Bar Association, Family Law Section, Continuing Legal Education, October 1996; "Appellate Procedure & Stay of Execution," Oklahoma Bar Association, Continuing Legal Education, May 1997; "Handling the High Income Case," Oklahoma Bar Association, Family Law Section, Continuing Legal Education, Fall 2000; "Custodial Parent Relocation," Oklahoma Bar Association, Family Law Section, Continuing Legal Education, Fall 2002; "Basic Divorce," Oklahoma Bar Association, Family Law Section, Continuing Legal Education, Fall 2004. *Member:* Oklahoma County Bar Association, Young Lawyers Division (Member: Board of Directors, 1991-1996; Vice-Chairman, 1993-1994; Chair-Elect, 1994-1995; Chairman, 1995-1996) Oklahoma Bar Association (Young Lawyers Division, Member: Board of Directors, 1995-1996). ***PRACTICE AREAS:*** Family Law; Civil Litigation. ***Email:*** mmullins@mhj-law.com

KARL F. HIRSCH, born Wilmington, Delaware, January 23, 1952; admitted to bar, 1978, Oklahoma; 1979, U.S. District Court, Western District of Oklahoma; 1985, Colorado. *Education:* University of Oklahoma (B.B.A., 1974; J.D., 1978). *Member:* Oklahoma County, Oklahoma (Member, Mineral Law Section) and Colorado Bar Associations; Oklahoma City Mineral Lawyers. ***REPORTED CASES:*** Brumark Corp. v. Corporation Commission, 864 P.2d 1287 (Okl. App. 1993); McClain v. Ricks Exploration Co., 894 P.2d 422 (Okl. App. 1994); RLM Petroleum Corp. v. Emmerich, 896 P.2d 531 (Okl. 1995); Vastar

(This Listing Continued)

MULLINS, HIRSCH & JONES, P.C., Oklahoma City—Continued

Resources, Inc. v. Howard, 38 P.3d 236 (Okl. App. 2001). ***PRACTICE AREAS:*** Oil and Gas Law; Civil Litigation; Corporation Commission Law; Real Estate Law; Wills; Trusts and Estates. ***Email:*** khirsch@mhj-law.com

K. NICHOLLE JONES, born Tulsa, Oklahoma, July 17, 1969; admitted to bar, 1997, Oklahoma; U.S. District Court, Northern and Western Districts of Oklahoma. *Education:* University of Oklahoma (B.B.A., 1991; J.D., 1997). Co-Author: "Qualified Domestic Relations Orders and Federal Civilian Retirement Orders," Oklahoma Bar Association, October 2001; "The Evolution of the Mentoring Program of the Ruth Bader Ginsburg American Inn of Court," The Bencher, January/February 2003. Ruth Bader Ginsburg American Inn of Court, Member, 1998-2000, 2001-2005, Mentoring Co-Chairperson, 2001-2005. *Member:* Oklahoma County (Co-Chairperson, Family Law Section, 2001-2002) and Oklahoma (Member: Diversity Committee; Family Law Section) Bar Associations. ***PRACTICE AREAS:*** Family Law; Labor and Employment; Civil Litigation. ***Email:*** njones@mhj-law.com

---

DONALD F. HEATH, JR., born Enid, Oklahoma, May 20, 1957; admitted to bar, 1982, Oklahoma; U.S. District Court, Eastern, Northern and Western Districts of Oklahoma; U.S. Court of Appeals, Tenth Circuit and U.S. Supreme Court. *Education:* Grinnell College (B.A., 1979); University of Oklahoma (J.D., 1982). Recipient: American Jurisprudence Award, Trusts, 1981; Chairman's Award, National Association of Royalty Owners, 1996. Author: "Oklahoma's New Summary Probate Act: Reducing the Time and Expense of Probate," 70 Oklahoma Bar Journal 2283, July 24, 1999; "Rebuttable Presumptions Under House Bill 2783," 66 Oklahoma Bar Journal 2964, September 30, 1995; "Force Pooling Mortgages: Due Process and Jurisdictional Considerations," 58 Oklahoma Bar Journal 1527, May 30, 1987; "Limited Liability Companies in Real Estate Titles: What Requirements Should the Examiner Make?" 65 Oklahoma Bar Journal 1112, March 26, 1994. President, National Association of Royalty Owners, Oklahoma Chapter, 1999-2000. *Member:* Oklahoma (Chairman, Real Property Law Section, 1995-1996) and American Bar Associations; Oklahoma City Mineral Lawyers Society (President, 2003-2004); Oklahoma City Real Property Lawyers Association (President, 1999). ***PRACTICE AREAS:*** Litigation; Oil and Gas; Real Property; Probate. ***Email:*** dheath@mhj-law.com

RICK J. HENTHORN, born Oklahoma City, Oklahoma, September 24, 1955; admitted to bar, 1998, Oklahoma; U.S. District Court, Northern, Eastern and Western Districts of Oklahoma. *Education:* University of Central Oklahoma (B.B.A., 1993); Oklahoma City University School of Law (J.D., 1998). Certified Family and Divorce Mediator. *Member:* Oklahoma County, Canadian County, Oklahoma (Member: Family Law Section; Outstanding Family Law Attorney, 2001; Co-Editor OBA/FLS Journal; Board Member, Young Lawyers Division) and American (Member, Family Law Section) Bar Associations; Luther Bohanon American Inn of Curt XXII. ***PRACTICE AREAS:*** Family Law; Juvenile Law; General Practice; Mediation; Civil Litigation. ***Email:*** rhenthorn@mhj-law.com

R. GREG ANDREWS, born Oklahoma City, Oklahoma, March 20, 1972; admitted to bar, 2001, Oklahoma; U.S. District Court, Eastern, Northern and Western Districts of Oklahoma. *Education:* University of Oklahoma (B.A., 1998; J.D., 2001); Brasenose College, Oxford University, Oxford, England (Legal Studies, 1999). Phi Delta Phi. Member, Ruth Bader Ginsburg American Inn of Court, 2003-2005. Recipient: Academic Achievement Award in Family Law. *Member:* Oklahoma County, Oklahoma (Member, Family Law Section and Mineral Law Section) and American Bar Associations; Fellow, Oklahoma Bar Foundation. ***PRACTICE AREAS:*** Banking Law; Labor and Employment Law; Oil and Gas Law; Federal Civil Litigation; Personal Injury; Insurance Bad Faith; Family Law. ***Email:*** gandrews@mhj-law.com

BLAKE C. PARROTT, born Oklahoma City, Oklahoma, August 22, 1973; admitted to bar, 2000, Oklahoma; U.S. Court of Appeals, Tenth Circuit; U.S. District Court, Western, Northern and Eastern Districts of Oklahoma. *Education:* University of Oklahoma (B.B.A., 1996; J.D., 2000). Phi Delta Phi. Member, Oklahoma Title Examination Standards Committee. *Member:* Oklahoma County, Oklahoma and American Bar Associations; Oklahoma County Title Lawyers Association; Ruth Bader Ginsburg Inn of Court. Fellow, Oklahoma Bar Foundation. ***REPORTED CASES:*** Smith v. Baptist Foundation of Oklahoma, 2002 OK 57, 50 P.3d 1132 (Okla. 2002). ***PRACTICE AREAS:*** Civil Litigation; Title Insurance Defense; Insurance Defense; Commercial Litigation; Real Estate Law; Collections; Personal Injury. ***Email:*** bparrott@mhj-law.com

NASH, COHENOUR & KELLEY, P.C.

4101 PERIMETER CENTER DRIVE
SUITE 200
OKLAHOMA CITY, OKLAHOMA 73112
Telephone: 405-917-5000
Fax: 405-917-5005
Email: INFO@NASHFIRM.COM
URL: http://www.NASHFIRM.COM

Commercial and Bankruptcy Law (Creditors only). Civil Litigation, Insurance Defense, Real Property, Foreclosures, Corporations, Partnerships, Fiduciary and Trust Litigation, Collections, Estate Planning and Probate, Trusts, Federal and State Taxation Law.

FIRM PROFILE: The firm strives to maintain two dedicated principles. The first is personalized service. We analyze your case and place you with the attorney who best suits your needs. The second principle is effectively maintaining cost control. We strive to ensure that every case or matter remains cost-effective and economically prudent.

While modest in size, the firm is able to provide its clients with personal and competent representation by attorneys experienced in their respective areas of practice. Every attorney in the firm has been a lecturer for continuing legal education seminars in their respective areas of expertise. The firm's regular clientele include numerous banks, finance companies, prominent corporations and varied business entities of substantial means.

(This Listing Continued)

MEMBERS OF FIRM

ROLLIN NASH, JR., born Oklahoma City, Oklahoma, May 5, 1955; admitted to bar, 1980, Oklahoma; U.S. District Court, Western, Northern and Eastern Districts of Oklahoma; U.S. Court of Appeals, Tenth Circuit; U.S. Tax Court; U.S. Supreme Court. *Education:* Oklahoma State University (B.S., 1977); University of Oklahoma (J.D., 1980). Former Adjunct Professor and Lecturer, CLE Seminars, Oklahoma City Community College and Oklahoma Banker's Association. *Member:* Oklahoma County and Oklahoma (Member: Bankruptcy, Real Property and Commercial Law Sections) Bar Associations; Oklahoma City Commercial Law Attorneys Association (Charter Member and Past President). ***PRACTICE AREAS:*** Civil Litigation; Corporate Law; Commercial Law; Bankruptcy Law; Real Property Law; Fiduciary and Trust Litigation. ***Email:*** RNash@NashFirm.com

CYNTHIA COHENOUR, born Ponca City, Oklahoma, May 5, 1952; admitted to bar, 1987, Oklahoma; U.S. District Court, Western District of Oklahoma. *Education:* University of Oklahoma (B.S., 1974; M.Ed., 1976; J.D, 1987). Phi Alpha Delta. Iota Tau Tau (Treasurer, Oklahoma City Alumnae Chapter). Member, Oklahoma City Estate Planning Council. Lecturer, CLE Seminars. *Member:* Oklahoma Bar Association. ***PRACTICE AREAS:*** Probate Law; Estate and Gift Tax Law; Estate Planning Law; Individual Taxation; Fiduciary Income Tax; Real Property Law. ***Email:*** cyndic@msn.com

KEVIN KELLEY, born Killeen, Texas, July 13, 1962; admitted to bar, 1988, Oklahoma; U.S. District Court, Western District of Oklahoma, U.S. Court of Appeals, Tenth Circuit. *Education:* Central State University (B.A., 1985); University of Oklahoma (J.D., 1988). Recipient, American Jurisprudence Award, Constitutional Law I, 1986. Lecturer, CLE Seminars. *Member:* Oklahoma Bar Association; Oklahoma City Commercial Law Attorneys Association (Charter Member; Past President). ***PRACTICE AREAS:*** Civil Litigation; Commercial Law; Bankruptcy Law; Real Property Law; Collections. ***Email:*** KKelley@NashFirm.com

DENNIS S. BOXEUR, born New York, New York, February 6, 1951; admitted to bar, 1978, Oklahoma; 1979, U.S. District Court, Western District of Oklahoma; 1984, U.S. District Court, Northern District Of Texas; 1987, U.S. District Court, Eastern and Northern District of Oklahoma; 1989, U.S. Court of Appeals, 10th Circuit; 1991, U.S. Claims Court. *Education:* St. Peter's College (B.S., 1975); University of Oklahoma (J.D., 1978). Phi Alpha Delta. Author: "An Overview of the Oklahoma Securities Act For the General Practitioner," 51 Oklahoma Bar Journal 9, 1980. Associate General Counsel, Oklahoma Securities Commission, 1978-1980. *Member:* Oklahoma Bar Association. [First Lt., U.S. Army- New York Army National Guard, 1969-1975]. ***LANGUAGES:*** French. ***PRACTICE AREAS:*** Civil Litigation; Commercial Law; Personal Injury Law; Arbitration. ***Email:*** DBoxeur@NashFirm.com

GARY L. GIESSMANN, born Parsons, Kansas, October 26, 1952; admitted to bar, 1985, Oklahoma and U.S. District Court, Western, Eastern and Northern Districts of Oklahoma; U.S. Court of Appeals, Tenth Circuit. *Education:* University of Oklahoma (B.A., 1975); Oklahoma City University (J.D., 1985). Phi Delta Phi. Member, OCU Moot Court Board, 1983-1984. *Member:* Cleveland County and Oklahoma Bar Associations; Oklahoma City Commercial Law Attorneys Association. ***PRACTICE AREAS:*** Civil Litigation; Civil Appeals; Commercial Law; Collections; Bankruptcy Law; Real Property. ***Email:*** GaryG@NashFirm.com

WILLIAM J. BERGNER, born Sidney, Nebraska, August 17, 1948; admitted to bar, 1981, Oklahoma and U.S. District Court, Western District of Oklahoma; 1982, U.S. District Court, Northern District of Oklahoma and U.S. Court of Appeals, 10th Circuit; 1985, U.S. District Court, Eastern District of Oklahoma; 1986, U.S. Supreme Court; 2000, U.S. Tax Court. *Education:* University of North Dakota at Williston and Grand Forks (B.S., 1970); University of Oklahoma (J.D., 1981). Phi Delta Phi (Vice Magistrate, 1980). Adjunct Faculty, Oklahoma City Community College, 1988-1991. *Member:* Oklahoma Bar Association (Member, Taxation Section); Oklahoma City Commercial Law Attorneys Association; American Society of IRS Problem Solvers. ***PRACTICE AREAS:*** Insurance Law; Insurance Defense; Civil Litigation; Mediation; Arbitration; IRS Disputes. ***Email:*** BBergner@NashFirm.com

REPRESENTATIVE CLIENTS: Safeco Insurance Company; Americrest Bank (Formerly Guaranty Bank & Trust Co.); American General Finance, Inc.; Oklahoma Pulmonary Physicians, Inc.; Million Air of Oklahoma City; Sundance Aviation, Inc.; Fidelity Financial Services, Inc.; Wells Fargo Financial Acceptance; Union Bank and Trust Company; Bank of Oklahoma, N.A.; Quail Creek Bank, N.A.; Roadway Express, Inc.; MAR-CO Sales, Inc.; Financial Management Services, Inc.; CitiFinancial Services, Inc.; Commercial Credit Plan; David Stanley Chevrolet, Inc.; Arcadia Financial Ltd.; Baxter Credit Union; Credit Union One of Oklahoma; David Stanley Dodge, Inc.; The Trust Company of Oklahoma; Heritage Trust Company; Oklahoma State Bank; Breathing Disorders Services, Inc.; StartSmart Solutions, L.L.C.; Cimmaron Women's Health Clinic, Inc.; Intrust Bank; Compton Orthopedic Services, Inc.; R&R Manufacturing and Supply Co.; MidAmerica Mortgage, L.L.C.; Sundance Airpark, Ltd.; Ace Group, L.L.C.; American Air, Inc.; PRN Medical Staffing, Inc.

NICHOLS, WOLFE, STAMPER, NALLY, FALLIS & ROBERTSON, INC.

OKLAHOMA CITY, OKLAHOMA

(See Tulsa)

Corporate Law, Business Law, Management Labor and Employment Law, Construction Law, Banks and Banking, Financial Institutions Law, Software Licensing (or Computer Law), Real Estate Law, Surety Law, Wills, Trusts, Estates and Probate, Product Liability Defense, Civil Litigation Practice in all Federal and State Courts and before Government Agencies.

NIEMEYER, ALEXANDER, AUSTIN & PHILLIPS

A PROFESSIONAL CORPORATION
Established in 1984
THREE HUNDRED NORTH WALKER
OKLAHOMA CITY, OKLAHOMA 73102
Telephone: 405-232-2725
Fax: 405-239-7185
Email: staff@niemeyerfirm.com
URL: http://www.niemeyerfirm.com

General Civil Practice. Products Liability Law, Environmental, Insurance, Casualty and Surety Law. Trials in all State and Federal Courts.

FIRM PROFILE: Since 1984, Niemeyer, Alexander, Austin & Phillips has been a small Firm of highly qualified attorneys with a broad range of experience. The Firm aggressively represents clients in a wide variety of civil litigation, with primary focus on insurance defense matters, including those involving novel coverage, "bad faith" issues, and product liability matters. The Firm litigates cases throughout Oklahoma, as well as on a regional basis in the States of Arizona, Arkansas, Colorado, Kansas, Nevada, New Mexico, and Texas for some of its clients. Through its reputation as a determined adversary and advocate for the interests of its clients, the Firm has gained credibility that benefits its clients in all phases of litigation, from pre-filing negotiations through appeals.

JOHN C. NIEMEYER, born La Grange, Texas, June 27, 1935; admitted to bar, 1962, Oklahoma, Texas; U.S. Supreme Court; U.S. Court of Appeals, Eighth and Tenth Circuits; U.S. District Court, Eastern, Northern and Western Districts of Oklahoma and Northern District of Texas; U.S. District Court, District of Arizona. *Education:* A. & M. College of Texas (B.B.A., 1957); Southern Methodist University (J.D., 1962). Phi Alpha Delta. *Member:* Oklahoma County, Oklahoma and American Bar Associations; State Bar of Texas; Oklahoma Trial Lawyers Association; The Association of Trial Lawyers of America. ***PRACTICE AREAS:*** Product Liability Law; Insurance Law; Torts; Personal Injury; Civil Litigation. ***Email:*** johnniemeyer@niemeyerfirm.com

LINDA G. ALEXANDER, born Winchester, Virginia, May 10, 1953; admitted to bar, 1978, Oklahoma; U.S. Court of Appeals, Fifth, Seventh, Eighth and Tenth Circuits; U.S. District Court, Eastern, Northern and Western Districts of Oklahoma; U.S. Court of Federal Claims; U.S. Supreme Court. *Education:* Madison College; George Mason University (B.A., 1975); University of Oklahoma (J.D., 1978). *Member:* Oklahoma County, Oklahoma and American Bar Associations; Oklahoma Trial Lawyers Association. ***PRACTICE AREAS:*** Insurance Law; Appellate Law; Environmental Law; Civil Litigation. ***Email:*** lindaalexander@niemeyerfirm.com

NORMAN F. AUSTIN, born Oklahoma City, Oklahoma, March 31, 1953; admitted to bar, 1989, Oklahoma; U.S. District Court, Eastern, Northern and Western Districts of Oklahoma. *Education:* University of Oklahoma (B.A., 1976); Oklahoma City University (J.D., 1988). *Member:* Oklahoma County and Oklahoma Bar Associations. ***PRACTICE AREAS:*** Torts; Personal Injury Law. ***Email:*** frankaustin@niemeyerfirm.com

HARRIS A. PHILLIPS, III, born Dallas, Texas, July 23, 1966; admitted to bar, 1991, Oklahoma and U.S. District Court, Eastern, Northern and Western Districts of Oklahoma; U.S. Court of Appeals, Seventh and Tenth Circuits. *Education:* Oklahoma State University (B.S., with honors, 1988); University of Oklahoma (J.D., with honors, 1991). *Member:* Oklahoma County, Oklahoma and American Bar Associations. ***PRACTICE AREAS:*** Civil Litigation; Insurance Law; Appellate Practice. ***Email:*** harrisphillips@niemeyerfirm.com

STEPHEN A. DOTTER, born Oklahoma City, Oklahoma, October 4, 1955; admitted to bar, 1998, Oklahoma and U.S. District Court, Eastern, Northern and Western Districts of Oklahoma. *Education:* Oklahoma State University; University of New Mexico (B.A., Political Science, magna cum laude, 1995); Oklahoma City University School of Law (J.D., 1998). Phi Delta Phi. *Member:* Oklahoma County and Oklahoma Bar Associations. ***Email:*** stephendotter@niemeyerfirm.com

CHARLES A. DICKSON, III, born Denton, Texas, January 26, 1969; admitted to bar, 1999, Oklahoma and U.S. District Court, Western, Northern and Eastern Districts of Oklahoma. *Education:* University of Central Oklahoma (B.A., 1994); Oklahoma City University (J.D., 1999). Phi Delta Phi. Moot Court Honors Board. *Member:* Oklahoma and American Bar Associations. ***Email:*** charlesdickson@niemeyerfirm.com

OF COUNSEL

RANDAL D. HOMBURG, born Omaha, Nebraska, September 15, 1958; admitted to bar, 1989, Oklahoma; U.S. District Court, Eastern, Western and Northern Districts of Oklahoma; registered to practice before U.S. Patent and Trademark Office. *Education:* Southeastern Oklahoma State University (B.S., 1982); Oklahoma City University (J.D., 1988). *Member:* Oklahoma and U.S. Patent and Trademark Bar Associations. ***PRACTICE AREAS:*** Intellectual Property; Contracts; Patent Licensing; Small Business Law. ***Email:*** rhomburg@cox.net

REGIONAL COUNSEL FOR: Bridgestone/Firestone North American Tire, LLC.
REPRESENTATIVE CLIENTS: Alderwoods Group, Inc.; American Family Insurance Co.; Canal Insurance Co.; Continental Tire North America; Pettibone Corporation; R.J. Reynolds Company; Underwriters at Lloyds, London; Dolese Bros. Co.; International Business Machines; RJR/Nabisco, Inc.; Western Heritage Insurance Co.; Western World Insurance Co.

NIX & McINTYRE LLP

1300 SOUTH MERIDIAN, SUITE 501
OKLAHOMA CITY, OKLAHOMA 73108-1700
Telephone: Toll Free: 866-917-5200
800-4-Injury (Oklahoma)
866-917-5200 (Nationwide)
Fax: 405-917-5405
URL: http://www.oklahomainjurylaw.com
Email: counsel@oklahoma-law.com
URL: http://www.oklahoma-law.com

Litigation practice including Personal Injury, Automobile Accidents and Injuries, Product Liability, Medical Malpractice, Nursing Home Negligence, Mass Torts.

MEMBERS OF FIRM

GLENDELL D. NIX, born Idabel, Oklahoma, 1964; admitted to bar, 1989, Oklahoma. *Education:* University of Tulsa; Central State University (B.B.A., 1986); University of Oklahoma (J.D., with highest honors, 1989). *Member:* Oklahoma Bar Association; The Association of Trial Lawyers of America. ***PRACTICE AREAS:*** Personal Injury; Nursing Home Negligence; Medical Malpractice; Pharmacy Negligence; Insurance Bad Faith. ***Email:*** glendell@oklahoma-law.com

NOBLE K. McINTYRE, born Fargo, North Dakota, 1970; admitted to bar, 1995, Oklahoma. *Education:* Oklahoma Baptist University (B.B.A.,1992); University of Oklahoma (J.D., 1995). *Member:* Oklahoma Bar Association. The Association of Trial Lawyers of America. ***PRACTICE AREAS:*** Automobile Accidents; Personal Injury; Products Liability; Mass Torts. ***Email:*** noble@oklahoma-law.com

ASSOCIATES

JACOB D. DIESSELHORST, born Peoria, Illinois, July 13, 1976; admitted to bar, 2002, Oklahoma. *Education:* Oklahoma State University (B.A., 1999); University of Oklahoma College of Law (J.D., 2002). *Member:* Oklahoma and American Bar Associations. ***PRACTICE AREAS:*** Personal Injury; Medical Malpractice; Nursing Home Abuse and Neglect; Insurance; Torts. ***Email:*** jacob@oklahoma-law.com

JEREMY A. THURMAN, born Paris, Texas, 1976; admitted to bar, 2002, Oklahoma. *Education:* Southeastern Oklahoma State University (B.S., 1998); University of Oklahoma (J.D., 2002). *Member:* Oklahoma and American Bar Associations. ***LANGUAGES:*** English. ***PRACTICE AREAS:*** Medical Malpractice; Personal Injury; Products Liability; Mass Torts. ***Email:*** jthurman@nkblaw.com

NORMAN & EDEM, P.L.L.C.

127 NORTHWEST 10TH STREET
OKLAHOMA CITY, OKLAHOMA 73103-4927
Telephone: 405-272-0200
Fax: 405-235-2949
Toll Free: 866-272-0201
URL: http://www.nemw.com

Civil Trial and Appellate Practice, Personal Injury, Negligence, Aviation, Products Liability and Professional Negligence.

JOHN W. NORMAN, born Duncan, Oklahoma, February 18, 1944; admitted to bar, 1968, Oklahoma and U.S. District Court, Western District of Oklahoma; 1972, U.S. Supreme Court. *Education:* University of Oklahoma (B.A., 1966; LL.B., cum laude, 1968). Order of the Coif. Member, Oklahoma Law Review, 1966-1968. Author: "Jury Analysis for the Plaintiff," Oklahoma Center for Continuing Education, 1971; "Trial Techniques—Opening Statements for the Plaintiff," Oklahoma Center for Continuing Education, April 1972; "Trial Techniques—Closing Statements for the Plaintiff," Oklahoma Center for Continuing Education, April 1972; "Availability and Use of FAA Aircraft Airmen and Accident Record," ABA National Institute on Small Aircraft Accident Legislation, 1974; "Crashworthiness Update, Law and Techniques," ATLA Annual Convention, Chicago, Illinois, 1985; "Discovery & Admissibility of Government Records and Depositions of Personnel in Aircraft Accident Cases," ABA Third National Institute on Litigation in Aviation, 1984 and ATLA Annual Convention, Seattle, 1984. Member, Governor's Advisory Committee, 1976. Vice-President, 1986-1987 and President, 1987-1988, Oklahoma Chapter of the American Board of Trial Advocates. *Member:* Oklahoma County, Oklahoma, Federal and American (Vice Chairperson, Section of Tort and Insurance Practice, Committee on Aviation and Space Law, 1986-1987) Bar Associations; Oklahoma Trial Lawyers Association (President, 1980); The Association of Trial Lawyers of America (Parliamentarian, 1974-1978; Secretary, 1980-1981; Treasurer, 1981-1982; Chairman, Home Office and Budget Committee, 1982-1984; Chairman, State Development Fund Board, 1985-1986); International Academy of Trial Lawyers; Inner Circle of Advocates (Vice President, 2001-2003; President, 2004-2006); American College of Trial Lawyers. ***REPORTED CASES:*** Hinds v. Warren Transport, Inc., 882 P.2d 1099 (Okla. Ct. App. 1994); Prettyman v. Halliburton Co., 841 P.2d 573 (Okla. 1992); Duane v. Oklahoma Gas & Elec. Co., 833 P.2d 284 (Okla. 1992); Manora v. Watts Regulator Co., 784 P.2d 1056 (Okla. 1989); Wilson v. Gipson, 753 P.2d 1349 (Okla. 1988); Lee v. Volkswagen of America, Inc., 743 P.2d 1067 (Okla. 1987); Lamke v. Futorian Corp., 709 P.2d 684 (Okla. 1985); Redwine v. Baptist Medical Center of Oklahoma, Inc., 679 P.2d 1293 (Okla. 1983); Lee v. Volkswagen of America, Inc., 688 P.2d 1283 (Okla. 1984); Vanderpool v. Oklahoma, 672 P.2d 1153 (Okla. 1983); Horst v. Sirloin Stockade, Inc., 666 P.2d 1285 (Okla. 1983); Scott v. Thunderbird Industries, Inc., 651 P.2d 1346 (Okla.Ct.App. 1982); Stephens v. Yamaha Motor Co., Ltd., Japan, 627 P.2d 439 (Okla. 1981); Hershel v. University Hospital Foundation, 610 P.2d 237 (Okla. 1980); Fields v. Volkswagen of America, Inc., 555 P.2d 48 (Okla. 1976); Fuller v. Rahill, 494 P.2d 785 (Okla. 1972); Repp v. Anadarko Municipal Hospital, 43 F.3d 519 (10th Cir. 1994); Blair v. Eagle-Picher Industries, Inc., 962 F.2d 1492 (10th Cir. 1992); Smith v. FMC Corp., 754 F.2d 873 (10th Cir. 1985); Needham v. Phillips Petroleum Co. of Norway, 719 F.2d 1481 (10th Cir. 1983); Callaway v. U.S., 568 F.2d 684 (10th Cir. 1978); Gates v. Ford Motor Co., 494

(This Listing Continued)

NORMAN & EDEM, P.L.L.C., Oklahoma City—Continued

F.2d 458 (10th Cir. 1974); Sade v. Northern Natural Gas Co., 483 F.2d 230 (10th Cir. 1973); Woolf v. Trans World Airlines, Inc., 443 F.2d 841 (10th Cir. 1971); Brown v. Wichita State University, 547 P.2d 1015 (Kan. 1976); Brown v. Wichita State University, 540 P.2d 66 (Kan. 1975). ***PRACTICE AREAS:*** Personal Injury; Products Liability; Aviation Law.

EMMANUEL E. EDEM, born Calabar, Nigeria, October 27, 1952; admitted to bar, 1982, Oklahoma, U.S. District Court, Western District of Oklahoma and U.S. Court of Appeals, Tenth Circuit. *Education:* Dalhousie University, Halifax, Nova Scotia, Canada (B.S., 1974); Oklahoma City University (J.D., 1982; L.L.D., 1998). Phi Alpha Delta. Member and Chairman, Moot Court Board. Member, Order of the Barristers. Outstanding Alumnus, 1989. Case Comment Editor, Oklahoma City University Law Review, 1981-1982. Author: "Alimony for Men: The Thrust of Recent Decisions of the Supreme Court of the United States," Oklahoma City University Law Review, Vol. 6:2, 1981; "Direct Examination of Expert Witnesses," Excellence in Advocacy, ATLA Press, 1992. OCU Adjunct Professor of Trial Practice, 1986—. Member: Uniform Jury Instruction Committee, Oklahoma Supreme Court, 1991-1996; Civil Justice Reform Act Committee, 1992-1994. Trustee, Oklahoma City University, 2000. Director, Appleseed Foundation, 2000. *Member:* Oklahoma County, Oklahoma (Member, Task Force on Advertising and Solicitation; Chair, Law Schools Committee, 1996) and American Bar Associations; National Bar Association; Oklahoma City Association of Black Lawyers; Oklahoma Trial Lawyers Association (Member, Board of Directors, 1984-1993; Treasurer, 1987-1989; Chair: Nominations and Awards Committee, 1990-1993; CLE Committee, 1989-1990; President, 1995); The Association of Trial Lawyers of America (State Delegate, 1987-1992; Chair, 1988-1993 and Member, 1993, Awards Committee; Co-Chair, Consumer Coalition Committee, 1993; Member: Election Committee; Public Affairs Committee, 1992—; Faculty Member and Diplomate, National College of Advocacy, 1986—; Vice President, Civil Justice Foundation, 1996-1997; President, 1998-1999); American Inn of Court CV (Master of the Bench, 1989—); American Board of Trial Advocates. ***REPORTED CASES:*** Beal v. McCann, 910 P.2d 1099 (Okla.Ct.App. 1995); Duane v. Oklahoma Gas & Elec. Co., 833 P.2d 284 (Okla. 1992); Repp v. Anadarko Municipal Hospital, 43 F.3d 519 (10th Cir. 1994); Intercon, Inc. v. Bell Atlantic Solutions, Inc., 205 F.3d. 1244 (10th Cir. 2000); Dodoo v. Seagate Technology, Inc. 235 F.3d 522 (10th Cir. 2000). ***PRACTICE AREAS:*** Personal Injury; Medical Negligence; Insurance; Civil Litigation.

THOMAS A. WALLACE, born Sapulpa, Oklahoma, October 12, 1923; admitted to bar, 1952, Oklahoma and U.S. District Court, Northern District of Oklahoma; 1953, U.S. District Court, Western District of Oklahoma; 1955, U.S. Court of Appeals, 10th Circuit. *Education:* Columbia University (B.S., 1951; J.D., 1953). Lecturer and Author: "Service of Process Under the Oklahoma General Corporation Act," Oklahoma Bar Association Continuing Legal Education Seminar, University of Oklahoma, Oklahoma City University, 1986, 1987; "Update on the Pleading Code," Oklahoma Bar Association Seminar, 1986; "Plaintiff's Preparation of the Second Impact Collision Case Under the Oklahoma Law of Products Liability," Oklahoma Trial Lawyers Association, 1987. Member: Supreme Court Senate Concurrent Resolution 69 Committee, Oklahoma Code of Evidence, 1976; Uniform Jury Instructions Committee, Oklahoma Supreme Court, 1979-1982; Supreme Court Standing Committee on Uniform Jury Instructions, 1993-2001. *Member:* Oklahoma Bar Association (Member, Sub-Committee, Oklahoma Evidence Code, 1973-1977; Member, 1979-2001 and Vice-Chair, 1994-1996, Civil Procedure Committee); Oklahoma Trial Lawyers Association (President, 1976); The Association of Trial Lawyers of America. [USMCR, 1943-1946]. ***REPORTED CASES:*** Intercon v. Bell Atlantic Internet Solutions, Inc., 205 F. 3rd 1244 (10th Cir. 2000); Kraszewski v. Baptist Medical Center of Oklahoma, Inc., 916 P.2d 241 (Okla. 1996); Hinds v. Warren Transport, Inc., 882 P.2d 1099 (Okla.Ct.App. 1994); Swick v. Swick, 864 P.2d 819 (Okla. 1993); Sigma Resources Corp. v. Norse Exploration, Inc., 852 P.2d 764 (Okla.Ct.App. 1992); Mott v. Carlson, 786 P.2d 1247 (Okla. 1990); Dodson v. Henderson Properties, Inc., 708 P.2d 1064 (Okla. 1985); Lee v. Volkswagen of America, Inc., 688 P.2d 1283 (Okla. 1984); Joyce v. M & M Gas Co., 672 P.2d 1172 (Okla. 1983); Liberty Nat. Bank & Trust Co. of Oklahoma City v. Kaibab Industries, Inc., 591 P.2d 692 (Okla. 1978); Shankle Equipment Co., Inc. v. Liberty Nat. Bank & Trust Co. of Oklahoma City, 569 P.2d 965 (Okla. 1977); Avco Corp. v. Swartzlander, 470 P.2d 340 (Okla. 1970); Gaddy v. Mid-Continent Freight Lines, Inc., 406 P.2d 479 (Okla. 1965); Wood v. Camp, 397 P.2d 890 (Okla. 1964); Tom P. McDermott, Inc. v. Birks, 395 P.2d 575 (Okla. 1964); Wellman v. Novak, 392 P.2d 377 (Okla. 1964); Automobile Owners Safety Ins. Co. v. Baker, 324 P.2d 867 (Okla. 1958); Barnett v. Newcomer, 307 P.2d 148 (Okla. 1957); Mitchell v. Williamson, 304 P.2d 314 (Okla. 1956); Riss & Co. v. Reed, 301 P.2d 208 (Okla. 1956); Moore v. Subaru of America, 891 F.2d 1445 (10th Cir. 1989); Looney v. Capital National Bank of Austin, Texas, 235 F.2d 436 (5th Cir. 1956); Smith v. FMC Corp., 754 F.2d 873 (10th Cir. 1985). ***Email:*** taw@nemw.com

JOHN B. NORMAN, born Norman, Oklahoma, July 13, 1964; admitted to bar, 1988, Oklahoma and U.S. District Court, Western District of Oklahoma. *Education:* Baylor University (B.A., 1985); University of Oklahoma (J.D., 1988). Phi Delta Phi. Recipient, American Jurisprudence Awards. American Inns of Court. *Member:* Oklahoma and American Bar Associations; Oklahoma Trial Lawyers Association; The Association of Trial Lawyers of America. ***REPORTED CASES:*** Kraszewski v. Baptist Medical Center of Oklahoma, Inc., 916 P.2d 241 (Okla. 1996); Grimes v. Swaim, 971 F.2d 622 (10th Cir. 1992). ***PRACTICE AREAS:*** Personal Injury; Products Liability; Aviation Law; Medical Negligence; Civil Litigation. ***Email:*** jbn@nemw.com

MARK A. COX, born Troy, Ohio, August 26, 1962; admitted to bar, 1990, Oklahoma and U.S. District Court, Western, Northern and Eastern Districts of Oklahoma. *Education:* Central State University (B.B.A., Finance, 1985); Oklahoma City University (J.D., 1990). Phi Delta Phi. Moot Court Board (Secretary-Treasurer, 1988-1989). Editor, SBA Newsletter, 1988. Faculty, Oklahoma College of Advocacy, 1994-1998. Writer/Director: "The Peoples Law School: Four-Part Television Program - For the Thomas Dee Frasier Educational Foundation (Episode 1 - Products Liability; Episode 2 - Medical Negligence; Episode 3 - Nursing Home Negligence; Episode 4 - Workers' Compensation, 1996, Aired on KOCO Channel 5 - Oklahoma City). Speaker: "Opening Statements" - Oklahoma Trial Lawyers Association, June 11, 1998, "Maximizing Automobile Accident Cases" - Grady County Bar Association, November 13, 1998, "Nursing Home Law in Oklahoma-Evaluation and Preparation of the Plaintiffs Case" - Oklahoma Bar Association, 2001. Publications: "The Hazards of Multipurpose Lighters," - The Association of Trial Attorneys of America (ATLA) Trial Magazine, November, 1998 pp. 55-60. Member, MENSA, 1983-2004. Member, City of Edmond Board of Appeals and Board of Adjustments, 1993-1994. Member: Presidents Advisory Council 1988; Dean's Advisory Board 1988. Recipient, Judge Raymond Naifeh Judicial Fellowship, 1987-1988; Dean's Service Award, 1988; Oklahoma City University School of Law Alumni Association Award of Merit, 1988. President, Student Bar Association, 1988-1989. Member: Board of Directors, 1996-1998; Advisory Board of Directors, 1995. Chair, People's Law School Committee, 1996-1998. Co-Chair, Awards Committee, 1995. Co-Chair, Membership Committee, 1994. Chair, Law Schools Committee, 1993. Member, Oklahoma City University School of Law Alumni Board of Directors, 1990-1996 (President, 1995; Vice-President, 1994; Secretary, 1992; Treasurer, 1991). *Member:* Oklahoma County (Community Law Week Committee, Chair, 1992; Vice-Chair, 1991) and Oklahoma Bar Associations; Oklahoma Trial Lawyers Association (Chair, Continuing Legal Education, 1997-1998). ***REPORTED CASES:*** Bowers v. Wimberly, et al, 933 P.2d 312 (Okla. 1997); Shugart v. Central Rural Electric Cooperative, 110 F.3d 1501 (10th Cir. 1997); Price v. TLC Healthcare, Inc. (2004 Okla. 8). ***PRACTICE AREAS:*** Personal Injury; Medical Negligence; Products Liability; Motor Vehicle Accidents and Injuries; Nursing Home Litigation; Defective Motorcycle Helmet Litigation; Insurance Bad Faith.

BRADLEY E. NORMAN, born Oklahoma City, Oklahoma, March 7, 1971; admitted to bar, 2000, Oklahoma and U.S. District Court, Western, Eastern, and Northern Districts of Oklahoma. *Education:* Malone College (B.A., 1996); Oklahoma City University (J.D., 2000). *Member:* Oklahoma County Bar Association; Oklahoma Trial Lawyers Association; The Association of Trial Lawyers of America.

JERRI K. BIRD, born Roswell, New Mexico, August 20, 1973; admitted to bar, 2001, Oklahoma and U.S. District Court, Eastern and Western District of Oklahoma. *Education:* Texas Christian University (B.S., 1995); Oklahoma City University (J.D., 2001). *Member:* Oklahoma and Oklahoma County Bar Associations; Oklahoma Trial Lawyers Association; The Association of Trial Lawyers of America.

MARK BONNER, born Beaver, Oklahoma, August 15, 1961; admitted to bar, 1992, Oklahoma; U.S. Supreme Court; U.S. Court of Appeals, Tenth Circuit; U.S. District Court, Northern, Eastern and Western Districts of Oklahoma. *Education:* University of Oklahoma (B.A., Journalism/Advertising, 1984; J.D., with highest honors, 1992). Order of the Coif. Member, University of Oklahoma Law Review. *Member:* Oklahoma County and Oklahoma Bar Associations; Oklahoma Trial Lawyers Association; The Association of Trial Lawyers of America.

REFERENCES: IBC Bank; Bank of Oklahoma.

DAVID L. NUNN, P.C.

OKLAHOMA CITY, OKLAHOMA

(See Edmond)

Commercial Law, Corporate Law, Commercial Collections, Bankruptcy (Creditors only), Automotive Warranty and Finance Law, Consumer Finance, Creditors Rights, Contracts, Litigation.

OGLE & WELCH, P.C.

117 PARK AVENUE, THIRD FLOOR
OKLAHOMA CITY, OKLAHOMA 73102
Telephone: 405-232-9800
Facsimile: 405-232-1608
Email: josh@joshwelchlaw.com
URL: http://www.joshwelchlaw.com

Criminal Trial and Appellate Practice in all State and Federal courts. Grand Jury Investigations, White Collar and Complex Crimes, Drugs, Driving Under the Influence, Murder, Sex Crimes, Obscenities, Security Fraud, Personal Injury, Auto Accidents, Trucking Accidents, Driving While Intoxicated, Criminal Record Expungements, Civil Rights.

FIRM PROFILE: The Firm practices in both criminal and civil trial law, with emphasis on grand jury, jury trial and appellate practice. Representation has taken the firm throughout the State of Oklahoma in both State and Federal court matters. Mr. Ogle is an active lecturer in continuing legal education seminars throughout the State of Oklahoma for various groups and bar associations. It is the objective of the firm to handle each client's case in a specialized approach that involves experienced lawyers, support staff and investigators.

Reported cases: United States v. Van Meter, 278 F.3rd 1156 (10th Cir. 2002); United States v. Day, 223 F.3rd 1225 (10th Cir. 2000); United States v. Dickerson, 195 F.3rd 1183 (10th Cir. 1999).

DAVID OGLE, born Kirksville, Missouri, March 23, 1968; admitted to bar, 1997, Oklahoma and U.S. District Court, Western and Northern Districts of Oklahoma; U.S. District Court, District of Colorado; U.S. Court of Appeals, Tenth Circuit; 2004, Texas; U.S. Supreme Court. *Education:* Oklahoma State University (B.S., 1991); Oklahoma City University (J.D., 1997). Board Member, Moot Court. Lecturer, Continuing Legal Education Seminars. Criminal Justice Act Panel, Western District of Oklahoma, 1998-present. *Member:* Oklahoma County (Board of Directors) and American (Member, Section: Criminal Justice) Bar Associations; National Association of Criminal Defense Lawyers (Life Member); Oklahoma Criminal Defense Lawyers Association (President); Oklahoma Trial Lawyers Association; Association of Trial Lawyers of America; Luther Bohanon American Inns of Court. ***PRACTICE AREAS:*** Criminal Defense; Grand Jury Practice; White Collar Crime; Drug Crimes; Driving While Intoxicated; Murder; Sex Crimes; Securities Fraud. ***Email:*** dogle@oglewelchlaw.com

JOSH T. WELCH, born Paris, Texas, December 28, 1968; admitted to bar, 1997, Oklahoma; 1998, U.S. District Court, Western District of Oklahoma. *Education:* Oklahoma State University (B.S., 1992); Oklahoma City University School of Law (J.D., 1997). Phi Delta Phi. Moot Court. *Member:* Oklahoma County, Oklahoma and American Bar Asso-

(This Listing Continued)

ciations; National Association of Criminal Defense Lawyers; Oklahoma Criminal Defense Lawyers Association; American Trial Lawyers Association. ***PRACTICE AREAS:*** Criminal Defense; Criminal Law; Drug Crimes; Driving While Intoxicated; Felonies; Personal Injury; Automobile Accidents and Injuries; Wrongful Death. ***Email:*** jwelch@oglewelchlaw.com

---

ANN K. HADRAVA, born Janesville, Wisconsin, August 20, 1970; admitted to bar, 2002, Texas; 2004, Oklahoma and U.S. District Court, Western, Northern and Eastern Districts of Oklahoma; U.S. Court of Appeals, Tenth Circuit. *Education:* Oklahoma State University (B.S., B.A.,1992); Oklahoma City University School of Law (J.D., summa cum laude, 2002). Editor, Law Review. *Member:* Oklahoma and American Bar Associations; Oklahoma Criminal Defense Lawyers Association. ***PRACTICE AREAS:*** Criminal Defense; Criminal Appeals; Habeas Corpus. ***Email:*** ahadrava@oglewelchlaw.com

OF COUNSEL

HACK WELCH, born Sherman, Texas, March 7, 1946; admitted to bar, 1973, Oklahoma. *Education:* University of Oklahoma (B.B.A., 1970); Tulsa University (J.D., 1973). *Member:* Oklahoma Bar Association.

OLDFIELD, COKER & GRAVES

4808 NORTH CLASSEN BOULEVARD
OKLAHOMA CITY, OKLAHOMA 73118
Telephone: 405-840-0555
Fax: 405-840-4808

General Civil Practice. Trials in all State and Federal Courts. Corporation, Insurance, Workers Compensation, Personal Injury and Oil and Gas Law.

MEMBERS OF FIRM

JOHN S. OLDFIELD, JR., born Alexandria, Virginia, January 7, 1945; admitted to bar, 1973, Oklahoma and U.S. District Court, Western District of Oklahoma. *Education:* Wheeling University (B.A., 1968); University of Oklahoma (J.D., 1973). Phi Alpha Delta. Order of the Coif. Adjunct Professor, University of Oklahoma College of Law, 1985—. Judge, Court of Appeals Temporary Division 220. *Member:* Oklahoma County, Oklahoma (Member, House of Delegates) and American Bar Associations; Oklahoma Association of Defense Counsel; American Inn of Court (President); The Association of Trial Lawyers of America; Oklahoma Trial Lawyers Association. Fellow, Oklahoma Bar Foundation. [1st Lt., USMC, ret.]. ***PRACTICE AREAS:*** Workers Compensation Law; Personal Injury Law; Insurance Law.

MICHAEL G. COKER, born Shawnee, Oklahoma, May 19, 1950; admitted to bar, 1975, Oklahoma. *Education:* University of Oklahoma (B.A., 1972; J.D., 1975). *Member:* Oklahoma County (Member, Workers Compensation Section), Oklahoma (Chairman and Director, Workers Compensation Section) and American (Member, Sections on: Tort and Insurance Practice; Natural Resources Law) Bar Associations; Oklahoma Association of Defense Counsel; The Association of Trial Lawyers of America (Associate Member); Association of Workers Compensation Defense Counsel. ***PRACTICE AREAS:*** Workers Compensation Law; Oil and Gas Law.

MATTHEW J. GRAVES, born Okarche, Oklahoma, November 20, 1962; admitted to bar, 1988, Oklahoma and U.S. District Court, Western District of Oklahoma; 1991, U.S. District Court, Northern District of Oklahoma; 1994, U.S. District Court, Eastern District of Oklahoma; U.S. Court of Appeals, Tenth Circuit. *Education:* Anderson College (B.A., 1985); University of Oklahoma (J.D., 1988). *Member:* Oklahoma and American (Member, Tort and Insurance Practice Section) Bar Associations. ***PRACTICE AREAS:*** Personal Injury Law; Product Liability Law; Workers Compensation Law.

ASSOCIATE

CYNTHIA WOOD WELCH, born Oklahoma City, Oklahoma, August 30, 1962; admitted to bar, 1990, Oklahoma. *Education:* University of Oklahoma (B.A., 1984; J.D., 1989). *Member:* Oklahoma (Member, Workers Compensation Section). and American Bar Associations. ***PRACTICE AREAS:*** Workers Compensation.

DOUGLAS L. PARR

228 ROBERT S. KERR, SUITE 550
OKLAHOMA CITY, OKLAHOMA 73102
Telephone: 405-528-1018
Fax: 405-528-1035
Email: douglas.parr@parrlawoffice.com
URL: http://www.parrlawoffice.com

Criminal Law, Criminal Defense, Post-Conviction Remedies, Police Misconduct, Civil Rights, Drug Trafficking, Assault and Battery, Sexual Assault, Homicide, Felonies, Misdemeanors, White Collar Crime, Forensic, DNA, Theft, Driving While Intoxicated.

DOUGLAS L. PARR, born 1951; admitted to bar, 1979, Oklahoma. *Education:* Oklahoma State University (B.S., 1973); University of Oklahoma (J.D., 1978). Cooperating Attorney, The Center for Constitutional Rights, New York City, 1980—. Legal Commentator, ABC News, "Nightline" and "Good Morning America". *Member:* Oklahoma Bar Association; Oklahoma Criminal Defense Lawyers Association (President, 2005—); National Association of Criminal Defense Lawyers. ***PRACTICE AREAS:*** Criminal Law; Criminal Defense; Post-Conviction Remedies; Police Misconduct; Civil Rights; Drug Trafficking; Assault and Battery; Sexual Assault; Homicide; Felonies; Misdemeanors; White Collar Crime; Forensic DNA; Theft; Driving While Intoxicated.

THE PARRISH LAW FIRM

A PROFESSIONAL CORPORATION
ONE NORTH HUDSON, SUITE 700
OKLAHOMA CITY, OKLAHOMA 73102
Telephone: 405-232-1985; Toll Free: 800-270-1980
Facsimile: 405-232-4679
Email: mparrish@parrishlaw.org

Personal Injury, Slip and Fall, Automobile Accidents, Trucking Accidents, Wrongful Death, Workers Compensation, Nursing Home Abuse.

MEMBER OF FIRM

MURRY J. PARRISH, born Stillwater, Oklahoma, December 2, 1969; admitted to bar, 1995, Arizona and U.S. District Court, District of Arizona; 1996, Oklahoma and U.S. District Court, Western District of Oklahoma. *Education:* Oklahoma State University (B.A., 1992); University of Oklahoma (J.D., 1995). Phi Alpha Delta. *Member:* Oklahoma County, Oklahoma and American Bar Associations; State Bar of Arizona; Arizona Trial Lawyers Association; The Association of Trial Lawyers of America. ***PRACTICE AREAS:*** Personal Injury; Health Law; Litigation; Insurance; Contracts.

PARSONS & ASSOCIATES LAW FIRM

A CORPORATION
OKLAHOMA CITY, OKLAHOMA
(See Norman)

Banking Litigation, Business Litigation, Business Torts, Commercial Collections, Commercial Litigation, Corporate Contracts, Creditors Rights, Lawsuits, Lender Liability, Internet Violations, Oklahoma Lottery, Employer Defense and Trial Practice in All Courts.

PATE, KEMPF & KNARR

A PROFESSIONAL CORPORATION
Established in 1968
TWO LEADERSHIP SQUARE
211 NORTH ROBINSON, SUITE 418
P.O. BOX 1907
OKLAHOMA CITY, OKLAHOMA 73102
Telephone: 405-235-4211
Fax: 405-232-3930
Email: sknarr@pkklawyers.com

Civil Practice which includes: Trial and Appellate Practice in State and Federal Courts. Insurance Defense, Banking Law, Telecommunication Law, Real Estate, Federal and State Taxation, Bankruptcy and Creditor's Rights, Probate, Oil and Gas.

COLLIER H. PATE, born Fort Worth, Texas, December 11, 1939; admitted to bar, 1969, Oklahoma, U.S. District Court, Western, Northern and Eastern Districts of Oklahoma, U.S. Court of Appeals, Fifth and Tenth Circuits and U.S. Supreme Court. *Education:* Texas Christian University (B.S., 1961); University of Oklahoma (M.B.A., 1965); Oklahoma City University (J.D., 1968). Phi Delta Phi. *Member:* Oklahoma County and Oklahoma Bar Associations; Oklahoma Association of Defense Counsel. ***PRACTICE AREAS:*** Civil Litigation. ***Email:*** cpate@pkklawyers.com

JOHN FREDERICK KEMPF, JR., born Oklahoma City, Oklahoma, August 24, 1951; admitted to bar, 1977, Oklahoma and U.S. District Court, Western District of Oklahoma; 1979, U.S. Court of Appeals, Tenth Circuit; 1980, U.S. Supreme Court; 1987, U.S. District Court, Eastern District of Oklahoma. *Education:* Oklahoma State University (B.A., 1973); Oklahoma City University (J.D., 1977). *Member:* Oklahoma County and Oklahoma Bar (Chair, Real Property Law Section, 2000; Member, Title Examination Standards Committee, 1994—) Associations; Oklahoma City Real Property Lawyers Association (Board Member, 2000—); Mineral Lawyers Society of Oklahoma City. ***PRACTICE AREAS:*** Real Estate; Real Estate Titles; Commercial Law; Civil Litigation; Probate; Telecommunications. ***Email:*** jfkempf@pkklawyers.com

STUART ALAN KNARR, born Kansas City, Kansas, December 22, 1961; admitted to bar, 1989, Oklahoma; U.S. District Court, Western, Eastern and Northern Districts of Oklahoma and U.S. District Court, Northern District of Texas; U.S. Court of Appeals, Tenth Circuit and U.S. Supreme Court. *Education:* University of Tennessee (B.S., in Mechanical Engineering, 1984); Oklahoma City University (J.D., 1989). Moot Court Board. *Member:* Oklahoma County and Oklahoma Bar Associations. ***PRACTICE AREAS:*** Civil Litigation; Insurance Law; Real Property Law; Bankruptcy; Corporate Law; Telecommunications. ***Email:*** sknarr@pkklawyers.com

KEN D. KERR, JR., born Oklahoma City, Oklahoma, October 6, 1966; admitted to bar, 1995, Oklahoma; U.S. District Court, Western and Northern Districts of Oklahoma and U.S. Supreme Court. *Education:* University of Oklahoma (B.B.A., 1991; J.D., 1995). Phi Delta Phi. Recipient, American Jurisprudence Award, Real Property Law. *Member:* Oklahoma County, Oklahoma and American Bar Associations; Oklahoma Association of Defense Counsel. ***PRACTICE AREAS:*** Civil Litigation; Commercial Law; Telecommunications. ***Email:*** kkerr@pkklawyers.com

OF COUNSEL

JOHN P. MARCH, born Oklahoma City, Oklahoma, August 2, 1940; admitted to bar, 1969, Oklahoma. *Education:* Oklahoma State University (B.S., 1962); Oklahoma City University (J.D., 1969). Phi Delta Phi. ***PRACTICE AREAS:*** State and Federal Taxation Law.

REPRESENTATIVE CLIENTS: Available Upon Request.
REFERENCES: Available Upon Request.

JIM PEARSON

Established in 1983

PENN PARK, SUITE 304
5001 NORTH PENNSYLVANIA
OKLAHOMA CITY, OKLAHOMA 73112
Telephone: 405-858-8500
Fax: 405-858-8585
Email: jpearsonpc@aol.com
URL: http://www.lawyers.com/jimpearson

Divorce and Family Law, including Child Law, Child Custody and Child Support.

FIRM PROFILE: Jim Pearson is listed in the Bar Register of Preeminent Lawyers in the Area of Family Law.

JIM PEARSON, born Oklahoma City, Oklahoma, May 25, 1946; admitted to bar, 1973, Oklahoma and U.S. District Court, Western District of Oklahoma. *Education:* Oklahoma State University (B.A., 1968); University of Oklahoma (J.D., 1973). Assistant Public Defender, 1976-1979. Special Judge, Oklahoma County, Oklahoma, 1979-1982. *Member:* Oklahoma (Member, Family Law Section) and American (Member, Family Law Section) Bar Associations. [1st. Lt., U.S. Army, 1968-1970]. ***PRACTICE AREAS:*** Family Law; Children.

BRIAN L. PETERSON, P.C.

101 PARK AVENUE, SUITE 275
OKLAHOMA CITY, OKLAHOMA 73102-7206
Telephone: 405-232-1857
Fax: 405-232-1665
Email: bpeterson@blppc.com

Aviation, Oil and Gas, Environmental Law, Civil Litigation, Litigation, Commercial, Corporate, Financing, Transactions.

BRIAN L. PETERSON, born Oklahoma City, Oklahoma, June 5, 1960; admitted to bar, 1985, Oklahoma and U.S. District Court, Western and Northern Districts of Oklahoma; 1989, U.S. Court of Appeals, Eighth and Tenth Circuits. *Education:* Yale University (B.A., 1982); Baylor University (J.D., 1985). Member: Order of the Barristers; Moot Court; Jessup International Law Moot Court; National Mock Trial Team. *Member:* Oklahoma and American Bar Associations. ***PRACTICE AREAS:*** Oil and Gas; Environmental; Civil Litigation; Commercial; Corporate; Financing; Transactions.

LANCE BOYD PHILLIPS

Established in 1998

1 NORTH HUDSON, SUITE 700
OKLAHOMA CITY, OKLAHOMA 73102
Telephone: 405-235-5944
Mobile: 405-641-3869
Fax: 405-232-4679
Email: lancebp2000@yahoo.com
URL: http://www.lawyers.com/lancephillips

Criminal Law, Family Law, Adoption Law, Civil Practice, Workers Compensation, Divorce, DUI, Auto Accidents.

LANCE BOYD PHILLIPS, born Oklahoma City, Oklahoma, May 12, 1971; admitted to bar, 1996, Oklahoma and U.S. District Court, Western District of Oklahoma. *Education:* Texas Christian University (B.B.A., 1993); University of Oklahoma (J.D., 1996). Phi Delta Phi (Vice President, 1996). Member, Rotary International. *Member:* Oklahoma County and Oklahoma Bar Associations. ***PRACTICE AREAS:*** Criminal Law; Family Law; Adoption Law; Civil Practice; Workers Compensation; Divorce; Driving While Intoxicated; Automobile Accidents and Injuries.

Language: Spanish.

PHILLIPS McFALL McCAFFREY McVAY & MURRAH, P.C.

Established in 1986

ONE LEADERSHIP SQUARE, 12TH FLOOR
211 NORTH ROBINSON
OKLAHOMA CITY, OKLAHOMA 73102
Telephone: 405-235-4100
Fax: 405-235-4133
URL: http://www.phillipsmcfall.com

Other Oklahoma City Office: 1001 N.W. 63rd Street, Suite 200, 73116. Telephone: 405-840-5240; Fax: 405-840-2136.
Norman, Oklahoma Office: 232 E. Main, Suite B., 73069. Telephone: 405-346-3346. Fax: 405-364-4666.
Other Norman Office: 401 W. Main, Suite 444, 72067. Telephone: 405-292-4445. Fax: 405-292-4446.

Administrative, Antitrust, Banking, Bankruptcy and Reorganization, Commercial, Consumer Financial Services, Corporate and Partnership, Employment, Environmental, Estate Planning and Probate, Federal and State Taxation, Financial Institution Regulation, Franchise, Health Care, Insurance Defense, International, Litigation, Municipal Finance, Oil and Gas, Product Liability, Public Pension, Real Estate, Securities Regulation and Telecommunications.

FIRM PROFILE: Phillips, McFall, McCaffrey, McVay and Murrah, P.C. is listed in the Preeminent Lawyers.

(This Listing Continued)

ELIZABETH KEMP BROWN, born Ada, Oklahoma, October 17, 1957; admitted to bar, 1983, Oklahoma; 1985, U.S. District Court, Western District of Oklahoma and U.S Tax Court. *Education:* East Central University; University of Oklahoma (B.A., 1979; J.D., 1983). Beta Gamma Sigma. Author: "Tax Consequences Associated with Intervivos Transfers of Encumbered Property Into Trust," Taxes, The Tax Magazine, September, 1980, page 659; "Fallout from the Take-or-Pay Wars," Gross Production Tax on Proceeds Received in Settlement, Take-or-Pay Litigation Okla. Law Review Vol. 43:457 (1990). Certified Public Accountant, Oklahoma, 1980. *Member:* Oklahoma County and Oklahoma Bar Associations; American Institute of Certified Public Accountants; Oklahoma Society of Certified Public Accountants; National Health Lawyers Association. ***PRACTICE AREAS:*** Federal Income Tax; State Income Tax; Estate and Gift Taxation; Estate Planning; Supplemental Needs Trust; Trust Litigation; Probate; Commercial Law; Real Estate; Health Care. ***Email:*** ekbrown@phillipsmcfall.com

ROBERT J. CAMPBELL, JR., born Oklahoma City, Oklahoma, June 22, 1952; admitted to bar, 1980, Oklahoma; 1983, U.S. District Court, Western, Eastern and Northern Districts of Oklahoma, U.S. Court of Appeals, Tenth Circuit and U.S. Supreme Court. *Education:* Oklahoma City Southwestern Junior College (A.A., 1972); University of Oklahoma (B.A., 1975); Oklahoma City University (J.D., with honors, 1980). Law Clerk (Attorney) Oklahoma Court of Appeals, 1981-1982. Recipient, American Jurisprudence Awards: Corporations, Remedies, Criminal Procedure, Wills & Estates I, Wills & Estates II. Legal Assistant (Attorney) Oklahoma Court of Criminal Appeals, 1980-1981, 1983-1984. *Member:* Oklahoma and American Bar Associations. ***PRACTICE AREAS:*** Commercial Litigation; Appellate; Corporate Law; Public Utility Law; Civil; Oil and Gas Law. ***Email:*** rjcampbell@phillipsmcfall.com

MARC EDWARDS, born Baytown, Texas, March 10, 1955; admitted to bar, 1983, Oklahoma; U.S. District Court, Western and Eastern Districts of Oklahoma; 1987, U.S. Court of Appeals, Tenth Circuit. *Education:* Southwest Missouri State University (B.S., 1979); University of Tulsa (J.D., 1983). Assistant Attorney General, Oklahoma, 1983-1987. Hearing Examiner, Oklahoma State Ethics Commission, 1995-1998. *Member:* Oklahoma County, Oklahoma and American Bar Associations; National Association of Public Pension Attorneys; Oklahoma State Board of Property and Casualty Rates. ***PRACTICE AREAS:*** Administrative Law; Civil Litigation; Public Pension Plans; Governmental Law; Telecommunications Regulation. ***Email:*** medwards@phillipsmcfall.com

LLOYD T. HARDIN, JR., born Oklahoma City, Oklahoma, March 13, 1949; admitted to bar, 1977, Oklahoma; U.S. Court of Appeals, Tenth Circuit and U.S. District Court, Western District of Oklahoma. *Education:* University of Oklahoma (B.A., 1971; J.D., 1977); Worcester College, Oxford University, England (Summer Term, 1975). Phi Delta Phi. Recipient, American Jurisprudence Awards in Creditors' Rights, Trusts and Estate Tax, 1976. Adjunct Professor, University of Oklahoma College of Law, 1985-1987. Vice President and Assistant General Counsel, Landmark Land Company, Inc., a New York publicly traded corporation located in Carmel, California, 1987-1992. *Member:* American College of Real Estate Lawyers (Elected, 1987). [1st Lt., USMC, 1971-1974]. ***PRACTICE AREAS:*** Commercial Transactions; Real Estate; International Law; Hotel and Resort Development; Construction Law; Architectural Law. ***Email:*** lthardin@phillipsmcfall.com

SALLY A. HASENFRATZ, born Perry, Oklahoma, October 30, 1960; admitted to bar, 1986, Oklahoma; 1987, U.S. District Court, Western District of Oklahoma and U.S. Tax Court. *Education:* University of Oklahoma (B.B.A., with honors, 1983); University of Oklahoma (J.D., 1986); Southern Methodist University (LL.M., Taxation, 1987). Phi Delta Phi. Law Clerk to Justice Marian P. Opala, Oklahoma Supreme Court. *Member:* Oklahoma (Member: AIDS Support Committee, 1996-1998; Probate Code Committee, 1997-1998) and American Bar Associations. ***PRACTICE AREAS:*** Real Estate; Taxation; Estate Planning. ***Email:*** sahasenfratz@phillipsmcfall.com

TERRY L. HAWKINS, born Hobart, Oklahoma, June 20, 1956; admitted to bar, 1981, Oklahoma. *Education:* Oklahoma State University (B.S., 1978); University of Oklahoma (J.D., 1981). Phi Delta Phi. Co-Author: "Oklahoma Municipal Bonds," 3rd edition, 1987; 4th edition, 1993; 5th edition, 1995, 6th edition, 1999. *Member:* Oklahoma County, Oklahoma and American Bar Associations; National Association of Bond Lawyers. ***PRACTICE AREAS:*** Municipal Finance. ***Email:*** tlhawkins@phillipsmcfall.com

FRED A. LEIBROCK, born Mexico City, Mexico, May 7, 1965; admitted to bar, 1990, Oklahoma and U.S. District Court, Eastern, Northern and Western Districts of Oklahoma; U.S. Supreme Court; U.S. Court of Appeals, Tenth Circuit. *Education:* Texas Christian University (B.A., 1987); Oklahoma City University (J.D., with honors, 1990). Phi Delta Phi (Magister, 1988-1989; Chairman, Fraternity Wide Committee on International Programs and Activities, 1989). Oklahoma City University Law Review (Staff Member, 1988-1989; Staff Editor, 1989-1990). Barrister, Ruth Bader Ginsburg American Inn of Court. Pupil, William J. Holloway, Jr. American Inn of Court. Author: "Lender Liability Under the Comprehensive Environmental Response, Compensation and Liability Act; Recent Developments and Proposed Precautions," 62 O.B.J. 2374 (1991). *Member:* Oklahoma County, Oklahoma and American Bar Associations. ***LANGUAGES:*** Spanish. ***PRACTICE AREAS:*** Litigation; Product Liability; Real Estate; Commercial Law. ***Email:*** faleibrock@phillipsmcfall.com

J. MARK LOVELACE, born Tyler, Texas, July 11, 1955; admitted to bar, 1982, Oklahoma; 1985, U.S. District Court, Western District of Oklahoma. *Education:* Duke University (B.A., cum laude, 1976); University of Oklahoma (J.D., 1982). *Member:* Oklahoma County, Oklahoma and American Bar Associations. ***PRACTICE AREAS:*** Real Estate; Commercial. ***Email:*** jmlovelace@phillipsmcfall.com

JAMES A. McCAFFREY, born Oklahoma City, Oklahoma, August 12, 1939; admitted to bar, 1964, Oklahoma; 1966, U.S. District Court, Eastern and Western Districts of Oklahoma and U.S. Court of Appeals, Tenth Circuit; 1969, U.S. Supreme Court. *Education:* University of Oklahoma (B.B.A., 1961; J.D., 1964). Phi Alpha Delta. Faculty Member, Oklahoma Bar Review, 1975-1996. Co-Author: "Truth-in-Lending Disclosure in Open and Closed End Credit," Oklahoma City University Law Review, Vol. 9, #1, 1984; "Practitioner's Guide to the Oklahoma Uniform Consumer Credit Code," Butterworths; "The U3C Manual: Users Guide to the Uniform Consumer Credit Code," Oklahoma Bankers Association Services Co, Inc., 1994. Professor of Law, Oklahoma City University Law School, 1972-1981. Special Instructor of Law, Tulsa University School of Law, 1975. *Member:* Oklahoma County, Oklahoma and American (Member: Business Law Section and Con-

(This Listing Continued)

sumer Financial Serivces Sub-Section; Consumer Financial Services Committee) Bar Associations. ***PRACTICE AREAS:*** Commercial Financial Services; Consumer Credit; Banking; Consumer Credit Compliance. ***Email:*** jamccaffrey@phillipsmcfall.com

D. KEITH McFALL, born Oklahoma City, Oklahoma, March 31, 1957; admitted to bar, 1982, Oklahoma; U.S. District Court, Eastern and Western Districts of Oklahoma. *Education:* University of Oklahoma (B.B.A., 1979; J.D., 1982). *Member:* Oklahoma County, Oklahoma (Banking and Commercial Law Sections, Chair 1991) and American (Member, Business Law Section) Bar Associations; Oklahoma Society of Title Attorneys. ***PRACTICE AREAS:*** Banking; Commercial; Corporate; Mergers and Acquisitions; Real Estate; Sports Law; Bankruptcy and Reorganization; Debtor-Creditor. ***Email:*** dkmcfall@phillipsmcfall.com

MELVIN R. McVAY, JR., born Cleveland, Ohio, December 27, 1954; admitted to bar, 1982, Oklahoma; U.S. Supreme Court; U.S. Court of Appeals, Tenth Circuit and U.S. District Court, Western, Eastern and Northern Districts of Oklahoma. *Education:* University of Missouri (B.S., 1977); University of Tulsa (M.B.A., 1982; J.D., 1982). Phi Alpha Delta. *Member:* Oklahoma County, Oklahoma and American Bar Associations; The Association of Trial Lawyers of America. ***PRACTICE AREAS:*** Commercial Litigation; Telecommunications Law; Commercial Law; Bankruptcy. ***Email:*** mrmcvay@phillipsmcfall.com

ROBERT O. O'BANNON, born Des Moines, Iowa, May 3, 1954; admitted to bar, 1979, Oklahoma. *Education:* University of Oklahoma (B.A., 1976); Oklahoma City University (J.D., 1979); Boston University (LL.M., Taxation, 1980). Phi Alpha Delta. Certified Public Accountant, Oklahoma, 1984. ***REPORTED CASES:*** W.H. Braum Family Partnership v. Commission T.C. Merro 1993-1994. ***PRACTICE AREAS:*** Corporate Law; Mergers, Acquisitions and Divestitures; Partnerships; Federal and State Taxation; Estate Planning and Probate; Civil and Criminal Tax Controversy. ***Email:*** roobannon@phillipsmcfall.com

MICHAEL R. PERRI, born New York, New York, February 24, 1961; admitted to bar, 1986, Oklahoma and U.S. District Court, Western and Northern Districts of Oklahoma and U.S. Court of Appeals, Tenth Circuit. *Education:* University of Notre Dame (B.B.A., with honors, 1983); University of Oklahoma (J.D., 1986). Phi Delta Phi. Member, American Inn of Court XXIII. *Member:* Oklahoma and American (Member, Public Utility Law Section) Bar Associations. ***PRACTICE AREAS:*** Commercial Law; Litigation; Oil and Gas Law; Wills; Trusts; Public Utility Law. ***Email:*** mrperri@phillipsmcfall.com

T. RAY PHILLIPS, III, born Oklahoma City, Oklahoma, December 22, 1939; admitted to bar, 1966, Oklahoma. *Education:* University of Oklahoma (B.B.A., 1963; J.D., 1966); New York University (LL.M., Taxation, 1967). Phi Delta Phi. *Member:* Oklahoma County, Oklahoma (Lawyers Helping Lawyers Committee) and American Bar Associations; National Association of Bond Lawyers. ***PRACTICE AREAS:*** Acquisitions, Divestitures and Mergers; Real Estate Development; Federal Income, Estate and Gift Taxation; Estate Planning; Probate. ***Email:*** trphillips@phillipsmcfall.com

SANDRA LEAH SCHOVANEC, born Enid, Oklahoma, June 21, 1959; admitted to bar, 1984, Oklahoma, U.S. District Court, Northern, Eastern and Western Districts of Oklahoma and U.S. Court of Appeals, Tenth Circuit. *Education:* Phillips University (B.S., magna cum laude, 1981); University of Oklahoma (J.D., with honors, 1984). Order of the Coif. Member and Editor, Oklahoma Law Review, 1983-1984. Author: "Manufacturer's Products Liability: Punitive Damage Awards in Strict Products Liability Cases in Oklahoma," 37 Oklahoma Law Review, 338, 1984; "Landlord and Tenant: Is Discrimination Against Children Permissible in Oklahoma," 36 Oklahoma Law Review, 361, 1983. *Member:* Oklahoma County, Oklahoma and American Bar Associations. ***PRACTICE AREAS:*** Employment; Products Liability; Litigation; Bankruptcy. ***Email:*** slschovanec@phillipsmcfall.com

ROBERT N. SHEETS, born St. Louis, Missouri, June 16, 1954; admitted to bar, 1979, Oklahoma; U.S. District Court, Western District of Oklahoma; U.S. District Court, Western District of Arizona; U.S. Court of Appeals, Tenth Circuit; U.S. Supreme Court. *Education:* Washington University (A.B., 1976); Oklahoma City University (J.D., with honors, 1979). Moot Court Board, 1977-1978. Member, Oklahoma City University Law Review, 1977-1979. Adjunct Professor of Law, Oklahoma City University, 1981-1984. Law Clerk, Chief Judge of the United States District Court, Western District of Oklahoma, 1979-1981. Lecturer, Southwestern Legal Foundation Institute for Petroleum Landmen, 1983. *Member:* Oklahoma County, Oklahoma and American Bar Associations; Oklahoma City Society of Title Attorneys Association. ***PRACTICE AREAS:*** Commercial Litigation; Oil and Gas; Real Estate. ***Email:*** rnsheets@phillipsmcfall.com

DOUGLAS M. TODD, born Rockledge, Florida, December 12, 1967; admitted to bar, 1993, Oklahoma, U.S. District Court, Western and Eastern Districts of Oklahoma; U.S. District Court, Northern District of Texas; U.S. Court of Appeals, Tenth Circuit. *Education:* University of Texas at Tyler (B.S., Computer Science, 1988); Oklahoma City University (J.D., summa cum laude, 1993). Phi Delta Phi; Alpha Chi; Theta Kappa; Phi Theta Kappa; Order of Barristers. Matton W. Summers Scholar. Member: National Moot Court Team, 1992; Jessup International Moot Court Team, 1991; Moot Court Board, 1991-1992. Recipient, American Jurisprudence Awards in: Civil Procedure, Conflicts, Contracts, Torts, Wills & Estates, and Legal Profession. Law Clerk to Honorable Sam Joyner, Magistrate Judge, U.S. District Court, Northern District of Oklahoma, 1995-2002. Adjunct Professor of Law, University of Tulsa, 2001-2002. *Member:* Oklahoma County, Oklahoma and American Bar Associations. ***PRACTICE AREAS:*** Litigation. ***Email:*** dmtodd@phillipsmcfall.com

THOMAS G. WOLFE, born Oklahoma City, Oklahoma, July 23, 1957; admitted to bar, 1985, Oklahoma; 1989, U.S. Court of Appeals, Tenth Circuit; U.S. District Court, Eastern, Northern and Western Districts of Oklahoma. *Education:* University of Oklahoma (B.S., 1980; J.D., with honors, 1985). Phi Delta Phi. Co-Author, Kirkland v. General Motors Corp. and Beyond: An Overview of Twenty Years of Oklahoma Product Liability Law," 65 Oklahoma Bar Journal 3593, Oklahoma 1994. *Member:* Oklahoma County, Oklahoma (Board of Directors, Young Lawyers Division, 1990-1991) and American Bar Associations. ***PRACTICE AREAS:*** Products Liability; Commercial Law; Oil and Gas Litigation. ***Email:*** tgwolfe@phillipsmcfall.com

RAY E. ZSCHIESCHE, born Oklahoma City, Oklahoma, April 16, 1959; admitted to bar, 1985, Oklahoma; 1989, U.S. Court of Appeals, Tenth Circuit; U.S. District Court, Eastern, Northern and Western Districts of Oklahoma. *Education:* Oklahoma State University (B.S., 1982); University of Oklahoma (J.D., with distinction, 1985). Phi Delta Phi. Recipient, George J. Fagin Municipal Law Endowment Award, 1984-1985. Author: "The Business Record Exception to the Hearsay Rule: An Overview," 61 Okla. Bar Journal 2047 (July, 1990). *Member:* Oklahoma County, Oklahoma and American Bar Associations. ***PRACTICE AREAS:*** Commercial Litigation; Products Liability; Insurance Defense. ***Email:*** rezschiesche@phillipsmcfall.com

---

VICKIE J. BUCHANAN, born Pittsburg, Kansas, September 12, 1973; admitted to bar, 1999, Oklahoma and U.S. District Court, Western District of Oklahoma. *Education:* Northeastern State University (B.S., summa cum laude, Criminal Justice, English, 1996); University of Oklahoma (J.D., with distinction, 1999). Phi Delta Phi; Kappa Alpha Theta. Recipient: Douglas W. Sanders, Sr., Memorial Law Scholarship; American Jurisprudence Award, Land Use Control. *Member:* Oklahoma County, Oklahoma and American Bar Associations; Oklahoma Association of Defense Counsel. ***PRACTICE AREAS:*** Litigation; Products Liability. ***Email:*** vjbuchanan@phillipsmcfall.com

CATHERINE L. CAMPBELL, born Boulder, Colorado, February 5, 1965; admitted to bar, 1991, Oklahoma; 1992, U.S. District Court, Western and Eastern Districts of Oklahoma and U.S. Supreme Court; 1993, U.S. District Court, Northern District of Oklahoma and U.S. Court of Appeals, Tenth Circuit; 2004, U.S. Supreme Court. *Education:* University of Colorado at Boulder (B.A., 1987); University of Oklahoma (J.D., with distinction, 1991). Member, University of Oklahoma Law Review. Author: "Updates to Statutes Governing Oklahoma Practice and Procedure," 74 O.B.J. 1477 (2003); "Evidence of Common Insurance to Show Expert Bias: The Rest of the Story," 68 O.B.J. 3001 (1997). *Member:* Oklahoma County, Oklahoma (Past Chair, Past Chair-Elect and Past Secretary, Appellate Practice Section) and American Bar Associations. ***REPORTED CASES:*** Trainor v. Apollo Metal Specialties, Inc., 318 F.3d 976; Parish v. Henry, 2004 OK 62, 97 P.3d 646; Conterez v. O'Donnell, 2002 OK 67, 68 P.3d 759; Anderson v. Boring, 2001 OK CIV APP 137, 39 P.3d 822; White v. Adoption of Baby Boy D., 2000 OK 44, 10 P.3d 212; Currens v. Hampton, 1997 OK 58, 939 P.2d 1138; Sparks v. Hicks, 1996 OK 20, 912 P.2d 331; Lykins v. St. Francis Hosp., Inc., 1995 OK 135, 917 P.2d 1; Crussel v. Kirk, 1995 OK 41, 894 P.2d 1116. ***PRACTICE AREAS:*** Litigation; Appellate Practice; Employment Law; Products Liability. ***Email:*** clcampbell@phillipsmcfall.com

DALE B. CAZES, born Queens, New York, October 13, 1972; admitted to bar, 1998, Oklahoma and U.S. District Court, Western District of Oklahoma. *Education:* University of Florida (B.S.B.A., 1994); Oklahoma City University (J.D., 1998); Southern Methodist University (LL.M., Taxation, 1999). Phi Delta Phi. *Member:* Oklahoma (Member, Sections on: Tax; Estate Planning, Probate and Trust; Member, Probate Committee) and American (Member, Sections on: Tax; Real Property, Probate and Trust) Bar Associations. ***PRACTICE AREAS:*** Taxation; Estate Planning; Wills; Probate; Corporate Law; Real Estate; Tax Controversies; Tax Litigation. ***Email:*** dbcazes@phillipsmcfall.com

JENNIFER K. GOLDEN, born Boulder, Colorado, July 17, 1956; admitted to bar, 1998, Oklahoma. *Education:* University of Colorado at Boulder (B.S., magna cum laude, 1988); University of Oklahoma (J.D., with honors, 1998). Academic Achievement Awards: Legal Research and Writing II; Professional Responsibility; Agricultural Environmental Law. *Member:* Oklahoma County, Oklahoma and American Bar Associations. ***PRACTICE AREAS:*** Federal Income Tax; Estate and Gift Taxation; State Taxation; Local Taxation; Estate Planning; Probate. ***Email:*** jkgolden@phillipsmcfall.com

BONNER J. GONZALES, born Oklahoma City, Oklahoma, December 28, 1977; admitted to bar, 2004, Oklahoma. *Education:* University of Oklahoma (B.B.A., 2000; J.D., 2004). Order of the Coif. *Member:* Oklahoma and American Bar Associations. ***PRACTICE AREAS:*** Taxation; Corporate Law; Mergers and Acquisitions; Trusts and Estates; Tax Controversies. ***Email:*** bjgonzales@phillipsmcfall.com

HEATHER L. HINTZ, born Downers Grove, Illinois, July 12, 1961; admitted to bar, 1988, Texas; 1990, Oklahoma. *Education:* St. Olaf College (B.A., 1983); Vanderbilt University (J.D., 1987). Member: Moot Court Board; Jessup International Moot Court Team. Recipient, G. Scott Briggs Transnational Legal Studies Award, 1986-1987. Author: "*Ex Parte* Communications with a Corporate Adversary's Former Employees: The Scope of Rule 4.2 of the Oklahoma Rules of Professional Conduct," 61 Okla. Bar Journal, No. 48 (December 29, 1990). Adjunct Professor of Law, Oklahoma City University Law School, 1993-1994. *Member:* State Bar of Texas; Oklahoma Bar Association. ***PRACTICE AREAS:*** Commercial Litigation; Securities Litigation; Intellectual Property; International Law. ***Email:*** hlhintz@phillipsmcfall.com

RODNEY KENT HUNSINGER, III, born Norman, Oklahoma, April 26, 1977; admitted to bar, 2003, Oklahoma and U.S. District Court, Western and Northern Districts of Oklahoma; 2004, U.S. District Court, Eastern District of Oklahoma. *Education:* Northeastern Oklahoma State University (B.B.A., Accounting, magna cum laude, 1999); University of Oklahoma (J.D., with distinction, 2003). *Member:* Oklahoma and American Bar Associations; Defense Research Institute. ***PRACTICE AREAS:*** Commercial Litigation; Products Liability; Employment Law. ***Email:*** rkhunsinger@phillipsmcfall.com

WILLIAM J. JARVIS, born Jackson, Mississippi, July 1, 1971; admitted to bar, 2003, Oklahoma. *Education:* University of Oklahoma (B.B.A., 1999); Oklahoma City University (J.D., 2003). *Member:* Oklahoma County, Oklahoma and American Bar Associations. ***PRACTICE AREAS:*** Real Estate. ***Email:*** wjjarvis@phillipsmcfall.com

CELESTE T. JOHNSON, born Fort Worth, Texas, October 9, 1970; admitted to bar, 2002, Oklahoma. *Education:* University of Texas at Austin (B.B.A., 1994); University of Oklahoma (J.D., 2002). *Member:* Oklahoma County, Oklahoma and American Bar Associations. ***PRACTICE AREAS:*** Consumer Law (20%); Commercial Law (20%); Banks and Banking (20%); Mergers, Acquisitions and Divestitures (20%); Health Care (20%). ***Email:*** ctjohnson@phillipsmcfall.com

ERIC L. JOHNSON, born Oklahoma City, Oklahoma, January 8, 1969; admitted to bar, 1994, Oklahoma. *Education:* Oklahoma State University (B.S., Accounting, 1991); Oklahoma City University (J.D., 1994). *Member:* Oklahoma and American (Member: Business Law Section; Aircraft Finance and Contracts Division of the Forum on Air and Space Law) Bar Associations. ***SPECIAL AGENCIES:*** Federal Aviation Administration; National Automotive Finance Association. ***PRACTICE AREAS:*** Banking; Commercial Fi-

(This Listing Continued)

PHILLIPS McFALL McCAFFREY McVAY & MURRAH, P.C., Oklahoma City—Continued

nancial Services Law; Consumer Financial Services Law; Financial Institution Regulation; E-Commerce; Information Technology; Aircraft Title Law; Aviation Law; Aircraft Finance; Commercial Aircraft Leasing. ***Email:*** eljohnson@phillipsmcfall.com

JENNIFER HEALD KIRKPATRICK, born Midwest City, Oklahoma, March 1, 1973; admitted to bar, 2002, Oklahoma and U.S. District Court, Western District of Oklahoma; 2003, U.S. District Court, Eastern and Northern Districts of Oklahoma; 2004, U.S. Court of Appeals, Tenth Circuit. *Education:* Cameron University (B.A., 1996); University of Oklahoma (M.A., 1999); Oklahoma City University (J.D., 2002). Phi Delta Phi; Order of the Barristers; Regional Finalist, American Bar Association National Appellate Advocacy Team, 2001. Recipient: LALI Award for Excellence in Litigation Practice; Merit Scholarship. *Member:* Oklahoma Bar Association (Member, Sections on: Bankruptcy, 2004—; Government and Administrative Law, 2004—). ***PRACTICE AREAS:*** Commercial Litigation; Creditors Rights; Bankruptcy; Administrative Law. ***Email:*** jhkirkpatrick@phillipsmcfall.com

JOAN LAMSON, born Oklahoma City, October 14, 1957; admitted to bar, 2000, Oklahoma and U.S. District Court, Eastern, Western and Northern Districts of Oklahoma. *Education:* University of Oklahoma (B.A., 1995); Oklahoma City University School of Law (J.D., 2000). *Member:* Oklahoma Bar Association. ***PRACTICE AREAS:*** Commercial Real Estate (100%). ***Email:*** jmlamson@phillipsmcfall.com

THOMAS P. MANNING, born Columbus, Ohio, April 15, 1957; admitted to bar, 1995, Oklahoma; U.S. District Court, Northern, Eastern and Western Districts of Oklahoma; U.S. Court of Appeals, Tenth Circuit. *Education:* University of Texas at Arlington (B.B.A., 1981); Oklahoma City University (J.D., cum laude, 1995). Phi Delta Phi. President, Moot Court Board, 1993-1994. Student Member, American Inns of Court, 1994-1995. *Member:* Oklahoma and American Bar Associations; Oklahoma County Bar Association; Oklahoma Association Defense Counsel; Defense Research Institute. ***PRACTICE AREAS:*** Litigation; Insurance Defense. ***Email:*** tpmanning@phillipsmcfall.com

JUNE E. MATCHETTE, born Cristobal, Panama Canal Zone, January 22, 1964; admitted to bar, 2001, Oklahoma and U.S. District Court, Western and Northern Districts of Oklahoma. *Education:* Indiana University (B.S., 1987); University of Oklahoma Health Sciences Center (M.S., 1990); University of Tulsa (J.D., 2001). Phi Delta Phi. Recipient, CALI Award for Excellence in Constitutional Law, Intellectual Property and Antitrust. *Member:* Oklahoma County and American Bar Associations; Oklahoma Bar Association. ***PRACTICE AREAS:*** Civil Rights Defense; Employment Law; Health Law. ***Email:*** jematchette@phillipsmcfall.com

BYRONA J. MAULE, born St. Joseph, Missouri, September 11, 1961; admitted to bar, 1986, Missouri; 1993, Alaska; 1994, Oklahoma. *Education:* University of Missouri (B.S., Political Science, summa cum laude, 1982; J.D., 1986). Phi Beta Kappa. Order of the Barristers. Recipient: Thomas E. Deacy, Jr. Prize in Advocacy; American Jurisprudence Award in Family Law. Assistant Attorney General, State of Missouri, 1986-1989. *Member:* Oklahoma, Alaska and American Bar Associations; The Missouri Bar. ***PRACTICE AREAS:*** Health Care Law; Litigation; Employment Law. ***Email:*** bjmaule@phillipsmcfall.com

JENNIFER LYNN MILLER, born Hollywood, California, February 2, 1976; admitted to bar, 2003, Oklahoma; U.S. District Court, Eastern, Western and Northern Districts of Oklahoma. *Education:* Oklahoma State University (B.S., Business Administration, 1999); Oklahoma City University (J.D., 2003). Phi Alpha Delta. Recipient: Roger Stephens Law Scholarship; CALI Awards, Excellence in Bankruptcy and Criminal Procedure; T. Hurley Jordan Award, Excellence in Criminal Procedure; 2003 Medal of Excellence, Bankrupty, American Bankrtuptcy Institute. *Member:* Oklahoma County, Oklahoma and American Bar Associations. ***Email:*** jlmiller@phillipsmcfall.com

A. V. PEOPLES, III, born Panama City, Florida, March 14, 1945; admitted to bar, 1975, Oklahoma. *Education:* Oklahoma City University (B.A., 1969; J.D., 1974). Land Manager and Corporate Counsel, Jones & Pellow Oil Co., 1975-1987. *Member:* Oklahoma Bar Association. ***PRACTICE AREAS:*** Oil and Gas; Real Estate. ***Email:*** avpeoples@phillipsmcfall.com

DAWN M. RAHME, born Ponca City, Oklahoma, December 31, 1975; admitted to bar, 2001, Oklahoma. *Education:* University of Tulsa (B.S.B.A., 1998); University of Oklahoma (J.D., 2001); New York University (LL.M., Taxation, 2002). *Member:* Oklahoma County, Oklahoma and American Bar Associations. ***PRACTICE AREAS:*** Taxation; Trusts and Estates; Corporate Law; Mergers and Acquisitions; Tax Controversies. ***Email:*** dmrahme@phillipsmcfall.com

MARCIA A. RUPERT, born Caldwell, Kansas, September 13, 1958; admitted to bar, 1987, Oklahoma; 1988, U.S. District Court, Western District of Oklahoma and U.S. Court of Appeals, 10th Circuit. *Education:* University of Oklahoma (B.A., 1980; M.S.W., 1981; J.D., 1987). Phi Beta Kappa; Order of the Coif. Note Editor, Oklahoma Law Review, 1986-1987. Law Clerk to the Hon. Carolyn Dineen King, U.S. Court of Appeals for the Fifth Circuit. Author, "Joint Custody In Oklahoma: Beyond Hornbeck," 39 Oklahoma Law Review 107, 1986. *Member:* Oklahoma and American Bar Associations. ***PRACTICE AREAS:*** Civil Litigation. ***Email:*** marupert@phillipsmcfall.com

BEVERLY I. VILARDOFSKY, born Warwick, Rhode Island, August 29, 1970; admitted to bar, 1995, Oklahoma; 1998, District of Columbia. *Education:* University of Rhode Island (B.A., 1991); Oklahoma City University (J.D., summa cum laude, 1995); Georgetown University (L.L.M., International and Comparative Law, 1996; L.L.M. Securities and Financial Regulation, with distinction, 1999). Recipient, West Publishing Outstanding Academic Achievement Award, 1995. Student Member, William J. Holloway, Jr. Inn of Court. *Member:* Oklahoma and American (Member, Sections on: Business Law; Intellectual Property); The District of Columbia Bar. ***PRACTICE AREAS:*** Corporate Law; Securities Regulation; Securities Offerings; High Technology Law. ***Email:*** bivilardofsky@phillipsmcfall.com

LYNDON W. WHITMIRE, born Shattuck, Oklahoma, May 13, 1971; admitted to bar, 1996, Oklahoma and U.S. District Court, Eastern, Western and Northern Districts of Oklahoma. *Education:* Oklahoma State University (B.A., with honors, 1993); University of Oklahoma (J.D., with highest honors, 1996). Member, Order of the Coif. *Member:* Oklahoma County, Oklahoma and American Bar Associations; Defense Research Institute. ***PRACTICE AREAS:*** Products Liability; Media Law; Tort Litigation; Commercial Litigation. ***Email:*** lwwhitmire@phillipsmcfall.com

OF COUNSEL

E. CAROLE BARNES, born Carnegie, Oklahoma, July 29, 1955; admitted to bar, 1980, Texas; 1981, Oklahoma. *Education:* University of Oklahoma (B.A., 1977); University of Texas (J.D., 1980). Phi Beta Kappa. *Member:* Oklahoma County, Oklahoma and American Bar Associations; State Bar of Texas. ***PRACTICE AREAS:*** Securities; Corporate; Commercial; Partnership Law. ***Email:*** ecbarnes@phillipsmcfall.com

DOUGLAS A. BRANCH, born Norman, Oklahoma, January 23, 1957; admitted to bar, 1982, Oklahoma and U.S. District Court, Western District of Oklahoma. *Education:* University of Oklahoma (B.B.A., in Finance, 1979; J.D., 1982). Phi Delta Phi. Chairman. Oklahoma Center for the Advancement of Science and Technology, 1991-1993. *Member:* Oklahoma County, Oklahoma (Chairman, Business and Corporate Law Section, 1995) and American Bar Associations. ***PRACTICE AREAS:*** Securities Law; Securities Offerings; Corporate Law; High Technology Law. ***Email:*** dabranch@phillipsmcfall.com

MICHAEL D. CARTER, born Wichita Falls, Texas, March 4, 1957; admitted to bar, 1982, Oklahoma, U.S. District Court, Northern, Eastern and Western Districts of Oklahoma and U.S. Court of Appeals, Fifth, Eighth and Tenth Circuits. *Education:* University of Oklahoma (B.A., Letters, 1979; J.D., 1982). Phi Delta Phi. *Member:* Oklahoma County, Oklahoma and American Bar Associations; Oklahoma Association of Defense Counsel (Director, 1998-2001); Defense Research Institute; Oklahoma Indigent Defense System (Board Member). ***PRACTICE AREAS:*** Employment Law; Asbestos Defense; Environmental Law. ***Email:*** mdcarter@phillipsmcfall.com

V. GLENN COFFEE, born Lubbock, Texas, January 20, 1967; admitted to bar, 1993, Oklahoma. *Education:* Northeastern Oklahoma State University (B.A., 1989); University of Oklahoma (J.D., 1992). Member, Oklahoma State Senate, 1998—. *Member:* Oklahoma and American Bar Associations. ***PRACTICE AREAS:*** Commercial Law; Corporate Law; High Technology Law. ***Email:*** vgcoffee@phillipsmcfall.com

SHANNON K. EMMONS, born Blackwell, Oklahoma, November 10, 1960; admitted to bar, 1990, Oklahoma; U.S. District Court, Western, Northern and Eastern Districts of Oklahoma; U.S. Court of Appeals, Tenth Circuit and U.S. Supreme Court. *Education:* University of Oklahoma (B.A. in Letters, 1987); University of Oklahoma College of Law (J.D., 1990). Phi Delta Phi. Oklahoma Law Review. Lawyer Pupil, William J. Holloway, Jr. American Inn of Court, 1994-1995. *Member:* Federal Bar Association (Member, Oklahoma City Chapter); Oklahoma County and American Bar Associations; Oklahoma Bar Association; Oklahoma Association of Defense Counsel; Defense Research Institute. ***PRACTICE AREAS:*** Employment Law; Insurance Litigation; Products Liability; Civil Litigation.

JOHN D. HASTIE, born Guthrie, Oklahoma, December 9, 1939; admitted to bar, 1964, Oklahoma. *Education:* University of Oklahoma (B.A., 1961; LL.B., 1964). Phi Delta Phi. Recipient, Hawes Award as Outstanding Law Graduate. Editor, Oklahoma Law Review, 1963-1964. Adjunct Professor, University of Oklahoma College of Law, 1982-1990, 2000—. Advisor, Restatement of the Law, Property - Servitudes and Restatement of the Law, Third Property Mortgages; Editorial Board, The Practical Real Estate Lawyer (2004—); American Law Institute. *Member:* Association of the Bar of the City of New York; Cleveland County, Oklahoma, American and International Bar Associations; American College of Real Estate Lawyers (Governor, 1990-2000; Member, Executive Committee, 1992-2000; President, 1999); American Law Institute; Anglo-American Real Property Institute; American College of Mortgage Attorneys. (Resident, Norman, Oklahoma Office). ***PRACTICE AREAS:*** Bankruptcy; Commercial Law; Business Organization; Real Estate. ***Email:*** jdhastie@hastielaw.com

KENNETH E. McBRIDE, born Abilene, Texas, June 8, 1948; admitted to bar, 1974, Oklahoma. *Education:* University of Central Oklahoma (B.A., 1971); Oklahoma City University (J.D., 1974). ***PRACTICE AREAS:*** Real Estate; Financial Institution Regulation; Corporate Law; Partnership Law. ***Email:*** kemcbride@phillipsmcfall.com

BRENT L. MILLS, born Oklahoma City, Oklahoma April 15, 1964; admitted to bar, 1989, Oklahoma. *Education:* University of Oklahoma (B.B.A., 1986; J.D., 1989). Phi Delta Phi. Adjunct Professor, Business Law, and Tort and Insurance Law, Tulsa Junior College, 1989-1996. Vice Chairman and Trustee, Tulsa Industrial Authority, 1990-1995. *Member:* Oklahoma Bar Association. ***PRACTICE AREAS:*** Banking Law; High Technology; Business Law; Finance; Mergers and Acquisitions; Real Estate; Employee Benefits. ***Email:*** blmills@phillipsmcfall.com

ALFRED P. MURRAH, JR., born Oklahoma City, Oklahoma, October 5, 1933; admitted to bar, 1961, Oklahoma. *Education:* Yale University (B.A., 1955); University of Oklahoma (LL.B., 1961). Phi Alpha Delta; Omicron Delta Kappa; Order of the Coif. Editor-in-Chief, Oklahoma Law Review, 1960. Author: "Application of Sullivan and its Progeny to Public Defamation Actions in Oklahoma," 51 Oklahoma Bar Journal 3073, 1980. Co-Author: "Royalty Payments-Who Owes How Much to Whom and When?" 35th Oil and Gas Inst., Matthew Bender, 1984. Adjunct Professor of Law, Civil Procedure, Trial Practice Courses, Oklahoma City University, 1973-1978. *Member:* Oklahoma County (Director, 1963-1966; 1973-1975; 1978-1981), Oklahoma and American Bar Associations. ***PRACTICE AREAS:*** Oil and Gas Litigation; Antitrust; Product Liability; Commercial Litigation. ***Email:*** apmurrah@phillipsmcfall.com

CINDY H. MURRAY, born Arlington Heights, Illinois, September 18, 1965; admitted to bar, 1998, Oklahoma. *Education:* University of Oklahoma (B.S., 1988; J.D., 1998). Associate Editor, American Indian Law Review, 1997-1998. Law Clerk to Justice Marian P. Opala, Oklahoma Supreme Court, 1999. Co-Author, "The ABC's of the UCC: Related and Supplementary Consumer Law," ABA, 1999. *Member:* Cleveland County, Oklahoma and American Bar Associations. (Resident, Norman, Oklahoma Office). ***PRACTICE AREAS:*** Commercial Law; Business Organization; Real Estate. ***Email:*** chmurray@hastielaw.com

SAM D. OTT, born Cherokee, Oklahoma, July 14, 1950; admitted to bar, 1974, Oklahoma; 1980, U.S. District Court, Western District of Oklahoma; 2004, Georgia; U.S. Supreme Court. *Education:* Oklahoma State University (B.S., 1972); University of Oklahoma (J.D., 1975). *Member:* Cleveland County, Oklahoma (Past Chairman: Banking and Finan-

(This Listing Continued)

cial Law Section; House Counsel Section; Member, Uniform Commercial Code Review Committee) and American Bar Associations; State Bar of Georgia. (Resident, Norman, Oklahoma Office). ***PRACTICE AREAS:*** Banking Law; Banking Regulation. ***Email:*** sam@dapape.com

MARTIN G. OZINGA, born Ridgewood, New Jersey, December 4, 1964; admitted to bar, 1990, Oklahoma; U.S. District Court, Northern, Eastern and Western Districts of Oklahoma; registered to practice before U.S. Patent and Trademark Office. *Education:* Southern Methodist University (B.S., 1987); Oklahoma City University (J.D., 1990). *Member:* Oklahoma County and Oklahoma Bar Associations. ***PRACTICE AREAS:*** Intellectual Property; Patents; Trademarks; Copyrights; Intellectual Property Licensing. ***Email:*** mgozinga@phillipsmcfall.com

DONALD A. PAPE, born Birmingham, Alabama, September 1, 1945; admitted to bar, 1974, Oklahoma and U.S. District Court, Western District of Oklahoma. *Education:* University of Oklahoma (B.A. in Journalism, 1967; J.D., 1973). Phi Delta Phi. Member: Article 8, Legislative Review Subcommittee of the Oklahoma Bar Association Financial Institutions and Commercial Law Section of the Uniform Commercial Code Committee; Oklahoma Banking Commissioners Banking Code Review Committee. *Member:* Cleveland County, Oklahoma and American Bar Associations; Oklahoma Bankers Association (Bank Attorneys Committee). [Capt., USAF, 1967-1971]. ***PRACTICE AREAS:*** Banking; Banking Regulation. ***Email:*** don@dapape.com

BILL PRICE, born Oklahoma City, Oklahoma, October 5, 1948; admitted to bar, 1973, Oklahoma, U.S. District Court, Western District of Oklahoma, U.S. Court of Appeals, Tenth Circuit and U.S. Supreme Court. *Education:* Georgetown University (B.S.F.S., 1970); University of Oklahoma (J.D., 1973). Recipient: U.S. Department of Justice Special Achievement Award for political corruption prosecutions, 1980; J.C. Penney Golden Rule Award, 1989; Man of the Year Award, Oklahoma State Association for Alcoholism and Drug Abuse, 1989; Coalition of Civil Leadership Award for Drug Education, 1989. Assistant to Judge Alfred P. Murrah, Assistant U.S. Attorney, Western District of Oklahoma, 1975-1982. U.S. Attorney, Western District of Oklahoma, 1982-1989. Lecturer: Federal Bureau of Prisons; Oklahoma State Bureau of Investigations; U.S. Department of Justice; Federal Bureau of Investigation; Oklahoma State School Board Association; Oklahoma Municipal League; Oklahoma Self-Insurers Association Seminar; Oklahoma Oil Marketers Association Seminar; Oklahoma College of Occupational and Environmental Medicine. Member: National Environmental Enforcement Council, 1983-1989; U.S. Attorneys' Advisory Committee to the U.S. Sentencing Commission; Public Corruption; Drug Education; Criminal Tax; Indian Affairs. *Member:* Oklahoma County, Oklahoma, Federal and American (Member, Tax Section) Bar Associations. ***PRACTICE AREAS:*** Criminal Litigation; Civil Litigation; Regulatory; Environmental; Energy; Insurance; Employment; Municipal Finance Law. ***Email:*** wsprice@phillipsmcfall.com

ELLEN K. SPIROPOULOS, born Bloomington, Indiana, April 5, 1964; admitted to bar, 1994, Oklahoma; U.S. District Court, Western and Northern Districts of Oklahoma. *Education:* Carleton College (B.A., cum laude, 1986); Northwestern University (J.D., 1994). *Member:* Oklahoma County, Oklahoma (Vice Chair, Young Lawyers Division Mock Trial, 1996-1998) and American (Business Law Section 1999—) Bar Associations; The Federalist Society (Member, Legal Intern Committee 2000—).Urban Land Institute. ***PRACTICE AREAS:*** Real Estate; Commercial Transactions; Mergers and Acquisitions; Zoning, Planning and Land Use. ***Email:*** ekspiropoulos@phillipsmcfall.com

D. CRAIG STORY, born Oklahoma City, Oklahoma, June 25, 1955; admitted to bar, 1980, Oklahoma. *Education:* Duke University (A.B., 1977); University of Oklahoma (J.D., 1980); Boston University (LL.M., Taxation, 1987). *Member:* Oklahoma County, Oklahoma and American Bar Associations; Oklahoma City Estate Planning Council, Inc. ***PRACTICE AREAS:*** Oil & Gas Title Examination Law; Federal and State Taxation; Estate Planning and Probate; Commercial Law. ***Email:*** cstory@swbell.net

REPRESENTATIVE CLIENTS: Aames Financial; Ace Cash Express; Aegis Mortgage Corp; American Bank Systems, Inc.; American General; American Home Products Corp.; The American Kennel Club; American National Bank of Lawton; An-son Company; ARKLA; Armstrong Bank; Atlantic Richfield Company; AT&T Communications of the Southwest, Inc.; Auto Marketing Network; Banc One Financial Services; Bank of America, N.A.; Bank of Oklahoma, N.A.; Bank One; Bank of Tokyo; Bell Finance; Benefit Services, Inc. Blue Quail Ridge Development Ltd.; Bombardier Capital, Inc.; Canaan Energy Corp.; Capital West Securities, Inc.; Carl E. Gungoll Exploration, Inc.; Chesapeake Operating, Inc.; Chubb Life Insurance Co.; The CIT Group; City National Bank and Trust Company of Lawton; Citicorp Dealer Finance; Citicorp Mortgage, Inc.; Communications Federal Credit Union; Community Bankers Association of Oklahoma; Cooperative Finance Association; Countywide Funding; Courtesy Insurance Agency; Cuna Mutual Group; Daimler Chrysler Corp.; Data Critical Corp.; Delco Remy International, Inc.; Duraclean International, Inc.Corporation; El Chico Corporation; EquiCredit Corporation; Ethos Communications Corp.; FAA Employees Credit Union; Farmland Industries, Inc.; Federal Employees Credit Union; First Bankers Mortgage Corp.; First Capital Mortgage Corp.; First Investors Financial Services, Inc.; First National Bank of Altus; First National Bank of McAlester; First National Bank of Midwest City; First State Bank of Hinton; First State Bank of Shawnee; First U.S.A. Bank; Fleetwood Credit Corp.; Fluid Technologies, Inc.; Fort Sill National Bank; Gannett Co., Inc. (KOCO-TV); Freightliner, L.L.C.; General Electric Credit Capital Corp.; Green Tree Financial Services; Heartland Care Group, Inc.; Home Savings and Loan Association of Oklahoma; Household Finance Corp.; HOW Insurance Co.; Indian Oil Company; Indian Meridian Vocational Technical School; InterSouth Partners; Jay Petroleum, Inc.; Kerr-McGee Corporation; Key Bank of New York; Kimray, Inc.; King Energy, L.L.C.; Life Insurance Company of the Southwest; Local Oklahoma Bank, N.A.; Longbranch Oil Company; Lucent Technologies; Mastermind Internet Services, Inc.; MetLife Financial Acceptance Corp.; Metro Bank, N.A.; MidFirst Bank, SSB; Moody National Bank; Mustang Fuel Corp.; Native American Asset Advisors; New York Life Insurance Co.; Nichols Energy Corp.; Nomadics, Inc.; Northpoint Communications, Inc.; Norwest Bank, Wisconsin, N.A. Novus Financial, Novazyume Pharmaceuticals, Inc.; Oklahoma City Airport Trust; Oklahoma Consumer Finance Association; The Oklahoma Development Finance Authority; Oklahoma Educators Credit Union; Oklahoma Firefighters Pension and Retirement System; Oklahoma Gas and Electric Co.; Oklahoma Law Enforcement Retirement System; Oklahoma Police Pension and Retirement System; Oklahoma State Insurance Fund; Olympus Corporation; Oxford Resources Corp; Parkside Medical Services, Inc.; Professional Association Services, Inc.; Prudential Securities, Incorporated; Pryor Oil Co., Inc.; R.N. Baker & Co.; Republic Bank of Norman; Rent Way; Rexworks, Inc.; School Employees Retirement System of Ohio; Sears Consumer Financial Corp.; Security Finance Corp.; Shoney's, Inc.; Sinclair Broadcast Group, Inc.; Small Loan Council of Oklahoma; Sonic Corp.; South Western Oklahoma Development Authority; Southern Plains Trust Company; Southwest Securities Group, Inc.; Sprint; Stillwater National Bank and Trust Company; Stone Credit Corp.; Sundown Energy, Inc.; Texas Independent Bankers; TMS, Inc.; Tomen America, Inc.; Trust Company of Texas; Turner Bros.Crane & Rigging; Turner Bros. Trucking, Inc.; Union Acceptance Corp.; Vastar Resources, Inc.; Western Financial Bank; World Acceptance Corp.; Zymetx, Inc. APPROVED TITLE EXAMINERS: Chicago Title Insurance Co.; Ticor Title Insurance Company.

PIERCE COUCH HENDRICKSON BAYSINGER & GREEN, L.L.P.

Established in 1923

1109 NORTH FRANCIS
P.O. BOX 26350
OKLAHOMA CITY, OKLAHOMA 73126
Telephone: 405-235-1611
Fax: 405-235-2904
URL: http://www.PierceCouch.com

Tulsa, Oklahoma Office: 624 South Boston, Suite 500, 74119. Telephone: 918-583-8100. Fax: 918-583-8107.

General Civil Practice. Insurance, Surety, Corporation, Aviation Law, Medical and Dental Malpractice, Professional Liability, Workers Compensation, Bad Faith Law, Arson, Construction Law, Municipal Liability, Civil Rights, Employment Law, Business Torts and Business Litigation, Insurance Coverage Issues and Automobile/Vehicle Liability. Trial of Cases in all Courts in Oklahoma.

FIRM PROFILE: The firm was founded in 1923 by Clayton B. Pierce and has always been recognized for its strong commitment to client service and expertise in the areas of insurance defense and trial practice. Its staff of over 30 lawyers, practicing in offices in Oklahoma City and Tulsa, represent prominent local, regional and national clients before almost every state court, all three federal district courts within Oklahoma, the Workers Compensation Court, the U.S. Tenth Circuit Court of Appeals, and the U.S. Supreme Court.

Pierce Couch Hendrickson Baysinger & Green, L.L.P. is listed in the Bar Register of Preeminent Lawyers.

CLAYTON B. PIERCE (1889-1981)
JOHN R. COUCH (1915-1993)
CALVIN W. HENDRICKSON (1921-2001)
JAMES B. DURANT (1934-2004)

MEMBERS OF FIRM

HUGH A. BAYSINGER, born Kansas City, Missouri, June 24, 1938; admitted to bar, 1966, Oklahoma. *Education:* Yale University (B.E., with honors, in Civil Eng., 1960; M.E., 1961); Oklahoma University (J.D., 1966). American Arbitration Association (Arbitrator, Commercial/Construction). *Member:* Oklahoma County, Oklahoma and American (Member, Sections on: Litigation; Tort and Insurance Practice and Science and Technology) Bar Associations; Oklahoma Association of Defense Counsel (Past President); International Association of Defense Counsel; Defense Research Institute. ***PRACTICE AREAS:*** Construction Law; General Tort and Contract Litigation; Surety Law; Professional Liability Law; Architects and Engineers Liability; Real Estate Brokers and Agents Liability; Accountants Liability; Products Liability. ***Email:*** hbaysinger@piercecouch.com

GERALD P. GREEN, born Oklahoma City, Oklahoma, January 22, 1952; admitted to bar, 1976, Oklahoma and U.S. District Court, Western, Eastern and Northern Districts of Oklahoma; Federal Circuit, Tenth Circuit Court of Appeals. *Education:* United States Air Force Academy and University of Oklahoma (B.A., 1973); University of Oklahoma College of Law (J.D., 1976). Member, Arbitration Panel, Western District Court of Oklahoma. *Member:* Oklahoma County and Oklahoma Bar Associations; Oklahoma Association of Defense Counsel (President Elect, 2002); Defense Research Institute (Chairman, Governmental Liability Committee, 1991-1994, State Representative, 1995-1997); Federation of Defense and Corporate Counsel; Oklahoma Association of Municipal Attorneys; American Employment Law Council. ***PRACTICE AREAS:*** Litigation; Civil Rights Law; Products Liability Law; Professional Liability; Employer Liability; Insurance. ***Email:*** jgreen@piercecouch.com

STEPHEN L. OLSON, born Oklahoma City, Oklahoma, April 2, 1951; admitted to bar, 1977, Oklahoma; U.S. District Court, Western, Eastern and Northern Districts of Oklahoma; U.S. Court of Appeals, Tenth Circuit. *Education:* University of Oklahoma (B.A., 1973; J.D., 1977). Author: "Is a Statute of Repose Comparable to, or is it Different from, a Statute of Limitations?" IADC Casualty Committee Newsletter, April 2002; "Is the Collateral Source Rule Applicable to Medicare and Medicaid Write-Offs?" IADC Defense Counsel Journal, April, 2004. *Member:* Oklahoma County and Oklahoma Bar Associations; Oklahoma Association of Defense Counsel (Board of Directors, 1995-1998); Defense Research Institute; International Association of Defense Counsel. ***PRACTICE AREAS:*** Litigation; Insurance Defense Law; Bad Faith Law; Products Liability Law; Employment Law. ***Email:*** solson@piercecouch.com

D. LYNN BABB, born Stillwater, Oklahoma, December 29, 1953; admitted to bar, 1980, Oklahoma and U.S. District Court, Western, Eastern and Northern Districts of Oklahoma; U.S. Court of Appeals, Tenth Circuit; U.S. Supreme Court. *Education:* U.S. Air Force Academy; Oklahoma State University (B.A., 1976); University of Oklahoma (J.D., 1980). *Member:* Oklahoma County, Oklahoma and American (Member, Section on Tort and Insurance Practice, Subcommittee on Property Law) Bar Associations; Tenth Circuit, Judicial Conference; International Association of Defense Counsel; Oklahoma Association of Defense Counsel; International Association of Arson Investigators; Defense Research Institute; Ruth Bader Ginsburg American Inn of Court (Co-Chair, Mentoring Committee, 2000-2001). ***PRACTICE AREAS:*** Bad Faith Law; Arson Law; Insurance Fraud Defense Law; Insurance Defense Law; Litigation. ***Email:*** lbabb@piercecouch.com

INONA JANE HARNESS, born Ponca City, Oklahoma, January 15, 1947; admitted to bar, 1981, Oklahoma; 1982, U.S. District Court, Western and Northern Districts of Oklahoma. *Education:* Oklahoma State University (B.S., Biology and Medical Technology, 1970); University of Oklahoma (J.D., 1980). Phi Delta Phi. Recipient, American Jurisprudence Award, Property I and Property II. *Member:* Oklahoma County (Member, Fee Grievance and Ethics Committee, 1984—), Oklahoma and American Bar Associations; Oklahoma Association of Defense Counsel; Defense Research Institute; International Association of Defense Counsel. ***PRACTICE AREAS:*** Medical Malpractice Law.

(This Listing Continued)

PIERCE COUCH HENDRICKSON BAYSINGER & GREEN, L.L.P., Oklahoma City—Continued

RUSSELL L. HENDRICKSON, born Oklahoma City, Oklahoma, October 19, 1959; admitted to bar, 1984, Oklahoma and U.S. District Court, Eastern, Northern and Western Districts of Oklahoma. *Education:* Oklahoma State University (B.S., 1981); University of Oklahoma (J.D., 1984). Phi Delta Phi. Author: "Physician's Liability: Don't Be Responsible For The Negligence of Others," The Professional Monitor, Vol. 1, No. 2, December, 1991; Editor, Oklahoma Law Review, 1982-1984. *Member:* Oklahoma County and Oklahoma Bar Associations; Oklahoma Association of Defense Counsel (Chairman, Legislative Committee); Defense Research Institute; Federation of Defense and Corporate Counsel. Master, Robert J. Turner, American Inn of Court, 1999-2001. ***PRACTICE AREAS:*** Medical Malpractice Law; Nursing Home Liability; Insurance Defense Law. ***Email:*** rhendrickson@piercecouch.com

JOHN ROGER HURT, born Tulsa, Oklahoma, December 22, 1958; admitted to bar, 1984, Oklahoma. *Education:* Oklahoma State University; University of Tulsa (B.S., 1981); University of Oklahoma (J.D., 1984). Member, Oklahoma Law Review, 1983-1984. *Member:* Oklahoma County and Oklahoma Bar Associations. ***PRACTICE AREAS:*** Medical Malpractice Law; Personal Injury Law; Employment Law; Drug and Medical Device Litigation. ***Email:*** rhurt@piercecouch.com

FRANCES E. PATTON, born Tulsa, Oklahoma, January 30, 1959; admitted to bar, 1984, Oklahoma and U.S. District Court, Western, Eastern and Northern Districts of Oklahoma; U.S. Court of Appeals, Tenth Circuit. *Education:* Oklahoma State University; University of Oklahoma (B.A., Econ., 1981; J.D., 1984). *Member:* Oklahoma County, Oklahoma and American Bar Associations (TIPS, Litigation); Defense Research Institute, Inc. ***PRACTICE AREAS:*** Litigation; Insurance Coverage; Employment Law; Products Liability; Consumer Law; Trademark Infringement. ***Email:*** fpatton@piercecouch.com

CHARLES A. BRANDT, born Oklahoma City, Oklahoma, November 8, 1943; admitted to bar, 1984, Oklahoma and U.S. District Court, Western, Northern and Eastern Districts of Oklahoma; U.S. Court of Appeals, Tenth Circuit. *Education:* Oklahoma City University (B.S., 1965; J.D., 1984). *Member:* Oklahoma County and Oklahoma Bar Associations; Oklahoma Association of Defense Counsel; Defense Research Institute. ***PRACTICE AREAS:*** Insurance Defense Law; Litigation; Products Liability Law; Insurance Law; Personal Injury; Trucking Law; Transportation; Bad Faith. ***Email:*** cbrandt@piercecouch.com

ROBERT S. LAFFERRANDRE, born Providence, Rhode Island, May 24, 1960; admitted to bar, 1986, Oklahoma and U.S. District Court, Western, Eastern and Northern Districts of Oklahoma; U.S. Court of Appeals, Tenth Circuit. *Education:* New Hampton School (Valedictorian, 1979); Franklin College, Switzerland; Wroxton College, Wroxton, England; University of Vermont (B.A., with honors, 1983); Paris Institute of International and Comparative Law, Paris, France (1984); ; University of Oklahoma (J.D., 1986). Phi Beta Kappa. President, University of Oklahoma International Law Society, 1983-1985. Author: "Legal and Practical Guidelines for Training and Supervision of Police Officers," DRI Governmental Liability Committee Newsletter, May/June 1990; "Limiting Municipal Exposure For Negligent Traffic Regulation Under The *Manual On Uniform Traffic Control Devices,*" DRI Governmental Liability Committee Newsletter, September/October 1990. Speaker, DRI Civil Rights Seminars, 1994, 1995, 1996, 1997, 1998 and 2000, Insurance Advisory Counsel, 1998-1999; World Research Group, 2000; New Mexico Defense Association, 2000. *Member:* Oklahoma County and Oklahoma Bar Associations; Oklahoma Association of Defense Counsel; Defense Research Institute; International Association of Defense Counsel. ***PRACTICE AREAS:*** Civil Rights; Labor and Employment Law; Education Law; Insurance Defense. ***Email:*** rlafferrandre@piercecouch.com

JOHN CHRISTOPHER CONDREN, born Pensacola, Florida, December 3, 1952; admitted to bar, 1976, Oklahoma and U.S. District Court, Western District of Oklahoma; 1984, U.S. Court of Appeals, Tenth Circuit; 1988, U.S. District Court, Eastern District of Oklahoma; 1996, U.S. District Court, Northern District of Oklahoma. *Education:* University of Kansas (B.A., 1973); University of Oklahoma (J.D., 1976). General Counsel, Oklahoma Department of Securities, 1985-1987. *Member:* Oklahoma County and Oklahoma Bar Associations; Oklahoma Association of Defense Counsel; Defense Research Institute; International Association of Defense Counsel. ***PRACTICE AREAS:*** Casualty Insurance Law; Insurance Defense Law; Litigation; Medical Malpractice Defense; Dental Malpractice Defense; Nursing Home Negligence. ***Email:*** ccondren@piercecouch.com

PETER L. WHEELER, born Norman, Oklahoma, April 29, 1960; admitted to bar, 1988, Oklahoma and U.S. District Court, Western District of Oklahoma; 1989, U.S. District Court, Eastern and Northern Districts of Oklahoma. *Education:* Oscar Rose Junior College; University of Oklahoma (B.A., in letters, 1985; J.D., 1988). Phi Delta Phi. *Member:* Oklahoma County and Oklahoma Bar Associations; Oklahoma Association of Defense Counsel; Defense Research Institute. ***PRACTICE AREAS:*** Insurance Defense Law; Personal Injury; Bad Faith; Litigation. ***Email:*** pwheeler@piercecouch.com

G. CALVIN SHARPE, born Oklahoma City, Oklahoma, October 2, 1960; admitted to bar, 1986, Oklahoma and U.S. District Court, Western, Northern and Eastern Districts of Oklahoma; U.S. Court of Appeals, Tenth Circuit. *Education:* University of Oklahoma (B.B.A., 1982; J.D., 1985). *Member:* Oklahoma County (Member: Social Committee, 1989-2001; Young Lawyers Division, 1986-1997; Outstanding Director, 1987-1988; Outstanding Young Lawyer, 1991-1992; Chairman, 1991-1992), Oklahoma, Federal and American (Member Sections on: Tort & Insurance Practice; Litigation) Bar Associations; Oklahoma Association of Defense Counsel (Secretary, 1999-2000); Defense Research Institute, Inc.; International Association of Defense Counsel. ***PRACTICE AREAS:*** Civil Litigation, Federal and State Courts; Medical Malpractice; Products Liability; Insurance Defense; Admiralty and Maritime Law; Premises Liability; Employment Law. ***Email:*** csharpe@piercecouch.com

TODD ESTES, born Oklahoma City, Oklahoma; admitted to bar, 1990, Oklahoma. *Education:* University of Oklahoma (B.A., Minor, Congressional Studies, 1986; J.D., 1989). *Member:* Oklahoma County and Oklahoma Bar Associations; Oklahoma Association of Defense Counsel; Workers' Compensation Defense Counsel; Defense Research Institute; USLaw. ***PRACTICE AREAS:*** Litigation; Workers' Compensation Law; Insurance Defense Law. ***Email:*** testes@piercecouch.com

(This Listing Continued)

LEAH P. KEELE, born Fort Smith, Arkansas, January 5, 1965; admitted to bar, 1994, Oklahoma. *Education:* Northeastern Oklahoma State University (B.S., 1986); University of Tulsa (J.D., 1993). Member, Tulsa Law Journal. Recipient, American Jurisprudence Award, Workers Compensation. Author: "The Aftermath of Dewsnup Lien Survival in Chapter 13," TLJ, Vol. 28, No. 4, Summer 1993. Member, National Self-Insured Association. Board Member, Oklahoma Self-Insured Association. *Member:* Defense Research Institute; Tulsa Claims Association; Oklahoma Association of Defense Counsel. (Resident, Tulsa Office). ***PRACTICE AREAS:*** Workers Compensation. ***Email:*** lkeele@piercecouch.com

SCOTT A. LAW, born Tulsa, Oklahoma, January 29, 1963; admitted to bar, 1988, Oklahoma, U.S. District Court, Western, Eastern and Northern Districts of Oklahoma and U.S. Court of Appeals, Tenth Circuit. *Education:* Oklahoma State University (B.S., 1985); University of Oklahoma (J.D., 1988). *Member:* Oklahoma County and Oklahoma Bar Associations; Oklahoma Defense Research Institute; Oklahoma Association of Defense Counsel; USLaw. ***PRACTICE AREAS:*** Medical Malpractice; Toxic Tort; Insurance Defense Law; Energy. ***Email:*** slaw@piercecouch.com

ASSOCIATES

HAVEN TOBIAS, born Chicago, Illinois, June 2, 1942; admitted to bar, 1974, Oklahoma; U.S. Supreme Court; U.S. Court of Appeals, Tenth Circuit; U.S. District Court, Western, Northern and Eastern Districts of Oklahoma. *Education:* University of New Mexico (B.A., magna cum laude, 1964); University of Oklahoma (J.D., 1973). Member, Oklahoma Supreme Court OUJI Committee, 1992—. ***PRACTICE AREAS:*** Appellate Practice. ***Email:*** htobias@piercecouch.com

VICTORIA D. TINDALL, born Texarkana, Arkansas, July 9, 1956; admitted to bar, 1997, Oklahoma and U.S. District Court, Western District of Oklahoma. *Education:* University of Oklahoma (B.A., 1994; J.D., 1997). Co-Author: "Demise of the General Release—Is It Mere Excess Verbiage?". *Member:* Oklahoma County and Oklahoma Bar Associations; Oklahoma Association of Defense Council; Defense Research Institute. ***PRACTICE AREAS:*** Commercial; Construction Contracts; Negligence; Professional Liability; Insurance Defense; ERISA. ***Email:*** vtindall@piercecouch.com

LINDA PRINE BROWN, born Vinita, Oklahoma, December 16, 1945; admitted to bar, 1989, Oklahoma, U.S. District Court, Western, Eastern and Northern Districts of Oklahoma and U.S. Court of Appeals, Tenth Circuit. *Education:* Oklahoma State University (B.S., 1969); Oklahoma City University (J.D., 1989). *Member:* Oklahoma County and Oklahoma Bar Associations; Oklahoma Association of Defense Counsel; Defense Research Institute. ***PRACTICE AREAS:*** Accountants Liability; Architects and Engineers Liability; Insurance; Torts; Contract Litigation. ***Email:*** lbrown@piercecouch.com

ANGELA REINSTEIN, born Hugo, Oklahoma, June 26, 1971; admitted to bar, 1997, Oklahoma. *Education:* University of Oklahoma (B.A., 1993; J.D., 1996). *Member:* Oklahoma County and Oklahoma Bar Associations. ***PRACTICE AREAS:*** Workers Compensation Defense. ***Email:*** areinstein@piercecouch.com

JOHN R. SCHNEIDER, born Connersville, Indiana, March 13, 1951; admitted to bar, 1983, Oklahoma. *Education:* Southern Illinois University (B.S., 1973; M.Sc., 1975); Oklahoma City University (J.D., 1983). *Member:* Oklahoma Count and Oklahoma (Workers' Compensation Section, Appellate Practice Section) Bar Associations; Oklahoma Association of Defense Counsel. ***PRACTICE AREAS:*** Workers Compensation Defense Law (100%, 2500). ***Email:*** jschneider@piercecouch.com

RANDI A. DONALDSON, born Kansas City, Missouri, September 29, 1974; admitted to bar, 1999, Missouri and U.S. District Court, Western District of Missouri; 2001, Oklahoma. *Education:* Drake University (B.A., cum laude, 1996; J.D., Highest Honors, 1999). Order of the Coif; Order of Barristers; Blackstone Inn of Court. *Member:* The Missouri Bar. ***PRACTICE AREAS:*** General Liability; Construction Litigation; Insurance Defense. ***Email:*** rdonaldson@piercecouch.com

JASON M. HENDERSON, born Tulsa, Oklahoma, September 24, 1968; admitted to bar, 1995, Oklahoma and U.S. District Court, Northern District of Oklahoma. *Education:* University of Oklahoma (B.A., 1991); University of Tulsa (J.D., 1994). Member, American Inns of Court. *Member:* Tulsa County and Oklahoma Bar Associations. (Resident, Tulsa Office). ***PRACTICE AREAS:*** Civil Litigation; Workers Compensation. ***Email:*** jhenderson@piercecouch.com

ROBERT B. HOUSTON, born Biloxi, Mississippi, July 10, 1965; admitted to bar, 1991, Oklahoma; 1993, U.S. District Court, Eastern District of Oklahoma; 1994, U.S. District Court, Northern District of Oklahoma. *Education:* Centre College of Kentucky (B.S., 1987); University of Tulsa (J.D., 1991). Licensed Realtor, Oklahoma, 1997. *Member:* Oklahoma County and Oklahoma Bar Associations. ***PRACTICE AREAS:*** Medical Malpractice; Insurance Defense; Products Liability; Litigation. ***Email:*** bhouston@piercecouch.com

JUSTON ROBERT GIVENS, born Guymon, Oklahoma, March 9, 1975; admitted to bar, 2001, Oklahoma. *Education:* Oklahoma State University (B.A., 1998); Oklahoma City University School of Law (J.D., 2001). *Member:* Oklahoma Bar Association. ***Email:*** jgivens@piercecouch.com

LESLIE DIANE GUAJARDO, born Weatherford, Oklahoma, August 15, 1976; admitted to bar, 2002, Oklahoma. *Education:* Southwestern Oklahoma State University (B.A., cum laude, 1997); Oklahoma City University School of Law (J.D., cum laude, 2002). *Member:* Oklahoma County and Oklahoma Bar Associations; Oklahoma Association of Defense Counsel. ***PRACTICE AREAS:*** Insurance Defense; Medical Malpractice Defense; Nursing Home Negligence Defense; Hospital Negligence Defense. ***Email:*** lguajardo@piercecouch.com

LARRY G. CASSIL, JR., born Oklahoma City, Oklahoma, July 27, 1963; admitted to bar, 1988, Texas and U.S. District Court, Northern District of Texas; 1990, U.S. Court of Appeals, Tenth Circuit and U.S. District Court, Western and Northern Districts of Oklahoma; 1991, Oklahoma; 1996, U.S. Court of Appeals, Fifth Circuit; 2003, U.S. District Court, Eastern District of Oklahoma. *Education:* Vanderbilt University (B.A., summa cum laude, 1985; M.A., 1994); Columbia University (J.D., 1988). *Member:* Oklahoma County

(This Listing Continued)

and Oklahoma Bar Association; State Bar of Texas; Oklahoma Association of Defense Counsel. ***LANGUAGES:*** Spanish. ***PRACTICE AREAS:*** Labor and Employment; Insurance Coverage; Insurance Defense. ***Email:*** lcassil@piercecouch.com

JAMIE MESSINA BELLER, born Oklahoma City, Oklahoma, March 9, 1977; admitted to bar, 2002, Oklahoma. *Education:* University of Tulsa (B.A., 1999; J.D., 2002). *Member:* Oklahoma and American Bar Associations. (Resident, Tulsa Office). ***PRACTICE AREAS:*** Workers Compensation; Insurance Defense; Employment Law. ***Email:*** jbeller@piercecouch.com

NANCY K ANDERSON, born Ames, Iowa, October 24, 1941; admitted to bar, 1981, Oklahoma. *Education:* Iowa State University (B.S., Journalism, 1963); University of Oklahoma (J.D., 1980). ***PRACTICE AREAS:*** Appellate Practice. ***Email:*** nanderson@piercecouch.com

JERROD S. GEIGER, born Born in Okeene, Oklahoma, October 30, 1976; admitted to bar, 2002, Oklahoma; U.S. District Court, Western District of Oklahoma. *Education:* University of Oklahoma (B.A., summa cum laude, Political Science, 1999); University of Oklahoma (J.D., 2002). *Member:* Oklahoma County, Oklahoma and American Bar Associations; Workers' Compensation Defense Counsel; Oklahoma Association of Defense Counsel. ***PRACTICE AREAS:*** Workers Compensation; Litigation. ***Email:*** jgeiger@piercecouch.com

CAREY C. CALVERT, born Tulsa, Oklahoma, April 9, 1968; admitted to bar, 1993, Oklahoma, U.S. District Court, Northern, Western and Eastern Districts of Oklahoma and U.S. Court of Appeals, Tenth Circuit. *Education:* Oklahoma State University (B.S., 1989); University of Oklahoma (J.D., 1993). *Member:* Tulsa County, Oklahoma and American Bar Associations; Oklahoma Association of Defense Counsel; Defense Research Institute. ***PRACTICE AREAS:*** Insurance Defense; Civil Litigation; Medical Malpractice; Nursing Home Liability. ***Email:*** ccalvert@piercecouch.com

AMY S. HAYES, born Albertville, Alabama, September 29, 1979; admitted to bar, 2003, Oklahoma and U.S. District Court, Western District of Oklahoma. *Education:* Auburn University (B.A., cum laude, 2000); Oklahoma City University (J.D., 2003). *Member:* Oklahoma County and Oklahoma Bar Associations; Oklahoma Association of Defense Counsel; Defense Research Institute. ***PRACTICE AREAS:*** Civil Litigation; Insurance Defense; Nursing Home Negligence. ***Email:*** ahayes@piercecouch.com

HEIDI M. NICHOLS, born Ithaca, New York, June 21, 1976; admitted to bar, 2002, Mississippi, U.S. District Court, Northern and Southern Districts of Mississippi and U.S. Court of Appeals, Fifth Circuit; 2004, Oklahoma. *Education:* Ithaca College (B.A., cum laude, with honors, 1998); St. Louis University (J.D., cum laude, 2002). *Member:* Oklahoma County and Oklahoma Bar Associations; The Mississippi Bar; Oklahoma Association of Defense Counsel; Defense Research Institute. ***LANGUAGES:*** Spanish. ***PRACTICE AREAS:*** Insurance Defense; Products Liability. ***Email:*** hnichols@piercecouch.com

LORI R. WHITWORTH, born Shawnee, Oklahoma, January 17, 1978; admitted to bar, 2003, Oklahoma and U.S. District Court, Western District of Oklahoma. *Education:* University of Oklahoma (B.A., Political Science, 2000; J.D., 2003). *Member:* Oklahoma County and Oklahoma Bar Associations; Oklahoma Association of Defense Counsel. (Resident, Tulsa Office). ***PRACTICE AREAS:*** Workers Compensation. ***Email:*** lwhitworth@piercecouch.com

JOHN L. SHEARS, born Ponca City, Oklahoma, July 4, 1975; admitted to bar, 2001, Oklahoma, U.S. District Court, Northern, Eastern and Western Districts of Oklahoma and U.S. Court of Appeals, Tenth Circuit. *Education:* Oklahoma State University (B.A., 1998); University of Oklahoma (J.D., 2001). *Member:* Oklahoma County, Oklahoma and American Bar Associations; Oklahoma Association of Defense Counsel; Defense Research Institute; William J. Holloway, Jr. American Inn of Court. ***PRACTICE AREAS:*** Workers Compensation; Insurance Defense; Personal Injury; Products Liability; Civil Litigation. ***Email:*** jshears@piercecouch.com

JEFFREY I. CRAIN, born Oklahoma City, Oklahoma, November 21, 1971; admitted to bar, 2004, Oklahoma and U.S. District Court, Western District of Oklahoma. *Education:* Davidson College (B.A., Psychology, 1994); Oklahoma City University (J.D., summa cum laude, 2003). Phi Alpha Delta. Recipient, CALI Awards in: Contracts; Juvenile Law; Secured Transactions; Law and Medicine. *Member:* Oklahoma County and Oklahoma Bar Associations; Oklahoma Association of Defense Counsel; Defense Research Institute. [Major, U.S. Army Reserves, 2000—; U.S. Army, 1994-2000]. ***PRACTICE AREAS:*** Insurance Defense; Medical Malpractice. ***Email:*** jcrain@piercecouch.com

MELISSA J. HOEHN, born Fort Hood, Texas, July 23, 1959; admitted to bar, 2004, Oklahoma, U.S. District Court, Western District of Oklahoma and U.S. Court of Appeals, Tenth Circuit. *Education:* University of Oklahoma (B.A., 1998); Oklahoma City University (J.D., 2003). *Member:* Oklahoma County, Oklahoma and American Bar Associations; Oklahoma Association of Defense Counsel; Defense Research Institute. ***PRACTICE AREAS:*** Civil Practice (100%). ***Email:*** mhoehn@piercecouch.com

WILLIAM J. BAZE, born Hugo, Oklahoma, July 17, 1972; admitted to bar, 2001, Oklahoma. *Education:* University of Oklahoma (B.A., 1995; J.D., with honors, 2001). Order of the Coif. *Member:* Oklahoma County and Oklahoma Bar Associations; Oklahoma Association of Defense Counsel; Defense Research Institute. ***PRACTICE AREAS:*** Appellate Practice. ***Email:*** bbaze@piercecouch.com

MATTHEW J.G. McDEVITT, born Cleveland, Ohio, January 24, 1979; admitted to bar, 2004, Texas; 2005, Oklahoma. *Education:* Texas A & M University (B.A., Political Science, 2001); Oklahoma City University (J.D., 2004). *Member:* Oklahoma County and Oklahoma Bar Associations; State Bar of Texas; Oklahoma Association of Defense Counsel; Defense Research Institute. ***PRACTICE AREAS:*** Medical Malpractice; Insurance Defense. ***Email:*** mmcdevitt@piercecouch.com

PATRICK S. PARR, born Aurora, Illinois, September 13, 1970; admitted to bar, 2000, Oklahoma; 2003, U.S. District Court, Northern District of Oklahoma. *Education:* Southeastern Oklahoma State University (B.A., Criminal Justice, 1997); University of Tulsa (J.D., 2000). Phi Delta Phi. *Member:* Oklahoma Bar Association (Board Member, Workers' Compensation Section, 2003—); Oklahoma Association of Defense Counsel. [Sergeant and Squad Leader, U.S. Marine Corps, 1988-1994]. ***PRACTICE AREAS:*** Workers Compensation (100%). ***Email:*** pparr@piercecouch.com

(This Listing Continued)

AMY R. STEELE, born Irving, Texas, November 10, 1978; admitted to bar, 2004, Oklahoma. *Education:* University of Texas at Dallas (B.A., 2001); University of Oklahoma (J.D., with distinction, 2004; M.P.A., 2004). Phi Alpha Delta. Certified Interpreter for the Deaf/Hard of Hearing, Texas Level 1, 2000—. *Member:* Oklahoma County, Oklahoma and American Bar Associations; The Association of Trial Lawyers of America; Oklahoma Association of Defense Counsel; Defense Research Institute. ***PRACTICE AREAS:*** Insurance Defense; Civil Litigation; Employment Law. ***Email:*** asteele@piercecouch.com

OF COUNSEL

JAMES E. GOLDEN, JR., born Dallas, Texas, February 21, 1955; admitted to bar, 1979, Texas; 1981, Oklahoma and U.S. Tax Court; 1982, U.S. Court of Appeals, Fifth and Tenth Circuits. *Education:* Southern Methodist University (B.A., with high honors, 1976; J.D., 1979). Member, National Association of Securities Dealers Arbitration Panel. *Member:* State Bar of Texas (Member, Sections on: Health Law; Labor and Employment Law); American Health Lawyers Association; Oklahoma Health Lawyers Association. (Also practicing individually). ***PRACTICE AREAS:*** Business Law; Commercial Litigation; Corporate Law; Insurance Law; Health Law; Banks and Banking; Creditor; Litigation; Securities Litigation; Trusts and Estates; Construction Law; Complex and Multi-District Litigation; Asset Protection; Insurance Bad Faith; Environmental Law; Business Transactions and Transfers; Personal Injury; Products Liability. ***Email:*** jgolden@piercecouch.com

MALINDA S. MATLOCK, born Tulsa, Oklahoma, February 2, 1966; admitted to bar, 1991, Oklahoma and U.S. District Court, Northern, Western and Eastern Districts of Oklahoma. *Education:* University of Oklahoma (B.B.A., 1988; J.D., 1991). Member, Defense Research Institute and Oklahoma Association of Defense Counsel, 1992-2003. *Member:* Oklahoma and American Bar Associations. ***PRACTICE AREAS:*** Medical Malpractice Defense; Health Law; Insurance Defense; Civil Litigation. ***Email:*** mmatlock@piercecouch.com

ROBERT M. ANTHONY, born Auburn, New York, April 2, 1954; admitted to bar, 1979, Oklahoma; 1980, U.S. District Court, Western District of Oklahoma and U.S. Court of Appeals, Tenth Circuit; 1990, U.S. District Court, Northern and Eastern Districts of Oklahoma. *Education:* Harvard University; University of Tulsa; Oklahoma State University (B.U.S., 1976); University of Oklahoma (J.D., 1979). Phi Alpha Delta (Justice, 1979). Partner, Pence, Housley & Anthony, Norman, Oklahoma, 1983-1990. Assistant Attorney General, State of Oklahoma, 1990-1992 and 1996-2001. Foreign Service Officer, U.S. Department of State, 1992-1996.*Member:* Oklahoma County and Oklahoma Bar Associations; Oklahoma Association of Defense Counsel; Defense Research Institute. ***LANGUAGES:*** Spanish. ***REPORTED CASES:*** Medina v. State, 871 P.2d 1379 (Okla. 1993). ***PRACTICE AREAS:*** Civil Litigation; Civil Rights; Employment Law; Personal Injury. ***Email:*** banthony@piercecouch.com

REPRESENTATIVE CLIENTS: Aetna Insurance Co.; AIG Insurance; American Modern Insurance Group; American Society of Composers, Authors and Publishers; Atlanta International Insurance Co.; Bethlehem Steel Corp.; Borg-Warner; Brotherhood Mutual Insurance Co.; Brown & Root; Cessna; Chubb Insurance Group; CIGNA Insurance; CNA/Insurance Group; Continental Insurance; Crawford & Co.; Federated Insurance Co.; Fireman's Fund Insurance; Foremost Insurance Co.; Halliburton Cos.; Highlands Insurance Co.; Housing Authority Risk Retention Group; Insurance Company of North America; Interstate Insurance; Kansas City Life Insurance Co.; Kemper Insurance Group; Lloyd's of London; Marriott Corp.; Michigan Mutual Insurance Co.; Midwest Mutual Insurance Co.; Oklahoma Municipal Assurance Group; Oklahoma Natural Gas Co.; Oklahoma Property & Casualty Guarantee Assn.; Owens Corning Fiberglass; PHICO; Physicians Liability Insurance Co.; Professional Medical Insurance Co.; Republic Western Insurance Co.; RLI Insurance; Ryder Corp.; Sentry Insurance Cos.; Shelter Insurance Companies; Texas Medical Liability Trust; The Hartford Insurance Co.; U-Haul Corp.; U.S.A.A.; Utica Mutual Insurance Co.; Van Waters and Rogers, Inc.; Welltech Corporation.
REFERENCES: MidFirst Bank; Stillwater National Bank & Trust Co.

PIGNATO & COOPER, P.C.

Established in 2001

1120 ROBINSON RENAISSANCE
119 NORTH ROBINSON
OKLAHOMA CITY, OKLAHOMA 73102
Telephone: 405-606-3333
Fax: 405-606-3334
Email: firm@pclaw.com
URL: http://www.pignatocooper.com

FIRM PROFILE: Pignato & Cooper, P.C. holds the highest rating established according to Martindale-Hubbell standards. The firm specializes in Complex Insurance Litigation, General Insurance Defense, Professional Liability, Medical Malpractice, Trucking Law, Negligence, Civil Rights Defense, Automobile and Garage Liability, Manufacturers' Products Liability and Employment Law with emphasis in Trial and Appellate Practice. The firm practices throughout the state of Oklahoma in state and federal court.

GERARD F. PIGNATO, born Meriden, Connecticut, April 22, 1959; admitted to bar, 1985, Oklahoma, U.S. District Court, Western, Northern and Eastern Districts of Oklahoma and U.S. Court of Appeals, Tenth Circuit. *Education:* Brown University (B.A., 1981); University of Oklahoma (J.D., 1984). Author: "When a Conflict of Interest Arising Out of A Reservation of Rights Allows an Insured to Select His Own Counsel and Control the Defense: An Oklahoma Forecast," 64 OBJ 1646 (1993); also Frequent Lecturer on Complex Insurance Issues and Litigation. *Member:* Oklahoma County, Oklahoma and American Bar Associations; Defense Research Institute. ***PRACTICE AREAS:*** Complex Insurance Litigation; Civil Rights; Transportation; Medical Negligence; Professional Liability. ***Email:*** jerry@pclaw.org

R. THOMPSON COOPER, born Little Rock, Arkansas, September 20, 1968; admitted to bar, 1993, Oklahoma, U.S. District Court, Western, Northern and Eastern Districts of Oklahoma and U.S. Court of Appeals, Tenth Circuit. *Education:* University of Oklahoma (B.A. in Letters, 1990; J.D., 1993). Recipient, American Jurisprudence Award in Evidence. Lecturer on Insurance Coverage Issues. *Member:* Oklahoma County, Oklahoma, Federal and American Bar Associations; Defense Research Institute. ***PRACTICE AREAS:*** Civil Litigation; Insurance Defense; Professional Liability. ***Email:*** tom@pclaw.org

(This Listing Continued)

PIGNATO & COOPER, P.C., Oklahoma City—Continued

PAUL M. KOLKER, born Elgin, Oklahoma, February 26, 1974; admitted to bar, 2000, Oklahoma and U.S. District Court, Western, Northern and Eastern Districts of Oklahoma. *Education:* Louisiana Tech University (B.A., 1997); University of Oklahoma (J.D., 2000). Author: "Expert Witness Fees as a Recoverable Item of Costs: Recent Litigation Trends," 57 Okla. L. Rev., 2005. *Member:* Oklahoma and American Bar Associations; Association of Trial Lawyers of America; Oklahoma Trial Lawyers Association; Robert J. Turner American Inn of Court; Federalist Society; Oklahoma Association of Defense Counsel; Defense Research Institute. ***PRACTICE AREAS:*** Insurance Defense; Professional Liability; Trucking Law. ***Email:*** paul@pclaw.org

BRAD L. ROBERSON, born Liberal, Kansas, August 17, 1975; admitted to bar, 2000, Oklahoma and District of Columbia; U.S. District Court, Northern, Eastern and Western Districts of Oklahoma; U.S. Court of Appeals, Tenth Circuit. *Education:* Bethany College (B.A., cum laude, 1997); University of Oklahoma College of Law (J.D., with honors, 2000). *Member:* Oklahoma and American Bar Associations; District of Columbia Bar. ***PRACTICE AREAS:*** Commercial Litigation; Insurance Defense; Professional Liability; Civil Rights Defense. ***Email:*** brad@pclaw.org

ADRIENNE BABETTE ROBERSON, born Tulsa, Oklahoma, July, 1975; admitted to bar, 2000, Oklahoma, U.S. District Court, Western, Eastern and Northern Districts of Oklahoma and the District of Columbia and U.S. Court of Appeals, Tenth Circuit. *Education:* University of Oklahoma (B.A., 1997); University of Oklahoma School of Law (J.D., 2000). *Member:* Oklahoma Bar Association; District of Columbia Bar. ***PRACTICE AREAS:*** Insurance Defense; Professional Liability.

PATRICK L. HULLUM, born Okmulgee, Oklahoma, May 14, 1977; admitted to bar, 2003, Oklahoma and U.S. District Court, Western District of Oklahoma. *Education:* Oklahoma State University (B.A., 1999); University of Oklahoma (J.D., 2003). *Member:* Oklahoma and American Bar Associations. ***PRACTICE AREAS:*** Insurance Defense; Bad Faith Litigation. ***Email:*** patrick@pclaw.org

OF COUNSEL

MICHAEL P. KELLY, born Pittsburgh, Pennsylvania, 1959; admitted to bar, 1985, Oklahoma and Texas. *Education:* University of Oklahoma (B.B.A., Finance, 1980); University of Oklahoma School of Law (J.D., 1985). ***PRACTICE AREAS:*** Insurance Defense; Professional Liability; Business Litigation.

D. BENHAM KIRK, JR., born Oklahoma City, Oklahoma, September 15, 1957; admitted to bar, 1982, Oklahoma; U.S. District Court, Northern, Eastern and Western Districts of Oklahoma; U.S. Court of Appeals, Tenth Circuit. *Education:* Trinity University (B.A., 1977); University of Oklahoma (J.D., 1982). *Member:* Oklahoma County and Oklahoma Bar Associations.

REPRESENTATIVE CLIENTS: American Bankers Insurance Group; American International Group, Inc.; Association of County Commissioners of Oklahoma-Self-Insured Group; Atlas Carriers, Inc.; Brotherhood Mutual Insurance Company; Budget Rent-A-Car Systems, Inc.; Champion Homes, Inc.; Claims Management Services, Inc.; Coregis Insurance Company; Cumis Insurance Society; Employers Reinsurance Corporation; First Guard Adjustment Co.; First Specialty Insurance Corporation; Frontier Insurance Company; Gallagher Bassett Services, Inc.; GreenPoint Credit Corp.; Government Employees Insurance Company; Legion Indemnity Company; Medical Protective Insurance Company; Modern Woodmen of America; National Casualty Company; Noble Rubber Products, Inc.; Oklahoma Farmers Union Mutual Insurance Company; Oklahoma Rural Water Association Assurance Group; Progressive Casulaty Insurance Company; Redman Building Products, Inc.; Reynolds Ford, Inc.; Ryder TRS, Inc.; Scottsdale Insurance Company; Smith Cogeneration; Tetco, Inc.; Tinker Industrial Developers; Travelers Insurance Company; Universal Insurance Agency, Inc.; Ward Strategic Claims Solutions; Western Heritage Insurance Company; Westport Insurance Company; Wind Degree Advertising; Bank of America.

PINKERTON & FINN, P.C.

OKLAHOMA CITY, OKLAHOMA

(See Tulsa)

Civil Trial and Appellate Practice, State and Federal Courts, Commercial, Securities and Intellectual Property Litigation, Securities Fraud, Health Law, Contract Litigation, Non-Compete Agreements, Business Litigation.

POSTIC & BATES

A PROFESSIONAL CORPORATION

2212 SHADOWLAKE DRIVE

OKLAHOMA CITY, OKLAHOMA 73159-7440

Telephone: 405-691-5080

Telecopier: 405-691-6329

URL: http://www.posticbates.com

Estate Planning, Real Estate Law, Adoption Law, Probate, Guardianship.

MARTIN POSTIC, JR., admitted to bar, 1980, Oklahoma. *Education:* University of Oklahoma (B.B.A., 1977; J.D., 1980). ***LANGUAGES:*** German. ***PRACTICE AREAS:*** Estate Planning Law (80%); Real Estate Law (20%). ***Email:*** posticm@posticbates.com

JULIE E. BATES, born Swindon, England, July 11, 1957; admitted to bar, 1983, Oklahoma, U.S. Court of Appeals, Tenth Circuit, U.S. District Court, Northern, Eastern and Western Districts of Oklahoma and U.S. District Court, Northern and Western Districts of Texas; 1986, U.S. Supreme Court. *Education:* Texas Christian University (B.A., with high honors, 1978); Queens College, Oxford University (1982); University of Oklahoma (J.D., 1983). Phi Delta Phi. Member, Order of the Barristers. Member, National Trial Advocacy Team, 1982 and 1983. Recipient: American Jurisprudence Award in: Professional Responsibility and Municipal Law; Special Recognition Award, 1997; President's Award, 1999; John Shipp Award for Professionalism, 2004. Co-Author: "Traffic Accident Reconstruction," Defense Counsel Journal, November, 1988; "Accident Reconstruction," The Briefcase, December 1988; "Driver's Viewpoint Important to Design," The Briefcase, January, 1989; "Civil Appeals to the Tenth Circuit: A General Overview of the Local Court Rules as Amended," The Briefcase, April and May, 1989; "Accident Reconstruction in Personal Injury Lawsuits," Accident Reconstruction Journal, Nov.-Dec., 1989; "Personal Injury Defense Litigation Treatise," Matthew Bender, 1990. Adjunct Professor, Civil Pretrial Litigation and Adoption Law, University of Oklahoma College of Law, 2002—. *Member:* Oklahoma County (Alternate Delegate to Annual Meeting, 2001-2003, Delegate, 2004—; Board of Directors, 2004-2007; Awards Committee, 2000—; Fee Grievance and Ethics Committee, 2000-2003; Committee on Professionalism, 2002) and Oklahoma (Member, Committees on: Model Rules of Professional Conduct, 1989-1990; Civil Procedure, 1989-1990; Legal Ethics, 1999; Awards, 2000—, Vice Chair, 2004-2005; Vice-Chief Master, Professional Responsibility Tribunal, 2004-2005; Parliamentarian for 2003 OBA Annual Meeting) Bar Associations; Ruth Bader Ginsburg American Inn of Court (Co-Founder, 1995; Master of the Bench and Administrator, 1995—). ***PRACTICE AREAS:*** Adoption Law; Probate; Guardianship. ***Email:*** batesj@posticbates.com

---

RAINEY, ROSS, RICE & BINNS, P.L.L.C.

Established in 1890

735 FIRST NATIONAL CENTER WEST

OKLAHOMA CITY, OKLAHOMA 73102-7405

Telephone: 405-235-1356

Telecopier: 405-235-2340

General Practice. Trials in all State and Federal Courts, Corporation, Public Utility, Commercial, Bankruptcy, Administrative, Probate, Negligence, Oil and Gas, Products Liability, Railroad, Aircraft Title Law.

ROBERT M. RAINEY (1882-1971)

STREETER BLANTON FLYNN (1892-1971)

GORDON F. RAINEY (1913-1975)

H. D. BINNS, JR. (1944-1997)

HUGH D. RICE, admitted to bar, 1964, Oklahoma; U.S. Supreme Court; U.S. District Court, Western, Eastern and Northern Districts of Oklahoma and U.S. Court of Appeals, Tenth Circuit. *Education:* University of Oklahoma (B.A., 1961); University of Virginia (LL.B., 1964). Phi Alpha Delta. *Member:* Oklahoma and American Bar Associations. ***PRACTICE AREAS:*** Aircraft Law; Decedent's Estates; Corporate Law; Real Estate Law; Public Utility Law; Railroad Law. ***Email:*** hrice@raineyfirm.com

RODNEY L. COOK, admitted to bar, 1974, Oklahoma, U.S. District Court, Western, Eastern and Northern Districts of Oklahoma and U.S. Court of Appeals, Tenth Circuit; U.S. District Court, Eastern and Western Districts of Arkansas. *Education:* University of Oklahoma (B.B.A., 1971; J.D., 1974). Phi Delta Phi. *Member:* Oklahoma Bar Association; National Association of Railroad Trial Counsel. ***PRACTICE AREAS:*** Civil Litigation; Electrical Injury; Federal Employers' Liability Act; General Trial Practice; Railroad Law; Public Utility Law. ***Email:*** cookr-ne@oge.com

ROBERTA BROWNING FIELDS, admitted to bar, 1984, Oklahoma, U.S. District Court, Northern, Eastern and Western Districts of Oklahoma, U.S. Court of Appeals, Tenth Circuit and U.S. Supreme Court. *Education:* Oral Roberts University (B.A., 1977); Oklahoma State University (M.S., 1981); University of Oklahoma (J.D., with distinction, 1984). Editor, Oklahoma Law Review, 1983-1984. *Member:* Oklahoma Bar Association. ***PRACTICE AREAS:*** Civil Litigation; Employment Law; Public Utility Law; Railroad Law. ***Email:*** fieldsr-ne@oge.com

---

WILLIAM P. TUNELL, JR., admitted to bar, 1996, Oklahoma; U.S. District Court, Northern and Eastern Districts of Oklahoma; U.S. Court of Appeals, Tenth Circuit. *Education:* University of Pennsylvania (B.A., 1992); University of Notre Dame (J.D., M.B.A., 1996). Symposium and Associate Articles Editor, Journal of Legislation, 1994-1996. Author: "Welfare Reform: The Case For a Systemic Approach," 21 J. Legis. 301, 1995. *Member:* Tulsa County, Oklahoma and Muscogee (Creek) Nation Bar Associations. ***LANGUAGES:*** Spanish. ***PRACTICE AREAS:*** Commercial Litigation; Banking Law; Intellectual Property; Commercial Transactions. ***Email:*** btunell@raineyfirm.com

PATRICIA L. FRANZ, admitted to bar, 1998, Oklahoma and U.S. District Court, Western District of Oklahoma, U.S. Court of Appeals, Tenth Circuit and U.S. Supreme Court. *Education:* Ohio Wesleyan University (B.A., 1986); The Ohio State University (M.S.W., 1990; J.D., with honors, 1998). Phi Beta Kappa. Author: "Ohio v. The Bank: An Historical Examination of Osborn v. Bank of the United States," 23 Journal of the Supreme Court History, No. 1, p. 112, 1999; "Habits of a Highly Effective Transformative Mediation Program," 13 Ohio State Journal on Dispute Resolution 1039, 1998. *Member:* Oklahoma Bar Association. ***PRACTICE AREAS:*** Defense Litigation; Utility Law; Railroad Law; Employment Law; Environmental Law. ***Email:*** pfranz@raineyfirm.com

KENNETH A. TILLOTSON, admitted to bar, 2001, Oklahoma and U.S. District Court, Western District of Oklahoma; U.S. District Court, Eastern and Western Districts of Arkansas. *Education:* Northeastern State University (B.A., 1998); University of Oklahoma (J.D., with distinction, 2001). Phi Delta Phi. *Member:* Oklahoma Bar Association. ***PRACTICE AREAS:*** Civil Litigation; Federal Employers Liability Act (FELA); Railroad Law; Public Utility Law. ***Email:*** ktillotson@raineyfirm.com

DUSTIN R. FREDRICK, admitted to bar, 2001, Oklahoma and U.S. District Court, Western, Northern and Eastern Districts of Oklahoma. *Education:* Oklahoma State University (B.A., cum laude, 1998); University of Oklahoma (J.D., 2001). Phi Kappa Phi; Psi Chi; Order of Omega; Phi Delta Phi. *Member:* Oklahoma County, Oklahoma and American Bar Associations. ***SPECIAL AGENCIES:*** Oklahoma Corporation Commission; Federal Energy Regulatory Commission. ***PRACTICE AREAS:*** Civil Litigation; Energy Law; Public Utility Law; Contract Law. ***Email:*** fredrid@oge.com

RACHEL L. BUSSETT, admitted to bar, 2003, Oklahoma; U.S. district Court, Western District of Oklahoma. *Education:* Oklahoma State University (B.S., 1997); Oklahoma City University School of Law (J.D., cum laude, 2003). Phi Delta Phi. Faculty Honor Roll.

(This Listing Continued)

Member: Jessup International Law Moot Court Team; Order of the Barristers; Ruth Bader Ginsberg Inn of Court. *Member:* Oklahoma Bar Association. ***PRACTICE AREAS:*** Civil Litigation; Federal Employers Liability Act (FELA); Railroad Law; Public Utility Law. ***Email:*** rbussett@raineyfirm.com

OF COUNSEL

WILLIAM J. ROSS, admitted to bar, 1954, Oklahoma. *Education:* University of Oklahoma (B.B.A., 1952; LL.B., 1954). Phi Alpha Delta. Assistant Municipal Counselor, Oklahoma City, 1955-60. *Member:* Oklahoma County, Oklahoma and American Bar Associations. ***PRACTICE AREAS:*** Trust Law. ***Email:*** williamjross@coxinet.net

ROBERT D. STEWART, JR., admitted to bar, 1972, Oklahoma, U.S. District Court, Eastern and Western Districts of Oklahoma, U.S. Court of Appeals, Tenth Circuit, U.S. Supreme Court. *Education:* University of Oklahoma (B.A., 1966; J.D., 1971). Phi Delta Theta. Municipal Judge, City of Wewoka, Oklahoma, 1973-1978. General Counsel, Oklahoma Corporation Commission, 1979-1982. *Member:* Oklahoma County, Oklahoma and American Bar Associations. [Lieutenant Colonel, U.S. Army (Retired)]. ***LANGUAGES:*** French. ***SPECIAL AGENCIES:*** Oklahoma Corporation Commission; Federal Energy Regulatory Commission. ***PRACTICE AREAS:*** Energy Law; Public Utility Law; Contract Law. ***Email:*** stewarrd@oge.com

GENERAL ATTORNEYS FOR OKLAHOMA: Burlington Northern & Santa Fe; Santa Fe Pacific Corp.; Santa Fe Railway System.
ATTORNEYS FOR: Bank of America; Bluebell Creameries; Burlington Northern and Santa Fe Railway Company; Circle K Stores, Inc.; J.P. Morgan Leasing Inc.; DeQueen & Eastern Railroad Company; Thyssen Dover Elevator; Enogex, Inc.; Enogex Products Corp.; Enogex Services Corp.; Excel Energy Inc; International Paper Company; JLG Industries, Inc.; OG&E Electric Services; OGE Energy Corp.; Oklahoma Gas and Electric Company; PIC USA; Pinkerton Group, Inc.; Provident Bank; Santa Fe Pacific Minerals Corporation; Southern Pacific Transportation Co.; Southwestern Electric Power Co.; Southwestern Public Service Co.; Union Pacific Railroad Co.; Texas, Oklahoma & Eastern Railroad Company; Weyerhaeuser.

RAMEY & THARP

OKLAHOMA CITY, OKLAHOMA

(See Yukon)

General Civil Trial and Criminal Practice in all State and Federal Courts. Real Property, Medical Malpractice, Personal Injury, Child Custody, Products Liability, Probate, Corporate, Banking and Commercial Law, Family Law.

DONELLE RATHEAL, P.C.

Established in 1993

5909 N.W. EXPRESSWAY, SUITE 300
OKLAHOMA CITY, OKLAHOMA 73132
Telephone: 405-842-6342
Fax: 405-842-6708
Email: donelleratheal@yahoo.com
URL: http://www.lawyers.com/donelleratheal

Domestic Relations/ Contested and Uncontested, Family Law Litigation, Family Law Mediation, Collaborative Divorce, Child Custody and Support.

FIRM PROFILE: The firm limits its Practice to issues relating to family law in litigation, mediation and collaborative divorce.

DONELLE H. RATHEAL, born Nowata, Oklahoma, January 11, 1957; admitted to bar, 1992, Oklahoma. *Education:* University of Denver (B.M., 1979); University of Texas at Austin (M.M., 1981); University of Oklahoma (J.D., 1992). Phi Delta Phi; Order of the Barristers, 1991. Member: National Moot Court Team, 1990; Law Day Moot Court Team, 1991. Recipient: Hardin Ballard Memorial Award, 1990; American Jurisprudence Award, Appellate Advocacy, 1990. Assistant Managing Editor, Oklahoma Law Review, 1991-1992. Adjunct Professor, University of Oklahoma College of Law, 2000-2002. Certified Family Law Mediator, 2005. Member: International Association of Collaborative Professionals; Oklahoma Association of Collaborative Professionals. *Member:* Oklahoma County, Oklahoma (Director, Family Law Section Continuing Legal Education, 2001; Editorial Board, Family Law Section, 2002) and American Bar Associations. ***LANGUAGES:*** Spanish and German. ***REPORTED CASES:*** Dorn v. Heritage Trust Co., 2001 OK Civ. App. 64, 24 P.3d 886; Smith v. Smith, 2003 OK Civ. App. 28, 67 P.3d 351; State v. Routt, 2001 OK Civ. App. 113, 30 P.3d 1180. ***PRACTICE AREAS:*** Child Custody and Support; Divorce; Collaborative Divorce; Trusts and Estates; Wills and Probate; Family Law; Mediation. ***Email:*** donelleratheal@yahoo.com

LEGAL SUPPORT PERSONNEL

ARLENE CAIN (Office Manager)

JULIE STAFFORD (Paralegal)

Languages: English and Spanish.

RESIDES & RESIDES, PLLC

Established in 2004

114 NW SIXTH STREET, SUITE 203
OKLAHOMA CITY, OKLAHOMA 73102
Telephone: 405-605-6547
Fax: 405-605-6577
Email: wdresides@resideslaw.com
URL: http://www.resideslaw.com

General Practice.

(This Listing Continued)

FIRM PROFILE: The law firm of Resides & Resides, PLLC serves Oklahoma City and its surrounding areas and is dedicated to providing the finest legal representation available. Our firm prides itself in its commitment to clients, offering personalized and professional attention to each matter.

W. DEVIN RESIDES, born Phoenix, Arizona, November 15, 1967; admitted to bar, 2002, Oklahoma. *Education:* Northern Arizona University (B.S., 1990); Oklahoma City University School of Law (J.D., 2002). Phi Delta Phi (President). Recipient, Merit Scholarship. Managing Editor, Oklahoma City University Law Review, 2001-2002. Author: "HMO Liability in the New Millennium: New Theories with and Old Twist," Oklahoma City University Law Review in Vol. 27, Spring 2002. Police Officer, 1990-1999. *Member:* Oklahoma Bar Association (Member, Mineral Law Section). ***PRACTICE AREAS:*** Civil Litigation; Wrongful Death; Oil and Gas Law; Insurance Defense; Workers Compensation; Employment Law; Criminal Defense. ***Email:*** wdresides@resideslaw.com

LAURE M. RESIDES, born Oklahoma City, Oklahoma, June 14, 1975; admitted to bar, 2002, Oklahoma. *Education:* Oklahoma State University (B.A., 1999); Oklahoma City University School of Law (J.D., magna cum laude, 2002). Phi Delta Phi. Recipient: CALI Award for Excellence in Constitutional Law; CALI Award for Excellence in Legal Research and Writing; Law Review Managing Editors Award. Research Editor of the Oklahoma City University Law Review. *Member:* Oklahoma Bar Association. ***PRACTICE AREAS:*** Real Estate; Commercial Law; Consumer Law; Constitutional Law; Insurance Defense; Estate Planning; Probate. ***Email:*** lmresides@resideslaw.com

OF COUNSEL

DR. BARBARA K. YUILL, born Tucson, Arizona, January 12, 1954; admitted to bar, 2002, Oklahoma; registered to practice before U.S. Patent and Trademark Office. *Education:* University of Arizona (B.S., Metallurgical Engineering, 1976; M.S., Metallurgy, 1981); University of Oklahoma (Ph.D., Chemical Engineering, 1995); Oklahoma City University (J.D., 2002). Merit Scholar. Staff Editor, Oklahoma City Law Review. Author and Speaker: "Economic Study of Surfactant-Enhanced Pump-and-Treat Remediation," Proceedings of the Water Environment Federation 69th Annual Conference, 1996; "Economic Considerations in Surfactant-Enhanced Pump-and-Treat Remediation," ACS Symposium Series, 1995; "Surfactant Enhanced Remediation of Residual Organic Contaminants," Ph.D. dissertation, University of Oklahoma, 1995; "Hydrometallugry: Progress Despite Shutdown," World Mining, 1982; "Copper Concentrate Enrichment Process," AIME 1984, "Biologically-Aided Heap Leaching of a Silver-Manganese Ore," AIME 1986; "Uranium Extraction From a Carbonaceous Uranium Ore," M. S. thesis, University of Arizona, 1981. Co-inventor of: U.S. Patent No. 4,579,598, Process For The Recovery of Precious Metals From A Roaster Calcine Leach Residue; U.S. Patent No. 4,752,332, Treating Manganese Containing Ores With A Metal Sulfide; U.S. Patent No. 4,740,243, Metal Value Recovery From Metal Sulfide Containing Ores; Canadian Patent No., 258,181, Process For Producing Enriched Mineral Ore Concentrates. *Member:* Oklahoma County Bar Association (Member, Intellectual Property Section) Oklahoma and American Bar Associations. ***PRACTICE AREAS:*** Intellectual Property; Patent Prosecution; Patent Infringement; Patent Validity; Trademark Clearence; Software Licensing; Patent Licensing; Copyrights. ***Email:*** bkyuill@resideslaw.com

REPRESENTATIVE CLIENTS: JMA Energy Company, L.L.C.; Tower Royalty Company, L.L.C.; Amundsen Food Equipment; GFLP Properties; Oklahoma Department of Human Services; TL Homes, LLC; PC Innovations; Fashion Cleaners and Laundry, Moore Girls Softball Association; Tew Testing, LLC; TL Properties LLC; Arbuckle Enterprises, L.L.C.; Aunt Samme's L.LC.

REYNOLDS, RIDINGS, VOGT & MORGAN

Established in 1926

2200 FIRST NATIONAL CENTER
120 NORTH ROBINSON
OKLAHOMA CITY, OKLAHOMA 73102
Telephone: 405-232-8131
Fax: 405-232-7911
Email: rrvm@rrvmlaw.com

Commercial and Civil Litigation, Bankruptcy, Collections, Business Law, Banks and Banking, Creditor Rights.

FIRM PROFILE: The firm was founded in 1926 by Norman Reynolds, Sr. and W. Otis Ridings. Since the firm began, it has specialized in the areas of bankruptcy, creditors' rights and commercial litigation. The bankruptcy practice consists primarily of representation of creditors in complex reorganization cases, creditors' committees and trustees. In the area of creditors' rights, the firm handles matters such as foreclosure on personal and real property, representation of banks and finance companies in loan transactions and litigation associated with troubled loans, and collection matters for creditors in diverse areas. Commercial litigation is primarily business related. Clients include large multi-state banks, several Fortune 500 companies and local banks and business entities.

MEMBERS OF FIRM

NORMAN E. REYNOLDS (1888-1953)

W. OTIS RIDINGS (1899-1970)

JAMES W. VOGT, born Corn, Oklahoma, September 27, 1950; admitted to bar, 1975, Oklahoma, U.S. District Court, Western, Northern and Eastern Districts of Oklahoma and Northern District of Texas, U.S. Court of Appeals, Tenth Circuit and U.S. Supreme Court. *Education:* Southwestern Oklahoma State University (B.A., 1972); Oklahoma City University (J.D., 1975). Phi Alpha Delta. President and Board of Directors, Edmond Public Schools Foundation. *Member:* Oklahoma County (Member, Bankruptcy Section, President, 1990-1991) and Oklahoma (Member: Legal Ethics Committee, 1987-1990; Administration of Justice Committee, 1994-1996; Civil Procedure Committee, 1997—; Bankruptcy Section) Bar Associations; Commercial Law League of America. (Certified in Business Bankruptcy Law by the American Board of Certification) (Certified in Creditors'

(This Listing Continued)

REYNOLDS, RIDINGS, VOGT & MORGAN, Oklahoma City—Continued

Rights Law by the American Board of Certification). ***PRACTICE AREAS:*** Bankruptcy; Collections; Commercial Litigation; Creditors Rights; Bank Collections. ***Email:*** jimvogt@rrvmlaw.com

FRED S. MORGAN, born St. Louis, Missouri, February 9, 1954; admitted to bar, 1980, Oklahoma, U.S. District Court, Eastern, Western and Northern Districts of Oklahoma and U.S. Court of Appeals, Tenth Circuit. *Education:* St. Louis University (B.A., 1976); Oklahoma City University (J.D., 1980). Phi Delta Phi. Member, Oklahoma House of Representatives, 1994—, Assistant Minority Leader, 1996-1998, Minority Leader, 1998-2002. Special Counsel to Governor Frank Keating, 1994-1995. *Member:* Oklahoma County (Member, Bankruptcy Law Section) and Oklahoma Bar Associations; Commercial Law League of America; American Inns of Court CV. Fellow, Oklahoma Bar Foundation. ***PRACTICE AREAS:*** Bankruptcy Reorganization; Collections; Debtor and Creditor; Banks and Banking; Business Law; Corporate Law; Commercial Litigation. ***Email:*** morganfs@rrvmlaw.com

ASSOCIATES

LISA A. ROBERTSON, born Oklahoma City, Oklahoma, June 20, 1965; admitted to bar, 1995, Oklahoma, U.S. District Court, Western, Northern and Eastern Districts of Oklahoma and U.S. Court of Appeals, Tenth Circuit. *Education:* University of Oklahoma (B.A., 1992); Oklahoma City University (J.D., 1995). Phi Delta Phi. *Member:* Oklahoma County (Member, Commercial Law Section) and Oklahoma Bar Associations; Commercial Law League of America. ***PRACTICE AREAS:*** Creditors Rights; Commercial Collections; Commercial Litigation; Secured Transactions; Bankruptcy.

BENJAMIN HARRIS, admitted to bar, 2000, Oklahoma, U.S. District Court, Western, Eastern and Northern Districts of Oklahoma and U.S. Court of Appeals, Tenth Circuit. *Education:* Oklahoma City University (B.S., 1997); University of Oklahoma (J.D., 2000). Recipient: American Jurisprudence Award: Trial Techniques.*Member:* Oklahoma County and Oklahoma Bar Associations. ***PRACTICE AREAS:*** Commercial Litigation; Bankruptcy; Collections; Creditors Rights. ***Email:*** benharris@rrvmlaw.com

REPRESENTATIVE CLIENTS: Bank of America; Unisource; US Bank; Whirlpool Financial Corp.; General Electric Capital Corp.; Performance Materials Supply; Hope Lumber & Supply; Petroleum Marketers Equipment Co.; Haliburton Cos.; Mercury Marine; Schlumberger; National Association of Credit Management; Textron Financial; Citicorp Vendor Finance, Inc.
REFERENCES: Bank One; Banc First; Dun & Bradstreet; Mill Creek Lumber Co.; Mill Creek Carpet & Tile; Gulf Industries, Inc.

RHODES, HIERONYMUS, JONES, TUCKER & GABLE, P.L.L.C.

OKLAHOMA CITY, OKLAHOMA

(See Tulsa)

General Civil Trial and Appellate Practice in all State and Federal Courts. General and Extra-contractual Liability Insurance, Negligence, Products Liability, Medical, Legal and Professional Liability, Employment, Workers' Compensation, Environmental, Aviation, Suretyship, Common Carriers, Toxic Torts, ERISA, Construction.

ELIZABETH A. RICHARDS

112 WEST COMMERCE
OKLAHOMA CITY, OKLAHOMA 73109-6020
Telephone: 405-319-9696
Fax: 405-319-9464
Email: richardslawfirm@aol.com
URL: http://www.lawyers.com/richardslawfirm

Probate, Bankruptcy, Family Law, Divorce, Child Support, Real Estate, Residential Real Estate, Guardianships, Adoptions, Child Custody, Wills, Workers Compensation, Collections.

ELIZABETH A. RICHARDS, born Oklahoma City, Oklahoma; admitted to bar, 1987, Oklahoma; U.S. District Court, Western, Northern and Eastern Districts of Oklahoma; U.S. Supreme Court. *Education:* Principia College (B.A.); Oklahoma City University School of Law (J.D., 1987). *Member:* Oklahoma County, Oklahoma and American Bar Associations. ***LANGUAGES:*** Spanish.

RIFE & WALTERS

Established in 1987
BANKONE CENTER
100 NORTH BROADWAY AVENUE, SUITE 2730
OKLAHOMA CITY, OKLAHOMA 73102
Telephone: 405-235-3800
Fax: 405-235-5800
Email: rwstaff@rifewalters.com

Medical, Legal and Professional Malpractice, Professional Discipline, Insurance Defense Law. Trial Practice State and Federal Courts.

MEMBERS OF FIRM

GARY A. RIFE, born Anadarko, Oklahoma, September 10, 1953; admitted to bar, 1978, Oklahoma; 1979, U.S. District Court, Western District of Oklahoma and U.S. Court of Appeals, Tenth Circuit; 1983, U.S. Supreme Court. *Education:* University of Oklahoma (B.B.A., 1975; J.D., 1978). Recipient, Award for Legal Ethics, 1997. Adjunct Professor of Law, Professional Responsibility, University of Oklahoma College of Law and Oklahoma City University School of Law. *Member:* Cleveland County (President, 1982-1983), Oklahoma County, Oklahoma (General Counsel, 1981-1983; Chairman, 1986-1990 and Member, 1984—, Legal Ethics Committee; Member, 1994—and Co-Chair, 2000-2005, Rules of Professional Conduct Committee; Outstanding Young Lawyer, 1984; Member, House of Delegates, 1980—; Member, Board of Governors, 1986-1988) and American Bar Associations; Association of Professional Responsibility Lawyers; Oklahoma Association of Defense Counsel; Robert J. Turner American Inn of Court. ***PRACTICE AREAS:*** Litigation; Legal Ethics; Medical and Legal Professional Malpractice Law; Professional Discipline; General Civil Practice.

HILTON H. WALTERS, born Bronxville, New York, July 11, 1955; admitted to bar, 1987, Oklahoma and U.S. District Court, Western District of Oklahoma; 1989, U.S. District Court, Eastern District of Oklahoma; U.S. Supreme Court and U.S. Court of Appeals, Tenth Circuit. *Education:* Furman University (B.S., Biology, 1978); Oklahoma City University (J.D., 1987). Phi Delta Phi. Member: Order of the Barrister; Benton National Moot Court Competition. Recipient, American Jurisprudence Award, Property and Professional Responsibility. Investigator, 1982-1987 and Computer Security Specialist, 1987, Federal Aviation Administration. *Member:* Oklahoma County and Oklahoma Bar Associations; Defense Research Institute; Robert J. Turner American Inn of Court. ***PRACTICE AREAS:*** Medical and Legal Professional Malpractice Law; Insurance Defense Law.

ASSOCIATES

JAMIE K. BRUEHL, born Shawnee, Oklahoma, October 8, 1976; admitted to bar, 2002, Oklahoma and U.S. District Court, Eastern and Western Districts of Oklahoma. *Education:* University of Oklahoma (B.B.A., Business, cum laude, 1999; J.D., with distinction, 2002). Recipient: American Jurisprudence Award, Business Office Practice. *Member:* Cleveland and Oklahoma Bar Associations; Defense Research Institute; Oklahoma Association of Defense Counsel. ***PRACTICE AREAS:*** Medical Malpractice Defense (100%). ***Email:*** jbruehl@rifewalters.com

TRAVIS K. SIEGEL, born Midwest City, Oklahoma, May 17, 1977; admitted to bar, 2002, Oklahoma and U.S. District Court, Western District of Oklahoma. *Education:* Oklahoma City University (B.S., magna cum laude, 1999); University of Oklahoma (J.D., 2002). *Member:* Oklahoma and American Bar Associations; Defense Research Institute; Oklahoma Association of Defense Counsel. ***PRACTICE AREAS:*** Medical Malpractice Defense (100%). ***Email:*** tsiegel@rifewalters.com

RIGGS, ABNEY, NEAL, TURPEN, ORBISON & LEWIS

A PROFESSIONAL CORPORATION
Established in 1972
5801 BROADWAY EXTENSION
PARAGON BUILDING, SUITE 101
OKLAHOMA CITY, OKLAHOMA 73118-7489
Telephone: 405-843-9909
Fax: 405-842-2913
URL: http://www.riggsabney.com

Tulsa, Oklahoma Office: 502 West Sixth Street, 74119. Telephone: 918-587-3161. Fax: 918-587-9708.
Muskogee, Oklahoma Office: 215 State Street, First National Severs Building, Suite 508. Telephone: 918-687-5404; 800-722-1332. Fax: 918-687-1128.
Denver, Colorado Office: 621 Seventeenth Street, Suite 1900. Telephone: 303-298-7392. Fax: 303-298-7398.

General Civil, Trial and Appellate Practice before all State and Federal Courts and Agencies, Alternative Dispute Resolution, Banking, Corporate, Securities, Anti-trust, Administrative, Government Relations, Real Estate, Commercial Transactions, Oil and Gas, Estate Planning, Probate, Taxation, Employment and Discrimination, Employee Benefits, Social Security, Bankruptcy and Reorganization, Family Law, Healthcare, Negligence, Personal Injury, Products Liability, Medical Malpractice, Transportation, and Indian Law.

MEMBERS OF THE FIRM

MICHAEL C. TURPEN, admitted to bar, 1975, Oklahoma; 1976, U.S. District Court, Eastern District of Oklahoma; 1983, U.S. Supreme Court and U.S. Court of Appeals, 10th Circuit; 1987, U.S. District Court, Northern and Western Districts of Oklahoma. *Education:* University of Tulsa (B.S., 1972; J.D., 1974). Member, The Order of the Barristers. Member, Moot Court Team. Author: "The Law of Warrantless Search & Seizure," Oklahoma Bar Journal, 1980. Instructor of Law: Oral Roberts University College of Law, 1980-1981; National College of District Attorneys, 1982-1986. Recipient, Oklahoma Bar Association Outstanding Young Lawyer Award, 1975. Police Legal Advisor, Muskogee, 1974-1975. District Attorney, Muskogee County, 1977-1982. President, Oklahoma District Attorneys Association, 1980-1981. Oklahoma Attorney General, 1982-1986. *Member:* Oklahoma County, Tulsa County, Oklahoma and American Bar Associations. Fellow: Oklahoma Bar Foundation. ***PRACTICE AREAS:*** Administrative Law; Civil Litigation; Corporate Law.

RICHARD A. MILDREN, admitted to bar, 1977, Oklahoma; 1987, U.S. District Court, Western District of Oklahoma; 1990, U.S. Court of Appeals, Tenth Circuit. *Education:* University of Oklahoma (B.A., 1974; J.D., 1977). *Member:* Oklahoma County and Oklahoma Bar Associations. ***PRACTICE AREAS:*** Administrative Law; Government Relations Law.

ROBERT A. NANCE, admitted to bar, 1978, Oklahoma; 1979, U.S. District Court, Western District of Oklahoma; 1981, U.S., District Court, Northern and Eastern Districts of Oklahoma and U.S. Court of Appeals, Fifth, Eighth, and Tenth Circuit Courts. *Education:* Oklahoma State University (B.A., with honors, 1975); Georgetown University Law Center (J.D., 1978). Assistant Attorney General, Chief, Federal Division, 1981-1992. *Member:* Oklahoma County and Oklahoma Bar Associations. ***REPORTED CASES:*** Saffle v. Parks, 494 U.S., 110S. CT., 108 L.Ed.2d 415 (1990); Ross v. Oklahoma, 487 U.S., 108S. CT., 101 L.Ed2d 80 (1988).

(This Listing Continued)

MELVIN C. HALL, admitted to bar, 1982, Oklahoma; 1983, U.S. District Court, Western District of Oklahoma; 1988, U.S. District Court, Northern District of Oklahoma; 1989, U.S. District Court, Eastern District of Oklahoma; 1990, U.S. Court of Appeals, Tenth Circuit. *Education:* Langston University (B.A., 1978); University of Oklahoma (J.D., 1981). Assistant District Attorney, Cleveland County District Attorneys Office, 1980-1983. Executive Director, Oklahoma Human Rights Commission, 1983-1987. Board Member: Legal Counsel, Oklahoma State Chamber of Commerce and Industry, 1989-1993; Southwest Center for Human Relations Studies, 1985—. Board Member, Progressive Independence, 1987. Regent, University of Oklahoma, 1992-1999. *Member:* Oklahoma Bar Association. ***PRACTICE AREAS:*** Civil Litigation; Employment and Civil Rights Law.

GEORGE MARVIN EMERSON, admitted to bar, 1989, Oklahoma; U.S. District Court, Western, Eastern and Northern Districts of Oklahoma. *Education:* University of Oklahoma (B.A., 1986; J.D., 1989). *Member:* Oklahoma County (Member, Young Lawyers Division, Board of Directors, 1991-1992, 1992-1993, 1993-1994 and Secretary, 1992-1993), Oklahoma (Member, Young Lawyers Division, Publications Committee Chair, 1993-1994) and American Bar Associations. ***PRACTICE AREAS:*** Civil Litigation.

ASSOCIATES

D. Sharon Gentry
Terry D. Kordelski, II
Janice Morrow
Gisele Perryman
Gary W. Wood

RISCHARD & PHIPPS P.C.

Established in 2004

120 N. ROBINSON AVENUE, SUITE 2320
OKLAHOMA CITY, OKLAHOMA 73102
Telephone: 405-235-2393
Fax 405-235-2347
Email: admin@rischardphipps.com

General Civil Litigation, Business Litigation, Health Care Law, Nursing Home Litigation, Contract Litigation, Corporate and Insurance Defense, Oil and Gas Litigation, Employment Litigation, Federal Civil Litigation, Estate Planning, Adoption Law.

DENIS P. RISCHARD, born Oklahoma City, Oklahoma, September 2, 1961; admitted to bar, 1986, Oklahoma, U.S. District Court, Western District of Oklahoma; 1987, U.S. Court of Appeals, Tenth Circuit; 1990, U.S. District Court, Northern District of Oklahoma; 1992, U.S. District Court, Southern District of Illinois; 1994, U.S. District Court, Eastern District of Oklahoma; 2004, U.S. District Court, Southern District of Texas. *Education:* University of Notre Dame (B.B.A., 1983); University of Oklahoma (J.D., 1986). Phi Alpha Delta. Author: "Mentoring Our Young Lawyers," For the Defense, Vol. 40, No. 1, Jan. 1998. Co-Author: "Taking Depositions, Why, Who, Where, When and How," For the Defense, Vol. 37, No. 1, Jan, 1995. *Member:* Oklahoma County (Member: Continuing Legal Education Committee, 1993-1994; Litigation Section), Oklahoma (Member, Health Law and Litigation Sections) Bar Associations; Oklahoma Association of Defense Counsel (Member, Legislative Committee, 1995-1996); Defense Research Institute (Member, Professionalism and Ethics Steering Committee; Member and Immediate Past Chairman, Long-Term Care Subcommittee of Medical Liability Committee, 1998-2003; Program Chair, Nursing Home Litigation Seminar, 2002-2003); Luther Bohannon American Inns of Court XXII (Barrister, 1996-1999). ***REPORTED CASES:*** Ardmore Mfg. vs. Jones, 837 P.2d 934 (Okla. App. 1992); Perrin v. Owens-Corning Fiberglas Corp., 871 F.Supp. 1092 (N.D. Iowa 1994). ***PRACTICE AREAS:*** General Civil Litigation; Health Care Law; Nursing Home Litigation; Corporate and Insurance Defence; Business Litigation; Employment Litigation. **Email:** drischard@rischardphipps.com

STEPHANIE L. PHIPPS, born Enid, Oklahoma, March 7, 1970; admitted to bar, 1995, Oklahoma and U.S. District Court, Eastern District of Oklahoma; 1999, Texas and U.S. District Court, Western and Northern Districts of Oklahoma; 2000, U.S. District Court, Northern District of Texas; 2001, U.S. District Court, Eastern District of Texas. *Education:* Oklahoma State University (B.S., 1992); University of Oklahoma (J.D., 1995). Pi Kappa Phi. Recipient, American Jurisprudence Award. Co-Author: *Fraud and Abuse Current Hospital Handbook,* 1998. Speaker, Medicare Fraud and Abuse Seminar, 1999. *Member:* Oklahoma Bar Association; State Bar of Texas; Defense Research Institute; Tulsa County Bar Association. ***REPORTED CASES:*** United States v. Foster, 104 F.3d 1228 (10th Cir. 1996); Darnaby v. Davis, 57 P.3d 100 (Okla. App. 2000); Medcalf v. Coleman, 71 P.3d 53 (Okla. App. 2003); Jones v. Khorsandi, 148 S.W. 3d 201 (Tex. App. 2004). ***PRACTICE AREAS:*** General Civil Litigation; Health Care Law; Nursing Home Litigation; Estate Planning; Adoption Law. **Email:** sphipps@rischardphipps.com

JAYNE JARNIGAN ROBERTSON, P.C.

Established in 1998

119 NORTH ROBINSON, SUITE 825
OKLAHOMA CITY, OKLAHOMA 73102
Telephone: 405-319-0400
Fax: 405-319-0404
Email: jaynerobertson@cs.com
URL: http://www.lawyers.com/jaynerobertson

Commercial Litigation, Environmental Law, Oil and Gas Law, Contracts.

FIRM PROFILE: After practicing 15 years with a medium sized firm in Oklahoma City, Ms. Robertson decided to open a solo practice in order to provide more personalized service to her clients. Currently focusing her practice in the areas of environmental and commercial law, Ms. Robertson also has extensive experience in oil and gas matters, including contracts and acquisitions.

(This Listing Continued)

Ms. Robertson's litigation experience is extremely diverse-- from securities fraud and RICO actions to products liability to contract disputes to environmental matters-- she has represented clients in Oklahoma state courts, before the Oklahoma Corporation Commission, in all three Oklahoma federal district courts, including bankruptcy courts, and in federal courts in Kansas and Texas where she was admitted pro hac vice. Ms. Robertson is also proud of her appellate record, most notably those Tenth Circuit Court of Appeals' decisions affirming dismissals she obtained at the preliminary motion stage. Jayne Jarnigan Robertson, P.C. is listed in the Martindale-Hubbell Bar Register of Preeminent Lawyers in the areas of Environmental and Commercial Law.

JAYNE J. ROBERTSON, born Oklahoma City, Oklahoma, May 26, 1958; admitted to bar, 1983, Oklahoma and U.S. District Court, Western District of Oklahoma; 1984, U.S. Court of Appeals, Tenth Circuit; 1985, U.S. District Court, Eastern and Northern Districts of Oklahoma. *Education:* University of Oklahoma (B.B.A., 1980; J.D., 1983). Phi Delta Phi. *Member:* Oklahoma County, Oklahoma and American Bar Associations. ***REPORTED CASES:*** Sac & Fox Tribe of Indians of Oklahoma vs. Apex Construction Co., 757 F.2d 221 (10th Cir. 1985); Home-Stake Production Co. vs. Talon Petroleum, C.A., 907 F.2d 1012 (10th Cir. 1990); Cobb vs. Saturn Land Co., Inc., 966 F.2d 1334 (10th Cir. 1992); Fox v. Maulding, 16F.3d 1079, appeal after remand 112 F.3d 453 (10th Cir. 1997).

ROBERTSON & WILLIAMS, INC.

Established in 1988

3033 N.W. 63RD STREET, SUITE 200
OKLAHOMA CITY, OKLAHOMA 73116-3607
Telephone: 405-848-1944
Fax: 405-843-6707
Email: marobert@robertsonwilliams.com

Business and Corporate Law, Oil and Gas, Civil Litigation, Securities, Mergers, Acquisitions and Divestitures, Commercial Law, Real Estate, Trusts and Estates, International Trusts, Franchising, Aircraft Title, Consumer Law.

FIRM PROFILE: Robertson & Williams are listed in the Bar Register of Preeminent Lawyers.

MARK A. ROBERTSON, born Vallejo, California, January 22, 1950; admitted to bar, 1975, Oklahoma. *Education:* University of Oklahoma, University of Edinburgh, Scotland and DePauw University (B.A., with honors, 1972); University of Oklahoma (J.D., 1975). *Member:* Oklahoma and American (Member: Law Practice Management Section; Business Law Section) Bar Associations. Fellow, College of Law Practice Management. ***PRACTICE AREAS:*** Business; Corporate Law; Corporate Financing Law; Securities Law; Mergers, Acquisitions and Divestitures; Franchising; Trusts and Estates; Nonprofit and Charitable Organizations. **Email:** marobert@robertsonwilliams.com

THOMAS C. WILLIAMS, born Oklahoma City, Oklahoma, June 25, 1951; admitted to bar, 1976, Oklahoma. *Education:* University of Oklahoma, University of the Americas, Mexico and Oklahoma City University (B.S., 1973); Oklahoma City University (J.D., 1976). *Member:* Canadian County and Oklahoma Bar Associations. ***PRACTICE AREAS:*** Oil and Gas Law; Probate Law; Civil Litigation. **Email:** tcw@robertsonwilliams.com

R. POPE VAN CLEEF, JR., born Oklahoma City, Oklahoma, September 14, 1952; admitted to bar, 1977, Oklahoma. *Education:* University of Oklahoma (B.A., 1974); Oklahoma City University (J.D., 1976). *Member:* Oklahoma County, Oklahoma and Federal Bar Associations. ***REPORTED CASES:*** Oklahoma Radio Associates vs FDIC 969 F.2d. 940 (10th cir. 1992); Oklahoma Radio Associates vs FDIC 987 F.2d. 685 (10th cir. 1993); Oklahoma Radio Associates vs. FDIC 3F.3rd.1436 (10th cir. 1993). ***PRACTICE AREAS:*** Litigation; Federal Practice; Corporate; Commercial; Real Estate; Collections. **Email:** popevan@robertsonwilliams.com

JAMES D. TACK, JR., born Wichita, Kansas, September 24, 1951; admitted to bar, 1978, Oklahoma. *Education:* Cornell University (B.S., 1973); Washburn University (J.D., cum laude, 1977). *Member:* Oklahoma County, Oklahoma and American Bar Associations; Mineral Lawyers of Oklahoma City. ***PRACTICE AREAS:*** Oil and Gas; Mining; Commercial Transactions; Commercial Litigation; Real Estate. **Email:** jtack@robertsonwilliams.com

KECIA KHAE COLE, born Oklahoma City, Oklahoma, August 5, 1968; admitted to bar, 1994, Oklahoma. *Education:* Oklahoma State University (B.S., 1989); Oklahoma City University (J.D., 1994). Certified Public Accountant, 1993. *Member:* Oklahoma Bar Association. ***PRACTICE AREAS:*** Oil and Gas Law; Commercial; Civil Litigation. **Email:** kcole@robertswilliams.com

CHARLES E. WETSEL, born Mangum, Oklahoma, December 16, 1956; admitted to bar, 1986, Oklahoma and U.S. District Court, Western and Northern Districts of Oklahoma. *Education:* Oklahoma Christian College (B.S., 1980); University of Oklahoma (J.D., 1986). ***PRACTICE AREAS:*** Banking; Bankruptcy Law; Business Law; Commercial Law; Corporate Law; Real Property; Wills; Probate. **Email:** cwestel@robertsonwilliams.com

A List of Representative Clients Available Upon Request.

RYAN, WHALEY & COLDIRON

119 N. ROBINSON AVENUE, SUITE 900
OKLAHOMA CITY, OKLAHOMA 73102-4617
Telephone: 405-239-6040
Fax: 405-239-6766
URL: http://www.ryanwhaley.com

Civil Litigation, Disability Insurance, Products Liability, Environmental and Energy Law and Litigation, Securities, Business Litigation, Drug and Medical Device Litigation, Complex Litigation, Franchise Litigation, Arbitration, Commercial Litigation, Employment Law, White Collar Criminal Defense, Civil Practice, Trial Practice, Appellate Practice, Medical Malpractice.

(This Listing Continued)

RYAN, WHALEY & COLDIRON, Oklahoma City—Continued

PATRICK M. RYAN, born Oklahoma City, Oklahoma, September 26, 1945; admitted to bar, 1969, Oklahoma and U.S. District Court, Western and Eastern Districts of Oklahoma; 1974, U.S. Court of Appeals, Tenth Circuit; 1985, U.S. Supreme Court. *Education:* University of Oklahoma (B.A., 1966; J.D., 1969). Order of the Coif; Phi Delta Phi. Editor, Oklahoma Law Review, 1967-1969. United States Attorney, Western District of Oklahoma. *Member:* Oklahoma County (President, 1988-1989; Director, 1981-1983, 1987-1993), Oklahoma (Trustee, Oklahoma Bar Foundation, 1978-1984; Member, Board of Governors At-Large, 1991-1994); American Board of Trial Advocates (President, Oklahoma Chapter, 1990-1991); American Inn of Court XXIII (Master). Fellow: American College of Trial Lawyers; International Academy of Trial Lawyers. ***PRACTICE AREAS:*** Business Litigation; Drug and Medical Device Litigation; Complex Litigation. ***Email:*** pryan@ryanwhaley.com

PHILLIP G. WHALEY, born Wichita, Kansas, August 3, 1961; admitted to bar, 1988, Oklahoma; U.S. District Court, Northern, Western and Eastern Districts of Oklahoma and U.S. Court of Appeals, Tenth Circuit. *Education:* University of Oklahoma (B.B.A., with special distinction, 1983; J.D., with highest honors, 1988). Beta Gamma Sigma; Order of the Coif. Recipient, Earl T. Warren Memorial Award. Research Editor, Oklahoma Law Review, 1986-1988. Teaching Assistant, Legal Research and Writing, University of Oklahoma College of Law, 1986-1988. *Member:* Oklahoma County, Oklahoma and American (Member, Sections on: Litigation, Tort and Insurance) Bar Associations; Luther Bohanon American Inn of Court (Barrister). ***PRACTICE AREAS:*** Civil Litigation; Disability Insurance; Products Liability; Securities; Business Litigation; Environmental Litigation. ***Email:*** pwhaley@ryanwhaley.com

MARK D. COLDIRON, born Fairfax, Oklahoma, September 4, 1945; admitted to bar, 1972, Oklahoma; U.S. District Court, Northern, Western and Eastern Districts of Oklahoma; U.S. Court of Appeals, Tenth Circuit; U.S. Supreme Court. *Education:* University of Oklahoma (B.S.Ch.E., 1968; J.D., 1972). Phi Delta Phi. Author: "Primer on Superfund," OBA, Sept., 1989; "A Practical Guide to Superfund Litigation," Dallas Energy Symposium, Jan., 1990; "Environmental Liability Arising from Ownership of Oil & Gas Properties," OCU/Oklahoma City Petroleum Landman's Association, June 1990; "An Attorney's Prospective: Working with Consultants," OBA, Nov., 1990; "Environmental Factors in Business Transactions and Bankruptcy, NBI, OK, March 1991; "Spill and Release Reporting," OBA, April 1994; Co-Author: "Use of Experts in Environmental Litigation and Enforcement Matters," ABA Section of Natural Resources and Environment, Summer, 1996, chosen as "Best of Best," by ABA. *Member:* Oklahoma (Member and Chairman, 1993, Natural Resources, Energy and Environmental Law Section) and American (Member, Natural Resources and Environment Section) Bar Associations. ***PRACTICE AREAS:*** Environmental Law; Environmental Litigation; Energy; Complex Business Litigation. ***Email:*** mcoldiron@ryanwhaley.com

JOE M. HAMPTON, born Borger, Texas, June 22, 1961; admitted to bar, 1986, Oklahoma, U.S. District Court, Western, Eastern and Northern Districts of Oklahoma, U.S. Court of Appeals, Tenth Circuit and U.S. Supreme Court. *Education:* University of Oklahoma (B.B.A., 1983; J.D., with distinction, 1986). Chief Note Editor, Oklahoma Law Review, 1984-1986. *Member:* Oklahoma County, Oklahoma and American Bar Associations; Robert J. Turner Inn of Court (Barrister). ***PRACTICE AREAS:*** Complex Civil Litigation; Arbitration. ***Email:*** jhampton@ryanwhaley.com

TIMOTHY J. BOMHOFF, born Okarche, Oklahoma, November 16, 1962; admitted to bar, 1988, Oklahoma, U.S. District Court, Western District of Oklahoma and U.S. Court of Appeals, Tenth Circuit; 1990, U.S. District Court, Northern District of Oklahoma; 2005, U.S. District Court, Eastern District of Oklahoma. *Education:* Oklahoma State University (B.S., 1984); University of Oklahoma (J.D., with honors, 1988). *Member:* Oklahoma County (Member, Employment Section), Oklahoma and American (Member, Sections on: Litigation and Employment Law) Bar Associations; National Institute of Trial Advocacy (Rocky Mountain Regional, 1990); Robert J. Turner Inn of Court (Barrister). ***PRACTICE AREAS:*** Civil Litigation; Commercial Litigation; Business Litigation; Securities Litigation; Arbitration; Environmental Litigation; Employment Law. ***Email:*** tbomhoff@ryanwhaley.com

ROBIN F. FIELDS, born Oklahoma City, Oklahoma, January 18, 1955; admitted to bar, 1984, Oklahoma; U.S. District Court, Northern and Western Districts of Oklahoma; U.S. Court of Appeals, Tenth Circuit; U.S. Supreme Court. *Education:* Old Dominion University (B.A., summa cum laude, 1977); University of Oklahoma (J.D., with honors, 1984). Phi Kappa Phi; Phi Delta Phi. Order of Barristers. Vice-President, Board of Advocates, 1983-1984. Teaching Assistant, Legal Research and Writing, University of Oklahoma College of Law, 1983-1984. Faculty, National Institute of Trial Advocacy (Dallas Region Program), Deposition Strategies, Preparing and Taking Depositions. Moderator and Speaker, "Taking and Defending Depositions," Oklahoma Bar Association, September 2000. First Chair of Coordinating Group on Alternate Dispute Resolution, Natural Resources, Energy and Environmental Law Section; Vice Chair, Nominating Committee, 1996; Vice Chair Strategic Planning Committee, 1997, American Bar Association. *Member:* Oklahoma County, Oklahoma and American (Chair, Energy and Natural Resources Litigation Committee of the Natural Resources Energy and Environmental Law Section) Bar Associations; Oklahoma Trial Lawyers Association; American Trial Lawyers Association. ***PRACTICE AREAS:*** Complex Business Law; Oil and Gas Litigation; Environmental Law; Qui Tam Litigation; Class Actions; Securities Law. ***Email:*** rfields@ryanwhaley.com

DANIEL G. WEBBER, JR., born Okarche, Oklahoma, February 14, 1966; admitted to bar, 1994, Oklahoma; 1995, U.S. District Court, Western District of Oklahoma and U.S. Court of Appeals, Tenth Circuit; 2003, U.S. District Court, Northern District of Oklahoma. *Education:* Oklahoma State University (B.S., 1988); Georgetown University (J.D., 1993). Co-Author: "When Homeland Security Comes Calling," 75 OK Bar J. 2557, 2004. U.S. Attorney, Western District of Oklahoma, 1999-2001. Assistant U.S. Attorney, 1995-1999. *Member:* Oklahoma County, Oklahoma and American Bar Associations; William J. Holloway American Inn of Court. [Captain, Judge Advocate, Oklahoma Army National Guard, 1997—]. ***PRACTICE AREAS:*** Civil Litigation; Criminal Law. ***Email:*** dwebber@ryanwhaley.com

(This Listing Continued)

KEITH J. KLEIN, born Rochester, New York, September 14, 1952; admitted to bar, 1984, California; 1999, Oklahoma; U.S. District Court, Western and Eastern Districts of Oklahoma; 2002, Missouri and U.S. District Court, Eastern District of Missouri. *Education:* Princeton University (B.A., cum laude, 1975); University of Southern California (M.S., Systems Management, 1981); University of San Diego (J.D., magna cum laude, 1984); George Washington University (LL.M., Environmental Law, with highest honors, 1994). Member, Law Review, University of San Diego, 1982-1984. Author, "Fear of Cancer — A Legitimate Claim in Toxic Tort Cases?" 31 A.F.L.Rev. 365 (1991). *Member:* Oklahoma County, Oklahoma and American Bar Associations. [Lt. Col., U.S. Air Force, 1979-1999]. ***PRACTICE AREAS:*** Environmental Law; Energy; Civil Litigation; Construction Litigation. ***Email:*** kklein@ryanwhaley.com

MICHAEL A. PETERS, born Stillwater, Oklahoma, March 7, 1966; admitted to bar, 1992, Oklahoma. *Education:* University of Oklahoma (B.A., 1989; J.D., 1992). Enforcement Attorney, Air Quality Division of the Oklahoma Department of Environmental Quality, 1992-1996. *Member:* Cleveland County, Oklahoma and American Bar Associations. ***PRACTICE AREAS:*** Environmental Law; Energy; Environmental Regulation; Litigation. ***Email:*** mpeters@ryanwhaley.com

STEPHEN L. JANTZEN, born Denver, Colorado, May 14, 1968; admitted to bar, 1994, Oklahoma; U.S. District Court, Western and Northern Districts of Oklahoma; U.S. Court of Appeals, District of Columbia Circuit. *Education:* Westminster College (B.A., Economics, 1990); Oklahoma City University (J.D., summa cum laude, 1994); George Washington University (LL.M., Environmental Law, 1997). Member: Moot Court Board; Merit Scholars Organization, Oklahoma City University School of Law. Member, Oklahoma City University Law Review. Author: "Environmental Regulation in Oklahoma: A Patchwork Green," Oklahoma Politics, Special Issue; "Environmental Policy in Oklahoma: Issues, Innovations, Insights," Dec. 2001. Assistant Attorney General, State of Oklahoma, 1998-2001. *Member:* Oklahoma County, Oklahoma and American Bar Associations. ***PRACTICE AREAS:*** Environmental; Energy; Litigation. ***Email:*** sjantzen@ryanwhaley.com

AMY J. PIERCE, born Durant, Oklahoma, October 26, 1974; admitted to bar, 1999, Oklahoma, U.S. District Court, Western, Eastern and Northern Districts of Oklahoma and U.S. Court of Appeals, Tenth Circuit. *Education:* Oklahoma State University (B.S., 1996); Oklahoma City University School of Law (J.D., cum laude, 1999). Phi Delta Phi. *Member:* Oklahoma County, Oklahoma and American Bar Associations. ***PRACTICE AREAS:*** Civil Practice; Employment Law; Disability Insurance; Trial Practice; Appellate Practice. ***Email:*** apierce@ryanwhaley.com

PATRICK R. PEARCE, JR., born Little Rock, Arkansas, September 14, 1975; admitted to bar, 2000, Oklahoma; U.S. District Court, Northern, Eastern and Western Districts of Oklahoma; U.S. Court of Appeals, Tenth Circuit. *Education:* University of Arkansas (B.A., summa cum laude, 1997); University of Tulsa (J.D., with highest honor, 2000). Chosen, "Outstanding Senior Law Student," Oklahoma Bar Association, 1999. Winner, MELPR National Writing Competition, 2000. Executive Editor, Energy Law Journal, 1999-2000. Author: "The Right of an Indirect Customer to Contest FERC-Approved Rate Settlements," 20 Energy Law Journal 99 (1999); "A Call for a New Policy Toward CERCLA Cleanup Costs in the Eighth Circuit: Is It Fair to Punish the PRP Who Initiates the Cleanup at a Superfund Site," 7 Missouri Environmental Law and Policy Review 126 (2000). *Member:* Oklahoma County, Oklahoma and American Bar Associations. ***PRACTICE AREAS:*** Environmental Law; Energy; Litigation. ***Email:*** rpearce@ryanwhaley.com

JASON A. RYAN, born Clark AFB, Philippines, November 2, 1973; admitted to bar, 2000, Oklahoma; U.S. Court of Appeals, Tenth Circuit; U.S. District Court, Western, Eastern and Northern Districts of Oklahoma. *Education:* Oklahoma City University (B.S., with honors, 1997; J.D., 2000). *Member:* Oklahoma County, Oklahoma and American Bar Associations. ***PRACTICE AREAS:*** Civil Litigation; Drug and Medical Device Litigation; Products Liability; Business Litigation; Employment Law; Medical Malpractice. ***Email:*** jryan@ryanwhaley.com

MATTHEW C. KANE, born New Orleans, Louisiana, November 21, 1976; admitted to bar, 2002, Oklahoma; U.S. District Court, Northern and Western Districts of Oklahoma; U.S. Court of Appeals, Tenth Circuit. *Education:* University of Oklahoma (B.A., 1998; J.D., with distinction, 2002); University of St. Andrews, Scotland. *Member:* Oklahoma County, Oklahoma and American (Vice Chair, International Criminal Law Committee) Bar Associations; Luther Bohanon Inn of Court; American Inns of Court; American Society of International Law; American Society of Political and Legal Philosophy. ***PRACTICE AREAS:*** Criminal Defense; Civil Litigation; International Law. ***Email:*** mkane@ryanwhaley.com

COREY A. NELLER, born Oklahoma City, Oklahoma, January 12, 1976; admitted to bar, 2002, Oklahoma and U.S. District Court, Western, Eastern and Northern Districts of Oklahoma. *Education:* University of Central Oklahoma (B.A., 1998); University of Oklahoma (J.D., 2002). *Member:* Oklahoma County, Oklahoma and American Bar Associations; Young Lawyer's Association; The Association of Trial Lawyers of America; Oklahoma Lawyers for Children. ***PRACTICE AREAS:*** Environmental and Energy Litigation. ***Email:*** cneller@ryanwhaley.com

COREE L. STEVENSON, born Oklahoma City, Oklahoma, July 20, 1973; admitted to bar, 1999, Oklahoma, U.S. District Court, Western, Northern and Eastern Districts of Oklahoma and U.S. Court of Appeals for the Tenth Circuit; 2004, U.S. Supreme Court. *Education:* Oklahoma State University (B.A., 1995); Oklahoma City University School of Law (J.D., cum laude, 1999). Phi Delta Phi. Merit Scholar. Research Editor, Oklahoma City University Law Review. Recipient: Oklahoma City University Law School Dean's Service Award, 1999; Oklahoma County Bar Association Pro Bono Award, 2004. *Member:* Oklahoma County, Oklahoma (Member, Bench and Bar Committee) and American Bar Associations; William J. Holloway American Inn of Court. ***PRACTICE AREAS:*** Business Litigation; Environmental Law; Energy Law. ***Email:*** cstevenson@ryanwhaley.com

LAW OFFICE OF PETER K. SCHAFFER

204 N. ROBINSON AVENUE SUITE 2305
OKLAHOMA CITY, OKLAHOMA 73102-6891
Telephone: 405-239-7707
Fax: 405-239-6800
Email: pschaffer@adoptionattorneys.org

Adoption Law.

PETER K. SCHAFFER, born September 20, 1943; admitted to bar, 1974, Oklahoma. *Education:* Babson College (B.S., 1965); Oklahoma City University (J.D., 1974). ***PRACTICE AREAS:*** Adoption Law.

SCHNEIDER & LABARTHE, P.A.

304 NORTHWEST 13TH STREET
SUITE 120
OKLAHOMA CITY, OKLAHOMA 73103
Telephone: 405-232-9990
Fax: 405-232-9992
URL: http://www.okielaw.com

Mailing Address: P.O. Box 1147, Oklahoma City, OK 73101

Civil Litigation in all State and Federal Courts, Transportation, Immigration Law, Motor Carrier, Truck Accidents, Cargo Claims, Products Liability, Bankruptcy, Estate Planning, Employment Law, Civil Business Litigation, Corporate Law, Real Estate Law, Estate and Trust Law.

DAVID B. SCHNEIDER, born 1944; admitted to bar, 1969, Texas; 1979, Oklahoma, U.S. District Courts, Northern, Eastern and Western Districts of Oklahoma; 1977, U.S. Supreme Court. *Education:* University of Texas at Austin (B.B.A.; J.D., 1969). Delta Theta Phi. Recipient, Distinguished Service Award, Transportation Lawyers Association. Attorney-Advisor, Washington, D.C., Interstate Commerce Commission, 1969-1973; Transportation Counsel, Yellow Freight System, Inc., 1973-1979. *Member:* American Bar Association; American Immigration Lawyers Association; Transportation Lawyers Association (Past President, 1996-1997); Conference of Freight Counsel; Defense Research Institute. ***PRACTICE AREAS:*** Transportation Law; Motor Carrier Law; Cargo Claims; Immigration Law; Administrative Law; Estate Planning; Employment Law; Litigation. ***Email:*** schnlaw@swbell.net

RICHARD C. LABARTHE, born Stillwater, Oklahoma, 1956; admitted to bar, 1985, Oklahoma. *Education:* Oklahoma State University (B.S., 1982); University of Oklahoma (J.D., magna cum laude, 1985). Order of the Coif; Phi Alpha Delta. *Member:* Oklahoma County, Oklahoma and American Bar Associations; American Immigration Lawyers Association. ***PRACTICE AREAS:*** Immigration Law; Bankruptcy; Civil Litigation; Corporate Law; Property Law; Transportation; Trusts; Employment Litigation; Products Liability. ***Email:*** rlab1@icon.net

REPRESENTATIVE CLIENTS: Furnished Upon Request.

SCOGGINS & CROSS, PLLC

Established in 2002
3100 CITY PLACE
204 N. ROBINSON
OKLAHOMA CITY, OKLAHOMA 73102
Telephone: 405-239-4300
Fax: 405-239-4305
URL: http://www.okhealthlawyer.com

Civil Litigation, Healthcare Law, Employment Law, Administrative Law, Regulatory Law, Employment Litigation, Bioethics, General Corporate Law, Mergers and Acquisitions, Guardianship, Elder Law.

MEMBERS OF FIRM

LINDA G. SCOGGINS, born Denison, Texas, November 2, 1947; admitted to bar, 1981, Oklahoma and U.S. District Court, Western, Eastern and Northern Districts of Oklahoma; 1982, U.S. Court of Appeals, Tenth Circuit; 1985, U.S. Supreme Court. *Education:* University of Oklahoma (B.A., 1969; J.D., 1981). Phi Delta Phi. Editor-in-Chief, Oklahoma Law Review, 1980-1981. Recognized in: The Best Lawyers in America (Health Law). Adjunct Professor of Employment Law, University of Oklahoma College of Law. *Member:* Oklahoma County (Board of Directors, 1991-1994; Vice President, 1995-1996), Oklahoma (Member, section on Health Law) and American (Member, Sections on: Labor and Employment Law; Health Law) Bar Associations; American Health Lawyers Association; Oklahoma Health Lawyers Association (President, 1995-1996); Ginsberg American Inn of Court (Master of the Bench). ***SPECIAL AGENCIES:*** Practitioner Licensure Boards; Oklahoma State Department of Health. ***PRACTICE AREAS:*** Civil Litigation; Healthcare Law; Employment Law; Administrative Law; Regulatory Law. ***Email:*** lscoggins@okhealthlawyer.com

LAURA L. CROSS, born Corpus Christi, Texas, October 6, 1945; admitted to bar, 1988, Oklahoma; U.S. Court of Federal Claims. *Education:* University of Oklahoma (B.S.N., 1979; M.S., 1981); Oklahoma City University School of Law (J.D., 1988). Hatton W. Sumners Scholar. Registered Nurse, Oklahoma, 1966. Founding President, Oklahoma Association for Healthcare Ethics, Inc. Principal Investigator, Community-State Partnership to improve end-of-life-care. Project Director, Oklahoma Alliance for Better Care of the Dying (OKABCD). Recognized in: Best Lawyers in America (Health Law). *Member:* American and Oklahoma Health Lawyers Associations. ***SPECIAL AGENCIES:*** Oklahoma State Department of Health; Oklahoma Health Care Authority, PRRB; and Practitioner Licensure Boards. ***PRACTICE AREAS:*** Health Law; Administrative Law; Regulatory Law; Employment Law; Bioethics; Mergers and Acquisitions; Probate; Estate Planning. ***Email:*** lauracross@okhealthlawyer.com

(This Listing Continued)

ASSOCIATES

HEATHER M. POOLE, born Ft. Ord., California, May 25, 1965; admitted to bar, 1998, Oklahoma and U.S. District Courts, Western and Northern Districts of Oklahoma; 2004, U.S. Supreme Court. *Education:* University of Oklahoma (B.S., 1990); University of Tulsa (J.D., 1998). Phi Delta Phi, Order of Barristers. *Member:* Oklahoma County (Member, YLD Board of Directors 2000-2003), Oklahoma (Member, Family Law Section) and American (Member, section on Health Law) Bar Associations; Ginsburg American Inn of Court. ***LANGUAGES:*** French. ***SPECIAL AGENCIES:*** Oklahoma Merit Protection Commission. ***PRACTICE AREAS:*** Collections; Civil Litigation; Family Law; Employment Law; Administrative Law. ***Email:*** hpoole@okhealthlawyer.com

ARLENE M. RANDALL, born Blackwell, Oklahoma, April 10, 1961; admitted to bar, 2003, Oklahoma. *Education:* Northwestern Oklahoma State University (B.S., 1982); Oklahoma City University School of Law (J.D., 2003). *Member:* Oklahoma County, Oklahoma and American Bar Associations. ***PRACTICE AREAS:*** Estate Planning; Probate; Guardianship; Elder Law; Corporate Law; Tax Law. ***Email:*** arandall@okhealthlawyer.com

AIMÉE D. M. SALALATI, born Norman, Oklahoma, February 2, 1974; admitted to bar, 1999, Oklahoma; U.S. District Court, Western District of Oklahoma. *Education:* University of Oklahoma (B.S., in Environmental Science, with distinction, 1996; J.D., 1999). Phi Delta Phi. Recipient, American Jurisprudence Award, Criminal Law and Criminal Procedure. *Member:* Oklahoma County, Oklahoma and American Bar Associations; Oklahoma Health Lawyers Association. ***PRACTICE AREAS:*** Civil Litigation; Health Law; Administrative Law. ***Email:*** asalalati@okhealthlawyer.com

REPRESENTATIVE CLIENTS: Oklahoma State Medical Association; Oklahoma State Nursing Association; Midwest Regional Medical Center; Pauls Valley General Hospital, Health Systems of Oklahoma, L.L.C., Health Care Innovations, Inc.; Individual Physicians, Practitioners and Clinics.

JOSEPH G. SHANNONHOUSE, IV

500 NORTH WALKER, SUITE C-100
OKLAHOMA CITY, OKLAHOMA 73102
Telephone: 405-415-1700
Fax: 405-415-1703
Email: JS@Shannonhouselaw.com
URL: http://www.lawyers.com/shannonhouse

Tax Controversies, Tax Litigation, Criminal Taxation, Taxation, White Collar Criminal Defense, Criminal Trial Practice - Federal.

FIRM PROFILE: Joseph G. Shannonhouse is listed in the Bar Register of Preeminent Lawyers under the area of Tax Law.

JOSEPH G. SHANNONHOUSE, IV, born Alexandria, Louisiana, May 27, 1945; admitted to bar, 1970, Oklahoma. *Education:* University of Central Oklahoma (B.S., 1967); University of Oklahoma (J.D., 1970); New York University (LL.M., in Taxation, 1972). Phi Delta Phi. Author: "Basic Tax For The Landman, Landman's Handbook on Basic Land Management," 1978. Co-Author: "The Money Laundering Control Act: An Attack On The Business Side of Organized Crime," The Oklahoma Bar Journal, 1988; "New Federal Legislation May Be A Trap For The Unwary," Oklahoma Business, 1988; "Attorney, Accountants and Clients: Roles In A Criminal Tax Fraud Investigation," The Oklahoma Bar Journal, 1991. *Member:* Oklahoma and American Bar Associations. ***PRACTICE AREAS:*** Tax Controversies; Tax Litigation; Criminal Taxation; Taxation; White Collar Criminal Defense.

SHELTON LAW GROUP

7701 S. WESTERN AVENUE, SUITE 201
OKLAHOMA CITY, OKLAHOMA 73139
Telephone: 405-605-8800
Fax: 405-601-0677
Email: dshelton@sheltonlawok.com
URL: http://www.okshelton.com

Litigation and Trial Practice, Personal Injury, Insurance Law, Insurance Defense, Construction Defects, Mold Litigation, Consumer Law, Employment Law, Real Estate, Trusts and Estates.

MEMBER OF FIRM

DOUGLAS J. SHELTON, born 1956; admitted to bar, 1981, Oklahoma. *Education:* Oklahoma University (B.A., 1978; J.D., 1981). *Member:* Cleveland County and Oklahoma Bar Associations; Oklahoma Association of Defense Counsel; Defense Research Institute. ***PRACTICE AREAS:*** Insurance Defense; Insurance Law; Products Liability; Negligence Law; Personal Injury Law. ***Email:*** dshelton@sheltonlawok.com

ASSOCIATES

M. DANIEL WEITMAN, born Lynbrook, New York, March 11, 1967; admitted to bar, 1997, Oklahoma. *Education:* University of Oklahoma (B.A. Communications, 1994; J.D., 1997). ***PRACTICE AREAS:*** Civil Defense; Domestic; Personal Injury; Workers Compensation; Consumer Law; Employment Law. ***Email:*** dweitman@sheltonlawok.com

MELISSA SHELTON BURGET, born Chariton, Iowa, July 23, 1973; admitted to bar, 1999, Oklahoma. *Education:* Oklahoma University (B.A., 1996; J.D., 1999). *Member:* Oklahoma Bar Association. ***PRACTICE AREAS:*** Civil Litigation; Insurance Defense; General Practice; Trusts and Estates; Real Estate; Family Law. ***Email:*** msburget@cox.net

ELIZABETH A. KERR, born Ada, Oklahoma, April 18, 1969; admitted to bar, 1993, Oklahoma. *Education:* Oklahoma State University (B.S., 1991); University of Oklahoma (J.D., 1993). *Member:* Oklahoma Bar Association. ***PRACTICE AREAS:*** Mediation; Civil Litigation; Family Law. ***Email:*** ekerr@sheltonlawok.com

STEPHEN A. SHERMAN & ASSOCIATES

117 PARK AVENUE BUILDING
FOURTH FLOOR
OKLAHOMA CITY, OKLAHOMA 73102
Telephone: 405-235-0707
Fax: 405-235-0712
Email: ssherman@shermanfirm.com

General Civil Practice, Real Estate, Landlord-Tenant, Commercial, Corporate, Partnership and Probate Law, Litigation, Business Litigation, Contracts.

FIRM PROFILE: Mr. Sherman is listed in the Bar Register of Preeminent Lawyers.

STEPHEN A. SHERMAN, born Omaha, Nebraska, August 22, 1953; admitted to bar, 1981, Oklahoma, U.S. District Court, Western District of Oklahoma, U.S. Court of Appeals, Tenth Circuit; U.S. Tax Court and U.S Supreme Court. *Education:* University of Michigan (B.G.S., with high distinction, 1975); University of Santa Clara (M.B.A.; J.D., 1979). Municipal Judge, Nichols Hills, Oklahoma. Adjunct Professor, Oklahoma City University, 1982-1984. Commissioner, Oklahoma Real Estate Commission. *Member:* Oklahoma County, Oklahoma and American Bar Associations.

REPRESENTATIVE CLIENTS: B.F. Saul Co.; Canadian Valley Medical Solutions; Citation Properties, Inc.; CMH Parks, Inc.; Cornhusker Packing Co.; First Commercial Management, Inc.; Flower City, Inc.; Gungoll Exploration; Hogan Property Company; Irish Realty Corp.; Kaiser-Francis Oil Co.; Liberty Group, Inc.; Manson Realty Co.; Maccini Construction Co.; Morrison Supply Company; Nicholas Investment Co.; Oxford Capital Partners; Price-Edwards; Realtech Development and Construction Co., Inc.; Realty Operating Company; Samis Oil Company; Bob Sullivan Group; U.S. Foodservice, Inc.; Vision for Life International; Western Industries Corp.

SHIPLEY & KELLOGG, P.C.

Established in 1983
TWO LEADERSHIP SQUARE
211 NORTH ROBINSON, SUITE 1300
OKLAHOMA CITY, OKLAHOMA 73102-7114
Telephone: 405-235-0808
Fax: 405-232-3746
Email: rkellogg@shipleylaw.net

Tulsa, Oklahoma Office: 1648 South Boston Avenue, Suite 100, 74119-4416. Telephone: 918-582-1720. Facsimile: 918-584-7681. Email: firm@shipleylaw.net

General Civil Practice in all State and Federal Courts, with emphasis in Environmental Law, Water Rights, Business and Commercial Litigation, Class Actions, Alternative Dispute Resolution and Native American Law.

FIRM PROFILE: This firm is the Oklahoma member of the Environmental Law Network which is comprised of select environmental law firms nationwide.

ROBERT D. KELLOGG, born Brooklyn, New York, August 18, 1946; admitted to bar, 1978, Oklahoma. *Education:* University of Oklahoma (B.S., 1972); Oklahoma City University (J.D., 1977). General Counsel, Oklahoma Department of Environmental Quality, 1993-1998. Member, Air and Waste Management Association, 1998. Registered Environmental Professional, No. 671, Oklahoma, 1976. *Member:* Oklahoma (Chair, Environmental Law Section) and American Bar Associations. [Staff Sergeant, U.S. Air Force, 1965-1969]. (Resident). ***REPORTED CASES:*** Toxic Waste Impact Group v. Leavitt, 755 P.2d 626 (Okl. 1988) and 890 P.2d 906 (Okl. 1994); Stewart v. Rood, 796 P.2d 321 (Okl. 1990). ***PRACTICE AREAS:*** Environmental Law; Administrative Law; Water Law. ***Email:*** rkellogg@shipleylaw.net

REPRESENTATIVE CLIENTS: Arbuckle Master Conservancy District; Ashland Chemical Co.; Atlantic Richfield Co.; ASARCO; Borg-Warner Corp.; Cherokee Nation Supreme Court; Cities of Blackwell and Chickasha, Oklahoma; Flintco; General Electric Co.; Georgia-Pacific Corp.; McDonnell Douglas Corp.; Oklahoma Department of Environmental Quality; Oklahoma Turnpike Authority; ONEOK, Inc.; Tulsa Metropolitan Utility Authority; Uniroyal-Goodrich Tire Co.
REFERENCE: Bank of America.

(For complete biographical data on all personnel, see Professional Biographies at Tulsa, Oklahoma)

SHIRK WORK & ROBINSON, P.C.

Established in 1904
15 NORTH ROBINSON AVENUE, SUITE 500
OKLAHOMA CITY, OKLAHOMA 73102
Telephone: 405-236-3571
FAX: 405-236-8028
Email: shirklawfirm@swbell.net

Municipal Bond, Corporate, Probate, Land Use and Real Property.

FIRM PROFILE: Shirk Work & Robinson, P.C. is listed in the Bar Register of Preeminent Lawyers.

JAMES E. WORK, born Wewoka, Oklahoma, January 16, 1927; admitted to bar, 1953, Oklahoma. *Education:* University of Oklahoma (B.A., 1952; LL.B., 1953). Phi Alpha Delta. Chair, Oklahoma Board of Bar Examiners, 1963-1971. *Member:* Oklahoma County, Oklahoma (Vice President, 1973) and American Bar Associations; American Judicature Society (Director, 1967-1971); National Association of Bond Lawyers. Fellow, American College of Bond Lawyers. ***PRACTICE AREAS:*** Commercial Litigation; Bond Law; Corporation Law; Real Estate Law; Real Estate Litigation. ***Email:*** shirklaw@swbell.net

OF COUNSEL

WILLIAM J. ROBINSON, born Pauls Valley, Oklahoma, July 28, 1931; admitted to bar, 1955, Oklahoma. *Education:* University of Oklahoma (A.B., 1953; LL.B., 1955). Phi

(This Listing Continued)

Alpha Delta. Adjunct Professor, "Public Finance," Oklahoma City University, School of Law, Fall 1986 and 1988. General Counsel: State Insurance Board of Oklahoma, 1957-1960; Oklahoma Turnpike Authority, 1987-1989. *Member:* Oklahoma County (Director, 1972-1975), Oklahoma and American Bar Associations. ***PRACTICE AREAS:*** Commercial Litigation; Mineral Law; Real Estate Property Law. ***Email:*** jrob91950@aol.com

J. KELLY WORK, born Oklahoma City, Oklahoma, February 25, 1955; admitted to bar, 1980, Oklahoma. *Education:* University of Oklahoma (B.B.A., 1977; J.D. 1980). Assistant Municipal Counselor, 1980-1982 and Legal Counsel to Board of Adjustment, 1981-1982, Oklahoma City. *Member:* Oklahoma County, Oklahoma and American Bar Associations. (Also Practicing Individually). ***PRACTICE AREAS:*** Real Property; Business Law; Commercial Law; Litigation; Employment Litigation; Municipal; Land Use; Administrative; Tax Exempt Finance. ***Email:*** jkwork@earthlink.com

REPRESENTATIVE CLIENTS: Denny's Restaurants; Black-Eyed Pea U.S.A.; BancFirst; Weyerhauser Co.; Federal Corp.; Little Giant Corp.; Hendershot Tool Co.; Oklahoma County Finance Authority; Oklahoma City Chamber of Commerce; South Eastern Oklahoma Industries Authority; Asplundh Tree Expert Co.

SHORT WIGGINS MARGO & BUTTS

Established in 1977
3100 OKLAHOMA TOWER
210 PARK AVENUE
OKLAHOMA CITY, OKLAHOMA 73102
Telephone: 405-232-1211
Telecopier: 405-235-7025
Email: swmb@swmb.net

General Civil Litigation Practice, Medical Liability, Products Liability, Employment Law, Appellate Practice. Trial of Cases in all Courts in Oklahoma.

MEMBERS OF FIRM

GEORGE F. SHORT, born Ponca City, Oklahoma, April 19, 1927; admitted to bar, 1950, Oklahoma; U.S. Court of Appeals, Tenth Circuit; U.S. District Court, Northern, Eastern and Western Districts of Oklahoma. *Education:* Southeastern State University; Louisiana Polytechnic Institute; University of Oklahoma (LL.B., 1950). Phi Alpha Delta. *Member:* Oklahoma County, Oklahoma (Member, Professional Responsibility Commission, 1977-1985; Chairman, 1983-1984; Member, Board of Governors, 1986-1989) and American Bar Associations; International Association of Defense Counsel; Federation of Defense and Corporate Counsel (Member, Malpractice Committee, 1977—); Trial Attorneys of America; Oklahoma Association of Defense Counsel. Fellow: American Board of Trial Advocates; International Academy of Trial Lawyers; American College of Trial Lawyers; American Inn of Court, Master of the Bench Emeritus. Fellow: American Bar Foundation. ***PRACTICE AREAS:*** Litigation Defense; Malpractice Defense; Professional Liability Law; Products Liability Law; Insurance Defense Law; Anti-Trust; Civil Rights; Bad Faith.

JOHN E. WIGGINS, born Bartlesville, Oklahoma, April 5, 1949; admitted to bar, 1974, Oklahoma; 1980, U.S. Tax Court; U.S. Supreme Court; U.S. Court of Appeals, Tenth Circuit; U.S. District Court, Northern, Eastern and Western Districts of Oklahoma. *Education:* Oklahoma State University (B.A., with honors, 1971); University of Oklahoma (J.D., 1974). Phi Kappa Phi; Pi Sigma Alpha; Phi Delta Phi. Trial Advisor, Oklahoma State Board of Medical Licensure and Supervision. Listed in Best Lawyers in America. Attorney of the Year (2001), Oklahoma Court Reporters Association. *Member:* Oklahoma County, Oklahoma and American Bar Associations; Oklahoma Association of Defense Counsel; International Association of Defense Counsel; Trial Attorneys of America; The Association of Trial Lawyers of America; American Board of Trial Advocates; American College of Barristers (Senior Counsel); Board Certifications: National Board of Trial Advocacy (Civil); American Board of Professional Liability Attorneys. Fellow, American College of Trial Lawyers. ***PRACTICE AREAS:*** Litigation; Medical and Legal Malpractice Defense; Professional Liability Law; Products Liability Law; Insurance Defense Law.

ROBERT C. MARGO, born Indianapolis, Indiana, March 1, 1949; admitted to bar, 1974, Oklahoma; U.S. Supreme Court; U.S. Court of Appeals, Tenth Circuit; U.S. District Court, Eastern and Western Districts of Oklahoma. *Education:* Southern Methodist University (B.A., 1971); Oklahoma City University (J.D., 1974). Phi Alpha Delta. *Member:* Oklahoma County (Director, 1992-1995), Oklahoma and American Bar Associations; Federation of Defense and Corporate Counsel (Member: Medical Malpractice Section; Professional Liability Section); American Board of Trial Advocates (President, Oklahoma Chapter, 1994); Oklahoma Association of Defense Counsel (Vice-President, 1983-1984); Trial Attorneys of America; American Inn of Court CV (Master). Fellow, American College of Trial Lawyers. ***PRACTICE AREAS:*** Litigation Defense; Malpractice Defense; Professional Liability Law; Products Liability Law; Insurance Defense Law. ***Email:*** rmargo@swmb.net

BENJAMIN J. BUTTS, born Columbia, Missouri, February 16, 1958; admitted to bar, 1983, Oklahoma; U.S. District Court, Western, Northern and Eastern Districts of Oklahoma; U.S. Court of Appeals, Tenth Circuit; U.S. Supreme Court. *Education:* Washington & Lee University (B.S., 1980); University of Oklahoma (J.D., 1983). *Member:* Oklahoma County, Oklahoma and American Bar Associations; Oklahoma Association of Defense Counsel (Vice President, 1991; Board of Directors, 1988-1991). Federation of Defense and Corporate Counsel. ***PRACTICE AREAS:*** Litigation Defense; Malpractice Defense; Insurance Defense; Professional Liability Law; Products Liability Law; Employment Law.

RANDALL L. SEWELL, born Oklahoma City, Oklahoma, March 23, 1959; admitted to bar, 1984, Oklahoma; U.S. District Court, Western and Eastern Districts of Oklahoma. *Education:* University of Oklahoma (B.A., 1981; J.D., 1984). *Member:* Oklahoma, Oklahoma County and American Bar Associations; International Association of Defense Counsel; Oklahoma Association of Defense Counsel (Secretary/Treasurer, 1993; Board of Directors, 1995-1997). ***PRACTICE AREAS:*** Litigation Defense; Medical Malpractice Defense; Premises Liability; Products Liability; Insurance Defense; Trucking Defense.

PERRY T. MARRS, JR., born Wurzburg, Germany, September 3, 1960; admitted to bar, 1986, Oklahoma; 1987, U.S. Court of Appeals, Tenth Circuit and U.S. District Court, Eastern and Western Districts of Oklahoma. *Education:* University of Oklahoma (B.A.,

(This Listing Continued)

1983; J.D., 1986). Phi Delta Phi. *Member:* Oklahoma County, Oklahoma and American Bar Associations; Oklahoma Association of Defense Counsel; International Association of Defense Counsel; Federation of Defense and Corporate Counsel. ***PRACTICE AREAS:*** Litigation Defense; Malpractice Defense; Professional Liability Law; Products Liability Law; Insurance Defense Law.

CYNTHIA L. SPARLING, born Cedar Rapids, Iowa, December 25, 1947; admitted to bar, 1978, Oklahoma; U.S. Supreme Court; U.S. Court of Appeals, Tenth Circuit; U.S. District Court, Western, Northern and Eastern Districts of Oklahoma. *Education:* Southern Methodist University (B.A., 1970; M.A., 1972); Oklahoma City University (J.D., 1978). Iota Tau Tau. Articles Editor, Oklahoma City University Law Review, 1978. Instructor, Legal Research and Writing, Oklahoma City University School of Law, 1978-1980. Director, Legal Research and Writing, Oklahoma City University School of Law, 1980-1983. Judicial Assistant, Oklahoma Supreme Court, 1982. *Member:* Oklahoma County (Vice President, 1997-1998), Oklahoma and American Bar Associations; Oklahoma Association of Defense Counsel; Oklahoma Health Lawyers Association; National Health Lawyers Association; Master of the Bench, American Inn of Court (President, 2004-2005); Oklahoma Bar Foundation (Member, Board of Trustees); Professional Responsibility Tribunal. ***PRACTICE AREAS:*** Litigation Defense Law; Malpractice Defense; Professional Liability Law; Products Liability Law; Insurance Defense Law; Civil Rights.

ASSOCIATES

L. EARL OGLETREE, born Jacksonville, Florida, November 3, 1971; admitted to bar, 1999, Oklahoma and U.S. District Court, Eastern, Northern and Western Districts of Oklahoma. *Education:* Valdosta State University (B.S., 1995); Oklahoma City University (J.D., 1999). *Member:* Oklahoma County, Oklahoma and American Bar Associations; Oklahoma Association of Defense Counsel. ***PRACTICE AREAS:*** Medical Malpractice Defense; Defense Litigation; Insurance Defense; Professional Liability; Products Liability.

KEVIN K. TROUT, born Waurika, Oklahoma, June 12, 1969; admitted to bar, 1994, Oklahoma. *Education:* University of Oklahoma (B.B.A., 1991; J.D., 1994). Recipient, American Jurisprudence Award in Agency and Partnership Law. ***PRACTICE AREAS:*** Medical Malpractice Defense.

GEREMY A. ROWLAND, born Oklahoma City, Oklahoma, May 10, 1972; admitted to bar, 2000, Oklahoma and U.S. District Court, Western and Eastern Districts of Oklahoma. *Education:* University of Oklahoma (B.A., 1996); Oklahoma City University School of Law (J.D., 2000). *Member:* Oklahoma County, Oklahoma and American Bar Associations; Oklahoma Association of Defense Counsel; American Inns of Court. ***PRACTICE AREAS:*** Litigation; Medical Malpractice Defense; Insurance Defense.

MELISSA A. COUCH, born Shawnee, Oklahoma, January 1, 1977; admitted to bar, 2002, Oklahoma and U.S. District Court, Northern and Western Districts of Oklahoma. *Education:* University of Oklahoma (B.A., 1999); Oklahoma City University School of Law (J.D., 2002). Member, Oklahoma City University Law Review, 2000-2002. *Member:* Oklahoma and American Bar Associations; Oklahoma Association of Defense Counsel; Luther Bohanon Inn of Court. ***PRACTICE AREAS:*** Medical Malpractice Defense; Insurance Defense.

W. TODD BLASDEL, born Oklahoma City, Oklahoma, March 28, 1977; admitted to bar, 2002, Oklahoma and U.S. District Court, Western District of Oklahoma. *Education:* Rhodes College (B.A., 1999); University of Oklahoma (J.D., 2002). *Member:* Oklahoma County, Oklahoma and American Bar Associations; Oklahoma Association of Defense Counsel; William Holloway Inn of Court. ***PRACTICE AREAS:*** Medical Malpractice Defense; Insurance Defense; Litigation.

LANE O. KRIEGER, born Edmond, Oklahoma, February 25, 1978; admitted to bar, 2004, Oklahoma and U.S. District Court, Western District of Oklahoma. *Education:* Oklahoma State University (B.B.A., 2000); University of Oklahoma (J.D., with distinction, 2004). *Member:* Oklahoma Bar Association. ***PRACTICE AREAS:*** Medical Malpractice; Products Liability. ***Email:*** lkrieger@swmb.net

REPRESENTATIVE CLIENTS: CIGNA Companies; Kemper Group Insurance Cos.; Physicians Liability Insurance Co.; Crown Cork & Seal; Corning Glass Works; Continental Insurance Co.; The Medical Protective Company; Ophthalmic Mutual Insurance Co.; Broadspire; The Doctors Company; St. Paul Fire and Marine.
REFERENCE: BancFirst, Oklahoma City, Oklahoma.

B. DAVID SISSON

OKLAHOMA CITY, OKLAHOMA

(See Norman)

Bankruptcy, Domestic, Probate and Estate Planning, Family Law, Divorce, Child Custody Modifications.

LEE SLATER

2601 NORTHWEST EXPRESSWAY, SUITE 210-WEST
P.O. BOX 14785
OKLAHOMA CITY, OKLAHOMA 73113-0785
Telephone: 405-608-0914
Fax: 405-608-0907
Email: leeslater@coxinet.net
URL: http://www.lawyers.com/leeslater

General Practice.

LEE SLATER, born Chandler, Oklahoma, October 27, 1943; admitted to bar, 1988, Oklahoma and U.S. District Court, Western District of Oklahoma. *Education:* University of Oklahoma (B.B.A., 1978); University of Central Oklahoma (M.B.A., 1984); Oklahoma City University (J.D., 1987). Member, Order of Barristers. Member, National Moot Court Team. Recipient, American Jurisprudence Award for Torts, Property, Constitutional Law and Family Law. Outstanding Graduate, 1988. Winner, CJS Award for Legal Scholarship, 1985 and 1987. Notes and Comments Editor, Oklahoma City University Law Review, 1987. Author: "Oklahoma's Legislative Veto: Combat Casualty in Separation of Powers War?" Oklahoma City University Law Review, Spring Issue, 1987; "The Preferred Communications Case: An Opportunity to Set a First Amendment Standard for Cable Television," Oklahoma City University Law Review, Summer Issue, 1986. Adjunct Professor and Lecturer on Election Trends, State Legislative Process, Political Science Department, University of Central Oklahoma, 1990-1996. Secretary of Oklahoma State Senate and Oklahoma State Election Board, 1971-1988. President, American Society of Legislative Clerks and Secretaries, 1983. Hearing Examiner, Oklahoma Public Employees Retirement System, 2002—. Co-owner, Campaign Technology Professionals, L.L.C., Campaign Finance Reporting Firm, Oklahoma City, Oklahoma. *Member:* Oklahoma County, Oklahoma and American Bar Associations. [With U.S. Air Force, 1967]. ***REPORTED CASES:*** Calvey v. Daxon, 997 P.2d 164 (Okla.2000); McKye v. State Election Board, 890 P.2d 954 (Okla.1995); In re Initiative Petition No. 358, 870 P.2d 782 (Okla. 1994). ***PRACTICE AREAS:*** Constitutional Law; Administrative Law; Governmental Law; Election Law; Initiative and Referendum; Employment Law; Municipal Law; Government Contracts; Legislative Law; Civil Litigation.

(This Listing Continued)

REPRESENTATIVE CLIENTS: Accenture; Chesapeake Energy Corporation; OGE; ONEOK; Oklahoma Association of Realtors; Oklahoma Bankers Association; Oklahoma Association of Health Care Providers; American Electric Power; CompSource Oklahoma; University Hospitals Authority; Oklahoma State Senate; Rural Enterprises of Oklahoma, Inc.

SMITH RHODES STEWART & ELDER, P.L.L.C.

Established in 1992

ROBINSON RENAISSANCE, SUITE 820
119 NORTH ROBINSON
OKLAHOMA CITY, OKLAHOMA 73102
Telephone: 405-236-8282
Fax: 405-236-2828
Email: lawyers@srselaw.com
URL: http://www.srselaw.com

Litigation in State and Federal Courts. Products Liability, Negligence, Aircraft Accident, Environmental, Insurance Law and Coverage, Asbestos Litigation, Employment Law, Commercial Transactions, Business and Corporate Law, Bankruptcy, Asset Protection, Entertainment Law, Mediation Services.

FIRM PROFILE: SMITH RHODES STEWART & ELDER, P.L.L.C., specializing in defense litigation and claims matters. The firm also has an established general business practice. The firm combines the personalized attention of a small-sized firm with the extensive litigation experience and capabilities of a large firm. This allows the flexibility to address the various needs and requirements of our clients, including a process of managing litigation costs with detailed billing reports and budgets.

SMITH RHODES STEWART & ELDER, P.L.L.C. is committed to Service-to its clients by providing excellent legal representation on a cost-effective basis, and to its community by pursuing the practice of law at the highest professional and ethical standards.

CURTIS L. SMITH, born Oklahoma City, Oklahoma, March 9, 1951; admitted to bar, 1976, Oklahoma and U.S. District Court, Western, Northern and Eastern Districts of Oklahoma; 1980, U.S. Court of Appeals, 10th Circuit. *Education:* University of Oklahoma (B.A., 1973; J.D., 1976). *Member:* Oklahoma County, Oklahoma and American Bar Associations; International Association of Defense Counsel; Oklahoma Association of Defense Counsel; Defense Research Institute. ***PRACTICE AREAS:*** State and Federal Trials; Products Liability Law; Negligence; Insurance Law; Employment Law; Commercial Transactions. ***Email:*** clsmith@srselaw.com

SCOTT M. RHODES, born Morgan City, Louisiana, September 16, 1952; admitted to bar, 1979, Oklahoma and U.S. District Court, Western, Eastern and Northern Districts of Oklahoma; U.S. Court of Appeals, Tenth Circuit; U.S. Supreme Court. *Education:* University of Oklahoma (B.A. in Letters, magna cum laude, 1975; J.D., 1979). Member, Legal Staff, Oklahoma Insurance Commission, 1979. Member, Arbitration Panel, U.S. District, Western District of Oklahoma. *Member:* Oklahoma County and Oklahoma Bar Associations; Oklahoma Association of Defense Counsel (Board of Directors, 1991-1994; President-Elect, 1994; President, 1995); Federation of Defense and Corporate Counsel. ***PRACTICE AREAS:*** Product Liability; Negligence; Insurance Law; Insurance Coverage; Employment Law. ***Email:*** srhodes@srselaw.com

JOHN DEXTER MARBLE, born Jacksonville, Florida, July 18, 1944; admitted to bar, 1988, Oklahoma and U.S. District Court, Western, Northern and Eastern Districts District of Oklahoma, U.S. Court of Appeals, 10th Circuit. *Education:* Stanford University (A.B., 1966); Texas Christian University (Ph.D., 1974); University of Oklahoma (J.D., with distinction, 1988). Member, University of Oklahoma Law Review, 1987-1988.*Member:* Oklahoma and American (Member, Torts and Insurance Practice Section; Vice Chair, Insurance Coverage Litigation Committee) Bar Associations. ***PRACTICE AREAS:*** Insurance Defense; Insurance Coverage; Appellate Practice; Product Liability; Negligence; Employment Law; Environmental Law. ***Email:*** jdmarble@srselaw.com

JAMES W. DOBBS, born Altus, Oklahoma, August 8, 1965; admitted to bar, 1991, Texas, Oklahoma and U.S. District Court, Western, Eastern and Northern Districts of Oklahoma and U.S. Court of Appeals, 10th Circuit. *Education:* University of Oklahoma (B.B.A., 1988; J.D., 1991). *Member:* Oklahoma County and Oklahoma Bar Associations; State Bar of Texas; Defense Research Institute; Oklahoma Association of Defense Counsel. ***PRACTICE AREAS:*** Civil Litigation; Insurance Defense; Insurance Coverage; Insurance Law; Products Liability; Employment Law. ***Email:*** jdobbs@srselaw.com

KELLY L. WHITWORTH, born Lawton, Oklahoma, January 19, 1978; admitted to bar, 2003, Oklahoma. *Education:* University of Tulsa (B.A., 2000); University of Oklahoma (J.D., 2003). *Member:* Oklahoma Bar Association. ***PRACTICE AREAS:*** Products Liability Defense; Aviation Law. ***Email:*** kwhitworth@srselaw.com

(This Listing Continued)

SMITH RHODES STEWART & ELDER, P.L.L.C., Oklahoma City—Continued

T. GRANT SEXTON, JR., born Montgomery, Alabama, 1979; admitted to bar, 2004, Oklahoma and U.S. District Court, Western District of Oklahoma. *Education:* Huntingdon College; University of Alabama (B.A., 2001); Oklahoma City University School of Law (J.D., 2004). ***Email:*** gsexton@srselaw.com

SUSAN F. KANE, born Dover, Delaware, 1976; admitted to bar, 2002, Oklahoma and U.S. District Court, Western and Northern Districts of Oklahoma. *Education:* University of Oklahoma (B.A., 1998; J.D., 2002). ***Email:*** skane@srselaw.com

OF COUNSEL

A. THOMAS ELDER, JR., born Sentinel, Oklahoma, November 5, 1943; admitted to bar, 1970, Oklahoma, U.S. District Court, Western and Eastern Districts of Oklahoma, and U.S. Court of Appeals, 10th Circuit; 1977, U.S. Supreme Court and U.S. District Court, Northern District of Oklahoma. *Education:* Oklahoma State University (B.S., 1967); University of Oklahoma (J.D., 1970). Phi Delta Phi. Member, Board of Editors, Defense Counsel Journal, 1985-1987. *Member:* Oklahoma County and Oklahoma Bar Associations; Lawyer-Pilots Bar Association; International Association of Defense Counsel (Faculty, Defense Counsel Trial Academy, 1992); National Board of Trial Advocacy (President-Elect, 2001-2002; Member, Board of Directors). Fellow, American College of Trial Lawyers. ***PRACTICE AREAS:*** Aviation; Products Liability; Litigation; Drug and Medical Device Defense. ***Email:*** telder@srselaw.com

DAVID C. JOHNSTON, JR., born Oklahoma City, Oklahoma, February 26, 1931; admitted to bar, 1960, Oklahoma; U.S. District Court, Western, Eastern and Northern Districts of Oklahoma; U.S. Supreme Court; U.S. Court of the Armed Forces. *Education:* public schools, Oklahoma City; New Mexico Military Institute; Oklahoma City University (B.S., 1956; J.D., 1960). Phi Delta Phi. *Member:* Oklahoma County, Oklahoma and American (Vice Chairman, Committee on Aviation and Space Law, 1970-1991) Bar Associations; International Bar Association; Lawyer-Pilots Bar Association; NTSB Bar Association; Oklahoma Association of Defense Counsel; International Association of Arson Investigators; International Society of Air Safety Investigators. ***PRACTICE AREAS:*** Aviation Law; Products Liability; Insurance Law; Labor and Employment Law; Corporation Law; Real Estate Law; Civil Litigation; Appeals. ***Email:*** dcjohnston@srselaw.com

MICHAEL C. STEWART, born Oklahoma City, Oklahoma, February 1, 1938; admitted to bar, 1964, Oklahoma and U.S. District Court, Western District of Oklahoma; 1965, U.S. Court of Appeals, 10th Circuit; 1973, U.S. Supreme Court; 1974, U.S. District Court, Northern and Eastern Districts of Oklahoma. *Education:* University of Oklahoma (B.S., 1961; LL.B., 1964). Recipient: Lawyers Lawyer Award, The Law and You Foundation. Assistant U.S. District Attorney, 1964-1967. *Member:* Oklahoma County, Oklahoma (Member, Uniform Jury Instruction Committee and Professional Responsibility Tribunal); Oklahoma Association of Defense Counsel; Federation of Insurance and Corporate Counsel. Fellow, American College of Trial Lawyers. ***PRACTICE AREAS:*** Products Liability; Property and Casualty; Nursing Home Liability; Electric Utilities. ***Email:*** mstewart@srselaw.com

REPRESENTATIVE CLIENTS: Acceptance Insurance Co.; AIG Aviation, Inc.; American Mercury Insurance Group; AON Corp.; Aramark; Archer-Daniels-Midland; Associated Aviation Underwriters, Inc.; Associated International Insurance Co.; American Empire Insurance; Atlanta Casualty Companies; Austin Company; Auto-Owners Insurance Co.; Avemco; Aventis Pharmaceuticals; Aviation Underwriters at Lloyds; Bell Helicopter Textron Inc.; Carpenter Manufacturing, Inc.; Cessna Aircraft Co.; Chubb Group of Insurance Companies; CIGNA Property and Casualty; CNA Insurance Company; COMAV Managers, Inc.; Conair Corp.; Cooper Industries, Inc.; Cornhusker Casualty Co.; Culligan International; Delahousie Lumbermen's Association; Dresser Industries Inc.; EMC Insurance Cos.; Empire Insurance Group; Federal Insurance Company; Federated Mutual Insurance Company; Federated Rural Electric Insurance Co.; Ford Motor Co.; The G.W. Van Keppel Company; Gibralter National Insurance Co.; Glock, Inc.; Greyhound Lines, Inc.; Gryphon Insurance Group; Gulfstream Aerospace Corp; Gulfstream Aerospace Technologies; The Hartford; Highway Carrier Corp.; Honeywell; Houston General Insurance Co.; Indiana Lumberman's Mutual Insurance Co.; Kansas Farm Bureau Cos.; Kumho Industrial Company, Ltd.; Kumho Tire U.S.A., Inc.; Kubota Tractor Corporation; Lear Jet Corp.; Lloyds of London; Loss Management Services, Inc.; Medeva Pharmaceuticals; Mid-Continent Casualty Company; Mitsui Marine and Fire Insurance Company, LTD.; Mitsui Marine Claims Service; National Fire & Marine Insurance Co.; National Indemnity Co.; National Transportation Adjusters; NEC Corporation; Northland Insurance Company; Oklahoma Attorneys Mutual Insurance Co.; Oklahoma Restaurant Association; Overhead Door Corporation; Piper Aircraft Corp.; Protective Insurance; Ranger Insurance; Redland Insurance Co.; The Redwood Fire and Casualty Insurance Co., The T.H. Rogers Lumber Co.; RegO Co.; Rheem Manufacturing Co.; Risk Administrative Services; Rockwell International Corp.; Ruan Truck Leasing Company; Ryder Truck Rental, Inc.; St. Paul Insurance; Scottsdale Insurance Co.; Scripto-Tokai Corp.; Sears, Roebuck and Co.; Sphere Drake Insurance Co.; State Industries, Inc.; The State Insurance Fund; Sumitomo Marine and Fire Insurance Company; Sunbeam Corp.; Teledyne Continental Motors Aircraft Products Division; Textron, Inc.; Textron Lycoming; Tokio Fire and Marine Insurance Company; UMC Corporation; United States Aviation Underwriters, Inc.; Universal Loss Management, Inc.; Universal Underwriters Group; Wilson Industries, Inc.; Yamaha Motor Company, LTD.; Yasuda Claims Services, Inc.; The Yasuda Fire and Marine Insurance Company; Yellow Freight System, Inc.; Zurich-American Insurance Co.

SNEED LANG, P.C.

OKLAHOMA CITY, OKLAHOMA

(See Tulsa)

Civil Litigation, White Collar Criminal Defense Litigation. Oil and Gas Law, Securities, Securities Fraud. Qui Tam Litigation, Antitrust, Bankruptcy, Negligence, Insurance, Banking, Corporate, Real Estate Law and Title Examination. Environmental Law, Health Care Law, Federal Indian Law and Policy. Family Law, Divorce, Child Custody. Guardianships, Probate, Estate Planning, Sports Law and Transportation.

LESLIE GENE SPARKS

3555 N.W. 58TH STREET, SUITE 510
OKLAHOMA CITY, OKLAHOMA 73112
Telephone: 405-946-8022
Fax: 405-942-8362
URL: http://www.lawyers.com/lessparks

Appellate Practice, Family Law, Divorce, Child Custody, Spousal Support, Guardianship, Adoption Law, Contracts.

LESLIE GENE SPARKS, admitted to bar, 2001, Oklahoma; U.S. District Court, Western District of Oklahoma. *Education:* University of Central Oklahoma (M.Ed., Counseling Psychology, 1978); Oklahoma City University (J.D., 2000). *Member:* Oklahoma and Oklahoma County Bar Associations. ***PRACTICE AREAS:*** Family Law; Divorce; Child Custody; Spousal Support; Guardianship; Adoption Law; Probate.

SPECK PHILBIN ATTORNEYS

A PROFESSIONAL CORPORATION

Established in 1963

204 NORTH ROBINSON, SUITE 800
OKLAHOMA CITY, OKLAHOMA 73102-6885
Telephone: 405-235-1603
FAX: 405-232-0587
Email: SPTFL1@aol.com

General Civil Practice in all State and Federal Courts. Corporation, Taxation, Probate, Estate Planning, Commercial, Real Estate, Employee Benefits Law, ERISA, Wills and Trusts, Litigation, Health Law.

FIRM PROFILE: The firm was founded by John K. Speck, deceased, in the late 1940s to practice primarily in the area of tax law. The firm still concentrates its practice in the tax-related areas of personal, business and tax planning for professionals, owners of closely held businesses and highly compensated individuals and the family law areas of estate planning, probate, trust and estate administration and litigation. The firm's practice also involves real estate law and tax and organizational planning for tax exempt organizations, private foundations and governmental units.

ARNOLD T. FLEIG (1902-1993)

JOHN K. SPECK (1904-1983)

JOSEPH A. ELBOW (1915-2001)

JOHN A. PHILBIN, born Shawnee, Oklahoma, July 2, 1934; admitted to bar, 1961, Oklahoma; 1963, U.S. Court of Appeals, Tenth Circuit and U.S. District Court, District of Oklahoma; 1971, U.S. Tax Court and U.S. Supreme Court. *Education:* University of Oklahoma; Oklahoma City University (J.D., 1961). Phi Delta Phi. Internal Revenue Agent, 1957-1960. Internal Revenue Estate & Gift Tax Examiner, 1960-1963. President, Oklahoma City Estate Planning Council, 1972. President, Oklahoma City Lawyers Tax Group, 1968. *Member:* Oklahoma County, Oklahoma (President, Oklahoma City Chapter, 1970-1971), Federal and American (Member, Tax Section) Bar Associations; American College of Trust and Estate Counsel. ***PRACTICE AREAS:*** Taxation Law; Estate Planning Law; Probate Law; Business Tax Planning Law. ***Email:*** JAPhilbin@aol.com

CHARLES B. LUTZ, JR., born Oklahoma City, Oklahoma, July 28, 1939; admitted to bar, 1968, Oklahoma and U.S. Tax Court; 1970, U.S. District Court, Western and Eastern Districts of Oklahoma and U.S. Court of Appeals, Tenth Circuit; 1976, U.S. Claims Court. *Education:* University of Oklahoma (B.A., 1965; LL.B., 1968). Phi Alpha Delta. Member, Oklahoma City Lawyers Tax Group. Municipal Judge, City of Nichols Hills, Oklahoma, 1986—. President, Oklahoma Municipal Judges Association, 1996. Mediator, American Arbitration Association, 1991—. *Member:* Oklahoma (Chairman, Probate and Estate Planning Sections, 1981), Oklahoma County (Member, Board of Directors, 1981) and American Bar Associations. ***PRACTICE AREAS:*** Real Estate Law; Probate Law; Trusts. ***Email:*** cblutz@aol.com

JIMANNE HARRIS MAYS, born Bonham, Texas, July 23, 1952; admitted to bar, 1978, Oklahoma. *Education:* Baylor University (B.A., 1973); University of Oklahoma (J.D., 1978). Public Defender, 1978-1981. Assistant District Attorney, 1981-1982. *Member:* Oklahoma County, Oklahoma and American Bar Associations; Oklahoma Trial Lawyers Association; The Association of Trial Lawyers of America. ***PRACTICE AREAS:*** Business Law; Trust Law; Tax Law; ERISA Litigation; Probate. ***Email:*** JHMays@aol.com

PATRICIA E. MAHONEY, born Evergreen Park, Illinois, November 2, 1957; admitted to bar, 1982, Oklahoma; 1990, U.S. District Court, Western District of Oklahoma. *Education:* University of New Mexico (B.B.A., 1979); University of Oklahoma (J.D., 1982). Phi Alpha Delta. Trust Officer, 1996-2000. *Member:* Oklahoma Bar Association; Oklahoma City Estate Planning Council. ***PRACTICE AREAS:*** Estate Planning Law; Probate Law; Trust Law.

REPRESENTATIVE CLIENTS: *Automobile:* National Car Rental of Okla. City; Western Equipment LLC. *Contractors and Construction:* Broce Construction Co., Inc.; Pier Drillers, Inc.; Modular Business Systems, Inc. *Investments. Manufacturing and Commercial:* Darby Mercantile Co.; Farming and Ranching Norris Cattle Co.; Midwest Decals, L.L.C.; Natkin and Co.; Drapery Manufacturing, Inc. *Medical:* Physicians Wellness, Inc. *Newspapers and Printing:* Anadarko Publishing Co.; Clinton Daily News; Engleman Newspaper, Inc. *Non-Profit: Oil and Gas:* TEC Resources; Speller Oil Corporation.

SPRADLING, KENNEDY & McPHAIL, L.L.P.

THE TOWER
1601 NW EXPRESSWAY, SUITE 1750
OKLAHOMA CITY, OKLAHOMA 73118
Telephone: 405-418-2700
Facsimile: 405-418-2705
Email: firm@spradlinglaw.com

General Civil Practice in all State and Federal Courts. Administrative, Aviation, Banking, Construction, Corporate Law, Business Organization, Employment, Health Care, Insurance, Lending, Product Liability, Real Estate, and Zoning Law.

MEMBERS OF FIRM

T. SCOTT SPRADLING, born Oklahoma City, Oklahoma, April 8, 1948; admitted to bar, 1975, Oklahoma and U.S. District Court, Western and Northern Districts of Oklahoma. *Education:* University of Virginia (B.A. with distinction, 1970); University of Oklahoma (J.D. with special distinction, 1975). Phi Delta Phi; Order of the Coif. Member, Board of Editors, 1973-1975 and Article and Book Review Editor, 1974, Oklahoma Law Review. Adjunct Professor of Law, University of Oklahoma College of Law, 1978. *Member:* Oklahoma County, Oklahoma (Chairman, Section of Savings and Loan Counsel, 1981-1982) and American Bar Associations; American Land Title Association (Associate-Legal Member, Lenders Counsel Section). [Lt. (jg), U.S. Navy, 1970-1972]. ***PRACTICE AREAS:*** Commercial Real Estate; Corporate Law; Business Organization; Lender Law. ***Email:*** tsspradling@spradlinglaw.com

DAVID D. KENNEDY, born Ann Arbor, Michigan, May 1, 1958; admitted to bar, 1984, Oklahoma. *Education:* Illinois Institute of Technology; Northeast Missouri State University (B.S., 1981); University of Oklahoma (J.D., with distinction, 1984). *Member:* Oklahoma County, Oklahoma and American Bar Associations; Oklahoma City Real Property Attorneys Association. ***PRACTICE AREAS:*** Commercial Real Estate; Zoning Law; Corporate Law; Business Organization. ***Email:*** ddkennedy@spradlinglaw.com

MARK R. McPHAIL, born Oklahoma City, Oklahoma, February 5, 1967; admitted to bar, 1992, Oklahoma and U.S. District Court, Western and Northern Districts of Oklahoma; U.S. Court of Appeals, Tenth Circuit. *Education:* University of Oklahoma (B.B.A., 1989; J.D., with honors, 1992). Phi Delta Phi. Member, 1990-1992 and Note Editor, 1991-1992, Oklahoma Law Review. Author, Note, "Environmental Law: CERCLA Liability of Parent Corporations for their Dissolved or Undercapitalized Subsidiaries," Oklahoma Law Review, Vol. 44-2, Summer 1991. *Member:* Oklahoma County, Oklahoma and American (Member, Sections on: Litigation; Employment Law) Bar Associations. ***PRACTICE AREAS:*** Civil Litigation; Employment Law; Business Law. ***Email:*** mrmcphail@spradlinglaw.com

APPROVED COUNSEL FOR: First American Title & Trust Company; Lawyers Title of Oklahoma City Inc.; American Guaranty Title Company.

STIPE, HARPER, LAIZURE, USELTON, EDWARDS & BELOTE, LLP

Established in 1954
4111 NORTH LINCOLN BOULEVARD
P.O. BOX 53567
OKLAHOMA CITY, OKLAHOMA 73105
Telephone: 405-524-2268
Fax: 405-525-3231
Email: jstipe@stipelawokc.com
URL: http://www.stipelaw.com

McAlester, Oklahoma Office: 343 East Carl Albert Parkway. Telephone: 918-423-0421.
Muskogee, Oklahoma Office: 384 S. 33rd St. Telephone: 918-683-5050. Telefax: 918-682-5700.
Tulsa, Oklahoma Office: 2417 E. Skelly Drive. Telephone: 918-749-0749.

General Civil and Criminal Trial Practice. Personal Injury, Workers Compensation, Probate, Real Estate, Federal Employers Liability, Medical Malpractice and Products Liability Law.

(For personnel at McAlester, Muskogee and Tulsa, see Professional Biographies McAlester)

STRONG, MARTIN & ASSOCIATES, P.L.L.C.

A Professional Limited Liability Company
Attorneys and Counselors at Law
Established in 2000
2700 FIRST NATIONAL CENTER
120 NORTH ROBINSON
OKLAHOMA CITY, OKLAHOMA 73102
Telephone: 405-604-7500
Fax: 405-604-7503
Toll Free: 1-866-859-7500
Email: info@strongmartin.com
URL: http://www.strongmartin.com

Nursing Home, Wrongful Death, Pharmaceutical and Personal Injury Litigation, Commercial and Insurance Litigation, Products Liability, Consumer, Corporate, Class Action and Multi Plaintiff Litigation and General Civil Litigation, Practice in State and Federal Courts in Oklahoma and other jurisdictions.

FIRM PROFILE: Strong, Martin & Associates, P.L.L.C. represents plaintiffs in complex personal injury, wrongful death and nursing home litigation, as well as plaintiffs and defendants in commercial and business litigation. The firm additionally is involved in class and federal multi-jurisdictional actions against national and international companies. The firm provides exceptional, cost-effective representation to corporate and individual clients through a "team approach" and a timeless commitment to building and fostering continuing attorney-client relationships.

Mr. Strong and Mr. Martin have each received the highest possible rating by Martindale-Hubbell.

DON S. STRONG, born Clinton, Oklahoma, September 8, 1947; admitted to bar, 1990, Oklahoma, U.S. District Court, Western District of Oklahoma and U.S. Court of Appeals, Tenth Circuit. *Education:* University of Oklahoma (B.A., History, 1984; M.A., Latin American Studies, 1986; J.D., 1990). Listed in Who's Who Among American Law Students, 1989-1990, 1990-1991. Recipient: Oklahoma Law Review Outstanding Third Year Author, 1989-1990; American Jurisprudence Awards in: Contracts I; Criminal Law; Trial Techniques. Member, Oklahoma Law Review, 1989-1990. Author: "Eiusdem Generis: Oklahoma's Approach to the Interpretation of Other Minerals After Commissioners of Land Office v. Butler," 42-3 Oklahoma Law Review, Fall 1989; "The Prospects for Future Oil and Gas Exploration Within a Municipality After the Amendment to 11 Oklahoma Stat. §44-104," 43-4 Oklahoma Law Review, Winter 1990. Member: Oklahoma University College of Law Board of Advocates, 1988-1990; The Oklahoma Historical Society (Lifetime); National Cowboy Hall of Fame and Western Heritage Center (Lifetime). *Member:* Oklahoma County, Oklahoma (Member, Lawyers Helping Lawyers, Disaster Response and Relief and Law Related Education Committees) and American Bar Associations; American Trial Lawyers Association. ***REPORTED CASES:*** Rider v. Independent School Dist. No. 89; 951 P.2d 951 (Okla. Ct. App. 1994). ***PRACTICE AREAS:*** Nursing Home Litigation; Personal Injury; Wrongful Death; Consumer Law; Torts; Products Liability; Class Actions; Pharmaceutical; Breach of Contract; Federal Litigation; State Litigation. ***Email:*** dss@strongmartin.com

G. STEPHEN MARTIN, II, born Muskogee, Oklahoma, December 17, 1969; admitted to bar, 1996, Oklahoma, U.S. District Court, Western and Eastern Districts of Oklahoma and U.S. Court of Appeals, Tenth Circuit. *Education:* Northeastern State University (B.S., 1992); Oklahoma City University School of Law (J.D., cum laude, 1996). Phi Delta Phi.*Member:* Oklahoma, Oklahoma County and American Bar Associations; Oklahoma Trial Lawyers Association; Outstanding Lawyers of America. Past Associate, Robert J. Turner American Inn of Court, 1999-2000. ***REPORTED CASES:*** Oklahoma Plaza Investors v. Wal-Mart Stores, Inc., 153 F.3d 728 (10th Cir. 1998). ***PRACTICE AREAS:*** Nursing Home Negligence; Pharmaceutical and Product Liability; Federal Litigation; State Litigation; Personal Injury; Commercial Litigation; Corporate Law. ***Email:*** gsm@strongmartin.com

REPRESENTATIVE CLIENTS: Furnished upon request.

TAWWATER & SLAMA, LLP

Established in 1972
SUITE 1950, ONE LEADERSHIP SQUARE
211 NORTH ROBINSON
OKLAHOMA CITY, OKLAHOMA 73102-7124
Telephone: 405-319-7300
Fax: 405-319-7350
Email: help@tawlaw.com
URL: http://www.tawlaw.com

Civil Trial Practice. Negligence, Products Liability, Medical Malpractice, Insurance Bad Faith, Personal Injury, Wrongful Death, HMO Law, Nursing Home Negligence, Automobile Accidents, Construction Injuries, Pharmaceutical Litigation, Mass Torts, Class Action Torts.

FIRM PROFILE: Tawwater & Slama, LLP is listed in the Bar Register of Preeminent Lawyers in the areas of Personal Injury, Medical Malpractice and Products Liability.

MEMBERS OF FIRM

LARRY A. TAWWATER, born Oklahoma City, Oklahoma, May 10, 1947; admitted to bar, 1972, Oklahoma, U.S. District Court, Northern, Eastern and Western Districts of Oklahoma and U.S. Court of Appeals, Fourth, Fifth and Tenth Circuits; 1975, U.S. Supreme Court. *Education:* University of Oklahoma (B.A., 1969; J.D., 1972). Phi Delta Phi. Member, Governor's Committee on Workers Compensation, 1985. Member, Select Committee on Insurance Rates and Tort Claims, 1986-1988. Member, Interim Advisory Committee on Judgments and Appeals, 1991-1992; Oklahoma Supreme Court Rules Revision Committee, 1993, 1994. Member, Governor's Task Force on Medical Malpractice Rates, 2003. Recipient, Earl Sneed CLE Award. Member, Judicial Selection Committee and Advisory Committee, Center for Constitutional Litigation. Member, Oklahoma Uniform Jury Instructions Committee. *Member:* Oklahoma County, Oklahoma (Member, Civil Procedure Committee, 1980-2002; Chairman, 1985, 1990, 1991, 1992, 1993; Member, House of Delegates, 1991, 1992), Federal and American (Member, Tort Reform Task Force) Bar Associations; Oklahoma Trial Lawyers Association (President, 1982; Legislative Chairman, 1985-1987; Member, Board of Directors, 1979-2002; Fellow, Roscoe Pound Foundation; Member, Trial Lawyers for Public Justice); The Association of Trial Lawyers of America (Member, Board of Governors, 1988-2006; Chairman, Labor Law Section, 1977-1979; Legal Affairs Committee; Budget Committee; Judicial Selection Committee; Advisory Committee, Center for Constitutional Litigation); American Society of Law, Medicine and Ethics; American Judicature Society; American Board of Trial Advocates; Master, American Inns of Court. Fellow: International Society of Barristers; Oklahoma Bar Foundation; American College of Trial Lawyers; International Academy of Trial Lawyers. ***PRACTICE AREAS:*** General Negligence Law; Personal Injury; Trials and Appeals; Products Liability Law; Insurance Bad Faith. ***Email:*** lat@tawlaw.com

JO LYNN SLAMA, born Wakefield, Nebraska, January 6, 1961; admitted to bar, 1990, Oklahoma, U.S. District Court, Western, Eastern and Northern Districts of Oklahoma and Northern District of Texas, U.S. Court of Appeals, Fifth and Tenth Circuits and U.S. Supreme Court. *Education:* University of Nebraska (B.S., 1982); Oklahoma City University (J.D., with high distinction, 1990). Phi Delta Phi; Order of the Barristers. Recipient: Oklahoma Bar Association Senior Law Student Award; Oklahoma Women's Lawyers Associa-

(This Listing Continued)

TAWWATER & SLAMA, LLP, Oklahoma City—Continued

tion Award; Corpus Juris Secundum Award; American Jurisprudence Awards; Phillips Allen Porta Memorial, Legal Ethics Award. President OCU School of Law, Alumni Board of Directors, 1995-1996. Adjunct Instructor, Trial Practice, Applied Evidence, Oklahoma City University, School of Law, 1996—. *Member:* Oklahoma County, Oklahoma and American Bar Associations; Oklahoma Trial Lawyers Association; The Association of Trial Lawyers of America. ***PRACTICE AREAS:*** Medical Malpractice Law; Nursing Home Negligence; General Negligence Law; HMO Law; Personal Injury; Products Liability Law. ***Email:*** joslama@tawlaw.com

ASSOCIATES

DARREN M. TAWWATER, born Midwest City, Oklahoma, September 13, 1972; admitted to bar, 2000, Oklahoma, U.S. District Court, Western, Northern and Eastern Districts of Oklahoma and U.S. Court of Appeals, Tenth Circuit. *Education:* Texas Christian University (B.S., 1997); Oklahoma City University (J.D., cum laude, 2000). Phi Delta Phi. Member, Moot Court Honors Board. Member, Merit Scholars Organization. Recipient: Oklahoma Bar Foundation Scholarship; W. Feagin Hood Endowed Scholarship; Law Performance Scholarship; American Jurisprudence Awards. *Member:* American Bar Association; Oklahoma Trial Lawyers Association; The Association of Trial Lawyers of America (Member, New Lawyer Board of Governors). ***PRACTICE AREAS:*** Insurance Bad Faith; Products Liability; Nursing Home Negligence; Medical Malpractice; Trucking Litigation; Negligence. ***Email:*** dtaw@tawlaw.com

STEVEN R. DAVIS, born Shawnee, Oklahoma, January 13, 1946; admitted to bar, 1992, Oklahoma and U.S. District Court, Western, Northern and Eastern Districts of Oklahoma. *Education:* University of Oklahoma (B.B.A., 1971); Oklahoma City University School of Law. Member, Moot Court Board. Recipient, American Jurisprudence Award, Trial Practice. *Member:* Oklahoma Bar Association; The Association of Trial Lawyers of America; Oklahoma Trial Lawyers Association. ***PRACTICE AREAS:*** Medical Negligence; Personal Injury; Nursing Home Negligence; Products Liability. ***Email:*** steved@tawlaw.com

MARY A. TRAVIS
ATTORNEY AT LAW

Established in 2004

500 COLCORD DRIVE
OKLAHOMA CITY, OKLAHOMA 73102
Telephone: 405-610-2280
Fax: 405-737-1595
Email: mary@marytravis.com

Bankruptcy, Family Law, Criminal Law and Insurance.

MARY A. TRAVIS, born Oklahoma City, Oklahoma, June 20, 1966; admitted to bar, 1992, Oklahoma; U.S. District Court, Eastern and Western Districts of Oklahoma; U.S. Court of Appeals, Tenth Circuit. *Education:* University of Oklahoma (B.A., 1988; J.D., 1991). Certified Mediator. *Member:* Oklahoma Bar Association. ***PRACTICE AREAS:*** Bankruptcy; Family Law; Criminal Law; Insurance.

REX K. TRAVIS

500 COLCORD DRIVE
OKLAHOMA CITY, OKLAHOMA 73102-2279
Telephone: 405-236-5400
Fax: 405-236-5499
Email: RexTravis@TravisLawOffice.com
URL: http://www.TravisLawOffice.com

Practice Limited to Plaintiffs Personal Injury and Insurance Litigation, Products Liability and Appellate.

REX K. TRAVIS, born Oklahoma City, Oklahoma, December 4, 1938; admitted to bar, 1962, Oklahoma, U.S. Supreme Court, U.S. Court of Appeals, Tenth Circuit, U.S. District Court, Western, Eastern and Northern Districts of Oklahoma. *Education:* University of Oklahoma (B.A., 1960; LL.B., 1962). Delta Theta Phi. Editor, Travis Oklahoma Law Summary, 1981-1983. Teacher, Legal Assistant Program, Insurance Law, University of Oklahoma College of Law, 1986-1992. Adjunct Professor: Insurance Law, Oklahoma City University Law School, 1993—; University of Oklahoma College of Law, 1994—. Columnist, Oklahoma Trial Lawyers Association Advocate, Insurance Law Column, 1984—. Contributing Author, Long, Law of Liability Insurance, Matthew Bender Co., 1988—. Lecturer and Author: "Oklahoma Uninsured/Underinsured Motorist Coverage, Cases and Tactics," Oklahoma County Bar Association Continuing Legal Education, December 13, 1979; "Proving Liability in Personal Injury and Wrongful Death Cases," The Oklahoma Institute of Continuing Legal Education, Inc., Fall, 1983; "Use of Structured Settlement Annuities in Personal Injury and Death Case Settlements," 54 Oklahoma Bar Journal 2463, September 30, 1983; "The Concept and Mechanics of Uninsured Motorist Coverage," Woodward Oklahoma County Bar Association, Boiling Springs Institute, September 25, 1984; "Commonly Overlooked Insurance Coverages," Oklahoma Trial Lawyers Association Continuing Legal Education, October 24, 1984; "Settlement: Factors Affecting Evaluation, Approaches, The Offer to Settle, Special Considerations," Oklahoma Trial Lawyers Association Continuing Legal Education, October 25, 1985; "Insurance Law -- Unfair Claim Practices Act," Oklahoma City University Continuing Legal Education, September 5, 1986; "The Unfair Claim Practices Act and the Claim Procedures Act," Oklahoma Trial Lawyers Association Continuing Legal Education, November 20, 1986; "Unfair Claim Practices Act and Claim Procedures Act," Oklahoma Association of Defense Counsel Continuing Legal Education, January 23, 1987; "Uninsured Motorist Coverage," Oklahoma Trial Lawyers Association Continuing Legal Education, November 12, 1987; "Uninsured Motorist and Bad Faith Seminar," University of Oklahoma Legal Assistant Course CLE Seminar, November 21, 1987; "Update of UM Insurance," Central Oklahoma Association of Legal Assistants, February 12, 1988; "Direct and Cross Examination of Expert Witnesses," Oklahoma City University School of Law CLE, April 15, 1988; "Oklahoma Uninsured Motorist Coverage," Oklahoma County Bar Association, April 20, 1988; "Advanced Personal Injury Law -- How to Recover Money and Stay Out of Trouble in Uninsured Motorist Cases," University of Oklahoma CLE and Oklahoma Trial Lawyers Association CLE, August 18, 1988; "The Ins & Outs of Insurance Law," Oklahoma Trial Lawyers Association, December 8, 1988; "Insurance Law Update," Oklahoma Bar Association CLE, December 9, 1988; "How to Evaluate & Settle Personal Injury Claims in Oklahoma -- Settlement from the Plaintiff's Perspective," Professional Education Systems, Inc., January 26 and January 27, 1989; "How To Try Hard To Win Cases -- Trying Slip & Fall Cases," Oklahoma Trial Lawyers Association, March 17, 1989; "Uninsured Motorist Law Update," Oklahoma Trial Lawyers Association, Tulsa, April 19, 1989; "Uninsured/Underinsured Motorist, Bad Faith and the Unfair Claim Settlement Practice Act," Oklahoma Claim Association, April 28, 1989; "Advanced Personal Injury; Uninsured Motorist, Underinsured Motorist Coverage and Cases," University of Oklahoma, College of Law CLE and Oklahoma Trial Lawyers Association CLE, June 1, 1989; "Oklahoma Uninsured Motorist Coverage," University of Oklahoma College of Law CLE, July 14, 1989; "Oklahoma Uninsured Motorist Law," Woodward County Bar Association CLE, Boiling Springs Institute, September 26, 1989; "The Current State of Uninsured Motorist Law," Oklahoma Trial Lawyers Association, Oklahoma City, November 16, 1989; "Recent Developments in Oklahoma Law-Insurance Law," Oklahoma Bar Association CLE, Oklahoma City, November 17, 1989, Tulsa, December 15, 1989; "Insurance Law in the 80's-Handling the UM Case," Oklahoma Bar Association CLE, December 1, 1989, Tulsa, December 8, 1989; "Uninsured and Underinsured Motorist Law," Oklahoma City Legal Secretaries Association, Oklahoma City, March 27, 1990; "Oklahoma UM Coverage-The First 30 Years," University of Oklahoma College of Law CLE, Oklahoma City, April 26, 1990; "Altering the Burden of Proving Notice in Slip & Fall Cases," Association of Trial Lawyers of America CLE, New Orleans, May 3, 1990; "Insurance Law-Automobile Insurance, Uninsured Motorist and Bad Faith Law" University of Oklahoma Law Center, Legal Assistant Program CLE, September 22, 1990; "Uninsured Motorist Update," University of Oklahoma College of Law CLE/Oklahoma Trial Lawyers Association CLE, Tulsa, November 15, 1990; "Avoiding Alligators-Malpractice Avoidance in Tort and Insurance Cases," University of Oklahoma College of Law CLE/Oklahoma Trial Lawyers Association CLE, November 15, 1990; "Recent Developments in Oklahoma Law-Insurance Law," Oklahoma Bar Association CLE, Tulsa, November 16, 1990; "How to Evaluate & Settle Personal Injury Claims in Oklahoma-Settlement from the Plaintiff's Perspective," Professional Education Systems, Inc., Tulsa, November 29, 1990, Oklahoma City, November 30, 1990; "Insurance Law in Oklahoma—Uninsured/Underinsured Motorist and Bad Faith Litigation Update," Oklahoma Bar Association, Tulsa, May 12, 1995, Oklahoma City, May 19, 1995; "Effective Legal Writing Workshop," Oklahoma Bar Association Appellate Practice Section, September 8, 1995; "UM & Bad Faith Update," Garfield County Bar Association, Enid, September 13, 1995; "1995 Insurance, Tort & Workers' Compensation Update," (Program Moderator-Presenter of "Insurance Law Update," "Uninsured Motorist Coverage 1995," and "Malpractice Avoidance," Oklahoma Trial Lawyers Association, Tulsa, November 9, 1995, Oklahoma City, December 14, 1994; "Auto Insurance and Accident Litigation," Lorman Education Services, October 26, 1995, Tulsa; "Uninsured Motorist Law Issues," Lorman Education Services, October 26, 1995, Tulsa; "Masters of the Courtroom," Moderator, Oklahoma Bar Association CLE and Oklahoma Trial Lawyers Association CLE, October 27, 1995, Oklahoma City; "Insurance, Tort & Workers' Compensation Update," (Program Moderator of Multi-speaker Program, presenter of "Insurance Law Update," "Uninsured Motorist Coverage 1994," and "Malpractice Avoidance," Oklahoma Trial Lawyers Association, Tulsa, November 17, 1994, Oklahoma City, December 8, 1994; "Avoiding Hostile Fire—Subrogation and Medical Claims Against Bodily Injury Recoveries," Oklahoma Trial Lawyers Association, Oklahoma City, January 19, 1995; "Changes in Insurance Law and Uninsured Motorist Coverage," Oklahoma Association of Defense Counsel, January 27, 1995; "Subrogation and Medical Claims Against Bodily Injury Recoveries," Muskogee County Bar, Muskogee, Oklahoma, March 1, 1995; "Liability Insurance Discovery and Trial Issues," (chapter), Long, Law of Liability Insurance, Matthew-Bender Co., December, 1990; "Subrogation," (chapter), Long, Law of Liability Insurance, Matthew-Bender Co., February, 1991; "Avoiding Alligators—Malpractice Avoidance in Tort and Insurance Cases," Tulsa Trial Lawyers Association, Tulsa, March 17, 1993; "Insurance Law in Oklahoma—Developments in Insurance Coverage," Oklahoma Bar Association CLE, Tulsa, April 30, 1993, Oklahoma City, May 7, 1993; "Oklahoma Insurance Law: First Party Bad Faith Claims—The Law Relating to Bad Faith," Lorman Education Services, Tulsa, September 9, 1993; "Insurance Law—Recent Developments and Uninsured Motorist Law," Oklahoma Trial Lawyers Association, Tulsa, November 14, 1993, Oklahoma City, November 11, 1993; "Recent Developments in Insurance Law—1993," Oklahoma Bar Association CLE, Tulsa, November 5, 1993; "Beware the New Summary Judgment Appeal Rules," Oklahoma Trial Lawyers Association Advocate, January-February, 1994; "Recent Developments in Insurance Law—Uninsured/Underinsured Motorist Update," Lorman Education Services, April 22, 1994; "A Short But Thoughtful Discussion of Recent Cases Involving UM and Bad Faith," Oklahoma Trial Lawyers Association CLE, April 28, 1994; "Insurance Law In Oklahoma—Uninsured/Underinsured Motorist Coverage," Oklahoma Bar Association, Tulsa, May 13, 1994, Oklahoma City, May 20, 1994. Program Chairman and Lecturer, "Uninsured-Underinsured Coverage and Bad Faith Cases Against Insurance Companies," Oklahoma Bar Association Continuing Legal Education, September 1983. Lecturer: "Pretrial Procedure in a Civil Case -- Discovery, Motions and Trial Preparation," Oklahoma Trial Lawyers Association College of Advocacy, 1986 and 1987; "Ethics and Malpractice Prevention," Oklahoma Trial Lawyers Association College of Advocacy, University of Oklahoma College of Law, Summer, 1995; "Medical Malpractice in the 1990's," Conference on Consumer Finance Law and Oklahoma City University School of Law, November 3, 1995, Oklahoma City; "Res Ipsa Loquitur—The Practitioner's View," Conference on Consumer Finance Law and Oklahoma City University School of Law, November 3, 1995, Oklahoma City; "Garvin County Bar Association Seventh Annual Bench & Bar CLE Seminar," Garvin County Bar Association, Pauls Valley, Oklahoma, February 2, 1996; "1996 UM Update," Garvin County Bar Association, Pauls Valley, Oklahoma, February 2, 1996; "UM Update, Ethics & Malpractice Avoidance," Oklahoma Trial Lawyers Association (Interactive Video presentation), Oklahoma City, March 1, 1996; "Update on UM Coverage," Oklahoma Bar Association CLE, Tulsa, May 10, 1996, Oklahoma City, May 17; "Trial Masters," Moderator, Oklahoma Bar

(This Listing Continued)

Association CLE and Oklahoma Trial Lawyers Association CLE, Oklahoma City, October 18, 1996, Tulsa, October 25, 1996; "1996 Insurance, Tort & Workers' Compensation Update," (Program Moderator, Presenter of "Insurance Law Update," Uninsured Motorist Coverage, 1995." and Malpractice Avoidance,", Oklahoma Trial Lawyers Association, Oklahoma City, November 15, 1996; Tulsa, November 22, 1996; "1996 UM Update," Oklahoma County Bar Association, December 3, 1996; Insurance Law Seminar "UM Insurance and Life Insurance Law Update 1996," Conference on Consumer Finance Law, Oklahoma City, December 6, 1996; "Subrogation," Oklahoma Trial Lawyers Association - Presenter "Health Insurance/ERISA Subrogation," Oklahoma City February 14, 1997; "1997 Insurance Law Update," - Oklahoma Bar Association CLE - Moderator and Presenter of Ethics and Malpractice Prevention Segment - Tulsa May 9, 1997 - Oklahoma City May 16, 1997; "The Future of Bad Faith in Oklahoma," Oklahoma Association of Defense Counsel - Moderator - Shangri-La Resort October 17, 1997; "1997 UM Update" - Oklahoma County Bar Association - Oklahoma City October 21, 1997; "1998 Insurance, Tort & Workers' Compensation Update" Oklahoma Trial Lawyers Association - Moderator and Presenter of segments on Insurance Law Update, UM Law Update and Malpractice Avoidance - Tulsa November 6, 1997, Oklahoma City December 12, 1997; "1998 Insurance Law Update," - Oklahoma Bar Association Continuing Legal Education - Moderator and Presenter of "Uninsured/Underinsured Motorist Coverage - Tulsa - April 17, 1998 - Oklahoma City - April 24, 1998; "Malpractice Prevention," - Tulsa Trial Lawyers Breakfast Continuing Legal Education - Tulsa - May 21, 1998; "Insurance Law Update," Oklahoma Trial Lawyers Association - Las Vegas - June 12, 1998; "Oklahoma Uninsured Motorist Law," - State Farm Automobile Insurance Company - Internal Training Program - Tulsa - August 12, 1998; "1998 Insurance, Tort & Workers' Compensation Update," - Program Moderator - Presenter of "Insurance Law Update," Uninsured Motorist Coverage 1998," and "Malpractice Avoidance," - Oklahoma Trial Lawyers Association - Tulsa - November 12, 1998 - Oklahoma City - December 11, 1998; "Oklahoma Uninsured - Underinsured Motorists Coverage," - Oklahoma Bar Association Continuing Legal Education - Tulsa - April 9, 1999 - Oklahoma City - April 16, 1999; "Trial Ethics and Malpractice Prevention", University of Oklahoma College of Advocacy, August 1,1999; "1999 Oklahoma Uninsured Motorist Coverage", Avoiding Alligators-Malpractice Avoidance in a Tort and Insurance Practice", Oklahoma Trial Lawyers Association, November 11, 1999, Tulsa, December 10, 1999 Oklahoma City; "General Insurance Law Update", Oklahoma Bar Association, December 1, 1999; "Recent Developments in Oklahoma Insurance Law 1999", Oklahoma County Bar Association, December 14, 1999. Oklahoma Trial Lawyers Association, May 19, 2000, Oklahoma City, "Ethics Discussion", "Corporate Discovery" . Oklahoma County Bar Association, October 17, 2000 "Insurance Law Update 2000". Oklahoma Trial Lawyers Association, November 16, 2000, Oklahoma City, December 8, 2000, Tulsa "2000 Oklahoma Uninsured Motorist Coverage"; "Avoiding Alligators-Malpractice Avoidance in a Tort and Insurance Practice"; "Insurance Law Update," Oklahoma Bar Association, Oklahoma City, April 13, 2001 and Tulsa, April 20, 2001; "Insurance, Tort and Workers Compensation Update," Oklahoma Trial Lawyers Association, Tulsa, November 15, 2001 and Oklahoma City, December 7, 2001; Oklahoma Bar Association, April 26, 2002, Tulsa, May 3, 2002, Oklahoma City, "Auto Insurance Developments,"; The Graduate School of Successful Trial Advocacy, August 4, 2002, Oklahoma City, "Ethics;" Oklahoma Trial Lawyers Association, November 21, 2002, Oklahoma City, December 13, 2002, Tulsa, "Insurance Law, General Tort Law, and Uninsured Motorist Coverage Update," "Avoiding Alligators-Malpractice Avoidance in a Tort and Insurance Practice;" Oklahoma Bar Association, April 25, 2003, Tulsa, May 2, 2003, Oklahoma City, "Recent Developments in Oklahoma Insurance Law-2003"; "The Best of the Best, Insurance, Tort and Workers Compensation Update," Oklahoma Trial Association, November 7, 2003, Oklahoma City, November 13, 2003, Tulsa. The University of Oklahoma Continuing Education, December 19, 2003, Oklahoma City, "Winning the Federal Case Before Trial." Oklahoma Bar Association, "2003 Insurance Case Law Update," April 30, 2004, Tulsa, and May 7, 2004, Oklahoma City. Woodward County Bar Association's 2004 Boiling Springs Institute Continuing Legal Education, "Insurance Law Update and a Discussion of Recent Changes in Bad Faith in Oklahoma. Oklahoma Trial Lawyers Association, November 11, 2004, Oklahoma City, November 19, 2004, Tulsa, "The Best of the Best, Insurance, Tort and Workers Compensation Update." Member, Oklahoma Legal Ethics Committee, 1985-1991. *Member:* Oklahoma County (Chairman: Bench and Bar Committee, 1976-1977; Prepaid Legal Services Committee, 1976-1977; Member, Board of Directors, 1978-1982 and 1983-1986; Vice-President, 1978-1979; General Counsel, 1979-1982; Vice President, 2001-2002; President-Elect, 2002-2003; President, 2004-2005), Oklahoma and American Bar Associations; Oklahoma Trial Lawyers Association (Member, Board of Directors, 1985-1987; Chairman, Amicus Curiae Committee, 1985-1987; 1989-2003); The Association of Trial Lawyers of America; Luther Bohanon American Inn of Court XXIII (Master). [Lieut. Col., USAFR-Ret.]. ***PRACTICE AREAS:*** Plaintiffs Personal Injury; Insurance Litigation; Uninsured Motorist; Products Liability; Appellate Practice.

MAX C. TUEPKER, P.C.

Established in 1987

204 NORTH ROBINSON, 25TH FLOOR
OKLAHOMA CITY, OKLAHOMA 73102
Telephone: 405-235-1700
Fax: 405-232-9114
URL: http://www.lawyers.com/tuepkerlaw

Civil Litigation Practice in State and Federal Courts. Commercial, Contracts, Corporate, Employment, Probate, Insurance, Oil and Gas Law, Creditors' Rights, Intellectual Property Litigation, Business Litigation.

MAX C. TUEPKER, born Oklahoma City, Oklahoma, October 21, 1953; admitted to bar, 1980, Oklahoma; 1981, Colorado; U.S. District Court, Western, Eastern and Northern Districts of Oklahoma; U.S. Court of Appeals, Tenth Circuit; U.S. Supreme Court. *Education:* Central State University (B.S., summa cum laude, 1976); University of Tulsa (J.D., 1980). Phi Delta Phi. Member, Order of the Curule Chair. Law Clerk, Hon. H. Dale Cook, Chief Judge, U.S. District Court, Northern District of Oklahoma, 1980-1981. *Member:* Oklahoma County, Oklahoma, Colorado and American Bar Associations. **Email:** mtuepker@swbell.net

(This Listing Continued)

SHAWNAE E. PROCTOR, born Oklahoma City, Oklahoma, November 30, 1975; admitted to bar, 2001, Oklahoma; U.S. District Court, Western, Eastern and Northern Districts of Oklahoma; U.S. Court of Appeals, Tenth Circuit. *Education:* Cameron University (B.S., 1998); Oklahoma City University (J.D., 2001). Phi Delta Phi. Hatton W. Sumners Scholar. Member, Oklahoma City University Law Review. *Member:* Oklahoma County, Oklahoma and American Bar Associations. **Email:** shawnaep@swbell.net

VAUGHT & CONNER

A Professional Limited Liability Company

50 PENN PLACE, SUITE 1300
OKLAHOMA CITY, OKLAHOMA 73118
Telephone: 405-848-2255
Fax: 405-840-4701
Email: sconner@vcokc.com

Commercial, Corporate and Business, Real Estate, Energy, Cogeneration, Utility Law, Employment, Healthcare Law, Estates and Trusts, Litigation in State and Federal Courts.

CHERYL A. VAUGHT, born White Plains, New York, June 7, 1959; admitted to bar, 1985, Oklahoma and U.S. District Court, Western District of Oklahoma. *Education:* University of Oklahoma (B.A. Journalism, 1981; J.D., 1984). Omicron Delta Kappa; Kappa Tau Alpha; Phi Alpha Delta. Recipient, University of Oklahoma Achievement Award. City Attorney, Purcell, Oklahoma, 1985-1988. President Board of Directors: Leadership Oklahoma City; The National Memorial Institute for Prevention of Terrorism; American Red Cross SW Regional VELD Committee; President Board of Director, The Arts Council of Oklahoma City; Energtix LLC; Oklahoma City Public Schools Foundation. *Member:* Oklahoma County, Oklahoma and American Bar Associations. ***PRACTICE AREAS:*** Regulatory Law; Independent Power Production; Administrative Law; Employment Law; Litigation. **Email:** cvaught@vcokc.com

SCOT A. CONNER, born Lawton, Oklahoma, February 20, 1957; admitted to bar, 1986, Oklahoma, U.S. District Court, Western District of Oklahoma, U.S. Tax Court and U.S. Court of Federal Claims. *Education:* University of Oklahoma (B.B.A., 1980; J.D., 1983). Phi Delta Phi. *Member:* Oklahoma County (Member, Board of Directors, Chairman and Vice-Chairman, Young Lawyers Division, 1986-1990), Oklahoma (Member, Board of Directors, Secretary, Young Lawyers Division 1988-1991; Member, Taxation Section) and American (Member, Sections on: Corporation, Banking and Business Law; Taxation) Bar Associations; National Health Lawyers Association; Oklahoma City Real Property Attorneys Association; Oklahoma City Lawyers Tax Group; Oklahoma City Estate Planning Council. [1st Lt., U.S. Army, Europe, 1984-1986]. ***PRACTICE AREAS:*** General Corporate Law; Commercial; Real Estate Law; Tax Law; Healthcare Law; Estate Planning Law; Probate Law. **Email:** sconner@vcokc.com

REPRESENTATIVE CLIENTS: Available Upon Request.
REFERENCES: Available Upon Request.

WAGNER & WAGNER, P.C.

4000 N. CLASSEN BOULEVARD, SUITE 101-N
P.O. BOX 60924
OKLAHOMA CITY, OKLAHOMA 73146-0924
Telephone: 405-521-9105; 1-800-453-9890
Fax: 405-521-8994
Email: rjw@wagnerfirm.com
Email: klw@wagnerfirm.com
Email: info@wagnerfirm.com

Family Law, Personal Injury, Automobile Accidents, Truck Accidents, Wrongful Death, Divorce, Alimony, Child Support, Workers Compensation, Social Security Disability, Employment, Employment Discrimination, Wrongful Termination, Adoptions.

KERRY L. WAGNER, born McAlester, Oklahoma, July 24, 1956; admitted to bar, 1992, Oklahoma; U.S. District Court, Northern, Eastern and Western Districts of Oklahoma. *Education:* University of Missouri, Columbia (B.S., 1981; M.Ed., 1983); Oklahoma City University (J.D., 1992). Iota Tau Tau. *Member:* Oklahoma County and American Bar Associations; Oklahoma Trial Lawyers Association; The Association of Trial Lawyers of America.

ROBERT J. WAGNER, born St. Louis, Missouri, January 12, 1960; admitted to bar, 1996, Oklahoma; U.S. Supreme Court; U.S. Court of Appeals, Tenth Circuit; U.S. District Court, Northern, Eastern and Western Districts of Oklahoma. *Education:* University of Missouri, Columbia; Oklahoma City University (B.S., Business Administration, 1992; J.D., 1995). Member, Environmental Law Student Association. *Member:* Oklahoma County and American Bar Associations; Oklahoma Trial Lawyers Association; The Association of Trial Lawyers of America.

WALKER, FERGUSON & FERGUSON

Established in 1973

SUITE 400
301 N.W. 63RD STREET
OKLAHOMA CITY, OKLAHOMA 73116
Telephone: 405-843-8855
Fax: 405-843-8934
Email: walkerl@okc.coxatwork.com

General Civil Practice. Insurance Defense, Banking and Commercial Law, Federal, State and Local Taxes, Real Estate, Oil and Gas, Probate, Administrative and Legislative Law. Transportation, Communications, Cable TV, Workers Compensation Law, Employer Liability Law, Employment (Management), Telecommunications, Commercial Litigation, Taxation, Subrogation, Trials in State and Federal Courts.

(This Listing Continued)

WALKER, FERGUSON & FERGUSON, Oklahoma City—Continued

MEMBERS OF FIRM

JAMES E. (JIM) WALKER, born Shawnee, Oklahoma, May 11, 1944; admitted to bar, 1974, Oklahoma and U.S. District Court, Western, Northern and Eastern Districts of Oklahoma; 1977, U.S. Tax Court; 1988, U.S. Court of Appeals, 10th Circuit; 1989, U.S. Supreme Court. *Education:* Oklahoma University (B.B.A., 1967; J.D., 1974). Phi Alpha Delta. Chairman, Oklahoma Tax Commission, 1977-1981. Director, Oklahoma Alcoholic Beverage Control Board, 1976-1977. *Member:* Oklahoma County, Oklahoma and American Bar Associations. [U.S. Army, 1967-1970; Army JAGC, 1974-1976; Brigadier General (retired), Oklahoma Army National Guard]. ***PRACTICE AREAS:*** State and Federal Lobbying; Transportation Law; Communications Law; Cable T.V. Law; Tax Law; Insurance Law. ***Email:*** walkerl@okc.coxatwork.com

THOMAS G. FERGUSON, JR., born Spokane, Washington, May 12, 1948; admitted to bar, 1973, Virginia; 1974, U.S. District Court, Western District of Oklahoma; 1976, U.S. Tax Court; 1977, West Virginia; 1979, Oklahoma; 1985, U.S. District Court, Northern and Eastern Districts of Oklahoma; 1988, U.S. Court of Appeals, 10th Circuit; 1989, U.S. Supreme Court. *Education:* Virginia Military Institute (B.A., 1970); Washington & Lee University (J.D., 1973). Phi Delta Phi. Assistant General Counsel, Oklahoma Tax Commission, 1978-1980. *Member:* Oklahoma County, Oklahoma, Virginia, West Virginia and American Bar Associations; Virginia State Bar; West Virginia State Bar; Defense Research Institute. [U.S. Army, 1973-1977; LTC., JAGC, U.S. Army Reserve (retired)]. ***PRACTICE AREAS:*** Insurance Defense Law; Insurance Bad Faith Defense; Cable TV; General Litigation; Employer Liability Law. ***Email:*** tferg@okc.coxatwork.com

JAMES C. FERGUSON, born Brussels, Belgium, December 13, 1951; admitted to bar, 1985, Oklahoma. *Education:* Washington & Lee University (B.S., 1974); University of Oklahoma (M.A., 1978; J.D., 1985). *Member:* Oklahoma and American Bar Associations. [US Army, 1974-1981; Col., Oklahoma Army National Guard (retired).]. ***PRACTICE AREAS:*** Workers Compensation Law; Employer Liability Law. ***Email:*** jimferg@okc.coxatwork.com

ASSOCIATES

TIMOTHY J. LAMIELL, born Chicopee Falls, Massachusetts, November 23, 1952; admitted to bar, 1976, Oklahoma. *Education:* University of Hawaii (B.B.A., 1973); University of Tulsa (J.D., 1976). *Member:* Oklahoma Bar Association. ***PRACTICE AREAS:*** Oil and Gas Law; Real Estate Law; Probate.

JON LOUIS DEROUEN, JR, born Atlanta, Georgia, August 1, 1970; admitted to bar, 1998, Oklahoma and U.S. District Court, Western District of Oklahoma; 1999, U.S. District Court, Eastern District of Oklahoma. *Education:* Texas A & M University (B.A., 1993); Oklahoma City University (J.D., 1998). *Member:* Oklahoma and American Bar Associations. ***PRACTICE AREAS:*** Workers Compensation.

CAROLYN K. HEBERT, born Madison, Wisconsin, December 4, 1966; admitted to bar, 1995, Oklahoma; U.S. District Court, Western and Eastern Districts of Oklahoma. *Education:* Marion College (B.A., Political Science, 1992); Oklahoma City University, School of Law (J.D., 1995). Assistant District Attorney, Oklahoma County, Oklahoma, 1994-1996. Formerly with Holloway, Dobson & Bachman. *Member:* Oklahoma County (Member, Worker's Compensation Section) and Oklahoma Bar Associations. ***PRACTICE AREAS:*** Workers Compensation Defense; Insurance Defense. ***Email:*** chebert@okc.coxatwork.com

SHEILA D. BARNES, born Guymon, Oklahoma, April 6, 1977; admitted to bar, 2002, Oklahoma and U.S. District Court, Western District of Oklahoma. *Education:* University of Central Oklahoma (B.A., Criminal Justice, magna cum laude, 1999); University of Oklahoma (J.D., 2002). Phi Delta Phi. Member, Oklahoma Law Review. *Member:* Oklahoma County, Oklahoma and American Bar Associations. ***PRACTICE AREAS:*** Insurance Law; Civil Litigation; Workers Compensation. ***Email:*** sbarnes@okc.coxatwork.com

OF COUNSEL

BRUCE V. WINSTON, born Oklahoma City, Oklahoma, April 19, 1947; admitted to bar, 1973, Oklahoma and U.S. District Court, Western District of Oklahoma; 1975, U.S. District Court, Eastern District of Oklahoma; 1979, U.S. District Court, Northern District of Oklahoma and U.S. Court of Appeals, 10th Circuit. *Education:* University of Oklahoma (B.B.A., 1970); Oklahoma City University (J.D., 1973). Phi Delta Phi. *Member:* Oklahoma Bar Association; International Association of Defense Counsel and Defense Research Institute. ***REPORTED CASES:*** Short v. Oklahoma Farmers Union, 619 P.2d 588 (Okla., 1980); Brown v. Wal-Mart Stores, Inc., 11 F.3d 1559 (10th Cir. 1993). ***PRACTICE AREAS:*** Civil Litigation; Insurance Defense Law; Employer Liability; Workers' Compensation; Insurance Bad Faith Defense. ***Email:*** brucewinston@hotmail.com

MIA C. ROPS, born Oklahoma City, Oklahoma, October 20, 1967; admitted to bar, 1993, Texas; 1994, Oklahoma. *Education:* University of Oklahoma (B.A. in Letters, 1989); University of Texas School of Law (J.D., 1993). *Member:* Oklahoma County and Oklahoma Bar Associations; State Bar of Texas; Oklahoma Association of Defense Counsel; Oklahoma Workers' Compensation Defense Counsel. ***PRACTICE AREAS:*** Workers' Compensation. ***Email:*** mrops@okc.coxatwork.com

REPRESENTATIVE CLIENTS: Accord Human Resources; AIG; Adjustco; American Interstate Insurance Co.; Argonaut-Great Central; BancFirst; Boldt Construction Co.; Braums Ice Cream Company; Browning-Ferris Industries; Cable Telecommunications Operators of Oklahoma; The City of Lawton; Claims and Risk Services; Consolidated Bureau Resources of the U.S.; Cox Communications, Inc.; Crawford & Co.; CNA Insurance; Crawley Petroleum Corporation; El Paso Production Company; E&O Professionals; Employers Ace-USA; Employers Mutual Companies; Essex Insurance Co.; Fanch Communications; First Data Corp; Fleming Companies; FPCO Oil & Gas Co.; Fort Howard Paper Co.; Galleger Bassett; Goodville Mutual Insurance Co.; Hobby Lobby; Homeland; Hydro Modular Systems, Inc.; Insurers Loss Management OKC; Jack Cooper Transport Co.; Love Box Co.; Love's Stores; Markel American Insurance Company; Mannix Oil Company; Marathon Oil, Inc.; Marriott; Loomis Fargo; Maryland Casualty Insurance Co.; Midlands Haskel Lemon Construction Co.; Remedy Staffing; Mustang Fuel Corporation; Oklahoma Bankers Association; Oklahoma County; Oklahoma Farmers Union Mutual Insurance Co.; Oklahoma Gas & Electric; Oklahoma Grocers Association; Oklahoma Municipal Assurance Group; Oklahoma Restaurant Group; Pool Company; Preferred Risk Insurance Co.; St. Mary Operating Company; St. Paul Insurance; SAFECO; Segwick James of Oklahoma Inc.; CompSource; State Farm Insurance Cos.; Stephens Production Company; Tempo, Inc.; The Tokio Marine and Fire Insurance Co., Ltd.; Union Standard Insurance Companies; Unit Parts Company; Universal Underwriters Insurance Group; Williams Energy Services; Willis Caroon; Yellow Freight Systems; Zenith Insurance.

(This Listing Continued)

REFERENCE: BancFirst.

WALKER & WALKER

Established in 1954

950 LANDMARK TOWERS EAST

3535 N.W. 58TH STREET

OKLAHOMA CITY, OKLAHOMA 73112

Telephone: 405-943-9693

Fax: 405-949-1505

URL: http://www.lawyers.com/walkerwalker

General Civil Practice. Trials. Oil and Gas including International Oil and Gas Transactions, Real Property, Environmental, Probate, Trusts, Corporations and Partnerships, Complex Litigation, Personal Injury and Products Liability.

FIRM PROFILE: Founded in 1954 by Barth P. Walker, a former All-American football player at The University of Oklahoma, and joined in 1974 by his son, Russell, the law firm of Walker and Walker is a renowned International Oil & Gas firm. Its practice includes civil litigation matters in addition to Oil and Gas law.

Walker & Walker is proud to be able to offer all the amenities and services of large law firms but within the comfortable setting of a small law firm.

MEMBERS OF FIRM

RUSSELL JAMES WALKER, born Camden, Arkansas, March 24, 1946; admitted to bar, 1974, Oklahoma. *Education:* Yale University (B.A., 1968); University of Oklahoma (J.D., 1974). Phi Delta Phi. Member, University of Oklahoma Law Review, 1972-1974. Author: "Can Rights Required to be Given Limited Partners Under New Tax Shelter Investment Regulations be Reconciled with Section 7 of the Uniform Limited Partners Act," 26 Oklahoma Law Review 289, 1973. Division L, Temporary Court of Appeals, State of Oklahoma, 1991.*Member:* Oklahoma Bar Association (Member, Sections on Real Property and Mineral Law); Oklahoma City Title Lawyers Association; Oklahoma City Mineral Lawyers Association. ***LANGUAGES:*** French and German. ***SPECIAL AGENCIES:*** Oklahoma Corporation Commission. ***REPORTED CASES:*** Atlantic Richfield Co. v. Tomlinson, 859 P. 2d 1088 (Okl., 1993); Kaneb Production Company vs GHK Exploration Company, 796 P.2d 1388 (Okl. 1989); Roberts vs Funk Exploration, Inc. 764 P.2d 147 (Okl. 1988); Calvert Drilling Company vs Corporation Commission, 589 P.2d 1064 (Okl. 1979); Amax Petroleum Corporation vs Corporation Commission, 552 P.2d 387 (Okl. 1976); Caudillo vs Corporation Commission, 551 P.2d 1110 (Okl. 1976); Eason Oil Company vs Corporation Commission, 535 P.2d 283 (Okl. 1975). ***PRACTICE AREAS:*** Real Property; Oil and Gas; Oil and Gas Conservation; International Oil and Gas Transactions; Partnerships; Corporation; Business Law. ***Email:*** rjwalker@walkerandwalker.com

ANDREW J. WALDRON, born San Jose, California, September 10, 1972; admitted to bar, 1997, Oklahoma, U.S. District Court, Eastern, Northern and Western Districts of Oklahoma, U.S. Court of Appeals, Tenth Circuit, U.S. Court of Appeals for the Federal Circuit and U.S Tax Court, U.S. Court of Claims; 2000, U.S. Supreme Court. *Education:* University of Central Oklahoma (B.A., magna cum laude, 1994); University of Oklahoma (J.D., with distinction, 1996). Phi Delta Phi. Recipient, American Jurisprudence Award in Contracts. *Member:* Oklahoma County, Oklahoma and American Bar Associations. ***REPORTED CASES:*** Scrivner v. Sonat, 242 F.3d 1288 (10th Circuit 2001); Palo Duro v. FDIC, 1999 U.S. App. LEXIS 29175. ***PRACTICE AREAS:*** Civil Litigation; Contract Law; Appellate Practice; Oil and Gas Law. ***Email:*** ajwaldron@walkerwalker.com

OF COUNSEL

GLENN J. SHRADER, JR., born Greenville, Ohio, January 14, 1952; admitted to bar, 1978, Oklahoma. *Education:* Miami University (A.B., 1974); University of Toledo; Oklahoma City University (J.D., 1977). Author: "Rule 533: Too Little Too Late," University of Toledo Law Review, Spring, 1976. *Member:* Oklahoma Bar Association; Oklahoma Trial Lawyers Association; The Association of Trial Lawyers of America. ***PRACTICE AREAS:*** Complex Litigation; Personal Injury; Products Liability Law.

STEPHEN O. CLARKE, born Ypsilanti, Michigan, May 19, 1967; admitted to bar, 1997, Oklahoma. *Education:* University of Oklahoma (B.A., 1994; J.D., 1997). *Member:* Oklahoma Bar Association. ***PRACTICE AREAS:*** Products Liability; Civil Litigation; Family Law.

EDWARD J. CLARKE, born Ypsilanti, Michigan, July 27, 1971; admitted to bar, 2000, Oklahoma. *Education:* California State University (B.S., 1997); University of Oklahoma (J.D., 2000). ***PRACTICE AREAS:*** Oil and Gas Conservation; Oil and Gas Law; Tax Law. ***Email:*** ejclarke@walkerandwalker.com

REPRESENTATIVE CLIENTS: Agate Petroleum, Inc.; Arapahoe Resources, LLC; Carroll D. Beaman; Berry Operating Co. Blake Production Company, Inc.; Buttram Energies, Inc.; Calvert Investments, Inc.; G.M. Oil Properties, Inc./Belt Properties, Inc.; Godfrey Oil Properties; William W. London, Inc.; Natural Gas Anadarko Co./Courson Oil & Gas, Inc.; Paraclifra Land & Minerals, Ltd./4-JW, Ltd; Patterson Oil Company, Inc.; Pure Energy Systems, Inc.; Michael Shearn/Sol West III; Spess Oil Company, Inc.; Stephens & Johnson Operating Co.; Te-Ray Energy, Inc.; Triad Energy, Inc./Sterling Exploration, Inc./Maple Street Corporation; Trimble Maclaskey Oil, LLC.

WALLACE & BERTMAN, PC

100 N. BROADWAY AVENUE, SUITE 2270
OKLAHOMA CITY, OKLAHOMA 73102
Telephone: 405-605-6100
Fax: 405-606-8403
Email: lawfirm@wallacebertman.com
URL: http://www.wallacebertman.com

Civil Litigation, Indian Law, Aircraft Finance and Leasing, Litigation, Commercial Law, Administrative Law, Contracts, Business, Construction Law, Corporate, Partnership, Family Business, Professional Licensing, Municipal Law, Native American Law, Appellate Practice.

R. BROWN WALLACE, born Granite, Oklahoma, December 5, 1944; admitted to bar, 1970, Oklahoma. *Education:* University of Oklahoma (B.A., 1967; J.D., 1970). ***REPORTED CASES:*** Kiowa Tribe of Oklahoma v. Manufacturing Technologies, Inc., 523 U.S. 751, 118 S. Ct. 1700, 140 L.Ed. 2d 981 (1998). ***PRACTICE AREAS:*** Civil Litigation; Indian Law; Aircraft Finance and Leasing; Litigation; Commercial Law; Administrative Law.

EUGENE K. BERTMAN, born Islip, New York, 1972; admitted to bar, 2002, Oklahoma, U.S. Court of Appeals, Tenth Circuit, U.S. Court of Appeals for the Federal Circuit, U.S. District Court, Eastern, Northern and Western Districts of Oklahoma and U.S. Tax Court. *Education:* Oklahoma State University (B.S., 1995); Oklahoma City University (J.D., cum laude, 2002). Phi Delta Phi. *Member:* Oklahoma County, Oklahoma and New York State Bar Associations. ***PRACTICE AREAS:*** Litigation; Commercial Law; Contracts; Business; Construction Law; Corporate; Partnership; Family Business; Administrative Law; Professional Licensing; Municipal Law; Native American Law; Appellate Practice.

WELCH LAW FIRM, P.C.

722 NORTH BROADWAY
SUITE 301
OKLAHOMA CITY, OKLAHOMA 73102-6025
Telephone: 405-236-5222
Fax: 405-231-5222
Email: RWelch@WelchLawPC.com

Corporate Law, Commercial Law, Financial Transactions, Commercial Litigation, Bankruptcy Law, Creditors Rights.

RUSTON C. WELCH, born Oklahoma City, Oklahoma, July 10, 1964; admitted to bar, 1989, Oklahoma; U.S. District Court, Western District of Oklahoma. *Education:* Southern Nazarene University (B.S., cum laude, 1986); University of Oklahoma (J.D., with honors, 1989). Phi Delta Lambda; Order of the Coif. *Member:* Oklahoma County, Oklahoma and American Bar Associations. ***PRACTICE AREAS:*** Corporate Law; Commercial Law; Financial Transactions; Commercial Litigation; Bankruptcy Law; Creditors Rights.

WELCH & SMITH, P.C.

6440 AVONDALE DRIVE, SUITE 206
OKLAHOMA CITY, OKLAHOMA 73116
Telephone: 405-286-0801
Fax: 405-286-0301
Email: mwelch@welchsmith.com
Email: ssmith@welchsmith.com

Civil Trial and Appellate Practice in all State and Federal Courts, including Insurance Coverage, Professional Liability, Business Torts, Employment, Products Liability and Negligence.

MORT G. WELCH, born De Queen, Arkansas, September 21, 1950; admitted to bar, 1975, Texas and U.S. District Court, Southern District of Texas; 1976, Oklahoma and U.S. District Court, Western District of Oklahoma; 1977, U.S. Court of Appeals, 10th Circuit; 1979, U.S. District Court, Northern District of Oklahoma; 1980, U.S. District Court, Eastern District of Oklahoma; 1999, U.S. Supreme Court. *Education:* University of Oklahoma (B.A., with special distinction, 1972); University of Texas (J.D., 1975). Phi Beta Kappa. *Member:* Oklahoma and American Bar Associations; Defense Research Institute; International Association of Defense Counsel. ***REPORTED CASES:*** Trinity Univ. Ins. Co. v. Broussard 932 F. Supp. 1307 (N.D. OK 1996); Angelo vs. Armstrong World Industries, 11 F.3d 957 (10th Cir. 1993); Beeman vs. Manville Corp. Asbestos Disease Compensation Fund, 496 N.W.2d 247 (Iowa 1993); Bristol vs. Fibreboard Corp., 789 F.2d 846 (10th Cir. 1986); Case vs. Fibre Board Corp., 743 P.2d 1062 (Okla) 1987); Cofer vs. Morton, 784 P.2d 67 (Okla 1989); Coleman vs. Turpen, 697 F.2d 1341 (10th Cir. 1982), app. after remand 827 F.2d 667 (10th Cir. 1987); Fisher vs. Owens Corning Fiberglass Corp., 868 F.2d 1175 (10th Cir. 1989); Fleming vs. Hall, 638 P.2d 1115 (Okla 1981); Horace Mann Ins. Co. vs. Johnson, 953 F.2d 575 (10th Cir. 1991); Oklahoma Farmers Union Mut. Ins. Co. v. John Deere Ins. Co., 967 P.2d 479 (Ok. Civ. App. 1998); Huff vs. Fibreboard Corp., 836 F.2d 473 (10th Cir. 1987); Lindsey vs. Dayton-Hudson Corp., 592 F.2d 1118 (10th Cir. 1979); Livengood vs. Thedford, 681 F. Supp. 695 (W.D. Okla 1988); Sargent vs. Central National Bank & Trust Co. of Enid, Oklahoma, 809 P.2d 1298 (Okla. 1991); State Farm Mut. Ins. Co. vs. Schwartz, 933 F.2d 848 (10th Cir. 1991); Tax Investments Concepts, Inc. vs. McLaughlin, 670 P.2d 981 (Okla 1982); Thiry vs. Armstrong World Industries, 661 P.2d 515 (Okla. 1983); Vilsick vs. Fibreboard Corp., 861 S.W.2d 659 (Mo. App. 1993); Wever vs. State ex rel. Dept. of Human Services, 839 P.2d 672 (Okla. App. 1990); Wilson & Co. vs. Reed, 603 P.2d 1172 (Okla. App. 1979); Wilson Foods Corp. vs. Noble 613 P.2d 485 (Okla. App. 1980); Wilson Foods Corp. vs. Porter, 612 P.2d 261 (Okla. 1980); Timberlake Construction Co. v. U.S.F.& G. Co., 71 F.3d 335 (10th Cir. 1995); Akin v. Ashland Chemical Co., 156 F.3d 1030 (10th Cir. 1998); Grain Dealers Mut. Ins. Co. v. Farmers All. Mut. Ins. Co., 298 F.3d 1178 (10th Cir. 2002). ***PRACTICE AREAS:*** Insurance Coverage; Insurance Bad Faith. **Email:** mwelch@welchsmith.com

(This Listing Continued)

SHERRY L. SMITH, born Baltimore, Maryland, June 13, 1956; admitted to bar, 1984, Oklahoma; 1985, U.S. District Court, Western District of Oklahoma; 1986, U.S. Court of Appeals, Tenth Circuit; 1988, U.S. District Court, Eastern District of Oklahoma. *Education:* Oklahoma City University (B.A., magna cum laude, 1981); University of Oklahoma (J.D., 1984). Phi Delta Phi. *Member:* Oklahoma County, Oklahoma and American Bar Associations; Oklahoma Association of Defense Counsel; Defense Research Institute. ***REPORTED CASES:*** Cimarron Pipeline Constr. v. U.S.F. & G. Co., 848 P.2d 1161 (Okla. 1983); Macy v. Oklahoma City School District, 961 P.2d 804 (Okla. 1998); Grain Dealers Mut. Ins. Co.v. Farmers All. Mut. Ins. Co., 298 F.3d 1178 (10th Cir. 2002). ***PRACTICE AREAS:*** First and Third Party Insurance Defense; Self Insured Defense. **Email:** ssmith@welchsmith.com

REPRESENTATIVE CLIENTS: American International Cos.; American Interstate Insurance Co.; Avis Rent-A-Car Systems Inc.; CIGNA Ins.Group; CNA Insurance Co.; Grain Dealers Mutual Insurance Co.; Great American Insurance Co.; Oklahoma Attorneys Mutual Insurance Co.; Oklahoma Farmers Union Mutual Insurance Company; Reliant American Group; Shand Morahan & Co.; The May Department Stores Co., Inc.
REFERENCE: National Bank of Commerce, Oklahoma City, Oklahoma.

WHITE, COFFEY & FITE, P.C.

Established in 1982

1001 N.W. 63RD ST., SUITE 100
OKLAHOMA CITY, OKLAHOMA 73116-7335
Telephone: 405-842-7545
Fax: 405-840-9890

General Civil Practice. Trials of Civil Cases in all State and Federal Courts. Corporation, Commercial, Oil and Gas, Environmental, Agriculture, Public Utility, Real Property, Title and Probate, Taxation, Banking and Bankruptcy Law.

JOHN M. COFFEY, born Oklahoma City, Oklahoma, October 29, 1941; admitted to bar, 1966, Oklahoma. *Education:* University of Oklahoma (B.B.A., 1963; J.D., 1966); New York University (LL.M. in Taxation, 1967). Phi Delta Phi (Exchequer, 1965). Editor, Oklahoma Law Review, 1964-1966. Certified Public Accountant, Oklahoma, 1972. *Member:* Oklahoma County and Oklahoma Bar (Former Chairman, Tax Section and Estate and Trust Section) Associations. ***PRACTICE AREAS:*** Corporate Law; Tax Law; Probate Law; Broadcasting Law; Automobile Dealership Law; Business and Reorganization Law. **Email:** jcoffey@wcgflaw.com

JACK P. FITE, born Norman, Oklahoma, February 16, 1951; admitted to bar, 1976, Oklahoma. *Education:* Oklahoma University (B.A., 1972); Oklahoma City University (J.D., 1975). *Member:* Oklahoma County and Oklahoma Bar Associations. ***PRACTICE AREAS:*** Public Utility; Communications Law. **Email:** jfite@wcgflaw.com

JAMES U. WHITE, JR., born Oklahoma City, Oklahoma, August 4, 1949; admitted to bar, 1974, Oklahoma. *Education:* Yale University (B.A., 1971); University of Oklahoma (J.D., 1974). *Member:* Oklahoma County, Oklahoma and American Bar Associations. ***PRACTICE AREAS:*** Trial Practice; Oil and Gas Law; Franchise Law; Real Property Law; Commercial Litigation. **Email:** jwhite@wcgflaw.com

REPRESENTATIVE CLIENTS: American Electric Power/Public Service Company of Oklahoma; Dr Pepper/Seven Up, Inc.; Big Red Incorporated; Oklahoma Liquefied Gas Co., Inc.; Oklahoma Rural Water Association; West Resources, Inc.; Raydon Exploration, Inc.; Zinke & Trumbo, Inc.; Tener's Western Outfitters; Canadian Oil & Gas Services, Inc.; Jamestown Office Park, LLC; Magnum Supply Company, Inc.; Queen Ann Cafeteria, Inc.; Intrust Bank, N.A.; Fox Broadcasting Co., Inc.; Hometown Auto Sales, Inc.; Motor City, Inc.; Knippelmier Chevrolet, Inc.; The Empire District Electric Company; LPM Parts & Service; Professional Animal Health, Inc.; Solidtech Animal Health, Inc.; The Veterinary Pharmacy, Inc.; Solidose, LLC; Dobbins Ranch; Rebel Oil Company; Covington Oil Co., Inc.; Green Transportation, Inc.; Martin-Foster's Fuel Service, Inc.; Platinum Equity, LLC; The Shoppes at North Pointe, LLC; Elder & Vaughn, Inc.; Legends Sports Complex; The Neiman Marcus Group, Inc.; Richardson Auto Group; NextiraOne, LLC; K.S. Oil Company, Inc.; Nutopicals, L.L.C.; Centerpoint Energy Resources Corp. dba Centerpoint Energy Oklahoma Gas.

WHITE & WEDDLE, P.C.

5532 NORTH WESTERN
OKLAHOMA CITY, OKLAHOMA 73118
Telephone: 405-858-8899
Fax: 405-858-8844

Criminal State and Federal, Personal Injury, Education Law, General Civil Practice.

JOE E. WHITE, JR., born Roswell, New Mexico, October 27, 1962; admitted to bar, 1988, Oklahoma and U.S. District Court, Eastern, Western and Northern Districts of Oklahoma; 1990, U.S. District Court, Eastern and Northern Districts of Texas; 1991, U.S. District Court, District of Colorado. *Education:* Central State University (B.A., 1985); University of Oklahoma (J.D., 1988). Trustee: Oklahoma Student Loan Authority, 1991-1996; University of Central Oklahoma Foundation, 1992-2000. *Member:* Oklahoma County and Oklahoma Bar Associations; American Trial Lawyers Association; Oklahoma Trial Lawyers Association. ***PRACTICE AREAS:*** Personal Injury; Wrongful Death; Class Actions; Insurance Bad Faith; Products Liability; Nursing Home Negligence; Medical Malpractice; General Civil Practice; Criminal Defense. **Email:** joewhite@coxinet.net

CHARLES C. WEDDLE III, born Oklahoma City, Oklahoma, November 14, 1973; admitted to bar, 2000, Oklahoma and U.S. District Court, Western and Eastern Districts of Oklahoma. *Education:* University of Oklahoma (B.A., 1997); Oklahoma City University (J.D., 2000). Phi Delta Phi. *Member:* Oklahoma County Bar Association; Oklahoma Bar Association; Oklahoma Trial Lawyers Association. ***PRACTICE AREAS:*** Personal Injury; Wrongful Death; Class Actions; Insurance Bad Faith; Products Liability; Medical Malpractice; General Civil Practice; Criminal Defense. **Email:** charlesweddle@coxinet.net

ASSOCIATES

MARVEL E. LEWIS, born El Paso, Texas, February 10, 1966; admitted to bar, 2002, Oklahoma and U.S. District Court, Western and Eastern Districts of Oklahoma. *Education:* Central State University (B.A., 1989); Oklahoma City University (J.D., 2002). *Member:*

(This Listing Continued)

WHITE & WEDDLE, P.C., Oklahoma City—Continued

Oklahoma Bar Association; Oklahoma County Bar Association; Oklahoma Trial Lawyers Association. ***PRACTICE AREAS:*** Personal Injury; Family Law; General Civil Practice; Criminal Defense. ***Email:*** marvellewis@coxinet.net

JOSHUA L. PARKINSON, born Deadwood, South Dakota, December 1, 1977; admitted to bar, 2004, Oklahoma; 2005, U.S. District Court, Western District of Oklahoma. *Education:* Northeastern State University (B.S., 2000); University of Oklahoma (J.D., 2004). *Member:* Oklahoma Bar Association. ***PRACTICE AREAS:*** Personal Injury; Family Law; General Civil Practice; Criminal Defense. ***Email:*** joshparkinson@coxinet.net

WHITTEN, NELSON, McGUIRE, TERRY & ROSELIUS

A Professional Limited Liability Company

SUITE 400, ONE LEADERSHIP SQUARE
211 NORTH ROBINSON
OKLAHOMA CITY, OKLAHOMA 73102
Telephone: 405-239-2522
Fax: 405-239-2573
Email: whitten@whitten-nelson.com
URL: http://www.whitten-nelson.com

Products Liability, Civil Rights, Business & Commercial Litigation, Casualty and Fire Loss Insurance, Underinsured Motorist Coverage, Labor and Employment Law, Environmental Law, Professional Liability, Personal Injury, RICO, ERISA, Workers' Compensation. Trials in all State, Federal and Appellate Courts, Automobile and Trucking Defense, Construction Accidents, Insurance Coverage Disputes; ERISA Litigation.

FIRM PROFILE: Whitten, Nelson, McGuire, Terry & Roselius is a broad based full service law firm that combines legal talent and up-to-date technology to produce high-quality, yet cost-effective, legal services for its clients. The firm's attorneys are supported by a staff of skilled and experienced managers, paralegals, investigators and legal secretaries, all using the latest in computerized equipment, services, and research capabilities.

The firm prides itself on conducting aggressive discovery in order to facilitate an early and cost-effective evaluation and settlement if necessary. However, negotiation from a position of strength is always best. The firm's philosophy is that the most favorable settlements are reached when the opposition is convinced the prospects of winning at trials are poor. Therefore, the firm prepares every case as if it were going to trial. The firm's track record in the courtroom is outstanding.

The firm is listed in The Bar Register of Preeminent Lawyers and is a Member of American Law Firm Associates, International (ALFA).

REGGIE N. WHITTEN, born Seminole, Oklahoma, May 23, 1955; admitted to bar, 1980, Oklahoma, U.S. District Court, Northern, Eastern and Western Districts of Oklahoma and U. S. Court of Appeals, Tenth Circuit. *Education:* University of Oklahoma (B.A., 1977; J.D., 1980). Author, Articles for, "The Defense Magazine" and "Am Jur." Listed in "Best Lawyers in America." *Member:* Oklahoma County and Oklahoma Bar Associations; Oklahoma Association of Defense Counsel; Oklahoma Association of Municipal Attorneys; Federation of Insurance and Corporate Counsel; Defense Research Institute; American Law Firm Association. ***PRACTICE AREAS:*** Insurance Defense; Products Liability Law; Uninsured and Underinsured Motorists; Appellate Practice; Transportation Law; Civil Rights; Labor and Employment Law; Complex Litigation; Insurance Bad Faith Coverage; Personal Injury; Arbitration; Business Law; Civil Trial Practice; Commercial Litigation; Constitutional Law; Construction Law; Medical Malpractice; Professional Liability; Legal Malpractice. ***Email:*** whitten@whitten-nelson.com

ROBERT W. NELSON, born Oklahoma City, Oklahoma, March 1, 1955; admitted to bar, 1980, Oklahoma. *Education:* East Central University (B.S., 1977); University of Oklahoma (J.D., 1980). *Member:* Canadian County, Oklahoma County and Oklahoma (Outstanding Young Lawyer, 1984) Bar Associations; Oklahoma Trial Lawyers Association; American Board of Trial Advocacy. ***PRACTICE AREAS:*** Insurance; Civil Litigation; Personal Injury; Defense Litigation; Federal Litigation. ***Email:*** nelson@whitten-nelson.com

KENT R. McGUIRE, born Duncan, Oklahoma, February 16, 1963; admitted to bar, 1989, Oklahoma, U.S. District Court, Northern, Eastern and Western Districts of Oklahoma and U.S. Court of Appeals, Tenth Circuit. *Education:* East Central State University (B.A., 1985); Oklahoma City University (J.D., 1989). *Member:* Oklahoma County and Oklahoma Bar Associations; Oklahoma Association of Defense Counsel. ***PRACTICE AREAS:*** Insurance Defense; Uninsured and Underinsured Motorists; Transportation Law; Civil Rights; Employment Law; Product Liability Law; Appellate Practice; Civil Trial Practice; Commercial Litigation; Constitutional Law; Labor and Employment Law; Medical Malpractice; Personal Injury; Professional Liability; Workers' Compensation. ***Email:*** mcguire@whitten-nelson.com

DOUGLAS A. TERRY, born Tahlequah, Oklahoma, December 4, 1967; admitted to bar, 1993, Oklahoma, U.S. District Court, Northern, Eastern and Western Districts of Oklahoma and U.S. Court of Appeals, Tenth Circuit. *Education:* Northeastern Oklahoma State University (B.A., summa cum laude, 1990); University of Oklahoma (J.D., with distinction, 1993). Member, Oklahoma Law Review, 1991-1993. *Member:* Oklahoma County and Oklahoma Bar Associations; Oklahoma Association of Defense Counsel; Defense Research Institute. ***PRACTICE AREAS:*** Insurance Defense Law; Transportation Law; Product Liability Law; Bad Faith; Insurance Coverage Disputes; Labor and Employment Law; Professional Liability; Appellate Practice; Civil Trial Practice; Commercial Litigation; Construction Law; Legal Malpractice; Personal Injury. ***Email:*** terryd@whitten-nelson.com

JASON E. ROSELIUS, born Amarillo, Texas, May 11, 1969; admitted to bar, 1995, Oklahoma, U.S. District Court, Northern, Eastern and Western Districts of Oklahoma and U.S. Court of Appeals, Tenth Circuit. *Education:* West Texas State University (B.A., magna cum laude, 1991); University of Oklahoma (J.D., 1995). Phi Delta Phi. *Member:* Oklahoma County and Oklahoma Bar Associations; Oklahoma Association of Defense Council; Defense Research Institute. ***PRACTICE AREAS:*** Insurance Defense Law; Automobile Accidents and Injuries; Products Liability Law; Personal Injury; Transportation Law; Labor and Employment Law; Insurance Bad Faith; Coverage Disputes; Civil Trial Practice; Appellate Practice; Civil Rights; Construction Law. ***Email:*** roselius@whitten-nelson.com

JIM T. PRIEST, born Syracuse, New York, June 3, 1955; admitted to bar, 1980, Oklahoma. *Education:* Houghton College (B.A., 1977); Syracuse University (J.D., 1980). Author: "Recent Developments in Oklahoma Class Action Law," University of Oklahoma Law Review, Volume 57, No. 4 (2005); "Watch Your Neck on White-Collar Exemption for Legal Assistants," Oklahoma Bar Journal, November 2004; "McKennon v. Nashville Banner, Two Wrongs Still Make a Civil Right," Oklahoma Bar Journal, 1995; "Pro Bono Aid Needed Now More Than Ever," American Bar Association Journal, June 1996; "The Wake of Hinson v. Cameron: Choppy Waters for the Law of Wrongful Discharge," Oklahoma Bar Journal, 1988; "Defending Police Misconduct Cases," Am Jur. Trials 2d, 1988; Defense of A Police Misconduct Suit, American Jurisprudence, Vol. 38, 1989. ***REPORTED CASES:*** E.E.O.C. v. W.H. Braum, Inc., 347 F.3d 1192 C.A.10 (Okla) 2003; Harris v. Allstate Ins. Co., 300 F.3d 1183 C.A.10 (Okla.) 2002; Lusk v. Ryder Intergrated Logistics, 238 F.3d 1237 C.A.10 (Okla.) 2001; Tsotaddle v. Absentee Shawnee Housing Authority, 20 P.3d 153 Okla-.Civ.App. Div. 4, 2000; Allen v. Muskogee, Okl., 19 F.3d 837 C.A.10 (Okl.) 1997; York v. American Tel. & Tel. Co., 95 F.3d 948 C.A.10 (Okl.) 1996; Anderson v. Oklahoma Temporary Services, Inc., 925 P.2d 574 Ok.App., 1996; Hayes v. Eateries, Inc., 905 P.2d 778 Okl. 1995; Banks v. Reynolds, 54 F.3d 1508 C.A.10 (Okl.) 1995; White v. York Intern. Corp., 45 F.3d 357 C.A.10 (Okl.) 1995; Metz v. Merrill Lynch, Pierce Fenner & Smith, Inc., 39 F.3d 1482 C.A.10 (Okl.) 1994; Berry v. Muskogee, 900 F.2d 1489 C.A.10 (Okl.) 1990. ***PRACTICE AREAS:*** Labor and Employment (80%); Civil Rights (15%); Insurance (5%). ***Email:*** jimpriest@whitten-nelson.com

G. PATRICK "PAT" O'HARA, born Elk City, Oklahoma, August 15, 1950; admitted to bar, 1992, Oklahoma. *Education:* Oklahoma State University (B.S., Accounting, 1972); University of Oklahoma (J.D., with highest honors, 1992). Order of the Coif. Recipient: American Jurisprudence Awards in Torts I and II, Civil Procedures I and II, Environmental Law, Criminal Procedure and Corporate Finance. Certified Public Accountant, 1973. Adjunct Professor of Law, University of Oklahoma College of Law, 1994-1996. *Member:* Oklahoma Bar Association; Oklahoma Society of Certified Public Accountants; American Institute of Certified Public Accountants. [U.S. Army Reserve, 1972-1978]. ***PRACTICE AREAS:*** Litigation (30%); Contracts (20%); Trusts and Estates (20%); Corporate Law (15%); Taxation (15%). ***Email:*** pat.ohara@whitten-nelson.com

PATRICK O'HARA, JR., born Stillwater, Oklahoma, November 27, 1969; admitted to bar, 1995, Oklahoma and U.S. District Court, Western, Northern and Eastern Districts of Oklahoma. *Education:* Oklahoma State University (B.S., Speech Communication, 1992); University of Oklahoma (J.D., with highest honors, 1995). Order of the Coif. Note Editor, Oklahoma Law Review, 1994-1995. Recipient: American Jurisprudence Awards in Torts I and II, Civil Procedure I, Antitrust, Legal Research and Writing and Trial Techniques; George B. Frasier Memorial Scholarship, 1993; Rayburn L. Foster Memorial Scholarship, 1994. *Member:* Oklahoma County, Oklahoma and American Bar Associations. ***PRACTICE AREAS:*** Class Actions; Oil and Gas Litigation; Personal Injury; Business Litigation; Health Care Litigation. ***Email:*** patrick.ohara@whitten-nelson.com

PHILIP W. ANDERSON, born San Francisco, California, December 17, 1948; admitted to bar, 1996, Oklahoma, U.S. District Court, Northern, Eastern and Western Districts of Oklahoma and U.S. Court of Appeals, Tenth Circuit. *Education:* Oklahoma City University (B.S., 1982; J.D., 1995). Phi Delta Phi. *Member:* Oklahoma County, Oklahoma and American Bar Associations. ***PRACTICE AREAS:*** Civil Practice; Appellate Practice; Construction Law; Insurance Defense; Labor and Employment Law; Civil Rights; Product Liability Law; Transportation Law; Personal Injury. ***Email:*** panderson@whitten-nelson.com

SIMONE GOSNELL FULMER, born Mesquite, Texas, October 14, 1967; admitted to bar, 1996, Oklahoma, U.S. District Court, Western District of Oklahoma and U.S. Court of Appeals, Tenth Circuit. *Education:* Oklahoma Baptist University (B.M.E., cum laude, 1989); University of Oklahoma College of Law (J.D., with distinction, 1996). Omicron Delta Kappa; The Order of Barristers. Member, Luther Bohannon American Inn of Court. Recipient, Academic Achievement in Trial Techniques, University of Oklahoma College of Law. *Member:* Oklahoma County and Oklahoma Bar Associations. ***PRACTICE AREAS:*** Uninsured and Underinsured Motorist Coverage; Life Insurance; Accident Insurance; Health Insurance; Insurance Bad Faith; Insurance Coverage Disputes; Civil Litigation; Appellate Practice. ***Email:*** sgfulmer@whitten-nelson.com

DERRICK T. DEWITT, born Beaver, Oklahoma, September 15, 1973; admitted to bar, 1998, Oklahoma. *Education:* Oklahoma State University (B.A., Economics, 1995); Oklahoma City University (J.D., cum laude, 1998). Phi Delta Phi. Oklahoma City University Law Review, 1996-1998. *Member:* Oklahoma County and Oklahoma Bar Associations. ***PRACTICE AREAS:*** Insurance Defense; Insurance Coverage; Civil Litigation; Personal Injury. ***Email:*** ddewitt@whitten-nelson.com

TIMOTHY DAVID EISEL, born Fort Belvoir, Virginia, April 7, 1966; admitted to bar, 1992, Oklahoma. *Education:* University of Oklahoma (B.S., Finance, 1988; J.D., 1992). Order of the Coif. ***PRACTICE AREAS:*** Employment Law (90%); Civil Rights Defense (10%). ***Email:*** teisel@whitten-nelson.com

---

R. GREGORY KIRBY, born Oklahoma City, Oklahoma, November 28, 1967; admitted to bar, 1996, Oklahoma, U.S. District Court, Western District of Oklahoma and U.S. Court of Appeals, Tenth Circuit. *Education:* University of Central Oklahoma (B.A., 1992); Oklahoma City University (J.D., 1996). Phi Delta Phi. *Member:* Oklahoma County and Oklahoma Bar Associations. ***PRACTICE AREAS:*** Insurance Defense; Insurance Coverage; Personal Injury; Civil Litigation; Products Liability; Administrative Law. ***Email:*** kirby@whitten-nelson.com

DERRICK L. MORTON, born Amarillo, Texas, January 28, 1973; admitted to bar, 1999, Oklahoma and U.S. District Court, Eastern, Western and Northern Districts of Oklahoma. *Education:* Texas Tech University (B.B.A., 1996); University of Oklahoma (J.D.,

(This Listing Continued)

1999). Phi Delta Phi. *Member:* Oklahoma County and Oklahoma Bar Associations. ***PRACTICE AREAS:*** Class Actions; Insurance; Torts; Products Liability; Personal Injury. ***Email:*** morton@whitten-nelson.com

THOMAS A. PARUOLO, born New Rochelle, New York, August 13, 1974; admitted to bar, 1999, Oklahoma and U.S. District Court, Western District of Oklahoma. *Education:* Baylor University (B.A., 1996); Syracuse University College of Law (J.D., 1999). ***PRACTICE AREAS:*** Insurance Defense; Construction Law; Title VII Discrimination. ***Email:*** tomp@whitten-nelson.com

KATHRYN D. TERRY, born Norman, Oklahoma, June 22, 1971; admitted to bar, 1996, Oklahoma, U.S. District Court, Western District of Oklahoma and U.S. Court of Appeals, Tenth Circuit; 1999, U.S. Court of Appeals for the Seventh and Eighth Circuit. *Education:* University of Oklahoma (B.A., summa cum laude, 1993; J.D., with honors, 1996). Phi Beta Kappa; Phi Kappa Phi; Order of the Coif. Member, William J. Holloway Inn of Court, 1999-2000. *Member:* Oklahoma County, Oklahoma and American Bar Associations; Defense Research Institute. ***PRACTICE AREAS:*** Insurance Defense; Employment Law; Products Liability Defense. ***Email:*** kterry@whitten-nelson.com

GUY R. WOOD, born Oklahoma City, Oklahoma, July 21, 1968; admitted to bar, 1993, Oklahoma and U.S. District Court, Northern, Western and Eastern Districts. *Education:* Cameron University (B.B.A., 1990); University of Oklahoma (J.D., 1993). Phi Delta Phi. *Member:* Oklahoma County and Oklahoma Bar Associations. ***PRACTICE AREAS:*** Oil and Gas Law; Insurance Bad Faith; Insurance Coverage Defense; Personal Injury. ***Email:*** guywood@whitten-nelson.com

CARIN L. MARCUSSEN, born Millington, Tennessee, October 31, 1977; admitted to bar, 2003, Tennessee and U.S. District Court, Western District of Oklahoma; 2004, U.S. District Court, Northern District of Oklahoma (Not admitted in Oklahoma). *Education:* Oklahoma State University (B.S., Finance and International Business, 2000); University of Oklahoma (J.D., 2004). Phi Alpha Delta. Recipient: Academic Achievement Awards in Evidence and International Trade Law, 2001; Academic Achievement Award in European Union Law, 2002; Albert C. Hunt Practice Court Award, 2003. Second Place, Intra-School Moot Court, University of Oklahoma, 2001. Regional Champions, Jessup International Moot Court, 2003. ***PRACTICE AREAS:*** Litigation. ***Email:*** cmarcussen@whitten-nelson.com

CHAD E. IHRIG, born Blackwell, Oklahoma, April 21, 1976; admitted to bar, 2002, Oklahoma and U.S. District Court, Western District of Oklahoma; 2003, U.S. District Court, Northern District of Oklahoma; 2004, U.S. Court of Appeals, Tenth Circuit. *Education:* Oklahoma State University (B.S., Business Administration, 1998); University of Oklahoma (J.D., 2002). *Member:* Oklahoma and American Bar Associations; Defense Research Institute (Member, Litigation Section, 2002—). ***PRACTICE AREAS:*** Class Actions (60%); Insurance Litigation (10%); Nursing Home Litigation (10%); Drug and Medical Device Litigation (10%); Medical Malpractice (10%). ***Email:*** cihrig@whitten-nelson.com

LAUREN F. GUHL, born Lawton, Oklahoma, May 15, 1979; admitted to bar, 2004, Oklahoma. *Education:* University of Oklahoma (B.A., Letters, 2001; J.D., 2004). *Member:* Oklahoma and American Bar Associations; Association of Trial Lawyers of America. ***PRACTICE AREAS:*** Insurance Bad Faith (33%); Employment Law (33%); Civil Litigation (34%). ***Email:*** lfguhl@whitten-nelson.com

REPRESENTATIVE CLIENTS: Crum & Forster Commercial Insurance Co.; OML Municipal Assurance Group; Biomet, Inc.; Ferno Manufacturing Co.; Great West Casualty; Liberty Mutual; Manhattan Construction Co.; Medmarc Associations; S.C. Johnson & Son, Inc.; U.S. Xpress Co.; Consolidated Freightways; St. Paul-Travelers Ins. Co.; Kemper Ins. Co.; Columbia Ins. Group; Sight'n'Sound Appliance Centers, Inc.; Weyerhaeuser Co.; Pharmacists Mutual Ins. Co.; J.P. Morgan Chase & Co.; Legacy Bank; OU Medical Center; Braum's Inc.

WILLIAMS, BOX, FORSHEE & BULLARD, P.C.

Established in 1991

522 COLCORD DRIVE
OKLAHOMA CITY, OKLAHOMA 73102-2202
Telephone: 405-232-0080
Telecopier: 405-236-5814

Municipal Law, Zoning, Planning and Land Use, Real Estate, Eminent Domain, Municipal Redevelopment, Municipal Bonds, Public Finance, Corporate Law, Banks and Banking, Trust Law, Commercial Law, Business Litigation, Utility Law, Telephone Utility Regulation, Administrative Law, Public Law.

FIRM PROFILE: Williams, Box, Forshee & Bullard, P.C. is listed in the Bar Register of Preeminent Lawyers.

JOHN MICHAEL WILLIAMS, born July 14, 1949; admitted to bar, 1974, Oklahoma. *Education:* Oklahoma State University (B.S., 1971) Omicron Delta Kappa; University of Oklahoma (J.D., 1973). Phi Delta Phi. Law Day Moot Court Team. Assistant Municipal Counselor, 1974-1977 and Head, Planning Division, 1976-1977, Office of Municipal Counselor, City of Oklahoma City. Member, Board of Regents, 1984-2000 and Chairman, 1987-1997, Oklahoma City Community College. Adjunct Professor, Land Use Law, Oklahoma City University School of Law, 1987, 1988, 1992. Lecturer: "Boundary Disputes in Oklahoma," 1990, 1992, 1993, 1994; "Oklahoma Land Use: Current Issues in Subdivision Annexation and Zoning Law," National Business Institute, 2000. *Member:* Oklahoma County, Oklahoma and American Bar Associations; American Planning Association; Oklahoma Association of Municipal Attorneys; National Association of Bond Lawyers. ***PRACTICE AREAS:*** Municipal Law; Zoning, Planning and Land Use; Real Estate; Municipal Bonds; Municipal Redevelopment. ***Email:*** williams@wbfblaw.com

DENNIS R. BOX, born Oklahoma City, Oklahoma, April 5, 1953; admitted to bar, 1978, Oklahoma. *Education:* Oklahoma State University (B.S., 1975); Oklahoma City University (J.D., 1978). Phi Delta Phi. Member, Oklahoma City University Law Review. Author: "A Guide to Local Initiative and Referendum," The Oklahoma Bar Journal, Vol. 70, No. 4, 3841, 1999. Co-Author: "Before the Bulldozer Comes: An Eminent Domain Guide for the Landowner," The Oklahoma Bar Journal, Vol. 72, No. 24, August 11, 2001; "Condemnation: A Special Statutory Proceeding," The Oklahoma Bar Journal, Vol. 73, No. 15, May 11, 2002. Adjunct Professor, Land Use Law, Oklahoma City University School of Law, 1986—. Frequent Lecturer for the Conference on Consumer Finance Law and the National Business Institute and Lorman Education Services. Assistant Municipal Counselor, 1977-1980 and Legal Counsel, Planning Commission, 1979-1980, City of Oklahoma City. Barrister, American Inns of Court. *Member:* Oklahoma County, Oklahoma and American Bar Associations; American Planning Association; Association of Municipal Attorneys. Fellow, Oklahoma Bar Foundation (Trustee, 1985-1986). ***PRACTICE AREAS:*** Eminent Domain; Municipal Law; Zoning, Planning and Land Use. ***Email:*** drbox@wbfblaw.com

RICHARD D. FORSHEE, born Oklahoma City, Oklahoma, November 13, 1951; admitted to bar, 1980, Oklahoma. *Education:* Oklahoma State University (B.S., 1974); Oklahoma City University (J.D., with distinction, 1979). Phi Delta Phi; Phi Eta Sigma. Adjunct Professor, Oklahoma City Community College, Negotiable Instruments, Letters of Credit, Banking Law, 1983-1985. Lecturer, "Letters of Credit," American Institute of Banking, 1983, 1984; "Banking Law," Oklahoma City University School of Law, 1983, 1984, "Commercial Loan Documentation," Oklahoma University School of Law, 1984. Member, Oklahoma State Credit Union Board, 2001. *Member:* Oklahoma County, Oklahoma (Member, Banking Law Section) and American (Member, Section of Corporation, Banking and Business Law) Bar Associations; National Association of Bond Lawyers. ***PRACTICE AREAS:*** Commercial Law; Banks and Banking; Credit Union Law; Trust Law; Public Finance Law. ***Email:*** forshee@wbfblaw.com

KEITH R. GIBSON, born Fulton, New York, February 24, 1954; admitted to bar, 1984, Oklahoma and U.S. District Court, Eastern, Western and Northern Districts of Oklahoma and Northern District of Texas, Dallas Division. *Education:* Lycoming College (B.A., 1976); Adelphi University (Paralegal Certificate, 1976); Oklahoma City University (J.D., 1984). Phi Delta Phi. Research Editor, Oklahoma City University Law Review, 1983-1984. Member, Moot Court Board. Recipient, American Jurisprudence Award, Agency, Partnerships and Corporations. Author: "Corporate Social Responsibility: Antithesis of Classical Capitalism," Vol. 10 Oklahoma City University Law Review 343, Summer, 1985. Law Clerk, Hon. Don Barnes, Chief Justice, Oklahoma Supreme Court, 1983-1984. Instructor, Real Estate Law: American Institute of Paralegal Studies, 1989; Oklahoma City University Legal Assistant Program, 1990-1998. Lecturer, Continuing Legal Education Seminars on the following topics: Successful Judgment Collection; Foreclosure and Repossession; Document Production and Organization; The Paralegal's Role in Real Estate Transactions, 1998-2000. *Member:* Oklahoma County (Member, Bankruptcy and Commercial Law Sections) and Oklahoma Bar Associations. ***PRACTICE AREAS:*** Bankruptcy; Real Estate; Commercial Litigation. ***Email:*** kgibson@wbfblaw.com

PAUL E. LEFEBVRE, born Oklahoma City, Oklahoma, May 8, 1952; admitted to bar, 1995, Oklahoma. *Education:* University of Oklahoma (B.A., 1976); American Graduate School of International Management (M.I.M., 1978); Oklahoma City University (J.D., magna cum laude, 1994). Phi Delta Phi. Recipient: American Jurisprudence Award, Contracts. Member, Law Review. *Member:* Oklahoma County and Oklahoma Bar Associations. ***PRACTICE AREAS:*** Real Estate; Zoning, Planning and Land Use; Municipal Law. ***Email:*** lefebvre@wbfblaw.com

AUDREY D. BLANK, born Montclair, New Jersey, September 20, 1952; admitted to bar, 2000, Oklahoma. *Education:* Elizabethtown College (B.A., cum laude, 1974); Oklahoma City University School of Law (J.D., magna cum laude, 2000). Member, Law Review. Co-Author: "Before the Bulldozer Comes: An Eminent Domain Guide for the Landowner," The Oklahoma Bar Journal, Vol. 72, No. 24, August 11, 2001; "Condemnation: A Special Statutory Proceeding," The Oklahoma Bar Journal, Vol. 73, No. 15, May 11, 2002. *Member:* Oklahoma County, Oklahoma and American Bar Associations; American Planning Association. ***PRACTICE AREAS:*** Land Use; Real Estate; Eminent Domain; Municipal Law. ***Email:*** ablank@wbfblaw.com

MICHAEL D. O'NEAL, born Thousand Oaks, California, October 2, 1977; admitted to bar, 2004, Oklahoma and California. *Education:* Oklahoma Christian College (B.S., 2001); Pepperdine University (Entrepreneurship and Technology Certificate, 2003); Pepperdine University School of Law (J.D., 2003). Phi Alpha Delta. *Member:* Oklahoma County and Oklahoma Bar Associations; State Bar of California. ***PRACTICE AREAS:*** Municipal Law; Land Use; Real Estate; Municipal Bonds. ***Email:*** moneal@wbfblaw.com

OF COUNSEL

WILLIAM J. BULLARD, born Oklahoma City, Oklahoma, November 24, 1948; admitted to bar, 1975, Oklahoma. *Education:* University of Oklahoma (B.B.A., 1971; J.D., 1975). Assistant Attorney General, Charitable Foundations, State of Ohio, 1976-1978. Administrative Assistant, U.S. Congressman Mike Synar, 1979-1982. Assistant Attorney General, Utility Regulation and Environment, State of Oklahoma, 1983-1985. First Assistant Attorney General, State of Oklahoma, 1985-1987. *Member:* Oklahoma County and Oklahoma Bar Associations. ***PRACTICE AREAS:*** Utility Law; Administrative Law; Telephone Utility Regulation.

WILSON, CAIN & ACQUAVIVA

Established in 1982

300 N.W. 13TH STREET, SUITE 100
OKLAHOMA CITY, OKLAHOMA 73103-3739
Telephone: 405-236-2600
Fax: 405-236-2607
Email: wcaokc@swbell.net
URL: http://www.wca-law.com

Tulsa Office: 1717 South Boulder Avenue, Suite 801, 74119-4805. Telephone: 918-583-4777. Fax: 918-583-0774.

General Civil Trial Practice State and Federal Courts. Products Liability, Fire and Casualty Insurance Defense, Insurance Coverage, Uninsured Motorist, Bad Faith Law, Professional Malpractice Defense, Veterinary and Insurance Defense, Workers Compensation, Subrogation Insurance Defense, including Personal Injury, Automobile Accidents, Wrongful Death.

(This Listing Continued)

WILSON, CAIN & ACQUAVIVA, Oklahoma City—Continued

MEMBERS OF FIRM

DAVID D. WILSON, born Oklahoma City, Oklahoma, October 6, 1944; admitted to bar, 1970, Oklahoma. *Education:* Westminster College; University of Oklahoma (B.B.A., 1967); University of Oklahoma (J.D., 1970). Phi Delta Phi. *Member:* Oklahoma County and Oklahoma Bar Associations; Oklahoma Association of Defense Counsel. (Also at Tulsa Office). ***PRACTICE AREAS:*** Insurance Defense; Insurance Coverage; Uninsured and Underinsured Motorists; Insurance Bad Faith; Products Liability; Fire and Casualty; Veterinary Law. ***Email:*** davidwca@swbell.net

TIMOTHY D. CAIN, born Oklahoma City, Oklahoma, February 7, 1961; admitted to bar, 1986, Oklahoma. *Education:* University of Oklahoma (B.B.A., 1983; J.D., 1986). American Inn of Court. *Member:* Oklahoma County, Oklahoma and American Bar Associations; Oklahoma School Board Attorneys Association; Oklahoma Association of Defense Counsel; Defense Research Institute; National Institute of Trial Advocacy. ***PRACTICE AREAS:*** Insurance Defense; Insurance Coverage; Products Liability; Fire and Casualty. ***Email:*** timcain@swbell.net

JOSEPH T. ACQUAVIVA, JR., born Queens, New York, May 25, 1959; admitted to bar, 1986, Oklahoma. *Education:* Long Island University (B.A., 1983); Oklahoma City University (J.D., 1986). Guest Lecturer, L.S.U. National Institute of Trial Advocacy Training Program. *Member:* Oklahoma County, Oklahoma and American Bar Associations; Oklahoma Association of Defense Counsel; National Institute of Trial Advocacy; Defense Research Institute. ***PRACTICE AREAS:*** Insurance Defense; Insurance Coverage; Products Liability; Fire and Casualty; Insurance Bad Faith. ***Email:*** jtacq@aol.com

ASSOCIATES

AMY L. LOUGHRIDGE, born Tulsa, Oklahoma, March 24, 1970; admitted to bar, 1998, Oklahoma. *Education:* Southern Methodist University (B.A., 1992); University of Tulsa (J.D., 1997). Delta Theta Phi. Recipient, Rogers Scholarship, 1996, 1997. *Member:* Oklahoma County and Oklahoma Bar Associations. ***PRACTICE AREAS:*** Insurance Defense. ***Email:*** Amol.Thomas@aol.com

BARBARA K. BURATTI, born New York, N.Y., May 8, 1951; admitted to bar, 1987, Oklahoma. *Education:* Temple University (B.A., cum laude, 1973); Georgia State University (M.Ed., 1981); University of Oklahoma (J.D., 1987). *Member:* Oklahoma County and Oklahoma Bar Associations; Oklahoma Association of Defense Counsel. ***PRACTICE AREAS:*** Insurance Defense; Insurance Coverage Law; Products Liability; Nursing Home Defense; Commercial Law. ***Email:*** barbarab@wcalaw.com

BILL M. ROBERTS, born Muskogee, Oklahoma, June 16, 1953; admitted to bar, 1980, Oklahoma, U.S. District Court, Northern, Western and Eastern Districts of Oklahoma and U.S. Court of Appeals, Tenth Circuit. *Education:* Central State University (B.B.A., 1976); Oklahoma City University (J.D., 1980). *Member:* Oklahoma County, Oklahoma and American Bar Associations; Oklahoma Association of Defense Counsel; Defense Research Institute; American Law Firm Association. ***PRACTICE AREAS:*** Products Liability Law; Environmental Litigation; Insurance Litigation. ***Email:*** billr@wcalaw.com

TRAVIS DUNN, born Pasadena, Texas, March 24, 1970; admitted to bar, 1995, Oklahoma and U.S. District Court, Western, Northern and Eastern Districts of Oklahoma. *Education:* Oklahoma State University (B.S., Accounting, 1992); University of Oklahoma (J.D., 1995). Phi Alpha Delta. *Member:* Oklahoma County and Oklahoma Bar Associations. ***REPORTED CASES:*** Harwick v. Purcell Municip. Hospital, et al., 975 P.2d 453 (Okla. 1999). ***PRACTICE AREAS:*** Medical Malpractice; Employment Law; Personal Injury. ***Email:*** travisd@wcalaw.com

FRANCES J. ARMSTRONG, born McAlester, Oklahoma, April 8, 1948; admitted to bar, 1987, Oklahoma, U.S. District Court, Northern, Western and Eastern Districts of Oklahoma and U.S. Court of Appeals, Tenth Circuit. *Education:* East Central State College; Central State College (B.S., 1969); University of Tulsa (J.D., 1987). Phi Delta Phi; Order of the Curule Chair. Staff Member, Energy Law Journal, 1985-1987. Recipient, American Jurisprudence Award, Civil Procedure II. *Member:* Tulsa County, Oklahoma County and Oklahoma Bar Associations; The Association of Trial Lawyers of America. ***PRACTICE AREAS:*** Insurance; Litigation; Personal Injury; Products Liability. ***Email:*** francesa@wcalaw.com

KEVIN M. WALOS, born Lewiston, New York, July 1, 1967; admitted to bar, 1993, Oklahoma; 1994, District of Columbia and U.S. District Court, Northern, Eastern and Western Districts of Oklahoma. *Education:* State University of New York at Buffalo (B.A., 1990); University of Oklahoma (J.D., 1993). *Member:* Oklahoma Bar Association; The District of Columbia Bar. ***PRACTICE AREAS:*** Insurance Defense; Insurance Subrogation. ***Email:*** kevinw@wcalaw.com

REPRESENTATIVE CLIENTS: State Farm Mutual Automobile Insurance Co.; The Ohio Casualty Insurance Companies; Oklahoma Farm Bureau Mutual Insurance Co.; American Mercury Insurance Company; Mid-Continent Casualty Company, USAA; National American Insurance Company; Progressive Northern Insurance Company; State Farm Fire and Casualty Co.; American States Insurance Company; The Dolese Company; Atlantic Mutual Insurance Co.; Northland Insurance Co.; American Fidelity Insurance Companies; Church Mutual Insurance Co.; Comanche County Memorial Hospital; Hobby Lobby; Trend Drilling; Advance Food Company, Inc.; State Insurance Fund; Clarendon National Insurance Co.; Monaco Coach Corporation; CNA Companies; Encompass Insurance Company; Kemper Insurance Company; Service Casualty Insurance Company; Union Standard Insurance Company; St. Anthony's Hospital; Today Homes, Inc.; 1st National Banks of Weatherford and Thamas; InterAmerican Manufacturing, Inc.; UICI.

E. VANCE WINNINGHAM

2200 N.W. 50TH STREET, SUITE 240

OKLAHOMA CITY, OKLAHOMA 73112

Telephone: 405-843-1037

Fax: 405-848-2463

URL: http://www.americanvisas.com

Immigration Law.

(This Listing Continued)

E. VANCE WINNINGHAM, born Oklahoma City, Oklahoma, April 23, 1942; admitted to bar, 1966, Oklahoma; 1971, U.S. Supreme Court. *Education:* Oklahoma State University (B.S., 1966); University of Oklahoma (J.D., 1966). Listed more than 10 consecutive years in The Best Lawyers in America (1994-2006). Member of the first Board of Trustees of the American Immigration Law Foundation based in Washington, D.C. Founder and Administrator of internet based network of nationally prominent immigration lawyers (www.AmericanVisas.com). *Member:* Oklahoma County, Oklahoma and Federal Bar Associations; American Immigration Lawyers of America (Former President, Texas - Oklahoma - New Mexico Chapter); Oklahoma Lawyers for Children. ***PRACTICE AREAS:*** Immigration and Naturalization.

J. KELLY WORK

HIGHTOWER BUILDING

105 N. HUDSON, SUITE 304

OKLAHOMA CITY, OKLAHOMA 73102

Telephone: 405-232-2790

Fax: 405-232-3966

Email: jkwork@sbcglobal.com

URL: http://www.lawyers.com/kellywork

Real Property, Business and Commercial, Employment, Litigation, Municipal, Land Use, Landlord/Tenant, Municipal Bond Law.

J. KELLY WORK, born Oklahoma City, Oklahoma, February 25, 1955; admitted to bar, 1980, Oklahoma. *Education:* University of Oklahoma (B.B.A., 1977; J.D. 1980). Assistant Municipal Counselor, 1980-1982 and Legal Counsel to Board of Adjustment, 1981-1982, City of Oklahoma City. *Member:* Oklahoma County, Oklahoma and American Bar Associations. (Also of Counsel to The Shirk Law Firm, P.C.). ***PRACTICE AREAS:*** Real Property; Business Law; Commercial Law; Employment Law; Litigation; Municipal; Land Use; Eminent Domain; Zoning Law; Tax Exempt Finance.

REPRESENTATIVE CLIENTS: Archon Group; Central Oklahoma United Methodist Retirement Facility (dba "Epworth Villa"); Family Dollar Stores; Horn Seed Co.; Little Giant Pump Co.; Locke Supply Co.; McDonald's Corp.; Sun Pipe Line Co.; Williams Pipe Line Co.

CLIFFORD A. WRIGHT, P.C.

SUITE 1300, TWO LEADERSHIP SQUARE

211 NORTH ROBINSON

OKLAHOMA CITY, OKLAHOMA 73102-7114

Telephone: 405-235-5880

Fax: 405-235-5664

Email: cawpclaw@aol.com

URL: http://www.cliffordawrightpc.com

General Civil Trial Practice, Appellate Practice in all Courts in Oklahoma, including Business, Commercial, Oil and Gas Contracts, Securities, Collections, Bankruptcy, Insolvency Law, Creditors Rights, Domestic Relations, Family Law, Real Estate, Corporations, Limited Liability Companies, Federal and State Taxation, Insurance, Estate Planning, Probate and Estate Administration, Health Care Law, Administrative Law, Torts (including Negligence, and Personal and Business Injuries), Taxing Agencies, Elder Law, Employment Law.

CLIFFORD A. WRIGHT, born Tulsa, Oklahoma, 1950; admitted to bar, 1977, Oklahoma, U.S. Tax Court and U.S. Claims Court; 1978, U.S. District Court, Western, Eastern and Northern Districts of Oklahoma and U.S. Court of Appeals, Tenth Circuit; U.S. Supreme Court. *Education:* University of Washington (B.A., 1974); Oklahoma City University (J.D., 1976); Boston University (LL.M. in Taxation, 1977). Phi Delta Phi. Author: "Use of Revocable Trusts in Business and Estate Planning," Oklahoma Home Builder and Builder Review, 1978; "Oil and Gas Drilling Programs: Preparing the Documentation," Clark Boardman Company, Ltd., 1984. Co-Author: "Tax Aspects of Oil and Gas Programs," The Institute for Energy Development, 1979; "Investor Oriented Lease Acquisition Funds," The Institute for Energy Development, 1980. Contributing Author: "Securities and Partnership Law for MLP's & Other Investment Limited Partnerships," Clark Boardman Company, Ltd., 1989. *Member:* Oklahoma and American Bar Associations; The Association of Trial Lawyers of America; Oklahoma Trial Lawyers Association. [U.S. Army, 1968-1970]. ***REPORTED CASES:*** Tenneco Oil Company v. Richard D. Bogert, et al., 630 F.Supp. 961 (W.D. Oklahoma, 1986); Peabody Coal Company v. State of Oklahoma ex rel Commissioners of the Land Office, 1992 OkCiv App 83, 884 P.2d 857; Texaco, Inc. V. Berry Petroleum Corporation et al, 869 F.Supp. 1523, 131 Oil & Gas Rep. 81 (W.D. Oklahoma, December 5, 1994); Oklahoma Employers Safety Group, SIA v. Colbert Nursing Home, Inc., 1997 OK 94, 954 P.2d 120; In re Magnolia Gas Company, LLC et al v. Compression Solutions Co., LLC, 255 B.R. 900 (United States Bankruptcy Court, W.D. Oklahoma, November 21, 2000); Rose Group, LLC v. Brian R. Miller, et al 2003 OK CIV APP 18 64 P.3d 573; State of Oklahoma, ex rel. State Insurance Fund v. Great Plains Care Center, Inc., 2003 OK 79, 78 P.3d 83; Chesapeake Exploration Limited Partnership v. Chesapeake Exploration Limited Partnership, Chespeake Operating, Inc. and Evok, Inc., 2004 Ok. Civ.App. 94, 103 P.3d 621. ***Email:*** cawpclaw@aol.com

REPRESENTATIVE CLIENTS: Carl Albert State College; Energy Fluids, Inc.; EXOK, Inc.; LTC Services, Inc.; Mitchell Health Care; Spectrum Investments, Inc.; Snake Creek; Manna, LLC; OTC Petroleum Corporation; MBO Video, Inc.

WYATT LAW OFFICE

501 NORTH WALKER AVENUE, SUITE 110
P.O. BOX 1947
OKLAHOMA CITY, OKLAHOMA 73101
Telephone: 405-234-5500
Fax: 405-232-4556
Email: bobwyatt@wyattlaw.com
URL: http://www.wyattlaw.com

Statewide criminal practice in Oklahoma and in federal courts nationwide. Focus on sex crimes and pornography, drug crimes, conspiracy, homicide and violence, white collar crimes (such as mail fraud, bank crimes, embezzlement), grand jury investigations, appeals and expungement.

ROBERT L. WYATT, IV, born Las Cruces, New Mexico, 1964; admitted to bar, 1989, Oklahoma, U.S. District Court, Eastern, Northern and Western Districts of Oklahoma, U.S. Court of Appeals, Eighth and Tenth Circuits, and U.S. Supreme Court. *Education:* Southeastern Oklahoma State University (B.S., with honors, 1986); University of Oklahoma College of Law (J.D., 1989). Alpha Chi; Phi Delta Phi. Listed in: Who's Who in American Law (9th—); Who's Who in America (1997—). Contributing Author, "Vernon's Oklahoma Forms, 2d: Criminal Practice and Procedure." Deputy Special Counsel to Governor of Oklahoma, 1995. *Member:* Oklahoma; American Inns of Court, Luther Bohanon Chapter; National Association of Criminal Defense Lawyers (Life Member); Oklahoma Criminal Defense Lawyers Association; National Institute for Trial Advocacy. ***REPORTED CASES:*** U.S. v. Avery, 34 F.3d 1517 (10th Cir. 1994); Creason v. Perry, 801 P.2d 715 (Okla. 1990). ***PRACTICE AREAS:*** Criminal Law; Drug Crimes; Sex Crimes; Federal Criminal Law; Criminal Conspiracy; Search and Seizure; Homicide; Grand Jury Practice; White Collar Crime; Medicare Fraud and Abuse; Mail Fraud; Criminal Appeals. ***Email:*** bobwyatt@wyattlaw.com

REPRESENATIVE CLIENTS: Associates Financial Services, Inc.; City of Enid; Crawford & Co.; E& O Professionals; Excel Corp.(Cargill, Inc.); Lowe's Home Improvement Warehouse; National American Insurance Company; Old Surety Life Insurance Company.
LOCAL COUNSEL FOR: Luckinbill, Inc. (Mechanical Contractors).

THE BARKSDALE LAW FIRM, P.C.

Established in 1947
310 EAST SEVENTH STREET
P.O. BOX 1366
OKMULGEE, OKLAHOMA 74447
Telephone: 918-756-0900
Fax: 918-756-0943
URL: http://www.barksdalelawfirm@hotmail.com
URL: http://www.lawyers.com/brwlaw

Civil Trial Practice, Business Organization and Litigation, Probate, Oil and Gas, Real Estate, Bankruptcy-Creditor only, Estate Planning-Trusts.

DALE F. RAINEY (1907-1987)

JOHN H. W. BARKSDALE (1915-1999)

BILL BARKSDALE, born Okmulgee, Oklahoma, November 7, 1947; admitted to bar, 1973, Oklahoma and U.S. District Court, Northern, Western and Eastern Districts of Oklahoma; 1974, U.S. Court of Appeals, Tenth Circuit; 1976, U.S. Supreme Court. *Education:* University of Oklahoma (B.A., 1970; J.D., 1973). Municipal Judge, City of Okmulgee, 1979—.

GENERAL COUNSEL FOR: Citizens Bank & Trust Co.; Okmulgee Memorial Hospital, Inc.; East Central Oklahoma Rural Electric Cooperative, Inc.

INGLISH & GAITHER

PROFESSIONAL CORPORATION
MCCULLOCH BUILDING
114 NORTH GRAND, SUITE 408
P.O. BOX 130
OKMULGEE, OKLAHOMA 74447
Telephone: 918-756-5274
Fax: 918-756-0502
Email: ig@inglishgaither.com

Henryetta, Oklahoma Office: 405 West Trudgeon Street, P.O. Box 1090, 74437. Telephone: 918-652-4402. Facsimile: 918-652-4487.

General Civil Practice in all State and Federal Courts. Probate, Oil and Gas, Real Estate, Banking, Bankruptcy (Creditor), Corporation, Mortgage Foreclosures, Estate Planning Law, Title Insurance, Family Law, Personal Injury.

GEORGE R. INGLISH (1912-1998)

ROBERT INGLISH, born Okmulgee, Oklahoma, January 8, 1954; admitted to bar, 1979, Oklahoma and U.S. District Court, Eastern and Northern Districts of Oklahoma; U.S. Court of Appeals, Tenth Circuit. *Education:* Oklahoma State University (B.S., 1976); University of Oklahoma (J.D., 1978). Title Insurance Agent: Lawyers Title; Land America; First American Title. City Attorney, Beggs, Oklahoma, 1979-1981. Municipal Judge, Morris, Oklahoma, 1980-1985. Adjunct Professor, University of Tulsa, 1989-1994; 1996. *Member:* Okmulgee County (President, 1992), Oklahoma (Recipient, Courageous Advocacy Award, 1988; Board of Directors, Bankruptcy Section, 1989-1994; Chairman, 1992) and American Bar Associations; American Civil Liberties Union of Oklahoma (Legal Counsel, 1989-1994). ***REPORTED CASES:*** Parents of Child v. Coker, et al, 676 F Supp 1072 (ED Okl. 1987); Matter of Estate of Maheras 897 P.2d 268 (Okl. 1995); In Re: Cluck, 101 BR 691 (BR ED Okl. 1989). In Re: Scott, 121 BR 605 (BR ED Okl. 1990). In Re: Treiber, 92 BR 930 (BR ND Okl. 1988). Fidelity Savings & Investment Co. v. New Hope Baptist, 880 F2d

(This Listing Continued)

1172 (CA 10 Okl. 1989). In Re: Jones, 107 BR 350 (BR ED Okl. 1989). In Re: Beck, 128 BR 571 (Br ED Okl. 1991). In Re: Johnston Energy, Inc., 101 BR 684 (Br ED Okl. 1988). Wade v. Bradford, 39 F3d 1126 (CA 10 Okl. 1994). ***PRACTICE AREAS:*** Probate; Trust Law; Oil and Gas Law; Real Estate Bankruptcy; Creditors Rights; Mortgage Foreclosure; Estate Planning. ***Email:*** robert@inglishgaither.com

LUKE GAITHER, born Okmulgee, Oklahoma, December 21, 1972; admitted to bar, 1998, Oklahoma. *Education:* Northeastern Oklahoma State University (B.A., summa cum laude, 1995); University of Tulsa (J.D., with highest honors, 1998). Phi Delta Phi; Order of the Curule Chair. Notes and Comments Editor, Tulsa Law Journal, 1997-1998. Associate Editor, Oklahoma Bar Journal, 2002—. *Member:* Okmulgee County and Oklahoma (Director, 2000— and Secretary, 2003, Young Lawyer Division) Bar Associations. Fellow, Oklahoma Bar Foundation. (Also at Henryetta Office). ***PRACTICE AREAS:*** Civil Practice; Trial Practice; Family Law; Contracts; Probate; Business Law; Real Estate; Trust Law; Banking Law; Personal Injury. ***Email:*** luke@inglishgaither.com

GENERAL COUNSEL FOR: The First National Bank and Trust Co. of Okmulgee, Okmulgee, Oklahoma; American Exchange Bank, Henryetta; First National Bank of Henryetta.
REPRESENTATIVE CLIENTS: Morris State Bank, Morris, Oklahoma; Okmulgee Ready-Mix Concrete Co.; Okmulgee Land Title Co.; Pine Properties, Inc.; American Heritage Bank, Beggs Branch; First United Bank, Durant; Sam K. Viersan Jr. Trust; First Family Credit Union, Henryetta.
APPROVED EXAMINING ATTORNEYS FOR: Rural Housing Service; Farm Service Agency; Lawyers Title; First American Title.

MICHAEL J. HESTER, INC.

OVERBROOK, OKLAHOMA

(See Ardmore)

General Civil Trial Practice. Corporate, Commercial, Farm, Ranch and Equine Law, Probate, Real Estate, Personal Injury, Wills, Trusts and Estate Planning.

SPENCE LAW OFFICE

OWASSO, OKLAHOMA

(See Tulsa)

Commercial and Civil Litigation, Construction Law, Real Property Law, General Practice Litigation, Trust and Estate Litigation, Bankruptcy.

GARVIN, AGEE, CARLTON & MASHBURN, L.L.P.

101 EAST GRANT AVENUE
PAULS VALLEY, OKLAHOMA 73075
Telephone: 405-238-5559; 888-238-5559
Fax: 405-238-5666
URL: http://www.attysatlaw.com

Oklahoma City Office: 2100 City Place Tower, 204 North Robinson Avenue, 73102. Telephone: 405-232-9996. Fax: 405-232-9979.

Litigation, Personal Injury, Medical Malpractice, Automobile Accidents, Slip and Fall, Wrongful Death, Nursing Home Abuse, Unsafe Products, Toxic Torts, Legal Malpractice, Insurance, Professional Liability, Business Law, Commercial Law, Contracts, Corporate Law, Education Law, Banking Law, Bankruptcy, Debtor and Creditor, Taxation, Tax Planning, Consumer Law, Consumer Fraud, Warranties, Natural Resources, Energy, Elder Law, Wills and Probate, Trusts and Estates, Estate Planning, Guardianship, Real Estate, Buying or Selling a Home, Construction Law, Landlord and Tenant, General Practice, Appellate Practice.

FIRM PROFILE: Further information available on website or upon request.

R.B. GARVIN (1906-1975)

ALAN AGEE, born 1934; admitted to bar, 1972, Oklahoma. *Education:* University of Oklahoma (B.B.A., 1956; J.D., 1972). ***PRACTICE AREAS:*** Litigation; Toxic Torts; Personal Injury; Medical Malpractice; Automobile Accidents; Slip and Fall; Wrongful Death; Nursing Home Abuse and Neglect; Legal Malpractice; Professional Liability; Business Law; Commercial Law; Contracts; Corporate Law; Banking Law; Bankruptcy; Debtor and Creditor; Consumer Law; Consumer Fraud; Warranty Law; Product Defects; Natural Resources; Energy Law; Elder Law; Real Estate; Construction Law; Landlord and Tenant Law; Insurance; Appellate Practice; General Practice.

BRETT AGEE, born 1963; admitted to bar, 1988, Oklahoma; 1996, Colorado. *Education:* University of Oklahoma (B.Acct., 1985; J.D., 1988). ***PRACTICE AREAS:*** Litigation; Unsafe Products; Toxic Torts; Personal Injury; Medical Malpractice; Automobile Accidents; Slip and Fall; Wrongful Death; Nursing Home Abuse and Neglect; Legal Malpractice; Professional Liability; Business Law; Commercial Law; Contracts; Corporate Law; Banking Law; Debtor and Creditor; Consumer Law; Consumer Fraud; Warranty Law; Construction Law; Insurance; Appellate Practice; General Practice.

JAMES W. CARLTON, JR., born 1962; admitted to bar, 1988, Oklahoma. *Education:* University of Oklahoma (B.Acct., 1985; J.D., 1988). ***PRACTICE AREAS:*** Business Law; Commercial Law; Contracts; Corporate Law; Education Law; Banking Law; Taxation; Tax Planning; Elder Law; Wills; Probate; Trusts and Estates; Estate Planning; Guardianship; Real Estate; Landlord and Tenant Law; General Practice.

JOHN D. MASHBURN, born 1959; admitted to bar, 1988, Oklahoma. *Education:* Virginia Polytechnic Institute and State University (B.S., 1981; M.S., 1983); University of Oklahoma (J.D., 1988). (Resident, Oklahoma City Office). ***PRACTICE AREAS:*** Litigation; Personal Injury; Medical Malpractice; Automobile Accidents; Slip and Fall; Wrongful Death; Nursing Home Abuse and Neglect; Toxic Torts; Legal Malpractice; Professional Liability; Business Law; Commercial Law; Contracts; Corporate Law; Banking Law; Bankruptcy; Debtor and Creditor; Consumer Law; Consumer Fraud; Warranty Law; Product Defects; Natural Resources; Construction Law; Landlord and Tenant Law; Insurance; Appellate Practice; General Practice.

(This Listing Continued)

GARVIN, AGEE, CARLTON & MASHBURN, L.L.P., Pauls Valley—Continued

STEVEN C. KENDALL, born 1966; admitted to bar, 1994, Oklahoma. *Education:* West Texas A & M (B.A., 1988); University of Oklahoma (J.D., 1994). ***PRACTICE AREAS:*** Litigation; Debtor and Creditor; Personal Injury; Automobile Accidents; Wrongful Death; Guardianship; General Practice.

B. DAVID SISSON

PAULS VALLEY, OKLAHOMA

(See Norman)

Bankruptcy, Domestic, Probate and Estate Planning, Family Law, Divorce, Child Custody Modifications.

BREWER, WORTEN, ROBINETT

Established in 1928

204 FIRST NATIONAL BANK BUILDING
PAWHUSKA, OKLAHOMA 74005
Telephone: 918-287-2200

Bartlesville, Oklahoma Office: 117 W. 5th Street, 500 Professional Building, P.O. Box 1066, 74005-1066. Telephone: 918-336-4132. Fax: 918-336-9009.

General Civil Practice. State and Federal Litigation. Corporate, Banking, Real Estate, Oil and Gas, Probate, Trust and Estate Planning, Family and Employment Law, Personal Injury and Insurance Defense.

(For complete biographical data on all personnel, see Professional Biographies at Bartlesville, Oklahoma)

WILLIAM J. PERRY

Established in 1966

522 ILLINOIS
P.O. BOX 372
PAWNEE, OKLAHOMA 74058-0372
Telephone: 918-762-2501
Fax: 918-762-2502

General Civil Trial Practice. Real Property, Probate, Wills, Corporate, Oil and Gas Law.

WILLIAM J. PERRY, born Carnegie, Oklahoma, April 3, 1941; admitted to bar, 1966, Oklahoma; 1967, New Mexico. *Education:* Oklahoma State University (B.S., 1963); University of Oklahoma (LL.B., 1966). Phi Alpha Delta. *Member:* Pawnee County (President, 1973-1987) and Oklahoma Bar Associations; State Bar of New Mexico.

REPRESENTATIVE CLIENT: First National Bank of Pawnee, Pawnee, Oklahoma.
REFERENCE: First National Bank of Pawnee, Pawnee, Oklahoma.

SPENCE LAW OFFICE

PERRY, OKLAHOMA

(See Tulsa)

Commercial and Civil Litigation, Construction Law, Real Property Law, General Practice Litigation, Trust and Estate Litigation, Bankruptcy.

ATKINS & MARKOFF

PONCA CITY, OKLAHOMA

(See Oklahoma City)

Personal Injury, Automobile Accidents, Wrongful Death, Trucking Accidents, Slip and Fall, Nursing Home Abuse, Head and Spinal Injuries, Dog Bites, Sexual Abuse, Criminal Law, Drug Crimes, DUI/DWI, Juvenile Crimes, General Practice, Family, Divorce, Adoptions, Child Custody, Child Support, Domestic Violence, Visitation Rights, Elder Law, Legal Malpractice, Medical Malpractice, Social Security, Social Security Disability, Taxation, IRS Audits, Property Tax Appeals, Tax Planning, Toxic Torts, Trust and Estate, Wills and Probate.

BAUMERT, CUMMINGS, HIATT & YOUNG

Established in 1949

HOME NATIONAL BANK BUILDING, SUITE 205
P.O. BOX 470
PONCA CITY, OKLAHOMA 74602
Telephone: 580-762-2403
Fax: 580-762-3166
URL: http://www.bchylawfirm.com

General Civil Practice in all Courts. Real Estate, Family Law, Probate, Banking, Taxation, Bankruptcy, Employment, Corporation, Insurance, Personal Injury and Negligence Law. Trials.

MEMBERS OF FIRM

L. ENLOE BAUMERT, born McAlester, Oklahoma, January 2, 1933; admitted to bar, 1959, Oklahoma. *Education:* Oklahoma State University (B.A., 1954); University of Oklahoma (LL.B., 1959). Phi Alpha Delta. President, Oklahoma Tax Institute, 1973. *Member:* Kay County (President, 1974), Oklahoma and American Bar Associations. ***PRACTICE AREAS:*** Estate Planning; Probate; Trust Law; Corporate Law.

(This Listing Continued)

DAVID S. CUMMINGS, born Ponca City, Oklahoma, October 27, 1952; admitted to bar, 1977, Oklahoma. *Education:* Central State University (B.S., 1974); University of Oklahoma (J.D., 1977). Phi Delta Phi. *Member:* Kay County (President, 1991), Oklahoma (Chairman, Banking and Commercial Law Section, 1984; Member, Board of Editors, Oklahoma Bar Journal, 1988-1990) and American Bar Associations. ***PRACTICE AREAS:*** Banking; Commercial; Real Estate; Business Organizations; Financing; Health Care; Litigation; Personal Injury; Estate Planning. ***Email:*** DavidCummings@cableone.net

DERRIN K. HIATT, born Blackwell, Oklahoma, September 24, 1964; admitted to bar, 1989, Oklahoma. *Education:* Oklahoma Christian College (B.A., magna cum laude, 1986); University of Oklahoma (J.D., 1989). Phi Delta Phi. *Member:* Kay County, Oklahoma and American Bar Associations. ***PRACTICE AREAS:*** Banking; Commercial; Real Estate; Family Law; Social Security; Personal Injury; Estate Planning. ***Email:*** Hiatt@cableone.net

LORI L. YOUNG, born Idabel, Oklahoma, July 8, 1960; admitted to bar, 1997, Oklahoma. *Education:* University of Central Oklahoma (B.S., 1993); Oklahoma City University School of Law (J.D., 1997). *Member:* Kay County, Oklahoma and American Bar Associations. ***PRACTICE AREAS:*** Employment Law; Family Law; Banking; Criminal Defense; Negligence; Personal Injury. ***Email:*** LoriYoung@cableone.net

REPRESENTATIVE CLIENTS: Home National Bank, Ponca City; Educational Data Services, Inc. (ADPC); Kay County Home Finance Authority; Kay County Development Authority; Via Christi Oklahoma Regional Medical Center-Ponca City; Doctor's Park of Ponca City; Moyer Car; Unitherm Food Systems, Inc.; Northpark Development Company; Ponca Plaza Shopping Center; Bowker Ford.
REFERENCE: Home National Bank, Ponca City.

KAREN L. CARMICHAEL P.C.

PONCA CITY, OKLAHOMA

(See Tulsa)

Estate Planning, Living Trusts, Living Wills, Wills and Probate, Trusts and Estates, Probate, Business Counseling, Irrevocable Trusts, Asset Protection, Charitable Giving, Health Care, Power of Attorney, HIPAA.

LAW OFFICE OF MELISSA DELACERDA

PONCA CITY, OKLAHOMA

(See Stillwater)

Family Law, Bankruptcy, Divorce, Child Custody, Adoptions, Criminal Law and Probate, Driving While Intoxicated, Wills Trusts and Estates.

BRIAN T. HERMANSON

620 E. COMANCHE, SUITE 3
P.O. BOX 2110
PONCA CITY, OKLAHOMA 74602
Telephone: 580-762-0020
Fax: 580-762-5620
Email: bhermanson@oklawhoma.com

Litigation, Criminal Law, Family Law, Divorce, Personal Injury.

BRIAN T. HERMANSON, born Milwaukee, Wisconsin, December 11, 1952; admitted to bar, 1978, Oklahoma, U.S. District Court, Western, Eastern and Northern Districts of Oklahoma, U.S. Court of Appeals, Tenth Circuit and U.S. Supreme Court. *Education:* Carroll College (B.A., 1975); University of Oklahoma (J.D., 1978). Phi Delta Phi (President, 1977-1978); Order of the Barristers. Member, National Moot Court Team, 1977-1978. Recipient: Sole Practitioner of the Year, 2004-2005, American Bar Association; Recipient: Clarence Darrow Award for Outstanding Trial Advocacy, Oklahoma Criminal Defense Lawyers Association, 1986. Lecturer: "Battered Woman's Syndrome, COALA, 1997; "Mastering Voir Dire and Jury Selection," ABA Annual Meeting, 1996; "Defense of Sex Crimes," OBA/CLE, 1996; "Ethics in Criminal Cases," OU/CLE, 1996; "Mastering Voir Dire and Jury Selections," ABA Annual Meeting, 1996; "The Use of a Psychiatrist in a Criminal Case," OU/CLE, 1995; "Battered Woman's Syndrome," OBA/CLE, 1995; "Discovery in Criminal Cases", OU/CLE, 1994; "Criminal Law for the General Practitioner", OBA/CLE, 1994; "Recent Developments in Criminal Law", OBA/CLE, 1994; "Dealing with the Jury in Criminal Cases," OBA/CLE, 1993; "Preliminary Hearings in Criminal Cases," OU/CLE, 1993; "Criminal Tactics and Evidence, OPA, 1993; "Personal Injury Litigation Up-Date," ABA Annual Meeting, 1992; "Significant Issues In Criminal Trial Practice," OBA/CLE, 1992; "The Science of Cross Examination," OCDLA/CLE, 1992; "Criminal Pretrial Motions and Discovery," OBA/CLE, 1991; "Developing Trial Skills Workshop-Auto Accidents," OBA/CLE, 1991; "Voir Dire in Tort Cases," ABA Annual Meeting, 1990; "Handling the Auto Accident Case," ABA Annual Meeting, 1988; "Representing Criminal Indigent," OBA/CLE, 1987; "New Child Support Guidelines," OBA/CLE, 1987; "Child Support Guidelines," OBA Family Law Section, 1987. Article Author: Reciprocal Discovery Under Allen v. District Court of Washington Co., Gauntlet (OCDLA) June, 1991. Lead Counsel, State of Oklahoma v. Terry Lynn Nichols, Oklahoma City Bombing Case, 1999-2004. *Member:* Kay County (President, 1989), Oklahoma (Vice President, 1988; Board of Governors, 1985-1988; 1997-1999; Chairman, Young Lawyers Division, 1981-1982; Oklahoma Court of Criminal Appeals Committee for Uniform Criminal Jury Instructions (1994-1997); Criminal Law Committee, 1994-1999; Board of Editors, 1994-1996; Member, Special Committee on Child Support Guidelines, 1987; Chair, Litigation Section, 1995-1997), American (Chair, 1986-1991, Tort and Insurance Committee, General Practice Section; Chair, Litigation Committee, General Practice Section, 1997-1998) Bar Associations; Oklahoma Trial Lawyers Association; The Association of Trial Lawyers of America; The National Association of Criminal Defense Lawyers; Oklahoma Criminal Defense Lawyers Association (President, 1993); American Board of Trial Advocates (National Board of Directors, 1997-1999); Oklahoma Bar Foundation

(This Listing Continued)

(President, 1993). Oklahoma Bar Association Young Lawyers Division (President, 1991, 1992). ***PRACTICE AREAS:*** Litigation; Criminal Law; Family Law; Personal Injury; Trusts and Estates; Probate; Wills.

NORTHCUTT, CLARK, GARDNER, HRON & TATE

FOURTH FLOOR, COMMERCIAL FEDERAL BANK
P.O. DRAWER 1669
PONCA CITY, OKLAHOMA 74602
Telephone: 580-762-1655
Fax: 580-765-4142
URL: http://www.northcuttlawfirm.com

General Civil Practice in all State and Federal Courts. Trials and Appeals. Personal Injury, Probate, Real Estate, Family Law, Corporate, Business and Business Litigation and Workers Compensation Law. No collections.

FIRM PROFILE: Our firm was founded in 1938 by our senior partner, C.D. Northcutt in Ponca City, Oklahoma and merged in 1977 with Clark & Hron. Our offices are located on the fourth floor of the Commercial Federal Bank building, corner of 4th Street and Central Ave., Ponca City, Oklahoma. The firm serves clients principally in northern Oklahoma and the Eastern, Western and Northern U.S. District Courts, U.S. Tenth Circuit Court of Appeals and the U.S. Supreme Court. The firm offers services in all areas of the law, except collections patents and maritime.

MEMBERS OF FIRM

CLARENCE D. NORTHCUTT, born Guin, Alabama, July 7, 1916; admitted to bar, 1938, Oklahoma. *Education:* University of Oklahoma (A.B., 1939; LL.B., 1938). *Member:* Oklahoma Bar Association (Past President). Fellow: American College of Trial Lawyers; International Society of Barristers; American Bar Foundation; American College of Trust and Estate Counsel; International Academy of Trial Lawyers. [Lt. Col., Field Artillery, European Theatre, World War II]. ***PRACTICE AREAS:*** Probate Law; Real Estate Law.

PAUL E. NORTHCUTT, born Lexington, Oklahoma, May 19, 1925; admitted to bar, 1950, Oklahoma. *Education:* University of Oklahoma (LL.B., 1950). [Tech. Sgt., U.S. Air Force, Pacific Theatre, World War II]. ***PRACTICE AREAS:*** Probate Law; Tax Law; Real Estate Law.

GUY P. CLARK, born Oklahoma City, Oklahoma, May 27, 1940; admitted to bar, 1965, Oklahoma. *Education:* Oklahoma State University (B.S., 1962); University of Oklahoma (J.D., 1965). Author: "Epilogue To The Due on Sale Storm," Oklahoma Bar Quarterly Journal, 1983. Member, Board of Governors, 1999-2002, Oklahoma Bar Association. Fellow: American College of Trial Lawyers; American Bar Foundation. [Capt., USMC, active duty, 1966-1970]. ***PRACTICE AREAS:*** Business Litigation; Commercial Litigation; Construction Litigation; Appeals; Probate; Real Estate Law.

JOHN J. GARDNER, II, born Newkirk, Oklahoma, October 9, 1946; admitted to bar, 1971, Oklahoma. *Education:* Oklahoma State University (B.S., 1968); University of Oklahoma (J.D., 1971). [1st Lt., U.S. Army Signal Corps, 1968-1976]. ***PRACTICE AREAS:*** Personal Injury; Insurance Defense; Family Law; Divorce; Child Custody; Litigation.

JOHN W. HRON, JR., born Ponca City, Oklahoma, October 20, 1947; admitted to bar, 1973, Oklahoma. *Education:* Oklahoma State University (B.S., 1970); University of Oklahoma (J.D., 1973). ***PRACTICE AREAS:*** Real Estate Law; Probate.

STUART L. TATE, born Oklahoma City, Oklahoma, May 24, 1962; admitted to bar, 1992, Oklahoma. *Education:* Central State University (B.A., 1986); Oklahoma City University (J.D., cum laude, 1991). Phi Delta Phi. *Member:* Kay County, Oklahoma and American Bar Associations. ***PRACTICE AREAS:*** General Civil Law; Bankruptcy; Tax Law; Family Law; Divorce; Child Custody; Elder Law; Probate; Corporate Law; Estate Planning. ***Email:*** state@northcuttlawfirm.com

OF COUNSEL

JOHN W. RALEY, JR., born Bartlesville, Oklahoma, May 23, 1932; admitted to bar, 1959, Oklahoma. *Education:* Oklahoma Baptist University (A.B., 1954); University of Oklahoma (J.D., 1959). Phi Alpha Delta. Assistant U.S. Attorney, Western District of Oklahoma, 1961-1969. U.S. Attorney, Eastern District of Oklahoma, 1990-1997. Member, Commission on Oklahoma Uniform Jury Instructions, State Ethics Commission, Criminal, 1971-1981. Mayor, Ponca City, Oklahoma, 1980-1983. Municipal Judge, Ponca City. Advocate, American Board of Trial Advocates. President, 1980, Kay County Bar Association; Member, Board of Governors, 1988—, Oklahoma Bar Association. *Member:* Oklahoma Association of Defense Counsel (State Vice-President, 1975, 1979). Fellow, American College of Trial Lawyers. [Capt., U.S. Naval Reserve, 1950-1984; active duty, 1952, 1954-1956]. ***PRACTICE AREAS:*** Litigation; Trial Practice.

All Members of The Firm are Members of the Kay County, Oklahoma and American Bar Associations.

REPRESENTATIVE CLIENTS: Mid America Door Co.; Freeman Ranches; Conoco Pipeline Co.; Harbor Insurance Co.; Continental Casualty Co.; Continental Carbon Co.; Ponca City Board of Realtors; Shelter Insurance Co.; Security Title.
REFERENCE: Commercial Federal Savings & Loan.

ATKINS & MARKOFF

POTEAU, OKLAHOMA

(See Oklahoma City)

Personal Injury, Automobile Accidents, Wrongful Death, Trucking Accidents, Slip and Fall, Nursing Home Abuse, Head and Spinal Injuries, Dog Bites, Sexual Abuse, Criminal Law, Drug Crimes, DUI/DWI, Juvenile Crimes, General Practice, Family , Divorce, Adoptions, Child Custody, Child Support, Domestic Violence, Visitation Rights, Elder Law, Legal Malpractice, Medical Malpractice, Social Security, Social Security Disability, Taxation, IRS Audits, Property Tax Appeals, Tax Planning, Toxic Torts, Trust and Estate, Wills and Probate.

HAMILTON, WARREN & BOVOS

A PROFESSIONAL CORPORATION
DELIVERY ADDRESS: 101 NORTH BROADWAY
P.O. BOX 660
POTEAU, OKLAHOMA 74953-9998
Telephone: 918-647-9171
Fax: 918-647-9175
URL: http://www.lawyers.com/hwb

General Civil and Trial Practice. Real Estate, Oil and Gas, Probate, Corporate, Negligence, Insurance and Mining Law. No collections under $25,000.00.

DEAN E. WARREN, born Lane, Oklahoma, September 2, 1939; admitted to bar, 1969, Oklahoma. *Education:* Northeastern Oklahoma State University (B.S., 1961); University of Oklahoma (M.S., 1962; J.D., 1969). Delta Theta Phi. Assistant District Attorney: Caddo County, 1970; Le Flore County, 1971-1974. District Attorney, Le Flore County and Latimer County, 1975-1977. Director, Oklahoma District Attorney Association, 1973-1976. Municipal Court Judge, City of Pocola, 1980-1983. *Member:* Le Flore County and Oklahoma Bar Association. [Lt. Cmdr., USNR, Retired]. ***PRACTICE AREAS:*** Civil Practice; Trial Practice; Real Estate; Oil and Gas Law; Probate; Trust Law; Insurance; Negligence; Estate Planning Law. ***Email:*** dwarren@clnk.com

MARC L. BOVOS, born Laramie, Wyoming, March 12, 1963; admitted to bar, 1988, Oklahoma; 1990, U.S. District Court, Eastern District of Oklahoma and U.S. Supreme Court. *Education:* Northeastern State University (B.S., 1985); Oklahoma City University (J.D., 1988). Legal Intern, 1987-1988, Assistant Attorney General, 1988, State Attorney General's Office. Municipal Judge: City of Pocola 1990-2000; City of Wister, 1995-2000. City Attorney, Town of Howe, 2000—. Member: Poteau School Board. City Attorney, City of Poteau, 1996—. *Member:* Le Flore County, Oklahoma and American Bar Associations; Oklahoma Trial Lawyers Association (Chairman, Law Day, 1989). ***PRACTICE AREAS:*** Civil Practice; Trial Practice; Real Estate; Oil and Gas Law; Probate; Trust Law; Insurance; Negligence; Estate Planning Law. ***Email:*** mbovos@clnk.com

ASSOCIATE

KEVIN S. MERRITT, born Poteau, Oklahoma, November 13, 1977; admitted to bar, 2003, Oklahoma. *Education:* Northeastern State University (B.S., 2000); University of Tulsa (J.D., 2003). Municipal Attorney, Town of Wister, Oklahoma, 2004—. *Member:* Le Flore County, Oklahoma and American Bar Associations. ***PRACTICE AREAS:*** Oil and Gas Law; Probate; Civil Practice; Corporate Law; Negligence; Trial Practice; Insurance; Real Estate; Mining Law. ***Email:*** kevinmerritt@clnk.com

REPRESENTATIVE CLIENTS: Central National Bank, Poteau; First National Bank, Heavener; Ollies Lumber Co., Poteau; Eastern Oklahoma Medical Center; Bob Smedley Chevrolet-Olds, Inc., Poteau; Wortz Co., Inc.; Caughern Const., Co.; Poteau Valley Improvement Authority.
APPROVED ATTORNEYS FOR: First American Title and Trust Co.; Farmers Home Administration (FHA).

DESMOND SIDES

100 FLEENER AVENUE
P.O. BOX 995
POTEAU, OKLAHOMA 74953
Telephone: 918-647-3442
Fax: 918-647-0649

General Civil and Criminal Practice. Real Estate, Probate, Wills and Trusts, Personal Injury, Corporation and Commercial, Matrimonial, Family Law, Bankruptcy.

DESMOND SIDES, born Bokoshe, Oklahoma, October 23, 1955; admitted to bar, 1994, Oklahoma and U.S. District Court, Western District of Oklahoma. *Education:* Northeastern Oklahoma State University (B.S., 1980); University of Tulsa (J.D., 1992). Certified Public Accountant, Arkansas, 1982; Oklahoma, 1986. Member, Alcohol Beverage Law Enforcement Commission, 1996—. *Member:* Oklahoma and American Bar Associations; American Institute of Certified Public Accountants; Oklahoma Society of Certified Public Accountants; Arkansas Society of Certified Public Accountants. ***PRACTICE AREAS:*** General Practice; Criminal Law; Real Estate; Probate; Wills; Trust Law; Personal Injury; Corporate Law; Commercial Law; Matrimonial Law; Family Law; Bankruptcy.

ELLIOTT & SHERRER, P.C.

Established in 1976
112 B NORTH VANN
P.O. BOX 1165
PRYOR, OKLAHOMA 74362
Telephone: 918-825-6711
Fax: 918-825-0080
URL: http://www.lawyers.com/elliott

Condemnation/Eminent Domain, Criminal Law, Family Law, Corporate Law, Estate Planning, Probate, Personal Injury and Real Estate.

FIRM PROFILE: Elliott & Sherrer, P.C. is a general practice firm.

RANDALL ELLIOTT, born Carnegie, Oklahoma, March 5, 1951; admitted to bar, 1976, Oklahoma. *Education:* Oklahoma State University (B.A., 1973); University of Oklahoma (J.D., 1976). Assistant General Counsel, 1978-1980 and Acting General Counsel, 1987-1988, Grand River Dam Authority. Assistant City Attorney, 1980-1981, and City Attorney, 1987-1991, Pryor Creek, Oklahoma. Attorney: Chouteau, 1983-1988 and 1994-1996; Salina, 1988-1989; Sportsmen Acres, Oklahoma, 2001—; Disney, Oklahoma, 2001—. Municipal Judge for Pryor, 1985-1987 and 2000—. *Member:* Mayes County, Oklahoma and American Bar Associations; Oklahoma Trial Lawyers Association; The As-

(This Listing Continued)

ELLIOTT & SHERRER, P.C., Pryor—Continued

sociation of Trial Lawyers of America. ***PRACTICE AREAS:*** Eminent Domain; Corporate Law; Estate Planning; Real Estate; Criminal Law; Family Law; Probate. ***Email:*** randy-e@swbell.net

R. BENJAMIN SHERRER, born Anchorage, Alaska, June 18, 1968; admitted to bar, 1997, Oklahoma. *Education:* Oklahoma State University (B.S., 1990); Oklahoma City University (J.D., 1997). William J. Holloway, Jr. American Inn of Court, 1997. LSEO Pro Bono Honoree, 1999. Assistant City Attorney, Pryor Creek, Oklahoma, 1998-2003. City Attorney, Pryor Creek, Oklahoma, 2003. Town Attorney, Chouteau, Oklahoma, 2001—. Member, Oklahoma House of Representatives, 2005—. *Member:* Mayes County, Tulsa County, Oklahoma and American Bar Associations; Oklahoma Trial Lawyers Association; American Trial Lawyers Association. ***PRACTICE AREAS:*** Family Law; Criminal Law; Personal Injury; Real Property. ***Email:*** bsherrer@swbell.net

DANNY L. LITTLEFIELD, JR., born Tulsa, Oklahoma, September 2, 1977; admitted to bar, 2002, Oklahoma. *Education:* Northeastern Oklahoma State University (B.S., 1999); University of Tulsa (J.D., 2002). Member, Tulsa Law Review, 2001-2002. *Member:* Mayes County (President, 2005) and American Bar Associations. ***PRACTICE AREAS:*** Criminal Law; Personal Injury; Family Law; Probate; Bankruptcy; Workers Compensation. ***Email:*** littlefieldd@swbell.net

LEGAL SUPPORT PERSONNEL

LINDA WALKER

MONICA EATON

REPRESENTATIVE CLIENTS: Mayes County Rural Water District #8; Oklahoma Turnpike Authority; Grand River Dam Authority; Mayes County Abstract Co.; Callison Construction; Honeycutt Construction; Oklahoma State University.
APPROVED EXAMINING ATTORNEYS FOR: American First Title & Trust Co.; Southwest Title & Trust Co.; Chicago Title & Trust Co.; Lawyers Title & Trust Co.; Insured Titles, Inc.
REFERENCE: RCB Bank.

LOGAN & LOWRY, LLP

PRYOR, OKLAHOMA

(See Vinita)

General Practice, Including Trials in all State and Federal Courts, Eminent Domain, Environmental and Coal, Banking, Commercial Transactions, Creditors' Rights and Bankruptcy, Corporation, Public Utility, Real Estate, Estate Planning and Probate, Criminal, Domestic Relations, Civil Rights, Employment, Appellate Practice and Administrative Law.

J. RALPH MOORE, PC

Established in 1953

COURT PLACE AT N. VANN

P.O. BOX 368

PRYOR, OKLAHOMA 74362

Telephone: 918-825-0332

Email: jrmpc@swbell.net

URL: http://www.jrmpclaw.com

Civil Litigation, Insurance Defense, Workers Compensation, Civil Rights, Litigation, Employment and Labor Law, Estate Planning, Medicaid Planning, Real Estate, Probate and Adoptions.

J. RALPH MOORE (Retired)

DARRELL L. MOORE, admitted to bar, 1979, Oklahoma; U.S. Court of Appeals, Tenth Circuit; U.S. Court of Military Appeals and U.S. Supreme Court. *Education:* University of Oklahoma (B.B.A.; J.D.); Georgetown University (LL.M., Labor Law). *Member:* Mayes County and Oklahoma Bar Associations. ***PRACTICE AREAS:*** Civil Litigation; Insurance Defense; Workers Compensation; Civil Rights; Labor and Employment.

JULIA L. NEFTZGER, admitted to bar, 1991, Oklahoma and U.S. Court of Appeals, Tenth Circuit. *Education:* Oklahoma State University (B.S.); University of Tulsa (J.D.). *Member:* Mayes County and Oklahoma Bar Associations. ***PRACTICE AREAS:*** Estate Planning; Medicaid Planning; Real Estate; Probate; Adoption Law.

K. ELLIS RITCHIE, P.C.

Established in 1992

2 1/2 SOUTH ADAIR

PRYOR, OKLAHOMA 74361

Telephone: 918-825-4558

Fax: 918-825-1623

Email: kim-kellispc@swbell.net

URL: http://www.ritchielawok.com

Mailing Address: P.O. Box 246, Pryor, OK 74362

Practice includes Eminent Domain/Condemnation/Property Rights.

FIRM PROFILE: The Ritchie Law Firm is a full service firm with particular extensive experience in real estate litigation. The Firm has represented over 250 landowners in eminent domain matter.

K. ELLIS RITCHIE, born Versailles, Missouri, November 23, 1962; admitted to bar, 1992, Oklahoma; U.S. District Court, Northern District of Oklahoma. *Education:* Northeastern Oklahoma State University (B.S., 1986); University of Tulsa (J.D., 1992). Phi Delta Phi. Municipal Court Judge, 1993—. Trained Civil Mediator. *Member:* Mayes County,

(This Listing Continued)

Oklahoma Bar Association and American Bar Associations. ***PRACTICE AREAS:*** Eminent Domain; Condemnation; Real Estate; Contracts; Divorce; Child Custody; Child Support; Civil Litigation. ***Email:*** kim-kellispc@swbell.net

SHAWN SCOTT TAYLOR, born Nowata, Oklahoma, October 17, 1965; admitted to bar, 1991, Oklahoma and U.S. District Court, Western District of Oklahoma. *Education:* Oklahoma State University (B.S., 1988); East Central University (1983-1985); University of Oklahoma (J.D., 1991). Registered Lobbyist, Oklahoma State Legislature. *Member:* Oklahoma County, Cleveland County, Oklahoma and American Bar Association; Oklahoma Trial Lawyers Association. ***PRACTICE AREAS:*** Civil Practice; Criminal Law; Administrative Law; Legislative Practice.

TAYLOR, BURRAGE, FOSTER, MALLETT, DOWNS & RAMSEY, P.C.

PRYOR, OKLAHOMA

(See Claremore)

Civil and Criminal Practice in all State and Federal Courts. Employment Law, Healthcare Law, Medical Malpractice, Professional Liability, Insurance Defense, Real Estate, Probate, Guardianships, Corporation, Commercial and Personal Injury Law.

LAW OFFICES OF JOHN T. CRIPPS, INC.

Established in 1975

104-A SOUTH OAK

P.O. BOX 606

SALLISAW, OKLAHOMA 74955

Telephone: 918-775-9142

Fax: 918-775-7588

Email: crippslaw@sbcglobal.net

General Civil Practice. Real Estate, Probate, Family, Workers Compensation, Bankruptcy and Commercial Law, Social Security.

JOHN T. CRIPPS, born Durham, North Carolina, December 20, 1945; admitted to bar, 1975, Oklahoma. *Education:* University of Oklahoma (B.S.Ed., 1967; J.D., 1975). Phi Delta Phi. City Judge: Vian, Oklahoma, 1978—; Sallisaw, Oklahoma, 1986—; Roland, Oklahoma, 1991-1993; Arkoma, Oklahoma, 1991—. City Judge, Panama, 1990—. District Judge of the Cherokee Nation, 1999—. *Member:* Sequoyah County, Oklahoma and American Bar Associations; The Association of Trial Lawyers of America; Oklahoma Criminal Defense Attorneys Association; Oklahoma Trial Lawyers Association. [Capt., U.S. Army Special Forces, 1968-1972]. ***Email:*** crippslaw@sbcglobal.net

A list of representative clients and references will be furnished upon request.

GEAN, GEAN & GEAN

SALLISAW, OKLAHOMA

(See Fort Smith, Arkansas)

General Civil Litigation, State and Federal Courts. Business, Corporate, Real Estate, Probate, Creditor Bankruptcy, Criminal, Family Law, Divorce, Personal Injury Law, Labor Law, Collections, Automobile Accidents, Wrongful Death, Wills, Probate, Workers Compensation, Social Security.

LAW OFFICES OF HARRY SCOUFOS, P.C.

Established in 1971

CREEK & ELM STREETS

P.O. BOX 787

SALLISAW, OKLAHOMA 74955

Telephone: 918-775-5546

Toll Free: 888-775-5546

Fax: 918-775-4990

Email: scoufos3@iamerica.net

Trial Practice. Negligence, Personal Injury, Products Liability, Medical Malpractice, Insurance, Workers Compensation, Family, Criminal Defense, Admiralty Law, Aviation Law, Class Action.

HARRY G. SCOUFOS, III, born Okemah, Oklahoma, August 17, 1943; admitted to bar, 1971, Oklahoma; U.S. District Court, Western District of Oklahoma; U.S. District Court, Eastern District of Oklahoma, U.S. Supreme Court and U.S. Court of Appeals, Tenth Circuit; U.S. District Court, Northern District of Oklahoma. *Education:* East Central State College (B.A., 1966); Oklahoma City University (J.D., 1970). *Member:* Sequoyah County (President, 1976-1977), Oklahoma and American Bar Associations; Oklahoma Trial Lawyers Association (Sustaining Member; Past Member, Board of Directors); Oklahoma Criminal Defense Lawyers Association (Member, Board of Directors); The Association of Trial Lawyers of America. ***SPECIAL AGENCIES:*** Health Planning Commission. ***PRACTICE AREAS:*** Consumer Class Actions; Personal Injury; Medical Malpractice; Workers Compensation; Family Law; Negligence; Civil Practice; Trial Practice. ***Email:*** hs3@scoufoslaw.com

(This Listing Continued)

THOMAS W. CONDIT, born San Francisco, California, August 7, 1941; admitted to bar, 1967, California; 1993, Oklahoma; U.S. Supreme Court; U.S. Court of Appeals, Tenth Circuit; U.S. District Court, Eastern District of California. *Education:* San Francisco State University (B.A., 1964); Hastings College of Law (J.D., 1967). Recipient, Distinguished Service Award, California District Attorneys Association, 1977. *Member:* Sequoyah County Bar Association. ***PRACTICE AREAS:*** Consumer Class Actions; Personal Injury; Civil Practice; Trial Practice; Criminal Defense. **Email:** tom@scoufoslaw.com

HARRY G. ("FOURTH") SCOUFOS, IV, born Oklahoma City, Oklahoma, November 15, 1970; admitted to bar, 1996, Oklahoma; 1998, Arkansas; U.S. Court of Appeals, 10th Circuit; U.S. District Court, Eastern and Western Districts of Oklahoma; U.S. District Court, Eastern and Western District of Arkansas. *Education:* University of Oklahoma (B.B.A., 1993); Oklahoma City University (J.D., 1996). *Member:* Sequoyah County, Oklahoma and American Bar Associations; Arkansas Bar Association; Oklahoma Trial Lawyers Association; The Association of Trial Lawyers of America; Oklahoma Criminal Defense Lawyers Association. ***PRACTICE AREAS:*** Family Law; Criminal Defense; Consumer Class Actions; Personal Injury; General Practice; Trial Practice. **Email:** fourth@scoufoslaw.com

REPRESENTATIVE CLIENTS: First National Bank of Sallisaw and Roland, OK; Armstrong Bank of Muldrow, OK and Vian, OK; Public Schools, Marble City, OK; Nix's Medical Supply, Inc., Sallisaw., OK; Central Arkansas Nursing Centers, Inc., Fort Smith AR.
REFERENCES: First National Bank of Sallisaw, OK; Armstrong Bank, Vian, OK.

TAYLOR, BURRAGE, FOSTER, MALLETT, DOWNS & RAMSEY, P.C.

SALLISAW, OKLAHOMA

(See Claremore)

Civil and Criminal Practice in all State and Federal Courts. Employment Law, Healthcare Law, Medical Malpractice, Professional Liability, Insurance Defense, Real Estate, Probate, Guardianships, Corporation, Commercial and Personal Injury Law.

ATKINS & MARKOFF

SAPULPA, OKLAHOMA

(See Oklahoma City)

Personal Injury, Automobile Accidents, Wrongful Death, Trucking Accidents, Slip and Fall, Nursing Home Abuse, Head and Spinal Injuries, Dog Bites, Sexual Abuse, Criminal Law, Drug Crimes, DUI/DWI, Juvenile Crimes, General Practice, Family , Divorce, Adoptions, Child Custody, Child Support, Domestic Violence, Visitation Rights, Elder Law, Legal Malpractice, Medical Malpractice, Social Security, Social Security Disability, Taxation, IRS Audits, Property Tax Appeals, Tax Planning, Toxic Torts, Trust and Estate, Wills and Probate.

KAREN L. CARMICHAEL P.C.

SAPULPA, OKLAHOMA

(See Tulsa)

Estate Planning, Living Trusts, Living Wills, Wills and Probate, Trusts and Estates, Probate, Business Counseling, Irrevocable Trusts, Asset Protection, Charitable Giving, Health Care, Power of Attorney, HIPAA.

RUSSELL D. CARSON, P.C.

SAPULPA, OKLAHOMA

(See Tulsa)

Family Law, Child Custody, High Conflict Divorce, Child Support, Adoptions, Step-Parent Adoption, Mediation.

LESTER D. HENDERSON, P.C.

Established in 1982
16 NORTH PARK
P.O. BOX 205
SAPULPA, OKLAHOMA 74067
Telephone: 918-227-2733
FAX: 918-227-2051

Probate, Estate Planning, Real Estate, General Civil, Municipal Law, Personal Injury, Oil and Gas and Contract Law.

LESTER D. HENDERSON, born Houston, Texas, September 28, 1937; admitted to bar, 1961, Oklahoma; 1970, U.S. District Court, Northern District of Oklahoma; U.S. Court of Appeals, 10th Circuit. *Education:* Oklahoma State University (B.S. in B.A., 1958); University of Oklahoma (LLB., 1961). Phi Alpha Delta. Managing Editor, Oklahoma Law Review, 1961. Member, 1968-1971 and President, 1969-1970, Sapulpa Board of Education. City Attorney, Sapulpa, Oklahoma, 1971-1976. District Judge, 24th Judicial District, 1978-1982. Sapulpa School Board Attorney, 1990—. *Member:* Creek County, Oklahoma and American Bar Associations. ***PRACTICE AREAS:*** Probate; Estate Planning; Real Estate; Mediation; Civil Litigation.

REFERENCE: American Heritage Bank, Sapulpa.

BROOKS & ISRAEL

119 EAST MAIN STREET
SAYRE, OKLAHOMA 73662-2913
Telephone: 580-928-5593
Fax: 580-928-2648

General Trial Practice, Domestic Relations, Divorce, Family, Adoption, Probate, Real Estate, Collections, Commercial and Criminal Law, Driving Under the Influence, Trusts and Estates, Estate Planning.

DAVID BROOKS, born Chickasha, Oklahoma, April 14, 1953; admitted to bar, 1978, Oklahoma; 1979, U.S. District Court, Western District of Oklahoma. *Education:* Southwestern Oklahoma State University (B.A., 1975); University of Tulsa (J.D., 1978). Phi Delta Phi. Associate District Judge, Greer County, Oklahoma, 1981-1991. Assistant District Attorney, Beckham County, 1991-1992. *Member:* Beckham County (President, 1993) and Oklahoma Bar Associations. ***PRACTICE AREAS:*** Civil Trial Practice; Domestic Relations; Divorce; Adoptions; Family Law; Probate; Real Estate; Commercial.

TIMOTHY P. ISRAEL, born Guymon, Oklahoma, January 8, 1954; admitted to bar, 1979, Oklahoma. *Education:* Southwestern Oklahoma State University; University of Oklahoma (B.A., 1976); University of Oklahoma College of Law (J.D., 1979). Phi Delta Phi. Assistant District Attorney, Beckham and Greer Counties, 1986-1991. *Member:* Beckham County (President, 1982-1983; Treasurer, 1983-1986) and Oklahoma Bar Associations; Southwest Legal Institute (Vice President, 1981-1982; President, 1982-1983). ***PRACTICE AREAS:*** Adoption Law; Probate; Real Estate; General Trial Practice; Domestic Relations; Custody; Family Law.

IVESTER, IVESTER & IVESTER

Established in 1927
115 W. MAIN STREET
P.O. BOX 160
SAYRE, OKLAHOMA 73662-0160
Telephone: 580-928-2116; 1-800-891-2319
Fax: 580-928-5353
Email: ivesterlaw@itlnet.net
URL: http://www.ivesterlaw.com

Elk City Office: 114 N. Adams, P.O. Box 1950, 73648-1950. Telephone: 580-225-6525. Fax: 580-225-2806.

Civil Litigation, Business Law, Commercial Law, Corporate Law, Partnership Law, Insurance, Real Estate, Family Law, Oil & Gas, Probate, Taxation, Trusts and Estates.

MEMBERS OF FIRM

H. C. IVESTER (1901-1975)

JOHN ED T. IVESTER, born Sayre, Oklahoma, 1933; admitted to bar, 1965, Oklahoma. *Education:* Oklahoma Baptist University and University of Oklahoma (B.A., 1957); Oklahoma City University (J.D., 1965). Phi Alpha Delta. *Member:* Beckham County and Oklahoma Bar Associations. ***PRACTICE AREAS:*** Adoptions; Elder Law; Trusts and Estates; Wills; Guardianship and Conservatorship; Probate. **Email:** jetivesteriii@itlnet.net

JACK W. IVESTER, born Sayre, Oklahoma, 1947; admitted to bar, 1973, Oklahoma. *Education:* University of Oklahoma (B.B.A., 1970; J.D., 1973). Delta Theta Phi. *Member:* Beckham County and Oklahoma Bar Associations. ***PRACTICE AREAS:*** Civil Litigation; Corporate Law; Partnership Law. **Email:** jwiivesteriii@itlnet.net

THOMAS S. IVESTER, born Sayre, Oklahoma, 1969; admitted to bar, 2000, Oklahoma. *Education:* Syracuse University; Texas Christian University (B.B.A., magna cum laude, 1992); University of Oklahoma (J.D., with honors, 2000). Note Editor, Oklahoma Law Review, 1998-2000. *Member:* Beckham County Bar Association; Oklahoma Bar Association. [Officer, U.S. Army, 1992-1997]. ***PRACTICE AREAS:*** Business Law; Civil Litigation; Taxation; Oil and Gas; Probate. **Email:** ivesterlaw@itlnet.net

REPRESENTATIVE CLIENTS: Beckham County Rural Water District; Northfork Electric Cooperative, Inc., Sayre, Oklahoma; Southwest State Bank, Sentinel, Oklahoma.
REFERENCES: Southwest State Bank, Sentinel Oklahoma; InterBank, Sayre, Oklahoma.

ELSENER & CADENHEAD, P.C.

300 EAST SEMINOLE
P.O. BOX 2067
SEMINOLE, OKLAHOMA 74818-2067
Telephone: 405-382-6341; 257-2773
Fax: 405-382-5513
Email: cadnhead@swbell.net
URL: http://www.lawyers.com/e&claw

General Civil Trial Practice. Probate, Real Estate, Indian Land Title, Oil and Gas Law, Foreclosure, Municipal.

G. DALE ELSENER, born Frederick, Oklahoma, March 26, 1951; admitted to bar, 1976, Oklahoma. *Education:* Oklahoma State University (B.S., 1973); University of Oklahoma (J.D., 1976). Phi Delta Phi. City Attorney, Wewoka, 1986—. *Member:* Seminole County (President, 1982) Bar Association; Oklahoma Bar Association. ***PRACTICE AREAS:*** Civil Litigation; Probate; Indian Land Title; Oil and Gas. **Email:** delsener@swbell.net

ED CADENHEAD, born Tulsa, Oklahoma, September 26, 1950; admitted to bar, 1980, Oklahoma. *Education:* University of Tulsa (B.S., 1972); Florida State University; Tulsa University (J.D., 1980). City Attorney, Seminole, 19852002. Municipal Judge, Seminole, 2002—. *Member:* Seminole County Bar Association; Oklahoma Bar Association. ***PRACTICE AREAS:*** Civil; Foreclosure; Insurance Defense; Real Estate. **Email:** cadnhead@swbell.net

HENSON, HENSON, HENSON, MARSHALL & MILBURN, LLP

Established in 1953

101 WEST NINTH
P.O. BOX 3488
SHAWNEE, OKLAHOMA 74802-3488
Telephone: 405-275-2550
Fax: 405-275-2588

General Civil Practice. Probate, Real Property, Family, Banking, Bankruptcy, Insurance, Oil and Gas and Negligence Law. Trials in State and Federal Courts.

MEMBERS OF FIRM

ALMON E. HENSON, born Pauls Valley, Oklahoma, March 3, 1919; admitted to bar, 1948, Oklahoma. *Education:* University of Oklahoma (LL.B., 1948). Phi Alpha Delta. Recipient, "Award of Ethics," Oklahoma Bar Association, 1998. County Attorney, Pottawatomie County, 1951-1952. President, Oklahoma Association of County Attorneys, 1952. Secretary, Pottawatomie County Election Board, 1972-1977. Justice of the Supreme Court, Citizen Pottawatomie Nation Tribal Court of Oklahoma, 1986-2004. *Member:* Pottawatomie County (President, 1955, 1956), Oklahoma and American Bar Associations. ***REPORTED CASES:*** Thompson v. Rorschach, 416 P.2d 898 (Okl., 1966); Hargrave v. Canadian Valley Elec. Coop., Inc., 792 P.2d 50 (Okl., 1990). ***PRACTICE AREAS:*** Probate; Real Estate; Estate Planning.

J. ROGER HENSON, born Shawnee, Oklahoma, March 10, 1951; admitted to bar, 1976, Oklahoma and U.S. District Court, Western District of Oklahoma; 1977, U.S. District Court, Eastern District of Oklahoma; 1991, U.S. District Court, Northern District of Oklahoma; 1990, U.S. Supreme Court; Judge of Tribal Court of Absentee Shawnee Tribe of Oklahoma. *Education:* Oklahoma Baptist University (B.A., 1973); University of Oklahoma (J.D., 1976). Phi Alpha Delta. Adjunct Instructor, Business Law, Oklahoma Baptist University. *Member:* Pottawatomie County, Oklahoma and American Bar Associations; The Association of Trial Lawyers of America. ***REPORTED CASES:*** Webster v. Woods, 586 P.2d 337 (Okl. App., 1978). ***PRACTICE AREAS:*** Litigation; Business Law; Commercial Law; Probate; Real Estate; Contracts. ***Email:*** rogerhenson@hhhmmlaw.com

KAREN ANN HENSON, born Shawnee, Oklahoma, April 19, 1954; admitted to bar, 1979, Oklahoma and U.S. District Court, Western and Eastern Districts of Oklahoma. *Education:* Oklahoma Baptist University (B.A., 1976); University of Oklahoma (J.D., 1979). Phi Delta Phi. Member, Board of Editors, Oklahoma Law Review, 1978-1979. *Member:* Pottawatomie County, Oklahoma and American Bar Associations. ***REPORTED CASES:*** Kittredge v. Kittredge 911 P.2d 903 (Okl. 1995) Matter of Will of Clem 692 P.2d 552 (Okl. 1984). ***PRACTICE AREAS:*** Probate; Civil Litigation; Family Law; Real Property; Estate and Trusts; Banking. ***Email:*** karenhenson@hhhmmlaw.com

JAMES R. MARSHALL, born Kitzingen, West Germany, March 7, 1950; admitted to bar, 1979, Oklahoma. *Education:* University of Oklahoma (B.A., 1972; J.D., 1979) Creighton University (M.A., International Relations, 1976). Phi Beta Kappa; Phi Delta Phi. Member, Board of Editors, Oklahoma Law Review, 1977-1979. *Member:* Pottawatomie County (President, 1988), Oklahoma and American Bar Associations; The Association of Trial Lawyers of America. [Brigadier General Air National Guard]. ***REPORTED CASES:*** State v. Patton 837 P.2d 483 (Okl. Cr. 1992). ***PRACTICE AREAS:*** Personal Injury; Civil Litigation; Real Estate; Probate. ***Email:*** jamesmarshall@hhhmmlaw.com

KERMIT M. MILBURN, born Shawnee, Oklahoma, July 17, 1959; admitted to bar, 1984, Oklahoma. *Education:* Oklahoma State University (B.S., 1980); University of Oklahoma (J.D., 1983). Phi Alpha Delta. Recipient: Young Lawyers Division Outstanding Service Award, Oklahoma Bar Association, 1989-1990; Hicks Epton Law Day Award, Oklahoma Bar Association, 1990. *Member:* Pottawatomie County (President, 2001), Oklahoma (Member, Board of Directors, Young Lawyers Division, 1991-1992) and American Bar Associations. ***PRACTICE AREAS:*** Civil Litigation; Banking; Real Estate. ***Email:*** kermit@hhhmmlaw.com

GENERAL COUNSEL FOR: Oklahoma Baptist University; Canadian Valley Electric Cooperative, Inc.; Tri-County Federal Credit Union; Liberty Bell Federal Credit Union; Carney State Bank.
REPRESENTATIVE CLIENTS: Arvest Bank; Arvest Mortgage Co.; Indaco Metals, LLC; Triangle Sales, Inc.; First United Bank and Trust Company.
APPROVED ATTORNEYS FOR: First American Title & Trust Co.; American First Title & Trust Co.; Lawyers Title Insurance Corp.; First American Title Insurance Co.

PARSONS & ASSOCIATES LAW FIRM

A CORPORATION

SHAWNEE, OKLAHOMA

(See Norman)

Banking Litigation, Business Litigation, Business Torts, Commercial Collections, Commercial Litigation, Corporate Contracts, Creditors Rights, Lawsuits, Lender Liability, Internet Violations, Oklahoma Lottery, Employer Defense and Trial Practice in All Courts.

STUART & CLOVER

Established in 1904

Formerly Miller, Peters, Diamond & Stuart

128 NORTH BROADWAY
P.O. BOX 1925
SHAWNEE, OKLAHOMA 74802-1925
Telephone: 405-275-0700
Telecopy: 405-275-6805
URL: http://www.lawyers.com/stuart&clover

General Corporate, Banking, Commercial Law and Litigation, Real Property, Probate, Oil and Gas, Estate Planning, General Civil Practice.

(This Listing Continued)

MEMBERS OF FIRM

JAMES T. STUART, born Shawnee, Oklahoma, March 18, 1953; admitted to bar, 1979, Oklahoma; 1981, U.S. District Court, Western District of Oklahoma. *Education:* Central State University (B.B.A., 1975); University of Tulsa (J.D., 1979). Phi Delta Phi. Temporary Panel, Oklahoma Court of Appeals, 1991. *Member:* Pottawatomie County and Oklahoma (Member, Real Property Law Section; Director, Young Lawyer's Division, 1985-1988) Bar Associations. ***REPORTED CASES:*** New Covenant Community Church v. Federal National Bank & Trust Co., 734 P2d 1318 (1987); Foye v. Eastover Bank for Savings, 811 P2d 108 (1991); McCully v Wil-Mc Oil Corp., 879 P2d 150 (1994). ***PRACTICE AREAS:*** Commercial Law; Commercial Litigation; General Corporate; Banking; Real Property; Oil and Gas; Probate. ***Email:*** jtstuart@swbell.net

MICHAEL D. CLOVER, born McAlester, Oklahoma, May 17, 1955; admitted to bar, 1990, Oklahoma and U.S. District Court, Western District of Oklahoma. *Education:* Northeastern Oklahoma A&M (A.A., 1975); Central State University (B.S., 1977); Oklahoma City University (J.D., 1990). Assistant City Attorney, City of Shawnee, 1995—. *Member:* Pottawatomie County and Oklahoma (Member, Real Property Law Section) Bar Associations. ***REPORTED CASES:*** Berry v. Mendenhall, 1998 OK Civ.App. 134, 964 P.2d 974. ***PRACTICE AREAS:*** Commercial Law; Commercial Litigation; General Corporate; Banking; Real Property; Oil and Gas; Probate; Municipal Law. ***Email:*** mdclover@swbell.net

GENERAL COUNSEL: BancFirst, Shawnee, OK; BancFirst, Prague, OK; Central Plastics Co.; First American Title & Trust Co.
REPRESENTATIVE CLIENTS: BancFirst, McLoud, OK; Arvest Bank, Shawnee, OK; Shawnee Urban Renewal Authority; Shawnee Economic Development Foundation; Town of Bethel Acres; Absentee Shawnee Housing Authority; Don Bodard Trust.
APPROVED EXAMINING ATTORNEYS FOR: First American Title & Trust Co.; Lawyers Title Insurance Corp.

ATKINS & MARKOFF

STILLWATER, OKLAHOMA

(See Oklahoma City)

Personal Injury, Automobile Accidents, Wrongful Death, Trucking Accidents, Slip and Fall, Nursing Home Abuse, Head and Spinal Injuries, Dog Bites, Sexual Abuse, Criminal Law, Drug Crimes, DUI/DWI, Juvenile Crimes, General Practice, Family , Divorce, Adoptions, Child Custody, Child Support, Domestic Violence, Visitation Rights, Elder Law, Legal Malpractice, Medical Malpractice, Social Security, Social Security Disability, Taxation, IRS Audits, Property Tax Appeals, Tax Planning, Toxic Torts, Trust and Estate, Wills and Probate.

LOWELL A. BARTO

A PROFESSIONAL CORPORATION

Established in 1985

SUITE 210 SEVENTH AVENUE CENTER
123 WEST SEVENTH AVENUE
STILLWATER, OKLAHOMA 74074
Telephone: 405-372-4371
Fax: 405-372-4420

General Civil Trial Practice. Commercial, Probate, Estate Planning and Real Estate Law, Elder Care Law.

LOWELL A. BARTO, born Stillwater, Oklahoma, May 26, 1956; admitted to bar, 1981, Oklahoma, U.S. District Court, Northern and Western Districts of Oklahoma and U.S. Court of Appeals, Tenth Circuit; 1984, U.S. Supreme Court. *Education:* Oklahoma State University (B.A., 1977); University of Tulsa (J.D., with honors, 1980). Phi Kappa Phi; Phi Delta Phi. Recipient, American Jurisprudence Award in Administrative Law. City Attorney, City of Stillwater, Oklahoma, 1981-1985. Municipal Judge, Ripley, Oklahoma, 1986—. Commissioner, 1985-1997 and Chairman, 1986-1997, Stillwater Public Housing Authority. *Member:* Payne County, Oklahoma (Member, Estate Planning and Probate Section) and American (Member, Real Property, Probate and Trust Section) Bar Associations. ***PRACTICE AREAS:*** Estate Planning; Real Estate; Elder Care; Probate; Commercial Law; Civil Practice; Trusts and Estates; Contracts; Business Transactions; Business Formation.

JOHN R. COUCH, JR.

123 W. 7TH, SUITE 102
P.O. BOX 984
STILLWATER, OKLAHOMA 74076
Telephone: 405-377-9383
Fax: 405-377-8187
Email: couchlaw@provalue.net
URL: http://www.couch-lawfirm.com

Probate, Estate Planning, Environmental Law, General Practice, Personal Injury.

JOHN R. COUCH, JR., born Oklahoma City, Oklahoma, August 18, 1942; admitted to bar, 1970, Oklahoma; 1971, U.S. District Court, Western District of Oklahoma and U.S. Court of Appeals, Tenth Circuit. *Education:* Rice University (B.A., 1964); University of Oklahoma (M.A., 1968; J.D., 1970); Oklahoma State University (Ph.D., Environmental Science, 1996). Phi Delta Phi. Special District Judge, 9th Judicial District, State of Oklahoma, 1974-1979. *Member:* Oklahoma and American Bar Associations. ***PRACTICE AREAS:*** Civil Practice; Environmental Law; Guardianship; Wills; Probate; Personal Injury.

LAW OFFICE OF MELISSA DeLACERDA

Established in 1979
301 SOUTH DUCK
P.O. BOX 1252
STILLWATER, OKLAHOMA 74076
Telephone: 405-624-8383
Fax: 405-624-8385
Email: melissde@aol.com
URL: http://www.stillwater-law.com

Family Law, Bankruptcy, Divorce, Child Custody, Adoptions, Criminal Law and Probate, Driving While Intoxicated, Wills Trusts and Estates.

MELISSA DeLACERDA, born St. Petersburg, Florida, March 17, 1952; admitted to bar, 1979, Oklahoma and U.S. District Court, Western District of Oklahoma; 1980, U.S. District Court, Northern District of Oklahoma. *Education:* Memphis State University (B.S., 1973); University of Tulsa, School of Law (J.D., 1979). Delta Theta Phi. Order of Curule. Recipient, American Jurisprudence Award, University of Tulsa, 1979. *Member:* Oklahoma (President, 2003; Member, Board of Directors, Young Lawyers Division, 1983-1986; Member, Board of Governors, 1996-1999) and American (Member, Standing Committee on Client Protection, 1999-2002, 2003—) Bar Associations. ***PRACTICE AREAS:*** Family Law; Bankruptcy; Personal Injury; Criminal Law; Probate.

REPRESENTATIVE CLIENTS: Will be Furnished Upon Request.
REFERENCES: Stillwater National Bank; Bank, N.A.; First National Bank of Pawnee.

ELLIS & DRUMMOND

An Association of Professional Limited Liability Companies.
711 SOUTH HUSBAND STREET
STILLWATER, OKLAHOMA 74074
Telephone: 405-743-3770
Fax: 405-743-3773
Email: hwellis@ellisanddrummond.com
URL: http://www.EllisandDrummond.com

Wills and Trusts, Tax and Estate Planning, Probate, Business Formations, Non-profit Organizations, Tax Litigation, Corporate and Business Law.

FIRM PROFILE: Hal Wm. Ellis is a fellow of the American College of Trust and Estate Counsel.

HAL WM. ELLIS, born Biloxi, Mississippi, November 4, 1948; admitted to bar, 1974, Oklahoma and U.S. Tax Court; U.S. District Court, Northern and Western Districts of Oklahoma; U.S. Court of Appeals, Tenth Circuit. *Education:* University of Central Oklahoma (B.B.A., 1971; M.B.A., 1974); University of Oklahoma (J.D., 1974). Phi Delta Phi. Member, Board of Editors, American Indian Law Review, 1973-1974. Author: "Exclusion of Earnings On Allotted Indian Land From Federal Income Taxation," Vol. II, No. 1, American Indian Law Review, p. 119, 1974; "Capital Gains On Sales Of Undeveloped Realty-Three Alternatives," The Tax Advisor, p. 162, March, 1977; "Tax Deferred Exchanges Under Internal Revenue Code Section 1031" Oklahoma Bar Journal, October 4, 2003 Vol. 74 No. 27 p.2619. Associate Professor, College of Business Administration, Oklahoma State University, 1975-1986. Member, Professional Responsibility Tribunal, State of Oklahoma, 1981-1988. Member, Court on the Judiciary Appellate Division, 1997-2003. *Member:* Payne County (President, 1986), Oklahoma (Board of Governors, 1993-1995) and American Bar Associations. Fellow, Oklahoma Bar Foundation (President 2006); American Bar Foundation; American College of Trust and Estate Counsel (State Chair 2002); Trustee, Oklahoma Bar Foundation. ***PRACTICE AREAS:*** Wills; Trusts; Tax Law; Estate Planning; Tax Deferred Exchanges; Buy-Sell Agreements; Tax Exempt Organizations; Tax Exempt Finance; Probate. ***Email:*** hwellis@ellisanddrummond.com

LeANN PAGE DRUMMOND, born Stillwater, Oklahoma, June 21, 1965; admitted to bar, 1991, Oklahoma, U.S. District Court, Western District of Oklahoma and U.S. Tax Court. *Education:* Oklahoma State University (B.S., Accounting, 1987); University of Oklahoma (J.D., with honors, 1991). Phi Delta Phi; Order of the Coif. Student Law Clerk to the Hon. Marian Opala, Oklahoma Supreme Court, 1989-1991. Special Assistant to United States Attorney, Western District of Oklahoma, 1991-1993. Staff Attorney, IRS District Counsel Office, 1991-1993. Board Member and President, Stillwater Education Foundation. Treasurer, OBA Estate Planning, Probate and Trust Section. *Member:* Payne County Bar Association. Fellow, Oklahoma Bar Foundation. ***PRACTICE AREAS:*** Wills; Trusts; Tax Law; Estate Planning; Tax Deferred Exchanges; Buy-Sell Agreements; Tax Exempt Organizations; Tax Exempt Finance; Probate. ***Email:*** lpdrum@ellisanddrummond.com

REPRESENTATIVE CLIENTS: Oklahoma State University Foundation; Warren Clinic, Stillwater; Kraybill Construction Co.; Benchmark Property Management Co.; Knotts Investment Co.; Kerns Construction Co.; OSUF Phase III Student Housing, L.L.C.; Wooden Nickel, Inc.; Greater Oklahoma Land Firm, L.L.C.; OSUF Okmulgee Student Housing, L.L.C.; Kicker Trucking, L.L.C.; Stillwater Surgery Center, L.L.C.; Drummond Eye Clinic, P.C.; OSU Center for Innovation and Economic Development, Inc.

FORSYTH, CUBBAGE & ASSOCIATES, P.C.

STILLWATER, OKLAHOMA

(See Cushing)

Mediation, Business Law, Estate Planning, Trusts, Probate, Real Estate, Commercial Law, Banking Law.

HERT, BAKER & KOEMEL

A PROFESSIONAL CORPORATION
Established in 1977
222 EAST SEVENTH
P.O. BOX 668
STILLWATER, OKLAHOMA 74076
Telephone: 405-377-8644
FAX: 405-377-6363

Civil Practice. Banking Law, Commercial Law, Family Law, Probate, Trusts and Estates, Wills, Real Estate, Corporate Law, Personal Injury, Oil and Gas Law, Labor and Employment, Criminal Law, Elder Law, Social Security, Franchise Law, Trademarks, Collections, General Practice.

ROBERT L. HERT, JR., born Colorado Springs, Colorado, June 21, 1944; admitted to bar, 1969, Oklahoma. *Education:* Oklahoma State University (B.A., 1966); University of Oklahoma (J.D., 1969). Phi Alpha Delta. Assistant City Attorney, Stillwater, 1970-1974. *Member:* Oklahoma and American Bar Associations. [LTC, USAR]. ***PRACTICE AREAS:*** Real Estate; Probate; Trusts and Estates; Wills; Elder Law. ***Email:*** bobhert@hertbaker.com

WILLIAM J. BAKER, born San Angelo, Texas, June 27, 1947; admitted to bar, 1972, Oklahoma; 1973, Hawaii and U.S. Court of Military Appeals; U.S. District Courts, Eastern, Northern and Western Districts of Oklahoma. *Education:* Oklahoma State University (B.A., 1969); University of Oklahoma (J.D., 1972). Chair, Oklahoma Judicial Evaluation Commission. *Member:* Oklahoma (President, 1997; Member, Board of Governors, 1984-1986, 1996-1998) and American Bar Associations; Oklahoma Bar Foundation (President and Trustee, 1988-1992). [LTC. USAR]. ***PRACTICE AREAS:*** Banks and Banking; Business Law; Corporate Law; Family Law; Real Estate; Litigation. ***Email:*** williebaker@hertbaker.com

TINA MOONEY KOEMEL, born Muskogee, Oklahoma, November 19, 1960; admitted to bar, 1986, Texas; 1988, U.S. District Court, Northern District of Texas; 1991, U.S. District Court, Southern, Eastern and Western Districts of Texas; 1993, Oklahoma. *Education:* Baylor University (B.B.A., cum laude, 1983; J.D., 1986). Mentor in the "I Have A Dream" Foundation. *Member:* Payne County and Oklahoma Bar Associations; State Bar of Texas. ***LANGUAGES:*** Spanish. ***PRACTICE AREAS:*** Banking Law; Collections; Real Estate; Social Security; Disabilities. ***Email:*** tinakoemel@hertbaker.com

JOHN E. KOEMEL, JR., born Beeville, Texas, February 5, 1963; admitted to bar, 1988, Texas and U.S. District Court, Northern District of Texas; 1991, U.S. District Court, Southern District of Texas and U.S. Court of Appeals, Fifth Circuit; 1992, U.S. District Court, Western District of Texas and U.S. Supreme Court; 1997, Oklahoma and U.S. District Court, Western District o f Oklahoma; 1998, U.S. District Court, Northern, and Eastern Districts of Oklahoma; 1999, U.S. Court of Appeals, Tenth Circuit. *Education:* Texas A & M University (B.S., summa cum laude, 1985); Baylor University (J.D., 1988); Oklahoma State University (M.S., 1996; Ph.D., 1999). *Member:* Payne County Bar Association; Oklahoma State Bar; State Bar of Texas (inactive). ***PRACTICE AREAS:*** Commercial Law; Litigation; Real Estate; Probate. ***Email:*** johnkoemel@hertbaker.com

REPRESENTATIVE CLIENTS: Stillwater National Bank and Trust Co.; Farm Credit Services; Lambert Construction Co., Inc.; The Stillwater Board of Realtors; Stillwater Medical Center Authority; Strode-Bernhart Funeral Home; Berry Operating Co.; DuPree Sports Equipment; Oklahoma State Development, Inc.; Ron Shirley Pontiac-Buick-GMC, Inc.; Owen Thomas Ford; Oklahoma State University; Stillwater Country Club, Inc.; Creative Labs, Inc.; Eskimo Joe', Inc.; Stan Clark Cos.; Pepin Oil, Inc.; Stillwater Women's Clinic, Inc.; Cimarron Internal Medicine, P.C.; Mahaffey Enterprises Inc.; Stillwater Radiology, Inc.

HOUSTON & OSBORN, PC

123 WEST 7TH AVENUE
P.O. BOX 1118
STILLWATER, OKLAHOMA 74076
Telephone: 405-377-7618; 377-8233
Telecopier: 405-377-8234
Email: losborn@Houston-Osborn.com
URL: http://www.houston-osborn.com

General Civil and Trial Practice. Probate, Estate Planning, Real Estate, Banking, Business, Commercial and Oil and Gas Law, Civil Litigation, Commercial Litigation, Business Law.

MEMBERS

WINFREY D. HOUSTON, born Stillwater, Oklahoma, June 1, 1926; admitted to bar, 1950, Oklahoma; 1952, U.S. District Court, Western District of Oklahoma; 1969, U.S. District Court, Eastern District of Oklahoma; 1972, U.S. Court of Appeals, Tenth Circuit; 1975, U.S. District Court, Northern District of Oklahoma; 1978, U.S. Supreme Court. *Education:* Oklahoma State University (B.A.); University of Oklahoma (J.D.). Phi Alpha Delta. *Member:* Payne County, Oklahoma (President, 1969) and American Bar Associations. Patron, Oklahoma Bar Foundation (President, 1983). Fellow, American Bar Foundation. ***PRACTICE AREAS:*** Civil Litigation; Banking Law; Probate; Estate Planning; Business Law. ***Email:*** whouston@Houston-Osborn.com

LYNN R. OSBORN, born Pawnee, Oklahoma, July 2, 1947; admitted to bar, 1972, Oklahoma and U.S. District Court, Western District of Oklahoma. *Education:* Oklahoma State University (B.S., 1969); Oklahoma University (J.D., 1972). Phi Delta Phi. *Member:* Payne County, Oklahoma and American Bar Associations. Fellow, Oklahoma Bar Foundation. ***PRACTICE AREAS:*** Civil Litigation; Real Estate; Probate; Business Law; Banking Law; Commercial Law. ***Email:*** losborn@Houston-Osborn.com

REPRESENTATIVE CLIENTS: BancFirst; Payne County Bank, Perkins, Okla.; Stillwater School District; Bates Bros. Mercantile, Inc.; Citizens State Bank of Morrison; Town of Morrison; Stillwater National Bank & Trust Co.; Frontier Electronic Systems Corp.; SpiritBank.
REFERENCES: BancFirst; Payne County Bank, Perkins, Okla.; Stillwater National Bank and Trust Co.; Citizens State Bank of Morrison.

G. MICHAEL SOLOMON

Established in 1983

711 SOUTH HUSBAND STREET
STILLWATER, OKLAHOMA 74074
Telephone: 405-743-3770
Fax: 405-743-3773
Email: gmsolomonlaw@aol.com

Woodland Hills, California Office: 22151 Ventura Boulevard, Suite 200. Telephone: 818-348-4470. Telecopier: 818-992-7687.

General Business, Transactions, Commercial Litigation, Banking Including Lending Practices, Creditor Bankruptcy, Commercial and Corporate Law.

G. MICHAEL SOLOMON, born Tulsa, Oklahoma, October 7, 1957; admitted to bar, 1982, Oklahoma and U.S. District Court, Northern District of Oklahoma; 1986, California and U.S. District Court, Central District of California; 1990, U.S. Tax Court; 1994, U.S. District Court, Western District of Oklahoma. *Education:* Oklahoma State University (B.S.B.A., 1979); University of Tulsa (J.D., 1982). Phi Delta Phi. *Member:* Los Angeles County, Payne County and Oklahoma Bar Associations; State Bar of California.

SZLICHTA & RAMSEY

Established in 1979

8 MAIN PLACE
P.O. BOX 1206
STILLWATER, OKLAHOMA 74076
Telephone: 405-377-3393
Fax: 405-377-4775
Email: ramseyc911@aol.com

General Practice. Trials. Family, School, Municipal, Administrative Law and Criminal Defense Law.

MEMBERS OF FIRM

CHRISTOPHER D. SZLICHTA, born Fort Dix, New Jersey, August 27, 1949; admitted to bar, 1976, Oklahoma; 1979, U.S. District Court, Western District of Oklahoma; 1981, U.S. Court of Appeals, Tenth Circuit; 1982, U.S. Supreme Court. *Education:* Oklahoma State University (B.A., 1972); Oklahoma City University (J.D., 1975). Phi Delta Phi. Faculty Member, Family Law, O.B.A./C.L.E., 1983-1985. Advisory and Faculty Member: Oklahoma Institute of C.L.E., Inc., 1983-1984; OBA/FLS, 1986-1992; Professional Education Systems, Inc., 1987; O.U., C.L.E., 1987-1993. Assistant District Attorney, Payne and Logan Counties, Oklahoma, 1976-1978. City Attorney, Stillwater, 1978-1979. Member, 1982-1987, Vice-President, 1983 and President, 1984, Stillwater Board of Education, Stillwater, Oklahoma. President, Stillwater Public Education Foundation, 1990. Member, Oklahoma Supreme Court Commission on Contempt Guidelines. *Member:* Pawnee County, Noble County, Payne County (Secretary-Treasurer, 1980; Vice-President, 1981; President, 1984), Oklahoma (Chairman, Family Law Section, 1984, 1985, 1987; named as Outstanding Oklahoma Family Lawyer, Family Law Section, 1987; Chairman, Board of Governors Special Committee on Child Support Guidelines, 1987) and American (Member, Family Law Section; Member, Ethics Committee) Bar Associations. Oklahoma Trial Lawyers Association; The Association of Trial Lawyers of America. Fellow: American Academy of Matrimonial Lawyers (President, Oklahoma Chapter, 1986, 1987; Member, Board of Governors, 1987-1989); Oklahoma Bar Foundation. ***PRACTICE AREAS:*** Family Law; School Law; Municipal Law; Administrative Law.

CHERYL A. RAMSEY, born Vinita, Oklahoma, June 6, 1951; admitted to bar, 1977, Oklahoma, U.S. District Court, Northern and Western Districts of Oklahoma, U.S. Court of Appeals, Tenth Circuit and U.S. Supreme Court. *Education:* Oklahoma State University (B.S., 1974); Oklahoma City University (J.D., 1976). Phi Alpha Delta. Special Judge, Ninth Judicial District, Payne County, Oklahoma, 1979-1984. Assistant District Attorney, Payne and Logan Counties, Oklahoma, 1978-1979. Member: Oklahoma Criminal Law Recodification Committee, 1991; Oklahoma Criminal Jury Instruction Committee, 1995; Oklahoma Sentencing Commission, 1997-2002. Appointed, Oklahoma Bar Association Professional Tribunal, December 2002. *Member:* Payne County (Secretary-Treasurer, 1986; President, 1987), Oklahoma and American (Member, Criminal Law Section) Bar Associations; National Association of Criminal Defense Lawyers; Oklahoma Criminal Defense Lawyers Association (Member, Board of Directors, 1988—; President, 1991, 1992). Oklahoma Bar Foundation. ***PRACTICE AREAS:*** Criminal Defense Law (100%).

REPRESENTATIVE CLIENTS: Moore Business Forms, Inc.; American National Bank, Cushing, Oklahoma; Oklahoma Nursing Home, Ltd.; Cushing Regional Hospital; Cushing Board of Education.
APPROVED ATTORNEYS FOR: First American Title Insurance Co.; Chicago Title Insurance Co.; Southwest Title and Trust Co.; Insurance Titles Inc.; Lawyers Title Insurance Corp.
REFERENCES: Stillwater National Bank and Trust Co.; Banc First, Stillwater.

GARRETT LAW OFFICE, P.C.

TAHLEQUAH, OKLAHOMA

(See Tulsa)

Personal Injury, Insurance Litigation, Products Liability, Workers Compensation, Securities, Bankruptcy.

LOCKE & MOORE

TAHLEQUAH, OKLAHOMA

(See Muskogee)

General Practice including Family Law, Criminal Law, Business Law, Bankruptcy, Personal Injury, Wills, Trusts and Estates, Probate.

YASODHARA "MITTY" MOHANTY MEANS P.C.

TAHLEQUAH, OKLAHOMA

(See Muskogee)

Mediation, Federal Litigation, Civil Litigation, Representation of Nurses and other Health Care Professionals, Administration Law, Corporate Law, Business Litigation, Estate Plan, Probate, Insurance and Surety Law.

OTTESON LAW PLLC

236 SOUTH MUSKOGEE AVENUE
TAHLEQUAH, OKLAHOMA 74464
Telephone: 918-456-7000
Fax: 918-456-5800
Email: ottesonlaw@sbcglobal.net

Civil and Criminal Trial Practice, Family Law, Bankruptcy and Employment Law. Licensed Family and Divorce Mediator.

MEMBER OF FIRM

PEGGY E. SHANNON OTTESON, born Lawton, Oklahoma, 1958; admitted to bar, 2001, Oklahoma and U.S. District Court, Northern, Eastern and Western Districts of Oklahoma; Cherokee Nation District Court. *Education:* University of St. Francis (B.S., magna cum laude, 1995); DePaul University (1996-1997); University of Tulsa (J.D., 2000). Oklahoma Indigent Defense Contractor, Cherokee County. *Member:* Oklahoma, Cherokee Nation and Cherokee County Bar Associations; Oklahoma Criminal Defense Lawyers Association; Oklahoma Trial Lawyers Association; American Association of University Women. ***Email:*** ottesonlaw@sbcglobal.net

COUNSEL FOR: Oklahoma Indigent Defense System; Cherokee County; Humane Society of Cherokee County.

ATKINS & MARKOFF

TECUMSEH, OKLAHOMA

(See Oklahoma City)

Personal Injury, Automobile Accidents, Wrongful Death, Trucking Accidents, Slip and Fall, Nursing Home Abuse, Head and Spinal Injuries, Dog Bites, Sexual Abuse, Criminal Law, Drug Crimes, DUI/DWI, Juvenile Crimes, General Practice, Family , Divorce, Adoptions, Child Custody, Child Support, Domestic Violence, Visitation Rights, Elder Law, Legal Malpractice, Medical Malpractice, Social Security, Social Security Disability, Taxation, IRS Audits, Property Tax Appeals, Tax Planning, Toxic Torts, Trust and Estate, Wills and Probate.

A. CRAIG ABRAHAMSON

Established in 1986

706 BEACON BUILDING
406 S. BOULDER AVENUE
TULSA, OKLAHOMA 74103
Telephone: 918-584-0318
Fax: 918-582-6106
Email: craiga@abrahamsonlaw.com
URL: http://www.abrahamsonlaw.com

Family Law, Divorce, Child Custody, Visitation Rights, Child Support, Alimony, Spousal Support, Post Decree Modification and Enforcement, Premarital Agreements, Bankruptcy Creditors, Bankruptcy Debtor Ch. 7, Bankruptcy Debtor Ch. 11, Bankruptcy Debtor Ch. 13, Business Law, Commercial Transactions, Business Litigation, Commercial Litigation, Real Estate Transactions, Landlords.

A. CRAIG ABRAHAMSON, born Washington, D.C., May 24, 1954; admitted to bar, 1979, Minnesota and U.S. District Court, District of Minnesota; 1982, Oklahoma; 1983, U.S. District Court, Northern District of Oklahoma; 1988, U.S. District Court, Eastern District of Oklahoma; 1990, U.S. Court of Appeals, Tenth Circuit; 1991, Missouri. *Education:* University of Minnesota (B.A., 1976); University of Tulsa (J.D., 1979). Listed in, Who's Who in American Law. Recipient, American Jurisprudence Award in Evidence. *Member:* Tulsa County (Family Law Section, Bankruptcy Section), Oklahoma (Family Law Section; Bankruptcy Section; Real Property Section) Bar Associations. Fellow, Tulsa County Bar Foundation. ***PRACTICE AREAS:*** Family Law; Divorce; Child Custody; Visitation Rights; Child Support; Alimony; Spousal Support; Premarital Agreements; Bankruptcy; Bankruptcy Creditors; Bankruptcy Debtor Ch. 7; Bankruptcy Debtor Ch. 11; Bankruptcy Debtor Ch. 13; Business Law; Commercial Transactions; Commercial Litigation; Real Estate Transactions; Landlords.

KEVIN D. ADAMS

1717 SOUTH CHEYENNE AVENUE
TULSA, OKLAHOMA 74119
Telephone: 918-587-8100
Fax: 918-582-7830
Email: kevin@oklahomacriminallaw.com
URL: http://www.oklahomacriminallaw.com

Criminal Defense, Felonies, White Collar, Drug Crimes, Driving While Intoxicated, Assault and Battery, Manslaughter, Sex Crimes, Murder.

KEVIN D. ADAMS, born Tulsa, Oklahoma, August 22, 1973; admitted to bar, 2001, Oklahoma, U.S. District Court, Northern District of Oklahoma and U.S. Court of Appeals, Tenth Circuit; 2003, U.S. District Court, Eastern District of Oklahoma. *Education:* Univer-

(This Listing Continued)

sity of Tulsa (B.S., 1998; J.D., 2000). Recipient, Clarence Darrow Award, Oklahoma Criminal Defense Lawyers Association, 2003. *Member:* Oklahoma Criminal Defense Lawyers Association; Tulsa Criminal Defense Lawyers Association; National Association of Criminal Defense Lawyers. ***REPORTED CASES:*** U.S. v. Solomon, 399 F.3d 1231 (10th Cir. 3/1/2005). ***PRACTICE AREAS:*** Criminal Defense.

ALBRIGHT, RUSHER & HARDCASTLE

A PROFESSIONAL CORPORATION

Established in 1986

2600 BANK OF AMERICA CENTER
15 WEST SIXTH STREET
TULSA, OKLAHOMA 74119
Telephone: 918-583-5800
Fax: 918-583-8665
Email: arhlaw@arhlaw.com
URL: http://www.arhlaw.com

General Civil Trial Practice, Trials and Appeals of Civil Cases in State and Federal Courts, Construction Litigation, Federal and State Taxation, Corporate and Securities, Mergers and Acquisitions, Bankruptcy and Creditors' Rights, Commercial Bankruptcy, Debtor and Creditor, Collections, Oil and Gas, Real Estate, Probate and Estate Planning, Family Law, Alternative Dispute Resolution, Limited Liability Company Law, Business Formation, Closely Held Business Law, Tax Exempt Organizations, Asset Protection.

KENNETH F. ALBRIGHT, born Memphis, Tennessee, July 28, 1956; admitted to bar, 1981, Oklahoma. *Education:* Oklahoma State University (B.A., 1978); University of Oklahoma (J.D., 1981); Southern Methodist University (LL.M., in Taxation, 1982). ***PRACTICE AREAS:*** Tax; Oil & Gas; Corporate Law; Securities; Estate Planning. ***Email:*** kfalbright@arhlaw.com

JAMES W. RUSHER, born Miami, Oklahoma, February 25, 1960; admitted to bar, 1985, Oklahoma. *Education:* Southern Methodist University (B.A., cum laude, 1982; J.D., 1985). *Member:* Oklahoma and American (Member, Construction Law Section, 1985) Bar Associations. ***PRACTICE AREAS:*** Commercial Litigation; Construction Defects; Civil Litigation; Estate Planning; Family Law; Divorce; Debtor and Creditor; Bankruptcy. ***Email:*** jwrusher@arhlaw.com

HEATH E. HARDCASTLE, born Orange, Texas, September 2, 1967; admitted to bar, 1990, Oklahoma. *Education:* University of Arkansas (B.A., 1986; J.D., 1990). Phi Alpha Delta. Articles Editor, Arkansas Law Review, 1989-1990. Author: "Holdway v. Duvoisin: Garnishment Payments as Preferences Under §547," 43 Arkansas Law Review 217, 1989. *Member:* Oklahoma, Arkansas and American Bar Associations. ***PRACTICE AREAS:*** Commercial Litigation; Business Tort Litigation; General Civil Litigation; Creditors' Rights; Collections; Commercial Bankruptcy. ***Email:*** hehardcastle@arhlaw.com

TODD ALEXANDER

Established in 1987

2121 SOUTH COLUMBIA
SUITE 500, PARKLAND PLAZA BUILDING
TULSA, OKLAHOMA 74114-3519
Telephone: 918-744-0201
Facsimile: 918-747-8820
Email: todd@toddalexanderlaw.com
URL: http://www.toddalexanderlaw.com

Family Law, Divorce, Child Custody, Adoptions, Guardianship, Visitation Rights, Premarital Agreements, Spousal Support, Probate, Wills, Trusts, Business Litigation, Civil Litigation.

TODD ALEXANDER, born Tulsa, Oklahoma, July 16, 1954; admitted to bar, 1980, Oklahoma; 1983, Texas, U.S. District Court, Northern District of Texas and U.S. District Court, Northern District of Oklahoma; U.S. Court of Appeals, Tenth and Seventh Circuits. *Education:* University of Nebraska at Lincoln; University of Chicago (B.A., 1977); University of Oklahoma (J.D., 1980). Phi Alpha Delta. Certified Mediator in Oklahoma and Texas. *Member:* Tulsa and Oklahoma Bar Associations; State Bar of Texas.

THE LAW OFFICE OF ROBERT H. ALEXANDER, JR.

ATTORNEYS AND COUNSELORS AT LAW, P.C.

TULSA, OKLAHOMA

(See Oklahoma City)

Pharmaceutical, Automotive, Mechanical and General Products Liability Defense, General Civil Trial and Appellate Practice.

CHARLES BRYAN ALRED, P.C.

3242 EAST 30TH PLACE
SUITE B
TULSA, OKLAHOMA 74114
Telephone: 918-745-9960
Fax: 918-745-9965
URL: http://www.tulsaautoaccidentslaw.com
Email: bryanalred@hotmail.com
URL: http://www.tulsaautoaccident.com

Automobile Accidents, Personal Injury, Wrongful Death, Insurance Disputes, Criminal Defense, Driving While Intoxicated, Workers' Compensation, Negligence, General Civil Litigation. Trial in State and Federal Courts, Trucking Accidents, Motorcycle Accidents, Boating Accidents, Dog Bites, Products Liability and Driving While Under the Influence.

(This Listing Continued)

CHARLES BRYAN ALRED, born Pawhuska, Oklahoma, October 26, 1958; admitted to bar, 1987, Oklahoma; 1989, U.S. District Court, Northern District of Oklahoma. *Education:* Oklahoma State University (B.S., 1980); University of Kansas (J.D., 1986). Kappa Beta Gamma (President, 1986). *Member:* Tulsa County, Osage County and Oklahoma Bar Associations; Association of Trial Lawyers of America; Oklahoma Trial Lawyers Association; The University of Oklahoma and the Oklahoma Trial Lawyers Association; Oklahoma College of Advocacy. [U.S. Marine Corp., 1982-1986]. ***PRACTICE AREAS:*** Personal Injury; Workers Compensation; Criminal Defense; Driving While Intoxicated. ***Email:*** bryanalred@hotmail.com

JOHN W. ANDERSON, JR., P.C.

Established in 1995

7318 SOUTH YALE AVENUE, SUITE A
TULSA, OKLAHOMA 74136-7000
Telephone: 918-481-5552
Fax: 918-481-5558
Email: johnanderson@abanet.org
URL: http://www.lawyers.com/johnanderson

General and Commercial Litigation in Federal and State Courts. Judgment Domestication and Collection, Contract Analysis, Drafting and Litigation, Contingency Business Litigation, Appellate Practice, General Corporate Work, White Collar Criminal Law, Grand Jury Practice, Insurance Defense, Insurance Coverage, International Contract and Distribution Agreements, Dealer and Distributor Termination, Risk Management and Legal Research and Writing on a contract basis.

JOHN W. ANDERSON, JR., born Salt Lake City, Utah, August 14, 1962; admitted to bar, 1989, Oklahoma, U.S. Court of Appeals, Eighth and Tenth Circuits and U.S. Federal District Courts, Northern, Eastern and Western Districts of Oklahoma. *Education:* University of Utah (B.S., 1985; J.D., 1989). Phi Delta Phi (Vice-Magister, 1988-1989). Author: "How to Spot a Conflict of Interest," Barrister Magazine, Winter, 1996. Seminar Participant: Paralegal Ethics in Oklahoma, 2002; Debt Collection from Start to Finish in Oklahoma, 2004. *Member:* Tulsa County (Member: Pictorial Directory Committee, 1991-1993; Law Day Committee, 1991-1993; Public Relations Committee, 1994-1996; Fee Arbitration Committee, 1996—; Professional Responsibility Committee, 1998—), Oklahoma and American (Member: Young Lawyers Division, Litigation Committee, 1989-1999; Planning Board Committee on Ethics and Professionalism, 1995-1998) Bar Associations; American Inn of Court. ***REPORTED CASES:*** A-Plus Janitorial & Carpet Cleaning v. The Employers' Workers Compensation Association, 936 P.2d 916 (Okla. 1997); Calvert v. Tulsa Public Schools, 932 P.2d 1087 (Okla. 1996). ***Email:*** johnanderson@abanet.org

ANDREW, WILLIAMS & IKENBERRY A PROFESSIONAL CORPORATION

125 WEST THIRD STREET
TULSA, OKLAHOMA 74103
Telephone: 918-583-1111
Fax: 918-587-4414
Email: info@awlaw.net
URL: http://www.awlaws.com

Labor Law, Equal Employment Law, Civil Trials.

STEPHEN L. ANDREW, born Tulsa, Oklahoma, November 23, 1944; admitted to bar, 1973, Oklahoma. *Education:* St. Lawrence University (B.S., 1968); University of Tulsa (J.D., 1972). ***PRACTICE AREAS:*** Employment Law; Civil Trial Practice. ***Email:*** steve@awlaw.net

RENEE WILLIAMS, born Garden City, Kansas, August 25; admitted to bar, 1988, Oklahoma, Texas and District of Columbia. *Education:* Wichita State University (B.G.S., magna cum laude, 1984); University of Arkansas (J.D., 1988). ***LANGUAGES:*** French and Spanish. ***Email:*** renee@awlaw.net

D. KEVIN IKENBERRY, born Clinton, Missouri, October 1, 1954; admitted to bar, 1983, Oklahoma, U.S. District Court, Northern District of Oklahoma; 1985, Virginia and U.S. Court of Appeals, Tenth Circuit. *Education:* Oral Roberts University (B.A., summa cum laude, 1980; J.D., cum laude, 1983).

REPRESENTATIVE CLIENTS: Warehouse Market, Inc.; Gatesway Foundation, Inc.; The Hardesty Co.; North American Galvanizing; Chandler Materials; EIS Communications; Fabricut, Inc.; O'Reilly Auto Parts, Inc.; Technotherm Corp.
LABOR RELATIONS CLIENTS: International Chemical Company; Metropolitan Tulsa Transit Authority; MidContinent Concrete Company; Tuloma Stevedoring, Inc.; Continental Industries, Inc.; Oklahoma Fixture Co.; Burgess-Norton Mfg. Co.; Oklahoma Installation Co.; The Nordam Group, Inc.; City of Muskogee; Flowserve Corp.

THE ASH LAW FIRM

Established in 1974

2500 MID-CONTINENT TOWER
401 SOUTH BOSTON AVENUE
TULSA, OKLAHOMA 74103-4016
Telephone: 918-599-0001;
1-800-700-0715
Fax: 918-599-0101
Email: info@ashlawfirm.net
URL: http://www.ash-law.com

Trials in all State and Federal Courts. Personal Injury, Medical Malpractice, Product Liability, Insurance, Workers' Compensation Law and Social Security Disability.

(This Listing Continued)

THE ASH LAW FIRM, Tulsa—Continued

FIRM PROFILE: The Ash Law Firm represents plaintiffs in all areas of personal injury litigation. The firm is headed by Edwin W. Ash who has served as lead counsel in over 400 jury trials. In addition to regularly trying cases before juries, M. Scott Ash is heavily involved in representing clients in Workers Compensation cases and Social Security Disability hearings. The bulk of the firms' clients are referred by other lawyers and former clients.

MEMBERS OF FIRM

EDWIN W. ASH, born Clarksburg, West Virginia, September 18, 1935; admitted to bar, 1965, Oklahoma; 1991, U.S. Supreme Court. *Education:* Salem College (B.S., 1961); University of Tulsa (J.D., 1965). Phi Delta Phi. City Attorney, Okmulgee, Oklahoma, 1971. Member, American Inns of Court, Hudson-Hall-Wheaton Chapter. *Member:* Tulsa County, Oklahoma and American Bar Associations; Oklahoma Trial Lawyers Association; The Association of Trial Lawyers of America; American Judicature Society; American Board of Trial Advocates. Fellow: Oklahoma Bar Foundation; American College of Trial Lawyers. ***PRACTICE AREAS:*** Personal Injury Law; Medical Malpractice; Products Liability; Insurance.

M. SCOTT ASH, born Tulsa, Oklahoma, August 15, 1963; admitted to bar, 1989, Colorado; 1992, U.S. Court of Appeals, Tenth Circuit; 1993, U.S. District Court, District of Colorado; 1994, Oklahoma. *Education:* University of Oklahoma (B.B.A, 1986); University of Tulsa (J.D., 1989). Delta Theta Phi. Member, American Inns of Court, Hudson-Hall-Wheaton Chapter. *Member:* Tulsa County, Colorado, Oklahoma and American Bar Associations; Oklahoma Trial Lawyers Association; Colorado Trial Lawyers Association; The Association of Trial Lawyers of America. ***PRACTICE AREAS:*** Personal Injury; Workers' Compensation; Social Security Disability.

ATKINS & MARKOFF

TULSA, OKLAHOMA

(See Oklahoma City)

Personal Injury, Automobile Accidents, Wrongful Death, Trucking Accidents, Slip and Fall, Nursing Home Abuse, Head and Spinal Injuries, Dog Bites, Sexual Abuse, Criminal Law, Drug Crimes, DUI/DWI, Juvenile Crimes, General Practice, Family , Divorce, Adoptions, Child Custody, Child Support, Domestic Violence, Visitation Rights, Elder Law, Legal Malpractice, Medical Malpractice, Social Security, Social Security Disability, Taxation, IRS Audits, Property Tax Appeals, Tax Planning, Toxic Torts, Trust and Estate, Wills and Probate.

ATKINSON, HASKINS, NELLIS, BRITTINGHAM, GLADD & CARWILE

Established in 1961

1500 PARKCENTRE
525 SOUTH MAIN STREET
TULSA, OKLAHOMA 74103
Telephone: 918-582-8877
Fax: 918-585-8096
Email: ahnmail@ahn-law.com

Medical and Legal Malpractice, Negligence, Insurance, General Civil Practice, Trials and Appeals, Product Liability, Environmental, Oil and Gas, Aviation, Corporation and Antitrust, Securities, Broker-Dealer Disputes, Workers' Compensation, Civil Rights, Employment Law, Pharmaceutical Defense, Commercial Litigation, Construction Litigation, Bankruptcy, Antitrust.

FIRM PROFILE: Atkinson, Haskins, Nellis, Brittingham, Gladd & Carwile is one of Oklahoma's premier litigation firms. The firm concentrates its practice in the area of insurance and corporate defense litigation, specializing in defense of legal and medical malpractice, insurance bad faith, manufacturer's products liability and general civil actions. The firm's clients cover the spectrum of the industry, and include some of the nation's largest insurers and corporations. The firm is recognized for its expertise in trial practice, quality of service, and client results. The firm is listed in the Bar Register of Preeminent Lawyers.

MICHAEL P. ATKINSON, P.C., born Fort Worth, Texas, February 19, 1946; admitted to bar, 1972, Oklahoma. *Education:* Westminster College and University of Oklahoma (B.A., 1968); University of Oklahoma (J.D., 1972); University of Texas (LL.M., 1975). Assistant Public Defender, 1973 and Assistant District Attorney, 1974, Oklahoma County, Oklahoma. Assistant Adjunct Professor of Law, University of Tulsa College of Law, 1976. Faculty Member, Insurance Counsel Trial Academy, Boulder, Colorado, 1986. *Member:* Tulsa County and Oklahoma Bar Associations; Diplomate, American Board of Trial Advocates (President, Oklahoma Chapter, 1995). Master Emeritus, American Inns of Court. Fellow, International Academy of Trial Lawyers. Fellow, American College of Trial Lawyers. ***PRACTICE AREAS:*** Medical and Legal Malpractice; Trial Advocacy; Complex Litigation; Insurance; Negligence; Insurance Bad Faith. ***Email:*** matkinson@ahn-law.com

WALTER D. HASKINS, P.C., born Kansas City, Kansas, April 1, 1956; admitted to bar, 1980, Oklahoma, U.S. District Court, Eastern, Western and Northern Districts of Oklahoma, U.S. District Court, Eastern and Western Districts of Arkansas, and U.S. Court of Appeals, 10th Circuit; 1988, U.S. Supreme Court. *Education:* Drury College (B.A., magna cum laude, 1977); University of Kansas (J.D., 1980); Insurance Counsel Trial Academy. Pi Kappa Delta; Omicron Delta Kappa. Panel Member, Criminal Justice Act, U.S. District Court, Northern District of Oklahoma. *Member:* Tulsa County and Oklahoma Bar Associations; Oklahoma Association of Defense Counsel; Lawyer-Pilots Bar Association; International Association of Defense Councel; American Board of Trial Advocates (Advocate). ***PRACTICE AREAS:*** Medical and Legal Malpractice; Trial Advocacy; Aviation; Insurance; Negligence; Insurance Bad Faith. ***Email:*** whaskins@ahn-law.com

(This Listing Continued)

GREGORY D. NELLIS, P.C., born Ottawa, Kansas, March 24, 1955; admitted to bar, 1980, Oklahoma; 1981, U.S. District Court, Eastern, Western and Northern Districts of Oklahoma; U.S. Court of Appeals, 10th Circuit; U.S. Supreme Court. *Education:* Southwestern Oklahoma State University (B.A., magna cum laude, 1976); University of Oklahoma (J.D., 1980); Insurance Counsel Trial Academy. Phi Delta Phi (Local President, Fall, 1979). Member: Tulsa County, Oklahoma and American Bar Associations; Defense Research Institute; Oklahoma Association of Defense Counsel; International Association of Defense Counsel; American Board of Trial Advocates. ***PRACTICE AREAS:*** Negligence; Products Liability; Insurance; Medical Malpractice; Civil Rights; Insurance Bad Faith. ***Email:*** gnellis@ahn-law.com

GALEN LEE BRITTINGHAM, P.C., born Nevada, Missouri, April 27, 1954; admitted to bar, 1987, Oklahoma. *Education:* Southwest Missouri State University (B.S., 1976); Central Missouri State University (M.S., 1983); Washburn University of Topeka (J.D., with honors, 1987). Phi Alpha Delta. Member, Washburn Law Journal, 1986-1987. *Member:* Tulsa County and Oklahoma Bar Associations. ***PRACTICE AREAS:*** Appeals; Medical Malpractice; Negligence; Insurance; Insurance Bad Faith. ***Email:*** gbrittingham@ahn-law.com

JOHN S. GLADD, born Kansas City, Missouri, July 27, 1961; admitted to bar, 1987, Oklahoma; 1988, U.S. District Court, Eastern, Western and Northern Districts of Oklahoma. *Education:* Oklahoma State University (B.S., 1983); University of Tulsa (J.D., 1987). Phi Alpha Delta. *Member:* Tulsa County, Oklahoma and American Bar Associations; Defense Research Institute; Oklahoma Association of Defense Counsel; DRI-Defense Counsel Trial Academy; International Association of Defense Counsel. ***PRACTICE AREAS:*** Negligence; Products Liability; Insurance; Premises Liability; Trial Advocacy; Insurance Bad Faith. ***Email:*** jgladd@ahn-law.com

JOHN J. CARWILE, born Escanaba, Michigan, August 3, 1954; admitted to bar, 1984, Oklahoma, U.S. District Court, Eastern, Western and Northern Districts of Oklahoma and U.S. Court of Appeals, Tenth Circuit. *Education:* United States Naval Academy (B.S., with highest honors, 1976); Harvard Law School (J.D., cum laude, 1984). Law Clerk to Hon. S. K. Seymour, Judge, U.S. Court of Appeals, Tenth Circuit, 1984-1985. Adjunct Professor, Tulsa University College of Law, 1985-1990. *Member:* Tulsa County and American Bar Associations. [Lt., U.S. Navy, 1976-1981]. ***PRACTICE AREAS:*** General Litigation; Business and Civil Litigation; Trial Advocacy; Bankruptcy Law; Commercial Litigation. ***Email:*** jcarwile@ahn-law.com

WILLIAM A. FIASCO, born Los Angeles, California, January 3, 1961; admitted to bar, 1988, Oklahoma; U.S. District Court, Eastern, Western and Northern Districts of Oklahoma. *Education:* University of Oklahoma (B.A., 1983; J.D., 1988). Order of the Barristers. Ungerman Scholar. National Trial Team, 1986-1988. Member, American Inns of Court. *Member:* Tulsa County, Oklahoma and American Bar Associations; Defense Research Institute; Oklahoma Association of Defense Counsel. ***PRACTICE AREAS:*** Medical Malpractice; Negligence; Products Liability; Insurance; Trial Advocacy; Insurance Bad Faith. ***Email:*** wfiasco@ahn-law.com

JAMES N. EDMONDS, born Paola, Kansas, July 6, 1961; admitted to bar, 1993, Oklahoma; U.S. District Court, Northern, Eastern and Western Districts of Oklahoma; U.S. Court of Appeals, 10th Circuit. *Education:* University of Kansas (B.A., 1987; M.A., 1990; J.D., 1993). Phi Kappa Phi. Order of the Coif. Recipient: American Jurisprudence Award in Evidence; Payne & Jones Appellate Advocacy Award. Member: Kansas Journal of Law and Public Policy, 1991-1992; Kansas Law Review, 1992-1993. *Member:* Tulsa County, Oklahoma and American (Member, Labor and Employment Law Section) Bar Associations; Oklahoma Association of Defense Counsel; Defense Research Institute. ***PRACTICE AREAS:*** Insurance Bad Faith; Employment Law; Negligence; Products Liability; Appellate Advocacy. ***Email:*** jedmonds@ahn-law.com

SCOTT R. HALL, born Oklahoma City, Oklahoma, November 29, 1968; admitted to bar, 1994, Oklahoma and U.S. District Court, Western, Eastern and Northern Districts of Oklahoma; 1995, U.S. Court of Appeals, Tenth Circuit; 1999, U.S. District Court, Western and Eastern Districts of Arkansas. *Education:* Oklahoma State University (B.S., 1991); University of Oklahoma (J.D., with honors, 1994). Phi Delta Phi; Order of the Coif. Member, Oklahoma Law Review. *Member:* Tulsa County, Oklahoma and American Bar Associations. ***PRACTICE AREAS:*** Negligence; Products Liability; Insurance; Trial Advocacy. ***Email:*** shall@ahn-law.com

MARK W. MAGUIRE, born Oklahoma City, Oklahoma, March 6, 1963; admitted to bar, 1989, Oklahoma; U.S. District Court, Northern, Eastern and Western Districts of Oklahoma. *Education:* Oklahoma State University (B.B.A., 1986); University of Oklahoma (J.D., 1989). Blue Key; Omicron Delta Kappa; Phi Kappa Phi. Member, American Inns of Court, 1991-1992. *Member:* Tulsa County, Oklahoma and American Bar Associations; Defense Counsel Trial Academy; Oklahoma Association of Defense Counsel; Defense Research Institute. ***PRACTICE AREAS:*** Negligence; Products Liability; Insurance; Trial Advocacy; Business Litigation; Civil Litigation; Commercial Litigation. ***Email:*** mmaguire@ahn-law.com

JENNIFER ANNIS, born Woodward, Oklahoma, June 27, 1972; admitted to bar, 1998, Oklahoma. *Education:* University of Oklahoma (B.A., 1994; J.D., 1998). Phi Delta Phi; Order of Barristers. Member: Association of Trial Lawyers of America Trial Team; National Trial Team. Recipient: Salem Civil Rights Award; McAfee Taft Award; American Jurisprudence Awards for Trial Techniques and Disability Law. Teaching Assistant, Legal Research and Writing, University of Oklahoma, 1996-1998. Member, American Inns of Court. ***LANGUAGES:*** German and French. ***PRACTICE AREAS:*** Insurance Defense; Medical Malpractice Defense. ***Email:*** jannis@ahn-law.com

MARTHA J. PHILLIPS, born Ranger, Texas, November 20, 1949; admitted to bar, 1986, Oklahoma and U.S. District Court, Eastern, Western and Northern Districts of Oklahoma and U.S. Court of Appeals, 10th Circuit. *Education:* Oklahoma State University (B.S., Med. Tech., 1971); University of Tulsa (J.D., 1986). Delta Theta Phi. Licensed Physician's Assistant, University of Oklahoma Health Sciences Center, 1978. *Member:* Tulsa County, Oklahoma and American Bar Associations; Defense Research Institute. ***PRACTICE AREAS:*** Medical Malpractice; Negligence; Insurance. ***Email:*** mphillips@ahn-law.com

JON D. STARR, born Stilwell, Oklahoma, August 15, 1964; admitted to bar, 1991, Oklahoma; U.S. District Court, Northern, Eastern and Western Districts of Oklahoma; U.S.

(This Listing Continued)

Court of Appeals, Tenth Circuit. *Education:* Oklahoma State University (B.S., 1986); University of Oklahoma (J.D., with distinction, 1991). Recipient, American Jurisprudence Award for Personal Property Security. Intern, Judge John TeSelle, U.S. Bankruptcy Court, Western District of Oklahoma, 1990. Author: "Attorney Lien Claimed: Is It Worth the Paper It Is Written On?" Oklahoma Bar Journal, 2000, and "Some Major Points About Minor's Claims," Oklahoma Bar Journal, 2002. *Member:* Tulsa County Bar Association; American Bar Association; Oklahoma Association of Defense Counsel (President, 2002); Defense Research Institute; American Board of Trial Advocates; Oklahoma Bar Association (Chairperson, Insurance Law Section, 2005). ***PRACTICE AREAS:*** Medical Malpractice; Negligence; Products Liability; Construction Law; Insurance; Trial Advocacy; Insurance Bad Faith. ***Email:*** jstarr@ahn-law.com

MARTHANDA J. BECKWORTH, born Muskogee, Oklahoma, January 16, 1949; admitted to bar, 1983, Oklahoma; U.S. District Court, Eastern and Northern Districts of Oklahoma; U.S. Court Appeals, 10th Circuit; U.S. Supreme Court. *Education:* Northeastern Oklahoma State University (B.A., with honors, 1971); University of Tulsa (J.D., with honors, 1983). Order of the Curule Chair. Ungerman Scholar. Recipient, Travis I. Milsten Award for Decedent's Estates and Trusts. Member, Tulsa Law Journal, 1981-1983. Law Clerk of Judge William W. Means, Oklahoma Court of Appeals, 1983-1989. Adjunct Professor of Law, University of Tulsa. *Member:* Tulsa County, Oklahoma and American Bar Associations. ***PRACTICE AREAS:*** Appeals; Insurance; Medical and Legal Malpractice; Employment Law; Health Care Law; Civil Rights. ***Email:*** mbeckworth@ahn-law.com

KIRSTEN E. PACE, born Oklahoma City, Oklahoma, July 31, 1965; admitted to bar, 1990, Oklahoma, U.S. District Court, Northern, Eastern and Western Districts of Oklahoma, U.S. Court of Appeals, Tenth Circuit and U.S. Supreme Court. *Education:* Duke University (A.B., 1987); University of Oklahoma (J.D., with distinction, 1990). Phi Delta Phi. Legal Research and Writing Teaching Assistant, University of Oklahoma College of Law, 1988-1990. *Member:* Tulsa County, Oklahoma and American Bar Associations. ***PRACTICE AREAS:*** Appeals; Medical and Hospital Negligence; Products Liability; Negligence; Insurance. ***Email:*** kpace@ahn-law.com

ERIC J. BEGIN, born Shawnee, Oklahoma, August 23, 1969; admitted to bar, 1994, Oklahoma; U.S. District Court, Northern, Eastern and Western Districts of Oklahoma. *Education:* Oklahoma Christian University (B.S., 1991); Oklahoma City University (J.D., 1994). Recipient, American Jurisprudence Award. *Member:* Tulsa County (Member: Professional Responsibility Committee, 2002-2003; Court Operation Committee, 2002-2003) and Oklahoma (Member, Sections on: Employment; Litigation) Bar Associations; Young Lawyers Division (Community Outreach Committee, 1995); Oklahoma Association of Defense Counsel. ***PRACTICE AREAS:*** Insurance Defense; Professional Malpractice Defense; Employment Litigation; Products Liability; Commercial Litigation. ***Email:*** ebegin@ahn-law.com

---

CAROL J. ALLEN, born New York, N.Y., July 11, 1965; admitted to bar, 1999, Oklahoma. *Education:* Northeastern Oklahoma State University (B.S., 1995); University of Tulsa (J.D., 1999). Recipient, CALI Excellence for Future Award, University of Tulsa. *Member:* Oklahoma and American Bar Associations. ***PRACTICE AREAS:*** Bankruptcy; Commercial Litigation. ***Email:*** callen@ahn-law.com

GABE W. LAWSON, born Denver, Colorado, September 4, 1976; admitted to bar, 2001, Oklahoma. *Education:* Southwestern University (B.A., 1998); University of Tulsa (J.D., 2000). ***PRACTICE AREAS:*** Insurance Defense; Civil Litigation; Medical Malpractice. ***Email:*** glawson@ahn-law.com

RACHEL D. PARRILLI, born Oklahoma City, Oklahoma, June 1, 1975; admitted to bar, 2000, Oklahoma. *Education:* Oral Roberts University (B.A., 1997); University of Tulsa (J.D., 2000). Phi Delta Phi. ***PRACTICE AREAS:*** Insurance Defense; Civil Rights; Negligence; Civil Appellate Research. ***Email:*** rmalone@ahn-law.com

ANDREW C. JAYNE, born Muskogee, Oklahoma, November 9, 1976; admitted to bar, 2002, Oklahoma. *Education:* Westminster College (B.A., 1999); University of Oklahoma College of Law (J.D., 2002). Order of the Coif. Chief Articles Editor, Oklahoma Law Review. Recipient: Robert J. Emery Scholarship; Frank C. Love Scholarship, Outstanding Legal Writing; OU Criminal Legal Clinic Outstanding Student Award; American Jurisprudence Award, Criminal Procedure. Author: "Affirmative Action in the Public Sector: The Admissibility of Post-Enactment Evidence of Discrimination to Provide a Compelling Governmental Interest," 55 Okla. L. Rev. 121, 2002. ***Email:*** ajayne@ahn-law.com

JAMES CRAIG BUCHAN, born Tulsa, Oklahoma, October 18, 1976; admitted to bar, 2002, Oklahoma; U.S. District Court, Northern, Eastern and Western Districts of Oklahoma. *Education:* University of Oklahoma (B.B.A., 1999; J.D., 2002). Member, Oklahoma Law Review. Member, National Trial Team. Author: "Boy Scouts of America v. Dale: The Scout Oath and Law Survive Government Intrusion," 55 Okla L. Rev. 153, 2002. *Member:* Oklahoma and American Bar Associations. ***PRACTICE AREAS:*** Medical Malpractice; Insurance Defense; Products Liability; Construction Law; Trial Advocacy. ***Email:*** jbuchan@ahn-law.com

STACIE L. HIXON, born Tulsa, Oklahoma, September 10, 1974; admitted to bar, 2002, Oklahoma. *Education:* Oklahoma State University (B.A., 1996; M.A., 1997); University of Tulsa (J.D., 2002). Phi Delta Phi. Editor-in-Chief, Energy Law Journal, 2001-2002. Author: Electric Deregulated in Oklahoma," 22, Energy L.J. 381 (2002). ***LANGUAGES:*** German. ***Email:*** shayes@ahn-law.com

JAMIE A. ROGERS, born Ponca City, Oklahoma, July 26, 1977; admitted to bar, 2003, Oklahoma. *Education:* Oklahoma State University (B.S., 1999); University of Oklahoma (J.D., 2003). ***Email:*** jrogers@ahn-law.com

BART JAY ROBEY, born Oklahoma City, Oklahoma, June 27, 1978; admitted to bar, 2003, Oklahoma. *Education:* American University (B.A., 2000); George Washington University (J.D., 2003). Phi Delta Phi. ***PRACTICE AREAS:*** Medical Malpractice; Negligence; Insurance Law; Trial Advocacy; Bad Faith. ***Email:*** brobcy@ahn-law.com

OF COUNSEL

K. CLARK PHIPPS, born Norman, Oklahoma, January 9, 1957; admitted to bar, 1986, Oklahoma; U.S. District Court, Eastern, Western and Northern Districts of Oklahoma; U.S. Court of Appeals, Tenth Circuit; 1995, Texas. *Education:* University of Oklahoma (B.S., 1979); Tulane University (J.D., cum laude, 1986). Member, Moot Court. Order of the Barristers. National Semifinalist, Craven Appellate Competition, 1986. *Member:* Tulsa County, Oklahoma and American Bar Associations; State Bar of Texas; American Board of Trial Advocates; International Association of Defense Counsel; Defense Research Institute; Defense Counsel Trial Academy; Oklahoma Association of Defense Counsel. ***PRACTICE AREAS:*** Trial Advocacy; Medical Malpractice; Securities/Business Litigation; Broker-Dealer Disputes; Product Liability; Pharmaceutical Defense. ***Email:*** cphipps@ahn-law.com

(This Listing Continued)

LEGAL SUPPORT PERSONNEL

BEVERLY J. RUBINO, M.D., born Ft. Worth, Texas, August 16, 1960. *Education:* Texas Woman's University (B.S., Chemistry, 1981); University of Texas (M.D., 1986). Alpha Chi (President). Continuing Education: Pathology Training, St. Paul Medical Center, Dallas, Texas, 1991; Pathology Training, Health Science Center, University of Texas, Dallas, Texas, 1991. Medical License: Texas, 1987; Oklahoma, 1997. Lecturer, OBGyn Pathology, St. Paul Medical Center, Dallas, Texas, 1988-1991. Previous Employment: Wallach and Moore, Ft. Worth, Texas, Consultant; Otstott and Andrews, Dallas, Texas, Consultant; Scanlon and Gearinger, Akron, Ohio, Consultant; Corning Clinical Labs, Irving, Texas, Associate Medical Director. Member: College of American Pathologists, 1997; Texas Medical Association, 1987; American Medical Association, 1987; American Society of Clinical Pathologists, 1987-1997; Dallas County Medical Society, 1994-1997. *Areas of Responsibility:* Medical Counsel; Medical Research to Legal Defense. (Medical Counsel). ***Email:*** brubino@ahn-law.com

REPRESENTATIVE CLIENTS: Alexsis Incorporated; Allianz Insurance Co.; Allied Group; Allstate Insurance Co.; American National Property & Casualty Co.; Atlantic Casualty Insurance Co.; Atlantic Indemnity Co.; Atlantic Security Insurance Co.; Automobile Club Interinsurance Exchange; AvisCorp.; Bank of Chelsea; Bank of Commerce (Catoosa); Bayer Corp.; Blue Cross/Blue Shield of Oklahoma; Boy Scouts of America; Brookhaven Hospital, Inc.; Cancer Treatment Centers of America; CNA-HealthPro; Central Insurance Cos.; Century Life Assurance Co.; Cigna Insurance Co.; Continental Insurance Healthcare; Coram Healthcare; Crum & Foster Insurance Co.; Economy Fire & Casualty Co.; Electric Mutual Insurance Co.; Employers Mutual Cos.; Federated Mutual Insurance Co.; Guaranty National Insurance Co.; Goodville Mutual Insurance Co.; Hanover Insurance Co.; Hartford Insurance Co.; Highlands Insurance Co.; Homeland Stores, Inc.; Insurance Company of North America; Interstate Insurance Group; John Deere Insurance Co.; Ion Laboratories, Inc.; Kemper Insurance Co.; Landmark American Insurance Co.; Liberty Mutual Insurance Co.; Majoil Co.; Matrix Service Co.; Medical Protective Co.; Memorial Medical Center; Metropolitan Tulsa Transit Authority; Miller Brewing Corp.of Oklahoma; Natasco Underwriters; National American Insurance Co.; National Chiropractic Mutual Insurance Co.; National Farmers Union Insurance Co.; National Union Fire Insurance Co.; Nationwide Insurance Co.; Northbrook Property & Casualty; Oklahoma Property & Casualty Insurance; Oregon Oil & Gas Co.; Physicians Liability Insurance Co.; Preferred Physicians Mutual; Reliance National; Renal Treatment Centers; Rhoads Operating Co.; Safeway Stores, Inc.; Shand Morahan & Company, Inc.; Shelter Insurance Cos.; St. Francis Hospital, Inc.; State Farm Mutual Automobile Insurance Co.; Sterling Drug, Inc.; Underwriters of Lloyd's of London; U.S. Insurance Group; U.S. Fire Insurance Co.; United States Aviation Underwriters; Unison Insurance Co.; Utica Mutual Insurance Co.; Vector Properties, Inc.; Viking County Mutual Insurance Co.; Viking Insurance Company of Wisconsin; Yellow Freight.

BARBER & BARTZ

A PROFESSIONAL CORPORATION

Established in 1983

525 SOUTH MAIN STREET, SUITE 800

TULSA, OKLAHOMA 74103

Telephone: 918-599-7755

Fax: 918-599-7756

Email: email@barberbartz.com

Oklahoma City, Oklahoma Office: 204 North Robinson, 25th Floor, 73102. Telephone: 405-235-6677. Fax: 405-235-6679.

Business Organizations and Transactions, Securities, Taxation, Estate Planning, Probate, Commercial Litigation, Real Property, Domestic Relations, Bankruptcy, Labor and Employment, Franchising and Civil Practice.

FIRM PROFILE: Barber & Bartz was founded in 1988 by Ron B. Barber and Robert J. Bartz, former classmates and graduates of the University of Tulsa College of Law. The firm began as a local general practice, and now serves clients from around the state through offices located in Tulsa and Oklahoma City. The firm supports the personal as well as professional development of its attorneys, integrating personal growth with the practice of law by encouraging family and community involvement. It measures its effectiveness in the representation of its clients by reference to the client's individual expectations.

RON B. BARBER, born Poteau, Oklahoma, December 16, 1954; admitted to bar, 1980, Oklahoma; 1981, U.S. District Court, Northern District of Oklahoma and U.S. Tax Court. *Education:* University of Arkansas (B.S.B.A., in Accounting, 1977); University of Tulsa (J.D., 1980). Phi Delta Phi. Certified Public Accountant, Oklahoma, 1980. *Member:* Tulsa County, Oklahoma and American Bar Associations; Oklahoma Society of Certified Public Accountants; American Institute of Certified Public Accountants. ***PRACTICE AREAS:*** Taxation Law; Estate Planning Law; Corporate Law; Real Estate Law; Business Organizations and Transactions. ***Email:*** rbarber@barberbartz.com

ROBERT J. BARTZ, born Chicago, Illinois, March 15, 1955; admitted to bar, 1980, Oklahoma; 1981, U.S. District Court, Northern, Eastern and Western Districts of Oklahoma. *Education:* University of Tulsa (B.S., 1977; J.D., 1980). Author: "Branch Banking: The Oklahoma Debate," 15 University of Tulsa Law Journal 348, 1979. Assistant District Attorney, Tulsa County, Oklahoma, 1981-1984. *Member:* Tulsa County and Oklahoma (Member, Section on Family Law) Bar Associations; The Association of Trial Lawyers of America; Oklahoma Trial Lawyers Association. (Also at: Oklahoma City, Oklahoma Office). ***PRACTICE AREAS:*** Civil Litigation; Commercial Litigation; Domestic Relations Law; Real Estate Law. ***Email:*** bbartz@barberbartz.com

NANCY HANANIA JONES, born Plainfield, New Jersey, April 15, 1956; admitted to bar, 1981, Pennsylvania; 1983, Oklahoma. *Education:* Moravian College (B.A., 1978);

(This Listing Continued)

BARBER & BARTZ, A PROFESSIONAL CORPORATION, Tulsa—Continued

University of Tulsa (J.D., 1981). Law Clerk, Third Judicial District of Pennsylvania, 1981-1982. Adjunct Instructor, University of Tulsa College of Law, 1990. *Member:* Tulsa County, Oklahoma and American Bar Associations. ***PRACTICE AREAS:*** Corporate Law; Business Organizations and Transactions; Securities Regulation; Employment Law. ***Email:*** njones@barberbartz.com

JOHN M. HICKEY, born St. Charles, Illinois, April 5, 1956; admitted to bar, 1985, Oklahoma, U.S. District Court, Northern, Eastern and Western Districts of Oklahoma; 1996, U.S. Tax Court. *Education:* Indiana University (B.A., 1978); University of Tulsa (J.D., 1984). *Member:* Tulsa County, Oklahoma (Member, Sections on: Bankruptcy; Labor and Employment); American (Member, Sections on: Litigation, Labor and Employment Law) Bar Associations; American Inns of Court, Council Oak Chapter. ***PRACTICE AREAS:*** Commercial Litigation; Civil Litigation; Commercial Law; Bankruptcy; Labor and Employment; Real Estate.

JOE M. FEARS, born Fort Smith, Arkansas, August 23, 1955; admitted to bar, 1980, Oklahoma; 1981, U.S. District Court, Northern, Eastern and Western Districts of Oklahoma and U.S. Court of Appeals, Tenth Circuit; 1983, U.S. Court of Appeals, Fifth Circuit. *Education:* Westark Community College and Northeastern Oklahoma State University (B.S., 1977); Boalt Hall School of Law, University of California (J.D., 1980). Adjunct Professor University of Tulsa School of Law, 1993, 1996. *Member:* Tulsa County and Oklahoma Bar Associations; Cherokee Nation Bar Association; Muscogee (Creek) Nation Bar Association. ***PRACTICE AREAS:*** Civil Litigation; Appellate Practice; Indian Law; Products Liability. ***Email:*** jfears@barberbartz.com

CURTIS J. SHACKLETT, born Jackson, Mississippi, November 22, 1944; admitted to bar, 1979, Oklahoma; 1980, U.S. District Court, Northern District of Oklahoma. *Education:* University of Tulsa (B.S., Zoology, 1967; J.D., 1979). *Member:* Tulsa County and Oklahoma Bar Associations; Tulsa Title and Probate Lawyers Association; Tulsa Estate Planning Forum; National Academy of Elder Law Attorneys. ***PRACTICE AREAS:*** Trusts and Estates Law; Elder Law; Charitable Planned Giving; Business Organizations and Transactions; Real Estate. ***Email:*** cshacklett@barberbartz.com

---

ROBERT LEE BEARER, born Bartlesville, Oklahoma, February 18, 1949; admitted to bar, 1982, Oklahoma. *Education:* University of Oklahoma (B.A., 1973); Université de Grenoble, Grenoble, France; Université de Rouen, Rouen, France; University of Pittsburgh (M.B.A., 1978); University of Tulsa (J.D., 1982). *Member:* Tulsa County and Oklahoma Bar Associations; Christian Legal Society. ***LANGUAGES:*** French and Hebrew. ***PRACTICE AREAS:*** Corporate Law; Business Organizations; Real Estate and Banking Law; Commercial and Consumer Law; Secured Transactions. ***Email:*** bbearer@barberbartz.com

LYNN SUMMERS LUGIBIHL, born Stillwater, Oklahoma, May 10, 1959; admitted to bar, 1984, Oklahoma and U.S. District Court, Northern and Eastern Districts of Oklahoma. *Education:* Oklahoma State University (B.S., 1981); Washington University (J.D., 1984). Assistant District Attorney, Tulsa, Oklahoma, 1986-1989. Assistant General Counsel, Oklahoma Tax Commission, 1989-1995. *Member:* Tulsa County (Member, Family Law Section) and Oklahoma Bar Associations. ***PRACTICE AREAS:*** Civil Litigation; Domestic Relations Law; Criminal Law.

MATT DAVID MATHESON, born Tulsa, Oklahoma, January 14, 1965; admitted to bar, 1990, Oklahoma. *Education:* Oklahoma State University (B.S., Accounting, 1987); University of Tulsa (M.S., Tax, with honors, 1990; J.D., with honors, 1990); University of Florida (LL.M., Taxation, 1991). Beta Alpha Psi; Beta Gamma Sigma. *Member:* Oklahoma Bar Association. ***PRACTICE AREAS:*** Estate Planning; Taxation; Adoptions; Non-Profit Organizations; Probate; Trusts and Estates. ***Email:*** mmatheson@barberbartz.com

RICHARD P. CLARKE, born Wichita, Kansas, June 20, 1960; admitted to bar, 1985, Oklahoma. *Education:* Wichita State University (B.B.A., 1982); University of Tulsa, College of Law (J.D., 1985). Special District Judge, Tulsa County, 1988-1998. ***PRACTICE AREAS:*** Family Law; Civil Litigation; Criminal Defense. ***Email:*** rclarke@barberbartz.com

COUNSEL

RICHARD D. WHITE, JR., born Long Beach, California, September 27, 1955; admitted to bar, 1980, Oklahoma and U.S. Court of Appeals, Fifth and Tenth Circuits; U.S. District Court, Northern, Eastern and Western Districts of Oklahoma. *Education:* Long Beach State University (B.S., 1977); University of Tulsa (J.D., 1980). *Member:* Tulsa County and Oklahoma Bar Associations; Commercial Law League. ***Email:*** rwhite@barberbartz.com

REFERENCE: Available upon request.

THE BARKLEY LAW FIRM

401 SOUTH BOSTON AVENUE, SUITE 2700
TULSA, OKLAHOMA 74103
Telephone: 918-599-9991
Fax: 918-584-1110
URL: http://www.thebarkleylaw.com

Trial Practice, Civil Litigation in State and Federal Courts. Hospital Law, Labor and Employment, Administrative, Corporate, Probate, Estate Planning, Real Estate, Litigation, Medical Malpractice, Securities, Drug and Products Liability Law, Environmental Law, Communications Law, Negligence, Insurance, Business Reorganization, Arbitration, Mediation, Alternative Dispute Resolution.

C. MICHAEL BARKLEY, born Tulsa, Oklahoma, June 16, 1948; admitted to bar, 1973, Oklahoma and U.S. District Court, Northern, Eastern and Western Districts of Oklahoma; 1979, U.S. Supreme Court. *Education:* Oklahoma State University (B.S., in Finance, 1970); University of Tulsa (J.D., 1973). Delta Theta Phi. *Member:* Tulsa County, Oklahoma

(This Listing Continued)

and American Bar Associations; Oklahoma Association of Defense Counsel; Defense Research Institute. ***PRACTICE AREAS:*** Medical Malpractice Law; Products Liability Law; Securities Law. ***Email:*** mike@thebarkleylawfirm.com

FRED WILL DeMIER, born Tulsa, Oklahoma, November 27, 1956; admitted to bar, 1989, Oklahoma; U.S. District Court, Northern District of Oklahoma. *Education:* University of Tulsa (B.S., 1979; J.D., 1988). *Member:* Tulsa County and Oklahoma Bar Association. ***PRACTICE AREAS:*** Medical Malpractice; Workers' Compensation. ***Email:*** wdemier@thebarkleylawfirm.com

DAVID G. GRAVES, born Fort Smith, Arkansas, July 9, 1966; admitted to bar, 1991, Oklahoma, U.S. District Court, Eastern and Northern Districts of Oklahoma and U.S. Court of Appeals, Tenth Circuit. *Education:* University of Oklahoma (B.B.A., with distinction, 1988); Washington & Lee University (J.D., 1991). Alpha Lambda Delta; Beta Gamma Sigma; Phi Delta Phi. Legal Assistance Program for the Federal Women's Prison Camp, Alderson, West Virginia. *Member:* Oklahoma and American Bar Associations. ***PRACTICE AREAS:*** Medical Malpractice Defense; Personal Injury; Civil Litigation; Insurance Defense; Products Liability Defense; Employment Law. ***Email:*** dgraves@thebarkleylawfirm.com

BRAD SMITH, born Oklahoma City, Oklahoma, April 28, 1951; admitted to bar, 1977, Oklahoma; U.S. Court of Appeals, Tenth Circuit; U.S. District Court, Northern District of Oklahoma; U.S. Supreme Court. *Education:* Oklahoma State University and University of Tulsa (B.S., 1974; J.D., 1977). *Member:* Tulsa County, Oklahoma and American Bar Associations; Oklahoma Association of Defense Counsel. ***REPORTED CASES:*** Tuller v. Shallcross, 886 P.2d 481 (Okla. 1994); Carney v. State Farm Mut. Auto, 877 P.2d 1113 (Okla. 1994); Hildebrand v. Gray, 866 P.2d 447 (Okla.App. 1993); Johnson v. Johnson, 848 P.2d 72 (Okla. App. 1993); Railhead Freight Systems, Inc. v. United States Fire Ins. Co., 924 F.2d 994 (10th Cir. 1991); Travelers Ins. Companies v. Dickey, 799 P.2d 625 (Okla. 1990); April v. City of Broken Arrow, 775 P.2d 1347 (Okla. 1989); Moses v. Haney, 725 P.2d 866 (Okla. 1986); Ellington v. Coca Cola Bottling, 717 P.2d 109 (Okl. 1986); Sisney v. Smalley, 690 P.2d 1048 (Okl. 1984); Moses v. Hoebel, 646 P.2d 601 (Okl. 1982); Berry v. Empire Indem. Ins. Co., 634 P.2d 718 (Okla. 1981); Canadian Public School Dist. vs. McGraw-Edison, No. 634 P.2d 782 (Okla. App. 1981); Boyles v. Oklahoma Natural Gas Co., 619 P.2d 613 (Okla. 1980); David v. Pennwalt Corp., 592 P.2d 980 (Okla. 1979); Lee v. Phillips & Lomax Agency, Inc., 11 P.3d 632 (Okla. 2000); Quantrill v. Warren, 998 P.2d 644 (Ok. Civ. App. 2000); Sturgeon v. Retherford Publications, Inc., 987 P.2d 1218 (Ok. Civ. App. 1998); Rhea v. Southwest Cupid, 969 P.2d 1000 (Ok. Civ. App. 1998); Green Bay Packaging, Inc. v. Preferred Packaging, Inc., 932 P.2d 1091 (Okla. 1996); Medlin v. Texaco, Inc., 926 P.2d 804 (Ok. Civ. App., 1996); Assalone v. Hartford Acc. & Indem. Co., 908 P.2d 812 (Ok. Civ. App., 1994); McKenzie v. Renberg's, Inc., 94 F.3d 151 (10th Cir. 1996); Pacificare of Oklahoma, Inc. v. Burrage, 59 F.3d 151 (10th Cir. 1995); Eck v. Parke, Davis, 256 F. 3d 1013 (10th Cir., 2001). ***PRACTICE AREAS:*** Appeals; Civil Defense; Insurance Litigation. ***Email:*** bsmith@thebarkleylawfirm.com

JEFFREY L. WILSON, born Tulsa, Oklahoma, September 14, 1961; admitted to bar, 1986, Oklahoma, U.S. District Court, Northern and Eastern Districts of Oklahoma and U.S. Court of Appeals, 10th Circuit, U.S. Supreme Court. *Education:* Oklahoma State University (B.S., 1983); University of Oklahoma (J.D., with distinction, 1986); University of Arkansas (LL.M., 1987). Phi Kappa Phi. Adjunct Professor, University of Tulsa, College of Law, 1991—. Member, City of Bixby Board of Adjustment, 1995—. *Member:* Tulsa County and Oklahoma Bar Associations. ***PRACTICE AREAS:*** Insurance Law; Personal Injury Defense; Insurance Bad Faith; Medical Malpractice; Appellate Practice. ***Email:*** jwilson@thebarkleylawfirm.com

LINDSEY E. ALBERS, born Stockton, California, November 24, 1975; admitted to bar, 2002, Oklahoma, U.S. District Court, Northern District of Oklahoma and U.S. Court of Appeals, Tenth Circuit. *Education:* University of California at Davis (B.A., 1997); University of Tulsa (J.D., with highest honors, 2002). Phi Delta Phi. American Inns of Court, Johnson-Sontag Chapter. Recipient: American Jurisprudence Award in Evidence; Kenneth L. Brune Award, 2001; George Kerr National Scholarship Award, 2001. Member, Energy Law Journal, 2000-2001. Executive Notes and Comments Editor, Energy Law Journal, 2001-2002. Executive Articles Editor, ABA Year in Review: Environment, Energy, and Resource Law, 2002. ***REPORTED CASES:*** Griffin v. Griffin, 94 P.3d 96 (Okla-.Civ.App.2004). ***PRACTICE AREAS:*** Civil Litigation; Medical Malpractice; Appellate Practice. ***Email:*** lalbers@thebarkleylawfirm.com

ASHLEY R. MELSON, born Tulsa, Oklahoma; admitted to bar, 2004, Oklahoma. *Education:* University of Oklahoma Health Sciences Center (B.S., Physical Therapy, with special distinction, 1997); University of Tulsa College of Law (J.D., with highest honors, 2003). Phi Delta Phi; Phi Kappa Phi. Member, Golden Key. Recipient: Valedictorian, University of Tulsa College of Law, 2003; Outstanding First and Third Year Law Student Award; American Jurisprudence Award for Civil Procedure, Constitutional Law, Evidence, Legal Writing, Property, Real Estate, Secured Transactions, Torts. Honors Legal Intern, Office of the Secretary of Defense, 2002. Judicial Extern to The Honorable Stephanie K. Seymour, Tenth Circuit Court of Appeals, 2002. Judicial Intern to: The Honorable Joe C. Taylor, Oklahoma Court of Civil Appeals, 2001; The Honorable Thomas R. Brett, U.S. District Court, Northern District, Oklahoma, 2001. Author: Bioterrorism, Biodefense and Biotechnology in the Military: A Comparative Analysis of Legal and Ethical Issues in the Research, Development and Use of Biotechnological Products on American and British Soldiers, 14 Alb. L.J. Sci. & Tech. 497 (2004). *Member:* Oklahoma and American Bar Associations. ***PRACTICE AREAS:*** Medical Malpractice; Civil Litigation. ***Email:*** amelson@thebarkleylawfirm.com

REPRESENTATIVE CLIENTS: Saint Francis Healthcare System; Saint Francis Hospital in Broken Arrow; Warren Clinic; Laureate Psychiatric Clinic and Hospital; St. John Health System; Warner-Lambert Co.; North American Refractories Company; American International Group; Physicians' Liability Insurance Co.; The Group Insurance Companies; AIG Technical Services; Property Company of America; Pfizer; Parke Davis Co.; The Atlanta Casualty Cos.; Reliance Insurance Co.; Travelers Group; The Guardian Insurance Company; Prison Health Services; Lincoln General Insurance Company, Orion Telecommunications Corporation.

BARROW & GRIMM, P.C.

Established in 1976

610 SOUTH MAIN, SUITE 300
TULSA, OKLAHOMA 74119-1258
Telephone: 918-584-1600
Fax: 918-585-2444
Email: EMAIL@BGGG.com
URL: http://www.BGGG.com

Civil Trial and Appellate Practice. General Business Practice. Corporate, Commercial Litigation, Employment Law, Finance, Bankruptcy, Contract, Insurance, Real Estate, Mineral, Probate, Taxation, Estate Planning and Health Law.

FIRM PROFILE: Barrow & Grimm, P.C. is listed in the Bar Register of Preeminent Lawyers in the areas of Civil Trial Practice, Tax Law, Bankruptcy Law, and Business Law.

ALLEN E. BARROW, JR., born Savannah, Georgia, December 14, 1944; admitted to bar, 1970, Oklahoma. *Education:* Oklahoma University (B.B.A., 1967); Tulsa University (J.D., 1969). Member, Legal Committee, Interstate Oil Compact Commission, 1982-1994. Member, Board of Corrections, State of Oklahoma, 1985-1989. *Member:* Tulsa County (Member, Board of Directors, 1990-1992), Oklahoma and American Bar Associations. ***PRACTICE AREAS:*** Business Law; Real Estate; Estate Planning. ***Email:*** barrow@bggg.com

WILLIAM R. GRIMM, born Kansas City, Missouri, May 30, 1947; admitted to bar, 1973, Oklahoma; 1976, U.S. District Court, Northern, Eastern and Western Districts of Oklahoma, U.S. Court of Appeals, Tenth Circuit and U.S. Supreme Court. *Education:* University of Oklahoma (B.B.A., Accounting and Finance, 1970; J.D., 1973). Recipient: OBA President's Award for Outstanding Leadership Service, 2004; Gary C. Clark TCBA Distinguished Service Award, 2003; Neil E. Bogan TCBA Professionalism Award, 2002; TCBA Distinguished Service Award, 1989 and 1990. Member: Vision 2000 Criminal Justice Task Force, 1993-1996; Law Enforcement Consolidation Task Force, 1992-1993. Trustee, Skiatook Reservoir Authority, 1981-1989. Author: "A Practical Approach to Professionalism," Tulsa Lawyer, June 1990. Co-Author: "Oklahoma Standards of Professionalism," adopted by OBA, 2002. Faculty Member: 2004 OBA Winter Judicial Conference. Member: Hudson Chapter, American Inns of Court, 1989-1992; Listed in: Who's Who in American Lawyers, 2000—; Strathmore's Who's Who in Law, Millennium Edition. *Member:* Tulsa County Bar Association (President, 1991-1992; Member, Board of Directors, 1988-1993; Chairman: Centennial Celebration, 2000-2003); Oklahoma Bar Association (President-Elect, 2005; Vice President, 2004; Board of Governors, 1996-1998; 2004—); American Bar Association (Delegate, 1992, 2005-2006; Member: National Conference of Bar Presidents, 1991-1993, 2005—); Tulsa Lawyers for Children, Inc.; American Board of Trial Advocates; Tulsa Title and Probate Lawyers Association. Fellow: American Bar Foundation; Tulsa County Bar Foundation (President, 1992-1993; Director, 1992-1998; Charter Fellow); Oklahoma Bar Foundation (Board of Trustees, 2005-2006; Benefactor Fellow, 2004). Certified as a Civil Trial Advocate by the National Board of Trial Advocacy. ***PRACTICE AREAS:*** Business Litigation. ***Email:*** grimm@barrowgrimm.com

WILLIAM E. FARRIOR, born Montgomery, Alabama, April 20, 1950; admitted to bar, 1976, Alabama; 1977, Oklahoma, U.S. Tax Court and U.S. Court of Appeals, Tenth Circuit. *Education:* Vanderbilt University (B.A., 1971); University of Alabama (J.D., 1976); Southern Methodist University (LL.M. in Taxation, 1977). *Member:* Tulsa County, Oklahoma and American Bar Associations. ***PRACTICE AREAS:*** Taxation Law; Estate Planning Law. ***Email:*** farrior@bggg.com

ROBERT B. SARTIN, born Tulsa, Oklahoma, August 20, 1963; admitted to bar, 1988, Oklahoma; U.S. District Court, Northern, Eastern and Western Districts of Oklahoma; U.S. Court of Appeals, Tenth Circuit; 1991, U.S. Supreme Court. *Education:* University of Oklahoma (B.B.A., Finance, 1985; J.D., 1988). *Member:* Tulsa County (President, 2002-2003; Outstanding Young Lawyer, 1995; Member: Executive Committee, 1996-1997, 1998-2004; Board of Directors, 1993-1994, 1996-2004; Member, 1988-1996 and Chairperson, 1993-1994, Young Lawyers Committee) and Oklahoma (Member: Board of Governors, 2004-2006, 1998; Civil Procedure Committee, 1990-1995; Administration of Justice Committee, 1991-1996; Member, 1993-1999 and Chairperson, 1998, Young Lawyers Division Board of Directors) Bar Associations; Tulsa County Bar Foundation (President, 2003-2004 and Member, Board of Directors, 1999-2004); Oklahoma Bar Foundation. ***PRACTICE AREAS:*** Business Litigation; Business Transactions; Commercial Litigation; Commercial Transactions; Health Care Litigation; Employment Litigation; Corporate Law; Estate Planning. ***Email:*** sartin@bggg.com

ASSOCIATES

WM. BRAD HECKENKEMPER, born Tulsa, Oklahoma; admitted to bar, 1980, Oklahoma; 1986, U.S. Supreme Court; U.S. District Court, Northern, Eastern and Western Districts of Oklahoma; U.S. Court of Appeals, Tenth Circuit. *Education:* Oklahoma State University (B.A., 1977); University of Oklahoma (J.D., 1979). Member: Oklahoma Court on the Judiciary, 2003-2007. Adjunct Settlement Judge, U.S. District Court, Northern District of Oklahoma and Tulsa County Court. *Member:* Oklahoma Bar Association (Member, Professional Responsibility Commission, 2004-2006). ***REPORTED CASES:*** Bayly, Martin & Fay, Inc. v. Pickard, 780 P2d 1168 (Okl. 1989). ***PRACTICE AREAS:*** Commercial Litigation; Business Law; Corporate Law; Bankruptcy Law; Employment Law. ***Email:*** brad@bggg.com

CHRISTOPHER A. BARROW, born Tulsa, Oklahoma, August 19, 1975; admitted to bar, 2001, Texas; 2004, Oklahoma; U.S. District Court, Eastern, Western, Northern and Southern Districts of Texas; U.S. District Court, Northern District of Oklahoma. *Education:* Indiana University, Bloomington (B.S., 1998); Emory University School of Law (J.D., 2001). Order of the Advocates. Member, Emory Moot Court Society. *Member:* Tulsa County and Oklahoma Bar Associations; State Bar of Texas. ***PRACTICE AREAS:*** Civil Litigation; Business Law. ***Email:*** cbarrow@bggg.com

ADAM K. MARSHALL, admitted to bar, 2003, Oklahoma. *Education:* University of Tulsa (B.A., magna cum laude, 1997); University of Oklahoma (M.B.A., 2003; J.D., with distinction, 2003). Phi Beta Kappa (Competition Director, Board of Advocates). Order of the Barristers. Member, Oklahoma Law Review. Vice President, Graduate Business Association. Author: "Oil & Gas Law: Royalty Valuation: Rogers v. Westerman Farm Co.: Burdening Lessees with an Implied Duty to Deliver Gas to a Marketable Location," 56 Okla L. Rev. 233 (2003). *Member:* Tulsa County, Oklahoma and American Bar Associations. ***Email:*** marshall@bggg.com

APPROVED ATTORNEYS FOR: Lawyers Title Insurance Corp.; American First Land Title Insurance Co.; Chicago/Security Union Title Insurance Co. (Agent).
REFERENCE: NationsBank, N.A.

BARBARA ANN BARTLETT

406 SOUTH BOULDER, SUITE 642
TULSA, OKLAHOMA 74103
Telephone: 918-584-1894
Fax: 918-584-1891
Email: bab@babartlett.com

Family Law.

FIRM PROFILE: Barbara Ann Bartlett is listed in the Bar Register of Preeminent Lawyers under Family Law.

BARBARA ANN BARTLETT, born Tulsa, Oklahoma, November 15, 1957; admitted to bar, 1985, Oklahoma; U.S. District Court, Northern District of Oklahoma; U.S. Court of Appeals, Tenth Circuit. *Education:* Utah State University (B.S., cum laude, 1979); University of Oklahoma (J.D., with distinction, 1985). Author: "Paternity: Defining Fatherhood in the Nineties," 64 Okla.Bar Journal 1680, 1993; "Parenting Coordination: A New Tool for Assisting High-Conflict Families," 75 Okla. Bar Journal 453, 2004. Oklahoma reporter for the Family Law Quarterly, ABA. Former Co-Editor, Oklahoma Family Law Journal. Presenter at conferences, including the Association of Family and Conciliation Courts, on the topic of Parenting Coordination. Former Executive Board Member, Family Law Section of the Oklahoma Bar Association. Former Chair, Family Law Section, Tulsa County Bar Association. Founding Member, Quality Assurance Panel, Families in Transition, domestic court reform program for Tulsa County. Former Chair, Rogers County Planning Commission. Formerly on Board of Directors, Catoosa Public Library.

BEELER, WALSH & WALSH P.L.L.C.

TULSA, OKLAHOMA

(See Oklahoma City)

Insurance Defense, Automobile Accidents, Personal Injury, Medical Malpractice, Products Liability, Nursing Home Negligence.

MARTIN BENJAMIN BERNERT

3314 EAST 51ST STREET, SUITE 218
TULSA, OKLAHOMA 74135-3527
Telephone: 918-749-4222
Fax: 918-743-3377
Email: mberlaw@aol.com

Estate Planning, Probate and Trust Law, Real Estate, Business, Commercial and Franchise Law.

MARTIN BENJAMIN BERNERT, born Oklahoma City, Oklahoma, November 7, 1949; admitted to bar, 1979, Oklahoma; 1980, U.S. District Court, Northern District of Oklahoma; 1981, U.S. District Court, Western District of Oklahoma and U.S. Court of Appeals, Tenth Circuit; 1983, U.S. Supreme Court. *Education:* University of Oklahoma (B.A., 1972; M.A.P.A., 1973); University of Tulsa (J.D., 1979). Adjunct Professor, University Center at Tulsa, 1980-1981. Author: "Redemption of Collateral From a Consumer Debt Under the Bankruptcy Act," Oklahoma Bar Journal, Vol. 52, No. 8 (1981). Director, American Society for Public Administration, 1973-1974. Director and Vice President, American Corporate Counsel Association, 1986-1989. Arbitrator, Panel of Commercial Arbitrators, American Arbitration Association, 1989-1996. Barrister, American Inns of Court, 1991-1993. *Member:* Tulsa County (Chairman, Arbitration Committee, 1991-1993; Director and Chairman, Budget Committee, 2000-2001), Oklahoma (Chairman, House Counsel Section, 1987-1988, Banking and Commercial Law Section and Business Associations Section) and American (Sections on: Business Law, Real Property, Probate and Trust Law) Bar Associations.

BEST & SHARP

A PROFESSIONAL CORPORATION

Established in 1987

ONEOK PLAZA
100 W. 5TH, SUITE 808
TULSA, OKLAHOMA 74103-4225
Telephone: 918-582-1234
Fax: 918-585-9447
URL: http://www.bestsharp.com

Medical Malpractice, Legal Malpractice, Professional Liability, Accountants Malpractice, Products Liability, Insurance Defense, Architects and Engineers Liability, General Civil Practice, Appellate Law, Labor and Employment, Directors and Officers Liability, Civil Rights Defense, Probate, Workers' Compensation, Environmental Law, Taxation and Estate Planning.

FIRM PROFILE: Best & Sharp is a solid and established defense firm with a reputation for excellence in the area of trial practice. The Firm's two senior partners, Joseph M. Best and Joseph A. Sharp, have practiced together for 40 years in the defense litigation field. Mr. Best has specialized for over 40 years in the trial practice area, while Mr. Sharp has specialized in

(This Listing Continued)

BEST & SHARP, A PROFESSIONAL CORPORATION, Tulsa—Continued

appellate review and litigation research. Since 1986, the attorneys of the Firm have tried over 300 complex cases which have been successfully defended over 90% of the time. With the Firm's trial experience and support staff, the Firm is well prepared to handle complex litigation in the courtroom.

The firm is listed in the Bar Register of Preeminent Lawyers.

JOSEPH M. BEST, born Minneapolis, Kansas, October 12, 1925; admitted to bar, 1950, Oklahoma; U.S. Court of Appeals, Tenth Circuit; U.S. District Court, Northern, Eastern and Western Districts of Oklahoma; U.S. District Court, Southern District of Ohio. *Education:* Oklahoma A. & M. College and Bethany Peniel College; University of Oklahoma and University of Tulsa (LL.B., 1950). Phi Beta Gamma. Named, Best Lawyer in America, 1983-1995. *Member:* Tulsa County, Oklahoma and American Bar Associations; Federation of Insurance Counsel (Secretary-Treasurer, 1970; President, 1971-1972; Chairman, Board of Directors, 1972-1973); Oklahoma Association of Defense Counsel; American Inns of Court (Master). Fellow, American College of Trial Lawyers. ***PRACTICE AREAS:*** Medical Malpractice; Defense Litigation; Personal Injury Litigation.

JOSEPH A. SHARP, born Enid, Oklahoma, June 4, 1921; admitted to bar, 1949, Oklahoma; U.S. Supreme Court; U.S. Court of Appeals, Tenth and Sixth Circuits; U.S. District Court, Northern, Eastern and Western Districts of Oklahoma. *Education:* George Washington University and University of Tulsa (B.A., 1950); University of Oklahoma (LL.B., 1950). Order of the Coif; Phi Delta Phi. *Member:* Tulsa County, Oklahoma and American Bar Associations; Oklahoma Association of Defense Counsel (President, 1971); Federation of Insurance and Corporate Counsel. ***PRACTICE AREAS:*** Appellate Law; Medical Malpractice; Environmental Law.

TIMOTHY G. BEST, born Tulsa, Oklahoma, August 9, 1960; admitted to bar, 1988, Oklahoma, U.S. Court of Appeals, Tenth Circuit and U.S. District Court, Northern, Eastern and Western Districts of Oklahoma. *Education:* Oklahoma State University (B.S., 1982); University of Tulsa (J.D., 1988). *Member:* Tulsa County, Oklahoma and American Bar Associations; Christian Legal Society; International Association of Defense Counsel; Oklahoma Association of Defense Counsel. ***PRACTICE AREAS:*** Medical Malpractice Law; Insurance Defense; Labor and Employment; Bad Faith. ***Email:*** tgb@bestsharp.com

DANIEL S. SULLIVAN, born Tulsa, Oklahoma, March 12, 1963; admitted to bar, 1988, Oklahoma; U.S. Court of Appeals, Tenth Circuit; U.S. District Court, Northern, Eastern and Western Districts of Oklahoma. *Education:* Northeastern State University (B.S., cum laude, 1985); University of Tulsa (J.D., 1988). Order of Barristers; Trial Team, 1986-1987, 1987-1988. *Member:* Tulsa County (Secretary, 1994-1995; Treasurer, 1995-1996; Vice President, 1996-1997) and Oklahoma Bar Associations; Oklahoma Association of Defense Counsel; International Association of Defense Counsel; Defense Research Institute; Christian Legal Society. ***PRACTICE AREAS:*** Medical Malpractice Law; Insurance Defense; Engineering Products Liability; Accountants Liability; Nursing Home Liability; Civil Rights Section 1983. ***Email:*** dsullivan@bestsharp.com

AMY E. KEMPFERT, born Beloit, Wisconsin, March 22, 1950; admitted to bar, 1981, Wisconsin; 1982, Oklahoma; U.S. Supreme Court; U.S. Court of Appeals, Tenth Circuit; U.S. District Court, Northern, Eastern and Western Districts of Oklahoma. *Education:* University of Wisconsin-Stevens Point (B.S., 1974); University of Tulsa (J.D., with honors, 1981). Order of the Curule Chair; Tulsa Law Journal, 1980-1981. Assistant District Attorney, Wood County, Wisconsin, 1981-1982. *Member:* Tulsa County, Oklahoma and American Bar Associations; American College of Trial Lawyers; Federation of Insurance and Corporate Counsel; Defense Research Institute; Oklahoma Association of Defense Counsel. ***PRACTICE AREAS:*** General Defense Litigation; Medical Malpractice; Products Liability; Healthcare; Employment. ***Email:*** akempfert@bestsharp.com

THOMAS A. LE BLANC, born Baton Rouge, Louisiana, April 9, 1965; admitted to bar, 1991, Oklahoma; U.S. Court of Appeals, Tenth and Eighth Circuits; U.S District Court, Northern, Eastern and Western Districts of Oklahoma. *Education:* Louisiana State University (B.A., 1987); University of Maryland (J.D., with honors, 1991). Recipient, American Jurisprudence Award for Complex Litigation. Author: *"Defending A 42 U.S.C. §1983 Claim for Police Misconduct,"* Oklahoma Bar Journal, Vol. 4, No. 30 (July 31, 1993). *Member:* Tulsa County, Oklahoma and American Bar Associations; Oklahoma Association of Defense Counsel; Defense Research Institute. ***PRACTICE AREAS:*** Insurance Defense; Medical Malpractice; Nursing Home Defense; Civil Law; Civil Rights Section 1983; Trucking Liability. ***Email:*** tleblanc@bestsharp.com

SEAN H. McKEE, born Iowa City, Iowa, June 15, 1965; admitted to bar, 1990, Oklahoma; U.S. Court of Appeals, Tenth Circuit; U.S. District Court, Northern District of Oklahoma. *Education:* Graceland College (B.A., 1987); University of Tulsa (J.D., 1990). Notes and Comments Editor, Tulsa Law Journal, 1989-1990. *Member:* Tulsa County (Chair, Young Lawyers Section, 1994-1995; Secretary, 1995-1996; Chair, Pro Bono Committee, 1997-1999; Outstanding Young Lawyer, 1996) and Oklahoma Bar Associations. ***PRACTICE AREAS:*** Medical Malpractice Defense; Products Liability; Labor and Employment; Insurance Defense; Civil Litigation; Trucking Liability. ***Email:*** smckee@bestsharp.com

DAN W. ERNST, born Middleburg Heights, Ohio, May 25, 1955; admitted to bar, 1980, Oklahoma; 1981, U.S. Court of Appeals, Tenth Circuit; U.S. District Court, Northern, Eastern and Western Districts of Oklahoma. *Education:* Miami University (B.S., cum laude, 1977); University of Tulsa (J.D., with honors, 1980). Beta Gamma Sigma; Phi Delta Phi. *Member:* Tulsa County and Oklahoma Bar Associations. ***PRACTICE AREAS:*** Medical Liability; Dental Liability Law. ***Email:*** dernst@bestsharp.com

---

MATTHEW B. FREE, born Ponca City, Oklahoma, April 16, 1973; admitted to bar, 1998, Oklahoma and U.S. District Court, Northern, Eastern and Western Districts of Oklahoma. *Education:* Oklahoma State University (B.S., with honors, 1995); University of Oklahoma (J.D., with honors, 1998). Phi Delta Phi. Assistant Managing Editor, Oklahoma Law Review, 1997-1998. Member, Board of Advocates. Author: *"Kravzewski v. Baptist Medical Center of Okla., Inc.-- The Oklahoma Supreme Court Recognizes the Tort of Intentional Infliction of Severe Emotional Distress in a New Context,"* Oklahoma Law Review, 1997. *Member:* Oklahoma and American Bar Associations; Oklahoma Association of Defense Counsel. ***PRACTICE AREAS:*** Appellate Practice; Medical Malpractice. ***Email:*** mfree@bestsharp.com

(This Listing Continued)

STEVEN W. SIMCOE, born Tulsa, Oklahoma, September 26, 1965; admitted to bar, 1992, Oklahoma and U.S. District Court, Northern and Eastern Districts of Oklahoma; U.S. Court of Appeals, Tenth Circuit. *Education:* University of Oklahoma (B.A., 1987); Georgetown University (J.D., 1992). *Member:* Tulsa, Oklahoma and American Bar Associations; Oklahoma Association of Defense Counsel; Oklahoma Health Lawyers Association. ***PRACTICE AREAS:*** Medical Malpractice Defense; Products Liability; Insurance Defense. ***Email:*** ssimcoe@bestsharp.com

BOB D. JAMES, born Tulsa, Oklahoma, June 17, 1965; admitted to bar, 1992, Oklahoma; U.S. District Court, Northern, Eastern and Western Districts of Oklahoma. *Education:* University of Oklahoma (B.A., 1989; J.D., 1992). *Member:* Tulsa County, Oklahoma and American Bar Associations; Oklahoma Association of Defense Counsel. ***PRACTICE AREAS:*** Medical Malpractice Defense; Nursing Home Negligence; Insurance Defense; Civil Litigation; Civil Rights Section 1983; Trucking Liability. ***Email:*** bjames@bestsharp.com

JOHN JAY BOWLING, born Jefferson City, Missouri, March 18, 1970; admitted to bar, 1996, Oklahoma; U.S. District Court, Northern, Western and Eastern Districts of Oklahoma. *Education:* Purdue University (B.A., 1992); University of Tulsa (J.D., 1995). Phi Delta Phi. Listed in Who's Who American Law Students, 1995. Senior Articles Editor, Tulsa Journal of Comparative and International Law, 1994-1995. Author, "When May a Sovereign Be Held Liable for the Acts of Her Instrumentalities Under the Foreign Sovereign Immunities Act? The Effect of the McKesson Decision," Tulsa Journal of Comparative and International Law, Vol. 1, No 2. Spring 1994. *Member:* Tulsa County, Oklahoma and American Bar Associations; Oklahoma Association of Defense Counsel; Defense Research Institute. ***PRACTICE AREAS:*** Medical Malpractice Defense; Nursing Home Negligence; Architects and Engineers Malpractice. ***Email:*** jbowling@bestsharp.com

J. SPENCER BRYAN, born Tulsa, Oklahoma; admitted to bar, 2002, Oklahoma and U.S. District Court, Northern and Western Districts of Oklahoma; U.S. District Court, Eastern District of Oklahoma; U.S. Court of Appeals, Tenth Circuit. *Education:* University of Arizona (B.A., 1998); University of Oklahoma College of Law (J.D., 2002). *Member:* Tulsa County, Oklahoma and American Bar Associations; National Association of Security Dealers. ***PRACTICE AREAS:*** Civil Rights Defense; Prisoners Rights; Employment Discrimination; Medical Malpractice Defense; Civil Litigation. ***Email:*** sbryan@bestsharp.com

TREVOR A. DENNIS, born New Cambria, Kansas, 1976; admitted to bar, 2003, Oklahoma and U.S. District Court, Northern and Western Districts of Oklahoma. *Education:* Kansas State University (B.S., 2000); University of Tulsa (J.D., with highest honors, 2003). Phi Delta Phi. Member, Order of Curule Chair. Recipient, CALI Excellence for the Future Awards for Basic Corporate Law, Civil Procedure, Civil Procedure II, Constitutional Law, Contracts, Criminal Law and Administration, and Evidence. Vice President, Board of Advocates, 2001. Executive Editor, Tulsa Journal of Comparative and International Law, 2002-2003. Author: "The Principality of Sealand: Nation Building by Individuals," Tulsa Journal of Comparative and International Law, Vol. 10, No. 1, Fall 2002. *Member:* Tulsa County, Oklahoma and American Bar Associations. ***PRACTICE AREAS:*** Medical Malpractice Defense; Insurance Defense; Insurance Bad Faith. ***Email:*** tdennis@bestsharp.com

OF COUNSEL

WILLIAM E. PATTEN, born Joplin, Missouri, June 1, 1948; admitted to bar, 1987, Missouri and Oklahoma; 1988, U.S. Tax Court; 1990, U.S. District Court, Northern District of Oklahoma. *Education:* Missouri Southern State College (B.S., 1971); University of Missouri (M.A., in Accounting, 1972); University of Tulsa (J.D., 1987); University of Denver (LL.M., in Taxation, 1988). Certified Public Accountant: Missouri, 1977; Oklahoma, 1978. *Member:* Tulsa County, Oklahoma and American (Member, Taxation Section) Bar Associations; The Missouri Bar (Member, Committee on Taxation). ***PRACTICE AREAS:*** Taxation Law; Estate Planning Law; Commercial Law; Probate Law. ***Email:*** wpatten@bestsharp.com

REPRESENTATIVE CLIENTS: AFLAC; AIG Technical Services; Akros Medico Enterprises, Inc.; American Suzuki Motor Corp.; Cargill, Inc.; Central Insurance Companies; Central National Insurance Company of Omaha; Church Mutual; CNA Healthpro, Inc.; Corporate Service, Inc.; Corrections Corporation of America; Crane Carrier Company; Crawford & Company; Crum & Forster Insurance Company; Cunningham-Lindsey; Deloitte & Touche; Economy Fire & Casualty Company; Electric Mutual Insurance Company; Employee Benefit Administration, Inc.; Employers Casualty Corporation; Employers Reinsurance; Fleming & Hall Administrators; Frontier Insurance; GAB Business Services; General Accident Company; GE Auto Ins.; General Casualty Insurance Company; General Electric Corporation; Hartford Insurance Company; Highlands Insurance Company; Home Depot; Interstate Insurance Group; Kingway General Ins. Co.; K&K Insurance Company; McDonald's Corporation; Members Insurance Company; National State Ins.; Nationwide Insurance Company; Occidental Fire & Casualty Company; Oklahoma State Insurance Fund; OMIC; Physicians Casualty Insurance Company; Physicians Liability Insurance Company; Pioneer Claims Management; Preferred Physicians Insurance Company; Reliance Insurance; Robbins GAB; RSKO; Saint Francis Health Systems; Schindler Elevator Company; Scottsdale Insurance; Seneca Insurance; Service Merchandise Stores; Shand Morahan & Company, Inc.; Shoney's; Statewide General Agency, Inc.; St. Francis Hospital; Texas Iron Works; The Doctors Company; The St. Paul Companies; TIG Insurance Company; Titan Insurance; United Teachers Association; Western Heritage Insurance Company.

MICHAEL J. BLASCHKE, P.C.

TULSA, OKLAHOMA

(See Oklahoma City)

Oil and Gas Litigation, Commercial Litigation, Oil and Gas Law.

BODENHAMER & LEVINSON, P.C.

Established in 1984

SOUTHBRIDGE OFFICE PARK
1743 E. 71ST STREET
TULSA, OKLAHOMA 74136-5108
Telephone: 918-492-4433
Fax: 918-492-6224
Email: ken@bodenhamer.com

General Civil Practice in all State and Federal Courts. Oil and Gas, Corporate, Construction, Administrative, Family, Divorce, Child Custody and Probate Law, Environmental.

FIRM PROFILE: The firm regularly practices in front of the Oklahoma Corporation Commission.

KENNETH D. BODENHAMER, born Bedford, Indiana, April 14, 1934; admitted to bar, 1982, Oklahoma and U.S. District Court, Eastern and Northern Districts of Oklahoma, and U.S. Court of Appeals, Tenth Circuit. *Education:* Troy State University (A.A., 1974); Hampton University (B.A., 1975); Oral Roberts University (J.D., 1982). Adjunct Settlement Judge, Tulsa County District Court, 1991—. *Member:* Tulsa County, Oklahoma and American Bar Associations. [Col. U.S. Air Force, Ret.]. ***PRACTICE AREAS:*** Corporate Law; Business Law; Construction Law; Administrative Law; Family Law; Probate Law; Litigation. ***Email:*** ken@bodenhamer.com

LEE I. LEVINSON, born Tulsa, Oklahoma, January 30, 1951; admitted to bar, 1976, Oklahoma and U.S. District Court, Northern District of Oklahoma. *Education:* Tulane University; University of Oklahoma (B.A., Economics, 1973); University of Tulsa (LL.B., 1976). *Member:* Tulsa County, Oklahoma and American (Member of Natural Resources Section) Bar Associations. ***PRACTICE AREAS:*** Oil and Gas Law; Environmental Law.

KATRINA S. BODENHAMER, born Fort Wayne, Indiana, March 29, 1958; admitted to bar, 1992, Oklahoma and U.S District Court, Northern District of Oklahoma; U.S. Court of Appeals, 10th Circuit. *Education:* University of Tulsa (B.A., 1989; J.D., 1992). *Member:* Tulsa County, Oklahoma and American Bar Associations. ***PRACTICE AREAS:*** General Practice; Appellate; Family Law; Divorce.

RICK D. WESTCOTT, born Tulsa, Oklahoma, October 15, 1954; admitted to bar, 1993, Oklahoma, U.S. District Court, Northern, Eastern and Western Districts of Oklahoma; U.S. Court of Appeals, Tenth Circuit. *Education:* Oral Roberts University (B.A., 1989); University of Tulsa (J.D., 1993). Faculty, Oral Roberts University, 1991-2004, American Government, Constitutional Law, Civil Rights, American Jurisprudence, Criminal Procedure. *Member:* Tulsa County, Oklahoma and American Bar Associations. ***PRACTICE AREAS:*** Civil Litigation; Insurance Defense; Trucking Defense; Appellate Practice.

OF COUNSEL

KENNY JOE SMITH, born Ft. Hood, Texas, June 25, 1954; admitted to bar, 1981, Oklahoma and U.S. District Court, Northern District of Oklahoma; 1982, U.S. District Court, Western District of Oklahoma. *Education:* Oklahoma State University (B.A., 1976); University of Tulsa (J.D., 1981). *Member:* Tulsa County, Oklahoma and American (Member, Section on Natural Resources Law) Bar Associations. ***PRACTICE AREAS:*** Oil and Gas; Real Property; Probate.

BOESCHE McDERMOTT LLP

Established in 1934

SUITE 800 ONEOK PLAZA
100 WEST FIFTH STREET
TULSA, OKLAHOMA 74103
Telephone: 918-583-1777
Fax: 918-592-5809
Email: bme@bme-law.com
URL: http://www.bme-law.com

General Civil Practice, State and Federal Civil Trials. Banking, Bankruptcy, Corporation, Oil and Gas, Probate, Real Property, Insurance, Employment, Sports Law, Aviation, Insurance, Negligence, Environmental, International, Estate Planning, Commercial Litigation, Mergers and Acquisitions.

FIRM PROFILE: The firm of Boesche McDermott LLP is dedicated to providing the highest quality of legal services to its clients, utilizing the knowledge and expertise gained through long experience. Ours is a traditional environment emphasizing integrity, respect for every client and professionalism. Because the firm understands the needs of businesses, our commitment is to serving the special needs of each client in an efficient and responsive manner.

MEMBERS OF FIRM

FENELON BOESCHE (1910-1993)

RICHARD B. McDERMOTT (1905-1977)

BRADLEY K. BEASLEY, born Tulsa, Oklahoma, January 18, 1956; admitted to bar, 1980, Oklahoma; 1994, Wyoming; 1998, Montana. *Education:* University of Oklahoma (B.A., summa cum laude, 1977); University of Tulsa (J.D., 1979). Phi Beta Kappa; Phi Delta Phi. Member, Order of the Curule Chair. *Member:* Tulsa County and Oklahoma Bar Associations; Wyoming State Bar; State Bar of Montana. ***PRACTICE AREAS:*** Litigation; Banking Law; Real Estate; Mergers and Acquisitions; Sports Law. ***Email:*** bbeasley@bme-law.com

DAVID A. JOHNSON, born Evansville, Indiana, September 6, 1944; admitted to bar, 1969, Oklahoma. *Education:* University of Oklahoma (B.A., 1966; J.D., 1969). Omicron Delta Kappa; Phi Alpha Delta. *Member:* Tulsa, Oklahoma and American Bar Associations. [Capt., Judge Advocate, USAF, 1969-1973]. ***PRACTICE AREAS:*** Corporate Law; International Law; Litigation; Estate Planning. ***Email:*** djohnson@bme-law.com

(This Listing Continued)

OF COUNSEL

LINDA McQUILLEN KULP, born Okmulgee, Oklahoma, March 16, 1944; admitted to bar, 1969, Oklahoma. *Education:* University of Oklahoma (B.S.,1966; J.D.,1969). Member: Oklahoma Bar Title Examination Standards Committee; Tulsa County Title & Probate Lawyers Association. *Member:* Oklahoma Bar Association. ***PRACTICE AREAS:*** Oil and Gas Law; Real Property; Probate Law. ***Email:*** lkulp@bme-law.com

MICHAEL S. FORSMAN, born Dayton, Ohio, February 22, 1945; admitted to bar, 1971, Oklahoma. *Education:* University of Oklahoma (B.B.A., 1967; J.D., 1971). *Member:* Oklahoma and American Bar Associations. ***PRACTICE AREAS:*** Business Transactions; Banking Law; Corporate Law. ***Email:*** mforsman@bme-law.com

RODGER A. RANDLE, born Tulsa, Oklahoma, October 26, 1943; admitted to bar, 1978, Oklahoma. *Education:* University of Oklahoma (B.A., 1967); University of Tulsa (J.D., 1978). Adjunct Faculty, Oklahoma City University Law School. Member, Oklahoma House of Representatives, 1970-1972. Member, Oklahoma State Senate, 1972-1988. Mayor, Tulsa, Oklahoma, 1988-1992. *Member:* Tulsa County (Director, 1998—; Member: Sections on, Banking and Commercial; Bankruptcy; Professional Responsibility Committee) and Oklahoma (Member, Legal Ethics Committee) Bar Associations. ***LANGUAGES:*** Spanish and Portuguese. ***PRACTICE AREAS:*** Administrative Law; Litigation; International Law; Employment Law.

REPRESENTATIVE CLIENTS: ADESA; Aetna Insurance Co.; Apache Corp.; Atlantic Richfield Co.; Bandera Petroleum; Bank of America; Barbre Group Invesments; Capitol Indemnity Corp.; The Chase Manhattan Bank (N.A.); Chrysler Corp.; CIGNA Corp.; Cogentrix Energy Inc.; Community Bank & Trust Co.; Ford Motor Co.; GAF Corp.; Grand Lake Bank; Helmerich & Payne, Inc.; Houlihan-Parnes; Landco Construction Co.; Local Oklahoma Bank, NA; Marathon Oil Co.; Metropolitan Life Insurance Co.; Morgan Stanley & Co.; OCV Control Valves; OXY USA, Inc.; Phoenix Home Life Mutual Insurance Co.; The Pillsbury Co.; Paragon Development; The Quaker Oats Co.; Shell Oil Co.; Superior Federal Bank; Tank Consultants, Inc.; TeleProcessors, Inc..; Transportation Leasing Company; TCI Services, Inc.; Williams Cos.; Williford Energy, Inc.; X Corp.
APPROVED ATTORNEYS FOR: Albright Title and Trust Co.; American First Title & Trust Co.; Lawyer's Title Insurance Corp.; Pioneer National Title Insurance Co.; Chicago Title Insurance Co.

BONHAM & HOWARD

An Association of Professional Associates
Not A Partnership

15 W. 6TH STREET
TULSA, OKLAHOMA 74119
Telephone: 918-744-7440
Fax: 918-744-9358
URL: http://www.bonhamandhoward.com

Oklahoma City Office: 3555 NW 58th Street, 73112. Telephone: 405-943-6650. Fax: 405-943-6655.

General, Civil and Trial Practice in Federal Courts and all State Courts, Insurance Defense, Property and Casualty, Workers' Compensation, Products Liability, Surety, Civil Rights Defense, Personal Injury, Regulatory and Administrative Law, Corporate, Estate Planning, Probate.

MEMBERS OF FIRM

GENE C. HOWARD, born Perry, Oklahoma, September 26, 1926; admitted to bar, 1950, Oklahoma; 1952, U.S. District Court, Northern District of Oklahoma; 1956, U.S. Supreme Court, U.S. District Court, Eastern District of Oklahoma and U.S. Court of Military Appeals; 1964, U.S. District Court, Western District of Oklahoma and U.S. Court of Appeals, Tenth Circuit. *Education:* University of Oklahoma (LL.B., 1951; J.D., 1970). Phi Delta Phi. State Representative, 1958-1962. State Senator, 1964-1982. President, Pro Tempore, 1975-1981. *Member:* Tulsa County and Oklahoma Bar Associations; Oklahoma Trial Lawyers Association. ***PRACTICE AREAS:*** Civil Litigation; Appellate Law; Commercial Law. ***Email:*** howardgc@swbell.net

P. GAE WIDDOWS, born Tulsa, Oklahoma, January 23, 1954; admitted to bar, 1979, Oklahoma and U.S. District Court, Eastern District of Oklahoma; 1980, U.S. District Court, Northern and Western Districts of Oklahoma; 1983, U.S. Court of Appeals, Tenth Circuit. *Education:* University of Arkansas (B.S.B.A., 1976); University of Tulsa (J.D., 1979); Queens College University of Cambridge, Cambridge, England (International Law Study, 1978). Phi Delta Phi. *Member:* Tulsa County, Oklahoma and American Bar Associations; Oklahoma Trial Lawyers Association; The Association of Trial Lawyers of America. ***PRACTICE AREAS:*** Family Law; Commercial Law; Probate; Wills; Trust Law. ***Email:*** hwbfirm@swbell.net

JOSEPH F. BUFOGLE, born Tokyo, Japan, July 1, 1953; admitted to bar, 1983, Oklahoma; U.S. Supreme Court; U.S Court of Appeals, Tenth Circuit; U.S. District Court, Northern, Eastern and Western Districts of Oklahoma. *Education:* Abilene Christian University (B.S., 1976); University of Tulsa (J.D., 1983). Phi Alpha Delta. *Member:* Tulsa County, Oklahoma and American Bar Associations; Oklahoma Trial Lawyers Association; The Association of Trial Lawyers of America. ***PRACTICE AREAS:*** Insurance Law; Federal Courts; Personal Injury.

ASSOCIATES

DAVID C. FISHER, born April 12, 1968; admitted to bar, 2002, Oklahoma. *Education:* Oklahoma State University (Business Management, 1990) University of Tulsa (J.D., 2001). *Member:* Oklahoma Bar Association. ***PRACTICE AREAS:*** Insurance Defense; Civil Litigation. ***Email:*** dcfisher@swbell.net

MARTIN FRANKLIN HALSTEAD, born Hethersett, Norfolk, U.K., May 15, 1959; admitted to bar, 2003, Oklahoma. *Education:* Northeastern Oklahoma State University (B.S., 1997); University of Tulsa (J.D., 2003). Recipient, CALI Awards for EU and Corporate Law. Editor, Tulsa Law Review, 2002-2003. Author: "The Regulated Become the Regulators - Problems and Pitfalls in the New World of Digital Copyright Legislation," 38 Tulsa

(This Listing Continued)

BONHAM & HOWARD, Tulsa—Continued

L.R. 195, 2002. *Member:* Oklahoma and Tulsa Bar Associations; Oklahoma Trial Lawyers Association; American Inns of Court. ***PRACTICE AREAS:*** Personal Injury; Property Law; Business Litigation; Insurance Law. ***Email:*** martinhalstead@bcglobal.net

ANDREW B. MORSMAN, born Tulsa, Oklahoma, March 18, 1959; admitted to bar, 1984, Oklahoma; 1985, U.S. Court of Appeals, 10th Circuit and U.S. District Court, Western District of Oklahoma; 1986, U.S. District Court, Northern and Eastern Districts of Oklahoma. *Education:* Oklahoma State University (B.S., 1981); University of Oklahoma (J.D., 1984). Pi Sigma Alpha; Phi Alpha Delta. *Member:* Oklahoma Bar Association (Member, Workers Compensation Section); Christian Legal Society; Oklahoma Association of Defense Counsel; Defense Research Institute; Rutherford Institute. ***PRACTICE AREAS:*** Defense Litigation; Workers Compensation Law; Premises Liability; Medical Malpractice; Dental Malpractice. ***Email:*** morsmanlaw@aol.com

KYMBERLY J. WATT, born Enid, Oklahoma, October 30, 1965; admitted to bar, 1993, Oklahoma. *Education:* University of Tulsa (B.S.B.A., magna cum laude, 1990; J.D., 1993). Beta Gamma Sigma; Phi Delta Phi. Recipient: Merit Scholarship; American Jurisprudence Award. ***PRACTICE AREAS:*** Nursing Home Negligence; Personal Injury. ***Email:*** k_watt@swbell.net

MALCOLM D. SMITH, JR., born Shreveport, Louisiana, August 30, 1948; admitted to bar, 1981, Oklahoma. *Education:* Oklahoma State University (B.S.B.A., 1974); University of Tulsa (J.D., 1981). Assistant City Prosecutor, Tulsa, 1981-1984; Municipal Judge, Healdton, 1987-1989. *Member:* Tulsa County, Oklahoma and American Bar Associations; Western Association of Workers' Compensation Boards and Commissions; Tulsa Claims Association. (Also practicing individually). ***LANGUAGES:*** French. ***REPORTED CASES:*** American Management Systems v. Burns, 903 P.2d 288 (Okl. 1995); Special Indemnity Fund v. Figgins, 831 P.2d 1379 (Okl. 1992); Hefner v. American Airlines, 888 P.2d 1 (Okla. Civ.App 1994); Smith v. City of Tulsa, 663P.2d 1237 (Okl. Cr. 1983). ***PRACTICE AREAS:*** Workers Compensation; Insurance Defense; Appellate Practice. ***Email:*** mdsmith@gbronline.com

MARK T. HAMBY, born Phoenix, Arizona, January 26, 1960; admitted to bar, 1989, Colorado; 1990, U.S. District Court, District of Colorado, U.S. Court of Appeals, Tenth Circuit; 1996, Oklahoma; 1997, U.S. District Court, Northern District of Oklahoma; 1998, U.S. District Court, Eastern and Western Districts of Oklahoma. *Education:* University of Denver (B.A., 1982; J.D., 1989). *Member:* Tulsa County, Colorado, Oklahoma and American Bar Associations. (Also practicing individually). ***PRACTICE AREAS:*** Employment Law; Civil Rights; Civil Litigation; Appellate Practice; Bankruptcy. ***Email:*** mthamby@swbell.net

REPRESENTATIVE CLIENTS: Oklahoma Safety Association; Claims Indemnity Services, Inc.; The Travelers Group; State Insurance Fund/CompSource Oklahoma; Texas County Mutual Insurance Co.; Dot-Line Transportation; Oklahoma Property & Casualty Insurance; Guaranty Assn.; The Chubb Group of Insurance Co.; Federal Insurance Group; Ranger Insurance Co.; D & M Surety, Inc.; MGI-Mechanical Breakdown Insurers; The Heritage Group, Inc.; Oklahoma County Sheriff, John Whetsel; Ensuro Holdings, Inc.; General Thomas P. Stafford and related Companies; Providence Property and Casualty Insurance Co.; Imperial Casualty and Indemnity Co.; Dallas General Insurance Co.; The Hartford Insurance Group; Oklahoma Manufactured Housing Association; Midlands Management Corp.; Dallas Fire and Safety Insurance Co.; AMS Staff Leasing; Claims and Risk Services; BancInsure Insurance Co.; International Fidelity Insurance Co.; American Surety Co.

BOONE, SMITH, DAVIS,
HURST & DICKMAN

A PROFESSIONAL CORPORATION

Established in 1920

500 ONEOK PLAZA

100 WEST 5TH STREET

TULSA, OKLAHOMA 74103

Telephone: 918-587-0000

Fax: 918-599-9317

URL: http://www.boonesmith.com

Litigation in State and Federal Courts, Employment and Labor, ERISA, Healthcare and Hospital Law, Antitrust, Product Liability, Municipal and Zoning, Securities Transactions and Litigation, Business Organization, Banking, Bankruptcy, Estate Planning, Probate, Energy Law, Environmental, Intellectual Property, Media Law, International Transactions, White Collar Crime, Arbitration/Mediation, Alternative Dispute Resolution, Trademarks, Copyrights, Telecommunications.

FIRM PROFILE: One of the oldest and most established law firms in Tulsa, Boone, Smith, Davis, Hurst & Dickman has long been recognized for its special expertise in civil litigation in federal and state courts. The firm has enjoyed an excellent reputation for providing high-quality legal services to major corporations, businesses and individuals locally, nationally and internationally.

We are pleased to represent corporations, individuals and small businesses including: Accounting Firms, Aircraft Manufacturers, Attorneys and Professional Corporations, Hospitals, Healthcare Providers, Insurance Companies, Automobile Manufacturers, Dealers and Rental Companies, Banks and Savings Associations, Estates and Trusts, Financial Institutions, Government Agencies, Manufacturers, Medical Providers, Nonprofit Organizations and Private Foundations, Oil and Gas Companies, Private Trusts and Foundations, Real Estate Developers, and Telecommunications Firms.

LAW FIRM ALLIANCES/ASSOCIATIONS: ***MERITAS***

BYRON V. BOONE (1908-1988)

TERESA MEINDERS BURKETT, born Okarche, Oklahoma, August 3, 1959; admitted to bar, 1985, Oklahoma. *Education:* University of Oklahoma (B.S.N., with honors, 1982; J.D., with honors, 1985). 2000 Golden Quill Award for *Conservation Easements-New Opportunities for Doing Well by Doing Good,* OBJ, Vol. 71, No. 14, May 6, 2000. Author: *Medical Records and Oklahoma Law, A Legal Manual,* Oklahoma Health Information Management Association; *End of Life Decision Making, OBJ* Vol. 72, No. 21, July 14, 2001. Registered Nurse, Oklahoma, 1982. *Member:* Tulsa County and Oklahoma (Chairman, Health Law Section, 1996-1997; Vice-Chairman, Uniform Law Committee. 2002) Bar Associations; American Health Lawyers Association; Oklahoma Health Lawyers Association (President, 1991-1992 and 2003-2005; Board of Directors, 1997-2003); Oklahoma Academy for State Goals (Member, Health Care Task Force). Listed in "Best Lawyers in America (Health Law Section," 1992—). ***SPECIAL AGENCIES:*** Professional Licensure Boards: Oklahoma Board of Medical Licensure and Supervision; Oklahoma Board of Nursing; Oklahoma State Department of Health; Oklahoma Human Rights Commission, Oklahoma Employment Security Commission; Equal Employment Opportunity Commission. ***PRACTICE AREAS:*** Healthcare and Hospital Law; Employment Law; Civil Litigation. ***Email:*** tburkett@boonesmith.com

JOHN A. BURKHARDT, born Sheboygan, Wisconsin, September 19, 1955; admitted to bar, 1980, Oklahoma. *Education:* University of Tulsa (B.A., 1977; J.D., 1980). Phi Delta Phi. National Registry of Who's Who. Board of Directors, 1994-2000 and Executive Committee, 1999, University of Tulsa Alumni Association. *Member:* Tulsa County (Member, Court Operations Committee), Oklahoma and American (Member, Litigation Section) Bar Associations; Barrister, American Inns of Court (W. Lee Johnson Chapter, 1996—). ***PRACTICE AREAS:*** Business Litigation; Banking Litigation; Commercial Litigation; Bankruptcy; Oil and Gas Litigation; Securities Litigation; Labor and Employment; Franchise Litigation; Dealership Law; Intellectual Property; Arbitration; Mediation. ***Email:*** jburkhardt@boonesmith.com

REUBEN DAVIS, born Muskogee, Oklahoma, November 5, 1943; admitted to bar, 1973, Oklahoma. *Education:* Westminster College (B.A., 1966); University of Oklahoma (J.D., 1973). Phi Delta Phi; Order of the Coif. Managing Editor, Oklahoma Law Review, 1971-1973. Recipient, 2003 and 2004, Businessman of the Year. Listed in: Outstanding Lawyers of America; The Best Lawyers in America. President, Tulsa County Sheriff's Association, 1993—; Chairman, Executive Committee Tulsa County Reserve Deputy Program, 1991—. Trustee: Mary C. Alexander Trust; Hillcrest Medical Center; Hillcrest Medical Center Foundation and The Tulsa Foundation. Senior Vice President, Indian Nations Council, Boy Scouts of America. Member, Board of Directors and Director of Camping, Southern Region, Boy Scouts of America. Member, Philmont Board of Directors, Boy Scouts of America. Director of Camping, Indian Nations Council, Boy Scouts of America. *Member:* Tulsa County (President, 1988-1989; President Elect, 1987-1988; Vice-President, 1986-1987; Chairman of Professional Responsibility Committee, 1984-1986), Oklahoma (Member, Ethics Committee, 1992-1994) and American (Member, Sections on: Labor and Employment Law; Litigation) Bar Associations; American Board of Trial Advocates; The Association of Trial Lawyers of America; National Health Lawyers Association; Oklahoma Trial Lawyers Association; Oklahoma Criminal Defense Lawyers Association; Propane and Gas Defense Association; American Inns of Court (Master), Hudson-Hall Wheaton Chapter; Oklahoma Association of Defense Counsel. [Captain, U.S. Army, 1966-1970]. ***PRACTICE AREAS:*** General Civil Litigation; Products Liability Defense; Medical Malpractice Law; Personal Injury; General Business Litigation; Trademark Litigation; Securities Litigation. ***Email:*** rdavis@boonesmith.com

GARRY M. GASKINS, born Okmulgee, Oklahoma, December 20, 1978; admitted to bar, 2004, Oklahoma. *Education:* University of Oklahoma (B.A., 2001); University of Tulsa (J.D., with highest honors, 2004). Order of Curule Chair. Editor, Tulsa Law Review. ***Email:*** ggaskins@boonesmith.com

CHARLES GREENOUGH, born Tulsa, Oklahoma, January 7, 1962; admitted to bar, 1987, Oklahoma. *Education:* Trinity University (B.A., summa cum laude, 1984); University of Oklahoma (J.D., with highest honors, 1987). Order of the Coif. Recipient, Nathan Scarritt Prize, University of Oklahoma, 1987. Member, Chapter 7 Trustee Panel, Eastern and Northern Districts of Oklahoma. Listed in "Best Lawyers in America". *Member:* Tulsa County and Oklahoma Bar Associations. ***PRACTICE AREAS:*** Business Law; Aviation Law; Civil Litigation; Commercial Litigation; Bankruptcy; Mergers and Acquisitions. ***Email:*** cgreenough@boonesmith.com

LARRY D. HENRY, born St. Paul, Minnesota, 1946; admitted to bar, 1970, Iowa; 1976, Oklahoma; U.S. Court of Military Appeals; U.S. Court of Appeals for the 10th Circuit; U.S. Supreme Court. *Education:* University of Iowa (LL.B., with distinction, 1970). Iowa Law Review. *Member:* Oklahoma and Iowa Bar Associations. ***PRACTICE AREAS:*** Consumer Credit; Fair Credit Reporting Act; Employment Discrimination; Equal Employment Opportunity Law; Fair Employment Practices; Wage and Hour Law; Litigation. ***Email:*** lhenry@boonesmith.com

GERALD L. HILSHER, born Houston, Texas, September 2, 1953; admitted to bar, 1979, Texas and Oklahoma; 1989, U.S. Supreme Court. *Education:* Northeastern Oklahoma State University (B.S., 1976); University of Texas (J.D., 1979). Assistant U.S. Attorney, Northern District of Oklahoma (Lead Attorney, Organized Crime Drug Enforcement Task Force, 1982-1985). Deputy Assistant Secretary for Law Enforcement, U.S. Treasury Department, 1987-1989. Member, Governor's Animal Waste and Water Quality Protection Task Force, 1997. Commissioner, Oklahoma Scenic River Commission, 1998—. Federal Adjunct Settlement Judge, Northern District of Oklahoma, 1992-2001, 2003—. *Member:* Tulsa County (Editor, Tulsa Lawyer, 1993-1994; Director, 1993-1994, 1996-1998, 2003—); Oklahoma Bar Associations; State Bar of Texas; American Bar Association; Environmental Law Institute; Environmental Federation of Oklahoma. ***REPORTED CASES:*** United States v. Whitaker, 152 F.3d 1238 (10th Cir. 1998) (Exceptional post-offense efforts at drug rehabilitation may be considered as a basis for downward departure under Sentencing Guidelines); Cardiovascular Surgical Specialists, Corp. v. Mammana, 2002 OK 27, 61 P.3d 210 (finding non-compete provisions of physician's employment agreement unenforceable under Oklahoma's restraint of trade statute and overruling arbitration award to the contrary). ***PRACTICE AREAS:*** Commercial Litigation; Business Litigation; Arbitration; Mediation; Environmental Law; White Collar Criminal Defense. ***Email:*** ghilsher@boonesmith.com

WILLIAM C. KELLOUGH, born Tulsa, Oklahoma, December 2, 1949; admitted to bar, 1975, Oklahoma and Texas. *Education:* University of Texas (B.A., with honors, 1972; J.D., 1975). Member, Board of Associate Editors, Texas International Law Journal, 1974-1975. President of the Firm, 1998-2004. Outstanding Junior Lawyer, Tulsa County, 1982.

(This Listing Continued)

Listed: Best Lawyers in America, 1995—; Leadership Oklahoma Class XVII. *Member:* Tulsa County (Chairman, Young Lawyers Section, 1982; Treasurer, 1984; Director, 1988; Member, Health Law Section, 2003—), Oklahoma and American Bar Associations; State Bar of Texas; American Health Lawyers Association; Oklahoma Health Lawyers Association (President, 1998-1999). ***TRANSACTIONS:*** Merger of two hospitals in Shawnee, OK (2002); Acquisition of two hospitals in Tulsa, OK (1998); Sale of hospital system, 2004. ***PRACTICE AREAS:*** Healthcare Law; Business Law; Probate; Estates and Trusts. ***Email:*** wkellough@boonesmith.com

DONALD A. LEPP, born Tahlequah, Oklahoma, October 10, 1967; admitted to bar, 1993, Michigan and U.S. District Court, Western District of Michigan; 1994, Oklahoma and U.S. District Court, Northern District of Oklahoma; 1995, U.S. District Court, Western District of Oklahoma; 1996, U.S. District Court, Eastern District of Oklahoma. *Education:* University of Oklahoma (B.B.A., 1990); University of Michigan (J.D., 1993). Contributing Editor, Michigan Journal of International Law (1991-1993). Semifinalist, Henry M. Campbell Moot Court Competition, 1992 and 1993. *Member:* Tulsa County, Oklahoma and American Bar Associations; State Bar of Michigan. ***PRACTICE AREAS:*** Civil Litigation; Corporate Law; Real Estate; Zoning, Planning and Land Use. ***Email:*** dlepp@boonesmith.com

MICHAEL J. McDANIEL, born Tulsa, Oklahoma, September 4, 1968; admitted to bar, 1999, Oklahoma; 2000, Kansas. *Education:* University of Tulsa (B.A., cum laude, 1990; J.D., with honors, 1999). Phi Delta Phi. Three-time recipient: CALI Excellence for the Future Award. Legal Certificate Programs, University of Tulsa College of Law: Health Law, 1999; Public Policy and Regulation, 1999; Resource, Energy and Environmental Law, 1999. Civil Service: Volunteer Patient Advocate Intern, Oklahoma State Department of Mental Health and Substance Abuse Services, 1998. Author: "Constitutionality of Oklahoma's Commitment Scheme for Incompetent Criminal Defendants," 70 Okla. B.J. 2989 (1999); "Regulation of Human Cloning: Implications for Biotechnological Advancement," 32 Val. U.L. Rev. 543 (1998). Member, Board of Directors, The Center for Individuals with Physical Challenge, Tulsa, Oklahoma, 2005—. Member, Institutional Review Board, Oklahoma State University Center for Health Sciences, Tulsa, Oklahoma, 2003—. *Member:* Tulsa County and Oklahoma (Member, Mental Health Committee, 1999-2003) Bar Associations; American Health Lawyers Association; Medical Group Management Association. ***LANGUAGES:*** Spanish. ***REPORTED CASES:*** Robinett v. The Haskell Company, 12 P.3d 411 (Kan. 2000). ***PRACTICE AREAS:*** Health Care; Labor and Employment. ***Email:*** mmcdaniel@boonesmith.com

ANGELA McSPADDEN PAULSEN, born Hominy, Oklahoma, August 13, 1961; admitted to bar, 1994, Texas; 2000, Oklahoma. *Education:* University of Tulsa (B.A., magna cum laude, 1991; J.D., with honors, 1994). Order of the Curule Chair. Board of Advocates, Tulsa Law Journal, 1991-1994. Judicial Internship, Hon. Thomas J. Crewson, 1993. *Member:* Oklahoma and American Bar Associations; State Bar of Texas; American Inns of Court. ***TRANSACTIONS:*** Successfully defended private and public employers nationwide in employment litigation and represented management in all aspects of the employment relationship. Extensive experience negotiating with organized labor and defending management at labor union arbitrations. ***PRACTICE AREAS:*** Labor and Employment; Civil Litigation. ***Email:*** apaulsen@boonesmith.com

FREDERIC N. (NICK) SCHNEIDER III, born Ada, Oklahoma, July 27, 1948; admitted to bar, 1973, Oklahoma. *Education:* University of Oklahoma and University of Tulsa (B.A., 1970); University of Tulsa (J.D., 1972). Phi Delta Phi. Member, Order of the Curule Chair. Member, Tulsa Law Journal, 1971-1972. Law-Clerk Bailiff for U.S. District Judge Allen E. Barrow, Northern District of Oklahoma, 1972-1974. Legislative Assistant to U.S. Senator Henry Bellmon, 1974-1975. *Member:* Tulsa County, Oklahoma and American Bar Associations. ***PRACTICE AREAS:*** Employment and Labor Law; General Civil Litigation; Employee Benefits; Family Law. ***Email:*** nschneider@boonesmith.com

STEPHEN A. SCHULLER, born North Carolina, 1951; admitted to bar, 1976, Oklahoma and U.S. District Court, Northern District of Oklahoma; 1977, Illinois; 1993, U.S. Court of Appeals, 10th Circuit. *Education:* Northwestern University (B.A., 1973); University of Tulsa (J.D., 1976). Member, Board of Trustees, Employees' Retirement System of Tulsa County, Oklahoma, 1990—; Member, City of Tulsa Sales Tax Overview Committee, 1991-1994. Trustee, 2002— and Vice Chairman 2005—, Tulsa Authority for the Recovery of Energy. Listed in "Best Lawyers in America." *Member:* Tulsa County, Oklahoma (Member, 1982-1992 and Chairman, 1986, Board of Directors, Real Property Section; Member, Title Examination Standards Committee, 1981-1991) and American Bar Associations; Tulsa Title and Probate Lawyers Association (President, 1989). ***LANGUAGES:*** German. ***PRACTICE AREAS:*** Real Estate; Zoning, Planning and Land Use Law; Business Law; Finance; International Trade. ***Email:*** sschuller@boonesmith.com

L. K. SMITH (1934-2001)

OF COUNSEL

EDWIN S. HURST, born Pawnee, Oklahoma, January 8, 1919; admitted to bar, 1942, Oklahoma; 1950, U.S. Supreme Court; 1963, Texas. *Education:* Oklahoma State University and University of Oklahoma (A.B., 1940); University of Oklahoma (LL.B., 1942). Phi Delta Phi; Order of the Coif. Adjunct Professor, Contracts, University of Tulsa College of Law, 1948-1954. Attorney, Gulf Oil Corporation Law Department, 1952-1978. *Member:* Tulsa County, Oklahoma and American Bar Associations; State Bar of Texas. [Major, U.S. Army, 1942-1945]. ***PRACTICE AREAS:*** Civil Litigation; Communications Law; Oil and Gas Law; Products Liability; General Business Litigation.

BILL FREUDENRICH, born Oklahoma City, Oklahoma, May 6, 1961; admitted to bar, 1988, Texas; 1991, Oklahoma. *Education:* Oklahoma State University (B.A., 1983); University of Tulsa (J.D., 1988). Member, Energy Law Journal, 1986-1988. *Member:* State Bar of Texas; Oklahoma and American Bar Associations. ***TRANSACTIONS:*** Due diligence for mergers and acquisitions; Representation of self-insured medical plans; Expert witness in ERISA litigation involving leased employees and breach of fiduciary duty; Termination of qualified retirement plans; Design and implementation of employee stock ownership plans for privately held corporations; Representation of clients and negotiations of settlements with the Department of Labor and Internal Revenue Service; Design and Implementation of executive bonus programs. ***PRACTICE AREAS:*** Employee Benefits Law; Employee Relations Law. ***Email:*** bfreudenrich@boonesmith.com

(This Listing Continued)

LEGAL SUPPORT PERSONNEL

CHRISTIE HAUGEN
BETTYE PAYNTER
PAMELA MAPPIN
JoANN SUPPES
KIM THORSEN

REPRESENTATIVE CLIENTS: Bank of America; Williams Employees Credit Union; City of Tulsa; Phillips Petroleum Company; The Whirlpool Corporation; BP Amoco Corporation; Chevron USA, Inc., Southwest Gas Corporation; Zebco Corporation; Brunswick Corporation, GEA Rainey Corporation; Hospital Casualty Company; Oklahoma Oncology, Inc.; PricewaterhouseCoopers, LLP; Pratt and Whitney; The Boeing Company; Ford Motor Company; Southwestern Bell Telephone Company; Southwestern Bell Wireless; Sears Roebuck and Company; Federal Express; PacifiCare of Oklahoma, Inc.; Matrix Services, Inc.; Williams-Scotsman; SecurityLink from Ameritech; Total Information Services; Xeta Corporation; QuikTrip Corporation; Spartan School of Aeronautics; Unit Corporation; State Farm Insurance Company; Hillcrest Healthcare System; Tahlequah City Hospital; Comanche County Memorial Hospital; Cimarron Memorial Hospital; Indian Health Care Resource Center; Utica Physicians Associates Limited.

BREWER, WORTEN, ROBINETT

TULSA, OKLAHOMA

(See Bartlesville)

General Civil Practice. State and Federal Litigation. Corporate, Banking, Real Estate, Oil and Gas, Probate, Trust and Estate Planning, Family and Employment Law, Personal Injury and Insurance Defense.

BREWSTER AND DE ANGELIS, P.L.L.C.

2617 EAST 21ST STREET
TULSA, OKLAHOMA 74114-1707
Telephone: 918-742-2021
Facsimile: 918-742-2197
URL: http://www.brewsterlaw.com

General Civil Trial Practice in State and Federal Courts. Personal Injury, Medical Malpractice, Products Liability, Taxation, Probate, Real Estate, Bankruptcy, Family Law, Selected Criminal Defense.

FIRM PROFILE: Since inception of this firm in 1982 it has been committed to champion the cause of those who deserve redress for injury to person or property; to promote the public good through concerted efforts to secure safe products, a safe workplace, competent medical treatment, and a clean environment; to further the rule of law and the civil justice system; to protect the rights of the accused; and to preserve the constitutional right to trial by jury.

In the course of meeting this Firm's objectives, the Firm and its constituent lawyers have earned a reputation of success in the preparation and trial of medical negligence, complex civil litigation and high profile criminal defense. The firm has a reputation for obtaining acquittals for the wrongfully accused criminal defendant. For an ever expanding client base, the Firm also provides general legal services, such as legal representation in contested matters in the bankruptcy, probate, and family courts, and before the IRS and the Oklahoma Tax Commission. The Firm is officed on the "21st Street Corridor" near Utica Square, approximately 10 minutes from the Tulsa County and Federal Courthouse.

MEMBERS OF FIRM

CLARK O. BREWSTER, born Marlette, Michigan, November 5, 1956; admitted to bar, 1981, Oklahoma and U.S. District Court, Northern, Eastern and Western Districts of Oklahoma; 2001, U.S. District Court, Northern District of Texas; U.S. Court of Appeals, Tenth Circuit. *Education:* Central Michigan University (B.S., cum laude, 1977); The University of Tulsa (J.D., with honor, 1980). Phi Delta Phi. Member: Order of Barristers; Order of the Curule Chair. *Member:* Oklahoma and American Bar Associations; The Association of Trial Lawyers of America (Sustaining Member); Oklahoma Trial Lawyers Association (Past President, 1998); National Association of Criminal Defense Lawyers. ***REPORTED CASES:*** Calvert v. Tulsa Public Schools, 932 P.2d 108 116 Ed. Law Rep. 815 (Okla App 1996); U.S.A. v. Staples, 971 F.2d 608 (10th Cir. 1992), 114 S. Ct. 1793 (1994); Tarabishi v. McAlester Regional Hospital, 951 F.2d 1558 (10th Cir. 1991); U.S.A. v. Songer, 655 F. Supp 861 and 842 F.2d 240 (10th Cir. 1988); Trinity Broadcasting Corporation v Eller, 827 F.2d 673 (10th Cir. 1987) and 835 F.2d 245 (10th Cir. 1987). U.S.A. v. Wood, 207 F.3d 1222 (10th Cir.2000). ***PRACTICE AREAS:*** Medical Malpractice; Criminal Defense; Complex Litigation. ***Email:*** cbrew@brewsterlaw.com

JENNIFER L. DE ANGELIS, born Whittier, California, August 1, 1962; admitted to bar, 1987, Oklahoma. *Education:* Oklahoma State University (B.S., 1984); University of Tulsa (J.D., 1987). Delta Theta Phi. Recipient, Jurisprudence Award in Agency and Partnership Law. *Member:* Oklahoma and American Bar Associations; Oklahoma Trial Lawyers Association. ***REPORTED CASES:*** U.S.A. v. Staples, 114 S.Ct 1793 (1994). ***PRACTICE AREAS:*** Medical Malpractice Law; Civil Litigation; Personal Injury. ***Email:*** jdeangel@brewsterlaw.com

GUY A. FORTNEY, born Tulsa, Oklahoma, May 21, 1964; admitted to bar, 1996, Oklahoma, U.S. District Court, Northern and Eastern District of Oklahoma and U.S. Court of Appeals, Tenth Circuit. *Education:* University of Tulsa (B.S., 1993; J.D., 1996). Phi Delta Phi. Order of Barristers. Recipient, Jerry M. Melone Award, Law and Medicine. Student Speaker, University of Tulsa Hooding, 1996. Editor In-Chief, Baculus, 1995-1996. *Member:* Tulsa County and Oklahoma and American Bar Associations; The Association of Trial Lawyers of America; Oklahoma Trial Lawyers Association. ***REPORTED CASES:*** U.S.A. v. Wood, 207 F.3d 1222 (10th Cir. 2000); Pierce v. Gilchrist, 359 F.3d 1279 (10th Cir. 2004). ***PRACTICE AREAS:*** Medical Malpractice; Complex Litigation; Civil Rights; Personal Injury. ***Email:*** gfortney@brewsterlaw.com

(This Listing Continued)

BREWSTER AND DE ANGELIS, P.L.L.C., Tulsa—Continued

MONTGOMERY LOYD LAIR, born Corpus Christi, Texas, February 11, 1972; admitted to bar, 1997, Oklahoma, U.S. District Court, Northern District of Oklahoma. *Education:* Oklahoma Baptist University (B.A., 1994); University of Tulsa (J.D., 1997). *Member:* Oklahoma Bar Association; Oklahoma and American Trial Lawyers Associations. ***PRACTICE AREAS:*** Medical Malpractice; Civil Litigation; Products Liability; Commercial Law; Business Litigation; Personal Injury; Criminal Defense. ***Email:*** mlair@brewsterlaw.com

CASSIE M. BARKETT, born Mt. Pleasant, Michigan, January 31, 1975; admitted to bar, 2000, Oklahoma; 2001, U.S. District Court, Northern District of Oklahoma and Northern District of Texas. *Education:* Texas Christian University (B.S., Political Science, minor, Psychology, 1997); University of Tulsa College of Law (J.D., with highest honors, 2000). Order of Barristers; Order of Curule Chair. Recipient, CALI Award for Excellence: Research, Analysis and Writing, Criminal Procedure I; Secured Transactions; Advanced Trial Practice. Student Member, Oklahoma Criminal Defense Lawyers Association and American Trial Lawyers Association. *Member:* Tulsa County Bar Association; Tulsa County Criminal Defense Lawyers; Oklahoma Trial Lawyers Association; Oklahoma Criminal Defense Lawyers Association; National Association of Criminal Defense Lawyers; The Association of Trial Lawyers of America. ***PRACTICE AREAS:*** Criminal Defense; Family Law; Civil Litigation. ***Email:*** cbarkett@brewsterlaw.com

ROBERT NIGH, JR., born Enid, Oklahoma, November 1, 1959; admitted to bar, 1986, Oklahoma; U.S. District Court, Northern, Eastern and Western Districts of Oklahoma and District of Nebraska; U.S Court of Appeals, Eighth and Tenth Circuits and U.S. Supreme Court. *Education:* William Jewell College (B.S., 1982); University of Oklahoma (J.D., 1985). *Member:* Tulsa County and Oklahoma Bar Associations; Tulsa County Criminal Defense Lawyer's Association; Oklahoma Criminal Defense Lawyer's Association (Member, Board of Directors, 1993-1999); National Association of Criminal Defense Lawyers. ***REPORTED CASES:*** U.S. V. McVeigh, 157 F.3d 809, 98 CJ C.A.R., 5176 (10th Cir. (Colo). Oct 05, 1998; U.S. v. McVeigh, 153 F.3d, 98 CJ C.A.R. 4652 (19th Cir. (Colo.), Sep 08, 1998; U.S. v. McVeigh, 119 F.3d 806, 25 Media L. Rep. 1937, 97 CJ C.A.R. 1124 (10th Cir. (Colo.), Jul 14, 1997; U.S. v. McVeigh, 106 F.3d 325, 65 USLW 2543, 97 CJ C.A.R. 196 (10th Cir. (Colo.), Feb. 04, 1997; U.S. V. Maines, 20 F.3d 1102 (10th Cir. (Okla), Apr 05, 1994; U.S. v. Zeigler, 19 F.3d 486 (10th Cir. (Okla.), Mar 07, 1994; U.S. v. Burtrum, 17 F.3d 1299, 38 Fed. R. Evid. Serv. 1377 (10th Cir. (Okla.), Feb 25, 1994; U.S. v. Smith, 13 F.3d 380 (10th Cir. (Okla.), Dec 30, 1993; U.S. v. Hernandez-Urista, 9 F.3d 82 (10th Cir. (Okla.), Nov 08, 1993; U.S. v. Johnson, 4 F.3d 904, 39 Fed. R. Evid. Serv. 527 (10th Cir. (Okla.), Sep 09, 1993; U.S. v. Butler, 980 F.2d 619, 61 USLW 2391 (10th Cir.. (Okla.), Nov 23, 1992; U.S. v. Battle, 117 F.Supp.2d 1175 (D.Kan., Oct 12, 2000; U.S. v. McVeigh, 118 F.Supp.2d 1137 (D.Colo., Oct 12, 2000); U.S. v. Glover, 43 F.Supp.2d 1217 (D.Kan., Mar 04, 1999); U.S. v. McVeigh, 964 F.Supp. 313, 25 Media L. Rep. 1697 (D.Colo., May 12, 1997); U.S. v. McVeigh, 958 F.Supp. 512 (D.Colo., Mar 25, 1997); U.S. v. McVeigh, 955 F.Supp. 1281 (D.Colo., Mar 17, 1997); U.S. v. McVeigh, 955 F.Supp. 1278 (D.Colo., Feb 26, 1997); U.S. v. McVeigh, 954 F.Supp. 1454 (D.Colo., Feb 14, 1997); Application of The Buffalo News, a Div. of Berkshire Hathaway, Inc., 969 F.Supp. 869 (W.D.N.Y., Feb 05, 1997); U.S. v. McVeigh, 954 F.Supp. 1441 (D.Colo., Jan 28, 1997); U.S. v. McVeigh, 169 F.R.D. 362, 65 USLW 2335 (D.Colo., Oct 25, 1996); U.S. v. McVeigh, 944 F.Supp. 1478 (D.Colo., Sep 25, 1996); U.S. v. McVeigh, 940 F.Supp. 1571 (D.Colo., Sep 09, 1996); U.S. v. McVeigh, 940 F.Supp. 1541, 45 Fed. R. Evid. Serv. 535 (D.Colo., Aug 14, 1996); U.S. v. McVeigh, 931 F.Supp. 756, 24 Media L. Rep. 1908 (D.Colo., Jun 13, 1996); U.S. v. McVeigh, 931 F.Supp. 753 (D.Colo., May 29, 1996); U.S. v. McVeigh, 923 F.Supp. 1310 (D.Colo., Apr 29, 1996); U.S. v. McVeigh, 918 F.Supp. 1467, 64 USLW 2534, 24 Media L. Rep. 1821 (W.D.Okla., Feb. 20, 1996); U.S. v. McVeigh, 918 F.Supp. 1452, 24 Media L. Rep. 1737 (W.D.Okla., Jan 24, 1996); U.S. v. McVeigh, 896 F.Supp. 1549 (W.D.Okla., Aug 07, 1995). ***PRACTICE AREAS:*** Criminal Defense. ***Email:*** rnigh@brewsterlaw.com

MARK B. JENNINGS, born Claremore, Oklahoma, October 12, 1954; admitted to bar, 1983, Oklahoma; U.S. District Court, Northern, Eastern and Western Districts of Oklahoma, U.S. District Court, Western District of Arkansas and U.S. Court of Appeals, Tenth Circuit. *Education:* University of Arkansas; Oklahoma State University (B.S., Electrical Engineering, 1978); University of Arkansas (J.D., 1983). *Member:* Oklahoma Bar Association. ***PRACTICE AREAS:*** Civil Litig; Environmental Law; Debtor and Creditor Litigation; Probate. ***Email:*** mjennings@brewsterlaw.com

REPRESENTATIVE CLIENTS: Alpha & Omega Professional Business Services, Inc.; Post Oak Oil Co.; The Employer's Workers Compensation Association; I-44 Auto Auction, Inc.; Pride Energy; Imperial Coffee Service, Inc.; Oklahoma General Contractors; United Steel Erectors, Inc.; Chaser Transportation; Custom Motors, Inc.; Worldlink; Amini Gallery.

BRUNE LAWYERS

Established in 1994

900 REUNION CENTER
NINE EAST FOURTH STREET
TULSA, OKLAHOMA 74103
Telephone: 918-599-8600
Facsimile: 918-599-8673
Email: nancypascoe@bruneneff.com

General Civil Litigation, International and Domestic Business Transactions, Commercial, Corporate and Contract Law, Securities and Finance, Trademarks, Energy, Transportation, Real Estate and Construction.

FIRM PROFILE: The firm is engaged in the general practice of law with emphasis in corporate law, complex litigation, business organization, securities and finance, international and domestic business transactions, commercial law, and trust and estate matters.

KENNETH L. BRUNE, born Fort Madison, Iowa, 1945; admitted to bar, 1975, Iowa and Oklahoma. *Education:* St. Ambrose University (B.A., 1967); University of Iowa (M.A., 1972); University of Tulsa (J.D., 1974). Delta Epsilon Sigma; Phi Delta Phi. Editor, Tulsa Law Journal, 1973-1975. Adjunct Professor of Law, University of Tulsa School of Law, 1984-1985. Law Clerk, U.S. District Court for the Northern District of Oklahoma, 1975-1977. Assistant District Attorney, Tulsa County, Oklahoma, 1977. Special District Judge, Tulsa County, Oklahoma, 1978-1979. President, University of Tulsa, College of Law Alumni Association, 1994-1995. President, Tulsa County Bar Association, 2000-2001. *Member:* Oklahoma, Iowa State and American Bar Associations. Fellow, American Bar Foundation. ***PRACTICE AREAS:*** Litigation; Energy; Business; Commercial Law; Trusts; Transportation; Trademarks. ***Email:*** kenbrune@bruneneff.com

(This Listing Continued)

DAVID M. MESSER, born Nashville, Tennessee, October 31, 1963; admitted to bar, 2001, Oklahoma. *Education:* Free Will Baptist Bible College (B.S., 1985); Southern Baptist Theological Seminary (M.C.M., 1987); University of Tulsa (J.D., with highest honors, 2000). Member: Order of Barrister; Order of Curule Chair. Articles Editor, Journal of International and Comparative Law, 1998-1999. Author: "The Harbor Maintenance Tax: All Dredged Up and No Place to Go" Vol. 6, No. 1. ***PRACTICE AREAS:*** Civil Litigation; International Business Law; Real Estate; Franchise Law. ***Email:*** davidmesser1@aol.com

OF COUNSEL

JONATHAN C. NEFF, born Vinita, Oklahoma, December 13, 1951; admitted to bar, 1985, Oklahoma. *Education:* Cornell University; University of California (B.A., 1974); University of Arkansas (J.D., 1984). Phi Alpha Delta. Member, University of Arkansas Law Review, 1983-1984. Lecturer, Oklahoma Bar Association and U.S. Dept. of Commerce. Founding Chair, Oklahoma Bar Association International Law Section, 1991-1992. Governor's International Team, 1994-2002; District Export Council, 1995-2002. *Member:* Tulsa County, Oklahoma and American Bar Associations. ***REPORTED CASES:*** Strickland Tower Maintenance, Inc. v. AT&T Communications, Inc., 128 F.3d 1422 (10th Cir. 1997). ***PRACTICE AREAS:*** International Business Transactions; Contract Law; Corporate; Securities; Franchise Law; Finance; Real Estate; Construction Law; Litigation. ***Email:*** jonneff@bruneneff.com

REPRESENTATIVE CLIENTS: Price Waterhouse Coopers; Medallion Petroleum, Inc.; Barrick Energy, Inc.; Nabholz Construction Corp.; Interface, Inc.; A&M Railroad Co.; Dyna Ten Corporation; Vatana Phaisal Engineering Co., Ltd.; Hodges Warehouse; Source Rock L.L.C.; Marjo Operating Co.; SCFM Compression Systems, Inc.; Coastal Hydrogen Energy, Inc.

JAMES D. BRYANT

7633 E. 63RD PLACE, SUITE 510
TULSA, OKLAHOMA 74133
Telephone: 918-392-1985
Fax: 918-392-1955
Email: jim@jbryantlaw.com
URL: http://www.jbryantlaw.com

Commercial Litigation, Family Law, Divorce, Taxation, Bankruptcy.

JAMES D. BRYANT, born Oklahoma City, Oklahoma, October 14, 1959; admitted to bar, 1987, Oklahoma. *Education:* Central State University (B.S., Accounting, 1983); University of Oklahoma (J.D., with honors, 1987). Order of the Barristers. Certified Public Accountant, Oklahoma, 1984. Member Oklahoma Society of Certified Public Accountants, 2004—. ***PRACTICE AREAS:*** Commercial Litigation; Family Law; Divorce; Taxation; Bankruptcy.

BRYANT LAW FIRM PLLC

Established in 1997

950 KENNEDY BUILDING
321 SOUTH BOSTON AVENUE
TULSA, OKLAHOMA 74103-3313
Telephone: 918-587-4200
Fax: 918-587-4217
URL: http://www.bryantlaw.com

Business Litigation and Trials in Federal and State Courts including Business Torts, Contract Litigation, Securities Litigation, Oil & Gas Litigation, Intellectual Property Litigation, Unfair Competition, Fraud and Deceit, Banking Litigation and Professional Liability.

FIRM PROFILE: Business litigation and trials. A small firm with extraordinary experience and surprising resources, often selected as counsel or co-counsel by some of America's leading law firms and Fortune 500 companies.

DAVID L. BRYANT, born Wichita, Kansas, 1955; admitted to bar, 1981, Oklahoma; U.S. Court of Appeals, 10th Circuit; U.S. District Court, Northern, Eastern and Western Districts of Oklahoma. *Education:* University of Oklahoma (B.A., 1977); University of Texas (J.D., 1981). Texas Law Review. Director, Trial Advocacy, Board of Advocates. *Member:* Tulsa County Bar Association; Oklahoma Bar Association (Vice-Chair, Law Office Management and Technology Section); Federal and American Bar Associations; American Inns of Court (Master, Hudson-Hall-Wheaton Chapter). ***PRACTICE AREAS:*** Business Litigation; Commercial Litigation; Business Torts; Contract Litigation; Executive Employment Litigation; Fraud and Deceit; Insurance Litigation; Insurance Bad Faith; Intellectual Property Litigation; Professional Liability Litigation; Securities Litigation; Unfair Competition; Federal Civil Practice; Trial Practice. ***Email:*** dbryant@bryantlaw.com

CRAIG A. FITZGERALD, born Stillwater, Oklahoma, November 17, 1967; admitted to bar, 1992, Oklahoma; 1993, U.S. District Court, Northern District of Oklahoma; 1997, U.S. District Court, Western District of Oklahoma and U.S. Court of Appeals, Tenth Circuit; 2000, U.S. Supreme Court. *Education:* Oklahoma Christian College (B.S., summa cum laude, 1989); Vanderbilt University (J.D., 1992). Memorialist, Jessup Team. *Member:* Tulsa County, Oklahoma and American Bar Associations. **PRACTICE AREAS:** Business Litigation; Commercial Litigation; Business Torts; Contract Litigation; Executive Employment Litigation; Fraud and Deceit; Insurance Litigation; Insurance Bad Faith; Intellectual Property Litigation; Securities Litigation; Unfair Competition; Federal Civil Practice; Trial Practice. ***Email:*** cfitzgerald@bryantlaw.com

(This Listing Continued)

LEGAL SUPPORT PERSONNEL

REAGAN N. DEWITT, born Albuquerque, New Mexico, May 23, 1973. *Education:* Colby College, Waterville, Maine (B.A., 1995); Université de Caen, Normandy, France; University of Tulsa (Certificate, Paralegal Studies, 1998). Certified Legal Assistant, Oklahoma, 1999. Certified Legal Assistant Specialist in Litigation, Oklahoma, 2001. *Member:* Tulsa Association of Legal Assistants; National Association of Legal Assistants. (Certified Legal Assistant). ***PRACTICE AREAS:*** Legal Research; Legal Pleadings; Document Analysis; Knowledge Management Systems; Trial Graphics; Multimedia Presentations. ***Email:*** rdewitt@bryantlaw.com

ANNA M. MITCHELL, born Joplin, Missouri, November 16, 1976. *Education:* Crowder College, Neosho, Missouri (A.A., 1996); Missouri Southern State University, Joplin, Missouri (B.S., 1999); University of Tulsa (Certificate, Paralegal Studies, 2002). Certified Legal Assistant, Oklahoma, 2005. *Member:* Tulsa Association of Legal Assistants; National Association of Legal Assistants. (Certified Legal Assistant). ***PRACTICE AREAS:*** Legal Research; Legal Pleadings; Document Analysis; Knowledge Management Systems. ***Email:*** amitchell@bryantlaw.com

REPRESENTATIVE CLIENTS: Ace Capital Re Corporation; AEGON USA Investment Management, Inc.; Blackrock Financial Management, Inc.; Commercial Guaranty Assurance, Ltd.; ExxonMobil; Financial Federal Credit, Inc.; First North American National Bank; Hyperion Capital Management, Inc.; ING Investment Management, Inc.; Johnson & Johnson; Kerr-McGee Corporation; Liberty Mutual Insurance Company; Matrix Power Development Co.; Mercury Mortgage Company; Merrill Lynch Asset Management, L.P.; National Farms, Inc.; ONEOK, Inc.; Shell Oil Company; Stein Roe & Farnham, Inc.; Texaco, Inc.; Union Oil Company of California; Ultramar, Inc.; Wal-Mart; Zeeco, Inc.

BUCKMAN & ROACH

A PROFESSIONAL CORPORATION

PARK CENTRE, SUITE 660
525 SOUTH MAIN STREET
TULSA, OKLAHOMA 74103-4521
Telephone: 918-587-1525
Fax: 918-587-1535
URL: http://www.lawyers.com/buckman&roach

General Civil and Trial Practice in all State and Federal Courts. Insurance, Negligence, Bad Faith Litigation, Trade Secrets, Products Liability, Fire, Life and Casualty, Employment Law, and Business Torts.

FIRM PROFILE: Firm Members are veteran trial attorneys recognized in the Martindale-Hubbell Bar Register of Preeminent Lawyers.

LOYAL J. ROACH, III, born Tulsa, Oklahoma, July 8, 1939; admitted to bar, 1970, Oklahoma. *Education:* University of Oklahoma (B.F.A., 1962; M.A., 1964; J.D., 1970). Editor, Oklahoma Law Review, 1969-1970. Author: "Life Insurance: Waiver of Premium Benefit Enforcement Before and After a Policy Lapse," 69 Oklahoma Bar Journal 2725, 1998; "Discovery: The Physician Patient Privilege, Waiver, and the Effect of Avery v. Nelson," 23 Oklahoma Law Review 115, 1970; "Admiralty Jurisdiction in Oklahoma: Exclusiveness and Choice of Forum," 42 Oklahoma Bar Association Supplement 68, 1971 (reprinted in Arkansas Lawyer, 1972). Adjunct Professor of Trial Practice, University of Tulsa School of Law, 1979-1981. *Member:* Tulsa County and Oklahoma Bar Associations. ***REPORTED CASES:*** Spears v. Shelter Mutual Ins. Co., 73 P.3d 865 (Okla. 2003); State ex rel. Board of Tax Roll Corrections Tulsa Cty. v. Mack Truck Sales of Tulsa, 620 P.2d 388 (Okl. 1980); Armour & Co. v. Jones, 84 F.R.D. 606 (E.D. Okl. 1978); Christian v. Metropolitan Life Insurance Co., 566 P.2d 445 (Okl. 1977). ***PRACTICE AREAS:*** Insurance; Employment Law; Trade Secrets; Business Torts; Life Insurance; Casualty Insurance. ***Email:*** lroach@buckmanroach.com

STEVEN V. BUCKMAN, born Tulsa, Oklahoma, July 16, 1960; admitted to bar, 1984, Oklahoma; 1985, Texas; 1988, U.S. Supreme Court, U.S. Court of Appeals, Tenth Circuit and U.S. District Court, Northern, Eastern and Western Districts of Oklahoma. *Education:* Oklahoma State University (B.S., 1981); Oklahoma City University (J.D., 1984). Member, Moot Court Board. Private Pilot's License, 1981. *Member:* Tulsa County, Oklahoma (Professional Responsibility Committee - investigation of bar complaints) and American Bar Associations. ***PRACTICE AREAS:*** Insurance Law; Fire Insurance; Casualty Insurance; Bad Faith Litigation; Civil Litigation; Negligence Law; Products Liability. ***Email:*** sbuckman@buckmanroach.com

---

DIANE M. BLACK, born Blue Island, Illinois, July 10, 1968; admitted to bar, 2000, Oklahoma and U.S. District Court, Northern and Eastern Districts of Oklahoma. *Education:* University of Tulsa (B.A., 1994; J.D., 1999). Recipient: CALI Award for Excellence; Native American Law Certificate. *Member:* Tulsa County, Oklahoma and American Bar Associations. ***PRACTICE AREAS:*** Insurance; Wage and Hour Law; Civil Practice. ***Email:*** dblack@buckmanroach.com

REPRESENTATIVE CLIENTS: Mendota Insurance Company; Alea London; BCS Insurance; The Hartford; St. Paul/Travelers Insurance; Shelter Mutual Insurance; American Bankers Insurance; Terra Nova Insurance; Gulf Insurance Group; Central Insurance Co.; Atlantic Insurance Co.; Associates Insurance Co.; National American Insurance Co.; Underwriters at Lloyd's London; Northland Insurance; Penn-America Insurance; Allied/Nationwide Insurance; St. Paul Reinsurance; American General Life & Accident Insurance Co.; Jefferson Insurance Co.; Gulf Life Insurance Company; Voyager Indemnity Insurance; One Beacon Insurance; Rent Quik.
REFERENCE: Bank of America, Tulsa.

BULLARD & HOEHNER, P.C.

TULSA, OKLAHOMA

(See Oklahoma City)

Workers Compensation Defense, Litigation, Insurance Coverage, Environmental, Products Liability.

ROBBIE EMERY BURKE

320 S. BOSTON AVENUE, SUITE 1030
TULSA, OKLAHOMA 74103
Telephone: 918-592-9003
Fax: 918-592-9006
Email: rburkelaw@aol.com
URL: http://www.robbieburke.com

Elder Law, Guardianship, Decedents Estates, Contested Wills, Contested Trusts and Estates, Estate Planning, Real Property, Real Estate Title Examination, Oil and Gas Law.

ROBBIE EMERY BURKE, born Duncan, Oklahoma, March 23, 1952; admitted to bar, 1982, Oklahoma. *Education:* University of Oklahoma (B.A., 1974); University of Tulsa (J.D., 1981). Lecturer, "The Disabled or Elderly Client," Oklahoma Bar Association, 1991; "Special Considerations for the Elderly", Oklahoma Bar Association, 1994; "Future Planning: Legal, Medical and Financial Issues," National Conference on Practice Management of Alzheimer's Disease, 2004. Co-Author: "Oklahoma Indian Titles", 29 Tulsa Law Journal 361, 1993. Past President, Tulsa Title and Probate Lawyers, 1994. *Member:* Oklahoma Bar Association (Member, Client Security Fund Committee, 1996—); National Academy of Elder Law Attorneys. ***PRACTICE AREAS:*** Elder Law; Guardianship; Decedents Estates; Estate Planning; Oil and Gas Law; Contested Wills; Contested Trusts and Estates; Real Property; Real Estate Title Examination.

KAREN L. CARMICHAEL P.C.

2727 E. 21ST., SUITE 402
TULSA, OKLAHOMA 74114
Telephone: 918-493-4939
Fax: 918-488-1573
Email: trustkaren@juno.com
URL: http://www.lawyers.com/karencarmichael

Estate Planning, Living Trusts, Living Wills, Wills and Probate, Trusts and Estates, Probate, Business Counseling, Irrevocable Trusts, Asset Protection, Charitable Giving, Health Care, Power of Attorney, HIPAA.

KAREN L. CARMICHAEL, born Ponca City, Oklahoma, May 16, 1958; admitted to bar, 1985, Oklahoma; 1996, Texas. *Education:* Oklahoma State University (B.A., 1980; M.A., 1982); University of Tulsa (J.D., 1985). *Member:* Tulsa County, Oklahoma and American Bar Associations. ***PRACTICE AREAS:*** Estate Planning; Living Trusts; Wills; Probate; Business Counseling; Irrevocable Trusts; Asset Protection; Charitable Giving; Long Term Care.

CARR & CARR

4416 S. HARVARD AVENUE
TULSA, OKLAHOMA 74135-2605
Telephone: 918-747-1000
Fax: 918-747-7284
URL: http://www.carrcarrlaw.com

Brain Injury, Personal Injury, Insurance Bad Faith, Nursing Home Negligence, Products Liability, Trucking Law, Toxic Exposure, Accidents, Wrongful Death, Negligence.

MEMBERS OF THE FIRM

PATRICK E. CARR, admitted to bar, 1973, Oklahoma; U.S. Supreme Court. *Education:* University of Oklahoma (B.A., History, with Special Distinction, 1970; J.D., 1973). Phi Beta Kappa. Former Judge, Oklahoma Temporary Court of Appeals. *Member:* Tulsa County, Oklahoma (Former Member, Rules of Professional Conduct Committee) and American Bar Associations; Oklahoma Trial Lawyers Association (Vice President, 2001; President, 2002; Member, Board of Directors); American Trial Lawyers Association. ***PRACTICE AREAS:*** Brain Injury; Personal Injury; Insurance Bad Faith. ***Email:*** pcarr@carrcarr.com

GUY A. THIESSEN, born Washington, D.C., March 28, 1963; admitted to bar, 1989, Oklahoma; U.S. District Court, Northern, Eastern and Western Districts of Oklahoma, U.S. Court of Appeals, Tenth Circuit and U.S. Supreme Court. *Education:* Oklahoma State University (B.S., Business Administration, 1985); Oklahoma City University (J.D., 1989). *Member:* Oklahoma Trial Lawyers Association (Member, Board of Directors, 1996—); The Association of Trial Lawyers of America. ***PRACTICE AREAS:*** Personal Injury; Nursing Home Negligence; Insurance Bad Faith; Products Liability; Trucking Law; Toxic Exposure. ***Email:*** gthiesse@carrcarr.com

RANDALL KENT GAUSE, born Elk City, Oklahoma, 1962; admitted to bar, 1990, Oklahoma; U.S. District Court, Northern and Eastern Districts of Oklahoma and U.S. District Court, Northern District of Alabama. *Education:* University of Oklahoma (B.A., Political Science, 1986; J.D., 1990). Member, Board of Advocates, University of Oklahoma College of Law, 1990. *Member:* Tulsa County, Madison County, Oklahoma, Alabama State and American Bar Associations; Oklahoma Trial Lawyers Association; Alabama Trial Lawyers Association. ***PRACTICE AREAS:*** Personal Injury; Wrongful Death; Products Liability; Negligence; Insurance. ***Email:*** rgause@carrcarr.com

A. LAURIE KOLLER, born St. Mary's, West Virginia, December 24, 1965; admitted to bar, 1991, Missouri; 1996, Oklahoma; 2001, Arkansas. *Education:* Duke University (B.A., Political Science, cum laude, 1988; J.D., 1991). *Member:* Tulsa County (Member, Court Operations Committee), Oklahoma and Arkansas Bar Associations; The Missouri Bar. ***PRACTICE AREAS:*** Personal Injury; Wrongful Death; Products Liability; Insurance. ***Email:*** lkoller@carrcarr.com

BRIAN R. HUDDLESTON, born Batesville, Arkansas, August 11, 1960; admitted to bar, 1988, Oklahoma; U.S. Court of Appeals, Tenth Circuit; U.S. District Court, Northern, Western and Eastern Districts of Oklahoma. *Education:* Vanderbilt University (B.A., 1984); University of Arkansas School of Law (J.D., 1988). Dean's List. Member, Moot

(This Listing Continued)

CARR & CARR, Tulsa—Continued

Court Board. Outstanding Oral Advocate, 1986. Student Writings Editor, Arkansas Law Review, 1987-1988. Vice President, Christian Legal Society, 2002. *Member:* Tulsa County, Oklahoma and American Bar Associations; Oklahoma Trial Lawyers Association; The Association of Trial Lawyers of America. ***PRACTICE AREAS:*** Accidents. ***Email:*** bhuddles@carrcarr.com

BRADLEY W. WALLACE, born Tacoma, Washington, October 3, 1973; admitted to bar, 2002, Arkansas. *Education:* Harding University (B.A., 1997; M.S.E., 1999); University of Arkansas (J.D., 2002). *Member:* Arkansas and American (Member, Labor and Employment Section) Bar Associations; Society of Human Resources Management. ***PRACTICE AREAS:*** Personal Injury; Torts; Employment Law.

ROBERT N. YLLA, JR., born Holdenville, Oklahoma, November 10, 1970; admitted to bar, 1997, Oklahoma; U.S. District Court, Western District of Oklahoma. *Education:* University of Oklahoma (B.A., 1994; J.D., 1997). Delta Phi. ***PRACTICE AREAS:*** Personal Injury; Insurance; Wrongful Death; Insurance Bad Faith. ***Email:*** rylla@carrcarrokc.com

TYE H. SMITH, born Oklahoma City, Oklahoma, October 16, 1967; admitted to bar, 1992, Oklahoma; U.S. District Court, Eastern and Western Districts of Oklahoma and U.S. Court of Appeals, Tenth Circuit. *Education:* University of Oklahoma (B.A., Political Science, 1989; J.D., with distinction, 1992). *Member:* Oklahoma Bar Association; Oklahoma Trial Lawyers Association (Member, Board of Directors; Former Co-Chair, Public Education Committee); American Trial Lawyers Association. ***PRACTICE AREAS:*** Personal Injury; Wrongful Death; Insurance Bad Faith. ***Email:*** tyesmith@carrcarrokc.com

JEREMY D. WEST, admitted to bar, 1996, Oklahoma. *Education:* Northeastern Oklahoma State University (B.S., Business Administration, 1993); University of Oklahoma School of Law (J.D., 1996). *Member:* Oklahoma Bar Association; Oklahoma Trial Lawyers Association; American Trial Lawyers Association. ***PRACTICE AREAS:*** Personal Injury; Insurance; Wrongful Death. ***Email:*** jwest@carrcarrokc.com

BRENT D. BERRY, admitted to bar, 1998, Oklahoma. *Education:* Southeastern Oklahoma State University (B.A., History, 1995); University of Oklahoma College of Law (J.D., 1998). *Member:* Cleveland County and Oklahoma Bar Associations; Oklahoma Trial Lawyers Association; American Trial Lawyers Association; Association for Advancement of Modern Professionals. ***PRACTICE AREAS:*** Personal Injury; Products Liability; Insurance; Wrongful Death. ***Email:*** bberry@carrcarrokc.com

PHILLIP VOTAW, admitted to bar, 1999, Oklahoma. *Education:* Northeastern Oklahoma State University (B.B.A., 1992); University of Oklahoma School of Law (J.D., 1999). *Member:* Oklahoma, Arkansas and American Bar Associations; Oklahoma Trial Lawyers Association; Arkansas Trial Lawyers Association; American Trial Lawyers Association. ***PRACTICE AREAS:*** Personal Injury; Products Liability; Premises Liability; Insurance. ***Email:*** pvotaw@carrcarr.com

CARROLL & MILLER

A Professional Limited Liability Company

Established in 2004

3130 N. WILD MOUNTAIN ROAD
TULSA, OKLAHOMA 74127
Telephone: 918-299-6914
Fax: 918-298-6915
Email: joemiller@jwmweb.com
URL: http://www.carroll-miller.com

Corporate Law, Commercial Transactions, Technology Transfer, Software Licensing, Telecommunications, Business Law, Energy, Due Diligence Reviews.

FIRM PROFILE: Carroll & Miller combines the experience and expertise derived from practicing at both large law firms and in-house legal departments. Our goal is to maintain low costs and charge our clients rates that are a fraction of those charged by attorneys with equivalent backgrounds. We have arrangements with other highly credentialed attorneys that allow us to provide low-cost, high-quality services to meet a client's specific needs.

MEMBERS OF FIRM

ROBERT W. CARROLL, born Anderson, Indiana, March 22, 1945; admitted to bar, 1971, Ohio; 1981 Oklahoma. *Education:* Indiana University at Bloomington (B.S., with high honors, 1967); University of Virginia (LL.B., 1971). Beta Gamma Sigma; Order of the Coif. Member, University of Virginia Law Review, 1969-1970. *Member:* Tulsa County, Oklahoma and American Bar Associations. ***PRACTICE AREAS:*** Corporate Law; Commercial Transactions; Technology Transfers; Software Licensing; Telecommunications Law. ***Email:*** bobcarroll@rwclaw.com

JOSEPH W. MILLER, born Huntington, West Virginia, August 7, 1956; admitted to bar, 1985, Oklahoma; 1991, U.S. Court of Appeals for the District of Columbia Circuit and U.S. Court of Appeals, Tenth Circuit; 1993, U.S. District Court, Northern District of Oklahoma. *Education:* University of Missouri (A.B., 1977; J.D., cum laude, 1985). Delta Theta Phi. Order of the Coif. Managing Editor, Missouri Law Review, 1984-1985. Adjunct Professor of Law, University of Tulsa College of Law, 1992. Instructor, Summerscape Gifted Program, Drury University, 1994, 2001, 2003. Author: "Applying a Public Benefit Requirement to Tax Exempt Organizations," 49 Missouri Law Review 253, 1984. Organizer and Panel Chair, Telecommunications Law 2001 Presentation, Tulsa County Bar Association. Volunteer Arbitrator of the Year, Tulsa Council of Better Business Bureaus, 1996. Listed in Who's Who in American Law. *Member:* Tulsa County, Oklahoma and Federal Communications Bar Associations. ***TRANSACTIONS:*** Spin off of Williams Communications by The Williams Companies, 2001 (lead attorney, transition agreements and telecommunications regulatory issues). Construction of Williams Communications nationwide fiber optic network, 1997-2000 (lead attorney). $2.5 billion sale of WilTel Network Services, 1995 (lead attorney, telecommunications regulatory issues and non-competition agreement). Agreements between WilTel and the Cuban telecommunications authority, 1994 (lead attorney, commercial issues). WilTel-MCI telecommunications capacity agreement (total capacity purchased exceeded $100 million), 1990 (co-lead attorney). ***PRACTICE AREAS:*** Telecommunications (1%); Commercial Contracts (10%); Right of Way Easements (10%); Telephone Utility Regulation (5%); Mergers and Acquisitions (10%); Spin-Offs (3%); Business Divestitures (3%); Business Acquisitions (3%); Mergers, Acquisitions and Divestitures (3%); Strategic Alliances (2%); Commercial Transactions (4%); Telecommunications Contracts (25%); Telecommunications Law (1%); Telecommunications Regulation (20%). ***Email:*** joemiller@jwmweb.com

(This Listing Continued)

REPRESENTATIVE CLIENTS: Telecommunications: WilTel Communications; McLeod USA; ITC Deltacom; ACN Inc.; AFN Telecom (Citynet). Energy: CenterPoint Energy; Kaneb Pipeline; Information/Technology/Automation: AETEQ, Inc.; Cicada Corp.; R.L. Hudson and Co.

RUSSELL D. CARSON, P.C.

THE ADAMS BUILDING PENTHOUSE
403 SOUTH CHEYENNE
TULSA, OKLAHOMA 74103
Telephone: 918-582-5490
Fax: 918-582-5063

Family Law, Child Custody, High Conflict Divorce, Child Support, Adoptions, Step-Parent Adoption, Mediation.

RUSSELL D. CARSON, born Pittsburg, Kansas, June 28, 1955; admitted to bar, 1985, Oklahoma; U.S. District Court, Northern, Eastern and Western Districts of Oklahoma and U.S. Court of Appeals, Tenth Circuit. *Education:* Kansas State University (B.S., 1977); Oral Roberts University (J.D., 1984). *Member:* Tulsa County, Oklahoma and American Bar Associations; The Association of Trial Lawyers of America; Oklahoma Trial Lawyers Association. Fellow, Oklahoma Bar Foundation.

CARUSO LAW FIRM, P.C.

Established in 2003

THE COLONIAL BUILDING
1325 EAST 15TH STREET, SUITE 201
TULSA, OKLAHOMA 74120
Telephone: 918-583-5900
Fax: 918-583-5902
Email: dcaruso@carusolawfirm.com
URL: http://www.carusolawfirm.com

Business and Commercial Trial and Appellate Practice in Federal and State Courts, including Arbitration, Contract Litigation, Energy Litigation, General Civil Litigation, Intellectual Property Litigation, Oil and Gas Litigation, Real Estate Litigation and Unfair Trade Practices Litigation; Business Organization, Planning and Review.

FIRM PROFILE: The firm provides legal representation in business trials and arbitrations. A small firm with extensive expertise and substantial resources, it has represented clients in local, state, regional and national forums. The firm's success arises from combining traditional trial practice methods with technical expertise and state of the art technology. The firm's founder, Dennis A. Caruso, has acted as lead trial counsel for numerous individuals and entities, including some of America's foremost corporations, and has been selected as counsel and co-counsel by leading law firms throughout the United States. The firm prides itself on delivering individualized attention to clients, the highest quality of legal experience and service, and cost-effective case management. The firm is listed in the Bar Register of Preeminent Lawyers.

DENNIS A. CARUSO, born Montclair, New Jersey, January 21, 1960; admitted to bar, 1986, Oklahoma, U.S. District Court, Northern, Eastern and Western Districts of Oklahoma, U.S. Court of Appeals, Tenth and Federal Circuits and U.S. Court of Federal Claims. *Education:* Colorado School of Mines (B.S., 1982); University of Tulsa (J.D., 1986). Member: Tulsa Law Journal, 1983-1984; Energy Law Journal, 1984-1986. Author, "Strategies and Techniques to Avoid, Minimize and Shift Risks and Costs Arising from Oil Field Pollution," 1997 Rocky Mountain Symposium on Environmental Issues in Oil and Gas Operations (Colorado School of Mines). *Member:* Tulsa County and Oklahoma Bar Associations; American Inns of Court. ***REPORTED CASES:*** East Texas Seismic Data, L.L.C. v. Seitel Data, Inc., 279 F.3d 915 (10th Cir. 2002); In re Stumpff, 109 B.R. 1014 (E.D. Okla. 1989); Cherokee Nation v. United States, 124 F.3d 1413 (Fed. Cir. 1997). ***TRANSACTIONS:*** Represented major creditor in the financial restructuring pursuant to a Plan of Reorganization of Columbia Gas Transmission, resulting in a $180 million payment (see website for additional information). ***PRACTICE AREAS:*** Business Law; Commercial Law; Trial Practice; Appellate Practice; Arbitration; Contract Litigation; Energy Litigation; Civil Litigation; Intellectual Property Litigation; Oil and Gas Litigation; Real Estate Litigation; Unfair Trade Practices Litigation; Business Organization; Business Planning. ***Email:*** dcaruso@carusolawfirm.com

LEGAL SUPPORT PERSONNEL

DAWN KIDDY, born Dallas, Texas, June 27, 1975. *Education:* Tulsa Community College (Associate of Applied Science, Legal Assistant, 2003). *Member:* National Association of Legal Assistants; Tulsa Association of Legal Assistants. ***PRACTICE AREAS:*** Litigation; Corporate Law; Oil and Gas Law.

REPRESENTATIVE CLIENTS: See website.

CATHCART & DOOLEY

A PROFESSIONAL CORPORATION

TULSA, OKLAHOMA

(See Oklahoma City)

Insurance Defense, Insurance and Subrogation, Property Insurance, Fire and Casualty and Insurance Law. Negligence Trial Practice.

CHEADLE & ASSOCIATES

7318 SOUTH YALE AVENUE SUITE A
TULSA, OKLAHOMA 74136-7000
Telephone: 918-585-8500
Fax: 918-592-3030
Email: gecesq@ionet.net

Estate Planning, Oil and Gas Law, Creditor and Debtor Bankruptcy, Probate, Real Estate, Contracts, Corporate Law, Civil Trial Practice.

FIRM PROFILE: Cheadle & Associates, Inc., in contrast to current trends, has continued the small firm tradition of emphasizing effective and cost-conscious legal representation. Over the years, individuals as well as small to medium size businesses have come to rely on personalized service and attention to detail to resolve critical issues requiring Federal and State court litigation. The firm maintains a diverse general practice, with emphasis placed on litigation matters involving real estate, oil and gas, bankruptcy, contracts, and collections as well as non-adversarial matters involving probate and estate planning, corporate formation, and operation and sale of businesses.

GRANT E. CHEADLE, born Seattle, Washington, July 9, 1957; admitted to bar, 1982, Oklahoma; 1983, U.S. District Court, Northern District of Oklahoma; 2003, U.S. District Court, Eastern District of Oklahoma; 2004, U.S. Court of Appeals, Tenth Circuit. *Education:* University of Washington (B.A., 1979); O.W. Coburn (J.D., 1982). *Member:* Tulsa County and Oklahoma Bar Associations. ***PRACTICE AREAS:*** Probate And Estate Planning; Oil and Gas Law; Bankruptcy; Real Estate; Contracts; Corporate Law. ***Email:*** gecesq@ionet.net

ASSOCIATE

DANA M. McDANIEL, born Tulsa, Oklahoma, December 23, 1966; admitted to bar, 2005, Oklahoma. *Education:* University of Phoenix (B.A., 2001); University of Tulsa (J.D., 2004). *Member:* Tulsa County and Oklahoma Bar Associations. ***PRACTICE AREAS:*** Probate; Estate Planning; Bankruptcy; Contracts; Collections; Corporate Law; Real Estate. ***Email:*** mcdanieldlaw@aol.com

CINOCCA & ASSOCIATES, P.C.

9710 E. 55TH PLACE
TULSA, OKLAHOMA 74146
Telephone: 918-488-9117
Facsimile: 918-488-9198
URL: http://www.cinoccalaw.com
Email: tcinocca@cinoccalaw.com
URL: http://www.lawyers.com/cinocca

Corporate and Business Law, Corporations and Limited Business Formations, Liability Companies, Contracts, Employment Law, Family, Divorce, Child Custody, Premises Liability, Auto Accidents, Personal Injury, and Criminal, Assault and Battery; DUI.

TRACY A. CINOCCA, born Tulsa, Oklahoma, March 23, 1972; admitted to bar, 1998, Oklahoma, U.S. District Court, Western and Eastern Districts of Oklahoma; 2002, U.S. Court of Appeals, 10th Circuit. *Education:* Villanova (Physics and Business Studies, 1989-1990); University of Oklahoma (B.A., Political Science, History, 1993); Oklahoma City University (M.B.A., 1994); University of Tulsa (J.D., 1997). College Memberships: Student Lobby Association; University of Oklahoma Student Government Association: At Large Chairman and Intern Coordinator; 1992 Intern U.S. House of Representatives. Law School Memberships: Phi Delta Phi; Twenty-Five percent of Class; Dean's Honor Roll; Student Bar Association Representative; Oklahoma Intercollegiate Legislature Delegate for TU. Oklahoma Supreme Court Certified Mediator - Early Settlement. Loyola Law School Chicago-Rome Center-International Legal Studies 1995. Health Law Certificate. Management Emphasis on Global Logistics Planning and International Studies in Business Abroad in England, Holland and Germany. Publications: Cinocca, Tracy, "The Need for a Family Decision Making Statute in Oklahoma," Oklahoma Bar Journal. Vol. 69, No. 48, 12/26/98; Cinocca, Tracy, "Careers in the Law: Success Without College," Barron's Educational Series, Inc. p. 184 (2001). Junior Great Books Leader, 2004-2006. Member, Oklahoma County Bar Association, 1998 -2000. *Member:* Tulsa County (Member, 1999—; Employment Law and Family Law Sections, the Tulsa County Professional Responsibility Commission, 2003—; Corporate, Criminal, Employment, Family, Young Lawyers and Litigation Sections, 2005-2006), Oklahoma (Member, 1998—; Young Lawyers Section, 1998-2007; Chair of Health Law Committee, 1998-2001) and American (Member, 2002—; Sections on: Business, Litigation and Family Law, 2004-2006; Young Lawyers, 2002—; Business Law Section Young Lawyers Forum, 2005-2006; Summer 2005 Chicago Annual Conference Attendee) Bar Associations; Association of Trial Lawyers of America (Member, 1999—; Sections on: Business Torts and Family Law, 2005-2006; Young Lawyers, 1999-Present; Summer 2005 Toronto Annual Conference Attendee). ***PRACTICE AREAS:*** Business Law (25%); Employment Law (5%); Consumer Law (2%); Criminal Law (2%); Premises Liability (2%); Contracts (25%); Family Law (37%); Personal Injury (2%). ***Email:*** tcinocca@cinoccalaw.com

CLARK & WILLIAMS

Established in 1977

SUITE 600 FOX PLAZA OFFICE CENTER
5416 SOUTH YALE AVENUE
TULSA, OKLAHOMA 74135
Telephone: 918-496-9200
Fax: 918-496-3851
Email: CLAWIL96@aol.com

General Civil and Criminal Trial Practice. Corporate, Oil and Gas, Personal Injury, Workers Compensation, Domestic Relations, Probate, Commercial, Real Estate, Corporate Real Estate, Commercial and Residential Landlord and Tenant Law, Zoning, Creditor's Rights, Bankruptcy, Family Law, Divorce, Wills and Trusts, and Child Custody.

FIRM PROFILE: Clark and Williams is listed in the Bar Register of Preeminent Lawyers.

MEMBERS OF FIRM

WENDELL W. CLARK, born Tulsa, Oklahoma, June 10, 1944; admitted to bar, 1968, Oklahoma. *Education:* University of Tulsa (B.A., 1966; J.D., 1968). Phi Alpha Delta; Phi Eta Sigma; Pi Gamma Mu. Member, Tulsa Law Journal, 1967-1968. Public Defender, Tulsa County, 1969-1970. *Member:* Tulsa County (Secretary, 1984) and Oklahoma Bar Associations; Oklahoma Trial Lawyers Association. [Capt., Air National Guard, 1972-1976]. ***REPORTED CASES:*** Austin vs. Wilkerson, 519 P.2d 899 (Okl. 1974); Case-Aimola Properties, Inc. vs. Thurman, 752 P.2d 1120 (Okl. 1988); Willow Creek Condominiums Second, Inc. vs. Andreyev, 798 P.2d 648 (Okl. App. 1990); Beale v. Beale, 78 P.3d 973, (2003 Okl. Civ.App. 90). ***PRACTICE AREAS:*** Civil Litigation; Commercial Landlord and Tenant; Family Law; Divorce. ***Email:*** wwclark@sbcglobal.net

DARRELL E. WILLIAMS, born Sapulpa, Oklahoma, December 6, 1947; admitted to bar, 1974, Oklahoma, U.S. District Court, Northern District of Oklahoma and U.S. Court of Appeals, Tenth Circuit. *Education:* Northeastern State College (B.A., 1969); University of Tulsa (J.D., 1974). Delta Theta Phi. Creek County Juvenile Officer, 1969-1970. *Member:* Tulsa County, Creek County, Oklahoma and American Bar Associations; Oklahoma Trial Lawyers Association. ***REPORTED CASES:*** Cleere vs. United Parcel Service, Inc., 669 P.2d 785 (Okl. App 1983); Sanders v. Crosstown Market, Inc., 850 P.2d 1061 (Okl. 1993). ***PRACTICE AREAS:*** Personal Injury; Tort Litigation; Corporate; General Civil Litigation. ***Email:*** CLAWIL96@aol.com

ASSOCIATES

MARK R. REENTS, born Chicago, Illinois, July 16, 1953; admitted to bar, 1978, Oklahoma and U.S. District Court, Northern District of Oklahoma; 1980, U.S. Court of Appeals, Tenth Circuit. *Education:* University of Tulsa (B.S., 1975; J.D., 1978). Phi Delta Phi. *Member:* Oklahoma Bar Association. ***REPORTED CASES:*** In re Morris, 302 B.R. 728. ***PRACTICE AREAS:*** Real Estate Acquisition; Finance and Development; Zoning; Bankruptcy; Residential Landlord and Tenant; General Civil Litigation. ***Email:*** CLAWIL96@aol.com

MICHAEL DeCARLO, born Lamar, Missouri, September 2, 1958; admitted to bar, 1988, Oklahoma; U.S. District Court, Northern District of Oklahoma. *Education:* University of Tulsa (B.S., 1981; J.D., 1988). *Member:* Tulsa County and Oklahoma Bar Associations. ***REPORTED CASES:*** Willow Creek Condominiums Second, Inc. vs. Andreyev, 798 P.2d 648 (Okl. App. 1990). ***PRACTICE AREAS:*** Commercial and Residential Landlord and Tenant; Civil Litigation; Family Law; Creditor's Rights; Corporate Law; Real Estate; Bankruptcy. ***Email:*** mdecarlo@sbcglobal.net

KATHRYN A. HERWIG, born Great Bend, Kansas, November 6, 1951; admitted to bar, 1990, Oklahoma and U.S. District Court, Northern District of Oklahoma; 1993, U.S. District Court, Western District of Oklahoma; 2004, U.S. District Court, Eastern District of Oklahoma. *Education:* University of Tulsa (B.S., 1986; J.D., 1990). Phi Delta Phi. Oklahoma Real Estate Broker, 1982-1996. *Member:* Tulsa County and Oklahoma Bar Associations. ***REPORTED CASES:*** King v. Neal, 19 P.3d 899 (Okl. 2001). ***PRACTICE AREAS:*** General Civil Litigation; Real Estate; Family Law; Probate; Wills; Trusts; Workers Compensation; Personal Injury. ***Email:*** CLAWIL96@aol.com

LEGAL SUPPORT PERSONNEL

REBECCA ARMSTRONG

CLAUDIA GARRETT

REPRESENTATIVE CLIENTS: Case and Associates Properties, Inc.; Phipps & Company Productions; Grand Bluffs Development Co.; Wilhoit Properties; ICAN Energy; Thermal Windows, Inc.; Advanced Plastics, Inc.; Crain Displays and Exhibits, Inc.; Tri Management, Inc.; Felco Auto Lease, Inc.; Simon Property Group LP; Tulsa Boat Sales; McDowell & Associates; Mid-Continent/Midco Concrete Companies; Admiral Properties, Inc.; Woods Enterprises; Elastomer Specialties Inc.; JEM Engineering and Manufacturing Co.; Burlingame Realtors; The Hardesty Co.; Kaiser-Francis Oil Co (Realty Operating Company); NOSAJ, Inc.; Wellsford Properties; Master Packaging, Inc.; National Restaurant Development, Inc.; Equity Residential Co.; Juno Systems, Inc.; American Opportunity Foundation; United States Aviation Company; Union Planters Bank; CB Richard Ellis, Oklahoma, Inc.; Capital Assets, Inc.; The American Opportunity Foundation; Sheltering Palms Foundation; Zimmerman Investments.
REFERENCES: Bank of Oklahoma; Peoples State Bank.

W. KIRK CLAUSING

2021 SOUTH LEWIS AVENUE, SUITE 240
TULSA, OKLAHOMA 74104
Telephone: 918-745-0417
Telecopier: 918-745-9909
Email: clausing@swbell.net

Taxation, Estate and Gift Taxation, Wills, Probate, Trusts and Estate Planning, Corporations, Business Transactions, Private Foundations; Non Profit, Asset Protection; Business Organization and Formation.

(This Listing Continued)

W. KIRK CLAUSING, Tulsa—Continued

W. KIRK CLAUSING, born Enid, Oklahoma, September 12, 1944; admitted to bar, 1969, Oklahoma, U.S. Court of Appeals, 10th Circuit and U.S. District Court, Northern District; 1974, U.S. Tax Court. *Education:* University of Oklahoma (B.B.A., 1966; J.D., 1969). Phi Alpha Delta. Certified Public Accountant, Oklahoma, 1969. *Member:* Tulsa County (Member, Fee Arbitration Committee, 1993—), Oklahoma and American Bar Associations; Oklahoma Society of Certified Public Accountants. [1st Lt., USAR, 1970-1971]

REPRESENTATIVE CLIENTS: Furnished Upon Request.

CONCORDIA BENEFITS GROUP, P.C.

Established in 2000

320 SOUTH BOSTON, SUITE 2000
TULSA, OKLAHOMA 74103-4713
Telephone: 918-583-5700
Fax: 918-583-5341
URL: http://www.concordiabenefits.com

ERISA, Employee Benefits Law.

FIRM PROFILE: Concordia Benefits Group, P.C. is a law practice focused on representing clients in the area of employee benefits law. Based in Tulsa, the firm has represented clients located largely in the Southwest ranging in size from 100 to 75,000 employees.

The firm's services include plan design and compliance advice on welfare and retirement plans, vendor contract review and negotiation for all types of plans and arrangements, assistance to litigation counsel concerning benefit plan litigation and advice on employee benefit issues in mergers and acquisitions.

DEBBIE L. BLACKWELL, born Kansas City, Missouri, July 1, 1956; admitted to bar, 1986, Texas; 1988, Oklahoma. *Education:* University of Tulsa (B.S., Philosophy, with honors, 1979; J.D., 1986). Past President, Southwest Benefits Association. Listed in Best Lawyers in America among employee benefit practitioners. *Member:* State Bar of Texas; Oklahoma and American (Member: Tax Section; Employee Benefits Committee) Bar Associations. ***PRACTICE AREAS:*** Employee Benefits; ERISA. ***Email:*** debbieblackwell@concordiabenefits.com

ERIC S. SMITH, born Kansas City, Kansas, 1973; admitted to bar, 1998, Oklahoma. *Education:* Oklahoma State University (B.S., Finance, 1995); University of Oklahoma (J.D., 1998). Order of the Coif. Managing Editor, Oklahoma Law Review, 1997-1998. *Member:* Oklahoma and American (Member, Tax Section) Bar Associations. ***PRACTICE AREAS:*** Employee Benefits; ERISA. ***Email:*** ericsmith@concordiabenefits.com

C. GORDON HARRIS, born Oklahoma City, Oklahoma, 1966; admitted to bar, 2005, Oklahoma. *Education:* University of Oklahoma (B.A., Philosophy, 1992); Washburn University (J.D., with honors, 2005). *Member:* Oklahoma and American Bar Associations. ***PRACTICE AREAS:*** Employee Benefits; ERISA. ***Email:*** gordonharris@concordiabenefits.com

CONNER & WINTERS, LLP

Established in 1933

3700 FIRST PLACE TOWER
15 EAST 5TH STREET
TULSA, OKLAHOMA 74103-4344
Telephone: 918-586-5711
Fax: 918-586-8982
Email: postmaster@cwlaw.com
URL: http://www.cwlaw.com

Oklahoma City, Oklahoma Office: One Leadership Square, 211 North Robinson, Suite 1700, 73102-7101. Telephone: 405-272-5711. Facsimile: 405-232-2695.
Fayetteville, Arkansas Office: 100 West Center Street, Suite 200, 72701-6081. Telephone: 479-582-5711. Facsimile: 479-587-1426.
Santa Fe, New Mexico Office: 303 Paseo De Peralta, 87501. Telephone: 505-983-6497. Facsimile: 505-983-6478.
Jackson, Wyoming Office: 155 East Pearl Street, Suite 200, P.O. Box 4099, 83001-4099. Telephone: 307-733-2547. Fax: 307-733-3947.
Washington, DC Office: 1627 I Street, N.W., Suite 900, 20006. Telephone: 202-887-5711. Fax: 202-887-6999.
Houston, Texas Office: 1000 Louisiana, Suite 1301, 77002-5005. Telephone: 713-355-5711. Fax: 713-651-3929.

General Civil Practice. Trial and Appeals of Civil Cases in all State and Federal Courts. Administrative Proceedings, Alternative Dispute Resolution, Bankruptcy and Reorganization, Construction, Corporate and Securities, Employee Benefits, Employment and Labor Relations, Energy, Environmental, Estate Planning, Trust and Probate, Federal and State Taxation, Federal White Collar Criminal Defense, Financial Services and Banking, Governmental Affairs, Insurance and Risk Management, International, Litigation and Antitrust, Products Liability, Propane, Real Estate, Tax Exempt Organizations and Charitable Foundations and Workers' Compensation.

FIRM PROFILE: Founded in 1933, Conner & Winters, LLP has become one of the largest and most diverse law firms in the South Central Region of the United States.

The Firm serves a broad range of clients in local, state, regional, national, and international arenas. Its clients include businesses of all sizes and types-locally-owned companies to multinational corporations, individuals, estates and trusts, municipalities and other public-sector organizations, institutions, and charitable foundations.

Conner & Winters, LLP is a full-service firm with numerous specialty groups. Many of its lawyers have experience in several practice areas and that diversity allows the Firm to provide a broad array of legal services to numerous and varied clients. The Firm's lawyers work together to perform legal services with expertise, consistent quality and in a cost-effective manner.

HENRY G. WILL, born Hutchinson, Kansas, May 25, 1940; admitted to bar, 1965, Colorado; 1966, Oklahoma; 1986, U.S. Tax Court; 1991, U.S. Supreme Court. *Education:* Yale University (B.A., magna cum laude, 1962; LL.B., 1965). Listed in The Best Lawyers in America (Trusts and Estates; Taxation). Adjunct Professor of Law, University of Tulsa, 1970-1982. Fellow, American College of Trust and Estate Counsel. ***PRACTICE AREAS:*** Estate Planning Law; Employee Benefits Law; Closely Held Business Law. ***Email:*** hwill@cwlaw.com

JOSEPH J. McCAIN, JR., born Pine Bluff, Arkansas, March 27, 1942; admitted to bar, 1967, Texas; 1968, Oklahoma. *Education:* Southern Methodist University (B.B.A., 1964; J.D., 1967). Recent Decisions Editor, Southwestern Law Journal, 1966-1967. Law Clerk to Chief Judge, Alfred P. Murrah, U.S. Court of Appeals, Tenth Circuit, 1967-1968. ***PRACTICE AREAS:*** Real Estate Law; Trusts and Estates; Oil and Gas Law. ***Email:*** jmccain@cwlaw.com

LYNNWOOD R. MOORE, JR., born Colorado Springs, Colorado, March 30, 1945; admitted to bar, 1970, Oklahoma. *Education:* Princeton University (A.B., 1967); University of Oklahoma (J.D., 1970). Order of the Coif. Member, Board of Editors, Oklahoma Law Review, 1968-1970. Listed in The Best Lawyers in America (Corporate Transactions). ***PRACTICE AREAS:*** Securities Regulation Law; Corporate Law; Mergers, Acquisitions and Divestitures. ***Email:*** lmoore@cwlaw.com

ROBERT A. CURRY, born Liberal, Kansas, December 14, 1947; admitted to bar, 1975, Oklahoma. *Education:* Kansas State University (B.S., Electrical Engineering, 1970); University of Texas (J.D., with honors, 1975). Phi Delta Phi; Sigma Tau; Eta Kappa Nu. Listed in The Best Lawyers in America (Corporate Transactions). ***PRACTICE AREAS:*** Corporate Law; Securities Regulation Law; Mergers, Acquisitions and Divestitures; International Business Transactions. ***Email:*** rcurry@cwlaw.com

STEVEN W. McGRATH, born Washington, D.C., June 6, 1948; admitted to bar, 1974, Pennsylvania; 1980, U.S. Tax Court; 1986, Oklahoma. *Education:* University of Maryland (B.S., 1970); College of William and Mary (J.D., 1974). Member, 1972-1974 and Research Editor, 1973-1974, William and Mary Law Review. Listed in The Best Lawyers in America (Employee Benefits Law). Chairperson, Flexible Benefits Advisory Council, State of Oklahoma, 1989-1991. Member, Board of Directors, SouthWest Benefits Association, 1997-2000. *Member:* American Bar Association (Member: Employee Benefits Committee; Section on Taxation); American College of Employee Benefits Counsel. ***PRACTICE AREAS:*** Employee Benefits; Executive Compensation; ERISA Litigation. ***Email:*** smcgrath@cwlaw.com

D. RICHARD FUNK, born Chestnut Hill, Pennsylvania, January 6, 1946; admitted to bar, 1973, Pennsylvania; 1988, Oklahoma. *Education:* Lehigh University (B.S., 1967; M.B.A., 1968); Dickinson School of Law (J.D., cum laude, 1973). Member, Dickinson Law Review, 1971-1973. ***PRACTICE AREAS:*** Commercial Litigation; General Civil Litigation; Antitrust Litigation. ***Email:*** rfunk@cwlaw.com

RANDOLPH L. JONES, JR., born Tacoma, Washington, February 15, 1947; admitted to bar, 1974, Minnesota; 1976, Texas; 1995, Oklahoma; 2003, Wyoming. *Education:* University of Minnesota (B.A., summa cum laude, 1969; J.D., 1974). Phi Beta Kappa. Recipient, Oklahoma Bar Association Pro Bono Service Award, 1999. Legal Department, El Paso Natural Gas Company, 1974-1979. Coal Attorney, General Manager Coal Sales, Assistant General Counsel, MAPCO, 1979-1987; Vice President, General Counsel and Secretary, MAPCO Petroleum Inc., 1987-1990. *Member:* The Maritime Law Association of the United States. (Also at Jackson, Wyoming Office). ***PRACTICE AREAS:*** Environmental Law and Litigation; Federal and State Energy Regulatory Law; Administrative Law and Litigation; Commercial Law and Litigation; General Civil Litigation and Appeals; International Arbitration and Litigation; Juvenile Litigation; Admiralty Law. ***Email:*** rjones@cwlaw.com

J. RONALD PETRIKIN, born Waynesville, Missouri, December 10, 1946; admitted to bar, 1973, Missouri; 1975, Tennessee; 1982, Oklahoma. *Education:* University of Missouri (B.A., 1968); St. Louis University (J.D., 1973). Listed in The Best Lawyers in America (Labor and Employment Law). Attorney, Region 14, National Labor Relations Board, 1973-1974. Chairman, 1988, Labor and Employment Law Section, Oklahoma Bar Association. Chairman, 1988-1990, Board of Oklahoma Bar Professional Liability Insurance Company. ***PRACTICE AREAS:*** Labor and Employment Law; Civil Rights Litigation. ***Email:*** rpetrikin@cwlaw.com

LARRY B. LIPE, born Fayetteville, Arkansas, July 11, 1951; admitted to bar, 1976, Arkansas; 1979, Oklahoma, U.S. District Court, Northern, Eastern and Western Districts of Oklahoma and, U.S. Court of Appeals, Fifth, Eighth and Tenth Circuits. *Education:* University of Arkansas (B.S., with honors in Public Administration, 1973); Southern Methodist University (J.D., 1976). Leading Articles Editor, Journal of Air Law and Commerce, 1975-1976. Member: Master, Hudson Hall, Wheaton Chapter, 1995. Barrister: Robert Hudson Chapter, 1987-1988; W. Lee Johnson Chapter, 1989-1990, American Inns of Court. ***PRACTICE AREAS:*** Commercial Litigation; Personal Injury; Construction Law. ***Email:*** llipe@cwlaw.com

JAMES E. GREEN, JR., born Wichita, Kansas, July 8, 1949; admitted to bar, 1977, Oklahoma and U.S. District Court, Northern, Western and Eastern Districts of Oklahoma; U.S. Court of Appeals, Fourth, Ninth, Tenth and Eleventh Circuits. *Education:* University of Tulsa (B.S., 1971; J.D., 1977). Order of the Curule Chair. Staff Member, Tulsa Law Journal, 1975-1977. Member, Master, The Council Oak Chapter, American Inns of Court, 1995—. ***PRACTICE AREAS:*** Insurance Coverage Law; Insurance Coverage Litigation; Products Liability; Personal Injury; Business Litigation. ***Email:*** jgreen@cwlaw.com

MARTIN R. WING, born Tulsa, Oklahoma, August 21, 1954; admitted to bar, 1978, Oklahoma; 1986, U.S. Tax Court; 1991, U.S. Supreme Court. *Education:* Rice University (B.A., cum laude, 1977); Columbia University (J.D., 1978). Adjunct Professor of Law, University of Tulsa, 1986-1990, 1993, 1996-1998. ***PRACTICE AREAS:*** Employee Benefits Law; State Taxation Law; Tax Exempt Organizations. ***Email:*** mwing@cwlaw.com

(This Listing Continued)

JOHN W. INGRAHAM, born Huntington, New York, July 28, 1948; admitted to bar, 1976, New York; 1980, Oklahoma. *Education:* Wesleyan University (B.A., 1970); Fordham University (J.D., 1975). Law Clerk to Chief Judge, U.S. District Court, Northern District of Oklahoma, 1975-1976. Assistant District Attorney, New York County, N.Y., 1976-1980. ***PRACTICE AREAS:*** Probate Law; Trusts and Estates; Wills. ***Email:*** jingraham@cwlaw.com

ANDREW R. TURNER, born Tulsa, Oklahoma, February 4, 1956; admitted to bar, 1981, Oklahoma; 1990, U.S. Supreme Court. *Education:* University of Oklahoma (B.A., with highest honors, 1978); Southern Methodist University (J.D., cum laude, 1981). Phi Beta Kappa; Order of the Coif. Editor, Journal of Air Law and Commerce, 1980-1981. Adjunct Professor of Law, University of Tulsa, 1988. Chairman, Bankruptcy Section, Tulsa County Bar Association, 1989-1990; Governor, Bankruptcy Section, Oklahoma Bar Association, 1999—. *Member:* American Bankruptcy Institute. (Certified in Business Bankruptcy Law by the American Board of Certification). ***PRACTICE AREAS:*** Commercial Bankruptcy; Commercial Litigation; Real Estate Liens. ***Email:*** aturner@cwlaw.com

GENTRA ABBEY SOREM, born Dodge City, Kansas, April 14, 1958; admitted to bar, 1983, Oklahoma. *Education:* University of Kansas (B.A., with highest distinction and honors, 1980; J.D., 1983). Phi Beta Kappa; Phi Kappa Phi; Order of the Coif. Member, 1981-1983 and Note and Comment Editor, 1982-1983, Kansas Law Review. ***PRACTICE AREAS:*** Real Estate Law; Banking Law. ***Email:*** gsorem@cwlaw.com

R. KEVIN REDWINE, born Hugo, Oklahoma, December 23, 1958; admitted to bar, 1984, Oklahoma. *Education:* University of Oklahoma (B.B.A., 1981; J.D., with highest honors, 1984). Order of the Coif. Member, Oklahoma Law Review, 1982-1984. ***PRACTICE AREAS:*** Corporate Law; Mergers, Acquisitions and Divestitures; Oil and Gas Law. ***Email:*** kredwine@cwlaw.com

TONY W. HAYNIE, born Houston, Texas, September 26, 1955; admitted to bar, 1985, Oklahoma; 1990, U.S. Tax Court, U.S. District Court, Northern, Western and Eastern Districts of Oklahoma, U.S. Court of Appeals, Fifth, Seventh, Tenth and District of Columbia Circuits and U.S. Supreme Court. *Education:* University of Oklahoma (B.A., 1978); University of Tulsa (J.D., 1984); Oklahoma State University (M.B.A., 1994). Phi Delta Phi; Order of the Barristers. Member, Tulsa Law Journal, 1982-1984; Master, Hudson Hall, Wheaton Chapter American Inns of Court, 1995—. Adjunct Professor of Law, University of Tulsa, 2002—. ***PRACTICE AREAS:*** Commercial Litigation; Trade Secrets; Securities Litigation; Complex Litigation; Bankruptcy; Trust and Estates Litigation; Employment Law. ***Email:*** thaynie@cwlaw.com

BRUCE W. FREEMAN, born Muskogee, Oklahoma, March 14, 1959; admitted to bar, 1984, Oklahoma, U.S. District Court, Northern and Eastern Districts of Oklahoma, U.S. District Court, Western and Eastern Districts of Arkansas and U.S. Court of Appeals, Eighth and Tenth Circuits. *Education:* Yale University (B.A., 1981); University of Oklahoma (J.D., with distinction, 1984). Member, 1982-1984 and Note Editor, 1983-1984, Oklahoma Law Review. ***PRACTICE AREAS:*** Litigation; Appellate Practice; Oil and Gas Law. ***Email:*** bfreeman@cwlaw.com

DAVID R. CORDELL, born Tulsa, Oklahoma, December 21, 1959; admitted to bar, 1985, Oklahoma; 1988, U.S. Tax Court. *Education:* Washington & Lee University (B.A., cum laude, 1982); University of Oklahoma (J.D., 1985). Member, 1983-1985 and Note Editor, 1985, Oklahoma Law Review. Adjunct Settlement Judge, U.S. District Court, Northern District of Oklahoma, 1990. American Inns of Court, Member Johnson - Sontag Inn. *Member:* Tulsa County Bar Association (Member, Committees on: Fee Arbitration and Professional Responsibility). ***PRACTICE AREAS:*** Employment; Litigation; Oil and Gas Law; Airline Labor Law. ***Email:*** dcordell@cwlaw.com

JOHN N. HOVE, born Kansas City, Missouri, August 16, 1947; admitted to bar, 1972, Oklahoma. *Education:* University of Tulsa (B.S.B.A., 1969); Southern Methodist University (J.D., 1972). Phi Alpha Delta. General Counsel, Willbros Group, Inc., 1999-2001. *Member:* Oklahoma District Export Council. ***PRACTICE AREAS:*** Corporate Law; Construction Law; International Business Transactions. ***Email:*** jhove@cwlaw.com

C. RAYMOND PATTON, JR., born Tulsa, Oklahoma, July 21, 1950; admitted to bar, 1976, Oklahoma. *Education:* University of Oklahoma (B.B.A., Finance, 1973; J.D., 1976). Adjunct Professor, University of Tulsa, College of Law, ADR, Securities Reg. and M&A, 1993—. Associate General Counsel, 1976-1977, General Counsel, 1977-1978 and Administrator, 1984-1986, Oklahoma Securities Commission. Chairman, Oklahoma Capital Investment Board, 1988-1991. Adjunct Settlement Judge, U.S.D.C. for the Northern District of Oklahoma 1988—. Listed in Best Lawyers in America for Securities, Corporate, and Mergers and Acquisitions. ***PRACTICE AREAS:*** Securities Law; Broker-Dealer Regulation; Investment Regulation; Corporate Law; Business Litigation. ***Email:*** rpatton@cwlaw.com

PAUL E. BRADEN, born Chicago, Illinois, January 29, 1942; admitted to bar, 1980, Kansas; 1981, Oklahoma and Florida. *Education:* MacMurray College (B.A., 1964); St. Louis University (M.S., USAF Program, 1968); Washburn University (J.D., cum laude, 1980); University of Miami (LL.M., in Estate Planning, 1981). Phi Delta Phi. ***PRACTICE AREAS:*** Employee Benefits Law. ***Email:*** pbraden@cwlaw.com

ROBERT J. MELGAARD, born Yankton, South Dakota, May 6, 1959; admitted to bar, 1985, Oklahoma. *Education:* Montana State University (B.S., with honors, 1982); University of Nebraska (J.D., with distinction, 1985). Beta Gamma Sigma; Order of the Coif. Executive Editor, 1984-1985 and Member, 1983-1985, Nebraska Law Review. Listed in The Best Lawyers in America: Corporate, Mergers and Acquisitions, and Securities Law. Chairman, Business and Corporate Law Section, 1998, Oklahoma Bar Association. *Member:* Tulsa County Bar Association (Chairman, Corporate Counsel Section, 1994-1995). ***PRACTICE AREAS:*** Securities Regulation Law; Corporate Law; Business Law. ***Email:*** rmelgaard@cwlaw.com

P. SCOTT HATHAWAY, born Oklahoma City, Oklahoma, February 3, 1964; admitted to bar, 1989, Oklahoma. *Education:* Vanderbilt University (B.A., 1986); Southern Methodist University (J.D., 1989). Recipient, Golberg & Alexander Award. ***PRACTICE AREAS:*** Employment Law; Construction Law; Complex Litigation; Commercial Litigation. ***Email:*** shathaway@cwlaw.com

(This Listing Continued)

LAWRENCE A. HALL, born Lawton, Oklahoma, May 28, 1965; admitted to bar, 1990, Oklahoma. *Education:* University of Oklahoma (B.B.A., with highest honors, 1987); Harvard University (J.D., 1990). ***PRACTICE AREAS:*** Corporate Law; Mergers, Acquisitions and Divestitures; Energy Law; Securities Law. ***Email:*** lhall@cwlaw.com

TIMOTHY T. TRUMP, born Lansing, Michigan, January 7, 1958; admitted to bar, 1984, Oklahoma, U.S. District Court, Northern, Eastern and Western Districts of Oklahoma and U.S. Court of Appeals, Tenth Circuit. *Education:* University of Kansas (B.S., 1980; J.D., 1983). Member, Client Security Fund Committee, 1991-1999, Oklahoma Bar Association. (Certified Specialist, Business and Consumer Bankruptcy Law, American Bankruptcy Board of Certification). ***PRACTICE AREAS:*** Bankruptcy Law; Commercial Litigation; Collections; Insurance Defense. ***Email:*** ttrump@cwlaw.com

MARK E. DREYER, born San Diego, California, September 8, 1963; admitted to bar, 1988, North Carolina; 1992, Oklahoma, U.S. District Court, Middle District of North Carolina, U.S. District Court, Northern, Eastern and Western Districts of Oklahoma and U.S. Court of Appeals, Third, Tenth and Eleventh Circuits. *Education:* Washington University (B.A., 1985); University of Tulsa (J.D., 1988). Notes and Comments Editor, Tulsa Law Journal, 1987-1988. ***PRACTICE AREAS:*** Insurance Coverage; Products Liability; Civil Litigation. ***Email:*** mdreyer@cwlaw.com

NANCY E. VAUGHN, born Los Angeles, California, September 5, 1947; admitted to bar, 1974, Oklahoma, U.S. District Court, Northern, Eastern and Western Districts of Oklahoma and U.S. Court of Appeals, Tenth and Fifth Circuits. *Education:* University of Southern California (A.B., cum laude, 1969); University of Tulsa (J.D., 1974). Phi Delta Phi. Member, Order of the Curule Chair. Member: Tulsa Law Journal, 1973-1974. ***PRACTICE AREAS:*** Employment Law; Civil Rights Litigation. ***Email:*** nvaughn@cwlaw.com

GREGORY D. RENBERG, born Tulsa, Oklahoma, 1957; admitted to bar, 1985, Oklahoma, U.S. District Court, Northern District of Oklahoma and U.S. Court of Appeals, Tenth Circuit. *Education:* University of Tulsa (B.S.B.A., 1981; J.D., 1985). Certified Public Accountant, Oklahoma, 1989. ***PRACTICE AREAS:*** Employee Benefits Law; Oil and Gas; Taxation Law; ERISA Litigation. ***Email:*** grenberg@cwlaw.com

MARK D. BERMAN, born Yonkers, New York, December 13, 1956; admitted to bar, 1981, Oklahoma; 1986, Texas; 1987, District of Columbia. *Education:* University of California at Santa Cruz (A.B., cum laude, 1978); University of Utah (J.D., 1981). Senior Editor, Utah Law Review, 1980-1981. *Member:* Tulsa County Bar Association (Chairman, Corporate Section, 2002-2003). ***PRACTICE AREAS:*** Securities Regulation; Corporate Law; Mergers, Acquisitions and Divestitures. ***Email:*** mberman@cwlaw.com

KATHERINE G. COYLE, born Tulsa, Oklahoma, February 8, 1947; admitted to bar, 1972, Oklahoma. *Education:* Hollins College (B.A. cum laude, 1969); University of Tulsa (J.D., 1972); New York University (LL.M., in Taxation, 1975). Order of the Curule Chair. Law Clerk, U.S. Court of Appeals, Tenth Circuit, 1972-1973. ***PRACTICE AREAS:*** Estate Planning Law; Charitable Trusts and Foundations Law; Trust Law. ***Email:*** kcoyle@cwlaw.com

BEVERLY K. SMITH, born Dallas, Texas, March 8, 1948; admitted to bar, 1988, Oklahoma. *Education:* University of Oklahoma (B.A., 1970); University of Tulsa (J.D., with honor, 1987). Order of the Curule Chair. Recipient, Outstanding Law Student Award, Oklahoma Bar Association, 1986. Member, Tulsa Law Journal, 1985-1987. ***PRACTICE AREAS:*** Real Estate; Estate Planning; Probate; Trusts and Estates; Business Transactions. ***Email:*** bsmith@cwlaw.com

MELODIE FREEMAN-BURNEY, born Tulsa, Oklahoma, October 26, 1954; admitted to bar, 1988, Oklahoma, U.S. District Court, Northern, Eastern and Western Districts of Oklahoma and U.S. Court of Appeals, Tenth Circuit. *Education:* Oklahoma Baptist University (B.A., magna cum laude, with honors, 1976); University of Tulsa (J.D., with honors, 1988). Order of the Curule Chair. Recipient, Ten American Jurisprudence Awards. Member, 1986-1988 and Articles Editor, 1987-1988, Tulsa Law Journal. ***PRACTICE AREAS:*** Commercial Litigation; Personal Injury; Insurance Litigation. ***Email:*** mburney@cwlaw.com

R. RICHARD LOVE, III, born Oklahoma City, Oklahoma, September 3, 1966; admitted to bar, 1991, Oklahoma; U.S. District Court, Northern and Western Districts of Oklahoma; U.S. Court of Appeals, Tenth and Fifth Circuits. *Education:* University of Oklahoma (B.A., 1988; J.D., with honors, 1991). Order of the Coif. Member, 1989-1991 and Note Editor, 1990-1991, Oklahoma Law Review. Assistant United States Attorney, Northern District of Oklahoma, 1999-2002. ***PRACTICE AREAS:*** Commercial Litigation; Federal White Collar Criminal Defense; Securities Litigation; Employment Litigation. ***Email:*** rlove@cwlaw.com

ROBERT D. JAMES, born Arkadelphia, Arkansas, September 12, 1968; admitted to bar, 1995, Oklahoma; 1996, Arkansas, U.S. District Court, Northern, Eastern and Western Districts of Oklahoma and U.S. Court of Appeals, Tenth Circuit; 2001, U.S. Court of Appeals, Third Circuit; 2003, U.S. District Court, Eastern and Western Districts of Arkansas; 2004, U.S. Supreme Court. *Education:* University of Arkansas (B.S.B.A., 1992; J.D., 1995). Phi Delta Phi; Order of the Barristers. Member, Board of Advocates, National Moot Court Team, Best Brief and Third Place Overall. ***PRACTICE AREAS:*** Civil Litigation; Commercial Litigation; Products Liability; Personal Injury; Insurance Law. ***Email:*** rjames@cwlaw.com

STEPHEN R. WARD, born Stillwater, Oklahoma, June 14, 1956; admitted to bar, 1990, Oklahoma; U.S. Supreme Court; U.S. Court of Appeals, Fifth, Eighth, Tenth, Eleventh and Federal Circuits; 1993, U.S. District Court, Northern, Western and Eastern Districts of Oklahoma. *Education:* Oklahoma State University (B.S., 1978); University of Tulsa (J.D., 1990). Editor in Chief, Tulsa Law Journal, Volume 25, 1989-1990. Author: Maynard v. Cartwright: "How the Supreme Court Killed the Catchall Category in Oklahoma Death Penalty," 25 Tulsa Law Journal 215 (1988). *Member:* Oklahoma Bar Association. ***PRACTICE AREAS:*** Federal Litigation; Appellate Practice; Energy; Public Lands Law; Native American Law; Indian Law; Environmental Law. ***Email:*** sward@cwlaw.com

JEFFREY R. SCHOBORG, born Marshalltown, Iowa, December 5, 1956; admitted to bar, 1984, Oklahoma and U.S. District Court, Northern, Eastern and Western Districts of Oklahoma. *Education:* University of Oklahoma (B.S., 1979); University of Tulsa (J.D., 1983). *Member:* Tulsa County, Oklahoma and American Bar Associations; The Association

(This Listing Continued)

CONNER & WINTERS, LLP, Tulsa—Continued

of Trial Lawyers of America; Oklahoma Trial Lawyers Association. ***PRACTICE AREAS:*** Workers Compensation Defense; Employment Defense; Commercial Litigation; Insurance Defense. ***Email:*** jschoborg@cwlaw.com

ANNE B. SUBLETT, born Mobile, Alabama, 1946; admitted to bar, 1980, Oklahoma. *Education:* University of Tulsa (B.A., cum laude, 1968); Georgetown University Law Center (J.D., 1980). Legal Seminars: Employee Benefits, Rendering Third Party Legal Opinions, Choice of Entities for Doing Business, Juvenile Law. Adjunct Professor of Law, Agency and Partnership Law, The University of Tulsa College of Law. President, Tulsa Lawyers for Children, Inc. *Member:* Tulsa County, Oklahoma and American Bar Associations. ***PRACTICE AREAS:*** Employee Benefits; Business Transactions. ***Email:*** asublett@cwlaw.com

J. RYAN SACRA, born Tulsa, Oklahoma, 1971; admitted to bar, 1996, Oklahoma; 1999, New York. *Education:* University of Oklahoma (B.B.A., with distinction, 1993; J.D., 1996). Phi Delta Phi. *Member:* Alternative Dispute Resolution Society. ***PRACTICE AREAS:*** Securities Regulation; Business Law; Corporate Law; Mergers and Acquisitions. ***Email:*** rsacra@cwlaw.com

JASON S. TAYLOR, born Denver, Colorado, December 8, 1970; admitted to bar, 1998, Texas; 1999, Oklahoma; 2000, U.S. District Court, Northern District of Texas, U.S. District Court, Northern and Eastern Districts of Oklahoma and U.S. Court of Appeals, Tenth Circuit. *Education:* University of Oklahoma (B.A., 1995; J.D., with distinction, 1998). Phi Delta Phi. ***PRACTICE AREAS:*** Civil Litigation; Securities Litigation; Employment Litigation; Commercial Litigation. ***Email:*** jtaylor@cwlaw.com

---

KATY DAY INHOFE, born Fayetteville, Arkansas, September 11, 1965; admitted to bar, 1992, Oklahoma. *Education:* Washington University (B.A., 1987); University of Tulsa (J.D., with honors, 1992). Member, Tulsa Law Journal, 1990-1992. Law Clerk, U.S. District Court, Northern District of Texas, 1992-1993. ***PRACTICE AREAS:*** Corporate Law; Mergers, Acquisitions and Divestitures; Securities Law. ***Email:*** kinhofe@cwlaw.com

JULIA FORRESTER-SELLERS, born Tulsa, Oklahoma, December 28, 1975; admitted to bar, 2000, Oklahoma and U.S. District Court, Eastern and Northern Districts of Oklahoma. *Education:* University of Oklahoma (B.A., Anthropology, 1997); University of Tulsa (M.A., Cultural Anthropology, with honors, 2000; J.D., with honors, 2000). Phi Delta Phi. CALI Award for Excellence in Arbitration. Author: "The 1921 Race Riot and the Politics of Memory," University of Tulsa, 2000. ***PRACTICE AREAS:*** Insurance Law; Civil Litigation. ***Email:*** jsellers@cwlaw.com

MELINDA L. KIRK, born New York, N.Y., February 3, 1964; admitted to bar, 2001, Oklahoma; 2005, U.S. District Court, Northern, Eastern and Western Districts of Oklahoma. *Education:* University of Tulsa (B.S., Accounting, 1986; J.D., with highest honors, 2001). Order of the Curule Chair; Order of the Barristers. Editor-in-Chief, Tulsa Law Journal, 2000-2001. Honorary Member *Scribes*. Author: "Employment Protection for Service Personnel," Tulsa Law Magazine, Spring 2004. ***PRACTICE AREAS:*** Civil Litigation; Commercial Litigation; Labor and Employment; Construction Litigation; Propane Litigation. ***Email:*** mkirk@cwlaw.com

P. BRADLEY BENDURE, born Tulsa, Oklahoma, December 21, 1976; admitted to bar, 2001, Oklahoma and U.S. District Court, Northern, Eastern and Western Districts of Oklahoma. *Education:* Knox College (B.A., magna cum laude, 1998); University of Oklahoma (J.D., with honors, 2001). Order of the Coif. ***PRACTICE AREAS:*** Civil Litigation; Insurance Law; Employment Law. ***Email:*** bbendure@cwlaw.com

KATHRYN J. KINDELL, born Okmulgee, Oklahoma, June 4, 1954; admitted to bar, 2001, Oklahoma. *Education:* Northeastern Oklahoma State University (B.S., 1976); University of Tulsa (J.D., with honors, 2001). *Member:* Tulsa County Bar Association. ***PRACTICE AREAS:*** Securities Registration; Corporate Law; Business Law. ***Email:*** kkindell@cwlaw.com

AMY MONSOUR SANTEE, born Oklahoma City, Oklahoma, July 2, 1971; admitted to bar, 2001, Oklahoma. *Education:* University of Oklahoma (B.A., with distinction, 1994; J.D., with honors, 2001). Order of the Coif. Member, 1999-2001 and Research Editor, 2000-2001, Oklahoma Law Review. ***PRACTICE AREAS:*** Real Estate. ***Email:*** asantee@cwlaw.com

CARA M. HAIR, born Stillwater, Oklahoma, October 26, 1976; admitted to bar, 2002, Oklahoma. *Education:* Oklahoma State University (B.S., summa cum laude, 1998); University of Oklahoma (J.D., with honors, 2002). Order of the Coif. ***PRACTICE AREAS:*** Civil Litigation; Employment Law; Commercial Litigation. ***Email:*** chair@cwlaw.com

ALISSA A. HURLEY, born Springfield, Missouri, July 7, 1977; admitted to bar, 2002, Oklahoma. *Education:* University of Tulsa (B.A., 1999; J.D., with highest honors, 2002). Order of Curule Chair; Order of the Barristers; Phi Delta Phi. Notes and Comments Editor, Tulsa Law Review, 2001-2002. ***PRACTICE AREAS:*** Employee Benefits Law; Tax Law. ***Email:*** ahurley@cwlaw.com

HEATHER HOLT BILDERBACK, born Fayetteville, Arkansas, February 23, 1974; admitted to bar, 2002, Oklahoma; 2003, Arkansas. *Education:* University of Arkansas (B.A., 1996; J.D., cum laude, 2002). Member, Arkansas Law Review, 2001-2002. Member, Board of Advocates, 2001-2002. ***PRACTICE AREAS:*** Real Estate Law; Financial Services and Banking; Bankruptcy; Reorganization Law. ***Email:*** hbilderback@cwlaw.com

DEBRA RENAE STOCKTON, born Tulsa, Oklahoma, April 29, 1969; admitted to bar, 1994, Oklahoma. *Education:* Northeastern Oklahoma State University (B.A., 1991); University of Tulsa (J.D., 1994). ***PRACTICE AREAS:*** Business Law; Corporate Law; Telecommunications Law. ***Email:*** dstockton@cwlaw.com

SHELLEY L. CARTER, born Fairfax, Virginia, May 23, 1978; admitted to bar, 2003, Oklahoma. *Education:* Duke University (B.A., magna cum laude, 2000); Georgetown University Law Center (J.D., 2003). Law Fellow 2001-2003. Member, Georgetown Journal of Legal Ethics. Recipient, CALI Award for Excellence in Class Actions Seminar. Author: "Driving on the Wrong Side of the Road: How Lawyers are Sanctioned for Vehicular Homicide," Georgetown Journal of Legal Ethics, Summer 2002. ***PRACTICE AREAS:*** Civil Litigation; Employment Law; Commercial Litigation. ***Email:*** scarter@cwlaw.com

JED W. ISBELL, born Enid, Oklahoma, February 14, 1975; admitted to bar, 2004, Oklahoma. *Education:* Oklahoma State University (B.S., 1997; M.S., 1999); University of Tulsa (J.D., with honors, 2004). Phi Delta Phi. Editor, Tulsa Law Review, 2003-2004. ***PRACTICE AREAS:*** Civil Litigation; Commercial Litigation. ***Email:*** jisbell@cwlaw.com

TRAVIS L. WRIGHT, born Gainesville, Florida, July 11, 1974; admitted to bar, 2005, Oklahoma. *Education:* University of Florida (B.A., with honors, 1997); University of Tulsa (J.D., with highest honors, 2003); New York University (LL.M., in Taxation, 2004). ***PRACTICE AREAS:*** Taxation; Corporate and Securities; Tax Exempt Organizations. ***Email:*** twright@cwlaw.com

JASON B. COUTANT, born Tulsa, Oklahoma, July 21, 1980; admitted to bar, 2005, Oklahoma. *Education:* Oklahoma State University (B.S., Accounting, magna cum laude, 2002); University of Texas (J.D., with honors, 2005). ***PRACTICE AREAS:*** Banks and Banking; Finance; Corporate Law; Securities; Regulatory Law; Taxation. ***Email:*** jcoutant@cwlaw.com

ALLISON C. McGRATH GARDNER, born Pittsburgh, Pennsylvania, May 3, 1980; admitted to bar, 2005, Oklahoma. *Education:* University of Virginia (B.A., 2002); University of Oklahoma (J.D., with distinction, 2005). ***PRACTICE AREAS:*** Estate Planning; Tax Exempt Organizations; Employee Benefit.

KERRILEE E. KOBBEMAN, born Lincoln, Kansas, January 22, 1975; admitted to bar, 2005, Oklahoma. *Education:* McPherson College (B.S., Biology, 1997); University of Arkansas (J.D., summa cum laude, 2005). Editor-in-Chief, Arkansas Law Review, 2004-2005. Author, "Hook, Line and Sinker: How Congress Swallowed the Domestic Catfish Industry's Narrow Definiton of This Ubiquitous Bottomfeeder," 57 Ark. L. Rev. 401, 2004. ***PRACTICE AREAS:*** Corporate Law. ***Email:*** kkobbeman@cwlaw.com

OF COUNSEL

BOB F. McCOY, born Hutchinson, Kansas, December 10, 1942; admitted to bar, 1972, Oklahoma; 1973, U.S. District Court, Eastern District of Oklahoma; 1975, U.S. District Court, Northern District of Oklahoma; 1983, U.S. Court of Appeals, Tenth Circuit. *Education:* United States Military Academy (B.S., 1964); University of Michigan (J.D., magna cum laude, 1971). Order of the Coif. *Member:* Tulsa County, Oklahoma and American Bar Associations; Federal Communications Bar Association. [Capt., U.S. Army, 1964-1969]. ***Email:*** bmccoy@cwlaw.com

WILLIAM G. VON GLAHN, born Bronxville, New York, August 29, 1943; admitted to bar, 1974, New York; 1984, Oklahoma. *Education:* University of North Carolina (B.A., 1965); Washington University (J.D., 1973). Managing Editor, Washington University Law Quarterly, 1972-1973. Chairman, State of Oklahoma Ethics Commission, 1993-1996. Adjunct Professor of Law, Tulsa University, 1990. Associate, Sullivan & Cromwell, 1973-1977. Attorney: W. R. Grace & Co., 1977-1981; Armco, Inc., 1981-1984. Associate General Counsel, 1984-1996. Senior Vice President and General Counsel, 1996-2002, The Williams Companies, Inc. [Capt., USMC, 1965-1974]. ***PRACTICE AREAS:*** Corporate Law; Securities Regulation Law; Banking; Finance; Commercial Transactions; International Business Transactions. ***Email:*** bvonglahn@cwlaw.com

(For Biographical Data of other Firm Personnel, See Professional Biographies in Tulsa, Oklahoma, Oklahoma City, Oklahoma, Jackson, Wyoming, Fayetteville, Arkansas, Santa Fe, New Mexico, Washington, D.C and Houston, Texas)

WILLIAM R. COOK II, PLLC

TULSA, OKLAHOMA

(See Oklahoma City)

Federal and State Income Taxation, Estate and Gift Taxation Law, Tax Controversies and Tax Litigation. Probate, Estate Planning, Trust Law, Wills.

COOPER, McKINNEY & WOOSLEY, PLLP

401 SOUTH BOSTON
TULSA, OKLAHOMA 74103
Telephone: 918-592-3302
Fax: 918-592-7816
URL: http://www.coopermckinney.com

General Civil Practice, Civil Litigation, Major Transactions, Business Organization, Employment Law, Health Care, Employee Benefits, Banking, Estate Planning, Education Law, Construction, Oil and Gas, Real Estate and Environmental Law.

FIRM PROFILE: Founded by three experienced lawyers, Cooper, McKinney & Woosley, PLLP is a firm which combines a sophisticated legal practice with a unique blend of flexibility, technology and professionalism allowing us to provide the highest level of service in both large and small matters in a responsive and cost effective manner.

The firm represents business entities and individuals in all aspects of a general, civil business practice. Areas of concentration include complex litigation in all state and federal courts, mergers and acquisitions, banking, health care, employee benefits, ERISA litigation, higher education law, commercial transactions, construction, oil and gas law, real estate, environmental law, insurance law, estate planning and probate.

We emphasizes integrity, quality, accessibility and value. We will not assign more lawyers or staff to a project than is justified. The assignment of each matter to a particular attorney facilitates communication and assures personal service. We are proud of our national, regional and local clients and our reputation for professionalism and innovation. Our experience and enthusiasm of our lawyers and staff allow us to provide the capabilities and resources of a large firm with the personal attention, value and other benefits of a smaller organization.

(This Listing Continued)

R. CASEY COOPER, born Tulsa, Oklahoma, January 20, 1943; admitted to bar, 1967, Oklahoma. *Education:* University of Tulsa (B.S., B.A., 1965; J.D., 1967). Phi Alpha Delta; Order of The Curule Chair. Editor-in-Chief, Tulsa Law Journal, 1967. *Member:* Oklahoma and American Bar Associations; The Mervin Bovaird Foundation (President and Trustee). [Lt., JAGC, USNR, active duty, 1967-1971]. ***PRACTICE AREAS:*** Complex Litigation; Environmental Law; Corporate Law. ***Email:*** casey.cooper@cmw-law.com

DAVID B. McKINNEY, born Tulsa, Oklahoma, June 22, 1951; admitted to bar, 1975, Oklahoma. *Education:* Rice University (B.A., 1974); Columbia University (J.D., 1975). Harlan Fiske Stone Scholar (1973 - 1975). *Member:* Tulsa County and Oklahoma Bar Associations; American Health Lawyers Association; Tulsa Pension Attorneys (Immediate past Moderator); Tulsa Employee Benefits Group (Immediate past Chair); OBA Health Law Section (Secretary); The Mervin Bovaird Foundation (Vice President and Trustee). Oklahoma Bar Foundation (Fellow and former Trustee). ***REPORTED CASES:*** Roe v. American Life Ins. Co., 712 F.2d 450 (10 Cir. 1983) U.S. v. Community Bank, 768 F.2d 34 (10 Cir. 1985) Kelso v. General American Life Ins. Co., 967 F.2d 388 (10 Cir. 1992). ***TRANSACTIONS:*** Sale of hospital, 1996; $480 million. Cogeneration facility financing. ***PRACTICE AREAS:*** Health Care; Pension and Profit Sharing Law; Corporation Law; Banking Law. ***Email:*** david.mckinney@cmw.law.com

CHRISTOPHER K. WOOSLEY, born Portsmouth, Virginia, September 8, 1969; admitted to bar, 1994, Oklahoma and Missouri; 1994, U.S. District Court, Eastern District of Missouri; 1996, U.S. District Court, Northern, Eastern and Western Districts of Oklahoma; 2004, Tenth Circuit Court of Appeals. *Education:* Oklahoma State University (B.S., with honors, 1991); Pepperdine University (J.D., 1994). Order of the Barristers. Terry M. Giles Honor Scholar. Leadership Tulsa Class XXVII. *Member:* Tulsa County, Oklahoma and American Bar Associations; The Missouri Bar. ***PRACTICE AREAS:*** Civil Litigation; Corporate Law; Oil and Gas Law. ***Email:*** chris.woosley@cmw-law.com

---

ANDREA D. STAILEY, born Rolla, Missouri, December 2, 1978; admitted to bar, 2005, Oklahoma. *Education:* Northeastern Oklahoma State University (B.A., cum laude, 2002); University of Tulsa College of Law (J.D., with highest honor, 2005). Order of the Curule Chair. Recipient, Oklahoma Bar Association Outstanding Graduating Student Award, 2004. Articles Research Editor, Tulsa Law Review, 2004-05. Author: "The Health Act's Same Old Story, Different Congress Dilemma: Overhauling the Health Act and Unifying Congress as a Remedy for Tort Reform," 40 Tulsa L. Rev. 187 (2004). Panel Speaker, National Conference of Law Reviews, 2005. *Member:* Oklahoma Bar Association. ***PRACTICE AREAS:*** Civil Litigation; Business Law; Corporate Law. ***Email:*** andrea.stailey@cmw-law.com

OF COUNSEL

T. HILLIS ESKRIDGE, born Elmore City, Oklahoma, July 8, 1920; admitted to bar, 1948, Oklahoma. *Education:* University of Oklahoma (B.S., 1942; LL.B., 1948); University of Washington. Phi Delta Phi; Order of the Coif. *Member:* Oklahoma and American Bar Associations.

C. ERIC PFANSTIEL, born Charlotte, North Carolina, October 10, 1968; admitted to bar, 1995, Oklahoma and U.S. District Court, Northern District of Oklahoma. *Education:* Hillsdale College (B.A., 1992); University of Tulsa (J.D., 1995). Member, Tulsa Law Journal, 1995. *Member:* Tulsa County and Oklahoma Bar Associations. ***PRACTICE AREAS:*** Civil Practice; Litigation; Real Estate. ***Email:*** eric.pfanstiel@cmw-law.com

KENNETH E. CRUMP JR., born Chickasha, Oklahoma, June 18, 1958; admitted to bar, 1986, Oklahoma and U.S. District Court, Northern District of Oklahoma; 1987, U.S. District Court, Eastern District of Oklahoma and U.S. Court of Appeals, Tenth Circuit; 1994, U.S. District Court, Western District of Oklahoma. *Education:* University of Oklahoma (B.A., 1981); University of Tulsa (J.D., 1986). Member, Energy Law Journal. Author: "Crackdown on Counterfeiting; The Trademark Counterfeiting Act of 1984," 56 Oklahoma Bar Journal 2175, 1985. Adjunct Settlement Judge, U.S. District Court, Northern District of Oklahoma. Member, National Arbitration Forum Panel of Arbitrators and Mediators. *Member:* Tulsa County, Oklahoma (Member, Civil Procedure Committee, 1992) and American Bar Associations; American Inns of Court (Barrister; Robert D. Hudson Chapter, 1987-1988; 1991-1994; Hudson-Hall-Wheaton Chapter, 1995-1998). ***PRACTICE AREAS:*** Business; General Civil Litigation; Arbitration; Mediation. ***Email:*** ken.crump@cmw-law.com

MONICA A. PLAKE, born Baton Rouge, Louisiana, March 9, 1966; admitted to bar, 1997, Oklahoma. *Education:* University of Texas at Arlington (B.A., 1990); University of Tulsa (J.D., with honors, 1997). *Member:* Tulsa County, Oklahoma and American Bar Associations; American Intellectual Property Law Association. (Senior Attorney) (With The Williams Companies, Inc.). ***PRACTICE AREAS:*** Intellectual Property; Information Technology; Commercial Transactions. ***Email:*** monica.plake@cmw-law.com

---

CORLEY & GANEM

Established in 1976

1809 EAST 15TH STREET
TULSA, OKLAHOMA 74104
Telephone: 918-745-9200
FAX: 918-747-4921
Email: cna@corleyganem.com
URL: http://www.corleyganem.com

Personal Injury, Products Liability, Medical Malpractice, Insurance, State and Federal Court Litigation, Nursing Home Negligence.

FIRM PROFILE: A law firm dealing exclusively in personal injury litigation. For many years Corley & Ganem had two state records, (1) largest settlement for single injured person ($8.7 Million), and (2) largest personal injury verdict ($22 Million).

The partners are frequent lecturers in CLE seminars in Oklahoma and numerous other states as well.

(This Listing Continued)

MEMBERS OF FIRM

E. TERRILL CORLEY, born Eufaula, Oklahoma, October 20, 1942; admitted to bar, 1972, Oklahoma; 1973, U.S. District Court, Western, Northern and Eastern Districts of Oklahoma; U.S. Court of Appeals, Tenth Circuit; U.S. Supreme Court. *Education:* University of Central Oklahoma (B.A., 1964; M.S., 1966); University of Tulsa (J.D., 1972). Delta Theta Phi. Distinguished former Student, University of Central Oklahoma, 1991. Law Journal Staff, University of Tulsa. Assistant Public Defender, Tulsa County, 1972-1976. Listed in Best Lawyers in America last 9 years. Member, Million Dollar Advocates Forum. *Member:* Tulsa County (Member: Fee Arbitration Committee, 1986; Professional Responsibility Committee, 1990-1991) and Oklahoma (House of Delegates, 1994-1998; Vice Chair, Legislative Committee, 1991) Bar Associations; Oklahoma Trial Lawyers Association (President, 1992; Member, Hall of Fame); The Association of Trial Lawyers of America (Sustaining Member); American Board of Trial Advocates; Roscoe Pound Foundation; Trial Lawyers for Public Justice. Fellow, American College of Trial Lawyers. ***PRACTICE AREAS:*** Negligence Law; Products Liability Law. ***Email:*** et@corleyganem.com

THOMAS F. GANEM, born Ray, Arizona, November 24, 1947; admitted to bar, 1975, Oklahoma and U.S. District Court, Northern and Western Districts of Oklahoma; 1989, U.S. District Court, Eastern District of Oklahoma. *Education:* University of Tulsa (B.S., 1969; J.D., 1975). Phi Delta Phi. *Member:* Tulsa County and Oklahoma Bar Associations; Oklahoma Trial Lawyers Association (President, 1997; Vice-President, 1995; Member: Hall of Fame; Board of Directors, 1989-1998; Executive Committee, 1991-1998; Secretary/Treasurer, 1992-1993; Chairman of Membership, 1990); The Association of Trial Lawyers of America (Sustaining Member). [U.S. Army, 1969-1971]. ***PRACTICE AREAS:*** Personal Injury; Products Liability; Medical Malpractice. ***Email:*** tfganem@corleyganem.com

ASSOCIATE

DONALD B. BOLT, III, born Lafayette, Louisiana, July 17, 1967; admitted to bar, 1993, Oklahoma; 1994, U.S. District Court, Eastern and Northern Districts of Oklahoma; 1997, U.S. Court of Appeals, Tenth Circuit; 1998, U.S. District Court, Western District of Oklahoma. *Education:* University of Oklahoma (B.A., 1990); University of Tulsa (J.D., 1993). Phi Delta Phi. Member: Energy Law Journal, University of Tulsa, 1991-1993; Institute on International and Comparative Law, Mexico, 1992. *Member:* Oklahoma Trial Lawyers Association. ***PRACTICE AREAS:*** Insurance Bad Faith; Plaintiffs Personal Injury; Nursing Home Negligence; Medical Malpractice; Products Liability. ***Email:*** cg@corleyganem.com

LEGAL SUPPORT PERSONNEL

CAROLYN ARKISON, born Tulsa, Oklahoma. *Education:* Southern Nazarene University (B.S., M.S.; Business Management, 1985).

COVINGTON & POE

Established in 1948

SUITE 740
111 WEST FIFTH STREET
TULSA, OKLAHOMA 74103-4267
Telephone: 918-585-5537
Fax: 918-585-5530

General Civil Practice. Insurance, Negligence and Products Liability. Trials and Appeals.

A. M. COVINGTON (1905-1992)

JAMES E. POE, born Garfield, Arkansas, February 21, 1935; admitted to bar, 1959, Oklahoma, U.S. District Court, Northern District of Oklahoma, U.S. Court of Appeals, Tenth Circuit, U.S. Court of Federal Claims, U.S. Tax Court and U.S. Supreme Court. *Education:* University of Tulsa (B.A., 1957; LL.B., 1959). Delta Theta Phi. *Member:* Tulsa County (President, 1980), Oklahoma (Board of Governors, 1981-1983) and American Bar Associations. Master, American Inns of Court. Advocate, American Board of Trial Advocates. Fellow, American College of Trial Lawyers. ***PRACTICE AREAS:*** Negligence Law; Insurance Defense; Insurance Coverage; Civil Litigation; Contract Litigation; Condemnation; Personal Injury. ***Email:*** covandpoe@sbcglobal.net

ASSOCIATE

STEPHEN R. CLOUSER, born Sioux City, Iowa, December 15, 1955; admitted to bar, 1981, Oklahoma; U.S. District Court, Northern District of Oklahoma; U.S. Court of Appeals, Tenth Circuit. *Education:* Oklahoma State University; University of Oklahoma (B.B.A., 1978); University of Tulsa (J.D., 1981). Delta Theta Phi. *Member:* Tulsa County (Outstanding Junior Lawyer, 1989), Oklahoma (Chairman of Young Lawyers Division, 1990, Member Board of Governors, 1990) and American (ABA/YLD Assembly Clerk, 1990-1991; Speaker of Assembly, 1991-1992) Bar Associations. ***PRACTICE AREAS:*** Negligence Law; Insurance Defense; Civil Litigation; Surety Law; Copyrights; Probate. ***Email:*** covandpoe@sbcglobal.net

REPRESENTATIVE CLIENTS: National General Insurance Co.; St. Paul Companies; Oklahoma Surety Co.; Mid Continent Casualty Co.; Farmers Insurance Companies; Church Mutual Insurance Co.; M.J. Lee Construction Co.; McIntosh Services Co.

CROWE & DUNLEVY

A PROFESSIONAL CORPORATION

Established in 1902

500 KENNEDY BUILDING
321 SOUTH BOSTON AVENUE
TULSA, OKLAHOMA 74103-3313
Telephone: 918-592-9800
Fax: 918-592-9801
Email: bryantd@crowedunlevy.com
URL: http://www.crowedunlevy.com

Oklahoma City, Oklahoma Office: 20 North Broadway, Suite 1800, 73102-8273. Telephone: 405-235-7700. Fax: 405-239-6651.

Norman, Oklahoma Office: 2500 South McGee, Suite 140, 73072-6705. Telephone: 405-321-7317. Fax: 405-360-4002.

General Practice. Litigation of all types in both state and federal court. All types of alternative dispute resolution methodologies. Administrative Law, Antitrust, Appellate, Aviation, Bankruptcy and Creditors' Rights, Business Organizations, Commercial Real Estate, Commercial Transactions, Consumer Credit, Corporate and Securities Finance, Environmental, ERISA, Estates and Trusts, Family Law, Financial Institutions and Finance, Franchising and Distribution, Healthcare, Initiative Petition, Insurance Litigation and Regulation, Intellectual Property and Technology, International Business, Labor and Employment, Medicare/Medicaid Fraud and Abuse, Medical Malpractice Defense, Mergers and Acquisitions, Oil and Gas, Oklahoma Corporation Commission, Patent, Trademark, Copyright and Related Matters, Products Liability, Public Finance, School Law, Small Business and Venture Capital, Taxation, White Collar Crime.

FIRM PROFILE: Crowe & Dunlevy, founded in 1902, is the largest and one of the oldest law firms in Oklahoma. The Firm was founded in Oklahoma City and has enjoyed steady and consistent growth, expanding in October of 1989 to include an office in Tulsa and September of 1991 to include an office in Norman. Crowe & Dunlevy is the Oklahoma member of Lex Mundi, an international association of 146 independent law firms, which provides contacts and relationships with leading law firms throughout the world.

Crowe & Dunlevy is organized as a professional corporation and is engaged in most areas of the practice of law. The Firm serves clients ranging from individuals to small businesses to large national and multi-national corporations. The diversity of legal representations within the Firm is underscored by the fact that the Firm's largest client represents less than five percent of its annual fee income.

The Firm is committed to a philosophy of providing on a timely basis high quality legal services to its clients at a reasonable cost. The Firm strives to maintain state of the art library, administrative and other services conducive to the realization of this objective. The Firm has consistently avoided the practice of staffing its cases in a manner in which lawyers provide unnecessary services at unnecessary expense to its clients.

Due to the wide range of experience, the Firm is able to respond to clients with its ability to assemble a legal team with the availability of knowledge and expertise necessary to maximize effective representation. This philosophy encourages timely solutions to client needs in a practical problem-solving environment and at a reasonable cost.

Crowe & Dunlevy is proud to recognize the leadership achievements of its members, both past and present, including: Presidents of the American, Oklahoma, Oklahoma County, Tulsa County and Cleveland County Bar Associations; President of the National Health Lawyers Association; President of the American College of Trial Lawyers; President of the American College of Mortgage Attorneys; Trustee of the United States Supreme Court Historical Society; Chief Judge, United States Court of Appeals, for the 10th Circuit; United States District Judge; Oklahoma Court of Appeals Judge; United States Tax Court Judge; United States Magistrate Judge; United States Attorneys; District Attorneys; United States Ambassador; Deputy Attorney General of the United States; Former Lead and Associate Counsels of the Office of Independent Counsel; Chair of the Murrah Federal Building Memorial Task Force, the Oklahoma City National Memorial Foundation and the Board of Trustees of the Oklahoma City National Memorial Trust; White House Fellow; Deans of the University of Oklahoma College of Law; Mayors; State Representative; Oklahoma Corporation Commissioner; Members of the Boards of Regents for major state universities, and numerous listings in Who's Who in America, Who's Who in American Law, Who's Who in the World and The Best Lawyers in America.

JAMES L. KINCAID, born Carthage, Missouri, 1936; admitted to bar, 1961, Oklahoma. *Education:* Harvard University (A.B., 1958; LL.B., 1961). Listed in the Best Lawyers in America (Business Litigation). ***PRACTICE AREAS:*** Federal Civil Litigation; Complex Litigation; Environmental Litigation; Oil and Gas Litigation; Securities Litigation. ***Email:*** kincaidj@crowedunlevy.com

CRAIG W. HOSTER, born Fort Worth, Texas, 1946; admitted to bar, 1973, Oklahoma. *Education:* University of Oklahoma (B.B.A., 1971; J.D., 1973). Order of the Coif; Phi Delta Phi. Editor, Oklahoma Law Review, 1971-1973. Chair, Public Employees Relations Board, State of Oklahoma, 2000—. *Member:* American Inns of Court (Master, Hudson-Hall-Wheaton Chapter). ***PRACTICE AREAS:*** Civil Litigation; Trial Practice; Employment Litigation; Franchise Litigation. ***Email:*** hosterc@crowedunlevy.com

GARY R. McSPADDEN, born Duncan, Oklahoma, 1947; admitted to bar, 1972, Oklahoma. *Education:* University of Oklahoma (B.A., 1969; J.D., 1972). Phi Beta Kappa; Order of the Coif; Phi Delta Phi. Editor, Oklahoma Law Review, 1970-1972. Chair, Financial Institutions and Commercial Law Section, Oklahoma Bar Association, 1993. Listed in The Best Lawyers in America (Banking Law). [Capt., JAGC, U.S. Army, 1972-1975]. ***PRACTICE AREAS:*** Banking Law; Oil and Gas Finance; Commercial Real Estate; Commercial Law; Mortgage Finance. ***Email:*** mcspaddg@crowedunlevy.com

GARY C. CLARK, born Flippin, Arkansas, 1947; admitted to bar, 1975, Oklahoma. *Education:* Oklahoma State University (B.S., 1969; M.S., 1972); University of Texas (J.D., with honors, 1975). Phi Kappa Phi; Phi Delta Phi; Order of the Coif. Notes and Comments Editor, Texas International Law Journal, 1974-1975. Outstanding Senior Lawyer, Tulsa County Bar Association (1996). Listed in The Best Lawyers in America (Bankruptcy Law and Trusts and Estates). Tulsa Title and Probate Lawyers Association (President, 1990); Tulsa County Bar Foundation (President, 1994-1995); Bankruptcy Section, Tulsa Estate Planning Forum., Tulsa County Bar Association (President, 1993-1994; Board of Directors, 1989-1995, 1997—). Oklahoma Bar Association (President-Elect, 2001; Board of Governors, 1997-1999); Past Member, Board of Directors, Oklahoma Bar Association Young Lawyers Division. Oklahoma State University AÆ Board of Regents, 1993-2001 (Chair, 1997-1998). Chair, Estate Planning and Probate Section, Oklahoma Bar Association, 1989; Delegate: Oklahoma Bar Association House of Delegates, 1980—. Fellow: Tulsa County Bar Foundation; Oklahoma Bar Foundation; American Bar Foundation. ***PRACTICE AREAS:*** Estate Planning; Probate; Commercial Law; Bankruptcy; Commercial Real Estate; Property; Oil and Gas Law. ***Email:*** clarkg@crowedunlevy.com

GARY L. BETOW, born Lake Charles, Louisiana, 1954; admitted to bar, 1979, Oklahoma. *Education:* University of Oklahoma (B.A., 1975); Harvard University (J.D., cum laude, 1979). Phi Beta Kappa. President, Legal Aid of Western Oklahoma, 1989; President, Legal Services of Eastern Oklahoma, Inc., 1994; Director, Tulsa Family & Children's Services, Inc., Tulsa Arts and Humanities Council, Community Action Project of Tulsa County, Inc.; Youth Services of Tulsa, Inc. Chair: Financial Institutions Section, Oklahoma Bar Association, 1992. Listed in Best Lawyers in America (Banking Law). *Member:* Oklahoma Hospital Lawyers Association; American Health Lawyers Association. ***PRACTICE AREAS:*** Banking Law; Consumer Law; Commercial Law; Health Care Law. ***Email:*** betowg@crowedunlevy.com

MALCOLM E. ROSSER IV, born Duncan, Oklahoma, 1955; admitted to bar, 1981, Oklahoma. *Education:* Oklahoma State University (B.S., Arch. Engr., 1977); University of Oklahoma (J.D., 1981). Tau Beta Pi; Delta Theta Phi. Recipient, Maurice Merrill Golden Quill Award, Oklahoma Bar Association, 2001. Member: Tulsa Title and Probate Lawyers Association; Real Property Law Section, Oklahoma Bar Association (Board of Directors, 1991-1995; Chair, 1995). Tulsa Chapter, National Association of Office and Industrial Properties (Board of Directors, 1999—). Author: "Adverse Possession in Oklahoma: An Idea Whose Time Has Come and Gone?" 72 Okla. Bar Journal 713 (2001) (with Elizabeth Moseley Guse). Winner, Leadership Tulsa, Paragon Award, 2001. ***PRACTICE AREAS:*** Commercial Real Estate Finance; Commercial Real Estate Acquisitions; Commercial Real Estate Workouts; Oil and Gas Finance. ***Email:*** rosserm@crowedunlevy.com

MICHAEL J. GIBBENS, born Honolulu, Hawaii, 1956; admitted to bar, 1981, Oklahoma, U.S. Court of Appeals, 5th and 10th Circuits and U.S. District Court, Northern, Eastern and Western Districts of Oklahoma. *Education:* Rice University (B.A., cum laude, 1978); University of Texas (J.D., with honors, 1981). Order of The Coif. Law Clerk to The Honorable William J. Holloway, Circuit Judge for The Tenth Judicial Circuit, 1981-1982. Member, Litigation Section, Forum on Franchising, American Bar Association. ***PRACTICE AREAS:*** Commercial Litigation; Franchise Litigation; Securities Litigation; Environmental Litigation; Construction Law; Antitrust. ***Email:*** gibbensm@crowedunlevy.com

TERRY M. THOMAS, born Muskogee, Oklahoma, 1951; admitted to bar, 1981, Oklahoma; U.S. Court of Appeals, Tenth Circuit; U.S. District Court, Northern and Eastern Districts of Oklahoma. *Education:* Southeastern Oklahoma State University (B.S., with honors, 1972; M.B.S., 1976); University of Texas (J.D., with honors, 1980). Order of the Coif. Listed in Best Lawyers in America, 2002-2003. ***PRACTICE AREAS:*** Commercial Litigation; Bankruptcy; Environmental Litigation. ***Email:*** thomast@crowedunlevy.com

MADALENE A. B. WITTERHOLT, born Providence, Rhode Island, 1959; admitted to bar, 1983, Oklahoma. *Education:* University of Tulsa (B.A., 1980; J.D., 1983). Delta Theta Phi (President, 1982-1983). Law Clerk to the Honorable James O. Ellison, Judge, U.S. District Judge, Northern District of Oklahoma, 1989-1990. Member: Labor and Employment Law Section, Oklahoma Bar Association (Chairperson, 1996); EEOC Committee, Labor and Employment Law Section, American Bar Association. ***PRACTICE AREAS:*** Labor and Employment; Workers' Compensation Defense; Civil Litigation. ***Email:*** witterhm@crowedunlevy.com

RANDALL J. SNAPP, born Newton, Kansas, 1959; admitted to bar, 1985, Oklahoma; 1988, U.S. District Court, Northern District of Oklahoma; 1990, U.S. Court of Appeals, 10th Circuit; 1991, U.S. District Court, Eastern District of Oklahoma; 1993, U.S. District Court, Western District of Oklahoma and U.S. Supreme Court. *Education:* University of Kansas (B.A., 1981; M.B.A. and J.D., 1985). Pi Sigma Alpha. Member: Tulsa County Bar Association (Board of Directors, 1992-1993), (Chair, Membership Services Committee, 1992-1993); Past President of Big Brothers and Sisters of Green County (1995-1996); Labor and Employment Section (Employee Rights and Responsibilities Committee), American Bar Association; Labor and Employment Section (Treasurer, 1997-1998, Chair. 1998-1999), Oklahoma Bar Association. Adjunct Instructor, Human Resources Law, Tulsa Community College (1998-2001). ***PRACTICE AREAS:*** Civil Litigation; Labor and Employment; Workers' Compensation Defense. ***Email:*** snappr@crowedunlevy.com

VICTOR E. MORGAN, born Wichita Falls, Texas, 1962; admitted to bar, 1987, Oklahoma. *Education:* University of Oklahoma (B.B.A., 1984; J.D., 1987). Phi Delta Phi; Order of the Coif. Editor, Oklahoma Law Review, 1985-1987. ***PRACTICE AREAS:*** Civil Litigation; Creditors Rights; Banking Litigation; Commercial Law; Bankruptcy. ***Email:*** morganv@crowedunlevy.com

JEFFREY T. HILLS, born Tulsa, Oklahoma, 1964; admitted to bar, 1991, Oklahoma. *Education:* Oklahoma State University (B.S., 1986); University of Tulsa (J.D., with honors, 1991). ***PRACTICE AREAS:*** Litigation; Corporate Law; Oil and Gas Law; Environmental Law; Securities Litigation. ***Email:*** hillsj@crowedunlevy.com

---

GERALD L. JACKSON, born Waynesville, Missouri, 1964; admitted to bar, 1990, Missouri; 1994, Maryland; 1996, Oklahoma. *Education:* Southwest Missouri State University (B.S., 1987); University of Tulsa (J.D., with honors, 1990). Formerly Assistant Counsel, Committee on Agriculture, U.S. House of Representatives. ***PRACTICE AREAS:*** Litigation. ***Email:*** jacksong@crowedunlevy.com

(This Listing Continued)

ALEXANDER F. KING, born Tulsa, Oklahoma, 1971; admitted to bar, 1998, Oklahoma. *Education:* University of Kansas (B.A. 1995); Georgetown University Law Center, (J.D., 1998). Member, Georgetown Immigration Law Journal. ***PRACTICE AREAS:*** Litigation. ***Email:*** kinga@crowedunlevy.com

KAYCI BAIR HUGHES, born Pittsburg, Kansas, 1974; admitted to bar, 1999, Oklahoma. *Education:* University of Oklahoma (B.A., 1996; J.D., 1999). Order of Barristers. Member, Oklahoma Law Review, Board of Advocates President, 1997-1998. Awards and Honors: Outstanding Note Editor Award; Second Place at National Native American Law Student Association Moot Court Competition. Recipient: Rayburn L. Foster Scholarship. ***PRACTICE AREAS:*** Litigation. ***Email:*** hughesk@crowedunlevy.com

SUSAN E. HUNTSMAN, born Conway, Arkansas, 1973; admitted to bar, 1999, Oklahoma; 2004, Illinois. *Education:* University of Arkansas (B.A., summa cum laude, 1996); Harvard University (J.D., cum laude, 1999). Deputy Editor-in-Chief, Harvard Journal of Law and Public Policy. Law Clerk to the Honorable Terry C. Kern, U.S. District Court, Northern District of Oklahoma, 1999-2000. ***PRACTICE AREAS:*** Litigation. ***Email:*** huntsmas@crowedunlevy.com

CHRISTOPHER J. KIRT, born Colorado Springs, Colorado, 1970; admitted to bar, 2000, Oklahoma. *Education:* Trinity University (B.B.A., 1993); University of Oklahoma (J.D., with highest honors, 2000). Order of the Coif; Phi Kappa Phi; Phi Delta Phi. Recipient: American Jurisprudence Awards in Corporations, Introduction to Commercial Law, Wills and Trusts, Employment Law, Land Use Controls; Oklahoma Business Associations Section's Award; Ray Teague Memorial Scholarship; William T. and James T. Comfort Scholarship. ***PRACTICE AREAS:*** Commercial Transactions; Financial Institutions; Finance; Corporate Law; Securities. ***Email:*** kirtc@crowedunlevy.com

CHRISTOPHER B. WOODS, born Oklahoma City, Oklahoma, 1974; admitted to bar, 2000, Oklahoma. *Education:* University of Oklahoma (B.B.A., Economics, 1996; J.D., with highest honors, 2000). Order of the Coif. Editor-in Chief, Oklahoma Law Review. Recipient: Nathan Scarritt Prize; Welcome D. Pierson Award; Phillips Allen Porta Legal Ethics Memorial Prize; West Publishing Company Award; McKinney, Stringer & Webster Scholarship; Robert B. Looper Scholarship; George B. Fraser Scholarship; Comfort Scholarship; American Jurisprudence Awards in Advanced Civil Procedure, Antitrust, Civil Procedure I, Corporations, Evidence, Land Use, Professional Responsibility, Property, Real Estate Transaction, Title Examination, Torts I and Legal Writing. Author: "Determining Repugnancy in an Electronic Age: Excluded Transactions Under Electronic Writing and Signature Legislation," 52 Okla. L. Rev. 411 (1999). ***PRACTICE AREAS:*** Banking Law; Secured Lending; Electronic Banking; Business Law; Commercial Real Estate. ***Email:*** woodsc@crowedunlevy.com

JENNIFER A. CHAMPLIN, born Oklahoma City, Oklahoma, 1977; admitted to bar, 2002, Massachusetts and U.S. District Court, District of Massachusetts; 2005, Oklahoma, U.S. District Court, Northern District of Oklahoma and U.S. Court of Appeals, Tenth Circuit. *Education:* Oklahoma State University (B.A., with honors, 1999); Cornell Law School (J.D., 2002). National Merit Scholar. Symposium Editor, Journal of Law and Public Policy. Author: "New Opportunities for Defense Lawyers: The Restatement's Treatment of Pharmaceuticals," Defense Research Institute, For the Defense, Vol 45 No. 7, July 2003. *Member:* Tulsa County, Oklahoma and American Bar Associations. ***PRACTICE AREAS:*** Litigation. ***Email:*** champlij@crowedunlevy.com

NORA R. O'NEILL, admitted to bar, 2003, Oklahoma. *Education:* University of Pittsburgh (B.A., 2000); University of Pennsylvania School of Law (J.D., 2003).

PAIGE N. SHELTON-VANDERYT, born Oak Ridge, Tennessee, 1976; admitted to bar, 2004, Oklahoma. *Education:* Vanderbilt University (B.A., Math and Economics, 1997); University of Tulsa (J.D., with highest honor, 2004). Phi Delta Phi (Treasurer); Order of the Curule Chair; Order of the Barristers. Recipient: Oklahoma Bar Association Mineral Law Section Writing Award; Tulsa Title & Probate Lawyer's Association Richard D. Cleverdon Scholarship; Paul F. McTighe, Jr. Award; International Academy of Trial Lawyers Student Advocacy Award; CALI Excellence for the Future Awards: Administrative Law; Evidence; Federal Income Taxation. Third Place: ATLA Regional Competition; ABA Negotiation Regional Competition. Managing Editor, Tulsa Law Review. ***PRACTICE AREAS:*** Litigation.

JERAN E. STEUART, born Moore, Oklahoma, 1978; admitted to bar, 2005, Oklahoma. *Education:* University of Oklahoma (B.A., 2002); University of Oklahoma College of Law (J.D., 2005). *Member:* Oklahoma County, Oklahoma and American Bar Associations. ***PRACTICE AREAS:*** Litigation. ***Email:*** steuartj@crowedunlevy.com

OF COUNSEL

THE HON. (RET.) THOMAS R. BRETT, born 1931; admitted to bar, 1957, Oklahoma. *Education:* University of Oklahoma (B.B.A., 1953; L.L.B., 1957; J.D., 1971). U.S. District Judge, 1979-2003. [Col., USAR, JAG, Retired]. ***PRACTICE AREAS:*** ADR; Mediation; Arbitration. ***Email:*** brett@crowedunlevy.com

All Lawyers listed are Members of the Tulsa County, Oklahoma and American Bar Associations.

REPRESENTATIVE CLIENTS: Atlantic Richfield Co.; Aetna Life Insurance Co.; AmCare; American National Insurance Co.; American Airlines, Inc.; Anadarko Petroleum Corp.; Armstrong World Industries; ASC Machine Tools, Inc.; BancFirst; Bank of America, N.A.; Bank of Oklahoma, N.A.; Bank One, Oklahoma, N.A.; Bechtel Group, Inc.; Blue Cross/Blue Shield of Oklahoma; The Boeing Company; Boston Mutual Life Insurance Company; BP/Amoco Corporation; Buford Properties, Inc.; Capital Cities/ABC, Inc.; Chevron Texaco U.S.A., Inc.; CHUBB Executive Risk Insurance; Commonwealth Life Insurance Company; Concentra; Connecticut Mutual Life Ins. Co.; Conoco, Inc.; Dollar Systems, Inc.; Dow Corning Corporation; Equitable Life Assurance Co. (N.Y.); Exxon Mobil Corporation; Flint Industries, Inc.; Ford Motor Co.; Fortis Insurance Co.; GMX Resources; Goodyear Tire & Rubber Company; Harold's Stores, Inc.; Helmerich & Payne, Inc.; Hillcrest Healthcare System; Homeland Stores, Inc.; Hunzicker Brothers, Inc.; Ins. Co. of North America, INAPRO/CIGNA; INTEGRIS Health, Inc.; J.C. Penney Life Ins. Co.; John Alden Life Ins. Co.; John Hancock Life Insurance Co.; Lawyers Title Insurance Corp.; Liberty Nat. Life. Ins. Co.; Life Insurance Company of Georgia; Lincoln National Life Insurance Co.; Lloyd's of London; Marathon Oil Company; Massachusetts Mutual Life Insurance Co.; Mercy Hospital; Metropolitan Life Insurance Co.; MONY Life Insurance Co.; New England Mutual Life; New York Life Insurance Co.; Norman Regional Hospital; Oklahoma Association of Health Plans; Oklahoma Foundation for Medical Quality; Phoenix Life Insurance Co.; Pre-Paid Legal Services; Protective Life Ins. Company; Sheffield Steel Corporation; Southwestern Bell Telephone Co.; St. Anthony Hospital; Thrifty Rent-A-Car System, Inc.; Trammell Crow Company; Transamerica Occidental Life; USAirways, Inc.; VHA of Oklahoma/Arkansas, Inc.; The Williams Companies; Williams Communications Group, Inc.

(For complete Client listing and Biographical Data on other Personnel, see Professional Biographies at Oklahoma City and at Norman for Crowe & Dunlevy)

CRUTCHMER, BROWERS & BARNES, P.L.L.C.

1112 S. BOSTON AVENUE
TULSA, OKLAHOMA 74119
Telephone: 918-382-8686
Fax: 918-382-8685
URL: http://www.cbb-law.com

Securities Law, Banking, Oil and Gas Law, Real Estate, Commercial Transactions.

FIRM PROFILE: The law firm of Crutchmer, Browers & Barnes was established in Tulsa, Oklahoma in 2001. Although a relatively new firm, all of the attorneys have previously practiced in large firms or large corporations. Our attorneys have extensive experience in their respective practice areas and all have attained Martindale-Hubbell's highest rating for legal ability and ethical standards. Our attorneys use their knowledge and experience to respond to client needs, providing high quality legal services at reasonable costs. Our clients are varied, ranging from individuals to small businesses to national and regional corporations. Our goal is to provide effective, creative and efficient solutions to the legal matters of our clients.

CLYDE V. CRUTCHMER, born Okmulgee, Oklahoma, January 10, 1953; admitted to bar, 1982, Oklahoma. *Education:* University of Colorado at Boulder (B.S., 1975); University of Tulsa (J.D., 1982). *Member:* Oklahoma Bar Association. ***PRACTICE AREAS:*** Securities Law; Banking Law; Real Estate Law; Commercial Transactions; Corporate Law; Estate Planning. ***Email:*** clyde@cbb-law.com

RONALD MERRILL BARNES, born Okmulgee, Oklahoma, November 16, 1953; admitted to bar, 1980, Oklahoma. *Education:* University of Oklahoma (B.B.A., 1977); Oklahoma City University (J.D., 1980). Phi Alpha Delta (Vice President, 1979-1980). Chief Trial Examiner, Oklahoma Corporation Commission, 1981. *Member:* Oklahoma Bar Association (Chair, Mineral Bar Section, 2004). ***PRACTICE AREAS:*** Oil and Gas Law; Corporate Law. ***Email:*** ron@cbb-law.com

DEBORAH B. BROWERS, born Tulsa, Oklahoma, July 31, 1954; admitted to bar, 1984, Oklahoma; 1988, U.S. District Court, Western District of Oklahoma; 1989, U.S. District Court, Northern District of Oklahoma and U.S. Court of Appeals, Tenth Circuit. *Education:* University of Oklahoma (B.A., Journalism, 1976); Oklahoma City University (J.D., with distinction, 1983). Phi Delta Phi. Recipient, American Jurisprudence Awards in Criminal Law, Torts, Civil Procedure, Property, Bankruptcy and Trusts; Order of Barristers Advocacy Award, 1983; National Moot Court Team, 1983; Woman's Law Caucus Award, 1983. Articles Editor for Law Review, 1982-1983. Author: "Corporate Attorney-Client Privilege-The Changing Tide," 7 Okla. City U. L. Rev. 419 (1982); "Interpretation of Corporation Commission Orders: The Dichotomous Court/Agency Jurisdiction," 8 Okla. City U. L. Rev. 311 (1983). Co-Author, with Mike Palmer, Natural Gas Marketing and Transportation Committee 1993 Annual Report: "Part III, Gathering," "Nominations and Allocation Under Section 8 of the PRSA," Update on Senate Bill 168: New Requirements for Royalty Payment and Revenue Sharing, sponsored by the University of Oklahoma College of Law Continuing Education Department, 1993; "Guide to Letters of Intent," presented at Central and South West Corporation legal conference, 1995; "New Applications of the Doctrine of the Implied Covenant to Market in Oil and Gas Leases," presented at the Eugene Kuntz Conference on Natural Resources Law and Policy, 1996, The Year in Review, Natural Resources, Energy and Environmental Law; "Restructuring of the Natural Gas Industry in Oklahoma," presented at the 1999 Oil and Gas Law Institute, The Conference on Consumer Finance Law, 1999; "Diversity in the Natural Gas Industry," presented at the Diversity Symposium sponsored by the Oklahoma Bar Association and Oklahoma City University School of Law, 2001. Staff Attorney, Oklahoma Supreme Court, 1985-1989. Private practice, 1984, 1989-1991. Vice President, Human Resources and Administration, 1996-1997. Attorney, Transok, Inc., 1991-1997 and Vice President, Secretary and Associate General Counsel, ONEOK, Inc., 1997-2001. *Member:* Tulsa County Bar Association (Chair, Court Operation Committee, 1996-1997), Oklahoma Bar Association (Chairperson, Mineral Law Section, 2000-2001) and American Bar Association; Oklahoma Defense Lawyers Association, 2002—; American Health Lawyers 2002—. Barrister, The Council Oak American Inn of Court (1996-1999); Oklahoma City University of Oklahoma School of Law (Executive Board, 2001—); Oklahoma Board of Bar Examiners, 2000—; Fellow, American Bar Foundation (Oklahoma). ***REPORTED CASES:*** Marathon Oil Company v. Corporation Commission of State of Oklahoma, 910 P.2d 966 (Okla. 1996); Fischer v. Atlantic Richfield Co., 774 F. Supp. 616 (W.D. Okla. 1989). ***PRACTICE AREAS:*** Employment Law; Health Care; Corporate Law. ***Email:*** debbie@cbb-law.com

REPRESENTATIVE CLIENTS: Bank of America; Bank of Oklahoma; Braum's Ice Cream & Dairy Stores; First Fidelity Bank; M-D Building Products, Inc.; MidFirst Bank; Samson Resources Company; Unit Petroleum Corporation; Vintage Petroleum Company.

SAM P. DANIEL III, P.L.L.C.

Established in 1995

1756 SOUTH UTICA AVENUE
TULSA, OKLAHOMA 74104-5336
Telephone: 918-749-9007
Telecopier: 918-749-9023
Email: sam.daniel@samdaniellaw.com
URL: http://www.samdaniellaw.com

General Civil Litigation, Family, Construction, Oil and Gas, Real Estate, Business, Condemnation, Employment, Mechanic's Liens, Collections.

SAMUEL P. DANIEL III, born Washington, D.C., October 29, 1953; admitted to bar, 1980, Oklahoma. *Education:* Georgetown University (B.A., 1975); University of Oklahoma (J.D., 1979). Adjunct Settlement Judge, U.S. District Court, Northern District of

(This Listing Continued)

SAM P. DANIEL III, P.L.L.C., Tulsa—Continued

Oklahoma. Certified Mediator. Civil Service Commissioner, City of Tulsa, 2003—. *Member:* Tulsa County (Director-at-Large, 1996-1997; Chairman, Committee for Professional Responsibility, 1998-1999), Oklahoma and Federal Bar Associations. ***SPECIAL AGENCIES:*** Oklahoma Department of Transportation Condemnation Trial Attorney. ***PRACTICE AREAS:*** Federal Practice; Civil Litigation; Family Law; Divorce; Child Custody. ***Email:*** sam.daniel@samdaniellaw.com

REPRESENTATIVE CLIENTS: Manhattan Construction Co.; Federal Bank Centre; Keith F. Walker Oil & Gas Company, LLC.; Oklahoma Department of Transportation.

DAY, EDWARDS, PROPESTER & CHRISTENSEN, P.C.

Established in 1982
320 SOUTH BOSTON AVENUE
805
TULSA, OKLAHOMA 74103
Telephone: 918-592-2121
Facsimile: 918-388-6601
URL: http://www.dayedwards.com

Oklahoma City, Oklahoma Office: 210 Park Avenue, 73102-5605. Telephone: 405-239-2121. Telecopier: 405-236-1012.

General Civil Trial. Trial of Civil Cases in all State and Federal Courts. Administrative Law, Agribusiness, Anti-Trust Law, Arbitration and Mediation of disputes, Banking Regulation and Transactions, Bankruptcy and Insolvency Law, Commercial Law, Corporate Law, Employment Law, Energy Law, Environmental Law, Franchising Regulation and Transactions, Health Care Law, Insurance Law, International Law, Labor Relations, Litigation, Mergers and Acquisitions, Natural Resources, Products Liability, Professional Malpractice, Real Estate Law, Securities Regulation and Transactions and Workers Compensation.

(For Complete Personnel and Biographical Data, see Professional Biographies at Oklahoma City, Oklahoma)

DOERNER, SAUNDERS, DANIEL & ANDERSON, L.L.P.

Established in 1896
SUITE 500
320 SOUTH BOSTON AVENUE
TULSA, OKLAHOMA 74103-3725
Telephone: 918-582-1211
Fax: 918-591-5360
URL: http://www.dsda.com

Oklahoma City, Oklahoma Office: One Leadership Square, Suite 501. Telephone: 405-319-3500. Fax: 405-319-3509. URL: http://www.dsda.com.

Federal Civil Practice, State Civil Practice, Administrative Law, Appellate Practice, Antitrust, Bankruptcy, Creditors' Rights and Loan Workouts, Construction Law, Consumer Credit, Corporate, Commercial and Securities, Employment and Labor, Environmental, ERISA and Employee Benefits, Estates, Trusts and Probate, Family Law, General Litigation, Health Care, Indian Law, Intellectual Property, Patents, Trademarks, Copyrights, International Business, Mediation and Arbitration, Media and First Amendment Law, Medicare/Medicaid Fraud and Abuse, Mergers and Acquisitions Law, Oil and Gas, Oklahoma Corporation Commission, Products Liability, Public Trust and Tax Exempt Financing, Real Estate, Rural Water District Competition, Securities Litigation, Small Business and Venture Capital, Taxation, Telecommunications, Toxic Tort Litigation and Workers' Compensation.

FIRM PROFILE: Doerner Saunders Daniel & Anderson, L.L.P. is one of Oklahoma's oldest law firms. Today, the Firm's lawyers engage in virtually every major area of civil practice in Tulsa, Oklahoma City and throughout the nation. The Firm has built a strong reputation for more than 100 years of commitment to its clients, its profession and its community. Service to its clients is and always has been the principal philosophy of Doerner Saunders, from the selective recruitment and hiring of attorneys to the day to day response to clients' opportunities and needs.

PARTNERS

ERWIN J. DOERNER (1897-1980)

DICKSON M. SAUNDERS (1920-2001)

SAM P. DANIEL, born Tulsa, Oklahoma, December 20, 1932; admitted to bar, 1959, Oklahoma. *Education:* Georgetown University (B.S., 1954); University of Oklahoma (LL.B., 1959). Master Emeritus, American Inns of Court, Hudson-Hall-Wheaton Chapter, Tulsa, Oklahoma. President, Tulsa County Bar Association, 1986-1987. Listed, Best Lawyers in America, Business Litigation and Family Law, 1983-2000. Adjunct Professor of Law, University of Tulsa, 1990, 1992. Fellow, American College of Trial Lawyers, 1981. Certified Fellow, American Academy of Matrimonial Lawyers, 1984-2000. [Capt., USAF, 1955-1957]. ***PRACTICE AREAS:*** Family Law; General Civil and Business Litigation. ***Email:*** sdaniel@dsda.com

WILLIAM C. ANDERSON, born Canton, Ohio, November 14, 1941; admitted to bar, 1966, Oklahoma. *Education:* Oberlin College (B.A., 1963); University of Michigan (J.D., 1966). Order of the Coif. Law Clerk to Hon. A.P. Murrah, Chief Judge, U.S. Court of Appeals, Tenth Circuit, 1966-1967. Listed in "Best Lawyers in America." Master Emeritus, American Inns of Court, Council Oaks Chapter, Tulsa, Oklahoma. Fellow, American College of Trial Lawyers. ***PRACTICE AREAS:*** Environmental Law; Civil Litigation; Appellate Practice. ***Email:*** wanderson@dsda.com

(This Listing Continued)

G. MICHAEL LEWIS, born Pampa, Texas, July 26, 1942; admitted to bar, 1967, Oklahoma. *Education:* University of Oklahoma (B.A., 1964; J.D., 1967). Associate Editor, Oklahoma Law Review, 1965-1967. [Capt., U.S. Army, JAGC, 1967-1971]. ***PRACTICE AREAS:*** Civil Litigation; Legal Ethics; Medical Ethics; Health & Hospital Law; Utility Law Litigation; Environmental Law Litigation; Motor Carrier Law; Broker-Dealer Regulation. ***Email:*** mlewis@dsda.com

LAWRENCE T. CHAMBERS, JR., born Altus, Oklahoma, February 26, 1945; admitted to bar, 1972, Oklahoma. *Education:* University of Oklahoma (B.B.A., 1967; J.D., 1972). Order of the Coif. Article and Book Review Editor, 1971 and Associate Editor, 1971-1972 Oklahoma Law Review. Listed in The Best Lawyers in America. [1st Lt., U.S. Army, 1967-1969]. ***PRACTICE AREAS:*** Corporate Law; Securities Law; Mergers and Acquisitions; Banking Law. ***Email:*** lchambers@dsda.com

DALLAS E. FERGUSON, born Blackwell, Oklahoma, December 20, 1945; admitted to bar, 1971, Oklahoma, U.S. District Court, Western District of Oklahoma and U.S. Court of Appeals, Tenth Circuit; 1973, U.S. District Court, Northern District of Oklahoma; 1978, U.S. District Court, Eastern District of Oklahoma. *Education:* Cornell College (B.A., 1968); Columbia University (J.D., 1971). Law Clerk to Hon. A.P. Murrah, Senior Circuit Judge, U.S. Court of Appeals, Tenth Circuit, 1971-1972. ***PRACTICE AREAS:*** General Civil Litigation; Telecommunications Law; Public Utility Law; Federal Practice. ***Email:*** dferguson@dsda.com

SAM G. BRATTON II, born New Haven, Connecticut, December 23, 1946; admitted to bar, 1974, Oklahoma. *Education:* University of New Mexico (B.B.A., 1969; J.D., 1974). National Moot Court Team, 1973. Adjunct Settlement Judge, Bankruptcy Court, Northern District of Oklahoma. Special Judge, Oklahoma Court of Appeals, Temporary Division, 1980-1982. Listed: Best Lawyers in America, 1987—; Who's Who in American Law. Director, 1994— and Chair, 1998, Bankruptcy and Reorganization Section, Oklahoma Bar Association, 1994—. Chair, Advisory Committee on Local Rules of Bankruptcy Procedure, Northern District of Oklahoma, 1995—. ***PRACTICE AREAS:*** Bankruptcy Law; Reorganization; Financial Restructuring; Workouts; Creditors Rights. ***Email:*** sbratton@dsda.com

GARY M. McDONALD, born Berlin, Germany, January 7, 1950; admitted to bar, 1975, Oklahoma. *Education:* University of Arkansas (B.A., 1972; J.D., 1975). Member, Arkansas Law Review, 1973-1975. Listed in Best Lawyers in America, 1987—. Chairman, Tulsa County Bar Professional Responsibility Grievance Committee, 1993-1994. *Member:* Tulsa County Bar Association (Board of Directors, 1994-1996; Secretary, 1997-1998); American Bankruptcy Institute. ***PRACTICE AREAS:*** Bankruptcy Law; General Civil Litigation. ***Email:*** gmcdonald@dsda.com

H. WAYNE COOPER, born Tulsa, Oklahoma, July 31, 1945; admitted to bar, 1975, Oklahoma. *Education:* University of Oklahoma (B.S.M.E., 1968); University of Nevada (M.B.A., 1971); University of Tulsa (J.D., with highest honors, 1975). Managing Editor, Tulsa Law Journal, 1974-1975. Law Clerk to Hon. William J. Holloway, Jr., Circuit Judge, U.S. Court of Appeals, 10th Circuit, 1975-1976. Co-author, Vols. 3A and 3B, Vernon's Oklahoma Forms 2d, Business Organizations (West Group). Listed in The Best Lawyers in America for Corporate, Mergers and Acquisitions and Securities Law. [Capt., USAF, 1968-1972]. ***PRACTICE AREAS:*** Corporate; Business Acquisitions; Securities; Franchising Law. ***Email:*** hwcooper@dsda.com

KEVIN C. COUTANT, born Manhattan, Kansas, July 17, 1952; admitted to bar, 1977, Oklahoma. *Education:* Oklahoma State University (B.S., 1974); University of Texas (J.D., 1977). ***PRACTICE AREAS:*** Real Estate; Zoning; Oil and Gas; Commercial Law. ***Email:*** kcoutant@dsda.com

RICHARD P. HIX, born Oklahoma City, Oklahoma, January 27, 1948; admitted to bar, 1977, Texas; 1978, Oklahoma. *Education:* University of Oklahoma (B.A., with highest honors, 1974) Phi Beta Kappa; Duke University (J.D., 1977). Editor, Law and Contemporary Problems, 1976-1977. Member, Moot Court Board, 1976-1977. Master, American Inns of Court, Hudson-Hall-Wheaton Chapter, Tulsa, Oklahoma. Adjunct Settlement Judge, Tulsa County District Court, 1993-1997; Adjunct Settlement Judge, U.S. District Court, Northern District of Oklahoma, 1998—. *Member:* State Bar of Texas. [With U.S. Air Force, 1967-1970]. ***PRACTICE AREAS:*** Complex Litigation; Contract Litigation; Business Litigation; Energy Litigation; State and Federal Practice. ***Email:*** rhix@dsda.com

WILLIAM F. RIGGS, born Pine Bluff, Arkansas, March 4, 1953; admitted to bar, 1979, Oklahoma. *Education:* University of Arkansas (B.A., with honors, 1976; B.S.P.A., with honors, 1976; J.D., with high honors, 1979). Phi Beta Kappa. Member, Arkansas Law Review, 1978-1979. ***PRACTICE AREAS:*** Corporate Law; Business Law; Securities Law; Uniform Commercial Code Law. ***Email:*** wriggs@dsda.com

LEWIS N. CARTER, born Wichita Falls, Texas, June 13, 1951; admitted to bar, 1980, Oklahoma. *Education:* Dartmouth College (B.A., 1973); University of Texas; University of Oklahoma (J.D., 1980). Member, Oklahoma Law Review, 1979-1980. Member: Order of the Coif; Order of the Barristers. Instructor, Legal Research and Writing, University of Oklahoma, 1979-1980. ***Email:*** lcarter@dsda.com

LINDA CROOK MARTIN, born Chattanooga, Tennessee, November 30, 1949; admitted to bar, 1980, Oklahoma; 1981, U.S. District Court, Northern, Eastern and Western Districts of Oklahoma, U.S. District Court, Western District of Arkansas, U.S. Court of Appeals, Tenth Circuit and U.S. Supreme Court. *Education:* University of Tennessee (B.A., with honors, 1972; J.D., 1980). Mining Commissioner, State of Oklahoma, 2000. *Member:* Tulsa County (Member, Board of Directors, 1986), Oklahoma (Co-Chair, Women in Law Conference, 1996-1997) and American (Member, Sections on: Natural Resources; Energy; Environment) Bar Associations; Tulsa Women's Lawyers Association (President, 1986-1987). ***PRACTICE AREAS:*** Environmental Law; Rural Water District Law; Rural Electric Cooperative Law; General Civil Litigation; Hospital Law. ***Email:*** lmartin@dsda.com

JAMES PATRICK McCANN, born Augusta, Georgia, October 8, 1951; admitted to bar, 1975, Iowa and U.S. Court of Military Appeals; 1976, California; 1979, Trust Territory of the Pacific Islands and U.S. Tax Court; 1981, Oklahoma and U.S. Court of Appeals, Tenth Circuit; U.S. District Court, Eastern, Northern and Western Districts of Oklahoma; 1995, U.S. Supreme Court. *Education:* University of San Francisco (B.A., 1973; J.D., 1975). Adjunct Faculty, University of Tulsa College of Law, 1989—. Senior Adjunct Settlement Judge, U.S. District Court, Northern District of Oklahoma, 1990—. Member, Panel of Me-

(This Listing Continued)

diators, U.S. District Court, Western District of Oklahoma. *Member:* State Bar of California; Iowa State Bar Association; American Inns of Court, Johnson-Sontag Chapter (Master). [Capt., JAGC, U.S. Army, 1973-1981]. ***PRACTICE AREAS:*** General Civil Litigation; Federal Practice; Mediation; Arbitration. ***Email:*** jmccann@dsda.com

RICHARD H. FOSTER, born Winchester, Kansas, September 4, 1957; admitted to bar, 1982, Oklahoma, U.S. Court of Appeals, Tenth Circuit and U.S. Court of Appeals for the Federal Circuit. *Education:* Kansas University (B.S., 1979); Duke University (J.D., 1982). Certified Public Accountant, Oklahoma, 1984. ***PRACTICE AREAS:*** General Civil Litigation. ***Email:*** rfoster@dsda.com

CHARLES S. PLUMB, born Columbus, Ohio, March 27, 1957; admitted to bar, 1982, Oklahoma. *Education:* Southern Methodist University (B.B.A., 1979); Ohio State University (J.D., with honors, 1982). Staff Member, 1980-1981 and Associate Editor, 1981-1982, Ohio State Law Journal; Editor, Oklahoma Employment Law Letter, 1991—(published monthly). Listed in "The Best Lawyers in America.". ***PRACTICE AREAS:*** General Civil Litigation; Employment and Labor Law (Management); Employment Discrimination Law. ***Email:*** cplumb@dsda.com

LEONARD I. PATAKI, born Palmerton, Pennsylvania, October 2, 1953; admitted to bar, 1978, Oklahoma and U.S. District Court, Northern District of Oklahoma; 1981, U.S. Court of Appeals, Tenth Circuit; 1985, U.S. Supreme Court. *Education:* University of Pittsburgh (B.S., 1975); Oklahoma City University (J.D., with honors, 1977). Research Editor, 1976 and Managing Editor, 1977, Oklahoma City University Law Review. Research Assistant, Oklahoma Uniform Civil Jury Instructions Committee, 1978. Crier/Law Clerk to Hon. Allen E. Barrow, Northern District of Oklahoma, 1978. Law Clerk to Hon. Fred Daugherty, Northern District of Oklahoma, 1978-1979. Senior Law Clerk to Hon. James O. Ellison, Northern District of Oklahoma, 1979-1982. Adjunct Settlement Judge, U.S. Bankruptcy Court, Northern District of Oklahoma, 1998—. Contributing author, Oklahoma Employment Law Newsletter. Trustee, Law Library, Tulsa County. Certified Mediator, Civil-Commercial Employment Law, Oklahoma Mediation Act, 2000—. *Member:* American Bankruptcy Institute; Commercial Law League of America; Tulsa County Bar Association (Chair, Bankruptcy Section, 1998-1999); American Bar Association (Occupational Safety and Health Law Committee). ***PRACTICE AREAS:*** Bankruptcy; Creditors' Rights; Labor Law (Management); General Civil Litigation; Contested Probate Matters; OSHA Compliance and Administrative Proceedings (State and Federal). ***Email:*** lpataki@dsda.com

S. DOUGLAS DODD, born Tulsa, Oklahoma, June 21, 1949; admitted to bar, 1982, Oklahoma. *Education:* University of Tulsa (B.S., 1971; J.D., 1981). Barrister, American Inns of Court, Johnson-Sontag Chapter, Tulsa, Oklahoma. Listed, Best lawyers in America, First Amendment Law, 1995-2000. Law Clerk to Hon. James O. Ellison, U.S. District Judge for the Northern District of Oklahoma, 1982. Member, National Diabetes Advisory Board, 1985-1987. Chairman of the Board, American Diabetes Association, Inc., 1987-1988. Member, Board of Directors, Tulsa County Bar Association, 1987-1988. Chairman, Bar Media Relations Committee, Oklahoma Bar Association. Member, Tulsa Public Schools Board of Education. [1st LT. USAF, Ret.]. ***PRACTICE AREAS:*** Media and First Amendment Law; General Civil; Personal Injury Defense. ***Email:*** sddodd@dsda.com

ELISE DUNITZ BRENNAN, born Dearborn, Michigan, June 29, 1954; admitted to bar, 1983, Oklahoma. *Education:* Newcomb College at Tulane University (B.A., magna cum laude, 1976); University of Michigan (M.S.W., 1978); Southern Methodist University (J.D., 1983). Phi Beta Kappa; Order of the Barristers. Listed in "The Best Lawyers in America." *Member:* American Health Lawyers Association (Chairman, Credentialing and Peer Review, 1997-2000 and Board of Directors, 2000-2001); American Bar Association Health Law Forum; AMA Doctors Advisory Network. ***PRACTICE AREAS:*** Managed Care; Health Care; Dispute Resolution; Employee Benefits. ***Email:*** ebrennan@dsda.com

JON E. BRIGHTMIRE, born Tulsa, Oklahoma, August 13, 1960; admitted to bar, 1986, Oklahoma. *Education:* Oklahoma State University (B.S., with honors, 1982); University of Texas (J.D., with honors, 1985). ***PRACTICE AREAS:*** General Civil Litigation; Federal Practice; Appellate Practice; Zoning Law. ***Email:*** jbrightmire@dsda.com

TOM Q. FERGUSON, born Tulsa, Oklahoma, June 13, 1962; admitted to bar, 1987, Oklahoma. *Education:* Northeastern Oklahoma State University (B.A., summa cum laude, 1984); University of Oklahoma (J.D., with highest honors, 1987). Order of the Coif. Order of the Barristers. Editor-in-Chief, Oklahoma Law Review. Member: National Moot Court Team, 1986; National Appellate Advocacy Team, 1986. Author: "Attorneys: Deterrence of Improper Pleading Practices By Awards of Attorneys' Fees," 39 Oklahoma Law Review 59, 1986. ***PRACTICE AREAS:*** Complex Litigation; General Civil Litigation; Oil and Gas Litigation; Employment Litigation; Intellectual Property Litigation; Media Law; Nonprofit Organizations Law; Religious Institutions; Municipal Law; Land Use. ***Email:*** tferguson@dsda.com

RICHARD J. EAGLETON, born Tulsa, Oklahoma, December 4, 1962; admitted to bar, 1988, Oklahoma. *Education:* Vanderbilt University (B.A., 1985; J.D., 1988). Member, American Inns of Court, Council Oaks Chapter, Tulsa, Oklahoma, 1994-1995. ***PRACTICE AREAS:*** Domestic Relations Law; General Civil Litigation. ***Email:*** reagleton@dsda.com

REBECCA McCARTHY FOWLER, born Kingsville, Texas, January 25, 1947; admitted to bar, 1989, Oklahoma, U.S. District Court, Northern, Eastern and Western Districts of Oklahoma, U.S. Court of Appeals, 5th and 10th Circuits and U.S. Supreme Court. *Education:* University of Houston (B.B.A., 1978); University of Tulsa (J.D., with highest honors, 1989). Phi Delta Phi. Order of the Curule Chair. Articles Editor, 1988-1989, Tulsa Law Journal. Regular Contributing Author to Oklahoma Employment Law Letter. Co-Author, Oklahoma Chapter of the ABA Sales and Use Tax Handbook, Member, OBA State Tax Legislative and Regulatory Review Committee. *Member:* Oklahoma (Member, Awards Committee; Long Range Planning Committee; Uniform Laws Committee) and American (Member, Labor and Employment Section, Tax Section) Bar Associations. ***PRACTICE AREAS:*** State Tax Controversies; Federal Tax Controversies; Tax Litigation; Employment Law; Employment Litigation; General Civil Litigation. ***Email:*** rfowler@dsda.com

MICHAEL C. REDMAN, born Miami, Florida, December 26, 1961; admitted to bar, 1988, Oklahoma; 1990, U.S. Court of Appeals, 10th Circuit; 1992, U.S. Court of Appeals, 7th Circuit. *Education:* University of Oklahoma (B.B.A., Economics, with honors, 1985; J.D., with distinction, 1988). American Inns of Court, W. Lee Johnson, Robert D. Hudson and Hudson-Hall-Wheaton, Chapters. Member, Oklahoma Law Review, 1986-1988. Law

(This Listing Continued)

Clerk to Hon. Thomas R. Brett, U.S. District Court, Northern District of Oklahoma, 1988-1990. Member, Advisory Panel, Overseeing Implementation of the Civil Justice and Reform Act of 1990, 1995-2000. Director: Young Lawyers' Division, Oklahoma Bar Association, 1993-1995. Contributing Author: Media Privacy and Related Law, 50 State Survey, Libel Defense Resource Center. ***PRACTICE AREAS:*** Employment Law; Antitrust; Unfair Competition. ***Email:*** mredman@dsda.com

STEVEN K. METCALF, born San Diego, California, February 10, 1958; admitted to bar, 1991, Oklahoma. *Education:* Oklahoma State University (B.S.E.T., 1980); University of Tulsa (J.D., with honors, 1991). Order of the Curule Chair. Senior Staff, 1989-1990 and Senior Editor, 1990-1991, Tulsa Law Journal. Pupil, American Inns of Court, Robert D. Hudson Chapter XXXII, 1990-1991. Author: "The Right to Vote of the Mentally Disabled in Oklahoma: A Case Study in Overinclusive Language and Fundamental Rights," 25 Tulsa Law Journal 171; "The Oklahoma Public Competitive Bidding Act of 1974: Ingenuity in Submitting to the Process," 25 Tulsa Law Journal 843. *Member:* Oklahoma and American Bar Associations. ***PRACTICE AREAS:*** Civil Litigation; Business Litigation; Construction Disputes; Construction Contract Drafting; Construction Contract Negotiation; Mechanics Liens; Materialmens Liens; Mechanic Foreclosure; Materialmen Foreclosure; Construction Mediation; Construction Arbitration; Construction Litigation; Payment Enforcement; Performance Bond Enforcement. ***Email:*** smetcalf@dsda.com

RUSSELL W. KROLL, born Tulsa, Oklahoma, June 25, 1959; admitted to bar, 1992, Oklahoma. *Education:* University of Tulsa (B.S., CHE, 1982); University of Tulsa Law School (J.D., with honors, 1992). Member, Order of the Curule Chair. Honorary Membership, Scribes. Articles Editor, Tulsa Law Journal. Staff Member, Tulsa Law Journal. Registered Professional Engineer, Oklahoma. ***PRACTICE AREAS:*** Environmental Law; General Civil Litigation; OSHA Compliance; State and Federal Administrative Proceedings. ***Email:*** rkroll@dsda.com

RACHEL BLUE, born Tulsa, Oklahoma, August 29, 1963; admitted to bar, 1988, Missouri; 1995, Oklahoma. *Education:* University of Texas (B.A., magna cum laude, 1984); University of Tulsa (J.D., 1988). Recipient, Outstanding Law Alumni Award, 1999 and Presidential Service Award, 2002, University of Tulsa. Trademark Examining Attorney, U.S. Patent and Trademark Office, 1988-1995. Past President, University of Tulsa College of Law Alumni, 2001-2002. *Member:* Tulsa County, Oklahoma (Past President, Intellectual Property Section, 1999-2001) and American (Member: Intellectual Property Section; Forum on Franchising Sections) Bar Associations; International Trademark Association. ***PRACTICE AREAS:*** Trademarks; Trademark Licensing; Internet Law; Trade Secrets; Trademark Infringement; Copyrights; Unfair Competition; Franchise Law. ***Email:*** rblue@dsda.com

JAMES C. MILTON, born McAlester, Oklahoma. June 27, 1966; admitted to bar, 1995, Oklahoma; 1996, U.S. Court of Appeals, 10th Circuit; 1998, U.S. Supreme Court. *Education:* Oklahoma State University (B.S.B.A., 1988); University of Texas (J.D., with honors, 1995). Omicron Delta Kappa. Phi Delta Phi. Executive Editor and Recipient, Outstanding Editor Award, Texas Law Review, 1994-1995. National Products Liability Moot Court Team (1st Place and Best Brief), 1994. Author: "An Appellate Practitioner's War Story: Fighting an Emergency Request for Injunction Pending Appeal," Appellate Advocacy Newsletter, TIPS Appellate Advocacy Committee, Tort and Insurance Practice Section, American Bar Association, at p. 1, Spring, 2000. Board of Advocates, 1994-1995. Associate Member, American Inns of Court, Hudson-Hall-Wheaton Chapter, 1996-2002. Oklahoma Bar Association Civil Procedure Committee, 2000—. ***REPORTED CASES:*** Pittsburg County Rural Water Dist. No. 7 v. McAlester, No. 97-CV-185-B, 1997 WL 835210 (E.D. Okla., Nov. 26, 1997). Pittsburg County Rural Water Dist. No. 7 v. McAlester, 211 F.3d 1279, 2000 WL 525942 (10th Cir.), cert. denied, 531 U.S. 1011 (2000). Sequoyah County Rural Water Dist. No. 7 v. Town of Muldrow, 191 F.3d 1192 (10th Cir., 1999), cert. denied, 529 U.S. 1037, 529 U.S. 1049 (2000). ***PRACTICE AREAS:*** Commercial Litigation; Products Liability; Municipal Competition; Antitrust; Appellate Practice; Consumer Credit; Elder Abuse; Insurance Coverage. ***Email:*** jmilton@dsda.com

ASSOCIATES

AUDRA K. HAMILTON, born Paragould, Arkansas, September 27, 1970; admitted to bar, 1996, Arkansas; 1998, Oklahoma. *Education:* Hendrix College (B.A., magna cum laude, with distinction, 1992); University of Arkansas (J.D., with high honors, 1996). Articles Editor, Arkansas Law Review, 1995-1996. Law Clerk to the Hon. Warren K. Urbom, U.S. Senior District Judge, District of Nebraska, 1996-1998. Editor and Contributing Author, Oklahoma Employment Law Newsletter. ***PRACTICE AREAS:*** Employment Law; General Civil Litigation. ***Email:*** ahamilton@dsda.com

WILLIAM H. SPITLER, born Princeton, Illinois, March 13, 1974; admitted to bar, 2000, Oklahoma. *Education:* Eastern Illinois University (B.A., 1996); University of Arkansas (J.D., cum laude, 2000). Staff Member, Arkansas Law Review, 1999-2000. ***PRACTICE AREAS:*** Litigation. ***Email:*** wspitler@dsda.com

YOUNG PEI, born Seoul, South Korea, December 24, 1971; admitted to bar, 2000, Oklahoma. *Education:* Boston University (B.A., magna cum laude, 1994); University of Oklahoma (J.D., 2000). ***LANGUAGES:*** Korean. ***PRACTICE AREAS:*** Commercial Litigation; Corporate. ***Email:*** ypei@dsda.com

CHAD M. HINRICHS, born Macon, Missouri, December 16, 1967; admitted to bar, 1995, Oklahoma; registered to practice before U.S. Patent and Trademark Office. *Education:* University of Kansas (B.S.M.E., 1991); University of Tulsa (J.D., 1995). Phi Delta Phi. Member, Energy Law Journal, 1993-1995. Board Member, University of Tulsa College of Law Alumni Association. *Member:* Tulsa County, Oklahoma (Director, Intellectual Property Section) and American Bar Associations. ***PRACTICE AREAS:*** Patents; Trademarks; Trade Secrets; Intellectual Property Licensing. ***Email:*** chinrichs@dsda.com

JOHNATHAN D. HORTON, born Harrison, Arkansas, July 29, 1976; admitted to bar, 2001, Oklahoma; 2002, Arkansas. *Education:* Lyon College (B.A., magna cum laude, 1998); University of Arkansas (J.D., magna cum laude, 2001). *Member:* Tulsa County, Oklahoma, Arkansas and American Bar Associations. ***PRACTICE AREAS:*** Civil Litigation; Employment Defense; General Practice. ***Email:*** jhorton@dsda.com

ROBERT SPOO, born Hornell, New York, July 24, 1957; admitted to bar, 2001, New York; 2003, Oklahoma. *Education:* Lawrence University (B.A, magna cum laude, 1979);

(This Listing Continued)

DOERNER, SAUNDERS, DANIEL & ANDERSON, L.L.P., Tulsa—Continued

Princeton University (M.A., 1984, Ph.D., English, 1986); Yale University (J.D., 2000). Phi Beta Kappa. Recipient, Best Student Contribution to Yale Law Journal Issue of Social Importance. Executive Editor, Yale Law Journal. Editor, James Joyce Quarterly. Copyright Editor: Journal of Modern Literature; James Joyce Quarterly. Law Clerk to Honorable Sonia Sotomayor, U.S. Court of Appeals, Second Circuit. Professor, English, University of Tulsa, 1988-2000. ***PRACTICE AREAS:*** Intellectual Property; Copyrights; Litigation. ***Email:*** rspoo@dsda.com

LESLEY FORD RICHER, born Rapid City, South Dakota, December 25, 1976; admitted to bar, 2002, Oklahoma. *Education:* University of Notre Dame (B.A., 1999); Southern Methodist University (J.D., 2002). Phi Delta Phi. Inns of Court. Articles Editor, Computer Law Review and Technology Journal. ***PRACTICE AREAS:*** Corporate Law; Health Law; Taxation; Litigation. ***Email:*** lricher@dsda.com

DAVID L. IANDIORIO, born Cooperstown, New York, March 17, 1970; admitted to bar, 2001, Oklahoma. *Education:* State University of New York at Oneonta (B.S., English Literature, 1995); Franklin Pierce Law Center (J.D., 2000). Attended "Intellectual Property Summer Institute," Franklin Pierce Law Center, 1998. Member: Leadership Tulsa Class of 2002; Board of Directors, Tulsa Economic Development Corp. *Member:* Tulsa County, Oklahoma and American Bar Associations; American Intellectual Property Law Association. ***PRACTICE AREAS:*** Trademarks; Trademark Infringement; Trademark Registration; Copyrights; Copyright Infringement; Copyright Registration; Unfair Competition; Trade Secrets Law; Domain Names; Internet Law; Licensing; Publishing Law; Entertainment Law. ***Email:*** dli@dsda.com

N. LANCE BRYAN, born November 28, 1977; admitted to bar, 2003, Oklahoma. *Education:* Oklahoma State University (B.A., Political Science and Economics, summa cum laude, 2000); University of Texas School of Law (J.D., with honors, 2003). Member, Mock Trial Team (two-time winner, regional competition of the Texas Young Lawyer's Association National Trial Competition). ***PRACTICE AREAS:*** Business Litigation; Commercial Law; Litigation; Appellate Practice. ***Email:*** lbryan@dsda.com

CHAD J. KUTMAS, born Kirksville, Missouri, November 28, 1975; admitted to bar, 2002, Oklahoma. *Education:* Unversity of Arkansas (B.A., 1999); University of Tulsa College of Law (J.D., 2002). Phi Delta Phi. Law Clerk to Hon. Terrence L. Michael, Chief Judge and Judge, Bankruptcy Appellate Panel, Tenth Circuit, U.S. Bankruptcy Court, Northern District of Oklahoma. *Member:* Oklahoma and American Bar Associations. ***PRACTICE AREAS:*** Bankruptcy; Civil Litigation.

HEATHER D. FLYNN, born Tulsa, Oklahoma, June 14, 1975; admitted to bar, 2002, Oklahoma. *Education:* University of Tulsa (B.S., Psychology, 1997); University of Oklahoma (M.P.H., 2002); University of Tulsa College of Law (J.D., 2002). Phi Delta Phi. Recipient: CALI Excellence of the Future Award; Community Health Foundation Scholarship. Named Outstanding Academic Student for the College of Public Health Policy and Administration. Notes and Comments Editor, Tulsa Law Review, 2001-2002. Author, Comment, "In Utero Endangerment and Mandatory Drug Testing: Public Health Issues from Conception," 26 Tulsa L.J. 649 (2001). *Member:* Tulsa County, Oklahoma and American Bar Associations. ***PRACTICE AREAS:*** Family Law. ***Email:*** hflynn@dsda.com

ELIZABETH W. CARROLL, born 1980; admitted to bar, 2005, Oklahoma. *Education:* University of Oklahoma (B.A., summa cum laude in History, minors in Political Science and German, 2002); University of Oklahoma College of Law (J.D., 2005). Phi Beta Kappa. Indexing Editor, Oklahoma Law Review. Research Assistant for Professor Steven Gensler on forthcoming Federal Rules of Civil Procedure (West 3d ed., 2006). Recognized as Third Best Oral Advocate in First Year Moot Court competition. Recipient, American Jurisprudence Awards in Legal Research and Writing and Torts III. ***LANGUAGES:*** German. ***PRACTICE AREAS:*** Litigation; Corporate Law.

E. McLAINE DeWITT HERNDON, born Albuquerque, New Mexico, March 8, 1975; admitted to bar, 2005, Oklahoma. *Education:* University of Malaga, Malaga, Spain (1995); University of Tulsa (B.A., majors in English Language and Literature and minor in Spanish Language and Literature, 1996); University of Tulsa School of Law (J.D. with Honors, 2005). Phi Delta Phi; Phi Kappa Phi; Kappa Delta Pi. Recipient, Norman-Hix Scholarship for Law; BNA Award for Excellence in the Study of Labor and Employment Law. Notes and Comments Editor, Tulsa Law Review. *Member:* Tulsa County, Oklahoma and American Bar Associations. ***PRACTICE AREAS:*** Litigation; Corporate Law. ***Email:*** mherndon@dsda.com

STEVEN P. TEPERA, born McKinney, Texas, September 12, 1979; admitted to bar, 2005, Oklahoma. *Education:* University of Texas (B.S., with honors in Aerospace Engineering, 2002); University of Texas School of Law (J.D., with honors, 2005); University of London, Queen Mary School of Law in London, United Kingdom (received merit). *Member:* Tulsa County, Oklahoma and American Bar Associations. ***PRACTICE AREAS:*** Corporate Law; Litigation. ***Email:*** stepera@dsda.com

RAYMOND H. TIPTON III, born 1979; admitted to bar, 2005, Oklahoma. *Education:* The University of Oklahoma (B.S., Business Administration, 2001); The University of Oklahoma College of Law (J.D. and M.B.A., 2005). Order of Barristers; Phi Delta Phi; Pi Kappa Phi. President, Interfraternity Council, University of Oklahoma, 2000. Member, Moot Court Team. Winner, First Year Moot Court Competition, University of Oklahoma College of Law. Regional Top 10 Speaker, ABA National Appellate Advocacy Competition, New Orleans, Louisiana. Business Development Editor, American Indian Law Review. Director Emeritus, Alliance of Emerging Professionals, Oklahoma City, Oklahoma. *Member:* Tulsa County, Oklahoma and American Bar Associations. ***PRACTICE AREAS:*** Civil Litigation; Corporate Organization; Mergers and Acquisitions. ***Email:*** rtipton@dsda.com

OF COUNSEL

MICHAEL MINNIS, born Wichita, Kansas, February 22, 1944; admitted to bar, 1969, Oklahoma; 1972, California; 1976, U.S. Supreme Court; 1981, District of Columbia. *Education:* University of Oklahoma (B.A., Journalism, 1966; J.D., 1969). Appointed, Judge, Court of Appeals Temporary Division No. 174, 1982. Chief Judge, Town of Valleybrook, 1982-1983. *Member:* Oklahoma and Federal (President, 1982-1983, Oklahoma City Chapter) Bar Associations; State Bar of California; The District of Columbia Bar. [Trial/Defense Counsel United States Marine Corp (1969-1972), Lieutenant Colonel (Retired), USAFR]. ***REPORTED CASES:*** Citizen Band Pottawatomie Indian Tribe of Okla. v. Okla. Tax Comm'n, 111 S.Ct. 905 (1991); Continental Casualty Co. v. Southwestern Bell Telephone Co., 860 F.2d 970 (10th Cir. Okl. 1988); McCain v. KTVY, Inc., 738 P.2d 960 (Okl. App.Ct. 1987); Miskovsky v. Okla. Pub. Co., 654 P.2d 587 (Okl. 1982), cert. denied, 459 U.S. 923 (1982); Okl. Pub. Co. v. Dist. Court of Okl. County, 430 U.S. 308 (1977). ***PRACTICE AREAS:*** Media Law; Indian Law. ***Email:*** mminnis@dsda.com

(This Listing Continued)

DAVID McCULLOUGH, born Anadarko, Oklahoma, January 6, 1953; admitted to bar, 1984, Oklahoma, U.S. Supreme Court, U.S. Court of Appeals, Tenth Circuit and U.S. District Court, Western District of Oklahoma; 1992, Texas. *Education:* Oxford University, Queens College, Oxford, England (1982); University of Oklahoma (B.A., Journalism, 1977; J.D., 1984). Advisory Board Member, Native American Alliance Foundation. Member, Board of Directors and Founding Member, FOI Oklahoma, Inc. *Member:* Oklahoma, Federal and American Bar Associations. ***PRACTICE AREAS:*** Media Law; Indian Law. ***Email:*** dmccullough@dsda.com

REPRESENTATIVE CLIENTS: AEP/Public Service Company of Oklahoma; United States Cellular Telephone Company; St. John Medical Center, Inc.; Community Care HMO, Inc.; Preferred Community Choice/CompMed, Inc.; St. Simeon's Nursing Home; Tulsa Psychiatric Center; Key Temporary Personnel, Inc.; Prudential Securities, Inc.; American Bank and Trust Co.; Flint Resources Company; The Rockland Corporation; Sanguine, Ltd.; Salomon Smith Barney Holdings, Inc.; Citigroup, Inc.; KOTV, Inc.; Sheehan Pipe Line Construction Company; Citgo Petroleum; Energy Transfer Partners, L.P.; Pro Quip Corp.; QuikTrip Corporation; Oklahoma Ordnance Works Authority; Unit Corp.; Pepsi Bottling Group; Piping Companies, Inc.; Bama Pie, Ltd.; Clifford Power Systems, Inc.; LCI International Communications; Paragon Films, Inc.; Aeromet, Inc.; Arrow Trucking Co.; Kmart Corporation; Dillard's, Inc.; Explorer Pipeline, Inc.; City of Broken Arrow; City of McAlester; City of Ponca City; Sequoyah Fuels Corp.; Baker Petrolite Corp.; City of Claremore; City of Guthrie; Labinel, Inc.; Griffin Communications; Northeast Oklahoma Electric Co-op., Inc.

(For complete biographical data on Oklahoma City Personnel, see Professional Biographies at Oklahoma City, Oklahoma)

FREDERIC DORWART

Established in 1994

OLD CITY HALL
124 EAST FOURTH STREET
TULSA, OKLAHOMA 74103-5010
Telephone: 918-583-9922
Fax: 918-583-8251
Email: fdorwart@fdlaw.com
URL: http://www.fdlaw.com

General Civil Practice including Oil and Gas, Banking and Business Planning, Securities Regulation, Technology Sales and Licensing, Mergers and Acquisitions, Corporation, White Collar Crime, Environmental, Employment Law, Health Care Law, Securities fraud, Securities Arbitration, Commercial Litigation, Business Litigation.

FIRM PROFILE: Our objective is to provide hands-on, timely, and cost-effective problem solving in both routine and difficult litigation, regulatory and transactional matters. We have substantial experience in banking, business planning, oil and gas, mergers and acquisitions, technology sales and licensing and securities matters. The firm serves as general counsel to Oklahoma's largest financial institution and to two of Oklahoma's larger independent oil and gas producers. The firm is listed in the Bar Register of Preeminent Lawyers.

FREDERIC DORWART, born Muskogee, Oklahoma, 1937; admitted to bar, 1966, Oklahoma. *Education:* United States Naval Academy (B.S., with distinction, 1959); Harvard University (LL.B., cum laude, 1966). [Lieut., USN, 1959-1963]. ***PRACTICE AREAS:*** Oil and Gas Law; Banking and Finance Law; Securities Law; Transactions and Litigation; Mergers and Acquisitions.

J. MICHAEL MEDINA, born New York, N.Y., 1950; admitted to bar, 1975, Oklahoma; U.S. Court of Appeals, Second, Fifth, Tenth Districts; District of Columbia and Federal Circuits, U.S. Supreme Court; U.S. District Court, Northern, Western and Eastern Districts of Oklahoma. *Education:* Southwestern College (B.A., summa cum laude, 1972); University of Oklahoma (J.D., with special distinction, 1975). Phi Delta Phi; Pi Gamma Mu; Order of the Coif. Editor, Oklahoma Law Review, 1973-1975. Author: "Pitfalls in Oklahoma Appellate Practice," 57 Okla. B.J. 741 (1986); Co-Author: "Take or Litigate: Enforcing the Plain Meaning of the Take-or-Pay Clause in Natural Gas Contracts," 40 Ark. L. Rev. 185 (1987); "The Take-or-Pay Wars: A Further Status Report," 41 Okla. L. Rev. 381 (1988); "Discretionary Review in the Oklahoma Supreme Court: A Practical Guide to the Court's Certiorari Jurisdiction," 13 Okla. City U. L. Rev. 257 (1988); "Ethical Concerns in Civil Appellate Practice," 43 Sw. L.J. 677 (1989); "Economic Duress As A Means of Avoiding Settlement Agreements in Oklahoma," 15 Okla. City U.L. Rev. 255 (1990); "The Emergency Clause And The Referendum in Oklahoma: Current Status and Needed Reform," 43 Okla. L. Rev. 401 (1990); Co-Author, "Recent Developments and Suggested Reforms in Oklahoma Civil Appellate Procedure," 26 Tulsa L.J. 489 (1991); "The Take-or-Pay Wars: A Cautionary Analysis for the Future," 27 Tulsa L.J. 897 (1991); "The Bible Annotated: Use of the Bible in Reported American Decisions," 12 N. Ill. L. Rev. 187 (1991); "The Interjurisdictional Certification of Questions of Law Experience: Federal, State and Oklahoma - Should Arkansas Follow?" 45 Ark. L. Rev. 99 (1992); "An Update on Pitfalls in Oklahoma Appellate Practice," 63 Okla. B.J. 897 (1992). Adjunct Professor of Law, University of Tulsa College of Law, 1992-1999. Judge, Oklahoma Court of Appeals, Temporary Div. XIV, 1991-1993, Alternate Judge, Municipal Court, City of Tulsa, 1993-1997. Member, Oklahoma Supreme Court Committee to Assist in Revision of Rules of the Supreme Court, Court of Appeals and on Certiorari. Treasurer, Appellate Practice Section, 1991, Chair, Continuing Legal Education Committee, 1992, Chair-Elect, Appellate Practice Section, 1992-1993 and Chair, 1993-1994, Oklahoma Bar Association. *Member:* Hispanic National Bar Association; American Academy of Appellate Lawyers; American Bar Association. ***PRACTICE AREAS:*** Appeals; Oil and Gas Law; Environmental Law; Employment Law. ***Email:*** mmedina@fdlaw.com

(This Listing Continued)

RICHARD J. CIPOLLA, JR., born Kansas City, Missouri, November 5, 1962; admitted to bar, 1989, Oklahoma. *Education:* University of Tulsa (B.S., Honors Program, Political Science, 1985) Pi Sigma Alpha; University of Kansas (J.D., 1989). Phi Delta Phi. Staff Member, University of Kansas Criminal Procedure Review, 1988-1989. Author: "Discovery Sanctions and the Compulsory Process Clause: *Taylor v. Illinois*," The University of Kansas Law Review, 1989 Criminal Procedure Edition; "A Practitioners' Guide to Oklahoma Trade Secrets Law, Past, Present & Future: The Uniform Trade Secrets Act," 27 Tulsa L.J. 137 (1991). ***PRACTICE AREAS:*** Business Litigation. ***Email:*** rcipolla@fdlaw.com

MATTHEW JAMES BROWNE, III, born Littlefield, Texas, May 28, 1952; admitted to bar, 1991, Oklahoma. *Education:* Centenary College (B.S., in Business, 1975); University of Arkansas (J.D., with honors, 1991). Phi Kappa Phi. Member, Law Review, University of Arkansas. (Also Practicing Individually). ***PRACTICE AREAS:*** Oil and Gas Litigation; Banking Law; Finance Law; Civil Litigation. ***Email:*** mbrowne@fdlaw.com

PAUL DeMURO, born Philadelphia, Pennsylvania, July 26, 1965; admitted to bar, 1993, New Mexico; 1997, Oklahoma; U.S. District Court, Districts of Arizona and New Mexico and Northern District of Oklahoma; U.S. Court of Appeals, Tenth Circuit. *Education:* Princeton University (B.A., 1987); University of New Mexico (J.D., magna cum laude, 1993). ***LANGUAGES:*** Spanish. ***PRACTICE AREAS:*** Criminal Defense; Commercial Litigation. ***Email:*** pdemuro@fdlaw.com

TAMARA R. WAGMAN, born Kearney, Nebraska, May 15, 1970; admitted to bar, 1995, Oklahoma. *Education:* University of Nebraska-Lincoln (B.A., Phi Beta Kappa, highest distinction, 1992); Vermont Law School (J.D., magna cum laude, 1995). Note Editor, Vermont Law Review, 1994-1995. Co-Author: "UCC Article 2B: Preliminary Report," 70 Okla. B.J. 443, 1999. *Member:* Tulsa County, Oklahoma and American Bar Associations. ***PRACTICE AREAS:*** Corporate; Securities; Technology Licensing; Internet Law. ***Email:*** twagman@fdlaw.com

JOHN D. CLAYMAN, born Tulsa, Oklahoma, February 5, 1960; admitted to bar, 1986, Oklahoma, U.S. District Court, Northern, Western and Eastern Districts of Oklahoma and U.S. Court of Appeals, Tenth Circuit. *Education:* University of Texas (B.B.A., with honors, 1982); University of Tulsa (J.D., 1986). Beta Alpha Psi. Chair, Order of the Curule. Member, Tulsa Law Journal, 1984-1985. Notes and Comments Editor, Energy Law Journal, 1985-1986. Certified Public Accountant, Oklahoma, 1984. Treasurer: Youth Services of Tulsa; Jewish Federation of Tulsa. *Member:* Tulsa County, Oklahoma (Member, Health Law Section) and American Bar Associations; National Health Lawyers Association; Oklahoma Society of Certified Public Accountants. ***PRACTICE AREAS:*** Business Litigation; Commercial Litigation; Estate Planning; Corporate Law; Health Care.

ERICA ANNE DORWART, born Tulsa, Oklahoma, June 7, 1968; admitted to bar, 1999, Oklahoma. *Education:* Vanderbilt University (B.A., 1990; M.Ed., 1992); University of Tulsa (J.D., with highest honor, 1999). ***LANGUAGES:*** Spanish, French, Portuguese. ***PRACTICE AREAS:*** Oil and Gas Law; Technology Law. ***Email:*** edorwart@fdlaw.com

TORI M. SNYDER, born Las Cruces, New Mexico, May 22, 1959; admitted to bar, 2000, Oklahoma; 2002, U.S. District Court, Northern District of Oklahoma. *Education:* Texas A & M University (B.B.A., 1981); University of Tulsa (J.D., with highest honors, 2000). Phi Delta Phi. CALI Award in Jurisprudence and Negotiating. *Member:* Tulsa County, Oklahoma and American Bar Associations. ***PRACTICE AREAS:*** Corporate Law. ***Email:*** tsnyder@fdlaw.com

KENNETH BENJAMIN WATT, born Tulsa, Oklahoma, 1965; admitted to bar, 1993, Oklahoma and U.S. District Court, Northern District of Oklahoma. *Education:* Washington University (B.S.B.A., 1987); University of Tulsa College of Law (J.D., 1993). Phi Delta Phi. Recipient, American Jurisprudence Award in Taxation of Corporation & Shareholders. Staff Member, Tulsa Law Journal. Certified Public Accountant, Texas, 1990. Author: "Piercing the Corporate Veil: A Need for Clarification of Oklahoma's Approach", 28 Tulsa Law J. No. 4. *Member:* Tulsa County (Member, Corporate Counsel Section) and Oklahoma (Member, Patent, Trademark and Copyright Law Section) Bar Associations.

STEVEN M. KOBOS, born Stillwater, Oklahoma, January 7, 1965; admitted to bar, 1990, Oklahoma, U.S. Court of Appeals, Tenth Circuit and U.S. District Court, Eastern, Northern and Western Districts of Oklahoma and Eastern District of Texas. *Education:* University of Oklahoma (B.A., 1986; J.D., with Highest Honors, 1990). Phi Alpha Delta (Justice, 1989-1990). Order of the Coif. Recipient: Oklahoma Bar Association Outstanding Senior Student Award; West Publishing Company Award. Adjunct Professor of Law, University of Tulsa College of Law, 1992-1995. *Member:* Tulsa County, Oklahoma and American Bar Associations. ***PRACTICE AREAS:*** Litigation; Employment Law; Trust Litigation; Banking Law; Business Transactions. ***Email:*** skobos@fdlaw.com

DEIRDRE O. DEXTER, born Stillwater, Oklahoma, April 15, 1956; admitted to bar, 1984, Oklahoma; 1985, U.S. District Court, Northern and Eastern Districts of Oklahoma; 1987, U.S. District Court, Western District of Oklahoma and U.S. Court of Appeals, Tenth Circuit. *Education:* Oklahoma State University; Phillips University (B.S., cum laude, 1981); University of Oklahoma (J.D., with highest honors, 1984). Delta Theta Phi; Order of the Coif; Order of the Barristers. Member 1982-1984 and Articles Editor 1983-1984, Oklahoma Law Review. Author, "Constitutional Law: The Equal Protection Clause: The Effect of Plyler v. Doe on Intermediate Scrutiny," 36 Okla. L.Rev. 321 (1983). Recipient: American Jurisprudence Awards for Outstanding Performance in Contracts Law, Criminal Law, Administrative Law and Uniform Commercial Law. Listed in Who's Who Among American Law Students; Who's Who in Finance and Industry; Who's Who in American Law; Who's Who in the South and Southwest; Who's Who Among American Women; Who's Who in the World. Life member for Who's Who National Registry. Associate District Judge, Tulsa County, Oklahoma, 2000-2003. *Member:* Tulsa County and Oklahoma Bar Associations; American Inns of Court (Master, Hudson-Hall-Wheaton Chapter). ***PRACTICE AREAS:*** Employment Law; Commercial Litigation; Complex Commercial Litigation; Complex Litigation; Securities Litigation; Securities Arbitration; Appellate Practice; Mediation. ***Email:*** ddexter@fdlaw.com

ERIC R. SCHELIN, born Butte, Montana, May 5, 1976; admitted to bar, 2002, Oklahoma. *Education:* Montana Tech of the University of Montana (B.S., 1998); University of Tulsa, College of Law (J.D., 2002). Representative, Curriculum Committee, University of Tulsa, 2002. *Member:* Tulsa County and Oklahoma (Member, CAP Committee, 2002) Bar Associations; American Inns of Court. ***LANGUAGES:*** German. ***PRACTICE AREAS:*** Commercial Litigation; Civil Litigation. ***Email:*** eschelin@fdlaw.com

(This Listing Continued)

REPRESENTATIVE CLIENTS: BOK Financial Corporation; Bank of Oklahoma, National Association; Bank of Arkansas, National Association; Bank of Texas, National Association; Bank of Albuquerque, National Association; Sooner Southwest Bancshares, Inc.; Fabricut, Inc.; Kaiser-Francis Oil Company; The Williford Companies; Williford Energy Company; Safety Training Systems, Inc.; Fountains Continuum of Care, Inc.; Bank of New York; Chase Bank; Family and Childrens Services, Inc.; Fell Oil and Gas Company; North American Palladium, Inc.; Realty Operating Company; Rougeot Oil and Gas Corporation; Albert Investment Co., Inc.; Grand Resources International; Taurus Exploration, Inc; Kaiser Energy, Ltd.; PetroCorp Incorporated; BOSC Securities Inc.

DOYLE HARRIS DAVIS & HAUGHEY

A PROFESSIONAL CORPORATION

Established in 1985

1350 BOULDER, SUITE 700

P.O. BOX 1679

TULSA, OKLAHOMA 74101-1679

Telephone: 918-592-1276

Fax: 918-592-4389

Email: D&H@CommerciaLaw.com

URL: http://www.CommerciaLaw.com

Federal Practice, Business Torts/Commercial Litigation, Anti-Trust, Securities, Environmental, Insurance Coverage Litigation, Patent and Copyright Litigation. Trial Practice.

STAN P. DOYLE, born Youngstown, Ohio, August 26, 1939; admitted to bar, 1964, Oklahoma; 1971, U.S. Supreme Court. *Education:* University of Tulsa (LL.B., 1964); New York University (LL.M., Corporation Law, 1975). Editor in Chief, Tulsa Law Journal, Vol. I, No. 1, 1963-1964. *Member:* Oklahoma Bar Association. (Also Of Counsel, James, Potts and Wulfers, Inc.). ***PRACTICE AREAS:*** Antitrust; Securities; Business Litigation. ***Email:*** D&H@commerciaLaw.com

STEVEN M. HARRIS, born Dodge City, Kansas, November 3, 1950; admitted to bar, 1975, Oklahoma, U.S. Supreme Court, U.S. Court of Appeals, Ninth and Tenth Circuit, U.S. Claims Court and U.S. District Court, Northern, Eastern and Western Districts of Oklahoma. *Education:* University of Kansas (B.A., 1972); University of Tulsa (J.D., 1974). *Member:* Tulsa County and Oklahoma and American Bar Associations; Commercial Law League of America; The Association of Trial Lawyers of America. ***PRACTICE AREAS:*** General Practice; Commercial Law; Business Torts; Professional Malpractice (Non-Medical). ***Email:*** steve.harris@CommerciaLaw.com

MICHAEL D. DAVIS, born Sallisaw, Oklahoma, September 11, 1956; admitted to bar, 1985, Oklahoma; 1986, U.S. Court of Appeals, Ninth and Tenth Circuit and U.S. District Court, Northern, Eastern and Western Districts of Oklahoma. *Education:* Northeastern Oklahoma State University (B.S., 1978); University of Tulsa (J.D., 1985). *Member:* Tulsa County and Oklahoma Bar Associations; The Association of Trial Lawyers of America. ***PRACTICE AREAS:*** Commercial Law; General Practice. ***Email:*** mike.davis@CommerciaLaw.com

DOUGLAS R. HAUGHEY, born Urbana, Illinois, August 23, 1956; admitted to bar, 1988, Oklahoma. *Education:* Illinois State University (B.A., 1978); University of Tulsa (J.D., 1981). Phi Alpha Delta. *Member:* Tulsa County and Oklahoma Bar Associations. ***PRACTICE AREAS:*** Commercial Litigation; Debtor and Creditor Rights. ***Email:*** doug.haughey@CommerciaLaw.com

---

C. MATTHEW BICKELL, born Claremore, Oklahoma, November 21, 1972; admitted to bar, 1998, Oklahoma. *Education:* University of Tulsa (B.B.A., 1994); University of Oklahoma (J.D., 1998). *Member:* Tulsa County and Oklahoma Bar Associations. ***PRACTICE AREAS:*** Patent Law; Commercial Law; Business Torts; Civil Litigation. ***Email:*** matt.bickell@commercialaw.com

LEGAL SUPPORT PERSONNEL

HOLLY BOBO DeBOER, (Office Administrator)

PHYLLIS PECK, (Legal Assistant)

REPRESENTATIVE CLIENTS: Bankers Trust Company of New York; Board of Public Utilities - City of Springfield, Missouri; Texas Oil & Gas Corp.; Delhi Gas Pipe Line Corp.; Wheatley/TXT Corp. (Division of Dresser Industries); St. Louis Bank; Wells Fargo Bank; Pyramid Energy Corp.; Copelco Leasing Corp.; Westinghouse Electric Corp.; Interstate Electric Corp.; Creek County Rural Water District No. 2; Jefferson Lines, Inc.; Ferguson Enterprises, Inc.; ABC Supply Co., Inc.; Tulsa Dynaspan, Inc.; ITT Commercial Finance Corp.; Henderson Brick (Division of Boral Brick); Commonwealth Financial Group (REIT - now Parkway Texas Corp.); Video Communications, Inc.; United Entertainment Corp.; Fortune Films, Inc.; Hope Lumber & Supply Co., Inc.; The Sherwin-Williams Co.; Rainbow Concrete Co.; Cherokee Building Materials, Inc.; Oil Capital Electric; Gilmore Sports Concepts, Inc.; The Lewis Companies; Mill Creek Lumber; Whitestar Machinery, Inc.; Pittsburg County Rural Water District #7; Tulsa County Rural Water District #2; Dona Ama Mutual Domestic Water Consumers Association; Salem Water Users Association; Pushmataha Rural Water District #2; Wagoner County rural Water District #8; Sequayah County rural Water District #7;Murray County Rural Water District #1; Butterfield Park Mutual Domestic Water Association.
REFERENCES: Stillwater National Bank; Peoples State Bank; American Bank and Trust Co.

DOYLE & SALISBURY

Established in 1985

100 WEST 5TH STREET, SUITE 550

TULSA, OKLAHOMA 74103-4288

Telephone: 918-583-7766

Fax: 918-583-9251

Real Estate, Employment Law and General Civil Litigation.

WILLIAM J. DOYLE III, born Tulsa, Oklahoma, January 28, 1938; admitted to bar, 1963, Oklahoma; 1964, Michigan, U.S. Court of Appeals, Tenth Circuit and U.S. District Court, Northern, Western and Eastern Districts of Oklahoma. *Education:* University of Oklahoma (B.A., 1960); University of Oklahoma and University of Tulsa (LL.B., 1963).

(This Listing Continued)

DOYLE & SALISBURY, Tulsa—Continued

Phi Alpha Delta. President, Tulsa Title and Probate Lawyers, 1981. *Member:* Tulsa County, Oklahoma and American Bar Associations. [Capt., U.S. Army, 1963-1965]. ***PRACTICE AREAS:*** Real Estate Law; General Civil Litigation. ***Email:*** bill@law-ok.com

HAROLD W. SALISBURY, born Clinton, Oklahoma, November 27, 1962; admitted to bar, 1988, Oklahoma; 1989, U.S. Court of Appeals, Tenth Circuit and U.S. District Court, Northern, Eastern and Western Districts of Oklahoma. *Education:* University of Oklahoma (B.B.A., 1985); University of Tulsa (J.D., 1988). Delta Theta Phi. *Member:* Tulsa County and Oklahoma Bar Associations. ***PRACTICE AREAS:*** Employment Law; Health and Welfare Benefits; General Civil Litigation. ***Email:*** hsalisbury@cbremail.com

APPROVED ATTORNEYS FOR: Lawyers' Title Insurance Corp.; Chicago Title Insurance Co.; Commonwealth Land Title Company; Standard Title Insurance Co.; Ticor Title Insurance Co.; Title Insurance Company of Minnesota.
REFERENCE: F & M Bank and Trust Company of Tulsa.

THE DRUMMOND LAW FIRM

Established in 1970

1500 SOUTH UTICA, SUITE 400
TULSA, OKLAHOMA 74104
Telephone: 918-749-7378
Fax: 918-749-7869
Email: gfd@drumlaw.com
URL: http://www.drumlaww.com

General Civil Practice in State and Federal Courts, Corporate, Banking, Insurance Defense, Bankruptcy, Estate Planning, Probate, Oil & Gas, Real Estate, Employment, Environmental, Indian and Criminal Law.

FIRM PROFILE: The Drummond Law Firm has provided quality regal services to northeastern Oklahoma individuals and businesses for over 30 years. With special emphasis on business litigation and transactions, the lawyers at Drummond offer expertise in a wide variety of disciplines.

THOMAS E. DRUMMOND, born Pawhuska, Oklahoma, April 3, 1945; admitted to bar, 1971, Oklahoma, U.S. District Court, Northern, Eastern and Western Districts of Oklahoma and U.S. District Court, Northern District of Texas. *Education:* Oklahoma University (B.B.A., 1967); Tulsa University (J.D., 1971). Delta Theta Phi. Assistant District Attorney, Osage County, 1971-1973. Commissioner, Oklahoma Horse Racing Commission. *Member:* Osage County, Tulsa and Oklahoma Bar Associations. [Bronze Star, U.S. Army, Vietnam, 1967-1969]. ***PRACTICE AREAS:*** Commercial Litigation; Agricultural Law; Probate; Domestic Relations. ***Email:*** ted@drumlaw.com

GENTNER F. DRUMMOND, born Stillwater, Oklahoma, October 1, 1963; admitted to bar, 1995, Oklahoma and U.S. District Court, Northern, Eastern and Western Districts of Oklahoma; U.S. Supreme Court. *Education:* Oklahoma State University (B.S., Agricultural Economics, 1984); Georgetown University (J.D., 1995). Member, The Tax Lawyer Law Journal, 1993-1995. Author: "Comm'r vs. Keystone," 47 Tax Lawyer 491, Winter 1994. Legislative Assistant, U.S. Senator Boren, 1993-1994. Assistant District Attorney, Osage and Pawnee Counties, 1995-1997. *Member:* Tulsa County, Osage County, Oklahoma, and American Bar Associations; National Lawyers Association. [Capt., U.S. Air Force, 1985-1992, Distinguished Flying Cross, Gulf War, 1991]. ***PRACTICE AREAS:*** Business Transactions; Commercial Litigation; Banking Law. ***Email:*** gfd@drumlaw.com

ASSOCIATES

MAX C. MYERS, JR., born Carney, Oklahoma, May 5, 1966; admitted to bar, 1997, Oklahoma. *Education:* Oklahoma State University (B.S., Agricultural Education, with honors, 1988); University of Tulsa (J.D., 1996).

WILL K. WRIGHT, JR., born Marlborough, Massachusetts, June 22, 1962; admitted to bar, 1994, Oklahoma. *Education:* Oral Roberts University (B.S., Business Administration, 1987); University of Tulsa (J.D., with honors, 1994).

LORETTA (LORI) K. ROBERTS, born Fort Worth, Texas, January 30, 1963; admitted to bar, 1996, Oklahoma. *Education:* University of Tulsa (B.A.,cum laude, 1991; J.D., with honors, 1996).

REBECCA R. HERT, born Tulsa, Oklahoma, December 1, 1970; admitted to bar, 2002, Oklahoma. *Education:* Oklahoma City University School of Law (J.D., 2002).

OF COUNSEL

RANDALL S. PICKARD, (P.C.), born Orange, California, September 28, 1958; admitted to bar, 1983, Oklahoma. *Education:* Willamette University; Southeastern Oklahoma State University (B.A., with honors, 1980); O.W. Coburn School of Law; Oral Roberts University (J.D., cum laude, 1983).

ALAN J. OXFORD, II, born Orlando, Florida, April 10, 1961; admitted to bar, 1997, Oklahoma. *Education:* Oklahoma Baptist University (B.A., Journalism, 1987); University Central Oklahoma (Accounting, 1991); University of Oklahoma (J.D., with honors, 1997).

MAX K. NAEGLER, born Springfield, Missouri, May 12, 1941; admitted to bar, 1966, Missouri and Florida; 1977, Oklahoma. *Education:* Southwest Missouri State University (B.A., Political Science/English, 1963); Washington School of Law (J.D., 1966). [Officer, *JAGC, U.S. Army, 1966-1970*]

J. PETER MESSLER, born Tulsa, Oklahoma, October 30, 1940; admitted to bar, 1971, Oklahoma. *Education:* Oklahoma State University (B.S., Marketing, 1962); University of Tulsa (J.D., 1971).

JAMES W. DUNHAM, JR.

Established in 1978

2112 BANK OF AMERICA CENTER
15 WEST 6TH STREET
TULSA, OKLAHOMA 74119
Telephone: 918-592-1144
Fax: 918-592-1149
Email: elawyer@swbell.net
URL: http://www.nursingneglect.com

Commercial Litigation, Personal Injury, Nursing Home Abuse and Neglect.

FIRM PROFILE: Priding ourselves on personal, one-to-one communications between client and lawyer, the Law Offices of James W. Dunham, Jr., have served the people of Oklahoma and surrounding states for 26 years.

JAMES W. DUNHAM, JR., born West Point, New York, November 19, 1952; admitted to bar, 1978, Oklahoma; 1979, U.S. District Court, Northern and Western Districts of Oklahoma; 1980, U.S. District Court, Eastern District of Oklahoma; 1982, U.S. District Court, Northern District of Texas; 1984, U.S. District Court, Northern District of Illinois. *Education:* United States Military Academy; University of Tulsa (B.S., 1974; J.D., 1978). *Member:* Oklahoma and American Bar Associations; Oklahoma Trial Lawyers Association; Association of Trial Lawyers of America. ***PRACTICE AREAS:*** Commercial Litigation; Personal Injury Law; Nursing Home Abuse and Neglect.

REPRESENTATIVE CLIENTS: The Rockland Corporation; Premiere Consulting, LLC; Parasol Communications, Inc.; Republic Metals, LLC.

EAGLETON, EAGLETON & HARRISON, INC.

SUITE 1700, 320 SOUTH BOSTON AVENUE
TULSA, OKLAHOMA 74103-4706
Telephone: 918-584-0462
Fax: 918-584-3724
Email: eaglelaw@swbell.net
URL: http://www.eehlaw.com

Administrative and Judicial Resolution of Tax Controversy, Civil and Criminal, State and Federal; Estate Planning and Probate, Business Transactions, Employee Benefits, Family Law.

FIRM PROFILE: Eagleton, Eagleton and Harrison, Inc. is listed in Martindale-Hubbell's Bar Register of Preeminent Lawyers.

E. JOHN EAGLETON, born Tulsa, Oklahoma, January 22, 1932; admitted to bar, 1956, Oklahoma and U.S. Supreme Court. *Education:* University of Oklahoma (B.B.A., 1955; LL.B., 1956). Phi Alpha Delta. Certified Public Accountant. Trial Attorney, Regional Counsel, Internal Revenue Service, 1957-1962. *Member:* Oklahoma Society of Certified Public Accountants; Tax Lawyers-Internal Revenue Service. Fellow, American College of Trust and Estate Counsel. ***PRACTICE AREAS:*** Tax Controversies; Criminal Taxation; Estate Planning; Business Transactions.

JAMES R. EAGLETON, born Tulsa, Oklahoma, October 9, 1924; admitted to bar, 1951, Oklahoma. *Education:* University of Oklahoma (A.B., 1949; J.D., 1951). Phi Alpha Delta. President, Tulsa County Bar Association, 1981-1982. President, Oklahoma Bar Association, 1986. *Member:* American College of Trust and Estate Counsel. ***PRACTICE AREAS:*** Probate; Oil and Gas Law.

CHARLES D. HARRISON, born Chicago, Illinois, June 10, 1954; admitted to bar, 1981, Oklahoma; U.S. Tax Court; U.S. District Court, Northern and Eastern Districts of Oklahoma; U.S. Court of Appeals, Tenth Circuit, U.S. Court of Federal Claims and U.S. Supreme Court. *Education:* Bradley University (B.S., 1976); University of Tulsa (J.D., 1981); Georgetown University Law Center (M.L.T., 1982). ***PRACTICE AREAS:*** Tax Controversies; Criminal Taxation; Estate Planning; Business Transactions; Taxation.

L. MICHELE NELSON, born Tulsa, Oklahoma, March 19, 1964; admitted to bar, 1996, Oklahoma; U.S. District Court, Northern District of Oklahoma; U.S. District Court, Eastern and Western Districts of Oklahoma and U.S. Tax Court. *Education:* University of Oklahoma (B.B.A., Marketing, 1985); University of Tulsa (J.D., 1996); Southern Methodist University (LL.M., Taxation, 1997). Phi Delta Phi. Production Editor, Tulsa Law Journal, 1994-1995. ***PRACTICE AREAS:*** Taxation; Estate Planning; Trusts; Probate; Business Transactions.

OF COUNSEL

NORMA EAGLETON, born Wewoka, Oklahoma, March 19, 1934; admitted to bar, 1988, Oklahoma. *Education:* Stephens College (A.A., 1954); University of Oklahoma (B.A., 1956); Oklahoma City University (J.D., 1988). Phi Beta Kappa. Commissioner, Finance & Revenue, City of Tulsa, 1976-1979; Oklahoma Corporation Commission, 1979-1989. Board of Regents, Rogers State College until 1996; Tulsa Airport Authority. ***PRACTICE AREAS:*** Mediation; Family Law; Guardianship; Probate Law; Estate Planning.

REPRESENTATIVE CLIENTS: Available upon request.

EDGAR & PERIGO, P.C.

Established in 1984

2615 EAST FIFTEENTH STREET
TULSA, OKLAHOMA 74104-4711
Telephone: 918-748-9444
Fax: 918-748-9464
Email: eph.law@cox.net
URL: http://www.lawyers.com/ephlaw

Family, Child Custody, Divorce, Adoptions, General Business, Guardianships, Real Estate, Probate, Estate Planning, Wills and Trusts, Civil Law, Juvenile Law.

(This Listing Continued)

STEVEN E. EDGAR, born Salina, Kansas, February 9, 1951; admitted to bar, 1977, Arkansas; 1979, Oklahoma; 1980, U.S. Tax Court. *Education:* Arkansas Tech University (B.S., 1974); University of Arkansas (J.D., 1977). Arbitrator, Better Business Bureau, 1987-1993. Assistant Municipal Judge: City of Owasso, 1990—; City of Broken Arrow, 2000—. Family Relations Mediator. *Member:* Tulsa County and Oklahoma Bar Associations. ***PRACTICE AREAS:*** Probate Law; General Business Law; Guardianships; Family Law; Juvenile Law. ***Email:*** steve-edgar@cox.net

JERRY E. PERIGO, born Houston, Texas, June 4, 1946; admitted to bar, 1976, Oklahoma. *Education:* University of Oklahoma (B.A., 1968); University of Tulsa (J.D., 1976). Phi Eta Sigma; Phi Delta Phi. Special Judge of the District Court, Tulsa County, 1979-1981. Alternate Municipal Judge, City of Tulsa, 1984—. Arbitrator, Better Business Bureau 1987-1993. State Certified Family Relations Mediator. *Member:* Tulsa County and Oklahoma Bar Associations. [With U.S. Coast Guard, 1968-1972]. ***PRACTICE AREAS:*** Family Law; Child Custody Law; Juvenile Law; Mediation; Alternative Dispute Resolution. ***Email:*** jerry-perigo@cox.net

REPRESENTATIVE CLIENTS: Reliance Wine & Spirits Company, Inc.; Mohawk Steel Company; Communicating Arts, Inc.; Odyssey Digital Printing; Valkenberg International; Vekamaf Holland, B.V.; Grand Lake Bank; Premium Brands Wine & Spirits Company.
REFERENCES: Security Bank; Guaranty Abstract Co., Tulsa, Oklahoma.

EDWARDS & MAILATH, L.L.P.

6226 EAST 101ST STREET, SUITE 100
TULSA, OKLAHOMA 74137
Telephone: 918-299-9360
Facsimile: 918-299-9369
URL: http://www.lawyers.com/edwards&huffman

Commercial Transactions, Commercial Litigation, Real Estate, Title Insurance, Banking, Bankruptcy Reorganizations and Creditor's Rights, Loan Documentation and Lending Transactions, Administrative, Public Utility, General Corporate Law and Estate Planning.

MEMBERS OF FIRM

RODNEY A. EDWARDS, born Washington, D.C., January 4, 1951; admitted to bar, 1976, Oklahoma. *Education:* Oklahoma State University (B.A., 1973); University of Tulsa (J.D., 1975). Delta Theta Phi. *Member:* Tulsa County, Oklahoma and American Bar Associations. ***PRACTICE AREAS:*** Civil Litigation; Banking Law; Loans; Lender Regulation; Creditors Rights; Bankruptcy. ***Email:*** redwards@edwardshuffman.com

MELISSA D. MAILATH, born Norman, Oklahoma, November 9, 1969; admitted to bar, 1997, Oklahoma and U.S. District Court, Northern, Eastern and Western Districts of Oklahoma. *Education:* Tulane University of Louisiana (B.A., 1992); University of Oklahoma (J.D., 1996). *Member:* Tulsa County and Oklahoma Bar Associations; American Inns of Court, Hudson-Hall-Wheaton Chapter. ***PRACTICE AREAS:*** Corporate Law; Corporate Litigation; Civil Litigation; Business Transactions; Real Estate; Employment Law. ***Email:*** mmailath@edwardshuffman.com

ELDRIDGE COOPER STEICHEN & LEACH P.L.L.C.

110 WEST SEVENTH STREET, SUITE 200
TULSA, OKLAHOMA 74119
Telephone: 918-388-5555
Fax: 918-388-5654
URL: http://www.ecsloklaw.com
Email: general_delivery@ecslok.com
URL: http://www.ecslok.com
Mailing Address: P.O. Box 3566, Tulsa, OK 74101-3566

Appellate Practice, Business Law, Civil Trial Practice, Class Actions, Commercial Litigation, Construction Law, Environmental Law, Insurance Law, Labor and Employment Law, Personal Injury, Product Liability Law.

FIRM PROFILE: Effective, efficient and innovative firm with extensive experience defending national clients in products liability and commercial litigation. Our specific emphasis on and vast experience in the litigation arena enables us to provide our clients with dynamic and productive representation. Experience does not translate into inflexibility, as we utilize state-of-the-art technology, from our near paperless document system, to our complex databases, to our custom computer animations. We approach litigation with the unwavering commitment to provide our clients a service that exceeds all expectations. The firm is listed in the Bar Register of Preeminent Lawyers.

RICHARD M. ELDRIDGE, born Okmulgee, Oklahoma, June 20, 1951; admitted to bar, 1976, Oklahoma, U.S. District Court, Northern, Eastern and Western Districts of Oklahoma, U.S. District Court, Eastern and Western Districts of Arkansas, U.S. Court of Appeals, Tenth Circuit. *Education:* Oklahoma State University (B.A., 1973); University of Tulsa (J.D., 1975). Phi Kappa Phi; Phi Delta Phi. Member: Order of the Barristers; Order of the Curule Chair. Staff Member, Tulsa Law Journal, 1974-1975. Special District Judge for Tulsa and Pawnee Counties, 1978-1981. Judge, Temporary Court of Appeals. Adjunct Settlement Judge, Tulsa County, 1990-1998. Publications: Contributed Oklahoma Chapter to American Bar Association, The Restatement Sections Specifically Applicable to Pharmaceutical and Medical Device Cases in State Court: A 50 State Survey; "Is Direct-to-Consumer Advertising Eroding the Learned Intermediary Doctrine?," 41 For The Defense 14 (No. 12, Dec. 1999); "Baker v. Arbor Drugs, Inc.: Pharmacists Beware of Voluntarily Assuming the Duty to Protect Against Harmful Drug Interactions," 141 J. Contemp. Health L. and Pol'y 41, (1997). *Member:* Tulsa County (Director at Large, 1985-1986, 1991-1992), Oklahoma and American (Member, Tort and Insurance Practice Section) Bar Associations; Defense Research Institute; Oklahoma Association of Defense Lawyers; American Judicature Society. Fellow, Oklahoma Bar Foundation. ***PRACTICE AREAS:*** Litigation; Product Liability Law; Medical Products Liability; Insurance Defense. ***Email:*** reldridge@ecslok.com

(This Listing Continued)

MARY QUINN COOPER, born Tulsa, Oklahoma, March 25, 1960; admitted to bar, 1986, Oklahoma; U.S. District Court, Northern, Eastern and Western Districts of Oklahama; U.S. Court of Appeals, Tenth Circuit. *Education:* University of Arkansas (B.A., 1982); University of Tulsa (J.D., 1986). Delta Theta Phi. Author: "The Use of Demonstrative Exhibits and Aids at Trial," *Tulsa L.J.* (Spring 1999). Chairman, Admission and Grievance Committee, U.S. District Court, Northern District of Oklahoma, 1998—. *Member:* Tulsa County, Oklahoma and American (Member, Products Liability and Tort Sections) Bar Associations; International Association of Defense Counsel; Products Liability Advisory Council; American Board of Trial Advocates; Defense Research Institute; Oklahoma Association of Defense Counsel. Fellow, Oklahoma Bar Foundation. ***PRACTICE AREAS:*** Products Liability; Complex Litigation. ***Email:*** mcooper@ecslok.com

THOMAS E. STEICHEN, born Norton, Kansas, January 3, 1948; admitted to bar, 1975, Oklahoma; U.S. District Court, Northern, Eastern and Western Districts of Oklahoma; U.S. Court of Appeals, Tenth Circuit. *Education:* St. Louis University (A.B., Honors Program, 1970; J.D., 1975); Indiana University (M.B.A., 1972). *Member:* Tulsa County (Chairman, Workers Compensation Section, 1993) Oklahoma (Chairman, Workers Compensation Section, 1989) and American Bar Associations; Defense Research Institute. Fellow, Oklahoma Bar Foundation. ***PRACTICE AREAS:*** Medical Products Liability; Products Liability; Civil Litigation. ***Email:*** tsteichen@ecslok.com

WILLIAM S. LEACH, born Amarillo, Texas, November 6, 1956; admitted to bar, 1982, Texas and Oklahoma; U.S. District Court, Northern, Eastern and Western Districts of Oklahama; U.S. District Court, Northern, Eastern and Western Districts of Texas; U.S. Court of Appeals, Fifth and Tenth Circuits; U.S. Supreme Court. *Education:* Oklahoma State University (B.S., 1979); University of Oklahoma (J.D., 1982). Editor, Oklahoma Law Review, 1981-1983. Member, National Mock Trial Team, 1981-1982. *Member:* Oklahoma Bar Association; State Bar of Texas; Texas Association of Defense Counsel; American Board of Trial Advocates (Advocate). Fellow, Oklahoma Bar Foundation. (Board Certified, Civil Trial Law and Personal Injury Trial Law, Texas Board of Legal Specialization). ***PRACTICE AREAS:*** Civil Litigation; Products Liability. ***Email:*** wleach@ecslok.com

HAROLD C. ZUCKERMAN, born Miami, Florida, January 17, 1959; admitted to bar, 1985, Oklahoma and U.S. District Court, Northern, Western and Eastern Districts of Oklahoma; 1989, U.S. Court of Appeals, Tenth Circuit. *Education:* University of Tulsa (B.S., 1981; J.D., 1984). *Member:* Tulsa County, Oklahoma and American (Tort and Insurance Practice Section) Bar Associations; Oklahoma Association of Defense Counsel. ***PRACTICE AREAS:*** Products Liability; Commercial Litigation; Environmental Law; Premises Liability. ***Email:*** hzuckerman@ecslok.com

ANDREW L. RICHARDSON, born Tulsa, Oklahoma, July 25, 1968; admitted to bar, 1994, Oklahoma, U.S. District Court, Northern, Eastern and Western Districts of Oklahoma; U.S. Court of Appeals, Tenth Circuit. *Education:* Baylor University (1989); Oklahoma State University (B.A., 1991); University of Oklahoma (J.D., 1994). Phi Delta Phi. Member, Oklahoma Law Review. Author, "Cohen v. Brown University: A Title IX Lesson for Colleges and Universities on Gender Equity," 47 Oklahoma Law Review 161 (1994). *Member:* Oklahoma Bar Association. ***PRACTICE AREAS:*** Products Liability; Civil Litigation. ***Email:*** arichardson@ecslok.com

KATHY R. NEAL, born Tulsa, Oklahoma, March 14, 1957; admitted to bar, 1982, Oklahoma; U.S. District Court, Northern, Eastern and Western Districts of Oklahoma; Oklahoma Supreme Court; U.S. Court of Appeals, Tenth Circuit; U.S. Supreme Court; Alberta, Canada. *Education:* University of Oklahoma (B.A., summa cum laude, 1979); University of Tulsa College of Law (J.D., 1982). Phi Beta Kappa. Barrister, American Inns of Court, Robert D. Hudson Chapter, 1987-1988. Barrister, American Inns of Court, W. Lee Johnson Chapter, 1991-1994. Law Clerk to Hon. Thomas R. Brett, United States District Judge, Northern District of Oklahoma, 1982-1984. Editor, Oklahoma Law Letter, 1993-2000. Author: "Is Your Client's Award or Settlement of an Employment Claim Taxable?" Oklahoma Bar Journal, Vol. 65, No. 48, December, 25 1993; "Consignments Under the Uniform Commercial Code," Oklahoma Bar Journal, Vol. 53, No. 21, May 1982. Associate Adjunct Professor of Law, Alternative Dispute Resolution, University of Tulsa College of Law, 1996. Master, Adjunct Settlement Judge, U. S. District Court, Northern District of Oklahoma, 1990-1996. Listed in "Best Lawyers in America," Labor and Employment Law, 1997-2001. Member: Leadership Tulsa Class XXI. *Member:* Tulsa County and Oklahoma Bar Associations; Canadian Bar Association; Law Society of Alberta. ***PRACTICE AREAS:*** Employment Litigation; Federal Civil Litigation; Commercial Litigation; Products Liability. ***Email:*** kneal@ecslok.com

MICHAEL F. SMITH, born Oklahoma City, Oklahoma, August 11, 1964; admitted to bar, 1991, Oklahoma; 1992, Illinois and U.S. District Court, Northern District of Illinois; 1994, U.S. District Court, Northern and Eastern Districts of Oklahoma and U.S. Court of Appeals, Tenth Circuit; 1998, U.S. Supreme Court; 2002, New York. *Education:* Oklahoma State University (B.S., 1987); University of Tulsa (J.D., 1991). Staff Member, 1989-1990 and Notes and Comments Editor, 1990-1991, Tulsa Law Journal. Publications: "Law and Practice of Insurance Coverage Litigation," Leitner, Simpson & Bjorkman, A.B.A. Tort & Ins. Practice Sec (Chapter 4, Duty to Defend); "Fifty State Construction Lien and Bond Law," Cushman & Butler, Oklahoma Chapter (2d ed. Aspen Law & Business 2000); "Is Direct-to-Consumer Advertising Eroding the Learned Intermediary Doctrine?," For The Defense, Vol. 41, No. 12, p. 14 (Defense Research Institute, December 1999); "State-by-State Guide to Architect, Engineer, and Contractor Licensing," Walker, Holderness & Butler, Oklahoma Chapter (Aspen Law & Business 1999); "Baker v. Arbor Drugs, Inc.: Pharmacies Beware of Voluntarily Assuming the Duty to Protect Against Harmful Drug Interactions," 14 J. Contemp. Health L. & Policy 41 (1997); "The Evolution of PRP Standing Under the Comprehensive Environmental Response, Compensation, and Liability Act of 1980, 21 Wm & Mary Env. L. & Policy Rev. 300 (1997); "Limiting Liability of the Passive Lender Under the Comprehensive Environmental Response, Compensation, and Liability Act of 1980," 26 Tulsa. L.J. 75 (1990). *Member:* Oklahoma, Illinois State and New York State Bar Associations. ***PRACTICE AREAS:*** Products Liability (75%); Appellate Practice (25%). ***Email:*** msmith@ecslok.com

FREDERICK CABELL CORNISH, born Ft. Worth, Texas, September 23, 1945; admitted to bar, 1974, Oklahoma; U.S. District Court, Northern, Eastern and Western Districts of Oklahoma; U.S. Court of Appeals, Tenth Circuit; U.S. Supreme Court. *Education:* St. Louis University (B.A., 1967; M.A., 1970; J.D., 1974). Oklahoma Commissioner, National Conference on Uniform State Laws, 1986-1995. Lawyer Member, and Chairman, Okla-

(This Listing Continued)

ELDRIDGE COOPER STEICHEN & LEACH P.L.L.C., Tulsa—Continued

homa Mental Health Board, 1980-1982. Judge by special appointment, Oklahoma Court of Appeals, 1982. Founding Member and President, Tulsa CASA, Inc. 1984-1994. *Member:* Tulsa County and Oklahoma Bar Associations. ***PRACTICE AREAS:*** Higher Education Law; Commercial Litigation; Employment Litigation; Small Business Law; Commercial Transactions; Probate.

ASSOCIATES

LYNDA DIANNE RIKER, born Oklahoma City, Oklahoma, July 30, 1957; admitted to bar, 2000, Oklahoma. *Education:* Oklahoma State University (B.S., Education, 1980); University of Tulsa (J.D., 1999). *Member:* Tulsa County and Oklahoma Bar Associations. ***PRACTICE AREAS:*** Products Liability; Civil Litigation; Employment Litigation. ***Email:*** lriker@ecslok.com

VANI SINGHAL, born Tulsa, Oklahoma, June 29, 1971; admitted to bar, 1996, Oklahoma; 1999, Illinois; U.S. District Court, Northern, Eastern and Western Districts of Oklahoma; U.S. District Court, Western and Eastern Districts of Wisconsin; U.S. District Court, Northern District of Illinois. *Education:* Oklahoma State University (B.A., 1992); Georgetown University (J.D., 1995). Author, "Renewal of Prescription Drug User Fee Act Raises Issues for Government, Public Groups, Pharmaceutical and Medical Device," Law Bulletin, January 2002. Co-Author: "Recent Developments in Medicine and Law," 37 Tort and Ins.L.J. 601, Winter 2002; FDA's Regulation of Dietary Supplements Fueled by Industry Growth, Pharmaceutical and Medical Device Law Bulletin, February 2001; "Products and Entities Subject to Strict Liability," 35 Tort and Ins.L.J. 553, Winter 2000. Chair, Committee on Diversity and the Profession, American Bar Associations Tort Trial and Insurance Practice Section, 2004—. *Member:* Oklahoma and American (Chair, Medicine and Law Committee, 2001-2003; Tort Trial and Insurance Practice Section) Bar Associations. ***LANGUAGES:*** Hindi. ***PRACTICE AREAS:*** Products Liability; Medical Device Liability; Pharmaceutical Litigation; Professional Liability; Asbestos Litigation; Mass Tort Litigation; Commercial Litigation. ***Email:*** vsinghal@ecslok.com

DWAIN S. SHAW, born Austin, Texas, August 30, 1962; admitted to bar, 2003, Oklahoma. *Education:* Austin Community College (L.P.N., 1982); Southwest Texas State University (B.S.H.P., 1985); University of Texas Health Science Center at Houston (M.P.H., 1987); University of Tulsa (J.D., 2003). Licensed Vocational Nurse, 1982. *Member:* Tulsa County (Vice Chair, Health Law Section) and American Bar Associations; American Health Lawyers Association; American Trial Lawyers Association; Defense Research Institute; Inns of Court. ***PRACTICE AREAS:*** Health Care; Employment Law; Products Liability; Civil Litigation; Mental Health Law. ***Email:*** dshaw@ecslok.com

JENNIFER D. LEE, born Hayes, Kansas, January 16, 1968; admitted to bar, 1993, Oklahoma and U.S. District Court, Western District of Oklahoma; 1996, U.S. District Court, Northern District of Oklahoma. *Education:* Vanderbilt University (B.A., 1990); Oklahoma City University (J.D., cum laude, 1993). Phi Delta Phi. Moot Court Competition. Oklahoma City University Law Review, 1991-1993. Recipient: American Jurisprudence Award, Eighth Amendment Law. *Member:* Oklahoma Bar Association. ***PRACTICE AREAS:*** Appellate Practice; Products Liability. ***Email:*** jlee@ecslok.com

SHELLY DALRYMPLE, born Los Angeles, California, May 11, 1958; admitted to bar, 1992, Oklahoma. *Education:* Dickinson College (B.A., cum laude, 1981); George Washington University National Law Center (J.D., 1992). Member, George Washington University Journal of International Law and Economics, 1990-1992. Contributing Author, *Oklahoma Employment Law Letter:* Administrator, American Inns of Court, W. Lee Johnson Chapter, 1995—. *Member:* Tulsa County (Court Operations Committee) and Oklahoma (Client Security Fund Committee; Treasurer, Health Law Section) Bar Associations; National Health Lawyers Association; Oklahoma Association for Healthcare Ethics (Charter Member); Tulsa Health Care Lawyers Group; Tulsa Women Lawyers Association (President, 1994-1996). ***PRACTICE AREAS:*** Complex Commercial Litigation; Class Actions; Employment Law. ***Email:*** sdalrymple@ecslok.com

SELIM K. FLAGOME, born Kpandu, Ghana, April 3, 1979; admitted to bar, 2004, Oklahoma. *Education:* University of Tulsa (B.A., 2001; J.D., 2004). Delta Theta Phi. Recipient, R. Steven Chandler Award, 2004. Staff Member, Tulsa Journal of Comparative and International Law, 2003-2004. *Member:* Tulsa County, Oklahoma and American Bar Associations; Muscogee (Creek) National Bar Association; North Eastern Oklahoma Black Lawyers Association; Oklahoma Bar Examiner. ***PRACTICE AREAS:*** Products Liability; Litigation; Civil Rights; Community Development Law; Economic Development Law; Nonprofit Organizations Law; Immigration; International Law; Native American Law; Administrative Law; Education Law; Employment Law; Insurance; Business Law; Commercial Transactions.

BARBARA ELLEN CIRDEKK, born Tulsa, Oklahoma, August 23, 1972; admitted to bar, 2004, Oklahoma, U.S. District Court, Northern and Western Districts of Oklahoma. *Education:* Vanderbilt University (B.A., 1994); University of Oklahoma (M.A., 1997); University of Tulsa College of Law (J.D., 2004). Phi Delta Phi. Staff Member, Energy Law Journal, 2002-2004. *Member:* Tulsa County, Oklahoma and American Bar Associations. ***PRACTICE AREAS:*** Products Liability; Employment Law; Native American Law. ***Email:*** ecordell@ecslok.com

OF COUNSEL

BRITA HAUGLAND-CANTRELL, born Muskogee, Oklahoma, April 24, 1962; admitted to bar, 1987, Oklahoma; U.S. District Court, Northern and Eastern Districts of Oklahoma; U.S. Supreme Court. *Education:* Wellesley College (B.A., 1984); University of Oklahoma (J.D., 1987). Note Editor, University of Oklahoma Law Review, 1985-1987. Executive Director, Oklahoma Chapter, The Nature Conservancy, 1994-2000. Author: "The Constitutional Tools of an Adequate Defense," Oklahoma Law Review, 1986. Assistant Attorney General, Oklahoma, 1989-1994. Executive Director, The Nature Conservancy Oklahoma Chapter, 1994-2000. *Member:* Oklahoma (Past Chairman, Environmental Law Section) Bar Association. ***PRACTICE AREAS:*** Environmental Law; Products Liability; Administrative Law; Civil Practice. ***Email:*** bcantrell@ecslok.com

(This Listing Continued)

REPRESENTATIVE CLIENTS: ACE USA; Accor North America, Inc.; American Medical Systems, Inc.; B.F. Ascher & Company, Inc.; Best Industries, Inc.; Boston Scientific Corporation; Boxer Property Management Corp.; Camelot Music, Inc.; Case New Holland, Inc.; Centerpulse USA Inc.; Chubb Services Corporation; Conley Corporation; Daimlerchrysler Corp.; Disetronic Medical Systems, Inc.; ESIS, Inc.; Ford Motor Company; Forest Pharmaceuticals, Inc.; Gallager Bassett Services; General Motors Corporation; Harley-Davidson Motor Company; Herbalife International of America, Inc.; Hilton Hotels, Inc.; Kia Motors America Inc.; Kimberly-Clark Corporation; Medmarc Insurance Group; Merrill Lynch, Pierce, Fenner & Smith, Inc.; Novartis Consumer Health, Inc.; Novartis Pharmaceuticals Corp.; Oklahoma Kenworth, Inc.; Pfizer Inc.; Republic American Insurance Co.; Royal & SunAlliance; Safeskin Corporation; Sanjel (U.S.A.) Inc.; Siemens, Inc.; Smith & Nephew, Inc.; Specialty Claims Management; St. Jude Medical, Inc.; Sutherland Lumber Company; Synthes, (U.S.A.) Inc.; Technothern, Inc.; Teva Pharmaceuticals USA, Inc.; The Raymond Corporation; Thomas L. Green Co.; The University of Tulsa; Valor Telecommunications, Inc.; Weyerhaeuser Company; XL Winterthur International; 3M Company.

ELLER AND DETRICH

A PROFESSIONAL CORPORATION

Established in 1979

MIDWAY BUILDING

2727 E. 21ST STREET, SUITE 200

TULSA, OKLAHOMA 74114-3533

Telephone: 918-747-8900

Toll Free: 866-547-8900

Fax: 918-747-2665

URL: http://www.ellerdetrich.com

General Civil Practice, Mergers and Acquisitions, Commercial Transactions, Real Property, Construction, Financial Services and Banking, Corporation, Employment, Oil and Gas, Estate Planning and Probate, Bankruptcy and Creditor's Rights, Commercial, Tort, Insurance and Zoning Law, Trials and Appeals in State and Federal Courts.

PHILIP J. ELLER, born Tulsa, Oklahoma, November 7, 1950; admitted to bar, 1976, Oklahoma, U.S. District Court, Northern and Western Districts of Oklahoma and U.S. Court of Appeals, Tenth Circuit. *Education:* University of Tulsa (B.S.B.A., 1973; J.D., 1976). ***PRACTICE AREAS:*** Real Estate Law; Commercial Transactions and Litigation. ***Email:*** peller@ellerdetrich.com

DONALD DETRICH, born Chicago, Illinois, March 26, 1951; admitted to bar, 1976, Oklahoma; U.S. District Court, Northern, Eastern and Western Districts of Oklahoma; U.S. Court of Appeals, Tenth Circuit. *Education:* University of Tulsa (B.S., with honors, 1973; J.D., 1976). ***PRACTICE AREAS:*** Real Estate Law; Corporate and Commercial Law. ***Email:*** ddetrich@ellerdetrich.com

KEVIN H. WYLIE, born El Dorado, Arkansas, October 27, 1957; admitted to bar, 1983, Oklahoma, U.S. District Court, Northern, Western and Eastern Districts of Oklahoma and U.S. Court of Appeals, Tenth Circuit. *Education:* Oklahoma State University (B.S., 1980); University of Tulsa (J.D., 1983). ***PRACTICE AREAS:*** Commercial and Civil Litigation; Bankruptcy; Commercial Law; Business Transactions. ***Email:*** kwylie@ellerdetrich.com

R. LOUIS REYNOLDS, born El Dorado, Arkansas, September 6, 1956; admitted to bar, 1982, Oklahoma; 1983, U.S. District Court, Northern District of Oklahoma; 1993, U.S. Federal Court of Claims. *Education:* University of Tulsa (B.S., 1978; J.D., 1982). ***PRACTICE AREAS:*** Real Estate Law; Commercial Law and Litigation; Oil and Gas Law. ***Email:*** rlreynolds@ellerdetrich.com

JAMES C. HODGES, born Sapulpa, Oklahoma, August 12, 1950; admitted to bar, 1975, Oklahoma; U.S. District Court, Northern, Eastern and Western Districts of Oklahoma; U.S. Court of Appeals, Tenth Circuit and U.S. Supreme Court. *Education:* College of Wooster (B.A., 1972); Southern Methodist University (J.D., 1975). ***PRACTICE AREAS:*** Civil Litigation; Commercial Transactions; Oil and Gas Law. ***Email:*** jhodges@ellerdetrich.com

SHANANN PINKHAM PASSLEY, born Eunice, New Mexico, September 28, 1949; admitted to bar, 1990, Oklahoma; U.S. District Court, Northern, Western and Eastern Districts of Oklahoma; U.S. Court of Appeals, Tenth Circuit; U.S. Supreme Court. *Education:* Ft. Hays State University (B.A., cum laude, 1971); University of Tulsa (J.D., 1990). ***LANGUAGES:*** Spanish. ***PRACTICE AREAS:*** Litigation; Employment Law; Insurance Law; Commercial Law. ***Email:*** spassley@ellerdetrich.com

PAUL A. KANE, born Tulsa, Oklahoma, April 5, 1966; admitted to bar, 1992, Oklahoma; U.S. District Court, Northern, Eastern and Western Districts of Oklahoma and U.S. Court of Federal Claims. *Education:* University of Notre Dame (B.A., 1989); University of Oklahoma (J.D., 1992). ***PRACTICE AREAS:*** Real Estate; Construction; Litigation. ***Email:*** pkane@ellerdetrich.com

ASSOCIATE

REBECCA W. HUNTER, born McAlester, Oklahoma, September 10, 1976; admitted to bar, 2002, Oklahoma, U.S. District Court, Northern, Eastern and Western Districts of Oklahoma. *Education:* University of Tulsa (B.S.B.A., 1999); University of Oklahoma (J.D., 2002). ***PRACTICE AREAS:*** Civil Practice. ***Email:*** rhunter@ellerdetrich.com

OF COUNSEL

JOHN H. LIEBER, born Ardmore, Oklahoma, November 19, 1953; admitted to bar, 1978, Oklahoma; U.S. District Court, Eastern, Northern and Western Districts of Oklahoma; U.S. Court of Appeals, Tenth Circuit; U.S. Supreme Court. *Education:* University of Tulsa (B.S., with honors, 1975; J.D., with honors, 1978). Private Mediator and Arbitrator, Oklahoma Mediation/Arbitration Service. *Member:* Oklahoma Bar Association. ***PRACTICE AREAS:*** Litigation; Tort and Insurance Law; Municipal Law; Employment Law; Civil Rights Law. ***Email:*** jlieber@ellerdetrich.com

PHILIP R. FEIST, born Coronado, California, October 25, 1950; admitted to bar, 1992, Oklahoma and California; U.S. District Court, Northern District of Oklahoma; U.S. District Court, Southern District of California; 1994, U.S. Tax Court; 1995, Kansas; 1996, Virgin Islands. *Education:* University of California, Davis (A.B., 1971); Dallas Theological

(This Listing Continued)

Seminary (Th.M., 1975); University of San Diego (J.D., 1991). *Member:* Oklahoma, Kansas and Virgin Islands Bar Associations; State Bar of California. (Certified Specialist, Estate Planning, Trust and Probate Law, The State Bar of California Board of Legal Specialization). ***PRACTICE AREAS:*** Estate Planning; International Estate Planning; Wealth Preservation; International Trusts; Wills; Trust Litigation. ***Email:*** pfeist@ellerdetrich.com

JERRY M. SNIDER, born Tulsa, Oklahoma, August 27, 1951; admitted to bar, 1976, Oklahoma and U.S. District Court, Northern and Eastern Districts of Oklahoma and U.S. Court of Appeals, 10th Circuit. *Education:* University of Oklahoma (B.S., 1972); University of Tulsa (J.D., 1975). ***PRACTICE AREAS:*** Real Estate; Title Insurance; Business Organization. ***Email:*** jsnider@ellerdetrich.com

All attorneys in firm are members of Tulsa County, Oklahoma and American Bar Associations.

REPRESENTATIVE CLIENTS: Federal National Mortgage Association; ABN Amro Mortgage; The Williams Companies; Trammell Crow Company; Senior Star Management Company; Gemini Properties; P & H Properties, L.L.C.; Jerry Gordon Development, Inc.; H W Allen Co.; Bank One, N.A.; Bank South; Arvest Bank; BancFirst; The F & M Bank & Trust Company; MidFirst Bank; Edward D. Jones & Co.; Cendant Mobility Services Corp.; Sabre Inc.; Mill Creek Lumber and Supply Co.; Home Builders Association of Greater Tulsa, Inc.; Spears World Travel, Inc.; Magellan Pipeline Company; Premium Beers of Oklahoma, L.L.C.; North American Galvanizing Company; Mercury Midstream, L.L.C.;Independent Tubular Corporation; Cameron Glass, Inc.; Reinforcing Services, Inc.; United Engines, L.L.C.; Western Technologies, Inc.; Silicone Specialties, Inc.; Kansas City Life Insurance Company; Gulf Insurance Group; Cumis Insurance Society; Municipal Assurance Group; Harbor Insurance Company; Oklahoma Attorneys Mutual Insurance Company; Statewide General Agency, Inc.
APPROVED ATTORNEYS FOR: First American Title Insurance Co.

JULIE A. EVANS, P.C.

Established in 1991

624 SOUTH DENVER, SUITE 202
TULSA, OKLAHOMA 74119
Telephone: 918-592-5566
Fax: 918-582-5022
Email: Julie@EvansEstateLaw.com
URL: http://www.lawyers.com/julieaevans

Practice includes Wills and Probate, Trust and Estates, Guardianship, Estate Litigation and Estate Planning.

JULIE A. EVANS, born Stillwater, Oklahoma; admitted to bar, 1989, Oklahoma. *Education:* Oklahoma State University (B.S., 1983); Central State University (M.B.A., 1986); University of Tulsa (J.D., 1989). *Member:* Tulsa County (Co-Chair, 2004-2005; Member, Probate and Elder Law Section; Chair, 2001 and 2004, Law School/Mentoring Committee; Director, 2000-2002; Library Trustee, 1998-1999), Oklahoma (Chair, 2001, Estate Planning, Probate and Trust Section; Member, 1996—, Probate Code Committee; Vice Chair, 2003-2005, Law Schools Committee) and American (Member, Real Property, Probate and Trust Law Section) Bar Associations; Tulsa Title and Probate Lawyers Association (President, 2002; Vice President, 2001; Secretary, 2000); Tulsa Estate Planning Forum (Director, 1996-1999); University of Tulsa College of Law Alumni Association (President, 1999-2000). ***PRACTICE AREAS:*** Wills; Probate; Guardianship; Estate Planning. ***Email:*** Julie@EvansEstateLaw.com

BENJAMIN C. FAULKNER

1111 PARK CENTRE BUILDING
525 SOUTH MAIN STREET
TULSA, OKLAHOMA 74103
Telephone: 918-582-8801
FAX: 918-582-8803
Email: benfaulkner@lawyers.com
URL: http://www.bcfaulkner.com

General Civil Practice, Business Litigation, Civil Litigation, Probate Litigation, Contested Trusts and Estates, Trust Litigation, Family Law, Divorce, Child Custody, Adoption Law, Private Adoptions, Indian Child Welfare Act.

FIRM PROFILE: Benjamin C. Faulkner is listed in The Bar Register of Preeminent Lawyers.

BENJAMIN C. FAULKNER, born Baker, Montana, November 21, 1946; admitted to bar, 1976, Oklahoma; 1977, U.S. District Court, Northern and Eastern Districts of Oklahoma; 1978, U.S. Court of Appeals, Tenth Circuit; 1990, U.S. Claims Court. *Education:* University of Oklahoma (B.A., 1972; J.D., 1976). Phi Delta Phi. *Member:* Tulsa County, Oklahoma and American (Member, Litigation Section) Bar Associations; American Inns of Court, Johnson-Sontag Chapter. ***REPORTED CASES:*** The Matter of Baby Boy W 1999 OK 74. ***PRACTICE AREAS:*** Civil Practice; Civil Litigation in State and Federal Courts; Probate Litigation; Contested Trusts and Estates; Adoption Law; Family Law.

FELDMAN, FRANDEN, WOODARD, FARRIS & BOUDREAUX

Established in 1953

1000 PARK CENTRE
525 SOUTH MAIN
TULSA, OKLAHOMA 74103-4514
Telephone: 918-583-7129
Telecopier: 918-584-3814
Email: feldman@tulsalawyer.com
URL: http://www.tulsalawyer.com

General Civil Practice. Trials. Corporation, Insurance, Negligence, Products Liability, Toxic Torts, Environmental Law, Securities, Oil and Gas, Real Estate, Probate, Fidelity and Surety, Aviation, School Law, Professional Liability. Estate Planning, Business, Bankruptcy and Medical Malpractice Law, Securities Fraud, Employment Law, White Collar Criminal Defense.

(This Listing Continued)

FIRM PROFILE: In 1953 W. E. Green and Raymond Feldman formed a law partnership and the firm's practice has continued to grow and diversify. Although still engaged primarily in the defense of businesses and professionals, through its emphasis on litigation, the firm has added other specialties such as oil and gas, real estate and toxic tort law. The firm's litigation practice encompasses trials and administrative hearings throughout the state in all federal trial and appellate courts. In addition to first party and third party litigation matters, the firm has an active corporate and real estate practice. Its members and associates offer a wide range of legal services. All partners and associates participate annually in continuing legal education seminars, professional association activities and civic affairs. This firm is listed in the Bar Register of Preeminent Lawyers.

MEMBERS OF FIRM

W. E. GREEN (1889-1977)

WILLIAM S. HALL (1930-1991)

ROBERT A. FRANDEN, born Chicago, Illinois, June 30, 1939; admitted to bar, 1964, Oklahoma and U.S. District Court, Northern, Eastern and Western Districts of Oklahoma; U.S. Court of Appeals, Tenth Circuit; U.S. Supreme Court. *Education:* University of Oklahoma (B.A., 1961; LL.B., 1964); University of Houston (Diploma, International Private Investment Law, 1970). Phi Alpha Delta. Commissioner of Streets and Public Property, City of Tulsa, 1976-1978. Chairman, Tulsa Performing Arts Center Trust Authority, 1976-1978. Vice-Chairman, Tulsa Metropolitan Transit Authority and Tulsa Energy Resource Recovery Authority, 1976-1978. Visiting Fellow, University of Tulsa, 1985—. Adjunct Professor, Business Law, University of Tulsa, 1986-1987. Chair, 2001-2002 and Chair Emeritus, 2002-2004, America Law Firm Association. *Member:* Tulsa County, Oklahoma and American Bar Associations. ***LANGUAGES:*** Spanish. ***PRACTICE AREAS:*** Business Law; Real Estate Law; Corporate Law; Civil Trial Law. ***Email:*** rfranden@tulsalawyer.com

JOHN R. WOODARD, III, born Tulsa, Oklahoma, September 23, 1943; admitted to bar, 1968, Oklahoma; 1971, U.S. District Court, Northern District of Oklahoma, U.S. Supreme Court, U.S. Court of Military Appeals and U.S. District Court, Eastern District of Oklahoma; 1974, U.S. Court of Appeals, Tenth Circuit; 1984, U.S. District Court, Western District of Oklahoma; 1990, U.S. District Court, Western District of Texas. *Education:* University of Tulsa (B.A., 1965; J.D., 1967). Phi Alpha Delta. Author: "Punitive Damages For Bad Faith Breach of An Insurance Contract: It's Unconstitutional," 54 OBJ 1125, 1983. Advocate, American Board of Trial Advocates. Master Emeritus, Council Oak Chapter, American Inns of Court. *Member:* Tulsa County (Outstanding Young Lawyer, 1975; Member: Continuing Legal Education Committee and Budget Committee, 1976-1976; Executive Committee, 1976-1976; Treasurer, 1976-1976; Outstanding Senior Lawyer, 2002), Oklahoma (Chairman, Insurance Section, 1983) and American (Member, Sections on: Tort and Insurance Practice; Litigation; Economics of Law Practice Law) Bar Associations; Oklahoma Association of Defense Counsel (President, 1983); Federation of Defense and Corporate Counsel (President, 1997-1998); Defense Research Institute (Director, 1994-2000); International Association of Defense Counsel. [Captain, Judge Advocate, U.S. Marine Corps, 1968-1971]. ***PRACTICE AREAS:*** Civil Trial Law; Insurance Law; Professional Liability Law; Products Liability Law; Transportation Law. ***Email:*** jwoodard@tulsalawyer.com

JOSEPH R. FARRIS, born Batesville, Arkansas, December 29, 1947; admitted to bar, 1976, Oklahoma and U.S. District Court, Northern District of Oklahoma; 1977, U.S. Court of Appeals, Tenth Circuit; 1980, U.S. Court of Appeals for the D.C. Circuit; 1983, U.S. Court of Appeals, Ninth Circuit. *Education:* University of Missouri (A.B., 1969); University of Tulsa (J.D., with honors, 1976). Phi Delta Phi (Magister, 1974-1975). Managing Editor, Tulsa Law Journal, 1975-1976. Member, Order of the Curule Chair. Recipient, American Jurisprudence Award. Author, "Recent Development, U.S. v. Toscanino," 10 Tulsa Law Journal 379, 1975. Fellow, American College of Trial Lawyers. Member, W. Lee Johnson Chapter, American Inns of Court. *Member:* Tulsa County, Oklahoma and American Bar Associations (Member, Section on Litigation); Oklahoma Association of Defense Counsel; Association of Defense Trial Attorneys. [1st Lt., U.S. Army, Military Intelligence, 1969-1973]. ***PRACTICE AREAS:*** Civil Trial Law; Insurance Law; Professional Liability Law; Transportation Law; Products Liability. ***Email:*** jfarris@tulsalawyer.com

PAUL T. BOUDREAUX, born Oklahoma City, Oklahoma, August 20, 1955; admitted to bar, 1980, Oklahoma; 1981, U.S. District Court, Eastern, Western and Northern Districts of Oklahoma; 1988, U.S. Court of Appeals, Tenth Circuit and U.S. Supreme Court. *Education:* St. Gregory's College (A.A., 1975); Oklahoma City University (B.A., magna cum laude, 1977); University of Oklahoma (J.D., 1980); Insurance Counsel Trial Academy, 1982. Phi Theta Kappa; Phi Delta Phi; Blue Key. Faculty Member, College of Advocacy, Norman, Oklahoma, 1992, 1993 and 1994. *Member:* Tulsa County, Oklahoma and American Bar Associations; The Association of Trial Lawyers of America; Defense Research Institute (Member, Steering Committee, 2001; State Liaison, Life, Health and Disability, 2002); International Association of Defense Counsel; Oklahoma Association of Defense Counsel (Vice President, 1984-1985, 1985-1986, 1986-1987, 1987-1988, Treasurer, 1988-1989); Tulsa Claim Association; American Inns of Court. ***PRACTICE AREAS:*** Civil Litigation; Business Litigation; Insurance; Insurance Bad Faith; Negligence; Premises Liability; Products Liability; Fire Loss; Personal Injury; Medical Malpractice; Employment Law. ***Email:*** pboudreaux@tulsalawyer.com

PAULA J. QUILLIN, born Okmulgee, Oklahoma, April ll, 1956; admitted to bar, 1981, Texas; 1982, Oklahoma, U.S. District Court, Northern, Eastern and Western Districts of Oklahoma and U.S. Court of Appeals, Tenth Circuit. *Education:* Oklahoma State University (B.S., 1978); University of Texas (J.D., 1981); University of Oklahoma (M.A., 1999). Pi Sigma Alpha. Member, American Journal of Criminal Law, 1980-1981. Instructor: Contracts, Oil and Gas, Legal Research, Paralegal Program, University of Tulsa, 1992-1994. Member, Tulsa Area Human Resources Association. Member, Tulsa Equal Employment Opportunity Commission Association. *Member:* Tulsa County and Oklahoma (Member, Employment Law Section) Bar Associations; State Bar of Texas; Defense Research Institute; International Association of Defense Counsel. ***PRACTICE AREAS:*** Appellate Practice; Civil Practice; Class Actions; Employee Benefits; General Practice; Insurance Defense; Labor and Employment Law; Personal Injury; Products Liability; Professional Liability. ***Email:*** pquillin@tulsalawyer.com

(This Listing Continued)

FELDMAN, FRANDEN, WOODARD, FARRIS & BOUDREAUX, Tulsa—Continued

ASSOCIATES

THAYLA PAINTER BOHN, born Fayetteville, Arkansas, October 14, 1972; admitted to bar, 1998, Oklahoma; 1999 Arkansas, U.S. District Court, Northern, Eastern and Western Districts of Oklahoma and U.S. Court of Appeals, Tenth Circuit. *Education:* University of Tulsa (B.A., with honors, Organizational Communications); University of Arkansas (J.D., with honors, 1998). Member, Arkansas Law Review, 1996-1998. *Member:* Tulsa County, Oklahoma, Arkansas and American Bar Associations; Defense Research Institute; Women's Law Student Association. ***REPORTED CASES:*** Hartley v. Williamson, 2001 OK CIV APP 6, 18 P.3d 355 (published by order of Oklahoma Supreme Court); Perigo v. Wiseman, 2000 OK 67, 11 P.3d 217; Hathcock v. Barnes, 2001 OK CIV APP 69, 25 P.3d 295; Allison v. UNUM Life Ins. Co of America 381 F.3d 1015 (10th Cir. 2004). ***PRACTICE AREAS:*** Civil Litigation; Insurance Law; Employment Law; Appellate Practice. ***Email:*** tpbohn@tulsalawyer.com

PAUL F. PRATHER, born Oklahoma City, Oklahoma, November 9, 1964; admitted to bar, 1990, Oklahoma and U.S. District Court, Northern District of Oklahoma; 1991, U.S. District Court, Eastern District of Oklahoma; 1994, U.S. Court of Appeals, Tenth Circuit. *Education:* Tulane University (B.A., 1987); University of Oklahoma (J.D., 1990). Phi Delta Phi. *Member:* Tulsa County Bar Association; Oklahoma Bar Association; American Bar Association. ***REPORTED CASES:*** Rucks v. Boergermann, 57 F.3d 978 (10th Cir. 1995). ***PRACTICE AREAS:*** Trial Practice; Insurance; Products Liability; Municipal Law; Telecommunications Law; Zoning Law. ***Email:*** pprather@tulsalawyer.com

F. JASON GOODNIGHT, born Crossett, Arkansas, December 8, 1975; admitted to bar, 2000, Oklahoma and U.S. District Court, Northern, Eastern and Western Districts of Oklahoma. *Education:* University of Arkansas (B.A., 1998; J.D., with honors, 2001). *Member:* Tulsa County, Oklahoma and American Bar Associations; Defense Research Institute. ***REPORTED CASES:*** Archer v. Kelly, 271 F.Supp.2d 1320 (N.D. Okla. June 19, 2003) (No. 03-CV-0283-EA (M); Whisenant v.First National Bank & Trust Co., 258 F.Supp.2d 1312, N.D.Okla, April 14, 2003. ***PRACTICE AREAS:*** Products Liability; Trucking Law; Insurance Bad Faith. ***Email:*** jgoodnight@tulsalawyer.com

CURTIS J. ROBERTS, born Liberal, Kansas, March 17, 1977; admitted to bar, 2003, Oklahoma. *Education:* University of Oklahoma (B.B.A., 1999); University of Tulsa (J.D., 2003). Phi Delta Phi. ***PRACTICE AREAS:*** Insurance Bad Faith; Trial Practice; Products Liability; Construction Law. ***Email:*** croberts@tulsalawyer.com

VICTOR R. WANDRES, born Tulsa, Oklahoma, March 5, 1974; admitted to bar, 2002, Oklahoma; 2003, U.S. District Court, Northern District of Oklahoma; 2004, U.S. District Court, Western and Eastern Districts of Oklahoma. *Education:* Tulane University (B.S., Escology, Evolution and Organismal Biology, 1996); University of Oklahoma (J.D., 2002). Recipient, Dolores K. Hanna Best Brief Award, Saul Lefkowitz Intellectual Property Moot Court Competition, 2002. Managing Editor and Co-Founder, Oklahoma Journal of Law and Technology, 2002. *Member:* Tulsa County, Oklahoma and American (Bar Associations; American Inns of Court; Defense Research Institute. ***PRACTICE AREAS:*** Trial Practice; Insurance; Products Liability; Intellectual Property Law; Copyrights; Trademarks.

JASEN R. CORNS, born Tulsa, Oklahoma, September 29, 1971; admitted to bar, 2004, Oklahoma; 2005, U.S. District Court, Northern and Eastern Districts of Oklahoma. *Education:* University of Nebraska at Omaha (B.A., 2001); University of Tulsa (J.D., with highest honors, 2004). Order of the Barristers. Member: ATLA Regional Trial Team; NTC Regional Trial Team; Criminal Justice National Trial Team. Recipient: International Academy of Trial Lawyers Student Advocacy Award, 2003, 2004; CALI Excellence for the Future Awards: Corporate Law, Administrative Law, Advanced Trial Practice. Notes and Comments Editor, Tulsa Law Review, 2002-2004. Author, "Pigskin Paydirt: The Thriving of College Football's Bowl Championship Series in the Face of Antitrust Law," 39 Tulsa L. Rev. 167. Judicial Intern, Dana L. Rasure, U.S. Bankruptcy Court, N.D. Okla. *Member:* Tulsa County, Oklahoma and American Bar Associations. ***PRACTICE AREAS:*** Business Litigation. ***Email:*** jcorns@tulsalawyer.com

OF COUNSEL

RAYMOND G. FELDMAN, born Tulsa, Oklahoma, January 10, 1922; admitted to bar, 1946, Oklahoma. *Education:* University of Tulsa and University of Oklahoma (B.S., 1942); University of Oklahoma and University of Chicago (J.D., 1945). *Member:* Tulsa County, Oklahoma and American Bar Associations. ***PRACTICE AREAS:*** Corporation Law; Oil and Gas Law; Real Estate Law. ***Email:*** rfeldman@tulsalawyer.com

REPRESENTATIVE CLIENTS: The Equitable Life Assurance Society of the United States; Browning-Ferris Industries, Inc.; Oklahoma Bar Professional Liability Insurance Co.; Aviation Underwriters, Inc.; Progressive Casualty Insurance Co.; Liberty Mutual Insurance Co.; ACE/USA; Schneider National Transportation; Arrow Trucking; Ford Motor Company; Eli Lilly & Co., Zurich Insurance; Stevens Transport; Allianz; Metropolitan Tulsa Transit Authority; AIG Companies; United Healthcare.

FELLERS, SNIDER, BLANKENSHIP, BAILEY & TIPPENS

A PROFESSIONAL CORPORATION

Established in 1964

THE KENNEDY BUILDING
321 SOUTH BOSTON, SUITE 800
TULSA, OKLAHOMA 74103-3318
Telephone: 918-599-0621
Fax: 918-583-9659
Email: fsbb&t@icnet.net
URL: http://www.fellerssnider.com

Oklahoma City, Oklahoma Office: Bank One Tower, 100 North Broadway, Suite, 1700. Telephone: 405-232-0621. Fax: 405-232-9659.

(This Listing Continued)

General Practice. Trial of all Cases in State and Federal Courts. Commercial, Corporate, Oil and Gas, Banking and Banking Regulation, Administrative, Probate, Estate Planning, Transportation, Bankruptcy, Securities, Insurance, Federal and State Taxation, Unfair Competition, Aircraft Title, Aircraft Finance and Leasing, Aircraft Sales, Real Property, Employment, Workers' Compensation, Intellectual Property, and Antitrust Law.

FIRM PROFILE: The law firm of Fellers, Snider, Blankenship, Bailey & Tippens was founded in Oklahoma City in 1963. In four decades, the Firm has grown in size, scope and reputation, attracting attorneys with a wide array of skills and experience. Our attorneys have held numerous leadership positions, including President of the American Bar Association, President of the Oklahoma Bar Association, President of the Oklahoma County Bar Association, President of the Oklahoma Bar Foundation, Professor of Law and Associate Dean of the University of Oklahoma College of Law, Professor of Law of the Oklahoma City University College of Law and others. Our common bond is our dedication to delivering the highest quality of legal service available. Fellers, Snider is listed in the Bar Register of Preeminent Lawyers.

ROY C. BREEDLOVE, born Kansas City, Kansas, October 16, 1952; admitted to bar, 1977, Oklahoma; 1981, U.S. Supreme Court and U.S. Court of Appeals, Tenth Circuit; 1995, U.S. Court of Appeals for the Federal Circuit. *Education:* Washburn University (B.A., magna cum laude, 1973; J.D., Deans Honors, 1977). Phi Kappa Phi. Member, Order of the Barristers. Member, National Moot Court Team; Master, Hudson Hall Wheaton American Inns of Court. Adjunct Settlement Judge, U.S. District Court for the Northern District of Oklahoma, 1995—. Member: Oklahoma Bar Association Long Range Planning Committee and Task Force on Specialization. ***PRACTICE AREAS:*** Intellectual Property Litigation; Business Litigation; Securities Litigation; Professional Liability Claims. ***Email:*** rbreedlove@fellerssnider.com

TODD A. NELSON, born Alva, Oklahoma, September 22, 1964; admitted to bar, 1992, Oklahoma; 1993, Kansas. *Education:* Kansas State University (B.S., 1987); University of Oklahoma (J.D., with honors, 1992). Phi Kappa Phi; Phi Delta Phi. Order of the Coif. Fellow, Oklahoma Bar Foundation. ***PRACTICE AREAS:*** Complex Civil Litigation; Business Law; Intellectual Property Litigation. ***Email:*** tnelson@fellerssnider.com

DENNIS D. BROWN, born Amarillo, Texas, November 26, 1957; admitted to bar, 1989, Oklahoma; 1990, U.S. District Court, Northern District of Oklahoma; 1995, U.S. District Court, Eastern District of Oklahoma; registered to practice before U.S. Patent and Trademark Office. *Education:* Texas A&M University (B.S.Ch.E., magna cum laude, 1980); Oklahoma State University (M.B.A., 1985); University of Tulsa (J.D., with honors, 1989). Order of the Curule Chair. Member, Tulsa Energy Law Journal, 1988-1989. Author: "Changes In U.S. Patent Law Resulting From The Uruguay Round Agreements Act," The Oklahoma Bar Journal, Vol. 66, No. 30, 8/5/95; "Software And Other Computer-Implemented Inventions: The Federal Circuit Strengthens Patentability," The Oklahoma Bar Journal, Vol. 66, No. 37, 10/21/95. *Member:* Oklahoma Bar Association (Member, Section on Patent, Trademark and Copyright Law). ***PRACTICE AREAS:*** Patents; Trademarks; Copyrights; Intellectual Property Licensing; Intellectual Property Litigation. ***Email:*** dbrown@fellerssnider.com

R. ALAN WEEKS, born Chitose, Japan, October 15, 1964; admitted to bar, 1990, Texas; 1994, Oklahoma; registered to practice before U.S. Patent and Trademark Office. *Education:* Texas A&M University (B.S., Biomedical Science, 1987); University of Texas at Austin (J.D., with honors, 1990). Adjunct Professor, University of Tulsa College of Law, 1994—. *Member:* Oklahoma Bar Association; State Bar of Texas. ***PRACTICE AREAS:*** Intellectual Property. ***Email:*** aweeks@fellerssnider.com

R. DANIEL SCROGGINS, born Houston, Texas, July 11, 1966; admitted to bar, 1993, Oklahoma; 1999, Texas. *Education:* University of North Texas (B.B.A., 1988); University of Tulsa (J.D., 1993). *Member:* Oklahoma Bar Association (Member, Board of Directors, Workers' Compensation Section, 1998—); Oklahoma Association of Defense Counsel; Defense Research Institute. ***PRACTICE AREAS:*** Workers' Compensation; Civil Trial Law. ***Email:*** dscroggins@fellerssnider.com

TERRY L. WATT, born Tulsa, Oklahoma, November 23, 1952; admitted to bar, 1995, Oklahoma and U.S. District Court, Northern District of Oklahoma; registered to practice before U.S. Patent and Trademark Office. *Education:* University of Tulsa (B.A., Mathematics, 1975); Princeton University (M.A., Statistics, 1977); University of Tulsa (Ph.D., Geophysics, 1984; M.B.A., Finance, 1988; J.D., 1995). Order of the Curule Chair. Solicitor/Research Editor for Articles, Tulsa University Law Review, 1994-1995; Staff, 1993-1994). Recipient, American Jurisprudence Awards in Constitutional Law, Legal Writing and Conflict of Laws. Adjunct Professor: University of Tulsa College of Arts & Sciences, 1983-1985, 1988-1989, 1990; College of Law, University of Tulsa, 1996, 1998—. Research Geophysicist: Cities Service Oil Company, Tulsa, Oklahoma, 1977-1984; Amerada Hess Oil Company, Tulsa, Oklahoma, 1984-1992. *Member:* American Intellectual Property Law Association; American Statistical Association. ***PRACTICE AREAS:*** Intellectual Property; Patents; Computer and Software Law. ***Email:*** tlwatt@fellerssnider.com

SCOTT R. ZINGERMAN, born Suffern, New York, March 8, 1963; admitted to bar, 1990, Oklahoma and U.S. District Court, Northern District of Oklahoma; 1995, U.S. Court of Appeals for the Federal Circuit; registered to practice before U.S. Patent and Trademark Office. *Education:* Oral Roberts University (B.S. Chem., 1987); University of Tulsa (J.D., 1990). Phi Delta Phi. Member, American Inns of Court, 1995-1996. *Member:* Tulsa County Bar Association; American Intellectual Property Law Association. ***PRACTICE AREAS:*** Intellectual Property. ***Email:*** szingerman@fellerssnider.com

CURTIS M. LONG, born Oklahoma City, Oklahoma, November 8, 1948; admitted to bar, 1974, Oklahoma. *Education:* University of Oklahoma (B.A., 1971; J.D., 1974). Phi Delta Phi. Author: "Corporate Political Contributions: What Activities are Prohibited in Oklahoma?" 59 Okla. B.J. 2039, 1988; "The New Ethics Commission Rules: They're Not Just for Politicians." 65 Okla. B.J. 3113, 1994. Chair: Mineral Law Section, Tulsa County Bar Association, 1990; Mineral Law Section, Oklahoma Bar Association, 1999. ***PRACTICE AREAS:*** Energy; Trial Practice; Telecommunications. ***Email:*** clong@fellerssnider.com

STEVEN J. ADAMS, born Fort Worth, Texas, May 19, 1953; admitted to bar, 1979, Oklahoma; 1980, U.S. District Court, Northern, Eastern and Western Districts of Oklahoma. *Education:* Oklahoma State University (B.S., 1976); University of Tulsa (J.D., 1979).

(This Listing Continued)

Order of Barristers. Named Outstanding District Judge, State of Oklahoma, 1992. Adjunct Professor of Law, University of Tulsa College of Law, 1990—. District Judge, State of Oklahoma, 1987-1993. Municipal Judge, City of Catoosa, 1981-1986. Member: Oklahoma Bar Foundation Board of Trustees, 1990-1991; Oklahoma Supreme Courts Committee on Civil Jury Instructions, 1991—. ***PRACTICE AREAS:*** Trial Practice; Energy Law; Environmental Law. ***Email:*** sadams@fellerssnider.com

JOHN D. RUSSELL, born Enid, Oklahoma, October 4, 1963; admitted to bar, 1988, Oklahoma; 1989, District of Columbia; U.S. District Court, District of Columbia, U.S. District Court, Northern and Western Districts of Oklahoma, U.S. Court of Appeals, Tenth and District of Columbia Circuits and U.S. Tax Court. *Education:* Oklahoma State University (B.S., with honors, 1985); University of Oklahoma (J.D., with distinction, 1988). Trial Attorney, Tax Division, United States Department of Justice, 1991-1993. Assistant U.S. Attorney, Northern District of Oklahoma, 1995-2002. *Member:* Tulsa County and American Bar Associations; American Inns of Court (Council Oak Chapter; Barrister). ***PRACTICE AREAS:*** Litigation; White Collar Criminal Defense; Telecommunications; Insurance. ***Email:*** jrussell@fellerssnider.com

JAMES F. LEA, born Fayetteville, Arkansas, August 12, 1967; admitted to bar, 1994, Oklahoma; registered to practice before U.S. Patent and Trademark Office. *Education:* University of Oklahoma (B.S., 1990; J.D., 1994). ***PRACTICE AREAS:*** Intellectual Property. ***Email:*** jlea@fellerssnider.com

TRACY A. POOLE, born Heilbronn, Germany, September 21, 1967; admitted to bar, 1993, Texas; U.S. District Court, Northern District of Texas, U.S. Court of Appeals, Fifth Circuit, U.S. District Court, Western and Northern Districts of Oklahoma and U.S. Court of Appeals, Tenth Circuit; 1996, Oklahoma. *Education:* Oklahoma State University (B.S., 1989); University of Oklahoma (J.D., with distinction, 1993). Phi Delta Phi. Recipient, American Jurisprudence Award in Bankruptcy. Shareholder, Fellers, Snider, Blankenship, Bailey & Tippens, P.C., Oklahoma City, Oklahoma, 1996-1999. Senior Attorney, The Williams Companies Inc., 1999-2002. Member: Board of Advocates, 1989-1990; American Inns of Court, 1996-1999. *Member:* Oklahoma and American Bar Associations; State Bar of Texas. ***PRACTICE AREAS:*** Commercial Transactions; Corporate Law; Mergers and Acquisitions; Structured Energy Commodity and Derivative Transactions; Gas and Power Marketing; Entity Formation; Project Finance; Commercial Litigation. ***Email:*** tpoole@fellerssnider.com

CHARLES R. WILLING, born Houston, Texas, September 22, 1962; admitted to bar, 1993, Oklahoma and U.S. District Court, Western District of Oklahoma; 1994, U.S. Court of Appeals, Tenth Circuit; 2002, U.S. District Court, Northern District of Oklahoma. *Education:* University of Oklahoma (B.S.P.E., 1985); Oklahoma City University (J.D., cum laude, 1993). Tau Beta Pi; Pi Epsilon Tau; Phi Delta Phi. Member, Oklahoma City University Law Review, 1991-1993. Member, 1998-2002, Social Chair, 2001-2002 and Outstanding Associate, 2000-2001, Ruth Bader Ginsburg American Inns of Court. Member, Society of Petroleum Engineers, 1983—. Senior Administrative Law Judge, Oklahoma Corporation Commission, 1997-2002. ***PRACTICE AREAS:*** Environmental Litigation; Oil and Gas; Commercial Litigation; Energy. ***Email:*** cwilling@fellerssnider.com

---

TRAVIS A. FULKERSON, born Oklahoma City, Oklahoma, August 7, 1975; admitted to bar, 2000, Oklahoma and U.S. District Court, Western District of Oklahoma. *Education:* University of Oklahoma (B.A., 1997; J.D., 2000). ***PRACTICE AREAS:*** Workers' Compensation; Insurance Defense. ***Email:*** tfulkerson@fellerssnider.com

ROBERT TODD WADDELL, born Norman, Oklahoma, January 18, 1963; admitted to bar, 1998, Oklahoma and U.S. District Court, Eastern, Western and Northern Districts of Oklahoma. *Education:* University of Oklahoma (B.S., 1986; M.S., 1996); Oklahoma City University (J.D., magna cum laude, 1997). ***PRACTICE AREAS:*** Environmental Law. ***Email:*** twaddell@fellerssnider.com

DEBORAH V. MELIKIAN, born Newton, Massachusetts, July 22, 1975; admitted to bar, 2004, Oklahoma. *Education:* University of Tulsa (B.A., 1999; J.D., 2004). Recipient, International Academy of Trial Lawyers Student Advocacy Award, 2003. Member: Competitive Trial Practice; Board of Advocates. *Member:* Tulsa County and Oklahoma Bar Associations; Association of Trial Lawyers of America (ATLA). ***LANGUAGES:*** Greek and French. ***PRACTICE AREAS:*** Commercial Litigation. ***Email:*** dmelikian@fellerssnider.com

OF COUNSEL

JACK E. PHILLIPS, born Durham, North Carolina, August 18, 1933; admitted to bar, 1961, Oklahoma; registered to practice before U.S. Patent and Trademark Office. *Education:* University of North Carolina at Chapel Hill (A.B., 1955); George Washington University (J.D., 1961). President, Patent, Trademark and Copyright Section, Oklahoma Bar Association, 2000. *Member:* Washington County Bar Association (Past President). ***PRACTICE AREAS:*** Patents; Trademarks; Copyrights. ***Email:*** jephill@fellerssnider.com

LON FOSTER, III, born Los Angeles, California, 1942; admitted to bar, 1968, California; 1970, Oklahoma; 1982, Texas. *Education:* University of Oklahoma (B.A., with distinction, 1964); University of Michigan (J.D., 1967). Phi Beta Kappa. Listed in Best Lawyers in America (Corporate Law). *Member:* State Bar of California; Oklahoma Bar Association; State Bar of Texas. ***PRACTICE AREAS:*** Corporate Law; Business Law; Mergers and Acquisitions; Entrepreneurial Business Law; Corporate Governance. ***Email:*** lfoster@fellerssnider.com

FRED H. HOLMES, born Tulsa, Oklahoma, April 6, 1957; admitted to bar, 1996, Oklahoma. *Education:* University of Oklahoma (B.S.E.E., 1979); University of Tulsa (J.D., 1995). ***PRACTICE AREAS:*** Intellectual Property. ***Email:*** fholmes@fellerssnider.com

All Attorneys are Members of the Tulsa County, Oklahoma and American Bar Associations.

REPRESENTATIVE CLIENTS: Aetna Life Insurance Co.; Adams Investment Company, Inc.; A.G. Edwards & Sons, Inc.; American Agency Systems; American Express Co.; Amoco Corporation; Archon Group L.P.; A.S.C. Incorporated; ATÆ Corp.; BancFirst; Bank One; Bank of America, N.A.; Bayliner Marine Corporation; BellSouth Communication Systems, Inc.; Bogo Energy Corp; BP America, Inc.; Brunswick Corporation; CenterPoint Energy Arkla, a division of CenterPoint Resources Group; Century Martial Arts Supply Inc.; Charter Com-

(This Listing Continued)

munications Corporation; Chevron U.S.A., Inc.; Chrysler Financial Corp.; Chubb Group Insurance; Cingular Wireless, LLC; City of Tulsa-Rogers County Port Authority; Connecticut General Life Insurance Co.; Conoco Inc.; Continental Resources, Inc.; Corken, Inc.; Cunningham Lindsey Claims Management; Dillon, Read & Co., Inc.; Doug Carson & Associates, Inc.; Ellsworth Motor Freight Lines, Inc.; Enogex Inc.; Exxon Mobil Corporation; Farmers Insurance; Farmland Industries; Filtrex, Inc.; Fleet National Bank; Follett Corporation; Frank's Tong Service, Inc.; Gallagher Bassett Claims Services; GatesMcDonald; General Electric Capital Corp.; Guaranty Bank and Trust Co.; Halliburton Co.; Harold Simpson, Inc.; Hertz Corp.; Hormel Foods Corporation; IBC Securities Corp.; Igloo Corporation; International Bank of Commerce; Jennie-O Turkey Store, Inc.; Johnson Controls World Services, Inc.; Kawasaki Motors Corp. USA; Life Insurance Company of North America; Kerr-McGee Corp.; LG&E Energy Marketing Inc.; Little Giant Pump Company; Magellan Midstream Partners, L.P.; Marathon Oil Co.; McKinley Properties, Inc.; Mercedes-Benz Credit Corporation; MetalFab, Inc.; Mosher-Adams Inc.; Motion Picture Association of America; Murphy Farms, Inc.; Northstar Presidio Management Companies, LLC; Oklahoma City Water Utilities Trust; Oklahoma Gas & Electric Corp.; Oklahoma State University; Outboard Marine Corporation; Panhandle Royalty Company; Phelps Dodge; Professional Cattle Consultants; Progress Energy, Inc.; Raptor Properties; Republic Insurance Group; Ritchie Capital Management, LLC; Richie Capital Management; RLI Insurance; Rupture Pin Technology, Inc.; Seagate Technology LLC; Service Corporation Intl.; Sharp Personnel; Sonic Corp.; Sonic Industries, Inc.; Sonic Restaurants, Inc.; Southwest Risk Management; Southwestern Bell Communications Services, Inc.; Southwestern Bell Telephone, L.P.; Stars Restaurants Corp.; Sykes Enterprises, Inc.; Taylor Valve Technology, Inc.; Tierra Vista; Torchmark Development Corp.; Tyson Foods, Inc.; United Parcel Service; UroCor, Inc.; USAA; USLife Corp.; VIP Foods, Inc.; Volvo Commercial Finance LLC The Americas; Wal-Mart Corporation; Wexford Capital, LLC; Wexford Management, LLC; The Williams Companies; Williams Power Company, Inc.; WilTel Communications Group, Inc.;Yamaha Motor Corporation USA; Zebco Corporation; ZEECO, Inc.

(For biographical data on other personnel, see Professional Biographies at Oklahoma City, Oklahoma)

FENTON, FENTON, SMITH, RENEAU & MOON

TULSA, OKLAHOMA

(See Oklahoma City)

General Civil Practice. Casualty, Surety and Insurance Law, Workers Compensation, Employers Liability, Medical and Hospital Malpractice, Products Liability, Toxic Tort and Environmental Law, School Law, Real Property, Title Examination, Title Insurance, Probate, Mortgage Foreclosure, Corporate, Commercial, Zoning, Planning and Subdivision, Real Estate Development, Municipal Law. Trials in all State and Federal Courts.

FISHER & FISHER

Established in 2004

8177 SOUTH HARVARD AVENUE, #333
TULSA, OKLAHOMA 74137
Telephone: 918-296-9898
Fax: 918-296-9880
Email: tfisheresq@sbcglobal.net
URL: http://www.tulsaattorneyslaw.com

Commercial Law, Commercial Collections, Litigation, Criminal Defense, General Practice, Workers Compensation, Products Liability, Insurance Law, Professional Liability Law, Appellate Practice, Medical Malpractice.

FIRM PROFILE: Civil Trial Practice in all State and Federal Courts. Commercial and Consumer Collections, Commercial Litigation, Professional Liability Litigation, Creditors' Rights and FDCPA Litigation, Bankruptcy Litigation, Legal Malpractice Law.

PARTNERS OF FIRM

TIMOTHY A. FISHER, admitted to bar, 1994, Oklahoma and U.S. District Court, Northern District of Oklahoma; 1995, U.S. District Court, Eastern District of Oklahoma; 2000, U.S. District Court, Western District of Oklahoma. *Education:* Richmond College, London, England; Gonzaga University; University of Tulsa (B.A., 1991; J.D., 1994). *Member:* Tulsa County and Oklahoma Bar Associations. Fellow, Oklahoma Bar Foundation. ***PRACTICE AREAS:*** Collections; Commercial Collections; Consumer Collections; Commercial Litigation; Creditors Rights; Bankruptcy Litigation; Post Judgment Collections; Professional Collections; Retail Collections; Secured Collections; Unsecured Collections; Creditor Bankruptcy; Creditors Rights in Bankruptcy; Fair Debt Collection Practices Act; Unsecured Creditors Rights; Secured Creditors Rights; Driving While Intoxicated. ***Email:*** tfisheresq@sbcglobal.net

KRISTIN BLUE FISHER, born Houston, Texas, April 27, 1969; admitted to bar, 1994, Oklahoma, U.S. District Court, Northern, Eastern and Western Districts of Oklahoma and U.S. Court of Appeals, Tenth Circuit. *Education:* Northwestern University; University of Tulsa (B.A., 1991; J.D., 1994). Recipient, American Jurisprudence Awards for Trial Practice and Legal Writing and Research. Tulsa County District Attorneys Office, Feldman, Franden, Woodward, Farris & Boudreaux. *Member:* Tulsa County (Member, Professional Responsibility Committee), Oklahoma and American Bar Associations; Defense Research Institute; Oklahoma Association of Defense Counsel (Member, Appellate Practice Section). ***REPORTED CASES:*** Nicholas v. Morgan, 2002 OK 88, 58 P.3d 775; Myers v. Weson Construction, Inc., 2002 OK CIV APP 116, 59 P.3d 1277; Woodral v. TEC, 2002 Westlaw 31236281; Wilkins v. Atlantic Richfield Co., 2002 OK CIV APP 76, 51 P.3d 595; Campbell v. Hunt JB Transport, 2002 OK CIV APP 33, 43 P.3d 421; Leach v. Hamilton Trucking, 2002 OK CIV APP 11, 39 P.3d 824; Weekly v. AAON, 2001 OK CIV APP 148, 38 P.3d 924; Emery v. Wal-Mart, 2000 OK CIV APP 4, 2 P.3d 898; Eastern State Hospital v. Swinehart, 2000 OK CIV APP 14, 996 P.2d 479; Richardson v. Bartlett Collins, Co., 1999 OK CIV APP 105, 990 P.2d 305; Mapp v. Stand-By Personnel, 1999 OK CIV APP 87, 988 P.2d 355; Moss v. Affiliated Food Stores, Inc., 1999 OK CIV APP 51, 982 P.2d 1089; Ferraton v. Bob Howard Auto Mall, 1998 OK CIV APP 154, 970 P.2d 196; Durham v. Wal-Mart, 1998 OK CIV APP 165, 966 P.2d 808; Furr v. Wal-Mart, 1998 OK CIV APP 147, 966 P.2d 1193; Eidschun v. Air-X-Changers, 1998 OK CIV APP 142, 964 P.2d 970; Favell v. Favell, 1998 OK CIV APP 22, 957 P.2d 556; Powell v. Nortex Investigation Services, 1997 OK CIV APP 63, 947 P.2d 614; Brazeal v. Citgo Petroleum Corp., 1997 OK CIV APP 61, 946 P.2d 680. ***PRACTICE AREAS:*** Appellate Practice; Commercial Litigation; Collections; Commercial Collections; Post Judgment Collections; Secured Collections; Unse-

(This Listing Continued)

FISHER & FISHER, Tulsa—Continued

cured Collections; Retail Collections; Professional Collections; Creditors Rights; Creditors Rights in Bankruptcy; Secured Creditors Rights; Bankruptcy Litigation; Fraudulent Conveyance. ***Email:*** kfisheresq@sbcglobal.net

REPRESENTATIVE CLIENTS: American Express Travel Related Services Co.; Discover Bank; American Express Centurion Bank; Wachovia Bank; A&B Engraving, Inc.; TransWestern Publishing, LLC; Chubb Group Insurance; Kansas Counselors, Inc.; NCO Financial Systems, Inc.; TBF Financial, LLC; First Call of Tulsa, Inc.; Toomey Oil Co., Inc.; Ball Legends, L.L.C.; Hygiene Systems, Inc. d/b/a Omnisystems.

LAW OFFICES OF FLOWERS & ASSOCIATES P.C.

810 SOUTH CINCINNATI, SUITE 400
TULSA, OKLAHOMA 74105
Telephone: 918-742-4000
Fax: 918-749-0164
Email: Info@flowersandfisher.com
URL: http://www.lawyers.com/flowerslaw

General Civil Practice. Civil Trial Practice in all State and Federal Courts. Collections, Commercial Law, Corporation, Probate, Guardianship Litigation, Taxation and Estate Planning, Wills and Trusts, Commercial Litigation.

STEVEN P. FLOWERS, born Champaign, Illinois, June 30, 1950; admitted to bar, 1975, Oklahoma and U.S. District Court, Northern District of Oklahoma; 1976, U.S. Court of Appeals, 10th Circuit, U.S. Tax Court and U.S. District Court, Eastern District of Oklahoma. *Education:* University of Tulsa (B.S., accounting, 1972; J.D., 1974). Omicron Delta Kappa. Certified Public Accountant, Oklahoma, 1976. *Member:* Tulsa County, Oklahoma (Member, Probate Code Committee, 1997-2000) and American Bar Associations. ***PRACTICE AREAS:*** Commercial Law; Corporate Law; Probate; Guardianship Litigation; Estate Planning; Taxation. ***Email:*** spflowers@flowersandfisher.com

REPRESENTATIVE CLIENTS: C&L Systems Corp.; Nu-Car Unloading Co.; Peppers Restaurants; Interior Concepts, Inc.; Toomey Oil Co.; Native Tulsan Eateries, Inc.; A & B Engraving; Route 66 Harley-Davidson, Inc.; Blue Sky Aviation, Inc.; American Express Travel Related Services, Inc.; Arrow Financial Services; Trans-Western Publishing LLC; Crestline Construction Co., Inc.; Route 66 Real Estate, LLC; Concrete Services Corp.; Alliance Title Inc.

FRANCY LAW FIRM

1861 EAST 15TH STREET
TULSA, OKLAHOMA 74104-4610
Telephone: 918-747-1295
Fax: 918-744-6300
Email: jkenton.francy@francylaw.com
URL: http://www.francylaw.com

Mailing Address: P.O. Box 2048, Broken Arrow, OK 74013

Broken Arrow, Oklahoma Office: 110 South Main Street, 74012. Telephone: 918-251-7373. Fax: 918-258-4606.

Collaborative Law, Family Law, Divorce, Child Support Collection, Visitation Rights, Protective Orders, Premarital Agreements, Grandparents Rights, Guardianship, Post Decree Modifications, Violations of Protection Orders, Criminal Law, Driving Under the Influence, Drug Crimes, Estate Planning, Trusts and Estates, Wills and Probate, Living Wills, Advanced Directives, Mediation, Arbitration.

FIRM PROFILE: Mr. Francy has received extensive training in high-conflict, including multi-issue, complex and domestic violence situations. In addition, the firm offers alternative dispute resolution and mediation services beyond the realm of family law and domestic relations, including corporate and civil litigation matters.

J. KENTON FRANCY, born Tulsa, Oklahoma, February 7, 1950; admitted to bar, 1976, Oklahoma and U.S. District Court, Northern District of Oklahoma; 1977, U.S. Court of Appeals, Tenth Circuit; 1988, U.S. District Court, Eastern District of Oklahoma. *Education:* University of Oklahoma; University of Tulsa (B.S., 1973; J.D., 1976). Phi Delta Phi. Authorship: "Divorce Mediation Process, Rules and the Role of Counsel", Oklahoma Bar Journal Vol. 62 Feb. 1991. Adjunct Professor, University of Tulsa College of Law, 2000—; Oklahoma State University Agricultural Mediation Program. *Member:* Tulsa County (Chairman, Alternative Dispute Resolution Committee, 1991-1993), Oklahoma (Vice Chairman, Alternative Dispute Resolution Committee, 1992-1993; Chair, 1993-1994) and American (Member, Family Law Advance Practitioners Section; Alternative Dispute Resolution Section) Bar Associations; The Association for Conflict Management; Oklahoma Academy of Mediators and Arbitrators (President, 1995-1996). ***REPORTED CASES:*** Robertson v. Robertson, 1982 OK 108,654 P.2nd 600 (1982) Wallis v. Wallis, 2003 OK Civ App 77, 78 P. 3rd 562 (2003). ***PRACTICE AREAS:*** Mediation; Arbitration; Divorce; Family Law; Child Support; Civil Trial; Collaborative Law.

ASSOCIATES

MICHAEL F. McCANN, born New Orleans, Louisiana, November 24, 1959; admitted to bar, 1992, Oklahoma. *Education:* Tulsa Junior College; Oklahoma State University (B.S., 1986); University of Tulsa College of Law (J.D., 1992). Member, Energy Law Journal, University of Tulsa College of Law, 1991-1992; W. Lee Johnson Chapter of the American Inns of Court, 1991-1992. Former Associate: Williams Communications; Hemphill Corporation Northwestern Mutual Insurance. *Member:* Tulsa County (Member, Alternative Dispute Resolution Section) and Oklahoma (Member, Sections on: Real Property; Family Law; Alternative Dispute Resolution; Legal Ethics Committee; Access to Justice Committee) Bar Associations; Collaborative Lawyers of Oklahoma. ***PRACTICE AREAS:*** Telecommunications Law; Easements; Construction Law; Business Transactions; Mediation; Collaborative Law. ***Email:*** mfmccann@francylaw.com

(This Listing Continued)

JOSEPH A. FLORES, born El Paso, Texas, November 10, 1960; admitted to bar, 2003, Oklahoma. *Education:* University of Texas at Austin (B.S., 1984); University of Tulsa (J.D., 2001). *Member:* Tulsa County, Oklahoma (Member, Sections on: Family Law, Criminal Law) and American Bar Associations. ***LANGUAGES:*** Spanish. ***PRACTICE AREAS:*** Adoption Law; Divorce; Civil Litigation; Tax Law; Juvenile Criminal Law. ***Email:*** jaflores@francylaw.com

DAVID G. FRANCY, born Tulsa, Oklahoma, November 11, 1975; admitted to bar, 2004, Oklahoma. *Education:* Northeastern State University (B.A., 2000); University of Tulsa (J.D., 2003). Delta Theta Phi. Member, Legal Fraternity, 2000-2003. ***PRACTICE AREAS:*** Family Law; Child Support Collection; Business Organization; Real Estate Transactions; Criminal Law; Driving While Intoxicated. ***Email:*** dgfrancy@francylaw.com

OF COUNSEL

LUCY S. KROBLIN, born St. Louis, Missouri, July 16, 1947; admitted to bar, 1987, Oklahoma; U.S. District Court, Northern District of Oklahoma. *Education:* St. Mary's College, Notre Dame, Indiana (B.A., 1969); University of Tulsa (J.D., 1987). Junior League of Tulsa, Oklahoma. *Member:* Tulsa County, Oklahoma (Member, Family Law Section) and American Bar Associations; Oklahoma Trial Lawyers Association; The Association of Trial Lawyers of America. ***PRACTICE AREAS:*** Civil Litigation; Estate Planning; Family Law. ***Email:*** lskroblin@francylaw.com

FRASIER, FRASIER & HICKMAN, LLP

1700 SOUTHWEST BOULEVARD
TULSA, OKLAHOMA 74107
Telephone: 918-584-4724
Fax: 918-583-5637
Email: frasier@tulsa.com
URL: http://www.frasierlaw.com

General Civil, Criminal and Trial Practice. Personal Injury, Medical Mal-practice, Labor, Products Liability, Workers Compensation, FELA, Transportation, Commercial, Probate, Corporate, Real Estate and Administrative Law.

FIRM PROFILE: Frasier, Frasier & Hickman, LLP is listed in the Bar Register of Preeminent Lawyers.

MEMBERS OF FIRM

THOMAS DEE FRASIER (1924-2001)

JAMES E. FRASIER, born Evergreen Park, Illinois, December 29, 1940; admitted to bar, 1965, Oklahoma; 1968, U.S. Supreme Court. *Education:* University of Tulsa (B.A., 1963; J.D., 1965). *Member:* Tulsa County, Oklahoma and American Bar Associations; Oklahoma Trial Lawyers Association; The Association of Trial Lawyers of America.

STEVEN R. HICKMAN, born Tulsa, Oklahoma, December 11, 1954; admitted to bar, 1981, Oklahoma. *Education:* Brigham Young University (B.S., magna cum laude, 1976; J.D., cum laude, 1980). *Member:* Tulsa County and Oklahoma Bar Associations; Oklahoma Trial Lawyers Association; The Association of Trial Lawyers of America. ***LANGUAGES:*** Swedish.

JOHN W. FLIPPO, born Tulsa, Oklahoma, November 8, 1948; admitted to bar, 1978, Oklahoma. *Education:* Oklahoma Baptist University (B.M., 1971); Central State University (M.Ed., 1973); University of Tulsa (J.D., 1978). Member, Selective Service Board, Tulsa County, Oklahoma. *Member:* Tulsa County and Oklahoma Bar Associations; Oklahoma Trial Lawyers Association; The Association of Trial Lawyers of America.

EVERETT R. BENNETT, JR., born Tulsa, Oklahoma, November 3, 1959; admitted to bar, 1985, Oklahoma. *Education:* Oklahoma State University; University of Oklahoma (B.S., 1982); University of Tulsa (J.D., 1985). Delta Theta Phi. Member, National Trial Advocacy Team, University of Tulsa, 1984 and 1985. *Member:* Tulsa County, Oklahoma and American Bar Associations; Oklahoma Trial Lawyers Association; The Association of Trial Lawyers of America; Oklahoma Criminal Defense Lawyers Association.

JERRY L. FRANKS, JR., born Ft. Smith, Arkansas, July 16, 1964; admitted to bar, 1990, Oklahoma, U.S. District Court, Northern, Eastern, Western Districts of Oklahoma. *Education:* University of Arkansas (B.S.B.A., 1986); University of Tulsa (J.D., 1990). *Member:* Tulsa County, Oklahoma and American Bar Associations; The Association of Trial Lawyers of America; Oklahoma Trial Lawyers Association.

FRANK W FRASIER, III, born Albuquerque, New Mexico, October 27, 1966; admitted to bar, 1998, Oklahoma. *Education:* George Washington University (B.A., 1989); District of Columbia School of Law (J.D., 1997). *Member:* Oklahoma and American Bar Associations; Oklahoma Trial Lawyers; American Trial Lawyers.

GEORGE M. MILES, born Tulsa, Oklahoma, May 25, 1960; admitted to bar, 1985, Oklahoma. *Education:* Oklahoma State University (B.S., 1982); University of Tulsa (J.D., 1985). Adjunct Professor, Tulsa Community College, 1998—. Alternate Municipal Judge, City of Glenpool, Oklahoma, 1989—. *Member:* Tulsa County and Oklahoma Bar Associations.

ASSOCIATES

MICHAEL A. SHIFLET, born Bartlesville, Oklahoma, July 29, 1969; admitted to bar, 2000, Oklahoma and U.S. District Court, Northern District of Oklahoma. *Education:* Phillips University (B.S., Business Administration, 1991); University of Tulsa College of Law (J.D., 2000). Phi Delta Phi. Member: Oklahoma Society and American Institute of Certified Public Accountants, 1995—. Certified Public Accountant, Oklahoma, 1995—. Recipient: Presidential Scholar, Phillips University; Dean John Rogers Scholar, University of Tulsa College of Law. *Member:* Oklahoma and American Bar Associations; Oklahoma Trial Lawyers Association.

TOMY W. McDONALD, admitted to bar, 2003, Oklahoma. *Education:* Langston University (B.A., 1999); University of Tulsa College of Law (J.D., 2002). *Member:* Oklahoma Bar Association.

(This Listing Continued)

LAURIE PHILLIPS, born Tulsa, Oklahoma, August 28, 1962; admitted to bar, 2003, Oklahoma. *Education:* University Center at Tulsa (B.A., History, 1996); University of Tulsa (J.D., 2003). *Member:* Oklahoma Bar Association; Oklahoma Trial Lawyers Association; The Association of Trial Lawyers of America.

REPRESENTATIVE CLIENTS: Communication Workers of America, Tulsa, Oklahoma; Transport Workers Union, Local 514, Tulsa, Oklahoma; United Steelworkers of America; Teamsters L.523; Machinists Union; IAFF; INITE; AFSCME; L.1180.
REFERENCES: Community State Bank, Tulsa, Oklahoma; The Bank of Oklahoma, Tulsa, Oklahoma.

FREESE & MARCH, P.A.

Established in 1955

4510 EAST 31ST STREET
TULSA, OKLAHOMA 74135
Telephone: 918-749-9331
Fax: 918-749-9336
Email: jackfreese@aol.com

General Civil Practice in all State and Federal Courts. Trials. Probate, Real Estate, Corporation, Oil and Gas, Family, Commercial, Administrative and Labor Law, Estate Planning.

CHARLES H. MARCH (1912-1997)

JOHN MARKHAM FREESE, born Tulsa, Oklahoma, February 12, 1928; admitted to bar, 1950, Oklahoma; 1954, U.S. Supreme Court. *Education:* Notre Dame, Williams College and University of Oklahoma (A.B., 1946); University of Oklahoma (LL.B.). Phi Alpha Delta. Governor's Appointee: Director, Oklahoma Drug and Alcohol Policy Board, 1991-1993; Oklahoma State and Education Employees Group Insurance Board, 1993-2002. *Member:* Tulsa County (Member, Committee on Professional Economics, 1967-1977), Oklahoma (Member, Committees on: Unauthorized Practice of Law 1969-1970; Member, 1965-1981 and Chairman, 1979-1981, Committee on Professional Economics; Member, 1968 and Chairman, 1969, Special Committee on Implementation of Judicial Reform) and American (Vice Chairman, Economics Committee, General Practice Section, 1975-1977; Co-Chairman, 1977-1978, Vice Chairman, 1979; Chairman: Committee for Solo Practitioners and Small Firms, Economics of Law Practice Section, 1978-1979) Bar Associations. ***PRACTICE AREAS:*** Business; Corporate; Real Estate; Estate Planning; Probate; Family Law; Divorce; Child Custody; Litigation.

REPRESENTATIVE CLIENTS: Aircraft Cylinders of America, Inc.; Associated Engine Remanufacturers Organization, Inc.; Boston Communications, Inc.; Bed Check Corporation; Eagan Landscape and Sprinkler Co.; Doss Properties, LLC; Preferred Pediatric; Corporate Secondary Strategies, Inc.; BENCO Mechanical, Inc.; Polysteel of Oklahoma, Inc.; Insulated Technologies, Inc.; Elliott Chiropratic Clinics; Cendac II, Inc.; Multicare of Oklahoma, Inc.; Fiber Plast Corp.; American Waste Management, Inc.; Judds Brothers Construction; Powers Radiology Group; Century Geophysical Corp.
REFERENCES: Bank of Oklahoma; Bank One; Triad Bank, N.A.; Security Bank.

FRY & ELDER

Established in 1991

906 SOUTH CHEYENNE
TULSA, OKLAHOMA 74119
Telephone: 918-585-1107
Fax: 918-592-2410

Family Law, Domestic Relations including Divorce, Custody, Marital Estates, Visitation.

MEMBERS OF FIRM

ROBERT G. FRY, JR., born Tulsa, Oklahoma, December 19, 1941; admitted to bar, 1968, Oklahoma and U.S. District Court, Northern District of Oklahoma; 1972, U.S. Court of Appeals, Tenth Circuit. *Education:* Michigan State University (B.A., 1964); University of Tulsa (J.D., 1967). Phi Alpha Delta. Chief Public Defender, Tulsa County, Oklahoma, 1968-1969. Outstanding Young Lawyer, Tulsa County, 1973. Certified Mediator and Arbitrator (certified by the American Academy of Matrimonial Lawyers). CLE Speaker: "Fundamentals of a Divorce Case," April 2000, May 2001; "How to Cross Examine a Psychological Expert," March 1998; "How to Examine a Custody Evaluation Report," May 2005. *Member:* Tulsa County (Chairman, Domestic Relations Section, 1984-1993) Oklahoma and American Bar Associations; American Academy of Matrimonial Lawyers (President, Oklahoma Chapter, 2001-2003). ***PRACTICE AREAS:*** Domestic Law; Divorce; Custody Law; Family Law. ***Email:*** halfdisme@tulsacoxmail.com

JAMES R. ELDER, born Tulsa, Oklahoma, August 16, 1946; admitted to bar, 1972, Oklahoma; 1973, U.S. District Court, Northern District of Oklahoma; 1975, U.S. Court of Appeals, 10th Circuit; 1977, U.S. Supreme Court. *Education:* Oklahoma Military Academy (A.A., 1967); Northeastern State College (B.A., 1969); University of Tulsa (J.D., 1971). Phi Alpha Delta (Chapter President, 1971). *Member:* Tulsa County (Chair, Family Law Section, 1995-1996) and Oklahoma (Member, Family Law Section) Bar Associations; Oklahoma Trial Lawyers Association (Contributing Editor, "The Advocate", 1986-1990). ***PRACTICE AREAS:*** Family Law; Business Law; Corporate Law; Civil Litigation.

FULLER, CHLOUBER & FRIZZELL, L.L.P.

TWENTY EAST FIFTH STREET, SUITE 200
TULSA, OKLAHOMA 74103-4407
Telephone: 918-585-9155
Facsimile: 918-585-9414
URL: http://www.legalok.com

Banking, Bankruptcy, Business Law, Commercial Transactions, Corporate, Creditor's Rights, Criminal Law, Energy and Regulatory Law, Family Law, Federal, General Civil Litigation, Health Care Law, Insurance Defense, Labor and Employment Law, Oil & Gas, Private Foundations, Probate, Products Liability, State and Local Taxation of Businesses and Individuals, Trial Practice, Wills and Estates, Workers' Compensation, Telecommunications and Real Estate.

(This Listing Continued)

FIRM PROFILE: This firm has achieved the highest rating for legal ability in Martindale-Hubbell.

BRAD D. FULLER, born San Antonio, Texas, August 29, 1962; admitted to bar, 1987, Oklahoma. *Education:* University of Oklahoma (B.B.A., 1984; J.D., 1987). Recipient, Oklahoma Bar Association Outstanding Young Lawyer, 1996. Member, City of Tulsa Board of Adjustment, 1989-1992. *Member:* Tulsa County, Oklahoma (Past Chair and Board of Directors, Young Lawyers Division, 1994) and American (District No. 24 Representative, Oklahoma and Arkansas, Young Lawyers Division, 1995-1997) Bar Associations; Oklahoma Liquefied Petroleum Gas Board (Chair, Rules Committee, 1998-2001). ***PRACTICE AREAS:*** Civil Litigation; Business Law; Real Estate. ***Email:*** BFuller@LegalOK.com

STEVEN E. CHLOUBER, born Winslow, Arizona, July 24, 1966; admitted to bar, 1991, Oklahoma. *Education:* Oklahoma State University (B.S., 1988); University of Oklahoma (J.D. with distinction, 1991). Phi Kappa Phi. Member, Oklahoma Law Review, 1989-1991. *Member:* Tulsa County and Oklahoma Bar Associations; American Trial Lawyers Association. ***PRACTICE AREAS:*** Trial Practice; Civil Litigation; Family Law; Creditors Rights. ***Email:*** SEC@LegalOK.com

BLAINE G. FRIZZELL, born Wichita, Kansas, December 7, 1962; admitted to bar, 1989, Oklahoma; U.S. District Court, Northern and Eastern Districts of Oklahoma; U.S. Tax Court. *Education:* Oklahoma State University (B.S., 1986); University of Tulsa (J.D., 1989); Southern Methodist University (LL.M., Taxation, 1995). Member: Blue Key; National Moot Court Team; Order of Barristers; Honorary Member of Scribes. Notes and Comments Editor, Tulsa Law Journal, 1988-1989. Author: "Aerial Surveillance Withstands Fourth Amendment Scrutiny," 23 Tulsa Law Journal 259, 1987; "Strict Liability in Tort for Builder-Vendors of Homes," 24 Tulsa Law Journal 117, 1988. *Member:* Tulsa, Oklahoma and American (Member, Sections of: Real Property, Probate and Trust Law and Taxation) Bar Associations. ***PRACTICE AREAS:*** Trusts and Estate Planning; Probate; Corporate Law; Business Organization; Nonprofit Organizations Law; Private Foundations. ***Email:*** BGF@LegalOK.com

GREGG G. FULLER, born Rochester, Minnesota, May 25, 1964; admitted to bar, 1992, Oklahoma and U.S. District Court, Northern, Eastern and Western Districts of Oklahoma. *Education:* Oklahoma State University (B.S.B.A., 1987); University of Tulsa (J.D., 1992). Assistant District Attorney, Tulsa County, 1992-1993. *Member:* Tulsa County, Oklahoma and American Bar Associations. ***PRACTICE AREAS:*** Workers' Compensation; General Liability. ***Email:*** GreggFuller@LegalOK.com

R. MICHAEL COLE, born Oklahoma City, Oklahoma, 1966; admitted to bar, 1991, Oklahoma; U.S. District Court, Northern and Eastern Districts of Oklahoma; U.S. Court of Appeals, Tenth Circuit. *Education:* University of Oklahoma (B.S., Letters, 1988); Harvard Law School (J.D., 1991). *Member:* Tulsa County, Oklahoma and American Bar Associations. ***PRACTICE AREAS:*** Civil Litigation; Complex Litigation; Family Law; Labor and Employment; Bankruptcy; Commercial Litigation. ***Email:*** mcole@LegalOK.com

REPRESENTATIVE CLIENTS: America First Insurance Company; American Airlines; Atrium Companies, Inc.; Auto Crane; Bank One Oklahoma, N.A.; Cactus Drilling; Crane Carrier Company; Crawford & Company; Eastern Commercial Credit Services, Inc.; Oklahoma Department of Transportation; Peachtree Telecommunications Internation, L.L.C.; ITT Hartford; Mid-America Land, Grain & Cattle; United Parcel Service, Inc.; Specialty Risk Services; Spectrum Paint Co., Inc.; The Broadhurst Foundation; WEIGAND - OMEGA Management, Inc.

GABLE & GOTWALS

A PROFESSIONAL CORPORATION

1100 ONEOK PLAZA
100 WEST FIFTH STREET
TULSA, OKLAHOMA 74103-4217
Telephone: 918-595-4800
Fax: 918-595-4990
Email: info@gablelaw.com
URL: http://www.gablelaw.com

Oklahoma City, Oklahoma Offices: Fifteenth Floor, One Leadership Square, 211 North Robinson, 73102-7101. Telephone: 405-235-5500. Fax: 405-235-2875.

Administrative Law, Alternative Dispute Resolution, Antitrust, Bankruptcy, Banks and Banking, Class Actions, Commercial Law, Communications and Media, Copyright, Corporate Law, Employee Benefits, Energy, Environmental Law, Family Law, Finance, Franchises and Franchising, General Practice, Guardianship and Conservatorship, Insurance, Intellectual Property, Labor and Employment, Litigation, Mergers, Acquisitions and Divestitures, Natural Resources, Patents, Personal Injury, Probate, Property Law, Real Estate, RICO, Regulatory Law, Securities, Software Licensing, Sports Law, Taxation, Technology Law, Torts, Trademarks, Utility Law, Workers Compensation.

FIRM PROFILE: Gable & Gotwals is a full-service law firm representing a diversified client base in Oklahoma, the Southwest and across the nation. The firm provides efficient, professional and ethical representation for all clients at competitive rates. With expertise ranging from energy litigation and labor law to the rapidly evolving specialties of ADR, technology and intellectual property -- ensure Gable & Gotwals has the depth to serve both small and large clients. Though Oklahoma-based, our connections and reach are global. Fortune 500 corporations, entrepreneurs, privately owned companies, foundations and individuals entrust us every day with the stewardship and strategic management of their legal challenges.

STEPHEN B. ALLEN, born Lawrence, Massachusetts, 1973; admitted to bar, 1998, Oklahoma. *Education:* Oklahoma Baptist University (B.A., magna cum laude, 1995); Vanderbilt University (J.D., 1998). ***PRACTICE AREAS:*** Technology Licensing; Software Licensing; Business Organizations; Securities; Banking Law; Real Estate Commercial Law. ***Email:*** sallen@gablelaw.com

GENE C. BUZZARD, born Vandalia, Illinois, 1946; admitted to bar, 1974, Oklahoma. *Education:* Yale University (B.A., 1969); Washington University (J.D., 1974). Urban Law

(This Listing Continued)

GABLE & GOTWALS, A PROFESSIONAL CORPORATION, Tulsa—Continued

Annual. Senior Adjunct Settlement Judge, U.S. District Court, Northern District of Oklahoma, 1990—. ***PRACTICE AREAS:*** Business Torts; Complex Litigation; Federal Practice. ***Email:*** gbuzzard@gablelaw.com

DENNIS C. CAMERON, born Tulsa, Oklahoma, 1962; admitted to bar, 1987, Oklahoma. *Education:* University of Oklahoma (B.S.M.E., with distinction, 1984; J.D., with honors, 1987). Tau Beta Phi. Chair, ABA-TIPS Automobile Law Committee, 1993-1994 and 1997-1998; Chair, ABA-TIPS National Trial Academy, 2000. Member, Rocky Mountain Mineral Law Foundation. ***PRACTICE AREAS:*** Civil Litigation; Oil and Gas Law; Products Liability; Railroads; Environmental Law. ***Email:*** dcameron@gablelaw.com

TIMOTHY A. CARNEY, born Indianapolis, Indiana, 1960; admitted to bar, 1986, Oklahoma. *Education:* Southwest Missouri State University (B.S., 1983); University of Tulsa (J.D., 1986). Tulsa Law Journal. Order of the Curule Chair. Listed in Best Lawyers in America, 2006 (Commercial Litigation). Adjunct Settlement Judge, U.S. District for the Northern District of Oklahoma, 1995—. ***PRACTICE AREAS:*** Litigation; Employment Law; Business Torts; ERISA; Insurance Law. ***Email:*** tcarney@gablelaw.com

PATRICK W. CIPOLLA, born Kansas City, Missouri, 1965; admitted to bar, 1992, Oklahoma. *Education:* Oklahoma State University (B.S., 1988); University of Oklahoma (J.D., with distinction, 1992). ***PRACTICE AREAS:*** Employment Discrimination Law; Management Employment Law; Litigation; Employer-Employee Relations Law; Occupational Safety and Health Law; Employee Drug Testing. ***Email:*** pcipolla@gablelaw.com

RENEE DeMOSS, born Enid, Oklahoma, 1958; admitted to bar, 1984, Oklahoma. *Education:* Oklahoma City University (B.A., summa cum laude, 1980); University of Oklahoma (J.D., with honors, 1984). Order of the Coif; Order of Barristers. Oklahoma Law Review. ***PRACTICE AREAS:*** Commercial Litigation; Insurance Law; Federal Practice; Civil Litigation; Class Action Administration. ***Email:*** rdemoss@gablelaw.com

THEODORE Q. ELIOT, born Tulsa, Oklahoma, 1954; admitted to bar, 1979, Oklahoma. *Education:* Drake University (B.A., 1976); University of Oklahoma (J.D., 1979). Book Review Editor, Oklahoma Law Review. ***PRACTICE AREAS:*** Complex Litigation; Oil and Gas Litigation; Bankruptcy. ***Email:*** teliot@gablelaw.com

AMELIA A. FOGLEMAN, born Tishomingo, Oklahoma, 1969; admitted to bar, 1994, Oklahoma. *Education:* Oklahoma State University (B.A., with honors, 1991); University of Virginia (J.D., 1994). Notes Editor, Virginia Law Review. Law Clerk to Hon. Stephanie Seymour, Chief Judge, U.S. Court of Appeals, Tenth Circuit, 1994-1995. Law Clerk to Hon. Sven E. Holmes, U.S. District Judge, Northern District of Oklahoma, 1995-1996. ***PRACTICE AREAS:*** Complex Litigation; Federal Practice; Appellate Practice. ***Email:*** afogleman@gablelaw.com

JEFFREY D. HASSELL, born Holdenville, Oklahoma, 1962; admitted to bar, 1987, Oklahoma. *Education:* University of Oklahoma (B.B.A., Finance, with special distinction, 1984; J.D., with honors, 1987). Order of the Coif. ***PRACTICE AREAS:*** Commercial Law; Probate and Trust Law; Bankruptcy; Real Estate; Banks and Banking. ***Email:*** jhassell@gablelaw.com

OLIVER S. HOWARD, born Oklahoma City, Oklahoma, 1945; admitted to bar, 1979, Oklahoma. *Education:* Oklahoma Christian College (B.A., summa cum laude, 1967); Abilene Christian University (M.A., 1970); Hebrew Union College (Ph.D., 1978); University of Cincinnati (J.D., 1979). Order of the Coif. Fellow, International Academy of Trial Lawyers. Listed in The Best Lawyers in America. Research Editor, University of Cincinnati Law Review. Adjunct Settlement Judge, U.S. District Court, Northern District of Oklahoma. Member, Oklahoma Fellows, America Bar Foundation. ***PRACTICE AREAS:*** Complex Litigation; Antitrust Litigation; Oil and Gas Litigation; Employment Discrimination Litigation; Intellectual Property Litigation; Securities Litigation. ***Email:*** ohoward@gablelaw.com

DAVID E. KEGLOVITS, born Syracuse, New York, 1963; admitted to bar, 1990, Oklahoma. *Education:* University of Notre Dame (B.B.A., with honors, 1985); University of Texas (J.D., with honors, 1990). Fellow: Oklahoma Bar Foundation; Tulsa County Bar Foundation. Member, Oklahoma Bar Association Civil Procedure Committee. Adjunct Settlement Judge for the U.S. District Court for the Northern District of Oklahoma. ***PRACTICE AREAS:*** Commercial Litigation; Trade Secrets; Professional Liability; Energy Law. ***Email:*** dkeglovits@gablelaw.com

THOMAS J. KIRBY, born Cherokee, Oklahoma, 1951; admitted to bar, 1976, Oklahoma. *Education:* University of Oklahoma (B.A., 1973; J.D., 1975). Board of Editors, Oklahoma Law Review. Member, Civil Procedure Committee, Oklahoma Bar Association. Past Chair, Mineral Law Section, Tulsa County Bar Association. Master Emeritus, Council Oak/Johnson-Sontag Inn, American Inns of Court. Fellow: Oklahoma Bar Foundation; Tulsa County Bar Foundation. ***PRACTICE AREAS:*** Litigation; Energy Law. ***Email:*** tkirby@gablelaw.com

STEPHEN W. LAKE, born Tulsa, Oklahoma, 1963; admitted to bar, 1991, Oklahoma. *Education:* Vanderbilt University (B.A., cum laude, with honors, Economics, 1987); University of Oklahoma (J.D., with highest honors, 1991). Order of the Coif. Editor-in-Chief, Oklahoma Law Review. ***PRACTICE AREAS:*** Mergers and Acquisitions; Securities; Corporate Finance; Corporate Law; Business Law. ***Email:*** slake@gablelaw.com

DOUGLAS J. MAY, born Eglin A.F.B., Florida, March 7, 1970; admitted to bar, 1995, Oklahoma; 1999, Texas. *Education:* University of Missouri, Columbia (B.A., summa cum laude, 1992); University of Tulsa (J.D., with honors, 1995). Order of the Curule Chair. Notes and Comments Editor, Tulsa Law Journal. *Member:* State Bar of Texas; Oklahoma Bar Association. ***PRACTICE AREAS:*** Finance; Securities; Commercial Transactions; Energy. ***Email:*** dmay@gablelaw.com

SHEPPARD F. MIERS, JR., born Tulsa, Oklahoma, 1941; admitted to bar, 1966, Oklahoma. *Education:* University of Oklahoma (B.A., 1963; J.D., 1966); Southern Methodist University (LL.M. in Taxation, 1979). Chairman, Oklahoma Bar Association Taxation Law Section, 1999-2000. Certified Public Accountant, Oklahoma. Listed in Best Lawyers in America (Tax Law). *Member:* Tulsa Pension Attorneys (Chairman, 1989-1997); Oklahoma Society of Certified Public Accountants; American Institute of Certified Public Accountants. ***PRACTICE AREAS:*** Taxation Law; Employee Benefits; Estate Planning Law; Wills; Trusts. ***Email:*** smiers@gablelaw.com

J. DANIEL MORGAN, born Spartanburg, South Carolina, 1950; admitted to bar, 1978, Tennessee; 1983, Oklahoma. *Education:* Vanderbilt University (B.A., cum laude, 1972); Florida State University (M.S., 1973); Memphis State University (J.D., 1978); University of Pennsylvania (LL.M., 1979). Memphis State University Law Review. Chief Master, Professional Responsibility Tribunal, Oklahoma Bar Association. Vice President, 1994, President-Elect, 1995 and President, 1996-1997, Tulsa County Bar Association. ***PRACTICE AREAS:*** Employment Discrimination Law; Equal Employment Law; Fair Employment Law; Labor Relations Law; Wage and Hour Law. ***Email:*** jmorgan@gablelaw.com

JOSEPH W. MORRIS, admitted to bar, 1947, Kansas; 1949, Oklahoma; 1978, Texas. *Education:* Washburn University (A.B., 1943; J.D., 1947); University of Michigan (LL.M., 1948; S.J.D., 1955). Order of the Coif. Legal Department, Shell Oil Co., 1948-1960. Associate General Counsel and General Counsel, Amerada Hess Petroleum Corporation, 1960-1969. Vice-President and General Counsel of Amerada Division, Amerada Hess Corporation, 1969-1971. Vice-President and Associate General Counsel, Amerada Hess Corporation, 1971-1972. Adjunct Professor, University of Tulsa College of Law, 1950-1972. Dean, University of Tulsa College of Law, 1972-1974. U.S. District Judge, 1974-1978 and Chief Judge, 1975-1978, Eastern District of Oklahoma. Vice President and General Counsel, Shell Oil Company, 1978-1983. Joined Gable & Gotwals, 1984. Chairman, Section of Natural Resources Law, American Bar Association, 1983-1984. President, Tulsa County Bar Association, 1971. Member, National Panel of Distinguished Neutrals of the CPR Institute for Dispute Resolution, American Arbitration Association. Member at Large, Complex Case Panel of Arbitrators. Fellow, American Bar Foundation. [Ensign, U.S. Navy Reserve, WW II]. ***PRACTICE AREAS:*** Alternative Dispute Resolution; Litigation; Oil and Gas Law. ***Email:*** jmorris@gablelaw.com

ELIZABETH R. MURATET, born Boston, Massachusetts, 1954; admitted to bar, 1983, Oklahoma. *Education:* Oklahoma State University (B.A., with honors, 1976); University of Tulsa (J.D., with honors, 1983). Tulsa Law Journal. Order of the Curule Chair. ***PRACTICE AREAS:*** Banking Law; Commercial Law; Real Estate Law; Title Examinations. ***Email:*** emuratet@gablelaw.com

RICHARD B. NOULLES, born Knoxville, Tennessee, 1949; admitted to bar, 1975, Oklahoma. *Education:* Rice University (B.A., 1970); University of Tulsa (J.D., 1975). Notes and Comments Editor, Tulsa Law Journal. Order of the Curule Chair. ***PRACTICE AREAS:*** Litigation; Federal Practice; Oil and Gas Law. ***Email:*** rnoulles@gablelaw.com

MICHAEL L. PATE, born 1953; admitted to bar, 1979, Texas; 1984, Oklahoma. *Education:* University of Michigan (A.B., with distinction, Economics, 1975); Indiana University (M.B.A., 1978; J.D., cum laude, 1978). Former Corporate Counsel, OXY USA, Inc. Vice President and Senior Legal Officer, Occidental Energy Marketing, Inc. *Member:* State Bar of Texas. ***PRACTICE AREAS:*** Energy Law; Derivative Products. ***Email:*** mpate@gablelaw.com

TERRY D. RAGSDALE, born Tulsa, Oklahoma, 1962; admitted to bar, 1992, Oklahoma. *Education:* University of Tulsa (B.S.P.E., summa cum laude, 1984); Southern Methodist University (J.D., magna cum laude, 1992). Tau Beta Pi. Order of the Coif. Editor-in-Chief, Southern Methodist University Law Review Association. Registered Professional Engineer, Petroleum Engineering, Louisiana. ***PRACTICE AREAS:*** Litigation; Oil and Gas Law. ***Email:*** tragsdale@gablelaw.com

JEFFREY C. RAMBACH, born Spokane, Washington, 1961; admitted to bar, 1986, Louisiana; 1989, Oklahoma, U.S. Tax Court and U.S. Court of Federal Claims. *Education:* Boston University (B.S., 1983); Tulane University (J.D., 1986); Georgetown University (LL.M. in Taxation, 1989). Law Clerk to the Hon. D. Irvin Couvillion, U.S. Tax Court, 1987-1989. Member, OBA Legal Ethics Committee, 2002-2003. ***PRACTICE AREAS:*** Mergers and Acquisitions Law; Corporate Law; Federal and State Taxation; Tax Controversies Law; Charitable Trusts and Foundations; Estate Planning. ***Email:*** jrambach@gablelaw.com

RONALD N. RICKETTS, born Tulsa, Oklahoma, 1943; admitted to bar, 1969, Oklahoma. *Education:* University of Oklahoma (B.A., 1965); University of Tulsa (J.D., 1968). Special District Judge, Tulsa County, 1969-1972. District Judge, Tulsa County, 1972-1979. Elected Member, 1993-1999 and Chairman, 1997-1998, Oklahoma Judicial Nominating Commission. Member, Oklahoma Supreme Court Standing Committee for Uniform Civil Jury Instructions, 1993—. Neutral, AAA Commercial Panel. ***PRACTICE AREAS:*** Litigation; Alternative Dispute Resolution; Environmental Law. ***Email:*** rricketts@gablelaw.com

SCOTT R. ROWLAND, born Snyder, Texas, March 12, 1960; admitted to bar, 1985, Oklahoma. *Education:* Texas A & M University (B.S., 1982); University of Tulsa (J.D., with highest honors, 1985). ***PRACTICE AREAS:*** Business Litigation; Antitrust; Complex Litigation; Civil Litigation. ***Email:*** srowland@gablelaw.com

LISA TRAYLOR SILVESTRI, born Orange, California, 1970; admitted to bar, 1996, Texas and U.S. District Court, Northern, Southern, Eastern and Western Districts of Texas; 2001, Oklahoma. *Education:* University of Texas at Austin (B.A., Government, with high honors, 1992; B.J., with high honors, 1992; J.D., with honors, 1996). Phi Beta Kappa. Member, The Review of Litigation. Member, Board of Advocates, 1995-1996. ***PRACTICE AREAS:*** Business Litigation; Commercial Litigation; Oil and Gas Litigation; Insurance Litigation. ***Email:*** lsilvestri@gablelaw.com

M. BENJAMIN SINGLETARY, born Roanoke Rapids, North Carolina, 1948; admitted to bar, 1977, Oklahoma. *Education:* University of North Carolina (B.A., 1971); University of Tulsa (J.D., 1977). Order of the Curule (Chair). Editor-in-Chief, Tulsa Law Review. Law Clerk to Joseph W. Morris, Chief U.S. District Judge, Eastern District of Oklahoma, 1977-1978. Assistant Editor of Committee on Energy Litigation Newsletter, Section of Litigation, American Bar Association, 1994—. Vice Chairman, Energy and Natural Resources Litigation Committee, American Bar Association, 1995-1997. ***PRACTICE AREAS:*** Oil and Gas Law; Mining or Mineral Law; Litigation; Federal Practice. ***Email:*** bsingletary@gablelaw.com

JAMES M. STURDIVANT, born Tulsa, Oklahoma, 1937; admitted to bar, 1964, Oklahoma. *Education:* University of Oklahoma (B.B.A., 1959; J.D., 1964). Order of the

(This Listing Continued)

Coif. Oklahoma Law Review. Vice President, Oklahoma Bar Association, 1976. Chairman, Professional Responsibility Commission, Oklahoma Bar Association, 1978. Elected Member, 1981-1987 and Chairman, 1985-1987, Oklahoma Judicial Nominating Commission. Member, House of Delegates, American Bar Association, 1992, State Delegate, 1995-2004. Member, Board of Governors, 2004—. Trustee, Center for American and International Law. Fellow: American Bar Foundation; American College of Trial Lawyers (State Chair, 2000-2002). ***PRACTICE AREAS:*** Litigation. ***Email:*** jsturdivant@gablelaw.com

SIDNEY K. SWINSON, born Wichita, Kansas, 1955; admitted to bar, 1980, Oklahoma. *Education:* University of Notre Dame (B.B.A., 1977); Tulsa University (J.D., 1980). Adjunct Assistant Professor of Law, 1983-1984, Adjunct Professor of Law, 1994—, University of Tulsa. Adjunct Settlement Judge, U.S. District Court and Bankruptcy Court, Northern District of Oklahoma, 1998—. Treasurer, 1993, Tulsa County Bar Association. Chair, Bankruptcy and Reorganization Section, Oklahoma Bar Association, 1994-1995, 2003-2004. Member, Professional Responsibility Tribunal, 2001—, Vice Chief Master, 2003-2004, Chief Master, 2004—. ***PRACTICE AREAS:*** Bankruptcy Law; Commercial Law. ***Email:*** sswinson@gablelaw.com

RAMON L. WATKINS, born 1970; admitted to bar, 1998, Oklahoma. *Education:* Cornell University (B.S., with distinction, 1992); Howard University (J.D., with honors, 1997). Recipient, American Jurisprudence Award. Howard Law National Moot Court Team Invitation. Member, Howard Law Journal. ***PRACTICE AREAS:*** Commercial Law; Real Estate; Sports Law. ***Email:*** rwatkins@gablelaw.com

ASSOCIATES

SARA E. BARRY, born Houston, Texas, 1974; admitted to bar, 2000, Oklahoma. *Education:* Oklahoma State University (B.A., Psychology, honors program, 1997); Baylor University (J.D., with highest honors, 2000). Recipient, Thomas M. Featherston, Jr., Estate Planning Award. Assistant Managing Editor, Notes and Comments; Managing Editor, Lead Articles; Executive Editor, Baylor Law Review. ***PRACTICE AREAS:*** Business Organizations; Securities; Estate Planning; Commercial Law. ***Email:*** sbarry@gablelaw.com

CASON P. CARTER, born Tulsa, Oklahoma, 1977; admitted to bar, 2003, Oklahoma. *Education:* Duke University (B.A., Public Policy and Economics, 2000); Georgetown University Law Center (J.D., 2003). ***PRACTICE AREAS:*** Business Litigation; RICO. ***Email:*** ccarter@gablelaw.com

ERIN K. DAILEY, born Cincinnati, Ohio, 1978; admitted to bar, 2004, Oklahoma. *Education:* University of Oklahoma (B.A., Letters, summa cum laude, 2000); University of Tulsa (J.D., with honors, 2004). Order of the Curule (Chair). Senior Candidates Editor, Tulsa Journal of Comparative and International Law, 2003-2004. Law Clerk to the Hon. Sven E. Holmes, U.S. District Judge, Northern District of Oklahoma, 2004-2005. *Member:* Oklahoma Bar Association. ***PRACTICE AREAS:*** Litigation; Natural Resources. ***Email:*** edailey@gablelaw.com

JOHN D. DALE, born Louisville, Kentucky, 1977; admitted to bar, 2003, Oklahoma. *Education:* Loyola University, New Orleans (B.A., Finance, 1999); University of Tulsa (J.D., with highest honors, 2003). Order of the Curule (Chair). Notes and Comments Editor, Tulsa Law Journal. ***PRACTICE AREAS:*** Bankruptcy; Creditors Rights; Commercial Law. ***Email:*** jdale@gablelaw.com

JOHN J. GRIFFIN, III, born Oklahoma City, Oklahoma, 1980; admitted to bar, 2005, Oklahoma. *Education:* University of Oklahoma (B.A., Finance, summa cum laude, 2000; J.D., 2005). *Member:* Oklahoma Bar Association. ***PRACTICE AREAS:*** Taxation; Corporate Law. ***Email:*** jgriffin@gablelaw.com

RANIA NASREDDINE, born Tulsa, Oklahoma, 1980; admitted to bar, 2005, Oklahoma. *Education:* Emory University (B.A., 2002); University of Oklahoma (J.D., 2005). Write-On Competition Editor, Oklahoma Law Review, 2004-2005. Law Clerk to the Hon. Joe Heaton, U.S. District Judge, Western District of Oklahoma, 2005. *Member:* Oklahoma Bar Association. ***PRACTICE AREAS:*** Litigation. ***Email:*** rnasreddine@gablelaw.com

MASON G. PATTERSON, born Pawhuska, Oklahoma, 1975; admitted to bar, 2000, Oklahoma. *Education:* Oklahoma State University (B.S., 1997); University of Virginia (J.D., 2000). Order of the Coif. Member, University of Virginia Law Review. ***PRACTICE AREAS:*** Commercial Litigation; Appellate Practice; Bankruptcy. ***Email:*** mpatterson@gablelaw.com

TYSON D. SCHWERDTFEGER, born Pratt, Kansas, 1976; admitted to bar, 2002, Oklahoma. *Education:* Oklahoma Christian College (B.A., History/Pre-Law, summa cum laude, 1999); Vanderbilt University (J.D., 2002). Law Clerk to Hon. Claire Eagan, U.S. District Court, Northern District of Oklahoma, 2002-2003. ***PRACTICE AREAS:*** Business Litigation. ***Email:*** tschwerdtfeger@gablelaw.com

MIA VAHLBERG, born Oklahoma City, Oklahoma, 1959; admitted to bar, 2004, Oklahoma. *Education:* University of Oklahoma (B.B.A., 1979); University of Tulsa (J.D., with highest honors, 2004). Order of Curule Chair. Editor, Tulsa Law Journal. Vice President, Board of Advocates. First Place, National Health Law Appellate Competition, 2003. Certified Public Accountant, Oklahoma, 1983. ***LANGUAGES:*** French. ***PRACTICE AREAS:*** Commercial Litigation. ***Email:*** mvahlberg@gablelaw.com

BRADLEY W. WELSH, born McAlester, Oklahoma, 1971; admitted to bar, 1999, Oklahoma. *Education:* University of Oklahoma (M.A., 1996); University of Texas at Austin (J.D., 1999). Articles Editor, Texas Law Review. ***PRACTICE AREAS:*** Commercial Litigation; Appellate Practice. ***Email:*** bwelsh@gablelaw.com

OF COUNSEL

JOHN L. ARRINGTON, JR., born Pawhuska, Oklahoma, 1931; admitted to bar, 1956, Oklahoma. *Education:* Princeton University (A.B., summa cum laude, 1953); Harvard University (J.D., magna cum laude, 1956; LL.M., 1957). Phi Beta Kappa. Member, Harvard Law School Board of Student Advisers. Treasurer, 1963 and President, 1970, Tulsa County Bar Association. Associate, 1957 and Partner, 1961, Arrington Kihle Gaberino & Dunn and predecessor firms 1957-1996. General Counsel, ONEOK, Inc., 1994-1998. ***PRACTICE AREAS:*** Corporate Law; Public Utilities; Litigation. ***Email:*** info@gablelaw.com

(This Listing Continued)

FRANK J. CATALANO, born New York, N.Y., 1942; admitted to bar, 1969, Michigan; 1990, Oklahoma; registered to practice before U.S. Patent and Trademark Office. *Education:* University of Detroit (B.E.E., 1964; J.D., cum laude, 1968). Gamma Eta Gamma. *Member:* State Bar of Michigan; Oklahoma and American (Member, Patent, Trademark and Copyright Sections) Bar Associations. ***PRACTICE AREAS:*** Intellectual Property; Patents; Trademarks; Unfair Competition; Copyrights. ***Email:*** fcatalano@gablelaw.com

G. ELLIS GABLE (1905-2001)

RICHARD W. GABLE, born Tulsa, Oklahoma, 1938; admitted to bar, 1963, Oklahoma. *Education:* University of Oklahoma (B.S.M.E., with distinction, 1960; J.D., 1963). Oklahoma Law Review. ***PRACTICE AREAS:*** Commercial Law; Real Estate Law; Domestic Relations. ***Email:*** rgable@gablelaw.com

CHARLES P. GOTWALS, JR., born Muskogee, Oklahoma, 1917; admitted to bar, 1940, Oklahoma. *Education:* University of Oklahoma (A.B., 1938; J.D., 1940). Phi Beta Kappa; Order of the Coif.

CHAD M. HINRICHS, admitted to bar, 1995, Oklahoma; registered to practice before U.S. Patent and Trademark Office. *Education:* University of Kansas (B.S.M.E., 1991); University of Tulsa (J.D., 1995). Member, Energy Law Journal, 1993-1995. Board Member, University of Tulsa School of Law Alumni Association. *Member:* Oklahoma Bar Association(Director, Intellectual Property Section). ***PRACTICE AREAS:*** Patents; Trademarks; Trade Secrets; Copyrights; Intellectual Property Licensing. ***Email:*** chinrichs@gablelaw.com

PAUL H. JOHNSON, born Tulsa, Oklahoma, 1926; admitted to bar, 1957, Oklahoma; registered to practice before U.S. Patent and Trademark Office. *Education:* Oklahoma State University (B.S.E.E., 1950); University of Tulsa (J.D., 1957). Co-Founder and Member, Head, Johnson & Kachigian, 1958-2001. Adjunct Settlement Judge, 1992—. Member, Will Rogers Memorial Commission, Claremore, Oklahoma; Director Emeritus, Thomas Gilcrease Museum Association, Tulsa, OK. Past-Chairman, Tulsa Housing Authority. Past-President, Green T Club of Tulsa. Member, International Lion's Club (Past-President, Tulsa Downtown Lion's Club). Member, Rotary Club of Tulsa; Hall of Fame Member, Intellectual Property Law Section, Oklahoma Bar Association. ***PRACTICE AREAS:*** Patents; Unfair Competition; Trade Secrets; Trademarks; Copyrights. ***Email:*** iplaw@gablelaw.com

DONALD A. KIHLE, born Noonan, North Dakota, 1934; admitted to bar, 1967, Oklahoma. *Education:* University of North Dakota (B.S. in I.E., 1957); University of Oklahoma (J.D., 1967). Order of the Coif. Oklahoma Law Review. ***PRACTICE AREAS:*** Business Law; Mergers and Acquisitions Law; Securities Regulation Law; Energy Law. ***Email:*** dkihle@gablelaw.com

MICHAEL E. SELLERS, born Dallas, Texas, 1962; admitted to bar, 1994, Tennessee; 2004, Oklahoma; registered to practice before U.S. Patent and Trademark Office. *Education:* University of Arkansas (B.S.E.E., 1984; J.D., with honors, 1994). Registered Professional Engineer, Texas, 1990. Member, Arkansas Law Review, University of Arkansas, 1993-1994. *Member:* Knoxville, Tennessee and American Bar Associations; American Intellectual Property Law Association; International Trademark Association. ***PRACTICE AREAS:*** Patent Prosecution; Trademark Prosecution; Unfair Competition; Technology Licensing. ***Email:*** msellers@gablelaw.com

(For complete biographical data on other personnel, see Professional Biographies at Oklahoma City, Oklahoma)

GARRETT LAW OFFICE, P.C.

111 WEST FIFTH STREET, SUITE 800
TULSA, OKLAHOMA 74103
Telephone: 918-622-9292
URL: http://www.garrettlawoffice.com

Muskogee, Oklahoma Office: 215 State Street, 10th Floor, Suite 1000 74401. Telephone: 918-683-3288. Fax: 918-683-8445.

Oklahoma City, Oklahoma Office: 4000 N. Classen Boulevard, Suite 110-S, 73118. Telephone: 405-634-2500.

Fayetteville, Arkansas Office: One West Mountain Street, Suite 302, 72701.

Personal Injury, Insurance Litigation, Products Liability, Workers Compensation, Securities, Bankruptcy.

DAVID M. GARRETT, born Oklahoma City, Oklahoma, September 20, 1941; admitted to bar, 1969, Texas; 1982, Oklahoma; U.S. District Court, Eastern District of Oklahoma; 1989, U.S. Court of Appeals, 10th Circuit; 1990, U.S. District Court, Northern District of Oklahoma. *Education:* Northeastern Oklahoma State University (B.S., 1964); University of Tulsa (J.D., 1967). Certified Public Accountant, Texas, 1969. *Member:* Muskogee County (Secretary, 1983; Vice President, 1993; President, 1994), Oklahoma and American Bar Associations; State Bar of Texas; Oklahoma Trial Lawyers Association (Director, 1983-1987 and 1989-2001); Texas Trial Lawyers Association; The Association of Trial Lawyers of America (Sustaining Member). ***REPORTED CASES:*** Heintz v. Trucks For You, Inc., 1999 OK CIV APP 64, 1999 OK CIV APP 67, 984 P.2d 255 (Okla.Civ.App. Div. 2, Apr 13, 1999, NO. 92215; Lyons v. Tollie Freightways, 1993 OK CIV APP 46, 851 P.2d 549 (Okla.App.Div. 1, Mar 16, 1993). ***PRACTICE AREAS:*** Personal Injury; Insurance Litigation; Mass Torts; Products Liability; Workers Compensation; Social Security; Securities; Bankruptcy. ***Email:*** david@garrettlawoffice.com

---

DOUGLASS R. ELLIOTT, born Tulsa, Oklahoma, June 13, 1962; admitted to bar, 1993, Oklahoma, U.S. District Court, Northern and Eastern Districts of Oklahoma; 1994, U.S. District Court, Western District of Oklahoma. *Education:* University of Oklahoma (B.B.A., Finance, 1985); University of Tulsa Law School (J.D., with honors, 1992). Phi Delta Phi. *Member:* Muskogee County and Oklahoma Bar Associations; Oklahoma Trial Lawyers Association; The Association of Trial Lawyers of America. ***PRACTICE AREAS:*** Personal Injury. ***Email:*** doug@garrettlawoffice.com

JARED A. DeSILVEY, born Slidell, Louisiana, December 18, 1970; admitted to bar, 1997, Oklahoma. *Education:* University of Southern Mississippi (B.S., 1993); University

(This Listing Continued)

GARRETT LAW OFFICE, P.C., Tulsa—Continued

of Tulsa (J.D., 1996). Phi Delta Phi. *Member:* Muskogee and Oklahoma Bar Associations; The Association of Trial Lawyers of America. ***PRACTICE AREAS:*** Personal Injury. ***Email:*** jared@garrettlawoffice.com

DAVID C. BEAN, born Philadelphia, Pennsylvania, June 12, 1945; admitted to bar, 1988, Oklahoma and U.S. District Court, Northern, Eastern and Western Districts of Oklahoma. *Education:* Wake Forest University (B.A., 1967); Westchester University; University of Tulsa (J.D., 1988). Phi Alpha Delta. Recipient, American Jurisprudence Award, Commercial Law, 1986. *Member:* Oklahoma and American Bar Associations; Oklahoma Trial Lawyers Association; The Association of Trial Lawyers of America. ***REPORTED CASES:*** Richard v. Halter, 131 F.Supp.2d 1261, 73 soc.Sec.Rep.Serv. 60 (N.DOkla. Feb. 09, 2001, NO. 00-C-573-M); Heintz v. Trucks For You, Inc., 1999 OK CIV App 64, 1999 OK CIV APP 67, 984 P.2d 255 (Okla.Civ.App. Div. 2, Apr 13, 1999, NO 92215). ***PRACTICE AREAS:*** Personal Injury Law; Products Liability; Professional Negligence; Workers' Compensation Law; Social Security; Civil Litigation. ***Email:*** dave@garrettlawoffice.com

JOHN FRANCIS BATES, born Chicago, Illinois, April 21, 1950; admitted to bar, 1979, Oklahoma; U.S. District Court, Western District of Oklahoma; 1995, U.S. District Court, Northern District of Oklahoma. *Education:* Southern Illinois University (B.A., 1972; M.A., 1976); Oklahoma City University School of Law (J.D., 1979). Phi Alpha Delta. Case Comment Editor, Law Review. *Member:* Oklahoma Bar Association (Treasurer, Workers Compensation Section, 1992-1994); Oklahoma Trial Lawyers Association. ***REPORTED CASES:*** Barnhill v. Multiple Injury Trust Fund, 37 P.3d 890, 2001 OK 114 (Okla., Dec. 11, 2001, NO. 94575); King v. Pillsbury Bakery Co., 2001 OK CIV App 38, 21 P.3d 82 (Okla.Civ.App. Div. 3, Mar 01, 2001, NO. 95298); Dixon v. Bhulyan, 10 P.3d 888, 141 Lab. Cas. P 59,053, 147 Ed. Law Rep. 1106, 2000 OK 56 (Okla., Jul 18, 2000, NO. 92303); Clanton v. American Airlines, 1999 OK CI APP 110, 990 P.2d 338 (Okla.Civ.App. Div. 3, Aug 27, 1999, NO. 92,752); Bailes v. Home of Hope, 1999 OK CIV APP 27, 977 P.2d 1145 (Okla.Civ.App. Div. 2, Feb 09, 1999, NO. 91, 833); Eidschun v. Air-X-Changers, 1998 OK CIV APP 142, 964 P.2d 970 (Okla.Civ.App. Div. 1, Aug. 28, 1998, NO. 91, 194); Southwest United Industries v. Polston, 964 P.2d 210, 1998 OK 78 (Okla., Jul 14, 1998, NO. 82, 471); Noble County v. Cross, 1991 OK CIV APP 31, 810 P.2d 380 (Okla.App. Div. 3, Apr 16, 1991, NO. 75, 899); Glenn v. State, 749 P.2d 121, 1988 OK CR 16 (Okla. Crim.App., Jan 13, 1988, NO F-85-750); Wilhelm v. Wilhelm, 1983 OK CIV APP 9, 678 P.2d 727 (Okla.App. Div. 4, Mar 01, 1983, NO. 57092; Richardson v. J.C. Penney co., Inc., 1982 OK CIV APP 35, 649 P.2d 565 (Okla.App. Div. 2, Jul 13, 1982; NO 56419). ***PRACTICE AREAS:*** Workers Compensation. ***Email:*** john@garrettlawoffice.com

AMBER PECKIO GARRETT, born Tulsa, Oklahoma; admitted to bar, 2003, Oklahoma. *Education:* Southeastern Oklahoma State University (B.S., Economics and Political Science, 1999); University of Tulsa College of Law (J.D., 2003). Phi Delta Phi. *Member:* Tulsa County and Oklahoma Bar Associations; The Association of Trial Lawyers of America; Oklahoma Trial Lawyers Association. ***PRACTICE AREAS:*** Personal Injury; Insurance Law; Products Liability. ***Email:*** amber@garrettlawoffice.com

STEVEN F. LANGER, born Bentonville, Arkansas; admitted to bar, 1992, Oklahoma and U.S. District Court, Western District of Oklahoma; 1993, U.S. Court of Appeals, Tenth Circuit; 1996, U.S. District Court, Eastern District of Oklahoma; 1998, U.S. District Court, Northern District of Oklahoma; 2000, U.S. Supreme Court. *Education:* University of Oklahoma (B.A., Journalism, 1989; J.D., 1992). *Member:* McClain County (President, 2004) and Oklahoma (Member, Committees on: Legal Ethics, 1999-2001; Civil Procedure, 2000-2001) Bar Associations. ***REPORTED CASES:*** Walker v. Elbert, et. al., 75 F.3d 592 (10th Cir. 1996); Rosen v. White Swan, Inc., et al., OK CIV App 44, 69 P.3d 1229, 2003. ***PRACTICE AREAS:*** Workers Compensation; Personal Injury; Social Security Disability. ***Email:*** stevenl@garrettlawoffice.com

TIA J. BAKER SURLES, born Fayetteville, Arkansas, December 20, 1970; admitted to bar, 1998, Arkansas; 2000, Oklahoma; 2003, U.S. District Court, Northern District of Oklahoma; 2004, U.S. District Court, Eastern District of Oklahoma. *Education:* Hendrix College; University of Arkansas (B.A., Business Administration, 1993); University of Arkansas School of Law (J.D., 1996). Phi Alpha Delta; Sigma Iota. Dean's List. Listed, Who's Who American Law Students, 1996. *Member:* Tulas County, Arkansas and Oklahoma Bar Associations; The Association of Trial Lawyers of America. ***PRACTICE AREAS:*** Personal Injury; Estate Planning; Probate; Contracts; Insurance Law. ***Email:*** tia@garrettlawoffice.com

JEFFREY A. HEATER, born Paducah, Kentucky, November 16, 1969; admitted to bar, 2005, Oklahoma. *Education:* University of Memphis (B.S., Finance, 1996; M.B.A., 1998); University of Tulsa (J.D., 2004). Order of Barristers. President, American Constitution Society. Recipient: Lawyering Skills Certificate. National Health Law Moot Court Competition (Second place finisher overall and winner, Best Brief in 2004); Criminal Law Trial Advocacy Competition (First place finisher, 2004); Health Law Appellate Advocacy Competition (Second place finisher, 2004); Hager Tort Appellate Advocacy Competition (Second place finisher, 2004); Criminal Law Trial Advocacy Competition (Second place finisher, 2003); Health Law Appellate Advocacy Competition (Third place finisher, 2003). *Member:* Tulsa County, Oklahoma and American Bar Associations; Association of Trial Lawyers of America. ***Email:*** jeffh@garrettlawoffice.com

LEGAL SUPPORT PERSONNEL

KAETHE D. WAINWRIGHT, born Bad Schlangenbad, Germany, October 15, 1944. *Education:* Connors State College (A.A., Sociology); Northeastern Oklahoma State University (B.A., Psychology). Interpreter, German Police and German Courts, 1973-1977. Representation of Social Security Claimants at all administrative appeal levels since 1979 (20 CFR 404. 1703(b) and 20 CFR 416. 1505(b)). Legal Advocacy Worker, Legal Services of Eastern Oklahoma, *specializing in Social Security Disability, Veterans Appeals, and* Welfare cases, 1979-1996. *Member:* National Organization of Social Security Claimants Representatives. [Nato Affairs Clerk/Court Clerk/Interpreter, US Army Staff Judge Advocate Office, 3rd Armored Division, Germany, 1973-1977]. (Social Security Claimants' Representative). ***PRACTICE AREAS:*** Social Security Disability. ***Email:*** kaethe@garrettlawoffice.com

(This Listing Continued)

D. MITCHELL GARRETT, JR. *Education:* Texas A & M University (B.A., 1993); University of Tulsa (J.D., 2004) (Business Manager)

OF COUNSEL

RICK PAYNTER, born Tulsa, Oklahoma; admitted to bar, 1985, Oklahoma. *Education:* University of Oklahoma (B.A., 1981; J.D., 1984). *Member:* Tulsa County, Oklahoma and American Bar Associations. ***PRACTICE AREAS:*** Workers Compensation; Personal Injury; Products Liability; Civil Practice.

GREGORY P. WILLIAMS, born Rockville, Connecticut, March 29, 1945; admitted to bar, 1981, Oklahoma; 1982, U.S. District Court, Northern District of Oklahoma; 1986, U.S. District Court, Eastern District of Oklahoma; 1988, U.S. District Court, Western District of Oklahoma and U.S. Court of Appeals, 10th Circuit. *Education:* University of Missouri, School of Journalism at Columbia (B.J., cum laude, 1972); University of Tulsa (J.D., 1981). Recipient, Bozell and Jacobs Fellowship, 1971-1972. Member, American Inns of Court, 1992—. Faculty Member, University of Oklahoma College of Law, Trial Practice, 1992-1993. *Member:* Tulsa County, Oklahoma (Member, Task Force on Lawyer Solicitations and Advertising, 1994) and American (Member, Sections on: Torts and Insurance Practice Law; Litigation) Bar Associations; Oklahoma Trial Lawyers Association (President, 1994; Vice President, 1991-9290; Political Action Committee Chair, 1989-1991; Member, Executive Committee, 1985—; Member, Board of Directors, 1984—; Outstanding Member of the Year, 1987; President's Citation, 1986; Public Information Chairman, 1985-1987; Member, Speaker's Bureau, 1985-1992); The Association of Trial Lawyers of America; Sustaining Member, New York State Trial Lawyers Association. [With USN, 1965-1969]

GARVIN, AGEE, CARLTON & MASHBURN, L.L.P.

TULSA, OKLAHOMA

(See Pauls Valley)

Litigation, Personal Injury, Medical Malpractice, Automobile Accidents, Slip and Fall, Wrongful Death, Nursing Home Abuse, Unsafe Products, Toxic Torts, Legal Malpractice, Insurance, Professional Liability, Business Law, Commercial Law, Contracts, Corporate Law, Education Law, Banking Law, Bankruptcy, Debtor and Creditor, Taxation, Tax Planning, Consumer Law, Consumer Fraud, Warranties, Natural Resources, Energy, Elder Law, Wills and Probate, Trusts and Estates, Estate Planning, Guardianship, Real Estate, Buying or Selling a Home, Construction Law, Landlord and Tenant, General Practice, Appellate Practice.

GASSAWAY LAW FIRM

Established in 1999

THOMPSON BUILDING
20 EAST FIFTH STREET, SUITE 600
TULSA, OKLAHOMA 74103-4441
Telephone: 918-592-6800
Fax: 918-592-1800
URL: http://www.lawyers.com/gassawaylaw

Civil Litigation, Family Law, Divorce Child Custody, Child Support, Visitation Rights, Domestic Violence, Alimony, Spousal Support, Premarital Agreements, Post Decree Modifications, Adoptions, Guardianships, Estate Planning, Trusts, Probate and Wealth Transfer.

KEVIN T. GASSAWAY, born Ada, Oklahoma, June 28, 1955; admitted to bar, 1980, Oklahoma; 1981, U.S. District Court, Northern District of Oklahoma; 1986, U.S. District Court, Eastern District of Oklahoma and U.S. Court of Appeals, Tenth Circuit ; 1989, U.S. District Court, Western District of Oklahoma. *Education:* Centre College of Kentucky; University of Oklahoma (B.A. in Letters, 1977; J.D., 1980). Phi Delta Phi. *Member:* Tulsa County and Oklahoma (Member: Professional Responsibility Tribunal, 1985-1988; 1989-1990; Professional Responsibility Commission, 1990-1993) Bar Associations. ***PRACTICE AREAS:*** Family Law; Divorce; Adoption Law; Child Custody; Child Support; Premarital Agreements; Post Divorce Modification; Civil Litigation. ***Email:*** ktg@gassawaylaw.com

RITA J. GASSAWAY, born Ponca City, Oklahoma, May 4, 1959; admitted to bar, 1984, Oklahoma, U.S. District Court, Northern, Western and Eastern Districts of Oklahoma and U.S. Court of Appeals, 10th Circuit. *Education:* Oklahoma State University (B.S., 1981); University of Oklahoma (J.D., 1984). American Inns of Court (Barrister, W. Lee Johnson Chapter, 1994-2004, Executive Committee, 1997-2004). *Member:* Tulsa County and Oklahoma Bar Associations; Oklahoma Association of Defense Counsel (Vice President, 1993-1994; President, 1996); Tulsa Title and Probate Lawyers Association (Executive Committee, 2000); Estate Planning Forum (Secretary, 2002; V.P., 2003-2004; President, 2005). ***PRACTICE AREAS:*** Trusts and Estate Planning; Probate. ***Email:*** rjg@gassawaylaw.com

JODI JOHNSON BAKER, born Tulsa, Oklahoma, May 15, 1977; admitted to bar, 2002, Oklahoma and U.S. District Court, Western, Eastern and Northern Districts of Oklahoma. *Education:* University of Oklahoma (B.A., 1999; J.D., 2002). Phi Beta Kappa. Member, Mortar Board. *Member:* Tulsa County and Oklahoma Bar Associations; American Inns of Court (Council Oak/Johnson-Sontag Chapter). ***PRACTICE AREAS:*** Family Law; Divorce; Adoption Law; Child Custody; Child Support; Premarital Agreements; Post Divorce Modification; Civil Litigation. ***Email:*** jjb@gassawaylaw.com

LEGAL SUPPORT PERSONNEL

DEBORAH J. LIPPERD. Email: djl@gassawaylaw.com

CHERRY D. MARSHALL, (admission pending). *Education:* Associates Degree. ***Email:*** cdm@gassawaylaw.com

(This Listing Continued)

REBEKAH L. TAPIA, born 1977; (admission pending). ***Email:*** rlt@gassawaylaw.com

GIBBON, BARRON & BARRON, P.A.

2 W. 6TH STREET, SUITE 320
TULSA, OKLAHOMA 74119-1215
Telephone: 918-745-0687
Fax: 918-745-0821

Okmulgee, Oklahoma Office: P.O. Box 1211. Telephone: 918-756-7772.

General Civil Practice in all Courts. Workers Compensation, Personal Injury, Products Liability, Surety, Aviation and Insurance Law. Trials.

RICHARD D. GIBBON, born Blackwell, Oklahoma, December 24, 1925; admitted to bar, 1954, Oklahoma. *Education:* Morningside College; University of Tulsa (LL.B., 1954). Phi Beta Gamma. *Member:* Tulsa County, Oklahoma and American Bar Associations; Oklahoma Trial Lawyers Association. ***PRACTICE AREAS:*** Personal Injury; Torts; Plaintiff; Workers Compensation.

CINDY L. McVEY, born Tulsa, Oklahoma, April 23, 1959; admitted to bar, 1988, Oklahoma and U.S. District Court, Northern District of Oklahoma; 1990, U.S. District Court, Western and Eastern Districts of Oklahoma; 1993, U.S. Court of Appeals, 10th Circuit. *Education:* University of Tulsa (B.S.B.A., 1982; J.D., 1987). Delta Theta Phi. *Member:* Tulsa County, Oklahoma and American (Member, Tort and Insurance Practice Section) Bar Associations.

BRADFORD D. BARRON, born Norman, Oklahoma, October 27, 1971; admitted to bar, 1997, Oklahoma; 1998, U.S. District Court, Northern and Eastern Districts of Oklahoma. *Education:* Emporia State University (B.S., psychology, 1994); University of Tulsa (J.D., 1997). Phi Delta Phi. *Member:* Tulsa County, Oklahoma and American Bar Associations. ***PRACTICE AREAS:*** Personal Injury Litigation; Insurance Law.

ZACHARY T. BARRON, born Tulsa, Oklahoma, February 19, 1976; admitted to bar, 2001, Oklahoma and U.S. District Court, Northern District of Oklahoma. *Education:* Baker University (B.S., 1998); University of Tulsa (J.D., 2000). ***PRACTICE AREAS:*** Personal Injury; Insurance; Torts; Plaintiffs Personal Injury. ***Email:*** zbarron@gbbfirm.com

REPRESENTATIVE CLIENT: Intersearch Gas Corp.

CHARLES A. GIBBS, III

Established in 1982
BEACON BUILDING-SW MEZZANINE
406 SOUTH BOULDER AVENUE
TULSA, OKLAHOMA 74103-3821
Telephone: 918-599-9000
Fax: 918-599-9001
Email: LAW4HIRE@morelaw.com
URL: http://www.law4hire.com

Construction Law, Corporate and Business Practice. Commercial Law, Real Estate, Leases, Evictions, Landlord/Tenant, Mechanics Liens. General Civil Practice State and Federal Courts, Indian Gaming Law.

CHARLES A. GIBBS, III, born Tulsa, Oklahoma, September 14, 1956; admitted to bar, 1982, Oklahoma and U.S. District Court, Northern District of Oklahoma. *Education:* Oklahoma State University (B.S.B.A., 1978); University of Tulsa (J.D., 1982). Phi Delta Phi. *Member:* Tulsa County, Oklahoma and American Bar Associations.

REPRESENTATIVE CLIENTS: Kirby-Smith Machinery; Mid-Continent Casualty/Oklahoma Surety; Transco Supply; Midwesco Ind.; Cherokee Builders; Third Day Properties; Met Games.

GIBBS ARMSTRONG BOROCHOFF MULLICAN & HART, P.C.

500 PETROLEUM CLUB BUILDING
601 SOUTH BOULDER AVENUE
TULSA, OKLAHOMA 74119
Telephone: 918-587-3939
Fax: 918-582-5504
Email: ggibbs@tulsacounsel.com
URL: http://www.gibbsandarmstrong.com

General Civil Trial Practice including Corporate, Commercial, Railroad, Personal Injury, Bad Faith, Professional Malpractice, Nursing Home Malpractice, Medical Malpractice, Premises Liability, Automobile Negligence, Private and Commercial Trucking Negligence, Catastrophic Injury cases; Environmental Liability, Domestic Law and Workers Compensation; Governmental Tort Claims; Civil Rights Litigation; Military Justice; Business Planning and Municipal Law.

FIRM PROFILE: Gibbs & Armstrong a prominent mid-sized law firm, offers more than fifty years of diverse trial experience in civil litigation, with its primary focus on railroad defense, insurance defense matters, including those involving bad faith, car accidents, private and commercial truck, nursing home, nursing malpractice, catastrophic injury, premises liability, breach of contract, governmental tort claims, civil rights litigation, environmental liability, military justice, domestic law, and workers' compensation. The firm tries lawsuits throughout Oklahoma, Arkansas, and the Central United States as well as practicing before the U.S. Supreme and U.S. Appeals Courts. The firm enjoys a well recognized reputation for a personalized, responsive, and cost-conscious practice through aggressive and ethical representation of its clients utilizing state-of-the-art technology that serves as the cornerstone of its commitment to build and maintain long-term attorney-client relationships.

(This Listing Continued)

GEORGE GIBBS, born Flint, Michigan, March 2, 1954; admitted to bar, 1986, Oklahoma; 1987, Arkansas, U.S. District Courts, Eastern, Northern and Western Districts of Oklahoma and Northern and Eastern Districts of Arkansas and U.S. Court of Appeals, Eighth and Tenth Circuits. *Education:* Southern Baptist College (A.A., 1974); Southwest Baptist University (B.A., 1976); Southwest Baptist Theological Seminary (Masters, 1980); Oklahoma City University (J.D., 1986). *Member:* Tulsa County, Oklahoma, and Arkansas Bar Associations; Oklahoma Defense Counsel Association; Association of Trial Lawyers of America; National Association of Railroad Trial Counsel. ***PRACTICE AREAS:*** Products Liability; Insurance Law; Torts; Personal Injury Law; Uninsured Motorist Coverage; Professional Malpractice; Nursing Home Litigation; Insurance Bad Faith; Railroad Law. ***Email:*** ggibbs@tulsacounsel.com

TOM L. ARMSTRONG, born Norman, Oklahoma, April 26, 1940; admitted to bar, 1971, Oklahoma and U.S. District Court, Western District of Oklahoma; 1972, California; 1973, U.S. Court of Appeals, Tenth Circuit; 1975, U.S. District Court, Eastern District of Oklahoma; 1976, U.S. District Court, Northern District of Oklahoma; 1979, U.S. Supreme Court; 1981, U.S. District Court, Northern District of Texas. *Education:* University of California at Santa Barbara (B.A., 1968); Boalt Hall School of Law, University of California at Berkeley (J.D., 1971). Phi Beta Kappa. Adjunct Assistant Professor of Law, Tulsa College of Law, 1977-1981. *Member:* Tulsa County, Oklahoma and American Bar Associations; State Bar of California; National Association of Railroad Trial Counsel. ***PRACTICE AREAS:*** Civil Litigation; Railroad Law; Corporate Law; Banking Law. ***Email:*** tarmstrong@tulsacounsel.com

DOUGLAS M. BOROCHOFF, born Tulsa, Oklahoma, February 24, 1955; admitted to bar, 1990, Oklahoma and U.S. District Court, Northern District of Oklahoma; 1992, U.S. District Court, Eastern District of Oklahoma; 1997, U.S. Court of Appeals, Tenth Circuit. *Education:* University of Oklahoma (B.A., 1986); University of Tulsa (J.D., 1990). Phi Alpha Delta. Member: Order of the Barristers; National Moot Court Team, 1989-1990; National Mock Trial Team, 1989-1990; Tulsa Law Journal, 1988-1990. Recipient, American Jurisprudence Awards in Alternative Methods of Dispute Resolutions and Advanced Advocacy. *Member:* Tulsa County and Oklahoma Bar Associations; Oklahoma Association of Defense Counsel; National Association of Railroad Trial Counsel. ***PRACTICE AREAS:*** General Tort and Insurance Defense; Products Liability; Premises Liability; Real Estate Transactions; Medical Malpractice; Nursing Home Negligence. ***Email:*** dborochoff@tulsacounsel.com

GEORGE ROBERT MULLICAN, born Oklahoma City, Oklahoma, April 2, 1970; admitted to bar, 1995, Oklahoma; 2000, U.S. District Court, Eastern, Western and Northern Districts of Oklahoma and U.S. Court of Appeals, Tenth Circuit. *Education:* Northeastern Oklahoma State University (B.B.A., cum laude, 1992); University of Oklahoma College of Law (J.D., with honors, 1995). Member, University of Oklahoma Law Review. Author: "Are Stepchildren within the meaning of 'Children' in Title 12 B.S.1053 47 Okla. L. Rev. 727 (1994). *Member:* Oklahoma Bar Association. [Capt., U.S. Army, JAGC, 1995-1999]. ***PRACTICE AREAS:*** Commercial Litigation; Tort Defense; Military Justice; Railroad Law. ***Email:*** gmullican@tulsacounsel.com

ROBERT D. HART, born Tulsa, Oklahoma, May 5, 1969; admitted to bar, 1995, Oklahoma and U.S. District Court, Northern, Eastern and Western Districts of Oklahoma; 2000, U.S. Court of Appeals, Tenth Circuit. *Education:* Northeastern Oklahoma State University (B.B.A., cum laude, 1992); University of Oklahoma (J.D., with distinction, 1995). Alpha Chi; Rho Theta Sigma. *Member:* Tulsa County and Oklahoma Bar Associations. ***PRACTICE AREAS:*** Civil Litigation; Railroad Law; Corporate Law; Nursing Home Litigation; Civil Rights; Employment Law; Workers Compensation. ***Email:*** rhart@tulsacounsel.com

CHRISTOPHER D. WOLEK, born Paterson, New Jersey, June 28, 1970; admitted to bar, 1995, Texas; 2002, Oklahoma. *Education:* Tulane University (B.S., Chemistry, cum laude, 1992); University of Oklahoma (J.D., with honors, 1995). Phi Delta Phi; Board of Advocates. Managing Editor, Oklahoma Law Review, 1994-1995. Author: "Practice and Procedure: The Safe Harbor Amendment to Rule 11 ... Any Port in a Storm?" 47 Oklahoma Law Review 319, 1995; "Hippocrates Enters the New Millennium-Texas Medical Privileges in the Year 2000," 41 South Texas Law Review 315, 2000. *Member:* State Bar of Texas. ***PRACTICE AREAS:*** Civil Litigation; Health Law; Railroad Litigation. ***Email:*** cwolek@tulsacounsel.com

---

JEFFREY G. FIELDS, born Hampton, Virginia, February 26, 1971; admitted to bar, 2000, Oklahoma. *Education:* Eastern Kentucky University (B.A., 1993); University of Tulsa (J.D., 2000). *Member:* Oklahoma Bar Association. ***PRACTICE AREAS:*** Personal Injury; Nursing Home Liability; Workers Compensation. ***Email:*** jfields@tulsacounsel.com

ROBERT E. COWAN, born Tulsa, Oklahoma; admitted to bar, 1995, Oklahoma; U.S. District Court, Northern District of Oklahoma. *Education:* Carl Albert State College (A.S., 1986); Oklahoma State University (B.S., 1990); University of Tulsa College of Law (J.D., 1994). Phi Delta Phi. Editor, Tulsa Law Journal. Recipient, American Jurisprudence Awards for Civil Procedure and Commercial Law. *Member:* Oklahoma Bar Association. ***PRACTICE AREAS:*** Insurance Defense; Personal Injury; Nursing Home Litigation; Criminal Law. ***Email:*** rcowan@tulsacounsel.com

CHARLES A. McSOUD, born Tulsa, Oklahoma, May 12, 1971; admitted to bar, 2000, Oklahoma; U.S. District Court, Northern, Eastern and Western Districts of Oklahoma; U.S. Court of Appeals, Tenth Circuit. *Education:* Westminster College (B.A., 1993); University of Tulsa (M.A., 1995); University of Tulsa (J.D., 1999). Member, Board of Advocates. Recipient, First Place Award, Client Counseling Competition, Board of Advocates. *Member:* Tulsa County (Member, Young Lawyers Division), Oklahoma and American Bar Associations; Oklahoma Bar Foundation; The Association of Trial Lawyers of America; Oklahoma Trial Lawyers Association. ***PRACTICE AREAS:*** Insurance Defense; Nursing Home Litigation; Employment Discrimination; Civil Rights; Premises Liability; Business Torts. ***Email:*** cmcsoud@tulsacounsel.com

KEVIN S. HOSKINS, born El Paso, Texas, May 25, 1966; admitted to bar, 1996, Oklahoma and U.S. District Court, Northern and Eastern Districts of Oklahoma. *Education:* Northwestern Oklahoma State University (B.S., Biology and Chemistry, 1989); University of Tulsa College of Law (J.D., 1996). Phi Delta Phi. Senior Staff, Tulsa Law Journal. *Mem-*

(This Listing Continued)

GIBBS ARMSTRONG BOROCHOFF MULLICAN & HART, P.C., Tulsa—Continued

ber: Tulsa County and Oklahoma Bar Associations. ***PRACTICE AREAS:*** Construction Litigation; Products Liability; Insurance Defense; Personal Injury; Wrongful Death; Professional Malpractice; Nursing Home Litigation; Hospital Law; Insurance Bad Faith; Fire Insurance; Explosions; Electrocution Litigation; Petroleum Law; Environmental Litigation; Class Actions. ***Email:*** khoskins@tulsacounsel.com

JONATHAN D. CARTLEDGE, born Atlanta, Georgia, June 29, 1976; admitted to bar, 2001, Oklahoma. *Education:* Oral Roberts University (B.A., 1998); University of Tulsa College of Law (J.D., with highest honors, 2001). Phi Delta Phi. Recipient, CALI Awards for Legal Research and Writing, Torts, Administrative Law, Federal Income Taxation, Introduction to Alternative Dispute Resolution and Civil Procedure I.*Member:* Tulsa County and Oklahoma Bar Associations. ***PRACTICE AREAS:*** Nursing Home Litigation; Insurance Defense; Personal Injury. ***Email:*** jcartledge@tulsacounsel.com

KARLA M. ROGERS, born Edmond, Oklahoma, December 6, 1967; admitted to bar, 2000, Oklahoma; U.S. District Court, Northern, Eastern and Western Districts of Oklahoma and U.S. Court of Appeals, Tenth Circuit. *Education:* Texas Tech University (B.S., 1991); University of Tulsa (J.D., 1999). Dean's List. Phi Delta Phi. Recipient, Cali Award, Excellence for Comparative Antitrust. Staff Member: International and Comparative Law Journal; Energy Law Journal. Member, Board of Advocates. *Member:* Tulsa County and Oklahoma Bar Associations. ***PRACTICE AREAS:*** Products Liability; Premises Liability; Employment Discrimination; Nursing Home Negligence; Insurance Defense; Personal Injury. ***Email:*** krogers@tulsacounsel.com

EDDIE L. CARR, born Lindsay, Oklahoma, October 26, 1961; admitted to bar, 1989, Oklahoma; U.S. District Court, Northern District of Oklahoma; 1990, U.S. Court of Federal Claims. *Education:* Central State University (B.S., 1984); Oklahoma City University (J.D., 1988). Phi Delta Phi. *Member:* Tulsa County and Oklahoma Bar Associations. ***PRACTICE AREAS:*** Nursing Home Abuse and Neglect; Medical Malpractice Defense. ***Email:*** ecarr@tulsacounsel.com

PETER C. ASTOR, born Hammond, Indiana, November 30, 1970; admitted to bar, 1997, Oklahoma; 2001, U.S. District Court, Northern District of Oklahoma and U.S. Court of Appeals, Tenth Circuit; 2002, U.S. District Court, Eastern District of Oklahoma. *Education:* University of Oklahoma (B.A., Journalism, 1994); University of Oklahoma College of Law (J.D., 1997). Special Features Editor, American Indian Law Review, 1996-1997. ***PRACTICE AREAS:*** Insurance Defense; Nursing Home Negligence; Medical Malpractice. ***Email:*** pastor@tulsacounsel.com

JANUARY J. WINDRIX, born Tulsa, Oklahoma, January 30, 1976; admitted to bar, 2004, Oklahoma. *Education:* Northeastern State University (B.S., cum laude, 2001); University of Tulsa (J.D. with honor, 2004). Phi Delta Phi. Recipient: CALI Awards for Corporate Law, Professional Responsibility. *Member:* Oklahoma Bar Association. ***PRACTICE AREAS:*** Railroad Law.

COREY CORNELISON, born Ft. Worth, Texas, April 26, 1972; admitted to bar, 2003, Oklahoma and U.S. District Court, Eastern District of Oklahoma; 2004, U.S. District Court, Northern District of Oklahoma. *Education:* Northeastern Oklahoma State University (B.S., cum laude, Criminal Justice, 1997); University of Tulsa (J.D., 2003). ***PRACTICE AREAS:*** Insurance Defense; Litigation; Contracts; Domestic Relations; Probate.

LAURA L. EAKENS, born November 15, 1979; admitted to bar, 2004, Oklahoma; U.S. District Court, Northern District of Oklahoma. *Member:* Tulsa and Oklahoma Bar Associations. ***PRACTICE AREAS:*** Railroad Law.

REPRESENTATIVE CLIENTS: Midwest Mutual Insurance Company; GuideOne Insurance Company; Brotherhood Mutual Insurance Company; CNA Ins. Co.; Country Companies Insurance Company; State Farm Insurance Company; CGU Insurance Company; Trans-General Insurance Company; One Beacon Ins. Co.; Gulf Insurance Company; Western Heritage Insurance Company; Philadelphia Insurance Company; Baptist General Convention of Oklahoma; Oklahoma Baptist University; Baptist Retirement Centers of Oklahoma; Bailey-Forristell; Met Life; Union Pacific Railroad; Chicago & Northwestern Trans. Co.; CNA Insurance; Coregis Insurance; International Pro Rodeo Association; McLarens Toplis; National Rail Passenger Corp. (AMTRAK); Norfolk Southern Corp; North American Van Lines; Sand Springs Railway Company; South Kansas & Oklahoma Railroad; State Auto Insurance Co.; Hospital Casualty Co.; Burlington Northern Santa Fe Railway Co.; FCI Logistics.

THE GLENDENING LAW FIRM

8816 SOUTH SHERIDAN ROAD
TULSA, OKLAHOMA 74133
Telephone: 918-494-7037
Fax: 918-494-0766

General Practice.

MEMBER OF FIRM

JEFFREY A. GLENDENING, born Tulsa, Oklahoma, March 22, 1960; admitted to bar, 1986, Oklahoma. *Education:* University of Oklahoma (B.A., 1982; J.D., 1985). Phi Alpha Delta. *Member:* Tulsa County, Oklahoma and American Bar Associations; Oklahoma Association of Defense Counsel. ***PRACTICE AREAS:*** Hospital Liability Defense; Physician Practices; Nursing Home Abuse and Neglect.

ASSOCIATES

JOHN D. BOGATKO, born Philadelphia, Pennsylvania, May 15, 1973; admitted to bar, 2002, Oklahoma; 2003, U.S. District Court, Eastern District of Oklahoma. *Education:* Southwest Missouri State University (B.A., 1996); University of Tulsa (M.A., 2002; J.D., 2002). Recipient: Certificate in Health Law: Boone, Smith, Davis, Hurst & Dickman Law, Medicine and Ethics Award; CALI Awards for: Civil Procedure II; Criminal Procedure: Police Practices; Domestic Violence; Evidence Workshop; Law, Medicine and Ethics Seminar; Protection of Minority and Indigenous Cultures. Author: "Stem Cell Research: A Comparative Legal Analysis," Journal of Medicine and Law, Michigan State University Detroit College of Law, Vol. 6, Issue 2, Spring 2002. *Member:* Oklahoma Bar Association. ***PRACTICE AREAS:*** Nursing Home Litigation.

(This Listing Continued)

JAMES A. HIGGINS, admitted to bar, 2000, Oklahoma and U.S. District Court, Northern and Eastern Districts of Oklahoma. *Education:* University of Tulsa (B.A., 1993; J.D., 1999). Editor, Tulsa Law Journal, 1998-1999. *Member:* Tulsa, Oklahoma and American Bar Associations. ***PRACTICE AREAS:*** Medical Malpractice; Insurance Defense; Appellate Practice.

ANGIE A. SUMNER, born Dallas, Texas, June 4, 1970; admitted to bar, 2002, Oklahoma. *Education:* Baylor University (B.B.A., 1992); University of Tulsa (J.D., 2000). *Member:* Oklahoma Bar Association.

JAMES R. GOTWALS AND ASSOCIATES, INC.

A PROFESSIONAL CORPORATION

Established in 1978

1130 PARK CENTRE, 525 SOUTH MAIN STREET
TULSA, OKLAHOMA 74103-4512
Telephone: 918-599-7088
Fax: 918-599-7153
URL: http://www.jrgotlaw.com
Email: jim.gotwals@jrgotlaw.com
URL: http://www.gotwalslaw.com

General Civil and Trial Practice. Family, Personal Injury, Real Estate, Probate, Corporate, Oil and Gas, Criminal Law, Business Formations, Business Litigation, Commercial Litigation, Contingent Business Litigation, Securities Litigation, Mediation.

FIRM PROFILE: James R. Gotwals and Associates, Inc. is listed in Martindale-Hubbell's Bar Register of Preeminent Lawyers.

JAMES R. GOTWALS, born Tulsa, Oklahoma, November 9, 1950; admitted to bar, 1975, Oklahoma, U.S. District Court, Northern and Eastern Districts of Oklahoma and U.S. Court of Appeals, Tenth Circuit. *Education:* Oklahoma University (B.B.A., 1972; J.D., 1975). Phi Delta Phi. Listed, Best Lawyers in America, 1992—. *Member:* Tulsa County (Chairman: Fitness and Mental Health Committee, 1993-1994, Fee Arbitration Committee, 1993-1994; Member, Professional Responsibility Committee, 1995—; Vice Chair, 2002-2003; Chair, 2003-2004; Member, 1996—; Chairman, 1999-2000, Tulsa County Bar Association Family Law Section; Tulsa County Bar Court Operations Committee, 1999—), Oklahoma (Member, Executive Board, Family Law Section, 1990-1995; Member, Real Property Section; Chairman, Family Law Section, 1995-1996) and American (Member, Family Law Section) Bar Associations; American Inns of Court, 1999—; Oklahoma Trial Lawyers Association; Association of Trial Lawyers of America; Quality Assurance Panel for the Families in Transition Program of the 14th Judicial District of Oklahoma, 1999-2004 (Certified Mediator). ***PRACTICE AREAS:*** Civil Litigation; Family; Real Estate; Mediation. ***Email:*** jim.gotwals@jrgotlaw.com

MARY L. GUTIERREZ, born Brownsville, Texas, December 17, 1951; admitted to bar, 1999, Oklahoma, U.S. District Court, Northern and Eastern Districts of Oklahoma and U.S. Court of Appeals, Tenth Circuit. *Education:* University of Tulsa (B.A., 1973); University of Tulsa College of Law (J.D., with honors, 1999). Phi Delta Phi. Recipient, CALI Awards for: Legal Authorities; Appellate Advocacy. Research Editor, Notes and Comments, Tulsa Law Journal, 1998-1999. Author: "Oklahoma's New Adoption Code and Disclosure of Identifying Information," 34 Tulsa LJ 133 (1998). Certified Mediator. *Member:* Tulsa County, Oklahoma and American (Member, TCBA Court Operations and Children and the Law Committees) Bar Associations; Oklahoma Trial Lawyers Association. ***PRACTICE AREAS:*** Family Law; Civil Litigation. ***Email:*** mary.gutierrez@jrgotlaw.com

OF COUNSEL

ARTHUR E. RUBIN, born Fairland, Oklahoma, 1921; admitted to bar, 1950, Oklahoma. *Education:* University of Oklahoma (J.D., 1950). Phi Delta Phi. Associate Editor, Oklahoma Bar Journal, 1978-1984. Author: "Property Division in Divorce," 54 Oklahoma Bar Journal 531, February 26, 1983. Assistant Professor of Law, University of Tulsa, 1951-1952. Member, Oklahoma Industrial Finance Authority, 1965-1973; Tulsa River Parks Authority, 1980-1986. Member, Board of Trustees, Oklahoma Public Employees Retirement System, 1989-1991. Member, Federal Judge Selection Committee, Northern District of Oklahoma. *Member:* Tulsa County and Oklahoma Bar Associations. ***PRACTICE AREAS:*** Family Law; Personal Injury.

GRAHAM & FREEMAN, PLLC

Established in 2003

6226 E. 101ST STREET, SUITE 300
TULSA, OKLAHOMA 74137
Telephone: 918-298-1716
Fax: 918-298-1728
Email: info@grahamfreeman.com
URL: http://www.grahamfreeman.com

Litigation, Business Litigation, Business Arbitration, Products Liability, White Collar Criminal Defense, Civil Trial Law, Insurance Bad Faith Litigation, Native American Law, Insurance Defense.

TONY M. GRAHAM, born Mexico, Missouri, May 17, 1949; admitted to bar, 1977, Oklahoma, U.S. District Court, Northern, Eastern and Western Districts of Oklahoma and U.S. Court of Appeals, Tenth Circuit. *Education:* University of Missouri at Rolla (B.S., 1971); University of Tulsa (J.D., 1976). Phi Delta Phi. Blue Key. Recipient, Conoco Scholarship. W. Lee Johnson Inn of Court (Master Emeritus, 1989—). Member: National Association of Former U.S. Attorneys, 1993; Tulsa Fed. Executives Association, 1988-1993. Au-

(This Listing Continued)

thor: 12 Tulsa Law Journal 194, Federal Courts, Remand, 1976. Adjunct Professor, University of Tulsa College of Law, Professional Responsibility, 1983. Faculty Advisor, National Judicial College, Reno, Nevada, 1982-1985; Special District Judge, Tulsa County, Oklahoma, 1978-1982; District Judge, Tulsa County, Oklahoma, 1982-1987; U.S. Attorney, Northern District of Oklahoma, 1987-1993. Former Partner, Feldman, Franden, Woodard, Farris & Boudreaux. Founder, Graham & Freeman, P.L.L.C. *Member:* Tulsa County and Oklahoma Bar Associations; International Association of Defense Counsel. ***PRACTICE AREAS:*** Litigation; Business Litigation; Business Arbitration; Business Mediation; Products Liability; Native American Law; Gaming Law; Complex Commercial Litigation; White Collar Criminal Defense; Federal Criminal Law. ***Email:*** tgraham@grahamfreeman.com

R. JACK FREEMAN, born Commerce, Oklahoma, November 14, 1948; admitted to bar, 1982, Oklahoma, U.S. District Court, Northern, Eastern and Western Districts of Oklahoma and U.S. Court of Appeals, Tenth Circuit. *Education:* Ozark Bible College (B.S.L., 1971); Pittsburgh State University (B.S., 1978); University of Tulsa College of Law (J.D., 1982). Formerly, Solo Practitioner; Partner, Feldman, Franden, Woodard, Farris & Boudreaux. Founder, Graham & Freeman, P.L.L.C. Member. *Member:* Tulsa County Bar Association; Oklahoma Bar Association; American Bar Association; Oklahoma Association of Defense Counsel. ***REPORTED CASES:*** Carson v. Specialized Concrete, Inc., 1990 OK 87, 801 P.2d 691 (Okla. 1990); Hartley v. Williamson, 2001 OK CIV APP 6, 18 P.3d 355. ***PRACTICE AREAS:*** Insurance Defense; Insurance Bad Faith; Commercial Litigation; Catastrophic Injury; Products Liability. ***Email:*** jfreeman@grahamfreeman.com

WILLIAM F. SMITH, born Lawton, Oklahoma, October 18, 1952; admitted to bar, 1977, Oklahoma, U.S. District Court, Northern, Eastern and Western Districts of Oklahoma and U.S. Court of Appeals, Tenth Circuit. *Education:* Oklahoma State University (B.A., 1974); University of Tulsa (J.D., 1977). Order of the Curule Chair. *Member:* Oklahoma Bar Association. ***PRACTICE AREAS:*** Personal Injury; Insurance Bad Faith; Medical Malpractice; Products Liability; Insurance Defense; Premises Liability. ***Email:*** bsmith@grahamfreeman.com

SHEILA M. BRADLEY, born Flushing, New York, July 17, 1940; admitted to bar, 1989, Oklahoma; U.S. District Court, Northern, Eastern and Western Districts of Oklahoma; U.S. Court of Appeals, Tenth Circuit and U.S. Supreme Court. *Education:* University of Pennsylvania (B.A., 1962); University of Tulsa (J.D., with honors, 1989). Phi Delta Phi; Order of the Curule Chair; Barrister, American Inns of Court, (Hudson-Hall-Wheaton Chapter, 1996—). Staff Member, Tulsa Law Journal, 1987-1989. Member, National Client Counseling Team, 1986-1987. *Member:* Oklahoma Bar Association; Tulsa County Bar Foundation. ***PRACTICE AREAS:*** Civil Practice; Litigation; Family Law; Probate; Trusts and Estates; Insurance Defense; Bankruptcy. ***Email:*** sbradley@grahamfreeman.com

---

GRAVES & BARKETT, PLLC

1010 BOULDER TOWERS
1437 SOUTH BOULDER AVENUE
TULSA, OKLAHOMA 74119
Telephone: 918-582-6900
Fax: 918-582-6907
Email: dgraves@webzone.net
URL: http://www.gblaw.org

Civil Practice, Medical Negligence, Personal Injury, Medical Malpractice, Products Liability, Business Litigation, Commercial Law, Employment Litigation, Criminal Defense.

DANIEL B. GRAVES, born Tulsa, Oklahoma, January 23, 1969; admitted to bar, 1995, Oklahoma and U.S. District Court, Northern, Western and Eastern Districts of Oklahoma. *Education:* University of Tulsa (B.A., 1991; J.D., 1995). Phi Delta Phi. Recipient, American Jurisprudence Awards: Professional Responsibility; Legal Research and Writing. Recipient, Philip Allen Porta Memorial Scholarship for Legal Ethics. Listed in, Who's Who in American Law Students. *Member:* Tulsa County, Oklahoma and American Bar Associations; Oklahoma Trial Lawyers Association; The Association of Trial Lawyers of America. ***LANGUAGES:*** Latin. ***REPORTED CASES:*** LCR, Inc. v. Linwood Properties, et al, 918 P.2d 1388 (Okla. 1996). ***PRACTICE AREAS:*** Civil Practice; Medical Negligence; Personal Injury.

MICHAEL L. BARKETT, born Oklahoma City, Oklahoma, October 1, 1968; admitted to bar, 1994, Oklahoma, U.S. District Court, Western District of Oklahoma and U.S. Court of Appeals, Tenth Circuit; 1995, U.S. District Court, Northern District of Oklahoma; 1999, U.S. District Court, Eastern District of Oklahoma; 2001, U.S. District Court, Northern District of Texas and U.S. Supreme Court. *Education:* University of Oklahoma (B.A., Political Science, 1990; J.D., with distinction, 1994). Phi Delta Phi. Recipient, American Jurisprudence Award in Trial Practice, 1993. Author and Presenter: "Medical Expert Testimony--Successful Deposition and Trial Testimony," Okla. Bar Assoc. Seminar October 2002; "Trying the Wrongful Death Case," National Business Institute Seminar, 1999. Co-Author: "Discovery Issues in Bad Faith Cases," Oklahoma Bar Association Seminar, 1995. *Member:* Oklahoma County, Tulsa County and American Bar Associations. ***REPORTED CASES:*** Shore Slurry Seal, Inc. v. CMI Corp., 964 F. Supp. 152 (D. N.J. 1997); Multimedia Games, Inc. v. WLGC Acquisition Corp., 214 F.Supp.2d 1131 (N.D. Okla. 2001). ***PRACTICE AREAS:*** Medical Malpractice; Personal Injury; Products Liability; Business Litigation; Commercial Law; Employment Litigation; Criminal Defense.

WILLIAM McLAIN, born Orangeburg, South Carolina, February 24, 1969; admitted to bar, 2002, Oklahoma; 2002, U.S. District Court, Northern and Western Districts. *Education:* Wofford College (B.A., Finance, 1991); University of Tulsa (J.D., 2001). Phi Delta Phi. Recipient, Cali Award for Insurance Law. *Member:* Tulsa County Bar Association; The Association of Trial Lawyers of America; Oklahoma Trial Lawyers Association. ***PRACTICE AREAS:*** Personal Injury; Civil Practice; Medical Negligence. ***Email:*** chad.mclain@sbcglobal.net

GRIFFIN, REYNOLDS & ASSOCIATES

TULSA, OKLAHOMA

(See Oklahoma City)

Personal Injury, Insurance Bad Faith, Family Law, Wills, Trust Law, Probate, Bankruptcy, Auto Accidents, Trucking Accidents, Motorcycle Accidents, Wrongful Death, Products Liability, Nursing Home Abuse, Medical Malpractice, Divorce, Child Custody, Adoptions, Child Support and Workers Compensation Law.

MARIJO COPELAND GRISSOM, P.C.

Established in 2002
TWO MAIN PLAZA
616 SOUTH MAIN, SUITE 301
TULSA, OKLAHOMA 74119
Telephone: 918-582-4848
Fax: 918-582-4846
Email: mcgrissom@sbcglobal.net

Family Law, Wills, Probate, Personal Injury.

FIRM PROFILE: After working in the federal sector in environmental and regulatory areas, Marijo Copeland Grissom launched Marijo Copeland Grissom, P.C., a solo practice that focuses on legal concerns of the family. The firm also offers divorce and family mediation.

MARIJO COPELAND GRISSOM, born Tulsa, Oklahoma, April 27, 1951; admitted to bar, 1996, Oklahoma. *Education:* University of Tulsa (B.S., 1977); University of Oklahoma (J.D., 1989). *Member:* Tulsa (Member: Lawyer Referral Panel; Diversity Committee; Family Law Section), Oklahoma (Member, Sections on: Family Law; Estate Planning and Probate; Member, Diversity Committee) and American Bar Associations. ***PRACTICE AREAS:*** Family Law; Adoption Law; Child Custody; Child Support; Paternity; Divorce; Wills; Probate; Guardianships; Family Mediation; Personal Injury. ***Email:*** mcgrissom@sbcglobal.net

---

HALL, ESTILL, HARDWICK, GABLE, GOLDEN & NELSON

A PROFESSIONAL CORPORATION
320 SOUTH BOSTON AVENUE, SUITE 400
TULSA, OKLAHOMA 74103
Telephone: 918-594-0400
Facsimile: 918-594-0505
URL: http://www.HallEstill.com

Oklahoma City Office: Bank One Center, Suite 2900, 100 North Broadway, 73102-8827. Telephone: 405-553-2828. Facsimile: 405-553-2855.

Washington, D.C. Office: Suite 700 North Building, 1120 20th Street N.W. 20036-3406. Telephone: 202-973-1200. Facsimile: 202-973-1212.

Fayetteville, Arkansas Office: One East Center Street, Suite 315, 72701. Telephone: 479-973-5200. Facsimile: 479-973-0520.

General Civil Practice. Trials and proceedings before all State and Federal Courts and Agencies. Antitrust, Bankruptcy, Banking, Construction, Corporate, Commercial, Securities, Employee Benefits, Executive Compensation, Energy, Natural Resources, Energy Regulatory, Environmental, Estate Planning, Probate, Family Law, Domestic, Healthcare, Medical Malpractice, Indian Law, Intellectual Property, International Law and Trade, Labor, Employment, Legislative, Administrative Law, Litigation, Media, Real Estate, Taxation, Telecommunications, Tort, Insurance Defense, Utility Law.

FIRM PROFILE: Hall, Estill, Hardwick, Gable, Golden & Nelson, P.C. is listed in Martindale Hubbell's Bar Register of Preeminent Lawyers.

WALTER B. HALL (1923-1986)

FRED S. NELSON (1928-1987)

JAMES C. T. HARDWICK, born Bartlesville, Oklahoma, February 23, 1938; admitted to bar, 1963, Oklahoma. *Education:* University of Oklahoma (B.S., with distinction, 1960; LL.B., 1963). Phi Delta Phi; Tau Beta Pi; Sigma Tau; Pi Epsilon Tau; Phi Eta Sigma. Member, Board of Editors, Oklahoma Law Review, 1961-1963. Author: "The 1982 Model Form Operating Agreement: Changes and Continuing Concerns," Special Institute on Oil and Gas Agreements, (Rocky Mountain Mineral Law Foundation), 1983; "Gas Royalty Issues Arising From Direct Gas Marketing," 43 Oil & Gas Inst., ch. 11, Sw. Legal Fdn. (Matthew Bender 1992); "Gas Marketing Royalty Issues in The 1990's," Special Institute on Oil And Gas Royalties On Non-Federal Lands (Rocky Mtn. Min. Law Fdn. 1993); "Indian Units And Indian Communitization Agreements," Special Institute on Onshore Pooling and Unitization (Rocky Mtn. Min. Law Fdn. 1997); "Response and Comment: Some Musings on Fiduciary Duties and Oil and Gas Relationships," 50 Oil & Gas Inst., ch. 4A, Appendix, Sw. Legal Fdn. (Matthew Bender 1999); "Something Old, Something New — Current Issues Under the Joint Operating Agreement," 51 Oil & Gas Inst. ch. 6, Sw. Legal Fdn. (Matthew Bender 2000); and "Private Landowner Royalties on Oil — Theory and Reality," Special Institute on Private Oil & Gas Royalties, (Rocky Mtn. Min. Law Fdn. 2003); "Market Value Royalties - Yesterday, Today and Tomorrow," (Energy & Mineral Law 25th Annual Institute, 2004). Oklahoma Reporter, "Mineral Law Newsletter," Rocky Mountain Mineral Law Foundation, 1984—. Past Trustee and Past Member of Executive Committee, Rocky Mountain Mineral Law Fdn. Vice-Chair of the Executive Committee of the Advisory Board of the Institute for Energy Law of The Center for American and International Law (formerly The Southwestern Legal Fdn). The 2004 recipient of the Eugene Kuntz Award for Leadership in Natural Resources Law and Policy. AAPL Committee on Revision of Form 610 Joint Operating Agreement, 1986-1989. *Member:* Tulsa County, Oklahoma and American Bar Associations. ***PRACTICE AREAS:*** Natural Resources Law; Federal and State Energy Regulatory Law; Partnership Law. ***Email:*** JHARDWICK@HallEstill.com

(This Listing Continued)

HALL, ESTILL, HARDWICK, GABLE, GOLDEN & NELSON, A PROFESSIONAL CORPORATION, Tulsa—Continued

LARRY W. SANDEL, born Huntington Park, California, January 20, 1943; admitted to bar, 1969, California; 1976, Oklahoma. *Education:* University of Southern California (B.A., 1964; J.D., 1968). Order of the Coif. Associate Editor, University of Southern California Law Review, 1967-1968. ***PRACTICE AREAS:*** Securities Law; Corporation Law; Partnership Law; Commercial Law. ***Email:*** LSANDEL@HallEstill.com

ANDREW M. WOLOV, born Philadelphia, Pennsylvania, December 10, 1941; admitted to bar, 1966, Pennsylvania; 1970, U.S. Tax Court; 1977, Oklahoma. *Education:* Pennsylvania State University (B.S., 1963); Villanova University (J.D., 1966); New York University (LL.M., Tax, 1969). Attorney in Office of Chief Counsel, Internal Revenue Service, 1966-1968. *Member:* Tulsa County, Oklahoma and American Bar Associations; American College of Trust and Estate Counsel. ***PRACTICE AREAS:*** Taxation Law; Estate Planning Law; Employee Benefits Law. ***Email:*** AWOLOV@HallEstill.com

FRANK M. HAGEDORN, born Morgantown, West Virginia, February 11, 1938; admitted to bar, 1968, Oklahoma; U.S. District Court, Northern, Eastern and Western Districts of Oklahoma; U.S. Court of Criminal Appeals, Tenth, Federal and District of Columbia Circuits; U.S. Supreme Court. *Education:* University of Tulsa (B.A., 1961; J.D., 1968). Delta Theta Phi. Assistant District Attorney, Tulsa, Oklahoma, 1968-1973. Director, Oklahoma Bureau of Investigation, 1973-1974. *Member:* Tulsa County, Oklahoma and American Bar Associations; The Association of Trial Lawyers of America; American Inns of Court (Council Oak/Johnson-Sontag Chapter); National Criminal Defense Association. ***PRACTICE AREAS:*** Commercial Law; General Civil Litigation; Selective Federal Criminal Practice; Labor Law. ***Email:*** FHAGEDORN@HallEstill.com

J. PATRICK CREMIN, born Tulsa, Oklahoma, November 18, 1944; admitted to bar, 1974, Oklahoma; U.S. District Court, Northern District of Michigan and U.S. Court of Appeals, Fifth, Eighth and Tenth Circuits. *Education:* University of Tulsa (B.S., 1966; J.D., 1973). Phi Delta Phi. Listed in: Best Lawyers in America; Who's Who in American Law. Cited as Leading Lawyer for Business, Chambers USA. Member: National Moot Court Team; Order of the Barristers. Order of the Curule Chair, 1973. Member, University of Tulsa Law Review, 1972-1973. Master, American Inns of Court. *Member:* Tulsa County, Oklahoma and American Bar Associations. The American College of Trial Lawyers. ***PRACTICE AREAS:*** Labor and Employment Law; Civil Litigation. ***Email:*** PCREMIN@HallEstill.com

J. KEVIN HAYES, born Tulsa, Oklahoma, April 22, 1950; admitted to bar, 1975, Oklahoma. *Education:* University of Tulsa (B.S., 1972; J.D., 1974). Phi Gamma Kappa; Phi Alpha Delta. *Member:* Tulsa County, Oklahoma and American Bar Associations; Federal Energy Bar Association; American Inns of Court (Master; President, Council Oak Chapter). ***PRACTICE AREAS:*** Energy; Commercial Litigation; Oil and Gas Pipeline Law; Telecommunications Law; Natural Resources Law. ***Email:*** KHAYES@HallEstill.com

MICHAEL D. GRAVES, born Randolph Field AFB, Texas, February 4, 1946; admitted to bar, 1973, Oklahoma; 1977, Kentucky. *Education:* Tulsa University (B.A., 1967; M.A., 1969); Washington University (J.D., 1973). Member, Order of the Coif. Author: "Attorneys' Fees: What Constitutes a 'Benefit' Sufficient to Award Fees From Third Party Beneficiaries," Washington University Law Quarterly 271, 1972. Co-Author: Note, "Introduction: The Insanity Defense in the District of Columbia," Washington University Law Quarterly 19, 1973; "Environmental Compliance Auditing," 21 Tulsa Lawyer 9, 1981. Co-Author: "Oklahoma" Chapter, 6 Environmental Law Practice Guide (Matthew Bender, 1997). Author: "Selected Environmental Issues in Bankruptcy Law," Oklahoma Environmental Law Handbook (Oklahoma Bar Association, 1997). Author: "Oklahoma" Chapter, Brownfields: A Comprehensive Guide To Redeveloping Contaminated Property (Section of Environment, Energy and Resources, American Bar Association, 2002). Trial Attorney, Pollution Control Section, Land and Natural Resources Division, U.S. Department of Justice, 1973-1977. Recipient, Award for Meritorious Service, Land and Natural Resources Division, U.S. Department of Justice, 1976. Lecturer, Environmental Law, University of Louisville School of Law, 1978. Adjunct Professor of Environmental Law, University of Tulsa, 1982. Chairman, Policy and Planning Committee, Governor's Council on Environmental Quality, 1990-1994. Former Chairman, Environmental Law Section, Oklahoma Bar Association. Former Chairman, and current Vice Chairman, Hazardous Waste Advisory Council, Oklahoma Department of Environmental Quality. *Member:* Tulsa County, Oklahoma, Kentucky and American (Member, Section on Natural Resources Law) Bar Associations. ***PRACTICE AREAS:*** Environmental Regulation; Environmental Litigation; Environmental Land Use; Water Law; Civil Appeals; Architectural Law. ***Email:*** MGRAVES@HallEstill.com

JAMES D. SATROM, born Lake Charles, Louisiana, March 31, 1952; admitted to bar, 1977, Virginia; 1980, Oklahoma. *Education:* Tulane University (B.A., cum laude, 1974); University of Virginia (J.D., 1977). Phi Beta Kappa. Attorney-Advisor, Office of the General Counsel, Secretary of the Air Force, 1977-1980. *Member:* Tulsa County, Oklahoma and Federal Energy Bar Associations. ***PRACTICE AREAS:*** Energy Law; Federal and State Regulatory Law; International Law. ***Email:*** JSATROM@HallEstill.com

RICHARD A. GROENENDYKE, JR., born Birmingham, Alabama, December 22, 1945; admitted to bar, 1970, Alabama; 1987, Oklahoma. *Education:* University of Alabama (B.A., 1967); Cumberland School of Law of Samford University (J.D., 1970). ***PRACTICE AREAS:*** Litigation; Family Law. ***Email:*** RGROENENDYKE@HallEstill.com

GRAYDON DEAN LUTHEY, JR., born Topeka, Kansas, September 18, 1955; admitted to bar, 1979, Oklahoma, U.S. Court of Appeals, Tenth Circuit, U.S. Claims Court, U.S. Tax Court and U.S. District Court, Northern, Eastern and Western Districts of Oklahoma; 1982, U.S. Supreme Court; 2000, U.S. Court of Appeals, Sixth Circuit. *Education:* University of Oklahoma (B.A. in Letters, with highest honors, 1976; J.D., 1979); Keble College of Oxford University, Oxford, England. Phi Beta Kappa; Omicron Delta Kappa. Visiting Research Fellow of Keble College, 1975. Author: "Chickasaw Nation v. United States: The Beginning of the End of the Indian Law Canons in Statuatory Cases and the Start of the Judicial Assault on the Trust Relationship?" 27 Am. Indian L. Law Review Rev. 553 (2003). Chancellor of the Episcopal Diocese of Oklahoma, 1985-1999. Adjunct Professor of Law, University of Tulsa, 1985—. Chairman, University Hospitals Authority of State of Oklahoma, 1993-1998. Chairman, State of Oklahoma Economic Future Board, 1998-2002. Chairman, Tulsa Public Facilities Authority, 1990-1993. Presiding Judge, Oklahoma Temporary Court of Appeals, 1991. *Member:* American Law Institute; American Inns of Court (Barrister, 1987-1989; Master, 1996—). Fellow, American Bar Foundation. ***PRACTICE AREAS:*** Commercial Litigation; Public Law; Indian Law; Appeals. ***Email:*** DLUTHEY@HallEstill.com

DEL L. GUSTAFSON, born Holdrege, Nebraska, March 18, 1954; admitted to bar, 1979, Oklahoma. *Education:* University of Nebraska at Lincoln (B.A., with high distinction, 1976); Vanderbilt University (J.D., 1979). Phi Beta Kappa. *Member:* Tulsa County and Oklahoma Bar Associations. ***PRACTICE AREAS:*** Corporate Law; Commercial Law; Securities Law. ***Email:*** DGUSTAFSON@HallEstill.com

MARK K. BLONGEWICZ, born Lincoln, Nebraska, March 13, 1955; admitted to bar, 1980, Oklahoma; 1985, Nebraska. *Education:* University of Nebraska (B.S., Education, 1977); Duke University (J.D., 1980). Master, American Inns of Court (Council Oak/Johnson-Sontag Chapter). *Member:* Tulsa County, Oklahoma and Nebraska State Bar Associations; Defense Research Institute; Oklahoma Association of Defense Counsel. ***PRACTICE AREAS:*** Tort Defense; Insurance Litigation; Indian Law. ***Email:*** MBLONGEWICZ@HallEstill.com

MICHAEL D. COOKE, born Beckley, West Virginia, November 6, 1951; admitted to bar, 1980, Oklahoma. *Education:* Drury College (B.A., 1974); University of Iowa; University of Tulsa (J.D., 1980). Phi Delta Phi (Exchequer, 1978-1979). Notes and Comments Editor, Tulsa Law Journal, 1979-1980. Member, Phillip C. Jessup International Moot Court Team, 1978. *Member:* Tulsa County, Oklahoma and American Bar Associations. ***PRACTICE AREAS:*** Corporate Law; Construction; Telecommunications; Intellectual Property. ***Email:*** MCOOKE@HallEstill.com

KENNETH L. HUNT, born Laramie, Wyoming, March 6, 1955; admitted to bar, 1981, Oklahoma. *Education:* Brigham Young University (B.S., summa cum laude, 1978; J.D., cum laude, 1980). J. Reuben Clark Scholar. Author: "Property Settlements," Brigham Young Law School Journal of Legal Studies—Family Law Summary, 1980; "Oklahoma Taxes," Baedeker Press, 2002. Correspondent on Taxes, Oklahoma State Tax Notes. *Member:* Tulsa County, Oklahoma and American (Member, Tax Section) Bar Associations. ***LANGUAGES:*** Japanese. ***PRACTICE AREAS:*** Federal and State Taxation Law; Estate Planning Law; Corporate Law. ***Email:*** KHUNT@HallEstill.com

B. KENNETH COX, JR., born Fayetteville, Arkansas, July 30, 1956; admitted to bar, 1981, Oklahoma. *Education:* University of Arkansas (B.S., with high honors, 1978); Duke University (J.D., 1981). *Member:* Tulsa County, Oklahoma and American (Member, Sections on: Real Property, Probate and Trust Law; Communications Industries) Bar Associations. ***PRACTICE AREAS:*** Commercial Real Estate; Leases and Leasing; Commercial Loans; Right of Way Easements; Telecommunications Contracts; Telecommunications Law; Telecommunications Leasing. ***Email:*** KCOX@HallEstill.com

D. KENYON WILLIAMS, JR., born Tulsa, Oklahoma, February 4, 1952; admitted to bar, 1977, Oklahoma; 1998, Arkansas. *Education:* University of Tulsa (B.S., 1974; J.D., 1977). Author, "Ethics and Environmental Justice," presented to the 1998 Joint Meeting of the Arkansas and Oklahoma Environmental Law Section; "Civil and Criminal Liability of Officers and Directors of Corporations under Current Environmental Law - Guidance through Summaries of Recent Cases," Environmental Law Section Handbook, 1997 Edition; "Oklahoma's Proposed Regulation of Naturally Occurring Radioactive Materials," Environmental Law Section Newsletter, 1994. Adjunct Professor: "Oil & Gas Law II," Tulsa Junior College, 1989; "Environmental Law," Tulsa University, 1992 and 1993. *Member:* Tulsa County (Chair, Mineral Law Section, 1988—), Oklahoma (Member, Environmental Law Section, 1991—; Chair, 1995-1996), Arkansas (Member, Environmental Law Section) and American (Member, Sections on: Natural Resources, Energy and Environmental Law, 1988—; Real Property, Probate and Trust Law, 1988—) Bar Associations; American Inns of Court (Master). ***PRACTICE AREAS:*** Environmental; Business; Oil and Gas; Litigation. ***Email:*** KWILLIAMS@HallEstill.com

THOMAS P. SCHROEDTER, born Milwaukee, Wisconsin, February 26, 1954; admitted to bar, 1979, Oklahoma and U.S. District Court, Northern District of Oklahoma. *Education:* Duke University (B.A., 1976); University of Tulsa (J.D., 1979). Delta Theta Phi. Author: "Oil and Gas Title Examination and Title Curative: Marketable v. Defensible Title," Comprehensive Land Practices, an AAPL Publication, 1984. Adjunct Professor, University of Tulsa School of Law, 1986-1989. Chairman, Legal Committee, Oklahoma Independent Petroleum Association, 1986-1990. *Member:* Tulsa County (Chairman, Mineral Law Section, 1984-1985), Oklahoma (Member, Mineral Law Section) and American (Member, Natural Resources Law Section) Bar Associations. ***PRACTICE AREAS:*** Natural Resources Law; Governmental Relations; Regulatory Law; Business Law. ***Email:*** TSCHROEDTER@HallEstill.com

JAMES J. PROSZEK, born Chicago, Illinois, July 19, 1953; admitted to bar, 1983, Oklahoma, U.S. Court of Appeals, Fourth, Ninth, Tenth and Eleventh Circuits, U.S. District Court, Eastern, Northern and Western Districts of Oklahoma and U.S. District Court, Central and Northern Districts of Illinois, including Trial Bar Cherokee Nation. *Education:* University of Tulsa (B.S., 1975; J.D., 1983). Phi Delta Phi (Secretary, 1981-1982; Chapter and Province Graduate of the Year, 1983); Order of the Barristers; Order of the Curule Chair. Member, National Moot Court Team. Staff Member, 1981-1982 and Articles Editor, 1982-1983, Tulsa Law Journal. Instructor, Tulsa Community College Paralegal Program, 1984-1989. Member, National Association of Legal Assistants Certifying Board, 1985-1987. Ad Hoc Board Member, Oklahoma One-Call Systems, Inc. 2005—. Barrister, American Inns of Court (Johnson-Sontag Chapter). *Member:* Tulsa County and Oklahoma Bar Associations. ***PRACTICE AREAS:*** Telecommunications Law; Indian Law; Civil Trials; Civil Appeals; Eminent Domain; Right of Way Easements. ***Email:*** JPROSZEK@HallEstill.com

JAMES M. REED, born Libertyville, Illinois, July 20, 1956; admitted to bar, 1982, Oklahoma, U.S. Court of Appeals, Tenth Circuit, and U.S. District Court, Northern, Western and Eastern Districts of Oklahoma. *Education:* Lake Superior State College (B.A., cum laude, 1978); University of Arkansas (J.D., 1982). Phi Delta Phi (President, 1981-1982). Adjunct Professor, Tulsa Community College, Paralegal Program, 1990-1991. *Member:* Tulsa County and Oklahoma Bar Associations. ***PRACTICE AREAS:*** General Civil Litigation; Securities Litigation; Bankruptcy Law; Antitrust; Debtor and Creditor; Commercial Law; Real Estate. ***Email:*** JREED@HallEstill.com

(This Listing Continued)

THOMAS A. CREEKMORE, III, born Tulsa, Oklahoma, July 15, 1957; admitted to bar, 1982, Oklahoma, U.S. District Court, Northern, Eastern and Western Districts of Oklahoma and U.S. Court of Appeals, Tenth Circuit. *Education:* University of Oklahoma (B.A., Journalism, 1978; J.D., 1982). Order of the Coif; Phi Delta Phi. Note Editor, Oklahoma Law Review, 1982. Adjunct Professor of Law, Real Estate Transactions, University of Tulsa College of Law, 1988. *Member:* Oklahoma Bar Association; American Bankruptcy Institute. ***PRACTICE AREAS:*** Bankruptcy; Business Law; Commercial Law; Debtor and Creditor; Finance. ***Email:*** TCREEKMORE@HallEstill.com

STEPHEN W. RAY, born Kittery, Maine, October 30, 1957; admitted to bar, 1982, Oklahoma; 1986, U.S. Tax Court. *Education:* University of Oklahoma (B.B.A., with distinction, 1979; J.D., 1982). Phi Eta Sigma; Beta Gamma Sigma; Phi Delta Phi. Editor, Oklahoma Law Review, 1981-1982. Secretary, Dollar Thrifty Automotive Group, Inc., 1997—. Member, American Society of Corporate Secretaries, 1999—. ***PRACTICE AREAS:*** Business Organizations and Transactions; Real Estate Law; Securities Law; Commercial Law; Estate Planning Law. ***Email:*** SRAY@HallEstill.com

MARGARET A. SWIMMER, born Stratford, Oklahoma, February 6, 1944; admitted to bar, 1983, Oklahoma. *Education:* University of Oklahoma (B.A., with distinction, 1966; M.S.W., 1969); University of Tulsa (J.D., 1983). Phi Beta Kappa; Phi Delta Phi; Order of the Curule Chair. Notes and Comment Editor, Tulsa Law Journal, 1982-1983. Author: "Indian Tribes: Self-Determination Through Effective Management of Natural Resources," 17 Tulsa Law Journal 507. Co-Author, "Indian and Federal Oil and Gas Leasing and Royalty Valuation," 20th Annual Institute Journal Vol. 5 (1993). *Member:* Tulsa County, Oklahoma and American Bar Associations. ***PRACTICE AREAS:*** Indian Law; Energy Law; General Civil Litigation. ***Email:*** MSWIMMER@HallEstill.com

MICHAEL T. KEESTER, born Lawton, Oklahoma, October 26, 1959; admitted to bar, 1984, Oklahoma, U.S. Court of Appeals, Tenth Circuit and U.S. District Court, Northern, Western and Eastern Districts of Oklahoma. *Education:* University of Oklahoma (B.A., with distinction, 1981; J.D., with honors, 1984). Order of the Coif; Phi Beta Kappa; Phi Delta Phi. Editor, Oklahoma Law Review, 1983-1984. Member, Board of Directors, Oklahoma University College of Law Alumni Association, 1988-2000; President, 1990. Member, American Bar Association Litigation and Construction Sections; Barrister, American Inns of Court. Member and Director, Oklahoma Association of Defense Counsel and Past Member, Oklahoma Bar Association Civil Procedure Committee. Past Chairman, Tulsa County Bar Association, Professionalism Committee. Tulsa County Bar Association, Distinguished Service Award, 1991. *Member:* Defense Research Institute. ***PRACTICE AREAS:*** Construction Law; Civil Litigation; Commercial and Business Litigation; Insurance Defense; Employment Law. ***Email:*** MKEESTER@HallEstill.com

RONALD O. RAY, JR., born Frederick, Oklahoma, November 1, 1958; admitted to bar, 1984, Oklahoma. *Education:* Oklahoma State University (B.A., 1980); University of Oklahoma (J.D., with distinction, 1984). *Member:* Oklahoma (Member, Mineral and Energy Law Sections) and American Bar Associations (Member, Mineral and Energy Law Sections). ***PRACTICE AREAS:*** Oil and Gas; Energy; Real Estate Law. ***Email:*** RRAY@HallEstill.com

FRED M. BUXTON, born Oklahoma City, Oklahoma, June 21, 1959; admitted to bar, 1987, Oklahoma; U.S. District Court, Eastern, Northern and Western Districts of Oklahoma, U.S. Court of Appeals, Tenth Circuit and U.S. Court of Federal Claims. *Education:* Oklahoma State University (B.S., 1983); University of Tulsa (J.D., 1987). Member, Order of the Curule Chair. Co-Author with Jeffrey D. Knight: "Coastal Oil & Gas v. FERC: Does the Natural Gas Act Control 'Dedication' Pursuant to Contract?" 22 Tulsa Law Journal 659, 1987. *Member:* Oklahoma Bar Association; Bar of the Cheyenne and Arapaho Tribal Court; Kickapoo Tribal Court; Ponca Tribal Court. ***PRACTICE AREAS:*** Oil and Gas Law; General Civil Litigation. ***Email:*** FBUXTON@HallEstill.com

STEVEN A. BROUSSARD, born Port Arthur, Texas, June 20, 1962; admitted to bar, 1988, Oklahoma. *Education:* Vanderbilt University (B.S., 1984); University of Tulsa (J.D., 1988). Staff Member, Energy Law Journal, 1987-1988. *Member:* Oklahoma Bar Association. ***PRACTICE AREAS:*** Employment Law; Civil Litigation; Labor and Employment; Litigation. ***Email:*** SBROUSSARD@HallEstill.com

STEVEN W. SOULÉ, born Santa Monica, California, September 7, 1964; admitted to bar, 1989, Oklahoma, U.S. Court of Appeals, Tenth Circuit, U.S. District Court, Northern, Eastern and Western Districts of Oklahoma, Southern District of Texas and District of Colorado. *Education:* University of Oklahoma (B.B.A., Accounting, 1986; J.D., with honors, 1989). Phi Delta Phi. Chapter 7 Panel Trustee, U.S. Bankruptcy Court for the Northern District of Oklahoma. *Member:* Tulsa County (Member, Bankruptcy Section) and Oklahoma (Member, Bankruptcy Section) Bar Associations; American Bankruptcy Institute; National Association of Bankruptcy Trustees. ***PRACTICE AREAS:*** Bankruptcy; Creditors Rights; Financial Institutions; Franchise; Real Estate; Commercial Law; Telecommunications Law. ***Email:*** SSOULE@HallEstill.com

MICHAEL L. NEMEC, born Tulsa, Oklahoma, August 1, 1949; admitted to bar, 1976, Oklahoma. *Education:* University of Tulsa (B.A., 1971; J.D., 1976). Phi Delta Phi. *Member:* Oklahoma Bar Association. ***PRACTICE AREAS:*** Probate Law; Estate Planning Law. ***Email:*** MNEMEC@HallEstill.com

JOSEPH D. FINCHER, born Lagunillas, Venezuela, May 18, 1959; admitted to bar, 1984, Oklahoma. *Education:* University of Notre Dame (B.A., with highest honors, 1981); Duke University (J.D., with honors, 1984). Phi Beta Kappa. *Member:* Oklahoma (Member, Business Associations Section; Chair-Elect, Indian Law Section) and American Bar Associations. ***PRACTICE AREAS:*** Indian Law; Franchise Law; Trademarks; Commercial Law; Corporate Law. ***Email:*** JFINCHER@HallEstill.com

ANGELYN L. DALE, born Wichita, Kansas, May 22, 1959; admitted to bar, 1984, Oklahoma; 1985, U.S. District Court, Northern District of Oklahoma and U.S. Court of Appeals, 10th Circuit; 1986, U.S. District Court, Western District of Oklahoma; 1991, U.S. District Court, Eastern District of Oklahoma. *Education:* University of Oklahoma (B.B.A., Statistics, with high honors, 1981); Southern Methodist University (J.D., 1984). Beta Gamma Sigma, Mortar Board. Editor, Southern Methodist University Journal of Air Law and Commerce, 1983-1984. Executive Committee, American Inns of Court, Johnson-Sontag Chapter, 1991—. Law Clerk, Honorable James O. Ellison, Northern District of Oklahoma, 1987-1991. Senior Adjunct Settlement Judge, Northern District of Oklahoma, 1992—. *Member:* Tulsa County, Oklahoma and American Bar Associations. ***PRACTICE AREAS:*** Litigation; Employment Law; Employment Litigation. ***Email:*** ADALE@HallEstill.com

R. MARK PETRICH, born Columbia, Missouri, May 5, 1959; admitted to bar, 1986, Oklahoma. *Education:* University of Hawaii (B.B.A., 1983); University of Tulsa (J.D., 1986). Delta Theta Phi. Member, Tulsa Law Journal, 1984-1986. *Member:* Tulsa County, Oklahoma and American Bar Associations. ***PRACTICE AREAS:*** Commercial Litigation; Bankruptcy Law. ***Email:*** MPETRICH@HallEstill.com

PAMELA H. GOLDBERG, born Brooklyn, New York, December 12, 1955; admitted to bar, 1987, Oklahoma; 1990, Colorado. *Education:* Brooklyn College (B.A., magna cum laude, 1976); University of Tulsa (M.A., 1981; J.D., 1987). Member, Order of the Curule Chair. Member, Tulsa Law Journal, 1985-1987. Author: "The Nuclear Waste Policy Act of 1982: Does Immigration & Naturalization Service v. Chadha Veto the Congressional Override?" Tulsa Law Journal, Vol. 21, No. 4, Summer, 1986. *Member:* Oklahoma and American Bar Associations. ***PRACTICE AREAS:*** Bankruptcy Law; Commercial Law; General Civil Litigation; Appellate Practice. ***Email:*** PGOLDBERG@HallEstill.com

MARK BANNER, born Rockville Centre, New York, April 7, 1958; admitted to bar, 1988, Oklahoma. *Education:* University of Oklahoma (B.A., 1983); Georgetown University (J.D., cum laude, 1988). Staff Member and Associate Editor, The Tax Lawyer, 1986-1988. *Member:* Tulsa County, Oklahoma and American Bar Associations; American Inns of Court. ***PRACTICE AREAS:*** Commercial Litigation; Oil and Gas Litigation; Telecommunications Law. ***Email:*** MBANNER@HallEstill.com

ROBERT F. DOUGHERTY, born Oklahoma City, Oklahoma, October 31, 1965; admitted to bar, 1991, Oklahoma; 1993, U.S. Tax Court; 1994, Missouri; 1995, Kansas. *Education:* University of Oklahoma (B.B.A., Accounting, 1988; J.D., 1991); Emory University (LL.M., Taxation, 1993). Oklahoma Law Review. Certified Public Accountant, Oklahoma, 1992. *Member:* Tulsa County, Oklahoma and American Bar Associations; The Missouri Bar. ***PRACTICE AREAS:*** Commercial Law; Real Estate; Telecommunications Law; Taxation. ***Email:*** RDOUGHERTY@HallEstill.com

T. LANE WILSON, born Rockford, Illinois, January 20, 1967; admitted to bar, 1994, Oklahoma, U.S. Court of Appeals, Second, Fifth, Seventh and Tenth Circuits, U.S. District Court, Western and Northern Districts of Oklahoma and Western and Southern Districts of Texas. *Education:* University of Tulsa (B.S., Electrical Engineering, 1989; J.D., with honors, 1994). Member, Order of the Curule Chair. Managing Editor, Tulsa Law Journal, 1993-1994. *Member:* Tulsa County, Oklahoma and American Bar Associations. ***PRACTICE AREAS:*** Intellectual Property; Trade Secrets; Unfair Competition; Securities; Antitrust; Telecommunications; Oil and Gas; Construction; Litigation. ***Email:*** LWILSON@HallEstill.com

BETSY GRABEL JACKSON, born Tulsa, Oklahoma, August 18, 1965; admitted to bar, 1991, Oklahoma; 1992, U.S. District Court, Northern District of Oklahoma; 1993, District of Columbia; 1994, Maryland and U.S. District Court, District of Maryland; 1995, U.S. District Court for the District of Columbia. *Education:* Southern Methodist University (B.B.A., 1987); University of Tulsa (J.D., 1990). Phi Alpha Delta. Recipient, American Jurisprudence Award in Contracts II. Author: "The Exemption of ERISA Qualified Pension Plans in Bankruptcy," 25 Tul. L.J. 799 (1990). *Member:* Oklahoma Bar Association. ***PRACTICE AREAS:*** Corporate; Securities; Commercial; Real Estate. ***Email:*** BJACKSON@HallEstill.com

ROBERT P. FITZ-PATRICK, born Arlington, Virginia, October 22, 1957; admitted to bar, 1991, Oklahoma. *Education:* Boston University (B.S., 1979); Massachusetts Institute of Technology (M.S., 1987); University of Tulsa (J.D., 1991). Member, Society of Petroleum Engineers, 1982-1988. *Member:* Tulsa County, Oklahoma and American Bar Associations. ***PRACTICE AREAS:*** Defense Litigation; Employment Law; Intellectual Property; White Collar Crime. ***Email:*** RFitzpatrick@HallEstill.com

SARAH JANE GILLETT, born Oklahoma City, Oklahoma, July 12, 1967; admitted to bar, 1993, New York; 1996, Oklahoma, U.S. District Court, Southern and Eastern Districts of New York, U.S. District Court, Northern, Eastern and Western Districts of Oklahoma and U.S. Court of Appeals, Tenth Circuit. *Education:* Wellesley College (B.A., with honors, 1989); Boston College (J.D., with honors, 1992). *Member:* Tulsa County, Oklahoma and American Bar Associations; American Inns of Court; Tulsa Women Lawyers Association. ***PRACTICE AREAS:*** Business Litigation. ***Email:*** SGILLETT@HallEstill.com

JOHN F. HEIL, III, admitted to bar, 1994, Oklahoma; 1995, U.S. District Court, Northern and Eastern Districts of Oklahoma; U.S. Court of Appeals, Eighth and Tenth Circuits. *Education:* Oklahoma State University (B.S., Finance, 1990); University of Tulsa (J.D., with honors, 1994). Phi Kappa Phi. Order of the Curule Chair. Recipient, American Jurisprudence Awards. Production Editor, Tulsa Law Journal, 1993-1994. *Member:* Tulsa County, Oklahoma and American Bar Associations; American Inns of Court. ***PRACTICE AREAS:*** Business Litigation; Intellectual Property; Trade Secrets; Unfair Competition; Telecommunications Law. ***Email:*** JHEIL@HallEstill.com

PAMELA S. ANDERSON, born Tulsa, Oklahoma, 1959; admitted to bar, 1986, Oklahoma. *Education:* University of Tulsa (B.A., magna cum laude, 1982; J.D., with honors, 1985). Tulsa Law Journal. Phi Delta Phi. Order of the Curule Chair. Author: "Gender-Based Determination Retirement Benefits. Arizona v. Norris," 19 Tulsa Law Journal 755 (1984). Co-Author, "Division of the Goodwill of a Medical Practice as a Marital Asset after Monik v. Monik," 63 Oklahoma Bar Journal 3851 (1992). *Member:* Tulsa County, Oklahoma and American Bar Associations. ***PRACTICE AREAS:*** Business Litigation; Commercial Litigation; Complex and Multi-District Litigation; Federal Practice; Telecommunications Law; Oil and Gas Litigation; Appellate Practice. ***Email:*** PANDERSON@HallEstill.Com

TIMOTHY S. POSEY, born Tulsa, Oklahoma, October 15, 1963; admitted to bar, 1989, Oklahoma; U.S. Court of Appeals, Tenth Circuit; U.S. District Court, Northern, Western and Eastern Districts of Oklahoma. *Education:* University of Oklahoma (B.A., with distinction, 1986); University of Oklahoma College of Law (J.D., 1989). Speaker, Doing Business in Indian Country, Oklahoma State University, Okmulgee Campus, 2003 and 2004. Supreme Court Justice, Sac and Fox Tribe of Indians of Oklahoma. ***REPORTED CASES:*** Kiowa Tribe of Oklahoma v. Manufacturing Technologies, 118 S. Ct. 1700 (May

(This Listing Continued)

HALL, ESTILL, HARDWICK, GABLE, GOLDEN & NELSON, A PROFESSIONAL CORPORATION, Tulsa—Continued

26, 1998); Muscogee (Creek) Nation v. American Tobacco Co., R.J. Reynolds, et al., Case No. CV 97-27 (1997), Oklahoma Bar Journal. ***PRACTICE AREAS:*** Federal Indian Law; Employment; Corporate; Litigation. ***Email:*** tposey@hallestill.com

MARSHALL J. WELLS, born Roanoke, Virginia, May 27, 1971; admitted to bar, 1996, Oklahoma, U.S. District Court, Eastern, Western and Northern Districts of Oklahoma and U.S. Court of Appeals, Fifth and Tenth Circuits. *Education:* DePauw University (B.A., 1993); University of Tulsa (J.D., 1996). Phi Alpha Delta. *Member:* Tulsa County and Oklahoma Bar Associations; Oklahoma Association of Defense Counsel. ***PRACTICE AREAS:*** Defense Litigation; Employment Discrimination; Insurance; Negligence; Products Liability. ***Email:*** MWELLS@HallEstill.com

ANTHONY J. JORGENSON, born Boone, Iowa, March 22, 1971; admitted to bar, 1996, Oklahoma; U.S. District Court, Northern, Western and Eastern Districts of Oklahoma and U.S. Court of Appeals, Fourth, Tenth and Eleventh Circuits. *Education:* Iowa State University (B.B.A., 1993); University of Oklahoma (J.D., 1996). *Member:* Oklahoma Bar Association. ***PRACTICE AREAS:*** Business Litigation; Antitrust; Intellectual Property; Telecommunications Law; Insurance Defense. ***Email:*** AJORGENSON@HallEstill.com

HEATHER L. CUPP, born Norman, Oklahoma, October 25, 1969; admitted to bar, 1997, Oklahoma, U.S. District Court, Northern and Western Districts of Oklahoma, U.S. District Court, District of Colorado and U.S. Court of Appeals, Tenth Circuit. *Education:* Northeastern Oklahoma State University (B.A., cum laude, 1994); University of Tulsa (J.D., 1997). Phi Delta Phi. Publishing Editor, Tulsa Journal of Comparative and International Law, 1996-1997. Author: Comment, "The Impact of the Trade Wars Between the United States and Japan on the Future Success of the World Trade Organization," 3 Tulsa Journal of Comparative and International Law 227 (1996). *Member:* Tulsa County, Oklahoma and American Bar Associations; American Inns of Court (W. Lee Johnson Chapter, 1997-1998, 2002-2003). ***PRACTICE AREAS:*** Commercial Litigation; Intellectual Property; Trade Secrets; Unfair Competition; Business Torts; Securities; Civil Litigation. ***Email:*** HCUPP@HallEstill.com

MICHAEL J. LISSAU, born Tulsa, Oklahoma, October 2, 1971; admitted to bar, 1998, Oklahoma, U.S. District Courts for the Northern, Eastern and Western Districts of Oklahoma and the U.S. Court of Appeals, Tenth Circuit. *Education:* Westminster College (B.A., 1994); University of Tulsa (J.D., 1998). *Member:* Tulsa County, Oklahoma and American Bar Associations. ***PRACTICE AREAS:*** Labor and Employment; Class Action Litigation; General Litigation; Health Law. ***Email:*** MLISSAU@HallEstill.com

KYLE D. FREEMAN, born Oklahoma City, Oklahoma, June 10, 1969; admitted to bar, 1998, Oklahoma. *Education:* University of Central Oklahoma (B.A., 1991); University of Tulsa (J.D., 1998). Phi Delta Phi; Order of the Curule Chair. Articles Editor, Tulsa Law Journal, 1997-1998. Corpus Juris Secundum Award, Civil Procedure. CALI Award, Civil Procedure. Author, "*Robinson v. City of Edmond:* Establishment Clause Jurisprudence and A Case for Governmental Acknowledgment of The Historical Role of Religion," 32 Tulsa L.J. 605 (1997). *Member:* Tulsa County and Oklahoma Bar Associations. ***PRACTICE AREAS:*** Commercial Transactions; Information Technology; Real Property; Telecommunications Law; Commercial Litigation. ***Email:*** KFREEMAN@HallEstill.com

W. DEKE CANADA, born Tulsa, Oklahoma, July 10, 1969; admitted to bar, 1998, Colorado; 2001, Oklahoma. *Education:* Evergreen State College (B.S., 1992); Tulane University (J.D., 1998); Georgetown University (LL.M., Taxation, 2000). Member, Journal of International and Comparative Law. *Member:* Tulsa County, Oklahoma and American Bar Associations. ***PRACTICE AREAS:*** Corporate Finance; Mergers and Acquisitions; Business Organization; Corporate Law; Commercial Law; Taxation. ***Email:*** DCANADA@HallEstill.com

BONNIE N. HACKLER, born Henryetta, Oklahoma, March 21, 1974; admitted to bar, 1999, Oklahoma, U.S. District Court, Western, Eastern, Northern and Southern Districts of Oklahoma and U.S. Court of Appeals, Tenth Circuit. *Education:* University of Oklahoma (B.A., with special distinction in Political Science, 1996; J.D., with special distinction, 1999). Phi Beta Kappa. Articles Editor, Oklahoma Law Review, 1998-1999. Recipient, Judge Harry L. S. Halley Memorial Scholarship. Teaching Assistant for the Legal Research and Writing Program, 1997-1998. Cortez A. H. Ewing, Washington D.C. Fellow. *Member:* Oklahoma and American Bar Associations; American Bankruptcy Institute. ***PRACTICE AREAS:*** Commercial Litigation; Bankruptcy; Debtor and Creditor Rights. ***Email:*** BHACKLER@HallEstill.com

KIMBERLY R. SCHUTZ, born St. Louis, Missouri, March 8, 1975; admitted to bar, 2000, Oklahoma; U.S. District Court, Northern and Eastern Districts of Oklahoma and U.S. Court of Appeals, Tenth Circuit. *Education:* University of Kansas (B.B.A., 1997); University of Oklahoma (J.D., 2000). Phi Delta Phi. Member, Board of Advocates, 1998-1999. Recipient, Dean's Honor Roll, 1997-1999. *Member:* Oklahoma and American Bar Associations. ***PRACTICE AREAS:*** Litigation. ***Email:*** KBIEDLER@HallEstill.com

MATTHEW T. CROOK, born Tulsa, Oklahoma, December 11, 1974; admitted to bar, 2002, Oklahoma. *Education:* University of Oklahoma (B.B.A., Accounting/Finance, 1997; J.D., 2002). Certified Public Accountant, Oklahoma, 2003. *Member:* Tulsa County, Oklahoma and American Bar Associations; Oklahoma Society of Certified Public Accountants; Tulsa County Society of Certified Public Accountants. ***PRACTICE AREAS:*** Business Organizations; Business Transactions; Commercial Law; Real Estate Law; Taxation; Securities Law. ***Email:*** MCROOK@HallEstill.com

JOHN T. RICHER, born Albuquerque, New Mexico, September 24, 1971; admitted to bar, 2002, Oklahoma and U.S. District Court, Northern, Eastern and Western Districts of Oklahoma and U.S. Court of Appeals, Tenth Circuit. *Education:* University of Tulsa (B.A., cum laude, 1995); University of Kansas (J.D., 2002). Member, Kansas Law Review. Law Clerk to the Honorable James A. Pusateri, Chief Judge, U.S. Bankruptcy Court for the District of Kansas. *Member:* Tulsa County (Member, Bankruptcy Section) and Oklahoma Bar Associations; American Bankruptcy Institute; American Inns of Court. ***PRACTICE AREAS:*** Bankruptcy; Debtor and Creditor Rights; Commercial Litigation. ***Email:*** JRicher@HallEstill.Com

(This Listing Continued)

GENEVIEVE L. SCHMOOK, born Tulsa, Oklahoma, October 25, 1975; admitted to bar, 2002, Oklahoma. *Education:* Oklahoma State University (B.S., Business Management, 1997); University of Tulsa (M.B.A., 1998; J.D., 2002). *Member:* Oklahoma Bar Association. ***PRACTICE AREAS:*** Business Organizations; Business Transactions; Commercial Law; Real Estate Law; Securities Law. ***Email:*** GSchmook@HallEstill.Com

STEPHANIE T. GENTRY, born Tucson, Arizona, May 5, 1973; admitted to bar, 1998, Texas; 2000, Oklahoma and Arizona. *Education:* University of Arizona (B.S./B.A., 1994; J.D., 1998). *Member:* Tulsa County Bar Association; Inns of Court. ***PRACTICE AREAS:*** Construction Law; Labor and Employment. ***Email:*** sgentry@hallestill.com

STEPHANIE A. HORTON, born Waterloo, Iowa, September 4, 1973; admitted to bar, 2003, Oklahoma. *Education:* University of Tulsa (B.A., 1995); University of Oklahoma College of Law (J.D., 2003). *Member:* Oklahoma Bar Association (Member, Litigation Section). ***PRACTICE AREAS:*** Litigation. ***Email:*** shorton@hallestill.com

MOLLY A. BIRCHER, born Ellsworth, Kansas, June 20, 1978; admitted to bar, 2003, Oklahoma; 2004, Kansas. *Education:* Fort Hays State University (B.A., 2000); University of Kansas (J.D., 2003). Member, Kansas Law Review. *Member:* Tulsa County, Oklahoma, Kansas and American Bar Associations. ***PRACTICE AREAS:*** Labor and Employment; Litigation. ***Email:*** mbircher@hallestill.com

KARISSA K. COTTOM, born Woodward, Oklahoma, August 18, 1974; admitted to bar, 2001, Texas; 2004, Oklahoma; U.S. District Court, Eastern, Northern and Southern Districts of Texas; U.S. District Court, Western and Northern Districts of Oklahoma. *Education:* Oklahoma State University (B.A., Psychology, 1996); Baylor University (J.D., magna cum laude, 2001). Member, Baylor Law Review. *Member:* Tulsa County, Oklahoma (Member: Litigation Section; Young Lawyers Division) and American Bar Associations; State Bar of Texas. ***PRACTICE AREAS:*** Litigation; Construction Law; Oil and Gas. ***Email:*** KWATERBURY@HallEstill.com

KIMBERLY L. WATKINS, born Monticello, Arkansas, August 29, 1977; admitted to bar, 2004, Oklahoma; U.S. District Court; Northern District of Oklahoma. *Education:* University of Arkansas at Pine Bluff (B.S., Biology, minor Chemistry, summa cum laude, 1999); University of Arkansas School of Law (J.D., magna cum laude, 2004). Associate Editor, Arkansas Law Review. Member: Tulsa County and Oklahoma Bar Associations; American Inns of Court (Johnson-Sontag Chapter). ***PRACTICE AREAS:*** Litigation; Environmental. ***Email:*** KWATKINS@HallEstill.com

MAREN K. MINNAERT, born Huron, South Dakota, November 20, 1978; admitted to bar, 2004, Oklahoma. *Education:* Oklahoma State University (B.S., Economics and Political Science, summa cum laude, 2001); Georgetown University (J.D., 2004). Author, Georgetown Journal of Gender & Law, Vol. IV, No. 1, Fall 2002 (Senior Notes and Articles Editor). Formerly with U.S. Department of Justice, U.S. Marshals, Office of General Counsel. *Member:* Tulsa County and Oklahoma Bar Associations; Johnson-Sontag Inns of Court. ***PRACTICE AREAS:*** Complex Commercial Litigation; Corporate Litigation. ***Email:*** MMINNAERT@HallEstill.com

BOBBI L. ALLEN, born Jamestown, North Dakota, 1977; admitted to bar, 2005, Oklahoma. *Education:* North Dakota State University; Oklahoma State University (B.S., 2000); University of Oklahoma (J.D., 2005). Phi Kappa Phi; Phi Delta Phi. Member, Golden Key National Honor Society. *Member:* Tulsa County, Oklahoma and American Bar Associations. ***PRACTICE AREAS:*** Corporate Law; Commercial Law; Business Transactions. ***Email:*** BALLEN@HallEstill.com

JOHNSON W. CUSTER, born Stillwater, Oklahoma, 1979; admitted to bar, 2005, Oklahoma. *Education:* Southern Methodist University (B.A., 2002); Vanderbilt University (J.D., 2005). *Member:* Tulsa County, Oklahoma and American Bar Associations; American Inns of Court (Johnson-Sontag Chapter). ***PRACTICE AREAS:*** Commercial Litigation; Corporate Litigation. ***Email:*** JCUSTER@HallEstill.com

ELISABETH R. HIGHAM, born Chicago, Illinois, 1976; admitted to bar, 2005, Oklahoma. *Education:* University of Kentucky (B.A., 1998); University of Arkansas, Fayetteville (J.D., 2005). *Member:* Tulsa County, Oklahoma and American Bar Associations; American Inns of Court (Johnson-Sontag Chapter). ***PRACTICE AREAS:*** Labor and Employment. ***Email:*** EHIGHAM@HallEstill.com

OF COUNSEL

JOHN S. ESTILL, JR., born Grapevine, Texas, January 20, 1919; admitted to bar, 1948, Texas; 1958, Kansas; 1966, Oklahoma; 1975, District of Columbia. *Education:* Texas Christian University (B.S., 1940); Southern Methodist University (J.D., 1948). Delta Theta Phi. Special Assistant to U.S. Attorney, Northern District of Texas, 1950-1953. *Member:* Tulsa County, Oklahoma, Kansas and American Bar Associations; District of Columbia Bar; State Bar of Texas. ***PRACTICE AREAS:*** Oil and Gas Law; Pipeline Law. ***Email:*** JESTILL@HallEstill.com

THOMAS D. GABLE, born Tulsa, Oklahoma, April 7, 1942; admitted to bar, 1967, Oklahoma. *Education:* University of Oklahoma (B.B.A., 1964; J.D., 1967). Order of the Coif; Phi Delta Phi; Beta Gamma Sigma. Member, Board of Editors, 1965-1967, Note Editor, 1966, Oklahoma Law Review. *Member:* Tulsa County and Oklahoma Bar Associations. ***PRACTICE AREAS:*** Corporate Law; Commercial Law; Real Estate Financing Law. ***Email:*** TGABLE@HallEstill.com

THOMAS F. GOLDEN, born New Orleans, Louisiana, May 24, 1942; admitted to bar, 1968, Oklahoma. *Education:* Oklahoma State University (B.S., Economics, 1966); University of Tulsa (J.D., 1968). Managing Editor, Tulsa Law Journal. Member, Federal Judicial Nominating Commission, all Federal Districts of Oklahoma, 1981-1992. Board of Directors of DTU, Eateries, Inc. and Midwesco Industries, Inc. *Member:* Tulsa County and Oklahoma Bar Associations; Full Member, Urban Land Institute. ***PRACTICE AREAS:*** Commercial Real Estate Transactions; Legislative Matters; Commercial Law. ***Email:*** TGOLDEN@HallEstill.com

WILLIAM W. PRITCHARD, born Tulsa, Oklahoma, March 20, 1951; admitted to bar, 1976, Oklahoma and U.S. District Court, Northern District of Oklahoma. *Education:* University of Kansas (B.A., with honors, 1973); University of Tulsa (J.D., 1975). Vice President and General Counsel, Parker Drilling Co. (NYSE). *Member:* Oklahoma and

(This Listing Continued)

American Bar Associations. ***PRACTICE AREAS:*** Commercial Transactions; Oil and Gas Contracts; Corporate Practice; Mergers and Acquisitions; Securities. ***Email:*** WPRITCHARD@HallEstill.com

CLIVE A. SEYMOUR, born Brighton, England, June 24, 1946; admitted to bar, 1978, Texas; 2000, Oklahoma. *Education:* University of Texas (B.A., 1974; J.D., 1978). Certified Public Accountant, 1985. *Member:* Oklahoma and American Bar Associations; State Bar of Texas. ***PRACTICE AREAS:*** Employee Benefits; Estate Planning; Executive Compensation; Tax. ***Email:*** CSEYMOUR@HallEstill.com

RONALD L. JONES, born Ames, Iowa, April 11, 1942; admitted to bar, 1973, Nebraska; 1979, U.S. Supreme Court; 1989, Texas; 1999, Oklahoma; U.S. District Court, District of Nebraska and U.S. Court of Appeals, Eighth Circuit. *Education:* Illinois Wesleyan University (B.A., 1965); Naval Justice School, 1968; California Western School of Law (J.D., 1972). Author, Books: "How to Counsel Corporate Clients: Ten Reasons Business People Don't Take Legal Advice, And What You Can Do About It," American Law Institute-American Bar Association (ALI-ABA), January 2000; "Practice Preventive Corporate Law," ALI-ABA, 1985, Law School Edition, 1986. Author, Articles: "Losing Business Clients the Hard Way," ABA Journal; "Small Companies and Preventive Law," ACCA Docket; Implementing Preventive Law Programs," Preventive Law Reporter. Employment: Senior Attorney, The Williams Companies, 1997-2002. Of Counsel, Texas Instruments Incorporated, 1997. Assistant General Counsel, Occidental Chemical Corporation, 1988-1996. Corporate Counsel, Peter Kiewet Sons, Inc., 1984-1988. Vice President and General Counsel, Royster Company, 1979-1983. Assistant General Counsel, Fluor, Inc., 1974-1979. Corporate Counsel, Gene Fuller, Inc., 1973-1974. Certified Mediator, Attorney-Mediators Institute. Awarded Preventive Law Prize by the National Center for Preventive Law. *Member:* Tulsa County, Oklahoma, Nebraska State and American (Member, Sections on: Corporation, Banking and Business Law; Natural Resources Law; Member, Forum Committee on the Construction Industry, 1975-1980) Bar Associations; State Bar of Texas. [Capt., USMC, 1965-1969]. ***PRACTICE AREAS:*** Energy Law; Natural Resources Law; Engineering Law; Construction Law; Offshore Oil and Gas Law; Corporation Law; Real Estate Law; Environmental Law; Chemical Regulation Law. ***Email:*** RJones@HallEstill.Com

REPRESENTATIVE CLIENTS: AES Shady Point, LLC; Allbritton Communications Company; America Online; Apache Corporation; Arby's; AUSCO; Bank of Oklahoma; Bank of Texas; Bank One; Berendson Fluid Power, Inc.; Blockbuster, Inc.; Blount, Inc.; Blue Cross/Blue Shield of Oklahoma; Burlington Resources Oil & Gas Company; Cherokee Nation Enterprises, Inc.; Chubb Insurance; City of Tulsa, Oklahoma; CNA Insurance; Conde Nast Publications, Inc.; ConocoPhillips; Denny's Restaurant; Dollar Thrifty Automotive Group; Dow Jones & Company; Eateries, Inc.; El Paso Energy Corporation; Fluor Corporation; Halliburton Company; Hearst- Argyle Television, Inc.; Hilton/Doubletree Hotels; Hormel Food Corporation; Leucadia National Corporation; Magellan Midstream Partners, LP; MCI; Multimedia Games, Inc.; National Steak & Poultry; Oklahoma Transportation Authority/Oklahoma Turnpike Authority; Oxy USA, Inc.; Southern Hills Country Club; St. Francis Health Systems; St. Paul Insurance; State Farm Insurance; State of Oklahoma; Terex Corporation; The Goodyear Tire & Rubber Company; The New York Times Company; The Seminole Group, LP; The Warren Foundation; The Williams Companies; Travelers Insurance Company; Wal-Mart Stores, Inc.; Williams Sonoma; WilTel Communications, LLC; Zurich North America.

PHILIP S. HANEY ASSOCIATES

1437 SOUTH BOULDER, SUITE 1050
BOULDER TOWERS
TULSA, OKLAHOMA 74119
Telephone: 918-744-1023
Facsimile: 918-583-7170
Email: pshaney@swbell.net
URL: http://www.lawyers.com/churchlaw

Tax Exempt, Nonprofit and Charitable Organizations, Public Charities, Churches, Religious Ministries, Charitable Giving, Estate Planning.

FIRM PROFILE: Philip S. Haney Associates is listed in the Bar Register of Preeminent Lawyers.

PHILIP S. HANEY, born Evanston, Illinois, September 26, 1946; admitted to bar, 1971, Oklahoma; 1990, Tennessee. *Education:* Oklahoma University (A.B., 1968; J.D., 1971); New York University (LL.M., Taxation, 1975). Author: "Publicly Traded Partnerships After the Revenue Act of 1987"; "Taxes - The Tax Magazine," Prentice Hall, May 1988; "Gas Balancing Refunds and Deficiencies: Taxpayers Playing 'Hide or Seek' "; "Oil & Gas Tax Quarterly," Matthew Bender, March 1990; "Church Tax Benefits and First Amendment Tensions"; "Tax Exempt Organizations," Maxwell Macmillian, May 1991; "Religion and the Constitution: When Is A 'Church' Really a Church?," The Oklahoma Bar Journal, October 1991. *Member:* Tulsa County, Oklahoma, Tennessee and American Bar Associations. ***PRACTICE AREAS:*** Tax Exempt; Nonprofit and Charitable Organizations; Charitable Giving; Estate Planning.

REPRESENTATIVE CLIENTS: Bread of Life Church; Chitwood & Chitwood; Church Management Tax Conference; Clergy, Tax & Law; Evangel Church; Don Meares Ministries; Faith Fellowship Ministries; Henry Fernandez Ministries; International Congress of Local Churches; International Faith Center; Joby Brady Ministries; John Avanzini Ministries; People United for Christ; Perfecting Church; Peter Popoff Evangelistic Association of Canada; Shore Christian Center; Strategic Compensation Group of America LLC; Straight Gate Church; The Wisdom Center; Mike Murdock Evangelistic Association.

HARRIS, McMAHAN, PETERS, THOMPSON & STALL P.C.

Established in 1980

SUITE 900
1800 SOUTH BALTIMORE
TULSA, OKLAHOMA 74119
Telephone: 918-743-6201
Fax: 918-747-2965
URL: http://www.hmptsfirm.com

General Civil and Federal Practice. Oil and Gas, Real Estate and Corporation Law.

(This Listing Continued)

RICHARD L. HARRIS, born Anson, Texas, February 14, 1932; admitted to bar, 1962, Colorado; 1963, Oklahoma. *Education:* Texas A & M University (B.B.A., 1954); University of Denver (LL.B., 1962). *Member:* Tulsa County, Oklahoma and American Bar Associations. [Capt., USAF, 1954-1956]. ***PRACTICE AREAS:*** Oil and Gas Law; Corporate; Estate Planning. ***Email:*** rharris@hmptsfirm.com

JOHN A. McMAHAN, born San Diego, California, January 15, 1953; admitted to bar, 1978, Oklahoma. *Education:* Southern Methodist University (B.S., 1975); University of Tulsa (J.D., 1978). Phi Delta Phi. *Member:* Tulsa County and Oklahoma Bar Associations. ***PRACTICE AREAS:*** Oil and Gas Law. ***Email:*** jmcmahan@hmptsfirm.com

STEPHEN Q. PETERS, born Tulsa, Oklahoma, October 27, 1958; admitted to bar, 1985, Oklahoma. *Education:* Southern Methodist University (B.A., 1981; B.B.A., 1981); University of Oklahoma (J.D., 1985). *Member:* Tulsa County and Oklahoma Bar Associations; The Association of Trial Lawyers of America; Oklahoma Trial Lawyers Association. ***PRACTICE AREAS:*** General Civil Litigation before all State and Federal Courts; Oil and Gas Litigation; Business Contract Litigation; Tort Litigation; Corporate Law; Employment Litigation. ***Email:*** speters@hmptsfirm.com

R. LYNN THOMPSON, born Hereford, Texas, May 18, 1962; admitted to bar, 1990, Oklahoma. *Education:* West Texas State University (B.A., 1985); University of Tulsa (J.D., 1989). *Member:* Tulsa County (Vice Chairman, Mental Health and Fitness Committee) and Oklahoma Bar Associations; The Association of Trial Lawyers of America; Oklahoma Trial Lawyers Association; Sports Lawyers Association. ***PRACTICE AREAS:*** Bad Faith Insurance Litigation; Personal Injury; Civil Litigation. ***Email:*** rlthompson@hmptsfirm.com

ERIC W. STALL, born Tulsa, Oklahoma, April 4, 1965; admitted to bar, 1990, Oklahoma. *Education:* Oklahoma State University (B.A., 1987); University of Tulsa (J.D., 1990). Assistant District Attorney, Tulsa County, 1990-1996. *Member:* Tulsa County and Oklahoma Bar Associations; Oklahoma Trial Lawyers Association. ***PRACTICE AREAS:*** Criminal Law; Civil Litigation; Business Contract Litigation; Tort Litigation. ***Email:*** estall@hmptsfirm.com

---

TODD WILLIAM SINGER, born Enid, Oklahoma, July 27, 1961; admitted to bar, 1990, Oklahoma. *Education:* Brandeis University (B.A., 1985); University of Tulsa (J.D., 1990). American Inns of Court. Adjunct Professor, University of Tulsa, 2002. Assistant Public Defender, 1990-1992. Assistant District Attorney, 1993-1996. Special District Judge, 1996-2001. *Member:* Tulsa County and Oklahoma Bar Associations. ***PRACTICE AREAS:*** Civil Litigation; Criminal Law; Litigation; Business Law; Divorce. ***Email:*** tsinger@hmptsfirm.com

RANDALL T. DUNCAN, born Tulsa, Oklahoma, December 27, 1963; admitted to bar, 1990, Oklahoma, U.S. Court of Appeals, Tenth Circuit and U.S. District Court, Northern District of Oklahoma. *Education:* Northeastern State University (B.S., 1987); University of Tulsa (J.D., 1990). *Member:* Tulsa County and Oklahoma Bar Associations. ***PRACTICE AREAS:*** Commercial Litigation; Business Contract Litigation; Tort Litigation; Family Law; Probate; Condemnation; Collections; Personal Injury; Trial Practice. ***Email:*** rduncan@hmptsfirm.com

KORT A. BESORE, born Omaha, Nebraska, January 10, 1967; admitted to bar, 1991, Oklahoma. *Education:* University of Oklahoma (B.A., 1988; J.D., 1991). Phi Delta Phi. *Member:* Tulsa County and Oklahoma Bar Associations; The Association of Trial Lawyers of America. ***PRACTICE AREAS:*** Civil Litigation; Business Torts; Personal Injury; Divorce; Child Custody; Child Support. ***Email:*** kort@hmptsfirm.com

OF COUNSEL

WILLIAM D. TONEY, born Sallisaw, Oklahoma, May 8, 1927; admitted to bar, 1957, Oklahoma; 1968, Texas; 1975, U.S. District Court, Northern District of Oklahoma; 1977, U.S. Court of Appeals, 5th, 10th and District of Columbia Circuits. *Education:* Oklahoma State University (B.S., 1954); University of Oklahoma (LL.B., 1957). *Member:* Tulsa County, Oklahoma (Member, Labor Law Section) and American (Member, Labor Relations Law Section) Bar Associations; State Bar of Texas (Member, Labor Law Section). Fellow, Southwest Legal Foundation. ***PRACTICE AREAS:*** Management Labor Law and Employment Law. ***Email:*** wtoney@hmptsfirm.com

JOHN W. MOODY, born Miami, Oklahoma, October 23, 1943; admitted to bar, 1969, Oklahoma. *Education:* Oklahoma State University (B.A., 1966); University of Tulsa (J.D., 1968). Phi Delta Phi. Articles Editor, 1967 and Notes and Comment Editor, 1968, Tulsa Law Journal. Member, 1975-1989, and Chairman, 1978-1989, Tulsa City-County Environmental Advisory Council. *Member:* Tulsa County and Oklahoma Bar Associations. ***PRACTICE AREAS:*** Zoning Law; Real Property Law. ***Email:*** jmoody@hmptsfirm.com

REPRESENTATIVE CLIENTS: Sterling Oil of Oklahoma, Inc.; HS Resources, Inc.; Newfield Exploration Mid-Continent, Inc.; Hyperion Energy, LP; Railroad Signal, Inc.; Weinkauf Petroleum, Inc.; South Memorial Properties, LLC; Delaware County Rural Water District No. 10; Town of West Siloam Springs, Oklahoma; El Dorado Chemical Co.; LSB Industries, Inc.; Scott Brass, Inc.; Interplastic Corp.; International Environmental Corp.
APPROVED ATTORNEYS FOR: Lawyers Title Co.
REFERENCE: F & M Bank and Trust Company.

MARTIN G. HART

Established in 1989
318 W. 14TH PLACE
TULSA, OKLAHOMA 74119
Telephone: 918-582-5888
Fax: 918-582-4443
Email: mgh9393@hotmail.com

Trial Practice State and Federal Courts, including Medical Malpractice, Personal Injury, Criminal Defense, Environmental Investigations and Defense.

MARTIN G. HART, born Ft. Worth, Texas, September 13, 1953; admitted to bar, 1979, Oklahoma, U.S. Court of Appeals, 10th Circuit and U.S. District Court, Northern and Eastern Districts of Oklahoma. *Education:* Oklahoma State University (B.S., 1975; M.S.,

(This Listing Continued)

MARTIN G. HART, Tulsa—Continued

1976); University of Tulsa (J.D., 1979). District Attorney, Muskogee County, 1979-1980. Member, Tulsa County Public Defenders Office, 1980-1984. Deputy Chief Public Defender, Tulsa County, 1984-1985. Member, Melone, Shepherd, Schroeder, Hart, Allred, Melone, 1988-1989. *Member:* Tulsa County (Member: Judicial Candidates Committee, 1985-1989; Grievance Committee, 1995—) and Oklahoma Bar Associations; Oklahoma Criminal Defense Lawyers Association (Member, Board of Directors, 1984-1986; President, 1986-1987). ***PRACTICE AREAS:*** Auto Accidents; Personal Injury; Criminal Defense; Products Liability; Social Security; Disability Benefits; Environmental Criminal Defense.

KIMBERLY K. HAYS

Established in 1998

248 WEST 16TH STREET
TULSA, OKLAHOMA 74119-4212
Telephone: 918-592-2800
Fax: 918-592-4143
Email: kimberlyhayslaw@aol.com
URL: http://www.divorcelaw-firm.com

Family Law, Divorce, Child Custody, Child Support, Paternity, Visitation Rights.

KIMBERLY K. HAYS, born Tulsa, Oklahoma, August 18, 1967; admitted to bar, 1993, Oklahoma. *Education:* Oklahoma State University (B.A., 1990); University of Kansas (J.D., 1993). *Member:* Tulsa County, Creek County, Oklahoma (Member, Family Law Section) and American (Member, Family Law Section) Bar Associations. ***PRACTICE AREAS:*** Family Law; Divorce; Child Custody; Child Support; Paternity; Visitation Rights; Alimony; Separation Agreements; Property Law; Premarital Agreements; Post Divorce Modification; Guardianship.

LEGAL SUPPORT PERSONNEL

STEPHANIE THOMPSON, Certified Legal Assistant.

HEAD, JOHNSON & KACHIGIAN

Established in 1958

228 WEST 17TH PLACE, MOORE MANOR
TULSA, OKLAHOMA 74119-4694
Telephone: 918-587-2000; 1-800-627-4323
Telefax: 918-587-5603
URL: http://www.lawyers.com/hjklaw
Email: hjklaw.com
URL: http://www.hjklaw.com

Domestic and International Patent, Trademark, Copyright and Intellectual Property Law.

FIRM PROFILE: Head, Johnson & Kachigian is a tradition in the ever changing intellectual property field. Head, Johnson & Kachigian has extensive worldwide experience in patent, trademark, copyright and related matters, including Federal and State Court litigation and proceedings before the U.S. Patent and Trademark Office.

JAMES R. HEAD (Retired)

MARK G. KACHIGIAN, admitted to bar, 1978, Oklahoma; 1980, New York; registered to practice before the U.S. Patent and Trademark Office. *Education:* Rider College (B.S., 1974); University of Tulsa (J.D., 1978). Delta Theta Phi. Author: "Cable Television and the New Copyright Bill," 7 Performing Arts Review 176, 1977; "Organizing and Operating a Corporation to Exploit a Patent," 77 Patent and Trademark Review 438, 1979. Adjunct Professor, University of Tulsa College of Law, 1994-1996. *Member:* Oklahoma (President, Patent, Trademark and Copyright Section, 1994-1995), New York State and American Bar Associations; American Intellectual Property Law Association. ***PRACTICE AREAS:*** Patents; Trademarks; Copyrights. ***Email:*** mkachigian@hjklaw.com

ALLEN BENNETT, admitted to bar, 2002, Arkansas; 2004, Oklahoma; registered to practice before the U.S. Patent and Trademark Office. *Education:* University of Arkansas at Fayetteville (B.S., Biochemistry, cum laude; J.D., 2001); Baylor College of Medicine. Recipient: Freidrich Kekule Award for Outstanding Chemistry Student; Kathy Nolan Award for Excellent Laboratory Work; A.C.S. Analytical Chemistry Award. Author, Publication in the scientific journal Biochemistry; Alpha Chi Sigma. ***PRACTICE AREAS:*** Patents; Trademarks; Copyrights. ***Email:*** abennet@hjklaw.com

LEGAL SUPPORT PERSONNEL

LORI SEARS, (Manager of International Patents and Trademarks). ***Email:*** lsears@hjklaw.com

TODD MAXWELL HENSHAW

Established in 1993

320 SOUTH BOSTON
SUITE 1130
TULSA, OKLAHOMA 74103
Telephone: 918-583-7500
Fax: 918-583-7542
Email: thenshaw@swbell.net
URL: http://www.henshawlaw.com

Bankruptcy, Commercial Litigation and Corporate Law, State and Federal Courts.

(This Listing Continued)

FIRM PROFILE: Listed in Martindale-Hubbell's Bar Register of Preeminent Lawyers in the area of Bankruptcy Law.

TODD MAXWELL HENSHAW, born Tulsa, Oklahoma, November 19, 1950; admitted to bar, 1976, Minnesota; 1978, U.S. District Court, District of Minnesota; 1981, Oklahoma, U.S. District Court, Northern, Eastern and Western Districts of Oklahoma and U.S. Court of Appeals, Tenth Circuit. *Education:* Carleton College (A.B., 1973); Washington University (J.D., 1976). Member, Order of the Coif. Citizen, Cherokee Nation of Oklahoma. Editor, Washington University Law Quarterly, 1975-1976. *Member:* American Bankruptcy Institute. ***PRACTICE AREAS:*** Bankruptcy; Bankruptcy Chapter 7; Bankruptcy Chapter 11; Bankruptcy Chapter 13; Commercial Litigation; Corporate Law.

DAVID W. HOLDEN

4146 S. BIRMINGHAM PLACE
TULSA, OKLAHOMA 74105
Telephone: 918-742-3985
Fax: 918-742-4617
Email: dwh@dwhweb.com
URL: http://www.dwhweb.com

Business Law, Mergers, Acquisitions and Divestitures, Corporate Law and Securities.

FIRM PROFILE: Timely and cost effective planning and implementation of business strategies.

DAVID W. HOLDEN, born Duncan, Oklahoma, 1942; admitted to bar, 1968, Oklahoma. *Education:* University of Oklahoma (B.A., 1965; J.D., 1968). Phi Delta Phi. *Member:* Tulsa County, Oklahoma and American Bar Associations. ***PRACTICE AREAS:*** Business Law; Mergers, Acquisitions and Divestitures; Corporate Law; Securities.

HOLDEN & CARR

Holden Professional Corporation

Established in 1998

200 REUNION CENTER
9 EAST FOURTH STREET, SUITE 200
TULSA, OKLAHOMA 74103
Telephone: 918-295-8888
Facsimile: 918-295-8889
Email: hm@holdenokla.com
URL: http://www.holden-okla.com

Insurance Defense, Medical Malpractice Defense, Nursing Home Defense, Toxic Mold Defense, Casualty Insurance, Commercial Litigation, Banking, Appeals, Coverage Opinions, Labor and Employment Litigation, Contracts.

FIRM PROFILE: Holden & Carr is listed in the Bar Register of Preeminent Lawyers under Insurance Defense.

STEVEN E. HOLDEN, born Willow Springs, Missouri, August 24, 1955; admitted to bar, 1981, Missouri and Oklahoma, U.S. District Court, Northern, Eastern and Western Districts of Oklahoma; U.S. District Court, Northern District of Texas. *Education:* Southwest Missouri State University (B.S., 1977); University of Tulsa (J.D., 1981). *Member:* Tulsa County, Oklahoma and American (Member, Sections on: Tort and Insurance Practice Law; Litigation) Bar Associations; Oklahoma Association of Defense Counsel; Federation of Insurance and Corporate Counsel; American Inns of Court (Barrister). ***PRACTICE AREAS:*** Medical Malpractice; Insurance Litigation; Employment Law. ***Email:*** sholden@holdenokla.com

MICHAEL L. CARR, born Tulsa, Oklahoma, April 9, 1972; admitted to bar, 1999, Oklahoma, U.S. District Court, Western, Eastern and Northern Districts of Oklahoma and U.S. Court of Appeals, Tenth Circuit. *Education:* University of Oklahoma (B.A., 1996; J.D., 1999). Recipient: American Jurisprudence Awards, Evidence and Employment Law. Author: "Defending Civil Wire-tapping Actions" For The Defense, July 1999. *Member:* Oklahoma Bar Association. ***PRACTICE AREAS:*** Insurance Defense; Insurance Bad Faith Defense; Medical Malpractice; Employment Law; Automobile Liability Defense; Civil Litigation. ***Email:*** mcarr@holdenokla.com

---

ROBERT E. APPLEGATE, born Tulsa, Oklahoma, February 1, 1972; admitted to bar, 1998, Oklahoma and U.S. District Court, Western, Northern and Eastern Districts of Oklahoma; 1999, U.S. Court of Appeals, Tenth Circuit; 2002, U.S. Supreme Court. *Education:* University of Oklahoma (B.B.A., 1994); Oklahoma City University School of Law (J.D., 1997). *Member:* Oklahoma County, Oklahoma and American Bar Associations. ***REPORTED CASES:*** Childress v. City of Arapaho, 210 F. 3d 1154 (10th Cir. 2000); Lowe v. Cantrell, 1 P. 3d 438, 2000 OK CIV App 27. ***PRACTICE AREAS:*** Governmental Liability; Insurance Defense; Civil Rights; Constitutional Law; Employment Litigation; Workers Compensation. ***Email:*** rapplegate@holdenokla.com

NANCY C. CURTIS, born Shawnee, Oklahoma, September 7, 1953; admitted to bar, 1991, Ohio; 1993, Oklahoma; 1994, U.S. District Court, Western District of Oklahoma; 2002, U.S. District Court, Northern District of Oklahoma and U.S. Court of Appeals, Sixth Circuit; 2003, U.S. District Court, Eastern District of Oklahoma and U.S. Court of Appeals, Tenth and Eleventh Circuits; U.S. Bankruptcy Court, Northern District of Oklahoma. *Education:* University of Oklahoma (B.A., Anthropology/Asian Studies, 1988); Case Western Reserve University Law School (J.D., 1991). Phi Beta Kappa. Recipient: Iva Schmidt Springstead Award, Outstanding Graduating Senior. *Member:* Oklahoma Bar Association. ***PRACTICE AREAS:*** Antitrust and Trade Regulation; Commercial Law; Litigation; Products Liability; Communications and Media.

(This Listing Continued)

DEREK S.A. LAWRENCE, born Detroit, Michigan, October 28, 1956; admitted to bar, 2002, Oklahoma and U.S. District Court, Western, Eastern and Northern Districts of Oklahoma. *Education:* University of Southwestern Louisiana (B.A., Political Science, 1986); University of Tulsa (J.D., 2002). Author: "Section 227 of the Urban Recovery Act of 1983: Pets Prove Positive Influence on Handicapped and Elderly Tenants," Maricopa Lawyer, March 1988 at 12. *Member:* Oklahoma and American Bar Associations. ***PRACTICE AREAS:*** Insurance Defense; Litigation; Commercial Law. ***Email:*** dlawrence@holdenokla.com

MICHELLE D. SKEENS, born Princeton, West Virginia, April 7, 1975; admitted to bar, 1999, West Virginia and U.S. District Court, Southern District of West Virginia; 2000, U.S. District Court, Northern District of West Virginia; 2001, U.S. Court of Appeals, Fourth Circuit; 2004, Oklahoma. *Education:* West Virginia University (B.A., cum laude, 1996, J.D., 1999). Author: "Ownership of Coalbed Methane Gas: Recent Developments in Case Law," West Virginia Law Review, Volume 100, Issue 3; cited in Energy Development Corp. v. Moss, 591 S.E.2d 135 (W.Va. 2003). *Member:* West Virginia State Bar; Oklahoma Bar Association; Defense Research Institute; Defense Trial Counsel of West Virginia. ***PRACTICE AREAS:*** Civil Practice; Insurance Law; Insurance Defense; Insurance Bad Faith; Personal Injury; Medical Malpractice Defense; Condemnation; Business Litigation. ***Email:*** mskeens@holdenokla.com

RHONDA G. THOMAS, born Midwest City, Oklahoma, June 17, 1967; admitted to bar, 1999, Oklahoma and U.S. District Court, Western District of Oklahoma. *Education:* Northwestern Oklahoma State University (B.S., Psychology, 1990); Oklahoma City University School of Law (J.D., 1998). *Member:* Oklahoma Bar Association (Member, Family Law Section). ***PRACTICE AREAS:*** Civil Litigation; Insurance Defense; Family Law; Entertainment Law; Criminal Defense; Real Estate; Employment Discrimination. ***Email:*** rthomas@holdenokla.com

REPRESENTATIVE CLIENTS: AIG; Albertson's; All American Fitness & Racquetball Centers; American Equity Insurance Company; AXA Assurances; Alternative Services Concepts; Alpha Insurance Company; Arch Insurance Group; Cancer Treatment Center; Carpet City; Clear Channel Communications; Chubb Group; CNA; Columbia Insurance Company; Continental Western; Coregis; Crawford & Company; Clarendon Insurance Company; E&O Professionals; Employers Reinsurance Corporation; First Mercury Insurance Company; Gulf Atlantic; K & K Insurance Group; Metropolitan Property & Casualty; Nautilus; Preferred Physicians; Reliance National; Scottsdale Insurance Company; Shoney's, Inc.; SPI Security; State Bank; The St. Paul; The Medical Protective Company; TIG; TRM; Tulsa National Bank; Universal Underwriters Group (Zurich); Utica Mutual; Wal-Mart; Westport Insurance Company.

HOLEMAN LAW FIRM, PLLC

320 SOUTH BOSTON AVENUE, SUITE 1500
TULSA, OKLAHOMA 74103
Telephone: 918-585-2225
Fax: 918-585-2224
Email: dholeman@holemanlaw.com
URL: http://www.lawyers.com/dholeman

Civil Litigation in all State and Federal Courts, Certified Mediator.

FIRM PROFILE: 20 Years Trial Experience.

DANIEL E. HOLEMAN, born Oklahoma City, Oklahoma, October 10, 1961; admitted to bar, 1986, Oklahoma; U.S. Court of Appeals, Tenth Circuit; U.S. District Court, Eastern, Western and Northern Districts of Oklahoma. *Education:* University of Oklahoma (B.A., 1983); University of Oklahoma, College of Law (J.D., 1986). Phi Beta Kappa; Pi Kappa Phi (President, 1982). Specialized Mediation Training; U.S. District Court Adjunct Settlement Judge Training; Straus Institute for Dispute Resolution, Pepperdine University School of Law; Certified Adjunct Settlement Judge, U.S. District Court, Northern District of Oklahoma. *Member:* Tulsa County, Oklahoma and American Bar Associations; Oklahoma Association of Defense Counsel; International Association of Defense Counsel; International Academy of Trial Lawyers; Defense Research Institute, Inc.; American Board of Trial Advocates (Advocate) American Inns of Court (Master, Council Oak Chapter). ***PRACTICE AREAS:*** Pharmaceutical; Medical Device; Products Liability Litigation; Personal Injury; Bad Faith Litigation; Business Litigation; Mediation; Medical Malpractice.

HOOD & RAYNOLDS, P.C.

Established in 1976
1914 SOUTH BOSTON
TULSA, OKLAHOMA 74119
Telephone: 918-583-5825
Fax: 918-583-6872
Email: info@hoodandraynoldspc.com
URL: http://www.hood-raynolds.com

Matrimonial Law, Family Law, Child Custody, Divorce, Child Support, Litigation, Trials and Appeals.

FIRM PROFILE: Hood & Raynolds, P.C. is pre-eminent among law firms concentrating in family law. The firm utilizes a team concept in which no family law problem is too large or too small.

Combining experience in trial practice, child custody and property division, the law firm offers a strong, well rounded attack on any family law problem.

Hood & Raynolds, P.C. has developed a staff which understands all aspects of family law, and can help the client going through tough financial and emotional aspects of separation and divorce.

In order to provide the highest quality of services available, Hood & Raynolds, P.C. accepts primarily family law cases and divorce.

(This Listing Continued)

Hood & Raynolds, P.C. is listed in the Bar Register of Preeminent Lawyers in the area of family law.

WILLIAM W. HOOD (1941-1999)

WILLIAM F. RAYNOLDS, II, born San Antonio, Texas, February 7, 1948; admitted to bar, 1976, Oklahoma. *Education:* University of Tulsa (B.S., 1973; J.D., 1976). Sigma Chi. Author: "Goodwill in Valuation of Professional Practices," 9 Okl. Family Law Journal 117, 1994; "Jurisdictional Issues in Child Custody Cases 64 Okl. Bar Journal 3351, 1993; "Psychological Examinations in Child Custody," 8 Okl. Family Law Journal 140, 1993; "Brief Look at MMPI," 5 OBA Family Law Journal 6, 1990. Adjunct Professor: University of Tulsa College of Law. Instructor, University of Tulsa Legal Assistant Program. Editor, Oklahoma Family Law Journal, 1995. *Member:* Tulsa County (Chairman, Family Law Section, 1993, 1994, 1996, 1997), Oklahoma and American Bar Associations; Catholic Lawyers Guild; St. Thomas More Society. Fellow, American Academy of Matrimonial Lawyers. ***PRACTICE AREAS:*** Matrimonial Law; Child Custody; Divorce; Equitable Distribution; Child Support. ***Email:*** billr@hoodandraynoldspc.com

HUCKABY, FLEMING, GREENWOOD & OLSSON, LLP

TULSA, OKLAHOMA

(See Oklahoma City)

State and Federal Civil Litigation and Appellate Practice. Insurance Defense, Subrogation, Arbitration, Mediation, Tort Law, Product Liability, Vehicular Negligence, Premises Liability.

JAMES, POTTS AND WULFERS, INC.

Established in 1994
SUITE 2600, MID-CONTINENT TOWER
401 SOUTH BOSTON AVENUE
TULSA, OKLAHOMA 74103-4015
Telephone: 918-584-0881
Fax: 918-584-4521
URL: http://www.jpwlaw.com

General Practice. Trial and Appellate Practice in Federal and State Courts, including Defense of Criminal and Civil State and Federal Tax Claims. Commercial Law, Commercial Litigation, Business Law, Corporation Law and Planning, Financial Institutions, Real Estate, Oil and Gas, Estate Planning, Trust Planning, Wealth Transfer Planning, Probate, Administrative and Tax Law.

FIRM PROFILE: James, Potts and Wulfers, Inc. is listed in the Bar Register of Preeminent Lawyers in the fields of Tax, Probate, Trusts, Estate Planning, Real Estate, Commercial and Business Law.

THOMAS G. POTTS, born Scott Air Force Base, Illinois, September 17, 1948; admitted to bar, 1977, Oklahoma and U.S. Tax Court; 1978, U.S. District Court, Northern District of Texas; 1980, U.S. District Court, Northern District of Oklahoma; 1981, U.S. Court of Federal Claims and U.S. Court of Appeals, Tenth Circuit; 1983, U.S. Supreme Court. *Education:* University of Oklahoma (B.A., 1970); Boston University (M.S.B.A., cum laude, 1974); University of Tulsa (J.D., 1976); Southern Methodist University (LL.M., Taxation, 1980). Phi Delta Phi. Staff Member, Tulsa Law Journal, 1976. The Best Lawyers in America (Tax), 1991, 1994—. Staff Attorney, Office of Chief Counsel, IRS, 1977-1980. Adjunct Federal Settlement Judge, DCND, Okla. 1992-2003. Tax Attorney, Cities Service Company, 1980-1982. *Member:* Oklahoma Bar Association. [1st Lt., Infantry, U.S. Army; Colonel, U.S. Air Force (Reserve, Ret.)]. ***PRACTICE AREAS:*** Tax Litigation; Criminal Taxation. ***Email:*** tpotts@jpwlaw.com

DAVID W. WULFERS, born Cape Girardeau, Missouri, December 19, 1954; admitted to bar, 1981, Oklahoma; U.S. District Court, Northern and Western Districts of Oklahoma; U.S. Court of Appeals, Tenth Circuit. *Education:* Southeast Missouri State University (B.S.B.A., 1977); University of Tulsa (J.D., 1981). Instructor, Civil Procedure, Tulsa Community College, 1984—. *Member:* Oklahoma and American Bar Associations. ***PRACTICE AREAS:*** Business Law; Real Estate Law; Commercial Law; Civil Litigation. ***Email:*** dwulf@jpwlaw.com

CORNELIUS P. DUKELOW, born Philadelphia, Pennsylvania, April 1, 1974; admitted to bar, 2001, Oklahoma; registered to practice before U.S. Patent and Trademark Office. *Education:* Kansas State University (B.S. in Biology, 1997); University of Tulsa (J.D., 2001). Articles Editor, University of Tulsa Law Review. *Tulsa County, Oklahoma and American Bar Associations.* ***PRACTICE AREAS:*** Intellectual Property. ***Email:*** cdukelow@jpwlaw.com

OF COUNSEL

DAVID F. JAMES, born Tulsa, Oklahoma, October 15, 1940; admitted to bar, 1964, Oklahoma; 2002, U.S. Supreme Court. *Education:* Tulsa University (B.S.B.A., 1962; LL.B., 1964). Phi Alpha Delta; Omicron Delta Kappa. Managing Editor, Tulsa Law Journal, 1963-1964. The Best Lawyers in America (Trust and Estates), 1991—. Adjunct Professor, Corporation Law, University of Tulsa College of Law, 1987-1998. Staff Attorney, Securities and Exchange Commission, 1964-1965. Assistant District Attorney, Tulsa, Oklahoma, 1965-1967. Secretary, 1967-1968; President, 1969-1970, Oklahoma Young Lawyers Conference. *Member:* Oklahoma Bar Association. ***PRACTICE AREAS:*** Corporate Law; Business Law; Estate Planning Law. ***Email:*** djames@jpwlaw.com

PAMELA K. WHEELER-NORBERG, born Tulsa, Oklahoma; admitted to bar, 1974, Oklahoma. *Education:* Randolph-Macon Woman's College (B.S., 1972); Oklahoma

(This Listing Continued)

JAMES, POTTS AND WULFERS, INC., Tulsa—Continued

University (J.D., 1974); University of Tulsa (M.T., 2001). Certified Public Accountant, Oklahoma, 1979. *Member:* Oklahoma and American Bar Associations. ***PRACTICE AREAS:*** Taxation. ***Email:*** pwnorberg@jpwlaw.com

REPRESENTATIVE CLIENTS: Arkansas Valley State Bank; Collins & Associates, Inc.; Deltat Limited; FasCast, Inc.; Fleming Building Company, Inc.; Hydrant Repair Parts, Inc.; T-G Excavating, Inc.; Utility Supply Company.

JARBOE & STOERMER

A PROFESSIONAL CORPORATION

Established in 1987

18TH FLOOR, MID-CONTINENT TOWER
401 SOUTH BOSTON, SUITE 1810
TULSA, OKLAHOMA 74103
Telephone: 918-582-6131
Fax: 918-584-4213

General Civil and Federal Practice. Antitrust, Bankruptcy and Reorganization, Corporate, Private and Public Contract, State and Federal Taxation, Tax Controversies, Estate Planning and Probate Law, Wills, Trusts, Business Organizations and Formation, State and Federal Administrative Law, Water Law, Real Estate, Commercial Litigation, Asset Protection.

JOHN B. JARBOE, born Tulsa, Oklahoma, March 28, 1940; admitted to bar, 1965, Oklahoma and U.S. Claims Court; 1966, U.S. Court of Military Appeals and U.S. Tax Court; 1967, Louisiana. *Education:* Oklahoma University (B.A., 1962); University of Tulsa (J.D., 1965). Phi Alpha Delta. Editor-in-Chief, Tulsa Law Journal, 1964-1965. Law Clerk for U.S. District Judge Allen E. Barrow, 1963-1965. Author: "Undue Influence and Gifts to Religious Organizations," The Catholic Lawyer, Vol. 35, p. 271, St. John's University, 1999. Trial Attorney, U.S. Department of Justice, 1965-1966. Member, Board of Regents, 1971-1979; Chairman of Regents, 1971-1972, University of Sciences and Arts of Oklahoma. Member, Oklahoma Water Resources Board, 1979-1983. Judge, Oklahoma Court of Appeals, Temporary Division, 1982. *Member:* Tulsa County (Vice-President, 1985), Oklahoma (Chairman, Bankruptcy and Reorganization Section, 1983-1984) and Louisiana State Bar Associations. ***PRACTICE AREAS:*** Antitrust Law; Bankruptcy Reorganization Law; Estate Planning; Probate. ***Email:*** jjarboe@jarboelaw.com

JEFFREY D. STOERMER, born Pittsburgh, Pennsylvania, April 28, 1952; admitted to bar, 1979, Oklahoma. *Education:* Dartmouth College (A.B., cum laude, 1974); University of Tulsa (J.D., 1979); Georgetown University (LL.M., in Taxation, 1982). Phi Delta Phi. Member, Tulsa Law Journal, 1977-1979. Author: "Cattle Breeding as a Tax-Sheltered Investment," 14 Tulsa Law Journal 410, 1978. Attorney, U.S. Department of Energy, Washington, D.C., 1979-1982. Director, 1987-1990 and President, 1989-1990, Tulsa Estate Planning Forum. Director, Oklahoma Planned Giving Council (1997-2000). Chairman, Entrepreneurs of Tulsa, Inc., 1987—. Director: Oklahoma Private Enterprise Forum, 1989-1997. Director and Chairman of Family Estate Planning Services Committee, Parent Child Center of Tulsa, 1996—. Member, 1995— and Secretary, 1997-1998, Friends of Finance. *Member:* Tulsa County (Chairman, Taxation Section, 1986-1987), Oklahoma and American (Member, Sections on: Taxation; Real Property, Probate and Trust Law; National Chairman, Task Force on Legislative Revision of Domestic Worker Taxes; Co-Chairman, Task Force on Legislative Revision of IRC § 6672, 100% Penalty) Bar Associations. ***PRACTICE AREAS:*** Taxation Law; Tax Controversies; Estate Planning; Probate Law; Business Organizations. ***Email:*** jdstoermer@jarboelaw.com

ASSOCIATE

F. BENNETT CALLICOAT, born Tulsa, Oklahoma, October 24, 1962; admitted to bar, 2000, Oklahoma. *Education:* University of Tulsa (B.A., 1994); University of Tulsa College of Law (J.D., 1998). Phi Delta Phi. *Member:* Oklahoma Bar Association. ***PRACTICE AREAS:*** Bankruptcy Litigation; Business Litigation; Employment Law; Landlord and Tenant Law. ***Email:*** fbcallicoat@jarboelaw.com

OF COUNSEL

THEODORE P. GIBSON, born Muskogee, Oklahoma, July 4, 1931; admitted to bar, 1960, Oklahoma, U.S. District Court, Northern, Eastern and Western Districts of Oklahoma and U.S. Court of Appeals, Tenth Circuit. *Education:* Brown University (A.B., 1953); University of Tulsa (LL.B., 1960). Phi Alpha Delta. Lecturer, Oklahoma Bar Association. Assistant City Attorney, Tulsa, 1970-1973. Member, 1982 and Judge, 1983, Oklahoma Court of Appeals, Temporary Division #79. *Member:* Tulsa County (Secretary, Vice President, Director at Large, Chairman Court Operations Committee; Member, Sections on: Professional Responsibility, Fee Arbitration, Bankruptcy and Insolvency) and Oklahoma (Director and Past Chairman, Bankruptcy and Insolvency Sections) Bar Associations; Commercial Law League (Lifetime Member); American Bankruptcy Institute. ***PRACTICE AREAS:*** Commercial Law; Bankruptcy; Creditors Rights; Family Law; Corporate Law.

REPRESENTATIVE CLIENTS: Campbell Wholesale Co.; The Catholic Diocese of Tulsa; C.H. Smith Construction Co., Inc.; Coweta Sand & Transportation, Inc.; Select Wines and Spirits Co.; U.S. Coating Applicators, LLC; Southwest Risk Management, Inc.; Earth Power Resources, Inc.
REFERENCE: American Bank & Trust.

JOHNSON, JONES, DORNBLASER, COFFMAN & SHORB

A Professional Corporation

2200 BANK OF AMERICA CENTER
15 WEST SIXTH STREET
TULSA, OKLAHOMA 74119-5416
Telephone: 918-584-6644
Fax: 918-584-6645

General Practice of Business Law with emphasis on Business Organizations, Business and Commercial Transactions and Planning, Non-Profit and Professional Corporations, Securities Law, Federal, State and Local Taxation, Tax Controversies, Health Law, Municipal Finance, Tax Exempt Bonds, Governmental Law, Real Estate, Estate Planning, Probate and Trust Administration.

W. THOMAS COFFMAN, born Alva, Oklahoma, 1940; admitted to bar, 1966, Oklahoma; 1972, U.S. Supreme Court; 1987, U.S. Tax Court. *Education:* University of Tulsa (B.S.B.A., 1963; J.D., 1966). Editor, Tulsa Law Journal, 1965-1966. President, University of Tulsa Alumni Association, 1988-1989, and Law Alumni Association, 1992-1994. Co-Author: "Oklahoma Estate Planning, Will Drafting and Estate Administration Forms," 1997, LEXIS Publishing. Chairman, Estate Planning and Probate Section, Oklahoma Bar Association, 1974 and 1990. President, Tulsa Estate Planning Forum, 1976-1977. President, Tulsa Title and Probate Lawyers Association, 1979. Outstanding Junior Member, 1972, Outstanding Senior Member, 1989 and President, 1997-1998, Tulsa County Bar Association. Fellow: American Bar Foundation; American College of Trust and Estate Counsel (Oklahoma State Chair, 1986-1992; Regent, 1992-1998; Foundation Board, 1995-2001; Membership Selection Committee, 2001-2006, Chair, 2005); Oklahoma Bar Foundation; Tulsa County Bar Foundation (President, 1998-1999). ***PRACTICE AREAS:*** Estate Planning; Charitable Trusts and Foundations; Probate Law; Trust Law; Will Contests; Trust Contests. ***Email:*** tcoffman@jjdcs.com

KENNETH E. DORNBLASER, born Bartlesville, Oklahoma, 1955; admitted to bar, 1980, Oklahoma. *Education:* Oklahoma State University (B.S., 1977); University of Oklahoma (J.D., 1980). Order of the Coif. Editor, Oklahoma Law Review, 1977-1980. Member, General Corporation Act Committee of the Business Association Section of the Oklahoma Bar Association, 1990—. Member, Revised Uniform Partnership Act Committee of the Business Association Section of the Oklahoma Bar Association, 1993-2002. ***PRACTICE AREAS:*** Corporate Law; Mergers, Acquisitions and Divestitures; Securities Law; Municipal Finance; Commercial Law; Sales and Use Tax. ***Email:*** kdornblaser@jjdcs.com

E. ANDREW JOHNSON, born Tulsa, Oklahoma, 1969; admitted to bar, 1995, Oklahoma. *Education:* Oklahoma State University (B.S., 1991); University of Oklahoma (J.D., with honors, 1995). Editor, Oklahoma Law Review, 1994-1995. Certified Public Accountant, Oklahoma 1993. *Member:* Tulsa County (Chairman, Young Lawyers Division, 2000-2001) and Oklahoma (Chairman, Business and Corporate Law Section, 2001-2002; Chairman, Section of Taxation, 2003-2004) Bar Associations. ***PRACTICE AREAS:*** Taxation; Mergers, Acquisitions and Divestitures; Corporate Law; Professional Corporations; Estate Planning; Health Law; Probate. ***Email:*** ajohnson@jjdcs.com

JOHN B. JOHNSON, JR., born Little Rock, Arkansas, 1933; admitted to bar, 1957, Oklahoma; 1961, U.S. Supreme Court. *Education:* University of Oklahoma (B.B.A., 1955; J.D., 1957); Harvard Law School (LL.M., 1961). Editor, Oklahoma Law Review, 1955-1957. Chairman, Metropolitan Tulsa Chamber of Commerce, 1989. ***PRACTICE AREAS:*** Corporate Law; Securities; Mergers, Acquisitions and Divestitures; Estate Planning. ***Email:*** jbjohnson@jjdcs.com

C. ROBERT JONES, born Enid, Oklahoma, 1936; admitted to bar, 1961, Oklahoma and U.S. Tax Court. *Education:* Oklahoma State University (B.S., 1958); Oklahoma University (J.D., 1961). Order of the Coif. Editor, Oklahoma Law Review, 1959-1961. Co-Author: "Oklahoma Estate Planning, Will Drafting and Estate Administration Forms," 1997, LEXIS Publishing. ***PRACTICE AREAS:*** Corporate Law; Professional Corporations; Charitable Trusts and Foundations; Employee Benefits Law; Estate Planning; Health Law. ***Email:*** crjones@jjdcs.com

RANDY R. SHORB, born Hardesty, Oklahoma, 1959; admitted to bar, 1985, Oklahoma. *Education:* Fort Hays State University (B.A., cum laude, 1982); Southern Methodist University (J.D., 1985). Editor, Southwestern Law Journal, 1984-1985. Chairman, Section of Taxation, Oklahoma Bar Association, 1992. ***PRACTICE AREAS:*** Mergers, Acquisitions and Divestitures; International Business Law; Business Organizations; Taxation; Municipal Finance; Tax Exempt Bonds. ***Email:*** rshorb@jjdcs.com

JESSE N. BOMER, born Tulsa, Oklahoma, 1978; admitted to bar, 2003, Oklahoma. *Education:* University of Tulsa (B.S.B.A., magna cum laude, 2000; J.D., with highest honor, 2003). Managing Editor, Tulsa Law Review, 2002-2003. ***PRACTICE AREAS:*** Business Organization; Corporate Law; Mergers, Acquisitions and Divestitures; Taxation; Health Law; Trusts and Estates. ***Email:*** jbomer@jjdcs.com

OF COUNSEL

RICHARD D. JONES, born Enid, Oklahoma, 1939; admitted to bar, 1964, Oklahoma; 1968, U.S. Supreme Court; 1973, U.S. Tax Court. *Education:* Oklahoma State University (B.S., 1961); University of Oklahoma (J.D., 1964). Order of the Coif. Editor, Oklahoma Law Review, 1962-1964. Certified Public Accountant, Oklahoma, 1968. ***PRACTICE AREAS:*** Corporate Law; Business Organizations; Contract Law; Taxation. ***Email:*** rdjones@jjdcs.com

PAUL D. KINGSOLVER, born Okemah, Oklahoma, July 15, 1958; admitted to bar, 1983, Oklahoma; 1984, Missouri; 1988, District of Columbia; 1999, U.S. Tax Court. *Education:* University of Tulsa (B.S., 1980; J.D., 1983). Law Clerk, Hon. Roy W. Harper, U.S. District Court Judge, Eastern District of Missouri, 1983-1984. ***PRACTICE AREAS:*** Litigation; Employment Law; Intellectual Property. ***Email:*** kingsolver@jjdcs.com

(This Listing Continued)

DIANA H. CLARK, born Tulsa, Oklahoma, November 5, 1950; admitted to bar, 1992, Oklahoma. *Education:* University of Tulsa (B.S., Industrial Sociology with honors, 1973); University of Tulsa Law School (J.D., 1992). Notes and Comments Editor, Tulsa Law Journal, 1991-1992. Professor of Law, University of Tulsa. ***PRACTICE AREAS:*** Employment Law; Trusts; Taxation; Litigation. ***Email:*** dclark@jjdcs.com

All Attorneys are Members of Tulsa County and Oklahoma Bar Associations.

REPRESENTATIVE CLIENTS: AAON, Inc.; Arena Resources, Inc.; City of Tulsa-Rogers County Port Authority; Hemphill Corporation; Hilti, Inc.; Holland Hall School; Hughes Lumber Company; International American Ceramics, Inc.; Internet Telemetry Corp.; Laufen International, Inc.; Lexus of Tulsa; LifeGuard America, LLC; Mazzio's; McElroy Manufacturing, Inc.; Metris Companies, Inc.; Mill Creek Lumber & Supply Company; Murphy Industries, Inc.; Neurological Associates of Tulsa, Inc.; Oklahoma Heart Institute; Radiology Consultants of Tulsa, Inc.; Red Man Pipe & Supply Co.; Regent Private Capital; Tayloe Paper Company; Tulsa Endoscopy Center; Tulsa Industrial Authority; Tulsa Radiology Associates, Inc.; United States Beef Corporation; Universal Field Services, Inc.; Wells, Nelson & Associates.

KENDALL W. JOHNSON, P.C.

601 SOUTH BOULDER, SUITE 600
TULSA, OKLAHOMA 74119
Telephone: 918-583-9000
Fax: 918-585-1079
Email: kwjohnson4@sbcglobal.net
URL: http://www.kwjohnsonlaw.com

Family Law, Divorce, Child Custody, Child Support, Spousal Support, Personal Injury, Auto Accidents, Wrongful Death, Estate Planning, Wills, Trusts, Probate, Bankruptcy, Criminal Law, Driving While Intoxicated, Driving Under the Influence, Traffic Violations, Garnerships, Adoptions, Business Law, Entertainment Law.

KENDALL W. JOHNSON, born Salem, Oregon, August 24, 1960; admitted to bar, 1994, Oklahoma; 1995, Missouri. *Education:* Oral Roberts University (B.S., Business Administration, 1988); University of Tulsa (J.D., 1993). Music Director, Oral Roberts University Basketball Band, 1994—. *Member:* Tulsa County (Member, Family Law Section, Professional Responsibility Committee) and Oklahoma Bar Associations; Christian Legal Society. ***PRACTICE AREAS:*** Family Law; Wills; Estates; Trusts; Personal Injury; Criminal Defense. ***Email:*** kwjohnson4@sbcglobal.net

JONES, GOTCHER & BOGAN

A PROFESSIONAL CORPORATION
Established in 1964
3800 FIRST PLACE TOWER
TULSA, OKLAHOMA 74103
Telephone: 918-581-8200
Fax: 918-583-1189 or 918-583-6652
URL: http://www.jonesgivens.com

General Civil Practice and Appeals before all State and Federal Courts. Corporate, Banking, Administrative, Bankruptcy, Probate, Employment Law, Insurance, Real Estate, Construction, Zoning, Oil and Gas, Family, Employee Relations, Communications, Trademark, Copyright, Environmental, E-Commerce and Estate Planning Law.

FIRM PROFILE: Jones, Gotcher & Bogan was formed by two senior members on March 16, 1964, as a general practice with emphasis on corporate, real estate transactions and commercial litigation law. Since its inception, four presidents of the Oklahoma Bar Association have been associated with the firm, and a like number of Tulsa County Bar presidents, accenting the firm's strong devotion to professional and ethical standards. The wide range of the firm's representative clients in banking, oil and gas production, insurance, governmental administration, real estate radio & television and manufacturing, illustrates the diverse specialties of its members. The firm takes pride in its reputation as a leader in the legal profession.

Jones, Gotcher & Bogan is listed in Martindale-Hubbell's Bar Register of Preeminent Lawyers.

DERYL LEE GOTCHER (1922-2001)

NEIL E. BOGAN (1945-1990)

WILLIAM B. JONES, born Mangum, Oklahoma, October 29, 1925; admitted to bar, 1951, Oklahoma, U.S. Court of Appeals, Tenth Circuit and U.S. District Court, Northern, Eastern and Western Districts of Oklahoma. *Education:* University of North Carolina; Harvard University; University of Oklahoma (LL.B., 1951). Phi Delta Phi. *Member:* American Bar Association. ***PRACTICE AREAS:*** Corporate; Contracts; Real Estate; Zoning. ***Email:*** bjones@jonesgivens.com

JAMES E. WEGER, born Denver, Colorado, September 11, 1956; admitted to bar, 1982, Oklahoma and U.S. Supreme Court; 1983, U.S. Court of Appeals, 10th Circuit and U.S. District Court, Northern, Western and Eastern Districts of Oklahoma. *Education:* University of Oklahoma (B.B.A., 1979; J.D., 1982); University of Oxford, Oxford, England; Queens College. Phi Delta Phi. Listed in Who's Who in American Law; Who's Who in Executives & Professionals. Adjunct Settlement Judge, United States District Court, Northern District of Oklahoma. *Member:* Tulsa County (Chairman, Employment Law Section, 2001-2002) and American Bar Associations (Member Sections on: Litigation and Antitrust). ***PRACTICE AREAS:*** Business Litigation; Real Estate; Antitrust; Communications Law; Employment Law; Environmental Law; Construction Litigation. ***Email:*** jweger@jonesgivens.com

THOMAS L. VOGT, born El Paso, Texas, August 24, 1959; admitted to bar, 1984, Oklahoma, U.S. District Court, Northern and Eastern Districts of Oklahoma and U.S. Court of Appeals, Tenth Circuit. *Education:* University of Oklahoma (B.B.A. in Accounting, 1981; J.D., with highest honors, 1984). Order of the Coif; Phi Eta Sigma; Beta Gamma Sigma. *Member:* American Bar Association (Member, Sections on: Labor and Employment Law; Real Estate, Probate and Taxes); National Association of College and University Attorneys. ***PRACTICE AREAS:*** Business Litigation; Employment Law; Real Estate; Education Law; Bankruptcy. ***Email:*** tvogt@jonesgivens.com

JACK L. BROWN, born Miami, Oklahoma, September 11, 1957; admitted to bar, 1984, Oklahoma, U.S. Supreme Court; U.S. Court of Appeals, Tenth Circuit and U.S. District Court,. Northern, Western and Eastern Districts of Oklahoma. *Education:* University of Oklahoma (B.A., 1979); University of Tulsa (J.D., 1984). Delta Theta Phi. Tulsa Metropolitan Utility Authority, 1988-1993, Chairperson, 1990. *Member:* Tulsa County, Oklahoma (Member, Young Lawyers Chairperson, 1991-1992; Board of Governors, 1992-1993; Chair, Bench & Bar Committee, 2005) and American (Member, Board of Governors, 1993-1996; Delegate, 1997-2005) Bar Associations; Oklahoma Bar Foundation (Member, Board of Trustees, 2005). Fellow, American Bar Foundation. ***PRACTICE AREAS:*** Commercial Law; Trusts; Probate. ***Email:*** jbrown@jonesgivens.com

WILLIAM G. LASORSA, born Lancaster, Pennsylvania, April 30, 1945; admitted to bar, 1974, Oklahoma and U.S. District Court, Northern District of Oklahoma; 1976, U.S. Court of Appeals, 10th Circuit; 1977, U.S. Supreme Court; 1985, U.S. Court of Military Appeals. *Education:* Marquette University (B.A., 1967); University of Tulsa (J.D., 1973). Assistant District Attorney, Tulsa County, Oklahoma, 1973-1980. Appointed Special Prosecutor, 1996. *Member:* Tulsa County (Member: Grievance Committee, 1984-1985; Judicial Nominating Committee, 1986-1987; Outreach Committee, 1990-1991; Fee Arbitration Committee, 1991-1993; Chair, 1992-1993, Member, Family Law Section), Oklahoma (Board of Governors, 1994-1996; Member, Executive Committee, Family Law Section, Programs Chair, 1991-1992; Fellow, Young Lawyers Division) and American (Member, Family Law Section) Bar Associations; Oklahoma Trial Lawyers Association; The Association of Trial Lawyers of America; American Inns of Court (Master Emeritus, Hudson-Hall-Wheaton Chapter). Fellow: Oklahoma Bar Foundation (Member, Board of Trustees, 1996—; President, 2004); American Bar Foundation. Charter Fellow, Tulsa County Bar Foundation. [Ret. Lieut. Col., JAGC, USAR]. ***LANGUAGES:*** German. ***PRACTICE AREAS:*** Family Law; Civil and Criminal Litigation. ***Email:*** blasorsa@jonesgivens.com

C. MICHAEL COPELAND, born Tulsa, Oklahoma, June 19, 1963; admitted to bar, 1988, Oklahoma, U.S. District Court, Northern, Eastern and Western Districts of Oklahoma and U.S. Court of Appeals, 10th Circuit. *Education:* University of Oklahoma (B.B.A., Finance, 1985; J.D., with honors, 1988). Member, Oklahoma Law Review, 1987-1988. Recipient, American Jurisprudence Award for Federal Securities Regulation. *Member:* Tulsa County, Oklahoma and American Bar Associations. ***PRACTICE AREAS:*** Commercial Litigation; Securities Litigation; Products Liability Litigation. ***Email:*** mcopeland@jonesgivens.com

ROBERT R. PETERS II, born Tulsa, Oklahoma, November 23, 1962; admitted to bar, 1992, Oklahoma; U.S. District Court, Northern, Eastern and Western Districts of Oklahoma and U.S. Supreme Court. *Education:* University of Kansas (B.A., 1987); University of Tulsa (J.D., 1991). *Member:* Tulsa County, Oklahoma and American (Member, Business, Sports and Entertainment Law Sections) Bar Associations; Sports Lawyers Association; American Inns of Court. ***PRACTICE AREAS:*** Commercial Litigation; Business Law; Real Estate; General Corporate Law; Sports Law. ***Email:*** rpeters@jonesgivens.com

MICHAEL ALAN JOYCE, born Tulsa, Oklahoma, March 16, 1962; admitted to bar, 1987, Oklahoma and U.S. District Court, Northern, Eastern and Western Districts of Oklahoma; 1988, Arkansas. *Education:* University of Oklahoma; University of Tulsa (B.S.B.A., 1984; J.D., 1987; M.B.A., 1999). Delta Theta Phi. Chairman, University of Tulsa Genave King Rogers Business Law Center Advisory Board (2001-2002). Real Estate Broker, Oklahoma, 1989-2002. Member: National Association of Realtors (1989-2004); Greater Tulsa Association of Realtors (1989-2004). *Member:* Arkansas, Oklahoma and American Bar Associations. ***PRACTICE AREAS:*** Real Estate; Corporate Law; Sports Licensing; Commercial Law; Trust Law; Probate; Limited Liability Company Law. ***Email:*** mjoyce@jonesgivens.com

---

ADAM J. STRANGE, admitted to bar, 2004, Oklahoma. *Education:* University of Dallas (B.A., cum laude, 2001); University of Oklahoma College of Law (J.D., 2004). National Dean's List. Phi Delta Phi. Recipient: Dean's Circle Merit Scholarship; Cecil L. Hunt Memorial Scholarship; CALI Award; Quarter Finalist, NTC Trial Competition. Student Member: Ruth Bader Ginsburg American Inns of Court; American Bar Association. Former Member: American Trial Lawyers Association (SBA Representative).

OF COUNSEL

JOHN W. CANNON, born Oklahoma City, Oklahoma, February 4, 1967; admitted to bar, 1993, Oklahoma, U.S District Court, Northern, Western and Eastern Districts of Oklahoma and U.S. Court of Appeals, Tenth Circuit. *Education:* Oral Roberts University (B.S., Finance, magna cum laude, 1989); University of Tulsa College of Law (J.D., with honors, 1993). Order of the Curule Chair; Phi Delta Phi. Recipient, American Jurisprudence Awards in Basic Corporate Law and Commercial Law. Research Editor, Tulsa Law Journal, 1992-1993. Author: "Resolving the Debtors and Creditors' Rights in Property Revested in Debtor Post-Confirmation Under Chapter 13," 69 OBJ 2316 (1998); "The Resurrection of Victim Impact Evidence in Capital Sentencing Hearings: *Payne v. Tennessee*," 27 Tulsa L. J. 453 (1992). Adjunct Faculty, University of Tulsa College of Law (Professional Responsibility UCC Articles 2 and 2A, and Agency/Partnership, 1999-2001). Partner, Moyers, Martin, Santee, Imel & Tetrick, LLP, 1999-2001. Senior Counsel: Koch Petroleum Group, LP; Flint Hills Resources LP, 2001-2002. Corporate Counsel and Assistant Secretary, John Zink Company, LLC, 2002-2004. *Member:* Tulsa County (Chairman, Corporate Counsel Section, 2004), Oklahoma and American Bar Associations; Association of Corporate Counsel; American Bankruptcy Institute; American Inns of Court (Barrister, Johnson-Sontag Chapter, 1999-2004). ***PRACTICE AREAS:*** Corporate Law; Corporate Compliance; Commercial Law; Commercial Litigation; Bankruptcy Law; Antitrust; Mergers and Acquisitions; Trusts; Probate.

All of the firm's attorneys are members of the Tulsa County and Oklahoma Bar Associations.

(This Listing Continued)

JONES, GOTCHER & BOGAN, A PROFESSIONAL CORPORATION, Tulsa—Continued

REPRESENTATIVE CLIENTS: *Communications & Entertainment:* Clear Channel Communications; Clear Channel Radio; Clear Channel TV; LeSea Broadcasting; Major League Baseball Players Association. *Energy:* American Natural Energy Corporation; Homestake Royalty Co.; Medallion Production Co.; Mobile Oil Co.; Nadel & Gussman. *Financial Services:* BankOne; Local America Bank of Tulsa; Tulsa National Bank; BancOklahoma Mortgage Corporation; Kansas City Life Insurance Company; Liberty Mortgage Company. *Government, Non-Profit, and Education:* Grand River Dam Authority; The University of Tulsa; Oklahoma State University; Tulsa County Public Facility Authority; Tulsa Community College; Oklahoma Christian University; McAlester Regional Health Center. *Insurance:* American International Group; Government Employees Insurance Co.; Oklahoma Attorneys Mutual Insurance Company; Travelers Insurance Company; GAB Robins North America, Inc.; AmeriClaim Adjustment Corporation; ITT Hartford. Safeco Insurance; Cres Insurance. *Manufacturing and Commerce:* Brunswick Corporation; Novartis; Flight Safety International; BOC Group; General Signal Corp.; Libby-Owens-Ford; Union Carbide Corp.; International Marine & Gaming; Bill's Dollar Stores; TGI Enterprises, Inc.; Arrow Trucking Company; W.C. Bradley; Zebco Holdings Inc.; Sportz Bruch, LLC; All-Sport Bruch LLC. *Professional Services:* KPMG, Peat Marwick; Williams Bros. Engineering; Air Cooled Exchangers, Inc. *Real Estate:* Gordona Duca Realtors; John Hausam Realtors; Leinbach Company; Prudential Detrick Realty; Prudential Alliance Realty; McGraw, Davisson & Stewart; Keller Williams Realtors; Lincoln Properties Co.; Property Company of America; Trammell Crow Company.

JOYCE, PAUL & McDANIEL, P.C.

Established in 2000

200 MAPCO PLAZA
1717 SOUTH BOULDER AVENUE
TULSA, OKLAHOMA 74119-4833
Telephone: 918-599-0700
Facsimile: 918-732-5370
URL: http://www.jpm-law.com

Administrative Law, Class Actions, Commercial Law, Construction Law, Contracts, Eminent Domain, Energy, Environmental Law, Labor and Employment, Litigation, Mergers, Acquisitions and Divestitures, Natural Resources, Oil and Gas Transportation, Natural Gas Pipelines, Hazardous Materials Transportation, Occupational Safety and Health, Real Estate, Regulatory Law, Torts, Transportation, Immigration and Nationality Law.

ROBERT J. JOYCE, born Tulsa, Oklahoma, August 19, 1958; admitted to bar, 1988, Oklahoma. *Education:* University of Tulsa (B.S., 1981; J.D., 1988). Tau Beta Pi; Delta Theta Pi. Order of the Curule Chair. Staff Member, 1987-1988 and Outstanding Staff Member, 1988, Energy Law Journal. Author: "Lender Liability Under the Comprehensive Environmental Response, Compensation and Liability Act (CERCLA) - EPA's Final Rule Interpreting the Security Interest Exemption," 63 Oklahoma Bar Journal 2702, Sept. 1992; "Drawing the Line on Rate Conditions Under Section 7 of the Natural Gas Act," 9 Energy Law Journal 113, 1988. *Professional Background:* Executive Partner, Gardere & Wynne, LLP, Tulsa Office; Senior Attorney and Environmental Manager, Hilti, Inc.; Chemical Engineer, OXY USA/Cities Service Co. *Member:* Tulsa County, Oklahoma (Member, Environmental Law Section) and American (Member, Natural Resources, Energy and Environmental Law Section) Bar Associations; American Institute of Chemical Engineers. ***PRACTICE AREAS:*** Administrative Law; Environmental; Occupational Safety and Health; Regulatory Law; Transportation; Litigation. ***Email:*** rjoyce@jpm-law.com

CHRIS A. PAUL, born Philadelphia, Pennsylvania, June 14, 1958; admitted to bar, 1983, Pennsylvania; 1984, U.S. Army Court of Military Review; 1988, U.S. District Court, Eastern District of Pennsylvania and U.S. Supreme Court; 1990, Oklahoma; 2001, U.S. District Court, Northern, Eastern and Western Districts of Oklahoma. *Education:* Dickinson College (B.A., 1980); College of William & Mary, Marshall-Wythe School of Law (J.D., 1983). Adjunct Instructor, Oklahoma State University Engineering Extension Hazardous Materials Management Program. National Trustee, Arthritis Foundation. Volunteer, Tulsa County Bar Association Military Families Assistance Project. Legal Advisor, Tulsa Affiliate of Susan G. Komen Foundation. Member, American Legion. *Professional Background:* Partner, Gardere & Wynne, L.L.P.; Environmental Department Manager, Tulsa Refinery, Sun Company, Inc.; Senior Attorney, Sun Pipe Line Company. *Member:* Tulsa County and Oklahoma Bar Associations; Transportation Lawyers Association. [Capt. U.S. Army; JAGC Trial Counsel and Special Assistant U.S. Attorney, 1984-1988]. ***PRACTICE AREAS:*** Transportation; Contracts; Environmental; Mergers, Acquisitions and Divestitures; Litigation. ***Email:*** cpaul@jpm-law.com

A. SCOTT McDANIEL, born Winston-Salem, North Carolina, July 24, 1958; admitted to bar, 1995, Oklahoma; U.S. District Court, Northern, Eastern and Western Districts of Oklahoma, U.S. Court of Appeals, Tenth Circuit and U.S. Supreme Court. *Education:* North Carolina State University (B.S., 1981); University of Tulsa College of Law (J.D., with highest honors, 1995). Order of the Curule Chair. Managing Editor, Tulsa Law Journal, 1994-1995. Author: Comment, "The Good, The Bad, The Unqualified: The Public Interest and The Unregulated Practice of General Contracting in Oklahoma," 29 Tulsa Law Journal, 1994. Member, Board of Education, Union Public Schools. Registered Professional Engineer, Oklahoma, 1992, North Carolina, 1985. *Professional Background:* Attorney, Gardere & Wynne, L.L.P. Certified Mediator. Adjunct Settlement Judge. Project Civil Engineer, Tennessee Valley Authority. *Member:* Tulsa County, Oklahoma and American (Member, Sections on: Dispute Resolution; Natural Resources, Energy and Environmental Law; Litigation; Construction Law; Torts and Insurance Practice) Bar Associations; Defense Research Institute; Transportation Lawyers Association; National Society of Professional Engineers. ***PRACTICE AREAS:*** Commercial Law; Construction Law; Contracts; Litigation; Environmental; Transportation; Labor and Employment; Torts. ***Email:*** smcdaniel@jpm-law.com

STACY L. ACORD, born Hugo, Oklahoma, July 14, 1974; admitted to bar, 2000, Oklahoma; U.S. District Court, Eastern, Northern and Western Districts of Oklahoma and U.S. Court of Appeals, Tenth Circuit. *Education:* Oklahoma State University (B.A., 1996); University of Oklahoma (J.D., 2000). Phi Delta Phi. Recipient, American Jurisprudence Awards in Trial Techniques, Capital Punishment and Professional Responsibility. Member: The Council Oak American Inn of Court, 2002—; Luther Bohannon American Inn of Court, 1999-2000. *Member:* Oklahoma, Tulsa County (Member, The Tulsa Lawyer Committee) and American (Member, Sections on: Litigation; Young Lawyers) Bar Associations; Oklahoma Association of Defense Counsel (Member, Board of Directors, 2005—; Vice Chairperson, Legislative Committee, 2004—; Chairperson, Young Lawyers Committee, 2002-2004; Nominating Committee, 2004—); Defense Research Institute, Inc. ***PRACTICE AREAS:*** Torts; Environmental Law; Education Law; Civil Litigation; Commercial Law. ***Email:*** sacord@jpm-law.com

NICOLE M. LONGWELL, born Garland, Texas, September 19, 1970; admitted to bar, 2000, Oklahoma. *Education:* Northeastern Oklahoma State University (B.S., Criminal Justice, 1996); University of Tulsa School of Law (J.D., with highest honors, 2000). Magistrate, Phi Delta Phi. Order of the Curule Chair. Member, The Order of the Barristers. Vice President, Board of Advocates, 1998-2000. Senior Staff, Tulsa Law Journal, 1999-2000. Research Assistant, Professor Martin A. Frey, 1998-2000. Former Member, University of Tulsa Trial Team, 1999; The Hudson Hall Wheaton American Inn of Court, 1999-2000. *Professional Background:* Attorney, Gardere, Wynne, Sewell, LLP. *Member:* Tulsa County, Oklahoma (Member, Sections on: Labor and Employment; Litigation; Vice Chairperson, Mock Trial Committee, Young Lawyers Division) and American (Member, Sections on: Labor and Employment; Litigation) Bar Associations; Defense Research Institute; The Council Oak American Inn of Court; Oklahoma Association of Defense Counsel. ***PRACTICE AREAS:*** Commercial Law; Construction Law; Environmental Law; Labor and Employment; Torts; Title Insurance Defense; Transportation; Civil Litigation; Real Estate Litigation. ***Email:*** nlongwell@jpm-law.com

PHILIP D. HIXON, born Stroud, Oklahoma, December 2, 1966; admitted to bar, 2001, Oklahoma; U.S. District Court, Northern, Eastern and Western Districts of Oklahoma and U.S. Court of Appeals, Tenth Circuit. *Education:* University of Central Oklahoma (B.B.A., summa cum laude, 1990); Oklahoma City University (M.B.A., high honors, 1992; J.D., summa cum laude, 2001). Phi Delta Phi. Recipient: Outstanding Note Award, Oklahoma City University Law Review, 2000; CALI Excellence for the Future Awards for Torts I and II, Property I, Criminal Law, Legal Research and Writing II, Constitutional Law I, Income Tax, Labor Law I, Consumer Law, Products Liability, Trial Practice; Outstanding Young Lawyer Award, 2003-2004 and President's Award, 2003-2004, Tulsa County Bar Association. Managing Editor, Oklahoma City Law Review, 2000-2001. Author: "Contingent Workers and ERISA: Should the Law Protect Workers with No Reasonable Pension Expectations?" 25 Okla. City U. L. Rev. 667 (2000). *Member:* Tulsa County (Chairperson, Young Lawyers Division, 2003-2004; Chairperson, SBLS Committee, 2004-2005), Oklahoma and American Bar Associations; Oklahoma Association of Defense Counsel; Tulsa Lawyers for Children; American Inns of Court (Council Oak Chapter). ***REPORTED CASES:*** Continential Industries, Inc. v. Integrated Logistics Solutions, LLC, 211 F.R.D. 442 (N.D. Okla. 2002). ***PRACTICE AREAS:*** Civil Practice; Commercial Law; Environmental Litigation. ***Email:*** phixon@jpm-law.com

MARTIN ALLEN BROWN, born Sarasota, Florida, May 11, 1970; admitted to bar, 2000, Oklahoma and U.S. District Court, Northern District of Oklahoma; 2004, U.S. District Court, Western and Eastern Districts of Oklahoma. *Education:* University of Tulsa (B.A., 1992; M.A., 1997; J.D., 1999); Universidad de Palermo, Argentina (International and Comparative Law Certificate); University of Oklahoma School of Successful Trial Advocacy (Graduate). Recipient: Eric B. Jensen Memorial Award, University of Tulsa College of Law, 1999; Gardere & Wynne Environmental Law Award, 1998. President, TU College of Law Chapter, Black Law Students Association (BLSA). Senior Staff, Tulsa Law Journal, 1997-1998. Author: "Spoils of the Cold War: U.S. Foreign Policy Toward Ghana, 1956-1963," University of Tulsa, Tulsa, Oklahoma, 1997. General Counsel, World Service Corporation. Attorney, Corporate Law Section, The Rode Law Firm. Associate, Hudson-Hall-Wheaton Chapter, American Inns of Court. Director At Large and Co-Chair, University of Tulsa Alumni Board of Directors. Mentor, Tulsa Jobs Partnership. Leadership Tulsa, Class 33. *Member:* Tulsa County, Oklahoma and American Bar Associations; Northeastern Oklahoma Black Lawyers Association (NOBLA) (President). [Yeoman, U.S. Navy, 1993]. ***REPORTED CASES:*** Roy C. Johnson, et al., v. City of Tulsa, and Fraternal Order of Police, Lodge No. 93, Case No.: 94-CV-39-H(M), U.S. District Court, Northern District of Oklahoma a.k.a. "The Black Officers Coalition's Lawsuit.". ***PRACTICE AREAS:*** Venture Capital; Equity Finance; Corporate Law; International Law; Commercial Law; Internet Law; International Banking Law; Securities Law; Complex Business Litigation; Complex Commercial Litigation. ***Email:*** mbrown@jpm-law.com

DAVID M. VONHARTITZSCH, born Wellington, New Zealand, March 18, 1970; admitted to bar, 2000, Oklahoma and U.S. District Court, Northern, Eastern and Western Districts of Oklahoma; 2001, U.S. Court of Appeals, Tenth Circuit. *Education:* Southern Methodist University (B.A., 1992); University of Tulsa (J.D., with highest honors, 2000). Phi Delta Phi. Recipient: Ronald M. Brochstein Award; CALI Excellence for the Future Awards for Research, Analysis and Writing II, Law of Professional Sports and Evidence Workship. Articles Editor, Tulsa Law Review, 1999-2000. *Professional Background:* Associate: Norman, Wohlgemuth, Chandler & Dowdell; Glass Law Firm; Latham, Stall, Wagner, Steele & Lehman. *Member:* Tulsa County and Oklahoma Bar Associations. ***PRACTICE AREAS:*** Commercial Litigation; Appellate Practice; Torts; Environmental Litigation. ***Email:*** dvonhartizsch@jpm-law.com

(This Listing Continued)

JOYCE AND POLLARD

515 SOUTH MAIN STREET, SUITE 300
TULSA, OKLAHOMA 74103-4475
Telephone: 918-585-2751
Fax: 918-582-9308
Email: contact@joycepollard.com
URL: http://www.joycepollard.com

Litigation, Trials, Appeals, Estate and Gift Taxation, Corporate Law, Business Law, Real Estate, Estate Planning, Wills and Probate, Trusts and Estates, First Amendment Law, Constitutional Law, Tax Exempt Organizations, Nonprofit and Charitable Organizations, Religious Ministries, Church Law.

DWAYNE C. POLLARD (1939-1999)

(This Listing Continued)

J. C. JOYCE, born Mansfield, Arkansas, January 23, 1940; admitted to bar, 1966, Oklahoma; 1967, Supreme Court of State of Oklahoma; 1971, U.S. Supreme Court; 1989, U.S. Court of Appeals for the District of Columbia Circuit; 1997, U.S. Court of Appeals, Fifth Circuit; 1988, U.S. Court of Appeals, Ninth Circuit; 1970, U.S. Court of Appeals, Tenth Circuit; 1994, U.S. Court of Appeals, Eleventh Circuit; 1999, U.S. Court of Appeals for the Federal Circuit; 1967, U.S. District Court, Northern District of Oklahoma; 1984, U.S. District Court, Northern District of Texas; 1997, U.S. District Court, Western District of Texas; 1988, U.S. Tax Court; 1999, U.S. Court of Federal Claims. *Education:* Oklahoma State University (B.A., 1962); University of Tulsa (J.D., 1966). Editor-in-Chief, Tulsa Law Journal, 1965. *Member:* Tulsa County Bar Association; Oklahoma Bar Association; District of Columbia Bar; U.S. Court of Federal Claims Bar Association. Fellow, The American College of Trust and Estate Counsel. ***PRACTICE AREAS:*** Constitutional Law; First Amendment Law; Litigation; Tax Exempt Organizations; Nonprofit and Charitable Organizations; Religious Ministries; Church Law; Estate Planning; Wills; Probate; Trusts and Estates. ***Email:*** jc.joyce@joycepollard.com

---

TED J. NELSON, born Fort Knox, Kentucky, October 15, 1955; admitted to bar, 1983, Oklahoma; U.S. District Court, Northern, Eastern and Western Districts of Oklahoma; U.S. District Court, District of Arizona; U.S. Court of Appeals, Tenth Circuit; U.S. Supreme Court; U.S. Tax Court. *Education:* Purdue University (B.A., 1978); Oral Roberts University (J.D., 1982). *Member:* Tulsa County (Continuing Legal Education Committee, 1995-1998) and Oklahoma Bar Associations. ***REPORTED CASES:*** Durant v. Changing, Inc., 891 P.2d 628 (Okl.App. 1995). ***PRACTICE AREAS:*** Litigation; Real Estate; Business Law; Tax Exempt Organizations; Religious Ministries; Church Law. ***Email:*** ted.nelson@joycepollard.com

JOHN C. JOYCE, born Tulsa, Oklahoma, September 14, 1966; admitted to bar, 1993, Oklahoma and U.S. District Court, Northern District of Oklahoma; 1995, U.S. Court of Appeals, Tenth Circuit; 1998, U.S. Supreme Court; 1999, U.S. Court of Appeals, Federal Circuit and U.S. District Court, Western District of Oklahoma. *Education:* Trinity University (B.A., 1988); University of Tulsa (J.D., 1992). *Member:* Tulsa County and Oklahoma Bar Associations. ***PRACTICE AREAS:*** Constitutional Law; Wills; Probate; Trusts and Estates; Litigation; Tax Exempt Organizations; Nonprofit and Charitable Organizations; Religious Ministries; Church Law; Corporate Law; Business Law; Real Estate. ***Email:*** john.joyce@joycepollard.com

MICHAEL A. POLLARD, born February 20, 1970; admitted to bar, 1998, Oklahoma and U.S. District Court, Northern District of Oklahoma. *Education:* University of Colorado (B.S., 1992); University of Tulsa (J.D., 1997). *Member:* Tulsa County and Oklahoma Bar Associations; American Inns of Court. ***PRACTICE AREAS:*** Litigation; Business Organization; Business Transactions; Limited Liability Company Law; Corporate Law; Real Estate; Contracts; Wills; Probate; Trusts and Estates. ***Email:*** michael.pollard@joycepollard.com

MARK K. GRADDY, born Columbus, Georgia, December 26, 1976; admitted to bar, 2004, Oklahoma and U.S. District Court, Northern District of Oklahoma; 2005, Texas. *Education:* Drury College (B.A., 2000); University of Tulsa (J.D., 2004). Member: Students in Free Enterprise; Motar Board; Board of Advocates, 2003-2004; Student Bar Association; Student Delegate and Academic Affairs Committee. *Member:* Tulsa County, Oklahoma and American Bar Association; State Bar of Texas; Muscogee (Creek) Nation Bar Association; American Trial Lawyers Association. ***PRACTICE AREAS:*** Litigation; Commercial Law; Tax Exempt Organizations; Insurance; Real Estate; Torts; Products Liability; Personal Injury. ***Email:*** mark.graddy@joycepollard.com

KEVIN B. JOYCE, born Tulsa, Oklahoma, September 7, 1977; admitted to bar, 2004, Oklahoma and U.S. District Court, Northern District of Oklahoma. *Education:* University of Colorado (B.A., 2001); University of Tulsa (J.D., 2004). *Member:* Tulsa County and Oklahoma Bar Associations. ***PRACTICE AREAS:*** Guardianship and Conservatorship; Wills; Probate; Trusts and Estates; Litigation; Business Organization; Nonprofit and Charitable Organizations; Products Liability; Torts. ***Email:*** kevin.joyce@joycepollard.com

CATHERINE J. GRADDY, born Tulsa, Oklahoma, November 25, 1975; admitted to bar, 2004, Oklahoma. *Education:* University of Colorado (B.A., 1998); University of Tulsa (J.D., 2004). Member: National Honor Society in Psychology: University of Colorado, Boulder, 1997-1998; Pepperdine University, 1998-2000. Certified Mediator, pursuant to Oklahoma District Court Mediation Act. *Member:* Tulsa County and Oklahoma Bar Associations. ***PRACTICE AREAS:*** Family Law; Divorce; Child Custody; Guardianship; Family Mediation; Divorce Mediation. ***Email:*** catherine.graddy@joycepollard.com

REPRESENTATIVE CLIENTS: Furnished Upon Request.

LAW OFFICES OF CHARLES J. KANIA

4860 SOUTH LEWIS AVENUE, SUITE 105
TULSA, OKLAHOMA 74105
Telephone: 918-743-2233
Fax: 918-743-2244
Email: cjkania@cox.net
URL: http://www.lawyers.com/charleskania

General Practice, Criminal Law, Personal Injury, Family Law, Business Law.

CHARLES J. KANIA, born Buffalo, New York, October 6, 1959; admitted to bar, 2005, Oklahoma. *Education:* Oklahoma State University (B.S., 1988); University of Tulsa (J.D., 2004). *Member:* Oklahoma Bar Association. ***PRACTICE AREAS:*** General Practice; Criminal Law; Personal Injury; Family Law; Business Law.

KIVELL, RAYMENT AND FRANCIS, P.C.

SUITE 240, TRIAD CENTER ONE
7666 EAST 61ST STREET
TULSA, OKLAHOMA 74133
Telephone: 918-254-0626
Fax: 918-254-7915
Email: tkivell@kivell.com
URL: http://www.kivell.com

General Civil Trial Practice. Commercial and Residential Real Estate, Corporations, Partnerships, Estate Planning, Bankruptcy, Mortgage Foreclosure, and Automobile Finance Law.

FIRM PROFILE: The firm has been heavily involved with national clientele in the areas of state-wide foreclosure, bankruptcy, eviction, replevin and creditor rights law. We are experienced in commercial and general litigation, including the areas of contracts, commercial law, bankruptcy, products liability and torts. The firm has been involved in real estate transactions, both residential and commercial, as well as significant bankruptcy matters. In 1991 the shareholders were appointed as Special Assistant United States Attorneys for the Northern District of Oklahoma to represent the Department of Housing and Urban Development on a statewide basis. The firm is an active member of the USFN, America's Mortgage Banking Attorneys.

The firm also conducts a general corporate, civil litigation, partnership and estate and business planning practice. It is experienced in corporate formation, governance and compliance matters. It has significant background in federal lending requirements.

THOMAS D. KIVELL, born Detroit, Michigan, February 29, 1948; admitted to bar, 1976, Oklahoma, U.S. District Court, Northern District of Oklahoma and U.S. Court of Appeals, Tenth Circuit. *Education:* Michigan State University (B.A., 1970); University of Tulsa (J.D., 1975). Delta Theta Phi (Bailiff, 1974-1975). Recipient, American Jurisprudence Award in Civil Procedures, 1973. Special Assistant U.S. Attorney, 1992—. *Member:* Tulsa County, Oklahoma (Member, Real Property Section) and American (Member, Real Property Section) Bar Associations; Tulsa Title and Probate Lawyers Association; Tulsa Mortgage Bankers Association. ***PRACTICE AREAS:*** Real Estate Transactions; Finance; Business Organization; Foreclosure Law. ***Email:*** tkivell@kivell.com

BRIAN J. RAYMENT, born Painesville, Ohio, April 3, 1957; admitted to bar, 1982, Oklahoma, U.S. District Court, Northern, Western and Eastern Districts of Oklahoma and U.S. Court of Appeals, Tenth Circuit. *Education:* Oklahoma State University (B.A., 1979); University of Tulsa (J.D., 1982). Phi Alpha Delta. Special Assistant U.S. Attorney, 1992—. *Member:* Tulsa County, Oklahoma and American Bar Associations. ***PRACTICE AREAS:*** Civil Litigation; Business Law; Bankruptcy; Automobile Finance Law. ***Email:*** brayment@kivell.com

JOE B. FRANCIS, born Wellington, Texas, March 4, 1956; admitted to bar, 1982, Oklahoma; 1989, New Mexico and U.S. Court of Appeals, Tenth Circuit. *Education:* Oklahoma State University (B.S., 1978); University of Tulsa (J.D., 1982). Phi Kappa Phi; Delta Theta Phi. Special Assistant, U.S. Attorney, 1992—. *Member:* Oklahoma and American (Member, Real Property and Probate Section) Bar Associations; State Bar of New Mexico. ***PRACTICE AREAS:*** Real Estate Transactions; Probate and Estate Planning; Business Organizations and Foreclosure Law. ***Email:*** jfrancis@kivell.com

---

KAREN M. FUNK, born Kansas City, Missouri, February 15, 1946; admitted to bar, 1976, Oklahoma; 1980, California; U.S. District Court, Northern District of Oklahoma. *Education:* Texas Christian University (B.A., 1964); University of Kansas; University of Tulsa (J.D., 1975); University of San Diego (LL.M., 1981). Phi Delta Phi. Adjunct Professor, Western State University, 1979. *Member:* Oklahoma Bar Association; State Bar of California. ***PRACTICE AREAS:*** Real Estate; Foreclosures. ***Email:*** kfunk@kivell.com

JEFFREY DARIN LOWER, born Tulsa, Oklahoma, August 23, 1961; admitted to bar, 1986, Oklahoma and U.S. District Court, Northern, Western and Eastern Districts of Oklahoma. *Education:* University of Tulsa (B.S., 1983; J.D., 1986). Delta Theta Phi (President, 1985-1986). *Member:* Tulsa County and Oklahoma (Member, Title Examination Standards Committee) Bar Associations; Tulsa Title and Probate Lawyers Association. ***PRACTICE AREAS:*** Commercial Real Estate; Residential Real Estate; Civil Litigation; Probate; Title Examinations. ***Email:*** jlower@kivell.com

JASON L. HOWELL, born Tulsa, Oklahoma, June 2, 1976; admitted to bar, 2001, Oklahoma. *Education:* Oklahoma State University (B.S., 1998); University of Oklahoma (J.D., 2001). *Member:* Oklahoma Bar Association (Member, Real Estate Section). ***PRACTICE AREAS:*** Real Estate Foreclosure; Real Estate Title Examination. ***Email:*** jhowell@kivell.com

AMY ELIZABETH COLLINS, admitted to bar, 1998, Oklahoma. *Education:* Oregon State University (B.S., Psychology, 1994); University of Tulsa (J.D., 1998). *Member:* Oklahoma Bar Association.

TEDDI LEWIS ALLEN, admitted to bar, 1990, Oklahoma. *Education:* University of Tulsa (B.A., 1987; J.D., 1990). *Member:* Tulsa County and Oklahoma Bar Associations.

MICHAEL W. McCOY, born Bellows Falls, Vermont, July 31, 1952; admitted to bar, 1995, Oklahoma; U.S. District Court, Northern, Eastern and Western Federal Districts of Oklahoma. *Education:* Oral Roberts University (B.S., magna cum laude, 1988); University of Tulsa (J.D., 1995).

A. GRANT SCHWABE, born Norman, Oklahoma, June 20, 1976; admitted to bar, 2005, Oklahoma. *Education:* University of Oklahoma (B.A., 2000); University of Tulsa College of Law (J.D., 2004). Delta Theta Phi. Recipient: Resources, Energy and Environmental Law Certificate; American Jurisprudence Award, Oil and Gas Law, 2003. Tulsa ABA Vice President, 2003-2004. ***PRACTICE AREAS:*** Commercial Litigation; Real Estate; Mortgage Banking Law. ***Email:*** grant@bridger-riley.com

SHANNON TAYLOR, born Tulsa, Oklahoma; admitted to bar, 2004, Oklahoma. *Education:* Oklahoma State University (B.S., Health Education, 1991); University of Tulsa (J.D., 2005).

(This Listing Continued)

KIVELL, RAYMENT AND FRANCIS, P.C., Tulsa—Continued

REPRESENTATIVE CLIENTS: FirstTitle & Abstract Services, Inc.; Smith Brothers Abstract & Title Co.; Bank of Oklahoma, N.A.; General Motors Acceptance Corp.; John Hausam Realtors; Chase Manhattan Mortgage Corp.; Countrywide Home Loans; Bank South N.A.; Ocwen Federal Bank; Irwin Mortgage Corp.; Aurora Loan Servicing, Inc.; GMAC Mortgage Corporation of Pennsylvania; Kan-Pak L.L.C.; DirecTV, Inc.; Rental Service Corp.; AmeriQuest Mortgage; Regions Mortgage; Litton Loan Servicing, Citifinancial; Wells Fargo Home Loan; Bank of America; Midland Mortgage; Select Servicing; Homecomings Financial.
APPROVED ATTORNEYS FOR: Stewart Title Insurance Co.; Commonwealth Land Title Insurance Co.
REFERENCES: Triad Bank, N.A.; Bank of Oklahoma; Bank South.

THOMAS M. KLENDA

Established in 1984

15 EAST 5TH STREET, SUITE 3900
TULSA, OKLAHOMA 74103-4306
Telephone: 918-587-9191
Fax: 918-587-3064
URL: http://www.tmklaw.com
Email: tklenda@shapexpress.com
URL: http://www.lawyers.com/tmklaw

Corporate, Business Transactions, Estate and Business Planning, Wills, Trust Law, Franchises, Real Estate, Probate and Commercial Litigation.

THOMAS M. KLENDA, born Wichita, Kansas, August 9, 1955; admitted to bar, 1980, Oklahoma; 1981, U.S. District Court, Northern District of Oklahoma; U.S. Court of Appeals, Tenth Circuit. *Education:* Oklahoma State University (B.S., 1977); University of Tulsa (J.D., 1980). Member, Tulsa Estate Planning Forum. *Member:* Tulsa County, Oklahoma and American Bar Associations; Tulsa Title and Probate Lawyers Association. ***PRACTICE AREAS:*** Corporate; Business Transactions; Estate and Business Planning; Franchise Law; Real Estate; Probate; Commercial Litigation.

REPRESENTATIVE FRANCHISE CLIENTS: Ron's Hamburgers & Chili, Inc.; ShapeXpress, Inc.

KORNFELD FRANKLIN RENEGAR & RANDALL

A PROFESSIONAL CORPORATION

TULSA, OKLAHOMA

(See Oklahoma City)

General Civil Practice. Class Action Litigation, Federal and State Taxation, Oil and Gas, Corporate, Estate Planning, Banking, Employment Law, Bankruptcy, Communications, Real Estate, Pollution Litigation, Railroad and Insurance Law. Trials and Appellate Practice in all State and Federal Courts before Mediation and Arbitration Panels and Administrative Agencies.

LACOURSE, DAVIS, COFFEY & GUDGEL, P.L.C.

Established in 2001

2250 EAST 73RD STREET, SUITE 600
TULSA, OKLAHOMA 74136
Telephone: 918-744-7100
Fax: 918-477-2299
URL: http://www.lacoursedavis.com
Email: administrator@lacoursedavis.com
URL: http://www.lacourse-davis.com

General Civil Trial Practice including Commercial Litigation, Business Transactions, Corporate Law, Wills and Trusts, Estate Planning, Securities Offerings, Employment Law, Insurance Defense, Family Law, Divorce, Commercial Transportation, Products Liability, Nursing Home Litigation.

JOEL A. LACOURSE, born Cambridge, New York, 1962; admitted to bar, 1996, Oklahoma; 1997, Kansas. *Education:* Oral Roberts University (B.S., Accounting, 1984); Oral Roberts University Graduate School of Business; Regent University School of Law (J.D., 1996). National Moot Court Team; American Inn of Courts. Federal Judicial Legal Intern, Hon. Stephen C. St. John, U.S. Bankruptcy Court, Eastern District of Virginia, Norfolk, 1996. Certified Public Accountant, Audit and Tax practice, PriceWaterhouseCoopers. Presenter: "Asset Protection - Mission Possible?" United Visions Seminar, 2002; "Estate Planning," University of Tulsa Financial Management Series, 2002. Executive Officer, Small Business Administration. Controller: Oral Roberts University, Regent University. *Member:* Oklahoma Bar Association; Kansas Bar Association; American Bar Association; Association of Trial Lawyers of America; Defense Research Institute; Christian Legal Society. ***PRACTICE AREAS:*** Commercial Litigation; Business Litigation; Corporate Law; Estate Planning; Business Planning; Tax Planning; Personal Injury; Family Law; Bankruptcy; Workers Compensation; Civil Litigation. **Email:** joel@lacoursedavis.com

J. CHRISTOPHER DAVIS, born Chanute A.F.B., Rantoul, Illinois, January 9, 1965; admitted to bar, 1995, Oklahoma. *Education:* Oral Roberts University (B.A., 1989; M.A., 1991; M.Ed., 1992); University of Oklahoma (J.D., 1995). Member: Order of Barristers; National Moot Court Team; National Trial Team; Jessup International Moot Court Team; Tulsa Area Human Resource Managers. Recipient, Teaching Fellowship for Legal Research and Writing Program, 1993-1995. Assistant Note Editor, American Indian Law Review. Law Clerk to U.S. District Judge Jimm Larry Hendren, U.S. District Court, Western District of Arkansas, *1995-1996. Co-Author: Is* Direct-To-Consumer Advertising Eroding the Learned Intermediary Doctrine?, Vol. 41, No. 12, "For the Defense," Defense Research Institute, December 1999; 2000 Annual Oklahoma Claims Adjusters' Convention, "A Broad Overview of Federal Employment Law"; 2000 OU-Texas Annual Dallas Claims Seminar, "What Constitutes Deceptive Acts and Unfair Trade Practices in the Insurance Industry under Texas Law?"; 2000 Lorman Business Institute Seminar, "Current Employment Law Seminar"; 1999 Dallas Area Employment Seminar, "An Employee's Right to Privacy in the Workplace"; 1998 OU-Texas Annual Dallas Claims Seminar, "Insurers' Duty to Defend"; 1997 OU-Texas Annual Dallas Claims Seminar, "Developments in Bad Faith Law in Oklahoma". Member, Tulsa Area Human Resource Managers. *Member:* Oklahoma and American Bar Associations; Defense Research Institute; Oklahoma Association of Defense Counsel. American Inns of Court. ***REPORTED CASES:*** First Marine Insurance Co. v. Scott, 2000 U.S.App.Lexis 23452 (10th Cir., Sept. 18, 2000). ***PRACTICE AREAS:*** Insurance Defense; Commercial Litigation; Employment Law; Contracts. **Email:** chris@lacoursedavis.com

ROBERT P. COFFEY, JR., born Norman, Oklahoma, November 25, 1966; admitted to bar, 1992, Oklahoma and U.S. District Court, Northern, Eastern and Western Districts of Oklahoma. *Education:* University of Oklahoma (B.B.A., 1989); University of Tulsa (J.D., 1992). Administrative Judge, Oklahoma Department of Labor, 1995-1997. Supreme Court Justice, Pottawatomie Indian Nation, 1992—. *Member:* Tulsa County, Oklahoma and American Bar Associations; Oklahoma Defense Association (Board Member); Trucking Industry Defense Association; Defense Research Institute; International Association of Defense Counsel; American Trucking Association (Litigation Center); Oklahoma Nursing Home Association. ***PRACTICE AREAS:*** Commercial Transportation; Personal Injury; Litigation; Insurance Defense; Corporate Law; Products Liability; Nursing Home Litigation. **Email:** robert@lacoursedavis.com

TOM H. GUDGEL, III, born Tulsa, Oklahoma, October 6, 1956; admitted to bar, 1990, Oklahoma and U.S. District Court, Northern, Eastern and Western Districts of Oklahoma. *Education:* University of Oklahoma (B.B.A., 1980); University of Tulsa (J.D., 1990). Phi Delta Phi (Exchequer, 1989-1990). Staff Member, Energy Law Journal, 1989-1990. Member, Christia Legal Society. *Member:* Tulsa County, Oklahoma and American Bar Associations. ***PRACTICE AREAS:*** Insurance; Oil and Gas Law; Corporate; Estate Planning. **Email:** tom@lacoursedavis.com

ASSOCIATES

DAVID A. GUTEN, born Tulsa, Oklahoma, January 12, 1978; admitted to bar, 2004, Oklahoma; 2005, U.S. District Court, Northern District of Oklahoma. *Education:* Oklahoma City University (B.S., 2000); University of Tulsa College of Law (J.D., 2003). President, Delta Theta Phi, 2002-2003. *Member:* Tulsa County, Oklahoma and American Bar Associations. ***PRACTICE AREAS:*** Family Law; Criminal Law; Civil Litigation. **Email:** dguten@lacoursedavis.com

NICHOLAS G. HAUGEN, born Madison, Wisconsin, June 12, 1977; admitted to bar, 2005, Oklahoma. *Education:* Illinois Wesleyan University (B.A., 1999); University of Tulsa (J.D., 2005). Phi Delta Phi; Order of the Curule (Chair). Recipient, Martin Fellow Smith Award. Member, Tulsa Law Review, 2003-2005. *Member:* Oklahoma Bar Association. ***PRACTICE AREAS:*** Health Law; Insurance; Business Litigation. **Email:** nick@lacoursedavis.com

LATHAM, STALL, WAGNER, STEELE & LEHMAN

Established in 1998

SPIRIT TOWER - SUITE 500
1800 SOUTH BALTIMORE
TULSA, OKLAHOMA 74119
Telephone: 918-382-7523
Fax: 918-382-7541
URL: http://www.lswsl.com

General Civil Litigation including Insurance Law, Corporate Law, Professional Liability Defense, Medical Malpractice Defense, Premises Liability Defense, Products Liability Defense, Commercial Litigation, Banking, Construction Litigation, Commercial Transactions, Nursing Home Litigation, Creditors Rights, Bankruptcy, Pharmacy Liability, Civil Rights, Media Law, Bad Faith Litigation, Real Estate Zoning, Automobile Liability, Class Action, Antitrust.

FIRM PROFILE: Latham, Stall, Wagner, Steele & Lehman is a civil litigation firm located in Tulsa, Oklahoma. Practicing in state and federal courts throughout Oklahoma, the firm represents businesses and professionals in a variety of legal matters.

Our goal is to obtain cost effective solutions for our clients. At the onset, each case is analyzed to determine whether alternative dispute resolution is appropriate. This approach eliminates "courthouse settlements" thereby reducing attorney fees. When settlement fails, cases are aggressively pushed to trial. Having tried in excess of 250 jury trials, the firm's partners are experienced trial attorneys.

The firm carries the highest legal ability rating in Martindale-Hubbell for legal expertise and integrity.

BOBBY L. LATHAM, JR., born Yazoo City, Mississippi, May 24, 1966; admitted to bar, 1993, Oklahoma; U.S. District Court, Northern, Eastern and Western Districts of Oklahoma and U.S. Court of Appeals, Tenth Circuit. *Education:* University of Oklahoma (B.A., Management Finance, 1989; J.D., 1993). *Member:* Tulsa County and Oklahoma Bar Associations. ***PRACTICE AREAS:*** Insurance Defense; Corporate Law; Professional Malpractice Defense; Bad Faith Litigation; Medical Malpractice; Nursing Home Litigation; Automobile Liability; Commercial Litigation. **Email:** blatham@lswsl.com

DOUGLAS E. STALL, born Tulsa, Oklahoma, March 24, 1963; admitted to bar, 1989, Oklahoma, U.S. Court of Military Appeals and U.S. District Court, Northern, Eastern and Western Districts of Oklahoma. *Education:* Oklahoma State University (B.S., 1985); University of Tulsa (J.D., 1989). *Member:* Oklahoma Bar Association. [U.S. Marine Corps, 1989-2000; 45th Infantry Brigade, Oklahoma Army National Guard, 2000—]. ***PRACTICE AREAS:*** Medical Malpractice Defense; General Insurance Defense; Products Liability Defense; Media Law; Nursing Home Litigation. **Email:** dstall@lswsl.com

KENNETH E. WAGNER, born Norman, Oklahoma, December 15, 1964; admitted to bar, 1994, Oklahoma and Arkansas; 1995, U.S. District Court, Northern and Eastern Districts of Oklahoma and U.S. Court of Appeals, 10th Circuit. *Education:* University of Oklahoma (B.A., Public Administration, 1988); University of Tulsa (J.D., 1993). *Member:* Okla-

(This Listing Continued)

homa, Arkansas and American Bar Associations. ***PRACTICE AREAS:*** Commercial Litigation; Banking Law; Professional Negligence; Commercial Transactions; Nursing Home Litigation; Medical Malpractice; Construction Law; Products Liability; Class Action; Insurance Bad Faith. ***Email:*** kwagner@lswsl.com

MARK T. STEELE, born Toledo, Ohio, October 17, 1965; admitted to bar, 1991, Oklahoma; 1992, U.S. District Court, Northern, Western and Eastern District of Oklahoma; U.S. Court of Appeals, Tenth Circuit. *Education:* University of Colorado (1984-1985); Oral Roberts University (B.A., 1988); University of Tulsa (J.D., 1991). *Member:* Tulsa County and Oklahoma Bar Associations; Defense Research Institute, Inc. ***PRACTICE AREAS:*** Premises Liability; Pharmacy Liability; Products Liability; Construction Litigation; Civil Rights Defense; Medical Malpractice Defense. ***Email:*** msteele@lswsl.com

SCOTT F. LEHMAN, born San Antonio, Texas, July 7, 1967; admitted to bar, 1995, Oklahoma and U.S. District Court, Northern, Western and Eastern Districts of Oklahoma. *Education:* University of Tulsa (B.A., 1990; J.D., 1994). *Member:* Tulsa County (Member, Board of Directors, 1995-1997 and Chair, 1997, Young Lawyers Division) and Oklahoma Bar Associations; Commercial Law League of America; American Bankruptcy Institute; National Association of Retail Collection Attorneys. ***PRACTICE AREAS:*** Civil Litigation; Banking Law; Creditors Rights; Bankruptcy; Collections; Foreclosures. ***Email:*** slehman@lswsl.com

RICK J. HORTON, born Little Rock, Arkansas, February 15, 1968; admitted to bar, 1995, Oklahoma, U.S. District Court, Northern, Eastern and Western Districts of Oklahoma and U.S. Court of Appeals, Tenth Circuit; 2002, Missouri and U.S. Supreme Court. *Education:* Baylor University (B.A., 1990); University of Tulsa (J.D., 1994). *Member:* Oklahoma and American Bar Associations; The Missouri Bar. ***PRACTICE AREAS:*** Insurance Defense; Products Liability Defense; Premises Liability Defense; Civil Litigation; Nursing Home Litigation. ***Email:*** rhorton@lswsl.com

ASSOCIATES

RONI S. RIERSON, born Bozeman, Montana, June 20, 1968; admitted to bar, 1997, Colorado and U.S. District Court, District of Colorado; 1999, Oklahoma, U.S. District Court, Eastern, Western and Northern Districts of Oklahoma and U.S. Court of Appeals, Tenth Circuit. *Education:* Texas Christian University (B.A., 1991); University of Oklahoma (J.D., 1996). Order of the Barristers. Member: American Bar Association Appellate Advocacy Team; Jessup International Moot Court Team. Recipient, American Jurisprudence Award for Torts (1994) and American Jurisprudence Award for International Human Rights (1995). *Member:* Tulsa County, Oklahoma and American Bar Associations. ***REPORTED CASES:*** Dubbs v. Head Start, Inc., et al., 336 F.3d 1194 (10th Cir. 2003). ***PRACTICE AREAS:*** Civil Litigation; Insurance Defense; Premises Liability Defense; Corporate Law; Medical Malpractice; Bad Faith Litigation. ***Email:*** rrierson@lswsl.com

BRIAN J. GOREE, born Killeen, Texas, March 18, 1964; admitted to bar, 1989, Oklahoma and U.S. District Court, Northern, Eastern and Western Districts of Oklahoma; registered to practice before U.S. Patent and Trademark Office. *Education:* University of Oklahoma (B.S., 1986); University of Tulsa (J.D., 1989). *Member:* Tulsa County and Oklahoma Bar Associations; Oklahoma Association of Defense Counsel; Defense Research Institute. ***REPORTED CASES:*** Wallace v. Bd. of County Commissioners, 2000 OK CIV APP 131, 15P.3d 985; Rush v. Brown, 1999 OK CIV APP 86, 987 P.2d 439; Armstrong v. Carr, 2003 OK CIV APP 80; Clem v. Leedey Public Works Authority, 2003 OK CIV APP93, 78 P.3d 969. ***PRACTICE AREAS:*** Insurance Defense; Civil Litigation; Employment Litigation; Medical Malpractice; Premises Liability; Products Liability; Bad Faith Litigation. ***Email:*** bgoree@lswsl.com

MARCUS N. RATCLIFF, born Monroe, Louisiana, June 6, 1975; admitted to bar, 2001, Oklahoma; U.S. District Court, Northern, Eastern and Western Districts of Oklahoma. *Education:* University of Louisiana, Monroe (B.A., 1998); University of Tulsa (J.D., with Honors, 2001). Phi Delta Phi. Recipient, Robert Butler Jr. Award. Articles Editor, Tulsa Law Journal, 2000-2001. Author: "The Good Character Requirement for Bar Admission: Proposal for a Uniform National Standard," 36 Tulsa L.J., 47, 2000. *Member:* Tulsa, Oklahoma and American Bar Associations. ***PRACTICE AREAS:*** Insurance Defense; Premises Liability Defense; Construction Litigation; Commercial Transactions; Commercial Litigation; Corporate Law; Banking Law; Media Law; Nursing Home Litigation. ***Email:*** mratcliff@lswsl.com

PINE G. DREWYOR, born Lansing, Michigan, May 28, 1974; admitted to bar, 2001, Arkansas and Oklahoma; U.S. District Court, Northern and Eastern Districts of Oklahoma. *Education:* University of Arkansas (B.S., Business Administration, 1996; J.D., 2000). Member, District Attorney's Counsel of Oklahoma, 2001-2002. *Member:* Tulsa County, Oklahoma and Arkansas Bar Associations. ***PRACTICE AREAS:*** Insurance Defense; Nursing Home Litigation; Medical Malpractice Defense; Premises Liability Defense; Civil Litigation; Products Liability Defense; Corporate Law. ***Email:*** pdrewyor@lswsl.com

ROBERT M. GALLANT, born Salem, Massachusetts, January 4, 1963; admitted to bar, 1994, Oklahoma and Colorado; U.S. District Court, Northern and Western Districts of Oklahoma and U.S. Court of Appeals, Tenth Circuit. *Education:* University of Cincinnati (B.A., Economics, 1987); University of Tulsa College of Law (J.D., 1994). Phi Delta Phi. Certificate of Native American Studies; Notes and Comments Editor, Energy Law Journal. *Member:* Tulsa County and Oklahoma Bar Associations; American Inns of Court. ***PRACTICE AREAS:*** Insurance Defense; Medical Malpractice Defense; Premises Liability Defense; Product Liability Defense; Civil Litigation. ***Email:*** rgallant@lswsl.com

SAMANTHA WEYRAUCH, born New York, New York, December 18, 1973; admitted to bar, 2001, Oklahoma and U.S. District Court, Northern District of Oklahoma. *Education:* University of Tulsa (B.A., Accounting, 1996; Masters, Business Administration, 2000; J.D., 2000). Beta Alpha Psi. Phi Delta Phi. *Member:* Tulsa County and Oklahoma Bar Associations; American Inns of Court. ***PRACTICE AREAS:*** Medical Malpractice Defense; Insurance Defense; Civil Litigation. ***Email:*** sweyrauch@lswsl.com

KANDI D. EPP, born Weatherford, Oklahoma, December 1, 1976; admitted to bar, 2003, Oklahoma, U.S. District Court, Northern, Western and Eastern Districts of Oklahoma and U.S. Court of Appeals, Tenth Circuit. *Education:* Northeastern Oklahoma State University (B.B.A., 1999); University of Tulsa (J.D., 2002). *Member:* Tulsa County and Oklahoma Bar Associations. ***PRACTICE AREAS:*** Civil Litigation; Creditors Rights; Insurance Defense; Banking Law; Commercial Transactions; Corporate Law; Commercial Litigation; Premises Liability. ***Email:*** kepp@lswsl.com

(This Listing Continued)

RUSSELL M. JACOBSON, JR., born Tulsa, Oklahoma, October 10, 1961; admitted to bar, 1991, Oklahoma, U.S. District Court, Northern, Western and Eastern Districts of Oklahoma and U.S. Court of Appeals, Tenth Circuit. *Education:* Oklahoma State University (B.S., 1985); University of Tulsa (J.D., 1991). Staff Member, Energy Law Journal, 1990-1991. *Member:* Tulsa County, Oklahoma and American Bar Associations. ***PRACTICE AREAS:*** Construction Law; Construction Litigation; Medical Malpractice Defense; Insurance Defense. ***Email:*** rjacobson@lswsl.com

LANCE FREIJE, born Wichita, Kansas, November 3, 1970; admitted to bar, 1996, Kansas and U.S. District Court, District of Kansas; 1999, U.S. District Court, Northern and Eastern Districts of Oklahoma; 2000, Oklahoma; 2001, U.S. District Court, Western District of Oklahoma. *Education:* University of Kansas (B.A., Political Science, 1993; J.D., 1995). Recipient, American Jurisprudence Excellence in Appellate Advocacy Award. *Member:* Oklahoma and Kansas Bar Associations. ***PRACTICE AREAS:*** Medical Malpractice Defense; Insurance Defense; Pharmacists Liability. ***Email:*** lfreije@rodolftodd.com

ALLISON L. THOMPSON, born Charleston, South Carolina; admitted to bar, 1997, Oklahoma and U.S. District Court, Western District of Oklahoma; 2000, North Carolina; 2002, U.S. District Court, Northern District of Oklahoma; 2004, U.S. District Court, Eastern District of Oklahoma. *Education:* University of Central Oklahoma (B.S., 1993); University of Tulsa (J.D., 1996). *Member:* Tulsa County, Oklahoma, South Carolina and American Bar Associations; Defense Research Institute. ***PRACTICE AREAS:*** Civil Appeals; Medical Malpractice Defense; Products Liability. ***Email:*** athompson@lswsl.com

OF COUNSEL

NEAL F. LEHMAN, born Bradford, Pennsylvania, June 29, 1943; admitted to bar, 1971, Texas; 1976, Oklahoma and U.S. District Court, Northern District of Oklahoma. *Education:* Grove City College (B.A., 1965); St. Mary's University (J.D., 1970). Delta Theta Phi. Trial Attorney, U.S. Department of Justice, Antitrust Division, 1972-1974. Former Senior Counsel, Phillips Petroleum Company. *Member:* Oklahoma and American Bar Associations; State Bar of Texas. ***PRACTICE AREAS:*** Antitrust; Commercial Transactions. ***Email:*** nlehman@lswsl.com

E. SCOTT PRUITT, born Danville, Kentucky, May 9, 1968; admitted to bar, 1993, Oklahoma. *Education:* Georgetown College (B.A., 1990); University of Tulsa College of Law (J.D., 1993). Elected to Oklahoma State Senate, 1998. *Member:* Oklahoma Bar Association. ***SPECIAL AGENCIES:*** Equal Employment Opportunity Commission, Department of Labor. ***PRACTICE AREAS:*** Employment Law; Civil Rights; General Civil Litigation. ***Email:*** spruitt@lswsl.com

LAWSON, KING & SHELTON, PLLC

10777 S. MEMORIAL DRIVE, SUITE C
TULSA, OKLAHOMA 74133-7351
Telephone: 918-369-9980
Fax: 918-369-9981

Oklahoma City, Oklahoma Office: 2501 North Stiles, 73105. Telephone: 405-523-2501. Fax: 405-523-2324.

General Civil Practice before all State and Federal Courts, Trials, Insurance Defense, Personal Injury, Negligence, Workers' Compensation, Products Liability.

(For complete biographical data on all personnel, see Professional Biographies at Oklahoma City, Oklahoma)

LAYMAN PADGETT BARNHART BECKERT & WILLIAMS

324 SOUTH MAIN, SUITE 818
TULSA, OKLAHOMA 74103
Telephone: 918-293-0903
Fax: 918-293-0901
Email: nlayman@lpblaw.com
Email: ppadgett@lpblaw.com
Email: jbarnhart@lpblaw.com
Email: landp@ionet.net

Workers Compensation Defense, Civil Practice and Insurance Defense Law.

MEMBERS OF FIRM

NEIL F. LAYMAN (1932-2004)

PAT A. PADGETT, born 1942; admitted to bar, 1987, Oklahoma. *Education:* University of Tulsa (B.S.B.A., 1964; J.D., 1986). Recipient, American Jurisprudence Award in Professional Ethics and Responsibility. *Member:* Tulsa County, Oklahoma and American Bar Associations. ***PRACTICE AREAS:*** Workers Compensation Defense. ***Email:*** ppadgett@lpblaw.com

JOHN G. BARNHART, born Madison, Wisconsin, October 3, 1962; admitted to bar, 1989, Texas; 1993, Oklahoma. *Education:* Oklahoma State University (B.S., 1986); University of Oklahoma (J.D., 1989). Recipient, American Jurisprudence Awards in Criminal Law and Contracts. Note Editor, Oklahoma Law Review, 1987-1989. Instructor, Legal Research and Writing, University of Oklahoma College of Law, 1988-1989. *Member:* Oklahoma Bar Association; State Bar of Texas. ***PRACTICE AREAS:*** Workers Compensation; Insurance Defense. ***Email:*** jbarnhartlaw@aol.com

JAMES A. BECKERT, born Chicago, Illinois, September 14, 1961; admitted to bar, 1987, Oklahoma. *Education:* University of Central Oklahoma (B.S., 1983; M.B.A., 1985); University of Tulsa (J.D., 1987). *Member:* Tulsa County and Oklahoma Bar Associations.

(This Listing Continued)

LAYMAN PADGETT BARNHART BECKERT & WILLIAMS, Tulsa—Continued

KIMBERLEE DAWN WILLIAMS, born 1962; admitted to bar, 1994, Oklahoma. *Education:* University of Oklahoma (B.A., 1985; J.D., 1994). *Member:* Oklahoma Bar Association.

REPRESENTATIVE CLIENTS: American Airlines; Association of County Commissioners; Boeing Corp.; Cannon Cochran Management Services; Ace, USA; ESIS; City of Broken Arrow; Crawford & Company; Gallagher Bassett Services; Kemper; Ohio Casualty Group; Oklahoma Natural Gas; RSKCo Management Solutions; Gulf Insurance Group; Specialty Risk Services (The Hartford); Terex Corporation; The Travelers Insurance Co.; Wausau Insurance Company; Zapata Industries; Hillcrest Medical Systems, Inc.; Rheem Corporation; Baldor Electric, Inc.; St. Johns Hospital; Centrilift/Baker Hughes; American Interstate; Old Republic; National Union Fire; Midwest Employers Casualty; Fintube; Bios.

LEBLANG, SOLANO & ASHBAUGH, P.L.L.P.

Established in 1979

7615 EAST 63RD PLACE, SUITE 200
TULSA, OKLAHOMA 74133
Telephone: 918-254-1414; 877 Visa Law
Fax: 918-254-1888; 888-650-1888
URL: http://www.tulsalaw.com
Email: leblang@tulsalaw.com
URL: http://www.lawyers.com/lsa

Citizenship, Immigration and Naturalization, Visa Law, International Law, Foreign Investors.

FIRM PROFILE: Experience, specialization, personal and business needs. This firm presents these attributes and more. The Partners have many years of serving the needs of clients. Immigration is the cornerstone of our practice. We serve your business and personal legal needs with competency and a caring attitude. Our clients come first.

MEMBERS OF FIRM

MARK J. LEBLANG, born Fort Dix, New Jersey, January 4, 1953; admitted to bar, 1977, Oklahoma; U.S. District Court, Northern District of Oklahoma and U.S. Court of Appeals, 10th Circuit. *Education:* Syracuse University (B.A. in Economics, 1974); University of Tulsa (J.D., 1977). *Member:* Tulsa County, Oklahoma, Federal and American Bar Associations; American Immigration Lawyers Association. ***PRACTICE AREAS:*** Immigration Law. ***Email:*** leblang@tulsalaw.com

R. MARK SOLANO, born Harrisonburg, Virginia, April 17, 1951; admitted to bar, 1981, Pennsylvania; 1985, Oklahoma. *Education:* State University of New York at Albany (B.A., magna cum laude, 1975; M.A., 1977); Union University, Albany Law School (J.D., cum laude, 1981). Justinian Society. Member, 1979-1980 and Articles Editor, 1980-1981, Albany Law Review. *Member:* Tulsa County and Oklahoma Bar Associations. (Also practicing individually in Tulsa). ***PRACTICE AREAS:*** Labor Law; Employment Discrimination Law; Immigration Law. ***Email:*** solano@tulsalaw.com

JUDITH A. ASHBAUGH, born Chicago, Illinois, March 18, 1939; admitted to bar, 1991, Oklahoma; U.S. District Court, Northern, Western and Eastern Districts of Oklahoma. *Education:* University of Oklahoma (B.A., 1960; M.C.D., 1965); University of Tulsa (J.D., 1990). Recipient, Order of Curule Chair; Achievement Award, Oklahoma Association of Women Lawyers. Licensed speech-language pathologist. *Member:* Tulsa County and Oklahoma Bar Associations; American Immigration Lawyers Association. ***PRACTICE AREAS:*** Immigration Law. ***Email:*** ashbaugh@tulsalaw.com

KEVIN Y. LITZ, born Preston, Idaho, December 27, 1961; admitted to bar, 1989, Oklahoma and U.S. District Court, Northern District of Oklahoma; 1994, U.S. Supreme Court. *Education:* Utah State University (B.A., cum laude, 1986); University of Utah (J.D., 1989). Moot Court Editor, Phi Delta Phi (Magister, 1988-1989; Vice-Magister, 1987-1988). Blue Key Honor Fraternity, Utah State University. Adjunct Professor, Civil Procedure, Tulsa Community College, 1992-1995. *Member:* Oklahoma and American (Member, Business Law, International Law and Practice, Labor and Employment Law and Intellectual Property Law Sections) Bar Associations; American Corporate Counsel Association. ***LANGUAGES:*** Japanese. ***PRACTICE AREAS:*** Commercial Law; Corporate; Intellectual Property; Labor and Employment; International Consulting; Litigation.

Languages: Spanish, Portuguese.

REPRESENTATIVE CLIENTS: Furnished Upon Request.

LEONARD & RINEER, P.C.

Established in 1998

1921 SOUTH BOSTON AVENUE
TULSA, OKLAHOMA 74119-5221
Telephone: 918-583-8700
Fax: 918-582-3838
URL: http://www.lawyers.com/leonardlaw
Email: thefirm@leonardrineer.com
URL: http://www.leonardrineer.com

General Civil and Appellate Practice. Business and Commercial Litigation, Business Planning, Estate Planning, Guardianship, Trust and Probate Law, Personal Injury Law, Environmental Law, Business, Corporate and Commercial Transactions, Real Estate Law, Domestic Relations, Mediation.

LARRY D. LEONARD, born Horton, Kansas, January 7, 1948; admitted to bar, 1974, Oklahoma and Kansas; U.S. District Court, Northern, Western and Eastern Districts of Oklahoma; U.S. District Court, District of Kansas; U.S. Court of Appeals, Tenth Circuit. *Education:* University of Kansas (B.S.Ed., 1971; J.D., 1974). Deputy District Attorney, Wyandotte County, Kansas, 1973. Outstanding Young Lawyer, Tulsa County, 1983. *Member:* Tulsa County (Treasurer, 1985; Secretary, 1990 and 2000; Vice President, 2001; President Elect, 2002-2003; President, 2003-2004); Tulsa County Bar Foundation (President, 2004-2005), Oklahoma, Kansas and American Bar Associations. ***PRACTICE AREAS:*** Business Litigation; Business Planning Law; Personal Injury Litigation; Commercial Law; Environmental Law; Domestic Relations. ***Email:*** ldleonard@leonardrineer.com

HUGH V. RINEER, born Norristown, Pennsylvania, May 20, 1948; admitted to bar, 1975, Oklahoma and U.S. District Court, Northern District of Oklahoma; 1977, U.S. Court of Appeals, Tenth Circuit. *Education:* East Stroudsburg University (B.A., 1971); University of Tulsa (J.D., 1975); National Judicial College, University of Nevada, Reno, 1985. Phi Delta Phi; Order of the Curule Chair. Member, University of Tulsa Law Journal, 1974-1975. Adjunct Faculty, University of Tulsa College of Law, 2000—. Co-Managing Attorney, Legal Services of Eastern Oklahoma, 1980-1984. Special District Judge, 14th Judicial District, Tulsa, Oklahoma, 1984-1988. Adjunct Settlement Judge, Northern District of Oklahoma, 2000—. Member, Board of Directors, Alumni Association, University of Tulsa College of Law, 1997-1998. *Member:* Tulsa County (Member, Board of Directors, 1988-1990, 2003-2004) and Oklahoma (Member, House of Delegate's, 1991-1994, 2004-2006; Member, Executive Committee, Family Law Section; Budget Officer, 1989-1990; Member, Alternate Dispute Resolution Section; Budget Officer, 2000) Bar Associations; Association for Conflict Resolution; Association of Attorney Mediators; Oklahoma Academy of Mediators and Arbitrators; Oklahoma Academy of Collaborative Professionals; International Academy of Collaborative Professionals. ***PRACTICE AREAS:*** Family Law; Divorce; Mediation; Collaborative Law. ***Email:*** hrineer@leonardrineer.com

REPRESENTATIVE CLIENTS: JOMC Properties, Inc.; Thermal Process Engineering & Services, Inc.; Merry Maids of Oklahoma, Inc.; Tradition Realty, Ltd.; Refractory Anchors, Inc.; Tulsa Overhead Door Co.; West Companies International; Airco Service, Inc.; Lancaster & Co.; City of McAlester, Oklahoma; Town of Muldrow, Oklahoma; Bluelincs HMO; M.C. Enterprises, Inc.; Ameriban, Inc.; Stokely Outdoor Advertising, Inc.; 3D Icon Corporation; Chattan Investments, L.L.C.
REFERENCES: Bank of America, N.A.; State Bank & Trust, N.A.; Bank of Oklahoma.

LOGAN & LOWRY, LLP

TULSA, OKLAHOMA

(See Vinita)

General Practice, Including Trials in all State and Federal Courts, Eminent Domain, Environmental and Coal, Banking, Commercial Transactions, Creditors' Rights and Bankruptcy, Corporation, Public Utility, Real Estate, Estate Planning and Probate, Criminal, Domestic Relations, Civil Rights, Employment, Appellate Practice and Administrative Law.

BRIAN T. LOUGHRIN

TULSA, OKLAHOMA

(See Oklahoma City)

Criminal Defense, Bankruptcy Chapter 7, Driving While Intoxicated, Felonies, Sexual Assault, Federal Criminal Law, Personal Bankruptcy, Criminal Law, Sex Crimes.

GEORGE H. LOWREY

Established in 1994

THE BEACON BUILDING
406 SOUTH BOULDER AVENUE
SUITE 400
TULSA, OKLAHOMA 74103-3800
Telephone: 918-599-9788
Fax: 918-582-6106
Email: glowlaw@mac.com
URL: http://www.georgelowrey.com

Civil Litigation including Arbitration. Civil Trial Practice and Commercial Litigation.

FIRM PROFILE: George H. Lowrey is listed in the Bar Register of Preeminent Lawyers under Commercial Litigation and Civil Trial Practice.

GEORGE H. LOWREY, born Woodward, Oklahoma, June 29, 1958; admitted to bar, 1984, Oklahoma, U.S. District Court, Northern, Eastern and Western Districts of Oklahoma and U.S. Court of Appeals, Tenth Circuit. *Education:* University of Oklahoma (B.A., summa cum laude, 1980); Cornell University (J.D., cum laude, 1984). Phi Beta Kappa; Phi Eta Sigma. Member, U.S. Supreme Court Historical Society. Barrister, Hudson-Hall Wheaton Chapter, American Inns of Court. *Member:* Tulsa County, Oklahoma and American Bar Associations. ***PRACTICE AREAS:*** Arbitration; Complex Commercial Litigation; Trial Practice; Oil and Gas Litigation; Securities Litigation; Trust Litigation; Contested Wills.

REFERENCES: Available Upon Request.

LYONS & CLARK

Established in 1986

TWO MAIN PLAZA
616 SOUTH MAIN, SUITE 201
TULSA, OKLAHOMA 74119
Telephone: 918-599-8844
Fax: 918-599-8585
URL: http://www.lawyers.com/lyons&clark

General Civil and Criminal Practice in Federal and State Courts. Commercial/Business Litigation, Construction Law, Negligence, Employment, Civil Rights, Probate, Appeals.

(This Listing Continued)

FIRM PROFILE: Lyons & Clark was established in 1986 when Mark Lyons and Cary Clark left the Tulsa County District Attorney's Office after a combined total of 17 years in the criminal and civil divisions. The firm continues its tradition of a litigation-based practice in federal and state court, representing businesses and individuals. This firm takes great pride in its dedication to providing personal service to the client. See web site for reported cases.

CARY W. CLARK (1950-1988)

MARK D. LYONS, born Holdenville, Oklahoma, February 19, 1954; admitted to bar, 1980, Oklahoma; 1982, U.S. District Court, Northern and Western Districts of Oklahoma and U.S. Court of Appeals, Tenth Circuit; 1989, Muscogee (Creek) Nation. *Education:* University of Oklahoma (B.S., Zoology, 1977); University of Tulsa (J.D., 1980). Order of the Barristers. Adjunct Professor, University of Tulsa, College of Law. Part-time Instructor: Paralegal Program, University of Tulsa and Tulsa Junior College. Author and Lecturer: Continuing Legal Education, Products Liability and Trial Practice Ethics, Tulsa County and Oklahoma Bar Associations. Assistant District Attorney, Tulsa County, Oklahoma (Criminal and Civil Divisions). Member, Civil Justice Reform Act Committee, Northern District of Oklahoma (Practitioner Subcommittee Chairman, 1995). Commissioner and Vice Chairman, Oklahoma Ethics Commission, 1996-2000. *Member:* Tulsa County (Member, Ethics Committee) and Oklahoma Bar Associations. ***PRACTICE AREAS:*** Commercial Litigation; Business Law; Labor and Employment; Construction Law; Criminal Law; Appellate Practice; Civil Rights; Products Liability; Medical Malpractice; Personal Injury.

ASSOCIATES

NICOLE A. KING, born Shreveport, Louisiana, July 5, 1973; admitted to bar, 2000, Oklahoma; 2002, U.S. District Court, Northern District of Oklahoma and U.S. Court of Appeals, Tenth Circuit. *Education:* University of Tulsa (B.S.B.A., 1995; M.B.A., 1997; J.D., 1999). Phi Delta Phi. Executive Editor, 1999 and Publications Editor, 1999, Tulsa Journal of Comparative and International Law. Assistant Attorney General, Public Utility Unit, Oklahoma Attorney General. Legal Consultant, The Williams Companies, Inc., International Legal Department. *Member:* Tulsa County (Member, Litigation and Corporate Sections) and American Bar Associations; Oklahoma Bar Association. ***PRACTICE AREAS:*** Public Utility Regulation; International Business Law; Corporate Law; Civil Litigation; Appellate Practice; Probate. **Email:** nking_lyonsclark@swbell.net

C. ALISON WADE, born Kansas City, Missouri, October 3, 1973; admitted to bar, 2001, Oklahoma; 2003, U.S. District Court, Northern District of Oklahoma. *Education:* Baylor University (B.A., Psychology and Sociology, 1997); University of Tulsa (M.A., Industrial Organizational Psychology, 2001; J.D., 2001). Phi Delta Phi. Highest Honors, Order of the Curule Chair, Order of Barristers. Executive Editor, Tulsa Law Review. President, Board of Advocates. *Member:* Tulsa County and Oklahoma Bar Associations; Oklahoma Criminal Defense Lawyers Association (Young Lawyers Division Executive Committee). ***PRACTICE AREAS:*** Criminal Law. **Email:** awade_lyonsclark@swbell.net

REPRESENTATIVE CLIENTS: Williams Construction Company; KeyBank; Furniture Factory Outlet, Inc.; Airgas-Mid South, Inc.; Industrial Controls of Oklahomas, Inc.; Mid-South Maintenance, Inc.

RONALD MAIN, P.C.

CENTER 2800, SUITE 821
2815 EAST SKELLY DRIVE
TULSA, OKLAHOMA 74105-6251
Telephone: 918-742-1990
Fax: 918-742-2004
Email: rmainbtl@aol.com

General Civil Trial and Appellate Practice in all State and Federal Courts. Real Estate, Financial Institutions, Corporations, Creditors' Rights, Insurance, Personal Injury, Probate, Guardianship and Estate Planning Law, Wills, Trusts, Matrimonial Law, Divorce, Employment.

FIRM PROFILE: Ronald Main is listed in the Bar Register of Preeminent Lawyers in the areas of Family and Business Law.

RONALD MAIN, born Woodhaven, New York, February 28, 1940; admitted to bar, 1964, Oklahoma. *Education:* University of Tulsa (B.A., 1962; J.D., 1964). Phi Alpha Delta (Justice, 1964). Associate Editor, Tulsa Law Journal, 1963-1964. Adjunct Assistant Professor of Law, University of Tulsa College of Law, 1969-1980. Author: Cases and Materials on Workers' Compensation Law, University of Tulsa Press. Editor, Okla. Bar Journal, 1996. Justice, Court of Appeals, State of Oklahoma (Temp. Div.), 1981. Vice President, Legal Services of Eastern Oklahoma, 1988, 2001. *Member:* Tulsa County (President, 1984-1985; Outstanding Lawyer, 1986; Golden Rule Award, 1998), Oklahoma (Member: Board of Governors, 1988-1990; Professional Responsibility Tribunal, 1993; Professional Responsibility Commission, 1995; Chair, 1997; Chair, Bench and Bar Committee, 1991; Vice-President, 1992) and American Bar Associations. Fellow: American Academy of Matrimonial Lawyers; Tulsa County Bar Foundation (President, 1986; Trustee, 1984-1995; Charter Fellow, 1994); Oklahoma Bar Foundation (Fellow, 1974; Trustee, 1991-1996). [Lt., JAGC, USNR]. **Email:** rmainbtl@aol.com

REPRESENTATIVE CLIENTS: Brumbaugh & Fulton, Co.; Miles Shipping Co.; H.S. Boyd, Co.; Kemco Fuels, Inc.; Sawyer Manufacturing Co.; Ultimate Development Corp.
REFERENCES: Bank of Oklahoma, N.A.; Tulsa National Bank.

MALLOY & MALLOY, INC.

Established in 1972
111 WEST FIFTH, SUITE 700
TULSA, OKLAHOMA 73103
Telephone: 918-747-3491
Fax: 918-743-6103
Email: psmiiim@aol.com

General Trial Practice. Civil Wrongful Termination, F.E.L.A., Insurance, Bankruptcy, Real Estate, Appellate Practice.

(This Listing Continued)

FIRM PROFILE: Malloy & Malloy, Inc., represents the continuation of three generations of legal service provided throughout the state of Oklahoma. The firm presently consists of a father and son combination, Pat Malloy Jr. and Patrick J. Malloy III. The original Pat Malloy was one of the state's earliest County Attorneys, serving as County Attorney of Tulsa County from 1910 to 1913. Thereafter he served as Assistant Attorney General in President Roosevelt's cabinet; General Counsel, Constantine Oil and Gas; Special Counsel, Sinclair Oil Company.

Pat Malloy, Jr. has been active in both the law and politics since the late 1940s after serving his country in the U.S. Navy during World War II. He served as Regional Solicitor for the Department of Interior, supervising 24 attorneys in six states representing various agencies of the department.

In addition to general personal injury, he represented a substantial number of employees in suits arising under the Federal Employer's Liability Act. Defendant litigation primarily involved representation of Reliance Insurance Company.

For many years he represented the Tulsa office of Ponca City Savings and Loan Association, later Frontier Federal Savings and Loan Association.

Patrick J. Malloy III joined his father in the practice of law in June 1972 and has specialized in bankruptcy and general litigation since that time. As noted below, Patrick J. Malloy III has been involved in a number of significant cases in the area of wrongful termination. He has participated in the jury trial of numerous wrongful termination cases, which have resulted in combined jury verdicts of in excess of $20,000,000.00.

Major Transactions: Cook, Miller and Lewis v. Northrop Worldwide Aircraft Services, Inc.; Oklahoma Court of Appeals Case No. 78,452; Comanche County District Court Case No. CJ-90-479.

1. Cook, Lewis and Miller v. Northrop, wrongful termination in violation of State Public Policy; State Supreme Court affirmed jury verdict worth $2.5 million at conclusion of the appeal.

2. Marshall v. TRW, Inc., Reda Pump Div., 900 F.2d 1517 (10th Cir. 1990), wrongful termination in violation of the Workers' Compensation Law of the State of Oklahoma; 10th Circuit Court of Appeals affirmed District Court jury verdict of approximately $350,000.00.

3. Mantha v. Liquid Carbonics Industries, 839 P.2d 200 (Okla. App. 1992), wrongful termination in violation of the Workers' Compensation law of the State of Oklahoma, jury verdict affirmed on appeal for approximately $400,000.00.

In addition to wrongful termination, Patrick J. Malloy III has been involved in significant Chapter Eleven bankruptcy proceedings. Most notable is the matter of In Re: Interchange, Case No. 92-01413-W United States Bankruptcy Court for the Northern District of Oklahoma. This case represented the Debtor's successful reorganization of an eight ($8) million dollar debt to the Resolution Trust Company (RTC) over the objection of the RTC.

PAT MALLOY, JR. (1916-2004)

PATRICK J. MALLOY, III, born Tulsa, Oklahoma, November 18, 1946; admitted to bar, 1972, Oklahoma; U.S. District Court, Northern, Eastern and Western Districts of Oklahoma; 1973, U.S. Court of Appeals, 10th Circuit and U.S. Supreme Court. *Education:* Cascia Hall, Tulsa and University of Notre Dame (B.A., 1968); Munich Institute for Study of the Soviet Union, Summer, 1971 and University of Oklahoma (J.D., 1972). Recipient, Golden Rule Award, Tulsa County Bar Association, February, 2002. Chapter 7 Panel Trustee for U.S. Bankruptcy Court for the Northern District of Oklahoma, 1972—. Adjunct Professor of Soviet Law, Tulsa University, College of Law, 1977. Speaker, University of Tulsa Law School Seminar, "Chapter 11 Basics," 1994. Speaker, "Advanced Bankruptcy," Oklahoma Bar Association Continuing Legal Education Seminar, 1994. *Member:* Tulsa County, Oklahoma and American Bar Associations; Oklahoma Trial Lawyers Association; The Association of Trial Lawyers of America. ***LANGUAGES:*** Russian. ***REPORTED CASES:*** Marshall v. TRW, Inc., Reda Pump Div., 900 F.2d 1517 (10th Cir. 1990); Mantha v. Liquid Carbonic Industries, 839 P.2d 200 (Okla. 1992); Shields, 85 B.R. 582 (N.D. Okla. 1982); Crussell v. Kirk, 894 P.2d 1116 (Okla. 1995); Groce v. Foster, 880 P.2d 902 (Okla. 1994); Malloy v. S. John Medical Center (In re: Woodward), 234 B.R. 519 (Bankr. N.D. Okla. 1999); In re: Limited Gaming of America v. Sunrise Island, Ltd., 228 B.R. 275 (Bkrtcy. N.D. Okla. 1998); In re Universal Factoring Co. Inc., 279 BR 297 (Bankr. N.D. of Okla. 2002). ***PRACTICE AREAS:*** Bankruptcy Law; Litigation; Wrongful Termination; Appellate Practice.

LEGAL SUPPORT PERSONNEL

TIMOTHY B. MALLOY, (Paralegal)

REPRESENTATIVE CLIENTS: Reliance Insurance Group; Reliance Insurance National; Aetna Insurance; Bituminous Insurance Co.; United Pacific Insurance Co.; Clarendon National Insurance Co.; Crawford & Co.; Verdigris Valley Rural Electric Coop.; Pinion Oil Co.; W.K. Warren Medical Research, Inc.; W.K. Warren Foundation; Schmoldt Engineering; R.H. Siegfried, Inc.; J.M. Hewgley, Jr.; Addison-Leyen Drilling, Co., Calgary, Alberta, Canada; Ramsey Industries Express Storage Management; Villareal & Associates, Inc.

MATTHIES LAW FIRM

A PROFESSIONAL CORPORATION
Established in 1978
SUITE 310, THOMPSON BUILDING
20 EAST FIFTH STREET
TULSA, OKLAHOMA 74103-4435
Telephone: 918-582-4400
Fax: 918-584-4453
Email: mattlawfrm@aol.com
URL: http://www.members.aol.com/mattlawfrm/mattlaw.htm

Labor and Employment Law (Management) and Corporate Civil Litigation, Employment Discrimination, ERISA.

(This Listing Continued)

MATTHIES LAW FIRM, A PROFESSIONAL CORPORATION, Tulsa—Continued

MARY CONSTANCE T. MATTHIES, (MS.), born Baton Rouge, Louisiana, March 22, 1948; admitted to bar, 1973, Oklahoma; 1974, U.S. Court of Appeals, Tenth Circuit; 1975, U.S. Court of Appeals, Eighth and District of Columbia Circuits; 1976, U.S. Supreme Court. *Education:* Oklahoma State University (B.S., 1969); University of Tulsa (J.D., 1972). Phi Delta Phi. Member, Rogers Inn (Exchequer, 1971-1972). Member of Staff, Tulsa Law Journal, 1971-1972. Author: Chapters 25 & 26, "Evidence and Discovery," Sexual Harassment in Employment Law, BNA (1992); "The Americans with Disabilities Act," 63 Oklahoma Bar Journal, 855 (1992). Chapter 27, "Title VII Coverage," Employment Discrimination Law, 2d Ed., BNA (1982); "The Developing Law on Equal Employment Opportunity," Vol. 5, Journal of Contemporary Business, 1976; "Personal Injuries: Should Non-Taxability of Judgments Decrease Awards?" Vol. 8, Tulsa Law Journal, 1973. Associate Trustee, Hillcrest Medical Center, 1986-1996. *Member:* Tulsa County, Oklahoma (Member, 1974—, Council Member, 1974-1981, Secretary, 1976-1977 and Chairperson, 1978-1979, Labor Law Section) and American (Member: Equal Employment Opportunity Committee, Labor Relations Law Section, 1973—; Special Subcommittee for Liaison with the Equal Employment Opportunity Commission, 1974—; Management Co-Chairperson, Subcommittees on: National Origin Discrimination, 1974-1975; Civil Rights Class Action and Remedies, 1975-1978) Bar Associations. Fellow, American College of Labor and Employment Lawyers. ***REPORTED CASES:*** Shell Oil Co. v. Dartt, 434 U.S. 98, 1977; NLRB v. Dover Corp., 429 U.S., 978, 1976; Nulf v. International Paper Co., 656 F. 2d 553, 10th Cir., 1981; Merrick v. Northern Natural Gas, 911 F. 2d 426, 10th Cir., 1990. ***PRACTICE AREAS:*** Employment Discrimination; ERISA; Wrongful Termination Defense; Labor Relations; Management Labor Law. ***Email:*** matllawfrm@aol.com

REPRESENTATIVE CLIENTS: Atlantic Richfield; General Motors Co.; Schlumberger Technology Corp.; Rockwell International; Shell Oil Co.; Hertz Corporation; Zurich American Ins. Co.; Allstate Insurance Co.

MCALISTER, MCALISTER, MCKINNIS & TUGGLE, P.C.

TULSA, OKLAHOMA

(See Edmond)

Estate and Gift Taxation, Business Law, Contracts, Commercial Law, Corporate Law, Partnership Law, Commercial Transaction, Civil Litigation, Estate Litigation, Trust Litigation, Probate, Real Estate, Mergers, Acquisitions and Divestures, Taxation, Wills, Labor and Employment Law, Estate Planning, Elder Law, Guardianship and Conservatorship, Nonprofit and Charitable Organizations.

MCATEE LAW OFFICE

Established in 2001

1115 SOUTH CINCINNATI
TULSA, OKLAHOMA 74119
Telephone: 918-746-4332
Fax: 918-746-4334
Email: jmcatee@mcateelawoffice.com
URL: http://www.mcateelawoffice.com

Mailing Address: P.O. Box 50611, Tulsa, OK 74150-0611

State Workers Compensation Law, Insurance Defense, Immigration Law.

R. JAY MCATEE, born Canyon, Texas, December 30, 1956; admitted to bar, 1983, Oklahoma and U.S. District Court, Northern District of Oklahoma. *Education:* Oklahoma State University (B.A., 1980); University of Tulsa (J.D., 1983). *Member:* Tulsa County and Oklahoma Bar Associations; Oklahoma Association of Defense Counsel; Defense Research Institute. ***PRACTICE AREAS:*** Workers Compensation; Insurance Defense; Immigration Law. ***Email:*** jmcatee@mcateelawoffice.com

ASSOCIATE

VALERIE L. SPARKS, born December 22, 1973; admitted to bar, 2004, Oklahoma. *Education:* Northeastern Oklahoma State University (B.S., 1999); University of Tulsa (J.D., 2003). Phi Delta Phi. *Member:* Tulsa County (Member, Sections on: Workers Compensation; Insurance), Oklahoma and American Bar Associations; Oklahoma Association of Defense Counsel; Defense Research Institute; Oklahoma Self Insured Association. ***LANGUAGES:*** French. ***PRACTICE AREAS:*** Workers Compensation; Immigration Law; Litigation. ***Email:*** vsparks@mcateelawoffice.com

REPRESENTATIVE CLIENTS: J.B. Hunt; Love's Country Stores; OK Foods; A.I.G.; John Christner Trucking; Risk Enterprise Management; Arrow Trucking; Sagamore Insurance; Med-Corp Plus; Cracker Barrel Old Country Stores; Gallagher Basset; Blueworks; Southwest Medical Center; Broadspire.

MCCORMICK FIELD & CINOCCA, P.L.L.C.

Established in 1994

BRIDGEPORT II, SUITE 100
6440 SOUTH LEWIS AVENUE
TULSA, OKLAHOMA 74136-1039
Telephone: 918-488-8000
Facsimile: 918-481-8751

General Trial Practice in all State and Federal Courts. Real Estate, General Corporate, Probate and Estate Planning, Wills and Probate, Trusts and Estates, Corporation, Commercial, Class Action Litigation, Bankruptcy, Civil Litigation, Personal Injury, Automobile Accidents, Wrongful Death and Products Liability.

(This Listing Continued)

MEMBERS OF FIRM

JOSEPH A. MCCORMICK, born Bartlesville, Oklahoma, August 4, 1942; admitted to bar, 1967, Oklahoma. *Education:* Northeastern Oklahoma A & M College; Oklahoma State University; University of Tulsa (LL.B., 1966). Phi Alpha Delta. *Member:* Tulsa County, Oklahoma and American Bar Associations; Tulsa Title and Probate Lawyers Association (President, 1985). [Capt., JAG, Military Judge, USAF, 1967-1972]. ***PRACTICE AREAS:*** Real Estate Law; Corporate Law; Trial Practice. ***Email:*** mylawyer@mindspring.com

STEWART E. FIELD, born Tulsa, Oklahoma, October 24, 1956; admitted to bar, 1982, Oklahoma; 1989, U.S. Supreme Court. *Education:* University of Tulsa (B.S.B.A., 1978; J.D., 1981). Phi Gamma Kappa. *Member:* Tulsa County, Oklahoma and American Bar Associations; Oklahoma Society of Certified Public Accountants (Member, Tulsa Chapter); Tulsa Title and Probate Lawyers Association. ***PRACTICE AREAS:*** Commercial; Probate and Estate Planning; Class Action Litigation. ***Email:*** sfieldesq@aol.com

JAMES EDWARD CINOCCA, JR., born Tulsa, Oklahoma, May 31, 1968; admitted to bar, 1995, Oklahoma. *Education:* University of Texas at Austin (B.B.A., Accounting, 1991); University of Tulsa (J.D., 1994). *Member:* Tulsa County and Oklahoma Bar Associations; Oklahoma Trial Lawyers Association. ***PRACTICE AREAS:*** Civil Litigation; Personal Injury; Products Liability; Real Estate. ***Email:*** jim.cinocca@cox.net

HOLLY BREESE CINOCCA, born Owasso, Oklahoma, March 21, 1969; admitted to bar, 1994, Oklahoma. *Education:* University of Tulsa (B.A., 1991; J.D., 1994). Phi Delta Phi; Order of the Barristers. *Member:* Tulsa County and Oklahoma Bar Associations. ***PRACTICE AREAS:*** Personal Injury; Insurance Defense; Civil Litigation. ***Email:*** holly.cinocca@cox.net

STEPHEN E. MCCORMICK, born Abilene, Texas, January 13, 1969; admitted to bar, 2002, Oklahoma. *Education:* Baylor University (B.B.A., 1992); Wake Forest University (M.B.A., 1994); University of Tulsa (J.D., 1997). Member, Tulsa Title and Probate Lawyers. *Member:* Tulsa County, Oklahoma Bar Associations. ***PRACTICE AREAS:*** Real Estate; Probate; Estate Planning; Civil Litigation; Corporate Law. ***Email:*** steveericmccormick@earthlink.net

REPRESENTATIVE CLIENTS: Warehouse Market, Inc.; Bauer and Associates Realtors; CitiCapital Commercial Corporation; Rush Truck Centers of Oklahoma, Inc.; Valmont Industries, Inc.; Gable Excavating Inc.; Graphic Electronics, Inc.

MCCORMICK, SCHOENENBERGER & GISH

A PROFESSIONAL ASSOCIATION

Established in 1986

1441 SOUTH CARSON AVENUE
TULSA, OKLAHOMA 74119-3417
Telephone: 918-582-3655
Facsimile: 918-582-3657
URL: http://www.tulsaoklawfirm.com

Oklahoma City, Oklahoma Office: 4312 Classen Drive, 73118. Telephone: 405-525-0777. Fax: 405-557-0777.

General Civil Practice before all State and Federal Courts including, Insurance Defense, Personal Injury, Business Litigation, Corporation, Oil and Gas Law and Acquisitions, Title Examination, Employment Law, Sports Law, Family Law, Guardianship, Adoption Law, Divorce, Child Custody, Paternity, Social Security Disability.

FIRM PROFILE: Founded in 1986 as McCormick & Weichman, PA, the firm of McCormick, Schoenenberger & Gish, PA continues its tradition of providing high-quality, personalized legal services. The principals of the firm have over 60 years of combined experience representing individual and business clients in the firm's various areas of practice including civil litigation, oil and gas law, disability and workers compensation.

TIMOTHY E. MCCORMICK, born Minneapolis, Minnesota, March 26, 1948; admitted to bar, 1977, Oklahoma, U.S. District Court, Northern, Western and Eastern Districts of Oklahoma, U.S. Court of Appeals, Tenth Circuit and U.S. Supreme Court. *Education:* University of Minnesota (B.A., 1970); University of Tulsa (J.D., 1977). Phi Delta Phi. Notes and Comment Editor, Tulsa Law Journal, 1976-1977. *Member:* Tulsa County and Oklahoma Bar Associations; Oklahoma Association of Defense Counsel; Oklahoma Trial Lawyers Association. ***LANGUAGES:*** Spanish. ***PRACTICE AREAS:*** Civil Practice; Insurance; Negligence; Labor and Employment Law; Personal Injury; Sports Law. ***Email:*** mccorlaw@aol.com

THOMAS R. SCHOENENBERGER, born Evanston, Illinois, May 15, 1950; admitted to bar, 1977, Oklahoma; 1978, U.S. District Court, Northern District of Oklahoma; 1990, U.S. Supreme Court. *Education:* Boston University (B.S., magna cum laude, 1972); University of Tulsa (J.D., 1977). Phi Delta Phi. Author: "Preparing Farmouts and Contribution Agreements," Practical Oil and Gas Law VII: Oil and Gas Contracts, University of Tulsa College of Law. Lecturer: Oil and Gas Contracts-University of Tulsa Continuing Legal Education and American Association of Petroleum Landmen Seminars, 1983-1985. *Member:* Tulsa County (Member, Mineral Law Section) and Oklahoma (Member, Mineral Law Section) Bar Associations; Tulsa Association of Petroleum Landmen. ***PRACTICE AREAS:*** Oil and Gas Law; Oil and Gas Title Examination; Oil and Gas Acquisitions; Oil and Gas Contracts; Corporate Contracts. ***Email:*** schoenlaw@aol.com

DANA L. GISH, born Midland, Michigan, October 4, 1965; admitted to bar, 1990, Oklahoma. *Education:* University of Oklahoma (B.A., 1983); University of Tulsa (J.D., 1990). Member, Oklahoma Workers' Compensation Board, 2002-2005; Chairman, 2004-2005. Certified Mediator. *Member:* Tulsa County, Oklahoma and American Bar Associations. ***PRACTICE AREAS:*** General Practice; Workers' Compensation; Social Security Disability Claims and Appeals. ***Email:*** dgish@msglawoffice.com

REPRESENTATIVE CLIENTS: Acme, Inc.; Alliance Specialties, Inc.; American and Foreign Insurance Co.; Americo, Inc.; Apex Industries, Inc.; BP Amoco, Inc.; Brighton Energy, L.L.C.; Connecticut Indemnity Co.; Daimsler Chrysler Corp.; Environmental Action, Inc.; Fire and Casualty Insurance Company of Connecticut; Globe Indemnity; Grocers Insurance Co.; KCS

(This Listing Continued)

Energy, Inc.; Marjo Operating Co.; Max True Fireproofing; Newfield Exploration; Oklahoma Comp Source Sedwick; Comp Source of Oklahoma; Sedgwich Claim Services; Oklahoma Nursing Homes Self Insurance Association; Republic Western Insurance Co.; Royal Indemnity; Royal Insurance Company of America; Security Insurance Company of Hartford; Strat Land Exploration Co.; Tidemark Exploration, Inc.; U-Haul Company of Oklahoma, Inc. and U-Haul International, Inc.
REFERENCE: Bank of Oklahoma, Bank of Oklahoma Tower.

McKINNEY & STRINGER

A PROFESSIONAL CORPORATION
MID CONTINENT TOWER
401 SOUTH BOSTON, SUITE 600
TULSA, OKLAHOMA 74103
Telephone: 918-582-3176
Telecopier: 918-582-1403
URL: http://www.McKinneyStringer.com

Oklahoma City, Oklahoma Office: Corporate Tower, 101 North Robinson, Suite 1300. Telephone: 405-239-6444. Telecopier: 405-239-7902.

Litigation; Appellate Practice; Alternate Dispute Resolution; Administrative Law; Antitrust and Trade Regulation; Aviation Law; Bankruptcy; Banks and Banking; Business Law; Civil Rights; Commercial Law; Computer and Technology Issues, Corporate Law; Mergers and Acquisitions; Energy; Oil and Gas Law; Environmental Law; Government Agency Practice; Health Care; Insurance; Intellectual Property; Trademarks; Patent Litigation; Labor and Employment; Workers Compensation; Medical Malpractice; Personal Injury; Toxic Torts; Products Liability; Probate; Real Estate; Securities Law; Taxation; Trusts and Estates; Wills.

FIRM PROFILE: Since its founding in 1971, McKinney & Stringer has grown into a multi-specialty firm serving clients in a wide range of business, industries and interest on both a local and national scale. Now one of Oklahoma's largest firms, McKinney and Stringer has continued to steadily expand not only the number of attorneys and professional support staff, but also the diversity of its practice areas, breadth of its client base, and the geographical location of its resources.

McKinney & Stringer maintains offices in both Oklahoma City and Tulsa. Its major practice areas focus on all aspects of corporate law and business transactions; intellectual property law; complex business litigation; insurance defense, product liability and personal injury law; environmental law; energy law and employment law. McKinney & Stringer provides clients, from individuals to large national corporations, with a full service law firm - a firm that combines up-to-date technological resources and a professional support staff with dedicated attorneys who are experienced in virtually every dimension of the legal profession. The firm has built its reputation on the pursuit of innovative, practical and cost-effective solutions for its clients' legal and business problems, and remains committed to this goal.

DIRECTORS

PATRICK H. KERNAN, born Stillwater, Oklahoma, March 2, 1948; admitted to bar, 1975, Oklahoma. *Education:* Oklahoma State University (B.S., 1970); Oklahoma City University (J.D., 1975). [U.S. Army, 1971-1973, 1st Lt. Infantry]. ***PRACTICE AREAS:*** Commercial Litigation; Personal Injury Litigation. ***Email:*** KernanP@McKinneyStringer.com

MICHAEL S. LINSCOTT, born Oklahoma City, Oklahoma, April 22, 1959; admitted to bar, 1991, Texas (inactive); 1997, Oklahoma. *Education:* University of Oklahoma (B.S., 1984); University of Tulsa College of Law (J.D., with honors, 1991). *Member:* Federal Bar Association. ***PRACTICE AREAS:*** Commercial Litigation; Insurance Defense; Creditor Bankruptcy; Commercial Transactions; Securities Arbitration. ***Email:*** LinscottM@McKinneyStringer.com

KRIS T. LEDFORD, born Lawton, Oklahoma, April 6, 1972; admitted to bar, 1997, Oklahoma. *Education:* Cameron University (B.A., magna cum laude, 1994); Tulsa University (J.D., 1997). Order of the Curule (Chair). ***PRACTICE AREAS:*** Insurance; Products Liability; Litigation. ***Email:*** LedfordK@McKinneyStringer.com

OF COUNSEL

CHRISTOPHER S. HEROUX, born Evanston, Illinois, December 13, 1958; admitted to bar, 1986, Oklahoma; 1988, Texas. *Education:* Loyola University of Chicago (A.B., 1981); University of Tulsa College of Law (J.D., with honors, 1986). ***PRACTICE AREAS:*** Business Formation; Business Transactions; Small Business; Business Consulting; Oil and Gas; Banking; Financial Institutions; Business Litigation; Creditors Rights; Real Estate. ***Email:*** herouxc@mckinneystringer.com

GARRY L. KEELE, II, born El Reno, Oklahoma, 1965; admitted to bar, 1994, Oklahoma. *Education:* University of Oklahoma (B.B.A., 1987); University of Tulsa (J.D., 1994). ***PRACTICE AREAS:*** Environmental Law.

ASSOCIATES

SCOTT R. HELTON, born Little Rock, Arkansas, 1976; admitted to bar, 2003, Oklahoma. *Education:* Oklahoma Baptist University (B.S., 2000); University of Tulsa (J.D., with honors, 2003). ***PRACTICE AREAS:*** Insurance Defense; Personal Injury.

LEAH P. CARPENTER, born Durant, Oklahoma, May 6, 1971; admitted to bar, 2004, Oklahoma. *Education:* University of Oklahoma (B.S., 1994); University of Tulsa (J.D., with highest honors, 2004). Phi Delta Phi. Editor-in-Chief, Tulsa Journal of Comparative and International Law, 2003-2004. Author, "The Status of the H1B Visa in These Conflicting Times," 10 Tul. J. Comp. & Int'l. L. 553 (2003). Speaker, Law Related Education Committee, Oklahoma Bar Association. ***PRACTICE AREAS:*** Employment Law; Corporate Law; Commercial Litigation. ***Email:*** CarpenterL@Mckinneystringer.com

(For Remainder of Firm Professional Biographies, See Oklahoma City)

McQUEEN, RAINS & TRESCH, LLP

6100 S. YALE AVENUE, SUITE 618
TULSA, OKLAHOMA 74136
Telephone: 918-728-7800
Fax: 918-728-7899

Commercial Law, Commercial Finance, Consumer Credit, Corporate Banking Law, Secured Lending, Emergency Response Transactions, General Civil Litigation, Commercial Litigation, Products Liability, Energy Litigation, Refining and Marketing, Contracts, International Transactions, Joint Ventures, Investment Funds, Energy Law, Oil and Gas Law, Labor and Employment, Litigation.

L. DRU McQUEEN, born Oklahoma City, Oklahoma, August 15, 1955; admitted to bar, 1983, Oklahoma and U.S. District Court, Northern and Western Districts of Oklahoma. *Education:* Southern Methodist University (B.F.A., in Journalism, with highest honors, 1976); University of Tulsa (J.D., with honors, 1982). Phi Delta Phi. Law Clerk to Hon. Thomas R. Brett, U.S. District Judge, Northern District of Oklahoma, 1983-1985. Tulsa County District Court Adjunct Settlement Judge. Served on Board of Directors and as President of the Child Abuse Network. *Member:* Tulsa County and Oklahoma Bar Associations. (Counsel). ***PRACTICE AREAS:*** Litigation; Complex and Multi-District Litigation; Commercial Litigation; Premises Liability Defense; Products Liability Defense; Toxic Tort Defense.

STUART A. RAINS, born Tulsa, Oklahoma, July 5, 1956; admitted to bar, 1981, Oklahoma. *Education:* University of Oklahoma (B.A., 1978; J.D., 1981). Phi Alpha Delta. *Member:* Tulsa and Oklahoma Bar Associations. ***PRACTICE AREAS:*** Advertising and Marketing; Business Law; Real Estate; Contracts; Corporate Law; Energy; International Law; Litigation.

W. KYLE TRESCH, born Nashville, Tennessee, 1964; admitted to bar, 1989, Oklahoma; 1995, Arizona. *Education:* Oklahoma Baptist University (B.A., 1986); Washington & Lee University (J.D., 1989). Member: Leadership Tulsa; Tulsa Habitat for Humanity, Inc. Board of Directors, Oklahoma Baptist University National Advisory Board. *Member:* Oklahoma and American Bar Associations; State Bar of Arizona. ***PRACTICE AREAS:*** Commercial Law; Commercial Finance; Consumer Credit; Corporate Banking Law; Secured Lending.

JACK P. GRIMALDI, born Newark, New Jersey, November 12, 1946; admitted to bar, 1973, Kansas; 1975, Oklahoma;. *Education:* St. Mary of the Plains (B.A., 1968); University of Kansas (J.D., 1973). *Member:* Tulsa County, Oklahoma and Kansas Bar Associations. ***LANGUAGES:*** Spanish. ***PRACTICE AREAS:*** International Transactions; Joint Ventures; Energy Law; Oil and Gas Law.

JULIE C. CHIEN, admitted to bar, 1998, California and U.S. District Court, Central District of California; 2005, Oklahoma. *Education:* Stanford University (B.A., with honors, 1994); Harvard Law School (J.D., 1997). Phi Beta Kappa. *Member:* Oklahoma and American Bar Associations; State Bar of California. ***LANGUAGES:*** Mandarin and Shanghainese. ***PRACTICE AREAS:*** Commercial Transactions; Energy; Oil and Gas Law.

EUGENE L. RICCETTI, born Cherry Hill, New Jersey, January 11, 1968; admitted to bar, 1994, Texas (Not admitted in Oklahoma). *Education:* University of Texas (B.A., Philosophy, 1991); South Texas College of Law (J.D., 1994). Formerly: Corporate Counsel - Petroleum Markets, El Paso Corporation, Houston, TX, 2001-2004; Corporate Counsel - Refining, Marketing and Marine Law Dept., The Coastal Corporation, Houston, TX, 1999-2001; Contract Attorney, Condea Vista Chemical Company, Houston, TX, 1998; Associate, Lorenz & Carter, Houston, TX, 1994-1998. ***PRACTICE AREAS:*** Corporate Law; Commercial Law; Refining and Marketing.

JENNIFER E. MUSTAIN, born Brussels, Belgium, June 7, 1966; admitted to bar, 1991, Oklahoma. *Education:* University of Oklahoma (B.A., 1988; J.D., 1991); University of Hawaii; Oxford University. *Member:* Tulsa County, Oklahoma and American Bar Associations; Oklahoma Association of Defense Counsel; Defense Research Institute. ***PRACTICE AREAS:*** General Civil Litigation; Commercial Litigation; Products Liability; Energy Litigation. ***Email:*** jmustain@mcqueenrains.com

AMIT K. MISRA, born St. Louis, Missouri, March 23, 1972; admitted to bar, 1996, Texas and U.S. District Court, Southern District of Texas; 2002, U.S. Court of Appeals, Fifth Circuit (Not admitted in Oklahoma). *Education:* George Washington University (B.A., 1992); University of Texas (J.D., 1995; M.P.Aff., 1995). Phi Beta Kappa. *Member:* Houston Bar Association; State Bar of Texas; South Asian American Bar Association of Houston. ***LANGUAGES:*** Hindi and German. ***PRACTICE AREAS:*** Labor and Employment; Litigation; Business Law; Nonprofit Organizations Law. ***Email:*** amisra@mcqueenrains.com

HOLLY CHASTAIN, admitted to bar, 1995, Alabama (Not admitted in Oklahoma). *Education:* University of Aix en Provence, France (Summer 1990); University of Alabama (B.S., Marketing, 1992; J.D., 1995). Schlumberger Regional Legal Counsel for North America, United Kingdom and Ireland, 1995-2004. *Member:* Alabama State Bar; American Bar Association; Association of Women Attorneys. ***LANGUAGES:*** French. ***PRACTICE AREAS:*** Business Law; Business Torts; Business Transactions; Buying and Selling of Businesses; Antitrust and Trade Regulation; Antitrust; Deceptive Trade Practices; Contracts; International Commercial Contracts; International Contracts; Energy; Energy Contracts; International Energy Law; International Law; Foreign Corrupt Practices Act.

MILLER, KEFFER & BULLOCK, PC

222 SOUTH KENOSHA AVENUE
TULSA, OKLAHOMA 74120
Telephone: 918-743-4460
Fax: 918-743-6689

Dallas, Texas Office: Miller, Keffer & Pedigo, P.C., 8401 North Central Expressway, Suite 630, 75225. Telephone: 214-696-2050. Fax: 214-696-2482.

Environmental, Oilfield Pollution, Expert Witness Support.

(This Listing Continued)

MILLER, KEFFER & BULLOCK, PC, Tulsa—Continued

J. RANDALL MILLER, born Springfield, Missouri, May 21, 1951; admitted to bar, 1977, Oklahoma. *Education:* University of Tulsa (B.S., 1974; J.D., 1977). Member, American Inns of Court. *Member:* Tulsa County, Oklahoma, Federal and American Bar Associations. ***PRACTICE AREAS:*** Environmental. ***Email:*** rmiller@mkblaw.net

LOUIS W. BULLOCK, born Selma, Alabama, September 15, 1948; admitted to bar, 1975, Oklahoma, U.S. District Court, Northern District of Oklahoma and U.S. Court of Appeals, Tenth Circuit; 1976, U.S. Supreme Court. *Education:* Oklahoma State University (B.S., 1971); University of Oklahoma (J.D., 1975). *Member:* Oklahoma Bar Association; Oklahoma Trial Lawyers Association; The Association of Trial Lawyers of America. ***PRACTICE AREAS:*** Federal Practice; Environmental Law; Water Quality. ***Email:*** lbullock@mkblaw.net

---

DAVID P. PAGE, born Fresno, California, December 22, 1954; admitted to bar, 1981, Oklahoma; U.S. District Court, Northern, Eastern and Western Districts of Oklahoma; U.S. Court of Appeals, Tenth Circuit. *Education:* San Jose State University (B.A., 1978); University of Tulsa (J.D., with honors, 1981). Member, Order of the Curule Chair. Contributing Author and Co-Editor, Oklahoma Bar Association Environmental Law Handbook. *Member:* Tulsa County, Oklahoma and American Bar Associations; Hudson-Hall-Wheaton Chapter (Master); American Inns of Court. ***PRACTICE AREAS:*** Environmental Litigation; Environmental Regulation; Civil Litigation; Employment Litigation. ***Email:*** dpage@mkblaw.net

SUSAN E. MAJOR, born San Antonio, Texas; admitted to bar, 1992, Oklahoma. *Education:* Oklahoma State University (B.S., Medical Technology, 1980); University of Tulsa (J.D., 1992). General Counsel for Newspaper Printing Corporation: World Publishing Company. *Member:* Oklahoma Bar Association. ***Email:*** smajor@mkblaw.net

ROBERT BLAKEMORE, born Tulsa, Oklahoma, January 4, 1973; admitted to bar, 2000, Oklahoma. *Education:* University of Oklahoma (B.A., 1997; J.D., 2000). Phi Delta Phi. *Member:* Oklahoma and American Bar Associations. ***Email:*** bblakemore@mkblaw.net

(For complete biographical data on all personnel, see Professional Biographies at Dallas, Texas)

STANLEY D. MONROE & ASSOCIATES

Established in 1995

BANK OF AMERICA CENTER, SUITE 2112
15 W. 6TH STREET
TULSA, OKLAHOMA 74119
Telephone: 918-592-1144
Fax: 918-592-1149
Email: sdmonroe@swbell.net
Email: stanley.monroe@monroe-associates.com
URL: http://www.monroe-associates.com

General Trial Practice in State and Federal Courts, Criminal Appellant Practice-10th Circuit; Criminal Law, Family Law, Juvenile Law, Personal Injury, Medical Malpractice.

FIRM PROFILE: Stanley D. Monroe & Associates is listed in the Bar Register of Preeminent Lawyers under Criminal Law.

STANLEY D. MONROE, born Jackson, Mississippi, April 9, 1953; admitted to bar, 1978, Oklahoma; 1979, U.S. District Court, Northern District of Oklahoma; 1981, U.S. Court of Appeals, Tenth Circuit; 1987, U.S. District Court, Eastern District of Oklahoma. *Education:* University of Oklahoma (B.A., 1975); University of Tulsa (J.D., with honors, 1978). Tulsa County Public Defender, 1977-1979. Federal Public Defender/Criminal Justice Panel-Northern District of Oklahoma. *Member:* Tulsa County and Oklahoma Bar Associations; Oklahoma Trial Lawyers Association; Oklahoma Criminal Defense Lawyers Association; National Association of Criminal Defense Lawyers; Tulsa Criminal Defense Lawyers Association (President, 1997). ***PRACTICE AREAS:*** Defense of Federal and State Criminal Cases; Appellate Practice; Traffic Violations; Driving While Intoxicated; Drug Crimes; White Collar Crime; Sex Crimes; Homicide; Plaintiffs Personal Injury; Automobile Accidents and Injuries; Motorcycle Accidents; Wrongful Death; Family Law; Divorce; Child Custody; Child Support; Medical Malpractice.

ASSOCIATE

TREVOR L. REYNOLDS, born Phoenix, Arizona, October 18, 1971; admitted to bar, 1999, Iowa; U.S. District Court, Northern and Southern Districts of Iowa; 2002, Oklahoma; U.S. District Court, Western and Northern Districts of Oklahoma and U.S. Court of Appeals, 10th Circuit. *Education:* University of Texas, El Paso (B.A., 1996); Drake University (J.D., 1999). Delta Theta Phi. Member, Howard Fellowship for Indigent Criminal Defense. *Member:* Iowa and Oklahoma Bar Associations. ***PRACTICE AREAS:*** Civil Litigation; Criminal Defense; Family Law. ***Email:*** trevorreynolds@sbcglobal.net

---

MORREL, WEST, SAFFA, CRAIGE & HICKS, INC.

Established in 1974

3501 SOUTH YALE AVENUE
TULSA, OKLAHOMA 74135-8014
Telephone: 918-664-0800
Fax: 918-663-1383
URL: http://www.law-office.com

General Civil, Criminal and Trial Practice in all State and Federal Courts. Taxation, Personal Injury, Administrative, Real Estate, Commercial, Corporate, Estate Planning, Pension and Profit Sharing, Bankruptcy, Corporate Reorganization, Oil and Gas, Family and Probate Law.

(This Listing Continued)

REECE B. MORREL, born Macomb, Oklahoma, March 20, 1940; admitted to bar, 1966, Oklahoma, 1972, U.S. Tax Court. *Education:* Central State University (B.S., 1961); Tulsa University (J.D., 1966). Delta Theta Phi (Treasurer, 1964-1966). Internal Revenue Agent, Internal Revenue Service, 1961-1966. Trust Officer, Bank of Oklahoma, N.A., 1966-1968. *Member:* Tulsa County (Member, Unlawful Practice of Law Committee, 1975), Oklahoma and American (Member: Taxation Section; Real Estate Committee) Bar Associations. ***PRACTICE AREAS:*** Taxation; Corporate Law; Estate Planning; Business Law. ***Email:*** reece@law-office.com

BARRY G. WEST, born Tulsa, Oklahoma, May 23, 1946; admitted to bar, 1974, Oklahoma, U.S. District Court, Northern and Eastern Districts of Oklahoma and U.S. Tax Court; 1979, U.S. Court of Appeals, Tenth Circuit; 1983, U.S. Court of Federal Claims and U.S. Supreme Court. *Education:* Oklahoma State University (B.S., 1969); University of Tulsa (J.D., 1973). Beta Alpha Psi; Delta Theta Phi (Secretary-Treasurer, 1971-1973). Certified Public Accountant, Oklahoma, 1975. Contributing Author: "Oklahoma Probate: Beyond the Basics," National Business Institute, 2002; "Support Custody Jurisdiction and Enforcement," Oklahoma Bar Association, Continuing Legal Education, 1998. *Member:* Tulsa County, Oklahoma and American (Member, Taxation Section) Bar Associations. ***PRACTICE AREAS:*** Probate; Taxation; Estate Planning; Real Estate; Business Law. ***Email:*** barry@law-office.com

RONALD J. SAFFA, born Tulsa, Oklahoma, July 14, 1948; admitted to bar, 1982, Oklahoma; 1983, U.S. District Court, Northern and Eastern Districts of Oklahoma, U.S. Court of Appeals, Tenth and Federal Circuits, U.S. Tax Court and U.S. Court of Federal Claims; 1985, U.S. Supreme Court. *Education:* Oklahoma State University (B.S., 1971; M.S., 1972); University of Tulsa (J.D., 1981). Phi Kappa Phi; Beta Alpha Psi. Editor, Research Institute of America. Certified Public Accountant, Oklahoma, 1974. Author: "Oklahoma Income Taxes", Research Institute of America, 1992. Lecturer: "Representing Small Businesses Before the Internal Revenue Service," 1997; "Offers and Settlements With Tax Authorities," Tulsa Chapter, Oklahoma Society of Certified Public Accountants, 2002. Certified Public Accountant, Oklahoma, 1974; "Representation of Clients During IRS Audits and Collections," Oklahoma Society of CP Certified Public Accountants, 2004. Director and Treasurer: Board of Directors, Morton Comprehensive Health Service, Inc.; Internal Revenue Service, 1974-1983. *Member:* Tulsa County, Oklahoma (Member, Committee on Corporate Law, 1983) and American Bar Associations. ***PRACTICE AREAS:*** Taxation; Estate Planning; Business Law; Corporate Law. ***Email:*** ron@law-office.com

MARK A. CRAIGE, born Durant, Oklahoma, June 8, 1957; admitted to bar, 1982, Oklahoma; U.S. Court of Appeals, Tenth Circuit; U.S. District Court, Northern and Eastern Districts of Oklahoma, U.S. District Court Eastern District of Texas and U.S. District Court Eastern and Western Districts of Arkansas and Eastern District of Wisconsin. *Education:* Southeastern Oklahoma State University (B.S., cum laude, 1979); University of Tulsa (J.D., 1981). Assistant District Attorney, Bryan county, 1983. Editor, "Banca Rotta," Oklahoma Bar Association Bankruptcy Section Newsletter, 1989-1990. Professional Awards: Earl Sneed Award for Outstanding contribution to continuing legal education, Oklahoma Bar Association, 1998; Meritorious Service Award, American Bankruptcy Institute, 1995; Distinguished Service Award, Tulsa County Bar Association, 1987. Lectures: "Recent Development in Bankruptcy Tax Issues," Law Education Institute, Vail, Colo., 2000; "Creditor's Rights in Bankruptcy," Lorman Business Institute, 2000; "Basic Bankruptcy for Creditors," National Business Institute, 2000; "Recent Development in Bankruptcy Tax Issues," Law Education Institute, Vail, Colo., 2001; "Creditor's Rights in Bankruptcy," Lorman Business Institute, 2001; "Basic Bankruptcy for Creditors," National Business Institute, 2001; "Creditor's Rights in Bankruptcy," Lorman Business Institute, 2002; "Basic Bankruptcy for Creditors," National Business Institute, 2002; "Current Development in Article 9," National Business Institute, 2003; Squeezing Blood from a Turnip, Bankruptcy Issues," Oklahoma Bar Association, 2003; Landlord/Tennant Issues in Bankruptcy," Oklahoma Bar Association, 2004; "Creditor Issues in Chapter 13 Bankruptcy," Oklahoma Bar Association, 2005; "Impact of Bankruptcy Reform and Consumer Protection Act on Creditor's Rights in Consumer Cases under Chapter 7 and 13," Oklahoma Credit Union League, 2005. Author: "The New Family Farms Bankruptcy Act," 58 Oklahoma Bar Journal 1505; "Pension Plans Are Not Property of Bankruptcy Estate," 63 Oklahoma Bar Journal 3341. Contributing Author, "Small Business Bankruptcy Reorganizations," Wylie Publishing Company, 1994. Lecturer: "Representation of Debtors in Bankruptcy," Oklahoma Bar Association Continuing Legal Education, 1990; "Representation of Debtors Criminal Considerations," Oklahoma Bar Association Continuing Legal Education, 1990; "Criminal Considerations in Bankruptcy," Oklahoma Bar Association, Continuing Legal Education, 1990; "Financing a Debtor in Chapter 12 including Use, Sale or Lease of Collateral," West Texas Bankruptcy Bar Association, Texas Tech University School of Law, 1991; "Basic Chapter 7," Oklahoma Bar Association Continuing Legal Education, 1991; "Chapter 12 Farm Reorganization," Farm Crisis Task Force, 1991; "Representation of Creditors in Bankruptcy," Oklahoma Bar Association, Continuing Legal Education, 1992; "Recent Developments in Bankruptcy," Oklahoma City University, 1992, 1993, 1994; "Representing Debtors in Consumers Bankruptcy," Oklahoma Bar Association, Continuing Legal Education, 1993; "Effect of Bankruptcy on Receiverships" and "Partnership Bankruptcy Issues," National Business Institute, 1994; "Small Business Chapter 11," University of Tulsa, 1994; "Recent Developments in Bankruptcy," Annual Bankruptcy Retreat, Bankruptcy and Reorganization Section, Oklahoma Bar Association; "The Impact of the 1994 Bankruptcy Reform Act," Oklahoma City University, 1995; "Cash Collateral and Adequate Protection", Oklahoma City University, 1995; "Discharge Issues under §523 &§727, Oklahoma City University, 1995; "The 1994 Bankruptcy Reform Act", Stetson University Law School, Continuing Legal Education, Tampa Florida; "Which Chapter for Small Business, Chapter 11 or Chapter 13?", Law Education Institute, Vail Colorado, 1997; "Creditors Rights in Bankruptcy". Lorman Business Institute, 1997; "Small Business Reorganizations", University of Arkansas, Continuing Legal Education, 1997; "Family Law Issues in Bankruptcy", National Business Institute, 1997; "Which Chapter for Small Business, Chapter 11 or Chapter 13?", Tulsa County Bar Association (Program Chair) 1997; "Recent Development in Bankruptcy Tax Issues", Law Education Institute, Vail Colorado, 1998; "Creditor's Rights in Bankruptcy", Lorman Business Institute, 1998; "Agricultural Bankruptcy Issues", American Bankruptcy Institute's Rocky Mountain Bankruptcy Conference, 1998; "Sanctions and Contempt Powers in Bankruptcy", Americans Bankruptcy Institute's Annual Meeting, 1998; "Creditor's Rights in Bankruptcy", National Business Institute, 1998; "Recent Development in Bankruptcy Tax Issues", Law Education Institute, Vail, Colorado, 1999;

(This Listing Continued)

"Creditor's Rights in Bankruptcy". Lorman Business Institute, 1999; "Small Business Reorganizations", 5th Annual Mid-South Bankruptcy Conference University of Arkansas et al., Memphis, Tennessee, 1999. *Member:* Tulsa County and Oklahoma (Board, 1985-1996; Chairman, 1986-1987 Bankruptcy and Reorganization Section; Public Information Committee, 1986-1988) Bar Associations; Oklahoma Trial Lawyers Association (Membership Committee, Chairman, 1994-1998; National Membership Network Sub-Committee, Chairman, 1992-1993); American Bankruptcy Institute (Rules Committee, Technology Sub-Committee, 1992-1993); American Board of Certification (Chairman, 2001; President, 2000; President-Elect, 1999; Vice-President, 1996-1998; Board of Directors, 1994-2002, Marketing Committee Chair, 1995-1997; Standard Committee, 1994-1998). Fellow, American College of Bankruptcy (Class of 2000). (Certified in Business Bankruptcy Law by the American Board of Certification). ***REPORTED CASES:*** In re Merrill, 246 B.R. 906 (Bankr.N.D.Okla. 2000); In re Tirey Distributing Co., 242 B.R. 717 (Bankr. E.D.Okla. 1999); Smolen v. Hatley, 227B.R. 757 (10th Cir. BAP, 1998), Diviney v. NationsBank, 225S B.R. 762 (10th Cir. BAP, 1998), In re Hermann 221 B.R. (Bankr. N.D. Okla. 1998), In Re Salina Speedway, Inc. 210 B.R. 851 (10th Cir. BAP 1997), Diviney v. NationsBank, 211 B.R. 951 (Bankr. N.D. Okla, 1997), Osborn v. Durant Bank & Trust Co. (In re Osborn), 24 F.3d 1199 (10th Cir., 1994), Rick v. United States of America, ex rel Internal Revenue Service, 97 B.R. 692 (Bankr. N.D. Okla. 1996), aff'd slip. op. 96-CV-007755K, (N.D. Okla. 1997), In re Osborn, 176 B.R. 217 (Bankr. E.D. Okla, 1994), In re Osborn 176 B.R. 941 (Bankr. E.D. Okla., 1994), In re Bulter, 139 B.R. 258 (Bankr. E.D. Okla., 1992), In re Seviski 161 B.R. (Bankr. N.D. Okla., 1993), In re Manley, 135 B.R. 137 Bankr. N.D. Okla., 1992), Marx v. Reeds 145 B.R. 703 (Bankr. N.D. Okla., 1992), In re Luker 1990 LEXIS 1539 (Bankr. N.D. Okla., 1990), In re Wood Comm fund 1, Inc., 116 B.R. 817 (Bankr. ND. Okla., 1990), In re Threet, 118 B.R. 805 (Bankr. N.D. Okla., 1990), In re Dodd, 97 B.R. 74 (Bankr. N.D. Okla., 1989), In re Wilford, 105 B.R. 992 (Bankr. N.D. Okla., 1989), In re Garrison, 108 B.R. 760 (Bankr. N.D. Okla., 1989); In re Elrs Loss Mitigation, LLC, 325 B.R. 604 (Bankr.N.D.Oklahoma., 2005); Sheehan Pipe Line Const. Co. v. Laney Directional Drilling Co., 228 F.Supp.2d 1271, (N.D.Okla., 2002); US v. Kroblin, 2004 WL 1747467, 94 A.F.T.R.2d 2004-5180, 2004-2USTCP 50,345 (N.D.Okla., 2004); In re Wallace, 316 B.R. 743 (10th Cir.BAP 2004); In re Wallace, 314 B.R. 904 (10th Cir.BAP 2004); In re Tiger Petroldeum Co. (Bankr. N.D.Okla. 2004); In re Wallace, 311 B.R. 601 (Bankr. N.D.Okla., 2004). ***PRACTICE AREAS:*** Bankruptcy; Debtor and Creditor. ***Email:*** mark@law-office.com

JAMES R. HICKS, born Blackwell, Oklahoma, April 30, 1960; admitted to bar, 1985, Oklahoma; 1989, U.S. Supreme Court. *Education:* University of Oklahoma (B.B.A., 1982); University of Tulsa (J.D., 1985). President: Tulsa County Law Library Board of Trustees, 1992; Legal Services of Eastern Oklahoma, 1997-2000. *Member:* Tulsa County (Chairman, Young Lawyers Committee), Oklahoma (Member, Board of Governors, 1994; Chairperson, Young Lawyers Division, 1994) and American (Director, 1995-1996; Chairperson, Young Lawyers Division, Awards of Achievement, 1995) Bar Associations; Oklahoma Trial Lawyers Association; The Association of Trial Lawyers of America. ***PRACTICE AREAS:*** Civil Litigation; Bankruptcy. ***Email:*** jim@law-office.com

REECE B. MORREL, JR., born Bartlesville, Oklahoma, March 2, 1962; admitted to bar, 1991, Oklahoma, U.S. District Court, Northern, Eastern and Western Districts of Oklahoma, U.S. Court of Appeals, Tenth and Federal Circuits and U.S. Tax Court. *Education:* Oklahoma State University (B.S.B.A., 1983); University of Tulsa (M.B.A., 1986; J.D., 1991). Phi Alpha Delta; Beta Alpha Psi. Author: "Recent Developments in Consumer Bankruptcy," Oklahoma City University College of Law Continuing Legal Education Seminar, 1993; "The 'Virtual' Bankruptcy Office-Part I," American Bankruptcy Institute Journal, Vol. XII No. 1, February 1994; "The 'Virtual' Bankruptcy Office" Part II (Reach Out and Touch Someone)," American Bankruptcy Institute Journal, Vol. XIII No. 4, May 1994; "The IRS's Knockout Punch: The 100 Percent Penalty For Failure To Collect Or Pay Over Tax," The Oklahoma Bar Journal, Vol. 65-No. 37, September 30, 1994. Lecturer: "Law Office Technology," Oklahoma Bar Association Continuing Legal Education, 1994. Served in Governor's Office as Director of Planning and Management Analysis, October 1992-August 1993. *Member:* Tulsa County, Oklahoma and American Bar Associations; Oklahoma Society of Certified Public Accountants; American Institute of Certified Public Accountants; American Bankruptcy Institute. ***PRACTICE AREAS:*** Taxation; Estate Planning; Bankruptcy; Business Law. ***Email:*** reecejr@law-office.com

OF COUNSEL

PAUL R. HODGSON, born Goodrich, Kansas, August 25, 1924; admitted to bar, 1963, Oklahoma; 1964, U.S. District Court, Northern District of Oklahoma; U.S. Tax Court; 1968, U.S. District Court, Western District of Oklahoma; 1974, U.S. Supreme Court. *Education:* University of Kansas (B.S., 1948); University of Tulsa (J.D., 1963). Certified Public Accountant, Oklahoma, 1950. Author: "Who is the Manufacturer for Excise Tax Purposes," Prentice Hall Tax Ideas, 1963; "How to Determine Earnings and Profits Distributions under Section 312 (of the Internal Revenue Code)," Prentice Hall Tax Ideas and Prentice Hall Oil and Gas Taxes, 1965. Member, State of Oklahoma Governor's Advisory Committee on Taxation. *Member:* Tulsa County, Oklahoma and American Bar Associations; Oklahoma Society of Certified Public Accountants. [USAF, 1943-1946]. ***PRACTICE AREAS:*** Estate Planning; Taxation.

MAC D. FINLAYSON, born Muskogee, Oklahoma, March 26, 1951; admitted to bar, 1976, Oklahoma, U.S. District Court, Eastern, Northern and Western Districts of Oklahoma and U.S. Court of Appeals, Tenth Circuit; 1979, U.S. District Court, Eastern and Western Districts of Arkansas and U.S. Supreme Court. *Education:* Drury College (B.A., cum laude, 1973); University of Tulsa (J.D., 1976). Phi Delta Phi. *Member:* Tulsa County (Member, Bankruptcy and Reorganization Section, 1983—), Oklahoma (Member: Bankruptcy and Reorganization Section, 1983—; Disaster Response and Relief Committee, 1989—; Chair, 1991-1994) and American (Member, Business Section, 1976—) Bar Associations; American Bankruptcy Institute; Commercial Law League of America; Association of Certified Fraud Examiners (Certified Fraud Examiner); American Board of Certification (Director, 2004—). (Certified in Consumer Bankruptcy Law, Business Bankruptcy Law and Creditors' Rights Law by the American Board of Certification). ***PRACTICE AREAS:*** Bankruptcy; Collections; Creditors' Rights; Commercial Law. ***Email:*** mac.finlayson@finlaysonlaw.com

A list of Representative Clients furnished upon request.

MOYERS, MARTIN, SANTEE, IMEL & TETRICK, L.L.P.

Established in 1910

Formerly Moyers, Martin, Conway, Santee & Imel

1100 MID-CONTINENT TOWER
401 SOUTH BOSTON AVENUE
TULSA, OKLAHOMA 74103
Telephone: 918-582-5281
Fax: 918-585-8318
Email: info@moyersmartin.com
URL: http://www.moyersmartin.com

Bixby, Oklahoma Office: 113 West Dawes, Suite 100, 74408. Telephone: 918-366-3935. Fax: 918-366-3936.

Civil Practice, Banks and Banking, Bankruptcy, Business Law, Commercial Law, Construction Law, Corporate Law, Education Law, Energy, Federal Practice, Insurance, Labor and Employment, Leases and Leasing, Litigation, Mergers, Acquisitions and Divestitures, Natural Resources, Personal Injury, Probate, Real Estate, Taxation, Trusts and Estates.

FIRM PROFILE: Moyers, Martin, Santee, Imel & Tetrick, L.L.P. has been engaged in the general civil practice of law since 1910 and is one of the oldest firms in Oklahoma. The firm has an extensive history of providing clients with exceptional legal representation in a personal, timely and cost efficient manner.

MEMBERS OF FIRM

VILLARD MARTIN (1889-1965)

GARRETT LOGAN (1901-1975)

DONALD P. MOYERS (1907-1995)

VILLARD MARTIN, JR. (1918-2002)

JACK H. SANTEE, born Skiatook, Oklahoma, January 11, 1931; admitted to bar, 1956, Oklahoma. *Education:* University of Oklahoma (B.S., 1953; LL.B., 1956). Phi Alpha Delta. Member, Board of Regents, University of Oklahoma, 1968-1975. *Member:* Tulsa County (Vice President, 1968), Oklahoma and American Bar Associations. ***PRACTICE AREAS:*** Corporate Law; Contracts; Business Litigation; Trusts and Estates; Non Profit and Charitable Organizations. ***Email:*** santee@moyersmartin.com

JOHN M. IMEL, born Cushing, Oklahoma, August 4, 1932; admitted to bar, 1959, Oklahoma. *Education:* University of Oklahoma (B.S. 1954; J.D., 1959). Municipal Judge, City of Tulsa, 1960-1961. United States Attorney, Northern District of Oklahoma, 1961-1967. Member, Board of Regents, University of Oklahoma, 1981-1988; Chairman, 1987-1988. Listed in: Best Lawyers in America. *Member:* Tulsa County, Oklahoma and American Bar Associations. Master, American Inns of Court. Fellow: American College of Trial Lawyers; American Bar Foundation. [Captain, USNR, retired]. ***PRACTICE AREAS:*** Civil Litigation; Complex Litigation; Defense Litigation; Federal Litigation; Business Litigation. ***Email:*** imel@moyersmartin.com

STEVEN A. STECHER, born Woodward, Oklahoma, March 16, 1948; admitted to bar, 1973, Oklahoma. *Education:* University of Oklahoma (B.B.A., 1970); University of Texas (J.D., 1973). Phi Delta Phi. *Member:* Tulsa County and Oklahoma Bar Associations. ***PRACTICE AREAS:*** Commercial Real Estate; Mortgages; Real Estate; Real Estate Finance; Real Estate Title. ***Email:*** stecher@moyersmartin.com

JAMES H. FERRIS, born Tulsa, Oklahoma, August 22, 1949; admitted to bar, 1975, Oklahoma. *Education:* University of Oklahoma (B.A., 1972); University of Tulsa (J.D., 1974). Phi Alpha Delta. Member, Tulsa Law Journal, 1973-1974. *Member:* Tulsa County, Oklahoma and American Bar Associations. ***PRACTICE AREAS:*** Business Law; Commercial Law; Secured Lending; Trusts and Estates. ***Email:*** ferris@moyersmartin.com

PATRICK D. O'CONNOR, born Iowa City, Iowa, August 25, 1952; admitted to bar, 1977, Oklahoma. *Education:* University of Iowa (B.G.S., 1974); University of Tulsa (J.D., 1977). Phi Delta Phi. *Member:* Tulsa County (President, 2004-2005; Vice President, 1990, 2003-2004; Treasurer, 2001-2002; Adjunct Settlement Judge), Oklahoma and Federal (Chairman, Tulsa County Bankruptcy Section, 2001-2004) Bar Associations. ***PRACTICE AREAS:*** Bankruptcy Law; Business Litigation; Business Transactions; Insurance Defense; Litigation. ***Email:*** pdo@moyersmartin.com

JOHN E. ROONEY, JR., born Tulsa, Oklahoma, July 23, 1956; admitted to bar, 1981, Oklahoma. *Education:* University of Notre Dame (B.A., with honors, 1978); Georgetown University (J.D., cum laude, 1981). *Member:* Tulsa County and Oklahoma Bar Associations. ***PRACTICE AREAS:*** Construction Law; Contract Litigation; Landlord and Tenant Law; Leases and Leasing; Noncompetition and Non-Solicitation Agreements. ***Email:*** rooney@moyersmartin.com

TERRY M. KOLLMORGEN, born Downers Grove, Illinois, July 24, 1964; admitted to bar, 1989, Oklahoma. *Education:* University of Oklahoma (B.B.A., with honors, 1986; J.D., with honors, 1989). Phi Delta Phi. Recipient, American Jurisprudence Award. Member, American Inns of Court. *Member:* Tulsa County, Oklahoma, Federal and American Bar Associations. ***PRACTICE AREAS:*** Employment Discrimination; Labor and Employment; Sexual Discrimination; Wrongful Termination Defense; Education Law. ***Email:*** tmk@moyersmartin.com

JAMES E. MAUPIN, born North Kansas City, Missouri, November 27, 1966; admitted to bar, 1992, Oklahoma. *Education:* Northeastern Oklahoma State University (B.A., summa cum laude, 1989); University of Tulsa (J.D., with honors, 1992). Phi Delta Phi; Order of Curule Chair. Recipient, American Jurisprudence Award. Law Clerk to the Honorable Thomas R. Brett, N.D. Oklahoma, 1992-1994. *Member:* Tulsa County and Oklahoma Bar Associations. ***PRACTICE AREAS:*** Appellate Practice; Commercial Litigation; Insurance; Insurance Bad Faith; Litigation. ***Email:*** maupin@moyersmartin.com

(This Listing Continued)

MOYERS, MARTIN, SANTEE, IMEL & TETRICK, L.L.P., Tulsa—Continued

MICHAEL E. ESMOND, born Tulsa, Oklahoma, May 29, 1972; admitted to bar, 2005, Oklahoma. *Education:* University of Oklahoma (B.B.A., 1994); Gonzaga University (M.B.A., 2000); University of Tulsa (J.D., with highest honor, 2004). Phi Delta Phi. Chair, Order of the Curie; American Inns of Court. Managing Editor, Tulsa Law Review, 2003-2004. Recipient: American Bankruptcy Institute Medal of Excellence; Sellers & Bryant Oil and Gas Award. *Member:* Oklahoma Bar Association. [Captain, U.S. Air Force, 1995-2000]. ***PRACTICE AREAS:*** Litigation. ***Email:*** esmond@moyersmartin.com

OF COUNSEL

CHARLES B. TETRICK, born Tulsa, Oklahoma, July 2, 1933; admitted to bar, 1965, Oklahoma. *Education:* University of Oklahoma (B.B.A., 1955); University of Tulsa (J.D., 1965); Washington University (LL.M., Taxation, 1971). Phi Delta Phi. Attorney, Office of the Chief Counsel, Internal Revenue Service, 1966-1971. Listed in: Best Lawyers in America. *Member:* Tulsa County, Oklahoma and American Bar Associations. ***PRACTICE AREAS:*** Decedents Estates; Estate Planning; Probate; Taxation. ***Email:*** tetrick@moyersmartin.com

LARRY E. EVANS, born Moline, Illinois, October 28, 1948; admitted to bar, 1975, Oklahoma. *Education:* University of Illinois (B.A., 1970); University of Tulsa (J.D., 1975). Phi Delta Phi. Member, Order of the Curule Chair. Associate Editor, University of Tulsa Law Journal, 1974-1975. *Member:* Tulsa County and Oklahoma Bar Associations. ***PRACTICE AREAS:*** Energy; Minerals; Natural Resources; Oil and Gas Contracts; Oil and Gas Title Examination.

REPRESENTATIVE CLIENTS: Allied Helicopter Services, Inc.; American Central Gas Companies; Anchor Gasoline Corp.; Apache Corp.; Atlas General Contractors; Bordens Dairy; Boswell Supply Co.; Chase Manhattan; Citizens Security Bank & Trust Co., Bixby; Cox Radio, Inc.; Deans Food, Inc.; Electrolux Home Products; Enercon Services, Inc.; Golden Eagle Communications, Inc.; Greater Tulsa Association of Realtors; H & M Pipe Beveling Machine Co., Inc.; Holland Hall School; The J.E. and L.E. Mabee Foundation, Inc.; Katharyn S. Cornell Trust; Lawson Petroleum Company; Lone Star Technologies, Inc.; May's Drug Store's, Inc.; Miratech Corporation; Monte Cassino School; Multiple Listing Service of Tulsa Realtors, Inc.; Nalco Chemical Co.; Natcom, Inc.; Oral Roberts University; Oxley Petroleum; Southern Food Group; Torchmark Corp.; Tower Realty Group, Inc.; United American Ins. Co.; University Broadcasting, Inc.; University Village, Inc.; Williams Energy Marketing & Trading Co.; WillTel.

MYSOCK & CHEVAILLIER, L.L.P.

Established in 1985

SUITE 700, 2021 SOUTH LEWIS
TULSA, OKLAHOMA 74104
Telephone: 918-747-6099
Telecopier: 918-747-6299

Practice includes Taxation, Tax Audits, Like Kind Exchanges, General Business Law, Estate Planning, Wills and Probate, Trusts and Estates, Employee Benefits, Asset Protection, Business Transactions, NASD Arbitration, Sports Law.

EDWARD J. MYSOCK, JR., born Akron, Ohio, September 4, 1947; admitted to bar, 1977, Oklahoma and U.S. District Court, Northern District of Oklahoma; 1979, U.S. Tax Court. *Education:* University of Pennsylvania (B.S., 1969); University of Tulsa (J.D., 1976). Member, University of Tulsa Law Journal, 1975-1976. *Member:* Oklahoma Bar Association; The Missouri Bar. [1st Lt., U.S. Marine Corps, 1969-1973]. ***PRACTICE AREAS:*** Corporate Law; Business Transactions; Estate Planning Law; Taxation Law. ***Email:*** ejm@mychev.com

WILLIAM C. CHEVAILLIER, JR., born Pine Bluff, Arkansas, December 27, 1955; admitted to bar, 1982, Oklahoma; 1988, U.S. Tax Court; 1989, U.S. District Court, Northern, Eastern and Western Districts of Oklahoma. *Education:* University of Arkansas (B.S.B.A., 1978; J.D., 1981). Phi Alpha Delta. Certified Public Accountant, 1985, Oklahoma. *Member:* Tulsa County (Member, Committee on Taxation) and Oklahoma Bar Associations; Oklahoma Society of Certified Public Accountants. ***PRACTICE AREAS:*** Taxation Law; Business Transactions; Estate Planning. ***Email:*** wcc@mychev.com

STEPHEN R. BOLDEN, born Tulsa, Oklahoma, May 30, 1966; admitted to bar, 1991, Arkansas; 1994, Oklahoma. *Education:* Hendrix College (B.A., 1988); University of Arkansas at Fayetteville (J.D., 1990); University of San Diego (LL.M., cum laude, 1992). Certified Public Accountant. *Member:* Arkansas, Oklahoma and American (Member, Tax Section) Bar Associations. ***PRACTICE AREAS:*** Taxation; Corporate Finance; Employee Benefits; Business Transactions. ***Email:*** srb@mychev.com

REPRESENTATIVE CLIENTS: Chimi's, Inc.; QuikTrip Corporation; Mc Graw Davisson Stewart, Inc.; Refrigerated Delivery Services, Inc.; Leaders Life Insurance Co.; Utica Physicians' Association, Ltd.; Carrera Gas Company, L.L.C.; ADDvantage Technology Group, Inc.; Advanced Plastics, Inc.; Consolidated Benefits Resources, L.L.C.; Tulsa Development Authority; Globestar International, Inc.; Advanced Companies; Chromium Plating Co.; Jenkin Lloyd Jones Foundation; Skinny Tours, LLC; The Great Divide, LLC; Dixon Real Estate Company; Cazcat.com, Inc.; Indian Territory Illuminating Gas Co., L.L.C.; Performance Petroleum, Inc.; U.S. Gas Gathering, Inc.; Tulsa Spine Hospital, L.L.C.; Omni Packaging Corp.; Qual-Tron Corp; Clifford Power Systems; K&E Field Services, Inc.; Natura Vineyards & Winery, L.L.C.; Stonecliff Vineyards & Winery, L.L.C.; Financial Advisory Service, Inc.

WILLIAM D. NAY

4444 EAST 66TH STREET
TULSA, OKLAHOMA 74136-4206
Telephone: 918-492-8481
Email: william.nay@lawoklahoma.com

Corporate, Business, Commercial, Wills and Probate, Trusts and Estate.

WILLIAM D. NAY, born Oklahoma City, Oklahoma, January 6, 1943; admitted to bar, 1971, Oklahoma. *Education:* Central State University and Oklahoma State University (B.S., 1965); University of Tulsa (J.D., with honors, 1970). Phi Delta Phi. Member, Order of the Curule. Editor-in-Chief, Tulsa Law Journal, 1970. *Member:* Tulsa County (Chairman, Corporate Counsel Section, 1993-1994 and 1996-1997), Oklahoma and American Bar Associations. ***PRACTICE AREAS:*** Commercial Law; Environmental Law; Real Estate Law; Business Law; Corporate; Probate.

K. S. NELSON LAW FIRM, P.L.L.C

320 SOUTH BOSTON AVENUE, SUITE 1030
TULSA, OKLAHOMA 74103
Telephone: 918-230-2708; Toll Free: 866-414-0529
Fax: 866-414-0529

Tulsa Office: 320 South Boston Avenue, Suite 1030, 74103.

Family Law.

KATHY SHERWOOD NELSON, born Cedar Rapids, Iowa, April 4, 1969; admitted to bar, 2003, Oklahoma. *Education:* University of Tulsa (B.A., 1998); University of Tulsa College of Law (J.D., 2001). *Member:* Tulsa County (Member, Sections on: Family Law, Probate, Lawyer Referral) and Oklahoma Bar Associations. ***PRACTICE AREAS:*** Family Law.

NEWTON, O'CONNOR, TURNER & KETCHUM

A PROFESSIONAL CORPORATION

Established in 1983

BANK OF AMERICA CENTER
15 WEST 6TH STREET, SUITE 2700
TULSA, OKLAHOMA 74119-5421
Telephone: 918-587-0101
Fax: 918-587-0102
Email: joconnor@newtonoconnor.com
URL: http://www.newtonoconnor.com

Employment counsel and training, Labor and Employment Litigation, Worker's Compensation, Business Law counsel and litigation, Business Formation, Business Development, Commercial Transactions, Business Succession Planning, Banking, Real Estate, Estate Planning, Probate and Adoption.

G. W. (BILL) NEWTON, born Perry, Oklahoma, January 24, 1937; admitted to bar, 1962, Oklahoma; 1964, U.S. District Court, Northern and Western Districts of Oklahoma; 1969, U.S. District Court, Northern District of Oklahoma; 1976, U.S. District Court, Eastern District of Oklahoma. *Education:* University of Oklahoma (B.A., 1959; LL.B., 1962). Phi Alpha Delta. Author and Lecturer: "Deficiency Judgments and Liability of Guarantor," Oklahoma Bar Association Continuing Legal Education Seminar, 1990; "Advanced Real Estate Law in Oklahoma," National Business Institute, 1991 and 1994; "Planning Opportunities with Living Trusts in Oklahoma," National Business Institute, 1994; "Recent Developments in Indian Law," Cleverdon Real Property Round Table Seminar, 2001.. Adjunct Professor, Real Estate, Tulsa University, 1985-1986. Assistant County Attorney, Stephens County, Oklahoma, 1962-1964. President, Stephens County Bar Association, 1963-1964. Assistant District Attorney, Tulsa County, Oklahoma, 1965-1970. Chief Civil Assistant District Attorney, Tulsa, 1967-1970. Sole Practitioner, 1971-1983. *Member:* Tulsa County (Member, Court Operations Committee; Estate and Probate Committee; Professional Responsibility Committee) and Oklahoma (Member: Real Property Section; Title Standards Committee) Bar Associations; Tulsa County Title and Probate Lawyers Association; Tulsa Estate Planning Forum. ***PRACTICE AREAS:*** Real Estate; Business Law; Commercial Transactions; Corporate Law; Nonprofit Corporations; Estate Planning Law; Wills and Trusts; Probate; Construction; Litigation; Constitutional Law; Mineral Law. ***Email:*** bnewton@newtonoconnor.com

JOHN M. O'CONNOR, born Tulsa, Oklahoma, December 5, 1954; admitted to bar, 1980, Oklahoma; 1981, U.S. District Court, Northern and Eastern Districts of Oklahoma; 1996, U.S. Tax Court. *Education:* Oklahoma State University (B.A., 1977); University of Tulsa (J.D., 1980). Delta Theta Phi (Vice-Dean, 1979). International Rotary Foundation Scholar, Friedrich Wilhelms Rheinische Universitat, Bonn, Germany, 1980-1981. President: Student Bar Association, Tulsa University, 1979-1980; President, Board of Directors, Ronald McDonald House, 1988-1990. Member: Oklahoma Dispute Resolution Advisory Board, State of Oklahoma, 1984-1986; Fee Arbitration Committee, Tulsa County, 1985; City of Tulsa, Human Rights Conciliator, 1985-1988; American Inns of Court, Council Oak Chapter, 1995-1997; 1997-2005, Presenter, OBA CLE: Probate; 1997, 2004 Presenter, University of Tulsa CLE: Adoption Litigation; American Academy of Adoption Attorneys, 1993—. Foundation Chairman: Rotary International District 6110, 1996-1997; Oklahoma Adoption Law Reform Committee, 1995-1998. President, Rotary Club of Tulsa, 2003-2004. Officer and Director: Dillon International, Inc., 1994—; OSU Alumni Association, 1994-1996; Tulsa Archives, Inc. 2004—. Commissioner, City of Tulsa Judicial Nominating Commission 2005—.*Member:* Tulsa County (Member, Professional Responsibility Committee, 2003—), Oklahoma (Director, Young Lawyers Division, 1983-1985) and American (Member, Sections on: Litigation; Business Law; Torts and Insurance Practice; Construction Litigation Committee) Bar Associations. ***LANGUAGES:*** German. ***PRACTICE AREAS:*** Business Formation; Business Transactions; Banking Law; Civil Litigation; Construction; Corporate; Commercial; Non-Profit Organizations; Adoption Law. ***Email:*** joconnor@newtonoconnor.com

W. KIRK TURNER, born Jacksonville, Arkansas, September 28, 1964; admitted to bar, 1989, Oklahoma and U.S. District Court, Northern, Eastern and Western Districts of Oklahoma; U.S. District Court for the Eastern and Western Districts of Arkansas; U.S. Court of Appeals, Tenth Circuit; U.S. Tax Court; U.S. Supreme Court. *Education:* Arkansas Tech University (B.S., 1986); University of Arkansas (J.D., 1989). Delta Theta Phi; Blue Key; Society for Human Resource Management (National Employment and Labor Relations Committee); Oklahoma State Council for Human Resource Management (Vice President, Legislative Affairs and General Counsel); Tulsa Area Human Resources Association

(This Listing Continued)

(Past President and General Counsel; Vice President of Legislative Affairs and General Counsel); Tulsa Equal Employment Opportunity Coordinators Association (Past Board Member); Industrial Relations Association; Oklahoma State Chamber of Commerce (Human Resources Committee); American Inns of Court, W. Lee Johnson Chapter, 1991, Council Oaks Chapter, 1995. *Member:* Tulsa County (Member, Labor and Employment Law Section), Oklahoma (Past Chairman, Labor and Employment Law Section) and American (Member, Labor and Employment Law Section). ***PRACTICE AREAS:*** Labor and Employment; Management Employment Law; Employment Litigation; Civil Rights. **Email:** kturner@newtonoconnor.com

DANIEL R. KETCHUM, II, born Elizabethtown, North Carolina, October 5, 1964; admitted to bar, 1993, Georgia and U.S. District Court, Northern District of Georgia; 1998, Oklahoma and U.S. District Court, Northern District of Oklahoma; 2002, U.S. District Court, Western District of Oklahoma. *Education:* Oklahoma State University (B.S., 1986); University of Oklahoma (J.D., with distinction, 1993). Certified Public Accountant, Georgia, 1989. Blue Key; Omicron Delta Kappa; Phi Kappa Phi. Member, Luther Bohanon American Inn of Court XXIII, 1992-1993. Recipient, Academic Achievement Award in Environmental Law. Member: American Indian Law Review, 1992-1993; Board of Advocates. *Member:* Tulsa County (Member, Sections on: Probate and Estate Planning) and Oklahoma (Member, Sections on: Estate Planning; Probate and Trust) Bar Associations; State Bar of Georgia; American Association of Attorney CPAs. ***PRACTICE AREAS:*** Estate Planning; Business Succession Planning; Business Formation; Business Transactions; Business Law; Nonprofit Organizations Law; Wills; Trust Law; Probate. ***Email:*** dketchum@newtonoconnor.com

KEITH A. WILKES, born Petaluma, California, September 5, 1962; admitted to bar, 1995, Oklahoma; U.S. District Court, Northern and Eastern Districts of Oklahoma and U.S. Court of Appeals, Tenth Circuit. *Education:* Oklahoma State University (B.S., 1988); University of Tulsa (J.D., 1995). Phi Delta Phi. Member, Board of Advocates. Staff Member, 1993-1994 and Production Editor, 1994-1995, Tulsa Law Journal. Recipient: Nichols, Wolfe, Nally, Stamper, Fallis & Robertson Award, Employment Discrimination; Ronald M. Brochstein Award, Sports Law; Additional Highest Class Grade: Trial Practice and Evidence Workshop; Oklahoma Bar Association Maurice Merrill Golden Quill Award, 1998. Author: "Teetering on the Brink of Litigation: Today's Perilous Balance Between Federal Employment and Oklahoma's Workers' Compensation Laws," 69 OBJ 3686, 1998. Adjunct Instructor, Human Resources Law, Tulsa Community College, 2001—. Member: Society for Human Resource Management; American Red Cross, Tulsa Area Chapter, Administrative Services Committee, 2001—; Veterans of Foreign Wars. *Member:* Tulsa County, Oklahoma (Chairman, Labor and Employment Law Section, 2004-2005) and American Bar Associations; Tulsa Equal Employment Opportunity Coordinators Association; American Inns of Court, Council Oaks Chapter; Defense Research Institute. [Sergeant, U.S. Army, 1980-1984; Army Commendation Medal, 1983]. ***PRACTICE AREAS:*** Labor and Employment; Management Employment Law; Commercial Litigation; Business Litigation; Civil Litigation. ***Email:*** kwilkes@newtonoconnor.com

---

CHRISTOPHER S. THRUTCHLEY, born Mt. Ayr, Iowa, January 7, 1967; admitted to bar, 1993, Oklahoma; U.S. District Court, Northern, Eastern and Western Districts of Oklahoma; U.S. District Court, Northern District of California; and U.S. Court of Appeals, Ninth and Tenth Circuits. *Education:* Graceland University (B.A., 1989); University of Tulsa (J.D., highest honors, 1993). Order of the Curule Chair. Recipient: American Jurisprudence Award in Property; Highest score, Legal Thought and Labor Law. Editor in Chief, Tulsa Law Review, 1992-1993. Certified Professional in Human Resources. Co-Author: "Conflicts of Interest in Benefits Appeals: Beware of Costly New Risks," SHRM Legal Report (Oct./Nov.2004); "Tenth Circuit Clarifies Types of FMLA Claims," 74 OBJ 1211 (2003); "Supreme Court Removes FMLA Regulatory Landmine: What are the Implications and How Should Employers Respond?" 73 O.B.J. 2065 (2002); "Supervisors Guide to HR Policies and Procedures," Interactive Web-Based Manual (2001); "Minnick v. Mississippi: Rationale of Right to Counsel Requires Reversal of Michigan v. Mosley's Right to Silence Ruling," 27 Tulsa Law Rev. 181 (1991). Member, Society for Human Resources Management. Vice President, Legal and Legislative Affairs, Tulsa Area Human Resources Association, 2002-2004; Human Resources Director, 2000-2002. *Member:* Oklahoma Bar Association (Secretary , Labor and Employment Section (2004-2005); Past Director, Young Lawyers Division; Vice President, Program Planning, Tulsa Equal Employment Opportunity Coordinators Association (2002 —). ***PRACTICE AREAS:*** Labor and Employment; Management Employment Law; Employment Defense. ***Email:*** cthrutchley@newtonoconnor.com

JENNIFER K. KERN, born Oakland, California, February 16, 1961; admitted to bar, 2003, Oklahoma; 2005, U.S. District Court, Northern District of Oklahoma. *Education:* California State University, Stanislaus (B.A., cum laude, 1984); University of Tulsa College of Law (J.D., 2002). Phi Delta Phi. Member, Board of Advocates. Recipient: CALI Highest Honors in Contracts and Appellate Brief Writing and Oral Argument; Native American Law Award; Lawyering Skills Certification. *Member:* Tulsa County Bar Association (Young Lawyer and Family Law Sections); Oklahoma and American Bar Associations; Christian Legal Society; American Inns of Court (Hudson-Hall-Wheaton Chapter, 2002—); Adoption Forum (Chair, Program Committee 2003-2005); Presenter, Tulsa Equal Employment Opportunity Coordinators Associations: Training the Trainers: Update on Employment Law. ***PRACTICE AREAS:*** Civil Litigation; Business Litigation; Adoption Law. ***Email:*** jkern@newtonoconnor.com

JON M. PAYNE, born Columbus, Mississippi, November 1, 1966; admitted to bar, 1992, Texas; 1998, Oklahoma; U.S. Court of Appeals, Fifth and Tenth Circuits; U.S. District Court, Northern District of Texas; U.S. District Court, Northern and Eastern Districts of Oklahoma. *Education:* Princeton University (A.B., 1989); Southern Methodist University (J.D., 1992). *Member:* Tulsa County and Oklahoma Bar Associations; State Bar of Texas; American Inns of Court (Barrister, Hudson Hall Wheaton Chapter, Tulsa, Oklahoma). ***PRACTICE AREAS:*** Civil Litigation; Labor and Employment.

RACHEL B. CRAWFORD, born Tulsa, Oklahoma, March 24, 1980; admitted to bar, 2005, Oklahoma. *Education:* University of Oklahoma (B.A., 2002; J.D., 2005). Recipient, American Jurisprudence Award: Evidence; Torts II; Legal Research; Writing. ***PRACTICE AREAS:*** Labor and Employment; Business Transactions; Civil Litigation.

(This Listing Continued)

OF COUNSEL

MICHAEL L. WILLIS, born Coffeyville, Kansas, March 20, 1967; admitted to bar, 1992, Oklahoma. *Education:* Oklahoma State University (B.S., 1989); University of Tulsa (J.D., highest honors, 1992). Phi Kappa Phi; Order of Barristers; Order of the Curule Chair. Recipient, American Jurisprudence Award: Contracts I; Commercial Law; Torts II; Lab. Member, Tulsa Law Journal. Chief of Staff, Congressman Steve Largent. *Member:* Tulsa County and Oklahoma Bar Associations; American Inns of Court. ***PRACTICE AREAS:*** Government Relations; Business Formation; Business Transactions; Corporate Law; Commercial Law. ***Email:*** mwillis@newtonoconnor.com

STEVEN K. BUNTING, born Lincoln, Nebraska, June 13, 1952; admitted to bar, 1977, Oklahoma; 1978, Texas; U.S. District Court, Northern District of Oklahoma. *Education:* University of Oklahoma (B.A., 1974; J.D., 1977). Phi Alpha Delta; Phi Beta Kappa. *Member:* Tulsa County, Oklahoma and American Bar Associations; State Bar of Texas; Oklahoma Association of Defense Counsel. ***PRACTICE AREAS:*** Workers Compensation; Personal Injury; Civil Trial Practice.

REPRESENTATIVE CLIENTS: Cintas Corporation; Ford Motor Company; Ford of Tulsa; Ford Investment Enterprises Corporation; Arrow Magnolia International LP; McDonald's Restaurants; Oklahoma National Bank; Orkin Exterminating Company; Rollins; Tyson Foods; Tulsa National Bank; Aircraft Fueling Systems; Air Liquide America; Baldwin Steel Company; Carter Excavating; Catholic Charities Community Care; Cyntergy; Dillon International; DP Manufacturing; Kaiser Francis Oil Company; Matrix Service Company; Norris, a Dover Resources Company; Oxford Healthcare; Tulsa Winch; Reco Enterprises, Inc.
REFERENCES: State Bank.; Stillwater National Bank; Oklahoma National Bank.

ROBERT J. NICHOLS

400 PETROLEUM CLUB BUILDING
601 SOUTH BOULDER AVENUE
TULSA, OKLAHOMA 74119
Telephone: 918-582-3222
Fax: 918-582-2705
Email: nicholsatty@worldnet.att.net

General Civil Practice before all State and Federal Courts. Trials, Eminent Domain, Condemnation, Municipal, Real Estate, Zoning, Real Estate Brokerage.

FIRM PROFILE: Sole Practitioner.

ROBERT J. NICHOLS, born Erie, Pennsylvania, October 7, 1949; admitted to bar, 1975, Oklahoma; 1983, New York. *Education:* Syracuse University (B.A., 1972); University of Tulsa (J.D., 1974). Adjunct Professor, University of Tulsa, Real Estate Transactions, 1995—. Vice President, 1979 and President, 1981-1982, Tulsa Land Use Lawyers Association. Tulsa County Alternate Delegate, Oklahoma Bar Convention, 1984-1985. *Member:* Tulsa County; Oklahoma (Member, Section on Real Property Law), New York State and American Bar Associations; Oklahoma Trial Lawyers Association (Editor, Real Estate Section of the Advocate, 1982-1984). Fellow, Oklahoma Bar Foundation. ***REPORTED CASES:*** Oklahoma Turnpike Authority vs. New Life Pentecostal Church 870 P2d 762. ***PRACTICE AREAS:*** Zoning Law; Condemnation Law; Brokerage Law; Eminent Domain.

REPRESENTATIVE CLIENTS: Greater Tulsa Association of Realtors; McGraw Davisson and Stewart Realtors; Oral Roberts Ministries; Sitrin Petroleum Corp.; State Bank; Wal-Mart Stores, Inc.
REFERENCES: State Bank; Bank IV; John Hausam Realtors.

NICHOLS, WOLFE, STAMPER, NALLY, FALLIS & ROBERTSON, INC.

Established in 1963

SUITE 400, OLD CITY HALL BUILDING
124 EAST FOURTH STREET
TULSA, OKLAHOMA 74103-5010
Telephone: 918-584-5182
Fax: 918-582-9321
URL: http://www.nicholswolfe.com

Corporate Law, Business Law, Management Labor and Employment Law, Construction Law, Banks and Banking, Financial Institutions Law, Software Licensing (or Computer Law), Real Estate Law, Surety Law, Wills, Trusts, Estates and Probate, Product Liability Defense, Civil Litigation Practice in all Federal and State Courts and before Government Agencies.

FIRM PROFILE: Nichols, Wolfe, Stamper, Nally, Fallis & Robertson, Inc., is a business-oriented law firm located in downtown Tulsa, in the restored historic city hall. Since 1965, the firm has assisted businesses and individuals in accomplishing their objectives and in advocating and protecting their rights. It concentrates its work in a general corporate and business practice, construction law, civil litigation and the representation of management in all aspects of labor and employment law. The firm has received the highest rating available from Martindale-Hubbell.

JERRY R. NICHOLS, born Los Angeles, California, March 24, 1942; admitted to bar, 1969, Oklahoma and U.S. District Court, Northern District of Oklahoma; 1972, U.S. Court of Appeals, Tenth Circuit; 1973, U.S. Supreme Court; 1974, District of Columbia; 1991, U.S. District Court, Eastern District of Oklahoma. *Education:* Oklahoma State University (B.S., 1964); University of Tulsa (J.D., 1969). Delta Theta Phi. *Member:* Tulsa County, Oklahoma (Member and Chairman, Corporate, Banking and Business Law Section, 1978-1979) and American (Member, Sections on: Corporation, Banking and Business Law) Bar Associations; The Bar Association of the District of Columbia. ***PRACTICE AREAS:*** Corporate Law; Business Law; Financial Institutions Law; Banks and Banking. ***Email:*** jnichols@nicholswolfe.com

FRANK B. WOLFE, III, born Flint, Michigan, February 23, 1939; admitted to bar, 1967, Oklahoma; 1972, U.S. Court of Appeals, Eighth and Tenth Circuits; 1974, U.S. Court

(This Listing Continued)

NICHOLS, WOLFE, STAMPER, NALLY, FALLIS & ROBERTSON, INC., Tulsa—Continued

of Appeals, Sixth Circuit; 1975, U.S. Court of Appeals, Fifth Circuit. *Education:* Washington & Lee University (B.S., 1961); University of Tulsa (J.D., 1966). Phi Alpha Delta. Guest Lecturer, Labor Law, University of Tulsa, College of Law, 1970-1973. Associate General Counsel, NLRB, 16th Region, 1967-1969. *Member:* Tulsa County, Oklahoma (Member, 1974— and Council Member, 1975—, Labor Law Section) and American (Member, Equal Employment Opportunity Committee, Labor and Employment Law Section, 1973-1976) Bar Associations. ***PRACTICE AREAS:*** Labor and Employment. **Email:** fwolfe@nicholswolfe.com

GERALD G. STAMPER, born Tulsa, Oklahoma, February 8, 1936; admitted to bar, 1959, Oklahoma; 1963, U.S. Court of Appeals, Tenth Circuit; 1965, U.S. District Court, Eastern and Northern Districts of Oklahoma; 1967, U.S. District Court, Western District of Oklahoma and U.S. Supreme Court; 1968, U.S. Tax Court and U.S. Court of Appeals, Fifth Circuit; 1973, U.S. District Court, Southern District of Alabama; 1977, U.S. District Court, Northern District of Alabama; 1983, U.S. District Court, Southern District of Texas; 1984, U.S. District Court, Western District of Tennessee; 2000, Courts of the Cherokee Nation; 2002, U.S. District Court, Middle District of Louisiana; 2003, Courts of the Muscogee (Creek) Nation. *Education:* University of Oklahoma (B.A., 1957; LL.B., 1959). Phi Alpha Delta. Judge, Oklahoma Temporary Court of Appeals, 1982-1984. Lecturer, Engineering Extension, Oklahoma State University. Construction and Commercial Disputes Arbitrator, American Arbitration Association, 1980-1998. Member, Board of Visitors, The College of Architecture, University of Oklahoma. Past Affiliate Director, AIA Northeastern Oklahoma. *Member:* Tulsa County, Oklahoma and American (Member, Sections on: Tort and Insurance Practice; Litigation; Member, Forum Committee on Construction Industry, 1976—) Bar Associations. [Lt., USNR, active duty, 1959-1964]. ***PRACTICE AREAS:*** Construction Law; Surety Law; Litigation; Business Law. **Email:** gstamper@nicholswolfe.com

THOMAS P. NALLY, born Juneau, Alaska, September 2, 1951; admitted to bar, 1976, Oklahoma, U.S. District Court, Northern, Eastern and Western Districts of Oklahoma and U.S. Court of Appeals, Tenth Circuit; 1978, U.S. District Court, Northern District of Texas; 1984, U.S. Supreme Court and U.S. Court of Appeals, Fifth Circuit. *Education:* University of Tulsa (B.S., 1973; J.D., 1976). Phi Delta Phi (Vice Magistrate, 1974). Judge, Oklahoma Temporary Court of Appeals, 1992. *Member:* Tulsa County, Oklahoma (Director, Young Lawyers Division, 1978; Member, Grievance Committee, 1993; Member, Service Committee, 2002; Chairman, Court Operations Committee, 2004; Member, Banking and Business Law Section) and American (Member, Corporation, Banking and Business Law Section) Bar Associations. ***PRACTICE AREAS:*** Corporate Law; Banking Law; Business Law; Litigation. **Email:** tnally@nicholswolfe.com

S. M. FALLIS, JR., born Tulsa, Oklahoma, December 19, 1934; admitted to bar, 1960, Oklahoma; 1961, U.S. District Court, Western, Eastern and Northern Districts of Oklahoma; 1981, U.S. District Court, Northern and Western Districts of Texas, U.S. Court of Appeals, Tenth Circuit and U.S. Supreme Court. *Education:* University of Tulsa (B.A., 1957; LL.B., 1960). Phi Alpha Theta; Pi Gamma Mu; Delta Theta Phi. Recipient, Distinguished Faculty Award. Instructor: Criminal Law, Tulsa Community College, 1971-1981; Adjunct Professor: O. W. Coburn School of Law, 1981-1982; University of Tulsa College of Law, 1997-2001. Instructor, National College of District Attorneys, 1969-1996. Assistant County Attorney, 1960-1967. District Attorney, Tulsa County, 1967-1981. Judge, Oklahoma Temporary Court of Appeals, 1982-1984. Master, American Inns of Court, W. Lee Johnson Chapter, 1991—. Advocate, American Board of Trial Advocates, 1993—. *Member:* Tulsa County (Chairman, Law Day Committee, 1980), Oklahoma (Chairman, Criminal Law Committee, 1967) and American Bar Associations. Fellow, American College of Trial Lawyers, 1994. [With USNR, 1953-1961]. ***PRACTICE AREAS:*** Litigation. **Email:** sfallis@nicholswolfe.com

THOMAS D. ROBERTSON, born Oklahoma City, Oklahoma, April 22, 1953; admitted to bar, 1978, Georgia and U.S. District Court, Northern District of Georgia; 1979, Oklahoma and U.S. District Court, Northern, Eastern and Western Districts of Oklahoma; 1980, U.S. Court of Appeals, Tenth Circuit; 1991, U.S. Court of Appeals, Fifth Circuit. *Education:* Austin College (B.A., 1975); Emory University (J.D., 1978). Phi Delta Phi. Member, Emory National Trial Competition Team, 1977. Trial Attorney, Equal Employment Opportunity Commission, Atlanta Regional Litigation Center, 1978-1979. Member, Planning Committee, ABOTA Multi-State Labor and Employment Seminar, 1984—. Adjunct Professor, Human Resources Law, Tulsa Community College, 1994-1998. *Member:* Tulsa County (Member: Board of Directors, 2002-2003; Grievance Committee, 1991-1995; Fee Arbitration Committee, 1988-1991; Employment Law Section), Oklahoma (Chairman, Labor and Employment Law Section, 1990) and American (Member, Sections on: Labor and Employment Law; Litigation) Bar Associations; State Bar of Georgia. ***PRACTICE AREAS:*** Management Employment Law; Management Labor Law; Management Employment Litigation; Commercial Litigation. **Email:** trobertson@nicholswolfe.com

SARAH E. HANSEL, born Alton, Illinois, March 3, 1961; admitted to bar, 1989, Oklahoma. *Education:* Eastern Illinois University (B.A., summa cum laude, 1983); University of Oklahoma (J.D., with honors, 1989). Phi Delta Phi. Recipient, Emory Scholarship, 1987. *Member:* Tulsa County, Oklahoma and American (Member, Section on: Business Law) Bar Associations. ***PRACTICE AREAS:*** Software Licensing; Electronic Commerce; Business Law; Commercial Law; Corporate Law; Banks and Banking; Financial Institutions Law. **Email:** shansel@nicholswolfe.com

TRENT A. GUDGEL, born Tulsa, Oklahoma, September 7, 1963; admitted to bar, 1990, Texas; 1991, U.S. District Court, Northern District of Texas; 1992, U.S. District Court, Eastern District of Texas; 1994, U.S. District Court, Western District of Texas and U.S. Court of Appeals, Fifth Circuit; 1995, U.S. District Court, Southern District of Texas; 1996, Oklahoma, U.S. District Court, Northern, Eastern and Western Districts of Oklahoma and U.S. Court of Appeals, Tenth Circuit. *Education:* University of Oklahoma (B.B.A., 1986; M.B.A., 1990; J.D., 1990). Phi Delta Phi. The Order of Barristers. Member, ATLA National Trial Team, 1989-1990. Student Member, American Inns of Court XXIII, 1989-1990. *Member:* Tulsa County, Oklahoma and American Bar Associations; State Bar of

(This Listing Continued)

Texas; American Inns of Court (Council Oak Chapter); Defense Research Institute. ***PRACTICE AREAS:*** Business Litigation; Construction Litigation; Real Estate Litigation; Defense Litigation; Business Law. **Email:** tgudgel@nicholswolfe.com

JOHN E. HARPER, JR., born Arlington, Texas, January 31, 1973; admitted to bar, 1997, Oklahoma and U.S. District Court, Western District of Oklahoma; 1998, U.S. District Court, Northern District of Oklahoma, U.S. Court of Appeals, Tenth Circuit; 2000, Courts of the Cherokee Nation; 2001, U.S. District Court, Eastern District of Oklahoma; 2003, Courts of the Muscogee (Creek) Nation. *Education:* University of Oklahoma (B.A., with special distinction, 1994; J.D., 1997). Recipient, R. Boyd Gunning Academic Scholarship. *Member:* Tulsa County, Oklahoma, Muscogee (Creek) Nation, Cherokee Nation and American Bar Associations. ***LANGUAGES:*** German. ***PRACTICE AREAS:*** Construction Litigation; Litigation; Surety Law; Business Law. **Email:** jharper@nicholswolfe.com

---

KAREN M. GRUNDY, born Dallas, Texas, October 1, 1964; admitted to bar, 1990, Oklahoma; U.S. Court of Appeals, Tenth Circuit; U.S. District Court, Northern, Eastern and Western Districts of Oklahoma. *Education:* Austin College (B.A., 1987); University of Notre Dame (J.D., 1990). Executive Editor, Notre Dame Journal of Law, Ethics and Public Policy, 1989-1990. Rules Editor, Appellate Practice Journal, 1995. Author: "Recent Developments in Federal Appellate Practice and Procedure," Tort and Insurance Law Journal, Winter, 1995; "Evidentiary Use (and Misuse) of the Civil Defendant's Financial Status," Oklahoma Bar Journal (1995). *Member:* Tulsa County, Oklahoma (Chairman, Appellate Practice Section, 1996) and American (Member, Sections on: Tort and Insurance Practice; Appellate Advocacy Committee; Chair, 1996; Litigation Section, Appellate Practice Committee; Civil Procedure Committee) Bar Associations; Oklahoma Association of Defense Counsel (President, 2000); Defense Research Institute. ***REPORTED CASES:*** Eastern Okla. Bldg. & Constr. Trades Council v. Pitts, 2003 OK 113, 82 P.3d 1008; Sisk v. J.B. Hunt Transport, Inc., 2003 OK 69, 81 P.3d 55; Christian v. Gray, 2003 OK 10, 65 P.3d 591. ***PRACTICE AREAS:*** Defense Litigation; Appellate Practice. **Email:** kgrundy@nicholswolfe.com

STUART E. VAN DE WIELE, born Tulsa, Oklahoma, April 20, 1972; admitted to bar, 1999, Oklahoma; 2003, Courts of the Muscogee (Creek) Nation. *Education:* University of Arkansas; University of Oklahoma (B.B.A., 1995); University of Tulsa (J.D., highest honors, 1999). *Member:* Tulsa County, Oklahoma and American Bar Associations. ***PRACTICE AREAS:*** Corporate Law; Business Law; Commercial Law; Wills; Trusts and Estates; Probate. **Email:** svandewiele@nicholswolfe.com

OF COUNSEL

TOM L. HOLLAND, born Delaware, Arkansas, September 11, 1938; admitted to bar, 1971, Oklahoma. *Education:* Friends University (B.A., 1961); University of Tulsa (J.D., 1970); University of Illinois (LL.M., 1976). Delta Theta Phi. Order of the Curule Chair Graduate teaching assistant, University of Illinois. Notes and Comments Editor, Tulsa Law Journal. Author: Uniform Commercial Code Series: Documents of Title (with Hawkland & Anzivino (Callaghan & Co. 1986); Uniform Commercial Code Series: Letters of Credit (with Hawkland) (1984). Lecturer: Professor of Law, The University of Tulsa College of Law, 1973—; Visiting Professor of Law, St. Mary's University of San Antonio, Spring, 1981. Adjunct Settlement Judge, Settlement Conference Program, Oklahoma Fourteenth Judicial District, 1990-1999. *Member:* Tulsa County (Member, Executive Committee, 1976-1979), Oklahoma (Member, Mandatory Continuing Legal Education Commission, 1988-1993) and American Bar Associations. [Sgt. E-5, U.S. Army Finance Corps, 1961-1964]. ***PRACTICE AREAS:*** Negotiable Instruments; Sales of Goods; Secured Transactions. **Email:** tom-holland@utulsa.edu

REPRESENTATIVE CLIENTS: Dover Resources, Incorporated; Acme Engineering & Manufacturing Corp.; Fintube Technologies, Inc.; The Boeing Company; Dal-Tile Corporation; Sweet Adelines International, Inc.; Paccar, Inc.; Wright Tree Service, Inc.; Anheuser-Busch Companies, Inc.; Pitney Bowes, Inc.; Wolverine Tube, Inc.; Exchange Bank; Associated General Contractors of America, Oklahoma Builders Chapter; Associated Builders & Contractors of Oklahoma, Inc.; Howard Management Group, Inc.; M.J. Lee Construction Co.; Osage County, Oklahoma; Comerica Bank; Darden Restaurants, Inc.; Remediation Services, Inc.; Ark Wrecking Company of Oklahoma, Inc.; CH2M Hill; SunGard Data Systems; SolArc, Inc.; Sportcraft; Bankers Trust/Deutsche Bank; The Facility Group, Inc.; Pepsico; Mid-Continent Group (insurance and bonds); Old Republic National Title Insurance Company; KAMO Power; Stewart Title Guarranty Company; The Crosby Group, Inc.; FRI Industries; Storey Wrecker Service, Inc.; City of Tulsa, Flint Energy Service, Inc.; Acme Architectural Products, Inc.; Summit Bank; OakTree Software, Inc.; Bridgelogix Corp.; The Weitz Company, LLC; Employers Mutual Casualty Co.; American Arbitration Association; Oliver Group, LLC (architects); Chase Fetters Hewitt Architects; Bovis Lend Lease, Inc.; T-K-O Equipment Co.; The Cust-O-Fab Companies; Hyde Park Hotels, Inc.; Federal Signal Corporation; The Ross Group Construction Corp.

NORMAN WOHLGEMUTH CHANDLER & DOWDELL

Established in 1970

2900 MID CONTINENT TOWER
TULSA, OKLAHOMA 74103
Telephone: 918-583-7571
Fax: 918-584-7846
Email: postmaster@nwcdlaw.com

General Civil Practice. Trials and Appeals in all State and Federal Courts. Business Organizations, General Corporate, Banking, Communications, Real Estate, Commercial Transactions, Oil and Gas, Energy Acquisitions, Municipal and Zoning, Antitrust, Probate, Arbitration and Mediation, Securities Fraud Litigation, Securities Arbitration, Commercial Litigation, Telecommunications, Energy Litigation, Insurance Litigation, Tort Litigation.

FIRM PROFILE: Established in Tulsa more than 30 years ago, Norman Wohlgemuth Chandler & Dowdell offers a wide range of legal services to local, regional, national and international clients. The firm provides diverse, creative and efficient experience in a number of practice areas, most notably appellate practice, business law, complex litigation, energy, real estate, telecommunications and zoning and municipal law.

(This Listing Continued)

MEMBERS OF FIRM

CHARLES E. NORMAN, born Quanah, Texas, September 2, 1930; admitted to bar, 1953, Oklahoma; 1957, U.S. Supreme Court. *Education:* Texas Tech University and University of Oklahoma (LL.B., 1951); University of Oklahoma (LL.B., 1953). Phi Alpha Delta. Assistant City Attorney, 1956-1959 and City Attorney, 1959-1968 City of Tulsa, Oklahoma. *Member:* Tulsa County, Oklahoma and American Bar Associations. ***PRACTICE AREAS:*** Real Estate; Zoning Law; Business Law; Corporate Law; Banking Law; Communications and Cable Television Law; Municipal. ***Email:*** cen@nwcdlaw.com

JOEL L. WOHLGEMUTH, born Chicago, Illinois, December 30, 1945; admitted to bar, 1970, Minnesota; 1971, Oklahoma, U.S. Court of Appeals, 10th Circuit and U.S. District Court, Northern District of Oklahoma; 1973, U.S. District Court, Western District of Oklahoma; 1976, U.S. Supreme Court. *Education:* Brown University (A.B., 1967); Washington University (J.D., 1970). Judge, Temporary Court of Appeals, Divisions 180 and 198, 1982-1983. Special Assistant Attorney General, State of Minnesota, 1970. Member, Committee on Admissions and Grievances, U.S. District Court, Northern District of Oklahoma, 1975—. Adjunct Settlement Judge, Northern District of Oklahoma, 2000 —. Associate Bar Examiner, 1976—. *Member:* Tulsa County (Member: Grievance Committee, 1976-1977; Fee Arbitration Committee, 1979-1982; Chairman, 1981), Oklahoma and American Bar Associations; Master, American Inns of Court (Johnson-Sontag Chapter). ***PRACTICE AREAS:*** Federal and Complex Litigation; Antitrust Litigation. ***Email:*** jlw@nwcdlaw.com

R. JAY CHANDLER, born Springfield, Missouri, January 15, 1949; admitted to bar, 1979, Oklahoma; 1980, U.S. District Court, Northern District of Oklahoma; 1981, U.S. Court of Appeals, Tenth Circuit. *Education:* Missouri Southern State College (B.A., cum laude, 1975); University of Tulsa (J.D., 1979). Phi Alpha Delta. Assistant District Attorney, Tulsa County, Oklahoma, 1979. *Member:* Tulsa County, Oklahoma and American (Member, Sections on: Business Law; Real Property) Bar Associations. [With U.S. Army, 1968-1970]. ***PRACTICE AREAS:*** Real Estate; General Corporate Law; Commercial Transactions; Litigation. ***Email:*** rjc@nwcdlaw.com

JOHN E. DOWDELL, born Tulsa, Oklahoma, January 22, 1955; admitted to bar, 1983, Oklahoma, U.S. Court of Appeals, Tenth Circuit and U.S. District Court, Northern, Eastern and Western Districts of Oklahoma; 1986, U.S. Supreme Court. *Education:* Wake Forest University (B.A., 1978); University of Tulsa (J.D., 1981). Law Clerk to the Honorable William J. Holloway, Jr., U.S. Circuit Judge, Tenth Circuit Court of Appeals, 1981-1983. Master, American Inns of Court (President, 2000-2001; Council Oak Chapter). Adjunct Settlement Judge, Northern District of Oklahoma, 1998. *Member:* Tulsa County (Court Operations Committee, Vice Chairman, 1997-1998; Chairman, 1998-1999), Oklahoma (Associate Editor, Oklahoma Bar Journal, 2003) and American Bar Associations. ***PRACTICE AREAS:*** Federal and Complex Litigation; Energy Litigation; Appellate Practice. ***Email:*** jed@nwcdlaw.com

THOMAS M. LADNER, born Lawrenceville, Illinois, December 15, 1955; admitted to bar, 1981, Oklahoma and U.S. District Court, Northern, Eastern and Western Districts of Oklahoma. *Education:* St. Louis University (A.B., magna cum laude, 1978; J.D., cum laude, 1981). Order of the Woolsack. Master, American Inns of Court (W. Lee Johnson Chapter). *Member:* Tulsa County and Oklahoma Bar Associations. ***PRACTICE AREAS:*** Commercial Law; Litigation; Arbitration Law; Oil and Gas Law; Energy Acquisitions. ***Email:*** tml@nwcdlaw.com

WILLIAM W. O'CONNOR, born Tulsa, Oklahoma, March 2, 1964; admitted to bar, 1989, Oklahoma; 1990, U.S. District Court, Northern, Western and Eastern Districts of Oklahoma and U.S. Court of Appeals, Tenth Circuit; U.S. Supreme Court. *Education:* Oklahoma State University (B.S., 1986); University of Oklahoma (J.D., 1989). Member, Oklahoma Law Review, 1988-1989. Barrister, American Inns of Court (Council Oak Chapter). Director, Tulsa County Bar Foundation Board of Directors. *Member:* Tulsa County (Member: Board of Directors; Professional Responsibility and Court Operations Committees; Chairman, Community Outreach Committee), Oklahoma and American Bar Associations (Member, Litigation and Antitrust Sections). ***PRACTICE AREAS:*** Federal Litigation; Complex Litigation; Securities and Antitrust Litigation; Energy Litigation; Arbitration Law; Insurance Litigation; Tort Litigation; Legal Malpractice Defense. ***Email:*** wwo@nwcdlaw.com

ROGER K. ELDREDGE, born Sapulpa, Oklahoma, November 24, 1962; admitted to bar, 1992, Oklahoma; U.S. District Court, Northern, Eastern and Western Districts of Oklahoma; U.S. Court of Appeals, Tenth Circuit. *Education:* Oklahoma State University (B.S., 1986); University of Tulsa (J.D., with honors, 1992). Member, Order of the Curule Chair. Staff Member, Tulsa Law Journal, 1989-1991. *Member:* Tulsa County, Oklahoma and American Bar Associations. ***PRACTICE AREAS:*** Real Estate; Commercial Law; Litigation; Probate Law. ***Email:*** rke@nwcdlaw.com

CHRISTINE D. LITTLE, born Wichita, Kansas, September 5, 1968; admitted to bar, 1995, Oklahoma; U.S. District Court, Northern and Western Districts of Oklahoma; U.S. Court of Appeals, Tenth Circuit. *Education:* University of Oklahoma (B.A., 1991; J.D., with highest honors, 1995). Phi Delta Phi. Order of the Coif. Member, Oklahoma Law Review, 1993-1995. Recipient: American Jurisprudence Awards in Professional Responsibility, Equal Employment Opportunity, Children and the Law, and Agricultural Environmental Law. *Member:* Tulsa County (Member, Professional Responsibility Section), Oklahoma and American Bar Associations. ***PRACTICE AREAS:*** Complex Litigation; Employment Litigation; Oil and Gas Litigation; Legal Malpractice Defense. ***Email:*** cdl@nwcdlaw.com

ANGELA F. PORTER, born Oklahoma City, Oklahoma, December 13, 1970; admitted to bar, 1997, Oklahoma; 1998, U.S. District Court, Northern District of Oklahoma. *Education:* Hollins University (B.A., 1993); University of Tulsa College of Law (J.D., 1996). Phi Delta Phi. Recipient: Robert C. Butler, Jr. Award. Articles Editor, Tulsa Law Journal, 1995-1996. Author: "Health Care and Retirement Corp. of America: Potential Broadening of the Test for Supervisory Status Under the NLRA," 31 Tulsa L.J. 323, 1995. *Member:* Tulsa County, Oklahoma and American Bar Associations; Associate, American Inns of Court, Hudson-Hall-Wheaton Chapter, 1998-2000. ***PRACTICE AREAS:*** Complex Litigation; Arbitration Law; Legal Malpractice Defense. ***Email:*** afp@nwcdlaw.com

(This Listing Continued)

ASSOCIATES

DAVID R. ROSS, born Nuremberg, Germany, October 7, 1976; admitted to bar, 2003, Oklahoma and U.S. District Court, Northern District of Oklahoma. *Education:* Indiana University (B.A., 2000); Washington University (J.D., 2003). Associate Editor, Washington University Journal of Law and Police, 2002-2003. *Member:* Tulsa County and Oklahoma Bar Associations. ***PRACTICE AREAS:*** Civil Litigation; State and Federal Law. ***Email:*** drr@nwcdlaw.com

J. PAUL BETZER, born Kansas City, Missouri, January 6, 1969; admitted to bar, 2003, Oklahoma and U.S. District Court, Eastern, Northern and Western Districts of Oklahoma; 2004, U.S. Court of Appeals, Tenth Circuit. *Education:* Oral Roberts University (B.A., summa cum laude, 1999); University of San Diego (J.D., 2002). Recipient: Dean's Merit Scholarship; Outstanding Brief Award, Regent One-L Moot Court Competition; Academic Excellence Awards in Contracts and Legal Writing. *Member:* Tulsa County, Oklahoma (Member, Young Lawyers Division Committee on Religion and the Law) and American Bar Associations. ***PRACTICE AREAS:*** Civil Litigation; Real Estate; Zoning Law; Legal Malpractice Defense. ***Email:*** jpb@nwcdlaw.com

JO LYNN JETER, born Sapulpa, Oklahoma, April 16, 1979; admitted to bar, 2004, Oklahoma. *Education:* Oklahoma State University (B.S., summa cum laude, 2001); University of Oklahoma (J.D., with honors, 2004). Phi Delta Phi. Order of the Coif. Recipient: Academic Achievement Awards in Property, Employment Law, Commercial Law, Federal Indian Law and Agricultural Biotechnology and the Law. Member, Oklahoma Journal of Law and Technology, 2003-2004. Author, Agricultural Biotechnology: United States Caselaw, 2 Okla. J.L. & Tech. 14 (2004); Agricultural Biotechnology: U.S. Policy Regarding Patent Applications, 2 Okla. J.L. & Tech. 20 (2004); Agricultural Biotechnology: United States Statutory Law, 2 Okla. J.L. & Tech 24 (2004). *Member:* Oklahoma and American Bar Associations. ***PRACTICE AREAS:*** Commercial Litigation. ***Email:*** jlj@nwcdlaw.com

MELANIE M. POUNCEY, born Hattiesburg, Mississippi, February 28, 1979; admitted to bar, 2004, Oklahoma and U.S. District Court, Northern and Eastern Districts of Oklahoma. *Education:* University of Southern Mississippi (B.S., B.A., with highest honors, 2001); University of Oklahoma (J.D., with honors, 2004). *Member:* Oklahoma and American Bar Associations. ***PRACTICE AREAS:*** Civil Litigation. ***Email:*** mmp@nwcdlaw.com

OF COUNSEL

MARICHIEL A. LEWIS, born Manila, Philippines, May 16, 1972; admitted to bar, 1999, Oklahoma; 2001, U.S. District Court, Northern District of Oklahoma; 2002, U.S. District Court, Eastern District of Oklahoma; U.S. Court of Appeals, Tenth Circuit. *Education:* University of Illinois (B.A., 1994); University of Oklahoma (J.D., with honors, 1999). Recipient: Academic Achievement Awards in Torts and Construction Contracts; Writing Award, Mineral Law Section, Oklahoma Bar Association. Outstanding Third Year Member and Indexing Editor, 1998-1999, Oklahoma Law Review. Outstanding Staff Member and Assistant Note Editor, 1998-1999, American Indian Law Review. Author: "Oil & Gas Top Leasing After Voiles v. Santa Fe Minerals: Unethical Claim-jumping or Prudent Business Practice?" 52 Okla. L. Rev. 127, 1999. Teaching Assistant, Legal Writing Program, University of Oklahoma College of Law. *Member:* Oklahoma and American Bar Associations. ***PRACTICE AREAS:*** Civil Litigation.

GENERAL COUNSEL FOR: The Hardesty Companies; Tulsa Parking Authority.
REPRESENTATIVE CLIENTS: Bethlehem Steel Corp.; BSW International; Citicorp Real Estate, Inc.; Crum & Forster; Mid-Continent Concrete Co.; Mid-Continent Energy, Inc.; Raytheon Co.; Sooner Pipe, Inc. and affiliates; Sovereign Insurance Life Insurance Company of California; St. John Medical Center; Cox Communications; Tulsa City-County Library System; Gemstar-TV Guide International, Inc.; T-Mobile USA, Inc.; Farmers Alliance Mutual Insurance; Duke Energy Field Services, Inc.; Hillcrest Health System; Warren Foundation.

THE OWENS LAW FIRM, P.C.

Established in 1959

234 W. 13TH STREET
TULSA, OKLAHOMA 74119-3026
Telephone: 918-587-0021
Fax: 918-587-6111
Email: olf@owenslawfirmpc.com

General Civil Trial Practice in all State and Federal Courts. Probate, Corporation, Real Estate, Oil and Gas, Taxation, International, Bankruptcy, Business Law, Estate Planning, Elder Law and Guardianship Law.

FIRM PROFILE: The Owens Law Firm was founded by Geo. W. Owens in 1959 as a sole proprietorship. The firm became the partnership of Owens & Goodman. In 1976 the firm name was changed to Eagleton, Eagleton & Owens. The partnership was incorporated under the same name which in 1981 was changed to Owens & McGill, Inc. In August, 1990 the present name was adopted. The firm engages in a general practice emphasizing corporate, business, tax planning, oil & gas, probate, estate planning, wills, trusts and estates, guardianships, estate, trust and guardianship litigation, civil trial, bankruptcy, health and elder law.

GEORGE W. OWENS, born Tulsa, Oklahoma, June 1, 1926; admitted to bar, 1951, Texas; 1959, Oklahoma; 1960, U.S. District Court, Northern, Eastern and Western Districts of Oklahoma; 1967, U.S. Court of Appeals, Tenth Circuit. *Education:* University of Texas (LL.B., 1951). Order of the Coif; Phi Delta Phi; Chancellors. Comment Editor, Texas Law Review, 1951. Presiding Judge, Court of Appeals, State of Oklahoma (Temp. Division), 1983. *Member:* Tulsa County and Oklahoma (Member, Law Office Management Section) Bar Associations; State Bar of Texas. ***REPORTED CASES:*** Clarence T. and Anna Thompson v. USA, 223 F 3d 1206 (10th Circuit 2000). ***PRACTICE AREAS:*** Tax Planning Law; Corporate Law; Business Law; Oil and Gas Law; Civil Litigation; Bankruptcy Reorganization Law. ***Email:*** gwo@owenslawfirmpc.com

ROBYN OWENS, born Tulsa, Oklahoma, July 28, 1954; admitted to bar, 1979, Oklahoma; 1980, U.S. District Court, Northern District of Oklahoma; U.S. Court of Appeals, Tenth Circuit. *Education:* Trinity University (B.A., cum laude, 1976); University of Tulsa

(This Listing Continued)

THE OWENS LAW FIRM, P.C., Tulsa—Continued

(J.D., 1979). Phi Alpha Delta. *Member:* Tulsa County (Member, Grievance and Fee Arbitration Committees) and Oklahoma (Member, OBA Client Security Fund Committee) Bar Associations. ***PRACTICE AREAS:*** Estate Planning Law; Probate Law; Elder Law; Business Law; Guardianship Law; Trusts and Estates Litigation; Guardianship Litigation. ***Email:*** ro@owenslawfirmpc.com

---

RANDALL E. ROSE, born Muskogee, Oklahoma, January 29, 1951; admitted to bar, 1978, Oklahoma; 1981, U.S. District Court, Northern District of Oklahoma; 1982, U.S. Supreme Court and U.S. Court of Appeals, Tenth Circuit; 1990, U.S. District Court, Western District of Oklahoma. *Education:* University of Tulsa (B.A., 1974; J.D., 1978); Université de Besançon, Besançon, France. Phi Delta Phi. *Member:* Tulsa County, Oklahoma and American Bar Associations. ***REPORTED CASES:*** Tulsa Professional Collection Services, Inc. vs. Pope, 485 US 478, 108 S. Ct. 1340, 99 L. Ed. 2nd 565 (1988); Tulsa Professional Collection Services, Inc. vs. Pope, 808 P. 2d 640 (Okla. 1991); Thompson v. United States, 223 F.3d 1206 (10th Cir. 2000). ***PRACTICE AREAS:*** Commercial Law; Business Law; Appellate Practice; Civil Litigation; Bankruptcy Law. ***Email:*** rer@owenslawfirmpc.com

REPRESENTATIVE CLIENTS: Electronic Sciences, Inc.; Zephyrus Electronics, Ltd.; Littlefield Marketing & Advertising, Inc.; Printed Products, Inc.; Ervin Electric, Inc.; Rangeline Field Services, Oklahoma Well Log Library; Limestone Investments Co.; Centrex Operating Co.; Hamilton Investments, L.P.; Ideal Aerosmith, Inc., East Grand Forks, MN.
LOCAL COUNSEL FOR: Stillbrooke Corporation; O.U. Medical School; Power Cleaning Specialists, Inc., Baton Rouge, LA.

THE PAUL LAW FIRM

A PROFESSIONAL CORPORATION

Established in 1971

SUITE 400, REUNION CENTER
9 EAST 4TH STREET
TULSA, OKLAHOMA 74103
Telephone: 918-584-2583
Telefax: 918-587-8521
URL: http://www.paulfirm.com
URL: http://www.paullawfirm.com

General Civil and Trial Practice in State and Federal Courts, including Medical Malpractice, Insurance Defense, Commercial, Negligence, Professional Liability, General Liability, Products Liability, Employment, Employee Discrimination, Insurance Law and Environmental Law.

E. LEE GRIGGS (Deceased)

JOHN R. RICHARDS (Deceased)

JOHN R. PAUL, born Tulsa, Oklahoma, 1949; admitted to bar, 1975, Oklahoma; U.S. District Court, Northern, Eastern and Western Districts of Oklahoma and U.S. Court of Appeals, Tenth Circuit; U.S. Supreme Court. *Education:* Centre College of Kentucky (B.A., 1971); University of Tulsa (J.D., 1974). *Member:* Tulsa County, Oklahoma and American Bar Associations; Oklahoma Association of Defense Counsel (Vice-President, 1983); International Association of Defense Counsel; American Inns of Court (Barrister). ***PRACTICE AREAS:*** Medical Malpractice; General Insurance Defense; Corporate; Medical/Legal; Hospital; Employment; Professional Liability; Negligence; Insurance Law. ***Email:*** john@paulfirm.com

---

LEAH McCASLIN KINSEY, born Tulsa, Oklahoma, April 9, 1970; admitted to bar, 1995, Oklahoma and U.S. District Court, Northern, Eastern and Western Districts of Oklahoma; U.S. Court of Appeals, Tenth Circuit. *Education:* Knox College (B.A., magna cum laude, 1992); University of Tulsa (J.D., with honors, 1995). Phi Beta Kappa; Order of the Curule Chair; Phi Delta Phi. Production Editor, Tulsa Law Journal, 1994-1995. Author: "Harris v. Forklift Systems, Inc.: Defining the Plaintiff's Burden in Hostile Environment Sexual Harassment Claims", 29 Tulsa L.J. 761 (1994). *Member:* Tulsa County and Oklahoma Bar Associations. ***PRACTICE AREAS:*** Insurance Defense Law; Medical Malpractice Defense; Litigation. ***Email:*** leah@paulfirm.com

PARALEGAL

Kathy A. Cooper

REPRESENTATIVE CLIENTS: St. Paul Insurance Co.; Caronia Corp.; Hillcrest Healthcare System; Hillcrest Medical Center; Integris Health System; The Medical Protective Co.; The Doctor's Co.; Baptist Healthcare Corp.; HealthSouth Rehabilitation Hospital; Grove General Hospital; Baptist Regional Health Center; Choctaw Memorial Hospital; Mayes County Medical Center; Bristow Memorial Hospital; Blackwell Regional Hospital; Medical Center of Southeastern Oklahoma; Stroud Municipal Hospital; Pawnee Municipal Hospital; Health Management Associates; Midwest Regional Medical Center; Bass Baptist Health Center; Cancer Treatment Center of Oklahoma; Children's Medical Center; Cleveland Municipal Hospital; Marshall Memorial Hospital; Green Country Mental Health Services, Inc. Rest Haven Nursing Home; Country Manor Nursing Home; Carewell Corporation of Oklahoma; Inola Health Care Center; OMH Medical Center; Physician's Surgical Center; Prison Health Services; Quik Trip Corp.; MSI Insurance Companies; Metropolitan Property & Casualty Insurance Co.; CNA Insurance Co.; Oklahoma Property & Casualty Insurance Guaranty Association; Oklahoma Farm Bureau; INAPRO; Cigna Companies; Republic Insurance Co.; Continental Insurance Co.; Preferred Physicians Mutual Insurance Co.; Northland Insurance Co.; Golden Eagle Insurance Co.; Reliance National Insurance Co.; The Traveler's Co.; Hospital Casualty Co.; Employer's Re-Insurance Co.; St. Paul Travelers; General Fire & Casualty; Oklahoma Turnpike Authority; Jackson Hewitt Tax Service; Myron F. Steves & Co.

PERRINE, McGIVERN, REDEMANN, REID, BERRY & TAYLOR, PLLC

Established in 2002

1437 SOUTH BOULDER AVENUE, SUITE 620
P.O. BOX 1710
TULSA, OKLAHOMA 74101-1710
Telephone: 918-382-1400
Fax: 918-382-1499
URL: http://www.pmrlaw.com
Email: rredemann@pmrlaw.net
URL: http://www.pmrlaw.net

Civil Litigation, Products Liability, Insurance Defense, Professional Liability, Workers Compensation, Toxic Tort Law, Insurance Receivership, Insurance Law, Insurance Bad Faith, Labor and Employment Law, Wrongful Death, Personal Injury, Social Security Appeals.

FIRM PROFILE: The firm was established by a highly experienced group of litigation attorneys who have expertise in complex civil cases and workers compensation. Personal contact, trial experience and efficiency through technology are the firms hallmarks. The firm represents international, national and local clients.

WILLIAM D. PERRINE, born Tulsa, Oklahoma, October 6, 1951; admitted to bar, 1986, Oklahoma. *Education:* University of Oklahoma (B.S., 1977); University of Tulsa (J.D., 1986). Delta Theta Phi. Order of the Curule Chair. Staff Member, Tulsa Law Journal, 1985-1986. *Member:* Tulsa County and Oklahoma Bar Associations; Oklahoma Association of Defense Counsel; Defense Research Institute. Fellow, Oklahoma Bar Foundation. ***REPORTED CASES:*** Southern Hospitality, Inc v. Zurich American Ins. Co., 393 F.3d 1137 (10th Cir. 2004); DeAnda v. AIU Ins., 2004 OK 54, 98 P.3d 1080; Graham v. Travelers, 2002 OK 95, 61 P.3d 225; May v. National Union Fire Ins. Co. of Pittsburgh, Pennsylvania, 1996 OK 52, 918 P.2d 43; Anglen v. E.L. Powell & Sons, 1991 OK 53, 812 P.2d 1364; Moore v. Subaru of America, 891 F.2d 1445 (10th Cir. 1989). ***PRACTICE AREAS:*** Civil Litigation; Products Liability Law; Insurance Defense; Insurance Bad Faith. ***Email:*** wperrine@pmrlaw.net

MICHAEL W. McGIVERN, born Tulsa, Oklahoma, February 11, 1952; admitted to bar, 1980, Oklahoma. *Education:* University of Tulsa (B.S., 1974; J.D., 1980). *Member:* Tulsa County and Oklahoma (Treasurer, 1989-1991, and President, 1997, Workers' Compensation Section) Bar Associations; Oklahoma Association of Defense Counsel. Fellow, Oklahoma Bar Foundation. ***REPORTED CASES:*** Heat Transfer & Equipment v. Cauthron, 2004 OK 80, 100 P.3d 722; Arrow Tool & Gauge v. Mead, 2000 OK 86, 16 P.3d 1120; Sneed v. McDonnell Douglas, 1999 OK 84, 991 P.2d 1001; Montgomery v. UNI-Steel, 1999 OK CIV. App. 87; 987 P.2d 451; Kirk v. American Airlines, 1998 OK CIV. APP. 168, 972 P.2d 883. ***PRACTICE AREAS:*** Workers Compensation; Civil Litigation. ***Email:*** mmcgivern@pmrlaw.net

ROBERT P. REDEMANN, born Ripon, Wisconsin, February 20, 1951; admitted to bar, 1978, Oklahoma and Wisconsin. *Education:* University of Wisconsin-Madison (B.S., 1973); University of Tulsa (J.D., 1978). Author: "The Evolution of PRP Standing Under the Comprehensive Environmental Response, Compensation, and Liability Act of 1980," 21 Wm. & Mary Env. & Policy L. Rev. 300 (1997); "Duty to Defend" chapter, Law and Practice of Insurance Coverage Litigation. Adjunct Settlement Judge, U.S. District Court, Northern District of Oklahoma. Master, American Inns of Court (Hudson-Hall-Wheaton Chapter). *Member:* Tulsa County, Oklahoma and American (Member, Trial Tort and Insurance Practice Section, 1984) Bar Associations; State Bar of Wisconsin; Defense Research Institute; Oklahoma Association of Defense Counsel. Fellow, Oklahoma Bar Foundation. ***REPORTED CASES:*** Timmons v. Royal Globe Ins. Co., 1982 OK 97, 653 P.2d 907; Hervey v. Dyer, 1998 OK CIV. 185, 972 P.2d 42; State ex rel. Crawford v. South Atlanta Standard Life & Acc. Ins. Co., 2001 OK CIV. App. 152, 37 P.3d 971; Sagona v. Sun Co., Inc., 2002 OK CIV. APP. 93, 57 P.3d 879; Sun Co., Inc., (R&M) v. Browing-Ferris, Inc., 124 F.3d 1187, 143 A.L.R. Fed. 755, (10th Cir. 1997). ***TRANSACTIONS:*** Mid-Continent Life Ins. Assumption Re-insurance Agreement. ***PRACTICE AREAS:*** Litigation; Product Liability Law; Toxic Tort Law; Insurance; Insurance Receivership; Insurance Bad Faith. ***Email:*** rredemann@pmrlaw.net

DAVID P. REID, born Tulsa, Oklahoma, July 4, 1954; admitted to bar, 1979, Oklahoma and U.S. District Court, Northern and Eastern Districts of Oklahoma; 1980, U.S. Court of Appeals, Tenth Circuit. *Education:* Dallas Baptist College (B.B.A., 1976); University of Oklahoma (J.D., 1979). Order of the Coif. Recipient, American Jurisprudence Awards. Staff Member, Oklahoma Law Review, 1977-1979. *Member:* Tulsa County (Past Chair, Workers Compensation Section), Oklahoma and American Bar Associations. ***REPORTED CASES:*** Berg v. Parker Drilling, 2004 OK 72, 98 P.3d 1099; Whiteside v. Braden Mfg. LLC, 2003 OK CIV. APP. 39, 68 P.3d 890; Big Four Foundries Corp. v. Davis, 2003 OK CIV. APP. 39, 68 P.3d 1000; Bama Pie Ltd., v. Raes, 1995 OK 122, 905 P.2d 811; Park Terrace v. Raska, 1994 OK CV. APP. 158, 887 P.2d 344. ***PRACTICE AREAS:*** Workers Compensation; Civil Litigation; Bankruptcy. ***Email:*** dreid@pmrlaw.net

KEVIN D. BERRY, born Wichita Falls, Texas, April 20, 1961; admitted to bar, 1986, Oklahoma; U.S. District Court, Northern, Eastern and Western Districts of Oklahoma and U.S. Court of Appeals Tenth Circuit. *Education:* University of Missouri (B.A., 1983); University of Tulsa (J.D., 1986). Delta Theta Phi. Staff Member, Tulsa Law Journal, 1985-1986. *Member:* Tulsa County (Member, Workers' Compensation Section), Oklahoma (Board of Governors and Secretary/Treasurer, Workers' Compensation Section, 1994-1996) and American Bar Associations. Fellow, Oklahoma Bar Foundation. ***REPORTED CASES:*** Gray v. Natkin Contracting, 2001 OK 73, 44 P.3d 547; Bailes v. Home of Hope, 1999 OK CIV. APP. 27, 977 P.2d 1145; Henson v. HOW Foundation-State Ins. Fund, 1998 OK 114, 970 P.2d 604; Frew v. McDonnell Douglas Indus. Indem. Co., 1996 OK 108, 932 P.2d 35; Coleman v. J.C. Penney, 1993 OK 21, 848 P.2d 1158; Brent v. Agrico Chemical Co., 1992 OK 132, 839 P.2d 189. ***PRACTICE AREAS:*** Civil Litigation; Bankruptcy; Workers Compensation. ***Email:*** kberry@pmrlaw.net

CATHERINE C. TAYLOR, born Oklahoma City, Oklahoma, November 1, 1961; admitted to bar, 1990, Oklahoma. *Education:* University of Oklahoma (B.A., 1983); Univer-

(This Listing Continued)

sity of Tulsa (J.D., 1990). Phi Alpha Delta (Historian, 1988-1989; Vice Justice, 1989-1990). Member, Board of Advocates, 1988-1989. Staff Member, Tulsa Law Journal, 1988-1990. *Member:* Tulsa County, Oklahoma (Member, Public Information Committee, 1993—; Secretary, Workers' Compensation Section, 1998-1999; President, 1999-2000) and American Bar Associations; Oklahoma Association of Defense Counsel; American Inns of Court, W. Lee Johnson Chapter. ***REPORTED CASES:*** Patterson v. Sue Estell Trucking Co., Inc., 2004 OK 66, 95 P.3d 1087; Cooper v. National Union Fire Ins. Co.of Pittsburgh, Pennsylvania, 1996 OK CIV. APP. 52, 921 P.2d 1297; Wolf v. Prudential Ins. Co. of America, 50 F.3d 793, 18 Employee Benefits Cas. 2915, (10th Cir. 1995); Langley v. Barnhart, 373 F.3d 1116 (10th Cir. 2004). ***PRACTICE AREAS:*** Workers Compensation; Employment. ***Email:*** ctaylor@pmrlaw.net

VICTOR R. SEAGLE, born Lynchburg, Virginia, March 28, 1945; admitted to bar, 1976, Oklahoma. *Education:* University of Tulsa (B.A., 1967; J.D., 1975). Phi Delta Phi. Judge, Workers' Compensation Court of Oklahoma, 1981-1991. *Member:* Oklahoma County, Tulsa and Oklahoma (Member, Workers' Compensation Section) Bar Associations; International Association of Industrial Accident Boards and Commissions; Western and Southern Associations of Workers' Compensation Administrators; Oklahoma Trial Lawyers Association (Member, Board of Editors, American Journal of Clinical Assessment); Defense Research Institute; Oklahoma Association of Defense Counsel. ***REPORTED CASES:*** Wal-Mart Stores, Inc. v. Berg, 2004 OK CIV. APP. 89, 99 P.3d 1205; Diversified Rubber v. Harvey, 2003 OK CIV. App. 67, 74 P.3d 619; Special Indemnity Fund v. Figgins, 1992 OK 59, 831 P.2d 1379; Richardson v. Bartlett Collins Co., 1999 OK CIV. APP. 105, 990 P.2d 305. ***PRACTICE AREAS:*** Workers Compensation (100%). ***Email:*** vseagle@pmrlaw.net

---

KELLY M. GREENOUGH, born Tulsa, Oklahoma; admitted to bar, 1992, Oklahoma. *Education:* Oklahoma State University (B.S., 1985); University of Tulsa (J.D., 1992). Author: "Workers' Compensation Reform in Oklahoma: Exclusion of Injuries Sustained at Recreational or Social Events," 26 Tulsa Law Journal 405 (1991). *Member:* Oklahoma Bar Association. ***REPORTED CASES:*** Heat Transfer & Equipment v. Cauthron, 2004 OK 80, 100 P.3d 722; Big Four Foundries v. Davis, 2003 OK CIV. APP. 39, 68 P.3d 1000; Sharitt v. American Airlines, 1998 OK CIV. APP. 74, 962 P.2d 663; Darco Transp. v. Dulen, 1996 OK 50, 922 P.2d 591. ***PRACTICE AREAS:*** Civil Appeals; Civil Litigation; Workers Compensation. ***Email:*** kgreenough@pmrlaw.net

CHERYL S. GAN, born Akron, Ohio, September 30, 1954; admitted to bar, 1991, Oklahoma and U.S. District Court, Northern District of Oklahoma; 1992, U.S. District Court, Eastern District of Oklahoma and U.S. Court of Appeals, 10th Circuit. *Education:* University of Oklahoma (B.A., 1976; M.P.H., 1988); Tulsa University (J.D., 1991). University of Tulsa Law Journal, 1990-1991. Author: Grandparental Visitation Rights in Oklahoma, Tulsa Law Journal, Vol. 26, Number 2, 1990. *Member:* Oklahoma and American (Member, Section on: Labor Law) Bar Associations; Oklahoma Trial Lawyers Association; American Inns of Court, 1992-1993. ***REPORTED CASES:*** Walter v. Morton, 33 F.3d 1240 (10th Cir. 1994). ***PRACTICE AREAS:*** Workers Compensation. ***Email:*** cgan@pmrlaw.net

L. BRAD TAYLOR, born Dallas, Texas, December 16, 1965; admitted to bar, 1994, Oklahoma; U.S. District Court, Northern District of Oklahoma. *Education:* Baylor University (B.B.A., 1989); University of Tulsa (J.D., 1994). Member, International Brotherhood of Magicians. Recipient: Most Outstanding Law Student Award and Class President Award, University of Tulsa, 1993-1994; Number One in the Nation, Student Bar Association, 1993-1994. Editor, Energy Law Journal, Tulsa University, 1994. Lecturer: Oklahoma Bar Association; Oklahoma Trial Lawyers Association; University of Tulsa; Oral Roberts University; Tulsa Community College; Baylor University; and numerous Fortune 500 companies on topics ranging from Complex Litigation to Worker's Compensation. *Member:* Tulsa County (Member, Workers' Compensation Section) and Oklahoma Bar Associations. ***REPORTED CASES:*** Eller v. County of Pittsburgh, 2003 OK CIV. APP. 65, 74 P.3d 605; Yaffee Metals v. Quick, 1996 OK CIV. APP. 16, 918 P.2d 1996. ***PRACTICE AREAS:*** Workers Compensation. ***Email:*** btaylor@pmrlaw.net

JENNIFER L. STRUBLE, born Stillwater, Oklahoma, January 27, 1971; admitted to bar, 2003, Oklahoma. *Education:* Oklahoma State University (B.S., 1993); University of Oklahoma (Master of Public Administration, 1995); University of Tulsa (J.D., 2003). Phi Delta Phi. Executive Editor, Tulsa Law Review, 2002-2003. *Member:* Tulsa county and Oklahoma Bar Associations. ***REPORTED CASES:*** Southern Hospitality, Inc. v. Zurich American Ins. Co., 393 F.3d 1137 (10th Cir. 2004); Victory v. Barnhart, 121 Fed. Appx. 819, 102 Soc. Sec. Rep. Serv. 565 (10th Cir. 2005); King v. Barnhart, 114 Fed. Appx. 968, 100 Soc. Sec. Rep. Serv. 377 (10th Cir. 2004); Timmons v. Barnhart, 118 Fed. Appx. 349, 102 Soc. Sec. Rep. Serv. 241 (10th Cir. 2004). ***PRACTICE AREAS:*** Social Security; Civil Litigation; Employment Law. ***Email:*** jstruble@pmrlaw.net

TIMOTHY C. EDWARDS, born Tulsa, Oklahoma, February 26, 1977; admitted to bar, 2002, Oklahoma and U.S. District Court, Western District of Oklahoma. *Education:* University of Oklahoma (B.A., 1998; J.D., 2002). *Member:* Oklahoma County and Oklahoma Bar Associations. ***PRACTICE AREAS:*** Workers Compensation; Litigation. ***Email:*** tedwards@pmrlaw.net

DAVID C. SENGER, born Tulsa, Oklahoma, March 17, 1974; admitted to bar, 2000, Oklahoma and U.S. District Court, Northern, Eastern and Western Districts of Oklahoma; U.S. Court of Appeals, Tenth Circuit; U.S. Supreme Court. *Education:* Langston University (B.S., 1997); University of Tulsa College of Law (J.D., 2000). *Member:* Tulsa County, Oklahoma and American Bar Associations; Council Oak Chapter, American Inns of Court (Associate Member). ***REPORTED CASES:*** Limerta v. Ashcroft, 88 Fed.Appx. 363 (10th Cir. 2004). ***PRACTICE AREAS:*** Civil Litigation; Insurance Defense; Insurance Bad Faith; Products Liability; Immigration. ***Email:*** dsenger@pmrlaw.net

JENNIFER A. JOHNSON, born Tulsa, Oklahoma; admitted to bar, 2003, Oklahoma and U.S. District Court, Eastern District of Oklahoma; 2004, U.S. District Court, Western and Northern Districts of Oklahoma and U.S. Court of Appeals, Tenth Circuit. *Education:* University of Tulsa (B.A., Political Science, cum laude, 1999; Certificates in International Relations and Jurisprudence; J.D., with highest honors, 2003; Certifications in International and Comparative Law). CALI Awards for Excellence in Evidence and Constitutional Law. *Member:* Tulsa County, Oklahoma and American Bar Associations; National Organization of Social Security Claimant Representatives (NOSSCR) (Sustaining Member). ***LANGUAGES:*** French. ***PRACTICE AREAS:*** Workers Compensation; Social Security; Administrative Law; Employment Law. ***Email:*** jjohnson@pmrlaw.net

OF COUNSEL

LAWRENCE W. ZERINGUE, born Evergreen Park, Illinois, October 23, 1946; admitted to bar, 1975, Iowa; 1978, Oklahoma; 1979, U.S. District Court, Northern District of Oklahoma; 1979, U.S. Supreme Court; 1998, U.S. District Court, Western District of Oklahoma and U.S. Court of Appeals, Tenth Circuit. *Education:* University of Iowa (B.S., 1971); University of Tulsa College of Law (J.D., 1974). Phi Delta Phi. *Member:* Tulsa County (Member, Board of Directors, 2000-2001; Chairman, 2000-2001 and Vice-Chairman, 1999-2000, Fee Arbitration Committee; Member, Grievance [Professional Responsibility] Committee, 2000—, 1997-1999, 1994-1996, 1988-1990; Member, Ethics and Unlawful Practice Committee, 1986-1988), Oklahoma, Iowa State and American Bar Associations; Johnson-Sontag Chapter, American Inns of Court (Barrister, 1999—). ***REPORTED CASES:*** Taylor v. Pepsi-Cola Co., 196 F.3d 1106 (10th Cir. 1999); Nordam v. Board of Review of Oklahoma Employment Sec. Com'n, 1996 OK 110, 925 P.2d 556; State v. Jaeger, 249 N.W.2d 688 (Iowa 1977). ***PRACTICE AREAS:*** Insurance Law; Employment Law; Business Litigation. ***Email:*** lzeringue@pmrlaw.net

REPRESENTATIVE CLIENTS: AIG; Bechtel; The Sherwin-Williams Company; Target Corporation; The Travelers; Zurich North America; Zurich Specialties London Limited; Krung Thai Bank; Wal-Mart Stores, Inc.; Crawford & Company; Gallagher-Bassett; Wackenhut Corporation; Crane Co.; Yamagki Co. Communications, Inc.

PEZOLD, BARKER & WOLTZ

A Partnership of Professional Corporations

Established in 1985

15 WEST SIXTH STREET, SUITE 2800
TULSA, OKLAHOMA 74119-5415
Telephone: 918-584-0506
Fax: 918-584-0720
Email: mail@pbwtulsa.com
URL: http://www.pbwtulsa.com

General Civil Practice. Business Litigation. Oil and Gas Law. Oil and Gas Litigation. Environmental Litigation. Class Actions. Corporation. Banking, Securities Regulation and Litigation. General Appellate Practice.

MEMBERS OF FIRM

R. K. PEZOLD, born Washington, D.C., August 4, 1944; admitted to bar, 1975, Oklahoma. *Education:* University of Virginia (B.S., 1967); University of Tulsa (J.D., 1974). Phi Delta Phi. Member: Raven Society; Order of the Curule Chair. Business Editor, Tulsa Law Journal, 1973-1974. Adjunct Associate Professor of Law, University of Tulsa School of Law, 1979-1981. Author: "The Effective Use of ADR," 42 Rocky Mountain Mineral Law Institute 20-1 (1996); "The 'Industry Deal' Among Oil and Gas Companies and The Federal Securities Acts," 16 Texas Tech Law Review 827, (1985); "The Demise of the Statute of Limitations as an Antitrust Defense," 33 Oklahoma Law Review; "The National Transport Safety Board--A Critical Review of Information Availability," 43 Journal of Air Law and Commerce; "Computerized Legal Research--An Arrival," Tulsa Law Journal. ***PRACTICE AREAS:*** Litigation; Energy Law; Oil and Gas Law. ***Email:*** bpezold@pbwtulsa.com

TERRY J. BARKER, born Miami, Oklahoma, June 14, 1960; admitted to bar, 1988, Oklahoma, U.S. District Court, Northern, Eastern and Western Districts of Oklahoma, U.S. Court of Federal Claims, U.S. Court of Appeals, Tenth and Federal Circuits and U.S. Supreme Court. *Education:* Oklahoma State University (B.S., 1984); University of Tulsa (J.D., 1988). Member, Energy Law Journal, 1987-1988. *Member:* Tulsa County, Oklahoma and American Bar Associations; The Association of Trial Lawyers of America. ***PRACTICE AREAS:*** Civil Litigation; Oil and Gas Litigation. ***Email:*** tbarker@pbwtulsa.com

JOSEPH C. WOLTZ, born Norman, Oklahoma, October 28, 1963; admitted to bar, 1990, Oklahoma, U.S. District Court, Northern, Western and Eastern Districts of Oklahoma, U.S. Court of Federal Claims and U.S. Court of Appeals, Tenth and Federal Circuits. *Education:* University of Oklahoma (B.A., with highest honors, 1985; M.A., 1987); University of Tulsa College of Law (J.D., with honors, 1990). Phi Beta Kappa. Order of the Curule Chair. Articles Editor, Tulsa Law Journal, 1989-1990. Author: "Possible Constitutional Limits on Punitive Damages: *Bankers Life & Casualty Co. v. Crenshaw,*" 24 Tulsa Law Journal 429 (1989); "The Excessive Fines Clause Revisited: Punitive Damages After *Browing-Ferris Industries v. Kelco Disposal, Inc.,*" 25 Tulsa Law Journal 337 (1989). *Member:* Tulsa County, Oklahoma and American Bar Associations. ***PRACTICE AREAS:*** Oil and Gas Law; Litigation; Civil Appeals. ***Email:*** jwoltz@pbwtulsa.com

ASSOCIATES

GENE G. BOERNER, III, born Baton Rouge, Louisiana, December 26, 1971; admitted to bar, 1997, Oklahoma. *Education:* University of Tulsa (B.A., cum laude, 1994); University of Oklahoma (J.D., 1997). Recipient: Dean's Honor Roll; American Jurisprudence Award in Bankruptcy. Author, "Roye Realty & Developing, Inc. v. Watson: Oklahoma Decides Royalty Obligations on Take-or-Pay Settlements Using 'Plain Terms' Analysis," 33 Tulsa Law Journal 891 (1998). *Member:* Tulsa County, Oklahoma and American Bar Associations. ***PRACTICE AREAS:*** Oil and Gas Law; Litigation. ***Email:*** gboerner@pbwtulsa.com

ROBERT NEIL LAWRENCE, born Escondido, California, December 19, 1970; admitted to bar, 1999, Oklahoma and U.S. District Court, Northern and Western Districts of Oklahoma. *Education:* University of Oklahoma (B.B.A., 1993); University of Texas (J.D., 1999). Member, The Review of Litigation. *Member:* Oklahoma Bar Association. ***PRACTICE AREAS:*** Energy Litigation; Corporate Law. ***Email:*** rlawrence@pbwtulsa.com

(This Listing Continued)

PEZOLD, BARKER & WOLTZ, Tulsa—Continued

REPRESENTATIVE CLIENTS: *Oil and Gas:* Dyco Petroleum Corporation; Ensign Operating Co.; Envirotek Fuel Systems, Inc.; Geodyne Production Co.; Grace Petroleum Corp.; Samson Investment Co.; The Rudman Partnership; D. Wagner & Co. *Commercial:* Consolidated Investment Co.

PIERCE COUCH HENDRICKSON BAYSINGER & GREEN, L.L.P.

624 SOUTH BOSTON, SUITE 500
TULSA, OKLAHOMA 74119
Telephone: 918-583-8100
Fax: 918-583-8107
URL: http://www.PierceCouch.com

Oklahoma City, Oklahoma Office: 1109 North Francis, P.O. Box 26350, 73126. Telephone: 405-235-1611. Fax: 405-235-2904.

General Civil Practice. Insurance, Surety, Corporation, Aviation Law, Medical and Dental Malpractice, Professional Liability, Workers Compensation, Bad Faith Law, Arson, Construction Law, Municipal Liability, Civil Rights, Employment Law, Business Torts and Business Litigation, Insurance Coverage Issues and Automobile/Vehicle Liability. Trial of Cases in all Courts in Oklahoma.

JAMES B. DURANT (1934-2004)

MEMBER OF FIRM

LEAH P. KEELE, born Fort Smith, Arkansas, January 5, 1965; admitted to bar, 1994, Oklahoma. *Education:* Northeastern Oklahoma State University (B.S., 1986); University of Tulsa (J.D., 1993). Member, Tulsa Law Journal. Recipient, American Jurisprudence Award, Workers Compensation. Author: "The Aftermath of Dewsnup Lien Survival in Chapter 13," TLJ, Vol. 28, No. 4, Summer 1993. Member, National Self-Insured Association. Board Member, Oklahoma Self-Insured Association. *Member:* Defense Research Institute; Tulsa Claims Association; Oklahoma Association of Defense Counsel. (Resident). ***PRACTICE AREAS:*** Workers Compensation. ***Email:*** lkeele@piercecouch.com

ASSOCIATES

JASON M. HENDERSON, born Tulsa, Oklahoma, September 24, 1968; admitted to bar, 1995, Oklahoma and U.S. District Court, Northern District of Oklahoma. *Education:* University of Oklahoma (B.A., 1991); University of Tulsa (J.D., 1994). Member, American Inns of Court. *Member:* Tulsa County and Oklahoma Bar Associations. ***PRACTICE AREAS:*** Civil Litigation; Workers Compensation. ***Email:*** jhenderson@piercecouch.com

JAMIE MESSINA BELLER, born Oklahoma City, Oklahoma, March 9, 1977; admitted to bar, 2002, Oklahoma. *Education:* University of Tulsa (B.A., 1999; J.D., 2002). *Member:* Oklahoma and American Bar Associations. ***PRACTICE AREAS:*** Workers Compensation; Insurance Defense; Employment Law. ***Email:*** jbeller@piercecouch.com

LORI R. WHITWORTH, born Shawnee, Oklahoma, January 17, 1978; admitted to bar, 2003, Oklahoma and U.S. District Court, Western District of Oklahoma. *Education:* University of Oklahoma (B.A., Political Science, 2000; J.D., 2003). *Member:* Oklahoma County and Oklahoma Bar Associations; Oklahoma Association of Defense Counsel. ***PRACTICE AREAS:*** Workers Compensation. ***Email:*** lwhitworth@piercecouch.com

(For complete biographical data on all personnel, see professional biographies at Oklahoma City)

PINKERTON & FINN, P.C.

2000 FIRST PLACE
15 EAST FIFTH STREET
TULSA, OKLAHOMA 74103-4367
Telephone: 918-587-1800
Facsimile: 918-582-2900
URL: http://www.pinkerton-finn.com

Civil Trial and Appellate Practice, State and Federal Courts, Commercial, Securities and Intellectual Property Litigation, Securities Fraud, Health Law, Contract Litigation, Non-Compete Agreements, Business Litigation.

LAURENCE L. PINKERTON, born Tulsa, Oklahoma, March 27, 1946; admitted to bar, 1976, Oklahoma. *Education:* University of Oklahoma (B.A., with honors, 1968); University of North Dakota (M.A., 1972); Columbia University School of Law (J.D., 1976). Greenbaum Prize for Oral Advocacy. Master, American Inns of Court. *Member:* Oklahoma and American Bar Associations. ***PRACTICE AREAS:*** Civil Trials; Breach of Contract Litigation; Commercial Law; Securities Fraud; Intellectual Property; Disputes.

JUDITH A. FINN, admitted to bar, 1981, Oklahoma; U.S. Supreme Court; U.S. Court of Appeals, Tenth Circuit. *Education:* University of Wisconsin (B.A.; M.A., English, M.A., Educational Psychology); Texas A & M University (Ph.D., English Lit.); University of Tulsa (J.D.; M.A., Urban Studies). Phi Delta Phi. Associate Professor, University of Tulsa, 1986-1991. Law Clerk, Honorable H. Dale Cook, U.S. District Court, Northern District of Oklahoma, 1980-1985. *Member:* Tulsa County, Oklahoma and American Bar Associations; American Trial Lawyers Association. ***PRACTICE AREAS:*** Commercial Litigation; Securities Fraud; Guardianship.

OF COUNSEL

J. DAVID JORGENSON, born Duncan, Oklahoma, September 23, 1953; admitted to bar, 1978, Oklahoma and U.S. District Court, Northern District of Oklahoma; 1980, U.S. Court of Appeals, Tenth Circuit; 1982, U.S. District Court, Western District of Oklahoma; 1992, U.S. Supreme Court. *Education:* Oklahoma Baptist University (B.A., summa cum laude, 1975); University of Texas at Austin (J.D., 1978). ***PRACTICE AREAS:*** Business Litigation; Oil and Gas Acquisitions; Telecommunications; Construction Law. ***Email:*** djorgenson@att.net

REPRESENTATIVE CLIENTS: Upon Request.

POSTIC & BATES

A PROFESSIONAL CORPORATION
TULSA, OKLAHOMA
(SeeOklahoma City)
Estate Planning, Real Estate Law, Adoption Law, Probate, Guardianship.

PRAY, WALKER, JACKMAN, WILLIAMSON & MARLAR

A PROFESSIONAL CORPORATION
900 ONEOK PLAZA
100 WEST 5TH STREET
TULSA, OKLAHOMA 74103-4218
Telephone: 918-581-5500
Fax: 918-581-5599
URL: http://www.praywalker.com

General Civil Trial Practice in all State and Federal Courts; Corporate, Oil and Gas, Taxation, Labor and Employment Law, Employee Benefits, Securities, Real Estate, Banking, Commercial, Probate, Trusts, Insurance, Bankruptcy, Personal Injury, Products Liability, Entertainment and Administrative Law.

J. WARREN JACKMAN (1934-2002)

W. BLAND WILLIAMSON, JR., born Selma, Alabama, April 6, 1938; admitted to bar, 1963, Georgia; 1969, Oklahoma. *Education:* Stetson University (B.S., 1959); Emory University (J.D., 1963). Phi Delta Phi. Member, Editorial Staff, Journal of Public Law, 1962-1963. Listed in, The Best Lawyers in American (Natural Resources Law). Chairman, Legal Committee, 1978-1985, General Counsel, 1986—, and Director, 1988—, Oklahoma Independent Petroleum Association. Coordinator, Energy Advocates, 1987-1988, 1991. Regional Vice President, Petroleum Association of America, 1991-1995; Member, Oklahoma Energy Resources Board, 1993-1994. *Member:* Tulsa County (Chairman, Mineral Law Section, 1978-1979), Oklahoma (Chairman, Mineral Law Section, 1981) and American (Co-Chair, Energy Committee, Section of Administrative Law and Regulatory Practice, 1997-1998; Vice-Chairman, Natural Gas, Marketing and Transportation Committee, National Resources Section, 1986-1987) Bar Associations. [Capt., J.A.G.C., U.S. Army, 1963-1967]. ***PRACTICE AREAS:*** Oil and Gas Law; Energy Regulatory Law; Corporate Law. ***Email:*** wbw@praywalker.com

DONALD F. MARLAR, born Little Rock, Arkansas, January 15, 1944; admitted to bar, 1969, Oklahoma. *Education:* Arkansas State University (B.S., 1966); University of Tulsa (J.D., 1968); George Washington University (LL.M., 1972). *Member:* Tulsa County, Oklahoma (Chairman, Taxation Law Section, 1979) and American Bar Associations. [Capt., J.A.G.C., U.S. Army, 1969-1973]. ***PRACTICE AREAS:*** Corporate Law; Tax and Estate Planning; Bankruptcy Law. ***Email:*** dfm@praywalker.com

TERRY R. DOVERSPIKE, born Tulsa, Oklahoma, October 20, 1951; admitted to bar, 1976, Oklahoma. *Education:* University of Oklahoma (B.A., 1973); University of Tulsa (J.D., 1976). Psi Chi; Phi Delta Phi. Member, Tulsa Law Journal, 1975-1976. Member, Marquis Who's Who in American Law (Corporate Section) 1992. Member and Chairman, Tulsa Zoning Board of Adjustment (1990-1996). City Councilor, Tulsa District 7 (1996-2000). *Member:* Tulsa County (Member, Corporate Law Section, 1980—) Oklahoma (Member, Business Associations Section, 1984) and American (Chairman, Committee of Real Property, Probate and Trust Law Section on Current Legislation, 1988-1993; Member, Section of Business Law, 1984-1994) Bar Associations. ***PRACTICE AREAS:*** Corporate Law; Banking Law; Real Estate Law; Trusts and Estates. ***Email:*** trd@praywalker.com

JOHN F. McCORMICK, JR., born Little Rock, Arkansas, March 13, 1944; admitted to bar, 1974, Oklahoma; 1975, California. *Education:* University of Notre Dame (B.A., 1966); University of Oklahoma (J.D., 1974). Phi Delta Phi. Senior Adjunct Settlement Judge, U.S. District Court, Northern District of Oklahoma, 1988—. American Inns of Court (Master Emeritus). *Member:* Tulsa County (Chairman, Ethics Committee, 1988; Vice Chairman, Grievance Committee, 1990; Chairman, Fee Arbitration Committee, 1991) and Oklahoma (Member, Professional Responsibility Tribunal, 1990-1993) Bar Associations; State Bar of California; The Association of Trial Lawyers of America; Oklahoma Trial Lawyers Association. [Capt., U.S. Marine Corps, 1967-1971; 1974-1976]. ***PRACTICE AREAS:*** Personal Injury Law; Medical Negligence Law; Products Liability Law; Insurance Law; Employment Law. ***Email:*** jfm@praywalker.com

FRANK D. SPIEGELBERG, born Washington, D.C., August 21, 1948; admitted to bar, 1973, Maryland; 1974, U.S. Court of Military Appeals; 1977, Texas; 1978, Oklahoma; 1985, U.S. Supreme Court. *Education:* Kent State University (B.A., with honors, 1970); Duke University (J.D., 1973). Phi Alpha Delta. Co-Author: "Unclaimed Property: A Primer on the Law of Escheat," 62 Ok. Bar J. 3821 (12-28-1991). Author: "Oilfield Pollution: Can There Be Settlement Without Remediation...," Society of Professional Engineers, Paper SPE 29750, March, 1995. Member, Board of Education, Union Public Schools, 1989-1999. *Member:* Tulsa County (President, Mineral Law Section, 1999-2000), Oklahoma and American Bar Associations; State Bar of Texas. [With USAF, 1974-1977; Capt. Staff Judge Advocate Corps]. ***PRACTICE AREAS:*** Oil and Gas Litigation; Environmental; Corporate Law. ***Email:*** fds@praywalker.com

JOHN L. RANDOLPH, JR., born Morganton, North Carolina, September 18, 1953; admitted to bar, 1979, Oklahoma. *Education:* Davidson College (B.A., 1975); Oxford University, Oxford, England; University of Tulsa (J.D., 1978). Member: Oklahoma Independent Petroleum Association, Legal Committee, 1991—; Chair, 1996-2000; Independent Petroleum Association of America (Litigation Task Force). *Member:* Tulsa County (Member,

(This Listing Continued)

Mineral Law Section), Oklahoma (Member, Sections on: Appellate Practice, Mineral Law and Environmental Law) and Energy (Judicial Review Committee, 1996—) Bar Associations. ***PRACTICE AREAS:*** Appellate Practice; Oil and Gas Law; Corporate Law; Environmental Law. ***Email:*** jlr@praywalker.com

WILLIAM L. EAGLETON, IV, born Tulsa, Oklahoma, December 11, 1955; admitted to bar, 1981, Oklahoma. *Education:* University of Oklahoma (B.A., 1978); University of Tulsa (J.D., 1981). Delta Theta Phi. Member, Tulsa Title and Probate Lawyers; President, 1992. *Member:* Tulsa County (Member, Mineral Law Section, President, 1990), Oklahoma (Member, Sections on: Real Property and Mineral Law) and American (Member, Sections on: Real Property, Probate, Trust and National Resources Law) Bar Associations. ***PRACTICE AREAS:*** Real Estate; Probate Law; Oil and Gas Law. ***Email:*** wle@praywalker.com

WM. GREGORY JAMES, born Milan, Tennessee, February 11, 1954; admitted to bar, 1982, Oklahoma and U.S. District Court, Northern, Eastern and Western Districts of Oklahoma. *Education:* The Citadel (B.A., 1977); University of Tulsa (J.D., 1982). Phi Delta Phi. Member, American Inns of Court (Barrister, Hudson-Wheaton-Hall Chapter, 1995). *Member:* Tulsa County, Oklahoma (Charter member, Litigation Section) and American Bar Associations; Oklahoma Association of Defense Counsel. ***PRACTICE AREAS:*** Civil Practice; Insurance Law; Personal Injury Law; Oil and Gas Litigation; Civil Litigation. ***Email:*** wgj@praywalker.com

DONALD S. SMITH, born St. Louis, Missouri, May 30, 1957; admitted to bar, 1982, Missouri; 1983, Illinois and U.S. Supreme Court; 1984, Oklahoma; 1993, Texas. *Education:* Southwest Missouri State University (B.A., 1979); University of Tulsa (J.D., 1982). Delta Theta Phi. Member, Tulsa Law Journal, 1981-1982. *Member:* Tulsa County, Oklahoma (Chairman, Mineral Law Section), Illinois, Missouri and American Bar Associations; Texas State Bar; Tulsa Association of Petroleum Landmen; Oklahoma Independent Petroleum Association (Chair, Legal Committee, 2003—). ***PRACTICE AREAS:*** Oil and Gas Law; Real Estate and Environmental Law; Title Examinations Law. ***Email:*** dss@praywalker.com

RANDALL G. VAUGHAN, born Okmulgee, Oklahoma, July 6, 1954; admitted to bar, 1985, Oklahoma. *Education:* Oral Roberts University (B.A., cum laude, 1976); Oklahoma University (M.A., 1981); University of Tulsa (J.D., with honors, 1985). Member: Order of the Barristers; Order of the Curule Chair; National Moot Court Team. Recipient: Martin, Fellows, Smith Outstanding Student Award, 1985; Robert C. Butler, Jr., Award for Best Publication, 1985. Articles Editor, Tulsa Law Journal, 1984-1985. Author: Comment, "Tax Issues of Personal Injury and Wrongful Death Awards," 19 Tulsa Law Journal 703 (1984); "Employee Termination for Wage Garnishment or Child Support Income Assignments," 59 Oklahoma Bar Journal 1425 (May 28, 1988). American Inns of Court (Hudson-Hall-Wheaton, 1990-2004; Master). *Member:* Tulsa County and Oklahoma Bar Associations. ***PRACTICE AREAS:*** Business Litigation. ***Email:*** rgv@praywalker.com

CHARLES BRETTON CRANE, born Salt Lake City, Utah, February 20, 1958; admitted to bar, 1984, Oklahoma. *Education:* University of Tulsa (B.S., 1980; J.D., 1984; M.B.A., 1985). Phi Delta Phi. Member, Order of Curule Chair. Staff Member, Tulsa Law Journal, 1981-1982; 1982-1983. Author: "Market Value and Long Term Purchase Contracts: Tara Petroleum Corporation v. Hughey," 17 Tulsa Law Journal 566, 1982. *Member:* Tulsa County (Chairman, Corporate Counsel Section, 1992-1993), Oklahoma (Chairman, Business Associations Section, 2000) and American Bar Associations. ***PRACTICE AREAS:*** Corporations; Partnership Law; Mergers and Acquisitions; Securities Law; Corporate Finance; Venture Capital. ***Email:*** cbc@praywalker.com

KEVIN PIERCE DOYLE, born Tulsa, Oklahoma, January 8, 1963; admitted to bar, 1988, Oklahoma; U.S. District Court, Northern, Eastern and Western Districts of Oklahoma; U.S. Court of Appeals, 6th and 10th Circuits. *Education:* University of Oregon; University of Oklahoma (B.A., 1985); University of Tulsa (J.D., 1988). Member, Tulsa Law Journal, 1987-1988. *Member:* Tulsa County, Oklahoma (Member, Sections on: Labor and Employment Law) and American (Member, Sections on: Labor and Employment Law) Bar Associations. ***REPORTED CASES:*** Lusk v. Ryder Integrated Logistics, 238 F.3d 1237 (10th Cir. 2001); Ferro Corporation v. Garrison Industries, Inc., 142 F.3d 926 (6th Cir. 1998). ***PRACTICE AREAS:*** Management Labor Relations Law; Employment Law; Wage and Hour Law; Bankruptcy Law. ***Email:*** kpd@praywalker.com

THOMAS M. ASKEW, born Kansas City, Missouri, August 14, 1964; admitted to bar, 1990, Oklahoma and U.S. District Court, Northern, Eastern and Western Districts of Oklahoma. *Education:* Oklahoma State University (B.S., 1986); University of Tulsa (J.D., 1990). Member, Energy Law Journal, 1989-1990. *Member:* Tulsa County (Director, 2002-2004) and Oklahoma (Charter Member, President, Insurance Law Section; Director, Young Lawyers Division, 1997-2001) Bar Associations; Oklahoma Association of Defense Counsel (Member, 1997— and Vice-President, 2001, Board of Directors); American Inns of Court (W. Lee Johnson Chapter, Pupil, 1989-1990; Hudson-Wheaton-Hall Chapter, Barrister, 1997-1998, Pupil, 1994-1995). ***PRACTICE AREAS:*** Insurance Law; Products Liability Litigation; General Civil Litigation; Commercial Litigation; Entertainment Law. ***Email:*** tma@praywalker.com

ROBERT J. WINTER, born Columbia, South Carolina, May 29, 1969; admitted to bar, 1995, Oklahoma; U.S. District Court, Northern, Eastern and Western Districts of Oklahoma and U.S. Court of Appeals, 10th Circuit. *Education:* Brigham Young University (B.A., 1992); University of Tulsa (J.D., 1995). Phi Delta Phi. Production Editor, Tulsa Law Journal. Author: Note, "Rodebush: Finding The Road To Strict Liability for the Intentional Torts of Employees," 30 Tulsa Law Journal 375 (1994). *Member:* Tulsa County, Washington County and Oklahoma Bar Associations; American Inns of Court (W. Lee Johnson Chapter, Pupil, 1994-1995; Hudson-Wheaton-Hall Chapter, Associate, 1996—); The Association of Trial Lawyers of America; Oklahoma Trial Lawyers Association. ***PRACTICE AREAS:*** General Civil Trial Practice; Business and Employment Litigation; Personal Injury Litigation. ***Email:*** rjw@praywalker.com

STEVEN B. BUTTERFIELD, born Tulsa, Oklahoma, December 7, 1964; admitted to bar, 1990, Oklahoma. *Education:* University of Oklahoma (B.B.A., with distinction, 1987; J.D., 1990). Beta Gamma Sigma. *Member:* Tulsa County and Oklahoma (Member, Mineral Law Section) Bar Associations; Tulsa Association of Petroleum Land Men. ***PRACTICE AREAS:*** Oil and Gas Law; Title Examination; Business Law; Corporate Law. ***Email:*** sbb@praywalker.com

(This Listing Continued)

PAMELA D. LANGSTON, born Stillwater, Oklahoma, June 18, 1964; admitted to bar, 1997, Oklahoma and U.S. Court of Appeals, Tenth Circuit. *Education:* University of Tulsa (B.S., 1988; J.D., 1997). Certified Public Accountant, Oklahoma, 1991. Author: "Revised UCC Article 9," 71 OK. Bar J. 3151 (12-9-2000). *Member:* Tulsa County (Member, Corporate Law Section) and Oklahoma Bar Associations. ***PRACTICE AREAS:*** Business Law; Corporate Law; Commercial Transactions; Oil and Gas Finance; Commercial Lending; Acquisitions and Divestitures; Joint Ventures. ***Email:*** pdl@praywalker.com

KIMBERLY A. VOJVODA, born Tacoma, Washington, April 30, 1962; admitted to bar, 1993, Oklahoma. *Education:* University of Oklahoma (B.B.A., 1984; J.D., 1993). Certified Public Accountant. *Member:* Tulsa County Bar Association; Oklahoma Society of Certified Public Accountants (Tulsa Chapter, Executive Vice President; President Elect); Tulsa Tax Forum (Past President, 2001-2003); Tulsa Title & Probate Lawyers Association. ***PRACTICE AREAS:*** Estate Planning; Tax Compliance; Guardianship; Elder Law; Probate. ***Email:*** kav@praywalker.com

HARRY A. PARRISH, born Tulsa, Oklahoma, May 8, 1951; admitted to bar, 1985, Oklahoma, U.S District Court, Northern, Eastern and Western Districts of Oklahoma. *Education:* University of Kansas (B.A., 1973); University of Tulsa (J.D., 1985). *Member:* Oklahoma Bar Association; Chartered Property Casualty Underwriters Society. ***PRACTICE AREAS:*** Insurance Coverage; Uninsured and Underinsured Motorists; Automobile Liability Defense; Insurance Coverage Defense; Workers Compensation; Appellate Practice; Personal Injury Law. ***Email:*** hap@praywalker.com

CHARLES R. HOLLADAY, born Tulsa, Oklahoma, January 13, 1958; admitted to bar, 1999, Oklahoma. *Education:* University of Tulsa (B.S., Applied Mathematics, magna cum laude, 1989; J.D. with highest honors, 1999). Tau Beta Pi; Kappa Mu Epsilon; Recipient: CALI Awards of Excellence in Legal Reasoning and Writing, Advanced Legal Writing, Taxation of Estates, Trusts & Gifts, Secured Transactions and Creditor's Rights and Bankruptcy; Oklahoma Bar Foundation; Chapman-Rogers Educational Fund Scholarship Award, 1998-1999; American Bankruptcy Institute 1999 Medal of Excellence Award; American Bankruptcy Law Journal Prize; TU-American Bankruptcy Institute Medal. Registered Professional Land Surveyor, Oklahoma, 1995. *Member:* Tulsa County and Oklahoma Bar Associations; Tulsa Title and Probate Lawyers; Oklahoma Society of Land Surveyors. ***PRACTICE AREAS:*** Real Estate; Business; Corporate; Litigation. ***Email:*** crh@praywalker.com

CHAD C. TAYLOR, born Tulsa, Oklahoma, September 1, 1971; admitted to bar, 1999, Oklahoma. *Education:* University of Oklahoma (B.B.A., 1995); University of Tulsa (J.D., 1998). Delta Theta Phi. Member, Journal of Comparative and International Law, 1997-1998. Representative: Young Lawyers Division. *Member:* Tulsa County, Oklahoma and American Bar Associations; Defense Research Institute; American Trial Lawyers Association; Oklahoma Association of Defense Counsel (Chair, OBA Committee, 2002). ***PRACTICE AREAS:*** Civil Litigation; Insurance Law; Commercial Litigation; Sports Law. ***Email:*** cct@praywalker.com

JILL GRIMSLEY DREWYOR, born Bentonville, Arkansas, January 11, 1976; admitted to bar, 2001, Oklahoma; 2002, Arkansas; U.S. Tax Court; U.S. District Court, Northern and Eastern Districts of Oklahoma. *Education:* Texas Christian University (B.S., 1998); Tulane University (J.D., 2001). Extern, United States Bankruptcy Court for the Eastern District of Louisiana. *Member:* Tulsa County, Oklahoma and Arkansas Bar Associations. ***PRACTICE AREAS:*** Corporations; Partnership Law; Mergers and Acquisitions; Securities Law; Corporate Finance; Venture Capital; Commercial Lending; Tax Law. ***Email:*** jgd@praywalker.com

SCOTT C. WEATHERHOLT, born Tulsa, Oklahoma, December 11, 1977; admitted to bar, 2003, Oklahoma. *Education:* University of Oklahoma (B.B.A., 2000; J.D., 2003). *Tulsa County and Oklahoma Bar Associations.* ***PRACTICE AREAS:*** Oil and Gas Law; Civil Litigation. ***Email:*** scw@praywalker.com

DAVID A. WARTA, born Davenport, Iowa, January 6, 1968; admitted to bar, 2004, Oklahoma. *Education:* University of Kansas (B.A., Eng. Lit., 1991); University of Tulsa (J.D., with honors, 2004). Executive Editor, Tulsa Law Review. Author: Comment, "Personal Foul: Unnecessary Restriction of Endorsement and Employment Opportunities for NCAA Student-Athletes," 39 Tulsa L. Rev. 419 (2003). *Member:* Tulsa County and Oklahoma Bar Associations. ***Email:*** daw@praywalker.com

OF COUNSEL

DONALD E. PRAY, born Tulsa, Oklahoma, January 16, 1932; admitted to bar, 1963, Oklahoma. *Education:* University of Tulsa (B.S., Petr. Eng., 1955); Oklahoma University (LL.B., with honors, 1963). Order of the Coif. Author: "Associations in Estate Planning," 16 Oklahoma Law Review 373, 1963; "Oklahoma Well Spacing Act and Its Interpretation," Vol. 36, Oklahoma Bar Journal 487, 1965; "Title Standards and Marketable Title Act," Vol. 38, No. 11, Oklahoma Bar Journal, 1967. *Member:* Tulsa County, Oklahoma and American Bar Associations. Fellow: American Bar Foundation. ***PRACTICE AREAS:*** Corporation Law; Estate Planning Law; Banking Law. ***Email:*** depray@home.com

FLOYD L. WALKER, born Kiefer, Oklahoma, March 27, 1919; admitted to bar, 1949, Oklahoma. *Education:* University of Tulsa (LL.B., 1949). Phi Beta Gamma. *Member:* Tulsa County (Chairman, Grievance Committee, 1971-1972; President, 1973), Oklahoma (Member, Board of Governors, 1979-1981) and American Bar Associations; Oklahoma Trial Lawyers Association; The Association of Trial Lawyers of America. Patron, Oklahoma Bar Foundation. Fellow, American College of Trial Lawyers. ***PRACTICE AREAS:*** Civil Practice; Personal Injury Law; Antitrust Law. ***Email:*** flw7abc@home.com

C. BRUCE JONES, born Stroud, Oklahoma, December 14, 1949; admitted to bar, 1976, Oklahoma and U.S. District Court, Western and Northern Districts of Oklahoma. *Education:* University of Tulsa and Oklahoma State University (B.A., 1972); University of Oklahoma (J.D., 1976). Phi Delta Phi. Member, Oklahoma Law Review, 1974-1976. *Member:* Tulsa County, Oklahoma and American Bar Associations. ***PRACTICE AREAS:*** Oil and Gas Law; Title Examination; Real Estate. ***Email:*** cbj@praywalker.com

RAINS & SAUNDERS, PLC

A Professional Limited Liability Company
MIDWAY BUILDING
2727 E. 21ST STREET, SUITE 402
TULSA, OKLAHOMA 74114
Telephone: 918-747-3727
URL: http://www.rstaxlaw.com
URL: http://www.tulsaestateplanner.com

Trusts and Estates, Wills, Probate, Guardianship and Conservatorship, Taxation, Medicare and Medicaid, Business Law, Contracts, Corporate Law, Partnership Law, Nonprofit and Charitable Organizations, International Law.

FIRM PROFILE: Rains & Saunders, PLC advises individuals and closely-held businesses in the areas of taxation, estate planning, business law, commercial transactions, estate and trust litigation, family philanthropy and international tax planning. The firm has offices in Oklahoma and New Mexico.

CHARLES E. RAINS, born Orlando, Florida, 1944; admitted to bar, 1969, Texas; 1975, District of Columbia; 1979, Oklahoma; 1989, New Mexico. *Education:* University of Oklahoma (B.B.A., Accounting, 1966); University of Texas (J.D., 1969); London School of Economics, London, England (LL.M., International Law, 1974); George Washington University (LL.M., Taxation, 1977). Phi Delta Phi. Adjunct Professor: International Law, Taxation, University of Tulsa; Estate Planning, Taxation, University of New Mexico. Fellow, American College of Trust and Estate Counsel (International Estate Planning Committee). ***PRACTICE AREAS:*** Trusts and Estates; Wills; Probate; Taxation; Business Law; Contracts; Corporate Law; Partnership Law; Nonprofit and Charitable Organizations; International Law. ***Email:*** chuck@rstaxlaw.com

KATHERINE SAUNDERS, born Tulsa, Oklahoma, 1954; admitted to bar, 1991, Oklahoma. *Education:* Trinity University (B.A., 1976; M.B.A., 1981); University of Tulsa (J.D., 1991). Phi Alpha Delta. Staff, Tulsa Law Journal. Member, Inns of Court (Hudson-Hall-Wheaton Chapter). Author: "Home Remedies: Tax Planning Opportunities with a Qualified Personal Residence Trust," 65 Oklahoma Bar Journal 1789 (1994). Lecturer: National Business Institute; Professional Education Systems, Inc. *Member:* Tulsa County (Corporate Counsel, Probate, Estate Planning and Elder Law Sections; Tulsa Lawyer, Community Outreach, Memberships and Nominating Chairs), Oklahoma and American Bar Associations; Tulsa Title and Probate Lawyers Association; National Association of Elder Law Attorneys (NAELA). ***PRACTICE AREAS:*** Trusts and Estates; Wills; Probate; Taxation; Business Law; Contracts; Corporate Law; Partnership Law; Adult Guardianship; Medicaid Planning; Elder Law. ***Email:*** katie@rstaxlaw.com

RHODES, HIERONYMUS, JONES, TUCKER & GABLE, P.L.L.C.

Established in 1931
ONEOK PLAZA
100 WEST 5TH STREET, SUITE 400
TULSA, OKLAHOMA 74103-4287
Telephone: 918-582-1173
Fax: 918-592-3390
URL: http://www.rhodesokla.com
Mailing Address: P.O. Box 21100, Tulsa, OK 74121-1100

General Civil Trial and Appellate Practice in all State and Federal Courts. General and Extra-contractual Liability Insurance, Negligence, Products Liability, Medical, Legal and Professional Liability, Employment, Workers' Compensation, Environmental, Aviation, Suretyship, Common Carriers, Toxic Torts, ERISA, Construction.

FIRM PROFILE: Rhodes Hieronymus is a civil trial and appellate law firm. We represent manufacturers, employers, insurers and health care providers throughout Oklahoma and in other states.

We emphasize the use of technology to manage files and for trial or appellate presentations. This, combined with our specific emphasis on trial practice, enables us to be very competitive while providing excellent representation.

Specific areas of concentration include: product liability; employment; toxic and environmental; professional liability; drug and medical device; fidelity and surety; negligence; ex-contract liability; insurance; workers' compensation; and construction.

Rhodes Hieronymus was founded in 1931. We are listed in the Bar Register of Preeminent Lawyers.

E. D. HIERONYMUS (1908 -1994)
GEORGE W. GABLE (1918-2000)

CHRIS L. RHODES, III, born Hartford, Connecticut, March 31, 1932; admitted to bar, 1959, Oklahoma. *Education:* University of Oklahoma (B.B.A., 1954; LL.B., 1959). Managing Partner, 1968—. Phi Alpha Delta. Oklahoma Deputy Insurance Commissioner, 1974-1982. Trustee, Oklahoma Bar Foundation, 1990-1995. Oklahoma Counsel for the ETSI Coal Slurry Pipeline Legal Project. Counsel for the Oklahoma Insurance Commissioner, as Receiver in Rehabilitations and Liquidations since 1971. Listed in Best Lawyers in America, Corporate Law. *Member:* Tulsa County, Oklahoma and American Bar Associations; Defense Research Institute; American Judicature Society. Fellow, American Bar Foundation (Oklahoma Chair, 1997-1999). [U.S.A.F., Pilot SAC, TAC]. ***PRACTICE AREAS:*** Corporate; Insurance and Damage Suit Defense; Insurance Rehabilitation and Liquidation; Construction; Suretyship. ***Email:*** crhodes@rhodesokla.com

(This Listing Continued)

BERT M. JONES, born Tulsa, Oklahoma, October 28, 1932; admitted to bar, 1959, Oklahoma. *Education:* University of Oklahoma (B.A., 1954; LL.B., 1959). Phi Alpha Delta. Staff Member, Oklahoma Law Review, 1958-1959. Author: "Fraud-Symposium on the Statutes of Limitations in Oklahoma," 12 Oklahoma Law Review 379, 1959; "Products Liability Defenses-Oklahoma," DRI Compendium, 1992 and 1999. Assistant County Attorney, Oklahoma County, 1960. Fellow, Oklahoma Bar Foundation. *Member:* Tulsa County, Oklahoma and American (Member, Products, General Liability and Consumer Law Committee, Tort and Insurance Practice Section, 1984) Bar Associations; Oklahoma Association of Defense Counsel (Director, 1974; Vice President, 1979); American Judicature Society; American Board of Trial Advocates; Defense Research Institute; Products Liability Advisory Council. [Capt., U.S.M.C.R.]. ***REPORTED CASES:*** Clark v. Mazda Motor Corp., 68 P.3d 207 (Okla. 2003); Ball v. Harnischfeger Corp., 877 P.2d 45 (Okla. 1994); Hinds v. General Motors Corp., 988 F.2d 1039 (10th Cir. 1993); Moore v. Subaru of America, 891 F.2d 1445 (10th Cir. 1989); Treadway v. Uniroyal Tire Co., 766 P.2d 938 (Okla. 1988); McMurray v. Deere and Co., Inc., 858 F.2d 1436 (10th Cir. 1988); Lee v. Volkswagen of America, Inc., 688 P.2d 1283 (Okla. 1984); Robinson v. Audi NSU Auto Union Aktiengesellschaft, 739 F.2d 1481 (10th Cir. 1984); World-Wide Volkswagen Corp. v. Woodson, 444 U.S. 559 (1980); Mayberry v. Akron Rubber Machinery Corp., 183 F. Supp. 407 (N.D. Okla. 1976); Duncan v. General Motors Corp., 499 F.2d 835 (10th Cir. 1974); Kirkland v. General Motors Corp., 521 P.2d 1353 (Okla. 1974); Hunt v. Firestone Tire & Rubber Co., 448 P.2d 1018 (Okla. 1968). ***PRACTICE AREAS:*** Products Liability; Appellate Practice. ***Email:*** bjones@rhodesokla.com

JOHN H. TUCKER, born Oklahoma City, Oklahoma, November 2, 1942; admitted to bar, 1966, Oklahoma. *Education:* University of Oklahoma (B.A., 1963; J.D., 1966). Member, PE-ET Society. U.S. Court of Appeals, Tenth Circuit Advisory Committee, Oklahoma Delegate, 2000-2004. Senior Adjunct Settlement Judge, Special Projects, U.S. District Court, Northern District of Oklahoma, 1988—. Chairman, Civil Justice Reform Act Advisory Committee, Northern District of Oklahoma. U.S. Supreme Court Historical Society, Region Chair 2004—; State Chair, 1999-2004; Historical Society of the 10th Judicial Circuit. *Member:* Tulsa County, Oklahoma and American Bar Associations; American Board of Trial Advocates; American Inns of Court (Master). Fellow: American College of Trial Lawyers (Regent 2004—; State Chairman, 1996-1998; Chairman, Samuel Gates Committee, 2000-2004); International Academy of Trial Lawyers; Oklahoma and American Bar Foundations. ***PRACTICE AREAS:*** Civil Litigation; Appellate Practice. ***Email:*** jtucker@rhodesokla.com

JO ANNE DEATON, born Tulsa, Oklahoma, July 15, 1955; admitted to bar, 1981, Oklahoma. *Education:* University of Oklahoma (B.A., 1978); University of Tulsa (J.D., 1981). Phi Delta Phi. Member, The Order of Barristers. Law Clerk Bailiff for U.S. District Judge James O. Ellison, Northern District of Oklahoma, 1981-1982. Adjunct Settlement Judge, U.S. District Court, Northern District of Oklahoma. Adjunct Settlement Judge, Tulsa County District Court. Member, Local Rules Committee, U.S. District Court, Northern District of Oklahoma. Vice-Chairperson, Board of Directors, Oklahoma Attorneys Mutual Insurance Company. Fellow, Oklahoma Bar Foundation. *Member:* Tulsa County, Oklahoma and American (Member, Tort and Insurance Practice Section, 1984) Bar Associations; American Inns of Court. ***PRACTICE AREAS:*** Employment; Products Liability; Insurance; Appellate Practice. ***Email:*** jdeaton@rhodesokla.com

DAN S. FOLLUO, born Keokuk, Iowa, August 6, 1960; admitted to bar, 1985, Oklahoma. *Education:* Southwest Missouri State University (B.S., 1982); University of Tulsa (J.D., 1985). Author: "Navigating the Troubled Waters of the Tripartite Relationship," OADC News, Spring 1999. Adjunct Settlement Judge, Tulsa County District Court. *Member:* Tulsa County and Oklahoma Bar Associations; Oklahoma Association of Defense Counsel (Vice President 1995-1996; President Elect 1997; President 1998); Defense Research Institute (Exceptional Performance Citation, 1998); Trucking Industry Defense Association. ***PRACTICE AREAS:*** Motor Carrier; Products Liability; Extra Contractual Insurance Defense; Professional Liability; Insurance. ***Email:*** dfolluo@rhodesokla.com

ANN E. ALLISON, born Tulsa, Oklahoma, January 10, 1963; admitted to bar, 1988, Oklahoma; U.S. District Court, Northern, Eastern and Western Districts of Oklahoma. *Education:* Oklahoma State University (B.S., 1985); University of San Diego; University of Oklahoma (J.D., 1988). *Member:* Tulsa County, Oklahoma and American Bar Associations; International Association of Defense Counsel; Oklahoma Association of Defense Counsel. ***PRACTICE AREAS:*** Products Liability; Professional Liability; Healthcare Liability; Insurance Defense; Litigation; Medical Malpractice Defense; Drug and Medical Device Defense; Employment. ***Email:*** aallison@rhodesokla.com

ANDREW D. DOWNING, born Tulsa, Oklahoma, March 19, 1969; admitted to bar, 1996, Oklahoma; U.S. District Court, Northern and Eastern Districts of Oklahoma; U.S. Court of Appeals, Tenth Circuit, U.S. Court of Federal Claims. *Education:* Rice University (B.A., 1991); University of Tulsa (J.D., 1995). Author: "Oklahoma Employers Beware: The Rock and A Hard Place Dilemma," Vol. 72, No. 21, Oklahoma Bar Journal (7/14/2001). Member, The University of Tulsa Division of Continuing Education, Advisory Board. Special Counsel for the Oklahoma Insurance Commissioner. Adjunct Professor, Advanced Torts, The University of Tulsa. *Member:* Oklahoma, Tulsa County and American (Member, Sections on: Tort; Insurance Practice) Bar Associations; Oklahoma Association of Defense Counsel. ***PRACTICE AREAS:*** Civil Litigation; Insolvency; Receiverships; ERISA; Workers' Compensation; Third Party Subrogation; Appellate Practice. ***Email:*** adowning@rhodesokla.com

BRADLEY A. JACKSON, born Terre Haute, Indiana, May 26, 1967; admitted to bar, 1992, Oklahoma; U.S. District Court, Northern, Eastern and Western Districts of Oklahoma. *Education:* Oklahoma State University (B.S., 1989); University of Tulsa (J.D., 1992). Phi Delta Phi. Recipient, American Jurisprudence Award in Professional Responsibility, 1992. *Member:* Tulsa County (Member: Law Related Education Committee; Court Operations Committee) and Oklahoma Bar Associations; Defense Research Institute; Oklahoma Association of Defense Counsel (President, 2006). ***PRACTICE AREAS:*** Commercial; General Liability; Products Liability; Professional Liability; Construction; Motor Carrier; Health Care Negligence. ***Email:*** bjackson@rhodesokla.com

COLIN H. TUCKER, born Tulsa, Oklahoma, April 12, 1967; admitted to bar, 1994, Oklahoma. *Education:* Dartmouth College (B.A., 1990); Columbia University (J.D., 1994). Articles Editor, Columbia Journal of Law and the Arts, 1993-1994. Director, Columbia Negotiation Competition, 1993. Judicial Law Clerk to: the Hon. James O. Ellison, U.S. District

(This Listing Continued)

Court for the Northern District of Oklahoma, 1994-1995; Hon. Sven Erik Holmes, U.S. District Court for the Northern District of Oklahoma, 1995. U.S. Supreme Court Historical Society, State Chair 2004—. *Member:* Tulsa County (Board of Directors; Outstanding Young Lawyer Award, 2000-2001), Oklahoma, Federal (Northern and Eastern Districts of Oklahoma, President 2001-2002) and American Bar Associations; American Inns of Court. ***PRACTICE AREAS:*** Environmental; Media and Entertainment; Commercial Litigation; Civil Litigation; Appellate Practice. ***Email:*** chtucker@rhodesokla.com

KERRY R. LEWIS, born Benton, Arkansas, September 20, 1965; admitted to bar, 1994, Texas; 1995, Oklahoma. *Education:* Southern Nazarene University (B.S., 1988); University of Tulsa (J.D., 1991); Tulane University of Louisiana (LL.M., 1992). Staff Member, Tulsa Law Journal, 1989-1990. Notes and Comments Editor, Tulsa Law Journal, 1990-1991. Recipient, Scribes Award as Outstanding Editor of a Law Journal, 1991. Author: Comment: "A Re-Examination of the Constitutional Right to a Jury Trial Under Title VII of the Civil Rights Act of 1964, 26 Tulsa Law Journal 571 (1992). *Member:* Tulsa County, Oklahoma and American (Member, Sections On: Tort & Insurance Practice; Litigation) Bar Associations. ***LANGUAGES:*** Spanish. ***PRACTICE AREAS:*** Commercial Litigation; Products Liability; Insurance Defense; Employment; Litigation; Appellate Practice. ***Email:*** klewis@rhodesokla.com

LESLIE J. SOUTHERLAND, born Bartlesville, Oklahoma, November 26, 1960; admitted to bar, 1987, Oklahoma. *Education:* University of Tulsa (B.A., 1984; J.D., 1987). Staff Member and Research Editor, Tulsa Law Journal. Recipient, American Jurisprudence Award in Constitutional Law. Graduate, DRI Trial Academy. Collaborator, Neighbor for Neighbor Legal Clinic. Participant, Tulsa Lawyers for Children. *Member:* Tulsa County, Oklahoma and American Bar Associations; Defense Research Institute. ***PRACTICE AREAS:*** Products Liability; Insurance Defense; Civil. ***Email:*** ljsoutherland@rhodesokla.com

---

NATHAN E. CLARK, born Tulsa, Oklahoma, September 12, 1971; admitted to bar, 1997, Oklahoma. *Education:* Baylor University (B.A., English Literature, 1994; J.D., 1997). Graduate, NITA Trial Academy. Phi Beta Kappa; Phi Delta Phi. *Member:* Tulsa County and Oklahoma Bar Associations; Oklahoma Association of Defense Counsel. ***PRACTICE AREAS:*** Products Liability; Health Care Negligence; Construction Litigation; Mold Litigation; Insurance Defense; Insurance Coverage. ***Email:*** nclark@rhodesokla.com

THERESA NOBLE HILL, born Lubbock, Texas, July 18, 1970; admitted to bar, 1999, North Carolina; 2001, Oklahoma. *Education:* University of Victoria (B.A., 1992); University of Oklahoma (J.D., 1999). *Member:* Tulsa County, Oklahoma and American Bar Associations. ***PRACTICE AREAS:*** Construction Litigation; Commercial Litigation; Insurance Defense; Toxic Torts. ***Email:*** thill@rhodesokla.com

CARLYE O. JIMERSON, born Tulsa, Oklahoma, April 10, 1957; admitted to bar, 1997, Oklahoma. *Education:* Oklahoma State University (B.S., 1979); University of Tulsa (J.D., 1995). *Member:* Tulsa County, Oklahoma and American Bar Associations; Federal Bar Association (President, Northern/Eastern Oklahoma Chapter, 2004); United States, American, and North Tulsa Tennis Associations. ***PRACTICE AREAS:*** Commercial Litigation; Civil Trial Practice; Employment Liability; Products Liability. ***Email:*** cjimerson@rhodesokla.com

BRADLEY S. SHELTS, born Bartlesville, Oklahoma, January 29, 1974; admitted to bar, 2002, Oklahoma. *Education:* Oklahoma State University (B.S., Business Administration, 1998); University of Tulsa (J.D., with highest honors, 2002). Phi Delta Phi; Order of the Curule Chair; Order of the Barristers. Recipient, CALI Excellence for the Future Award in Advanced Legal Writing; Merit Scholarship Winner. *Member:* Tulsa County, Oklahoma and American Bar Associations. ***PRACTICE AREAS:*** Products Liability; Insurance Defense; Civil Litigation; Employment Law; Appellate Practice. ***Email:*** bshelts@rhodesokla.com

LINDSAY J. McDOWELL, born Tulsa, Oklahoma, January 4, 1977; admitted to bar, 2003, Oklahoma. *Education:* Oklahoma State University (B.A., Journalism, 1999); University of Oklahoma (J.D., 2003). Member, Whittier Moot Court Team, 2002-2003. Member and Class President, 2002-2003, Student Bar Association. *Member:* Tulsa County (Member, Executive Committee, Young Lawyers Division 2005-2006), Oklahoma and American Bar Associations; Oklahoma Association of Defense Counsel; Hudson-Hall-Wheaton Chapter of American Inns of Court (Associate). ***PRACTICE AREAS:*** Employment Arbitration; Insurance Defense. ***Email:*** ljmcdowell@rhodesokla.com

MARGARET M. CLARKE, born Bronx, New York, January 25, 1971; admitted to bar, 1996, Oklahoma. *Education:* University of Oklahoma (B.A., 1993); Oklahoma City University (J.D., 1996). *Member:* Tulsa County, Oklahoma and American Bar Associations; Defense Research Institute. ***PRACTICE AREAS:*** Products Liability; Insurance Law; Civil Litigation; Health Care Litigation; Medical Law; Professional Liability. ***Email:*** mclarke@rhodesokla.com

DENELDA L. RICHARDSON, born Tulsa, Oklahoma, December 13, 1963; admitted to bar, 2004, Oklahoma. *Education:* Southern Nazarene University (B.S., Human Resources, 1996); University of Tulsa (J.D., 2003). Phi Delta Phi; Order of the Curule Chair. *Member:* Tulsa County and Oklahoma Bar Associations. ***LANGUAGES:*** American Sign Language. ***PRACTICE AREAS:*** Civil Litigation; Appellate Practice. ***Email:*** drichardson@rhodesokla.com

GREGG J. LYTLE, born New Haven, Connecticut, September 20, 1978; (admission pending). *Education:* Oklahoma State University (B.S., Management, 2001); University of Tulsa (J.D., 2005). *Member:* Tulsa County Bar Association. ***PRACTICE AREAS:*** Insurance Defense; Products Liability; Civil Litigation. ***Email:*** glytle@rhodesokla.com

LEGAL SUPPORT PERSONNEL

JOHN GREGORY MADDEN, III, born Tulsa, Oklahoma, May 29, 1951. *Education:* University of Tulsa (B.S., Business Administration, 1974); Oklahoma State University (M.S., Business Administration, 1978). Member, Association of Legal Administrators (Regional Officer, 2005-2007; President, Tulsa Chapter, 2002-2003). *Member:* American Bar Association (Associate Member). [Lt. Colonel, USMC Reserve, Retired]. (Administrator). ***Email:*** gmadden@rhodesokla.com

GAY WAID SELLERS, born Miami, Oklahoma, March 22, 1951. Member, NALS... the association for legal professionals (1972—; President, NALS of Oklahoma, 2004-2006). Certified Professional Legal Secretary, 1980. Certified Professional Paralegal, 2004. (Administrator). ***Email:*** gsellers@rhodesokla.com

REPRESENTATIVE CLIENTS: ACE USA; Air Products & Chemicals; AIG; AGCO; APAC-Oklahoma Inc. a division of Ashland Oil; Atlantic Companies; Audi NSU; Bechtel; Cancer Care Associates; Chubb Group; Circle International, Inc.; Clorox; CNA Surety; Contract Freighters Inc.; Crown Equipment; Deere & Co.; Dresser Industries; Dresser-Rand/Halliburton; EGL, Inc.; Fireman's Fund; General Motors; Global Aerospace/AAU; The Hanover Insurance Company; Highlands Insurance; Kemper Insurance; Kraft General Foods; Lancer Insurance; Mazda; MEDMARC; Mid-Continent Insurance; Mid-Continent Pipeline; Mitsubishi; Nationwide Group; Navistar/International Harvester; Nissan; PFT Roberson Transportation; PPG Industries; Phillip Morris; Protective Insurance; Republic Insurance; RLI Insurance; Royal & SunAlliance; Service Corporation International; The Shaw Group; Solkatronic Chemical, Inc.; Spirit Homes Inc.; Sun Companies, Inc. (R & M); Sunoco, Inc.; Sunoco Pipeline Partners, LLP; Tokio Marine & Fire; Transport Insurance; Travelers; United Dominion Industries; Volkswagen, A.G.; YMCA of Greater Tulsa; Zurich.

(This Listing Continued)

RICHARDS & CONNOR

Established in 1997

12TH FLOOR, PARK CENTRE BUILDING
525 SOUTH MAIN, SUITE 1250
TULSA, OKLAHOMA 74103-4509
Telephone: 918-585-2394
Fax: 918-585-1449
Email: prichards@richardsconnor.com
URL: http://www.richardsconnor.com

General Civil and Trial Practice in State and Federal Courts, including Medical Malpractice, Insurance Defense, Commercial, Negligence, Professional Liability, General Liability, Physical Damage, Bodily Injury, Products Liability, Employment, Insurance Law and Environmental Law.

FIRM PROFILE: Richards & Connor is a firm primarily devoted to the handling of complex litigation involving insurance, medical, personal injury and commercial issues. Representing both insurance industry and business, Richards & Connor provides trial representation through experienced and respected trial lawyers assisted by associates skilled in litigation support. The firm also has a research group recognized for its capabilities to the degree that they are utilized by companies to handle appellate work and assist with legal issues even in cases not tried by the firm. The scope of cases handled by Richards & Connor is truly diverse, but the single constant and guiding principle in all of its representation is an intense focus on excellence with unwavering integrity.

MEMBERS OF FIRM

PHIL R. RICHARDS, born Tulsa, Oklahoma, 1958; admitted to bar, 1983, Oklahoma, U.S. District Court, Northern, Eastern and Western Districts of Oklahoma, U.S. Court of Appeals, Tenth Circuit and U.S. Supreme Court. *Education:* University of Oklahoma (B.A., 1980; J.D., 1983). Phi Alpha Delta. Recipient, American Jurisprudence Award, Criminal Procedure. District Attorneys Office, Stephens and Grady Counties, 1982-1984. *Member:* Tulsa County, Oklahoma and American Bar Associations; Oklahoma Association of Defense Counsel (Vice President, 2002; President-Elect, 2003; President, 2004); Defense Research Institute; Federation of Insurance and Corporate Counsel; American Inns of Court. Fellow, American College of Trial Lawyers. ***PRACTICE AREAS:*** Medical/Legal; Professional Liability; Products Liability; Insurance Law; Insurance Bad Faith Defense; Commercial; General Liability. ***Email:*** prichards@richardsconnor.com

JAMES W. CONNOR, JR., born Bartlesville, Oklahoma, March 11, 1961; admitted to bar, 1987, Oklahoma and U.S. District Court, Northern, Eastern and Western Districts of Oklahoma; 1988, U.S. Court of Appeals, Tenth Circuit. *Education:* University of Tulsa (B.S.B.A., 1984; J.D., 1987). Delta Theta Phi. Author: "Civil RICO—The Pattern of Racketeering Requirement: Louisiana Power and Light v. United Gas Pipeline," 8 Energy Law Journal 105, 1987. Law Clerk to Honorable Layn R. Phillips, U.S. District Judge, Western District of Oklahoma, 1987-1988. *Member:* Oklahoma County, Tulsa County and Oklahoma Associations; Defense Research Institute; Oklahoma Association of Defense Counsel. ***PRACTICE AREAS:*** Medical Malpractice Defense; Products Liability; Employment Law; Insurance; Civil Litigation. ***Email:*** jconnor@richardsconnor.com

RACHEL CARVER MATHIS, born Sapulpa, Oklahoma, 1970; admitted to bar, 1995, Oklahoma and Arkansas; U.S. District Court, Northern, Eastern and Western Districts of Oklahoma; 1996, U.S. Court of Appeals, Tenth Circuit. *Education:* Oklahoma State University (B.S., 1992); University of Oklahoma (J.D., 1995). Phi Delta Phi. *Member:* Tulsa County, Oklahoma and Arkansas Bar Associations; Defense Research Institute; Oklahoma Association of Defense Counsel. ***REPORTED CASES:*** Williams v. Tulsa Motels, No. 89,857, Supreme Court of Oklahoma, May 21, 1998; Heintz v. Trucks For You, Inc., 1999 OK CIV. APP. 64,984 P.2d 255. ***PRACTICE AREAS:*** Insurance Defense; General Liability; Products Liability; Employment Law; Contract Litigation; Business Litigation. ***Email:*** rmathis@richardsconnor.com

THOMAS D. HIRD, born Wichita, Kansas, 1962; admitted to bar, 1990, Oklahoma; 1993, California, U.S. District Court, Northern, Eastern and Western District of Oklahoma; U.S. Court of Appeals, Tenth Circuit and U.S. Supreme Court. *Education:* Oklahoma Christian University (B.S., 1985); University of Oklahoma (J.D., 1990). Member, Oklahoma Law Review. Judicial Law Clerk for the United States District Courts for the District of Nevada, Northern and Eastern Districts of Oklahoma and Central District of California. *Member:* Tulsa County and Oklahoma Bar Associations; State Bar of California; Oklahoma Association of Defense Counsel. ***PRACTICE AREAS:*** Appellate Practice; Insurance Defense. ***Email:*** third@richardsconnor.com

(This Listing Continued)

RICHARDS & CONNOR, Tulsa—Continued

ASSOCIATES

JASON L. GLASS, born McAlester, Oklahoma, 1971; admitted to bar, 1997, Oklahoma; U.S. District Court, Northern, Eastern and Western Districts of Oklahoma; U.S. Court of Appeals, Tenth Circuit; U.S. Supreme Court. *Education:* Southern Methodist University (B.A., magna cum laude, 1993; B.B.A., magna cum laude, 1993); University of Texas School of Law (J.D., 1997). *Member:* Tulsa County and Oklahoma Bar Associations; Defense Research Institute; Oklahoma Association of Defense Counsel. ***PRACTICE AREAS:*** Insurance Defense; Medical Malpractice Defense; Employment Law; Civil Litigation; Products Liability. ***Email:*** jglass@richardsconnor.com

JOHN A.L. CAMPBELL, born Palmerton, Pennsylvania, September 8, 1967; admitted to bar, 1997, Oklahoma; 1998, U.S. District Court, Northern, Eastern and Western Districts of Oklahoma. *Education:* Oklahoma State University (B.S., 1990); University of Tulsa (J.D. with honors, 1997). Phi Delta Phi. Recipient, CALI Excellence for the Future Award for Evidence. *Member:* Tulsa County and Oklahoma Bar Associations; Oklahoma Association of Defense Counsel; Defense Research Institute. [USMC, 1991-1994; USAR, 2005—]. ***REPORTED CASES:*** Stade v. Bodycote Thermal Processing, Inc., 99 P.3d 733, 2004 OK CIV APP 70. ***PRACTICE AREAS:*** Civil Trial Practice; Criminal Defense; Family Law. ***Email:*** jcampbell@richardsconnor.com

RICHARD L. HATHCOAT, born Stillwater, Oklahoma, 1963; admitted to bar, 1991, Oklahoma; 1996, U.S. District Court, Northern and Eastern Districts of Oklahoma; 1998, U.S. Court of Appeals, Tenth Circuit. *Education:* University of Tulsa (B.S.B.A., 1988; J.D., 1991). *Member:* Tulsa County and Oklahoma Bar Associations; Oklahoma Association of Defense Counsel. ***PRACTICE AREAS:*** Litigation. ***Email:*** rhathcoat@richardsconnor.com

JEFFREY C. BAUM, born Oklahoma City, Oklahoma, September 26, 1969; admitted to bar, 1996, Oklahoma; 1997, U.S. District Court, Western District of Oklahoma; 2000, U.S. District Court, Northern and Eastern Districts of Oklahoma and U.S. Court of Appeals, Tenth Circuit. *Education:* University of Oklahoma (B.A., 1992; J.D., 1995). *Member:* Oklahoma County, Tulsa County (Chair, Young Lawyers Division, 2001-2002), Oklahoma (Member, Real Property Section) and American (Member, Estate, Property and Trusts Sections) Bar Associations; American Inns of Court; Oklahoma Association of Defense Counsel; Defense Research Institute. ***PRACTICE AREAS:*** Civil Litigation; Business Law; Corporate Law; Real Property; Estate Planning. ***Email:*** jbaum@richardsconnor.com

STEPHANIE R. COATES, born Birmingham, Alabama, February 14, 1969; admitted to bar, 1996, Texas and U.S. District Court, Northern, Southern, Eastern and Western Districts of Texas; 1999, Oklahoma; 2001, U.S. District Court, Northern, Eastern and Western Districts of Oklahoma. *Education:* Baylor University (B.A., English, 1991); South Texas College of Law (J.D., 1995). *Member:* Tulsa County and Oklahoma Bar Associations; State Bar of Texas; Oklahoma Association of Defense Counsel. ***LANGUAGES:*** Spanish. ***PRACTICE AREAS:*** Insurance Defense; Insurance Law; General Liability; Products Liability; Civil Litigation. ***Email:*** scoates@richardsconnor.com

ELIZABETH A. HART, born Rogers, Arkansas, March 11, 1975; admitted to bar, 2000, Oklahoma and U.S. District Court, Northern, Eastern and Western Districts of Oklahoma; U.S. Court of Appelas, Tenth Circuit. *Education:* University of Arkansas (B.A., 1997); University of Tulsa (J.D., 1999). *Member:* Tulsa County and Oklahoma Bar Associations; Oklahoma Health Care Lawyers Association; Oklahoma Association of Defense Counsel; Association of Trial Lawyers of America. ***PRACTICE AREAS:*** Medical Malpractice; Insurance Bad Faith; Commercial Litigation. ***Email:*** ehart@richardsconnor.com

OLIVER L. SMITH, born Tulsa, Oklahoma, September 30, 1978; admitted to bar, 2003, Oklahoma. *Education:* University of Oklahoma (B.A., 2000); University of Tulsa (J.D., with highest honors, 2003). Editor, Tulsa Law Review, 2002-2003. Recipient: Order of the Curule Chair; CALI Excellence for the Future Awards for Civil Procedure I, Federal Income Taxation and Jurisprudence. *Member:* Oklahoma Bar Association; Oklahoma Association of Defense Counsel. ***PRACTICE AREAS:*** Insurance Defense; Civil Litigation. ***Email:*** osmith@richardsconnor.com

AMY E. HAMPTON, born Tulsa, Oklahoma, 1976; admitted to bar, 2004, Oklahoma. *Education:* University of Tulsa (B.A., 1999; J.D., 2004). Phi Delta Phi. Recipient: CALI Excellence for the Future Awards in Constitutional Law II and International Energy & Natural Resources. Senior Articles Editor, Tulsa Journal of Comparative & International Law, 2003-2004. Judicial Law Clerk for Superior Court of New Jersey, Family Division, 2004-2005. Author: "Population Control in China: Sacrificing Human Rights for the Greater Good?", 11 Tulsa J. Comp. & Int'l L.321 (2003). *Member:* Oklahoma Bar Association. ***PRACTICE AREAS:*** Civil Litigation; Insurance Defense. ***Email:*** ahampton@richardsconnor.com

OF COUNSEL

JOHN W. KELSON, born Ponca City, Oklahoma, November 25, 1947; admitted to bar, 1979, Oklahoma; 1984, U.S. District Court, Western District of Oklahoma; 1996, U.S. District Court, Northern District of Oklahoma. *Education:* Central State University (B.A., 1972); Oklahoma City University (J.D., 1978). Member, District Attorney's Office, Oklahoma, Tulsa, Stephens, Delaware Counties. *Member:* Oklahoma Bar Association. ***PRACTICE AREAS:*** Criminal Defense. ***Email:*** jkelson@richardsconnor.com

REPRESENTATIVE CLIENTS: St. Paul Travelers Companies; Physicians Liability Insurance Company; Gulf Insurance Company; The Hartford Insurance Group; Electric Insurance Company; American Mercury Insurance Cos.; Mazzio's Corporation; General Electric Company; Conseco Companies; Admiral Insurance Co.; NCMIC Insurance Company; Interstate Insurance Group; Shand Morahan & Company; Target Corp.; American National Property & Casualty Companies; Miller Insurance Group; Sunshine Homes; Lexington Insurance Company; One Beacon Insurance; American Family Insurance Group; American Commerce Ins. Co.; RSA Surplus Lines Ins. Serv.; ACE USA; Summit Risk Services, Inc.; Pacer International, Inc.; Rental Services Corp.; Texas All-Risk General Agency, Inc.; American Modern Home Insurance Company; American Specialty Insurance Company; Gateway Insurance Company; Nationwide Mutual Insurance Co.; State Auto Insurance Company; Fleet Boston Financial Corp.; SecurCare Properties; Viking Packing Specialist; Deutz of America Corp.; Honeywell International, Inc.; Deep South Insurance.

RIGGS, ABNEY, NEAL, TURPEN, ORBISON & LEWIS

A PROFESSIONAL CORPORATION

Established in 1972

502 WEST SIXTH STREET

TULSA, OKLAHOMA 74119

Telephone: 918-587-3161

Fax: 918-587-9708

URL: http://www.riggsabney.com

Oklahoma City, Oklahoma Office: The Paragon Building, Suite 101, 73118-7489. Telephone: 405-843-9909. Fax: 405-842-2913.

Muskogee, Oklahoma Office: 215 State Street, First National Severs Building, Suite 508, 74402. Telephone: 918-687-5404; 800-722-1332. Fax: 918-687-1128.

Denver, Colorado Office: 621 Seventeenth Street, Suite 1900, 80293. Telephone: 303-298-7392. Fax: 303-298-7398.

General Civil, Trial and Appellate Practice before all State and Federal Courts and Agencies, Alternative Dispute Resolution, Banking, Corporate, Securities, Anti-trust, Administrative, Government Relations, Real Estate, Commercial Transactions, Oil and Gas, Estate Planning, Probate, Taxation, Employment and Discrimination, Employee Benefits, Social Security, Bankruptcy and Reorganization, Family Law, Healthcare, Negligence, Personal Injury, Products Liability, Medical Malpractice, Transportation and Indian Law.

MEMBERS OF FIRM

M. DAVID RIGGS, admitted to bar, 1969, Oklahoma. *Education:* Phillips University (B.A., 1959); University of Oklahoma (M.A., 1962); University of Tulsa (J.D., 1968). Graduated First in Class, University of Tulsa. Member: Oklahoma House of Representatives, 1971-1987; Oklahoma Senate, 1987-1988. ***PRACTICE AREAS:*** Personal Injury Law; Medical Malpractice Law; General Litigation.

GARY L. NEAL, admitted to bar, 1975, Oklahoma. *Education:* Northeastern Oklahoma State University (B.A., 1968); University of Oklahoma (J.D., 1975). [U.S. Navy, 1968-1972]. ***PRACTICE AREAS:*** Real Estate Law; Corporate; Banking Law; Commercial Transactions.

C.S. LEWIS, III, admitted to bar, 1971, Oklahoma. *Education:* Washington University (B.A., 1968); University of Oklahoma (J.D., 1971). Member, University of Oklahoma Board of Regents, 1991—. Member and Secretary, 1985-1987 and Vice Chairman, 1987-1988, Board of Trustees, University Center at Tulsa. Member, Zoning Board of Adjustment, City of Tulsa, 1978-1982. ***PRACTICE AREAS:*** Litigation; Banking Law; Bankruptcy Law.

JAMES C. ORBISON, admitted to bar, 1968, Oklahoma. *Education:* Oklahoma State University; University of Tulsa (B.A., 1966; J.D., 1968). Member, Board of Directors, Federal Home Loan Bank of Topeka, 1998—. Vice Chairman, Tulsa County Public Facilities Authority, 1983—. Chairman, Oklahoma Turnpike Authority, 1991-1995. ***PRACTICE AREAS:*** Corporate Law; Banking Law; Real Estate Law; Employment Law; Government Relations.

DONALD M. BINGHAM, admitted to bar, 1977, Oklahoma. *Education:* Princeton University (A.B., cum laude, 1970); University of Tulsa (J.D., 1976). Special Judge, Oklahoma Court of Appeals, 1982, 1993. Adjunct Professor, Trial Practice and Pre-Trial Practice, University of Tulsa College of Law, 1984-1992. ***PRACTICE AREAS:*** Civil Litigation; Employment Law; ERISA.

JOSEPH P. LENNART, admitted to bar, 1981, Oklahoma and U.S. Tax Court. *Education:* University of Tulsa (B.S., 1969; J.D., 1981). Certified Public Accountant, Oklahoma, 1973. Adjunct Professor of Law, University of Tulsa, 1985-1986. ***PRACTICE AREAS:*** Taxation Law; Corporate Law; Securities Law; Estate Planning.

KENNETH M. SMITH, admitted to bar, 1972, Oklahoma. *Education:* Oklahoma State University (B.S.C.E., 1965); University of Tulsa (J.D., 1972). Licensed Professional Engineer, Oklahoma, 1972. [Lt. (J.g.), USN, 1966-1969]. ***PRACTICE AREAS:*** Real Estate; Corporate; Title Insurance Law; Real Estate Litigation; Business Litigation; Commercial Litigation.

STEPHEN B. RILEY, admitted to bar, 1972, Oklahoma. *Education:* University of Oklahoma (B.S., 1967; J.D., 1972). Assistant District Attorney, 1972-1973. ***PRACTICE AREAS:*** Civil Litigation; Bankruptcy Law.

SCOTT P. KIRTLEY, admitted to bar, 1985, Oklahoma. *Education:* Oklahoma State University (B.S., 1981); O. W. Coburn School of Law, Oral Roberts University (J.D., 1985). Law Clerk to the Honorable Mickey D. Wilson, United States Bankruptcy Judge, Northern District of Oklahoma, 1986-1988. Panel Chapter 7 and 11 Trustee for the Northern and Eastern Districts of Oklahoma, since 1988. ***PRACTICE AREAS:*** Bankruptcy Law; Commercial Law.

RICHARD A. GANN, admitted to bar, 1975, Oklahoma. *Education:* Oklahoma State University (B.S., 1971); Tulsa University (J.D., 1974). Assistant District Attorney, Tulsa County, 1975-1978. ***PRACTICE AREAS:*** General Civil Litigation; Personal Injury.

HARLEY W. THOMAS, admitted to bar, 1980, Oklahoma. *Education:* Vanderbilt University (B.A., 1976); University of Tulsa (J.D., 1979). ***PRACTICE AREAS:*** Banking Law; Corporate Law; Real Estate Law; Commercial Transactions.

JANET S. DUMONT, admitted to bar, 1987, Oklahoma. *Education:* University of Oklahoma (B.F.A., 1974; M.Ed., 1975); University of Tulsa (J.D., 1987). ***PRACTICE AREAS:*** Employee Benefits; Employment Law; Health Care; Insurance Law; Corporate Law.

LISA R. RIGGS, admitted to bar, 1987, District of Columbia; 1988, Maryland; 1996, Oklahoma; 1998, Colorado. *Education:* University of Oklahoma (B.S., 1982; M.A., 1984); Georgetown University (J.D., 1987). ***PRACTICE AREAS:*** Medical Malpractice; Product Safety; Catastrophic Injury; Construction Accidents; Wrongful Death.

(This Listing Continued)

J. LYON MOREHEAD, admitted to bar, 1976, Oklahoma. *Education:* Westminster College and University of Tulsa (B.A., 1973; J.D., 1976). President, Tulsa Title and Probate Lawyers Association, 1994. ***PRACTICE AREAS:*** Title Examination; Real Estate Law.

RICHARD T. GARREN, admitted to bar, 1975, Oklahoma. *Education:* University of Tulsa (B.A., 1971; J.D., 1974). ***PRACTICE AREAS:*** Family Law; Civil Litigation.

JACK R. ANDERSON, admitted to bar, 1968, Oklahoma. *Education:* University of Tulsa (B.S., 1966; J.D., 1968). *Member:* Motor Carrier Lawyers Association. [U.S. Army, 1968-1970]. ***PRACTICE AREAS:*** Transportation Law; Bankruptcy Law; Probate and Estate Planning Law.

STEPHANIE L. JONES THEBAN, admitted to bar, 1983, Oklahoma. *Education:* Cameron University; Oklahoma State University (B.A., with honors, 1980); University of Tulsa (J.D., 1983). Member, Order of Curule Chair. ***PRACTICE AREAS:*** Civil Appellate Practice; Civil Litigation.

FRED RAHAL, JR., admitted to bar, 1963, Oklahoma. *Education:* University of Tulsa (B.A., 1961; J.D., 1963). [Capt., U.S. Army, 1963-1966]. ***PRACTICE AREAS:*** Corporate Law; Civil Litigation; Transportation Law.

GRETCHEN M. WIDDIG SCHILLING, admitted to bar, 1992, Oklahoma. *Education:* Cameron University (B.Acct., highest honors, 1987); University of Tulsa (J.D., 1992). ***PRACTICE AREAS:*** Civil Litigation; Civil Appeals.

REX WADE THOMPSON, admitted to bar, 1989, Oklahoma. *Education:* University of Tulsa (B.A., 1986; J.D., 1989). ***PRACTICE AREAS:*** Employment Law; Family Law; Administrative Law.

BEVERLY A. STEWART, admitted to bar, 1988, Oklahoma. *Education:* Southern Methodist University-Methodist Hospital (R.N., 1957); University of Tulsa (B.A. in Sociology, with honor, 1983; J.D., 1988). ***PRACTICE AREAS:*** Social Security Disability; Disability Insurance; Insurance Law; Employment Law; Civil Litigation.

JAMES R. POLAN, admitted to bar, 1987, Oklahoma; 1994, New Mexico. *Education:* University of Tulsa (B.F.A., 1973; M.A., 1983); Cornell University (J.D., 1987). ***PRACTICE AREAS:*** Employment; Workers Compensation; Contracts; Civil Litigation.

KAREN CARDEN WALSH, admitted to bar, 1991, Oklahoma. *Education:* University of Tulsa (B.S., cum laude, 1988); University of Oklahoma (J.D., with highest honors, 1991). Order of the Coif. ***PRACTICE AREAS:*** Bankruptcy; Commercial Law.

DOUGLAS A. WILSON, admitted to bar, 1989, Oklahoma. *Education:* Oklahoma State University (B.A., 1986); University of Tulsa (J.D., 1989).

DAVID C. CAMERON, admitted to bar, 1980, Oklahoma. *Education:* University of Oklahoma (B.A., 1977; J.D., 1980). ***PRACTICE AREAS:*** Real Estate; Corporate.

IRA L. EDWARDS, JR., admitted to bar, 1976, Texas; 1978, Oklahoma. *Education:* Central State University (B.S., 1973); University of Oklahoma (J.D., 1976). ***PRACTICE AREAS:*** Civil Litigation.

ROBERT P. SKEITH, admitted to bar, 1994, Oklahoma. *Education:* University of Tulsa (B.A., 1991; J.D., with honors, 1994). ***REPORTED CASES:*** Hurlbut v. Morrow, 2002 OK CIV APP 83, 55 P.3d 455; In the Matter of O.L.P., 2002 OK CIV APP 17, 41 P.3d 999; Meghan Coves Association, Inc. v. Meghan Coves Property, Inc., 2002 OK CIV APP 63, 50 P2d 226; Wyatt-Doyle & Butler Engineers, Inc. v. City of Eufaula, 2000 OK 74, 13 P.3d 474; Mid America Ag Network, Inc. v. Monkey Island Development Authority, 2004 WL 1529284 (10th Cir.). ***PRACTICE AREAS:*** Civil Litigation; Commercial; Banking; Real Estate.

ASSOCIATES

Greg Alberty
Ryan James Assink
Jack Steven Barker
William A. Bowles
Kelly L. Bratcher
James R. Briggs
Peter W. Brolick
Scott Wallace Byrd
Michelle M. Carter
Colby Cook
Glenna S. Dorris
Stephen E. Hale
Zachery R. Hargis
Erik Houghton
Robert E. Howard
Deborah Johnstone
Kiemonn Jones
Kristopher Koepsel
G. Diane Lee
Tyler D. Leonard
Michelle Lester
Mary Jean Little
Lori T. Lovoi-Nieves
Janet G. Mallow
John R. Maloy
Mark L. Nelms
Mary J. Rounds
William C. Searcy
Linda Van Arkel-Greubel
Sharon K. Weaver
Jerry Witt
Courtney Wolin
Michael P. Womack

REPRESENTATIVE CLIENTS: Pre-Paid Legal Services, Inc.; Bank of Oklahoma, N.A.; BancOklahoma Mortgage Corp.; Arvest Bank; American State Bank; Bank One; Oklahoma State Banking Commission; SpiritBank; State Bank & Trust, N.A.; Oklahoma Central Credit Union; RCB Bank; Anheuser Busch, Inc.; Amway Corp.; SBC Communications, Inc.; Southwestern Bell Telephone Co.; Southwestern Bell Wireless; Builders Square; B.P. America, Inc.; Case & Associates Properties, Inc.; Intervest Properties, Ltd.; Calumet Oil Co.; Emergency Medical Services Authority; Tulsa County Criminal Justice Authority; PowerSmith Cogeneration Project, L.P.; Power Resource Group, Inc.; Verdigris Valley Electric Cooperative; Sand Springs Public Schools; Quarles Agency, Inc.; National Steak and Poultry, Inc.; Whitlock Packaging Corp.; Member Service Life Insurance Co.; Webco Industries, Inc.; Capital Assets, Inc.; Frisco Title and Abstract Co.; University Hospital Authority; Amica Mutual Insurance Co.; Air Tulsa, Inc.; Oklahoma Association of Realtors; Oklahoma State Board of Registered Dentists; State Board of Osteopathic Examiners; Oklahoma Board of Public Accountancy; Oklahoma Educational Television Authority; Oklahoma State Insurance Dept.; Oklahoma Department of Transportation; Oklahoma Public Employees Association.

(This Listing Continued)

K. ELLIS RITCHIE, P.C.

TULSA, OKLAHOMA

(See Pryor)

Practice includes Eminent Domain/Condemnation/Property Rights.

THE ROBERTSON LAW FIRM, PLLC

2000 BANK OF AMERICA CENTER
15 E. 6TH STREET
TULSA, OKLAHOMA 74119
Telephone: 918-382-9332
Fax: 918-382-9319
Email: moura@robertsonlawfirm.net
URL: http://www.tulsadivorce.com

Matrimonial and Family Law, including Antenuptial Agreements, Divorce, Child Custody, Domestic Torts, Adoption, Guardianship.

MOURA A.J. ROBERTSON, born Kingston, New York, April 8, 1960; admitted to bar, 1992, Oklahoma and U.S. District Court, Northern District of Oklahoma; 1993, U.S. District Court, Eastern District of Oklahoma; 1994, U.S. District Court, Western District of Oklahoma. *Education:* State University of New York College at New Paltz (B.A., 1982); University of Tulsa College of Law (J.D., 1992). Phi Alpha Delta. Board of Advocates. Energy Law Journal. *Member:* Tulsa County Bar Association (Family Law Section); Oklahoma Bar Association (Family Law Section); American Bar Association (Family Law Section). ***PRACTICE AREAS:*** Divorce; Divorce Mediation; Domestic Torts; Domestic Violence; Premarital Agreements; Post Divorce Modification. ***Email:*** moura@robertsonlawfirm.net

ROBINETT & MURPHY

624 SOUTH BOSTON, SUITE 900
TULSA, OKLAHOMA 74119
Telephone: 918-592-3699
Fax: 918-592-0963

General Civil Practice Before all State and Federal Courts.

TRACY W. ROBINETT, born Enid, Oklahoma, July 7, 1964; admitted to bar, 1989, Oklahoma. *Education:* University of Oklahoma (B.B.A., 1986); University of Tulsa (J.D., 1989). *Member:* Tulsa County and Oklahoma Bar Associations; American Inns of Court (Robert D. Hudson Chapter, 1993-1994; Hudson-Hall Wheaton Chapter, 1995-1996). ***PRACTICE AREAS:*** Civil Litigation. ***Email:*** trobinett@robinettmurphy.com

LAWRENCE R. MURPHY, JR., born Waterbury, Connecticut, April 21, 1972; admitted to bar, 1997, Oklahoma. *Education:* Saint Anselm College (B.A., 1994); University of Tulsa (J.D., 1997). Phi Delta Phi. Articles Editor, Tulsa Law Journal, 1996-1997. ***PRACTICE AREAS:*** Civil Litigation; Banking Law; Construction Law; Insurance Defense; Products Liability. ***Email:*** lmurphy@robinettmurphy.com

GREGORY A. CALVERT, born Tulsa, Oklahoma, November 5, 1966; admitted to bar, 1993, Oklahoma and U.S. District Court, Northern District of Oklahoma; 1996, U.S. District Court, Eastern District of Oklahoma; 2000, U.S. District Court, Western District of Oklahoma and U.S. Court of Appeals, Tenth Circuit. *Education:* Oklahoma State University (B.S., Economics, 1990); University of Oklahoma (J.D., with honors, 1993). *Member:* Tulsa County and Oklahoma Bar Associations; National Association of Railroad Trial Counsel. ***PRACTICE AREAS:*** Civil Litigation; Products Liability; Railroad Law. ***Email:*** gcalvert@robinettmurphy.com

KELLY A. SMAKAL, born Berwyn, Illinois, December 28, 1970; admitted to bar, 1997, Oklahoma and U.S. District Court, Eastern District of Oklahoma; 1998, U.S. District Court, Northern District of Oklahoma. *Education:* University of Arkansas at Fayetteville (B.A., 1994; J.D., 1996). Phi Delta Phi. Author: "Pro Bono Legal Services for the Poor," OBA Desk Manual, 1998, 1999. Adjunct Clinical Professor of Law, Elder Law Clinic, University of Tulsa, 2002. *Member:* Tulsa County and Oklahoma Bar Associations; Court Operations Committee; Professional Responsibility Committee. ***PRACTICE AREAS:*** Family Law; Domestic Relations; Adoption Law; Guardianship; Probate; Traffic Violations. ***Email:*** ksmakal@robinettemurphy.com

STEPHAN S. MATHIS, born Sapulpa, Oklahoma, June 18, 1968; admitted to bar, 2001, Oklahoma, U.S. District Court, Northern and Eastern Districts of Oklahoma; 2002, U.S. District Court, Western District of Oklahoma. *Education:* Oklahoma State University (B.S.B.A., 1990); University of Tulsa (J.D., with highest honors, 2001). Order of Curule Chair. Phi Delta Phi. Recipient, CALI Award for Civil Procedure and Agency and Partnership. Member, Tulsa Law Journal, 2000-2001. Certified Public Accountant, Oklahoma, 1992. *Member:* Tulsa County and Oklahoma Bar Associations; American Inns of Court; Defense Research Institute; Oklahoma Association of Defense Counsel. ***PRACTICE AREAS:*** Civil Litigation; Medical Malpractice; Municipal Liability; Products Liability. ***Email:*** smathis@robinettmurphy.com

PANSY C. MOORE-SHRIER, born Tulsa, Oklahoma, July 28, 1976; admitted to bar, 2004, Oklahoma and U.S. District Court, Northern and Western Districts of Oklahoma; 2005, U.S. District Court, Eastern District of Oklahoma. *Education:* St. Mary-of-the-

(This Listing Continued)

ROBINETT & MURPHY, Tulsa—Continued

Woods College (B.S., 2000); University of Tulsa (J.D., 2004). *Member:* Tulsa County and Oklahoma Bar Associations. ***PRACTICE AREAS:*** Civil Litigation; Insurance Defense; Products Liability. ***Email:*** pmoore-shrier@robinettmurphy.com

REPRESENTATIVE CLIENTS: ABBCO Roofing; ABC Supply Company; Addco Electric; ARC Supply Company; Black Gold Concrete; BSW Architects & Engineers; Commerce Bank N.A.; Emergency Care, Inc.; George & George Safety and Glove; Gold Bank; Harp Electric; Hi-Tech Systems; Kansas & Oklahoma Railroad; Midwest Truck; Murphy Industries, Inc.; Oklahoma Department of Transportation; Oklahoma Municipal Assurance Group; Paragon Painting; PSS World Medical, Inc.; Roofing & Sheet Metal Supply Co.; Scoggins Roofing; South Kansas & Oklahoma Railroad; Spec Building Materials; State Auto Insurance Cos.; Stillwater Central Railroad; Superior Stucco; Thompson Metal Fab; Turner Roofing & Sheet Metal, Inc.; Utter & Associates; WATCO Cos., Inc.; Wilco Guttering Co.

THE ROBINSON LAW FIRM

5810 EAST SKELLY DRIVE
SUITE 1100
TULSA, OKLAHOMA 74135
Telephone: 918-587-2311
Fax: 918-587-2317
Email: grobinson@webzone.net
URL: http://www.grobinson.com

Insurance Defense, Premises Liability, Tort, General Civil Practice in all courts.

FIRM PROFILE: The Robinson Law Firm is listed in the Bar Register of Preeminent Lawyers.

EUGENE ROBINSON, born Wichita Falls, Texas, June 11, 1957; admitted to bar, 1983, Oklahoma and U.S. District Court, Northern, Eastern and Western Districts of Oklahoma. *Education:* Northeastern Oklahoma A & M (A.A., 1977); University of Tulsa (B.S., 1979; J.D., 1983). Recipient, American Jurisprudence Award for Trial Practice. Listed in the Bar Register of Preeminent Lawyers. *Member:* Tulsa County, Oklahoma and American (Member, Section on: Tort and Insurance Practice Law; Litigation) Bar Associations; Oklahoma Association of Defense Counsel; American Inns of Court; Defense Research Institute; American Board of Trial Advocates. ***PRACTICE AREAS:*** General Tort; Appellate Practice; Insurance Law; Civil Litigation.

ASSOCIATES

KENNETH M. YATES, born Tulsa, Oklahoma, October 22, 1966; admitted to bar, 1992, Oklahoma. *Education:* Oklahoma Christian College (B.S., 1989); University of Tulsa (J.D., 1992). Oklahoma Attorney General Office, Creek Nation Department of Justice. ***PRACTICE AREAS:*** Insurance Law; Civil Litigation.

STEPHEN L. McCLELLAN, born McAlester, Oklahoma, August 14, 1967; admitted to bar, 1994, Oklahoma. *Education:* University of Oklahoma (B.A., 1991; J.D., 1994). (Also Associate, Boettcher, Ryan & Martin). ***PRACTICE AREAS:*** Workers' Compensation; Insurance Defense.

RODOLF & TODD

401 SOUTH BOSTON, 20TH FLOOR
TULSA, OKLAHOMA 74103
Telephone: 918-295-2100

General Civil Practice, Trials in all State and Federal Courts. Medical Malpractice Defense, Products Liability, Employment Litigation.

STEPHEN J. RODOLF, born Chicago, Illinois, August 9, 1948; admitted to bar, 1979, Oklahoma; 1981, U.S. District Court, Northern, Eastern and Western Districts of Oklahoma; 1989, U.S. Court of Appeals, Tenth Circuit; U.S. Supreme Court. *Education:* University of Oklahoma (B.A., 1976; J.D., 1979). Phi Delta Phi. Judge, Fourteenth Judicial District, Oklahoma, 1984-1985. Listed in The Best Lawyers in America. *Member:* Oklahoma and American Bar Associations; American Board of Trial Advocates (Advocate); Defense Research Institute; International Association of Defense Counsel (Member, Medical Malpractice Committee); International Association for Insurance Law; Oklahoma Health Lawyers Association; American Inns of Court (Master), Hudson Wheaton Hall Chapter. Fellow, American College of Trial Lawyers. ***PRACTICE AREAS:*** Medical Malpractice; Products Liability; Employment Litigation. ***Email:*** srodolf@rodolftodd.com

TERRY TODD, born Whittier, California, September 5, 1953; admitted to bar, 1979, Oklahoma; 1990, U.S. District Court, Northern and Eastern Districts of Oklahoma and U.S. Court of Appeals, Tenth Circuit. *Education:* Oklahoma State University (B.S., 1975); Oklahoma City University (J.D., 1979). Phi Delta Phi. *Member:* Creek County, Tulsa County and Oklahoma Bar Associations; Oklahoma Health Lawyers Association. ***PRACTICE AREAS:*** General Civil Litigation; Medical Malpractice; Products Liability; Employment Litigation. ***Email:*** ttodd@rodolftodd.com

KAREN L. CALLAHAN, born Tulsa, Oklahoma, August 12, 1965; admitted to bar, 1991, Oklahoma, U.S. District Court, Northern, Eastern and Western Districts of Oklahoma and U.S. Court of Appeals, Tenth Circuit; U.S. Supreme Court. *Education:* University of Tulsa (B.A., 1988; J.D., 1991). Phi Alpha Delta. Recipient, American Jurisprudence Award in Corporate Law. *Member:* Tulsa County and Oklahoma Bar Associations; Oklahoma Health Care Lawyers Association; Defense Research Institute. ***REPORTED CASES:*** Elledge v. Stillwater Medical Center 62 P.2d 793 (Okla. App. 2002). ***PRACTICE AREAS:*** Medical Malpractice Law; Employment Litigation. ***Email:*** kcallahan@rodolftodd.com

LESLIE CUSTER WEEKS, born Tulsa, Oklahoma, March 9, 1966; admitted to bar, 1991, Texas; 1994, Oklahoma and U.S. District Court, Northern and Eastern Districts of Oklahoma; U.S. Court of Appeals, Tenth Circuit; U.S. Supreme Court. *Education:* Texas Christian University (B.S., summa cum laude, 1988); University of Texas (J.D. with honors, 1991). *Member:* Tulsa County, Oklahoma and American Bar Associations; State Bar of Texas. ***PRACTICE AREAS:*** Medical Malpractice; Employment Law; Appellate Practice. ***Email:*** lweeks@rodolftodd.com

(This Listing Continued)

ELIZABETH K. HALL, born Lawton, Oklahoma, November 18, 1969; admitted to bar, 1995, Oklahoma and U.S. District Court, Northern, Eastern and Western Districts of Oklahoma; U.S. Court of Appeals, Tenth Circuit. *Education:* University of Oklahoma (B.B.A., Accounting, 1992; J.D. with distinction, 1995). Phi Delta Phi. *Member:* Tulsa County, Oklahoma and American Bar Associations; American Inns of Court. ***REPORTED CASES:*** Ballard v. Muskogee Regional Medical Center, 238 F3d 1250 (Okla. 2001); Walking Stick v. Muskogee Regional Medical Center, 992 P2d 924 (Okla. App. 1999). ***PRACTICE AREAS:*** Medical Malpractice; Insurance Defense; Product Liability; Appellate Practice; Employment Law. ***Email:*** ehall@rodolftodd.com

DAVID A. RUSSELL, born Bartlesville, Oklahoma, February 13, 1968; admitted to bar, 1993, Oklahoma and U.S. District Court, Northern, Eastern and Western Districts of Oklahoma. *Education:* University of Kansas (B.A., 1990); University of Oklahoma (J.D., 1993). Phi Delta Phi. Certified Mediator and Arbitrator, Oklahoma, 1996. *Member:* Tulsa County, Oklahoma and American Bar Associations; The Association of Trial Lawyers of America; Oklahoma Association of Defense Council. ***REPORTED CASES:*** Fair Meadows & The State Insurance Fund v. Roger D. Ward, 950 P.2d 885. ***PRACTICE AREAS:*** Medical Malpractice; Nursing Home Negligence; Employment Law; Torts. ***Email:*** drussell@rodolftodd.com

ASSOCIATES

ELIZABETH S. REYNOLDS, born Aurora, Illinois, June 17, 1974; admitted to bar, 2000, Iowa; 2002, Oklahoma, U.S. District Court, Northern and Eastern Districts of Oklahoma and U.S. Court of Appeals, Tenth Circuit. *Education:* University of Illinois (B.A., 1996); Drake University (J.D., 1999). Delta Theta Phi. Member, Drake Journal of Agricultural Law. *Member:* Iowa State and Oklahoma Bar Associations. ***PRACTICE AREAS:*** Medical Malpractice; Employment Law; Appellate Practice. ***Email:*** breynolds@rodolftodd.com

MARK EDWARD HARDIN, born Oklahoma City, Oklahoma, April 26, 1968; admitted to bar, 1993, Oklahoma; 1994, Colorado; U.S. District Court, Northern and Eastern Districts of Oklahoma; U.S. Court of Appeals, Tenth Circuit; U.S. Supreme Court. *Education:* Oklahoma State University (B.S., 1990); University of Oklahoma (J.D. with distinction, 1993). Phi Alpha Delta. *Member:* Oklahoma and Colorado Bar Associations. ***PRACTICE AREAS:*** Medical Malpractice; Employment Law. ***Email:*** mhardin@rodolftodd.com

ERIC M. JORDAN, born Logansport, Indiana, December 9, 1968; admitted to bar, 1997, Oklahoma and U.S. District Court, Northern District of Oklahoma. *Education:* Southern Methodist University (B.A., 1991); University of Tulsa (J.D., 1997). Phi Delta Phi. *Member:* Oklahoma Bar Association. ***PRACTICE AREAS:*** Medical Malpractice. ***Email:*** ejordan@rodolftodd.com

BRENT L. THOMPSON, born McAlester, Oklahoma, July 3, 1970; admitted to bar, 1995, Oklahoma and U.S. District Court, Eastern, Western and Northern Districts of Oklahoma; 1996, U.S. Court of Appeals, Tenth Circuit. *Education:* University of Oklahoma (B.B.A., 1992); University of Tulsa (J.D., 1995). Phi Delta Phi. Notes and Comments Editor, Energy Law Journal, 1994-1995. Primary ABA Editor, American Bar Association Natural Resources, Energy, and Environmental Law Year in Review, 1994. *Member:* Oklahoma and American Bar Associations; Defense Research Institute. ***REPORTED CASES:*** Beville v. Curry, 39 P. 3d 754 (Okla. 2001). ***PRACTICE AREAS:*** Medical Malpractice Defense; Products Liability Defense; Insurance Defense. ***Email:*** bthompson@rodolftodd.com

CHAD H. MOODY, born San Angelo, Texas, December 9, 1970; admitted to bar, 1998, Oklahoma. *Education:* University of Tulsa (B.S., 1994; J.D., 1997). Delta Theta Phi. *Member:* Oklahoma Bar Association; Defense Research Institute. ***PRACTICE AREAS:*** Medical Malpractice. ***Email:*** cmoody@rodolftodd.com

BETH ANNE WILKENING, born Jefferson City, Tennessee, March 2, 1968; admitted to bar, 1993, Oklahoma; 1997, U.S. District Court, Northern and Western Districts of Oklahoma and U.S. Court of Appeals, 19th Circuit. *Education:* University of Oklahoma (B.A., 1990; J.D., 1993). ***REPORTED CASES:*** US Cellular v. City of Broken Arrow, 340 F.3d 1122 (10th Cir. 2003). ***PRACTICE AREAS:*** Medical Malpractice Defense; Insurance Defense; Employment Law. ***Email:*** bwilkening@rodolftodd.com

REPRESENTATIVE CLIENTS: Bay Area Medical Center, Corpus Christi, TX; Bartlett Memorial Medical Center; Broken Arrow Medical Center; Children's Hospital of Oklahoma City; Childrens Medical Center; Children's Medical Center of Tulsa; Claremore Regional Hospital; Cleveland Area Hospital; CNA; HCA HealthCare Corp.; Comanche Memorial Hospital; Craig General Hospital; Cushing Regional Hospital; Doctors Hospital; Doctors Regional Hospital, Corpus Christi, TX; Eastern Oklahoma Medical Center; Employer's Reinsurance Corp.; Hillcrest HealthCare Systems; Hillcrest Medical Center; Holdenville General Hospital; Hospital Casualty Co.; Tahlequah City Hospital; Jane Phillips Medical Center; McAlester Regional Health Center; Medical Protective Co.; Muskogee Regional Medical Center; Osteopathic Founders Foundation; Southcrest Hospital; Southwestern Medical Center; Specialty Hospital/Tulsa; St. John Medical Center; Stillwater Medical Center; Stilwell Memorial Hospital; SurgiCare of Tulsa; Tulsa Regional Medical Center; University of Oklahoma Medical Center; Wagoner Hospital; Wesley Medical Center, Wichita, KS.

ROGERS & BELL

Established in 1913
320 SOUTH BOSTON BUILDING
SUITE 801
TULSA, OKLAHOMA 74103
Telephone: 918-582-5201
Fax: 918-582-1751

Probate, Wills, Trusts, Estate Planning, Oil and Gas, Real Estate and Taxation Law, Charitable Organizations.

FIRM PROFILE: With roots dating from early statehood, Rogers and Bell has served as general counsel for the Chapman-McFarlin Interests since 1912. John Rogers, and later William H. Bell, established a firm philosophy based on quality, integrity and personalized service to our clients, to the bar, and to the community. Over the years, Rogers and Bell has evolved into

(This Listing Continued)

a law firm concentrating in the areas of trust administration, charitable organizations, estate planning, probate, guardianships, oil and gas, real estate, and related trial practice and appeals.

MEMBERS OF FIRM

JOHN ROGERS (1890-1977)

WILLIAM H. BELL (1926-1988)

SHARON J. BELL, born Tulsa, Oklahoma, April 26, 1951; admitted to bar, 1985, Oklahoma. *Education:* Connecticut College (B.A., magna cum laude, 1974); University of Pennsylvania (M.C.P., 1978); The University of Tulsa (J.D., 1985). Staff Member, Tulsa Law Journal, 1983-1985. Editorial Board Member and Office Manager of "Planning Comment," 1975. Judicial Intern, for The Honorable Thomas R. Brett, U.S. District Judge, Northern District of Oklahoma, 1983. Teaching Assistant in Legal Writing, The University of Tulsa, College of Law, 1983-1984. Trustee: Hillcrest Medical Center, Oklahoma, 1988—; Holland Hall School, Oklahoma, 1988—; Oklahoma Medical Research Foundation, 1988—; Children's Medical Center, 1988—; The University of Tulsa, 1988—; Trinity University, Texas, 1988—; John Brown University, Arkansas, 1988—. Director: Bank of Oklahoma Financial Corp., 1993—; National Conference for Community and Justice (Chair, 1999-2001). Tulsa Metropolitan Ministry Foundation, 1995-2001. *Member:* Tulsa County, Oklahoma and American Bar Associations; Tulsa Title and Probate Lawyers Association; American Institute of Certified Planners; American Planning Association (Chair, AICP Review Course for Oklahoma Chapter/APA, 1980-1982; President, Oklahoma Chapter, 1983, Executive Committee, 1980-1983); Leadership Oklahoma, Class VIII 1994-1995. ***PRACTICE AREAS:*** Trust Administration Law; Charitable Organizations Law; Estate Planning Law. ***Email:*** sjbell@rogersandbell.com

ROBERT S. FARRIS, born Tulsa, Oklahoma, January 22, 1950; admitted to bar, 1976, Oklahoma; 1979, U.S. Supreme Court. *Education:* University of Tulsa (B.S.M.E., 1972; J.D., 1975). Tau Beta Pi. Member: American College of Trust and Estate Counsel; Tulsa Title and Probate Lawyers Association; National College of Probate Judges; Tulsa Estate Planning Forum. Adjunct Professor, Decedents' Estates and Trusts, University of Tulsa College of Law, 1992—. Special Judge, District Court, Tulsa County, 1981-1990. Trustee: Presbyterian Children's Services, 1991—; Tulsa Psychiatric Center, 1992—. Director: St. John Medical Center, 1996—; Mental Health Association in Tulsa, 2000—; Parkside, Inc., 1993—. *Member:* Tulsa County, Oklahoma (Member: Probate Code Committee) and American (Member, Real Property, Probate and Trust Law Section) Bar Associations. ***PRACTICE AREAS:*** Probate Law and Estate Planning Law. ***Email:*** rsfarris@rogersandbell.com

GREGORY A. GRAY, born Muskogee, Oklahoma, October 2, 1954; admitted to bar, 1986, Oklahoma. *Education:* University of Tulsa (B.S.B.A., 1976; J.D., 1985). Trustee, St. Simeon's Episcopal Home, 1992—. Director, 1988-1992 and 1994-1999, Oklahoma Special Olympics; Planned Parenthood of Eastern Oklahoma and Western Arkansas, 1990-1995. Director, Project Get Together, 1991-1993. Director, 1991 and Chairman, 1993-1995, Town & Country School. Director, Thomas Gilcrease Museum Association, 1999—. *Member:* Tulsa County, Oklahoma and American Bar Associations. ***PRACTICE AREAS:*** Charitable Organization Law. ***Email:*** gagray@rogersandbell.com

GENERAL COUNSEL FOR: Chapman-McFarlin Interests.
REPRESENTATIVE CLIENT: BancOklahoma Trust Co.

ROSENSTEIN, FIST & RINGOLD

A PROFESSIONAL CORPORATION

Established in 1920

525 SOUTH MAIN, SUITE 700
TULSA, OKLAHOMA 74103
Telephone: 918-585-9211
Facsimile: 918-583-5617
URL: http://www.rfrlaw.com

Oklahoma City Office: 2801 N. Lincoln Blvd., Suite 224, 73105. Telephone: 405-521-0202. Facsimile: 405-521-1515.

General Civil Practice in all State and Federal Courts. Corporation, Bankruptcy Reorganization, Education, Environmental, Health Care, Labor and Employment, Oil and Gas, Real Estate, Taxation, Wills and Probate, Workers' Compensation Law and Estate Planning.

MEMBERS OF FIRM

DAVID L. FIST, born Tulsa, Oklahoma, July 28, 1931; admitted to bar, 1955, Oklahoma. *Education:* University of Oklahoma (B.A., 1952; LL.B., 1955). Order of the Coif. Editor-in-Chief, Oklahoma Law Review, 1954-1955. ***PRACTICE AREAS:*** Education Law; Oil and Gas Law; Real Estate Law. ***Email:*** davidf@rfrlaw.com

A. F. RINGOLD, born Tulsa, Oklahoma, August 6, 1931; admitted to bar, 1955, Oklahoma. *Education:* University of Michigan (A.B., 1953; LL.B., 1955); University of Tulsa (M.A., 1972). ***PRACTICE AREAS:*** Corporate Law; Health Care Law. ***Email:*** tonyr@rfrlaw.com

COLEMAN L. ROBISON, born Ardmore, Oklahoma, January 7, 1943; admitted to bar, 1967, Oklahoma. *Education:* University of Oklahoma (B.B.A., 1964; J.D., 1967). Order of the Coif. Editor, Oklahoma Law Review, 1965-1967. ***PRACTICE AREAS:*** Corporate Law; Real Estate Law; Finance Law. ***Email:*** colemanr@rfrlaw.com

J. DOUGLAS MANN, born Tulsa, Oklahoma, November 16, 1948; admitted to bar, 1973, Oklahoma. *Education:* Oklahoma State University (B.A., 1970); University of Texas (J.D., 1973). ***PRACTICE AREAS:*** Commercial Law; Civil Litigation; Education Law. ***Email:*** dougm@rfrlaw.com

JOHN G. MOYER, JR., born Columbia, Pennsylvania, July 11, 1945; admitted to bar, 1975, Oklahoma. *Education:* University of Tulsa (B.S., 1972; J.D., 1975). ***PRACTICE AREAS:*** Administrative Law; Municipal Law; Civil Litigation; Education Law. ***Email:*** johnm@rfrlaw.com

(This Listing Continued)

JOHN E. HOWLAND, born Broken Arrow, Oklahoma, December 20, 1950; admitted to bar, 1978, Oklahoma. *Education:* Washington University; University of Oklahoma (B.A., 1974; J.D., 1978). *Member:* American Bankruptcy Institute. ***PRACTICE AREAS:*** Bankruptcy Law; Education Law; Civil Litigation; Commercial Law. ***Email:*** johnh@rfrlaw.com

JERRY L. ZIMMERMAN, born Chicago, Illinois, January 2, 1954; admitted to bar, 1979, Oklahoma; 1980, U.S. Tax Court. *Education:* Cornell College (B.A., 1976); University of Tulsa (J.D., 1979); Boston University (LL.M., Taxation, 1980). ***PRACTICE AREAS:*** Estate Planning Law; Taxation Law; Mergers and Acquisitions Law; Health Care Law. ***Email:*** jerryz@rfrlaw.com

MARK S. RAINS, born Des Moines, Iowa, December 26, 1958; admitted to bar, 1984, Oklahoma. *Education:* University of Iowa (B.A. with distinction, 1981); University of Tulsa (J.D., 1984). Articles Editor, Tulsa Law Journal, 1983-1984. ***PRACTICE AREAS:*** Civil Litigation; Appellate Practice; Construction Law; Special Education. ***Email:*** markr@rfrlaw.com

FREDERICK J. HEGENBART, born Sioux City, Iowa, January 23, 1959; admitted to bar, 1984, Oklahoma. *Education:* Iowa State University (B.S., 1981); University of Tulsa (J.D., 1984). Member, Panel of Arbitrators, American Arbitration Association. *Member:* Defense Research Institute. ***PRACTICE AREAS:*** Contract Law; Education Law; Tort Law; Litigation. ***Email:*** fredh@rfrlaw.com

ANDREA R. KUNKEL, born Tulsa, Oklahoma, October 29, 1961; admitted to bar, 1986, Oklahoma. *Education:* University of Tulsa (B.A. with honors, 1983; J.D. with honors, 1986). Order of the Curule Chair. Member, 1984-1986 and Articles Editor, 1985-1986, Tulsa Law Journal. ***PRACTICE AREAS:*** Special Education for Handicapped Children Law; Education Law. ***Email:*** andreak@rfrlaw.com

ERIC P. NELSON, born Fayetteville, Arkansas, October 19, 1957; admitted to bar, 1986, Oklahoma; 2002, Texas. *Education:* University of Arkansas (B.A., 1983); University of Tulsa (J.D., 1986). Order of the Curule Chair. Member, Tulsa Law Journal. *Member:* National Association of Bond Lawyers. ***PRACTICE AREAS:*** Real Estate; Public Finance; Education Law; Health Care Law. ***Email:*** ericn@rfrlaw.com

KAREN L. LONG, born Joplin, Missouri, February 21, 1952; admitted to bar, 1979, Oklahoma; 1984, U.S. Supreme Court. *Education:* Drury College; Christopher Newport College of William and Mary (B.A., 1975); Oklahoma City University (J.D., 1978). ***PRACTICE AREAS:*** Employment Law; Labor Law; Education Law. ***Email:*** karenl@rfrlaw.com

JOHN E. PRIDDY, born Oklahoma City, Oklahoma, June 30, 1963; admitted to bar, 1990, Oklahoma. *Education:* University of Oklahoma (B.S., 1987); University of Tulsa (J.D., 1990). ***PRACTICE AREAS:*** Civil Litigation; Education Law; Municipal Law; Law Enforcement Defense. ***Email:*** jpriddy@rfrlaw.com

BRYAN K. DRUMMOND, born Great Falls, Montana, February 8, 1967; admitted to bar, 1995, Oklahoma. *Education:* Oklahoma State University (B.S., 1991); University of Oklahoma (J.D., with honors, 1995). Order of the Coif. Member, Oklahoma Law Review. ***PRACTICE AREAS:*** Education Law; Employment Law; Civil Litigation; Civil Rights Litigation; Probate; Guardianship. ***Email:*** bryand@rfrlaw.com

OF COUNSEL

Jerry A. Richardson
Larry A. Lewis
Kent "Bo" Rainey
Catharine M. Bashaw
Jana R. Burk (Not admitted in OK)

Matt P. Cyran
Eric D. Wade
Cassandra L. Wilkinson

All Attorneys are Members of the Oklahoma Bar Association.

LAW OFFICE OF HARRY V. ROUSE, P.C.

1408 SOUTH DENVER
TULSA, OKLAHOMA 74119
Telephone: 918-583-2227
Fax: 918-584-1129
Email: hvrouse@aol.com
URL: http://www.harryvrouse.com

Tax, Estate Planning, Probate, Wills, Complex Trusts and Estates, Trusts, Elder Law, Guardianships, ERISA, Employee Benefits, Medicaid Planning, Non Profit Organizations, Business Formations.

HARRY V. ROUSE, born Tulsa, Oklahoma, March 14, 1955; admitted to bar, 1985, Oklahoma; 1996, U.S. Tax Court; 1997, U.S. District Court, Northern District of Oklahoma. *Education:* United States Naval Academy (B.S., with distinction, 1977); Harvard University (J.D., 1985); Georgetown University Law Center (LL.M., Taxation and Certificate in Employee Benefits Law, 1996). Member, Military Officers Association of America, 1997—. *Member:* Tulsa County and Oklahoma Bar Associations; National Academy of Elder Law Attorneys. [Active duty, U.S. Navy, 1977-1995, CDR, JAGC, USN (Ret.)]. ***PRACTICE AREAS:*** Tax; Estate Planning; Probate; Employee Benefits; Non Profit Organizations; Trusts; Business Formations; Complex Trusts and Estates; ERISA; Elder Law; Medicaid Planning.

SANDERS & ASSOCIATES, P.C.

2727 E. 21ST STREET, SUITE 303
TULSA, OKLAHOMA 74114
Telephone: 918-745-2000; 800-745-2006
Fax: 918-745-0575
Email: esther@sanderslawoffice.com

Personal Injury, Workers Compensation, Social Security, Automobile Insurance Coverage.

ESTHER M. SANDERS, born Macks Creek, Missouri, December 30, 1964; admitted to bar, 1993, Oklahoma. *Education:* Drury College (B.A., 1989); Oklahoma City University School of Law (J.D., 1992). *Member:* Oklahoma and American Bar Associations; The Association of Trial Lawyers of America; Oklahoma Trial Lawyers Association.

TANA FREDRICK SMITH, born 1957; admitted to bar, 1995, Oklahoma. *Education:* Northeastern Oklahoma State University (B.S., 1979); University of Tulsa (J.D., 1994).

SANDERS & SANDERS, P.C.

Established in 1957
DENVER BUILDING
624 SOUTH DENVER
TULSA, OKLAHOMA 74119
Telephone: 918-582-5181
Fax: 918-582-5022
Email: dsandersjr@sandersok.com

General Civil Practice, Commercial Real Estate, Commercial Loans, Bank Law, Corporation, Wills, Probate, Surety Law.

DAVID H. SANDERS (1915-2004)

DAVID H. SANDERS, JR., born Tulsa, Oklahoma, June 2, 1943; admitted to bar, 1969, Oklahoma. *Education:* University of Oklahoma (B.A., 1965); University of Tulsa (J.D., 1968). *Member:* Tulsa County and Oklahoma Bar Associations. ***PRACTICE AREAS:*** Real Estate; Bank Law.

REPRESENTATIVE CLIENTS: First National Bank, Chelsea, Oklahoma; Lakeside State Bank, Oologah, Oklahoma; Holiday Mortgage Corp.; Businessmen's Assurance Company of America; Guaranty Abstract Company, Lawyers Title Insurance.

SECREST, HILL & BUTLER

Established in 1984
7134 SOUTH YALE, SUITE 900
TULSA, OKLAHOMA 74136-6342
Telephone: 918-494-5905
Fax: 918-494-2847
Email: rbutler@secresthill.com
URL: http://www.secresthill.com

General Civil Practice. Trials. Insurance, Negligence, Corporation, Aviation, Medical/Dental Malpractice, Architectural/Engineer Malpractice, Products Liability Law, Accounting Malpractice, Construction Defect, Insurance Coverage, Insurance Bad Faith, Nursing Home/Long Term Care Malpractice, Employment Practice, Appellate Oractice, Nursing Malpractice, Environmental Law, Mass Tort Litigation. .

FIRM PROFILE: Since its formation, the philosophy of Secrest, Hill & Butler has been to provide exceptional, aggressive and ethical legal representation to its clients in the civil judicial system. There are three principles underlying our philosophy.

First, the firm is committed to providing personalized service to our clients, always keeping them informed as to the status of their cases. Dialogue is constantly promoted between the firm and our clients, focusing upon their personal involvement in the legal process.

Second, we endeavor to perform only truly productive and meaningful discovery. Through such discovery, we seek to bring legal matters to an early resolution if possible, and if not, thoroughly and aggressively prepare them for successful resolution at trial or on appeal.

Third, in representing our clients, we are committed to maintaining the ethical standards of our profession, as officers of the court. This includes providing exceptional legal services at fair and reasonable rates.

Although Secrest, Hill & Butler has historically provided legal counsel to named defendants through assignments from insurance carriers, and continues to do so, the changing insurance climate has resulted in many corporations and companies becoming self-insured. As a result, a growing percentage of our legal services are provided directly to named defendants.

MEMBERS OF FIRM

JAMES K. SECREST, II, born Pana, Illinois, March 23, 1947; admitted to bar, 1972, Oklahoma; 1976, U.S. District Court, Northern District of Oklahoma; 1977, U.S. Supreme Court; 1979, U.S. District Court, Western District of Oklahoma. *Education:* University of Tulsa (B.S.B.A., 1969; J.D., 1972). Phi Delta Phi. Member of Commercial Panel, American Arbitration Association. *Member:* Tulsa County, Federal and Oklahoma (Chairman-Elect, Insurance Section, 1985) Bar Associations; Oklahoma Association of Defense Counsel (Member, Board of Directors, 1980-1982; Secretary-Treasurer, 1983-1985; President, 1986); American Inns of Court (Barrister); International Association of Defense Counsel; American Society of Law and Medicine; American Board of Trial Advocates (President, Oklahoma Chapter). Fellow: The American College of Trial Lawyers. [Capt., Judge Advocate, U.S. Air Force, 1972-1976]. ***PRACTICE AREAS:*** Products Liability Law; Medical

(This Listing Continued)

and Dental Liability; Nursing Liability; Architectural Law; Accounting; Engineering Professional Liability; Bad Faith; Employment Law; Directors and Officers Liability; General Liability Defense; Environmental Law. ***Email:*** jsecrest@secresthill.com

W. MICHAEL HILL, born Norman, Oklahoma, July 14, 1947; admitted to bar, 1974, Oklahoma; 1976, U.S. District Court, Northern, Western and Eastern Districts of Oklahoma and U.S. Supreme Court; 1979, U.S. Court of Appeals, Eighth and Tenth Circuits. *Education:* Baylor University (B.A., 1969); University of Tulsa (J.D., 1973). Delta Theta Phi. Law Clerk for Chief U.S. District Judge Allen E. Barrow, Northern District of Oklahoma, 1974-1975. Counsel, Federation of Insurance & Corporation Counsel. *Member:* Tulsa County and Oklahoma Bar Associations; Oklahoma Association of Defense Counsel (Member, Board of Directors, 1986-1988; Vice President, 1989); American Board of Trial Advocates (Charter Member); Defense Research Institute (Member, Medical Professional Liability Committee); American Inns of Court (Barrister). ***PRACTICE AREAS:*** Medical and Dental Malpractice; Products Liability; Negligence; Architectural Liability; Engineering Liability; Professional Liability; Nursing Home Negligence; Insurance Bad Faith; Insurance Coverage; Employment Law; Directors and Officers Liability; General Liability Defense; Environmental Law. ***Email:*** wmhill@secresthill.com

ROGER N. BUTLER, JR., born Idabel, Oklahoma, February 15, 1964; admitted to bar, 1989, Oklahoma and U.S. District Court, Northern and Eastern Districts of Oklahoma; 1992, U.S. District Court, Western District of Oklahoma and U.S. Court of Appeals, Tenth Circuit; 1993, Arkansas and U.S. District Court, Western and Eastern Districts of Arkansas; 1995, U.S. Court of Appeals, Eighth Circuit. *Education:* University of Oklahoma (B.A., Journalism, 1986; J.D., 1989). Phi Delta Phi. Author, "Piercing Worker's Compensation Exclusivity Through the Independent Legal Relationship Doctrine," 61 Oklahoma Bar Journal 3436, (12-29-90). *Member:* Tulsa County, Oklahoma and Arkansas Bar Associations; Oklahoma Association of Defense Counsel. ***PRACTICE AREAS:*** Insurance; Bad Faith Litigation; Insurance Coverages; Employment Law; Medical Malpractice; Appellate Practice; Environmental Law; General Liability Defense; Directors and Officers Liability. ***Email:*** rbutler@secresthill.com

RICHARD C. HONN, born Hutchinson, Kansas, December 20, 1934; admitted to bar, 1963, Oklahoma; U.S. District Court, Northern, Eastern and Western Districts of Oklahoma. *Education:* Fort Hays Kansas State College (B.A., 1959); University of Tulsa (LL.B., 1963). Phi Delta Phi. *Member:* Oklahoma and Tulsa County Bar Associations; Oklahoma Association of Defense Counsel; Association of Defense Trial Attorneys (Oklahoma Chairman, 1979-1992). ***PRACTICE AREAS:*** Insurance Defense; Products Liability; Negligence; Professional Malpractice; Premises Liability. ***Email:*** rhonn@secresthill.com

EDWARD JOHN MAIN, born Tulsa, Oklahoma, May 5, 1947; admitted to bar, 1986, Oklahoma; 1988, U.S. District Court, Northern District of Oklahoma and U.S. Court of Appeals, Tenth Circuit; 1990, U.S. Supreme Court; 1992, U.S. District Court, Eastern District of Oklahoma; 1995, U.S. Court of Appeals, Eighth Circuit; 1997, U.S. District Court, Western District of Oklahoma. *Education:* University of Tulsa (B.A., 1969; J.D., with honors, 1986); Southern Illinois University at Carbondale (M.A., 1974; Ph.D., 1982). Author: "The Neglected Prong of the Miller Test for Obscenity: Serious Literary, Artistic, Political, or Scientific Value," 11 Southern Illinois University Law Journal 1159, 1987; "The Relevance of a Biological Definition of Life to Fundamental Rights," 6 Medicine and Law 189, 1987; "The Current State of Landowner Liability in Oklahoma," 63 Oklahoma Bar Journal 2723 (9/30/92); "Bad Faith in the Workers' Compensation Context: A Cause in Search of an Action," 30 Tulsa Law Journal 507, 1995; "Removal, Remand & Review of 'Bad Faith' Workers' Compensation Claims," 13 Thomas M. Cooley Law Review 121, 1996; "Who Owns a Nursing Facility?", 75 Oklahoma Bar Journal 111 (1/17/04); "The Perfected Appeal," 75 Oklahoma Bar Journal 749 (3/13/04). *Member:* Tulsa County, Oklahoma and American Bar Associations. ***PRACTICE AREAS:*** Appellate. ***Email:*** emain@secresthill.com

JAMES KEITH SECREST, III, born Tulsa, Oklahoma, May 31, 1972; admitted to bar, 2000, Oklahoma; U.S. District Court, Northern, Eastern and Western District of Oklahoma. *Education:* Oklahoma State University (M.I.S., 1996); Tulsa University (J.D., 2000). *Member:* Tulsa and Oklahoma Bar Associations; Oklahoma Association of Defense Counsel. ***PRACTICE AREAS:*** Medical Malpractice Defense; Professional Negligence; Insurance Defense; Products Liability; Aircraft Defense; Aviation Law; Dental Malpractice; Construction Defect; Environmental Law; Nursing Home Abuse and Neglect; Insurance Bad Faith; Premises Liability; Subrogation; Contract Law. ***Email:*** jsecrest3@secresthill.com

JASON A. ROBERTSON, born Muskogee, Oklahoma, October 6, 1971; admitted to bar, 1997, Oklahoma and U.S. District Court, Northern Districts of Oklahoma; 1999, U.S. District Court, Eastern and Western Districts of Oklahoma; 2002, U.S. District Court, Eastern and Western, Districts of Arkansas and U.S. Court of Appeals, Tenth Circuit. *Education:* Northeastern Oklahoma State University (B.S., 1994); Oklahoma City University School of Law (J.D., 1997). Graduate of the International Association of Defense Counsel (IADC) Trial Academy, 2001. *Member:* Tulsa County, Oklahoma and American Bar Associations; Oklahoma Association of Defense Counsel. ***PRACTICE AREAS:*** Litigation. ***Email:*** jrobertson@secresthill.com

---

SYMA S. AZAM, born Lahore, Pakistan, September 2, 1972; admitted to bar, 1998, Oklahoma; 2000, U.S. District Court, Northern District of Oklahoma; 2001, U.S. District Court, Eastern District of Oklahoma. *Education:* Southwest Missouri State University (B.A., English, 1994); University of Tulsa-College of Law (J.D., 1997). *Member:* Oklahoma Bar Association; Oklahoma Association of Defense Counsel; Defense Research Institute. ***LANGUAGES:*** Urdu. ***REPORTED CASES:*** Wallace v. Board of Commissioners of Tulsa County, 2000 OK Civ App. 131, 15 P.3d 985. ***PRACTICE AREAS:*** Insurance Defense; Nursing Home Negligence; Medical Malpractice Defense; Professional Negligence; Attorney Discipline. ***Email:*** sazam@secresthill.com

TIMOTHY S. HARMON, born Meridian, Mississippi, August 27, 1960; admitted to bar, 1985, Oklahoma; 1986, U.S. District Court, Northern and Eastern Districts of Oklahoma; 1987, U.S. District Court, Western District of Oklahoma. *Education:* Oral Roberts University (B.A., 1982); O.W. Coburn School of Law, Oral Roberts University (J.D., 1985). *Member:* Oklahoma Bar Association; Oklahoma Association of Defense Counsel. ***PRAC-***

(This Listing Continued)

TICE AREAS: Insurance Law; Insurance Defense; Products Liability; Nursing Home Negligence; General Liability; Construction Liability; Premises Liability; Insurance Bad Faith; Personal Injury; Subrogation. **Email:** tharmon@secresthill.com

DON W. DANZ, born Bangkok, Thailand, March 11, 1966; admitted to bar, 1992, Oklahoma; 1993, Missouri, Kansas, U.S. District Court, Northern, Eastern and Western Districts of Oklahoma, U.S. Court of Appeals, Tenth Circuit and U.S. Tax Court; 1994, Minnesota; 1996, U.S. Supreme Court. *Education:* University of Illinois (B.A., 1989); University of Tulsa (J.D., 1992); University of Missouri-Kansas City (LL.M., Taxation, 1993). Legal Research Teaching Assistant, Energy Law Journal, University of Tulsa. Member, Representative: Oklahoma IRS/Bar Liaison Conference, 1994-2000; National Association of State Bar Tax Sections, 1997. Former, Insurance Company In-House Counsel. *Member:* Oklahoma Bar Association (Chairperson, Taxation Section, 1997-1998; Founding Editor, OBA Taxation Journal, 1994-1997); Oklahoma Association of Defense Counsel. **PRACTICE AREAS:** Insurance Defense; Insurance Coverage; Insurance Bad Faith; Transactional; Contract Law; Taxation. **Email:** ddanz@secresthill.com

JACK Y. GOREE, born Shawnee, Oklahoma, February 13, 1939; admitted to bar, 1970, Oklahoma, U.S. District Court, Northern, Eastern and Western Districts of Oklahoma, U.S. Court of Appeals, Tenth Circuit and U.S. Supreme Court. *Education:* University of Tulsa and Northeastern State College (B.A., 1961); University of Tulsa (J.D., 1969). Delta Theta Phi. *Member:* Oklahoma Bar Association. Oklahoma Association of Defense Counsel; Defense Research Institute. [U.S. Army, 1961-1964]. **PRACTICE AREAS:** Liability; Insurance Defense. **Email:** jgoree@secresthill.com

MICHAEL D. GOSS, born St. Joseph, Missouri, August 11, 1968; admitted to bar, 1995, Oklahoma and U.S. District Court, Northern District of Oklahoma; 1996, Kansas and U.S. District Court, District of Kansas. *Education:* Northwest Missouri State University (B.S., Accounting, 1992); University of Tulsa (J.D., 1995). Blue Key National Honor Fraternity (President, 1991-1992).*Member:* Tulsa and Oklahoma Bar Associations; Oklahoma Association of Defense Counsel. **PRACTICE AREAS:** Litigation; Medical Negligence; Professional Negligence; Products Liability. **Email:** mgoss@secresthill.com

ERIC A. MARESHIE, born Belleville, Illinois, July 25, 1966; admitted to bar, 1999, Oklahoma; U.S. District court, Northern, Eastern and Western Districts of Oklahoma; U.S. Court of Appeals, Tenth Circuit. *Education:* Southern Illinois University at Edwardsville (B.S., 1996); University of Tulsa College of Law (J.D., 1998). Phi Alpha Delta. Member, Board of Advocates. Recipient: Merit Scholarship Award; Cali Award; Health Law Certificate; Honorable Discharge Achievement and Good Conduct Medals, U.S. Air Force, 1989. Winner, Client Counseling Competition. Former Associate: Joe L. White P.C.; Bridger-Riley, Stallard & Associates. *Member:* Tulsa County and Oklahoma Bar Associations. [U.S. Air Force, 1985-1989]. **PRACTICE AREAS:** Nursing Home Negligence; Medical Negligence; Employment Discrimination; Civil Litigation; Appellate Practice. **Email:** tmareshie@secresthill.com

JENNY R. EBERSOLE, born El Paso, Texas, December 26, 1973; admitted to bar, 1999, Oklahoma; 2002, U.S. District Court, Northern, Western and Eastern Districts of Oklahoma. *Education:* Clarion University of Pennsylvania (B.A., with honors, English Literature, 1996); University of Tulsa (J.D., 1999). Recipient, CALI Award, Introductions to Alternative Dispute Resolution. Certificates: Native American Law; Public Interest Law. Member, Women's Law Caucus, Native American Law Students Association. Former Associate: Feldman, Franden, Woodard & Farris; McGivern, Gilliard & Curthoys. **PRACTICE AREAS:** Insurance Defense; Workers Compensation; Pharmaceutical Law; Product Defects; Products Liability; Medical Negligence; Dental Malpractice. **Email:** jebersole@secresthill.com

KIMBERLY N. CLARK, born De Queen, Arkansas, November 19, 1971; admitted to bar, 1999, Oklahoma; 2002, U.S. District Court, Eastern, Northern and Western Districts of Oklahoma. *Education:* Northeastern Oklahoma State University (B.A., B.S., 1996); University of Tulsa (J.D., 1999). Recipient, CALI Award, Intro. to Advocacy; Certificate of Public Policy. Former General Counsel, Wal-Mart Stores. *Member:* Oklahoma Association of Defense Counsel. **PRACTICE AREAS:** Insurance Defense; Nursing Home Negligence; Litigation. **Email:** kclark@secresthill.com

W. JOSEPH PICKARD, born Tulsa, Oklahoma, February 19, 1975; admitted to bar, 2002, Oklahoma; 2004, U.S. District Court, Northern and Western Districts of Oklahoma; 2005, U.S. District Court, Eastern District of Oklahoma. *Education:* University of Oklahoma (B.A., 1997; J.D., 2002). President, Board of Advocates, 2001-2002. *Member:* Tulsa County and Oklahoma Bar Associations; Oklahoma Association of Defense Counsel. **PRACTICE AREAS:** Insurance Defense; Litigation. **Email:** jpickard@secresthill.com

MICHAEL W. BOUTOT, born Miami, Oklahoma, April 13, 1967; admitted to bar, 2002, Oklahoma; 2003, U.S. District Court, Northern and Eastern Districts of Oklahoma; 2004, U.S. District Court, Western District of Oklahoma. *Education:* University of Tulsa (B.A., Political Science, 1999; M.A., Russian History, 2002); University of Tulsa College of Law (J.D., 2002). Phi Delta Phi; Order of Barristers. Recipient: College of Law Merit Scholarship; CALI Awards, Constitutional Law and Advanced Legal Writing. Regional Champion, National Trial Competition, 2002. Author: "Hot Coffee as a Defective Products in the Liebeck v. McDonald's Case," Law of Russia, United States of American and European Union: Problems and Prospectives of the Development, Mari State University, Russian Federation, 2001. Vice President, Board of Advocates, Fall 2000. Member, Tulsa Committee on Foreign Relations. *Member:* Tulsa County, Oklahoma and American Bar Associations; American Inns of Court (Member, Hudson Hall Wheaton Chapter). **LANGUAGES:** Russian. **PRACTICE AREAS:** Civil Litigation; Insurance Defense. **Email:** mboutot@secresthill.com

TARA P. GOODNIGHT, born Dallas, Texas, September 10, 1975; admitted to bar, 2001, Oklahoma. *Education:* University of Arkansas (B.A., 1998; J.D., 2001). **PRACTICE AREAS:** Drug and Medical Device Litigation; Insurance Defense. **Email:** tgoodnight@secresthill.com

REPRESENTATIVE CLIENTS: OMS Mutual Insurance Co.; Alexsis Insurance Co.; Allied Fidelity Insurance Co.; Allstate Insurance Co.; Safeco; Avis Rent-A-Car; Best Buy; Burlington Insurance Group; Canal Insurance Co.; Cigna Insurance Co.; Contract Freighters, Inc.; Cooper Tire & Rubber Co.; CNA Insurance Cos.; Crawford & Co.; First National Insurance Co.; Freightliner Corp.; The Hanover Insurance Company; Hartford Insurance Group; Kemper Group; Kentucky Fried Chicken; Lawyer's Surety Corp.; National American Insurance Co.; National RV; National Tank Co.; Northbrook Property and Casualty Insurance Company; Park, Davis & Company; Pennsylvania Lumbermen's Mutual Insurance Co.; Pepsi-Cola Co.; Philadelphia Indemnity Insurance Co.; Physicians Liability Insurance Co.; Podiatry Insurance Company of America; Raytheon Company, Inc.; Reliance National Insurance Co.; Sears, Roebuck and Company; Shand Morahan & Company, Inc.; Speed Queen Co.; State Volunteer Mutual Insurance Company; Transcontinental Insurance Co.; Tupperware Services; United Services Automobile Assn.; Warner Lambert Co.; Mid-Continent Casualty Group; Associated Aviation Underwriters; Chubb Group of Insurance Companies; Cessna Aircraft Company; North American Physicians Insurance Risk Retention Group; Prefab Transit, Inc.; Insurance Co. of the State of Pennsylvania; Zurich U.S.; Guide One Insurance; GEICO; AutoZone; Western Heritage; Capital Indemnity; Columbia Casualty; Prudential; Jacobsen/Textron, a division of Textron, Inc.; Fortress Insurance Co.

SEYMOUR LAW FIRM

Established in 1982

100 WEST FIFTH STREET, SUITE 550
TULSA, OKLAHOMA 74103-4288
Telephone: 918-583-5791
FAX: 918-583-9251
Email: rtseymour1@aol.com
Email: robtburton@aol.com
URL: http://www.seymourlawfirm.com

General Civil Practice in all State and Federal Courts. Trials and Appeals. White Collar Criminal, Corporate, Bankruptcy, Securities, Securities Fraud, Commercial Litigation, Banking Law, Civil RICO Litigation, Civil Rights.

R. THOMAS SEYMOUR, born Tulsa, Oklahoma, July 13, 1942; admitted to bar, 1967, Oklahoma; U.S. District Court, Northern District of Texas; U.S. District Court, Northern, Eastern and Western Districts of Oklahoma; U.S. Court of Appeals, Fifth, Tenth and Federal Circuits; U.S. Supreme Court. *Education:* Harvard University (A.B., 1964; LL.B., cum laude, 1967). Adjunct Professor of Law, Securities Regulation and Real Estate Transactions, Oral Roberts University, 1982-1986. *Member:* Tulsa County, Oklahoma (Chairman, Business Associations Section, 1979-1980) and American Bar Associations; National Association of Criminal Defense Lawyers. **REPORTED CASES:** Samson Inv. Co. v. Chevaillier, 988 P.2d 327 (Okla. 1999); GAIA Technologies, Inc. v. Recycled Products Corp., 175 F.3d 365 (5th Cir. 1999); GAIA Technologies, Inc. v. Recycled Products Corp., 93 F.3d 774 (Fed. Cir. 1996); Resolution Trust Corp. v. Stone, 998 F.2 1534 (10th Cir. 1993); In re CFS (CFS v. Brady), 261 B.R. 49 (N.D.Okla. 2000); United States v. Richard Clark Gardner, 23 F.Supp.2d 1283 (N.D.Okla. 1998); Samson Resources Co. v. International Business Partners, Inc., 906 F.Supp.624 (N.D.Okla. 1995). **PRACTICE AREAS:** Litigation; Appeals; Securities; Corporate Law; Banking; Bankruptcy; White Collar Criminal Law; Criminal Law; Civil RICO. **Email:** rtseymour1@aol.com

C. ROBERT BURTON, IV, born Fort Worth, Texas, 1965; admitted to bar, 1990, Oklahoma; U.S. District Court, Northern, Eastern and Western Districts of Oklahoma; U.S. Court of Appeals, Fifth, Tenth and Federal Circuits; U.S. Supreme Court. *Education:* Cornell College (B.A., 1987); Willamette University (J.D., 1990). Member, Moot Court Board, 1988-1989. Staff Member, 1988-1989 and Editorial Board, 1989-1990, Willamette Law Review. Recipient: Oklahoma Bar Association Young Lawyers Division "Outstanding Service to the Legal Profession Award" (1992). *Member:* Tulsa County Bar Association Lawyers (ABA/YLD Liaison 1993-1994); Oklahoma Bar Association Young Lawyers Division (Board of Directors 1992-1996); American Bar Association Young Lawyers Division (Member, Affiliate Assistance Program 1994-1995; Chair, Affiliate Assistance Subgrant Program, 1995-1996; Liaison, Standing Committee on Professionalism, 1996-1998). **PRACTICE AREAS:** Litigation; Appeals; Director and Officer Liability Litigation; White Collar Criminal Law; Securities Litigation; Oil and Gas Litigation; Civil RICO Litigation. **Email:** robtburton@aol.com

ASSOCIATE

SCOTT A. GRAHAM, born Columbus, Ohio, April 6, 1970; admitted to bar, 2003, Oklahoma; U.S. District Court, Northern and Western Districts of Oklahoma; U.S. Court of Appeals, Tenth Circuit. *Education:* Old Dominion University (B.S., 2000); University of Tulsa (J.D., 2003). Delta Theta Phi. Member, Golden Key National Honor Society. *Member:* Oklahoma, Tulsa and American Bar Associations. **PRACTICE AREAS:** Litigation; Appellate Practice; Securities Litigation; White Collar Criminal Law; Civil Rights Litigation. **Email:** sgraham-tulsa@sbcglobal.net

REPRESENTATIVE CLIENTS: Furnished Upon Request.

SHALLCROSS LAW FIRM

Established in 1982

THE WRIGHTSMAN MANOR
1645 SOUTH CHEYENNE
TULSA, OKLAHOMA 74119
Telephone: 918-592-1645
Fax: 918-585-9137
Email: ADVOCATUS@AOL.COM
URL: http://www.shallcrosslaw.com

General Civil Trial Practice in State and Federal Courts. Personal Injury and Medical Malpractice.

FIRM PROFILE: Richard A. Shallcross has maintained a civil trial practice in Tulsa, Oklahoma for the past 23 years. He is committed to champion the cause of those who deserve redress for injury to person or property; to promote the public good through concerted efforts to secure safe products, a safe workplace, competent medical treatment, and a clean environment; to further the rule of law and the civil justice system; to protect the rights of the accused; and to preserve the constitutional right to trial by jury.

(This Listing Continued)

SHALLCROSS LAW FIRM, Tulsa—Continued

Mr. Shallcross specializes in complex civil litigation, representing plaintiffs in medical negligence, products liability, and wrongful death claims. The firm also provides general legal services such as representation in contested matters in the bankruptcy, probate, and family courts, and before the I.R.S. and the Oklahoma Tax Commission. The firm is officed in the historic Wrightsman Manor, a mere five minute drive to the Federal and County Courthouses.

RICHARD A. SHALLCROSS, born Champaign, Illinois, December 9, 1947; admitted to bar, 1982, Oklahoma; 1983, U.S. District Court, Northern, Eastern and Western Districts of Oklahoma. *Education:* Rose-Hulman Institute of Technology (B.S., 1970); Georgia State University (M.B.A., 1973); The University of Tulsa (J.D., 1981). Certified Public Accountant, Texas and Oklahoma, 1978. Advocate, National College of Advocacy, 1992-2004. Member, Legal/Medical Interdisciplinary Sub-Committee of The Oklahoma Bar Association Ethics Committee, 1998-1999. *Member:* Tulsa County and Oklahoma (Member, Ethics Committee, 2003-2004) Bar Associations; The Association of Trial Lawyers of America; The Oklahoma Trial Lawyers Association; American Association of Attorneys and C.P.A.'s, Inc. (Lifetime Member). [Capt., U.S. Army Infantry, 1971-1974]. ***REPORTED CASES:*** Standefer v. Standefer, 26P.3d104(Okl. 2001); Estate of Bell, 13 P.3d 86 (Okl. App. 2000); Drllevich Construction, Inc. v. Stock, 958 P.2d 1277 (Okla. 1998); Polymer Fabricating, Inc. v. TEWCA, 980 P.2d 109 (Okl. 1998); Durocher v. Nelson Stone Co., Inc., 978 P.2d 371 (Okl. App. 1998); Mills v. Grotheer, 1998 Ok 33, 957 P.2d 540 (Okla., 1998); In re Stewart, 215 B.R. 456 (10th Cir. B.A.P. 1997); In re Stewart, 201 B.R. 996 and 204 B.R. 780 (Bankr. N.D. Okla., 1996); In re Stewart, 175 F.3d 796 (10th Cir. 1999); In re Kelly, 194 B.R. 258 (Bankr. N.D. Okl. 1996) (rev'd. on appeal); In re Kelley, 215 B.R. 468 (10th Cir. B.A.P., 1997); Weatherly v. Flournoy, 929 P.2d 296 (Okla. App., 1996); TEWCA v. W.P. Industries, 925 P.2d 1225 (Okla. App. 1996); Post Oak Oil Company v. Joe Dancy, Esq., et al., 913 P.2d 1311 (Okla., 1996); Rossen v. Dr. Tom Coburn, 876 P.2d 731 (Okla. App., 1994); Three "M" Investments, Inc. v. The Ahrend Company, 827 P.2d 1324 (Okla., 1992); Broadwater v. Courtney, 809 P.2d 1310 (Okla., 1991). ***PRACTICE AREAS:*** Medical Malpractice.

REPRESENTATIVE CLIENTS: Injured Workers, Patients, and Consumers.

SHARMA LAW FIRM, PLLC

Established in 2004

403 SOUTH CHEYENNE
SUITE 1100
TULSA, OKLAHOMA 74103
Telephone: 918-398-0327
Fax: 918-516-0232
Email: rohit@sharmalawfirm.com
URL: http://www.sharmalawfirm.com

General Practice. Business Organization, Business Transactions, Securities Litigation, Securities Arbitration, Bankruptcy, Estate Planning, Family Law, Divorce, Immigration and Criminal Law.

ROHIT C. SHARMA, admitted to bar, 2003, Oklahoma, U.S. District Court, Northern and Eastern Districts of Oklahoma and U.S. Tax Court. *Education:* Rochester Institute of Technology (B.S., Accounting, 1994); University of Tulsa (J.D., 2002). Phi Delta Phi. Articles Editor, Energy Law Journal. Certified Public Accountant, Oklahoma. Author: Note, "Niagra Mohawk Power Corp. v. FERC," 23 Energy L.J. 157, 2002. *Member:* Tulsa and Oklahoma Bar Associations; The Association of Trial Lawyers of America; American Inns of Court; American Association of Attorneys Certified Public Accountants. ***LANGUAGES:*** Hindi. ***PRACTICE AREAS:*** Business Organization; Business Transactions; Securities Litigation; Estate Planning; Securities Arbitration; Family Law; Divorce; Immigration Law; Criminal Law. ***Email:*** rohit@sharmalawfirm.com

SHIPLEY & KELLOGG, P.C.

Established in 1983

1648 SOUTH BOSTON AVENUE, SUITE 100
TULSA, OKLAHOMA 74119-4416
Telephone: 918-582-1720
Fax: 918-584-7681
Email: firm@shipleylaw.net

Oklahoma City, Oklahoma Office: Two Leadership Square, 211 North Robinson, Suite 1300, 73102-7114. Telephone: 405-235-0808. Facsimile: 405-232-3746. Email: rkellogg@shipleylaw.net

General Civil Practice in all State and Federal Courts, with emphasis in Environmental Law, Water Rights, Business and Commercial Litigation, Class Actions, Alternative Dispute Resolution and Native American Law.

FIRM PROFILE: This firm is the Oklahoma member of the Environmental Law Network which is comprised of select environmental law firms nationwide.

CHARLES W. SHIPLEY, born Dallas, Texas, March 9, 1943; admitted to bar, 1971, Virginia; 1972, Oklahoma; 1973, District of Columbia; 1975, U.S. Supreme Court and U.S. Court of Appeals, First, Fifth, Sixth, Ninth and Tenth Circuits. *Education:* George Washington University (J.D., 1971; LL.M., Environmental Law, 1972). Assistant District Counsel, U.S. Army Corps of Engineers, Tulsa Office, 1972-1973. Trial Attorney, U.S.D.O.J. Pollution Control Section, 1974-1977. Master, W. Lee Johnson Chapter, American Inns of Court. Executive Editor, Oklahoma Environmental Law Handbook. ***PRACTICE AREAS:*** Environmental Law; Commercial Law; Litigation; Water Rights; Native American Law. ***Email:*** cshipley@shipleylaw.net

JAMIE TAYLOR BOYD, born Oklahoma City, Oklahoma, June 21, 1964; admitted to bar, 1989, Oklahoma. *Education:* Oklahoma State University (B.S., 1986); University of Tulsa (M.B.A., 1989; J.D., with honors, 1989). Recipient, American Jurisprudence Award in Administrative Law. Author: "Brownfields Redevelopment in Oklahoma," and "Citizens Suits Under Environmental Statutes," Oklahoma Environmental Law Handbook, Fall, 1997. *Member:* Oklahoma (Chair, Environmental Law Section, 2003-2004) and American Bar Associations. ***PRACTICE AREAS:*** Environmental Law; Litigation. ***Email:*** jboyd@shipleylaw.net

OF COUNSEL

D. E. DISMUKES, born Uvalde, Texas, November 3, 1952; admitted to bar, 1986, Oklahoma, U.S. District Court, Northern, Eastern and Western Districts of Oklahoma and U.S. Court of Appeals, Tenth Circuit. *Education:* University of Tulsa (J.D., 1986). Term Master, American Inns of Court, Council Oak Chapter. Administrative Law Judge, Oklahoma Department of Labor. Oklahoma Certified Mediator. ***PRACTICE AREAS:*** Civil Litigation; Oil and Gas Litigation; Bankruptcy; Products Liability Litigation; Arbitration; Mediation; Employment Litigation. ***Email:*** ndismukes@earthlink.net

REPRESENTATIVE CLIENTS: Arbuckle Master Conservancy District; Ashland Chemical Co.; Atlantic Richfield Co.; ASARCO; Borg-Warner Corp.; Cherokee Nation Supreme Court; Cities of Blackwell and Chickasha, Oklahoma; Flintco; General Electric Co.; Georgia-Pacific Corp.; McDonnell Douglas Corp.; Oklahoma Department of Environmental Quality; Oklahoma Turnpike Authority; ONEOK, Inc.; Tulsa Metropolitan Utility Authority; Uniroyal-Goodrich Tire Co.
REFERENCE: Bank of America.

SLICKER LAW FIRM, P.C.

Established in 2000

4444 EAST 66TH, SUITE 201
TULSA, OKLAHOMA 74136-4206
Telephone: 918-496-9020
Facsimile: 918-496-9024
URL: http://www.tulsalaw-firm.com
Email: fslicker@swbell.net
URL: http://www.slickerlawfirm.com

Mergers, Acquisitions, Business Purchases and Sales, Corporate Finance, Securities Offerings and Compliance, Franchise Compliance, Corporations, Partnerships, LLCs, Joint Ventures, General Business Law, Problem Solving and Dispute Resolution.

FREDERICK K. SLICKER, born Tulsa, Oklahoma, August 21, 1943; admitted to bar, 1968, Kansas; 1972, U.S. Supreme Court, 1973, Texas; 1980, Oklahoma. *Education:* University of Kansas (B.A., 1965; J.D., with highest distinction, 1968); Harvard University (LL.M., 1973). Order of the Coif; Phi Delta Phi (Graduate of the Year). Associate Editor, Kansas Law Review, 1967-1968. Frequent Continuing Legal Education speaker on Business Law and Professional Ethics issues. *Member:* Tulsa County (Chairman, Business Law Section, 2000-2002; Chairman, Professional Grievance Committee, 2004-2005), Oklahoma and American Bar Associations. [Capt., JAGC, U.S. Army, 1968-1972]. ***PRACTICE AREAS:*** Business Combinations; Securities Regulation; Business Law; Franchise Law; Alternative Dispute Resolution. ***Email:*** fslicker@swbell.net

SMILING, BENDER & ROUNDS, P.A.

BRADFORD PLACE
9175 SOUTH YALE AVENUE, SUITE 300
TULSA, OKLAHOMA 74137
Telephone: 918-477-7500
Fax: 918-477-7510
URL: http://www.smilinglaw.com
Email: slf@smilinglaw.com
URL: http://www.smilinglawfirm.com

General Insurance Defense in all State and Federal Courts, Insurance Law with First and Third Party Claims, Products Liability, Medical and Legal Malpractice, Hospital, Nursing Home and Health Care Law, Civil Rights, Employment Law, Workers' Compensation, Premises Liability, Subrogation, Environmental Law, Transportation and Common Carriers, Arson, Property and Casualty, Commercial Litigation, Mediation/Arbitration, Construction Law, Estate Planning, Business Planning, Charitable Gift Tax Planning, Business Litigation, Personal Injury, Wrongful Death, Wills, Trusts and Estates, Contracts, Transactions, Equine Law, Aviation Law.

A. MARK SMILING, born Clinton, North Carolina, February 14, 1958; admitted to bar, 1984, Oklahoma, U.S. District Court, Northern, Eastern and Western Districts of Oklahoma and U.S. Court of Appeals, Tenth Circuit; 1998, North Carolina; 2003, U. S. District Court, Eastern and Western Districts of Arkansas. *Education:* Lee College (B.S., 1980); O. W. Coburn Law School (J.D., 1983). *Member:* Tulsa County (Member, Professional Responsibility Committee), Oklahoma and American Bar Associations; American Board of Trial Advocates (Diplomat); Oklahoma Association of Defense Counsel; Defense Research Institute; International Association of Defense Counsel; Federation of Insurance and Corporate Counsel; National Association of Subrogation Professionals. ***PRACTICE AREAS:*** Personal Injury Litigation; Insurance Defense Law; Corporate Law; Bad Faith; Wrongful Termination; Premises Liability; Mediation; Arbitration; Products Liability; Civil Rights; Health Law; Hospital Law; Professional Liability; Medical Malpractice; Workers' Compensation; Nursing Home Litigation; Business Litigation.

GERALD M. BENDER, born Denver, Colorado, December 21, 1953; admitted to bar, 1991, Oklahoma; U.S. District Court, Northern, Eastern and Western Districts of Oklahoma and U.S. Court of Appeals, Tenth Circuit; 2003, U.S. District Court, Eastern and Western Districts of Arkansas. *Education:* Washburn University (B.A., cum laude, 1987; J.D., with honors, 1990). Phi Delta Phi. Appointed Adjunct Settlement Judge, 14th Judicial District. *Member:* Tulsa County and Oklahoma Bar Associations; American Board of Trial Advocates; Oklahoma Association of Defense Counsel; Defense Research Institute. ***PRAC-***

(This Listing Continued)

TICE AREAS: Personal Injury Litigation; Insurance Defense; Medical Malpractice; Legal Malpractice; Products Liability; Mediation; Arbitration; Equine Law; Aviation Law; Workers' Compensation; Civil Litigation.

PHILARD L. ROUNDS, JR., born Tokyo, Japan, February 22, 1952; admitted to bar, 1977, Oklahoma; 1978, U.S. Tax Court and U.S. District Court, Northern District of Oklahoma; 1979, U.S. Court of Appeals, Tenth Circuit; 1980, U.S. District Court, Western District of Oklahoma; 1981, U.S. Supreme Court; 1983, U.S. District Court, Eastern District of Oklahoma; 2003, U.S. District Court, Eastern and Western Districts of Arkansas. *Education:* Oral Roberts University (B.A., 1974); Oklahoma City University (J.D., 1977). Phi Alpha Delta. President, Student Bar Association, 1976-1977. Assistant District Attorney, Tulsa County, 1977-1979. Assistant U.S. Attorney, Northern District of Oklahoma, 1980-1983. *Member:* Tulsa County, Oklahoma and American Bar Associations; Oklahoma Association of Defense Counsel; Defense Research Institute. ***LANGUAGES:*** Japanese. ***PRACTICE AREAS:*** Personal Injury; Insurance Bad Faith; Medical Malpractice; Products Liability; Insurance Defense; Law Enforcement; Litigation; Insurance; Nursing Home Defense; Hospital Law; Health Care; Premises Liability.

STEPHAN A. WANGSGARD, born Stillwater, Oklahoma, September 4, 1967; admitted to bar, 1997, Arizona; 1998, U.S. District Court, District of Arizona; 1999, Oklahoma; 2000, U.S. District Court, Northern District of Oklahoma; 2002, U.S. District Court, Eastern District of Oklahoma. *Education:* Arizona State University (B.A., 1993); University of Tulsa College of Law (J.D., 1996). Phi Delta Phi; Golden Key. Listed, Who's Who American Law Students, 1997. Author: "Secession, Humanitarian Intervention, and Clear Objectives: When to Commit U.S. Military Forces," 3 Tulsa J.Comp. & Int'l L 313, 1996. *Member:* State Bar of Arizona; Oklahoma and American Bar Associations. ***PRACTICE AREAS:*** Civil Litigation; Insurance Litigation; Insurance Coverage Law; Personal Injury; Insurance Defense; Business Litigation.

JANE R. COWDERY, born Washington, D.C., January 9, 1947; admitted to bar, 1990, Oklahoma, U.S. District Court, Northern, Eastern and Western Districts of Oklahoma and U.S. Court of Appeals, Tenth Circuit. *Education:* University of Oklahoma (B.A., 1968); University of Tulsa (J.D., 1990). Phi Beta Kappa; Phi Delta Phi; Mortar Board. *Member:* Tulsa County and Oklahoma Bar Associations; Oklahoma Association of Defense Counsel. ***PRACTICE AREAS:*** Insurance Defense; Personal Injury; Litigation; Bad Faith; Civil Rights; Wrongful Termination; Medical Malpractice; Products Liability; Nursing Home Litigation; Appellate Practice.

J. KENT FREDENBERGER, born Tulsa, Oklahoma, February 2, 1959; admitted to bar, 1993, Texas; 1995, Oklahoma and U.S. District Court, Northern, Eastern and Western Districts of Oklahoma. *Education:* University of Oklahoma Health Science Center (B.S., 1982; B.S., with special distinction, 1983); University of Houston (J.D., 1992). Phi Delta Phi. Alpha Eta Honor Society for Allied Health. Registered Diagnostic Cardiac Sonographer, 1983. *Member:* Tulsa County and Oklahoma Bar Associations; Texas Bar Association. ***PRACTICE AREAS:*** Personal Injury; Insurance Defense; Medical Malpractice; Nursing Home Litigation; Environmental Law. ***Email:*** kfredenberger@smilinglaw.com

JASON C. MESSENGER, admitted to bar, 2003, Oklahoma. *Education:* University of Arkansas (B.S., 2000); University of Tulsa College of Law (J.D., 2003). Phi Delta Phi. Listed, Who's Who American Law Students, 2000-2002. Managing Editor, Tulsa Journal of Comparative and International Law. Author: "Opening the U.S.-Mexico Border: Problems and Concerns for the Bush Administration, the Countries, and the Legal System to Consider," 9 Tulsa J. Comp. & Int'l L. 607 (2002). *Member:* Tulsa County, Oklahoma and American Bar Associations; American Inns of Court, Hudson Hall Wheaton Inn. ***PRACTICE AREAS:*** Insurance Defense; Civil Litigation; Workers Compensation; Probate.

REPRESENTATIVE CLIENTS: Farmers Insurance Company, Inc.; Mid-Century Insurance Company; Truck Insurance Exchange; Farmers Insurance Exchange; Fire Insurance Exchange; Atlanta Casualty Companies; American Premier Insurance Company; Prudential Property & Casualty; Universal Underwriters Insurance Company; Universal Underwriters Life Insurance Company; Universal Underwriters Acceptance Corporations; Mountain Insurance Agency, Inc.; Shelter Insurance Company; Employers Mutual Insurance Company; Windsor Group; Markel Insurance Company; Zurich Insurance Company; Nautilus Insurance Company; Nationwide Insurance Company; Fulcrum Insurance Company; Traders Insurance Company; Burlington Insurance Company; Berkley Risk Administrators Company; St. Paul Reinsurance Company; Republic Insurance Company; Great West Casualty Company; XL Environmental Claims; Western Heritage Insurance Company; Swift Transportation Company; Dairyland Insurance Company; Progressive Insurance Company; Siemens Westinghouse Corporation; Foremost Insurance Company; Ohio Casualty Group; Claims Indemnity Service; Old Dominion Freight Line; Freymiller Trucking; Sedgwick Claims; USAA Insurance Company; International Paper Company; Liberty Mutual Insurance Company.

DIANNE L. SMITH

2502 EAST 21ST STREET
TULSA, OKLAHOMA 74114-1706
Telephone: 918-743-5151
Telecopier: 918-743-4695
Email: dsmith@gutheryandsmith.com

Banking Law, Bankruptcy, Real Estate, Business Law, Corporate, Contracts, Commercial and Probate Law.

DIANNE L. SMITH, born Orlando, Florida, January 5, 1947; admitted to bar, 1979, Oklahoma. *Education:* Agnes Scott College and Hendrix College (B.A., 1969); University of Tulsa (J.D., with honors, 1979). Member, Order of the Curule Chair. Notes and Comments Editor, Tulsa Law Journal, 1978-1979. Adjunct Settlement Judge, Tulsa County District Court, 1998—. Term Master, American Inns of Court, Council Oak Chapter, Tulsa, Oklahoma. Director, Pet Assistance and Welfare Society, Tulsa, Oklahoma. *Member:* Tulsa County, Oklahoma and American Bar Associations.

REPRESENTATIVE CLIENTS: BancFirst, Tulsa, Oklahoma and BancFirst branches throughout northeastern Oklahoma; Robinson Glass; Sooner Southwest Bankshares Inc., Tulsa, Oklahoma; Security First National Bank, Hugo, Oklahoma; Community Bank, Bristow Oklahoma; First National Bank, Heavener, Oklahoma.
REFERENCE: BancFirst, Tulsa, Oklahoma.

SNEED LANG, P.C.

Established in 1970
1700 WILLIAMS CENTER TOWER I
ONE WEST THIRD STREET
TULSA, OKLAHOMA 74103
Telephone: 918-583-3145
Telecopier: 918-582-0410
URL: http://www.sneedlang.com

Civil Litigation, White Collar Criminal Defense Litigation. Oil and Gas Law, Securities, Securities Fraud. Qui Tam Litigation, Antitrust, Bankruptcy, Negligence, Insurance, Banking, Corporate, Real Estate Law and Title Examination. Environmental Law, Health Care Law, Federal Indian Law and Policy. Family Law, Divorce, Child Custody. Guardianships, Probate, Estate Planning, Sports Law and Transportation.

FIRM PROFILE: Sneed Lang, P.C. is listed in The Bar Register of Preeminent Lawyers.

Sneed Lang was founded on January 1, 1970, when a group of exceptional young lawyers established a new law firm dedicated to technological innovation and to the delivery of quality legal services.

Sneed Lang is a unique law firm in that it represents Fortune 500 corporations, oil and gas companies, individuals and companies charged with business crimes, injured plaintiffs, insurance companies, Native American interests and individuals with a wide variety of legal problems. It is the consistent delivery of high quality services in diverse areas of law that for over 30 years has made Sneed Lang a highly respected firm in both litigation and transactional matters.

JAMES C. LANG, born Tulsa, Oklahoma, November 10, 1940; admitted to bar, 1964, Oklahoma; 1966, U.S. Tax Court and U.S. Supreme Court. *Education:* Oklahoma State University and University of Tulsa (B.A., 1962; M.A., 1970); University of Tulsa (J.D., 1964). Phi Alpha Theta; Phi Alpha Delta. Author: "The Legislative History of the Federal Trade Commission Act," 13 Washburn Law Journal 6, 1974; "An Overview of Prosecutions in the Health Care Industry for False Claims for Reimbursement from Medicare, Medicaid and Private Insurance Companies," 67 Oklahoma Bar Journal 1747 (1996); "Federal Grand Jury Practice," 74 Oklahoma Bar Journal 855 (2003). Member, National Moot Court Team, 1963. Special Agent, Federal Bureau of Investigation, U.S. Department of Justice, 1966-1969. Assistant District Attorney, Tulsa County, 1969-1971. Master Emeritus, American Inns of Court, 1992—. Member, American Board of Trial Advocates. President, University of Tulsa College of Law Alumni Association, 1997-1998. Member: Interstate Oil Compact Commission, 1982-1995; Executive Committee, 1984-1986, Tulsa County Bar Association. ***PRACTICE AREAS:*** Complex Business Litigation; Commercial Litigation; Federal Civil Litigation; White Collar Criminal Defense; Business Crimes. ***Email:*** jlang@sneedlang.com

D. FAITH ORLOWSKI, born Cape Girardeau, Missouri, July 28, 1954; admitted to bar, 1978, Oklahoma; 2000, Texas. *Education:* University of Texas (B.A., with highest honors, 1975; J.D., 1978). Phi Beta Kappa; Phi Kappa Phi. Associate Editor, Texas International Law Journal, 1977-1978. Lecturer: "Oklahoma Indian Titles." Speaker: National Association of Division Order Analysts, 1999, National Association of Lease & Title Analysts, 2002; "Real Property Forms," Oklahoma Bar Association, Form Book, 1995 and 2001. Co-Author: "Oklahoma Indian Titles," 29 Tulsa Law Journal 361, 1993. *Member:* Tulsa County Bar Association (Secretary, 2001); Oklahoma Bar Association (Chair, Real Property Section, 2001; Chair, Women in Law, 1997-2001; Member, Title Examinations Standards Committee); Tulsa Mineral Lawyers Association (President, 1999). ***PRACTICE AREAS:*** Oil and Gas Law; Oil and Gas Acquisitions; Real Estate; Oil and Gas Contracts; Estate Planning; Probate; Guardianship. ***Email:*** forlowski@sneedlang.com

BRIAN S. GASKILL, born Greenville, South Carolina, January 14, 1944; admitted to bar, 1968, Massachusetts; 1969, Oklahoma. *Education:* Hendrix College (B.A., 1965); Harvard University (J.D., 1968). Public Defender, Tulsa County, 1969-1971. ***PRACTICE AREAS:*** Complex Business Litigation; Oil and Gas Litigation; Federal Civil Litigation; Commercial Litigation; Corporate Criminal Law. ***Email:*** bgaskill@sneedlang.com

G. STEVEN STIDHAM, born Muskogee, Oklahoma, March 16, 1954; admitted to bar, 1979, Oklahoma; 1989, U.S. Supreme Court; 1990, U.S. Tax Court. *Education:* Colorado College (B.A., magna cum laude, 1976); University of Michigan (J.D., 1979). Special Prosecutor, Southern District of Florida, 1981. Assistant U.S. Attorney, Eastern District of Oklahoma, 1980-1982. Member, American Board of Trial Advocates. Member, Oklahoma Scenic Rivers Commission, 1992-1998; Chairman, 1996-1998. *Member:* Tulsa County Bar Association (Member, Professional Responsibility Committee, 2000-2001); American Inns of Court. ***PRACTICE AREAS:*** Complex Commercial Litigation; Manufacturers Liability; Environmental Litigation; White Collar Criminal Defense; Federal Civil Litigation. ***Email:*** gstidham@sneedlang.com

STEPHEN R. McNAMARA, born Tulsa, Oklahoma, March 12, 1953; admitted to bar, 1979, Oklahoma. *Education:* University of Notre Dame (B.A., 1976); University of Tulsa (J.D., 1978). Chief Counsel, Reading & Bates Petroleum Co., 1982-1988. Member, Legal Advisory Group, Oklahoma Independent Petroleum Association, 1985-1988. Author: "Oklahoma's Production Revenue Standards Act Post FERC Order 636 - Measurement, Delivery and Quantity Issues," 29 Tulsa Law Journal 639, 1994, *Member:* Tulsa County (Chairman, Mineral Law Section, 1987-1988) and International Bar Associations (Member, Section on Energy and Natural Resources Law). ***PRACTICE AREAS:*** Oil and Gas Law; Oil and Gas Litigation; Class Actions; Corporate Law. ***Email:*** smcnamara@sneedlang.com

PATRICK O. WADDEL, born Tulsa, Oklahoma, 1941; admitted to bar, 1967, Oklahoma; 1968, Missouri; 1969, Texas. *Education:* University of Pittsburgh; University of Tulsa (B.A., 1964); Southern Methodist University (LL.B., 1967). Member, Journal of Air Law and Commerce. Law Clerk to William H. Becker, Chief Judge, U.S. District Court, Western District of Missouri, 1967-1969. *Member:* The Missouri Bar; State Bar of Texas; Oklahoma Bar Association. ***PRACTICE AREAS:*** Corporate Commercial Law; Corporate Finance; Public Offerings; Business Syndication; Broker-Dealer Regulation. ***Email:*** pwaddel@sneedlang.com

(This Listing Continued)

SNEED LANG, P.C., Tulsa—Continued

DOUGLAS L. INHOFE, born Des Moines, Iowa, July 8, 1946; admitted to bar, 1971, Oklahoma and District of Columbia; 1974, U.S. Court of Appeals, Tenth Circuit; 1988, U.S. Supreme Court. *Education:* University of Oklahoma (B.A. in Letters, 1968); Cornell University (J.D., 1971); Harvard University (M.Div., 2001). Phi Kappa Phi. Editor, Cornell Law Review, 1969-1970. Assistant to The General Counsel, Office of The Secretary of the Air Force, The Pentagon, 1972-1974. Law Clerk to Chief Judge, U.S. Court of Appeals, Tenth Circuit, 1974-1975. Adjunct Professor of Law, University of Tulsa, 1988-1989. Visiting Professor of Law, Civil Procedure, Torts and Trial Practice, University of Tulsa, 1989-1990. Judge, Oklahoma Temporary Court of Appeals. Master Emeritus, The Council Oak Chapter, American Inns of Court. Appointed by Governor to Board, Oklahoma Indigent Defense System, 1994-1999. *Member:* Tulsa County, Oklahoma and American Bar Associations; District of Columbia Bar. ***PRACTICE AREAS:*** Federal Litigation; Complex Litigation; Business Litigation; Environmental Litigation; Securities Litigation; Antitrust; Unfair Competition. ***Email:*** dinhofe@sneedlang.com

STEVEN K. BALMAN, born Wichita, Kansas, November 2, 1956; admitted to bar, 1981, Oklahoma. *Education:* Harvard University (A.B., cum laude, 1978); University of Texas (J.D., with honors, 1981). Master Emeritus, American Inns of Court. Adjunct Professor, Appellate Advocacy, Pretrial Litigation, Evidence, Corporations, University of Tulsa College of Law, 1991—. Note and Comment Editor, 1979-1980 and Editor-in-Chief, 1980-1981, American Journal of Criminal Law. Judge, Oklahoma Court of Appeals, Temporary Div., Panel LXI, 1992-1993. Adjunct Settlement Judge, United States District Court, Northern District of Oklahoma, 1998—. *Member:* Tulsa County, Oklahoma and American Bar Associations; American Law Institute; Supreme Court Historical Society (State Membership Chairman, 1992-1993). Fellow, Oklahoma Bar Foundation. ***PRACTICE AREAS:*** Business Litigation; Appellate Practice. ***Email:*** sbalman@sneedlang.com

DAVID J. HYMAN, born Chattanooga, Tennessee, February 9, 1952; admitted to bar, 1981, Tennessee; 1985, Oklahoma. *Education:* Vanderbilt University (B.A., 1974); Cumberland School of Law of Samford University (J.D., 1981). Member, 1979-1980 and Articles Editor, 1980-1981, American Journal of Trial Advocacy. Articles: "Gainsharing 01-1: The OIG's latest word," Physician Organizations 4:1 (2001). Adjunct Professor, Healthcare Law, University of Tulsa School of Law, 1996—. *Member:* Tulsa County and Oklahoma (Chair, Health Law Section, 2004-2005) Bar Associations; American Health Lawyers Association (Vice-Chair, Physician Organization Practice Group, 2004-2005). ***PRACTICE AREAS:*** Health Care Law; Business Law; Corporate Law. ***Email:*** dhyman@sneedlang.com

SHARON L. CORBITT, born Prague, Oklahoma, November 13, 1946; admitted to bar, 1982, Oklahoma. *Education:* Northeastern State University (B.S., 1979); University of Tulsa (J.D., 1982). Outstanding Family Lawyer, Oklahoma Bar Association, 1993 and 1995. Member, Board of Directors, Alumni Association, University of Tulsa College of Law, 1997-2000. *Member:* Tulsa County (Member, Board of Directors, 1985-1993; Member, House of Delegates, 1989-2000; Treasurer, 1989-1990), Oklahoma (Member, Executive Committee, Family Law Section; Chair 1992) and American (Chair, Family Law Section, 2001-2002; House of Delegates, 2002—) Bar Associations. Fellow, American Academy of Matrimonial Lawyers (President, Oklahoma Chapter, 1999-2001). Fellow: American Bar Foundation; Oklahoma Bar Foundation; Tulsa County Bar Foundation. ***PRACTICE AREAS:*** Family Law; Divorce; Child Custody. ***Email:*** scorbitt@sneedlang.com

STUART D. CAMPBELL, born Houston, Texas, 1960; admitted to bar, 1985, Oklahoma. *Education:* Phillips University (B.S., 1982); University of Oklahoma (J.D., 1985). *Member:* Transportation Lawyers Association; Trucking Industry Defense Association. Licensed with the National Basketball Players Association. ***PRACTICE AREAS:*** Transportation Law; Sports Law; Litigation; Energy Law. ***Email:*** scampbell@sneedlang.com

BRIAN T. INBODY, born New York, New York, October 12, 1964; admitted to bar, 1990, Texas; 1996, Oklahoma. *Education:* University of Oklahoma (B.B.A., Finance, 1986; M.B.A., 1990; J.D., 1990). Assistant City Attorney, Dallas, Texas (Criminal and Civil Litigation Divisions), 1991-1997. Barrister, American Inns of Court, 1997—. ***PRACTICE AREAS:*** Federal Civil Litigation; Business Litigation; Commercial Litigation; Manufacturers Liability; Governmental Liability. ***Email:*** binbody@sneedlang.com

D. MICHAEL McBRIDE III, born Bartlesville, Oklahoma, November 24, 1965; admitted to bar, 1993, Oklahoma and Indian Nation Tribal Courts; U.S. Court of Federal Claims, U.S. Court of Appeals, Tenth Circuit and U.S. Supreme Court. *Education:* Trinity University (B.A., Philosophy and Political Science, 1989); University of Oklahoma (J.D., 1993). Phi Delta Phi. Editor, American Indian Law Review, 1991-1993. Judicial Legal Intern for Justice Yvonne Kauger, Oklahoma Supreme Court, 1991. Law Clerk to Magistrate Arvo Q. Mikkanen, Court of Indian Appeals, 1992. Special District Judge, 1995-1999 and Associate Justice, 1999—, Kaw Nation, a Federally-recognized Indian Tribe. Author: Articles, 19 Okla.C.U. L.Rev. 81 (1994); 67 Okla. B.J. 3183 (1996); 68 Okla. B.J. 379 (1997); 36 Tulsa L.J. 641 (2001); Sovereignty Symposium VIII to XIII. Adjunct Law Professor, University of Tulsa College of Law, 1996—. Member, Leadership Tulsa, Class 26. General Counsel, Tulsa Workforce Investment Board, 2002—. *Member:* Tulsa County (Director, Diversity Chair, 2002—; Alternate Delegate to Oklahoma Bar Association House of Delegates, 1999-2001), Oklahoma (Section Officer, Indian Law, 2000-2004; Chairman, General Practice, Solo and Small Firm Section, 1998-1999; Director, Young Lawyers Division, 1999-2001; Member, Long Range Planning and Civil Procedure Committees), Federal (Vice President, Tenth Circuit, 2002-2003; Council Member, 2001-2002; Board Member and Editor, Indian Law Section; President, Northeast Oklahoma Chapter, 2000-2001) and American (Member, Sections on: General Practice, Solo and Small Firm; Chair, GP Link Committee, 2001—; Council Member, 2001-2004; Vice-Chair, Membership, Native American Resources Committee of Natural Resources Section, 1999-2000) Bar Associations; Oklahoma Trial Lawyers Association (Board Member and Chair of Membership, 1997). Fellow, Oklahoma Bar Foundation. ***PRACTICE AREAS:*** Federal Indian Law; Gaming Law; Complex Federal Litigation; Business Law. ***Email:*** mmcbride@sneedlang.com

N. SCOTT JOHNSON, born Tulsa, Oklahoma, July 18, 1966; admitted to bar, 1992, Oklahoma. *Education:* Oklahoma State University (B.S., 1988); University of Tulsa (J.D., with honors, 1992). Phi Alpha Delta. Recipient, American Jurisprudence Award, Family Law. President, Student Bar Association, University of Tulsa, 1991-1992. Member, Board of Directors, Alumni Association, University of Tulsa College of Law, 1997-1999. Associate Member, American Inns of Court, 2000—. *Member:* Tulsa County (Member, Professional Responsibility Committee; Secretary, Family Law Section, 2000—), Oklahoma (Member, Board of Directors, Young Lawyers Division, 1996-2001) and American (Chair, Family Law Committee, ABA/YLD, 1996-1998; Member, AOP National Conference Team, 1998-1999; Vice Chair, AOP National Conference Team, 1999-2000; District Representative-OK/AR, 1999-2001; Member, Executive Council, ABA/YLD) Bar Associations. Fellow, American Academy of Matrimonial Lawyers. ***PRACTICE AREAS:*** Family Law; Divorce; Child Custody; Appellate Practice. ***Email:*** sjohnson@sneedlang.com

RONALD W. LITTLE, born Denton, Texas, May 9, 1963; admitted to bar, 1992, Oklahoma; 1994, Texas. *Education:* Texas A & M University (B.B.A., 1986); University of Tulsa (J.D., with honors, 1992). Order of the Curule Chair. Order of the Barristers. Member, Tulsa Law Journal, 1990-1991. Recipient: American College of Trial Lawyers Medal for Excellence in Advocacy, 1991; American College of Trial Lawyers Award for Outstanding Advocacy Skills, 1992. *Member:* State Bar of Texas; Tulsa County, Oklahoma and American Bar Associations; American Inns of Court. ***PRACTICE AREAS:*** Litigation. ***Email:*** rlittle@sneedlang.com

TIFFANY AREND CAMPBELL, born Memphis, Tennessee, 1968; admitted to bar, 1996, Oklahoma. *Education:* Texas Christian University (B.S., magna cum laude, 1991); Tulane University (J.D., magna cum laude, 1996). Order of the Coif. *Member:* Tulsa County, Oklahoma and American Bar Associations. ***PRACTICE AREAS:*** Litigation. ***Email:*** tarendcampbell@sneedlang.com

OF COUNSEL

JAMES L. SNEED, born Tulsa, Oklahoma, June 24, 1938; admitted to bar, 1963, Oklahoma. *Education:* Harvard University (A.B., cum laude, 1960); University of Oklahoma (J.D., 1963). Order of the Coif; Phi Delta Phi. Oklahoma Law Review. ***PRACTICE AREAS:*** Trusts and Estates Taxation; Charitable Trusts and Foundations; Oil and Gas Law; Estate Planning; Family Business Law; Nonprofit Organizations Law; Wills; Trust Law; Probate. ***Email:*** jlsneedlaw@sbcglobal.net

REPRESENTATIVE CLIENTS: Apache Corporation; Bank of America Illinois; Bank One, Texas; BP Pipeline N.A., Inc.; Cherokee Tribal Counsel; Danzas Corporation; Global Natural Resources; Halliburton Energy Services; Helmerich & Payne, Inc.; International Steel Services, Inc.; Lafarge/Mineral Solutions, Inc.; Osage Nation; RAM Energy, Inc.; Sac and Fox Nation; Seneca-Cayuga Tribe of Oklahoma; ChevronTexaco Corporation; Thlopthlocco Tribal Town; Torch Energy Advisors, Incorporated; Tyson Foods, Inc.; The Washington Group International, Inc.; Wells Fargo Bank; The Williams Companies; The University of Tulsa.

SPENCE LAW OFFICE

Established in 1994

1440 SOUTH HARVARD AVENUE
SUITE 100
TULSA, OKLAHOMA 74112
Telephone: 918-582-3266
Fax: 918-582-3271
Email: brucespence@sbcglobal.net
URL: http://www.tulsaconstructionlaw.com

Commercial and Civil Litigation, Construction Law, Real Property Law, General Practice Litigation, Trust and Estate Litigation, Bankruptcy.

FIRM PROFILE: The Firm primarily works with Contractors, Owners, Architects and Engineers in Construction related legal services. Principle was a practicing architect, and concentrates in construction, real estate, and commercial litigation, trusts, and bankruptcy.

MANAGING ATTORNEY

BRUCE A. SPENCE, born Kansas City, Missouri, August 27, 1956; admitted to bar, 1994, Oklahoma. *Education:* Kansas State University (B.S., 1981); University of Tulsa (J.D., 1994). Architect.: Texas, 1984; Missouri, 1987. Member, American Institute of Architects, 1981-1991. *Member:* Tulsa and Oklahoma Bar Associations. ***PRACTICE AREAS:*** Construction and Design Law; Construction Liens; Construction Litigation; Fair Debt Collection Practices Act; Trusts and Estates; Estate Litigation; Family Trusts; Real Estate; Real Estate Contracts; Real Estate Foreclosure; Real Estate Litigation; Probate; Contract Litigation; Family Law; Civil Litigation; Federal Litigation.

STANLEY, MANDEL & IOLA, L.L.P.

1323 EAST 71ST STREET, SUITE 315
TULSA, OKLAHOMA 74136-5068
Telephone: 918-524-5005
Fax: 918-524-5006
URL: http://www.smi-dallas.com

Asbestos Litigation.

MARK H. IOLA, born Kansas City, Missouri, August 1, 1958; admitted to bar, 1982, Oklahoma; 1995, Texas and Michigan. *Education:* George Washington University (B.A., 1979); University of Oklahoma (J.D., 1982). Phi Delta Phi. Legal Research and Writing Instructor, University of Oklahoma, 1981. Appellate Advocacy Instructor, University of Oklahoma, 1982. *Member:* Oklahoma and American Bar Associations; State Bar of Texas; State Bar of Michigan; Oklahoma Trial Lawyers Association; The Association of Trial Lawyers of America. (Certified as a Civil Trial Specialist by the National Board of Trial Advocacy) (Also Member, Stanley, Mandel & Iola, L.L.P., Dallas, Texas). ***PRACTICE AREAS:*** Asbestos Litigation. ***Email:*** miola@smi-law.com

(This Listing Continued)

OF COUNSEL

RANDALL L. IOLA, born Tulsa, Oklahoma, April 13, 1964; admitted to bar, 1989, Oklahoma; 2000, Illinios; 2001, Texas. *Education:* University of Pennsylvania (B.A., 1986); University of Oklahoma (J.D., 1989). Member: Order of Barristers; Board of Advocates, 1986-1989. *Member:* Tulsa County, Oklahoma, Illinois State and American Bar Associations; State Bar of Texas; The Association of Trial Lawyers of America; National Employment Lawyers Association; Oklahoma Trial Lawyers Association; Texas Trial Lawyers Association. ***Email:*** riola@smi-law.com

STAUFFER, GRAVES & NATHAN

Established in 1990

2816 EAST 51ST STREET, SUITE 200
TULSA, OKLAHOMA 74105
Telephone: 918-592-7070
Facsimile: 918-592-7071
URL: http://www.nealstaufferlawyers.com
Email: nstauffer@staufferlaw.com
URL: http://www.lawyers.com/nealstauffer

Mailing Address: P.O. Box 702860, Tulsa, OK 74170-2860

Insurance coverage, including First and Third Party Claims, Bad Faith Claims, Insurance Defense, Products Liability Defense, Personal Injury, Commercial Litigation, and General Civil Litigation. Trial and Appellate practice in State and Federal Courts.

FIRM PROFILE: Since 1990, Stauffer, Graves & Nathan has been providing its clients with excellent quality legal services at a reasonable price. The firm litigates and tries insurance coverage issues, complex personal injury cases, first and third party claims, bad faith claims, and products liability claims. Personal, professional service is the key to our success, and we prove it every day by winning our clients' cases.

NEAL E. STAUFFER, born Tulsa, Oklahoma, February 29, 1956; admitted to bar, 1989, Oklahoma, U.S. District Court, Eastern and Northern Districts of Oklahoma and U.S. Court of Appeals, Tenth Circuit. *Education:* University of Oklahoma (B.B.A., 1979; J.D., 1989). Phi Eta Sigma; Phi Delta Phi. *Member:* Tulsa County, Oklahoma and American Bar Associations. ***REPORTED CASES:*** ANB Bankcorp, Inc. v. Equitable Life Assurance Society, 86 F.Supp.2d 1113 (N.D. Okla. 2000); Lawrence v. State Farm, 166 F.3d 1221 (10th Cir. 1999), 1999 WL 26880; State Farm v. Van Horn, 139 F.3d 912 (10th Cir. 1998), 1998 WL 58187; Travel Stop, Inc. v. Alliance Gen. Ins. Co., 950 P.2d 834 (Okla. 1997); Truesdell v. State Farm Fire & Cas. Co., 960 F.Supp. 1511 (N.D. Okla. 1997); Wagnon v. Sate Farm Fire & Cas. Co., 146 F.3d 764 (10th Cir. 1998); Wagnon v. State Farm Fire & Cas. Co., 951 P.2d 641 (Okla. 1997); Weldon v. Dunn, 962 P.2d 1273 (Okla. 1998); Wilson v. Glancy, 913 P.2d 286 (Okla. 1995). ***PRACTICE AREAS:*** Insurance Defense; Insurance Coverage Defense; Surety Bonds; Commercial Litigation.

GREGG L. GRAVES, born Oklahoma City, Oklahoma, October 18, 1960; admitted to bar, 1989, Oklahoma; U.S. District Court, Northern and Eastern Districts of Oklahoma. *Education:* University of Oklahoma (B.B.A., 1984); University of Tulsa (J.D., 1989). Staff Member, University of Tulsa Law Journal. Recipient, American Jurisprudence Award Constitutional Law I. *Member:* Tulsa County, Oklahoma and American Bar Associations; American Inns of Court. ***PRACTICE AREAS:*** Civil Litigation; Criminal Law; Insurance Defense; Torts. ***Email:*** ggraves@staufferlaw.com

JODY R. NATHAN, born Hugo, Oklahoma, 1957; admitted to bar, 1986, Oklahoma, U.S. District Court, Northern, Eastern and Western Districts of Oklahoma, U.S. Court of Appeals, Eighth and Tenth Circuits and U.S. Supreme Court. *Education:* Reed College (B.A., 1979); University of Oklahoma (J.D., 1986). Phi Alpha Delta. Member, University of Oklahoma Law Review, 1982-1986. Recipient: American Jurisprudence Award for Wills and Contracts; Oklahoma Bar Association Earl Sneed Award, 2004. Judicial Intern, Oklahoma Supreme Court, 1983-1984. ABA and TIPS Vice Chair and Editor, Trial Techniques Committee Newsletter, 1990. Regional Editor, Covered Events, 1994-2002. Author: "Erisa Nuts and Bolts," 23 Fall Brief 61 (1993). *Member:* Oklahoma Bar Association (Member, Civil Procedure Committee, 1990-2005; Technology Committee, 2004; Vice Chair, Benefits Committee, 2005); Tulsa County Bar Association; American Bar Association. ***REPORTED CASES:*** State Farm Automobile Ins. Co. v. Hubbard, 763 P2d 720 (Okla. App. 1988); Roark v. Shelter Mutual Ins. Co., 731 P2d 389 (Okla. 1987); Neece v. IRS, 922 F2d 573 (10th Cir. 1990); Neece v. IRS, 41 P.3d 1396 (10th Cir. 1994); Neece v. IRS, 96 F.3d 460 (10th Cir. 1996); First Bank of Turley v. Fidelity & Deposit Inc. Co., 1996 OK 105, 928 P.2d 298; Kaye v. Ronson Consumer Products Corp., 1996 OK CIV APP 57, 921 P.2d 1300; Choate v. Champion Home Builders Co., 222 F.3d 788 (10th Cir. 2000); Osgood v. State Farm Mut. Auto. Ins. Co, 848 F2d 141 (10th Cir. 1988); Tilton v. Richardson, 6 F.3d 683 (10th Cir. 1993) Lyons v. Tollie Freightways, 851 P.2d 549 (Okla. App. 1993); Weavel v. U.S. Fidelity & Guar. Co., 848 P.2d 54 (Okla. App. 1993); Weavel v. U.S. Fidelity & Guar. Co., 852 P.2d 783 (Okla. App. 1992); Elsken v. Network Multi-Family Sec. Corp., 838 P.2d 1007 (Okla. 1992); In Matter of Application of Bankoff (Juluis)(2 cases) Browning-Ferris, Inc. v. Board of County Commissioners of County of Wagoner, Board of Adjustment of Wagoner County, Williamson (David), Robson (Nick), Vestal (Jim), Wagoner County Citizens for a Clean Environment, 875 P.2d. 1138 (Okl. 1994); Aven v. Reeh, 878 p.2d 1069 (Okla. 1994); Elsken v. Network Multi-Family Sec. Corp., 49 F.3d 1470 (10th Cir. 1994); Mustain v. Grand River Dam Authority, 68 P.3d 991, 2003 OK 43 (Okla., Apr 22, 2003); Bishop v. Takata Corp., 12 P.3d 459, Prod.Liab.Rep. (CCH) P 15,903, 2000 OK 71; Gallagher v. Enid Regional Hosp., 910 P.2d 984, 1995 OK 137 (Okla., Dec 12, 1995); Exchange Bank v. Director of the Office of Thrift Supervision, 29 F.Supp.2d 1272 (N.D.Okla., November 23, 1998); Millsap v. McDonnell Douglas Corp., 368 F.3d 1246, Pens. Plan Guide (CCH) P 23988N, 32 Employee Benefits Cas. 2586 (C.A.10, May 21, 2004); Reed v. Landstar Ligon, Inc., 314 F.3d 447 (C.A.10 (Okla.), December 11, 2002). ***PRACTICE AREAS:*** Insurance; Automobile Insurance; Automobile Insurance Coverage; Automobile Liability; Casualty Insurance; Commercial Insurance; Commercial Property Insurance; Extra Contractual Insurance Claims; Fire Insurance; Fire Loss; First and Third Party Insurance; General Liability; Indemnity; Insurance Bad Faith; Insurance Contracts; Insurance Coverage; Insurance Litigation; Life and Health Insurance; Property Damage; Property Insurance; Property Insurance Coverage; Unfair Insurance Practices; Uninsured and Underinsured Motorists; Professional Liability Defense; Professional Liability Insurance Coverage; Professional Malpractice; Professional Negligence.

(This Listing Continued)

NATHAN GUY PARRILLI, born Park Ridge, Illinois, November 10, 1975; admitted to bar, 2000, Oklahoma. *Education:* University of Illinois (B.A., 1997); University of Tulsa (J.D., 2000). Phi Delta Phi. Member, Delegate and Committee Chairman, Student Bar Association. ***PRACTICE AREAS:*** Insurance Defense; Insurance Coverage Defense; Civil Litigation; Torts. ***Email:*** nathan@staufferlaw.com

DALINDA J. JEFFERS, admitted to bar, 1991, Oklahoma; U.S. District Court, Northern and Eastern Districts of Oklahoma. *Education:* University of Tulsa (B.A., 1980; J.D., 1991).

OF COUNSEL

JOHN A. COATES, born Oklahoma City, Oklahoma, April 22, 1959; admitted to bar, 1987, New York and U.S. District Court, Southern District of New York; 1990, Tennessee and U.S. District Court, Middle District of Tennessee; 1991, U.S. Court of Appeals, Sixth Circuit and U.S. District Court, Eastern District of Tennessee; 1999, Oklahoma; 2002, U.S. District Court, Northern District of Oklahoma. *Education:* Yale University (B.A., 1982); Vanderbilt University (J.D.,1986). Associate Editor, Vanderbilt Law Review, 1985-1986. *Member:* Oklahoma Bar Associations. ***REPORTED CASES:*** Brooks v. Toyotom Company, Ltd., 86 F.3d 582 (6th Cir. 1996); Investors Credit Corp. v. Batie (In re Batie), 995 F.2d 85 (6th Cir. 1993); Lee v. Toshiba Machine Company of America, 804 F.Supp. 1029 (E.D. Tenn. 1992). ***PRACTICE AREAS:*** Litigation. ***Email:*** jcoates@staufferlaw.com

JOSEPH R. ROBERTS, born Bartlesville, Oklahoma, January 31, 1931; admitted to bar, 1960, Oklahoma. *Education:* University of Tulsa (B.A., 1957; J.D., 1960). Phi Delta Phi. Public Defender, Tulsa County, 1962. *Member:* Tulsa County, Oklahoma and American Bar Associations. [U.S. Navy, 1949-1953]. ***Email:*** jroberts@staufferlaw.com

REPRESENTATIVE CLIENTS: Mt. Hawley Insurance Company; RLI Insurance Company; National American Insurance Company; Shelter Insurance Companies; Oklahoma Attorneys Mutual Insurance Company; State Farm Fire and Casualty Company; Oklahoma Farm Bureau Mutual Insurance Company; State Farm Mutual Insurance Company.

STEIDLEY & NEAL

EXCHANGE TOWER, SUITE 800
4500 SOUTH GARNETT ROAD
P.O. BOX 1165
TULSA, OKLAHOMA 74146
Telephone: 918-664-4612
Fax: 918-664-4133

McAlester, Oklahoma Office: 100 East Carl Albert Parkway, P.O. Box 1165, 74502. Telephone: 918-423-4611. Fax: 918-423-4620

Civil Litigation in all State and Federal Courts. Insurance Defense and Personal Injury Law.

REPRESENTATIVE CLIENTS: AAA Inter-Insurance Exchange; AI Transport; Acceptance Insurance Co.; American Indemnity Group; AMOCo; Arkansas Farm Bureau Mutual Insurance Co.; Atlanta Casualty Companies; Baker-Hughes Oilfield Operations, Inc.; Brotherhood Mutual Insurance Co.; Choctaw Nation of Oklahoma; COREGIS Insurance Company; Crawford & Company; Deep South Insurance; Enogex, Incorporated; ESIS/CIGNA; Farmers Alliance Mutual Insurance Co.; Farrell-Cooper Mining; Federated Rural Electric Insurance Corp.; First State Management Group; Genesis Insurance Co.; Gibraltar National Insurance Co.; Great West Casualty Co.; Harbor Insurance Co.; Housing Authority of Creek Nation of OK; Imperial Casualty & Indemnity Co.; Johne Deere Insurance Company; John Deere transportation Services; Marathon Oil Company; Maryland Insurance Company; Mid-Continent Group; Midland Risk Insurance Co.; Mustang Fuel Corporation; National American Insurance Co.; National Farmers Union; National Security Fire & Casualty Co.; North Star Mutual Ins.; Northwestern Mutual Life; Oklahoma Attorneys Mutual Insurance Co.; Oklahoma Municipal Assurance Group; Oklahoma Farm Bureau Mutual Insurance Co.; Oklahoma Farmers Union Mutual Insurance Co.; Preferred Risk; Progressive Insurance; Prudential Insurance; Royal Maccabees Life Insurance; Sedgwick Claims Management Service; Sentry Insurance Co.; Shelter Insurance Company; Southern Marine Aviation, Inc.; Texas Farm Bureau; Titan Indemnity Company; Transportation Claims, Inc.; Tri-State Insurance; Union Mutual Insurance Co.; United Fire Casualty; United Southern Assurance Co.; Utica National Insurance Group; Vanliner Insurance Co.; Volunteer Firemen's Insurance Services; Western Heritage Insurance.

(For complete biographical data on all personnel, see Professional Biographies at McAlester, Oklahoma).

STIPE, HARPER, LAIZURE, USELTON, EDWARDS & BELOTE, LLP

Established in 1954

2417 EAST SKELLY DRIVE
TULSA, OKLAHOMA 74114
Telephone: 918-749-0749
URL: http://www.stipelaw.com

McAlester, Oklahoma Office: 343 East Carl Albert Parkway. Telephone: 918-423-0421.
Muskogee, Oklahoma Office: 384 South 33rd Street. Telephone: 918-683-5050. Telefax: 918-682-5700
Oklahoma City, Oklahoma Office: 4111 North Lincoln Boulevard. Telephone: 405-524-2268.

General Civil and Criminal Trial Practice. Personal Injury, Workers Compensation, Probate, Real Estate, Federal Employers Liability, Medical Malpractice and Products Liability Law.

REPRESENTATIVE CLIENTS: Sooner Federal Savings & Loan Assn.; Safeway Stores, Inc.; U.M.W.A. (State); AFL-CIO (State); Kiamichi Electric Cooperative.

(For personnel at Muskogee, Oklahoma City and Tulsa, see Professional Biographies at those locations)

STONE JESSUP, P.C.

Established in 1972

320 SOUTH BOSTON

TULSA, OKLAHOMA 74103-4736

Telephone: 918-583-1178

Fax: 918-583-0277

Email: stonejes@sw.bell.net

Municipal Law, Public Authority Financing, Tax Exempt Finance, Economic Development, Project Finance, Real Estate, Financing, Mortgage Law and Indian Law.

SAMUEL C. STONE, born El Dorado, Kansas, October 2, 1942; admitted to bar, 1966, Kansas and Oklahoma; 1968, U.S. Tax Court. *Education:* University of Kansas (B.A., 1963); University of Tulsa (J.D., 1966). Phi Delta Phi. Assistant Tulsa City Attorney, 1968-1972. Member, Board of Trustees: Philbrook Art Center, 1973-1993; Tulsa Philharmonic Society, 1976-1981. Trustee, 1979-2001, President, 1985-1987 and Chairman, 1988-1990, Tulsa Psychiatric Center. *Member:* Tulsa County, Kansas, Oklahoma and American Bar Associations; National Association of Bond Lawyers (Chairman, Special Assessment Committee, 1981; Member, 1978 and Chairman, 1983, Bond Attorneys Workshop Steering Committee; Member, Board of Directors, 1983). ***PRACTICE AREAS:*** Municipal Bonds; Public Authority Finance.

JAMES R. JESSUP (1936-1991)

REPRESENTATIVE CLIENTS: University Center at Tulsa Authority; Greater Sand Springs Trust Authority; Broken Arrow Economic Development Authority; Washington County Medical Authority; Craig County Hospital Authority.
REFERENCES: Bank of Oklahoma, National Association, Tulsa, Oklahoma; Commerce Bank, El Dorado, Kansas.

STRECKER & ASSOCIATES, P.C.

2150 MID-CONTINENT TOWER

401 SOUTH BOSTON AVENUE

TULSA, OKLAHOMA 74103-4009

Telephone: 918-582-1716; 918-582-1734

Fax: 918-582-1780

Email: mail@streckerlaborlaw.com

URL: http://www.streckerlaborlaw.com

Labor and Employment Law (Management).

FIRM PROFILE: Strecker & Associates, P.C. represents management in all aspects of labor and employment law. It is widely recognized, both in Oklahoma and in several surrounding states, as a leader and innovator in this area of practice. The firm was founded on the principle that clients are entitled to responsive attorneys who give accurate, business-oriented advice, which will help clients achieve their business goals and satisfy their legal obligations.

DAVID E. STRECKER, born Carthage, Missouri, November 29, 1950; admitted to bar, 1976, New York and U.S. District Court, Northern District of New York; 1981, Oklahoma; U.S. District Court, Northern, Eastern and Western Districts of Oklahoma; U.S. District Court, Eastern and Western Districts of Arkansas; U.S. Supreme Court and U.S. Court of Appeals, Sixth and Tenth Circuits. *Education:* Westminster College (B.A., magna cum laude, 1972); Cornell University (J.D., cum laude, 1975; Masters Industrial Labor Relations, 1976). Adjunct Instructor, Labor Relations, Oklahoma State University. Vice President and General Counsel, Tulsa Area Human Resources Association, 1990-1999. Barrister, Robert D. Hudson Chapter, American Inns of Court, 1989-1991; Master, Hudson-Hall-Wheaton Chapter, American Inns of Court, 1995—. Member, Society for Human Resource Management. *Member:* Tulsa County, Oklahoma (Chairman: Labor and Employment Law Section, 1990-1991; CLE Committee, 2000-2001) and American Bar Associations. [Capt. U.S. Army Judge Advocate General's Corps, 1976-1980]. ***PRACTICE AREAS:*** Labor and Employment Law. ***Email:*** david.strecker@streckerlaborlaw.com

---

JAMES E. ERWIN, born Fayetteville, Arkansas, November 8, 1961; admitted to bar, 1997, Oklahoma; U.S. District Court, Northern, Eastern and Western Districts of Oklahoma; U.S. District Court, Eastern and Western Districts of Arkansas; U.S. Court of Appeals, Tenth Circuit. *Education:* University of Central Oklahoma (B.A., 1994); University of Tulsa (J.D., with honors, 1997). Member, Phi Delta Phi, 1996-1997. Production Editor, University of Tulsa Law Journal, 1996-1997. *Member:* Tulsa County, Oklahoma and American (Member, Labor and Employment Law Section) Bar Associations; American Immigration Lawyers Association; Tulsa Area Human Resources Association; American Inns of Court (Member, Council Oak Chapter). ***PRACTICE AREAS:*** Labor and Employment; Immigration Law. ***Email:*** ed.erwin@streckerlaborlaw.com

YVETTE B. HART, born Mesa, Arizona, November 16, 1974; admitted to bar, 2002, Oklahoma. *Education:* Our Lady of the Lake University (B.S.W., Social Work, cum laude, 1997); University of Tulsa (J.D., 2002). Articles Editor, Tulsa Journal of Comparative and International Law, 2000-2001. Former Assistant District Attorney, District 14 (Tulsa Co.). *Member:* Oklahoma and American (Member, Labor and Employment Law Section) Bar Associations. ***LANGUAGES:*** Spanish. ***PRACTICE AREAS:*** Labor and Employment Law. ***Email:*** yvette.hart@streckerlaborlaw.com

REPRESENTATIVE CLIENTS: Allegheny Ludlum Corp.; Associated Wholesale Grocers, Inc.; ASARCO; Bob Moore Cadillac; Cardinal Health; Chimi's Restaurants; City of Cushing, Oklahoma; City of Coffeyville, Kansas; Columbus McKinnon Corp.; CompSource Oklahoma; Cordell Memorial Hospital; Crane Carrier Co.; Dollar Thrifty Automotive Group; Emoteq, Corp.; Family & Childrens Service; Fresenius Medical Care North America; Gas Processors Association; Graphic Electronics, Inc.; Hale-Halsell Co.; Homeland, Inc.; Jane Phillips Memorial Hospital; LeSEA Broadcasting, Inc.; Marriott Corp.; Magellan Midstream Partners; Newell Coach Corp.; Nextep, Inc.; Plymouth Pharmaceuticals, Inc.; Rail Services, Inc.; Regis Corp.; Route 66 Harley-Davidson; Samson Investment Co.; Sodexho Marriott Services, Inc.; Spears Mfg. Co.; SpiritBank; Taylor Crane & Rigging; Thermal Engineering Int'l; Trust Co. of Oklahoma; U.S. Pioneer; Valtimet, Inc.; Washington Group Int'l, Inc.; Webco Industries, Inc.

THE STRICKLAND LAW FIRM, P.C.

Established in 1994

320 SOUTH BOSTON, SUITE 1107

TULSA, OKLAHOMA 74103

Telephone: 918-584-3744

Fax: 918-584-3745

Email: Gray@strickland-law-firm.com

URL: http://www.Strickland-Law-Firm.com

Insurance Defense, Personal Injury, Construction, Commercial Transactions and Litigation, Bankruptcy and Real Estate.

GRAY M. STRICKLAND, born Lawton, Oklahoma, February 23, 1961; admitted to bar, 1987, Oklahoma, U.S. District Court for the Northern, Eastern and Western Districts of Oklahoma and U.S. Court of Appeals, Tenth Circuit. *Education:* University of Oklahoma (B.A., 1984; J.D., 1987). Phi Alpha Delta. Recipient, American Jurisprudence Award in Trusts. Speaker, Oklahoma Bar Association Insurance Law Seminar, 1997, 1998. Member: Governors Conference on Small Business, 1993; NACM Advanced Bonds & Liens, 2001; Cleverdon Real Property Round Table Seminar, 2001; Oklahoma Bar Association Annual Convention, 2001; NBI Evictions and Landlord/Tenant Law in Oklahoma, 2001; PESI Boundary Law & Landowner Disputes, 2002; Lorman Oklahoma Construction Lien Law, 2002; Lorman Solving Water Intrusion & Mold Problems, 2002-2003; Lorman What You Really Need to Know About Mold and Your Legal Liabilities, 2003. *Member:* Tulsa County, Oklahoma and American Bar Associations; Oklahoma Association of Defense Counsel; Defense Research Institute. ***LANGUAGES:*** French. ***REPORTED CASES:*** Jones v. Tubbs, 860 P.2d 234 (Okla. 1993); Okla. City Urban Renewal Authority v. Borelli, 848 P.2d 33 (Okla. App. 1992); United Okla. Bank v. Moss, 793 P.2d 1359 (Okla. 1990). ***PRACTICE AREAS:*** Insurance Defense; Construction Law; Business Litigation; Bankruptcy; Real Estate. ***Email:*** Gray@strickland-law-firm.com

ASSOCIATES

ELIZABETH C. NICHOLS, born Independence, Missouri, May 3, 1971; admitted to bar, 2002, Oklahoma, U.S. Court of Appeals, Tenth Circuit, U.S. District Courts, Northern, Eastern and Western Districts of Oklahoma. *Education:* Northeastern Oklahoma State University (B.A., 1999); University of Tulsa (J.D., 2001). Winner, Negotiation Competition, American Bar Association, Fall, 2000. Recipient, CALI Award, Advance Trial Practice, 2001. Executive Counsel. American Board of Trial; Advocates, 2001. *Member:* Oklahoma County, Tulsa County, Oklahoma and American Bar Associations; Oklahoma Association of Defense Counsel. ***Email:*** Elizabeth@strickland-law-firm.com

RUSSELL D. ABBOTT, born Tulsa, Oklahoma, August 19, 1971; admitted to bar, 1998, Oklahoma, U.S. District Court, Northern, Eastern and Western Districts of Oklahoma. *Education:* University of Kansas (B.A., 1993); University of Oklahoma College of Law (J.D., 1997). *Member:* Oklahoma Bar Association(Member, Civil Procedure Committee, 1998-1999). ***LANGUAGES:*** Spanish and French. ***PRACTICE AREAS:*** Insurance Defense; Construction Litigation; Business Litigation; Family Law; Criminal Defense; Products Liability. ***Email:*** Russell@strickland-law-firm.com

OF COUNSEL

J. BARAK WHITE, born September 22, 1959; admitted to bar, 1983, Kansas; 1984, Oklahoma; 1989, Missouri; 2000, Illinois; U.S. District Court for the District of Kansas; U.S. District Court for the Northern, Eastern and Western Districts of Oklahoma. *Education:* University of Kansas (B.S., 1980; J.D., 1983). *Member:* The Missouri Bar; Illinois State and Oklahoma Bar Associations. ***LANGUAGES:*** Spanish. ***REPORTED CASES:*** Seaberg v. Lockard, 800 P.2d 230 (Okla. 1990); Snowden v. Connaught Laboratories, Inc., 137 F.R.D. 325 (D.Kan. 1991). ***PRACTICE AREAS:*** Personal Injury; Products Liability; Legal Malpractice; Commercial Litigation; Contract Litigation. ***Email:*** Jay@strickland-law-firm.com

Languages: French and Spanish.

REPRESENTATIVE CLIENTS: American Home Assurance; Broce Construction Co., Inc.; Consolidated Electric Distributors; Davis Construction Company; Farmers Alliance Mutual Insurance Company; Flintco, Inc.; H&H Plumbing & Utilities, Inc.; Hajoca Corporation; Horace Mann Insurance Co.; Horizon Construction Company, Inc.; Messer Construction, Inc.; NCS Construction Services; Oakridge Builders, Inc.; Reiss Painting Co.; Stuart C. Irby Co.; The University Club, LLC.

STUART, BIOLCHINI & TURNER

FIRST PLACE TOWER

SUITE 3300

15 EAST 5TH STREET

TULSA, OKLAHOMA 74103-4334

Telephone: 918-582-3311

Fax: 918-582-3033

General Civil Practice, State and Federal Courts, Aviation, Aerospace, Corporation, Securities, Joint Ventures, Mergers and Acquisitions, Banking, Taxation, Estates and Trusts, Oil and Gas, Antitrust, Intellectual Property, Internet and E-Business, Technology, False Advertising, Secured Transactions, Labor Relations and Bankruptcy.

FIRM PROFILE: From Indian Territory to today, the firm traces its origins in the practice of law from 1896, when Judge C.B. Stuart, the first United States District Judge and the first Circuit Judge in Indian Territory, founded his law firm prior to Oklahoma statehood.

C. B. STUART (1857-1936)

MEMBERS OF FIRM

HAROLD C. STUART, born Oklahoma City, Oklahoma, July 4, 1912; admitted to bar, 1936, Oklahoma; 1952, District of Columbia. *Education:* University of Virginia; University of Virginia Law School (J.D., LL.B., 1936). Judge of Court of Common Pleas, Tulsa

(This Listing Continued)

County, Oklahoma, 1941-1942. Assistant Secretary of the Air Force, 1949-1951. Oklahoma State Highway Commissioner, 1959-1963. *Member:* District of Columbia Bar; Tulsa County and Oklahoma Bar Associations. [Army Air Forces, 1942-1946, Colonel, U.S.A.F.R.]. **Email:** stuart28@ibm.net

ROBERT F. BIOLCHINI, born Detroit, Michigan, September 22, 1939; admitted to bar, 1965, Oklahoma and Michigan. *Education:* University of Notre Dame (B.A., 1962); George Washington University (LL.B., 1965). Member, National Moot Court Team, 1964-1965. Member, Advisory Council for University of Notre Dame Law School, 1982—. Trustee, University of Notre Dame, 2001—. *Member:* State Bar of Michigan; Tulsa County and Oklahoma Bar Associations. [Capt., U.S. Army, 1965-1967]. **Email:** robert.biolchini@sbtlaw.com

JOHN B. TURNER, born Oklahoma City, Oklahoma, July 9, 1943; admitted to bar, 1967, Oklahoma and U.S. Court of Military Appeals; 1971, U.S. Tax Court. *Education:* University of Tulsa (B.A., 1965; J.D., 1967); Washington University (LL.M., 1975). Associate Editor, Tulsa Law Journal, 1966-1967. Adjunct Professor, Partnership Taxation, Southern Methodist University, 1976. *Member:* Tulsa County and Oklahoma Bar Associations. Fellow, American College of Trust and Estate Counsel. [LCDR, U.S. Navy, 1967-1970]. **Email:** jturner@tulsacoxmail.com

ASSOCIATES

WILLIAM D. MOELLER, born Davenport, Iowa, November 17, 1957; admitted to bar, 1985, Iowa; 1986, Oklahoma; 1990, Texas. *Education:* Iowa State University (B.S., 1980); University of Iowa (J.D., with distinction, 1985); Georgetown University (LL.M., Taxation, with distinction, 1995). Phi Delta Phi. *Member:* Houston, Tulsa County, Oklahoma and American Bar Associations; State Bar of Texas. **Email:** william.moeller@sbtlaw.com

DAVID P. LIMEKILLER, born Yonkers, New York, January 30, 1963; admitted to bar, 1989, New York; 1990, U.S. District Court, Southern District of New York; 1998, Oklahoma. *Education:* Boston University (B.A., 1985); Georgetown University (J.D., 1988). *Member:* Tulsa County, Oklahoma and New York State Bar Associations. ***PRACTICE AREAS:*** Commercial Litigation; Employment Law; Bankruptcy. **Email:** david.limekiller@sbtlaw.com

TONI TURNER BUDD, born Albany, Oregon, December 9, 1963; admitted to bar, 1997, Oklahoma. *Education:* Northeastern State University (B.B.A., with distinction, 1991); University of Notre Dame (J.D., cum laude, 1997). *Member:* Tulsa County and Oklahoma Bar Associations. ***PRACTICE AREAS:*** Business Transactions; Business Litigation; Corporate Law. **Email:** toni.turnerbudd@sbtlaw.com

TOBIN M. BIOLCHINI, born Tulsa, Oklahoma, August 15, 1974; admitted to bar, 2001, Oklahoma. *Education:* University of Notre Dame (B.A., 1996; M.B.A., J.D., 2000). ***PRACTICE AREAS:*** Corporate Litigation; Corporate Law. **Email:** tobin.biolchini@sbtlaw.com

REPRESENTATIVE CLIENTS: The NORDAM Group, Inc.; Oil & Gas Journal; PennWell Corporation; Valley National Bank; Bank of the Lakes; Bank of Jackson Hole; Lumen Energy Corporation; Sullivan and Company Oil & Gas; Petroleum International, Inc.; Great Empire Broadcasting, Inc.; Sooner Pipe and Supply Corp.; Prime Actuator Control Systems, Inc.; Transok, Inc.; Fireman's Fund Insurance Company; Americare Complete Care, Inc.; Labatt USA; First Stuart Corp.; Pratt & Whitney; World Publishing Company; Merkel Family Foundation; Harold C. Stuart Foundation; Frances Langford Foundation; Manhattan Construction Company; Deloitte & Touche; OAI Electronics; Falcon Express Cargo Airlines; Ameritrust Holding Company; PennEnergy; Alliance Resource Partners; Oxley Petroleum.

THOMAS, GLASS, ATKINSON, HASKINS, NELLIS & BOUDREAUX

TULSA, OKLAHOMA

(See Atkinson, Haskins, Nellis, Brittingham, Gladd & Carwile)

THORNTON AND THORNTON

A PROFESSIONAL CORPORATION

Established in 1974

SUITE 660, 525 SOUTH MAIN
TULSA, OKLAHOMA 74103-4507
Telephone: 918-587-2544
Fax: 918-582-0551
Email: dmthornton@sbcglobal.net

Business Law, Commercial Law, Civil Litigation, Probate, Real Estate, Trust and Estates, Family Law.

DAVID M. (MIKE) THORNTON, JR., born South Bend, Indiana, November 8, 1948; admitted to bar, 1974, Oklahoma; 1975, U.S. Court of Appeals, Tenth Circuit; 1976, U.S. District Court, Northern District of Oklahoma and U.S. Court of Appeals, Fifth Circuit; 1977, District of Columbia Court of Appeals; 1978, U.S. District Court, Western District of Oklahoma; 1980, U.S. District Court, Eastern District of Oklahoma. *Education:* Georgetown University College of Arts & Sciences (A.B., 1971); Georgetown University Law Center (J.D., 1974). *Member:* The District of Columbia Bar; Tulsa County and Oklahoma Bar Associations; The Association of Trial Lawyers of America. ***REPORTED CASES:*** Uricam Corporation N.V. v. W.R. Grace & Co., 739 F. Supp. 1493 (W.D. Okl. 1990). ***PRACTICE AREAS:*** Real Estate; Business; Estates and Trusts; Family Law.

REPRESENTATIVE CLIENTS: Aberdeen Dynamics Supply, Inc.; American Central Gas Technologies, Inc.; The Bank of Bloomfield Hills; Bank Tower, Ltd. Partnership; Brook Plaza Shopping Center; DiCarlo Construction Co.; Estro Incorporated, N.V.; European Investment Management Services, Inc.; Fluid Specialties; Fox Real Estate Investments, L.L.C.; Gateway Building Products of Missouri, Inc.; Hart Housing Group, Inc.; JP Mann Construction Co.; JSPP Corporation; Madison Square Townhomes Owners' Association; Midwest Marble Co.; Rent Quik Enterprises, Inc.; Stonelake Title Company; Sunset Plaza Apartments; Triplett Enterprises, Inc.; Wiggin Properties, L.L.C.

THE TILLY LAW FIRM

Established in 1987

ONE WEST THIRD STREET, SUITE 109
P.O. BOX 3645
TULSA, OKLAHOMA 74101-3645
Telephone: 918-583-8868
Facsimile: 918-584-3162
Email: jwtilly@tilly.com
URL: http://www.tilly.com

General Civil Trial Practice in State and Federal Courts. Corporate Representation, Commercial Litigation, Intellectual Property, Insurance, Bankruptcy, Real Property and Oil and Gas Law.

JAMES W. TILLY, born Pryor, Oklahoma, October 22, 1953; admitted to bar, 1979, Oklahoma. *Education:* Oklahoma State University (B.A., 1976); University of Tulsa (J.D., 1979). Articles Editor, Tulsa Law Journal, 1979; Adjunct Professor, Trial Practice, University of Tulsa College of Law, 1992-1994. *Member:* Tulsa County, Oklahoma and American Bar Associations. ***REPORTED CASES:*** Cardtoons, L.C. v. Major League Baseball Players Association, 868 F. Supp. 1266 (N.D. Okla 1994) aff'd, 95 F.3d 959 (10th Cir. 1996). ***PRACTICE AREAS:*** Commercial Litigation; Intellectual Property; Computers and Software; First Amendment Law; Civil Litigation; Federal Civil Litigation; Civil Appeals; Torts; Contracts. **Email:** jwtilly@tilly.com

REPRESENTATIVE CLIENTS: Prudential Relocation Management; Nelson Nissan Mazda; Western Petroleum Company, Inc.; General Electric Company; Allegheny Teledyne, Inc.; Sanditen Investments, Ltd.; LVV International, Inc.; Precious Moments, Inc.; Featherlite, Inc., Vogue Division; American HomePatient, Inc.; Hawkins-Smith; The Pump & Motor Works, Inc.; Selser Schaefer Architects.
REFERENCE: Bank of Oklahoma.

TITUS HILLIS REYNOLDS DICKMAN & McCALMON

FIRST PLACE TOWER, SUITE 2750
15 EAST 5TH STREET
TULSA, OKLAHOMA 74103-4334
Telephone: 918-587-6800
Facsimile: 918-587-6822
URL: http://www.titushillis.com

Trial Practice, Civil Litigation, Federal Litigation, Labor and Employment, Hospital Law, Banking Law, Administrative, Corporate, Probate, Estate Planning, Real Estate, Securities Litigation, Medical Malpractice, Products Liability Law, Environmental Law, Aviation Law, Oil and Gas Law, Communications Law, Negligence, Insurance, Antitrust, Mergers and Acquisitions, Bankruptcy, Business Reorganization, Arbitration, Mediation, Alternative Dispute Resolution.

FIRM PROFILE: Titus Hillis & Reynolds, P.C. was established on June 1, 1998 by four former partners from what was one of the oldest and well-established Tulsa law firms. Titus Hillis & Reynolds strives to provide legal services in numerous areas of law, including banking law and litigation, labor and employment law, commercial law and litigation, real property law and litigation, securities litigation, insurance defense litigation, healthcare law, drug and products liability law, environmental law, aviation law, communications law, negligence, mergers and acquisitions, bankruptcy, business reorganization, arbitration, mediation, alternative dispute resolution, probate, estate planning, oil and gas law. The firm has represented numerous companies and individuals in both state and federal courts.

J SCHAAD TITUS, born Casper, Wyoming, June 8, 1953; admitted to bar, 1978, Oklahoma. *Education:* Southern Methodist University (B.F.A., 1975); University of Oklahoma (J.D., 1978). Phi Delta Phi; Order of the Coif. Managing Editor, Oklahoma Law Review, 1977-1978. Adjunct Professor, Oral Roberts University, 1983-1984. Member: Robert D. Hudson Chapter, American Inns of Court, 1987-1989; Hudson Hall, Wheaton American Inns of Court, 1998-2003. Named: Best Lawyers in America, 1997-2003; Woodward/White, Inc., Tulsa's Best Lawyers, Tulsa People Magazine. *Member:* Tulsa County, Oklahoma and American Bar Associations. ***PRACTICE AREAS:*** Banking Law; Bankruptcy; Commercial; Securities; First Amendment; Insurance Litigation. ***Email:*** stitus@titushillis.com

R. TOM HILLIS, born Tulsa, Oklahoma, September 29, 1962; admitted to bar, 1987, Oklahoma. *Education:* Oklahoma University (B.B.A., 1984; J.D., with honors, 1987). Member, Order of the Coif. Phi Alpha Delta. Member, Oklahoma Law Review, 1985-1987. Pupil, W. Lee Johnson Chapter, American Inns of Court (1989-1990). Adjunct Settlement Judge, Northern District of Oklahoma. *Member:* Tulsa County and Oklahoma Bar Associations. ***PRACTICE AREAS:*** Corporate Law; Commercial Litigation; Labor and Employment Law. ***Email:*** thillis@titushillis.com

BARRY G. REYNOLDS, born Miami, Oklahoma, November 22, 1963; admitted to bar, 1989, Oklahoma. *Education:* N.E.O. A & M Jr. College (A.A., 1984); University of Southern Mississippi (B.S., with highest honors, 1986); University of Oklahoma (J.D., 1989). Phi Theta Kappa; Sigma Chi. Member, University of Oklahoma National Jury Trial Team. Barrister of Hudson Hall Wheaton American Inns of Court. *Member:* Tulsa County (Membership Committee), Oklahoma and American Bar Associations. ***PRACTICE AREAS:*** Commercial Litigation; Banking; Personal Injury; Negligence; Insurance Litigation; Probate; Domestic Relations. ***Email:*** reynolds@titushillis.com

J. SCOTT DICKMAN, born Tulsa, Oklahoma, September 7, 1960; admitted to bar, 1992, Oklahoma. *Education:* University of Tulsa (B.A., 1986; J.D., 1992). Member, Board of Directors, Pinnacle Packaging Company, Inc. Member: Young Presidents Organization; Tulsa Chapter, and a Trustee of the Tulsa Industrial Authority. *Member:* Tulsa County, Oklahoma and American Bar Associations. ***PRACTICE AREAS:*** Debt and Equity Finance. ***Email:*** scott@pinnaclepkg.com

(This Listing Continued)

TITUS HILLIS REYNOLDS DICKMAN & McCALMON, Tulsa—Continued

JACK S. McCALMON, born Oklahoma City, Oklahoma, February 25, 1964; admitted to bar, 1989, New Mexico and U.S. District Court, District of New Mexico; 1991, Oklahoma. *Education:* University of Oklahoma (B.A., 1986; J.D., 1989). Phi Beta Kappa. President's Leadership Scholar. Author: "Effective Loss Control Techniques for Employment Practices," Western New England Law Review, Vol. 21, Issue 2, 1999. *Member:* Oklahoma Bar Association; State Bar of New Mexico. ***PRACTICE AREAS:*** Employment Law; Civil Rights Law. ***Email:*** jmccalmon@mccalmon.com

---

KELLEY G. LOUD, born Miami, Oklahoma, September 28, 1964; admitted to bar, 1989, Texas; 1993, Oklahoma; U.S. District Court, Northern, Eastern and Southern Districts of Texas; U.S. District Court, Northern, Western and Eastern Districts of Oklahoma. *Education:* Oklahoma City University (B.A., 1986); University of Oklahoma (J.D., 1989). *Member:* Tulsa County and Oklahoma Bar Associations; State Bar of Texas. ***PRACTICE AREAS:*** Bankruptcy; Commercial Litigation; Banking Law; Labor and Employment. ***Email:*** kloud@titushillis.com

JESSICA E. RAINEY, born Tulsa, Oklahoma, February 10, 1974; admitted to bar, 1999, Oklahoma; U.S. District Court, Northern, Eastern and Western Districts of Oklahoma; U.S. Court of Appeals, Tenth and Eighth Circuits. *Education:* Drake University (B.A., 1996; J.D., 1998). Phi Alpha Delta. Associate Editor: Drake Law School Newspaper, The Gavel; Drake Law Review, 1997-1998. Recipient, Charles and Joseph Howard Fellowship, 1998. *Member:* Tulsa County, Creek County and American Bar Associations. ***PRACTICE AREAS:*** Business Law; Insurance; Employment Litigation; Banking Law; Negligence; Contracts.

REPRESENTATIVE CLIENTS: The F & M Bank & Trust Company; The Tulsa World; World Publishing Company; Airborne Express Corporation; The Bama Companies, Inc; CIT Financial Group; US Bancorp; Property Company of America; Hillcrest Healthcare System; Security Bank; Community Bank & Trust Company; The Guardian Insurance Company; Pinnacle Packaging Company; Oracle Packaging Company; American Bank of Baxter Springs; E-Z Mart Stores, Inc.; Gold Bank; The Trust Company of Oklahoma; First State Bank of Porter; Household Automotive Finance Corporation; Labor Consultants of America; NEO Federal Credit Union; The City of Commerce; Avalon Oil P.L.C.; Rib Crib, Inc; Avalon Exploration Company; Avalon International P.C.; The Grange Insurance Companies; Guardian Insurance Company; Fireman's Fund Insurance; Tulsa Center for Fertility; J.D. Young Company; Sonic Drive-In, Inc.; Mr. Ed's Auction Company; Carl's Jr.; Taco Bueno; Medical Information Bureau, Inc.; UBS Financial Services, Inc.

TOMLINS & GOINS

A PROFESSIONAL CORPORATION

Established in 1993

UTICA PLAZA BUILDING
2100 SOUTH UTICA AVENUE, SUITE 300
TULSA, OKLAHOMA 74114
Telephone: 918-747-6500
Fax: 918-749-0874
URL: http://www.tomlinsandgoins.com

Litigation Practice, State and Federal Courts, Bankruptcy, Corporate, Employment and Commercial.

NEAL TOMLINS, born Tulsa, Oklahoma, September 25, 1958; admitted to bar, 1983, Oklahoma. *Education:* Southern Methodist University (B.B.A., 1980); University of Oklahoma (J.D., 1983). Note Editor, 1982 and 1983, Oklahoma Law Review. Certified Public Accountant, Oklahoma, 1982. *Member:* Tulsa County (Treasurer, 1990-1991; 1991-1992; Budget Chairman, 1992-1993) and Oklahoma Bar Associations; Oklahoma Society of Certified Public Accountants; American Bankruptcy Institute. ***REPORTED CASES:*** In re Commercial Financial Services, Inc., 246 F.3d 1291; NI Fuel Co., Inc. v. Jackson, et al., 257 B.R. 600 (N.D. Okla. 2000); NationsBank, N.A. v. Commercial Financial Services, Inc., 268 B.R. 579 (Bankr. N.D. Okla. 2001); In re Nichols. 221 B.R. 275 (Bankr. N.D. Okla. 1998). ***PRACTICE AREAS:*** Commercial Law; Bankruptcy Law; Corporate Law. ***Email:*** ntomlins@tglaw.com

RONALD E. GOINS, born Fort Smith, Arkansas, March 16, 1957; admitted to bar, 1982, Oklahoma. *Education:* Georgia Institute of Technology (B.S., with highest honors, 1979); University of Arkansas (J.D., 1982). Phi Kappa Phi. Member, Arkansas Law Review, 1981-1982. *Member:* Tulsa County and Oklahoma Bar Associations; Council Oak Inn, American Inns of Court. ***PRACTICE AREAS:*** Litigation; Commercial Law; Employment Law. ***Email:*** rgoins@tglaw.com

OF COUNSEL

EDWARD E. TOMLINS, JR., born Oklahoma City, Oklahoma, April 26, 1928; admitted to bar, 1956, Oklahoma. *Education:* University of Oklahoma (B.S., 1953); University of Tulsa (J.D., 1956). Phi Alpha Delta. Certified Public Accountant, 1953. Retired Tax Partner, Touche Ross & Co. *Member:* Oklahoma Bar Association. [Army Air Force, 1946-1947]

REPRESENTATIVE CLIENTS: Associated Wholesale Grocers, Inc.; Bank of Oklahoma, N.A.; Beautyco, Inc.; Capital One Financial Corp.; Commercial Financial Services, Inc., Debtor; EnMark Gas Corp.; F&M Bank and Trust Company; Oklahoma Methodist Manor, Inc.; Struthers Industries, Inc., Trustee; Sheffield Steel Corporation, Reorganized Debtor.

WAGNER AND GRUNDY, L.L.P.

Established in 1988

2000 BANK OF AMERICA CENTER
FIFTEEN WEST SIXTH
TULSA, OKLAHOMA 74119-5414
Telephone: 918-587-2547
Fax: 918-587-2886
Email: wagnerandgrundy@aol.com

Family and Matrimonial Law.

FIRM PROFILE: Wagner & Grundy, L.L.P. exclusively engages in the practice of family and matrimonial law. With forty five years of combined experience, the members of the firm have the enhanced ability to provide the highest quality legal service to their clientele, whether in marital agreements, jurisdictional disputes, settlement negotiations, mediation, or at the trial and appellate levels of divorce and family law litigation.

Firm members have served twice as President of the Oklahoma Bar Association, Family Law Section, President and Fellow of the Oklahoma Chapter of the American Academy of Matrimonial Lawyers, and twice as Editor in Chief of the Oklahoma Family Law Journal. The members have taught family law both in law school and frequently in continuing legal education seminars. Likewise, they are often published for their views on family law issues in the Oklahoma Bar Journal and other noted national and state legal publications.

Martindale-Hubbell has chosen Wagner & Grundy, L.L.P. for inclusion in its Bar Register of Preeminent Lawyers. The Best Lawyers in America has included a Wagner & Grundy, L.L.P. firm member in its publication. The National Board of Trial Advocacy has certified a Wagner & Grundy, L.L.P. firm member in family law.

MEMBERS OF FIRM

RICHARD A. WAGNER, II, born Tulsa, Oklahoma, March 18, 1947; admitted to bar, 1972, Oklahoma and U.S. District Court, Eastern District of Oklahoma; 1973, U.S. Court of Appeals, Tenth Circuit; 1974, U.S. District Court, Northern District of Oklahoma and U.S. Court of Appeals, Fifth Circuit; 1975, U.S. Supreme Court; 1978, U.S. District Court, Western District of Oklahoma. *Education:* Oklahoma State University; University of Tulsa (B.S.B.A., 1969); University of Notre Dame (J.D., 1972). Listed in, Best Lawyers in America, 1997—. Editor, Oklahoma Family Law Journal, 1991. Associate Editor, Tulsa Lawyer, 1976. Author: "Are Employment Severance Benefits Marital Property?" Vol. 66 Oklahoma Bar Journal, p. 1795, June 3, 1995; "The Family Lawyer's Ethical Dilemma", Vol. 65 Oklahoma Bar Journal, p. 1093, March 26, 1994; "Valuation of a Professional Practice in a Divorce Proceeding," Vol. 6 Oklahoma Family Law Journal, Sept. 30, 1991; "Support Alimony: Family Law's Ever Evolving Enigma," Vol. 60 Oklahoma Bar Journal, p. 3197, Dec. 30, 1989. Adjunct Professor of Family Law, O.W. Coburn School of Law, 1985-1986. *Member:* Tulsa County (Member, Grievance Committee, 1977-1980), Oklahoma (Budget Officer, Family Law Section, 1991, Chairman, 1993; Member, Grievance Committee, 1978-1980; Associate Bar Examiner, 1980—) and American Bar Associations; Oklahoma Trial Lawyers Association; The Association of Trial Lawyers of America. Fellow, American Academy of Matrimonial Lawyers (Chair, Oklahoma Chapter, 1997; National Board of Governors, 2000-2003). (Board Certified in Family Law by the National Board of Trial Advocacy). ***REPORTED CASES:*** Thielenhaus v. Thielenhaus, 890 P.2d 925 (Okl. 1995). ***PRACTICE AREAS:*** Family Law. ***Email:*** wagnerandgrundy@aol.com

BRADLEY A. GRUNDY, born Tulsa, Oklahoma, February 2, 1965; admitted to bar, 1990, Oklahoma. *Education:* University of Tulsa; Southern Methodist University (B.A., cum laude, 1987); University of Notre Dame (J.D., magna cum laude, 1990). Staff Member, 1988-1989 and Managing Editor, 1989-1990, The Journal of College and University Law. Co-Author: "Shannon v. Bepko: Public Colleges and Universities as State Agencies: Standards for Eleventh Amendment Protection," 16 J.C.U.L. 151, Summer, 1989; "Support Alimony: Family Law's Ever Evolving Enigma," 60 Oklahoma Bar Journal 3197, Dec. 30, 1989. Author: "Equitable Division of Personal Injury or Worker's Compensation Awards," Oklahoma Bar Association Family Law Journal, Vol. 6, No. 2, June 30, 1991; "The Trial: Proposing Relocation," 20 Family Advocate 36, Fall, 1997. Editor, Oklahoma Bar Association Family Law Journal, 1993. *Member:* Tulsa County (Chair, Continuing Legal Education, 1998; Board of Directors, 1998), Oklahoma (Chair, Family Law Section, 1999; Budget Officer, Family Law Section, 1996; Programs Chair, 1995; Programs Co-Chair, 1997) and American Bar Associations. ***REPORTED CASES:*** Colclasure v. Colclasure, 892 P.2d 676 (Okl. App. 1995). ***PRACTICE AREAS:*** Family Law. ***Email:*** wagnerandgrundy@aol.com

ASSOCIATE

MELISSA F. CORNELL, born Colorado Springs, Colorado, May 31, 1967; admitted to bar, 2004, Oklahoma. *Education:* Metropolitan State College (B.S., 2001); University of Tulsa (J.D., with honors, 2004). Phi Delta Phi. Order of the Barristers. Editor, University of Tulsa Law Review, 2003-2004. *Member:* Tulsa County, Oklahoma and American Bar Associations; Inns of Court (Hudson-Hall-Wheaton Chapter, 2003—). ***PRACTICE AREAS:*** Family Law (100%). ***Email:*** wagnerandgrundy@aol.com

LEGAL SUPPORT PERSONNEL

JANICE MURRAY
KATHY WAGNER
TAMMY CREED

REFERENCE: F & M Bank & Trust.

WALKER, FERGUSON & FERGUSON

TULSA, OKLAHOMA

(See Oklahoma City)

General Civil Practice. Insurance Defense, Banking and Commercial Law, Federal, State and Local Taxes, Real Estate, Oil and Gas, Probate, Administrative and Legislative Law. Transportation, Communications, Cable TV, Workers Compensation Law, Employer Liability Law, Employment (Management), Telecommunications, Commercial Litigation, Taxation, Subrogation, Trials in State and Federal Courts.

WILBURN & MASTERSON

Established in 1953

5800 E. SKELLY DRIVE, SUITE 250
TULSA, OKLAHOMA 74135-6439
Telephone: 918-494-0414
Fax: 918-493-3455
Email: mike.masterson@wilburnmasterson.com
URL: http://www.wilburnandmasterson.com

General Civil Practice in all Courts. Insurance (Every Aspect), Personal Injury, Insurance Defense, Bad Faith, Property and Casualty, Products Liability, Premises Liability, Defamation, Appellate Practice, Nursing Home Law, Civil Rights, Wrongful Termination, Workers Compensation, Subrogation, Sexual Harassment, Wrongful Death.

MICHAEL J. MASTERSON, born Tulsa, Oklahoma, May 17, 1956; admitted to bar, 1981, Oklahoma; U.S. District Court, Northern, Eastern and Western Districts of Oklahoma; U.S. Court of Appeals, Tenth Circuit. *Education:* Northeastern Oklahoma State University (B.S., 1978); University of Oklahoma (J.D., 1981). Past President, Oklahoma Association of Defense Counsel. *Member:* Tulsa County and Oklahoma Bar Associations; Defense Research Institute. ***Email:*** mike.masterson@wilburnmasterson.com

OF COUNSEL

RAY H. WILBURN

ASSOCIATE

D. RUSTIN SMITH, born Ardmore, Oklahoma, September 9, 1976; admitted to bar, 2002, Oklahoma. *Education:* University of Oklahoma (B.A., 1999; J.D., 2002). ***PRACTICE AREAS:*** Insurance Defense; Subrogation; Labor and Employment; Products Liability; Workers Compensation; Litigation. ***Email:*** rusty.smith@wilburnmasterson.com

REPRESENTATIVE CLIENTS: Farmers Ins. Co., Inc.; National Indemnity Ins. Co.; Scottsdale Ins. Co.; Gryphon Ins. Co.; Country Mutual Ins. Co.; Western Heritage Ins. Co.; Prudential Ins. Co.; Windsor Group; Mid-Century Ins. Co.; Acceptance Ins. Co.; Empire Fire & Marine Ins. Co.; Vesta/Shelby Ins. Co.; Zurich Ins. Group; Universal Underwriters Ins. Co.; Truck Ins. Exchange; Grange Ins. Co.; Standard Guaranty Ins. Co.; Associated Claims Enterprises; Fire Ins. Exchange; Vanliner Ins. Co.; Fulcrum Ins. Co.; American Equity Ins. Co.; Northland Ins. Co.; Clarendon Ins. Co.; All Risk Claims Services; AXA Global Risk U.S. Ins. Co.; Daimler Chrysler Ins. Co.; OneBeacon Ins. Co.; America First Ins. Co.; Everest National Ins. Co.; Farmland Ins. Co.; Paratransit Ins. Co.; T.H.E. Ins. Co.; Trinity Universal Ins. Co.; Florists' Ins. Co.; North Pacific Ins.; National Security Group, Inc.; Gulf Ins. Co.; Travelers Ins. Co.; Croft Claim Works; Commercial General Agency; Home State County Mutual Ins. Co.; Carl Warren & Co.; Berkley Risk Administrators Co.; American Commerce Ins. Co.; Ins. Corp. of Hanover; Nationwide Companies; Colony Insurance Co.; Oklahoma Farm Bureau Mutual Ins. Co.; MCM Group.

THE WILKINSON LAW FIRM

Established in 1970

SUITE 400
7625 EAST 51ST STREET
TULSA, OKLAHOMA 74145
Telephone: 918-663-2252
Fax: 918-663-2254
URL: http://www.wilklaw.com
Email: wilklaw@wilklaw.com
URL: http://www.wilkinson-law.com

General Civil Trial Practice, State and Federal Courts. Education, Franchise, Commercial and Employment Law, Employment Discrimination, Harassment, Wrongful Discharge, Wrongful Termination, Covenants Not to Compete.

FIRM PROFILE: Wilkinson Law Firm is committed to excellence in employment law and education law litigation matters. Martindale-Hubbell, the only national publication which rates attorneys based on peer evaluations, has recognized the Wilkinson Law Firm as having the highest legal abilities and highest ethical standards.

MEMBER OF FIRM

BILL V. WILKINSON, born Comanche, Oklahoma, March 28, 1944; admitted to bar, 1969, Oklahoma and U.S. District Court, Northern District of Oklahoma; 1976, U.S. Court of Appeals, Tenth Circuit; 1979, U.S. Supreme Court; 1988, U.S. District Court, Eastern District of Oklahoma and pro hoc vice, U.S. District Court, Central District of California; U.S. District Court, Western District of Arkansas. *Education:* University of Oklahoma (B.S., 1966); University of Tulsa (J.D., 1968). Member, Tulsa Law Journal, 1965-1966. Member, Moot Court Board. Adjunct Professor, Trial Practice, University of Tulsa College of Law, 1982-1983. *Member:* Tulsa County (Member, Judicial Appointments Committee and Public Schools Committee, 1974-1983), Oklahoma (Chairman, Committee on Law and Citizenship Education, 1975-1980) and American (Member, Section on Litigation, 1974-1975) Bar Associations; The National School Boards Association Council of School Attorneys. ***PRACTICE AREAS:*** Trial Practice; Business Litigation; Commercial Law; Education Law; Employment Law. ***Email:*** wilklaw@wilklaw.com

WILSON, CAIN & ACQUAVIVA

Established in 1982

1717 SOUTH BOULDER AVENUE, SUITE 801
TULSA, OKLAHOMA 74119-4410
Telephone: 918-583-4777
Fax: 918-583-0774
Email: wcatulsa@swbell.net
URL: http://www.wca-law.com

Oklahoma City Office: 300 N.W. 13th, Suite 100, 73103-3739. Telephone: 405-236-2600. Fax: 405-236-2607.

General Civil Trial Practice State and Federal Courts. Products Liability, Fire and Casualty Insurance Defense, Insurance Coverage, Uninsured Motorist, Bad Faith Law, Professional Malpractice Defense, Veterinary and Insurance Defense, Workers Compensation, Subrogation Insurance Defense, including Personal Injury, Automobile Accidents, Wrongful Death, Mediation and Settlement Services.

MEMBER OF FIRM

DAVID D. WILSON, born Oklahoma City, Oklahoma, October 6, 1944; admitted to bar, 1970, Oklahoma. *Education:* Westminster College; University of Oklahoma (B.B.A., 1967); University of Oklahoma (J.D., 1970). Phi Delta Phi. *Member:* Oklahoma County and Oklahoma Bar Associations; Oklahoma Association of Defense Counsel. (Also at Oklahoma City Office). ***PRACTICE AREAS:*** Insurance Defense; Insurance Coverage; Uninsured and Underinsured Motorists; Insurance Bad Faith; Products Liability; Fire and Casualty; Veterinary Law. ***Email:*** davidwca@swbell.net

ASSOCIATES

JOHN BRIAN DES BARRES, born Tulsa, Oklahoma, November 5, 1961; admitted to bar, 1987, Oklahoma and U.S. District Court, Northern District of Oklahoma; 1990, U.S. District Court, Eastern and Western Districts of Oklahoma and U.S. Court of Appeals, Tenth Circuit; U.S. Supreme Court. *Education:* Western State College of Colorado; University of Tulsa (B.S.B.A., 1984; J.D., 1987). Delta Theta Phi. American Inns of Court (Barrister Member, W. Lee Johnson, Santag Chapter). *Member:* Tulsa County (Member, Fee Arbitration Committee) and Oklahoma (Member, Legal Ethics Committee) Bar Associations; Defense Research Institute; Oklahoma Association of Defense Counsel. ***PRACTICE AREAS:*** Insurance Defense; Uninsured and Underinsured Motorists; Insurance Bad Faith; Breach of Contract; Products Liability; Insurance Coverage; Fire Insurance; Casualty Insurance. ***Email:*** mrjbdb@msn.com

STEPHEN M. COATES, born 1967; admitted to bar, 1996, Oklahoma. *Education:* University of Kansas (B.A., 1990); University of Oklahoma (M.S., 1995; J.D., 1995). *Member:* Tulsa County, Oklahoma, Federal and American Bar Associations. ***PRACTICE AREAS:*** Business Litigation; Insurance Litigation; Employment Litigation; ERISA Litigation. ***Email:*** stephenc@wcalaw.com

CHAD MICAH KIRK, born 1975; admitted to bar, 2001, Oklahoma. *Education:* Oklahoma State University (B.S., 1998); University of Oklahoma (J.D., 2001). ***PRACTICE AREAS:*** Civil Litigation; Personal Injury; Contracts. ***Email:*** chadk@wcalaw.com

OF COUNSEL

TRUMAN B. RUCKER, JR., born Tulsa, Oklahoma, October 16, 1950; admitted to bar, 1977, Oklahoma and U.S. District Court, Northern and Western Districts of Oklahoma; 1983, U.S. Supreme Court; 1986, U.S. District Court, Eastern District of Oklahoma and U.S. Court of Appeals, Tenth Circuit. *Education:* University of Tulsa (B.S., 1972; J.D., 1977). Certified Mediator, Oklahoma Supreme Court. Adjunct Settlement Judge, Tulsa County District Court. *Member:* Tulsa County and Oklahoma Bar Associations. ***PRACTICE AREAS:*** Civil Litigation; Insurance Defense; Personal Injury; Probate; Mediation; Wills; Trusts and Estates; Products Liability; Negligence; Surety; Commercial Law. ***Email:*** canoer44@aol.com

REPRESENTATIVE CLIENTS: Allstate Insurance Company; Atlantic Mutual Insurance Company; CNA Companies; Encompass Insurance Company; Kemper Insurance Company; Mid-Continent Casualty Company; The Ohio Casualty Insurance Company; Oklahoma Farm Bureau Mutual Insurance Company; Progressive Northern Insurance Company; Service Casualty Insurance Company; State Farm Fire and Casualty Company; State Farm Mutual Automobile Insurance Company; USAA Insurance Company; Union Standard Insurance Company; GuideOne Insurance Group; Oklahoma Surety Company; Oklahoma Farmers Union Mutual Insurance Company; Equity Insurance Company; Benchmark Insurance Companies.

WORKS & LENTZ, INC.

A PROFESSIONAL CORPORATION

Established in 1968

1437 SOUTH BOULDER, SUITE 900
TULSA, OKLAHOMA 74119-8609
Telephone: 918-582-3191
Fax: 918-592-2709
Email: wl@workslentz.com
URL: http://www.workslentz.com

Oklahoma City, Oklahoma Office: Union Plaza, Suite 225, 3030 Northwest Expressway. Telephone: 405-942-2211. Fax: 405-942-2370.

General Civil Practice in all State and Federal Courts, Probate, Trust and Estates, Real Estate, Title Examination, Mortgage Foreclosure, Landlord Tenant, Bankruptcy, Creditors Rights, Business, Family, Personal Injury, Corporate and Commercial Law, Retail Collections, Commercial Collections, Fair Debt Collection Practices Act, Construction, Creditors Rights.

(This Listing Continued)

WORKS & LENTZ, INC., A PROFESSIONAL CORPORATION, Tulsa—Continued

FIRM PROFILE: Works & Lentz, Inc. serves the entire state and maintains fully staffed offices in both Tulsa and Oklahoma City, offering a wide range of legal services. While maintaining a general practice, the firm's areas of emphasis include commercial and retail collections, real estate transactions, representation of creditors in bankruptcy proceedings, probate, and estate planning.

WILTON W. WORKS (1925-2004)

HARRY A. LENTZ, JR., born Washington, D.C., August 2, 1944; admitted to bar, 1969, Oklahoma. *Education:* Sterling College (B.S., 1966); University of Tulsa (J.D., 1969). *Member:* Tulsa County and Oklahoma Bar Associations. ***PRACTICE AREAS:*** Commercial Collections; Retail Collections; Fair Debt Collection Practices Act; Subrogation; Probate. ***Email:*** hlentz@workslentz.com

FRED A. POTTORF, born Tulsa, Oklahoma, June 25, 1946; admitted to bar, 1975, Oklahoma. *Education:* Oberlin College (B.A., 1968); University of Tulsa (J.D., 1974). *Member:* Tulsa County and Oklahoma Bar Associations; Tulsa Title and Probate Lawyers Association. ***PRACTICE AREAS:*** Trust and Estates; Real Estate Title Examination; Mortgage Foreclosure; Collections; Garnishments. ***Email:*** fpottorf@workslentz.com

MARK W. DIXON, born Portsmouth, Virginia, June 28, 1950; admitted to bar, 1982, Oklahoma. *Education:* University of Iowa (B.A., 1972); University of Tulsa (J.D., 1981). Alternate Judge, Tulsa Municipal Court, 1997—. *Member:* Tulsa County (President, 1994), Oklahoma (Member, Board of Governors 1991-1993; Chief Master, Professional Responsibility Tribunal, 1998-2001; Professional Responsibility Commission, 2005—) and American Bar Associations. Fellow: Tulsa County Bar Foundation; Oklahoma Bar Foundation. ***PRACTICE AREAS:*** Landlord/Tenant; Commercial Real Estate; Litigation. ***Email:*** mdixon@workslentz.com

B. JACK SMITH, born Tulsa, Oklahoma, January 11, 1957; admitted to bar, 1982, Oklahoma. *Education:* University of Oklahoma (B.A., 1979; J.D., 1982). *Member:* Tulsa County and Oklahoma Bar Associations. ***PRACTICE AREAS:*** Bankruptcy; Business Fraud; Commercial Law; Contracts; Creditors Rights.

DANIEL M. WEBB, born Enid, Oklahoma, March 28, 1957; admitted to bar, 1984, Oklahoma. *Education:* University of Oklahoma (B.A., 1979); University of Tulsa (J.D., 1984). *Member:* Tulsa County and Oklahoma Bar Associations. ***PRACTICE AREAS:*** Consumer Law; Commercial Law; Probate; Creditors Rights in Bankruptcy; Secured Creditors Rights.

SUSAN LENTZ RATCLIFF, born Tulsa, Oklahoma, August 2, 1974; admitted to bar, 2000, Oklahoma. *Education:* Oklahoma Baptist University (BB.A., 1997); University of Oklahoma (J.D., 2000). *Member:* Oklahoma Bar Association. ***PRACTICE AREAS:*** Collections; Garnishments; Creditors Rights. ***Email:*** sratcliff@workslentz.com

---

ROGER M. COIL, born San Francisco, California, October, 1963; admitted to bar, 1996, Oklahoma and U.S. District Court, Western District of Oklahoma. *Education:* University of Oklahoma (B.A., 1991; J.D., 1995). ***PRACTICE AREAS:*** Collections; Commercial Law; Contract Law; Personal Injury; Administrative Law. ***Email:*** rcoil@workanlentz.com

LESLIE EDWARD LENZ, born Tulsa, Oklahoma, August 7, 1964; admitted to bar, 1991, Oklahoma and U.S. District Court, Western District of Oklahoma; 1999, U.S. District Court Eastern District of Oklahoma. *Education:* Oklahoma State University (B.S., 1987); University of Oklahoma (J.D., 1991). ***PRACTICE AREAS:*** Retail Collections; Commercial Collections; Creditors Rights; Fair Debt Collection Practices Act. ***Email:*** lelenz@worksandlentz.com

REPRESENTATIVE CLIENTS: Tulsa Regional Medical Center; Hillcrest Medical Center; Emergency Medical Services Authority; The University of Tulsa; St. Francis Hospital; Arvest Bank; Oklahoma Natural Gas.
APPROVED ATTORNEYS FOR: First American Title Insurance Co.; Lawyers Title Insurance Corp.
REFERENCES: Bank One; MidFirst Bank.

MARK A. ZANNOTTI

525 SOUTH MAIN, SUITE 1111
TULSA, OKLAHOMA 74103-4512
Telephone: 918-583-6964
Fax: 918-582-8803
Email: mark.zannotti@jrgotlaw.com

Family Law, Adoptions, Probate, Commercial, Collections, Criminal, White Collar Crime, General Litigation.

FIRM PROFILE: Mr. Zannotti successfully represented Oklahoma State University in negotiations with the NCAA concerning eligibility questions and structural settlement transfers for 321 Henderson & Stone Street Capitol, Inc.

MARK A. ZANNOTTI, born Malden, Massachusetts, September 10, 1961; admitted to bar, 1994, Oklahoma and U.S. District Court, Northern and Eastern Districts of Oklahoma. *Education:* Oklahoma State University (B.S., 1983); University of Tulsa (J.D., 1993). Articles Editor, Tulsa Journal of Comparative and International Law, 1993. Former President, St. Thomas More Society. *Member:* Tulsa County (Former Chair, Family Law Section), Oklahoma and American Bar Associations. ***PRACTICE AREAS:*** Family Law; Civil; Criminal Litigation; Children; Guardianship; Probate; Collections; NCAA Regulation.

PHYLLIS L. ZIMMERMAN

1220 BANK OF AMERICA CENTER
15 WEST 6TH STREET
TULSA, OKLAHOMA 74119-5406
Telephone: 918-582-6151
Fax: 918-582-6153
Email: phyzim@swbell.net
Adoptions, General Civil Practice.

PHYLLIS L. ZIMMERMAN, born Arkansas City, Kansas, March 24, 1931; admitted to bar, 1963, Oklahoma; 1964, U.S. Court of Claims; 1973, U.S. Supreme Court. *Education:* University of Tulsa (B.S. in B.A., 1952); American University (J.D., 1963). Phi Beta Kappa; Phi Alpha Delta. *Member:* Tulsa County, Oklahoma (Chairman, Real Property Section, 1971) and American Bar Associations; Tulsa Title and Probate Lawyers Association; Oklahoma Association of Women Lawyers (President, 1967); National Association of Women Lawyers. ***PRACTICE AREAS:*** Adoption; Probate; Real Estate.

APPROVED ATTORNEY FOR: American-First Title & Trust Co.; Commercial Standard Insurance Co.; Standard Title Insurance Co.; Chicago Title Insurance Co.; Lawyers Title Insurance Corp.
REFERENCE: Bank One.

JONES & GARDNER

244 SOUTH SCRAPER
P.O. BOX 866
VINITA, OKLAHOMA 74301
Telephone: 918-256-8791
Fax: 918-256-8794
Email: karl@junct.com

Real Estate, Probate, Wills and Trusts, Estate Planning, Banking Law, Condemnation.

KARL D. JONES, born Vinita, Oklahoma, September 19, 1960; admitted to bar, 1986, Oklahoma. *Education:* University of Oklahoma (B.A., 1983); University of Tulsa (J.D., 1986). Member, Order of the Curule Chair. Notes and Comments Editor, Tulsa Law Journal, 1985-1986. Recipient, American Jurisprudence Award: Torts, Civil Procedure I and Civil Procedure II. *Member:* Craig County and Oklahoma Bar Associations. ***PRACTICE AREAS:*** Real Estate; Probate; Banking Law; Zoning Law; Condemnation.

JOSEPH M. GARDNER, born Joplin, Missouri, December 3, 1967; admitted to bar, 1993, Oklahoma. *Education:* University of Tulsa (B.A., 1990; J.D., 1993). *Member:* Oklahoma and American Bar Associations. ***PRACTICE AREAS:*** Adoption Law; Eminent Domain; Family Law; Personal Injury; Probate.

ASSOCIATES

TAMARA E. JAHNKE, born Council Bluffs, Iowa, November 3, 1968; admitted to bar, 1994, Oklahoma; U.S. District Court, Northern District of Oklahoma. *Education:* Central College (B.S., 1991); University of Tulsa (J.D., 1994). Phi Delta Phi. Member, Energy Law Journal, 1993-1994. President, Women's Law Caucus, 1993-1994. Formerly with Logan & Lowry, LLP. *Member:* Craig County (Secretary Treasurer, 1999-2002; President, 2003-2005) and Oklahoma (Member, Estate Planning, Probate and Trust Sections) Bar Associations; Oklahoma Bar Foundation. ***PRACTICE AREAS:*** Probate; Estate Planning; Family Law; Civil Practice.

ADRIAN M. WILKERSON, born Hammond, Indiana, November 18, 1977; admitted to bar, 2003, Oklahoma. *Education:* University of Notre Dame (B.B.A., 2000); Marquette University Law School (J.D., 2003). Alpha Sigma. *Member; Oklahoma Bar Association.* ***PRACTICE AREAS:*** Family Law; Civil Litigation; Criminal Law.

LOGAN & LOWRY, LLP

Established in 1963
101 SOUTH WILSON STREET
P.O. BOX 558
VINITA, OKLAHOMA 74301-0558
Telephone: 918-256-7511
Fax: 918-256-3187
Email: vinitaoffice@loganlowry.com

Grove, Oklahoma Office: 19 East 3rd Street. P.O. Box 452469. 74345-2469. Telephone: 918-786-7511. Fax: 918-786-5687.

General Practice, Including Trials in all State and Federal Courts, Eminent Domain, Environmental and Coal, Banking, Commercial Transactions, Creditors' Rights and Bankruptcy, Corporation, Public Utility, Real Estate, Estate Planning and Probate, Criminal, Domestic Relations, Civil Rights, Employment, Appellate Practice and Administrative Law.

FIRM PROFILE: J. Duke Logan and Richard W. Lowry founded the law firm in 1963. The firm has grown through lateral recruitment and in-house training of new associates. The firm's practice is regional in scope, covering all of northeast Oklahoma. The firm regularly tries commercial and tort cases in both federal and state courts throughout the Midwest, and has tried eminent domain cases throughout Oklahoma.

MEMBERS OF FIRM

J. DUKE LOGAN, born Norman, Oklahoma, February 4, 1931; admitted to bar, 1955, Oklahoma; 1959, U.S. District Court, Western District of Oklahoma; 1962, U.S. District Court, Eastern District of Oklahoma; 1966, U.S. District Court, Northern District of Oklahoma; 1972, U.S. Court of Appeals, Tenth Circuit. *Education:* University of Oklahoma (B.A., 1953; LL.B., 1955). Phi Alpha Delta. City Attorney, Vinita, Oklahoma, 1956-1966. Chairman, Oklahoma Employment Security Commission, 1959-1964. Member, Vinita School Board, 1968-1973. General Counsel, Grand River Dam Authority, 1969-1970. Di-

(This Listing Continued)

rector, University of Oklahoma College of Law Association; Oklahoma Council Judicial Complaint, 1989-1995; Chairman, 1992-1994; General Counsel, Council on Judicial Complaints, 1996—; Board of Directors, Oklahoma Historical Society, 1990-1993. *Member:* Craig County (President, 1961-1966), Oklahoma (Professional Responsibility Commission, 1997-1998; Chairman, 1999; Board of Governors, 1989-1996; President, 1995) and American Bar Associations; The Association of Trial Lawyers of America. Fellow and Trustee, Oklahoma Bar Foundation, 1994-1995. Fellow, American Bar Foundation. Fellow, American College of Trial Lawyers. Master Emeritus, American Inns of Court. ***PRACTICE AREAS:*** Civil Litigation; Utility Law.

O. B. JOHNSTON, III, born Tulsa, Oklahoma, October 1, 1941; admitted to bar, 1966, Oklahoma; 1970, U.S. District Court, Western District of Oklahoma and U.S. Court of Appeals, Tenth Circuit; 1975, U.S. District Court, Northern District of Oklahoma; 1982, U.S. Supreme Court;. *Education:* Baylor University (B.B.A., 1963); University of Tulsa (J.D., 1966). Associate Editor, Tulsa Law Journal, 1964-1966. Assistant U.S. Attorney, Western District of Oklahoma, 1970-1976. *Member:* Craig County (President, 1986-1988), Delaware County, Mayes County, Oklahoma (Member, Finance Commission; Associate Editor and Member, Board of Editors, Oklahoma Bar Journal, 2000—) and American (President, Federal Oklahoma City Chapter, 1975) Bar Associations; Fellow: Oklahoma Bar Foundation (Member, Board of Trustees, 1988-1996; President, 1995); American Bar Foundation (State Chair, 2001-2003). [Capt., U.S. Army, JAGC, 1966-1970]. ***PRACTICE AREAS:*** Family Law; Civil Litigation; Personal Injury Litigation. ***Email:*** objohnston@loganlowry.com

THOMAS J. McGEADY, born Bethlehem, Pennsylvania, March 1, 1951; admitted to bar, 1976, Virginia; 1982, Oklahoma. *Education:* University of Virginia (B.A., magna cum laude, 1973); Georgetown University (J.D., 1976). *Member:* Craig County (President, 1992-1995) and American (Member, Sections on: Litigation; Natural Resources Law) Bar Associations. ***PRACTICE AREAS:*** Civil Litigation; Environmental Law; Debtor/Creditor Litigation. ***Email:*** tjmcgeady@loganlowry.com

MARK W. CURNUTTE, born Vinita, Oklahoma, May 28, 1954; admitted to bar, 1979, Oklahoma. *Education:* University of Oklahoma (B.B.A., Accounting, 1976; J.D., 1979). *Member:* Craig County, Oklahoma and American Bar Associations. Fellow: Oklahoma Bar Foundation (Member, Board of Trustees, 2000—); American College of Trust and Estate Counsel. ***PRACTICE AREAS:*** Estate Planning Law; Probate and Trust Law; Real Property Law; Business Transactions; Business Planning. ***Email:*** mcurnutte@loganlowry.com

LEONARD M. LOGAN, IV, born Vinita, Oklahoma, December 5, 1957; admitted to bar, 1985, Oklahoma; U.S. District Court, Northern District of Oklahoma; U.S. District Court, Eastern District of Oklahoma. *Education:* University of Oklahoma (B.B.A., 1981); University of Tulsa (J.D., 1984). Recipient, American Jurisprudence Award in Criminal Procedure. *Member:* Craig County, Oklahoma and American Bar Associations; Oklahoma Trial Lawyers Association; The Association of Trial Lawyers of America. ***PRACTICE AREAS:*** Condemnation; Debtor Creditor Litigation; Criminal Law; Personal Injury Litigation; Utility Law. ***Email:*** llogan@loganlowry.com

DONNA L. SMITH, born Vinita, Oklahoma, May 6, 1950; admitted to bar, 1988, Oklahoma. *Education:* Pittsburgh State University (B.S.Ed., 1973; M.S.Ed., 1981); University of Tulsa (J.D., with honors, 1988). *Member:* Craig County (Secretary Treasurer, 1992-1998, 2003—; President, 1999-2000), Oklahoma (Associate Bar Examiner, 1988-2001; Civil Procedure Committee, 1995-1997; Bar Examiner, 2002—) and American Bar Associations; Oklahoma Bar Foundation. ***PRACTICE AREAS:*** Civil Litigation; Debtor/Creditor Litigation; Appellate Practice; Employment Law. ***Email:*** dsmith@loganlowry.com

ROBERT ALAN RUSH, born Omaha, Nebraska, February 27, 1963; admitted to bar, 1988, Oklahoma. *Education:* Kearney State College (B.S., magna cum laude, 1985); University of Kansas (J.D., 1988). Member: Moot Court Council; Kansas Law Review. *Member:* Craig County Bar Association (President, 2000-2003). ***PRACTICE AREAS:*** Civil Litigation; Bankruptcy; Condemnation. ***Email:*** rrush@loganlowry.com

DAVID E. JONES, born Kansas City, Missouri, April 30, 1965; admitted to bar, 1990, Oklahoma; 1991, Kansas and U.S. District Court, Northern and Eastern Districts of Oklahoma; U.S. Court of Appeals, Tenth Circuit. *Education:* University of Kansas (B.S., with honors, 1987; J.D., 1990). Phi Kappa Phi. Recipient, American Jurisprudence Award, Property II. Certified Public Accountant (Silver Medalist, May 1997 Oklahoma CPA Exam). *Member:* Delaware County, Oklahoma (Member: Uniform Laws Committee, 1995-1997; Law Related Education Committee, 1995-1997) and Kansas Bar Associations; Oklahoma Bar Foundation. ***PRACTICE AREAS:*** Civil Litigation; Business Law; Municipal Law; Appellate Practice. ***Email:*** djones@loganlowry.com

TODD E. KOLCZUN, born Takoma Park, Maryland, March 8, 1969; admitted to bar, 1994, Oklahoma; 1995, Texas; U.S. District Court, Eastern, Western and Northern Districts of Oklahoma; U.S. Court of Appeals, Fifth and Tenth Circuits. *Education:* Fordham University (B.S., 1991); Southern Methodist University (J.D., 1994). Phi Delta Phi. Articles Editor, 1992-1994, The International Lawyer. *Member:* Delaware County and Oklahoma Bar Associations; State Bar of Texas (Director, Young Lawyers Division, 2001-2004; Outstanding Committee Chair, 1996) Oklahoma Bar Foundation. ***PRACTICE AREAS:*** Civil Litigation; Business Law; Commercial Transactions; Oil and Gas. ***Email:*** tkolczun@loganlowry.com

ASSOCIATES

STEVE NEAS, born Tulsa, Oklahoma, August 4, 1974; admitted to bar, 2003, Oklahoma. *Education:* University of Tulsa (B.S., 1997; J.D., 2002). *Member:* Oklahoma Bar Association. ***PRACTICE AREAS:*** General Practice. ***Email:*** sneas@loganlowry.com

MARTHA L. LONDAGIN, born Oklahoma City, Oklahoma, June 20, 1965; admitted to bar, 1993, Arkansas, Oklahoma and U.S. District Court, Western District of Arkansas; 1994, U.S. District Court, Northern District of Oklahoma. *Education:* University of Arkansas (B.S., 1987; J.D., 1993). ***PRACTICE AREAS:*** General Practice. ***Email:*** mlondagin@loganlowry.com

RYAN P. LANGSTON, born Tulsa, Oklahoma, November 6, 1977; admitted to bar, 2005, Oklahoma. *Education:* Oklahoma State University (B.S.B.A., magna cum laude, 2000); University of Tulsa (J.D., Entrepreneurial Law Certificate, with highest honors, M.B.A., with honors, 2004). Phi Delta Phi. *Member:* Oklahoma Bar Association. ***Email:*** rlangston@loganlowry.com

OF COUNSEL

RICHARD W. LOWRY, born Oklahoma City, Oklahoma, December 19, 1937; admitted to bar, 1963, Oklahoma; 1965, U.S. District Court, Northern and Eastern Districts of Oklahoma; 1971, U.S. District Court, District of Kansas; U.S. Court of Appeals, Tenth Circuit. *Education:* University of Oklahoma (B.A., 1960); University of Oklahoma and University of Tulsa (LL.B., 1963). *Member:* Craig County Bar Association (President, 1967-1968). Fellow, Oklahoma Bar Foundation. ***PRACTICE AREAS:*** Litigation; Corporate Law; Mining Law; Probate Law.

CHARLES E. WEST, born Vinita, Oklahoma, September 8, 1947; admitted to bar, 1978, Oklahoma. *Education:* Oklahoma State University and Northeastern State College (B.S., 1969); University of Tulsa (J.D., 1978). Phi Delta Phi. *Member:* Craig County and Oklahoma Bar Associations. [Capt., U.S. Air Force, 1969-1975]. ***PRACTICE AREAS:*** Real Estate Law; Probate Law; Real Estate Foreclosure Law. ***Email:*** cwest@loganlowry.com

REPRESENTATIVE CLIENTS: Northeast Oklahoma Electric Cooperative, Inc.; Grand Bank; First National Bank & Trust Company of Vinita; American Cancer Society; Heartland Division, Inc.; C & L Supply, Inc.; Garland Coal and Mining Inc.; Anchor Industries, Inc.; Tower Components, Inc.; Farrell-Cooper Mining Co.; Northeast Area Vo-Tech Schools; Oklahoma Wildlife Federation; Advanced Medical Instruments Inc.; Doctor's Optical Supply, Inc.; Inter Tribal Council, Inc.; Nautilus Insurance Co.; Hanover Insurance Cos.; AXA Equitable Life Insurance Company; Har-Ber Village Foundation; Triangle Insurance Company; Blitz, USA; ROCMND Area Youth Services, Inc.
GENERAL COUNSEL: First National Bank & Trust Company of Vinita; Northeast Oklahoma Electric Cooperative, Inc.; C & L Supply, Inc.; Franks and Son, Inc.; Franks Operating Company; OK Freight Brokers, Inc.; Northeast Holding Company, Inc.; Diesel Services, Inc.; Granite Investments, Inc.; Craig County Hospital Authority.
REFERENCE: First National Bank and Trust Company of Vinita, Oklahoma.
APPROVED ATTORNEYS FOR: Lawyer's Title Insurance Co.; Chicago Title Insurance Co.; First American Title Insurance Co.; Farmers Home Administration.

TAYLOR, BURRAGE, FOSTER, MALLETT, DOWNS & RAMSEY, P.C.

VINITA, OKLAHOMA

(See Claremore)

Civil and Criminal Practice in all State and Federal Courts. Employment Law, Healthcare Law, Medical Malpractice, Professional Liability, Insurance Defense, Real Estate, Probate, Guardianships, Corporation, Commercial and Personal Injury Law.

A. CRAIG ABRAHAMSON

WAGONER, OKLAHOMA

(See Tulsa)

Family Law, Divorce, Child Custody, Visitation Rights, Child Support, Alimony, Spousal Support, Post Decree Modification and Enforcement, Premarital Agreements, Bankruptcy Creditors, Bankruptcy Debtor Ch. 7, Bankruptcy Debtor Ch. 11, Bankruptcy Debtor Ch. 13, Business Law, Commercial Transactions, Business Litigation, Commercial Litigation, Real Estate Transactions, Landlords.

SPENCE LAW OFFICE

WAGONER, OKLAHOMA

(See Tulsa)

Commercial and Civil Litigation, Construction Law, Real Property Law, General Practice Litigation, Trust and Estate Litigation, Bankruptcy.

TAYLOR, BURRAGE, FOSTER, MALLETT, DOWNS & RAMSEY, P.C.

WAGONER, OKLAHOMA

(See Claremore)

Civil and Criminal Practice in all State and Federal Courts. Employment Law, Healthcare Law, Medical Malpractice, Professional Liability, Insurance Defense, Real Estate, Probate, Guardianships, Corporation, Commercial and Personal Injury Law.

MICHAEL C. FLANAGAN

ATTORNEY AT LAW

Not a Partnership

Established in 1946

217 NORTH BROADWAY
P.O. BOX 5
WALTERS, OKLAHOMA 73572-0005
Telephone: 580-875-2121, 875-3113
Fax: 580-875-2135
Email: michaelcflanagan@sbcglobal.net

General Practice in all Federal and State Courts. Trials. Probate, Real Estate, Taxation, Bankruptcy, Estate Planning, Family Law, Education Law, Oil and Gas Law, Commercial Law.

MICHAEL C. FLANAGAN, born Walters, Oklahoma, July 1, 1954; admitted to bar, 1980, Oklahoma, U.S. District Court, Western District of Oklahoma, U.S. Tax Court and

(This Listing Continued)

MICHAEL C. FLANAGAN, ATTORNEY AT LAW, Walters—Continued

U.S. Court of Appeals, 10th Circuit; 1993, Colorado. *Education:* Oklahoma State University (B.S., 1976); Oklahoma City University (J.D., 1979). *Member:* Cotton County (President, 1985-1991, 1998,2001) and Oklahoma (Member, Probate Code Committee, 1990-1999) Bar Associations. ***PRACTICE AREAS:*** Probate; Real Estate; Estate Planning; Commercial Law; Taxation; Domestic Relations.

REPRESENTATIVE CLIENTS: Walters Bank and Trust Co.; Rural Water District No. 2, Cotton County, Oklahoma; J. David Schumpert, C.P.A; F.J. Lashley Jr., M.D.; City of Walters.
APPROVED ATTORNEY FOR: First American Title Insurance Co.; Farm Service Agency; Stewart Title & Trust Co.
REFERENCE: Walters Bank and Trust Co.

ATKINS & MARKOFF

WEATHERFORD, OKLAHOMA

(See Oklahoma City)

Personal Injury, Automobile Accidents, Wrongful Death, Trucking Accidents, Slip and Fall, Nursing Home Abuse, Head and Spinal Injuries, Dog Bites, Sexual Abuse, Criminal Law, Drug Crimes, DUI/DWI, Juvenile Crimes, General Practice, Family , Divorce, Adoptions, Child Custody, Child Support, Domestic Violence, Visitation Rights, Elder Law, Legal Malpractice, Medical Malpractice, Social Security, Social Security Disability, Taxation, IRS Audits, Property Tax Appeals, Tax Planning, Toxic Torts, Trust and Estate, Wills and Probate.

STEPHEN D. BEAM

Established in 1982

110 SOUTH BROADWAY
P.O. BOX 31
WEATHERFORD, OKLAHOMA 73096
Telephone: 580-772-2900
Telecopier: 580-772-6879
Email: sbeam@ionet.net
URL: http://www.lawyers.com/beamlaw

General Civil and Criminal Practice in all State and Federal Courts. Trusts and Estates, Real Estate, Commercial, Banking, Oil and Gas, Personal Injury, Bankruptcy, and Family Law.

STEPHEN D. BEAM, born Pampa, Texas, May 10, 1958; admitted to bar, 1982, Oklahoma; U.S. District Court, Western District of Oklahoma, U.S. District Court, Northern District of Texas, U.S. Court of Appeals, Fifth Circuit, U.S. Supreme Court. *Education:* Trinity University; Oklahoma State University (B.A., 1979); University of Oklahoma (J.D., 1982). Phi Delta Phi. Recipient, Solo Lawyer of the Year, 2003. *Member:* Custer County (President, 1992), Oklahoma (Member: Board of Governors, 1995-1997, 2004—; Vice President, 2003—; Board of Editors, Oklahoma Bar Journal, 1997-2003; Professional Responsibility Tribunal, 2000—; Chair, Solo and Small Firm Committee, 1999-2002; Treasurer, 1998-1999, Secretary, 1999-2000, Vice-Chair, 2000-2001, Chair, 2001-2002, General Practice Section) and American (Deputy Chair, Communications Division, Sole Practitioners and Small Firms Committee, 1998-1999; Chair, Sole Practitioners and Small Firms Committee, 1999—; Division Director, Solo and Small Firm Practice Division, General Practice, Solo and Small Firm Section, 2001-2002. Member, General Practice, Solo and Small Firm Section, Council, 2000—) Bar Associations; Oklahoma Trial Lawyers Association; Oklahoma Criminal Defense Lawyers Association.

REPRESENTATIVE CLIENTS: BancFirst, Weatherford, Oklahoma; Southwest National Bank, Weatherford, Oklahoma; Bank of Hydro, Hydro, Oklahoma; First Bank and Trust Co., Clinton, Oklahoma; Chesapeake Energy Corp.; Baptist General Convention; Federal Deposit Insurance Corp.; ANR Pipeline Co.; Transok, Inc.; Southern Natural Gas; Texaco; United Auto Workers; Public Service Company of Oklahoma; Unit Corporation; Feist Publications, Inc.; Gold Bank, Weatherford, Oklahoma; Oneok, Inc.
APPROVED EXAMINING ATTORNEY FOR: American First Title & Trust Co.; First National Bank and Trust Co. of Weatherford; BancFirst, Weatherford, Oklahoma; Bank of Hydro, Hydro, Oklahoma; Federal Deposit Insurance Corp.; Gold Bank, Weatherford, Oklahoma.

EDMONDS, COLE, HARGRAVE, GIVENS, RYAN & WOODSON, P.C.

Established in 1985

117 1/2 S. WEWOKA
P.O. BOX 1342
WEWOKA, OKLAHOMA 74884
Telephone: 405-257-5550
Email: jhargrave@edmonds-cole.com

Oklahoma City Office: One North Hudson, Suite 200, 73102. Telephone: 405-272-0322. Fax: 405-235-4654.

General Civil Practice. Insurance, Casualty and Surety Law, Negligence Trial Practice, Environmental Law, Employment Law, Civil Rights Law, Lender Liability Law.

(For complete biographical data on all personnel, see Professional Biographies at Oklahoma City, Oklahoma)

DUKE HALLEY LAW FIRM, P.L.L.C.

1703 MAIN STREET
P.O. BOX 509
WOODWARD, OKLAHOMA 73802-0509
Telephone: 580-254-9131
Facsimile: 580-254-2738
Email: dukehalley@sbcglobal.net
URL: http://www.lawyers.com/dukehalley

Oklahoma City, Oklahoma Office: 500 Colcord Drive, 73102. Telephone: 405-602-5600. Facsimile: 405-236-5499.

(This Listing Continued)

Civil Trial Practice, Appellate Practice in all State and Federal Courts, Personal Injury, Workers' Compensation, Product Defects, Insurance, Oil and Gas, Iodine Law, Environmental Law, Toxic Litigation.

DUKE HALLEY, born Vici, Oklahoma, July 7, 1948; admitted to bar, 1973, Oklahoma; 1989, U.S. District Court, Western District of Oklahoma, U.S. Court of Appeals, Tenth Circuit and U.S. Supreme Court. *Education:* Southwestern Oklahoma State University (B.A., cum laude, 1970); University of Oklahoma (J.D., 1973). Member: Oklahoma Crime Commission, 1975-1977; United States District Judge Selection Advisory Commission, 1979; Professional Responsibility Tribunal, 1990-1996; Judicial Nominating Committee, 1997—. *Member:* Woodward County (President, 1989), Oklahoma and American Bar Associations; Oklahoma Trial Lawyers Association (Current President; Member, Board of Directors, 1996—; President-Elect, 2004); The Association of Trial Lawyers of America. Fellow: American Board of Trial Advocacy (President, Oklahoma Chapter, 1989); American College of Trial Lawyers. (Certified as a Civil Trial Advocate by the National Board of Trial Advocacy)

REPRESENTATIVE CLIENT: Woodward Production Credit Assn.
REFERENCE: First State Bank of Mooreland.

HODGDEN, HALLREN, SMITHTON & HODGDEN, P.L.L.C.

Established in 1954

1002 NINTH STREET
P.O. BOX 529
WOODWARD, OKLAHOMA 73802
Telephone: 580-256-5517
Fax: 580-256-8459
Email: hodgdenh@sbcglobal.net

General Civil and Criminal Practice, State and Federal Courts. Trials. Real Property, Probate, Oil and Gas, Personal Injury, Workers Compensation, Family Law, Pollution, Environmental, Iodine, Personal Injury.

FIRM PROFILE: The firm succeeds Hieronymus, Hodgden & Hallren and its predecessors, which have practiced law in Woodward continuously since 1954.

BRYCE HODGDEN, born Enid, Oklahoma, January 1, 1942; admitted to bar, 1967, Oklahoma; 1970, U.S. Court of Appeals, Tenth Circuit and U.S. District Court, Western District of Oklahoma. *Education:* Oklahoma State University (B.S., 1964); University of Oklahoma (J.D., 1967). Phi Alpha Delta. *Member:* Woodward County, Oklahoma and American Bar Associations; American Judicature Society; Oklahoma Trial Lawyers Association. ***PRACTICE AREAS:*** Real Estate; Natural Resources; Oil and Gas; Environmental Law; Probate; Litigation; Personal Injury; Iodine.

KATHLEEN LIES HALLREN, born Pittsburgh, Pennsylvania, August 17, 1957; admitted to bar, 1982, Oklahoma and U.S. District Court, Western District of Oklahoma. *Education:* Worcester Polytechnic Institute (B.S., 1979); University of Oklahoma (J.D., 1982). Phi Alpha Delta. *Member:* Woodward County, Oklahoma and American (Member, Family Law Section) Bar Associations. ***PRACTICE AREAS:*** Real Estate; Probate; Litigation; Debtor and Creditor; Family Law.

W. SHANE SMITHTON, born Laverne, Oklahoma, August 19, 1966; admitted to bar, 1991, Oklahoma and U.S. District Court, Western District of Oklahoma. *Education:* Oklahoma State University (B.S., Business/Marketing, 1988); University of Notre Dame (J.D., 1991). *Member:* Woodward County, Oklahoma County, Oklahoma and American Bar Associations. ***PRACTICE AREAS:*** Real Estate; Commercial Transactions; Litigation; Personal Injury; Family Law; Estate Planning; Probate; Bankruptcy.

CODY B. HODGDEN, born Woodward, Oklahoma, October 17, 1970; admitted to bar, 1995, Oklahoma and U.S. District Court, Western District of Oklahoma. *Education:* Oklahoma State University (B.S., with honors, in Economics, 1992); University of Oklahoma (J.D., with highest honors, 1995). Order of the Coif. Recipient, American Jurisprudence Awards in: Contracts II; Civil Procedure II; Property II. Member, Oklahoma Law Review. Note, "The Evolving Liability Framework of the Comprehensive Environmental Response, Compensation & Liability Act," 47 Okla. L. Rev. 139, 1994. *Member:* Woodward County and Oklahoma Bar Associations. ***PRACTICE AREAS:*** Real Estate; Litigation; Oil and Gas; Collections; Estate Planning; Probate; Bankruptcy.

APPROVED EXAMINING ATTORNEYS FOR: Chicago Title Co.; Lawyers Title Insurance Co.; American First Title & Trust Co.; Farmers Home Administration; Federal Land Bank of Western Oklahoma.
ATTORNEYS FOR: First American Bank; John Hancock Mutual Life Insurance Co.
REFERENCES: Central National Bank of Alva, Woodward, Oklahoma; Stock Exchange Bank, Woodward, Oklahoma; First American Bank, Woodward, Oklahoma.

MITCHEL, GASTON, RIFFEL & RIFFEL, P.L.L.C.

1725 OKLAHOMA AVENUE
WOODWARD, OKLAHOMA 73801
Telephone: 580-254-3447
Fax: 580-254-5314
Email: lawyers@westoklaw.com
URL: http://www.westoklaw.com

Mailing Address: P.O. Box 887, Woodward, OK 73802-0887

Enid, Oklahoma Office: 201 N. Grand, Fourth Floor, 73701. Telephone: 580-234-8447.
Fairview, Oklahoma Office: 124 E. Broadway, Suite 6, 73737. Telephone: 580-234-8447.
Alva, Oklahoma Office: 907 Oklahoma Boulevard, 73717. Telephone: 580-254-3447.

Banks and Banking, Bankruptcy, Civil Rights, Collections, Contracts, Corporate Law, Criminal Law, Family Law, Federal Estate and Gift Taxation, Income Tax, Insurance, Oil and Gas Law, Personal Injury, Probate, Real Estate, Torts, Utility Law, Workers Compensation. .

(This Listing Continued)

FIRM PROFILE: The firm is Northwest Oklahoma's only regional law firm with offices in Woodward, Enid, Alva and Fairview and is comprised of seven attorneys. The firm has a general civil and criminal trial practice in all state and federal courts. The firm has over 30 years experience in the practice of law.

MICHAEL W. MITCHEL, born Perryton, Texas, October 12, 1948; admitted to bar, 1973, Oklahoma. *Education:* Northwestern State College of Oklahoma (B.S., 1970); University of Oklahoma (J.D., 1973). Delta Theta Phi (Vice Dean, 1971-1972; Secretary, 1972-1973). Member: Oklahoma State Board of Vocational and Technical Education, 1988-2000; Oklahoma State Board of Education, 1994-2000. *Member:* Woodward County (President, 1977) and Oklahoma (Member, Board of Governors, 1980-1982; Chairman, Commission on Continuing Legal Eduction, 1982-1985; Vice-President, 1983) Bar Associations; Oklahoma Criminal Defense Lawyers Association; Oklahoma Trial Lawyers Association; The Association of Trial Lawyers of America. Fellow, Oklahoma Bar Foundation. ***PRACTICE AREAS:*** Banks and Banking; Children; Civil Rights; Criminal Law; Family Law; Insurance Defense; Personal Injury; Real Estate; Workers Compensation. ***Email:*** mike@westoklaw.com

DONALD C. GASTON, born Britton, Oklahoma, May 23, 1942; admitted to bar, 1975, Oklahoma. *Education:* Oklahoma State University (B.S., 1965); Oklahoma City University (J.D., 1975). Certified Public Accountant, Oklahoma, 1965. *Member:* Oklahoma Bar Association (Member: Real Estate Section; Mineral Law Section). ***PRACTICE AREAS:*** Corporate Law; Bankruptcy; Federal Estate and Gift Taxation; Oil and Gas Leasing; Oil and Gas Title Examination; Probate; Real Estate; Trusts and Estates; Wills. ***Email:*** don@westoklaw.com

KATRESA J. RIFFEL, born Fairview, Oklahoma, May 29, 1967; admitted to bar, 1992, Oklahoma; U.S. District Court, Northern, Eastern and Western Districts of Oklahoma; U.S. Court of Appeals, Tenth Circuit. *Education:* Oklahoma State University (B.S., 1989); Oklahoma City University (J.D., cum laude, 1992). Phi Delta Phi. Law Review Editor, 1990-1992. *Member:* Garfield County and Oklahoma Bar Associations; American Inn of Courts. ***PRACTICE AREAS:*** Personal Injury; Products Liability; Insurance Defense; Bank Litigation; Divorce. ***Email:*** katresa@westoklaw.com

CRAIG RIFFEL, born Woodward, Oklahoma, November 11, 1967; admitted to bar, 1995, Oklahoma; U.S. District Court, Western and Eastern Districts of Oklahoma and U.S. Tax Court. *Education:* Oklahoma State University (B.S., 1990); Oklahoma City University (J.D., 1995). Certified Public Accountant, Oklahoma, 1995. *Member:* Garfield County, Oklahoma and American Bar Associations; Oklahoma Society of Certified Public Accountants; National Academy of Elder Law Attorneys. ***PRACTICE AREAS:*** Estate Planning; Medicaid Planning; Trusts; Probate; Tax Controversies; Tax Collection. ***Email:*** craig@westoklaw.com

ASSOCIATES

LYNN M. RETZ, born Ogden, Utah, May 1, 1966; admitted to bar, 1992, Oklahoma; 1993, Kansas and U.S. District Court, Western and Eastern Districts of Kansas. *Education:* Wichita State University (B.S., 1989); Oklahoma City University (J.D., 1992). *Member:* Garfield County, Oklahoma and Kansas Bar Associations. ***PRACTICE AREAS:*** Bankruptcy; Corporate Law; Debt Workouts; Medicaid Planning; Estate Planning. ***Email:*** lynn@westoklaw.com

ARIC A. ALLEY, born Shattuck, Oklahoma, 1976; admitted to bar, 2005, Oklahoma. *Education:* Brigham Young University (B.A., 2002); University of Oklahoma (J.D., 2005). Member, J. Reuben Clark Law Society, 2004-2005. *Member:* Woodward County and Oklahoma Bar Associations. ***PRACTICE AREAS:*** General Practice; Family Law; Real Estate; Civil Practice; Estate Planning. ***Email:*** aric@westoklaw.com

DALEN D. McVAY, born Greensburg, Kansas, 1977; admitted to bar, 2005, Oklahoma. *Education:* University of Central Oklahoma (B.S., 1999); Oklahoma City University

(This Listing Continued)

(J.D., 2005). Phi Alpha Delta. *Member:* Garfield County and Oklahoma Bar Associations. ***PRACTICE AREAS:*** Personal Injury; Probate; Estate Planning; Family Law; General Practice. ***Email:*** dalen@westoklaw.com

REPRESENTATIVE CLIENTS: Barby Energy, Inc.; Boomer Well Service; Latigo Oil and Gas, Inc.; Woodward Iodine; Woodward Regional Hospital; Oklahoma Farm Bureau Mutual Insurance Co.; U.S.F. & G.; Cheyenne Drilling, Inc.; Prudential Insurance Co.; Northwestern Electric Cooperative Corp.; Central National Bank of Alva, Woodward. OK; First State Bank of Camargo, Oklahoma.
APPROVED ATTORNEYS FOR: American First Title & Trust Co.; Federal National Mortgage Assn.; Farmers Home Administration.
REFERENCES: Central National Bank of Enid, Woodward, OK; Stock Exchange Bank, Woodward, OK; Central National Bank of Alva, Woodward, OK.

RAMEY & THARP

Established in 1969

3 SOUTH FIFTH STREET
YUKON, OKLAHOMA 73099
Telephone: 405-354-1987
Telecopier: 405-354-1992
Email: rameytharp@msn.com
URL: http://www.lawyers.com/rameytharp

General Civil Trial and Criminal Practice in all State and Federal Courts. Real Property, Medical Malpractice, Personal Injury, Child Custody, Products Liability, Probate, Corporate, Banking and Commercial Law, Family Law.

FIRM PROFILE: The firm is a general law practice with several areas of expertise. The firm is well known for its excellence in the quality of its work and meeting each particular client's needs.

MEMBERS OF FIRM

GEORGE H. RAMEY, born Oklahoma City, Oklahoma, April 23, 1943; admitted to bar, 1969, Oklahoma; U.S. District Court, Western and Northern Districts of Oklahoma and U.S. Court of Appeals, 10th Circuit. *Education:* Oklahoma State University (B.A., 1967); Tulsa University (J.D., 1969). Delta Theta Phi. Notes and Comments Editor, Tulsa Law Review, 1968-1969. Municipal Judge, Yukon, Oklahoma, 1974—. Judge of the Court of Appeals, Temporary Division, Number 88, Supreme Court, Oklahoma, 1982—. *Member:* Canadian County, Oklahoma County and Oklahoma Bar Associations. ***REPORTED CASES:*** Dave Markley Ford, Inc. v. Lair, 565 P.2d 671 (Okla. 1977); Adair State Bank v. American Casualty Company of Reading, PA, 949 F.2d 1067 (10th Cir. 1991); O'Petro Energy Corporation v. Canadian State Bank, 837 P.2d 1391 (Okla. 1992); Robert G. Boren v. Leah Dawn Kirk, 878 P2 1059 (Okla. 1994). ***PRACTICE AREAS:*** Personal Injury Law; Banking Law; Litigation; Family Law; Commercial Law. ***Email:*** rameytharp@msn.com

WILLIAM D. THARP, born Ponca City, Oklahoma, February 18, 1962; admitted to bar, 1990, Oklahoma; 1991, U.S. District Court, Western District of Oklahoma. *Education:* Oklahoma State University; University of Oklahoma (B.B.A. in Accounting, 1985; J.D., 1990). *Member:* Canadian County, Oklahoma County and Oklahoma Bar Associations. ***PRACTICE AREAS:*** Bankruptcy Litigation; Probate Law; Corporate Law; Employment Discrimination Law; Family Law; Personal Injury. ***Email:*** rameytharp@msn.com

REPRESENTATIVE CLIENTS: Canadian State Bank of Yukon, OK; Bank of Commerce, Catoosa, OK; Jackie Cooper BMW, Inc. of Oklahoma City; Title Insurance Company of Minnesota; Joe Cooper Ford of Midwest City and Yukon Oklahoma; Jackie Cooper Mercedes Benz and Volvo of Tulsa, Oklahoma.
APPROVED ATTORNEYS FOR: Oklahoma City Abstract and Title Co.; Lawyers Title Insurance Corp.; Capitol Abstract & Title Co.; Chicago Title Insurance Co.; Stewart Title Guaranty Co.; Title Insurance of Minnesota; Warranty Title & Abstract, Inc. of El Reno, Oklahoma.

TIM BRITTLE
ATTORNEY AT LAW

ALBANY, OREGON

(See Corvallis)

Elder Law, Trusts and Estates, Estate Planning, Estate Litigation, Wills, Probate, Insurance, Nursing Home Abuse, Guardianship and Conservatorship, Asset Protection, Business Law, Corporate Law, Closely Held Business, Limited Liability Company Law, Partnership Law, Small Business Law, Buying or Selling a Business, Contracts, Business Start-Ups, Business Planning, Real Estate, Buying or Selling a Home, Residential Real Estate, Landlord and Tenant, Commercial Leasing.

CLARK, LINDAUER, FETHERSTON, EDMONDS, LIPPOLD & COLLIER, LLP

ALBANY, OREGON

(See Salem)

Trial and Business Practice in State and Federal Courts including Business Litigation, Insurance Law, Agricultural Law, Automobile, Premises Liability, Professional Negligence, including Legal and Medical Malpractice, Product, Toxic Tort and Environmental Liability, Employment Discrimination, Wrongful Discharge and Defamation, Arbitration and Mediation, Business, Real Estate, and Estate Law, Probate.

PETERSON LAW OFFICES, PC

ALBANY, OREGON

(See Portland)

Personal Injury, Premises Liability, Automobile Accidents and Injuries, Dog Bites and Wrongful Death.

WEATHERFORD, THOMPSON, COWGILL, BLACK & SCHULTZ, P.C.

Established in 1875

130 WEST FIRST AVENUE
P.O. BOX 667
ALBANY, OREGON 97321
Telephone: 541-926-2255
Fax: 541-967-6579
Email: legal@wtlegal.com
URL: http://www.wtlawyer.com

General Civil and Trial Practice, Business and Corporate Law, Pension and Profit Sharing, Banks and Banking, Taxation, Probate, Estate Planning, Elder Law, Real Property, Agricultural Law, Land Use and Zoning, Securities, Creditors Rights, Commercial Law, Personal Injury, Environmental and Natural Resources.

FIRM PROFILE: In July, 1875, James K. Weatherford was admitted to practice law in Oregon. He chose to settle in Albany, and so began 60 years of continuous legal service to the citizens of Linn and Benton Counties. Now in its second century, James K. Weatherford's law firm continues to provide legal services and individual contributions to the community of Albany and the entire state.

MICHAEL G. COWGILL, born Albany, Oregon, January 3, 1953; admitted to bar, 1978, Oregon. *Education:* Oregon State University (B.S., 1975); University of Oregon (J.D., 1978). Phi Kappa Phi; Blue Key. *Member:* Linn County (President, 1983-1984) and American Bar Associations; Oregon State Bar (Member, Local Professional Responsibility Committee, 1984-1987); Oregon Trial Lawyers Association. ***PRACTICE AREAS:*** Business; Agricultural Law; Personal Injury; Civil Litigation; Real Property. ***Email:*** mcowgill@wtlegal.com

THOMAS L. BLACK, born Los Angeles, California, November 11, 1947; admitted to bar, 1977, Oregon. *Education:* California State University at Long Beach (B.A., 1970); University of California at Santa Barbara State University (M.A., 1974); Lewis and Clark College (J.D., 1977); University of Florida (LL.M., in Taxation, 1978). Member, Lewis and Clark College Law Review, 1976-1977. Author: "Population Criteria of Oregon and the United States in the Siting of Nuclear Power Plants," 6 Environmental Law Review 897, 1976. *Member:* Linn County and American Bar Associations; Oregon State Bar. ***PRACTICE AREAS:*** Business; Pension and Profit Sharing Plans; Wills; Estate Planning. ***Email:*** tblack@wtlegal.com

EDWARD F. SCHULTZ, JR., born Livingston, Montana, March 28, 1946; admitted to bar, 1972, Oregon; 1981, U.S. District Court, District of Oregon. *Education:* University of Oregon (B.S., 1968; J.D., 1972). District Attorney, Jefferson County, Madras, Oregon, 1975-1977. Linn County Counsel, Albany, Oregon, 1977-1981. *Member:* Linn County and American Bar Associations; Oregon State Bar. ***PRACTICE AREAS:*** Real Estate; Land Use; Governmental; Environmental; Civil Litigation; Appellate Practice. ***Email:*** eschultz@wtlegal.com

MICHAEL B. BRINK, born Hillsboro, Oregon, June 24, 1953; admitted to bar, 1979, Oregon and North Carolina. *Education:* Lewis and Clark College (B.A., 1975); Willamette University (J.D., 1978). *Member:* Linn County (President, 1991-1992) and American Bar Associations; Oregon State Bar. ***PRACTICE AREAS:*** Elder Law; Business; Real Estate; Probate. ***Email:*** mbrink@wtlegal.com

(This Listing Continued)

ASSOCIATES

JOEL D. KALBERER, born Mexicali, Mexico, October 20, 1972; admitted to bar, 2001, Oregon; 2002, Oregon Federal District Court. *Education:* Whitman College (B.A., Politics, 1994); University of Oregon (J.D., 2001). Moot Court. Member, Journal of Environmental Law and Litigation. *Member:* Linn County Bar Association (Member, Sections on: Government Law; Real Estate; Land Use; Member, Legislative Committee, 2004—); Oregon State Bar. ***PRACTICE AREAS:*** Business Law; Real Estate; Land Use; Landlord and Tenant Law; Housing Law; Litigation. ***Email:*** jdk@wtlegal.com

ANDREW J. BEAN, born Yakima, Washington, November 25, 1969; admitted to bar, 1999, Oregon. *Education:* Santa Clara University (B.S., 1992); Willamette University (J.D., magna cum laude, 1999). Business Manager, Willamette Law Review, 1998-1999. ***PRACTICE AREAS:*** Land Use; Real Estate; Business Law; Estate Planning. ***Email:*** abean@wtlegal.com

COUNSEL

BRETT R. CHYTRAUS, born Fullerton, California, January 28, 1961; admitted to bar, 1990, Oregon; 1992, U.S. District Court, District of Oregon and U.S. Federal Court of Appeals. *Education:* Montana State University (B.A., History, 1985); Northwestern School of Law of Lewis & Clark College (J.D., 1990). Regional Winner, National Competitor, Moot Court Client Counseling; Moot Court Honor Board. *Member:* Linn County and American Bar Associations; Oregon State Bar. ***PRACTICE AREAS:*** Business Law; Mergers and Acquisitions; Real Estate; Construction Law; Estate Planning. ***Email:*** bchytraus@wtlegal.com

DENNIS D. ASHENFELTER, born The Dalles, Oregon, April 16, 1944; admitted to bar, 1971, Oregon; 1978, U.S. District Court, District of Oregon; 1979, U.S. Tax Court. *Education:* Oregon State University (B.S., 1968); Willamette University (J.D., 1971); College of William & Mary (L.L.M., in Taxation, 1978). Phi Delta Phi. Editor, Willamette Law Journal, 1971. *Member:* Linn County Bar Association; Oregon State Bar (Member, Executive Committee, Business Law Section, 1986-1990). ***PRACTICE AREAS:*** Estate Planning; Trust Administration; Wills; Business Law; Mergers and Acquisitions; Taxation; Income Tax; Estate and Gift Taxation. ***Email:*** dashenfelter@wtlegal.com

REPRESENTATIVE CLIENTS: Morse Bros., Inc.; Weyerhaeuser Company; Willamette Community Bank; Greater Albany Public School District; ATI Wah Chang; DLF International Seeds, Inc.; Corvallis Radiology; Wilbur-Ellis Company; Oregon State University Alumni Association; Timberhill Corporation; Hart's Nursery of Jefferson, Inc.; Cala Farms, Inc.
REFERENCES: Linn-Benton Bank; Key Bank of Oregon; U.S. National Bank of Oregon, Albany Branch; First Interstate Bank of Oregon, Albany Branch.

FOSTER DENMAN, LLP

ASHLAND, OREGON

(See Medford)

Business Litigation in all State and Federal Courts. Corporate Law, Business Law, Real Property, Land Use, Estate Planning, Estate Administration, Probate, Trusts Law, Nonprofit Organizations Law, Health Law, Construction Law, Tax Law.

THOMAS C. HOWSER, P.C.

Established in 1972

607 SISKIYOU BOULEVARD
P.O. BOX 640
ASHLAND, OREGON 97520
Telephone: 541-482-2621
Fax: 541-482-1512
Email: info@ashlandlaw.com
URL: http://www.ashlandlaw.com

Accidents, Adoptions, Appeals, Assault and Battery, Auto Accidents, Business Law, Civil Practice, Commercial Litigation, Corporations, Criminal Damages, Damages, Easements, Elder Law, Employment Discrimination, Estate Planning, General Practice, Insurance, Land Use, Landlord Tenant Law, Leasing, Litigation, Malpractice, Medical Malpractice, Modification, Municipal Law, Partnerships, Personal Injury, Probate Law, Property, Real Estate, Trial Practice, Trusts, Water Rights, Wills Wrongful Death, Zoning.

THOMAS C. HOWSER, admitted to bar, 1961, Oregon. *Education:* University of Oregon (B.S., 1959; J.D., 1961); Netherlands Institute for Foreign Trade (1958). *Member, Oregon State Bar.*

JUDITH H. UHERBELAU, admitted to bar, 1981, California; 1982, Oregon. *Education:* Ball State University (B.S., 1978); University of California at Los Angeles (J.D., 1981). *Member:* Oregon State Bar; State Bar of California.

JACOBSON, THIEROLF & DICKEY, P.C.

ASHLAND, OREGON

(See Medford)

General Litigation and Office Practice, Civil and Criminal Trials and Appeals in State and Federal Courts, Bankruptcy and Collections, Real Estate and Land Use, Probate, Estate Planning, Business, Domestic Relations, Indian and Environmental Law, Water Law, Immigration, Patents, Trademarks, Copyrights, Licensing, Wills, Trusts.

CHARLES GEORGE KOCHLACS

ASHLAND, OREGON

(See Medford)

Family Law, Divorce, Child Custody, Child Support, Spousal Support, Domestic Violence, Premarital Agreements, Criminal Law and Juvenile Law, Driving While Intoxicated, Drug Crimes, Felonies, Misdemeanors, Sexual Assault, Traffic Violations, Parole and Probation.

KUENZEL & ASSOCIATES

98 PINE STREET
ASHLAND, OREGON 97520
Telephone: 541-552-0142
Fax: 541-552-0145
Email: kuenzel@aol.com
URL: http://www.lawyers.com/kuenzel&associates

San Rafael, California Office: 4040 Civic Center Drive, Suite 200, 94903. Telephone: 415-492-8100. Fax: 415-492-8174.

Business Law, Business Litigation, Employment Law, Intellectual Property, Arbitration and Mediation.

FIRM PROFILE: Providing sophisticated legal skills and judgment honed over more than 25 years solving problems for major national clients, with the friendly, personal service to be expected from a neighbor.

ROBERT V. KUENZEL, born Evanston, Illinois, November 16, 1949; admitted to bar, 1976, Illinois; 1979, California; 1996, Oregon. *Education:* Princeton University (A.B., 1971); Northwestern University (J.D., summa cum laude, 1976). Order of the Coif. Member, Northwestern University Law Review. Law Clerk to Judge Wilbur F. Pell, Jr., U.S. Court of Appeals, Seventh Circuit, 1976-1978. Associate, Latham & Watkins, 1979-1983. Associate (2 years) and then Partner-in-Charge, Business Litigation Practice Groups, Proskauer Rose Goetz & Mendelsohn, Los Angeles and San Francisco, 1983-1995. Publications: "Alternative Dispute Resolution: Why All the Fuss?" Employment & Benefits Review, July 1996; "Employment 'at Will', Employers at Risk," Prentice Hall Law & Business; "Making Sense of Robinson-Patman," 62 Va. L. Rev. 1211; "Defamation Law in the Wake of Gertz," 69 N.W.U.L.Rev. Lecturer: ABA Litigation Section Annual Meeting, 1994 (video technology in trials); 28th and 26th Corporate Counsel Institutes (employment); California State Bar Convention, 1988 (employment). Member, American Arbitration Association National Panel of Commercial Arbitrators. ***PRACTICE AREAS:*** Business Law; Business Litigation; Employment Law; Intellectual Property; Arbitration; Mediation.

COREY, BYLER, REW, LORENZEN & HOJEM, L.L.P.

BAKER CITY, OREGON

(See Pendleton)

General Civil and Trial Practice. Agriculture and Agricultural Cooperatives, Domestic Relations, Banking, Business, Municipal, Zoning, Condemnation, School, Corporation, Insurance, Tax, Estate Planning, Probate, Water and Real Estate Law.

PETERSON LAW OFFICES, PC

BAKER CITY, OREGON

(See Portland)

Personal Injury, Premises Liability, Automobile Accidents and Injuries, Dog Bites and Wrongful Death.

YERVASI POPE, P.C.

Established in 1998
1990 THIRD STREET
P.O. BOX 50
BAKER CITY, OREGON 97814-0050
Telephone: 541-523-7973
Fax: 541-523-7993
URL: http://www.lawyers.com/yervasicoltman

Personal Injury, Civil and Criminal Litigation, Wrongful Death, Probate, Estate Planning, Bankruptcy.

DAMIEN R. YERVASI, born Rochester, New York, August 14, 1966; admitted to bar, 1995, Oregon; 1999, U.S. District Court, District of Oregon. *Education:* The Citadel (B.S., 1988); Northwestern School of Law at Lewis and Clark College (J.D., 1995). *Member:* Association of Trial Lawyers of America; Oregon Trial Lawyers Association; National College of Advocacy (Advocate); National Crime Victims Bar Association. [Lt., USN, 1988-1992]. ***PRACTICE AREAS:*** Personal Injury; Wrongful Death; Civil Litigation; Criminal Litigation; Insurance. ***Email:*** dyervasi@eoni.com

MILO POPE, born Hoquiam, Washington, July 18, 1936; admitted to bar, 1961, Idaho and U.S. District Court of Idaho; 1967, Oregon and U.S. District Court, District of Oregon; 1973, U.S. Court of Appeals, Ninth Circuit. *Education:* Boise Junior College; University of Oregon; University of Idaho (LL.B., 1961). Member: State Professional Responsibility Board, 1981-1983; Board of Governors, Oregon State Bar, 1984-1987. Vice-President, Oregon State Bar, 1987. Circuit Court Judge, 1989-2000. *Member:* Oregon Criminal Defense Lawyers Association; Oregon Trial Lawyers Association. ***PRACTICE AREAS:*** Litigation; Probate; Criminal Defense. ***Email:*** mpope@bakervalley.net

(This Listing Continued)

LISE F. YERVASI, born Nelsonville, Ohio, March 29, 1964; admitted to bar, 1993, Oregon; 1995, U.S. District Court, District of Oregon. *Education:* University of Wyoming (B.S., with honors, 1990); Northwestern School of Law (J.D., 1993). *Member:* Baker County and Multnomah County Bar Associations; Oregon State Bar (Member, Young Lawyers Division); Oregon Trial Lawyers Association. ***PRACTICE AREAS:*** Domestic Relations; Business Litigation; Employment Law.

LEGAL SUPPORT PERSONNEL

THERESA CURTIS
HEIDI JOHNSON

ATHERTON & ALLEN

Established in 1925
P.O. BOX 1256
BANDON, OREGON 97411
Telephone: 541-347-8315
Fax: 541-347-7620
Email: daveallen@estplanlaw.com

Chula Vista, California Office: 210 Towne Centre Professional Building, 345 "F" Street, 91910. Telephone: 619-420-6869.

General Civil Practice. Estate Planning, Trusts and Estates, Wills, Probate Law, Corporate and Real Estate Law.

(For complete biographical data on all personnel, see Professional Biographies at Chula Vista, California)

ADAMS & UFFELMAN LLP

Established in 1952
HALL STREET STATION
4500 S.W. HALL BOULEVARD
BEAVERTON, OREGON 97005-0504
Telephone: 503-644-2146
Fax: 503-646-2227
Email: info@beavertonlaw.com
URL: http://www.beavertonlaw.com

General Civil and Trial Practice in all State and Federal Courts. Business, Corporate, Estate Planning and Probate Law, Entertainment Law, Family Law, Divorce, Real Estate Law, Contracts, Criminal Law, Criminal Trials and Appeals in all State and Federal Courts.

FIRM PROFILE: Adams & Uffelman LLP is the oldest Law Firm in the City of Beaverton. One of the firm's founding partners, James B. Castles, incorporated Tektronix, Inc., in 1946. The firm has dedicated itself to providing its clients with the finest quality legal services at a reasonable cost. The present members of the firm have continued this tradition of professional excellence and service to their community.

MEMBERS OF FIRM

RODNEY C. ADAMS, born Roseburg, Oregon, September 14, 1935; admitted to bar, 1960, Oregon; 1961, U.S. District Court, District of Oregon. *Education:* Willamette University and University of Oregon (B.A., 1957); Willamette University (J.D., 1960). Phi Delta Phi; Phi Eta Sigma; Eta Mu Pi. City Attorney, 1965-1970. *Member:* Washington County (President, 1968) and American Bar Associations; Oregon State Bar (Member, Committee on Professional Responsibility, 1972-1982, 1987-1989; Treasurer, Real Estate Section, 1980). ***PRACTICE AREAS:*** Real Estate; Municipal; General Business; Estate Planning and Probate; Family Law; Guardianship and Conservatorship. ***Email:*** rodney.adams@beavertonlaw.com

JOHN E. UFFELMAN, born Portland, Oregon, April 28, 1948; admitted to bar, 1973, Oregon; 1974, U.S. District Court, District of Oregon; 1986, U.S. Court of Appeals, Ninth Circuit; 1991, U.S. Supreme Court. *Education:* Gonzaga University (B.A., 1970); University of Oregon (J.D., 1973). Associate Editor, Oregon Law Review, 1972-1973. Trustee, Pacific Coast Outward Bound School, 1978-1985. *Member:* Oregon State Bar; American Bar Association; Oregon Trial Lawyers Association; The Association of Trial Lawyers of America. ***PRACTICE AREAS:*** Civil and Commercial Litigation; Personal Injury; Wrongful Death; Medical Malpractice; Drug and Medical Device Litigation; Automotive Products Liability; Automobile Accidents and Injuries; Wills; Trusts and Estates; Probate. ***Email:*** john.uffelman@beavertonlaw.com

REPRESENTATIVE CLIENTS: Culver Glass Co.; Hinditron International; Prier Pipe and Supply, Inc.; Tualatin Hills Park & Recreation District; Lithtex, Inc.
REFERENCE: United States National Bank of Oregon (Beaverton Branch).

BLAKELY, SOKOLOFF, TAYLOR & ZAFMAN

A Limited Liability Partnership
Established in 1975
1925 NW AMBERGLEN PARKWAY, SUITE 230
BEAVERTON, OREGON 97006
Telephone: 503-439-8778
Facsimile: 503-439-6073
Email: BSTZ_mail@bstz.com
URL: http://www.bstz.com

Sunnyvale, California Office: 1279 Oakmead Parkway. Telephone: 408-720-8300. Facsimile: 408-720-8383.

Los Angeles, California Office: 7th Floor, 12400 Wilshire Boulevard. Telephone: 310-207-3800. Facsimile: 310-820-5988.

(This Listing Continued)

Costa Mesa, California Office: 3200 Park Center Drive, Suite 700. Telephone: 714-557-3800. Facsimile: 714-557-3347.
Denver, Colorado Office: 8055 E. Tufts Avenue, 13th Floor. Telephone: 303-740-1980. Facsimile: 303-740-6962.
Seattle, Washington Office: 601 Union Street, Suite 3000. Telephone: 206-292-8600. Facsimile: 206-292-8606.
San Jose, California Office: 60 S. Market Street, Suite 510. Telephone: 408-947-8200. Facsimile: 408-947-8280.

Intellectual Property Law, including Patents, Trademarks, Copyrights, Related Prosecution and Litigation.

GREGORY D. CALDWELL, born Montreal, Quebec, Canada, July 25, 1963; admitted to bar, 1995, California and Oregon; registered to practice before U.S. Patent and Trademark Office. *Education:* Oregon Institute of Technology (B.S., cum laude, 1986); Santa Clara University (J.D., 1994). *Member:* American Bar Association. ***Email:*** greg.d.caldwell@bstz.com

PAUL A. MENDONSA, born Sacramento, California, January 11, 1971; admitted to bar, 1997, California; 1998, Oregon; registered to practice before U.S. Patent and Trademark Office. *Education:* Brigham Young University (B.S.E.E., 1994); Santa Clara University (J.D., 1997). ***Email:*** paul_mendonsa@bstz.com

---

MARK C. VAN NESS, born Wahoo, Nebraska, July 8, 1958; admitted to bar, 1983, Colorado; registered to practice before U.S. Patent and Trademark Office (Not admitted in Oregon). *Education:* University of Colorado at Boulder (B.A., cum laude, 1980); Georgetown University (J.D., 1983); University of Colorado at Denver (B.S., Electrical Engineering, 1999). ***Email:*** mark_van_ness@bstz.com

VINCENT H. ANDERSON, born Oxnard, California, March 6, 1974; admitted to bar, 2003, Oregon; registered to practice before U.S. Patent and Trademark Office. *Education:* Brigham Young University (B.S.E.E., 2000); Willamette University (J.D., cum laude, 2003). ***Email:*** vincent_anderson@bstz.com

REPRESENTATIVE CLIENTS: Apple Computer, Inc.; Applied Materials, Inc.; eBay Inc.; Guidant Corporation; Intel Corporation; Patagonia, Inc.; OPI Products, Inc.; Sony Corporation of America; Sun Microsystems, Inc.

(For complete biographical data on personnel at Los Angeles, Sunnyvale, Costa Mesa, San Jose, California, Denver, Colorado and Seattle, Washington, see Professional Biographies at those locations)

CASE & DUSTERHOFF, LLP

Established in 1980

9800 SW BEAVERTON HILLSDALE HIGHWAY, SUITE 200
BEAVERTON, OREGON 97005
Telephone: 503-641-7222
Facsimile: 503-643-6522
Email: info@case-dusterhoff.com
URL: http://www.case-dusterhoff.com

Business and Business Litigation, Insurance, Asbestos Defense, Construction Litigation, Probate and Real Property Law, Taxation. General Civil and Trial Practice, Products Liability, Casualty, Surety and Fidelity, Errors and Omissions, Employment, Estate Planning and Wills and Trusts, Personal Injury, Medical and Legal Malpractice, Family Law and Mediation.

FIRM PROFILE: The law firm of Case & Dusterhoff, LLP is listed in the Bar Register of Preeminent Lawyers.

JAMES D. CASE, born Seattle, Washington, October 2, 1945; admitted to bar, 1973, Oregon; 1984, Washington. *Education:* Washington State University (B.S., 1967); Northwestern School of Law of Lewis and Clark College (J.D., 1973). *Member:* Oregon State Bar; Washington State Bar Association; American, Multnomah County and Washington County Bar Associations; Oregon Association of Defense Counsel; Defense Research Institute. ***PRACTICE AREAS:*** Casualty; Surety and Fidelity; Errors and Omissions; Products Liability Law; Asbestos Defense; Business Litigation. ***Email:*** jcase@case-dusterhoff.com

R. BRUCE DUSTERHOFF, born Cut Bank, Montana, April 17, 1945; admitted to bar, 1975, Oregon. *Education:* University of Oregon (B.A., 1967; J.D., 1975); University of Washington (M.B.A., 1970). *Member:* Oregon State Bar; Multnomah County Bar Association; American Trial Lawyers Association; Oregon Trial Lawyers Association. ***PRACTICE AREAS:*** Products Liability; Professional Malpractice; Business Law; Real Property; Personal Injury; Criminal Law; Domestic Relations; Contracts. ***Email:*** bruce@case-dusterhoff.com

---

LEO A. REINIKKA, born Vancouver, Washington, July 15, 1945; admitted to bar, 1970, Oregon; 1973, U.S. Tax Court. *Education:* Western Washington State University (B.A., cum laude, 1967); Willamette University (J.D., 1970). Delta Theta Phi. Associate Editor, Willamette Law Journal, 1969-1970. Attorney, Office of Chief Counsel, IRS, 1970-1981. *Member:* Oregon State Bar (Member, Taxation Section; IRS Liaison Committee); Washington County Bar Association. ***PRACTICE AREAS:*** Business and Individual Taxation; Estate and Tax Planning; Probate; Real Property; Domestic Relations. ***Email:*** lreinikka@case-dusterhoff.com

MARGARET H. LEEK LEIBERAN, born Eugene, Oregon, April 27, 1950; admitted to bar, 1977, Oregon; U.S. District Court, District of Oregon; U.S. Court of Appeals; 1980, U.S. Supreme Court. *Education:* University of Oregon (B.S., 1972); Harvard University (J.D., 1976). Staff Attorney, Oregon Court of Appeals, 1983-1985. Pro-Tem Hearing Referee, Workers Compensation Board, 1987. *Member:* Oregon State Bar. ***PRACTICE AREAS:*** Appeals.

(This Listing Continued)

REPRESENTATIVE CLIENTS: Gateway, Inc.; Streimer Sheet Metal Works, Inc.; International Wood Industries, Inc.; Paninkret Chem-Pharm; Goodrich Trading Company, Inc.; Alterra Health Care Corporation; Metalclad Insulation Corporation; Inductotherm Industries, Inc.; Admiral Insurance Co.; Duro Dyne Corporation.

DEBAST, MCFARLAND & RICHARDSON, LLP

BEAVERTON, OREGON

(See Portland)

Family Law, Divorce, Premarital Agreements, Child Support, Property Settlements, Spousal Support, Child Custody, Domestic Violence, Visitation Rights, Estate Planning, Wills, Trusts, Probate, Civil Litigation, Criminal Law, Personal Injury, Driving While Intoxicated, Drug Crimes, Guardianships and Conservatorship.

DRAKULICH & CARLSON, P.C.

BEAVERTON, OREGON

(See Portland)

General Civil and Trial Practice. Family Law, Child Custody, Child Support, Divorce, Domestic Violence, Visitation Rights, Personal Injury, Automobile Accidents, Dog Bites, Sexual Abuse, Slip and Fall, Wrongful Death, Medical Malpractice, Insurance, Health Care, Construction Law, Contracts, Lawsuits, Real Estate Buying and Selling, Residential Real Estate, Commercial Real Estate, Criminal Law, Driving While Intoxicated, Drug Crimes, Parole and Probation.

HELZER & CROMAR, LLP

4900 S.W. GRIFFITH DRIVE, SUITE 245
BEAVERTON, OREGON 97005
Telephone: 503-626-2889
Fax: 503-626-9944
URL: http://www.helzercromar.com
URL: http://www.helzercromarlaw.com

Criminal Law, Family Law, Divorce, Child Custody, Spousal Support, Personal Injury, Automobile Accidents, Criminal Law, Driving While Intoxicated, Felonies, Drug Crimes, Juvenile Crimes, Parole and Probation, Sexual Abuse, Traffic Violations, Estate Litigation, Guardianship and Conservatorship, Employment Law, Discrimination, Sexual Harassment.

RICHARD G. HELZER, born Oregon City, Oregon, June 19, 1939; admitted to bar, 1969, Oregon. *Education:* Oregon State University (B.S., 1961); Portland State University (B.S., 1962); Northwestern School of Law, Lewis & Clark College (J.D., 1969). Delta Theta Phi. *Member:* Multnomah County, Washington County (Secretary, 1991) and American (Member, Sections on: Economics of Law Practice; Family Law; Litigation; Member, Forum Committee on Entertainment and Sports Industry, 1980—) Bar Associations; Oregon State Bar (Member, Committees on: Economics of Law Practice, 1977-1978; Ad Hoc Annual Meetings, 1977-1978; Unauthorized Practice of Law, 1982-1985; Local Professional Responsibility Committee, 1990-1991; Washington and Yamhill County Professional Responsibility). ***PRACTICE AREAS:*** Criminal Law; Driving While Intoxicated; Felonies; Misdemeanors; Drug Crimes; Juvenile Criminal Law; Parole and Probation; Sexual Assault; Traffic Violations; Entertainment Law; Family Law; Divorce; Child Custody; Child Support; Personal Injury; Automobile Accidents and Injuries; Civil Litigation; Business Law; Real Estate; Contracts; Probate; Wills. ***Email:*** rgh@helzercromar.com

JAMES S. CROMAR, born Flint, Michigan, August 17, 1964; admitted to bar, 1991, Oregon; 1992, U.S. District Court, District of Oregon. *Education:* University of Michigan, Ann Arbor (B.A., Film and Political Science, 1987); Washington University (J.D., 1991). *Member:* Washington County and Multnomah County Bar Associations; Oregon State Bar. ***PRACTICE AREAS:*** Family Law; Divorce; Civil Litigation; Contracts; Personal Injury; Collaborative Family Law; Domestic Partnerships; Premises Liability; Wills; Employment Law; Business Law; General Practice; Real Estate; Trusts and Estates. ***Email:*** jsc@helzercromar.com

ASSOCIATES

ROGER DALE SCARBROUGH, born Lubbock, Texas, 1955; admitted to bar, 1991, Texas; 1999, North Carolina; 2001, Oregon. *Education:* Texas Tech University (B.A., 1981); Thurgood Marshall School of Law (J.D., 1991). ***Email:*** rds@helzercromar.com

SARA D. CIVEY, born Pullman, Washington, September 17, 1976; admitted to bar, 2002, Oregon. *Education:* Lewis and Clark College (B.A., 1998); Willamette University (J.D., 2002). *Member:* Oregon State Bar. ***PRACTICE AREAS:*** Personal Injury; Civil Litigation; Family Law; Probate. ***Email:*** sdc@helzercromar.com

MCNEIL LAW OFFICE LLC

BEAVERTON, OREGON

(See Hillsboro)

Family, Criminal, Wills, Personal Injury, Business Litigation.

PETERSON LAW OFFICES, PC

BEAVERTON, OREGON

(See Portland)

Personal Injury, Premises Liability, Automobile Accidents and Injuries, Dog Bites and Wrongful Death.

RAIVIO, KOHLMETZ & STEEN, P.C.

BEAVERTON, OREGON

(See Portland)

Criminal Law, Personal Injury, Civil Rights, Driving While Intoxicated, Weapons Charges, Drug Crimes, Auto Accidents, Slip and Fall, Dog Bites, Wrongful Death, Assault, Homicide, Robbery, Measure II, White Collar Crime, Sexual Accusations.

LAURIE SHERTZ LLC

BEAVERTON, OREGON

(See Portland)

Criminal Defense, Trial Practice, Felonies, Homicide and Assault, Self Defense, Weapons Charges, Sex Offenses, Drug Crimes, Theft and Fraud. Practice in Federal and State Courts.

THE THOMPSON LAW FIRM

BEAVERTON, OREGON

(See Portland)

Wills, Trusts and Estates, Estate Planning, Probate, Taxation, Tax Planning, Guardianship, Conservatorships, Contracts, Closely Held Business, Small Business Law, Partnership Law, Limited Liability Company Law, Business Planning.

BAOQIN WANG AND TANYA P. SHEPHERD

Established in 1997

4900 SW GRIFFITH DRIVE, SUITE 165
BEAVERTON, OREGON 97005
Telephone: 503-626-7051
Fax: 503-626-7950
Email: immigration@askwang.com
URL: http://www.askwang.com

Immigration Law, Corporate Law.

FIRM PROFILE: Immigration Specialist: We devote our practice exclusively to immigration law. We have represented our clients in different types of immigration cases such as H-1B, L-1, E-1, E-2, Employment and Family Based Green Card applications, Asylum, Fiancé Visa etc.

Diverse: We deal with all aspects of U.S. Immigration and Nationality Law and represent individual and corporate clients across the United States and around the world in immigration related matters.

Personalized Service: Each case is unique and requires different levels of attention. Thus, we take time to analyze each individual case in order to find the best solutions for our clients.

Communication: We believe communication is a key element in practicing immigration law. We take the time to properly and thoroughly explain the immigration process to our clients, and we promptly update our clients with the progress of their case.

Reasonable Fixed Fee: Our fee is based on the complexity of the case which will vary based on circumstances. The fee will be reasonably fixed based on the work and research required for the specific case.

BAOQIN WANG, born Weinan, Shaanxi, China, August 30, 1968; admitted to bar, 2000, California; 2005, Oregon. *Education:* Jilin University, Jilin, China (LL.B., 1990); Brigham Young University (J.D., 1999). *Member:* State Bar of California; Oregon State Bar; American Immigration Lawyers Association. ***LANGUAGES:*** Chinese. ***SPECIAL AGENCIES:*** U.S. Citizenship and Immigration Services; U.S. Department of Labor. ***PRACTICE AREAS:*** Immigration Law (100%). ***Email:*** immigration@askwang.com

TASANEEYA P. SHEPHERD, born Bangkok, Thailand, June 21, 1976; admitted to bar, 2002, Oregon. *Education:* Chulalongkorn University, Bangkok, Thailand (LL.B., 1998); Gonzaga University (J.D., cum laude, 2002). *Member:* Oregon State Bar. ***LANGUAGES:*** Thai. ***SPECIAL AGENCIES:*** U.S. Citizenship and Immigration Services; U.S. Department of Labor. ***PRACTICE AREAS:*** Immigration Law (90%); Corporate Law (10%). ***Email:*** tanya@askwang.com

Languages: Chinese, Thai, Japanese.

BABB HEATHERMAN LLP

960 SW DISK DRIVE
P.O. BOX 8
BEND, OREGON 97709
Telephone: 541-389-1010
Fax: 541-382-6875
Email: paul@bendattorneys.com
URL: http://bendattorneys.com

Business Law, Commercial Law, Contracts, Collections, Construction Law, Real Estate, Commercial Leasing, Family Law, Divorce, Child Custody, Estate Planning, Wills, Probate, Personal Injury, Lawsuits, Litigation.

PARTNERS

RAY A. BABB, born Eugene, Oregon, May 21, 1940; admitted to bar, 1965, Oregon and U.S. District Court, District of Oregon. *Education:* Colorado College (B.A., 1962); University of Oregon (J.D., 1965). Former Chairman, Oregon State Bar Continuing Legal Education Committee. ***PRACTICE AREAS:*** Estate Planning; Real Estate; Business Law; Construction Law; Personal Injury; Litigation. ***Email:*** ray@bendattorneys.com

(This Listing Continued)

PAUL B. HEATHERMAN, born Napa, California, September 5, 1962; admitted to bar, 1993, Oregon and U.S. Court of Appeals, Ninth Circuit; 1996, U.S. District Court, District of Oregon. *Education:* Humboldt State University (B.S., 1985); Willamette University College of Law (J.D., 1993). Editor, Willamette University Law Review, 1992-1993. Law Clerk to the Honorable Paul De Muniz, Oregon Court of Appeals, 1993-1995. Author: "Collection of Vendee Installment Payments and the Law of Waiver in Light of Alderman v. Davidson," Oregon Debtor-Creditor Newsletter XVI, No.1, 1997; "Smoothing the Rough Edges of Arbitration," Trial Lawyer, Fall 1997; "Physical Injury to or Loss of Chattels," Damages, Oregon State Bar, 2002; "Attorney Fees," Civil Litigation Manual, Oregon State Bar, 2004. Co-author: "Residential Landlord-Tenant Disputes," Real Estate Disputes, Oregon State Bar, 2002; "Reexamining the Definition of a Prevailing Party: The Attorney Fee Conundrum," Litigation Journal, 19, No. 2 Aug. 2000. *Member:* Oregon State Bar (Chairperson, Trial Ethics Panel, Region One, 2003-2004). ***PRACTICE AREAS:*** Real Estate; Real Estate Litigation; Business Law; Construction Law; Contracts; Personal Injury; Litigation; Commercial Litigation; Landlord and Tenant Law. ***Email:*** paul@bendattorneys.com

ASSOCIATE

LILLAH McBRIDE, born Tupelo, Mississippi, January 10, 1977; admitted to bar, 2003, Oregon. *Education:* University of Southern Mississippi (B.A., 2003); Willamette University (J.D., 2003). ***PRACTICE AREAS:*** Construction Law; Family Law; Divorce; Adoption Law; Child Custody; Child Support; Civil Litigation. ***Email:*** lillah@bendattorneys.com

OF COUNSEL

KATHARINE A. MILLER, born Los Angeles, California, June 24, 1955; admitted to bar, 1987, California, U.S. District Court, Central District of California and U.S. Court of Appeals, Eighth Circuit; 1995, U.S. Court of Appeals, Ninth Circuit; 1999, Oregon; 2002, U.S. District Court, District of Oregon. *Education:* University of Puget Sound (B.S., magna cum laude, 1977); Whittier College School of Law (J.D., summa cum laude, 1986). Phi Kappa Phi. Mortar Board. Editor, Whittier Law Review, 1985-1986. Recipient: American Jurisprudence Awards. Judicial Clerkship, U.S. Court of Appeals, Eighth Circuit, 1986-1987. *Member:* State Bar of California; Oregon State Bar. (Also Member, King & Miller LLP, Pasadena, California). ***PRACTICE AREAS:*** Municipal Law; Civil Litigation; Business Law; Real Estate. ***Email:*** katharine@bendattorneys.com

BALL JANIK LLP

15 SW COLORADO AVENUE, SUITE 3
BEND, OREGON 97702
Telephone: 541-617-1309
Telecopy: 541-617-8824
Email: info@balljanik.com
URL: http://www.balljanik.com

Portland, Oregon Office: One Main Place, 101 SW Main Street, Suite 1100, 97204-3219. Telephone: 503-228-2525. Telecopy: 503-295-1058.
Washington, D.C. Office: 1455 F Street, NW, Suite 225, 20005-1004. Telephone: 202-638-3307. Telecopy: 202-783-6947.

Real Estate and Land Use Law, Business and Corporate Law, Construction, Environmental and Natural Resources Law, Zoning Law, Health Care, Securities.

PARTNERS OF FIRM

NANCY CRAVEN, born Springfield, Illinois, 1954; admitted to bar, 1979, Oregon. *Education:* Lawrence University (B.A., 1976); Southern Illinois University (J.D., 1979). Law Clerk to Chief Judge George Joseph, Oregon Court of Appeals, 1979-1981. County Counsel, Lincoln County, Oregon, 1981-1986. *Member:* Oregon State Bar. (Also at Portland, Oregon Office). ***PRACTICE AREAS:*** Land Use; Natural Resources; Zoning; Environmental. ***Email:*** ncraven@balljanik.com

LAURA CRASKA COOPER, born Munich, Germany, 1966; admitted to bar, 1991, California; 1993, Pennsylvania (inactive); 1999, Oregon. *Education:* University of Missouri (B.J., summa cum laude, 1988; B.A., summa cum laude, 1988); University of California, Boalt Hall School of Law (J.D., 1991). Phi Beta Kappa. Senior Note and Comment Editor, California Law Review, 1990-1991. Law Clerk to Hon. Charles E. Wiggins, U.S. Court of Appeals, Ninth Circuit, 1991-1992. *Member:* Oregon State Bar; State Bar of California. (Also at Portland, Oregon Office). ***PRACTICE AREAS:*** Real Estate; Land Use; Corporate Law; Environmental; Construction. ***Email:*** lcooper@balljanik.com

SPECIAL COUNSEL

ROBERT A. STOUT, born Cambridge, Massachusetts, 1946; admitted to bar, 1974, Oregon. *Education:* Michigan State University (B.A., 1968); Yale University (J.D., 1974). *Member:* Multnomah (Past Chair, CLE Committee) and Lane County (Member, CLE Committee) Bar Associations; Oregon State Bar (Member, Executive Committee, Business Law Section; Past Chair and Executive Committee Member, Securities Section; Past Executive Committee Member, Corporate Counsel Section; Past Executive Committee Member, Estate Planning and Administration Section; Member, Sections on: Securities Law; Business Law). [Lt. SC USN, 1968-1971]. (Also at Portland, Oregon Office). ***PRACTICE AREAS:*** Corporate Finance; Corporate Law; Mergers and Acquisitions; Securities; Real Estate; Health Care Law. ***Email:*** rstout@balljanik.com

ASSOCIATES

REAGAN L.B. DESMOND, born Lancaster, Pennsylvania, 1967; admitted to bar, 1997, Utah; 2001, California; 2004, Oregon. *Education:* Indiana University of Pennsylvania (B.S., 1990); University of Utah Law School (J.D., 1997). *Member:* Oregon State Bar; State Bar of California; Utah State Bar; American Bar Association (Member, Natural Resources, Energy and Environmental Law Section). (Also at Portland, Oregon Office).

(This Listing Continued)

PRACTICE AREAS: Land Use; Environmental; Water Quality; Water Rights; Public Agency Law; California Environmental Quality Act (CEQA). ***Email:*** rdesmond@balljanik.com

KRISTIN L. UDVARI, born Hanover, New Hampshire, 1974; admitted to bar, 1999, Oregon; 2004, Washington. *Education:* Yale University (B.A., 1996); Northwestern School of Law of Lewis & Clark College (J.D., cum laude, 1999). Articles Editor, Environmental Law, Northwestern School of Law, Lewis and Clark Law Review, 1998-1999. Co-Chair, Environmental Law Caucus, 1997-1998. *Member:* Oregon State Bar; Washington State Bar Association. (Also at Portland, Oregon Office). ***PRACTICE AREAS:*** Land Use; Environmental; Natural Resources. ***Email:*** kudvari@balljanik.com

(For Complete Biographical Data on Personnel at Washington, D.C., and Portland, Oregon, see Professional Biographies at those locations)

BRYANT, LOVLIEN & JARVIS, P.C.

Established in 1915

591 SW MILL VIEW WAY

P.O. BOX 1151

BEND, OREGON 97709-1151

Telephone: 541-382-4331

Fax: 541-389-3386

Email: bljadmin@bljlawyers.com

URL: http://www.bljlawyers.com

General Civil and Trial Practice, Corporations, Creditor's Rights in Bankruptcy, Taxation, Estate Planning, Probate, Elder Law, Real Estate, Land Use Planning, Natural Resource Law, Water Rights, Insurance Defense and Family Law.

NEIL R. BRYANT, born Spokane, Washington, July 8, 1948; admitted to bar, 1973, Oregon and U.S. District Court, District of Oregon. *Education:* Pacific Lutheran University (B.A., 1970); Willamette University (J.D., 1973). Oregon State Senator, District #27, 1993-2000. Chair, Senate Judiciary Committee. Board Member, Central Oregon, Independent Health Services, 1998— (Health Insurance Company). Member: Board of Regents, Pacific Lutheran University, 1987-1996; National Conference of State Legislators (Executive Committee, 1996-1999); Board Member, OMSI (Oregon Progress Board). Chair, Board of Advisors, Oregon State University, 2000-2003. Board Member, High Desert Museum. Government Affairs Consultant, Oregon State Board of Higher Education, 2004—. *Member:* Oregon State Bar (Executive Committee, Corporate and Business Law Section, 1978-1982; Executive Committee, Debtor-Creditor Section, 1983-1987; Labor Law Section Executive Committee, 1987-1989); American Bar Association. ***PRACTICE AREAS:*** Business Law; Corporate Law; Labor Law; Real Estate; Water Law. ***Email:*** bryant@bljlawyers.com

ROBERT S. LOVLIEN, born Klamath Falls, Oregon, May 8, 1949; admitted to bar, 1974, Oregon and U.S. District Court, District of Oregon. *Education:* University of Washington (B.A., 1971); University of Oregon (J.D., 1974). Phi Beta Kappa; Phi Delta Phi. *Member:* Oregon State Bar (Board of Bar Examiners, 1984-1987; Chairperson, 1986-1987; Executive Committee, Real Estate and Land Use Section, 1988-1990; State Professional Responsibility Board, 1988-1991; Board of Examiners Review Board, 1991-1993; Chairperson, 1993). ***PRACTICE AREAS:*** Land Use Law; Real Estate Law; Business Law; Corporate Law. ***Email:*** robert@bljlawyers.com

LYNN F. JARVIS, born Portland, Oregon, October 11, 1943; admitted to bar, 1979, Oregon; 1989, Idaho (inactive) and U.S. District Court, District of Oregon. *Education:* Oregon State University (B.S., 1966); University of Idaho School of Law (J.D., 1978). University of Idaho Law Review, 1976-1978. *Member:* Oregon State Bar (Chair, 2002, and Current Member of Executive Committee, Family Law Section; Debtor-Creditor Section and Former Member, Executive Committee; Lawyer Representative, Bankruptcy Section, 9th Circuit Judicial Conference, 1994-1997); Central Oregon Matrimonial Lawyers. ***PRACTICE AREAS:*** Family Law; Creditors Rights in Bankruptcy. ***Email:*** jarvis@bljlawyers.com

JOHN A. BERGE, born Santa Cruz, California, June 17, 1961; admitted to bar, 1987, Oregon; 1988, U.S. District Court, District of Oregon. *Education:* Oregon State University (B.S., 1983); Willamette University (J.D., cum laude, 1987). Past President, Central Oregon Bar Association. *Member:* Oregon State Bar (Member: Debtor/Creditor Section; Litigation Section Executive Committee; Former Member and Chair, Local Professional Responsibility Committee; Executive Committee, OSB Ethics Trial Panel Member). ***PRACTICE AREAS:*** Civil Practice; General Civil Litigation; Insurance Defense. ***Email:*** berge@bljlawyers.com

SHARON R. SMITH, born Lansing, Michigan, April 25, 1958; admitted to bar, 1986, Oregon. *Education:* University of Oregon (B.S., 1983; J.D., 1986). Order of the Coif. City Land Use Hearings Officer, 2002—; Municipal Judge, Pro Tem. *Member:* Oregon State Bar (Executive Committee, Real Estate and Land Use Section, 1995-1996; Treasurer, 1996-1997; Secretary, 1997-1998; Chair, 1999-2000; Business Law Section; Local Professional Responsibility Committee, 1993-1996); Oregon Women Lawyers (Board Member, 1988-1992; Vice President, 1989; Executive Committee, 1990-1993; Secretary, 1992-1993). ***PRACTICE AREAS:*** Land Use Law; Real Estate Law; School Law; Public Law. ***Email:*** smith@bljlawyers.com

JOHN D. SORLIE, born Fort Jackson, South Carolina, September 22, 1963; admitted to bar, 1993, Illinois (inactive); 1995, Oregon and Idaho (inactive); 1998, U.S. District Court, District of Oregon. *Education:* Carleton College (B.A., 1986); Northwestern School of Law, Lewis & Clark College (J.D., 1993). Editor, International Legal Perspectives, Northwestern School of Law, 1992-1993. *Member:* Oregon State Bar (Sections on: Business Law; Estate Planning); American Bar Association. ***PRACTICE AREAS:*** Business Law; Real Estate; Probate Law; Estate Planning. ***Email:*** sorlie@bljlawyers.com

MARK G. REINECKE, born New Canaan, Connecticut, August 6, 1962; admitted to bar, 1991, Oregon; 1997, U.S. District Court, District of Oregon. *Education:* John Carroll University (B.S.B.A., 1986); Washington & Lee University School of Law (J.D., 1991).

(This Listing Continued)

Member: Oregon State Bar (Sections on: Litigation; Business Litigation; Debtor/Creditor; Environmental and Natural Resources). ***PRACTICE AREAS:*** General Civil Litigation; Water Law. ***Email:*** reinecke@bljlawyers.com

MELISSA P. LANDE, born Thessaloniki, Greece, September 28, 1966; admitted to bar, 1991, Oregon. *Education:* New York University (B.A., 1988); Washington & Lee University School of Law (J.D., 1991). *Member:* Deschutes County Bar Association (Member, Family Law Advisory Committee); Oregon State Bar (Family Law Section; Former Member, Local Professional Responsibility Committee); Central Oregon Matrimonial Attorneys. ***LANGUAGES:*** French. ***PRACTICE AREAS:*** Family Law. ***Email:*** lande@bljlawyers.com

KITRI C. FORD, born Vancouver, Washington, December 11, 1952; admitted to bar, 1989, Washington; 1991, Oregon. *Education:* Oregon State University (B.S., with high honors, 1975); University of Alaska (B.S., cum laude, Nursing Science, 1981); University of Utah (J.D., 1989). Order of the Coif. *Member:* Oregon State Bar; Washington State Bar Association; Oregon Association of Defense Counsel. ***PRACTICE AREAS:*** Estate Planning; Probate; Guardianship and Conservatorship; Insurance; Insurance Defense. ***Email:*** ford@bljlawyers.com

---

PAUL J. TAYLOR, born Tachikawa, Japan, May 22, 1968; admitted to bar, 1998, Oregon; 1999, Washington. *Education:* University of Oregon (B.A., 1993; J.D., 1998). *Member:* Oregon State Bar (Sections on: Business Law; Real Estate and Land Use; Estate Planning and Administration); Washington State Bar Association; American Bar Association. ***PRACTICE AREAS:*** Business Law; Corporate Law; Real Estate; Estate Planning. ***Email:*** taylor@bljlawyers.com

CHRISTOPHER A. BAGLEY, born Portland, Oregon, November 18, 1971; admitted to bar, 1997, Oregon. *Education:* University of Oregon (B.A., cum laude, 1994); University of Minnesota (J.D., cum laude, 1997). *Member:* Oregon State Bar (Sections on: Litigation; Family Law). ***PRACTICE AREAS:*** Civil Litigation; Insurance Defense; Family Law. ***Email:*** bagley@bljlawyers.com

JEREMY M. GREEN, born Columbus, Ohio, November 2, 1977; admitted to bar, 2004, Oregon. *Education:* Warner Pacific College (B.S., 2000); University of Oregon (J.D., 2003). ***PRACTICE AREAS:*** Business Law; Real Estate; Taxation; Estate Planning. ***Email:*** green@bljlawyers.com

KELLY L. SCHUKART, born Grande Prairie, Alberta, February 28, 1979; admitted to bar, 2005, Oregon. *Education:* University of Oregon (B.A., 2001); University of Cincinnati (J.D., 2005). *Member:* Oregon State Bar (Member, Litigation and Family Law Sections).

REPRESENTATIVE CLIENTS: Bend-LaPine School District; Eagle Crest Resort; Bob Thomas Chevrolet-Cadillac-Honda-Geo; Robberson Ford Sales; Jack Robinson and Sons Construction, Inc.; 4-R Equipment, L.L.C; Arnold Irrigation District; State Farm Insurance Co.; Mt. Bachelor Village, Inc.; Idatech, LLC; Pieratt Bros., Inc.; Reed Bros., Inc.; Kerr, Oliver & Co.; Steve Scott & Co.; Re/Max Manzanita Land Co.; Western Communications, dba The Bulletin; Cascade Pumice, Inc.; East Cascade Women's Clinic; Barber Barrett & Turner, Architects, Inc.; Neal Huston & Assoc., Architects; City of Madras; Sisters School District; Bend Metro Parks & Recreation District; LaPine Rural Fire Protection District; Western Title & Escrow Company; KTVZ 21; Swalley Irrigation District; Desert Bone and Joint Specialists, LLP; Horizon Broadcasting Group, LLC; United Communications, Inc. (Unicom); Community First Bank; Bend Broadband; Summit Accomodators, Inc.
REFERENCE: Bank of the Cascades.

CLARK, LINDAUER, FETHERSTON, EDMONDS, LIPPOLD & COLLIER, LLP

BEND, OREGON

(See Salem)

Trial and Business Practice in State and Federal Courts including Business Litigation, Insurance Law, Agricultural Law, Automobile, Premises Liability, Professional Negligence, including Legal and Medical Malpractice, Product, Toxic Tort and Environmental Liability, Employment Discrimination, Wrongful Discharge and Defamation, Arbitration and Mediation, Business, Real Estate, and Estate Law, Probate.

D'AMORE & ASSOCIATES, P.C.

BEND, OREGON

(See Portland)

Medical Malpractice, Plaintiff's Personal Injury, Wrongful Death, Automobile Collisions and Injuries, Consumer Class Actions, Automobile Negligence, Insurance Litigation, Automobile Insurance Coverage, Insurance Bad Faith, Insurance Fraud, Insurance Premium Fraud, Unfair Insurance Practices, Uninsured Motorists, Property Damage Insurance Coverage, Brain Injury, Catastrophic Injury, Vehicular Homicide, Premises Liability, Medical Negligence. Motorcycle and Bicycle Accidents, Toxic Torts, ERISA and HMO Litigation, Employment Law and Discrimination, Wrongful Termination, Sexual Harassment, Workers Compensation, Dog Bites, Nursing Home Abuse, Trucking Accidents.

ROXANNE L. FARRA, P.C.

17 N.W. IRVING AVENUE
BEND, OREGON 97701
Telephone: 541-385-3017
Fax: 541-330-1556
Email: rfarra@bendbroadband.com
URL: http://www.lawyers.com/roxannefarra

Employment Litigation and Consultation, Business Litigation, Employment Law, Wage and Hour Law, Discrimination, Sexual Harassment, Wrongful Termination and Disability Accommodation.

ROXANNE L. FARRA, born Newport Beach, California, October 20, 1962; admitted to bar, 1990, Oregon. *Education:* Oregon State University (B.A., 1984); Northwestern School of Law (J.D., 1989). Law Clerk to the Hon. William M. Dale, Jr., U.S. District Court Magistrate, 1989-1992. Law Clerk to the Hon. Edward Leavy, U.S. Circuit Court of Appeals, Ninth Circuit, 1992-1993. Featured Speaker: Drafting Severance Agreements, May 1999; Human Resource Audits in Oregon, March 2003. *Member:* Oregon State Bar (Member, Executive Committee, Business Litigation Section, 2001—; Judicial Conference of the Ninth Circuit Lawyer Delegate, 2003-2005; Junior Co-Chair, 2003-2004; Senior Co-Chair, 2004-2005); J.R. Campbell American Inns of Court (2000—). ***PRACTICE AREAS:*** Employment Law; Employment Litigation; Business Law. ***Email:*** rfarra@bendbroadband.com

FRANCIS, HANSEN & MARTIN, LLP

Established in 1980
1148 N.W. HILL STREET
BEND, OREGON 97701
Telephone: 541-389-5010
Fax: 541-382-7068
URL: http://www.francishansenmartin.com

Real Estate, Probate, Personal Injury, Workers Compensation, Business, Corporate, Limited Liability Companies, Estate Planning, Homeowners Association Law and Civil Litigation.

FIRM PROFILE: The firm fully serves its business and real estate clients. C.E. "Win" Francis is responsible for business consulting and estate planning. Gerald A. Martin is responsible for all litigation, including contract disputes, workers compensation claims, labor disputes and personal injury. Martin E. Hansen is responsible for commercial and complex civil litigation, bank law and utility law.

MEMBERS OF FIRM

C. E. "WIN" FRANCIS, born Portland, Oregon, August 25, 1948; admitted to bar, 1977, Oregon and U.S. District Court, District of Oregon. *Education:* Stanford University (A.B., 1970); Lewis and Clark College (LL.B., 1976). Member, Central Oregon Board of Realtors, 1983. Member, Board of Trustees, The Tower Theater Foundation, Inc. Member, AAA Oregon/Idaho. *Member:* Oregon State Bar (Member: Committee on Professionalism, 1987-1990; Board of Directors, Real Estate and Land Use Section, 1990-1993; Treasurer, 1992-1993). ***PRACTICE AREAS:*** Business Law; Commercial Real Estate; Construction Law; Wills; Trusts and Estates; Probate; Real Estate Foreclosure; Real Estate Leasing; Right of Way Easements; Boundary Disputes; Homeowners Association Law; Property Management; Real Estate Development; Family Limited Partnerships; Nonprofit and Charitable Organizations; Contracts; Corporate Law; Limited Liability Company Law; Small Business Law; Business Sales; Real Estate Sales; Agricultural Law; Farm and Ranch Law; Leases and Leasing; Partnership Law. ***Email:*** win@francishansenmartin.com

MARTIN E. HANSEN, born San Francisco, California, February 13, 1955; admitted to bar, 1979, Washington and U.S. District Court, Western District of Washington; 1980, Oregon, U.S. District Court, District of Oregon and U.S. Court of Appeals, Ninth Circuit; U.S. Claims Court. *Education:* Southern Oregon State College (B.S., cum laude, 1975); University of Puget Sound School of Law (J.D., cum laude, 1978). Municipal Judge, Rainier, Washington, 1980. Council on Court Procedures, 2003—. *Member:* Thurston-Mason County, Central Oregon (President, 1992-1993; Member, Bench Bar Committee, 1986—), Washington State and American Bar Associations; Oregon State Bar (Member: Professional Liability Fund Defense Panel, 1985—; State Professional Responsibility Committee, 1995-1998; Chair 1997-1998; Special Counsel for Commission on Judicial Fitness and Disability, 1999—; Oregon State Bar, Trial Counsel, 1999—; Chair, 11th and 22nd Judicial District Pro-Tem Screening Committee, 1990—; Committee on Civil Jury Instructions, 1984-1987; Procedure and Practice Committee, 1988-1991); Local Professional Responsibility Committee (Chairman, 1987-1988), 1985-1988; Association of Defense Counsel (Member: Executive Committee, Debtor-Creditor Section, 1991-1993; Legal Ethics Committee, 1991-1993); The Association of Trial Lawyers of America; Oregon Trial Lawyers Association. ***PRACTICE AREAS:*** Civil Practice; Commercial Litigation; Insurance Law; Banking Law; Land Use Law; Legal Malpractice Defense. ***Email:*** meh@francishansenmartin.com

GERALD A. MARTIN, born Iowa City, Iowa, March 3, 1943; admitted to bar, 1969, Oregon; 1970, U.S. District Court, District of Oregon; 1985, U.S. Court of Appeals, Ninth Circuit. *Education:* University of Iowa (B.A., with honors, 1966; J.D., with distinction, 1969). Phi Delta Phi. Member, Oregon Community College Budget Committee, 1983-1991. *Member:* Oregon State Bar (Member: Uniform Civil Jury Instructions, 1982-1983; Board of Bar Examiners, 1978-1981). ***PRACTICE AREAS:*** Civil Litigation; Business Litigation; Personal Injury; Insurance Defense; General Litigation; Commercial Law; Labor and Employment Law. ***Email:*** Jerry@francishansenmartin.com

---

MICHAEL H. McGEAN, born Salt Lake City, Utah, May 27, 1970; admitted to bar, 2000, Oregon. *Education:* Reed College (B.A., 1992); University of California, Hastings College of the Law (J.D., 2000). J.R. Campbell American Inns of Court, 2001-2003. *Member:* Oregon State Bar (Member, Civil Jury Instructions Committee). ***PRACTICE AREAS:*** Commercial Litigation; Real Property; Debtor and Creditor; Contracts; Zoning, Planning and Land Use. ***Email:*** mike@francishansenmartin.com

GREGORY J. STUMAN, born Honolulu, Hawaii, April 18, 1967; admitted to bar, 1993, California and U.S. District, Southern District of California; 2004, Oregon;. *Education:* Willamette University (B.S., 1989); University of San Diego School of Law (J.D., 1992). MT Bachelor Rotary Club. *Member:* State Bar of Oregon; State Bar of California. ***PRACTICE AREAS:*** Business Law; Real Estate; Estate Planning; Securities Regulation; Securities; Trademark Licensing; Technology Licensing. ***Email:*** greg@francishansenmartin.com

REPRESENTATIVE CLIENTS: Wells Fargo Bank; Central Electric Cooperative Inc.; Advanced Power Technologies; Quantum Communications; CoEnergy LLC; R.A. Brownrugg Investments Inc.; Bank of The Cascades; Broken Top Community Association; Professional Liability Fund; Town of Lakeview; Mt. High Homeowners Association; Sanderson Co.; Central Oregon Board of Realtors; Duke Warner Realty; Federated Rural Electric Insurance; American Modern Ins.; Nationwide Ins. Co.; Appraisal Associated of Oregon; Bancroft Appraisal Company; Bev-Art Kitchen Countertops, Inc.; D.E. Rink Construction, Inc.; Hoyt's Hardware and Building Supply, Inc.; Sound Construction, Inc.; Tumalo Rim Property Owners Association; Starwood Homeowners Association, Inc.; Sundance Meadows Property Owners Association; Wild River Homeowner Association; Rudy's Market's, Inc.; Bend Property Management, Inc.; Computerized Property Management, Inc.; W.L. Perkins Construction Company, Inc.; Winderemere/Central Oregon Real Estate LLC; Eagle Crest Estate Homesite Association; AmeriTitle.
REFERENCE: Wells Fargo & Co.

LAW OFFICES OF BETHANY FLINT GROENER

360 NORTHWEST VERMONT PLACE
SUITE 500
BEND, OREGON 97701
Telephone: 541-318-0221
Fax: 541-318-7274
Email: beth@bendfamilylaw.com

Litigation, Family Law, Domestic Relations, Divorce, Child Custody.

BETHANY FLINT GROENER, born Tucson, Arizona, March 18, 1976; admitted to bar, 2003, Oregon. *Education:* University of California, Irvine (B.A., English, magna cum laude, 1999); Whittier College School of Law (J.D., summa cum laude, 2003). Whittier College Law Review. Chair, Appellate Advocacy Honors Board. Recipient: Association of Southern California Defense Counsel Excellence in Oral Advocacy Award; California State Bar Commitment to Law Serving the Exploited and Disadvantaged Award. Extern to: the Honorable Florence-Marie Cooper, United States District Court. ***PRACTICE AREAS:*** Litigation; Family Law; Domestic Relations; Divorce; Child Custody.

HENDRIX, BRINICH & BERTALAN, LLP

Established in 1988
716 N.W. HARRIMAN STREET
BEND, OREGON 97701
Telephone: 541-382-4980
Fax: 541-382-9060
Email: gh@bendcable.com
URL: http://www.hxbri.com

General Civil and Trial Practice, Business, Corporate, Real Estate, Construction Law, Land Use, Trademarks, Copyrights, Intellectual Property, Probate and Estate Planning.

GREG HENDRIX, born San Diego, California, July 19, 1953; admitted to bar, 1983, Oregon; 1985, U.S. District Court, District of Oregon. *Education:* San Diego State University (A.B., honors, 1979); Willamette University (J.D., 1983). Member, 1981-1982 and Executive Editor, 1982-1983, Willamette Law Review. Author: "Public Sector Union Security in Oregon and Washington," 19 Willamette L. Rev. 75, 1983. Crook County Deputy District Attorney, 1983-1987. Deschutes County Juvenile Referee, 1988-1992. Arbitrator for Deschutes County Courts Arbitration Program. *Member:* Deschutes County Bar Association (Chair, 1995-1996); Oregon State Bar (Member, Real Estate and Land Use Section). ***PRACTICE AREAS:*** Real Estate; Civil Litigation; Business Law; Construction Law. ***Email:*** gh@bendcable.com

KEN BRINICH, born Lakewood, Ohio, July 11, 1955; admitted to bar, 1982, Oregon; 1996, U.S. District Court, District of Oregon; registered to practice before U.S. Patent and Trademark Office. *Education:* University of Utah (B.S., Geology, 1977); Lewis and Clark College of Law (J.D., 1982). Deschutes County Deputy District Attorney, 1990-1995. Chief Felony Deputy District Attorney, 1994-1995. Arbitrator for Deschutes County Courts Arbitration Program. *Member:* Oregon State Bar (Member: Intellectual Property Section; Business Law Section); Deschutes County Bar Association. ***PRACTICE AREAS:*** Land Use and Real Estate; Intellectual Property; Business Litigation; Trials. ***Email:*** kb@bendcable.com

LISA N. BERTALAN, born Detroit, Michigan, November 22, 1965; admitted to bar, 1991, Oregon and U.S. District Court, District of Oregon. *Education:* University of Colorado (B.A., 1987); University of Sevilla, Sevilla, Spain; University of Oregon (J.D., 1991). Order of the Coif. Member, Attorney General Elder Abuse Task Force Committee. *Member:* Oregon State Bar (Editorial Board, Estate Planning and Administration Section Newsletter; Former Member, Elder Law Executive Committee). ***LANGUAGES:*** Spanish. ***PRACTICE AREAS:*** Estate Planning; Probate; Elder Law. ***Email:*** lisabertalan@bendcable.com

REPRESENTATIVE CLIENTS: The Academy at Sisters; Agate Water Systems; Cascade Mortgage; Heinrichs Architecture; Hagerty Construction; First Choice Computer Services; G.D. Construction; Hickman Williams & Assoc. Engineering; Hospice of Bend La Pine; J Bar J Youth Services; Lorenz Appraisal Services; Property Systems; Summers Wood Floors; Sunriver Country Store; Dent Instruments Inc.; Cascade Court Reporters, Inc.

(This Listing Continued)

HURLEY, LYNCH & RE, P.C.

Established in 1995

747 S.W. MILL VIEW WAY
BEND, OREGON 97702
Telephone: 541-317-5505
Fax: 541-317-5507
Email: info@hlr-law.com
URL: http://www.hlandr.com

Prineville Office: 446 NW 3rd Street, Suite 230, 97754. Telephone: 541-447-5777. Fax: 541-447-5755.

General Civil and Trial Practice, Business, Corporate, Real Estate and Land Use, Leasing, Insurance Defense, Commercial Litigation, Water Rights Law, Taxation, Intellectual Property, Licensing, Probate and Estate Planning, Health Law, Employment Law.

GREGORY P. LYNCH, born Crawfordsville, Indiana, January 8, 1949; admitted to bar, 1975, Oregon, U.S. District Court, District of Oregon, U.S. Court of Appeals, Ninth Circuit and The U.S. Supreme Court. *Education:* University of San Francisco (B.A., 1971); Northwestern School of Law of Lewis and Clark College (J.D., 1975). Teaching Assistant, Legal Writing Honors Program, Northwestern School of Law of Lewis and Clark College, Portland, Oregon, 1973-1975. Oregon Circuit Judge, Pro Tempore. *Member:* Oregon State, Central Oregon (Vice President, 1988; President, 1989) and American Bar Associations; Oregon Association of Defense Counsel; Oregon Association of Hospital Attorneys. ***PRACTICE AREAS:*** Litigation; Personal Injury Law; Insurance Defense Law; Health Law; Public Entity Law; Professional Liability Defense. ***Email:*** gplynch@hlr-law.com

DANIEL C. RE, born Vancouver, Washington, January 21, 1949; admitted to bar, 1980, Oregon. *Education:* University of Oregon (B.S., 1974); Gonzaga University (J.D., cum laude, 1980); University of Florida (LL.M., Taxation, 1981). *Member:* Oregon State Bar (Former Chair, Executive Committee, Estate Planning and Administration Section). ***PRACTICE AREAS:*** Probate Law; Estate Planning Law; Gift and Estate Taxation Law; Trust Administration. ***Email:*** dcre@hlr-law.com

BRYAN W. GRUETTER, born Portland, Oregon, November 15, 1958; admitted to bar, 1986, Oregon and U.S. District Court, District of Oregon. *Education:* Portland State University (B.S., 1980); Willamette University College of Law (J.D., 1985); Oxford University (Institute of International and Comparative Law). Author, "Oregon Discovery Law" and "Defense Guidelines and Billing Audit Services: Growing Risks Involving Ethics and the Duty to Defend," 1998; "Careers in the Balance: The Changing Face of Insurance Defense," Oregon Association of Defense Counsel Journal 1998 and 2000. Past Instructor, Fire Law, Central Oregon Community College. Member, Institutional Review Board- St. Charles Hospital. *Member:* Central Oregon and American (Member Torts and Insurance Sections) Bar Associations; Oregon State Bar (Treasurer, New Lawyers Division, Executive Committee, 1992-1994; Secretary, Ethics Committee, 1995, Chair, 1996; State Bar Delegate, 1996; Judicial Administration Committee, 1996-1999); Oregon Association of Defense Counsel (Chair, Trial Practice Group, 1999-2000; Member, Board of Directors, 2002-2004); International Association of Arson Investigators-Secretary-Treasurer, 2000-2001; Defense Research Institute; J.R. Campbell Inns of Court (Vice-President, 1999 and President, 2000). ***PRACTICE AREAS:*** Insurance Law; Fire Law; Personal Injury; Wrongful Death; Commercial Law; General Litigation; Arbitration; Mediation. ***Email:*** bwgruetter@hlr-law.com

WILLIAM E. FLINN, born Minneapolis, Minnesota, May 27, 1942; admitted to bar, 1967, Oregon; 1992, New Mexico (inactive). *Education:* San Jose State College (B.A., 1964); University of Oregon (J.D., 1967). Member: Board of Bar Examiners, 1979-1982; SPRB, 1987-1990. *Member:* Oregon State Bar; Oregon Association of Defense Counsel. ***PRACTICE AREAS:*** Insurance Defense (60%); Insurance Law (10%); Commercial Litigation (20%); Personal Injury (10%). ***Email:*** weflinn@hlr-law.com

CHRISTOPHER D. HATFIELD, born Eugene, Oregon, May 25, 1959; admitted to bar, 1987, Oregon. *Education:* University of Oregon (B.S., 1983); Northwestern School of Law (J.D., 1987). Member, Law Review, Northwestern School of Law, 1985-1987. Author: "Multiple Vehicles in One Household: Confusion on Stacking of PIP Benefits," Oregon Association of Defense Counsel Journal, 1999. *Member:* Oregon State Bar; Oregon Association of Defense Counsel. ***PRACTICE AREAS:*** Creditors Rights; Business Law; Tax Planning; Tax Litigation; Real Estate. ***Email:*** cdhatfield@hlr-law.com

OF COUNSEL

JAMES V. HURLEY, born St. Paul, Minnesota, January 8, 1934; admitted to bar, 1961, Oregon. *Education:* Loyola University (B.S.C., 1956); University of Wisconsin (M.B.A., 1957; LL.B., 1961). Phi Delta Phi; Order of the Coif. Member, Board of Editors, Wisconsin Law Review, 1960-1961. *Member:* Oregon State Bar; American Bar Association. ***PRACTICE AREAS:*** Business Law; Corporate Law; Real Estate Law; Leasing; Water Law; Intellectual Property; Licensing. ***Email:*** jvhurley@hlr-law.com

BRIAN J. MacRITCHIE, born Hillsdale, Michigan, October 26, 1952; admitted to bar, 1979, Oregon; 1980, Washington. *Education:* Michigan State University (B.S., 1975); Willamette University (J.D., 1979). *Member:* Washington State Bar Association; Oregon State Bar. ***PRACTICE AREAS:*** Litigation. ***Email:*** brian@merrill-osullivan.com

---

STANLEY D. AUSTIN, born Seattle, Washington, September 11, 1961; admitted to bar, 1991, Oregon; 1992, Washington and U.S. District Court, District of Oregon. *Education:* Western Washington University (B.A., 1985; M.S., 1987); Northwestern School of Law (J.D., 1991). Instructor, Business Law, Central Oregon Community College. *Member:* Oregon State Bar; Washington State Bar Association. ***PRACTICE AREAS:*** Litigation; Management Employment Law; Appellate Law. ***Email:*** sdaustin@hlr-law.com

ELIZABETH A. DICKSON, born Santa Rosa, California, March 31, 1957; admitted to bar, 1996, Oregon; 1998, U.S. District Court, District of Oregon. *Education:* Lewis & Clark College (B.S., 1979); Northwestern School of Law (J.D., 1995). *Member:* Deschutes County Bar Association; Oregon State Bar; Women's Lawyers Association. ***PRACTICE AREAS:*** Real Estate; Land Use Law; Business Law. ***Email:*** eadickson@hlr-law.com

TODD J. WINEGAR, born Ontario, Oregon, March 6, 1968; admitted to bar, 1998, Idaho; 1999, Oregon. *Education:* Brigham Young University (B.A., 1995); University of Arkansas (J.D., cum laude, 1998); University of Washington (LL.M., Taxation, 2001). *Member:* Oregon State Bar. ***PRACTICE AREAS:*** Business Law; Taxation; Real Estate; Estate Planning; Probate; Trust Administration. ***Email:*** twinegar@hlr-law.com

GARY R. JOHNSON, admitted to bar, 1993, Oregon; 1996, Washington. *Education:* University of Washington (B.S., 1987); Lewis and Clark (J.D., 1993). ***PRACTICE AREAS:*** Plaintiffs Personal Injury. ***Email:*** grjohnson@hlr-law.com

REPRESENTATIVE CLIENTS: Sunriver Resort; Arrier Title Co.; Bend Research; Deschutes County; Consep, Inc.; Scootsdale Insurance; Armed Forces Insurance; USAA; Redmond School District; A.I. Management; CUMIS Insurance; David Evans & Associates, Inc.; Central Oregon Irrigation; District Squaw Creek Irrigation District; Swalley Irrigation District; Hap Taylor & Sons, Inc.; High Desert Beverage; Overbay Development Co., Inc.; Bachelor Beverage Co. Inc.; Micromonitors, Inc.; Drew Paints, Inc.; Bend Memorial Clinic; Bend Orthopedic and Fracture Clinic; Central Oregon Radiology Associates; East Cascade Women's Group; St. Charles Medical Center; Bend Neurological Group; Bend Urology Associates; Central Oregon Women's Clinic; Cascade Medical Clinic; Central Oregon Pathology Consultants; Central Oregon Pediatrics Associates; Woodward Companies; Ochoco Mint Growers, Inc.; Brown's Insurance Company; Farmer's Insurance Co.; North Pacific Insurance; Colonial Insurance Co.; Mutual of Enumclaw; Grocers Insurance Group; Oregon Mutual Insurance Co.; Truck Insurance Exchange; Atlanta Casualty Insurance Co.; Country Companies; Mid-Century Insurance Co.; Brooks Resource Co.; JAL, Inc.; Fidelity and Deposit Company of Maryland; Ranger Insurance; Insurance Company of the West; Fidelity & Deposit Insurance; State Farm Insurance Co.

(This Listing Continued)

KARNOPP PETERSEN LLP

Established in 1950

1201 NW WALL STREET, SUITE 300
BEND, OREGON 97701
Telephone: 541-382-3011
Fax: 541-388-5410
Email: mail@karnopp.com
URL: http://www.karnopp.com

General Civil, Trial and Appellate Practice, including Plaintiff's Personal Injury and Tort Litigation. General Business, Banking, Creditor Bankruptcy, Tax, Estate Planning, Probate, Real Estate and Land Use, Employment Law, Water Law, Utility/Energy, Environmental and Indian Affairs Law.

FIRM PROFILE: The founders of Karnopp Petersen began serving the legal needs of Central Oregon in 1950 when Owen M. Panner (now a senior federal district judge) joined in partnership with Duncan McKay. While the scope of the firm's practice has expanded, many of those early clients are still with the firm today. In addition to its unique expertise in Indian law matters, the firm practices extensively in the areas of business law, general litigation, plaintiff's personal injury, real property and land use, taxation, estate planning and probate. Members of the firm have been and continue to be leaders in community and bar activities.

LYMAN C. JOHNSON (1929-1986)

DENNIS C. KARNOPP, born Lincoln, Nebraska, July 9, 1942; admitted to bar, 1967, Nebraska and Oregon. *Education:* University of Nebraska (B.A., 1965; J.D., 1967). Phi Delta Phi. Member, Board of Editors, Nebraska Law Review, 1965-1967. Commissioner, 1984-1990; Chairman, 1988-1990, Oregon Land Conservation and Development Commission. Lawyer Representative, 9th Circuit Judicial Conference, 1986-1988. President, Western State Bar Conference, 2000-2001. Co-Chair, Campaign For Equal Justice, 1998-2000. Trustee, The Nature Conservancy of Oregon, 2001—. *Member:* Central Oregon (President, 1973-1974), Nebraska State and American Bar Associations; Oregon State Bar (President, 1995-1996, Member, Board of Governors, 1993-1996; Chairman, Unauthorized Practice Committee, 1977; Chairman, General Practice Section, 1978-1979; Executive Committee, Estate Planning and Administration Section, 1978-1981; Chair, Disciplinary Review Taskforce, 2000—; House of Delegates, 1998—). Fellow, American Bar Foundation. ***PRACTICE AREAS:*** Indian Law; Energy Law; Real Estate Law; Business Law; Corporate Law. ***Email:*** dck@karnopp.com

JAMES E. PETERSEN, born Portland, Oregon, April 12, 1940; admitted to bar, 1964, Oregon. *Education:* University of Oregon (B.A., 1962; J.D., 1964). Chairman, Cross-Media Advisory Committee, State of Oregon Department of Environmental Quality, 1992. Commissioner, 1982 and Chairman, 1983-1988, State of Oregon Environmental Quality Commission. President, Oregon Law Institute, 1983. Fellow, The American College of Trust and Estate Counsel (State Chair, 1999-2005). *Member:* Central Oregon and American Bar Associations; Oregon State Bar (Chairman, Continuing Legal Education Committee, 1978). ***PRACTICE AREAS:*** Business Law; Corporate Law; Estate Planning Law; Probate Law; Real Estate Law. ***Email:*** jep@karnopp.com

JAMES D. NOTEBOOM, born Williston, North Dakota, September 19, 1945; admitted to bar, 1977, Oregon. *Education:* Oregon State University (B.S., 1967; M.B.A., 1968); University of Oregon (J.D., 1977); U.S. Army War College (M.S.S., 2002). Phi Kappa Phi; Phi Eta Sigma; Beta Gamma Sigma; Phi Delta Phi. Author: "Counterclaims and Cross-Claims," Pleading and Practice, Oregon State Bar, 1985; "The Origins of the Militia Provisions in the United States Constitution" The Judge Advocate General's School of the Army 1986; "Security Implications of Water Conflict in The Nile Basin" U.S. Army War College, 2002; "A Principled Approach - Doing Justice in the War on Terrorism", Oregon State Bar Bulletin, Nov. 2002. Adjunct Instructor, Defense Institute of International Legal Studies, 1997—. State Judge Advocate, State of Oregon, 1989-1993. *Member:* Central Oregon (President, 1989-1990) Bar Association; Oregon State Bar (Member, Executive Committee, Debtor/Creditor Section, 1980-1982; Chair, Executive Committee, Military Law Section, 1990-1991). [USMC 1964-1974, U.S. Army, 1975-2002]. ***PRACTICE AREAS:*** Indian Law; Water Law; Legislative Affairs Law; Military Law. ***Email:*** jdn@karnopp.com

HOWARD G. ARNETT, born Portland, Oregon, January 4, 1947; admitted to bar, 1977, Oregon; 1978, Arizona. *Education:* Stanford University (B.A., 1970); London School of Economics (M.Sc., 1971); University of Oregon (J.D., 1977). Author: "Written Discovery," Federal Civil Litigation in Oregon, Oregon State Bar, 1994; "Amended and Supplemental Pleadings," Oregon Civil Pleading and Practice Manual, Oregon State Bar, 1994. Adjunct Professor, Federal Indian Law: Northwestern School of Law, Lewis and

(This Listing Continued)

KARNOPP PETERSEN LLP, Bend—Continued

Clark College (1991-2003); University of Oregon School of Law (2005—). Lawyer Representative, 9th Circuit Judicial Conference, 2000-2003, University of Oregon School of Law, Dean's Advisory Council. *Member:* Oregon State Bar (Member, 1988-1991, and Vice-Chair, 1990-1991, Board of Bar Examiners; Member, 1994-1996, and Chair, 1995-1996, Bar Examiners Review Board; Indian Law Section Executive Committee (Chair, 2000-2001); Appellate Practice Section Executive Committee, 1998-2000; Committee on Low Income Legal Services, Chair, 2005); State Bar of Arizona; Navajo Nation Bar Association. ***PRACTICE AREAS:*** Indian Law; Civil Litigation; Appellate Practice. ***Email:*** hga@karnopp.com

THOMAS J. SAYEG, born Fresno, California, November 3, 1956; admitted to bar, 1982, California and US District Court, Northern District of California; 1983 U.S. Tax Court; 1987, Oregon; 1988, U.S. District Court, Eastern District of California. *Education:* University of Santa Clara (B.S.C., 1978); University of California, Hastings College of the Law, University of California, San Francisco (J.D., 1982); New York University (LL.M., Taxation, 1983). Beta Gamma Sigma. Extern to Hon. Stanley W. Weigel, U.S. District Court, Northern District of California, Summer, 1981. *Member:* The State Bar of California (Member, Estate Planning, Taxation, Trust, Probate and Business Law Sections); Oregon State Bar (Member: Estate Planning, Taxation and Business Law Sections; Past Chair, Executive Committee, Taxation Section; Past Chair, Executive Committee, Business Law Section; Member, Executive Committee, Estate Planning and Administration Section). Fellow, The American College of Trust and Estate Counsel. ***PRACTICE AREAS:*** Business Law; Estate Planning; Real Estate; Taxation. ***Email:*** tjs@karnopp.com

RONALD L. ROOME, born Lindsay, California, July 2, 1951; admitted to bar, 1982, California and U.S. District Court, Northern District of California; 1983, U.S. Court of Appeals, 9th Circuit and U.S. District Court, Eastern District of California; 1988, Oregon; 1989, U.S. District Court, District of Oregon. *Education:* California State University at Sacramento (B.A., 1979); Hastings College of Law, University of California (J.D., 1982). *Member:* Oregon State Bar (Member: Procedure and Practice Committee, 1994-1997; State Bar Disciplinary Board, 2005); State Bar of California; Deschutes County Bar Association (President, 1997-1998); J.R. Campbell American Inns of Court (President, 2002-2003). ***PRACTICE AREAS:*** Personal Injury; Commercial Litigation; Civil Litigation; Insurance Law; Employment Law; Land Use. ***Email:*** rlr@karnopp.com

MICHAEL L. DILLARD, born San Jose, California, February 13, 1948; admitted to bar, 1973, California; 1985, U.S. District Court, Eastern District of California; 1986, Oregon; 1998, U.S. District Court, Northern District of California; 2000, U.S. District Court, District of Oregon; 2001, U.S. District Court, Central District of California; 2003, U.S. Court of Federal Claims and U.S. District Court, District of Columbia. *Education:* University of California, Davis (B.A., Economics, 1970); Trinity College, Dublin, Ireland (Honors Economics and Politics, 1969-1970); University of California School of Law, Los Angeles (J.D., 1973). Associate Editor, UCLA Law Review, 1972-1973. Fellow, American College of Trial Lawyers, 1998—. Supervising Assistant and Assistant Public Defender, Sacramento County, 1974-1984. Judge Pro Tem, Superior Court of Sacramento County, California, 1988-1999; Judge Pro Tem, Superior Court of Placer County, California, 1993-1999. Member, J.R. Campbell, American Inns of Court. *Member:* Oregon State Bar (Member, Litigation Section); State Bar of California (Member, Litigation Section; Financial Institutions Committee, 1994-1997). ***PRACTICE AREAS:*** Business Litigation; Business Law; Banking Law; Real Estate; Civil Litigation; Commercial Law; Corporate Law. ***Email:*** mld@karnopp.com

BRENT S. KINKADE, born Spokane, Washington, October 22, 1966; admitted to bar, 1993, Oregon. *Education:* Brigham Young University (B.A., cum laude, 1990); University of Washington (J.D., with honors, 1993). Phi Kappa Phi. Member, Order of the Coif, Golden Key National Honor Society. Author: "Municipal Antitrust Liability After City of Columbia v. Omni Outdoor Advertising," Washington Law Review, April, 1992. Articles Editor, Washington Law Review, 1992-1993. *Member:* Oregon State Bar. ***LANGUAGES:*** French. ***PRACTICE AREAS:*** Estate Planning; Business Law; Corporate Law; Real Property Law; Securities. ***Email:*** bsk@karnopp.com

WILLIAM F. BUCHANAN, born Bend, Oregon, November 25, 1966; admitted to bar, 1993, Oregon and U.S. District Court, District of Oregon. *Education:* Oregon State University (B.S., 1990); George Washington University (J.D., 1993). Director, Indian Law Section, Oregon State Bar. *Member:* Deschutes County Bar Association; Oregon State Bar. ***PRACTICE AREAS:*** Complex Business Litigation; Condemnation; Antitrust; Creditors Rights; Real Estate Litigation. ***Email:*** wfb@karnopp.com

TAMARA E. MacLEOD, born Reno, Nevada, June 1, 1968; admitted to bar, 1995, Oregon; 1999, U.S. District Court, District of Oregon; 2005, Washington and U.S. District Court, Western District of Washington. *Education:* University of Nevada, Reno (B.A., Political Science, 1991); Willamette University College of Law (J.D., cum laude, 1995). Willamette Law Review: Staff Member, 1993-1994; Note and Comment Editor, 1994-1995. Author: "Excessiveness Review: Giving Substance to a Standardless Tool," Willamette Law Review, Vol. 31, No. 4, 1995. *Member:* American Bar Association; Deschutes County Bar Association (President, 2002-2003); Oregon State Bar (Member, Litigation Section and Real Estate/Land Use Section); J.R. Campbell American Inns of Court (Secretary-Treasurer, 2005-2006). ***PRACTICE AREAS:*** Land Use; Civil Litigation; Commercial Litigation. ***Email:*** tem@karnopp.com

OF COUNSEL

A. REED MARBUT, born Denver, Colorado, 1934; admitted to bar, 1987, Oregon; 1988, Washington and Montana. *Education:* Colorado State University (Doctor of Veterinary Medicine/D.V.M., 1960); Northwestern School of Law at Lewis and Clark College (J.D., 1987). Licensed Doctor of Veterinary Medicine in Colorado, Montana, Idaho and Washington. Managing Partner of the Grant Creek Ranch, Missoula, Montana. Adjunct Professor of Range Management at the University of Montana. Montana State Senate. Adjunct Professor of Water Law at Willamette University College of Law. Administrator and Intergovernmental Coordinator for the Oregon Water Resources Department. Author/Lecturer: "Legal Aspects of Upper Basin Water Allocation," Oregon State University/University of California Special Report 1037; "Determination of Federal Reserved Water Rights and Summary of Klamath Basin Adjudication, U.S. v. Adair and U.S v. Oregon," Dividing the Waters Conference; "Water Allocation - The States' View," United States Forest Service Officer Training ;"Real Property and Water Rights - Crisis in the West," International Right-of-Way Seminar; "Benefits and Liabilities of Negotiating Indian Water Rights," Western States Adjudication Conference. ***PRACTICE AREAS:*** Water Law (80%).

(This Listing Continued)

JOSH NEWTON, born Yreka, California, January 15, 1972; admitted to bar, 1998, Oregon. *Education:* Oregon State University (B.S., 1995); Willamette University (J.D., 1998). Judicial Clerk to the Honorable David V. Brewer, Oregon Court of Appeals. Judicial Clerk to the Honorable David V. Brewer.*Member:* Oregon State Bar; J.R. Campbell American Inns of Court. ***PRACTICE AREAS:*** Civil Litigation; Commercial Litigation; Appellate Law; Natural Resources; Water Law. ***Email:*** jn@karnopp.com

JON J. NAPIER, born Ashland, Oregon, January 19, 1972; admitted to bar, 1998, Oregon. *Education:* Linfield College (B.S., cum laude, 1994); Atkinson Graduate School of Management (M.B.A., 1998); Willamette University (J.D., cum laude1998). *Member:* Oregon State Bar; American Bar Association. ***PRACTICE AREAS:*** Business Law; Corporate Law; Estate Planning; Real Estate Law; Employment Law. ***Email:*** jjn@karnopp.com

ELLEN H. GROVER, born Traverse City, Michigan, 1970; admitted to bar, 1999, Oregon. *Education:* College of Charleston (B.A., 1993); Northwestern School of Law Lewis and Clark College (J.D., 1998). Judicial Clerk, the Honorable Robert Wollheim, Oregon Court of Appeals. *Member:* Oregon State Bar. ***PRACTICE AREAS:*** Land Use Planning; Natural Resource Law; Litigation; Appellate Law; Real Estate. ***Email:*** ehg@karnopp.com

CYNTHIA J. STARKE, born Yuba City, California, January 13, 1971; admitted to bar, 2001, Oregon. *Education:* University of Maryland-Asian Division (B.A., English, 1996); Harvard University (J.D., 2000). *Member:* Oregon State Bar; Federal Bar Association; National Native American Bar Association. ***PRACTICE AREAS:*** Indian Law. ***Email:*** cjs@karnopp.com

HEATHER J. HEPBURN, born Carmel, California, February 19, 1977; admitted to bar, 2003, Oregon and U.S. District Court, District of Oregon. *Education:* University of Oregon (B.S., 1999; J.D., 2003). *Member:* Oregon State Bar; J.R. Campbell American Inns of Court. ***PRACTICE AREAS:*** Business Law; Civil Litigation. ***Email:*** hjh@karnopp.com

JEFFREY T. EAGER, born Aberdeen, Washington, January 8, 1975; admitted to bar, 2004, Oregon. *Education:* Willamette University (B.A., 1997); University of Oregon (J.D., with honors, 2004). Order of the Coif. *Member:* Oregon State Bar; J.R. Campbell American Inns of Court. ***PRACTICE AREAS:*** Civil Litigation. ***Email:*** jte@karnopp.com

REPRESENTATIVE CLIENTS:Confederated Tribes of the Warm Springs Reservation of Oregon; Cascade Bankcorp; Advanced Power Technology, Inc.; Black Butte Ranch; Sunriver Owner"s Association; Deschutes Brewery, Inc.; First American Title Insurance Co. of Oregon; J.L. Ward Co.; Century West Engineering Corp; Innoprise Software, Inc.; PV Powered, Inc.; Taurus Development, Inc.; Central Oregon Hospice and Central Oregon Home Health Care; GEICO; Nature"s General Store, Inc.
REFERENCES: Bank of the Cascades; Indoff; Pepsi; Microwing, Inc.

LAW OFFICES OF ROBERT D. LOWRY

BEND, OREGON

(See Eugene)

Insurance Defense, Products Liability Defense, Medical Malpractice, Hospital Malpractice, Business Litigation, Construction Law and Civil Litigation.

SAALFELD GRIGGS PC

Established in 1932

1001-B SW DISK DRIVE, SUITE 102
BEND, OREGON 97702-1995
Telephone: 541-322-1822
Fax: 541-322-1823
Email: contactus@sglaw.com
URL: http://www.sglaw.com

Salem, Oregon Office: 250 Church Street, SE, P.O. Box 470, 97308. Telephone: 503-399-1070. Fax: 503-371-2927.

Business, Taxation, Intellectual Property, Real Estate and Land Use, Employment, Construction, Banking, Creditors' Rights, Estate Planning and Probate Law, Pension and Profit Sharing, Environmental Law, Labor and Employment, Commercial and Tax Litigation in all Courts.

FIRM PROFILE: Founded in 1932, the firm is a respected and expanding business law firm providing high-quality and timely legal services to entrepreneurs and businesses in Oregon, and is the only Oregon member of the Network of Leading Law Firms, a worldwide association of prestigious medium-sized independent law firms. The firm is divided into five practice groups who work exclusively on business and estate planning issues: Corporate - handles business formations and sales, tax planning, tax litigation, pension benefits and intellectual property; Employment - provides management with preventative advice, training, and litigation defense; Real Property - advises regarding land use development, commercial leases, and complex real property transactions; Estate Planning - provides complex estate planning, asset management, and tax reduction; Litigation - handles complex business disputes, creditors' rights, and civil appeals.

(For Complete Biographical Data on all Personnel, see Professional Biographies at Salem, Oregon)

SCHWABE, WILLIAMSON & WYATT, P.C.

A Partnership including Professional Corporations

Established in 1892

354 SW UPPER TERRACE DRIVE, SUITE 101

BEND, OREGON 97702

Telephone: 541-749-4044

Fax: 541-330-1153

Email: info@schwabe.com

URL: http://www.schwabe.com

Portland, Oregon Office: Suites 1600-1900 Pacwest Center, 1211 S.W. Fifth Avenue. Telephone: 503-222-9981.

Seattle, Washington Office: U.S. Bank Centre, Suite 3010, 1420 Fifth Avenue. Telephone: 206-622-1711. Fax: 206-292-0460.

Vancouver, Washington Office: Suite 410, Main Place Building, 1111 Main Street. Telephone: 360-694-7551; 696-0241.

Admiralty and Maritime Law, Antitrust, Appellate, Bankruptcy and Creditor's Rights, Business Law, Condemnation, Commercial Litigation, Complex Litigation, Construction Law, Energy and Environmental Law, Financial Institutions, Forest Products, Health Care Industry, Intellectual Property, International Law, Labor Relations, Land Use, Malpractice and Insurance Defense, Product Liability, Real Estate, Securities, Taxation, Workers' Compensation.

FIRM PROFILE: Schwabe, Williamson & Wyatt, P.C. is one of the top law firms serving the needs of businesses in the Pacific Northwest. The firm's attorneys provide a broad range of transaction and litigation services to many of the Northwest's leading companies, from Fortune 500 industry leaders, to emerging and small, family-owned businesses. With over 140 attorneys, Schwabe, Williamson & Wyatt is the second largest law firm in Oregon, with offices in Portland and Bend. The firm also serves clients from offices in Seattle and Vancouver, Washington.

SHAREHOLDERS

DONALD JOE WILLIS, born Richmond, Indiana, July 24, 1940; admitted to bar, 1971, Oregon; 1983, Washington. *Education:* University of Oregon (B.S., 1969; J.D., 1971). ***PRACTICE AREAS:*** Condemnation; Commercial Law; Securities Litigation; Civil Litigation. ***Email:*** jwillis@schwabe.com

KIRK JOHANSEN, born Coos Bay, Oregon, April 27, 1949; admitted to bar, 1974, Oregon. *Education:* University of Oregon (B.S., 1971; J.D., 1974). ***PRACTICE AREAS:*** Business Law; Forest Industry Law; Natural Resources. ***Email:*** kjohansen@schwabe.com

TIA M. LEWIS, born Asheville, North Carolina, October 13, 1965; admitted to bar, 1993, Oregon; U.S. District Court, District of Oregon. *Education:* North Carolina State University (B.A., 1987); Northwestern School of Law (J.D., cum laude, 1993). ***PRACTICE AREAS:*** Real Estate; Land Use. ***Email:*** tlewis@schwabe.com

KATHERINE C. TANK, born 1962; admitted to bar, 1988, Oregon; 1992, Alaska. *Education:* University of Oregon (B.S., 1984; J.D., 1988). ***PRACTICE AREAS:*** Labor and Employment. ***Email:*** ktank@schwabe.com

THOMAS M. TRIPLETT, born Palo Alto, California, August 18, 1940; admitted to bar, 1965, Oregon. *Education:* Yale University (A.B., 1962); Stanford University (LL.B., 1965). ***PRACTICE AREAS:*** Labor law; Employment Law; Business Litigation; Antitrust. ***Email:*** ttriplett@schwabe.com

MYLES A. CONWAY, born San Francisco, California, March 21, 1960; admitted to bar, 1988, Oregon; 1992, Alaska. *Education:* University of California at Berkeley (B.A., 1982); University of Oregon (J.D., 1988). ***PRACTICE AREAS:*** Environmental Law; Real Estate; Land Use. ***Email:*** mconway@schwabe.com

BRIAN L. GINGERICH, born Athabasca, Alberta, Canada, September 30, 1964; admitted to bar, 1992, Oregon, U.S. District Court, District of Oregon, U.S. Court of Appeals, 9th Circuit and U.S. Court of Federal Claims. *Education:* Willamette University (B.A., 1987); University of Oregon (J.D., 1991). ***PRACTICE AREAS:*** Commercial Litigation. ***Email:*** bgingerich@schwabe.com

ASSOCIATES

BETHANY C. GRAHAM, born Missoula, Montana, May 14, 1973; admitted to bar, 2002, Montana (inactive) and Oregon. *Education:* Pacific Lutheran University (B.A., 1995); University of Montana School of Law (J.D., 2000). ***PRACTICE AREAS:*** Employment Relations. ***Email:*** bgraham@schwabe.com

ISA A. TAYLOR, born Portland, Oregon, April 10, 1977; admitted to bar, 2004, Oregon. *Education:* University of Oregon (B.A., 1999); University of Colorado at Boulder (J.D., 2004). ***PRACTICE AREAS:*** Real Estate; Land Use. ***Email:*** itaylor@schwabe.com

RETIRED SHAREHOLDER

ROCKNE GILL, born Lebanon, Oregon, December 14, 1931; admitted to bar, 1955, Oregon. *Education:* University of Oregon (B.S., 1953; LL.B., 1955). ***Email:*** rgill@schwabe.com

(For complete biographical data on personnel at Portland, Oregon, Seattle, Washington, Vancouver, Washington and Washington, D.C., see Professional Biographies at those locations)

PAUL J. SPECK

1123 N.W. BOND STREET

BEND, OREGON 97701

Telephone: 541-388-1107

Fax: 541-388-7370

Email: pspeck@youroregonlawyer.com

URL: http://www.lawyers.com/pauljspeck

General Practice. Criminal Law, Driving While Intoxicated, Drug Crimes, Juvenile, Parole and Probation, Traffic Violations. Employment Law, Sexual Harassment and Wrongful Termination. Family Law including Adoptions, Child Custody, Child Support, Divorce, Domestic Violence and Visitation Rights. Real Estate including Buying or Selling, Commercial Leasing, Construction, Eminent Domain, Environmental, Landlord and Tenant, Zoning and Land Use. Trusts and Estates, Estate Planning, Guardianship, Wills and Probate. Business Enterprises, Closely Held Businesses, Corporate, Franchises, Limited Liability Companies, Partnerships, Small Business, Buying or Selling a Business, General Business, Business Planning, Contracts, Lawsuits. Debt and Credit, Collections and Creditors Rights.

PAUL J. SPECK, born Washington, D.C., December 16, 1945; admitted to bar, 1972, Oregon. *Education:* University of California at Davis (B.A., 1967); University of Oregon (J.D., 1971). Associate Editor, Oregon Law Review, 1970-1971. Recipient, Oregon State Bar Presidents Public Service Award. Editor and Author, Senior Law Manual. Assistant County Counsel, 1972-1974 and County Counsel, 1974, Coos County. Deputy District Attorney, Deschutes County, 1974-1977. *Member:* Deschutes County Bar Association; Oregon State Bar (Former Member: Legal Ethics Committee; Public Service Committee); Oregon Trial Lawyers Association; J.R. Campbell Inns of Court. ***PRACTICE AREAS:*** Real Estate; Land Use; Business Law; Employment Law; Water Law; Construction Law; Trial Practice.

STAHANCYK, KENT, JOHNSON & HOOK P.C.

225 NW FRANKLIN AVENUE, SUITE 3

BEND, OREGON 97701

Telephone: 541-318-9115

Fax: 541-318-9116

Email: info@stahancyk.com

URL: http://www.oregondivorce.com

Portland, Oregon Office: Athena Plaza, 808 S.W. 15th Avenue, 97205-1907. Telephone: 503-222-9115. Facsimile: 503-222-4037.

Astoria, Oregon Office: 552 Commercial Street, 97103. Telephone: 503-325-9117.

Prineville, Oregon Office: 105 SW Beaver Street, 97754. Telephone: 541-416-9312.

Vancouver, Washington Office: 411 West 11th Street, 98660. Telephone: 360-750-9115.

Adoptions, Child Custody, Child Support, Divorce, Domestic Violence, Visitation Rights, Wills and Probate, Trusts and Estates, Asset Protection, Guardianship, Family Law, Estate Planning.

FIRM PROFILE: Practicing Family Law & Estate Planning with offices in Portland, Bend, Astoria and Prineville, Oregon and Vancouver, Washington.

JOEL J. KENT, born Seattle, Washington, August 11, 1969; admitted to bar, 1996, Oregon and Washington. *Education:* University of Puget Sound (B.S., Economics, 1991); Seattle University School of Law (J.D., 1996). Recipient, Seattle University Client Counseling Award. Member, Junior Executive Board, Doernbecher Hospital, 1997. *Member:* Washington County Bar Association; Oregon State Bar. (Resident). ***PRACTICE AREAS:*** Family Law; Estate Planning; Child Custody; Guardianship; Adoption Law. ***Email:*** joel@stahancyk.com

RONALD M. JOHNSON, born Lebanon, Oregon, June 15, 1956; admitted to bar, 1988, Oregon. *Education:* Lewis and Clark College (B.A., 1984; J.D., 1988). *Member:* Clackamas County, Multnomah County and Washington County Bar Associations; Oregon State Bar (Member, International Section). (Resident). ***LANGUAGES:*** German and Italian. ***PRACTICE AREAS:*** Family Law. ***Email:*** ron@stahancyk.com

---

GORDON E. PHILLIPS, born Fort Dix, New Jersey, July 9, 1972; admitted to bar, 2000, Oregon. *Education:* University of Washington (B.A., 1996); Northwestern School of Law (J.D., 2000). *Member:* American Bar Association. ***PRACTICE AREAS:*** Family Law. ***Email:*** gordon@stahancyk.com

KRISTIN M. LARSON, born Salem, Oregon, March 9, 1970; admitted to bar, 2002, Oregon. *Education:* Pomona College (B.A., American Studies, 1992); Northwestern College of Law (J.D., cum laude, 2002). *Member:* Deschutes County Bar Association; Oregon State Bar (Member, Sections on:, Estate Planning; Family Law). ***PRACTICE AREAS:*** Trusts and Estates; Wills; Probate; Guardianship; Conservatorship; Premarital Agreements; Family Law. ***Email:*** kristin@stahancyk.com

(For complete biographical data on all personnel see Portland, Oregon)

HUTCHISON & WALSH

A PROFESSIONAL CORPORATION

CANBY, OREGON

(See West Linn)

General Civil and Trial Practice. Estate Planning, Probate, Trusts and Estates, Business Law, Contracts, Real Estate, Corporate, Personal Injury, Automobile Accidents, Wrongful Death, Financial Abuse of the Elderly.

FITZWATER & MEYER, LLP

Established in 1934

THREE TOWN CENTER
10121 S.E. SUNNYSIDE ROAD, SUITE 140
CLACKAMAS, OREGON 97015
Telephone: 503-786-8191
Fax: 503-786-3785
Email: wfitzwater@fitzwatermeyer.com
URL: http://www.fitzwatermeyer.com

Estate Planning, Trusts and Estate, Estate and Gift Taxation, Wills and Probate, Elder Law, Medicaid.

MEMBERS OF FIRM

WESLEY D. FITZWATER, born Portland, Oregon, February 24, 1955; admitted to bar, 1981, Oregon. *Education:* Willamette University (B.S., 1977); University of Pudget Sound School of Law (J.D., 1981). Co-Editor, "The Elder Law Handbook," Oregon State Bar Publication, a reference book for Oregon Attorneys. Member: Clackamas County Adult Abuse Response and Prevention Team; Oregon Attorney General's Task Force on Elder Abuse; Multnomah and Clackamas County Probate Court Advisory Committees. *Member:* Oregon State Bar (Member, Sections on: Elder Law; Estate Planning; Estate Administration; Law Practice Management; Current Chair, Elder Law Section; Past Chair, Estate Planning, Estate Administration); Multnomah and Clackamas Bar Associations; National Academy of Elder Law Attorneys. ***PRACTICE AREAS:*** Elder Law; Guardianship and Conservatorship; Incapacity Planning; Long Term Care; Probate; Estate Planning; Medicaid Planning. ***Email:*** wfitzwater@fitzwatermeyer.com

DONNA R. MEYER, born Oakland, California, October 6, 1951; admitted to bar, 1976, Oregon; 1977, U.S. District Court, District of Oregon; 1981, U.S. Court of Appeals, Ninth Circuit. *Education:* Portland State University (B.S., 1973); University of Oregon (J.D., 1976). Order of the Coif. Co-Author: "SSI and Medicaid Treatment of Trusts," Advanced Issues for Elder Law Practitioners, 1997. Member, Estate Planning Council of Portland. *Member:* Multnomah Bar Association; Oregon State Bar (Member, Sections on: Elder Law; Estate Planning and Administration; Disability Rights; Health Law; Chair, Administrative Law; Agency and Professional Relations Committee; Past Chair, Elder Law); National Academy of Elder Law Attorneys. ***PRACTICE AREAS:*** Estate Planning; Special Needs Trusts; Medicaid Planning; Wills. ***Email:*** dmeyer@fitzwatermeyer.com

THE JAMES LAW GROUP LLC

CLACKAMAS, OREGON

(See Portland)

Business Law and Planning, Corporate Law, Corporate Finance, Mergers and Acquisitions, Real Estate, Securities, Banking, Employment Litigation, Emerging Companies, Software Licensing, Corporate Finance, Commercial Leasing, Business Litigation.

FOSS, WHITTY, LITTLEFIELD, McDANIEL & BODKIN, LLP

Established in 1880

444 NORTH FOURTH STREET
P.O. BOX 1120
COOS BAY, OREGON 97420-2222
Telephone: 541-267-2156
Fax: 541-269-0839
Email: info@coosbaylaw.com
URL: http://www.coosbaylaw.com

General Civil and Trial Practice in all State and Federal Courts. Business, Corporation and Commercial Law, Estate Planning, Probate and Taxation Law, Real Property, Timber, Creditor's Rights, Personal Injury Law.

FIRM PROFILE: The firm is one of Oregon's oldest, dating back to 1880 when the firm's founder, J.W. Bennett, began the practice of law. Approximately 25% of the firm's work is in litigation, including commercial, real estate and personal injury cases. About 30% of the practice involves business, corporate and commercial law. Estate, trust, probate and taxation law comprise another 35%. Real property and timber law account for about 10% of the firm's work.

MEMBERS OF FIRM

JOHN T. FOSS, born Inwood, Iowa, May 5, 1929; admitted to bar, 1956, Iowa and Oregon. *Education:* Augustana College (B.A., 1951); State University of Iowa (J.D., 1956). Phi Delta Phi. *Member:* Coos County (President, 1972) and Iowa State Bar Associations; Oregon State Bar (Member, Executive Committee, Litigation Section, 1980-1983); Oregon Association of Defense Counsel. Fellow, American College of Trial Lawyers. ***PRACTICE AREAS:*** Litigation; Business Law; Corporate Law. ***Email:*** johnfoss@coosbaylaw.com

JOHN W. WHITTY, born North Bend, Oregon, January 18, 1933; admitted to bar, 1956, Oregon. *Education:* University of Oregon (B.S., 1954; LL.B., 1956). Author: "Income Tax Consequences of Transferring Real Property," Oregon CLE Handbook on Real Property, 1981; "Covenants Not To Compete in Oregon," Oregon Business Law Institute CLE, 1983; "Selling A Business," Oregon CLE Practical Skills Course, 1990, 1992, 1993; "Business Succession Planning - Golfers And Slaves," Oregon CLE, 1995; "Estate Planning for Transfers Of Business Interests," Oregon CLE, 1998; "Business Succession Planning-Transfers Within The Family," Oregon CLE, 1999. Co-Author: "Estate Tax Deductions for Timberland," Probate and Property, March/April 2005. *Member:* Coos County Bar Association; Oregon State Bar (Member, Executive Committee, Sections on: Taxation, 1977-1981; Estate Planning and Administration, 1979-1982 and Corporate and Business Law, 1980-1984; Chairman, 1983-1984). Fellow, American College of Trust and Estate Counsel. ***PRACTICE AREAS:*** Estate Planning; Estate Administration; Trust Law; Business Law; Commercial Law; Real Estate. ***Email:*** johnwhitty@coosbaylaw.com

JON R. LITTLEFIELD, born Oakland, California, September 20, 1944; admitted to bar, 1974, Oregon. *Education:* Stanford University (A.B., with distinction, 1967); Johns Hopkins University; Willamette University (J.D., 1974). Member, Board of Education, Southwestern Oregon Community College, 1982-1994. Pro Tempore Judge, 1995-1998. *Member:* Coos County Bar Association; Oregon State Bar. ***PRACTICE AREAS:*** Civil Practice; Real Estate; Real Estate Foreclosure; Business Formation; Wills; Trust Law; Probate; Elder Law; Estate Administration; Estate Litigation; Mediation; Arbitration. ***Email:*** jonlittlefield@coosbaylaw.com

WILLIAM A. McDANIEL, born Modesto, California, February 12, 1950; admitted to bar, 1976, Oregon. *Education:* University of California at Berkeley (A.B., 1972); University of Oregon (J.D., 1976). Order of the Coif. *Member:* Coos County Bar Association; Oregon State Bar; Oregon Trial Lawyers Association. ***PRACTICE AREAS:*** Litigation; Personal Injury. ***Email:*** billmcdaniel@coosbaylaw.com

MICHAEL N. BODKIN, born Oklahoma City, Oklahoma, June 26, 1954; admitted to bar, 1979, Oregon. *Education:* Denver University (B.S.B.A., summa cum laude, 1976); University of Oregon (J.D., 1979). Beta Gamma Sigma. Recipient, Alonzo P. May Economics Award. Co-Author: "Estate Tax Deductions for Timberland," Probate and Property, March/April 2005. *Member:* Coos County and American Bar Associations; Oregon State Bar. ***PRACTICE AREAS:*** Estate Planning; Trust Law; Business Law; Health Law. ***Email:*** mikebodkin@coosbaylaw.com

REPRESENTATIVE CLIENTS: Al Peirce Co.; Bay Clinic; Tower Motor Co.; D.B. Western, Inc.; Fred Messerle & Sons, Inc.; Stuntzner Engineering & Forestry, LLC; North Bend Medical Center, Inc.; Romtec, Inc.; Oregon State Bar Professional Liability Fund; Ticor Title Insurance Co.; Sweet Cranberries, LLC; Mahaffy Tree Farm, Inc.; North Bend Lanes, Inc.; Dement Ranch, LLC.; Juul Insurance; Farr's Hardware, Inc.; Southport Forest Products, LLC; Bay Area Medical Center; Events Management and Consulting, LLC; Hargens Construction Company; Heritage Hills Home Owners Association; Oregon Coast Spine Institute; Sweet Timber Company; Verger Chrysler-Plymouth-Dodge.

HUTCHINSON, COX, COONS, DuPRIEST, ORR & SHERLOCK, P.C.

COOS BAY, OREGON

(See Eugene)

General Practice in all Courts. Business Law, Contracts, Corporate Law, Environmental Law, Land Use, Real Estate, International Business, Civil Litigation, Personal Injury, Probate, Estate Planning, Copyright and Trademark, Family Law, Arbitration and Mediation, Tax Law, Creditors Rights.

JAQUA & WHEATLEY, LLC

COOS BAY, OREGON

(See Eugene)

General Practice in all Courts. Insurance Defense, Casualty and Surety Insurance Law. Litigation, Corporate Law, Partnerships, Business Litigation, Products Liability, Construction Law, Environmental Law, Professional Malpractice, Premises Liability, Estate Planning, Employment Law.

LAW OFFICES OF ROBERT D. LOWRY

COOS BAY, OREGON

(See Eugene)

Insurance Defense, Products Liability Defense, Medical Malpractice, Hospital Malpractice, Business Litigation, Construction Law and Civil Litigation.

MUHLHEIM BOYD

COOS BAY, OREGON

(See Eugene)

Creditor/Debtor Representation; Commercial Litigation; Workouts and Bankruptcy Reorganizations; Bankruptcy Litigation; Creditors' Rights; Foreclosure; Commercial Law; Business Litigation; Business Transactions; Litigation; Estate and Probate.

BARNHISEL, WILLIS, BARLOW & STEPHENS, P.C.

Established in 1970

123 N.W. SEVENTH STREET
P.O. BOX 396
CORVALLIS, OREGON 97339
Telephone: 541-757-0575
Fax: 541-757-2031
Email: barnhisel@bwbslaw.com
URL: http://www.bwbslaw.com

General Civil and Trial Practice in State and Federal Courts and Administrative Agencies. Appeals, Arbitration and Dispute Resolution. Banking, Business and Corporate, Charitable Trusts and Foundations, Communications, Construction, Estate Planning and Administration, Living Trusts, Family, Labor and Employment Relations and Real Estate Law.

FIRM PROFILE: This firm consistently offers high quality legal services, responsiveness to clients, and reasonable fees. The members of the firm have excellent educational backgrounds and extensive and diverse legal experience, each frequently assumes leadership roles in state, bar association, and community activities.

(This Listing Continued)

PETER L. BARNHISEL, born Portland, Oregon, June 30, 1939; admitted to bar, 1966, Oregon and U.S. District Court, District of Oregon; 1989, U.S. Court of Appeals, Ninth Circuit; 1992, U.S. Supreme Court. *Education:* Stanford University (B.S., Engineering, 1961); University of Oregon (J.D., 1966). Associate Editor, Oregon Law Review, 1965-1966. Author: "Relationship between State and Federal Courts," Federal Civil Litigation in Oregon, Oregon CLE, 1994, 1998, 2002; "Guardianship, Conservatorships and Transfers to Minors," Oregon CLE, 1993, 1996, 2000, 2004. Lawyer Representative, Ninth Circuit Judicial Conference, 1989-1992, Chair, 1991-1992. Commissioner, Oregon Fish and Wild Life Commission, 1990-1995, Chair, 1993-1995. Panel of Arbitrators and Mediators, American Arbitration Association. *Member:* Benton County (President, 1977-1978) and American Bar Associations; Oregon State Bar (Member: Board of Governors, 1974-1977, Treasurer, 1976-1977; State Professional Responsibility Board, 1977-1978, 1988-1991, Chair, 1977-1978, 1990-1991; Board of Bar Examiners, 1979-1982, Vice-Chair, 1981-1982; Bar Examination Review Board, 1987-1989, Chair, 1988-1989; Executive Committee, Estate Planning Section, 1981-1983; Executive Committee, Construction Law Section, 1985-1987, 1992-1994). ***PRACTICE AREAS:*** Trial Practice; Business Law; Real Estate; Estate Planning; Alternative Dispute Resolution. ***Email:*** barnhisel@bwbslaw.com

R. TIM WILLIS, born Lake City, Iowa, April 19, 1948; admitted to bar, 1976, Oregon and U.S. District Court, District of Oregon. *Education:* Cornell College (B.A., cum laude, 1970); University of Iowa (M.A.T., 1972); Willamette University (J.D., 1976). Phi Beta Kappa. Associate Editor, Willamette Law Journal, 1975-1976. *Member:* Benton County Bar Association (President, 1992-1993); Oregon State Bar (Member: Board of Bar Examiners, 1982-1985, Chair, 1984-1985; Bar Examination Review Board, 1991-1993, Chair, 1992-1993; Joint Committee on Trial Court Judicial Resources, 2000— Chair, 2004—). ***PRACTICE AREAS:*** Business; Real Estate; Estate Planning. ***Email:*** willis@bwbslaw.com

JOHN L. BARLOW, born Portland, Oregon, June 22, 1955; admitted to bar, 1981, Oregon and U.S. District Court, District of Oregon. *Education:* Lewis and Clark College and University of Oregon (B.A., 1978); Stanford University (J.D., 1981). Phi Beta Kappa. Member, Management Advisory Panel to National Labor Relations Board, 1994-1998. *Member:* Benton County (President, 2001-2002) and American (Member, Section on Labor and Employment Law) Bar Associations; Oregon State Bar (Member, Board of Bar Examiners, 1988-1991, Chairman, 1990-1991; Member, State Professional Responsibility Board, 1994-1997). ***PRACTICE AREAS:*** Labor Management Law; Employment Law; Personnel Law; Family Law; Trial Practice. ***Email:*** barlow@bwbslaw.com

CARY B. STEPHENS, born Elko, Nevada, March 24, 1969; admitted to bar, 1995, Oregon and U.S. District Court, District of Oregon. *Education:* University of Oregon (B.S., cum laude, 1991; J.D., 1995). Associate Editor, University of Oregon Law Review. *Member:* Benton County and American Bar Associations; Oregon State Bar. ***PRACTICE AREAS:*** General Practice; Real Estate; Business Law; Trial Practice. ***Email:*** stephens@bwbslaw.com

---

MARK R. MAY, born Salem, Oregon, July 2, 1971; admitted to bar, 2005, Oregon. *Education:* Willamette University (B.A., 1995); Lewis and Clark College (J.D., 2004). Associate Editor, Lewis and Clark Law Review, 2004-2005. *Member:* Oregon State Bar. ***PRACTICE AREAS:*** Business Law; Real Estate; Estate Planning. ***Email:*** may@bwbslaw.com

REPRESENTATIVE CLIENTS: CH2M/Hill, Inc. (Consulting Engineers); Truax Corp.; Town and Country Realtors; Oregon State University Foundation; Hewlett-Packard, Inc.; Videx, Inc.; TRC Communications, Inc.; Woodstock's Enterprises, Inc.; Cellular One; Evanite Fiber Corp.; Endex Engineering; Allann Brothers Coffee Co.; OSU Federal Credit Union; Corvallis Clinic, P.C.; Lee Enterprises, Inc.; Corvallis Gazette Times; Evergreen Technologies, Inc.; Citizens Bank; U.S. Intec.
REFERENCE: Citizens Bank, Corvallis, Oregon.

TIM BRITTLE
ATTORNEY AT LAW

343 N.W. 7TH STREET
CORVALLIS, OREGON 97330
Telephone: 541-738-8303
Fax: 541-753-2009
URL: http://www.brittle-law.com
Email: tim@brittle-law.com
URL: http://www.lawyers.eom/brittlelaw

Elder Law, Trusts and Estates, Estate Planning, Estate Litigation, Wills, Probate, Insurance, Nursing Home Abuse, Guardianship and Conservatorship, Asset Protection, Business Law, Corporate Law, Closely Held Business, Limited Liability Company Law, Partnership Law, Small Business Law, Buying or Selling a Business, Contracts, Business Start-Ups, Business Planning, Real Estate, Buying or Selling a Home, Residential Real Estate, Landlord and Tenant, Commercial Leasing.

TIM BRITTLE, born Los Angeles, California, August 30, 1949; admitted to bar, 1977, Oregon; 1985, Washington; 1994, Idaho. *Education:* University of Utah (B.S., magna cum laude, 1970); University of Santa Clara (J.D., magna cum laude, 1977). Author: "Avoiding Insurer's Excess Liability," Vol. 28, No. 3, Federation of Insurance Counsel Quarterly, Spring, 1978. *Member:* Benton County and American Bar Associations; Oregon State Bar (Member: Sections on: Elder Law, Estate Planning & Administration, Business Law); National Academy of Elder Law Attorneys. ***PRACTICE AREAS:*** Trusts and Estates; Wills; Business Law.

CABLE HUSTON BENEDICT HAAGENSEN & LLOYD LLP

Established in 1980

582 N.W. VAN BUREN
CORVALLIS, OREGON 97339
Telephone: 541-754-7477
Facsimile: 541-754-0051
URL: http://www.cablehuston.com

Portland, Oregon Office: Suite 2000, 1001 S.W. Fifth Avenue, 97204. Telephone: 503-224-3092. Facsimile: 503-224-3176.

Administrative, Agricultural, Banking, Bankruptcy, Commercial, Corporate, Complex Litigation, Creditors' Rights, Legislative, Employment, Energy, Environmental, Estate Planning, General Business, Land Use, Mining, Municipal, Natural Resource, Probate, Real Property, Taxation, Telecommunications, Trust Administration, Utility and Water Law.

OF COUNSEL

GEORGE B. HEILIG, born Portland, Oregon, June 5, 1944; admitted to bar, 1973, Oregon; U.S. District Court, District of Oregon. *Education:* Portland State University (B.S., 1970); Willamette University (J.D., cum laude, 1973). Chairman, Corvallis City Planning Commission, 1976-1985. *Member:* Benton County Bar Association; Oregon State Bar (Member, Executive Committee, Real Estate and Land Use Committee, 1990—). (Resident). ***PRACTICE AREAS:*** Real Estate Law; Business Litigation; Land Use Law. ***Email:*** lawyerg@peak.org

DAN C. ARMSTRONG, born Fergus Falls, Minnesota, October 19, 1960; admitted to bar, 1988, Oregon. *Education:* Boise State University (B.A., cum laude, 1985); Willamette University (J.D., magna cum laude, 1988). *Member:* Benton County and Multnomah County Bar Associations; Oregon State Bar. ***PRACTICE AREAS:*** Real Estate; Land Use; Business Litigation; Family Law. ***Email:*** darmstrong@peak.org

REPRESENTATIVE CLIENTS: Ace; Bank of Tokyo-Mitsubishi, Ltd.; Bayer Cropscience; Canby Utility Board; Chemical Waste Management of the Northwest, Inc.; The Chubb Group of Insurance Companies; City of Albany; City of Corvallis; City of Hermiston; City of McMinnville Water & Light; Clackamas County Bank; Clackamas County Department of Water Environment Services; Clackamas River Water District; Clatskanie People's Utility District; Emerald Christmas Tree Company; Eugene Water & Electric Board; Everfresh Fruit Co.; Exxon Mobil; Holiday Tree Farms; John Holmlund Nursery Inc.; Intel; J.H. Baxter & Co.; Liberty Insurance; Louisiana-Pacific Corp.; Oak Lodge Sanitary District; Merchants Bank; Oregon Dairy Farmers Association; Pacific Insurance Investment Company; Portland Trail Blazers; PRM Finance Inc.; Public Utility District No.1 of Cowlitz County, Washington; Safety-Kleen Systems, Inc.; Stewart Title Guarantee Company; Summit Real Estate Management Corp.; Surface Water Management Agency of Clackamas County; Tillamook People's Utility District; St. Paul Travelers; Tri City Service District; Tualatin Valley Water District; Union Carbide Corporation; Waste Management, Inc.
REFERENCES: Bank of America (Premier Banking); Union Bank of California, N.A. (trust Dept.); U.S. Bank, NA (Main Office-Commercial Dept. and Trust Dept.); U.S. Trust Company, NA (Portland Office); Wells Fargo Bank (Trust Dept); West Coast Trust Co., Inc.

(For complete biographical data on all attorneys in Portland, Oregon, see Professional Biographies at Portland, Oregon)

CLARK, LINDAUER, FETHERSTON, EDMONDS, LIPPOLD & COLLIER, LLP

CORVALLIS, OREGON

(See Salem)

Trial and Business Practice in State and Federal Courts including Business Litigation, Insurance Law, Agricultural Law, Automobile, Premises Liability, Professional Negligence, including Legal and Medical Malpractice, Product, Toxic Tort and Environmental Liability, Employment Discrimination, Wrongful Discharge and Defamation, Arbitration and Mediation, Business, Real Estate, and Estate Law, Probate.

LAW OFFICES OF ROBERT D. LOWRY

CORVALLIS, OREGON

(See Eugene)

Insurance Defense, Products Liability Defense, Medical Malpractice, Hospital Malpractice, Business Litigation, Construction Law and Civil Litigation.

PETERSON LAW OFFICES, PC

CORVALLIS, OREGON

(See Portland)

Personal Injury, Premises Liability, Automobile Accidents and Injuries, Dog Bites and Wrongful Death.

RINGO, STUBER, ENSOR & HADLOCK, P.C.

Established in 1951

605 S.W. JEFFERSON AVENUE
P.O. BOX 1108
CORVALLIS, OREGON 97339
Telephone: 541-757-1414
FAX: 541-753-0884
Email: ringoseh@peak.org
URL: http://www.ringostuber.com

General Civil and Trial Practice. Plaintiff's Personal Injury, Family, Malpractice, Products Liability, Negligence, Criminal.

(This Listing Continued)

RINGO, STUBER, ENSOR & HADLOCK, P.C., Corvallis—Continued

FIRM PROFILE: Ringo, Stuber, Ensor & Hadlock, P.C. emphasizes Tort Litigation in State and Federal Court.

ROBERT G. RINGO, born Spokane, Washington, August 18, 1924; admitted to bar, 1951, Oregon; 1969, U.S. Court of Military Appeals; 1970, U.S. Supreme Court and U.S. Court of Appeals, Ninth Circuit. *Education:* University of Oregon (B.S., 1949); Northwestern College of Law (LL.B., 1951). Delta Theta Phi. Member: Judicial Administration Committee, 1995—; State Professional Responsibility Board, 1979-1980; 1984-1988. Member, State of Oregon Judicial Fitness Commission, 1984—. Member, 21st District Arbitration Committee, 1984—. Member, 1969-1970, 1972-1974 and 1976-1978 and Chairman, 1978, Committee on Function and Organization of Bar. *Member:* Benton County (President, 1964-1965) and American Bar Associations; Oregon State Bar (Member, Board of Governors, 1980-1983; Secretary, 1982-1983); Oregon Trial Lawyers Association, (President, 1979-1980; Member, Board of Governors, 1980-1988); The Association of Trial Lawyers of America (Member, Board of Governors, 1982-1988; State Delegate, 1980-1982); American Board of Trial Advocates (Diplomat, National Executive Committee, 1982-1988). [Lieut. Col., USAFR, Retired, 1972]. ***PRACTICE AREAS:*** Personal Injury Litigation; Products Liability Litigation.

LARRY W. STUBER, born Tiffin, Ohio, February 1, 1952; admitted to bar, 1978, Oregon and U.S. District Court, District of Oregon. *Education:* University of Washington (B.A., 1974); University of Oregon (J.D., 1978). Phi Delta Phi (Magister, 1977-1978). *Member:* Linn County, Benton County (Secretary, 1982-1983; President, 1998-1999) and American Bar Associations; Oregon State Bar (Member: Corrections and Detention Committee, 1979-1981; Future of the Legal Profession, 1982-1984); American Academy of Matrimonial Lawyers; Oregon Trial Lawyers Association; The Association of Trial Lawyers of America. ***PRACTICE AREAS:*** Personal Injury Litigation; Family Law; Divorce. ***Email:*** stuber@ringostuber.com

STEPHEN R. ENSOR, born Evanston, Illinois, September 4, 1955; admitted to bar, 1981, Oregon; 1986, U.S. District Court, District of Oregon. *Education:* Indiana University (B.A., 1977); University of Oregon (J.D., 1980). Deputy District Attorney: Crook County, 1981-1984; Benton County, 1984-1985. *Member:* Oregon State Bar (Member, Local Professional Responsibility Committee, 1988-1991); Oregon Criminal Defense Attorneys Association; Oregon Trial Lawyers Association. ***PRACTICE AREAS:*** Personal Injury Litigation; Family Law. ***Email:*** ensor@ringostuber.com

PATRICK L. HADLOCK, born Boise, Idaho, October 8, 1956; admitted to bar, 1983, Oregon; 1986, U.S. District Court, District of Oregon; 1989, U.S. Court of Appeals, Ninth Circuit. *Education:* Linfield College; Reed College (B.A., 1978); University of Washington; University of Oregon (J.D., 1983). Co-Author: Chapters on Ejectment and Quiet Title, Oregon Civil Pleading and Practice, Continuing Legal Education, 1985. Author: Chapter on, "Suits to Quiet Title Real Estate Disputes," OSB Continuing Legal Education, 1993. *Member:* Benton County Bar Association (Secretary-Treasurer, 1986-1987); Oregon State Bar (Member: Uniform Civil Jury Instruction Committee, 1995-1998; Uniform State Laws Committee, 1986-1989); Oregon Trial Lawyers Association; The Association of Trial Lawyers of America. ***PRACTICE AREAS:*** Personal Injury Litigation; Appellate Practice. ***Email:*** hadlock@ringostuber.com

REFERENCES: Wells Fargo Bank (Corvallis Branch); Citizens Bank of Corvallis.

WEATHERFORD, THOMPSON, COWGILL, BLACK & SCHULTZ, P.C.

CORVALLIS, OREGON

(See Albany)

General Civil and Trial Practice, Business and Corporate Law, Pension and Profit Sharing, Banks and Banking, Taxation, Probate, Estate Planning, Elder Law, Real Property, Agricultural Law, Land Use and Zoning, Securities, Creditors Rights, Commercial Law, Personal Injury, Environmental and Natural Resources.

CLARK, LINDAUER, FETHERSTON, EDMONDS, LIPPOLD & COLLIER, LLP

DALLAS, OREGON

(See Salem)

Trial and Business Practice in State and Federal Courts including Business Litigation, Insurance Law, Agricultural Law, Automobile, Premises Liability, Professional Negligence, including Legal and Medical Malpractice, Product, Toxic Tort and Environmental Liability, Employment Discrimination, Wrongful Discharge and Defamation, Arbitration and Mediation, Business, Real Estate, and Estate Law, Probate.

SOMERS & WOLF

Established in 1962
106 EAST FOURTH STREET
P.O. BOX 1578
THE DALLES, OREGON 97058
Telephone: 541-296-2181
FAX: 541-296-9382
URL: http://www.somersandwolf.com
Email: susanchof@sbcglobal.net
URL: http://www.lawyers.com/somersandwolf

General Civil and Trial Practice. Family Law, Civil Litigation, Business Law, Real Estate, Probate, Trusts and Estates, Wills, Guardianships and Conservatorships, Partnership Law, Bankruptcy, Criminal Law, Personal Injury and Civil Drug Forfeiture.

(This Listing Continued)

RONALD M. SOMERS, born Buffalo, New York, November 9, 1937; admitted to bar, 1962, Oregon; 1963, U.S. District Court, District of Oregon; 1992, U.S. Supreme Court. *Education:* Lewis & Clark College (B.S., 1959); Willamette University (LL.B., 1962). Phi Delta Phi. Member, Environmental Quality Commission, 1974-1982. *Member:* Mid-Columbia and American Bar Associations; Oregon State Bar (Member: Grievance Committee, 1969-1986; Practice and Procedure Committee, 1986-1989; Lawyer Referral Committee, 1989-1991; Unauthorized Practice Committee, 1991-1993). ***PRACTICE AREAS:*** General Civil Law; Trial Practice; Business Law; Real Estate; Probate; Insurance; Personal Injury; Criminal Law; Partnership Law; Wills; Bankruptcy; Civil Litigation; Trusts and Estates; Family Law. ***Email:*** somers@somersandwolf.com

JOHN A. WOLF, born The Dalles, Oregon, April 30, 1970; admitted to bar, 1995, Oregon. *Education:* Oregon State University (B.S., 1992); Willamette University (J.D., 1995). *Member:* Mid-Columbia and American Bar Associations; Oregon State Bar. ***PRACTICE AREAS:*** Family Law; Civil Litigation; Business Law; Civil Drug Forfeiture; Guardianships and Conservatorships; Leases and Leasing; Mortgages; Partnership Law; Probate; Real Estate; Trusts and Estates; Wills. ***Email:*** wolf@somersandwolf.com

REFERENCE: United States National Bank.

KENT ANDERSON & ASSOCIATES

Established in 1978
888 WEST PARK STREET
EUGENE, OREGON 97401
Telephone: 541-683-5100
Telefax: 541-484-1754
URL: http://www.kentandersonlaw.com
Email: kentanderson@compuserve.com
URL: http://www.lawyers.com/kentanderson

Bankruptcy, Business Transactions, Construction, Creditor's Rights, Real Estate, Taxation, Tax Liens, Business Law, Contracts, Mechanics Liens, Foreclosures, Small Business, Buying or Selling a Business, Commercial Leasing, IRS Audits.

KENT ANDERSON, born Eugene, Oregon, August 17, 1949; admitted to bar, 1978, Oregon; 1979, U.S. District Court, District of Oregon and U.S. Court of Appeals, Ninth Circuit and U.S. Tax Court. *Education:* University of Oregon (B.S., in Biology, 1975; J.D., 1978). Barrister, Roland K. Rodman American Inn of Court. *Member:* Oregon State Bar; National Association of Consumer Bankruptcy Attorneys; National Association of Consumer Advocates. ***PRACTICE AREAS:*** Bankruptcy; Tax Liens; Taxation; Foreclosures; Business Transactions; Construction; Debtors Rights; Mortgage Bankruptcy; Mortgage Workouts; Individual Taxation; State Taxation.

ARNOLD GALLAGHER SAYDACK PERCELL ROBERTS & POTTER, P.C.

800 WILLAMETTE STREET, SUITE 800
P.O. BOX 1758
EUGENE, OREGON 97440-1758
Telephone: 541-484-0188
Fax: 541-484-0536
Email: info@agsprp.com
URL: http://www.arnoldgallagher.com

General Civil Practice, Banking, Business, Mergers and Acquisitions, Construction, Corporate, Creditors' Rights and Commercial Bankruptcy, Labor and Employment, Environmental, Estate Planning and Probate, Insurance, Media, Real Estate, Partnerships, Taxation, Timber and Trial Practice in Oregon State and Federal Courts.

FIRM PROFILE: Formed in 1993, Arnold Gallagher Saydack Percell Roberts & Potter represents clients doing business in Oregon and throughout the western states. Based in Eugene, we provide a broad array of legal services to business, ranging in size from startups to several of the largest privately-held companies in the state. We also serve as local counsel for various publicly-held companies. Recognized for our expertise, judgment, and the results we obtain, our focus on client service begins with the outstanding quality of our lawyers and staff. We regularly handle major complex business transactions and litigation. While we are large enough to handle such complex matters skillfully and efficiently, our clients appreciate the close working relationships and personal attention they receive from us, treatment more commonly associated with smaller firms. The members of our firm have long-standing roots in the community. We know and understand our region, its decision makers and how to get things done.

JOHN B. ARNOLD, born Ft. Sill, Oklahoma, March 29, 1947; admitted to bar, 1973, Oregon. *Education:* Stanford University (A.B., 1969); University of Michigan (J.D., cum laude, 1973). Special Instructor in Law, Advanced Appellate Advocacy, 1980-1981, Trial Practice, 1984, University of Oregon School of Law. Editor, Appeal and Review, Oregon State Bar, CLE, 1986. *Member:* Oregon State Bar. ***REPORTED CASES:*** Hammond v. Central Lane Communications Center, 816 P2d 593 (1991); Banks v. Hendershott, 719 P2d 484 (1986); Amfac Foods, Inc. v International Systems and Control Corp., 654 P2d 1092 (1982). ***PRACTICE AREAS:*** Business Law; Corporate Law; Real Estate; Construction Law; Banking Law; Commercial Law; Mergers and Acquisitions. ***Email:*** jarnold@agsprp.com

DONALD A. GALLAGHER, JR., born Corvallis, Oregon, September 13, 1946; admitted to bar, 1974, Oregon. *Education:* Oregon State University (B.S., 1968); University of Oregon (J.D., 1974). Member, Managing Board, Oregon Law Review, 1973-1974. Author: "The Right of Oregon Citizens to Inspect Public Records," Oregon Law Review, Vol. 53, 1974; "Economic and Personal Conflicts," Oregon State Bar, 1991; "Conveyances," Oregon State Bar, 1995. *Member:* Oregon State Bar (Chairman, Legal Ethics Committee, 1988-1989; Member, Real Estate and Land Use Executive Committee, 1993-1994); Ameri-

(This Listing Continued)

can Bar Association. ***PRACTICE AREAS:*** Banking Law; Business Law; Corporate Law; Estate Planning; Probate; Real Estate Law; Timber and Logging Law; Closely Held Business Estate Planning; Business Succession Planning. ***Email:*** dgallagher@agsprp.com

ROGER M. SAYDACK, born Detroit, Michigan, May 11, 1947; admitted to bar, 1980, Oregon. *Education:* Oakland University (B.A., 1971); University of Oregon (J.D., 1980). Recent Developments Editor and Member of the Managing Board, Oregon Law Review, 1979-1980. Recipient, Distinguished Service Award, Oregon Law Review, 1980. Co-Author: "Summons and Service," Oregon State Bar, 1985; "Defamation," Oregon State Bar, 1985. Adjunct Professor, Business Planning, University of Oregon School of Law. *Member:* Oregon State Bar (Revised Uniform Partnership Act, Legislative Committee, 1994-1997). ***PRACTICE AREAS:*** Business Law; Business Planning; Mergers, Acquisitions and Divestitures; Corporate Law; Intellectual Property Law; Commercial Real Estate. ***Email:*** rsaydack@agsprp.com

DENNIS W. PERCELL, born Portland, Oregon, April 3, 1950; admitted to bar, 1975, Oregon. *Education:* United States International University (B.A., summa cum laude, 1972); Willamette University (J.D., cum laude, 1975). Co-Author: "Insurance," Continuing Legal Education Handbook, 1983. *Member:* Oregon State Bar; Oregon Association of Defense Counsel; American Board of Trial Advocates. ***PRACTICE AREAS:*** Commercial Litigation; Employment Law; Employment Litigation; Insurance Defense. ***Email:*** dpercell@agsprp.com

ROHN M. ROBERTS, born Durham, North Carolina, August 18, 1954; admitted to bar, 1979, Oregon. *Education:* University of Oregon (B.S., 1976; J.D., 1979). *Member:* Lane County Bar Association (Past President, 1990-1991); Oregon State Bar. ***PRACTICE AREAS:*** Business Law; Creditors' Rights; Commercial Litigation; Real Estate; Timber and Logging Law. ***Email:*** rroberts@agsprp.com

WILLIAM R. POTTER, born Springfield, Minnesota, January 25, 1953; admitted to bar, 1978, Oregon. *Education:* Oregon State University (B.S., 1975); University of Oregon (J.D., 1978). Phi Kappa Phi; Order of the Coif. Adjunct Professor, University of Oregon School of Law. *Member:* Oregon State Bar (Member, Business Section). ***PRACTICE AREAS:*** Business Law; Corporate Law; Mergers and Acquisitions; Business Planning; Commercial Transactions; Real Property Law. ***Email:*** wpotter@agsprp.com

BRADLEY S. COPELAND, born Oceanside, California, March 29, 1956; admitted to bar, 1987, Oregon. *Education:* University of Delaware (B.A., 1982); Northwestern School of Law of Lewis and Clark College (J.D., 1987). Managing Editor, Environmental Law, 1986-1987. Author: "Town of Hallie v. City of Eau Claire, Expanding Antitrust Immunity Under The State Action Exemption," 17 Envtl. L. 275 (1986). *Member:* Oregon State Bar. ***PRACTICE AREAS:*** Bankruptcy; Creditors' Rights; Commercial Litigation. ***Email:*** bcopeland@agsprp.com

BRYON L. LAND, born Lebanon, Oregon, December 27, 1966; admitted to bar, 1994, Oregon. *Education:* Willamette University (B.S., cum laude, 1989; J.D., magna cum laude, 1992); University of Florida (LL.M., Taxation, 1996). Associate Editor, Willamette Law Review, 1991-1992. Graduate Editor, Florida Tax Review. Judicial Clerk to the Honorable Kurt C. Rossman, Oregon Court of Appeals, 1992-1994. Author: "Grady v. Corbin, Increased Double Jeopardy Protection for the Criminal Defendant," 27 Willamette Law Review 913 (1991); "Secondary Liability of a Broker-Dealer in the Ninth Circuit: A Strict Liability Approach," 28 Willamette Law Review 879 (1992). *Member:* Oregon State Bar. ***PRACTICE AREAS:*** State Taxation; Federal Taxation; Business Law; Corporate Law; Business Acquisitions; Business Sales; Estate Planning; Probate. ***Email:*** bland@agsprp.com

JOSEPH G. SCHWARTE, born Alton, Illinois, October 22, 1963; admitted to bar, 1992, Oregon. *Education:* University of Colorado (B.A., 1988); Willamette University (J.D., 1992). *Member:* Oregon State Bar; Oregon Association of Defense Counsel. ***PRACTICE AREAS:*** Commercial Litigation; Insurance Defense. ***Email:*** jschwarte@agsprp.com

CATHERINE D. SUSMAN, born Shreveport, Louisiana, May 8, 1972; admitted to bar, 1997, Louisiana; 2000, Oregon. *Education:* Northwestern State University (B.A., cum laude, 1994); Louisiana State University (J.D., 1997). Phi Alpha Delta. *Member:* Oregon State Bar; Louisiana State Bar Association; American Bar Association; Lane County Bar Association; Oregon Women Lawyers. ***PRACTICE AREAS:*** Business Law; Real Estate; Corporate Law; Commercial Transactions; Computers and Software. ***Email:*** csusman@agsprp.com

---

SUSAN B. BOCK, born Philadelphia, Pennsylvania, February 5, 1968; admitted to bar, 1993, Pennsylvania; 1996, North Carolina; 1999, Oregon. *Education:* Bryn Mawr College (A.B., magna cum laude, 1990); Duke University (J.D., with high honors, 1993; LL.M., 1993). Order of the Coif. Technical Editor, *Law and Contemporary Problems. Member:* Oregon State Bar. ***LANGUAGES:*** Russian. ***PRACTICE AREAS:*** Trusts and Estates; Wills; Probate. ***Email:*** sbock@agsprp.com

GREGORY T. LUSBY, born Eugene, Oregon, February 22, 1967; admitted to bar, 1993, Oregon. *Education:* University of Washington (B.A., 1989); Willamette University College of Law (J.D., 1993). Phi Alpha Delta. Order of the Barristers. Chairman, Willamette University College of Law Moot Court Board, 1992-1993. *Member:* Oregon State Bar; Oregon Association of Defense Counsel. ***PRACTICE AREAS:*** Insurance Defense; Commercial Litigation. ***Email:*** glusby@agsprp.com

ANDREW P. PARKS, born Salem, Oregon, April 9, 1974; admitted to bar, 2002, Oregon. *Education:* University of Puget Sound (B.A., 1996); University of Oregon (J.D., 2002). Member, Oregon Law Review. *Member:* Oregon State, Federal and American (Member, Litigation Section) Bar Associations. ***PRACTICE AREAS:*** Commercial Litigation; Land Use; Real Estate; Insurance Defense. ***Email:*** aparks@agsprp.com

MEGAN McALPIN, born Lewiston, Idaho, April 9, 1978; admitted to bar, 2003, Oregon. *Education:* Western Oregon University (B.S., 2000); Willamette University (J.D., 2003). Member, Willamette Law Review. *Member:* Oregon State Bar. ***PRACTICE AREAS:*** Business Law; Estate Planning; Real Estate. ***Email:*** mmcalpin@agsprp.com

DIANE M. WEISHEIT, born Portland, Oregon, March 29, 1979; admitted to bar, 2004, Oregon. *Education:* Wagner College (B.A., 2001); University of Oregon (J.D., 2004). Senior Editor, Journal of Environmental Law and Litigation, 2002-2004. *Member:* Lane County Bar Association (Member, Debtor-Creditor Section); Oregon State Bar. ***PRACTICE AREAS:*** Bankruptcy; Commercial Litigation; Creditors Rights. ***Email:*** dweisheit@agsprp.com

AARON J. NOTEBOOM, born Rochester, New York, April 30, 1973; admitted to bar, 2003, Oregon. *Education:* Oregon State University (B.A., summa cum laude, 1995); University of Oregon School of Law (J.D., 2003). Author: "A Principled Approach: Doing Justice on the War on Terrorism," Oregon State Bar Bulletin, November 2002; "Terrorism: I Know It When I See It," Oregon Law Review, 2002. *Member:* Oregon State Bar. [United States Marine Corps, 1996-2000; Artillery Officer, Oregon National Guard, 2001-2005; Infantry Officer, Baghdad, Iraq]. ***PRACTICE AREAS:*** Business Law. ***Email:*** anoteboom@agsprp.com

REPRESENTATIVE CLIENTS: Abby's, Inc.; Bi-Mart, Inc.; Cascade Title; Casey Industrial, Inc.; Cawood Communications; Chambers Communications Group; Chambers Construction Co.; Commercial Equipment Lease Corp.; Dari-Mart Stores; Davidson Industries, Inc.; Duco-Lam; EcoNorthwest; Lane Metropolitan Partnership; Evergreen Development Group; Farmers Insurance Group; Fifth Street Public Market; Flightcraft, Inc.; Gonyea & Associates; Hayworth Farms; Hayworth Seed Warehouse; Hinman Vineyards; Industrial Finance Co.; Jerry's Building Materials; KDKF TV; KDRF TV; Kendall Automotive Group; KEZI TV; KPD Insurance; Lane Transit District (Municipal Corporation); L.H. Morris Electric; LibertyBank; Lochmead Dairy; Lochmead Farms; MBM Group; McKenzie Forest Products; Mercedes Benz of Eugene; Michigan-California Lumber Co.; Obie Industries, Inc.; Papé Material Handling, Inc.; Papé Machinery, Inc.; The Papé Group Inc.; PeaceHealth Oregon Region; Pleasant Hill Corp.; Premier Distributors; Prudential Preferred Properties; Roger Langeliers Construction Co.; Ross Investments; Sanipac, Inc.; State Farm Mutual Automobile Insurance Co.; Superior Lumber; Swanson Bros. Lumber Co., Inc.; Swanson Group; Timber Products Group; Tyree Oil, Inc.; Umpqua Bank; Washington Mutual Bank; Western Pneumatics, Inc.; Willamette Pass Ski Corp.; The Willamette Valley Co.; Zip-O-Log Mills.
LOCAL COUNSEL: Christian Brothers of Illinois; General Growth Companies; First American Title Company; Lamar Advertising Company; Lorig Associates, LLC; PeaceHealth Corporation.
REFERENCE: LibertyBank.

BECKLEY & LONGTIN, P.C.

1257 HIGH STREET, SUITE 2
P.O. BOX 11098
EUGENE, OREGON 97440-3298
Telephone: 541-683-0888
Fax: 541-683-0889
Email: lawyers@beckleyandlongtin.com
URL: http://www.beckleyandlongtin.com

Federal Criminal Law and State Criminal Defense. Corporate Law, Family Practice, Divorce, Child Support, Domestic Violence, Drug Crimes, Felonies, Sexual Assault, Commercial, Estate Planning, Probate Law, and Domestic Relations.

KELLY R. BECKLEY, born Colville, Washington, February 19, 1949; admitted to bar, 1974, Oregon; 1975, U.S. Court of Military Appeals; 1977, U.S. Tax Court; 1979, U.S. District Court, District of Oregon; 1980, U.S. Court of Appeals, Ninth Circuit; 1984, U.S. Supreme Court. *Education:* Washington State University (B.A., with honors, 1971); University of Oregon (J.D., 1974). Omicron Delta Kappa; Phi Delta Phi. Instructor: Business Law, University of Maryland, European Division, 1977-1979; Trial Advocacy, University of Oregon School of Law, 1992, 1994. *Member:* American Bar Association; National Association of Criminal Defense Lawyers. [USAF, JAG, 1974-1979; Col. USAFR, JAG, 1980-2004]. ***PRACTICE AREAS:*** Federal and State Criminal Defense; Corporate Law; Commercial Law; Estate Planning; Probate. ***Email:*** kbeckley@beckleyandlongtin.com

MATTHEW D. LONGTIN, born Oregon City, Oregon, July 4, 1965; admitted to bar, 1998, Oregon, U.S. District Court, District of Oregon and U.S. Court of Appeals, Ninth Circuit. *Education:* Pacific University (B.A., 1994); University of Oregon (J.D., 1997). Member, Moot Court Board. *Member:* Lane County Bar Association; Oregon State Bar; Roland K. Rodman American Inns of Court. [2nd Class Petty Officer, U.S. Navy, 1986-1991]. ***PRACTICE AREAS:*** Federal and State Criminal Defense; Family Law; Divorce; Child Support; Domestic Violence; Domestic Relations. ***Email:*** mlongtin@beckleyandlongtin.com

REPRESENTATIVE CLIENTS: Lane Forest Products, Inc.; New Horizons Home Care Resources, Inc.; Reed's Fuel & Trucking; Papa's Pizza, Inc.; Professional Credit Services, Inc.; H&J Construction, Inc.; Gateway Assisted Living, Inc.

BROWN, ROSETA, LONG, McCONVILLE & KILCULLEN

210 NORTHBANK BUILDING
44 CLUB ROAD
EUGENE, OREGON 97401
Telephone: 541-686-1883
Fax: 541-686-2008
Email: lawfirm@brownroseta.com

Civil Trial and Appellate Practice. Insurance Defense. Insurance Law.

MEMBERS OF FIRM

LARRY A. BROWN, born Glendale, California, September 29, 1942; admitted to bar, 1968, Oregon. *Education:* University of Oregon (B.S., 1965; J.D., 1968). *Member:* Lane County Bar Association; Oregon State Bar; Oregon Association of Defense Counsel; Defense Research Institute. ***PRACTICE AREAS:*** Insurance Defense; Insurance Law. ***Email:*** larrybrown@brownroseta.com

MICHAEL H. LONG, born Portland, Oregon, April 10, 1951; admitted to bar, 1976, Oregon. *Education:* Lewis and Clark College and University of Oregon (B.S., with honors, 1973); University of Oregon (J.D., 1976). Phi Beta Kappa. *Member:* Lane County Bar Association; Oregon State Bar; Oregon Association of Defense Counsel; Defense Research Institute. ***PRACTICE AREAS:*** Insurance Defense; Insurance Law. ***Email:*** michaelhlong@brownroseta.com

(This Listing Continued)

BROWN, ROSETA, LONG, McCONVILLE & KILCULLEN, Eugene—Continued

PHILIP R. McCONVILLE, born Salem, Oregon, September 25, 1952; admitted to bar, 1978, Oregon. *Education:* Lewis & Clark College and University of Oregon (B.A., 1974); University of Oregon (J.D., 1978). Phi Alpha Delta. *Member:* Lane County Bar Association; Oregon State Bar; Oregon Association of Defense Counsel; Defense Research Institute. ***PRACTICE AREAS:*** Insurance Defense; Insurance Law. ***Email:*** philmcconville@brownroseta.com

JOHN F. KILCULLEN, born San Diego, California, March 11, 1946; admitted to bar, 1983, Oregon. *Education:* University of Oregon (B.S., with honors, 1980); University of Oregon (J.D., 1983). *Member:* Lane County Bar Association; Oregon State Bar; Oregon Association of Defense Counsel; Defense Research Institute. ***PRACTICE AREAS:*** Insurance Defense; Insurance Law. ***Email:*** johnkilcullen@brownroseta.com

OF COUNSEL

RICHARD A. ROSETA, born Seattle, Washington, February 23, 1947; admitted to bar, 1972, Oregon. *Education:* University of Oregon (B.S., 1969); University of Oregon School of Law (J.D., 1972). *Member:* Lane County Bar Association; Oregon State Bar; Oregon Association of Defense Counsel; Defense Research Institute; Advocate, American Board of Trial Advocates. Fellow, American College of Trial Lawyers. ***PRACTICE AREAS:*** Insurance Defense; Insurance Law. ***Email:*** rickroseta@brownroseta.com

REPRESENTATIVE CLIENTS: All Nation Insurance Co.; Allstate Insurance Co.; American States Insurance Co.; Crawford & Co.; Grange Mutual Insurance; Hanover Insurance Co.; Heritage Life Insurance Co.; Insurance Corp. of America; Mutual of Enumclaw; Northwest Physicians Mutual Insurance Co.; Oregon Mutual Insurance Co.; Professional Liability Fund; Royal Insurance Cos.; Safeco Insurance Cos.; State Farm Fire & Casualty Co.; State Farm Mutual Auto Insurance Co.; Transamerica Insurance Services; Travelers/Aetna Insurance Co.; Unigard Insurance Group; United Pacific/Reliance Cos.; USAA; Wausau Insurance Cos; Weyerhaeuser Co.

CALKINS & CALKINS

101 EAST 14TH AVENUE
EUGENE, OREGON 97401-3517
Telephone: 541-345-0371
FAX: 541-342-1220
Email: win@calkinslaw.com
URL: http://www.lawyers.com/calkinslaw

General Litigation including Civil Trial, Medical Malpractice Defense, Insurance Defense, Contracts, Construction Law, Construction Defense, Hospital Law, Utility Law, Trusts and Estates, Asset Protection, Charitable Giving, Estate Litigation, Estate Planning, Guardianship and Conservatorship, Wills and Probate.

FIRM PROFILE: Calkins & Calkins is a premier law firm listed in the Martindale-Hubbell Bar Register of Preeminent Lawyers.

MEMBERS OF FIRM

WINDSOR CALKINS (1910-1989)

S. M. CALKINS (1872-1969)

W. W. CALKINS (1860-1945)

WIN CALKINS, born Eugene, Oregon, December 18, 1944; admitted to bar, 1971, Oregon. *Education:* University of Oregon (B.A., with honors, 1967); Willamette University (J.D., 1971). Member, Willamette Moot Court Team, 1970. Associate Editor, Willamette Law Journal, 1970-1971. *Member:* Lane County and American Bar Associations; Oregon State Bar (Chair, Litigation Section, 1985-1986; Chair, CLE Committee, 2001); Oregon Association of Defense Counsel (Board Member, 1989-1992). Fellow: American College of Trial Lawyers; American Bar Foundation. ***PRACTICE AREAS:*** General Litigation; Medical Malpractice; Insurance Defense; Hospital and Utility Law. ***Email:*** win@calkinslaw.com

JUDY ANN CALKINS, born Eugene, Oregon, August 11, 1949; admitted to bar, 1991, Oregon. *Education:* University of Oregon (B.A., 1988; J.D., 1991). Kappa Tau Alpha. *Member:* Lane County and American Bar Associations; Oregon State Bar; Eugene Estate Planning Council; Oregon Association of Defense Counsel. ***PRACTICE AREAS:*** Trusts and Estates; Wills and Probate; Estate Planning; Hospital and Utility Law. ***Email:*** judy@calkinslaw.com

---

ERIC S. DEFREEST, born Akron, Ohio, February 10, 1963; admitted to bar, 1992, Oregon. *Education:* University of Miami (B.S., with honors, 1985); University of Oregon (J.D., 1991); Texas A & M University (M.S., 1992). Judicial Clerk, Lane County Circuit Court of Oregon. *Member:* Lane County and American Bar Associations; Oregon State Bar; Oregon Association of Defense Counsel. ***PRACTICE AREAS:*** General Litigation; Medical Malpractice; Insurance Defense; Hospital Law; Utility Law. ***Email:*** eric@calkinslaw.com

OF COUNSEL

JOSEPHINE H. MOONEY, born Waukesha, Wisconsin, May 16, 1962; admitted to bar, 1988, Oregon. *Education:* University of Wisconsin (B.A., with honors, 1984); University of Oregon (J.D., 1988). *Member:* Lane County and American Bar Associations; Oregon State Bar; Oregon Association of Defense Counsel. ***PRACTICE AREAS:*** General Litigation; Medical Malpractice; Insurance Defense; Hospital and Utility Law. ***Email:*** jodie@calkinslaw.com

COUNSEL FOR: Eugene Water & Electric Board; Sacred Heart Medical Center; Lane County Medical Society; Oregon Automobile Insurance Co.; North Pacific Insurance Co.; One Beacon Insurance; St. Paul Insurance Cos.; Safeco; Northwest Physicians Mutual Insurance Co.; General Accident Insurance Co.; Farmers Insurance Group; PeaceHealth; PeaceHealth Medical Group.

(This Listing Continued)

COIT & DEAN, P.C.

EUGENE, OREGON

(See Portland)

Family Law, Divorce, Child Custody, Child Support, Visitation Rights, Spousal Support, Modifications, Restraining Orders, Criminal Law, Personal Injury.

DON CORSON

101 EAST BROADWAY, SUITE 303
EUGENE, OREGON 97401
Telephone: 541-484-2525
Fax: 541-484-2929
Email: dcorson@doncorsonlaw.com
URL: http://www.doncorsonlaw.com

Personal Injury, Wrongful Death, Products Liability, Medical Negligence, Industrial Accidents, Electrical Injury.

DON CORSON, born San Fernando, California, March 29, 1956; admitted to bar, 1985, Oregon; 1986, U.S. District Court, District of Oregon; 1987, U.S. Court of Appeals, Ninth Circuit. *Education:* University of Oregon (B.S., 1976; J.D., 1985). Phi Beta Kappa; Order of the Coif. Recipient, American Jurisprudence Award. *Member:* Lane County and Multnomah County Bar Associations; Oregon State Bar; American College of Trial Lawyers; American Board of Trial Advocates; The Association of Trial Lawyers of America; Oregon Trial Lawyers Association (Past President, 1999); American Inns of Court; National Crime Victim Bar Association. ***PRACTICE AREAS:*** Personal Injury; Wrongful Death; Products Liability; Medical Negligence; Industrial Accidents; Electrical Injury.

DIMENT & WALKER

Established in 1975

SUITE 208, 767 WILLAMETTE STREET
EUGENE, OREGON 97401
Telephone: 541-484-2422
FAX: 541-484-9395
URL: http://www.dimentwalker.com

Civil Litigation, Criminal Law, Driving While Intoxicated, State and Federal Courts, Corporate, Construction, Personal Injury Automobile Accidents, Family Law, Divorce, Child Custody, Visitation Rights, Child Support, Real Estate Law, Probate Law.

MEMBERS OF FIRM

DONALD D. DIMENT, JR., born Portland, Oregon, May 15, 1942; admitted to bar, 1968, Oregon; 1969, U.S. District Court, District of Oregon; 1975, U.S. Supreme Court; 1980, U.S. Court of Appeals, Ninth Circuit. *Education:* Portland State College (B.S., 1965); Willamette University (J.D., 1968). Listed, Best Lawyers in America, 2002-2003. *Member:* Lane County Bar Association; Oregon State Bar; Oregon Trial Lawyers Association; Oregon Criminal Defense Lawyers Association; American Inns of Court. ***PRACTICE AREAS:*** Family Law; Divorce; Criminal Defense; Civil Litigation; Personal Injury. ***Email:*** ddiment@pcinw.com

THEODORE L. WALKER, born Eugene, Oregon, September 23, 1956; admitted to bar, 1983, Oregon; 1987, U.S. Supreme Court. *Education:* University of Oregon (B.S., 1978; J.D., 1983). Articles Editor, Oregon Law Review, 1982-1983. *Member:* Lane County Bar Association; Oregon State Bar. ***PRACTICE AREAS:*** Real Estate Law; Civil Litigation; Family Law; Small Business Law; Construction Law; Probate Law. ***Email:*** twalker@pcinw.com

DOYLE, GARTLAND, NELSON, McCLEERY & WADE, P.C.

Established in 1984

44 CLUB ROAD, SUITE 200
EUGENE, OREGON 97401
Telephone: 541-344-2174
Fax: 541-344-0209

Mailing Address: P.O. Box 11230, Eugene, OR 97440

General Civil and Trial Practice in all State and Federal Courts. Corporate, Business Litigation, Bankruptcy, Creditors Rights, Family, Mediation, Real Property, Construction, Estate Planning and Probate Law, Intellectual Property Law.

MICHAEL W. DOYLE, born Rochester, Minnesota, August 6, 1943; admitted to bar, 1969, California; 1979, Oregon and U.S. District Court, District of Oregon; 1984, U.S. Court of Appeals, Ninth Circuit. *Education:* University of California at Davis (B.A., 1966); University of California, Berkeley (J.D., 1969). Member, Moot Court Board. Senior Lecturer, University of Auckland, Auckland, New Zealand, 1972-1978. Author: "Criminal Procedure in New Zealand," Sweet and Maxwell Ltd., July, 1978; 3rd ed., 1991. *Member:* Lane County Bar Association; Oregon State Bar (Member, Debtor/Creditor Section). ***PRACTICE AREAS:*** Real Property; Corporate; Business Transactions; Creditor's Rights; Bankruptcy. ***Email:*** mwdoyle@dgnmw.com

JOHN C. GARTLAND, born Portland, Oregon, June 11, 1952; admitted to bar, 1977, Oregon; 1978, U.S. District Court, District of Oregon. *Education:* Oregon State University (B.A., 1974); University of Oregon (J.D., 1977). Associate Editor, Oregon Law Review, 1976-1977. *Member:* Lane County Bar Association (President, 1995-1996); Oregon State Bar (Member, Sections on: Family Law; Estate Planning and Administration; Alternative

(This Listing Continued)

Dispute Resolution); Association for the Resolution of Conflict (Practitioner Member). Fellow, American Academy of Matrimonial Lawyers (President, Oregon Chapter, 2004-2005). **PRACTICE AREAS:** Mediation; Family; Estate Planning; Probate. **Email:** jgartland@dgnmw.com

DOUGLAS A. NELSON, born Eugene, Oregon, May 11, 1949; admitted to bar, 1978, California; 1980, Oregon. *Education:* University of Oregon (B.S., 1971); Pepperdine University (J.D., cum laude, 1978). Member, Pepperdine Law Review, 1977-1978. *Member:* Lane County Bar Association (Executive Committee, Probate Section, 1993-1997, Chairman, 1995-1996); Oregon State Bar (Member: Estate Planning Section); Eugene Estate Planning Council (Board Member, 2000—; President, 2003-2004). **PRACTICE AREAS:** Estate Planning; Probate; Business Law; Family Business Entities; Business Acquisition and Sale; Real Property. **Email:** dnelson@dgnmw.com

P. SCOTT McCLEERY, born Germany, November 29, 1952; admitted to bar, 1985, Oregon; 1986, U.S. District Court, District of Oregon. *Education:* University of California at Santa Barbara (B.A., 1975); University of Oregon at Eugene (J.D., 1985). Law Clerk to Oregon Court of Appeals, 1984-1985. *Member:* Lane County Bar Association (Member, Debtor/Creditor and Real Estate Sections); Oregon State Bar. **PRACTICE AREAS:** Business Litigation; General Civil and Trial Practice; Real Property and Business Transactions; Creditors Rights; Business Workouts; Bankruptcy Litigation. **Email:** psmccleery@dgnmw.com

DAVID WADE, born New Orleans, Louisiana, June 2, 1951; admitted to bar, 1977, California; 1980, U.S. Supreme Court; 1982, New York; 1993, Oregon; 1984, U.S. District Court, Southern and Eastern Districts of New York; 1985, U.S. District Court, Central District of California and U.S. Court of Appeals for the Ninth Circuit; 2003, U.S. District Court, Northern District of California and U.S. Court of Federal Claims. *Education:* Harvard University (A.B., cum laude, 1973; J.D., cum laude, 1976). Law Clerk to U.S. District Judge James B. McMillan, Charlotte, North Carolina, 1976-1977. Attorney, Antitrust Division, U.S. Department of Justice, Washington, D.C., 1977-1981. Associate: John Doar Law Offices, New York, NY, 1981-1985. Associate, Hoecker & McMahon and Partner, Hoecker, McMahon & Wade, Los Angeles, Ca., 1985-1992. *Member:* Lane County, Oregon State and New York State Bar Associations; State Bar of California. **PRACTICE AREAS:** Business Litigation; Real Estate Litigation; Construction Law; Bankruptcy Litigation; Environmental Litigation; Business Formation; Business Transactions; Antitrust; Trade Regulation. **Email:** dwade@dgnmw.com

---

MINDY L. WITTKOP, born Eugene, Oregon, May 21, 1971; admitted to bar, 1997, Oregon; 1998, Washington and U.S. District Court, District of Oregon. *Education:* University of Portland (B.S., 1993); University of Oregon (J.D., 1997). Law Clerk to David V. Brewer, Lane County Circuit Court, 1997-1998. *Member:* Lane County Bar Association; Oregon State Bar; Oregon Women Lawyers. **PRACTICE AREAS:** Business Litigation; Creditor's Rights; Business Transactions; Real Property Transactions; Construction Law. **Email:** mwittkop@dgnmw.com

HEATHER M. WALLOCH, born Oklahoma City, Oklahoma, November 8, 1971; admitted to bar, 1996, Oregon; 1997, U.S. District Court, District of Oregon; 1999, District of Columbia and U.S. District Court for the District of Columbia; 2001, U.S. Court of Appeals for the Federal Circuit. *Education:* University of Puget Sound (B.A., 1993); University of Oregon (J.D., 1996). Law Extern to U.S. Bankruptcy Court, Eugene, Oregon, 1995. *Member:* Lane County Bar Association; Oregon State Bar; The District of Columbia Bar; Lane County Women Lawyers; Oregon Women Lawyers. **PRACTICE AREAS:** Commercial Litigation; Business Litigation; Real Estate Litigation; Construction Law; Business Transactions. **Email:** hwalloch@dgnmw.com

EMILY S. HILL, born Ithaca, New York, October 25, 1979; admitted to bar, 2004, Oregon and U.S. District Court, District of Oregon. *Education:* University of California, Berkeley (B.A., 2001; J.D., 2004). Law and Technology Certificate Program. *Member:* Lane County Bar Association; Oregon State Bar; Lane County Women Lawyers; Oregon Women Lawyers. **PRACTICE AREAS:** Business Litigation; Business Transactions; Intellectual Property Law; Real Property Transactions; Real Estate Litigation.

REPRESENTATIVE CLIENTS: Blixseth Group, Inc.; Yellowstone Mountain Club; Yellowstone Development; Western Pacific Timber; Kiefer's KIA; TexTron; BMW Financial Services; Pacific Continental Bank; Professional Liability Fund; Murphy Co.; Clarkes Sheet Metal, Inc.; Weber Enterprises, Inc.; Tangent Business Park; Oregon Development LLC; KBTC, Inc.; Essex General Construction, Inc.; Ramsay-Gerding Construction, Inc.; C & K Market, Inc.; Spanish Peaks Holdings.
REFERENCE: Pacific Continental Bank.

HUBERT G. DUVALL, JR.

CITIZENS BUILDING
975 OAK STREET, SUITE 610
EUGENE, OREGON 97401
Telephone: 541-349-9909
Fax: 541-349-9799
URL: http://www.oregoncriminalattorney.com
Email: hughduvall@oregoncriminalattorney.com
URL: http://www.lawyers.com/hgduvall

Criminal Law, Drug Crimes, Measure II, Sex Offenses, Stalking, Assault, Harassment, Theft, Forgery, Drug Crimes, DUI, Shoplifting, Driving While Intoxicated, Felonies, Juvenile Law, Misdemeanors, Parole and Probation, Sexual Assault, Business Crimes, Juvenile, Traffic Violations, Sexual Abuse, Sexual Harassment.

HUBERT G. DUVALL, JR., born Corvallis, Oregon, September 5, 1960; admitted to bar, 1988, Oregon. *Education:* Oregon State University (B.S., 1984) University of Oregon (J.D., 1988). Co-Author, Oregon State Bar Continuing Legal Education Update, "Pretrial Practice," 1990. Author: "Oregon Driver Restriction Guide"; "Oregon Expungement Guide"; "Collateral Consequences Guide"; "Family Law Practitioner's Guide to Restraining Orders and Gun Rights"; "Oregon Stalking Law Guide." Instructor, Trial Practice, University of Oregon School of Law, 1991, 2002, 2003, 2005. Speaker: Oregon Criminal Defense Lawyers Association, Summer Conference, 1990 and 2001, Spring Conference, 1998; Oregon State Bar, DUII Conference, October, 1998. Trial Practice Judge, University of Oregon School of Law, 1990, 1991 and 2000. Former Member, Roland K. Rodman Inn of Court, 2002. *Member:* Lane County Bar Association (Member, Board of Directors, 1995-1996, 1996-1997; Secretary/Treasurer, 1997-1998; President, 1999-2000; Criminal Law Section Chair, 2004-2005); Oregon State Bar; Oregon Criminal Defense Lawyers Association (Member, Board of Directors). **PRACTICE AREAS:** Drug Crimes; Sex Crimes; Assault and Battery; Harassment; Theft; Forgery; Driving While Intoxicated; Felonies; Juvenile Criminal Law; Juvenile Law; Misdemeanors; Parole and Probation; Sexual Assault; Business Crimes.

DAVID C. FORCE

96 EAST BROADWAY, SUITE 2
P.O. BOX 10972
EUGENE, OREGON 97440
Telephone: 541-343-2956
Fax: 541-686-1594
Email: forcelaw@aol.com
URL: http://www.lawyers.com/forcelaw

Government Agency Practice, Civil Rights, Libel, Slander and Defamation, Employment Law, Wrongful Termination, Discrimination, Gay and Lesbian Rights, Workers Compensation, Sexual Harassment, Family and Medical Leave Act, Employee Rights, Appellate Law, Federal Civil Law, Administrative Law.

DAVID C. FORCE, born Medford, Oregon, November 15, 1946; admitted to bar, 1982, Oregon. *Education:* University of Oregon (B.S., 1968; J.D., 1982). *Member:* Lane County Bar Association; Oregon State Bar (Member, Sections on: Workers' Compensation; Employment); Oregon Trial Lawyers Association; American Trial Lawyers Association. **REPORTED CASES:** Coszalter v. City of Salem; Boynton-Burns v. University of Oregon.

GAYDOS, CHURNSIDE & BALTHROP, P.C.

440 EAST BROADWAY, SUITE 300
P.O. BOX 1499
EUGENE, OREGON 97440
Telephone: 541-343-8060
Fax: 541-343-1599
Email: gcb@gcbpc.com
URL: http://www.gcb@gcbpc.com

General Civil and Trial Practice in State and Federal Courts. Business, Commercial, Banking, Corporate, Construction, Real Property, Bankruptcy, Estate Planning, Trusts, Probate, Alternate Dispute Resolution.

SHERYL BALTHROP, born Baker City, Oregon, December 29, 1965; admitted to bar, 1991, Oregon and U.S. District Court, District of Oregon. *Education:* University of Oregon (B.A., with honors, 1988; J.D., 1991). *Member:* Lane County Bar Association (Member, Sections on: Employment Law and Family Law); Oregon State Bar (Member, Construction Section); American Inns of Court. **LANGUAGES:** French. **PRACTICE AREAS:** Business; Contracts; Construction; Real Estate; Employment; Family Law; Litigation. **Email:** sheryl@gcbpc.com

DONALD J. CHURNSIDE, born Seattle, Washington, August 2, 1954; admitted to bar, 1979, Oregon; 1980, U.S. District Court, District of Oregon. *Education:* Linfield College (B.A., 1976); University of Oregon (J.D., 1979). *Member:* Lane County Bar Association; Oregon State Bar (Member, Business and Corporate Law, Debtor/Creditor, Litigation Sections; Chair, Legal Ethics Committee, 1991-1992 and CLE, 1991). **PRACTICE AREAS:** Real Estate; Business Law; Debtor & Creditor; Litigation; Commercial; Banking Law. **Email:** don@gcbpc.com

GERRY GAYDOS, born Columbus, Ohio, March 30, 1947; admitted to bar, 1972, Ohio; 1973, U.S. Court of Military Appeals; 1976, Oregon; 1980, U.S. District Court, District of Oregon. *Education:* Allegheny College and The Ohio State University (B.A., 1969); Case Western Reserve University (J.D., 1972). Assistant District Attorney, Lane County, 1977-1978. Member, Board of Directors, Lane Transit District. *Member:* Lane County and American (Member, Corporation, Banking and Business Law Section) Bar Associations; Oregon State Bar (Member, Sections on: Business and Corporate; Estate Planning and Administration; Real Estate and Land Use; Board of Bar Governors, 2002). [Capt., USAF, JAGC, 1972-1977]. **PRACTICE AREAS:** Business; Commercial; Corporate; Trusts; Estates; Probate. **Email:** gerry@gcbpc.com

---

P. REBECCA KAMITSUKA, (admission pending). *Education:* University of Oregon School of Law (1993); University of Missouri (Medical Technology and Food Science and Nutrition). Former Senior Assistant Attorney General, State of Oregon Department of Justice. **PRACTICE AREAS:** Civil Litigation; Commercial Litigation; Real Property; Regulation; Bankruptcy; Creditors Rights.

OF COUNSEL

JONATHAN R. MIKO, born Ridgewood, New Jersey, March 10, 1971; admitted to bar, 1998, New Jersey, New York and U.S. District Court, District of New Jersey; 2000, U.S. District Court, Northern and Southern Districts of New York; 2002, Oregon and U.S. District Court, District of Oregon. *Education:* Rutgers University (B.A., 1993); New York Law School (J.D., 1998). Associate: Melli Guerin & Melli, P.C., Paramus, N.J., 1998-1999; Landman Corsi Ballaine & Ford PC, Newark, N.J., 1999-2001. **PRACTICE AREAS:** Civil Litigation; Insurance Defense.

REPRESENTATIVE CLIENTS: Wells Fargo Bank N.A.; Key Bank of Oregon; Pacific Continental Bank; Spec Industries, Inc.; Paradise Homes, Inc.; Balzhiser & Hubbard Engineering, Inc.; McPheeters Electric; Reynolds Electric, Inc.; U.S. Allegiance, Inc.; Paradise Development Co.; Auto-Chlor System of Oregon; JCK Restaurants, Inc.; Howling Coyote, Inc.; KWK

(This Listing Continued)

GAYDOS, CHURNSIDE & BALTHROP, P.C., Eugene—Continued

Foods, LLC; Curtis Restaurant Equipment, Inc., Medford Pacific; The Athletic Club of Bend, Inc.; Shadow Hills Country Club; KVAL TV; Hyundai Semi-Conductor of America.

GLEAVES SWEARINGEN POTTER & SCOTT LLP

Established in 1924

975 OAK STREET, 8TH FLOOR
EUGENE, OREGON 97401
Telephone: 541-686-8833
Fax: 541-345-2034
Email: info@orbuslaw.com
URL: http://www.orbuslaw.com

General Civil Practice. Trial and Appellate Practice in all State and Federal Courts and Administrative Agencies, Antitrust, Banking, Bankruptcy, Business and Commercial, Construction, Computer, Corporations and Corporate Financing, Partnerships, Creditors Rights, Domestic Relations, Estate Planning, Government Contract, Labor and Employment, Media, Municipal, Probate, Trusts, Professional Negligence Defense, Real Property, Taxation, Timber, Trade Regulation and Natural Resource Law.

MEMBERS OF FIRM

FREDERICK A. BATSON, born Denver, Colorado, December 20, 1957; admitted to bar, 1982, Oregon. *Education:* Northern Arizona University (B.S., cum laude, 1979; B.S., 1980); Lewis & Clark College (J.D., cum laude, 1982). *Member:* Lane County and American Bar Associations; Oregon State Bar (Treasurer, 1990-1991; Secretary, 1991-1992; Chair-Elect, 1992-1993; Chair, 1993-1994, Construction Law Section). ***PRACTICE AREAS:*** General Business Litigation; Construction; Real Estate; Product Distribution Law; Secured Transactions. ***Email:*** batson@orbuslaw.com

JON V. BUERSTATTE, born Walla Walla, Washington, December 20, 1956; admitted to bar, 1982, Oregon. *Education:* Washington State University (B.A., summa cum laude, 1979); University of Oregon (J.D., 1982). Phi Beta Kappa; Phi Kappa Phi. *Member:* Lane County and American Bar Associations; Oregon State Bar. ***PRACTICE AREAS:*** Employment; Business Transactions; Transportation Law. ***Email:*** buerstatte@orbuslaw.com

JOSHUA A. CLARK, born Eugene, Oregon, April 14, 1969; admitted to bar, 1998, Oregon. *Education:* University of Washington (B.A., 1991); University of Oregon (J.D., 1998). Alpha Kappa Psi. Member, Moot Court Board. Recipient, Dean's Scholarship. ***PRACTICE AREAS:*** Business Law; Real Estate; Business Planning. ***Email:*** clark@orbuslaw.com

THOMAS P. E. HERRMANN, born Ann Arbor, Michigan, March 22, 1963; admitted to bar, 1988, Washington; 1991, Oregon. *Education:* University of Oregon (B.S., 1985; J.D., 1988). Executive Editor, Oregon Law Review, 1987-1988. Order of the Coif. *Member:* Lane County, Washington State and American Bar Associations; Oregon State Bar; Eugene-Springfield Tax Association. ***PRACTICE AREAS:*** Business Law; Tax Law; Real Estate Law; Estate Planning. ***Email:*** herrmann@orbuslaw.com

KRISTIN E. KERNUTT, born Seattle, Washington, May 31, 1965; admitted to bar, 1999, Oregon. *Education:* University of Puget Sound (B.A., 1987); Seattle University (M.B.A., 1995); University of Oregon (J.D., 1999). Beta Gamma Sigma. Managing Editor, Journal of Environmental Law & Litigation, 1997-1999. Life and Disability Agent's License, Washington State, 1992. ***PRACTICE AREAS:*** Business Law; Employment Law; Health Law. ***Email:*** kernutt@orbuslaw.com

STEPHEN O. LANE, born Portland, Oregon, July 18, 1947; admitted to bar, 1975, Oregon. *Education:* Whitman College (B.A., 1969); Willamette University (J.D., 1975). Associate Editor, Willamette Law Journal, 1974-1975. Listed in: The Best Lawyers in America, 2001-2002. *Member:* Lane County and American Bar Associations; Oregon State Bar. Fellow: American College of Trust and Estate Counsel. ***PRACTICE AREAS:*** Estate Planning; Probate; Qualified Retirement Plans; Business Tax Planning Law. ***Email:*** lane@orbuslaw.com

WILLIAM H. MARTIN, born Yakima, Washington, November 4, 1948; admitted to bar, 1974, Oregon. *Education:* University of Puget Sound (B.S., 1971); Northwestern School of Law of Lewis and Clark College (J.D., 1974). Assistant District Attorney, 1976-1979. Pro tem Judge, Lane County Circuit Court, 1986-1990; 1996—. Member: Board of Bar Examiners, 2002—; State Professional Responsibility Board, 2002—. *Member:* Lane County (Member, Board of Directors, 1981-1982 and 1991-1992) and American (Member, Litigation Section) Bar Associations; Oregon State Bar (Member, Litigation Section; Board of Directors of Professional Liability Fund, 1996-2001). ***PRACTICE AREAS:*** Commercial Litigation; Real Estate Litigation; Employment Litigation. ***Email:*** martin@orbuslaw.com

LAURA T.Z. MONTGOMERY, born East Lansing, Michigan, May 7, 1966; admitted to bar, 1993, Oregon and U.S. District Court, District of Oregon and U.S. Court of Appeals, Ninth Circuit. *Education:* University of Oregon (B.A., with honors, 1988; J.D., 1993). Managing Editor, Journal of Environmental Law and Litigation. *Member:* Lane County and American Bar Associations; Oregon State Bar; Roland K. Rodman American Inn of Court; Oregon Trial Lawyers Association; Oregon Women Lawyers. ***LANGUAGES:*** Italian. ***PRACTICE AREAS:*** Trial Practice; General Litigation; Commercial Business Litigation; Employment Litigation; Real Property and Construction Litigation. ***Email:*** montgomery@orbuslaw.com

STANDLEE G. POTTER, born Vancouver, Washington, July 25, 1940; admitted to bar, 1965, Oregon. *Education:* University of Oregon (B.S., 1962; LL.B., 1965). Listed in: The Best Lawyers in America, 2001-2005. *Member:* Lane County and American Bar Associations; Oregon State Bar. ***PRACTICE AREAS:*** Real Property; Timber; Estate Planning; Probate; Corporation; Partnership; Nonprofit Organizations. ***Email:*** spotter@orbuslaw.com

IAN T. RICHARDSON, born Baton Rouge, Louisiana, March 29, 1965; admitted to bar, 1997, Oregon. *Education:* University of California at Berkeley (B.A., 1987); Northwestern School of Law of Lewis and Clark College (J.D., cum laude, 1997). *Member:* Lane County Bar Association; Oregon State Bar. ***PRACTICE AREAS:*** Business; Taxation; Estate Planning; Probate. ***Email:*** richardson@orbuslaw.com

MARTHA J. RODMAN, born Eugene, Oregon, September 1, 1951; admitted to bar, 1977, Oregon. *Education:* Pomona College; University of Oregon (B.A., 1974; J.D., 1977). Phi Beta Kappa; Order of the Coif. *Member:* Lane County (Member, Board of Directors, 1980) and American Bar Associations; Oregon State Bar (Member, Council on Court Procedures, 1987-1989); Inns of Court. ***PRACTICE AREAS:*** Creditors Rights; Bankruptcy; Domestic Relations Law. ***Email:*** rodman@orbuslaw.com

DOUGLAS R. SCHULTZ, born Oakland, California, April 7, 1945; admitted to bar, 1973, Oregon. *Education:* University of Oregon (B.A., with honors, 1967; J.D., 1973). Phi Beta Kappa; Order of the Coif; Phi Eta Sigma. Co-Author: "Mortgage Foreclosure in Oregon," Oregon State Bar, 1976, 1981, 1984, 1988, 1997 and 2001. *Member:* Lane County (Chairman, Bankruptcy Committee, 1989—) and American Bar Associations; Oregon State Bar (Executive Committee, Debtor/Creditor Section). ***PRACTICE AREAS:*** Debtor and Creditor Bankruptcy; Creditors Rights Law; Foreclosures. ***Email:*** schultz@orbuslaw.com

MALCOLM H. SCOTT, born Eugene, Oregon, April 7, 1935; admitted to bar, 1964, Oregon. *Education:* University of Oregon (B.S., Accounting, 1957; LL.B., 1964). Beta Alpha Psi; Phi Alpha Delta. Chief Editor, Foreclosing Security Interests (Oregon State Bar, 1997 and 2001). Listed in: The Best Lawyers in America. Co-author: "Mortgage Foreclosure in Oregon," Oregon State Bar, 1971, 1976, 1981, 1984, 1988, 1992, 1997 and 2001. President, Oregon Law Institute, 1979-1981. *Member:* Lane County and American Bar Associations; Oregon State Bar; American College of Real Estate Lawyers. ***PRACTICE AREAS:*** Real Estate; Foreclosure; Corporate; Business Law. ***Email:*** scott@orbuslaw.com

JAMES W. SPICKERMAN, born The Dalles, Oregon, July 10, 1943; admitted to bar, 1968, Oregon; 1969, U.S. District Court, District of Oregon. *Education:* University of Oregon (B.S., 1965; J.D., 1968). Assistant Municipal Judge, City of Eugene, 1984-1998; City of Eugene Land Use Hearings Official, 1973-1998. *Member:* Oregon State Bar (Member, Real Estate and Land Use Section). ***PRACTICE AREAS:*** Land Use; Real Estate; Administrative Law. ***Email:*** spickerman@orbuslaw.com

KATE A. THOMPSON, born Chicago, Illinois, February 17, 1968; admitted to bar, 1998, Wisconsin; 2000, Oregon. *Education:* Colorado College (B.A., 1990); University of Wisconsin - Madison (J.D., cum laude, 1998). Order of the Coif. Member, University of Wisconsin Law Review. *Member:* Oregon State Bar; State Bar of Wisconsin. ***PRACTICE AREAS:*** Business Law; Litigation. ***Email:*** thompson@orbuslaw.com

ASSOCIATES

SEAN M. BANNON, born South Bend, Indiana, 1969; admitted to bar, 2005, Oregon. *Education:* University of Oregon (B.A., 1991; J.D., 2000). *Member:* Lane County and American Bar Associations; Oregon State Bar. ***PRACTICE AREAS:*** Litigation; Business Law. ***Email:*** bannon@orbuslaw.com

TANYA C. O'NEIL, born San Jose, California, August 7, 1975; admitted to bar, 2004, Oregon. *Education:* University of the Pacific (B.A., 1998); Willamette University (J.D., 2004). *Member:* Oregon State Bar. ***PRACTICE AREAS:*** Litigation; Business. ***Email:*** oneil@orbuslaw

JANE M. YATES, born Castro Valley, California, March 15, 1965; admitted to bar, 2005, Oregon. *Education:* American University of Paris (B.A. cum laude, 2001); University of Oregon (J.D., 2004). *Member:* Lane County and American Bar Associations; Oregon State Bar. ***LANGUAGES:*** French, Italian. ***PRACTICE AREAS:*** Civil Litigation; Business Law. ***Email:*** yates@orbuslaw.com

SPECIAL COUNSEL TO THE FIRM

ANSEL J. GIUSTINA, born Eugene, Oregon, August 17, 1943; admitted to bar, 1973, Oregon. *Education:* Oregon State University (B.S., Forest Products, B.A., Business, 1967); University of Pavia, Pavia, Italy; Willamette University (J.D., 1973). *Member:* Lane County Bar Association; Oregon State Bar (Member, Sections on: Business and Corporate Law; Real Estate and Land Use Law). ***PRACTICE AREAS:*** Business; Real Estate; Timber; Probate; Estate Planning. ***Email:*** giustina@orbuslaw.com

REPRESENTATIVE CLIENTS: ATS Systems Oregon Inc.; American Medical Concepts, Inc.; Brookings-Harbor Shopping Center; Cascade Timber Consulting, Inc.; Cascade Exchange Services, Inc.; Cascade Title Co.; Central Oregon & Pacific Railroad, Inc.; Chambers Communication, Inc.; Citizens Buuilding, LLC; Coastal Farm & Home Supply, Inc.; Corvallis Tool Company; D.R. Johnson Lumber Co.; Engineering and Geological Resources, Inc.; Eugene Association of Realtors; Giustina Land and Timber Co.; Green Diamond Products; Hult & Associates LLC; Internal Medicine Associates of Lane County, P.C.; JELD-WEN, INC.; Kerr Concentrates, Inc.; King Estate Winery Limited Partnership; Menasha Forest Products Corporation; Mid-Valley Glass & Millwork Co.; Monaco Coach Corporation; Dynea U.S.A. Inc..; Northwest Stamping and Precision; OBEC Consulting Engineers; Oregon Imaging Centers; Orthopedic Spine Association; Pacific Continental Bank; Pepsi-Cola Bottling Company of Eugene; PWPipe; Portland & Western Railroad, Inc.; Rexius Forest By-Products, Inc.; Rosen Sunvisor Systems, LLC; Seneca Sawmill Co.; Shelton-Turnbull Printers; Sherman Bros. Heavy Trucking; States Industries, Inc.; Ronald R. Sticka, U.S. Bankruptcy Trustee; Sweet Home School District; Tripod Data Systems, Inc.; Transition Management, Inc.; University of Oregon Foundation; Valley River Center; VersaLogic, Inc.; Westbrook Land & Timber, LLC; Westwood Industries, Inc.;Willamette & Pacific Railroad, Inc.; Whittier Wood Products.
LOCAL COUNSEL FOR: Advanstar Communications; Associates Commercial Corp.; Automatic Data Processing, Inc.; ATS Automation Tooling Systems, Inc.; C.I.T. Group/Equipment Financing, Inc.; Erin Truckways, Ltd. dba Digby Truckline Inc.; RailAmerica, Inc.; Rauma Corporation; Fisher Broadcasting, Inc dba KVAL TV; Timberjack Corporation; Washington Mutual Bank; Willis Corporation.

HARRANG LONG GARY RUDNICK P.C.

Established in 1957

360 EAST 10TH AVENUE, SUITE 300
EUGENE, OREGON 97401
Telephone: 541-485-0220
Fax: 541-686-6564
URL: http://www.harrang.com
Mailing Address: P.O. Box 11620, Eugene, OR 97440-3820

(This Listing Continued)

Portland, Oregon Office: 1001 S.W. 5th Avenue, Suite 1650. Telephone: 503-242-0000. Fax: 503-241-1458.
Salem, Oregon Office: 333 High Street, N.E., Suite 200. Telephone: 503-371-3330. Fax: 503-371-5336.

General Civil Trial and Appellate Practice in all State and Federal Courts, Governmental and Business Law, Corporate Law, Administrative Law, Financial Services, Securities Law, Creditors Rights, Partnership Law, Real Estate, State and Local Government Law, Environmental Law, Zoning, Planning and Land Use, Estate Planning and Probate, Insurance Law, Civil, Business, Complex and Tort Litigation, Alternative Dispute Resolution, Labor and Employment Law, Employee Benefits, Intellectual Property, Health Law, Nonprofit Law.

FIRM PROFILE: Harrang Long Gary Rudnick P.C. was organized as a partnership on July 1, 1957. It has offices in Eugene, Salem and Portland, Oregon. The firm conducts a diversified general practice with particular emphasis in municipal and public law, trial and appellate practice, intellectual property law and corporate, business and real estate law.

JILLIAN R. BRUCE, born Eugene, Oregon, September 23, 1959; admitted to bar, 1985, California; 1994, Oregon; 2004, Washington. *Education:* Lewis & Clark College (B.S., 1981); McGeorge School of Law, University of the Pacific (J.D., 1985). Member, Moot Court Honors Board. *Member:* Washington State Bar Association; State Bar of California; Oregon State Bar. ***Email:*** jillian.bruce@harrang.com

WILLIAM F. GARY, born Palo Alto, California, December 4, 1950; admitted to bar, 1976, California; 1977, Oregon; 1980, U.S. Supreme Court. *Education:* University of Oregon (B.A., 1973); University of California, Hastings College of Law (J.D., 1976). Member: Order of the Coif; Thurston Society. Editor, Hastings Law Journal, 1975-1976. Law Clerk, Oregon Court of Appeals, 1976-1978. Solicitor General of Oregon, 1981-1983. Deputy Attorney General of Oregon, 1983-1988. Special Assistant Attorney General, State of Oregon, 1989-1994, 1998-1999. City Attorney of Eugene, 1989-1996. Member, Oregon Criminal Justice Commission, 1996—. Governor's Special Task Force on Public Employees Retirement System, 2002. *Member:* Oregon State Bar (Executive Committee, Appellate Practice Section); State Bar of California; American Bar Association. Fellow, American Academy of Appellate Lawyers, 2001—. ***PRACTICE AREAS:*** Civil Litigation; Appellate Law; Municipal Law; Administrative Law. ***Email:*** william.f.gary@harrang.com

JAMES P. HARRANG, born Lebanon, Oregon, October 15, 1923; admitted to bar, 1951, Oregon. *Education:* University of Oregon (B.S., 1948; LL.B., 1951). Special Lecturer in Law, Oregon School of Law, Domestic Relations, 1958, 1959, 1960, 1963 and Contracts, 1960. Editor, Advising Oregon Businesses, Oregon State Bar, CLE, 1971-1972. *Member:* Oregon State Bar; American Bar Association. ***PRACTICE AREAS:*** Business Law; Corporate Law; Partnership Law; Trusts and Estates; Organizations; Operation and Transactions. ***Email:*** james.p.harrang@harrang.com

EMILY NEWTON JEROME, born Rock Falls, Illinois, October 30, 1970; admitted to bar, 1995, Oregon. *Education:* Western Illinois University (B.A., magna cum laude, 1992); University of Oregon (J.D., 1995). Member, Oregon Law Review. Assistant Instructor, Trial Practice, University of Oregon School of Law, 1998. *Member:* Lane County (Member, Sections on: Environmental Law and Land Use) and Oregon State (Member, Sections on: Government Law, Real Estate and Land Use) Bar Associations; Oregon Women Lawyers Association; Oregon City Attorneys Association. ***PRACTICE AREAS:*** Local Government Law; Land Use Permitting; Rezoning; Land Development; Land Use; Environmental Land Use; Land Use Litigation; Public Law; Fifth Amendment Law; Land Annexation; Inverse Condemnation; Subdivision; Zoning Law; Zoning Variances. ***Email:*** emily.n.jerome@harrang.com

GLENN KLEIN, born Santa Monica, California, September 28, 1956; admitted to bar, 1983, Oregon; U.S. District Court, District of Oregon and U.S. Court of Appeals, Ninth Circuit. *Education:* University of California at Irvine (B.A. 1978); University of Oregon (M.S., 1980; J.D. 1982). Certificates of Completion in Environmental and Natural Resources Law, and in Ocean and Coastal Law, Law Clerk to U.S. District Court Judge, 1982-1984. Honors Attorney, Oregon Department of Justice, 1984-1985. Assistant Attorney General, Oregon Department of Justice, General Counsel Division, 1985-1986, Special Litigation Unit, 1986-1989. Author: "Environmental Audits and Site Assessments," 1994 Update, Environmental Law C.L.E., December 1994. Past President, Oregon City Attorneys Association; City Attorney of Eugene, 1996—. *Member:* Oregon State Bar; American Bar Association. ***PRACTICE AREAS:*** Environmental Law; Government Law; Municipal Law; Zoning, Planning and Land Use. ***Email:*** glenn.klein@harrang.com

JEROME LIDZ, born Baltimore, Maryland, August 7, 1947; admitted to bar, 1977, Oregon; 1979, U.S. District Court, District of Oregon, U.S. Court of Appeals, Ninth Circuit and U.S. Supreme Court. *Education:* Yale University (B.A., 1968); University of Wisconsin (M.A., 1973); University of Oregon (J.D., 1977). Order of the Coif. Author, Comment, "Official Immunity from Damages in Section 1983 Suits: *Wood v. Strickland,*" 56 Oregon Law Review 124, 1977. Adjunct Professor, Willamette University College of Law, Fall, 1978; University of Oregon College of Education, 1987; University of Oregon School of Law, 1988, 1999. *Member:* Oregon State Bar; American Bar Association. ***PRACTICE AREAS:*** Local Government Law; Public Law; Administrative Law; Appellate Practice; Natural Resources Law. ***Email:*** jerome.s.lidz@harrang.com

STANTON F. LONG, born Forest Grove, Oregon, November 3, 1941; admitted to bar, 1967, Oregon. *Education:* Clark College; Oregon State University; University of Oregon (B.S., 1964); Willamette University (J.D., 1967). Oregon Deputy Attorney General, 1981-1983. Director, Oregon Department of Commerce, 1987. President, SAIF Corporation, 1988-1992. Vice President, Domestic General Claims of American International Group and President of AIGCS, Inc. a wholly owned subsidiary of AIG, 1992-1996. Vice Chairman of Travelers Property and Casualty Co., 1996-1998. Chairman of Claims Services for Travelers Property and Casualty Co., 1998—. Director and General Counsel of Project Time & Cost, an Atlanta, Georgia cost engineering and internet Co., 1999—. *Member:* Oregon State Bar; American Bar Association. ***PRACTICE AREAS:*** Insurance Law; Administrative Law; Litigation; Business Law. ***Email:*** stanton.f.long@harrang.com

JEFFERY J. MATTHEWS, born Honolulu, Hawaii, May 13, 1954; admitted to bar, 1989, Missouri and U.S. District Court, Western District of Missouri; 1992, U.S. Court of Appeals, Eighth Circuit; 1994, U.S. Court of Appeals, Tenth Circuit; 1995, U.S. District Court, Central District of Illinois; 1997, Oregon, U.S. Court of Appeals, Federal Circuit and U.S. District Court, District of Oregon; 2000, U.S. Court of Appeals, Ninth Circuit; 2002, Washington. *Education:* Southern Oregon State College (B.S., 1977); University of Nevada-Reno (M.A., 1984); University of Missouri-Kansas City (J.D., 1989). Order of the Bench & Robe; National Moot Court Board. Member, UMKC Law Review, 1988-1989. Law Clerk, Hon. Scott O. Wright, U.S. District Court Judge, Western District of Missouri, 1989-1991. *Member:* Lane County, Washington State, Federal and American Bar Associations; Oregon State Bar; The Missouri Bar. ***PRACTICE AREAS:*** Civil Litigation; Local Government Defense; Construction Law. ***Email:*** jeffery.j.matthews@harrang.com

WALTER W. MILLER, born Chicago, Illinois, May 6, 1954; admitted to bar, 1982, Illinois; 1987, U.S. Tax Court; 1995, Oregon. *Education:* Loyola University (B.B.A, 1977); DePaul University (J.D., 1982; M.S.T., 1983). Author, Journal of Taxation of Employee Benefits: Health and Welfare Benefits Law: Constant Refinement Means Practitioner Awareness is Critical," 2000; "IRS Finally Issues New Cobra Regulations," 1999; "Adoption Assistance: The Newest Tax-Favored Employee Benefit," 1998; "Creditable Coverage Certification Rules Under HIPAA Impose Another Administrative Burden for Employers," 1997; "New Cafeteria Plan Regulations Remove Conflicts with FMLA Mandates," 1996; "Employee Benefits Claim Litigation: Staying One Step Ahead of Your Adversary," 1996; "Avoiding the Welfare Benefit Plan Annual Reporting Landmines," 1996; Co-Author, "Welfare Plans Increasingly Require ERISA Expertise," 1993. Author: VEBAs, Cafeteria Plans and Other Fringe Benefit Plans, AICPA Coursebook, 1999; Designing Severance Packages, RIA Group, 1998; *Taxation of Health and Welfare Benefits,* Warren Gorham Lamont, 1994 "Debunking the Myths About Severance Pay," Journal of Compensation and Benefits, 1992; "Revised Age-Discrimination Law Covers Plans for Older Workers," The National Law Journal, 1991. Revenue Agent, Internal Revenue Service, 1977-1981; Member, Editorial Advisory Board, Journal of Taxation of Employee Benefits, 1996-2000. *Member:* Illinois State and American Bar Associations; Oregon State Bar. ***PRACTICE AREAS:*** Employee Benefits Law; ERISA; Pension and Profit Sharing; Flexible Benefits; Health Benefits; Executive Compensation; Retirement Plans. ***Email:*** wally.miller@harrang.com

CHRISTINE CUSICK NESBIT, born Vermillion, South Dakota, September 2, 1966; admitted to bar, 1995, California and U.S. District Court, Eastern District of California; 1996, U.S. District Court, Northern District of California and U.S. Court of Appeals, Ninth Circuit; 1997, Oregon and U.S. District Court, District of Oregon. *Education:* University of California, Santa Cruz (B.A., honors, 1989); University of California, Davis (J.D., 1995). Associate, Diepenbrock, Wulff, Plant & Hannegan LLP, Sacramento, California, 1995-1997. Associate, Anthony M. Kennedy Inn of Court, 1996-1997. Barrister, Roland K. Rodman Inn of Court, 1999 —. *Member:* Lane County and American Bar Associations; National Council of School Attorneys; Oregon State Bar; State Bar of California; Oregon City Attorneys Association; Oregon Council of School Attorneys. ***PRACTICE AREAS:*** Labor and Employment; Employment Litigation; Wage and Hour Law; Employee Discipline; Employment Arbitration; Employment Discrimination; Family and Medical Leave Act; Personnel Policies; Public Sector Employment Law; Nonprofit and Charitable Organizations. ***Email:*** christine.nesbit@harrang.com

ARDEN J. OLSON, born Wilmington, Delaware, June 21, 1952; admitted to bar, 1978, Washington and U.S. District Court, Western District of Washington; 1982, Pennsylvania and U.S. District Court, Eastern District of Pennsylvania; 1983, U.S. Court of Appeals, Third Circuit; 1987, Oregon, U.S. District Court, District of Oregon and U.S. Court of Appeals, Ninth Circuit; 2001, California; 2002, U.S. District Court, Eastern District of Washington. *Education:* Pacific Lutheran University (B.A., summa cum laude, 1974); University of Washington (J.D., 1978). Order of the Coif. Executive Editor, Washington Law Review. Oregon Assistant Attorney General, 1987-1992. General Counsel, Oregon State Accident Insurance Fund Corp, 1989-1992. Select Care Health Plans, 1993-1997. *Member:* Washington State and American Bar Associations; Oregon State Bar (Member, Federal Practice and Procedure Committee, 1993-1996; Ethics Committee, 1999); State Bar of California; American Judicature Society (Member, Executive Committee, 1982-1985, Board of Directors, 1980-1986). ***PRACTICE AREAS:*** Health Law; Insurance; Professional Responsibility; Litigation; Administrative Adjudications. ***Email:*** arden.j.olson@harrang.com

SHARON A. RUDNICK, born North Adams, Massachusetts, October 10, 1956; admitted to bar, 1981, California; 1983, Oregon, U.S. Court of Appeals, Ninth Circuit; 1985, U.S. District Court, District of Oregon; 2002, Washington and U.S. Supreme Court. *Education:* Middlebury College (B.A., magna cum laude, 1978); University of California at Los Angeles (J.D., 1981). Phi Beta Kappa; Order of the Coif. Associate Editor, University of California at Los Angeles Law Review, 1980-1981. Law Clerk, Senior U.S. District Court Judge William G. East, District of Oregon, 1981-1983. Special Assistant Attorney General, State of Oregon, 1989-1994. *Member:* Oregon State Bar; State Bar of California; Washington State and American Bar Associations. ***PRACTICE AREAS:*** Litigation and Appellate Practice; Labor and Employment; Employment Litigation. ***Email:*** sharon.a.rudnick@harrang.com

JENS SCHMIDT, born Hamburg, West Germany, March 15, 1958; admitted to bar, 1984, Oregon; 1987, U.S. Court of Appeals, Ninth Circuit; 1988, U.S. District Court, District of Oregon; 1994, U.S. Supreme Court. *Education:* University of Oregon (B.S., 1981; J.D., 1984). Associate Editor, Oregon Law Review, 1983-1984. Law Clerk to Judge William L. Richardson, Oregon Court of Appeals, 1984-1986. Assistant Attorney General, Oregon Department of Justice Honors Program, 1986-1987. *Member:* Lane County Bar Association; Oregon State Bar. ***REPORTED CASES:*** Knee Deep Cattle Co. v. Bindana Investments Co., 94 F.3d 514, 1996; Hunter v. City of Eugene, 309 or 298, 787 P2d 881, 1990; City of Eugene v. Nalven, 152 or App 720, 955 P2d 263, 1998; Yokum v. Farmers Ins. Co., 117 or App 546, 844 P2d 937, 1993; Bakr v. Elliot, 125 or App 1, 864 P2d 1340, 1993, rev den 318 or 381, 1994. ***PRACTICE AREAS:*** Appellate Practice; Administrative Law; Civil Rights; Commercial Law; Constitutional Law; Environmental Litigation; Governmental Liability; Insurance Defense; Employment Litigation; Police Liability; Litigation. ***Email:*** jens.schmidt@harrang.com

---

KARLA H. ALDERMAN, born Portland, Oregon, September 20, 1956; admitted to bar, 1999, Oregon. *Education:* Oregon State University (B.S., summa cum laude, 1994); Willamette University (J.D., magna cum laude, 1999). Recipient, International Academy of Trial Lawyers Award; West Group Outstanding Scholastic Achievement Award. Member

(This Listing Continued)

HARRANG LONG GARY RUDNICK P.C., Eugene—Continued

and Articles Editor, Willamette Law Review. Author: "Making Sense of Oregon's Equitable Exception to the American Rule of Attorney Fees After Armatta v. Kitzhaber," 35 Willamette Law Review, 407, 1999. *Member:* Lane County and American Bar Associations; Oregon State Bar. ***PRACTICE AREAS:*** Municipal Law; Litigation; Government. ***Email:*** karla.alderman@harrang.com

WENDY J. BAKER, born Butte, Montana, January 22, 1953; admitted to bar, 2002, Oregon. *Education:* University of Washington (B.A., 1975); University of Oregon (J.D., 2002). *Member:* Lane County and American Bar Associations; Oregon State Bar. ***PRACTICE AREAS:*** Labor and Employment. ***Email:*** wendy.baker@harrang.com

KATHRYN P. BROTHERTON, born Springfield, Oregon, October 16, 1972; admitted to bar, 1998, Oregon; 1999, U.S. District Court, District of Oregon; 2000, U.S. Court of Appeals, Ninth Circuit. *Education:* University of Arizona (B.A., magna cum laude, 1993); University of Oregon (J.D., 1997). Order of the Coif. Member, Oregon Law Review, 1995-1997. Law Clerk to Justice Allen T. Compton, Alaska Supreme Court, 1997-1998. Author: "Three Years After Campbell v. Acuff-Rose Music, Inc.: What is Fair Game for Parodists?" Loyola of Los Angeles Entertainment Law Journal, Vol. 18, 1997; "Sabelko v. City of Phoenix: Ninth Circuit Refuses to Burst 'Bubble' Protecting Women Entering Health Care Facilities," Oregon Law Review, Winter 1996. Adjunct Assistant Professor, University of Oregon, College of Education, 2000. Litigation Associate, Law Office of Robert E. Franz, 1998-2000. *Member:* Lane County and American Bar Associations; Oregon State Bar; Lane County Women Lawyers Association; Oregon City Attorneys Association. ***PRACTICE AREAS:*** Municipal Law; Land Use. ***Email:*** kathryn.brotherton@harrang.com

CRAIG J. CAPON, born Huntington, New York, October 5, 1973; admitted to bar, 1998, Oregon. *Education:* University of California, Irvine (B.A., 1995); University of Washington (J.D., 1998). Phi Alpha Delta. Author: "The Threat of Oil Pollution in the Malacca Strait: Arguing for a Broad Interpretation of the United Nations Convention on the Law of the Sea," 7 Pacific Rim Law and Policy Journal, 1998. *Member:* Lane County and American Bar Associations; Oregon State Bar. ***PRACTICE AREAS:*** Civil Rights; Commercial Law; Constitutional Law; Government Liability; Police Liability; Civil Litigation. ***Email:*** craig.j.capon@harrang.com

NICOLE R. COMMISSIONG, born Southampton, England, March 19, 1973; admitted to bar, 2002, Oregon; 2003, U.S. District Court, District of Oregon. *Education:* University of Oregon (B.A., cum laude, 1997); University of Oregon School of Law (J.D., 2001). Phi Beta Kappa. *Member:* Multnomah County and American Bar Associations; Oregon State Bar. ***LANGUAGES:*** French. ***PRACTICE AREAS:*** Litigation. ***Email:*** nicole.commissiong@harrang.com

ANDREA M. DAVIS, born Springfield, Oregon, January 11, 1974; admitted to bar, 1999, Louisiana, U.S. District Court, Eastern, Western and Middle Districts of Louisiana and U.S Court of Appeals, Fifth Circuit; 2000, Oregon and U.S. District Court, District of Oregon; U.S. Court of Appeals, Ninth Circuit. *Education:* Louisiana University (B.A., cum laude, 1995); Louisiana State University (J.D., 1999). Order of the Coif. ***PRACTICE AREAS:*** Insurance Defense; Commercial Litigation; Appellate Practice. ***Email:*** andrea.davis@harrang.com

KIRK A. MOORE, admitted to bar, 2004, Oregon. *Education:* Willamette University (B.S., Business Economics, 1997); University of Oregon School of Law (J.D., 2004). *Member:* Oregon State Bar. ***PRACTICE AREAS:*** Employee Benefits; Insurance; Health Care. ***Email:*** kirk.moore@harrang.com

ROSS M. WILLIAMSON, born Seattle, Washington, March 23, 1973; admitted to bar, 2001, Oregon. *Education:* Western Washington University (B.A., 1995); University of Oregon (J.D., 2001). Order of the Coif. Member, Oregon Law Review. *Member:* Lane County and American Bar Associations; Oregon State Bar. ***PRACTICE AREAS:*** Civil Litigation; Appellate Practice; Municipal Law. ***Email:*** ross.williamson@harrang.com

JUSTIN WIRTH, born 1972; admitted to bar, 2000, Oregon. *Education:* University of Colorado at Boulder (B.A., Philosophy, 1994); University of West Los Angeles, School of Paralegal Studies, 1995; University of Oregon School of Law (J.D., 2000; Certificate of Completion in Environmental and Natural Resources Law; Pro Bono Certificate). *Member:* Oregon State Bar. ***PRACTICE AREAS:*** Government. ***Email:*** justin.wirth@harrang.com

OF COUNSEL

J. DAVID GIBBS, admitted to bar, 1979, Georgia; 1985, District of Columbia; 1990, Maryland; 1992, New Hampshire; 1993, Massachusetts (Not admitted in Oregon). *Education:* University of Richmond (B.A., 1976); Emory University (J.D., 1979). Member: Federation of Defense and Corporate Counsel; Board of Associates of the University of Richmond; Board of Trustees of the Klingberg Family Centers (Vice Chairman); Board of Alacrity Insurance Services, LLC (Vice Chairman and General Counsel). *Member:* American Bar Association. ***PRACTICE AREAS:*** Insurance Law; Complex Commercial Litigation. ***Email:*** david.gibbs@harrang.com

JUDITH A. RECCHIO, born Santa Clara, California, November 21, 1964; admitted to bar, 1992, California; 1994, U.S. District Court, Northern District of California; 2004, Oregon. *Education:* University of California, Davis (B.A., International Relations, 1987); Santa Clara University School of Law (J.D., summa cum laude, 1992). *Member:* State Bar of California; Oregon State Bar. ***PRACTICE AREAS:*** Labor and Employment; Litigation. ***Email:*** judith.recchio@harrang.com

REPRESENTATIVE CLIENTS: SUMCO USA Corporation; SUMCO USA Sales Corporation; SUMCO Oregon Corporation; SUMCO Phoenix Corporation; Philip Morris USA Inc.; Schering-Plough Corporation; Altria Group Inc.; Providence Health Plan; PeaceHealth; Oregon Association of Hospitals and Health Systems; Oregon Health and Science University; Les Schwab Tire Centers, Inc.; Monterey Mushrooms, Inc.; Amycel, Inc.; Spawn Mate, Inc.; Amfac, Inc.; Northbrook Corporation; Crimson Trace Corporation; Ecotrust; Professional Liability Fund of the Oregon State Bar; Jefferson Behavorial Health; University of Oregon Bookstore; The Register-Guard; Cities of Eugene, Portland, Roseburg and Florence; Counties of Lincoln, Lane and Washington; Tualatin Valley Water District; Coquille Indian Gaming Commission; Eugene Water & Electric Board; Lane County Fair Board; Abby's Inc.; Harvest House Publishers; Lane Regional Air Pollution Authority; Lane Council of Governments; Tom Rogers Distributor, Inc.; City County Insurance Services; Oregon Freeze Dry, Inc.; Whittier Wood Products Co.; League of Oregon Cities; Oregon Self-Insurers Association.

(For Complete Biographical Data on all Atorneys see Professional Biographies at Portland and Salem Oregon Offices)

(This Listing Continued)

HERSHNER HUNTER, LLP

Established in 1944

180 EAST 11TH AVENUE
P.O. BOX 1475
EUGENE, OREGON 97440
Telephone: 541-686-8511
Fax: 541-344-2025
Email: info@hershnerhunter.com
URL: http://www.hershnerhunter.com

Florence, Oregon Office: 1441 7th Street. Telephone: 541-997-1997. Fax: 541-344-2025.

Business, Banking, Corporate, Timber, Estate Planning, Probate Trust Administration, Taxation, Creditors' Rights, Bankruptcy, Construction, Real Property, Land Use, Employee Benefits, Health Care, Employment and Litigation.

FIRM PROFILE: Hershner Hunter, LLP celebrates over 60 years of providing outstanding client service and sound legal counsel. We represent businesses and individuals in planning, compliance, transactional, commercial and litigation matters. A hallmark of the firm is a strong emphasis on specialization. We believe that limiting and focusing each attorney's practice areas allows us to provide superior legal services. The firm has active practices in Oregon, Washington, Alaska and other states.

MEMBERS OF FIRM

DAVID N. ANDREWS, born St. Francis, Kansas, August 27, 1930; admitted to bar, 1959, Oregon. *Education:* University of Oregon (B.S., 1957; J.D., 1959). Member, Sections on: Estate Planning and Administration; Taxation; Business Law (Chairman, 1979-1980), Oregon State Bar. Fellow: American College of Trust and Estate Counsel; American Bar Foundation. ***PRACTICE AREAS:*** Estate Planning; Probate; Federal Estate and Gift Taxation. ***Email:*** dandrews@hershnerhunter.com

WILLIAM D. BREWER, born Washington, D.C., June 28, 1947; admitted to bar, 1985, Oregon. *Education:* Cornell University; Willamette University (B.A., 1971); Northwestern School of Law of Lewis and Clark College (J.D., magna cum laude, 1985). *Member:* Oregon State Bar(Member, Executive Committee, Estate Planning and Administration Sections). Fellow, American College of Trust and Estate Counsel. ***PRACTICE AREAS:*** Estate Planning; Business Planning; Probate; Trust Administration; Estate and Gift Taxation; Trusts and Estates; Charitable Giving. ***Email:*** wbrewer@hershnerhunter.com

NANCY K. CARY, born Toledo, Oregon, September 29, 1962; admitted to bar, 1990, Oregon; 2002, Washington. *Education:* Willamette University (B.A., 1987; J.D., 1990). *Member:* Oregon State Bar (Member, Executive Committee, Construction Law Section); National Association of Women in Construction; Construction Financial Management Association. ***PRACTICE AREAS:*** Construction Law; Creditors' Rights; Bankruptcy. ***Email:*** ncary@hershnerhunter.com

PATRICIA L. CHAPMAN, born California, January 16, 1956; admitted to bar, 1983, California and U.S. District Court, Northern District of California; 1988, Oregon. *Education:* University of California at Berkeley (B.A., summa cum laude, 1979); University of San Francisco (J.D., 1982). Phi Beta Kappa. Member, University of San Francisco Law Review, 1981-1982. *Member:* Lane County and American Bar Associations; State Bar of California; Oregon State Bar (Executive Committee - Business Law Section; Treasurer, Real Estate and Land Use Section). ***PRACTICE AREAS:*** Business Law; Commercial Law; Contracts; Corporate Law; Nonprofit and Charitable Organizations; Finance; Mergers, Acquisitions and Divestitures; Real Estate. ***Email:*** pchapman@hershnerhunter.com

ARTHUR J. CLARK, born Eugene, Oregon, July 21, 1950; admitted to bar, 1976, Oregon. *Education:* University of Oregon (B.A., 1973; J.D., 1976). Phi Beta Kappa; Order of the Coif. ***PRACTICE AREAS:*** Business Planning; Estate Planning; Probate; Trust Administration. ***Email:*** aclark@hershnerhunter.com

WILL FORSYTH, born Seattle, Washington, December 19, 1970; admitted to bar, 1999, Oregon. *Education:* University of Notre Dame (B.A., 1993); University of Oregon (J.D., 1999). Order of the Coif. ***PRACTICE AREAS:*** Business Transactions; Corporate Law; Real Estate; Telecommunications Law. ***Email:*** wforsyth@hershnerhunter.com

JEFFREY D. KIRTNER, born Chicago, Illinois, March 19, 1959; admitted to bar, 1996, Oregon. *Education:* University of Chicago (B.A., 1981); University of Texas at Austin (J.D., 1995). Order of the Coif. ***PRACTICE AREAS:*** Employee Benefits; Corporate Law; Health Care Law. ***Email:*** jkirtner@hershnerhunter.com

ANDREW G. LEWIS, born Milwaukee, Wisconsin, October 13, 1963; admitted to bar, 1990, Oregon; 2002, Washington; U.S. District Court, District of Oregon; U.S. District Court, Western District of Washington; U.S. Court of Appeals, Ninth Circuit. *Education:* University of California, Davis (B.S., 1986); University of Oregon (J.D., 1990). ***PRACTICE AREAS:*** Labor and Employment; Employment Litigation. ***Email:*** alewis@hershnerhunter.com

SHERYL S. McCONNELL, born Indianapolis, Indiana, November 29, 1960; admitted to bar, 1995, Oregon. *Education:* Oregon State University (B.S., with honors, 1983); University of California at Los Angeles (J.D., 1995). ***PRACTICE AREAS:*** Estate Planning; Business Planning; Federal Estate and Gift Taxation Law; Charitable Giving. ***Email:*** smcconnell@hershnerhunter.com

EVERETT R. MORELAND, born Portland, Oregon, July 21, 1946; admitted to bar, 1976, Oregon. *Education:* Portland State University (B.S., with honors, 1973); Willamette University (J.D., cum laude, 1976); University of Florida (LL.M., Taxation, 1978). Form Editor, Willamette Law Journal, 1975-1976. ***PRACTICE AREAS:*** Employee Benefits Law; ERISA; Pensions. ***Email:*** emoreland@hershnerhunter.com

(This Listing Continued)

K. PATRICK NEILL, born Salem, Oregon, May 25, 1946; admitted to bar, 1971, Oregon. *Education:* Hiram College (B.A., summa cum laude, 1968); University of Southern California (J.D., 1971). Order of the Coif. ***PRACTICE AREAS:*** Commercial and Business Litigation. ***Email:*** kneill@hershnerhunter.com

ROBERT S. QUINNEY, born Inglewood, California, November 12, 1943; admitted to bar, 1971, Oregon. *Education:* Brigham Young University (B.S., 1965); University of California at Berkeley (M.B.A., 1968); University of Oregon (J.D., 1971). Certified Public Accountant, Oregon, 1968. *Member:* Association of Attorneys Certified Public Accountants. ***PRACTICE AREAS:*** Corporate Law; Estate Planning; Business Planning; Probate; Trust Administration; Tax Disputes. ***Email:*** rquinney@hershnerhunter.com

CRAIG A. SMITH, born Waterloo, Iowa, March 9, 1945; admitted to bar, 1973, Oregon. *Education:* University of Minnesota (B.S., with distinction, 1967); University of Michigan (J.D., cum laude, 1972). ***PRACTICE AREAS:*** Corporate Law; Employee Benefits Law; Health Care Law. ***Email:*** csmith@hershnerhunter.com

WM. RANDOLPH TURNBOW, born Eugene, Oregon, July 27, 1952; admitted to bar, 1980, Oregon; 1989, Alaska; 1990, Washington, U.S. District Court, District of Oregon, U.S. District Court, District of Alaska, U.S. District Court, Eastern and Western Districts of Washington, U.S. Court of Appeals, Ninth and Tenth Circuits and U.S. Court of Federal Claims. *Education:* Stanford University (B.A., 1974); University of Oregon (J.D., 1980). Order of the Coif. Member, Sections on: Litigation and Construction, Oregon State Bar. Member, Sections on: Litigation and Construction, Washington State Bar. *Member:* Alaska and Washington State Bar Associations; Oregon Trial Lawyers Association. ***PRACTICE AREAS:*** Commercial and Business Litigation; Construction Law. ***Email:*** rturnbow@hershnerhunter.com

PAUL V. VAUGHAN, born Denver, Colorado, September 4, 1955; admitted to bar, 1980, Oregon. *Education:* University of Colorado (B.A., 1977); University of Oregon (J.D., 1980). Phi Beta Kappa; Order of the Coif. ***PRACTICE AREAS:*** Transactions; Real Estate; Zoning, Planning and Land Use. ***Email:*** pvaughan@hershnerhunter.com

OF COUNSEL

MARLIN D. ARD, born St. Anthony, Idaho, August 29, 1948; admitted to bar, 1976, California; 1993, Oregon. *Education:* Pacific University (B.S., 1973); University of Oregon (J.D., 1976). Order of the Coif. House Counsel to Pacific Teleis. *Member:* State Bar of California. ***PRACTICE AREAS:*** Telecommunications Law; Antitrust; Business Transactions. ***Email:*** maratty@qwest.net

P. STEVE CORNACCHIA, born Eugene, Oregon, April 11, 1950; admitted to bar, 1980, Oregon. *Education:* University of Oregon (B.S., 1976; J.D., 1980). Lane County Commissioner, 1986-1999. President, Association of Oregon Counties, 1996-1997. [U.S. Army, Special Forces, 1968-1972]. ***PRACTICE AREAS:*** Real Estate; Land Use; Government. ***Email:*** scornacchia@hershnerhunter.com

JUDITH A. GIERS, born Chicago, Illinois, 1960; admitted to bar, 1991, Oregon; 1992, U.S. Court of Appeals, Ninth Circuit. *Education:* University of Colorado at Boulder (B.A., cum laude, 1982); Suffolk University Law School (J.D., cum laude, 1990). Instructor, University of Oregon School of Law, 2000-2004. Board Member, Lane County Legal Aid. Board Member, Oak Hill School. Member, Executive Committee for Constitutional Law. Member, Executive Committee, Appellate Section, 1995-1997. *Member:* Oregon State Bar; American Bar Association; American Inns of Court. ***PRACTICE AREAS:*** Appellate Practice; Litigation; Public Law. ***Email:*** jgiers@hershnerhunter.com

JANICE C. GOLDBERG, born Roswell, New Mexico, December 2, 1944; admitted to bar, 1982, Oregon. *Education:* University of Oregon (B.A., 1976; J.D., 1981). Order of the Coif. ***PRACTICE AREAS:*** Employment Law. ***Email:*** jgoldberg@hershnerhunter.com

LINDA J. KESSEL, born Oregon City, Oregon, February 18, 1951; admitted to bar, 1990, Oregon; 1994, U.S. District Court, District of Oregon and U.S. Court of Appeals, Ninth Circuit. *Education:* University of Oregon (B.S., with honors, 1987; J.D., 1990). Order of the Coif. Recipient, American Jurisprudence Awards in: Commercial Law; Trusts and Estates II; Conflict of Laws. Judicial Law Clerk to the Hon. William Riggs, Oregon Court of Appeals, 1990-1992. Adjunct Professor, Judicial Externship Program, 2003-2004 and Assistant Instructor, Legal Research and Writing Program, 1990, University of Oregon School of Law. Senior Assistant Attorney General, Labor and Employment Section, General Counsel, Department of Justice, State of Oregon, 2003-2005. *Member:* Lane County and American Bar Associations; Oregon State Bar; Lane County Women Lawyer's Association. ***PRACTICE AREAS:*** Labor and Employment.

NORMAN J. LeCOMPTE, JR., born San Francisco, California, December 8, 1950; admitted to bar, 1976, Oregon. *Education:* University of Washington (B.A., 1973); University of Oregon (J.D., 1976). ***PRACTICE AREAS:*** Banks and Banking; Business Law; Commercial Law; Commercial Real Estate; Finance; Mergers, Acquisitions and Divestitures. ***Email:*** nlecompte@hershnerhunter.com

PATRICK W. WADE, born Santa Monica, California, May 30, 1944; admitted to bar, 1984, Oregon. *Education:* University of California at Riverside (A.B., 1971); University of Oregon at Eugene (J.D., 1984). Phi Delta Phi. ***Email:*** pwade@hershnerhunter.com

ASSOCIATES

TODD R. JOHNSTON, born Portland, Oregon, January 18, 1974; admitted to bar, 1999, Oregon. *Education:* The Colorado College (B.A., 1995); University of Oregon School of Law (J.D., 1999). Author: "The Role of International Equity in a Sustainable Future, The Continuing Problem of Third World Debt and Development," 6 Buff. Envir.L.J. 1, 35 (1998). ***PRACTICE AREAS:*** Litigation. ***Email:*** tjohnston@hershnerhunter.com

SYLVIA M. VAN DYKE, born Everett, Washington, December 2, 1978; admitted to bar, 2003, Oregon. *Education:* College of the Redwoods (A.A., 1997); Seattle University (B.A., summa cum laude, 1999); University of Oregon (J.D., 2003). Phi Theta Kappa; Phi Alpha Delta. Order of the Coif. ***PRACTICE AREAS:*** Employment Law; Employment Litigation. ***Email:*** svandyke@hershnerhunter.com

GABRIELA SANCHEZ-AMPARAN, born El Paso, Texas, April 13, 1974; admitted to bar, 2003, Oregon. *Education:* University of Texas at El Paso (B.S., 1998); University of Oregon School of Law (J.D., 2003). *Member:* Lane County Women Lawyers (Member: Steering Committee; Debtor/Creditor Section). ***LANGUAGES:*** Spanish. ***PRACTICE AREAS:*** Bankruptcy; Creditors Rights. ***Email:*** gsanchez@hershnerhunter.com

NATHAN S. SNOW, born Salem, Oregon, March 9, 1977; admitted to bar, 2004, Oregon. *Education:* Willamette University (B.A., 2000); University of Oregon (J.D., 2004; M.B.A., 2004). ***PRACTICE AREAS:*** Business Law. ***Email:*** nsnow@hershnerhunter.com

VICKI L. REES, born Springfield, Missouri, March 6, 1966; admitted to bar, 2004, Oregon. *Education:* University of Memphis (M.S., 1989); University of Oregon (J.D., 2004). Recipient, Outstanding Student in Criminal Justice. *Member:* Oregon Women Lawyers. ***PRACTICE AREAS:*** Employee Benefits Law; ERISA; Pension Plans; Health Care Law; Business Law.

MELISSA F. BUSLEY, born Longview, Washington, February 27, 1979; admitted to bar, 2004, Oregon. *Education:* Washington State University (B.A., magna cum laude, 2000); University of Oregon (J.D., 2003); University of Washington (LL.M., 2004). Phi Kappa Phi; Pi Sigma Alpha. Golden Key. Recipient, Outstanding Graduating Senior in the College of Liberal Arts; Outstanding Sophomore in Political Science, Washington State University. ***PRACTICE AREAS:*** Employee Benefits; Estate Planning; Taxation; Trusts and Estates. ***Email:*** mbusley@hershnerhunter.com

KATHERINE C. FISHER, born New York, N.Y., 1973; admitted to bar, 2005, Oregon. *Education:* University of Montana (B.A., 1996); University of Oregon (J.D., 2005). Member, Oregon Law Review, 2003-2005. *Member:* Lane County Bar Association; Oregon State Bar. ***PRACTICE AREAS:*** Litigation.

All Partners and Associates are members of the Lane County Bar Association and the Oregon State Bar.

REPRESENTATIVE CLIENTS: AMC Mortgage Services, Inc.; Bank of America; Belfor USA Group, Inc.; The Jerry Brown Co., Inc.; Bulk Handling Systems, Inc.; Clarke Sheer Metal, Inc.; Country Coach Inc.; Delta Sand & Gravel co.; Farwest Steel Corporation; Flanagan Farms, Inc.; Forrest Paint Co.; Guard Publishing Company; Heceta Water District; John Hyland Construction, Inc.; Hynix Semiconductor Manufacturing America, Inc.; J. L. Jones & Associates, Inc.; Junction City Water Control District; Linn County Federal Credit Union; Marshall's Oil; Marty's River Lumber Co.; Miles Oil Company, Inc.; North Coast Electric Co.; Northwest Anesthesia Physicians, P.C.; Oregon Community Credit Union; Oregon Industrial Lumber Products, Inc.; Oregon Medical Group, P.C.; Oregon Pacific Banking Co., Pak Tech; pathology Consultants, P.C.; R & R King Logging, Inc.; Radiology Associates, P.C.; Random Lengths Production, Inc.; Realvest Corporation; Ridgeline Management Company; Sruslaw Valley Bank; Sterling Savings Bank; Sunbelt Rentals, Inc.; Terrain Tamers Land Development Company; Total Communications Co.; Twin Rivers Plumbing, Inc.; U.S. Bank National Association; Umpqua Bank; The Wildish Group of Companies; Washington Federal Savings; Western Coating, Inc.; World Savings Bank.

HUTCHINSON, COX, COONS, DuPRIEST, ORR & SHERLOCK, P.C.

Established in 1970

200 FORUM BUILDING
777 HIGH STREET
EUGENE, OREGON 97401-2782
Telephone: 541-686-9160
Fax: 541-343-8693
Email: info@eugene-law.com
URL: http://www.eugene-law.com

General Practice in all Courts. Business Law, Contracts, Corporate Law, Environmental Law, Land Use, Real Estate, International Business, Civil Litigation, Personal Injury, Probate, Estate Planning, Copyright and Trademark, Family Law, Arbitration and Mediation, Tax Law, Creditors Rights.

JAMES K. COONS, born St. Louis, Missouri, October 27, 1949; admitted to bar, 1976, Oregon; 1981, U.S. District Court, District of Oregon. *Education:* Harvard University (A.B., cum laude, 1972); University of Oregon (J.D., 1976). Member, Order of the Coif. Law Clerk to the Hon. F. Gordon Cottrell, Lane County Circuit Court, 1976-1977. *Member:* Oregon State Bar (Member, Sections on: Business and Corporate Law; Estate Planning and Administration; Intellectual Property Law). ***PRACTICE AREAS:*** Business Law; Corporate Law; Business Transactions; Probate; Estate Planning; Trademarks; Copyrights. ***Email:*** jcoons@eugene-law.com

JOHN G. COX, admitted to bar, 1969, Oregon; 1972, U.S. District Court, District of Oregon. *Education:* University of Oregon (B.A., 1964); Willamette University (J.D., summa cum laude, 1969). President, Eugene Chapter Estate Planning Council, 1984-1985. *Member:* Oregon State Bar (Member, Sections on: Business Law; Computer Law; Estate Planning and Administration; International Law; Elder Law); Rotary Club of Eugene (President, 2002-2003). [U.S. Army, Active and Reserves, 1964-1994; Col., (Retired), JAGC]. ***PRACTICE AREAS:*** Taxation; Business Law; Copyright and Trademark Law; Estate Planning Law; Probate Law; International Business; Elder Law. ***Email:*** johngcox@eugene-law.com

DOUGLAS M. DuPRIEST, admitted to bar, 1977, Oregon, U.S. District Court, District of Oregon. *Education:* Oberlin College (A.B., with high honors in Philosophy, 1974); University of Oregon (J.D., 1977). Recipient: Distinguished Service Award, Oregon Environmental Council, 1988. Articles Editor, Oregon Law Review, 1976-1977. Co-Author: Chapters in Continuing Legal Education: "Land Use," 1982 and 2000; "Administrative Law," 1985. Adjunct Assistant Professor, Real Estate Transactions, University of Oregon School of Law, 1986. ***PRACTICE AREAS:*** Real Estate; Land Use; Natural Resource; Foreclosures; Probate. ***Email:*** dupriest@eugene-law.com

FRANK C. GIBSON, born Greenville, Michigan, March 3, 1950; admitted to bar, 1979, Oregon. *Education:* University of California, Irvine (B.A., 1976); University of Oregon School of Law (J.D., 1979). Member, Managing Board, Oregon Law Review, 1978-1979. *Member:* Lane County Bar Association (President, 1989-1990); Oregon State Bar (Chair, Procedure and Practice Committee, 1985-1986; Member, Uniform Civil Jury In-

(This Listing Continued)

HUTCHINSON, COX, COONS, DuPRIEST, ORR & SHERLOCK, P.C., Eugene—Continued

structions Committee, 1986-1989; Member, Federal Procedure and Practice Committee, 1989-1992). ***PRACTICE AREAS:*** Civil Practice; Trial Practice; Business Law; Corporate Law; Real Estate; Family Law; Mediation. ***Email:*** fgibson@eugene-law.com

STEPHEN A. HUTCHINSON, admitted to bar, 1967, Oregon; 1968, U.S. District Court, District of Oregon; 1988, U.S. Court of Appeals, 9th Circuit. *Education:* Oregon State University (B.A.; B.S., 1963); University of Pavia, Italy; University of Oregon (J.D., 1967). Recipient, Outstanding Citizen Award, Lane County, 1986. Author: Speaker, "Effective Trial Advocacy," 1987, "Civil Litigation," 1990. Adjunct Professor of Law, Trial Practice, University of Oregon. President, Marist High School Board, 1992-1993. Rotary President, 2003-2004. Deputy District Attorney, Lane County, 1967-1970. *Member:* Oregon State Bar; Oregon Trial Lawyers Association. ***PRACTICE AREAS:*** Litigation; Personal Injury; Business Law; International Business Law; Probate; Real Estate. ***Email:*** shutchinson@eugene-law.com

THOMAS MICHAEL ORR, born Oswego, New York, June 23, 1955; admitted to bar, 1988, Oregon; 1989, U.S. District Court, District of Oregon; 1992, U.S. Court of Appeals, Ninth Circuit. *Education:* University of Alabama (B.A., 1977; J.D., 1981). President, Lane County Legal Aid, 1997-2001. Board of Directors, Lane County Legal Aid, 1995-2001. Pro-Tem Judge, State of Oregon, 1995—. *Member:* Lane County Bar Association (Member: Board of Directors, 1996-1999, President, 2000-2001); Oregon MCLE Board, 1996—; Chair, MCLE Board, 1998-1999; Oregon State Bar. ***PRACTICE AREAS:*** Civil Litigation; Bankruptcy; Business Law; Real Estate; Family Law; Creditors' Rights; Probate. ***Email:*** torr@eugene-law.com

WILLIAM H. SHERLOCK, born Mt. View, California, March 16, 1962; admitted to bar, 1990, Oregon. *Education:* University of California at Santa Cruz (B.A., 1986); University of Oregon (J.D., 1990). Executive Editor, Journal of Environmental Law and Litigation, 1988-1990. *Member:* Lane County Bar Association (Member, Environmental and Land Use Section, 1998—); Oregon State Bar (Member, Executive Committee, Environmental and Natural Resources Section, 1998—; Member, Sections on: Real Estate; Land Use; Alternative Dispute Resolution). ***LANGUAGES:*** Spanish. ***PRACTICE AREAS:*** Natural Resources; Land Use Law; Administrative Law; Civil Litigation; Business Law; Mediation. ***Email:*** lsherlock@eugene-law.com

---

E. BRADLEY LITCHFIELD, born Taber, Alberta, Canada, October 12, 1965; admitted to bar, 1993, British Columbia; 1999, Oregon and U.S. District Court, District of Oregon. *Education:* Brigham Young University (B.A., 1989); University of British Columbia (LL.B., 1993); J. Reuben Clark School of Law, Brigham Young University (LL.M., cum laude, 1999). Managing Editor, University of British Columbia Law Review, 1993. *Member:* Lane County, Oregon State, American and Canadian Bar Associations; Law Society of British Columbia. ***LANGUAGES:*** English and Spanish. ***PRACTICE AREAS:*** Civil Litigation; Commercial Leasing; Creditors Rights. ***Email:*** brad.litchfield@eugene-law.com

ZACK P. MITTGE, born Centralia, Washington, January 23, 1976; admitted to bar, 2004, Oregon. *Education:* University of Washington (B.A., 1998); University of Oregon (J.D., 2004). McNair Scholar. Member, O.R. Bankruptcy Moot Court Team. ***PRACTICE AREAS:*** Land Use (75%); Civil Litigation (15%); Administrative Law (5%); Estate Planning (5%). ***Email:*** zmittge@eugene-law.com

PATRICK L. STEVENS, born Houston, Texas, April 12, 1971; admitted to bar, 1998, Oregon and U.S. District Court, District of Oregon. *Education:* Texas A & M University (B.B.A., magna cum laude, 1994); University of Oregon School of Law (J.D., 1997). *Member:* Lane County Bar; Lane County Bankruptcy Association; Oregon Trial Lawyers Association. ***PRACTICE AREAS:*** Civil Litigation; Construction Law; Bankruptcy; Creditors Rights. ***Email:*** pstevens@eugene-law.com

All Attorneys are Members of the Lane County Bar Association and Oregon State Bar.

A list of Representative Clients is available upon request.

JAQUA & WHEATLEY, LLC

Established in 1962

825 EAST PARK

EUGENE, OREGON 97401-2909

Telephone: 541-686-8485

Fax: 541-343-0701

Email: bwheatley@jaquawheatly.com

URL: http://www.jaquawheatley.com

Portland, Oregon

General Practice in all Courts. Insurance Defense, Casualty and Surety Insurance Law. Litigation, Corporate Law, Partnerships, Business Litigation, Products Liability, Construction Law, Environmental Law, Professional Malpractice, Premises Liability, Estate Planning, Employment Law.

FIRM PROFILE: Established in 1962, the firm has built a reputation for statewide leadership. Jaqua & Wheatley's attorneys serve a wide range of litigants in corporate and business disputes. Our attorneys also serve clients requiring assistance with transactional, estate planning, and employment law related issues. The firm's lawyers have a long tradition of service to the Oregon State Bar and other professional organizations.

JOHN E. JAQUA (Inactive)

WILLIAM G. WHEATLEY, born Oakland, California, October 8, 1933; admitted to bar, 1959, Oregon; U.S. District Court, District of Oregon; U.S. Supreme Court; U.S. Claims Court. *Education:* Portland State College and University of Oregon (B.A., 1956); University of Oregon (J.D., 1959). Member, Board of Governors, 1991-1994, Board of Bar Examiners, 1967-1970. *Member:* Oregon State Bar (President, 1993-1994); International Association of Insurance Counsel; Federation of Insurance and Corporate Counsel; Oregon Association of Defense Counsel. Fellow, American College of Trial Lawyers. ***PRACTICE AREAS:*** Business Litigation; Insurance Defense Law; Products Liability Law. ***Email:*** bwheatley@jaquawheatley.com

---

HOLLI FROEMMING, born Eugene, Oregon; admitted to bar, 2005, Oregon and Michigan. *Education:* Austin Peay State University (B.A., magna cum laude, 2002); University of Michigan Law School (J.D., 2004). ***LANGUAGES:*** Spanish. ***PRACTICE AREAS:*** Civil Litigation; Legal Malpractice; Professional Malpractice; Insurance Defense. ***Email:*** hfroemming@jaquawheatley.com

ELIZABETH WATSON, admitted to bar, 1994, Hawaii; 2001, District of Columbia; 2002, Washington; 2005, Oregon, U.S. District Court, District of Oregon. *Education:* Western Washington University (B.A. 1990); University of Oregon School of Law (J.D., 1993). [Lieutenant Commander, U.S. Coast Guard, U.S. Coast Guard Reserve, 1995—]

PATRICK A. LYND, born Fresno, California, April 27, 1961; admitted to bar, 1998, Oregon; 2000, Washington, U.S. District Court, District of Oregon, U.S. Court of Appeals, Ninth Circuit and U.S. Court of Federal Claims. *Education:* University of Oregon (B.A., Journalism, 1995; J.D., 1998). Staff Member, 1996-1997, Associate Editor, 1997-1998, Oregon Law Review. Author: "Recent Developments Regarding Mandatory Arbitration of Statutory Employment Disputes," 77 Or. L. Rev. 287, 1998. *Member:* Lane County Bar Association (Member, Board of Directors, 2003-2006; Chairman, Program Committee, 2002-2003); American Bar Association; Oregon Association of Defense Counsel. ***PRACTICE AREAS:*** Insurance Defense; Business Litigation; Construction Law. ***Email:*** plynd@jaquawheatley.com

REPRESENTATIVE INSURANCE CLIENTS: 21st Century Insurance; American Family Insurance Group; Acceptance Insurance Co.; Affinity Insurance Services, Inc.; AIG Specialty Auto; American Family Insurance Group; ANPAC General Insurance Co.; BMW Financial Services; Cincinnati Insurance Companies; Crusader Insurance; CUNA Mutual Insurance Group; Canal Insurance Co.; Colonial Insurance Company of California; Continental Insurance Health Care; Crawford & Co.; Empire Fire & Marine; Employer's Reinsurance; Federated Insurance; Foremost Insurance Co.; GEICO; Houston General Ins. Co.; Industrial Indemnity Co.; Jefferson Insurance Group; Kemper Group; League General Insurance Co.; Maryland Casualty Co.; North Pacific Insurance Co.; Professional Liability Fund; Safeco Insurance Companies; Scottsdale Insurance Co.; State Farm Mutual Insurance Companies; United States Fidelity & Guaranty Co.; Zurich-American Insurance.
REPRESENTATIVE CORPORATE CLIENTS: American International Companies; Bucyrus-Erie Co.; Eli Lilly & Co.; Ford Motor Co.; General Motors Group; Hyundai Motors America; International Paper Co.; Mack Trucks, Inc.; Michelin Tire Corp.; Mutual of Omaha; OUM & Associates.

JOHNSON CLIFTON LARSON & SCHALLER, P.C.

10TH FLOOR, CITIZENS BUILDING

975 OAK STREET

EUGENE, OREGON 97401-3124

Telephone: 541-484-2434

Fax: 541-484-0882

Email: jclc@jclc.com

URL: http://www.jclc.com

Civil Litigation Practice in Personal Injury, Product Liability, Environmental Law, Employment Law, Civil Rights, Medical Malpractice, Taxation, Appellate, Real Estate, Trusts and Estates, Wills and Probate, Business Law.

ARTHUR C. JOHNSON, born Akron, Ohio, February 26, 1928; admitted to bar, 1953, Oregon; U.S. Supreme Court; U.S. Court of Appeals, Ninth and Fourth Circuits. *Education:* University of Oregon (B.S., 1950); Harvard Law School (LL.B., 1953). Recipient: Oregon Trial Lawyers Association Distinguished Trial Lawyer, 1990, University of Oregon School of Law Meritorious Service Award, 1994; TLPJ Public Justice Award, 1991. Listed in Best Lawyers in America, 1991. Co-Editor: Oregon Law of Torts, 1981 and Revised Editions, 1987, 1993, 1996, 2000; Insurance Practice in Oregon, Part III, 1969; Damages, 1965. Member, Oregon Land Conservation and Development Commission, 1991-1994; Governor's Willamette Greenway Commission, Chairman, 1975-1978. *Member:* Lane County (President, 1971-1972) and American (Member, House of Delegates, 1982-1987) Bar Associations; Oregon State Bar (Member, Board of Governors, 1979-1982; President, 1981-1982; Chairman, Procedure and Practice Committee, 1970; Chairman, Uniform Jury Instruction Committee, 1975; Director, Professional Liability Fund, 1977-1979; 1982-1985); American Judicature Society (Member, Board of Directors, 1983-1985); The Association of Trial Lawyers of America (Oregon Governor, 1989-1996); Oregon Trial Lawyers Association (President, 1988-1989); American Board of Trial Advocates (Oregon Chapter President, 1978). Fellow: American Bar Foundation; American College of Trial Lawyers; Lawyers Representation, Ninth Circuit Judicial Conference, 1986-1989; American Inns of Court. ***PRACTICE AREAS:*** Personal Injury; Products Liability; Medical Malpractice; Industrial Accidents; Construction Accidents; Aircraft Litigation.

JACOB K. CLIFTON, JR., born Auburn, Washington, August 2, 1945; admitted to bar, 1974, Oregon. *Education:* Portland State University (B.A., 1967); University of Oregon (J.D., 1974); New York University (LL.M., in Taxation, 1975). Adjunct Instructor in Accounting, University of Oregon College of Business Administration, 1976-1978, 1989-1990. Adjunct Professor: Estate and Gift Taxation, 1990, University of Oregon School of Law. *Member:* Lane County Bar Associations; Oregon State Bar. ***PRACTICE AREAS:*** Estate Planning; Taxation.

RICHARD L. LARSON, born Eugene, Oregon, November 16, 1951; admitted to bar, 1977, Oregon and U.S. District Court for the District of Oregon. *Education:* Stanford University (B.A., 1974); University of Oregon (J.D., 1977); New York University (LL.M., in Taxation, 1980). Adjunct Professor: Partnership and Corporate Taxation, 1982; Business Planning, 1986; Estate and Gift Taxation, 1986-1987, 1990-1991, University of Oregon School of Law. *Member:* Lane County and American (Taxation Section) Bar Associations; Oregon State Bar. ***PRACTICE AREAS:*** Estate Planning; Probate; Real Estate; Business Law.

(This Listing Continued)

DOUGLAS G. SCHALLER, born Sacramento, California, March 29, 1952; admitted to bar, 1985, Oregon; 1989, U.S. District Court, District of Oregon; 1990, U.S. Court of Appeals, Ninth Circuit. *Education:* University of California at Davis (B.A., 1974); University of Oregon (J.D., 1985). Order of the Coif. Law Clerk to: Hon. John H. Buttler, Oregon Court of Appeals, 1985-1986; Hon. Kurt C. Rossman, Oregon Court of Appeals, 1986-1987. *Member:* Oregon State Bar; Oregon Trial Lawyers Association; The Association of Trial Lawyers of America; American Inns of Court. ***PRACTICE AREAS:*** Personal Injury; Products Liability; Medical Malpractice; Wrongful Death; Truck Liability; Appellate Law.

DEREK C. JOHNSON, born Eugene, Oregon, February 26, 1959; admitted to bar, 1985, California; 1986, Washington; 1988, Oregon; 1989, U.S. District Court, District of Oregon; 1990, U.S. District Court, Northern District of California; 1993, U.S. Court of Appeals, Ninth Circuit; 1995, U.S. District Court, Eastern District of California. *Education:* Williams College (B.A., cum laude, 1981); Universite de Poitiers (B.A., 1982); University of California at Los Angeles (J.D., 1985); University of Washington (LL.M., 1987). Member, Oregon Governmental Ethics Commission (Commissioner, 1989-1993; Chair, 1992-1993). Board of Directors, The Child Center, 1994—. Member, Oregon State Bar Disciplinary Board (1995-2000; Chair, 2000-2001). *Member:* Oregon State Bar; State Bar of California; Washington State Bar Association; Oregon Trial Lawyers Association (Member, Board of Governors, 2000—); The Association of Trial Lawyers of America; American Inns of Court. ***LANGUAGES:*** French. ***PRACTICE AREAS:*** Personal Injury; Products Liability; Medical Malpractice; Motor Vehicle Accidents and Injuries; Bicycle Accidents; Environmental Law; Wrongful Death; Electrical Injury.

DENNIS M. GERL, born Torrance, California, July 21, 1954; admitted to bar, 1985, Oregon; 1986, California; 1988, U.S. District Court, Central District of California and U.S. District Court, District of Oregon. *Education:* University of California at Santa Barbara (B.A., 1975); University of Oregon (J.D., 1985). Order of the Coif. Recipient: American Jurisprudence Award in Administrative Law; Colyer Scholarship. Law Clerk to the Honorable Douglas Spencer, Oregon Circuit Court, 1985-1986. *Member:* Lane County Bar Association; Oregon State Bar; State Bar of California; Oregon Trial Lawyers Association; The Association of Trial Lawyers of America. ***PRACTICE AREAS:*** Personal Injury; Products Liability; Medical Malpractice; Wrongful Death; Industrial Accidents.

SCOTT C. LUCAS, born Livorno, Italy, May 11, 1965; admitted to bar, 1997, Oregon; 1998, U.S. District Court, District of Oregon. *Education:* University of California at San Diego (B.A., 1988); University of Oregon (J.D., 1996). Author: "The Meaning of Harm Under the Endangered Species Act," Journal of Environmental Law & Litigation, 1995. *Member:* Lane County Bar Association; Association of Trial Lawyers of America; Oregon Trial Lawyers Association. ***PRACTICE AREAS:*** Personal Injury; Products Liability; Motor Vehicle Accidents and Injuries; Medical Malpractice.

MARILYN HEIKEN, born Detroit, Michigan, June 26, 1961; admitted to bar, 1992, Oregon; 1998, U.S. District Court, District of Oregon. *Education:* University of Oregon (B.A., English, summa cum laude, 1987; J.D., 1992). Recipient, Anna E. Wood Award, 1992. Law Clerk to the Honorable Pierre Van Rysselberghe, Circuit Court Judge, Lane County, Oregon, 1992-1993. *Member:* Lane County Bar Association; Oregon State Bar; Oregon Trial Lawyer's Association; The Association of Trial Lawyers of America. ***LANGUAGES:*** Spanish. ***PRACTICE AREAS:*** Products Liability; Wrongful Death; Medical Malpractice; Truck Accidents; Environmental Law.

MICHELE C. SMITH, born La Jolla, California, February 14, 1964; admitted to bar, 2002, Oregon. *Education:* University of Oregon (B.A., summa cum laude, 1997; J.D., 2001). Phi Beta Kappa. Order of the Coif. Recipient, Dean Orlando John Hollis Scholar Award. *Member:* Lane County Bar Association; Oregon State Bar; Oregon Trial Lawyers Association; The Association of Trial Lawyers of America. ***PRACTICE AREAS:*** Products Liability; Wrongful Death; Medical Malpractice; Truck Accidents; Environmental Law.

PATRICK J. KOUBA

A PROFESSIONAL CORPORATION

Established in 1993

158 EAST 14TH AVENUE

EUGENE, OREGON 97401

Telephone: 541-687-0409

Fax: 541-687-0293

URL: http://www.sharkesq.com

Civil Litigation, including Insurance Defense and Plaintiff's Personal Injury, Contracts, Commercial Litigation, Small Business Formation, and Estate Planning.

PATRICK J. KOUBA, born Houston, Texas, March 7, 1958; admitted to bar, 1983, Oregon. *Education:* Stanford University (B.A., 1980) Boalt Hall School of Law, University of California (J.D., 1983). Associate, Atherly, Butler & Burgott, Eugene, Oregon, 1983-1990; Partner, 1990-1993. *Member:* Lane County Bar Association; Oregon State Bar; Oregon Association of Defense Counsel.

REPRESENTATIVE CLIENTS: Allstate Insurance Co.; Lloyds of London; Ladder Management Services; Greater Oregon Travel; Meridian Corp.; Global Focus Digital Media, LLC; Turtles Bar & Grill; Best Services.

KURTZ, FORD & JOHNSON, LLP

400 EAST 2ND AVENUE, SUITE 101

EUGENE, OREGON 97401

Telephone: 541-484-1273

Fax: 541-683-1815

Civil Litigation, Insurance Law, Insurance Defense, Legal Malpractice Defense, Product Liability Defense, Construction Law, Domestic Relations, Real Estate Law.

LOUIS L. KURTZ, born Des Moines, Iowa, December 7, 1947; admitted to bar, 1974, Nebraska; 1976, Oregon. *Education:* Regis College (B.S.B.A., 1970); Creighton University (J.D., cum laude, 1974). Law Clerk to the Honorable Leslie Boslaugh, Associate Justice, Nebraska Supreme Court, 1974-1976. *Member:* Lane County Bar Associations; Oregon State Bar; Oregon Association of Defense Counsel; Defense Research Institute. ***PRACTICE AREAS:*** Civil Practice; Insurance Defense. ***Email:*** lou@kfjllp.com

ROBERT A. FORD, born Oakland, California, February 19, 1949; admitted to bar, 1974, Oregon. *Education:* Pomona College (A.B., 1971); University of Oregon (J.D., 1974). *Member:* Lane County Bar Association; Oregon State Bar; Oregon Association of Defense Counsel; Defense Research Institute. ***PRACTICE AREAS:*** Insurance Defense Law; Civil Litigation. ***Email:*** bob@kfjllp.com

DONALD E. JOHNSON, born McMinnville, Oregon, February 11, 1959; admitted to bar, 1986, Oregon. *Education:* University of Oregon (B.A., 1982; J.D., 1985). *Member:* Lane County and American Bar Associations; Oregon State Bar; Oregon Association of Defense Counsel. ***LANGUAGES:*** German. ***PRACTICE AREAS:*** Insurance Defense; Civil Litigation; Real Estate Litigation; Medical Malpractice Litigation. ***Email:*** don@kfjllp.com

ASSOCIATE

R. SCOTT WEILAND, born Eugene, Oregon, February 1, 1974; admitted to bar, 2002, Oregon. *Education:* University of Oregon (B.S., 1996; J.D., 2000). Law Clerk to the Honorable Karsten H. Rasmussen, Lane County Circuit Court, 1999. *Member:* Lane County Bar Association; Oregon State Bar (Member, Sections on: Litigation; Construction Law; Estate Planning Law; Administration Law); Oregon Association of Defense Counsel. ***PRACTICE AREAS:*** Insurance Defense; Civil Litigation; Construction Law. ***Email:*** scott@kfjllp.com

---

LOOMIS & HOLLAND

Established in 1989

801 EAST PARK STREET

EUGENE, OREGON 97401-2980

Telephone: 541-344-8333

Fax: 541-344-8075

Trial practice in State and Federal Courts, Medical Malpractice, Professional Liability, Insurance, Products Liability, Pharmaceutical and Toxic Tort Litigation, Business Litigation, Real Property, Family, Probate Law, Unsafe Products, Legal Malpractice, Personal Injury, Wrongful Death.

MEMBERS OF FIRM

DANIEL M. HOLLAND, born Kansas City, Missouri, September 1, 1948; admitted to bar, 1973, Florida; 1980, Oregon and U.S. District Court, District of Oregon; 2002, Washington; 2003, U.S. Supreme Court. *Education:* University of Missouri (A.B, 1970; J.D., 1972). *Member:* Lane County and American Bar Associations; The Florida Bar; Oregon State Bar; Washington State Bar; Oregon Trial Lawyers Association; Federation of Insurance and Corporate Counsel; Association of Trial Lawyers of America. [USAF, JAG, 1973]. ***PRACTICE AREAS:*** Medical, Legal and Professional Liability; Products Liability; Toxic Torts; Civil Litigation; Personal Injury; Wrongful Death. ***Email:*** hollaw@continet.com

DONALD A. LOOMIS, born Roseburg, Oregon, March 22, 1941; admitted to bar, 1969, Oregon. *Education:* Oregon State University (B.S., in Pharmacy, 1965); Willamette University (J.D., 1968). Phi Delta Phi. Registered Pharmacist, Oregon, 1965. Municipal Judge, City of Florence, Oregon, 1992-1997. Assistant Municipal Judge, City of Eugene, Oregon. Municipal Judge, Junction City, Oregon, 1997—. *Member:* Lane County Bar Association; Oregon State Bar; Oregon Association of Defense Counsel; American Society of Pharmacy Lawyers. ***PRACTICE AREAS:*** Civil Litigation; Personal Injury; Employment Litigation; Business Litigation; Probate Law; Pharmacist Professional Liability. ***Email:*** dloomis@continet.com

RONALD B. TERZENBACH, born Compton, California, March 20, 1952; admitted to bar, 1978, Oregon and U.S. District Court, District of Oregon. *Education:* University of Oregon (B.A., 1974; J.D., 1977). *Member:* Lane County and American Bar Associations; Oregon State Bar; Oregon Association of Defense Counsel; Defense Research Institute. ***PRACTICE AREAS:*** Insurance Defense Law; Civil Litigation; Professional Liability. ***Email:*** rbt@continet.com

REPRESENTATIVE CLIENTS: Albertsons, Inc.; CNA Insurance Companies; Miller Group; Motorist Mutual Ins., Co.; Phico Ins., Co.; Colonial Insurance Company of California; Oregon Professional Liability Fund; North Pacific Insurance Co.; Horace Mann Insurance Co.; Capitol Indemnity Corporation; Orion Group; Zurich Insurance Co.; Fleetwood Enterprises; American Hardware Mutual Ins. Co.; National General Ins. Co.; Oregon Rubber Co.; Markel Ins. Company of Canada; Farmland Insurance Co.; Northland Ins. Co.; University of Washington.

LAW OFFICES OF ROBERT D. LOWRY

CITIZENS BUILDING

975 OAK STREET, SUITE 790

P.O. BOX 12010

EUGENE, OREGON 97440

Telephone: 541-687-7592

Cellular: 541-954-4451

Fax: 541-687-0805

Email: rdlowry@lowry-law.com

Insurance Defense, Products Liability Defense, Medical Malpractice, Hospital Malpractice, Business Litigation, Construction Law and Civil Litigation.

ROBERT D. LOWRY, born Washington, D.C., April 12, 1949; admitted to bar, 1980, Oregon, U.S. District Court, District of Oregon, U.S. Court of Appeals, Ninth and Federal Circuits, U.S. Claims Court and U.S. Supreme Court. *Education:* University of Oregon (B.A., 1971; J.D., 1980). Phi Delta Phi. Member, Rotary International, Honorary Paul Harris Fellow for Lifesaving; Lawyer Representative/Delegate, U.S. Courts for the Ninth Circuit Judicial Conference, 1996-1998. Law Clerk to Justices Edwin J. Peterson, Edward H.

(This Listing Continued)

LAW OFFICES OF ROBERT D. LOWRY, Eugene—Continued

Howell and J.R. Campbell, Oregon Supreme Court, 1980-1981. Chair, Regional Area Trauma Advisory Board, 1988—. Member, Board of Directors, Ninth Judicial Circuit Historical Society, 2003—. Chair, Lawyer Representatives, 9th Circuit, 2001. *Member:* Oregon State Bar (Chairman, Medical Profession Committee, 1988-1989); American Bar Association; The Association of Trial Lawyers of America; National Health Lawyers Association; Oregon Association of Defense Counsel; Oregon Association of Hospital Attorneys; Defense Research Institute; Inns of the Court; Propane Gas Defense Association.

REPRESENTATIVE CLIENTS: Safeco American States Insurance Co.; CNA; Farmers Insurance Group; Cumis Insurance Co.; ITT/Hartford Life; Protective Life; Pinnacle Risk Management; Crawford & Co.; Fred Meyer, Inc.; RiteAid; Willamette Industries; Blue Cross/Blue Shield of Oregon; Special Districts Association of Oregon; Federal Express Corp.; Trillium Family Services; Health Future, LLC; American Continental Insurance Co.; American Bankers Insurance Co.; Gulf Insurance; Kemper Insurance; GAB Robbins North America, Inc.; UGI-AmeriGas; SELCO Credit Union; Royal & SunAlliance; Morse Bros., Inc.; MMI Insurance; St. Paul Ins.; HealthFuture; Canal Ins.; Travelers Ins.; Continental Western Ins.; Financial Ind.; Jeld-Wen Corp.; 21st Century Ins.; Burlington Ins. Co.; City of GrantsPass; Old Republic Ins.; AIG; Effective Claims Management; Oregon Insurance Guarantee Fund; Clarion Insurance; Sedgwick CMS; Alberta Motor Assn.

LUVAAS COBB, P.C.

Established in 1955

300 FORUM BUILDING
777 HIGH STREET
P.O. BOX 10747
EUGENE, OREGON 97401
Telephone: 541-484-9292
Fax: 541-343-1206
URL: http://www.luvaascobb.com

General Civil Trial and Appellate Practice in all State and Federal Courts and Administrative Agency. Taxation, Business, Domestic Relations, Corporate, Commercial, Computer, Construction, Environmental, Media, Probate, Insurance, Estate Planning, Real Estate and Municipal Law. Legal and Medical Malpractice Defense. Intellectual Property, Copyright and Trademark.

JOHN L. LUVAAS (Retired)

ROBERT H. FRASER (Retired)

RALPH F. COBB, born Sioux City, Iowa, December 9, 1921; admitted to bar, 1948, South Dakota; 1949, Oregon; 1950, U.S. District Court, District of Oregon; 1961, U.S. Supreme Court. *Education:* Yankton College (B.A., 1948); University of South Dakota (LL.B., 1948). Delta Theta Phi. State of Oregon Junior First Citizen, 1953. Named Trial Lawyer of the Year, American Board of Trial Advocates, Oregon Chapter, 1998. Member, Governing Board, Sacred Heart General Hospital, 1974-1996. Chairman, Eugene Airport Commission, 1978. *Member:* Lane County (President, 1958) and American Bar Associations; Oregon State Bar (Member, Board of Governors, 1976-1979; Secretary, 1979); State Bar of South Dakota; American College of Trial Lawyers; American Board of Trial Advocates; Oregon Association of Defense Counsel. ***PRACTICE AREAS:*** Insurance Defense; Litigation. ***Email:*** rcobb@luvaascobb.com

JOE B. RICHARDS, born Colfax, Washington, June 12, 1929; admitted to bar, 1954, Oregon and U.S. District Court, District of Oregon; 1959, U.S. Court of Appeals, Ninth Circuit. *Education:* University of Oregon (B.A., 1951); Willamette University (LL.B., 1954). Representative, Oregon State Legislature, 1965-1970. Chairman: Oregon Environmental Quality Commission, 1975-1983; Oregon Water Policy Review Board, 1984-1986. President, Oregon School Lawyers Association, 1998-1999; State Bar Affirmative Action Committee, 1998-1999. *Member:* Lane County (President, 1969) and American Bar Associations; Oregon State Bar; Oregon Association of Defense Counsel. ***PRACTICE AREAS:*** Administrative Law; Employment Law; School Law; Business Law; Insurance Defense. ***Email:*** jbrichards@luvaascobb.com

J. DOMINIC MONAHAN, born Heppner, Oregon, October 19, 1938; admitted to bar, 1968, District of Columbia; 1994, Oregon, U.S. District Court, District of Columbia, U.S. Court of Appeals, District of Columbia Circuit and U.S. District Court, District of Oregon. *Education:* University of Portland (B.A. Economics, cum laude, 1961); Georgetown University (J.D., 1968). Law Clerk to Senior Judge Charles F. McLaughlin, U.S. District Court, District of Columbia, 1968-1969. *Member:* Lane County, American and Federal Communications Bar Associations; Oregon State Bar; District of Columbia Bar. [Capt., U.S.A.F., 1961-1964]. ***SPECIAL AGENCIES:*** Federal Communications Commission. ***PRACTICE AREAS:*** Administrative Law; Corporate Law; Business Law; Media Law; Communications Law; Government Relations. ***Email:*** dmonahan@luvaascobb.com

VARNER JAY JOHNS, III, born Los Angeles, California, February 17, 1953; admitted to bar, 1979, Oregon. *Education:* Loma Linda University (B.A., with honors, 1975); Willamette University (J.D., 1978); College of William and Mary (LL.M., Taxation, 1979). Order of Barristers. Co-Author, "Charitable Trusts, Oregon State Bar, Administering Trusts in Oregon," Oregon State Bar, 1995. *Member:* Lane County and American (Member, Sections on: Taxation; Real Property, Probate and Trust Law) Bar Associations; Oregon State Bar (Member, Sections on: Business and Corporate Law; Estate Planning; Taxation). ***PRACTICE AREAS:*** Probate; Estate Planning; Taxation; Business Law. ***Email:*** vjohns@luvaascobb.com

JOEL S. DEVORE, born Burlington, Iowa, June 10, 1951; admitted to bar, 1982, Oregon; 1984, U.S. District Court, District of Oregon; 1988, U.S. Court of Appeals, Ninth Circuit; 1993, U.S. Supreme Court. *Education:* Alaska Methodist University; Antioch College (B.A., 1974); University of Oregon (J.D., 1982). Associate Editor, Oregon Law Review, 1981-1982. Law Clerk to Judge Thomas F. Young, Oregon Court of Appeals, 1982-1983. *Member:* Lane County Bar Association (President-Elect, 2000); Oregon State Bar (Member, Executive Committee, Appellate Practice Section; Past Chair, Uniform Civil Jury Instruction Committee); Oregon Association of Defense Counsel. ***PRACTICE AREAS:*** Personal Injury Defense; Legal Malpractice Defense; Insurance Coverage; Civil Appeals; School Law. ***Email:*** devore@luvaascobb.com

(This Listing Continued)

DAVID A. JACOBS, born Champaign, Illinois, January 2, 1963; admitted to bar, 1994, Oregon; 1996, U.S. District Court, District of Oregon. *Education:* Middlebury College; University of Oregon (B.A., magna cum laude, 1988; J.D., 1993). Order of the Coif. Law Clerk to Judge Gregory G. Foote, Lane County Circuit Court, 1993-1994. *Member:* Lane County and American Bar Associations; Oregon State Bar; Oregon Association of Defense Counsel; Construction Specifications Institute. ***PRACTICE AREAS:*** Commercial Litigation; Construction Law; Insurance Defense; Personal Injury. ***Email:*** djacobs@luvaascobb.com

LANN D. LESLIE, born Oakland, California, March 27, 1955; admitted to bar, 1982, Oregon. *Education:* University of Oregon (B.S., Phi Beta Kappa, 1978; J.D., 1982). *Member:* Lane County Bar Association; Oregon State Bar; Oregon Association of Defense Counsel. ***PRACTICE AREAS:*** Insurance Defense; Personal Injury; Construction Litigation; Professional Liability; Real Estate. ***Email:*** lleslie@luvaascobb.com

GEORGE A. BURGOTT, born South Bend, Indiana, January 24, 1949; admitted to bar, 1974, Iowa; 1975, Michigan; 1976, Oregon. *Education:* University of Michigan (B.S., Ch.E., cum laude, 1971; J.D., cum laude, 1974). *Member:* Lane County Bar Association; Oregon State Bar; Oregon Association of Defense Counsel. ***PRACTICE AREAS:*** Insurance Defense; Insurance Law; Personal Injury; Products Liability; Trademark; Copyrights. ***Email:*** gburgott@luvaascobb.com

WENDY L. LAING, born Eugene, Oregon, March 18, 1966; admitted to bar, 1995, Oregon. *Education:* University of Chicago (A.B., 1988); University of Oregon (J.D., M.B.A., 1994). Managing Editor, "University of Oregon Journal of Environmental Law and Litigation," 1993-1994. *Member:* Lane County and American Bar Associations; Oregon State Bar. ***PRACTICE AREAS:*** Business Law; Estate Planning; Real Property. ***Email:*** wlaing@luvaascobb.com

FRANK E. BOCCI, JR., born Eugene, Oregon, November 24, 1955; admitted to bar, 1981, Oregon; 1982, U.S. District Court, District of Oregon. *Education:* Oregon State University (B.S., 1978); Willamette University (J.D., 1981). Phi Kappa Phi. *Member:* Lane County Bar Association; Oregon State Bar. ***PRACTICE AREAS:*** Civil Litigation; School Law; Construction Law; Real Property; Domestic. ***Email:*** fbocci@luvaascobb.com

GREG M. WOMER, born Klamath Falls, Oregon, April 17, 1970; admitted to bar, 2003, Oregon. *Education:* University of Oregon (B.S., 1992); University of Oregon Law School (J.D., 2003). *Member:* Oregon State Bar Association. ***PRACTICE AREAS:*** Estate Planning; Elder Law; Business Law; Corporate Law; Trust Administration; Probate Administration; Real Estate. ***Email:*** gwomer@luvaaccobb.com

OF COUNSEL

RICHARD W. BUTLER, born San Mateo, California, December 30, 1934; admitted to bar, 1960, Oregon. *Education:* Willamette University; University of Oregon (B.S., 1957; LL.B., 1960). Phi Delta Phi. *Member:* Lane County Bar Association (President, 1984-1985); Oregon State Bar; American Board of Trial Advocates; Oregon Association of Defense Counsel (Member, Board of Directors, 1983-1985). ***PRACTICE AREAS:*** Insurance Defense; Health Insurance; Electric Utility Law.

REPRESENTATIVE CLIENTS: Admiral Ins. Co.; Atlanta Casualty; Austin Mutual Insurance Co.; Blachly-Lane County Cooperative Electric Assn.; Capps Broadcast Group; Carolina Casualty; Champion Enterprises; CitiGroup; Colonial Penn Insurance Co.; Columbia Basin Electric Cooperative; Eugene Association of Realtors; Farmers Insurance Group; Firemen's Fund Insurance Cos; Greater Lane County Multiple Listing Service; Jamar Media; Liberty Mutual Insurance Co.; Millers Group; Motorists/American Hdwe. Ins. Cos.; Northland Insurance Co.; Northwest Physicians Mutual Insurance Co.; Ohio Casualty Group; Oregon Rural Electric Cooperative Assn.; Pacific Source; Professional Liability Fund of the Oregon State Bar; Reliance Insurance Co.; St. Paul Travelers; Sunbelt Broadcasting Company; Unitrin; Universal Underwriters Insurance Co.; USAA; Wausau Insurance Companies.
GENERAL COUNSEL FOR: Peterson Pacific Corp.; Vik Construction Co.; Sheppard Motors Ltd.; Newood Products, Inc.; Combined Communications, Inc. (KBND, KTWS/FM); Golden Temple of Oregon, Inc.; Oregon Association of Broadcasters; Starfire Lumber Company; Looking Glass Youth and Family Services, Inc.; Head Start of Lane County; Pearl Buck Center, Inc.; Casey Jones Well Drilling, Inc.
PUBLIC CORPORATION CLIENTS: School Districts: Eugene 4J; Corvallis 509J; Pleasant Hill 1; Creswell 40; Florence 97J; Bethel 52; Crow-Appelgate 66; Fern Ridge 28J; Marcola 79; Junction City 69; South Lane School District 45; Lane Education Service District; Central Linn School District 552-C; Harrisburg School District; Yoncalla School District.

MUHLHEIM BOYD

A Partnership of Professional Corporations

88 EAST BROADWAY
EUGENE, OREGON 97401
Telephone: 541-868-8005
Fax: 541-868-8004
Email: linen@mbclawoffice.com
URL: http://www.mbclawoffice.com

Creditor/Debtor Representation; Commercial Litigation; Workouts and Bankruptcy Reorganizations; Bankruptcy Litigation; Creditors' Rights; Foreclosure; Commercial Law; Business Litigation; Business Transactions; Litigation; Estate and Probate.

KEITH Y. BOYD, born Portland, Oregon, March 5, 1950; admitted to bar, 1976, Oregon. *Education:* Oregon State University (B.S., 1973); University of Oregon School of Law (J.D., 1976). Judge Pro Tempore, Oregon Circuit Court, Josephine County, 1996-2001. Listed, Best Lawyers in America, Bankruptcy. *Member:* Oregon State Bar (Member, Debtor-Creditor Section). ***PRACTICE AREAS:*** Bankruptcy; Real Estate; Business Transactions; Estate Planning; Business Planning. ***Email:*** boyd@mbclawoffice.com

WILSON C. MUHLHEIM, born Hays, Kansas, June 26, 1944; admitted to bar, 1968, Oregon. *Education:* Claremont Men's College; University of Oregon (J.D., 1968). Order of the Coif. *Member:* Oregon State Bar (Member, Sections on: Business and Corporate Law; Debtor-Creditor Law); American Bankruptcy Institute. Certified in Business Bankruptcy

(This Listing Continued)

by the American Board of Certification. ***PRACTICE AREAS:*** Workouts and Bankruptcy Reorganization; Bankruptcy Litigation and Creditors' Rights; Commercial Transactions; Real Estate Transactions. ***Email:*** muhlheim@mbclawoffice.com

ASSOCIATES

JULIA I. MANELA, born Eugene, Oregon, November 15, 1972; admitted to bar, 2002, Oregon; 2003, US. District Court, District of Oregon. *Education:* University of Oregon (B.A., 1995; J.D., 2002). Basic Mediation Training, University of Oregon, 2000. Certificate in Estate Planning, University of Oregon, 2002. *Member:* Lane County Bar Association; Oregon State Bar. ***PRACTICE AREAS:*** Bankruptcy; Creditors Rights; Real Estate; Business Transactions; Estate Planning; Probate. ***Email:*** manela@mbclawoffice.com

LOREN S. SCOTT, born Durham, North Carolina, February 2, 1976; admitted to bar, 2002, Oregon and U.S. District Court, District of Oregon. *Education:* Arizona State University (B.A., summa cum laude, 1998); University of Oregon (J.D., 2002). Order of the Coif. *Member:* Lane County Bar Association (President, Debtor/Creditors Section, 2005-2006); Oregon State Bar. ***PRACTICE AREAS:*** Bankruptcy; Commercial Litigation; Creditors Rights. ***Email:*** scott@mbclawoffice.com

OF COUNSEL

TODD H. TINKER, born Greenville, Michigan, June 5, 1962; admitted to bar, 1989, Texas, U.S. Court of Appeals for the Fifth Circuit and U.S. District Court, Northern and Southern Districts of Texas; 2002, Oregon; U.S. District Court, District of Oregon. *Education:* University of Michigan (B.G.S., 1986); Southern Methodist University (J.D., 1989). Phi Delta Phi (Historian, 1986-1987). *Member:* Dallas Bar Association; State Bar of Texas; Oregon State Bar. ***PRACTICE AREAS:*** Labor and Employment; Litigation; Commercial Litigation. ***Email:*** tinker@mbclawoffice.com

LEGAL SUPPORT PERSONNEL

DAWNNE L. LINENBRINK, (CLAS, CBA), born Riverton, Wyoming, 1959. *Education:* Northeastern Junior College (Intensive Paralegal Certificate, 1988). Certified by the National Association of Legal Assistants, 1995. Specialty Certification in Bankruptcy by the National Association of Legal Assistants, 1997. Specialty Certification in Real Estate by the National Association of Legal Assistants, 2000. Certified Bankruptcy Assistant Certification by the Association of Bankruptcy Judicial Assistants, 2002. *Member:* Pacific Northwest Legal Assistants, 1992—; National Association of Legal Assistants, 1993—; Debtor/Creditor Section, Oregon State Bar 1993—. (Senior Certified Paralegal Specialist) (Bankruptcy, Real Estate and Civil Litigation Paralegal). ***PRACTICE AREAS:*** Bankruptcy; Civil Litigation; Creditors Rights; Real Estate. ***Email:*** linen@mbclawoffice.com

MELISSA A. ARNOLD, CLA, born Jacksonville Beach, Florida, March 31, 1975. *Education:* University of Denver (B.S.B.A., 1997). Certified by the National Association of Legal Assistant, 2004. *Member:* National Association of Legal Assistants. ***PRACTICE AREAS:*** Bankruptcy; Probate; Estate Planning. ***Email:*** arnold@mbclawoffice.com

LAURA A. PARRISH

975 OAK STREET, SUITE 670
EUGENE, OREGON 97401
Telephone: 541-485-6162
Fax: 541-686-0114
URL: http://www.parrishor.com

Family Law, Divorce, Spousal Support, Child Support, Child Custody, Domestic Relations, Mediation, Collaborative Law, Negotiation and Settlement, Arbitration, Wills.

LAURA A. PARRISH, born Takoma Park, Maryland, 1951; admitted to bar, 1976, Oregon; 1977, U.S. District Court, District of Oregon. *Education:* University of Hawaii; University of Oregon (B.S., with honors, 1973; J.D., 1976). Phi Beta Kappa. Former Adjunct Professor, Family Law and the Child, University of Oregon School of Law. Judge, City of Eugene Municipal Court, 1998—. Director, NW Collaborative Law Institute. *Member:* Lane County (President, 1985-1986) and American (Member, Family Law Section) Bar Associations; Oregon State Bar (Member, Sections of: Family Law, Trial Practice and Alternative Dispute Resolution); Association for Conflict Resolution. Fellow, American Academy of Matrimonial Lawyers.

PETERSON LAW OFFICES, PC

EUGENE, OREGON

(See Portland)

Personal Injury, Premises Liability, Automobile Accidents and Injuries, Dog Bites and Wrongful Death.

SCOTT HOOKLAND LLP

Established in 1984
423 LINCOLN STREET
EUGENE, OREGON 97401
Telephone: 541 284-5820; 503 754-4700
Fax: 541 284-5821
Email: dlg@scott-hookland.com
URL: http://www.scott-hookland.com

Tigard, Oregon Office: 9185 S.W. Burnham Street, P.O. Box: 23414, 97223. Telephone: 503-620-4540. Toll Free: 800-334-8986. Fax: 503-620-4315.

Construction, Design, Civil and Trial Practice. Commercial Collections, Business, Real Estate, Mediations, Arbitrations, Creditors Rights.

(This Listing Continued)

ASSOCIATE

DOUGLAS L. GALLAGHER, born Portland, Oregon, July 19, 1972; admitted to bar, 1997, Oregon and U.S. District Court, District of Oregon. *Education:* University of Oregon (B.A., Departmental honors in Political Science, 1994; J.D., 1997). *Member:* Washington County and Multnomah County Bar Associations; Oregon State Bar (Member, Sections on: Debtor/Creditor; Construction; Real Estate and Land Use). ***PRACTICE AREAS:*** Construction; Collections; Real Property; Litigation; Creditors Rights. ***Email:*** dlg@scott-hookland.com

REPRESENTATIVE CLIENTS: United Rentals; Southwest Readymix Co.; Suburban Door Co.; Consolidated Electrical Distributors, Inc. (Oregon, Washington, Idaho and Alaska); National Water Works (Oregon and Washington); H&A Construction, Co.; Star Rentals, Inc.

SPEER, HOYT, JONES, FEINMAN, POPPE, WOLF & GRIFFITH, P.C.

975 OAK STREET
SUITE 700
EUGENE, OREGON 97401
Telephone: 541-485-5151
Fax: 541-485-5168
Email: inquiry@speerhoyt.com
URL: http://www.speerhoyt.com

Business Law, Formation of Business Entities, Business Buying and Selling, Employee Benefits, Conflict Resolution, Taxation, Trusts and Estates, Wills and Probate, Estate Planning, Real Estate, Tax Planning, Estate Tax, Tax Conflict Resolution, Collaboration, Family Law, Divorce, Separation, Prenuptial Agreements, Adoption, Custody, Paternity, Municipal Law, Government.

FIRM PROFILE: Speer, Hoyt, Jones, Feinman, Poppe, Wolf & Griffith, P.C., is a law firm focused upon personal, responsive, cost effective representation that works. Our goal is to keep our business, family, and municipal clients out of court through careful drafting, documentation, and common sense. We are skilled in alternative dispute resolution and are experienced in federal and state courts. Inquiries regarding fees are welcome.

HOWARD E. SPEER, born Newberg, Oregon, February 23, 1936; admitted to bar, 1961, Oregon; 1964, U.S. District Court, District of Oregon, U.S. Supreme Court and U.S. Tax Court. *Education:* Willamette University (B.A., 1958; LL.B., 1961) Phi Delta Phi; Georgetown University (LL.M., in Taxation, 1964). *Member:* Lane County Bar Association (Member, Probate Section); Oregon State Bar (Member, Sections on: Business and Corporate Law; Real Estate and Land Use Law; Treasurer, 1980-1981, Estate Planning and Administration Section; Chair, 1990-1991, Taxation Section; Secretary, 1994-1995, Legal Management Section); Oregon Estate Planning Council (President, Eugene Chapter, 1980-1981). ***PRACTICE AREAS:*** Taxation Law; Estate Planning; Business Planning; Real Estate Transactions; Business Transactions; Business Law; Real Estate Law; Probate; Trust Administration. ***Email:*** speer@speerhoyt.com

THOMAS H. HOYT, born Corvallis, Oregon, November 25, 1940; admitted to bar, 1966, Oregon; 1967, U.S. District Court, District of Oregon; 1971, U.S. Supreme Court. *Education:* University of Oregon (B.S., 1963); Willamette University (J.D., 1966). Phi Delta Phi. *Member:* Lane County Bar Association (Member: Probate Committee; Alternative Dispute Resolution); Oregon State Bar (Member, Sections on: Business Law; Estate Planning and Administration; Litigation; Real Estate and Land Use; Alternative Dispute Resolution; Construction Law; Debtor-Creditor; Legal Management). ***PRACTICE AREAS:*** Trusts and Estates; Wills; Real Estate; Property Law; Business Law; Commercial Real Estate; Contracts; Probate; Corporate Law; Leases and Leasing. ***Email:*** thoyt@speerhoyt.com

J. KENNETH JONES, born Prairie Grove, Arkansas, March 30, 1947; admitted to bar, 1972, Oregon and Washington; 1973, Alaska. *Education:* Washington State University (B.A., 1969); University of Oregon (J.D., 1972). Phi Alpha Delta. *Member:* Lane County and Washington State Bar Associations; Oregon State Bar (Member, Sections on: Municipal Law; Real Estate and Land Use Law; Board of Directors, Construction Law, 1997; Board of Directors, 1986-1993 and Chair, 1992, Government Law Section). ***PRACTICE AREAS:*** Municipal Law; Real Estate; Estate and Business Planning; Business Law; Wills. ***Email:*** jkj@speerhoyt.com

HOWARD F. FEINMAN, born Jersey City, New Jersey, October 18, 1949; admitted to bar, 1975, Oregon. *Education:* Lafayette College (B.A., Mathematics, cum laude, 1971); Washington University (J.D., 1975). Phi Beta Kappa. Member, Eugene Estate Planning Council (President, 2002-2003). *Member:* Lane County Bar; Multnomah County Bar; Oregon State Bar (Member, Estate Planning, Business and Corporate Law Sections). ***PRACTICE AREAS:*** Wills; Trusts and Estates; Business Law; Business Planning; Business Transactions; Probate; Trust Administration; Real Estate. ***Email:*** hfeinman@speerhoyt.com

RUSSELL D. POPPE, born Wichita, Kansas, May 11, 1953; admitted to bar, 1980, Oregon. *Education:* University of Kansas (B.A., with high honors, 1977); University of Oregon (J.D., 1980). Law Clerk to the Honorable William G. East, Senior U.S District Court Judge, 1980-1982. *Member:* Lane County Bar Association (Member, Committees on: Insurance; Attorney-Realtor, Chair, 1997-1998); Oregon State Bar. ***PRACTICE AREAS:*** Business Sales; Employment Law; Real Estate Litigation; Real Estate Sales; Business Litigation. ***Email:*** rpoppe@speerhoyt.com

JOHN A. WOLF, born Eugene, Oregon, March 26, 1948; admitted to bar, 1980, Oregon. *Education:* Oregon State University (B.S., 1970); Lewis and Clark College (J.D., 1980). Phi Eta Sigma; Blue Key. *Member:* Lane County Bar Association (Member, Family Law Section); Oregon State Bar (Member, Law Office Management Section). ***REPORTED CASES:*** Shinn v. Vaughn, 83 Or. App. 251, 730 P.2d 1290 (1986); Ladum v. City of Reedsport, 83 Or. App. 666, 733 P.2d 66 (1987); Markus v. Clark, 150 Or. App. 331, 946 P.2d 303 (1987). ***PRACTICE AREAS:*** Alternative Dispute Resolution; Business Law; Civil Practice; Collections; Commercial Law; Commercial Real Estate; Construction Law;

(This Listing Continued)

SPEER, HOYT, JONES, FEINMAN, POPPE, WOLF & GRIFFITH, P.C., Eugene—Continued

Contracts; Debtor and Creditor; Family Law; General Practice; Health Care; Leases and Leasing; Litigation; Mortgages; Municipal Law; Partnership Law; Property Law; Real Estate; Taxation; Wills. **Email:** jaw@speerhoyt.com

GWENDOLYN GRIFFITH, born Memphis, Tennessee, July 21, 1957; admitted to bar, 1981, California; 1983, Texas; 1991, Oregon. *Education:* Rollins College (B.A., 1978); Stanford University (J.D., 1981). Associate Editor, Stanford Law Review, 1980-1981. Editor-in-Chief, Stanford Journal of International Law, 1980-1981. Professor of Law, Willamette University College of Law, 1988-1999. Visiting Professor, University of Oregon School of Law, 2001-2004. *Member:* State Bar of California; Oregon State Bar. ***PRACTICE AREAS:*** Taxation; Trusts and Estates; Business Law; Copyrights; Contracts; Nonprofit and Charitable Organizations. **Email:** gwengriff@speerhoyt.com

ELLEN D. ADLER, born Brooklyn, New York, March 4, 1956; admitted to bar, 1989, Oregon; 1992, U.S. District Court, District of Oregon and U.S. Court of Appeals, Ninth Circuit. *Education:* University of Florida (B.A., 1977) Phi Kappa Phi National Scholarship Society; University of Oregon (M.S., 1979; J.D., 1989). Associate Editor, Oregon Law Review, 1988-1989. Judicial Law Clerk to the Honorable R. William Riggs, Oregon Court of Appeals, 1989-1991. *Member:* Lane County Bar Association (Member, Probate Section); Oregon State Bar (Member, Section on Estate Planning and Administration). ***PRACTICE AREAS:*** Trusts and Estates; Wills; Estate Planning for Domestic Partners; Probate Administration; Trust Administration; Real Estate; Property Law; Contracts; Business Law. **Email:** eadler@speerhoyt.com

---

CAROLYN H. CONNELLY, born Denver, Colorado, January 27, 1968; admitted to bar, 1995, Oregon; 1996, Washington. *Education:* Dartmouth College (B.A., 1990); Vermont Law School (J.D., M.S.L., 1995). Law Clerk to the Honorable Donald W. Hull, Hood River County Circuit Court and the Honorable John V. Kelly, Wasco County Circuit Court. *Member:* Lane County Bar Association; Oregon State Bar (Member, Sections on: Municipal Law; Environmental Law; Land Use); Lane County Women Lawyers. ***PRACTICE AREAS:*** Municipal Law; Environmental Law; Natural Resources; Zoning, Planning and Land Use. **Email:** chc@speerhoyt.com

SARAH R. HILDERBRAND, born Corvallis, Oregon, June 7, 1973; admitted to bar, 1997, Oregon. *Education:* University of Oregon (B.S., 1993); Williamette University (J.D., 1997). *Member:* Oregon State Bar. ***PRACTICE AREAS:*** Municipal Law (80%); Land Use (10%); Business Law (10%).

REPRESENTATIVE CLIENTS: U.S. Bank National Association; Wells Fargo Bank, N.A.; Market of Choice; Champion Friction Co.; City of Veneta; City of Junction City; Cramer & Giles Insurance, Inc.; Oregon Fire District Directors' Assoc.; Carter & Carter Financial, Inc.; Palo Alto Software, Inc.; Burley Design Cooperative; Jackson's Complete Auto Care; Soft-Tech Design and Construction; Cramer's Grinding and Tooling, Inc.; Double S Foods, Inc. (Sizzler Restaurants); Engelmann-Becker Corporation; NIFDI (National Institute for Direct Instruction); ORCAS (Oregon Center for Applied Science); Decision Research; Green Gear Cycling, Inc. (Bike Friday).

SPOONER, MUCH & AMMANN, P.C.

EUGENE, OREGON

(See Salem)

General Civil and Trial Practice in State and Federal Courts. Insurance, Products Liability and Personal Injury Law.

VERALRUD & ASSOCIATES, ATTORNEYS, P.C.

Established in 1967

625 CITIZENS BUILDING
975 OAK STREET
EUGENE, OREGON 97401
Telephone: 541-345-3333
Fax: 541-342-1908
URL: http://www.oregonattorney.com
Email: Veralrud@Oregonattorney.com
URL: http://www.EugeneAttorney.com

Plaintiff's Personal Injury. Automobile Accidents, Aviation Accidents, Wrongful Death, Slip and Fall, Medical Malpractice, Products Liability, Legal Malpractice, Civil Rights, Business Litigation, Criminal Law, White Collar Crime, Drug Defense, Sex Offenses, DUI.

FIRM PROFILE: The firm was established in 1967 by William F. Frye following two terms as Lane County District Attorney. Mr. Veralrud became a partner in the firm in 1981, following his service as felony deputy with the District Attorney. An active civil and criminal litigation practice developed.

The firm aims to provide highly personalized quality representation in plaintiffs' litigation and criminal defense.

WILLIAM F. FRYE (1929-1988)

GREGORY E. VERALRUD, born San Rafael, California, September 6, 1952; admitted to bar, 1978, Oregon; 1979, U.S. District Court, District of Oregon, U.S. Court of Appeals, 9th Circuit and U.S. Supreme Court. *Education:* University of New Mexico and University of Oregon (B.A., 1974); University of Oregon (J.D., 1978). Trial Practice Instructor, University of Oregon Law School, 1984-1998. Deputy District Attorney, Lane County, Oregon, 1978-1981. *Member:* Lane County Bar Association; Oregon State Bar; Oregon Trial Lawyers Association; Oregon Criminal Defense Lawyers Association (President, 1984-1986); National Association of Criminal Defense Attorneys. ***LANGUAGES:*** Spanish. ***PRACTICE AREAS:*** Plaintiffs' Litigation; Criminal Defense. **Email:** Veralrud@Oregonattorney.com

(This Listing Continued)

LINDSAY H. FOWLER, born Charleston, West Virginia, July 10, 1974; admitted to bar, 2002, Oregon. *Education:* West Virginia University (B.A., 1998; J.D., 2001). Law Clerk, Hon. Karsten Rasmussen, Lane County Circuit Court, Oregon, 2001-2002. Public Defender, Jackson County, Oregon, 2002-2005. *Member:* Lane County Bar Association; Oregon State Bar; Oregon Criminal Defense Lawyers Association; National Association of Criminal Defense Lawyers Association. ***PRACTICE AREAS:*** Criminal Defense; Personal Injury; Juvenile Law.

WATKINSON LAIRD RUBENSTEIN BALDWIN & BURGESS, P.C.

Established in 1994

101 EAST BROADWAY, SUITE 200
P.O. BOX 10567
EUGENE, OREGON 97440
Telephone: 541-484-2277
Fax: 541-484-2282
URL: http://www.wlrlaw.com

FIRM PROFILE: The firm was established in 1994 by experienced business and litigation attorneys with over 90 years of combined service to clients throughout Oregon. The firm provides a wide range of legal services to individual and business clients, with a special concentration in representation of physicians and other health care providers. Legal subjects of particular emphasis include business organization and operation; real estate; securities; estate planning and probate; taxation; executive compensation and employee benefits; employment law; family law and litigation in state and federal courts.

STEVE C. BALDWIN, born Portland, Oregon, September 21, 1952; admitted to bar, 1983, Oregon. *Education:* University of Oregon (B.S., 1978); University of Utah (M.S., 1980); University of Oregon (J.D., 1983). Law Clerk to Oregon Court of Appeals, 1983-1985. *Member:* Oregon State Bar. ***PRACTICE AREAS:*** Litigation; Family Law. **Email:** SBaldwin@wlrlaw.com

B. KEVIN BURGESS, born South Bend, Indiana, March 21, 1954; admitted to bar, 1988, Oregon. *Education:* St. Johns College (B.A., 1978); University of Oregon (J.D., 1988). Order of the Coif. Recipient, American Jurisprudence Awards in Contracts I and II, Civil Procedure, Jurisprudence and Criminal Practice II. *Member:* Oregon State Bar. ***PRACTICE AREAS:*** Employee Benefits; Litigation; Employment Law. **Email:** KBurgess@wlrlaw.com

DONALD R. LAIRD, born Eugene, Oregon, July 3, 1947; admitted to bar, 1975, Oregon. *Education:* Oregon State University (B.S., 1970); Temple University; University of Oregon (J.D., 1975). *Member:* Oregon State Bar (Chair, Section on Health Law, 2002—); American Health Lawyers Association. (Also at Roseburg Office). ***PRACTICE AREAS:*** Corporate Law; Employee Benefits; Health Law. **Email:** DLaird@wlrlaw.com

R. SCOTT PALMER, born Longmont, Colorado, July 24, 1951; admitted to bar, 1976, Oregon. *Education:* University of Colorado at Boulder (B.A., summa cum laude, 1973); University of Oregon (J.D., 1976). Phi Beta Kappa. Articles Editor, Oregon Law Review, 1975-1976. Municipal Judge, Creswell, Oregon, 1984—. Fellow, Paul K. Harris, Eugene Rotary Club. Member, Roland K. Rodman Inn of Court. *Member:* Lane County (Member, Debtor-Creditor Law Section) and Federal Bar Associations; Oregon State Bar (Member, Sections on: Litigation; Business; Law Practice Management; Debtor-Creditor). ***PRACTICE AREAS:*** Commercial Litigation; Bankruptcy Litigation; Creditors' Rights; Commercial Collection; Foreclosures; Commercial Law. **Email:** RSPalmer@wlrlaw.com

BARRY RUBENSTEIN, born Eugene, Oregon, May 21, 1942; admitted to bar, 1968, California; 1975, Oregon. *Education:* University of Washington (B.S., 1964); Hastings College of Law, University of California (J.D., 1967); Boston University (LL.M., in Taxation, 1976). Adjunct Professor, University of Oregon, 1978-1992. *Member:* Oregon State Bar; State Bar of California. (Also at Roseburg Office). ***PRACTICE AREAS:*** Estate Planning; Retirement Planning; Probate; Taxation; Non-Profit and Charitable Organizations; Corporate Law. **Email:** BRubenstein@wlrlaw.com

JOHN C. WATKINSON, born Seattle, Washington, July 28, 1943; admitted to bar, 1968, Indiana; 1971, Oregon. *Education:* Oregon State University (B.S., 1965); Indiana University (J.D., 1968). Editor and Chapter Author, Foreclosing Security Interests, Oregon State Bar, CLE. Chapter Author, Real Property, Oregon State Bar CLE. *Member:* Oregon State Bar (Member, Executive Committee, Business Law Section, 1980-1985, Chair, 1984-1985; Member, Executive Committee, Real Estate and Land Use Section, 1983-1984 and 1988-1990, Secretary, 1983-1984). ***PRACTICE AREAS:*** Real Estate; Business Law; Business Transactions. **Email:** JWatkinson@wlrlaw.com

---

STEPHANIE T. CHANDLER, born Virginia Beach, Virginia, May 8, 1969; admitted to bar, 1999, Oregon. *Education:* Whitman College (B.S., 1991); University of Oregon (J.D., 1999). *Member:* Oregon State Bar. ***PRACTICE AREAS:*** Family Law; Employment Law; Trademarks. **Email:** SChandler@wlrlaw.com

DEREK D. SIMMONS, born Denver, Colorado, December 15, 1969; admitted to bar, 2000, Oregon. *Education:* University of Kansas (B.S., 1992); Northwestern School of Law (J.D., 2000). Phi Delta Phi; Cornelius Honor Society. National Merit Scholar, University of Kansas. Author: Comment, "No Seconds on Spam: A Legislative Prescription to Harness Unsolicited Commercial E-Mail," 3 Journal of Small and Emerging Business Law 389, 1999. Law Clerk to the Honorable David V. Brewer, Oregon Court of Appeals, 2000-2002. *Member:* Lane County Bar Association; Oregon State Bar. ***PRACTICE AREAS:*** Business Law; Health Law; Commercial Litigation. **Email:** DSimmons@wlrlaw.com

ABIGAIL A. KLINECT, born Moline, Illinois, May 29, 1976; admitted to bar, 2002, Oregon. *Education:* Colorado State University (B.A., 1998); University of Oregon (J.D., 2002). *Member:* Lane County Bar Association (Member: New Lawyers Committee; Law

(This Listing Continued)

Mentoring Committee); Oregon State Bar (Member: New Lawyers Committee; Law School Outreach Subcommittee). ***PRACTICE AREAS:*** Real Property; Business Law. ***Email:*** aklinect@wlrlaw.com

ELIZABETH W. BAUER, born Chicago, Illinois, June 26, 1977; admitted to bar, 2003, Oregon. *Education:* University of Oregon (B.A., 1999; M.B.A., 2003; J.D., 2003). *Member:* Oregon State Bar; Lane County Bar Association. ***PRACTICE AREAS:*** Health Law; Business Law; Estate Planning; Litigation. ***Email:*** ebauer@wlrlaw.com

GLENDA R. SLOAN, born Canby, Oregon, March 24, 1977; admitted to bar, 2002, Oregon. *Education:* Oregon State University (B.S., 1999); University of Oregon School of Law (J.D., 2002). *Member:* Lane County Bar Association; Oregon State Bar. ***PRACTICE AREAS:*** Litigation. ***Email:*** gsloan@wlrlaw.com

OF COUNSEL

R. Sande Tomlinson (Also practicing individually in Eugene)

REPRESENTATIVE CLIENTS: Lane Individual Practice Association; Whittaker Realty Group; Douglas County Independent Practice Association, Inc.; Women's Health Care Associates, P.C.; East Earth Herb, Inc.; Oregon Research Institute; Far West Fibers, Inc.; Treasure Valley Physicians' Management Corp.; Emerald Kidsports; Keifer, Braunger & Co., Inc.; Quality Care Associates, Inc.; Roseburg Dental Services, L.L.C.; Advantage Dental Plan, Inc.; AlphaShop Network Services, Inc.; McKay Investment Co.; Valley River Plaza Shopping Center; Oakway Shopping Center; Coastwide Laboratories, Inc.

HERSHNER HUNTER, LLP

Established in 1944

1441 7TH STREET
P.O. BOX K
FLORENCE, OREGON 97439
Telephone: 541-997-1997
Fax: 541-344-2025
Email: info@hershnerhunter.com
URL: http://www.hershnerhunter.com

Eugene, Oregon Office: 180 East 11th Avenue. Telephone: 541-686-8511. Fax: 541-344-2025.

Business, Banking, Timber, Estate Planning, Probate and Trust Administration, Taxation, Creditors' Rights, Bankruptcy, Construction, Real Property, Land Use, Employee Benefits, Health Care, Employment and Litigation.

PARTNERS

SHERYL S. McCONNELL, born Indianapolis, Indiana, November 29, 1960; admitted to bar, 1995, Oregon. *Education:* Oregon State University (B.S., with honors, 1983); University of California at Los Angeles (J.D., 1995). ***PRACTICE AREAS:*** Estate Planning Law; Business Planning; Federal Estate and Gift Taxation Law. ***Email:*** smcconnell@hershnerhunter.com

WILLIAM D. BREWER, born Washington, D.C., June 28, 1947; admitted to bar, 1985, Oregon. *Education:* Cornell University; Willamette University (B.A., 1971); Northwestern School of Law of Lewis and Clark College (J.D., magna cum laude, 1985). *Member:* Oregon State Bar(Member, Executive Committee, Estate Planning and Administration Sections). Fellow, American Counsel of Trust and Estate Counsel. ***PRACTICE AREAS:*** Estate Planning; Business Planning; Probate; Trust Administration; Estate and Gift Taxation; Trusts and Estates. ***Email:*** wbrewer@hershnerhunter.com

PATRICIA L. CHAPMAN, born California, January 16, 1956; admitted to bar, 1983, California and U.S. District Court, Northern District of California; 1988, Oregon. *Education:* University of California at Berkeley (B.A., summa cum laude, 1979); University of San Francisco (J.D., 1982). Phi Beta Kappa. Member, University of San Francisco Law Review, 1981-1982. *Member:* Lane County and American Bar Associations; State Bar of California; Oregon State Bar (Executive Committee - Business Law Section; Treasurer, Real Estate and Land Use Section). ***PRACTICE AREAS:*** Business Law; Commercial Law; Contracts; Corporate Law; Nonprofit and Charitable Organizations; Finance; Mergers, Acquisitions and Divestitures; Real Estate. ***Email:*** pchapman@hershnerhunter.com

ASSOCIATE

TODD R. JOHNSTON, born Portland, Oregon, January 18, 1974; admitted to bar, 1999, Oregon. *Education:* The Colorado College (B.A., 1995); University of Oregon School of Law (J.D., 1999). Author: "The Role of International Equity in a Sustainable Future, The Continuing Problem of Third World Debt and Development," 6 Buff. Envir.L.J. 1, 35 (1998). ***PRACTICE AREAS:*** Litigation. ***Email:*** tjohnston@hershnerhunter.com

(For complete biographical data on all personnel, see Professional Biographies at Eugene, Oregon)

SPEER, HOYT, JONES, FEINMAN, POPPE, WOLF & GRIFFITH, P.C.

FLORENCE, OREGON

(See Eugene)

Business Law, Formation of Business Entities, Business Buying and Selling, Employee Benefits, Conflict Resolution, Taxation, Trusts and Estates, Wills and Probate, Estate Planning, Real Estate, Tax Planning, Estate Tax, Tax Conflict Resolution, Collaboration, Family Law, Divorce, Separation, Prenuptial Agreements, Adoption, Custody, Paternity, Municipal Law, Government.

TIMOTHY M. DOLAN

206 GARIBALDI AVENUE
GARIBALDI, OREGON 97118
Telephone: 503-322-3742
Fax: 503-322-3238
Email: timothymdolan@oregoncoast.com

Real Estate, Trusts and Estates, General Litigation, Criminal Law, Bankruptcy.

TIMOTHY M. DOLAN, born Portland, Oregon, July 14, 1957; admitted to bar, 1984, Oregon and U.S. District Court, District of Oregon. *Education:* Oregon State University (B.S., 1980); Northwestern School of Law of Lewis and Clark College (J.D., 1983). *Member:* Tillamook County (President, 1993-1994) and American Bar Associations; Oregon State Bar (Chairman, Local Professional Responsibility Committee, 1992-1993; State Uniform Trial Court Committee, 2002-2005). ***PRACTICE AREAS:*** Real Estate (20%, 60); Trusts and Estates (20%, 50); Litigation (20%, 25); Criminal Law (20%, 100); Bankruptcy (20%, 60).

PETERSON LAW OFFICES, PC

GLADSTONE, OREGON

(See Portland)

Personal Injury, Premises Liability, Automobile Accidents and Injuries, Dog Bites and Wrongful Death.

BROWN, HUGHES, BIRD, ROTE, WETMORE & BROUHARD, LLP

Established in 1948

612 N.W. FIFTH STREET
P.O. BOX 10
GRANTS PASS, OREGON 97528
Telephone: 541-479-2678
Fax: 541-479-7485
URL: http://www.southernoregonlawyer.com
Email: brown_hughes@charterinternet.com
URL: http://www.lawyers.com/bhbrw

General Civil and Trial Practice. Appellate Practice. Personal Injury, Family Law, Divorce, Custody, Child Support, Trusts and Estates, Wills and Probate, Contracts, Business, Corporate, Commercial, Employment Law, Real Estate, Bankruptcy, Land Use, Mining, Estate Planning, Federal and State Taxation, Civil Litigation, Creditors Rights, Landlord-Tenant.

GENE L. BROWN (1921-1999)

MEMBERS OF FIRM

DANIEL F. HUGHES, born Richmond, California, August 28, 1943; admitted to bar, 1969, Oregon; 1970 California. *Education:* Mankato State University; Colorado State College (B.A., 1966); Willamette University (J.D., 1969). *Member:* Oregon State Bar (Member: Real Estate Section; Fee Arbitration Committee, 1979—); State Bar of California. ***PRACTICE AREAS:*** Estates; Wills; Probate; Real Estate Law; Estate Planning; Guardianship and Conservatorship. ***Email:*** dan_hughes@charterinternet.com

MICHAEL J. BIRD, born Hays, Kansas, March 1, 1942; admitted to bar, 1971, Oregon. *Education:* Ft. Hays State University (B.S., 1968); University of Oregon (J.D., 1971). Circuit Judge Pro Tem. *Member:* Oregon State Bar (Member, Business Law, Business Litigation, Estate Planning and Administration and Litigation Sections). ***PRACTICE AREAS:*** Business Law; Commercial Law; Civil Litigation; Probate. ***Email:*** mike_bird@charterinternet.com

FRANK C. ROTE, III, born Pittsburgh, Pennsylvania, February 16, 1954; admitted to bar, 1983, U.S. District Court, Northern District of Ohio, U.S. Court of Appeals, Sixth Circuit and U.S. Tax Court; 1989, Oregon, U.S. District Court, District of Oregon and U.S. Court of Appeals, Ninth Circuit. *Education:* Xavier University (B.S., 1976); University of Akron School of Law (J.D., 1982). Phi Alpha Delta. Circuit Court Judge Pro Tem. *Member:* Oregon State Bar (Member, Sections on: Taxation and Appellate Practice). ***PRACTICE AREAS:*** Federal and State Taxation; Bankruptcy; Commercial Law; Appellate Practice; Estates and Trusts. ***Email:*** frank_rote@charterinternet.com

LADONNA S. WETMORE, admitted to bar, 1995, Oregon; 1996, U.S. District Court, District of Oregon. *Education:* University of Wyoming (B.S., 1992; J.D., 1995). *Member:* Josephine County Bar Association (President, 2001); Oregon State Bar (Member, Family Law Section). ***PRACTICE AREAS:*** Family Law; Divorce; Child Custody; Child Support; Estate Planning; Wills; Trust Law; Probate. ***Email:*** ladonna_wetmore@charterinternet.com

JASON BROUHARD, admitted to bar, 1998, Oregon; U.S. District Court, District of Oregon. *Education:* Willamette University (B.S., 1994; M.B.A.;, J.D., 1998). *Member:* Oregon State Bar (Member, Labor and Employment Section); American Bar Association (Member, Litigation and Labor and Employment Section). ***PRACTICE AREAS:*** Employment Law; Civil Litigation; Business Law; Corporate Law; Estate Planning; Wills; Trust Law; Probate. ***Email:*** jason_brouhard@charterinternet.com

REPRESENTATIVE CLIENTS: Southern Oregon Federal Credit Union; Farmers Building Supply; Hillebrand Paradise Ranch Resort, Inc.; Ram South Fork, Inc.; American Fuijino Enterprise, Co., Ltd.; Ausland Construction Company; Budget Internet; Idea Cafe; Southern Oregon Sanitation; Grants Pass Sanitation; Oregon Optometric Group Provider; onlineauction.com; Hull & Hull Funeral Home, Inc.
REFERENCES: Wells Fargo Bank; Umpqua Bank.

CAUBLE, DOLE & SORENSON

ONE ELEVEN BUILDING
111 S.E. 6TH STREET
P.O. BOX 398
GRANTS PASS, OREGON 97526
Telephone: 541-476-8825
Fax: 541-471-1704
Toll Free: 888-870-8825
Email: rvlaw@qwest.net
URL: http://www.roguevalleylaw.com

General Civil and Trial Practice in State and Federal Courts. Business, Construction Law, Corporate, Creditors' Rights, Elder Law, Employment Law, Estate Planning, Land Use Law, Mining, Probate, Real Property, School Law, Timber and Logging, Water and Natural Resources Law.

MEMBERS OF FIRM

WALTER L. CAUBLE, born Juneau, Alaska, April 10, 1941; admitted to bar, 1967, Oregon, U.S. District Court, District of Oregon and U.S. Court of Appeals, Ninth Circuit. *Education:* Willamette University (B.A., 1963; J.D., 1967). Delta Theta Phi. Member, Josephine-Jackson Counties Local Professional Responsibility Committee, 1984-1985. Member, Continuing Legal Education Committee, 2005—. *Member:* Josephine County (Past President) Bar Association; Oregon State Bar (Member, Procedure and Practice Committee, 1975-1976; Disciplinary Board Region 3, 1988-1993, Chairman, 1989-1990). [Capt., USAF, JAG, 1967-1971]. ***Email:*** rvlaw@qwest.net

JAMES R. DOLE, born Roseburg, Oregon, July 24, 1964; admitted to bar, 1989, Oregon, U.S. District Court, District of Oregon and U.S. Court of Appeals, Ninth Circuit. *Education:* University of Oregon (B.A., cum laude, 1986; J.D., 1989). Member, Editorial Board, Journal of Environmental Law and Litigation. Member, Board of Education, Rogue Community College. *Member:* Josephine County Bar Association; Oregon State Bar (Member, Local Professional Responsibility Committee, 2000-2003). ***Email:*** jdole@qwest.net

CHRISTOPHER L. CAUBLE, born Denver, Colorado, November 29, 1970; admitted to bar, 1996, Oregon, U.S. District Court, District of Oregon; U.S. Court of Appeals, Ninth Circuit and U.S. Supreme Court; 2002, Washington; 2004, U.S. District Court, Western District of Washington. *Education:* Willamette University (B.A., 1993); Gonzaga University (J.D., cum laude, 1996). Phi Alpha Delta. Circuit Court Judge Pro Tem, 2003—. *Member:* Josephine County Bar Association (Past President); Oregon State Bar (Member, Legal Ethics Committee). ***LANGUAGES:*** French. ***Email:*** clcauble@qwest.net

DEBORAH L. SORENSON, born Selah, Washington, November 25, 1977; admitted to bar, 2002, Oregon; U.S. District Court, District of Oregon; U.S. Court of Appeals, Ninth Circuit. *Education:* Washington State University (B.A., 1998); Gonzaga University School of Law (J.D., 2001). *Member:* Josephine County Bar Association; Oregon State Bar. ***Email:*** dlsorenson@qwest.net

ASSOCIATE

WILLARD L. RANSOM, born Kansas City, Kansas, January 12, 1978; admitted to bar, 2003, Oregon; 2005, U.S. District Court, District of Oregon. *Education:* Kansas State University (B.A., 2000); University of Kansas (J.D., 2002); University of the Pacific McGeorge School of Law (LL.M., 2004). *Member:* Oregon State Bar; Jackson County Bar Association. ***Email:*** wlransom@qwest.net

REPRESENTATIVE CLIENTS: Bentwood Furniture; Bridgeview Vineyards, Inc.; Copeland Paving/Copeland Sand & Gravel; Core-Mark Distributors, Inc.; Environmental Container Systems; Equi=Tech Inc.; Frist International Bank & Trust; Fourply, Inc.; Grants Pass School District; Indian Hill LLC; Jantzer & Sons Logging, Inc.; Jim Sigel Automotive Center; First American Title Company of Oregon; Lawless Roofing Co.; Riverside Ready Mix; Triple A RV Center, Inc.; Umpqua Bank; Perpetua Forest Products; Wells Fargo Bank Private Client Services; Wild River Brewing & Pizza Company; 221 Property Services, Inc.; Oregon's Best Cars, Inc.

JACOBSON, THIEROLF & DICKEY, P.C.

GRANTS PASS, OREGON

(See Medford)

General Litigation and Office Practice, Civil and Criminal Trials and Appeals in State and Federal Courts, Bankruptcy and Collections, Real Estate and Land Use, Probate, Estate Planning, Business, Domestic Relations, Indian and Environmental Law, Water Law, Immigration, Patents, Trademarks, Copyrights, Licensing, Wills, Trusts.

PETERSON LAW OFFICES, PC

GRANTS PASS, OREGON

(See Portland)

Personal Injury, Premises Liability, Automobile Accidents and Injuries, Dog Bites and Wrongful Death.

JAMES F. O'ROURKE JR. & ASSOCIATES

GRESHAM, OREGON

(See Portland)

Criminal Law, Driving While Intoxicated, Drug Crimes, Parole and Probation, Major Traffic Violations, Assault, Property Crimes, Domestic Violence, Personal Injury, Automobile Accidents, Wrongful Death, Truck, Motorcycle, Bicycle, Pedestrian Accidents, Asset Protection, Estate Planning, Guardianship, Wills, Trusts and Probate, Elder Law.

PETERSON LAW OFFICES, PC

GRESHAM, OREGON

(See Portland)

Personal Injury, Premises Liability, Automobile Accidents and Injuries, Dog Bites and Wrongful Death.

HALLMAN & DRETKE

HEPPNER, OREGON

(See Pendleton)

Civil Litigation, Personal Injury and Wrongful Death Litigation and Appellate Practice.

ANDERSON HANSELL, P.C.

Established in 1976

475 EAST MAIN STREET
HERMISTON, OREGON 97838
Telephone: 541-567-7800
Fax: 541-567-7656
Email: sally@andersonhansell.com

General Civil and Trial Practice, Agriculture, Business Litigation, Creditor's Rights, Real Estate, Estate Planning and Probate.

FIRM PROFILE: Formerly named George L. Anderson, P.C.

GEORGE L. ANDERSON, admitted to bar, 1976, Oregon. *Education:* Whitman College (B.A., 1967); University of Oregon (M.A., 1972); Lewis & Clark College (J.D., 1976). Associate Editor, Lewis and Clark Law Review, 1975 & 1976. *Member:* Oregon State Bar (Agricultural Law Section, Executive Committee Member). [U.S. Army Counter-Intelligence Agent, 1969-1971]. (Managing Partner). ***PRACTICE AREAS:*** Agricultural Law; Business Law; Creditors Rights; Civil Litigation; Real Estate. ***Email:*** george@andersonhansell.com

SALLY ANDERSON-HANSELL, admitted to bar, 2000, Oregon. *Education:* University of Oregon (B.A., 1997; J.D., 2000). *Member:* Oregon State Bar (Member, Business Law Section, Executive Committee); Oregon Women Lawyers Rebecca J. Bloom Chapter (President). ***PRACTICE AREAS:*** Business Law; Real Property; Agricultural Law; Probate; Estate Planning; Civil Litigation. ***Email:*** sally@andersonhansell.com

---

ADAMS & UFFELMAN LLP

HILLSBORO, OREGON

(See Beaverton)

General Civil and Trial Practice in all State and Federal Courts. Business, Corporate, Estate Planning and Probate Law, Entertainment Law, Family Law, Divorce, Real Estate Law, Contracts, Criminal Law, Criminal Trials and Appeals in all State and Federal Courts.

SHELLEY K. EDLING

Established in 1994

134 S.E. 5TH AVENUE, SUITE A
P.O. BOX 728
HILLSBORO, OREGON 97123
Telephone: 503-648-2900
Fax: 503-846-9110
Email: info@shelleyedling.com
URL: http://www.shelleykedling.com

Practice Limited to Workers Compensation Law.

FIRM PROFILE: Attorney Edling has handled workers' compensation matters for over 25 years, opening her office in Hillsboro specifically to assist injured workers with all issues relating to on the job injuries.

SHELLEY K. EDLING, born Hood River, Oregon, July 13, 1951; admitted to bar, 1980, Oregon and U.S. District Court, District of Oregon. *Education:* Utah State University; Universidad de las Americas, Mexico; Oregon State University; Brigham Young University (B.S., 1974; J.D., 1979). Delta Theta Phi. *Member:* Washington County Bar Association; Oregon State Bar (Member, Workers' Compensation Section Executive Committee, 2002-2005). ***LANGUAGES:*** French. ***PRACTICE AREAS:*** Workers Compensation.

Language: French.

BARBARA J. GARLAND LAW OFFICE, P.C.

Established in 1999

230 NORTHEAST SECOND AVENUE, SUITE H
HILLSBORO, OREGON 97124
Telephone: 503-615-8233
Fax: 503-693-0139
Email: bjgarland@verizon.net
URL: http://www.lawyers.com/bgarlandlaw

Family Law, Divorce, Child Custody, Paternity, Parenting Rights, Grandparents Visitation Rights, Support, Criminal Law, All State Court Offenses (non-Federal) including Aggravated Murder.

(This Listing Continued)

FIRM PROFILE: Barbara J. Garland has been practicing criminal and domestic relations law in Oregon since 1990, including 5 years of indigent criminal defense at the beginning of her career.

BARBARA J. GARLAND, born Portland, Oregon; admitted to bar, 1990, Oregon. *Education:* Portland State University (B.S., 1984); Lewis & Clark College, Northwestern School of Law (J.D., 1989). *Member:* Washington County Bar Association; Oregon State Bar; Oregon Criminal Defense Lawyers Association. ***PRACTICE AREAS:*** Domestic Relations; Criminal Law. ***Email:*** bjgarland@verizon.net

LEGAL SUPPORT PERSONNEL

MARY MUTSCHLER

HELZER & CROMAR, LLP

HILLSBORO, OREGON

(See Beaverton)

Criminal Law, Family Law, Divorce, Child Custody, Spousal Support, Personal Injury, Automobile Accidents, Criminal Law, Driving While Intoxicated, Felonies, Drug Crimes, Juvenile Crimes, Parole and Probation, Sexual Abuse, Traffic Violations, Estate Litigation, Guardianship and Conservatorship, Employment Law, Discrimination, Sexual Harassment.

McNEIL LAW OFFICE LLC

Established in 2003

1323 N.E. ORENCO STATION, SUITE 310
HILLSBORO, OREGON 97124
Telephone: 503-615-8336
Fax: 503-726-2220
Email: ken@mcneillawoffice.com
URL: http://www.mcneillawoffice.com

Family, Criminal, Wills, Personal Injury, Business Litigation.

FIRM PROFILE: The McNeil Law Office LLC is Orenco Station's first and only law firm. We are dedicated to counsel our clients with integrity, respect, quality and efficiency to secure the best possible result. We are close to many Hillsboro neighborhoods and businesses, and we are conveniently close to the Orenco MAX light rail stop.

KENNETH W. McNEIL, born Pullman, Washington, May 25, 1965; admitted to bar, 1991, Oregon and U.S. District Court, District of Oregon. *Education:* Whitman College (B.A., with honors, 1987); University of Oregon (J.D., 1990). *Member:* Washington County Bar Association (Member Board of Directors); Oregon State Bar (Member, Family Law Section); Oregon Criminal Defense Lawyers Association. ***PRACTICE AREAS:*** Criminal Law; Family Law; Personal Injury. ***Email:*** ken@mcneillawoffice.com

---

KEVIN D. BRENDEN, admitted to bar, 2002, Oregon. *Education:* University of Alaska (B.A., 1995); Northwestern School of Law, Lewis and Clark College (J.D., 2002). *Member:* Washington County Bar Association; Oregon State Bar (Member, Estate Planning Section); Oregon Criminal Defense Lawyers Association. ***PRACTICE AREAS:*** Estate Planning; Criminal Defense; Family Law. ***Email:*** kevin@mcneillawoffice.com

ERIK M. BUCHÉR, born Albany, Oregon, July 30, 1974; admitted to bar, 2000, Oregon. *Education:* Oregon State University (B.A., cum laude, 1997); University of Oregon School of Law (J.D., 2000). *Member:* Washington County Bar Association; Oregon State Bar (Member, Family Law Section); Oregon Criminal Defense Lawyers Association. ***PRACTICE AREAS:*** Family Law; Juvenile Law; Criminal Defense. ***Email:*** erik@mcneillawoffice.com

JAMES A. GOLDSTEIN, JR., born Elizabeth, New Jersey, March 29, 1968; admitted to bar, 1995, Oregon; 2001, New Jersey and New York. *Education:* Binghamton University (B.A., 1990); Northwestern School of Law, Lewis and Clark College (J.D., 1995). *Member:* Washington County, New Jersey State (Member, Family Law Section) and New York State Bar Associations; Oregon State Bar (Member, Sections on: Family Law; Business Litigation). ***PRACTICE AREAS:*** Family Law; Matrimonial Law; Child Custody; Domestic Violence; Criminal Law; Business Litigation. ***Email:*** jim@mcneillawoffice.com

---

SCOTT HOOKLAND LLP

HILLSBORO, OREGON

(See Tigard)

Construction, Design, Civil and Trial Practice. Commercial Collections, Business, Real Estate, Mediations, Arbitrations, Creditors Rights.

LAURIE SHERTZ LLC

HILLSBORO, OREGON

(See Portland)

Criminal Defense, Trial Practice, Felonies, Homicide and Assault, Self Defense, Weapons Charges, Sex Offenses, Drug Crimes, Theft and Fraud. Practice in Federal and State Courts.

MERLIN D. WILKINSON
ATTORNEY AT LAW

100 S.W. BASELINE
HILLSBORO, OREGON 97123
Telephone: 503-693-6641
Fax: 503-615-8687
Email: merlinwilkinson@att.net
URL: http://www.merlinwilkinson.com

Divorce, Child Custody, Child Support, Visitation Rights and Family Law.

MERLIN D. WILKINSON, born American Fork, Utah, February 25, 1957; admitted to bar, 1991, Oregon. *Education:* Brigham Young University (B.S., 1987); Northwestern School of Law (J.D., 1990). *Member:* Oregon State Bar (Member, Sections on: Family Law; Wills, 1995—). ***PRACTICE AREAS:*** Family Law; Divorce; Child Custody; Child Support; Visitation Rights.

WILLIAMS, ZOGRAFOS & PECK

A PROFESSIONAL CORPORATION

HILLSBORO, OREGON

(See Lake Oswego)

Limited Exclusively to the representation of Employers in Labor and Employment Matters, including Union-Management Relations, Labor Negotiations, Employment Discrimination, Wrongful Discharge, Wage and Hour, Preventive Labor Relations, Before Federal and State Courts and Administrative Agencies.

WISEMAN LAW OFFICE, P.C.

473 S. FIRST AVENUE
HILLSBORO, OREGON 97123
Telephone: 503-681-4626
Fax: 503-681-2171
URL: http://www.charleswiseman.com
Email: wisemancj@aol.com
URL: http://www.lawyers.com/wisemanlawoffices

Bankruptcy, Business Start-Ups, Personal Injury, Automobile Accidents, Dog Bites, Slip and Fall, Wrongful Death, Domestic Relations, Child Custody, Child Support, Divorce, Premarital Agreements, Business Law, Criminal Law, Driving While Intoxicated, Drug Crimes, Aviation Law.

CHARLES J. WISEMAN, born Tillamook, Oregon, October 30, 1942; admitted to bar, 1973, Oregon; U.S. Court of Appeals, Ninth Circuit; U.S. Supreme Court. *Education:* Lewis and Clark College (B.S., 1970); Northwestern School of Law of Lewis and Clark College (J.D., 1973). Deputy District Attorney: Multnomah County District Attorney's Office, 1971-1976; Lane County District Attorney's Office, 1976-1977. *Member:* Oregon State Bar. ***Email:*** wisemancj@aol.com

---

BOIVIN, UERLINGS & DIIACONI, P.C.

Established in 1915

803 MAIN STREET, SUITE 201
KLAMATH FALLS, OREGON 97601-6070
Telephone: 541-884-8101
FAX: 541-884-8498
Email: bud2025@qwest.net

General Civil and Trial Practices in State and Federal Courts. Arbitration, Business Law, Bankruptcy, Banking and Commercial Law, Corporate Law, Trusts and Estates, Wills and Probate, Estate and Trust Planning, Family Law, Divorce, Health Care Law, Hospital Defense, Insurance Defense, Municipal Law, Professional Liability Defense, Real Estate, Foreclosures, Collections.

FIRM PROFILE: The firm was founded in 1915 by Claude McColloch. Harry D. Boivin became an associate in 1923. Mr. McColloch was appointed to the U.S. District Court for the District of Oregon in the 1930's and left the firm at that time. Mr. Boivin continued in solo practice, becoming Speaker of the Oregon House in 1937 and President of the Oregon Senate for two terms in the 1960's. Robert D. Boivin joined the firm in 1964. James R. Uerlings became a partner in 1984. Barbara DiIaconi joined the firm in 1991. The firm has a regional practice in southern Oregon in the specialty areas listed above.

HARRY D. BOIVIN (1903-1999)

ROBERT D. BOIVIN (1937-1999)

JAMES R. UERLINGS, born Klamath Falls, Oregon, April 25, 1950; admitted to bar, 1976, Oregon; 1979, U.S. District Court, District of Oregon; 1987, U.S. Court of Appeals, Ninth Circuit. *Education:* Southern Oregon University (B.S., 1972); Seattle University (J.D., with honors, 1975). Municipal Judge, City of Klamath Falls, 1984—. Land Use Hearing Officer, Klamath County, 1979-1987. Deputy County Counsel, Klamath County, 1980-1987. *Member:* Klamath County Bar Association (President, 1980-1981 and 2003-2004); Oregon State Bar (Member: Disciplinary Board for Legal Ethics, 1988-1991; State Professional Responsibility Board, 1999-2003; Chairman, 2001-2003). ***PRACTICE AREAS:*** Business Law; Corporate Law; Bankruptcy; Foreclosure; Commercial; Probate; Banks and Banking; Municipal Law; Wills; Trust Law; Estate Planning; Real Estate; Collections; Family Law. ***Email:*** juerlings@qwest.net

BARBARA M. DIIACONI, born Portland, Oregon, December 3, 1949; admitted to bar, 1989, Nevada; 1990, U.S. District Court, District of Nevada and U.S. Court of Appeals, Ninth Circuit; 1991, Oregon; 1995, U.S. District Court, District of Oregon. *Education:*

(This Listing Continued)

BOIVIN, UERLINGS & DiIACONI, P.C., Klamath Falls—Continued

Gonzaga University (B.A., 1971); University of Oregon (M.A., 1977); Creighton University (B.S.N., 1979); Gonzaga University School of Law (J.D., cum laude, 1989). Registered Nurse, Washington State, 1979 and Nevada, 1989. Ninth Circuit Court Lawyer Representative, 2000-2002. *Member:* Klamath County Bar Association (Past President); Oregon State Bar; Southern Oregon Federal Bar Association (Treasurer, 2000-2003; President, 2003-2004); Defense Research Institute; National Health Lawyers Association; Oregon Association of Defense Counsel. ***REPORTED CASES:*** World Wide Underwriters Ins. Co. v. Jackson, 121 Or. App 292, 855 P2d 166, (1995). ***PRACTICE AREAS:*** Hospital Law (Hospital Counsel); Professional Malpractice; Medical Malpractice; Insurance Defense; Civil Litigation; Real Property; Timber and Logging; Family Law. ***Email:*** bdiiaconi@qwest.net

REPRESENTATIVE CLIENTS: Allied Insurance Co.; Basin Transit Service Transportation District; Capital Indemnity; Carolina Casualty Insurance Co.; Carriage Works; City of Malin; Church Mutual Insurance; Grange Mutual Insurance Co.; Klamath County School District; Klamath First Federal Savings & Loan Association; Merle West Medical Center; Oregon Professional Liability Fund; Sykes Industries; Standard Insurance Co.; St. Paul Insurance Co.; Worldwide Insurance Co.; Shasta View Irringration District; Swan Lake Moulding Co.; Gulf Insurance Group.

BRANDSNESS, BRANDSNESS, RUDD & BUNCH, P.C.

411 PINE STREET
KLAMATH FALLS, OREGON 97601-6020
Telephone: 541-882-6616
FAX: 541-882-8819
Email: info@brandsnessrudd.com
URL: http://www.brandsnessrudd.com

Trusts and Estates, Wills and Probate, Estate Planning, Real Estate, Zoning, Planning and Land Use, Corporate Law, Business Law, Buying and Selling of Businesses, Partnership Law, Commercial Law, Banking, Business Acquisitions, Timber Law, Contracts, Financial, Construction Law, Creditors Rights, Bankruptcy, Collections, Complex Civil Litigation.

WILLIAM P. BRANDSNESS, born Stanley, Wisconsin, December 9, 1933; admitted to bar, 1962, Oregon. *Education:* University of Oregon (B.S., 1955; LL.B., 1962). Phi Delta Phi (President, 1961-1962). City Attorney, Klamath Falls, Oregon, 1968-1975. *Member:* Klamath County Bar Association; Oregon State Bar. ***PRACTICE AREAS:*** Banking Law; Commercial Law; Business Law; Estates and Estate Planning; Real Estate Law; Business Acquisitions Law; Probate; Wills; Trust Law. ***Email:*** bill@brandsnessrudd.com

ANDREW C. BRANDSNESS, born Sacramento, California, September 30, 1957; admitted to bar, 1983, Oregon and U.S. District Court, District of Oregon; 1997, U.S. Court of Appeals, Ninth Circuit. *Education:* University of Oregon (B.S., 1979; J.D., 1983). Member, Oregon Bankers Association. *Member:* Klamath County Bar Association; Oregon State Bar; American Bankruptcy Institute. ***PRACTICE AREAS:*** Commercial Litigation; Creditor's Rights; Foreclosures and Secured Transactions; Construction Law. ***Email:*** andy@brandsnessrudd.com

MICHAEL PATRICK RUDD, born Colorado Springs, Colorado, October 10, 1967; admitted to bar, 1993, Oregon and U.S. District Court, District of Oregon. *Education:* University of Washington (B.A., 1989); Willamette University (J.D., 1993). *Member:* Klamath County Bar Association; Oregon State Bar. ***PRACTICE AREAS:*** Acquisitions; Business Law; Commercial Law; Trusts and Estates; Estate Planning; Real Estate; Land Use. ***Email:*** mike@brandsnessrudd.com

WILLIAM D. BUNCH, born Richmond, Virginia, March 29, 1965; admitted to bar, 1990, Virginia; 1998, Alaska; 1999, Oregon. *Education:* Hampden-Sydney College (B.A., 1987); University of Virginia School of Law (J.D., 1990). Phi Beta Kappa. [Lt., U.S. Navy, 1990-1994; U.S. Air Force, 1994-1998; U.S. Air Force Reserves, 1998-2000; Air National Guard, 2000—]. ***LANGUAGES:*** French. ***PRACTICE AREAS:*** Personal Injury; Criminal Law; Trial Practice; Real Property; Family Law. ***Email:*** dan@brandsnessrudd.com

REFERENCES: Klamath Falls, Oregon; U.S. National Bank of Oregon; South Valley State Bank, Klamath Falls, Oregon.

JACOBSON, THIEROLF & DICKEY, P.C.

KLAMATH FALLS, OREGON

(See Medford)

General Litigation and Office Practice, Civil and Criminal Trials and Appeals in State and Federal Courts, Bankruptcy and Collections, Real Estate and Land Use, Probate, Estate Planning, Business, Domestic Relations, Indian and Environmental Law, Water Law, Immigration, Patents, Trademarks, Copyrights, Licensing, Wills, Trusts.

LAW OFFICES OF ROBERT D. LOWRY

KLAMATH FALLS, OREGON

(See Eugene)

Insurance Defense, Products Liability Defense, Medical Malpractice, Hospital Malpractice, Business Litigation, Construction Law and Civil Litigation.

MUHLHEIM BOYD

KLAMATH FALLS, OREGON

(See Eugene)

Creditor/Debtor Representation; Commercial Litigation; Workouts and Bankruptcy Reorganizations; Bankruptcy Litigation; Creditors' Rights; Foreclosure; Commercial Law; Business Litigation; Business Transactions; Litigation; Estate and Probate.

RATLIFF & RATLIFF, P.C.

905 MAIN STREET, SUITE 200
KLAMATH FALLS, OREGON 97601
Telephone: 541-882-6331; 882-6334
Fax: 541-883-8494
URL: http://www.ratliffandratliff.com

General Civil and Criminal Trial Practice. Real Estate, Family, Divorce, Probate, Corporate. Traffic Matters. Personal Injury.

MEMBERS OF FIRM

DONALD M. (MIKE) RATLIFF, born Klamath Falls, Oregon, April 23, 1949; admitted to bar, 1975, Oregon and U.S. District Court, District of Oregon. *Education:* Oregon State University (B.S., 1972); Northwestern School of Law of Lewis and Clark College (J.D., 1975). Municipal Judge Pro-Tem, City of Merrill, 1979-1980. *Member:* Oregon State Bar Association; Oregon Trial Lawyers Association; The Association of Trial Lawyers of America; Oregon Criminal Defense Lawyers Association; National Association of Criminal Defense Lawyers. ***PRACTICE AREAS:*** Criminal Defense; Real Property; Probate; Family Law; Personal Injury; Liability; Civil Litigation; Product Liability. ***Email:*** dmratlif@aol.com

NATHAN J. RATLIFF, born Klamath Falls, Oregon, September 7, 1977; admitted to bar, 2003, Oregon and U.S. District Court, District of Oregon. *Education:* Oregon State University (B.A., summa cum laude, 1999); University of Oregon School of Law (J.D., 2003). Order of the Coif. *Member:* Oregon Criminal Defense Lawyers Association. ***LANGUAGES:*** Spanish. ***PRACTICE AREAS:*** Criminal Law (40%); Civil Litigation (30%); Personal Injury (20%); Family Law (10%).

Language: Spanish.

COREY, BYLER, REW, LORENZEN & HOJEM, L.L.P.

LA GRANDE, OREGON

(See Pendleton)

General Civil and Trial Practice. Agriculture and Agricultural Cooperatives, Domestic Relations, Banking, Business, Municipal, Zoning, Condemnation, School, Corporation, Insurance, Tax, Estate Planning, Probate, Water and Real Estate Law.

HALLMAN & DRETKE

LA GRANDE, OREGON

(See Pendleton)

Civil Litigation, Personal Injury and Wrongful Death Litigation and Appellate Practice.

MAUTZ BAUM & O'HANLON, LLP

Established in 1973

1902 4TH STREET
P.O. BOX 967
LA GRANDE, OREGON 97850
Telephone: 541-963-3104
Fax: 541-963-9254
Email: mbolg@mautzeltal.com

Pendleton, Oregon Office: 101 S.E. Byers Avenue, P.O. Box 628. 97801. Telephone: 541-276-2811. Fax: 541-276-0543.

General Litigation and Appellate Practice in all State and Federal Courts. Administrative, Agriculture, Bankruptcy, Business, Commercial, Creditors' Rights, Estate Planning and Probate, Insurance, Personal Injury, Professional Malpractice Defense and Real Estate.

FIRM PROFILE: Mautz Baum & O'Hanlon, LLP, is a regional firm offering business, estate and litigation services to lawyers and clients throughout northeastern Oregon from offices in Pendleton and La Grande.

RESIDENT PARTNER

DAVID C. BAUM, born La Grande, Oregon, August 14, 1949; admitted to bar, 1975, Oregon. *Education:* Eastern Oregon College (B.A., cum laude, 1972); Willamette University (J.D., 1975). *Member:* Union County and American Bar Associations; Oregon State Bar; Oregon Association of Defense Counsel; Oregon Trial Lawyers Association. ***PRACTICE AREAS:*** Litigation; Business Law; Estate Planning. ***Email:*** dcb@mautzetal.com

REPRESENTATIVE CLIENTS: Barenbrug USA (Imbler); Blue Mt. Seeds, Inc.; (Imbler); Royces Grass Seeds, Inc. (Imbler); Idaho Timber; Smith Frozen Foods; Louisiana Pacific; Mutual of Enumclaw; Cities of Cove, Elgin, North Powder; Union Education Service District; Designated Counsel Brotherhood of Locomotive Engineers; LaGrande School District; City of LaGrande; City of Imbler; Union County; City of Wallowa; City of Union; Joseph School District; Omnitrac, LLC; Oregon Mutual; Marr Flat Cattle Co., LLC.
REFERENCES: Pioneer Federal Savings & Loan Assn. (La Grande Branch); United States National Bank (La Grande Branch).

(For complete biographical data on all personnel, see Professional Biographies at Pendleton, Oregon).

PETERSON LAW OFFICES, PC

LA GRANDE, OREGON

(See Portland)

Personal Injury, Premises Liability, Automobile Accidents and Injuries, Dog Bites and Wrongful Death.

BITTNER & HAHS, P.C.

Established in 1983

4949 SW MEADOWS ROAD, SUITE 260
LAKE OSWEGO, OREGON 97258-2085
Telephone: 503-228-5626
FAX: 503-228-8566
URL: http://www.bittner-hahs.com

General Civil and Trial Practice in all State and Federal Courts. Corporate, Business, Employment, Construction, Estate Planning, Probate and Real Estate Law.

FIRM PROFILE: J. Terrence Bittner has been practicing since 1971. The firm was formed in 1983. Andrew D. Hahs has been with the firm since its inception.

J. TERRENCE BITTNER, born Portland, Oregon, March 20, 1946; admitted to bar, 1971, Oregon; 1972, U.S. District Court, District of Oregon and U.S. Court of Appeals, Ninth Circuit; 1997, U.S. Court of Federal Claims; 2003, Washington. *Education:* University of Oregon (B.S., 1968); Hastings College of Law, University of California (J.D., 1971). Order of the Coif. Member, Thurston Society. Author: "Bond Claims," Construction Handbook, Oregon State Bar CLE, 1986; "Rights and Liabilities of Sureties," Ch. 18, Construction Law, Oregon State Bar CLE, 1989. Associate Member, Oregon-Columbia AGC Legal Committee, 1984-1991. *Member:* Oregon State Bar (Member, Economics of Law Committee, 1983-1986; Member and Secretary, 1984, and Chairman, 1986, Construction Law Section; Lawyer Alcohol & Drug Dependencies Committee, 1986-1988); American Bar Association. ***PRACTICE AREAS:*** Business Law; Estate Planning Law; Wills; Probate; Surety Law; Construction Law; Commercial Banking; Business Succession Planning. ***Email:*** tbittner@bittner-hahs.com

ANDREW D. HAHS, born New London, Connecticut, April 15, 1956; admitted to bar, 1981, Oregon and U.S. District Court, District of Oregon; 1984, Washington and U.S. District Court, Eastern and Western Districts of Washington. *Education:* California State University at Sacramento (B.A., 1978); University of California at Davis (J.D., 1981). Phi Kappa Phi; Order of the Coif. Recipient, American Jurisprudence Awards in Real Property and Commercial Paper. *Member:* Oregon State Bar (Member, Future of the Legal Profession Committee, 1986-1989); Washington State and American Bar Associations. ***PRACTICE AREAS:*** Business Law; Property Management; Real Estate Law; Surety Law; Construction Law. ***Email:*** ahahs@bittner-hahs.com

---

BRANDON C. BITTNER, born October 23, 1971; admitted to bar, 2000, Oregon. *Education:* Whitworth College (B.S. in Biology, 1995); University of Oregon School of Law (J.D., 2000). Member, Lake Oswego Chamber of Commerce. *Member:* Oregon State Bar. ***PRACTICE AREAS:*** Estate Planning; Wills; Probate; Taxation; Business Law; Trust Law; Real Property; Intellectual Property. ***Email:*** bbittner@bittner-hahs.com

MARK J. McGRANAGHAN, born Geneva, New York, October 4, 1954; admitted to bar, 1995, Oregon; 1996, U.S. District Court, District of Oregon; 2003, Washington. *Education:* Sonoma State University (B.A., cum laude, 1991); Lewis and Clark College (J.D., 1995). *Member:* Oregon State Bar. ***PRACTICE AREAS:*** Litigation; Business Law; Landlord and Tenant Law; Plaintiffs Personal Injury. ***Email:*** mmcgranaghan@bittner-hahs.com

LEAH COLETTE SYKES, born Edmonton, Alberta, Canada, March 12, 1974; admitted to bar, 2002, Oregon. *Education:* Simon Fraser University (B.A., Criminology, 1997); Northwestern School of Law (J.D., 2001). Member: Ambassadors and Latino Business Advisory Councils. *Member:* Oregon State Bar; Federal and American Bar Associations; American Immigration Lawyers Association. ***PRACTICE AREAS:*** Immigration and Naturalization; International Law; Domestic Relations; Wills; Civil Litigation; Personal Injury. ***Email:*** lsykes@bittner-hahs.com

REPRESENTATIVE CLIENTS: Alliance Residential Company; Background Investigations; Bakemark Ingrediants (West), Inc.; Caddies 4 Cure; Clackamas Golf, LLC; Computer Forms, Inc.; DeLap White Caldwell & Croy, LLP; The Dischinger Team; Employers Mutual Casualty Co.; Essex Property Trust, Inc.; FSA Network, Inc.; Guardian Management, LLC; Harsch Investment Corp.; H.D. Fowler Company; Hollabaugh Bros. & Associates, Inc.; Housing Authority of Portland; Hoyt Northwest, Inc.; Huser Integrated Technologies; International Fidelity Insurance Co.; J.F. Shelton Co.; M & T Real Estate Trust; Maddox Airfreight; Mario's; Metro Multifamily Housing Association; Nomad International, Inc.; North Portland Chiropractic Clinic; Northwest Small Business Finance Corp; Onecreditsource.com; Pacific Lumber Resource, Inc.; Parker Johnstone's; Pile Contractors, Inc.; Pinnacle Property Management; S2 Contractors, Inc.; Sealant Specialists (John Latta & Associates, Inc.); Sentinel Property Management; Stagecraft Industries, Inc.; Stone Eagle Equity Partners, LLC; Temp Control Mechanical Corporation; Washington Trust Bank; Wilf's Restaurant; Wilsonville Honda.

BLUNCK & WALHOOD, LLC

LAKE OSWEGO, OREGON

(See West Linn)

Arbitration, Automobile Accidents, Construction Claims, Contracts, Personal Injury, Insurance.

BUCKLEY LeCHEVALLIER, P.C.

THREE CENTERPOINTE DRIVE, SUITE 250
LAKE OSWEGO, OREGON 97035
Telephone: 503-620-8900
Telecopier: 503-620-4878
Email: ncp@buckley-law.com
URL: http://www.buckley-law.com

Business, Real Estate, Commercial, Corporate, Land Law, Environmental Law, Bankruptcy, Trusts, Probate, Wills.

DENNIS P. BROOKSHIRE, born Prineville, Oregon, December 16, 1956; admitted to bar, 1982, Oregon. *Education:* Oregon State University (B.S., 1979); University of Oregon (J.D., 1982). *Member:* Gresham and Multnomah County Bar Associations; Oregon State Bar. ***PRACTICE AREAS:*** Real Estate; Commercial Law; Zoning, Planning and Land Use; Mortgages; Civil Practice. ***Email:*** dpb@buckley-law.com

WILLIAM T. BUCKLEY, born 1943; admitted to bar, 1973, Oregon. *Education:* University of Oregon (B.S., 1967); Lewis and Clark College (J.D., 1973). ***PRACTICE AREAS:*** Real Estate; Business Law; Environmental Law.

WILLIAM E. GAAR, born Kansas City, Kansas, November 17, 1961; admitted to bar, 1989, Oregon; 1998, Washington; 1999, U.S. District Court, District of Oregon. *Education:* Kansas State University (B.A., 1985); Northwestern School of Law (J.D., 1988). Cornelius Honor Society, Northwestern School of Law. *Member:* Washington State Bar Association (Member, Litigation Section); Oregon State Bar (Member, Sections on: Disability Law; Labor and Employment Law; Civil Rights; Business Law). ***LANGUAGES:*** Spanish. ***PRACTICE AREAS:*** Employment Law; Commercial Law.

ROBERT LeCHEVALLIER, born Euclid, Ohio, August 10, 1953; admitted to bar, 1978, Oregon; 1979, U.S. District Court, District of Oregon. *Education:* Willamette University (B.A., cum laude, 1975); University of Oregon (J.D., 1978). *Member:* Oregon State Bar (Member, Unlawful Practice of Law Committee, 1984-1987; Member, 1990-1995 and Chair, 1995, Joint Council on Legal Assistants; Member, 1994-1998 and Chair, 1998, Law Practice Management Section; Member, OSB Continuing Legal Education Committee, 2002-2004; Member, Region 6, House of Delegates, 2002—; Member, Business Law Section; Member, Estate Planning Section; Member, Securities Section; Member, International and Law Practice Management Section). ***LANGUAGES:*** French. ***PRACTICE AREAS:*** Business Law (45%); Estate Planning (40%); Real Estate (10%); Securities (5%). ***Email:*** rlc@buckley-law.com

RICHARD A. MARIO, born 1952; admitted to bar, 1979, Oregon; 1983, Arizona. *Education:* Oregon State University (B.A., 1976); Gonzaga University (J.D., 1979). ***PRACTICE AREAS:*** Real Estate; Commercial Law; Securities Litigation.

JAYE WICKHAM TAYLOR, born Oxnard, California, April 20, 1951; admitted to bar, 1994, Oregon. *Education:* University of California at Irvine (B.A., 1974); Northwestern College of Law (J.D., 1994). ***PRACTICE AREAS:*** Family Law; Trial Practice.

RICHARD A. UFFELMAN, born Portland, Oregon, February 14, 1941; admitted to bar, 1966, Oregon; 1967, U.S. Tax Court. *Education:* Reed College and Lewis and Clark College (B.A., 1963); Willamette University (J.D., 1966); New York University (LL.M., Taxation, 1967). Phi Delta Phi. Assistant Attorney General, Tax Division, Oregon State Department of Justice, 1967-1971. *Member:* Multnomah County Bar Association; Oregon State Bar. ***PRACTICE AREAS:*** Tax Law; Real Estate.

KAY WAKEFIELD ABRAMOWITZ, born St. Anthony, Idaho, September 17, 1940; admitted to bar, 1984, Oregon. *Education:* University of Utah (B.S., 1963); Northwestern School of Law of Lewis and Clark College (J.D., 1984). *Member:* Multnomah County and American Bar Associations; Oregon State Bar. ***PRACTICE AREAS:*** Estate Planning; Business Planning; Business Organization.

OF COUNSEL

JAY A. RICHARDSON, born Vernal, Utah, June 24, 1957; admitted to bar, 1982, Oregon. *Education:* Brigham Young University (B.S., Accounting, 1979); Willamette University College of Law (J.D., 1982). Member, Willamette Law Review. Certified Public Accountant, Oregon. Certified Management Accountant. Certified Financial Management. Former Co-Chair, Oregon State Bar Joint Committee. Member, Oregon Small Business Fair Planning Committee. *Member:* Oregon State Bar; Oregon Society of CPA's; Institute of Certified Management Accountants. ***PRACTICE AREAS:*** Corporate Taxation; Employment Law; Employee Benefit Taxation; Estate Planning; Financial Planning; Corporate Law; Business Law.

ASSOCIATES

AARON BLANKENSHIP, born Portland, Oregon, September 7, 1972; admitted to bar, 1999, Oregon; 2000, Washington. *Education:* Linfield College (B.A., 1995); Lewis and Clark College (J.D., 1999). Member, 1997-1998 and Articles Editor, 1998-1999, The Journal of Small and Emerging Business Law. *Member:* Multnomah County, Washington County and Washington State (Member, Sections on: Construction Law, Debtor/Creditor, and Business) Bar Associations; Oregon State Bar (Member, Sections on: Construction Law and Debtor/Creditor). ***PRACTICE AREAS:*** Construction Law; Debtor and Creditor; Commercial Collections.

LAURA J. BRADY, born Portland, Oregon, January 27, 1972; admitted to bar, 1997, Oregon. *Education:* California State University (B.S., 1994); Willamette University College of Law (J.D., 1997). *Member:* Multnomah County and American Bar Associations; Oregon State Bar (Member, Sections on: Business Law; Real Estate and Land Use); American Inn of Court. ***PRACTICE AREAS:*** Real Estate; Business Law; Water Law.

SHAWN A. NOLAN, born Milford, Connecticut, January 30, 1974; admitted to bar, 2001, Oregon. *Education:* Appalachian State University (B.S., 1996); Georgetown University (M.A.L.S., 1998); Lewis and Clark College (J.D., 2001). ***LANGUAGES:*** Japanese, French. ***PRACTICE AREAS:*** Litigation.

JUNE M. WIYRICK, born Spokane, Washington, July 17, 1972; admitted to bar, 1997, Oregon. *Education:* Eastern Washington University (B.A., 1994); Northwestern School of Law (J.D., 1997). *Member:* Oregon State Bar; Oregon Women Lawyers Association. ***PRACTICE AREAS:*** Business Law; Estate Planning; Probate; Trust Administration. ***Email:*** jmw@buckley-law.com

---

CLARK, LINDAUER, FETHERSTON, EDMONDS, LIPPOLD & COLLIER, LLP

LAKE OSWEGO, OREGON

(See Salem)

Trial and Business Practice in State and Federal Courts including Business Litigation, Insurance Law, Agricultural Law, Automobile, Premises Liability, Professional Negligence, including Legal and Medical Malpractice, Product, Toxic Tort and Environmental Liability, Employ-

(This Listing Continued)

CLARK, LINDAUER, FETHERSTON, EDMONDS, LIPPOLD & COLLIER, LLP, Lake Oswego—Continued

ment Discrimination, Wrongful Discharge and Defamation, Arbitration and Mediation, Business, Real Estate, and Estate Law, Probate.

COONEY & CREW, LLP

Established in 1981

4949 MEADOWS ROAD
SUITE 460
LAKE OSWEGO, OREGON 97035
Telephone: 503-607-2700
Fax: 503-607-2702

General Insurance and Civil Trial Practice, Professional Liability, Products Liability, General Corporate, Aviation, Real Property, Motor Carrier Law, Health and Employment Law and Administrative Law.

FIRM PROFILE: Cooney & Crew, LLP was established in 1981 and specializes in litigating all types of insurance claims, with particular emphasis on defending professional liability cases. Health and employment law are a large part of our practice. Cooney & Crew, LLP is one of the few law firms in the state with extensive experience representing the motor carrier industry.

MEMBERS OF FIRM

PAUL A. COONEY, born Portland, Oregon, March 18, 1960; admitted to bar, 1992, Oregon; 1995, Washington. *Education:* Oregon State University (B.S., 1987); University of Oregon (J.D., 1992). Recipient, William Fyre Scholarship. *Member:* Multnomah County and Washington State Bar Associations; Oregon State Bar; Oregon Association of Defense Counsel. ***PRACTICE AREAS:*** Insurance Defense; Indian Law; Litigation; Mental Health Law; Health Care; Professional Licensing. ***Email:*** pcooney@cooneyllc.com

THOMAS E. COONEY, born Portland, Oregon, July 16, 1931; admitted to bar, 1956, Oregon. *Education:* University of Portland (B.A., 1953); Willamette University (J.D., 1956). Recipient: American Board of Trial Lawyers Distinguished Trial Lawyer of the Year, 1996; Multnomah Bar Professionalism Award, 1996. *Member:* Multnomah County and American Bar Associations; Oregon State Bar; American Board of Trial Advocates; International Association of Defense Counsel; Defense Research Institute; Oregon Association of Defense Counsel; Society of Medical Association Counsel; Oregon Society of Hospital Attorneys. Fellow, American College of Trial Lawyers. ***PRACTICE AREAS:*** Insurance Defense; Professional Liability; Health Law. ***Email:*** tecooney@cooneyllc.com

THOMAS M. COONEY, born Portland, Oregon, May 15, 1957; admitted to bar, 1987, Oregon. *Education:* Lewis and Clark College (B.S., 1980); Northwestern School of Law (J.D., 1986). *Member:* Multnomah County Bar Association; Oregon State Bar; Oregon Association of Defense Counsel. ***PRACTICE AREAS:*** Insurance Defense; Personal Injury; Litigation; Indian Law. ***Email:*** tmcooney@cooneyllc.com

MICHAEL D. CREW, born Caldwell, Idaho, July 12, 1946; admitted to bar, 1972, Oregon, U.S. District Court, District of Oregon and U.S. Court of Appeals, Ninth Circuit. *Education:* Albertson College of Idaho (B.A., 1969); Willamette University (J.D., cum laude, 1972). *Member:* Multnomah County, Clackamas County and American Bar Associations; Oregon State Bar; Oregon Association of Defense Counsel; American Health Lawyers Association; Oregon Society of Hospital Attorneys; Society of Medical Association Counsel; Oregon Health Lawyers Association. ***PRACTICE AREAS:*** Health Law; Motor Carrier Law; Business Transactions; Business Litigation. ***Email:*** mcrew@cooneycrew.com

CHARLES A. SINSEL, born Clarksburg, West Virginia, September, 16, 1968; admitted to bar, 1999, Oregon. *Education:* West Virginia University (B.A., 1991; M.A., 1994); Willamette University (J.D., 1997). Recipient, Oregon State Bar New Lawyers Division Volunteer of the Year Award, 2001. *Member:* Multnomah County and American Bar Associations; Oregon State Bar; Oregon Association of Defense Counsel; American Health Lawyers Association. ***PRACTICE AREAS:*** Health Law; Employment Law; Business Transactions; Business Litigation; Construction Law. ***Email:*** csinsel@cooneycrew.com

DAVID J. MADIGAN, born Portland, Oregon, August 17, 1964; admitted to bar, 2001, Oregon; 2002, U.S. District Court, District of Oregon. *Education:* Portland State University (B.S., 1995); Northwestern School of Law (J.D., 2001). *Member:* Multnomah County Bar Association; Oregon State Bar. ***PRACTICE AREAS:*** Insurance Defense; Personal Injury; Litigation; Health Law; Business Transactions; Business Litigation. ***Email:*** dmadigan@cooneyllc.com

BRENT M. CREW, born Caldwell, Idaho, February 18, 1965; admitted to bar, 1992, Oregon. *Education:* Willamette University (B.S., 1987); Northwestern School of Law (J.D., 1992). *Member:* Oregon State Bar. ***PRACTICE AREAS:*** Health Law; Business Law; Estate Planning; Contracts; Real Estate. ***Email:*** bcrew@cooneycrew.com

JEFFREY M. BROWN, born Appleton, Wisconsin, July 24, 1969; admitted to bar, 1997, Oregon. *Education:* University of Wisconsin-Madison (B.A., 1991); Willamette University (J.D., cum laude, 1997). *Member:* American Bar Association; Oregon State Bar. ***PRACTICE AREAS:*** Government; Entertainment Law; Business Transactions. ***Email:*** jbrown@cooneycrew.com

REPRESENTATIVE CLIENTS: Underwriters at Lloyds; Amica Mutual Insurance Co.; Oregon Medical Assn.; Oregon Psychological Assoc.; Oregon State Bar Professional Liability Fund; Southwestern Aviation Underwriters; Gresham Transfer, Inc.; Canal Insurance Co.; Oregon Insurance Guaranty Association; NORCAL Mutual Insurance Co.; The Doctors' Co.; Matlack, Inc.; Walsh Trucking, Ltd.; Electric Mutual Liability Insurance Co.; Northwest Physicians Mutual Insurance Co.; Everest National Ins. Co.; The Church Ins. Co.

SARA L. GABIN, P.C.

Established in 1984

FIVE CENTERPOINTE DRIVE - SUITE 400
LAKE OSWEGO, OREGON 97035
Telephone: 503-620-3171
Fax: 503-620-3365
Email: slgabin@pacifier.com
URL: http://www.lawyers.com/gabinlaw

Social Security Disability and SSI, Personal Injury, Workers Compensation, Family Law.

SARA L. GABIN, born Detroit, Michigan, September 24, 1957; admitted to bar, 1981, Oregon; 1982, U.S. District Court, District of Oregon. *Education:* University of Michigan (B.A., 1978); Willamette University (J.D., 1981). *Member:* Oregon State Bar; Oregon Trial Lawyer's Association; National Organization of Social Security Claimant's Representatives; Oregon Women Lawyers. ***PRACTICE AREAS:*** Social Security Disability; Personal Injury; Workers Compensation; Family Law. ***Email:*** slgabin@pacifier.com

GARRETT, HEMANN, ROBERTSON, JENNINGS, COMSTOCK & TRETHEWY, P.C.

LAKE OSWEGO, OREGON

(See Salem)

Bankruptcy and Creditors' Rights, Business and Corporate Law, Civil Litigation, Employment and Labor Law, Estate Planning, Trusts and Probate, Family Law, Government Relations, Insurance and Workers' Compensation Defense, Real Estate Transactions and Development, School Law, Tax Law.

R. ERICK JOHNSON PC

Established in 2001

5285 S.W. MEADOWS ROAD, SUITE 230
LAKE OSWEGO, OREGON 97035
Telephone: 503-684-9658
Fax: 503-968-6159
Email: EJohnson@rejpc.com

Energy and Telecommunications, Regulatory, Administrative and Environmental Law, Directors and Officers, Complex Litigation.

FIRM PROFILE: The firm has extensive experience in federal energy contracts, rates, administrative and regulatory matters under the Northwest Power Act and related laws. The firm specializes in representing cooperatives in a wide range of matters. The firm is very experienced in matters involving directors and officers and in complex litigation.

R. ERICK JOHNSON, born Bay City, Michigan, July 1, 1952; admitted to bar, 1980, Oregon, U.S. District Court, District of Oregon and U.S. Court of Appeals, Ninth Circuit; 1988, U.S. Supreme Court; 1994, U.S. Court of Federal Claims. *Education:* Delta College (A.A., 1972); University of Michigan (A.B. with high distinction, 1974); Stanford University (J.D., 1978); European University Institute, Florence, Italy (Fulbright Scholar, 1979). *Member:* Multnomah and American Bar Associations; Oregon State Bar; Energy Bar Association; Electric Cooperative Bar Association. ***Email:*** EJohnson@rejpc.com

REPRESENTATIVE CLIENTS: PNGC Power; Power Resources Cooperative; Oregon Rural Electric Cooperative Association; Blachly-Lane County Cooperative Electric Association; Central Electric Cooperative; Clearwater Power Co.; Consumers Power, Inc.; Coos-Curry Electric Cooperative, Inc.; Douglas Electric Cooperative; Fall River Electric Cooperative, Inc.; Lane Electric Cooperative; Lost River Rural Electric Cooperative; Northern Lights, Inc.; Okanogan County Electric Cooperative, Inc.; Raft River Rural Electric Cooperative; Salmon River Electric Cooperative, Inc.; Umatilla Electric Cooperative Association; West Oregon Electric Cooperative, Inc.

JORDAN SCHRADER PC ATTORNEYS AT LAW

LAKE OSWEGO, OREGON

(See Portland)

Business, Construction Contracting and Claims, Real Estate Law, Land Use and Development, Environmental and Natural Resources Law, Water Law, Bankruptcy Creditors' Rights Law, Employment Law, Municipal Law, General Corporate and Commercial Law, Banking and Finance, Mediation, Arbitration and Litigation in all Federal and State Courts.

RAYBURN LAW OFFICES

17685 S.W. 65TH AVENUE, SUITE 300
LAKE OSWEGO, OREGON 97035
Telephone: 503-968-5820
Fax: 503-670-0441
Email: rayburn@pacifier.com

Litigation, Personal Injury, Automobile Accidents and Injuries, Wrongful Death Employment Law, Sexual Harassment.

RALPH F. RAYBURN, born Evansville, Indiana, April 6, 1954; admitted to bar, 1980, Nebraska; U.S. District Court, District of Nebraska; 1982, Oregon, U.S. District Court, District of Oregon; 1987 Washington, U.S. District Court, Eastern District of Washington. *Education:* University of Wisconsin (B.A., 1976); University of Nebraska (J.D., 1980). Executive Editor, Nebraska Law Review, 1978-1979. Law Clerk to the Honorable Judge, Leslie Boslaugh, Nebraska Supreme Court, 1980-1981. *Member:* Multnomah County, Nebraska State, Washington State and American (Member, Litigation Section) Bar Associations; Or-

(This Listing Continued)

egon State Bar; The Association of Trial Lawyers of America; Oregon Trial Lawyers Association. ***PRACTICE AREAS:*** Litigation; Employment Law; Personal Injury. ***Email:*** rayburn@pacifier.com

LAURIE SHERTZ LLC

LAKE OSWEGO, OREGON

(See Portland)

Criminal Defense, Trial Practice, Felonies, Homicide and Assault, Self Defense, Weapons Charges, Sex Offenses, Drug Crimes, Theft and Fraud. Practice in Federal and State Courts.

PRISCILLA TAYLOR ATTORNEY AT LAW

4248 GALEWOOD STREET
LAKE OSWEGO, OREGON 97035
Telephone: 503-675-4340
Fax: 503-675-4399
URL: http://www.ptaylorlawfirm.com
Email: prismt_53@yahoo.com
URL: http://www.ptaylorlaw.com

Trusts and Estates, Estate Planning, Wills, Probate and Corporate Law.

PRISCILLA TAYLOR, born Whittier, California, October 1, 1953; admitted to bar, 1986, Oregon; 1990, Washington. *Education:* California State University, Fullerton (B.A., 1975); Chapman College (M.A., 1977); Northwest School of Law, Lewis & Clark College (J.D., 1985). *Member:* Multnomah County, Washington State and American Bar Associations; Oregon State Bar (Member, Section on: Estate Planning Law, 2000—); Oregon Self-Insurers' Association; Association of Workers Compensation Defense Attorneys. ***PRACTICE AREAS:*** Trusts and Estates; Wills; Probate; Estate Planning; Corporate Law.

JAY URBAN

4248 GALEWOOD STREET
LAKE OSWEGO, OREGON 97035
Telephone: 503-655-1800
Fax: 503-675-8651
Email: jayurban@comcast.net
URL: http://www.jayurban.com

Mailing Address: P.O. Box 1947; Lake Oswego, Or 97035

Taxation, Domestic Relations, Business Law, Financial Law, Business Planning, Personal Injury.

JAY URBAN, born San Antonio, Texas, July 27, 1944; admitted to bar, 1992, Oregon. *Education:* University of California at Santa Barbara (B.A., 1968); Golden Gate University (M.B.A., Tax, 1984); Lewis and Clark Northwestern School of Law (J.D., 1992). ***PRACTICE AREAS:*** Taxation; Domestic Relations; Business Law; Financial Law; Business Planning; Personal Injury.

WILLIAMS, ZOGRAFOS & PECK

A PROFESSIONAL CORPORATION
Established in 1978
334 THIRD STREET
P.O. BOX 547
LAKE OSWEGO, OREGON 97034
Telephone: 503-699-1300
Fax: 503-699-4111
URL: http://www.wzplaborlaw.com

Limited Exclusively to the representation of Employers in Labor and Employment Matters, including Union-Management Relations, Labor Negotiations, Employment Discrimination, Wrongful Discharge, Wage and Hour, Preventive Labor Relations, Before Federal and State Courts and Administrative Agencies.

FIRM PROFILE: The firm's practice is limited exclusively to representation of employers in labor and employment matters and was founded in 1978 by Ronald J. Williams and Dean T. Zografos. The firm has grown from representation of a single, small employer to a firm representing major private and public sector employers throughout the western United States. Among the firm's clients are nationally recognized companies such as Tree Top, Inc. Offices are located in Lake Oswego, Oregon, a suburb of Portland. We are committed to providing our clients with the highest quality of legal service possible. We strive to learn as much as possible about the business objectives and operations of our clients, including their special legal needs and concerns, in order to enable us to anticipate and prevent problems and develop a full range of available legal options, including innovative solutions. Our goal is to obtain the most favorable result possible for our clients within the bounds of the law and professional ethics in a prompt, efficient and economic manner.

RONALD J. WILLIAMS, born Salem, Oregon, February 13, 1948; admitted to bar, 1973, Oregon, U.S. District Court, District of Oregon, U.S. Court of Appeals, Ninth Circuit and U.S. Supreme Court. *Education:* University of Oregon (B.A., 1970); Lewis and Clark College (J.D., 1973). *Member:* Multnomah County and American Bar Associations; Oregon State Bar (Member, Section on: Labor Relations Law). ***PRACTICE AREAS:*** Collective Bargaining; Contract Administration; National Labor Relations Act; Employment Contracts; Labor Arbitration; Union Organizing Matters; Personnel Policies; Labor and Employment Law; Labor Relations. ***Email:*** rwilliams@wzplaborlaw.com

(This Listing Continued)

DEAN T. ZOGRAFOS, born Spokane, Washington, November 3, 1950; admitted to bar, 1976, Oregon, U.S. District Court, District of Oregon, U.S. Court of Appeals, Ninth Circuit and U.S. Supreme Court. *Education:* Washington State University (B.A., 1973); Willamette University (J.D., 1976). Phi Beta Kappa. Adjunct Professor, Labor Law, Willamette University College of Law, 1985. *Member:* Multnomah County Bar Association; Oregon State Bar (Member, Section on Labor Relations Law). ***PRACTICE AREAS:*** Collective Bargaining; Contract Administration; National Labor Relations Act; Employment Contracts; Labor Arbitration; Union Organizing Matters; Personnel Policies; Labor and Employment Law; Labor Relations. ***Email:*** dzografos@wzplaborlaw.com

KATHY A. PECK, born Everett, Washington, September 7, 1952; admitted to bar, 1977, Oregon, U.S. District Court, District of Oregon and U.S. Court of Appeals, Ninth Circuit. *Education:* Washington State University (B.A., 1974); Willamette University (J.D., 1977). Phi Beta Kappa. Author: Oregon State Bar Continuing Legal Education Employer/Employee Relations, 1986; Employee Issues, 1989; Employment Law, 1990; Labor and Employment Law, 1994; Civil Rights, 1995; ADA, 1996; Private Sector Labor Law, 1997; Sexual Harassment, 1998. Presenter: American Arbitration Association; Oregon Law Institute; Council on Education; American Society of Public Administrators. Adjunct Professor, Willamette University College of Law, 1985. *Member:* Oregon State Bar (Member and Former Officer, Labor Relations Section). ***PRACTICE AREAS:*** Labor and Employment; Labor Arbitration; Personnel Policies; Public Sector Employment Law; Private Business Law. ***Email:*** kpeck@wzplaborlaw.com

DIAN S. RUBANOFF, born Van Nuys, California, September 12, 1961; admitted to bar, 1991, Oregon, U.S. District Court, District of Oregon and U.S. Court of Appeals, Ninth Circuit. *Education:* Whittier College School of Law (J.D., 1991). Member, Oregon State Bar Board of Bar Examiners. *Member:* Mutlnomah and Federal Bar Associations; Oregon State Bar (Member, Sections on: Labor and Employment; Civil Rights and Disability Law); Oregon Women's Lawyers Association. ***PRACTICE AREAS:*** Labor and Employment Law; Employment Termination; Wrongful Termination; Litigation; Preventive Personnel Policies. ***Email:*** drubanoff@wzplaborlaw.com

---

CHANDRA R. HATFIELD, admitted to bar, 2002, Oregon; U.S. District Court, District of Oregon. *Education:* Pacific University (B.S., 1998); Willamette University (J.D., 2002). *Member:* Multnomah County Bar Association; Oregon State Bar (Member: Sections on, Labor and Employment; Litigation). ***PRACTICE AREAS:*** Labor and Employment; Personnel Policies. ***Email:*** chatfield@wzplaborlaw.com

KRISTIN R. BINKLEY, born West Islip, New York, April 23, 1974; admitted to bar, 2001, Michigan, U.S. District Court, Eastern and Western Districts of Michigan and U.S. Court of Appeals, 6th Circuit; 2005, Oregon and U.S. District Court, District of Oregon. *Education:* State University of New York at Albany (B.A., 1996); University of Detroit Mercy School of Law (J.D., 2001). *Member:* Oregon State Bar; State Bar of Michigan. ***PRACTICE AREAS:*** Labor and Employment; Employment Termination; Wrongful Termination; Litigation. ***Email:*** kbinkley@wzplaborlaw.com

REPRESENTATIVE CLIENTS: Tree Top, Inc.; BE Aerospace/DELCO; Oregon State Bar; Utility Vault Co./Oldcastle Precast, Inc.; Amcor, Inc.; Rinker Materials; California Concrete Pipe; Christy Concrete; Concrete Technology, Inc.; Hanson Pipe & Products, Inc.; Walling Sand & Gravel; IDC-CH2M Hill; Columbia Distributing Company; Mt. Hood Beverage Company; Maletis Beverage; RM Beverage Washington; Western Beverage Co.; McDonald Wholesale, Inc.; Springfield Utility Board; Morrow Equipment Company; Parr Lumber Company; Knez Building Supply; Deluxe Ice Cream; Tillamook County Creamery Assn. (Tillamook Cheese); Kettle Foods; Sunshine Dairy; Umpqua Dairy; Snokist Growers; Capitol Auto Group; Don Rasmussen Mercedes; Sause Bros. Ocean Towing Co.; Accutel, Inc.; Waste Control Systems; Allied Waste of North America; Sanipac, Inc.; Rogue Disposal & Recycling; Bend Garbage Company; Holiday Retirement Corp.; Salem Clinic; Coast Rehabilitation; Oregon Hematology Oncology Association; West Coast Bancorp; GMAC Mortgage Corporation; First Pacific Corporation; Partnerships in Community Living; ;Norcom 911; Pacific Cast Technologies; Peco Manufacturing Co., Inc.; Rogue Valley County Club.
CITIES OF: Albany, Ashland, Astoria, Bend, Boardman, Canby, Corvallis, Dallas, Falls City, Forest Grove, Gladstone, Gresham, Hillsboro, Keizer, Lake Oswego, Lebanon, Lincoln City; McMinnville, Medford, Monmouth, Mt. Angel, Newport, Oregon City; Portland, Springfield, Tigard, Troutdale, West Linn, Wilsonville, Woodburn.
COUNTIES OF: Clackamas, Douglas, Hood River, Klamath, Multnomah, Marion County Fire Dist.; Morrow, Thurston, Washington; Union.
COMMUNITY COLLEGES: Clackamas Community College; Chemeketa Community College; Linn-Benton Community College; Southwestern Oregon Community College; Tillamook Bay Community College; Umpqua Community College.

RALPH E. WISER, III

Established in 1981
KRUSE WOODS ONE
5285 S.W. MEADOWS ROAD, SUITE 333
LAKE OSWEGO, OREGON 97035
Telephone: 503-620-5577
Fax: 503-598-4646
URL: http://www.ralphwiser.com
Email: ralph@wiserlaw.com
URL: http://www.lawyers.com/ralphewiser

Personal Injury, Medical Malpractice, Disability Insurance Issues, Sexual Abuse, Products Liability, Automobile Accidents and Injuries, Wrongful Death, Negligence, Torts, Employment Law, ERISA, Discrimination, Labor Law, Professional Licensing Issues, Civil Litigation, Business Litigation, Professional Sports Agency Issues, Trial Practice.

FIRM PROFILE: The firm concentrates its practice helping Oregon families in the area of wrongful death, injuries stemming from automobile collisions, defective products, medical or doctor negligence, insurance disputes, and general civil litigation. The firm combines its injury practice uniquely with representing Oregon's teachers and classified personnel throughout the state. Ralph E. Wiser is a preeminent trial lawyer with the highest rating from Martindale-Hubbell.

RALPH E. WISER, III, born Portland, Oregon, May 19, 1952; admitted to bar, 1981, Oregon; 1987, U.S. Supreme Court. *Education:* Portland State University (B.A., with hon-

(This Listing Continued)

RALPH E. WISER, III, Lake Oswego—Continued

ors, 1975); University of Oregon (M.A., 1978; J.D., 1981). Speaker, "Third Party Liability in Workers Compensation Cases," Oregon State Bar, Continuing Legal Education, 1996—. *Member:* Oregon State Bar (Member, Litigation and Employment Law Sections); Oregon Trial Lawyers; The Association of Trial Lawyers of America. ***LANGUAGES:*** Spanish. ***PRACTICE AREAS:*** Automobile Accidents and Injuries; Personal Injury; Medical Malpractice; Labor Law; Employment Law; Professional Sports Law.

Languages: Spanish.

REPRESENTATIVE CLIENTS: Oregon Education Association; Portland Firefighters Association; Carpenters Union.

BRANDSNESS, BRANDSNESS, RUDD & BUNCH, P.C.

LAKEVIEW, OREGON

(See Klamath Falls)

Trusts and Estates, Wills and Probate, Estate Planning, Real Estate, Zoning, Planning and Land Use, Corporate Law, Business Law, Buying and Selling of Businesses, Partnership Law, Commercial Law, Banking, Business Acquisitions, Timber Law, Contracts, Financial, Construction Law, Creditors Rights, Bankruptcy, Collections, Complex Civil Litigation.

LYNCH & VANDENBERG

620 NORTH FIRST STREET
P.O. BOX 351
LAKEVIEW, OREGON 97630
Telephone: 541-947-2196
Fax: 541-947-5234

General Practice. Probate, Trusts and Estate Planning. Real Estate and Water Law. Corporate, and Government Law.

JAMES C. LYNCH, born Lakeview, Oregon, February 2, 1936; admitted to bar, 1961, Oregon, U.S. District Court, District of Oregon and U.S. Court of Military Appeals. *Education:* University of Oregon (B.S., 1958; LL.B., 1961). Phi Beta Kappa; Phi Delta Phi. Recipient, Paul Patterson Award. Fellow, American College of Trust and Estate Counsel. *Member:* Lake County Bar Association; Oregon State Bar (Former Member, Executive Committee of Estate Planning and Administration Section). [U.S. Army, Judge Advocate General Corp., 1962-1964, Capt.]. ***PRACTICE AREAS:*** Probate Law; Trusts Law; Estate Planning Law; Corporate Law; Business Law; Real Property Law; Water Law; School Law; Hospital Law.

DAVID M. VANDENBERG, born Portland, Oregon, April 16, 1963; admitted to bar, 1989, Oregon. *Education:* Southern Oregon University (B.S., 1985); Willamette University (J.D., 1989). *Member:* Lake County Bar Association; Oregon State Bar. ***PRACTICE AREAS:*** General Litigation Practice; Personal Injury; Domestic Relations; Criminal.

REPRESENTATIVE CLIENTS: Fremont Sawmill Co.; Lake County Education Service District; Lake District Hospital; Lakeview Water Users, Inc.; Summer Lake Irrigation District; Dan Collins Ford.
REFERENCES: Sterling Savings Bank, Lakeview, Oregon.

RATLIFF & RATLIFF, P.C.

LAKEVIEW, OREGON

(See Klamath Falls)

General Civil and Criminal Trial Practice. Real Estate, Family, Divorce, Probate, Corporate. Traffic Matters. Personal Injury.

PETERSON LAW OFFICES, PC

LEBANON, OREGON

(See Portland)

Personal Injury, Premises Liability, Automobile Accidents and Injuries, Dog Bites and Wrongful Death.

CLARK, LINDAUER, FETHERSTON, EDMONDS, LIPPOLD & COLLIER, LLP

McMINNVILLE, OREGON

(See Salem)

Trial and Business Practice in State and Federal Courts including Business Litigation, Insurance Law, Agricultural Law, Automobile, Premises Liability, Professional Negligence, including Legal and Medical Malpractice, Product, Toxic Tort and Environmental Liability, Employment Discrimination, Wrongful Discharge and Defamation, Arbitration and Mediation, Business, Real Estate, and Estate Law, Probate.

CUMMINS, GOODMAN, FISH, DENLEY & VICKERS, P.C.

McMINNVILLE, OREGON

(See Newberg)

Insurance Defense, Employment Law, Workers' Compensation Defense, OSHA Defense, General Litigation, Business Law.

HAUGEBERG, RUETER, GOWELL, FREDRICKS, HIGGINS & McKEEGAN, P.C.

620 NE FIFTH STREET, P.O. BOX 480
McMINNVILLE, OREGON 97128
Telephone: 503-472-5141
Fax: 503-472-4713
URL: http://www.haugebergandrueter.com

General, Civil and Trial Practice, State and Federal Courts. Municipal, Insurance, Corporation, Timber and Logging, Federal and State Taxation, Estate Planning and Probate Law, Family Law, School Law.

DAVID C. HAUGEBERG, born Longview, Washington, April 10, 1940; admitted to bar, 1965, Oregon. *Education:* Willamette University (B.A., 1962); University of Oregon (LL.B., 1965). Phi Alpha Delta. Chair, Willamette University College of Law Board of Visitors, 1988-1992. *Member:* Oregon State Bar. ***PRACTICE AREAS:*** Corporate Law; Real Estate Law; School Law. ***Email:*** hrgfh@onlinemac.com

GARY A. RUETER, born Orlando, Florida, February 21, 1945; admitted to bar, 1969, Oregon. *Education:* Willamette University (B.A., 1966; J.D., 1969). Phi Mu Alpha; Phi Delta Phi. District Attorney, Yamhill County, 1972-1975. *Member:* Oregon State Bar; Oregon Association of Defense Counsel; Defense Research Institute; Willamette Valley American Inn of Court (President, 1999-2000). ***PRACTICE AREAS:*** Trial Practice; Real Property Law; Business Law; Commercial Litigation. ***Email:*** garyr@onlinemac.com

WALTER R. GOWELL, born Washington, D.C., August 22, 1952; admitted to bar, 1979, Oregon; 1981, U.S. District Court, District of Oregon. *Education:* Reed College (B.A., 1974); Lewis and Clark College (J.D., 1979). *Member:* Oregon State Bar (Chair, Real Estate and Land Use Section, 1998; Executive Committee of Ag Law Section, 2000-2001 and Government Law Section, 2003). ***PRACTICE AREAS:*** Real Estate Law; Municipal Law; Agriculture Law; Debtor and Creditor Law. ***Email:*** waltgowell@onlinemac.com

DOUGLAS S. FREDRICKS, born McMinnville, Oregon, January 16, 1953; admitted to bar, 1980, California; 1983, Oregon. *Education:* University of Oregon (B.S., 1975); University of San Fernando Valley (J.D., 1979); University of San Diego (L.L.M., in Taxation, 1983). *Member:* State Bar of California; Oregon State Bar. ***PRACTICE AREAS:*** Estate Planning; Probate Administration; Trust Administration; Business Planning; Federal Income, Estate and Gift Taxation. ***Email:*** dfred@onlinemac.com

ROBERT G. HIGGINS, born Ranchi, India, March 1, 1952; admitted to bar, 1982, Oregon. *Education:* Loma Linda University (B.A., 1975); Willamette University (M.M., 1981; J.D., 1981). *Member:* Oregon State Bar. ***PRACTICE AREAS:*** Family Law; Business Law. ***Email:*** rhiggins@onlinemac.com

JOHN N. McKEEGAN, born Harrisburg, Pennsylvania, July 12, 1962; admitted to bar, 1988, Arizona; 1998, Oregon. *Education:* Bucknell University (B.A., with honors, 1984); University of Notre Dame (J.D., 1987). *Member:* State Bars of Arizona and Oregon; Public Investors Arbitration Bar Association. ***PRACTICE AREAS:*** Civil Litigation; Employment Law; Securities Arbitration. ***Email:*** mckeegs@aol.com

DIANNE L. HAUGEBERG, born McMinnville, Oregon, May 5, 1975; admitted to bar, 2000, California; 2003, Oregon. *Education:* Willamette University (B.S., 1997); Santa Clara University School of Law (J.D., 2000); University of San Diego School of Law (LL.M., in Taxation, with honors, 2001). *Member:* State Bar of California; Oregon State Bar. ***PRACTICE AREAS:*** Estate Planning; Probate; Administration; Trust Administration; Federal Estate and Gift Taxation. ***Email:*** dianneh@onlinemac.com

JOHNSTONE & GOODFELLOW

Established in 1972
1215 NORTH ADAMS
P.O. BOX 626
McMINNVILLE, OREGON 97128-0626
Telephone: 503-472-9555; 800-409-3555
Fax: 503-472-9550
Email: rmjohnstone@johnstone-law.com
URL: http://www.johnstone-law.com

Moscow, Russia Office: Novoslabodskaya #33, Suite 17, Moscow 130030, Russia. Telephone: 972-61-84.

General Practice, Litigation, Federal and State Courts, Business, Corporate, Probate, Family Law, Divorce, Child Custody Law, Personal Injury, Alternative Dispute Resolution, Mediation and Arbitration, Construction Law, Debtor/Creditor Law, School, Insurance Law, Real Estate, International Law, Wills and Estate Planning,.

ROBERT M. JOHNSTONE, P.C., born Bellingham, Washington, April 20, 1944; admitted to bar, 1972, Oregon, Washington, U.S. District Court, District of Oregon and U.S. Claims Court. *Education:* University of Washington (B.A., 1966); Willamette University (J.D., 1972). *Member:* Oregon State Bar; Washington State Bar Association. [Lt. Col., USMCR, ret.; Judge Advocate, USMCR]. ***LANGUAGES:*** Spanish and Russian. ***Email:*** rmjohnstone@johnstone-law.com

BRENT GOODFELLOW, P.C., born Provo, Utah, January 23, 1975; admitted to bar, 2003, Oregon. *Education:* Brigham Young University (B.A., 2000); Willamette University (J.D., 2003). *Member:* Yamhill County, Multnomah County and American Bar Associations; Oregon State Bar. ***PRACTICE AREAS:*** Business Litigation; Real Estate; Family Law; Contracts; Landlord and Tenant Law. ***Email:*** bgoodfellow@johnstone-law.com

REPRESENTATIVE CLIENTS: Please see our Web Site.

LAW OFFICE OF GARY G. NORRIS

Established in 1996

2235 N.E. EVANS STREET
McMINNVILLE, OREGON 97128
Telephone: 503-472-3770
Fax: 503-472-2349
Email: garyg.norris@verizon.net

General Civil Trial Practice, Automobile and General Liability Insurance Defense, Insurance Coverage Disputes, Products Liability Defense, Business Litigation, Insurance Litigation and Commercial Litigation .

GARY G. NORRIS, born New York, New York, May 23, 1953; admitted to bar, 1982, Oregon; 1984, U.S. District Court, District of Oregon; 2003, Washington. *Education:* University of Oregon (B.S., Journalism, 1978; J.D., 1982). Lead Counsel, American States Insurance Company, 1991-1996. *Member:* Yamhill County Bar Association; Oregon State Bar; Oregon Association of Defense Counsel; Oregon Casualty Adjusters Association. ***PRACTICE AREAS:*** Civil Litigation.

ASSOCIATE

RYAN HUNT, born Mt. Ayr, Iowa, August 6, 1976; admitted to bar, 2002, Oregon. *Education:* Washington State University, Vancouver (B.A., Public Affairs, 1999); University of Oregon (J.D., 2002). ***PRACTICE AREAS:*** Civil Practice; Automobile Liability; Insurance Defense; Business Litigation; Land Use; Real Estate. ***Email:*** ryan.hunt2@verizon.net

REPRESENTATIVE CLIENTS: Safeco Insurance; Ohio Casualty Group; Oregon Mutual Insurance; Federated Rural Electric Insurance Exchange; American Family Insurance; Zurich North America Insurance; Travelers Insurance; Fleetwood Retail Corp.; A&E Safe and Alarm Co.; Oregon Pride Nurseries; Willamette West Realty; Lyle Farrow Construction, Inc.; D-Stake Mill; Ocean Terrace Condominium Assn.; Four Winds Vineyard.

KELLY L. ANDERSEN, P.C.

Established in 1979

1730 E. MCANDREWS ROAD, SUITE A
MEDFORD, OREGON 97504-5575
Telephone: 541-773-7000
Fax: 541-608-0535
URL: http://www.lawyers.com/klandersenlaw
Email: kelly@andersenlaw.com
URL: http://www.andersenlaw.com

Plaintiff's Personal Injury, Product Liability, Medical Malpractice, Wrongful Death, Sexual Abuse.

KELLY L. ANDERSEN, born Provo, Utah, March 30, 1952; admitted to bar, 1979, Oregon and U.S. District Court, District of Oregon; 1995, U.S. Court of Appeals, Ninth Circuit; 1998, U.S. Court of Claims. *Education:* Brigham Young University (B.A., 1976; J.D., 1979). Author: "The Genie is Out of the Bottle and the Jury is Out of the Box" Oregon State Bar Bulletin, Feb/March, 2000; "Remembering Lincoln the Lawyer" Clark Memorandum, Brigham Young University Law School Magazine, Spring/Summer, 1998. Circuit and District Court Judge Pro Tem. 1999—. Bar Counsel for Board of Governors in Lawyers Discipline Cases, 1999. Admitted to "Million Dollar Advocates Forum", 1997. *Member:* Oregon State Bar; Oregon Trial Lawyers Association; The Association of Trial Lawyers of America; Southern Oregon Federal Bar Association (President, 2000—). ***REPORTED CASES:*** Pierce v. Allstate, 316 OR 31 (1993); Roberts v. Drew, 105 OR App 251 (1991); Wick v. Viking Insurance, 105 OR App 33 (1990); Davis v. Vesely, 75 OR App 591 (1985). ***PRACTICE AREAS:*** Personal Injury; Product Liability; Wrongful Death; Medical Malpractice; Sexual Harassment; Auto; Sex Abuse. ***Email:*** kelly@andersenlaw.com

---

BROPHY, MILLS, SCHMOR, GERKING, BROPHY & PARADIS, LLP

A Limited Liability Partnership

Established in 1942

PARK PLACE BUILDING, FIFTH FLOOR
201 WEST MAIN STREET
P.O. BOX 128
MEDFORD, OREGON 97501
Telephone: 541-772-7123
Fax: 541-772-7249
URL: http://www.brophymills.com

General Practice. Trial Practice in all State and Federal Courts. Corporations, Business Transactions, Insurance, Trusts, Estate Planning and Probate, Real Property and Land Use, Real Estate, Timber Law, Creditors' Rights, Construction Law, Employment Law and School Law.

FIRM PROFILE: The firm was founded in 1942 by William M. McAllister, who had served as Speaker of the Oregon House of Representatives and later as a member of the Oregon State Senate and Chief Justice of the Oregon Supreme Court. Its distinguished alumni have included Robert B. Duncan, now retired, who also served as Speaker of the Oregon House of Representatives and served several terms in the United States Congress and Carl M. Brophy who retired in 2003 after 53 years of practice with the firm. Mr. Brophy received the Oregon State Bar Association's highest honor, the Award of Merit, in 1999. The firm provides southern Oregon and northern California with a wide range of legal services, and emphasizes continuing legal education of all partners and associates and the development by them of areas of concentration. It also encourages their participation in civic and professional association affairs. Brophy, Mills, Schmor, Gerking, Brophy & Paradis, LLP is a Martindale-Hubbell Bar Register of Preeminent Lawyers Firm.

MEMBERS OF FIRM

LEE A. MILLS, born Bellingham, Washington, October 31, 1948; admitted to bar, 1975, Oregon. *Education:* Oregon State University (B.S., in Engineering, 1970); Willamette University (J.D., 1975). Phi Delta Phi. Recipient, Oregon Parks Association Distinguished Service Award, 1997. Member, MENSA. *Member:* Jackson County (Member, 1981 and Chairman, 1982, Court Liaison Committee) and American Bar Associations; Oregon State Bar (Member, 1980-1982 and 1990-1992, Executive Committee, Debtor-Creditor Section; Chairman, CLE Committee, 1989). [U.S. Army, 1970-1972]. ***PRACTICE AREAS:*** Creditors' Rights Law; Bankruptcy; Commercial Law; Real Estate Law; Civil Litigation; Accident. ***Email:*** lmills@brophymills.com

DOUGLASS H. SCHMOR, born Klamath Falls, Oregon, September 25, 1951; admitted to bar, 1976, Oregon. *Education:* Willamette University (B.A., cum laude, 1973); Harvard Law School (J.D., 1976). President, Medford Chamber of Commerce, 1990-1992. *Member:* Jackson County and American Bar Associations; Oregon State Bar (Member, House of Delegates, 1996-1997 and 2005-2008; Executive Committee, Business Law Section, 1984-1988, and Chairman, 1989). ***PRACTICE AREAS:*** Business Formation; Mergers and Acquisitions; Closely Held Business Law; Estate Planning; Commercial Contracts; Land Use Law; Employment Law; Corporate Law. ***Email:*** dschmor@brophymills.com

TIMOTHY C. GERKING, born Bloomington, Indiana, March 12, 1949; admitted to bar, 1974, Arizona; 1979, Oregon. *Education:* Indiana University; University of Arizona (B.A., 1971); Arizona State University (J.D., 1974). Comment Editor, Arizona State Law Journal, 1973-1974. *Member:* Jackson County, Federal and American Bar Associations; Oregon State Bar (Member, Function and Organization of the Bar Committee, 1987-1990; Member 1990-1993 and Chairman, 1992-1993, Mandatory CLE Board; Member, State Professional Responsibility Board, 1993-1996; Board of Governors, 2005—); State Bar of Arizona; Southern Oregon Federal Bar Association; Oregon Association of Defense Counsel; Defense Research Institute; Oregon School Board Lawyers Association; National School Board Lawyers Association. ***PRACTICE AREAS:*** Insurance Defense; Insurance Coverage; Employment Litigation; Commercial Litigation; Products Liability; Public School Law. ***Email:*** tgerking@brophymills.com

TIMOTHY E. BROPHY, born Medford, Oregon, January 5, 1952; admitted to bar, 1978, Oregon. *Education:* Stanford University (B.A., in History, with honors, 1974); University of Oregon (J.D., 1978). Phi Delta Phi. Contributing Author: *Civil Litigation Manual,* Oregon State Bar CLE, 1982. *Member:* Jackson County and American Bar Associations; Oregon State Bar (Member: Executive Committee, Business Law Section, 1999-2003; Procedure and Practice Committee, 1984-1987); Southern Oregon Federal Bar Association. ***LANGUAGES:*** German and Swedish. ***PRACTICE AREAS:*** Business Law; Business Transactions; Commercial Real Estate; Employment Law; Land Use; Estate Planning; Probate. ***Email:*** tbrophy@brophymills.com

DAVID B. PARADIS, born Medford, Oregon, August 19, 1959; admitted to bar, 1985, Oregon. *Education:* Southern Oregon State College (B.A., cum laude, Spanish and Political Science, 1982); Guanajuato University, Guanajuato, Mexico; Willamette University College of Law (J.D., cum laude, 1985). Speaker: Debtor Creditor CLE, Collecting Money Judgments, 1998; Employment Law Issues, OADC Convention, 1998. Member, Providence Hospital Board, 2003—. *Member:* Jackson County, Federal (Board Member, Southern Oregon Chapter, 1998—) and American Bar Associations; Oregon State Bar (Member, Council on Court Procedures, 1995-1998; Member, 1995-1998 and Chairperson, 1998, Federal Practice and Procedure Committee); Southern Oregon Federal Bar Association; Oregon Association of Defense Counsel. ***LANGUAGES:*** Spanish. ***PRACTICE AREAS:*** Commercial Litigation; Construction Law; Insurance Litigation; Products Liability; Foreclosures; Real Estate; Professional Liability Defense. ***Email:*** dparadis@brophymills.com

TODD B. MADDOX, born Fairbanks, Alaska, August 12, 1957; admitted to bar, 1991, Oregon. *Education:* University of Oregon, 1975; Southern Oregon State College (B.S., History, 1981); Willamette University College of Law (J.D., 1991). Member and Past President, Southern Oregon Estate Planning Council. *Member:* Jackson County and American Bar Associations; Oregon State Bar. ***PRACTICE AREAS:*** Estate Administration; Estate and Gift Taxation; Trust Planning; Trust Administration; Fiduciary Law; Elder Law. ***Email:*** tmaddox@brophymills.com

MARK R. WEAVER, born Tucson, Arizona, December 3, 1969; admitted to bar, 1996, Oregon. *Education:* Willamette University (B.A., Spanish and Int'l Studies, 1992; J.D., cum laude, 1996). Certificate in Dispute Resolution. Member, Willamette Law Review, 1995-1996. *Member:* Jackson County (Member and Secretary) and American Bar Associations; Oregon State Bar; Southern Oregon Federal Bar Association; Oregon Association of Defense Counsel. ***LANGUAGES:*** Spanish. ***PRACTICE AREAS:*** Collections; Commercial Litigation; Contract Litigation; Debtor and Creditor; Insurance; OSHA. ***Email:*** mweaver@brophymills.com

THADDEUS G. PAUCK, born Ashland, Oregon, October 5, 1968; admitted to bar, 1998, Oregon. *Education:* Southern Oregon State College (B.S., History, 1990); University of Oregon School of Law (J.D., 1998). Order of the Coif. *Member:* Jackson County Bar Association; Oregon State Bar; Southern Oregon Estate Planning Council (Board Member). ***PRACTICE AREAS:*** Business Organization; Business Sales; Intellectual Property; Real Estate Contracts; Limited Liability Company Law. ***Email:*** tpauck@brophymills.com

ASSOCIATES

TAMARA L. GLEDHILL, born Medford, Oregon, November 24, 1975; admitted to bar, 2002, Oregon. *Education:* Southern Oregon State College (B.S., Business Management, 1998; M.B.A., Business Administration, 1999); Gonzaga University, School of Law (J.D., summa cum laude, 2002). Phi Delta Phi, 1999-2002. National Jesuit Honors Society. ***PRACTICE AREAS:*** Business Start-Ups; Buying and Selling of Businesses; Small Business Corporations; Real Estate; Trust Law; Wills. ***Email:*** tgledhill@brophymills.com

(This Listing Continued)

BROPHY, MILLS, SCHMOR, GERKING, BROPHY & PARADIS, LLP, Medford—Continued

DOMINIC M. CAMPANELLA, born Des Plaines, Illinois, September 18, 1976; admitted to bar, 2004, Oregon. *Education:* Eckerd College (B.A., with honors, 1998); University of Oregon (J.D., 2004). Order of the Coif. **PRACTICE AREAS:** Insurance Defense; Commercial Litigation; Collections. **Email:** dcampanella@brophymills.com

GENERAL COUNSEL FOR: Butte Falls School Dist. No. 91; California Oregon Broadcasting, Inc.; Cedar Links Golf Club, Inc.; Central Point School Dist. No. 6; Eagle Point School Dist. No. 9; Grange Cooperative Supply Association; Home Medical, Inc.; Kathrein Inc., Scala Division; Medford Moulding Co.; Medford School District 549C; Oregon Hydrangea Co.; Phoenix-Talent School Dist. No. 4; Rogue Community College; Rogue Valley Sewer Services; Southern Oregon Sales, Inc.; Southern Oregon Linen Service Cooperative; Wagner Electronic Products, Inc
LOCAL COUNSEL FOR: Acceptance Insurance Group; AIG Insurance; Allstate Insurance Company; American Hardware Insurance Group; Boise Cascade, Inc.; Charter Communications; Colonial Insurance Co. of California; Land America Lawyers Title Insurance Co.; Continental Western Insurance Co.; Country Companies; CNA; Crusader Insurance Co.; Cuna Mutual Insurance Group; Empire Insurance Cos.; Executive Risk Management Associates; Farmers Insurance Group; Foremost Insurance Company; First American Title Insurance Co.; First State Insurance Co.; Government Employees Insurance Co.; Great American Insurance Company; Gulf Insurance Company; Interstate Distributors Co.; John Deere Co.; MSI Insurance; National Claims Management; Omaha Indemnity Co.; Omaha Property and Casualty Co.; Oregon State Bar Professional Liability Fund; Smurfit-Stone Container Corporation; State Farm Fire & Casualty Co.; State Farm Mutual Automobile Insurance Co.; Swift Transportation; Transnation Title Insurance Company; Union Standard Insurance Group; United States Liability Insurance Group; Zurich-American Insurance Group.

FOSTER DENMAN, LLP

3521 EAST BARNETT ROAD
P.O. BOX 1667
MEDFORD, OREGON 97501
Telephone: 541-770-5466
Facsimile: 541-770-6502
URL: http://www.fosterdenman.com

Business Litigation in all State and Federal Courts. Corporate Law, Business Law, Real Property, Land Use, Estate Planning, Estate Administration, Probate, Trusts Law, Nonprofit Organizations Law, Health Law, Construction Law, Tax Law.

MEMBERS OF FIRM

DONALD K. DENMAN, born Medford, Oregon, June 13, 1933; admitted to bar, 1962, Oregon; 1993, U.S. District Court, District of Oregon. *Education:* Oregon State University (B.S., 1955); Willamette University (J.D., 1962). Phi Delta Phi. Chairman, Jackson County Planning Commission, 1964-1968. Member, Oregon Fish and Wildlife Commission, 1998—; Vice Chair, 1999—. *Member:* Jackson County Bar Association (Secretary, 1965-1966; President, 1980); Oregon State Bar (Member, Legal Ethics Committee, 1976-1979; Chairman, 1978; Member; Disciplinary Review Board, 1982-1985; Disciplinary Board, 1990). [U.S. Air Force, 1st. Lieutenant, 1956-1959]. **PRACTICE AREAS:** Estate Planning; Trusts and Estates; Estate Administration; Business Law; Real Estate. **Email:** ddenman@fosterdenman.com

STUART E. FOSTER, born The Dalles, Oregon, March 23, 1942; admitted to bar, 1967, Oregon. *Education:* University of Oregon (B.S., 1964); Willamette University (J.D., 1967). Phi Delta Phi. Member, Oregon Transportation Commission, 1995—, Chair, 2003—. *Member:* Jackson County and American Bar Associations; Oregon State Bar (President, 1989-1990; Member, Board of Governors, 1987-1990; Chairman, Business Law Section, 1985-1986; Chairman, Professional Liability Fund, 1995-1996). Fellow, American College of Trust and Estate Counsel. **PRACTICE AREAS:** Business Law; Corporate Law; Real Estate; Trusts and Estates; Business Litigation. **Email:** sfoster@fosterdenman.com

KAREN C. ALLAN, born Tulsa, Oklahoma, January 26, 1943; admitted to bar, 1975, Oregon; U.S. Court of Appeals, Ninth Circuit. *Education:* Radcliffe College (B.A., 1964); Reed College (M.A.T., 1965); University of Oregon (J.D., 1975). Order of the Coif. Law Clerk: Court of Appeals, State of Oregon, 1975-1976; Supreme Court, State of Oregon, 1976. Chair, 2002 and Director, 1997-2002, Professional Liability Fund. *Member:* Jackson County and American Bar Associations; Oregon State Bar (Member, Executive Committee, Estate Planning Section, 2003—). **PRACTICE AREAS:** Estate Planning; Estate Administration; Health Law; Appellate Practice; Nonprofit and Charitable Organizations. **Email:** kallan@fosterdenman.com

GARY C. PETERSON, born Portland, Oregon, October 2, 1945; admitted to bar, 1977, Oregon. *Education:* Lewis and Clark College (B.S., 1967; J.D., 1977). Member, Lewis and Clark Law Review, 1976-1977. Law Clerk, Supreme Court, State of Oregon, 1977-1978. *Member:* Jackson County and American Bar Associations; Oregon State Bar. **PRACTICE AREAS:** Labor and Employment; Construction Law; Real Estate; Commercial Real Estate; Zoning, Planning and Land Use; Contracts; Business Law; Corporate Law. **Email:** gpeterson@fosterdenman.com

LEWIS W. DAHLIN, born Bend, Oregon, March 14, 1947; admitted to bar, 1972, Oregon; U.S. District Court, District of Oregon; U.S. Tax Court. *Education:* Oregon State University (B.S., 1969); University of Oregon (J.D., 1972). Jackson County Deputy District Attorney, 1976-1988. *Member:* Jackson County Bar Association (President, 1993); Oregon State Bar (Member, State Professional Responsibility Board, 2002—; Chair, 2005; Vice President, 1995-1996; Member, Board of Governors, 1993-1996; Chair, Judicial Administration Committee, 1992-1993). [With U.S. Marine Corps, Judge Advocate Division, 1972-1976]. **PRACTICE AREAS:** Business Litigation; Construction Law; Employment Law. **Email:** ldahlin@fosterdenman.com

JASON M. ANDERSON, born Inglewood, California, January 4, 1970; admitted to bar, 1995, Oregon. *Education:* University of Oregon (B.A., 1992; J.D., 1995). *Member:* Jackson County and American Bar Associations; Oregon State Bar; Medford Planning Commission (Member, 1999-2003); Medford City Council (2003—). **LANGUAGES:** Spanish. **PRACTICE AREAS:** Business Law; Corporate Law; Trusts and Estates; Estate Administration; Real Estate; Land Use. **Email:** janderson@fosterdenman.com

(This Listing Continued)

TIMOTHY L. JACKLE, born Portland, Oregon, April 5, 1970; admitted to bar, 1998, Oregon; U.S. District Court, District of Oregon; U.S. Court of Appeals, Ninth Circuit. *Education:* Linfield College (B.S., magna cum laude, 1992); University of Oregon (J.D., 1998). Order of the Coif. Member, Editorial Board, Journal of Environmental Law and Litigation. *Member:* Jackson County Bar Association; Oregon State Bar. **PRACTICE AREAS:** Business Law; Corporate Law; Real Property; Estate Planning; Business Litigation. **Email:** tjackle@fosterdenman.com

ASSOCIATE

ERIC R. FOSTER, born Medford, Oregon, November 25, 1974; admitted to bar, 2002, Oregon and Washington; U.S. Tax Court. *Education:* University of Oregon (B.A., History/Japanese, 1997; J.D., 2001); University of Washington (LL.M., Taxation, 2002). Managing Editor, Journal of Environmental Law and Litigation, 2000-2001. *Member:* Oregon State Bar; Washington State and Jackson County Bar Associations. **LANGUAGES:** Japanese. **PRACTICE AREAS:** Business Law; Corporate Law; Real Property; Estate Planning; Taxation. **Email:** efoster@fosterdenman.com

REPRESENTATIVE CLIENTS: Alsthom USA, Inc. (Manufacturing); Asante Health System; Britt Festivals; Burrill Real Estate Co.; Burrill Resources, Inc.; Cardiology Consultants, P.C.; The Carpenter Foundation; Cascade Wood Products, Inc.; Cataract & Laser Institute of Southern Oregon, P.C.; Gordon Elwood Foundation; LTM, Incorporated (construction); Mail Tribune; Medical Eye Center, Inc.; Metal Masters, Inc.; R.A. Murphy Construction Co.; Oregon Shakespeare Festival; Profile Grinding & Machine, Inc.; Pulver & Leever Real Estate, Inc.; Raven Maps & Images; Renal Care Consultants, P.C.; Rogue Aggregates, Inc.; Rogue Valley Medical Center; Straus Ranches; Tucker Sno-Cat.

FOWLER & McNAIR, LLP

Established in 1972
705 WEST TENTH STREET
P.O. BOX 1746
MEDFORD, OREGON 97501
Telephone: 541-779-4075
Fax: 541-779-8742

Business Transactions, Real Property, Creditors Rights, Estate and Trust Planning and Administration, Arbitration, Commercial and Family Law.

FIRM PROFILE: One of the older continuously established Rogue Valley law firms. Former partner of Fowler, Alley & McNair, Frank R. Alley III retired from the firm in 1995 to accept an appointment to the U.S. Bankruptcy Court for the District of Oregon.

MEMBERS OF FIRM

WILLIAM H. FOWLER, born Scobey, Montana, March 13, 1943; admitted to bar, 1968, Oregon. *Education:* University of Oregon (B.S., 1965); Willamette University College of Law (J.D., 1968). *Member:* Jackson County and American Bar Associations; Oregon State Bar. **PRACTICE AREAS:** Complex Business Problems; Business Litigation; Family Law.

CHARLES M. McNAIR, born Riverside, California, December 7, 1943; admitted to bar, 1975, Oregon. *Education:* University of Oregon (B.A., 1967); Northwestern School of Law (J.D., 1975). Speaker, Article 9 and Commercial Practice, Continuing Legal Education. *Member:* Jackson County Bar Association; Oregon State Bar (Chair, Legal Management Section, 1995—; Chair, Debtor Creditor Section, 1988-1989). **REPORTED CASES:** Moorman v. Hall on Article 2 Statute of Limitations. **PRACTICE AREAS:** Estate and Trust Planning and Administration; Business and Corporate Planning; Creditor's Rights; Private and Court ordered Arbitrations. **Email:** cmm@fowlermcnair.com

ASSOCIATE

KIMBERLY S. T. BOLEN, born Hartford, Connecticut, October 13, 1969; admitted to bar, 1996, Oregon and U.S. District Court, District of Oregon. *Education:* Hartwick College (B.A., 1991); Gonzaga University (J.D, 1996). President, Moot Court Council, Gonzaga University, 1995-1996. *Member:* Oregon State Bar (Executive Committee Member, Family Law Section, 1999-2001). **PRACTICE AREAS:** Family Law; Civil Litigation. **Email:** kimstbolen@fowlermcnair.com

GENERAL COUNSEL: Capital Associates, Inc.; Roguejets, Inc.; Freeman Marine, Inc.; Southern Oregon Urology, Women's Health, Inc.; Medford Pathologists, P.C.; Rogue Pacific Lumber, Co.; Associated Fruit Co.

FROHNMAYER, DEATHERAGE, PRATT, JAMIESON, CLARKE & MOORE, P.C.

Established in 1910
LARSON CREEK PROFESSIONAL CENTER
2592 E. BARNETT ROAD
MEDFORD, OREGON 97504
Telephone: 541-779-2333
Fax: 541-779-6379
Email: fdfirm@fdfirm.com
URL: http://www.lawyers.com/fdfirm

General Civil and Trial Practice in all State and Federal Courts. Corporate Law, Business Law, Real Estate, Probate, Trust, Estate Planning, Federal Tax Law, Construction Law, Civil Rights, Commercial Litigation, Insurance Law, Professional Malpractice, Medical Malpractice, Personal Injury, Products Liability, Premises Liability, Wrongful Death, Criminal Law, Domestic Relations, Employment Law, Divorce, Family Law.

FIRM PROFILE: Founded in 1910, the firm has continuously provided high quality legal services to its clients throughout southwestern Oregon. Large enough to be a full service law firm, yet small enough to maintain a personal relationship with its clients, the firm provides excellent

(This Listing Continued)

legal representation to every client every day. Besides their commitment to provide high quality legal services, members of the firm actively support community work, charitable service, and professional activities.

OTTO J. FROHNMAYER (1905-2000)

WILLIAM V. DEATHERAGE, born Drumright, Oklahoma, April 17, 1927; admitted to bar, 1954, Oregon. *Education:* University of Oregon (B.S., 1952; LL.B., 1954). Delta Theta Phi. *Member:* Jackson County and American Bar Associations; Oregon State Bar (Chairman, Committee on Procedure and Practice, 1972-1973); Oregon Association of Defense Counsel (President, 1974); American Board of Trial Advocates. Fellow: International Academy of Trial Lawyers; American College of Trial Lawyers. ***PRACTICE AREAS:*** Civil Litigation; Business Law. ***Email:*** deatherage@fdfirm.com

STEVEN H. PRATT, born Sioux City, Iowa, July 26, 1946; admitted to bar, 1977, Oregon; U.S. District Court, District of Oregon; U.S. Court of Appeals, Ninth Circuit. *Education:* Iowa State University and University of Nebraska (B.S., 1973); University of Virginia (J.D., 1977). *Member:* Jackson County and Federal Bar Associations; Oregon State Bar (Member, Council on Court Procedures, 1985-1989; Member, 1987-1990 and Chairperson, 1990, Continuing Legal Education Committee; Judicial Administration Committee, 1992-1993; Jackson/Josephine County Local Professional Responsibility Committee, 1991-1992); Oregon Association of Defense Counsel (Board Member, 1993-1995); Association of Defense Trial Attorneys; Defense Research Institute; Advocate, American Board of Trial Advocates. Fellow, American College of Trial Lawyers. ***PRACTICE AREAS:*** Civil Litigation; Professional Liability Defense; Commercial Litigation. ***Email:*** pratt@fdfirm.com

STEPHEN G. JAMIESON, born Rochester, New York, December 26, 1944; admitted to bar, 1971, Washington; 1977, New York; 1980, U.S. Tax Court; 1983, Oregon. *Education:* Amherst College (B.A., 1967); Boston University (J.D., cum laude, 1971); New York University (LL.M., in Taxation, 1977). *Member:* Jackson County, Washington State and New York State Bar Associations; Oregon State Bar. ***PRACTICE AREAS:*** Probate; Trust; Tax and Estate Planning Law; Business and Corporate Law. ***Email:*** jamieson@fdfirm.com

MARK D. CLARKE, born Salem, Oregon, May 23, 1956; admitted to bar, 1983, Oregon. *Education:* Southern Oregon State College (B.S., magna cum laude, 1980); University of Oregon (J.D., 1983). *Member:* Jackson County Bar Association; Oregon State Bar (Member, Uniform Civil Jury Instruction Committee, 1991-1993; Civil Practice and Procedure Committee, 1993-1997; Federal Practice and Procedure Committee, 1998); Oregon Association of Defense Counsel (President, 2005; President Elect, 2004); Defense Research Institute; Federation of Insurance and Corporate Counsel; Southern Oregon Federal Bar Association (President, 1998); American Board of Trial Advocates. ***PRACTICE AREAS:*** Civil Litigation; Insurance Defense; Construction Law; Commercial Litigation; Employment Law; Personal Injury. ***Email:*** clarke@fdfirm.com

BERNARD S. MOORE, born Bay City, Michigan, April 28, 1958; admitted to bar, 1984, Oregon; 1986, U.S. District Court, District of Oregon; 1989, U.S. Court of Appeals, Ninth Circuit. *Education:* Alma College (B.A., 1980); Northwestern School of Law of Lewis and Clark College (J.D., 1984). Phi Alpha Theta. Deputy District Attorney, Jackson County, 1984-1985. Member: Jackson/Josephine County Local Professional Responsibility Committee, 1988-1990; Committee on Uniform Civil Jury Instructions, 1990-1993. Jackson County Circuit Court Judge Pro Tem. *Member:* Jackson County and American Bar Associations; Oregon State Bar; Oregon Association of Defense Counsel; Defense Research Institute; Association of Defense Trial Attorneys (Attorney Delegate, 9th Circuit Judicial Conference, 2003-2006). ***PRACTICE AREAS:*** Commercial Litigation; Insurance Defense; Employment Litigation; Personal Injury; Domestic Relations. ***Email:*** moore@fdfirm.com

THOMAS F. ARMOSINO, JR., born Oakland, California, February 18, 1965; admitted to bar, 1991, Oregon. *Education:* California State University, Chico (B.A., 1988); California Western School of Law, San Diego (J.D., 1991). *Member:* Jackson County and American Bar Associations; Oregon State Bar; Oregon Association of Defense Counsel; Defense Research Institute. ***PRACTICE AREAS:*** Civil Litigation; Insurance Defense; Commercial Litigation; Personal Injury; Divorce; Medical Malpractice; Products Liability. ***Email:*** armosino@fdfirm.com

TRACY M. McGOVERN, born Lakewood, New Jersey, November 11, 1967; admitted to bar, 1993, Oregon. *Education:* Catholic University of America (B.A., summa cum laude, 1990); George Washington University (J.D., 1993). Phi Beta Kappa. Member, Arbitration and Mediation Committees, Jackson County Circuit Court. *Member:* Jackson County and American Bar Associations; Oregon State Bar; Defense Research Institute; Oregon Association of Defense Counsel; Southern Oregon Women Lawyers; Oregon Women Lawyers (Member, Judicial Endorsement Committee). ***PRACTICE AREAS:*** Civil Litigation; Employment Law; Insurance Defense; Domestic Relations; Criminal Law. ***Email:*** mcgovern@fdfirm.com

---

KENNETH M. THARP, born Phoenix, Arizona, November 4, 1971; admitted to bar, 2000, Oregon. *Education:* University of Washington (B.A., cum laude, 1994); Willamette University (J.D./M.B.A., 1999). Phi Beta Kappa. *Member:* Jackson County Bar Association; Oregon State Bar. ***PRACTICE AREAS:*** Civil Litigation; Real Estate; Insurance Defense; Commercial Litigation; Divorce; Estate Planning. ***Email:*** tharp@fdfirm.com

EDWARD H. TALMADGE, born Lemoore A.N.S., California, October 19, 1968; admitted to bar, 2001, Oregon. *Education:* University of Oregon (B.A., 1995; J.D., 2001). Order of the Coif. *Member:* Jackson County Bar Association; Oregon State Bar; Oregon Association of Defense Counsel. ***LANGUAGES:*** Japanese. ***PRACTICE AREAS:*** Civil Litigation; Insurance Defense; Creditors Rights; Bankruptcy; Employment Law; Probate Litigation. ***Email:*** talmadge@fdfirm.com

ARNE I. CHERKOSS, born Los Angeles, California, September 9, 1971; admitted to bar, 2003, Oregon. *Education:* California State University, Dominguez Hills (B.A., 1993); University of Oregon School of Law (J.D., 2003). *Member:* Jackson County Bar Association; Oregon State Bar. ***PRACTICE AREAS:*** Civil Litigation; Insurance Defense; Divorce; Employment Law. ***Email:*** cherkoss@fdfirm.com

(This Listing Continued)

JODEE L. SCOTT, born Medford, Oregon, April 30, 1977; admitted to bar, 2005, Oregon. *Education:* University of Tennessee, Knoxville (1995-1997); Northern Michigan University (B.S., 2000); University of Oregon (J.D., 2003). *Member:* Jackson County Bar Association; Oregon State Bar. ***Email:*** scott@fdfirm.com

LOCAL COUNSEL FOR: Allstate Insurance Company; CNA; Country Companies; Farmers Insurance Group; Health Future, Inc.; Northwest Physicians Mutual Insurance Company; Oregon Auto/North Pacific Insurance; Oregon Mutual Insurance Company; Progressive Insurance Co.; Professional Liability Fund; St. Paul Insurance Companies; Self Insured Management Services; State Farm Ins. Co.; State Farm Mutual Company; Sublimity Ins. Co.; USAA; Unigard Insurance Group; Unitrin Insurance Group; American Family Insurance.
GENERAL COUNSEL FOR: Advanced Electrical Contractors; Lithia Motors Inc.; Musician's Friend, Inc.; Radiation Oncology Group, P.C.; Hematology Oncology Assoc. P.C., OB/Gyn Health Center; Premier West Bank.

HORNECKER, COWLING, HASSEN & HEYSELL, L.L.P.

717 MURPHY ROAD
MEDFORD, OREGON 97504
Telephone: 541-779-8900
Fax: 541-779-2982; 541-773-2635
Email: hchh@roguelaw.com
URL: http://www.roguelaw.com

Hornecker, Cowling, Hassen & Heysell, L.L.P., is the largest firm in Southern Oregon and endeavors to be a full service provider of legal services for all of our clients. The firm specializes in Business, Estate Planning and Probate, Real Estate, Land Use, Workers Compensation, Medical and Professional Malpractice, Products Liability, Premises Liability, Automobile, Commercial Litigation and Employee/Employer Relations, Personal Injury, Domestic Relations and Adoption, Municipal and Government, Health Care, Intellectual Property, Computer Law and Civil Trial and Appellate Practice in all State and Federal Courts.

FIRM PROFILE: Hornecker, Cowling, Hassen & Heysell, L.L.P. law firm has received the highest rating in ability and ethical standards.

In response to the needs of their clients for a full service legal provider, two of the largest, respected and experienced firms in the Rogue Valley merged in 1998. As with the original founders in the early 1900's, the firm continues its' dedication to providing quality legal assistance to the residents of the Rogue Valley and Southern Oregon.

Hornecker, Cowling, Hassen & Heysell's goal is to excel in producing experienced, personal and aggressive representation in its' specialized fields of business.

MEMBERS OF FIRM

GREGORY T. HORNECKER, born Portland, Oregon, September 5, 1933; admitted to bar, 1958, Oregon. *Education:* Oregon State University (B.S., 1955); University of Oregon (LL.B., 1958). Member, District Advisory Council, Small Business Administration, 1971-1978. *Member:* Oregon State Bar (Member, Board of Bar Examiners, 1973-1976); American Bar Association. ***PRACTICE AREAS:*** Business Law; Corporate Law; Estate Planning; Probate; Real Estate; Property Law. ***Email:*** gth@roguelaw.com

ROBERT L. COWLING, born Portland, Oregon, September 24, 1940; admitted to bar, 1965, Oregon. *Education:* University of Oregon (B.S., 1962; LL.B., 1965). Phi Delta Phi. Member, 1987-1990, Chair and Member, 1989-1990, Oregon State Professional Responsibility Board. Member, 1993-1995 and Lawyer Representative, Oregon District, Chair, 1995, Ninth Circuit Judicial Conference *Member:* Jackson County, Federal (Member, Board of Directors, 1996—); and American Bar Associations; Oregon State Bar; Oregon Association of Defense Counsel (Member, Board of Directors, 1981-1985); Defense Research Institute; American Board of Trial Advocates; Federation of Insurance and Corporate Counsel; American College of Trial Lawyers. ***PRACTICE AREAS:*** Medical Malpractice; Professional Malpractice; Products Liability; Civil Litigation; Health Care. ***Email:*** rlc@roguelaw.com

JOHN R. HASSEN, born Ahoskie, North Carolina, November 13, 1939; admitted to bar, 1965, Oregon. *Education:* Harvard University (A.B., cum laude, 1961); Stanford University (LL.B., 1965). Member, National Panel of Arbitrators, American Arbitration Association. *Member:* Jackson County and American Bar Associations; Oregon State Bar; American Academy of Adoption Attorneys. ***PRACTICE AREAS:*** Land Use; Land Development; Real Property; Corporate Law; Adoption Law; Estate Planning; Probate; Health Care Law. ***Email:*** jrh@roguelaw.com

R. RAY HEYSELL, born Vancouver, Washington, April 19, 1945; admitted to bar, 1973, Oregon. *Education:* University of Arizona; Lewis and Clark College (B.S., 1967); Northwestern School of Law (J.D., 1973). Member, Environmental Law Review, Northwestern School of Law of Lewis and Clark College, 1971. Member, Joint Committee, Oregon Medical Association and Oregon State Bar Association, 1980—. Member, State Professional Responsibility Board, 1997-1999. *Member:* Jackson County and American Bar Associations; Oregon State Bar (Member: Workers Compensation Referee Review Committee, 1980-1981; Member, Executive Committee, 1981-1984, 1986-1988 and Chairman, 1982-1983, Worker's Compensation Section; Committee on Uniform Civil Jury Instruction, 1984-1986;); Oregon Association of Defense Counsel; Association of Workers Compensation Defense Attorneys (Member, Executive Committee, 1985-1986). ***PRACTICE AREAS:*** Workers Compensation; Occupational Safety; Employment Law. ***Email:*** rrh@roguelaw.com

H. SCOTT PLOUSE, born Long Beach, California, December 12, 1951; admitted to bar, 1982, Oregon. *Education:* The Ohio State University (B.A., 1974); Capital University (J.D., cum laude, 1982). Member, Order of the Curia. Member, Board of Editors, Capital University Law Review, 1981-1982. Licensed Real Estate Salesman, Ohio, 1974. Author, "Branti v. Finkel, Spoiling the Spoils System," 10 Cap. Univ. Law Review, 1981; *Introduction to Workers' Compensation,* Oregon State Bar, Workers' Compensation 1988; Appellate Update, Oregon State Bar, Workers' Compensation Section, 1998. *Responsibility Law,* Oregon State Bar, Workers' Compensation Section CLE, 1990, 1995; . *Member:* Oregon State Bar (Member, Workers Compensation Section Nominating Committee, 1986-1988); Asso-

(This Listing Continued)

HORNECKER, COWLING, HASSEN & HEYSELL, L.L.P., Medford—Continued

ciation of Workers Compensation Defense Attorneys. [Lt., U.S. Navy, 1974-1978]. ***LANGUAGES:*** German. ***PRACTICE AREAS:*** Workers Compensation. ***Email:*** hsp@roguelaw.com

P. DAVID INGALLS, born Eugene, Oregon, March 8, 1951; admitted to bar, 1978, Oregon. *Education:* University of California at Santa Cruz (A.B., 1973); Northwestern School of Law of Lewis and Clark College (J.D., 1978). Member, Environmental Law Review, Northwestern School of Law of Lewis and Clark College, 1977-1978. *Member:* Jackson County Bar Association; Oregon State Bar (Member, Committee on Uniform Civil Jury Instructions, 1986-1990); Defense Research Institute; Oregon Association of Defense Counsel. ***PRACTICE AREAS:*** Employment Law; Civil Litigation. ***Email:*** pdi@roguelaw.com

ADAM T. STAMPER, born San Francisco, California, March 3, 1964; admitted to bar, 1989, Oregon; 1990, California. *Education:* California State University at Long Beach (B.S., 1986); Hastings College of the Law, University of California (J.D., 1989). Phi Alpha Delta. Associate Editor, Constitutional Law Quarterly. *Member:* Oregon State Bar; State Bar of California; Oregon Association of Defense Counsel. ***PRACTICE AREAS:*** Workers Compensation; Occupational Safety and Health; Employment Law. ***Email:*** ats@roguelaw.com

JOSEPH E. KELLERMAN, born Philadelphia, Pennsylvania, September 3, 1965; admitted to bar, 1992, Oregon. *Education:* University of Florida (B.A., 1987); University of Oregon (J.D., 1991); University of Washington (LL.M., 1992). Ford Foundation Fellowship. *Member:* Oregon State Bar. ***PRACTICE AREAS:*** Business Litigation; Real Estate Litigation; Municipal Law; Employment Law. ***Email:*** jek@roguelaw.com

JAMES A. WALLAN, born Bend, Oregon, December 8, 1957; admitted to bar, 1986, Oregon; 1990, U.S. District Court, District of Oregon; 1994, U.S. Court of Appeals, Ninth Circuit. *Education:* Oregon College of Education (B.A., 1981); Willamette University (J.D., 1985). Deputy District Attorney, Jackson County, 1986-1990. Oregon State Bar Counsel, 1991—. *Member:* Oregon State Bar; Jackson County Bar Association; Oregon Association of Defense Counsel. ***LANGUAGES:*** German. ***PRACTICE AREAS:*** Insurance Defense; Civil Litigation; Domestic Relations. ***Email:*** jaw@roguelaw.com

BENJAMIN M. BLOOM, born Philadelphia, Pennsylvania, December 14, 1966; admitted to bar, 1993, Oregon, U.S. District Court, District of Oregon; 1994, U.S. Court of Appeals, Ninth Circuit. *Education:* University of Edinburgh, Scotland (1988-1989); Hamilton College (A.B., 1990); Northwestern School of Law of Lewis and Clark College (J.D., 1993). *Member:* Jackson County (Member, Court Liaison Committee) and Federal (Director, 1999-2002; Council on Court Procedures, 1999-2003) Bar Associations; Oregon State Bar (Member, Executive Committee, Products Liability Section, 1999-2001); Oregon Association of Defense Counsel. ***PRACTICE AREAS:*** Insurance Defense; Medical Malpractice; Professional Malpractice; Municipal Law; Civil Rights; Civil Litigation. ***Email:*** bmb@roguelaw.com

CHARLES E. BOLEN, born Washington, D.C., March 17, 1966; admitted to bar, 1996, Oregon. *Education:* St. Mary's College of Maryland (B.A., summa cum laude, 1990); Gonzaga University (J.D., cum laude, 1996). Thomas More Scholar. *Member:* Oregon State Bar. ***PRACTICE AREAS:*** Civil Litigation; Medical Malpractice; Professional Malpractice; Insurance Defense; Workers Compensation. ***Email:*** ceb@roguelaw.com

ALAN D.B. HARPER, born Wallace, Idaho, September 7, 1967; admitted to bar, 1994, Oregon. *Education:* Willamette University (B.A., 1989; J.D., 1994). *Member:* Oregon State Bar. ***PRACTICE AREAS:*** Business Law; Corporate Law; Real Property. ***Email:*** adbh@roguelaw.com

RYAN J. VANDERHOOF, born Portland, Oregon, November 19, 1972; admitted to bar, 1998, Oregon. *Education:* Texas Tech University School of Law (1995-1996); University of Oregon (B.S., 1995); Northwestern School of Law at Lewis and Clark College (J.D., 1998). Law Clerk to Honorable Gregory G. Foote, 1998-1999. *Member:* Jackson County Bar Association; Oregon State Bar. ***PRACTICE AREAS:*** Employment Law; Civil Litigation; Insurance Defense. ***Email:*** rjv@roguelaw.com

OF COUNSEL

FRED M. AEBI, born Portland, Oregon, March 22, 1941; admitted to bar, 1967, Oregon. *Education:* Portland State University; Lewis & Clark College (J.D., 1967). Circuit Court Judge Pro Tem, 1982, 1984-1985, 1991. Gus J. Solomon Chapter American Inns of Court (Master Bencher, President, 1990). *Member:* Jackson County and American Bar Associations; Oregon State Bar (Committee Chair, Uniform Jury Instructions, Specialization, Federal Practice and Procedure); Federation of Defense and Corporate Counsel; Oregon Association of Defense Counsel (Member, Executive Board and Secretary-Treasurer). ***PRACTICE AREAS:*** Commercial Litigation; Insurance Litigation; Mediation; Arbitration. ***Email:*** fma@roguelaw.com

ASSOCIATES

RICHARD L. BILLIN, born San Jose, California, January 8, 1965; admitted to bar, 1990, Oregon. *Education:* Whitman College (B.A., 1987); Willamette University (J.D., cum laude, 1990). *Member:* Oregon State Bar (Member, Securities Division). ***PRACTICE AREAS:*** Civil Litigation; Business Law; Corporate Law. ***Email:*** rlb@roguelaw.com

SHANE J. ANTHOLZ, LL.M., born Atwood, Kansas, March 8, 1975; admitted to bar, 2002, Washington; 2003, Oregon. *Education:* Kansas State University (B.S., 1998); University of Oregon (J.D., 2001); University of Washington (LL.M. in Taxation, 2002). Associate Editor, 2000-2001 and Staff Editor, 1999-2000, Oregon Law Review. *Member:* Washington State Bar Association; Oregon State Bar. ***PRACTICE AREAS:*** Business Law; Corporate Law; Estate Planning; Probate; Guardianship; Conservatorship; Land Use Planning; Real Property. ***Email:*** sja@roguelaw.com

STEFANIE L. BURKE, born West Covina, California; admitted to bar, 2003, Oregon. *Education:* San Diego State University (B.S., 1999); Thomas Jefferson School of Law (J.D., 2003). Past Member: San Diego County Bar Association; Lawyers Club of San Diego. *Member:* American Bar Association. ***PRACTICE AREAS:*** Domestic Relations; Adoption Law. ***Email:*** slb@roguelaw.com

MARK S. BARTHOLOMEW, born San Francisco, California, September 26, 1975; admitted to bar, 2003, Oregon; 2005, U.S. District Court, District of Oregon. *Education:* Oregon State University (B.S., 1998); Northwestern School of Law of Lewis and Clark College (J.D., 2003). *Member:* Oregon State Bar. ***PRACTICE AREAS:*** Business Law; Corporate Law; Real Property; Land Use Planning. ***Email:*** msb@roguelaw.com

REPRESENTATIVE CLIENTS: Aetna Life & Casualty; Airport Chevrolet, Inc.; Alexis Risk Management; Allstate Insurance Co.; American Star Ins. Co.; American States Ins. Group; AMEX Assurance Co.; ANS Corp.; Anesthesia Associates of Medford, P.C.; Atlanta Casualty; Atlantic Mutual Insurance Co.; Austin Mutual; Bear Creek Corp.; Black Oak Village Shopping Center; Boise Cascade Corp.; City of Eagle Point; Civil Service Employees Ins. Co.; CNA; Coldwell Banker Pro West Real Estate, Inc.; Colonial Penn Ins. Co.; Commercial Union Ins. Co.; Continental Ins. Companies; Continental Lawyers Title Co.; Country Companies; Crawford and Co.; Crystal Springs Packing Co.; Darex Corp.; Farmers Ins. Group; Fireman's Fund Ins. Cos.; Fund a Rogue Valley; Gates, McDonald & Company; Gordon Trucking, Inc.; Grange Insurance Group; Great West Casualty; Gre/Talbot, Bird & Co., Inc.; Gulf Insurance Co.; Harbor Rural Water P.U.D.; Hartford Insurance Group; Health Future, Inc.; InfoStructure; Jackson County Title; Jeld-Wen of Oregon; K-Mart Administrative Services; Liberty Mutual Group; Liberty Northwest Ins. Corp.; Maryland Insurance Co.; Medford Clinic, P.C.; Medford Corp.; Medford Steel; Mutual of Enumclaw; New York Life Insurance Co.; North American Insurance Co. of California; Northwest News Co.; Northwest Physicians Mutual Ins. Co.; Ohio Casualty Group; Old Republic Insurance Co.; Open Door Networks; Oregon State Bar; Orion Group, Inc.; Pacific Trend Building Co.; Professional Liability Fund; Protectors Insurance, Inc.; Providence Medford Medical Center; R.A. Cook Construction; Realestaters/Better Homes and Gardens; Reter Fruit Co.; Rogue Valley Mall Shopping Center; Rogue Valley Medical Center; Roseburg Forest Products; Safeco Co.; Safeway Stores, Inc.; St. Paul's Insurance Co.; Samis, Inc.; Scott Wetzel Services; Sedgwick James Co.; Seibels, Bruce & Co.; Southern Oregon Subaru; Standard Fire Insurance Co.; Sterling Business Forms, Inc.; Steve Wilson Lumber Co.; St. Paul Insurance; Stone Forest Industries; Sublimity Insurance Co.; Talent Irrigation District; Timberland Logging; Town & Country Chevrolet; Town of Butte Falls; Travelers Ins. Co.; Triad Health Care Systems; Underwriters at Lloyd's London; Unigard Ins. Group; United Pacific/Reliance Ins. Co.; USAA; U.S.F. & G. Group; Western Transportation Lines; Weyerhaeuser Co.; Workmen's Auto Insurance Co.

JACOBSON, THIEROLF & DICKEY, P.C.

Established in 1980

TWO NORTH OAKDALE AVENUE
P.O. BOX 4687
MEDFORD, OREGON 97501
Telephone: 541-773-2727
Fax: 541-734-7269
URL: http://www.jacobsonthierolfdickey.com

General Litigation and Office Practice, Civil and Criminal Trials and Appeals in State and Federal Courts, Bankruptcy and Collections, Real Estate and Land Use, Probate, Estate Planning, Business, Domestic Relations, Indian and Environmental Law, Water Law, Immigration, Patents, Trademarks, Copyrights, Licensing, Wills, Trusts.

JERRY A. JACOBSON, born Lebanon, Oregon, August 29, 1948; admitted to bar, 1976, Oregon; 1977, California, U.S. District Court, District of Oregon and U.S. Court of Appeals, Ninth Circuit; 1980, U.S. District Court, Northern District of California; 1984, U.S. Supreme Court. *Education:* Oregon State University (B.S., 1970); Northwestern School of Law of Lewis and Clark College (J.D., 1976). Managing Editor, Environmental Law Review, 1975-1976. *Member:* Jackson County and American Bar Associations; Southern Oregon Estate Planning Council; Crater Lake Natural History Association (President, 1986—). Member, Board of Directors, Center for Nonprofit Legal Services, Inc., 2004—. ***PRACTICE AREAS:*** Real Estate; Business Law; Corporate Law; Business Litigation; Estate Planning; Probate; Domestic Relations.

RICHARD B. THIEROLF, JR., born Medford, Oregon, October 27, 1948; admitted to bar, 1976, Oregon and U.S. District Court, District of Oregon; 1977, U.S. Court of Appeals, Ninth Circuit; 1980, U.S. District Court, Northern District of California; 1993, U.S. Court of Federal Claims and U.S. Supreme Court. *Education:* Columbia University (B.A., 1970); University of Oregon (J.D., 1976). Interim City Attorney, City of Ashland, Oregon, 1991. Member, Planning Commission, City of Medford, 1990-1992. Member, Planning Commission, Jackson County, Oregon, 2001—. Panel Attorney, Criminal Justice Act (CJA), for federal criminal cases. *Member:* Jackson County (Secretary, 1988), Federal and American Bar Associations; Oregon State Bar (Representative to House of Delegates, 1999-2000; Member: Low Income Legal Services Committee, 1990-1993; Federal Practice and Procedure Committee, 1994-1997; Secretary, 1995-1997; Judicial Administration Committee, 1998-2001); Southern Oregon Estate Planning Council (Member, 2001— and President, 2004-2005, Board of Directors); American Immigration Lawyers Association (Vice Chair, 2003). ***REPORTED CASES:*** Decker v. Wiman, 288 Or 687, 607 P2d 1370 (1980); Shermoen, et al. v. United States, 982 F2d 1312 (9th Cir. 1992) cert. den. 509 U.S. 903 (1993). ***PRACTICE AREAS:*** Federal Practice; Bankruptcy; Immigration Law; Civil Practice; Criminal Law.

ROBERT R. DICKEY, JR., born Medford, Oregon, February 19, 1953; admitted to bar, 1978, Oregon. *Education:* University of Oregon (B.S., 1975; J.D., 1978). *Member:* Jackson County Bar Association; Oregon State Bar; Southern Oregon Estate Planning Council. ***PRACTICE AREAS:*** Family Law; Child Custody; Estate Planning; Probate.

GERALD D. HAYNES, born Medford, Oregon, March 2, 1958; admitted to bar, 1985, California; 1993, Oregon; registered to practice before U.S. Patent and Trademark Office. *Education:* Lewis and Clark College (B.A., Mathematics, 1980); Washington University (B.S., Chemical Engineering, 1981); George Washington University (J.D., with honors, 1985). George Washington Journal of International Law, 1983-1985. Professional Positions: Counsel, Intel Corporation, 1999-2005; Vice President, General Counsel and Secretary, Acres Gaming, Inc., 1997-1999; Vice President and General Counsel, OXIS International, Inc., 1996-1997; Patent Counsel, Kaiser Aluminum & Chemical Corp., 1994-1996.

(This Listing Continued)

(Senior Attorney). *PRACTICE AREAS:* Technology Law; Patents; Trademarks; Copyrights; Trade Secrets; Technology Licensing; Real Estate; Land Use; Business Transactions; Corporate Law; Mergers and Acquisitions.

OF COUNSEL

JOHN E. FERRIS, born Lewiston, Idaho, August 21, 1941; admitted to bar, 1966, Oregon. *Education:* University of Idaho (B.S., 1963); University of Michigan (J.D., 1966). Member, Board of Directors, 1971-1989, and President, 1985, Oregon Pre-Paid Legal Insurance. *Member:* Oregon State Bar (Member, Taxation Committee, 1970-1971; Member, 1986-1989 and Chairman, 1988-1989, Alternative Dispute Resolution Committee; Member, Future of the Legal Profession Committee, 1976-1979). ***PRACTICE AREAS:*** Family Law; Business Law; Corporate Law.

KELLINGTON & KELLINGTON

Established in 1997

901 WEST 8TH STREET
P.O. BOX 357
MEDFORD, OREGON 97501
Telephone: 541-773-8436
Fax: 541-773-8940
Email: dkellingtn@aol.com
URL: http://www.lawyers.com/kellington&kellington

Personal Injury, Automobile Accidents, Wrongful Death, Criminal Law, Felonies, Drug Crimes, Wills, Probate, Estate Planning.

FIRM PROFILE: A family team of lawyers, Michael has worked with Dan since 1984 as his legal assistant. Upon completing law school, Michael moved home to set up a partnership.

MEMBERS OF FIRM

DANIEL F. KELLINGTON, born Medford, Oregon, December 3, 1936; admitted to bar, 1965, Oregon. *Education:* University of Oregon (B.S., Prelaw, 1959); Lewis and Clark College (J.D., 1964). *Member:* Jackson County and Oregon State Bar Associations; Oregon Trial Lawyers Association. ***LANGUAGES:*** Spanish. ***PRACTICE AREAS:*** Personal Injury; Probate; Wills; Wrongful Death. ***Email:*** dkellingtn@aol.com

MICHAEL E. KELLINGTON, born Pasadena, California, December 29, 1966; admitted to bar, 1996, Washington; 1997, Oregon. *Education:* Southern Oregon State College (B.A., 1992); Seattle University School of Law (J.D., 1996). *Member:* Jackson County and American Bar Associations; Oregon State Bar; Oregon Trial Lawyers Association. ***LANGUAGES:*** Spanish and some Russian. ***PRACTICE AREAS:*** Personal Injury; Automobile Accidents; Drug Crimes; Criminal Law. ***Email:*** dkellingtn@aol.com

LEGAL SUPPORT PERSONNEL

Teresa Galindo (Legal Assistant)
Linda Fonseca (Legal Assistant)

KELLINGTON, KRACK, RICHMOND, BLACKHURST & GLATTE, LLP

Established in 1962

23 NEWTOWN STREET
MEDFORD, OREGON 97501
Telephone: 541-779-5175
Fax: 541-779-5585
URL: http://www.kkrbg.com

General Civil and Trial Practice. Corporation, Business, Real Property, Land Use Planning, Construction, Trusts, Estate Planning, Probate, Negligence, Creditor's Rights, Collections, Family Law, Employment Law, Appellate Practice and Wireless Communications.

MEMBERS OF FIRM

BRUCE KELLINGTON, born Medford, Oregon, May 7, 1938; admitted to bar, 1962, Oregon. *Education:* University of Oregon (B.S., 1960; J.D., 1962). ***Email:*** bkellington@kkrbg.com

CARL R. KRACK, born Evanston, Illinois, January 29, 1946; admitted to bar, 1972, Oregon. *Education:* Valparaiso University (B.A., 1968; J.D., 1972). ***Email:*** ckrack@kkrbg.com

DOUGLAS J. RICHMOND, born Roseburg, Oregon, February 9, 1950; admitted to bar, 1976, Oregon and U.S. District Court, District of Oregon; 1991, U.S. Court of Appeals, Ninth Circuit; 1992, U.S. Supreme Court. *Education:* Oregon State University (B.S., 1972); University of Oregon (J.D., 1976). ***Email:*** drichmond@kkrbg.com

JOHN BLACKHURST, born Medford, Oregon, July 10, 1953; admitted to bar, 1979, Oregon. *Education:* University of Oregon (B.S., 1975); Northwestern College of Law (J.D., 1978). ***Email:*** jblackhurst@kkrbg.com

ERIK J. GLATTE, born Seattle, Washington, March 15, 1963; admitted to bar, 1992, Idaho; 1995, Oregon. *Education:* University of Puget Sound (B.A., 1985); University of Oregon (J.D., 1992). ***Email:*** eglatte@kkrbg.com

CHARLES GEORGE KOCHLACS

308 HOWARD STREET
MEDFORD, OREGON 97504
Telephone: 541-608-9122
Fax: 541-779-0705
Email: divorce@cdsnet.net
URL: http://www.lawyers.com/kochlacs

Family Law, Divorce, Child Custody, Child Support, Spousal Support, Domestic Violence, Premarital Agreements, Criminal Law and Juvenile Law, Driving While Intoxicated, Drug Crimes, Felonies, Misdemeanors, Sexual Assault, Traffic Violations, Parole and Probation.

CHARLES GEORGE KOCHLACS, born Los Angeles, California, August 14, 1962; admitted to bar, 1989, Oregon; U.S. District Court, District of Oregon; U.S. Court of Appeals, Ninth Circuit. *Education:* University of California at Santa Barbara (B.A., 1984); University of Oregon (J.D., 1988). Associate Editor, Oregon Law Review, 1987-1988. Graduate, National Criminal Defense College. Jackson County Public Defenders Office, 1989-1997. NHTSA certificate: Standard Field Sobriety Testing. *Member:* Oregon State Bar (Member, Sections on: Family Law; Criminal Law; Juvenile Law and President, Criminal Law Section, 1997-1998; Member, House of Delegates, 1996-1998); American Bar Association (Member, Family Law Section); National Association of Criminal Defense Lawyers (Life Member); Oregon Criminal Defense Lawyers Association (Life Member).

KUENZEL & ASSOCIATES

MEDFORD, OREGON

(See Ashland)

Business Law, Business Litigation, Employment Law, Intellectual Property, Arbitration and Mediation.

LOOMIS & HOLLAND

MEDFORD, OREGON

(See Eugene)

Trial practice in State and Federal Courts, Medical Malpractice, Professional Liability, Insurance, Products Liability, Pharmaceutical and Toxic Tort Litigation, Business Litigation, Real Property, Family, Probate Law, Unsafe Products, Legal Malpractice, Personal Injury, Wrongful Death.

LAW OFFICES OF ROBERT D. LOWRY

MEDFORD, OREGON

(See Eugene)

Insurance Defense, Products Liability Defense, Medical Malpractice, Hospital Malpractice, Business Litigation, Construction Law and Civil Litigation.

MUHLHEIM BOYD

MEDFORD, OREGON

(See Eugene)

Creditor/Debtor Representation; Commercial Litigation; Workouts and Bankruptcy Reorganizations; Bankruptcy Litigation; Creditors' Rights; Foreclosure; Commercial Law; Business Litigation; Business Transactions; Litigation; Estate and Probate.

DAVID M. ORF

900 W. EIGHTH STREET
MEDFORD, OREGON 97501
Telephone: 541-772-8494
Fax: 541-773-6790
Email: davidorf@charterinternet.com
URL: http://www.lawyers.com/dmorf

Criminal Defense in all State and Federal Courts. Criminal Law, Driving While Intoxicated, Drug Crimes, Sexual Assault, Felonies, Misdemeanors.

DAVID M. ORF, born Los Angeles, California, August 20, 1950; admitted to bar, 1976, Mississippi and U.S. District Court, District of Mississippi; 1978, Oregon and U.S. District Court, District of Oregon; 1980, U.S. Court of Appeals, Ninth Circuit. *Education:* University of Mississippi (B.A., 1972; J.D., 1976). Jackson County Public Defender, Medford, Oregon, 1987-1994. Member: OSB Indigent Defense Task Force, 1989-1992; Oregon Supreme Court Task Force on Gender Fairness, 1995-1998. Speaker: CLE, Oregon Criminal Defense Lawyers Association Conference of Forensics Topic DNA, 1993; CLE, Oregon Municipal Court Judges Association, Gender Fairness in Courts, 2001. *Member:* Oregon State Bar (Member, Corrections Committee, 1985-1988; Board of Governors, 1996-2000; Vice President, 1999-2000; Member, Committee for Indigent Defense, 1981-1984, 1988-1990; Executive Director, Search Committee, 1994; Member, Gender Fairness Task Force, 1996-2000; PLF Executive Director, Search Committee, 2000); Oregon Criminal Defense Lawyers Association (Presidents Award, 1999); National Association of Criminal Defense Lawyers. ***LANGUAGES:*** Spanish. ***PRACTICE AREAS:*** Criminal Law.

PETERSON LAW OFFICES, PC

MEDFORD, OREGON

(See Portland)

Personal Injury, Premises Liability, Automobile Accidents and Injuries, Dog Bites and Wrongful Death.

STARK AND HAMMACK, P.C.

Established in 1958

201 WEST MAIN STREET, SUITE 1B
MEDFORD, OREGON 97501
Telephone: 541-773-2213; 779-2133
Fax: 541-773-2084
Email: ers@starkhammack.com
URL: http://www.lawyers.com/starkhammack

Corporate Commercial Law, Corporate Real Estate, Commercial Leasing, Real Property, Real Estate Development, Employment Defense, Estate Planning, Elder Law, Mechanics Liens, Contracts, Corporate Law, Divorce, Foreclosures, Business Law, Partnership Law, Landlord and Tenant Law, Mortgages, Commercial Real Estate, Wills and Probate, Zoning, Planning and Land Use.

RICHARD A. STARK, born San Francisco, California, October 8, 1943; admitted to bar, 1969, Oregon and U.S. District Court, District of Oregon. *Education:* University of Oregon (B.S., 1965; J.D., 1969). *Member:* Jackson County Bar Association (Secretary, 1971); Oregon State Bar. ***PRACTICE AREAS:*** Corporate Commercial Law; Corporate Real Estate; Commercial Leasing; Real Property; Real Estate Development; Estate Planning. ***Email:*** ras@starkhammack.com

LARRY C. HAMMACK, born Vancouver, Washington, December 15, 1942; admitted to bar, 1969, Oregon and U.S. District Court, District of Oregon. *Education:* University of Oregon (B.S., 1965; J.D., 1969). *Member:* Jackson County Bar Association; Oregon State Bar (Member, Committee on Unauthorized Practice of Law, 1974-1979). ***PRACTICE AREAS:*** Corporate Commercial Law; Corporate Real Estate; Commercial Leasing; Real Property; Real Estate Development; Employment Defense; Estate Planning. ***Email:*** lch@starkhammack.com

ERIC R. STARK, born Oakland, California, April 11, 1966; admitted to bar, 1992, Oregon and U.S. District Court, District of Oregon. *Education:* University of Oregon (B.A., 1988; J.D., 1991). Public Defender, Jackson County, 1992-1995. Planning Commissioner, 1992-1997, City of Medford. *Member:* Jackson County Bar Association (President, 1999); Oregon State Bar. ***PRACTICE AREAS:*** Corporate Commercial Law; Corporate Real Estate; Commercial Leasing; Landlord Tenant Law; Real Property; Real Estate Development; Land Use; Estate Planning. ***Email:*** ers@starkhammack.com

REPRESENTATIVE CLIENTS: North's Restaurants, Inc.; Providence Medford Medical Center; Horton Bros., Inc.; Farm Credit Services; Rogue Waste Systems, Inc.; Dry Creek and South Stage Landfill, Inc.; Micro-Trains, Inc.; Naumes Equipment & Fuel; Interim Health Care; Hawk Oil Co.; Recycle Solutions, Inc.; North West Sheet Metal.
REFERENCES: Washington Mutual, Medford Branch; South Valley Bank and Trust.

MONAHAN, GROVE & TUCKER

Established in 1947

105 NORTH MAIN STREET
MILTON-FREEWATER, OREGON 97862
Telephone: 541-938-3377
FAX: 541-938-6112
Email: tuckers@bmi.net
URL: http://www.lawyers.com/monahangrovetucker

General Trial Practice, State Courts. Corporation, Probate, Real Estate, Water, Municipal Law, Estate Planning, Criminal Law, Domestic Relations.

FIRM PROFILE: Firm established in the 1940s, represents numerous banks, public entities and major businesses in Milton-Freewater, Oregon area.

MEMBER OF FIRM

SAMUEL E. TUCKER, born Walla Walla, Washington, August 22, 1951; admitted to bar, 1976, Oregon. *Education:* Willamette University (B.A., 1973); Duke University (J.D., with distinction, 1976). Executive Editor, Duke Law Journal, 1975-1976. Director, Walla Walla Valley Estate Planning Association, 1985—, President, 1989-1990. Judge, Milton-Freewater Municipal Court, 1987—. *Member:* Oregon State Bar (Member, 1981-1984 and Chairman, 1984, Board of Bar Examiners; Chairman, Local Professional Responsibility Committee, 1988; Member, Disciplinary Board, 1992-1996); American Bar Association. ***PRACTICE AREAS:*** Estate and Gift Taxation; Probate Law; Business Law; Real Estate; Wills; Contracts. ***Email:*** tuckers@bmi.net

ASSOCIATE

JONATHAN S. LIEUALLEN, born Walla Walla, Washington, July 17, 1968; admitted to bar, 2000, Oregon. *Education:* Pacific University (B.A., Business Administration/Accounting 1990); University of Idaho (J.D., 1999). *Member:* Oregon State Bar (Member, Sections on: Family Law; Business Litigation; Debtor-Creditor; Litigation). ***PRACTICE AREAS:*** Criminal Law; Family Law; Property Law; Wills; Debtor and Creditor. ***Email:*** lieuallenj@bmi.net

REPRESENTATIVE CLIENTS: Baker Boyer Bank, Milton-Freewater, Oregon; O'Brien Construction Co.; Jim Waliser Orchards, Inc.; Roloff Farms, Inc.; Earl E. Brown & Sons, Inc.; Port of Morrow; Milton-Freewater, Athena-Weston and Helix School Districts; Greater Eastern Oregon Development Corp.; Hospital Authority of Umatilla County, Oregon; Roloff Brothers Inc.
REFERENCE: Baker Boyer Bank, Milton-Freewater, Oregon.

SARA L. GABIN, P.C.

MILWAUKIE, OREGON

(See Lake Oswego)

Social Security Disability and SSI, Personal Injury, Workers Compensation, Family Law.

REDMAN LAW FIRM

Established in 1963

10565 S.E. 23RD AVENUE
MILWAUKIE, OREGON 97222
Telephone: 503-659-5335
Fax: 503-659-5568
Email: mail@redmanlaw.com

Personal Injury, Automobile Accidents, Wrongful Death, Trusts and Estates, Business Law, Corporate Law, Wills and Probate, Guardianship and Conservatorship, Real Estate, Eminent Domain and Condemnation Law.

JAMES E. REDMAN, born Portland, Oregon, September 5, 1932; admitted to bar, 1963, Oregon; 1972, U.S. Supreme Court and U.S. Court of Appeals, 9th Circuit; 2002, Washington. *Education:* Lewis and Clark College (B.A., 1954); Northwestern School of Law of Lewis and Clark College (J.D., 1963). Deputy District Attorney, Clackamas County, 1965-1967. Member, Council on Court Procedures, State of Oregon, 1983-1989. *Member:* Clackamas County (President, 1976) and American Bar Associations; Oregon State Bar (Vice President, 1982-1983; Member, Board of Governors, 1980-1983; Member, Real Property Committee, 1968-1972; Chairman, 1971-1972; Member, Probate Committee, 1972-1976). ***PRACTICE AREAS:*** Personal Injury; Estate Planning; Automobile Accidents and Injuries; Probate; Real Estate; Trusts; Guardianship and Conservatorship. ***Email:*** mail@redmanlaw.com

MARI REDMAN IVES, born Oregon City, Oregon, April 21, 1954; admitted to bar, 2000, Oregon. *Education:* Oregon State University (B.A., 1976); Northwestern School of Law of Lewis and Clark College (J.D., 2000). Phi Delta Phi. *Member:* Clackamas County Bar Association (Treasurer, 2003); Oregon State Bar. (Managing Partner). ***PRACTICE AREAS:*** Municipal Law; Real Estate; Automobile Accidents and Injuries; Estate Planning; Probate; Guardianship and Conservatorship. ***Email:*** mari@redmanlaw.com

---

CUMMINS, GOODMAN, FISH, DENLEY & VICKERS, P.C.

100 S. COLLEGE STREET
P.O. BOX 609
NEWBERG, OREGON 97132
Telephone: 503-476-8200
Fax: 503-476-8201
Email: lat@cumminsgoodman.com

Insurance Defense, Employment Law, Workers' Compensation Defense, OSHA Defense, General Litigation, Business Law.

ELLIOTT C. CUMMINS, born 1941; admitted to bar, 1979, Oregon; 1979 U.S. District Court, District of Oregon. *Education:* Linfield College (B.A., 1963); Northwestern School of Law of Lewis and Clark College (J.D., 1979). ***PRACTICE AREAS:*** Mediator. ***Email:*** ecc@cumminsgoodman.com

GEORGE W. GOODMAN, born 1949; admitted to bar, 1979, Oregon. *Education:* University of Wisconsin-Madison (B.A., 1971); University of Southern California (M.F.A., 1973); Northwestern School of Law of Lewis and Clark College (J.D., 1979). ***Email:*** gwg@cumminsgoodman.com

REUEL K. FISH, born 1950; admitted to bar, 1986, Oregon. *Education:* University of Wisconsin-Madison (B.A., 1973); New York University (M.B.A., 1979); Northwestern School of Law of Lewis and Clark College (J.D., 1984). ***Email:*** rkf@cumminsgoodman.com

MATTHEW F. DENLEY, born 1959; admitted to bar, 1986, Oregon; 2001, District of Columbia; 2002, Washington. *Education:* Concordia College (B.A., 1982); Willamette University (J.D., 1986). ***Email:*** mfd@cumminsgoodman.com

DAMON L. VICKERS, born 1966; admitted to bar, 1992, Oregon; 2001, District of Columbia and Washington; 2002, Idaho. *Education:* Gonzaga University (B.A., 1988); Willamette University (J.D., 1992). ***Email:*** dlv@cumminsgoodman.com

---

STEPHEN E. VEROTSKY, born 1975; admitted to bar, 2001, Oregon. *Education:* Pennsylvania State University (B.S., 1997); University of Tennessee at Knoxville (J.D., 2001). ***Email:*** sev@cumminsgoodman.com

SAMUEL A. KUBERNICK, born 1973; admitted to bar, 2001, Illinois; 2004, Oregon. *Education:* University of California, Santa Barbara (B.A., 1995); Georgetown University Law Center (J.D., 2001). ***Email:*** sak@cumminsgoodman.com

REPRESENTATIVE CLIENTS: Allegheny Technologies; Allied Building Products Corp.; Associated Oregon Loggers, Inc.; Broadspire; Bruce Pac; Cambridge Integrated Services Group, Inc.; Cascade Steel, Inc.; Central Oregon Building Supply, Inc.; City County Insurance Services; City of Ashland; City of Grants Pass; City of Klamath Falls; City of Roseburg; CNA; CNA Claims Plus; Columbia Helicopters, Inc.; Copenhagen Utilities & Construction, Inc.; Croman Corporation; Crown Pacific Limited Partnership; DPR Construction, Inc.; Douglas County, Oregon; ESIS; Floragon Forest Products; Fred Meyer Stores; Frito-Lay, Inc.; Hoffman Construction, Inc.; Huffman & Wright Logging Co.; Huntleigh USA Corporation; Jackson County, Oregon; Jeld-Wen; Kraft Foods, Inc.; Lincoln County, Oregon; McDonald's Corporation; McKenzie Forest Products, LLC; MYR Group; Nabisco Biscuit Company; Northwest Earthmovers, Inc.; OIGA; Oregon Self-Insurers Association; Pinnacle Risk Management Services; Port of Portland; Public Risk Consultants; Rexius Forest By-Products, Inc.; Royal & SunAlliance Insurance Companies; Schnitzer Steel; Sedgwick CMS; Skyline Corporation; Special Districts Association of Oregon; Specialty Risk Services; Tualatin Valley Irrigation District; Wah Chang; Washington County, Oregon; Weyerhaeuser Co.; Yamhill County, Oregon.

JOHNSTONE & GOODFELLOW

NEWBERG, OREGON

(See McMinnville)

General Practice, Litigation, Federal and State Courts, Business, Corporate, Probate, Family Law, Divorce, Child Custody Law, Personal Injury, Alternative Dispute Resolution, Mediation and Arbitration, Construction Law, Debtor/Creditor Law, School, Insurance Law, Real Estate, International Law, Wills and Estate Planning,.

BARTON AND STREVER, P.C.

214 SOUTH WEST COAST HIGHWAY
P.O. BOX 870
NEWPORT, OREGON 97365
Telephone: 541-265-5377
Fax: 541-265-5614
URL: http://www.bartonstrever.com
Email: attorneys@bartonstrever.com
URL: http://www.lawyers.com/barton&strever

Civil Litigation, Plaintiffs Trial Practice. Psychological and Physical Injury Claims including Sexual Exploitation. Sexual Abuse, Personal Injury, Insurance Bad Faith, Wrongful Death, Medical Malpractice, Psychiatric Malpractice. Criminal Defense, DUI Defense.

WILLIAM A. BARTON, born March 15, 1948; admitted to bar, 1972, Oregon and U.S. District Court for the District of Oregon. *Education:* Pacific University (B.S., 1969); Willamette University (J.D., 1972). Author: "Recovering for Psychological Injuries," Second Ed. published by Association of Trial Lawyers of America. Member, Oregon Commission on Judicial Fitness and Disability, 1999—. Listed in Best Lawyers of America. *Member:* Oregon State Bar (Vice President, 1986); Oregon Trial Lawyers Association (President, 1983); Western Trial Lawyers Association (President, 1985); The Association of Trial Lawyers of America (Member, Board of Governors, 1988-1991); Oregon Professional Liability Fund (Chairman, 1992). Fellow: American College of Trial Lawyers; American Board of Trial Advocates (Member, State Executive Committee); International Society of Barristers; International Academy of Trial Lawyers. ***PRACTICE AREAS:*** Serious Injury Claims; Personal Injury; Medical Malpractice; Automobile Accidents and Injuries; Criminal Defense. ***Email:*** attorneys@bartonstrever.com

KEVIN K. STREVER, born July 4, 1960; admitted to bar, 1985, Oregon and U.S. District Court for the District of Oregon. *Education:* Southern Oregon State College (B.S., cum laude, 1982); University of Oregon (J.D., 1985). Author, Chapter 4, "Torts Arising from Sexual Misconduct," 1 Torts (Oregon CLE 1992). Listed in Best Lawyers of America. *Member:* Lincoln County Bar Association (President, 1989); Oregon State Bar (Board of Governors, 1995-1998; President, 1997-1998 and Member, Professional Responsibility Committee, 1993-1995); Oregon Trial Lawyers Association (Board of Governors, 1991-1996; Member, President's Club); The Association of Trial Lawyers of America; Oregon Law Foundation (Member: Board of Directors, 2000—; Joint Bench/Bar Commission on Professionalism, 2000—). ***PRACTICE AREAS:*** Psychological and Physical Injury Claims; Personal Injury; Medical Malpractice; Psychiatric Malpractice. ***Email:*** kevin@bartonstrever.com

LEGAL SUPPORT PERSONNEL

GREG A. ESTEP, born June 21, 1952. Police Officer, 1974-1989; Diplomate, Federal Law Enforcement Training Center, 1987. (Legal Investigator). ***Email:*** greg@bartonstrever.com

REFERENCE: Bank of the West, Newport, Oregon.

CLARK, LINDAUER, FETHERSTON, EDMONDS, LIPPOLD & COLLIER, LLP

NEWPORT, OREGON

(See Salem)

Trial and Business Practice in State and Federal Courts including Business Litigation, Insurance Law, Agricultural Law, Automobile, Premises Liability, Professional Negligence, including Legal and Medical Malpractice, Product, Toxic Tort and Environmental Liability, Employment Discrimination, Wrongful Discharge and Defamation, Arbitration and Mediation, Business, Real Estate, and Estate Law, Probate.

LAW OFFICES OF ROBERT D. LOWRY

NEWPORT, OREGON

(See Eugene)

Insurance Defense, Products Liability Defense, Medical Malpractice, Hospital Malpractice, Business Litigation, Construction Law and Civil Litigation.

RODNEY J. BECK, P.C.

Established in 1985

16239 SE MCLOUGHLIN BOULEVARD, SUITE 204
OAK GROVE, OREGON 97267
Telephone: 503-656-5888
Fax: 503-656-0588
Email: beckrodneyjpc@qwest.net

Mailing Address: P.O. Box 68447, Oak Grove, OR 97268-0447

Probate, Guardianship and Conservatorship, Estate Planning, Agricultural Law, Wills, Elder Law, Real Property, Contracts and General Litigation.

(This Listing Continued)

RODNEY J. BECK, born Portland, Oregon, November 23, 1948; admitted to bar, 1975, Oregon and U.S. District Court, District of Oregon. *Education:* Oregon State University (B.S., 1971); Cornell University (M.S., in Natural Resource Economics, 1972); Northwestern School of Law of Lewis and Clark College (J.D., 1975). Alpha Zeta Honor Society. Multnomah County Circuit Court Litigation Arbitrator (1982-1986). Clackamas County Circuit and District Court Arbitration Program (1984—). *Member:* Clackamas County and Multnomah County Bar Associations; Oregon State Bar (Member, Pro Bono Committee 1989-1992 and Ethics Committee 1983-1986).

REPRESENTATIVE CLIENT: Senior Citizens Council of Clackamas County, Inc.

OKAI LAW OFFICE, P.C.

475 SOUTHWEST 12TH STREET
ONTARIO, OREGON 97914
Telephone: 541-889-7810
Fax: 541-889-7840
Email: tokai@qwest.net
URL: http://www.lawyers.com/okai

Civil Litigation, Employment Law, Sexual Harassment, Discrimination, Business Law, Government Law, Agriculture, Personal Injury Law.

THOMAS K. OKAI, born Nyssa, Oregon, December 25, 1957; admitted to bar, 1985, Oregon; 1986, Idaho; U.S. District Court, District of Idaho; 1987, U.S. District Court, District of Oregon. *Education:* International College of Commerce and Economics, Kawagoe, Japan; Willamette University (B.S., 1981); California Western School of Law (J.D., 1984). *Member:* Federal and American Bar Associations; Oregon State Bar; Idaho State Bar. ***PRACTICE AREAS:*** Litigation; Labor and Employment Law; Business Law.

REPRESENTATIVE CLIENTS: Waldo Insurance Company; Adrian School District; Lifeways Behavioral Health; Professional Fishing Prodacto, Inc.; Waldo Real Estate; Kris Yano, Inc.; Kitamura Farms; C & J Farms, Inc.

PETERSON LAW OFFICES, PC

ONTARIO, OREGON

(See Portland)

Personal Injury, Premises Liability, Automobile Accidents and Injuries, Dog Bites and Wrongful Death.

YTURRI ROSE, LLP

89 S.W. THIRD AVENUE
P.O. BOX S
ONTARIO, OREGON 97914-2721
Telephone: 541-889-5368
Telecopier: 541-889-2432
Email: law@yturrirose.com
URL: http://www.yturrirose.com

General Civil and Trial Practice. Medical and Legal Malpractice, Insurance Defense, Insurance Law, Personal Injury, Business Litigation, Commercial Law, Corporations, Estate Administration, Estate Planning, Foreclosures, Debtor and Creditor, Zoning and Land Use, Real Estate, Farm and Ranch Law, Labor and Employment Law.

FIRM PROFILE: Licensed to practice in State and Federal Court in Oregon and Idaho.

CARL BURNHAM, JR., admitted to bar, 1964, Oregon. *Education:* University of Oregon (B.S., 1961; LL.B., 1964). Member of Council on Court Procedure, 1979-1983. Member, Panel of Arbitrators, American Arbitration Association. *Member:* Malheur County and American Bar Associations; Oregon State Bar (Member, Board of Governors, 1974-1978; Treasurer, 1978; Member, Procedure and Practice Committee, 1974-1977; Chairman, Federal Practice and Procedure Committee, 1984-1985); Oregon Association of Defense Counsel (Member, Board of Directors, 1982-1985; President, 1988); American Board of Trial Advocates; International Association of Defense Counsel. ***PRACTICE AREAS:*** Medical and Legal Malpractice; Insurance Defense; Insurance Law; Personal Injury; Civil Litigation. ***Email:*** cburnham@yturrirose.com

CLIFF S. BENTZ, admitted to bar, 1977, Oregon; 1985, Idaho. *Education:* Eastern Oregon College (B.S., cum laude, 1974); Lewis and Clark College Northwestern School of Law (J.D., 1977). Member, 1988-1996 and Chairman, 1994-1996, Oregon Water Resources Commission. Member, Board of Directors: Oregon Historical Society, 2003—; Eastern Oregon University Foundation, 2001—; Project Dove (Domestic Violence Eliminated), 2002—. *Member:* Malheur County and American Bar Associations; Oregon State Bar; Idaho State Bar. ***PRACTICE AREAS:*** Corporate; Business Transaction Planning; Real Estate; Foreclosure; Farm Law; Ranch Law; Water Law; Business Litigation. ***Email:*** cbentz@yturrirose.com

TIMOTHY J. HELFRICH, admitted to bar, 1976, Oregon; 1985, Idaho. *Education:* University of Oregon (B.A., 1973; J.D., 1976). Member, Moot Court. *Member:* Oregon State Bar (Chair, Executive Committee, Litigation Section, 1994-1995; Member, Executive Committee, Products Liability Section, 1999—); Idaho State Bar; Oregon Trial Lawyers Association; The Association of Trial Lawyers of America; Oregon Association of Defense Counsel. American Board of Trial Advocates. Certified Civil Trial Advocate by the National Board of Trial Advocacy. ***PRACTICE AREAS:*** Personal Injury Litigation; Personal Injury Defense; Trucking Law. ***Email:*** thelfrich@yturrirose.com

BRUNO J. JAGELSKI, admitted to bar, 1990, Oregon; 1991, Idaho. *Education:* Eastern Oregon State College (B.S., 1985); Willamette University College of Law (J.D., 1990). *Member:* Malheur County Bar Association (President, 2000 and 2001); Oregon State Bar; Idaho State Bar; Oregon Association Defense Counsel; Defense Research Institute. ***PRACTICE AREAS:*** Personal Injury; Civil Litigation; Employment Litigation; Insurance Litigation; Professional Liability Defense. ***Email:*** bjagelski@yturrirose.com

(This Listing Continued)

YTURRI ROSE, LLP, Ontario—Continued

SCOTT K. WARNER, admitted to bar, 1993, Oregon; 1994, Idaho. *Education:* Oregon State University (B.S., 1988); University of Oregon (J.D., 1993). *Member:* Malheur County Bar Association; Oregon State Bar; Idaho State Bar. ***PRACTICE AREAS:*** Civil Litigation; Real Estate; Corporate Law; Business Law; Commercial Law; Debtor and Creditor. ***Email:*** swarner@yturrirose.com

DAVID R. AUXIER, admitted to bar, 1990, Oregon; 2004, Idaho. *Education:* University of Idaho (B.S., 1987); Willamette University (J.D., 1990). *Member:* Multnomah County Bar Association; Association of Trial Lawyers of America. ***PRACTICE AREAS:*** Personal Injury; Civil Litigation; Insurance Defense. ***Email:*** dauxier@yturrirose.com

---

JEFFREY R. WHEELER, admitted to bar, 2002, Oregon; 2003, Idaho. *Education:* Western Oregon University (B.S., 1994); Willamette University (J.D., 2002). *Member:* Oregon State Bar; Idaho State Bar. ***PRACTICE AREAS:*** Civil Litigation; Real Estate; Corporate Law; Business Law; Commercial Law; Debtor and Creditor. ***Email:*** jwheeler@yturrirose.com

SHAWNA D. PETERSON, admitted to bar, 2002, Nebraska; 2004, Oregon; 2005, Idaho. *Education:* Gonzaga University (B.A., magna cum laude, 1998); Northwestern School of Law (J.D., 2002). *Member:* Omaha and Nebraska State Bar Associations; Oregon and Idaho State Bars. ***PRACTICE AREAS:*** Estate Planning; Estate Administration; Civil Litigation; Business Law.

M. GREGORY EMBREY, admitted to bar, 2000, Idaho (Not admitted in Oregon). *Education:* Whitman College (B.A., 1990); Gonzaga University Law School (J.D., magna cum laude, 1999). *Member:* Idaho State Bar. [U.S. Army, 1990-1993]. ***LANGUAGES:*** Russian, German. ***PRACTICE AREAS:*** Land Use; Real Estate Transactions; Commercial Litigation; Corporate Law. ***Email:*** gembrey@yturrirose.com

REPRESENTATIVE CLIENTS: Cascade Natural Gas Co.; Allied Insurance Co.; Farmers Insurance Exchange; Country Companies; Northwest Mutual Insurance Co.; Idaho Power Co.; State Farm Insurance Co.; Mutual of Enumclaw Insurance Co.; Professional Liability Fund of the Oregon State Bar Association; Intermountain Community Bank; Ontario School District 8C; Catholic Health Initiatives; Treasure Valley Community College; Northwest Physicians Insurance; Farmland Insurance; Farmers National Union Insurance; Prudential Insurance; Washington Mutual Bank; Gentry Ford Sales; Hollingsworth, Inc.; City of Ontario; City of Cove; Murikami Produce Co.; Farm Bureau Insurance; Continental Western Insurance.
REFERENCES: Intermountain Community Bank; Idaho Power.

RODNEY J. BECK, P.C.

OREGON CITY, OREGON

(See Oak Grove)

Probate, Guardianship and Conservatorship, Estate Planning, Agricultural Law, Wills, Elder Law, Real Property, Contracts and General Litigation.

BLUNCK & WALHOOD, LLC

OREGON CITY, OREGON

(See West Linn)

Arbitration, Automobile Accidents, Construction Claims, Contracts, Personal Injury, Insurance.

SARA L. GABIN, P.C.

OREGON CITY, OREGON

(See Lake Oswego)

Social Security Disability and SSI, Personal Injury, Workers Compensation, Family Law.

HELZER & CROMAR, LLP

OREGON CITY, OREGON

(See Beaverton)

Criminal Law, Family Law, Divorce, Child Custody, Spousal Support, Personal Injury, Automobile Accidents, Criminal Law, Driving While Intoxicated, Felonies, Drug Crimes, Juvenile Crimes, Parole and Probation, Sexual Abuse, Traffic Violations, Estate Litigation, Guardianship and Conservatorship, Employment Law, Discrimination, Sexual Harassment.

HUTCHISON & WALSH

A PROFESSIONAL CORPORATION

OREGON CITY, OREGON

(See West Linn)

General Civil and Trial Practice. Estate Planning, Probate, Trusts and Estates, Business Law, Contracts, Real Estate, Corporate, Personal Injury, Automobile Accidents, Wrongful Death, Financial Abuse of the Elderly.

SCOTT HOOKLAND LLP

OREGON CITY, OREGON

(See Tigard)

Construction, Design, Civil and Trial Practice. Commercial Collections, Business, Real Estate, Mediations, Arbitrations, Creditors Rights.

COREY, BYLER, REW, LORENZEN & HOJEM, L.L.P.

Established in 1945

222 SOUTHEAST DORION STREET
P.O. BOX 218
PENDLETON, OREGON 97801
Telephone: 541-276-3331
Facsimile: 541-276-3148
URL: http://www.corey-byler.com

General Civil and Trial Practice. Agriculture and Agricultural Cooperatives, Domestic Relations, Banking, Business, Municipal, Zoning, Condemnation, School, Corporation, Insurance, Tax, Estate Planning, Probate, Water and Real Estate Law.

FIRM PROFILE: For 60 years, the law firm has provided legal assistance to large and small businesses, public entities and individuals throughout eastern Oregon. The firm is dedicated to providing cost-effective solutions to complex legal problems. As one of the largest law firms in eastern Oregon, it provides lawyers experienced in nearly all facets of civil law, from complex litigation to estate and business planning to domestic relations.

MEMBERS OF FIRM

STEVEN H. COREY, born Pendleton, Oregon, July 11, 1946; admitted to bar, 1972, Oregon. *Education:* Yale University (A.B., 1968); Stanford University (J.D., 1972). Managing Editor, Stanford Law Review, 1971-1972. Chair, Oregon Transportation Commission. *Member:* Oregon State Bar; American Bar Association. Fellow: American College of Trial Lawyers; American Bar Foundation; International Society of Barristers. [Lt., Oregon National Guard, 1968-1974]. ***PRACTICE AREAS:*** Complex Litigation; Litigation; Real Estate; Land Use Law; Corporate Law; Business Law; Water Rights Law; Agricultural Law; Estate Planning. ***Email:*** corey@corey-byler.com

HENRY C. LORENZEN, born Pendleton, Oregon, July 3, 1944; admitted to bar, 1976, Oregon. *Education:* Oregon State University (B.S.E.E., with honors, 1966); Harvard University (M.B.A., 1968); Northwestern School of Law of Lewis and Clark College (J.D., cum laude, 1976). Blue Key; Phi Kappa Phi; Tau Beta Pi; Sigma Tau; Eta Kappa Nu. Member, 1974-1976 and Managing Editor, 1975-1976, Northwestern School of Law of Lewis and Clark College Law Review. Law Clerk Hon. James M. Burns, U.S. District Court, District of Oregon, 1976-1977. Licensed Real Estate Broker (Inactive), Oregon, 1972. Licensed Professional Engineer, Oregon, 1973. Licensed Certified Water Rights Examiner, Oregon, 1992. Assistant U.S. Attorney, U.S. Department of Justice, 1977-1983. Member, 1991-1998, and Chair, 1996-1998, Oregon Environmental Quality Commission, 1998-2003. Member, Oregon Fish and Wildlife Commission. Member and President, Oregon State Board of Higher Education. *Member:* Umatilla County and American Bar Associations; Oregon State Bar. [Lt., U.S. Public Health Service, 1968-1970]. ***PRACTICE AREAS:*** Condemnation Law; Public Utility Law; Business Law. ***Email:*** lorenzen@corey-byler.com

DOUGLAS E. HOJEM, born Ketchikan, Alaska, January 11, 1951; admitted to bar, 1980, Oregon. *Education:* Western Washington University (B.A., with distinction, 1973); University of Washington (J.D., 1980). Member and Chairman of Local Professional Responsibility Committee, 1991-1993. *Member:* Oregon State Bar (Past Member: Executive Committee, Appellate Practice Section; Executive Committee, Litigation Section; Present Member, House of Delegates); American Bar Association; Oregon Association of Defense Counsel. ***PRACTICE AREAS:*** Litigation; Appellate Law; Municipal Law; Employment Law; Legal Malpractice Defense. ***Email:*** hojem@corey-byler.com

DAVID M. BLANC, born Walla Walla, Washington, May 31, 1960; admitted to bar, 1986, Oregon; 1987, U.S. District Court, District of Oregon; 2003, Washington. *Education:* Whitman College (B.A., 1982); Gonzaga University (J.D., 1985). Author: "The NBA's Washington Bullets Win the Right to Change Their Name to the Wizards," The Sports Lawyer, March/April, 1997. President, Pendleton Chamber of Commerce, 1994. *Member:* Oregon State Bar; American Bar Association; Sports Lawyer Association; Oregon City Attorneys Association; Umatilla Tribal Court (CTUZR). ***PRACTICE AREAS:*** Commercial Law; Creditors Rights Law; Municipal Law; Litigation. ***Email:*** blanc@corey-byler.com

TIMOTHY P. O'ROURKE, born Oklahoma City, Oklahoma, December 9, 1958; admitted to bar, 1987, Oregon. *Education:* University of Portland (B.B.A., 1981); Willamette University (J.D., 1987). Certified Public Accountant, Oregon, 1983. *Member:* Oregon State Bar (Member, Executive Committee; Income Tax Section; Business Law Section); Oregon Society of Certified Public Accountants; American Institute of Certified Public Accountants. ***PRACTICE AREAS:*** Trusts and Estates; Estate and Gift Tax Planning Law; Business Law; Corporate Law; Real Estate; Tax Law. ***Email:*** orourke@corey-byler.com

STEVEN N. THOMAS, born Oakland, California, May 18, 1954; admitted to bar, 1980, Oregon. *Education:* Sierra College; University of California at Berkeley (B.A., magna cum laude, 1977); University of California at Los Angeles (J.D., 1980). Phi Beta Kappa. Municipal Court Judge, Pilot Rock, Oregon, 1989-1994. *Member:* Oregon State Bar (Past Chair, Executive Committee, Family Law Section); Umatilla Tribal Court (CTUZR). ***LANGUAGES:*** Spanish. ***PRACTICE AREAS:*** Domestic Relations Law; Tort Law; Landlord and Tenant Law; Litigation; Civil; Criminal. ***Email:*** thomas@corey-byler.com

JUSTIN J. BURNS, born Pendleton, Oregon, March 7, 1973; admitted to bar, 2000, Oregon and Washington. *Education:* Oregon State University (B.A., 1995); Willamette University College of Law (J.D., 2000). ***PRACTICE AREAS:*** Agricultural Law; Water Rights; Insurance Law; Complex Litigation; Environmental Law; Real Property Law. ***Email:*** jburns@corey-byler.com

ASSOCIATES

PATRICIA SULLIVAN, born Moline, Illinois, July 26, 1946; admitted to bar, 1978, Georgia; 1984, Oregon. *Education:* Loyola University (B.S., 1973); Washington University; University of Georgia (J.D., cum laude, 1978). Instructor, Business Law, Farm Law, Blue Mountain Community College, 1984-1985. Member: Georgia Legal Services Corporation, 1978-1980; Law Clerk for Hon. John W. Sognier, Georgia Court of Appeals, 1980-

(This Listing Continued)

1983. Member, State of Oregon Advisory Committee on Historic Preservation, 1992-1996. Member, 1994-1998 and Chair, 1996-1998, Joint Bench/Bar Commission Professionalism. Lawyer Representative, Ninth Circuit Court of Appeals, 2001-2004. *Member:* Sixth Judicial District (President, 1988-1989), Federal Bar Association (Member, Oregon Board of Directors, 2001-2004); American Bar Association; State Bar of Georgia (Member, Legal Aid Committee, 1982-1983); Oregon State Bar (Member, Lawyers' Assistance Committee, 1988-1990; Task Force on Professionalism, 1992-1996); Oregon Women Lawyers (Member: Board of Directors, 1991-1995, 200-2004; Judicial Endorsement Committee, 2001-2004); Oregon Legal Services (Member, Board of Directors, 1996-1998). ***PRACTICE AREAS:*** General Civil Litigation. ***Email:*** sullivan@corey-byler.com

J. T. LIEUALLEN, born Walla Walla, Washington, March 14, 1978; admitted to bar, 2004, Oregon. *Education:* Linfield College (B.S., 2000); University of Oregon (J.D., 2003). ***PRACTICE AREAS:*** Domestic Relations; Wills; Trust Law; Business Law. ***Email:*** jt@corey-byler.com

OF COUNSEL

LAWRENCE B. REW, born Eugene, Oregon, June 22, 1936; admitted to bar, 1961, Oregon. *Education:* Whitman College (B.A., 1958); Willamette University College of Law (J.D., 1961). *Member:* Oregon State Bar (President, 2001; Board of Governors, 1996-2000; Board of Bar Examiners, 1975-1979; Public Service Award, 1991); American Bar Association. Fellow, American Bar Foundation. ***PRACTICE AREAS:*** Agricultural Law; Estate Planning; Probate; Business Organization; Real Estate. ***Email:*** rew@corey-byler.com

ROBERT E. O'ROURKE, born Pendleton, Oregon, September 29, 1937; admitted to bar, 1961, Oregon. *Education:* University of Portland; Northwestern College of Law (LL.B., 1961). Member, Port of Umatilla Commission, 1966-1970. Director, Inland Empire Waterways Association, 1969-1971. Director, Oregon Water Resources Association, 1969-1976. *Member:* Oregon State Bar (Member, Natural Resources Committee, 1968-1970; Chairman, 1970); American Bar Association. ***PRACTICE AREAS:*** Business Law; Estate Planning Law.

REPRESENTATIVE CLIENTS: Cunningham Sheep Co.; Port of Umatilla; Blue Mountain Community College; Nelson Irrigation Corporation; endleton Grain Growers; Double M Ranch; Pendleton Medical Center; East Oregonian Publishing Co.; Pendleton Bottling Co.; Pendleton School District 16R; Umatilla Electric Cooperative Assn.; Hermiston School District; Stanfield School District; Oregon Trail Electric Coop.; City of Milton-Freewater; Mid Columbia Producers; Krebs Ranches; Port of Arlington; Cities of: Boardman, Granite, Haines, North Powder, Pilot Rock; Banner Bank; Umatilla County Federal Credit Union; Turner Ranch, Inc.; Umatilla Reservation Housing Authority; Cities of Athena, Weston, Adams; Professional Liability Fund; City County Insurance Services.
LOCAL COUNSEL FOR: Boise Cascade Corp.; Wells Fargo Bank; Union Pacific Railroad Company.

HALLMAN & DRETKE

Established in 2000

104 S.E. 5TH STREET
P.O. BOX 308
PENDLETON, OREGON 97801
Telephone: 541-276-3857
FAX: 541-276-7620
Email: Office@hallmandretke.com
URL: http://www.lawyers.com/hallmandretke

Civil Litigation, Personal Injury and Wrongful Death Litigation and Appellate Practice.

MEMBERS OF FIRM

W. EUGENE HALLMAN, born Seattle, Washington, January 2, 1949; admitted to bar, 1974, Oregon; 1975, U.S. District Court, District of Oregon; 1983, U.S. Court of Appeals, Ninth Circuit and U.S. Supreme Court. *Education:* University of San Francisco; Portland State University (B.S., 1971); Willamette University (J.D., magna cum laude, 1974). Editor-in-Chief, Willamette Law Journal, 1973-1974. Author: Comment, "Wrongful Death Actions in Oregon: New Developments," 10 Willamette Law Journal 217, 1974. Law Clerk to Justice Edward H. Howell of the Oregon Supreme Court, 1974-1975. Commissioner, 1987-1988 and Chairman, 1988-1989, Oregon Liquor Control Commission. Regional Chair, Supreme Court Disciplinary Board, 1992-1998. Member, State Professional Responsibility Board, 2003—. *Member:* Sixth Judicial District (President, 1983-1984) and American Bar Associations; Oregon State Bar; The Association of Trial Lawyers of America; Oregon Trial Lawyers Association; American Board of Trial Advocates. Fellow, American College of Trial Lawyers. (Certified as a Civil Trial Advocate by the National Board of Trial Advocacy). ***PRACTICE AREAS:*** Personal Injury; Wrongful Death; Appellate Practice. ***Email:*** Gene@hallmandretke.com

BRIAN CRAIG DRETKE, born Riverside, California, November 21, 1959; admitted to bar, 1993, Oregon; 1995, Oklahoma. *Education:* Louisiana State University (B.G.S., 1983); University of Tulsa (J.D., 1992). *Member:* Union County (Vice-President, 1996-1997; President, 1997-1998) and Umatilla County Bar Associations; Oregon State Bar (Member, State Procedure and Practice Committee); The Association of Trial Lawyers of America; Oregon Trial Lawyers Association (Board Member, 2004—). ***PRACTICE AREAS:*** Personal Injury; Wrongful Death. ***Email:*** brian@hallmandretke.com

LAW OFFICES OF ROBERT D. LOWRY

PENDLETON, OREGON

(See Eugene)

Insurance Defense, Products Liability Defense, Medical Malpractice, Hospital Malpractice, Business Litigation, Construction Law and Civil Litigation.

MAUTZ BAUM & O'HANLON, LLP

Established in 1973

101 S.E. BYERS AVENUE
P.O. BOX 628
PENDLETON, OREGON 97801
Telephone: 541-276-2811
Fax: 541-276-0543
Email: mbo@mautzetal.com
URL: http://www.mautzetal.com

La Grande, Oregon Office: 1902 4th Street, P.O. Box 967. 97850. Telephone: 541-963-3104. Fax: 541-963-9254. Email: mbolg@mautzeltal.com.

General Litigation and Appellate Practice in all State and Federal Courts. Administrative, Agriculture, Bankruptcy, Business, Commercial, Creditors' Rights, Estate Planning and Probate, Insurance, Personal Injury, Professional Malpractice Defense, Real Estate and Wrongful Death.

FIRM PROFILE: Mautz Baum & O'Hanlon, LLP, is a regional firm offering business, estate and litigation services to clients and lawyers throughout Northeastern Oregon from offices in Pendleton and La Grande.

MEMBERS OF FIRM

ROBERT T. MAUTZ, born Portland, Oregon, March 21, 1940; admitted to bar, 1964, Oregon and U.S. District Court, District of Oregon; 1983, U.S. Court of Appeals, Ninth Circuit and U.S. Supreme Court; 2003, Washington. *Education:* Harvard University; University of Oregon; Stanford University (B.S., 1963; J.D., 1964). *Member:* Oregon State Bar; Association of Defense Trial Attorneys; International Academy of Trial Lawyers; The Defense Research Institute; Oregon Association of Defense Counsel (President, 1978); Federation of Insurance and Corporate Counsel; American Board of Trial Advocates (Advocate); American Bar Foundation; Lawyer-Pilots Bar Association. ***PRACTICE AREAS:*** Civil Litigation; Business Litigation; Business Entities; Real Estate; Agriculture; Estate Planning. ***Email:*** rtm@mautzetal.com

TIMOTHY J. O'HANLON, born Portland, Oregon, June 30, 1962; admitted to bar, 1987, Oregon; 1989, Washington and U.S. District Court, District of Oregon; 1990, U.S. Court of Appeals, 9th Circuit. *Education:* University of Santa Clara (B.S., 1984); Northwestern School of Law of Lewis and Clark College (J.D., 1987). Deputy District Attorney, Multnomah County, 1987-1988. Member, President, Board of Directors, Pendleton Round Up and Happy Canyon Hall of Fame, 2004—; Pendleton Chamber of Commerce, 2001-2003. Board of Directors, St. Anthony Hospital Foundation, 2002—. Author: Oregon State Bar Civil Litigation Manual, Chapter 8, Summons (1993, 1996 and 1999), Oregon State Bar Damages CLE, Chapter 25, Contracts for The Sale of Goods (1995, 1998 and 2002). Municipal Judge Pro Tempore, 1999—. *Member:* Sixth Judicial District (President, 1991-1992; Secretary, 1991-1992), Washington State and American Bar Associations; Oregon State Bar (Member: Oregon State Bar Business Law Section, Executive Committee, 1999-2005; President, 2005; Uniform Civil Jury Instructions Committee, 1990-1993; Minimum Continuing Legal Education Board, 1995-1998); The Association of Trial Lawyers of America; Oregon Trial Lawyers Association. ***PRACTICE AREAS:*** Civil Litigation; Business Law; Business Litigation; Creditor Bankruptcy; Insurance Law; Banking Law; Personal Injury Litigation; Wrongful Death. ***Email:*** tjo@mautzetal.com

DAVID C. BAUM, born La Grande, Oregon, August 14, 1949; admitted to bar, 1975, Oregon. *Education:* Eastern Oregon College (B.A., cum laude, 1972); Willamette University (J.D., 1975). *Member:* Union County and American Bar Associations; Oregon State Bar; Oregon Association of Defense Counsel; Oregon Trial Lawyers Association. (Resident Partner, La Grande Office). ***PRACTICE AREAS:*** Litigation; Personal Injury; Insurance Defense; Commercial Litigation; Environmental Litigation; Real Property Transactions; Construction Law. ***Email:*** dcb@mautzetal.com

---

EVA JO TEMPLE, born Madras, Oregon, December 5, 1968; admitted to bar, 1996, Oregon; 2002, U.S. District Court, District of Oregon; 2003, Washington. *Education:* Carnegie Melon University; University of Oregon (B.A., 1993; J.D., 1996). Member, Pendleton Planning Commission; Criminal Justice Commission. *Member:* Oregon State Bar; Washington State Bar Association; Oregon Women Lawyers Society (Board of Directors); Oregon Trial Lawyers Association. ***PRACTICE AREAS:*** Civil Litigation; Business Litigation; Business Law; Real Estate; Land Use; Estate Planning. ***Email:*** ejt@mautzetal.com

BRANDON J. EYRE, born Pocatello, Idaho, January 13, 1973; admitted to bar, 2001, Oregon. *Education:* Brigham Young University (B.A., 1997; J.D., 2001). *Member:* Union County Bar Association; Oregon State Bar; Oregon Trial Lawyers Association; Oregon City Attorney Association. ***PRACTICE AREAS:*** Municipal Law; School Law; Litigation; Family Law; Real Property Transactions. ***Email:*** bje@mautzetal.com

REPRESENTATIVE CLIENTS: American Onion, Inc.; Logan International, Ltd.; Northwest Physicians Mutual Insurance Company; Oregon State Bar Professional Liability Fund; Western Empires Corporation; Pearson Ranches; Pine Creek Federal Credit Union; United Marketing, Inc.; Smith Frozen Foods; Mutual of Enumclaw; Canal Insurance; Blue Mountain Seeds, Inc.; Union County; La Grande School District; City of Wallowa; City of Union; Joseph School District; Omnitrac, LLC; Oregon Mutual; Marr Flat Cattle Co., LLC; R.D. Offutt Co.-Northwest; Albertson's, Inc.; Wells Fargo Home Mortgage, Inc.; Crusader Insurance Co.; Chief Industries, Inc.; Grange Insurance Group.
REFERENCE: Banner Bank.

PETERSON LAW OFFICES, PC

PENDLETON, OREGON

(See Portland)

Personal Injury, Premises Liability, Automobile Accidents and Injuries, Dog Bites and Wrongful Death.

ABBOTT & PRANGE, P.C.

Established in 2004

111 SW FIFTH AVENUE, SUITE 2650
PORTLAND, OREGON 97204
Telephone: 503-241-1254
Fax: 503-241-1245
URL: http://www.abbottprange.com

FIRM PROFILE: The Principals in our firm have collectively been practicing law for 48 years in Oregon and Washington. The firm is dedicated to providing quality legal representation to those involved in litigation with emphasis in the following areas: General Liability Defense, Insurance Coverage/Defense of Insurers, Environmental Litigation, Defense of Professionals, Construction Litigation, Employment Litigation, Products Liability and Commercial Litigation.

GARY V. ABBOTT, born Portland, Oregon, December 31, 1943; admitted to bar, 1972, Oregon; 1973, U.S. District Court, District of Oregon; 1975, U.S. Court of Appeals, Ninth Circuit; 1986, Washington. *Education:* Portland State University (B.S., 1969); Northwestern School of Law of Lewis and Clark College (J.D., 1972). Editor-in-Chief, Environmental Law, Law Review, 1971-1972. Law Clerk to Justice Thomas H. Tongue, Oregon Supreme Court, 1972-1973. *Member:* Oregon State Bar; Washington State and American Bar Associations; Defense Research Institute; Oregon Association of Defense Counsel; Washington Defense Trial Lawyers Association. ***PRACTICE AREAS:*** Professional Malpractice; Insurance Coverage; Personal Injury; Employment Law; Construction Law; Environmental Law; Toxic Torts; Products Liability; Intellectual Property. ***Email:*** gabbott@abbottprange.com

DAVID E. PRANGE, born Chapel Hill, North Carolina, July 3, 1959; admitted to bar, 1987, Oregon; 2002, Washington. *Education:* Colorado State University (B.S., with honors, 1984; M.S., 1986); Northwestern School of Law of Lewis and Clark College (J.D., 1987). Xi Sigma Pi. Recipient, American Jurisprudence Award in Constitutional Law. Author: "Regional Water Scarcity and the Galloway Proposal," 17 Environmental Law 81, 1986. *Member:* Multnomah County, Washington State and American (Member, Sections on: Health Law; Environmental Law) Bar Associations; Oregon State Bar; Oregon Association of Defense Counsel (Chair, Insurance Coverage Section); Washington Defense Trial Lawyers Association; Defense Research Institute; Northwest Environmental Claims Association. ***PRACTICE AREAS:*** Insurance Defense and Coverage; Environmental Litigation; General Litigation; Construction Litigation. ***Email:*** dprange@abbottprange.com

---

ANNALIE M. FADDIS, born Portland, Oregon, 1972; admitted to bar, 1999, Oregon; 2000, Washington. *Education:* Willamette University; University of Oregon (J.D., 1999). Member, 1997-1998, and Associate Editor, 1998-1999, Oregon Law Review. Law Clerk, Antitrust Division, Oregon Department of Justice, Consumer Protection Section. *Member:* Multnomah County, Washington State and American Bar Associations; Oregon State Bar; Oregon Association of Defense Counsel; Washington Defense Trial Lawyers Association. ***PRACTICE AREAS:*** Civil Litigation; Products Liability; Construction Defects; Insurance Defense. ***Email:*** afaddis@abbottprange.com

NICHOLAS A. NARDI, born Cleveland, Ohio, 1972; admitted to bar, 1998, Oregon; 2001, District of Columbia. *Education:* Tufts University (B.A., cum laude, 1994); Northwestern School of Law, Lewis and Clark College (J.D., 1998). *Member:* Multnomah County Bar Association; Oregon State Bar; Oregon Association of Defense Counsel. ***LANGUAGES:*** French. ***PRACTICE AREAS:*** Environmental; Construction Defects; Insurance Coverage; Appellate Practice; General Liability. ***Email:*** nnardi@abbottprange.com

KLARICE A. KOLBE, born Bellevue, Washington, July 20, 1978; admitted to bar, 2003, Oregon. *Education:* University of Washington; University of North Carolina School of Law (J.D., 2003). *Member:* Multnomah Bar Association (Committee Member, Young Lawyers Section); Oregon State Bar; Oregon Women Lawyers Society. ***PRACTICE AREAS:*** Environmental; Insurance Coverage; Construction Defects; Professional Liability; General Liability. ***Email:*** kkolbe@abbottprange.com

JENNIFER L. GATES, born Oconomowoc, Wisconsin, 1975; admitted to bar, 2001, Virginia; 2002, District of Columbia; 2005, Oregon. *Education:* University of Iowa (B.A., 1997); University of Iowa Graduate College (M.A., Urban & Regional Planning, 2001); University of Iowa College of Law (J.D., with honors, 2001). Previously with Ross, Dixon & Bell, LLP; Thompson, Loss & Judge, LLP. *Member:* American Bar Associations; Virginia State Bar; The District of Columbia Bar. ***PRACTICE AREAS:*** Environmental Law; Insurance Coverage; Litigation. ***Email:*** jgates@abbottprange.com

KEVIN BRAGUE, born Fullerton, California, March 31, 1967; admitted to bar, 2005, Oregon. *Education:* Arizona State University (B.A., English, cum laude, 1998); Pepperdine University School of Law (J.D., 2002). Publications: Brague K. "Relationship Disintegration: The Respective Rights of General and Sub-Contractors," Construction Executive, September 2004; Brague, K. & Carno, A. "Construction Debris and Hazardous Waste: How Trash can be an Environmental Liability," Construction Executive pgs.24-30, February 2004; Haight, C. & Brague, K., "The International Transfer of Business Personnel Into The United States," Southwestern Journal of Law and Trade in the Americas, Fall 1995. *Member:* Oregon State Bar. ***PRACTICE AREAS:*** Litigation. ***Email:*** kbrague@abbottprange.com

THEODORE F. SUMNER, born Seattle, Washington, July 5, 1969; admitted to bar, 2000, Oregon and U.S. District Court, District of Oregon; 2001, U.S. Court of Appeals, 9th Circuit. *Education:* United States Coast Guard Academy (B.S., with honors, 1993); Northwestern School of Law (J.D., 2000). Client Security Fund Member, 2005-2008. Previous Employment, Rosenthal & Greene, P.C., 1999-2004; U.S. Coast Guard, 1987-1996 (Deck Watch Officer, Damage Control Training Team Member, Navigation Officer, Search and Rescue Small Boat Crewman). *Member:* Multnomah County Bar Association; Oregon State Bar. ***Email:*** tsumner@abbottprange.com

(This Listing Continued)

REPRESENTATIVE CLIENTS: CNA; Boy Scouts of America; Fireman's Fund Insurance Company; Great American Insurance; Liberty Northwest Insurance; Nautilus Insurance; Oregon State Bar Professional Liability Insurance; Oregon Insurance Guaranty Association; Safeco Select Markets; Scotsdale Insurance Company; USAA Insurance & Unigard.

ADAMS & UFFELMAN LLP

PORTLAND, OREGON

(See Beaverton)

General Civil and Trial Practice in all State and Federal Courts. Business, Corporate, Estate Planning and Probate Law, Entertainment Law, Family Law, Divorce, Real Estate Law, Contracts, Criminal Law, Criminal Trials and Appeals in all State and Federal Courts.

ALTSCHUL LAW OFFICE, PC

117 SW TAYLOR STREET, SUITE 200
PORTLAND, OREGON 97204
Telephone: 503-417-0444
Fax: 503-417-0501
Email: andrew@portlandemploymentlaw.com
URL: http://www.portlandemploymentlaw.com

Employment Law, Human Resources, Employment Contracts, Employee Benefits.

FIRM PROFILE: Portland, Oregon based law firm providing employment law advice for Oregon, California and Washington employers and employees. This includes harassment investigation, training, employment litigation and ERISA litigation.

ANDREW ALTSCHUL, born Brooklyn, New York, November 27, 1970; admitted to bar, 1995, Illinois; 1998, Oregon; 2000, Washington; 2003, California. *Education:* Grinnell College (B.A., 1992); University of Michigan (J.D., 1995). *Member:* American Bar Association (Member, Labor and Employment Section, 1995—). ***PRACTICE AREAS:*** Employment Law; Employment Contracts; Employee Benefits. ***Email:*** andrew@portlandemploymentlaw.com

---

MARTIN L. ALVEY, P.C.

SUITE 100
140 S.W. ARTHUR STREET
PORTLAND, OREGON 97201
Telephone: 503-229-0895
Fax: 503-229-1094
URL: http://www.martinalveylaw.com
Email: malvey@qwest.net
URL: http://www.martinalvey.com

Astoria, Oregon Office: #1 Portway, Port of Astoria Building, Suite 3A, 97103. Telephone: 503-325-5509.

Personal Injury, Automobile Accidents, Workers Compensation, Longshore and Harbor Workers Compensation Act, Social Security Disability.

FIRM PROFILE: Representing injured people since 1987.

MARTIN L. ALVEY, born McMinnville, Oregon, December 30, 1959; admitted to bar, 1987, Oregon and U.S. District Court, District of Oregon. *Education:* Willamette University (B.A., 1982); Lewis and Clark College (J.D., 1986). Co-Author: "Permanent Disabilities," Chapter 1994, Oregon State Bar Treatise on Workers' Compensation, 1996 and 2000 cumulative supplements. *Member:* Multnomah County Bar Association; Oregon State Bar (Chair, 2005-2006 and Member, Workers' Compensation Section; Member, Sections on: Litigation; Small Firm and Law Office Management; Admiralty); Oregon Trial Lawyers Association (Chair, 2004-2005 and Member, Worker's Compensation Section); Oregon Workers Compensation Attorneys; Association of Trial Lawyers of America (ATLA); Trial Lawyers for Public Justice (TLPJ); National Organization of Social Security Claimant's Representatives. ***LANGUAGES:*** German. ***REPORTED CASES:*** Foster Wheeler Corporation v. Marble, 188 Or App 579, 72 P2d 645 (2003); SAIF v. Kurcin, 334 Or 399, 50 P3d 1167 (2002); SAIF v. Wolff, 138 Or App 579, 908 P2d 954 (1996); Liberty Northwest v. Potts, 119 Or App 252, 850 P2d 1135 (1993); Precision Cast Parts v. Lewis, 115 Or App 732, 840 P2d 104 (1992); Astoria Plywood Corp. v. Culp, 115 Or App 579, 840 P2d 99 (1992). ***PRACTICE AREAS:*** Personal Injury; Workers Compensation; Social Security Disability. ***Email:*** malvey@qwest.net

---

AMBROSE LAW GROUP LLC

An Oregon Limited Liability Company

Established in 1991

1670 KOIN CENTER
222 S.W. COLUMBIA STREET
PORTLAND, OREGON 97201-6616
Telephone: 503-222-0552
Facsimile: 503-222-0984
Email: admin@ambroselaw.com
URL: http://www.ambroselaw.com

Banking, Business and Corporate Transactions, Business Tax and Estate Planning, Finance, Real Estate Secured Finance, Asset-Based Lending, Real Estate Transactions, Technology, Internet and E-Commerce Strategies.

MEMBERS

DAVID R. AMBROSE, born Chicago, Illinois, April 30, 1953; admitted to bar, 1979, Oregon; 1983, Washington; U.S. District Court, District of Oregon; U.S. District Court,

(This Listing Continued)

Western District of Washington; U.S. Court of Appeals, Ninth Circuit. *Education:* University of Notre Dame (B.S., 1975); Northwestern School of Law of Lewis and Clark College (J.D., 1979). *Member:* Multnomah County, Clark County, King County, Washington State and American Bar Associations; Oregon State Bar; American Bankers Association; National Association of Mortgage Brokers; Oregon Mortgage Bankers Association; Oregon Association of Mortgage Brokers; Washington Mortgage Brokers Association. **PRACTICE AREAS:** Real Estate Finance; Business Transactions; Real Estate Transactions; Banking Law. **Email:** drambrose@ambroselaw.com

CHRISTOPHER R. AMBROSE, born Michigan City, Indiana, April 28, 1961; admitted to bar, 1987, California; 1988, U.S. District Court, Central and Southern Districts of California; 1996, Oregon and U.S. District Court, District of Oregon; 1997, Washington and U.S. District Court, Western District of Washington. *Education:* University of California at San Diego (B.A., Economics, 1983); University of California, San Diego School of Law (J.D., 1987). San Diego Law Review, 1986-1987. *Member:* San Diego County, Multnomah County; Washington State and American Bar Associations; State Bar of California; Oregon State Bar; Internet Professionals NW; Software Association of Oregon. **PRACTICE AREAS:** Real Estate; Mortgage Banking and Broker Litigation; Technology Law; Internet Law. **Email:** crambrose@ambroselaw.com

SENIOR COUNSEL

DOUGLAS B. GORDON, born Cleveland, Ohio, August 22, 1947; admitted to bar, 1973, Oregon and U.S. District Court, District of Oregon; 1981, U.S. Court of Appeals, Ninth Circuit; 1992, U.S. Claims Court; 2003, Washington. *Education:* Ohio University (A.B., 1969); University of Wisconsin (J.D., 1973). Phi Beta Kappa. Order of the Coif. Note and Comment Editor, University of Wisconsin Law Review, 1972-1973. Adjunct Professor, Commercial Law, UCC Article 9, Northwestern School of Law of Lewis and Clark College, 1978. *Member:* Washington County (President, 2000-2001; Member, Board of Directors, 1995-2001) and Multnomah County Bar Associations; Oregon State Bar (Member, Sections on: Litigation, Business Litigation, Real Estate and Land Use, Alternative Dispute Resolution, Debtor-Creditor; Committee on Uniform Laws, 1984-1987); Washington State Bar Association; Oregon Mediation Association. **PRACTICE AREAS:** Civil Litigation; Real Estate Transactions; Boundary Disputes. **Email:** dbgordon@ambroselaw.com

CHIEF OPERATIONS OFFICER

JANIS K. ALEXANDER, born Lebanon, Oregon, May 27, 1959. *Education:* Judson Baptist College, Portland, Oregon. *Member:* American Bar Association (Co-Chair, Computer & Technology Division); Oregon State Bar; Association of Legal Administrators (Regional Officer); Oregon Legal Management Association (Former Board Member and Chair of Legal Technology Section). **Email:** jkalexander@ambroselaw.com

REPRESENTATIVE CLIENTS: Bank of New York; First Tennessee Bank; Aurora Loan Services, Inc.; Mortgage Market, Inc.; Willamette Mortgage Services, Inc.; Fairway Commercial Mortgage Services, LLC; Summit Mortgage Corp.; Lime Financial Services, Ltd.; Financial Center Mortgages & Investment, Inc.; Valentine Lender Services, Inc.; Pacific Guaranty Mortgage Co.; Prism Mortgage Company; Accurate Installation Services, Inc.; C2F, Inc.; Longevity Labs, Inc.; Integrated Utilities Group, Inc.; Zmation, Inc.

AMBURGEY & RUBIN, P.C.

RIVERPLACE OFFICE BUILDING
1750 S. W. HARBOR WAY, SUITE 450
PORTLAND, OREGON 97201-0104
Telephone: 503-221-0309
Fax: 503-242-2457
Email: general@amburgeyrubin.com

Practice Limited to Representing Management in Labor and Employment Law, including Practice before State and Federal Courts and Administrative Agencies, and Business Immigration.

LARRY K. AMBURGEY, born Burlington, Washington, December 13, 1947; admitted to bar, 1975, Oregon and U.S. District Court, District of Oregon; 1976, U.S. Court of Appeals, Ninth Circuit; 1980, U.S. Supreme Court. *Education:* Whitman College (B.A., 1969); Northwestern School of Law of Lewis and Clark College (J.D., magna cum laude, 1975). Adjunct Professor, Labor Law, 2002. Co-Author: "The Americans with Disabilities Act," Oregon State Bar, 1994. Member, Board of Visitors, 1995—, Member, Alumni Board, 1999— and Alumni President, 2002-2003, Northwestern School of Law of Lewis and Clark College. Member, Employment Committee, 2000-2002 and General Counsel, Portland Chapter, 2001—, Society for Human Resource Management. Listed in Best Lawyers in America, 2001—; Chambers USA-America's Leading Lawyers. *Member:* Oregon State Bar (Member, Labor Relations Law Section; Chair-Elect, 1981-1982; Chair, 1982-1983; Secretary, 1983-1984; Member, Executive Committee, Civil Rights Law Section, 1979-1985). **PRACTICE AREAS:** Labor; Employment Law. **Email:** larry@amburgeyrubin.com

HOWARD RUBIN, born Chicago, Illinois, July 24, 1955; admitted to bar, 1983, Oregon and U.S. District Court, District of Oregon; 1989, U.S. Court of Appeals, Ninth Circuit. *Education:* University of Illinois; Northwestern University (B.A., 1978); Northwestern School of Law of Lewis and Clark College (J.D., 1983). *Member:* Oregon State Bar (Member, Sections on: Civil Rights; Labor Relations Law). **PRACTICE AREAS:** Labor; Employment Law. **Email:** hrubin@amburgeyrubin.com

AMY R. ALPERN, born Pittsfield, Massachusetts, May 3, 1958; admitted to bar, 1984, Oregon; 1987, U.S. District Court, District of Oregon and U.S. Court of Appeals, Ninth Circuit. *Education:* University of Southern California (B.A., 1980); Northwestern School of Law of Lewis and Clark College (J.D., 1983). Participant, Regional Moot Court Competition, 1983. Chair, Judges Committee National High School Mock Trial Competition, 1990. Author: "Request for Admissions," Oregon State Bar Civil Litigation Manual, 1994. Program Director, Gus J. Solomon American Inn of Court, 1993-1998. Arbitrator, Multnomah County, 1992-1998. *Member:* Multnomah Bar Association (Member, 1994-1997 and Secretary, 1999-2000, Board of Directors, Member, 1994-1997, Judicial Screening Committee,); Oregon State Bar (Member, Disciplinary Board, 1994-1999 and Chair, Region 5, 2000). **PRACTICE AREAS:** Employment Litigation. **Email:** aalpern@amburgeyrubin.com

PATRICIA ANN HAIM, born New York, N.Y., November 14, 1948; admitted to bar, 1984, Ohio and U.S. District Court, Northern District of Ohio; 1985, U.S. Court of Appeals, Sixth Circuit; 1988, Oregon, U.S. District Court, District of Oregon and U.S. Court of Appeals, Ninth Circuit. *Education:* University of Melbourne, Melbourne, Australia (B.A. with honors, 1970); Duke University (A.M., 1973; Ph.D., 1978); University of Notre Dame (J.D., summa cum laude, 1984). Articles Editor, Notre Dame Law Review, 1983-1984. Editor, "Computer Law," Oregon State Bar, 1992 and 1996. Co-Author: "Intentional Interference with Contractual and Business Relations," Oregon State Bar, 1990 and 1992; "An Overview of the Federal Courts in Oregon," Oregon State Bar, 1994, 1998 and 2002; "Civil Rights and Damages," Oregon State Bar, 1995, 1998, 2001; Equal Employment Opportunity: Disabilities, 1996, 1997, 2002. *Member:* Oregon State Bar (Chair, Committee on Balancing Career, Family, and Personal Life, 1992-1994; Member, Executive Committee, 1997-1999 and Chair, 1998-1999, MCLE Board; Member, Executive Committee, 1997-2000 and Chair, 1999-2000, Disability Law Section); American Immigration Lawyers Association. **PRACTICE AREAS:** Labor and Employment Law; Business Immigration. **Email:** phaim@amburgeyrubin.com

SCOTT TALMAGE CLIFF, born Honolulu, Hawaii, December 12, 1957; admitted to bar, 1987, Oregon and U.S. District Court, District of Oregon. *Education:* University of California, San Diego; Lewis and Clark College (B.S., 1979); Northwestern School of Law, Lewis & Clark College (J.D., 1987). Contributor, Evidence, Oregon Continuing Legal Education, 1984. Regional Moot Court Finalist and National Qualifier, National Moot Court Competition, 1985. Recipient: American College of Trial Lawyers, Medal for Excellence in Advocacy, National Moot Court Competition, 1985; American Jurisprudence Award in Employment Discrimination, 1987. Author: "Regulation of Agents and Adjusters," Oregon State Bar Continuing Legal Education, 1992. Co-Author: "Equal Employment Opportunity: Disabilities," Labor & Employment Law, Private Sector," Oregon State Bar Continuing Legal Education, 2002; "Standard Provisions and Conditions," Oregon State Bar Continuing Legal Education, 1992. Contributing Editor: *The Developing Labor Law,* 2nd Ed., 5th Supp., 1982-1988 (BNA). Instructor, Legal Writing, Portland State University, Spring Term 1993. Court-appointed Arbitrator, Circuit Courts of Clackamas, Multnomah and Washington Counties, 1999—. *Member:* Oregon State Bar (Member, Sections on: Labor; Litigation, 1987—; Member, Executive Committee, Civil Rights Section, 1989-1990, and Member, 1996-1998 and Chair Elect, 1999, Sole and Small Firm Practitioners Section). **PRACTICE AREAS:** Employment Litigation; Labor Law; Employment Arbitration; Mediation. **Email:** scliff@amburgeyrubin.com

URSULA A. KIENBAUM, born Grosse Pointe, Michigan, August 29, 1974; admitted to bar, 2004, Oregon. *Education:* University of Montana (B.A., with honors, 1998); Lewis and Clark Law School (J.D., 2004). Recipient, Lewis and Clark Legal Clinic, Outstanding Client Advocate Award, 2004. *Member:* Oregon State Bar. **PRACTICE AREAS:** Labor and Employment Law. **Email:** ursula@amburgeyrubin.com

REPRESENTATIVE CLIENTS: American Red Cross; Associated Builders and Contractors, Inc.; AT & T Alascom; Banner Corp.; Cascade Steel Rolling Mills, Inc.; Central Oregon Independent Health Services (Clear Choice Health Plans); CenturyTel; City of Portland; The Collins Companies; Community Medical Center (Missoula, MT); ConAgra Foods/Lamb-Weston; Cowlitz County, WA; FEI Co,; Friendsview Retirement Community; Gray's Harbor PUD; J. R. Simplot Company; City of Lacey, WA.; Lourdes Health Network; Madden Industrial Craftsmen, Inc.; National Frozen Foods Corp.; OSF International, Inc. (Old Spaghetti Factory); Oregon Bankers Association; Oregon Potato Company; Oregon Transfer; OrePac Building Products; Pathology Associates Medical Laboratories; Perkins & Co., P.C., CPAs; Port of Portland; Powell's Books, Inc.; Professional Liability Insurance Services (PLIS); Self-Enhancement, Inc.; Smurfit-Stone Container Corp.; Tillamook PUD; Toyota Logistics Services, Inc.; Tri-Cities Laboratory; Tri-Quint Semiconductor; Trus Joist (A Weyerhaeuser Business); Western Boxed Meats; Willamette Dental Group.

SUSAN K. ANDERSEN

2686 SOUTHWEST VISTA AVENUE
PORTLAND, OREGON 97201-1777
Telephone: 503-222-1996
Fax: 503-274-9945
Email: suzyander@aol.com
URL: http://www.lawyers.com/ska

Wills and Probate, Asset Protection, Trust Law, Estate Planning, Guardianship and Conservatorship.

SUSAN K. ANDERSEN, born Long Beach, California, June 3, 1947; admitted to bar, 1985, Oregon. *Education:* Willamette University (B.A., 1968); University of Southern California (M.S., Ed., 1969; M.A., English, 1972); Northwestern School of Law at Lewis and Clark College (J.D., 1985). Cornelius Honor Society. Associate Editor, Environmental Law, 1983-1985. *Member:* Multnomah County and American Bar Association; Oregon State Bar. **PRACTICE AREAS:** Estate Planning; Wills; Trust Law; Probate; Real Estate.

ATER WYNNE LLP

222 S.W. COLUMBIA, SUITE 1800
PORTLAND, OREGON 97201-6618
Telephone: 503-226-1191
Telecopier: 503-226-0079
URL: http://www.aterwynne.com

Seattle, Washington Office: Two Union Square, 601 Union Street, Suite 5450, Seattle, WA 98101-2327. Telephone: 206-623-4711. Telecopier: 206-467-8406.
Menlo Park, California Office: 525 Middlefield Road, Suite 150, Menlo Park, CA 94025-3441. Telephone: 650-566-1443. Telecopier: 650-325-2340.

Business, Civil Litigation, Corporation Law, Emerging Business, Employment and Labor Law, Energy, Environmental, Global Trade, Indian Law, Intellectual Property, International Law, Mergers and Acquisitions, Public/Private Ventures and Finance, Real Estate, Securities and Corporate Finance, Tax, Technology, Telecom, Venture Capital.

(This Listing Continued)

ATER WYNNE LLP, Portland—Continued

FIRM PROFILE: At Ater Wynne LLP our clients make the future happen. That's why we focus our legal services on the strategic needs, business and future of growing, innovative companies. Ater Wynne has been serving business, litigation and regulated industries clients along the West Coast for more than 50 years.

PARTNERS/SHAREHOLDERS

JONATHAN A. ATER, born Chicago, Illinois, September 14, 1940; admitted to bar, 1966, Oregon and U.S. District Court, District of Oregon. *Education:* Yale University (B.A., 1962); Yale Law School (LL.B., 1965). Order of the Coif. Member, Board of Editors, Yale Law Journal, 1963-1965. Law Clerk to U.S. District Judge Gus J. Solomon, 1965-1966. *Member:* Multnomah County and American Bar Associations; Oregon State Bar (Member, Board of Bar Examiners, 1971-1974; Vice-Chair, 1973-1974; Member, Bar Examination Review Board, 1986-1988; Chair, 1987-1988). ***SPECIAL AGENCIES:*** Member and Vice-Chair, Oregon Health Policy Commission, 2004—. Co-Chair, Governor's Mental Health Task Force, 2003-2004. Chair, Oregon Commission on Children and Families, 1994-1998. Member, Oregon Board of Higher Education, 1976-1980. Member: Governor's Juvenile Crime Prevention Task Force, 1997-1998; Hazardous Waste Steering Committee, U.S. Environmental Protection Agency (Region X), 1987-1988. Director, Albertina Kerr Centers, 2002—. Director, Metropolitan Public Defender, Inc., 2003—. ***PRACTICE AREAS:*** Health Law; Energy Law; Business Law; Strategy. ***Email:*** jaa@aterwynne.com

STEVEN K. BLACKHURST, born Cokato, Minnesota, November 10, 1946; admitted to bar, 1973, Oregon. *Education:* Pomona College (B.A., 1968); University of Oregon (J.D., 1973). Order of the Coif. Associate Editor, Oregon Law Review, 1972-1973. Attorney, U.S. Department of Justice, 1973-1978. Attorney General's Honors Program, Civil Rights Division, 1973-1975. Assistant Special Counsel for Intelligence, 1975-1976. Attorney General's Deputy Counsel on Professional Responsibility, 1976-1978. Lawyer Representative to Ninth Circuit Judicial Conference, 1986-1988. Oregon Law Commissioner, 1999-2003. President, Oregon Association of Defense Counsel, 2002. Chair, Multnomah Bar Association Judicial Screening Committee, 2005—. *Member:* Multnomah County, Federal and American (Member, Litigation Section) Bar Associations; Oregon State Bar. ***PRACTICE AREAS:*** Litigation. ***Email:*** skb@aterwynne.com

ERNEST G. BOOTSMA, born Long Beach, California, June 23, 1964; admitted to bar, 1990, Oregon; 1993, Washington. *Education:* Oregon State University (B.S., with high honors, 1986); Willamette University College of Law (J.D., cum laude, 1990). Phi Delta Phi. Member, Beaverton School District, Local Schools Committee, Jacob Wismer Elementary. Ater Wynne LLP, Portland, Oregon, Partner, 2004—; White & Lee LLP, Portland, Oregon, Partner, 2000-2004; Dunn Carney Allen Higgins & Tongue LLP, Portland, Oregon, Partner, 1998-2000, Associate 1992-1998; Miller Nash LLP, Portland, Oregon, Associate, 1990-1992*Member:* Oregon State Bar (Member, Business Section: CLE Committee Chair; Member, Taskforce to Draft Multi-Entity Merger Statutes); American Bar Association; American Electronics Association; Oregon Council (Membership Committee); Software Association of Oregon; Oregon Entrepreneurs Forum. ***PRACTICE AREAS:*** Emerging Business Law; Intellectual Property; Corporate Finance; Mergers and Acquisitions. ***Email:*** egb@aterwynne.com

LESLIE G. BOTTOMLY, born Portland, Oregon, November 28, 1962; admitted to bar, 1991, Oregon. *Education:* Stanford University (B.A., with honors and distinction, 1985); Northwestern School of Law of Lewis and Clark College (J.D., summa cum laude, 1990). Extern, Hon. Otto Skopil, Ninth Circuit Court of Appeals. *Member:* Oregon State Bar. ***PRACTICE AREAS:*** Litigation; Employment Law. ***Email:*** lgb@aterwynne.com

WILLIAM C. CAMPBELL, born Portland, Oregon, March 5, 1954; admitted to bar, 1979, Oregon. *Education:* Yale University (B.A., 1975); Yale Law School (J.D., 1979). Chair, Ater Wynne LLP, 2001-2005. Editor, Yale Law Journal, 1978-1979. Author: "Groundless Litigation and the Malicious Prosecution Debate: A Historical Analysis," 88 Yale Law Journal 1218, 1979; "Venture Capital Financing," Chapter 20 of Advising Oregon Business, Oregon State Bar Continuing Legal Education, 2001 Edition. Member, AeA Oregon Chapter Executive Committee, 1996-1998; 2003—. Board Member, Entrepreneur's Foundation of the Northwest, 2003—. Board Member, Oregon Biotechnology Association, 1993-1998. Chair, Oregon Higher Education Technology Transfer Board, 2002. Board Member, Software Association of Oregon, 1995-1996. Board Member, Oregon Trade & Marketing Center, Inc., 1988-1991 (Chair, 1990-1991). Director, 1981-1987, and Chair, 1981-1984, Northwest Regional China Council. Director, World Affairs Council of Oregon (President, 1987-1988). Member, Oregon China Committee, 1986-1989. Listed in:"Best of the Bar" peer survey, Portland Business Journal, 2005; "Chambers USA, America's Leading Lawyers for Business," 2004 and 2005. *Member:* Multnomah County, American and International Bar Associations; Oregon State Bar (Chair, Committee on Foreign and International Law, 1982-1983). ***LANGUAGES:*** German (conversational). ***PRACTICE AREAS:*** Corporate Law; Trade Law; International Transactions; Technology Law; Business Law. ***Email:*** wcc@aterwynne.com

FRED J. COCCODRILLI, born Brooklyn, New York, March 6, 1959; admitted to bar, 1985, New York and U.S. District Court, Southern District of New York; 1988, Washington; 1989, Oregon. *Education:* New York University (B.S., 1981); Fordham University (J.D., 1984). Adjunct Professor, Corporate Law, Lewis & Clark College, Northwestern School of Law, 1989. *Member:* Multnomah County, Washington State and American Bar Associations; Oregon State Bar. ***PRACTICE AREAS:*** Technology Law; Mergers and Acquisitions Law; Corporate Finance Law. ***Email:*** fjc@aterwynne.com

L. DAVID CONNELL, born St. Louis, Missouri, March 8, 1968; admitted to bar, 1995, Oregon. *Education:* Brigham Young University (B.S., 1992); J. Reuben Clark Law School, Brigham Young University (J.D., magna cum laude, 1995). *Member:* Multnomah County and American Bar Associations; Oregon State Bar; National Association of Bond Lawyers. ***PRACTICE AREAS:*** Taxation; Limited Liability Company Law; Nonprofit and Charitable Organizations; Pass-Through Entities. ***Email:*** ldc@aterwynne.com

ALICE CUPRILL-COMAS, born Wiesbaden, Germany, April 26, 1970; admitted to bar, 1995, Oregon; 1998, Texas. *Education:* University of Texas at Austin (B.A., with honors, 1992); Lewis and Clark College (J.D., 1995). Golden Key Honor Society. Member, Editorial Board, Environmental Law Review, Lewis and Clark, Northwestern School of Law, 1993-1995. ***LANGUAGES:*** Spanish. ***Email:*** amc@aterwynne.com

JAMES B. DAVIDSON, born Chicago, Illinois, August 8, 1950; admitted to bar, 1975, Illinois and U.S. District Court, Northern District of Illinois including Trial Bar; 1982, U.S. Court of Appeals, Seventh Circuit and U.S. Supreme Court; 1990, U.S. Court of Appeals, Ninth Circuit; 1991, U.S. District Court, Central District of Illinois and U.S. District Court, Eastern District of Wisconsin; 1992, U.S. Court of Appeals, Tenth Circuit; 2001, Oregon and U.S. District Court, District of Oregon; 2002, Washington. *Education:* University of Illinois (B.A., 1972); Washington University (J.D., 1975). Associate Editor, Washington Univeristy Law Quarterly, 1973-1975. Of Counsel, 2001-2003 and Partner, 2003, Ater Wynne LLP, Portland, Oregon. Davidson Mandell Menkes & Surdyk, LLP, Chicago, Illinois, Founding Partner, 1994-2001. Peterson & Ross, Chicago, Illinois, Partner, 1980-1994. Assistant State's Attorney, Cook County State's Attorney's Office, Chicago, Illinois, 1976-1980. Felony Repeat Offender Court, 1979-1980. *Member:* Multnomah County, Federal and American (Member, Sections on: Litigation; Tort Insurance Practice) Bar Associations; Oregon Association of Defense Counsel. American Inns of Court, Gus J. Solomon Chapter. ***PRACTICE AREAS:*** Litigation; Employment Law; Intellectual Property; Insurance. ***Email:*** jbd@aterwynne.com

VALERIE D. FISHER, born Evanston, Illinois, May 28, 1949; admitted to bar, 1974, Oregon and U.S. District Court, District of Oregon. *Education:* Stanford University (B.A., 1971); University of Oregon School of Law (J.D., 1974). Order of the Coif. Associate Editor, Oregon Law Review, 1973-1974. Member and Vice Chair, Board of Visitors, University of Oregon School of Law. Secretary and Member, Commercial Real Estate and Legislative Committees, Oregon Mortgage Bankers' Association. Winner, Award for Distinguished Service to Oregon Mortgage Bankers' Association. *Member:* American Bar Association (Member, Real Property, Probate and Trust Law Section); Oregon State Bar (Former Chair, Debtor-Creditor Section; Former Chair, Real Estate and Land Use Section; Member, Business and Corporate Law Section; Former Chair, State Bar Financial Institutions Committee; Member, State Bar Business Law and Real Estate Law Committees on Opinion Letters). ***PRACTICE AREAS:*** Commercial Mortgage Lending Law; Secured Transactions; Real Estate Law; Commercial Transactions; Contracts. ***Email:*** vdf@aterwynne.com

KIRK H. GIBSON, born York, Pennsylvania, November 16, 1953; admitted to bar, 1985, Oregon; 1986, Nevada; 1988, Washington; 1994, Florida; 1996, Alaska. *Education:* Rider University (B.S., 1975); Boston College (M.B.A., 1977); Franklin Pierce Law Center (J.D., 1984). *Member:* Multnomah County, Washington State and American Bar Associations; Oregon State Bar; State Bar of Nevada; The Florida Bar; Alaska State Bar. ***PRACTICE AREAS:*** Energy Project Development; Energy; Utility Law; Electric and Gas; Oil Pipelines. ***Email:*** khg@aterwynne.com

WALLACE A. GLAUSI, born Portland, Oregon, August 16, 1963; admitted to bar, 1992, Oregon; 1994, U.S. Tax Court. *Education:* University of Oregon (J.D., 1991); Georgetown University (LL.M., 1993). Ater Wynne LLP, Portland, Oregon, Partner, 2004—; White & Lee LLP, Portland, Oregon, Partner, 2000-2004; Dunn Carney Allen Higgins & Tongue, 1998-2000. *Member:* Oregon State Bar; American Electronics Association; Oregon Council (Legislative Committee). ***LANGUAGES:*** French. ***PRACTICE AREAS:*** Emerging Business Law; Corporate Finance; Tax Law. ***Email:*** wag@aterwynne.com

GREGG D. JOHNSON, born Hinsdale, Illinois, June 14, 1953; admitted to bar, 1983, Oregon. *Education:* University of Colorado (B.A., 1975); University of Chicago (M.A., 1980); Georgetown University (J.D., 1983). Co-Author: "Review of Risks to Indenture Trustees," J. Bankr. Law (June 2005). Author: "Lender Workouts: The Process Upon Default," Oregon Law Institute, 2003; "Structuring Transactions to Minimize the Impact of a Bankruptcy Case," Oregon State Bar Bankruptcy Law Manual, 1999; "Recovering a Creditor's Expenses and Legal and Accounting Fees as an Administrative Claim," 5 Bkrptcy. Dev. J. 463, 1988 (cited in *Cybergenics Corp. v. Chinery,* 330 F.3d 548, 584 3d.Cir. 2003); *In re Lease-A-Fleet, Inc.* , 148 B.R. 419 (Bkrptcy. E.D. Pa. 1992); *In re Brown* , 147 B.R. 55 (Bkrptcy . D. Mass. 1992). Co-Author: "Receivership or Custodianship Involving Corporate Assets," Prentice-Hall Law & Pub., 1993; "Secured Transactions," Oregon Law Institute, 1991; "Drafting Settlement Agreements on the Eve of Bankruptcy," 7 Bkrptcy. Dev. J. 360, 1990. Adjunct Professor of Secured Transactions, Lewis & Clark Law School, 1992. *Member:* Oregon State Bar (Chairman, Joint CPA Committee). ***REPORTED CASES:*** Spieker Properties v. Bank of New York, et al., 268 F.3d 712 (9th Cir. 2001); In re Allen Care Centers, 96 F.3d 1328 (9th Cir. 1996); Safeco Credit Co. v. U.S. Bancorp Leasing & Financial, 833 F. Supp. 833 (D. Or. 1993). ***TRANSACTIONS:*** Insolvency of Metropolitan Mortgage & Securities Co. and insurance affiliates, 2004 (representing custodian holding several hundred million dollars in securities); Bankruptcy of Southern Pacific Funding Corporation, 2001 (representing indenture trustee on $100 million bond debt); Bankruptcy of WTD Industries, et al., 1991 (representing debtor); Bankruptcy of Smith's Home Furnishings, Inc., 1995 (representing landlords and inventory suppliers). ***PRACTICE AREAS:*** Commercial Law; Creditors Rights; Bankruptcy. ***Email:*** gdj@aterwynne.com

RANDAL A. JOHNSON, born Marquette, Michigan, August 11, 1961; admitted to bar, 1987, Michigan; 1989, Oregon. *Education:* Michigan State University (B.A., 1983); University of South Carolina (J.D., 1987). Order of the Coif. Law Clerk to the Hon. James C. Harrison, Jr., Columbia, South Carolina, 1986-1987. *Member:* Oregon State Bar; State Bar of Michigan; American Bar Association. ***PRACTICE AREAS:*** Real Estate Law; Real Estate Finance; Real Estate Development; Land Use Law. ***Email:*** raj@aterwynne.com

FRANK V. LANGFITT, III, born Augusta, Georgia, July 14, 1947; admitted to bar, 1973, Oregon. *Education:* Stanford University (B.A., 1969); University of Oregon (J.D., 1973). *Member:* Multnomah County and American Bar Associations; Oregon State Bar (Treasurer, Real Estate Section, 1978-1979; Member, Editorial Board, Litigation, Section, 1993-1996); Oregon Association of Defense Counsel. ***PRACTICE AREAS:*** Business Litigation; Environmental Litigation; Insurance Coverage and Defense; Tort and Product Liability Defense. ***Email:*** fvl@aterwynne.com

DANIEL P. LARSEN, born Milwaukee, Wisconsin, July 2, 1968; admitted to bar, 1994, Oregon; U.S. District Court, District of Oregon. *Education:* University of Wisconsin-Madison (B.S., 1990); Northwestern School of Law of Lewis and Clark College (J.D., cum laude, 1994). Recipient: American Jurisprudence Awards for Torts II and Evidence, "Best Brief" in Moot Court Environmental Appellate Advocacy, Environmental Law Certificate,

(This Listing Continued)

1994. Law Clerk to Federal District Judge, Robert E. Jones, 1994-1996. Author: "Combatting the Exotic Species Invasion: The Role of Tort Liability," 5 Duke Environmental Law & Policy Forum 21 (1995); "Ownership of Historic Shipwrecks in U.S. Law," 9 International Journal of Marine and Coastal Law 31 (1994). *Member:* Multnomah County and American Bar Associations; Oregon State Bar (Chair, Membership Services Committee, 1996-1999 and Member, Executive Committee, 1999—New Lawyers Division). The Owen M. Panner American Inn of Court. ***PRACTICE AREAS:*** Commercial Litigation; Dispute Resolution. ***Email:*** dpl@aterwynne.com

DOUGLAS C. MacCOURT, born Savage, Minnesota, October 3, 1959; admitted to bar, 1989, Oregon and U.S. District Court, District of Oregon; 1991, U.S. Court of Appeals, Ninth Circuit. *Education:* Humboldt State University (B.S., cum laude, 1983); University of Oregon (J.D., 1988). Author: "Solid Waste Law and Regulation," Environmental Law for Oregon Practitioners (Oregon Law Institute, forthcoming 1999); "Portland's North Marine Drive: A Road to Jobs Through Brownfields Redevelopment," Engineering News Record, Oct. 26, 1998 at E-4; "National Brownfields Conference—Brownfields 98," Oregon Insider, 1998; "Portland Livable Community Showcase Project," Oregon Insider, 1998; "One Call for Brownfields," Oregon Insider, 1998; "Law and Regulation of Infectious Waste," Environmental Law for Oregon Practitioners (Oregon Law Institute, 1991). *Member:* Oregon State Bar (Member, Sections on: Real Estate and Land Use; Environmental and Natural Resources; Indian Law). ***REPORTED CASES:*** Leaco Enterprises, Inc. v. General Electric Co., 737 F.Supp. 605 (D.Or. 1990); Rebmann v. Linn County, 21 Or. LUBA 542 (1991). ***PRACTICE AREAS:*** Environmental; Land Use; Natural Resources; Indian Law. ***Email:*** dcm@aterwynne.com

STACEY E. MARK, born Wilmington, Delaware, May 15, 1956; admitted to bar, 1987, Oregon; 1988, U.S. District Court, District of Oregon; 1989, District of Columbia; 1990, U.S. Court of Appeals, Ninth Circuit; 2001, Washington; 2002, U.S. District Court, Eastern District of Washington. *Education:* Temple University (B.F.A., 1977); Northwestern School of Law of Lewis and Clark College (J.D., magna cum laude, 1987). *Member:* Oregon State Bar; Washington State, American and Federal Bar Associations. ***PRACTICE AREAS:*** Employment Law; Employment Litigation. ***Email:*** sem@aterwynne.com

BRENDA L. MELTEBEKE, born Hillsboro, Oregon, October 21, 1956; admitted to bar, 1987, Massachusetts; 1992, Oregon. *Education:* Portland State University (B.S., with honors, 1983); Boston University School of Law (J.D., 1986). Chair, Business Department, Ater Wynne LLP. Member, Start-Up Services Committee of Oregon Entrepreneurs Forum (OEF). Emeritus Member, Board of Software Association of Oregon. Member: Board of Trustees, Literary Arts, Inc.; Steering Committee, Womens' Investment Network; Advisory Board, The Link for Women. *Member:* Multnomah County and Massachusetts Bar Associations; Oregon State Bar (Member, Sections on: Business Law; Securities Regulation; Secretary, Executive Committee,. ***PRACTICE AREAS:*** Corporate Law; Business Law; Securities Law; Mergers, Acquisitions and Divestitures; Health Care; Alcoholic Beverages; Equity Finance; Business Formation; Business Organization; Business Planning; Business Start-Ups; Buy-Sell Agreements; Buying and Selling of Businesses; Closely Held Business Law; Emerging Growth Companies; Entrepreneurial Business Law; Limited Liability Company Law; Closely Held Corporations; Corporate Finance; Corporate Formation; Corporate Governance; Corporate Organization; Corporate Planning; Incorporation; Professional Corporations; Public Corporations; S Corporations; Small Business Corporations; Takeovers; Tender Offers; Health Care Corporate Law; Health Care Mergers and Acquisitions; Business Acquisitions; Business Divestitures; Mergers and Acquisitions Finance; Premerger Notification; Spin-Offs; Securities; Blue Sky Law; Initial Public Offerings; Private Placement; Public Offerings; Securities Disclosure; Securities Finance; Securities Offerings; Securities Registration; Securities Regulation; Shareholder Agreements; Shareholder Disputes; Shareholder Rights. ***Email:*** blm@aterwynne.com

CLAUDIA KAY POWERS, born Coos Bay, Oregon, February 15, 1947; admitted to bar, 1983, Oregon; 1984, U.S. District Court, District of Oregon. *Education:* University of Oregon (B.S. 1970); Northwestern School of Law of Lewis and Clark College of Law (J.D., 1982). *Member:* Multnomah County, Federal Energy and American (Member, Section on Natural Resources, Energy and Environmental Law) Bar Associations; Oregon State Bar (Member, Environmental and Natural Resources Section). ***PRACTICE AREAS:*** Environmental Law; Natural Resources Law. ***Email:*** ckp@aterwynne.com

LISA RACKNER, born Minneapolis, Minnesota, September 13, 1958; admitted to bar, 1987, Oregon. *Education:* Reed College (B.A., 1981); New York University (J.D., 1987). New York University Law Review, 1985-1986. Recipient, Arthur Garfield Hays Civil Liberties Fellow, 1986-1987, New York University Law School. Author: Law and Rackner, "Gender Equality and the Mexico City Policy," 20 Journal of International Law and Policy 193, 1987; Note, "Against Forfeiture of Attorney Fees under RICO: Protecting the Constitutional Rights of Criminal Defendants," 61 New York University Law Review, 124, 1986. *Member:* Multnomah County Bar Association; Oregon State Bar; Oregon Association of Defense Counsel. ***PRACTICE AREAS:*** Telecommunications and Energy Law; Labor and Employment Law; Internet Law; Administrative Law; Civil Litigation. ***Email:*** lfr@aterwynne.com

MICHAEL J. "SAM" SANDMIRE, born Green Bay, Wisconsin, October 9, 1961; admitted to bar, 1990, Oregon. *Education:* Stanford University (A.B., with distinction, 1985; J.D., 1990). Managing Editor, Stanford Law and Policy Review, 1988-1990. *Member:* Oregon State Bar; District of Columbia Bar; American Bar Association; Defense Research Institute; Oregon Association of Defense Counsel. ***PRACTICE AREAS:*** Civil Litigation; Products Liability Law; Employment Law. ***Email:*** mjs@aterwynne.com

RONALD L. SAXTON, born Albany, Oregon, May 5, 1954; admitted to bar, 1979, Oregon; 1988, U.S. Supreme Court. *Education:* Willamette University (B.S., 1976); University of Virginia (J.D., 1979). Named as an Outstanding Lawyer of America, 2003. *Member:* Multnomah County and American Bar Associations; Oregon State Bar; U.S. Supreme Court Bar. ***PRACTICE AREAS:*** Corporate Law; Business Law; Energy Law; Regulatory Law; Administrative Law; Public Utility Law. ***Email:*** rls@aterwynne.com

JOHN M. SCHULTZ, born Bloomington, Indiana, April 9, 1949; admitted to bar, 1978, Virginia; 1988, District of Columbia; 1991, Oregon; 2002, Washington. *Education:* Yale University (B.A., 1973); University of Virginia (J.D., 1977). *Member:* The District of Columbia Bar; Oregon State Bar (Member, Environmental and Natural Resources Section; Treasurer, Indian Law Section); American Bar Association (Member, Section on Natural

(This Listing Continued)

Resources, Energy and Environmental Law). ***LANGUAGES:*** French and Swedish. ***PRACTICE AREAS:*** Environmental Law; Natural Resources Law; Occupational Safety and Health Law; Federal Indian Law; Mining Law; Water Rights. ***Email:*** jms@aterwynne.com

MICHAEL W. SHACKELFORD, born Albany, Oregon, May 21, 1956; admitted to bar, 1981, Oregon. *Education:* Willamette University (B.S., cum laude, 1978; J.D., magna cum laude, 1981). *Member:* Multnomah County and American Bar Associations; Oregon State Bar. ***PRACTICE AREAS:*** Corporate Law; Securities Law; Business Law; Trusts and Estates Law. ***Email:*** mws@aterwynne.com

GREGORY E. STRUXNESS, born McMinnville, Oregon, December 6, 1952; admitted to bar, 1983, Oregon; 1989, District of Columbia. *Education:* Oregon State University (B.S., 1976); Willamette University (J.D., 1982). Member, Editorial Board, Willamette Law Review, 1981-1982. Author: "State Taxation of Foreign Source Dividend Income: Mobil Oil Corporation v. Commissioner of Taxes of Vermont," 17 Willamette Law Review 475, 1981; "A Review of Current Developments in Shareholder Rights Plans," Mergers & Acquisitions Law Reporter, April 1989. Staff Attorney, 1982-1984 and Special Counsel, 1985-1986, Division of Corporation Finance, Securities and Exchange Commission. *Member:* The District of Columbia Bar; Oregon State Bar; American Bar Association. ***PRACTICE AREAS:*** Corporate Law; Securities Law; Mergers and Acquisitions. ***Email:*** ges@aterwynne.com

MARK A. TURNER, born Pensacola, Florida, October 12, 1959; admitted to bar, 1986, Oregon. *Education:* University of Chicago (A.B., 1981; J.D., 1986). Phi Beta Kappa. Comment Editor, University of Chicago Legal Forum. Author: "Basics of Securities Arbitration," 12 Litigation Journal No. 1, Oct. 1992. Co-Author: "Securities Arbitration," Arbitration Mediation, 1992 (Oregon State Bar); "Attorney Fees and Costs," Federal Civil Litigation in Oregon 1994 (Oregon State Bar). *Member:* Multnomah and American Bar Associations; Oregon State Bar. ***PRACTICE AREAS:*** Securities Litigation; General Commercial Litigation; Employment Litigation. ***Email:*** mat@aterwynne.com

RETIRED PARTNER

STEVEN E. WYNNE, born Klamath Falls, Oregon, March 27, 1952; admitted to bar, 1977, Oregon. *Education:* Willamette University (B.A., in History, 1974); University of Oregon and Willamette University (J.D., cum laude, 1977). President and CEO, SBI International, New York, New York, March 2004 to present. Partner, Ater Wynne LLP, August 2001 to February 2004; Partner, 1985 to January 1995. Member, Boards of Directors: Planar Systems, Inc., 1996—; FLIR Systems, Inc., 2000—. Acting Vice President and General Counsel, FLIR Systems, Inc., Portland, Oregon, April 2002 to March 2003. Chairman and Chief Executive Officer, eteamz.com, Portland, Oregon, June 2000 to January 2001. President and Chief Executive Officer, Adidas America, Inc., Portland, Oregon, February 1995 to March 2000. *Member:* Multnomah County and American Bar Associations; Oregon State Bar (Member, Sections on: Business and Corporate Law; Securities Regulation; International Law). ***PRACTICE AREAS:*** Business Law; Mergers and Acquisitions; Corporate Governance; Public and Private Finance.

ASSOCIATES

RUKAIYAH ADAMS, admitted to bar, 2000, California. *Education:* Carleton College (B.A., with distinction, 1995); Stanford University (J.D., 1999). *Member:* State Bar of California. (Resident, Menlo Park, California Office). ***TRANSACTIONS:*** Represented Yahoo! Inc. in its $750,000,000 zero-zero debt offering. Represented Pixelworks, Inc. in its acquisition of Equator Technologies, Inc. ***PRACTICE AREAS:*** Corporate; Securities; Emerging Business; Mergers and Acquisitions.

JAMES M. BARRETT, admitted to bar, 2001, Oregon. *Education:* University of Washington (B.A., 1994); University of Virginia (J.D., 2001). [Lieutenant, United States Navy, 1994-1998]. ***PRACTICE AREAS:*** Litigation; Corporate. ***Email:*** jmb@aterwynne.com

JAMES C. BRADSHAW, born Salt Lake City, Utah, January 18, 1971; admitted to bar, 2001, Oregon. *Education:* University of Utah (B.S., 1996); Willamette University (J.D., cum laude, 2001). *Member:* Oregon State Bar. ***PRACTICE AREAS:*** Commercial Transactions; Sale of Goods; Intellectual Property Licensing; Foreign Military Sales; Defense Contracts; Government Procurement; Government Contracts. ***Email:*** jcb@aterwynne.com

AMIE JAMIESON, born Vernon, Connecticut, December 23, 1975; admitted to bar, 2005, Oregon. *Education:* University of Maine (B.A., Sociology, summa cum laude, 1997); Florida State University (M.S., Sociology, 1999); Lewis and Clark College (J.D., cum laude, 2005). Phi Beta Kappa. Recipient, Natural Resources Scholarship; University of Maine Presidential Scholarship, 1997; Lewis and Clark Law School Scholar List; Outstanding Oral Advocate; First Year Appellate Advocacy; Pro Bono Honors Award. Law Clerk to U.S. Attorney's Office, District of Oregon, 2003-2005. Managing Editor, Lewis and Clark Law School Environmental Law Review, 2004-2005. Member, Ninth Circuit Review, 2003-2004. Author: "Will Bald Eagles Remain Compelling Enough to Validate the Bald and Golden Eagle Protection Act After ESA Delisting? The Ninth Circuit's Analysis in United States v. Antoine," 34 Environmental Law 929 (2004). *Member:* Oregon State Bar; Oregon Women Lawyers. ***PRACTICE AREAS:*** Electric Utilities; Utility Contracts; Energy; Energy Acquisitions; Energy Contracts. ***Email:*** alj@aterwynne.com

NATHAN A. KARMAN, admitted to bar, 2004, Oregon. *Education:* University of Wisconsin at Milwaukee (B.A., 2001); Duke University (J.D., 2004). ***PRACTICE AREAS:*** Litigation; Business. ***Email:*** nak@aterwynne.com

JAMES N. McDERMOTT, born Los Angeles, California, July 29, 1971; admitted to bar, 2000, California; 2002, Oregon. *Education:* University of California, Irvine (B.A., 1993); University of California, Hastings College of the Law (J.D., 2000). Recipient, American Jurisprudence Award in American Legal History. Ater Wynne LLP, 2004—; Ball Janik LLP, 2002-2004; Brobeck Phleger & Harrison, 2000-2002; Travelocity.com, 1995-1997. *Member:* Multnomah Bar Association; Oregon State Bar; State Bar of California. ***LANGUAGES:*** Spanish. ***PRACTICE AREAS:*** Corporate Law; Mergers and Acquisitions; Securities; Business Law. ***Email:*** jnm@aterwynne.com

(This Listing Continued)

ATER WYNNE LLP, Portland—Continued

ALIA S. MILES, born Boston, Massachusetts, November 4, 1970; admitted to bar, 1998, Oregon. *Education:* University of California at San Diego (B.A., cum laude, 1992); Lewis and Clark College (J.D., 1998). Phi Beta Kappa. *Member:* Oregon State Bar (Executive Committee Member, Environmental and Natural Resources Section); American Bar Association. ***LANGUAGES:*** Italian. ***PRACTICE AREAS:*** Environmental Law; Natural Resources; Energy Project Development; Indian Economic Development. ***Email:*** am@aterwynne.com

DOUGLAS D. MORRIS, born California; admitted to bar, 1996, Oregon; 1997, Washington and U.S. District Court, Western District of Washington; 1998, U.S. District Court, Eastern District of Washington and District of Oregon; 1999, U.S. Court of Appeals, Ninth Circuit. *Education:* University of California at Berkeley (B.A., 1991); Lewis and Clark Law School (J.D., cum laude, 1996). *Member:* Oregon State Bar; Washington State Bar Association. ***PRACTICE AREAS:*** Corporate Law; Securities; Business Law. ***Email:*** ddm@aterwynne.com

JENNY L. TRIEU, admitted to bar, 2001, Oregon; 2002, Alaska. *Education:* Bryn Mawr College (B.A., magna cum laude, 1996); University of Michigan (J.D., 2000). ***LANGUAGES:*** Chinese and Russian. ***PRACTICE AREAS:*** Business Law; Intellectual Property; Energy Law; International Transactions. ***Email:*** jlt@aterwynne.com

SARAH K. WALLACE, admitted to bar, 1996, California; 2000, Oregon and Washington. *Education:* University of California at San Diego (B.A., 1992); University of San Diego (J.D., cum laude, 1996); Northwestern School of Law, Lewis & Clark College (LL.M., Environmental and Natural Resources Law, cum laude, 2004). Member, Editorial Board, San Diego Law Review, 1996. ***PRACTICE AREAS:*** Energy; Environmental; Telecommunications. ***Email:*** sek@aterwynne.com

OF COUNSEL

LORI IRISH BAUMAN, born Alexandria, Virginia, August 18, 1959; admitted to bar, 1984, California and U.S. District Court, Northern District of California; 1987, Oregon; 1989, U.S. District Court, Eastern District of California; 2004, U.S. District Court, Central District of California. *Education:* Princeton University (A.B., magna cum laude, 1981); University of Chicago (J.D., 1984). Staff Member, University of Chicago Law Review, 1983-1984. Author: "Alibi Notice Rules: The Preclusion Sanction As Procedural Default," 51 University of Chicago Law Review 254, 1984; "Familial Status Discrimination Under the Fair Housing Act," Oregon Real Estate and Land Use Digest, April 1992; "Legal Update on Familial Status," Journal of Property Management, July/August 1992; "Personal Jurisdiction and Internet Advertising," The Computer Lawyer, January 1997; "Split Over Splitting: Impasse Persists on Proposal to Split the 9th Circuit Court of Appeals," Oregon State Bar Bulletin, April 2004. *Member:* Oregon State Bar; State Bar of California. ***PRACTICE AREAS:*** Civil Litigation; Appeals; Antitrust and Trade Regulation. ***Email:*** lib@aterwynne.com

AKANA K. J. MA, born October 13, 1956; admitted to bar, 1985, Massachusetts and District of Columbia; 1995, Oregon. *Education:* Tufts University (B.A., 1979); Boston College (J.D., 1984); Harvard Law School, East Asian Legal Studies. Author: "Export of U.S. Microchip Technologies to China - The U.S. Government's Misplaced Concern," Portland Business Journal, May 20, 2005; "Importers' Compliance with U.S. Laws - When a Dusting of Flour Could Save Your Business," Oregon State Bar International Law Section Newsletter, March 2005; "What Is It? And Where Is It Going? The U.S. Government Wants to Know - U.S. Exports and Encryption," Oregon State Bar International Law Section Newsletter, March 2005; "Helping Clients Succeed with International Trade," Oregon State Bar Bulletin, November 2002; "Counsel's Role in the Export Sales Transaction - Harmonizing Competing Interests," Oregon State Bar International Law Section Newsletter, 1998, Vol. XII, No. I; Pacific Northwest International Trade Association Trade Winds, December 1997; International Lawyer's Newsletter Kluwer Law, Vol. XX, No. 1, 1998. *Member:* American (Member, International Law and Practice Section), International and InterPacific Bar Associations; Oregon State Bar (Member, International Law Section); Legal Counsel International (Founding Member). ***PRACTICE AREAS:*** International Commercial Transactions; Intellectual Property. ***Email:*** akm@aterwynne.com

JOHN D. WALCH, born Springfield, Oregon, April 24, 1960; admitted to bar, 1988, Utah; 1989, California; 1990, U.S. District Court, District of California and U.S. Court of Appeals, Ninth Circuit; 1996, Oregon, Washington, U.S. District Court, District of Oregon and U.S. Tax Court. *Education:* Brigham Young University (B.S., 1984); J. Reuben Clark School of Law, Brigham Young University (J.D., 1987). Senior Pension Attorney, Standard Insurance Company's Retirement Plans Division, 1998-2002. Formerly with: Benner & Associates, P.C., 2002-2004; Samuels, Yoelin and Kantor, LLP, 1996-1998. Member, Western Pension and Benefits Conference. *Member:* Oregon State Bar (Sections on: Taxation; Labor), American Bar Association. ***REPORTED CASES:*** PM Group v. Western Growers Assurance Trust, 953 F.2d. 543 (9th Cir. 1992). ***PRACTICE AREAS:*** ERISA; Employee Benefits. ***Email:*** jdw@aterwynne.com

LAURIE M. YOUNGER, born Corvallis, Oregon, January 15, 1969; admitted to bar, 1997, California; 2001, Oregon. *Education:* University of Oregon (B.A., 1991); Cornell University (J.D., 1997). ***PRACTICE AREAS:*** Intellectual Property; General Business. ***Email:*** lmy@aterwynne.com

REPRESENTATIVE CLIENTS: Advanced Silicon Materials LLC; Arkema Inc.;Bank of America, N.A.; Bank of New York; Bechtel Enterprises, Inc.; BOC Group; Cascade Microtech, Inc.; Cascade Station Development, LLC; Credence Systems, Corp.; Crownover Construction Co.; Columbia River People's Utility District; Columbia Ventures Corporation; Dine' Power Authority; FLIR Systems, Inc.; Golden Valley Electric Association, Inc.; Jack in the Box Inc.; *Idaho Power; Metro One Telecommunications, Inc.;* Mt. Hood Beverage Company; NoaNet Oregon; Northwest Pipe Company; ODS Companies; Open Source Development Labs; The Oregon Clinic; Oregon Health & Sciences University; Pacific Northern Inc.; Pixelworks, Inc.; Planar Systems, Inc.; Plum Creek Timber Co.; The Port of Portland; Portland Family Practice, Inc.; Schnitzer Steel Industries, Inc.; Time Warner Telecom of Oregon; Toyo Tanso USA, Inc.; TriQuint SemiConductor, Inc.; Union Bank of California.

BABENER & ASSOCIATES

Established in 1974

1020 BANK OF AMERICA FINANCIAL CENTER
121 S.W. MORRISON
PORTLAND, OREGON 97204-3140
Telephone: 503-226-6600
FAX: 503-226-4290
Email: contact@mlmlegal.com
URL: http://www.mlmlegal.com

General Civil and Trial Practice in all State and Federal Courts. Direct Selling, Marketing and Distribution, Commercial, Trade Regulation, Taxation, International, Corporation, Intellectual Property, Food and Drug, International Expansion.

FIRM PROFILE: The firm represents leading corporations in the Direct Selling Industry headquartered throughout the U.S. and abroad. The firm also focuses on representation of Pacific Rim Companies in the U.S. and abroad.

JEFFREY A. BABENER, born Seattle, Washington, April 19, 1948; admitted to bar, 1974, California, Oregon, U.S. District Court, District of Oregon, U.S. District Court, Central District of California and U.S. Court of Appeals, Ninth Circuit. *Education:* Occidental College (B.A., cum laude, 1970); University of Southern California (J.D., 1973). Phi Beta Kappa. Member, Board of Editors, Southern California Law Review, 1972-1973. Author: "Durational Residence Requirements for State and Local Office: A Violation of Equal Protection?" 45 Southern California Law Review, 996, 1972; MLM/Direct Seller's Corporate Handbook, Tax Guide for MLM/Direct Sellers; "Network Marketing: Window of Opportunity," Network Marketer's Guide to Success; "Network Marketing: What You Should Know". "Representative Published Articles: Is This Network Marketing Opportunity for Real?; The Inside Track on Network Marketing; MLM Earnings - How Much?; Marketing Discount Services; Network Marketing: Is It For You?; New Protection for MLM Distributors; Value Is The "In" Thing; Planning A Great Meeting; Co-op Advertising: Get the Word Out; Network Marketing: Future Opportunities; Successful Long Distance Sponsoring; Networking and Time Management; Networking Through Mail Lists; Networkers on the Information Highway; Networking Through Nonprofit; Changing Face of Network Marketing; Investigating a Network Marketing Company; ABC - Three-Way Calling; MLM Earnings Projections; Promote Sales Presentations with Gifts; FDA and MLM; Look for Buy-Back Policies; MLM Pyramid Legislation; MLM Management and Training; Incorporating Your MLM Business; Tax Deductions for Your MLM Home Office; Financing Growth for Your MLM Business; FDA Approval for MLM Products; MLM Retirement and Benefit Planning; MLM and the Postal Service; MLM and Credit Card Fraud - Be Careful; Your Personal MLM Legal Dictionary; What's in a Name?: MLM Trademarks; Marketing Through Nonprofit Organizations; New Life for MLM Services in Missouri; MLM Statutes: Georgia Adopts Legislation; Electronic Fund Transfers; FTC and Advertising; The FTC Cooling Off Rule; The Business Plan: A Valuable Tool for Success; Missouri's MLM Struggles; The MLM/Franchise; MLM Buyback Rules; Your MLM Home Office and Taxes; Who Owns the Downline?; FDA Nutritional Health Claims; MLM and Sales Taxes; Future of the MLM Industry; The MLM Distributor's Guide to Incorporation; When the Postman Knocks; MLM Taxes: Entertainment Deductions; Network Marketing v. Pyramid Schemes; MLM and Franchising; Organizing Your MLM Business; How Many Levels?; Boost Sales with Nonprofits; MLM National Expansion; MLM to Europe - 1992; Noncompetition Agreements: Enforceable?; MLM in Canada; Underage Distributors; Involving Your Family in Business; MLM Statutes: Washington Continues the Trend; MLM Cross-Sponsoring Rules; Changes in the Marketing Plan; Selling Sales Tools; MLM Sales Taxes and Corporate Taxes: The Multistate Tax Commission; MLM and Business Opportunity Statutes; Buenos Dias Mexico; NuSkin Troubles: Light in the Tunnel; The Saga of MLM Investigations; Earnings Hype - What Can You Say?; Say It Again Sam: Making the Most of Great Press; IRS Audits and Network Marketers; Canada-Welcome-Bienvenu; Proposed FDA Legislation Helps MLM; Network Marketing: Legal Issues; Knock! Knock! It's the FDA; The SEC Awakens; Electronic Fund Transfers; New Rules on Home Office Deductions; State AG's Applaud Industry; Buy-back Standards; MLM Nutraceuticals! -- Say What?; NSA Settlement: Enormous Industry Impact; Is the U.S. Postal Service in Your Future?; You Too Can Incorporate; SEC: We Hate Pyramids; Opportunity Goes South: Mexico MLM; FDA v. Health Industry: Showdown; Forget the Saturation Theory; Network Marketing Reaches Maturity; New Proposals For Home Office Deductions; Chasing the Competition; Networkers and Credit Card Fraud; NuSkin and the FTC: A Message on Earnings Claims; Network Marketing Management and Training; Cancel This Sale! - The Three-Day Rule; Looking for the Right Compensation Plan; Too Young to Play." Member, Lawyer's Council, Government Relations Committee, Internet Task Force of the Direct Selling Association, 1983—. Member, Board of Directors, Multilevel Marketing International Association, 1985—; Conference Sponsor: "University of Texas MLM Academic Conference," "The MLM Entrepreneur Series," and "Starting and Running the Successful MLM Company". *Member:* Multnomah County (Chairman, Speakers Bureau, 1977-1978) and American (Member, Commercial Transactions Litigation Committee, 1982—) Bar Associations; Oregon State Bar (Chairman, Committee on Judicial Administration, 1981-1982; Member, Professional Responsibility Committee, 1982-1985). ***PRACTICE AREAS:*** Commercial Litigation; Marketing Law; Franchising Law.

MITCHELL A. GOLDSTEIN, born Hartford, Connecticut, January 24, 1959; admitted to bar, 1987, Oregon. *Education:* Denison University (B.A., 1982); Northwestern School of Law of Lewis and Clark College (J.D., 1986). *Member:* Oregon State Bar.

REPRESENTATIVE CLIENTS: Nikken Inc.; Noevir, Inc.; Avon Products, Inc.; Discovery Toys; Kaire International, Inc.; Cell Tech; BeautiControl Cosmetics; Trek Alliance, Inc.; Tianshi Health Products, Inc.; Everest International, Inc.; At Home With Mr. Food; Legacy DCV; direcConnect, Inc; GMX Corp.; Oxyfresh; Pola International; Altwell USA, Inc.; Custom Corner; Money Maker's Monthly, Inc.; Multi-Level Marketing International Association; Envion International; Cell Tech; Amazon Herbs, Inc.; New Vision, Inc.; Tele-Sales, Inc.; Rachael Cosmetics, Inc.; IMPaX HealthPrime, Inc.; TravelMax International, Inc.; EssantéInternational; Worldconnect Communications; Intelligent Nutrients, Inc.; Global Village Market; Zig Ziglar Network; Dr. Nona International; Intracell; 21st Century Nutraceuticals; International Teamworks, Inc.; OneDotCom; Online Exchange; Unison Quest International.

BALL JANIK LLP

Established in 1982

ONE MAIN PLACE
101 SW MAIN STREET, SUITE 1100
PORTLAND, OREGON 97204-3219
Telephone: 503-228-2525
Telecopy: 503-295-1058
Email: info@balljanik.com
URL: http://www.balljanik.com

Washington, D.C. Office: 1455 F Street, NW, Suite 225, 20005-1004. Telephone: 202-638-3307. Telecopy: 202-783-6947.

Bend, Oregon Office: 15 SW Colorado Avenue, Suite 3, 97702. Telephone: 541-617-1309. Telecopy: 541-617-8824.

Real Estate, Land Use, Commercial Litigation, Business, Corporate, Government Relations, Financing, Bankruptcy, Business Workouts and Reorganizations, Environmental, Natural Resources, Creditors' Remedies, Taxation, Estate Planning and Probate, Administrative, Health Care, Employment, Construction, Insurance Recovery.

PARTNERS OF FIRM

DINA E. ALEXANDER, born Cheyenne, Wyoming, 1970; admitted to bar, 1996, Washington; 1999, California; 2003, Oregon. *Education:* University of Washington (B.A., 1992); Willamette University (J.D., 1996). Member, Willamette Law Review, 1994-1996. *Member:* Oregon State Bar; State Bar of California; Washington State and American Bar Associations. ***PRACTICE AREAS:*** Real Estate; Project Finance; Construction Law. ***Email:*** dalexander@balljanik.com

RICHARD H. ALLAN, born San Mateo, California, 1959; admitted to bar, 1988, Oregon; 1992, U.S. District Court, District of Oregon and U.S. Court of Appeals, Ninth Circuit; 2003, Washington. *Education:* University of California, Berkeley (B.S., with highest honors, 1982); Boalt Hall School of Law, University of California (J.D., 1988). Phi Beta Kappa; Order of the Coif. Editor-in-Chief, Ecology Law Quarterly, 1987-1988. Law Clerk to Chief Justice Malcolm M. Lucas, California Supreme Court, 1988-1989. *Member:* Oregon State Bar; Washington State Bar Association. ***PRACTICE AREAS:*** Land Use; Environmental; Natural Resources. ***Email:*** rallan@balljanik.com

JAMES A. BEALL, born Corvallis, Oregon, 1950; admitted to bar, 1976, Oregon; 1981, District of Columbia; 1990, U.S. Supreme Court. *Education:* Oregon State University (B.A., 1972); University of Oregon (J.D., 1976); Georgetown University (M.T.L., 1981). Member, Board of Editors, Oregon Law Review, 1975-1976. Legislative Coordinator to Congressman Al Ullman, 1977-1978. Professional Staff, House Committee on Ways and Means, 1979-1980. *Member:* Oregon State Bar; District of Columbia Bar; American Bar Association (Member, Section on Taxation). (Also at Washington, D.C. Office). ***PRACTICE AREAS:*** Government Affairs; Legislative Lobbying; Administrative Lobbying Law. ***Email:*** jbeall@dc.balljanik.com

BRUCE H. CAHN, born Los Angeles, California, 1963; admitted to bar, 1990, California and U.S. District Court, Central District of California; 1992, U.S. Court of Appeals, Ninth Circuit and U.S. District Court, Northern, Eastern and Southern Districts of California; 1993, Oregon; 1994, U.S. District Court, District of Oregon; 2003, Washington and U.S. District Court, Eastern District of Washington. *Education:* California State University at Northridge (B.A., 1986); Loyola Marymount University (J.D., 1990). Staff Member, Loyola of Los Angeles, International & Comparative Law Journal, 1988-1989. Member, St. Thomas More Law Honor Society. Co-Author, with Curt Roy Hineline: "Asset Freeze Injunctions in Securities Litigation: A New Tool for Plaintiffs?" ABA Committee on Class Actions & Derivative Suits, Vol. 5, No. 3, July 1995. *Member:* Oregon State Bar; State Bar of California; Washington State Bar Association. ***PRACTICE AREAS:*** Business Litigation; Construction Litigation; Commercial Litigation; Coverage Litigation. ***Email:*** bcahn@balljanik.com

LAURA CRASKA COOPER, born Munich, Germany, 1966; admitted to bar, 1991, California; 1993, Pennsylvania (inactive); 1999, Oregon. *Education:* University of Missouri (B.J., summa cum laude, 1988; B.A., summa cum laude, 1988); University of California, Boalt Hall School of Law (J.D., 1991). Phi Beta Kappa. Senior Note and Comment Editor, California Law Review, 1990-1991. Law Clerk to Hon. Charles E. Wiggins, U.S. Court of Appeals, Ninth Circuit, 1991-1992. *Member:* Oregon State Bar; State Bar of California. (Also at Bend, Oregon Office). ***PRACTICE AREAS:*** Real Estate; Land Use; Corporate Law; Environmental; Construction. ***Email:*** lcooper@balljanik.com

NANCY CRAVEN, born Springfield, Illinois, 1954; admitted to bar, 1979, Oregon. *Education:* Lawrence University (B.A., 1976); Southern Illinois University (J.D., 1979). Law Clerk to Chief Judge George Joseph, Oregon Court of Appeals, 1979-1981. County Counsel, Lincoln County, Oregon, 1981-1986. *Member:* Oregon State Bar. (Also at Bend, Oregon Office). ***PRACTICE AREAS:*** Land Use; Natural Resources; Zoning Law; Environmental. ***Email:*** ncraven@balljanik.com

DAVID W. CRISWELL, born Beloit, Wisconsin, 1963; admitted to bar, 1989, Illinois (Inactive), Wisconsin (Inactive), and U.S. District Court, Northern District of Illinois; 1991, U.S. District Court, Eastern District of Wisconsin; 1992, Oregon and U.S. District Court, District of Oregon; 2003, Washington and U.S. District Court, Western District of Washington. *Education:* Dartmouth College (B.A., 1986); University of Wisconsin-Madison (J.D., cum laude, 1989). *Member:* Oregon State Bar; Washington State Bar Association. ***PRACTICE AREAS:*** Business Reorganizations; Bankruptcy; Creditors' Rights; Fiduciary Litigation. ***Email:*** dcriswell@balljanik.com

JOHN J. DUNBAR, born Binghamton, New York, 1957; admitted to bar, 1984, Oregon; 1985, Washington; 1987, Illinois (Inactive), and U.S. District Court, Northern District of Illinois; 1989, U.S. Court of Appeals, Seventh Circuit; 1991, U.S. District Court, District of Oregon, and U.S. Tax Court; 1995, U.S. Court of Appeals, Ninth Circuit; 2001, U.S. District Court, Western District of Washington. *Education:* University of Notre Dame (A.B., with high honors, 1979); University of Washington (J.D., with honors, 1984). Executive Managing Editor, Washington Law Review, 1983-1984. Law Clerk, Hon. Owen M. Panner, Chief Judge, U.S. District Court, District of Oregon, 1984-1986. Special Assistant

(This Listing Continued)

Cook County State's Attorney, 1990-1991. *Member:* Oregon State Bar; Washington State Bar Association. ***PRACTICE AREAS:*** Litigation; Franchise and Distribution; Trade Secrets; Environmental Litigation; Construction. ***Email:*** jdunbar@balljanik.com

JEFFREY C. GARDNER, born Portland, Oregon, 1952; admitted to bar, 1998, Oregon and Washington; 2004, Idaho. *Education:* University of Portland (B.A., 1976; M.B.A., 1982); Pacific Coast Banking School at University of Washington (1987); Northwestern School of Law of Lewis & Clark College (J.D., cum laude, 1990). Recipient, American Jurisprudence Award in Alternative Dispute Resolution. Author: "Problem Loan Strategies" and "Problem Loan Workouts," RMA: The Risk Management Association. Formerly Senior Vice President and Group Manager Special Assets, U.S. Bancorp, 1991-1997. *Member:* Oregon State Bar; Washington State Bar Association; Idaho State Bar. ***PRACTICE AREAS:*** Business Reorganizations; Bankruptcy; Commercial Loan Workouts; Commercial Loan Transactions. ***Email:*** jgardner@balljanik.com

ROBERT G. HAYES, born Boston, Massachusetts, 1946; admitted to bar, 1974, Vermont; 1985, District of Columbia (Not admitted in Oregon). *Education:* Boston University (B.S., 1968); Catholic University (J.D., 1974). *Member:* Vermont Bar Association; The District of Columbia Bar. (Resident, Washington, D.C. Office). ***PRACTICE AREAS:*** Government Relations Law; International Trade Law; Natural Resources. ***Email:*** rhayes@dc.balljanik.com

STEPHEN T. JANIK, born Portland, Oregon, 1947; admitted to bar, 1974, Oregon. *Education:* Harvard College (A.B., magna cum laude, 1969); Harvard Business School (M.B.A., with distinction, 1974); Harvard Law School (J.D., cum laude, 1974). Editor, Real Estate Law, Oregon State Bar, 1982. Member, Executive Department, State of Oregon, 1970-1971. Special Assistant Attorney General, 1978, 1998. Chairman, Real Estate Land Use Section, Oregon State Bar, 1979. Listed in Best Lawyers in America. *Member:* Multnomah County Bar Association; Oregon State Bar; American College of Real Estate Lawyers. ***PRACTICE AREAS:*** Business; Real Estate; Land Use; Environmental. ***Email:*** sjanik@balljanik.com

PHILLIP E. JOSEPH, born Anchorage, Alaska, 1960; admitted to bar, 1988, Oregon; 2000, District of Columbia; 2001, Washington. *Education:* University of Oregon (B.A., summa cum laude, 1984); University of Washington (J.D., 1988). Law Clerk to Chief Judge Robert J. McNichols, Eastern District of Washington, 1988-1989. *Member:* Oregon State Bar; District of Columbia Bar; Washington State Bar Association. ***LANGUAGES:*** French. ***PRACTICE AREAS:*** Litigation; Construction; Real Estate. ***Email:*** pjoseph@balljanik.com

SALLY C. LANDAUER, born Bellingham, Washington, 1939; admitted to bar, 1978, Oregon and U.S. District Court, District of Oregon; 1987, U.S. Tax Court. *Education:* Whitman College (A.B., magna cum laude, 1961); Northwestern School of Law of Lewis and Clark College (J.D., 1978). Phi Beta Kappa. Editor, Oregon Probate System, Oregon State Bar, 1987. *Member:* Multnomah County and American Bar Associations; Oregon State Bar (Member, Executive Committee, Estate Planning and Administration Section, 1987-1993). American College of Trust and Estate Counsel. ***PRACTICE AREAS:*** Estate Planning; Taxation; Probate Law; Trust Administration; Antenuptial; Conservatorship Law. ***Email:*** slandauer@balljanik.com

JAMES T. McDERMOTT, born Newburgh, New York, 1960; admitted to bar, 1986, Pennsylvania (Inactive) and District of Columbia; 1987, U.S. District Court, District of Columbia and U.S. Court of Appeals, District of Columbia Circuit; 1993, Oregon, U.S. District Court, District of Oregon and U.S. Court of Appeals, Ninth Circuit; 1994, U.S. Tax Court, U.S. Court of Federal Claims, U.S. Court of Appeals, Federal Circuit and U.S. Supreme Court; 2000, Washington; 2001, U.S. District Court, Eastern and Western Districts of Washington; 2002, Idaho and U.S. District Court, District of Idaho. *Education:* Syracuse University (B.S., summa cum laude, 1982); University of Virginia (J.D., 1985). Syracuse Scholar Recipient and Excellence in Accounting Award, Syracuse University. Recipient: Taylor Tazwell Memorial Scholarship, University of Virginia. Member, Virginia Law Review, 1983-1985. Judicial Law Clerk to Hon. James L. Latchum, U.S. District Judge for the District of Delaware, 1985-1986. *Member:* Oregon State Bar; Washington State Bar Association; District of Columbia Bar; Idaho State Bar. ***PRACTICE AREAS:*** Commercial Litigation; Construction Litigation; Insurance Recovery. ***Email:*** jmcdermott@balljanik.com

BRADLEY S. MILLER, born Washington, D.C., 1961; admitted to bar, 1987, California; 1989, District of Columbia (Inactive); 1995, Oregon; 1997, Washington. *Education:* Swarthmore College (B.A., with high honors, 1983); University of Chicago (J.D., 1987). *Member:* Oregon State Bar; Washington State Bar Association; State Bar of California; International Council of Shopping Centers; National Association of Industrial and Office Properties. ***PRACTICE AREAS:*** Real Estate; Corporate; Project Finance. ***Email:*** bmiller@balljanik.com

JACK L. ORCHARD, JR., born Renton, Washington, 1947; admitted to bar, 1972, Oregon and U.S. District Court, District of Oregon; 1976, U.S. Court of Appeals, Ninth Circuit. *Education:* Washington State University (B.A., with distinction, 1969); University of Oregon (J.D., 1972). Phi Kappa Phi; Order of the Coif. Member, Board of Editors, Oregon Law Review, 1971-1972. Interim General Counsel, Legacy Health System, 1997-1998. *Member:* Multnomah County and American Bar Associations; Oregon State Bar. ***PRACTICE AREAS:*** Real Estate; Land Use; Zoning; Health Care; Hospital; Media. ***Email:*** jorchard@balljanik.com

TIMOTHY M. PARKS, born Eugene, Oregon, 1966; admitted to bar, 1993, Oregon. *Education:* Willamette University (B.S., cum laude, 1989; J.D., summa cum laude, 1993). *Member:* Oregon State Bar. ***PRACTICE AREAS:*** Real Estate; Corporate; Business. ***Email:*** tparks@balljanik.com

BARBARA W. RADLER, born Lancaster, Wisconsin, 1957; admitted to bar, 1982, Oregon. *Education:* University of Iowa (B.A., with highest distinction, 1978); George Washington University (J.D., 1982). Phi Beta Kappa; Phi Eta Sigma; Pi Sigma Alpha. Chair, 1994-1995, and Member, 1990-1996, Executive Committee, Real Estate and Land Use Section, Oregon State Bar. Editor, Supplement to Fundamentals of Real Estate Transactions and Documentation of Real Estate Transactions, Oregon State Bar, 1996 and 2001. *Member:* Multnomah County and American (Member, Sections on: Real Estate; Business Law) Bar Associations; Oregon State Bar (Member, Sections on: Real Estate; Business

(This Listing Continued)

BALL JANIK LLP, Portland—Continued

Law; Construction Law); American College of Real Estate Lawyers. ***PRACTICE AREAS:*** Lease Law; Real Estate; Real Estate Finance; Construction. ***Email:*** bradler@balljanik.com

IRENE RINGWOOD, born Spokane, Washington, 1958; admitted to bar, 1984, Washington; 1990, District of Columbia (Not admitted in Oregon). *Education:* Washington State University (B.A., cum laude, 1980); Gonzaga University School of Law (J.D., cum laude, 1984). *Member:* Washington State and American Bar Associations; District of Columbia Bar. (Resident, Washington, D.C. Office). ***PRACTICE AREAS:*** Government Relations; International Trade Law. ***Email:*** iringwood@dc.balljanik.com

SARAH J. RYAN, born Omaha, Nebraska, 1958; admitted to bar, 1983, Oregon; 2001, District of Columbia and Washington. *Education:* University of Nebraska (B.A., with honors, 1979); University of Oregon (J.D., 1982). Recipient, Am Jur Award in Torts, 1979. Law Clerk to Hon. George J. Woodrich, Lane County Circuit Court, 1982-1983. Lawyer Representative, Ninth Circuit Judicial Conference, 1995-1997. Director, U.S. District Court Historical Society, 1995—. Founding Director, Oregon Lawyers Against Hunger, 1997-2001. Director, Legal Aid Services of Oregon and Oregon Law Center, 2001—. *Member:* Multnomah County, Washington State and Federal (Member and Past President, Oregon Chapter) Bar Associations; Oregon State Bar (Member, Sections on: Business Litigation; Labor and Employment Law; Civil Litigation); District of Columbia Bar. ***PRACTICE AREAS:*** Litigation; Employment Law; Discrimination; Sexual Harassment; Civil Rights Actions. ***Email:*** sryan@balljanik.com

LEON SIMSON, born Eschwege, Germany, 1946; admitted to bar, 1975, Wisconsin (Inactive), and Oregon. *Education:* Oberlin College (B.A., 1968); University of Wisconsin (M.A., 1971; J.D., 1975). Order of the Coif. Member, Editorial Board, Wisconsin Law Review, 1974-1975. Instructor, Sales, Lewis and Clark Law School, 1977. Law Clerk to Oregon Supreme Court, 1975-1976. *Member:* Oregon State Bar; American Bar Association. ***PRACTICE AREAS:*** Business Reorganizations; Business; Corporate; Bankruptcy; Buying and Selling of Businesses. ***Email:*** lsimson@balljanik.com

BRAD T. (TONY) SUMMERS, born Auburn, Indiana, 1957; admitted to bar, 1983, California; U.S. District Court, Southern, Northern, Eastern and Central Districts of California; 1991, Oregon and U.S. District Court, District of Oregon; 2004, Washington. *Education:* University of Notre Dame (B.B.A., summa cum laude, 1979); University of California at Los Angeles (J.D., 1982). Beta Gamma Sigma; Order of the Coif. Law Clerk to Justice Warren W. Matthews, Supreme Court of the State of Alaska, 1982-1983. *Member:* Oregon State Bar; State Bar of California; Washington State Bar Association. ***PRACTICE AREAS:*** Business Reorganizations; Bankruptcy; Creditors Rights; Litigation. ***Email:*** tsummers@balljanik.com

CHRISTOPHER M. WALTERS, born Santa Monica, California, 1961; admitted to bar, 1986, California (Inactive); 1990, Oregon. *Education:* Stanford University (A.B., with honors, 1983); Boalt Hall School of Law, University of California (J.D., 1986). Phi Beta Kappa. Associate Editor, California Law Review, 1986. Judicial Extern to Chief Justice Malcolm Lucas, California Supreme Court, 1985. Author, "Suits for Partition," *Real Estate Disputes,* Oregon State Bar, 1993. *Member:* Oregon State Bar; State Bar of California (Executive Committee Officer, Section on Real Estate and Land Use). ***PRACTICE AREAS:*** Real Estate; Construction; Finance; Commercial; Corporate. ***Email:*** cwalters@balljanik.com

CHRISTEN CARLSON WHITE, born Coronado, California, 1966; admitted to bar, 1995, Oregon. *Education:* University of California (B.A., 1990); Boalt Hall School of Law, University of California, Berkeley (J.D., 1995). Order of the Coif. Environmental Law Certificate. Executive Editor, Ecology Law Quarterly, 1994-1995. Author: "Regulation of Leaky Underground Fuel Tanks: An Anatomy of Regulatory Failure," UCLA Envtl. Law & Pol'y Rev., 1995. *Member:* Oregon State Bar. ***PRACTICE AREAS:*** Environmental; Land Use; Natural Resources. ***Email:*** cwhite@balljanik.com

SENIOR COUNSEL

ROBERT S. BALL, born Red Lodge, Montana, 1941; admitted to bar, 1967, Oregon. *Education:* Whitman College (B.A., 1964); Boalt Hall School of Law, University of California (J.D., 1967). Editor, Real Estate Law, Oregon State Bar, 1982, 1985. Chairman, Continuing Legal Education Committee, 1979-1980; Member, Executive Committee, Section on Real Estate and Land Use, Oregon State Bar, 1981. *Member:* Multnomah County and American Bar Associations; Oregon State Bar; American College of Real Estate Lawyers. ***PRACTICE AREAS:*** Business Law; Real Estate. ***Email:*** rball@balljanik.com

SPECIAL COUNSEL

CRAIG A. CROTTEAU, born Sandpoint, Idaho, 1954; admitted to bar, 1987, Pennsylvania; 1988, District of Columbia; 1997, Oregon; 2002, Washington; registered to practice before U.S. Patent and Trademark Office. *Education:* Gonzaga University (B.S., Civil Engineering, 1976); University of Denver (M.B.A., 1978); George Washington University (J.D., 1987). Trial Attorney, European District, USACE, Germany, 1990-1993. Project Manager, Spring Valley Chemical Weapons Cleanup, Baltimore District, USACE, 1993-1995. Deputy Program Manager, Environmental Division, HQ, USACE, 1995-1997. Vice President: The IT Group, Inc., 1997-2002; MWH, Inc., 2002-2004. Chief Operating Officer, CMI, LLC, 2004-2005. Member, National Board of Directors, Society of American Military Engineers, 1987-1989. Member, Board of Directors, Hazardous Waste Action Coalition, 1998- 2002. Registered Professional Engineer, Virginia, 1988. Member, Board of Trustees, University of Findlay, 2000—. Member, Board of Advisors, National Infrastructure Institute, 2003—. Member, Army Engineer Association. *Member:* Pennsylvania, Washington State and American Bar Associations; The District of Columbia Bar; Oregon State Bar. [Attorney, Office of the Chief Counsel, H.Q., U.S. Army Corps of Engineers (USACE), Washington, D.C., 1987-1989; Combat Engineer, Company Commander, Pentagon and Battalion Staff Officer, U.S. Army, 1978-1987; Officer and Retired Lieutenant Colonel, U.S. Army, 1976-1997]. (Also at Washington, D.C. Office). ***PRACTICE AREAS:*** Government Relations; Litigation; Construction Litigation. ***Email:*** ccrotteau@balljanik.com

(This Listing Continued)

ROBERT A. STOUT, born Cambridge, Massachusetts, 1946; admitted to bar, 1974, Oregon. *Education:* Michigan State University (B.A., 1968); Yale University (J.D., 1974). *Member:* Multnomah (Past Chair, CLE Committee) and Lane County (Member, CLE Committee) Bar Associations; Oregon State Bar (Member, Executive Committee, Business Law Section; Past Chair and Executive Committee Member, Securities Section; Past Executive Committee Member, Corporate Counsel Section; Past Executive Committee Member, Estate Planning and Administration Section; Member, Sections on: Securities Law; Business Law). [Lt. SC USN, 1968-1971]. (Also at Bend, Oregon Office). ***PRACTICE AREAS:*** Corporate Finance; Corporate Law; Mergers and Acquisitions; Securities; Real Estate; Health Care Law. ***Email:*** rstout@balljanik.com

OF COUNSEL

WILLIAM H. PERKINS, born Houston, Texas, 1951; admitted to bar, 1979, District of Columbia (Inactive); 1983, Oregon. *Education:* Williams College (B.A., magna cum laude, 1973); Georgetown University Law Center (J.D., magna cum laude, 1979) Phi Beta Kappa. *Member:* Oregon State Bar; American Bar Association. ***PRACTICE AREAS:*** Complex Real Estate; Commercial Transactions; Business; Financing. ***Email:*** wperkins@balljanik.com

RICHARD J. STONE, born Chicago, Illinois, 1945; admitted to bar, 1971, California and U.S. District Court, Central District of California; 1977, U.S. District Court, Northern District of California and U.S. Court of Appeals, District of Columbia Circuit; 1986, U.S. Court of Appeals, Federal Circuit; 1987, U.S. Court of Appeals, Ninth Circuit; 1994, Oregon and U.S. District Court, Southern District of California; 1998, U.S. District Court, District of Oregon; 2000, District of Columbia; 2004, Washington. *Education:* University of Chicago (B.A., 1967); University of California at Los Angeles (J.D., 1970). Editor-in-Chief, UCLA Law Review, 1969-1970. Adjunct Professor of Law, Northwestern School of Law of Lewis & Clark College, 1998-1999. Deputy Assistant General Counsel, Intelligence, International and Investigative Programs, U.S. Department of Defense, 1978-1979. Assistant to the Secretary, U.S. Department of Energy, 1979-1980. General Counsel and Staff Director, Study and Report by the Special Advisor to the Los Angeles Board of Police Commissioners on the Civil Disorder in Los Angeles, 1992. Director, 1991-1998 and President, 1997-1998, Legal Aid Foundation of Los Angeles. Lawyer Representative, Ninth Circuit Judicial Conference, 1997-1998. Fellow, American Bar Foundation. *Member:* Los Angeles County (Trustee, 1986-1988; Chair, Antitrust Section, 1987-1988; Chair, Federal Courts Practices and Procedures Committee, 1987-1988), Multnomah County and American Bar Associations; State Bar of California; Oregon State Bar (Member: Ethics Committee, 2002-2003; Special Committee on Professional Rules, 2002); District of Columbia Bar; Washington State Bar Association. ***PRACTICE AREAS:*** Litigation. ***Email:*** rstone@balljanik.com

ASSOCIATES

AMY S. CAMPBELL, born Tillamook, Oregon, 1971; admitted to bar, 2002, Oregon and U.S. District Court, District of Oregon; 2004, U.S. Court of Appeals, Ninth Circuit. *Education:* University of Portland (B.A., Political Science, 1994); Northwestern School of Law of Lewis & Clark College (J.D., cum laude, 2002). *Member:* Oregon State Bar. ***PRACTICE AREAS:*** Labor and Employment; Commercial Litigation. ***Email:*** acampbell@balljanik.com

DENISE R. CASE, born Phoenix, Arizona, 1978; admitted to bar, 2003, New Jersey and Pennsylvania (Not admitted in Oregon). *Education:* University of Washington (B.A., 2000); Rutgers University School of Law (J.D., 2003). Notes and Casenotes Editor, Rutgers Law Journal, 2002-2003. Recipient, Rutgers-Camden Pro Bono Award, 2003. Author: "The USA Patriot Act: Adding Bite to the Fight Against Animal Rights Terrorism?" 34 Rutgers Law Journal 187, Fall 2002. ***PRACTICE AREAS:*** Commercial Finance; Real Estate Sales; Real Estate Acquisitions; Real Estate Leasing; Real Property Finance. ***Email:*** dcase@balljanik.com

DWAIN M. CLIFFORD, born Albuquerque, New Mexico, 1966; admitted to bar, 2000, Texas (inactive); 2002, Oregon and U.S. District Court, District of Oregon. *Education:* New Mexico State University (B.A., English, with honors, 1988); University of New Mexico (M.A., Secondary Education, 1990); University of Texas at Austin (J.D., with honors, 2000). Order of the Coif. Associate Editor, Texas Law Review. *Member:* Oregon State Bar; Texas Young Lawyers Association. ***PRACTICE AREAS:*** Commercial Litigation; Construction Law. ***Email:*** dclifford@balljanik.com

REAGAN L.B. DESMOND, born Lancaster, Pennsylvania, 1967; admitted to bar, 1997, Utah; 2001, California; 2004, Oregon. *Education:* Indiana University of Pennsylvania (B.S., 1990); University of Utah Law School (J.D., 1997). *Member:* Oregon State Bar; State Bar of California; Utah State Bar; American Bar Association (Member, Natural Resources, Energy and Environmental Law Section). (Also at Bend, Oregon Office). ***PRACTICE AREAS:*** Land Use; Environmental; Water Quality; Water Rights; Public Agency Law; California Environmental Quality Act (CEQA). ***Email:*** rdesmond@balljanik.com

RENEE M. FRANCE, born Boulder, Colorado, 1972; admitted to bar, 2000, Oregon. *Education:* University of California at Santa Barbara (B.A., with honors, 1995); Northwestern School of Law of Lewis & Clark College (J.D., cum laude, 2000). Associate Editor, 1999-2000, Member, 1998-1999, Environmental Law. ***PRACTICE AREAS:*** Land Use; Environmental; Natural Resources. ***Email:*** rfrance@balljanik.com

AARON D. GOLDSTEIN, born Portland, Oregon, 1977; admitted to bar, 2003, Washington and U.S. District Court, Western District of Washington (Not admitted in Oregon). *Education:* Cornell University (B.A., Government, 2000); University of Southern California (J.D., 2003). Order of the Coif. Executive Articles Editor, Southern California Law Review, 2002-2003. Author, "Race, Reasonableness and the Rule of Law," 76 So. Cal. L. Rev. 1189 (Notes 2003). *Member:* Washington State Bar Association (Member, UCC Committee on Revised Article 1 and Amended Article 2, Business Law Section). ***PRACTICE AREAS:*** Employment Law; Commercial Litigation. ***Email:*** agoldstein@balljanik.com

JESSICA T. HAMILTON, born Evanston, Illinois, 1974; admitted to bar, 2003, Oregon and U.S. District Court, District of Oregon. *Education:* University of California at San Diego (B.A., 1996); University of Washington (J.D., with honors, 2003). Order of the Barristers. Editor-in-Chief, Pacific Rim Law & Policy Journal, 2002-2003. Author, "Rescued at Sea, But Nowhere to Go: The Cloudy Legal Waters of the Tampa Crisis," 11 Pac. Rim L. &

(This Listing Continued)

Pol'y J. 461 (2002). *Member:* Oregon State Bar. ***LANGUAGES:*** Spanish and Russian. ***PRACTICE AREAS:*** Commercial Litigation; Employment. ***Email:*** jhamilton@balljanik.com

DANA L. KRAWCZUK, born Plantation, Florida, 1974; admitted to bar, 1999, Oregon. *Education:* University of Georgia (B.A., cum laude, 1996); Northwestern School of Law (J.D., 1999). Recipient: Environmental Ethics Certificate, University of Georgia, 1996; Environmental and Natural Resources Certificate, Northwestern School of Law of Lewis & Clark College, 1999. Co-Author: "The Antidegradation Policy of the Clean Water Act: A Primer and Case Law Update," 4 West. Water L. & Pol'y Rptr 241, 2000. *Member:* Oregon State Bar (Member, Sections on: Real Estate; Land Use; Environmental and Natural Resources). ***PRACTICE AREAS:*** Land Use; Environmental; Natural Resources. ***Email:*** dkrawczuk@balljanik.com

KEVIN S. MAPES, born Portland, Oregon, 1967; admitted to bar, 1994, California and U.S. District Court, Central, Northern, Eastern, and Southern Districts of California; 2002, Oregon. *Education:* University of Puget Sound (B.A., 1989), Phi Beta Kappa; Northwestern School of Law of Lewis & Clark College (J.D., cum laude, 1994). *Member:* Oregon State Bar; State Bar of California. ***PRACTICE AREAS:*** Commercial Litigation; Insurance Recovery; Environmental Litigation; Construction Law. ***Email:*** kmapes@balljanik.com

JEANA M. McGLASSON, born Fargo, North Dakota, 1971; admitted to bar, 2003, Oregon. *Education:* Oregon State University (B.S., Business Administration, 1993); University of Oregon (J.D., 2003); University of Washington (LL.M., Taxation, 2004). *Member:* Oregon State Bar (Member, Sections on: Tax; Estate Planning and Administration); American Bar Association (Member, Tax Section); American Association of Attorneys - Certified Public Accountants; American Institute of Certified Public Accountants; Oregon Society of Certified Public Accountants. ***PRACTICE AREAS:*** Probate; Taxation; Estate Planning; Trust Administration. ***Email:*** jmcglasson@balljanik.com

JAMES C. PRICHARD, born Ashland, Oregon, 1974; admitted to bar, 1999, Oregon; 2000, Washington, U.S. Court of Appeals, Ninth Circuit, and U.S. District Court, District of Oregon; 2001, California, U.S. District Court, Northern District of California, and U.S. District Court, Western District of Washington; 2002, U.S. District Court, Southern District of California and U.S. District Court, Central District of California; 2003, U.S. District Court, Eastern District of Washington. *Education:* University of Oregon (B.S., magna cum laude, 1995; J.D., 1999). Recipient, Otto Frohnmayer Scholarship. *Member:* Multnomah County, Washington State and American Bar Associations; Oregon State Bar; State Bar of California. ***PRACTICE AREAS:*** Construction; Surety; Commercial Litigation; Bankruptcy. ***Email:*** jprichard@balljanik.com

ROBERT L. TAYLOR, born Grants Pass, Oregon, 1977; admitted to bar, 2004, Oregon. *Education:* Brown University (B.A., with honors, Public Policy, 1999); Willamette University (J.D., magna cum laude, 2004). *Member:* Oregon State Bar. ***PRACTICE AREAS:*** Commercial Litigation; Construction Law; Insurance Recovery; Environmental Litigation. ***Email:*** rtaylor@balljanik.com

REBECCA BIERMANN TOM, born Portland, Oregon, 1967; admitted to bar, 1995, Oregon. *Education:* University of Washington (B.A., with honors, 1989); Willamette University (J.D., magna cum laude, 1995). Member, Golden Key Honor Society. Willamette Law Review Form Editor, 1994-1995 and Member, 1993-1994. *Member:* Oregon State Bar; American Bar Association. ***PRACTICE AREAS:*** Real Estate; Corporate; Business; Estate Planning; Construction Law. ***Email:*** rtom@balljanik.com

KRISTIN L. UDVARI, born Hanover, New Hampshire, 1974; admitted to bar, 1999, Oregon; 2004, Washington. *Education:* Yale University (B.A., 1996); Northwestern School of Law of Lewis & Clark College (J.D., cum laude, 1999). Articles Editor, Environmental Law, Northwestern School of Law, Lewis and Clark Law Review, 1998-1999. Co-Chair, Environmental Law Caucus, 1997-1998. *Member:* Oregon State Bar; Washington State Bar Association. (Also at Bend, Oregon Office). ***PRACTICE AREAS:*** Land Use; Environmental; Natural Resources. ***Email:*** kudvari@balljanik.com

ROBERT W. WILKINSON, born Chicago, Illinois, 1969; admitted to bar, 1999, Oregon; 2002, U.S. Court of Appeals, Ninth Circuit and U.S. District Court, District of Oregon. *Education:* Northwestern University (B.A., 1991); University of Oregon School of Law (J.D., 1999). Law Clerk to Hon. Janice M. Stewart, Magistrate Judge, U.S. District Court, District of Oregon, 1999-2001. *Member:* Multnomah County Bar Association; Oregon State Bar. ***PRACTICE AREAS:*** Commercial Litigation; Construction. ***Email:*** rwilkinson@balljanik.com

GOVERNMENT RELATIONS SPECIALISTS

MICHELLE GIGUERE, born Whittier, California, 1956. *Education:* Linfield College (1978). Legislative Director, Congressman Les AuCoin, 1979-1988. (Also at Washington, D.C. Office). ***PRACTICE AREAS:*** Government Relations; Specializing in Federal Legislative Appropriations and Authorizations Issues. ***Email:*** mgiguere@balljanik.com

DANIEL M. JAMES, born Missoula, Montana, 1964. *Education:* Pacific University (B.A., 1987). Legislative Staff, Congressman Les AuCoin, Washington, D.C., 1986-1989. Director of Alumni Relations, Pacific University, 1989-1991. Federal Affairs Representative, Pacific Northwest Waterways Association, Vancouver, Washington, 1992-2000. (Also at Washington, D.C. Office). ***PRACTICE AREAS:*** Government Relations; Specializing in Federal Legislative Appropriation and Authorization Issues. ***Email:*** djames@balljanik.com

REPRESENTATIVE CLIENTS: American Forest Resource Council; Aspen Hotel Management Group; Brooks Resources; Capital Crossing Bank; Centex Real Estate Corporation; City Center Parking; City of Las Vegas; City of Vancouver; Clackamas Co.; Coastal Conservation Association; Community Bank; Downtown Development Group; EC Company; Eagle Crest Partners; Fidelity National Title Company; Homestreet Bank; Hoyt Street Properties, LLC; Legacy Health System; Marsh & McLennan Companies, Inc.; Matrix Homes; May Department Stores Company; Melvin Mark Companies; Mount Hood Meadows; NAI; Norris, Beggs & Simpson; Northwest Container Services; Opus Northwest; Oregon Health & Science University (OHSU); Oregon Ironworks; Oregon Museum of Science & Industry; Oregon Newspaper Publishers Assn.; Oregon Scientific, Inc.; Pacific Crest Technology, Inc.; Polygon Northwest Company; Pronghorn Resort; Schnitzer Investment Corp.; Shipbuilders Council of America; Sunriver Resort Limited Partnership; Taiwan Semiconductor; Temp Control Mechanical; The Greenbrier Companies; The State of Oregon; Trammell Crow Co.; Trammell Crow Residential; Twin Star International; WaferTech LLC; Washington State Public Stadium Authority; William Felton & Associates; William Smith Properties; Williams & Dame Development Company, Inc.; WSCO Petroleum Corporation.

(For Complete Biographical Data on Personnel at Washington, D.C., and Bend, Oregon, see Professional Biographies at those locations)

BANKS LAW OFFICE, P.C.

Established in 1985

200 S.W. MARKET STREET, SUITE 1600
PORTLAND, OREGON 97201
Telephone: 503-222-7475
Telecopier: 503-248-0138
URL: http://www.investordefender.com
Email: info@investordefender.com
URL: http://www.lawyers.com/investordefender

Securities Fraud, Stockbroker Arbitration, Investor Rights, Investment Fraud, Business Torts, Securities Arbitration, Legal Malpractice in State and Federal Courts and before NASD, NYSE and AAA Arbitration Panels.

FIRM PROFILE: The firm emphasizes plaintiff-oriented litigation in the areas of stockbroker arbitration, securities fraud, business torts and shareholder rights. The firm has a national practice with clients throughout the United States.

ROBERT S. BANKS, JR., born Newark, New Jersey, June 5, 1955; admitted to bar, 1982, Wisconsin and Oregon; 1984, Massachusetts. *Education:* Reed College (B.A., 1977); University of Wisconsin Law School (J.D., 1982). Recipient, Distinguished Service Award, 1988 and President's Award, 1991, Federal Bar Association. Author: "Clearing Firms and the 2002 Uniform Securities Act: What you Didn't Know Could Have Hurt You," Practicing Law Institute Securities Arbitration 2003; "Judgments in Federal Court," Oregon State Bar Federal Civil Litigation in Oregon, 1993; "Of Bucket Shops and Boiler Rooms: A Primer on Micro-Cap Stock Fraud," Oregon Trial Lawyers Magazine, Fall 1998; "Investor Protection-Not SIPC and the Securities Investor Protection Act," Practicing Law Institute Securities Arbitration 2000; "Clearing Firms, The Uniform Securities Act and Koruga v. Fiserv Correspondent Services, Inc," Practicing Law Institute Securities Arbitration 2001; "Technology Market Woes" Oregon Trial Lawyers Magazine, Winter, 2002. Speaker: "Cross Examining Expert Witnesses" (PIABA Annual Meeting, 2003); "New Developments In Securities Arbitration" (Oregon State Bar Securities Section, May, 2004); Northwest Securities Institute, 1995-1998, 2002; Oregon State Bar, New Lawyers Section, "Deposition Basics," 1995, 1996 and 1998; Practicing Law Institute Securities Arbitration Program, 2001. Legal Writing Instructor, University of Wisconsin Law School, 1980-1981, 1981-1982. Member, Board of Directors, Public Investors Arbitration Bar Association (PIABA) (Board Member, Executive Committee, 2002-2003). Member, National Arbitration and Mediation Committee, NASD, 2002-2004. *Member:* Multnomah County, Massachusetts and Federal (President, Oregon Chapter, 1991-1992) Bar Associations; State Bar of Wisconsin; Oregon State Bar (Member: Securities Regulation Section; Chairperson, Executive Committee; Litigation Section, 1997-1998; Executive Committee, Antitrust Section, 1999-2001); Oregon Trial Lawyers Association (Chair, Business Litigation Section, 1993-1995). ***PRACTICE AREAS:*** Broker-Dealer Arbitration; NASD Arbitration; Securities Arbitration; Securities Fraud; Securities Litigation; Shareholder Rights. ***Email:*** RBanks@bankslawoffice.com

REFERENCE: Bank of America.

BANNER & WITCOFF, LTD.

Established In 1920 - Predecessor Parent

601 SW SECOND AVENUE
SUITE 1900
PORTLAND, OREGON 97204
Telephone: 503-425-6800
Fax: 503-425-6801
Email: info@bannerwitcoff.com
URL: http://www.bannerwitcoff.com

Chicago, Illinois Office: Ten South Wacker Drive, Suite 3000. Telephone: 312-463-5000. Facsimile: 312-463-5001.

Washington, D.C. Office: 1001 G Street, N.W., Suite 1100 Telephone: 202-824-3000. Facsimile: 202-824-3001.

Boston, Massachusetts Office: 28 State Street, 28th Floor. Telephone: 617-720-9600. Fax: 617-720-9601.

Intellectual Property including Procurement of Patents, Trademarks, Copyrights, Trade Secrets, Counseling & Opinions, Unfair Competition, Interferences, Licensing, Antitrust and International Trade Matters. Litigation including Trials and Appeals in Federal and State Courts and International Trade Commission.

FIRM PROFILE: Banner & Witcoff, Ltd. is dedicated to excellence in the specialized practice of intellectual property law, including patent, trademark, copyright, trade secret, computer, franchise and unfair competition law. The firm provides legal representation in obtaining, commercializing and litigating intellectual property rights in the United States and abroad. Firm attorneys practice in all technologies, including the electrical, mechanical and chemical arts as well as computer hardware and software, internet and e-commerce, and biotechnology.

THOMAS L. EVANS, admitted to bar, 1994, Virginia; 1996, District of Columbia; 2001, Oregon; registered to practice before U.S. Patent and Trademark Office. *Education:* University of Virginia (B.S.E.E., 1989); George Mason University School of Law (J.D., 1994). *Member:* The District of Columbia Bar; American Bar Associations; American Intellectual Property Law Association. ***PRACTICE AREAS:*** Intellectual Property Law; Patents; Patent Prosecution; International Trade; Electronic Intellectual Property Law. ***Email:*** tevans@bannerwitcoff.com

(This Listing Continued)

BANNER & WITCOFF, LTD., Portland—Continued

BYRON S. KUZARA, admitted to bar, 2000, Oregon; registered to practice before the U.S. Patent and Trademark Office. *Education:* University of Wyoming (B.S.M.E., 1996; J.D., 2000). *Member:* American Intellectual Property Law Association. ***PRACTICE AREAS:*** Intellectual Property; Patents. ***Email:*** bkuzara@bannerwitcoff.com

(For Complete Biographical Data on other Personnel, see Professional Biographies at Boston, Massachusetts, Chicago, Illinois and Washington, D.C.)

LAW OFFICE OF LAWRENCE BARON, PC

1515 S.W. FIFTH AVENUE, SUITE 808
PORTLAND, OREGON 97201
Telephone: 503-417-1117
Fax: 503-417-1118
URL: http://www.lawyers.com/baron
Email: baron@baronlawfirm.com
URL: http://www.baronlawfirm.com

Product Liability, Medical Malpractice, Lasik Eye Surgery, Air Bag Injuries, Automobile Defect Claims (Crash Worthiness) Wrongful Death, Maritime and Railroad Injuries.

LAWRENCE BARON, born Detroit, Michigan, April 9, 1950; admitted to bar, 1975, Michigan and U.S. District Court, Eastern District of Michigan; 1978, U.S. Court of Appeals, Sixth Circuit; 1981, Oregon; 1984, U.S. District Court, District of Oregon. *Education:* Kalamazoo College (B.A., cum laude, 1972); Wayne State University (J.D., 1974); National Institute for Trial Advocacy. Phi Beta Kappa. Recipient 1997 National Trial Lawyer of The Year Award (Trial Lawyers for Public Justice). Lecturer, Product Liability and Medical Malpractice. *Member:* Multnomah Bar Association; Oregon State Bar (Member, Product Liability Section; Former Member, Uniform Civil Jury Instruction Committee; Federal Practice and Procedure Committee); Oregon Trial Lawyers Association; The Association of Trial Lawyers of America; Attorney Information Exchange Group (Member, former Board of Directors); State Bar of Michigan (inactive). ***REPORTED CASES:*** Fulmer v. Timber Inn Restaurant and Lounge, Inc., 330 Or. 413, 9 P.3d 710 (2000); Gaussoin v. Port of Portland, 927 P2d 601; Trabosh v. Washington County, 915 P2d 1011; Whitley v. Southern Pacific Transp. Co., 902 P2d 1196. ***PRACTICE AREAS:*** Product Liability; Medical Malpractice; Lasik Eye Surgery; Air Bag Injuries; Automobile Defect Claims (crashworthiness); Wrongful Death; Maritime and Railroad Injuries. ***Email:*** baron@baronlawfirm.com

BARRACK LAW FIRM, P.C.

1675 S.W. MARLOW AVENUE
SUITE 340
PORTLAND, OREGON 97225
Telephone: 971-222-3646
Fax: 971-275-1023
Email: info@barrack.net
URL: http://www.barrack.net

Technology and Computer Law, Outsourcing, Strategic Alliances, Corporate Law, Finance, Real Estate, Intellectual Property, Mergers, Acquisitions and Divestitures, Arbitration, Mediation and Corporate Training.

MARTIN J. BARRACK, born Brooklyn, New York, February 28, 1961; admitted to bar, 1989, California and Washington; 1991, Colorado and Alaska; 2004, Oregon. *Education:* Cornell University (B.S., 1983); University of California at Los Angeles (J.D., 1988); Vanderbilt University (M.B.A., 1999). Beta Gamma Sigma. Dean's Award. Order of the Coif. Law Clerk to Judge Andrew J. Kleinfeld, U.S. District Court, District of Alaska, 1988-1989. Adjunct Professor, University of Alaska - Anchorage, School of Business, 1992. *Member:* State Bar of California; Oregon State Bar; Washington State, The Colorado and Alaska (inactive) Bar Associations. ***PRACTICE AREAS:*** Technology; Computer Law; Outsourcing; Strategic Alliances; Corporate Law; Finance; Real Estate; Intellectual Property; Mergers, Acquisitions and Divestitures; Arbitration; Mediation; Corporate Training. ***Email:*** marty@barrack.net

REPRESENTATIVE CLIENTS: The TriZetto Group, Inc.; Bridgespan Capital; Dealer Technology Group. *Of Counsel to:* Tindall Bennett & Shoup, Anchorage, AK.

BARRAN LIEBMAN LLP

Established in 1998
601 SW SECOND AVENUE, SUITE 2300
PORTLAND, OREGON 97204-3159
Telephone: 503-228-0500
Fax: 503-274-1212
Email: clientservices@barran.com
URL: http://www.barran.com

Labor and Employment Law.

MEMBERS OF FIRM

NELSON D. ATKIN II, born Syracuse, New York, January 1, 1949; admitted to bar, 1974, Oregon. *Education:* State University of New York at Albany (B.S., 1970); Syracuse University (J.D., cum laude, 1974). Phi Alpha Delta; Order of the Coif. Survey Editor, Syracuse Law Review, 1973-1974. *Member:* Oregon State Bar (Member, Executive Committee, Labor and Employment Section, 1981-1982, 1983-1984, 1995-1997; Treasurer, 1997-1998; Secretary, 1998-1999; Chair-Elect, 1999-2000; Chair, 2001); American Bar Association (Member, Section of the Labor and Employment Law Committee on the Development of the Law Under the NLRA; Associate Editor, The Developing Labor Law 4th Ed., Supps.). Fellow, College of Labor and Employment Lawyers. ***PRACTICE AREAS:*** Management Labor Law; Wage and Hour Law; Affirmative Action; Collective Bargaining. ***Email:*** natkin@barran.com

PAULA A. BARRAN, born Warren, Ohio, March 21, 1949; admitted to bar, 1980, Oregon; 1984, Washington. *Education:* College of William & Mary (B.A., summa cum laude, 1971); Cornell University (M.A., 1973); University of British Columbia (Ph.D., 1976); Osgoode Hall (LL.B., with honors, Silver Medal, 1979); University of Oregon (M.B.A., 1991). Phi Beta Kappa. Listed in: Best Lawyers In America, 2001—. Adjunct Professor, Willamette University College of Law, 2000-2001. *Member:* Life Fellow, American Bar Foundation. ***PRACTICE AREAS:*** Employment Law; Employment Discrimination; Wrongful Termination Defense; Management Labor Law; Defense Litigation. ***Email:*** pbarran@barran.com

BRENDA K. BAUMGART, born Lewiston, Idaho, January 17, 1973; admitted to bar, 1999, Oregon. *Education:* Williamette University (B.A., 1995; J.D., 1999). Phi Delta Phi. Note/Comment Editor, Willamette Law Review, 1997-1999. Member, Moot Court Board, 1997-1999. *Member:* Oregon State Bar; American and Federal Bar Associations. ***PRACTICE AREAS:*** Employment Litigation; Appellate Practice. ***Email:*** bbaumgart@barran.com

LISA C. BROWN, born Salt Lake City, Utah, May 28, 1954; admitted to bar, 1979, Oregon. *Education:* Swarthmore College and Northwestern University (B.A., 1976); George Washington University (J.D., 1979). Phi Beta Kappa. Barrister, American Inn of Court, XXVIII, 1987-1991. Speaker, Oregon Law Institute. Assistant Attorney General, Oregon Department of Justice, 1979-1981. Member, Multnomah County Arbitration Panel. Arbitrator, American Arbitration Association. *Member:* Multnomah County Bar Association; Oregon State Bar (Member: Local Professional Responsibility Committee for Multnomah County, 1988-1991); Oregon Association of Defense Counsel; Defense Research Institute (Council on Court Procedures). ***PRACTICE AREAS:*** Employment Law; Commercial Litigation; Alternative Dispute Resolution. ***Email:*** lbrown@barran.com

ROBERT L. CAREY, born La Grande, Oregon, November 8, 1961; admitted to bar, 1987, Oregon; 2001, District of Columbia; 2002, Washington. *Education:* Harvard University (B.A., Economics, 1984); Willamette University (J.D., 1987). Member, Willamette Law Review, 1986-1987. The Order of Barristers. [Maj., U.S. Army, JAGC, 1987-1993; USAR, 1994-1996]. ***PRACTICE AREAS:*** Complex Litigation; Employment Discrimination; Wrongful Termination Defense; Employment Law; Professional Liability Insurance Coverage. ***Email:*** rcarey@barran.com

TODD A. HANCHETT, born Plant City, Florida, October 3, 1974; admitted to bar, 1999, Oregon. *Education:* Walla Walla College (B.S., cum laude, 1996); Willamette University (J.D., 1999). *Member:* Multnomah and American Bar Associations; Oregon State Bar. ***PRACTICE AREAS:*** Employment Law; Employment Discrimination; Employment Litigation; Retaliatory Discharge; Management Labor Law. ***Email:*** thanchett@barran.com

EDWIN A. HARNDEN, born Medford, Oregon, November 13, 1946; admitted to bar, 1972, Oregon; 2000, District of Columbia; 2002, Washington; 2003, Idaho. *Education:* Columbia University (B.A., 1969; J.D., 1972). Harlan Fiske Stone Scholar. Recipient: 1990 Merit Award, Multnomah County Bar Association; 2002 Merit Award, Oregon State Bar Association. Member, Board of Directors, President, 1992, Oregon Law Related Education. Member: Portland Business Alliance; Board, Japan-American Society of Oregon. Ninth Circuit Membership Chairman, U.S. Supreme Court Historical Society. Member, Board of Directors, President, Oregon Courts Historical Society. Director, 1994-1995; Chair, Professional Liability Fund. Co-Chair, Annual Campaign for Equal Justice, 2002. Chair, State of Access to Justice in Oregon, 2002. *Member:* Multnomah County Bar Association (Director; President, 1996-1997); American and Federal Bar Associations; Oregon State Bar (President, 2001; Board of Governors; Board of Examiners); Oregon Association of Defense Counsel; Defense Research Institute; Federation of Insurance Counsel. Life Fellow, American Bar Foundation. (Managing Partner). ***PRACTICE AREAS:*** Employment Litigation; Executive Employment Law; Employer Liability; Professional Liability Insurance Coverage; Complex Commercial Litigation. ***Email:*** eharnden@barran.com

RICHARD C. HUNT, born Palo Alto, California, March 20, 1942; admitted to bar, 1967, California; 1968, Oregon; 1984, Washington; 2003, Idaho. *Education:* Stanford University (B.A., 1964); Boalt Hall School of Law, University of California (J.D., 1967). Associate Editor, California Law Review, 1966-1967. Law Clerk, Oregon Supreme Court, 1967-1968. Adjunct Professor of Law, Labor, Lewis & Clark Law School, 1986. ***PRACTICE AREAS:*** Management Labor Law; Employment Litigation; Executive Employment Law; Contract Litigation; Trade Secrets; Noncompetition and Non-Solicitation Agreements; Agency and Distributorships. ***Email:*** rhunt@barran.com

ALLYSON S. KRUEGER, born Harbor City, California, May 9, 1965; admitted to bar, 1996, Oregon; 1997, Washington. *Education:* University of California, Irvine (B.A., magna cum laude, 1993); University of Oregon (J.D., 1996). Order of the Coif. Recipient, American Jurisprudence Award, Legal Research and Writing. *Member:* Oregon State Bar; Washington State and American Bar Associations. ***PRACTICE AREAS:*** Employment Law; Employment Discrimination; Wrongful Termination Defense; Management Labor Law; Defense Litigation. ***Email:*** akrueger@barran.com

RICHARD F. LIEBMAN, born Medford, Oregon, September 11, 1947; admitted to bar, 1972, Hawaii; 1976, Oregon and District of Columbia. *Education:* University of California at Berkeley (B.A., 1969); Boalt Hall School of Law, University of California (J.D., 1972). Instructor, Equal Employment Opportunity Law, Portland State University. Listed in Best Lawyers in America, 1995—. Management Editor, Oregon Employment Law, Oregon State Bar. *Member:* Tri-County Affirmative Action Association (Chair, 1985-1986 and Board Member, 1983-1993; Management Editor, Labor and Employment Law-Private Sector, published by Oregon State Bar, 1989, 1994, 1997, 2002); Oregon State Bar (Member, Executive Committee, 1987-1992; Chair, Labor Section, 1990-1991; Member, Civil Rights Section Executive Committee). Fellow, College of Labor and Employment Lawyers. ***PRACTICE AREAS:*** Employment Law; Collective Bargaining; Equal Employment Opportunity Law; Management Labor Law; Wage and Hour Law. ***Email:*** rliebman@barran.com

BRADLEY F. TELLAM, born Wimpole Park, England, April 8, 1957; admitted to bar, 1982, Washington; 1984, Oregon. *Education:* Claremont Men's College (B.A., 1979);

(This Listing Continued)

Loyola University (J.D., 1982). Law Clerk, U.S. District Court, Southern District of California, 1982-1984. **PRACTICE AREAS:** Employment Litigation; Attorney Discipline; Legal Ethics; Federal Employment Law; Professional Liability Insurance Coverage. **Email:** btellam@barran.com

RICHARD N. VANCLEAVE, born Ontario, Oregon, November 20, 1953; admitted to bar, 1980, Oregon. *Education:* Oregon State University (B.S., with honors, 1977); Willamette University (J.D., cum laude, 1980). **PRACTICE AREAS:** Management Labor Relations Law; Employment Law; Employment Discrimination Law. **Email:** rvancleave@barran.com

MARYANN YELNOSKY, born Paterson, New Jersey, April 3, 1954; admitted to bar, 1986, Oregon; 1996, Washington. *Education:* University of Oregon (B.S., 1976; J.D., 1986). Order of the Coif. *Member:* Oregon State Bar; Multnomah County, Washington State and American Bar Associations. **PRACTICE AREAS:** Employment Litigation; Employment Law; Federal Employment Law; Wrongful Termination. **Email:** myelnosky@barran.com

---

KRISTIN L. BREMER, born New Braunfels, Texas, September 18, 1973; admitted to bar, 2003, Oregon. *Education:* University of Texas at Austin (B.A., 1997); Willamette University (J.D., cum laude, 2003). **PRACTICE AREAS:** Employment Law; Employment Litigation. **Email:** kbremer@barran.com

KIMBERLY C. CAPOBIANCO, born Lake Charles, Louisiana, June 18, 1976; admitted to bar, 2001, Massachusetts; 2004, Oregon. *Education:* Texas A & M University (B.A., cum laude, 1998); New York University (J.D., 2001). Golden Key International Honor Society. **PRACTICE AREAS:** Employment Law; Employment Litigation; Employment Discrimination. **Email:** kcapobianco@barran.com

KAREN L. O'CONNOR, born Lafayette, Indiana, March 20, 1966; admitted to bar, 1995, Oregon; 1997, Washington. *Education:* Mount Holyoke College (B.A., 1988); University of Oregon (J.D., 1995). Editor-in-Chief, Oregon Law Review, 1994-1995. Law Clerk to Honorable Malcolm F. Marsh, U.S. District Judge, 1995-1997. **LANGUAGES:** German. **PRACTICE AREAS:** Employment Litigation; Noncompetition and Non-Solicitation Agreements; Trade Secrets. **Email:** koconnor@barran.com

ANDREW M. SCHPAK, born Los Angeles, California, January 2, 1980; admitted to bar, 2004, Oregon. *Education:* Reed College (B.A., 2001); Cornell University Law School (J.D., 2004). *Member:* Multnomah County Bar Association (Membership Committee, Young Lawyers Section); Oregon State Bar. **LANGUAGES:** French. **PRACTICE AREAS:** Employment Law; Employment Litigation; Employment Discrimination; Management Labor Law. **Email:** aschpak@barran.com

KIMBERLY A. SORDYL, born Flint, Michigan, June 8, 1969; admitted to bar, 1999, Michigan; 2003, Oregon. *Education:* University of Michigan (B.A., with honors, 1994); University of Detroit Mercy (J.D., magna cum laude, 1998). Member, Justice Frank Murphy Honor Society. Case/Comment Editor, 1997-1998, Associate Editor, 1996-1997, University of Detroit Law Review. Recipient, Dean's Scholarship for Academic Excellence, 1996-1998. Law Clerk, Justice Michael F. Cavanagh, Michigan Supreme Court, 1998-2000. *Member:* State Bar of Michigan; Oregon State Bar. **PRACTICE AREAS:** Employment Litigation; Labor Law; Appellate Practice. **Email:** ksordyl@barran.com

REPRESENTATIVE CLIENTS: Frito-Lay; Health Future LLC; Hollywood Entertainment Corp.; Intel Corp.; Lloyds of London; Louisiana-Pacific Corporation; Pacific Maritime Association; The Oregonian; Tri-Met; Xerox Corporation.

BARTON AND STREVER, P.C.

PORTLAND, OREGON

(See Newport)

Civil Litigation, Plaintiffs Trial Practice. Psychological and Physical Injury Claims including Sexual Exploitation. Sexual Abuse, Personal Injury, Insurance Bad Faith, Wrongful Death, Medical Malpractice, Psychiatric Malpractice. Criminal Defense, DUI Defense.

BAUMGARTNER, NELSON & PRICE, P.L.L.C.

PORTLAND, OREGON

(See Vancouver, Washington)

General Civil, Trial and Appellate Practice, Automobile Accidents, Personal Injury, Insurance, Medical Malpractice, Professional Negligence, Products Liability, Commercial Litigation, Criminal Defense, Legal Malpractice, Slip and Fall, Dog Bites, Wrongful Death, Nursing Home Abuse and Neglect, Domestic Violence, Driving While Intoxicated, Traffic Violations, Consumer Law, Unsafe Products.

BRETT N. BENDER

1000 S.W. BROADWAY, SUITE 2400
PORTLAND, OREGON 97205-3054
Telephone: 503-223-6337
Fax: 503-241-2249
Email: brett@benderlaw.us
URL: http://www.lawyers.com/brettbender

Family Law, Child Custody, Child Support, Divorce, Visitation Rights, Domestic Violence.

BRETT N. BENDER, born Mankato, Minnesota, August 23, 1957; admitted to bar, 1988, Washington; 1994, Oregon. *Education:* University of Oregon (B.S., 1980); Northwestern School of Law (J.D., 1987). Cornelius Honor Society. Author: Washington State Bar, Civil Procedure Desk Practice Manual on Pleading and Pleading-Special Matters, 1994. *Member:* Multnomah County, Clackamas, Clark County, Washington County and Washington State Bar Associations; Oregon State Bar. **PRACTICE AREAS:** Family Law.

CARMEL BENDER PC

610 S.W. BROADWAY, SUITE 303
PORTLAND, OREGON 97205
Telephone: 503-222-3116
Fax: 503-222-3116
Email: carmelbender@comcast.net
URL: http://www.lawyers.com/carmelbender

General Practice.

CARMEL BENDER, born December 23, 1964; admitted to bar, 2002, Oregon. *Education:* University of Oregon (B.A., Sociology, 1993; J.D., 1996).

BIRDWELL & JANKE LLP

Established in 1991

1400 STANDARD PLAZA
1100 S.W. SIXTH AVENUE
PORTLAND, OREGON 97204-1221
Telephone: 503-228-1841
Fax: 503-228-2635
Email: portland@birdwelljanke.com
URL: http://www.birdwelljanke.com

Tucson, Arizona Office: 2301 E. Seventh Street, 85719. Telephone: 520-795-1446.

Intellectual Property including: Patent, Trademark, Copyright, Trade Secret and Unfair Competition Law, Licensing, Trials in State and Federal Courts, Practice before U.S. Patent and Trademark Office.

WILLIAM A. BIRDWELL, born Portland, Oregon, December 16, 1946; admitted to bar, 1973, Oregon and U.S. District Court, District of Oregon; 1982, U.S. Court of Appeals for the Federal Circuit; 1991, California; 1997, U.S. Court of Appeals, Ninth Circuit; 1998, U.S. District Court, Northern District of California; 1999, Arizona; registered to practice before U.S. Patent and Trademark Office. *Education:* Oregon State University (B.S.E.E., 1969); University of Colorado (J.D., 1973). Sigma Tau. Member, Board of Editors, University of Colorado Law Review, 1972-1973. Author: "Exhaustion of Rights and Patent Licensing Market Restrictions," 60 Journal of the Patent Office Society 203, 1978; "Business Names," Advising Oregon Businesses, 1985. Co-editor, Contract Law in Oregon, 1991. Co-Author, Chapters on Patent, Trademark and Copyright Law, Advising Small Business, Clark Boardman Callaghan, 1994. *Member:* Multnomah County and American Bar Associations; Oregon State Bar (Chairman, Patent and Trademark Section, 1981-1982; Member, Committee on Continuing Legal Education, 1985-1988); State Bar of California (Member, Intellectual Property Law Section); Oregon Patent Law Association; American Intellectual Property Law Association; Licensing Executives Society; Institute of Electrical and Electronics Engineers (Member, Lasers and Electro-Optics Society). **REPORTED CASES:** Kockums Industries Ltd. v. Salem Equipment, Inc., 561 F. Supp 168 (D. Or. 1983); Sun Studs, Inc. v. Applied Theory Associates, Inc., 772 F. 2d 1557 (Fed. Cir, 1985); Sun Studs, Inc. v. ATA Equipment Leasing, Inc. 655 F. Supp. 1013 (D.Or. 1987); inj. dissolved, 710 F. Supp. 1297; aff'd in part, rev'd in part, 8 72 F. 2d 987 (Fed. Cir. 1989); reh'g den., sug. for reh'g en banc accepted, 882 F. 2d 1583 (Fed. Cir. 1989); reh'g declined, opin. reinstated, 892 F. 2d 73 (Fed. Cir. 1989); John P. Jaqua v. Nike, Inc., 125 Or. App 294 (1993). **PRACTICE AREAS:** Patent; Trademarks; Trade Secrets; Copyrights; Unfair Competition; Litigation. **Email:** birdwell@birdwelljanke.com

GARTH JANKE, born Santa Monica, California, July 3, 1955; admitted to bar, 1994, Oregon; registered to practice before U.S. Patent and Trademark Office. *Education:* University of California at Davis (B.S. Mechanical Engineering, high honors, 1978; M.S., Materials Science and Electrical Engineering, 1980); Stanford University (J.D., 1994). Tau Beta Pi. Stanford Law Review. 1993-1994. *Member:* Oregon State Bar. (Resident). **PRACTICE AREAS:** Patent; Trade Secret; Trademark; Copyright; Unfair Competition. **Email:** janke@birdwelljanke.com

ASSOCIATES

ALLEN W. FIELD, born Kansas City, Missouri, August 9, 1960; admitted to bar, 1988, Oregon, U.S. District Court, District of Oregon, U.S. Court of Appeals, Ninth Circuit and U.S. Court of Appeals for the Federal Circuit. *Education:* Reed College (B.A., 1983); University of Oregon (J.D., 1988). Order of the Coif. Recipient, American Jurisprudence Award for: Real Property; Admiralty; Federal Income Tax. Law Clerk to Hon. John Jelderks, Hood River County, Oregon, 1988-1989. *Member:* Multnomah and American Bar Associations; Oregon State Bar; Oregon Trial Lawyers Association. **PRACTICE AREAS:** Intellectual Property Litigation. **Email:** allen@birdwelljanke.com

RICHARD A. WILHELM, born Spokane, Washington, December 15, 1954; admitted to bar, 1984, Oregon and U.S. District Court, District of Oregon; registered to practice before the U.S. Patent and Trademark Office. *Education:* University of Oregon (B.S., 1978); Northwestern School of Law of Lewis and Clark College (J.D., 1983); Portland State University (B.S., Electrical Engineering, 2000). *Member:* Oregon State Bar; American Bar Association. **PRACTICE AREAS:** Patents; Copyrights; Trademarks; Trade Secrets; Intellectual Property Licensing; Computer Law; Internet Law. **Email:** rwilhelm@birdwelljanke.com

GEOFFREY K. COOPER, born New York, New York, October 31, 1949; admitted to bar, 2003, Oregon, U.S. District Court, District of Oregon and U.S. Court of Appeals for the Federal Circuit; registered to practice before the U. S. Patent and Trademark Office. *Education:* University of Oregon (Ph.D, 1977; J.D., 2003). Member, American Chemical Society. Member, Planning Commission, Pleasanton, CA., 1996-1999. *Member:* American Bar Association; American Intellectual Property Law Association. **LANGUAGES:** Russian. **PRACTICE AREAS:** Patents; Trademarks; Copyrights; Trade Secrets. **Email:** gcooper@birdwelljanke.com

(This Listing Continued)

BIRDWELL & JANKE LLP, Portland—Continued

LEGAL SUPPORT PERSONNEL

CHRISTINE A. PELLECHI, born Bronx, New York, November 16, 1959. *Education:* University of California, Los Angeles (B.A., 1995); Lewis and Clark Law School (J.D., 1999). Alumni Scholar, University of California, Los Angeles. Recipient, Chancellor's Humanitarian Award, University of California, Los Angeles. (Office Manager). ***PRACTICE AREAS:*** All aspects of firm management. ***Email:*** chris@birdwelljanke.com

BIRMINGHAM & MACKESON, LLP

1001 SW FIFTH AVENUE, SUITE 2175
PORTLAND, OREGON 97204
Telephone: 503-224-2310
Fax: 503-224-4533
Email: pmbirm@teleport.com
URL: http://www.lawyers.com/patbirmingham

Criminal Trial Practice in State and Federal Courts. Drug Crimes, Felonies, Misdemeanors, Juvenile Law, White Collar Crime.

PAT BIRMINGHAM, born St. Paul, Minnesota, April 2, 1947; admitted to bar, 1975, California and U.S. District Court, Central District of California; 1978, Oregon; 1979, U.S. District Court, District of Oregon and U.S. Supreme Court. *Education:* Portland State University (B.S., 1970); Western State University (J.D., 1975). Trial Attorney Riverside County Public Defender, Riverside, California, 1975-1978. Deputy in Charge, Juvenile Court, 1977, Satellite Offices Corona & Banning, California. Former Member, Board of Directors for the Metropolitan Public Defenders, Portland, Oregon. Member, Multnomah County Bar Association's Mentor Program. Listed in: National Directory of Criminal Lawyers; Best Lawyers in America. Speaker/Lecturer: Defense of Homicides, Forfeiture, Evidence, Grand Jury and Criminal Trial Preparation, Oregon Criminal Defense Lawyers Association, Continuing Legal Education, Oregon State Bar Association. *Member:* Multnomah County and Clackamas County Bar Associations; Oregon State Bar; Oregon Criminal Defense Lawyers Association; California Attorneys for Criminal Justice; National Association of Criminal Defense Lawyers. ***PRACTICE AREAS:*** Criminal Defense; Murder; Sex Crimes; Search and Seizure; Driving While Intoxicated. ***Email:*** pmbirm@teleport.com

WAYNE MACKESON, born London, England, February 5, 1953; admitted to bar, 1982, Oregon; 1988, U.S. District Court, District of Oregon. *Education:* Northwest Nazarene College (B.S., 1976); Northwestern School of Law of Lewis and Clark College (J.D., 1982). *Member:* Multnomah County and Clackamas County Bar Associations; State Bar of Oregon; Oregon Criminal Defense Lawyers Association. ***REPORTED CASES:*** State v. Hansen, 295 Or. 635, 664 P.2d 1095 (1983); State v. Tweed, 62 Or. App. 711, 663 P.2d 38 (1983); State v. Tucker, 62 Or. App. 512, 662 P.2d 345 (1983); State v. Pearson, 83 Or. App. 624, 732 P.2d 937 (1987); State v. Tucker, 86 Or. App. 413, 740 P.2d 182 (1987); remanded 305 Or. 307, 749 P.2d 576 (1988), reaffirmed 90 Or. App. 506, 753 P.2d 427 (1988), affirmed 307 Or. 386, 768 P.2d 386 (1989); Highfield v. Hoffman Construction Company, 87 Or. App. 328, 742 P.2d 68, review denied 304 Or. 547 (1987); DeAngelo v. Schiedler, 306 Or. 91, 757 P.2d 1355 (1988); State v. Freund, 102 Or. App. 647, 796 P.2d 656 (1990); State v. Stockfleth, 311 Or. 40, 804 P.2d 471 (1991); State v. Durant, 122 Or. App. 380, 857 P.2d 891 (1993); Warren v. Baldwin, 140 Or. App. 318, 915 P.2d 1016 (1996); Cole v. DMV, 336 Or. 565, 87 P.3d 1120 (2004); Key West Retaining Systems, Inc. v. Holm II, Inc., 185 Or. App. 182, 59 P.3d 1280 (2002). ***PRACTICE AREAS:*** Criminal Defense; Plaintiffs Personal Injury; Appellate Practice. ***Email:*** wayne@epuerto.com

BITTNER & HAHS, P.C.

PORTLAND, OREGON

(See Lake Oswego)

General Civil and Trial Practice in all State and Federal Courts. Corporate, Business, Employment, Construction, Estate Planning, Probate and Real Estate Law.

BLACK HELTERLINE LLP

Established in 1898
1900 FOX TOWER
805 S.W. BROADWAY
PORTLAND, OREGON 97205-3359
Telephone: 503-224-5560
Telecopier: 503-224-6148
URL: http://www.bhlaw.com

Banking, Bankruptcy, Business and Corporate, Computer, Construction, Creditors' Rights, Employee Benefits, Employment and Discrimination, Environmental, Forest Products, Immigration, Insurance, International Transactions, Land Use and Development, Litigation in all Courts, Probate, Real Estate, Securities, Taxation, Technology Licensing, Trade Regulation and Antitrust, Trust and Estate Law, Venture/Technology Law.

MEMBERS OF FIRM

STARK ACKERMAN, born Jersey City, New Jersey, February 4, 1951; admitted to bar, 1979, District of Columbia; 1982, Oregon; 2000, Washington. *Education:* Amherst College (B.A., with honors, 1973); Yale University School of Forestry (M.F.S., 1975); George Washington University (J.D., with honors, 1978). Author: "Observations on the Transformation of Forest Service: The Effects of the National Environmental Policy Act on the U.S. Forest Service Decision Making," 20 Environmental Law 703, 1990. Editor, "1991, The Year in Review," Forest Resources Chapter, American Bar Association Section of Natural Resources, Energy and Environmental Law. Adjunct Professor, Northwestern School of Law, 1979-1998. *Member:* Oregon State Bar; Washington State Bar Association; The District of Columbia Bar. ***PRACTICE AREAS:*** Real Estate; Land Use; Land Development; Environmental Regulation Law; Forestry Law; Natural Resources Law. ***Email:*** sa@bhlaw.com

RONALD T. ADAMS, born Detroit, Michigan, October 6, 1942; admitted to bar, 1976, Oregon. *Education:* University of Colorado (B.S., 1964); University of Illinois (M.S., 1966); University of Santa Clara (J.D., magna cum laude, 1976). C.S. Marvel Firestone Fellow, Phi Lambda Upsilon Honorary. Co-Author: "Construction Law Bankruptcy Issues," for Oregon State Bar CLE. Engineer, Sylvania Electronic Defense Labs and Electromagnetic Systems Lab, Inc., 1967-1976. *Member:* Multnomah County and American (Member, Intellectual Property Section) Bar Associations; Oregon State Bar; Commercial Law League of America. ***PRACTICE AREAS:*** Computer Law; Construction Law; Debtor and Creditor Rights; Intellectual Property Licensing; Trademark; Copyrights. ***Email:*** rta@bhlaw.com

REMI A. BAPTISTE, born Lihue, Hawaii, December 10, 1965; admitted to bar, 1994, Oregon; 2002, Washington. *Education:* Manhattan College (B.A., magna cum laude, 1987); Northwestern School of Law at Lewis and Clark College (J.D., 1993). *Member:* Oregon State Bar; Washington State Bar Association; American Bar Association. ***PRACTICE AREAS:*** Business Law; Mergers and Acquisitions; Corporate Law; Real Estate; Intellectual Property; Commercial Transactions. ***Email:*** rab@bhlaw.com

JAMES M. BAUMGARTNER, born Waltham, Massachusetts, June 10, 1958; admitted to bar, 1986, Oregon. *Education:* Western Oregon State College (B.S., 1981); Willamette University (J.D., 1986). Order of the Barristers. *Member:* Oregon State Bar; American Bar Association; Oregon Association of Defense Counsel; Transportation Lawyers Association. ***PRACTICE AREAS:*** Employment Law; Family Business Law; Closely Held Business Law; Commercial Litigation. ***Email:*** jmb@bhlaw.com

ROBERT W. DONALDSON, born Portland, Oregon, January 10, 1946; admitted to bar, 1974, Oregon. *Education:* Oregon State University (B.S., 1968); Willamette University (J.D., 1974). Phi Delta Phi. Honorary Consul General for Korea (ROK) for Oregon. *Member:* American Immigration Lawyers Association (Chapter Chair, 1986-1988). [With U.S. Army Military Intelligence, Special Agent, 1968-1971]. ***PRACTICE AREAS:*** Immigration Law; International Law; Corporate Planning. ***Email:*** rwd@bhlaw.com

CLARENCE H. GREENWOOD, born Glasgow, Montana, December 9, 1947; admitted to bar, 1975, Montana; 1979, Oregon. *Education:* University of Montana (B.A., with honors, 1970; J.D., with high honors, 1975); New York University (LL.M. in Taxation, 1977). Phi Alpha Theta; Phi Kappa Phi. Staff Member, 1973-1974 and Business Manager, 1974-1975, Montana Law Review. Law Clerk to Judge Shiro Kashiwa, U.S. Court of Claims, 1977-1979. Oregon Tax Research (Director, 1990—;President, 1997-1999). *Member:* Multnomah County and American (Member, Section of Taxation) Bar Associations; Oregon State Bar; Montana State Bar; American Judicature Society. ***PRACTICE AREAS:*** Federal, State and Local Taxation; Tax Litigation; Business Law; Trust Law; Estate Planning and Administration. ***Email:*** chg@bhlaw.com

JOHN A. HIRSCHY, born Fort Wayne, Indiana, September 11, 1953; admitted to bar, 1982, Florida; 1983, Oregon and U.S. Tax Court. *Education:* Miami University (B.S., 1975); University of Florida (J.D., with honors, 1982; LL.M. in Taxation, 1983). Beta Alpha Psi; Phi Kappa Phi. Order of the Coif. Tax Editor, University of Florida Law Review, 1981-1982. Certified Public Accountant, Florida, 1982-1998. *Member:* The Florida Bar; Oregon State Bar; American Bar Association. [Lt., U.S. Navy, 1975-1979]. ***PRACTICE AREAS:*** Taxation; Estate Planning; Corporate; Business Law. ***Email:*** jah@bhlaw.com

PAUL R. HRIBERNICK, born La Grande, Oregon, October 28, 1954; admitted to bar, 1980, Oregon and U.S. Supreme Court. *Education:* University of Oregon (B.S., 1977; J.D., 1980). Fulbright Scholar. Law Clerk, U.S. District Court, Eastern District of Louisiana, 1983-1984. Contributing Editor, Oregon Real Estate and Land Use Digest, 1988-2002. Chapter Author and Editor, Oregon Law Institute Environmental Law Deskbook. Land Use Hearings Officer, City of Hillsboro, Oregon, 1989-1997. Visiting Professor, University of Oregon School of Law (Immigration). Faculty, AILA National and Northwest Regional Seminars, 1993-2006. Member, AILA/CIS Lincoln Liaison Team, 1998-2001. *Member:* Oregon State Bar; American Immigration Lawyers Association (Member, Board of Governors, 1992-1994). ***LANGUAGES:*** Spanish. ***PRACTICE AREAS:*** Immigration and Nationality Law; Land Development Law; Environmental Regulation Law; Real Estate Law. ***Email:*** prh@bhlaw.com

JOHN M. McGUIGAN, born Portland, Oregon, July 27, 1954; admitted to bar, 1979, Oregon; 1988, Washington. *Education:* University of Oregon (B.S., 1976; J.D., 1979). Executive Editor, Oregon L. Rev., 1978-1979. Chair, Board of Directors, LaSalle High School Foundation. Special Assistant Attorney General, State of Oregon, 1999—. *Member:* Multnomah County, Washington State and American Bar Associations; Oregon State Bar (Member, Executive Committee, 1989-1990; Treasurer, 1990-1991; Task Force on Close Corporations and Shareholder Rights, 1999-2001 and Corporation Act Committee, 2002, Business Law Section; Member, 1986-1990 and Chairman, 1988-1989, Financial Institutions Executive Committee; Member, Executive Committee, International Law Section, 1992-1994). ***PRACTICE AREAS:*** Domestic and International Business Transactions; Corporate and Finance; Securities; Mergers and Acquisitions; Banking. ***Email:*** jmm@bhlaw.com

MICHAEL B. MERCHANT, born Mineral Wells, Texas, April 24, 1963; admitted to bar, 1988, Oregon and U.S. District Court, District of Oregon; 1989, Washington and U.S. District Court, Eastern and Western Districts of Washington; 1999, U.S. Court of Federal Claims. *Education:* University of Washington (B.A., 1985); University of Oregon (J.D., 1988). Phi Delta Phi. Recipient, Business Law Certificate. Business Editor, Oregon Law Review, 1987-1988. Author: "Settlement And Compromise," OSB Civil Pleading And Practice CH. 29, 1994, 1998, 2000. *Member:* Clark County, Multnomah County and Washington State Bar Associations; Oregon State Bar; Defense Research Institute; Oregon Association of Defense Counsel. ***PRACTICE AREAS:*** Business; Commercial; Construction; Employment; Insurance; Personal Injury; Products Liability; Property Litigation; Securities; Trial Practice. ***Email:*** mbm@bhlaw.com

MICHAEL O. MORAN, born Portland, Oregon, March 16, 1945; admitted to bar, 1976, Oregon. *Education:* Reed College (B.A., 1967); University of California at Berkeley (M.S., 1969; J.D., 1976). Phi Beta Kappa. Woodrow Wilson Fellow. *Member:* Multnomah County and American Bar Associations; Oregon State Bar (Member, Financial Institutions

(This Listing Continued)

Committee, 1996—); American Chemical Society. ***PRACTICE AREAS:*** Civil Litigation; Creditors' Rights Law; Securities Law; Financial Institutions Law; Employment Law; Corporate Governance; Shareholders Law; Construction Law. ***Email:*** mom@bhlaw.com

DAVID G. NEWHALL, born Portland, Oregon, March 18, 1956; admitted to bar, 1987, Oregon; 1990, Guam. *Education:* Occidental College (B.A., 1979); Lewis and Clark College; Northwestern School of Law (J.D., 1986). Phi Beta Kappa. Member, Environmental Law Journal. Faculty, AILA National and N.W. Regional Immigration Law Seminars, 1998-2003. *Member:* Oregon State Bar; American Bar Association; American Immigration Lawyers Association (Member, Nebraska Service Center Liaison Committee, 2003-2004; Oregon Chapter Chairman, 1998-2000; Member, National Board of Governors, 1998-2000). ***PRACTICE AREAS:*** Immigration and Nationality Law. ***Email:*** dgn@bhlaw.com

ADAM S. RITTENBERG, born Perth Amboy, New Jersey, August 4, 1962; admitted to bar, 1993, Oregon and U.S. District Court, District of Oregon; 2002, Washington. *Education:* University of Oregon (B.A., 1984); Portland State University (M.A., 1988); Lewis and Clark College (J.D., cum laude, 1993). Associate Editor, Environmental Law Review. *Member:* Oregon State Bar; Washington State Bar Association. ***PRACTICE AREAS:*** Business Law; Estate Planning; Employee Benefits. ***Email:*** asr@bhlaw.com

DAVID P. ROY, born Yakima, Washington, June 6, 1951; admitted to bar, 1976, Oregon. *Education:* Washington State University (B.A., 1973); Harvard University (J.D., 1976). Pi Sigma Alpha; Phi Beta Kappa. Member: Panel of Arbitrators, American Arbitration Association; Arbitration Service of Portland. *Member:* Multnomah County and American (Member, Sections on: Business Law; Real Property) Bar Associations; Oregon State Bar. ***PRACTICE AREAS:*** Business Law; Corporate Law; Finance Law; Real Estate Law; Agricultural Law; Arbitration. ***Email:*** dpr@bhlaw.com

STEVEN R. SCHELL, born Portland, Oregon, April 12, 1939; admitted to bar, 1968, Oregon. *Education:* University of Oregon (B.A., 1961; J.D., 1968); University of Denver (M.A., 1965). Phi Delta Phi. Author: "Land Use Meets Populism: Citizen Control of Growth in Oregon," Oregon Law Review, Fall 1998; "Resolving Permit Conflicts in Oregon's Coastal Zone," Coastal Zone 87, Publication of the American Society of Civil Engineers; "How Far Can Local Government Go to Regulate State Agency Activities Affecting Land Use?" Twelfth Annual Oregon Planning Institute Publication (September 18, 1986); "Living with the Legacy of the 1970's: Federal/State Coordination in the Coastal Zone," 14 Env. Law 751 (1984); "1981 Legislative Changes in Oregon's Land Use System," 18 Will. L. Rev. 49 (1982). Co-Editor: "Construction Law," Oregon State Bar Cont. Leg. Ed. Publication (1997, 2003). Lecturer, 1989 and 1990 Wetlands Cont. Leg. Ed. Seminar, Environmental and Natural Resources Law Section, Oregon State Bar. Lecturer: Land Use Seminars, 1992, 1994, 1995, 1996 and 1999 (NBI); Wetlands Seminar, 1995 (NBI); Land Use Seminar, 1997 (LSI). Lecturer: Walter Law in Oregon, 2001 (NBI); Oregon State Bar Real Estate and Land Use 2002 and 2004 Annual Meetings. Vice-Chairman and Commissioner, Land Conservation and Development Commission, State of Oregon, 1973-1976. Member, Oregon Energy Facility Siting Council, 1990-1998. Chairman and President, Energy Trust of Oregon, 2000—. *Member:* Multnomah County and American (Member, Real Estate Financing Committee, Section of Real Property, Probate and Trust Law) Bar Associations; Oregon State Bar (Member, 1984-1986 and Chairman, 1985-1986, Continuing Legal Education Committee; Co-Editor, Continuing Legal Education Publication, Construction Law, 1987 and 1997; Secretary, 1986-1987, Mandatory Continuing Legal Education Committee; Chairman, 1980-1981, Real Estate and Land Use Section); Home Builders Association of Metropolitan Portland (Member, Government and Legal Affairs Committee). ***PRACTICE AREAS:*** Land Development Law; Environmental Regulation Law; Real Estate Law; Construction Law; Natural Resources Law; Energy. ***Email:*** srs@bhlaw.com

DAVID R. SIMON, born Toledo, Ohio, November 28, 1956; admitted to bar, 1982 Oregon. *Education:* Whitman College (B.A., cum laude, with honors in history, 1979); Vanderbilt University (J.D., 1982). Associate Editor, Vanderbilt Journal of Transnational Law, 1980-1982. Author: "Cooperatives," Advising Oregon Businesses (Oregon State Bar), 1989, 1994, 1997, 2001; "Worker Cooperatives," Journal of Employee Ownership Law and Finance, Vol. III, No. 3, 1991. Chair, Cooperative Corporations Task Force (Oregon State Bar), 1994-1995 . Member, National Council of Farmer Cooperatives (Legal, Tax and Accounting Committee). *Member:* Multnomah County and American (Member, Committee on Credit Unions, Business Law Section) Bar Associations; Oregon State Bar; National Health Lawyers Association; American Financial Services Association (Member, Law Committee). ***PRACTICE AREAS:*** Business Law; Consumer Law; Real Estate; Agricultural Law; Trusts and Estates; Health Care. ***Email:*** drs@bhlaw.com

KENNETH A. WILLIAMS, born Grangeville, Idaho, March 31, 1950; admitted to bar, 1980, Oregon, U.S. District Court, District of Oregon, U.S. Court of Appeals, Ninth Circuit and U.S. Tax Court; 1986, California; 2005, Washington. *Education:* University of Oregon (B.S., in Economics, cum laude, 1972; J.D., 1980). Phi Delta Phi. Forms Author, Advising Oregon Businesses, Oregon State Bar, 1984-2004. Former Vice President and General Counsel, American Home Savings, Federal Savings Bank. *Member:* Multnomah County and Washington State Bar Associations; Oregon State Bar (Member, Sections on: Business, Real Estate and Debtor/Creditor); State Bar of California. ***PRACTICE AREAS:*** Real Estate; Leasing; Mergers and Acquisitions; Commercial Lending. ***Email:*** kaw@bhlaw.com

ASSOCIATES

MARGARET E. SCHROEDER, born Clearwater, Florida, June 4, 1974; admitted to bar, 2002, Oregon. *Education:* Furman University (B.A., 1995); University of Oregon (J.D., 2002). *Member:* Oregon State Bar; Oregon Women Lawyers. ***LANGUAGES:*** Japanese. ***Email:*** mes@bhlaw.com

ANDREW T. REILLY, born Ridgewood, New Jersey, November 24, 1967; admitted to bar, 1996, Oregon; 2002, Washington. *Education:* University of South Carolina (B.S., 1993); Lewis and Clark College (J.D., 1996). Member and Associate Editor, Environmental Law, The Law Review of Lewis and Clark Law School, 1994-1996. *Member:* Multnomah County and Washington State Bar Associations; Oregon State Bar (Member, Federal Practice and Procedure Committee, 2001—; Panel Counsel, Disciplinary Board, 2001—).

(This Listing Continued)

PRACTICE AREAS: General Litigation; Construction Law; Environmental Law; Insurance Coverage; Trusts and Estates; Alternative Dispute Resolution. ***Email:*** atr@bhlaw.com

DAVID C. STREICHER, born Portland, Oregon, August 29, 1957; admitted to bar, 1984, Oregon. *Education:* Portland State University (B.S., 1979); University of Oregon (J.D., 1984). Certified Public Accountant, Oregon, 1984. Author, "Fixing Estate Planning Errors With Disclaimers," PLF, 1999. Speaker: "Drafting LLC and LLP Agreements," OSB, 2001; "Successful Wealth Transfer Techniques in Oregon," NBI, 2000; "Choice of Business Entity in Oregon," NBI, 2000; "Family Limited Partnerships and LLCs in Oregon, "NBI, 1999. *Member:* Oregon State Bar (Member: Taxation Section and Estate Planning and Administration Section); Oregon Society of Certified Public Accountants; Rotary Club of Portland. ***PRACTICE AREAS:*** Taxation; Estate Planning; Business Law. ***Email:*** dcs@bhlaw.com

KELLY R. TILDEN, born Reading, Pennsylvania, October 2, 1971; admitted to bar, 2001, Oregon. *Education:* Universite Paris-Sorbonne (1992); Muhlenberg College (A.B., cum laude, 1993); Willamette University College of Law (J.D., 2001). *Member:* Multnomah, Washington State and American Bar Associations; Oregon State Bar. ***LANGUAGES:*** French. ***PRACTICE AREAS:*** Employment Law; Immigration and Naturalization; Land Development; Business Litigation; Commercial Litigation. ***Email:*** krt@bhlaw.com

STEVEN M. ZIPPER, born Detroit, Michigan, March 17, 1970; admitted to bar, 1996, Oregon; 2004, Washington. *Education:* University of Michigan (B.A., 1992); Willamette University (J.D., 1996). Member, Willamette Law Review. *Member:* Oregon State Bar; Washington State Bar Association. ***PRACTICE AREAS:*** Corporate Law; Business Law; Taxation; Estate Planning; Estate Administration. ***Email:*** smz@bhlaw.com

JENNIFER M. MORRISSEY, born Portland, Oregon, January 14, 1971; admitted to bar, 2003, Oregon. *Education:* University of Iowa (B.A., 1993); Lewis and Clark College (J.D., 2003). Member, Lewis and Clark Law Review. Recipient: First Year Moot Court Honors Brief; Best Oralist. *Member:* Oregon State Bar; American Bar Association; American Immigration Lawyer's Association. ***LANGUAGES:*** Spanish. ***PRACTICE AREAS:*** Immigration Law; Civil Litigation; Business Law; Employment Law. ***Email:*** jm@bhlaw.com

BROOKE M. BURNS, born Moscow, Idaho, April 12, 1975; admitted to bar, 2000, Oregon. *Education:* Oregon State University (B.A., 1997); University of Oregon (J.D., 2000). Member, Oregon Law Review, 1998-2000. *Member:* Oregon State Bar; Multnomah County Bar Association; Oregon Association of Defense Counsel. ***PRACTICE AREAS:*** Commercial Litigation; Business Litigation; Consumer Law.

NATHAN R. GERHARDT, born Portland, Oregon, June 15, 1972; admitted to bar, 2003, Oregon. *Education:* University of Washington (B.A., 1994); University of Oregon (J.D., 2003; M.B.A., 2003). Order of the Coif. *Member:* Multnomah County and American Bar Associations; Oregon State Bar. [Lieutenant, U.S. Navy, 1994-1999]. ***PRACTICE AREAS:*** Business Law; Corporate Law.

ERIN L. DONALD, born Portland, Oregon, February 2, 1975; admitted to bar, 2004, Oregon. *Education:* Macalester College (B.A., 1997); University of Oregon (J.D., 2004). Order of the Coif. *Member:* Oregon State Bar. ***PRACTICE AREAS:*** Business Law. ***Email:*** eld@bhlaw.com

OF COUNSEL

ROBERT E. GLASGOW, born Portland, Oregon, November 13, 1944; admitted to bar, 1969, Oregon. *Education:* George Washington University (B.A., 1966; J.D., with honors, 1969). Member, Board of Trustees, 1972-1977 and Treasurer, 1976, Jewish Family and Child Service. Member, Board of Trustees, 1974-1976 and Chairman, 1976, Legal Aid Service Multnomah Bar Association, Inc. Member, Portland Art Museum Activities Council, 1984-1987. Member, Board of Trustees, 1986-1997 and President, 1991-1993, Mittleman Jewish Community Center. Member, Board of Trustees, Portland Jewish Community Foundation, 1989-1991; Board of Directors, Jewish Federation of Portland, 1991-1993. Board of Directors, 1996—, Treasurer, 1998-1999, Vice President, 1999-2000, and President, 2000-2002, Oregon Chapter, American Jewish Committee. Board of Directors, 2002-2004 and Vice President, 2003-2004, Oregon Uniting. Member, Board of Directors, Uniting to Understand Racism, 2004—. *Member:* Multnomah County and American Bar Associations; Oregon State Bar (Member, Corporate and Family Law Sections). ***PRACTICE AREAS:*** Business Law; Commercial Law; Real Estate; Family/Domestic Relations Law. ***Email:*** reg@bhlaw.com

LEWIS B. HAMPTON, born Squilchuck, Washington, June 12, 1933; admitted to bar, 1960, Oregon; 1961, U.S. District Court, District of Oregon; 1965, U.S. Court of Appeals, Ninth Circuit; 1971, U.S. Supreme Court. *Education.* Willamette University (B.A., 1955; J.D., 1960). Phi Delta Phi. Contributing Author and Authority: "Legacy Plan, Protect and Preserve Your Estate," 1996; "Ways and Means, Maximize the Value of Your Retirement Savings," 1999; "Generations," 1999; "Strictly Business," 2002. Contributing Reviewer for Conspectus Current. *Member:* American Bar Association (Member, Sections on: Business Law; Real Property; Probate and Trust Law; Wealth Counsel); Oregon State Bar (Member, Sections on: Taxation; Business Law; Real Estate and Land Use; Estate Planning and Administration). Fellow of the Esperti-Peterson Institute. [With U.S. Air Force, 1955-1958; Col. U.S. Air Force Reserve]. ***PRACTICE AREAS:*** Wealth Planning; Estate Planning; Commercial Law; Business Law. ***Email:*** lbh@bhlaw.com

GERALD H. ROBINSON (Retired)

REPRESENTATIVE CLIENTS: Arnold Worldwide, Inc.; Capital Pacific Bank; Capitol Auto Group; CH2M Hill Industrial Design & Construction, Inc.; CNF; Columbia Corridor Association; Cristom Vineyards, Inc.; Eagle-Picher Minerals, Inc.; Encompass Mechanical Services; Ensequence, Inc.; Erath Vineyards Winery, L.L.C.; ESCO Corp.; Georgia-Pacific Corp.; Glenn Walters Nursery, Inc.; HSBC Bank USA, N.A.; Inspiration Software, Inc.; International Wood Products, LLC; Johnstone Supply; LifeStyles, Senior Housing Managers, L.L.C.; Lime Financial; Linsco/Private Ledger Corp.; McKinstry Co.; MDU Resources Group, Inc.; Melvin Mark Properties; Morse Bros., Inc.; The Mountain Group; NACCO Materials Handling Group, Inc.; NIKE, Inc.; Northwest Technology Ventures, Limited Partnership; Northwest Tire Factory, LLC; Pixelworks, Inc.; Pope & Talbot, Inc.; Printingforless.com, Inc.; Property Investment Financial Corp.; Reliable Credit Association, Inc.; John L. Scott, Inc.; S.E.H. America, Inc.; Senco Products, Inc.; The Sivers Companies; State of Oregon; Tektronix, Inc.; Summit Research Network Management, Inc.; Union Bank of California, N.A.; U.S. Bank, N.A.

BLAKELY, SOKOLOFF, TAYLOR & ZAFMAN

PORTLAND, OREGON

(See Lake Oswego)

Intellectual Property Law, including Patents, Trademarks, Copyrights, Related Prosecution and Litigation.

MICHAEL H. BLOOM

522 SOUTH WEST 5TH AVENUE, SUITE 1125
PORTLAND, OREGON 97204-2128
Telephone: 503-223-2128
Email: bloompc@easystreet.com

Personal Injury, Medical Malpractice, Products Liability, Construction Law, Business Litigation.

MICHAEL H. BLOOM, born Portland, Oregon, May 31, 1954; admitted to bar, 1981, Oregon; 1987, U.S. Court of Appeals, Ninth Circuit; 1989, U.S. Supreme Court; 2000, District of Columbia and Washington; 2002, U.S. Tax Court. *Education:* University of Oregon (B.S., 1976; J.D., 1980). Phi Alpha Delta. Editor, Oregon Law Review, 1979-1980. Member, Moot Court Honor Board. Honors Attorney, United States Department of Transportation, Washington, D.C., 1980-1981. Recipient, 2001 MBA Award for Merit. *Member:* Washington State Bar Association; Oregon State Bar; District of Columbia Bar; Oregon Trial Lawyers Association; Association of Trial Lawyers of America.

BLUNCK & WALHOOD, LLC

PORTLAND, OREGON

(See West Linn)

Arbitration, Automobile Accidents, Construction Claims, Contracts, Personal Injury, Insurance.

BODYFELT MOUNT STROUP & CHAMBERLAIN LLP

Established in 1978
707 S.W. WASHINGTON STREET, SUITE 1100
PORTLAND, OREGON 97205
Telephone: 503-243-1022
Fax: 503-243-2019

Civil Trial and Appellate Practice in all State and Federal Courts, Products Liability, Professional Liability including Medical Malpractice, Insurance and Commercial Litigation.

MEMBERS OF FIRM

BARRY M. MOUNT, born Portland, Oregon, February 16, 1944; admitted to bar, 1969, Oregon. *Education:* Lewis and Clark College (B.A., 1966); University of Oregon (J.D., 1969). Recent Cases Editor, University of Oregon Law Review, 1968-1969. *Member:* Multnomah County and American Bar Associations; Oregon State Bar (Member, Procedure and Practice Committee, 1980-1982; Chairman, 1982; Uniform Civil Jury Instructions Committee, 1996-2000; Chairman, 2000); Oregon Association of Defense Counsel (Board of Directors, 1984-1986). [Lieut., U.S. Navy, JAGC, 1969-1973]. ***PRACTICE AREAS:*** Products Liability; Construction Defects; Premises Liability; Insurance Defense; Insurance Coverage; Professional Liability; Medical Litigation; Commercial Litigation; Toxic Torts. ***Email:*** mount@bmsc-law.com

PETER R. CHAMBERLAIN, born Palo Alto, California, August 12, 1950; admitted to bar, 1978, Oregon. *Education:* California Polytechnic State University (B.S., 1972); Lewis & Clark College, Northwestern School of Law (J.D., 1978). Member, Cornelius Honor Society. Managing Editor, Environmental Law Review, 1977-1978. Member, Board of Directors, Lewis & Clark Law School Alumni Association, 1992-1995. Member, Board of Directors, 1994-1999 and Secretary-Treasurer, 1997-1998, Professional Liability Fund. Member, 1992-1997, and Chair, 1993-1995, Uniform Trial Court Rules Committee. Member: Multnomah County and American Bar Associations; Oregon State Bar (Member: Uniform Civil Jury Instructions Committee, 1987-1990; Member, 1990-1992, and Secretary, 1991-1992, Prepaid Legal Committee; Bar Counsel Panel, 1986-1998; 2004—); Oregon Association of Defense Counsel (Member, Board of Directors, 2000-2003). ***PRACTICE AREAS:*** Products Liability; Appeals; Insurance Litigation; Medical Litigation; Commercial Litigation. ***Email:*** chamberlain@bmsc-law.com

RICHARD A. LEE, born Indianola, Iowa, July 16, 1958; admitted to bar, 1984, Oregon; 1987, Washington. *Education:* Grinnell College (B.A., 1981); University of Oregon (J.D., 1984). Order of the Coif. *Member:* Multnomah County, Clark County, Washington State and American (Member, Tort and Insurance Practice Section) Bar Associations; Oregon State Bar (Member, Litigation Section, Legal Assistants Council, 1991-1993, Federal Practice and Procedure Committee, 1995-1997); Oregon Association of Defense Counsel; Washington Defense Trial Lawyers; Oregon State Board of Bar Examiners (Member, 1995-1998; Chair, 1997-1998). ***PRACTICE AREAS:*** Environmental Litigation; Insurance; Products Liability; Commercial Litigation; Professional Liability. ***Email:*** lee@bmsc-law.com

MARK A. HIEFIELD, born Portland, Oregon, July 27, 1951; admitted to bar, 1977, Oregon; 1984, Washington. *Education:* Washington State University (B.S., 1973); Gonzaga University (J.D., 1977). *Member:* Multnomah County, Washington State and American Bar Associations; Oregon State Bar; Oregon Association of Defense Counsel; Defense Research Institute. ***PRACTICE AREAS:*** Automobile Law; Personal Injury Defense Litigation; Casualty Insurance Law; Toxic Torts. ***Email:*** hiefield@bmsc-law.com

MOLLY JO MULLEN, born Lexington, Kentucky, December 11, 1965; admitted to bar, 1991, Oregon. *Education:* University of Oregon (B.A., 1988); University of San Francisco (J.D., 1991). *Member:* Multnomah County, Federal and American Bar Associations; Oregon State Bar; Oregon Association of Defense Counsel; Oregon Women Lawyers; Defense Research Institute. ***LANGUAGES:*** Russian and German. ***PRACTICE AREAS:*** Civil Litigation; Products Liability; Drug and Medical Device; Employment. ***Email:*** mullen@bmsc-law.com

ERIC "SKIP" WINTERS, born Portland, Oregon, June 30, 1969; admitted to bar, 1994, Oregon; 1997, Washington. *Education:* University of Washington (B.A., 1991); Willamette University (J.D., 1994). *Member:* Multnomah County, Washington State and Federal Bar Associations; Oregon State Bar (Member: President's Task Force on Future Issues, 2002-2004; Oregon New Lawyers Division, Executive Committee, 1997-2003; Treasurer, 1999-2001; Chair-elect, 2002; Chair, 2003; Membership Services Committee, 1995-1997); Oregon Association of Defense Counsel; Defense Research Institute. ***PRACTICE AREAS:*** Construction Defects; Insurance; Civil Litigation; Commercial Litigation. ***Email:*** winters@bmsc-law.com

ASSOCIATES

ANDREW D. GLASCOCK, born Weiser, Idaho, November 28, 1973; admitted to bar, 1999, Oregon; 2005, Washington. *Education:* Idaho State University (B.B.A., 1996); Willamette University (J.D., 1999). *Member:* Multnomah County and American Bar Associations; Oregon State Bar; Oregon Association of Defense Counsel; Defense Research Institute. ***PRACTICE AREAS:*** Civil Litigation; Products Liability; Environmental Litigation. ***Email:*** glascock@bmsc-law.com

DEANNA L. WRAY, born Norfolk, Virginia, January 29, 1968; admitted to bar, 1997, Oregon; 2003, Washington; registered to practice before the U.S. Patent and Trademark Office. *Education:* North Carolina State University (B.S., 1990); Northwestern School of Law at Lewis & Clark College (J.D., 1997). *Member:* Oregon State Bar; Multnomah and Washington State Bar Associations; Defense Research Institute; Oregon Association of Defense Counsel; Oregon Women Lawyers (Member, Board of Directors, 2001-2005). ***PRACTICE AREAS:*** Civil Litigation; Product Liability; Personal Injury. ***Email:*** wray@bmsc-law.com

VICKI M. SMITH, born Spokane, Washington, April 6, 1975; admitted to bar, 2001, Oregon; 2005, Washington. *Education:* Eastern Washington University (B.A., 1998); Willamette University (J.D., 2001). *Member:* Multnomah County and Washington State Bar Associations; Oregon State Bar; Oregon Association of Defense Counsel; Oregon Women Lawyers; Defense Research Institute. ***PRACTICE AREAS:*** Civil Litigation; Insurance; Personal Injury. ***Email:*** smith@bmsc-law.com

JENNIFER A. DURHAM, born Wagner, South Dakota, September 23, 1979; admitted to bar, 2005, Oregon. *Education:* Buena Vista College (B.S., 2001); Northwestern School of Law (J.D., 2005). *Member:* Oregon State Bar. ***PRACTICE AREAS:*** Products Liability; Civil Litigation; Personal Injury; Insurance Defense; Employment Claims.

OF COUNSEL

CATHY E. CRANDALL, born Long Beach, California, June 5, 1957; admitted to bar, 1985, Oregon; 1986, Washington. *Education:* University of Utah (B.S., 1981); Northwestern School of Law of Lewis and Clark College (J.D., 1985). *Member:* Multnomah County and Washington State Bar Associations; Oregon State Bar; Oregon Women Lawyers; Oregon Association of Defense Counsel. ***PRACTICE AREAS:*** General Liability Litigation; Insurance Coverage Litigation; Appeals. ***Email:*** crandall@bmsc-law.com

FARRAND "RANDY" M. LIVINGSTON, born Mitchell, South Dakota, November 25, 1941; admitted to bar, 1967, Ohio; 1972, Oregon. *Education:* Kenyon College (B.A., cum laude, with high honors in Economics, 1964); Duke University (J.D., 1967). *Member:* Multnomah County and American Bar Associations; Oregon State Bar (Member, Sections on: Business Law; Construction Law; Debtor/Creditor; Estate Planning; Real Estate and Land Use). [Capt., JAG, USAF, 1968-1972]. ***PRACTICE AREAS:*** Transactions; Business; Estate Planning; Real Estate; Probate. ***Email:*** livingston@bmsc-law.com

REPRESENTATIVE CLIENTS: Ace Insurance Co.; A.J. Gerrard & Co.; BMW AG; Budget Rent-A-Car; Catholic Health Initiatives; Contractors Bonding and Insurance Company; Daimler Chrysler Corp.; CIGNA; CNA Insurance Companies; Coachmen Industries, Inc.; Eon Labs Manufacturing, Inc.; Federated Mutual Insurance Co.; Financial Indemnity Co.; Genuine Parts Co.; Georgia Pacific Corp; Harco Manufacturing Co.; Hartford Insurance Co.; Landmark Ford, Inc.; Markel Insurance Co.; Mutual of Enumclaw Insurance Co.; Oregon Mutual Insurance Co.; Otis Elevator Co.; PBS Environmental Building Consultants, Inc.; PPG Industries; Safeway Stores, Inc.; Sentry Insurance Co.; Simplex Time Recorder Co.; Skyline Corp.; St. Paul Insurance Co.; Tokio Marine Insurance Co.; Vanguard Car Rental Claims, Inc.; Zurich Insurance Co.

BORG STROM & GREENLICK

400 SW 6TH AVENUE, SUITE 600
PORTLAND, OREGON 97204
Telephone: 503-224-2595
Fax: 503-224-3203
URL: http://www.bsg-attys.com

Criminal Law and Criminal Defense, Driving While Intoxicated, Drug Crimes, Juvenile Crimes, Parole and Probation, Traffic Violations, Family Law, Adoptions, Child Custody, Child Support, Divorce, Domestic Violence, Visitation Rights, Business Law, Business Planning, Buying or Selling a Business, Contracts, Starting a Business and Small Business Law.

MEMBERS

C. LANE BORG, born San Francisco, California, August 6, 1959; admitted to bar, 1985, Oregon. *Education:* Pomona College (B.A., 1981); Northwestern College of Law (J.D., 1984). *Member:* Oregon State Bar; Clackamas County and American Bar Associations; Oregon Criminal Defense Lawyers Associations. ***PRACTICE AREAS:*** Business Law; Criminal Law. ***Email:*** lane@bsg-attys.com

TRINA J. STROM, born Craigmont, Idaho, March 15, 1959; admitted to bar, 1987, Oregon. *Education:* American University, Washington, D.C. (B.A., 1981); Lewis and Clark

(This Listing Continued)

College (J.D., 1986). *Member:* Oregon State Bar (Member, Family Law Section); American Bar Association (Continuing Legal Education Committee, 2000-2003). ***PRACTICE AREAS:*** Family Law. ***Email:*** tstrom@bsg-attys.com

MICHAEL A. GREENLICK, born Detroit, Michigan, September 7, 1959; admitted to bar, 1985, Oregon. *Education:* Pomona College (B.A., 1981); Lewis and Clark College (J.D., 1985). *Member:* Oregon State Bar; Multnomah County and American Bar Associations; Oregon Criminal Defense Lawyers Association; National Association of Criminal Defense Lawyers. ***PRACTICE AREAS:*** Criminal Defense. ***Email:*** mike@bsg-attys.com

BRADACH LAW OFFICES

LLOYD 700 BUILDING, SUITE 900
700 N.E. MULTNOMAH STREET
PORTLAND, OREGON 97232
Telephone: 503-238-7170
Facsimile: 503-238-7127
URL: http://www.bradachlaw.com

Construction and Design Law, Contracts, Government Contracts, Real Estate, Land Use, Arbitration, Mediation and General Litigation in State and Federal Courts.

JOHN F. BRADACH, SR., born Burns, Oregon, June 19, 1951; admitted to bar, 1979, Oregon, Washington and U.S. District Court, District of Oregon; 1982, U.S. Claims Court; 1985, U.S. District Court, Western District of Washington; 1990, U.S. Court of Appeals, Ninth Circuit and U.S. Supreme Court. *Education:* Portland State University and University of Oregon (B.A., Business Administration/ Accounting, 1974); Northwestern School of Law of Lewis and Clark College (J.D., 1979). Staff Member, Environmental Law, 1977-1978. Author: "Bid Disputes," Construction Law (Oregon State Bar CLE, 1989; updated, 1993, 1997); "Construction Contracts for the Project Owner: Use of the New AIA Contract Forms," Real Estate and Land Use Seminar, Oregon State Bar CLE (1988); "AIA Owner/ Contractor and Owner/Architect Agreements," Current Issues in Land Use and Real Estate Law Seminar, Oregon State Bar CLE (1998). Member: Oregon-Columbia Chapter Associated General Contractors: Construct by Contract Committee, 1980-1995, Chair, Legal Committee, 1999; Legislative Committee, 1986-2003; Public Contracting Steering Committee, 1998; Board of Directors, 2000; Executive Committee, 2000; ORS 279 Rewrite Task Group, 2002. Chairman, Oregon-Columbia Chapter, Associated General Contractors, Construct by Contract Task Force, 1985-1986; National Associated General Contractors: Construct by Contract Committee, 1989-1998; Special Contracting Preferences and Minority Business Enterprise Committees, Equal Business Access, 1991-2003; Dredging Committee, 1991-1998; Contract Documents, 1998-2003; Marine Contractors, 2000-2003; Risk Management, 1998-2003. Private Building Owners Committee, 1991-1999, Project Delivery Systems Committee, 1991-2003. Oregon-Columbia Chapter, Associated General Contractors National Committee Member of the Year, 1992; Northwest Construction Consumers Council, 1990-1993; Public Contract Law and Litigation Sections, American Bar Association, 1984-2003; Committee T, International Construction Contracts, Section on Business Law, International Bar Association, 1984-1992. *Member:* Multnomah County and American (Member, Construction Industry Forum, Sections on: Dispute Resolution, Tort and Insurance Practice, Litigation and Public Contract Law) Bar Associations; Oregon State Bar (Construction Law Section, 1984-2003; Chairman, 1984-1985; Executive Committee, 1985-1989; Alternative Dispute Resolution Section, 1992-2003; Real Estate and Land Use Section, 1992-2003; Litigation, 1979-2003); American Arbitration Association Panel of Arbitrators (Member, 1993-2003); Dispute Review Board Foundation, Inc., 1997- 1998. ***REPORTED CASES:*** Coral Construction v. King County, 941 F2d 910 (9th Cir 1991), cert denied, 112 S Ct 875 (1992). ***PRACTICE AREAS:*** Construction and Design Law; Litigation; Arbitration; Mediation; Contracts; Government Contracts; Land Use. ***Email:*** jbradach@bradachlaw.com

ASSOCIATE

DANELLE C. FORSETH, born State College, Pennsylvania, April 18, 1973; admitted to bar, 2004, Oregon; 2005, Idaho. *Education:* Washington State University (B.S., Civil Engineering, 1996); Lewis and Clark Law School (J.D., cum laude, 2004). *Member:* Multnomah County Bar Association; Oregon State Bar; Idaho State Bar. ***PRACTICE AREAS:*** Construction and Design Law; Litigation; Contracts.

REPRESENTATIVE CLIENTS: A.C. Schommer & Sons, Inc.; Chemeketa Community College; Columbia Northwest Recycling; Direct Marketing Solutions, Inc.; Evan House Co.; Excel Excavation, Inc.; Freese Precast Products, Inc.; Henkles & McCoy, Inc.; Hi-Tech Rockfall Construction, Inc.; Hodge Companies, Inc.; Inland Sea Maritime Group, LLC; J.P. Contractors, Inc.; James W. Fowler, Co.; KinderCare Learning Centers, Inc.; Merrill Contractors, Inc.; Pacific Northwest Aggregates; Portland State Bookstore; Precision Automotion, Inc.; Ross Island Sand & Gravel, Co.; Skyward Construction LLC; Southern Bleacher Construction Co.

BRAYTON PURCELL, LLP

THE AMERICAN BANK BUILDING
621 SOUTHWEST MORRISON, SUITE 950
PORTLAND, OREGON 97205-3824
Telephone: 503-295-4931
Fax: 503-241-2573
Email: portland@braytonlaw.com
URL: http://www.braytonlaw.com

Novato, California Office: 222 Rush Landing Road, 94948. Telephone: 415-898-1555. Fax: 415-898-1247. Email: novato@braytonlaw.com.
Los Angeles, California Office: 2401 El Segundo Boulevard, Suite 440, 90245. Telephone: 310-727-1900. Fax: 310-727-1904. Email: elsegundo@braytonlaw.com.
Salt Lake City, Utah Office: Parkview Tower, 215 S. State Street, Suite 900. 84111. Telephone: 801-366-9100. Fax: 801-350-0065.

Personal Injury including Asbestos, Toxic Torts, Automobile Accidents, Products Liability, Premises Liability.

(This Listing Continued)

ASSOCIATE

ELAINE J. BROWN, born London, England, November 2, 1955; admitted to bar, 1993, Oregon. *Education:* University of Nevada (B.A., 1988); Northwestern School of Law (J.D., 1992). Associate Editor, Northwestern Law Review, 1990-1992. *Member:* Oregon State Bar; Oregon Trial Lawyers Association; Trial Lawyers for Public Justice. ***PRACTICE AREAS:*** Personal Injury; Toxic Torts; Products Liability; Premises Liability.

(For complete Biographical Data on all personnel, see Professional Biographies at Novato, California)

BROWNSTEIN, RASK, SWEENEY, KERR, GRIM, DESYLVIA & HAY, LLP

Established in 1971
1200 S.W. MAIN BUILDING
PORTLAND, OREGON 97205
Telephone: 503-221-1772
Facsimile: 503-221-1074
Email: general@brownrask.com

General Practice. Trial Practice in all State and Federal Courts. Antitrust, Cooperatives, Corporations, Securities, Taxation, Real Estate, Insurance, Municipal, Pension and Profit Sharing, Estate Planning, Probate, Family, Television and Radio Law.

MEMBERS OF FIRM

JOHN H. ARENZ (1940-1999)

RICHARD J. BROWNSTEIN, born June 29, 1930; admitted to bar, 1953, Oregon; U.S. Supreme Court. *Education:* Reed College; Willamette University (LL.B., 1953);. *Member:* Oregon State Bar. [Colonel, JAGC, USAR, 1948-1981]. ***PRACTICE AREAS:*** Business; Real Estate; Housing and Urban Development. ***Email:*** rjb@brownrask.com

RAYMOND M. RASK, born April 1, 1936; admitted to bar, 1961, Oregon; 1970, U.S. Supreme Court. *Education:* Portland State University; Northwestern College of Law of Lewis and Clark College (J.D., 1961). *Member:* Oregon State Bar. ***PRACTICE AREAS:*** Civil Litigation; Business; Real Estate. ***Email:*** rmr@brownrask.com

MILES SWEENEY, born February 15, 1941; admitted to bar, 1966, Oregon. *Education:* Portland State College; Northwestern College of Law of Lewis and Clark College (J.D., 1966). *Member:* Oregon State Bar; Oregon Association of Defense Council. ***PRACTICE AREAS:*** Civil Litigation. ***Email:*** ms@brownrask.com

ANDREW P. KERR, born May 4, 1944; admitted to bar, 1969, Oregon. *Education:* Dartmouth College (A.B., 1966); Willamette University (J.D., 1969). *Member:* Oregon State Bar. ***PRACTICE AREAS:*** Business; Real Estate; Estate Planning. ***Email:*** apk@brownrask.com

DOUGLAS R. GRIM, born December 15, 1944; admitted to bar, 1970, Oregon; 2002, Washington. *Education:* Washington State University (B.S., 1967); Willamette University (J.D., 1970). *Member:* Oregon State Bar; Washington State Bar Association. ***PRACTICE AREAS:*** Business; Real Estate; Estate Planning. ***Email:*** drg@brownrask.com

TERRY DESYLVIA, born April 5, 1943; admitted to bar, 1969, Oregon. *Education:* University of Oregon and Stanford University (A.B., 1964); Stanford University (J.D., 1969). *Member:* Oregon State Bar. ***PRACTICE AREAS:*** Business; Real Estate; Tax and Estate Planning. ***Email:*** td@brownrask.com

DAVID J. SWEENEY, born November 19, 1948; admitted to bar, 1975, Oregon; U.S. District Court, District of Oregon; U.S. Court of Appeals, Ninth Circuit; U.S. Supreme Court; 2004, Washington. *Education:* Columbia University (A.B., 1971); Northwestern School of Law of Lewis and Clark College (J.D., 1975). *Member:* Oregon State Bar; Washington State Bar Association. ***PRACTICE AREAS:*** Civil Litigation; Appellate. ***Email:*** djs@brownrask.com

KIRKHAM E. HAY, born April 2, 1948; admitted to bar, 1975, Oregon; 1981, U.S. Tax Court. *Education:* University of New Mexico and University of Oregon (B.B.A., 1971); McGeorge College of the Law (J.D., 1975); Boston University (LL.M., Taxation, 1976). *Member:* Oregon State Bar. ***PRACTICE AREAS:*** Estate Planning; Business; Taxation; Transactions; Real Estate. ***Email:*** keh@brownrask.com

SCOTT L. JENSEN, born May 19, 1955; admitted to bar, 1986, New York and Oregon; 1987, Washington. *Education:* Western Oregon State College (B.S., 1977); New York Law School (J.D., 1985). *Member:* Oregon State Bar; New York State and Washington State Bar Associations. ***PRACTICE AREAS:*** Construction; Real Estate; Business; Debtor Creditor; Bankruptcy; Civil Litigation. ***Email:*** slj@brownrask.com

JAMES W. HENDRY, born May 16, 1958; admitted to bar, 1983, Oregon; 1984, U.S. District Court, District of Oregon; 2003, Washington. *Education:* California Polytechnic State University (B.S., 1980); Williamette University (J.D., 1983). *Member:* Oregon State Bar; Washington State Bar Association. ***PRACTICE AREAS:*** Civil Litigation; Securities and Business; Personal Injury; Workers Compensation; Domestic Relations; Criminal. ***Email:*** jwh@brownrask.com

PAUL G. DODDS, born April 28, 1960; admitted to bar, 1987, Oregon and U.S. District Court, District of Oregon; 1989, U.S. Court of Appeals, Ninth and Federal Circuits; 1995, U.S. Court of Appeals, Eleventh Circuit; 2003, U.S. Court of International Trade. *Education:* Portland State University (B.S., 1983); Northwestern School of Law of Lewis and Clark College (J.D., 1987). *Member:* Oregon State Bar. ***PRACTICE AREAS:*** Civil Litigation; Appellate; Insurance. ***Email:*** pgd@brownrask.com

STEPHEN E. BLACKMAN, born May 18, 1955; admitted to bar, 1991, Oregon; 1992, Washington. *Education:* Portland State University (B.A., 1978); Northwestern School of Law of Lewis and Clark College (J.D., summa cum laude, 1991). *Member:* Oregon State Bar; Washington State Bar Association. ***PRACTICE AREAS:*** Business; Bankruptcy; Real Estate. ***Email:*** seb@brownrask.com

DOUGLAS J. RAAB, born April 6, 1968; admitted to bar, 1993, Oregon; U.S. District Court, District of Oregon. *Education:* University of Oregon (B.S., 1990); Willamette Uni-

(This Listing Continued)

BROWNSTEIN, RASK, SWEENEY, KERR, GRIM, DeSYLVIA & HAY, LLP, Portland—Continued

versity College of Law (J.D., 1993). *Member:* Oregon State Bar. ***PRACTICE AREAS:*** Civil Litigation; Business; Personal Injury; Domestic Relations. ***Email:*** djr@brownrask.com

STEPHEN H. BUCKLEY, born Moline, Illinois, August 13, 1955; admitted to bar, 1980, Oregon; 1981, U.S. District Court, District of Oregon. *Education:* Colorado State University (B.A., 1976); Willamette University (J.D., 1980). *Member:* Oregon State Bar. ***PRACTICE AREAS:*** Employee Benefits; Labor. ***Email:*** shb@brownrask.com

THOMAS J. ARENZ, born December 1, 1968; admitted to bar, 1996, Oregon. *Education:* Occidental College and University Of Oregon (B.S., 1992); Gonzaga University School of Law (J.D., cum laude, 1994). *Member:* Oregon State Bar. ***PRACTICE AREAS:*** Business; Real Estate Transactions; Commercial Litigation; Civil Litigation. ***Email:*** tja@brownrask.com

ASSOCIATES

FRANK O. DIARMIT, born August 18, 1949; admitted to bar, 1981, Oregon. *Education:* Western Oregon State College (B.S.Ed., 1971); Portland State University (M.B.A., 1977); Willamette University (J.D., 1981); New York University School of Law (LL.M., in Taxation, 1987). Certified Public Accountant, Oregon, 1977. *Member:* Oregon State Bar. ***PRACTICE AREAS:*** Taxation; Pension and Profit Sharing; Trusts and Estate Planning. ***Email:*** fod@brownrask.com

CARY R. CADONAU, born November 29, 1972; admitted to bar, 2000, Oregon. *Education:* Loyola Marymount University (B.A.D.M., 1995); Northwestern School of Law of Lewis and Clark College (J.D., 2000). *Member:* Oregon State Bar. ***PRACTICE AREAS:*** Land Use; Employment; Criminal. ***Email:*** crc@brownrask.com

ENGRED K. CHAI, born December 12, 1968; admitted to bar, 2001, Oregon. *Education:* Oregon State University (B.S., 1993); Northwestern School of Law of Lewis and Clark College (J.D., 2001). *Member:* Oregon State Bar. ***PRACTICE AREAS:*** Business; Real Estate; Estate Planning. ***Email:*** ekc@brownrask.com

ANGELA M. RUSSELL, born July 12, 1976; admitted to bar, 2000, Oregon. *Education:* Southern Oregon State University (B.A., 1997); Northwestern School of Law of Lewis and Clark College (J.D., 2000). *Member:* Oregon State Bar. ***PRACTICE AREAS:*** Corporate; Employment; Estate Planning. ***Email:*** amr@brownrask.com

JAY B. DERUM, born Redding, Pennsylvania, August 28, 1963; admitted to bar, 1997, Oregon. *Education:* University of Oregon (B.A., 1988); Northwestern School of Law (J.D., 1996). *Member:* Oregon State Bar. ***PRACTICE AREAS:*** Personal Injury; Medical Malpractice; Litigation. ***Email:*** jbd@brownrask.com

REBEKAH L. STILES, born Springfield, Illinois, November 10, 1977; admitted to bar, 2003, Oregon. *Education:* Washington University (A.B., 1999); Lewis and Clark College (J.D., 2003). *Member:* Oregon State Bar. ***PRACTICE AREAS:*** Business; Corporate; Civil. ***Email:*** rls@brownrask.com

JOSEPH M. MABE, born Portland, Oregon, February 17, 1975; admitted to bar, 2001, Connecticut; 2004, Oregon. *Education:* University of Oregon (B.S., Political Science, Economics, 1997); University of Connecticut School of Law (J.D., 2000). *Member:* Oregon State Bar; Connecticut Bar Association. ***PRACTICE AREAS:*** Civil Litigation; Commercial Litigation; Administrative; Construction Litigation; Insurance Litigation. ***Email:*** jmm@brownrask.com

KENT D. JOHNSON, born Billings, Montana, January 22, 1965; admitted to bar, 1996, Montana and Oregon; 2001, Washington. *Education:* St. Olaf College (B.A., Mathematics, 1987); University of Montana (J.D., with honors, 1995); New York University (LL.M., Taxation, 1996). *Member:* Oregon State Bar; Washington State Bar Association; State Bar of Montana. ***PRACTICE AREAS:*** Real Estate; Corporate; Tax; Estate Planning.

REPRESENTATIVE CLIENTS: Alpenrose Dairy, Inc.; Carolina Tobacco Company; HMF Food Service, Inc.; IBU National Pension Trust; Jewett, Barton, Leavy & Kern, Inc.; Kaady Car Wash; Multnomah Athletic Club; Pacific Fence & Wire Co.; Pendleton Flour Mills; Plumbers Trust Funds; Radio Cab Co.; Reser's Fine Foods; R.M. Wade & Co.; Rodda Paint Co.; Space Age Fuels, Inc.; Sunshine Dairy Foods, Inc.; Wentworth Chevrolet, Co.; Western Family Foods, Inc.; West Hills Development Company; Wilsonville Chevrolet, Inc.; Zepak Corporation.

BULLARD SMITH JERNSTEDT WILSON

A PROFESSIONAL CORPORATION

Established in 1977

1000 S.W. BROADWAY, SUITE 1900

PORTLAND, OREGON 97205

Telephone: 503-248-1134

Fax: 503-224-8851

Email: laborlaw@bullardlaw.com

URL: http://www.bullardlaw.com

Practice Restricted to Labor and Employment Law, representing management and Business Interests including Litigation Practice before Federal and State Courts and Administrative Agencies.

FIRM PROFILE: We are Management's Choice for Labor and Employment Law. Our firm practices management labor and employment law exclusively. We provide advice and representation to clients in both the public and private sectors. OUR PRACTICE INCLUDES: labor and employment litigation before federal and state agencies and courts; NLRB charges and elections; and labor contract negotiations, arbitrations and administration. Our practice is regional in scope, including clients in Alaska, California, Montana, Idaho and Washington as well as Oregon. Affiliate of Worklaw Network: A Nationwide Network of Management Labor and Employment Law Firms.

(This Listing Continued)

GARRY R. BULLARD, born Chicago, Illinois, August 27, 1934; admitted to bar, 1959, Oregon. *Education:* Northwestern University (B.A., 1956; J.D., 1959). Phi Delta Phi; Phi Beta Kappa. Member, Board of Editors, Northwestern University Law Review, 1958-1959. *Member:* Multnomah County and American (Labor and Employment Law) Bar Associations; Oregon State Bar (Labor Relations Law). ***PRACTICE AREAS:*** Collective Bargaining; Union Contract Negotiations; Labor Law.

JIM D. KORSHOJ (Retired)

LESTER V. SMITH, JR., born Mt. Pleasant, Pennsylvania, May 10, 1940; admitted to bar, 1965, North Carolina; 1972, Illinois; 1973, Oregon; 1980, U.S. Supreme Court. *Education:* Duke University (A.B., 1962); University of North Carolina (J.D., 1965). Delta Theta Phi. Member, Editorial Board, Oregon Business and Corporate Law Digest, 1982—. Attorney, National Labor Relations Board, Peoria, Illinois, 1965; 1969-1972. *Member:* Multnomah County and Illinois State Bar Associations; Oregon State Bar (Chairman Section on Labor Relations Law, 1982-1983). [Capt., U.S. Army, 1966-1969, Judge Advocate USAR]. ***PRACTICE AREAS:*** Collective Bargaining; Union Organization; Labor Law. ***Email:*** lsmith@bullardlaw.com

KENNETH E. JERNSTEDT, born Rockville Centre, New York, February 27, 1944; admitted to bar, 1970, California and Oregon; 1977, U.S. Supreme Court. *Education:* Stanford University (A.B., 1966); Boalt Hall School of Law, University of California (J.D., 1969). *Member:* Multnomah County and American (Member, Labor and Employment Law Section) Bar Associations; State Bar of California; Oregon State Bar (Member, Sections on: Labor Relations Law; Civil Rights Law; Commissioner, 1987-1992 and Chair, 1987-1990, Oregon Fish and Wildlife Commission). ***PRACTICE AREAS:*** Collective Bargaining; Employee Discipline; Family and Medical Leave Act; Labor Relations; Labor Strikes; Union Organization; Labor Law; Management Employment Law; Management Labor Law; National Labor Relations Act; Fair Labor Standards; Union Elections. ***Email:*** kjernstedt@bullardlaw.com

DAVID H. WILSON, JR., born Corning, New York, March 9, 1945; admitted to bar, 1973, Wisconsin; 1974, Oregon. *Education:* Princeton University (B.A., 1967); University of Wisconsin-Madison (J.D., 1972). Order of the Coif. Law Clerk, U.S. District Court, Western District of Wisconsin, 1972-1973. Author: Note, "Criminal Law-Waiver of Jury in Wisconsin Criminal Cases," Wisconsin Law Review 626, 1971: Comment, "State and Local Regulation of Nonreturnable Beverage Containers," Wisconsin Law Review 536, 1972. Lecturer at Law, University of Wisconsin Law School, 1973-1974. Adjunct Professor, Willamette School of Law, 1991. *Member:* Oregon State Bar. ***REPORTED CASES:*** Forsberg v. Pacific Northwest Bell Telephone Co. 840 F2d 1409, 9th Cir. 1988; Koch v. City of Portland, 306 Or 444, 760 P2d 252, on remand 94 Or App 484 766P2d 405, 1988; Spurgeon v. Stayton Canning Co., 92 Or App 566, 759 P2d 1104, 1988; Karren v. Far West Federal Savings, 79 Or App 131 717 P2d 1271, rev den 301 Or 666, 725 P2d 1293, 1986; Claimants Members of Boilermakers v. Employment Division, 73 Or App 470, 699 P2d 203, rev den 299 Or 583, 1985; Paddack v. Dave Christensen, Inc., 745 F2d 1254, 9th Cir. 1984. ***PRACTICE AREAS:*** Employment Litigation; Wrongful Termination; Employment Benefit Litigation; Labor Law; Employment Law; Employment Class Actions. ***Email:*** dwilson@bullardlaw.com

RICHARD J. ALLI, JR., born Mckeesport, Pennsylvania, April 16, 1954; admitted to bar, 1980, Oregon and U.S. District Court, District of Oregon. *Education:* University of Oregon (B.S., 1977); Willamette University (J.D., 1980). *Member:* Multnomah County and American (Labor and Employment Law) Bar Associations; Oregon State Bar (Labor Relations Law; Civil Rights Law; Workers Compensation Law). ***PRACTICE AREAS:*** Collective Bargaining; Union Organization; Labor Law; Union Contract Negotiations; Labor Arbitration; Employment Law. ***Email:*** ralli@bullardlaw.com

ROBERT J. LEE, born Vancouver, Washington, August 14, 1956; admitted to bar, 1981, Oregon. *Education:* University of Washington (B.A., 1978); Northwestern School of Law of Lewis and Clark College (J.D., 1981). *Member:* Oregon State Bar (Labor Relations Law). ***PRACTICE AREAS:*** Collective Bargaining; Union Organization; NLRB and Employment Arbitration; Bureau of Labor Proceedings and Employee Handbooks; Labor Law; Employment Law. ***Email:*** rlee@bullardlaw.com

FRANCIS T. BARNWELL, born Greenville, Michigan, November 29, 1954; admitted to bar, 1981, District of Columbia; 1984, Oregon. *Education:* Dartmouth College (B.A., 1977); George Washington University (J.D., 1981). Adjunct Professor, Willamette School of Law, 1991. *Member:* Oregon State Bar. ***PRACTICE AREAS:*** Management Employment Law; Employment Contracts; Employee Drug Testing; Reductions in Force; Employment Class Actions; Employment Litigation. ***Email:*** fbarnwell@bullardlaw.com

ALAN M. LEE, born Portland, Oregon, December 25, 1942; admitted to bar, 1968, Oregon; 1969, U.S. District Court, District of Oregon. *Education:* Willamette University (B.S., 1966); Willamette University College of Law (J.D., 1968). *Member:* Oregon State Bar (Labor Relations Law; Civil Rights Law; Workers' Compensation Law); American Bar Association (Litigation; Labor and Employment Law); Oregon Association of Defense Counsel; Defense Research Institute. ***PRACTICE AREAS:*** Employment Law; Employment Litigation; FMLA; Employment Disability Discrimination. ***Email:*** alee@bullardlaw.com

DAVID J. RIEWALD, born Pasadena, California, September 12, 1958; admitted to bar, 1983, Michigan; 1988, Oregon; 1989, Washington. *Education:* Albion College (B.A., 1980); University of Oregon (J.D., 1983). Associate Editor, University of Oregon Law Review, 1982-1983. Adjunct Professor, Willamette University School of Law, 1992-1993. *Member:* State Bar of Michigan; Oregon State Bar; Washington State and American Bar Associations. ***PRACTICE AREAS:*** Employment Discrimination; Wrongful Termination; Employment Law; Employment Litigation. ***Email:*** driewald@bullardlaw.com

KATHRYN M. HINDMAN, born Eugene, Oregon, April 26, 1958; admitted to bar, 1987, Washington; 1988, Oregon. *Education:* Washington State University; University of Washington (B.A., 1981); Gonzaga University (J.D., with honors, 1986). Executive Editor, Gonzaga Law Review, 1985-1986. *Member:* Washington State Bar Association; Oregon State Bar. ***PRACTICE AREAS:*** Wage and Hour Law; Family and Medical Leave Act; Personnel Training; Personnel Policies; Harassment; Employment Litigation; COBRA; Employment Law; Employment Disability Discrimination. ***Email:*** khindman@bullardlaw.com

(This Listing Continued)

KENNETH E. BEMIS, born Baltimore, Maryland, June 27, 1964; admitted to bar, 1989, Oregon. *Education:* Principia College (B.A., 1986); Williamette University (J.D., 1989). Phi Alpha Delta. Member, 1987-1988, Associate Editor, 1988-1989, Williamette Law Review. Author: Comment, "Probation of Pencil and Paper Honesty Tests: Is Honesty the Best Policy?" 25 Williamette Law Review 571, 1989; "Application of Rule 11 Sanctions in the Ninth Circuit: Weapon or Nuisance?" 24 Williamette Law Review 801, 1988; Development: "Oregon Expands the Protections of the Attorney-Client Privilege for Corporations and Other Business Entities," 24 Williamette Law Review 157, 1988. *Member:* Oregon State Bar. ***PRACTICE AREAS:*** Collective Bargaining; Public Sector Collective Bargaining; Union Organization; Labor Law. ***Email:*** kbemis@bullardlaw.com

C. AKIN BLITZ, born Honolulu, Hawaii, September 2, 1949; admitted to bar, 1975, Oregon. *Education:* Willamette University (B.A., 1972); Lewis and Clark College (J.D., 1975); Georgetown University (LL.M., Labor, 1979). Chair, Portland Civil Service Reform Task Force, 1988. [Maj., USMCR]. ***PRACTICE AREAS:*** Labor Law; Public Sector Employment Law; Collective Bargaining; Municipal Labor Law; Municipal Liability; Police Labor Law. ***Email:*** ablitz@bullardlaw.com

BARBARA A. BLOOM, born Ridgewood, New Jersey, July 24, 1967; admitted to bar, 1992, Oregon. *Education:* Santa Clara University (B.S., 1989); Willamette University (J.D., 1992). Vice Justice, Phi Alpha Delta, 1991-1992. *Member:* Multnomah County and American Bar Associations; Oregon State Bar. ***PRACTICE AREAS:*** Union Organization; Collective Bargaining; Public Sector Collective Bargaining; Employment Arbitration; Labor Law; Employment Law. ***Email:*** bbloom@bullardlaw.com

KIRK S. PETERSON, born St. Paul, Minnesota, June 12, 1955; admitted to bar, 1993, Oregon and U.S. District Court, District of Oregon. *Education:* Eastern Montana College (B.S., 1979); University of Nebraska at Lincoln (J.D., with distinction, 1993). Order of the Coif. Member, Nebraska Law Review, 1992-1993. Moot Court Executive Committee, UNL College of Law, 1991-1993. *Member:* Multnomah County and American (Member, Sections on: Labor and Employment Law) Bar Associations; Oregon State Bar. ***PRACTICE AREAS:*** Employment Law; Labor Law; Public Sector Employment Law; Employment Arbitration; Employment Litigation. ***Email:*** kpeterson@bullardlaw.com

DANIEL R. BARNHART, born Portland, Oregon, October 19, 1964; admitted to bar, 1991, Washington; 1992, U.S. District Court for the Western and Eastern Districts of Washington and U.S. Court of Appeals, Ninth Circuit; 1995, Oregon and U.S. District Court, Oregon. *Education:* University of Oregon (B.A., 1988; J.D., 1991). Order of the Coif. Executive Editor, Oregon Law Review, 1990-1991. ***PRACTICE AREAS:*** Employment Litigation; Noncompete Litigation; Employment Contracts; Noncompetition and Non-Solicitation Agreements; Prevailing Wage Litigation. ***Email:*** dbarnhart@bullardlaw.com

MICHAEL G. McCLORY, born Torrance, California, December 24, 1963; admitted to bar, 1989, Indiana; 1990, U.S. District Court, Northern District of Indiana; 1991, California; 1992, U.S. District Court, Northern and Central Districts of California; 1993, Illinois; 1995, U.S. District Court, Southern District of California; 1997, Oregon and U.S. District Court, District of Oregon. *Education:* University of Notre Dame (B.A., 1986; J.D., 1989); University of Southern California Law Center. *Member:* American Bar Association (Labor and Employment Law, Equal Employment Opportunity Committee); State Bar of California; Oregon State Bar. ***PRACTICE AREAS:*** Employment Law. ***Email:*** mmcclory@bullardlaw.com

JACQUELINE M. DAMM, born Chicago, Illinois, March 2, 1965; admitted to bar, 1992, Illinois; 1993, U.S. District Court, Northern District of Illinois; 2001, Oregon. *Education:* University of Wisconsin (B.A., 1987); University of Minnesota (J.D., cum laude, 1992). *Member:* Chicago and American (Labor and Employment Law) Bar Associations. ***PRACTICE AREAS:*** Labor Law; Labor Arbitration; Union Contract Negotiations; Employment Law. ***Email:*** jdamm@bullardlaw.com

J. KENT PEARSON, JR., born Raleigh, North Carolina, May 6, 1957; admitted to bar, 1982, Oregon; 1985, U.S. District Court, District of Oregon; 1986, New Hampshire; 1988, U.S. Court of Appeals, First Circuit; 1991, U.S. Court of Appeals, Ninth Circuit. *Education:* Wake Forest University (B.A., cum laude, 1979); Washington and Lee University (J.D., 1982). Note and Comment Editor, Washington and Lee Law Review, 1981-1982. *Member:* Oregon State Bar (Member, Civil Rights; Labor and Employment Law Sections); American Bar Association (Member, Labor and Employment Law Section). ***PRACTICE AREAS:*** Labor Law; Employment Law; WARN Act; Fair Employment Practices; Employee Discipline.

THOMAS I. KRAMER, born Boston, Massachusetts, September 11, 1954; admitted to bar, 1981, Oregon; U.S. Court of Appeals, Ninth Circuit. *Education:* University of St. Andrews, St. Andrews, Scotland; Claremont McKenna College (B.A., summa cum laude, 1976); Yale University (J.D., 1980). Instructor, Law, Yale Law School, 1978-1979. Law Clerk to Hon. Otto R. Skopil, Jr., U.S. Court of Appeals, Ninth Circuit, 1980-1982. Chair, Portland Pension Study Group, 1989-1991. Member, Western Pension and Benefits Conference, 1984—. Co-Author: "Employee Health Benefits," Oregon Continuing Legal Education, 2000; "Health Insurance and Health Plans," 2 Insurance §40A, Oregon Continuing Legal Education, 1987; "Welfare Benefits Under the Tax Reform Act of 1986," Advanced Law of Pensions and Deferred Compensation After TRA 86 (ALI-ABA, 1987, 1988). *Member:* Oregon State Bar; American Bar Association. ***PRACTICE AREAS:*** Employee Benefits Law; Executive Compensation; Health Benefits; Qualified Retirement Plans; ERISA.

ADAM S. COLLIER, born Alhambra, California, October 20, 1970; admitted to bar, 1997, Oregon. *Education:* Brigham Young University (B.A., 1994); University of Southern California (J.D., 1997). *Member:* Multnomah County and American Bar Associations; Oregon State Bar. ***PRACTICE AREAS:*** Labor Law; Employment Law. ***Email:*** acollier@bullardlaw.com

JENNIFER LYN BOUMAN, born Durango, Colorado, November 8, 1971; admitted to bar, 1998, Texas; 2000, Oregon; 2004, Washington. *Education:* Texas Tech University (B.A., 1994); Texas Tech University School of Law (J.D., 1998). ***PRACTICE AREAS:*** Age Discrimination; Non-Competition and Non-Solicitation Agreements; Covenants Not To Compete; Employment Litigation; Employment Law; Labor Arbitration; Labor Law. ***Email:*** jbouman@bullardlaw.com

(This Listing Continued)

REPRESENTATIVE CLIENTS: *Corporate Labor:* American Steel; Avista Corporation; Chubb Group; Conagra, Inc.; Empire Health Services; EC Company; Executive Risk Management; Express Personnel Services; Federal Express; Fred Meyer, Inc.; Goodwill Industries; Hoffman Construction Co.; Interstate Distributor; Jeld-Wen, Inc.; Lanphere Enterprises; Legacy Health System; Lloyd's of London; Mercer Industries; Microchip Technology, Inc.; Mid-Columbia Medical Center; Nike, Inc.; Norpac Foods, Inc.; N.W Natural; Portland General Electric Co.; Rite-Aid; Schnitzer Industries; Savin; Silver Eagle Industries; Standard Insurance; Trillium Family Services; Union Pacific Railroad; Xenium Resources.
REPRESENTATIVE CLIENTS: *Public Labor:* Bay Area District Hospital; City of Hillsboro; City of Pendleton; City of Tigard; City of Tualatin; Clallam County; Clean Water Services; Coos County; Douglas County; Jackson County; Metropolitan Public Defenders; Olympic Memorial Hospital; Oregon State Sheriff's Association; St. Helens Rural Fire District; Tri-Met; Tulatin Valley Fire and Rescue; Umatilla County; Washington County; Washington County Consolidated Communications Agency.

BULLIVANT HOUSER BAILEY PC

Established in 1938
300 PIONEER TOWER
888 S.W. FIFTH AVENUE
PORTLAND, OREGON 97204-2089
Telephone: 503-228-6351
Facsimile: 503-295-0915
URL: http://www.bullivant.com

Seattle, Washington Office: 1601 Fifth Avenue, Suite 2300, 98101-1618. Telephone: 206-292-8930. Facsimile: 206-386-5130.
Vancouver, Washington Office: 805 Broadway Street, Suite 400, 98660-3310. Telephone: 360-693-2424. Facsimile: 360-695-8504.
Gold River, California Office: 11335 Gold Express Drive, Suite 105, 95670-6310. Telephone: 916-852-9100. Fax: 916-852-5777.
San Francisco, California Office: 601 California Street, Suite 1800, 94108-2823. Telephone: 415-352-2700. Fax: 415-352-2701.
Las Vegas, Nevada Office: 3980 Howard Hughes Parkway, Suite 550, 89109. Telephone: 702-650-6565. Facsimile: 702-650-2995.

Multiservice Business and Trial law firm offering Civil Litigation and Appellate Practice in all State and Federal Courts. Alternative Dispute Resolution, Mediation and Arbitration. Commercial Litigation; Bankruptcy, Finance and Banking; Creditors' Rights; Intellectual Property; International Business; Food and Beverage; Securities; Insurance Coverage and Insurance Defense; Bad Faith; Environmental; Products Liability; Life, Health and Disability; Errors and Omissions; Directors and Officers; Professional Liability, Fire, Inland Marine, Fidelity and Surety, Municipal Liability; Insurance Regulation; General Business and Corporate; S Corporations and Limited Liability Partnerships; Tax; Real Estate and Construction; Estate Planning and Probate; Employment Law; ERISA.

LAW FIRM ALLIANCES/ASSOCIATIONS: **MULTILAW**

SHAREHOLDERS

DOUGLAS R. ANDRES, born Staten Island, New York, July 13, 1952; admitted to bar, 1978, Oregon. *Education:* Bucknell University (B.A. in Japanese Studies, cum laude, 1974); George Washington University (J.D., 1978). ***PRACTICE AREAS:*** Employment Discrimination; Civil Rights; Municipal Liability; Litigation. ***Email:*** doug.andres@bullivant.com

RANDY L. ARTHUR, born Sullivan, Indiana, February 19, 1955; admitted to bar, 1985, Oregon. *Education:* Occidental College (A.B., 1977); University of California at Berkeley (M.S.W., 1983); Hofstra University (J.D., with distinction, 1985). ***PRACTICE AREAS:*** First-Party Insurance Coverage Law; Fidelity and Surety; Commercial Litigation. ***Email:*** randy.arthur@bullivant.com

JOHN P. ASHWORTH, born Seattle, Washington, May 20, 1954; admitted to bar, 1982, Oregon; 1983, U.S. District Court, District of Oregon; 1984, Washington; 1985, U.S. District Court, Western District of Washington; 1988, U.S. Supreme Court; 1989, U.S. Court of Appeals, Ninth Circuit. *Education:* Stanford University (B.A., with distinction, 1976); New York University (J.D., 1982). ***PRACTICE AREAS:*** Environmental Litigation; Commercial Litigation. ***Email:*** john.ashworth@bullivant.com

RONALD E. BAILEY, born Portland, Oregon, August 12, 1937; admitted to bar, 1963, Oregon. *Education:* University of Oregon (B.S., 1959); Willamette University (J.D., 1963). ***PRACTICE AREAS:*** Insurance Litigation; Product Liability Defense; Drug and Medical Device Defense. ***Email:*** ron.bailey@bullivant.com

JOHN A. BENNETT, born The Dalles, Oregon, October 7, 1950; admitted to bar, 1975, Oregon; 1979, U.S. District Court, District of Oregon. *Education:* University of Oregon (B.A., 1972); Northwestern School of Law of Lewis and Clark College (J.D., 1975). ***PRACTICE AREAS:*** Commercial Litigation; Insurance Coverage. ***Email:*** john.bennett@bullivant.com

SCOTT A. BROOKSBY, born Eugene, Oregon, August 13, 1962; admitted to bar, 1994, Pennsylvania; 1995, Oregon; 1996, U.S. District Court, District of Oregon. *Education:* Brigham Young University (B.A., 1987); Catholic University of America (J.D., 1994). ***PRACTICE AREAS:*** Products Liability; Commercial Litigation. ***Email:*** scott.brooksby@bullivant.com

HOWARD W. CARSMAN, born Glendale, California, January 4, 1953; admitted to bar, 1979, Idaho and U.S. District Court, District of Idaho; 1984, U.S. Court of Appeals, Ninth Circuit; 1987, Oregon and U.S. District Court, District of Oregon. *Education:* California State University at Northridge (B.A., magna cum laude, 1975); University of California School of Law at Davis (J.D., 1979). ***PRACTICE AREAS:*** Construction Law; Alternative Dispute Resolution. ***Email:*** howard.carsman@bullivant.com

RONALD J. CLARK, born Walla Walla, Washington, March 15, 1960; admitted to bar, 1988, Oregon. *Education:* Western Oregon State College (B.S., 1983); Northwestern School of Law of Lewis and Clark College (J.D., cum laude, 1987). ***PRACTICE AREAS:*** Insurance Coverage and Litigation; Products Liability; Tort Law. ***Email:*** ron.clark@bullivant.com

(This Listing Continued)

BULLIVANT HOUSER BAILEY PC, Portland—Continued

STEPHEN F. COOK, born Chicago, Illinois, June 18, 1958; admitted to bar, 1983, Oregon. *Education:* Dartmouth College (B.A., magna cum laude, 1980); Stanford University (J.D., 1983). ***PRACTICE AREAS:*** Corporate Law; International Trade; Intellectual Property; Mergers and Acquisitions; Real Estate and Land Use. ***Email:*** steve.cook@bullivant.com

CLAY D. CREPS, born Detroit, Michigan, January 17, 1960; admitted to bar, 1986, Montana and U.S. District Court, District of Montana; 1988, Michigan and U.S. Court of Appeals, Sixth Circuit; 1989, U.S. District Court, Eastern District of Michigan; 1992, Oregon and U.S. District Court, District of Oregon. *Education:* University of Notre Dame (B.A., summa cum laude, 1982); Harvard Law School (J.D., cum laude, 1985). ***PRACTICE AREAS:*** Employment Counseling and Litigation. ***Email:*** clay.creps@bullivant.com

DIANNE K. DAILEY, born Great Falls, Montana, October 10, 1950; admitted to bar, 1982, Oregon; 1984, Washington. *Education:* Montana State University; Portland State University (B.S., with honors, 1977); Northwestern School of Law of Lewis and Clark College (J.D., 1982). ***PRACTICE AREAS:*** Insurance Litigation; Commercial Litigation; Environmental Litigation. ***Email:*** dianne.dailey@bullivant.com

JAMES G. DRISCOLL, born Boston, Massachusetts, June 17, 1948; admitted to bar, 1977, Oregon and U.S. District Court, District of Oregon; 1980, U.S. Court of Appeals, Ninth Circuit; 1989, U.S. Supreme Court; 1992, California and U.S. District Court, Eastern, Northern, Central and Southern Districts of California. *Education:* Columbia College, Columbia University (B.A., 1971); Northwestern School of Law, Lewis and Clark College (J.D., 1977). ***PRACTICE AREAS:*** Commercial Litigation; Environmental; ERISA/Employee Benefits; Insurance Coverage. ***Email:*** jim.driscoll@bullivant.com

JEFFREY S. EDEN, born Portland, Oregon, August 1, 1960; admitted to bar, 1985, Oregon; 1986, U.S. District Court, District of Oregon; 1990, Washington and U.S. District Court, Western District of Washington; 1992, U.S. Supreme Court. *Education:* University of Delaware; University of Oregon (B.S., 1982); Northwestern School of Law of Lewis and Clark College (J.D., magna cum laude, 1985). ***PRACTICE AREAS:*** Personal Injury; Products Liability Defense. ***Email:*** jeff.eden@bullivant.com

STEPHEN F. ENGLISH, born Portland, Oregon, January 17, 1948; admitted to bar, 1973, Oregon and U.S. District Court, District of Oregon; 1980, U.S. Court of Appeals, Ninth Circuit; 1982, U.S. Supreme Court. *Education:* University of Oregon, Honors College (B.A., with honors, 1970); Hastings College of Law, University of California (J.D., 1973). ***PRACTICE AREAS:*** Commercial Litigation; Products Liability; Intellectual Property; Environmental. ***Email:*** steve.english@bullivant.com

DAVID A. ERNST, born Portland, Oregon, October 2, 1960; admitted to bar, 1985, Oregon and U.S. District Court, District of Oregon; 1990, Washington; U.S. District Court, Western District of Washington. *Education:* Oregon State University (B.S., 1982); Northwestern School of Law of Lewis and Clark College (J.D., cum laude, 1985). ***PRACTICE AREAS:*** Food Products Liability; Federal Civil Litigation; Church Law; Employment Claims. ***Email:*** dave.ernst@bullivant.com

KIMBALL H. FERRIS, born Princeton, New Jersey, September 11, 1947; admitted to bar, 1978, Oregon. *Education:* Yale University (B.A., 1969); University of Massachusetts (M.R.P., 1974; M.L.A., 1975); Willamette University (J.D., 1978). ***PRACTICE AREAS:*** Real Property; Finance and Banking; Corporate and General Business; International Law. ***Email:*** kimball.ferris@bullivant.com

DAVID R. FOSTER, born Galesburg, Illinois, May 22, 1952; admitted to bar, 1979, Arizona and U.S. District Court, District of Arizona; 1980, Oregon and U.S. District Court, District of Oregon; 1985, Washington and U.S. District Court, Western District of Washington. *Education:* New College (B.A., 1974); University of Arizona (J.D., 1979). ***PRACTICE AREAS:*** Commerical Litigation; Products Liability. ***Email:*** david.foster@bullivant.com

DOUGLAS G. HOUSER, born Oregon City, Oregon, July 11, 1935; admitted to bar, 1960, Oregon; 1974, U.S. Supreme Court; 1980, U.S. Court of International Trade. *Education:* Willamette University (B.A., 1957); Stanford University (J.D., 1960). ***PRACTICE AREAS:*** Insurance Coverage; Products Liability; Commercial Litigation; International Practice. ***Email:*** doug.houser@bullivant.com

THOMAS L. HUTCHINSON, born Dallas, Texas, September 24, 1963; admitted to bar, 1992, Louisiana; 1999, Oregon; 2001, U.S. District Court, District of Oregon. *Education:* University of Minnesota (B.S., 1985); Louisiana State University (J.D., 1992). ***PRACTICE AREAS:*** Commercial Litigation; Professional Liability; International Practice. ***Email:*** tom.hutchinson@bullivant.com

STUART D. JONES, born Portland, Oregon, July 12, 1954; admitted to bar, 1984, Oregon; 1986, U.S. District Court, District of Oregon; 1987, U.S. District Court, Northern District of California; 1992, U.S. Court of Appeals, Ninth Circuit. *Education:* Lewis and Clark College (B.S., 1977; J.D., 1984). ***PRACTICE AREAS:*** Commercial Litigation; Insurance Coverage. ***Email:*** stuart.jones@bullivant.com

JOHN M. JUNKIN, born 1949; admitted to bar, 1974, Oregon; U.S. District Court, District of Oregon; U.S. Court of Appeals, Ninth Circuit. *Education:* Oregon State University (B.S.); University of the Pacific, McGeorge School of Law (J.D., 1974). ***PRACTICE AREAS:*** Governmental Law; Real Estate and Land Use; Corporate Law. ***Email:*** john.junkin@bullivant.com

JOHN T. KAEMPF, born Portland, Oregon, November 23, 1966; admitted to bar, 1992, Oregon; 1993, U.S. District Court, District of Oregon and U.S. Court of Appeals, Ninth Circuit. *Education:* Portland State University (B.S., with honors, 1989); Northwestern School of Law of Lewis and Clark College (J.D., cum laude, 1992). ***PRACTICE AREAS:*** Personal Injury Defense; Products Liability; Commercial Litigation. ***Email:*** john.kaempf@bullivant.com

LISA E. LEAR, born Denver, Colorado, July 7, 1959; admitted to bar, 1985, Oregon; 1989, U.S. Court of Appeals, Ninth Circuit; 1992, U.S. Supreme Court. *Education:* University of Colorado (B.A., magna cum laude, 1981); Northwestern School of Law, Lewis and Clark College (J.D., summa cum laude, 1985). ***PRACTICE AREAS:*** Appellate Practice. ***Email:*** lisa.lear@bullivant.com

R. DANIEL LINDAHL, born Portland, Oregon, October 5, 1958; admitted to bar, 1984, Oregon and Washington; 1985, U.S. District Court, District of Oregon, U.S. Court of Appeals, Ninth Circuit; 1986, U.S. District Court, Western District of Washington; 1988, U.S. Supreme Court; 1993, U.S. District Court, Eastern District of Washington; 1996, U.S. Court of Appeals, Fourth Circuit. *Education:* University of Oregon (B.S., 1980); Northwestern School of Lewis and Clark College (J.D., cum laude, 1984). ***PRACTICE AREAS:*** Civil Appeals. ***Email:*** dan.lindahl@bullivant.com

JEANNE F. LOFTIS, born Minneapolis, Minnesota, June 20, 1963; admitted to bar, 1991, Oregon; 1991, U.S. District Court, District of Oregon; 1992, California. *Education:* University of California at Davis (B.S., 1985); McGeorge School of Law, University of the Pacific (J.D., 1991). ***PRACTICE AREAS:*** Products Liability; Construction and Development; Toxic Tort; Food and Beverage. ***Email:*** jeanne.loftis@bullivant.com

ROBERT B. LOWRY, born Medford, Oregon, December 1, 1951; admitted to bar, 1985, Oregon, U.S. District Court, District of Oregon and U.S. Court of Appeals, Ninth Circuit. *Education:* University of Portland (B.A., Communications, maxima cum laude, 1974); Northwestern School of Law of Lewis and Clark College (J.D., magna cum laude, 1985). ***PRACTICE AREAS:*** Commercial Litigation; Environmental Products Liability; RICO. ***Email:*** bob.lowry@bullivant.com

FRANCIS J. MALONEY, III, born Ronceverte, West Virginia, May 28, 1967; admitted to bar, 1995, Oregon. *Education:* Boston College (B.A., 1989); University of Oregon (J.D., 1995). ***PRACTICE AREAS:*** Insurance Coverage and Litigation. ***Email:*** fj.maloney@bullivant.com

CHRYS A. MARTIN, born Portland, Oregon, June 18, 1953; admitted to bar, 1981, Oregon. *Education:* Oregon State University (B.A., with honors, 1975) Phi Kappa Phi; Northwestern School of Law at Lewis & Clark College (J.D., cum laude, 1981). Member, Cornelius Honor Society. *Member:* Multnomah County and American (Member, Tort and Insurance Practice Section; Chair, Health Insurance Committee, 1992-93; Member and Former Vice Chair, Employer-Employee Relations Committee; Member: Life Insurance Committee; Section of Labor and Employment Law; Vice Chair, Employee Benefits Committee) Bar Associations; Oregon State Bar; Defense Research Institute (Member, Law Institutes); Oregon Association of Defense Counsel. ***PRACTICE AREAS:*** Employment Counseling and Litigation; ERISA/Employee Benefits. ***Email:*** chrys.martin@bullivant.com

STANLEY E. MARTINSON, born Clatskanie, Oregon, September 11, 1935; admitted to bar, 1970, Oregon. *Education:* Lewis and Clark College and University of Florida (B.S., 1957); Northwestern School of Law of Lewis and Clark College (J.D., 1970). ***PRACTICE AREAS:*** Real Property; Corporate Law. ***Email:*** stan.martinson@bullivant.com

DANIEL F. McNEIL, born Burlington, Vermont, December 12, 1954; admitted to bar, 1980, Oregon and U.S. District Court, District of Oregon; 1986, Washington and U.S. District Court, Western District of Washington. *Education:* University of Vermont (B.S., 1976); University of Notre Dame (J.D., 1979). ***PRACTICE AREAS:*** Commercial Litigation. ***Email:*** daniel.mcneil@bullivant.com

ROBERT B. MILLER, born Richmond, Indiana, March 18, 1959; admitted to bar, 1991, Florida; 1993, Colorado and District of Columbia; 1994, U.S. Supreme Court; 1996, Oregon and U.S. District Court, District of Oregon; 2000, Washington; 2001, U.S. District Court, Eastern District of Washington. *Education:* University of Central Florida (B.A., summa cum laude, 1987); University of Miami (J.D., 1990). ***PRACTICE AREAS:*** ERISA/Employee Benefits; Life, Health and Disability; Commercial Litigation. ***Email:*** bob.miller@bullivant.com

ROBERT A. MOORE, born San Francisco, California, January 1, 1955; admitted to bar, 1982, California; 1984, Oregon; 1986, Washington (inactive). *Education:* University of California at Berkeley (A.B., magna cum laude, 1977); University of Virginia (J.D., 1982). ***PRACTICE AREAS:*** Corporate Law; Intellectual Property; Mergers and Acquisitions. ***Email:*** robert.moore@bullivant.com

JOHN R. OSBURN, born Tacoma, Washington, August 25, 1955; admitted to bar, 1989, Oregon; 1991, U.S. District Court, District of Oregon and U.S. Court of Appeals, Ninth Circuit. *Education:* University of Oregon (B.S., with honors, 1986; J.D., 1989). ***PRACTICE AREAS:*** Real Estate and Land Use; Government Law; Asbestos Litigation. ***Email:*** john.osburn@bullivant.com

LOREN D. PODWILL, born Monticello, New York, February 21, 1956; admitted to bar, 1984, Oregon, Washington and U.S. District Court, District of Oregon; 1992, U.S. District Court, Eastern and Western Districts of Washington and U.S. Court of Federal Claims. *Education:* Colorado State University (B.A., 1979); Willamette University (J.D., cum laude, 1984). ***PRACTICE AREAS:*** Commercial Litigation; Construction Law; Fidelity and Surety Law; Professional Liability Litigation; Intellectual Property Law. ***Email:*** loren.podwill@bullivant.com

RENÉE E. ROTHAUGE, born Enid, Oklahoma, February 27, 1963; admitted to bar, 1990, Oregon; 1991, Washington. *Education:* Georgetown University (B.S.F.S., 1986); Willamette University (J.D., cum laude, 1990). ***PRACTICE AREAS:*** Intellectual Property; Commercial Litigation. ***Email:*** renee.rothauge@bullivant.com

BETH SKILLERN, born Pasadena, California, August 25, 1944; admitted to bar, 1986, Oregon; 1987, U.S. District Court, District of Oregon. *Education:* Southern Oregon State College (B.A., 1966); Northwestern School of Law of Lewis and Clark College (J.D., 1986). ***PRACTICE AREAS:*** Insurance Coverage; Commercial Litigation. ***Email:*** beth.skillern@bullivant.com

KATHERINE S. SOMERVELL, born Oakland, California, August 6, 1963; admitted to bar, 1995, Oregon; 1997, U.S. District Court, District of Oregon. *Education:* University of California at Berkeley (B.A., 1985); University of Virginia (M.A., 1988); Northwestern School of Law of Lewis & Clark College (J.D., 1995). ***PRACTICE AREAS:*** Life, Health, and Disability; Employment Law; ERISA/Employee Benefits. ***Email:*** katherine.somervell@bullivant.com

(This Listing Continued)

RONALD G. STEPHENSON, born Seattle, Washington, June 12, 1942; admitted to bar, 1967, Oregon. *Education:* Lewis & Clark College (B.S., 1964); Willamette University (J.D., 1967). ***PRACTICE AREAS:*** Products Liability; Professional Liability. ***Email:*** ron.stephenson@bullivant.com

DAVID D. VANSPEYBROECK, born Cambridge, Massachusetts, July 12, 1962; admitted to bar, 1989, Massachusetts; 1995, Oregon; U.S. District Court, District of Oregon; U.S. District Court, District of Massachusetts. *Education:* Hamilton College (B.A., 1984); Boston University Law School (J.D., cum laude, 1989). ***PRACTICE AREAS:*** Insurance Coverage; Special Investigations Unit. ***Email:*** david.vanspeybroeck@bullivant.com

MARGARET M. VAN VALKENBURG, born Seattle, Washington, May 6, 1957; admitted to bar, 1983, Washington; 1993, Oregon. *Education:* University of Washington (B.A., 1979); University of Oregon (J.D., 1983). ***PRACTICE AREAS:*** Commercial Litigation; Insurance Coverage. ***Email:*** megge.vanvalkenburg@bullivant.com

KAREN M. VICKERS, born Portland, Oregon, March 2, 1966; admitted to bar, 1991, Oregon; 1992, U.S. District Court, District of Oregon. *Education:* University of Oregon (B.S., 1988); Willamette University College of Law (J.D., cum laude, 1991). ***PRACTICE AREAS:*** School Law; Employment Counseling and Litigation. ***Email:*** karen.vickers@bullivant.com

PETER J. VITEZNIK, born San Francisco, California, February 2, 1965; admitted to bar, 1994, Oregon; 1995, Washington; 1997, U.S. District Court, District of Oregon. *Education:* Oregon State University (B.S., 1987); Willamette University (J.D. cum laude, 1994). ***PRACTICE AREAS:*** Construction Law; Commercial Litigation; Products Liability. ***Email:*** pete.viteznik@bullivant.com

TIMOTHY J. WACHTER, born Salem, Oregon, August 18, 1962; admitted to bar, 1987, Oregon; 1990, Washington. *Education:* Washington State University (B.A., cum laude, 1984); Willamette University (J.D., 1987). ***PRACTICE AREAS:*** Trusts and Estates; Probate; Taxation. ***Email:*** tim.wachter@bullivant.com

JOSEPH W. WEST, born Portland, Oregon, December 8, 1959; admitted to bar, 1985, Oregon and U.S. District Court, District of Oregon. *Education:* Willamette University (B.S., 1982); University of Oregon School of Law (J.D., 1985). ***PRACTICE AREAS:*** Real Estate and Land Use; Banks and Banking; Corporate Law. ***Email:*** joe.west@bullivant.com

RICHARD J. WHITTEMORE, born Portland, Oregon, January 19, 1956; admitted to bar, 1982, Oregon and U.S. District Court, District of Oregon; 1983, U.S. Court of Appeals, Ninth Circuit. *Education:* Colorado College (B.A., cum laude, 1978); Lewis and Clark, Northwestern School of Law (J.D., 1982). ***PRACTICE AREAS:*** Commercial Litigation; Products Liability; Environmental. ***Email:*** dick.whittemore@bullivant.com

JOEL WILSON, born Martin, Tennessee, October 8, 1950; admitted to bar, 1976, Missouri and U.S. District Court, Western District of Missouri; 1980, U.S. Supreme Court and Oregon; 1982, U.S. Court of Appeals, Ninth Circuit. *Education:* Southeast Missouri State University (B.A., 1972); University of Missouri (J.D., 1976). ***PRACTICE AREAS:*** Professional Liability Defense; Commerical Litigation. ***Email:*** joel.wilson@bullivant.com

ASSOCIATES

KEVIN E. BARTON, born Westminster, California; admitted to bar, 2002, Oregon. *Education:* Gonzaga University (B.A., cum laude, 1999); University of Notre Dame Law School (J.D., 2002). ***PRACTICE AREAS:*** General Litigation. ***Email:*** kevin.barton@bullivant.com

LLOYD BERNSTEIN, born Framingham, Massachusetts, July 11, 1969; admitted to bar, 1996, California; 2000, Oregon. *Education:* State University of New York at Plattsburg (B.A., 1991); California Western School of Law (J.D., 1996). ***PRACTICE AREAS:*** Litigation; Insurance Coverage. ***Email:*** lloyd.bernstein@bullivant.com

RYAN P. BOYLE, born 1979; admitted to bar, 2005, Oregon. *Education:* University of Puget Sound (B.A., 2001); University of Oregon, School of Law (J.D., 2005). ***PRACTICE AREAS:*** Products Liability. ***Email:*** ryan.boyle@bullivant.com

TIMOTHY J. CALDERBANK, born Tacoma, Washington, January 6, 1964; admitted to bar, 1997, Oregon; 1998, U.S. District Court, District of Oregon; 2001, U.S. Court of Federal Claims. *Education:* Western Washington University (B.A., with honors, 1994); Northwestern School of Law of Lewis & Clark College (J.D., cum laude, 1997). ***PRACTICE AREAS:*** Commercial Litigation; Construction and Development. ***Email:*** tim.calderbank@bullivant.com

MATTHEW CRAIG CASEY, born Portland, Oregon, August 24, 1973; admitted to bar, 1998, Oregon. *Education:* University of Santa Clara (B.S., in Political Science, 1995); Willamette University (J.D., 1998). ***PRACTICE AREAS:*** Personal Injury; Products Liability; Construction and Development. ***Email:*** matt.casey@bullivant.com

DARIN CHRISTENSEN, born Provo, Utah, May 23, 1967; admitted to bar, 1997, Oregon; 1998, U.S. Tax Court and U.S. Court of Appeals, Ninth Circuit. *Education:* Brigham Young University (B.S., with honors, 1991; J.D., cum laude, 1996); University of Florida (LL.M., Taxation, 1997). ***PRACTICE AREAS:*** Federal and State Tax; Business Planning; Estate Planning. ***Email:*** darin.christensen@bullivant.com

DAYNA J. CHRISTIAN, admitted to bar, 2003, Oregon and Washington; U.S. District Court, District of Oregon. *Education:* American University (B.A., Justice, 1993); Northwestern School of Law, Lewis & Clark College (J.D., Environmental Law Certificate, 1997). ***PRACTICE AREAS:*** Commercial Litigation. ***Email:*** dayna.christian@bullivant.com

NANCY M. COOPER, born 1958; admitted to bar, 1995, Oregon, U.S. Court of Appeals, Ninth Circuit and U.S. District Court, District of Oregon. *Education:* University of Arizona (B.S., 1980); Northwestern School of Law (J.D., 1995). ***PRACTICE AREAS:*** Labor and Employment; Employment Counseling. ***Email:*** nancy.cooper@bullivant.com

BETH CUPANI, admitted to bar, 1996, Oregon. *Education:* California State University, Fresno (B.A., cum laude, 1992); Northwestern School of Law (J.D., 1995). ***PRACTICE AREAS:*** Insurance Coverage; Special Investigations Unit. ***Email:*** beth.cupani@bullivant.com

(This Listing Continued)

NICHOLAS L. DAZER, born Ann Arbor, Michigan, May 23, 1974; admitted to bar, 2000, Oregon; 2001, U.S. District Court, District of Oregon. *Education:* University of Alaska (B.A., cum laude, 1996); Northwestern School of Law of Lewis and Clark College (J.D., with certificate in Environmental and Natural Resources Law, 2000). ***PRACTICE AREAS:*** Commercial Litigation; Products Liability. ***Email:*** nick.dazer@bullivant.com

STEPHEN FORREST DEATHERAGE, born Corona, California, April 9, 1969; admitted to bar, 1998, Oregon. *Education:* University of Oregon (B.A., 1991); Willamette University (J.D., cum laude, 1998). ***PRACTICE AREAS:*** Commercial Litigation; Environmental Litigation. ***Email:*** stephen.deatherage@bullivant.com

ALLEN E. ERAUT, admitted to bar, 1999, Oregon; 2000, Washington. *Education:* Santa Clara University (B.S., Political Science, 1996); University of Oregon School of Law (J.D., 1999). ***PRACTICE AREAS:*** Commerical Litigation; Insurance Coverage; Products Liability. ***Email:*** allen.eraut@bullivant.com

SUSAN L. FORD, born Iowa City, Iowa, September 27, 1965; admitted to bar, 1994, District of Columbia; 1995, Maryland; 1997, Oregon; 1998, Washington; 2000, U.S. District Court, District of Oregon. *Education:* Northwestern University (B.S., 1988); Georgetown University (J.D., 1994). ***PRACTICE AREAS:*** Construction Litigation; Commercial Litigation; Intellectual Property. ***Email:*** susan.ford@bullivant.com

MARIANNE M. GHIM, born Seattle, Washington, July 22, 1964; admitted to bar, 1992, Washington, Oregon; 1993, U.S. District Court, District of Oregon. *Education:* University of Oregon (B.A., 1987); Willamette University (J.D., 1991). ***PRACTICE AREAS:*** Insurance Coverage. ***Email:*** marianne.ghim@bullivant.com

LETA E. GORMAN, born Portland, Oregon, October 10, 1967; admitted to bar, 1994, Washington; 1997, U.S. District Court, Western District of Washington; 1998, Oregon, U.S. District Court, Eastern District of Washington and U.S. Court of Appeals, Ninth Circuit; 1999, U.S. District Court, District of Oregon and U.S. Supreme Court. *Education:* University of Washington (B.A., with honors, 1989); Seattle University (J.D., cum laude, 1994). ***PRACTICE AREAS:*** Commercial Litigation; Products Liability. ***Email:*** leta.gorman@bullivant.com

CHELSEA L. GRIMMIUS, admitted to bar, 2003, Oregon. *Education:* Brigham Young University (B.A., 2000); George Washington School of Law (J.D., 2003). ***PRACTICE AREAS:*** Employment Litigation. ***Email:*** chelsea.grimmius@bullivant.com

KRISTA N. HARDWICK, born 1979; admitted to bar, 2005, Oregon. *Education:* University of Nevada, Las Vegas (B.A., cum laude, 2002); Willamette University, College of Law (J.D., magna cum laude, 2005). ***PRACTICE AREAS:*** Business Litigation. ***Email:*** krista.hardwick@bullivant.com

DELYNE KLEIN, born December 28, 1968; admitted to bar, 2004, Oregon and Washington; 2005, U.S. District Court, District of Oregon. *Education:* Linfield College (B.S.N., summa cum laude, 1997); Northwestern School of Law, Lewis & Clark College (J.D., cum laude, 2003). [Staff Judge Advocate, U.S. Army Reserve, 2005]. ***PRACTICE AREAS:*** Asbestos Litigation; Litigation; Products Liability. ***Email:*** delyne.klein@bullivant.com

JOHN M. KREUTZER, born Portland, Oregon, April 14, 1966; admitted to bar, 1997, Oregon; 1998, U.S. District Court, District of Oregon; 1999, U.S. Court of Appeals, Ninth Circuit; 2000, Washington; 2002, U.S. District Court, Western District of Washington. *Education:* Oregon State University (B.S., 1989); Willamette University (J.D., 1997). ***PRACTICE AREAS:*** Employment Litigation and Counseling. ***Email:*** john.kreutzer@bullivant.com

J. RILEY LAGESEN, admitted to bar, 2003, Oregon. *Education:* University of Southern California at Los Angeles (B.F.A., 1993); Northwestern School of Law of Lewis & Clark College (J.D., 2003). ***PRACTICE AREAS:*** Commerical Litigation; Food and Beverage. ***Email:*** jriley.lagesen@bullivant.com

ANDREW C. LAUERSDORF, born Madison, Wisconsin, June 26, 1966; admitted to bar, 1998, Oregon; 2000, U.S. District Court, District of Oregon. *Education:* University of Wisconsin-Madison (B.A., 1992); Northwestern School of Law, Lewis and Clark College (J.D., 1997). ***PRACTICE AREAS:*** Insurance Coverage; Special Investigations Unit. ***Email:*** andrew.lauersdorf@bullivant.com

BRAD J. LEWIS, born Portland, Oregon, October 31, 1959; admitted to bar, 1989, Oregon. *Education:* Oregon State University (B.S., with honors, 1982); Lewis and Clark College (J.D., 1986). ***PRACTICE AREAS:*** Property Casualty Litigation; First Party Insurance Litigation. ***Email:*** brad.lewis@bullivant.com

MICHAEL J. MAYERLE, admitted to bar, 2003, Oregon. *Education:* Lewis and Clark College (B.S., Biology, 1990); Boston University, Center for Energy and Environmental Studies (M.A., International Relations and Resource and Environmental Management, 1996); Northwestern School of Law, Lewis & Clark College (J.D., cum laude, 2003). ***PRACTICE AREAS:*** Construction and Development; Surety. ***Email:*** michael.mayerle@bullivant.com

ROBERT C. MUTH, born Lechlade, England, December 22, 1963; admitted to bar, 1988, Texas; 1990, North Carolina; 1997, Oregon. *Education:* Millsaps College (B.A., cum laude, with honors, 1985); Washington and Lee University (J.D., 1988). ***PRACTICE AREAS:*** Commercial Litigation; ERISA/Employee Benefits; Products Liability. ***Email:*** robert.muth@bullivant.com

KRISTIN L. OLSON, admitted to bar, 2003, Oregon. *Education:* Gonzaga University (B.A., cum laude, Political Science, 1999); University of Oregon, School of Law (J.D., 2002). ***PRACTICE AREAS:*** ERISA/Employee Benefits; Life, Health and Disability. ***Email:*** kristin.olson@bullivant.com

DAIN PAULSON, born July 5, 1970; admitted to bar, 1997, Oregon. *Education:* University of Oregon (B.A., 1993); University of Oregon, School of Law (J.D., 1997). ***Email:*** dain.paulson@bullivant.com

TODD M. PECK, born Evansville, Indiana, June 11, 1967; admitted to bar, 1992, Oregon; 1994, U.S. District Court, District of Oregon. *Education:* Washington State University (B.A., with honors, 1989); Syracuse University (J.D., magna cum laude, 1992). ***PRACTICE AREAS:*** Commercial Litigation; Construction Litigation. ***Email:*** todd.peck@bullivant.com

(This Listing Continued)

BULLIVANT HOUSER BAILEY PC, Portland—Continued

HOLLY E. PETTIT, born Portland, Oregon, 1975; admitted to bar, 2000, Oregon. *Education:* Lewis and Clark College (B.A., 1997); Northwestern School of Law (J.D., summa cum laude, 2000). ***PRACTICE AREAS:*** Insurance Coverage. ***Email:*** holly.pettit@bullivant.com

SHEILA H. POTTER, born Washington, D.C., July 2, 1971; admitted to bar, 1999, Oregon. *Education:* College of William & Mary (B.A., 1993); University of Colorado (J.D., 1999). ***PRACTICE AREAS:*** Insurance Coverage Litigation. ***Email:*** sheila.potter@bullivant.com

ANTHONY REINER, born 1965; admitted to bar, 1996, Oregon; 1999, U.S. District Court, District of Oregon. *Education:* Lewis and Clark College (B.S., 1987); Willamette University College of Law (J.D., cum laude, 1996). ***PRACTICE AREAS:*** Insurance Coverage; Special Investigations Unit. ***Email:*** tony.reiner@bullivant.com

BLAKE ROBINSON, born 1979; admitted to bar, 2005, Oregon. *Education:* Eastern Oregon University (B.A., cum laude, 2002); Willamette University, College of Law (J.D., 2005). ***PRACTICE AREAS:*** Insurance Coverage. ***Email:*** blake.robinson@bullivant.com

SARA VAN LOH, born August 28, 1977; admitted to bar, 2004, Oregon and U.S. District Court, District of Oregon. *Education:* University of Oregon (B.A., Psychology, magna cum laude, 2001) Phi Beta Kappa; University of California, Berkeley, Boalt Hall School of Law (J.D., 2004). ***PRACTICE AREAS:*** Litigation; Special Investigations and Coverage Unit. ***Email:*** sara.vanloh@bullivant.com

TONYA VAN WALLEGHEM, admitted to bar, 1998, Oregon; 1999, U.S. District Court, District of Oregon. *Education:* University of Alberta (B.S., 1992); Willamette University College of Law (J.D., cum laude, 1998). ***PRACTICE AREAS:*** International Practice; Commercial Litigation. ***Email:*** tonya.vanwalleghem@bullivant.com

SHANNON VINCENT, born 1980; (admission pending). *Education:* Willamette University (B.A., cum laude, 2002); University of Pennsylvania Law School (J.D., 2005). ***PRACTICE AREAS:*** Business Litigation.

MICHAEL YIMESGEN, born December 13, 1975; admitted to bar, 2004, Oregon. *Education:* University of California, Davis (B.A., 1998); Willamette University, College of Law (J.D., 2004). ***LANGUAGES:*** Italian. ***PRACTICE AREAS:*** Commercial Litigation. ***Email:*** michael.yimesgen@bullivant.com

OF COUNSEL

THOMAS A. GERBER, born Portland, Oregon, September 27, 1947; admitted to bar, 1974, Oregon and U.S. District Court, District of Oregon; 1979, U.S. Supreme Court; 1987, U.S. Court of Appeals, Ninth Circuit. *Education:* Portland State University (B.S., 1971); Northwestern School of Law, Lewis and Clark College (J.D., 1974). ***PRACTICE AREAS:*** Debtor/Creditor Relations; Commercial Litigation; Personal Injury; Estate Planning and Probate. ***Email:*** thomas.gerber@bullivant.com

STEPHEN B. HILL, born Bluefield, West Virginia, July 17, 1941; admitted to bar, 1966, Oregon. *Education:* Northern Illinois University and University of Illinois (B.Sc., Accountancy, magna cum laude, 1963); Stanford University (LL.B., 1966). ***PRACTICE AREAS:*** Taxation; Mergers, Acquisitions and Divestitures; Corporate Law. ***Email:*** steve.hill@bullivant.com

HENRY "CHIP" LAZENBY, admitted to bar, 1982, Oregon. *Education:* Harvard University (A.B.); University of Oregon (M.B.A.; J.D.). *Member:* Multnomah County Bar Association; Oregon State Bar. ***PRACTICE AREAS:*** Real Estate; Land Use. ***Email:*** chip.lazenby@bullivant.com

WALTER H. PENDERGRASS, born Portland, Oregon, January 26, 1925; admitted to bar, 1950, Oregon. *Education:* Stanford University (A.B., 1947; J.D., 1950). ***PRACTICE AREAS:*** Probate; Estate Planning; Business Law. ***Email:*** walter.pendergrass@bullivant.com

JEFFREY G. ROBERTSON, born Medford, Oregon, October 19, 1973; admitted to bar, 2000, Washington; 2003, Oregon. *Education:* University of Washington (B.A., 1995); Indiana University School of Law (J.D., magna cum laude, 2000). ***PRACTICE AREAS:*** ERISA/ Employee Benefits; Tax Law; Fiduciary Advice. ***Email:*** jeffrey.robertson@bullivant.com

DONALD R. STARK, born Portland, Oregon, April 1, 1928; admitted to bar, 1954, Oregon. *Education:* University of Oregon (B.S., 1951) University of Oregon School of Law (J.D., 1954). ***PRACTICE AREAS:*** Real Estate and Land Use. ***Email:*** don.stark@bullivant.com

MARK L. STERMITZ, born August 29, 1953; admitted to bar, 1983, Montana; 2004, Oregon. *Education:* University of Montana (B.A., 1980); University of Montana, School of Law (J.D., 1983). ***PRACTICE AREAS:*** Commercial Litigation; Environmental Law; Real Estate; Land Use. ***Email:*** mark.stermitz@bullivant.com

REPRESENTATIVE CLIENTS: Acrymed; Association of Bay Area Governments; Archway Cookies LLC; Bear Creek Corporation (Harry & David); Boykin Lodging (Doubletree Inns); Casco Communications; Caterpillar, Inc.; Chubb Group of Insurance Companies; Clarity Visual Systems; Deere & Company; Dr. Martens AirWair USA; The Hartford; KinderCare Learning Centers; Louisiana-Pacific Corporation; MacKay & Sposito; McDonald's Corp.; The Nautilus Group; Nerve; Norcal Waste Systems; Pacific Coast Restaurants; The Salvation Army; The Standard; Sumitomo Electric Semiconductor Materials, Inc.; T-Mobile USA, Inc.; WaferTech LLC; Wieden + Kennedy; Walsh Construction Company.

(For complete biographical data on personnel at Gold River, California, San Francisco, California, Seattle, Washington and Vancouver, Washington, see Professional Biographies at those locations)

GARY M. BULLOCK AND ASSOCIATES, P.C.

1001 S.W. FIFTH AVENUE, SUITE 1500
PORTLAND, OREGON 97204
Telephone: 503-228-6277
Fax: 503-228-6280
Email: garybullock@qwest.net
URL: http://www.lawyers.com/bullockandregier

General Civil and Trial Practice. Family Law, Personal Injury, Negligence, Corporate, Real Estate and Condemnation Law.

GARY M. BULLOCK, born Roseburg, Oregon, April 22, 1937; admitted to bar, 1966, Oregon; 1971, U.S. Supreme Court; U.S. Claims Court; 1992, Washington; 1996, California; 2003, Idaho. *Education:* Oregon State University (B.S., 1959); Lewis and Clark College (J.D., 1966). *Member:* Washington State and American (Member, Sections on: Corporation, Banking and Business Law; Torts and Insurance Practice) Bar Associations; Oregon State Bar; Oregon Trial Lawyers Association; Idaho State Bar; Washington Trial Lawyers Association; The Association of Trial Lawyers of America. ***PRACTICE AREAS:*** Business; Real Estate; Personal Injury; Family; Condemnation Law.

ARTHUR BAIRD FOWLER, V, born Ridgewood, New Jersey, May 19, 1970; admitted to bar, 1998, Oregon. *Education:* Gettysburg College (B.A., cum laude, honors in Political Science, 1992); Northwestern School of Law (J.D., 1997). ***PRACTICE AREAS:*** Estate Administration; Domestic Relations; General Practice.

ERIC S. POSTMA, born Artesia, California, September 13, 1972; admitted to bar, 1999, Oregon; 2004, California. *Education:* California State University, Fullerton (B.A., 1995); Willamette University (J.D., 1999). Willamette Journal of International Law and Dispute Resolution, 1997-1999 (Editor-in-Chief, 1998-1999). *Member:* Multnomah Bar Association. ***PRACTICE AREAS:*** Civil Litigation; Family Law; Business Law; Trusts and Estates.

JOANNA L. DORCHUCK, born Las Vegas, Nevada, June 6, 1974; admitted to bar, 2001, Oregon. *Education:* Pacific University (B.A., 1996); University of South Dakota (J.D., 2001). Production Editor, South Dakota Law Review. ***PRACTICE AREAS:*** Personal Injury; Domestic Relations.

REPRESENTATIVE CLIENTS: A-1 Tri-City Taxi, Inc.; Autotec, Inc.; BR&R Insurance; Bagett, Griffith & Blackman/Professional Surveyors; Boitano Sanitary Services, Inc.; C and C Construction; Chinook Mini Storage; Columbia Enterprises Northwest; Condor Enterprises Inc.; Courtesy Auto Body, Inc.; Cygnet, Inc.; Derek L. Brown & Assoc., Inc.; EME Funding Corp.; Enway, Inc.; Four Star Distributing, Inc.; Ferguson Surveying Engineering; Frontier Resources, LLC; Great Western Restoration; Hal Kinion & Associates; Haralmer, Inc.; LLC-Heritage Roofing; JB Insulation; Jaciva's Chocolate Ltd.; Joseph Enterprises; Kasch's Nursery; Kohr's Auto Body, Inc.; Lent's Body Shop, Inc.; McDougal Bros., Inc.; Michael's Precast Concrete, LLC; Mike Becker General Contractor; Pioneer Resources, LLC; Sierra West Realty Advisors, Inc.; Stardust/Magna Corporation; Tomassene & Son Insurance, LLC; US Trading Co.; Upper V Painting; Wordsmith Services.

ROBERT G. BURT, P.C.

Established in 1992

THE 1515 BUILDING, SUITE 600
1515 S.W. FIFTH AVENUE
PORTLAND, OREGON 97201-5449
Telephone: 503-223-3600
Fax: 503-274-0778
Email: rgb@burtfirm.com
URL: http://www.burtfirm.com

Tax Law (including Business Tax Planning, Tax-Exempt Charitable Organizations, Administrative Proceedings with the Internal Revenue Service and Oregon Department of Revenue, and Tax Litigation (Civil and Criminal)); Business Law (including Corporations, Partnerships, Limited Liability Companies/Partnerships, Business Trusts, Cooperatives and Sole Proprietorships, particularly Closely-Held and Emerging Growth Businesses); Corporate Law; Partnership Law; Mergers (and other Major Business Transactions including Acquisitions, Reorganizations, and Sales); Nonprofit and Tax Exempt Organizations; Intellectual Property Law; Trademark, Copyright and Unfair Competition (including Registrations, Trade Secret Agreements, Non-Compete Agreements and Licensing Agreements); Trusts and Estates, Wills and Probate (including Wills, Trusts, Probates, Guardianships, Conservatorships, and Asset Protection/Preservation).

ROBERT G. BURT, born Tucson, Arizona, September 7, 1944; admitted to bar, 1972, Arizona; 1973, U.S. Court of Appeals, Eighth and Ninth Circuits; 1974, District of Columbia, U.S. Court of Appeals, First, Second, Fourth, Fifth and Sixth Circuits and U.S. Court of Appeals for the District of Columbia Circuit; 1975, U.S. Supreme Court and U.S. Court of Appeals, Third and Tenth Circuits; 1976, U.S. District Court, District of Oregon; 1977, Oregon, U.S. Tax Court and U.S. Court of Claims; 1978, U.S. Court of International Trade; 1981, U.S. Court of Custom and Patent Appeals; 1991, U.S. Court of Appeals, Seventh, Eleventh and Federal Circuits; 2002, Washington. *Education:* New Mexico Military Institute (A.A., 1964); University of Arizona (B.A., 1965; J.D., 1972); Georgetown University Law Center (LL.M., in Taxation, 1973). Appellate Attorney and Special Assistant to the Assistant Attorney General, Tax Division, U.S. Department of Justice, Washington, D.C., 1973-1975. Trial Attorney, Tax Division, U.S. Department of Justice, Washington, D.C., 1975-1977. Adjunct Professor of Law, Business Taxation, Northwestern School of Law at Lewis and Clark College, 1978 and 1982. Editor, Oregon State Bar, Professional Insight column, 1989-1994. Author: *Statute of Limitation Rules for Assessment of Federal Income Taxes,* Oregon State Bar Bulletin, September, 1989; *Attorney Fee Awards in Federal Tax Litigation,* Oregon State Bar Bulletin, July, 1990; *Discharge of Federal Tax Liabilities in Personal Bankruptcies,* Oregon Certified Public Accountant, May, 1991; *When to Advise the Filing of an Amended Federal Tax Return,* Oregon Certified Public Accountant, March,

(This Listing Continued)

1992; *Tax-Exempt Organizations' Audit, Organizational, and Administrative Issues,* Oregon State Bar Bulletin, January, 1993; *Accountant-Client Disclosures,* Oregon Certified Public Accountant, January, 1994; *Nonfilers: You Can Run, But You Cannot Hide,* Oregon State Bar For the Record, March, 1994; *How to Handle Deductions for Charitable Contributions,* Oregon State Bar Bulletin, May, 1995. *Member:* Multnomah County, Washington State (Member, Sections on: Business Law; Taxation Law) and American (Member: Business Law Section; Committee on Partnerships and Unincorporated Business Organizations, 1989—; Senior Lawyers Division Section; Taxation Section; Exempt Organizations, Closely-Held Businesses and Personal Service Organizations Committee, 1989—) Bar Associations; Oregon State Bar (Member: Business Law Section; Taxation Section; Executive Committee, 1985-1987 and Chair, 1987; Certified Public Accountants Joint Committee, Secretary, 1987-1989, Chair, 1989 and Special Advisor, 1990-1994; Continuing Legal Education Committee, 2002-2004 and Local Professional Responsibility Committee, Multnomah County, 2003-2005 and Chair, 2005); State Bar of Arizona; District of Columbia Bar. [Capt. U.S. Army Special Forces, 1967-1971]. ***PRACTICE AREAS:*** Taxation; Mergers, Acquisitions and Divestitures; Business Acquisitions; Business Divestitures; Mergers and Acquisitions; Business Law; Business Organization; Business Transactions; Buying and Selling of Businesses; Corporate Law; Partnership Law; Partnership Taxation; Nonprofit and Charitable Organizations; Nonprofit Organizations Law; Public Charities; Tax Exempt Organizations; Federal Estate and Gift Taxation; Trusts and Estates; Wills; Probate; Guardianship and Conservatorship; Guardianship; Trademarks; Copyrights; Copyright Licensing; Copyright Registration; Intellectual Property; Intellectual Property Licensing; Trade Secrets. ***Email:*** rgb@burtfirm.com

BUSSE & HUNT

Established in 1981

521 AMERICAN BANK BUILDING
621 SW MORRISON STREET
PORTLAND, OREGON 97205
Telephone: 503-248-0504
Fax: 503-248-2131
URL: http://www.busseandhuntlaw.com
URL: http://www.busseandhunt.com

Employment Law.

RICHARD C. BUSSE, JR., born Philadelphia, Pennsylvania, September 18, 1948; admitted to bar, 1974, Oregon and U.S. District Court, District of Oregon. *Education:* San Diego State University (B.S., 1971); University of California, Hastings College of the Law (J.D., 1974). Listed in: Best Lawyers in America for Labor and Employment Law, 1989-. Publications-Books: "Employees' Rights: Your Practical Handbook To Workplace Law," (Sphinx Publishing 2004); "Fired, Laid Off, or Forced Out," (Sphinx Publishing 2005); "Your Rights At Work," (Sphinx Publishing 2005); Articles: "Sexual Harassment Under Oregon and Federal Law," Litigating Sexual Harassment Claims, Oregon State Bar, 1998. Chief Deputy County Counsel, Multnomah County, Oregon, 1978-1981. ***REPORTED CASES:*** Albertson's, Inc. v. Kirkingburg, 527 U.S. 555 (1999); Meade v. Cedarapids, Inc., 164 F.3d 1219 (9th Cir. 1999); Wallulis v. Dymowski, 323 Or. 337, 918 P.2d 755 (1996); Dias v. SkyChefs, Inc. 919 F.2d 1370 (9th Cir. 1990); Leggett v. First Interstate Bank of Oregon, 86 Or. App. 523, 739 P.2d 1083 (1987). ***PRACTICE AREAS:*** Employment Law.

SCOTT N. HUNT, born Minneapolis, Minnesota, July 9, 1954; admitted to bar, 1992, Oregon; 1993, U.S. District Court, District of Oregon. *Education:* Grinnell College (B.A., 1976); Northwestern School of Law (J.D., magna cum laude, 1992). Phi Beta Kappa. Co-Author: "Reinstatement Rights of Injured and Disabled Workers," Oregon State Bar, CLE Workers' Compensation, 1994; "Settlement Conferences and Settlements," Oregon State Bar, Federal Civil Litigation in Oregon, 1994; "Complaints of Union Unfair Labor Practices," Oregon State Bar, CLE Labor and Employment Law: Public Sector, 1997. ***REPORTED CASES:*** Albertson's, Inc., v. Kirkingburg, 527 U.S. 555 (1999); Affolter v. Baugh Construction Oregon, Inc., 183 Or App 198, 51 P3d 642 (2002); Lansford v. Georgetown Manor, Inc., 192 Or App 261, 84 P3d 1105, adh'd to as modified, 193 Or App 59, 88 P3d 305, rev den 337 Or 182 (2004); Head v. Glacier Northwest, Inc., 413 F.3d 1053 (9th Cir. 2005); Meade v. Cedarapids, Inc., 164 F.3d 1218 (9th Cir. 1999); Johnsen v. Mel-Ken Motors, Inc., 134 Or. App. 81, 894 P.2d 540 (1995). ***PRACTICE AREAS:*** Employment Law; Defamation.

ASSOCIATE

MATTHEW B. DUCKWORTH, born Des Moines, Iowa, August 17, 1971; admitted to bar, 2002, Oregon and U.S. District Court, District of Oregon. *Education:* Stanford University (B.A., 1994); Northwestern School of Law, Lewis & Clark College (J.D., cum laude, 2002). ***PRACTICE AREAS:*** Employment Law. ***Email:*** mduckworth@busseandhunt.com

CABLE HUSTON BENEDICT HAAGENSEN & LLOYD LLP

Established in 1990

1001 S.W. FIFTH AVENUE, SUITE 2000
PORTLAND, OREGON 97204
Telephone: 503-224-3092
Facsimile: 503-224-3176
URL: http://www.cablehuston.com

Corvallis, Oregon Office: 582 N.W. Van Buren, 97339. Telephone: 503-754-7477. Facsimile: 503-754-0051.

Administrative, Agricultural, Banking, Bankruptcy, Commercial, Corporate, Complex Litigation, Creditors' Rights, Legislative, Employment, Energy, Environmental, Estate Planning, General Business, Land Use, Mining, Municipal, Natural Resource, Probate, Real Property, Taxation, Telecommunications, Trust Administration, Utility and Water Law.

(This Listing Continued)

FIRM PROFILE: Experienced attorneys from several of the largest law firms in the Pacific Northwest formed Cable Huston Benedict Haagensen & Lloyd LLP with the goal of providing high-quality, specialized legal services in a prompt and personal manner. The firm provides a full range of legal services to meet the needs of its clients, with the heaviest areas of concentration in energy and environmental law.

MEMBERS OF FIRM

CLARK I. BALFOUR, born Oakland, California, September 30, 1954; admitted to bar, 1979, Oregon; U.S. District Court, District of Oregon. *Education:* Linfield College (B.A., 1976); Northwestern School of Law of Lewis and Clark College (J.D., 1979). *Member:* American Bar Association; Oregon State Bar. ***PRACTICE AREAS:*** Public Contract Law; Public Construction Law; Municipal Law; Eminent Domain; Natural Resource Law; Environmental Law; Land Use Law; Water Law. ***Email:*** cbalfour@chbh.com

JAMES E. BENEDICT, born Ontario, Oregon, May 3, 1946; admitted to bar, 1976, Texas and Oregon; U.S. District Court, District of Oregon; U.S. Court of Appeals, Ninth Circuit; U.S. Supreme Court. *Education:* Oregon State University (B.S., Chem. Engr., with honors, 1968); University of Houston (J.D., magna cum laude, 1975). Phi Kappa Phi; Order of the Barons; Tau Beta Pi; Sigma Tau; Phi Alpha Delta. Chair, Associated Oregon Industries, Hazardous Waste Committee, 1996—. *Member:* Multnomah County and American Bar Associations; Oregon State Bar. ***PRACTICE AREAS:*** Environmental Law; Energy Law; Natural Resource Law. ***Email:*** jbenedic@chbh.com

J. LAURENCE CABLE, born Hannibal, Missouri, February 17, 1945; admitted to bar, 1971, Oregon; U.S. District Court, District of Oregon; U.S. Court of Appeals, Ninth Circuit; U.S. Supreme Court. *Education:* Stanford University (B.A., 1967); Willamette University College of Law (J.D., cum laude, 1971). Editor-in-Chief, Willamette Law Journal, 1970-1971. *Member:* Multnomah County and American Bar Associations; Oregon State Bar. ***PRACTICE AREAS:*** Utility Law; Energy Law; Complex Litigation; Environmental Law. ***Email:*** lcable@chbh.com

SUSAN TRUMP FELSTINER, born Boston, Massachusetts, February 19, 1965; admitted to bar, 1994, Oregon; 1998, Washington; U.S. District Court, District of Oregon; U.S. District Court, Eastern and Western Districts of Washington. *Education:* Lewis and Clark College (B.A., 1988); Northwestern School of Law of Lewis and Clark College (J.D., 1994). *Member:* Multnomah County Bar Association; Oregon State Bar; Washington State Bar; Chair, Oregon Hispanic Bar Association, Oregon Women Lawyers; Hispanic Metropolitan Chamber of Commerce. ***LANGUAGES:*** Spanish. ***PRACTICE AREAS:*** Environmental Litigation; Business Litigation; Telecommunications Law; Construction Law; Municipal Law; Employment Law; Probate Litigation; Real Property. ***Email:*** sfelstin@chbh.com

EDWARD A. FINKLEA, born Minneapolis, Minnesota, October 25, 1951; admitted to bar, 1984, Oregon and District of Columbia; U.S. District Court, District of Oregon; U.S. Court of Appeals for the District of Columbia Circuit; U.S. Court of Appeals, Ninth Circuit;. *Education:* University of Minnesota (B.A., 1974); Northwestern School of Law of Lewis & Clark College (J.D., 1980). Assistant General Counsel, Northwest Natural Gas Company. Trial Attorney, Bonneville Power Administration. Attorney, Federal Energy Regulatory Commission. Law Clerk, Council on Wage and Price Stability. Adjunct Professor, Economic Regulation of Energy, Northwestern School of Law, Lewis and Clark College, 1984-1989. Author: "Bonneville Power Administration Ratemaking: An Analysis of Substantive Standards and Procedural Requirements," 13 Envir. L. 927. *Member:* Multnomah County, Federal Energy and American Bar Associations; Oregon State Bar. ***PRACTICE AREAS:*** Energy Law; Environmental Law; Utility Law; Natural Resource Law. ***Email:*** efinklea@chbh.com

THOMAS M. GRIM, born Santa Clara, California, July 17, 1962; admitted to bar, 1988, Oregon; U.S. District Court, District of Oregon; U.S. Court of Appeals, Ninth Circuit ; U.S. Supreme Court. *Education:* University of California at Santa Barbara (B.A., with honors, 1984); University of Santa Clara (J.D., cum laude, 1988). Phi Beta Kappa. *Member:* Multnomah County Bar Association; Oregon State Bar. ***PRACTICE AREAS:*** Energy Law; Utility Law; Telecommunications Law; Municipal Law; Environmental Law; Water Law; Natural Resource Law; Complex Litigation. ***Email:*** tgrim@chbh.com

ANITA H. GRINICH, born San Francisco, California, December 2, 1956; admitted to bar, 1983, Oregon; 1996, Washington. *Education:* Lewis and Clark College (B.A., 1978); Northwestern School of Law of Lewis and Clark College (J.D., cum laude, 1983); University of Washington School of Law (LL.M., in Taxation, 1996). *Member:* Washington State Bar Association; Oregon State Bar; Portland Estate Planning Council. ***PRACTICE AREAS:*** Estate Planning Law; Taxation; Probate Law; Business Law; Real Property Law. ***Email:*** agrinich@chbh.com

DONALD A. HAAGENSEN, born Vancouver, Washington, May 7, 1945; admitted to bar, 1977, Oregon; U.S. District Court, District of Oregon; U.S. Court of Appeals, Ninth Circuit; U.S. Supreme Court. *Education:* College of Idaho (B.S., Zoology, 1967); University of Miami (M.S., Marine Biology, 1974; J.D., cum laude, 1977). Sigma Xi; Wig and Robe. Survey Editor, Miami Law Review, 1975-1977. *Author:* "Caribbean Zooplankton," Office of Naval Research, Department of the Navy; "Environmental Cleanup Liability," Oregon State Bar, CLE, Environmental and Natural Resources Law (2002). Member and Chair, Governing Board, Oregon Department of Geology & Mineral Industries, 1981-1990 and 2001—. Chair, Oregon Mined Land Reclamation Advisory Committee, 1983-1986. Member and Chair, Oregon Department of Environmental Quality, Hazardous Waste and Toxic Use Reduction Advisory Committee, 1991-1994; Member, Oregon Department of Environmental Quality, Environmental Enforcement Advisory Committee, 1992-1993, 2003—2005; Chair, Oregon Department of Environmental Quality, Environmental Cleanup Advisory Committee, 1995-2003; Member, Oregon Department of Environmental Quality, Hazardous Waste Program Development Advisory Committee, 1996-1997. *Member:* Multnomah County and American Bar Associations; Oregon State Bar. [Lieut., U.S. Coast Guard, 1969-1972]. ***PRACTICE AREAS:*** Environmental Law; Natural Resource Law; Mining Law; Administrative Law; Hazardous Waste Law; Energy Law. ***Email:*** dhaagens@chbh.com

G. FRANK HAMMOND, born Spokane, Washington, December 3, 1959; admitted to bar, 1985, Oregon; 1986, Washington; U.S. District Court, District of Oregon; U.S. District

(This Listing Continued)

CABLE HUSTON BENEDICT HAAGENSEN & LLOYD LLP, Portland—Continued

Court, Western District of Washington; U.S. Court of Appeals, Ninth Circuit; U.S. Supreme Court. *Education:* Lewis and Clark College (B.S., with honors, 1982); Cornell University (J.D., magna cum laude, 1985). Articles Editor, Cornell Law Review, 1984-1985. Co-Chair, Water Committee, Columbia Corridor Association, 1998. Chair, CLE Committee, Federal Bar Association, 1991. Member, Oregon Refuse and Recycling Association, 1999—. *Member:* Multnomah County and American Bar Associations; Oregon State Bar; Westside Economic Alliance Land Use Committee; Portland Metropolitan Homebuilders Association. ***PRACTICE AREAS:*** Land Use Law; Municipal Law; Solid Waste Law; Hazardous Waste Law; Appellate Litigation. ***Email:*** fhammond@chbh.com

ROBERT T. HUSTON, born Denver, Colorado, September 25, 1941; admitted to bar, 1968, Oregon. *Education:* University of Oregon (B.A., 1965; J.D., 1968). Comment Editor, Oregon Law Review, 1967-1968. *Member:* Multnomah County and American Bar Associations; Oregon State Bar; Portland Estate Planning Council. ***PRACTICE AREAS:*** Estate Planning Law; Probate Law. ***Email:*** rhuston@chbh.com

G. KEVIN KIELY, born Salem, Oregon, March 7, 1958; admitted to bar, 1983, Oregon; 1986, Washington; U.S. District Court, District of Oregon; U.S. District Court, Eastern and Western Districts of Washington; U.S. Court of Appeals, Ninth Circuit; U.S. Court of Appeals for the Federal Circuit; U.S. Court of Federal Claims; U.S. Supreme Court. *Education:* University of Oregon (B.A., 1980; J.D., 1983). Phi Delta Phi (Magister, 1983). *Author:* "Consolidation, Merger," in The Commercial Blanket Bond Annotated, ABA Press, 1985. *Member:* Washington State and American (Member: Litigation Section, Tort and Insurance Practice Section, Fidelity and Surety Law Committee; Public Contract Law Section) Bar Associations; Oregon State Bar (Past Chair, Construction Law Section); Board of Contract Appeals Bar Association; International Association of Defense Counsel. ***PRACTICE AREAS:*** Business Litigation; Construction Law; Insurance Coverage Law; Environmental Litigation. ***Email:*** gkkiely@chbh.com

JAMES S. KINCAID, born Portland, Oregon, May 4, 1961; admitted to bar, 1987, Oregon; U.S. District Court, District of Oregon; U.S. Supreme Court. *Education:* University of Oregon (B.S., 1983); Northwestern School of Law of Lewis and Clark College (J.D., magna cum laude, 1987). *Author:* "Invasions of Real Property Including Environmental Damage," Oregon State Bar, CLE, *Damages:* (1990 Revision). Member and Chair, Dry Cleaner Advisory Committee, Oregon Department of Environmental Quality, 1998—. Member, Willamette River TMDL Advisory Council, Oregon Department of Environmental Quality, 2001—. *Member:* Multnomah County and American Bar Associations; Oregon State Bar. ***PRACTICE AREAS:*** Environmental Law; Energy Law; Natural Resource Law; Land Use Law; Administrative Law. ***Email:*** jkincaid@chbh.com

WILLIAM J. LEHMAN, born Wilkes Barre, Pennsylvania, October 10, 1969; admitted to bar, 1998, Connecticut; 2002, Oregon. *Education:* University of Scranton (B.A., 1991); University of Notre Dame School of Law (J.D., 1997). *Member:* Oregon State Bar. ***PRACTICE AREAS:*** Telecommunications Law; Complex Commercial Litigation; Administrative Law; Energy. ***Email:*** wlehman@chbh.com

DON K. LLOYD, born American Falls, Idaho, August 7, 1944; admitted to bar, 1973, Oregon. *Education:* Portland State University (B.A., 1970); Northwestern School of Law of Lewis and Clark College (J.D., magna cum laude, 1973). Law Review, 1971-1972. *Author:* Ohio v. Wyandotte Chemicals Corp.: Restatement of the Original Jurisdiction of the Supreme Court of the United States, 2 Env. Law 358 (1972); Chapter on Estates in Land, Oregon State Bar Handbook on Real Property. President, Troutdale Area Chamber of Commerce, 1991-1994. City of Troutdale Planning Commission, 1991-1993. Member, City Council, City of Troutdale, 1993-1996. *Member:* Multnomah County and American Bar Associations; Oregon State Bar. [U.S. Marine Corps, 1966-1968]. ***PRACTICE AREAS:*** Real Property Law; Finance Law; Business Law. ***Email:*** dklloyd@chbh.com

RICHARD G. LORENZ, born San Bernardino, California, October 14, 1975; admitted to bar, 2000, Oregon; 2001, Washington; U.S. Court of Appeals, Ninth Circuit. *Education:* Linfield College (B.A., magna cum laude, 1997); Harvard University (J.D., cum laude, 2000). Deputy Editor in Chief, Harvard Negotiation Law Review. *Author:* "Good Fences Make Bad Neighbors," 33 The Urban Lawyer No. 1, 45-117 (Winter 2001). *Member:* Oregon State Bar. ***PRACTICE AREAS:*** Energy Law; Municipal Law; Utility Law; Environmental Law; Telecommunications Law. ***Email:*** rlorenz@chbh.com

MARGARET B. STERN, born Portland, Oregon, January 7, 1965; admitted to bar, 1993, New York; 1994, District of Columbia; 1998, Oregon; 2000, Washington; U.S. District Court, District of Oregon. *Education:* Georgetown University (B.S., 1987; J.D., 1992). *Member:* American Bar Association (Member, Section on Natural Resources, Energy and Environmental Law); Oregon State Bar. ***PRACTICE AREAS:*** Business Litigation; Employment Litigation; Environmental Litigation. ***Email:*** mstern@chbh.com

LAURA J. WALKER, born Fayetteville, Arkansas, October 16, 1953; admitted to bar, 1979, Oregon; 1995, Washington. *Education:* University of Arkansas (B.A., 1975); Georgetown University (J.D., cum laude, 1979). Phi Beta Kappa. *Member:* Multnomah County, Washington State and American Bar Associations; Oregon State Bar (Member, Executive Committee, Debtor-Creditor Section, 1986-1992 and 2002-2003, Chair, 1990-1991). ***PRACTICE AREAS:*** Creditors' Rights Law; Bankruptcy Law; Commercial Law. ***Email:*** lwalker@chbh.com

J. STEPHEN WERTS, born Seattle, Washington, January 26, 1945; admitted to bar, 1971, Washington; 1974, Oregon; U.S. District Courts, District of Oregon, Eastern and Western Districts of Washington, U.S. Court of Appeals, Ninth Circuit. *Education:* University of Washington (B.A., 1967); University of Oregon (J.D., 1971). Managing Editor, Oregon Law Review, 1970-1971. Vice-President, Secretary and General Counsel, Northwest Acceptance Corporation, Portland, Oregon, 1975-1981. *Member:* Washington State Bar Association (Member, Creditor Debtor Section); Oregon State Bar (Member: Debtor Creditor Section; Business Litigation Section, Executive Committee); American Bankruptcy Institute. Fellow, American College of Mortgage Attorneys. (Certified Specialist, Business Bankruptcy Law, American Bankruptcy Board of Certification). ***PRACTICE AREAS:*** UCC; Bankruptcy Law; Bankruptcy Litigation; Debtor Creditor Litigation; Real Property Litigation; Condemnation; Commercial Litigation; Workouts; Dispute Resolution; Secured Finance; Unsecured Finance. ***Email:*** swerts@chbh.com

(This Listing Continued)

ASSOCIATES

GRETCHEN S. BARNES, born Butte, Montana, February 11, 1971; admitted to bar, 2003, Oregon. *Education:* Gonzaga University (B.A., summa cum laude, 1993); Northwestern School of Law of Lewis & Clark College (J.D., cum laude, 2003). *Member:* Oregon State Bar (Member, Real Estate and Land Use Section, 2003—). ***LANGUAGES:*** French. ***PRACTICE AREAS:*** Real Estate; Real Estate Finance; Business Law. ***Email:*** gbarnes@chbh.com

LINDSAY R. KANDRA, born Klamath Falls, Oregon, June 4, 1977; admitted to bar, 2004, Oregon and California; 2005, Washington. *Education:* Linfield College (B.A., magna cum laude, 1999); University of Oregon (J.D., 2003). Order of the Coif. *Author:* "Questioning the Legal Foundation of Ashcroff's Attempt to Invalidate Oregon's Death With Dignity Act," Oregon Law Review (2003). *Member:* Oregon State Bar. ***PRACTICE AREAS:*** Energy; Natural Resources; Water Law; Utility Law; Environmental Law. ***Email:*** lkandra@chbh.com

CARLA S. RHODEN, born Eugene, Oregon, 1971; admitted to bar, 2002, California; 2005, Oregon; U.S. Court of Appeals, Ninth Circuit. *Education:* University of Oregon (B.A., 1994; J.D., 2002). Moot Court Board. Member, of Environmental Law & Litigation. Author: "Challenging Searches and Seizures of Computers at Home or in the Office: From a Reasonable Expectation of Privacy to Fruit of the Poisonous Tree," 30 Am. J. Crim. L. 107 (2002). ***PRACTICE AREAS:*** Litigation. ***Email:*** crhoden@chbh.com

CHAD M. STOKES, born Los Angeles, California, July 14, 1971; admitted to bar, 2000, Oregon. *Education:* University of California at Santa Barbara (B.A., Environmental Studies, 1996); Northwestern School of Law of Lewis and Clark College (J.D., 2000). Certificate in Environmental and Natural Resource Law. Phi Delta Phi. *Member:* Multnomah County and American Bar Associations; Oregon State Bar. ***PRACTICE AREAS:*** Energy Law; Environmental Law; Telecommunications; Natural Resource Law; Utility Law; Telecommunications Law. ***Email:*** cstokes@chbh.com

ROBIN BELLANCA, born Beaverton, Oregon, August 20, 1978; admitted to bar, 2005, Oregon. *Education:* Bowdoin College (B.A., 2000); Harvard Law School (J.D., 2005). *Member:* Oregon State Bar; American Bar Association (Member, Sections on: Environment Energy and Resources; Administrative Law and Regulatory Practice). ***PRACTICE AREAS:*** Energy; Public Utility Law; Natural Resources; Municipal Law. ***Email:*** rbellanca@chbh.com

OF COUNSEL

DAN C. ARMSTRONG, born Fergus Falls, Minnesota, October 19, 1960; admitted to bar, 1988, Oregon. *Education:* Boise State University (B.A., cum laude, 1985); Willamette University (J.D., magna cum laude, 1988). *Member:* Benton County and Multnomah County Bar Associations; Oregon State Bar. ***PRACTICE AREAS:*** Real Estate; Land Use; Business Litigation; Family Law. ***Email:*** darmstrong@peak.org

TAMARA L. FAUCETTE, born El Paso, Texas, January 7, 1969; admitted to bar, 1995, Oregon; 2001, District of Columbia and Texas; U.S. Court of Appeals, Ninth Circuit. *Education:* Brigham Young University (B.A., 1991); Northwestern School of Law of Lewis and Clark College (J.D., magna cum laude, 1995). *Member:* Multnomah County and American Bar Associations; Oregon State Bar (Natural Resources, Energy and Environmental and Governmental Law Sections). ***PRACTICE AREAS:*** Project Finance Law; Environmental Law; Natural Resource Law; Energy Law. ***Email:*** tfaucette@chbh.com

GEORGE B. HEILIG, born Portland, Oregon, June 5, 1944; admitted to bar, 1973, Oregon; U.S. District Court, District of Oregon. *Education:* Portland State University (B.S., 1970); Willamette University College of Law (J.D., cum laude, 1973). Chair, Corvallis City Planning Commission, 1976-1985. *Member:* Benton County Bar Association; Oregon State Bar (Member, Executive Committee, Real Estate and Land Use Section, 1990—). (Resident, Corvallis Office). ***PRACTICE AREAS:*** Real Estate Law; Business Litigation; Land Use Law. ***Email:*** lawyerg@peak.org

DAVID K. McADAMS, born Hillsboro, Oregon, July 27, 1945; admitted to bar, 1975, Oregon; U.S. Tax Court. *Education:* Oregon State University; University of Oregon (B.B.A., 1967; J.D., 1974); Boston University (LL.M. in Taxation, 1975). Beta Alpha Psi; Order of the Coif. Visiting Assistant Professor of Taxation, Portland State University, 1980-1982. *Member:* Multnomah County and American Bar Associations; Oregon State Bar; Portland Estate Planning Council. [1st Lt., USMC Reserve, active duty, 1967-1970]. ***PRACTICE AREAS:*** Estate Planning Law; Taxation; Probate Law; Business Law. ***Email:*** dmcadams@chbh.com

REPRESENTATIVE CLIENTS: Ace; Bank of Tokyo-Mitsubishi, Ltd.; Bayer Cropscience; Canby Utility Board; Chemical Waste Management of the Northwest, Inc.; The Chubb Group of Insurance Companies; City of Albany; City of Corvallis; City of Hermiston; City of McMinnville Water & Light; Clackamas County Bank; Clackamas County Department of Water Environment Services; Clackamas River Water District; Clatskanie People's Utility District; Emerald Christmas Tree Company; Eugene Water & Electric Board; Everfresh Fruit Co.; Exxon Mobil; Holiday Tree Farms; John Holmlund Nursery Inc.; Intel; J.H. Baxter & Co.; Liberty Insurance; Louisiana-Pacific Corp.; Oak Lodge Sanitary District; Merchants Bank; Oregon Dairy Farmers Association; Pacific Insurance Investment Company; Portland Trail Blazers; PRM Finance Inc.; Public Utility District No.1 of Cowlitz County, Washington; Safety-Kleen Systems, Inc.; Stewart Title Guarantee Company; Summit Real Estate Management Corp.; Surface Water Management Agency of Clackamas County; Tillamook People's Utility District; St. Paul Travelers; Tri City Service District; Tualatin Valley Water District; Union Carbide Corporation; Waste Management, Inc.

REFERENCES: Bank of America (Premier Banking); Union Bank of California, N.A. (trust Dept.); U.S. Bank, NA (Main Office-Commercial Dept. and Trust Dept.); U.S. Trust Company, NA (Portland Office); Wells Fargo Bank (Trust Dept); West Coast Trust Co., Inc.

LAW OFFICES OF
VINCENT P. CACCIOTTOLI

A PROFESSIONAL CORPORATION
121 SOUTHWEST MORRISON STREET
SUITE 1010
PORTLAND, OREGON 97204
Telephone: 503-220-1933
Facsimile: 503-220-1974
Email: vince@vpcpc.com

Employee Benefits Law, Executive Compensation, Employment Law and Corporate and Business Planning.

VINCENT P. CACCIOTTOLI, born New York, N.Y., April 18, 1950; admitted to bar, 1976, New York; 1979, Oregon. *Education:* New York University (B.A., 1972); Fordham University (J.D., 1975). Listed in *The Best Lawyers in America* (Employee Benefits). President, Western Pension and Benefits Conference, 1997-1998, Director, 1991-1996. Editor-in-Chief, *Benefits Bulletin*, 1991-1995. Co-Author, "Employee Health Benefits," *Oregon Health Law Manual.* Contributing Author, *Schwab Institutional Compliance Newsletter. Member:* Multnomah County, New York State and American (Member, Labor and Employment Law, Taxation and Business Law Sections) Bar Associations; Oregon State Bar. (Also Special Counsel to Benner and Associates, P.C. at same address). ***PRACTICE AREAS:*** Employee Benefits Law; Executive Compensation; Employment Law; Business Planning.

REPRESENTATIVE CLIENTS: Alcatel; Alyeska Resort; Americh Massena & Associates, Inc., Associated Oregon Industries; City of Lake Oswego; Clackamas River Water District; Clark Public Utilities; Evergreen International Aviation; Golden Valley Electric Association, Inc.; The Holland (Burgerville); Kerr Pacific Corp.; Lake District Hospital; Lane County; Mitsubishi Silicon America Corp.; Montana Rail Link; National Bank of Alaska; Oregon Education Association; OEA Choice Welfare Benefit Trust; Ounalashka Corp.; PacifiCorp.; Pendleton Flour Mills, LLC; Planar Systems, Inc.; Platt Electric Supply, Inc.; Portland Rose Festival Association; Rockwood Water PUD; Swift Newspapers, Inc.; Tualatin Valley Water District; Warn Industries, Inc.; West Coast Bancorp.
REFERENCES: Union Bank of California, N.A.; Deloitte & Touche, LLP; U.S. National Bank of Oregon N.A.; West Coast Bank.

CALLAHAN & SHEARS, P.C.

Established in 1990
4215 SOUTHEAST KING ROAD
P.O. BOX 22677
PORTLAND, OREGON 97269-2677
Telephone: 503-513-5130
Fax: 503-513-5915
URL: http://www.callahanandshears.com

Insurance Coverage Litigation, Professional Liability and Personal Injury Defense. General Civil and Trial Practice.

JAMES M. CALLAHAN, born Lebanon, Oregon, July 19, 1950; admitted to bar, 1978, Oregon; 1984, Washington. *Education:* University of Rochester (B.A., 1972); Syracuse University (J.D., cum laude, 1977). Author: "Avoiding Bad Faith Claims," Oregon Law Institute, 1988. *Member:* Multnomah County and Washington State Bar Associations; Oregon State Bar (Member: Board of Bar Examiners, 1983-1986; Procedure and Practice Committee, 1991-1995); Oregon Association of Defense Counsel (Member, Amicus Curiae Committee, 1991-1995); Defense Research Institute. ***PRACTICE AREAS:*** Professional Liability; Insurance Litigation; Commercial Litigation; Insurance Coverage Disputes. ***Email:*** jcallahan@callahanandshears.com

MELIA M. SHEARS, born Portland, Oregon, January 30, 1957; admitted to bar, 1986, Oregon. *Education:* University of Washington (B.A., 1979); University of Puget Sound (J.D., 1985). *Member:* Multnomah County and American Bar Associations; Oregon State Bar; Oregon Association of Defense Counsel; Defense Research Institute. ***PRACTICE AREAS:*** Professional Liability; Insurance Litigation; Commercial Litigation. ***Email:*** mshears@callahanandshears.com

---

SUSAN D. CARDONI, born Marquette, Michigan, September 27, 1946; admitted to bar, 1983, Oregon; 1987, U.S. District Court, District of Oregon; 1990, U.S. Supreme Court. *Education:* Northern Michigan University; Michigan State University (B.A., 1968); University of Michigan; Northwestern School of Law of Lewis and Clark College (J.D., 1983). Phi Beta Kappa. *Member:* Multnomah County Bar Association; Oregon State Bar. ***PRACTICE AREAS:*** Professional Liability; Insurance Litigation; Commercial Litigation. ***Email:*** scardoni@callahanandshears.com

REPRESENTATIVE CLIENTS: The St. Paul Insurance Companies; Met-Life Auto & Home; Employers Reinsurance Corporation; Westport Insurance Corporation; First Specialty Insurance Corporation; Coregis Insurance Company; Nautilus Insurance Company; Scottsdale Insurance Company; Transamerica Insurance Company; Utica Mutual Insurance Company; 7-Eleven, Inc.; Kemper Insurance Companies; Safeco Select Markets; Zurich North America; Farmers Mutual Insurance Company of Nebraska.

CANN LAWYERS

1300 S.W. FIFTH AVENUE, SUITE 2750
PORTLAND, OREGON 97201-5617
Telephone: 503-226-6529
Fax: 503-228-6529
Email: fec@cannlawyersusa.com
URL: http://www.cannlawyersusa.com

Construction Contract Litigation, Construction Defect Litigation.

(This Listing Continued)

MEMBER

FREDERIC E. CANN, born 1953; admitted to bar, 1978, Oregon; 1986, Washington; 2000, New South Wales. *Education:* Dartmouth College (B.A., cum laude, 1975); Boston College (J.D., magna cum laude, 1978). Author: "What to Do When There is No Miller Act Payment Bond," 23 Public Contract Law Journal 413 (Spring 1994), and 14 The Construction Lawyer No. 2, p.1, April 1994; "Insurance Coverage for Construction Defects: An Oregon Breakthrough," 19 Oregon State Bar Construction Law Newsletter (August 2001); "United States: 2003 Decisions Under the New York Convention: Conflicting Post Award Enforcement Litigation in National Courts," 2004 International Arbitration Law Review 145. *Member:* Oregon State Bar (Member, Construction Law Section); Washington State (Member, Construction Law Section) and American (Member, Forum Committee on the Construction Industry) Bar Associations; International Bar Association. ***PRACTICE AREAS:*** Construction Contracts; Construction Defects; Litigation. ***Email:*** fec@cannlawyersusa.com

REPRESENTATIVE CLIENTS: Turner Construction Company; Northridge Custom Homes.

M. CAROLINE CANTRELL & ASSOC., PC

Established in 2000
1500 NE IRVING STREET, SUITE 100
PORTLAND, OREGON 97232
Telephone: 503-236-9211
Fax: 503-236-0209
URL: http://www.bankruptcyoregon.com
Email: info@bankruptcyoregon.com
URL: http://www.lawyers.com/ccantrell

Bankruptcy Chapter 7, Bankruptcy Chapter 13.

FIRM PROFILE: Small firm offering professional courteous service to those in financial difficulty.

M. CAROLINE CANTRELL, born Coos Bay, Oregon, August 17, 1947; admitted to bar, 1991, Oregon. *Education:* Portland State University (B.S., 1980); Northwestern School of Law (J.D., 1990). Instructor, "Introduction to Bankruptcy," Portland Community College. *Member:* Oregon State Bar (Member, Debtor-Creditor Section); Oregon Pro Bono Bankruptcy Clinic. ***PRACTICE AREAS:*** Bankruptcy. ***Email:*** ccantrell@bankruptcyoregon.com

---

MICHAEL S. SCOTT, born Jackson, Michigan, October 9, 1970; admitted to bar, 1997, Oregon; 1998, Washington. *Education:* Miami University (B.A., 1993); Northwestern School of Law (J.D., 1997). *Member:* Oregon State Bar (Member, Debtor-Creditor Section; Chair, Consumer Bankruptcy Subcommittee, 2003; Pro Bono Bankruptcy Clinic); Washington State Bar Association (Member, Debtor-Creditor Section). ***PRACTICE AREAS:*** Bankruptcy. ***Email:*** mscott@bankruptcyoregon.com

---

GORDON T. CAREY, JR., P.C.

A Partnership of Professional Corporations
721 SOUTHWEST OAK, SECOND FLOOR
PORTLAND, OREGON 97205
Telephone: 503-222-1415
FAX: 503-222-1923
URL: http://www.careylaw-firm.com

Civil Trial and Appellate Practice in State and Federal Courts. Personal Injury, Business, Commercial, Maritime, Environmental, Securities Litigation.

GORDON T. CAREY, JR., born McMinnville, Oregon, May 14, 1950; admitted to bar, 1975, Washington and U.S. District Court, District of Washington; 1977, Oregon, U.S. Court of Appeals, 9th Circuit and U.S. District Court, District of Oregon; 1984, U.S. Supreme Court. *Education:* University of Oregon (B.A., 1972); University of Michigan (J.D., cum laude, 1975). Phi Beta Kappa. Editor, "Oregon Civil Pleading and Practice," published by Oregon State Bar. Author: Chapter on Default, "Oregon Civil Pleading and Practice," published by Oregon State Bar. Contributing Author: "Evidence," published by Oregon State Bar. *Member:* Oregon State Bar (Member, Continuing Legal Education Committee, 1992-1995). ***REPORTED CASES:*** Providence Health Plan v. McDowell, 361 F.3d 1243 (9th Cir. 2004), amended by, 385 F.3d 1168 (9th Cir. 2004), cert denied, - US -, 125 S Ct 1726, 1735, - LEd2d - (2005); FEDERAL: Stevedoring Services of America v. Ancora Transport, 506 U.S. 1043, 122L. Ed. 2d 112, 113 S. Ct. 955 (1993), reversing opinion at 884 F.2d 1250 (9th Cir., 1989), as modified in 941 F.2d 1378 (9th Cir., 1991); Stevedoring Services of America v. Armilla Intern., 889 F. 2d 919 (9th Cir., 1989); Marine Fuels v. M/V KEN LUCKY, 859 F.2d 1405 (9th Cir., 1988). STATE: City of Hillsboro v. Purcell, 306 Or. 547, 761 P.2d 510 (1988); Schlimgen v. May Trucking Co., 335 OR 143, 61 P3d 923 (2003), modifying opinion at 178 Or. App 397, 37 P3d 1005 (2001); Graham v. State of Oregon, 164 Or. App. 747, 995 P.2d 1167 (2000); Egner v. City of Portland, 103 Or. App. 623, 798 P.2d 721 (1990); The Oregon Bank v. Nautilus Crane and Equipment Corp., 68 Or. App. 131, 683 P.2d 95 (1984). ***PRACTICE AREAS:*** Personal Injury Litigation; Business Litigation; Commercial Litigation; Maritime Litigation; Securities Litigation; Environmental Litigation.

REPRESENTATIVE CLIENTS: Stevedoring Services of America; Paula Insurance Corp.; Shaver Transportation, Inc.; May Trucking Co.; Montinove Vineyards; Astoria Metal Corp.

CARON COLVEN ROBISON & SHAFTON P.S.

PORTLAND, OREGON

(See Vancouver)

Litigation: Personal Injury, Commercial, Municipal, Real Estate; Commercial Law, Insurance, Appellate Practice, Probate, Construction Law, Trial Practice, Automobile Accidents and Injuries, Slip and Fall, Dog Bites, Wrongful Death, Products Liability, ERISA.

CASE & DUSTERHOFF, LLP

PORTLAND, OREGON

(See Beaverton)

Business and Business Litigation, Insurance, Asbestos Defense, Construction Litigation, Probate and Real Property Law, Taxation. General Civil and Trial Practice, Products Liability, Casualty, Surety and Fidelity, Errors and Omissions, Employment, Estate Planning and Wills and Trusts, Personal Injury, Medical and Legal Malpractice, Family Law and Mediation.

BOB CASEY ATTORNEY

1205 NW 25TH AVENUE
PORTLAND, OREGON 97210-2422
Telephone: 503-221-9700
Fax: 503-226-3131
Email: bcasey@rsblaw.net
URL: http://www.bobcaseylaw.com

Estate Planning, Probate, Trust Administration, Contested Wills, Guardianships and Conservatorships.

BOB CASEY, born Salt Lake City, Utah, August 17, 1954; admitted to bar, 1983, Utah; 1984, Alaska; 1986, Washington; 1987, Oregon. *Education:* Whitman College (B.A., 1977); Seattle University (J.D., 1981). Member, Estate Planning Council of Portland, Inc., 1996—. *Member:* Alaska and Washington State Bar Associations; Utah State Bar; Oregon State Bar (Board Member, Estate Planning and Administration Section). ***PRACTICE AREAS:*** Estate Planning (50%, 100); Probate (20%, 20); Trust Administration (10%, 8); Contested Wills (10%, 4); Guardianship and Conservatorship (10%, 4).

CASTEEL & CARSON

Established in 1972
2035 N.E. 42ND AVENUE
PORTLAND, OREGON 97213
Telephone: 503-288-9291
FAX: 503-288-4576

Business, Business Enterprises, Buying and Selling a Business, Real Estate, Contracts, Probate, Estate Planning and Trusts, Wills, Conservatorships, Guardianships, Commercial Law, Collections, Personal Injury, Automobile Accidents, Slip and Fall, Dog Bites, Wrongful Death, Professional Liability, Family Law, Step-Parent Adoptions, Divorce, Child Custody, Child Support, Visitation Rights, Elder Law, Neglect, Elder Abuse, Medical Malpractice, Trademarks, Tax Planning,.

MEMBERS OF FIRM

JAMES L. CASTEEL, born Salem, Oregon, March 1, 1945; admitted to bar, 1971, Oregon; 1973, U.S. District Court, District of Oregon. *Education:* Oregon State University (B.S., 1967); University of Illinois and University of Oregon (J.D., 1971). Phi Kappa Phi; Beta Gamma Sigma. Estate Tax Attorney, I.R.S., U.S. Treasury Department, 1971-1973. *Member:* Multnomah County Bar Association; Oregon State Bar (Member: Executive Committee, Estate Planning and Administration Sections, 1984-1987; Litigation and Taxation Sections). ***PRACTICE AREAS:*** Commercial Law; Business Law; Probate Law; Real Estate Law; Estate Planning; Trusts.

BRETT S. CARSON, born Sheridan, Wyoming, October 31, 1952; admitted to bar, 1979, Oregon and U.S. District Court, District of Oregon. *Education:* Colorado College and University of Oregon (B.S., 1976); Gonzaga University (J.D., cum laude, 1979). Director, Oregon State Council for Senior Citizens, 1989—. *Member:* Multnomah County Bar Association; Oregon State Bar (Member: Realtors Joint Committee, 1991-1993; Real Estate, Land Use, Business, Corporate and Debtor-Creditor Sections). ***PRACTICE AREAS:*** Commercial Law; Collections; Business Law; Probate Law; Estate Planning; Real Estate Law; Contracts.

ASSOCIATE

RANDALL H. BAKER, born Ann Arbor, Michigan, June 9, 1959; admitted to bar, 1991, Oregon; 1992, Washington; 1993, U.S. District Court, District of Oregon. *Education:* Lewis and Clark College (B.A. in Economics, 1981); University of Oregon (J.D., 1990). Managing Board Editor, University of Oregon Law Review, 1989-1990. *Member:* Multnomah County and Washington State Bar Associations; Oregon State Bar. ***LANGUAGES:*** Spanish and French. ***PRACTICE AREAS:*** Litigation; Collections; Business Law; Domestic Relations; Real Estate Law; Personal Injury.

CHERNOFF, VILHAUER, McCLUNG & STENZEL, LLP

Established in 1970
1600 ODS TOWER
601 S.W. SECOND AVENUE
PORTLAND, OREGON 97204
Telephone: 503-227-5631
Facsimile: 503-228-4373
Email: postmaster@chernofflaw.com
URL: http://www.chernofflaw.com

Intellectual Property Law and Litigation Relating to Patent, Trademark, Copyright, Trade Secrets, Licensing, Computer Technology. Franchising, Unfair Competition, Trade Dress and False Advertising.

FIRM PROFILE: Chernoff, Vilhauer, McClung & Stenzel, LLP, was founded in 1970 and currently consists of ten partners averaging over twenty-five years experience and twenty years longevity with the firm. The partners and associates of the firm all have technical degrees in the physical or biological sciences.

The firm practices all phases of acquisition, commercialization and enforcement of domestic and foreign intellectual property rights. Particular emphasis is placed on patent and trademark prosecution and litigation. Specialized expertise is available in the biological, chemical, mechanical, electrical, electronic and computer fields.

The firm has an active litigation practice, representing its clients effectively in federal court trials of the highest complexity with respect to the enforcement and defense of patent, trademark, unfair competition and false advertising claims.

MEMBERS OF FIRM

DANIEL P. CHERNOFF (1935-1995)

JACOB E. VILHAUER, JR., born Portland, Oregon, January 22, 1940; admitted to bar, 1964, Oregon; 1971, U.S. District Court, District of Oregon; 1972, U.S. Court of Appeals, Ninth Circuit; 1974, U.S. Court of Appeals for the Federal Circuit; registered to practice before U.S. Patent and Trademark Office. *Education:* Oregon State University (B.S., Mech.E., 1961); University of Oregon (LL.B., 1964). Phi Delta Phi. Author: "Intellectual Property: Avoiding the Common Pitfalls," Oregon Business and Corporate Law Digest, September, 1984. *Member:* Multnomah County Bar Association; Oregon State Bar (Chairman, Committee on Patent, Trademark and Copyright Law, 1974-1975); Oregon Patent Law Association (Secretary, 1977-1978; Vice President, 1978-1979; President, 1979-1980); American Intellectual Property Law Association; Association of Trial Lawyers of America. [Capt., U.S. Army, 1964-1966]. ***PRACTICE AREAS:*** International Patents; International Trademarks; Trade Secrets; Intellectual Property Infringement; Intellectual Property Licensing. ***Email:*** jev@chernofflaw.com

DENNIS E. STENZEL, born Detroit, Michigan, January 31, 1942; admitted to bar, 1972, California, Oregon and U.S. District Court, District of Oregon; 1982, U.S. Court of Appeals for the Federal Circuit; 1990, U.S. Court of Appeals, Ninth Circuit; 1993, U.S. District Court, Western District of Washington; registered to practice before U.S. Patent and Trademark Office. *Education:* Whitman College; Brigham Young University (B.S., 1967); George Washington University (J.D., with honors, 1971). Phi Kappa Phi. Member, George Washington University Law Review, 1970-1971. Examiner, U.S. Patent Office, 1967-1970. *Member:* Multnomah County Bar Association; Oregon State Bar (Chairman, Patent and Trademark Section, 1985-1986); State Bar of California; Oregon Patent Law Association (Board Member); American Intellectual Property Law Association. ***LANGUAGES:*** Finnish and Russian. ***REPORTED CASES:*** Western Food Equipment Co. v. Foss America, Inc. 1980 WL 30367, 205 U.S.P.Q. 835 (D. Or., 1980); Hammerquist v. Clark's Sheet Metal, Inc. 658 F.2d 1319 (9th Cir. 1981); Moore International Corp. v. Lumber Systems, Inc. 1982 WL 51056, 217 U.S.P.Q. 2d 1278 (D.Or., 1982); Wedgwood Homes, Inc. v. Lund, 294 Or. 493 (1983) (Or., 1982); Sowa & Sons v. American Hoist & Derrick, 725 F.2d 1350 (Fed. Cir. 1984), cert. denied, 469 US 821 (1984); Classic Instruments, Inc. v. VDO-Argo Instruments, Inc. 73 Or.App. 732, 700 P.2d 677, 266 U.S.P.Q. 894 (Or.App. 1985); Sun Studs, Inc. v. Applied Theory Associates, Inc., 772 F.2d 1557 (Fed. Cir. 1985); Official Airline Guides, Inc. v. Goss, 856 F.2d 85, 8 U.S.P.Q. 2d 1157 (9th Cir. 1988); Official Airline Guides, Inc. v. Churchfield Publications, Inc., 756 F.2d 1393, 17 U.S.P.Q. 2d 1897 (D.Or., 1990); Gemini Industries, Inc. v. Labtec Enterprises, Inc., 1993 WL 580807, 31 U.S.P.Q. 2d 1776 (W.D. Wash. 1993); Official Airline Guides, Inc. v. Goss, 6 F.3d 1385, 28 U.S.P.Q. 2d 1641 (9th Cir. 1993); Oregon Precision Industries, Inc. v. International Omni-Pac Corp., 889 F. Supp. 412, 36 U.S.P.Q. 2d 1708 (D.Or., 1995); Moore International Corp. v. Lumber Systems, Inc., 217 U.S.P.Q. 1278 (D.Or., 1982). ***PRACTICE AREAS:*** Intellectual Property; Unfair Competition; Litigation; Trademarks; Intellectual Property Licensing; Chemical Patents; Pharmaceutical Patents. ***Email:*** des@chernofflaw.com

CHARLES D. McCLUNG, born Seattle, Washington, December 26, 1939; admitted to bar, 1975, Washington and Oregon and U.S. District Court, District of Oregon and Western District of Washington; U.S. Court of Appeals, Federal and Ninth Circuits; registered to practice before U.S. Patent and Trademark Office. *Education:* University of Washington (B.S.M.E., 1962; M.S.M.E., 1964); Gonzaga University (J.D., cum laude, 1974). *Member:* Multnomah County, Washington State and American (Member: Committee on Inventors, 1976-1977; Patent, Trademark and Copyright Law Section) Bar Associations; Oregon State Bar (Chairman, Patent and Trademark Section, 1979-1980); Oregon Patent Law Association (President, 1995); American Intellectual Property Law Association (Member, Public Information Committee, 1975-1977); American Society of Mechanical Engineers. ***PRACTICE AREAS:*** Patents; Trademarks; False Advertising; Trade Dress; Intellectual Property Licensing. ***Email:*** chuck@chernofflaw.com

DONALD B. HASLETT, born Geneva, New York, June 16, 1945; admitted to bar, 1977, Oregon; U.S. District Court, District of Oregon; U.S. Court of Appeals for the Federal Circuit; U.S. Court of Appeals, Ninth Circuit; registered to practice before U.S. Patent and Trademark Office. *Education:* United States Naval Academy (B.S., 1966); Cornell Univer-

(This Listing Continued)

sity (J.D., 1977). *Member:* Multnomah County, Federal and American Bar Associations; Oregon State Bar (Secretary, Computer Law Section, 1996-1997); American Intellectual Property Law Association; Oregon Patent Law Association (President, 1983-1984). [Capt., USNR, Ret.]. ***PRACTICE AREAS:*** Patents; International Patents; Trademarks; Design Patents; Unfair Competition; Intellectual Property Infringement; Intellectual Property Licensing. ***Email:*** don@chernofflaw.com

J. PETER STAPLES, born Newburgh, New York, April 16, 1947; admitted to bar, 1979, Oregon; 1985, Washington; U.S Supreme Court; U.S. Court of Appeals, Ninth Circuit; U.S. Court of Appeals for the Federal Circuit; registered to practice before U.S. Patent and Trademark Office. *Education:* United States Military Academy (B.S., 1969); Northwestern School of Law of Lewis and Clark College (J.D., 1979). Listed, Best Lawyers in America, 2005-2006. Author: "Changes in Trademark Law Provide Protection, Certainty," Daily Journal of Commerce, May 1, 1990. Attorney, Salem City Attorney's Office, 1980. *Member:* Multnomah County and Washington State Bar Associations; Oregon State Bar (Member, Patent and Trademark Section; Treasurer, 1985-1986; Secretary, 1986-1987; Chairman, 1988-1989); Oregon Patent Law Association. [Capt., U.S. Army, 1969-1974]. ***REPORTED CASES:*** Sodima v. International Yogurt Co., 662 F. Supp. 839 (D. Or. 1987); Tse, et al. v. Gentlecare Systems, Inc., 17 U.S.P.Q.2d 1571 (D. Or. 1990); Soloflex, Inc. v. Nordic Track, Inc., 31 U.S.P.Q.2d 1721 (D. Or. 1994); Nelson/Weather-Rite, Inc. v. Leatherman Tool Group, Inc., 40 U.S.P.Q.2d 1239 (N.D. Ill. 1995); Woodstock's Enterprises, Inc. (California) v. Woodstock's Enterprises, Inc. (Oregon), 43 U.S.P.Q2d 1440 (TTAB 1997); Leatherman Tool Group, Inc. v. Cooper Industries, Inc., 44 U.S.P.Q.2d 1045 (D.Or. 1997); Leatherman Tool Group, Inc. v. Cooper Industries, Inc., 199 F.3d 1009 (9th Cir. 1999); Cooper Industries, Inc. v. Leatherman Tool Group, Inc.; 532 U.S. 424 (2001); Tillamook County Smoker, Inc. v. Tillamook County Creamry Assn., 311 F.Supp.2d 1023 (D. Or. 2004); Tillamook County Smoker, Inv. v. Tillamook County Creamery Assn., 333 F.Supp. 2d 975 (D.Or. 2004). ***PRACTICE AREAS:*** Intellectual Property Litigation; Trademarks; Patents; Trade Dress; False Advertising; Unfair Competition; Copyrights; Intellectual Property Licensing. ***Email:*** pete@chernofflaw.com

WILLIAM O. GENY, born Tennessee, February 12, 1947; admitted to bar, 1974, Tennessee (inactive); 1975, U.S. Court of Federal Claims and U.S. Court of Customs and Patent Appeals; 1983, Oregon; registered to practice before U.S. Patent and Trademark Office. *Education:* Tulane University of Louisiana (B.S., 1969); Vanderbilt University (J.D., 1973). Trial Attorney, Patent Section, Civil Division, U.S. Dept. of Justice, 1974-1982. *Member:* Oregon State Bar; Oregon Patent Law Association (Treasurer, 1986-1987; Vice President, 1987-1988). ***REPORTED CASES:*** Alexey T. Zacharin v. The United States, 34 Fed. Cl. 609; Dynamics Corporation of America v. The United States, 5 Cl. Ct. 591; Charles P. Fogarty v. The United States, 5 Cl. Ct. 402; Motorola, Inc. v. The United States, 1 Cl. Ct. 131; James N. Constant v. The United States, 1 Cl. Ct. 600; Norris Industries, Inc. v. The United States, 681 F.2d 751; McDonnell Douglas Corporation v. The United States, 670 F.2d 156; Rel-Reeves Inc. v. The United States, 606 F.2d 949; T. H. Egley v. The United States, 576 F.2d 309. ***PRACTICE AREAS:*** Copyright Law; Intellectual Property Licensing; Patent Litigation; Computer and Software Patents; Electrical Patents. ***Email:*** bill@chernofflaw.com

NANCY J. MORIARTY, born Concord, California, March 27, 1952; admitted to bar, 1984, Iowa (inactive); 1987, Oregon and U.S. District Court, District of Oregon; 1988, U.S. Court of Appeals, Ninth Circuit; 1996, U.S. Court of Appeals for the Federal Circuit; 1999, U.S. Court of Appeals, Eighth Circuit; registered to practice before U.S. Patent and Trademark Office. *Education:* University of California at Riverside (B.S., 1974; M.A, 1975); University of Iowa (J.D., with high distinction, 1984). Associate Editor, Iowa Law Review, 1983-1984. Law Clerk to Judge Edward J. McManus, U.S. District Court, Northern District of Iowa, 1984-1987. United States Magistrate, Selection Panel, 2005. President, Pioneer Courthouse Historical Society. President, U.S. District Court of Oregon Historical Society, 2000-2001. Chair, United States District Court, District of Oregon, Local Rules Advisory Committee, 1996-2000. Ninth Circuit Lawyer Representative Coordinating Committee, 1999-2000. Lawyer Representative to the Ninth Circuit Judicial Conference, 1998-2000. *Member:* Oregon State Bar (Chair, Ethics Committee, 1999); Federal Bar Association (President, 2002-2003, Oregon Chapter); Oregon Patent Law Association. ***REPORTED CASES:*** Woodstock's Enterprises, Inc. (California) v. Woodstock's Enterprises, Inc. (Oregon), 43 U.S.P.Q.2d 1440 (TTAB 1997). ***PRACTICE AREAS:*** Trademarks; Trademark Litigation; Intellectual Property Litigation; False Advertising; Copyright. ***Email:*** nancy@chernofflaw.com

KEVIN L. RUSSELL, born Auburn, Washington, November 18, 1967; admitted to bar, 1993, Oregon, U.S. District Court, District of Oregon and U.S. Court of Appeals for the Ninth and Federal Circuits; registered to practice before U.S. Patent and Trademark Office. *Education:* Washington State University (B.S.E.E., 1990); Willamette University (J.D., 1993). Candidate for Master of Science in Electrical Engineering, Portland State University. Tau Beta Pi. Author: Federal Circuit Patent Case Digests, West Group Legal Publishing, 1995—. *Member:* Multnomah County, Federal Circuit and American Bar Associations; Oregon State Bar (Executive Committee, Intellectual Property Section, 1994-1997); Oregon Patent Law Association; Computer Law Association; Institute of Electrical and Electronics Engineers. ***PRACTICE AREAS:*** Intellectual Property; Patents; Trademarks; Electronic Intellectual Property; Electrical Patents. ***Email:*** kevin@chernofflaw.com

---

TIM A. LONG, born Pasadena, California, June 14, 1945; admitted to bar, 1974, Oregon; registered to practice before U.S. Patent and Trademark Office. *Education:* University of Idaho (B.S.M.E., 1968); Northwestern School of Law of Lewis and Clark College (J.D., 1974); Portland State University (B.S.E.E., 1998). *Member:* Multnomah County Bar Association; Oregon State Bar; Oregon Patent Law Association. ***PRACTICE AREAS:*** Intellectual Property; Patents; Trademarks. ***Email:*** tal@chernofflaw.com

KURT A. ROHLFS, born Lincoln, Nebraska, April 30, 1967; admitted to bar, 1997, Oregon; 1999, U.S. District Court, District of Oregon; registered to practice before U.S. Patent and Trademark Office. *Education:* University of Nebraska (B.S., 1990); Lewis and Clark College (J.D., 1996). *Member:* Oregon State Bar. ***PRACTICE AREAS:*** Intellectual Property; Patents; Trademarks; Copyrights. ***Email:*** kurt@chernofflaw.com

BRENNA K. LEGAARD, born Omaha, Nebraska, December 14, 1973; admitted to bar, 2000, Oregon and U.S. District Court, District of Oregon; U.S. Court of Appeals for the Ninth Circuit; registered to practice before U.S. Patent and Trademark Office. *Education:* Idaho State University (B.A., with high honors, 1995; B.S., with honors, 2000); Case Western Reserve University (J.D., cum laude, 1999). ***LANGUAGES:*** Spanish and Japanese. ***REPORTED CASES:*** Tillamook Country Smoker, Inc. v. Tillamook County Creamery Assn., 333 F.Supp.2d 975 (D.Or.2004); Tillamook Country Smoker, Inc. v. Tillamook County Creamery Assn., 311 F.Supp2d 1023 (D.Or. 2004). ***PRACTICE AREAS:*** Intellectual Property; Litigation. ***Email:*** brenna@chernofflaw.com

SUSAN D. PITCHFORD, born Anchorage, Alaska, August 17, 1971; admitted to bar, 1996, Washington; 1998, Oregon; 2004, U.S. District Court, Eastern District of Washington, U.S. District Court, District of Oregon; registered to practice before U.S. Patent and Trademark Office. *Education:* Gonzaga University (B.S., B.A., 1993; J.D., 1996). Intern, Hon. Justice Philip Talmadge, Washington Supreme Court, 1995. *Member:* Clark County, Multnomah County, Washington State and Federal Bar Associations; Oregon State Bar; Clark County Young Lawyers Bar Association (President); Washington Bar Association Young Lawyers Division (Trustee); Oregon Federal Bar Association Young Lawyers (Chair). ***REPORTED CASES:*** Brewer v. Brewer, 976 P.2d 102 (1999). ***PRACTICE AREAS:*** Intellectual Property; Patents; Trademarks; Copyrights; Litigation. ***Email:*** sdp@chernofflaw.com

J. DOUGLAS WELLS, born Visalia, California, June 28, 1965; admitted to bar, 2004, Oregon; registered to practice before U.S. Patent and Trademark Office. *Education:* Purdue University (B.S.E.E., 1989; M.S.I.A., 1991); Northwestern School of Law at Lewis and Clark College (J.D., 2003). *Member:* Oregon State Bar; Oregon Patent Law Association; National Association of Patent Practioners Institute of Electrical and Electronics Engineers. ***PRACTICE AREAS:*** Intellectual Property; Patents; Trademarks; Trade Secrets; Copyrights. ***Email:*** doug@chernofflaw.com

LEGAL SUPPORT PERSONNEL

DAVID SYLVAN FINE, born Wilmington, Delaware, March 18, 1952. *Education:* University of Delaware (B.A., magna cum laude, 1981); University of Oregon (J.D., 1984). Co-Recipient, Ulin Award, University of Delaware, 1981. *Member:* Oregon Patent Law Association. ***Email:*** dsf@chernofflaw.com

REPRESENTATIVE CLIENTS: Allerderm Laboratories, Inc.; Benchmade Knife Company, Inc.; Bend Research, Inc.; Brandt Fruit Trees, Inc.; Cascade Corp.; Cascade Microtech, Inc.; Columbia Sportswear Co.; Entek, Inc.; ESCO Corporation; Evergreen Technologies, Inc.; The Greenbrier Cos.; Gunderson, Inc.; International Yogurt Co.; Iseli Nursery; InFocus Corporation; Leatherman Tool Group, Inc.; Longview Fibre Co.; Magno-Humphries Laboratories, Inc.; Microsound Systems, Inc.; NF Formulas, Inc.; Nutrition Now, Inc.; O'Loughlin Trade Shows; Planar Systems, Inc.; Pfizer, Inc.; Random Lenths Publications, Inc.; SAE, Inc.; Sartorius A.G.; Sharp Laboratories of America, Inc.; Soloflex, Inc.; Stash Tea Company; Tekmax Inc.; Tidland Corp.; Universal Enterprises, Inc.; University of Tennessee Research Corporation; U.S. Software; Western Graphics & Data, Inc.; White's Electronics, Inc.

JAMES D. CHURCH

1001 S.W. FIFTH AVENUE, SUITE 1520
PORTLAND, OREGON 97204
Telephone: 503-228-6449
Fax: 503-228-1058
URL: http://www.lawyers.com/jamesdchurch

General Trial Practice, Family Law, Domestic Relations, Interstate Child Custody, Mediation, Personal Injury, Probate Law, Adoptions, Child Custody, Child Support, Divorce, Domestic Violence, Visitation Rights, Automobile Accidents, Wills and Probate.

JAMES D. CHURCH, born Toccoa, Georgia, April 2, 1943; admitted to bar, 1973, Oregon and U.S. District Court, District of Oregon; 1983, U.S. Court of Appeals, Ninth Circuit. *Education:* Willamette University (B.A., 1965); Lewis and Clark College (J.D., 1973). Certified Mediator, State of Oregon, 1992—. *Member:* Oregon State Bar (Member, Family Law Section).

CLARK, LINDAUER, FETHERSTON, EDMONDS, LIPPOLD & COLLIER, LLP

PORTLAND, OREGON

(See Salem)

Trial and Business Practice in State and Federal Courts including Business Litigation, Insurance Law, Agricultural Law, Automobile, Premises Liability, Professional Negligence, including Legal and Medical Malpractice, Product, Toxic Tort and Environmental Liability, Employment Discrimination, Wrongful Discharge and Defamation, Arbitration and Mediation, Business, Real Estate, and Estate Law, Probate.

COIT & DEAN, P.C.

1211 SW 5TH AVENUE, SUITE 2350
PORTLAND, OREGON 97204
Telephone: 503-546-3178
Fax: 503-213-6023
Email: adeanattorneyatlaw@hotmail.com
URL: http://www.lawyers.com/adamldean

Family Law, Divorce, Child Custody, Child Support, Visitation Rights, Spousal Support, Modifications, Restraining Orders, Criminal Law, Personal Injury.

ADAM L. DEAN, born April 21, 1967; admitted to bar, 1995, Oregon and U.S. District Court, District of Oregon; Wisconsin and U.S. District Court, Eastern District of Wisconsin; 2000, Washington. *Education:* University of Wisconsin (B.S.W., 1990); Marquette University (J.D., 1995). *Member:* Oregon State Bar; State Bar of Wisconsin; Washington State Bar Association; Oregon Criminal Defense Lawyers Association. ***PRACTICE***

(This Listing Continued)

COIT & DEAN, P.C., Portland—Continued

AREAS: Family Law; Criminal Law; Driving While Intoxicated; Personal Injury; Divorce; Child Custody; Visitation Rights; Child Support; Spousal Support; Post Divorce Modification; Restraining Orders.

ANDREW COIT, admitted to bar, 1997, Oregon. *Education:* University of California at Santa Barbara (B.A., 1993); Northwestern School of Law (J.D., 1997). ***PRACTICE AREAS:*** Criminal Defense; Personal Injury; Family Law.

DES & SHANNON CONNALL, LLP

Established in 1974

1000 SW BROADWAY, SUITE 1220
PORTLAND, OREGON 97205
Telephone: 503-227-2688
Fax: 503-227-2687
URL: http://www.des-shannonconnall-llp.com

Federal and State Criminal Trial and Appellate Practice, Family Law including Divorce, Child Custody, Visitation Rights, Spousal Support, Child Support, Pre-nuptial Agreements, Domestic Relations, Juvenile Law.

MEMBERS OF FIRM

DES CONNALL, born Newbridge, Oregon, September 3, 1930; admitted to bar, 1957, Oregon; U.S. Supreme Court and U.S. Court of Appeals, Ninth Circuit. *Education:* University of Oregon; Lewis and Clark Law School (J.D., 1957). Former District Attorney, Multnomah County. *Member:* Multnomah County Bar Association; Oregon State Bar; Oregon Criminal Defense Lawyers Association; Oregon Association of Criminal Defense Lawyers. ***PRACTICE AREAS:*** Criminal Defense; Juvenile Law; Murder; Sex Crimes; Search and Seizure; Driving While Intoxicated. ***Email:*** desdconnall@msn.com

SHANNON K. CONNALL, born Portland, Oregon, August 10, 1968; admitted to bar, 1997, Oregon; 2003, Washington. *Education:* Lewis and Clark Law School. *Member:* Multnomah County Bar Association; Oregon State Bar; Washington State Bar; Oregon Association of Criminal Defense Lawyers Association. ***PRACTICE AREAS:*** Family Law; Child Custody; Juvenile Law; Murder; Sex Crimes; Search and Seizure; Driving While Intoxicated.

COSGRAVE VERGEER KESTER LLP

Established in 1934

805 S.W. BROADWAY, 8TH FLOOR
PORTLAND, OREGON 97205
Telephone: 503-323-9000
Fax: 503-323-9019
Email: cvk@cvk-law.com
URL: http://www.cvk-law.com

Civil, Trial and Appellate Practice. Casualty, Corporate, Construction, Environmental Law, Labor, Employment and Discrimination, Occupational Health and Safety, Probate, Trusts and Estates, Fire. Insurance Defense, Liability and Coverage. Life, Professional Malpractice, Products Liability, Railroad Federal Employer's Liability Act, Transportation Law and Business and Corporate Law.

FIRM PROFILE: Cosgrave Vergeer Kester LLP traces its beginning to the 1930's. The firm has always had a very strong trial practice in the state and federal courts of Oregon and Washington, with emphasis on personal injury, environmental contamination, medical and legal malpractice, insurance coverage, railroad transportation (FELA), Americans with Disabilities Act (ADA), hazardous substances, construction, employment, commercial, securities litigation and business and products cases. The firm has developed over the last five years a very strong business group involved in a wide range of business transactions. The firm is listed in the Bar Register of Preeminent Lawyers. See the website for more information.

MEMBERS OF FIRM

RANDALL B. KESTER, admitted to bar, 1940, Oregon. *Education:* Willamette University (A.B., 1937); Columbia University (J.D., 1940). Phi Delta Phi. Instructor, Northwestern College of Law, 1947-1956. Associate Justice, Oregon Supreme Court, 1957-1958. General Solicitor and Senior Counsel, Union Pacific Railroad, 1958-1981. *Member:* National Association of Railroad Trial Counsel; American Law Institute (Life Member); American Academy of Appellate Lawyers; Defense Research Institute. ***PRACTICE AREAS:*** Transportation; Appellate Practice; Personal Injury; Products Liability. ***Email:*** rkester@cvk-law.com

WALTER H. SWEEK, admitted to bar, 1962, Oregon; 1972, U.S. Supreme Court. *Education:* Southern Oregon College and University of Oregon (B.A., 1959); University of Oregon (LL.B., 1962). Phi Delta Phi. Law Clerk, Honorable John F. Kilkenny, U.S. District Court for Oregon, 1962-1963. *Member:* Oregon Association of Defense Counsel (President, 1982-1983); American Judicature Society. Fellow, American College of Trial Lawyers; Defense Research Institute; Federation of Insurance and Corporate Counsel. ***PRACTICE AREAS:*** Business Law; Products Liability; Professional Liability; Employer Liability; Trucking Law. ***Email:*** wsweek@cvk-law.com

FRANK H. LAGESEN, admitted to bar, 1969, Oregon; 1987, Washington. *Education:* Portland State College (B.S., 1963); University of Oregon (J.D., 1969). Phi Delta Phi. Certified Public Accountant, Oregon, 1965. *Member:* Federation of Defense and Corporate Counsel; Oregon Association of Defense Counsel (Past President); American and Oregon Societies of Certified Public Accountants. ***PRACTICE AREAS:*** Professional Liability; Construction; Employment Law; Securities; Business Litigation. ***Email:*** flagesen@cvk-law.com

EUGENE H. BUCKLE, admitted to bar, 1976, Oregon. *Education:* Duke University (B.A., Phi Beta Kappa; magna cum laude, 1971); University of Virginia (J.D., 1976). *Member:* National Association of Railroad Trial Counsel. ***PRACTICE AREAS:*** Personal Injury; Products Liability; Construction Litigation. ***Email:*** ebuckle@cvk-law.com

DAVID P. MORRISON, admitted to bar, 1977, Oregon. *Education:* University of Oregon (B.A., 1974); Northwestern School of Law, Lewis & Clark College (J.D., 1977). Phi Beta Kappa. Member, Environmental Law Review, Lewis & Clark Law School, 1976-1977. *Member:* National Association of Railroad Trial Counsel. ***PRACTICE AREAS:*** Construction Law; Real Estate; Personal Injury. ***Email:*** morrison@cvk-law.com

THOMAS W. BROWN, admitted to bar, 1980, Oregon; 2002, Washington. *Education:* University of Texas (B.S., 1974); Northwestern School of Law, Lewis and Clark College (J.D., 1980). Law Clerk to Hon. William L. Richardson, Judge of the Oregon Court of Appeals, 1980-1981. *Member:* Fellow, American Academy of Appellate Lawyers. ***PRACTICE AREAS:*** Civil Appeals; Insurance Coverage; Insurance Litigation; Professional Liability Defense. ***Email:*** tbrown@cvk-law.com

DAVID H. WILLIAMS, admitted to bar, 1975, Oregon. *Education:* Lake Forest College (B.A., 1970); Northwestern School of Law, Lewis and Clark College (J.D., cum laude, 1975). Supervising Attorney, Northwestern School of Law Legal Clinic, 1978-1979. *Member:* American Bar Association. ***PRACTICE AREAS:*** Professional Liability Defense; Business Transactions; Real Estate; Estate Planning. ***Email:*** williams@cvk-law.com

JEFFREY A. JOHNSON, admitted to bar, 1982, Oregon. *Education:* University of Oregon (B.S., magna cum laude, 1973; J.D., 1982). *Member:* American Bar Association; American Society of Safety Engineers. ***PRACTICE AREAS:*** Business Litigation; Employment Litigation; Products Liability; OSHA; Catastrophic Injury; Trucking Law; Transportation. ***Email:*** jjohnson@cvk-law.com

ROBERT E. BARTON, admitted to bar, 1972, California; 1981, Oregon. *Education:* St. Louis University (B.A., 1969); University of Notre Dame (J.D., 1972). Deputy Attorney General, California, 1972-1973. Deputy District Attorney, Orange County, California, 1973-1981. Assistant Attorney General, Oregon, 1981-1984. *Member:* Federal Bar Association; Oregon Association of Defense Counsel; National Lawyers Association. ***PRACTICE AREAS:*** Personal Injury; Products Liability; Trucking Litigation. ***Email:*** rbarton@cvk-law.com

CHARLES J. HUBER, admitted to bar, 1976, Oregon. (President Elect). ***PRACTICE AREAS:*** Corporate Law; Real Estate Transfers. ***Email:*** chuber@cvk-law.com

TIMOTHY J. COLEMAN, admitted to bar, 1984, Oregon. *Education:* University of Oregon (B.S., Economics and History, 1980; J.D., 1984). Phi Delta Phi. Member, Moot Court Board. *Member:* National Association of Railroad Trial Counsel. ***PRACTICE AREAS:*** Railroad Law; Personal Injury; Products Liability. ***Email:*** tcoleman@cvk-law.com

MICHAEL C. LEWTON, admitted to bar, 1987, Oregon; 1992, Nevada; 2003, Washington. *Education:* North Arizona University (B.S., 1970); University of Nevada (M.Ed., 1975); Willamette University (J.D., 1987). Phi Alpha Delta. ***PRACTICE AREAS:*** Professional Liability; Discrimination; Sexual Abuse; Litigation. ***Email:*** mlewton@cvk-law.com

ANDREW T. BURNS, admitted to bar, 1988, Oregon. *Education:* University of Portland; University of Oregon (B.S., 1983); Northwestern School of Law, Lewis & Clark College (J.D., 1987). *Member:* American Bar Association. ***PRACTICE AREAS:*** Construction Litigation; Personal Injury. ***Email:*** aburns@cvk-law.com

PHILIP R. BENNETT, admitted to bar, 1984, Oregon; 1985, U.S. District Court, District of Oregon. *Education:* University of Oregon (B.A., 1981; J.D., 1984). Member, Gus Solomon American Inn of Court, 1990-1994. *Member:* American Bar Association. ***PRACTICE AREAS:*** Personal Injury; Products Liability; Premises Liability; Construction Litigation. ***Email:*** pbennett@cvk-law.com

THOMAS M. CHRIST, admitted to bar, 1983, Oregon. *Education:* University of Oregon (B.S., 1979; J.D., 1983). Author: "Responsive Pleadings," Oregon State Bar, CLE on Civil Pleadings and Practice, 1991, 1994 and 1998. Co-Author: "Excess Liability," Oregon State Bar, CLE on Insurance, 1987 and 1992; "Technical Requirements for Briefs," Oregon State Bar, CLE on Appeal and Review, 1993 and 1998. Circuit Judge, Pro Tempore, Multnomah County, 1991—. Member, Board of Directors, American Civil Liberties Union of Oregon, 1994-1997. Member, Commission on Judicial Fitness and Disability, 1999—. *Member:* Oregon State Bar (Member, House of Delegates). ***PRACTICE AREAS:*** Insurance Coverage; Appellate Practice. ***Email:*** tchrist@cvk-law.com

KENNETH J. ABERE, JR, admitted to bar, 1994, Oregon; 2004, Washington. *Education:* Trinity College (B.A., 1986); Willamette University (J.D., 1994). Member, Moot Court Board. *Member:* Multnomah County Bar Association; Oregon State Bar; Oregon Association of Defense Counsel. ***PRACTICE AREAS:*** Personal Injury; Products Liability; Premises Liability; Real Estate Litigation; Business Litigation. ***Email:*** kabere@cvk-law.com

WENDY M. MARGOLIS, admitted to bar, 1994, Oregon, 1995, Washington. *Education:* University of California at Santa Barbara (B.A., 1983); University of Washington (M.S., 1985); University of Oregon (J.D., 1993). Order of the Coif. Law Clerk to the Honorable Mary J. Deits, Oregon Court of Appeals, 1993-1995. Member, American Speech, Language and Hearing Association, 1985—. ***PRACTICE AREAS:*** Civil Appeals; Litigation. ***Email:*** margolis@cvk-law.com

MICHAEL K. WALTON, admitted to bar, 1994, California and U.S. District Court, Northern District of California; 1999, Oregon; 2005, Washington. *Education:* University of Southern California (B.A., 1987); McGeorge School of Law, University of the Pacific (J.D., 1994). *Member:* National Association of Railroad Trial Counsel. ***PRACTICE AREAS:*** Railroad Law; Transportation; Products Liability. ***Email:*** mwalton@cvk-law.com

CHRISTINE COERS-MITCHELL, admitted to bar, 1992, Oregon. *Education:* University of California at Santa Cruz (B.A., with honors, 1982); Cambridge University (M.Phil, Social Anthropology, 1984); Gonzaga University (J.D., summa cum laude, 1992). Law Clerk to Chief Judge William Richardson, Oregon Court of Appeals, 1992-1994. ***PRACTICE AREAS:*** Civil Appeals; Professional Liability; Products Liability; Creditors Rights; Bankruptcy Litigation. ***Email:*** ccoersmitchell@cvk-law.com

(This Listing Continued)

JILL D. LANEY, admitted to bar, 1993, Oregon; 2004, Washington. *Education:* University of Portland (B.S., Nursing, maxima cum laude, 1982); Willamette University (J.D., cum laude, 1993). ***PRACTICE AREAS:*** Corporate Law; Property Law; Real Estate.

RICHARD MILLER, born Nice, France, December 27, 1950; admitted to bar, 1976, Oregon; 1983, U.S. Tax Court; 2004, Washington. *Education:* Colorado College (B.A., magna cum laude, 1973); Willamette University (J.D., 1976). Co-Author, "Federal Estate Tax and Generation Skipping Transfer Tax," Administering Oregon Estates, 1991. *Member:* Multnomah Bar Association; Oregon State Bar (Member, Sections of Business and Corporate Law, Taxation, Estate Planning and Administration and Solo and Small Firms). (Also practicing individually). ***PRACTICE AREAS:*** Tax Law; Estate Planning, Probate and Trust Law; Business Law; Real Estate Law. ***Email:*** rmiller@cvk-law.com

ASSOCIATES

ROBERT E. SABIDO, admitted to bar, 1996, Oregon; 1997, U.S. Court of Appeals, Ninth Circuit; 1998, U.S. District Court, District of Oregon; 1999, Washington. *Education:* University of Southern California at Los Angeles (B.A., 1993); Pepperdine University (J.D., 1996). Associate Editor, Pepperdine Law Review, 1995-1996. Author: "California Supreme Court Surveys," Pepperdine Law Review, Volume 22, pp. 1190,1233 & 1752; Volume 23, pp. 1038 & 1409. Assistant Attorney General, Oregon, 1996-1998. *Member:* Multnomah County and American Bar Associations; Oregon State Bar; Oregon Association of Defense Counsel. ***PRACTICE AREAS:*** Civil Appeals; Insurance Coverage; Insurance Litigation. ***Email:*** rsabido@cvk-law.com

PETER S. WILLCOX-JONES, admitted to bar, 1999, Oregon. *Education:* Roanoke College (B.A., 1995); University of Oregon School of Law (J.D., 1999). ***PRACTICE AREAS:*** Construction Law; Premises Liability; Personal Injury. ***Email:*** pwillcoxjones@cvk-law.com

JASON PISTACCHIO, admitted to bar, 2000, Oregon. *Education:* Washington State University (B.A., cum laude, 1996); University of Oregon (J.D., 2000). *Member:* American Bar Association. ***PRACTICE AREAS:*** Construction Law; Products Liability; Employment Litigation; Business Litigation. ***Email:*** jpistacchio@cvk-law.com

J. NICHOLAS BALDWIN-SAYRE, admitted to bar, 1997, Oregon. *Education:* University of California at Los Angeles (B.A., 1992); Northwestern School Law, Lewis and Clark College (J.D., 1997). Formerly with Marvin, Chorzempa & Associates.*Member:* Oregon State Bar (Chairman, Law Related Education Committee, 2000—); Oregon Association of Defense Counsel. ***PRACTICE AREAS:*** Construction Law; Products Liability; Property Law; Personal Injury. ***Email:*** nbaldwinsayre@cvk-law.com

GLENN W. ROBLES, admitted to bar, 1996, Guam; 1997, Commonwealth of the Northern Mariana Islands; 2001, Oregon. *Education:* University of California at Santa Cruz (B.A., 1987); Northwestern School of Law, Lewis & Clark College (J.D., 1996). ***PRACTICE AREAS:*** Transportation; Commercial Law; Construction Litigation; Automobile Litigation. ***Email:*** grobles@cvk-law.com

DEREK J. ASHTON, admitted to bar, 1987, Oregon. *Education:* University of Oregon (B.S., Finance, 1983; J.D., 1987). Listed in Dean's List, University of Oregon. District Attorney, Multnomah District Attorney's Office, 1987-2002. ***PRACTICE AREAS:*** Catastrophic Injury; Products Liability; Insurance Fraud; Insurance Defense; White Collar Criminal Defense. ***Email:*** dashton@cvk-law.com

AMITY L. CLAUSEN, admitted to bar, 2004, Oregon. *Education:* University of Oregon (B.S., magna cum laude, 2001); University of Utah (J.D., 2004). ***PRACTICE AREAS:*** Personal Injury; Commercial Litigation; Contract Litigation; Railroad Litigation; Professional Liability. ***Email:*** aclausen@cvk-law.com

GRETCHEN L. MANDEKOR, born Vancouver, British Columbia, January 13, 1973; admitted to bar, 2000, Oregon and U.S. District Court, District of Oregon. *Education:* McGill University (B.A., first class honours, 1994); University of Oregon (J.D., 1999). *Member:* American Bar Association. ***LANGUAGES:*** French, Latin. ***PRACTICE AREAS:*** Employment Litigation; Personal Injury; Premises Liability; Products Liability; Medical Malpractice.

NICHOLAS E. WHEELER, admitted to bar, 2004, Oregon. *Education:* Oregon State University (B.S., cum laude, 2001); University of Oregon (J.D., 2004). ***PRACTICE AREAS:*** Personal Injury; Commercial Litigation; Contract Litigation; Railroad Litigation; Professional Liability. ***Email:*** nwheeler@cvk-law.com

REPRESENTATIVE CLIENTS: AIG; AT&T; Bally Total Fitness; The Boise Cascade Corp.; Burlington Northern Railroad Co.; Cambridge Transportation; Contact Lumber; Farmers Insurance Group; Grove Worldwide; International Line Builders; MDU Resources, Inc.; Mollett Printing, Inc.; Morrison Companies; Mutual of Enumclaw Insurance Co.; Norris & Stevens; North Pacific Insurance Co.; Ochoco Lumber; Panel Equipment Company; Pinnacle Exhibits LLC; Professional Liability Fund; SAFECO; S.C. Johnson; St. Paul Fire & Marine Insurance Co.; Standard Insurance.; State Farm Mutual Automobile Insurance Co.; Swift Transportation; Taylor Lumber Co.; The Hartford; Tosco/Circle L Stores; Tosoh Quartz; Union Pacific Railroad Co.; U-Haul, Inc.

CRISPIN RUSSELL RISSBERGER ROHNY PC

d/b/a Crispin Employment Lawyers

Established in 1992

9600 SOUTHWEST OAK STREET
SUITE 500
PORTLAND, OREGON 97223
Telephone: 503-293-5770
Fax: 503-293-5766
URL: http://www.lawyers.com/employmentlaw-nw
Email: crispin@employmentlaw-nw.com
URL: http://www.employmentlaw-nw.com

Employment and Civil Rights Litigation before State and Federal Agencies and Courts of Oregon and Washington, including Americans with Disabilities Act, Sexual Harassment, Discrimination, Wage and Hour, Employee Benefits, Executive Employment Law, Executive Severance Contracts, Wrongful Termination, Civil Rights, Disability Accommodation, Personal Injury.

(This Listing Continued)

FIRM PROFILE: Crispin Russell Rissberger Rohny PC devotes its practice exclusively to employment and labor matters, representing individuals and employers in a broad range of services related to the employer-employee relationship. We strive to identify and serve the interests of our clients in the most professional way possible and to provide creative, forceful and effective advice, counsel and representation. Members of the firm are experienced trial lawyers, who believe in resolving our clients' claims in the most favorable way possible, including before federal and state court juries. The firm is committed to aggressive and strategic representation.

CRAIG A. CRISPIN, born Albany, Oregon, October 13, 1951; admitted to bar, 1981, Washington; 1982, Oregon and U.S. Court of Appeals, Ninth Circuit; 1983, U.S. District Court, District of Oregon; 1985, U.S. District Courts, Eastern and Western Districts of Washington and U.S. Supreme Court. *Education:* Southern Illinois University (B.S., University Honors, 1978); Willamette University (J.D., magna cum laude, 1981). Editor-in-Chief, Willamette Law Review, 1980-1981. Judicial Clerk, Circuit Judge Eugene A. Wright, Ninth Circuit Court of Appeals, 1981-1982. Member, National Employment Lawyers Association. *Member:* Washington State Bar Association; Oregon State Bar (Member, Sections on: Labor & Employment (Executive Committee, 2001-2002); Disabilities; Secretary, 1995-1996; Member, Executive Committee, 1996-1998); Oregon Trial Lawyers Association; Washington State Trial Lawyers Association. ***REPORTED CASES:*** Clackamas Gastroenterology Associates, P.C. v. Wells, 538 U.S. 440 (2003); Fraser v.Goodale, 342 F3d 1032 (9th Cir. 2003); Pavon v. Swift Transp. Co., 192 F.3d 902 (9th Cir. 1999); Wells v. Clackamas Gastroenterology, 271 F.3d 903 (9th Cir. 2001); Heller v. Columbia Edgewater Country Club, 195 F. Supp 2d 1212 (D.Or., 2002) (NO. CIV. 01-316-JE); Cornier v. Paul Tulacz, DVM PC, 176 Or.App. 245, 30 P.3d 1210, 7 Wage & Hour Cas.2d (BNA) 541 (2001); Janee Wilson v. Tarr, Inc., 2000 WL 1292590, 79 Empl. Prac. Dec. P.40,222, 141 Lab.Cas. P34,145,142 Lab.Cas. P 34, 153 (D.Or., Sep 08, 2000) (NO. CV-99-1412-HU); Sims v. Besaw's Cafe, 165 Or.App. 180, 997 P.2d 201, 81 Fair Empl. Prac.Cas. (BNA) 1411 (2000); Line Drivers, Pickup and Delivery Local Union No. 81 v. Roadway Exp. Inc., 152 F.3d 1098, 158 L.R.R.M. (BNA) 3082, 135 Lab.Cas. P 10,213 (9th Cir.1998); Stanich v. Precision Body and Paint, Inc., 151 Or.App.446,950 P.2d 328 (1997). ***PRACTICE AREAS:*** Executive Employment Law; Employment Discrimination; Wage and Hour Law; Americans with Disabilities Act; Civil Rights; Executive Severance Contracts; Sex Discrimination; Labor Relations; Discrimination; Sexual Harassment; Professional Malpractice. ***Email:*** crispin@employmentlaw-nw.com

SHELLEY D. RUSSELL, born Portland, Oregon, May 25, 1967; admitted to bar, 1994, Oregon and U.S. District Court, District of Oregon; 1998, U.S. Court of Appeals, Ninth Circuit; 2003, U.S. Supreme Court. *Education:* Pomona College (B.A., 1989); Lewis and Clark College (J.D., 1994). *Member:* Federal Bar Association (Member, Young Lawyers Section Committee, 1997-2001 and Chair, 2001-2002; Board Member, Oregon Chapter, 2002-2005); Oregon State Bar (Member, Council on Court Procedures, 2002—; Continuing Education Committee 1998-2001; Washington County Local Professional Responsibility Committee, 2001-2004); Oregon Women Lawyers; Oregon Trial Lawyers Association (Member, Board of Governors, 2001—; Member, Education Committee, 1996-1999, 2001—; Co-chair, 2001-2002); Co-Chair, Women's Caucus 1999-2001; Association of Trial Lawyers of America; National Employment Lawyers Association. ***LANGUAGES:*** French. ***REPORTED CASES:*** Goodman Herron v. Advanced Nav. and Positioning Corp., 940 F.Supp.288 (D.Or. 1996); Thoreson v. Competition Specialties, Inc., 2001 WL 950815 (D.Or. 2001); Heller v. Columbia Edgewater Country Club, 195 F.Supp.2d 1212 (D.Or. 2002); Volm v. Legacy Health Systems, Inc., 237 F.Supp.2d 1166 (D.Or. 2002); Sims v. Besaw's Cafe, 165 Or.App. 180, 997 P.2d 201 (2000). ***PRACTICE AREAS:*** Employment Litigation; Sex Discrimination; Americans with Disabilities Act; Age Discrimination in Employment; Employee Rights; Employment Contracts; Employment Discrimination; Employment Law; Executive Employment Law; Sexual Harassment; Personal Injury. ***Email:*** shelley@employmentlaw-nw.com

PATTY T. RISSBERGER, born Buffalo, New York, October 23, 1960; admitted to bar, 1987, Oregon; 1990, U.S. District Court, District of Oregon; 2003, U.S. Supreme Court. *Education:* Canisius College (B.A., 1982); Syracuse University College of Law (J.D., 1986). Author: Note, "Legalization of Illegal Aliens," 12 Syr. J. Int'l. L. & Com. 572. *Member:* Multnomah County Bar Association; Oregon State Bar; Oregon Trial Lawyers Association; National Employment Lawyers Association. ***REPORTED CASES:*** Manqual v. Home Depot USA, 2004 WL 1839191, D. Or., August 16, 2004; EL-Hakem v. Bjy, Inc., 262 F.Supp 2nd 1139 (D. Or. 2003); Perri v. Certified Languages, 187 App 76, 66 P3d 531 (2003); Reich v. Dunhy 2002, WL 31470392 (D. Or. 2002); Weiss-Clark v. Kaiser Foundation Health Plan of the Northwest, 2001 WL 204823 (Feb. 7, 2001); Holbrook v. Precision Helicopter, Inc. 16 Or. App 538, 916 P2d 646 (1999); Lamonts Apparel Inc. v. Si-Lloyd Associates, 158 Or. App 227, 956 P2d 1024 (1998). ***PRACTICE AREAS:*** Employment Law; Employment Litigation; Sex Discrimination; Age Discrimination; Employment Discrimination; Sexual Harassment; Wage and Hour Law; Appellate Practice; Race Discrimination. ***Email:*** Patty@employmentlaw-nw.com

CHARESE A. ROHNY, born Buffalo, New York, December 17, 1965; admitted to bar, 1995, Oregon; 2003, California; U.S. District Court, District of Oregon; U.S. District Court, Northern and Southern Districts of California. *Education:* Humboldt State University (B.A., 1987); Bradford University, England, United Kingdom, 1985-1986; Willamette University (J.D., and Certificate in Dispute Resolution, 1995). Order of the Barristers. Moot Court Board. Member, Willamette University Center for Dispute Resolution Fellowship. Co-Founder/Chair, Willamette University Public Interest Law Project. Co-author/Lecturer, "Damages," CLE Publication and One-Day Seminar, National Business Institute, 2003. Instructor, Jury Selection, Willamette University, Trial Practice Seminar 2003, and Teaching Assistant, Negotiations Course, 1994, Willamette University College of Law. Commissioner, Human Rights and Relations Advisory Commission, City of Salem, 1999-2001. Board Member, Oregon Lawyers Against Hunger, 2001—. Member, Stand for Children, 1998—. *Member:* Multnomah County, Marion County and American Bar Associations; Oregon State Bar (Member, House of Delegates, 1996-1997; Employment and Civil Rights Sections); Oregon Trial Lawyers Association; Willamette Valley American Inns of Court, 1996-2000. ***REPORTED CASES:*** Shoup v. Wal-Mart Stores, Inc., 335 Or. 164, 61 P.2d 928 (2003); State of Washington v. Heckel, 143 Wash. 2d 824, 24 P.3 404 (2001), Cert denied, 534 U.S. 997 (2001). ***PRACTICE AREAS:*** Employment Litigation; Employment Discrimination; Race Discrimination; Age Discrimination; Whistleblower Litigation;

(This Listing Continued)

CRISPIN RUSSELL RISSBERGER ROHNY PC, Portland—Continued

Equal Pay Act Claims; Sexual Harassment; Retaliatory Discharge; Civil Rights; Wrongful Termination; Personal Injury; Wrongful Death. ***Email:*** charese@employmentlaw-nw.com

JOHN P. CROWELL

870 PIONEER TOWER
888 S.W. FIFTH AVENUE
PORTLAND, OREGON 97204-2019
Telephone: 503-222-4455
Facsimile: 503-243-2717
Email: john@jpcrowell.com

General Civil Law; Trial Practice in State and Federal Courts. Commercial, Securities, Personal Injury and Pension Litigation.

JOHN P. CROWELL, born Boston, Massachusetts, March 21, 1955; admitted to bar, 1982, Oregon; 1984, Washington. *Education:* Dartmouth College (B.A., 1977); University of Oregon (J.D., 1982). *Member:* Multnomah County and Washington State Bar Associations; Oregon State Bar.

CURTIS & CORRELL

4300 NORTH EAST FREMONT STREET, SUITE 230
PORTLAND, OREGON 97213-1100
Telephone: 503-230-9285
Fax: 503-282-4106
URL: http://www.curtiscorrell.com

Criminal Law, Sex Crimes, Sexual Abuse, Sexual Assault, Parole and Probation, Homicides, Death Penalty, Drug Crimes, Felonies, Post Conviction, Juvenile.

MEMBERS OF FIRM

MICHAEL CURTIS, born Albuquerque, New Mexico, August 11, 1949; admitted to bar, 1977, Oregon and U.S. District Court, District of Oregon. *Education:* Columbia University (B.A., 1971); Willamette University (J.D., 1977). *Member:* American Bar Association; National Association of Criminal Defense Lawyers (life member); Oregon Criminal Defense Lawyers Association (life member); National Legal Aid and Defender Association; American Academy of Forensic Sciences. ***PRACTICE AREAS:*** Criminal Law; Sex Crimes; Sexual Abuse; Sexual Assault; Parole and Probation; Homicide; Death Penalty; Drug Crimes; Felonies. ***Email:*** curtismichael@qwest.net

KATHLEEN M. CORRELL, born Pennsylvania, December 25, 1961; admitted to bar, 1987, Oregon, U.S. District Court, District of Oregon, U.S. Court of Appeals, Ninth Circuit and U.S. Supreme Court. *Education:* Oberlin College (B.A., 1983); Northeastern University School of Law (J.D., 1987). *Member:* Multnomah County and American Bar Associations; Oregon State Bar; National Association of Criminal Defense Lawyers; Oregon Criminal Defense Lawyers Association; National Legal Aid and Defender Association. ***PRACTICE AREAS:*** Criminal Law; Death Penalty; Criminal Appeals. ***Email:*** defender@pacifier.com

ROBERT D. DAMES, JR.

Established in 1978

1000 S.W. BROADWAY, SUITE 1510
PORTLAND, OREGON 97205
Telephone: 503-228-2700
FAX: 503-228-5341
Email: damesjr@aol.com

Plaintiff's Medical Malpractice and Pharmaceutical Liability.

ROBERT D. DAMES, JR., born Jamestown, North Dakota, January 26, 1948; admitted to bar, 1975, Oregon; U.S. District Court, District of Oregon; U.S. District Court, Northern District of California; U.S. Court of Appeals, Ninth Circuit. *Education:* UCLA (B.A., 1971); Northwestern School of Law (J.D., 1975). *Member:* Oregon State Bar; Association of Trial Lawyers of America; Oregon Trial Lawyers Association; American Board of Trial Advocates. ***PRACTICE AREAS:*** Medical Malpractice; Pharmaceutical Liability; Products Liability; Drug and Medical Device Litigation.

D'AMORE & ASSOCIATES, P.C.

506 S.W. 6TH AVENUE, SUITE 700
PORTLAND, OREGON 97204
Telephone: 503-222-6333
Vancouver Telephone: 360-696-3437
Fax: 503-224-1895
URL: http://www.damorelaw.com
Email: help@damorelaw.com
URL: http://www.lawyers.com/damorelaw

Medical Malpractice, Plaintiff's Personal Injury, Wrongful Death, Automobile Collisions and Injuries, Consumer Class Actions, Automobile Negligence, Insurance Litigation, Automobile Insurance Coverage, Insurance Bad Faith, Insurance Fraud, Insurance Premium Fraud, Unfair Insurance Practices, Uninsured Motorists, Property Damage Insurance Coverage, Brain Injury, Catastrophic Injury, Vehicular Homicide, Premises Liability, Medical Negligence, Motorcycle and Bicycle Accidents, Toxic Torts, ERISA and HMO Litigation, Employment Law and Discrimination, Wrongful Termination, Sexual Harassment, Workers Compensation, Dog Bites, Nursing Home Abuse, Trucking Accidents.

(This Listing Continued)

THOMAS D. D'AMORE, born Hollywood, Florida, October 7, 1961; admitted to bar, 1990, California; 1992, Oregon; 1993, Washington. *Education:* University of Nevada (B.A., 1984; B.S., 1985); Pepperdine University School of Law (J.D., 1990). Beta Alpha Psi (President). Certified Public Accountant, Oregon (inactive). Lecturer and Instructor, Becker CPA Review, 1993-1994. *Member:* Oregon State Bar; State Bar of California; Washington State Bar Association; Washington State Trial Lawyers Association (Eagle Member); Oregon Trial Lawyers Association (Member: President's Circle, 1997—; Board of Governors, 1998—; Chairperson, Motor Vehicles Section, 1998-2000); Association of Trial Lawyers of America (Oregon State Delegate; Member, President's Circle). (Certified as a Civil Trial Advocacy Specialist by the National Board of Trial Advocacy). ***PRACTICE AREAS:*** Plaintiffs Personal Injury; Automobile Accidents and Injuries; Wrongful Death; Consumer Class Actions; Medical Malpractice; Brain Injury; Spinal Injury; Insurance Bad Faith; Insurance Fraud; Insurance Premium Fraud; Unfair Insurance Practice; Uninsured and Underinsured Motorists; Property Insurance Coverage; Catastrophic Injury; Vehicular Homicide; Premises Liability; Motorcycle Accidents; Bicycle Accidents; ERISA Litigation; Health Maintenance Organizations; Workers Compensation. ***Email:*** tom@damorelaw.com

LINDA M. WEIMAR, born Albany, Oregon, November 18, 1954; admitted to bar, 1997, Oregon. *Education:* Portland State University (B.S., with honors, 1992); Lewis & Clark College Northwestern School of Law (J.D., 1997). *Member:* Oregon State Bar; Washington State Bar; Oregon Trial Lawyers Association (Member: President's Circle, 2000—; Membership Committee, 1998—); Washington Trial Lawyers Association; American Trial Lawyers Association; Oregon Women Lawyers; Washington County Women Lawyers. ***PRACTICE AREAS:*** Plaintiff's Personal Injury; Automobile Accidents and Injuries; Medical Malpractice; Pharmacists Liability; Employment Law; Employment Discrimination; Civil Litigation; Wrongful Deaths; Workers Compensation. ***Email:*** lweimar@damorelaw.com

DAVIS ROTHWELL EARLE & XOCHIHUA P.C.

1900 WELLS FARGO CENTER
1300 SOUTHWEST FIFTH AVENUE
PORTLAND, OREGON 97201-5604
Telephone: 503-222-4422
Telecopier: 503-222-4428
Email: inquiry@davisrothwell.com
URL: http://www.davisrothwell.com

Seattle, Washington Office: 2850 Bank of America Tower, 701 Fifth Avenue, 98104-7047. Telephones: 206-622-2295; Toll-Free: 1-800-370-8399. Telecopier: 206-340-0724.

Litigation Practice Concentrating on Insurance Defense, Personal Injury and Tort Claims, Environmental Law, Construction, Products Liability, Employment Law and the Defense of Professionals.

HEATHER C. BEASLEY, born Waterbury, Connecticut, June 21, 1966; admitted to bar, 1991, Pennsylvania; 1996, Oregon and U.S. District Court, District of Oregon; 2000, Massachusetts; 2001, Washington. *Education:* Tufts University (B.A., cum laude, 1988); Washington College of Law, American University (J.D., 1991). Senior Notes and Comments Editor, Administrative Law Journal. [Lt., U.S. JAG Corps., U.S. Navy 1991-1996; LCDR, JAG Corps., U.S. Navy Reserve, 2000—]. ***PRACTICE AREAS:*** Insurance Defense Litigation; Personal Injury; Products Liability; Premises Liability; Liquor Liability; Construction; Landlord and Tenant Law; Unlawful Trade Practices Act; Uninsured and Underinsured Motorists. ***Email:*** hbeasley@davisrothwell.com

WILLIAM ALAN DAVIS, born Olympia, Washington, May 8, 1952; admitted to bar, 1977, Oregon and U.S. District Court, District of Oregon; 1984, Washington and U.S. Court of Appeals, Ninth Circuit; 1989, U.S. District Court, Western and Eastern Districts of Washington. *Education:* Stanford University (B.A., 1974); University of Oregon (J.D., 1977). Order of the Coif. ***PRACTICE AREAS:*** Personal Injury; Construction; Employment; Professional Malpractice. ***Email:*** wdavis@davisrothwell.com

CHRISTOPHER J. DROTZMANN, born Yankton, South Dakota, August 9, 1971; admitted to bar, 1996, Oregon; 1997, Washington and U.S. District Court, District of Oregon. *Education:* Washington State University (B.A., 1993); Willamette University (J.D., cum laude, 1996). Form Editor, 1995-1996, Member, 1994-1995, Willamette Law Review. Chair and Vice-Chair, Oregon Association of Defense Counsel's Construction Defect Practice Group, 2002-2004. ***PRACTICE AREAS:*** Insurance Defense; Professional Liability Defense; Errors and Omissions Defense; Construction Defect; Commercial Litigation. ***Email:*** cdrotzmann@davisrothwell.com

WILLIAM G. EARLE, born Worcester, Massachusetts, December 14, 1955; admitted to bar, 1983, Oregon; 1985, U.S. District Court, District of Oregon; 1995, Washington and U.S. Court of Appeals, Ninth Circuit. *Education:* University of California at Riverside (A.B., with honors, 1978; M.A., 1980); Northwestern School of Law of Lewis and Clark College (J.D., 1983). Associate Editor, Environmental Law Journal, 1982-1983. ***PRACTICE AREAS:*** Insurance Coverage Litigation; Insurance Defense; Professional Malpractice; Environmental; Employment Litigation. ***Email:*** wearle@davisrothwell.com

ALAN GLADSTONE, born New York, N.Y., August 20, 1948; admitted to bar, 1994, Oregon and U.S. District Court, District of Oregon; U.S. Court of Appeals, Ninth Circuit. *Education:* Cooper Union (B.S., 1969); Northwestern School of Law of Lewis and Clark College (J.D., magna cum laude, 1994). Recipient: West Publishing Award for Outstanding Academic Achievement. Law Clerk to the Hon. Susan M. Leeson, Oregon Court of Appeals, 1994-1996. ***PRACTICE AREAS:*** Insurance Defense; Appellate Practice; Environmental Law. ***Email:*** agladstone@davisrothwell.com

JOHN S. KNOWLES, born Macomb, Illinois, October 18, 1950; admitted to bar, 1984, Colorado; 1994, Oregon. *Education:* Western Illinois University (B.S., 1977); Northwestern School of Law of Lewis and Clark College (J.D., 1984). Student Representative, Cornelius Honor Society. Extern, Honorable Otto R. Skopil, Jr., U.S. Court of Appeals, Ninth Circuit. ***PRACTICE AREAS:*** Litigation. ***Email:*** jknowles@davisrothwell.com

(This Listing Continued)

NICOLE M. RHOADES, born Palo Alto, California, April 8, 1973; admitted to bar, 1999, Oregon and U.S. District Court, District of Oregon; 2003, Washington. *Education:* Oregon State University (B.S., magna cum laude, 1996); Willamette University College of Law (J.D., 1999). Certificate in Dispute Resolution, 1999. Member, Willamette Law Review, 1997-1998. Articles Editor, Willamette Law Review, 1998-1999. Author: "The Constitutional Shaping of Oregon's Trade Secret Law: State ex rel. Sports Management News v. Nachtigal," Willamette Law Review, Vol. 35, No. 2 (1999). ***PRACTICE AREAS:*** Insurance Defense; Litigation. ***Email:*** nrhoades@davisrothwell.com

PAUL R. XÓCHIHUA, born Braham, Minnesota, November 24, 1961; admitted to bar, 1988, Oregon and U.S. District Court, District of Oregon; 1989, Washington and U.S. District Court, Eastern and Western Districts of Washington. *Education:* Lewis and Clark College (B.S., 1983; M.P.A., 1984); Northwestern School of Law of Lewis and Clark College (J.D., 1988). ***PRACTICE AREAS:*** Insurance Defense Litigation; Agricultural Law; Commercial; Fraud; Medical Malpractice; Personal Injury; Products Liability; Professional Liability. ***Email:*** pxochihua@davisrothwell.com

---

SAMUEL K. ANDERSON, born Cambridge, Massachusetts, January 3, 1975; admitted to bar, 2003, Oregon; 2004, U.S. District Court, District of Oregon; U.S. Court of Appeals, Ninth Circuit. *Education:* University of California at Santa Cruz (B.A., with honors, 1997); University of Oregon School of Law (J.D., 2003). Associate Editor, Oregon Law Review, 2002-2003. *Member:* Oregon State Bar. ***PRACTICE AREAS:*** Insurance Defense; Construction Law. ***Email:*** sanderson@davisrothwell.com

BRIAN F. CHURCH, born Portland, Oregon, January 25, 1973; admitted to bar, 2000, Oregon. *Education:* Oregon State University (B.S., cum laude, 1995); University of Oregon (J.D., 2000). ***PRACTICE AREAS:*** Insurance Defense; Construction Defects Litigation; Professional Liability Defense; Architects and Engineers Errors and Omissions; Personal Injury; Products Liability. ***Email:*** bchurch@davisrothwell.com

GINA M. DELAHUNT, born Salem, Oregon, July 14, 1965; admitted to bar, 2004, Oregon. *Education:* University of Portland (B.B.A., Academic Honors, 1987; M.B.A., 1992); Insurance Institute of America (A.R.M., 2001); Northwestern School of Law at Lewis & Clark College (J.D., 2004). Business Law Roundtable Scholar. Member, Risk & Insurance Management Society, 1998-2001. Author, Journal of Small and Emerging Business Law, 7 J. Small & Emerging Bus L. 501 (2003). ***Email:*** gdelahunt@davisrothwell.com

KEVIN A. EIKE, born Monroe, Wisconsin, August 12, 1975; admitted to bar, 2001, Oregon. *Education:* Iowa State University (B.S., 1997); University of Nebraska at Lincoln (J.D., cum laude, 2001). Phi Alpha Delta. Recipient: CALI Excellence for The Future Cyber Law, 1999; CALI Excellence for Administrative Law, 2001. Vice President, International Legal Society, 1999-2000. *Member:* American Bar Association; Oregon State Bar. ***PRACTICE AREAS:*** Litigation; Professional Liability; Construction Litigation; Commercial Litigation; Products Liability. ***Email:*** keike@davisrothwell.com

DANIEL S. HASSON, born Portland, Oregon, June 7, 1978; (admission pending). *Education:* Georgetown University (B.S., 2000); University of Oregon (J.D., 2005). Order of the Coif. ***LANGUAGES:*** Japanese. ***PRACTICE AREAS:*** Insurance Defense; Construction Defects. ***Email:*** dhasson@davisrothwell.com

ELIZABETH E. LAMPSON, born San Francisco, California, September 15, 1967; admitted to bar, 1993, California; 1997, Oregon; 1998, Washington. *Education:* University of California, Berkeley (B.A., 1990); Southwestern University School of Law (J.D., 1993). *Member:* Multnomah County and Washington State Bar Associations; State Bar of California; Oregon State Bar; Oregon Association of Defense Counsel; Washington Defense Trial Lawyers. ***PRACTICE AREAS:*** Construction Defects; Products Liability; Trademarks; Environmental Law; Toxic Torts; Commercial Litigation; Insurance Coverage. ***Email:*** elampson@davisrothwell.com

CARI WATERS, born Grass Valley, California, June 28, 1977; admitted to bar, 2003, Nevada and U.S. District Court, District of Nevada; 2004, Oregon. *Education:* Willamette University (B.A., 1999); University of Nevada (J.D., magna cum laude, 2003). Member, National Negotiation Team, American Bar Association, 2002-2003. Member, Nevada Law Journal, 2001-2003. Author, "Nevada's Failure to Secure Its Future," 3 Nev. L.J. 115. *Member:* State Bar of Nevada; Oregon State Bar. ***Email:*** cwaters@davisrothwell.com

REPRESENTATIVE CLIENTS: Admiral Insurance Company; CNA Insurance Companies; COREGIS (Westport Insurance Corp.); Crawford & Company; Crum & Forster; ECS Claims Administrators; Farmers Insurance Group; Federal Express; Fireman's Fund Insurance Companies; GAB Business Services, Inc.; Hertz Corporation; Lancer Claims Services, Inc.; Locating, Inc.; Lowe's Home Stores; Mitsui Sumitomo Insurance Group; Mutual of Enumclaw Insurance Co.; Oregon State Bar Professional Liability Fund; Oregon Mutual Insurance Co.; Oregon Life & Health Insurance Guaranty Assn.; PETCO; Physicians Insurance; Sentry Insurance Company; AIG Insurance Companies; Ohio Casualty Group; One Beacon Insurance Company; Monitor Liability Managers, Inc.; Borg-Warner Corporation; Oregon School Boards Association; Kingsmen Plastering, Inc.

DAVIS WRIGHT TREMAINE LLP

SUITE 2300, 1300 S.W. FIFTH AVENUE
PORTLAND, OREGON 97201-5682
Telephone: 503-241-2300
FAX: 503-778-5299
URL: http://www.dwt.com

Offices also at: Anchorage, Alaska, Bellevue, Washington, Los Angeles, California, New York, New York, San Francisco, California, Washington, D.C., Seattle, Washington, Shanghai, China.

Antitrust, Business and Corporate, Communications, Media and Information Technologies, Construction and Government Contracts, Credit Recovery and Bankruptcy, Education, eHealth Law, Emerging Business and Technology, Employee Benefits, Employment, Energy, Environmental and Natural Resources, Finance and Commercial Transactions, Food and Agriculture, Government Contracts, Healthcare, Hospitality, Immigration, Intellectual Property, International Law, Internet and eCommerce, Legislation, Litigation, Mergers and Acquisitions, Municipal Finance, Newspapers and Publishing, Real Estate and Land Use, Retail, Securities, Shanghai and China, State and Local Tax, Tax Exempt Organizations, Taxes, Technology, Telecommunications and Regulatory, Trusts and Estates.

FIRM PROFILE: Since its founding in the early 1900s in Seattle, Washington, Davis Wright Tremaine has continued to grow and change in response to the needs of its clients. Today the firm is organized by practice industry groups, and offers a wide range of legal services to regional, national and international clients through offices in Washington, Oregon, Alaska, California, Washington D.C., New York and Shanghai, China. A state-of-the-art communications network provides our clients the benefit of immediate access to shared knowledge, experience and resources of attorneys firm-wide. Dedicated to a tradition of public and professional service, the people of Davis Wright Tremaine are active in professional groups at the national, state and local levels.

LAW FIRM ALLIANCES/ASSOCIATIONS: ***LEX MUNDI***
PACIFIC RIM ADVISORY COUNCIL

PARTNERS

JAMES F. AMBROSE, admitted to bar, 1979, Oregon; 1980, California. *Education:* University of Notre Dame (B.B.A., cum laude, 1975); Loyola University of Los Angeles (J.D., cum laude, 1978). ***PRACTICE AREAS:*** Taxation and Business; Executive Compensation; Qualified Benefit Plans; Estate Planning. ***Email:*** jimambrose@dwt.com

DAVID C. BACA, admitted to bar, 1982, Oregon. *Education:* Linfield College (B.A., summa cum laude, 1978); Harvard University (J.D., magna cum laude, 1981). ***PRACTICE AREAS:*** Corporate Finance; Securities; Corporate Law. ***Email:*** davebaca@dwt.com

ANNE L. BARRAGAR, admitted to bar, 1987, Oregon. *Education:* Pomona College (B.A., 1982); University of Washington (J.D., 1987). ***PRACTICE AREAS:*** Business Transactions; Finance; Municipal Law. ***Email:*** annebarragar@dwt.com

MERRILL J. BAUMANN, JR., admitted to bar, 1986, California; 1999, Oregon. *Education:* Dartmouth College (A.B., with distinction, 1981); University of Southern California (J.D., 1985). Hale Moot Court Honors Program, 1984-1985. ***PRACTICE AREAS:*** Business; Corporate; Technology Law. ***Email:*** merrillbaumann@dwt.com

CAROL J. BERNICK, admitted to bar, 1989, Oregon; 1990, Washington. *Education:* Roanoke College (B.A., magna cum laude, 1985); University of Virginia (J.D., 1989). Pi Gamma Mu; Phi Alpha Theta. ***PRACTICE AREAS:*** Labor and Employment Law; Discrimination Defense; Wage and Hour. ***Email:*** carolbernick@dwt.com

DUANE A. BOSWORTH, II, admitted to bar, 1982, Oregon. *Education:* Yale University (B.A., 1975); University of Oregon (J.D., 1982). Editor-in-Chief, Oregon Law Review, 1981-1982. Law Clerk to Hon. T. Emmet Clarie, U.S. District Court Judge, District of Connecticut, 1982-1983. ***PRACTICE AREAS:*** Communications; Media Law; Litigation; Advertising Law; Entertainment Law. ***Email:*** duanebosworth@dwt.com

LAWRENCE B. BURKE, admitted to bar, 1989, Oregon; 1990, California. *Education:* University of Notre Dame (B.S., cum laude, 1978); Loyola Law School (J.D., cum laude, 1989). Order of the Coif. California Registered Environmental Assessor. ***PRACTICE AREAS:*** Environmental Litigation; Environmental Law; Environmental Insurance Litigation; Engineering Malpractice; Civil Litigation. ***Email:*** larryburke@dwt.com

JOHN A. CAMERON, JR., admitted to bar, 1973, Connecticut; 1975, District of Columbia; 1980, U.S. Supreme Court; 1992, Oregon. *Education:* University of Michigan (B.A., 1970); George Washington University (J.D., with distinction, 1973). ***PRACTICE AREAS:*** Energy Contract and Finance Law; Administrative Litigation; Appellate Practice; Natural Resources Law; Utility Rate Law. ***Email:*** johncameron@dwt.com

E. MICHAEL CONNORS, admitted to bar, 1995, Oregon. *Education:* University of California at San Diego (B.A., 1991); University of Oregon (J.D., 1995). ***PRACTICE AREAS:*** Land Use; Real Estate Development. ***Email:*** michaelconnors@dwt.com

GUSTAVO J. CRUZ, JR., admitted to bar, 1993, Oregon. *Education:* University of Santa Clara; University of Oregon (B.S., cum laude, 1983); Northwestern School of Law of Lewis and Clark College (J.D., 1993). ***PRACTICE AREAS:*** Corporate Finance; Secured Transactions. ***Email:*** gustavocruz@dwt.com

ERIC L. DAHLIN, admitted to bar, 1996, Oregon. *Education:* Grinnell College (B.A., Economics, 1989); University of Oregon School of Law (J.D., 1996). ***PRACTICE AREAS:*** Media Law; Government Litigation; Commercial Litigation. ***Email:*** ericdahlin@dwt.com

KATHLEEN DENT, admitted to bar, 1996, Oregon. *Education:* Willamette University (B.A., 1992); University of Nebraska (M.A., 1996; J.D., 1996). ***PRACTICE AREAS:*** Labor and Employment; Litigation; Civil Rights. ***Email:*** kathydent@dwt.com

JOHN DiLORENZO, admitted to bar, 1980, Oregon, U.S. District Court, District of Oregon and U.S. Court of Appeals, Ninth Circuit; 1984, U.S. Supreme Court; 1997, District of Columbia. *Education:* Willamette University (B.S., cum laude, 1977; J.D., 1980). ***Email:*** johndilorenzo@dwt.com

TIMOTHY DOZOIS, admitted to bar, 1989, Oregon. *Education:* Oregon State University (B.S., 1985); University of Oregon (J.D., 1989). Order of the Coif. ***PRACTICE AREAS:*** Securities; Mergers and Acquisitions; Healthcare. ***Email:*** timdozois@dwt.com

RICHARD M. GLICK, admitted to bar, 1976, California; 1979, Oregon. *Education:* University of California at Berkeley (B.A., with distinction, 1973); University of Southern California (J.D., 1976). ***PRACTICE AREAS:*** Environmental Law; Water Law; Energy Law. ***Email:*** rickglick@dwt.com

EUGENE GRANT, admitted to bar, 1979, Oregon. *Education:* University of Oregon (B.A., with honors, 1976; J.D., 1979). ***PRACTICE AREAS:*** Real Estate; Land Use. ***Email:*** genegrant@dwt.com

PATRICK J. GREEN, admitted to bar, 1974, Oregon; 1975, U.S. Tax Court. *Education:* University of Oregon (B.S., 1970; J.D., 1973); University of Miami (LL.M., in Taxation, 1974). Fellow: American College of Tax Counsel; American College of Trust and Estates Counsel. ***PRACTICE AREAS:*** Taxation; Business; Estate Planning Law. ***Email:*** patgreen@dwt.com

(This Listing Continued)

DAVIS WRIGHT TREMAINE LLP, Portland—Continued

MARK J. HACKETT, admitted to bar, 1992, Oregon. *Education:* Georgetown University; University of California, Davis (A.B., 1989); Cornell Law School (J.D., 1992). ***PRACTICE AREAS:*** Employment Law. ***Email:*** markhackett@dwt.com

STUART C. HARRIS, admitted to bar, 1986, Washington; 1992, Oregon. *Education:* Brigham Young University (B.A., 1983); Cornell University (J.D., cum laude, 1986). ***PRACTICE AREAS:*** Employee Benefits; Taxation; Business. ***Email:*** stuartharris@dwt.com

GREGORY S. HATHAWAY, admitted to bar, 1973, Oregon and U.S. District Court, District of Oregon. *Education:* Willamette University (B.A., Economics, 1970); Northwestern School of Law of Lewis and Clark College (J.D., 1973). ***PRACTICE AREAS:*** Land Use; Real Estate Development Law. ***Email:*** gregoryhathaway@dwt.com

THOMAS S. HILLIER, admitted to bar, 1980, Oregon. *Education:* University of Oregon (B.S., 1977; J.D., 1980). Law Clerk to Hon. James R. Hargreaves, Lane County Circuit Court, Lane County, Oregon, 1980-1981. ***PRACTICE AREAS:*** Transactional Real Estate; Real Estate Exchanges; Commercial Leasing; Construction Liens; Real Estate Finance. ***Email:*** tomhillier@dwt.com

JAY D. HULL, admitted to bar, 1984, Oregon. *Education:* Reed College (B.A., 1978); University of Chicago Divinity School (M.A., 1979); Lewis and Clark Law School (J.D., 1984). ***PRACTICE AREAS:*** Communications Company Corporate Matters; Communications Company Transactional Matters; Mergers and Acquisitions; Joint Ventures; Corporate Finance. ***Email:*** jayhull@dwt.com

EVERETT W. JACK, JR., admitted to bar, 1989, Oregon; 2000, Texas. *Education:* University of Portland (B.B.A., cum laude, 1986); South Texas College of Law (J.D., 1989). Order of the Lytae. ***PRACTICE AREAS:*** Litigation-Plaintiff and Defense. ***Email:*** everettjack@dwt.com

CHRISTOPHER P. KOBACK, admitted to bar, 1988, Wisconsin and Illinois; 1991, Oregon. *Education:* University of Wisconsin-Stevens Point (B.A., with honors, 1985); University of Wisconsin-Madison (J.D., cum laude, 1988). ***PRACTICE AREAS:*** Land Use; Land Use Regulation; Real Estate Litigation; Commercial Litigation. ***Email:*** chriskoback@dwt.com

WENDELL G. KUSNERUS, admitted to bar, 1979, Oregon; 1985, Washington. *Education:* Michigan State University (B.S., Mathematics, 1974; M.S., Mathematics, 1976); University of Oregon (J.D., 1979). ***PRACTICE AREAS:*** Creditors Rights; Bankruptcy; Financial Transactions; Negotiable Instruments; Litigation; Commercial Transactions. ***Email:*** wendellkusnerus@dwt.com

PETER S. LEICHTFUSS, admitted to bar, 1995, Oregon. *Education:* University of Wisconsin (B.A., 1990); University of Oregon (J.D., 1995). ***PRACTICE AREAS:*** Litigation; Real Estate; Construction Law; Fair Housing. ***Email:*** peterleichtfuss@dwt.com

RODNEY E. LEWIS, JR., admitted to bar, 1974, Oregon. *Education:* Stanford University (B.A., 1971); University of Oregon (J.D., 1974). Order of the Coif. ***PRACTICE AREAS:*** Contracts Litigation; Creditors Rights Litigation; Banking Litigation; Real Estate Litigation; Defamation Litigation; Trust and Probate Litigation. ***Email:*** rodlewis@dwt.com

JESSE D. LYON, admitted to bar, 1998, Oregon. *Education:* Washington State University (B.S., cum laude, 1992); Purdue University (M.S., 1995); George Mason University School of Law (J.D., with high honors, 1998). ***PRACTICE AREAS:*** Business Transactions; Food and Agriculture; Hospitality; Wine Law; Real Estate. ***Email:*** lyonj@dwt.com

GEORGE M. MARDIKES, admitted to bar, 1984, Missouri; 1989, Oregon. *Education:* University of Chicago (A.B., 1979); University of Missouri-Kansas City (J.D., 1984). *Member:* National Association of Bond Lawyers. ***PRACTICE AREAS:*** Public Finance. ***Email:*** georgemardikes@dwt.com

D. CHARLES MAURITZ, admitted to bar, 1969, Texas; 1970, Oregon. *Education:* Colorado College (B.A., 1966); University of Texas (J.D., 1969). Fellow, American College of Trust and Estate Counsel. ***PRACTICE AREAS:*** Estate Planning; Business Succession Planning; Business Organizations and Reorganizations; Mergers and Acquisitions. ***Email:*** chuckmauritz@dwt.com

MICHAEL McARTHUR-PHILLIPS, admitted to bar, 1982, Oregon. *Education:* University of Michigan (B.A., in Economics, 1978; B.A., in Political Science, 1978); Northwestern School of Law of Lewis and Clark College (J.D., 1982). ***PRACTICE AREAS:*** Securities; Mergers and Acquisitions; Business Law; Corporate Law. ***Email:*** mcp@dwt.com

CHRISTOPHER F. McCRACKEN, admitted to bar, 1989, Oregon. *Education:* Kenyon College (B.A., cum laude, 1986); University of Oregon (J.D., 1989). Order of the Coif. ***Email:*** chrismccracken@dwt.com

PATRICIA McGUIRE, admitted to bar, 1996, Oregon. *Education:* Oregon State University (B.A., 1983); Northwestern School of Law, Lewis and Clark College (J.D., 1995). ***PRACTICE AREAS:*** Commercial Litigation; Antitrust; Construction. ***Email:*** patriciamcguire@dwt.com

JOHN F. McGRORY, JR., admitted to bar, 1981, Oregon. *Education:* Carleton College and University of Minnesota (B.A., 1978); Lewis and Clark Law School (J.D., 1981). ***PRACTICE AREAS:*** Antitrust; Securities; Commercial Litigation. ***Email:*** johnmcgrory@dwt.com

JAMES M. MEI, admitted to bar, 1989, Oregon; 1990, Washington. *Education:* Shanghai University (B.A., 1983); Willamette University (J.D., 1988). ***LANGUAGES:*** Chinese. ***PRACTICE AREAS:*** International Law; Corporate Law; Business Immigration. ***Email:*** jimmei@dwt.com

WILLIAM R. MILLER, JR., admitted to bar, 1975, Oregon. *Education:* Pomona College (B.A., 1969); Claremont Graduate School (M.A., 1972); Northwestern School of Law of Lewis and Clark College (J.D., cum laude, 1975). ***PRACTICE AREAS:*** Banking; Commercial Finance; Real Estate. ***Email:*** billmiller@dwt.com

(This Listing Continued)

JAMES K. NEILL, admitted to bar, 1971, Oregon. *Education:* Oregon State University (B.S., 1967); Willamette University (J.D., 1971). ***PRACTICE AREAS:*** Administrative Law; Government Relations; Hospitality Law; Gaming Law; Corporate Law; Real Estate Law; Alcoholic Beverage Control; Intellectual Property Licensing; Regulatory Law; Licensing and Regulation. ***Email:*** jimneill@dwt.com

ROBERT D. NEWELL, admitted to bar, 1977, California; 1979, Oregon. *Education:* Harvard College (A.B., 1969); University of Oregon (J.D., 1976). ***PRACTICE AREAS:*** Commercial Litigation; Trade Secrets Litigation; Securities Litigation; Insurance Litigation. ***Email:*** bobnewell@dwt.com

DENNIS M. PATERSON, III, admitted to bar, 1982, Oregon. *Education:* Sacramento State University (B.A., 1971); Lewis and Clark College (J.D., 1982). ***PRACTICE AREAS:*** Creditor's Rights; Real Property Litigation; Financial Institution Regulation; General Business Litigation. ***Email:*** dennispaterson@dwt.com

PHILLIP C. QUERIN, admitted to bar, 1972, Oregon. *Education:* University of Oregon (B.S., 1968; J.D., 1971). Phi Beta Kappa; Phi Alpha Delta. ***PRACTICE AREAS:*** Real Estate Litigation; Broker Liability; Lessor-Lessee; Manufactural Housing; Real Estate Transactions. ***Email:*** philquerin@dwt.com

CONI S. RATHBONE, admitted to bar, 1988, Oregon. *Education:* Boise State University; University of Idaho (B.S. in General Business cum laude, 1978); Willamette University (J.D., 1988). ***PRACTICE AREAS:*** Real Estate Development; Mergers and Acquisitions; Securities; International; Corporate. ***Email:*** conirathbone@dwt.com

CARMEN J. SANTAMARIA, admitted to bar, 1976, Pennsylvania; 1982, Oregon. *Education:* University of Pittsburgh (B.S., 1972); Gonzaga University (J.D., 1976). ***PRACTICE AREAS:*** Business Organizations; Business Transactions; Tax Planning and Litigation; Estate Planning. ***Email:*** carmensantamaria@dwt.com

ERIK S. SCHIMMELBUSCH, admitted to bar, 1995, California; 1997, Oregon. *Education:* Brigham Young University (B.A., 1992); McGeorge School of Law, University of the Pacific (J.D., 1995; LL.M., 1997). ***PRACTICE AREAS:*** Taxation; Estate Planning; Business Planning. ***Email:*** erikschimmelbusch@dwt.com

MICHAEL H. SCHMEER, admitted to bar, 1959, Oregon. *Education:* Stanford University (B.A., 1957; LL.B., 1959). Phi Alpha Delta. Member, Board of Editors, Stanford Law Review, 1957-1958. ***PRACTICE AREAS:*** Secured and Unsecured Credit Transactions; Syndicated Credit Transactions; Purchases and Sales of Businesses. ***Email:*** mikeschmeer@dwt.com

PETER A. SERGIENKO, admitted to bar, 1988, Oregon. *Education:* Harvard University (A.B., cum laude, 1982); University of Oregon (J.D., 1988). ***PRACTICE AREAS:*** Environmental Law; Natural Resources Law; Water Law; Real Estate Law; Real Estate Development. ***Email:*** petersergienko@dwt.com

JAMES STUART SMITH, admitted to bar, 1984, Oregon and Washington. *Education:* Portland State University (B.A., summa cum laude, 1979); University of Southern California (J.D., 1983). Phi Alpha Delta. ***PRACTICE AREAS:*** Civil Litigation; Land Use; Energy Litigation. ***Email:*** jimsmith@dwt.com

MILTON R. STEWART, admitted to bar, 1971, Oregon. *Education:* Indiana University (A.B., 1968; J.D., summa cum laude, 1971). Phi Alpha Delta; Order of the Coif. ***PRACTICE AREAS:*** Corporations and Business Law; Mergers and Acquisitions; Secured Transactions and Finance. ***Email:*** miltstewart@dwt.com

KENT B. THURBER, admitted to bar, 1975, Oregon. *Education:* Stanford University (B.A., 1971); Willamette University (J.D., 1975). ***PRACTICE AREAS:*** Health Care Reimbursement; Health Care Licensure; Fraud and Abuse; Regulatory Matters; Commercial Litigation. ***Email:*** berniethurber@dwt.com

MARK P. TRINCHERO, admitted to bar, 1988, Oregon. *Education:* University of California at Berkeley (B.A., summa cum laude); Hastings College of Law (J.D. cum laude, 1988). ***PRACTICE AREAS:*** Telecommunications; Energy; Regulated Industries. ***Email:*** marktrinchero@dwt.com

JOSEPH VANCE, admitted to bar, 1995, Washington; 1999, Oregon. *Education:* Brigham Young University (B.S., 1992); University of Washington (J.D., 1995). ***PRACTICE AREAS:*** Employment Law; Litigation. ***Email:*** joevance@dwt.com

JOSEPH M. VANLEUVEN, admitted to bar, 1982, Oregon. *Education:* Reed College (B.A., 1978); University of Michigan (J.D., cum laude, 1982). ***PRACTICE AREAS:*** Bankruptcy; Creditors Rights. ***Email:*** joevanleuven@dwt.com

TIMOTHY R. VOLPERT, admitted to bar, 1981, Oregon. *Education:* Earlham College (B.A., 1978); Willamette University College of Law (J.D., 1981). Law Clerk to Hon. W. Michael Gillette, Judge of the Oregon Court of Appeals, 1981-1982. ***PRACTICE AREAS:*** Appeals; Telecommunications Law; Education Law. ***Email:*** timvolpert@dwt.com

JAMES C. WAGGONER, admitted to bar, 1974, Oregon. *Education:* Reed College (B.A., 1968); London School of Economics; University of Oregon (J.D., 1974). Phi Beta Kappa; Order of the Coif. Fulbright Scholar. Clerk to Chief Justice O'Connell, Supreme Court of Oregon, 1974-1975. ***PRACTICE AREAS:*** Financial Institutions; Bankruptcy; Real Estate; Commercial and Consumer Credit. ***Email:*** jimwaggoner@dwt.com

JAMES D. ZUPANCIC, admitted to bar, 1979, California; 1986, Oregon. *Education:* Brigham Young University (B.S., 1975); McGeorge School of Law, University of the Pacific (J.D., 1979). ***PRACTICE AREAS:*** Corporate; Finance; Securities; International/Pacific Rim; High Technology; Intellectual Property; Real Estate; Land Use. ***Email:*** jimzupancic@dwt.com

RESIDENT ASSOCIATES

Elleanor H. Chin (Not admitted in OR)
Jessica Crone
Anne E. Denecke
Jeff N. Evans
Kristen M. Gurdin
Thomas M. Jones
Nanci Klinger
Elizabeth Knight
Kevin Kono
Jeni L. Lassell

(This Listing Continued)

RESIDENT ASSOCIATES (Continued)

Devon T. Lyon (Not admitted in OR)
Sean B. Malcolm (Not admitted in OR)
Joe Mattoon
P. Andrew McStay, Jr.
William D. Miner
Rita Molina
Jenna Leigh Mooney
Sheila Fox Morrison (Not admitted in OR)
Carol Noonan
David C. Rocker
Aaron K. Stuckey
Trinh Tran
Scott E. Warnick (Not admitted in OR)

COUNSEL

INGRID BRYDOLF, admitted to bar, 1993, Oregon. *Education:* Willamette University (B.A., 1985); Northwestern School of Law (J.D., cum laude, 1993). Author, "Takings," 22 Environmental Law 1115 (1992). ***PRACTICE AREAS:*** Health Care.

GREGORY A. CHAIMOV, admitted to bar, 1982, Oregon. *Education:* Carleton College (B.A., magna cum laude, 1978); Northwestern School of Law of Lewis and Clark College (J.D., cum laude, 1982).

JACOB A. HETH, admitted to bar, 1994, California; 1997, Oregon. *Education:* University of California, Davis (B.A., 1991); Willamette University College of Law (J.D., 1994); McGeorge School of Law, University of the Pacific (LL.M. in Taxation, 1997).

DAVID J. KRIEGER, admitted to bar, 1958, Oregon. *Education:* University of Oregon (B.A., 1953; J.D., 1958). Member, Editorial Staff, Oregon Law Review, 1957-1958. *Member:* Multnomah County and American Bar Associations. ***PRACTICE AREAS:*** Real Estate. ***Email:*** davekrieger@dwt.com

MILTON C. LANKTON, admitted to bar, 1957, Oregon. *Education:* Wabash College (A.B., 1950); Yale University (J.D., 1957). ***PRACTICE AREAS:*** Real Estate; Construction; Corporate; Business; Business Litigation; Construction Litigation; Arbitration; Mediation. ***Email:*** miltlankton@dwt.com

DANIEL E. O'LEARY, admitted to bar, 1963, Oregon. *Education:* Gonzaga University (B.A., 1959); Northwestern School of Law of Lewis and Clark College (LL.B., 1963; LL.M., Environmental, 1993). Fellow, American College of Trial Lawyers. ***PRACTICE AREAS:*** Natural Resources Litigation; Civil Litigation; Mediation and Arbitration. ***Email:*** danoleary@dwt.com

DEAN M. PHILLIPS, admitted to bar, 1975, Oregon. *Education:* Portland State University (B.S., 1972); Lewis and Clark College (J.D., 1975). ***PRACTICE AREAS:*** Construction Law; Government Contracts; Real Estate; Real Estate Development. ***Email:*** deanphillips@dwt.com

RONALD K. RAGEN, admitted to bar, 1961, Oregon. *Education:* Yale University (B.A., 1957); Stanford University (J.D., 1961). *Member:* National Association of Bond Lawyers. ***PRACTICE AREAS:*** Corporate; International Business Transactions; Municipal Bond; Finance Law; Securities. ***Email:*** ronaldragen@dwt.com

THOMAS S. SMITH, admitted to bar, 1978, California; 1982, Nevada; 1999, Oregon. *Education:* University of California, Berkeley (B.A., 1974); Hastings College of the Law, University of California (J.D., 1977). President, Graduating Class, Hastings. Author, "Taking the Stress Out of Distressed Property," Real Estate Issue, Winter 2000-2001. Member, Quality of Life Committee, Oregon State Bar. *Member:* Multnomah County and American Bar Associations; State Bar of California; State Bar of Nevada; International Council of Shopping Centers. [US Army, 1966-1970; Viet Nam Veteran]. ***PRACTICE AREAS:*** Business Law; Real Estate.

H. STEWART TREMAINE, admitted to bar, 1947, Washington and Oregon. *Education:* University of Washington (B.A., 1940); Yale University (LL.B., 1946). Phi Delta Phi. (Retired). ***PRACTICE AREAS:*** Corporation; Business; Estate Planning; Securities Law. ***Email:*** stewarttremaine@dwt.com

All Portland Attorneys are Members of the Oregon State Bar.

REPRESENTATIVE CLIENTS: adidas America, Inc.; AT&T Wireless; Bank of America; Belo Corporation; Cmedia; Evergreen International Aviation, Inc.; Freightliner LLC; Intel Corporation; Legacy Health System; McCormick & Schmick Holding Corp.; Microsoft; Oregon Health & Science University; Rite Aid Corporation; Shell Oil Co.; Starbucks Coffee Company; The Reserve Vineyards and Golf Club; TriMet; U.S. Bancorp; XO Communications.

(For complete biographical data on personnel at Anchorage, Alaska, Los Angeles and San Francisco, California, Washington, D.C., Bellevue and Seattle, Washington, New York, N.Y. and Shanghai, China, see Professional Biographies at those locations)

DEBAST, MCFARLAND & RICHARDSON, LLP

9600 BUILDING
9600 SOUTHWEST BARNES ROAD, SUITE 325
PORTLAND, OREGON 97225
Telephone: 503-297-9600
Fax: 503-297-9500
URL: http://www.dmr-law.com

Family Law, Divorce, Premarital Agreements, Child Support, Property Settlements, Spousal Support, Child Custody, Domestic Violence, Visitation Rights, Estate Planning, Wills, Trusts, Probate, Civil Litigation, Criminal Law, Personal Injury, Driving While Intoxicated, Drug Crimes, Guardianships and Conservatorship.

PARTNERS OF FIRM

PAUL J. DEBAST, born Vancouver, Washington, December 31, 1946; admitted to bar, 1972, Oregon and U.S. District Court, District of Oregon. *Education:* University of Washington (B.A., 1969); Willamette University (J.D., 1972). *Member:* Washington County Bar Association (President, 1981); American Bar Association; Oregon State Bar (Director, Family Law Section, 1981-1983 and 1989-1991); American Academy of Matrimonial Lawyers; Oregon Academy of Family Law Practitioners. (Managing Partner). ***PRACTICE AREAS:*** Family Law; Divorce. ***Email:*** debast@dmr-law.com

(This Listing Continued)

BARBARA P. MCFARLAND, born Kansas City, Missouri, February 20, 1934; admitted to bar, 1974, Oregon and U.S. District Court, District of Oregon. *Education:* Sweet Briar College; Portland State University (B.S., 1971); Northwestern School of Law at Lewis and Clark College (J.D., 1974). *Member:* Multnomah County and Washington County (Member, Board of Directors, 1991-1994) Bar Associations; Oregon State Bar (Member: Sections on: Family and Juvenile Law, 1975—); Oregon Academy of Family Law Practitioners (Board Chairman, 2003—). ***PRACTICE AREAS:*** Family Law; Divorce. ***Email:*** mcfarland@dmr-law.com

JAMES B. RICHARDSON, born Portland, Oregon, March 4, 1947; admitted to bar, 1977, Oregon, U.S. District Court, District of Oregon and U.S. Court of Appeals, Ninth Circuit. *Education:* University of California at Los Angeles; Portland State University (B.S., 1969; M.A., 1972); University of Wisconsin-Madison; Lewis and Clark College, Northwestern School of Law (J.D., 1977). Instructor, Juvenile Law, Portland State University, 1983-1985. Judge Pro Tem, Washington County Justice Court. Arbitrator, Multnomah County and Washington County Circuit and District Courts. *Member:* Multnomah County and Washington County (Officer, 1982, Member, Board of Directors, 1988, 1989, 1990) Bar Associations; Oregon State Bar (Member, Local Professional Responsibility Committee, 1986-1989; Elected Member, House of Delegates, 1996-1998); Oregon Criminal Defense Lawyers Association. ***LANGUAGES:*** German. ***PRACTICE AREAS:*** Family Law; Divorce; Estate Planning; Probate; Wills; Trust Law; Personal Injury; Criminal; Civil Litigation; Domestic Torts. ***Email:*** richardson@dmr-law.com

DELO & BOWERS, LLP

2400 SW FOURTH AVENUE, SUITE 210
PORTLAND, OREGON 97201
Telephone: 503-228-3299
Fax: 503-228-1890
URL: http://www.delo-bowers.com

General Business, E-commerce, Computer and Internet Law, Intellectual Property and Business, Tax and International Commercial Litigation.

FIRM PROFILE: Delo & Bowers, LLP, provides general business and high technology companies with personal attention and high quality representation in the areas of general business, computer and Internet law, and business, tax and international litigation.

MEMBERS OF FIRM

LEW E. DELO, born Bremerton, Washington, April 29, 1944; admitted to bar, 1974, Oregon; 1982, U.S. District Court, District of Oregon; 1989, U.S. Tax Court. *Education:* Washington State University (B.A., 1966); University of Washington (B.A., 1971); Northwestern School of Law of Lewis and Clark College (J.D., 1974). Author: "The English Doctrine of Custom in Oregon Property Law, Thornton v. Hay," 1974. Member, Tax Department, Peat Marwick Mitchell & Co., 1974-1975. *Member:* Multnomah County Bar Association; Oregon State Bar (Member, Sections on: International Law; Business Law, Tax Law). [Capt., U.S. Army, 1966-1969]. ***LANGUAGES:*** Conversational German. ***SPECIAL AGENCIES:*** Internal Revenue Service. ***PRACTICE AREAS:*** Business Law; Business Litigation; Federal Tax Controversies; Tax Litigation; International Litigation. ***Email:*** lew@delo-bowers.com

CHARLES R. BOWERS, born Chicago, Illinois, August 30, 1956; admitted to bar, 1985, Oregon, U.S. District Court, District of Oregon and U.S. Court of Appeals, Ninth Circuit; 1986, U.S. Court of Appeals, Seventh Circuit. *Education:* University of Oregon (B.S., 1978; J.D., 1985). Associate Editor, Oregon Law Review, 1984-1985. Author: "Semiconductor Chip Design Protection — A New Intellectual Property Right," 65 Oregon Law Review 789, 1986. *Member:* Multnomah County Bar Association; Oregon State Bar (Member, Sections on: Business Law; Intellectual Property Law Real Estate; International Law; Member and Former Chair, Computer and Internet Law Section). ***PRACTICE AREAS:*** Business Law; Corporate Law; Computer and Software; Internet Law; Intellectual Property; Technology and Science; Trademarks. ***Email:*** charles@delo-bowers.com

DONNA S. DELO, born Norman, Oklahoma, January 13, 1944; admitted to bar, 1980, Oregon; 1982, U.S. District Court, District of Oregon. *Education:* University of Washington (B.S., magna cum laude, 1966); Northwestern School of Law of Lewis and Clark College (J.D., cum laude, 1980). Phi Beta Kappa. Oral Historian for U.S. District Court of Oregon Historical Society, 1988-1989. *Member:* Multnomah County and American Bar Associations; Oregon State Bar. ***PRACTICE AREAS:*** Business Formation; Closely Held Business Law; Limited Liability Company Law; Corporate Contracts. ***Email:*** donna@delo-bowers.com

REPRESENTATIVE CLIENTS: Pre1.com; CSK Auto, Inc.; Time Domain Analysis, Inc.; Hollywood Entertainment, Inc.; Portland Music Co.; Shiels Obletz Johnsen, Inc.; Fireman's Fund Insurance Co.; American Insurance Company; H&R Block (Regional Franchise); Internet Technologies, Inc.; Bek-Tel, Inc.; allMRO Products, Inc.; Wise Software Solutions, Inc.; Wespak, Inc.; CT3, Inc.; Anderson-McConaughey Design; Leisure Sales, Inc.; Oregon Soccer Center, Inc.; Machinery Sales Corporation, Inc.; Fulfillment Corporation of America; Multnomah Athletic Club; Seder Architects; West Coast Bancorp; Waking Dream Productions; Elk Horn Ridge Estates, LLC.; Arthur Anderson (Germany); Industrial Alloy Fabricators, Inc.; Pacific Metering, Inc.; Fireside Distributors of Oregon, Inc.; NW Vein Specialists, P.C.; Online Meal Pros, LLC; Webcoach Internet Services, Inc.; Advanced Lending, Inc.; Wilderness Cabins of America; KPMG (Germany).
REFERENCES: Wells Fargo Bank; United States National Bank of Oregon.

HELEN C. DILLON

Established in 1980
210 S.W. MORRISON, SUITE 600
PORTLAND, OREGON 97204-3150
Telephone: 503-223-7884
FAX: 503-273-8591
Email: helen@helendillon.com
URL: http://www.lawyers.com/hdillon

Family, Domestic Relations, Divorce, Child Custody, Parenting Time, Visitation Rights, Child Support Modifications, Spousal Support, Adoption, Premarital Agreements, Domestic Violence.

(This Listing Continued)

HELEN C. DILLON, Portland—Continued

HELEN C. DILLON, born Iowa City, Iowa, August 28, 1944; admitted to bar, 1980, Oregon; 1981, U.S. District Court, District of Oregon. *Education:* George Washington University; Lewis and Clark College (B.A., 1965); Northwestern School of Law of Lewis and Clark College (J.D., 1980). Editor: Chapter, "Marriage; Annulment; Separation," Oregon Family Law Continuing Legal Education, Supplements, 1983, 1986, 1997 and 2001. Speaker: Ethics in Family Law, Oregon Law Institute, July 29, 1988; Spousal Support, National Business Institute, Inc., July 30, 1992. *Member:* Multnomah County and American (Member, Family Law Section) Bar Associations; Oregon State Bar (Member, Section of Family Law).

THE DOBSON LAW FIRM LLC

1000 S.W. BROADWAY, SUITE 2400
PORTLAND, OREGON 97205
Telephone: 503-295-6888
Fax: 503-241-2249
Email: ken@oregonenvironmentallaw.com
URL: http://www.oregonenvironmentallaw.com

Environmental Law, Complex Litigation, Solid and Hazardous Waste, Indian Law, Water Law, Toxic Torts, Zoning, Planning and Land Use, Bankruptcy, Commercial, Business Law, Business Litigation, Construction Law, Construction Defects, Mechanics Liens, Debtor and Creditor, Creditors Rights, Real Estate, Commercial Real Estate, Landlord and Tenant Law, Residential Real Estate, Agricultural Law, Eminent Domain, Condemnation, Natural Resources Law, Endangered Species Law, Contaminated Site Litigation.

MEMBER OF FIRM

KENNETH P. DOBSON, born Tallahassee, Florida, September 6, 1969; admitted to bar, 2000, Oregon; U.S. District Court, District of Oregon; U.S. Court of Appeals, Ninth Circuit. *Education:* University of Wyoming (B.S., 1993); Vermont Law School (J.D., cum laude, 2000; M.S.E.L., cum laude, 2000). Member: Environmental Moot Court Advisory Board, 1998-1999; Civil Trial Team, 1999-2000. Senior Managing Editor, Vermont Law Review, 1999-2000. Publications: Co-Author: Chapter on Hazardous Waste Management, Environmental Law Deskbook (OSB ed. 2001). Author, *Courts Define When Landowners Must Be Compensated for Restrictions on Timber Harvesting on Private Lands,* Outlook (OSB ENR section ed. Summer 2004). Author, Note, *Methods and Motives for Imposing Strict Liability on Parties Hiring Independent Contractors to Transport Hazardous Materials in the State of Florida,* 24 VT. L. REV. 1297 (2000). *Member:* Multnomah County and American Bar Associations; Oregon State Bar (Member: Executive Committee, Environmental and Natural Resources Section; Indian Law Section); The Association of Trial Lawyers of America; Oregon Trial Lawyers Association. ***PRACTICE AREAS:*** Environmental Law; Complex Litigation; Solid Waste; Hazardous Waste; Indian Law; Water Law; Toxic Torts; Zoning, Planning and Land Use; Bankruptcy; Commercial Law; Business Law; Business Litigation; Construction Law; Construction Defects; Mechanics Liens; Debtor and Creditor; Creditors Rights; Real Estate; Commercial Real Estate; Landlord and Tenant Law; Residential Real Estate; Agricultural Law; Eminent Domain; Condemnation; Natural Resources; Endangered Species; Environmental Contamination; Toxic Mold. ***Email:*** ken@oregonenvironmentallaw.com

SEAN DONAHUE

Established in 1992
SUITE 1625, BENJ. FRANKLIN PLAZA
ONE S.W. COLUMBIA
PORTLAND, OREGON 97258-2098
Telephone: 503-226-1084
Fax: 503-227-6366
Email: sdonalaw@aol.com

General Business, Labor Law and Civil Litigation including Employment and Commercial Litigation, Employment Discrimination, Sexual Harassment, Wrongful Termination.

SEAN DONAHUE, born Bethesda, Maryland, April 26, 1954; admitted to bar, 1979, Oregon. *Education:* Columbia University (B.A., cum laude, 1976); University of Paris; University of Oregon (J.D., 1979). Author: "Semiotic Interpretation of Statutes," 8 UCLA Alaska Law Review 218, 1978; "Semiotic Interpretation-II," 9 UCLA Alaska Law Review 2, 1979. *Member:* Multnomah County and American Bar Associations; Oregon State Bar.

REPRESENTATIVE CLIENTS: Melvin Simon & Associates; Metropolitan Disposal & Recycling Corp.; Herbert Malarkey Roofing Co.; Ron Tonkin Chevrolet Co.; Lloyd Properties, Ltd.; Biotronik, Inc.; Micro Systems Engineering, Inc.

DRAKULICH & CARLSON, P.C.

Established in 1980
1500 SOUTHWEST 1ST AVENUE, SUITE 1170
PORTLAND, OREGON 97201
Telephone: 503-224-0871
Fax: 503-224-4215
URL: http://www.drakulichcarlson.com
Email: rich@teleport.com
URL: http://www.lawyers.com/drakulich&carlson

General Civil and Trial Practice. Family Law, Child Custody, Child Support, Divorce, Domestic Violence, Visitation Rights, Personal Injury, Automobile Accidents, Dog Bites, Sexual Abuse, Slip and Fall, Wrongful Death, Medical Malpractice, Insurance, Health Care, Construction Law, Contracts, Lawsuits, Real Estate Buying and Selling, Residential Real Estate, Commercial Real Estate, Criminal Law, Driving While Intoxicated, Drug Crimes, Parole and Probation.

(This Listing Continued)

NICK A. DRAKULICH, born Portland, Oregon, April 20, 1950; admitted to bar, 1975, Oregon. *Education:* Willamette University (B.A., 1972); Northwestern School of Law of Lewis and Clark College (J.D., 1975). *Member:* Multnomah County Bar Association; Oregon State Bar; Oregon Trial Lawyers Association; The Association of Trial Lawyers of America. ***PRACTICE AREAS:*** Personal Injury; Construction Law; Business Litigation; Family Law. ***Email:*** NAD@teleport.com

RICHARD A. CARLSON, born Chicago, Illinois, September 24, 1949; admitted to bar, 1975, Oregon and U.S. District Court, District of Oregon. *Education:* University of Illinois (B.A., 1972); Northwestern School of Law of Lewis and Clark College (J.D., 1975). Member and Book Review Editor, Lewis and Clark College Law Review, 1974-1975. School Law Instructor, Portland State University, 1995—. Deputy District Attorney, Multnomah County, 1975-1978. Member, Tigard-Tualatin School Board, 1989-2001. *Member:* Multnomah County Bar Association; Oregon State Bar; Oregon Trial Lawyers Association; Oregon Criminal Defense Lawyers Association; The Association of Trial Lawyers of America; National Association of Criminal Defense Lawyers. ***PRACTICE AREAS:*** Construction Law; Family Law; Business Litigation; Personal Injury; Criminal Law; School Law. ***Email:*** rich@teleport.com

THE DuBOFF LAW GROUP, LLC

Established in 1994
6665 S.W. HAMPTON STREET, SUITE 200
PORTLAND, OREGON 97223
Telephone: 503-968-8111
Fax: 503-968-7228
Email: info@dubofflaw.com
URL: http://www.dubofflaw.com

General Business, Art Law, Publishing Law, Copyright, Trademark and High Tech Law, Estate Planning, Civil Litigation, Intellectual Property, Licensing Agreements, Trade Secrets, Trademarks, Internet, E-Commerce, Business Planning, Contracts, Lawsuits, Entertainment, Starting A Business.

FIRM PROFILE: The firm specializes in general business law with an emphasis on the intellectual property disciplines of copyright, trademark, and trade dress, and in intellectual property and commercial litigation.

MEMBERS OF FIRM

LEONARD D. DuBOFF, born Brooklyn, New York, October 3, 1941; admitted to bar, 1972, New York; 1974, U.S. District Court, Southern and Eastern Districts of New York, U.S. Court of Appeals, Second Circuit and U.S. Court of International Trade; 1975, U.S. Supreme Court; 1977, Oregon; 1990, U.S. District Court, District of Oregon, U.S. Court of Appeals, Ninth Circuit; 1995, U.S. District Court, Northern and Central Districts of California, U.S. Tax Court and U.S. District Court, District of Hawaii. *Education:* Brooklyn Poly Tech (A.A.S., 1964); Hofstra University (B.E.S., magna cum laude, 1968); Brooklyn Law School (J.D., summa cum laude, 1971). Sigma Pi Sigma. Author: *The Deskbook of Art Law*, Oceana Publications, 1993, revised 2000; *Art Law In A Nutshell*, West Publishing Co., 2000; *Art Law: In A Nutshell*, trans. into Mandarin by Zhou Lin, West Publishing Co., 1995; *The Book Publisher's Legal Guide*, 2d ed., Fred B. Rothman & Co., 1991; *The Law (In Plain English) For Small Businesses*, Allworth Press, 1998; *The Law (In Plain English) For Health Care Professionals*, John Wiley & Sons, Inc., 1993; *The Performing Arts Encyclopedia*, Allworth Press, 1996; *The Art Business Encyclopedia*, Allworth Press, 1994; *The Law (In Plain English) for Photographers*, Allworth Press, 2001; *The Law (In Plain English) For Writers*, John Wiley & Sons, Inc., 1992; *The Law (In Plain English) for Galleries*, Allworth Press, 1999; *The Law (In Plain English) For Crafts*, Allworth Press, 1999; *High-Tech Law (In Plain English)*, Copyright Information Services/Association for Educational Communication and Technology, 1991. Teaching Fellow, Stanford Law School, 1971-1972. Professor of Law, Lewis and Clark Law School, 1972-1994. Chairman of the Board, Oregon Commission for the Blind, 1979-1987, 1990-1994. *Member:* Multnomah County, New York State and American Bar Associations; Oregon State Bar; National Native American Bar Association. ***PRACTICE AREAS:*** Business; Art Law; Intellectual Property; Copyright; Trademark; Trade Dress; Trade Secrets; Corporate; Commercial Litigation; High Technology. ***Email:*** lduboff@dubofflaw.com

CHRISTY O. KING, born Dallas, Texas, June 18, 1969; admitted to bar, 1993, Oregon; 2000, U.S. District Court, District of Oregon. *Education:* Louisiana State University (B.A.J., 1989); Lewis and Clark College (J.D., cum laude, 1993). Co-Editor in chief, Critical Issues Newsletters; Co-author: "Art Law in a Nutshell," West Publishing Co., 2000; "Deskbook of Art Law," Oceana, revised 2000; "First Amendment and Censorship," Oceana, 2005. *Member:* Oregon State Bar. ***PRACTICE AREAS:*** Business; Corporate; Intellectual Property; Copyright; Trademark; Trade Dress; Trade Secrets; Commercial Leases. ***Email:*** cking@dubofflaw.com

ASSOCIATES

ABIGAIL R. MICHELS, born Washington, October 17, 1975; admitted to bar, 2001, Oregon; 2005, Washington. *Education:* University of Washington (B.A., 1997); Willamette University, College of Law (J.D., 2001). Member, Willamette Law Review. Author: Article published in Entertainment Law Review and Oregon Law Journal. *Member:* Oregon State Bar; Washington State Bar Association. ***PRACTICE AREAS:*** Civil Litigation; Complex Litigation; Commercial Litigation; Trademarks; Trademark Infringement; Intellectual Property Litigation. ***Email:*** amichels@dubofflaw.com

CHRISTOPHER W. BROWN, born Covina, California, November 21, 1974; admitted to bar, 2002, Oregon. *Education:* Oregon State University (B.S., 1997); Lewis and Clark Law School (J.D., 2002). Phi Delta Phi. *Member:* Oregon State Bar (Member, Intellectual Property Section). ***PRACTICE AREAS:*** Litigation; Intellectual Property; Business Law. ***Email:*** cbrown@dubofflaw.com

MARISA N. JAMES, born Portland, Oregon, August 10, 1977; admitted to bar, 2002, Oregon. *Education:* Carleton College (B.A., 1999); Lewis and Clark College (J.D., 2002). *Member:* Oregon State Bar. ***PRACTICE AREAS:*** Intellectual Property.

DUFFY KEKEL LLP

Established in 1930

1200 STANDARD PLAZA
1100 S.W. SIXTH AVENUE
PORTLAND, OREGON 97204
Telephone: 503-226-1371
Telecopier: 503-226-3574
URL: http://www.duffykekel.com

Taxation, Estate Planning, Tax Planning, Tax Litigation, Business Law, Timber Matters, Probate, Real Property, Wills, Trusts, Deferred Compensation, Exempt Organizations, Elder Law, Estate and Trust Litigation, Commercial Litigation, Special Education, Guardianships, Conservatorships.

MEMBERS OF FIRM

CHARLES P. DUFFY (1915-2001)

DAVID A. KEKEL (1938-1999)

PHILIP N. JONES, born Seattle, Washington, May 5, 1951; admitted to bar, 1976, Oregon; 1993, Washington. *Education:* Lewis and Clark College (B.A., 1973); Northwestern School of Law of Lewis and Clark College (J.D., 1976). Member, Estate Planning Council of Portland. *Member:* Oregon State Bar; Washington State Bar Association. ***PRACTICE AREAS:*** Tax Litigation; Estate Planning; Probate; Estate Litigation; Trust Litigation; Taxation; Tax Controversies; Appeals. ***Email:*** pjones@duffykekel.com

STEVEN A. NICHOLES, born Eugene, Oregon, September 29, 1952; admitted to bar, 1980, Oregon. *Education:* Oregon State University (B.A., 1975); Gonzaga University (J.D., 1980); University of Florida (LL.M., Taxation, 1981). *Member:* Oregon State Bar. ***PRACTICE AREAS:*** Taxation; Real Estate; Business Law; Trusts and Estates; Real Estate Exchanges; Estate and Gift Taxation. ***Email:*** snicholes@duffykekel.com

DONNA M. MUEHLECK, born Riverside, California, May 6, 1953; admitted to bar, 1986, Oregon; 1988, Washington. *Education:* Portland State University (B.S., 1980); New York University (J.D., 1983). Member: Estate Planning Council of Portland. *Member:* Oregon State Bar; Washington State Bar Association. ***PRACTICE AREAS:*** Estate Planning; Probate; Wills; Trusts; Taxation. ***Email:*** dmuehleck@duffykekel.com

PETER J. DUFFY, born Portland, Oregon, October 5, 1958; admitted to bar, 1987, Oregon; 1993, Washington. *Education:* University of Washington (B.A., 1980); University of Oregon (J.D., 1986); University of Florida (LL.M., Taxation, 1987). *Member:* Oregon State Bar; Washington State Bar Association. ***PRACTICE AREAS:*** Taxation; Estate Planning; Wills; Trusts; Probate; Business Law; Retirement Benefit Plans. ***Email:*** pduffy@duffykekel.com

ERIC H. VETTERLEIN, born Boston, Massachusetts, January 30, 1954; admitted to bar, 1987, Oregon. *Education:* University of Oregon; University of Colorado (B.A., 1977); Northwestern School of Law of Lewis and Clark College (J.D., 1986). Member, Estate Planning Council of Portland. *Member:* Oregon State Bar. ***PRACTICE AREAS:*** Estate Planning; Probate; Wills; Trusts; Taxation; Business Law. ***Email:*** evetterlein@duffykekel.com

ASSOCIATE

HOLLY N. MITCHELL, born Vancouver, Washington, December 18, 1952; admitted to bar, 1984, Oregon. *Education:* Lewis and Clark College (B.A., 1975); Northwestern School of Law (J.D., 1984). *Member:* Oregon State Bar. ***PRACTICE AREAS:*** Estate Planning; Probate; Wills; Trusts. ***Email:*** hmitchell@duffykekel.com

OF COUNSEL

DANA R. TAYLOR, born Burbank, California, September 30, 1950; admitted to bar, 1977, Oregon and U.S. District Court, District of Oregon; 1981, U.S. Court of Appeals, Ninth Circuit; 1982, U.S. Tax Court and U.S. Supreme Court; 1993, U.S. Court of Federal Claims; 1999, U.S. Court of Appeals for the Federal Circuit. *Education:* University of Southern California (B.A., 1973); Northwestern School of Law at Lewis & Clark College (J.D., 1977). *Member:* Multnomah County and American Bar Associations; Oregon State Bar. ***PRACTICE AREAS:*** Tax Law; Commercial Litigation; Special Education. ***Email:*** dtaylor@duffykekel.com

RON D. BAILEY, born Klamath Falls, Oregon, January 21, 1936; admitted to bar, 1966, Oregon. *Education:* Oregon State University (B.S., 1957); Northwestern College of Law of Lewis and Clark College (J.D., 1966). Received Presidents membership service award For Outstanding (legislative) Volunteer Related Services to the Public, 1997. *Member:* Multnomah County Bar Association; Oregon State Bar (Chair, Committee on Corporation and Partnership Law, 1974-1975; Member, Administrative Law Committee, 1977-1979; Chair, 1978-1979; Member, Trust Legislation Committee, 1981-1984; Chair, 1983-1984; Secretary, Taxation Section, 1986-1987; Legislative Chair, Estate Planning and Administration Section, 1993-1997; Chair, Estate Planning and Administration Section, 2002); Executive Secretary, Oregon State Board of Dentistry, 1974-1982). ***PRACTICE AREAS:*** Trust Law; Estate Planning; Wills; Guardianships; Conservatorships; Probate; Tax Planning; Business Law. ***Email:*** rbailey@duffykekel.com

DUNN CARNEY ALLEN HIGGINS & TONGUE LLP

Established in 1930

PACIFIC FIRST FEDERAL BUILDING
851 S.W. SIXTH AVENUE
SUITE 1500
PORTLAND, OREGON 97204
Telephone: 503-224-6440
FAX: 503-224-7324
Email: info@dunn-carney.com
URL: http://www.dunncarney.com

General Civil and Trial Practice in all State and Federal Courts. General Business, Antitrust, Appellate Practice, Banking Law, Bankruptcy, Construction Law, Contracts, Corporate, Creditors Rights, Employee Benefits,Employment Law, ERISA, Estate Planning, Federal and State Tax Law, Guardianship and Conservatorship, Health Care, Insurance, Intellectual Property, Medical Malpractice, Mergers, Acquisitions and Divestitures, Nonprofit and Charitable Organizations, Partnership Law, Probate, Products Liability, Real Estate, Retirement Plans, Trust Administration, and Zoning, Planning and Land Use.

FIRM PROFILE: The firm was founded in 1930 by William H. Morrison. Recognized nationally as an outstanding trial attorney, he served as President of the American College of Trial Lawyers. Today the firm maintains a business, real estate and trial practice representing corporate and individual clients at the local, national and international levels. Lawyers at Dunn Carney retain accesssibility and responsiveness often associated with a smaller firm but, unlike smaller firms, Dunn Carney has the talent and resources to handle the most complex and demanding legal problems. Firm lawyers are admitted to practice law in Oregon, Washington, California and other states. The firm was selected to become the only Oregon member of Meritas, a global affiliation of independent law firms in major cities worldwide. For more information about Meritas see www.meritas.org.

LAW FIRM ALLIANCES/ASSOCIATIONS: **MERITAS**

PARTNERS OF FIRM

ROBERT L. ALLEN, born Upland, California, August 13, 1937; admitted to bar, 1965, Oregon. *Education:* Stanford University (A.B., 1960); Boalt Hall School of Law, University of California (LL.B., 1965). *Member:* Multnomah County and American Bar Associations; Oregon State Bar. ***PRACTICE AREAS:*** General Business Law; Unfair Competition; Business Litigation. ***Email:*** RLA@dunn-carney.com

KENNETH S. ANTELL, born Duluth, Minnesota, March 22, 1959; admitted to bar, 1986, Oregon; 1988, U.S. District Court, District of Oregon; 1993, Washington. *Education:* University of Michigan (B.A., 1981); University of Oregon (J.D., 1986). Co-Author: "Negligent Misrepresentation in Oregon, the Elusive Claim," Oregon State Bar Litigation Journal, Volume 12, Number 3, May 1993. *Member:* Multnomah County, Washington State and American Bar Associations; Oregon State Bar; Building Owners and Managers Association; International Council of Shopping Centers. ***PRACTICE AREAS:*** Real Estate; Commercial Transactions; Real Estate Acquisition and Financing; Construction; Leasing. ***Email:*** KSA@dunn-carney.com

JONATHAN A. BENNETT, born Portland, Oregon, August 11, 1959; admitted to bar, 1986, Oregon; 1988, Washington. *Education:* University of Oregon (B.S., 1981; J.D., 1986). *Member:* Multnomah County and Washington State Bar Associations; Oregon State Bar; Oregon Association of Defense Counsel. ***PRACTICE AREAS:*** Business Law; Real Estate Law; Commercial Law; General Litigation. ***Email:*** JAB@dunn-carney.com

DAVID J. BUONO, born Portland, Oregon, October 5, 1943; admitted to bar, 1968, Oregon; 1970, U.S. District Court, District of Oregon and U.S. Court of Appeals, Ninth Circuit; 1989, U.S. Tax Court; U.S. Court of Federal Claims. *Education:* University of Oregon (B.S., 1965; J.D., 1968). Speaker: "Probate," The Oregon Escrow Council, Inc., 1987; Business Forms and Construction Liens and Bond Claims, Pacific Northwest Steel Fabricators Association, 2002. Member, Panel of Arbitrators, American Arbitration Association. *Member:* Multnomah County and American (Member, Sections on: Construction; Real Estate; Probate) Bar Associations; Oregon State Bar (Secretary, Chairman, 1981-1982 and Member, Economics of Law Practice Committee, 1980-1982; Member: Certified Public Accountants Joint Committee, 1989-1990; Sections on: Business Litigation; Construction Law; Corporate; Real Estate and Land Use; Probate; Litigation; Member, 1992—, Secretary, 1993-1994 and Chairman, 1994-1995, Client Security Fund). ***PRACTICE AREAS:*** Business Law; Commercial Law; Business Organization; Construction Law; Contracts; Debtor and Creditor; Eminent Domain; Management Employment Law; Estate Planning; Probate; Estate Administration; Real Estate; Trademarks; Trusts and Estates; Wills. ***Email:*** DJB@dunn-carney.com

MADELEINE S. CAMPBELL, born Glencoe, Scotland, May 21, 1955; admitted to bar, 1981, Oregon; U.S. District Court, District of Oregon. *Education:* University of British Columbia (B.A., 1976; LL.B., 1979). Author, "Insurance Coverage for Directors & Officers," Oregon Law Institute, 1991. Co-Author: "Case Comment on California Asbestos Insurance Coverage Cases," Tort and Insurance Law Journal, 1989; "Practical Problems in Complex Coverage Litigation," DRI Insurance Law, 1989; "Comprehensive General Liability Policy Forms..." Oregon Law Institute, 1988. *Member:* Multnomah and American (Member, Tort and Insurance Practice Section, 1989) Bar Associations; Oregon State Bar; Defense Research Institute. ***PRACTICE AREAS:*** Professional Liability; Insurance Coverage; Insurance Bad Faith; Litigation. ***Email:*** MSC@dunn-carney.com

JOHN H. CHAMBERS, born Mountain View, California, January 22, 1965; admitted to bar, 1992, Oregon and California; 1993, U.S. District Court, District of Oregon. *Education:* University of Michigan (B.A., 1987); University of Oregon (J.D., 1991). Associate Editor, Oregon Law Review, 1990-1991. *Member:* State Bar of California; Oregon State Bar. ***PRACTICE AREAS:*** Litigation; Construction Law; Construction Litigation; Commercial Litigation; Business Litigation; Design Professionals Law; Collections; Creditors Rights. ***Email:*** jhc@dunn-carney.com

(This Listing Continued)

DUNN CARNEY ALLEN HIGGINS & TONGUE LLP, Portland—Continued

JAY R. CHOCK, born York, Pennsylvania, February 24, 1955; admitted to bar, 1983, Oregon; 1986, U.S. District Court, District of Oregon. *Education:* Pennsylvania State University (B.A., 1977); Lewis and Clark College Northwestern School of Law (J.D., 1982). *Member:* Multnomah County Bar Association; Oregon State Bar; Oregon Association of Defense Counsel; Defense Research Institute. ***REPORTED CASES:*** Allstate v. SafeCo, 99 Oregon App. 162 (1989). ***PRACTICE AREAS:*** Insurance Defense; Personal Injury; Insurance Coverage; Business Litigation. ***Email:*** jrc@dunn-carney.com

GEORGE J. COOPER, born Seattle, Washington, August 12, 1947; admitted to bar, 1972, Oregon. *Education:* Willamette University (B.A., 1969); Duke University (J.D., 1972). *Member:* Multnomah County and American Bar Associations; Oregon State Bar. ***PRACTICE AREAS:*** Employment Law; Antitrust Law. ***Email:*** GJC@dunn-carney.com

I. KENNETH DAVIS, born Portland, Oregon, November 28, 1950; admitted to bar, 1988, Oregon. *Education:* Columbia College (A.B., 1972); Lewis and Clark College Northwestern School of Law (J.D., summa cum laude, 1988). *Member:* Multnomah County Bar Association; Oregon State Bar. ***PRACTICE AREAS:*** Corporate; Commercial; Estate Planning; Probate and Trust Administration; Business Succession Planning. ***Email:*** IKD@dunn-carney.com

RANDALL L. DUNCAN, born San Francisco, California, September 18, 1957; admitted to bar, 1985, Oregon, California and U.S. District Court, Northern, Central and Southern Districts of California; 1986, U.S. Court of Appeals, Ninth Circuit and U.S. Tax Court; 1989, U.S. District Court, District of Oregon; 2002, Washington. *Education:* University of California at Los Angeles (B.A., cum laude, 1980); McGeorge School of Law, University of the Pacific (J.D., 1983). Master, Gus J. Solomon Chapter, American Inns of Court, 1990—. *Member:* Los Angeles County (Member, Litigation Section), Multnomah County (Director, 1991-1993 and Treasurer, 1992-1993, Young Lawyers Section; Director, Volunteer Lawyer's Project, 1994-1996), Washington State and American (Member, Section on Business Law) Bar Associations; Oregon State Bar; State Bar of California; American Inns of Court. ***PRACTICE AREAS:*** Business Law; Real Estate Law; Civil Litigation; Estate Planning; Construction Law; Asset Protection; Collections; Franchise Law. ***Email:*** rd@dunn-carney.com

SUSAN C. GLEN, born San Mateo, California, July 28, 1964; admitted to bar, 1994, Oregon; 1997, Washington. *Education:* Carleton College (B.A., cum laude, 1986); University of Minnesota (J.D., cum laude, 1994). Article Editor, Minnesota Law Review, 1993-1994. Author: Comment, "Central States v. Personnel, Inc.: When Real Estate Ownership Creates Personal Liability Under the Multiemployer Pension Plan Act of 1980," 78 Minn. L. Rev. 501, 1993. *Member:* Multnomah County, Washington State and American Bar Associations; Oregon State Bar; Oregon Women Lawyers; Commercial Real Estate Women. ***PRACTICE AREAS:*** Real Estate; Corporate; Business Law; Construction; Leasing. ***Email:*** SCG@dunn-carney.com

JAMES M. HILLAS, born Morristown, New Jersey, January 2, 1966; admitted to bar, 1994, Oregon. *Education:* Hampshire College (B.A. 1989); Lewis and Clark College Northwestern School of Law (J.D., 1994). Phi Delta Phi. Student Materials Editor, 1993-1994 and Law Review Member, 1992-1993, Environmental Law Review. Co-Instructor, Southwestern Oregon Community College, Criminal Law, 1995. Adjunct Faculty, Portland Community College, Construction Law, 2002. *Member:* Multnomah and Federal Bar Associations; Oregon State Bar; Oregon Association of Defense Counsel. ***PRACTICE AREAS:*** General Litigation; Business Litigation; Commercial Litigation; Bankruptcy; Construction Law; Construction Liens; Employment Contracts; Wage and Hour Law; Residential Real Estate; Bankruptcy Litigation; Complex Litigation. ***Email:*** JMH@dunn-carney.com

FRANK H. HILTON, JR., born Portland, Oregon, October 29, 1941; admitted to bar, 1966, Oregon. *Education:* Stanford University (A.B., 1963); University of Oregon (LL.B., 1966). Phi Delta Phi; Order of the Coif. Editor, University of Oregon Law Review, 1965-1966. *Member:* Multnomah County Bar Association; Oregon State Bar (Member, 1972-1976 and Vice-Chairman, 1974-1976, Board of Bar Examiners; Chairman: Bar Admissions Study Committee, 1978-1979; Bar Examination Board of Review, 1980-1982; Member, Committees on: Uniform Jury Instructions, 1978-1981; Multnomah County Professional Responsibility Committee, 1978-1983). ***PRACTICE AREAS:*** Business Law; Business Litigation; Real Estate. ***Email:*** FHH@dunn-carney.com

JACK D. HOFFMAN, born August 23, 1947, Richland, Washington; admitted to bar, 1976, Oregon. *Education:* Washington State University (B.S., 1969; M.S., 1973); Lewis and Clark College Northwestern School of Law (J.D., 1976). Issue Editor, Environmental Law Review, 1975-1976. *Member:* Multnomah County and American Bar Associations; Oregon State Bar; Oregon Association of Defense Counsel. ***PRACTICE AREAS:*** Insurance Law; Land Use; Zoning, Planning and Land Use Litigation; Litigation. ***Email:*** JDH@dunn-carney.com

CHARLES SCOTT HOWARD, born Los Angeles, California, November 14, 1953; admitted to bar, 1978, California; 1979, Oregon. *Education:* Occidental College (B.A., 1975); Whittier College School of Law (J.D., 1978). *Member:* Multnomah County and American (Member, Corporation, Banking and Business Law Section) Bar Associations; State Bar of California; Oregon State Bar. ***PRACTICE AREAS:*** Real Property Acquisitions; Foreclosures; Corporate. ***Email:*** CSH@dunn-carney.com

SCOTT A. JONSSON, born Portland, Oregon, May 19, 1951; admitted to bar, 1983, Washington; 1984, U.S. District Court, Western and Eastern Districts of Washington; 1986, Oregon and U.S. District Court, District of Oregon; 1987, U.S. Court of Appeals, 9th Circuit; 1989, U.S. Claims Court; 1990, U.S. Supreme Court. *Education:* University of Oregon (B.S., with honors, 1974; J.D., 1983). Member: National Moot Court Team; National Civil Trial Team. Instructor, National Institute for Trial Advocacy (NITA). Law Clerk for Hon. William H. Erickson, Colorado State Supreme Court, Summer, 1982. Past President: Eastern Washington Jaycees; American Lung Association. Board Member, Catholic Charities. Chair, Program Committee, Easter Seals Society. *Member:* Multnomah County, Washington State and American Bar Associations; Oregon State Bar (Member, Unlawful Practice of OSB Bar Committee, 1994-1997); Defense Research Institute (Author and Speaker). ***PRACTICE AREAS:*** Business Litigation; Commercial Litigation; Insurance Coverage; Antitrust; Class Action Defense; Labor and Employment; Business Torts; Professional Liability Defense; Federal Litigation; Complex and Multi-District Litigation. ***Email:*** SAJ@dunn-carney.com

JoDEE K. KEEGAN, born Ogden, Utah, November 14, 1971; admitted to bar, 1997, Oregon. *Education:* Boise State University (B.A., 1994); Willamette University (J.D., 1997). *Member:* Multnomah County and American Bar Associations; Oregon State Bar. ***PRACTICE AREAS:*** Mergers, Acquisitions and Divestitures; Commercial Transactions; Corporate Law; Business Law; Commercial Law; Securities; Business Succession Planning; Taxation; Contracts; Partnership Law. ***Email:*** JKK@dunn-carney.com

ERIC A. KEKEL, born National City, California, November 10, 1961; admitted to bar, 1992, Oregon; 1993, Washington. *Education:* Oregon State University (B.S., 1983); Willamette University (J.D., 1992). Phi Delta Phi. Associate Editor, 1990-1991 and Note Editor, 1991-1992, Willamette Law Review. Author: Comment, "Oregon Products Liability Law and the Problem of Economic Loss," 28 Willamette Law Review 565, 1992. *Member:* Multnomah County and Washington State Bar Associations; Oregon State Bar. ***PRACTICE AREAS:*** General Civil Litigation; Insurance Law; Construction Disputes; Construction Law; Products Liability; Corporate Law; Business Law; Contracts. ***Email:*** EAK@dunn-carney.com

ROBERT A. KERR, born Portland, Oregon, June 25, 1970; admitted to bar, 1996, Oregon; 1999, Washington; 2000, U.S. District Court, District of Oregon. *Education:* Brigham Young University (B.A., 1993; J.D., 1996). *Member:* Multnomah Bar Association; Oregon State Bar; Washington State Bar. ***PRACTICE AREAS:*** Business Law; Collections; Civil Litigation; Probate; Real Estate Law; Employment Law. ***Email:*** RAK@dunn-carney.com

MARSHA MURRAY-LUSBY, born Missoula, Montana, May 10, 1957; admitted to bar, 1984, Oregon. *Education:* University of Montana (B.A., with high honors, 1980); Willamette University (J.D., cum laude, 1984). Managing Editor/Production, Willamette Law Review, 1982-1984. Author: "State Action Immunity For Local Land Use Decisions: Oregon & Washington Systems Provide Broad Contrasts," 20 Willamette Review 755, 1984. *Member:* Multnomah County Bar Association; Oregon State Bar. ***PRACTICE AREAS:*** Estate Planning; Probate and Trust Administration; General Business Law. ***Email:*** MML@dunn-carney.com

GILBERT E. PARKER, born Los Angeles, California, August 27, 1950; admitted to bar, 1975, Oregon. *Education:* Lewis and Clark College (B.A., 1972); Hastings College of Law, University of California (J.D., 1975). *Member:* Multnomah County and American Bar Associations; Oregon State Bar. ***PRACTICE AREAS:*** Real Estate; Real Estate Leasing; Commercial Real Estate; Condominium Law; Real Estate Title Insurance; Real Estate Foreclosure; Conveyancing; Real Estate Development; Banking Law; Commercial Law; Business Law; Secured Lending; Closely Held Business Law; Limited Liability Company Law; Joint Ventures; Business Formation. ***Email:*** GEP@dunn-carney.com

RENEE R. STINEMAN, born Yuba City, California, September 6, 1968; admitted to bar, 1994, California and U.S. District Court, Eastern District of California; 1999, Oregon; 2000, U.S. District Court, District of Oregon. *Education:* California State University, Sacramento (B.A., 1990); McGeorge School of Law, University of the Pacific (J.D., 1994). [Lieutenant Commander, Judge Advocate Generals Corps, U.S. Navy, 1994-2000]. ***PRACTICE AREAS:*** Employment Litigation; Commercial Litigation; Business Litigation; Real Estate Litigation. ***Email:*** RRS@dunn-carney.com

BRIAN R. TALCOTT, born Glendora, California, November 19, 1968; admitted to bar, 1996, Oregon. *Education:* University of California at San Diego (B.A., 1991); University of Oregon (J.D., 1996). Managing Editor, Oregon Law Review, 1995-1996. *Member:* Multnomah County and American Bar Associations; Oregon State Bar (Member, Appellate Practice Section); Oregon Association of Defense Counsel; Oregon Board of Bar Examiners. ***REPORTED CASES:*** Safeco v. Laskey, 162 Or. App.1, 985P.2d 878 (1999); Hollister v. Tuttle, 201 F.3d 1033 (9th Cir. 2000); Robinson v. Lamb's Wilsonville Thriftway, 162 Or.App.632, 986 P2d 661. (1999), reversed, 332 Or.453 (2001); Bingham v. Employment Div., 163 Or.App.381, 987 P.2d 578 (1999). ***PRACTICE AREAS:*** Appellate Law; Insurance Coverage; Insurance Litigation; Commercial Litigation; Business Litigation. ***Email:*** BRT@dunn-carney.com

DONALD E. TEMPLETON, born Portland, Oregon, May 12, 1959; admitted to bar, 1984, Washington; 1986, Oregon. *Education:* University of Oregon (B.S., 1981); University of Washington (J.D., 1984). Author: Insurance, Chapter 28, "Comprehensive Personal Liability Coverage," Oregon State Bar Association, CLE 1996 Revision and 1999 Supplement; Damages, Chapter 7, "Medical Expenses," Oregon State Bar Association, CLE 1998; Arbitration and Mediation, Chapter 11, "Arbitration Under PIP/UM/UIM Provisions in Automobile Insurance Policies," Oregon State Bar Association, CLE, 1996 and 2000 update. *Member:* Multnomah County, Oregon State, Washington State and American Bar Associations; Oregon Association of Defense Counsel; Oregon Board of Bar Examiners (Member, 1999-2002; Chairperson, 2001-2002); Multnomah County Local Professional Responsibility Committee (Member, 1993-1995; Chairperson, 1995-1996). ***PRACTICE AREAS:*** Civil Litigation; Insurance Law. ***Email:*** DET@dunn-carney.com

THOMAS HEALY TONGUE, born Portland, Oregon, November 27, 1943; admitted to bar, 1968, Oregon; 1970, U.S. District Court, District of Oregon; 1971, U.S. Court of Appeals, Ninth Circuit; 1973, U.S. Supreme Court. *Education:* University of Oregon (B.S., 1965); University of Wisconsin-Madison (J.D., 1968). Phi Delta Phi. Recipient: Owen Panner Professionalism Award, 2002; Exceptional Performance Citation, Defense Research Institute, 1999; President's Membership Service Award, Oregon State Bar Board of Governors, 1992; Professionalism Award, Multnomah County Bar Association, 1990. Delegate, U.S. Court of Appeals, 9th Circuit Judicial Conference, 1992-1994. Member, 1993 and Chair, 1997, Merit Selection Panel for Selection of U.S. Magistrate Judges. Recommended for U.S. District Court Judge by Merit Selection Panel, 2003. *Member:* Multnomah County (President, 1976) and American Bar Associations; Oregon State Bar (Member, Litigation Section); American Judicature Society; Oregon Association of Defense Counsel (Member, Board of Directors, 1993—); International Association of Defense Counsel; American College of Trial Lawyers (Regent, Northwest Region, 2003-2007). Fellow, American College of Trial Lawyers. ***PRACTICE AREAS:*** General Litigation; Complex Litigation; Arbitration; Mediation; Insurance Law; Health Care Law; Products Liability. ***Email:*** THT@dunn-carney.com

(This Listing Continued)

DANIEL F. VIDAS, born Davenport, Iowa, September 7, 1942; admitted to bar, 1977, Oregon. *Education:* University of Illinois (B.S., 1968; M.S./ABD-Ph.D., 1974; J.D., 1977). Phi Delta Phi. Assistant Professor, Business Law, Oregon State University, College of Business, 1977-1978. Staff Attorney, U.S. Bankruptcy Court, 1984-1988. *Member:* Multnomah County and American Bar Associations; Oregon State Bar (Member, Executive Committee, Debtor-Creditor Section). ***PRACTICE AREAS:*** Bankruptcy Law; Creditors Rights Law; Commercial Litigation. ***Email:*** DFV@dunn-carney.com

ROBERT K. WINGER, born Corvallis, Oregon, January 19, 1948; admitted to bar, 1973, Oregon. *Education:* University of Oregon (B.A., 1970; J.D., 1973). Phi Beta Kappa. Member, Editorial Board, Oregon Law Review, 1972-1973. Author: "Public School Finance in Oregon and Serrano v. Priest," Oregon Law Review, Vol. 52, 1972. *Member:* Multnomah County and American Bar Associations; Oregon State Bar (Member, Executive Committee, Tax Section; Chairman, 1991; Member, Joint Task Force on LLC). ***PRACTICE AREAS:*** Corporate; Tax; LLC; ERISA. ***Email:*** RKW@dunn-carney.com

---

CYNTHIA CROFT ADAMS, born Philadelphia, Pennsylvania, April 17, 1953; admitted to bar, 1983, Oregon; 1987, Washington; 1995, U.S. District Court, District of Oregon and U.S. District Court, Western District of Washington. *Education:* West Chester State College (B.A., summa cum laude, 1977); Lewis and Clark College Northwestern School of Law (J.D., 1982). *Member:* Multnomah County and Washington State Bar Associations; Oregon State Bar. ***PRACTICE AREAS:*** Consumer Law; Employment Law; Insurance Law.

RICHARD THEODORE ASHE, born May 5, 1971; admitted to bar, 2002, Oregon. *Education:* Southwest Missouri State University (B.A., Philosophy, 1996); Northwestern School of Law of Lewis and Clark College (J.D., cum laude, 2001). Recipient, "2000-2001 Award for Law Review Excellence," for work of Associate Editor, Environmental Law Review. Associate Editor, Environmental Law Review, 1999-2001. *Member:* Multnomah Bar Association; Oregon State Bar. ***PRACTICE AREAS:*** Business Litigation; Commercial Litigation; Litigation; Intellectual Property; Copyrights; Computer Law. ***Email:*** rta@dunn-carney.com

BRIAN R. CABLE, born Palm Springs, California, January 19, 1971; admitted to bar, 2001, Oregon. *Education:* Washington State University (B.A., 1993); Northwestern School of Law (J.D., cum laude, 2001). *Member:* Oregon State Bar (Member, Sections on: Business; Securities); American Bar Association; Multnomah Bar Association. ***PRACTICE AREAS:*** Business Law; Commercial Law; Securities; Mergers and Acquisitions. ***Email:*** brc@dunn-carney.com

DELOS R. CLARK, born Salem, Oregon, August 21, 1969; admitted to bar, 1996, Oregon. *Education:* Washington & Lee University (B.S., 1990); Willamette University (J.D., 1993); University of Washington (LL.M., Taxation, 1999). Member: Order of Barristers; Moot Court Board. *Member:* Multnomah County, Washington State and American (Member: Tax Section; Business Section) Bar Associations; Oregon State Bar (Member, Tax Section, 1996—). ***PRACTICE AREAS:*** Taxation; Business Law; Corporate Law; Trusts and Estates; Employee Compensation; Employee Benefits; Real Estate; Intellectual Property. ***Email:*** DRC@dunn-carney.com

W. TODD CLEEK, born Beckley, West Virginia, July 4, 1968; admitted to bar, 1994, Oregon. *Education:* University of Delaware (B.A., 1990); Willamette University (J.D., 1994). Executive Editor, Willamette Bulletin of International Law. Member, City Club of Portland, 1995—. *Member:* Multnomah County Bar Association; Oregon State Bar. ***PRACTICE AREAS:*** Civil Litigation.

DANIEL J. DRAZAN, born Walla Walla, Washington, March 21, 1973; admitted to bar, 1998, Oregon; 1999, U.S. District Court, District of Oregon; 2003, Washington. *Education:* Lewis and Clark College (B.A., 1995); Willamette University (J.D., magna cum laude, 1998). Articles Editor, Willamette Law Review, 1996-1998. Author: "Siting of Cellular Relay Towers: Are Prohibitive Land Use Regulations Consistent With Oregon's Constitutional Guarantee of Free Expression" 34 Willamette L.Rev. (1998). *Member:* Multnomah County, Clark County and Washington State Bar Associations; Oregon State Bar (Member, Unlawful Practice Committee). ***PRACTICE AREAS:*** Real Estate; Business Law; Commercial Law; Land Use; Leasing. ***Email:*** DJD@dunn-carney.com

PAUL G. ELLIS, admitted to bar, 1985, Oregon; 1988, U.S. District Court, District of Oregon; 1998, U.S. Court of Appeals, Ninth Circuit. *Education:* University of Iowa (B.B.A., 1971); Lewis and Clark College (J.D., 1984). *Member:* Oregon State Bar. ***PRACTICE AREAS:*** Civil Litigation; Business Law; Personal Injury. ***Email:*** PGE@dunn-carney.com

SAMANTHA FAIR, born Jackson, Michigan, August 6, 1964; admitted to bar, 1990, Oregon. *Education:* Reed College (B.A., 1986); Lewis and Clark College (J.D., cum laude, 1990). *Member:* Oregon State Bar. ***PRACTICE AREAS:*** Criminal Law; Family Law; Consumer Law; Real Estate Law; Landlord and Tenant Law. ***Email:*** SAF@dunn-carney.com

STEFAN FEUERHERDT, born New York, N.Y., May 31, 1963; admitted to bar, 1992, Florida; 1996, Oregon; 2004, U.S. District Court, District of Oregon. *Education:* University of South Florida (B.A., Finance, 1985); Florida State University (J.D., 1992). Member, The Florida Bar, 1992-2000. *Member:* Oregon State Bar. [Captain, U.S. Marine Corps, 1990-1996]. ***PRACTICE AREAS:*** Civil Litigation; Family Law; Consumer Law; Criminal Law. ***Email:*** SLF@dunn-carney.com

ANNE D. FOSTER, born Coos Bay, Oregon, 1970; admitted to bar, 1999, Oregon and U.S. District Court, District of Oregon; 2000, Washington; 2002, U.S. Court of Appeals, 9th Circuit. *Education:* University of Oregon (B.A., Major in Political Science and Sociology, 1993; J.D., 1999). Associate Editor, Journal of Environmental Law and Litigation, 1997-1999. *Member:* Multnomah County, Clark County, Oregon State, Washington State and American Bar Associations; Oregon Women Lawyers; Defense Research Institute. ***PRACTICE AREAS:*** General Litigation; Product Liability; Professional Malpractice; Personal Injury; Construction Law; Premises Liability. ***Email:*** adf@dunn-carney.com

HEATHER L. GUTHRIE, born Detroit, Michigan, November 19, 1968; admitted to bar, 2000, Oregon and Washington. *Education:* Portland State University (B.A., 1995); Lewis and Clark College Northwestern School of Law (J.D., 1999). Recipient, Federal Income Tax Certificate, Northwestern School of Law. *Member:* Multnomah County, Washington State and American Bar Associations; Oregon State Bar. ***LANGUAGES:*** French, Spanish. ***PRACTICE AREAS:*** Estate Planning; Business Transactions; Mergers, Acquisitions and Divestitures; Federal Taxation; Business Law; Corporate Law; Guardianship and Conservatorship; Nonprofit and Charitable Organizations; Taxation; Trusts and Estates; Wills. ***Email:*** HLG@dunn-carney.com

TIM HERING, born Agana, Guam; admitted to bar, 2005, Oregon. *Education:* University of Washington (B.A., with honors, 1997); University of Oregon (J.D., 2005). Recipient, Maxine Lee Award for Editorial Excellence, University of Oregon. Executive Editor, Oregon Law Review, 2004-2005. *Member:* Oregon State Bar. ***PRACTICE AREAS:*** Litigation; Civil Litigation. ***Email:*** TBH@dunn-carney.com

MISTI K. JOHNSON, born Springfield, Oregon; admitted to bar, 2001, Oregon. *Education:* Oregon State University (B.A., 1994); University of Oregon (J.D., 2000). *Member:* Oregon State Bar (Member, Real Estate and Land Use Section). ***PRACTICE AREAS:*** Real Estate; Land Use; Business Transactions. ***Email:*** MKJ@dunn-carney.com

TAMARA B. MAHER, born Orangeville, Ontario, Canada; admitted to bar, 1991, Oregon; 1992, U.S. District Court, District of Oregon; 1997, Washington and U.S. District Court, Western District of Washington. *Education:* State University of New York at Binghamton (B.A., 1980); American University (M.P.A., 1982); Willamette University College of Law (J.D., 1991). *Member:* Oregon State Bar (Member, Elder Law and Family Law Sections). ***PRACTICE AREAS:*** Estate Planning and Probate; Family Law; Guardianship and Conservatorship; Bankruptcy. ***Email:*** TBM@dunn-carney.com

JOHN G. O'NEIL, born Portland, Oregon, December 19, 1970; admitted to bar, 2001, California, U.S. District Court, Northern District of California and U.S. Court of Appeals, Ninth Circuit (Not admitted in Oregon). *Education:* Portland State University (B.S., Physics, 1998); Hastings College of the Law, University of California (J.D., 2001). *Member:* State Bar of California. [Sergeant, U.S. Marine Corps, 1989-1993]. ***PRACTICE AREAS:*** Business Law; Commercial Law; Intellectual Property; Litigation. ***Email:*** JGO@dunn-carney.com

PIERRE L. ROBERT, born October 11, 1958; admitted to bar, 1992, Oregon. *Education:* Kalamazoo College (B.A., 1980); Willamette University (J.D., 1992). *Member:* Multnomah and Oregon Bar Associations. ***PRACTICE AREAS:*** Criminal Law; Family Law; Trusts and Estates; Real Estate. ***Email:*** PLR@dunn-carney.com

DAVID P. ROSSMILLER, born Wildrose, North Dakota, October 18, 1961; admitted to bar, 1998, Oregon; 2000, U.S. District Court, District of Oregon. *Education:* Minot State University (B.A., cum laude, 1984); University of Michigan (J.D., cum laude, 1998). Former Reporter, Phoenix Gazette. *Member:* Multnomah, Federal and American Bar Associations; Oregon State Bar. ***PRACTICE AREAS:*** Litigation; Insurance Coverage; Securities Litigation; Employment Discrimination; Contracts. ***Email:*** dpr@dunn-carney.com

MELISSA M. RYAN, born Milwaukee, Wisconsin, 1969; admitted to bar, 1998, Oregon. *Education:* Boston College (B.A., cum laude, 1991); University of Wyoming School of Law (J.D., 1998). *Member:* Oregon State Bar; Wyoming State Bar; Friends of Columbia Gorge (Director). ***PRACTICE AREAS:*** Real Estate Law; Zoning, Planning and Land Use; Condominium Law; Business Law; Commercial Law. ***Email:*** mmr@dunn-carney.com

DAMIEN J. SINNOTT, born Seattle, Washington, September 2, 1971; admitted to bar, 1996, North Carolina; 1999, Oregon, U.S. District Court, District of Oregon and U.S. Court of Appeals, Ninth Circuit. *Education:* Whitman College (B.A. with honors, 1993); Syracuse University (M.A./J.D., cum laude, 1996). *Member:* Oregon State Bar. [1st. Lt., U.S. Marine Corps, 1993-1996]. ***REPORTED CASES:*** Briley v. Farabow, 348 N.C. 537, 501 S.E.2d 649 (1998). ***PRACTICE AREAS:*** Litigation; Personal Injury Defense; Insurance Defense; Products Liability; Commercial Torts. ***Email:*** djs@dunn-carney.com

ERIC A. SMITH, born Coos Bay, Oregon; admitted to bar, 1999, Oregon and Washington. *Education:* University of Oregon (B.A., 1991; J.D., 1998). *Member:* Oregon State Bar (Member, Business Section); Washington State Bar Association. ***PRACTICE AREAS:*** Business Transactions; Business Formation; Closely Held Business Law; Small Business Law; Private Business Law; Admiralty and Maritime Law; Commercial Contracts. ***Email:*** eas@dunn-carney.com

KYLE J. STINCHFIELD, born Salem, Oregon, January 23, 1975; admitted to bar, 2002, Washington, Oregon and U.S. Tax Court. *Education:* University of Puget Sound (B.A., Psychology, 1997); University of Oregon (J.D., 2001; M.B.A., 2001); New York University (LL.M., Taxation, 2002). *Member:* Washington State Bar Association. ***PRACTICE AREAS:*** Taxation; Business Law; Employee Benefits; Corporate Law; Mergers, Acquisitions and Divestitures; Partnership Law. ***Email:*** KJS@dunn-carney.com

KJERSTEN H. TURPEN, born Rotorua, New Zealand; admitted to bar, 2000, California; 2002, Oregon; 2003, U.S. District Court, District of Oregon. *Education:* University of Oregon (B.A., English, with honors, 1996); Santa Clara University (J.D., International Law, 1999). *Member:* Multnomah and Federal Bar Associations; Oregon State Bar; Oregon Association of Defense Counsel, Owen M. Panner American Inn of Court. ***PRACTICE AREAS:*** Commercial Litigation; Employment Litigation; Insurance Coverage; Contract Disputes; Business Litigation. ***Email:*** kht@dunn-carney.com

GAIL P. VORE, admitted to bar, 1989, Oregon and U.S. District Court, District of Oregon; 1993, Commonwealth of the Northern Mariana Islands. *Education:* Whitman College (B.A., Political Science, 1985); Northwestern School of Law of Lewis and Clark College (J.D., 1989). *Member:* Oregon State Bar. ***PRACTICE AREAS:*** Family Law; Guardianship; Conservatorship; Adoption Law; Civil Litigation. ***Email:*** gpv@dunn-carney.com

OF COUNSEL

TY K. WYMAN, born Ann Arbor, Michigan, January 30, 1964; admitted to bar, 1992, Oregon. *Education:* University of California, Berkeley (B.A., 1987); University of Oregon (J.D., 1992). *Member:* Oregon State Bar (Member, Real Estate and Land Use Sections, 1992—). ***PRACTICE AREAS:*** Zoning, Planning and Land Use. ***Email:*** tkw@dunn-carney.com

(This Listing Continued)

DUNN CARNEY ALLEN HIGGINS & TONGUE LLP, Portland—Continued

J. DAVID ZEHNTBAUER, born 1969; admitted to bar, 1996, Oregon; 2000, U.S. District Court, District of Oregon. *Education:* University of California at Santa Barbara (B.A., 1991); Willamette University, Atkinson Graduate School of Management (M.B.A, Beta Gamma Sigma, 1996); Willamette University College of Law (J.D., cum laude, 1996). *Member:* Oregon State Bar; Multnomah County, Federal and American Bar Associations. ***PRACTICE AREAS:*** Real Estate; Corporate Law; Business Law; Commercial Law; Construction Law. ***Email:*** jdz@dunn-carney.com

REPRESENTATIVE CLIENTS: Allstate Insurance Co.; Costa Pacific Homes; Country Companies Insurance; Eastern Western Corp.; Gerding/Edlen Development Co.; Hollywood Entertainment; Kuni Enterprises, Inc.; Leatherman Tool Group, Inc.; North Pacific Group, Inc.; Oregon Medical Professional Review Organization; Oregon State Bar Professional Liability Fund; OTAK, Inc.; Pan Pacific Retail Properties, Inc.; Rose City Moving & Storage; Safeco Insurance Co.; Shelter Products, Inc.; South Coast Lumber Co.; The RREEF Funds; US Bank Trust Group; Weyerhaeuser Co.; YMCA of Columbia-Willamette Oregon, Inc.

DWYER & MILLER, LLP

215 S.W. WASHINGTON STREET, SUITE 200
PORTLAND, OREGON 97204
Telephone: 503-241-9456
Fax: 503-241-7708
Email: attys@dwyermiller.com
URL: http://www.dwyerandmiller.com

Arbitration and Mediation, Family Law, Domestic Relations, Personal Injury.

FIRM PROFILE: The firms practice is focused on Arbitration and Litigation. Ms. Jayson's extensive experience in handling such matters throughout the country has led her to the representation of Brokerage firms, as well as arguing before state and family courts.

J. MICHAEL DWYER, born Los Angeles, California, April 28, 1952; admitted to bar, 1977, California; 1982, Hawaii; 1989, Oregon. *Education:* University of California at Los Angeles (B.A., magna cum laude, 1974); Loyola Marymount University (J.D., 1977). Chief Ninth Circuit Editor, Loyola Law Review, 1976-1977. Assistant U.S. Attorney, U.S. Attorneys Office, Los Angeles, California, 1979-1981. *Member:* Multnomah County (Board of Directors, 2005—; Chair, Judicial Liaison Committee, 2004; Chair, Judicial Selection Committee; Chair, Legal Services for the Poor) and American Bar Associations; Oregon State Bar; Oregon Trial Lawyers Association; Master, Owen M. Panner Inns of Court. ***PRACTICE AREAS:*** Mediation; Family Law; Domestic Relations; Personal Injury. ***Email:*** michael@dwyermiller.com

LISA ALMASY MILLER, born Evanston, Illinois, July 30, 1955; admitted to bar, 1983, Oregon; 1985, U.S. District Court, District of Oregon. *Education:* University of California at Santa Barbara (B.A., magna cum laude, 1977); University of Santa Clara School of Law (J.D., 1983). Member, National Moot Court Competition. Member, Multnomah County Arbitration Commission, 2004—. *Member:* Clackamas County and Multnomah County (Member and Chair, Professional Responsibility Committee, 1999-2002) Bar Associations; Oregon State Bar (Board of Directors, Professional Liability Fund, 2003—); Oregon Trial Lawyers Association. ***PRACTICE AREAS:*** Arbitration; Mediation; Family Law; Plaintiffs Personal Injury. ***Email:*** lisa@dwyermiller.com

SUSAN K. EGGUM, P.C.

ATTORNEYS AT LAW
621 SW ALDER, SUITE 600
PORTLAND, OREGON 97205
Telephone: 503-228-9607
Fax: 503-228-5790
Email: susan@eggum.com
Email: catherine@eggum.com
Email: stephen@eggum.com
URL: http://www.eggum.com

Trial and Appellate Practice in Federal and State Courts. Employment Litigation, Age Discrimination, Sexual Harassment, Construction Defect Litigation, Contract Litigation and Professional Malpractice.

SHAREHOLDER

SUSAN K. EGGUM, born Portland, Oregon, December 16, 1953; admitted to bar, 1982, Oregon; 1983, U.S. District Court, District of Oregon and U.S. Court of Appeals, Ninth Circuit; 1988, U.S. Supreme Court. *Education:* University of California at Berkeley (B.A., with highest honors, 1976; M.A., with honors, 1977); Georgetown University (J.D., 1982). Phi Beta Kappa. Member, 1980-1981 and Editor, 1981-1982, Law and Policy in International Business. Author: "Should You Sue A Party Who You Have a Good Faith and Reasonable Basis for Believing Is Not Liable?" Oregon State Bar Litigation Section, Litigation Journal, November 1998; "Is the Mere Giving of a Tort Claim Notice the Equivalent of Discovery of a Claim for Relief?" Oregon State Bar Litigation Section, Litigation Journal, July 1998; "What Showing Must a Plaintiff Make to Avoid Summary Judgment in a Federal Age Discrimination Case?" Oregon State Bar Litigation Section, Litigation Journal, June 1997; "Trial Practice," Chapter 22, Federal Civil Litigation in Oregon, Oregon State Bar, 1994 and 1998 and 2002 Supplement; "Trial Notebooks," Chapter 23, Civil Litigation Manual, Oregon State Bar, 1993, 1999 and 2004 Supplements; "Problems In The Formation of Contracts," Chapter 6, Contract Law in Oregon, 1991 Edition and 1999 and 2002 Supplement, Oregon State Bar. *Member:* Multnomah County Bar Association (Director, 1985 and President, 1986, Young Lawyers Section; Chair, Continuing Legal Education Committee, 1991-1992; Member, Local Professional Responsibility Committee, 1987-1990); Oregon State Bar (Member: Litigation Section; Litigation Journal Editorial Board, 1996—; Continuing Legal Education Committee, 1994-1997; Federal Practice and Procedure Committee, 1991-1994; Ad Hoc Committee on Specialization, 1986-1987; Member, Executive Committee, Litigation Section; Elected to House at Delegates for Region 5); Oregon Women Lawyers (Charter Member); The Owen M. Panner American Inn of Court (Master and Member, Executive Committee, 1997—; President, 2002-2004). ***REPORTED CASES:*** Bramel, et. al. v. Brandt, et. al., 190 Or App. 432 (2003); Machado-Miller v. Mersereau & Shannon, 180 Or App. 586, 43 P3d 1207 (2002); Lowery v. City Liquidators, Inc., et. al., 334 Or 631 (2002); Joey Uruo, et.al. v. Clackamas County, et. al., 166 Or App 133 (2000); Columbia Forest Products, Inc. v. AON Risk Services, Inc. of Oregon, 164 Or App 586 (1999); Walleri v. The Federal Home Loan Bank of Seattle, et. al., 83 F3d 1575 (9th Cir 1996); Poole v. Frank, Fed. Sec. L. Rptr. (CCH) 95,751 (D Or 1990); Computer Concepts v. Brandt, 98 Or App 618, aff'd 310 Or 706 (1990); Northwest Food Processors Ass'n v. Reilly, 869 F2d 543 (9th Cir 1989) (without opinion), 886 F2d 1075 (9th Cir 1989) (with opinion); Love v. Thomas, 668 F Supp 1443, aff'd in part, rev in part 838 F2d 1059, am and superseded 858 F2d 1347 (1988), cert den American Federation of Labor and Congress of Industrial Organizations v. Love, 109 S Ct 1932, 104 L Ed 2d 403, aff'd in part, rev in part 858 F2d 1347 (1988); Investors Mort. Ins. Co. v. Dykema, 598 F. Supp 666 (DC Or 1984); Beebe v. Pacific Trust Realty, 578 F. Supp 1128 (DC Or 1984). ***PRACTICE AREAS:*** Federal and State Trial and Appellate Practice; Employment Litigation; Professional Negligence; Torts; Construction Defect Litigation. ***Email:*** susan@eggum.com

(This Listing Continued)

ASSOCIATE

CATHERINE D. LAWSON, admitted to bar, 1985, Oregon; 1988, U.S. District Court, District of Oregon; 1998, U.S. Court of Appeals, Ninth Circuit and U.S. Court of Veterans' Affairs. *Education:* University of Oregon (B.A., 1969); Willamette University (J.D., cum laude, 1985). Dean's Honor List. Recipient: Trustee Scholarship; Butler Scholarship. *Member:* Oregon Women Lawyers. ***PRACTICE AREAS:*** Real Estate Litigation; Construction Defect Litigation; Employment Litigation; Legal Malpractice Defense Litigation. ***Email:*** catherine@eggum.com

OF COUNSEL

STEPHEN D. LEGGATT, admitted to bar, 2003, Oregon; 2000, California, U.S. Court of Appeals, Sixth Circuit; 2001, U.S. Court of Appeals, Ninth Circuit;. *Education:* Brown University (A.B., magna cum laude, 1993); University of Pennsylvania (M.A., 1994); University of California at San Diego (M.S., 1996); University of Michigan Law School (J.D., cum laude, 1999). Order of the Coif. Clarence Darrow Fellow. Two-time Winner, Wiley W. Manuel Award for Pro Bono Legal Services, State Bar of California. Contributing Editor, Michigan Journal of International Law, University of Michigan Law School, 1998-1999. Judicial Clerk to the Hon. James L. Ryan, Sixth Circuit Court of Appeals, 1999-2000. *Member:* Oregon State Bar. ***LANGUAGES:*** French. ***PRACTICE AREAS:*** Employment Litigation; Legal Malpractice Defense Litigation. ***Email:*** stephen@eggum.com

REPRESENTATIVE CLIENTS: Northwest Stucco & Construction, Inc.; Geopier Foundation Company Northwest, Inc.; Professional Liability Fund; Oregon Coalition Against Domestic & Sexual Violence.

ELLIOTT, OSTRANDER & PRESTON, P.C.

Established in 1995
UNION BANK OF CALIFORNIA
707 S.W. WASHINGTON STREET, SUITE 1500
PORTLAND, OREGON 97205
Telephone: 503-224-7112
Fax: 503-224-7819
Email: attorneys@eoplaw.com
URL: http://www.eoplaw.com

Seattle, Washington Office: 707 East Harrison Street, 98102. Telephone: 206-325-2171. Fax: 206-325-3269.

General Civil, Trial, and Appellate Practice in State and Federal Courts. Business and Finance Law, Mergers and Acquisitions, Real Estate, Employment, Commercial, Environmental, Insurance, Intellectual Property, Internet Law, Entertainment Law, Personal Injury, Trusts and Estates, and Taxation, Insurance, Copyrights, Licensing, Trademarks, Immigration and Nationality.

KAREN WETHERELL DAVIS, born Sodus, New York, June 8, 1966; admitted to bar, 1991, Washington; 2003, Oregon. *Education:* Syracuse University (B.Mus., summa cum laude, 1988); Stanford Law School (J.D., 1991). Adjunct Professor: Entertainment Law, Copyright Law; Seattle University Law School, 1997-1999. *Member:* Clark County and Washington State (Chair, Intellectual Property Section, 1999-2000) Bar Associations; Oregon State Bar (Executive Committee, Intellectual Property Section, 2004); Computer Law Association; International Trademark Association; Oregon Media Production Association. ***PRACTICE AREAS:*** Intellectual Property; Copyrights; Trademarks; Entertainment; Arts; Internet. ***Email:*** karen@eoplaw.com

WILLIAM A. DREW, born Hillsboro, Oregon, September 23, 1966; admitted to bar, 1995, Oregon. *Education:* Willamette University (B.S., cum laude, 1989); Harvard Law School (J.D., cum laude, 1994). Judicial Law Clerk to Hon. W. Michael Gillette, Oregon Supreme Court, 1994-1995. *Member:* Washington County, Multnomah County and Federal Bar Associations; Oregon State Bar; Owen M. Panner Inn of Court. ***PRACTICE AREAS:*** Civil Appeals; Civil Litigation; Federal Practice; Insurance Disputes; Real Estate; Intellectual Property Disputes; Trademark Disputes; Business Disputes; General Liability Defense. ***Email:*** billd@eoplaw.com

JEROME F. ELLIOTT, born Malta, Montana, April 5, 1959; admitted to bar, 1985, California; 1992, Oregon; 1993, Washington. *Education:* University of Illinois (B.S., with high honors, 1981); University of Michigan (J.D., 1985). Tau Beta Pi; Order of the Barristers. *Member:* Multnomah County, Washington State and American Bar Associations; State Bar of California; Oregon State Bar. ***PRACTICE AREAS:*** Business Law; Mergers and Acquisitions; Finance; Real Estate; Commercial Law. ***Email:*** jerry@eoplaw.com

(This Listing Continued)

MATTHEW W. McCLELLAN, born Walla Walla, Washington, February 11, 1965; admitted to bar, 1992, Pennsylvania; 1995, District of Columbia (Not admitted in Oregon). *Education:* Georgetown University (B.A., 1987); Catholic University of America (J.D., 1992). *Member:* American Immigration Lawyers Association. ***PRACTICE AREAS:*** Immigration and Nationality (100%). ***Email:*** matthew@eoplaw.com

JOHN D. OSTRANDER, born Ann Arbor, Michigan, September 4, 1962; admitted to bar, 1987, Oregon; 1990, Washington. *Education:* London School of Economics, London, England; Grinnell College (B.A., 1984); Washington University (J.D., 1987). *Member:* Multnomah County, Clark County and Washington State Bar Associations; Oregon State Bar. ***PRACTICE AREAS:*** Civil Litigation; Employment; Intellectual Property; Insurance; Personal Injury; General Liability Defense; Transportation. ***Email:*** john@eoplaw.com

ROBERT J. PRESTON, born Santa Monica, California, March 16, 1957; admitted to bar, 1985, Oregon; 1986, Washington; 1987, Alaska; 1998, Ohio. *Education:* University of California at Berkeley (A.B., 1980); University of Washington (J.D., 1985). Author: "Tax Court Rebuffs IRS View that Power to Remove Trustee is Retained Control," 80 Journal of Taxation No. 3 (March 1994); "Spouse's Stock in a Divorce Can Be Redeemed Tax Free," 78 Journal of Taxation No. 6 (June 1993); "When Will Crummey Transfers to Contingent Beneficiaries Be Excludable Present Interests?" 76 Journal of Taxation No. 2 (Feb. 1992). *Member:* Oregon State Bar; Washington State, Alaska, Ohio State and American Bar Associations. ***PRACTICE AREAS:*** Estate Planning; Tax Planning; Tax Controversies; Business Planning; Executive Compensation. ***Email:*** robert@eoplaw.com

ASSOCIATES

HARSHI M. LIYANAGE, born Kandy, Sri Lanka, September 4, 1967; admitted to bar, 1991, Sri Lanka; 2003, Oregon. *Education:* Sri Lanka Law College, Colombo (J.D., equivalant, 1991); Open University of Sri Lanka, Colombo (LL.B., Bachelor of Law, 1996). *Member:* Multnomah County and American Bar Associations; Oregon State Bar (Member, Committees on: New Lawyers Division CLE; Pro Bono); American Immigration Lawyers Association; Oregon Women Lawyers; Oregon Minority Lawyers Association. ***PRACTICE AREAS:*** Immigration and Nationality. ***Email:*** harshi@eoplaw.com

SONIA A. MONTALBANO, born Jamaica, Queens, New York, August 22, 1969; admitted to bar, 1997, Oregon; 2002, Washington. *Education:* Hunter College of the City University of New York (B.A., magna cum laude, 1992); American Academy of Dramatic Arts; Northwestern School of Law (J.D., 1996). Member, Cornelius Honor Society. *Member:* Multnomah County, Washington State and American Bar Associations; Oregon State Bar (Bar Counsel); Oregon Trial Lawyers Association; Oregon Women Lawyers. ***REPORTED CASES:*** Mantia v. Hanson, 190 Or. App. 36 (2003); Mantia v. Hanson, 190 Or. App. 412 (2003). ***PRACTICE AREAS:*** Civil Litigation; Employment Law; Business Law; Misdemeanors.

JENNIFER L. ROLLINS, born Smithtown, New York, July 27, 1971; admitted to bar, 2000, Oregon. *Education:* Wittenberg University (B.A., 1993); University of Virginia (J.D., 2000). *Member:* Multnomah County and American Bar Associations; Oregon State Bar. ***PRACTICE AREAS:*** Business Law; Real Estate; Finance. ***Email:*** jennifer@eoplaw.com

ELLIOTT & PARK

0324 SW ABERNETHY STREET
PORTLAND, OREGON 97239-4356
Telephone: 503-227-1690
Fax: 503-274-8384

General Civil and Trial Practice in State and Federal Courts. Business Litigation, Personal Injury, Communications, Commercial Law, Professional Negligence, Product Liability, Consumer and Securities Fraud, Wrongful Termination, Employment, Auto Accidents, Wrongful Death, Civil Rights.

MEMBERS OF FIRM

DENNIS H. ELLIOTT, born Newport News, Virginia, October 31, 1946; admitted to bar, 1974, Oregon; 1979, U.S. Court of Appeals, Ninth Circuit and U.S. Supreme Court. *Education:* Pomona College (B.A., 1968); Northwestern School of Law of Lewis and Clark College (J.D., cum laude, 1974). Member: Board of Bar Examiners, 1980-1983; Executive Committee, Section on Litigation, 1980-1982; Executive Committee and Past Chair, Section on Business Litigation, 1995-2001; Practice and Procedure Committee, 1984-1987, Oregon State Bar. *Member:* Multnomah County and American Bar Associations; Oregon Trial Lawyers Association; The Association of Trial Lawyers of America. ***REPORTED CASES:*** Hatcher vs. U.S. National Bank, 643 p2d 359; Pape Inv. Co. vs. Knoll, 687 p2d 1087; Bray vs. American Property Management Corp., 988 p2d 933. ***PRACTICE AREAS:*** Civil and Business Litigation; Personal Injury; Commercial; Communications Law; Professional Negligence; Product Liability; Consumer Fraud; Securities Fraud. ***Email:*** dennis@elliott-park.com

DAVID D. PARK, born Seattle, Washington, May 15, 1955; admitted to bar, 1980, Oregon and U.S. District Court, District of Oregon. *Education:* University of California at Berkeley (B.A., with distinction, 1977); Northwestern School of Law of Lewis and Clark College (J.D., 1980). Member, Northwestern School of Law of Lewis and Clark College Law Review, 1979-1980. *Member:* Multnomah County Bar Association; Oregon State Bar; Oregon Trial Lawyers Association. ***PRACTICE AREAS:*** Business Litigation; Personal Injury; Product Liability; Civil Rights; Employment Discrimination; Construction Defects. ***Email:*** dave@elliott-park.com

ESLER, STEPHENS & BUCKLEY

Established in 1980
700 PIONEER TOWER
888 SW FIFTH AVENUE
PORTLAND, OREGON 97204-2021
Telephone: 503-223-1510
Fax: 503-294-3995

General Civil, Trial and Appellate Practice. Complex Litigation, Private, Business and Non-Profit Corporations, Securities, Franchises, Banking, Energy and Telecommunications, Patent Litigation and Intellectual Property Law, Antitrust, Public Utility, Municipal, Real Estate, Administrative and Commercial Law.

MEMBERS OF FIRM

MICHAEL J. ESLER, born Chicago, Illinois, October 8, 1945; admitted to bar, 1971, Oregon, U.S. District Court, District of Oregon and Northern District of California; 1974, U.S. Court of Appeals, Ninth Circuit; 1982, U.S. Supreme Court. *Education:* St. Mary of the Lake and University of Illinois (B.A., 1967); University of Chicago (J.D., 1971). Instructor: Nonprofit Law, Uniform Securities Act Task Force; Depositions, Current Developments in RICO. Arbitrator, National Association of Securities Dealers, 1981—. ***PRACTICE AREAS:*** Complex Litigation; Securities Litigation; Franchise Litigation; Business Law; Non-Profit Law. ***Email:*** esler@eslerstephens.com

JOHN W. STEPHENS, born Portland, Oregon, April 9, 1952; admitted to bar, 1977, Oregon, U.S. District Court, District of Oregon and Northern District of California; U.S. Court of Appeals, Ninth Circuit and Federal Circuit. *Education:* Stanford University (A.B., with honors, 1974); University of California at Los Angeles (J.D., 1977). Member, UCLA Law Review, 1975-1977. Member, 1990-1997 and Chair, 1992-1993, 1995-1996, Governing Board, Oregon State Department of Geology and Mineral Industries. Member: U.S. District Court Local Rules Committee, 2000—; Executive Committee, 2000—, Governor's Task Force to Study Public Utility Commission, 2000-2001; Oregon Seismic Safety Policy Commission, 1998-2002. *Member:* Oregon State Bar (Chair, Public Utility Law Section, 1989-1992); American Bar Association. ***PRACTICE AREAS:*** Trade Regulation; Public Utility Regulation; Intellectual Property Litigation. ***Email:*** stephens@eslerstephens.com

KIM T. BUCKLEY, born Seattle, Washington, April 8, 1948; admitted to bar, 1978, Oregon, U.S. District Court, District of Oregon and U.S. Court of Appeals, Ninth Circuit; 1979, U.S. Claims Court; 1982, Washington; 1983, U.S. District Court, Western District of Washington; 1986, U.S. Court of Appeals, Seventh Circuit; 1988, U.S. Supreme Court; 1995 U.S. Court of Appeals, Federal Circuit. *Education:* University of Washington (B.A., 1970; B.S., 1974; J.D., 1978). Member, Board of Editors, Washington Law Review, 1977-1978. Author: "Remedies for Breach of Contract," *Contract Law in Oregon,* 1991 and 1994 Supplement. Editor: 1999 and 2003 Supplement to *Contract Law in Oregon;* 2003 Revision to *Contract Law in Oregon.* Arbitrator: National Association of Securities Dealers, 1989—. ***PRACTICE AREAS:*** Investment Litigation; Complex Litigation; Appellate Practice. ***Email:*** buckley@eslerstephens.com

REPRESENTATIVE CLIENTS: Various Securities Investor Groups; AMP Life, Ltd.; Reliant Energy, Inc.; City of Bend; Metro One Communications, Inc.; Moving Floors, Inc.; American Diabetes Association, Inc.; Pewag Chain, Inc.; Citizens Utility Board; Lacey-Harmer, Inc.; Chase International Inc.; Pacific Northern Oil, Inc.; Hallco Manufacturing Co.; Ochoco Lumber Co.; Shamrock Building Materials, Inc.; Various National and Local Church Organizations; The Harris Soup Co..

KATHLEEN A. EVANS
ATTORNEY AT LAW

PORTLAND, OREGON

(See Salem)

FARLEIGH WITT

ATTORNEYS AT LAW
121 SW MORRISON STREET, SUITE 600
PORTLAND, OREGON 97204
Telephone: 503-228-6044
FAX: 503-228-1741
Email: farleighwitt.com
URL: http://www.farleighwitt.com

Banking, Bankruptcy, Commercial Litigation, Corporate, Electronic Commerce, Employment, Environmental, Estate Planning and Administration, Financial Services, Insurance Defense, Mediation/Arbitration, Real Estate, Securities, Trademark and General Business Practice.

F. SCOTT FARLEIGH, born Renton, Washington, September 11, 1946; admitted to bar, 1974, Oregon; 1976, U.S. District Court, District of Oregon; 1977, U.S. Court of Appeals, Ninth Circuit. *Education:* University of Oregon (B.S., 1968; LL.B., 1974). Member, University of Oregon Law Review, 1973-1974. *Member:* Multnomah County and American Bar Associations (Member, Sections on: Corporation, Banking and Business Law; Antitrust Law); Oregon Association of Defense Counsel. [1st Lt., Military Intelligence, 1968-1971]. ***PRACTICE AREAS:*** Corporate; Securities Regulation; Civil Litigation; Environmental. ***Email:*** SFarleigh@fwwlaw.com

BRIAN R. WITT, born Malta, Montana, May 10, 1957; admitted to bar, 1982, Oregon; 1991, Washington. *Education:* Montana State University (B.S., 1979); Willamette University (J.D., 1982). Phi Delta Phi (Magister, 1981-1982). Associate Editor, Willamette Law Review, 1981-1982. Author: Business Lawyer: "Federal Preemption of Consumer Lending Law: A Focus On Credit Unions;" "The Oregon Business Corporation Act: Revisions of Corporate Procedure and Liability," 18 Willamette Law Review 123, 1982. *Member:* Oregon State Bar (Member, Sections on: Business and Corporate Law; Financial Institutions Committee); Washington State and American (Member: Corporation, Banking and Busi-

(This Listing Continued)

FARLEIGH WITT, ATTORNEYS AT LAW, Portland—Continued

ness Law Section; Consumer Financial Services Committee; Chairman, Credit Union Committee; Cyberspace Committee) Bar Associations. ***PRACTICE AREAS:*** Financial Institutions; Corporate; Electronic Commerce. ***Email:*** BWitt@fwwlaw.com

KAREN E. SAUL, born Salem, Oregon, December 9, 1957; admitted to bar, 1983, Oregon; 1984, U.S. District Court, District of Oregon; 1985, Washington; 1986, U.S. District Court, Western District of Washington; 1993, U.S. District Court, Eastern District of Washington. *Education:* Lewis and Clark College (B.A., 1980); Willamette University (J.D., 1983). *Member:* Multnomah County, Washington State (Member, Section on: Labor/Employment) and American (Member, Sections on: Litigation; Labor/Employment) Bar Associations; Oregon State Bar (Member, Sections on: Litigation; Labor/Employment), Gus J. Solomon American Inn of Court. ***PRACTICE AREAS:*** Employment; Civil Litigation. ***Email:*** KSaul@fwwlaw.com

DEAN T. SANDOW, born San Jose, California, May 7, 1958; admitted to bar, 1984, Oregon; 1993, Washington. *Education:* Pacific Union College (B.S., 1981); Willamette University (J.D., cum laude, 1984). Member, 1982-1983 and Form Editor, 1983-1984, Willamette Law Review. *Member:* Multnomah County, Washington State (Member, Sections on: Real Property, Probate and Elder Law) and American (Member, Sections of: Business Law; Real Property, Probate and Trust) Bar Associations; Oregon State Bar (Member, Sections of: Estate Planning and Administration, Computer Law, Business and Corporate Law). ***PRACTICE AREAS:*** Financial Institutions; Estate Planning; Estate Administration; Corporate; General Business; Technology. ***Email:*** DSandow@fwwlaw.com

VALERIE TOMASI AUERBACH, born Staten Island, New York, February 18, 1958; admitted to bar, 1984, Oregon and U.S. District Court, District of Oregon. *Education:* University of Rhode Island (B.A., High distinction, 1979); Northwestern School of Law (J.D., 1984). Phi Beta Kappa; Phi Kappa Phi. *Member:* Multnomah County and American (Member, Business and Real Property Sections) Bar Associations; Oregon State Bar (Member, Sections on: Real Estate and Land Use; Debtor/Creditor). ***PRACTICE AREAS:*** Real Estate; Construction; Creditors' Rights and Remedies; Collections; Financial Institutions. ***Email:*** VAuerbach@fwwlaw.com

PETER C. McKITTRICK, born St. Louis, Missouri, June 8, 1959; admitted to bar, 1985, Oregon and U.S. District Court, District of Oregon. *Education:* Lewis and Clark College (B.S., 1981); Willamette University College of Law (J.D., cum laude, 1985). Certified Business Bankruptcy Specialist, 2002. Co-Author: "Chapter 7 Overview: Redemption and Reaffirmation," Bankruptcy Law (Oregon CLE 1999). *Member:* Multnomah County and American (Member, Business and General Sections) Bar Associations; Oregon State Bar (Member, Debtor/Creditor and Business Law Sections; Chair, 2005 and Member, Executive Committee); American Bankruptcy Institute. ***PRACTICE AREAS:*** Commercial and Consumer Bankruptcy; Creditors' Rights and Remedies; Corporate. ***Email:*** PMckittrick@fwwlaw.com

BRAD C. STANFORD, born Oakland, California, February 1, 1959; admitted to bar, 1985, Oregon; 1991, U.S. District Court, District of Oregon and U.S. Court of Appeals, Ninth Circuit; 1994, Washington. *Education:* University of California at Berkeley; University of Oregon (B.S., 1981); University of Washington (J.D., 1985). Phi Beta Kappa. Member, Mortar Board. *Member:* Multnomah County, Oregon State and Washington State Bar Associations; Oregon State Bar; Association of Ski Defense Attorneys; Federation of Defense and Corporate Counsel. (Certified in Civil Trial Advocacy by the National Board of Trial Advocacy). ***PRACTICE AREAS:*** Business and Tort Litigation; General Litigation. ***Email:*** BStanford@fwwlaw.com

HAROLD B. SCOGGINS, III, born Oklahoma City, Oklahoma, July 10, 1962; admitted to bar, 1991, Oregon; 1992, Washington. *Education:* Hampden-Sydney College (B.A., 1984); George Mason University (J.D., 1991). *Member:* Washington State (Member, Creditor/Debtor Section) and American (Member: Business Law Section; Consumer Finance and Credit Union Committees) Bar Associations; Oregon State Bar (Member, Debtor/Creditor Section). ***PRACTICE AREAS:*** Financial Services Law; Commercial; Business and Consumer Collections; Bankruptcy. ***Email:*** HScoggins@fwwlaw.com

DAVID R. LUDWIG, born Chicago, Illinois, May 8, 1952; admitted to bar, 1978, Oregon; 1980, U.S. Court of Appeals, Ninth Circuit and U.S. District Court, District of Oregon; 1981, U.S. Tax Court. *Education:* University of Oregon (B.A., 1975; J.D., 1978). Phi Delta Phi. Oregon Survey Editor, Oregon Law Review, 1977-1978. Author: Casenote, 57 Oregon Law Review 602, 1978. *Member:* Multnomah County and American (Member, Sections on: Business; Real Property, Probate and Trust; Tax) Bar Associations; Oregon State Bar (Member, Sections on: Business Law; Securities Regulation; Real Estate and Land Use; Member, Executive Committee, 1996-2002, and Chair, 2001, Securities Regulation, 1996-2002). ***PRACTICE AREAS:*** Corporate; Securities; Real Estate; Merger and Acquisitions. ***Email:*** DLudwig@fwwlaw.com

KATHRYN P. SALYER, born Rich Hill, Missouri, June 11, 1959; admitted to bar, 1988, Oregon. *Education:* University of Maryland (B.A., 1985); University of Oregon (J.D., 1988). Order of the Coif. Associate Editor, Oregon Law Review, 1988. Author: Casende, 67 Oregon Law Review 901 (1988). *Member:* Federal Bar Association; Oregon Association of Defense Counsel. ***PRACTICE AREAS:*** Litigation; Creditors' Rights; Insurance Defense; Fraud; Securities Litigation. ***Email:*** KSalyer@fwwlaw.com

TARA J. SCHLEICHER, admitted to bar, 1995, Oregon. *Education:* Oregon State University (B.S., 1990); Willamette University (J.D., cum laude; M.M., 1995). Associate Editor, Willamette University Law Review, 1994-1995. Author: "A Tale of Two Courts: Differences between Oregon's Approach and the United States Supreme Court's Approach to Fifth Amendment Takings Claims," 31 Willamette L.R. 817 (Fall, 1995); "Post-Chicago Antitrust Theory: Implications for Marketing Practice, " 16 Journal of Public Policy and Marketing 310 (Fall, 1997). ***PRACTICE AREAS:*** Creditors' Rights; Bankruptcy; Litigation; Estate Planning. ***Email:*** TSchleicher@fwwlaw.com

---

MICHELLE M. BERTOLINO, born San Diego, California, September 9, 1963; admitted to bar, 1991, Oregon; 1996, U.S. District Court, District of Oregon; 1997, Washington and U.S. District Court, Western and Eastern District of Washington. *Education:* Willamette University (B.S., 1986; J.D., 1991). *Member:* Multnomah County and Washington State Bar Associations; Oregon State Bar (Member, Pro Bono Subcommittee, Debtor/Creditor Section). ***PRACTICE AREAS:*** Collections; Debtor and Creditor; Bankruptcy; Creditors' Rights. ***Email:*** mbertolino@fwwlaw.com

ROBERT N. MURASKI, admitted to bar, 2000, Oregon. *Education:* DePaul University (B.S., 1995); University of Oregon (M.B.A., 1998; J.D., 2000). Associate Editor, Oregon Law Review, 1998-2000. Author, "Multidisciplinary Practices and The Legal Profession: An Uncertain Future," Oregon Law Review, Spring, 2000. *Member:* Multnomah and American (Member, Business Law Section) Bar Associations; Oregon State Bar (Member: Business, Tax, and Securities Sections). ***PRACTICE AREAS:*** Corporate Law; Business Law; Securities; Tax Law. ***Email:*** rmuraski@fwwlaw.com

KIMBERLEY A. HANKS MC GAIR, born Dayton, Ohio, April 20, 1973; admitted to bar, 1998, Oregon; 1999, U.S. District Court, District of Oregon and U.S. Court of Appeals, Ninth Circuit; 2000, Washington. *Education:* University of Oregon (B.A., cum laude, 1994); Northwestern School of Law (J.D., cum laude, 1998). *Member:* Multnomah County and American Bar Associations; Oregon State Bar; Oregon Association of Defense Counsel; America Inns of Court. ***PRACTICE AREAS:*** Civil Litigation; Employment Law; Creditors' Rights. ***Email:*** kmcgair@fwwlaw.com

MICHELLE HOLMAN KERIN, admitted to bar, 1996, Oregon; 1997, Washington, U.S. District Court, District of Oregon and U.S. District Court, Western District of Washington. *Education:* University of California at San Diego (B.A., 1993); Northwestern School of Law (J.D., 1996). Member, Northwestern School of Law Review. *Member:* Multnomah County Bar Association (Member: Federal Practice and Procedure Committee); Oregon State Bar (Member: Executive Committee, Civil Rights Section; Uniform Jury Instructions-Civil Committee, Employment & Labor Section); Washington State Bar (Member, Employment & Labor Section); Oregon Women Lawyers. ***PRACTICE AREAS:*** Commercial Litigation; Employment and Labor. ***Email:*** MKerin@fwwlaw.com

CONNIE L. SPECK, born Eugene, Oregon, March 22, 1963; admitted to bar, 1996, Oregon. *Education:* University of Oregon (B.S., magna cum laude, 1993; J.D., 1996). Student Bar Representative, 1995-1996. *Member:* Oregon State Bar (Member, Procedure and Practice Committee); Oregon Women Lawyers (Member, Board of Directors). ***PRACTICE AREAS:*** Employment Law; Financial Services Law; Commercial Law.

OF COUNSEL

LAURY H. HENNINGS, born Fresno, California, May 1, 1946; admitted to bar, 1976, Oregon; 1977, U.S. District Court, District of Oregon and U.S. Court of Appeals, Ninth Circuit. *Education:* Williamette University (B.A., 1967); Northwestern School of Law of Lewis and Clark College (J.D., 1976). *Member:* Multnomah County Bar Association, Oregon State Bar. ***PRACTICE AREAS:*** Financial Institutions; Corporate; Securities; Real Estate; Commercial Law. ***Email:*** lhennings@fwwlaw.com

REPRESENTATIVE CLIENTS: Bank of the West; JP Morgan Chase Bank, National Association; Citicorp Vendor Finance, Inc.; City of Vancouver; City of Battle Ground; Clackamas County Bank; IQ Credit Union; Credit Union Association of Oregon; CWS Corp.; Digimarc Corporation; Dimera Incorporated; Emmert International; Eurobest Food Industries, Inc.; Evanite Fiber Corp.; First Bank System; First Technology Credit Union; First Citizens Bank; Hampton Affiliates; Harland Financial Services; Health Care Services, LLC; Hillsboro Garbage Disposal, Inc.; Home Street Bank; Key Bank; Mt. Ashland Ski Area; Mt. Hood Meadows; Northwest Nordic, Inc.; Northwest Community Credit Union; Park Place Wood Products, Inc.; Peco Manufacturing Co., Inc.; Portland Teachers Credit Union; Protection One Alarm Monitoring, Inc.; Rainier Pacific Bank; S.A. Piazza & Associates, LLC; SICO America, Inc.; Silicon Valley Bank; Ski Bowl; S/B Systran Financial Services Corp.; Textron Financial Corporation; Timberline Lodge; Tualatin Hotel Partners LLC; U.S. Bancorp Equipment Finance; U.S. Bank; Umpqua Bank; Washington State Employees Credit Union; Washington Credit Union League; Wells Fargo Bank; Willamette Pass Ski Area.

MARY ELLEN PAGE FARR

0324 S.W. ABERNETHY STREET
PORTLAND, OREGON 97239
Telephone: 503-224-9133
Fax: 503-827-5060
Email: mefarr@qwest.net

Litigation, Business Litigation, Employment Law, Sexual Harassment, Wrongful Termination, Personal Injury, Insurance Coverage, Discrimination, Automobile Accidents, Premises Liability, Negligence, Wrongful Death, Slip and Fall, Contracts, Business Law.

MARY ELLEN PAGE FARR, born Portland, Oregon, December 18, 1948; admitted to bar, 1982, Oregon, U.S. District Court, District of Oregon and U.S. Court of Appeals, Ninth and Federal Circuits; U.S. Supreme Court. *Education:* Portland State University (B.A., with honors, 1970); University of Pennsylvania (Ph.D., 1977); Lewis and Clark College (J.D., cum laude, 1982). Member, American Judicature Society; U.S. District Court of Oregon Historical Society. *Member:* Oregon State Bar; Oregon Trial Lawyers Association; National Lawyers Guild. ***LANGUAGES:*** Persian.

MARGARET FIORINO

Established in 1999
P.O. BOX 14068
PORTLAND, OREGON 97293-0068
Telephone: 503-224-1551
Facsimile: 503-233-0785
Email: mfiorino@easystreet.com
URL: http://www.lawyers.com/fiorinolaw
Mailing Address: P.O. Box 14068, Portland, OR 97293-0068

Trust and Estate Litigation, Insurance Coverage Litigation, Elder Financial Abuse Litigation, Guardianship and Conservatorship Litigation, Contested Wills, Medical Malpractice, Appellate Practice, Wrongful Death, Probate Litigation.

(This Listing Continued)

FIRM PROFILE: Margaret Fiorino is a sole practitioner after having worked as a general litigator for ten years in one of Portland's largest and most prestigious law firms. She is well-respected by lawyers as her client base is primarily based on referrals from other attorneys. Her experience is wide-ranging, from serving as counsel for insurers in environmental insurance coverage litigation to handling a nationally reported murder trial in federal court trying to establish that her clients' mother was murdered by her third husband in 1992 (Gorham v. Schlosser, US Dist Ct. Case No. 01-CV-1763-ST) to establishing the tort of intentional interference with prospective inheritance in the Oregon Supreme Court. She is efficient, easy-going, well-respected by judges as well as lawyers, and well-liked by her clients, who range from corporations and financial institutions to individuals in difficult situations.

MARGARET FIORINO, born Tacoma, Washington, September 25, 1949; admitted to bar, 1982, Oregon. *Education:* Oregon State University (B.A., 1972); Oregon State University (MBA Program) and University of Oregon (Graduate Philosophy Program) (1972 - 1978); University of Oregon (J.D., 1981). Judicial Clerk to Chief Judge George M. Joseph, Oregon Court of Appeals, 1981-1983. Author: Oregon State Bar 1999 CLE Aviation Insurance Supplement; "Recent Developments and Current Issues in Probate Litigation," Oregon Law Institute, July 24, 1998; "Premediation Considerations," Oregon Law Institute, July 30, 1999; "No Contest Clauses," Oregon Law Institute October 2, 2002; "Statute of Limitations Issues in Estate Claims," Oregon Law Institute, March 12, 2004. Associate, 1983-1990 and Partner, 1990-1993, Miller, Nash, Wiener, Hager & Carlsen. *Member:* Multnomah County Bar Association; Oregon State Bar; Ninth Circuit Court of Appeals Bar; Oregon Women Lawyers. ***REPORTED CASES:*** Allen v. Hall, 139 F3d 716 (9th Cir 1998), 328 Or276, 974 P2d 199 (Or Supreme Ct 1999). ***PRACTICE AREAS:*** Trust and Estate Litigation; Insurance Litigation; Contested Wills; Medical Malpractice; Appellate Practice; Elder Abuse; Guardianship and Conservatorship; Probate Litigation.

JUSTINE FISCHER

Established in 1989

720 S.W. WASHINGTON STREET, SUITE 750
PORTLAND, OREGON 97205
Telephone: 503-222-4326
Telecopier: 503-222-6567
Email: jfattyor@aol.com

Securities, Antitrust and Business Litigation and Class Actions in Federal and State Courts.

JUSTINE FISCHER, born Albany, New York, May 17, 1946; admitted to bar, 1972, District of Columbia; 1981, Oregon. *Education:* Smith College (B.A., 1968); University of Chicago (J.D., 1971). Editor, Federal Civil Litigation in Oregon; Oregon State Bar, 1994. Author: Unauthorized Practice Handbook, American Bar Foundation, 1972. Clinical Instructor and Assistant Director, Legal Technician Program, Antioch School of Law, 1974-1975. Senior Trial Attorney, U.S. Department of Transportation, Washington, D.C., 1976-1980. *Member:* Multnomah County (Member, Committee on Professionalism, 1986-1988) Bar Association; The District of Columbia Bar; Oregon State Bar (Member: Executive Committee, Antitrust Section, 1983-1992; Federal Practice and Procedure Committee, 1988-1992; Executive Committee, Securities Regulation Section, 1995-2003; Chair, 2002).

ANN L. FISHER

AF Legal and Consulting Services

Established in 1996

2005 SW 71ST AVENUE
PORTLAND, OREGON 97225-3705
Telephone: 503-721-0181
Fax: 503-223-2305
Email: afisherl@qwest.net
Email: enerGlaw@aol.com
URL: http://www.lawyers.com/annfisher

General Business and Commercial Law, Contracts and Litigation, Real Estate, Energy and Utility Law, Mediation Services.

ANN L. FISHER, born Reading, Pennsylvania, March 31, 1948; admitted to bar, 1984, Oregon; 1987, Washington, U.S. District Court, District of Oregon, U.S. District Court, Eastern and Western Districts of Washington and U.S. Court Of Appeals 9th and Federal Circuits. *Education:* Oregon State University (B.S., 1975); Willamette University (J.D., 1983). Author and Speaker: Ethics, Energy and Restructuring Issues, Course Materials, 1993-2002. Pro tem Judge, 1995—. *Member:* Oregon State Bar (Member: MCLE, Chair, 1992-1997; Disciplinary Board, 1993-1998, Region 5 Chair, 1995-1997; Ethics Committee, 1998-2001; Chair, Utility Section, 2001-2002); Federal Energy Bar Association (Member, Ethics Committee).

GEORGE P. FISHER, ATTORNEY AT LAW

3635 S.W. DOSCH ROAD
PORTLAND, OREGON 97239-1427
Telephone: 503-224-7730
Fax: 503-227-2429
Email: george.fisher@gpf-law.com
URL: http://www.gpf-law.com

Labor Law, Employment Law, Contracts.

GEORGE P. FISHER, born Huntington, New York, February 17, 1949; admitted to bar, 1991, Oregon. *Education:* Hope College (B.A., 1972); University of North Dakota (J.D., 1990); North Dakota State University. *Member:* Multnomah County, Washington County and American Bar Associations; Oregon State Bar; National Employment Lawyers Association; Oregon Trial Lawyers Association (Member, Employment Section). ***PRACTICE AREAS:*** Labor Law (60%); Employment Law (30%); Contracts (10%).

(This Listing Continued)

FISHER & PHILLIPS LLP

Established in 1943

SUITE 1600, 1001 S.W. FIFTH AVENUE
PORTLAND, OREGON 97204
Telephone: 503-242-4262
Fax: 503-242-4263
Email: fp@laborlawyers.com
URL: http://www.laborlawyers.com

Atlanta, Georgia Office: 1500 Resurgens Plaza, 945 East Paces Ferry Road, 30326-1125. Telephone: 404-231-1400. Fax: 404-240-4249.
Charlotte, North Carolina Office: Suite 2020, 227 West Trade Street, 28202. Telephone: 704-334-4565. Fax: 704-334-9774.
Chicago, Illinois Office: 1000 Marquette Building, 140 South Dearborn Street, 60603. Telephone: 312-346-8061. Fax: 312-346-3179.
Columbia, South Carolina Office: Suite 1400, 1901 Main Street, 29201. Telephone: 803-255-0000. Fax: 803-255-0202.
Dallas, Texas Office: 4343 Thanksgiving Tower, 1601 Elm Street, 75201. Telephone: 214-220-9100. Fax: 214-220-9122.
Fort Lauderdale, Florida Office: Suite 800, 450 East Las Olas Boulevard, 33301. Telephone: 954-525-4800. Fax: 954-525-8739.
Irvine, California Office: Suite 400, 18400 Von Karman Avenue, 92612. Telephone: 949-851-2424. Fax: 949-851-0152.
Kansas City, Missouri Office: Suite 400, 104 West Ninth Street, 64105. Telephone: 816-842-8770. Fax: 816-842-8767.
Las Vegas, Nevada Office: Suite 650, 3993 Howard Hughes Parkway, 89109. Telephone: 702-252-3131. Fax: 702-252-7411.
New Orleans, Louisiana Office: Suite 3710, 201 St. Charles Avenue, 70170. Telephone: 504-522-3303. Fax: 504-529-3850.
Oakland, California Office: City Center, Suite 200, 501 Fourteenth Street, 94612. Telephone: 510-763-4411. Fax: 510-763-4418.
Orlando, Florida Office: 1250 Lincoln Plaza, 300 South Orange Avenue, 32801. Telephone: 407-541-0888. Fax: 407-541-0887.
San Diego, California Office: 4225 Executive Square, Suite 950, La Jolla, California, 92037. Telephone: 858-597-9600. Fax: 858-597-9601.
Somerset, New Jersey Office: Corporate Park III, Third Floor, 580 Howard Avenue, 08873. Telephone: 732-560-7100. Fax: 732-560-0788.
Tampa, Florida Office: Suite 2525, 401 East Jackson Street, 33602. Telephone: 813-769-7500. Fax: 813-769-7501.

Labor and Employment, Alternative Dispute Resolution, Arbitration, Business Immigration, Collective Bargaining, Employment Discrimination, Labor Relations, Mergers, Acquisitions and Divestitures, Occupational Safety and Health, Pension and Benefits, Sexual Harassment, Wage and Hour, Whistleblower Litigation, Wrongful Termination.

FIRM PROFILE: Fisher & Phillips LLP, a national law firm founded in 1943, was one of the first law firms to center its practice on representing employers in labor and employment matters. Now one of the largest in the field, the firm has maintained its commitment to helping employers find innovative legal and practical solutions to their business needs by offering management preventive advice and litigation defense. Working in many areas of employment law, the firm's attorneys offer a wide breadth of expertise covering such traditional subjects as NLRB practice, EEOC, wage and hour, and disability law, as well as business immigration, pension and benefits, education law and occupational safety and health. In addition to defending employers in labor cases, Fisher & Phillips attorneys help their clients to minimize litigation risks through the development of effective contracts, policies and procedures and through training supervisors and administrators in practical compliance strategies and dispute resolution. The firm's integrated communications systems and network of ten offices from coast to coast enable its attorneys to handle matters promptly and efficiently in any state. Its focus on labor law permits the firm to provide cost-effective services to employers ranging from large multi-national companies to small, family-owned businesses. Firm attorneys participate actively in state and local bar associations and in many charitable organizations and public service activities.

Fisher & Phillips LLP represents employers in a broad range of industries including hospitality, health care, automotive, manufacturing, transportation and logistics, credit unions, banks and financial institutions, private schools, colleges and universities, state and local governments, legal and professional service firms, insurance and related services, and non-profit organizations.

MEMBERS OF FIRM

CLARENCE M. BELNAVIS, born Kingston, Jamaica, January 17, 1969; admitted to bar, 1994, Oregon (active); 1996, District of Columbia (inactive). *Education:* Florida Atlantic University (B.A., 1991); Howard University (J.D., 1994). Moot Court Team; Howard University Law Journal; Named: Top 40 Under 40, Portland Business Journal, 2003. Co-Author, "The Impact of Medical Marijuana Laws on Employment in the Wild, Wild West", Oregon Civil Rights Newsletter (October, 2000). Board Member, Morrison Child and Family Services, 2002-2005. Member, Owen M. Panner Chapter of the American Inns of Court, 1998-2002. Panelist, Panel Discussion of Grutter v. Bolinger, ABA Equal Justice Seminar, 2003. *Member:* National Bar Association (Assistant Executive Director, Region 9, 2001-2002; President, Oregon Chapter, 1997); Association of Oregon Black Lawyers (President, 1997). ***PRACTICE AREAS:*** Labor and Employment Law (Counseling and Litigation); Collective Bargaining; Employment Investigations; Employment Law Training. ***Email:*** cbelnavis@laborlawyers.com

RICHARD R. MENEGHELLO, born Jersey City, New Jersey, September 29, 1971; admitted to bar, 1996, Oregon. *Education:* Syracuse University (A.B., 1993); Georgia State

(This Listing Continued)

FISHER & PHILLIPS LLP, Portland—Continued

University College of Law (J.D., cum laude, 1996). *Member:* Oregon State Bar (Past Chair, Executive Committee, Disability Law Section; Executive Committee, Civil Rights Section). ***PRACTICE AREAS:*** Labor and Employment; Americans with Disabilities Act (ADA); Employment Discrimination; Employment-Related Torts; Grievance Arbitration; Non-Compete and Trade Secrets Litigation; Race Discrimination; Retaliation; Sex and Same Sex Harassment; Trial Practice; Workplace Violence. ***Email:*** rmeneghello@laborlawyers.com

SENIOR COUNSEL

CORBETT GORDON, born Chicago, Illinois, September 16, 1946; admitted to bar, 1982, Oregon; 2003, Washington; U.S. Supreme Court. *Education:* Antioch College (B.A., 1969); Harvard University (J.D., 1980). Named: Best Lawyers in America, 2001—; Named: Chambers USA America's Leading Business Lawyers, 2003—. Past Master and Member, Executive Committee, Gus J. Solomon Inns of Court. Judicial Clerk, Chief Judge Frank J. Battisti, Northern District of Ohio, 1980-1981. Co-Author: "The Departing Employee," Oregon State Bar, 1983—; "Appearing Before the Bureau of Labor and Industries," Oregon State Bar, 1995. Adjunct Professor, Employment Law, Willamette University College of Law, 1992-1996. *Member:* Oregon State Bar (Member, Diversity Section, Past Best Practices Committee Chair; Past Member: Executive Committee, Labor Law and Employment Section; Executive Committee, Rights of the Handicapped and Rights of Persons with Disabilities Section; Executive Committee, Civil Rights Section: Past Chair, Editorial Board); Washington State Bar Association (Appointed by the Board of Governors, Civil Rights Committee, 2004—). ***PRACTICE AREAS:*** Labor and Employment Defense; Appeals; Collective Bargaining and Arbitration; Diversity and Cultural Competency Awareness and Training; Drug and Alcohol Testing; Employment Policies and Procedures; Fair Labor Standards Act (FLSA); Litigation; Non-Competition and Trade Secrets Agreements; Personnel and Supervisor Training; Sexual Harassment. ***Email:*** cgordon@laborlawyers.com

OF COUNSEL

MITCHELL C. BAKER, born Tacoma, Washington, February 12, 1970; admitted to bar, 1998, Oregon. *Education:* Western Washington University (B.A., 1994); Lewis and Clark College (J.D., 1997). ***PRACTICE AREAS:*** Labor and Employment; Breach of Employment Contract; Complex Litigation; Confidentiality Agreements; Employment Counseling; Harassment in the Workplace; Manager Training; Non-Competition Law; Reductions in Force (RIF); Retaliatory Discharge; Trade and Unfair Competition; Worker Adjustment and Retraining Notification Act (WARN). ***Email:*** mbaker@laborlawyers.com

ASSOCIATES

RACHELLE HONG BARTON, admitted to bar, 2002, California; 2005, Oregon. *Education:* University of California, Berkeley (B.A., 1999); University of Notre Dame (J.D., 2002). ***PRACTICE AREAS:*** Labor and Employment; Employment Termination; Labor and Employment Litigation; Race and Gender Discrimination; Wrongful Termination. ***Email:*** rbarton@laborlawyers.com

HEIDI GUETTLER, born Portland, Oregon, February 8, 1966; admitted to bar, 1994, Oregon. *Education:* Gonzaga University (B.A., 1988); Willamette University College of Law (J.D., 1993). ***PRACTICE AREAS:*** Labor and Employment; Appellate Practice; Compliance Audits and Counseling; Defense Litigation; Education Law; I-9 Compliance; Independent Contractor/Employee Status; Recordkeeping Obligations; Religious Discrimination; Sex Discrimination; Title VII. ***Email:*** hguettler@laborlawyers.com

JOSEPH J. HADDAD, born Portland, Oregon, May 20, 1974; admitted to bar, 2000, Oregon. *Education:* University of Michigan (B.A., 1996); University of Oregon (J.D., 2000). ***PRACTICE AREAS:*** Labor and Employment; Age Discrimination in Employment Act (ADEA); Alternative Dispute Resolution (ADR); Employment Litigation; Family and Medical Leave Act (FMLA); National Origin Discrimination; Preventive Labor and Employment Law; Wage and Hour Litigation; Wrongful Discharge. ***Email:*** jhaddad@laborlawyers.com

(For complete biographical data on attorneys in other offices, see Professional Biographies at those locations)

JEFFREY FOOTE & ASSOCIATES, P.C.

Established in 1988

1515 S.W. FIFTH AVENUE, SUITE 808
PORTLAND, OREGON 97201
Telephone: 503-228-1133
Fax: 503-228-1556
Email: jfoote@footelaw.com
URL: http://www.footelaw.com

Civil Trial Practice including Personal Injury, Vehicle Rollover and Auto Products Liability, Professional Negligence, Medical Malpractice, Products Liability, Automobile Accidents, Wrongful Death, Legal Malpractice.

JEFFREY P. FOOTE, born Portland, Oregon, August 11, 1949; admitted to bar, 1974, Oregon and U.S. District Court, District of Oregon. *Education:* University of Oregon (B.S., 1971); Lewis and Clark College (J.D., 1974). Recipient, Public Justice Award, Oregon Trial Lawyers Association, 1993; Steven J. Sharp Public Service Award, Association of Trial Lawyers of America, 1998. Finalist, Trial Lawyer of the Year, Trial Lawyer for Public Justice, 1998. Author: "Wilderness—A Question of Purity," 3 Environmental Law 255, 1973; "The Bonneville Power Administration: Northwest Power Broker," 6 Environmental Law 831, 1976; "Natural Disaster Claims," Trial Magazine, Vol. 21, No. 4, April 1, 1985, p. 36; "Stock Exchange Rules," Trial Magazine, Vol. 21, No. 12, December, 1985, p. 33; "Representing Catastrophically Injured Clients," Trial Magazine, Vol. 35. No. 4, April, 1999. p. 36; "When Your Client is a Grieving Family," Trial Magazine, Vol. 40, No. 2 p. 24, February 2003; "Rescission and Cancellation," Oregon *Civil Pleading and Practice,* Chapter 60, 1985 Revision, Oregon State Bar; "Medical Expenses," Oregon State Bar Damages, Chapter 7, 1990; "Interstate Trucking Litigation, "Personal Injury Handbook: Forms and procedures, James Publishing Co., 1991. Professor (Part-Time), Lewis and Clark Law School, 1975-1977. Lecturer on Civil Trial issues, including Personal Injury, Products Liability, Trial Strategy and Securities law, in conjunction with Continuing Legal Education programs before the Association of Trial Lawyers of America, Attorney's Information Exchange Group (Member, Board of Directors, 2001—), Oregon Trial Lawyers Association, Washington State Trial Lawyers Association, California Trial Lawyers Association, Idaho Trial Lawyers Association, Louisiana Trial Lawyers Association, New Mexico Trial Lawyers Association, Oklahoma Trial Lawyers Association, Montana Trial Lawyers Association, Wyoming Trial Lawyers Association, Oregon Law Institute and the Oregon State Bar. Executive Director, Natural Resources Law Institute, 1974-1977. Deputy City Attorney, City of Portland, Oregon, 1977-1979. Member, 1984-1986 and Vice Chairman, 1985-1986, Oregon Council on Court Procedures. Trustee, Citizens Oregon Lawyers Trust, 1988-1991. Recipient, Public Justice Award, Oregon Trial Lawyers Association, 1993. *Member:* Multnomah County and Washington State Bar Associations; Oregon State Bar (Member, Procedure and Practice Committee, 1988-1989; House of Delegates, 1996-2000); The Association of Trial Lawyers of America (State Delegate, 1983-1990; Board of Governors, 1991-2000); Oregon Trial Lawyers Association (Member, Board of Governors, 1981-2000; President, 1990-1991); Washington State Trial Lawyers Association; Trial Lawyers for Public Justice (Founder, Member, Board of Directors, 1986—; President, 1992-1993); Roscoe Pound Foundation (Fellow, 1992—). ***PRACTICE AREAS:*** Personal Injury; Professional Negligence; Products Liability; Toxic Torts. ***Email:*** jfoote@footelaw.com

RONALD F. WEBSTER, born Centralia, Washington, July 10, 1968; admitted to bar, 2001, Oregon. *Education:* Portland State University (B.A., 1993); Temple University School of Law (J.D., 2001). Member, Temple Law Review. *Member:* Multnomah County Bar Association; Oregon State Bar; The Association of Trial Lawyers of America (Member, Board of Governors, New Lawyer Division, 2004—); Trial Lawyers for Public Justice. ***PRACTICE AREAS:*** Personal Injury; Medical Negligence; Products Liability; Professional Negligence. ***Email:*** rwebster@footelaw.com

FOSTER PEPPER TOOZE LLP

Established in 1904

601 S.W. SECOND AVENUE, SUITE 1800
PORTLAND, OREGON 97204-3171
Telephone: 503-221-0607
Facsimile: 503-221-1510
URL: http://www.foster.com

New Address Effective October 25, 2003: 601 SW Second Avenue, Suite 1800, Portland, Oregon 97204-3171.

Seattle, Washington Office: Foster Pepper & Shefelman PLLC, 34th Floor, 1111 Third Avenue. Telephone: 206-447-4400. Facsimile: 206-447-9700.

Spokane, Washington Office: Foster Pepper & Shefelman PLLC, W. 422 Riverside Avenue, Suite 1310. Telephone: 509-777-1600. Facsimile: 509-777-1616.

Banks and Banking, Business Law, Business Acquisitions, Divestitures and Reorganizations, Civil Litigation, Cooperative Law, Corporate Finance, Corporate Law, Creditor's Rights and Bankruptcy, Emerging Companies and High Growth Companies, Environmental Law, Estate Planning, Health Care, Intellectual Property, Labor and Employment, Land Use, Real Estate, Securities, Sports Law, Taxation.

FIRM PROFILE: Foster Pepper & Shefelman PLLC is one of the larger law firms in the Pacific Northwest maintaining a strong regional presence in Washington and Oregon. Our tradition of service dates from early in the century. Since 1904 our lawyers have been shaping the development of the region by providing creative, practical advice.

We have developed a broad base of 30 major practice areas in which our lawyers focus their legal talent. These practice groups, which are listed above, are concentrated in particular industries or areas of law. We actively promote the integration of these specialties to ensure a cohesive, interdepartmental approach to client representation. We have the necessary experience to concentrate resources quickly on large projects requiring fast turn-around as well as efficiently staff smaller less complex matters.

Foster Pepper is a member of Interlaw, an international network of independent law firms from around the world. Interlaw has approximately 60 member firms with more than 3,200 attorneys in 100 major commercial centers located in North, Central and South America, Europe and the Middle East, Africa, Asia and the Pacific. We are the representative firm in the Pacific Northwest.

JAMES P. WETER (1877-1959)

F. M. ROBERTS (1880-1973)

W. V. TANNER (1881-1953)

JOHN P. GARVIN (1888-1972)

HAROLD S. SHEFELMAN (1898-1984)

JAMES C. HARPER (1915-1993)

ARTHUR S. QUIGLEY, admitted to bar, 1942, Washington (Not admitted in Oregon). (Retired)

THOMAS B. FOSTER (1915-1999)

WILLARD HATCH (Not admitted in Oregon; Retired)

RESIDENT PARTNERS OF FIRM

NEALE E. CREAMER, born Los Angeles, California; admitted to bar, 1961, California; 1978, Oregon. *Education:* Stanford University (A.B., 1958; LL.B., 1960). *Member:*

(This Listing Continued)

Multnomah County and American Bar Associations; State Bar of California (Member, Tax Section); Oregon State Bar. ***PRACTICE AREAS:*** Taxation; Estate Planning; Cooperative Law; Corporate Law. ***Email:*** crean@fosterpdx.com

GORDON E. CRIM, born Hartford, Connecticut, 1954; admitted to bar, 1993, Oregon; 2003, Washington. *Education:* Stanford University (B.A., 1977); Lewis & Clark College, Northwestern School of Law (J.D., cum laude, 1993). Associate Editor, Environmental Law, 1993. Member, Bank Counsel Division, Oregon Bankers Association. *Member:* Oregon State Bar; Multnomah and Washington State Bar Associations. ***LANGUAGES:*** German. ***PRACTICE AREAS:*** Business Law; Corporate Finance; Securities; Banks and Banking; Banking Regulation. ***Email:*** crimg@fosterpdx.com

MICHAEL J. GENTRY, admitted to bar, 1971, Oregon. *Education:* University of Missouri (B.S., 1968); University of Michigan (J.D., 1971). *Member:* Multnomah and American Bar Associations; Oregon State Bar; Oregon Association of Defense Counsel. ***PRACTICE AREAS:*** Insurance Defense; Business Litigation; Employment Law; Products Liability. ***Email:*** gentm@fosterpdx.com

PAUL B. GEORGE, born Twin Falls, Idaho, March 8, 1947; admitted to bar, 1973, California; 1999, Oregon; U.S. District Court, Central, Northern and Southern Districts of California. *Education:* University of Oregon (B.S., with honors, 1969); University of San Francisco (J.D., 1972). Phi Alpha Delta. Instructor: Hastings College of Trial Advocacy, University of California, 1986-1991; Federal Bar Association, Bankruptcy Seminar Panelist on trying cases in Bankruptcy Court and Complex Litigation. Lecturer: "Contracts and Litigation in U.S. Courts," le Centre de Formation Profesionelle de Barreaux de Paris, presented by the CFPP, 1992; "Closing Arguments," presented by the Hastings Center for Trial and Appellate Advocacy, Advocacy Fundamentals Program, Irvine, California, 1989; "Opening Statements," presented by the Center for Trial and Appellate Advocacy, Hastings College of the Law, Advocacy Fundamentals Program, Los Angeles, California, 1986. Moderator and Speaker, "A Workshop in Trial Strategy and Technique," Orange County Bankruptcy Forum, 1995. Moderator: "Bankruptcy and Complex Litigation, The Interplay Between Bankruptcy and Non-Bankruptcy Courts," presented by the Federal Bar Association, Orange County Bankruptcy Forum, Orange County Bar Association, 1994; "The Impact of Bankruptcy on Complex Litigation" more of "What Civil Litigators Need to Know About Bankruptcy," Federal Bar Association, Orange County Chapter, 1993. Panelist: "Basic Bankruptcy for the California Attorney," Orange County Bar Association, 1993; "What Civil Litigators Need to Know About Bankruptcy," Orange County Federal Bar Association, 1991; "Trial Workshop and Trial Techniques," Orange County Bankruptcy Forum; "Handling the Short, Non-Jury Civil Case," California Continuing Education of the Bar, 1986; "Using Documentary and Demonstrative Evidence Effectively," California Continuing Education of the Bar, 1984. Faculty Leader, "Advanced Advocacy Program, Business Tort Litigation, Hastings College of the Law, Center for Trial and Appellate Advocacy, 1985-1989. Elliott Inn of Court (Master of the Bench). *Member:* Orange County Bar Association; State Bar of California; Oregon State Bar; American Inns of Court. ***Email:*** georp@fosterpdx.com

CURT B. GLEAVES, born Portland, Oregon, February 20, 1957; admitted to bar, 1982, Oregon; 2003, Washington. *Education:* Stanford University (A.B., 1979), Phi Beta Kappa; University of California, Hastings College of the Law (J.D., 1982). Order of the Coif. Executive Committee, Securities Regulation Section, Oregon State Bar, 1984-1990. Chair, Securities Regulation Section, Oregon State Bar, 1988-1989. Adjunct Professor, Securities Regulation, Lewis & Clark College, Northwestern School of Law, 1990. ***PRACTICE AREAS:*** Business Law; Corporate Law; Corporate Finance; Securities; Mergers, Acquisitions and Divestitures. ***Email:*** gleac@fosterpdx.com

WILLIAM P. HUTCHISON, born Portland, Oregon; admitted to bar, 1969, Oregon. *Education:* University of Oregon (B.S., 1963); Willamette University (J.D., 1969). Member, Oregon Board of Forestry, 2002—. Member, Legal, Tax and Accounting Committee and Executive Committee, 2002-2004, National Council of Farmer Cooperatives. *Member:* Multnomah and American Bar Associations; Oregon State Bar. ***PRACTICE AREAS:*** Cooperative Law; Corporate Law; Real Property; Environmental Law. ***Email:*** hutch@fosterpdx.com

JOEL S. KAPLAN, born Newark, New Jersey, August 26, 1954; admitted to bar, 1979, Oregon and U.S. District Court, District of Oregon. *Education:* California State University, Fullerton (B.A., with high honors, 1976); University of Oregon (J.D., with honors, 1979). Author: "Contract Law in Oregon," Oregon State Bar, 1991*Member:* Oregon State Bar. ***PRACTICE AREAS:*** Securities; Real Estate; Corporate Law. ***Email:*** jsk@fosterpdx.com

JANET KNAUSS LARSEN, admitted to bar, 1995, Oregon and U.S. District Court, District of Oregon; 1996, Washington. *Education:* Whitman College (B.A., 1988); Obirin College, International Society and Business Program, Tokyo, Japan (1989); Lewis and Clark College, Northwestern School of Law (J.D., 1993). Judicial Clerk, Honorable Ellen F. Rosenblum, Multnomah County Circuit, Portland, Oregon, 1995-1996. Kilmer, Voorhees & Laurick, Portland, Oregon, 1996-2001. *Member:* Multnomah, Oregon State (Member, Sections on: Litigation; Business Litigation),Washington State (Member, Litigation Section) and Federal Bar Associations; Oregon Women Lawyers; Owen M. Panner American Inns of Court; Oregon Historical Society. ***PRACTICE AREAS:*** Commercial and Complex Litigation; Alternative Dispute Resolution; Business Torts; Business Contracts; Employment Law. ***Email:*** larja@fosterpdx.com

CARTER M. MANN, born Orlando, Florida, May 23, 1962; admitted to bar, 1992, New York; 1996, Oregon and Washington. *Education:* Colgate University (B.A., 1984); State University of New York at Buffalo (J.D., cum laude, 1991). Member, Buffalo Law Review. ***PRACTICE AREAS:*** Litigation; Creditors' Rights; Labor and Employment. ***Email:*** mannc@fosterpdx.com

WALTER W. McMONIES, JR., born Portland, Oregon, May 11, 1947; admitted to bar, 1973, California; 1974, Oregon. *Education:* Yale University (B.A., cum laude, 1969; J.D., 1972). Member, Yale Law Journal, 1970-1971. Adjunct Professor, Securities Law, Lewis & Clark College, Northwestern School of Law, 1987. *Member:* Oregon State Bar (Member, Real Estate and Land Use Section); American Bar Association. ***PRACTICE AREAS:*** Real Estate Law. ***Email:*** mcmow@fosterpdx.com

ANDREW J. MORROW, JR., born Bend, Oregon, April 8, 1952; admitted to bar, 1980, Oregon; 2003, Washington. *Education:* Columbia University and University of Oregon (B.A., 1974); Stanford University (J.D., 1980). Phi Beta Kappa. Section Chair, 1992-1993, Executive Committee Member, 1990-1994, Legislative Committee Chair, 2000—, Oregon State Bar, Business Law Section. Executive Committee Member, 1990-1992, Oregon State Bar, Securities Regulation Section. Chair, 1989-1993 and Secretary, 1985-1987, Business Corporation Act Task Force, Oregon State Bar, Business Law Section. Recipient: Oregon State Bar President's Membership Service Award, 1992; Oregon State Bar Business Law Section James B. Castles Leadership Award, 2001. ***PRACTICE AREAS:*** Banks and Banking; Business Law; Corporate Law; Mergers, Acquisitions and Divestitures; Finance; Securities; Health Care. ***Email:*** morra@fosterpdx.com

TOD A. NORTHMAN, born Bend, Oregon, June 17, 1966; admitted to bar, 1994, Oregon; 1995, Washington; U.S. District Court, District of Oregon and U.S. District Court, Western District of Washington; U.S. Court of Appeals, 9th Circuit. *Education:* Portland State University (B.A., 1988); New York University (M.A., 1991); Case Western Reserve University School of Law (J.D., cum laude, 1994). *Member:* Multnomah, Clark County, Washington State (Member, Business Law Section) and American Bar Associations; Oregon State Bar (Member, Business Law Section). ***PRACTICE AREAS:*** Corporate Law; Aviation Law; Telecommunications Law. ***Email:*** nortt@fosterpdx.com

NANCIE K. POTTER, born Portland, Oregon, September 3, 1953; admitted to bar, 1979, New York and U.S. District Court, Southern and Eastern Districts of New York; U.S. Court of Appeals, Second Circuit; 1980, Oregon and U.S. District Court, District of Oregon; U.S. Court of Appeals, Ninth Circuit. *Education:* Lewis and Clark College (B.A., 1974); Northwestern School of Law of Lewis & Clark College (J.D., 1978). Cornelius Honor Society. *Member:* New York State and Federal Bar Associations; Oregon State Bar (House of Delegates, 2001-2004; Litigation Section Executive Committee, 2002-2006, Treasurer, 2004-2005; Securities Regulation Section Executive Committee, 2003-2005); Multnomah County Bar Association (Professionalism Committee, 2001-2004, Chair, 2003-2004); Oregon Women Lawyers; National Association of Securities Dealers Arbitration Panel; Multnomah County Circuit Court Arbitration Panel. ***PRACTICE AREAS:*** Business Litigation; Complex Commercial Litigation; Securities Litigation; Bankruptcy Litigation; Arbitration. ***Email:*** pottn@fosterpdx.com

GREGORY L. POWELL, born Portland, Oregon, May 30, 1963; admitted to bar, 1990, Oregon; 2003, Washington. *Education:* University of Oregon (B.A., 1985); Lewis and Clark College (J.D., 1988). Counsel, U.S. Senate Committee on Finance-Tax, 1991-1994. Associate, 1994-1996, Weiss Jensen Ellis & Howard. Associate, 1996-1998, Partner, 1998, Managing Partner, 2002, Foster Pepper & Shefelman. ***PRACTICE AREAS:*** Real Estate Finance; Real Estate Development; Partnership Law; Limited Liability Partnerships; Business Law; Income Tax; General Business. ***Email:*** poweg@fosterpdx.com

KENNETH E. ROBERTS, born Lebanon, Oregon, October 2, 1944; admitted to bar, 1969, Oregon. *Education:* Oregon State University (B.S., 1966); Harvard University (J.D., 1969). Listed in The Best Lawyers in America, Banking Law Section, 1997-2003. Author, Chapters, "Public Financing" and "Financing the Purchase," in "Advising Oregon Businesses," Oregon State Bar. Member: Oregon Bankers Association; Washington Bankers Association; Washington Financial League. President, Columbia-Willamette Chapter of the Association of Corporate Growth, Board Member 1999-2002. *Member:* Multnomah and American (Member, Business Law Section) Bar Associations; Oregon State Bar (Securities Regulation Section; Business Law Section). ***PRACTICE AREAS:*** Business Law; Financial Institutions Law; Mergers and Acquisitions; Securities. ***Email:*** robek@fosterpdx.com

MICHAEL R. SILVEY, born San Mateo, California, April 13, 1945; admitted to bar, 1972, California; 1990, Oregon; 1996, Washington. *Education:* University of California at Santa Barbara (A.B., cum laude, 1967); Hastings College of the Law, University of California (J.D., 1971). Order of the Coif. Note and Comment Editor, Hastings Law Journal, 1970-1971. Author: "Judicial Foreclosure," California Real Property Journal, April, 1990; "How to Execute a Slam Dunk in Public/Private Negotiations, The Oregon Arena Project Experience," Development Magazine, Spring 1995. Partner, Crosby, Heafey, Roach & May, Oakland, California, 1977-1990. *Member:* Oregon State Bar (Real Estate and Land Use Section); State Bar of California (Member, Executive Committee, California Conference of Delegates, 1986-1989); National Association of Industrial and Office Properties (Oregon Chapter President, 1998); Counselors of Real Estate (CRE; Chair, 2002). ***PRACTICE AREAS:*** Real Estate Leasing; Real Estate Finance; Real Estate Development; Sports Facilities Development; Land Use Regulation. ***Email:*** silvm@fosterpdx.com

RESIDENT ASSOCIATES

JEREMY R. BADER, admitted to bar, 2002, California and U.S. District Court, Northern District of California; 2004, Oregon. *Education:* University of Washington (B.A., 1996); University of San Francisco Law School (J.D., 2002). *Member:* State Bar of California; Oregon State Bar. ***PRACTICE AREAS:*** Litigation; Real Estate. ***Email:*** badej@fosterpdx.com

H. FAITH GRAHAM, born Tacoma, Washington, March 31, 1973; admitted to bar, 2001, Massachusetts; 2003, Oregon. *Education:* University of Washington (B.A., English Literature, cum laude, 1994); Northeastern University School of Law (J.D., 2000). *Member:* Oregon State Bar; American Bar Association; Commercial Real Estate Women; Commercial Association of Realtors. ***PRACTICE AREAS:*** Real Estate; Real Estate Finance; Land Use. ***Email:*** grahh@fosterpdx.com

ANDREW H. OGNALL, born Yorkshire, England, November 18, 1971; admitted to bar, 1997, Oregon. *Education:* Cornell University (B.A., 1993); Lewis and Clark College, Northwestern School of Law (J.D., cum laude, 1997). Co-Editor, Advising Oregon Businesses CLE, 2002—. Committee Chair Oregon State Bar Business Law Section and Co-Editor of Oregon Business Lawyer, 2002—. Member, Oregon State Bar House of Delegates, 2001-2003. President, Cornell Club of Oregon, 2003-2004. Form and Style Editor, Law Review, 1997. *Member:* Oregon State Bar; Multnomah and American Bar Associations. ***PRACTICE AREAS:*** Corporate Finance; Banking; Securities; Business. ***Email:*** ognaa@fosterpdx.com

ELIA E. POPOVICH, born Minneapolis, Minnesota; admitted to bar, 1998, Oregon. *Education:* Middlebury College (B.A., 1991); The Graduate Institute, St. Johns College, Sante Fe, New Mexico (M.A., 1997); William Mitchell College of Law (J.D., cum laude,

(This Listing Continued)

FOSTER PEPPER TOOZE LLP, Portland—Continued

1998). Law Review, Staff Member and Associate Editor, 1995-1997. *Member:* Multnomah Bar Association; Oregon State Bar. ***PRACTICE AREAS:*** Real Estate; Real Estate Finance. ***Email:*** popoe@fosterpdx.com

KATHLEEN PROFITT, admitted to bar, 2004, Oregon. *Education:* Lewis and Clark College (B.A., 2000; J.D., 2003). ***PRACTICE AREAS:*** Litigation. ***Email:*** profk@fosterpdx.com

MARISOL RICOY, born Albuquerque; admitted to bar, 2002, Oregon. *Education:* Michigan State University (B.S., 1994); Willamette University College of Law (J.D., cum laude, 2002); Willamette University Atkinson School of Management (M.B.A., 2002). *Member:* Multnomah Bar Association; Oregon State Bar; Hispanic Metropolitan Chamber; Oregon Women Lawyers. ***PRACTICE AREAS:*** Corporate Law. ***Email:*** ricom@fosterpdx.com

CHARMIN B. SHIELY, admitted to bar, 2000, Oregon. *Education:* Duke University (B.A., magna cum laude, 1996); University of North Carolina at Chapel Hill (J.D., high honors, 2000). Order of the Coif. Member, North Carolina Law Review. Author: "United States v. Bajakajian: Will A New Standard for Applying the Excessive Fines Clause to Criminal Forfeitures Affect Civil Forfeiture Analysis?", 77 N C L Rev 1595 (1999). *Member:* Multnomah Bar Association; Oregon State Bar (Member, Securities Regulation Section). ***PRACTICE AREAS:*** Business Law; Finance; Securities. ***Email:*** shiec@fosterpdx.com

CLIFF E. SPENCER, born Billings, Montana; admitted to bar, 1995, Oregon; 2003, Washington. *Education:* Montana State University (B.S., Business Administration, 1991); Atkinson Graduate School of Management, Willamette University (M.B.A., 1995; J.D., 1995). Associate Editor, Willamette Law Review, 1995. Recipient, Trustees' Merit Scholarship, Willamette University College of Law. Listed in: Who's Who: American Law Student. Author: "The Oregon Supreme Court Grants Majority Shareholders in Close Corporations a License to Steal: Stringer v. Car Data Systems, Inc.," Willamette Law Review, Vol. 30, No. 2; "Oregon's Independent Contractor Statute: A Legislative Placebo for Employers," Willamette Law Review, Vol. 31, No. 3; "CERCLA: Indirect Regulation Dictating Lending Policy," Oregon Business Law Digest, Vol. 12, No. 1. *Member:* Multnomah and American Bar Associations; Oregon State Bar. ***PRACTICE AREAS:*** Business Law; Corporate Law; Securities; Mergers and Acquisitions. ***Email:*** spenc@fosterpdx.com

REPRESENTATIVE CLIENTS: Albina Community Bank; Benenson Capital Company; BPM Development Company; CarrAmerica Realty Corporation; Chase Manhattan Bank; Citation Mortgage Corp.; Cornus Corporation; Critical Path Software, Inc.; Danielson's Fresh Marketplace; Eagle Crest, Inc.; Edwards Manufacturing, Inc.; e-Ference, Inc.; Equity Residential Properties; Essex Property Trust; Fabric Depot, Inc.; First & Goal, Inc.; HealthNotes, Inc.; Heller Financial, Inc.; Holiday Retirement Corp.; Independent Financial Network, Inc.; Inform Graphics, Inc.; Intel Corporation; JELD-WEN, Inc.; Lithia Motors, Inc.; Marquis Quality Health Care, Inc.; National Golf Operating Partnership, L.P.; Oregon Arena Corporation; Oregon Trail Financial Corp.; Papa Murphy's International, Inc.; Parallel Communication Incorporated; Park Place Development Company; Plaid Pantries, Inc.; Portland Trail Blazers; PremierWest Bancorp; Prestige Assisted Living, L.L.C.; Prestige Care, Inc.; Private Consulting Group; Pro Sports Systems, Inc.; Ralph Schlesinger Company; Rose City Radio Corporation; Saba Investments, Inc.; Seedling Technologies, Inc.; Sekidenko, Inc.; Silver Mountain Corporation; Technology, Inc.; Timberline Software, Inc.; Transamerica Equipment Financial Services Corp.; Umpqua Holding Corp.; Unico Properties, Inc.; Washington Mutual, Inc.; Wright Runstad & Co.; Xyron Corporation; YOCREAM International, Inc.

SARA L. GABIN, P.C.

PORTLAND, OREGON

(See Lake Oswego)

Social Security Disability and SSI, Personal Injury, Workers Compensation, Family Law.

GARRETT, HEMANN, ROBERTSON, JENNINGS, COMSTOCK & TRETHEWY, P.C.

PORTLAND, OREGON

(See Salem)

Bankruptcy and Creditors' Rights, Business and Corporate Law, Civil Litigation, Employment and Labor Law, Estate Planning, Trusts and Probate, Family Law, Government Relations, Insurance and Workers' Compensation Defense, Real Estate Transactions and Development, School Law, Tax Law.

GARVEY SCHUBERT BARER

Established in 1966

ELEVENTH FLOOR
121 S.W. MORRISON STREET
PORTLAND, OREGON 97204
Telephone: 503-228-3939
Fax: 503-226-0259
URL: http://www.GSBlaw.com

Beijing, China Office: 820 South Tower, Beijing Kerry Center, 1 Guang Hua Road, Chaoyang District, Beijing, PRC 100020. Telephone: 8610-8529-9880. Fax: 8610-8529-9881.

New York, New York Office: Eighth Floor, 599 Broadway, 10012. Telephone: 212-431-8700. Fax: 212-334-1278.

Seattle, Washington Office: 1191 Second Avenue, 18th Floor, 98101. Telephone: 206-464-3939. Fax: 206-464-0125.

Washington, D.C. Office: Fifth Floor, 1000 Potomac Street, N.W., 20007. Telephone: 202-965-7880. Fax: 202-965-1729.

General Practice in Business, Litigation and Government Relations. Administrative, Admiralty, Affordable Housing and Community Development, Antitrust, Banking, Bankruptcy and Creditors' Rights, Class Action Litigation, Commercial and Secured Transactions, Communications and Media Law, Construction Law, Corporate Finance and Securities, E-Commerce and Emerging Technologies, Employee Benefits, Entertainment, Sports and Arts, Environmental, Estate Planning and Probate, Federal Taxation, Global Customs and Trade, Government Contracts, Health and Safety Regulation, Healthcare Law, Immigration, Indian Law, Insurance Coverage and Defense, Intellectual Property, International Practice, Labor and Employment Law, Land Use and Condemnation, Maritime, Mergers and Acquisitions, Municipal, Natural Resources, Nonprofit and Tax-Exempt Organizations, Products Liability, Public Policy, Lobbying and Political Law, Real Estate, State and Local Taxation, Sustainable Business, Transportation Law, White-Collar Criminal Defense.

FIRM PROFILE: Garvey Schubert Barer offers a sophisticated, full service business practice complemented by a zealous team of litigators. We serve as outside general counsel to established market leaders and newly-launched enterprises. Our attorneys are active in many different industry sectors including high technology, labor and employment, trade and transportation, real estate, entertainment and healthcare. On behalf of our clients, we handle such varied matters as customs disputes, software licensing, employment litigation, class-action lawsuits, property tax appeals and federal government relations.

This listing provides information about our attorneys' educational backgrounds, bar admissions and practice areas. For more detailed biographical information, please consult our Web site at www.GSBlaw.com.

OWNERS

RICHARD BAROWAY, born 1958; admitted to bar, 1983, Oregon; 2002, Washington; U.S. District Court, District of Oregon; U.S. District Court, Western District of Washington; U.S. Court of Appeals, Ninth Circuit; U.S. Supreme Court. *Education:* Humboldt State University (B.A., magna cum laude, 1980); Willamette University (J.D., cum laude, 1983). ***PRACTICE AREAS:*** Appellate Litigation; Corporate Law; Commercial Law; Real Estate; Nonprofit Organizations Law; Tax Exempt Organizations; Maritime Law; Maritime Litigation; Bankruptcy; Creditors Rights. ***Email:*** rbaroway@gsblaw.com

A. JEFFERY BIRD, born 1955; admitted to bar, 1981, District of Columbia; 1988, U.S. Supreme Court; 1990, Washington; 1996, Oregon. *Education:* Washington & Lee University (B.A., cum laude, 1978); University of Virginia (J.D., 1981). ***PRACTICE AREAS:*** Corporate Law; Securities Law; Mergers and Acquisitions; Corporate Finance; Venture Capital Transactions. ***Email:*** jbird@gsblaw.com

LARRY J. BRANT, born 1959; admitted to bar, 1984, Oregon and U.S. District Court, District of Oregon; 1985, Washington; 1991, U.S. Tax Court. *Education:* Portland State University (B.S., cum laude, 1981); Willamette University (J.D., cum laude, 1984); University of Florida College of Law (LL.M., Taxation, 1987). ***PRACTICE AREAS:*** Taxation; Business Law; Mergers and Acquisitions; Real Estate. ***Email:*** lbrant@gsblaw.com

KATHLEEN C. BRICKEN, born 1968; admitted to bar, 1994, Oregon; 1995, Washington; 1997, U.S. District Court, District of Oregon. *Education:* University of California at Santa Barbara (B.A., 1990); University of Notre Dame (J.D., 1994). ***PRACTICE AREAS:*** Complex Civil Litigation; Professional Liability. ***Email:*** kbricken@gsblaw.com

CHRISTINE P. BROWN, born 1951; admitted to bar, 1977, District of Columbia; 1980, Oregon; 1981, U.S. Court of Appeals, Ninth Circuit, U.S. Tax Court and U.S. District Court, District of Oregon. *Education:* Wheeling College (B.A., cum laude, 1972); Columbus School of Law, Catholic University of America (J.D., 1977). ***PRACTICE AREAS:*** Estate Planning and Probate; Tax Law; Corporate Law; Commercial Law. ***Email:*** cbrown@gsblaw.com

DAVID L. CANARY, born 1950; admitted to bar, 1976, Oregon; 1981, U.S. District Court, District of Oregon; 1983, U.S. Tax Court; 1986, U.S. Court of Appeals, Ninth Circuit. *Education:* Linfield College (B.A., cum laude, 1972); Lewis and Clark College, Northwestern School of Law (J.D., 1976). ***PRACTICE AREAS:*** State Tax Litigation; Property Tax Litigation; Commercial Litigation. ***Email:*** dcanary@gsblaw.com

STEPHEN J. CONNOLLY, born 1952; admitted to bar, 1978, Oregon and U.S. District Court, District of Oregon. *Education:* Oregon State University (B.S., magna cum laude, 1974); Gonzaga University School of Law (J.D., magna cum laude, 1977). ***PRACTICE AREAS:*** Business Law; Commercial Law; Mergers and Acquisitions; Health Care; Real Estate. ***Email:*** sconnolly@gsblaw.com

KEITH S. DUBANEVICH, born 1957; admitted to bar, 1983, Texas; 1984, U.S. District Court, Southern District of Texas and U.S. Court of Appeals, Fifth Circuit; 1985, U.S. District Court, Eastern District of Texas; 1989, Massachusetts and U.S. District Court, Western District of Wisconsin; 1997, Oregon and U.S. Supreme Court. *Education:* Northeastern University (B.S., Public Administration, high honors, 1980); Tulane University (J.D., cum laude, 1983). ***PRACTICE AREAS:*** Litigation; Professional Liability; Antitrust; Intellectual Property Litigation. ***Email:*** kdubanevich@gsblaw.com

MARK E. FRIEDMAN, born 1947; admitted to bar, 1973, Oregon and U.S. District Court, District of Oregon. *Education:* University of Illinois (B.S., Accountancy with honors, 1970; J.D., 1973). Certified Public Accountant, Illinois, 1970. ***PRACTICE AREAS:*** Complex Commercial Litigation; Professional Liability Litigation; Employment Law; Employment Litigation; Failed Financial Institutions Litigation; Construction Litigation. ***Email:*** mfriedman@gsblaw.com

ROBERT R. GRIFFITH, born 1952; admitted to bar, 1985, Oregon and U.S. District Court, District of Oregon; 1986, U.S. Court of Appeals, Ninth Circuit; 1992, Washington; U.S. District Court, Western and Eastern Districts of Washington. *Education:* Oregon State University (B.S., 1974); Northwestern School of Law of Lewis and Clark College (J.D., 1985). ***PRACTICE AREAS:*** Real Estate; Business Law; Commercial Law; International Transactions; Financial Institutions Law; Sustainable Business. ***Email:*** rrgriffi@gsblaw.com

ERIC A. LINDENAUER, born 1953; admitted to bar, 1983, Oregon; 1984, U.S. District Court, District of Oregon; 1985, U.S. Court of Appeals, Ninth Circuit; 1986, Washington; 1992, U.S. District Court, Western District of Washington. *Education:* University of California at Berkeley (A.B. Political Science, 1976); Willamette University (J.D., summa cum laude, 1983). ***PRACTICE AREAS:*** Litigation; Health Care; Employment Law; Insurance Law; Construction Law; Bankruptcy Law. ***Email:*** elindenauer@gsblaw.com

(This Listing Continued)

JEFFREY F. NUDELMAN, born 1961; admitted to bar, 1986, Oregon; 1988, Washington. *Education:* University of Oregon (B.S., Political Science, 1983); Northwestern School of Law (J.D., 1986). ***PRACTICE AREAS:*** Business Law; Commercial Transactions; Secured Transactions; Corporate Transactions; Labor and Employment; Real Estate; Mergers and Acquisitions; Construction Law; Sustainable Business. ***Email:*** jnudelman@gsblaw.com

MICHAEL M. RATOZA, born 1951; admitted to bar, 1976, Oregon; U.S. District Court, District of Oregon; U.S. Court of Appeals, Ninth Circuit; U.S. Tax Court. *Education:* University of Oregon (B.S., 1973); University of Oregon School of Law (J.D., 1976). ***PRACTICE AREAS:*** Intellectual Property; Prosecution; Licensing; Anti-piracy; Litigation. ***Email:*** mratoza@gsblaw.com

ALEC J. SHEBIEL, born 1967; admitted to bar, 1994, Oregon. *Education:* University of Wisconsin at Madison (B.S., 1991); Boston University (J.D., 1994). ***PRACTICE AREAS:*** Business Law; Civil Litigation; International Business Law; E-Commerce and Technology. ***Email:*** ashebiel@gsblaw.com

EDWARD J. SULLIVAN, born 1945; admitted to bar, 1969, Oregon; 1978, District of Columbia; 2001, Washington. *Education:* St. John's University (B.A., 1966); Willamette University College of Law (J.D., 1969); Portland State University (M.A., History, 1973; Urban Studies Cert., 1974); University College, London (LL.M., 1978); University College, Oxford (Diploma in Law, 1984); University of Durham (M.A., Political Thought, 1999). ***PRACTICE AREAS:*** Land Use; Condemnation; Municipal Law; Administrative; Housing Law; Real Estate. ***Email:*** esullivan@gsblaw.com

ROBERT C. WEAVER, JR., born 1950; admitted to bar, 1975, Ohio; 1979, District of Columbia; 1980, Oregon; U.S. District Court, District of Oregon; U.S. Court of Appeals, 9th and 5th Circuits; U.S. Tax Court. *Education:* University of Notre Dame (B.A., cum laude, 1972; J.D., cum laude, 1975). ***PRACTICE AREAS:*** Complex Civil Litigation; White Collar Criminal Defense; Tax Litigation. ***Email:*** rweaver@gsblaw.com

OF COUNSEL

CYNTHIA M. FRASER, admitted to bar, 1987, Oregon; 1988, U.S. District Court, District of Oregon. *Education:* University of Oregon (B.A., 1980; J.D., 1987). ***PRACTICE AREAS:*** Eminent Domain; Condemnation; Inverse Condemnation; Property Rights; Litigation; Arbitration and Mediation. ***Email:*** cfraser@gsblaw.com

WILLIAM K. KABEISEMAN, admitted to bar, 1994, Oregon. *Education:* College of William & Mary (B.A. in Economics, 1987); University of Oregon (J.D., 1993). Order of the Coif. ***PRACTICE AREAS:*** Appellate Practice; Environmental Law; Municipal Law; Natural Resources; Land Use; Condemnation. ***Email:*** billkab@gsblaw.com

SAMUEL C. KAUFFMAN, born 1967; admitted to bar, 1994, Oregon, U.S. District Court, District of Oregon and U.S. Court of Appeals, 9th Circuit. *Education:* Colorado State University (B.S., Finance, 1989); Willamette University (J.D., 1994). (Also practicing individually). ***PRACTICE AREAS:*** Litigation; White Collar Criminal Defense. ***Email:*** skauffman@gsblaw.com

PAUL J. KELLY, JR., admitted to bar, 1970, Oregon; 1971, U.S. District Court, District of Oregon; U.S. Court of Appeals, Ninth Circuit. *Education:* University of Notre Dame (A.B., 1967); Georgetown University (J.D., 1970). ***PRACTICE AREAS:*** International Law; Government Relations; Public Policy; Alternative Dispute Resolution. ***Email:*** pkelly@gsblaw.com

TIMOTHY D. SMITH, born 1964; admitted to bar, 1991, Oregon. *Education:* University of Notre Dame (B.A., magna cum laude, 1986); Harvard Law School (J.D., cum laude, 1991). ***PRACTICE AREAS:*** Litigation; Sustainable Business. ***Email:*** tsmith@gsblaw.com

ASSOCIATES

JOY ELLIS, born 1969; admitted to bar, 1995, Oregon; 1996, Washington; U.S. Court of Appeals, Ninth Circuit; U.S. District Court, District of Oregon; U.S. District Court, Western District of Washington. *Education:* Yale University (B.A. in American Studies and Environmental Studies, magna cum laude, 1991); Northwestern School of Law of Lewis and Clark College (J.D., magna cum laude, 1995). ***PRACTICE AREAS:*** Labor and Employment; Litigation; Sustainable Business. ***Email:*** jellis@gsblaw.com

ADAM R. KELLY, born 1975; admitted to bar, 2002, Oregon; U.S. District Court, District of Oregon; U.S. Court of Appeals, Ninth Circuit. *Education:* University of Colorado (B.A., History, 1997); University of Oregon School of Law (J.D., 2002). ***PRACTICE AREAS:*** Commercial Litigation. ***Email:*** akelly@gsblaw.com

MICHAEL R. O'CONNOR, born 1972; admitted to bar, 1997, Oregon; 1998, Washington; 1999, U.S. District Court, District of Oregon and U.S. District Court, Western District of Washington; 2005, U.S. Court of Appeals, Ninth Circuit. *Education:* Yale University (B.A., Political Science, 1994); University of Oregon (J.D., 1997). ***PRACTICE AREAS:*** Commercial Litigation; Employment Litigation; Class Action Litigation. ***Email:*** moconnor@gsblaw.com

CARRIE A. RICHTER, admitted to bar, 2000, Oregon. *Education:* Lewis and Clark College (B.A. in History, 1992); University of Utah (M.S. in Historic Preservation, 1997); Northwestern School of Law of Lewis and Clark College (J.D. and Environmental Law Certificate, 2000). ***LANGUAGES:*** Italian. ***PRACTICE AREAS:*** Land Use; Municipal Law; Environmental Law; Natural Resources; Real Estate. ***Email:*** crichter@gsblaw.com

LAURA CALDERA TAYLOR, born 1968; admitted to bar, 1999, Oregon; U.S. District Court, District of Oregon; U.S. Court of Appeals, Ninth Circuit. *Education:* California State University (B.A., Political Science, 1995); Willamette University (J.D., 1999). ***PRACTICE AREAS:*** Intellectual Property Litigation; Commercial Litigation. ***Email:*** ltaylor@gsblaw.com

ADRIENNE W. WHITWORTH, born 1976; admitted to bar, 2002, Oregon; U.S. District Court, District of Oregon. *Education:* Willamette University (B.A., Political Science, with honors, 1998); University of Oregon School of Law (J.D., 2002). Order of the Coif. ***PRACTICE AREAS:*** Commercial Litigation; Labor and Employment. ***Email:*** awhitworth@gsblaw.com

(This Listing Continued)

REPRESENTATIVE CLIENTS: American Steamship Owners Mutual Protection and Indemnity Association, Inc.; Assisted Living Concepts, Inc.; Cascade AIDS Project; Christenson Oil; City of Oregon City; Coverall of Oregon; Columbia Sportswear; Federal Deposit Insurance Corporation; Foss Environmental Services Company; Foss Maritime Company; Fujitsu Microelectronics America, Inc.; Great American Insurance Companies; H.J. Heinz; InFocus Corporation; K2 Corporation; Anthony Robbins & Associates, Inc.; LaCrosse Footwear, Inc.; Land O'Lakes, Inc.; Maco Wood Products, Inc.; Mitsubishi Silicon America; NIKE, Inc.; Ore-Ida Foods, Inc.; Oregon Health & Science University; Pacific Coast Fruit Company; Parr Lumber Company; PeaceHealth; Plumb Creek Manufacturing, L.P.; Portland State University Foundation; Regence BlueCross BlueShield of Oregon; Regence HMO Oregon; Sacred Heart Medical Center; St. John Medical Center; Ste. Michelle Wine Estates Ltd.; Taco Bell Corp.; Tetra Tech; Teufel Nursery; Trailblazers, Inc.; The Nautilus Group, Inc.; The North of England P& I Association; The Port of Portland; The Regence Group; Totem Ocean Trailer Express, Inc.; Transamerica Commercial Finance Corporation; TriQuint Semiconductor, Inc.; United Kingdom Mutual Steam Ship Assurance Association.

(For other data on firm personnel see Beijing, New York, New York, Seattle, Washington and Washington, D.C.)

THE GARY LAW GROUP

Established in 1992

2000 ONE MAIN PLACE
101 SW MAIN STREET
PORTLAND, OREGON 97204
Telephone: 503-227-8424
Facsimile: 503-227-8412
Email: rachel@prgarylaw.com
URL: http://www.prgarylaw.com

Litigation and Management of Construction, Product Defects and Business Claims, Insurance and Insurance Coverage.

PAUL R. GARY, born Chicago, Illinois, June 8, 1950; admitted to bar, 1976, Illinois; 1983, Oregon, U.S. District Court, Northern District of Illinois, U.S. District Court, District of Oregon and U.S. Court of Appeals, Seventh and Ninth Circuits. *Education:* Northwestern University (B.A., 1973; J.D., 1976). Law Clerk to The Hon. John Powers Crowley, U.S. District Court, Northern District of Illinois. Author: "Federal Civil Litigation in Oregon", Oregon State Bar Association. Past Chair and Member, Judicial Selection Task Force and Employment Practices Committee, Associated Oregon Industries. *Member:* Multnomah Bar, Oregon State (Past Chair, Joint CPA Committee), Federal (Past President, Oregon Chapter) and American Bar Associations; American Architectural Manufacturer's Association (AAMA Window Defect Panel). ***PRACTICE AREAS:*** Construction Law; Construction Litigation; Products Liability; Insurance Coverage; Business Litigation. ***Email:*** paul@prgarylaw.com

STEVE NORMAN, born Longview, Washington, July 4, 1969; admitted to bar, 1996, Oregon; 1997, California. *Education:* University of Oregon (B.S., cum laude, 1991); University of California at Davis (J.D., 1995). ***PRACTICE AREAS:*** Business Litigation; Construction Litigation; Commercial Litigation; Real Estate Litigation; Business Formation. ***Email:*** steve@prgarylaw.com

SUSAN MACKAY, (admission pending), *Member:* Multnomah and American Bar Associations; Oregon Women Lawyers Association.

GEARING, RACKNER & ENGEL LLP

811 SW NAITO PARKWAY
PORTLAND, OREGON 97204
Telephone: 503-222-9116
Fax: 503-222-9118
URL: http://www.gre-lawfirm.com

Family Law, Custody Law, Juvenile Law, Estate Planning.

MEMBERS OF FIRM

DAVID C. GEARING, born Chicago, Illinois, May 14, 1957; admitted to bar, 1984, Oregon. *Education:* State University of New York at Buffalo (B.A., cum laude, 1980); University of Oregon (J.D., 1983). *Member:* Clackamas County, Multnomah County, Clatsop County and Washington County Bar Associations; Oregon State Bar. ***PRACTICE AREAS:*** Family Law; Custody Law; Juvenile Law; Estate Planning.

LAURA E. RACKNER, born Minneapolis, Minnesota, September 10, 1956; admitted to bar, 1984, Oregon. *Education:* University of Oregon (B.S., 1979; J.D., 1984). Deputy District Attorney, Marion County District Attorneys Office. Assistant Attorney General, Oregon Department of Justice. Staff, United States Department of Justice, Office of Chief Counsel, Drug Enforcement Administration. *Member:* Clackamas County, Multnomah County and Washington County Bar Associations; Oregon State Bar (Member, Family Law Section). ***PRACTICE AREAS:*** Family Law; Juvenile Law; Custody Law; Estate Planning.

BRETT E. ENGEL, born Oak Park, Illinois, October 30, 1965; admitted to bar, 1995, Oregon. *Education:* University of Vermont (B.A., 1988); Willamette University (J.D., 1995). ***PRACTICE AREAS:*** Family Law.

CRAIG WYMETALEK, born Portland, Oregon, November 19, 1970; admitted to bar, 1996, Oregon. *Education:* University of Oregon (B.A., 1993); Northwestern School of Law (J.D., 1996). *Member:* Multnomah and Washington County Bar Associations; Oregon State Bar (Member, Family Law Section). ***PRACTICE AREAS:*** Family Law; Guardianship; Appellate Practice.

MICHAEL T. McGRATH, born Homestead, Florida, July 30, 1976; admitted to bar, 2001, Oregon; 2002, Washington. *Education:* Linfield College (B.A., Political Science, 1998); Lewis and Clark College (J.D., 2001). *Member:* Multnomah County, Washington County and Washington State Bar Associations; Oregon State Bar. ***PRACTICE AREAS:*** Family Law.

GEVURTZ, MENASHE, LARSON & HOWE, P.C.

Established in 1981

111 S.W. FIFTH AVENUE
SUITE 900
PORTLAND, OREGON 97204-3604
Telephone: 503-227-1515
Fax: 503-243-2038
URL: http://www.gevurtzmenashe.com

Practice Limited to Family Law, including Divorce Spousal Support, Prenuptial Agreements, Palimony, Paternity, Parenting, Custody and Visitation Issues, Adoption and Surrogacy, Name Changes, International Custody, Domestic Partnerships, Juvenile Issues, Grandparents Rights.

FIRM PROFILE: For Complete Information on the Firm and Attorneys, Please see www.gevurtzmenashe.com. Practice in Oregon and South West Washington.

ALBERT A. MENASHE, born Portland, Oregon, April 24, 1950; admitted to bar, 1977, Oregon; 1980, U.S. Supreme Court. *Education:* University of Oregon (B.S., 1971); Willamette University (J.D., 1976).

ERIC C. LARSON, born Portland, Oregon, March 17, 1947; admitted to bar, 1972, Oregon; 1978, U.S. Supreme Court and U.S. Court of Appeals, Ninth Circuit. *Education:* University of Oregon (B.A., 1969; J.D., 1972).

WILLIAM J. HOWE, III, born Chicago, Illinois, November 28, 1948; admitted to bar, 1975, Oregon; 1986, U.S. Supreme Court. *Education:* University of Washington (B.A., 1970); Willamette University (J.D., 1975).

MARSHAL P. SPECTOR, born Washington, D.C., April 28, 1960; admitted to bar, 1986, Maryland; 1991, Oregon. *Education:* University of Maryland (B.A., 1982); University of Baltimore School of Law (J.D., 1985). (Resident). ***LANGUAGES:*** Hebrew.

RUTH E. PEKELDER, born Paterson, New Jersey, April 16, 1957; admitted to bar, 1984, Oregon; 1985, Michigan (inactive). *Education:* Calvin College (B.A., 1979); Northwestern School of Law of Lewis and Clark College (J.D., 1983). ***PRACTICE AREAS:*** Divorce; Spousal Support; Domestic Relations; Matrimonial Law.

ANDREA J. ANDERLY, born Pendleton, Oregon, November 30, 1948; admitted to bar, 1990, Oregon; 2004, Washington. *Education:* University of Oregon (B.S., 1972); Northwestern School of Law of Lewis and Clark College (J.D., 1988).

JULIA M. HAGAN, born Sacramento, California, December 25, 1956; admitted to bar, 1985, Oregon. *Education:* Santa Clara University (B.S., 1979); Lewis and Clark College (J.D., 1984).

KATHRYN L. VILLA-SMITH, born Espanola, New Mexico, June 25, 1952; admitted to bar, 1982, Oregon. *Education:* New Mexico State University (B.A., 1974); Lewis and Clark College (J.D., 1982).

CRAIG M. COWLEY
SAVILLE W. EASLEY
CATHERINE A. TAPPEL
DRAKE A. LIGHTLE
RICHARD W. FUNK
ZACHARY J. FRUCHTENGARTEN
ROBIN J. WRIGHT
SHAWN N. MENASHE
SARAH B. CREEM

GORDON & MENEGHELLO, P.C.

PORTLAND, OREGON

(See Fisher & Phillips LLP)

GORDON & POLSCER, LLC

9755 SW BARNES ROAD, SUITE 650
PORTLAND, OREGON 97225
Telephone: 503-242-2922
Fax: 503-242-1264
URL: http://www.gordon-polscer.com

Seattle, Washington Office: 1000 Second Avenue, Suite 1500, 98104. Telephone: 206-223-4226; Fax: 206-223-5459.

Insurance Coverage and Defense Law, Bad Faith Law, Professional Liability Law, Products Liability Law, General Civil Litigation and Appellate Practice.

FIRM PROFILE: From our offices in Portland and Seattle, Gordon & Polscer, LLC represents insurers and other corporate clients in complex insurance coverage and defense litigation and in connection with novel risk management issues. Our partners share an interest in partnering with clients to reduce the high cost of litigation through stringent cost management, creative approaches to settlement, prompt and effective use of ADR, and pro-active and high quality representation. We encourage "alternative" billing arrangements and detailed litigation planning. We advise clients on national programs, and we are active in litigation throughout the Western U.S.

(This Listing Continued)

MEMBERS OF FIRM

THOMAS A. GORDON, born Portland, Oregon, October 20, 1948; admitted to bar, 1974, Oregon. *Education:* Portland State University (B.S., 1971); Northwestern College of Law of Lewis & Clark College (J.D., 1974). Member, Northwestern Law Review, 1973-1974. *Member:* Multnomah County and American (Member, Torts and Insurance Practice Section; Vice Chairman, Professional Officer and Director, Liability Committee, 1986) Bar Associations; Oregon State Bar; Oregon Association of Defense Counsel; Defense Research and Trial Lawyers Association (Chairman, Insurance Law Committee, 1986-1989; Law Institute Committee, 1995-2000; Board of Directors, 1996-1999); International Association of Defense Counsel. ***PRACTICE AREAS:*** Insurance Coverage; Commercial Litigation; Professional Liability Defense Law; Hazardous Substances Law. ***Email:*** tgordon@gordon-polscer.com

DIANE L. POLSCER, born Allentown, Pennsylvania, September 12, 1960; admitted to bar, 1984, Washington, U.S. District Court, Eastern District of Washington and U.S. Court of Appeals, Ninth Circuit; 1987, Oregon and U.S. District Court, District of Oregon; 1989, U.S. District Court, Western District of Washington. *Education:* The Pennsylvania State University (B.A., with distinction, 1981); University of Oregon (J.D., 1984). Phi Alpha Delta. Associate Editor, University of Oregon Law Review, 1982-1984. Recipient, American Jurisprudence Award. Law Clerk for Hon. Robert J. McNichols, Chief Judge, United States District Court, Eastern District of Washington, 1984. *Member:* Multnomah County (Chair, Committee on the Status of Women, 1989-1990), Washington State, Federal and American (Past Chair, Tort and Insurance Practice Self Insurers and Risk Managers Committee) Bar Associations; Oregon State Bar (Member Sections on: Litigation; Natural Resources Law; Member, Oregon State Bar Judicial Administration Committee, 1989-1992; Member, Oregon State Bar Board of Bar Examiners, 1991-1994); Defense Research Institute (Chair, Excess and Reinsurance Subcommittee); Federation of Defense & Corporate Counsel; Oregon Women Lawyers (Member, Board of Directors, 1989-1991; Secretary, 1989-1990; Treasurer, 1990-1991); Gus J. Solomon American Inns of Court. ***PRACTICE AREAS:*** Insurance Coverage Litigation; Construction Defect; Toxic Tort; Technology Claims; Products Liability; Commercial Law; Environmental Litigation. ***Email:*** dpolscer@gordon-polscer.com

GREGORY L. BAIRD, born Castro Valley, California, December 8, 1964; admitted to bar, 1992, Oregon. *Education:* Portland State University (B.S., high honors, 1988); Northwestern School of Law (J.D., magna cum laude, 1992). Recipient, American Jurisprudence Awards in Corporations and Contracts. *Member:* Multnomah County, Federal and American Bar Associations; Oregon State Bar; Owen M. Panner, American Inns of Court. ***PRACTICE AREAS:*** Insurance Coverage Litigation; Products Liability; Toxic Torts; Civil Litigation; Appellate Practice. ***Email:*** gbaird@gordon-polscer.com

ASSOCIATES

RUSSELL W. PIKE, born Carbondale, Illinois, October 22, 1946; admitted to bar, 1981, California; U.S. Court of Appeals, Fifth and Ninth Circuits; 1984, Texas; 1985, Oregon; 1987, Washington. *Education:* University of California at Los Angeles (B.A., 1968; M.B.A., 1970); Loyola University of Los Angeles (J.D., 1981). *Member:* Multnomah, Clark County Federal and Washington State Bar Associations; Oregon State Bar; State Bar of Texas; State Bar of California. ***PRACTICE AREAS:*** Environmental Law; Litigation; Commercial Law. ***Email:*** rpike@gordon-polscer.com

ANDREW S. MOSES, born May 24, 1969; admitted to bar, 1998, Oregon. *Education:* Stanford University (B.S., 1991; M.S., 1992); University of Oregon (J.D., 1998). *Member:* Multnomah County Bar Association; Oregon State Bar. ***PRACTICE AREAS:*** Insurance Coverage Litigation; Products Liability; Environmental Litigation; Construction Defects. ***Email:*** amoses@gordon-polscer.com

JEFFREY C. DAHL, born Salt Lake City, Utah, November 13, 1960; admitted to bar, 1985, Florida; 1986, U.S. District Court, Southern District of Florida; U.S. Court of Appeals, Eleventh Circuit; 1996, Oregon. *Education:* University of Colorado at Boulder (B.A., 1982); University of Miami School of Law (J.D., 1985). *Member:* The Florida Bar (Member, Admiralty Committee). ***LANGUAGES:*** Spanish and French. ***PRACTICE AREAS:*** Insurance Coverage; Insurance Defense; Construction Accidents; Products Liability; Construction Defects.

ROBERT SPAJIC, born New York, N.Y., January 16, 1964; admitted to bar, 1993, Washington; 1996, Oregon. *Education:* San Jose State University (B.A., with honors, Political Science, 1989); Gonzaga University School of Law (J.D., 1992). *Member:* Oregon State Bar; Washington State Bar Association; Hood River County Bar Association (President). ***LANGUAGES:*** Croatian. ***PRACTICE AREAS:*** Insurance Coverage; Insurance Defense; Construction; Commercial Transactions; Litigation. ***Email:*** bspajic@gordon-polscer.com

HEATHER A. BRANN, born Pocatello, Idaho; admitted to bar, 2000, Idaho; 2001, Washington; 2004, Oregon (Not admitted in Oregon). *Education:* Idaho State University (B.A., with high honors, Philosophy and French, 1996); University of Utah (J.D., 2000). Phi Kappa Phi; Order of the Coif. Clyde Fellow. Recipient: Rotary International Ambassadorial Exchange Scholarship, 1992-1993; CALI Outstanding Achievement Awards in Torts, International Environmental Law, Water Law and Business Organizations. Staff Editor, 1999-2000 and Member, 1998-1999, Utah Law Review. Law Clerk to the Hon. Edward F. Shea, U.S. District Judge, Eastern District of Washington, 2000-2002. Author: Comment, "Utah's Medical Malpractice Pre-litigation Panel: Exploring State Constitutional Arguments Against a Non-binding Inadmissible Procedure," 2000 Utah L. Rev. 359, 2000. *Member:* Washington State Bar Association; Idaho State Bar; Trial Lawyers for Public Justice. ***LANGUAGES:*** French. ***PRACTICE AREAS:*** Civil Litigation; Insurance Coverage; Defense Litigation. ***Email:*** hbrann@gordon-polscer.com

SPENCER S. ADAMS, born January 25, 1973; admitted to bar, 2001, California (Not admitted in Oregon). *Education:* Brigham young University (B.A., 1998); J. Reuben Clark Law School, B.Y.U. (J.D., cum laude, 2001). *Member:* American Bar Association. ***LANGUAGES:*** Italian. ***PRACTICE AREAS:*** Litigation; Construction; Eminent Domain; Labor and Employment; Insurance Coverage.

GORDON & REES LLP

1001 S.W. FIFTH AVENUE, SUITE 1100
PORTLAND, OREGON 97204
Telephone: 503-220-1679
Fax: 503-907-6636
Email: info@gordonrees.com
URL: http://www.gordonrees.com

Phoenix, Arizona Office: 2375 E. Camelback Road, Suite 500. Telephone: 602-265-4700. Fax: 602-265-4700.
San Francisco, California Office: Embarcadero Center West, Twentieth Floor, 275 Battery Street. Telephone: 415-986-5900. Fax: 415-986-8054; 415-296-9287; 415-677-9673.
San Diego, California Office: 101 West Broadway, Suite 1600. Telephone: 619-696-6700. Fax: 619-696-7124.
Los Angeles, California Office: 633 West Fifth Street, Suite 4900. Telephone: 213-576-5000. Fax: 213-680-4470.
Sacramento, California Office: 655 University Avenue, Suite 200. Telephone: 916-565-2900. Fax: 916-920-4402.
Newport Beach, California Office: 4675 MacArthur Court, Suite 800. Telephone: 949-255-6950. Fax: 949-474-2060.
Las Vegas, Nevada Office: 221 North Buffalo Drive, Suite A. Telephone: 702-577-9300. Fax: 702-255-2858.
New York, New York Office: One Liberty Plaza, 14th Floor. Telephone: 212-201-6777. Fax: 212-201-6778.
Houston, Texas Office: 3D/International Tower, 1900 West Loop South, Suite 1100. Telephone: 713-961-3366. Fax: 713-961-3938.

Business and Corporate Litigation, Business and Technology, Construction, Commercial, Environmental Law, Estate Planning and Probate, Health Care, International, Maritime, Intellectual Property, Product Liability, Property Insurance, Real Estate, Real Property Litigation, Reinsurance, Tort Injury Defense, Toxic Tort, Insurance Coverage and Bad Faith, Medical Device Litigation, Professional Liability, Employment Law.

FIRM PROFILE: Gordon & Rees, LLP is best known as a firm of successful trial attorneys. Our clients know us as that, and more.

Founded in 1974 by Stuart Gordon and Donald Rees as a San Francisco-based litigation firm, Gordon & Rees has developed into a dynamic law firm of more than 220 attorneys with offices in San Francisco, San Diego, Los Angeles, Sacramento, San Diego and Orange County, California; Las Vegas, Nevada; Portland, Oregon; Houston, Texas; Phoenix, Arizona and New York, N.Y. The firm offers litigation expertise with an established reputation for success and a full range of business and transactional legal services.

PARTNERS OF FIRM

STUART M. BROWN, born Portland, Oregon, July 3, 1945; admitted to bar, 1976, Oregon, U.S. District Court, District of Oregon and U.S. Court of Appeals, Ninth Circuit; 1994, California and U.S. District Court, Southern, Northern and Middle Districts of California; 2004, Washington. *Education:* Oregon State University (B.S., 1968); University of Oregon (J.D., 1976). Editor-in-Chief, Oregon Law Review, 1975-1976. Adjunct Professor, Advanced Appellate Advocacy, University of Oregon Law School, 1979-1982. *Member:* Multnomah County, Washington State and American Bar Associations; Oregon State Bar; State Bar of California. [Captain, U.S. Army, 1968-1973]. ***PRACTICE AREAS:*** Employment Law; Litigation. ***Email:*** smbrown@gordonrees.com

THOMAS A. PACKER, born Fresno, California, September 18, 1957; admitted to bar, 1982, California; 1994, Oregon. *Education:* University of California at Los Angeles (B.A., 1979); Hastings College of Law, University of California (J.D., 1982). Note Editor, Hastings Constitutional Law Quarterly, 1981-1982. Author: "Defense Of Agricultural Chemical Contamination Cases Under The EPA Safe Drinking Water Act," presented to American Agricultural Law Association 1993 Annual Meeting; "Products Liability Law and Complex Litigation in the United States: Considerations for Foreign Companies," presented at 1995 Annual Conference of Multinational Association of Independent Law Firms, Manila, Philippines; "The Sins Of The Fathers-Liability of Descendents' Estates and Trusts Under CERCLA," Defense Research Institute, For The Defense, April, 1996; "Effective Use Of The Pesticide Exception To CERCLA," BNA Toxic Liability Reporter, June, 1996; "Defending Physicians Against Allegations of Financial Conflicts of Interest," Defense Research Institute, For The Defense, August 1996; "Insurer Liability under CERCLA: No Good Deed Goes Unpunished," Environmental Claims Journal, Autumn 1996; *Pesticide Litigation Manual*, Contributing Author, 1999 Ed.; "Defending Health Care: A Noble Pursuit," For The Defense, Defense Research Institute, February, 2002; "Defending Health Care Providers," For The Defense, Defense Research Institute, October, 2003. Extern, Hon. Thelton E. Henderson, U.S. District Court for the Northern District of California, 1981. *Member:* Defense Research Institute (Past Chair, Medical Liability and Health Care Law Committee; Member, Drug and Medical Device and Environmental and Toxic Tort Law Committees; Elected to National Board of Directors, 2003; Outstanding Chair of Year Award, 2003); Association of Defense Counsel of Northern California and Nevada (Member, Board of Directors); American Agricultural Law Association; Food and Drug Law Institute. (Also at San Francisco, California Office). ***PRACTICE AREAS:*** Environmental; Toxic Torts; Health Care; Drug and Medical Device; Professional Liability. ***Email:*** tpacker@gordonrees.com

SENIOR COUNSEL

MARK P. PIHL, born Portland, Oregon, November 30, 1956; admitted to bar, 1990, Oregon and U.S. District Court, District of Oregon; 1992, U.S. Court Appeals, Ninth Circuit; 2001, Illinois. *Education:* Portland State University (B.S., 1982); Willamette University (J.D., 1989). *Member:* Multnomah County and Illinois State Bar Associations; Oregon State Bar. ***LANGUAGES:*** Danish. ***PRACTICE AREAS:*** Employment; Business; Technology; Litigation. ***Email:*** mpihl@gordonrees.com

HALA J. GORES

621 S.W. MORRISON, SUITE 1218
PORTLAND, OREGON 97205
Telephone: 503-295-1940
Fax: 503-295-2651
Email: hala@goreslaw.com
URL: http://www.goreslaw.com

Personal Injury, Wrongful Death, Medical Malpractice, Therapy Malpractice, Automobile Accidents and Catastrophic Injuries, Dog Bites, Sexual Abuse, Insurance Law.

HALA J. GORES, born Nazareth, Israel, May 13, 1963; admitted to bar, 1989, Oregon. *Education:* Portland State University (B.S., with highest honors, 1983); Northwestern School of Law at Lewis and Clark College (J.D., 1987). ***PRACTICE AREAS:*** Personal Injury (100%); Wrongful Death; Medical Malpractice; Therapy Malpractice; Automobile Accidents and Injuries; Catastrophic Injury; Dog Bites; Sexual Abuse; Insurance Law.

RICHARD L. GRANT

THE GADSBY HOUSE
1205 NW 25TH AVENUE
PORTLAND, OREGON 97210-2497
Telephone: 503-222-7343
Fax: 503-226-3131
Email: rgrant@rsblaw.net

Business Law, Creditor Rights, Collections, Business Enterprises, Corporate, Limited Liability Companies, Partnerships, Small Business, Debt and Credit, General Business, Business Planning, Lawsuits, Contracts, Wills and Probate, Trusts and Estates, Estate Planning, Civil Litigation.

RICHARD L. GRANT, born Arlington, Virginia, December 25, 1952; admitted to bar, 1983, Oregon; 1984, U.S. District Court, District of Oregon; 1984, Washington; 1986, U.S. District Court, Western District of Washington; 1991, U.S. Court of Appeals, 9th Circuit. *Education:* University of Michigan (B.S., with honors, 1978); Northwestern School of Law of Lewis and Clark College (J.D., 1983). *Member:* Multnomah County, Washington State, Federal and American Bar Associations; Oregon State Bar.

GREENE & MARKLEY, P.C.

Established in 1985

1515 S.W. FIFTH AVENUE, SUITE 600
PORTLAND, OREGON 97201
Telephone: 503-295-2668
Fax: 503-224-8434
URL: http://www.greenemarkley.com

All Facets of Bankruptcy and Commercial Law including Reorganization, Trustee Representation, Litigation, Creditors' Rights and UCC, Real Estate, Tax Controversy, Collection, Corporate Matters, Appellate Law.

S. WARD GREENE, born Boston, Massachusetts, February 7, 1947; admitted to bar, 1973, Wisconsin; 1977, Oregon and U.S. District Court, District of Oregon. *Education:* Florida State University (B.S. in Bus., 1969); Duke University (J.D., 1973). Editorial Board, Oregon State Bar Debtor-Creditor Newsletter, 1986-2005. Author: "Understanding the Interplay Between Domestic Relations and Bankruptcy Law," Debtor-Creditor Newsletter, Vol. X, No. 4, 1990; "Pre-Bankruptcy Planning: A Lawyer's Duty or Death Wish?" Debtor-Creditor Newsletter, 2000. Co-Editor, Oregon Commercial Practice Manual, 1988-1994 Supplement. Past President, Owen M. Panner Inn of Court; Oregon Law Institute. *Member:* Multnomah County Bar Association (President, 1998-1999); Oregon State Bar, Board of Governors; American Bankruptcy Institute. American College of Bankruptcy. ***PRACTICE AREAS:*** Business Transactions; Bankruptcy; Commercial Litigation; Employment Law; Real Estate. ***Email:*** ward.greene@greenemarkley.com

CHARLES R. MARKLEY, born Sacramento, California, December 30, 1944; admitted to bar, 1975, Oregon; 1984, Washington, U.S. Supreme Court, U.S. Court of Appeals, Ninth Circuit, U.S. District Court, District of Oregon and U.S. District Court, Eastern and Western District of Washington; U.S District Court, Northern District of California. *Education:* University of Washington (B.A., 1972); Lewis and Clark Law School (J.D., cum laude, 1975). Editor in Chief, Environmental Law, 1974-1975. Author: Note, "Constitutional Limits on Enforcement of Air Pollution Laws," 5 Env. Law 147, 1974; "Conflicts in the Courts: NLRB Decisions as Res. Judicata in Section 303 Suits," 27 Admin. Law Rev. 83, 1975; "Damages," Continuing Legal Education, Oregon State Bar, 1986. Editor, Debtor-Creditor Newsletter, Oregon State Bar, 1981-1983. Adjunct Professor of Law, Advanced Bankruptcy, Lewis and Clark Law School, 1987-1989. *Member:* Multnomah County and American Bar Associations; Oregon State Bar; Washington State Bar Association. ***PRACTICE AREAS:*** Commercial Law; Real Estate; Litigation; Creditor; Corporate Law. ***Email:*** charles.markley@greenemarkley.com

DAVID A. FORAKER, born Minneapolis, Minnesota, February 22, 1956; admitted to bar, 1981, Oregon and U.S. District Court, District of Oregon; U.S. Court of Appeals, Ninth Circuit. *Education:* St. Cloud State University (B.S., summa cum laude, 1978); University of Oregon (J.D., 1981). Phi Kappa Phi; Beta Gamma Sigma; Phi Delta Phi. Editor, 1986-1995 and Editor-in-Chief, 1988, Debtor-Creditor Newsletter, Oregon State Bar. Planning Committee Member, 2001-2003 and Chair, 2002, Northwest Bankruptcy Institute. Author: "Marital Dissolution and the Consequences of Bankruptcy," Oregon State Bar Family and Juvenile Law Newsletter, Vol. 6, Nos. 1 and 2, 1986. Co-Author: "Avoidance Powers of Trustee and Debtor," Bankruptcy Law Handbook (OSB/CLE, 1988-1989, 1992 and 1995 Supplements); "Foreclosure of Real Property as a Fraudulent Conveyance Under § 548 of the Bankruptcy Code: The Rebirth of Durett in the Ninth Circuit," Oregon State Bar Debtor-Creditor Newsletter, Vol. V, No. 1, 1985. *Member:* Multnomah County and American Bar Associations; Oregon State Bar (Member, 1986-1995 and Chair, 1992, Bankruptcy

(This Listing Continued)

GREENE & MARKLEY, P.C., Portland—Continued

Rules and Forms Subcommittee; Fast Track Chapter 11 Subcommittee); American Bankruptcy Institute; Turnaround Management Association, Northwest Chapter. (Board Certified in Business Bankruptcy Law-American Board of Certification). ***PRACTICE AREAS:*** Bankruptcy Law; Business Reorganization; Commercial Law; Buying and Selling of Businesses. ***Email:*** david.foraker@greenemarkley.com

SANFORD R. LANDRESS, born Ventura, California, May 13, 1953; admitted to bar, 1981, Oregon; 1986, U.S. District Court, District of Oregon; 1987, U.S. Court of Appeals, Ninth Circuit. *Education:* University of Oregon (B.S., 1976; J.D., 1981). Associate Editor, Oregon Law Review, 1980-1981. Co-Author: "Avoidance Powers of Trustee and Debtor," Bankruptcy Law Handbook (OSB/CLE 1988-1989, 1992 and 1995) Supplement; "Priorities," Oregon Commercial Practice Handbook (OSB/CLE 1988-1989); "Bankruptcy and Local Government," District Attorney Handbook, 1988. *Member:* Multnomah County Bar Association; Oregon State Bar. ***PRACTICE AREAS:*** Business Law; Bankruptcy Law; Commercial Litigation. ***Email:*** sanford.landress@greenemarkley.com

STEPHEN T. BOYKE, born Chicago, Illinois, October 30, 1952; admitted to bar, 1988, Oregon; 1989, U.S. District Court, District Of Oregon; 1994, U.S. Tax Court. *Education:* University of Illinois (B.M., 1979); University of Oregon (J.D., 1988). Member, Order of the Coif. Recipient, American Jurisprudence Awards in Commercial Law, Business Planning, Corporate and Partnership Taxation, 1986-1987. Adjunct Professor, Business Law, Linfield College, 1988-1989. Member, Board of Directors, Northwest Lawyers and Artists, 1990-1991. Speaker and Author: "Bankruptcy Issues for County Tax Collectors," Oregon Association of County Tax Collectors Annual Meeting, 1994. Speaker and Co-Author: "Tax Issues Affecting Debtor-Creditor Practice," Annual Meeting of the Debtor-Creditor Section of the Oregon State Bar, 1994; "Paper, Rock & Scissors: Priorities - Who Wins?" Annual Meeting of the Debtor-Creditor Section of the Oregon State Bar, 1998. Co-Author: "Tax Aspects of Bankruptcy," Bankruptcy Law Handbook (OSB/CLE, 1998-1999). Speaker and Co-Author: "E-Commerce Bankruptcy," 18th Annual Northwest Bankruptcy Institute, 2005. *Member:* Multnomah County and American Bar Associations; Oregon State Bar. ***PRACTICE AREAS:*** Bankruptcy; Commercial Law; Taxation. ***Email:*** stephen.boyke@greenemarkley.com

GARY L. BLACKLIDGE, born San Pedro, California, April 3, 1954; admitted to bar, 1990, Oregon; 1991, U.S. District Court, District of Oregon. *Education:* Oregon State University (B.A., 1977); Northwestern School of Law of Lewis & Clark College (J.D., 1990). *Member:* Multnomah County and American Bar Associations; Oregon State Bar (Past Chair, Legislative Subcommittee of Debtor-Creditor Section). ***PRACTICE AREAS:*** Land Title Law; Creditor Rights; Bankruptcy; Real Estate. ***Email:*** gary.blacklidge@greenemarkley.com

JEFFREY M. WONG, born Honolulu, Hawaii, November 1, 1956; admitted to bar, 1984, Oregon, Washington and U.S. Tax Court. *Education:* Reed College (B.A., 1978); University of Oregon (J.D., 1984). Recipient, Commendation for Academic Excellence. Author: "The After-Acquired Property Rule with Federal Tax Liens," Oregon State Bar Debtor-Creditor Newsletter, Spring, 1992; "Federal Tax Claims," Chapter 5 of materials for Oregon Law Institute CLE on Governmental Claims In an Out of Bankruptcy, September 1993. Speaker and Co-Author: "Paper, Rock & Scissors: Priorities - Who Wins," Oregon State Bar Debtor-Creditor Section CLE in Lien Priorities, 1998. Co-Author: "Tax Aspects of Bankruptcy," Bankruptcy Law Handbook, Oregon State Bar, 1998-1999; "An Overview of Tax Administration," "Federal Tax Lien Priorities," "The New IRS CDP Appeal Process," "Offers in Compromise, A Kindler, Gentler Alternative to Bankruptcy," A Four Part Series of Articles for the Debtor-Creditor Section Newsletter of the Oregon State Bar; "Joint or Separate Income Tax Returns with Debt-Troubled Households,"; "Spousal Relief from Joint Tax Liabilities," a Two-Part Series for the Oregon State Bar Debtor-Creditor Newsletter, Winter and Spring, 2001. Speaker and Author: "Tax Issues in Bankruptcy for the Small Business," Oregon State Bar CLE, July, 2001; "Tax Issues with Damage Awards," Oregon State Bar CLE, September, 2001; "Resolving Tax Collection Controversies," Oregon Society of Public Accountants and Oregon Society of Licensed Tax Consultants Continuing Professional Education, Summer 2003; "Tax Planning Opportunities and Pitfalls in Bankruptcy Cases," Northwest Bankruptcy Institute CLE, April 2003. Trial Attorney, Office of Chief Counsel, Internal Revenue Service, 1984-1998. Special Assistant U.S. Attorney, District of Oregon, representing U.S. Government in tax controversies before the Oregon Bankruptcy Court and U.S. Tax Court, 1988-1998. *Member:* Oregon State Bar (Member, Debtor-Creditor Section). ***REPORTED CASES:*** In re Moore, 200 B.R. 687 (Bankr. D. Or. 1996); In re Goude, 201 B.R. 275 (Bankr. D. Or. 1996); Van Eck v. Commissioner, Tax Court Memo, 1995-570; 85 Gorgonio Wind Generating Co. v. Commissioner, Tax Court Memo 1994-544; TJE Enterprises v. Commissioner, 101 Tax Court 39 (1993); Hoffman et al v. Commissioner, Tax Court Memo 1989-154. ***PRACTICE AREAS:*** Taxation; Bankruptcy. ***Email:*** jeffrey.wong@greenemarkley.com

---

M. ELIZABETH DUNCAN, born Warrenton, Virginia, August 10, 1957; admitted to bar, 1987, Oregon; 1988, U.S. District Court, District of Oregon, U.S. Court of Appeals, Ninth Circuit and U.S. Supreme Court. *Education:* University of Virginia (B.A., 1979); Northwestern School of Law of Lewis and Clark College (J.D., cum laude, 1987). Recipient, President's Membership Service Award, Oregon State Bar, 1999. *Member:* Multnomah County and American Bar Associations; Oregon State Bar (Member, 1993-1998 and Chair, 1998, Executive Committee, Appellate Practice Section). ***PRACTICE AREAS:*** Appellate Litigation; Complex Litigation; Business Law. ***Email:*** elizabeth.duncan@greenemarkley.com

HEATHER E. HARRIMAN, born Portland, Oregon, September 29, 1974; admitted to bar, 1999, Oregon; 2000, U.S. District Court, District of Oregon and U.S. Court of Appeals, Ninth Circuit; 2001, U.S. Tax Court. *Education:* University of Oregon (B.A., 1996); Western New England College (J.D., cum laude, 1999). Member and Note Editor, Western New England Law Review. Author: "Manufactured Dwellings: Realty or Personalty," Oregon State Debtor-Creditor Newsletter, Summer 2000; "Reclamation Rights: The Practicalities of a Seller's Right to Reclaim Its Goods," Oregon State Bar Debtor-Creditor Newsletter, Winter, 2001; "Supreme Court and Court of Appeals Case Notes," Oregon State Bar Debtor-Creditor Newsletter, Spring 2002-Fall 2004. *Member:* Multnomah County (Young Lawyers Section, Professional Development Committee, 2004—); Federal and American Bar Associations; Oregon State Bar (Member, Sections on: Debtor-Creditor; Business and Litigation). ***PRACTICE AREAS:*** Commercial, Business and Tax Litigation; Commercial Real Estate; Debtor and Creditor. ***Email:*** heather.harriman@greenemarkley.com

DANIEL L. STEINBERG, born Portland, Oregon, October 8, 1971; admitted to bar, 1999, Oregon; U.S. District Court, District of Oregon; 2000, Washington; U.S. District Court, Western and Eastern Districts of Washington and U.S. Court of Appeals, Ninth Circuit. *Education:* Portland State University (B.S., 1996); University of Oregon (J.D., 1999). Judicial Extern to Honorable Frank Alley, U.S. Bankruptcy Court, District of Oregon, 1998-1999. Co-Author: "Preference Defense in Bankruptcy," NACM Newsletter, January 2002. Speaker: "When Counties Should Consider Retaining Bankruptcy Counsel," Oregon County Counsels Associations' Annual Meeting, November 2003. *Member:* Multnomah County and Washington State (Member, Sections on: Debtor/Creditor; Litigation) Bar Associations; Oregon State Bar (Member, Sections on: Debtor/Creditor; Litigation). ***PRACTICE AREAS:*** Commercial Litigation; Creditor Rights; Maritime Lien Litigation; Bankruptcy. ***Email:*** daniel.steinberg@greenemarkley.com

AARON M. WIGOD, born Detroit, Michigan, March 10, 1975; admitted to bar, 2002, Oregon and U.S. District Court, District of Oregon. *Education:* Michigan State University (B.S., 1997); Northwestern School of Law of Lewis and Clark College (J.D., 2002). Law Review Research Editor, Journal of Small and Emerging Business Law at Northwestern School of Law of Lewis and Clark College. Author: "The AOL-Time Warner Merger: An Analysis of the Broadband Internet Access Market, 6 J. Small and Emerging Bus. L. 349 (2002). Co-Author: "Taxation of Damage Awards," Oregon State Bar CLE, October 2001. *Member:* Multnomah County Bar Association; Oregon State Bar. ***PRACTICE AREAS:*** Commercial Litigation; Bankruptcy; Real Estate. ***Email:*** aaron.wigod@greenemarkley.com

OF COUNSEL

RIDGWAY K. FOLEY, JR., born Portland, Oregon, October 7, 1937; admitted to bar, 1963, Oregon; 1971, U.S. Supreme Court; 1972, U.S. Court of Appeals, Ninth Circuit. *Education:* Lewis and Clark College (B.S., magna cum laude, special honors in study, 1959); University of Oregon (J.D., 1963). Order of the Coif. Editor-in-Chief, Oregon Law Review, 1962-1963. *Member:* Multnomah County (Director, 1993-1997) and American Bar Associations; Oregon State Bar. ***PRACTICE AREAS:*** Appellate Litigation; Complex Litigation; Insurance Coverage; Business and Estate Planning. ***Email:*** ridgway.foley@greenemarkley.com

DAVID P. WEINER, (P.C.), born Portland, Oregon, February 9, 1948; admitted to bar, 1972, Oregon; 2002, Washington. *Education:* Claremont McKenna College (B.A., 1969); Willamette University (J.D., magna cum laude, 1972). Delta Theta Phi. Author: 7 Willamette Law Journal 481, 1971. *Member:* Multnomah County (Professional Responsibility Committee, 1984-1986), Washington State and American (Member, Real Property, Probate and Trust Section Committee on Opinion Letters in Real Estate Transactions, 1992—) Bar Associations; Oregon State Bar (Member: Oregon Supreme Court Committee on Disciplinary Rules and Procedures, 1986-2000; Joint Committee-Realtors, 1986-1989, Chairman, 1988-1989; Section on Real Property and Land Use Executive Committee, 1985-1987; Standing Committee on Opinion Letters in Oregon Real Estate Transactions, Chairman, 1988—; Committee on Real Property, 1974-1977; Chairman, 1976-1977). ***PRACTICE AREAS:*** Real Estate Law; General Business Law; Corporate Law. ***Email:*** david.weiner@greenemarkley.com

REPRESENTATIVE CLIENTS: American International Group Insurance.; Diesel Cast West, Inc.; Exel Direct, Inc.; Foress Sign Co.; Freeway Transport Inc.; Garden Fresh Restaurant Corp.; Marathon Management Co., Inc.; Robert K. Morrow, Inc. (Bankruptcy Trustee); NIKE USA, Inc.; Pacific Coast Investment Company; Pacific Continental Bank; Realvest Corporation (Real Estate Developer); RTM Portland, Inc.; Shilo Management Corporation; Suburban Auto Group; United Salad Co.; Wells-CTI, LLC; PPR Washington Square, LLC; Hanjin Shipping Company, Ltd.

THOMAS J. GREIF, P.C.

4519 S.W. CORONADO
P.O. BOX 80458
PORTLAND, OREGON 97280
Telephone: 503-244-4822
Fax: 503-244-5745
Email: GreifPC@aol.com
URL: http://www.lawyers.com/tjgreif

General Business, Corporations, Partnerships, Franchises, Licensing Agreements, Joint Ventures, Limited Liability Companies, Transactions, Real Estate Purchases/Sales, Commercial Leases, Construction Liens, Partitions, Commercial Litigation, Debtor-Creditor, Probate and Estate Planning, Will Contests, Guardianship/Conservatorships, Elder Law, Vessel Documentation Sales, and Maritime Ship Financing.

THOMAS J. GREIF, born Cleveland, Ohio, May 31, 1944; admitted to bar, 1970, Oregon. *Education:* University of Oregon (B.A., 1966); Willamette University (J.D., 1970). Member, Attorney Information Network, 1985—. *Member:* Multnomah County Bar Association; Oregon State Bar (Member, Sections on: Business Law, Debtor/Creditor; Real Estate and Land Use; Elder Law; Consumer Law; Estate Planning). ***LANGUAGES:*** Spanish. ***REPORTED CASES:*** In re Barge Ceres, _/A.M.C._ (1981). ***TRANSACTIONS:*** Closed largest commercial loan transaction in Portland Metropolitan area in 1974 between Citicorp and Williamette-Western Corp., together with numerous additional multi-million dollar maritime financing transactions involving Chemical Bank, Chase Manhattan Bank, US Bancorp, First Interstate Bank (now Wells Fargo). ***PRACTICE AREAS:*** General Business; Transactions; Real Estate Law; Commercial Litigation; Debtor and Creditor; Probate and Estate Planning; Corporations.

LEGAL SUPPORT PERSONNEL

SHARON TIMMEN-SHAHA

(This Listing Continued)

REPRESENTATIVE CLIENTS: ATM Data Corp.; Advanced Wiring Services, Allied International Credit Corp.; BZB Properties; Barnard Commercial Real Estate; Columbia Benefits Group; Contractor Management Workplace; Cottman Transmissions; Elke's Originals Ltd.; Extended Stay America/Homestead Studio Suites Hotels; Finishing First, Inc.; First A.M.E. Zion Church; Fleur de Lis Bakery; Immunology Consultants Laboratory, Inc.; Lyon Share Investment Clubs; Magnum Boats; Mortgage You; Multnomah Anglers and Hunters; Nestucca Anglers; North Rim Development Group, LLC; North Rim Properties, LLC; Northwest Redevelopment; Russell Marine & Fuel LLC; Schoppert Logging, Inc.; Synertex; Taylor Boiler & Equipment; Tri-County Plumbing, Inc.; Wellness Marketing International, Inc.; Windermere North Rim Commercial Realty.

GRENLEY, ROTENBERG, EVANS, BRAGG & BODIE, P.C.

Established in 1980

SUITE 1100 PACWEST CENTER
1211 S.W. FIFTH AVENUE
PORTLAND, OREGON 97204-3737
Telephone: 503-241-0570
Facsimile: 503-241-0914
URL: http://www.grebb.com

Business and Corporate Law, Real Estate and Land Use, Taxation (State and Federal), Pension and Profit Sharing, Estate Planning and Probate, Employment Relations and Benefits, Securities and Venture Capital, Franchising and Trade Regulation, Intellectual Property, Government and Regulatory Affairs, Municipal Law, Charitable Organizations, Alternative Dispute Resolution and related Commercial, Business, Class Actions and Civil Trial and Appellate Litigation in State and Federal Courts in Oregon and Washington.

FIRM PROFILE: Grenley, Rotenberg, Evans, Bragg & Bodie, P.C. is a full service, highest Martindale-Hubbell rated, business law firm providing a broad range of transaction and litigation legal services. The firm was formed in 1980, and it is devoted to assisting its clients in an increasingly complex and competitive business world.

The experience of the firm assures a complete package of legal services involving business transactions and planning, employment relations and benefits, taxation, pension and profit-sharing, personal financial and estate and retirement planning, business succession planning, real estate, government and regulatory affairs, land use, municipal law, technology licensing, charitable organizations, dispute resolution, and commercial and general civil litigation in state and federal courts in Oregon and Washington.

Our goal is to provide our clients with superior legal services in a prompt and cost efficient manner from experienced attorneys who specialize in their areas of practice. We are also committed to the zealous representation of our clients within the bounds of ethics, as well as the obligation to hold our clients' trust and confidences above all else. We hope that the enclosed information will be of interest and look forward to the opportunity to be of service.

JEFFREY C. BODIE, born Brooklyn, New York, February 24, 1951; admitted to bar, 1978, Oregon; U.S. District Court, District of Oregon; 1989, Washington. *Education:* Northwestern University (B.A., Psy., 1973); Northwestern School of Law, Lewis and Clark College (J.D., 1978). Member, Northwestern Law Review. Author: "The Irradiated Plaintiff: Tort Recovery Outside Price-Anderson," 6 Environmental Law 859, 1976. *Member:* Multnomah County and Washington State (Member, Sections on: Real Estate, Business Law, Intellectual Property) Bar Associations; Oregon State Bar (Member, Sections on: Real Estate and Land Use; Intellectual Property; Computer and Internet Law; Business Law). ***LANGUAGES:*** Spanish. ***REPORTED CASES:*** Lincoln Loan v. City of Portland, 158 OR App 574, 976 P.2d 60 (1999); rev. den. 330 OR 138 (2000); Witzig v. Chou, 62 OR App 479, 661, P.2d 587 (1983); rev.den. 295 OR 446 (1983). ***TRANSACTIONS:*** Purchase and development of manufacturing facility for Benchmade Knife Co., Inc.; Various commercial property purchases and sales; various asset or stock purchase agreements; various licensing transaction. ***PRACTICE AREAS:*** Business Litigation; Real Estate Litigation; Business Transactions; Business Planning; Real Estate Development; Patent Licensing; Trademark Licensing; Trade Secrets. ***Email:*** jbodie@grebb.com

MICHAEL J. BRAGG, born Clarksburg, West Virginia, November 15, 1949; admitted to bar, 1976, Oregon; 1980, U.S. Tax Court. *Education:* Oregon State University (B.S., 1971); University of the Pacific, McGeorge School of Law (J.D., 1975); Southern Methodist University (LL.M., 1976). Member: Western Pension Conference; Estate Planning Council of Portland, Inc. *Member:* Multnomah County Bar Association (Past Chair, Insurance Committee, Continuing Legal Education Committee, Certified Public Accountants Joint Committee); Oregon State Bar (Member: Sections on Taxation; Agriculture; Business). ***PRACTICE AREAS:*** Federal Taxation; Business Law; Executive Compensation; Business Transition Planning; Family Wealth Planning. ***Email:*** mbragg@grebb.com

DAVID E. DEAN, born Kansas City, Missouri, January 4, 1956; admitted to bar, 1981, Oregon and U.S. District Court, District of Oregon. *Education:* Kalamazoo College (B.A., cum laude, 1978); Northwestern School of Law of Lewis and Clark College (J.D., 1981). *Member:* Multnomah County and American Bar Associations; Oregon State Bar (Chair, Quality of Life Committee, 1999-2000; Member, Federal Practice and Procedures Committee, 1985-1986); Oregon Trial Lawyers Association; The Association of Trial Lawyers of America. ***PRACTICE AREAS:*** Commercial Litigation; Construction Law; Employment Law; Personal Injury Law. ***Email:*** ddean@grebb.com

LAWRENCE EVANS, born Portland, Oregon, October 16, 1950; admitted to bar, 1975, Oregon. *Education:* University of Oregon (B.A., 1972); Northwestern School of Law of Lewis and Clark College (J.D., 1975). Author and Lecturer: "Church Liability in the 90's - 'Practical Prevention'," Western Evangelical Seminary, 1993; "Uncontested Adoptions—A Practical Guide," Oregon Law Institute, 1988 Family Law Practice; "Strategic Alliances," Oregon State Bar CLE: Advising Business Entrepreneurs, 1996; Article and Seminar: "Church Liability in the 90's-Practical Prevention," Western Evangelical Seminary, 1993. *Member:* Multnomah Bar Association; Oregon State Bar (Member, Executive Committee, Business Law Section, 1996-1998; Chair, Continuing Legal Education Committee, Business Law Section; Ethics Committee, 1984-1985; Disciplinary Rules and Procedures Committee, 1981-1984; Executive Committee, Computer Law Section); Christian Legal Society. ***PRACTICE AREAS:*** Mergers and Acquisitions; Commercial Real Estate; General Business; Nonprofit and Charitable Organizations. ***Email:*** levans@grebb.com

GARY I. GRENLEY, born Tacoma, Washington, January 29, 1947; admitted to bar, 1975, Oregon and U.S. District Court, District of Oregon; 1976, U.S. Court of Appeals, Ninth Circuit. *Education:* University of Puget Sound (B.A., 1972); Northwestern School of Law of Lewis & Clark College (J.D., 1975). Member, Environmental Law Review, 1974-1975. Author: "The Oregon Remedy for Securities Fraud and the Federal Remedy Under Rule 10b-5: A Comparative Analysis," 14 Willamette Law Journal 127, 1978; "Liquidated Damages," Oregon State Bar Continuing Legal Education, Chapter 30, 1980. Author and Lecturer: "Accountant Professional Malpractice," Oregon State Bar Continuing Legal Education, 1987; Planner: "Alternative Dispute Resolution," Conference, Oregon Law Institute, 1990. Member, Panel of Commercial Arbitrators, American Arbitration Association. Court Appointed Special Advocate for Children. *Member:* Multnomah County (Judicial Screening Committee, 2002—), Federal (Chair, Dispute Resolution Committee, 1993-1994) and American Bar Associations; Oregon State Bar (Chair: Business Litigation Section, 1991-1992; Securities Section, Executive Committee, 1978-1981; Alternative Dispute Resolution Section, Executive Committee, 1992-1993; Chair, Antitrust and Trade Regulation Section, 2000-2001); Oregon Trial Lawyers Association (Chair: Business Litigation Section, 1991-1992). ***PRACTICE AREAS:*** Business Litigation; Securities Litigation; Real Estate Litigation; Antitrust Litigation; Class Actions. ***Email:*** ggrenley@grebb.com

LAURA L. HAMMOND, born Honolulu, Hawaii, January 31, 1970; admitted to bar, 1995, Oregon. *Education:* University of Oregon (B.A., 1991; J.D., 1994). Recipient: International Baccalaureate Degree; American Jurisprudence Award, Family Law. *Member:* Multnomah County Bar Association; Oregon State Bar (Member, Taxation Section). ***PRACTICE AREAS:*** Estate Planning; Corporate Law; Qualified Plans; Business Succession Planning. ***Email:*** lhammond@grebb.com

KELLY MELTZER, born Mesa, Arizona, July 2, 1969; admitted to bar, 1997, Oregon. *Education:* University of Colorado at Boulder (B.S., 1992); Northwestern School of Law, Lewis and Clark College (J.D., 1997). Member, Northwestern Law Review. Recipient, Environmental Law Certificate. Author: "Liquidated Damages," Chapter Revision, DAMAGES, Oregon CLE, 1998; "Warranties in Real Estate Sales," Chapter Revision, Fundamentals of Real Estate Transactions, Oregon CLE, 2001. *Member:* Multnomah County Bar Association; Oregon State Bar (Member, Business Law Section). ***PRACTICE AREAS:*** Mergers and Acquisitions; General Business; Employment Law. ***Email:*** ekmeltzer@grebb.com

STAN N. ROTENBERG, born Portland, Oregon, December 28, 1949; admitted to bar, 1977, Oregon. *Education:* University of Oregon (B.S., 1973); University of Puget Sound (J.D., 1976). Author: "Warranties In Real Estate Sales," Oregon State Bar Continuing Legal Education, Fundamentals of Real Estate Transactions, Chapter 8, 1991. *Member:* Multnomah County Bar Association; Oregon State Bar (Member: Real Estate and Land Use Section; Business and Corporate Law Section; Chairman, Joint Realtors Committee, Portland Board of Realtors Legal Committee, 1990). ***PRACTICE AREAS:*** Commercial Real Estate Transactions; General Business. ***Email:*** stanrote@grebb.com

---

JAMES F. MARRON, born Moscow, Idaho, October 5, 1972; admitted to bar, 2000, Oregon and U.S. District Court, District of Oregon. *Education:* Pacific Lutheran University (B.A., 1995); Drake University (J.D., with honors, 1998). *Member:* Oregon State Bar (Member, Sections on: Business Law; Litigation; New Lawyer's Division). ***PRACTICE AREAS:*** General Litigation; Arbitration; Mediation; Construction Defect Litigation; Insurance Coverage. ***Email:*** jmarron@grebb.com

DAVID L. SHAWCROSS, born Portland, Oregon, May 21, 1975; admitted to bar, 2004, Oregon. *Education:* Washington State University (B.A., 2000); Northwestern School of Law (J.D., 2004). [U.S. Army, 1994-1997, E-4]. ***PRACTICE AREAS:*** Business; Estate Planning; Estate Administration. ***Email:*** dshawcross@grebb.com

NICHOLAS J. SLINDE, born Minneapolis, Minnesota, December 23, 1974; admitted to bar, 2000, Oregon; 2002, U.S. District Court, District of Oregon. *Education:* University of Iowa (B.A., 1997); University of Oregon (J.D., 2000). *Member:* Oregon State Bar (Member, New Member Division; Member, Sections on Business; Construction); Oregon Trial Lawyers Association. ***PRACTICE AREAS:*** General Practice; Business; Employment; Construction; Litigation. ***Email:*** nslinde@grebb.com

PAUL H. TRINCHERO, born Mountain View, California, December 24, 1971; admitted to bar, 2001, Oregon; 2002, U.S. District Court, District of Oregon. *Education:* University of California, Davis (B.S.C., 1995); Northwestern School of Law of Lewis & Clark College (J.D., 2001). Associate Editor, Environmental Law Review, 1999-2001. *Member:* Multnomah County and American Bar Associations; Oregon State Bar. ***PRACTICE AREAS:*** Business Litigation; Securities Litigation; Employment Litigation; Intellectual Property. ***Email:*** ptrinchero@grebb.com

JOSEPH A. TRIPI, born Rochester, New York, August 11, 1966; admitted to bar, 1992, Oregon; 1993, U.S. District Court, District of Oregon. *Education:* University of Rhode Island (B.S., 1988); University of Oregon (J.D., 1992). *Member:* Multnomah County Bar Association (Sections on: Construction Law; Business Litigation); Oregon State Bar; Associated General Contractors; American Builders and Contractors; American Institute of Architects; Home Builders Association. ***PRACTICE AREAS:*** Construction Litigation; Franchise Litigation; Business Litigation. ***Email:*** jtripi@grebb.com

OF COUNSEL

NORMAN A. RICKLES, born Portland, Oregon, December 15, 1950; admitted to bar, 1979, Oregon. *Education:* University of Oregon (B.A., 1974); Northwestern School of Law of Lewis and Clark College (J.D., 1979). Member, Panel of Arbitrators, American Arbitration Association, Multnomah County Circuit Court. *Member:* Multnomah County Bar Association; Oregon State Bar (Member: Sections on: Business and Corporation, Real Estate and Land Use, Estate Planning and Administration). (Also practicing individually). ***PRACTICE AREAS:*** Real Estate Law; Business Law; Estate Planning Law; Probate Administration. ***Email:*** nrickles@grebb.com

(This Listing Continued)

GRENLEY, ROTENBERG, EVANS, BRAGG & BODIE, P.C., Portland—Continued

REPRESENTATIVE CLIENTS: Action Equipment Co., Inc.; Air Flow Systems, Inc.; All Star Ford; All Star Toyota; Apothecary Software, Inc.; Astoria Ford; Autowerks NW, Inc.; Beacon Homes, LLC; Beaverton Foursquare Church; Beaverton Nissan; Bees Knees Honey Factory; Benchmade Knife Company, Inc.; Boyland Honda; C & R Real Estate Services, Co.; Central Pacific Bank; Christian Copyright Licensing, Inc.; Clark's Discount, Inc.; Coast Services, Inc.; Columbia Ultimate Business Systems, Inc.; CoreMedia Training Solutions; CSL Farms, Inc.; Custom Cast Corporations; Davis Agency, Inc.; DCI International; East Hill Church; Emerald Commodities, Inc.; Encounter Collaborative Corporation; Equity Development, Inc.; E/S Chase Company, Inc.; Fast Break, Inc.; Fidelity National Title Insurance Co.; First Pacific Mortgage, Inc.; Food Management Corporation; Gresham Dodge, Inc.; The Hasson Company; Hearing Aid Counselors, Inc.; Hoffman, Stewart & Scmidt, P.C.; Hot Off The Press, Inc.; J & L Nursery Company; JHI Engineering, Inc.; Jim Fisher Volvo; Johnson Sheen Advertising, Inc.; Karakas, Parmley-Eisner & Associates, LLC; Lakeside Lumber, Inc.; Leo Gentry Wholesale Nursery, Inc.; Leopold Ketel, LLC; Lincoln Loan Co.; Mentor Group; Metro Metals NW, Inc.; Moffatt Rosenthal Advertising, Inc.; Mountain Fresh Bottled Water Co.; McCormack Pacific Company; Nautamatic Marine Systems; Northstar Glassworks, Inc.; Pal Joey Sport Pub, LLC; Platinum Construction Service, Inc.; R & R Textiles, Inc.; Martha E. Rich, DMD, PC; Rosen Brown Direct, Inc.; Shamrock Lumber; Sentinel Group, LLC; Simms Fine Homes, Inc.; Sounds of Life Hearing Centers; Specialty Polymers Products, Inc.; Symonds, Evans & Company, P.C.; Town & Country Dealerships; Vintage House Merchants, Inc.; WatchTV, Inc.; West Coast Wallboard, Inc.

GREGORY L. GUDGER

140 SW ARTHUR STREET, SUITE 200
PORTLAND, OREGON 97201
Telephone: 503-228-1170
Fax: 503-228-1173
Email: dcglg@hotmail.com

Family Law, Criminal Law, Civil Rights Law, Employment Law, Torts, DUI, Real Estate, Litigation, Probate.

GREGORY L. GUDGER, born Washington, D.C., November 3, 1951; admitted to bar, 1987, Oregon; U.S. Court of Appeals for the District of Columbia; U.S. Supreme Court; U.S. District Court, District of Oregon; U.S. Court of Federal Claims. *Education:* University of Oregon (B.S., 1975); Willamette University (J.D., 1986). *Member:* Multnomah County Bar Association.

HAGEN O'CONNELL LLP

Established in 2003
BANK OF AMERICA BUILDING
SUITE 1500
121 SW MORRISON STREET
PORTLAND, OREGON 97204-3160
Telephone: 503-227-2900
Fax: 503-227-3870
URL: http://www.hagenoconnell.com
Email: shval@hagenoconnell.com
URL: http://www.lawyers.com/hagenoconnell

Taxation Law, Corporate Law, Mergers and Acquisitions, Business Law, Estate Planning, Executive Compensation, Estate Administration, Probate, Business Transactions, Real Estate, Litigation.

JOSEPH T. HAGEN, born Chicago, Illinois, January 24, 1945; admitted to bar, 1972, Oregon; 1974, California and U.S. Supreme Court. *Education:* Mt. Angel College (B.A., 1967); University of Innsbruck; Georgetown University Law Center (J.D., 1971); New York University (LL.M. in Taxation, 1972). Member, Georgetown Journal of International Law and Policy, 1970-1971. Editor, Partnership Section of Advising Oregon Business, Continuing Legal Education, 1978-1979. Adjunct Professor, Northwestern School of Law at Lewis and Clark College, 1976-1983. Co-founder, Member, Board of Directors, Portland Tax Forum, 1987—and Chairman, Portland Tax Forum, 1988. *Member:* Multnomah County, Washington State and American Bar Associations; Oregon State Bar (Treasurer, 1979-1980; Secretary, 1980-1981, Tax Section); State Bar of California. ***PRACTICE AREAS:*** Taxation Law; Corporate Law; Mergers and Acquisitions; Business Law; Estate Planning; Executive Compensation. ***Email:*** jhagen@hagenoconnell.com

KEVIN P. O'CONNELL, born Brooklyn, New York, January 7, 1942; admitted to bar, 1966, Oregon, U.S. District Court, District of Oregon and U.S. Court of Appeals, Ninth Circuit. *Education:* Fordham University (B.A., 1963); Fordham University Law School (LL.B., 1966); New York University (LL.M. in Taxation, 1970). Law Clerk to Hon. Arno H. Denecke, Associate Justice, Supreme Court of Oregon, 1966-1967. *Member:* Multnomah County and American Bar Associations; Oregon State Bar. ***PRACTICE AREAS:*** Taxation; General Corporate Law; Tax and Business Litigation. ***Email:*** koconnell@hagenoconnell.com

STEVEN B. HVAL, born Portland, Oregon, November 15, 1965; admitted to bar, 1993, Oregon; 1995, U.S. District Court, District of Oregon, U.S. Court of Federal Claims and U.S. Tax Court. *Education:* University of Washington (B.A., 1988); University of Oregon (J.D., 1992); University of Miami (LL.M., 1993). *Member:* Multnomah County and American Bar Associations; Oregon State Bar. ***PRACTICE AREAS:*** Taxation; Corporate Law; Tax Litigation; Business Litigation; Estate Planning. ***Email:*** shval@hagenoconnell.com

THOMAS J. FRASER, born West Point, Mississippi, January 16, 1951; admitted to bar, 1985, Oregon. *Education:* University of Kansas; University of Oregon (B.S., with honors, 1981; J.D., 1985); George Washington University (LL.M. in Taxation, 1987). *Member:* Multnomah County Bar and American Bar Associations; Oregon State Bar. ***PRACTICE AREAS:*** Taxation; General Corporate Law; Estate Planning and Administration. ***Email:*** tfraser@hagenoconnell.com

---

PAUL D. MIGCHELBRINK, born Goldendale, Washington, December 13, 1965; admitted to bar, 1993, Oregon; 1995, U.S. District Court, District of Oregon. *Education:* University of Idaho (B.S., 1988); Willamette University (J.D., cum laude, 1993). *Member:* Multnomah County and American Bar Associations; Oregon State Bar (Member, Debtor Creditor and Business Law Sections). ***PRACTICE AREAS:*** Business Transactions; Corporate Law; Corporate Finance; Mergers and Acquisitions; Intellectual Property; Real Estate. ***Email:*** pmigchelbrink@hagenoconnell.com

OF COUNSEL

JOHN C. RAMIG, born North Platte, Nebraska, June 10, 1958; admitted to bar, 1985, Oregon. *Education:* Harvard University (A.B., magna cum laude, 1980); University of Virginia Law School (J.D., 1984). Author: Case Comment, "Winpisinger v. Watson: Challenging the Incumbency Advantage in Presidential Elections," Virginia Journal of Law & Politics, Fall, 1983. *Member:* Multnomah County Bar Association (Member, Section on Administrative Law and Practice; Vice Chairman, Forestry Committee, 1989—); American Bar Association; Oregon State Bar. ***PRACTICE AREAS:*** Government Relations; Administrative Law; International Law; Sports Law; Entertainment Law; Business Law; Nonprofit Corporations; Nonprofit Organizations Law. ***Email:*** jramig@hagenoconnell.com

DIANE C. KERNS, born Minneapolis, Minnesota, January 6, 1949; admitted to bar, 1978, Oregon; 2002, Washington. *Education:* Marquette University (B.A., magna cum laude, 1971); Northwestern School of Law of Lewis & Clark College (J.D., 1978). Phi Beta Kappa. Author: "Mergers and Consolidations, The A Reorganization," Advising Oregon Businesses (Ore. State Bar CLE, 1979, 1989, 1994); "Tax Aspects of Intellectual Property," Advising Oregon Businesses (Ore. State Bar CLE); "Income Tax Consequences of Incorporation," Advising Oregon Businesses 1989 (Ore. State Bar CLE, 1989, 1994, 2001). Member, School Advisors Council for St. John the Baptist School. *Member:* Oregon State Bar (Member, Sections on: Taxation; Estate Planning and Administration; Business Law); Multnomah County and Washington State Bar Associations; Estate Planning Council of Portland; Oregon Women Lawyers. ***PRACTICE AREAS:*** Taxation Law; Corporate Law; Estate Planning; Administrative Law. ***Email:*** dkerns@hagenoconnell.com

HAGLUND, KELLEY, HORNGREN & JONES LLP

Established in 1988
ONE MAIN PLACE
101 S.W. MAIN, SUITE 1800
PORTLAND, OREGON 97204
Telephone: 503-225-0777
Facsimile: 503-225-1257
URL: http://www.hk-law.com
URL: http://www.lawyers.com/hk-law

Commercial Litigation, Business (including Forest Products Industry), Contracts, Antitrust, Public Lands, Land Use, Products Liability, Personal Injury, Probate, Admiralty, Administrative Law, Employment Law, Indian Law.

MEMBERS OF FIRM

MICHAEL E. HAGLUND, born Portland, Oregon, March 28, 1952; admitted to bar, 1977, Oregon. *Education:* Western Oregon University (B.A., 1974); Boston University (J.D., 1977). Note and Comment Editor, Boston University Law Review, 1976-1977. Adjunct Professor of Law, Willamette University College of Law, 1982-1983. Lawyer Delegate, Ninth Circuit Judicial Conference, 1991—. *Member:* Multnomah Bar Association (President, Board of Directors, 1989-1990); Oregon State Bar. ***PRACTICE AREAS:*** Antitrust; Commercial Litigation; Admiralty Law; Administrative Law; Natural Resources Law; Forestry Law; Personal Injury. ***Email:*** haglund@hk-law.com

MICHAEL K. KELLEY, born Spokane, Washington, February 25, 1959; admitted to bar, 1985, Oregon. *Education:* Carroll College (B.A., 1981); University of Notre Dame (J.D., 1984). *Member:* Multnomah and American Bar Associations; Oregon State Bar; The Association of Trial Lawyers of America. ***PRACTICE AREAS:*** Commercial Litigation; Admiralty Law; Antitrust. ***Email:*** kelley@hk-law.com

SCOTT W. HORNGREN, born Chicago, Illinois, February 15, 1955; admitted to bar, 1988, Oregon. *Education:* Stanford University; Oregon State University (B.S., in Forestry, 1977); University of San Francisco; Northwestern School of Law of Lewis and Clark College (J.D., cum laude, 1988). Co-Author: "The Minimum Management Requirements of Forest Planning," Environmental Law, Vol. 17, 1987. *Member:* Oregon State Bar; Society of American Foresters. ***PRACTICE AREAS:*** Forestry Law; Timber and Logging Law; Environmental Law; Public Lands Law; Commercial Litigation; Administrative Law; Government Contracts; Endangered Species. ***Email:*** horngren@hk-law.com

TIMOTHY J. JONES, born Stayton, Oregon, February 4, 1958; admitted to bar, 1989, Oregon. *Education:* Willamette University; Oregon State University (B.S., 1982); Willamette University (J.D., 1988). *Member:* Multnomah County and American Bar Associations; Oregon State Bar; Oregon Trial Lawyers Association; The Association of Trial Lawyers of America. ***PRACTICE AREAS:*** Plaintiffs Personal Injury; Catastrophic Injury; Wrongful Death; Construction Accidents; Maritime Personal Injury; Motor Vehicle Accidents and Injuries; Medical Malpractice; Products Liability. ***Email:*** timjones@hk-law.com

MICHAEL G. NEFF, born Great Falls, Montana, August 16, 1960; admitted to bar, 1992, Oregon. *Education:* Whitman College (B.A., 1982); University of Oregon (J.D., 1992). Member, National Moot Court Team; Tigard Planning Commission, 1996-1998; the Oregon Investment Board. ***LANGUAGES:*** Russian. ***PRACTICE AREAS:*** Real Property; Boundary Disputes; Easements; Real Estate Valuation; Zoning Law; Land Use; Administrative Law; Commercial Litigation. ***Email:*** neff@hk-law.com

SHAY S. SCOTT, born Eugene, Oregon, January 4, 1964; admitted to bar, 1993, Oregon. *Education:* Arizona State University (B.M., Music Theory, 1987); University of Oregon (J.D., 1993). Executive Editor, Oregon Law Review, 1992-1993. *Member:* Oregon State Bar; Washington State Bar Association. ***PRACTICE AREAS:*** Litigation; Antitrust; Public Lands Law. ***Email:*** shay@hk-law.com

(This Listing Continued)

JULIE A. WEIS, born Wilmington, Delaware, September 26, 1962; admitted to bar, 1997, Oregon. *Education:* Baylor University (B.A., 1987; M.S., 1990); University of Georgia (Doctoral Program in Ecology, 1990-1994); Northwestern School of Law (J.D., 1997). Cornelius Honor Society. Articles Editor, Environmental Law, 1996-1997. Author: "Eliminating the National Forest Management Act's Diversity Requirement as a Substantive Standard," Environmental Law, Vol. 27. *Member:* American Bar Association (Member, Sections of Natural Resources, Energy and Environmental Law). ***PRACTICE AREAS:*** Commercial Litigation; Natural Resources; Trademarks; Administrative Law; Environmental Law. ***Email:*** weis@hk-law.com

LEROY W. WILDER, born Eureka, California, July 15, 1944; admitted to bar, 1973, California; 1977, District of Columbia; 1980, Oregon. *Education:* Oregon State University (B.S., 1967); Golden Gate University (J.D., 1973). Editor-in-Chief, Golden Gate Law Review, 1972-1973. Member, Karuk Tribe of California Indians. One of the first two California Indians admitted to California Bar. [Captain, U.S. Army, Infantry 1967-1970]. ***PRACTICE AREAS:*** Indian Law. ***Email:*** lwilder@hk-law.com

WILLIAM K. BARQUIN, born Lander, Wyoming, August 27, 1973; admitted to bar, 1998, Oregon; 2003, U.S. District Court, District of Oregon and U.S. Court of Appeals, Ninth Circuit. *Education:* Gonzaga University (B.A., 1995; J.D., cum laude, 1998). *Member:* Multnomah Bar Association; Oregon State Bar (Member, Indian Law Section, Executive Committee, 2001-2002); Federal Bar Association. ***PRACTICE AREAS:*** Federal Indian Law. ***Email:*** wbarquin@hk-law.com

ASSOCIATES

DANICA K. HIBPSHMAN, born Silverton, Oregon, December 31, 1976; admitted to bar, 2003, Oregon. *Education:* University of Alaska (B.A., 1999); Willamette University College of Law (J.D., 2003). *Member:* Multnomah Bar Association; Oregon State Bar. ***PRACTICE AREAS:*** Civil Litigation; Probate. ***Email:*** dhibpshman@hk-law.com

CHRISTOPHER G. LUNDBERG, born Iowa City, Iowa, March 20, 1966; admitted to bar, 1994, Oregon. *Education:* University of Wisconsin; Southern Methodist University (B.A., 1988); Northwestern College of Law (J.D., 1993). Judicial Clerk, Honorable Paul J. DeMuniz, Oregon Court of Appeals, 1997-1999. Staff Attorney, Oregon Supreme Court Racial/Ethnic Task Force Implementation Committee, 1994-1996. ***PRACTICE AREAS:*** Civil Litigation; Employment Law; Whistleblower Litigation; Business Torts; Trademark Litigation. ***Email:*** clundberg@hk-law.com

COUNSEL

JAMES L. FRANCESCONI, born Eureka, California, July 15, 1952; admitted to bar, 1978, Oregon and U.S. District Court, District of Oregon; 1994, U.S. Court of Appeals, Fourth Circuit. *Education:* Stanford University (B.A., Humanities, with honors, 1974); University of Oregon (J.D., 1978). Member: Portland City Commissioners, 1997-2004; Oregon Workers Compensation Committee, 1985-1986. *Member:* Oregon State Bar (Member, Executive Committee on Worker's Compensation, 1983); Oregon Trial Lawyers Association (Member, Board of Governors, 1987-1988). ***LANGUAGES:*** Italian. ***PRACTICE AREAS:*** Personal Injury (40%); Government Affairs (30%); Workers Compensation (30%). ***Email:*** jfrancesconi@hk-law.com

LEGAL SUPPORT PERSONNEL

Kent S. Kelly (Staff Forester) ***Scott A. Rathbone*** (Legal Assistant)

REPRESENTATIVE CLIENTS: Columbia Helicopters, Inc.; Ellett Construction Co. Inc.; Mt. View Public Golf Course; American Forest Resource Council; Portland Saturday Market; Roseburg Forest Products; SDS Lumber Co.; United Agri Products.

LAW OFFICES OF A. ALEXANDER HAMALIAN

714 SW 20TH PLACE
PORTLAND, OREGON 97205
Telephone: 503-222-3641
Fax: 503-274-7975
Email: mistrial@teleport.com
URL: http://www.lawyers.com/ahamalian

Criminal Defense.

A. ALEXANDER HAMALIAN, admitted to bar, 1996, Oregon and Washington. *Education:* California State University (B.A., 1992); Lewis and Clark College (J.D., 1995). ***PRACTICE AREAS:*** Criminal Defense.

LAW OFFICES OF MICHAEL G. HANLON

A PROFESSIONAL CORPORATION
1300 CONGRESS CENTER
1001 S.W. FIFTH AVENUE
PORTLAND, OREGON 97204
Telephone: 503-228-9787
Facsimile: 503-224-4200
Email: mgh@hanlonlaw.com
URL: http://www.hanlonlaw.com

Business Litigation including Antitrust, Securities and other Complex Business Litigation. General Corporate, Business and Real Estate. Creditors Rights, Bankruptcy and Commercial Law.

MICHAEL G. HANLON, born Palo Alto, California, May 7, 1953; admitted to bar, 1979, Oregon, U.S. District Court, District of Oregon and U.S. Court of Appeals, Ninth Circuit; 1995, U.S. District Court, Northern District of California and U.S. Supreme Court.

(This Listing Continued)

Education: University of Oregon (B.A., 1975); Northwestern School of Law of Lewis and Clark College (J.D., 1979). Member, Moot Court Board. Assistant Attorney General, Antitrust Division, State of Oregon Department of Justice, 1980. Recipient, Award of Merit, Multnomah Bar Association, 2001. Author: "Permanent Injunctions, Temporary Restraining Orders, and Preliminary Injunctions," Chapter 30 (2001 Supp.), Oregon Civil Pleading & Practice, Oregon State Bar. Co-Author: "Attorney Fees and Costs," Chapter 26 (2002 Supp.), Federal Civil Litigation in Oregon, Oregon State Bar. *Member:* Multnomah County (Member, 1998-2001, Co-Chair, 2000-2001, Professionalism Committee; Legislative Committee, 1986-1989; Multnomah Arbitration Panel, 1985—), Federal and American (Private Antitrust Litigation Committee, 1999-2000; Member, Sections on: Antitrust, Litigation, Business Law) Bar Associations; Oregon State Bar (Federal Practice and Procedure Committee, 1988-1991, 2001-2004; Chair, 2004; Member, 1996-2001, Chair, 1999-2000, Antitrust Section, Executive Committee; Member, Sections on: Antitrust, Securities, Litigation, Real Estate, Appellate). ***REPORTED CASES:*** Vogl v. Dept. of Rev., 327 Or. 193, 960 P.2d 373 (1998) ($340 million recovery); Wong v. Wong, 134 Or. App. 13, 894 P. 2d 519, rev. denied 322 Or. 167, 903 P. 2d 885 (1995); Sims Snowboards, Inc. v. Kelly, 863 F. 2d 643 (9th Cir. 1988); ; In Re Coordinated Pretrial Proceedings In Petroleum Products Antitrust Litigation, 497 F. Supp. 218 (C.D. Cal. 1980). ***PRACTICE AREAS:*** Litigation; Business Law; Antitrust; Securities Litigation; Class Actions. ***Email:*** mgh@hanlonlaw.com

OF COUNSEL

JOHN H. DURKHEIMER, born Portland, Oregon, February 10, 1953; admitted to bar, 1979, Oregon, U.S. District Court, District of Oregon and U.S. Court of Appeals, Ninth Circuit. *Education:* Pomona College (B.A., 1975); University of Copenhagen, Denmark; University of Oregon (J.D., 1978). Chair, Northwest Bankruptcy Institute, 1988. *Member:* Oregon State Bar (Chair, Debtor/Creditor Section, 1991-1992); American Bankruptcy Institute. ***PRACTICE AREAS:*** Creditors Rights; Bankruptcy; Business Law; Commercial Law. ***Email:*** jhd@hanlonlaw.com

REPRESENTATIVE CLIENTS: Coos-Curry Electric Cooperative, Inc.; Comotir, Inc.; Kai-Perm Northwest Federal Credit Union; Pacific Northwest Land Investments, LLC.

LAW OFFICES OF PETER O. HANSEN

620 S.W. FIFTH AVENUE, SUITE 1210
PORTLAND, OREGON 97204
Telephone: 503-228-6040
Fax: 503-226-0457
URL: http://www.peterohansenlawyers.com

Workers Compensation, Personal Injury, Maritime Law, Social Security Disability.

PETER O. HANSEN, born North Bend, Oregon, July 29, 1950; admitted to bar, 1975, Oregon, U.S. District Court, District of Oregon and U.S. Court of Appeals, Ninth Circuit; 2000, District of Columbia; 2001, Washington. *Education:* University of Oregon (B.S., 1972); Willamette University (J.D., 1975). President, Oregon Workers Compensation Attorneys, 1984-1989. *Member:* Multnomah County and American Bar Associations; Oregon State Bar (Member, Executive Committee, 1991-1993; Workers Compensation Section); The District of Columbia Bar; The Association of Trial Lawyers of America; Oregon Trial Lawyers Association.

CHRISTOPHER R. HARDMAN

909 SOUTHWEST ST. CLAIR
PORTLAND, OREGON 97205
Telephone: 503-916-1787
Fax: 503-916-1789
Email: crhardman@crhardman.com
URL: http://www.lawyers.com/crhardman

Attorney Professional Responsibility and Ethics Defense, Professional Licensing, Corporate Planning, Business Litigation, Consumer Fraud, Litigation, Insurance Defense, Criminal Defense.

CHRISTOPHER R. HARDMAN, born Salem, Oregon, October 10, 1954; admitted to bar, 1979, Oregon; 1980, U.S. District Court, District of Oregon; 1983, U.S. Supreme Court; 1990, U.S. Court of Appeals, Ninth Circuit; 1991, Washington. *Education:* Hanover College (B.A., 1976); Willamette University (J.D., 1979). Deputy District Attorney, Multnomah County, 1980-1989. Assistant Disciplinary Counsel, Oregon State Bar, 1989-1990. Associate, Holmes and Rickles, 1990-1997. Member: American Trial Lawyers Association, 1997-1999; Oregon District Attorneys Association, 1980-1989; Oregon Association of Defense Counsel, 1990-1998; Washington Defense Trial Lawyers Association, 1991-1998; Defense Research Institute, 1990-1998. Arbitrator, State Attorney General's Consumer Arbitration Program. *Member:* Multnomah, Washington State and American (Member, Litigation, Tort and Insurance Practice & Business Sections; Young Lawyers Division (Fellow); YLD Executive Council and YLD Assembly; ABA Center for Professional Responsibility) Bar Associations; Oregon State Bar; Oregon Young Lawyers Association (President, 1985-1986); Association of Professional Responsibility Lawyers; Oregon Trial Lawyers Association;. ***PRACTICE AREAS:*** Professional Licensing; Corporate Planning; Business Litigation; Consumer Fraud; Litigation; Insurance Defense; Criminal Defense.

HARRANG LONG GARY RUDNICK P.C.

Established in 1957

1001 S.W. 5TH AVENUE, SUITE 1650
PORTLAND, OREGON 97204
Telephone: 503-242-0000
Fax: 503-241-1458
URL: http://www.harrang.com

Eugene, Oregon Office: 300 East 10th Avenue, Suite 300. Telephone: 541-485-0220. Fax: 541-686-6564.

Salem, Oregon Office: 333 High Street, N.E., Suite 200. Telephone: 503-371-3330. Fax: 503-371-5336.

General Civil Trial and Appellate Practice in all State and Federal Courts, Governmental and Business Law, Corporate Law, Administrative Law, Financial Services, Securities Law, Creditors Rights, Partnership Law, Real Estate, State and Local Government Law, Environmental Law, Zoning, Planning and Land Use, Estate Planning and Probate, Insurance Law, Civil, Business, Complex and Tort Litigation, Alternative Dispute Resolution, Labor and Employment Law, Employee Benefits, Intellectual Property, Health Law, Nonprofit Law.

FIRM PROFILE: Harrang Long Gary Rudnick P.C. was organized as a partnership on July 1, 1957. It has offices in Eugene, Salem and Portland, Oregon. The firm conducts a diversified general practice with particular emphasis in municipal and public law, trial and appellate practice, intellectual property law and corporate, business and real estate law.

DAVID R. DENECKE, born Portland, Oregon, May 31, 1949; admitted to bar, 1978, Oregon, U.S. District Court, District of Oregon and U.S. Court of Appeals, Ninth Circuit; U.S. District Court, Northern District of California. *Education:* Oregon State University, University of Pavia in Pavia, Italy and University of Oregon (B.A., 1971); Northwestern School of Law of Lewis and Clark (J.D., 1978). Former Vice President, Assistant General Counsel, Amfac, Inc., 1982-1989. Assistant to the Chairman and General Counsel, Onsite Energy, (energy services subsidiary of Pacificorp). *Member:* Oregon State Bar; American Bar Association. ***PRACTICE AREAS:*** Food and Agriculture; Antitrust and Trade Regulation; Business Law; Commercial Law; Commercial Real Estate; Corporate Law; Copyrights; Intellectual Property; International Trade; Patent Licensing; Real Estate; Resorts and Leisure; Trademarks. ***Email:*** david.denecke@harrang.com

WILLIAM F. GARY, born Palo Alto, California, December 4, 1950; admitted to bar, 1976, California; 1977, Oregon; 1980, U.S. Supreme Court. *Education:* University of Oregon (B.A., 1973); University of California, Hastings College of Law (J.D., 1976). Member: Order of the Coif; Thurston Society. Editor, Hastings Law Journal, 1975-1976. Law Clerk, Oregon Court of Appeals, 1976-1978. Solicitor General of Oregon, 1981-1983. Deputy Attorney General of Oregon, 1983-1988. Special Assistant Attorney General, State of Oregon, 1989-1994, 1998-1999. City Attorney of Eugene, 1989-1996. Member, Oregon Criminal Justice Commission, 1996—. Governor's Special Task Force on Public Employees Retirement System, 2002. *Member:* Oregon State Bar (Executive Committee, Appellate Practice Section); State Bar of California; American Bar Association. Fellow, American Academy of Appellate Lawyers, 2001—. ***PRACTICE AREAS:*** Civil Litigation; Appellate Law; Municipal Law; Administrative Law. ***Email:*** william.f.gary@harrang.com

CAROLINE R. GUEST, born Fort Bragg, North Carolina, April 3, 1959; admitted to bar, 1994, Oregon. *Education:* Smith College (A.B., 1981); University of Oregon (J.D., 1994). Order of the Coif. *Member:* Oregon State Bar (Member, Labor and Employment Section); American Bar Association (Member, Labor and Employment Law Section). ***PRACTICE AREAS:*** Employment Litigation. ***Email:*** caroline.guest@harrang.com

SUSAN D. MARMADUKE, born Boston, Massachusetts, March 3, 1952; admitted to bar, 1978, California; 1979, Pennsylvania (inactive); 1984, Oregon; 1985, U.S. Court of Appeals, Ninth Circuit; 1989, U.S. Court of Appeals, Fourth Circuit; 1995, U.S. Court of Appeals for the Federal Circuit and U.S. Supreme Court. *Education:* Portland State University (B.A., cum laude, 1974); University of Tunis, Tunisia (Arabic Language, 1974); Boalt Hall School of Law, University of California, Berkeley (J.D., 1977). Author, "Jurisdiction, Removal and Remand," Federal Civil Litigation in Oregon, Oregon State Bar CLE, 2002 Supplement. *Member:* Multnomah and American Bar Associations; Oregon State Bar; State Bar of California; United States District Court for the District of Oregon (Member, Local Rules Advisory Committee); Oregon Association of Defense Counsel (Member, Amicus Committee). Fellow, American Bar Foundation. ***PRACTICE AREAS:*** Civil Litigation; Appellate Practice. ***Email:*** susan.marmaduke@harrang.com

FRANK A. MOSCATO, born Stockton, California, February 10, 1943; admitted to bar, 1972, Oregon, U.S. District Court, District of Oregon and U.S. Court of Appeals, Ninth Circuit; 2002, Washington. *Education:* Portland State University (B.S., 1969); Willamette University (J.D., 1972). *Member:* Multnomah County, Washington State, Federal (Member, Oregon Chapter) and American (Member, Sections on: Insurance, Negligence and Compensation Law) Bar Associations; Oregon State Bar; The Defense Research Institute; Oregon Association of Defense Counsel; Federation of Defense and Corporate Counsel; United States Arbitration and Mediation Panel (1994—); American Board of Trial Advocates. ***PRACTICE AREAS:*** Complex Civil Litigation; Medical and Legal Malpractice Defense; Products Liability and Insurance Defense. ***Email:*** frank.moscato@harrang.com

JAMES E. MOUNTAIN, JR., born Seattle, Washington, June 24, 1948; admitted to bar, 1975, Oregon and U.S. District Court, District of Oregon; 1977, U.S. Court of Appeals, Ninth Circuit; 1980, U.S. Supreme Court. *Education:* University of Oregon (B.A., 1970); Lewis & Clark College, Northwestern School of Law (J.D., 1975). Recipient: American Jurisprudence Award in Labor Law; National Association of Attorneys General, President's Distinguished Service Award, 1988. Solicitor General, State of Oregon, 1983-1986. Special Counsel to the Attorney General, State of Oregon, 1986-1988. The Deputy Attorney General, State of Oregon, 1988-1990. Member, Board of Directors, Marion-Polk Legal Aid Society. *Member:* Marion County Bar Association (President, 2000); Oregon State Bar (Member: Judicial Administration Committee, 1990-1993; Continuing Legal Education Committee, 1984-1987; Board of Bar Examiners, 1981-1984; Government Law Section; Litigation Section). (Resident). ***PRACTICE AREAS:*** Appellate Law; Civil Litigation; Administrative Law; Regulatory Law; Government Law. ***Email:*** james.e.mountain@harrang.com

(This Listing Continued)

MARK R. WADA, born Ontario, Oregon, January 17, 1953; admitted to bar, 1978, Oregon and U.S. District Court, District of Oregon; 1981, U.S. Court of Appeals, Ninth Circuit. *Education:* University of Oregon (B.B.A., Business Administration, 1975); Cornell Law School, (J.D., cum laude, with honors, 1978). *Member:* Multnomah County and American (Member, Business Law Section) Bar Associations; Oregon State Bar (Member, Business and Corporations and Debtor-Creditor Sections); Equipment Leasing Association. ***PRACTICE AREAS:*** Business Law; Banks and Banking; Finance. ***Email:*** mark.wada@harrang.com

---

AUDREY A. BAKER, admitted to bar, 1996, Colorado; 2000, Arizona; 2005, Oregon. *Education:* California State University (B.A., Journalism/Advertising, 1985); Gonzaga University (J.D., summa cum laude, 1996). *Member:* Oregon State Bar; American Bar Association. ***PRACTICE AREAS:*** Business Law; Real Estate. ***Email:*** audrey.baker@harrang.com

JOLYNN M. BROWN, admitted to bar, 1999, Kansas; 2000, Oregon and U.S. District Court, District of Oregon; 2002, Colorado. *Education:* University of Colorado at Boulder (B.A., Environmental, Population, Organism Biology, 1985); Washburn University of Topeka (J.D., 1998). *Member:* Multnomah and American Bar Associations; Oregon State Bar; Oregon Women Lawyers Association. ***PRACTICE AREAS:*** Insurance Defense. ***Email:*** jolynn.brown@harrang.com

SIVHWA GO, admitted to bar, 2003, Oregon. *Education:* Willamette University (B.A., 1995); Linfield College (B.S., cum laude, 2000); University of Oregon (J.D., 2003). Staff Editor, Oregon Law Review. Moot Court Board. *Member:* Asian Pacific American Law Student Association; Minority Law Student Association (Co-Director). ***LANGUAGES:*** Chinese (Tiachu) and Spanish. ***Email:*** sivhwa.go@harrang.com

CRAIG L. LEIS, born Columbus, Ohio; admitted to bar, 2002, Ohio and U.S. District Court, Southern District of Ohio; 2005, Oregon. *Education:* The Ohio State University (B.A., Psychology, 1998); Capital University (J.D., summa cum laude, 2002). Order of the Curia. *Member:* Ohio State and American Bar Associations; Oregon State Bar. ***PRACTICE AREAS:*** Labor and Employment. ***Email:*** craig.leis@harrang.com

ADINA MATASARU, admitted to bar, 2003, Oregon. *Education:* University of Portland, Oregon (B.A., Interdisciplinary Studies, 1997); Bucerius Law School, Hamburg, Germany (2002); Willamette University College of Law (J.D., 2003). *Member:* Multnomah Bar Association; Oregon State Bar; Oregon Minority Lawyers Association; Oregon Women Lawyers Association. ***LANGUAGES:*** Romanian, German. ***PRACTICE AREAS:*** Litigation; Appellate Practice. ***Email:*** adina.matasaru@harrang.com

JONA J. MAUKONEN, admitted to bar, 2004, Oregon. *Education:* Oregon State University (B.S., Environmental Science, cum laude, 1999); University of Oregon (J.D., 2004). *Member:* Oregon State Bar. ***PRACTICE AREAS:*** Litigation.

C. ROBERT STERINGER, born 1969; admitted to bar, 1998, Oregon; 2002, U.S. District Court, District of Oregon. *Education:* University of Oregon (B.A., cum laude, 1994; J.D., 1998). Member, Beaverton Area Chamber of Commerce, 2001—. *Member:* Multnomah and Federal Bar Associations. ***PRACTICE AREAS:*** Complex Litigation and Appeals; Business Transactions; Real Estate; Government Affairs. ***Email:*** bob.steringer@harrang.com

SEAN T. WATERS, admitted to bar, 2000, Nevada; 2005, Oregon; U.S. District Court, District of Nevada; U.S. Court of Appeals, Ninth Circuit. *Education:* Willamette University (B.S. Political Science and Rhetoric/Media Studies, 1996); University of Oregon (J.D., 2000). Order of the Coif. *Member:* Oregon State Bar; American Bar Association. ***PRACTICE AREAS:*** Litigation. ***Email:*** sean.waters@harrang.com

OF COUNSEL

DOUGLAS S. CHIAPUZIO, born North Bend, Oregon, 1960; admitted to bar, 1985, Oregon; 1991, Washington and U.S. Tax Court. *Education:* Lewis and Clark College (B.S., 1982); Willamette University (J.D., 1985). Certified Public Accountant, Oregon State Board of Accountancy, 1990. *Member:* Multnomah County Bar Association (Member, Sections on: Taxation, Real Property and Probate and Trust, Business Law, Estate Planning, Oregon Law), American Bar Association (Member, Sections on: Real Property, Taxation); Oregon State Bar (Member, Taxation Section); Washington Bar Association (Member, Sections: Business Law, Taxation Section, Real Estate, Probate and Trust). (Also practicing individually). ***PRACTICE AREAS:*** Estate Planning; Trusts; Probate and Administration; Business Law; Corporate and Entity Organization; Taxation; Like Kind Exchanges; Real Estate Transactions. ***Email:*** doug.chiapuzio@harrang.com

K. BRUCE KNIVILA, born Orofino, Idaho, November 4, 1962; admitted to bar, 1992, Oregon. *Education:* George Mason University (B.A., with distinction, 1989); Georgetown University Law Center (J.D., magna cum laude, 1992). Order of the Coif. *Member:* Oregon State Bar. ***PRACTICE AREAS:*** Litigation; Trials and Appeals; Appeals; Business Law; Administrative Law; Employment; Real Estate; Commercial Law; Education Law. ***Email:*** bruce.knivila@harrang.com

REPRESENTATIVE CLIENTS: US - SUMCO USA Corporation; SUMCO USA Sales Corporation; SUMCO Oregon Corporation; SUMCO Phoenix Corporation; Hynix Semiconductor America; Philip Morris Companies, Inc.; CheckPoint Software Tech Inc.; Providence Health Plan; Kaiser Foundation Health Plan of the Northwest; PeaceHealth; Les Schwab Tire Centers, Inc.; Wal-Mart Stores; Sysco Food Services of Portland; Foodbrands America, Inc.; Gunderson Partners LLC; Monterey Mushrooms, Inc.; Amyeel, Inc.; Spawn Mate; Development Group, Inc.; Amfac, Inc.; Northbrook Corporation; Crimson Trace Corporation; Process Facility Group, LLC.; Ecotrust; May Department Store (Meier and Frank); Fred Meyer; Professional Liability Fund of the Oregon State Bar; Day Management, Inc.; Jefferson Behavorial Health; Oregon Health and Services University; University of Oregon Bookstore; The Register-Guard; Cities of Eugene, Roseburg and Florence; Counties of Lincoln, Lane and Washington; Tualatin Valley Water District; Coquille Indian Gaming Commission; Eugene Water & Electric Board; Lane County Fair Board; Abby's Inc. (Abby's Legendary Pizza); West Coast Wire Rope & Rigging; Associated Oregon Industries; Harvest House Publishers; Lane Regional Air Pollution Authority; Lane Council of Governments; Tom Rogers Distributor, Inc.; Travelers Property Casualty; Farmers Ins. Co.; Standard Ins. Co.; City County Ins. Services; American International Group; Oregon Freeze Dry, Inc.; Taco Time International; Armored

(This Listing Continued)

Transport, Inc.; Whittier Wood Products Co.; League of Oregon Cities; Oregon Self-Insurers Association.

(For Complete Biographical Data on All Personnel, See Professional Biographies at Eugene)

HEEKIN LAW FIRM

121 SW MORRISON STREET, SUITE 600
PORTLAND, OREGON 97204
Telephone: 503-222-5578
Fax: 503-914-1889
Email: katherine@heekinlawoffice.com
URL: http://www.heekinlawoffice.com

Commercial Litigation, Employment Law, Electronic Discovery.

KATHERINE R. HEEKIN, born Ann Arbor, Michigan, September 3, 1967; admitted to bar, 1994, Oregon; 1996, U.S. District Court, District of Oregon; 1997, U.S. Court of Appeals, Ninth Circuit; 1999, Washington and U.S. District Court, Eastern District of Washington; 2000, U.S. District Court, Western District of Washington. *Education:* Princeton University (A.B., 1989); University of Oregon (J.D., 1994). Member and Executive Editor, University of Oregon Law Review, 1992-1994. Law Clerk to Hon. Ann Aiken, 1994-1995 and 2000. *Member:* Oregon State Bar; Washington State, American and Federal (Board Member, Oregon Chapter, 2002-2005) Bar Associations; Oregon Women Lawyers Association (Board Member, 1996-1998); Oregon State Bar House of Delegates (Delegate, 1997-1998). ***PRACTICE AREAS:*** Commercial Litigation; Employment Law.

HELZER & CROMAR, LLP

PORTLAND, OREGON

(See Beaverton)

Criminal Law, Family Law, Divorce, Child Custody, Spousal Support, Personal Injury, Automobile Accidents, Criminal Law, Driving While Intoxicated, Felonies, Drug Crimes, Juvenile Crimes, Parole and Probation, Sexual Abuse, Traffic Violations, Estate Litigation, Guardianship and Conservatorship, Employment Law, Discrimination, Sexual Harassment.

LEE M. HESS, P.C.

1000 S.W. BROADWAY, SUITE 1780
PORTLAND, OREGON 97205
Telephone: 503-273-8674
Fax: 503-273-8803
Email: lee@lmhpc.net
URL: http://www.lawyers.com/leehess

Business and Commercial Litigation. Creditors Rights, Secured Transactions, Real Estate. Trial and Appellate Practice, Corporate, Contracts, Debt and Credit Collections, Commercial Leasing, Construction, Environmental, Trusts and Estates, Wills and Probate.

LEE M. HESS, born Danbury, Connecticut, May 12, 1948; admitted to bar, 1977, Washington and Oregon; 1987, U.S. Court of Appeals, Ninth Circuit; 1992, U.S. Supreme Court. *Education:* University of Washington (B.S., cum laude, 1970; J.D., 1976); University of Chicago (M.S., 1974). Phi Beta Kappa; Order of the Coif. *Member:* Multnomah County, Washington State and American (Member, Sections on: Banking and Business Law; Litigation) Bar Associations; Oregon State Bar (Member: Sections on: Business Law; Creditor Debtor Law; Newsletter Committee). ***PRACTICE AREAS:*** Business Law; Commercial Litigation; Secured Transactions; Creditors Rights; Bankruptcy. ***Email:*** lee@lmhpc.net

LEGAL SUPPORT PERSONNEL

MARY D. McCOURT. *Education:* Oregon State University (B.A.). Recipient, President's Award, Oregon Paralegal Association, 2004. Paralegal Assistant to the Administrative Assistant to the Governor of the State of Oregon, 1975-1979. Court Reporter, Circuit and Federal Courts, 1990-1993. Experience in Business Law, Bankruptcy, Insurance Defense, Probate, Personal Injury, Complex Real Estate Law, Family Law, Corporate Law, Complex Litigation, Tax Law, Collection. Member, National Federation of Paralegal Associations; Oregon Paralegal Association. Board Member, Outstanding Member, 2000-2001 and 2002-2003, Oregon Paralegal Association. Chairperson, Oregon Paralegal Litigation Specialty Group. Past President, 1982-1986, Selected Legal Secretary of the Year, 1982 and 1983, Washington County Legal Secretaries. *Member:* Oregon State Bar (Member, Fee Arbitration Panel; Quality of Life Committee). (Paralegal) (CLA, CLI, CSR)

SHONDA FORMAN, Assistant, Bookkeeper and Bankruptcy. (CLA). ***PRACTICE AREAS:*** Business Law; Bankruptcy; Corporate Law; Complex Litigation; Probate; Real Estate.

REPRESENTATIVE CLIENTS: Daimler Chrysler Services North America L.L.C. (successor by merger to Mercedes-Benz Credit Corporation and successor by merger to Chrysler Financial Company, L.L.C.); The CIT Group/Sales Financing, Inc.; The CIT Group/Consumer Financing, Inc.; CIT Group/Equipment Financing, Inc.; CIT Small Business Lending Corporation; CIT Technology Financing Services, Inc.; Long Beach Acceptance, Inc.; IOS Capital; People First Auto Finance; Hardwater Scale Control Northwest, Inc.; Professional Restaurant Equipment Repair Service, Inc.; Pacific Fire and Smoke Cleaning Company; J.R. Elliot Design Limited; Fanno Creek Calicos, Inc.; Square Nail Design, Inc.

HINSHAW & CULBERTSON LLP

Hinshaw & Culbertson LLP is an Illinois registered limited liability partnership that has elected to be governed by the Illinois Uniform Partnership Act (1997)

Established in 1934

1000 SW BROADWAY
SUITE 1950
PORTLAND, OREGON 97205-3078
Telephone: 503-243-3243
Fax: 503-243-3240
Telex: 880248
Email: kfox@hinshawlaw.com
URL: http://www.hinshawlaw.com

Other Office Locations: Chicago, Illinois; Appleton, Wisconsin; Belleville, Illinois; Boston, Massachusetts; Champaign, Illinois; Crystal Lake, Illinois; Edwardsville, Illinois; Fort Lauderdale, Florida; Jacksonville, Florida; Joliet, Illinois; Lisle, Illinois; Los Angeles, California; Miami, Florida; Milwaukee, Wisconsin; Minneapolis, Minnesota; New York, New York; Peoria, Illinois; Phoenix, Arizona; Providence, Rhode Island; Rockford, Illinois; St. Louis, Missouri; San Francisco, California; Schererville, Indiana; Springfield, Illinois; Tampa, Florida; Waukegan, Illinois.

Appellate, Banking & Financing, Bankruptcy & Creditors' Rights, Class Action Litigation, Civil Rights Defense, Commercial Litigation, Corporate, Construction Law, Director & Officer Liability, Employee Benefits, Environmental, Fidelity & Surety, General Liability Litigation, Government, Health Care, Insurance Coverage, Insurance and Reinsurance, Labor & Employment, Legal Malpractice, Medical Malpractice, Mergers & Acquisitions, Municipal Liability, Personal Injury Defense, Public Law, Products Liability Litigation, Professional Liability, Regulatory, Real Estate, School Law, Securities, Taxation, Transportation, White Collar Crime and Workers' Compensation Defense.

FIRM PROFILE: Hinshaw & Culbertson LLP is a national AMLaw 200 firm with 425 lawyers in 27 offices coast-to-coast. The firm offers a full-service practice, with an emphasis in commercial and defense litigation, corporate, environmental, employment and construction law, as well as the representation of professionals in their liability and risk management matters.

Hinshaw provides services to a range of clients in financial services, construction, health care, not-for-profit, insurance, legal, manufacturing, real estate, transportation and other industries. Firm clients also include government agencies, municipalities and schools.

Hinshaw was founded in 1934. The firm is headquartered in Chicago, and maintains offices in 12 states: Arizona, California, Florida, Illinois, Indiana, Massachusetts, Minnesota, Missouri, New York, Oregon, Rhode Island and Wisconsin.

PARTNER

PETER R. JARVIS, born New York, N.Y., July 19, 1950; admitted to bar, 1976, Oregon and U.S. District Court, District of Oregon; 1977, U.S. Court of Appeals, Ninth Circuit; 1983, Washington and U.S. District Court, Western District of Washington; 1984, U.S. Court of Federal Claims; 1985, U.S. District Court, Eastern District of Washington; 1992, U.S. Tax Court; 2002, California; 2003, Alaska. *Education:* Harvard University (B.A., Economics, magna cum laude, 1972); Yale University (J.D., 1976; M.A., Economics, 1976). Phi Beta Kappa. Editor, Yale Law Journal, 1975-1976. *Member:* Washington State, Alaska and American Bar Associations; State Bar of California; Oregon State Bar; American Law Institute. ***PRACTICE AREAS:*** Legal Ethics and Professional Responsiblity; Attorney Discipline; Commercial Litigation; Lawyer Risk Management. ***Email:*** pjarvis@hinshawlaw.com

ASSOCIATES

DAVID J. ELKANICH, born Huntington, West Virginia, September 5, 1973; admitted to bar, 1999, Oregon; 2004, U.S. District Court, District of Oregon; 2005, Washington and U.S. District Court, Western District of Washington. *Education:* University of Arizona (B.A., magna cum laude, 1996); University of Oregon (J.D., 1999). Phi Beta Kappa; Phi Kappa Phi. Graduate Teaching Fellowship. Operations Editor, Oregon Law Review. Appointed by the Oregon State Bar to the Uniform Jury Instructions - Civil Committee, 2005—. Member, Center for Professional Responsibility. *Member:* Multnomah and Washington State Bar Associations; Oregon State Bar; American Bar Association. ***PRACTICE AREAS:*** Commercial Litigation; Employment Litigation; Labor and Employment Law; Legal Malpractice; Professional Liability Litigation; Professional Responsibility and Ethics. ***Email:*** delkanich@hinshawlaw.com

RENÉ C. HOLMES, born Minnesota, December 30, 1972; admitted to bar, 1998, Oregon; 2004, U.S. District Court, District of Oregon. *Education:* Western Oregon State College (B.A., Spanish, 1995); Willamette University (J.D., 1998). Deputy District Attorney, Marion County, Oregon (1998-2004); Adjunct Professor, Western Oregon University (2002-2003). *Member:* Oregon State Bar. ***LANGUAGES:*** Spanish. ***PRACTICE AREAS:*** Professional Liability; Legal Malpractice Defense; Attorney Disciplinary Defense; Legal Ethics and Professional Responsibility; Risk Management; Litigation; Civil Litigation. ***Email:*** rholmes@hinshawlaw.com

REPRESENTATIVE CLIENTS: ServiceMaster; PPG; Hobart; Schindler; Westinghouse; Textron; Laidlaw; Menards; BMW; CNA Insurance Company; Chubb Insurance Group; Cigna Corp.; Continental Insurance; Farmers Insurance; Aetna Life & Casualty Co.; Allstate Insurance Co.; Facial, Plastic and Reconstructive Surgery, Inc.; Chicago Hospital Risk Pooling; Conco, Inc.; Duplex Group; Fireman's Fund American; General Accident Group; Hartford Insurance Group; Maryland Casualty Co.; Prudential Insurance Co.; St. Mary of Nazareth Hospital; St. Therese Hospital; INRYCO, Inc.; Switchcraft, Inc.; University of Illinois; Holy Cross Hospital; Northwestern Memorial Hospital; St. Bernards; Shand, Morahan & Co., Inc.; U.S.F.&G.; American Academy of Orthopaedic Surgeons; First Federal Savings Bank of Champaign-Urbana; Inland Steel Co.; Condell Memorial Hospital; Illinois State Medical Insurance Services.

HITT HILLER & MONFILS LLP

510 SOUTHWEST THIRD AVENUE, SUITE 309
PORTLAND, OREGON 97204
Telephone: 503-228-8870
Fax: 503-228-4250
URL: http://www.hittandhiller.com

Civil Litigation, Personal Injury, Wrongful Death, Insurance Coverage, Products Liability, Transportation, Employment Law, Discrimination, and Business Litigation.

DANNY L. HITT, JR., born Richmond, Virginia, June 27, 1957; admitted to bar, 1983, Oregon. *Education:* University of Wisconsin (B.A., 1979); University of Oregon (J.D., 1983). *Member:* Multonah County Bar Association; Oregon State Bar; Oregon Association of Defense Counsel; Oregon Casualty Adjusters Association; Trucking Industry Defense Association. ***PRACTICE AREAS:*** Litigation; Insurance; Employment; Construction Law; Intellectual Property; Transportation. ***Email:*** dhitt@hittandhiller.com

JAMES L. HILLER, born New York, N.Y., September 28, 1952; admitted to bar, 1977, Oregon. *Education:* State University of New York at Buffalo (B.A., summa cum laude, 1974); University of Michigan (J.D., cum laude, 1977). Phi Beta Kappa; Phi Alpha Delta. Recipient: 1993 Merit Award, Multnomah County Bar Association; 2002 Federal Practice Award, Federal Bar Association. Chair, Local Rules Advisory Committee, U.S. District Court, District of Oregon, 2001—. *Member:* Multnomah County (Chairman, Court Liaison Committee, 1987-1990) and Federal (President, Oregon Chapter, 1998) Bar Associations; Association of Defense Trial Attorneys; National Association of Railroad Trial Counsel. ***PRACTICE AREAS:*** Litigation; Employment; Insurance; Transportation; Construction. ***Email:*** jhiller@hittandhiller.com

SCOTT P. MONFILS, born Portland, Oregon, January 21, 1951; admitted to bar, 1980, Oregon and Washington. *Education:* Portland State University (B.S., 1975); Gonzaga University (J.D., magna cum laude, 1980). *Member:* Oregon Self-Insurers Association; Oregon Law Institute; Defense Research Institute; Washington Self-Insurers Association. ***PRACTICE AREAS:*** Litigation; Workers Compensation; Employment. ***Email:*** smonfils@hittandhiller.com

BRIAN B. WILLIAMS, born Eugene, Oregon, March 24, 1971; admitted to bar, 1996, Oregon and Washington. *Education:* Willamette University (B.S. in Economics, cum laude, 1993); University of Oregon (J.D., 1996). Order of the Coif. Author: "Dolan v. Tigard: A New Era of Takings Clause Analysis," Oregon Law Review, Vol. 79. *Member:* Oregon and Washington Associations of Defense Trial Lawyers. ***PRACTICE AREAS:*** Litigation; Insurance; Construction; Transportation. ***Email:*** bwilliams@hittandhiller.com

REPRESENTATIVE CLIENTS: Great West Casualty; Liberty Mutual; St. Paul/Travellers; Nike; Amtrak; J.R. Simplot; Les Schwab Companies; USF Reddaway; Genesee & Wyoming Railroad.

HOEVET, BOISE & OLSON, PC

1000 S.W. BROADWAY, SUITE 1500
PORTLAND, OREGON 97205
Telephone: 503-228-0497
Fax: 503-228-7112
Email: attys@hoevet-boise.com

Criminal Defense in State and Federal Court, White Collar/Business Crimes, Drug Crimes, Vehicular Homicide, Sex Crimes, Tax and Securities Fraud, Civil Forfeiture.

RONALD H. HOEVET, born San Mateo, California, April 27, 1946; admitted to bar, 1975, Oregon; 1976, U.S. District Court, District of Oregon; 1978, U.S. Court of Appeals, Ninth Circuit; 1981, U.S. Tax Court. *Education:* Willamette University (B.A., Economics, 1968); Duke University (J.D., cum laude, 1975). Trial Attorney, Criminal Section, Tax Division, U.S. Department of Justice, 1975-1977. Assistant U.S. Attorney, District of Oregon, 1977-1981. Member, Board of Directors, Oregon Halfway House, Inc., 1984—. National Directory Criminal Defense Lawyers; Best Lawyers in America (Criminal Defense). *Member:* Oregon State Bar (Executive Committee, Criminal Law Section, 1992-1996); Oregon Criminal Defense Lawyers Association; National Association of Criminal Defense Lawyers. ***PRACTICE AREAS:*** Criminal Defense; Federal Criminal Law; Tax Fraud; Securities Fraud; Business Crimes; Drug Crimes; Civil Forfeiture. ***Email:*** rhoevet@hoevet-boise.com

WHITNEY P. BOISE, born Salem, Oregon, June 6, 1958; admitted to bar, 1985, Oregon; 1991, U.S. District Court, District of Oregon; 1992, U.S. Court of Appeals, Ninth Circuit. *Education:* University of Oregon; New York University (B.A., 1981); Willamette University (J.D., 1985). Member, 1983-1984 and Associate Editor, 1984-1985, Willamette Law Review. "Development In the Law, Rights Of The Institutionalized Mentally Ill Regarding Neuroleptic Medication and Electroconvulsive Therapy," 20 Willamette Law Review 384, 1984. Law Clerk, Oregon Court of Appeals, 1985-1986. United States Department of Justice-Special Attorney, 1986-1987; Metropolitan Public Defender 1987-1991. Member, Advisory Board, Federal Indigent Fund Trust, 2000—. *Member:* Multnomah County Bar Association; Oregon State Bar (Executive Committee, Criminal Law Section, 2001-2004, Chair, 2002-2003); Oregon Criminal Defense Lawyers Association (Education Committee, 2001-2002). ***PRACTICE AREAS:*** Criminal Defense; Federal Criminal Law; Drug Crimes; Sex Crimes; Business Crimes. ***Email:*** wboise@hoevet-boise.com

---

PER C. OLSON, born Spooner, Wisconsin, September 27, 1966; admitted to bar, 1993, Oregon; 1998, U.S. District Court, District of Oregon; 2000, U.S. Supreme Court; 2002, U.S. Court of Appeals, Ninth Circuit; 2003, Washington. *Education:* Willamette University (B.A., magna cum laude, 1988); Northwestern School of Law (J.D., cum laude, 1993). Law Clerk to: Hon. Supreme Court Justice George A. Van Hoomissen, Oregon, 1995-1997; Hon. Robert W. Redding, Oregon, 1994-1995. Author: "Oregon Adverse Possession Law," 23 Environmental Law 1297, 1993. *Member:* Multnomah County and Federal Bar Associations; Oregon State Bar (Member, Pro Bono Committee, New Lawyers Division, 1993-2000); Oregon Trial Lawyers Association; Oregon Criminal Defense Lawyers Association; Washington Association of Criminal Defense Lawyers. ***PRACTICE AREAS:*** Criminal Defense; Civil Litigation. ***Email:*** polson@hoevet-boise.com

JANET LEE HOFFMAN

1000 S.W. BROADWAY
SUITE 1500
PORTLAND, OREGON 97205
Telephone: 503-222-1125
Fax: 503-222-7589
Email: janet@jhoffman.com
URL: http://www.janetleehoffman.com

Criminal Trial and Appellate Practice in State and Federal Courts. Administrative Defense of Professional Licenses. Civil Forfeiture.

JANET LEE HOFFMAN, born Santa Monica, California, March 20, 1951; admitted to bar, 1977, Massachusetts; 1978, Oregon; 1981, U.S. District Court, District of Oregon. *Education:* Edinburgh University, Edinburgh, Scotland; University of Redlands (B.A., 1973); Boston College (J.D., 1977). Listed in: Best Lawyers in America, 2001—; International Society of Barristers, 2000—; National Directory of Criminal Lawyers, editor Barry Tarlow, Category 1. Carries the highest legal ability rating in Martindale-Hubbell. Author, "The Ethical and Practical Consideration of the Internal Investigation," Litigation Journal, Oregon State Bar; Technique: "Demonstrative Evidence," Oregon Law Institute, Advanced Litigation; "Rape Shield Law," OSB Evidence, Chapter 14; "Examination of for Cause Challenges Under the 'New' Time Limited Voir Dire," OSB Litigation Journal. Speaker/Instructor: Multi-states, including Oregon Trial Advocacy College, 2000-2005; Oregon Trial Practice: "The Right to a Fair and Impartial Jury Under Modern Voir Dire Methods," Oregon Law Institute; Jury Selection - Method Not Madness, "Designing a Jury Selection Strategy," Oregon State Bar. Member, Board of Trustees, Metropolitan Public Defender, 1977-2000. Member, Uniform Trial Court Rules Committee, 1989-1991. Former Member, Northern District, American Civil Liberties Union Lawyers Committee. Federal Defender Services, 1982-1983. *Member:* Oregon State Bar (Member: House of Delegates, 1997—; Board of Governors, 1991-1994; Treasurer, 1993-1994); Multnomah County Bar Association (Member, Board of Directors, 1989-1994; Secretary, 1989-1990; Treasurer, 1990-1991). ***PRACTICE AREAS:*** White Collar Crime; SEC Enforcement; Felonies; Professional Licensing.

ASSOCIATES

CARRIE MENIKOFF, born Honolulu, Hawaii, February 8, 1967; admitted to bar, 1997, Ohio; 2003, Oregon. *Education:* University of Pennsylvania (B.A., 1989); Case Western Reserve University (J.D., 1996). Member, Order of the Barristers. *Member:* Multnomah County, Oregon State and Federal Bar Associations; Oregon Criminal Defense Lawyers Association; National Association of Criminal Defense Lawyers. ***Email:*** carrie@jhoffman.com

CATHERINE M. TOSSWILL, born Concord, Massachusetts, August 19, 1965; admitted to bar, 1997, New York; 2004, Oregon; 2005, U.S. District Court, District of Oregon. *Education:* Yale University (B.A., 1987); Rutgers University School of Law (J.D., 1996). *Member:* Association of the Bar of the City of New York; Multnomah County, Oregon State and Federal Bar Associations; Oregon Criminal Defense Lawyers Association; National Association of Criminal Defense Lawyers. ***Email:*** kate@jhoffman.com

NICHOLAS CROPP, born Caerfryddin, Wales, August 9, 1977; admitted to bar, 1999, England and Wales; 2003, Oregon. *Education:* University College, London (LL.B., first class honours and Dean's list, 1998); Inns of Court School of Law (B.V.Q., 1999); Pembroke College, Oxford (B.C.L., 2000). *Member:* Oregon State Bar; Honourable Society of Gray's Inn; UK Lawyers for Liberty; University College London Bentham Society; Tanfield Barrister's Chambers, Warwick Court, London. ***Email:*** nick@jhoffman.com

HOLLAND & KNIGHT LLP

2300 U.S. BANCORP TOWER
111 SOUTHWEST FIFTH AVENUE
PORTLAND, OREGON 97204
Telephone: 503-243-2300
Telecopier: 503-241-8014
URL: http://www.hklaw.com

Annapolis, Maryland Office: State Circle Building, 47 State Circle, Suite 400, 21401. Telephone: 410-263-7800. Fax: 410-263-3768.

Atlanta, Georgia Office: One Atlantic Center, 1201 West Peachtree Street, N.E., Suite 2000, 30309. Telephone: 404-817-8500. Fax: 404-881-0470.

Beijing, China Office: No. 33, 14th Floor, IBM Tower, Pacific Century Place, 2 A Workers Stadium Road North, Chaoyang District, 100027. Telephone: 86-10-653-91232. Fax: 86-10-653-91060.

Bethesda, Maryland Office: 3 Bethesda Metro Center, Suite 800, 20814. Telephone: 301-654-7800. Fax: 301-656-3978.

Boston, Massachusetts Office: 10 St. James Avenue, 11th Floor, 02116. Telephone: 617-523-2700. Fax: 617-523-6850.

Bradenton, Florida Office: Bradenton Financial Center, 1401 West Manatee Avenue, Suite 1200, 34205. Telephone: 941-748-7076. Fax: 941-747-9774.

Chicago, Illinois Office: 131 South Dearborn Street, 30th Floor, 60603. Telephone: 312-263-3600. Fax: 312-578-6666.

Fort Lauderdale, Florida Office: One East Broward Boulevard, Suite 1300, 33301. Telephone: 954-525-1000. Fax: 954-463-2030.

Jacksonville, Florida Office: 50 North Laura Street, Suite 3900, 32202. Telephone: 904-353-2000. Fax: 904-358-1872.

Lakeland, Florida Office: 92 Lake Wire Drive, 33815. Telephone: 863-682-1161. Fax: 863-688-1186.

(This Listing Continued)

Los Angeles, California Office: 633 West Fifth Street, 21st Floor, 90071. Telephone: 213-896-2400. Fax: 213-896-2450.
Mexico City, Mexico Office: Holland & Knight - Gallastegui y Lozano, S.C., Edificio Arcos Bosques Corporativo, Paseo de los Tamarindos 400-B, Piso 2, Delegación Cuajimalpa, Bosques de las Lomas, 05120. Telephone: 525-55-261-1866. Fax: 525-55-261-1867.
Miami, Florida Office: 701 Brickell Avenue, Suite 3000, 33131. Telephone: 305-374-8500. Fax: 305-789-7799.
New York, New York Office: 195 Broadway, 10007. Telephone: 212-513-3200. Fax: 212-385-9010.
Northern Virginia: 1600 Tysons Boulevard, Suite 700, McLean, Virginia, 22102. Telephone: 703-720-8600. Fax: 703-720-8610.
Oakbrook Terrace, Illinois Office: One Mid America Plaza, Suite 1000, 60181. Telephone: 630-954-2100. Fax: 630-954-2112.
Orlando, Florida Office: SunTrust Building, Suite 2600, 200 South Orange Avenue, 32801. Telephone: 407-425-8500. Fax: 407-244-5288.
Providence, Rhode Island Office: One Financial Plaza, Suite 1800, 02903. Telephone: 401-751-8500. Fax: 401-553-6850.
Rancho Santa Fe, California Office: 6050 El Tordo, 92067. Telephone: 858-756-4410. Fax: 858-756-4386.
Sacramento, California Office: 1215 K Street, 17th Floor, 95814. Telephone: 916-503-1695. Fax: 916-503-2401.
San Antonio, Texas Office: Weston Centre, 112 East Pecan Street, Suite 2700, 78205. Telephone: 210-229-3000. Fax: 210-229-1194.
San Francisco, California Office: 50 California Street, Suite 2800, 94111. Telephone: 415-743-6900. Fax: 415-743-6910.
Seattle, Washington Office: 2600 Pike Tower, 520 Pike Street, 98101. Telephone: 206-340-1825. Fax: 206-623-4363.
St. Petersburg, Florida Office: 200 Central Avenue, Suite 1600, 33701. Telephone: 727-896-7171. Fax: 727-822-8048.
Tallahassee, Florida Office: 315 South Calhoun Street, Suite 600, 32301. Telephone: 850-224-7000. Fax: 850-224-8832.
Tampa, Florida Office: 100 North Tampa Street, Suite 4100, 33602-3644. Telephone: 813-227-8500. Fax: 813-229-0134.
Tokyo, Japan Office: Tokyo Ginko Kyokai Building, 15th Floor, 1-3-1 Marunouchi, Chiyoda-ku, 100-0005. Telephone: 813-3216-7206. Fax: 813-3216-7286.
Washington, D.C. Office: 2099 Pennsylvania Avenue, N.W., Suite 100, 20006. Telephone: 202-955-3000. Fax: 202-955-5564.
West Palm Beach, Florida Office: 222 Lakeview Avenue, Suite 1000, 33401. Telephone: 561-833-2000. Fax: 561-650-8399.
Representative Offices:
Caracas, Venezuela Office: Tinoco, Travieso, Planchart & Núñez, Avenida Francisco De Miranda, Torre Country Club, Pisos 1 y 2, Chacaito, 1050. Telephone: 582-12-952-9033 (Master). Fax: 582-12-953-1053/8365/7583. Email: ttpn@ttpn.com.ve.
Helsinki, Finland Office: Holland & Knight Oy, Pohjoisesplanadi 33, FIN-00100. Telephone: 358-9-684-1520. Fax: 358-9-6841-5252.
Tel Aviv, Israel Office: Haim Samet, Steinmetz, Haring & Co. Advocates, 23 Begin Road, 18th Floor, 66814. Telephone: 972-3-567-0100. Fax: 972-3-567-01010.

Litigation, Government Law, Business Law, Real Estate Law and Private Wealth Services.

FIRM PROFILE: At Holland & Knight we leverage the talents and resources of our entire firm to provide effective advocacy and comprehensive, integrated solutions in virtually all areas of the law, across the U.S., and around the world. The firm's infrastructure, along with its collaborative approach, enables clients to benefit fully from the size of our team, the depth of our experience and our extensive geographic footprint.

Holland & Knight's "one firm" structure allows the firm to support the most complex matters at all levels. The firm is organized into five practice Sections—Litigation, Government, Business, Real Estate and Private Wealth Services. Through integrated practice groups and industry-based teams, we can provide efficient and responsive legal representation anywhere in the world. We serve clients on the basis of their needs, not merely location. Holland & Knight's interdisciplinary approach assures that clients have access to the lawyers with the most appropriate experience.

PORTLAND MEMBERS

CHRISTOPHER W. ANGIUS, born Phoenix, Arizona, March 6, 1953; admitted to bar, 1981, Massachusetts; 1984, Oregon; 1996, Washington. *Education:* Columbia University (B.A., summa cum laude, 1978); Harvard Law School (J.D., 1981). Phi Beta Kappa. ***PRACTICE AREAS:*** Litigation; Products Liability; Corporate Law; Environmental. ***Email:*** christopher.angius@hklaw.com

CHRISTOPHER CLINE, born August 11, 1960; admitted to bar, 1991, California; 1996, Oregon. *Education:* San Francisco State University (B.A., 1987); Hastings College of the Law, University of California (J.D., 1991). Listed in the Best Lawyers in America. Fellow, American College of Trust and Estate Counsel. Author: Tax Management Portfolio: Powers of Appointment. Member, Editorial Advisory Board, Tax Management Estates, Gifts and Trusts Journal. President-Elect, Executive Committee of Estate Planning and Administration Section, Oregon State Bar. Secretary of the Board, Estate Planning Council of Portland, Inc. ***PRACTICE AREAS:*** Estate Planning; Estate Administration; Nonprofit and Charitable Organizations; Fiduciary Representation; Family Business Succession Planning. ***Email:*** chris.cline@hklaw.com

C. PAUL DAGLE, born Hawarden, Iowa, September 7, 1944; admitted to bar, 1969, Iowa; 1973, New York; 1975, Oregon. *Education:* University of Iowa (B.A., 1966; J.D., with distinction, 1969). Phi Delta Phi. Author: Note, "Rights of First Refusal Appendant to a Lease," 53 Iowa Law Review 1305, 1968; "Securities Regulation: SEC Regulation D—New Private Offering Rules," Vol. III, No. 2, Oregon Business and Corporate Law Digest, June 1982; "Corporate Buy-Sell Agreements," Advising Oregon Business, Oregon State Bar, 1984, 1988. *Member:* Multnomah County and American Bar Associations; Oregon State Bar (Member, Business Law, Construction Law and Real Estate and Land Use). [Capt., Judge Advocate, USAF, 1969-1972]. ***PRACTICE AREAS:*** Housing and Community Development; Low-income Housing Tax Credit; Securities; Corporate; Corporate Finance; Affordable Housing; Business Law; Limited Liability Company Law; Construction Law; Investments; Financial Services; Real Estate; Commercial Real Estate. ***Email:*** paul.dagle@hklaw.com

GEORGE J. GREGORES, born Portland, Oregon, July 17, 1948; admitted to bar, 1973, Oregon; 1978, U.S. Court of Appeals, Second Circuit; 1982, U.S. Court of Appeals, Ninth Circuit and U.S. District Court, District of Oregon. *Education:* University of Oregon (B.S., 1970); Northwestern School of Law (J.D., 1973). Staff Attorney, Federal Trade Commission, Los Angeles Regional Office, 1973-1975 and San Francisco Regional Office, 1975-1978. *Member:* Multnomah County and American Bar Associations; Oregon State Bar (Member, Sections on: Antitrust, Business and Corporate Law and Real Estate). ***PRACTICE AREAS:*** Business Law; Business Litigation; Real Estate Law; Construction Law; Contracts; Trusts and Estates; Mergers and Acquisitions. ***Email:*** george.gregores@hklaw.com

J. ALAN JENSEN, born Cedar Falls, Iowa, July 27, 1938; admitted to bar, 1963, Minnesota; 1968, California; 1972, Oregon. *Education:* Carleton College (B.A., 1960); University of Michigan (LL.B., 1963); New York University (LL.M. in Taxation, 1967). Listed in The Best Lawyers in America. Author: "Current Developments in Funding, Financing, Buying and Selling Life Insurance," Southern Federal Tax Institute; "Primer on the New Regime for Taxation of Split Dollar: Notice 2001-10 and Its Successor Notice 2002-8," West Group's Estate & Personal Financial Planning, April 2002; O.S.P.I.R.G.; "Tax Problems for Private Colleges and Universities," Environmental Law Review, 1972; "Tax Problems for Artists & Art," Law & the Visual Arts, Fred B. Rothman, Inc., 1974. Assistant Professor, 1970-1973, Associate Professor, 1973-1974, Professor of Law, 1974-1976 and Adjunct Professor of Law, 1977, 1989, 1999-2001, Northwestern School of Law of Lewis and Clark College. Fellow, American College of Trust and Estates Counsel. *Member:* State Bar of California; Oregon State Bar (Past Chairman, Probate, Administration and Estate Plan); American Bar Association (Member: Tax Section; Estate and Gift Tax Committee; Partnership Committee; Chairperson, Subcommittee on Life Insurance). ***PRACTICE AREAS:*** Taxation; Estate Planning; Family Business Law; Successions; International Taxation; Agricultural Law; Trusts and Estates; Nonprofit and Charitable Organizations; Charitable Giving. ***Email:*** alan.jensen@hklaw.com

JOEL P. LEONARD, born Natchez, Mississippi, October 17, 1961; admitted to bar, 1988, Wisconsin (Inactive); 1992, Massachusetts (Inactive); 1996, Oregon; 2002, Washington. *Education:* Harvard University (A.B., cum laude, 1983); University of Dar Es Salaam, Tanzania (post-graduate diploma, laws, 1987); University of Wisconsin Law School (J.D., 1988). Order of the Coif. Articles Editor, Wisconsin Law Review, 1987-1988. Law Clerk, Wisconsin Supreme Court, 1988-1989. *Member:* Multnomah County and Washington State Bar Associations; Oregon State Bar. ***REPORTED CASES:*** Department of Revenue v. IBM, 15 OTR 162 (2000). ***PRACTICE AREAS:*** Commercial Litigation; Appellate; Construction Law; Health Care; Products Liability; Trade Secrets. ***Email:*** joel.leonard@hklaw.com

LOUIS A. SANTIAGO, born New York, N.Y., August 15, 1950; admitted to bar, 1978, Oregon; 1979, U.S. District Court, District of Oregon, U.S. Court of Appeals, Ninth Circuit and U.S. Court of Federal Claims; 1994, Washington; 1997, U.S. District Court, Western and Eastern Districts of Washington. *Education:* University of Florida (B.S., Engineering, 1972); Northwestern School of Law of Lewis and Clark College (J.D., 1978). Alpha Pi Mu (Engineering Honor Society). Member, Law Review, Northwestern School of Law. *Member:* Multnomah County, Clark County and Washington State Bar Associations; Oregon State Bar; Defense Research Institute. ***PRACTICE AREAS:*** Employment Law; Employment Litigation; Commercial Litigation; Real Estate Litigation; Business Torts; Alternative Dispute Resolution. ***Email:*** louis.santiago@hklaw.com

MARK A. VON BERGEN, born Portland, Oregon, March 3, 1951; admitted to bar, 1979, Oregon. *Education:* Princeton University (A.B., 1974); University of Chicago (J.D., 1978). Phi Beta Kappa. Woodrow Wilson Scholar. Author: "Powers, Duties and Liabilities of Corporate Directors and Officers," Oregon State Bar Continuing Legal Education, Advising Oregon Businesses, 2001. Member, Editorial Committee, Oregon Business and Corporate Law Digest, 1981-1987. Co-Chair, Northwest Securities Institute, 1989. Chair, Oregon Securities Regulation Section, 1989-1990. Member, Oregon Task Forces on: Model Business Corporation Act, 1985-1988; Third-Party Legal Opinions, 1991-1994. *Member:* Oregon State Bar (Chair, Securities Regulation Section, 1989-1990; Member: Executive Committee, Business Law Section, 1987-1989; Sections on: Securities Regulation; Business Law); American Bar Association (Member, Corporation, Banking and Business Law Section). ***PRACTICE AREAS:*** Securities; Business; Venture Capital; Corporate; Contracts. ***Email:*** mark.vonbergen@hklaw.com

SENIOR COUNSEL

SUSAN BURTON, born Pasadena, California, February 9, 1962; admitted to bar, 1987, Oregon; 1994, Colorado; 2000, Washington; U.S. District Court, District of Oregon. *Education:* University of California at Los Angeles (B.A., 1982); Willamette University (J.D., 1986). Member, Willamette Law Review. *Member:* Oregon State Bar; The Colorado Bar; Washington State Bar Association. ***PRACTICE AREAS:*** Real Estate Finance; Real Estate Development. ***Email:*** susan.alterman@hklaw.com

CHARLES P. STARKEY, born New York, N.Y., April 26, 1949; admitted to bar, 1975, California; 1979, Oregon. *Education:* Columbia University (B.A., 1972); Hastings College of Law, University of California (J.D., 1975). *Member:* Oregon State Bar; State Bar of California; American Bar Association. ***PRACTICE AREAS:*** Mortgage Financing; Secured Transactions; Real Estate; Commercial Law; Business Law; Contracts; Debtor and Creditor; Banking; Legal Ethics. ***Email:*** charles.starkey@hklaw.com

ASSOCIATES

COURTNEY C. DIPPEL, born Oconomowoc, Wisconsin, August 20, 1976; admitted to bar, 2002, Oregon and Wisconsin. *Education:* Hope College (B.A., 1999); University of

(This Listing Continued)

HOLLAND & KNIGHT LLP, Portland—Continued

Wisconsin, Madison (J.D., 2002). *Member:* Oregon State Bar; State Bar of Wisconsin. ***PRACTICE AREAS:*** Commercial Litigation; Labor and Employment. ***Email:*** courtney.dippel@hklaw.com

AMELIA HEATH, born Portland, Oregon; admitted to bar, 2002, Oregon. *Education:* Seattle Pacific University (B.A., summa cum laude, 1994); Willamette University (J.D., summa cum laude, 2002). ***PRACTICE AREAS:*** Family Business Law; Trusts and Estates; Estate and Gift Taxation. ***Email:*** amelia.heath@hklaw.com

SARA C. HESKETT, born Newton, Massachusetts, August 1, 1966; admitted to bar, 2000, Florida; 2001, Massachusetts; 2004, Oregon. *Education:* Wellesley College (B.A., 1988); University of Florida (J.D., 2000). Order of the Coif. *Member:* Boston, Massachusetts and American Bar Associations; The Florida Bar; Oregon State Bar. ***PRACTICE AREAS:*** Syndication. ***Email:*** sara.heskett@hklaw.com

JOSHUA E. HUSBANDS, born Manzanillo, Colima, Mexico, May 1, 1973; admitted to bar, 1999, Oregon. *Education:* University of Texas (B.B.A., 1995); Northwestern School of Law, Lewis & Clark College (J.D., cum laude, 1999). Law Review - Managing Editor, 1998-1999, and Research Editor, 1997-1998, Journal of Small and Emerging Business Law. Author: "The Elusive Meaning of Small Business," Journal of Small and Emerging Business Law, Vol. 2:2. Member, Cornelius Honor Society. Member, Executive Committee, Oregon State Bar Taxation Section, 2003-2004. Member, Executive Committee, Oregon State Bar Securities Regulation Section, 2001-2004. *Member:* Oregon State Bar. ***LANGUAGES:*** Spanish. ***PRACTICE AREAS:*** Federal Taxation; Estate Planning; Business; Corporate; Securities. ***Email:*** joshua.husbands@hklaw.com

DAVID A. KOEMPEL, admitted to bar, 2001, Oregon. *Education:* Georgetown University (B.S., 1989); Northwestern School of Law, Lewis and Clark College (J.D., 2001). Member, Cornelius Honor Society. Research Editor, 1999-2000, and Editor-in-Chief, 2000-2001, The Journal of Small and Emerging Business Law. *Member:* Multnomah County Bar Association; Oregon State Bar. ***PRACTICE AREAS:*** Affordable Housing; Low Income Housing Tax Credits; Real Estate Syndication; Federal Taxation; Corporate Law; Business Formation; Historic Rehabilitation Tax Credits; Multi-Family Housing; Business Syndication; Business Start-Ups; Pass-Through Entities; Limited Liability Company Law; Entrepreneurial Business Law; Corporate Taxation; Partnership Law; Limited Partnerships; Partnership Syndication; Partnership Taxation. ***Email:*** david.koempel@hklaw.com

BENJAMIN LEEDY, born Seattle, Washington, October 5, 1978; admitted to bar, 2005, Oregon. *Education:* University of Portland (B.A., magna cum laude, 2001); Lewis and Clark College (J.D., cum laude, 2005). ***PRACTICE AREAS:*** Real Estate Estate. ***Email:*** benjamin.leedy@hklaw.com

DAVID C. WANG, admitted to bar, 1996, California; 2004, Oregon. *Education:* University of California, Berkeley (B.S., 1993); Cornell University (J.D., 1996); London School of Economics and Political Science (M.Sc., 2002). ***PRACTICE AREAS:*** Corporate; Securities; Intellectual Property. ***Email:*** david.wang@hklaw.com

(For Biographical Data of other firm Personnel, see Professional Biographies at other offices indicated in the heading of this card).

HOOPER, ENGLUND & WEIL LLP

Established in 1975

SUITE 1507, STANDARD PLAZA
1100 SOUTHWEST SIXTH AVENUE
PORTLAND, OREGON 97204-1016
Telephone: 503-226-0500
Fax: 503-226-7192

General Civil and Trial Practice in all State and Federal Courts. Corporate, Business and Commercial Law, Uniform Commercial Code, Mergers and Acquisitions, Securities, Estate Planning and Probate, Bankruptcy Litigation, Personal Injury.

MEMBERS OF FIRM

THOMAS K. HOOPER, born Ely, Nevada, July 17, 1952; admitted to bar, 1977, Oregon. *Education:* University of Utah (B.S., 1974); University of Oregon (J.D., 1977). *Member:* Multnomah County Bar Association; Oregon State Bar; Oregon Trial Lawyers Association. ***PRACTICE AREAS:*** Civil Law; Personal Injury; Commercial Litigation; Business Litigation; Corporate Law; Estate Planning; Uniform Commercial Code. ***Email:*** thooper@hooplaw.com

GREGORY J. ENGLUND, born Portland, Oregon, January 30, 1956; admitted to bar, 1981, Oregon; 2003, Washington; U.S. District Court, District of Oregon, U.S. Court of Appeals, Ninth Circuit and U.S. Tax Court. *Education:* Willamette University (B.S., 1978; J.D., 1981). Omicron Delta Kappa. Associate Editor, Willamette Law Review. Author: Note, 16 Willamette Law Review 165, 1979. *Member:* Multnomah County Bar Association; Oregon State Bar; Washington State Bar. ***REPORTED CASES:*** Morasch Meats v. Western Boxed Meats, 157 Or. App. 253, 971 P.2d 426 (1998). ***PRACTICE AREAS:*** Corporate Law; Business Law; Professional Practices; Mergers and Acquisitions; Securities Law; Estate Planning. ***Email:*** genglund@hooplaw.com

JOHN W. WEIL, born Chicago, Illinois, January 11, 1951; admitted to bar, 1980, Oregon; 1984, Washington; 1987, U.S. Court of Appeals, Ninth Circuit; U.S. District Court, District of Oregon and U.S. District Court, Western and Eastern Districts of Washington. *Education:* Oberlin College (B.A., 1973); University of Wisconsin-Milwaukee (M.S., 1976); Willamette University (J.D., cum laude, 1980). *Member:* Multnomah County and Washington State Bar Associations; Oregon State Bar. ***PRACTICE AREAS:*** Debtor Creditor Law; Commercial Law; Bankruptcy. ***Email:*** jweil@hooplaw.com

---

CHELSEA S. LEWANDOWSKI, born Houston, Texas, March 11, 1972; admitted to bar, 1999, Oregon; U.S. District Court, District of Oregon. *Education:* University of Wisconsin-Green Bay (B.S., 1995); Lewis and Clark College Northwestern School of Law (J.D., 1998). *Member:* Multnomah County Bar Association; Oregon State Bar. ***PRACTICE AREAS:*** Debtor and Creditor; Commercial Litigation; Bankruptcy. ***Email:*** clewandowski@hooplaw.com

REPRESENTATIVE CLIENTS: Greenwood International, Inc.; North Pacific Supply Company, Inc.; Oregon Screen Impressions, Inc.; Fidelity Financial Services; Jennett Investments; Fahey Machinery, Inc.; Enclume Design Products, Inc.; Portland Lines Bureau, Inc.; Chemwest Systems, Inc.; International Rehabilitive Sciences, Inc. dba RS Medical.
LOCAL COUNSEL FOR: Ford Motor Credit Co.; General Motors Acceptance Corp.; Nissan Motor Acceptance Corp.; New Holland Credit Company; Valley National Financial Services Co.; Hyundai Motor Finance Co.; Primus Automotive; World Omni Financial Services; Mazda American Credit; Volvo Commercial Finance LLC; The Americas; Associates Commercial Corporation; American Investment Bank; Accutel, Inc.; Chase Automotive Finance; Wells Fargo Financial; Harley Davidson; US Bank (Bankruptcy Department); 21st Mortgage Corporation; Vanderbilt Mortgage Corp.; Citicorp Vendor Finance; G.E. Commercial Distribution Finance Corporation.

HUNT & ASSOCIATES, PC

805 ONE MAIN PLACE
101 S.W. MAIN STREET
PORTLAND, OREGON 97204
Telephone: 503-226-1162
FAX: 503-223-5442
Email: admin@huntpc.com

Business and Commercial Litigation. Commercial and Creditors Rights Law, Real Estate, Trial and Appellate Practice, Corporate, Contract, Employment Law, Negligence, Plaintiffs Personal Injury, Wills, Probate, and Family Law.

LAWRENCE B. HUNT, born Portland, Oregon, January 30, 1950; admitted to bar, 1975, Oregon; 1976, U.S. Tax Court; 1986, Washington. *Education:* Northwestern University (B.A., with honors, 1971); University of Oregon (J.D., 1975). Contributing Author: "Survey on Uniform Commercial Code, General Provisions, Sales," Business Lawyer, 1985, 1987 and 1988. *Member:* Multnomah County, Federal and American (Member: Section on Corporation, Banking and Business Law; Subcommittee on Uniform Commercial Code) Bar Associations; Oregon State Bar (Member: Section on Debtor-Creditor Law; Debtor-Creditor Section Newsletter Subcommittee, 1985-1988; Multnomah County Local Professional Responsibility Committee, Past Member); Washington State Bar Association (Member, Sections on: Trial Practice; Corporation, Banking and Business Law; Creditor-Debtor Law); Oregon Trial Lawyers Association; The Association of Trial Lawyers of America. ***PRACTICE AREAS:*** Business Law; Commercial Litigation; Employment Law; Contracts Law; Personal Injury; Corporate Law and Transactions. ***Email:*** lbh@huntpc.com

MILLARD M. BECKER (Retired)

ASSOCIATES

BRAD A. MACOMBER, born Fullerton, California, December 10, 1975; admitted to bar, 2003, California, Oregon and U.S. District Court, District of Oregon. *Education:* University of Utah (B.S., Marketing, 1999); Willamette University (J.D., 2002). Editor, Willamette Journal of International Law. Co-Chair, Willamette University Computer Law and International Property Society, 2001-2002. Member, Oregon Entrepreneurs Forum, 2003. *Member:* Mutlnomah (Member, Young Lawyers Section, 2003) and American (Member, Young Lawyers Section, 2003) Bar Associations; Oregon Trial Lawyers Association; California Young Lawyers Association (Member: Business Law Section, 2003; Labor and Employment Section, 2003). ***PRACTICE AREAS:*** Business Law; Civil Practice; Commercial Law; Commercial Real Estate; Contracts; Family Law; Labor and Employment; Litigation; Real Estate. ***Email:*** brad@huntpc.com

KEVIN J. TILLSON, born San Francisco, California, June 28, 1977; admitted to bar, 2003, Oregon and U.S. District Court, District of Oregon. *Education:* University of Arizona (B.S., Renewable Natural Resources, 1999); Willamette University (J.D., 2003). *Member:* Multnomah County (Member, Young Lawyers Section) and American Bar Associations; Oregon Trial Lawyers Association. ***PRACTICE AREAS:*** Estate Planning; Probate; Business Planning; Civil Practice; Criminal Practice; Labor and Employment Law; Contracts Law; Litigation; Real Estate Law. ***Email:*** tillson@huntpc.com

REPRESENTATIVE CLIENTS: Mr. Formal, Inc.; Quality Plus Roofing; Metrica Labs, Inc.; G. F. Webb, Inc.; Fluid Connector Products, Inc.; Concannon Paper; Action Motor Sports, Inc.; worldcellar.net, Inc.; Elliott Powell Baden & Baker, Inc.; American Retro, Inc.; Boring Bark; Columbia River Staple & Lumber Wrap, Inc.; Sun Alliance, LLC; Wilhelm Funeral Home; Waste Connections, Inc.

HUTCHISON & WALSH

A PROFESSIONAL CORPORATION

PORTLAND, OREGON

(See West Linn)

General Civil and Trial Practice. Estate Planning, Probate, Trusts and Estates, Business Law, Contracts, Real Estate, Corporate, Personal Injury, Automobile Accidents, Wrongful Death, Financial Abuse of the Elderly.

KATHRYN E. JACKSON LAW OFFICE

1515 SOUTHWEST 5TH AVENUE, SUITE 1010
PORTLAND, OREGON 97201
Telephone: 503-222-4070
Fax: 503-399-9315
URL: http://www.kathrynjacksonlawfirm.com

Personal Injury, Wrongful Death, Premises Liability.

FIRM PROFILE: Salem, Oregon Office: Jackson Professional Building, 145 Wilson Street South, 97302. Telephone: 503-399-7648. Fax: 503-399-9315.

(This Listing Continued)

KATHRYN E. JACKSON, born Chicago, Illinois; admitted to bar, 1987, Oregon and Washington; 1988, Illinois; 1990, U.S. Court of Appeals, Ninth Circuit. *Education:* University of Illinois (B.S.); University of Oregon (J.D.). Phi Delta Phi. Member: International Moot Court Team; SBA Class Representative; Panhellenic Judicial Board. Recipient: Centurion Leadership Awards, 1984, 1985, 1986; Additional Certificates: Ocean, Coastal Law; Environmental Law. JELL Oregon Law Review Executive Board. University of Oregon's President's Advisory Board, 1984-1986. Elected, two terms to Oregon State Bar House of Delegates. Appointed: Legislative Committee, Oregon Trial Lawyers Association; Disciplinary Board Trial Panel, OSB Bar Press Broadcasters Council, Pro Tem Appointment Committee, Salem Kaizer Teen Court. *Member:* Marion County, Multnomah County, Washington State, Illinois State and American Bar Associations; Oregon State Bar; Oregon Trial Lawyers Association. ***PRACTICE AREAS:*** Personal Injury Law; Wrongful Death Law; Premises Liability Law.

THE JAMES LAW GROUP LLC

121 SOUTHWEST MORRISON STREET, SUITE 900
PORTLAND, OREGON 97204
Telephone: 503-228-5380
Fax: 503-228-5381
Email: info@jameslawgroup.com
URL: http://www.jameslawgroup.com

Business Law and Planning, Corporate Law, Corporate Finance, Mergers and Acquisitions, Real Estate, Securities, Banking, Employment Litigation, Emerging Companies, Software Licensing, Corporate Finance, Commercial Leasing, Business Litigation.

MEMBERS OF THE FIRM

CHRISTOPHER JAMES, born Portland, Oregon; admitted to bar, 1974, Oregon and U.S. District Court, District of Oregon; 1983, U.S. Court of Appeals, Ninth Circuit. *Education:* University of Oregon (B.S., 1970; J.D., 1974). *Member:* Multnomah County and American Bar Associations; Oregon State Bar. ***PRACTICE AREAS:*** Business Formation; Corporate Formation; Corporate Finance; Corporate Governance; Family Business Succession Planning; Fiduciary Duty; Business Litigation; Mergers and Acquisitions; Real Estate Development. ***Email:*** cjames@jameslawgroup.com

RONALD J. MILLER, born Munich, Germany; admitted to bar, 1995, Illinois; 2003, Oregon. *Education:* Washington State University (B.A., 1986); University of Notre Dame Law School (J.D., 1995). *Member:* Multnomah County and American Bar Associations; Oregon State Bar. ***PRACTICE AREAS:*** Business Law; Emerging Growth Companies; Corporate Finance; Mergers and Acquisitions; Real Estate. ***Email:*** rmiller@jameslawgroup.com

PHILIP S. GRIFFIN, born Shreveport, Louisiana; admitted to bar, 1987, Oregon; 1988, Washington. *Education:* University of Oregon (B.A., 1976; J.D., 1987); University of Nebraska at Lincoln (M.A., 1984). Phi Alpha Theta. Recipient, United States-Asia Environmental Fellowship, 1995. Author, "Singapore's Environmental Regulatory Regime: A Model for the Rest of Southeast Asia?" *Member:* Multnomah County and Washington State Bar Associations; Oregon State Bar; Oregon Association of Defense Counsel; Oregon Trial Lawyers Association. [Lt. Cmdr., U.S. Navy, 1977-1984]. ***PRACTICE AREAS:*** Complex Commercial Litigation; Aviation Products Liability; Insurance; Toxic Torts; Construction Defects. ***Email:*** pgriffin@jameslawgroup.com

ASSOCIATES

DYLAN T. BECKER, born Portland, Oregon; admitted to bar, 2002, Oregon and U.S. District Court, District of Oregon. *Education:* Western Washington University (B.A., cum laude, 1999); University of Oregon (J.D., 2002). Operations Editor, Oregon Law Review, 2001-2002. *Member:* Multnomah County and American Bar Associations; Oregon State Bar. ***PRACTICE AREAS:*** Business Litigation; Employment Law. ***Email:*** dbecker@jameslawgroup.com

MANDY M. PARKINSON BAKER, born San Diego, California; admitted to bar, 2002, California and U.S. District Court, Northern and Eastern Districts of California; 2003, Oregon and U.S. District Court, District of Oregon. *Education:* San Diego State University (B.A., 1998); Northwestern School of Law of Lewis and Clark College (J.D., 2001). *Member:* Oregon State Bar; State Bar of California. ***PRACTICE AREAS:*** Environmental Law; Employment Law; Real Estate; Business Transactions. ***Email:*** mparkinson@jameslawgroup.com

OF COUNSEL

MARY JO NAPLES MILLER, born Cleveland, Ohio; admitted to bar, 1995, Illinois (Not admitted in Oregon). *Education:* John Carroll University (B.S., magna cum laude, 1980); University of South Carolina (M.I.B., 1982); University of Notre Dame (J.D., cum laude, 1995). ***LANGUAGES:*** Spanish and French. ***PRACTICE AREAS:*** Banking Law; Securities; Corporate Finance. ***Email:*** mmiller@jameslawgroup.com

LISANNE M. BUTTERFIELD, born Brooklyn, New York; admitted to bar, 1991, Oregon; 1992, District of Columbia and U.S. District Court, District of Oregon; 1993, Guam and U.S. District Court of Guam. *Education:* University of Denver (B.A., 1987); Willamette University (J.D., 1991). President, International Law Society, Willamette University College of Law, 1989-1991. Contributing Editor, "The Business Judgment Rule: Fiduciary Duties of Corporate Directors," Prentice Hall Law & Business (3 ed. 1989). Author, "Enforcing Foreign Judgments," Willamette Int'l. L.J. (May 1991). *Member:* Multnomah County, Guam (Inactive Member), Federal and American Bar Associations; Oregon State Bar; The District of Columbia Bar (Inactive Member). ***LANGUAGES:*** Italian and French. ***PRACTICE AREAS:*** Insurance Defense; Construction Defects; Commercial Litigation; Products Liability; Employment Law; Copyright Infringement; Trademark Infringement. ***Email:*** lbutterfield@jameslawgroup.com

JOHNSON CLIFTON LARSON & SCHALLER, P.C.

PORTLAND, OREGON
(See Eugene)

Civil Litigation Practice in Personal Injury, Product Liability, Environmental Law, Employment Law, Civil Rights, Medical Malpractice, Taxation, Appellate, Real Estate, Trusts and Estates, Wills and Probate, Business Law.

JOHNSON & SHERTON, P.C.

2303 S.E. GRANT STREET
PORTLAND, OREGON 97214
Telephone: 503-233-1533
Fax: 503-236-8216
Email: js@orlanduse.com
URL: http://www.orlanduse.com

Salem, Oregon Office: 247 Commercial Street, N.E., Suite 205, 97301. Telephone: 503-391-7446. Fax: 503-391-7403. Email: sherton@teleport.com.

Land Use Law, Plan and Zone Changes, Environmental Law, Resource Regulation, Water Law.

ALLEN L. JOHNSON, born Peoria, Illinois, July 10, 1943; admitted to bar, 1973, Oregon and U.S. District Court, District of Oregon; U.S. Supreme Court and U.S. Court of Appeals, Ninth Circuit. *Education:* Carleton College (A.B., 1965); University of Oregon (J.D., 1973). Order of the Coif. Law Clerk to Justice Thomas H. Tongue, Oregon Supreme Court, 1973-1974. Former editor: OSB Administrative Law Handbook. Contributor: Oregon Land Use, Administrative Law and Pleading and Practice Handbooks. Former Hearings Official: Oregon Land Conservation and Development Commission; Oregon Health Planning and Development Agency; Metro Wastewater Management Commission; Lane Regional Air Pollution Authority. Former Member: Oregon State Bar Continuing Legal Education Committee, Executive and Legislative Committees of Real Estate and Land Use Section; Legal Aid Board of Directors. *Member:* Oregon State Bar; American Planning Association. ***PRACTICE AREAS:*** Land Use; Land Development; Zoning Law. ***Email:*** aljohnson@orlanduse.com

CORINNE C. SHERTON, born New York, N.Y., January 18, 1949; admitted to bar, 1981, Oregon. *Education:* University of Chicago (B.S., 1968; Ph.D., Biochemistry, 1973); Willamette University (J.D., 1980). Director, Oregon Environmental Council, 1982-1987; Referee, Oregon Land Use Board of Appeals, 1987-1995. Contributor: Oregon Land Use and Administrative Law Handbooks. Author: "Preserving Instream Flows in Oregon's River and Streams," Environmental Law, 1981. *Member:* Marion County Bar Association; Oregon State Bar (Member, Real Estate and Land Use Section; Executive Committee, Environmental and Natural Resources Section, 1989-1992); Mary Leonard Law Society (Treasurer, 1994-2003). (Resident, Salem Office). ***PRACTICE AREAS:*** Land Use; Land Development; Zoning Law. ***Email:*** sherton@teleport.com

JOHNSTON, ROOT & LEIBENGUTH, P.C.

920 CROWN PLAZA
1500 S.W. FIRST AVENUE
PORTLAND, OREGON 97201
Telephone: 503-226-7986
Fax: 503-223-0743
URL: http://www.johnstonroot.com
Email: lawoffice@johnstonroot.com
URL: http://www.lawyers.com/johnston&rootlaw

Family Law, Interstate and International Custody and Support, Marital Dissolution, Modifications, Child and Spousal Support, Property, Father's and Mother's Rights, Pre-Marriage Agreements, Appeals, Family Law Practice.

FIRM PROFILE: Each attorney has excellent technical expertise in family law. We also have the experience to guide distressed clients through family law cases. When necessary, we are effective litigators. A better result for most clients, however, is to resolve the case prior to trial. In this regard, we pride ourselves at being creative and innovative negotiators and "finders of solutions".

RONALD ALLEN JOHNSTON, born Vancouver, Washington, October 23, 1950; admitted to bar, 1976, Oregon, U.S. District Court, District of Oregon and U. S. Court of Appeals, Ninth Circuit. *Education:* Whitman College; Pacific University (B.A., with honors, 1972); Catholic University of America (J.D., 1976). Member, Moot Court Board. Member, Catholic University Law Review. Lecturer, Oregon State Bar Continuing Legal Education Programs. Former Family Law Reference Judge. *Member:* Oregon State Bar (Family Law Section, Chair-2005; Committee on Combining Family and Career, 1989-1990; Chairman, 1991-1992; Joint Custody Task Force, 1985; Support Guidelines Task Force, 1990); American Bar Association (Member, Family Law Section); Oregon Academy of Family Law Practitioners. ***PRACTICE AREAS:*** Family Law; Custody Law; Interstate Child Custody. ***Email:*** rjohnston@johnstonroot.com

KATHRYN SMITH ROOT, born Santa Monica, California, June 25, 1958; admitted to bar, 1985, Oregon and U.S. District Court, District of Oregon; 1987, U.S. Court of Appeals, Ninth Circuit. *Education:* Lewis and Clark College (B.S., 1980); Northwestern School of Law (J.D.,1984). Member, Cornelius Honor Society. Member, Cornelius Honor Society. Lecturer: American Bar Association, Oregon State Bar Association and Professional Liability Fund CLE Programs on Family Law, Child Custody and Interstate and International Custody, 1986—; Divorce Law Update Program on Interstate and International Custody Law, 1996. *Member:* Multnomah County (Chairman, Membership Committee, 1987-1989; Member, Committee on the Status of Women in the Practice of Law, 1987-1991) and American (Chair, International Law Committee, 2004— and Member, Family Law Section) Bar Associations; Oregon State Bar (Member: Family Law Section; Executive Committee, 1990-1991; Procedure and Practice Committee, 1987-1990; Chairman, 1991-1992); Oregon Academy of Family Law Practitioners (Secretary/Treasurer, 1994-

(This Listing Continued)

JOHNSTON, ROOT & LEIBENGUTH, P.C., Portland—Continued

1998; President, 1998-1999); Oregon Women Lawyers (Vice President, 1990-1991). ***PRACTICE AREAS:*** Family Law; Custody Law; Interstate Child Custody; International Family Law. ***Email:*** kroot@johnstonroot.com

M. SCOTT LEIBENGUTH, born Bloomington, Indiana, December 14, 1962; admitted to bar, 1994, Oregon. *Education:* Indiana University (B.S., Business and Economics, 1989); Willamette University (J.D., 1993). Past Speaker, Family Law Conference, Oregon State Bar. Past Director, Gresham Rotary Club. Past Member, Fairlawn Retirement Village Ethics Committee. Formerly with: Marion County District Attorney's Office; Trial Division, Oregon Department of Justice. *Member:* Multnomah (Past Member, CLE Committee) and American Bar Associations; Oregon State Bar (Member, Section on Family Law); Oregon Academy of Family Law Practitioners. ***PRACTICE AREAS:*** Family Law; Estate Planning; Wills; Probate Litigation; Property Rights; Child Custody; Trusts; Business Rights; Corporate Rights. ***Email:*** sleibenguth@johnstonroot.com

JOHNSTONE & GOODFELLOW

PORTLAND, OREGON

(See McMinnville)

General Practice, Litigation, Federal and State Courts, Business, Corporate, Probate, Family Law, Divorce, Child Custody Law, Personal Injury, Alternative Dispute Resolution, Mediation and Arbitration, Construction Law, Debtor/Creditor Law, School, Insurance Law, Real Estate, International Law, Wills and Estate Planning,.

JORDAN SCHRADER PC
ATTORNEYS AT LAW

Established in 1963

P.O. BOX 230669
PORTLAND, OREGON 97281-0669
Telephone: 503-598-7070
Fax: 503-598-7373
Email: info@jordanschrader.com
URL: http://www.jordanschrader.com

Business, Construction Contracting and Claims, Real Estate Law, Land Use and Development, Environmental and Natural Resources Law, Water Law, Bankruptcy Creditors' Rights Law, Employment Law, Municipal Law, General Corporate and Commercial Law, Banking and Finance, Mediation, Arbitration and Litigation in all Federal and State Courts.

FIRM PROFILE: Jordan Schrader PC, founded in 1963, serves businesses throughout Oregon and southwest Washington. The firm provides full business law services, including litigation in state, federal, and bankruptcy courts. Its extensive use of paralegals and alternative dispute resolution techniques allows it to offer cost-effective, timely results to its clients.

E. ANDREW JORDAN, born Portland, Oregon, August 3, 1944; admitted to bar, 1972, Oregon; 1975, U.S. District Court, District of Oregon. *Education:* University of Oregon (B.S., 1966; J.D., 1972). *Member:* Oregon State Bar. ***PRACTICE AREAS:*** Land Use; Real Estate; Employment; Municipal Law.

CHARLES R. SCHRADER, born Portland, Oregon, February 18, 1947; admitted to bar, 1977, Oregon; 1978, Washington and U.S. Claims Court; 1985, U .S. Supreme Court; 1991, California. *Education:* Stanford University (B.S., Civil Engineering, with distinction, 1969; M.S., Construction Engineering and Management, 1970); University of Oregon (J.D., 1977). *Member:* Oregon State Bar; State Bar of California; Washington State Bar Association. ***PRACTICE AREAS:*** Construction Law; Public Contracts; Surety; Design Professional Malpractice; Business Transactions; Construction Claims; Corporate Law; Construction Labor Law.

JEFFREY J. BENNETT, born Waupun, Wisconsin, July 4, 1952; admitted to bar, 1981, Oregon and U.S. District Court, District of Oregon; 1984, U.S. Court of Appeals, Ninth Circuit; 1993, Washington; 1994, U.S. District Court, Western District of Washington. *Education:* University of Wisconsin-Madison (B.S., Landscape Architecture, 1975); Northwestern School of Law of Lewis & Clark College (J.D., 1981). *Member:* Oregon State Bar; Washington State Bar Association. ***PRACTICE AREAS:*** Real Estate Development; Environmental Law; Land Use Law; Business Law; Civil Appeals.

CHRISTOPHER L. REIVE, born Kansas City, Missouri, October 16, 1951; admitted to bar, 1983, Oregon, U.S. District Court, District of Oregon and U.S. Court of Appeals, Ninth Circuit; 1984, Washington and U.S. District Court, Western and Eastern Districts of Washington; 1998, U.S. Court of Appeals for the Federal Circuit. *Education:* University of Michigan (B.S., 1973; M.P.H., 1976); Northwestern School of Law, Lewis and Clark College (J.D., 1983). *Member:* Oregon State Bar; Washington State Bar Association. ***PRACTICE AREAS:*** Environmental Law; Environmental Litigation; Natural Resources; Commercial Litigation; Insurance Coverage.

JOHN H. BAKER, JR., born Englewood, New Jersey, December 20, 1946; admitted to bar, 1986, Oregon; 1989, U.S. District Court, District of Oregon; 1993, Washington and U.S. District Court, Western District of Washington. *Education:* Cornell University (B.Arch., 1979); University of Oregon (J.D., 1986). Order of the Coif. Registered Professional Architect, Wyoming, 1981. *Member:* Oregon State Bar; Washington State Bar Association. ***PRACTICE AREAS:*** Construction Law; Contracts and Claims; Design-Build Contracting; Design Professionals.

ROBERT F. BLACKMORE, born Portland, Oregon, April 30, 1952; admitted to bar, 1981, Oregon. *Education:* University of Oregon (B.S., Finance, 1974; M.B.A., 1977); Northwestern School of Law, Lewis and Clark College (J.D., 1981). *Member:* Oregon State Bar. ***PRACTICE AREAS:*** Business Law; Business Litigation; Corporate Law; Commercial Transactions; Real Estate; Municipal Law.

(This Listing Continued)

THOMAS B. ERIKSEN, born Redmond, Oregon, April 17, 1957; admitted to bar, 1984, Oregon and Washington. *Education:* Oregon State University (B.S., 1979); Willamette University (M.S., J.D., 1984). *Member:* Oregon State Bar; Washington State Bar Association. ***PRACTICE AREAS:*** Business Law; Corporate Law; Mergers and Acquisitions; Succession Planning; Employee Benefits Law; ERISA.

HARLAN E. JONES, born Walla Walla, Washington, December 21, 1948; admitted to bar, 1979, Washington; 1985, Oregon. *Education:* Whitman College (A.B., 1975); Columbia University (J.D., 1978). *Member:* Washington State Bar Association; Oregon State Bar. ***PRACTICE AREAS:*** Commercial Litigation; Business Litigation; Construction Litigation.

DOUGLAS P. CUSHING, born Portland, Oregon, December 15, 1945; admitted to bar, 1970, Oregon; 1971, U.S. District Court, District of Oregon; 1979, U.S. Supreme Court; 1993, Washington. *Education:* Stanford University (B.A., 1967); Willamette University (J.D., magna cum laude, 1970). *Member:* Oregon State Bar; Washington State Bar Association. ***PRACTICE AREAS:*** Business; Creditors Rights; Real Estate; Probate; Estate Planning.

JANICE L. HOLTORF HIRSCH, born Agana, Guam, March 21, 1950; admitted to bar, 1993, Oregon. *Education:* Washington State University (B.A., 1989); Lewis and Clark College (J.D., 1993). Phi Delta Phi (Magister, 1992-1993; Exchequer, 1991-1992); Pi Sigma Alpha. Member, Cornelius Honor Society. *Member:* Oregon State Bar (Member, Sections on: Labor Relations and Civil Rights). ***PRACTICE AREAS:*** Labor and Employment Law; Preventive Personnel Policies.

EDWARD H. TROMPKE, born Holyoke, Massachusetts, August 16, 1952; admitted to bar, 1984, Oregon; 1988, U.S. District Court, District of Oregon. *Education:* Portland State University (B.S., 1979); Northwestern School of Law of Lewis and Clark College (J.D., 1984). *Member:* Oregon State Bar. ***PRACTICE AREAS:*** Business; Real Estate; Land Use; Corporations; Partnership Law; Limited Liability Company Law; Cooperative Association Law.

CHRISTINE M. MEADOWS, born Moline, Illinois, January 25, 1969; admitted to bar, 1996, Oregon, U.S. District Court, District of Oregon and U.S. Court of Appeals, Ninth Circuit. *Education:* University of Illinois at Urbana (B.S., 1991); Northwestern School of Law of Lewis and Clark College (J.D., 1996). *Member:* Oregon State Bar. ***PRACTICE AREAS:*** Employment Law; Civil Litigation; Education Law.

STEVEN L. SHROPSHIRE, born Greeley, Colorado, September 27, 1967; admitted to bar, 1994, Oregon; 1995, Colorado; 2001, Washington. *Education:* University of Colorado (B.A., 1991); Lewis and Clark College, Northwestern School of Law (J.D., with Certificate in Environmental and Natural Resources Law, 1994). *Member:* Washington State Bar Association; Oregon State Bar. ***PRACTICE AREAS:*** Water Law; Land Reclamation; Natural Resources; Water Quality; Real Estate; Land Use.

JEREMY T. VERMILYEA, born South Laguna, California, October 25, 1969; admitted to bar, 1997, Alaska; 2000, Oregon. *Education:* University of Alaska (B.A., 1992); Vermont Law School (J.D., cum laude, 1996). Law Clerk, Alaska Court of Appeals, 1996-1997. *Member:* Alaska Bar Association; Oregon State Bar. ***PRACTICE AREAS:*** Construction Law; Business Law; Real Estate.

EILEEN G. EAKINS, born Harvard, Illinois, June 23, 1962; admitted to bar, 1994, Oregon. *Education:* California State University, Sacramento (B.A., 1983); Northwestern School of Law, Lewis and Clark College (J.D., 1994). *Member:* Oregon State Bar. ***PRACTICE AREAS:*** Municipal Law; Employment Law; Business Law.

PETER O WATTS, born Portland, Oregon, January 28, 1977; admitted to bar, 2002, Oregon. *Education:* University of Mississippi (B.A., 1999); University of Oregon (J.D., 2002); University of Washington (LL.M., 2003). *Member:* Oregon State Bar. ***PRACTICE AREAS:*** Business Law; Taxation Law; Estate Planning; Probate Law.

JUSTIN D. GERICKE, born Gary, Indiana, December 27, 1968; admitted to bar, 1999, Oregon and U.S. District Court, District of Oregon. *Education:* DePauw University (B.A., Biology, 1991); Indiana University (M.P.A., Public Affairs, 1994; M.S. Environmental Science, 1994); Northwestern School of Law, Lewis and Clark College (J.D., 1997). *Member:* Multnomah and American Bar Associations; Oregon State Bar. ***PRACTICE AREAS:*** Water Law; Environmental Law; Natural Resources; Agribusiness.

REPRESENTATIVE CLIENTS: 7-Eleven, Inc.; AmberJack Ltd; Asphalt Pavement Assoc. of Oregon; Associated General Contractors; Benge Construction, Inc., Benge Equipment, Inc.; Birtcher Commercial Development Group; City of Forest Grove; City of Lafayette; City of Scappoose; Clatsop County; Colamette Construction Company; Community Financial Group; Covert Engineers, Inc.; Dice Properties; D.R. Horton, Inc.; Eugene Sand and Gravel, Inc.; Hilton Hotels Corporation; Hunter Davisson, Inc.; Interface Engineering, Inc.; J.C. Compton Contractor, Inc.; Legend Homes; LTM, Inc.; Matrix Development Corp.; McDonald's Corporation; Meridian Technology Group, Inc.; Multnomah Oil, Inc.; New Tradition Homes, Inc.; Oregon Association of Nurserymen; Oregon Landscape Contractors; Oregon Public Ports Association; Port of Tillamook; Rite Aid Corporation; R&W Engineering, Inc.; Salem Road & Driveway Co.; Slayden Construction, Inc.; Specht Properties, Inc.; Special Districts Association of Oregon; Sunbelt Rentals; Timberline Software Corporation; Todd Construction, Inc.; Transamerica Commercial Finance Company; Tualatin Valley Fire & Rescue; Tuefel Nursery, Inc.; Wacker Siltronic Corp.; Walgreen Co.; Washington Mutual Bank.

JOSSELSON, POTTER & ROBERTS

Established in 1983

425 NW 10TH AVENUE, SUITE 306
PORTLAND, OREGON 97209
Telephone: 503-228-1455
Facsimile: 503-228-0171
Email: office@jprlaw.com

Real Estate, Finance, Land Use, Environmental, Administrative, Municipal, Health Care, General Business, Surety, Construction, Business Litigation.

MEMBERS OF FIRM

FRANK JOSSELSON (1944-1998)

(This Listing Continued)

IRVING W. POTTER, born Portland, Oregon, March 28, 1948; admitted to bar, 1974, Oregon; 1975, U.S. District Court, District of Oregon; 1983, Washington. *Education:* Claremont Men's College (B.A., cum laude, 1970); Willamette University (J.D., magna cum laude, 1974). Contributing Editor, "Oregon Real Estate and Land Use Digest," 1978-1979. Member, Oregon Board of Maritime Pilots, 1992-1996; Chair, 1994-1996. *Member:* Multnomah County, Washington State and American Bar Associations; Oregon State Bar. ***PRACTICE AREAS:*** Real Estate Law; Finance; General Business Law; Environmental Law. ***Email:*** irving@jprlaw.com

LESLIE M. ROBERTS, born Vanport, Oregon, September 17, 1947; admitted to bar, 1972, Oregon; 1974, U.S. District Court, District of Oregon; 1977, U.S. Court of Appeals, Ninth Circuit; 1979, U.S. Supreme Court. *Education:* Reed College (B.A., 1969); Yale University (J.D., 1972). Phi Beta Kappa. Author: "Arbitration," Civil Pleading and Practice Handbook, Oregon CLE, 1985 and 1991 Supplement and Supplement, 1995; "Judgements," Real Estate Handbook, Oregon CLE, 1983 and 1984 Supplements; "Judgements and Execution," Real Estate, Oregon CLE, 1993. Co-Editor and Co-author: *Arbitration and Mediation,* Oregon CLE, 1987, 1992 Supplement, 1996. Co-Editor, *Oregon Health Law Manual,* Health Law Section, 1990 and 1992 supplement. Law Clerk, Oregon Supreme Court, 1972-1974. Commissioner, Fourth Judicial District Arbitration Program, 1982-1987. *Member:* Multnomah County and American Bar Associations; Oregon State Bar (Member: Executive Committee of Real Estate and Land Use Section, 1978-1980; Chair, Health Law Section, 1991-1992; Chair, Alternative Dispute Resolution Section, 1990-1991; Member, Legal Ethics Committee, 1994-1997 and Chair, 1996-1997; Member, Disciplinary Board, 1996-2000). ***PRACTICE AREAS:*** Business Litigation; Real Property Litigation; Health Care Administrative Law; Municipal Law. ***Email:*** leslie@jprlaw.com

OF COUNSEL

LAWRENCE R. DERR, born Philadelphia, Pennsylvania, February 22, 1944; admitted to bar, 1969, Oregon; 1980, U.S. Supreme Court. *Education:* University of Oregon (B.A., Honors College, 1966); Willamette University (J.D., 1969). Phi Delta Phi. Co-Author: "Elections," Local Government Handbook, 1979 and "Legislative Developments in Energy and Environmental Law," 1983, Oregon Continuing Legal Education. Program Planner and Lecturer, "Commercial Real Property Leasing," 1984, Oregon Law Institute. County Counsel, Washington County, 1975-1978. Land Use Hearings Officer, Oregon Land Conservation and Development Commission, Washington County, Multnomah County and City of Hillsboro. Member, Portland Metropolitan Regional Government Charter Committee, 1991-1992. *Member:* Oregon State Bar (Member: Professional Insurance Committee, 1973-1976; Local Government Committee, 1977-1980; Member, 1981-1984 and Chairman, 1982, Environment and Natural Resources Committee; Member, 1977— and Secretary, 1980 and Chair, 1984, Real Estate and Land Use Section; Chairman, Editorial Committee, Government Law Section, 1981-1982); American Bar Association (Member, Sections on: Urban, State and Local Government Law; Real Property, Probate and Trust Law). ***PRACTICE AREAS:*** Administrative Law; Real Estate Law; Land Use Law. ***Email:*** larry@jprlaw.com

---

KAHN & KAHN, P.C.

Established in 1991

1210 CASCADE BUILDING
520 S.W. SIXTH AVENUE
PORTLAND, OREGON 97204-1510
Telephone: 503-227-4488
Fax: 503-227-0753
URL: http://www.kahnattorneys.com
Email: steven@kahnattorneys.com
URL: http://www.lawyers.com/kahn&kahn

Civil Trials, Negligence, Products Liability, Professional Liability, Premises Liability, Personal Injury, Auto Accidents, Wrongful Death, Slip and Fall, Insurance Claims.

GARRY L. KAHN, born San Francisco, California, April 20, 1936; admitted to bar, 1962, Oregon and U.S. District Court, District of Oregon; 1971, U.S. Supreme Court and U.S. Court of Appeals, Ninth Circuit. *Education:* University of Portland; Portland State University; Northwestern College of Law (LL.B., 1962). Distinguished Trial Lawyer, Oregon Trial Lawyers Association, 1991. Distinguished Graduate, Northwestern School of Law of Lewis and Clark College, 1999. Circuit Court Judge, 1992-1993. *Member:* Oregon State Bar (President, 1988-1989); Multnomah County Bar Association; Western Trial Lawyers Association (President, 1972-1973); The Association of Trial Lawyers of America (President, Oregon Chapter, 1968-1969; State Delegate, 1982-1985). Fellow, American College of Trial Lawyers. ***PRACTICE AREAS:*** Personal Injury; Wrongful Death; Products Liability; Medical Malpractice; Professional Liability. ***Email:*** garry@kahnattorneys.com

STEVEN A. KAHN, born Portland, Oregon January 28, 1963; admitted to bar, 1988, Oregon and U.S. District Court, District of Oregon; U.S. Court of Appeals, Ninth Circuit. *Education:* University of California at Berkeley (B.A., 1985); Northwestern School of Law of Lewis and Clark College (J.D., magna cum laude, 1988). President, Board of Directors, Northwestern School of Law of Lewis and Clark Alumni, 1998-2000. *Member:* Multnomah Bar Association; Oregon State Bar; Oregon Trial Lawyers Association; The Association of Trial Lawyers of America; The Owen M. Panner American Inn of Court (Barrister, 1987-1993). ***PRACTICE AREAS:*** Personal Injury; Products Liability; Medical Malpractice; Premises Liability. ***Email:*** steven@kahnattorneys.com

KAMINASH & ASSOCIATES, LLC

805 SW BROADWAY, SUITE 2440
PORTLAND, OREGON 97205
Telephone: 503-224-3241
Fax: 503-224-3581
Email: bkaminash@kaminashlaw.com
URL: http://www.kaminashassociates.com

Intellectual Property, Copyrights, Trade Secrets, Trademarks, Intellectual Property Licensing, Advertising, Internet Law, E-Commerce, Business Law, Business Formation, Venture Capital, Acquisitions, Breach of Contract, Antitrust and Trade Regulation.

BENJAMIN H. KAMINASH, born Brooklyn, New York, May 5, 1950; admitted to bar, 1982, California and U.S. District Court, Central District of California; 1983, U.S. District Court, Northern District of California; 1989, Oregon. *Education:* University of Wisconsin-Madison; College of New Rochelle (B.A., 1977); University of Texas (J.D., 1982). *Member:* Multnomah County and American (Member, Sections on: Business Law; Patent, Trademark and Copyright Law; Science and Technology) Bar Associations; State Bar of California; Oregon State Bar (Member, Sections on: Business Law; Patent and Trademark Law; Antitrust, Trade Regulation and Unfair Business Practice; Chairman, Patent and Trademark Law Section, 1995-1996); Computer Law Association; Oregon Film and Video Foundation (Board Member, 1994-2000). ***Email:*** bkaminash@kaminashlaw.com

---

KARNOPP PETERSEN LLP

PORTLAND, OREGON

(See Bend)

General Civil, Trial and Appellate Practice, including Plaintiff's Personal Injury and Tort Litigation. General Business, Banking, Creditor Bankruptcy, Tax, Estate Planning, Probate, Real Estate and Land Use, Employment Law, Water Law, Utility/Energy, Environmental and Indian Affairs Law.

KEATING JONES BILDSTEIN & HUGHES, P.C.

Established in 1997

800 BENJAMIN FRANKLIN PLAZA
ONE SOUTHWEST COLUMBIA
PORTLAND, OREGON 97258-2095
Telephone: 503-222-9955
Fax: 503-796-0699

Civil Litigation Practice Concentrating on the Defense of Professionals, including Physicians, Hospitals and other Health Care Providers and Attorneys, Health Care Antitrust, Medical Device and Drug Products Liability Claims, Health Care Law, Employment Law.

JEFFREY W. BILDSTEIN, born Port Lyautey, Morocco, April 19, 1957; admitted to bar, 1982, Oregon; 1984, U.S. District Court, District of Oregon; 1985, Washington; 1994, U.S. District Court, Eastern and Western Districts of Washington. *Education:* Bloomsburg State College; West Virginia University (B.S., magna cum laude, 1979); University of Oregon (J.D., 1982). Phi Delta Phi. *Member:* Multnomah County, Clark County, Washington State and American Bar Associations; Oregon State Bar; Oregon Association of Defense Counsel; Washington Defense Trial Lawyers Association; Oregon Academy of Healthcare Attorneys. ***PRACTICE AREAS:*** Health Care Law; Medical Malpractice. ***Email:*** jbildstein@keatingjones.com

SHERI C. BROWNING, born San Antonio, Texas, June 12, 1969; admitted to bar, 1997, Oregon; 1999, Washington. *Education:* University of North Texas (B.A., 1991); Northwestern School of Law of Lewis and Clark (J.D., cum laude, 1997). Teaching Assistant, Legal Research & Writing, 1995-1996, 1996-1997. *Member:* Multnomah County (Member, Young Lawyers Division, CLE Committee, 1997-1999) and American Bar Associations; Oregon State Bar. Owen M. Panner American Inn of Court, 1998—. ***PRACTICE AREAS:*** Medical Malpractice Defense; Insurance Defense. ***Email:*** sbrowning@keatingjones.com

LINDSEY H. HUGHES, born Boise, Idaho, May 26, 1956; admitted to bar, 1981, Idaho; 1983, Oregon; 1985, Washington; U.S. Supreme Court; U.S. District Court, Districts of Oregon, Idaho and Western District of Washington; U.S. Court of Appeals, Ninth Circuit. *Education:* University of Idaho (B.A., 1978); Willamette University (J.D., cum laude, 1981). Casenote Editor, Willamette Law Review, Fall, 1981. Law Clerk to Chief Justice Robert E. Bakes, Idaho Supreme Court, 1981-1983. Member, Oregon Board of Bar Examiners, 1993-1996, Chair, 1995-1996. *Member:* Oregon State Bar (CLE Committee, 1990-1993; Chair, 1992-1993); Idaho State Bar; Washington State, Federal and American Bar Associations; Oregon Association of Defense Counsel (Amicus Brief Committee, 1995—). ***PRACTICE AREAS:*** Appellate Law; Health Care Law; Medical Malpractice Defense; Legal Malpractice Defense. ***Email:*** lhughes@keatingjones.com

STEVEN P. JONES, born Salem, Oregon, January 2, 1951; admitted to bar, 1978, Oregon and U.S. District Court, District of Oregon. *Education:* Oregon State University (B.S., 1973); Northwestern School of Law of Lewis and Clark College (J.D., 1978). *Member:* Multnomah County and American Bar Associations; Oregon State Bar; Oregon Association of Defense Counsel; Oregon Academy of Healthcare Attorneys; Defense Research Institute. ***PRACTICE AREAS:*** Medical Malpractice; Professional Malpractice; Complex Litigation; Health Care Law. ***Email:*** sjones@keatingjones.com

ROBERT M. KEATING, born Rockford, Illinois, August 20, 1943; admitted to bar, 1968, Wisconsin; 1969, U.S. Court of Military Appeals; 1973, Oregon and U.S. District Court, District of Oregon; 1974, U.S. Court of Appeals, Ninth Circuit; 1992, U.S. Supreme Court. *Education:* University of Notre Dame (B.A., 1965); Northwestern University (J.D., cum laude, 1968). Order of the Coif. Founding Director, The Foundation for Medical Excellence. Fellow, American College of Trial Lawyers, 2003. *Member:* Multnomah County and American Bar Associations; Oregon State Bar; Oregon Academy of Healthcare Attorneys; American Society of Hospital Attorneys; American Society of Law, Medicine and

(This Listing Continued)

KEATING JONES BILDSTEIN & HUGHES, P.C., Portland—Continued

Ethics; Oregon Association of Defense Counsel (Board Member, 1997-2000); The Defense Research Institute; American Board of Trial Advocates; International Association of Defense Counsel. [Lt., JAGC, USNR, 1969-1973]. ***PRACTICE AREAS:*** Medical Malpractice; Health Care Law; Complex Litigation. ***Email:*** rkeating@keatingjones.com

SCOTT G. O'DONNELL, born Albany, Oregon, January 19, 1966; admitted to bar, 1993, Oregon; 1997, U.S. District Court, District of Oregon; 1998, Washington. *Education:* University of Oregon (B.S., 1988; J.D., 1993). Recipient, American Jurisprudence Award in Conflict of Laws, 1992. Author: "New Plan For Oregon Based on New Oregon Constitution," 30 Willamette Law Review 103, 1994. *Member:* Multnomah County, Washington State and American Bar Associations; Oregon State Bar; Oregon Association of Defense Counsel; Washington Defense Trial Lawyers. ***PRACTICE AREAS:*** Health Care; Medical Malpractice; Litigation. ***Email:*** sodonnell@keatingjones.com

---

KIRSTIN L. ABEL, born 1977; admitted to bar, 2003, Oregon; U.S. District Court, District of Oregon. *Education:* Linfield College (B.A., 1999); John Marshall Law School (J.D., 2003). Chief Justice, 2002-2003, and Member, 2002, Moot Court Board. Law Clerk to, Hon. Ellen F. Rosenblum, Multnomah County Circuit Court, 2004-2005. *Member:* Oregon State Bar; Owen M. Panner American Inns of Court. ***PRACTICE AREAS:*** Medical Malpractice Defense. ***Email:*** Kabel@keatingjones.com

CAROLINE COPPOCK, admitted to bar, 2002, Oregon and U.S. District Court, District of Oregon. *Education:* University of South Carolina (B.S., 1996); Northwestern School of Law of Lewis and Clark College (J.D., 2001). Outstanding Oral Advocate. ***PRACTICE AREAS:*** Medical Malpractice Defense; Complex Litigation. ***Email:*** ccoppock@keatingjones.com

JASON H. DAYWITT, born 1968; admitted to bar, 1999, Oregon; 2000, U.S. District Court, District of Oregon; 2001, Washington; 2002, U.S. District Court, District of Western Washington. *Education:* Washington and Lee University (B.A., 1995); University of Oregon (J.D., 1999). Editor-in-Chief, Journal of Environmental Law and Litigation, 1998-1999. *Member:* Multnomah County, Washington State and American Bar Associations; Oregon State Bar; Oregon Association of Defense Counsel; Defense Research Institute. ***LANGUAGES:*** Arabic and German. ***PRACTICE AREAS:*** Medical Malpractice Defense; Professional Malpractice; Complex and Multi-District Litigation; Products Liability. ***Email:*** jdaywitt@keatingjones.com

MONICA A. WELLS, born Medford, Oregon, May 21, 1978; admitted to bar, 2003, Oregon and U.S. District Court, District of Oregon. *Education:* Seattle University (B.A., magna cum laude, 2000); University of Oregon (J.D., 2003). Order of the Coif. *Member:* Multnomah County Bar Association; Oregon State Bar (Member, Young Lawyers Section); Oregon Association of Defense Counsel. ***PRACTICE AREAS:*** Medical Malpractice Defense; Litigation. ***Email:*** mwells@keatingjones.com

DEVON ZASTROW NEWMAN, born Denver, Colorado, July 9, 1972; admitted to bar, 2001, Oregon; 2002, U.S. District Court, District of Oregon; U.S. Court of Appeals, Ninth Circuit; registered to practice before the U.S. Patent and Trademark Office. *Education:* New Mexico State University (B.S., B.A., 1994); University of Colorado Health Sciences Center (M.S., 1998); Cornell Law School (J.D., 2001). Member, Moot Court Board. Executive Editor, 2000-2001 and Editor, 1999-2001, Legal Information Institute. *Member:* Multnomah County Bar Association; Oregon State Bar; Oregon Women Lawyers Association; American Intellectual Property Law Association; Gus J. Solomon American Inn of Court. ***PRACTICE AREAS:*** Medical Malpractice Defense; Litigation; Intellectual Property.

PETER O. TUENGE, born Boulder, Colorado, March 31, 1977; admitted to bar, 2003, Oregon. *Education:* Gonzaga University (B.A., 1999); University of Oregon (J.D., 2003). Order of the Coif. Member, Moot Court Board, 2001-2003. Associate Editor, 2001-2002 and Articles Editor, 2002-2003, Oregon Law Review. Law Clerk to Justice Richard B. Sanders, Washington State Supreme Court, 2003-2004. *Member:* Oregon State Bar; Multnomah County Bar Association; Oregon Association of Defense Counsel. ***PRACTICE AREAS:*** Appellate Practice; Medical Malpractice Defense.

OF COUNSEL

MOLLY K. MARCUM, born Portland, Oregon, January 16, 1954; admitted to bar, 1983, Oregon; 1984, U.S. District Court, District of Oregon. *Education:* University of Oregon, Nursing School (B.S., cum laude, 1978); Portland State University (B.A., 1978); Northwestern School of Law of Lewis and Clark College (J.D., 1983). Sigma Theta Tau. Registered Nurse, Oregon, 1978. Law Clerk to Hon. George E. Juba, U.S. Magistrate, District of Oregon, 1983-1984. *Member:* Multnomah County Bar Association; Oregon State Bar; The American Association of Nurse Attorneys; Oregon Association of Defense Counsel; Oregon Society of Hospital Attorneys. ***PRACTICE AREAS:*** Medical Malpractice. ***Email:*** mmarcum@keatingjones.com

RICKEE N. ARNTZ, born Billings, Montana, April 28, 1955; admitted to bar, 1992, Oregon; 1993, Washington and U.S. District Court, District of Oregon. *Education:* University of Arizona (B.A., 1978; M.S., Speech and Hearing Sciences, 1981); Creighton University School of Law (J.D., summa cum laude, 1992). Member, Creighton University Law Review. *Member:* Multnomah County and Washington State Bar Associations; Oregon State Bar. ***PRACTICE AREAS:*** Medical Malpractice Defense; Litigation. ***Email:*** rarntz@keatingjones.com

REPRESENTATIVE CLIENTS: CNA Insurance Companies; Farmers Insurance Group; Truck Insurance Exchange; Health Future, LLC; Legacy Health System; Northwest Physicians Mutual Insurance Company; Oregon State Bar Professional Liability Fund; Physicians Insurance Exchange; Peace Health; St. Paul Fire and Marine Insurance Company; Washington Casualty Company.

KELL, ALTERMAN & RUNSTEIN, LLP

Established in 1929

520 S.W. YAMHILL, SUITE 600
PORTLAND, OREGON 97204
Telephone: 503-222-3531
Fax: 503-227-2980
Email: webmaster@kelrun.com
URL: http://www.kelrun.com

General Business and Trial Practice, including Corporate, Tax and Real Estate Law, Litigation in all State and Federal Courts of Business, Personal Injury, Employment, Environmental, Divorce and Maritime cases, Estate Planning and Probate Law, Health Care Law, Construction Law, Bankruptcy, Debtor-Creditor Law, Government Relations, Secured Transactions, Business Acquisitions and Mergers and Franchise Law.

FIRM PROFILE: Kell, Alterman & Runstein has been serving the legal needs of businesses and individual clients in Oregon for over 70 years. We emphasize the high quality personal service to solve problems and create opportunities in the most practical, efficient and effective manner possible.

MEMBERS OF FIRM

RAYMOND M. KELL (1911-1991)

CLIFFORD B. ALTERMAN (1925-1995)

TED E. RUNSTEIN, born Portland, Oregon, December 1, 1939; admitted to bar, 1966, Oregon. *Education:* University of Washington (B.A., 1963); Willamette University (J.D., 1966). Trial Attorney, U.S. Department of Justice, Criminal Division. Honorary Consul for The Netherlands. *Member:* Multnomah County Bar Association; Oregon State Bar; Oregon Trial Lawyers Association; Association of Trial Lawyers of America. Fellow, American College of Trial Lawyers. ***PRACTICE AREAS:*** Personal Injury Litigation; Business Litigation; General Litigation; Family Law. ***Email:*** trunstein@kelrun.com

LEE DAVIS KELL, born Washington, D.C., March 17, 1939; admitted to bar, 1967, California and Oregon. *Education:* University of Oregon (B.A., 1962); New York University (LL.B., 1965). Certified Public Accountant: California, 1967; Oregon, 1968. *Member:* Multnomah County and American Bar Associations; The State Bar of California; Oregon State Bar. ***PRACTICE AREAS:*** Business Law; Closely Held Businesses; Estate Planning and Administration; Solid Waste Management. ***Email:*** lkell@kelrun.com

WAYNE D. PALMER, born Portland, Oregon, August 17, 1955; admitted to bar, 1981, Oregon. *Education:* Portland State University (B.S., with honors, 1977); Lewis and Clark College (J.D., 1981). *Member:* Multnomah County Bar Association; Oregon State Bar; Oregon Trial Lawyers Association; The Association of Trial Lawyers of America; Maritime Law Association of the United States. ***PRACTICE AREAS:*** Maritime/Foreclosure; Employment; Family Law; Business Litigation; Debtor Creditor. ***Email:*** wpalmer@kelrun.com

WILLIAM D. DICKAS, born Columbus, Ohio, November 26, 1941; admitted to bar, 1974, Ohio; 1975, Oregon. *Education:* St. Charles College (A.B., 1963); University of Innsbruck (M.A., 1967); Ohio State University (J.D., cum laude, 1974). *Member:* Oregon State Bar. ***PRACTICE AREAS:*** Business Law; Commercial Litigation; Real Estate; Government Regulation. ***Email:*** wdickas@kelrun.com

GARY P. COMPA, born Teaneck, New Jersey, May 13, 1945; admitted to bar, 1973, New Jersey; 1981, Oregon. *Education:* Georgetown University (A.B., 1967); Washington College of Law (J.D., 1972); New York University (LL.M. in Taxation, 1976). Co-Author: "Repeal of Unitary Tax and Revision of Corporate Income Tax in Oregon," Journal of Japanese Institute of International Business Law, 1985. Estate and Gift Taxation Attorney, Internal Revenue Service, 1976-1981. *Member:* New Jersey State Bar Association; Oregon State Bar. ***PRACTICE AREAS:*** Taxation; Business Law. ***Email:*** gcompa@kelrun.com

CHARLES R. WILLIAMSON, born Boston, Massachusetts, January 2, 1944; admitted to bar, 1968, Massachusetts; 1970, Oregon; 1977, U.S. Supreme Court. *Education:* Colgate University (B.A., 1965); Suffolk University (LL.B., 1968). Member, Editorial Staff, Suffolk University Law Review, 1967-1968. *Member:* Multnomah County Bar Association; Oregon State Bar (President, 2003; Member, Sections on: Litigation; Real Estate and Land Use; Debtor-Creditor; Business and Corporations; Estate Planning; Construction Law; Health Law; Government Law, Labor and Employment Law); Oregon Trial Lawyers Association; The Association of Trial Lawyers of America; American Bankruptcy Institute. ***PRACTICE AREAS:*** Legislative Advocacy; Arbitration; Mediation; Bankruptcy; Debtor Creditor Law; Business Litigation. ***Email:*** charlie@kelrun.com

ERIC SOGGE, born Ellensburg, Washington, January 23, 1943; admitted to bar, 1972, Oregon; 1973, U.S. District Court, District of Oregon and U.S. Court of Appeals, Ninth Circuit. *Education:* Harvard University (A.B., 1964); University of Oregon (J.D., 1972). Executive Editor, Oregon Law Review, 1971-1972. *Member:* Oregon State Bar (Member, Sections on: Antitrust, Trade Regulation and Unfair Business Practices; Debtor-Creditor Law; Corporate Law); American Bar Association (Member, Sections on: Antitrust Law; Business Law; Committee on Negotiated Acquisitions). ***PRACTICE AREAS:*** Secured Financial Transactions; Business Acquisitions and Mergers; Real Estate Law. ***Email:*** esogge@kelrun.com

THOMAS R. RASK, III, born Portland, Oregon, October 27, 1968; admitted to bar, 1993, Oregon and U.S. District Court, District of Oregon. *Education:* University of Notre Dame (B.B.A., 1990); Willamette University (J.D., 1993). Phi Delta Phi. Trustee, Oregon Association of Children With Learning Disabilities, 1993—. President, University of Notre Dame Alumni Club of Portland, 1996-1998. Director, American Red Cross, Oregon Trial Chapter. *Member:* Multnomah County and American Bar Associations; Oregon State Bar. ***PRACTICE AREAS:*** General Civil Litigation; General Business Law. ***Email:*** trask@kelrun.com

ROBERT E. KABACY, born Oakland, California, May 30, 1968; admitted to bar, 1993, Oregon, Wisconsin and U.S. District Court, Eastern District of Wisconsin; 1994, Washington and U.S. District Court, District of Oregon. *Education:* University of Puget Sound (B.A., honors, 1990); Marquette University Law School (J.D., cum laude, 1993).

(This Listing Continued)

Member: Oregon State Bar; Washington State Bar Association; State Bar of Wisconsin. ***PRACTICE AREAS:*** General Business; Estate Planning. ***Email:*** rkabacy@kelrun.com

DENNIS STEINMAN, born New York, N.Y., May 20, 1955; admitted to bar, 1995, Oregon; 1996, U.S. Court of Appeals, Ninth Circuit and U.S. District Court, District of Oregon. *Education:* Temple University (B.A., cum laude, 1976); Northwestern School of Law (J.D., 1995). Phi Delta Phi. Recipient: Best Oralist and Honors Brief, First Year Moot Court Competition; Best Trial Memorandum and Notebook, Mock Trial Competition; ASCAP Nathan Burke Award, National Copyright Competition. Author: "Disability Law in the Twenty-First Century," Lawyers and the ADA, 2001 Oregon State Bar Convention; "Reasonable Accomodation Under the ADA," Fair Housing Act and Oregon Law, Lorman Education Services, 2001; "Reasonable Accomodation Under the ADA," Fair Housing Act and State Law, Oregon Law Institute Continuing Legal Education, 2000; "The Undiscovered ADA," Oregon Law Institute Continuing Legal Education, 1999; "ADA Update: Reasonable Accomodation Beyond Physical Access," Associational Discrimination, Conflict of Laws, and Damages, 1999 Oregon State Bar Convention; "Sharpening Your Skills: The ADA's Application to Oregon's Regulatory and Licensing Programs," Oregon Law Institute Continuing Legal Education, 1999. Adjunct Professor, Northwestern School of Law, 2001—. Formerly with Steinman Cooper Wiscarson LLC. *Member:* Multnomah County and Federal Bar Associations; Oregon State Bar (Member: Civil Rights Section Executive Committee, 2001—; Disability Law Section Executive Committee, 2001—). ***LANGUAGES:*** American Sign Language, Italian, French. ***REPORTED CASES:*** State Farm Fire & Cas. Co. v. Finch, 2001 U.S. Dist. LEXIS 14438, September 6, 2001; Glass v. Hillsboro Sch. Dist. 1J, 142 F. Supp. 2d 1286 (D. Or. 2001); Alford v. City of Cannon Beach, 2000 WL 33200554 (D. Or. 2001); Sherwood v. Finch, 2000 WL 1862562 (D. Or. 2000); Glass v. Hillsboro School Dist. 1J, 2000 WL 1877647 (D.Or. 2000); Cornilles v. Regal Cinemas, Inc., 2000 U.S. Dist. LEXIS 15465, September 15, 2000, Decided, September 18, 2000; Cornilles v. Regal Cinemas, Inc., 2000 U.S.Dist. LEXIS 15464, August 2, 2000, Decided, August 2, 2000, Filed, Adopting Order of September 15, 2000; LaFore v. Housing Authority of Portland, 1999 WL 1058992 (D.Or. 1999); Drew v. Merrill, CV 99-810 KI, Consent Decree (D. Or. 1999); Green v. Housing Authority of Clackamas County, 994 F.Supp. 1253 (D. Or. 1998). ***PRACTICE AREAS:*** Civil Rights; Americans with Disabilities Act; Business Law; Corporate Law; Commercial Law; Litigation; Franchise Law. ***Email:*** dsteinman@kelrun.com

---

DANA L. BARNES, born Long Beach, California, February 24, 1958; admitted to bar, 1985, Oregon and U.S. District Court, District of Oregon. *Education:* Lewis and Clark College (B.S., with honors, 1980); Northwestern School of Law of Lewis and Clark College (J.D., 1984). *Member:* Multnomah County and Washington County Bar Associations; Oregon State Bar; Oregon Women Lawyers Association; Oregon Trial Lawyers Association. ***PRACTICE AREAS:*** Family Law. ***Email:*** dbarnes@kelrun.com

JENNIFER KAMPSULA, born Vancouver, Washington, November 21, 1972; admitted to bar, 1999, Washington; 2000, Oregon. *Education:* Seattle University (B.A., magna cum laude, 1995); University of Washington (J.D., 1999). Alpha Sigma Nu; Phi Alpha Delta. *Member:* Washington State and Oregon State Bar Associations; Oregon Trial Lawyers Association; Oregon Women Lawyers; Washington State Trial Lawyers Association. ***PRACTICE AREAS:*** Personal Injury; Employment Law; General Civil Litigation. ***Email:*** jkampsula@kelrun.com

JOHN A. KODACHI, born Portland, Oregon, February 20, 1966; admitted to bar, 1992, Hawaii; 1999, Oregon. *Education:* Oberlin College (B.A., 1988); Northwestern School of Law of Lewis and Clark College (J.D., 1992). Director: Japan-America Society of Oregon, 2001—; Japanese American Citizens League, Portland Chapter, 2002. *Member:* Multnomah County, Hawaii State and American Bar Associations; Oregon State Bar; American Immigration Lawyers Association. ***Email:*** jkodachi@kelrun.com

OF COUNSEL

LLOYD R. SUMMERS, born Colorado, June 28, 1939; admitted to bar, 1967, Colorado and U.S. District Court, District of Colorado; 1977, Oregon. *Education:* Walla Walla College (B.S., 1961); University of Colorado (J.D., 1967). *Member:* Oregon State Bar (Member, Estate Planning and Tax Section); Colorado Bar Association. ***PRACTICE AREAS:*** Estate Planning Law; Probate Law; Medical-Legal. ***Email:*** lsummers@kelrun.com

REPRESENTATIVE CLIENTS: Albina Fuel; The Ash Organization; The Bank of Tokyo-Mitsubishi, Ltd.; Baxter Auto Parts, Inc.; Carlton Chain Co.; Chase Manhattan Bank; Columbia Wire & Iron Works, Inc.; Consulate General of Japan in Oregon; Fibrex & Shipping; Hallmark Inns & Resorts, Inc.; Independent Dispatch, Inc.; NEC America, Inc.; Nordisk Skibi; Oregon Metal Slitters, Inc.; Portland Adventist Medical Center; Rose City Label Co.; Shokookai of Portland; Soderstrom Architects, P.C.; TMT Development Co., Inc.; Waste Control Systems, Inc.; Yamasa Corporation USA; Tudatin Valley Builders' Supply.
REFERENCES: Union Bank of California, N.A. (Portland Branch); The Bank of Tokyo-Mitsubishi, Ltd. (Portland Branch); U.S. Bank, (Portland Branch).

KENNEDY & KENNEDY LLP

601 SW SECOND AVENUE, SUITE 2050
PORTLAND, OREGON 97204
Telephone: 503-226-6555
Telecopier: 503-226-6466

Business and Corporate Law, Acquisitions, Insurance Regulation and Real Estate.

MEMBERS OF FIRM

JAMES M. KENNEDY, born Portland, Oregon, September 26, 1950; admitted to bar, 1976, Oregon. *Education:* University of Michigan (B.A., magna cum laude, 1972; J.D., cum laude, 1976). Phi Beta Kappa. Recipient, Oregon State Bar Membership Service Award, 2002. Co-Editor: Advising Oregon Businesses, Volumes 1-5, Oregon State Bar, 1984-1985, 1996-2004. Oregon Task Forces on: Model Business Corporation Act, 1985-1988, 1991-1993; Uniform Limited Partnership Act, 1983-1985; Third Party Legal Opinions, 1991-1994; Revised Uniform Partnership Act and Limited Liability Partnerships,

(This Listing Continued)

1993-1997. *Member:* Oregon State Bar; Federation of Regulatory Counsel. ***PRACTICE AREAS:*** Business Law; Corporate Law; Business Acquisitions; Insurance Regulatory Law. ***Email:*** jkennedy@kennedy-kennedylaw.com

RHONDA W. KENNEDY, born Poughkeepsie, New York, September 11, 1951; admitted to bar, 1976, Oregon. *Education:* University of Michigan (B.A., magna cum laude, 1972; J.D., cum laude, 1976). Author: Chapters in "Advising Oregon Businesses" and "Real Property," Oregon State Bar. Executive Committee and General Counsel, 1991-1994 and Board of Directors, 1991-1996, Portland Chamber of Commerce; Director, 1992-1997 and Chairperson, 1996-1997, Professional Liability Fund. *Member:* Oregon State Bar. ***PRACTICE AREAS:*** Business Law; Corporate Law; Business Acquisitions; Insurance Regulatory Law; Real Estate. ***Email:*** rkennedy@kennedy-kennedylaw.com

REPRESENTATIVE CLIENTS: Campbell Crane & Rigging Service, Inc.; Farmers Insurance Group; Housing Authorities Risk Retention Pool; Liberty Northwest Insurance Corporation; Northwest Physicians Mutual Insurance Co.; ODS Health Plan, Inc.; Oregon Contractors Workers Compensation Trust, Inc.; Oregon Dental Service; Oregon Mutual Insurance Co.; Pacific LightNet, Inc.; Twist.

KENNEDY, WATTS, ARELLANO & RICKS LLP

Established in 1971
(As Kennedy & King)
2850 PACWEST CENTER
1211 S.W. FIFTH AVENUE
PORTLAND, OREGON 97204
Telephone: 503-228-6191
FAX: 503-228-0009
Email: kwar@kwar.com
URL: http://www.kwar.com

Civil Litigation in State and Federal Courts including Business, Securities, Professional Liability, Products Liability, Drug and Medical Device Defense, Insurance and Family Law.

OF COUNSEL

JACK L. KENNEDY, born Portland, Oregon, January 30, 1924; admitted to bar, 1951, Oregon; U.S. District Court, District of Oregon; U.S. Court of Appeals, Ninth Circuit; U.S. Supreme Court. *Education:* United States Maritime Commission Academy; Southwestern University; Northwestern School of Law of Lewis and Clark College (J.D., 1951). Fellow, American College of Trial Lawyers. ***PRACTICE AREAS:*** General Civil Litigation; Family Law. ***Email:*** kennedy@kwar.com

MEMBERS OF FIRM

SUSAN E. WATTS, born Chilliwack, British Columbia, January 10, 1952; admitted to bar, 1977, Oregon and U.S. District Court, District of Oregon; U.S. Court of Appeals, Ninth Circuit. *Education:* University of Oregon (B.A., 1974; J.D., 1977). Phi Beta Kappa. ***PRACTICE AREAS:*** Business Litigation; Drug and Medical Device Defense; Products Liability; Professional Liability Litigation. ***Email:*** watts@kwar.com

JOSEPH C. ARELLANO, born Chicago, Illinois, July 13, 1953; admitted to bar, 1979, New York; 1980, Oregon and U.S. District Court, District of Oregon; U.S. Court of Appeals, Ninth Circuit; U.S. Supreme Court. *Education:* De Paul University (B.A., 1975); Northwestern School of Law of Lewis and Clark College (J.D., 1978). ***PRACTICE AREAS:*** Securities Litigation; Professional Liability Litigation; Business Litigation. ***Email:*** arellano@kwar.com

DANIEL M. RICKS, born Vincennes, Indiana, October 12, 1951; admitted to bar, 1978, Oregon and U.S. District Court, District of Oregon; U.S. Court of Appeals, Ninth Circuit. *Education:* Franklin & Marshall College (A.B., 1973); Northwestern School of Law of Lewis and Clark College (J. D., 1978). ***PRACTICE AREAS:*** Commercial Litigation; Business Litigation; Federal Litigation; Qualified Domestic Relations Orders (QDROs); Professional Liability Defense. ***Email:*** ricks@kwar.com

TODD L. VAN RYSSELBERGHE, born Eugene, Oregon, April 30, 1960; admitted to bar, 1988, Oregon; 1991, U.S. District Court, District of Oregon; 2003, U.S. Court of Appeals, Ninth Circuit. *Education:* University of Oregon (B.S., 1983); Northwestern School of Law of Lewis and Clark College (J.D., 1988). ***PRACTICE AREAS:*** General Civil Litigation; Family Law; Professional Liability Defense. ***Email:*** van@kwar.com

DANIEL L. KEPPLER, born Charleston, Illinois, January 8, 1967; admitted to bar, 1992, Oregon; U.S. District Court, District of Oregon; U.S. Court of Appeals, Ninth Circuit; 2000, Washington. *Education:* Williamette University (B.A., 1989); Gonzaga University (J.D., magna cum laude, 1992). ***PRACTICE AREAS:*** Civil Litigation; Commercial Litigation; Contract Litigation; Business Litigation; Employment Law; Personal Injury. ***Email:*** keppler@kwar.com

ASSOCIATES

XIN XU, born Anhui, China, March 20, 1975; admitted to bar, 2000, Oregon and Washington; U.S. District Court, District of Oregon and U.S. Court of Appeals, Ninth Circuit. *Education:* University of Oregon (B.A., Psychology, 1996; J.D., 2000). ***LANGUAGES:*** Chinese. ***PRACTICE AREAS:*** Professional Liability Defense; Family Law; Business Litigation. ***Email:*** xinxu@kwar.com

MELISSA BUDDEN KELLEIGH, born Grand Haven, Michigan, October 29, 1972; admitted to bar, 2000, Oregon; U.S. District Court, District of Oregon. *Education:* University of Chicago (B.A., 1995); Northwestern School of Law, Lewis and Clark College (J.D., cum laude, 2000). ***PRACTICE AREAS:*** Professional Liability; Business Litigation; Family Law. ***Email:*** kelleigh@kwar.com

REFERENCE: United States National Bank of Oregon.

KENT CUSTIS LLP

1500 S.W. TAYLOR STREET
PORTLAND, OREGON 97205
Telephone: 503-220-0717
Facsimile: 503-220-4299
URL: http://www.kentlaw.com

Civil Litigation emphasizing Business, Commercial, First Party Insurance, Real Estate, Construction, Shareholder Disputes, Franchise and Securities, Business Organizations and Transactions, Accountant and Attorney Malpractice and Employment Law, General Business, Discrimination, Wrongful Termination, Employment Contracts, Wrongful Death, Personal Injury, Eminent Domain, Commercial Leasing, Buying or Selling A Business, Business Enterprises, Closely Held Business, Limited Liability Companies, Partnerships, Small Business, Business Planning, Contracts, Intellectual Property, Licensing Agreements, Trade Secrets, Trademarks, Strategic Alliances, Joint Ventures, Mergers, Internet, E-Commerce.

CHRISTOPHER H. KENT, born Richmond, Virginia, August 11, 1955; admitted to bar, 1985, Oregon; U.S. Supreme Court; U.S. Court of Appeals, Ninth Circuit; U.S. District Court, District of Oregon; U.S. District Court, Westen District of Washington; U.S. Court of Federal Claims; U.S. Tax Court. *Education:* Virginia Commonwealth University (B.A., with high honors, 1977); State University of New York (A.A.S., with honors, 1979); University of Oregon (J.D., 1985). Co-Author: "Concurrent Causation in First-Party Insurance Claims," 21 Tort & Insurance L.J. 573 (1986), cited with approval in Garvey v. State Farm Fire and Cas. Co., 770 P2d 704, 707 (Cal. 1989). *Member:* Oregon State Bar. ***REPORTED CASES:*** Stewart v. FBI, U.S. District Court, OR, $6 million settlement; KPI v. Weyerhausen, U.S. District Court, OR, $12.1 million verdict; Hickey v. Sloy, arbitration award, $1.4 million. ***PRACTICE AREAS:*** Civil Litigation; Business; Commercial; Insurance; Real Estate; Construction; Franchise; Securities. ***Email:*** ckent@kentlaw.com

ROBERT J. CUSTIS, born Cleveland, Ohio, December 21, 1953; admitted to bar, 1979, Oregon; 1980, U.S. District Court, District of Oregon; U.S. Court of Appeals, Ninth Circuit. *Education:* University of Evansville (B.S., Economics, 1976); Williamette University (J.D., 1979). Associate Editor, Williamette Law Review. *Member:* Marion County Bar Association; Oregon State Bar; Oregon Trial Lawyers Association. ***PRACTICE AREAS:*** Civil Litigation; Business; Commercial; Insurance; Real Estate; Construction; Securities; Business Formation; Forest Industries. ***Email:*** bcustis@kentlaw.com

LESLIE S. JOHNSON, born Hood River, Oregon, September 2, 1956; admitted to bar, 1995, Oregon and U.S. District Court, District of Oregon; 1996, Washington; 1999, U.S. District Court, Western District of Washington. *Education:* Portland State University (B.S., 1991); Northwestern School of Law of Lewis and Clark College (J.D., 1995). *Member:* Multnomah County, Clark County, Washington State Bar Associations; Oregon State Bar; American Inns of Court. ***PRACTICE AREAS:*** Business Litigation; Employment Litigation; Professional Malpractice; Business Law; Franchise Insurance; Corporate Governance. ***Email:*** ljohnson@kentlaw.com

REPRESENTATIVE CLIENTS: Advantage Point, Inc.; Aesthetic Environments; Collectors Press, Inc.; Conwood Products; Grove Development, Inc.; Horizon Electric; Izzy's; Keith Brown Lumber; Lightspeed Technologies, Inc.; Oklahoma Points of Knowledge; OTAK; Pacific Bells, Inc.; Papa Murphy's, Inc.; Pogy's International, Inc.; PRCo., Inc.; Rolex; Sterling Jewelers, Inc.; Schmizza International, Inc.; Thomas C. Stewart; Unifirst Corp.; Washington Alder, LLC; WSCO Petroleum.

KILMER, VOORHEES & LAURICK

A PROFESSIONAL CORPORATION
Established in 1985
732 N.W. NINETEENTH AVENUE
PORTLAND, OREGON 97209
Telephone: 503-224-0055
FAX: 503-222-5290
Email: kvl@teleport.com
URL: http://www.lawyers.com/kvl

Civil litigation in State and Federal courts, including Business, Construction, Insurance, ERISA, Professional Liability, Banking, Product Liability and General Casualty.

JEFFREY M. KILMER, born Norwalk, Ohio, June 15, 1941; admitted to bar, 1969, Oregon; 1970, U.S. District Court, District of Oregon; 1983, Washington; 1984, U.S. District Court, Eastern and Western Districts of Washington; 1985, U.S. Court of Appeals, Ninth Circuit and U.S. Supreme Court. *Education:* Ohio Wesleyan University; Oberlin College (B.A., 1963); University of Cincinnati (J.D., 1969). Order of the Coif. Note Editor, University of Cincinnati Law Review, 1968-1969. Law Clerk to Oregon Supreme Court Justice Gordon Sloan, 1969-1970. Chief Deputy District Attorney, Multnomah County District Attorney's Office, 1971-1973. Chief Trial Deputy District Attorney, Lane County District Attorney's Office, 1974. *Member:* Oregon State Bar; Washington State and American Bar Associations; Oregon Association of Defense Counsel; Defense Research Institute. ***PRACTICE AREAS:*** Insurance Defense; Employment Litigation; Commercial Litigation. ***Email:*** jkilmer@kilmerlaw.com

STEPHEN C. VOORHEES, born Portland, Oregon, March 6, 1951; admitted to bar, 1979, Oregon; 1980, U.S. District Court of Oregon; 1987, Washington and U.S. Court of Appeals, Ninth Circuit; 1989, U.S. District Court, Western and Eastern Districts of Washington. *Education:* University of Oregon Honors College (B.S., 1973); Northwestern School of Law of Lewis and Clark College (J.D., 1979). Member, Northwestern Law Review, 1978-1979. Law Clerk to the Honorable Robert C. Belloni, U.S. District Judge, 1980. *Member:* Multnomah County and Washington State Bar Associations; Oregon State Bar; Oregon Association of Defense Counsel (Board of Directors). ***PRACTICE AREAS:*** Insurance Defense Law; Commercial Law; Business Litigation. ***Email:*** svoorhees@kilmerlaw.com

JAMES P. LAURICK, born Omaha, Nebraska, April 19, 1954; admitted to bar, 1982, Oregon and U.S. District Court, District of Oregon; U.S. Court of Appeals, Ninth Circuit. *Education:* University of Northern Colorado (B.S., 1976); Northwestern School of Law of Lewis and Clark College (J.D., 1981). Member, Environmental Law Review, 1979-1981. Author: "Recent Development," 11 Environmental Law 187, 1980. Associate Counsel, The Oregon Bank and Orbanco, 1982-1984. Associate Editor, ABA, 1990-1994. Editor, Oregon's Construction Law Newsletter, 1988. *Member:* Multnomah County Bar Association; Oregon State Bar. ***PRACTICE AREAS:*** Banking Law; Commercial Business Litigation; Insurance Defense Law; Product Liability Law. ***Email:*** jlaurick@kilmerlaw.com

GREGORY B. SNOOK, born Portland, Oregon, March 19, 1950; admitted to bar, 1977, Oregon; 1978, U.S. District Court, District of Oregon; 1987, U.S. Court of Appeals, Ninth Circuit. *Education:* Portland State University (B.S., with honors, 1974); Harvard University (J.D., cum laude, 1977). ***REPORTED CASES:*** Holduer v. Oregon Trout, Inc., 173 Or App 344, 22 P3d 244 (2001); Sutherland v. Brennan, 131 Or App 25, 883 P2d 1318 (1994); State v. x rel; Sam's Texaco v. Gallagher, 314 Or 652, 842 P2d 2383 (1992). ***PRACTICE AREAS:*** Appellate Practice; Insurance Defense; Insurance Coverage. ***Email:*** gsnook@kilmerlaw.com

CAROLYN L. LARSON, admitted to bar, 1977, Oregon and U.S. District Court, District of Oregon; 1999, Washington. *Education:* Kalamazoo College; Ubuversite' de Strasbourg; University of Colorado (B.A., 1972); University of Denver (J.D., 1976). Order of St. Ives. Corporate Counsel, Union Pacific Railroad Company, 1977-1989. *Member:* Oregon State Bar (Member: Business Law Section; Real Estate and Land Use Section, Estate Planning and Administrative Section); Washington State Bar Association; National Association of Railroad Trial Counsel. ***PRACTICE AREAS:*** Transportation Law; Real Estate; Business; Probate; Estate Planning. ***Email:*** clarson@kilmerlaw.com

CHRISTOPHER T. CARSON, born Alamosa, Colorado, September 25, 1958; admitted to bar, 1984, Oregon and U.S. District Court, District of Oregon; 1985, Washington and U.S. District Court, Western District of Washington; 1986, U.S. District Court, Eastern District of Washington. *Education:* Colorado College (B.A., 1980); Willamette University (J.D., cum laude, 1984). Associate Editor, Willamette Law Review, 1983-1984. Author: "State Constitutional Analysis of Equal Protection and Privileges or Immunities: Gender Discrimination in Oregon," 19 Willamette Law Review, 757, 1983. *Member:* Oregon State Bar (Chair, Construction Law Section, 1998; Chair-elect, Business Litigation Section, 2005; Federal Practice and Procedure Committee, 2003—); Washington State Bar Association. ***PRACTICE AREAS:*** Business Litigation; ERISA Litigation; Construction Litigation; Commercial Litigation; Insurance Coverage Litigation. ***Email:*** ccarson@kilmerlaw.com

PAMELA J. STENDAHL, born 1961; admitted to bar, 1989, Oregon; 1990, U.S. District Court, District of Oregon; 1992, U.S. Circuit Court of Appeals, Ninth Circuit; 1995, Washington and U.S. District Court, Western District of Washington. *Education:* University of California at Irvine (B.A., 1983); Northwestern School of Law of Lewis and Clark College (J.D., cum laude, 1989). Recipient: American Jurisprudence Awards in Property, 1986, and Civil Procedure, 1987. Author: Air Carrier's Liability for Passenger's Aerotitis, The Air and Space Lawyer, Volume F, Number 4 (Spring, 1993). Teaching Assistant, Northwestern School of Law, Lewis and Clark College, Legal Writing, Research and Reasoning, 1987-1988. *Member:* Multnomah County and Washington State Bar Associations; Oregon State Bar; Oregon Women Lawyers; Oregon Association of Defense Counsel. ***REPORTED CASES:*** Gardner v. Cox, 117 Or App 57 (1992). ***PRACTICE AREAS:*** Employment Litigation; Medical Malpractice; Products Liability; Casualty Insurance. ***Email:*** pstendahl@kilmerlaw.com

---

MARY L. POOL, born Chicago, Illinois, November 21, 1962; admitted to bar, 1992, Illinois and U.S. District Court, Northern District of Illinois; 1993, U.S. Court of Appeals, Seventh Circuit; 1996, Oregon; 1997, U.S. District Court, District of Oregon; 1999, Washington. *Education:* University of Illinois (B.S., 1986); DePaul University (J.D., 1992). Hearings Officer, Multnomah County Animal Control, 1998—. *Member:* Multnomah County and American Bar Associations; Oregon State Bar (Member, House of Delegates, Region 5 Delegate, 2000-2003; Medical Profession Joint Committee, 2003—); Oregon Association of Defense Counsel; Oregon Women Lawyers. ***REPORTED CASES:*** Dausch v. Rykse, 9 F.3d 1244 (7th Cir. 1993); Dausch v. Rykse, 52 F.3d 1425 (7th Cir. 1994). ***PRACTICE AREAS:*** Insurance Defense; Professional Liability; Commercial Litigation; Banking Litigation; Business Litigation; Products Liability. ***Email:*** mpool@kilmerlaw.com

THOMAS V. CUPANI, born Hollomand A.F.B., New Mexico, July 31, 1960; admitted to bar, 1989, California and U.S. District Court, Eastern District of California; 1992, Oregon; 2003, U.S. District Court, District of Oregon. *Education:* George Washington University (B.A., 1986); Pepperdine University School of Law (J.D., cum laude, 1989). California Survey Editor, Pepperdine University Law Review, 1988-1989. Associate, Burger & Flaherty, 1989-1992. Deputy District Attorney, Multnomah County District Attorney's Office, 1992-2002. *Member:* State Bar of California; State Bar of Oregon; Oregon Association of Defense Counsel. ***PRACTICE AREAS:*** Insurance Defense; Commercial Litigation; Business Litigation. ***Email:*** tcupani@kilmerlaw.com

CATHERINE B. BRINKMAN, born Havre de Grace, Maryland, July 2, 1974; admitted to bar, 2000, Oregon; 2001, U.S. District Court, District of Oregon. *Education:* Randolph-Macon College (B.A., Political Science, with honors, magna cum laude, 1996); Northwestern School of Law of Lewis and Clark College (J.D., 2000). Phi Bata Kappa; Phi Delta Phi. Co-Author, "Bid Disputes," Construction Law, Oregon CLE, 2004. Commissioner, Milwaukie Planning Commission, 2005-2009. *Member:* Multnomah County Bar Association (Member, Service to Public Committee, Young Lawyers Section, 2001-2003; President-Elect, 2005-2006, Treasurer, 2004-2005, Director, 2003-2004, Board of Directors, Young Lawyers Section; Member, Budget and Finance Committee, 2004-2005); Oregon State Bar (Member, Land Use and Real Estate Section; Environmental and Natural Resources Section) Oregon Association of Defense Counsel; Oregon Women Lawyers. ***PRACTICE AREAS:*** Commercial Litigation; Insurance Defense; Construction Law. ***Email:*** cbrinkman@kilmerlaw.com

LEGAL SUPPORT PERSONNEL

MEDICAL LEGAL ASSISTANT

KATHRYN A. SCHMITT, R.N., born Salem, Oregon, January 31, 1953. *Education:* Good Samaritan School of Nursing (1974); Linfield College (B.S.N., cum laude, 1986).

(This Listing Continued)

Registered Nurse, Oregon, 1974. ***PRACTICE AREAS:*** Medical Malpractice Defense; Medical Product Liability Claims; Chart Review; Retention and Coordination of Experts; Medical Research. ***Email:*** kschmitt@kilmerlaw.com

REPRESENTATIVE CLIENTS: ARG Enterprises, Inc.; ABC Supply Co., Inc.; Cushman & Wakefield of Oregon; Freightliner Corp.; Portland Traction Co.; Bank of America Oregon; Union Pacific Railroad Co.; West One Bank, Oregon; Seafirst National Bank, Reebok International, Taft-Hartley Plans; Washington Mutual.
REPRESENTATIVE SURETY & INSURANCE CLIENTS: Argonaut Insurance Co.; Aries Insurance Co.; AIG; Great American Ins. Co.; Kaiser Foundation Hospitals; North American Specialty Insurance Co.; Unigard Insurance Group; General Fire and Casualty Insurance Co.; Sedgwick James, Broadspace; Hanover Insurance Company; Liberty Northwest Insurance; Liberty Insurance Services; St. Paul/Travelers; Oregon Professional Liability Fund.

KIRKLIN FOLAWN LLP

1125 YEON BUILDING
522 SW 5TH AVENUE
PORTLAND, OREGON 97204
Telephone: 503-222-1640
Fax: 503-227-5251
URL: http://www.lawyers.com/lawyercomkirklinfolawnllp

Securities, Intellectual Property, Lender Liability, Business Torts, Contracts, Finance, Accounting and Auditing, Personal Injury, Product Liability, Professional Liability, Commercial Litigation, Civil Litigation, Probate, Wills.

GEORGE L. KIRKLIN, admitted to bar, 1962, Oregon. *Education:* Harvard University (A.B., 1959; LL.B., cum laude, 1962). Listed in Best Lawyers in America, Personal Injury and Commercial Litigation, 1990—. Member, Panel of Arbitrators, American Arbitration Association. Member, 1976-1979 and Chairman, 1978-1979, Oregon State Board of Bar Examiners. *Member:* National Association of Railroad Trial Counsel. Fellow: International Society of Barristers; American College of Trial Lawyers. ***PRACTICE AREAS:*** Litigation; Business Torts; Securities; Lender Liability; Finance; Contracts; Personal Injury; Patents; Antitrust; Defamation; Taxation; Employment Law.

JOHN S. FOLAWN, admitted to bar, 1971, California; 1973, Oregon. *Education:* University of Oregon (B.S., 1967); Hastings College of Law, University of California (J.D., 1970). *Member:* Professional Liability Underwriting Society (Co-Chair, Northwest Chapter, 1996). [Capt., JAGC, U.S. Army, 1967-1975]. ***PRACTICE AREAS:*** Business Law; Professional Liability; Environmental Law; Contested Wills; Personal Injury.

BONNIE RICHARDSON, admitted to bar, 1997, Oklahoma and U.S. District Court, Western District of Oklahoma; 1998, Oregon and U.S. District Court, District of Oregon. *Education:* University of Oklahoma (B.A., 1994; J.D., 1997). ***PRACTICE AREAS:*** Business Law; Complex Commercial Litigation; Real Estate Litigation; Product Liability.

KLARQUIST SPARKMAN, LLP

Established in 1941
ONE WORLD TRADE CENTER, SUITE 1600
121 S.W. SALMON STREET
PORTLAND, OREGON 97204
Telephone: 503-226-7391
FAX: 503-228-9446
Email: inquiry@klarquist.com
URL: http://www.klarquist.com

Reno, Nevada Office: 800 South Meadows Parkway, Suite 700. Telephone: 775-824-0104. Fax: 775-824-0107.
Seattle, Washington Office: Wells Fargo Center, 999 Third Avenue, Suite 4200. Telephone: 206-264-2960.

Patent, Trademark, Copyright Law, Trials, Unfair Competition Law.

FIRM PROFILE: For over 55 years, we have provided prompt top quality IP services for many of the foremost companies in the Pacific Northwest. On that foundation, we have built one of the West Coast's leading intellectual property practices, with special expertise in patenting computer hardware and software, biotechnology and other technical fields; trademark prosecution; licensing; and nationwide patent, trademark and copyright trial and appellate work.

MEMBERS OF FIRM

LISA M. CALDWELL, born Vancouver, Washington, January 23, 1962; admitted to bar, 1994, Oregon; registered to practice before U.S. Patent and Trademark Office. *Education:* California State University, San Jose (B.S., chemistry, 1984); Willamette University College of Law (J.D., summa cum laude, 1994). *Member:* American Bar Association; Oregon State Bar; Federal Patent Bar; Oregon Patent Law Association; American Chemical Society. ***PRACTICE AREAS:*** Patent Prosecution; Trademark Prosecution; Licensing; Chemical Semiconductor Device; Process Patent Prosecution. ***Email:*** lisa.caldwell@klarquist.com

J. CHRISTOPHER CARRAWAY, born Greenville, North Carolina, April 29, 1970; admitted to bar, 1996, Oregon; U.S. Court of Appeals, Federal Circuit; 1997, U.S. District Court, Eastern and Western Districts of Wisconsin, U.S. Court of Appeals, Seventh Circuit; 1999, Colorado; 2000, U.S. District Court, District of Oregon. *Education:* Wharton School, University of Pennsylvania (B.S., magna cum laude, Economics, 1992); Duke University School of Law (J.D., with high honors, 1995). Order of the Coif. Editor-in-Chief, Law and Contemporary Problems, 1994-1995. Law Clerk, Hon. William C. Bryson, U.S. Court of Appeals, Federal Circuit, 1995-1996. Author: "In the Wake of Knorr-Bremse: Opinions of Counsel are as Important as Ever," Practicing Law Institute (PLI), Patent Litigation 2005; "International Protection for Trademarks Is Now Easier Under the Madrid Protocol," Multnomah Lawyer, May 2004; "The Uncertain Future of Enforcing Patents Broadened through Reissue," 8 Federal Circuit Bar Journal 63 (1998); "Offer to Sell Amendment Expands Forum Options for Patent Infringement Actions," National Law Journal, Jan. 26, 1998 at C8; "Color as a Trademark Under the Lanham Act," 57 Law & Contemp. Probs. 243 (Autumn 1994). Associate, Michael Best & Friedrich, LLP, Milwaukee, Wisconsin, 1996-1999. Associate Editor, Federal Circuit Bar Journal, 1998—. *Member:* Federal Circuit and American (Member, Intellectual Property Law Section) Bar Associations; American Intellectual Property Law Association. ***LANGUAGES:*** French. ***REPORTED CASES:*** Motionless Keyboard Corp. v. Microsoft, 2005 WL 1113818 (D. Or. 2005) (summary judgment of non-infringement); Soverain Software, LLC v. Amazon.com, Inc., 2005 WL 2008504 (E.D. Tex. 2005) (summary judgment on patent marking); Network Commerce v. Microsoft, 260 F. Supp. 2d 1042 (W.D. Wash. 2003) (summary judgment of non-infringement); 260 F. Supp. 2d 1034 (W.D. Wash. 2002) (favorable claim construction); Forcier v. Microsoft Corp., 123 F. Supp. 2d 520 (N.D. Cal. 2000) (summary judgment on trade secret claims); Goldtouch Tech., Inc. v. Microsoft Corp., 102 F. Supp. 2d 722 (W.D. Tex. 2000) (summary judgment of non-infringement); Marquip, Inc. v. Fosber America, Inc., 198 F.3d 1363 (Fed. Cir. 1999); Toro Co. v. Ariens Co., 1998 U.S. Dist. LEXIS 22856 (D. Minn. Sep. 2, 1998) (summary judgment of non-infringement); Promega Corp. v. Novagen, Inc., 6 F. Supp. 2d 1004 (W.D. Wis. 1997) (JMOL of patent validity). ***PRACTICE AREAS:*** Patent Litigation; Trademark Litigation. ***Email:*** chris.carraway@klarquist.com

KRISTIN L. CLEVELAND, born Honolulu, Hawaii, September 18, 1969; admitted to bar, 1996, California; 1997, District of Columbia; 2000, Oregon. *Education:* Bard College (B.A., 1991); George Washington University (J.D., 1996). *Member:* American Bar Association; American Intellectual Property Law Association. ***PRACTICE AREAS:*** Intellectual Property; Litigation. ***Email:*** kristin.cleveland@klarquist.com

JAMES E. GERINGER, born Oak Lawn, Illinois, 1961; admitted to bar, 1990, New York; 1995, Oregon. *Education:* University of California at Berkeley (B.A., 1984); Deep Springs College (1982); Harvard University (J.D., cum laude, 1989). Phi Beta Kappa. ***PRACTICE AREAS:*** Patent, Trademark, and Copyright Law; Trade Secret Law; Litigation and Licensing. ***Email:*** james.geringer@klarquist.com

MICHAEL P. GIRARD, born Endicott, New York, April 18, 1968; admitted to bar, 1994, Virginia; 1999, Oregon; registered to practice before U.S. Patent and Trademark Office. *Education:* State University of New York at Buffalo (B.S.M.E., magna cum laude, 1990); University of Virginia (J.D., 1994). Tau Beta Pi. Articles Editor, Virginia Environmental Law Journal, 1993-1994. *Member:* American Intellectual Property Law Association. ***PRACTICE AREAS:*** Patent Prosecution; Litigation; Licensing. ***Email:*** michael.girard@klarquist.com

JOSEPH T. JAKUBEK, born Youngstown, Ohio, March 11, 1962; admitted to bar, 1988, California and U.S. District Court, Central District of California; 1992, U.S. Court of Appeals for the Federal Circuit; 1995, Oregon, and U.S. Court of Appeals for the Eleventh Circuit; 1996, U.S. District Court, District of Oregon; registered to practice before U.S. Patent and Trademark Office. *Education:* Youngstown State University (B.E. Chem. Eng., 1984); Ohio State University College of Law (J.D., 1987). Tau Beta Pi; Omega Chi Epsilon; Phi Delta Phi. *Member:* Oregon State Bar; American Bar Association; Oregon Patent Law Association; American Intellectual Property Law Association. ***PRACTICE AREAS:*** Patent; Trademark; Copyright; Litigation. ***Email:*** joseph.jakubek@klarquist.com

MICHAEL D. JONES, born Bartlesville, Oklahoma, March 25, 1950; admitted to bar, 1997, Oregon. *Education:* Washington University (A.B., 1972; A.M., 1974); Oregon Graduate Institute (Ph.D., 1980); Northwestern School of Law (J.D., cum laude, 1996). *Member:* Oregon State Bar. ***PRACTICE AREAS:*** Patent; Trademark; Copyright. ***Email:*** michael.jones@klarquist.com

RAMON A. KLITZKE, II, born Indianapolis, Indiana, July 5, 1955; admitted to bar, 1980, Wisconsin and Oregon; registered to practice before U.S. Patent and Trademark Office. *Education:* University of South Carolina (B.S.M.E., magna cum laude, 1977); Marquette University (J.D., 1980). Phi Beta Kappa; Tau Beta Pi; Phi Delta Phi. St. Thomas More Scholar. Member, Marquette Law Review, 1978-1980. *Member:* Oregon State Bar (Secretary, 1981-1982 and Chairman, 1983-1984, Patent and Trademark Section); State Bar of Wisconsin; American Bar Association; Oregon Patent Law Association. ***PRACTICE AREAS:*** Patent Prosecution; Trademark Prosecution; Copyright Law; Litigation and Licensing. ***Email:*** ray.klitzke@klarquist.com

GREGORY L. MAURER, born Columbia, Pennsylvania, January 8, 1967; admitted to bar, 1996, Virginia (inactive); 1997, Oregon; registered to practice before the U.S. Patent and Trademark Office. *Education:* Old Dominion University (B.S., Computer Science, magna cum laude, 1988); University of Virginia (J.D., 1996); Martin Luther University, Halle an der Saale, Germany. Phi Kappa Phi. Founder, Virginia Society of Law and Technology, University of Virginia. *Member:* American Intellectual Property Law Association; Association for Computing; American Radio Relay League. ***PRACTICE AREAS:*** Patent, Trademark and Copyright. ***Email:*** gregory.maurer@klarquist.com

DR. WILLIAM D. NOONAN, born Kansas City, Missouri, October 18, 1955; admitted to bar, 1980, Missouri; 1986, Oregon; registered to practice before U.S. Patent and Trademark Office, 1982. *Education:* Princeton University (A.B., 1977); Tulane University; University of Missouri-Kansas City (J.D., 1980); Oregon Health Sciences University (M.D., magna cum laude, 1991). Alpha Omega Alpha. Licensed Physician, Oregon. Member: American Medical Association. *Member:* Missouri Bar; Oregon State Bar. ***PRACTICE AREAS:*** Patent, Trademark and Copyright Law. ***Email:*** william.noonan@klarquist.com

DAVID P. PETERSEN, born Eugene, Oregon, May 24, 1950; admitted to bar, 1975, Oregon; registered to practice before U.S. Patent and Trademark Office. *Education:* Oregon State University (B.S.E.E., with highest honors, 1972); University of Oregon (J.D., 1975). Eta Kappa Nu; Order of the Coif. *Member:* Oregon State Bar; Oregon Patent Law Association. ***PRACTICE AREAS:*** Patent, Trademark and Copyright Law; Unfair Competition. ***Email:*** david.petersen@klarquist.com

RICHARD J. POLLEY, born Los Angeles, California, August 21, 1948; admitted to bar, 1975, Oregon; registered to practice before U.S. Patent and Trademark Office. *Education:* Willamette University (B.A. in Chem., 1971; J.D., 1975). Phi Delta Phi. *Member:* American Bar Association; Oregon State Bar (Chairman, Patent and Trademark Section, 1982-1983); American Intellectual Property Law Association; Oregon Patent Law Association (President, 1981-1982); American Chemical Society. ***PRACTICE AREAS:*** Patent, Trademark and Copyright Law; Unfair Competition. ***Email:*** richard.polley@klarquist.com

(This Listing Continued)

KLARQUIST SPARKMAN, LLP, Portland—Continued

KYLE B. RINEHART, born Kansas City, Missouri, November 1, 1971; admitted to bar, 1998, Oregon; registered to practice before the U.S. Patent and Trademark Office, 2000. *Education:* University of Kansas (B.A., Computer Science, with highest distinction, 1994); Harvard University (J.D., cum laude, 1998). Phi Beta Kappa. ***PRACTICE AREAS:*** Patent Prosecution; Patent Litigation. ***Email:*** kyle.rinehart@klarquist.com

WAYNE W. RUPERT, born Oil City, Pennsylvania, April 17, 1963; admitted to bar, 1989, Virginia; 2001, Oregon; registered to practice before the U.S. Patent and Trademark Office. *Education:* Pennsylvania State University (B.S. in Chemical Engineering, 1985); George Washington University (J.D., with honors, 1989). *Member:* Oregon State Bar; American Intellectual Property Lawyers Association. ***PRACTICE AREAS:*** Intellectual Property. ***Email:*** wayne.rupert@klarquist.com

STACEY C. SLATER, born Del Norte, Colorado, March 21, 1961; admitted to bar, 1990, Oregon; 1994, U.S. Court of Appeals, Federal Circuit; 1992, registered to practice before U.S. Patent and Trademark Office. *Education:* University of Colorado (B.A., Biochemistry, magna cum laude, 1984); Oregon State University (Ph.D. Program, Organic Chemistry, 1984-1987); University of Oregon (J.D., 1990). Phi Lambda Upsilon. *Member:* Oregon State Bar (Chair, Intellectual Property Section); American Bar Association (Member, Committee 108 on Intellectual Property); Oregon Patent Law Association (President, 2002). ***PRACTICE AREAS:*** Patent, Trademark and Copyright Law; Unfair Competition. ***Email:*** stacey.slater@klarquist.com

DONALD L. STEPHENS, JR., born New Orleans, Louisiana, September 30, 1949; admitted to bar, 1990, Oregon; registered to practice before U.S. Patent and Trademark Office. *Education:* California State University at Fullerton (B.S., 1976); McArdle Laboratory for Cancer Research; University of Wisconsin; Northwestern School of Law of Lewis and Clark College (J.D., 1990). Phi Delta Phi. *Member:* Oregon State Bar; American Bar Association (Member, Section of Patent, Trademark and Copyright); Oregon Patent Law Association; New York Academy of Sciences; American Optical Society; Society of Photo-optical Instrumentation Engineers (SPIE). ***PRACTICE AREAS:*** Patent, Trademark and Copyright Law; Unfair Competition; Physics; Biotechnology; Chemical and Medical Technologies. ***Email:*** donald.stephens@klarquist.com

JOHN D. VANDENBERG, born New Rochelle, New York, January 13, 1958; admitted to bar, 1984, New York; 1989, Oregon; registered to practice before U.S. Patent and Trademark Office. *Education:* Princeton University (B.S.E., Mechanical and Aerospace Engineering, with honors, 1979); New York University School of Law (J.D., with honors, 1983). Order of the Coif. *Member:* Oregon State Bar. ***PRACTICE AREAS:*** Patent Litigation. ***Email:*** john.vandenberg@klarquist.com

STEPHEN A. WIGHT, born Salt Lake City, Utah, January 21, 1965; admitted to bar, 1992, Oregon; registered to practice before the U.S. Patent and Trademark Office. *Education:* Brigham Young University (B.S., 1989); University of Washington (J.D., 1992); Lewis and Clark College. Tau Beta Pi. *Member:* Oregon State Bar; American Bar Association; American Intellectual Property Law Association. ***PRACTICE AREAS:*** Patent, Trademark and Copyright Law; Unfair Competition. ***Email:*** stephen.wight@klarquist.com

GARTH A. WINN, born Ozark, Alabama, September 26, 1960; admitted to bar, 1987, California (inactive); 1992, Oregon; registered to practice before U.S. Patent and Trademark Office. *Education:* Utah State University (B.S., cum laude, 1984); Brigham Young University (J.D., cum laude, 1987). Tau Beta Pi. Member: Brigham Young Law Review, 1986-1987. *Member:* State Bar of California (Inactive); Oregon State Bar. ***LANGUAGES:*** Korean. ***PRACTICE AREAS:*** Patent, Trademark and Copyright Law; Unfair Competition. ***Email:*** garth.winn@klarquist.com

SENIOR COUNSEL

KENNETH S. KLARQUIST, born Minneapolis, Minnesota, August 17, 1921; admitted to bar, 1950, District of Columbia; 1952, Oregon; registered to practice before U.S. Patent and Trademark Office. *Education:* University of Minnesota (B.Ch.E., 1943); Georgetown University (J.D., 1950). Gamma Eta Gamma. *Member:* Multnomah County and American Bar Associations; Oregon State Bar; American Intellectual Property Law Association. ***PRACTICE AREAS:*** Patent, Trademark and Copyright Law; Unfair Competition. ***Email:*** kenneth.klarquist@klarquist.com

JAMES S. LEIGH, born Lansing, Michigan, May 16, 1935; admitted to bar, 1961, Oregon; registered to practice before U.S. Patent and Trademark Office. *Education:* Michigan State University (B.S. in C.E., with high honors, 1957); University of Michigan (J.D., with distinction, 1960). Tau Beta Pi; Chi Epsilon; Phi Kappa Phi. Member, Michigan Law Review, 1958-1960. *Member:* Multnomah County and American Bar Associations; Oregon State Bar (Member: State Disciplinary Board, 1994-1999; State Professional Responsibility Board, 1988-1991; Member, 1984-1987, and Chairman, 1985-1986, County Professional Responsibility Committee; Member, Unauthorized Practice of Law Committee, 1974-1977; Disciplinary Rules and Procedures Committee, 1971-1974; Legal Ethics Committee, 1970-1971); American Intellectual Property Law Association; Oregon Patent Law Association; Computer Law Association. ***PRACTICE AREAS:*** Patent, Trademark and Copyright Law; Unfair Competition; Trade Secret Law; Licensing; Litigation; Arbitration; Mediation. ***Email:*** james.leigh@klarquist.com

ARTHUR L. WHINSTON, born New York, N.Y., February 5, 1925; admitted to bar, 1957, New York; 1964, Oregon; registered to practice before U.S. Patent and Trademark Office. *Education:* Cornell University (B.C.E., with distinction, 1945); Princeton University (M.S.E., 1947); New York University (J.D., cum laude, 1957). Registered Professional Engineer: New York, 1950; Oregon, 1964. President, Oregon Patent Law Association, 1977-1978. *Member:* Multnomah County and American Bar Associations; Oregon State Bar (Member, 1966-1969, 1975-1978 and Chairman, 1968-1969, 1977-1978, Committee on Patents and Trademarks; Member, 1970-1973 and Chairman, 1972-1973, Committee on Unauthorized Practice of Law; Member: Committee on Professional Responsibility, 1973-1975; Disciplinary Board, 1987-1989); American Intellectual Property Law Association. ***PRACTICE AREAS:*** Patent, Trademark and Copyright Law; Unfair Competition. ***Email:*** arthur.whinston@klarquist.com

(This Listing Continued)

COUNSEL

JEFFREY S. LOVE, born Portland, Oregon, June 23, 1958; admitted to bar, 1987, Oregon; 1998, California. *Education:* University of California at Santa Cruz (B.A., 1980); Boalt Hall School of Law, University of California at Berkeley (J.D., 1987). *Member:* Oregon State Bar (Executive Committee Member, Section on Antitrust and Trade Regulation, 1999-2001; Federal Practice and Procedure Committee). ***PRACTICE AREAS:*** Patent Litigation; Copyright Litigation; Trademark Litigation. ***Email:*** jeffrey.love@klarquist.com

OF COUNSEL

MICHAEL N. ZACHARY, born Boston, Massachusetts, December 18, 1956; admitted to bar, 1984, California; 1997, Washington; 2004, Oregon. *Education:* Columbia University (B.A., cum laude, 1978); Harvard University (J.D., cum laude, 1983). *Member:* Washington State Bar Association; Oregon State Bar. ***PRACTICE AREAS:*** Intellectual Property Litigation.

ASSOCIATES

THEODORE W. BAKER, born Austin, Texas, July 27, 1976; admitted to bar, 2003, Oregon; registered to practice before U.S. Patent and Trademark Office. *Education:* University of Arizona (B.S., magna cum laude, 1999; J.D., summa cum laude, 2003). Tau Beta Pi; Order of the Coif. Recipient, National Merit Scholar. Editor, Arizona Law Review. ***PRACTICE AREAS:*** Patent; Trademark; Copyright. ***Email:*** ted.baker@klarquist.com

PATRICK M. BIBLE, born April 27, 1974; admitted to bar, 1999, Nevada; 2002, Oregon; 2004, California. *Education:* Willamette University (B.A., magna cum laude, 1996); University of Colorado (J.D., 1999). ***LANGUAGES:*** German. ***PRACTICE AREAS:*** Patent Prosecution. ***Email:*** patrick.bible@klarquist.com

MICHAEL L. BUCKLER, born Leonardtown, Maryland, September 25, 1974; admitted to bar, 2000, Maryland; 2002, Oregon. *Education:* Cornell University (B.S., 1996); Duke University (J.D., 2000). Law Clerk to: U.S. Magistrate Judge Theresa C. Buchanan, Eastern District of Virginia, 2000-2001; U.S. District Judge Jon P. McCalla, Western District of Tennessee, 2001-2002. *Member:* Multnomah County and American Bar Associations; American Intellectual Property Law Association; Oregon Patent Lawyers Association. ***PRACTICE AREAS:*** Intellectual Property Litigation. ***Email:*** michael.buckler@klarquist.com

LANE M. CHITWOOD, (admission pending). *Education:* Northwest Nazarene University (B.S., summa cum laude, 2002); Georgetown University Law Center (J.D., cum laude, 2005). Recipient: Leon Robbin Patent Award for the graduate having done the best work in the field of patent law at the Georgetown University Law Center; CALI Award for International Protection of Intellectual Property. Patent Examiner Intern, U.S. Patent and Trademark Office, 2001. Legal Clerk, Board of Patent Appeals and Interferences, 2003. Legal Intern, U.S. International Trade Commission, Office of Unfair Import Investigations, 2004. ***PRACTICE AREAS:*** Intellectual Property; Patents. ***Email:*** lane.chitwood@klarquist.com

GENIE LYONS, born Biloxi, Mississippi, July 21, 1958; registered to practice before U.S. Patent and Trademark Office; (admission pending). *Education:* University of Utah (B.S., Computer Science, 1984; J.D., 2004). William H. Leary Scholar. Articles Editor, University of Utah Law Review, 2003-2004. Recipient: "Outstanding Achievement Award," Civil Procedure, Fall, 2001; Law, Language and Ethics, Spring, 2002; "Outstanding Woman Law Student 2004," University of Utah, National Association of Women Lawyers. Author: "Shaken Baby Syndrome: A Questionable Scientific Syndrome and a Dangerous Legal Concept," 2003 Utah L. Rev. 1009. ***PRACTICE AREAS:*** Patent Prosecution; Patent Litigation. ***Email:*** genie.lyons@klarquist.com

SCOTT E. DAVIS, born November 26, 1973; admitted to bar, 2000, California and U.S. Court of Appeals, Ninth Circuit; 2002, Oregon and U.S. District Court, District of Oregon; 2004, U.S. Court of Appeals for the Federal Circuit; 2005, U.S. District Court, Central District of California. *Education:* Oregon State University (B.S., Chemistry, summa cum laude, 1996); University of California, Los Angeles (M.S., Chemistry, 1997; J.D., 2000). Order of the Coif. Law Clerk to U.S. District Judge A. Howard Matz, Central District of California. *Member:* American Bar Association (Member, Section on Intellectual Property Law); Oregon Patent Law Association; American Chemical Society. ***PRACTICE AREAS:*** Intellectual Property Litigation; Intellectual Property Transactional Matters. ***Email:*** scott.davis@klarquist.com

BRIAN CASEY FITZPATRICK, born Coeur d'Alene, Idaho, September 16, 1973; admitted to bar, 2001, Oregon. *Education:* University of Oregon (B.A., 1995); University of Idaho (J.D., cum laude, 1999). ***PRACTICE AREAS:*** Intellectual Property. ***Email:*** casey.fitzpatrick@klarquist.com

JARED S. GOFF, born Milford, Utah, March 18, 1972; admitted to bar, 1999, Arizona and U.S. District Court, District of Arizona (inactive); 2001, U.S. Court of Appeals for the Federal Circuit; 2002, Colorado and U.S. District Court, District of Colorado (inactive); 2003, Oregon and U.S. District Court, District of Oregon; registered to practice before U.S. Patent and Trademark Office. *Education:* Brigham Young University (M.E., magna cum laude, 1996; J.D., summa cum laude, 1999). Order of the Coif. Law Clerk to Honorable Randall R. Radeer, U.S. Court of Appeals, Federal Circuit, 2000-2001. Author: "The Unpredictable Scope of the Waiver Resulting from the Advice-of-Counsel Defense to Willful Patent Infringement," 1998 BYU L. Rev. 213. *Member:* Federal Circuit Bar Association; American Intellectual Property Law Association. ***REPORTED CASES:*** Network Commerce, Inc. v. Microsoft Corp., —F.3d —, 2005 WL 2160089 (Fed.Cir. 2005); Hoffer v. Microsoft Corp., 405 F.3d 1326 (Fed. Cir. 2005); New Railhead Mfg., L.L.C. v. Vermeer Mfg. Co., 298 F.3d 1290 (Fed. Cir. 2002). ***PRACTICE AREAS:*** Intellectual Property Litigation. ***Email:*** Jared.Goff@klarquist.com

DEBRA A. GORDON, born Lima, Ohio; admitted to bar, 1998, Arizona; 2002, Oregon. *Education:* Western Washington University (B.S., Biology/Chemistry, cum laude, 1981; M.S., Chemistry, 1983); University of Arizona (Ph.D., Physiology, 1988; J.D., magna cum laude, 1998). ***PRACTICE AREAS:*** Intellectual Property. ***Email:*** debra.gordon@klarquist.com

(This Listing Continued)

JEFFREY BRIAN HAENDLER, born Baltimore, Maryland, February 12, 1971; admitted to bar, 2000, Oregon; registered to practice before the U.S. Patent and Trademark Office. *Education:* University of Maryland (B.S., Mechanical Engineering, 1993); Willamette University (J.D., cum laude, 2000). ***PRACTICE AREAS:*** Patent Prosecution; Litigation; Trademark. ***Email:*** jeffrey.haendler@klarquist.com

TANYA M. HARDING, PH.D., born Las Vegas, Nevada, November 28, 1968; admitted to bar, 1999, Oregon; registered to practice before U.S. Patent and Trademark Office. *Education:* Cook College, Rutgers University (B.S., Biotechnology, magna cum laude, 1991); University of California at Davis (Ph.D., Plant Biology, 1996); Cornell Law School (J.D., cum laude, 1999). *Member:* Multnomah and American Bar Associations; Oregon Women Lawyers; American Intellectual Property Law Association. ***PRACTICE AREAS:*** Intellectual Property Law; Biotechnology Patent Prosecution and Opinions. ***Email:*** tanya.harding@klarquist.com

KEVIN M. HAYES, admitted to bar, 2001, Oregon. *Education:* University of Puget Sound (B.S., Natural Science, 1997); University of Oregon (J.D., 2001). Order of the Coif. ***PRACTICE AREAS:*** Patent Prosecution; Trademark Prosecution; Intellectual Property Litigation. ***Email:*** kevin.hayes@klarquist.com

STEPHEN J. JONCUS, born Hartford, Connecticut, August 9, 1959; admitted to bar, 1995, Texas (inactive); 2001, Oregon and U.S. District Court, District of Oregon; registered to practice before U.S. Patent and Trademark Office, 1999. *Education:* University of Rochester (B.S.C.H.E., 1981); University of Houston (J.D., 1995). *Member:* Multnomah County, Federal Circuit, Federal and American Bar Associations; Oregon State Bar; American Intellectual Property Law Association;. ***PRACTICE AREAS:*** Patent Litigation. ***Email:*** stephen.joncus@klarquist.com

RICHARD D. McLEOD, admitted to bar, 2000, Texas and U.S. District Court, Eastern District of Texas; 2001, U.S.District Court, Northern, Southern and Western Districts of Texas, U.S. Court of Appeals for the Federal Circuit and U.S. Court of Appeals, Fifth Circuit; registered to practice before U.S. Patent and Trademark Office (Not admitted in Oregon). *Education:* University of Houston (B.S., 1981); Stanford University (M.S., 1987); University of Texas at Austin (J.D., 2000); University of New South Wales (LL.M., 2000). Order of Barristers. Judicial Clerk, Hon. Wendell C. Radford, U.S. Magistrate Judge, Eastern District of Texas, May 2000 - August 2001. ***PRACTICE AREAS:*** Intellectual Property Litigation.

SUNJAY Y. MOHAN, born Mysore, India; March 12, 1966; admitted to bar, 2001, Georgia (Not admitted in Oregon). *Education:* Georgia Institute of Technology (B.S.E.E., 1990); University of Georgia (J.D., 2001). ***PRACTICE AREAS:*** Intellectual Property. ***Email:*** sunjay.mohan@klarquist.com

TODD SIEGEL, born Crystal City, Missouri, 1969; admitted to bar, 1996, Missouri; 1997, U.S. District Court, Eastern District of Missouri; 2000, Oregon; 2001, U.S. District Court, District of Oregon; 2002, U.S. Court of Appeals for the Federal Circuit. *Education:* University of Missouri-Columbia (B.S., magna cum laude, 1991; J.D., 1996). ***PRACTICE AREAS:*** Patent Litigation. ***Email:*** todd.siegel@klarquist.com

A. JONATHAN VANCE, born Salt Lake City, Utah, February 20, 1977; admitted to bar, 2004, Oregon; registered to practice before U.S. Patent and Trademark Office, 2004. *Education:* Brigham Young University (B.S., Electrical Engineering, 2001); University of Texas School of Law (J.D., 2004). *Member:* American Intellectual Property Law Association; Oregon Patent Law Association. ***LANGUAGES:*** German. ***PRACTICE AREAS:*** Intellectual Property; Patents. ***Email:*** jonathan.vance@klarquist.com

JUSTIN D. WAGNER, born Danbury, Connecticut, April 10, 1974; admitted to bar, 2003, Oregon; registered to practice before U.S. Patent and Trademark Office. *Education:* Northwestern University (B.S., Electrical Engineering, 1997); University of California, Davis (J.D., 2003). ***PRACTICE AREAS:*** Patent, Trademark and Copyright Law; Unfair Competition. ***Email:*** justin.wagner@klarquist.com

GWYNEDD WARREN, PH.D., admitted to bar, 2004, Oregon; registered to practice before U.S. Patent and Trademark Office, 1999. *Education:* University of Michigan (B.S., 1983); Yale University (M.Phil., Ph.D., 1994), University of California, Berkeley (J.D., 2004). ***SPECIAL AGENCIES:*** United States Patent and Trademark Office. ***PRACTICE AREAS:*** Intellectual Property; Intellectual Property Procurement; Intellectual Property Prosecution; Medical Intellectual Property; Pharmaceutical Intellectual Property. ***Email:*** gwynedd.warren@klarquist.com

PATENT AGENTS

CHRISTOPHER ANDON, born Merced, California, March 2, 1977; registered to practice before U.S. Patent and Trademark Office. *Education:* University of Californiat at San Diego (B.S., Biology, cum laude, 1999); Oregon Health & Science University (Masters in Biomedical Infomatics). Phi Beta Kappa. ***LANGUAGES:*** Spanish. ***PRACTICE AREAS:*** Patent Prosecution; Biomedical Informatics. ***Email:*** chris.andon@klarquist.com

DANIEL H. BELL, born Chicago, Illinois, August 3, 1960; admitted to bar, 2005, Washington; registered to practice before U.S. Patent and Trademark Office, 2004 (Not admitted in Oregon). *Education:* Arizona State University (B.S., summa cum laude, Computer Science, 1997; J.D., cum laude, 2000). Phi Kappa Phi; Upsilon Pi Epsilon. William A. Pedrick Scholar. Member, Computer Law Association, 1998. ***Email:*** daniel.bell@klarquist.com

GILLIAN BUNKER, born Boston, Massachusetts, January, 5 1971; registered to practice before U.S. Patent and Trademark Office. *Education:* Bryn Mawr College (B.A., 1993); Oregon Health and Science University (Ph.D., 2001). ***Email:*** gillian.bunker@klarquist.com

ANNE CARLSON, born Montreal, Quebec, Canada, June 4, 1960. *Education:* McGill University (B.S., 1982; M.S., 1985); University of California, Los Angeles (Ph.D., 1994). Registered Patent Agent, United States, 2001. ***LANGUAGES:*** French. ***PRACTICE AREAS:*** Biotechnology Patent Prosecution. ***Email:*** anne.carlson@klarquist.com

SHEREE LYNN RYBAK, born Annapolis, Maryland, June 7, 1968; (admission pending). *Education:* Lebanon Valley College (B.S., magna cum laude, Biology, 1990); Carnegie Mellon University (Ph.D., Biological Sciences, 1997); Northwestern University School of Law of Lewis and Clark College. Phi Delta Phi. Phi Kappa Phi. (Patent Agent). ***PRACTICE AREAS:*** Biotechnology Patent Prosecution; Chemistry Patent Prosecution. ***Email:*** sheree.rybak@klarquist.com

SUSAN ALPERT SIEGEL, born Princeton, New Jersey, March 22, 1960. *Education:* University of California at Davis (B.S., 1982); Massachusetts Institute of Technology; Cold Spring Harbor Laboratory, State University of New York at Stonybrook (Ph.D., 1988). Phi Kappa Phi. Registered Patent Agent, 1998. (Patent Agent, Technology Consultant). ***PRACTICE AREAS:*** Patent Prosecution. ***Email:*** susan.alpert.siegel@klarquist.com

TRAVIS YOUNG, born Bloomington, Indiana, April 30, 1973. *Education:* Indiana University, Bloomington (B.S., Chemistry, 1995); University of Wisconsin (Ph.D., Organic Chemistry, 2001). (Technical Support). ***LANGUAGES:*** German. ***PRACTICE AREAS:*** Preparation and Prosecution of Patent Applications. ***Email:*** travis.young@klarquist.com

Clients available upon request.

JAMES L. KNOLL P.C.

1500 S.W. TAYLOR STREET
PORTLAND, OREGON 97205
Telephone: 503-222-9000
Fax: 503-222-9003
Email: Jim@knollmediation.com
URL: http://www.knollmediation.com

Mediation and Arbitration.

JAMES L. KNOLL, born Chicago, Illinois, October 5, 1942; admitted to bar, 1967, Illinois; 1971, Oregon; 1984, Washington; 1993, Alaska. *Education:* Brown University (A.B., 1964); University of Chicago (J.D., 1967). Adjunct Professor of Law, Northwestern School of Law of Lewis and Clark College, 1982-1991. *Member:* Washington State, Oregon State (Member, Alternate Dispute Resolution Section; Editor, Alternate Dispute Resolution CLE Book; Editor, 2 Volume Text on Insurance, 1996); Alaska Bar and American (Member, TIPS Council, 1989-1992; TIPS Advisor to the Uniform Law Commissions Drafting Committee of the Uniform Arbitration Act, 1998-2000; Chair, TIPS Alternate Dispute Resolution Committee); Bar Associations. ***PRACTICE AREAS:*** Mediation; Alternative Dispute Resolution; Commercial Law; Insurance; Construction Law; Health Care; Environmental Law; Securities. ***Email:*** Jim@knollmediation.com

LACHENMEIER ENLOE RALL & HEINSON

9600 S.W. CAPITOL HIGHWAY
PORTLAND, OREGON 97219
Telephone: 503-768-9600
FAX: 503-768-9133
Email: ler@lerlaw.com
URL: http://www.lerlaw.com

General Civil, Trial and Appellate Practice in all State and Federal Courts. Insurance Law. Products Liability and Professional Liability.

FIRM PROFILE: Lachenmeier Enloe Rall & Heinson concentrates its practice in the area of insurance defense litigation, automobile and general liability, insurance coverage analysis as well as general civil litigation. The firm's attorneys have handled a broad range of insurance litigation matters, asbestos defense, personal injury, wrongful death, general commercial and property liability, and coverage questions for over 25 years. Although based in Portland, the firm practices throughout the states of Washington and Oregon, and routinely handles cases outside of the Portland and Vancouver metropolitan areas. The firm's goal is to provide top quality legal counsel, and to promote the expeditious, economical and fair resolution of cases, through private negotiation, alternative dispute resolution and trial.

MEMBERS OF FIRM

JAY D. ENLOE, born Portland, Oregon, July 24, 1951; admitted to bar, 1976, Oregon; 1977, U.S. District Court for the District of Oregon and U.S. Court of Appeals for the Ninth Circuit. *Education:* University of Oregon (B.A., Journalism, 1973; J.D., 1976). *Member:* Multnomah County and Washington County Bar Associations; Oregon State Bar; Oregon Association of Defense Counsel; Defense Research Institute. ***PRACTICE AREAS:*** Automobile; General Liability; Insurance Defense; Products Liability. ***Email:*** jay@lerlaw.com

RUDY R. LACHENMEIER, born McMinnville, Oregon, April 5, 1950; admitted to bar, 1975, Oregon; 1976, U.S. District Court for the District of Oregon; 1977, U.S. Court of Appeals, Ninth Circuit. *Education:* University of Oregon (B.S. Pol. Sci., 1972); Drake University; Northwestern School of Law of Lewis and Clark College (J.D., 1975). Associate Editor, Lewis and Clark Law Review, 1974-1975. Author: "DDT And The Tussock Moth: The E.P.A. in a Crisis Situation," 4 Environmental Law, Vol 2, 1974; "The Endangered Species Act of 1973: Preservation or Pandemonium?" 5 Environmental Law, Vol. 1, 1974. *Member:* Multnomah County Bar Association; Oregon State Bar; Oregon Association of Defense Counsel; Defense Research Institute. ***PRACTICE AREAS:*** General Liability; Asbestos Defense; Discrimination; Insurance; Professional Liability; Environmental. ***Email:*** rudy@lerlaw.com

MARTIN M. RALL, born Seattle, Washington, August 23, 1956; admitted to bar, 1984, Oregon and Washington; 1988, U.S. District Court, District of Oregon and U.S. Court of Appeals, 9th Circuit; 1989, U.S. District Court, Western District of Washington. *Education:* Seattle University (B.S., Political Science, 1978); Willamette University (J.D., 1982). Phi Delta Phi. Deputy District Attorney, Washington County District Attorneys Office, 1985-1986. *Member:* Multnomah County and Washington State (Member, Trial Practice Section) Bar Associations; Oregon State Bar; Oregon Association of Defense Counsel; Washington Defense Trial Lawyers; The Association of Trial Lawyers of America. ***PRACTICE AREAS:*** Automobile; General Liability; Construction Law; Insurance; Professional Liability; Insurance Coverage. ***Email:*** marty@lerlaw.com

(This Listing Continued)

LACHENMEIER ENLOE RALL & HEINSON, Portland—Continued

TIMOTHY J. HEINSON, born Tillamook, Oregon, May 5, 1958; admitted to bar, 1987, Oregon; 1989, U.S. District Court, District of Oregon; 2002, Washington. *Education:* University of Portland (B.B.A., magna cum laude, 1983); Northwestern School of Law (J.D., cum laude, 1987). Beta Gamma Sigma. *Member:* Multnomah County Bar Association; Oregon State Bar; Oregon Association of Defense Counsel. ***PRACTICE AREAS:*** Litigation; Insurance; Automobile; Construction Law; Asbestos Defense. ***Email:*** tim@lerlaw.com

---

JULIE E. DUTTON, born Seattle, Washington, July 4, 1968; admitted to bar, 2000, Oregon; 2001, Washington and U.S. District Court, District of Oregon. *Education:* University of Oregon (B.A., 1990); Willamette University (J.D., 1999). Form Editor, Law Review, 1998-1999. *Member:* Multnomah County (Young Lawyers Section; Membership Committee, 2001-2002) and Washington State Bar Associations; Oregon State Bar; Oregon Association of Defense Counsel. ***PRACTICE AREAS:*** Litigation; General Liability; Automobile; Insurance Defense. ***Email:*** julie@lerlaw.com

BRIAN S. RUFF, born West Covina, California, December 29, 1970; admitted to bar, 1998, Oregon; 2005, U.S. District Court, District of Oregon. *Education:* California State Polytechnic University (B.A., 1994); Willamette University (J.D., 1997). *Member:* Multnomah Bar Association; Oregon State Bar. ***PRACTICE AREAS:*** Automobile Accidents and Injuries; General Liability; Insurance Defense; Products Liability; Premises Liability. ***Email:*** brian@lerlaw.com

LORI K. DEDOBBELAERE, born Portland, Oregon, November 24, 1965; admitted to bar, 1994, Oregon; 1997, U.S. District Court, District of Oregon; 1999, U.S. Court of Appeals, Ninth Circuit; 2000, U.S. Supreme Court; 2005, Washington. *Education:* University of Oregon (B.A., summa cum laude, 1988); Northwestern School of Law at Lewis and Clark College (J.D., cum laude, 1993). Phi Beta Kappa. *Member:* Multnomah Bar Association; Washington Bar Association; Oregon State Bar; Oregon Women Lawyers. ***PRACTICE AREAS:*** Litigation; Insurance; Asbestos Defense; Automobile Accidents and Injuries; Construction Defects. ***Email:*** lori@lerlaw.com

REPRESENTATIVE CLIENTS: State Farm Fire & Casualty Co.; State Farm Mutual Automobile Insurance Co.; Safeco Insurance; Grange Mutual Insurance Co.; Mutual of Enumclaw.

CLAYTON LANCE LLP

610 S.W. ALDER STREET, SUITE 915
PORTLAND, OREGON 97204
Telephone: 503-241-2242
Fax: 503-227-4136
Email: clayton_lance@qwest.net
Criminal Defense, Family Law.

CLAYTON J. LANCE, admitted to bar, 1983, Oregon. *Education:* University of Oregon (B.A., 1979; J.D., 1983). ***PRACTICE AREAS:*** Criminal Defense; Family Law. ***Email:*** clayton_lance@qwest.net

---

LANDYE BENNETT BLUMSTEIN LLP

Established in 1955
1300 SOUTHWEST FIFTH AVENUE, SUITE 3500
PORTLAND, OREGON 97201
Telephone: 503-224-4100
Facsimile: 503-224-4133
Email: info@landye-bennett.com
URL: http://www.landye-bennett.com

Anchorage, Alaska Office: 701 West Eighth Avenue, Suite 1200, 99501. Telephone: 907-276-5152. Facsimile: 907-276-8433.

Wasilla, Alaska Office: 1981 E. Palmer Wasilla Highway, Suite 220, 99654. Telephone: 907-746-5971. Facsimile: 907-746-5972.

General Practice and Litigation in State and Federal Courts. Business Entities and Business Finance, Real Estate, Taxation, Securities, Bankruptcy, Administrative Practice before Governmental Departments, Agencies and Commissions, Land Use Planning, Federal Land Law, Condominium and Community Association Law, Products Liability, Personal Injury and Aviation Law, Environmental and Hazardous Substances Law, Intellectual Property and Computer Law.

FIRM PROFILE: History: Founded in Portland, Oregon on July 1, 1955. Landye Bennett Blumstein initially focused on corporate securities law, finance and bankruptcy law, and mergers and acquisitions. In 1976, the firm established an office in Anchorage, Alaska, and in 2004, the firm established an office in Wasilla, Alaska. The firm has expanded its expertise to meet the needs of its clients.

Areas of Emphasis and Growth: The primary practice areas of Landye Bennett Blumstein include aviation, banking, bankruptcy, business, corporate, environmental law, business and environmental litigation, class action litigation, estate planning, finance, fisheries, intellectual property, litigation, mergers and acquisitions, mining, Native American law, personal injury and products liability litigation, executive compensation and termination, public law, real estate, tax, timber, transportation and utilities regulation. The firm has twenty-five lawyers and a support staff of twenty-five.

Client Base: Landye Bennett Blumstein serves individuals and businesses. The firm represents Pacific Northwest and Alaska corporations and businesses and acts as local counsel to a variety of national financial institutions and corporations, multi-national corporations, start-up businesses, municipalities, condominium homeowner associations, construction firms, real estate developers, and businesses which work with governmental agencies.

(This Listing Continued)

J. DAVID BENNETT, born Vancouver, Washington, August 15, 1941; admitted to bar, 1971, Oregon; 2002, Washington. *Education:* Linfield College (B.A., 1963); Willamette University (J.D., cum laude, 1971). Delta Theta Phi. *Member:* Multnomah County, Washington State and American Bar Associations; Oregon State Bar (Member, Sections on: Real Estate and Land Use; Estate Planning and Administration; Business and Corporate Law); Homebuilders Association of Metropolitan Portland; Oregon Chapter, Community Associations Institute (Director, 1980-1994 and President, 1986 and 1991); Portland Board of Realtors; Westside Economic Alliance (formerly Tualatin Valley Economic Development Corporation) (Director, 1988—, and Chairman, 1989-1991, 1995); National Association of Industrial and Office Properties. [Capt., U.S. Air Force, 1964-1968]. ***PRACTICE AREAS:*** Real Property Law; Estate Planning and Probate; Condominium and Community Association Law; Land Use Planning Law. ***Email:*** dbennett@landye-bennett.com

DAVID L. BLOUNT, born Columbia, Missouri, July 14, 1954; admitted to bar, 1980, Oregon; 1984, U.S. District Court, District of Oregon; 1986, U.S. Court of Appeals, Ninth Circuit; 2002, Washington. *Education:* College of William and Mary (B.S., 1975); Lewis & Clark Law School (J.D., 1980). Member, Environmental Law Review, 1979. Author: "Individual Liability for Release of Hazardous Substances," Environmental and Natural Resources Bar Section Newsletter, 1986; "Private Party Cost Recovery", Chapter 19, OLI-OSB Environmental Law Desk Reference, 1995, 2002. Enforcement Attorney, U.S. Environmental Protection Agency, Washington, D.C., 1980-1982. Assistant District Attorney, Clackamas County, Oregon, 1983. Chair, Environmental Cleanup Advisory Committee to Oregon Department of Environmental Quality, 1991. *Member:* Multnomah County (Member, Medical-Legal Committee, 1986—), Washington State, Federal and American (Member, Environmental and Natural Resources Law Section) Bar Associations; Oregon State Bar (Member, Sections on: Environmental and Natural Resources, Chair, 1988-1989); Oregon Trial Lawyers Association; The Washington State Trial Lawyers Association; The Association of Trial Lawyers of America. ***SPECIAL AGENCIES:*** Environmental Protection Agency. ***REPORTED CASES:*** Rhone-Poulenc, Inc. v. Gould Electronics, Inc, WL 704420 (N.D. Cal 1998). ***TRANSACTIONS:*** Belmont Dairy Brownfield Development Project, 1996; Union Station Brownfield Development Project, 2000; McCormick Pier Acquisition and Condo Conversion, 2002. ***PRACTICE AREAS:*** Environmental Litigation; Environmental Penalties; Environmental Permitting; Environmental Real Estate; Environmental Regulation; Hazardous Waste Liability; Superfund. ***Email:*** dblount@landye-bennett.com

PHILIP BLUMSTEIN, born New York, N.Y., April 5, 1957; admitted to bar, 1982, Alaska, U.S. District Court, District of Alaska and U.S. Court of Appeals, Ninth Circuit; 1986, U.S. Court of International Trade; 1989, U.S. Court of Federal Claims. *Education:* State University of New York at Binghamton (B.A., 1979); Boston University (J.D., 1982). *Member:* Alaska Bar Association (Member, Alaska Native Law Section). (Resident, Anchorage, Alaska Office). ***PRACTICE AREAS:*** Corporate Law; Real Estate; Municipal Law; Commercial Transactions; Alaska Native Law. ***Email:*** philb@lbblawyers.com

DAVID S. CASE, born Seattle, Washington, September 12, 1944; admitted to bar, 1974, Washington; 1975, Alaska. *Education:* Whitman College (B.A., 1966); University of Washington (J.D., 1974). Author: "Alaska Natives and American Laws," University of Alaska Press, 1984, 2002 Eds. Associate Professor, Native Studies and Political Science, University of Alaska at Fairbanks, 1982-1984. Member: Alaska Legal Services Corporation (Board Member, 1985-1991, Secretary-Treasurer, 1986-1987 and President); Anchorage Opera (Board Member, 1999—, Secretary, 2000-2002 and Board President, 2002-2005); Board of Visitors, Lewis & Clark Law School (Member, 1994—). Chief Counsel, Berger Commission, 1984-1985. Recipient, Alaska Federation of Natives Denali Award, 1998. *Member:* Alaska Bar Association. (Resident, Anchorage, Alaska Office). ***PRACTICE AREAS:*** Native Law; Corporate Law; Municipal Law. ***Email:*** dcase@lbblawyers.com

MITCHEL R. COHEN, born Portland, Oregon, March 15, 1951; admitted to bar, 1976, Oregon; 1979, District of Columbia; 2002, Washington. *Education:* Colgate University (B.A., 1973); Gonzaga University (J.D., magna cum laude, 1976); New York University (LL.M., 1977). Editor, Gonzaga Law Review, 1975-1976. Graduate Editor, Tax Law Review, 1976-1977. *Member:* Oregon State Bar (Member, Sections on: Taxation, Executive Committee, 1986-1990 and Estate Planning and Administration); District of Columbia Bar; Washington State Bar Association; American Bar Association (Member, Sections on: Taxation and Real Property, Probate and Trust Law; Secretary, 2001, Vice-Chair, 2002 and Chair, 2003, Western States-Internal Revenue Service Liaison Committee); Estate Planning Council of Portland. ***PRACTICE AREAS:*** Taxation Law; Business Law; Estate Planning; Probate Law. ***Email:*** mcohen@landye-bennett.com

STUART K. COHEN, born Redwood City, California, February 13, 1960; admitted to bar, 1985, Oregon. *Education:* Whitman College (B.A. in Economics, 1982); Lewis & Clark Law School (J.D., cum laude, 1985). Recipient: Award for Outstanding Oral Advocacy, 1983; American Jurisprudence Awards for Torts, 1984 and Wills/Trusts and Future Interests, 1985. *Member:* Multnomah County and American Bar Associations; Oregon State Bar (Member, Section on Computer and Internet Law, Past Chair and Board Member, 1989—, Section on Real Estate, 1989—); Pacific Rim Computer and Internet Law Institute (Member, Planning Committee, Chair and Speaker, 1989-2003); Community Association Institute (President, Oregon Chapter, 2004). ***PRACTICE AREAS:*** Intellectual Property; Real Estate; Community Association Law; Computer Law; Probate; Litigation. ***Email:*** scohen@landye-bennett.com

JAMES S. CRANE, born Chicago, Illinois, December 19, 1948; admitted to bar, 1976, Alaska; 1990, Oregon; 2002, Washington. *Education:* University of California at Santa Cruz (B.A., cum laude, 1970); University of Toronto, Toronto, Canada (M.A., 1971); Northeastern University (J.D., 1976). *Member:* Oregon State Bar (Member, Sections on: Litigation and Business Litigation); Alaska (Member, Torts Section), Washington State and American (Member, Sections on: Litigation; Tort and Insurance Practice; Business Law; Natural Resources and Environment) Bar Associations; Washington Trial Lawyers Association; The Association of Trial Lawyers of America. ***PRACTICE AREAS:*** Civil Litigation; Environmental Law; Insurance Law. ***Email:*** jcrane@landye-bennett.com

KIM DUNN, born Anchorage, Alaska, August 24, 1959; admitted to bar, 1985, Alaska; U.S. District Court, District of Alaska and U.S. Court of Appeals, Ninth Circuit. *Education:* Dartmouth College (B.A., magna cum laude, 1981); Boalt Hall School of Law, University of California (J.D., 1985). *Member:* Alaska (Member, Employment Law Section) and

(This Listing Continued)

American (Member, Construction Law Section) Bar Associations. (Resident, Anchorage, Alaska Office). ***PRACTICE AREAS:*** Employment Law; Health Care Corporate Law; Construction Law; Housing Law. ***Email:*** kimd@lbblawyers.com

DAVID N. GOULDER, born Natick, Massachusetts, May 11, 1950; admitted to bar, 1979, Oregon. *Education:* Brandeis University (B.A., summa cum laude, 1972); Harvard University (J.D., cum laude, 1979). Phi Beta Kappa. Member, Harvard University Environmental Law Review, 1978-1979. *Member:* American Bar Association; Oregon State Bar; The Association of Trial Lawyers of America. ***PRACTICE AREAS:*** Business Litigation; Real Estate Litigation; Appellate Law. ***Email:*** dgoulder@landye-bennett.com

KARNA R. GUSTAFSON, born Arlington, Virginia, March 30, 1968; admitted to bar, 1994, Oregon; 2002, Washington. *Education:* James Madison University (B.S., summa cum laude, 1990); Willamette University (J.D., cum laude, 1994). Phi Alpha Delta. *Member:* Multnomah County, Washington State and American Bar Associations; Oregon State Bar; Home Builders Association of Metropolitan Portland (Director, 2000 and 2002-2005); National Association of Home Builders (Director 2004-2005); Community Associations Institute (President, 2001); Portlandia Club, Inc. (President, 1999); Commercial Real Estate Women; Portland Metropolitan Association of Realtors; Oregon Women Lawyers; National Association of Industrial and Office Properties. ***PRACTICE AREAS:*** Real Property Law; Condominium and Community Association Law; Business Law. ***Email:*** kgustaf@landye-bennett.com

ROBERT B. HOPKINS, born Spring Valley, Illinois, July 2, 1948; admitted to bar, 1973, Oregon. *Education:* Oberlin College (B.A., magna cum laude, 1970); University of Chicago (J.D., 1973). Phi Beta Kappa. *Member:* American Bar Association (Member, Sections on: Litigation; Individual Rights and Responsibilities, Aviation and Space Law, and Tort and Insurance Practice); Oregon State Bar (Member, Sections on: Aviation, Secretary, 1984-1986, Chairman, 1987-1988, Executive Committee Member, 1984-2005; Litigation); The Association of Trial Lawyers of America; Oregon Trial Lawyers Association. ***PRACTICE AREAS:*** Business Litigation; Personal Injury Litigation; Aviation Law; Environmental Law; Products Liability Law. ***Email:*** rhopkins@landye-bennett.com

ROBERT H. HUME, JR., born Ann Arbor, Michigan, March 9, 1952; admitted to bar, 1977, Oregon; 1978, Alaska. *Education:* Colorado State University and University of Michigan (B.G.S., with high distinction, 1974); University of Michigan (J.D., cum laude, 1976). *Member:* Oregon State Bar; Alaska (Previous Co-Chair, Business Law Section; Member: Real Estate, Bankruptcy, and Native Law Sections; Member, Fee Arbitration Committee) and American (Member, Sections on: Business Law and Real Property, Probate and Trust Law) Bar Associations. (Resident, Anchorage, Alaska Office). ***PRACTICE AREAS:*** Business Law; Commercial Transactions; Corporate Law; Limited Liability Company Law; Alaska Native Law; Real Property Law; Bankruptcy Law. ***Email:*** bobh@lbblawyers.com

JODEE K KELLY, born Boise, Idaho; admitted to bar, 1995, Oregon; 1996, Idaho; 2003, Washington. *Education:* Oregon State University (B.S., 1992); Willamette University College of Law (J.D., 1995). *Member:* Washington State and American Bar Associations; Oregon State Bar (Member, Sections on: Real Estate & Land Use Law; Business and Corporate Law); Idaho State Bar (Section on Business and Corporate Law). ***PRACTICE AREAS:*** Business Transactions; Real Estate Transactions; Business Law. ***Email:*** jkelly@landye-bennett.com

THOMAS M. LANDYE, born San Francisco, California, March 20, 1939; admitted to bar, 1969, Oregon. *Education:* Reed College (A.B., 1960); University of Chicago (A.M., 1963; J.D., 1968). Member: Multnomah County Investment Advisory Board; Board of Visitors, University of Oregon Law School; Social Sciences Visiting Committee, University of Chicago; Citizens Crime Commission. *Member:* Multnomah County and American (Member, Sections on: Business Law and Taxation) Bar Associations; Oregon State Bar. ***PRACTICE AREAS:*** Corporate Law; Securities Law; Mergers and Acquisitions. ***Email:*** tlandye@landye-bennett.com

MICHELLE K. McCLURE, born Berkeley, California, May 19, 1968; admitted to bar, 1995, Oregon; 2000, Washington. *Education:* Claremont McKenna College (B.A., cum laude, 1990); Santa Clara University (J.D., 1995). Santa Clara University Law School, High Technology Law Journal. *Member:* Oregon State Bar (Member, Executive Committe, Product Liability Section); Washington State Bar Association; Oregon Trial Lawyers Association; The Association of Trial Lawyers of America. ***PRACTICE AREAS:*** Civil Litigation; Products Liability; Complex Construction Disputes; Health Care; Personal Injury. ***Email:*** mmcclure@landye-bennett.com

ORLANDO MEDINA, born Mastic, New York, July 31, 1974; admitted to bar, 2000, Oregon; 2003, Texas. *Education:* Texas A & M University (B.B.A., 1997); Northwestern School of Law, Lewis and Clark College (J.D., 2000). ***PRACTICE AREAS:*** Business Law; Commercial Law; Corporate Law; Mergers, Acquisitions and Divestitures; Partnership Law; Taxation. ***Email:*** omedina@landye-bennett.com

JEFFREY S. MUTNICK, born New York, N.Y., August 26, 1947; admitted to bar, 1972, Oregon; 1973, U.S. District Court, District of Oregon; U.S. Court of Appeals, Ninth Circuit; U.S. Supreme Court. *Education:* Tulane University of Louisiana (B.A., 1969); Northwestern University (J.D., 1972). Author: "Occupational Diseases," Oregon State Bar Handbook, 1984; "Pain and Suffering: Loss of Earnings and Earning Capacity," Oregon State Handbook, 1985. Co-Author: "Epidemic Type Claims in the Maritime Workplace," University of San Francisco Maritime Law Journal, Vol 4, Summer, 1992. Member, Board of Editors, Journal of Criminal Law, Criminology and Police Science, 1971-1972. Member, 1988—. *Member:* Oregon State Bar; The Association of Trial Lawyers of America; American Board of Trial Advocates. ***PRACTICE AREAS:*** Products Liability Law; Asbestos Litigation; Admiralty Law. ***Email:*** jmutnick@landye-bennett.com

GLEN PRICE, born 1955; admitted to bar, 1990, Alaska. *Education:* University of Alaska, Fairbanks (B.S., 1981); Vermont Law School (M.S.E.L., 1982); Lewis & Clark Law School (J.D., 1989; Certificate in Environmental and Natural Resources Law, 1989). (Resident, Wasilla, Alaska Office). ***PRACTICE AREAS:*** Commercial Law; Business Law; Corporate Law; Real Estate; Alaska Native Law. ***Email:*** glenp@lbblawyers.com

P. STEPHEN RUSSELL, III, born Galveston, Texas, April 17, 1956; admitted to bar, 1981, Oregon. *Education:* Georgetown University (B.S.F.S., 1978); Willamette University (J.D., cum laude, 1981). *Member:* Multnomah County and American (Member, Sections

(This Listing Continued)

on: Real Property, Probate and Trust Law; Business Law) Bar Associations; Oregon State Bar (Member, Sections on: Past Chairman, Real Estate and Land Use; Business and Corporate Law). ***PRACTICE AREAS:*** Real Property Law; Land Use; Condominium and Community Association Law; Corporate Law. ***Email:*** srussell@landye-bennett.com

THANE W. TIENSON, born Astoria, Oregon, August 22, 1946; admitted to bar, 1977, Oregon; 1983, Washington. *Education:* Santa Clara University (B.A., 1968); Golden Gate University (M.P.A., 1973); Lewis & Clark Law School (J.D., 1977). Member, 1975-1977 and Issue Editor, 1976-1977, Environmental Law Review. Author: "Alyeska v. Wilderness Society, Demise of the Private Attorney General," 6 ENV Law Review 243, 1976; "EU Fishery Trade Policies: A Case Study," 3 EEZ Technology 161, 1998; 2002 and 2005 Oregon State Bar Environmental and Natural Resources Law Deskbook Fisheries Law section. *Member:* Oregon State Bar; Washington State Bar Association; American Bar Association. [U.S. Army, Vietnam, 1968-1970]. ***PRACTICE AREAS:*** Civil Litigation; Employment Law; Fisheries Law; Environmental Law; Government Affairs. ***Email:*** ttienson@landye-bennett.com

RICHARD S. YUGLER, born Passaic, New Jersey, September 5, 1955; admitted to bar, 1980, Oregon; 1981, U.S. District Court, District of Oregon; 1982, U.S. Court of Appeals, Ninth Circuit; 1983, U.S. Supreme Court; 1985, U.S. Court of Appeals for the Federal Circuit; 2002, Washington. *Education:* Syracuse University (B.A., 1977); Lewis & Clark Law School (J.D., 1980). Member, Law Review, Lewis & Clark Law School, 1979-1980. Author: "Civil Racketeering," Chapter 28 Torts, Oregon State Bar; "Handbook for Jurors," "Piercing the Corporate Veil," Trial Lawyer, 1999. Recent Seminar Presentations: Insurance Bad Faith, Punitive Damages, Class Action Litigation, Mediation Techniques. Certified Mediator, Oregon Court of Appeals. Past President, Oregon Jury Project Foundation. *Member:* Multnomah County Bar Association (Past Secretary, Board of Directors, 1990-1992, Award of Merit); Oregon State Bar (Board of Governors, 2005—; Past Chair, Disciplinary Board; Past Member, Procedure and Practice Committee, Uniform Jury Instruction Committee); Oregon Trial Lawyers Association (Past President and Board of Governors, 1996-2003; Past Chairs, Business Litigation Section, Amicus Committee; Continuing Legal Education Committee; OTLA-PAC Trustee); Owen Panner Inn at Court (Master); The Association of Trial Lawyers of America (Past Member, Council of Presidents). ***REPORTED CASES:*** Computer Concepts v. Brandt, 310 OR 706, 801 P.2d 800 (1990). ***PRACTICE AREAS:*** Business Litigation; Securities Litigation; Personal Injury; Employment Litigation; Class Action; Insurance Litigation; Real Estate Litigation; Products Liability; Professional Malpractice. ***Email:*** ryugler@landye-bennett.com

ASSOCIATES

CYNTHIA M. HORA, born Chicago, Illinois, March 28, 1956; admitted to bar, 1980, Illinois; 1983, Alaska; 1994, U.S. District Court, Disrtict of Alaska; 1996, U.S. Court of Appeals, Ninth Circuit; 1996, U.S. Supreme Court. *Education:* University of Illinois (B.A., high distinction, summa cum laude, 1977) Phi Beta Kappa; Harvard University (J.D., 1980). Assistant Attorney General, 1982-1990, Chief Assistant Attorney General, 1990-1996, Deputy Attorney General, Criminal Division, 1996-2002, Alaska. National District Attorneys Association. *Member:* Alaska Bar Association. (Resident, Anchorage, Alaska Office). ***REPORTED CASES:*** Thompson v. Keohane, 516 US 99 (1995); Smith v. Doe, 123 Sch 1140 (2003); Krantz v. Briggs, 983 F.2d 961 (9th Cir. 1993); Ostrosky v. State, 913 F.2d 590 (9th Cir. 1990); State v. Hazelwood, 866 P.2d 827 (Alaska 1993); State v. J.R.N., 861 P.2d 578 (Alaska 1993). ***PRACTICE AREAS:*** Civil Litigation; Corporate Law. ***Email:*** cindyh@lbblawyers.com

CHERYL L. McKAY, born Warwick, Rhode Island; admitted to bar, 1998, Alaska; 1999, U.S. District Court, District of Alaska. *Education:* University of Alaska, Anchorage (B.A., Journalism, 1994); University of Colorado (J.D., 1998). Finalist, Moot Court Competition 1996. Member, Moot Court Advisory Board, 1997-1998. Recipient: American Indian Graduate Center Fellowship; Excellence in Trial Advocacy Award, 1998. Named to "Alaska's Top 40 Under 40," 2002. Law Clerk for the Hon. David C. Stewart, Alaska Court of Appeals, 1998-1999. Presenter, "School Law in Alaska," National Business Institute, 2002. *Member:* Anchorage (Director, 2002—; President, 2005), Alaska (Member, Sections on: Alaska Native Law; Labor and Employment Law) and American (Member, Sections on: Business Law; Labor and Employment Law) Bar Associations; Anchorage Association of Women Lawyers. (Resident, Anchorage, Alaska Office). ***PRACTICE AREAS:*** Employment Law; Education Law; Corporate Law; Business Transactions; Alaska Native Law. ***Email:*** cherylm@lbblawyers.com

KYLE D. SCIUCHETTI, born Spokane, Washington, March 1, 1970; admitted to bar, 1996, Oregon and Washington; 1999, U.S. District Court, Western District of Washington; 2000, U.S. District Court, District of Oregon, U.S. Court of Appeals, Ninth Circuit and U.S. Supreme Court. *Education:* University of Washington (B.A., 1992); Lewis & Clark Law School (J.D., 1996). Member, Dean's Fellowship, Lewis & Clark Law School. Assistant City Attorney, City of Spokane, Washington, 1997-1999. Senior Counsel, Public Power Council, 1999-2001. Session Attorney, Washington State Legislature, Office of Code Reviser, 1996-1997. *Member:* Oregon State Bar; Washington State (Legislative Committee) and American Bar Associations; Oregon Corporate Counsel. ***REPORTED CASES:*** Kaiser Aluminum & Chemical v. Bonneville Power Admin., 261 F.3d 843 (9th Cir. 2001). ***PRACTICE AREAS:*** Civil Litigation; Business Law; Administrative Law; Products Liability; Employment Law. ***Email:*** kyle@landye-bennett.com

REPRESENTATIVE CLIENTS: Canterbury Real Estate Services, Inc.; Cascade Corporation; condominium homeowners associations throughout Oregon and Washington; Container Properties, LLC; Emerging Markets of North America, Inc.; Frank A. Bitar & Associates; Generation Development, Inc.; Gould Electronics, Inc.; Herbert Malarkey Roofing Company; JELD-WEN, inc.; Keith L. Wilson Construction; Mentor Graphics Corporation; Metro Metals Northwest; National Cooperative Bank (AK); NuPark Development LLC; Ouzinkie Native Corporation (AK); Pacific Coast Shredding, LLC; Portland Development Commission; Regency Centers; Regional Multiple Listing Service, Inc.; Sealaska Corporation (AK); Sharp Laboratories of America, Inc.; United Agri Products; Veritas Investment Co., LLC; Walter West Construction Co.

LANE POWELL PC

Established in 1875

601 SW SECOND AVENUE, SUITE 2100
PORTLAND, OREGON 97204-3158
Telephone: 503-778-2100
Facsimile: 503-778-2200
Email: information@lanepowell.com
URL: http://www.lanepowell.com

Other Offices at: Seattle, Washington; Anchorage, Alaska; Olympia, Washington; and London, England.

Alternative Dispute Resolution; Admiralty and Maritime Law; Antitrust and Trade Regulation; Appellate Practice; Aviation; Banking; Bankruptcy and Reorganizations; Business Law; Creditor Rights; Architects; Engineers; Construction and Design Law; Class Actions; Corporate Finance and Securities; Emerging Companies and Venture Investment; Director and Officer Liability; Employee Benefits; Employment; ERISA Litigation; Energy Law; Environmental Law; Estate and Gift Taxation; Estate Planning; Federal and State Tax Planning, Litigation and Controversies; Franchising; Governmental Law; Hospital and Healthcare; Immigration and Naturalization; Intellectual Property and Technology; International Business, Trade Regulation; Labor and Employment Law, Counseling and Litigation; Land Use; Litigation; Local Government; Long-Term Care and Senior Housing; Mergers and Acquisitions; Natural Resources; Products Liability; Professional Liability; Real Estate, Land Use Development and Finance; Securities Litigation; Taxation and Tax Controversies; Toxic Torts; Transportation; Trusts and Estates; Trademarks; Utilities; White Collar Criminal Defense and Regulatory Compliance; Wood Products and Forest Resources.

FIRM PROFILE: Law firm of 175 attorneys providing business, employment and litigation services since 1875. Five offices are located in Washington, Oregon, Alaska and London, England.

SHAREHOLDERS

DEAN N. ALTERMAN, admitted to bar, 1989, Oregon. *Education:* Harvard University (A.B., 1981); Northwestern School of Law of Lewis and Clark College (J.D., magna cum laude, 1989). ***PRACTICE AREAS:*** Real Estate; Business; Land Use. ***Email:*** altermand@lanepowell.com

CRAIG D. BACHMAN, admitted to bar, 1978, Oregon; 1990, Washington. *Education:* Portland State University (B.S., 1972); Lewis & Clark College, Northwestern School of Law (J.D., 1978). ***PRACTICE AREAS:*** Trials; Trade Regulation Law; Insurance; Intellectual Property. ***Email:*** bachmanc@lanepowell.com

ROBERT R. CALO, admitted to bar, 1985, Massachusetts; 1986, California and U.S. District Court, Northern District of California; 1997, District of Columbia (Not admitted in Oregon). *Education:* Bryant College (B.S.B.A., 1981); Boston University (J.D., 1985). ***PRACTICE AREAS:*** White Collar Crime (80%); Regulatory Law (20%). ***Email:*** calor@lanepowell.com

KENNETH RAY DAVIS, II, admitted to bar, 1992, Washington; 1997, Oregon; U.S. District Court, Western District of Washington; U.S. District Court, District of Oregon; U.S. Court of Appeals, Ninth and Third Circuits. *Education:* Whitman College (B.A., 1989); University of Puget Sound (J.D., cum laude, 1992). ***PRACTICE AREAS:*** Intellectual Property Litigation; Patent and Trademark; Internet and E-Commerce; Antitrust; Complex Commercial Litigation. ***Email:*** davisk@lanepowell.com

JOHN H. GADON, admitted to bar, 1983, Washington; 1989, Oregon. *Education:* Brown University (A.B., 1979); University of Washington (J.D., with honors, 1983). ***PRACTICE AREAS:*** Tax Law; Federal and State Tax Litigation; Project Finance. ***Email:*** gadonj@lanepowell.com

ANNE W. GLAZER, admitted to bar, 1992, Washington; 1996, Oregon. *Education:* Wesleyan University; University of Washington (B.A., magna cum laude, 1989; J.D., with honors, 1992). ***PRACTICE AREAS:*** Trademark and Copyright Law; Advertising Law; Intellectual Property and Unfair Competition Litigation; Distribution Law; Internet Law. ***Email:*** glazera@lanepowell.com

BRUCE C. HAMLIN, admitted to bar, 1979, Oregon. *Education:* Whitman College (B.A., cum laude, 1976); University of Oregon (J.D., 1979). ***PRACTICE AREAS:*** Litigation; Products Liability Law; Commercial Law; Insurance Law. ***Email:*** hamlinb@lanepowell.com

TIMOTHY R. HARMON, admitted to bar, 1979, Oregon. *Education:* Elmhurst College (B.A., cum laude, 1971); University of Minnesota (J.D., magna cum laude, 1979). ***PRACTICE AREAS:*** Litigation; Real Property; Banking, Business and Transportation Disputes; Alternative Dispute Resolution. ***Email:*** harmont@lanepowell.com

LEWIS M. HOROWITZ, admitted to bar, 1985, Pennsylvania; 1986, District of Columbia and Maryland; 1993, Oregon. *Education:* Columbia University (B.A., 1981); Georgetown University (J.D., cum laude, 1985). ***PRACTICE AREAS:*** Taxation (Federal, State and International). ***Email:*** horowitzl@lanepowell.com

DAVID G. HOSENPUD, admitted to bar, 1983, Oregon; 1990, California. *Education:* University of California at Santa Barbara (B.A., with highest honors, 1978); University of Oregon (J.D., 1983). ***PRACTICE AREAS:*** Commercial Litigation; Employment Litigation; Products Liability. ***Email:*** hosenpudd@lanepowell.com

CHARLES F. HUDSON, admitted to bar, 1983, Oregon; 1984, Washington. *Education:* University of Virginia (B.A., with distinction, 1978; J.D., 1982). ***PRACTICE AREAS:*** Commercial Litigation; Eminent Domain; Securities. ***Email:*** hudsonc@lanepowell.com

NEIL D. KIMMELFIELD, admitted to bar, 1979, District of Columbia (inactive); 1994, Oregon. *Education:* Vassar College (A.B., with general and departmental honors, 1976); Harvard University (J.D., cum laude, 1979). ***PRACTICE AREAS:*** Taxation. ***Email:*** kimmelfieldn@lanepowell.com

(This Listing Continued)

ROBERT G. KOURY, II, admitted to bar, 1998, Oregon. *Education:* University of Southern California (B.A., 1993); Willamette University (J.D., 1997; M.B.A., 1997). ***PRACTICE AREAS:*** Real Estate; Real Estate Finance; Commercial Law. ***Email:*** kouryr@lanepowell.com

ROBERT E. MALONEY, JR., admitted to bar, 1967, Oregon; 1984, Washington. *Education:* University of Portland (B.A., magna cum laude, 1964); Willamette University (J.D., summa cum laude, 1967). ***PRACTICE AREAS:*** Complex Business Litigation; Condemnation Law; Lender Liability; Employment Discrimination; Products Liability Law. ***Email:*** maloneyr@lanepowell.com

STEPHEN P. McCARTHY, admitted to bar, 1985, California, 1989, Oregon. *Education:* California Polytechnic State University at San Luis Obispo (B.S., 1981); McGeorge School of Law (J.D., 1985). ***PRACTICE AREAS:*** Litigation; Insurance; Products Liability. ***Email:*** mccarthys@lanepowell.com

LEE C. NUSICH, admitted to bar, 1977, Oregon. *Education:* University of North Dakota (B.S. in Geological Engineering, 1972); University of Oregon (J.D., 1977). ***PRACTICE AREAS:*** Commercial Litigation; Environmental Litigation; Loan Workouts; Loan Restructuring. ***Email:*** nusichl@lanepowell.com

PAUL M. OSTROFF, admitted to bar, 1975, California; 1995, Oregon. *Education:* University of California at Berkeley (A.B., 1972); University of California, Hastings College of the Law (J.D., 1975). ***SPECIAL AGENCIES:*** NLRB; EEOC; U.S. Department of Labor; Oregon Bureau of Labor and Industries. ***PRACTICE AREAS:*** Labor; Employment. ***Email:*** ostroffp@lanepowell.com

MILO P. PETRANOVICH, admitted to bar, 1977, California; 1981, Oregon. *Education:* American University (B.A., magna cum laude, 1972); University of Michigan (J.D., 1976). ***PRACTICE AREAS:*** Litigation; Trade Regulation Law; Antitrust Law; Securities Law; Professional Liability Law. ***Email:*** petranovichm@lanepowell.com

CLAIRE J. PHILPOTT, admitted to bar, 1992, California; 1999, Oregon. *Education:* University of California, Davis (B.A., 1988); University of California, Los Angeles (J.D., 1992). ***PRACTICE AREAS:*** Corporate Finance; Mergers and Acquisitions; Technology Law; Real Estate; Real Estate Finance; Tax; Venture Capital. ***Email:*** philpottc@lanepowell.com

BRYAN E. POWELL, admitted to bar, 1988, California; 1995, Oregon. *Education:* University of Washington (B.A., cum laude, 1982); Hastings College of the Law, University of California (J.D., 1988). ***PRACTICE AREAS:*** Real Estate Law; Real Estate Finance; Secured Lending; Corporate Law. ***Email:*** powellb@lanepowell.com

DONALD H. PYLE, admitted to bar, 1976, Oregon. *Education:* Princeton University (A.B., magna cum laude, 1972); Temple University (J.D., 1976); Northwestern School of Law at Lewis and Clark College (LL.M. in Environmental and Natural Resources Law, 1999). ***PRACTICE AREAS:*** Complex Litigation; Environmental Litigation; Regulatory Practice. ***Email:*** pyled@lanepowell.com

VICKI L. SMITH, admitted to bar, 1985, Oregon; 1994, Washington. *Education:* University of Oregon (B.A., 1980, Phi Beta Kappa); American University (J.D., 1985). ***PRACTICE AREAS:*** Litigation. ***Email:*** smithv@lanepowell.com

THOMAS W. SONDAG, admitted to bar, 1984, Oregon. *Education:* University of California at Berkeley (A.B., with high honors, 1980); Boalt Hall School of Law, University of California (J.D., 1984). ***PRACTICE AREAS:*** Appellate Law. ***Email:*** sondagt@lanepowell.com

LEIGH D. STEPHENSON-KUHN, admitted to bar, 1962, New York and Oregon. *Education:* Yale University (A.B., 1958); Columbia University (LL.B., 1961). ***PRACTICE AREAS:*** Employee Benefit Law; Executive Compensation Law. ***Email:*** stephenson-kuhnl@lanepowell.com

JOHN C. STEVASON, admitted to bar, 1975, Oregon. *Education:* Princeton University (A.B., 1967); New York University (J.D., 1973). ***PRACTICE AREAS:*** Computer and Internet Law; Intellectual Property Law; Labor Relations Law; Employment Law. ***Email:*** stevasonj@lanepowell.com

CATHERINE S. TRAVIS, admitted to bar, 1981, Oregon; 1984, U.S. District Court, District of Oregon. *Education:* Vassar College (B.A., 1970); Lewis and Clark Law School (J.D., 1981). ***PRACTICE AREAS:*** Bankruptcy; Creditors; Commercial Litigation; Banking Law; Financial Services Law; Contracts; Arbitration; Mediation. ***Email:*** travisc@lanepowell.com

STEVEN B. UNGAR, born St. Louis, Missouri, December 14, 1954; admitted to bar, 1979, Missouri; 1982, Montana; 1995, Oregon; 1998, New York. *Education:* University of Wisconsin; College of William and Mary; Washington University (B.A., with honors, 1975); University of Missouri, Kansas City (J.D., with honors, 1979). ***PRACTICE AREAS:*** Criminal Law; White Collar Crime; Corporate Compliance; Regulatory Law; Professional Licensing. ***Email:*** ungars@lanepowell.com

JACK WALSH, admitted to bar, 1992, Oregon. *Education:* New York University; University of Dayton (B.S., cum laude, 1987); Hastings College of the Law, University of California (J.D., 1992). ***PRACTICE AREAS:*** ERISA; Employee Benefits; Executive Compensation. ***Email:*** walshj@lanepowell.com

KAREN M. WILLIAMS, admitted to bar, 1990, Washington; 1992, Oregon. *Education:* Antioch University (B.A., 1987); University of Puget Sound (J.D., cum laude, 1989). ***PRACTICE AREAS:*** Real Estate; Environmental Law; Public Private Partnerships; New Markets Tax Credits. ***Email:*** williamsk@lanepowell.com

RICHARD H. WILLIAMS, admitted to bar, 1972, Oregon. *Education:* Colgate University (A.B., 1969); Harvard University (J.D., cum laude, 1972). ***PRACTICE AREAS:*** Commercial Law; Corporate Law; Real Estate Law. ***Email:*** williamsr@lanepowell.com

JEFFREY C. WOLFSTONE, admitted to bar, 1977, Oregon. *Education:* Stanford University (A.B., 1974); Boalt Hall School of Law, University of California (J.D., 1977). ***PRACTICE AREAS:*** Corporate; Mergers and Acquisitions; Emerging Companies; Real Estate; Tax. ***Email:*** wolfstonej@lanepowell.com

(This Listing Continued)

EMERITUS MEMBERS

JOHN P. BLEDSOE, admitted to bar, 1948, Oregon. *Education:* University of Arkansas (B.A., 1941); Harvard University (LL.B., cum laude, 1948). ***PRACTICE AREAS:*** General Business Law. ***Email:*** morrisonk@lanepowell.com

JOHN B. CROWELL, JR., admitted to bar, 1958, New Jersey; 1959, Oregon. *Education:* Dartmouth College (A.B., 1952); Harvard University (LL.B., 1957). ***PRACTICE AREAS:*** Business Law; Forest Products; Real Property. ***Email:*** crowellj@lanepowell.com

STANLEY R. LOEB, admitted to bar, 1960, Oregon; 1984, Washington. *Education:* Harvard College (A.B., 1954); Harvard Law School (LL.B., 1960). ***PRACTICE AREAS:*** Estate Planning Law; Probate Law. ***Email:*** loebs@lanepowell.com

WILLIAM F. LUBERSKY, admitted to bar, 1940, Oregon; 1946, Washington. *Education:* University of Oregon (A.B., 1938; LL.B., 1940). ***PRACTICE AREAS:*** Employment Law; Labor Relations. ***Email:*** luberskyw@lanepowell.com

FRANK H. SPEARS, admitted to bar, 1939, Oregon. *Education:* University of Oregon (B.S., 1936); Harvard University (LL.B., 1939); Linfield College (LL.D., 1988). ***PRACTICE AREAS:*** Forest Products Industry Law; Business Law; Real Estate Law. ***Email:*** trussellp@lanepowell.com

COUNSEL

JEFFREY W. KNAPP, admitted to bar, 1989, Oregon. *Education:* Washington & Lee University (B.A., summa cum laude, 1984); University of Pennsylvania (J.D., cum laude, 1989). ***PRACTICE AREAS:*** ERISA; Employee Benefits; Executive Compensation. ***Email:*** knappj@lanepowell.com

ASSOCIATES

BETH A. ALLEN, admitted to bar, 1996, Oregon; 2000, Washington. *Education:* Portland State University (B.S., 1992); Williamette University College of Law (J.D., 1996). ***PRACTICE AREAS:*** Labor and Employment; Civil Litigation. ***Email:*** allenb@lanepowell.com

SUSAN J. BAIRD, admitted to bar, 2001, California (Not admitted in Oregon). *Education:* University of California at San Diego (B.A., 1998); University of California at Los Angeles (J.D., 2001). ***PRACTICE AREAS:*** Land Use; Real Estate; Water; Environmental Law; Administrative Law. ***Email:*** bairds@lanepowell.com

JOHN R. BARHOUM, admitted to bar, 2004, Oregon. *Education:* Lewis and Clark Law School (J.D., 2004). ***PRACTICE AREAS:*** Products Liability; Premises Liability. ***Email:*** barhoumj@lanepowell.com

VICTORIA D. BLACHLY, admitted to bar, 1997, Oregon; 2000, Washington; 2001, U.S. District Court, Western District of Washington. *Education:* Washington State University (B.S., 1993); Northwestern School of Law of Lewis & Clark (J.D., 1997). ***PRACTICE AREAS:*** Litigation; Estate Litigation; Trust Litigation; Fiduciary Litigation; Insurance Defense. ***Email:*** blachlyv@lanepowell.com

BRADY M. BUSTANY, admitted to bar, 2001, California, U.S. District Court, Central District of California; U.S. Court of Appeals, Ninth Circuit; 2002, U.S. District Court, Northern, Eastern and Southern Districts of California; 2003, Minnesota (inactive) and District of Columbia; 2004, Oregon; U.S. District Court, District of Oregon. *Education:* University of Michigan, Ann Arbor (A.B., 1995); University of California at Los Angeles (J.D., 2001). ***PRACTICE AREAS:*** Labor and Employment; Commercial Litigation; Health Care Litigation. ***Email:*** bustanyb@lanepowell.com

LEAH B. CRONN, admitted to bar, 1998, Oregon; 2002, U.S. District Court, District of Oregon; 2003, U.S. Court of Appeals, Ninth Circuit. *Education:* University of Michigan (B.A., with distinction, 1994); Northwestern School of Law of Lewis and Clark College (J.D., 1997). ***PRACTICE AREAS:*** Commercial Litigation; White Collar Criminal Defense; Government. ***Email:*** cronnl@lanepowell.com

LORNE O. DAUENHAUER, admitted to bar, 2002, Oregon. *Education:* Gonzaga University (B.S., 1990); Northwestern School of Law, Lewis and Clark College (J.D., cum laude, 2002). ***PRACTICE AREAS:*** Employee Benefits; Executive Compensation; Deferred Compensation; Equity Compensation; ERISA Compliance; Qualified Retirement Plans; Taft-Hartley Plans. ***Email:*** dauenhauerl@lanepowell.com

PILAR CORTWRIGHT FRENCH, admitted to bar, 1996, Oregon; 2003, Washington. *Education:* Northwestern University (B.A., with honors, 1992); Indiana University (J.D., 1996). ***PRACTICE AREAS:*** Commercial Litigation; Securities Litigation; Employment Litigation; Torts. ***Email:*** frenchp@lanepowell.com

JEFFRY S. GARRETT, admitted to bar, 2000, Oregon. *Education:* University of Oregon (B.A., 1993); Willamette University College of Law (J.D., cum laude, 2000). ***PRACTICE AREAS:*** Business Litigation; Appellate Practice; Securities Litigation. ***Email:*** garrettj@lanepowell.com

STEPHANIE HENDRICKS, admitted to bar, 2003, Oregon. *Education:* Georgia State University (B.I.S., 1998); Willamette University (J.D., 2002). ***PRACTICE AREAS:*** Litigation. ***Email:*** hendrickss@lanepowell.com

BENJAMIN G. LENHART, admitted to bar, 1996, Oregon. *Education:* Whitman College (B.A., 1991); Northwestern School of Law of Lewis & Clark College (J.D., cum laude, 1996). ***PRACTICE AREAS:*** Corporate Law; Mergers and Acquisitions; Emerging Growth Companies; Securities; Corporate Finance. ***Email:*** lenhartb@lanepowell.com

PARNA A. MEHRBANI, admitted to bar, 2005, Oregon. *Education:* University of Illinois (B.A., 2000); Lewis and Clark College (J.D., 2005). ***PRACTICE AREAS:*** Intellectual Property; Litigation. ***Email:*** mehrbanip@lanepowell.com

WILLIAM T. PATTON, admitted to bar, 1997, Oregon. *Education:* Occidental College (B.A., cum laude, 1993); George Washington University (J.D., 1997). ***PRACTICE AREAS:*** Class Actions; ERISA Litigation; Life, Health and Disability Insurance Litigation; Commercial Litigation. ***Email:*** pattonw@lanepowell.com

(This Listing Continued)

CHRISTOPHER B. STOREY, admitted to bar, 2000, New York; 2002, California; 2004, Oregon. *Education:* Willamette University (B.S., 1996); New York University (J.D., 1999). ***PRACTICE AREAS:*** Business; Finance; Corporate; Banking. ***Email:*** storeyc@lanepowell.com

REPRESENTATIVE CLIENTS: Advanced H2O, Inc.; Aramark Corporation; Associated Aviation Underwriters; Callison Architecture, Inc.; Chevron Corporation; CNF, Inc.; Coffman Engineers, Inc.; Cutter & Buck, Inc.; ERA Aviation, Inc.; Exxon Mobil Corporation; The Fishing Company of Alaska; Fred Hutchinson Cancer Research Center; Frito-Lay, Inc.; General Electric Capital Corp.; Georgia-Pacific Corporation; Home Depot U.S.A., Inc.; IBP, Inc.; Key Bank; Les Schwab Tire Centers; Monsanto Company; The MONY Group, Inc.; Morgan Stanley Dean Witter & Co.; Mowat Construction Company; Nike, Inc.; Nordstrom, Inc.; Norm Thompson Outfitters, Inc.; Northwest Biotherapeutics, Inc.; Novartis Consumer Health, Inc.; Oregon Public Employees Retirement System; Oremet-Wah Chang; Portland Development Commission; Premera Blue Cross; Prudential Securities; Quinton Inc.; Shell Oil Company; Simpson Investment Company; Sound Transit; Starbucks Coffee Company; T-Mobile Corporation; Tokai Carbon Co., Ltd.; TransAlta Corporation; Triad Hospitals, Inc.; Tri-County Metropolitan Transportation (District of Oregon (Tri-Met)); Underwriters at Lloyd's; Union Pacific Railroad Corp.; Verisign, Inc.; Wal-Mart Stores, Inc.; Washington Mutual Bank; Wells Fargo & Company; Weyerhauser Company.

(For complete biographical data on personnel at Anchorage, Alaska; Olympia, Seattle, Washington; and London, England, see Professional Biographies at those locations)

JAMES D. LANG

1020 S.W. TAYLOR, SUITE 375
PORTLAND, OREGON 97205-2554
Telephone: 503-227-4533
Facsimile: 503-248-9776
Email: jlang@teleport.com
URL: http://www.lawyers.com/jlang

Criminal and Juvenile Law. Trials in all State and Federal Courts.

JAMES D. LANG, born New York, N.Y., April 30, 1953; admitted to bar, 1981, Oregon; 1982, U.S. District Court, District of Oregon and U.S. Court of Appeals, 9th Circuit. *Education:* Ohio Wesleyan University; The Evergreen State College (B.A., 1976); Northwestern School of Law of Lewis and Clark College (J.D., 1981). Member, Cornelius Honor Society. Associate Editor, Environmental Law Review, 1981. Multnomah County Public Defender, 1982-1986; Metropolitan Public Defenders, 1987-1990; Federal Public Defenders, 1986-1987. *Member:* Multnomah County (Member, Corrections Committee and Committee on Fairness and Equality) and American Bar Associations; Oregon State Bar (Member, Sections on: Juvenile Law; Solo Practitioners; Criminal Law and Criminal Jury Instruction Committee); Oregon Criminal Defense Lawyers Association (Member, Board of Directors, 1983-1984); National Association of Criminal Defense Lawyers. ***PRACTICE AREAS:*** Criminal Law; Juvenile Law.

LARKINS VACURA, LLP

Established in 1999
808 S.W. THIRD AVENUE, SUITE 540
PORTLAND, OREGON 97204
Telephone: 503-222-4424
Facsimile: 503-827-7600
Email: jvacura@larkinsvacura.com
Email: wlarkins@larkinsvacura.com
URL: http://www.lawyers.com/vacuralarkins-llp

Litigation Practice in Federal and State Courts, emphasizing Business and Real Estate Disputes, Real Estate and Banking Transactions.

WILLIAM L. LARKINS, JR., born San Rafael, California, April 17, 1955; admitted to bar, 1981, Oregon; 2003, Washington; U.S. District Court, District of Oregon, U.S. District Court, Western District of Washington and U.S. Court of Appeals, Ninth Circuit. *Education:* Stanford University (B.A., with distinction, 1977); University of California at Berkeley (J.D., 1981). Phi Beta Kappa. Associate General Counsel, U.S. Bancorp, 1997-1999 (In-house Corporate Counsel, 1988-1996). *Member:* Oregon State Bar (Member, Executive Committee, Financial Institutions Committee of Business Law Section, 1992-1994; Executive Committee, Corporate Counsel Section, 1994-1996); Washington State Bar Association; Multnomah County Bar Association (Member, Judicial Screening Committee, 2002-2005). ***PRACTICE AREAS:*** Business Litigation; Banking Law; Creditors Rights. ***Email:*** wlarkins@larkinsvacura.com

JULIE R. VACURA, born Fairbanks, Alaska, April 29, 1959; admitted to bar, 1984, Oregon; 2003, Washington. *Education:* University of Santa Clara (B.S., cum laude, 1981); Willamette University (J.D., cum laude, 1984). Executive Editor, Willamette Law Review, 1983-1984. Author: Casenote, "Moore v. State: Drunk Driving and Talking the Fine Line in Oregon," 19 Willamette Law Review, 803, 1983; Comment, "Arbitration and NLRB Deferral: From Spielberg to Suburban Motor Freight and Beyond," 20 Willamette Law Review, 785, 1984; Oregon CLE on Damages, "Attorney Fees and Costs," 1998 (Supplements 1990, 1995). Judicial Clerk to Hon. Otto R. Skopil, Ninth Circuit Court of Appeals, 1984-1986. Member, Oregon State Bar Examiners, 1992-1995 (Chair, 1995). *Member:* Multnomah (Board of Directors, 1999-2002; Professionalism Committee, 1995-1998; Chair, 1998) and Washington State Bar Associations; Oregon State Bar (Member, Executive Committee, 1998-2005, Secretary, 2002, Treasurer, 2003, President-Elect, 2004 and President, 2005, Business Litigation Section Chair, Region Five, 2000 and Member, 1993-2000, Disciplinary Board); National Conference of Bar Examiners (Member, MPT Policy Committee, 1995-1997). ***REPORTED CASES:*** Allen v. Hall, 139 F3d 716 (9th Cir. 1998); Principal Life Ins. Co. v. Robinson, 394 F3d 665 (9th Cir. 2005). ***PRACTICE AREAS:*** Real Estate Litigation; Business Litigation; Banking Litigation. ***Email:*** jvacura@larkinsvacura.com

ASSOCIATES

LAINIE BLOCK, born Brooklyn, New York, September, 1, 1968; admitted to bar, 1994, Oregon; 1995, Washington; 2001, U.S. Court of Appeals, Ninth Circuit; 2002, U.S.

(This Listing Continued)

LARKINS VACURA, LLP, Portland—Continued

District Court, District of Oregon; 2005, U.S. District Court, Eastern District of Washington. *Education:* University of California, Los Angeles (B.A., 1990); University of Oregon (J.D., 1994). Associate Editor, Oregon Law Review, 1993-1994. Assistant Attorney General, Oregon Department of Justice, 1998-2000. *Member:* Multnomah and Washington State Bar Associations; Oregon State Bar. ***PRACTICE AREAS:*** Business Litigation; Banking Litigation; Construction Litigation; Civil Appeals. ***Email:*** lblock@larkinsvacura.com

PERRY S. HEITMAN, born Baton Rouge, Louisiana, April 18, 1958; admitted to bar, 2003, Oregon. *Education:* Louisiana State University (B.S., in Accounting, 1982); Northwestern School of Law at Lewis and Clark College (J.D., 2003). Articles Editor, Journal of Small and Emerging Business, 2002-2003. Recipient, Cornelius Honor Society Award. Certified Public Accountant, 1983. *Member:* Multnomah Bar Association (Member, Professional Development & Education Committee, 2005—); Oregon State Bar. ***PRACTICE AREAS:*** Business Litigation; Banking Law; Creditors Rights; Real Estate. ***Email:*** pheitman@larkinsvacura.com

REPRESENTATIVE CLIENTS: U.S. Bank; Nike, Inc.; Dryvit Systems; The Coffman Company; Oregon Central Credit Union; GMAC Mortgage Corp.; Spiegel Holdings, Inc.; Beal Bank.

LAYNE & LEWIS, LLP

111 SW COLUMBIA STREET, SUITE 1000
PORTLAND, OREGON 97201
Telephone: 503-295-1882
Facsimile: 503-295-2057
Email: mlayne@layne-lewis.com
URL: http://www.layne-lewislaw.com

Securities Arbitration and Litigation, Legal Malpractice, Shareholder Litigation.

RICHARD M. LAYNE, born Louisville, Kentucky, April 11, 1946; admitted to bar, 1978, Oregon, U.S. District Court, District of Oregon and U.S. Tax Court; 1979, Washington. *Education:* Boise State University (B.A., 1975); Willamette University (J.D., 1978). Assistant Corporation Commissioner, Oregon, 1980-1981. *Member:* Oregon State Bar; Washington State and American Bar Associations. [Capt., Armor, U.S. Army, 1966-1974]. ***Email:*** mlayne@layne-lewis.com

LEHNER & RODRIGUES, PC

Established in 1988
SUITE 1015 CROWN PLAZA
1500 S.W. FIRST AVENUE
PORTLAND, OREGON 97201
Telephone: 503-226-2225
Facsimile: 503-226-2418

Insurance Defense Practice including Civil Trial and Appellate Practice, Casualty, Fire, Auto, Insurance Coverage, Products Liability, Professional Liability, Environmental and Hazardous Waste, Motor Carrier and Transportation Insurance Law, Municipal and Governmental Liability.

FIRM PROFILE: Lehner & Rodrigues is listed in the Bar Register of Preeminent Lawyers in the area of Insurance Defense Law.

MICHAEL A. LEHNER, born Portland, Oregon, November 8, 1942; admitted to bar, 1974, Oregon and U.S. District Court of Oregon; 1978, U.S. Court of Appeals, 9th Circuit; 1980, U.S. Supreme Court; 1984, Washington. *Education:* University of Oregon (B.S., 1964); Northwestern School of Law of Lewis and Clark College (J.D., 1974). Editor-in-Chief, Environmental Law, 1972-1973. Author: "Excess Liability," Oregon State Bar CLE, 1983. Co-Author: "Parties and Jurisdiction," Insurance Section, Oregon State Bar CLE, 1983. Law Clerk to Justice Arno Denecke, Oregon Supreme Court, 1974-1975. Adjunct Professor of Law, Northwestern School of Law, 1979-1981. *Member:* Clark County, Multnomah County, Washington State and Federal Bar Associations; Oregon State Bar; Oregon Association of Defense Counsel; Defense Research Institute. ***PRACTICE AREAS:*** Insurance Defense. ***Email:*** lehnerm@lmrs.com

CARL R. RODRIGUES, born Hong Kong, September 7, 1951; admitted to bar, 1982, Oregon, U.S. District Court, District of Oregon and U.S. Court of Appeals, Ninth Circuit; 2003, Iowa and Washington. *Education:* California State University (B.A., 1973); Northwestern School of Law of Lewis and Clark College (J.D., 1982). *Member:* Multnomah County Bar Association; Oregon State Bar; Washington State Bar Association; Oregon Association of Defense Counsel; Defense Research Institute. ***PRACTICE AREAS:*** Insurance Defense. ***Email:*** rodriguesc@lmrs.com

THOMAS C PATTON, born California, 1959; admitted to bar, 1996, Oregon; 1999, U.S. Court of Appeals, Ninth Circuit; 2001, U.S. District Court, District of Oregon. *Education:* Sonoma State University (B.A., 1983); Lewis and Clark College Law School (J.D., 1996). [Lt. Col., Oregon Air National Guard, 1985—]. ***PRACTICE AREAS:*** Civil Litigation; Appellate Practice. ***Email:*** tpatton@lmrs.com

SHELLY M. DAMORE, admitted to bar, 2002, Oregon and Washington. *Education:* Northern Arizona University (B.A., 1998); Northwestern School of Law (J.D., 2002). *Member:* Oregon State Bar; Washington State Bar Association. ***PRACTICE AREAS:*** Insurance Defense. ***Email:*** sdamore@lmrs.com

LEGAL SUPPORT PERSONNEL

JULIE K. WEST, born Corvallis, Oregon, April 24, 1962. *Education:* Linn Benton Community College; Oregon State University. *Member:* Oregon Legal Assistants Association, 1988. (Paralegal). ***Email:*** westj@lmrs.com

PATRICIA A. NEAL, born Bishop, California, April 16, 1953. *Education:* University of Idaho, Boise State College (A.A.); College of Legal Arts (A.A. Paralegal Studies). ***Email:*** pneal@lmrs.com

REPRESENTATIVE CLIENTS: Allied Ins.; North Pacific/Oregon Auto Ins. Co.; City of Portland; The Hartford Ins. Group; The Infinity Group; Metro; Nationwide Ins. Group; Ohio Casualty; Pinnacle Risk Mgmt.; Progressive Ins. Co.; SAFECO Ins. Co's.; Scottsdale Ins.; State Farm Ins. Co's.; Trinity Universal Ins.; Valley Ins.

LAW OFFICE OF MICHAEL R. LEVINE

400 SW SIXTH AVENUE, SUITE 600
PORTLAND, OREGON 97204
Telephone: 503-546-3927
Fax: 503-224-3203
URL: http://www.lawyers.com/michaelrlevine
Email: michael@levinedefenders.com
URL: http://www.levinedefenders.com

Criminal Law, Drug Crimes, Trial Practice, Appellate Practice, Post-Conviction Remedies.

MICHAEL R. LEVINE, born Boston, Massachusetts, March 20, 1944; admitted to bar, 1974, California; 1975, U.S. District Court, Central District of California; 1976, U.S. Court of Appeals, Ninth Circuit; 1983, Hawaii and District of Columbia; 1993, Oregon. *Education:* University of Freiburg, Germany; Rollins College (A.B., 1965); Columbia University (B.S., 1966); University of California at Berkeley, Boalt Hall School of Law (J.D., 1974). Recipient, Outstanding Defender Award. Professor: Legal Writing, UCLA; Criminal Law, Richardson School of Law, University of Hawaii. Formerly: Prosecutor for the City of Los Angeles; Assistant Federal Public Defender in California; District of Hawaii's First Federal Public Defender, having been appointed by the Ninth Circuit Court of Appeals, 1982-1990; Assistant Federal Public Defender for the District of Oregon, 1990-2002; Law Office of Michael R. Levine, 2002. *Member:* Oregon State Bar (Former State Chair, Disciplinary Board), State Bar of California, Hawaii State and Federal Bar Associations; Hawaii Association of Criminal Defense Lawyers (Former President).

ASSOCIATE

MATTHEW G. McHENRY, born Adrian, Michigan, March 25, 1975; admitted to bar, 2004, Oregon and U.S. District Court, District of Oregon; 2005, U.S. Court of Appeals, Ninth Circuit. *Education:* University of Michigan Business School (B.B.A., cum laude, 1997); Lewis and Clark Law School (J.D., magna cum laude, 2004). Law Clerk, Federal Public Defenders Office, Portland, Oregon. *Member:* Oregon State Bar. ***PRACTICE AREAS:*** Criminal Law; Criminal Defense; Federal Criminal Law; Drug Crimes; Trial Practice; Appellate Practice; Post-Conviction Remedies; Civil Drug Forfeiture; Drug Forfeiture. ***Email:*** matthew@levinedefenders.com

LINDSAY, HART, NEIL & WEIGLER, LLP

Established in 1935
3400 WELLS FARGO CENTER
1300 S.W. FIFTH AVENUE
PORTLAND, OREGON 97201-5640
Telephone: 503-226-7677
Telecopier: 503-226-7697
Email: LHNW@lindsayhart.com
URL: http://www.lindsayhart.com

Washington, D.C. Office: 1201 Pennsylvania Avenue, N.W., Suite 315, 20004. Telephone: 202-783-3333. Fax: 202-783-4422.

Litigation, Products Liability, Corporate, Maritime, Employment, Professional Liability, Regulatory and Insurance.

FIRM PROFILE: A mid-sized firm of experienced, effective attorneys serving the litigation and transactional needs of local and international clientele since 1935.

MEMBERS OF FIRM

GUNTHER F. KRAUSE (1895-1967)

CARMIE R. DAFOE, JR. (1920-1975)

DONALD G. KRAUSE (1921-1986)

C. ALLAN HART, JR. (1909-2002)

LESLIE F. DARBY (1958-2002)

DENNIS J. LINDSAY, born Winnipeg, Manitoba, March 22, 1918; admitted to bar, 1941, Michigan; 1945, New York; 1948, Oregon; 1981, District of Columbia; 1979, U.S. Supreme Court. *Education:* Oberlin College (B.A., 1938); University of Michigan (J.D., 1941). Phi Beta Kappa. Attorney, U.S. Department of Interior, District of Columbia, 1941-1943. Associate, Cahill, Gordon & Reindel, New York City, 1943-1948. Deputy District Attorney, Multnomah County, Oregon, 1948-1950. Commissioner, 1957-1969; President, 1958-1961; 1965-1966; 1968-1969, Port of Portland Commission. Member, Portland Development Commission, 1974-1979. Special Counsel, U.S. Secretary of Transportation, Washington, D.C., 1979-1980. Commissioner, International Port of Coos Bay, 1988-1992. Governor's Task Force on Lower Columbia River, 1984-1985. Director, Inland Empire Waterways Association, 1959-1962. Board of Directors: Governor's Task Force for Portland Waterfront Development, 1971-1974; Oregon Association of Port Authorities, 1988-1991; Portland Metropolitan Chamber of Commerce, 1989-1995; Portland State University Foundation, 1990—. *Member:* Multnomah County and American Bar Associations; Oregon State Bar; Maritime Law Association of the United States (Member, Committee on Stevedores and Terminals); American Association of Average Adjusters; American Judicature Society. ***PRACTICE AREAS:*** Collective Bargaining; Labor Relations; Trade Associations Law; Maritime Law. ***Email:*** dlindsay@lindsayhart.com

(This Listing Continued)

CARL R. NEIL, born Boise, Idaho, October 1, 1933; admitted to bar, 1958, Oregon; 1971, U.S. Supreme Court. *Education:* Yale University (B.A., magna cum laude, 1955); Columbia University (LL.B., 1958). Phi Beta Kappa. Adjunct Professor of Admiralty, Northwestern School of Law of Lewis and Clark College, 1969—. Co-Chair, Pacific Northwest Admiralty Institute, 1985. Co-Editor, Oregon State Bar Handbook on Arbitration and Mediation, 1987, 1992, 1996, and 2001. Supp. Law Clerk to Justice Hall S. Lusk, Supreme Court of Oregon, 1958-1959. Member, Board of Directors: Portland Community College, 1968-1973; Portland Community College Foundation, 1982-1986; Oregon Law Foundation, 1982-1985; Oregon Liquor Control Commission, 1978-1981; Urban League of Portland, 2000—. *Member:* Multnomah County and American Bar Associations; Oregon State Bar (Member, Board of Governors, 1974-1977; President, 1976-1977); Maritime Law Association of the United States. ***PRACTICE AREAS:*** Civil Litigation; Arbitration; Maritime Law; Insurance; Forest Products Law. ***Email:*** cneil@lindsayhart.com

JERARD S. WEIGLER, born New York, N.Y., October 14, 1933; admitted to bar, 1960, Oregon; 1970, U.S. Supreme Court. *Education:* Colgate University (B.A., 1954); Yale University (LL.B., 1960). Assistant Instructor, Yale Law School, 1959-1960. Law Clerk to U.S. District Court Chief Judge Gus J. Solomon. *Member:* Multnomah County and American (Member, Section of Tort and Insurance Practice) Bar Associations; Oregon State Bar (Continuing Legal Education Author; Insurance Practice); Maritime Law Association of the United States; The Defense Research Institute; Oregon Association of Defense Counsel; Pacific Northwest Admiralty Institute; Oregon Lawyers for Children (Director; President, 1989-1990). [1st Lt., USAF]. ***PRACTICE AREAS:*** Civil Litigation; Products Liability Defense; Maritime; Casualty; Employer Liability. ***Email:*** jweigler@lindsayhart.com

JAMES H. BEAN, born Klamath Falls, Oregon, January 25, 1934; admitted to bar, 1967, District of Columbia; 1968, Oregon; 1987, U.S. Supreme Court. *Education:* Brigham Young University (B.A., 1962); George Washington University (J.D., 1966). Phi Delta Phi; Blue Key. Co-Author, with Douglas D. Smith: "Franchise Legal Documents," *Franchising,* (a textbook/handbook on franchising) compiled by Robert Justis and Richard Judd, published by South/Western Publishing Co., 1986. President, Oregon City Stake, 1972-1981 and Regional Representative of the Council of The Twelve, 1981-1987, The Church of Jesus Christ of Latter-Day Saints. Member, Board of Visitors, J. Rueben Clark School of Law, Brigham Young University, 1975-1979; Member, Board of Directors, Brigham Young University Alumni Association, 1975-1979. Member: Cascade Pacific Council, 1978—; Western Region Executive Board, 1986—, President, Area One, 1986-1991 and President, National Council, 1980—, Boy Scouts of America. *Member:* Oregon State Bar; The District of Columbia Bar; American Bar Association. ***PRACTICE AREAS:*** Business Law; Franchises; Real Estate; Land Use; Probate. ***Email:*** jbean@lindsayhart.com

GLEN P. McCLENDON, born Portland, Oregon, December 12, 1948; admitted to bar, 1973, Oregon. *Education:* Portland State University (B.S., 1970); University of Oregon (J.D., 1973). *Member:* Multnomah County Bar Association; Oregon State Bar. ***PRACTICE AREAS:*** Commercial; Casualty; Employment; General Business Litigation, all Courts. ***Email:*** gmcclendon@lindsayhart.com

ROBERT W. PALMER, born Ann Arbor, Michigan, July 28, 1946; admitted to bar, 1974, Oregon; 1975, U.S. Tax Court; 1985, Washington. *Education:* University of Michigan (B.B.A., with honors, 1970; J.D., 1973). Certified Public Accountant, Oregon, 1974. *Member:* Multnomah County and American (Member, Real Property, Probate and Trust Law Section; State of Oregon Chairman, Membership Committee, 1975-1976; Member, Professional Services Corporations Committee, 1977-1979; Taxation Section) Bar Associations; Oregon State Bar; Oregon Society of Certified Public Accountants (Chairman, Tax Forum Committee, 1977); American Institute of Certified Public Accountants. ***PRACTICE AREAS:*** Corporate; Real Estate; General and Business Law; Estate Planning. ***Email:*** rpalmer@lindsayhart.com

THOMAS E. McDERMOTT, born Darby, Pennsylvania, November 16, 1947; admitted to bar, 1976, Oregon. *Education:* Villanova University (A.B., 1969); Hastings College of the Law, University of California (J.D., 1976). Member: Thurston Society; Order of the Coif. Associate Editor, Hastings Law Journal, 1975-1976. Law Clerk to Justice Frank K. Richardson, California Supreme Court, 1975. *Member:* Oregon State Bar; Maritime Law Association of the United States. [Lt., U.S. Navy, 1969-1973]. ***PRACTICE AREAS:*** Civil Litigation; Maritime; Professional; Health Care. ***Email:*** tmcdermott@lindsayhart.com

WILLIAM M. TOMLINSON, born Paris, France, September 2, 1948; admitted to bar, 1974, Oregon; 1986, Washington. *Education:* Princeton University (B.A., 1970); University of Oregon (J.D., 1974). *Member:* Multnomah County and American (Member, Torts and Insurance Practice Section) Bar Associations; Oregon State Bar; Washington State Bar Association; Oregon Association of Defense Counsel. ***PRACTICE AREAS:*** Litigation; Labor; Longshore and Harborworkers Compensation Act; Products Defense; Maritime. ***Email:*** wtomlinson@lindsayhart.com

JAY W. BEATTIE, born Arcata, California, May 15, 1957; admitted to bar, 1987, Oregon; 1988, U.S. District Court, District of Oregon and U.S. Court of Appeals, Ninth Circuit; U.S. Supreme Court. *Education:* San Jose State University (B.A., with distinction, 1979); Northwestern School of Law of Lewis and Clark College (J.D., magna cum laude, 1987). Co-Author and Speaker: "Insurance Coverage Law in Oregon," N.B.I. Author, Chapter on Marine Insurance, OSB CLE Insurance Law. Co-Author Chapter "Compendium of Relevant Case Law," OSB CLE Appeal & Review, 2002. "Bad Faith Litigation in Oregon," N.B.I. Committee Member, *Multnomah Lawyer. Member:* Multnomah County and American Bar Associations; Oregon State Bar (Member, Executive Committee, Products Liability Section); Defense Research Institute. ***PRACTICE AREAS:*** Appeals; Products Liability; Insurance Defense; Maritime. ***Email:*** jbeattie@lindsayhart.com

ROY E. PULVERS, born New York, August 31, 1955; admitted to bar, 1983, Oregon, U.S. District Court, District of Oregon and U.S. Court of Appeals, Ninth and Tenth Circuits. *Education:* University of Michigan (B.A., 1980); Columbia University (J.D., 1983). Harlan Fiske Stone Scholar. Honors Attorney, Oregon Department of Justice, 1983-1984. Law Clerk to Judge Jonathan U. Newman, Oregon Court of Appeals, 1984-1985. Staff Attorney to the Oregon Supreme Court, 1989-1997. Adjunct Faculty (Constitutional Law and Law of Appellate Practice) Northwestern School of Law, Lewis & Clark College. Numerous speeches and publications, including the following. Author: "Separation of Powers Under the Oregon Constitution: A User's Guide," 75 Oregon Law Review 443 (1996). Co-Author:

(This Listing Continued)

"Compendium of Relevant Case Law" in Appeal and Review (Oregon State Bar 1993, 1998 Supp.) Member: Oregon State Board of Bar Examiners, 1990-1993; Director, Oregon Chapter, A.C.L.U. *Member:* Multnomah Bar Association; Oregon State Bar. ***PRACTICE AREAS:*** Civil Litigation; Appellate Practice; Antitrust. ***Email:*** rpulvers@lindsayhart.com

PAUL SILVER, born Detroit, Michigan, August 12, 1951; admitted to bar, 1978, Oregon and U.S. District Court, District of Oregon. *Education:* Michigan State University; Alma College (B.A., 1973); Willamette University (J.D., 1978). *Member:* Multnomah County Bar Association; Oregon State Bar. ***PRACTICE AREAS:*** Civil Litigation; Medical Malpractice; Products Liability. ***Email:*** psilver@lindsayhart.com

NIKOLA LYN JONES, born Anaheim, California, October 18, 1967; admitted to bar, 1994, Oregon; 1996, Colorado. *Education:* University of Colorado (B.A., 1989); Thomas M. Cooley Law School (J.D., 1994). ***PRACTICE AREAS:*** Civil Litigation; Medical Malpractice Defense; Professional Liability Defense. ***Email:*** njones@lindsayhart.com

ASSOCIATES

EDWARD T. TYLICKI, born September 17, 1967; admitted to bar, 1997, Oregon, U.S. District Court, District of Oregon and U.S. Court of Appeals, Ninth Circuit; 2000, Washington and U.S. District Court, Western District of Washington. *Education:* Georgetown University (B.S.F.S., 1989); Northwestern School of Law of Lewis and Clark College (J.D., 1997). Moot Court Honor Board. *Member:* Multnomah County Bar Association; American Inns of Court-Gus J. Solomon Chapter. ***PRACTICE AREAS:*** Civil Litigation. ***Email:*** etylicki@lindsayhart.com

DANIEL W. HOWARD, born Spokane, Washington, June 20, 1969; admitted to bar, 2000, Oregon and Washington. *Education:* University of Nebraska at Lincoln (B.A., with high distinction, 1997); University of Oregon (J.D., 2000). *Member:* Multnomah County Bar Association; Washington State Bar; Oregon State Bar. [U.S. Navy, 1987-1994]. ***PRACTICE AREAS:*** Civil Litigation; Products Liability; Maritime Law. ***Email:*** dhoward@lindsayhart.com

CORINNE SAM, born Harbor City, California, August 17, 1973; admitted to bar, 2000, Oregon. *Education:* University of California at Santa Barbara (B.A., with honors, 1995); Northwestern School of Law, Lewis & Clark (J.D., 1999). Managing Editor, Environmental Law, 1998-1999. Author, Environmental Law, Volume 29, Issue 1, 1999. *Member:* Oregon State Bar; Multnomah County Bar Association. ***PRACTICE AREAS:*** Civil Litigation. ***Email:*** csam@lindsayhart.com

JENNI E. MARSH, born Jackson, Michigan, July 10, 1976; admitted to bar, 2002, North Carolina; 2005, Oregon. *Education:* University of Oregon (B.S., Accounting, 1999); Boston College Law School (J.D., 2002). ***PRACTICE AREAS:*** Medical Malpractice; Professional Malpractice. ***Email:*** jmarsh@lindsayhart.com

JAMES P. McCURDY, born Brooklyn, New York, 1973; admitted to bar, 2004, Oregon. *Education:* Seattle University (B.A., 1996); University of Oregon (J.D., 2004).

OF COUNSEL

PAUL S. COSGROVE, born Seattle, Washington, August 5, 1952; admitted to bar, 1981, Oregon; 1984, Washington; 1986, U.S. Supreme Court. *Education:* Antioch College and Fairhaven College, Western Washington University (B.A., with honors, 1974); Northwestern School of Law of Lewis and Clark College (J.D., 1981). *Member:* Multnomah County and Washington State Bar Associations; Oregon State Bar. ***PRACTICE AREAS:*** Commercial Law; Consumer Finance Law; Bankruptcy Law; Government Relations; Regulatory; General Business. ***Email:*** pcosgrove@lindsayhart.com

PETER A. FRIEDMANN, born Seattle, Washington, September 13, 1952; admitted to bar, 1978, Washington; 1984, Oregon; 1986, District of Columbia. *Education:* University of Washington (B.A., 1975; J.D., 1978). (Resident, Washington, D.C. Office). ***PRACTICE AREAS:*** Federal Policy and Administration. ***Email:*** ourmanindc@aol.com

REPRESENTATIVE CLIENTS: Abbott Laboratories; ACI Corp.; Aluma Systems USA, Inc.; American Forest & Paper Association; American Honda Motor Co., Inc.; American International Insurance Group; American Isuzu Motors, Inc.; American Suzuki Motor Corp.; Archstone Communities Trust; Reebok International, Inc.; BP Amoco Corporation; Cardiac Pacemakers, Inc.; Cargill, Inc.; CNA Insurance Companies; The Church of Jesus Christ of Latter-Day Saints; Columbia Grain; Crowley Marine Services; Distilled Spirits Council of the U.S.; Firemen's Fund Insurance; Forest City Trading Group, Inc.; Foss Maritime; Guidant Corp.; Honda of American Manufacturing, Inc.; Honda Motor Co., Ltd.; Honeywell, Inc.; Insurance Corporation of British Columbia; JMJ Associates, Inc.; Jones Oregon Stevedoring Co.; Kawasaki Motors Corp., U.S.A.; Liberty International Underwriters; Lorillard Tobacco Company; Louis Dreyfus Corp.; Marine Office of America Corp.; Master Contracting Stevedore Association of the Pacific Coast, Inc.; Michelin North America, Inc.; Nationwide Insurance Company; Norcal Mutual Insurance Co.; Northwest Physicians Mutual Insurance Co.; Oregon Financial Services Assn.; Owens-Corning Fiberglas; Parks Corporation; Philip Morris USA Inc.; Port of Portland; Procter & Gamble Co.; R.J. Reynolds Tobacco Co.; Red Shield Insurance Co.; St. Paul Fire and Marine Ins. Co.; Sause Bros. Ocean Towing Co.; SC Johnson & Co.; Shipowners Mutual; Specialized Bicycle Components, Inc.; Stihl, Inc.; Suzuki Motor Corp.; Takata Corp.; TIG Insurance; Tracker Marine, L.P.; Trek Bicycle Co.; Uniroyal Goodrich Tire Company; United Grain Corp.; Utah Medical Insurance Association; Walsh Construction Co.; Washington Casualty; Westates Wood Products Co.; Woodbridge Financial.

LOOMIS & HOLLAND

PORTLAND, OREGON

(See Eugene)

Trial practice in State and Federal Courts, Medical Malpractice, Professional Liability, Insurance, Products Liability, Pharmaceutical and Toxic Tort Litigation, Business Litigation, Real Property, Family, Probate Law, Unsafe Products, Legal Malpractice, Personal Injury, Wrongful Death.

MARGER JOHNSON & McCOLLOM, P.C.

210 S.W. MORRISON STREET, SUITE 400
PORTLAND, OREGON 97204
Telephone: 503-222-3613
FAX: 503-274-4622
Email: info@techlaw.com
URL: http://www.techlaw.com

Vancouver, Washington Office: 5123 N.E. 94th Avenue, Suite C, 98662. Telephone: 360-260-3613. Fax: 360-695-0271.

Intellectual Property Law, Patents, Trademarks, Copyrights, Computers and Software, Trade Secrets, Licensing Agreements, Nanotechnology, Technology Licensing and Litigation.

FIRM PROFILE: Marger Johnson & McCollom, P.C. is a leading full-service intellectual property law firm specializing in patents, trademarks, copyrights, trade secrets and technology licensing, with particular expertise in prosecution, litigation and opinion work. With a stellar 18-year track record of securing intellectual property and transforming invention into advantage, the firm provides a visionary and comprehensive strategic counsel to top-tier clients in a wide variety of U.S. and foreign industries. With offices in Portland, Oregon and Vancouver, Washington, the firm's 20 attorneys are admitted to practice before the United States Patent and Trademark office, U.S. District Courts, Courts of Appeals, and the U.S. Supreme Court.

ALEXANDER C. JOHNSON, JR., born Richmond, Virginia, August 1, 1948; admitted to bar, 1978, Oregon and U.S. District Court, District of Oregon; 1983, U.S. Court of Appeals, Eighth Circuit; 1984, U.S. Court of Appeals for the Ninth and Federal Circuits; 2002, U.S. Supreme Court; registered to practice before U.S. Patent and Trademark Office. *Education:* The Citadel (B.S.E.E., 1970); Purdue University (M.S.E.E., 1974); Brigham Young University (J.D., cum laude, 1978). Tau Beta Pi. Member, The Order of Barristers (Member, Board of Advocates, 1976-1978). Author: "IC Design: Legal Protection, Pitfalls and Safe Harbors," IEEE Proceedings, 1986, Custom Circuits Conference and Journal of Semicustom ICs, Vol. 4, No. 4, June 1987; "Drafting Patents With a View To Litigation," Chapter 2, Intellectual Property Counseling and Litigation, edited by Horwitz and Horwitz, 1988, 1990 and 1997; *Intellectual Property Protection in the Semiconductor Industry,* Electronic Trend Publications, 1989. *Member:* Oregon State Bar (Member, Uniform State Laws Committee, 1983-1988; Chairman, 1988-1989); American Bar Association (Member, Sections on: Intellectual Property Law; Litigation); Oregon Patent Law Association; American Intellectual Property Lawyers Association; Institute of Electrical and Electronics Engineers. [U.S. Air Force (Active Duty, 1971-1975; Active Reserves, 1976-1982) Captain]. ***REPORTED CASES:*** In re Alappat, 31 USPQ 2d 1545 (Fed. Cir. 1994). ***PRACTICE AREAS:*** Patents; Trademarks; Copyrights; Unfair Competition; Trade Secrets; Litigation; Appellate Practice; Technology and Science. ***Email:*** alex@techlaw.com

ALAN T. McCOLLOM, born Bartlesville, Oklahoma, March 10, 1950; admitted to bar, 1977, Oklahoma; 1979, Oregon; registered to practice before U.S. Patent and Trademark Office. *Education:* Oklahoma State University (B.S.E.E., 1972); University of Oklahoma (J.D., 1977). Member, 1975-1977 and Research Editor, 1976-1977, Oklahoma Law Review. President: Oklahoma Patent Law Association (1987); Oregon Patent Law Association (1992). Author: "Protection of Intellectual Property Rights in Computer Programs," Computer Law, Oregon State Bar, 1992 (supplement 1994); "Litigating Copyright in Computer Programs," Litigation Journal, Oregon State Bar, 1991. Author and Speaker: "Drafting Dispute Resolution Clauses: International/Technology Focus," AAA CLE Seminar, 2003; "Patent, Copyright and Trade Secret Protection for Electronic Technology," IEEE NORTHCON/89, 1989. Speaker and Panelist: "Patent Opinion Letters," Fifth Lewis & Clark Law School Intellectual Property Conference, February, 2002. Special Master, Sole Arbitrator and Chair of Arbitration Panels. *Member:* Multnomah County, Oklahoma and American (Member, Sections on: Intellectual Property Law; Dispute Resolution) Bar Associations; Oregon State Bar (Member, ADR Section); American Intellectual Property Law Association (Member, ADR Committee); CPR Institute (Member, Technology and Oregon Panels); National Arbitration Forum (Member, Patent Panel); American Arbitration Association (Member, Technology and Domain Name Dispute Panels). ***PRACTICE AREAS:*** Patent Applications; Computer and Software Patents; Electronic Patents; Semiconductor Technology; Patent Litigation; Trademark Litigation; Copyright Litigation; Trade Secrets; Patent Prosecution; Patent Licensing; Patent Registration; Circuit and Network Patents; International Patents. ***Email:*** alan@techlaw.com

STEPHEN S. FORD, born Walla Walla, Washington, June 5, 1960; admitted to bar, 1992, Oregon and U.S. District Court, District of Oregon; 1993, Washington and Court of Appeals, Federal Circuit; registered to practice before U.S. Patent and Trademark Office. *Education:* Washington State University (B.S.E.E., 1983); University of Texas (M.S.E.E., 1988); Willamette University College of Law (J.D., 1992). Member, Institute of Electrical and Electronic Engineers, 1983. *Member:* Washington State, Federal and American (Member, Intellectual Property Law Section) Bar Associations; Oregon State Bar; Oregon Patent Law Association. ***PRACTICE AREAS:*** Patents; Trademarks; Copyrights; Intellectual Property; Litigation; Electronic Patents; Patent Applications. ***Email:*** steve@techlaw.com

SCOTT A. SCHAFFER, born Seattle, Washington, February 3, 1967; admitted to bar, 1994, Oregon; 1995, California, U.S. District Court, District of Oregon and U.S. Court of Appeals, Federal Circuit; registered to practice before U.S. Patent and Trademark Office. *Education:* Stanford University (B.S., Physics, 1989); University of Oklahoma (J.D., 1994). Member, Board of Editors, Oklahoma Law Review, 1992-1994. Extern, The Honorable Bana Blasedale of the U.S. District Court, Western District of Oklahoma. Lecturer, Computer Science Department, Portland State University. Author: "Domain Names Holders Bit by Trademark Law," Daily Journal of Commerce, 2003; "Startup gets small with archival technology," The Business Journal 20 (2004). Board Member, Oregon National History Museum. *Member:* Multnomah County and American (Member, Section on: Intellectual Property Law) Bar Associations; Oregon State Bar (Member, IP and Computer Law Sections); California State Bar (Member, Sections on: Intellectual Property Law; Litigation); Oregon Patent Legal Association (President, 1999-2000). ***PRACTICE AREAS:*** Patents; Trademarks; Copyrights; Unfair Competition; Intellectual Property; Trade Secrets; Internet Law; Litigation; Technology Licensing. ***Email:*** scott@techlaw.com

(This Listing Continued)

JOSEPH S. MAKUCH, born May 31, 1965; admitted to bar, 1995, Oregon and U.S. District Court, District of Oregon; 1999, U.S. Court of Appeals, Ninth Circuit; registered to practice before U.S. Patent and Trademark Office. *Education:* Case Western Reserve University (B.S.E.E., 1988); Lewis and Clark, Northwestern School of Law (J.D., 1995). Recipient, American Jurisprudence Award, first year appellate advocacy. Member, Oregon Patent Law Association, 1996—. *Member:* Oregon State Bar; Institute of Electrical and Electronics Engineers; Federal Bar Association; American bar Association (Member, Intellectual Property Law Section); American Intellectual Property Law Association. ***PRACTICE AREAS:*** Patents; Trademarks; Copyrights; Intellectual Property Litigation. ***Email:*** joe@techlaw.com

GRACIELA GOMEZ COWGER, born Mexicali, Mexico, March 14, 1966; admitted to bar, 1997, Oregon; registered to practice before the U.S. Patent and Trademark office. *Education:* San Diego State University (B.S.E.E., 1989); University of Washington (J.D., 1997). Member, Pacific Rim Law and Policy Journal, July 1996. *Member:* Hispanic and American Bar Associations; Institute of Electrical and Electronics Engineers. ***LANGUAGES:*** Spanish. ***PRACTICE AREAS:*** Patents; Trademarks; Copyrights; Intellectual Property. ***Email:*** graciela@techlaw.com

CRAIG R. ROGERS, born 1970; admitted to bar, 1998, Oregon; 1999, U.S. Court of Appeals, Federal Circuit; 2000, U.S. Court of Appeals, Ninth Circuit; registered to practice before U.S. Patent and Trademark Office; 2002, U.S. Supreme Court. *Education:* Brigham Young University (B.S.M.E, magna cum laude, 1994; J.D., summa cum laude, 1998). Law Clerk to the Honorable Randall Rader, U.S. Court of Appeals for the Federal Circuit. *Member:* Oregon State Bar. ***LANGUAGES:*** Afrikaans. ***PRACTICE AREAS:*** Intellectual Property; Litigation; Patents; Trademarks; Copyrights; Intellectual Property Licensing; Unfair Competition. ***Email:*** craig@techlaw.com

JULIE L. REED, born Richland, Washington, September 6, 1966; admitted to bar, 1995, Texas; 2001, Washington; registered to practice before the U.S. Patent and Trademark Office (Not admitted in Oregon). *Education:* Washington State University (B.S.E.E., 1988); University of Dallas (M.B.A., 1994); Southern Methodist University (J.D., 1995). Author: "Strategic Planning for IP," Oregon State Bar IP Newsletter Vol.3, No.1, Spring 2002. Adjunct Associate Professor, Portland State University School of Engineering and Technology Management, Portland State University, 2004. *Member:* American Intellectual Property Law Association; Washing State and American Bar Associations; Washing State Patent Law Association; National Association of Female Executives; IEEE. ***PRACTICE AREAS:*** Intellectual Property; Intellectual Property Portfolio Management; Patents; Electronics; Telecommunications Law; Wireless Communications; Digital Communications. ***Email:*** julie.reed@techlaw.com

ARIEL S. ROGSON, born Redwood City, California, September 2, 1969; admitted to bar, 1997, California; 1999, Oregon and Washington; registered to practice before U.S. Patent and Trademark Office. *Education:* California State University; University of California, Irvine (B.S./B.S., 1989); University of California, Los Angeles (M.S., 1992); University of California Davis School of Law (J.D., 1997). Phi Beta Kappa; Phi Delta Phi. Editor, Newsletter for the Los Angeles Chapter of ACM, 1992-1994. Member, Institute of Electrical and Electronics Engineers, 1995. Member, Association for Computing Machinery, 1989. *Member:* State Bar of California; Oregon State Bar; Washington State and American Bar Associations; American Intellectual Property Law Association. ***LANGUAGES:*** Spanish and Hebrew. ***PRACTICE AREAS:*** Patents; Intellectual Property; Trademarks; Copyrights; Trade Secrets; Internet Law. ***Email:*** ariel@techlaw.com

HOSOON LEE, born Seoul, Korea, November 8, 1964; admitted to bar, 1998, Oregon; registered to practice before the U.S. Patent and Trademark Office. *Education:* Yonsei University (B.S., 1991; M.S., 1993); Pierce Franklin Law Center (J.D., 1998). *Member:* Oregon State Bar. [Sgt., 8th Army, 1986-1988]. ***LANGUAGES:*** Korean and Japanese. ***PRACTICE AREAS:*** Patents; Intellectual Property; Trademarks; Intellectual Property Licensing; Copyrights; Trade Secrets. ***Email:*** hosoon@techlaw.com

HILLARY ANNE BROOKS, born Wiesbaden, Germany, January 17, 1970; admitted to bar, 1995, Texas; 1999, U.S. District Court, Northern District of Texas; 2000, U.S. Supreme Court; 2001, Oregon, Washington and U.S. District Court, District of Oregon; registered to practice before U.S. Patent and Trademark Office. *Education:* University of Washington (B.A., 1992); Southern Methodist University (J.D., 1995). Phi Beta Kappa; Phi Delta Phi. Winner, Jackson Walker Moot Court Competition. Articles Editor, The International Lawyer. ***PRACTICE AREAS:*** Patents; Copyrights; Trademarks; Litigation. ***Email:*** hillary@techlaw.com

---

TODD J. IVERSON, admitted to bar, 2002, Oregon. *Education:* University of Colorado at Boulder (B.S.E.E., 1994); University of Dayton (M.S., Electro-Optics, 1998); University of Oregon (J.D., 2002). [Captain, U.S. Air Force, 1995-1999]. ***PRACTICE AREAS:*** Intellectual Property; Patents; Trademarks. ***Email:*** todd@techlaw.com

JEFFREY JOHN RICHMOND, born Eugene, Oregon; admitted to bar, 2001, Oregon. *Education:* Oregon State University (B.S., 1998); Willamette University (J.D., 2001). ***PRACTICE AREAS:*** Intellectual Property. ***Email:*** jeff.richmond@techlaw.com

BRIAN G FORREST, born Alturas, California; admitted to bar, 2002, Oregon. *Education:* University of Washington (B.S., 1998); Northwestern School of Law (J.D., 2001). [U.S.M.C., 1988-1996]. ***LANGUAGES:*** English. ***PRACTICE AREAS:*** Patent Law; Copyright Law; Trademark Law. ***Email:*** brian@techlaw.com

JAMES A. HILSENTEGER, born Portland, Oregon; (admission pending); admitted to bar, registered to practice before U.S. Patent and Trademark Office. *Education:* Cornell University (B.S.M.E., 1989); Northwestern School of Law (J.D., 2004). ***Email:*** jimhilsenteger@techlaw.com

BRYAN D. KIRKPATRICK, born December 17, 1969; admitted to bar, 2004, Oregon. *Education:* Oregon State University (B.S., Nuclear Engineering, 1994); Lewis and Clark College (J.D., 2001). ***PRACTICE AREAS:*** Patents; Intellectual Property.

OF COUNSEL

JEROME S. MARGER, born Newark, New Jersey, January 17, 1941; admitted to bar, 1971, Oregon and U.S. District Court, District of Oregon; 1972, U.S. Court of Appeals, 9th

(This Listing Continued)

Circuit; registered to practice before U.S. Patent and Trademark Office. *Education:* New Jersey Institute of Technology (B.S.Ch. E., 1965); University of Louisville Law School (1965); Akron State University (J.D., 1970). *Member:* Multnomah County and American (Member, Intellectual Property Law Section) Bar Associations; Oregon State Bar (Member: Patent, Trademark and Copyright Section; Anti-Trust and Trademark Regulation Section); Oregon Patent Law Association (Secretary/Treasurer, 1975; Vice President 1976; President, 1977; Chairman, OPLA-WSPLA Joint Meeting, 1974-1993); American Chemical Society; Licensing Executives Society. ***PRACTICE AREAS:*** Intellectual Property; Patents; Trademarks; Copyrights; Intellectual Property Licensing. ***Email:*** jerry@techlaw.com

ELMER W. GALBI, born Vineland, New Jersey; admitted to bar, 1961, New York; 1962, District of Columbia; 1964, California; registered to practice before U.S. Patent and Trademark Office (Not admitted in Oregon). *Education:* Rutgers University (B.S., 1956); University of Illinois, Champaign/Urbana (M.S., 1957); Georgetown University (J.D., 1961). Tau Beta Pi; Eta Kappa Nu. Author: "Proposal for New Legislation to Protect Computer Programming," Bulletin-Copyright Society of the USA, pg. 280, 1971; "Unfair Competition Law in Protection of Program" IBM International Patent Quarterly, October, 1970; "Software and Patents: A Status Report," Communications of the ACM, April, 1971; "The Aftermath of the Benson & Tabbot Decision," Proceedings of the National Computer Conference, New York, N.Y., June, 1973; "Copyright and Unfair Competition Law as Applied to the Protection of Computer Programming," Computer Law Service, 1972; "The Prospect of Future Legislation and Court Action Concerning the Protection of Programming," Jurimetrics Journal, Summer, 1973; "The Aftermath of the Benson and Tabbot Decision," Computer Law Service, 1973. *Member:* New York State and American Bar Associations; The State Bar of California; District of Columbia Bar; Computer Law Association. ***PRACTICE AREAS:*** Intellectual Property (100%). ***Email:*** info@techlaw.com

PATENT AGENT

BRIAN D. WICHNER, born Los Angeles, California; admitted to bar, registered to practice before U.S. Patent and Trademark Office. *Education:* Oregon State University (PhD., 1998). Member, Lincoln County Planning Commission, 1994-1998. ***Email:*** wichner@techlaw.com

REPRESENTATIVE CLIENTS: Acres Gaming; Advanced Power Technology; Agilent; Analog Devices; Baker Hughes Inc.; Battelle Pacific Northwest Laboratories; Cisco Systems; Columbia Machine, Inc.; Cypress Semiconductor, Inc.; Digimarc Corporation; Elmers Restaurants, Inc.; Guillemot (formerly Thrustmaster, Inc.); Hanson Natural Resources Co.; Hewlett-Packard Co.; iMove; InControl Solutions, Inc.; Integrated Device Technology; Intel; Lattice Semiconductor Corp.; LaValley Industries, Inc.; Louisiana-Pacific Corp.; LSI Logic Corp.; McMenamins Pubs & Breweries; Novell; NSI; Oregon Health & Sciences University; Oregon State University; Osmetech plc; Oregon Graduate Institute; Oregon Medical Laser (Providence Health Systems); Samsung Electronics; Sharp Labs of America; Shurfine Foods; StanCorp: Tektronix, Inc.; Webridge; WebTrends; WebTrends/NetIQ; Western Wire Works.

MARKOWITZ, HERBOLD, GLADE & MEHLHAF, P.C.

3000 PACWEST CENTER
1211 SW FIFTH AVENUE
PORTLAND, OREGON 97204-3730
Telephone: 503-295-3085
FAX: 503-323-9105
URL: http://www.MarkowitzHerbold.com

Civil Litigation including Commercial, Insurance, Employment and Real Estate.

FIRM PROFILE: Markowitz, Herbold, Glade & Mehlhaf, P.C. is a specialty litigation firm with the professional resources and staffing to represent its clients effectively and efficiently in the mediation, arbitration, trial and appeal of the most demanding cases in both state and federal courts. The firm has represented diverse individuals and businesses in the prosecution and defense of all types of civil litigation ranging from extremely complex securities and professional malpractice actions to more conventional commercial and employment claims. Markowitz, Herbold, Glade & Mehlhaf, P.C. takes great pride in the quality of its legal services, which are designed to meet the specific needs of its clients.

SHAREHOLDERS

DAVID B. MARKOWITZ, born Chicago, Illinois, July 27, 1949; admitted to bar, 1974, Oregon and U.S. District Court, District of Oregon; 1983, U.S. Court of Appeals, Ninth Circuit; 1988, U.S. Supreme Court. *Education:* California State Polytechnic College (B.S., 1971); University of the Pacific, McGeorge School of Law (J.D., 1974). Special Legal Assistant, Nevada Supreme Court, 1974. Circuit Court Judge Pro Tem (civil cases only). *Member:* Multnomah County (Member, Board of Directors, 1990-1993) and Federal (Member, Oregon Chapter) Bar Associations; Oregon State Bar; Oregon Association of Defense Counsel; Oregon Trial Lawyers Association; American Inns of Court (Master, 1989—; President, 1991-1992); American Board of Trial Advocates. Fellow, American College of Trial Lawyers. Listed in Best Lawyers in America in Business Litigation, 1991—. ***PRACTICE AREAS:*** Commercial Litigation; Professional Malpractice Law; Employment Litigation; Employment Relations Litigation; Real Estate Litigation; Insurance Litigation; Trust Litigation. ***Email:*** DavidMarkowitz@mhgm.com

PETER H. GLADE, born Lafayette, Indiana, May 19, 1951; admitted to bar, 1979, Oregon and U.S. District Court, District of Oregon; 1980, U.S. Court of Appeals, Ninth Circuit; 1985, Washington; 1986, U.S. District Court, Western and Eastern Districts of Washington. *Education:* Indiana University (A.B., 1973); Northwestern School of Law of Lewis and Clark College (J.D., 1978). *Member:* Multnomah County, Washington State and American Bar Associations; Oregon State Bar; The Association of Trial Lawyers of America. ***PRACTICE AREAS:*** Commercial Litigation; Securities Litigation; Professional Malpractice Litigation; Business Torts; Real Estate Litigation. ***Email:*** PeterGlade@mhgm.com

WILLIAM N. MEHLHAF, born Corvallis, Oregon, June 11, 1950; admitted to bar, 1975, Oregon; 1977, U.S. District Court, District of Oregon; 1982, U.S. Court of Appeals, Ninth Circuit; 1985, Washington; 1986, U.S. Supreme Court and U.S. District Court, Western and Eastern Districts of Washington. *Education:* Oregon State University (B.A., 1972); Northwestern School of Law of Lewis and Clark College (J.D., 1975). *Member:* Multnomah County and Washington State Bar Associations; Oregon State Bar. ***PRACTICE AREAS:*** Commercial Litigation; Business Torts; Petroleum Marketing Law; Medical Law; Business Law; Corporate Law; Real Estate Litigation. ***Email:*** BillMehlhaf@mhgm.com

LYNN R. STAFFORD, born Portland, Oregon, July 9, 1949; admitted to bar, 1980, Virginia and Vermont; 1982, Oregon; 1984, U.S. District Court, District of Oregon. *Education:* University of California at Davis (B.A., 1970); George Mason University (J.D., cum laude, 1980). Editor, George Mason University Law Review, 1979. Adjunct Faculty, Northwestern School of Law, 1991. *Member:* Multnomah County Bar Association (Board of Directors, 1998-1999; Managing Shareholder, 1999—); Oregon State Bar. ***PRACTICE AREAS:*** Commercial Litigation; Professional Malpractice Litigation; Real Estate Law; Real Estate Litigation; Business Law. ***Email:*** LynnStafford@mhgm.com

LISA A. KANER, born Two Rivers, Wisconsin, December 14, 1960; admitted to bar, 1986, Pennsylvania; 1988, Oregon and U.S. District Court, District of Oregon; 2000, U.S. Court of Appeals, Ninth Circuit. *Education:* University of Edinburgh, Scotland; University of Pennsylvania (B.A., cum laude, 1983); Villanova University (J.D., magna cum laude, 1986). Associate Editor, Villanova Law Review. American Inns of Court (Master, Executive Committee). Law Clerk to Chief Judge Owen M. Panner, U.S. District Court, District of Oregon, 1986-1988. *Member:* Oregon State Bar. ***PRACTICE AREAS:*** Commercial Litigation; Securities Litigation; Professional Malpractice Litigation; Business Torts; Employment Litigation; Insurance Litigation; Civil Litigation. ***Email:*** LisaKaner@mhgm.com

LYNN R. NAKAMOTO, born Los Angeles, California, May 24, 1960; admitted to bar, 1986, New York; 1987, U.S. District Court, Southern and Eastern Districts of New York; 1988, Oregon and U.S. District Court, District of Oregon; 1991, U.S. Court of Appeals, Ninth Circuit. *Education:* University of California; Wellesley College (A.B., with honors, 1982); New York University (J.D., 1985). *Member:* Oregon State Bar; Oregon Trial Lawyers Association. ***PRACTICE AREAS:*** Employment Litigation; Civil Litigation; Civil Appeals. ***Email:*** LynnNakamoto@mhgm.com

JEFFREY M. EDELSON, born Philadelphia, Pennsylvania, January 14, 1961; admitted to bar, 1986, Pennsylvania and U.S. District Court, Eastern District of Pennsylvania; 1987, U.S. Court of Appeals, Third Circuit; 1988, Oregon and U.S. District Court, District of Oregon; 1993, U.S. Court of Appeals, Ninth Circuit. *Education:* Lafayette College (A.B., 1983); Villanova University (J.D., 1986). Law Clerk: Hon. George E. Juba (U.S. Magistrate); Hon. Robert C. Belloni (U.S. District Judge); Hon. Owen M. Panner (U.S. District Judge). Staff Attorney, Delaware County Legal Assistance Association, Chester, Pennsylvania. Staff Attorney, Marion-Polk Legal Aid Service, Salem, Oregon. Volunteer Attorney, Community Legal Services, Philadelphia, Pennsylvania. Member, Advisory Committee to Campaign for Equal Justice. *Member:* Multnomah County Bar Association (Member, Judicial Selection Committee); Oregon State Bar (Member, Oregon Bar Counsel on Disciplinary Matters). ***PRACTICE AREAS:*** Commercial Litigation; Trade Secrets; Noncompetition and Non-Solicitation Agreements; Employment Litigation. ***Email:*** JeffEdelson@mhgm.com

KERRY J. SHEPHERD, born Salem, Oregon, December 2, 1963; admitted to bar, 1989, Washington; 1994, Oregon. *Education:* Western Oregon State College (B.S., Business Admin., 1986); Willamette University College of Law (J.D., magna cum laude, 1989). Editor-in-Chief, Willamette Law Review, 1988-1989. *Member:* Oregon State Bar; Washington State Bar Association. ***PRACTICE AREAS:*** Commercial Litigation; Securities Litigation; Real Property Disputes; Product Liability; Professional Malpractice Litigation. ***Email:*** KerryShepherd@mhgm.com

JEFFREY M. BATCHELOR, born Portland, Oregon, February 20, 1946; admitted to bar, 1972, Oregon. *Education:* Oklahoma State University; Brigham Young University (B.S., 1969); Willamette University (J.D., cum laude, 1972). Member, Alternative Dispute Resolution Section, Executive Committee, 2004—. Member, Owen M. Panner American Inn of Court. Member, Oregon Rules of Appellate Procedure Committee, 1990-1996. Mediator, Oregon Court of Appeals Settlement Conference Program, 1995—. Oregon Circuit Judge Pro Tempore, 1993-2000. Fellow, American Academy of Appellate Lawyers (Member, Board of Directors, 1996-2000). Listed, *The Best Lawyers in America. Member:* Oregon State Bar (Member, Appellate Practice Section, Chair, 2002). ***REPORTED CASES:*** Pool v. VanRheen, 297 F.3d 899 (9th Cir. 2002); Westar Electric Co. v. Westar Acquisition Corp., 177 Or. App. 174, 33 P.3d 718 (2001); Portland 76 Auto/Truck Plaza, Inc. v. Union Oil Co. of California, 153 F.3d 938 (9th Cir. 1998); Ainslie v. First Interstate Bank of Oregon, 148 Or. App. 162, 939 P.2d 125 (1997); McGanty v. Staudenraus, 321 Or. 532, 901 P.2d 841 (1995); In Re Bergsoe Metal Corp., 910 F.2d 668 (9th Cir. 1990). ***Email:*** JeffBatchelor@mhgm.com

PAUL S. BIERLY, born La Grande, Oregon, July 16, 1960; admitted to bar, 1990, Washington; 1994, Alaska and U.S. District Court, District of Alaska; 1995, Oregon, U.S. District Court, District of Oregon; 1998, U.S. District Court, Western District of Washington, U.S. Court of Appeals, Ninth Circuit and U.S. Tax Court. *Education:* University of Washington (B.A., 1982); University of Puget Sound (J.D., cum laude, 1990). Law Clerk to Hon. H. Russel Holland, Chief Judge, District of Alaska, 1991-1994. Law Clerk to Hon. Charles K. Cranston, Superior Court Judge, Kenai, Alaska, 1990-1991. Member, Oregon Board of Bar Examiners, 2002-2004. *Member:* Washington State and Alaska Bar Associations; Oregon State Bar. ***REPORTED CASES:*** Hofsheier v. Farmers Insurance Exchange, 154 Or. App. 538, 963 P.2d 48 (1998); Chale v. Allstate, 353 F.3d 742 (9th Cir 2003); Truck Ins. Exch. v. BRE Properties, Inc., 81 P.2d 929 (Wash. App. 2003). ***PRACTICE AREAS:*** Litigation; Appellate Practice. ***Email:*** PaulBierly@mhgm.com

MATTHEW A. LEVIN, born Detroit, Michigan, December 18, 1968; admitted to bar, 1995, Michigan and U.S. District Court, Eastern District of Michigan; 2000, Oregon and Washington. *Education:* University of Michigan at Ann Arbor (B.S., 1991; J.D., cum laude, 1994). *Member:* Oregon State Bar; Washington State and Oakland County Bar Associations; State Bar of Michigan; Owen Panner Inns of Court. ***PRACTICE AREAS:*** Litigation; Real Estate; Corporate Law. ***Email:*** MattLevin@mhgm.com

(This Listing Continued)

MARKOWITZ, HERBOLD, GLADE & MEHLHAF, P.C., Portland—Continued

CHARLES J. PATERNOSTER, born Elmira, New York, May 17, 1971; admitted to bar, 1998, New York and U.S. District Court, Western and Northern Districts of New York; 2002, Oregon and U.S. District Court, District of Oregon. *Education:* Colgate University (B.A., 1993); University of Pittsburgh at Pittsburgh (J.D., 1998). *Member:* Oregon State Bar; New York State Bar Association. ***PRACTICE AREAS:*** Commercial Litigation. ***Email:*** ChipPaternoster@mhgm.com

MATTHEW D. LARSON, born Portland, Oregon, September 17, 1975; admitted to bar, 2003, Oregon. *Education:* Washington State University (B.A., 1997); Northwestern School of Law of Lewis and Clark College (J.D., 2003). ***PRACTICE AREAS:*** Business Litigation. ***Email:*** MattLarson@mhgm.com

OF COUNSEL

CHRISTINE T. HERRICK, born New York, N.Y., October 20, 1949; admitted to bar, 1975, Oregon. *Education:* Mount Holyoke College; Sarah Lawrence College (B.A., 1971); Northwestern School of Law of Lewis and Clark College (J.D., 1975). Lecturer, Fundamentals of Collective Bargaining, University of Oregon, Eugene, Oregon, 1982. Hearings Officer, Oregon Employment Relations Board, 1975-1982. Labor Arbitrator, 1982-1984. *Member:* Multnomah County Bar Association; Oregon State Bar (Member, Executive Committee, 1978-1980, Labor Law Section). ***PRACTICE AREAS:*** Commercial Litigation; Employment Law. ***Email:*** ChrisHerrick@mhgm.com

REPRESENTATIVE CLIENTS: Agassi Enterprises, Inc.; Assoociated Business Systems; AVIA International Group, Inc.; Boise Cascade Corporation; The Durst Organization, Inc.; 7-Eleven, Inc.; Equifax, Inc.; First Health Group, Corp.; Fleishman-Hillard Co.; Hollywood Entertainment Corp.; Home Depot; D.R. Horton, Inc.; International Association of Machinists and Aerospace Workers; Industrial Lumber Co.; Kpff Consulting Engineers; Matsushita Electronic Materials, Inc.; The May Department Stores Co. dba Meier & Frank Company; Medical Management Online, Inc.; Medtronic Sofamor Danek, Inc.; Mittleman Properties; National Food Processors Assn.; Nations Bank; Oakley, Inc.; Oil Can Henry's; Paragano Enterprises; Portland General Corporation; Property Management Services, Inc.; Reebok; S&W Fine Foods, Inc.; Scott USA; SONY Online Entertainment Corp.; SONY Pictures Entertainment, Inc.; United Western Grocers, Inc.; Vancouver Mall.

MARSH, HIGGINS, BEATY & HATCH, P.C.

PORTLAND, OREGON

(See Vancouver, Washington)

General Civil and Criminal Trial Practice. Negligence and Personal Injury, Domestic Relations, Probate, Estate Planning, Real Estate, Corporation, Workers Compensation and Bankruptcy Law. Employment and Labor Law, Auto Accidents, Slip and Fall, Discrimination, Wrongful Termination, Sexual Harassment, Wills, Trusts, Elder Law, Wrongful Death, Dog Bites, Divorce, Child Custody, Child Support, Visitation Rights, Adoption Law.

MARTIN, BISCHOFF, TEMPLETON, LANGSLET & HOFFMAN, LLP

Established in 1918

900 PIONEER TOWER
888 S.W. FIFTH
PORTLAND, OREGON 97204
Telephone: 503-224-3113
Fax: 503-224-9471
URL: http://www.martinbischoff.com

Anchorage, Alaska Office: 425 G Street, Suite 910, 99501. Telephone: 907-276-1277.

General Civil and Trial Practice in all State and Federal Courts of Oregon, Washington and Alaska. Insurance Defense and Coverage, Aviation, Products Liability, Business Planning, Employment, Estate Planning and Probate, Tax, Real Estate, Financial Institutions, Creditors Rights, Admiralty, Commercial and Real Property Litigation and Transactions and Federal and State Civil Appeals.

MEMBERS OF FIRM

JOHN L. LANGSLET, born Portland, Oregon, July 16, 1944; admitted to bar, 1972, Oregon and U.S. District Court, District of Oregon; 1973, U.S. Court of Appeals, 9th Circuit; 1975, U.S. Claims Court; 1984, U.S. Supreme Court. *Education:* University of Oregon and Portland State University (B.S., with honors, 1966); Boalt Hall School of Law, University of California (J.D., with honors, 1972). Order of the Coif. Member, 1989-1991 and Chairman, 1991-1992, Oregon State Board of Bar Examiners. *Member:* Multnomah County and American Bar Associations; Oregon State Bar (Member, Disciplinary Board, 2002-2004); American Judicature Society; Oregon Association of Defense Counsel (Federal Practice and Procedure Committee). ***PRACTICE AREAS:*** Insurance Coverage; Insurance Defense; Commercial Litigation; Financial Institutions Litigation. ***Email:*** jlangslet@martinbischoff.com

JONATHAN M. HOFFMAN, born Oakland, California, February 7, 1948; admitted to bar, 1975, Oregon; 1988, Alaska; U.S. Court of Appeals, 6th, 9th and 10th Circuits; U.S. District Court, District of Oregon; U.S. District Court, District of Alaska. *Education:* Harvard College (A.B., magna cum laude, 1970); University of Oregon (J.D., 1975). *Member:* Multnomah County, Federal (President, Portland Chapter, 1988-1989), Alaska and American (Chair, Automobile Law Committee, Tort and Insurance Practice Section, 1990-1991) Bar Associations; Oregon State Bar (Chair, Aviation Section, 1990-1991); Oregon Association of Defense Counsel (President, 2000); Product Liability Advisory Council; Northwest Aviation Insurance Association (Chair, 1991-1993). ***PRACTICE AREAS:*** Products Liability; Aviation Law; Tort Defense. ***Email:*** jhoffman@martinbischoff.com

(This Listing Continued)

JAMES C. HOWE, born Sturgeon Bay, Wisconsin, November 8, 1955; admitted to bar, 1980, Oregon and U.S. District Court, District of Oregon, 1988,U.S. Tax Court. *Education:* University of Oregon (B.S., 1977); University of Washington (J.D., with high honors, 1980). Phi Beta Kappa; Order of the Coif; Order of the Barristers. Editor-in-Chief, Washington Law Review, 1979-1980. Vice-Chair, Moot Court Honor Board, 1979-1980. *Member:* Multnomah County Bar Association; Oregon State Bar; Estate Planning Counsel of Portland. ***PRACTICE AREAS:*** Trusts and Estates; Business Law; Real Estate. ***Email:*** jhowe@martinbischoff.com

JOHN W. KNOTTNERUS, born Havre, Montana, February 29, 1964; admitted to bar, 1989, Oregon; U.S. District Court, District of Oregon; 1993, Washington; 1994, U.S. District Court, District of Washington, U.S. District Court, District of Alaska and U.S. Court of Appeals, Ninth Circuit; 2000, Alaska and U.S. District Court, District of Alaska. *Education:* University of Montana (B.A., with honors, 1986); University of Oregon (J.D., 1989). Order of the Coif. *Member:* Oregon State Bar; Washington State, Alaska and American Bar Associations; Defense Research Institute; Product Liability Advisory Council; Oregon Association of Defense Counsel (Chair, Product Liability Committee); Washington Defense Trial Lawyers Association. ***PRACTICE AREAS:*** Products Liability; Litigation; Insurance. ***Email:*** jknottnerus@martinbischoff.com

MARY-ANNE S. RAYBURN, born Detroit, Michigan, November 2, 1955; admitted to bar, 1980, Oregon; U.S. District Court, District of Oregon; 1990, Washington. *Education:* Portland State University (B.A., 1977); Willamette University (J.D., 1980). *Member:* Multnomah County, Washington State and American Bar Associations; Oregon State Bar (Member, Board of Bar Examiners, 1993-1995); Oregon Association of Defense Counsel; Defense Research Institute. ***PRACTICE AREAS:*** Products Liability; Tort Defense; Wrongful Termination Defense. ***Email:*** mrayburn@martinbischoff.com

JAMES T. DUNN, born Lawrence, Massachusetts, September 8, 1946; admitted to bar, 1971, Oregon; 1972, U.S. District Court, District of Oregon and U.S. Tax Court. *Education:* Boston College (B.S., cum laude, 1968); University of Notre Dame (J.D., 1971). Beta Gamma Sigma. Member, Notre Dame Law Review, 1970-1971. *Member:* Multnomah County and American Bar Associations; Oregon State Bar. ***PRACTICE AREAS:*** Business Law; Banking Law; Trusts and Estates; Real Estate; Tax Law. ***Email:*** jdunn@martinbischoff.com

DOUGLAS G. PICKETT, born Enid, Oklahoma, March 12, 1953; admitted to bar, 1981, Oregon and U.S. District Court, District of Oregon; 1986, Washington, U.S. Court of Appeals, Ninth Circuit and U.S. District Court, Eastern District of Washington; 1987, U.S. District Court, Western District of Washington. *Education:* Portland State University (B.A., 1975); University of Texas at Austin (M.A., 1978); University of Oregon (J.D., 1981). Phi Kappa Phi. *Member:* Washington State and American Bar Associations; Oregon State Bar. ***PRACTICE AREAS:*** Real Estate; Commercial Transactions; Creditors Rights; Commercial Litigation. ***Email:*** dgpickett@martinbischoff.com

PHILIP A. RUSH, born Washington, D.C., April 25, 1956; admitted to bar, 1988, California; 1989, Oregon and U.S. District Court, District of Oregon; 1990, Washington; 2002, Alaska. *Education:* California Maritime Academy (B.S., 1979); Golden Gate University (J.D., 1988); Tulane University of Louisiana (LL.M., Admiralty Law, 1989). Second Mate, Unlimited, U.S. Merchant Marine. Adjunct Professor, Aviation Law, Lewis Clark School of Law. *Member:* Washington State, Alaska and American Bar Associations; Oregon State Bar; State Bar of California. ***PRACTICE AREAS:*** Aviation Law; Products Liability; Admiralty Law; Tort Defense. ***Email:*** prush@martinbischoff.com

MICHAEL J. FARRELL, born Washington, D.C., April 2, 1964; admitted to bar, 1989, Washington; 1990, Oregon; U.S. District Court, District of Oregon; U.S. District Court, Eastern and Western Districts of Washington. *Education:* University of Oregon (B.A., 1986); University of London; Columbus School of Law, Catholic University (J.D., 1989); Georgetown University Law Center (LL.M., 1990). *Member:* Washington State (Member, Sections on: Taxation; Creditor/Debtor) and American Bar Associations; Oregon State Bar (Member, Sections On: Taxation; Creditor/Debtor). ***PRACTICE AREAS:*** Litigation; Financial Institutions Law; Creditors Rights; Commercial Transactions; Real Estate. ***Email:*** mfarrell@martinbischoff.com

SCOTT A. KAMIN, born Portland, Oregon, July 1, 1948; admitted to bar, 1976, Oregon, U.S. District Court, District of Oregon and U.S. Tax Court; 2003, Washington. *Education:* University of Oregon (B.S.); Northwestern School of Law (J.D., with honors, 1976). Member, MENSA. Listed, Who's Who in American Law. *Member:* Oregon State Bar (Member, Sections on: Business; Debtor-Creditor; Estate Planning and Administration; Real Estate and Land Use; Taxation; Member, IRS Liaison Subcommittee, Tax Section, 1990-2001; Elder Law Section; Computer Technology Subcommittee, 1998-2000; Continuing Legal Education Advising Professionals, 1992); Multnomah County and Washington State (Member, Real Property, Probate and Trust Section) Bar Associations. ***PRACTICE AREAS:*** Taxation; Commercial Real Estate; Trusts and Estates; Business Law. ***Email:*** skamin@martinbischoff.com

JUSTIN M. THORP, born Eugene, Oregon, June 9, 1972; admitted to bar, 1997, Oregon; 1998, U.S. District Court, District of Oregon and U.S. Court of Appeals, Ninth Circuit; 1999, Washington. *Education:* Willamette University (B.A., cum laude, 1994); University of Oregon (J.D., 1997). Order of the Coif. *Member:* Oregon State Bar; Washington State Bar Association. ***PRACTICE AREAS:*** Litigation; Products Liability; Insurance Coverage; Appellate Practice. ***Email:*** jthorp@martinbischoff.com

ASSOCIATES

JESSICA CARPENTER, born Shreveport, Louisiana, May 25, 1962; admitted to bar, 1997, Arizona; 2001, Oregon and U.S. District Court, District of Oregon. *Education:* University of Kansas (B.A., with honors and distinction, 1984; M.A., 1987); Arizona State University (J.D., cum laude, 1997). Phi Beta Kappa. *Member:* Multnomah County and American Bar Associations; Oregon Women Lawyers Association; Defense Research Institute; Oregon Association of Defense Counsel. ***LANGUAGES:*** French and Spanish. ***PRACTICE AREAS:*** Commercial Litigation; Insurance Coverage; Employment Law; ERISA Litigation. ***Email:*** jcarpenter@martinbischoff.com

MARJA E. SELMANN, born Williston, North Dakota, January 26, 1970; admitted to bar, 1996, Washington; 1998, Alaska; 2003, Oregon. *Education:* Pacific Lutheran Univer-

(This Listing Continued)

sity (B.A., magna cum laude, 1992); University of Washington (J.D., with honors, 1995). Order of the Coif. Articles Executive Editor, Washington Law Review. *Member:* Multnomah County and American Bar Associations; Oregon Women Lawyers. ***PRACTICE AREAS:*** Litigation; Products Liability; Insurance Coverage; Employment Law. ***Email:*** mselmann@martinbischoff.com

AARON C. DENTON, born Camp Lejeune, North Carolina, April 24, 1971; admitted to bar, 2002, Oregon. *Education:* University of Kansas (B.A., 1994); University of Minnesota, Minneapolis (J.D., cum laude, 2002). *Member:* Multnomah Bar Association; Oregon State Bar. ***PRACTICE AREAS:*** Insurance Coverage; Products Liability; Insurance Defense. ***Email:*** adenton@martinbischoff.com

CAMILLE TOURJÉ, born Minneapolis, Minnesota, August 7, 1974; admitted to bar, 2001, Oregon and U.S. District Court, District of Oregon. *Education:* Oberlin College (B.A., 1996); Case Western Reserve University (J.D., cum laude, 2001). *Member:* Multnomah Bar Association; Oregon Association of Defense Counsel; Oregon Women Lawyers. ***PRACTICE AREAS:*** Insurance Defense; Litigation; Products Liability; Insurance Coverage; Civil Litigation. ***Email:*** ctourje@martinbischoff.com

STEPHEN P. YOSHIDA, born Honolulu, Hawaii, November 6, 1978; admitted to bar, 2004, Oregon. *Education:* University of Portland (B.A., 2001); University of Oregon School of Law (J.D., 2004). Order of the Coif. ***PRACTICE AREAS:*** Insurance Defense; Products Liability. ***Email:*** syoshida@martinbischoff.com

REPRESENTATIVE CLIENTS: *Insurance:* Allianz Insurance Company; British Aviation Insurance Company Ltd; CIGNA Property and Casualty Insurance Company; Global Aerospace Underwriting Managers Limited; Lexington Insurance Company; Media/Professional Insurance Agency, Inc.; Liberty Northwest/North Pacific Insurance Company; Old Republic Surety Company; OneBeacon Insurance; Oregon Insurance Guaranty Association; St. Paul Reinsurance Company Limited; Terra Nova Insurance Company Limited; TM Claims Service, Inc.; Tokio Marine and Fire Insurance Company, Ltd.; Tokio Marine Management, Inc.; The Travelers; Underwriters at Lloyd's London; United States Aviation Underwriters, Inc.; Universal Loss Management, Inc.; Zurich London, Ltd.
GENERAL: Alpha Community Development; Andersen Windows, Inc.; Bank of America; Baxter Healthcare, Inc.; Bell Helicopter Textron, Inc.; Black & Decker (U.S.), Inc.; BMW Motor Cars; Chase Manhattan Bak USA, N.A.; Chase Manhattan Mortgage Corporation; Chrysler Corporation; Citigroup; Citicorp; Continental Tire; Ease Software, Inc.; Electronic Diversified, Inc.; Farwest Electric, Inc.; FMC Corporation; Fuji Heavy Industries; General Electric Co.; General Motors Corporation; H.W. Metal Products, Inc.; Harley Davidson Motor Co. Group, Inc.; Hessell Enterprises, Inc.; Honda North America, Inc.; J.B. Hunt Transport, Inc.; Hyundai Motor America; Mazda Motor Corp.; Mercedes-Benz of North America, Inc.; Mitsubishi Motor Sales of America; Multnomah County; National Mortgage Co.; Nissan North America; Ocwen Federal Bank, FSB; Porsche Cars North America, Inc.; Robinson Helicopter Co., Inc.; Rockwell International Corp.; Shore Bank Pacific; Subaru of America; Suzuki Motor Co., Ltd.; Toyota Motor Sales, USA; TRW, Inc.; Tyco International, Inc.; Volvo Trucks North America; Warn Industries; Yamaha Motor Corporation, U.S.A.

MARVIN, CHORZEMPA & LARSON, P.C.

Established in 1990

SELLWOOD BUILDING, SUITE 300
380 S.E. SPOKANE STREET
PORTLAND, OREGON 97202-6464
Telephone: 503-232-1410
Fax: 503-234-1824
Email: jhmarvin@mca-law.com
URL: http://www.lawyers.com/marvinchorzempa

Civil Trial in Federal And State Courts representing the Design and Construction Industry, Products Liability, Subsurface Litigation, Toxic Torts, Professional Liability, Estate Planning, Personal Injury, Mediation and Arbitration.

FIRM PROFILE: Marvin, Chorzempa & Larson, P.C., was formed as James H. Marvin P.C. in 1990 as a firm specializing in architects and engineers professional liability, construction and contract litigation, insurance defense and negligence. We are a four lawyer firm emphasizing construction law, contract drafting and negotiation, architect and engineer professional liability, insurance defense, litigation, arbitration and mediation. We practice in both state and federal courts with licenses in Oregon, Washington, Arizona and Massachusetts. The firm provides a wide range of legal services for the design and construction community as well as services for small businesses and individuals. Our services include forming businesses, general business advice, collection and litigation. All members of the firm participate in continuing education classes, professional organizations and are active in the community.

We work with our clients as a team. It is our goal to keep our clients informed during all phases of legal representation by providing legal analysis and day-to-day correspondence so they can make informed decisions. Clients are provided status letters and participate in making decisions as to how their legal matters will be handled. While our firm does litigation, arbitrations and mediations, we also work with our clients in legal risk management by providing seminars addressing specific client needs.

JAMES H. MARVIN, admitted to bar, 1972, Oregon and U.S. District Court, District of Oregon; U.S. Court of Appeals, Ninth Circuit; 2003, Washington and U.S. District Court, District of Washington. *Education:* Washington State University (B.S., 1965); Northwestern College of Law, Lewis and Clark College (J.D., 1972). *Member:* Multnomah County and American Bar Associations; Oregon State Bar (Member, Construction Law and Litigation Sections); Oregon Association of Defense Counsel; American Council of Engineering Companies of Oregon. ***PRACTICE AREAS:*** Construction and Design Law; Insurance Law; Tort Law; Mediation; Arbitration; Oil and Gas Leases. ***Email:*** jhmarvin@mca-law.com

JANELLE E. CHORZEMPA, admitted to bar, 1990, Oregon and U.S. District Court, District of Oregon; 2002, Washington and U.S. District Court, District of Washington. *Education:* University of Minnesota (B.A., 1972); University of Oregon (Masters of Architecture, 1976); Northwestern School of Law, Lewis and Clark College (J.D., 1990). *Member:* Multnomah County Bar Association; Oregon State Bar (Chairperson, Construction Law Section; Member, Law Practice Management and Estate Planning Sections); American Institute of Architects; Construction Specifications Institute. ***PRACTICE AREAS:*** Construction and Design Law; Personal Injury; Estate Planning; Business Law; Products Liability. ***Email:*** chorzempa@mca-law.com

JON C. LARSON, admitted to bar, 1989, Arizona and U.S. District Court, District of Arizona; 1997, Oregon and U.S. District Court, District of Oregon; 2003, Washington and U.S. District Court, District of Washington. *Education:* St. John's University (B.A., 1986); University of Minnesota (J.D., 1989). *Member:* Multnomah County, Washington State and American Bar Associations; Oregon State Bar (Member, Construction Law Section); Arizona State Bar; American Council of Engineering Companies of Oregon. ***PRACTICE AREAS:*** Commercial Litigation; Insurance Litigation; Tort Litigation; Construction Litigation; Design Professional Liability. ***Email:*** jclarson@mca-law.com

---

LISA M. GRAMP, admitted to bar, 2004, Oregon and Massachusetts. *Education:* Graduate School of Design at Harvard University (M.A., Architecture, Landscape, 1997); Northeastern University (J.D., 2002). *Member:* Multnomah County Bar Association; Oregon State Bar (Member, Sections on: Construction Law; Real Estate Land Use); Commonwealth of Massachusetts Bar; American Institute of Architects; American Planning Association; American Society of Landscape Architects. ***PRACTICE AREAS:*** Land Use; Real Estate; Construction Law.

REPRESENTATIVE CLIENTS: *Insurance Clients:* Admiral Insurance Company; C.R. Vince & Associates; Great American Insurance Services; Hartford Insurance; Horace Mann Insurance Company; Kemper Insurance Company; Lloyds of London; Shand Morahan; Risk Administration & Management (RA&MCO) Insurance Company; Terra Insurance Company; XL Design Professional and Zurich-North American. *Design Professional Clients:* Alpha Community Development, Inc.; AMEC Earth and Environmental, Inc.; CBG Consulting Engineers; Dull Olson Weekes Architects, P.C.; Fletcher, Farr, Ayotte Architecture Planning Interiors, P.C.; Kleinfelder, Inc.; LRS Architects; Moffatt, Nichol & Bonney, Inc.; Northwest Geotech, Inc.; Seton, Johnson & Odell Consulting Engineering, Inc.; Sienna Architecture; Squier\Kleinfelder, Inc.

HARRIS S. MATARAZZO

121 S.W. MORRISON AVENUE, SUITE 1020
PORTLAND, OREGON 97204
Telephone: 503-226-0306
FAX: 503-226-4290

Mental Health Issues related to Criminal Defense; Administrative Law; Appellate; Probate and Estate Planning.

HARRIS S. MATARAZZO, born Portland, Oregon, July 24, 1957; admitted to bar, 1986, Oregon, U.S. District Court, District of Oregon and U.S. Court of Appeals, Ninth Circuit; 1992, U.S. Supreme Court. *Education:* Brown University (A.B., 1979); Northwestern School of Law (J.D., 1983). Co-Author, "Mental Illness and Incapacity," in Continuing Legal Education "Criminal Law" Handbook, Oregon State Bar, 1994, 1998, 2005. Speaker, "State of Mind" Conference, Oregon Criminal Defense Lawyers Association, 1990; "Mental Health and the Law," Conference, 1995, 1996; "Mental Health and Ethical Issues in Dealing with the Mentally Ill," OLDLA Conference, 1999. *Member:* Multnomah County, Federal and American Bar Associations; Oregon State Bar; Oregon Criminal Defense Lawyers Association. ***REPORTED CASES:*** Ventris v. Maas, 781 P2d 381 (1989); Lovette v. PSRB, 795 P2d 587 (1990); Martin v. PSRB, 797 P2d 587 (1990); Bahrenfus, et al. v. Bachik, 806 P2d 170 (1991); Martin v. PSRB, 312 Or 157, 818 P2d 1264 (1991); Hodgin v. PSRB, 833 P2d 351 (1992); Garcia v. PSRB, 843 P2d 465 (1992); Strecker v. PSRB, 116 Or App 553 (1992), rev'd 120 Or App 178 (1993); Brumnett v. PSRB, 315 Or 402, 949 P2d 1194 (1991); Osborn v. PSRB, 851 P2d 1151 (1993); Strecker v. PSRB, 851 P2d 1151 (1993); Cramer v. PSRB, 857 P2d 232 (1993); Cook v. PSRB, 860 P2d 855 (1993); Stewart v. PSRB, 864 P2d 880 (1993); Hodgin v. PSRB, 873 P2d 466 (1994); Osborn v. PSRB, 898 P2d 789 (1995); Rios v. PSRB, 898 P2d 799 (1995); Drew v. PSRB, 322 Or 491, 909 P2d 211 (1996); McGowan v. PSRB, 324 Or 17, 920 P2d 153 (1996); ; State v. Bozman, 929 P2d 1019 (1996); McGowen v. PSRB, 934 P2d 609 (1997); Menzl v. PSRB, 325 Or 159, 934 P2d 431 (1997); Rios v. PSRB, 325 Or 151, 934 P2d 399 (1997); Osborn v. PSRB, 325 Or 332, 937 P2d 1028 (1997); Mueller v. PSRB, 325 Or 332, 937 P2d 1028 (1997); Einstein v. PSRB, 958 P2d 843 (1998); Strecker v. PSRB, 960 P2d 893 (1998); Hanson v. PSRB, 156 Or App 198 (1998); Beiswenger v. PSRB 970 P.2d 229 (1998); Osborn v. PSRB, 15 P.3d 80 (2000); Hanson v. PSRB, 19 P.3d 350 (2001); State v. Hedgecock, 21 P.3d 137 (2001); Rios v. PSRB, 30 P.3d 1227 (2001); Romanov v. PSRB 38 P.3d 965 (2002); Tharp v. PSRB 72 P.3d 1011 (2003); Beiswenger v. PSRB 84 P.3d 180 (2003); Laing v. PSRB 86 P.3d 100 (2004); Ashcroft v. PSRB 86 P.3d 102 (2004); Steward v. PSRB (Aug. 2004). ***PRACTICE AREAS:*** Administrative and Mental Health; Appellate; Business; Criminal; Probate; Estate Planning.

LAWRENCE MATASAR, P.C.

SUITE 1025
621 SOUTHWEST MORRISON STREET
PORTLAND, OREGON 97205
Telephone: 503-222-9830
Fax: 503-274-8575
Email: larry@pdxlaw.com
URL: http://www.lawyers.com/matasar

Criminal Defense, Fraud Environmental Crimes, White Collar Crimes, Narcotics Drug Crimes, Appellate Practice.

LAWRENCE MATASAR, born Chicago, Illinois, September 25, 1949; admitted to bar, 1974, Oregon and U.S. District Court, District of Oregon; 1977, U.S. Court of Appeals, Ninth Circuit; 1986, U.S. Supreme Court. *Education:* Wharton School of Finance and Commerce, University of Pennsylvania (B.S., cum laude, 1971); University of Pennsylvania Law School (J.D., 1974). Staff Attorney, Legal Services of Portland, 1974-1976; Senior Staff Attorney, Prisoners Legal Services, 1976-1979; Trial Attorney, Metropolitan Public Defender, 1979-1981; Partner, Hoffman & Matasar, 1981-1997. Speaker at numerous con-

(This Listing Continued)

(This Listing Continued)

LAWRENCE MATASAR, P.C., Portland—Continued

ferences, including: trial tactics, ethics; search and seizure; computers; discovery and legal research. Leader, Public Defender and Legal Services Delegation to China, 1981. Oregon State Bar Uniform Jury Instruction (Criminal) Committee, 1993-1996; Executive Committee, Criminal Law Section, 1991-1996 (Chair, 1994-1995); Uniform Trial Court Rules Committee, 1991-1996; Computers and Information Technology Committee, 1987-1990 (Chair, 1989-1990); Judicial Selection Committee, 1986-1988; State Medical Examiner Advisory Board, 1995—; State Professional Responsibility Board, 1997-2000 (Chair, 1999-2000). Listed in The Best Lawyers in America, 2003-2004. *Member:* Oregon State Bar; Multnomah County Bar Association; Oregon Criminal Defense Lawyers Association; National Association of Criminal Defense Lawyers. ***PRACTICE AREAS:*** Fraud Environmental Crimes; White Collar Crimes; Narcotics Drug Crimes. ***Email:*** larry@pdxlaw.com

McEWEN GISVOLD LLP

(Founded as Cake & Cake-1886)

1600 STANDARD PLAZA
1100 S.W. SIXTH AVENUE
PORTLAND, OREGON 97204
Telephone: 503-226-7321
FAX: 503-243-2687
Email: contact@mcewengisvold.com
URL: http://www.mcewengisvold.com

Real Estate, Real Estate Finance, Commercial Real Estate, Leases and Leasing, Corporate Law, Business Law, Bankruptcy, Debtor and Creditor, Low Income Housing, Estate Planning, Probate, Taxation, Nonprofit and Charitable Organizations, Litigation, Commercial Litigation, Legal Malpractice Defense, Products Liability Defense, Real Estate Litigation, Real Estate Title Insurance, Construction, Public Contracts, Surety Bond Claims and Defense and Mechanic's Liens.

DONALD W. McEWEN (1920-2000)

SENIOR PARTNERS

DEAN P. GISVOLD, born Minnesota, 1941; admitted to bar, 1966, Oregon. *Education:* Iowa State University (B.S., 1963); University of Minnesota (LL.B., 1966). Listed in "The Best Lawyers in America." Recipient, Portland's Junior First Citizen, 1972; George Russell Community Service Award, 1990. *Member:* Oregon State Bar; American College of Real Estate Lawyers; American Land Title Association Lenders Counsel Group. ***PRACTICE AREAS:*** Real Estate; Real Estate Finance; Real Estate Foreclosure; Real Estate Workouts. ***Email:*** deang@mcewengisvold.com

F. GORDON ALLEN, III, born Maryland, 1947; admitted to bar, 1974, Illinois; 1977, Oregon, U.S. District Court, District of Oregon, U.S. District Court, District of Illinois, U.S. Claims Court and U.S. Supreme Court. *Education:* Amherst College (B.A., 1969); University of Chicago (J.D., 1974). Author: "Punitive Damages" and "Nominal Damages" chapters in Oregon State Bar Continuing Legal Education, Damages Vol. 1. *Member:* Illinois State Bar Association; Oregon State Bar. ***REPORTED CASES:*** Argued Lampf v. Gilbertson, 111 Sup. Ct. 2773 (1991). ***PRACTICE AREAS:*** Employment Litigation; Securities Litigation; Construction Law; Commercial Law; Surety Law; Business Litigation. ***Email:*** gordya@mcewengisvold.com

PARTNERS

DON G. CARTER, born Oregon, 1953; admitted to bar, 1979, Oregon. *Education:* Oregon State University (B.S., with highest honors, 1975); University of Oregon (J.D., 1979). Phi Kappa Phi. Listed in The Best Lawyers in America. Business Manager, Oregon Law Review, 1978-1979. Law Clerk to the Honorable Edwin J. Peterson, Associate Justice, Oregon Supreme Court, 1979-1980. Chairman, Arthritis Foundation of Oregon, 1991-1992. Member, Board of Trustees, George Fox University, 1996—. *Member:* Multnomah Bar Association; Oregon State Bar (Member, 1987-1991 and Chair, 1989-1990, Real Estate and Land Use Section). ***PRACTICE AREAS:*** Real Estate; Real Estate Finance; Business Law. ***Email:*** donc@mcewengisvold.com

JAMES RAY STREINZ, born Ohio, 1955; admitted to bar, 1979, Oregon; 1985, Washington. *Education:* Linfield College (B.A., summa cum laude, 1976); Harvard University (J.D., cum laude, 1979). Author: "Receivers," Oregon Pleading and Practice (Oregon State Bar, Continuing Legal Education, 1985, 1994, 1997 and 2001). Adjunct Professor, Debtor-Creditor Law, Willamette University, 1995-1997. *Member:* Oregon State Bar (Chair, 1992-1993, and Executive Committee, 1986-1994, Debtor-Creditor Section); Washington State Bar Association. ***PRACTICE AREAS:*** Bankruptcy; Real Estate Foreclosure; Debtor and Creditor Collections; Debtor and Creditor Workouts; Legal Malpractice Defense. ***Email:*** rays@mcewengisvold.com

JANET M. GRAVDAL, born Wisconsin, 1959; admitted to bar, 1987, Oregon. *Education:* Pacific Lutheran University; Washington State University (B.A., cum laude, 1984); University of Idaho (J.D., 1987). Member and Executive Editor, 1986-1987, Idaho Law Review. Author: "Malpractice Traps Involving Loans," Oregon State Bar, Professional Liability Fund, C.L.E., 1994; "Fixtures," Oregon State Bar, C.L.E., 1994. Co-Author: "Subordinations," Multnomah Bar Association, C.L.E., 1994. *Member:* Multnomah Bar Association; Oregon State Bar; Oregon Women Lawyers. ***PRACTICE AREAS:*** Real Estate; Real Estate Finance; Real Estate Workouts. ***Email:*** jang@mcewengisvold.com

BARRY L. GROCE, born New York, 1954; admitted to bar, 1980, Oregon; 1981, U.S. District Court, District of Oregon; 1983, U.S. Court of Appeals, Ninth Circuit; 1986, Washington; 1988, U.S. District Court, Western District of Washington; 1999, U.S. Court of Appeals, Federal Circuit. *Education:* University of California, Berkeley (B.A., with distinction, 1976; M.P.P., 1979; J.D., 1980). *Member:* Oregon State Bar; Washington State Bar Association. ***PRACTICE AREAS:*** Commercial Leasing; Commercial Litigation; Trademark Licensing. ***Email:*** barryg@mcewengisvold.com

JONATHAN M. RADMACHER, born Oregon, 1965; admitted to bar, 1992, Oregon. *Education:* Willamette University (B.S., 1988); George Washington University (J.D., with high honors, 1992). Moot Court Board. Order of the Coif. Member, Board of Trustees, Willamette University. *Member:* Oregon State Bar (Member, Executive Board, Business Litigation Section). ***PRACTICE AREAS:*** Real Estate Litigation; Legal Malpractice Defense; Real Estate Title Insurance; Commercial Litigation; Appellate Practice. ***Email:*** jonathanr@mcewengisvold.com

JANICE NYSTROM TURNER, born Washington, 1964; admitted to bar, 1990, Oregon; 1991, Washington. *Education:* Central Washington University (B.A., 1986); Willamette University (J.D., 1990). *Member:* Oregon State Bar; Washington State Bar Association. ***PRACTICE AREAS:*** Real Estate; Real Estate Finance; Real Estate Foreclosure. ***Email:*** janicet@mcewengisvold.com

JOHNSTON A. MITCHELL, born California, 1959; admitted to bar, 1992, Oregon; 1999, Washington. *Education:* University of California at Irvine (B.A., cum laude, 1981), Phi Beta Kappa; University of Cambridge, England (M.Phil., 1984); Gonzaga University (J.D., magna cum laude, 1992). Author: "What Kind of Reform: The Bankruptcy Reform Act of 1994," Oregon State Bar Bulletin (June, 1995). Judicial Clerk to Hon. Elizabeth Perris, 1993-1995 and Hon. Donal Sullivan, 1995. ***PRACTICE AREAS:*** Bankruptcy; Business Law; Creditors Rights; Commercial Litigation. ***Email:*** johnstonm@mcewengisvold.com

ROBERT L. O'HALLORAN, born Maryland, 1957; admitted to bar, 1982, Oregon, U.S. District Court, District of Oregon and U.S. Claims Court; 1986, U.S. Court of Appeals, Ninth Circuit; 1992, U.S. Tax Court. *Education:* University of Oregon (B.S., 1979); Northwestern School of Law (J.D., 1982). Staff Member, 1980-1981 and Associate Editor, 1981-1982, Environmental Law Review. Member, Associated General Contractors. *Member:* Oregon State Bar (Member, Construction Law Section); American Bar Association (Member: Sections on: Torts and Insurance Practice; Fidelity and Surety; Member, Forum Committee on the Construction Industry); Owen M. Panner American Inn of Court (1988-1992). ***PRACTICE AREAS:*** Public Contracts Law; Construction Law; Surety Law. ***Email:*** roberto@mcewengisvold.com

OF COUNSEL

ROBERT D. RANKIN, born Missouri, 1943; admitted to bar, 1968, Oregon. *Education:* Iowa State University (B.S., 1965); Northwestern University (J.D., 1968). Member, National Association of Securities Dealers and Multnomah County Arbitration Panels. *Member:* Oregon State Bar. ***PRACTICE AREAS:*** Real Estate; Real Estate Finance; Securities; Insurance; Banks and Banking. ***Email:*** robertr@mcewengisvold.com

ASSOCIATES

J. KURT KRAEMER, born Alberta, Canada, 1971; admitted to bar, 1998, Oregon; 1999, Washington. *Education:* Gonzaga University (B.A., 1994; J.D., 1998). Recipient, CALI Excellence for the Future Award. *Member:* Oregon State Bar; Washington State Bar Association. ***PRACTICE AREAS:*** Real Estate Litigation; Business Litigation. ***Email:*** kurtk@mcewengisvold.com

HERTSEL SHADIAN, born Netanya, Israel, 1967; admitted to bar, 1998, Washington; 2000, Oregon. *Education:* University of Hawaii (B.A., 1993); Gonzaga University (J.D., with Tax/Business Concentration, 1997); University of Washington (LL.M., Taxation, 1998). Editorial Contributor: "Representation Before the Appeals Division of the IRS," "Tax Penalties and Interest," "Representing the Bankrupt Taxpayer," West Group, 1998-2004 Supplements, Arthur H. Boelter, Author. *Member:* Multnomah County and Washington State Bar Associations; Oregon State Bar; Oregon Minority Lawyers Association. ***PRACTICE AREAS:*** Taxation; Estate Planning; Business Formation; Business Planning; Nonprofit and Charitable Organizations. ***Email:*** hertsels@mcewengisvold.com

TRUNG D. TU, born Phan Thiet, Vietnam, 1973; admitted to bar, 2000, Oregon; 2001, U.S. Court of Appeals, Ninth Circuit; 2003, California and U.S. District Court, District of Oregon. *Education:* University of Notre Dame (B.A., 1995); Lewis and Clark Law School (J.D., 2000). Phi Delta Phi. *Member:* Oregon State Bar; State Bar of California; Federal Bar Association. ***LANGUAGES:*** Vietnamese. ***PRACTICE AREAS:*** Commercial Litigation. ***Email:*** trungt@mcewengisvold.com

JOHN B. BENAZZI, born New York, 1976; admitted to bar, 2004, Oregon. *Education:* Washington & Lee University (B.S., 1998); University of Oregon (J.D., 2004). *Member:* Oregon State Bar. ***PRACTICE AREAS:*** Real Estate; Land Use; Environmental. ***Email:*** johnb@mcewengisvold.com

ERIN MOAK LILLIS, born California, 1979; admitted to bar, 2005, Oregon. *Education:* University of Notre Dame (B.A., 2001); Georgetown University Law Center (J.D., 2005). ***PRACTICE AREAS:*** Real Estate; Real Estate Finance; Business Law. ***Email:*** erinl@mcewengisvold.com

GENERAL COUNSEL FOR: Standard Insurance Co.; Northwest Food Processors Assn.; North Pacific Homes, Inc.; Rainbow Mortgage Co.; Professional Liability Fund - Oregon State Bar; Oregon School Activities Assn.; S and H Incorporated; Homewood Corporation; Western Seminary.
LOCAL COUNSEL FOR: Safeway Inc.; John Deere Co.; TheTravelers Insurance Co. (Real Estate Investment Dept.); Transnation Title Insurance Co.; Bank of America, N.A.; Allianz Life Insurance Company of North America; Protective Life Insurance Company; Oregon Public Employee's Retirement Fund (Real Estate Sales, Acquisitions and Leasing Management); Sun Life Assurance Company of Canada; Deere Credit, Inc.; Bank of Hawaii; Artesia Mortgage Capital Corp.; Chicago Title Insurance Co.; Stewart Title Guaranty Company; Banner Bank; Sunbelt Rentals, Inc.; GE Security, Inc.; U.S. Bank National Association; M&T Real Estate Trust; CIT Equipment Rental and Finance.
REPRESENTATIVE CLIENTS: Anchor Insurance & Surety, Inc.; Berge Bros. Enterprises; Chubb Group of Insurance Companies; CNA Surety Companies; Colson and Colson General Contractor, Inc.; Federal Insurance Co.; First Union Management Co.; Klamath Pacific Corp.; Lakeside Industries; Ohio Casualty Insurance Co.; Pacific Retirement Services, Inc.; Pacific Wallboard; Pacific Northern Environmental Corp.; Performance Contracting Group; Star Insurance Co.; Tidewater Contractors, Inc.; Turner Construction Company; Walsh Construction Company.

(This Listing Continued)

ROBERT J. McGAUGHEY

Established in 1982

111 S.W. COLUMBIA STREET, SUITE 1000
PORTLAND, OREGON 97201-5855
Telephone: 503-223-7555
Fax: 503-525-4833
Email: bob@law7555.com

Securities, Shareholder, Partnership, LLC Litigation.

ROBERT J. McGAUGHEY, born Cambridge, Massachusetts, June 15, 1949; admitted to bar, 1980, Oregon and U.S. District Court, District of Oregon; 1985, Washington, U.S. District Court, Western District of Washington and U.S. Court of Appeals, Ninth Circuit. *Education:* Lowell Technological Institute (B.S.E.E., 1971); University of Akron (M.A., 1975; J.D., 1980). Author: "Oregon Corporate Law Handbook," 1999; "Washington Corporate Law Handbook," 2000, 1993; "Oregon Securities Law Handbook," 1991, 1985, 1982; "Oregon Securities Law," Advising Oregon Businesses, Oregon State Bar (2001, 1993, 1989). *Member:* Oregon State Bar (Past-Chair, Business Litigation Section, 1997-1998; Past Chair, Securities Regulation Section, 1994-1995; Member: Task Force on Uniform Securities Act, 2004-2005; Business Law Section Task Force on Changes to Corporation Act, 2001; Business Law Section, Task Force on Close Corporation Legislation, 1999). ***REPORTED CASES:*** Computer Concepts, Inc. v. Brandt, 137 Or App 572,905 P2d 1177 (1995); Chrome Data Systems v. Stringer, 109 Or App 513,820 P2d 831 (1991); Stringer v. Car Data Systems, 314 Or 576,841 P2d 1183 (1992); reconsidered denied, 315 Or 308,844 P2d 905 (1993); Computer Concepts, Inc. v. Brandt, 310 Or 706, 801 P2d 800 (1990); Prince v. Brydon, 307 Or 146,764 P2d 1370 (1988); In re Mettler, 305 Or 12,748 P2d 1010 (1988). ***PRACTICE AREAS:*** Securities; Shareholder; Partnership & LLC Litigation.

McNEIL LAW OFFICE LLC

PORTLAND, OREGON

(See Hillsboro)

Family, Criminal, Wills, Personal Injury, Business Litigation.

MICHAEL W. MELTZER, P.C.

Established in 2000

4225 S.W. HUBER STREET, SUITE 410
PORTLAND, OREGON 97219
Telephone: 503-892-6615
Fax: 503-892-8851
URL: http://www.immigrationcases.com
Email: mmeltzer@firstam.com
URL: http://www.lawyers.com/meltzer

Immigration and Naturalization.

FIRM PROFILE: Michael W. Meltzer, P.C. represents businesses, educational institutions, nonprofit organizations, and individuals regarding all aspects of United States immigration, consular, and nationality law. The firm's clients include the full range of business clients from large publicly held corporations with thousands of employees all over the world to small startup businesses with only a few employees. We assist our clients and their employees with all varieties of immigrant and non-immigrant work-related visas including H-1B, L and E, visas, investor green cards, and labor certification, reduction in recruitment, special handling, and national interest waivers. We advise employers on employer sanctions and I-9 audits, and represent individuals with respect to family based immigration, naturalization, deportation, and political asylum.

MICHAEL W. MELTZER, P.C., born Brooklyn, New York; admitted to bar, 1985, Oregon. *Education:* Williams College (B.A., magna cum laude, 1970); University of California at San Diego (Ph.D., 1978); Yale University (J.D., 1981). Phi Beta Kappa. *Member:* Oregon State Bar (Past Member: Executive Committee, International Law Section; Executive Committee, Securities Regulation Section; Board of Directors, Latin America Trade Organization (LATCO); Legal Ethics Committee); American Immigration Lawyers Association. ***LANGUAGES:*** Spanish. ***SPECIAL AGENCIES:*** Bureau of Citizenship Immigration Services; Executive Office of Immigration Review; Administrative Appeals Office. ***PRACTICE AREAS:*** Immigration and Naturalization Law. ***Email:*** mmeltzer@firstam.com

Languages: Spanish and Vietnamese.

MEYER & WYSE LLP

Established in 1985

AMERICAN BANK BUILDING
621 S.W. MORRISON STREET
SUITE 1300
PORTLAND, OREGON 97205-3816
Telephone: 503-228-8448
Fax: 503-273-9135
Email: law@meyerwyse.com
URL: http://www.meyerwyse.com

General Civil Trial and Appellate Practice in State and Federal Courts. Business, Real Property, Estate Planning, Probate, Mediation, Family Law, Creditors' Rights, Bankruptcy, Secured Transactions, Community Associations and Architectural, Engineering and Construction Law.

(This Listing Continued)

MEMBERS OF FIRM

ROGER L. MEYER, born St. Louis, Missouri, July 1, 1932; admitted to bar, 1957, Oregon; 1970, U.S. Supreme Court. *Education:* Oberlin College (B.A., 1954); Yale Law School (LL.B., 1957). Corbey Court. Assistant Instructor of Law, Yale Law School, 1956-1957. Member, 1977-1986, 1995— and Chairman, 1999-2000, Oregon State Board of Architect Examiners. Chairman, Western Conference, 1985-1986 and Director, 1986-1988, National Council of Architectural Registration Boards. Member, Panel of Arbitrators: American Arbitration Association; Arbitration Service of Portland. *Member:* Multnomah County and American Bar Associations; Oregon State Bar. ***PRACTICE AREAS:*** Corporate Law; Business Law; Litigation; Architectural Law; Construction Law. ***Email:*** rlm@meyerwyse.com

SCOTT C. WYSE, born Portland, Oregon, July 20, 1948; admitted to bar, 1974, Oregon. *Education:* University of Pennsylvania (B.A., 1970); University of California at Los Angeles and University of Oregon (J.D., 1974). Member, Board of Directors, Oregon Downtown Development Association, 1986-1994. Member, Livable Oregon, Inc., 1995—. *Member:* Multnomah County Bar Association; Oregon State Bar. ***PRACTICE AREAS:*** Business Law; Real Estate Law; Litigation. ***Email:*** scw@meyerwyse.com

JOSHUA KADISH, born New York, N.Y., June 28, 1951; admitted to bar, 1979, California; 1980, Oregon. *Education:* Haverford College (B.A., magna cum laude, 1973); Stanford University (J.D., 1979). Phi Beta Kappa. Associate Editor, Stanford Law Review, 1978-1979. Clementine Cope Fellow. Law Clerk to the Honorable Hans A. Linde, Oregon Supreme Court, 1979-1980. Adjunct Professor, Northwestern School of Law of Lewis and Clark College, 1989—. Public Member, Oregon Board of Licensed Professional Counselors and Therapists, 1989-1996. *Member:* State Bar of California (inactive); Oregon State Bar; Oregon Mediation Association. ***PRACTICE AREAS:*** Business Law; Trusts and Estates Law; Mediation Law; Family Law. ***Email:*** jdk@meyerwyse.com

BRUCE H. ORR, born Los Angeles, California, June 27, 1954; admitted to bar, 1981, Oregon; 1985, U.S. District Court, District of Oregon; 1989, Washington and U.S. District Court, Western District of Washington. *Education:* California Polytechnic State University, San Luis Obispo (B.S., with highest honors, 1976); University of California at Santa Barbara (M.A., 1977); Northwestern School of Law of Lewis and Clark College (J.D., 1981). Author, "Rights and Remedies of Secured Creditors and Non-Debtor Parties to Executory Contracts," Bankruptcy, Oregon State Bar CLE, 1989. ***PRACTICE AREAS:*** Bankruptcy; Commercial Law; Litigation; Creditors' Rights; Secured Transactions. ***Email:*** bho@meyerwyse.com

HELEN RIVES PRUITT, born Berkeley, California, October 6, 1954; admitted to bar, 1980, Oregon; 1984, Washington. *Education:* Wellesley College (A.B., 1976); Cornell University; University of Oregon (J.D., 1980). Associate Editor, Oregon Law Review, 1979-1980. *Member:* Washington State Bar Association; Oregon State Bar. ***PRACTICE AREAS:*** Trusts and Estates; Probate Law; Business Law. ***Email:*** hrp@meyerwyse.com

JAMES E. BARTELS, born St. Marys, Missouri, April 6, 1947; admitted to bar, 1974, Oregon, U.S. District Court, District of Oregon, U.S. District Court, Northern District of California and U.S. Court of Appeals, Ninth Circuit. *Education:* St. Louis University (B.S., Phi Beta Kappa, 1968); University of Chicago (J.D., 1974). Member, American Bar Association Forum on Franchising. *Member:* Oregon State Bar; Oregon Association of Defense Counsel. ***PRACTICE AREAS:*** Litigation (General and Complex); Trade Regulation and Business Practices Law; Trust Litigation; Estate Litigation; Securities Law; Professional Liability Law; Franchise Law. ***Email:*** jeb@meyerwyse.com

NICHOLAS S. FISH, born New York, N.Y., September 30, 1958; admitted to bar, 1987, New York; 1989, U.S. District Court, Southern District of New York; 1992, U.S. District Court, Eastern District of New York and U.S. Court of Appeals, Second Circuit; 1997, Oregon; 2000, U.S. District Court, District of Oregon. *Education:* Harvard College (B.A., 1981); Northeastern University School of Law (J.D., 1986). *Member:* Oregon State Bar; National Employment Lawyers Association. ***PRACTICE AREAS:*** Employment; Civil Litigation; Labor. ***Email:*** nf@meyerwyse.com

---

STEVEN JAMES KUHN, born Portland, Oregon, April 25, 1970; admitted to bar, 1998, Oregon; 1999, Washington. *Education:* Earlham College (B.A., 1992); The Ohio State University (M.A., 1995); Willamette University (J.D., 1998). Phi Beta Kappa. Note and Comment Editor, Willamette Law Review, 1997-1998. *Member:* Multnomah County, Washington State and American Bar Associations; Oregon State Bar. ***PRACTICE AREAS:*** Corporate Law; Business Law. ***Email:*** sjk@meyerwyse.com

DAVID I. BEAN, born Detroit, Michigan, July 13, 1972; admitted to bar, 2001, Oregon. *Education:* University of Colorado at Boulder (B.A., 1996); Lewis and Clark College, Northwestern School of Law (J.D., 2001). ***PRACTICE AREAS:*** Family Law; Civil Litigation. ***Email:*** dib@meyeruyse.com

REPRESENTATIVE CLIENTS: The Benkendorf Associates Corp.; Benner, Stange & Associates, Architects; BMW of North America LLC; Bushwacker, Inc.; Cascadian Landscapers, Inc.; Cascadian Nurseries, Inc.; Chevalier Advertising, Inc.; Eli Lilly & Co.; Everest Consultants, Inc.; Genoa Healthcare, LLC; Homes Association of Cedar Hills; Hydra-Power Systems, Inc.; KMD, Architects/Planners A.I.A.; Mackenzie and Dowd, Architects; MCM Architects, P.C.; Mel Corp.; Molecular Technologies, Inc.; Northwest Natural Co.; Northwest Energy Efficiency Alliance, Inc.; Northwest Power Planning Council; Pharmacare Prescriptions, Inc; Ross Island Sand & Gravel Co.; SAIF Corporation; Thomas Hacker Architects Inc.; Thompson Vaivoda & Associates Architects, Inc.; Vanport Manufacturing, Inc.; Walker Macy Landscape Architects; Western States Sales, Inc.; Wilcox Estates Homeowners Association; Yost Grube Hall, Architects and Planners, P.C.; Zaik/Miller Associates, Architects/Planners.

CAROLYN W. MILLER, P.C.

Established in 2001

THE RIVER FORUM, SUITE 525
4380 S W MACADAM
PORTLAND, OREGON 97239
Telephone: 503-241-2801
Fax: 503-241-2811
Email: carolyn@cwmillerpc.com
URL: http://www.lawyers.com/cwmillerlaw

Estate Planning, Probate, Trusts, Taxation, Tax Exempt Organization.

CAROLYN W. MILLER, born Ridgecrest, California, August 9, 1953; admitted to bar, 1978, Oregon; 1993, Washington. *Education:* University of California at Santa Barbara (B.A., 1975); Williamette University (J.D., 1978). Fellow, American College of Trust and Estate Counsel. Member, Estate Planning Council of Portland (President, 1995). Listed, Best Lawyers in America, 2002-2005. *Member:* Oregon State Bar (Chair, Taxation Section, 1998); Washington State Bar Association. ***PRACTICE AREAS:*** Estate Planning; Probate; Trusts; Taxation; Tax Exempt Organizations. ***Email:*** carolyn@cwmillerpc.com

MILLER NASH LLP

A Limited Liability Partnership including Professional Corporations

Established in 1873

111 S.W. FIFTH AVENUE, SUITE 3400
PORTLAND, OREGON 97204-3699
Telephone: 503-224-5858
Facsimile: 503-224-0155
Email: clientservices@millernash.com
URL: http://www.millernash.com

REVISER OF THE OREGON LAW DIGEST FOR THIS DIRECTORY.

Seattle, Washington Office: 4400 Two Union Square, 601 Union Street, 98101-2352. Telephone: 206-622-8484. Facsimile: 206-622-7485.
Vancouver, Washington Office: 500 East Broadway, Suite 400, P.O. Box 694, 98660-3324. Telephone: 360-699-4771; 503-289-2643. Facsimile: 360-694-6413.

General Civil Practice and Litigation in all State and Federal Courts and before Federal and State Administrative Tribunals. Agricultural Cooperatives; Antitrust and Trade Regulation; Appellate Practice; Banking and Financial Institutions; Bankruptcy; Biotechnology; Business; Communications and Media; Computers and Software; Construction; Contracts; Corporate Governance Litigation; Corporate; Debtor/Creditor; Education; Employee Benefits; Employment and Labor Relations Litigation; Energy; Entity Structuring; Environmental and Natural Resources; Finance; Gaming; Government; Healthcare and Hospitals; High-Tech; Homeland Security; Housing; Immigration; Insurance, Intellectual Property; International Litigation and Arbitration; International Trade; Land Use; Litigation, Arbitration and Mediation; Maritime; Mergers and Acquisitions; Municipal; Nonprofit and Charitable Organizations; Products Liability; Public Finance and Bonds; Real Estate; Securities, Corporate, Shareholder Disputes Litigation; Taxation; Technology and Science; Telecommunications; Trademarks; Transportation and Utilities; and Trusts and Estates.

FIRM PROFILE: Miller Nash LLP is one of the Pacific Northwest's largest and most respected multi-service law firms. We have provided legal services since 1873. Miller Nash has approximately 125 lawyers serving clients through our offices in Portland, Oregon, and Seattle and Vancouver, Washington. Our ever-expanding local, national, and international network of resources enables us to offer comprehensive, creative, and innovative services.

We serve a wide range of leading businesses, nonprofit organizations, public entities, individuals as well as pro bono activities. Our clients work in a variety of significant industries in our region, including banking, biotech, construction, food production, forest products, government, healthcare, high technology, higher education, public school districts, regulatory and government affairs, telecom, and utilities.

Miller Nash represents the states of Oregon and Washington in the world-wide Employment Law Alliance (http://www.employmentlawalliance.com) and is a member of the Institute for Transnational Arbitration.

PORTLAND, OREGON PARTNERS

CRAIG R. ARMSTRONG, P.C., born Toronto, Ontario, Canada, October 22, 1966; admitted to bar, 1992, Oregon; 2003, Washington. *Education:* University of California at Berkeley (B.A., 1988); Loyola Law School (J.D., 1992). Phi Delta Phi; Order of the Coif. Member, St. Thomas More Law Honor Society. *Member:* Oregon State Bar (Member, Executive Committee, Labor and Employment Law Section); Washington State and American Bar Associations. ***PRACTICE AREAS:*** Business Law; Labor and Employment. ***Email:*** craig.armstrong@millernash.com

JEFFREY D. AUSTIN, P.C., born Berkeley, California, May 10, 1951; admitted to bar, 1983, Oregon. *Education:* Portland State University (B.A., 1977); Northwestern School of Law of Lewis and Clark College (J.D., cum laude, 1983). *Member:* Multomah County and American (Member, Sections on: Litigation; Tort Trial and Insurance Practice) Bar Associations; Oregon State Bar; Defense Research Institute; Oregon Association of Defense Counsel; National School Boards Association Council of School Attorneys. ***PRACTICE AREAS:*** Education Law; Civil Litigation; Arbitration; Personal Injury Defense; Products Liability Defense; Employment Litigation; Commercial Litigation; Complex Litigation. ***Email:*** jeff.austin@millernash.com

DAVID G. BRISTOL, P.C., born Portland, Oregon, June 29, 1961; admitted to bar, 1992, Oregon. *Education:* University of Oregon (B.S., Finance, summa cum laude, 1983); Vanderbilt University (J.D., 1992). Order of the Coif. Associate Editor, Vanderbilt Law Review. *Member:* Multnomah County and American Bar Associations; Oregon State Bar.

(This Listing Continued)

PRACTICE AREAS: Business; Real Estate; Corporate; Mergers and Acquisitions; International; Product Distribution; Banking; Intellectual Property; Entertainment. ***Email:*** david.bristol@millernash.com

DONALD A. BURNS, P.C., born Memphis, Michigan, October 27, 1946; admitted to bar, 1973, Oregon. *Education:* Michigan State University (B.A., with high honors, 1968); Duke University (J.D., with distinction, 1973). Member, Duke Law Journal, 1972-1973. Listed in: Best Lawyers in America for Employee Benefits since 1995. Special Assistant Attorney General, State of Oregon, 1999— as outside employee benefits counsel to the Oregon Department of Justice. Member, Governor's Task Force on Oregon Public Employees Retirement System, 2002. Member, Oregon Department of Insurance and Finance Task Forces on Multiple Employer Welfare Arrangement legislation and Oregon Health Plan. Member, Board of Trustees, 1993-1996 and Treasurer, 1995-1996, Multnomah Athletic Club. Member, Board of Directors, 1983-1987 and President, 1985-1987, Portland Chapter, Western Pension and Benefits Conference. Chairman, Washington County Planning Commission, 1976-1979 and Member 1975-1979. Member, Washington County Property Rights Commission and Board of Adjustment in 1975-1979. Member, Board of Directors, Washington County Employees Federal Credit Union, 1974-1978. *Member:* Multnomah County and American Bar Associations; Oregon State Bar. [U. S. Army, Specialist 5th Class, Legal Clerk, Staff Judge Advocate, Fort Polk, Louisiana, 1969-1971]. ***PRACTICE AREAS:*** Employee Benefits Law. ***Email:*** don.burns@millernash.com

J. FRANKLIN CABLE, P.C., born Hannibal, Missouri, December 22, 1941; admitted to bar, 1967, Oregon. *Education:* Stanford University (A.B., with distinction, 1964); Harvard University (LL.B., 1967). Member, Executive Committee: Securities Regulation Section, Oregon State Bar, 1984-1985; Executive Committee, Business Law Section, Oregon State Bar, 1987-1988. Listed in: Best Lawyers in America. *Member:* Oregon State Bar. ***PRACTICE AREAS:*** Business Law; Corporate Finance; Acquisitions and Dispositions. ***Email:*** frank.cable@millernash.com

BRUCE L. CAMPBELL, P.C., born Portland, Oregon, December 4, 1957; admitted to bar, 1990, Washington; 1992, Oregon. *Education:* University of Oregon (B.S., 1980); Northwestern University (M.M., 1982); University of Michigan (J.D., cum laude, 1988). Law Clerk to the Honorable Cecil F. Poole, Circuit Judge, U.S. Court of Appeals, Ninth Circuit, 1988-1989. *Member:* Oregon State Bar; Washington State Bar Association. ***PRACTICE AREAS:*** Commercial Litigation; Appeals; Securities Litigation; Arbitration; Antitrust. ***Email:*** bruce.campbell@millernash.com

RICHARD A. CANADAY, born Alton, Illinois, August 26, 1947; admitted to bar, 1973, Oregon; 1987, Washington. *Education:* University of Washington and Stanford University (A.B., 1969); University of California, Boalt Hall School of Law (J.D., 1973). *Member:* Washington State and American Bar Associations; Oregon State Bar. ***PRACTICE AREAS:*** Commercial Law; Business Law; Commercial Finance Law; Real Estate Law. ***Email:*** rich.canaday@millernash.com

D. GARY CHRISTENSEN, P.C., born Richfield, Utah, April 8, 1962; admitted to bar, 1988, Oregon. *Education:* Brigham Young University (B.A., cum laude, 1985; J.D., magna cum laude, 1988). Phi Kappa Phi; Phi Delta Phi. Member: Order of the Coif; Order of Barristers; American Inns of Court Alumnus. Recipient, Presidential Award, Associated General Contractors, 2004. Counsel to Board, 2003-2004 and Member, Oregon-Columbia Chapter, Associated General Contractors. Member: Associated Builders and Contractors; Westside Economic Alliance. *Member:* Multnomah County and American (Member, Forum on the Construction Industry; Litigation Section) Bar Associations; Oregon State Bar (Member: Executive Committee, Construction Law Section; Sections on: Debtor/Creditor; Litigation; Business Litigation); J. Reuben Clark Law Society. ***PRACTICE AREAS:*** Commercial Litigation; Construction Law; Creditors Rights; Public Procurement Law. ***Email:*** gary.christensen@millernash.com

JEFFREY G. CONDIT, born Yakima, Washington, September 10, 1956; admitted to bar, 1982, Oregon; 2000, Washington. *Education:* University of Washington (B.A., cum laude, with distinction, 1979); Willamette University (J.D., 1982). Staff Member, Willamette Law Review. Co-Author: Chapter 4, "Land Use," Oregon State Bar, 1994, 2000 (Supplement). Benton County Counsel, 1986-1990. Lake Oswego City Attorney, 1991-1998. *Member:* Oregon State Bar (Member, Land Use Legislative Subcommittee, 1994—); International Municipal Lawyers Association (State Chair, 1998—); Oregon City Attorneys Association (Executive Committee, 1994-2000, President, 1999). ***PRACTICE AREAS:*** Municipal Law; School Law; Higher Education Law; Land Use Planning Law; Administrative Law; Appellate Practice. ***Email:*** jeff.condit@millernash.com

DAVID C. CULPEPPER, P.C., born Quantico, Virginia, March 15, 1946; admitted to bar, 1974, Oregon. *Education:* University of Santa Clara (B.A., 1968); University of Oregon (J.D., 1974). Order of the Coif. Fellow, American College of Tax Counsel, 2000—. Author: "Executive Compensation Matters," Advising Oregon Businesses, 1991, 1994, 1998 and 2001; "Tax Considerations in Drafting Partnership Allocation Provisions," Journal of Partnership Taxation, Winter, 1986; "Acquisitive Corporate Reorganizations," Advising Oregon Businesses, 1989, 1993, 1997, 2001 and 2004; "Limited Liability Companies," Advising Oregon Businesses, 1994, 1997, 2001 and 2004; "Tax Aspects of Limited Liability Companies," University of Oregon Law Review, 1994. Member, Committee on Partnerships, Tax Section of the American Bar Association, 1984—. Chair, Executive Committee, Oregon State Bar Taxation Section, 1992-1993. Co-Chair, Oregon State Bar's Task Force on Limited Liability Company Legislation. Listed in: Best Lawyers in America. *Member:* Oregon State Bar; American Bar Association (Member, Section of Taxation). ***PRACTICE AREAS:*** Federal Taxation; State Taxation; Executive Compensation; Partnership Law; Partnership Law Taxation; Limited Liability Company Law; Limited Liability Company Law Taxation. ***Email:*** david.culpepper@millernash.com

DEAN D. DeCHAINE, P.C., born Lake Oswego, Oregon, December 12, 1936; admitted to bar, 1964, Oregon, Virginia and U.S. District Court, District of Oregon; 1966, U.S. Court of Appeals, Ninth Circuit; 1986, Washington and U.S. District Court, Western District of Washington; 1996, U.S. Court of International Trade; 2004, U.S. Supreme Court. *Education:* Portland State University (B.S., 1959); University of Virginia (LL.B., 1964) Order of the Coif. President, Associated Students of Portland State University, 1958-1959. Research Assistant to U.S. Senator Richard L. Neuberger, 1959-1960. Research Assistant to U.S. Senator Hall S. Lusk, 1960-1961. Member, Editorial Board, University of Virginia Law Review, 1962-1964. Author: "Product Liability and the Disclaimer," 4 Willamette Law

(This Listing Continued)

Journal 364 (1967). President, Portland State University Alumni Association, 1967-1968. Program Co-Chairperson, Oregon Continuing Legal Education on Legislation, 1971. Secretary and Director, World Forestry Center, 1971—. Author: "Federal Documentation or State Registration: Requirements and Procedures," Pacific Northwest Admiralty Law Institute, 1979. Chairperson, Admiralty Section, Oregon State Bar, 1983-1984 and 1997-1998. Scout Master, Troop 127, Lake Oswego, Oregon, Boy Scouts of America, 1984-1986. President (first), Portland State University Alumni Board, 1987-1989. Author: "Evidence Problems in Coverage Litigation," Aviation Law Seminar presented by The Aviation Section, Seattle-King County Bar Association, Aviation Section, Oregon State Bar and The Federal Aviation Administration of the Northwest Mountain Region, 1988. Chairperson, Aviation Section, Oregon State Bar, 1989-1990. Listed in: Best Lawyers in America, 1989—. Trustee, Oregon College of Oriental Medicine, 2004—. *Member:* Oregon State Bar; Virginia State Bar; Washington State Bar Association; Maritime Law Association of the United States; Oregon Association of Defense Counsel. ***PRACTICE AREAS:*** Admiralty and Maritime Law; Aviation; Insurance Litigation; Environmental Litigation; Legal Malpractice; Commercial Litigation; Arbitration; Mediation. ***Email:*** dean.dechaine@millernash.com

JULIA A. DEWITT, P.C., born Livermore, California, April 6, 1969; admitted to bar, 1994, California; 1996, Oregon. *Education:* University of Oregon (B.S., summa cum laude, 1991); University of California, Hastings College of the Law (J.D., magna cum laude, 1994). Phi Beta Kappa. Order of the Coif. Recipient, American Jurisprudence Award in Evidence. Member, Western Pension & Benefits Conference, 1996—. Co-Author: 1995 Update to *Attorney's Guide to Pension and Profit-Sharing Plans,* 3rd Edition published by California Continuing Education of the Bar; "Executive Compensation Matters, Advising Oregon Businesses," Oregon State Bar, Committee on Continuing Legal Education, 1998. *Member:* State Bar of California; Oregon State Bar. ***PRACTICE AREAS:*** Employee Benefits. ***Email:*** julie.dewitt@millernash.com

BRIAN B. DOHERTY, P.C., born Portland, Oregon, January 13, 1952; admitted to bar, 1978, Oregon; 1979, U.S. Court of Appeals, Ninth Circuit. *Education:* Notre Dame University (B.A., 1974); Northwestern School of Law of Lewis and Clark College (J.D., 1978). Author/Editor: "Employer Incentives and Retroactive Reserve and Reemployment Funds" and "Covered Employers and Employees," Oregon CLE Handbook on Workers' Compensation, 1990, 1994; "OSHA Compliance in Oregon," 1992-2001. Law Clerk, Hon. John F. Kilkenny, Senior Circuit Judge, U.S. Court of Appeals, Ninth Circuit, 1978-1979. *Member:* Multnomah County and American Bar Associations; Oregon State Bar (Past Member, Executive Committee, Administrative Law Section; Member, Sections on: Labor and Employment Law; Government Law; Member, OSB House of Delegates, 1997—; Member, Board of Trustees, Classroom Law Project, 2002—). ***PRACTICE AREAS:*** Government Relations; OSHA; Labor and Employment; Administrative Lobbying; Election, Campaign and Political Law; Legislative Lobbying; Executive Lobbying; Election and Campaign Finance; Campaign Ethics; Occupational Safety and Health; Industrial Accidents; Occupational Disease; Occupational Injuries; Employer Intentional Torts; Employment Defense; Workplace Violence; Wrongful Termination Defense; Regulatory Agency Practice. ***Email:*** brian.doherty@millernash.com

C. MARIE ECKERT, born Buffalo, New York, October 7, 1957; admitted to bar, 1988, Oregon. *Education:* University of Michigan (B.A., 1985); Northwestern School of Law, Lewis and Clark College (J.D., magna cum laude, 1988). Research and Development Editor, Environmental Law, 1987-1988. Extern to the Hon. Joseph T. Sneed, U.S. Court of Appeals, Ninth Circuit, 1988. Author: "Tort or Contract," Oregon Statutory Time Limitations (Oregon CLE, 1998); "Actions Against Insurers," Chapter 11, Insurance (Oregon CLE, 1996). Speaker, "Watching for Sharks While Surfing: Navigating Difficult Attorney-Client Privilege and Waiver Issues," OSB Litigation Institute and Retreat, March 2005. Moderator: "What's Important to In-House Counsel," OSB Business Litigation Section, February 2004; "Working With In-House Counsel to Effectively Defend Litigation," OADC CLE, February 1999. Speaker, "Discovery of Electronic Evidence," Oregon Women Lawyers' Technology Conference, September 1998. Panelist, "Electronic Discovery of Computer-Based Evidence," OADC Annual Convention, June 1997. *Member:* Oregon State Bar (Representative, House of Delegates, 2003—; Member, Executive Board, Business Litigation Section, 1996-2003; Chair, 2002; Planning Committee, Litigation Institute and Retreat, 1997—); Oregon Association of Defense Counsel (Member, Board of Directors, 2000-2002; Chair, Commercial Litigation Practice Group, 1998-1999). ***PRACTICE AREAS:*** Complex Business Litigation; Financial Institutions Litigation. ***Email:*** marie.eckert@millernash.com

MARY ANN FRANTZ, P.C., born Bloomington, Indiana, July 15, 1953; admitted to bar, 1978, Oregon. *Education:* Stanford University (B.A., with honors, 1975; J.D., 1978). Phi Beta Kappa. Member, Oregon Nonprofit Corporation Law Task Force, 1988-1991. Listed in: Best Lawyers in America. *Member:* Oregon State Bar (Chairperson, Executive Committee, Securities Regulation Section, 1990-1991); American Bar Association (Chair, Subcommittee on the Annual Review of Federal Securities Regulation, Business Law Section). ***PRACTICE AREAS:*** Securities Regulation Law; Mergers and Acquisitions; Corporate Law. ***Email:*** maryann.frantz@millernash.com

JONATHON L. GOODLING, P.C., born October 28, 1953; admitted to bar, 1979, Oregon. *Education:* University of Oregon (B.S., 1976; J.D., 1979). Order of the Coif. Co-Author: "Perfection of Security Interests in Personal Property and Fixtures," Oregon Law Institute, 1988; "Lawyers' Opinions in Oregon Real Estate Transactions," Oregon State Bar, 1992; "Oregon Legal Guide for International Businesses—Real Estate Law and Practices," Oregon State Bar, 1993. Judicial Clerk to: Hon. Edward Leavy, U.S. District of Oregon, 1979-1980. Listed in: Best Lawyers in America. *Member:* Oregon State Bar (Chair: Financial Institutions Committee, 1991-1992; Chair: Committee on Rights of Persons With Disabilities, 1988-1989; Chair: Real Estate and Land Use Law Section, 1998-1999). ***PRACTICE AREAS:*** Real Estate Law; Commercial Lending Law; General Business Law. ***Email:*** jon.goodling@millernash.com

PHILLIP E. GRILLO, P.C., born Detroit, Michigan, March 24, 1956; admitted to bar, 1985, Oregon and Washington. *Education:* Michigan State University (B.A., 1978); Northwestern College of Law, Lewis and Clark College (J.D., 1984). Land Use Hearings Officer: City of Portland, Oregon, 1990-1994; City of Gresham, Oregon, 1992-1999; Multnomah County, Oregon, 1992-1997; City of Molalla, Oregon, 1993-1997. Land Use Hearings Examiner, Clark County, Washington, 1992-1997. *Member:* Oregon State Bar (Member, Real Estate and Land Use Section Executive Committee); Washington State Bar Association; American Planning Association; Oregon Planning Association. ***PRACTICE AREAS:*** Zoning; Planning; Land Use; Environmental Law; Municipal Law; Administrative Law; Appellate Practice. ***Email:*** phil.grillo@millernash.com

M. CHRISTIE HELMER, P.C., born Portland, Oregon, October 8, 1949; admitted to bar, 1974, Oregon; 2001, U.S. Court of International Trade. *Education:* Washington State University (B.A., magna cum laude, 1970) Phi Beta Kappa; Northwestern School of Law of Lewis and Clark College (J.D., cum laude, 1974); Columbia University, Parker School of Comparative and Foreign Law (LL.M., 1998). Chair, World Affairs Council of Oregon, 2004-2005. Adjunct Professor of Law, Transnational Litigation and Arbitration, Northwestern School of Law of Lewis and Clark College, 1999—. Special Instructor, International and Admiralty Law, Xiamen University, PRC, 1995. Author: "Arrest of Ships," Lloyd's of London Press, 1985. Lawyer Delegate: Ninth Circuit Judicial Conference, 1983-1985; Ninth Circuit Judicial Conference Executive Committee, 1986-1989. Member, Board of Bar Examiners, 1978-1981. Listed in: Best Lawyers in America, 1993—. *Member:* Oregon State Bar (Member, Board of Governors, 1981-1984; Member, House of Delegates, 2003—); International Bar Association; Maritime Law Association of the United States. ***PRACTICE AREAS:*** Business Litigation; International Litigation; International Arbitration; International Trade; Admiralty Law. ***Email:*** chris.helmer@millernash.com

LOUIS G. HENRY, P.C., born Portland, Oregon, June 2, 1955; admitted to bar, 1981, Oregon. *Education:* University of Oregon (B.S., 1977); Northwestern School of Law of Lewis and Clark College (J.D., 1981). Listed in: Best Lawyers in America. *Member:* Oregon State Bar; American Bar Association; American Bankruptcy Institute. ***PRACTICE AREAS:*** Commercial Lending; Secured Financing; Commercial Loan Workouts; Corporate Reorganization. ***Email:*** lou.henry@millernash.com

DAVID W. HERCHER, P.C., born Medford, Oregon, February 15, 1955; admitted to bar, 1981, Oregon; 1992, Washington. *Education:* University of Oregon (B.A., Clark Honors College, 1977); University of California, Boalt Hall School of Law (J.D., 1981). Phi Beta Kappa. Managing Editor, Ecology Law Quarterly, 1980-1981. Member, Editorial Board of Oregon State Bar Debtor/Creditor Section Newsletter, 1984-1989. Author: "Chapter 11 Overview" in Bankruptcy (Oregon State Bar, 1999 rev.). Co-Author: "Bankruptcy Issues for Real Estate Practitioners," in Fundamentals of Real Estate Transactions (Oregon State Bar 1992 and Supp 1996). *Member:* Washington State (Member, Creditor-Debtor Section) and American (Member, Business Law Section) Bar Associations; Oregon State Bar (Member, Debtor-Creditor Section). Certified in Business Bankruptcy Law by the American Board of Certification (Certification not recognized or required in Washington). ***PRACTICE AREAS:*** Bankruptcy Law; Reorganization Law; Out of Court Debt Restructuring. ***Email:*** dave.hercher@millernash.com

GRAHAM M. HICKS, P.C., born Salem, Oregon, February 9, 1949; admitted to bar, 1973, Oregon; 2005, Washington. *Education:* Willamette University (B.A., cum laude, 1970; J.D., magna cum laude, 1973). Articles Editor, Willamette Law Journal, 1972-1973. Past Chair, Oregon State Bar Disability Law Section. Program Committee, Pacific Northwest Institute on Special Education and the Law. *Member:* Oregon State Bar; Washington State and American Bar Associations; NSBA Council of School Attorneys; Education Law Association; Oregon Council of School Attorneys. ***PRACTICE AREAS:*** Litigation; School Law. ***Email:*** graham.hicks@millernash.com

STEVEN F. HILL, born Portland, Oregon, July 11, 1960; admitted to bar, 1993, Oregon; 1994, Washington; 1999, U.S. District Court, District of Oregon and U.S. District Court, Western and Eastern Districts of Washington. *Education:* Furman University (B.S., 1982); University of Southern California (M.M.A., 1983); Northwestern School of Law (J.D., cum laude, 1993). *Member:* Multnomah, Clark County, Washington State (Member, Environmental and Land Use Law Section) and American (Member, Environment, Energy and Resources Section) Bar Associations; Oregon State Bar (Member, Sections on: Admiralty; Environmental and Natural Resources Law; Real Estate Law and Land Use). (Also at Vancouver, Washington Office). ***PRACTICE AREAS:*** Environmental Law; Environmental Litigation; Admiralty; Insurance; Land Use; Real Estate. ***Email:*** steve.hill@millernash.com

SUZANNE C. LACAMPAGNE, P.C., born Turlock, California; admitted to bar, 1983, California; 1990, District of Columbia; 1995, Oregon. *Education:* Wellesley College (B.A.); Boston College Law School (J.D., 1983). Member, Boston College International Law Review. Author: "Bankruptcy Estimation of CERCLA Claims," 12 VA Envir. Law Journal 235 (1993). *Member:* State Bar of California (inactive); The District of Columbia Bar (inactive); Oregon State Bar; Womens Bar Association of District of Columbia (President, 1994-1995). ***PRACTICE AREAS:*** Environmental Law; Litigation; Administrative Law. ***Email:*** suzanne.lacampagne@millernash.com

JOHN A. LUSKY, born Louisville, Kentucky, October 30, 1951; admitted to bar, 1977, Oregon. *Education:* Harvard University (B.A., 1973); Stanford University (J.D., 1977). Author: "Regulations Affecting Real Estate Loans and Sales," Regulation and Taxation of Real Estate (Oregon State Bar 1995 and 1999 Supplement). *Member:* Oregon State Bar. ***PRACTICE AREAS:*** Business Law; Financial Institutions Law; Consumer Credit Law; Insurance Regulation Law. ***Email:*** john.lusky@millernash.com

WILLIAM S. MANNE, P.C., born Oceanside, New York, December 11, 1951; admitted to bar, 1985, Oregon; 2003, Washington. *Education:* Rochester Institute of Technology (B.S., 1975); Northwestern School of Law of Lewis and Clark College (J.D., 1984). Certified Public Accountant, Oregon, 1987. Partner in Charge, Tax Department. *Member:* Multnomah County Bar Association; Oregon State Bar (past Chair, Tax Section); Oregon Society of CPAs (Past Chair, Not-for-Profit Committee); American Institute of CPAs; Healthcare Financial Manager's Association. ***PRACTICE AREAS:*** Taxation; Corporate Law; Business Law; Nonprofit and Charitable Organizations. ***Email:*** bill.manne@millernash.com

COLLEEN L. McMULLEN, P.C., born Lebanon, Oregon, March 19, 1967; admitted to bar, 1995, Oregon. *Education:* Carleton College (B.A., magna cum laude, 1989); Northwestern School of Law of Lewis & Clark College (J.D., summa cum laude, 1995). Environmental Law, 1993-1994. *Member:* Multnomah County and American Bar Associations; Oregon State Bar. ***PRACTICE AREAS:*** Business Law; Corporate Law; Mergers and Acquisitions; Lease Financings; Securities Regulation. ***Email:*** colleen.mcmullen@millernash.com

(This Listing Continued)

MILLER NASH LLP, Portland—Continued

ERICH W. MERRILL, JR., P.C., born Memphis, Tennessee, May 18, 1957; admitted to bar, 1983, Oregon; registered to practice before U.S. Patent and Trademark Office. *Education:* Vanderbilt University (B.E., summa cum laude, 1979); Harvard University (J.D., 1983). Tau Beta Pi. Editor-in-Chief, Harvard Law Record, 1982-1983. Member, Program Committee, Software Association of Oregon, 1997-2002. Member and Chair, Emerging Business Committee, AeA Oregon Chapter, 2003-2004. Speaker: Thirteenth Annual Seattle Computer Law Conference, 2002; Drafting Business Documents, Oregon State Bar, 2003. Commentator, Venture Capital After the Bubble Symposium, Portland, Oregon, 2004. Listed in: Best Lawyers in America. *Member:* Oregon State Bar (Chair, Business Law Section, 1994-1995; Past Member, Executive Committee, Computer Law Section); International Trademark Association. ***PRACTICE AREAS:*** Mergers and Acquisitions; Securities Offerings; Emerging Growth Companies; Intellectual Property Law. ***Email:*** erich.merrill@millernash.com

JOHN CASEY MILLS, P.C., born Los Angeles, California, February 1, 1958; admitted to bar, 1984, Oregon and Washington. *Education:* Brown University (B.A., 1980); Northwestern School of Law of Lewis and Clark College (J.D., cum laude, 1984). Author: "Hazardous Substance Contamination Claims in Bankruptcy," Environmental Law for General Practitioners, J. Morford ed., 1991. Contributor, Oregon State Bar CLEs, Bankruptcy 1995, Environmental and Natural Resources Law 2002, Real Estate 1996 and 2001. *Member:* Oregon State Bar (Member, Debtor/Creditor Section); Washington State (Member, Creditor/Debtor Section) and American Bar Associations; American Bankruptcy Institute. Certified in Business Bankruptcy Law by the American Board of Certification (Certification not recognized or required in Washington). ***PRACTICE AREAS:*** Creditors Rights; Bankruptcy Law. ***Email:*** casey.mills@millernash.com

CONRAD L. MOORE, born Worland, Wyoming, March 9, 1937; admitted to bar, 1962, Oregon; 1963, California (inactive). *Education:* Willamette University (A.B., 1959); University of California, Boalt Hall School of Law, Berkeley (J.D., 1962). Listed in Best Lawyers in America for more than 10 consecutive years. Member, Board of Trustees, Maybelle Clark Macdonald Fund and Willamette View Foundation. *Member:* State Bar of California; Oregon State Bar; American Bar Association (Former Supervisory Council Member and Chairman, Committee on Administration and Distribution of Estates of the Section of Real Property, Probate and Trust Law); Oregon Law Institute (Former Director); Estate Planning Council of Portland. Fellow, American College of Trust and Estate Counsel. ***PRACTICE AREAS:*** Estate Planning Law; Estate Administration; Trust Administration; Fiduciary Income Law; Estate and Gift Taxation. ***Email:*** conrad.moore@millernash.com

DAVID M. MUNRO, born Portland, Oregon, July 9, 1941; admitted to bar, 1966, Oregon. *Education:* Stanford University (A.B., 1963; J.D., 1966); New York University (LL.M. in Taxation, 1967). *Member:* Oregon State Bar; American Bar Association (Member, Sections on: Real Property, Probate and Trust Law; Taxation Law). ***PRACTICE AREAS:*** Estate Planning; Probate Law; Charitable Trusts and Foundations. ***Email:*** dave.munro@millernash.com

JOHN F. NEUPERT, P.C., born Portland, Oregon, August 4, 1952; admitted to bar, 1978, Oregon. *Education:* University of Oregon (B.S., 1974; J.D., 1978). Phi Beta Kappa; Order of the Coif. Listed in "Chambers USA: America's Leading Business Lawyers". *Member:* Oregon State Bar. ***PRACTICE AREAS:*** Federal Practice; Complex Commercial Litigation; Corporate Litigation; Corporate Control Contests; Foreign Sovereign Immunities Act Litigation; Transnational Litigation. ***Email:*** john.neupert@millernash.com

TERESA H. PEARSON, P.C., born Portland, Oregon, October 30, 1970; admitted to bar, 1995, Oregon; 1996, Washington; U.S. Court of Appeals, Ninth Circuit, U.S. District Court, District of Oregon, Western and Eastern Districts of Washington, and U.S. Supreme Court. *Education:* University of California at Berkeley (B.A., highest honors, 1992); Duke University (J.D., high honors, 1995). Phi Beta Kappa. Robert Netherland Miller Scholar, Duke University Law School. *Member:* Multnomah County and Washington State Bar Associations; Oregon State Bar; American Inns of Court. ***PRACTICE AREAS:*** Insolvency; Reorganization; Creditors Rights; Business Law; Corporate Law; Appellate Practice. ***Email:*** teresa.pearson@millernash.com

DAVID G. POST, P.C., born Wichita Falls, Texas, September 15, 1967; admitted to bar, 1996, Oregon. *Education:* Cornell University (B.A., magna cum laude, 1990); Harvard Law School (J.D., 1996). *Member:* Multnomah County Bar Association; Oregon State Bar (President, Executive Committee, Securities Regulation Section); Northwest Securities Institute (Planning Co-Chair, February 2005). ***PRACTICE AREAS:*** Corporate Law; Mergers and Acquisitions; Securities Regulation; Emerging Business Law. ***Email:*** david.post@millernash.com

JOHN F. PURCELL, P.C., born Bellingham, Washington, April 25, 1954; admitted to bar, 1980, Oregon. *Education:* Stanford University (A.B., with honors, 1976); Northwestern School of Law of Lewis and Clark College (J.D., 1980). Co-Author: "Arbitration of Construction Disputes," Oregon Continuing Legal Education Handbook for Construction Law, 1989, 1997, 2004. Member, Panel of Arbitrators, American Arbitration Association. *Member:* Oregon State Bar (Member, Sections on: Construction Law; Commercial Litigation); American Bar Association (Member: Forum of the Construction Industry; Construction Litigation Committee, Litigation Section). ***PRACTICE AREAS:*** Construction Law; Arbitration; Mediation; Commercial Litigation. ***Email:*** john.purcell@millernash.com

DENNIS P. RAWLINSON, P.C., born Portland, Oregon, March 1, 1947; admitted to bar, 1976, Oregon. *Education:* University of Notre Dame (A.B., magna cum laude, 1969); Cornell University (M.B.A., 1976; J.D., 1976). Oregon State Bar President-Elect, 2005. Oregon State Bar President, 2006. Member, Board of Governors, Oregon State Bar, 2003—. Recommended in Best Lawyers in America, 2006, and Best Lawyers in American Commercial Litigation, 2005, Corporate Counsel and the American Lawyer of the Association of Corporate Counsel. Recommended Commercial Litigation Lawyer, Chambers USA, 2005. Chair, Litigation Section, Oregon State Bar, 1997-1998; Planning Committee, Oregon State Bar Litigation Institute and Retreat, 1994—. Member, Executive Committee, Litigation Section, Oregon State Bar, 1992—; Executive Committee, Debtor/Creditor Section, Oregon State Bar, 1987-1990; U.S. District Court of Oregon Historical Society Board of Directors and Executive Committee, November 1997-1999; Task Force on Civil Trial Practice Standards and Supplement, Section of Litigation, American Bar Association, 1997-1998 and 2003-2004. Co-Chair, Trial Evidence Committee, Section of Litigation, American Bar Association, 2003—; Commercial and Business Litigation Committee, Litigation Section, American Bar Association, 1999-2003; Creditors' Rights Subcommittee, Section of Litigation, American Bar Association, 1992-1998; American Bar Association Discovery Task Force, May 1997-2000. Managing Editor, Oregon Commercial Practice Manual, 1988 and 1994 and Oregon Commercial Practice Manual Supplement, 1990; Oregon State Bar Litigation Journal, 1992—; American Bar Association Commercial and Business Litigation newsletter, 1998-2003; American Bar Association Trial Evidence Journal, 2003—. Recipient, Oregon State Bar Membership Service Award, September 1995; Membership Service Award, Litigation Section, Oregon State Bar, 1999; Membership Service Award, Multnomah Bar Association, May 2000. Faculty Member, National Institute for Trial Advocacy Northwest Deposition Program, August 1996. Master in Owen M. Panner American Inn of Court, August 1996—. Past Chair, Member, Multnomah Bar Association Judicial Screening Committee, June 1997-2000. Speaker: "Old Dogs and New Tricks for Direct Examination, American Bar Association, Section of Litigation Annual Meeting, April 2005; "Written in Stone: A Fresh Look at 10 Commandments of Trial Practice," American Bar Association, Section of Litigation Annual Meeting, May 2004; "Resurrecting the Smoking Gun—How to Find and Recover Deleted Evidence" and "Litigating in the 21st Century: The Admissibility and Persuasion of Electronic Evidence," Section of Litigation Annual Meeting, American Bar Association, April, 2003; "The Internet Games" (mock trial on introduction into evidence of Internet information), American Bar Association Section of Litigation Annual Meeting, April 2002; "The Internet Olympics," American Bar Association Section of Litigation Annual Meeting, May 2001. Speaker and Author, "Depositions," Oregon State Bar, September 2001; Accountant Liability CPE for CPAs, September 1997, May 1998; "Anatomy of a Trial," Oregon State Bar Fundamentals of Oregon Civil Trial Procedure Seminar, November 1999—; "Professionalism in Federal Court," Oregon Law Institute Federal Practice and Procedure Seminar, December 1998—; "Provisional Process and Other Prejudgment Remedies," Oregon State Bar Fundamentals of Collecting Money Judgments Seminar, March 1998—; Economic Damages and the Use of Experts for Challenging Damages Seminar, Oregon State Bar, October 1998; Review of Agency and Contract Law for National Association of Credit Managers, October 1998. Author: "Execution on Unusual Property," Oregon State Bar Debtor-Creditor Section Annual Meeting, Summer 1986; "Collecting Money Judgments," Oregon State Bar, Multnomah Bar Association, February 1988; "UCC Article 2 Sales Remedies," Oregon Law Institute, 1989; "Garnishments," Oregon State Bar Debtor-Creditor Section newsletter, Winter 1990; "Fair Debt Collection Practices," Oregon State Bar Debtor-Creditor Section newsletter, February 1991; "Lessor's Remedies," Oregon State Bar Debtor-Creditor Section, November 15, 1991; "Enforcing Lessor's Interests Under Uniform Commercial Code Article 2A," Oregon State Bar Debtor-Creditor Section, February 1992; "Postjudgment Collection," Professional Education Systems, Inc., April 30, 1992; "Prejudgment Remedies," Oregon Law Institute, May 14, 1993; "Preparing for and Defending Depositions," Lorman Education Services, September 28, 1993; articles for the Oregon State Bar Litigation Journal, 1992—, including numerous columns dealing with litigation topics, such as opening statements, direct examinations, cross-examinations, deposition practice, new federal civil procedural rules, cases on evidentiary law, and dealing with the media; "Old Dogs and New Tricks for Direct Examination," American Bar Association Litigation magazine, Spring 2005; "Direct Examination: Old Dogs and New Tricks," Oregon State Bar Litigation Journal, Summer 2004; "Much Ado About Nothing New: Despite All the Commotion, Jones v. Emerald Pacific Homes, Inc., Adds Little to Oregon Law Regarding Construction Defect Claims," Oregon State Bar Construction Law Journal, 2004; "Distinctions Between State and Federal Practice," 1995 Litigation Institute and Retreat; "Fair Debt Collection Practices Act Revisited," American Bar Association Bankruptcy Litigation newsletter, January 1994; "Unfair Debt Collection Practices Notices Must Be Included in Pleadings," American Bar Association Bankruptcy Litigation newsletter, January 1995; "Provisional Process," Oregon State Bar Consumer and Commercial Collection Law in Oregon seminar, May 1995; "Buyer and Sellers Remedies in Real Estate Transactions," Law Seminars International, May 1996; "Dealing With the Media," Oregon Association of Defense Counsel, November 1996; "Lessor's Remedies," Law Seminars International, April 1997. *Member:* Oregon State Bar; American Bar Association; Multnomah Bar Association; Federal Bar Association; Oregon Association of Defense Counsel. American Bar Foundation, 2005. [1st Lieutenant, Army Medical Services Corps, Active Duty, 1970-1972 including Ambulance Company Commander and Service Officer, 44th MASH Hospital and Service Officer, 121 Evac Hospital, Camp Yongson, Korea. Brigade Commander, ROTC, University of Notre Dame]. (Board Certified in Civil Law by the National Institute for Trial Advocacy). ***PRACTICE AREAS:*** Commercial Litigation; Trial Practice; Real Estate Litigation; Creditors Rights Litigation; Employment Litigation; Contract Litigation; Shareholder Litigation; Tort Litigation. ***Email:*** dennis.rawlinson@millernash.com

PETER C. RICHTER, P.C., born Opava, Czechoslovakia, June 13, 1944; admitted to bar, 1971, Oregon. *Education:* University of Oregon (B.S., 1967; J.D., 1971). Adjunct Professor of Law, Trial Advocacy, Northwestern School of Law of Lewis and Clark College, 1987—. Pro Tem Judge, 1985-2001. Listed in: Best Lawyers in America; Chambers USA: America's Leading Business Litigation Lawyers. *Member:* Oregon State Bar; American Bar Association; International Association of Defense Counsel; American Board of Trial Advocates. American Bar Foundation. ***PRACTICE AREAS:*** Advocate; Trial Practice. ***Email:*** peter.richter@millernash.com

BRUCE A. RUBIN, P.C., born Pittsburgh, Pennsylvania, September 12, 1951; admitted to bar, 1976, Oregon. *Education:* Yale University (B.A., magna cum laude, 1973); Stanford University (J.D., 1976). Recipient, Clifford N. Carlsen, Jr. Award for Outstanding Pro Bono Service. *Member:* Oregon State Bar (Member: Judicial Administration Committee; Affirmative Action Committee; Task Force on Close Corporations); American Bar Association (Member: Task Force on the Judiciary; Steering Committee on Judicial Independence Project; Co-Chair, Subcommittee on Practical Ethical Considerations, Committee on Corporate Counsel); International Association of Defense Counsel. ***PRACTICE AREAS:*** Trial Practice; Appellate Practice; Corporate Governance; Employment Litigation; ERISA Litigation; Real Estate Litigation.

THOMAS C. SAND, P.C., born Portland, Oregon, June 4, 1952; admitted to bar, 1977, Oregon. *Education:* University of Oregon (B.A., 1974); Northwestern School of Law of Lewis & Clark College (J.D., 1977). Recipient, Distinguished Graduate, Northwestern School of Law of Lewis & Clark College, 2004. Member, U.S. Bank of Oregon Advisory

(This Listing Continued)

Board, 2002—. Listed in: Best Lawyers in America, 2005; Who's Who in American Law, 1996-2004; Who's Who in America, 1993-2003. Secretary, President, Board of Directors, Alumni Association of Northwestern School of Law of Lewis & Clark College, 1992-1997. Member, U.S. District Court of Oregon Historical Society, 1990—. President and Member Board of Directors, Portland Area Council of Camp Fire Inc., 1984-1985. Special Assistant Attorney General, Wasco County voter registration hearings, 1984. Volunteer, Northeast Legal Clinic Volunteer Lawyers Project. *Member:* Multnomah County (Chair, Professionalism Committee, 1988), Federal and American (Member, Litigation Section, Committee on Securities Litigation) Bar Associations; Oregon State Bar (Chair and Executive Board Member, Securities Regulation Section, 1999; Federal Practice and Procedure Committee, 1998-2001; Chair, Professionalism Committee, 1990); American Judicature Society (Oregon Chapter); Securities Industry Association (Member, Compliance and Legal Division). ***PRACTICE AREAS:*** Trial Practice; Securities Fraud; Shareholder Litigation; Employment Litigation; Broker-Dealer Regulation; Arbitration; Mediation. ***Email:*** tom.sand@millernash.com

JOSHUA M. F. SASAKI, P.C., born Portland, Oregon, July 1, 1971; admitted to bar, 1996, Oregon. *Education:* Dartmouth College (A.B., magna cum laude and with high honors, 1993); Northwestern School of Law of Lewis and Clark College (J.D., cum laude, 1996). Associate Editor, Environmental Law Review. *Member:* Oregon State Bar; American Bar Association; Japan-America Society of Oregon. ***PRACTICE AREAS:*** Commercial Litigation; Trial Practice; Real Estate Litigation; Shareholder Litigation; Corporate Litigation; Tort Litigation; Contract Litigation; Creditors Rights Litigation; Employment Litigation; Litigation. ***Email:*** josh.sasaki@millernash.com

CATHERINE A. SHAW, P.C., born Seattle, Washington, January 18, 1961; admitted to bar, 1988, Oregon; 2003, Washington. *Education:* University of Washington (B.A., magna cum laude, 1984; M.B.A., 1988; J.D., 1987). Phi Beta Kappa; Beta Gamma Sigma. *Member:* Multnomah County, Washington State and American Bar Associations; Oregon State Bar; National Association of Bond Lawyers; Nationally Recognized Bond Counsel. ***PRACTICE AREAS:*** Business Law; Public Finance; Commercial Finance; Real Estate; Mergers and Acquisitions. ***Email:*** catherine.shaw@millernash.com

RONALD A. SHELLAN, P.C., born Everett, Washington, October 17, 1949; admitted to bar, 1975, Oregon; 1979, U.S. District Court, District of Oregon; 1982, U.S. Tax Court. *Education:* University of Washington (B.A., magna cum laude, 1972); Willamette University (J.D., 1975). Beta Gamma Sigma. Associate Editor, Willamette Law Journal, 1975. Author: "Advising Oregon Businesses, The 'G' Reorganization - Tax Free Acquisition of the Financially Distressed Corporation," Oregon State Bar Continuing Legal Education, 1984; "Structuring Development Services Agreements in Section 42 Projects," 5 J Affordable Housing & Community Dev L 175 (1996); "Tax-Free Exchanges," 47 Major Tax Plan (MB) ch 14 (1995); "Negotiating Low-Income Housing Tax-Credit Venture Agreements: Beyond the Basics," 86 J of Taxation 140 (1997); "First Look: New Reverse-Starker Exchange Revenue Procedure," 41 Tax Management Memorandum 528 (2000); "Like Kind Exchanges," Documentation of Real Estate Transactions, Oregon State Bar, 2001; "Thinking About Year Fifteen of a Low-Income Tax Credit Partnership," 11 J Affordable Housing & Community Dev L 175 (2001); "Tax Issues in Capitalizing Low-Income Housing Tax-Credit Partnerships," 13 J. Affordable Housing No. 4 (2004). Law Clerk to Honorable Carlisle B. Roberts, Judge, Oregon Tax Court, 1975-1976. Certified Public Accountant, Oregon, 1978. Lecturer, University of Southern California Tax Institute, 1995. *Member:* Oregon State Bar (Member, Taxation Section; Chairman, 1984-1985; Member: Corporate Section; Executive Committee, 1988-1990, Estate Planning Section); American Bar Association (Member, Section on Taxation; Member, Committee on Sales, Exchanges and Basis, 1992—); Portland Tax Forum (Chairperson, 1988); Oregon Society of Certified Public Accountants (Member, Board of Directors, 1985-1987 and 1995-1997; Chairman, State and Local Taxation Committee, 1981-1982). ***PRACTICE AREAS:*** Corporate Law; Taxation Law; Estate Planning Law; Real Estate. ***Email:*** ron.shellan@millernash.com

MICHELLE SLATER, P.C., born Salt Lake City, Utah, January 31, 1969; admitted to bar, 1996, Oregon. *Education:* Vassar College (B.A., 1991); Northwestern School of Law of Lewis and Clark College (J.D., 1996). *Member:* Multnomah and American Bar Associations; Oregon State Bar. ***PRACTICE AREAS:*** Corporate Law; Mergers and Acquisitions; Business Law; Insolvency; Asset Based Finance. ***Email:*** michelle.slater@millernash.com

JEFFREY C. THEDE, P.C., born Santa Barbara, California, August 3, 1954; admitted to bar, 1979, Oregon; 1985, Washington. *Education:* University of Oregon (B.S., 1976); Willamette University (J.D., 1979). Associate Editor, Willamette Law Review, 1978-1979. Listed in: Best Lawyers in America. *Member:* Oregon State Bar; Washington State Bar Association. Fellow, American College of Trust and Estate Counsel. ***PRACTICE AREAS:*** Business Law; Estate Planning Law; Probate Law; Charitable Trusts and Foundations Law. ***Email:*** jeff.thede@millernash.com

PORTLAND, OREGON OF COUNSEL

JOHN D. BURNS, born Portland, Oregon, March 3, 1936; admitted to bar, 1962, Oregon. *Education:* University of Notre Dame (B.A., 1958); Georgetown University Law Center (J.D., 1961). President, Oregon Historical Society, 2001-2004. District Attorney, Gilliam County, 1999-2002. Managing Partner, Miller Nash LLP, 1997-1999. Oregon State Senator, 1967-1975. President, Oregon State Senate, 1971-1973. Deputy District Attorney, Multnomah County, 1962-1965. *Member:* Oregon State Bar. ***PRACTICE AREAS:*** Agricultural Law; Public Law; Petroleum Law; Trusts and Estates. ***Email:*** john.burns@millernash.com

PORTLAND, OREGON SPECIAL COUNSEL

WILLIAM R. KNUTHS, born Albany, Oregon, October 9, 1955; admitted to bar, 1983, Oregon and U.S. District Court, District of Oregon; 1985, District of Columbia; 1986, California. *Education:* University of Oregon (B.A., with honors, 1976; J.D., 1983). Associate Editor, Oregon Law Review, 1982-1983. Author: "*Harp v. Loux:* ORCP Permits Default Judgment Without Notice," 62 Oregon L. Rev. 465, 1983. *Member:* Multnomah County and American Bar Associations; Oregon State Bar. ***LANGUAGES:*** German and Serbo-Croatian. ***PRACTICE AREAS:*** Taxation; Business Law. ***Email:*** william.knuths@millernash.com

(This Listing Continued)

WILLIAM H. WALTERS, born Huntington, New York, February 19, 1942; admitted to bar, 1982, Oregon. *Education:* Occidental College (B.A., 1963); Princeton University (M.A., 1965); University of Massachusetts (Ph.D., 1975); University of Oregon (J.D., 1982). *Member:* Oregon State Bar. ***PRACTICE AREAS:*** Appellate Practice. ***Email:*** bill.walters@millernash.com

PORTLAND, OREGON COUNSEL

VICTORIA L. MACPHERSON, born Salem, Oregon, June 4, 1956; admitted to bar, 1986, Oregon; 1993, U.S. Court of Appeals, Ninth Circuit. *Education:* Oregon State University (B.A., 1981); Willamette University (J.D., magna cum laude, 1986). Editor, Developments in the Law, Willamette Law Review, 1985-1986. Judicial Clerk to the Honorable W. Michael Gillette, Oregon Supreme Court, 1986-1988. Co-Author: 2001 Labor and Employment Law: Public Sector, Chapter 16, "PERS and Related Programs," published by the Oregon State Bar. Listed in: Best Lawyers in America. Assistant Attorney General, Oregon Department of Justice, 1995-1999. *Member:* Oregon State Bar; American Bar Association. ***PRACTICE AREAS:*** Employee Benefits; Public Law. ***Email:*** tory.macpherson@millernash.com

PORTLAND, OREGON RETIRED PARTNERS

JOHN W. HILL, born Portland, Oregon, May 22, 1925; admitted to bar, 1949, Oregon. *Education:* Colorado College, University of Oklahoma and University of Oregon (B.S., 1947); University of Oregon (J.D., 1949). Co-Chairman: International Labor Law Committee, American Bar Association, 1990-1992; Committee on Practice and Procedure Before the National Labor Relations Board, American Bar Association, 1986-1989. *Member:* Oregon State Bar. ***PRACTICE AREAS:*** Management Labor Law; Employee Benefits Law.

NORMAN J. WIENER, born Portland, Oregon, September 10, 1919; admitted to bar, 1947, Oregon. *Education:* University of Oregon (B.S., 1941; J.D., 1947). Member, Environment, Energy and Resources Law Section, American Bar Association. *Member:* Oregon State Bar. Fellow, American Bar Foundation. ***PRACTICE AREAS:*** Complex Litigation; Antitrust; Forest Products Law; General Practice.

PORTLAND, OREGON ASSOCIATES

MICHELLE E. BARTON, born Garden Grove, California; admitted to bar, 2004, Oregon. *Education:* University of Notre Dame (B.A., magna cum laude, 2001; J.D., cum laude, 2004). Executive Editor, Notre Dame Law Review, 2003-2004. Law Clerk to the Hon. Frederick J. Martone, U.S. District Court, District of Arizona, 2004-2005. ***PRACTICE AREAS:*** Litigation. ***Email:*** michelle.barton@millernash.com

PAMELA T. BLACKWELL, born Brooklyn, New York, April 18, 1966; admitted to bar, 1993, England and Wales; 2000, Oregon. *Education:* University of St. Andrews, Scotland (M.A., magna cum laude, 1989); Northwestern School of Law of Lewis & Clark College (J.D., cum laude, 2000). Research Editor, Journal of Small and Emerging Business Law. ***PRACTICE AREAS:*** Business Law; Real Estate Law. ***Email:*** pamela.blackwell@millernash.com

ABRAHAM J.B. CABLE, born Portland, Oregon, September 8, 1975; admitted to bar, 2000, Oregon. *Education:* University of Puget Sound (B.A., magna cum laude, 1997); Harvard Law School (J.D., cum laude, 2000). Editor, Harvard Law Review. ***PRACTICE AREAS:*** Business Law. ***Email:*** abe.cable@millernash.com

HEATHER K. CAVANAUGH, born Tualatin, Oregon, December 14, 1974; admitted to bar, 2002, Washington; 2003, Oregon. *Education:* Oregon State University (B.S., 1998); University of Oregon (J.D., 2002). Order of the Coif. *Member:* Multnomah County and Clark County Bar Associations. ***PRACTICE AREAS:*** Litigation; Business Litigation; Real Estate Litigation. ***Email:*** heather.cavanaugh@millernash.com

STEVEN L. CHRISTENSEN, born Oklahoma City, Oklahoma, April 6, 1967; admitted to bar, 1997, Oregon and U.S. Tax Court; 1998, Washington. *Education:* Brigham Young University (B.S., magna cum laude, 1991); Georgetown University Law Center (J.D., cum laude, 1997). Phi Delta Phi (Excheqher). Certified Public Accountant, Oregon, 1994. *Member:* Oregon State Bar; American Institute of Certified Public Accountants. ***LANGUAGES:*** Portuguese. ***PRACTICE AREAS:*** Business Transactions; Partnership Law; Joint Ventures; Taxation; Private Equity. ***Email:*** steve.christensen@millernash.com

KIERAN J. CURLEY, born New York, N.Y., February 17, 1970; admitted to bar, 2001, Oregon. *Education:* Loyola College (B.B.A., 1992); University of Washington (J.D., 2001). *Member:* Oregon State Bar. ***PRACTICE AREAS:*** Litigation. ***Email:*** kieran.curley@millernash.com

KORNELIA DORMIRE, admitted to bar, 2001, Oregon. *Education:* University of Colorado at Boulder (B.A., 1995); Middlebury College (M.A., 1996); Lewis & Clark College (J.D., 2001). *Member:* Oregon State Bar. ***PRACTICE AREAS:*** Trusts and Estates. ***Email:*** kornelia.dormire@millernash.com

MAREESA M. ELMQUIST, admitted to bar, 1999, Oregon. *Education:* University of Utah (B.A., 1994); Lewis and Clark College Law School (J.D., cum laude, 1998). Phi Delta Phi. *Member:* Oregon State Bar; American Health Lawyers Association. ***LANGUAGES:*** Spanish. ***PRACTICE AREAS:*** Health Law; Hospital Law; Corporate Law; Commercial Law. ***Email:*** mareesa.elmquist@millernash.com

KY FULLERTON, born Eugene, Oregon, November 11, 1974; admitted to bar, 2002, Oregon. *Education:* Georgetown University (A.B., cum laude, 1997); University of Oregon (J.D., 2002). Editor-in-Chief, Oregon Law Review, 2001-2002. Co-Author: with M. Christie Helmer, "Jones Act: Still Safely Afloat," Propeller Club Q. at 4, Spring 2004; with Norman J. Wiener, "Does Oregon's Appellate Court System Need Fixing?" 81 Oregon Law Review 477, 2002. Author: "Bush, Gore, and the 2000 Presidential Election: Time for the Electoral College to Go?" 80 Oregon Law Review 717, 2001. ***PRACTICE AREAS:*** Litigation; Admiralty and Maritime Law. ***Email:*** ky.fullerton@millernash.com

CHRISTINE GIBERT, born Webster, Texas, February 9, 1978; admitted to bar, 2004, Oregon. *Education:* Rice University (B.A., cum laude, 2000); Harvard Law School (J.D., 2004). *Member:* Oregon State Bar; American Bar Association. ***PRACTICE AREAS:*** Employee Benefits. ***Email:*** christine.gibert@millernash.com

(This Listing Continued)

MILLER NASH LLP, Portland—Continued

PAUL L. HAVEL, born Detroit, Michigan, February 14, 1968; admitted to bar, 1996, Illinois; 1998, Oregon; 1999, Washington. *Education:* Denison University (B.A., 1990); Chicago-Kent College of Law (J.D., 1996). *Member:* Multnomah County, Washington State and American Bar Associations; Oregon State Bar (Member, Sections on: Intellectual Property; Computer Law; Business Law). ***PRACTICE AREAS:*** Intellectual Property; Trademarks; Copyrights; Business Law. ***Email:*** paul.havel@millernash.com

ASHLEY S. HOHIMER, born Seattle, Washington, September 14, 1977; admitted to bar, 2003, Oregon. *Education:* University of Oregon (B.A., 1999); Emory University School of Law (J.D., 2003). Author: "Constructive Trusts in Bankruptcy: Is an Equitable Interest in Property More Than Just a 'Claim'," 19 Bankruptcy Developments Journal 499 (2003). *Member:* Oregon State Bar (Member, Debtor-Creditor Section). ***LANGUAGES:*** Spanish. ***PRACTICE AREAS:*** Real Estate; Insolvency; Reorganization; Bankruptcy. ***Email:*** ashley.hohimer@millernash.com

KELLY SHAFER HOSSAINI, born Hillsboro, Oregon, May 15, 1964; admitted to bar, 2001, Oregon. *Education:* Portland State University (B.A., 1990; MURP (Masters of Urban and Regional Planning), 1993); Northwestern School of Law at Lewis & Clark (J.D., 2000). ***PRACTICE AREAS:*** Land Use; Public Law. ***Email:*** kelly.hossaini@millernash.com

HONG N. HUYNH, born Rach Gia, Vietnam, July 24, 1973; admitted to bar, 1998, Oregon. *Education:* Pacific University (B.S., 1995); University of Oregon (J.D., 1998). Executive Editor, Journal of Environmental Law and Litigation. Co-Author: "Environmental Liability Issues," Administering Trusts in Oregon 2000 supplement, Oregon State Bar; "Environmental Liability and Real Estate Transactions," in Fundamentals of Real Estate Transactions 2001 supplement, Oregon State Bar. *Member:* Oregon State Bar; American Bar Association (Member, Section on: Environment, Energy and Resources Law). ***LANGUAGES:*** Vietnamese. ***PRACTICE AREAS:*** Environmental Law; Natural Resources Law; Environmental Litigation; Telecommunications; Energy. ***Email:*** hong.huynh@millernash.com

DUSTIN R. KLINGER, born Spokane, Washington, May 21, 1970; admitted to bar, 1999, Washington; 2000, Oregon. *Education:* University of Notre Dame (B.A., 1992); University of Washington (J.D./LL.M., 1999). Editor-in-Chief, Pacific Rim Law & Policy Journal. Author, "Comparing Apples to Oranges: Lessons from the Failure of U.S. Apple Exports to Japan," 8 Pacific Rim Law & Policy Journal 121. *Member:* Oregon State Bar; Washington State Bar Association; American Immigration Lawyers Association. ***LANGUAGES:*** Japanese. ***PRACTICE AREAS:*** Business Law; Immigration; Real Estate. ***Email:*** dustin.klinger@millernash.com

KEVIN M. KOLINER, born Yankton, South Dakota, July 8, 1975; admitted to bar, 2001, Oregon; 2002, U.S. District Court, District of Oregon. *Education:* University of Minnesota (B.A., summa cum laude, 1997); University of Virginia (J.D., 2001). *Member:* Multnomah County and American Bar Associations; U.S. District Court of Oregon Historical Society. ***PRACTICE AREAS:*** Litigation; Mediation; Arbitration. ***Email:*** kevin.koliner@millernash.com

SABRINA P. LOISELLE, born Klamath Falls, Oregon, January 25, 1967; admitted to bar, 1992, Oregon. *Education:* Willamette University (B.S., cum laude, 1989); University of Oregon School of Law (J.D., 1992). Order of the Coif. Associate Editor, Oregon Law Review. *Member:* Multnomah County and American Bar Associations; Oregon State Bar (Member, Sections on: Litigation; Debtor-Creditor). ***PRACTICE AREAS:*** Commercial Litigation; Creditors Rights; Insolvency; Reorganization. ***Email:*** sabrina.loiselle@millernash.com

SARAH LOWINGER, born Haifa, Israel, October 3, 1971; admitted to bar, 2002, Oregon. *Education:* University of Oregon (B.A., 1995); University of Virginia (J.D., 2002). Phi Beta Kappa. ***PRACTICE AREAS:*** Litigation. ***Email:*** sarah.lowinger@millernash.com

CLIFTON MOLATORE, born Klamath Falls, Oregon, January 11, 1975; admitted to bar, 2000, California; 2004, Oregon. *Education:* University of Oregon (B.A., 1997); University of Oregon School of Law (J.D., 2000). Order of the Coif. ***PRACTICE AREAS:*** Bankruptcy; Banks and Banking; Debtor and Creditor; Finance. ***Email:*** clifton.molatore@millernash.com

RYAN R. NISLE, born Whittier, California, June 10, 1975; admitted to bar, 2001, Oregon. *Education:* Iowa State University (B.S., 1998); University of Oregon (J.D., 2001). Order of the Coif. *Member:* Oregon State Bar. ***PRACTICE AREAS:*** Business Law; Federal Taxation; State Taxation. ***Email:*** ryan.nisle@millernash.com

J. MICHAEL PORTER, born Kansas City, Missouri, August 9, 1970; admitted to bar, 2000, Oregon. *Education:* Kansas State University (B.S., 1993); University of South Carolina (M.Ed., 1995); University of Kansas School of Law (J.D., 2000). Order of the Coif. *Member:* National Association of College and University Attorneys; National School Boards Association Council of School Attorneys; Oregon School Boards Association Council of School Attorneys. ***PRACTICE AREAS:*** Labor and Employment; School Law; College and University Law; Litigation; Arbitration; Mediation. ***Email:*** michael.porter@millernash.com

JENNIFER J. ROOF, born Seattle, Washington, May 3, 1972; admitted to bar, 2000, Oregon; 2001, U.S. District Court, District of Oregon and U.S. Court of Appeals, Tenth Circuit; 2002, U.S. Court of Appeals, Ninth Circuit. *Education:* University of Washington (B.S., 1995); University of Oregon (J.D., 1999). Phi Alpha Delta; Order of the Coif. Member, Inns of Court, 1999-2001. Law Clerk to the Hon. Bobby R. Baldock, Tenth Circuit Court of Appeals. Associate Editor, Journal of Environmental Law & Litigation, 1997-1999. *Member:* Multnomah County (Member, Young Lawyer Section Pro Bono Committee), American (Member, Litigation Section and Young Lawyers Division) and Federal (Member, Younger Lawyers Division) Bar Associations; Oregon State Bar. ***PRACTICE AREAS:*** Litigation. ***Email:*** *jennifer.roof@millernash.com*

TAMARA E. RUSSELL, born Gresham, Oregon, August 25, 1970; admitted to bar, 1997, Oregon and U.S. District Court, District of Oregon; 1998, Washington and U.S. District Court, Western District of Washington; 1999, U.S. District Court, Eastern District of Washington. *Education:* Simmons College (B.A., 1992); Boston University (J.D., 1997).

(This Listing Continued)

Edward F. Hennessey Distinguished Scholar. Editor, the American Journal of Law and Medicine. *Member:* Multnomah and Washington State Bar Associations; Oregon State Bar; Oregon Association of Defense Counsel. ***PRACTICE AREAS:*** Labor and Employment; Litigation. ***Email:*** tamara.russell@millernash.com

JEFFREY T. SAGALEWICZ, born Encino, California, July 30, 1971; admitted to bar, 2005, Oregon. *Education:* University of Oregon (B.S., 1993; J.D., 2005). Order of the Coif. Author: "The Martha Duty: Protecting Shareholders from the Criminal Behavior of Celebrity Corporate Figures," 83 Oregon Law Review 331 (2004). ***PRACTICE AREAS:*** Litigation. ***Email:*** jeff.sagalewicz@millernash.com

JUSTIN CLARK SAWYER, born Amarillo, Texas, July 29, 1975; admitted to bar, 2001, Oregon. *Education:* Colorado College (B.S., 1998); Northwestern School of Law (J.D., 2000). Member, Regional Mock Trial Team, 1999 and Member, Moot Court Board, 2000, Northwestern School of Law. Certified Law Student, Multnomah County District Attorney's Office, 2000. *Member:* Oregon State Bar. ***PRACTICE AREAS:*** Commercial Litigation; Securities Litigation; Products Liability. ***Email:*** justin.sawyer@millernash.com

AMY SILLIMAN, born Madison, Wisconsin, September 18, 1968; admitted to bar, 1996, Oregon. *Education:* Stanford University (B.A., 1991); Harvard Law School (J.D., cum laude, 1994). Phi Beta Kappa. ***PRACTICE AREAS:*** Estate Planning; Probate Law; Charitable Trusts and Foundations. ***Email:*** amy.silliman@millernash.com

GENA A. STONE, born Portland, Oregon; admitted to bar, 2002, Oregon. *Education:* Walla Walla College (B.A., summa cum laude, 1998); Willamette University (J.D., magna cum laude, 2002). Member, Western Pension and Benefits Conference, 2003—. *Member:* Oregon State Bar. ***PRACTICE AREAS:*** Employee Benefits. ***Email:*** gena.stone@millernash.com

ALYSSA EVE THIRSK TORMALA, born Salt Lake City, Utah, February 12, 1976; admitted to bar, 2001, Oregon; 2004, U.S. District Court, District of Oregon. *Education:* University of Utah (B.A. in English, with honors, 1998; B.A. in News-Editorial Journalism, with honors, 1998); Stanford University (J.D., 2001). Phi Beta Kappa. Co-Chair, Women of Stanford Law, 2000, 2001. *Member:* Oregon State Bar; American Bar Association. ***PRACTICE AREAS:*** Labor and Employment; Alternative Dispute Resolution; Employment Litigation. ***Email:*** alyssa.tormala@millernash.com

ERIN E. TRUAX, born Portland, Oregon, July 15, 1976; admitted to bar, 2003, Oregon. *Education:* University of Nevada (B.A., cum laude, 1998); Lewis and Clark College (J.D., summa cum laude, 2003). *Member:* Multnomah County Bar Association; Oregon State Bar. ***PRACTICE AREAS:*** Litigation; Labor and Employment. ***Email:*** erin.truax@millernash.com

CONNIE TSAI, born Akron, Ohio, April 24, 1978; admitted to bar, 2005, Oregon. *Education:* Harvard University (B.A., 1999); University of Virginia (J.D., 2005). ***PRACTICE AREAS:*** Business Law. ***Email:*** connie.tsai@millernash.com

PORTLAND, OREGON LEGAL SUPPORT PERSONNEL

LESLIE M. MESERVE, born Kearny, New Jersey, December 27, 1942; admitted to bar, 1983, Oregon. *Education:* Upsala College (A.B., 1967); Rutgers University (M.L.S., 1969); Lewis & Clark Law School (J.D., 1983). *Member:* Oregon State Bar; American Association of Law Libraries. (Director of Library Services). ***Email:*** leslie.meserve@millernash.com

REPRESENTATIVE CLIENTS: Beaverton School District; ConocoPhillips; Express Personnel Services; Gardenburger, Inc.; HemCon, Inc.; Hyundai Motor America; InSport International, Inc.; Johnson & Johnson, Inc.; Kalispel Tribe of Indians; Louisiana-Pacific Corp.; McMorgan & Company; Merck & Co., Inc.; Merrill Lynch; Oregon Public Broadcasting; Pacific Seafood Group; Pacific University; Portland Community College; Portland Public Schools; Potlatch Corp.; Providence Health System; R.B. Pamplin Corporation; Rentrak Corp; Rockmore International, Inc.; Seattle University; Siltronic Corp.; Skanska USA; Smith Barney; Southwest Washington Medical Center; Sprint Spectrum, LP; The Oregon Community Foundation; Trendwest Resorts, Inc.; U.S. Bancorp; UBS Financial Services, Inc.; University of Portland; USF Reddaway; USFreightways; Weyerhaeuser; West Coast Bancorp; Western States Petroleum Association; Widmer Brothers Brewing Co.; WilTel Communications, LLC; WinCo Foods, Inc.

REVISER OF THE OREGON LAW DIGEST FOR THIS DIRECTORY.

(For Complete Biographical Data on Personnel in Seattle, WA or Vancouver, WA, see Professional Biographies at those locations).

MITCHELL, LANG & SMITH

A Law Firm Partnership

2000, ONE MAIN PLACE
101 S.W. MAIN STREET
PORTLAND, OREGON 97204
Telephone: 503-221-1011
Fax: 503-248-0732
Email: portlandoffice@mls-law.com
URL: http://www.MLS-law.com

Seattle, Washington Office: 1001 Fourth Avenue, Suite 3714, 98154. Telephone: 206-292-1212. Fax: 206-682-4687.

General Civil Trial and Appellate Practice in all State and Federal Courts. General Insurance Defense Practice, including Auto, Bad Faith Fire Coverage, Casualty, Professional Liability, Products Liability, Toxic Tort, Environmental Liability, Hazardous Waste, Uninsured and Underinsured Motorists, Trucking Liability, Premises Liability, Employment Defense, Insurance Coverage, Insurance Litigation, Liquor Liability.

MEMBERS OF FIRM

CHARLES T. SMITH, born Portland, Oregon, November 19, 1937; admitted to bar, 1965, Oregon. *Education:* Oregon State University (B.S., 1959); Northwestern School of Law (J.D., 1965). Delta Theta Phi. Member, Northwestern School of Law Alumni Board of Directors, 1980-1983. Circuit Judge, Pro Tempore, Multnomah County, 1981, 1987-1997, 2000-2003. Member, Panel of Arbitrators, American Arbitration Association. Past Mem-

(This Listing Continued)

ber, Committee on Client Security Fund, Oregon State Bar. *Member:* Oregon State Bar. ***PRACTICE AREAS:*** Insurance Defense Law; General Liability Defense. ***Email:*** csmith@mls-law.com

WM. KELLY OLSON, born Portland, Oregon, June 9, 1948; admitted to bar, 1974, Oregon; 1984, Washington. *Education:* University of Oregon (B.A., 1970); Northwestern School of Law of Lewis and Clark College (J.D., 1974). Member, Northwestern Law Review, 1973-1974. ***PRACTICE AREAS:*** Insurance Defense; Civil Litigation; Products Liability. ***Email:*** kolson@mls-law.com

BRUCE M. WHITE, born Seattle, Washington, September 29, 1950; admitted to bar, 1976, Oregon; 1984, Washington. *Education:* Whitman College (B.A., 1972); Northwestern School of Law of Lewis and Clark College (J.D., 1976). Associate Editor, Environmental Law Journal, 1975-1976. ***PRACTICE AREAS:*** Civil Litigation; Insurance Defense; Fire Litigation; Professional Malpractice; Toxic Torts; Asbestos Defense. ***Email:*** bwhite@mls-law.com

SCOTT J. MEYER, born Quincy, Illinois, September 9, 1956; admitted to bar, 1981, Oregon. *Education:* University of Illinois (B.S., 1978); Northwestern School of Law of Lewis and Clark College (J.D., cum laude, 1981). Author: "Compensating Hazardous Waste Victims," 11 Environmental Law 689, 1981; "Relevancy," Oregon State Bar CLE on Evidence, 1992 and 1995. Law Clerk to the Hon. George E. Juba, U.S. Magistrate, U.S. District Court, District of Oregon, 1981-1982. Adjunct Professor of Law, Northwestern School of Law, Lewis and Clark College, 1991-1994. Circuit Judge Pro Tempore, Multnomah County, 1992-1993. ***PRACTICE AREAS:*** Civil Litigation; Insurance Defense; General Liability Defense. ***Email:*** smeyer@mls-law.com

CHARLES D. HARMS, born Portland, Oregon, July 20, 1952; admitted to bar, 1977, Oregon. *Education:* Portland State University (B.S., with honors, 1974); University of Oregon (J.D., 1977). Phi Alpha Theta. *Member:* Oregon State Bar; Trucking Industry Defense Association (Charter Member); American Truck Association Litigation Center. ***PRACTICE AREAS:*** Civil Litigation; Trucking Litigation; Insurance Defense Law; General Liability Defense. ***Email:*** charms@mls-law.com

CANDACE H. WEATHERBY, born San Mateo, California, December 30, 1942; admitted to bar, 1985, Oregon. *Education:* University of Oregon (B.A., 1965); Northwestern School of Law of Lewis and Clark College (J.D., 1985). Co-Chairman, Moot Court Board, 1984-1985. Recipient, Justice Robert E. Jones Award for Excellence in Trial Advocacy, Spring, 1985. *Member:* Oregon State Bar (Member: Joint Committee on Medical Profession, 1992-1994; Judicial Administration Committee, 1996-1999, Chair, 1998-1999; Multnomah County Lawyers Professional Responsibility Committee, 1996-2000; 2004—; Multnomah County Court Liaison Committee, 2003—; Defense Research Institute). ***PRACTICE AREAS:*** Insurance Defense Law; General Liability Defense; Professional Liability. ***Email:*** cweatherby@mls-law.com

SHAWN M. O'NEIL, born Atlanta, Georgia, March 10, 1963; admitted to bar, 1991, Oregon; 1993, U.S. District Court, District of Oregon; 1994, District of Columbia; 2001, Washington; 2002, U.S. Court of Appeals, Ninth Circuit. *Education:* Boston University (B.A., 1986); Willamette University College of Law (J.D., 1991). Phi Delta Phi. Past Member, Gus J. Soloman Inns of Court. *Member:* Multnomah County and Washington State Bar Associations; Oregon State Bar; Oregon Association of Defense Counsel; Association of Trial Lawyers of American; Oregon Casualty Adjusters Association (Associate Member). ***PRACTICE AREAS:*** Civil Litigation; Insurance Defense; General Liability Defense. ***Email:*** soneil@mls-law.com

MATTHEW T. BOYLE, (P.S.C.) (Not admitted in Oregon; Resident at Seattle, Washington Office)

ROBERT C. LEVIN (Not admitted in Oregon; Resident at Seattle, Washington Office)

WILLIAM H. MITCHELL (Retired)

RICHARD L. LANG (Retired)

ASSOCIATES

JAMES E. OLIVER, born Shreveport, Louisiana, November 27, 1961; admitted to bar, 1994, Oregon; 1998, U.S. District Court, District of Oregon; 2000, Washington. *Education:* Louisiana State University (B.S., 1986); Willamette University (J.D., CDR, 1994). Order of the Barristers. *Member:* Multnomah County Bar Association; Oregon State Bar (Member: Environmental and Natural Resources Section); Oregon Association of Defense Counsel. ***PRACTICE AREAS:*** Construction; Environmental; Insurance Defense. ***Email:*** joliver@mls-law.com

RAYLYNNA J. PETERSON, born Manson, Iowa, August 23, 1967; admitted to bar, 1997, California; 1998, U.S. District Court, Central District of California; 2002, Oregon and U.S. District Court, District of Oregon. *Education:* University of Oregon (B.A., 1990); Whittier College School of Law (J.D., 1996). *Member:* Multnomah County Bar Association (Young Lawyers CLE Committee, 2003-); Oregon State Bar. ***Email:*** rpeterson@mls-law.com

LOWELL P. MCKELVEY, born Ann Arbor, Michigan, June 13, 1971; admitted to bar, 1999, Oregon; 2003, U.S. District Court, District of Oregon. *Education:* Southwestern University (B.A., 1994); University of Montana (J.D., 1999). *Member:* Oregon State Bar; Oregon Association of Defense Counsel; Defense Research Institute. ***PRACTICE AREAS:*** Civil Litigation; Criminal Defense. ***Email:*** lmckelvey@mls-law.com

WILLIAM R. JOSEPH, born Cleveland, Ohio, February 19, 1969; admitted to bar, 1996, California, U.S. District Court, Northern District of California and U.S. Court of Appeals, Ninth Circuit; 2000, Oregon and U.S. District Court, District of Oregon. *Education:* Boston University (B.A., cum laude, with distinction, 1992); George Washington University (J.D., with honors, 1996). Contributing Writer: Oregon State Bar Real Estate and Land Use Digest; Intellectual Property Newsletter; Legislative Alerts Newsletter; 2003 Legislative Update. *Member:* Multnomah Bar Association; Oregon State Bar (Member: Real Estate and Land Use; Environmental Law; Construction; Administrative Law Sections). ***PRACTICE AREAS:*** Insurance Defense; Civil Litigation; Environmental; Construction. ***Email:*** wjoseph@mls-law.com

BARTON J. WACHSTETER, born Jacksonville, Florida, October 18, 1969; admitted to bar, 1996, Oregon; 1997, U.S. District Court, District of Oregon. *Education:* Vanderbilt

(This Listing Continued)

University (B.A., 1992); Lewis and Clark College (J.D., 1996). Recipient, Moot Court Appellate Brief Honors Award. *Member:* Multnomah and Federal Bar Association; Oregon State Bar; Oregon Association of Defense Counsel. ***PRACTICE AREAS:*** Commercial Litigation; Products Liability; Insurance Defense. ***Email:*** bwachsteter@mls-law.com

THOMAS A. HEINRICH, born Oakland, California, June 16, 1965; admitted to bar, 1990, Washington; 2004, Oregon. *Education:* Lewis and Clark College (B.A., Political Science, Communications, 1987); University of Washington School of Law (J.D., 1990). Member, Order of the Barrister, 1990. Member, University of Washington Moot Court Honor Board, 1989, 1990. Law Clerk, Special Assistant U.S. Attorney Donald M. Reno, Jr., 1989-1990. Former Associate, Fallon & McKinley. *Member:* Washington State Bar Association. ***PRACTICE AREAS:*** Insurance Defense; Construction Defects; Products Liability. ***Email:*** theinrich@mls-law.com

REPRESENTATIVE CLIENTS: Allianz Insurance Co.; American Eagle Ins. Co.; American Hardware Insurance Co.; American National Insurance Co.; AON Corp.; Boise-Cascade Corp.; Burlington Insurance Corp.; Burlington Motor Carriers, Inc.; Chubb/Pacific Ind. Group; CIGNA; Civil Service Employees Insurance Co.; CNA Ins. Cos.; Crawford & Co.; Crusader Ins. Co.; Degussa Corp.; Dentists Benefits Insurance Co.; Farmers Insurance Group; Fireman's Fund Insurance Co.; First Financial Insurance Co.; Foremost Insurance Co.; GAB/Rollins; Grange Mutual Insurance Co.; Kemper Insurance Group; Liberty Northwest Insurance Company; Mutual of Enumclaw Insurance Co.; National American Insurance Co.; North Pacific Insurance Co.; Oregon Mutual Insurance Co.; Professional Risk Management Services, Inc.; Safeco Insurance Co.; Spartan Motors, Inc.; St. Paul Ins. Co.

MOORE SMITH BUXTON & TURCKE, CHARTERED

PORTLAND, OREGON

(See Boise, Idaho)

Business, Employment, Environmental, General Municipal Law, Mining, Municipal Bond, Natural Resource, Public Utility, Land Use, Telecommunications, Water Law, General Civil Trial and Appellate Practice in State and Federal Courts and before Various Federal and State Administrative Tribunals.

LYNNE B. MORGAN

1 SW COLUMBIA STREET, SUITE 1110
PORTLAND, OREGON 97258
Telephone: 503-417-7746
Fax: 503-227-7829
Email: lbmorgan@worldnet.att.net
URL: http://www.lawyers.com/lynnebmorgan

Federal Crimes, White Collar Crimes, Murder, Aggravated Murder, Sex Crimes, Drug Crimes, Parole and Probation, Fraud.

FIRM PROFILE: Solo practitioner whose practice is limited to criminal law with a special emphasis on defending those accused of all crimes in federal court, including white collar crimes, and on allegations of serious felony crimes in state court, including capital murder cases. The firm carries the highest legal ability rating in Martindale-Hubbell.

LYNNE B. MORGAN, born Oakland, California, May 3, 1960; admitted to bar, 1989, Oregon. *Education:* University of Oregon (B.A., 1982); Lewis and Clark College (J.D., 1988). Board of Bar Examiners, 1995-1997 (Vice Chair, 1997). Frequent Speaker, Criminal Law CLE's. *Member:* Oregon State Bar; Multnomah County Bar Association; National Association of Criminal Defense Lawyers; Oregon Criminal Defense Lawyers Association; American Inns of Court. ***PRACTICE AREAS:*** Criminal Defense; Federal Criminal Law; Capital Offenses.

MUHLHEIM BOYD

PORTLAND, OREGON

(See Eugene)

Creditor/Debtor Representation; Commercial Litigation; Workouts and Bankruptcy Reorganizations; Bankruptcy Litigation; Creditors' Rights; Foreclosure; Commercial Law; Business Litigation; Business Transactions; Litigation; Estate and Probate.

MURPHY & BUCHAL, LLP

2000 S.W. FIRST AVENUE, SUITE 320
PORTLAND, OREGON 97201
Telephone: 503-227-1011
Fax: 503-227-1034
Email: pmurphy@mbllp.com

Electric Energy, Utility, Commercial Litigation, Contracts, Natural Resources, Administrative Law, Appellate Litigation and Endangered Species Law.

MEMBERS OF FIRM

PAUL M. MURPHY, born Oakland, California, January 21, 1946; admitted to bar, 1974, Wisconsin, Illinois, U.S. District Court, Northern District of Illinois, U.S. District Court, Western District of Wisconsin; 1976, U.S. Court of Appeals, Seventh and Tenth Circuits; 1984, Oregon; 1985, U.S. District Court, District of Oregon and U.S. Court of Appeals, Ninth Circuit; 1986, U.S. Claims Court; 1991, U.S. Supreme Court. *Education:* University of Wisconsin-Madison (B.A., with distinction, 1971; J.D., summa cum laude, 1974). Order of the Coif. *Member:* Oregon State Bar; Energy Bar Association. ***PRACTICE AREAS:*** Energy and Utility Law; Administrative Law; Contracts; Appellate Litigation. ***Email:*** pmurphy@mbllp.com

JAMES L. BUCHAL, born Madison, Wisconsin, August 19, 1959; admitted to bar, 1986, New York and U.S. District Court, Eastern and Southern Districts of New York; 1992,

(This Listing Continued)

MURPHY & BUCHAL, LLP, Portland—Continued

Oregon and U.S. District Court, District of Oregon; 1994, U.S. Court of Appeals, Ninth Circuit; 2001, District of Columbia. *Education:* Harvard University (A.B., 1981); Yale University (J.D., 1985). Author: "Some Fallacies About Salmon Restoration," 25 Environmental Law 375, 1995; "*The Great Salmon Hoax,*" Iconoclast, 1997. *Member:* Oregon State Bar; Washington State Bar Association; The District of Columbia Bar. ***PRACTICE AREAS:*** Complex Litigation; Environmental Law. ***Email:*** jbuchal@mbllp.com

NELLOR RETSINAS & CRAWFORD

PORTLAND, OREGON

(See Vancouver)

Adoption, Bankruptcy and Business Reorganization, Business and Commercial Transactions, Business and Commercial Litigation, Business Law, Child Custody, Child Support, Commercial Law, Contracts, Corporate Law, Divorce, Family Law, Partnership Law, Probate, Real Estate, Trusts and Estates, Wills.

NELSON & NELSON

Established in 1975

SUITE 1620, UMPQUA BANK PLAZA
ONE S.W. COLUMBIA
PORTLAND, OREGON 97258-2098
Telephone: 503-222-1081
FAX: 503-222-6441
Email: mail@roscoecnelson.com

General Civil, Criminal and Trial Practice. Probate and Estate Planning, Wills, Trusts, Guardianship, Asset Protection, Corporate, Business and Real Estate Law.

MEMBERS OF FIRM

ROSCOE C. NELSON (1913-1987)

ROSCOE C. NELSON, JR., born Portland, Oregon, October 13, 1948; admitted to bar, 1973, Oregon and U.S. District Court, District of Oregon; U.S. Court of Appeals, Ninth Circuit. *Education:* Whitman College (B.A., 1970); Willamette University (J.D., 1973). Phi Delta Phi. Deputy District Attorney, Multnomah County, 1973-1975. *Member:* Multnomah County and American Bar Associations; Oregon State Bar; Oregon Criminal Defense Lawyers Association.

LEGAL SUPPORT PERSONNEL

Lola Cline

REFERENCES: Wells Fargo Bank of Oregon; U.S. Bank of Oregon.

ROBERT J. NEUBERGER

700 JACKSON TOWER
806 SW BROADWAY
PORTLAND, OREGON 97205-3309
Telephone: 503-228-1221
Toll Free: 877-631-5126
Fax: 503-228-2556
Email: rjn@robertneuberger.com
URL: http://www.lawyers.com/neuberger

Personal Injury, Dog Bites, Slip and Fall, Automobile Accidents, Wrongful Death, Products Liability, Automotive Products Liability, Professional Liability, Admiralty and Maritime, Maritime Injuries, Medical Malpractice, Insurance, Legal Malpractice, Consumer, Unsafe Products.

FIRM PROFILE: Plaintiff's personal injury and wrongful death cases throughout the State of Oregon.

ROBERT J. NEUBERGER, born Baker, Oregon, August 6, 1953; admitted to bar, 1980, Oregon and U.S. District Court, District of Oregon; 1981, U.S. Court of Appeals, 9th Circuit. *Education:* Colorado College (B.A., 1976); Lewis and Clark College (J.D., 1980). Member, Lewis and Clark College Law Review, 1978-1979. Author: Chapter 13: "Liability Insurance, Evidence," Oregon CLE, 1986; Chapters on: "Evidence and Civil Procedure and Practice in 1987 Oregon Legislation," Oregon CLE, 1987; Chapters on: "Evidence and Civil Procedure and Practice in 1989 Oregon Legislation," Oregon CLE, 1989; "Overview of Oregon Personal Injury Protection Law, Solving PIP Problems," Oregon CLE, 1994; "Senate Bill 601: Joint & Several Liability Law in Oregon, Torts and Civil Practices: Oregon Legislative Changes," Oregon CLE, 1995; "49 Practical Solutions to Real Problems in Insurance Cases," Oregon CLE, 1999; "Hold Harmless Clauses: Why a Plaintiff Should Just Say "No"," Oregon State Bar Litigation Journal, March, 1996; "Joint and Several Liability: The 1995 Amendments Four Years Later," Oregon State Bar Litigation Journal, March 1999; "Why Factual Disputes Should Be Decided by Jurors, Not Politicians," Oregon State Bar Bulletin, Vol. 60, No. 5, February/March, 2000; "How Dennis Rodman Messed with Your Client's Settlement," Oregon State Bar Litigation Journal, Fall 2004. *Member:* Multnomah County (Member, Board of Directors, 1999-2005 and President, 2003-2004; Committees on Judicial Selection, 1989-1992; Court Liaison, 1992-1995) and American Bar Associations; Oregon State Bar (Member, Committees on: Uniform Jury Instructions, 1981-1984; Procedure and Practice, 1984-1987 and 1993-1996; Litigation Section, Chair, 2001; Executive Committee, 1995-2002; Former Member, Committee on Statutory Revision); Oregon Trial Lawyers Association (Member: Board of Governors, 1991-1995); The Association of Trial Lawyers of America; American Board of Trial Advocates. ***REPORTED CASES:*** Estate of Greenslitt v. Farmers Insurance Company of Oregon, 1998, 964 P.2d 1129; Faverty v. McDonalds Restaurants of Oregon, Inc., 1995, 892 P.2d 703; Collins v. Farmers Insurance Company of Oregon, 1990, 791 P.2d 498; State ex rel. Stephens v. Londer, 1991, 811 P.2d 1375; Osborne v. International Harvester Company, 1982, 654 P.2d 1148; Osborne v. International Harvester Company, 1984, 688 P.2d 390. ***PRACTICE AREAS:*** Plaintiffs Personal Injury; Admiralty; Maritime Injuries; Consumer Law; Unsafe Products; Products Liability; Insurance; Medical Malpractice; Legal Malpractice; Personal Injury; Automobile Accidents and Injuries; Dog Bites; Slip and Fall; Wrongful Death.

(This Listing Continued)

NEWCOMB, SABIN, SCHWARTZ & LANDSVERK, LLP

Established in 1892

SUITE 4040, 111 S.W. FIFTH AVENUE
PORTLAND, OREGON 97204
Telephone: 503-228-8446
Fax: 503-228-5472
Email: office@nsslaw.com
URL: http://www.nsslaw.com

General Civil and Trial Practice. Emphasizing Corporations and General Business, Labor and Employment Law, Employee Benefits, Business Litigation, Real Property, Estate Planning and Insurance Coverage Litigation. Federal and State Tax Planning.

MEMBERS OF FIRM

ROBERT L. SABIN (1894-1985)

JOHN R. SABIN (1927-1990)

VERNE W. NEWCOMB, born Bakersfield, California, September 26, 1924; admitted to bar, 1951, Oregon; U.S. Court of Appeals, Fifth, Sixth, Seventh and Ninth Circuits; U.S. District Court, Central District of Illinois and Southern District of Ohio; U.S. Supreme Court and U.S. Tax Court. *Education:* University of California (A.B., 1947); Columbia University (LL.B., 1950). Lecturer in Law, University of Oregon, 1954-1956. Instructor, Corporation Law, Northwestern School of Law of Lewis and Clark College, 1952-1976. Visiting Scholar, Boalt Hall, University of California, 2003-2005. ***Email:*** newcomb@nsslaw.com

JACK B. SCHWARTZ, born Portland, Oregon, February 18, 1937; admitted to bar, 1961, Oregon. *Education:* Stanford University (A.B., 1958); Harvard Law School (LL.B., 1961). Phi Beta Kappa. ***Email:*** schwartz@nsslaw.com

WAYNE D. LANDSVERK, born LaCrosse, Wisconsin, April 25, 1946; admitted to bar, 1972, Wisconsin; 1973, Oregon; 1984, U.S. Supreme Court; 1985, Washington; U.S. Court of Appeals, Seventh and Ninth Circuits; U.S. District Court, Central District of Illinois, Eastern and Western Districts of Wisconsin and Western District of Washington. *Education:* University of Wisconsin (B.A., 1968; J.D., cum laude, 1972). Phi Alpha Theta. Note and Comment Editor, Wisconsin Law Review, 1970-1971. Author: "Tort Law—Statute of Limitations in Medical Malpractice Actions," 1970 Wisconsin Law Review 915; "Informed Consent as a Theory of Medical Liability," 1970 Wisconsin Law Review 879. Co-Author: "Labor Disputes," Labor and Employment Law, Private Sector, Oregon State Bar, 1990, 1994, 1997, 2002; "Labor Arbitration and Mediation," Oregon State Bar, 1987, 1992. Adjunct Faculty Member, Employment Discrimination Law, Lewis and Clark Law School, 1982-1984. Law Clerk to Hon. Robert Foley and Hon. Jacob Tanzer, Oregon Court of Appeals, 1972-1974. Deputy City Attorney, Portland, Oregon, 1974-1975. *Member:* Washington State Bar Association; State Bar of Wisconsin. ***Email:*** wlandsverk@nsslaw.com

RICHARD S. POPE, born Abington, Pennsylvania, October 8, 1952; admitted to bar, 1979, Illinois, U.S. Court of Appeals, Seventh Circuit and U.S. District Court, Central District of Illinois; 1980, Oregon; U.S. Court of Appeals, Ninth Circuit. *Education:* University of Illinois (B.S., 1974; J.D., magna cum laude, 1979). Order of the Coif. Editor, University of Illinois Law Forum. Law Clerk, Honorable Harold A. Baker, U.S. District Judge, Central District of Illinois, 1979-1980. *Member:* Federal Bar Association; Oregon Trial Lawyers Association; Oregon Association of Defense Counsel; Owen M. Panner American Inn of Court. ***PRACTICE AREAS:*** Business Litigation; Insurance Coverage Litigation; Employment Litigation. ***Email:*** rpope@nsslaw.com

JEFFREY P. CHICOINE, born Decatur, Illinois, June 4, 1956; admitted to bar, 1981, Illinois; 1990, Oregon; 2003, Washington. *Education:* University of Illinois (B.A., summa cum laude, 1977; M.A., 1981; J.D., 1981). Phi Beta Kappa. Articles Editor, University of Illinois Law Review. Author: "Privatization of State and Local Government Functions," Government Perspectives (October 1999); "Labor and Employment Law," 1999 and 2001 Oregon Legislative Highlights; "How to Take a Case Before the Employment Relations Board: Unfair Labor Practice Complaints," Labor and Employment Law: Public Sector Ch. 4 (Oregon State Bar Supplement); "Advocates as Witnesses In Hearings Before the Employment Relations Board," Annual Meeting Materials of Oregon State Bar Labor Law Section (1992); "Business Necessity as a Defense to an Employer's Breach of Its Bargaining Duty Under the PECBA," 28 Willamette Law Review 259 (Winter 1992); "Joint Campaigning by State and Federal Candidates: A Practical Legal Guide," 72 Illinois Bar Journal 354 (March 1984); Comment, "Res Judicata in Successive Employment Discrimination Suits," 1980 University of Illinois Law Forum 1049. Adjunct Associate Professor, Portland State University, 1990-1992. Hearing Officer, Employment Relations Board, 1990-1993. Director, West Linn-Wilsonville School Board, 1996-2001. Member, 2000 and Chair, 2001, State Bar Lawyer/Accountant Committee. Executive Committee, 1997-2004 and Chair, 2004, State Bar Labor Law Section. ***PRACTICE AREAS:*** Labor Relations; Employment Litigation; Administrative Law. ***Email:*** jchicoine@nsslaw.com

COUNSEL

BRIAN S. THOMPSON, born Portland, Oregon, September 10, 1959; admitted to bar, 1986, Oregon; 1987, Washington. *Education:* Oregon State University (B.S., highest honors, 1981); University of Oregon (J.D., 1986). Order of the Coif. Certified Public Accountant, Oregon, 1983 (inactive). *Member:* Oregon State Bar (Member, Executive Committee,

(This Listing Continued)

Corporate Counsel Section); Washington State Bar Association. ***PRACTICE AREAS:*** Corporate Law; Mergers and Acquisitions; Securities Regulation. ***Email:*** bthompson@nsslaw.com

OF COUNSEL

SIDNEY I. LEZAK, born Chicago, Illinois, November 8, 1924; admitted to bar, 1949, Oregon. *Education:* University of Chicago (Ph.B., 1946; J.D., 1949). Co-Editor; "Arbitration and Mediation," Oregon State Bar, 1987, 1992. U.S. Attorney for Oregon, 1961-1982. Adjunct Professor, Negotiation and Mediation, Dispute Resolution Center, Willamette University College of Law and Northwestern School of Law of Lewis and Clark College, 1985. Chair, Oregon Dispute Resolution Advisory Council, 1987—. Member, Mediation Panel, U.S. District Court of Oregon, 1987—. Consulting Council, Standing Committee on Dispute Resolution, American Bar Association, 1987—. Co-Chair, Public Affairs Committee, Society of Professionals in Dispute Resolution, 1992. Fellow, International Academy of Mediators. ***Email:*** lezak@nsslaw.com

LAWRENCE R. BROWN, born Ann Arbor, Michigan, April 6, 1947; admitted to bar, 1972, California; 1979, Oregon. *Education:* Stanford University (A.B., 1969); University of California at Berkeley (J.D., 1972). Order of the Coif. Note and Comment Editor, California Law Review, 1971-1972. Professor of Law, Lewis and Clark Law School, 1978—. Legislation Attorney, U.S. Congress, Joint Committee on Taxation, 1976-1978. *Member:* American Law Institute; American Institute of Certified Public Accountants. ***Email:*** lbrown@nsslaw.com

ASSOCIATE

THOMAS E. BAHRMAN, admitted to bar, 2000, Oregon; 2001, Washington. *Education:* University of Puget Sound (B.A., Computer Science and Business, 1995); Willamette University (M.B.A., 2000; J.D., 2000). Beta Gamma Sigma; Pi Alpha Alpha. Member, Tigard Tualatin School District Budget Committee, 2002-2004. Board of Directors, Orchard Hill Condominium Association, 2002—. *Member:* Oregon State Bar (Executive Committee, Computer and Internet Law Section, 2001—). ***Email:*** tbahrman@nsslaw.com

All Attorneys are Members of The Multnomah County and American Bar Associations and The Oregon State Bar.

GENERAL OR SPECIAL COUNSEL FOR: Adair Homes, Inc.; American Family Insurance Co.; American Metal Products Co.; Beall Corp.; Cascade Corp.; Clackamas County; Cummins Northwest, Inc.; Dependable Pattern Works; DigitalVision, Inc.; ESCO Corp.; Lucky Distributing Co., Inc.; NACCO Materials Handling Group, Inc.; Oregon Restaurant Services, Inc.; Peninsula Iron Works, Inc.; Premier Equipment, Inc.; Selmet, Inc.; Simpson Timber Co.; Steel and Wire Fabricators Assn.; SAPA Anodizing, Inc.; Sulzer Pumps; United Employers' Assn.; UMTA Trust; US Benefits; Western Machine Works, Inc.; Williams Controls, Inc.

SUZANNE J. NOLAND

1000 S. W. BROADWAY
SUITE 2400
PORTLAND, OREGON 97205
Telephone: 503-228-7591
Fax: 503-241-2249
Email: nolandsuzannej@qwest.net
URL: http://www.lawyers.com/portlandfamilylaw

Family Law, Divorce, Premarital Agreements, Child Support, Child Custody, Guardianships, Spousal Support, Domestic Relations, Visitation Rights.

SUZANNE J. NOLAND, born Adams, Minnesota, December 23, 1945; admitted to bar, 1975, Oregon and U.S. District Court, District of Oregon. *Education:* University of Oregon (B.A., 1966; M.A., 1970); Northwestern School of Law (J.D., 1974). *Member:* Multnomah County Bar Association (Member, Chair, Court Liaison Committee, 1991-1994; Membership Committee, 1997-2000; Judicial Selection Committee, 1999-2002); Oregon State Bar (Member: Family Law Section); Oregon Association of Family Law Practitioners. ***PRACTICE AREAS:*** Family Law; Divorce; Premarital Agreements; Child Support; Child Custody; Guardianship; Spousal Support; Domestic Relations; Visitation Rights.

O'DONNELL & CLARK LLP

Established in 1999

FREMONT PLACE II, SUITE 302
1650 NW NAITO PARKWAY
PORTLAND, OREGON 97209-2534
Telephone: 503-306-0224
Fax: 503-306-0257
URL: http://www.oandc.com
URL: http://www.odonnellclark.com
Email: wendyd@oandc.com
URL: http://www.lawyers.com/odonnellandclark

Administrative Law, Agency and Distributorships, Business Law, Business Transactions, Commercial Law, Commercial Real Estate, Consumer Law, Contracts, Corporate Law, Debtor and Creditor, Education Law, Election Campaign and Political Law, Estate Planning, Franchises and Franchising, Government Agency Practice, Government Law, Labor and Employment Law, Litigation, Nonprofit Corporations, Nonprofit Charitable Organizations, Real Estate, Resorts and Leisure, Taxation, Hospitality Law, Trade Associations.

MEMBERS OF FIRM

MARK P. O'DONNELL, born Portland, Oregon, April 14, 1943; admitted to bar, 1968, Oregon, U.S. District Court, District of Oregon and U.S. Supreme Court. *Education:* Gonzaga University (B.A., cum laude, 1965); Willamette University (J.D., 1968). *Member:* Multnomah County and Oregon State Bar; American Bar Association (Committees on Dispute Resolution, Nonprofit Corporations and Small Business; Subcommittees on Trade Associations and Closely Held Business Entities). ***REPORTED CASES:*** Hightech Inn.com v. EDC Development, LLC, 192 Or. App. 487, 89 P3d 95 (2004) Petition for Review Denied, Sept. 28, 2004; Anderson v. Peden, SC No. 25641, Supreme Court of Oregon, 284 Ore. 313, 587 P2d 59, 1978 Ore. LEXIS 1162, April 4, 1978, Argued, November 22, 1978; Clackamas County v. Dunham, SC No. 25644, Supreme Court of Oregon, 282 Ore. 419, 579 P2d 223, 1978 Ore. LEXIS 913, March 6, 1978, Argued, May 23, 1978, Rehearing Denied June 21, 1978; Anderson v. Peden, CA No. 7198, Court of Appeals of Oregon, 30 Ore. App. 1063, 569 P2d 633, 1977 Ore. App. LEXIS 1865, May 17, 1977, Argued, September 26, 1977, Reconsideration Denied November 2, 1977, Petition for Review Pending; Clackamas County v. Dunham, CA No. 6817, Court of Appeals of Oregon, 30 Ore. App. 595, 567 P2d 605, 1977 Ore. App. LEXIS 1635, May 25, 1977, Argued, August 17, 1977; Yates v. Schumacher, No. 90820, CA 6818, Court of Appeals of Oregon, 29 Ore. App. 449, 563 P2d 771, 1977 Ore. App. LEXIS 2330, May 16, 1977, Argued May 4, Affirmed May 16, 1977; Clackamas County v. Ague, No. 90259, CA 5803, Court of Appeals of Oregon, 27 Ore. App. 515, 556 P2d 1386, 1976 Ore. App. LEXIS 1482, September 27, 1976, Argued, November 29, 1976, Reconsideration Denied January 12, 1977, Petition for Review Denied March 15, 1977; Russell v. Jackson County, No. 75-176-E-2, CA 5720, Court of Appeals of Oregon, 26 Ore. App. 429, 552 P2d 578, 1976 Ore. App. LEXIS 1725, July 26, 1976, Argued, August 9, 1976, Reconsideration Denied, September 15, 1976, Petition for Review Denied, October 12, 1976; Columbia County v. Kelly, CA No. 5018, Court of Appeals of Oregon, 25 Ore. App. 1, 548 P2d 163, 1976 Ore. App. LEXIS 1917, February 17, 1976, Argued, April 5, 1976, Reconsideration Denied May 12, 1976, Petition for Review Denied June 2, 1976; Kristensen v. Eugene Planning Com., CA No. 4710, Court of Appeals of Oregon, 24 Ore. App. 131, 544 P2d 591, 1976 Ore. App. LEXIS 2255, December 18, 1975, Argued, January 19, 1976; Salem v. Trussell, (No Number in Original), Court of Appeals of Oregon, Department Two, 3 Ore. App. 465, 474 P2d 371, 1970 Ore. App. LEXIS 545, July 22, 1970, Argued, September 10, 1970, Petition for Rehearing Denied September 30, 1970, Petition for Review Denied November 17, 1970. ***PRACTICE AREAS:*** Business Law; Taxation; Real Estate; Debtor and Creditor; Tax Exempt Entities; Governmental Representation; Economic Development; Estate Planning. ***Email:*** marko@oandc.com

KELLY (W.G.) CLARK, born Little Rock, Arkansas, August 9, 1957; admitted to bar, 1983, Oregon and U.S. District Court, District of Oregon. *Education:* Northern Arizona University; Lewis and Clark College (B.S., 1980); Northwestern School of Law of Lewis and Clark College (J.D., 1983); Fuller Theological Seminary, Portland (Graduate Study, 1984-1985); Trinity College Theological School, Melbourne, Australia (M.Div. Candidate, 2004—). Staff of U.S. Senate Mark O. Hatfield, 1982. Outstanding Young Alumnus, Lewis and Clark College, 1991. Frequent Lecturer and Author on Professional and Political Topics. See Website for Complete List. Adjunct Professor, George Fox University, 2004. Member, Oregon State House of Representatives, 1989-1993. ***REPORTED CASES:*** Frevach Land Co. v. Multnomah County, No. CV-99-1295-HU, UNITED STATES DISTRICT COURT FOR THE DISTRICT OF OREGON, 2001 U.D. Dist. LEXIS 22255, December 18, 2001; Nelson v. Myers, SUPREME COURT OF OREGON, 330 Ore. 92, 996 P.2d 975, 2000 Ore. LEXIS 186, March 9, 2000; Lourim v. Swensen, 328 Or. 380 (Or. 1999); Fearing v. Bucher, 328 Or. 367 (Or. 1999); Checkley v. Boyd, CA A96887, Court of Appeals of Oregon, 170 Ore. App. 721, 14 P3d 81, 2000 Ore. App. LEXIS 1869; State v. Stoneman, 323 Or. 536, 920 P.2d 535 (Or., Jul 18, 1996) (NO. A70085, S42085); Lohman v. Bradbury, 333 Or, 231m 37 P.3d 989 (2002); League of Oregon cities v. state, 334 Or, 645, 56 P.3d 892 (2002); Employment Div., Dept. of Human Resources v. Bible Temple, 101 Or.App. 497, 790 P.2d 561 (Or.App., May 2, 1990) (NO. 86-T-106, CA A46818); Employment Div., Dept. of Human Resources v. Rogue Valley Youth for Christ, 307 Or. 490, 770 P.2d 588 (Or., Mar 7, 1989); Kay v. David Douglas School Dist. No. 40, 303 Or. 574, 738 P.2d 1389, 40 Ed. Law Rep. 1027 (Or., Jul 8, 1987) (NO. TC A8404-02438, CA A32742, SC S33089); Seattle-First Nat. Bank v. Umatilla County, 77 Or.App. 283, 713 P.2d 33; Ecumenical Ministries of Oregon v. Paulus, 298 Ore. 62, 688 P2d 1339, 1984 Ore. LEXIS 1832. ***PRACTICE AREAS:*** Civil Litigation; Commercial Litigation; Psychological Injury; Child Abuse and Neglect; Constitutional Law; Administrative Law; Education Law; Election Law. ***Email:*** kellyc@oandc.com

ASSOCIATES

MATTHEW D. LOWE, born Palo Alto, California, June 2, 1969; admitted to bar, 2000, Oregon and Washington. *Education:* Villanova University (B.A., 1991); Willamette University (J.D., 2000). Member, 1998-1999 and Associate Editor, 1999-2000, Willamette University Law Review. Part-time Instructor, Hotel, Restaurant and Travel Law, Mt. Hood Community College. Board Member, Dorchester Conference. Legislative Assistant to U.S. Senator Bob Packwood, 1993-1995. Chief of Staff to Oregon State Senator Tom Hartung, 1997. *Member:* Multnomah County, Washington State and American (Member, Sections on: Taxation; Business Law; Employment) Bar Associations; Oregon State Bar (Member, Sections on: Taxation; Business Law). ***PRACTICE AREAS:*** Business Transactions; Corporate Law; Employment Law; Taxation; Nonprofit Corporations; Trade and Professional Associations; Real Estate; Hospitality Law; Charter School Law. ***Email:*** mattl@oandc.com

KRISTIAN SPENCER ROGGENDORF, admitted to bar, 2001, Oregon; 2002, U.S. District Court, District of Oregon. *Education:* University of South Florida (B.A., cum laude, 1996); Northwestern School of Law, Lewis & Clark College (J.D., Environmental Law, 2001). Federalist Society, President, 1999-2000, Member, 1998-1999, 2000-2001, Northwestern School of Law at Lewis & Clark College. Phi Delta Phi Legal Fraternity, 1999-2001. Recipient: First Place NRA Civil Rights Legal Defense Fund Scholarship Essay, 2000; Dean's Fellowship, Northwestern School of Law at Lewis & Clark College, 1998-2001. Author: Environmental Law 30:3 Case Notes *(for attribution see Errata* 30:4 Editor's Note): Case Note, *Aluminum Co. of America v. Administrator, B.P.A.*, 175 F.3d 1156 (9th Cir. 1999), Case Note, *American Rivers v. Federal Energy Regulatory Comm'n*, 201 F.3d 1186 (9th Cir. 2000), Case Note, *Boeing Co. v. Cascade Corp.*, 207 F.3d 1177 (9th Cir. 2000), Case Note, *United States v. Griefen*, 200 F.3d 1256 (9th Cir. 2000). ***REPORTED CASES:*** Li v. Oregon, 338 Or. 376, 110 P3d 91 (2005); Starrett v. City of Portland, 196 Or. App. 534, 102 P3d 728 (2004); Langlotz v. Noelle, 179 Or. App. 317, 39 P3d 271 (2002); Wyant v. Meyers, 336 Or. 128, P3d 692 (2003). ***PRACTICE AREAS:*** Land Use Litigation; Property Rights; Firearms Litigation; Environmental Litigation; Condemnation; Takings; Administrative Law. ***Email:*** ksr@oandc.com

(This Listing Continued)

O'DONNELL & CLARK LLP, Portland—Continued

JONATHAN A. CLARK, born Portland, Oregon, September 1, 1965; admitted to bar, 2002, Oregon. *Education:* Western Oregon State College (B.S., 1989); Willamette University (J.D., 2002). ***PRACTICE AREAS:*** Civil Rights; Sexual Abuse; Elder Abuse; Abortion Injury Litigation; Civil Litigation. ***Email:*** jonathanc@oandc.com

REPRESENTATIVE CLIENTS: Aloha Produce, Inc.; Northwest Brainstorm Foundation; Brian Clopton Excavating, Inc.; Broadband IP Networking Solutions; Buggsi Hospitality Group, LLC; Clark Sprinkler Supply Co., Inc.; Columbia River Hardwoods, Inc.; Conser Homes, Inc.; Davis Amusement Cascadia, Inc.; Delta Fire, Inc.; The Emerson School, Inc.; Eric Gambee Construction, Inc.; Frevach Land Company; Floor Factors, Inc.; Gatto and Sons, Inc.; Hayden Island Manufactured Home Company; H.S.I. Security Systems, Inc.; Jamestown Ranch; Lautrec, Ltd.; The Lourdes School; Matrix Communications Corporation; McCuddy's Marina; Midland Investment Company; Monarch Hotel; National Federation of Independent Business; National Intramural-Recreation Sports Association; New Horizon Communications, Inc.; Northwest Medical, Inc.; Oregon Council of the Blind; Oregon Electronic Security Association; Oregon Family Council Association; Oregon Firearms Educational Foundation; Oregon Flower Growers Association; Oregon Flowers, Inc.; Oregonians For Fair Housing; Oregonians In Action; Oregon Lodging Association; Oregon Lien Service LLC; Oregon Small Business Association: Oregon Optometric Physicians Association; Oregon State Pharmacists Association; Oregon Taxpayers United Education Foundation; Oregon Republican Leadership Institute; Oregon Perennial Company; Oregon Remodelers Association; Permanent Employment, Inc.; Plibrico Sales & Service, Inc.; Portland Door Controls, Inc.; Rose Auto Wrecking, Inc.; Sauvie Island Moorage Company; Slater Architecture; Three Rivers Charter School; Tualatin Valley Television; US Term Limits; Wright's Custom Products, Inc.; Retriever Towing; Fleet Sales West; Oregon Connections Academy; TVTV; Foundation Works, Inc.; National Association of College and University Mail Services; Trillium Charter School; Emerson Charter School; Gordon Laboratory Charter School; Three Rivers Charter School.

STEVEN Y. ORCUTT, P.C.

Established in 1992
SUITE 500 RIVER FORUM I
4380 SW MACADAM AVENUE
PORTLAND, OREGON 97239-6412
Telephone: 503-228-9350
Fax: 503-228-6993
Email: yaleo@aol.com
URL: http://www.lawyers.com/stevenyorcutt

Real Estate (Buying or Selling), Commercial Real Estate, Commercial Leasing, Starting a Business, General Business, Contracts, Business Planning, Closely Held Business, Corporate, Limited Liability Companies, Small Business, Family Business, Estate Planning, Guardianship and Conservatorships, Trusts and Estates, Asset Protection, Wills and Probate, Elder Law.

STEVEN Y. ORCUTT, born Olympia, Washington, September 29, 1947; admitted to bar, 1975, Oregon and U.S. District Court, District of Oregon; 1977, California and U.S. District Court, Northern District of California; 1978, U.S. Tax Court; 1984, U.S. Court of Appeals, Ninth Circuit; 1988, Washington; 1990, U.S. District Court, Western District of Washington. *Education:* Lewis and Clark College (B.A., 1969); Seattle University School of Law (J.D., 1975). *Member:* Multnomah County, Washington State (Member, Sections on: Real Estate; Land Use; Business; Elder Law) and American (Member, Sections on: Real Estate; Land Use; Business) Bar Associations; Oregon State Bar (Member, Sections on: Real Estate; Land Use; Debtor and Creditor; Business; Elder Law); State Bar of California. [U.S. Naval Security Group, Okinawa, 1970-1972]. ***LANGUAGES:*** Japanese. ***PRACTICE AREAS:*** Real Estate; Estate Planning; Business Law; Wills; Trust Law; Probate; Elder Law. ***Email:*** yaleo@aol.com

REPRESENTATIVE CLIENTS: Mitsu Company; JPS Properties, Inc.; Hokkaido International School, Sapporo, Japan; MCM Architects, PC; Mister Piñata, Inc.; Quality Homes International LLC; Sibata Scientific Technology, Ltd.; Laser Masterpieces, LLC; Webster's Power Wash Co.

JAMES F. O'ROURKE JR. & ASSOCIATES

522 SOUTHWEST 5TH AVENUE, SUITE 710
PORTLAND, OREGON 97204
Telephone: 503-221-1425
Fax: 503-221-1497
Email: jfo@jfolaw.com
URL: http://www.lawyers.com/jfolaw

Criminal Law, Driving While Intoxicated, Drug Crimes, Parole and Probation, Major Traffic Violations, Assault, Property Crimes, Domestic Violence, Personal Injury, Automobile Accidents, Wrongful Death, Truck, Motorcycle, Bicycle, Pedestrian Accidents, Asset Protection, Estate Planning, Guardianship, Wills, Trusts and Probate, Elder Law.

JAMES F. O'ROURKE, JR., born Portland Oregon, September 14, 1951; admitted to bar, 1978, Oregon. *Education:* University of Oregon (B.A., 1974); Gonzaga University (J.D., 1978). *Member:* Oregon State Bar; American Bar Association; Oregon Trial Lawyers Association; The Association of Trial Lawyers of America. ***LANGUAGES:*** Russian. ***PRACTICE AREAS:*** Criminal Law; Personal Injury.

ORRICK, HERRINGTON & SUTCLIFFE LLP
PACIFIC NORTHWEST OFFICE

Established in 1863
1125 N.W. COUCH STREET, SUITE 800
PORTLAND, OREGON 97209
Telephone: 503-943-4800
Telecopier: 503-943-4901
URL: http://www.orrick.com

San Francisco, California Office: The Orrick Building, 405 Howard Street. Telephone: 415-773-5700. Telecopier: 415-773-5759.

(This Listing Continued)

Los Angeles, California Office: 777 South Figueroa Street, Suite 3200. Telephone: 213-629-2020. Telecopier: 213-612-2499.
New York, New York Office: 666 Fifth Avenue. Telephone: 212-506-5000. Telecopier: 212-506-5151.
Sacramento, California Office: 400 Capitol Mall. Telephone: 916-447-9200. Telecopier: 916-329-4900.
Washington, D.C. Office: Washington Harbour, 3050 K Street, N.W. Telephone: 202-339-8400. Telecopier: 202-339-8500.
Menlo Park, California Office: 1000 Marsh Road. Telephone: 650-614-7400. Telecopier: 650-614-7401.
Tokyo, Japan Office: Izumi Garden Tower, 28th Floor, 6-1 Roppongi 1-Chome, Minato-ku. Telephone: +81-3-3224-2900. Telecopier: +81-3-3224-2901.
London, England Office: Tower 42, 25 Old Broad Street. Telephone: +44-20-7562-5000. Telecopier: +44-20-7628-0078.
Pacific Northwest Office: Seattle, Washington Office: 719 Second Avenue, Suite 900. Telephone: 206-839-4300. Telecopier: 206-839-4301.
Irvine, California Office: 4 Park Plaza, Suite 1600. Telephone: 949-567-6700. Telecopier: 949-567-6710.
Paris, France Office: 47 rue de Monceau. Telephone: +33-1-53-53-7500. Telecopier: +33-1-53-53-7501.
Milan, Italy Office: Via Visconti di Modrone, 12. Telephone: +39-02-45-41-3800. Telecopier: +39-02-45-41-3801.
Rome, Italy Office: Via del Consolato, 6. Telephone: +39 0668600751. Telecopier: +39 0668192393.

General Practice, including Corporate and Municipal Finance, Domestic and International Commercial Law, Banking and Commercial Finance, Project Finance, Structured Finance, Mergers and Acquisitions, Commercial Litigation, Insurance, Insurance Insolvency, White Collar Criminal Defense, Tax, Employee Benefits and Personal Estates, Antitrust, Distribution, and Trade Regulation, Intellectual Property, Real Estate, Environmental and Energy, Labor and Employment Law and Bankruptcy.

RESIDENT PARTNERS

DOUGLAS E. GOE, admitted to bar, 1981, Oregon; 1988, Washington. *Education:* Lewis and Clark College (B.S., 1977); Willamette University College of Law (J.D., cum laude, 1981). Executive Editor, Willamette Law Review, 1980-1981. Law Clerk, Hon. George A. Van Hoomissen, Oregon Court of Appeals, 1981-1982. *Member:* Multnomah County, Washington State and American Bar Associations; Oregon State Bar; National Association of Bond Lawyers. ***PRACTICE AREAS:*** Municipal Bonds Law; Banking Law; Securities Law; Federal Indian Law; Public Finance Law. ***Email:*** dgoe@orrick.com

TOWNSEND HYATT, admitted to bar, 1989, Oregon. *Education:* University of North Carolina at Chapel Hill (B.A., cum laude, 1984); University of Copenhagen, Denmark (1986); Doshisha University, Kyoto, Japan (1988); Duke University (J.D., LL.M., International Law, 1989). *Member:* Oregon State Bar. ***LANGUAGES:*** Japanese. ***PRACTICE AREAS:*** Municipal Finance; Federal Indian Law; Public Finance. ***Email:*** thyatt@orrick.com

RESIDENT ASSOCIATES

COURTNEY C. MURASKI, admitted to bar, 1999, Oregon. *Education:* Cornell University (B.A., 1996); University of Oregon (J.D., 1999). Order of the Coif. ***LANGUAGES:*** Spanish. ***PRACTICE AREAS:*** Public Finance. ***Email:*** cmuraski@orrick.com

CHRISTINE REYNOLDS, admitted to bar, 2001, Oregon. *Education:* University of Washington (B.A., 1996); Lewis and Clark College, Northwestern School of Law (J.D., 2001). ***PRACTICE AREAS:*** Public Finance. ***Email:*** creynolds@orrick.com

MELISSA M. ROBERTSON, admitted to bar, 1997, Texas; 1999, Oregon. *Education:* University of Texas, Austin (B.A., 1994); University of Texas School of Law (J.D., 1997). *Member:* Oregon State Bar. ***PRACTICE AREAS:*** Public Finance. ***Email:*** mrobertson@orrick.com

OF COUNSEL

SCOTT E. SCHICKLI, admitted to bar, 1981, Illinois; 1984, Indiana; 1989, New York; 1994, Oregon; 1996, Alaska. *Education:* Carleton College (B.A., 1973); University of Minnesota (J.D., magna cum laude, 1981); New York University (LL.M., 1987). *Member:* Oregon State Bar; National Association of Bond Lawyers. ***PRACTICE AREAS:*** Taxation; Public Finance; Municipal Bonds. ***Email:*** sschickli@orrick.com

MICHAEL E. SCHRADER, admitted to bar, 1991, Indiana; 1998, Oregon. *Education:* Brigham Young University (B.A., cum laude, 1986); Indiana University, Bloomington (J.D., magna cum laude, 1990). Phi Kappa Phi; Order of the Coif. Assistant Editor, Indiana Law Journal, 1990. ***PRACTICE AREAS:*** Public Finance Law; Banking Law; Secured Lending; Mergers and Acquisitions. ***Email:*** mschrader@orrick.com

DAVID W. OWENS, P.C. & ASSOCIATES

101 SW MAIN STREET, SUITE 700
PORTLAND, OREGON 97201
Telephone: 503-224-3100
Fax: 503-274-8660
URL: http://www.lawyers.com/owens-law
General Practice.

DAVID W. OWENS, born 1945; admitted to bar, 1975, Oregon. *Education:* Portland State University (B.S., 1972); Lewis and Clark College (J.D., 1975).

PARISI & PARISI, P.C.

SUITE 100, THE ANNAND BUILDING
1630 SW MORRISON STREET
PORTLAND, OREGON 97205
Telephone: 503-417-1144
Fax: 503-721-2300
Email: admin@parisi-parisi.com

Finance, Antitrust, Real Estate, Land Use, Environmental, Business Transactions, Mining, Commercial Leasing, Zoning and Land Use.

ROBIN B. PARISI, born Redlands, California, July 7, 1954; admitted to bar, 1981, Idaho and U.S. District Court, District of Idaho; 1984, Oregon. *Education:* Stanford University (A.B., 1976); University of Idaho (J.D., cum laude, 1981). Member, Idaho Law Review, 1980-1981. Member, Oregon State Board of Bar Examiners, 1988-1991. ***PRACTICE AREAS:*** Transactions Law; Business Law; Finance Law; Real Estate Law. ***Email:*** robin@parisi-parisi.com

FRANK M. PARISI, born Oakland, California, March 31, 1948; admitted to bar, 1979, Oregon. *Education:* Reed College (B.A., 1971); University of Edinburgh, Scotland (Ph.D., Marshall Scholar, 1975); University of Oregon (J.D., 1978). ***PRACTICE AREAS:*** Appellate Law; Administrative Law; Antitrust Law; Environmental Law; Land Use Law; Natural Resources Law; Mining Law. ***Email:*** frank@parisi-parisi.com

REPRESENTATIVE CLIENTS: Home Depot U.S.A., Inc.; Scanlankemper Bard Companies; Ness Holding Company; Northwest Refrigerated Services, Inc.; Oregon Concrete and Aggregate Producers Association; Parker Northwest Paving Company; H. William Advisors, Inc.; Morse Bros., Inc.

PARSONS FARNELL & GREIN LLP

805 S.W. BROADWAY, SUITE 1560
PORTLAND, OREGON 97205
Telephone: 503-222-1812
Fax: 503-274-7979
URL: http://www.pfglaw.com

Appellate Practice, Business and Corporate Law, Commercial Litigation, Construction Litigation, Estate Planning, Insurance Coverage Litigation, Probate and Trust Administration and Litigation, Real Estate, Tax Planning and Controversies.

FIRM PROFILE: The law firm of Parsons Farnell & Grein LLP focuses on commercial litigation and transactions with expertise in critical areas such as tax, real estate, construction, probate, wills and trusts, estate planning, litigation, mergers and acquisitions, insurance coverage and appeals. The founding partners Michael Farnell, David Grein and John Parsons, have practiced successfully together for many years. Their success is the product of synergistic expertise that translates into effective and comprehensive legal services to Oregon and Washington businesses and individuals.

The firm is committed to a team approach, whether in solving problems or avoiding them. Having come from one of Portland's larger law firms, each of the firm's attorneys possess the kind of complete and refined skill fostered by such experience - skill that is now coupled with the responsiveness and accessibility only a small firm can provide.

PARTNERS

MICHAEL E. FARNELL, born Santa Maria, California, August 2, 1964; admitted to bar, 1992, Oregon and U.S. District Court, District of Oregon; 1994, Washington and U.S. District Court, Western District of Washington; 1996, U.S. Court of Appeals, Ninth Circuit; 2003, U.S. District Court, District of Colorado. *Education:* Willamette University (B.A., 1986); Seattle University (J.D., 1992). *Member:* Oregon State Bar; Multnomah County and Washington State Bar Associations. ***LANGUAGES:*** Spanish. ***PRACTICE AREAS:*** Insurance Coverage; Appellate Practice; Commercial Litigation. ***Email:*** mfarnell@pfglaw.com

DAVID E. GREIN, born Minneapolis, Minnesota, September 18, 1962; admitted to bar, 1990, Oregon; 2002, Washington. *Education:* Carleton College (B.A., 1985); University of Kansas School of Law (J.D., 1990); University of Denver Graduate Tax Program (LL.M., in Taxation, 1993). *Member:* Oregon State Bar; Washington State Bar Association. ***PRACTICE AREAS:*** Taxation; Business Planning; Business Transactions; Mergers and Acquisitions; Real Estate; Real Estate Finance; Estate Planning. ***Email:*** dgrein@pfglaw.com

JOHN D. PARSONS, born Brigham City, Utah, November 28, 1964; admitted to bar, 1992, Oregon; 1995, U.S. District Court, District of Oregon; 2002, Washington; 2003, U.S. District Court, Western District of Washington. *Education:* Utah State University (B.A., cum laude, 1989); Brigham Young University (J.D., 1992). Pi Sigma Alpha; Phi Delta Phi; Golden Key. Articles Editor, Brigham Young Environmental Law Forum, 1991-1992. Member, Gus J. Solomon Chapter, American Inns of Court. *Member:* Oregon State Bar (Member, Sections on: Litigation, Construction, and Debtor/Creditor); Multnomah County, Washington State and American (Member, Sections on: Litigation and Construction Law Forum) Bar Associations; The Association of Trial Lawyers of America. ***LANGUAGES:*** Spanish. ***PRACTICE AREAS:*** Commercial Litigation; Construction Litigation; Probate and Trust Litigation. ***Email:*** jparsons@pfglaw.com

OF COUNSEL

MARK A. GOLDING, born New York, New York, August 21, 1946; admitted to bar, 1976, Washington; 1978, U.S. Tax Court; 1985, Oregon and U.S. Court of Appeals, Ninth Circuit; 1994, U.S. Court of Federal Claims and U.S. Supreme Court. *Education:* Lafayette College (B.S., in Math, 1968); University of Southern California (M.B.A., 1971); Brooklyn Law School (J.D., 1975); New York University (LL.M. in Taxation, 1976). Author: "Tax Aspects of Converting a Partnership or Corporation into an Oregon Limited Liability Company," 73 Or. L. Rev. 25 (1994); "Financial Aspects of Oregon Limited Liability Companies," 73 Or. L. Rev. 55 (1994). Drafted Oregon Limited Liability Company Act and subsequent amendments to the same. Member, Board of Directors and Executive Committee, 1988—and Chairperson, 1994, Portland Tax Forum. *Member:* Oregon State Bar (Member, Executive Committee, 1987-1997, and Chair, 1995-1996, Tax Section; Member, Business Law Section, 1993—; Member, 1993—, and Co-Chair, 1995 and 1997, Limited Liability Task Force); Multnomah County and Washington State (Member, Tax Section) Bar Associations. ***PRACTICE AREAS:*** Federal and State Taxation; Business Law; Real Estate Taxation; Mergers and Acquisitions. ***Email:*** mgolding@pfglaw.com

ASSOCIATES

SAMANTHA L. MENDER, born New York, New York, February 11, 1972; admitted to bar, 2001, Oregon. *Education:* University of Pennsylvania (B.A., 1994); University of San Francisco (M.A., 1997); University of Arizona (J.D., cum laude, 2001). *Member:* Oregon State Bar (Member, Sections on: Business Litigation; Construction Law, Labor and Employment; Litigation); Multnomah Bar Association; American Inns of Court (Member, Gus Solomon Chapter). ***PRACTICE AREAS:*** Insurance Coverage Litigation; Employment Litigation; Commercial Litigation; Probate Litigation. ***Email:*** sgeboff@pfglaw.com

JAMES L. GUSE, born Richland, Washington, August 16, 1974; admitted to bar, 1999, Oregon. *Education:* University of Portland (B.A., 1996); University of Notre Dame (J.D., cum laude, 1999). *Member:* Oregon State Bar; Multnomah Bar Association. ***PRACTICE AREAS:*** Civil Litigation; Insurance Coverage; Entity Formation; Employment Litigation; Civil Rights Litigation. ***Email:*** jguse@pfglaw.com

CANDICE Y. KIM, born Seattle, Washington, December 30, 1977; admitted to bar, 2004, New York; 2005, Oregon. *Education:* University of Washington (B.A., 1999); Boston University School of Law (J.D., 2003). *Member:* Oregon State Bar; New York State Bar Association (Member, Tax Section). ***LANGUAGES:*** Korean. ***PRACTICE AREAS:*** Estate Planning; Probate. ***Email:*** ckim@pfglaw.com

AMY L. LARSON, born St. Louis Park, Minnesota, October 30. 1970; admitted to bar, 1999, Oregon and Wisconsin. *Education:* Carleton College (B.A., cum laude, 1993); University of Wisconsin-Madison (J.D., cum laude, 1999). Member, Public Interest Law Foundation (1996-1998). Member, National Lawyers Guild (1996-1998). *Member:* Oregon State Bar; Multnomah Bar Association. ***PRACTICE AREAS:*** Employment Law; Real Estate; Commercial Transactions; Mergers and Acquisitions; Trademark; Probate. ***Email:*** alarson@pfglaw.com

JUSTIN D. LEONARD, born Silverton, Oregon, March 31, 1977; admitted to bar, 2003, Oregon. *Education:* Stanford University (B.A., 1998); Northwestern School of Law of Lewis & Clark College (J.D., 2003). *Member:* Oregon State Bar; Multnomah Bar Association. ***PRACTICE AREAS:*** Insurance Coverage; Bankruptcy. ***Email:*** jleonard@pfglaw.com

EMILY S. ROBERTSON, born Eugene, Oregon, May 10, 1977; admitted to bar, 2003, Oregon. *Education:* University of Oregon (B.A., 1999); Boston University School of Law (J.D., 2003). *Member:* Oregon State Bar; Multnomah Bar Association. ***PRACTICE AREAS:*** Business Litigation; Insurance Coverage Disputes. ***Email:*** erobertson@pfglaw.com

---

PAULSON LAW FIRM

1000 S.W. BROADWAY, SUITE 1660
PORTLAND, OREGON 97205-3068
Telephone: 503-226-6361
Fax: 503-226-6276
Email: chuck@paulsonlawfirm.com
URL: http://www.lawyers.com/paulsonlawfirm

Civil Trials in all State and Federal Courts. Personal Injury, Medical and Dental Malpractice, Negligence, Products Liability, Wrongful Death, Automobile and Trucking Accidents, Sexual Abuse, Nursing Home Abuse, Unsafe Products.

FIRM PROFILE: Paulson Law Firm has the experience needed to be successful at trial.

When we walk into a courtroom or a settlement conference, we bring with us the credibility we have built representing plaintiffs in this community for four decades. We bring a highly skilled understanding of the law and the commitment to do the right thing for the right reasons.

CHARLES PAULSON, born Portland, Oregon, June 25, 1931; admitted to bar, 1958, Oregon and U.S. District Court, District of Oregon. *Education:* Portland State College; Reed College; Northwestern School of Law of Lewis and Clark College (J.D., 1958). Named Distinguished Lawyers of the Year, Oregon Trial Lawyers Association, 2000. Listed in "Best Lawyers in America." Distinguished Graduate, Northwestern School of Law of Lewis and Clark College, 1998. Member, Oregon Public Defenders Committee, 1974-1978. Member, Oregon Council on Court Procedures, 1977-1981. *Member:* Oregon State Bar (Member, Joint Committee with Medical Profession, 1968-1971; Chairman, 1970-1971; Member, Board of Governors, 1987-1990; Treasurer, 1989-1990); American Judicature Society; The Association of Trial Lawyers of America (President, Oregon Chapter, 1961-1962; 1967-1968; Member, Board of Governors, 1972-1974); Western Trial Lawyers Association (Vice President, 1962-1963; Parliamentarian, 1964-1965; 1966-1967; Treasurer, 1967-1968); Oregon Trial Lawyers Association. Fellow, American College of Trial Lawyers. ***PRACTICE AREAS:*** Personal Injury; Medical Malpractice; Wrongful Death. ***Email:*** chuck@paulsonlawfirm.com

JANE PAULSON, born Portland, Oregon, September 2, 1965; admitted to bar, 1991, Oregon, California and U.S. District Court, District of Oregon; 1995, Washington. *Education:* Arizona State University (1983-1985); Indiana University (B.S., 1987); University of Virginia (J.D., 1990). Law Clerk to the Honorable James M. Burns, U.S. District Court, District of Oregon, 1990-1991. Board Member, Oregon Law Institute, 1998-1999. Member, Gus Solomon Inn of Court, 1994-1997 and 2000-2002. *Member:* State Bar of California; Oregon State Bar (Member: Affirmative Action Committee, 1994-1997; Procedure and Practice Committee, 1997-2000); Washington State Bar Association; Oregon Trial Lawyers Association (President, 2004-2005; Board Member, 1995—); The Association of Trial Lawyers of America (State Delegate, 2000-2004). ***PRACTICE AREAS:*** Personal Injury;

(This Listing Continued)

PAULSON LAW FIRM, Portland—Continued

Medical Malpractice; Dental Malpractice; Wrongful Death; Products Liability. ***Email:*** jane@paulsonlawfirm.com

PERKINS COIE LLP

1120 N.W. COUCH STREET, 10TH FLOOR
PORTLAND, OREGON 97209-4128
Telephone: 503-727-2000
Facsimile: 503-727-2222
Email: perkins@perkinscoie.com
URL: http://www.perkinscoie.com

REVISER OF THE WASHINGTON LAW DIGEST FOR THIS DIRECTORY.

Other Offices: Anchorage, Alaska; Bellevue, Washington; Boise, Idaho; Chicago, Illinois; Denver, Colorado; Los Angeles, California; Menlo Park, California; Olympia, Washington; Phoenix, Arizona; San Francisco, California; Seattle, Washington; Washington, D.C.

General Civil Trial and Appellate Practice in Federal and State Courts and before various Federal and State Administrative Tribunals. Administrative; Antitrust and Trade Regulation; Aviation and Aerospace; Banks and Banking; Bankruptcy; Biotechnology; Business Law; Corporate Law; Employee Benefits; Energy; Environmental; Estate Planning; Federal Indian Law; Franchising; General Litigation; Government Contracts; Government Relations; Immigration; Intellectual Property; International Trade; International Law; Internet and Electronic Commerce; Labor and Employment; Land Use; Life Sciences; Mergers, Acquisitions and Divestitures; Municipal/Public Finance; Natural Resources; Nonprofit and Charitable Organizations; Probate; Patents; Product Liability; Project Finance; Political Law; Public Utility; Real Estate; School Law; Securities Law and Litigation; Taxation; Technology; Telecommunications; Toxic Torts; Trademarks and Copyrights; Venture Capital and Investment Funds; Water Rights; White-Collar Criminal Representation; Workers' Compensation.

FIRM PROFILE: Perkins Coie LLP is a leading, full-service international law firm. With more than 600 lawyers in 13 offices across the United States, the firm represents clients that range in size from Fortune 100 companies to start-ups, and has historically represented market leaders in traditional and cutting-edge technology industries.

PARTNERS

ALLAN R. ABRAVANEL, born New York, N.Y., March 11, 1947; admitted to bar, 1972, New York; 1976, Oregon. *Education:* Yale University (B.A., magna cum laude, 1968); Harvard University (J.D., cum laude, 1971). ***LANGUAGES:*** Spanish. ***PRACTICE AREAS:*** Corporation Law; International Law.

ROBERT L. ALDISERT, born Pittsburgh, Pennsylvania, April 3, 1956; admitted to bar, 1989, California (inactive); 1994, Oregon. *Education:* Columbia College (A.B., 1978); Loyola of Los Angeles Law School (J.D., magna cum laude, 1989). Order of the Coif. Law Clerk to the Honorable Charles Clark, Chief Judge, Fifth Circuit, 1989-1990. ***PRACTICE AREAS:*** Business Torts; Complex Commercial Litigation; Products Liability Defense.

PETER B. ARCHIE, born Nashville, Tennessee, March 3, 1940; admitted to bar, 1966, District of Columbia; 1999, Oregon; 2000, Washington. *Education:* University of North Carolina (B.S., 1962); Duke University (LL.B., cum laude, 1965). Order of the Coif. Member, Board of Editors, Duke Law Journal. (Also at Seattle, Washington Office). ***PRACTICE AREAS:*** Finance; Aircraft Finance and Leasing; Project Finance; Corporate; Real Estate. ***Email:*** archp@perkinscoie.com

RICHARD L. BAUM, born Brooklyn, New York, November 14, 1956; admitted to bar, 1982, Washington; 1998, Oregon. *Education:* Colgate University (B.A., cum laude, 1978); Georgetown University (J.D., 1982). Executive Editor, American Criminal Law Review. ***PRACTICE AREAS:*** Intellectual Property Litigation; Antitrust; Accountants Liability; Commercial Litigation; Trademark Litigation; Unfair Competition. ***Email:*** baumr@perkinscoie.com

DAVID A. BLEDSOE, born Portland, Oregon, November 28, 1954; admitted to bar, 1985, Oregon; 1989, Washington. *Education:* Harvard University (A.B., magna cum laude, 1978); Boalt Hall, University of California (J.D., 1985). Law Clerk to Hon. James A. Redden, District of Oregon, 1985-1987. ***LANGUAGES:*** Spanish, French. ***PRACTICE AREAS:*** Complex Litigation; Environmental Liability Law; Contamination Law; Business Torts; Insurance Coverage Litigation.

JEFFREY W. BOCK, born Minneapolis, Minnesota, March 26, 1950; admitted to bar, 1975, Oregon. *Education:* Dartmouth College (A.B. honors major with highest distinction, magna cum laude, 1972); University of Chicago (J.D., 1975). ***PRACTICE AREAS:*** Intellectual Property; Electronic Commerce; Internet Law; Corporate Finance.

BRENTLEY M. BULLOCK, born Roseburg, Oregon, May 24, 1961; admitted to bar, 1986, Oregon. *Education:* Oregon State University (B.S., with highest scholarship, 1983); Stanford University (J.D., 1986). Executive Editor, Stanford Journal of International Law. ***PRACTICE AREAS:*** Corporate Finance; Mergers and Acquisitions; Commercial Finance and Leasing.

RICHARD A. CANTLIN, born Buffalo, New York, August 21, 1946; admitted to bar, 1973, New York; 1975, Oregon. *Education:* Georgetown University (B.A., 1968); Columbia University (J.D., 1972). Council Member, Section of Real Property, Probate and Trust Law of the American Bar Association, 1985-1992. *Member:* American College of Real Estate Lawyers (Vice President and Member, Board of Governors). ***PRACTICE AREAS:*** Real Estate Development; Reorganizations.

AUSTIN W. CROWE, JR., born Boston, Massachusetts, December 21, 1939; admitted to bar, 1965, Oregon. *Education:* Tufts University (B.A., 1961); Cornell University (LL.B., 1964; J.D., 1969). Phi Delta Phi. Fellow, American College of Trial Lawyers. ***PRACTICE AREAS:*** Civil Litigation; Complex Litigation; Products Defense; Legal Malpractice. ***Email:*** crowa@perkinscoie.com

(This Listing Continued)

SCOTT D. EADS, born Somerset, Kentucky, May 27, 1956; admitted to bar, 1991, Oregon; 1992, U.S. District Court, District of Oregon; 1997, U.S. Court of Appeals, Ninth Circuit; 1998, U.S. District Court, Southern District of Texas and U.S., Court of Appeals, Fifth Circuit; 1999, Texas; registered to practice before U.S. Patent and Trademark Office. *Education:* Tennessee Technological University (B.S., Biology, summa cum laude, 1979); University of Texas at Austin (J.D., with honors, 1990); Portland State University (M.S.T., Molecular Biology, 1994). Editor, *Texas Environmental Law Journal*, 1989-1990. *Member:* Houston Young Lawyers Association. ***REPORTED CASES:*** Clontech Laboratories, Inc. v. Life Technologies, Inc., 2000 U.S. Dist. LEXIS 19320 (D. Md.); Pioneer Hi-Bred Int'l, Inc. v. DeKalb Genetics Corp., 1999 U.S. Dist. LEXIS 21393 (S.D. Iowa); Playboy Enterprises, Inc. v. Webbworld, Inc., 991 F.Supp. 543 (N.D. Tex. 1997); Playboy Enterprises, Inc. v. Webbworld, Inc., 968 F. Supp. 1171 (N.D. Tex. 1997); Lifting Technologies v. Dixon Industries, 1997 U.S. Dist. LEXIS 21517 (D. Mont.). ***PRACTICE AREAS:*** Patent Litigation; Trade Secrets; Copyright Litigation; Trademark Litigation; Unfair Competition. ***Email:*** eadss@perkinscoie.com

GEORGE K. FOGG, born Darby, Pennsylvania, May 17, 1947; admitted to bar, 1973, Ohio; 1991, Oregon. *Education:* Colgate University (A.B., honors, 1969); University of Wisconsin (J.D., cum laude, 1973). ***PRACTICE AREAS:*** Finance; Mergers, Acquisitions and Divestitures; Commercial Law; Business Law; Contracts; Debtor and Creditor. ***Email:*** foggg@perkinscoie.com

PAUL T. FORTINO, born Grand Haven, Michigan, November 13, 1945; admitted to bar, 1975, Michigan; 1980, Washington; 1983, Oregon. *Education:* University of Michigan (B.B.A., 1967); University of Notre Dame (J.D., summa cum laude, 1975). Notes Editor, Notre Dame Law Review. Representative to Ninth Circuit Judicial Conference, 1998—. *Member:* Oregon Association of Defense Counsel (President, 1997-1998); American College of Trial Lawyers. ***PRACTICE AREAS:*** Complex and Multi-District Litigation; Products Liability; Labor and Employment; Environmental Law.

JAMES H. GIDLEY, born Fergus Falls, Minnesota, January 10, 1942; admitted to bar, 1967, Oregon; 1987, Washington. *Education:* University of Wyoming (B.S., 1964); University of Oregon (J.D., 1967). Associate Editor, Oregon Law Review. *Member:* American College of Trial Lawyers; American Board of Trial Advocates. ***PRACTICE AREAS:*** Civil Litigation; Complex Litigation; Insurance; Construction Defects; Business Litigation; Premises Liability. ***Email:*** gidlj@perkinscoie.com

IVAN GOLD, born Pittsburgh, Pennsylvania; admitted to bar, 1972, New York and Oregon; 1979, District of Columbia. *Education:* University of Pittsburgh (B.A., 1968); New York University (J.D., 1971). Managing Editor, Annual Survey of American Law. Law Clerk to the Hon. Gus J. Solomon, 1971-1972. Deputy Public Utility Commissioner, Oregon, 1975-1976. Special Assistant to Chairman Civil Aeronautics Board, 1977-1978. ***PRACTICE AREAS:*** Energy; Utility Law; Business Transactions. ***Email:*** igold@perkinscoie.com

M. CHRISTOPHER HALL, born Livonia, Michigan, October 4, 1967; admitted to bar, 1997, New York; 2001, Oregon. *Education:* Michigan State University (B.A., 1989); Boston University (J.D., magna cum laude, 1996). ***PRACTICE AREAS:*** Corporate; Securities; Mergers and Acquisitions; Venture Capital. ***Email:*** hallc@perkinscoie.com

STEVEN M. HEDBERG, born Coeur d'Alene, Idaho, December 30, 1958; admitted to bar, 1984, Oregon; 1985, Washington. *Education:* Portland State University (B.A., 1981); Northwestern School of Law of Lewis & Clark College (J.D., 1984). Certified in Business Bankruptcy Law by the American Board of Bankruptcy Certification; Certified in Creditor's Rights by the Commercial Law League of America Academy of Commercial and Bankruptcy Law Specialists. (Also at Seattle, Washington Office). ***PRACTICE AREAS:*** Bankruptcy Law; Financial Restructuring; Commercial Loans; Lender Liability; Loan Workouts.

THOMAS RUSSELL JOHNSON, born Ann Arbor, Michigan, May 3, 1971; admitted to bar, 1998, New York; 2001, Oregon. *Education:* University of Michigan (B.B.A., 1993); University of North Carolina at Chapel Hill (J.D., high honors, 1997). ***PRACTICE AREAS:*** Commercial Litigation. ***Email:*** johnh@perkinscoie.com

CALVIN L. KEITH, born Norfolk, Virginia, September 20, 1952; admitted to bar, 1978, California; 1981, Oregon. *Education:* University of Arizona (B.S., 1975); University of Michigan (J.D., magna cum laude, 1978). Member, Executive Committee (1991-1993), Labor Law Section, Oregon State Bar. ***PRACTICE AREAS:*** Employment Law; Employment Litigation.

THOMAS E. LINDLEY, born Danville, Illinois, July 15, 1948; admitted to bar, 1977, Illinois; 1985, Oregon; 1987, Washington. *Education:* University of Illinois (B.A., cum laude, 1970); Vanderbilt University (J.D., 1977). Member, United States Delegation, Ninth Conference of Parties of the Convention on International Trade in Endangered Species (CITES) (1994). *Member:* Oregon State Bar; Washington State and American Bar Associations. ***PRACTICE AREAS:*** Environmental Law; Natural Resources Law. ***Email:*** lindt@perkinscoie.com

DAVID S. MATHESON, born Logan, Utah, January 23, 1964; admitted to bar, 1991, California; 1996, Oregon. *Education:* Stanford University (B.A., with distinction, 1987); The John E. Anderson Graduate School of Management at UCLA (M.B.A., 1991); University of California at Los Angeles School of Law (J.D., 1991). Executive Editor, Federal Communications Law Journal. ***LANGUAGES:*** Spanish. ***PRACTICE AREAS:*** Corporate Finance; Mergers and Acquisitions; Emerging Growth Companies; Business Transactions.

CHRISTOPHER T. MATTHEWS, born New Haven, Connecticut, August 25, 1954; admitted to bar, 1989, Oregon. *Education:* San Francisco State University (B.A., 1986); Hastings College of the Law (J.D., magna cum laude, 1989). Senior Research Editor, Hastings Law Journal. Law Clerk to Hon. Robert C. Belloni, District of Oregon, 1989-1990. ***PRACTICE AREAS:*** Real Estate; Land Use. ***Email:*** mattc@perkinscoie.com

NEIL NATHANSON, born Detroit, Michigan, October 26, 1960; admitted to bar, 1992, California; 1997, Oregon. *Education:* University of Michigan (B.S., 1982; M.S., 1984); Stanford University (J.D., 1992). Order of the Coif. Member, Stanford Law Review. Law Clerk to the Hon. Saundra Brown Armstrong, Northern District of California, 1992-1993. ***PRACTICE AREAS:*** Corporate Law; Securities; Computers and Software; Internet Law. ***Email:*** nathn@perkinscoie.com

(This Listing Continued)

DOUGLAS R. PAHL, born Pendleton, Oregon, November 3, 1963; admitted to bar, 1995, Oregon. *Education:* Central Washington University (B.A., 1986); Willamette University (J.D., 1992). Legislative Assistant to U.S. Senator Mark O. Hatfield (Washington, D.C.), 1990-1996; Legal Counsel, 1995-1996. Law Clerk to Chief Judge Michael R. Hogan, District of Oregon, 1996-1998. ***PRACTICE AREAS:*** Business and Civil Litigation; Bankruptcy; Debtor and Creditor; Regulatory Law; Government Relations. **Email:** pahld@perkinscoie.com

STEVEN L. PFEIFFER, born Klamath Falls, Oregon, August 13, 1953; admitted to bar, 1981, Oregon. *Education:* Lewis & Clark College (B.S., cum laude, 1975); University of Oregon School of Law (J.D., 1981). Member, Oregon Land Conservation and Development Commission, 1993—. ***PRACTICE AREAS:*** Land Use Law; Environmental Law. **Email:** pfeis@perkinscoie.com

LAWRENCE H. REICHMAN, born New York, N.Y., January 28, 1959; admitted to bar, 1985, New York; 1986, Oregon. *Education:* Cornell University (B.A., with distinction, 1980; J.D., magna cum laude, 1984). Order of the Coif. Associate, Cornell International Law Journal, 1982-1983. Law Clerk to the Hon. Edward H. Warren, Oregon Court of Appeals, 1984-1986. Associate Counsel, Northwest Natural Gas Co., 1995-1997. *Member:* Oregon State Bar. ***LANGUAGES:*** French. ***PRACTICE AREAS:*** Public Utility Regulation; Telecommunications Law; Energy Law; Antitrust and Unfair Competition. **Email:** reicl@perkinscoie.com

MICHAEL C. ROBINSON, born Kansas City, Missouri, June 14, 1955; admitted to bar, 1989, Wisconsin; 1991, Oregon. *Education:* University of Oklahoma (B.A., 1977; M.R.C.P., 1979); Northwestern School of Law of Lewis & Clark College (J.D., cum laude, 1988). *Member:* American Planning Association; American Institute of Certified Planners. ***PRACTICE AREAS:*** Land Use; Highway Access; Municipal Law. **Email:** robim@perkinscoie.com

ELIZABETH SCHWARTZ, born Houston, Texas, May 31, 1968; admitted to bar, 1994, Texas; 1996, Oregon. *Education:* Rice University (B.A., magna cum laude, 1990); University of Texas (J.D., with honors, 1994). Law Clerk to the Honorable Ferdinand F. Fernandez, Ninth Circuit, 1994-1995. ***PRACTICE AREAS:*** Litigation; Appellate Practice; Commercial Litigation; Environmental Litigation. **Email:** schwe@perkinscoie.com

MICHAEL H. SIMON, born New York, N.Y., December 1, 1956; admitted to bar, 1986, Oregon. *Education:* University of California at Los Angeles (B.A., summa cum laude, 1978); Harvard University (J.D., cum laude, 1981). Listed in Best Lawyers in America. Trial Attorney, Antitrust Division, U.S. Department of Justice, 1981-1986. Chair, 1992-1993, Member, 1990-1992, Oregon State Board of Bar Examiners. Chair, Antitrust Section, Oregon State Bar, 1990-1991. ***PRACTICE AREAS:*** Antitrust; Unfair Trade; Complex Litigation; First Amendment Law.

PATRICK J. SIMPSON, born Glendale, California, September 26, 1944; admitted to bar, 1971, Oregon. *Education:* University of California at Berkeley (A.B., 1967); Hastings College of Law, University of California and Boalt Hall, University of California (J.D., 1971). ***PRACTICE AREAS:*** Corporate Law; Securities Law.

DAVID P. R. SYMES, born Ardmore, Oklahoma, March 25, 1966; admitted to bar, 1996, Oregon. *Education:* St. Olaf College (B.A., magna cum laude, 1988); Manchester College, Oxford University; Washington University (J.D., 1992). Editor, Washington University Law Quarterly. Law Clerk to Judge Rene J. Gonzalez, Superior Court, State of Alaska, 1992-1993. ***PRACTICE AREAS:*** Employment Law; Employment Litigation; Equal Employment Opportunity Law; Wage and Hour Law; Wrongful Termination Defense.

ROY W. TUCKER, born Buffalo, New York, August 31, 1952; admitted to bar, 1980, New York; 1985, Oregon. *Education:* Kenyon College (B.A., magna cum laude, 1974); State University of New York at Buffalo (J.D., 1979). Senior Editor, Buffalo Law Review. Law Clerk to the Hon. Reid S. Moule, Appellate Division, New York State Supreme Court, 1979-1980. ***PRACTICE AREAS:*** Corporate Law; Business Law; Securities.

MARK D. WHITLOW, born Kansas City, Missouri, October 10, 1946; admitted to bar, 1975, Oregon; 1976, U.S. District Court, District of Oregon; 1977, U.S. Claims Court. *Education:* Memphis State University (B.S., 1971; J.D., 1974). [Member of U.S. Navy Reserve, 1965-1971]. ***PRACTICE AREAS:*** Real Estate; Land Use Law. **Email:** whitm@perkinscoie.com

JAY A. ZOLLINGER, born Stillwater, Oklahoma, September 4, 1967; admitted to bar, 1997, Oregon. *Education:* Boston University (B.A., cum laude, 1992); University of Utah (M.A., 1994); Boalt Hall School of Law, University of California (J.D., 1997). Articles Editor, California Law Review. ***PRACTICE AREAS:*** Litigation. **Email:** zolljc@perkinscoie.com

OF COUNSEL

AARON C. COURTNEY, born Istanbul, Turkey, February 7, 1967; admitted to bar, 1993, Oregon. *Education:* University of Virginia (B.A., 1989; J.D., 1992; M.S., 1993). Speeches and Publications: "American Bar Association 2002 Year in Review," Marine Resources Law Chapter; "Challenging NMFS' 2000 Biological Opinion," The Osprey (Federation of Fly Fishers) No. 40 (September 2000); "Individual-Area Relationships: The Relationship Between Animal Population Density and Area," Ecology 81(3), 2000, pp. 734-748 (2000). *Member:* Multnomah County, Federal and American Bar Associations. ***PRACTICE AREAS:*** Environmental; Natural Resources; Land Use; Real Estate Transactions. **Email:** acourtney@perkinscoie.com

FRANK M. FLYNN, born Philadelphia, Pennsylvania, May 4, 1948; admitted to bar, 1992, Oregon. *Education:* Beaver College (B.A., 1976); Oregon State University (M.A., 1988); Northwestern School of Law of Lewis & Clark College (J.D., 1992). ***PRACTICE AREAS:*** Land Use; Environmental Permitting. **Email:** flynnf@perkinscoie.com

MILTON T. JONES, born Coronado, California, February 16, 1948; admitted to bar, 1977, Oregon. *Education:* University of Oregon (B.A., 1970; M.A., 1972; J.D., 1977). ***PRACTICE AREAS:*** Environmental Law; Natural Resources; Energy; Occupational Safety and Health; Regulatory Law. **Email:** jonem@perkinscoie.com

JEANETTE THOMAS, admitted to bar, 1994, New York; 1998, Oregon. *Education:* Long Island University (B.A., summa cum laude, 1990); Hofstra University School of Law (J.D., 1993). *Member:* American Bankruptcy Institute; Turnaround Management Association. ***PRACTICE AREAS:*** Bankruptcy; Creditor's Rights; Secured Transactions. **Email:** jthomas@perkinscoie.com

RESIDENT ASSOCIATES

ROGER A. ALFRED, born Tucson, Arizona, September 27, 1966; admitted to bar, 1993, Oregon. *Education:* University of Arizona (B.A., 1989); Lewis and Clark College (J.D., cum laude, 1993). Associate Editor, Environmental Law. ***PRACTICE AREAS:*** Land Use; Environmental. **Email:** alfrr@perkinscoie.com

DANIELLE BENDERLY, born Washington, D.C., April 19, 1969; admitted to bar, 1996, Oregon. *Education:* Wellesley College (B.A., cum laude, 1991); Boalt Hall School of Law, University of California (J.D., 1996). ***PRACTICE AREAS:*** Corporate Law; Initial Public Offerings; Public Offerings; Securities Offerings; Securities Regulation; Business Law; Mergers and Acquisitions. **Email:** bendd@perkinscoie.com

DEENA B. BOTHELLO, admitted to bar, 2002, California (Not admitted in Oregon). *Education:* College of William & Mary (B.A., 1994); University of Oregon (J.D., 2002). Order of the Coif. Managing Editor, University of Oregon Law Review. ***PRACTICE AREAS:*** Venture Finance; Corporate Finance; Mergers and Acquisitions. **Email:** dbothello@perkinscoie.com

PEGGY L. CRANE, born Jonesboro, Arkansas, September 19, 1977; admitted to bar, 2001, Oregon. *Education:* Baylor University (B.A., 1997); Tulane University of Louisiana (J.D., 2001). Order of the Coif. ***PRACTICE AREAS:*** Environmental Law. **Email:** cranp@perkinscoie.com

SARAH J. CROOKS, born Las Vegas, Nevada, May 18, 1971; admitted to bar, 1996, Nevada; 1997, Oregon. *Education:* University of Nevada (B.S., 1992); University of Oregon (J.D., 1996). ***PRACTICE AREAS:*** Litigation. **Email:** croos@perkinscoie.com

JEFFREY C. DOBBINS, admitted to bar, 1994, West Virginia; 2002, Oregon. *Education:* Harvard University (A.B., magna cum laude, 1989); Duke University School of Environment (M.E.M., 1994); Duke University School of Law (J.D., with highest honors, 1994). Order of the Coif. Law Clerk to: Hon. John Paul Stevens; Hon. David S. Tatel. ***PRACTICE AREAS:*** Litigation; Environmental Litigation. **Email:** jdobbins@perkinscoie.com

STEPHEN M. FELDMAN, born New York, New York, April 16, 1967; admitted to bar, 1995, Oregon. *Education:* Brown University (B.A., 1989); Northwestern School of Law, Lewis & Clark College (J.D., summa cum laude, 1993). Law Clerk to the Hon. Ancer L. Haggerty, District of Oregon, 1994-1996. ***PRACTICE AREAS:*** Civil Appeals; Civil Litigation; Insurance Litigation. **Email:** felds@perkinscoie.com

MICHAEL S. GADD, born Wilmington, Ohio, July 1, 1964; admitted to bar, 1990, New York; 1994, Oregon; 1998, Washington. *Education:* University of South Carolina (B.A., magna cum laude, 1986); University of Michigan (J.D., with honors, 1989). ***PRACTICE AREAS:*** Corporate; Corporate Finance; Mergers and Acquisitions; Securities; International. **Email:** gaddm@perkinscoie.com

CHRISTOPHER L. GARRETT, born Portland, Oregon, December 26, 1973; admitted to bar, 2001, New York (Not admitted in Oregon). *Education:* Reed College (B.A., 1996); University of Chicago (J.D., with honors, 2000). Phi Beta Kappa. ***PRACTICE AREAS:*** Litigation; Labor and Employment; Appellate Practice. **Email:** cgarrett@perkinscoie.com

DINA GLASSMAN, born Baku, Azerbaijan, July 3, 1973; admitted to bar, 1999, New York; 2001, Oregon. *Education:* Colgate University (B.A., magna cum laude, 1995); New York University (J.D., 1998). ***LANGUAGES:*** Russian. ***PRACTICE AREAS:*** Labor and Employment; Commercial Litigation. **Email:** glasd@perkinscoie.com

SHANNON HARTWELL, born Portland, Oregon, July 19, 1970; admitted to bar, 2000, Oregon. *Education:* The Evergreen State College (B.A., 1995); Northwestern School of Law (J.D., cum laude, 2000). ***PRACTICE AREAS:*** Corporate; Securities. **Email:** harts@perkinscoie.com

ERICK J. HAYNIE, admitted to bar, 1998, Oregon. *Education:* University of Portland (B.A., summa cum laude, 1995); Northwestern University School of Law (J.D., cum laude, 1998). Executive Editor, Journal of Criminal Law and Criminology. ***PRACTICE AREAS:*** Civil Litigation. **Email:** hayne@perkinscoie.com

STEPHANIE K. HINES, admitted to bar, 2002, Oregon. *Education:* University of Sioux Falls (B.A., summa cum laude, 1999); Northwestern School of Law, Lewis & Clark College (J.D., magna cum laude, 2002). ***PRACTICE AREAS:*** Business; Litigation. **Email:** shines@perkinscoie.com

JULIA E. MARKLEY, born Portland, Oregon, January 19, 1974; admitted to bar, 2000, Oregon. *Education:* Stanford University (B.A., 1995); University of Washington (J.D., with honors, 1999). Order of the Coif. Notes and Comments Editor, Washington Law Review, 1998-1999. Law Clerk to the Hon. R. William Riggs, Associate Justice, Oregon Supreme Court, 1999-2001. ***PRACTICE AREAS:*** Litigation. **Email:** markj@perkinscoie.com

GWYNETH McALPINE, born Stanford, California, February 25, 1971; admitted to bar, 2000, California; 2004, Oregon. *Education:* University of California, Berkeley (B.A., 1994); University of California, Los Angeles School of Law (J.D., 2000). ***PRACTICE AREAS:*** Venture Finance; Corporate Finance; Mergers and Acquisitions. **Email:** gmcalpine@perkinscoie.com

LYNNE M. PARETCHAN, admitted to bar, 2002, Oregon; 2002, New Mexico. *Education:* University of California at Berkeley (B.S., Civil Engineering, 1980; M.S.,Construction Engineering, 1981; Master of Water Resources, 2003); University of New Mexico School of Law (J.D., cum laude, 2001). Order of the Coif. Lead Articles Editor, Natural Resources Journal. ***PRACTICE AREAS:*** Environmental; Natural Resources Law; Water Law. **Email:** lparetchan@perkinscoie.com

KEVIN SALI, admitted to bar, 2004, Oregon. *Education:* Wheaton College (B.S., 1994); Duke University Law School (J.D., 2004). Order of the Coif. Research Editor, Duke Law Journal. ***PRACTICE AREAS:*** Litigation. **Email:** ksali@perkinscoie.com

(This Listing Continued)

PERKINS COIE LLP, Portland—Continued

ANDREW H. SOLOMON, born Philadelphia, Pennsylvania, April 1, 1968; admitted to bar, 2001, Oregon. *Education:* Bowdoin College (B.A., 1990); Northwestern School of Law (J.D., 2001). ***PRACTICE AREAS:*** Real Estate; Land Use. ***Email:*** soloa@perkinscoie.com

CODY WESTON, born 1969; admitted to bar, 1998, Oregon. *Education:* Harvard University (B.A., Government, 1991); University of Oregon (J.D., 1998). Order of the Coif. Associate Editor, Oregon Law Review. [Infantry Officer and Lawyer, U.S. Marine Corps]. ***PRACTICE AREAS:*** Commercial Litigation. ***Email:*** cweston@perkinscoie.com

REVISER OF THE WASHINGTON LAW DIGEST FOR THIS DIRECTORY.

(For biographical data on other Perkins Coie personnel, see Professional Biographies for those offices)

R.W. (REG) PERRY

7420 SW BRIDGEPORT ROAD
SUITE 204
PORTLAND, OREGON 97224
Telephone: 503-670-0443
Fax: 503-443-3793
Email: rwperry@perrywingar.com
URL: http://www.perrywinegar.com

General Civil Litigation, Arbitration and Mediation, Construction, Business Law, Real Estate, Estate Planning and Probate, Wills, Trusts, Guardianships.

MEMBER

R.W. PERRY, born 1938; admitted to bar, 1969, Oklahoma; 1970, Nebraska; 1974, Oregon; U.S. District Court, District of Oregon. *Education:* Oklahoma State University (B.S.C.E., 1961); Oklahoma City University (J.D., 1969). Registered Professional Engineer, Oklahoma. Vice President and General Counsel, Hoffman Construction Company, 1973-1992. Arbitrator: American Arbitration Association; Court Panels for Multnomah, Washington and Clackamas Counties. *Member:* Oregon State Bar (Past Member, Executive Committee, Construction Section; Past-Chairman, Lawyer Referral Services).

PETERSON LAW OFFICES, PC

Established in 2000
825 NE 20TH AVENUE, SUITE 340
PORTLAND, OREGON 97232
Telephone: 503-280-0888
Fax: 503-231-9500
URL: http://injurylaworegon.com
Email: toddpeterson@coho.net
URL: http://injurylawfirmoregon.com

Personal Injury, Premises Liability, Automobile Accidents and Injuries, Dog Bites and Wrongful Death.

TODD A. PETERSON, born Cleveland, Ohio, November 13, 1963; admitted to bar, 1991, Oregon and U.S. District Court, District of Oregon; 1994, Washington. *Education:* Ohio University (B.A., 1986); Northwestern School of Law (J.D., 1991). Rotarian, 1991-1997. Previous employment: Bullock & Regier, Portland, Oregon, 1991-1996; Lygo & Peterson, Portland, Oregon, 1996-2000; Peterson Law Offices PC, Portland, Oregon, 2000—. *Member:* Oregon State Bar; Washington State Bar Association; Oregon Trial Lawyers Association. ***PRACTICE AREAS:*** Personal Injury; Premises Liability; Automobile Accidents and Injuries; Dog Bites; Wrongful Death. ***Email:*** info@injurylaworegon.com

DAVID J. ARTZ, born St. Paul, Minnesota, June 27, 1950; admitted to bar, 1975, California; 1993, Oregon. *Education:* University of California at Berkeley (B.A., 1972); Hastings College of Law (J.D., 1975). ***PRACTICE AREAS:*** Personal Injury; Litigation; Transportation. ***Email:*** david@injurylaworegon.com

MARGARET MADISON PHELAN P.S.

PORTLAND, OREGON

(See Vancouver)

Elder Law, Long Term Care Planning and Asset Preservation, Medicaid, Estate Planning, Probate and Trust Administration, Guardianship, Special Needs Trusts.

PICKETT DUMMIGAN RHODES LLP

621 SW MORRISON STREET, SUITE 900
PORTLAND, OREGON 97205
Telephone: 503-223-7770
Fax: 503-227-2530
URL: http://www.pickettdummiganrhodes.com

Litigation Practice including Personal Injury, Products Liability, Professional Liability and Toxic Tort Litigation.

PARTNERS

J. RANDOLPH PICKETT, born Eugene, Oregon, October 26, 1946; admitted to bar, 1972, Oregon; 1982, U.S. District Court, District of Oregon; 2003, U.S. Supreme Court. *Education:* University of Arizona (B.A., 1968); University of Oregon (J.D., 1972). Co-Author, "Torts and Products Liability," Oregon Legislation, 1991. Pro Bono Attorney, ATLA September 11 Victim Compensation Fund. *Member:* Multnomah County Bar Association; Oregon State Bar (Member, Toxic Tort Committee, 1989-1991; Chair, 1990-1991); Oregon Trial Lawyers Association (Member, President's Circle); The Association of Trial Lawyers of America (Member, President's Club). Supporting Fellow, Roscoe Pound Institute. ***REPORTED CASES:*** Wegener v. Walter Kidde & Co., 697 P 2d 981, 730 App 22; O'Donnell v. Floan, 728 P 2d 956, 820 App 656; Blizzard v. State Farm Auto Ins. Co., 738 P 2d 983, 860 App 56. ***PRACTICE AREAS:*** Products Liability; Medical Negligence; Premises Liability. ***Email:*** randy@pickettlaw.com

R. BRENDAN DUMMIGAN, born Boulder, Colorado, April 9, 1965; admitted to bar, 1993, Oregon; 2002, Washington; 2004, U.S. District Court, District of Oregon; 2005, U.S. District Court, District of Washington. *Education:* University of Colorado, Boulder (B.A., 1987); Lewis and Clark College (J.D., 1993). *Member:* Multnomah County Bar Association; Oregon State Bar; Oregon Lawyers Association (Member, President's Circle); Washington State Trial Lawyers Association; The Association of Trial Lawyers of America. ***LANGUAGES:*** Spanish. ***PRACTICE AREAS:*** Motor Vehicle Accidents and Injuries; Products Liability; Medical Negligence. ***Email:*** brendan@pickettlaw.com

LAURA LEE RHODES, admitted to bar, 1991, New Mexico, Colorado and U.S. District Court, District of New Mexico; 1993, U.S. District Court, District of Colorado; 1998, Oregon; 1999, U.S. District Court, District of Oregon; 2003, Washington. *Education:* University of New Mexico (B.A., 1987; J.D., 1991). *Member:* Multnomah Bar Association (Member, Products Liability Executive Committee); Oregon State Bar; Oregon Trial Lawyers Association. ***PRACTICE AREAS:*** Personal Injury; Products Liability; Nursing Home Litigation; Medical Malpractice. ***Email:*** laura@pickettlaw.com

ELVIA AGUILAR, born Chila, Michoacan, Mexico, September 24, 1973; admitted to bar, 2000, Oregon. *Education:* University of Oregon (B.A., 1996; J.D., 1999). *Member:* Multnomah County Bar Association; Oregon State Bar; Oregon Trial Lawyers Association. ***LANGUAGES:*** Spanish. ***PRACTICE AREAS:*** Personal Injury; Motor Vehicle Accidents and Injuries; Criminal Defense. ***Email:*** elvia@pickettlaw.com

PITZER LAW

101 S.W. MAIN STREET, SUITE 805
PORTLAND, OREGON 97204
Telephone: 503-227-1477
Fax: 503-227-5839
Email: jpitzer@pitzerlaw.net
URL: http://www.pitzerlaw.net

Complex Commercial Litigation, Intellectual Property Litigation (Patents, Trademarks, Copyrights), Technology Law, White Collar Criminal Defense, Antitrust, Eminent Domain, Products Liability Defense, Employment Litigation.

JEFF S. PITZER, born Pittsburg, Kansas, September 8, 1963; admitted to bar, 1990, Illinois; 2002, Oregon; U.S. District Court, District of Oregon; U.S. District Court, Northern District of Illinois, including Trial Bar, U.S. Court of Appeals, Seventh Circuit, and U.S. Supreme Court. *Education:* University of Kansas (B.A., Chemistry, 1986); University of Wisconsin (J.D., cum laude, 1990). Formerly with Jenner & Block, Chicago, Illinois, 1990-2001 (Partner, 1997-2001). Founder, Pitzer Law, 2002. *Member:* Multnomah County Bar Association; Oregon State Bar; Gus T. Solomon Inn of Court. ***PRACTICE AREAS:*** Complex Commercial Litigation; Intellectual Property Litigation; Technology Law; White Collar Criminal Defense; Products Liability Defense; Antitrust; Eminent Domain.

MARILYN R. PODEMSKI

2477 S.W. ARDEN ROAD
PORTLAND, OREGON 97201
Telephone: 503-228-5229
Fax: 503-224-5451
Email: mrp@podemski.com
URL: http://www.lawyers.com/podemski

Bankruptcy, Collections, Commercial Law, Litigation.

MARILYN R. PODEMSKI, born Los Angeles, California, December 12, 1946; admitted to bar, 1976, California; 1979, Oregon; 1994, Washington. *Education:* University of Oregon (B.A., Honors, College Literature, 1968; M.A., Literature, 1969); University of Chicago (J.D., 1976). Associate Editor, University of Chicago Law Review, 1975-1976. Mock Trial Coach, Oregon State Bar Competition. *Member:* Oregon State Bar (Debtor Creditor Section; Elected Delegate, Region 5, Oregon State Bar House of Delegates, 2001-2004); Washington State Bar Association; State Bar of California (inactive). ***PRACTICE AREAS:*** Commercial Law; Bankruptcy Collections.

POWERS, McCULLOCH & BENNETT, LLP

Established in 1973
3000 WELLS FARGO CENTER
1300 S.W. FIFTH AVENUE
PORTLAND, OREGON 97201
Telephone: 503-228-8588
Facsimile: 503-228-0057
URL: http://www.lawyers.com/pmblaw

Appellate Practice; Business Law; Construction Law; Family Law; Guardianship and Conservatorship; Insurance; Litigation; Medical Malpractice; Personal Injury; Probate; Products Liability; Professional Liability; Real Estate; Trusts and Estates; Wills.

PARTNERS OF FIRM

MARK M. McCULLOCH, born Portland, Oregon, May 20, 1942; admitted to bar, 1967, Oregon. *Education:* University of Oregon (B.A., Honors College, 1964; J.D., 1967). Phi Delta Phi. *Member:* Multnomah County and American Bar Associations; Oregon State

(This Listing Continued)

Bar; American Inns of Court (President, Gus Soloman Chapter, 1992-1993). ***PRACTICE AREAS:*** Arbitration; Mediation; Federal Civil Practice; Civil Fraud; Guardianship and Conservatorship; Insurance; Legal Malpractice; Civil Litigation; Complex Litigation; Medical Malpractice; Dental Malpractice; Personal Injury; Catastrophic Injury; Wrongful Death; Probate; Products Liability; Accountants Liability; Agents and Brokers Liability; Contested Wills. ***Email:*** mm@pmblaw.com

STEVEN R. BENNETT, born Tacoma, Washington, November 19, 1952; admitted to bar, 1978, Oregon. *Education:* University of Oregon (B.A., 1975); University of Santa Clara (J.D., 1978). *Member:* Multnomah County Bar Association; Oregon State Bar. ***PRACTICE AREAS:*** Business Litigation; Business Transactions; Commercial Real Estate; Leases and Leasing; Commercial Landlord and Tenant Law; Probate Administration; Probate Litigation; Real Estate Contracts; Shareholder Disputes; Federal Estate and Gift Taxation; Like Kind Exchanges; Contested Trusts and Estates; Estate Planning; Living Trusts; Trust Administration; Wills. ***Email:*** srb@pmblaw.com

ASSOCIATES

ARTHUR E. COYNE, born Knox, Indiana, March 30, 1970; admitted to bar, 1997, Oregon. *Education:* Butler University (B.A., 1992); Indiana University (J.D., 1996). Order of the Barristers. Member: Moot Court; Moot Court Board; Champion Team, Intramural Moot Court Competition. *Member:* Multnomah County Bar Association; Oregon State Bar. ***PRACTICE AREAS:*** Commercial Litigation; Commercial Transactions; Intellectual Property Licensing; Labor and Employment; Employer Liability; Employment Contracts; Non-Competition Agreements; Non-Solicitation Agreements; Personnel Policies; Wrongful Termination; Mortgage Foreclosure; Real Estate Leasing; Real Estate Litigation; Residential Real Estate Sales; Zoning; Planning; Land Use; Land Development. ***Email:*** ac@pmblaw.com

WALTER WEISS, JR., born Portland, Oregon, May 26, 1970; admitted to bar, 2001, Oregon. *Education:* Slippery Rock University (B.A., 1997); Willamette University (J.D., 2000). *Member:* Multnomah County Bar Association; Oregon State Bar. ***PRACTICE AREAS:*** Construction Claims; Contract Litigation; Property Rights; Family Law; Federal Practice; Management Employment Law; Employment Termination; Sexual Harassment; Civil Litigation; Products Liability; Estate Administration. ***Email:*** ww@pmblaw.com

REPRESENTATIVE CLIENTS: Stevens-Ness Law Publishing Co.; Steven Preece Investments, Inc.; Hardwood Industries; Robert Baily Design Group; DP Northwest; Isler and Co., CPA's; H & W Emergency Vehicles; A-Lazer; Pull-It Corporation; Paramount Graphics; Oak Grove Autobody; VLMK Engineers.

PRESTON GATES & ELLIS LLP

1400 KOIN TOWER
222 S.W. COLUMBIA STREET
PORTLAND, OREGON 97201-6632
Telephone: 503-228-3200
Facsimile: 503-248-9085
Email: info@prestongates.com
URL: http://www.prestongates.com

Anchorage, Alaska Office: 420 L Street, Suite 400, 99501-1937. Telephone: 907-276-1969. Facsimile: 907-276-1365.

Coeur d'Alene, Idaho Office: 1200 Ironwood Drive, Suite 315, 83814. Telephone: 208-667-1839. Facsimile: 208-765-2494.

Washington, D.C. Office: Preston Gates Ellis & Rouvelas Meeds LLP, 1735 New York Avenue, N.W., Suite 500, 20006-5209. Telephone: 202-628-1700. Facsimile: 202-331-1024.

Irvine, California Office: 1900 Main Street, Suite 600, 92614-7319. Telephone: 949-253-0900. Facsimile: 949-253-0902.

San Francisco, California Office: 55 Second Street, Suite 1700, 94105. Telephone: 415-882-8200. Facsimile: 415-882-8220.

Seattle, Washington Office: 925 Fourth Avenue, Suite 2900, 98104-1158. Telephone: 206-623-7580. Facsimile: 206-623-7022.

Spokane, Washington Office: 601 West Riverside Avenue, Suite 1400, 99201-0636. Telephone: 509-624-2100. Facsimile: 509-456-0146.

Beijing, China Office: Preston Gates & Ellis, Suite 1003, Tower E3, Oriental Plaza, No. 1 East Chang An Avenue. Telephone: +86 10 8518 8528. Facsimile: +86 10 8518 9299.

Hong Kong Office: Preston Gates & Ellis, 35th Floor, Two International Finance Centre, 8 Finance Street, Central, Hong Kong. Telephone: 852-2511-5100. Facsimile: 852-2511-9515.

Taipei, Taiwan Office: Preston Gates & Ellis, 2/F, No. 131, Min Sheng E. Rd., Sec. 3. Telephone:+886 (2) 2717 6657. Facsimile:+886 (2) 2712-8264.

General Practice. Administrative, Affordable Housing Finance, Americans with Disabilities Act, Bankruptcy Litigation, Business Transactions and Business Planning, Business Reorganization and Bankruptcy, Commercial Transactions and Litigation, Construction, Corporate, Corporate Financing, Creditors' Rights, Emerging Business, Employment, Environmental, Governmental Relations, Insurance, Technology and Intellectual Property (domestic and international, includes copyrights, trademarks, trade secrets, licensing and internet/e-commerce); International Business Transactions, Internet/E-Commerce Law, Labor, Land Use, Leasing, Legislative, Litigation, Mergers and Acquisitions, Municipal (general and finance), Natural Resources, Probate, Products Liability, Public Law, Real Estate, Real Estate Financing and Leasing, Securities, Solid Waste, Tax, Telecommunications, Uniform Commercial Code, Energy, Utilities and Transportation Law.

RESIDENT PARTNERS

ELLEN C. BACHMAN, born Portland, Oregon, March 22, 1949; admitted to bar, 1974, Oregon; 1980, U.S. Supreme Court; 1981, U.S. District Court, District of Oregon; 1982, U.S. Court of Appeals, Ninth Circuit. *Education:* Stanford University (A.B., with distinction, 1971); University of Washington (J.D., 1974). Phi Beta Kappa. Past President, Queen's Bench. Past Member, Oregon Appraiser Certification and Licensure Board. *Member:* Oregon State Bar (Past Chair, Financial Institutions Subcommittee, Business Law Section; Past Executive Committee and Secretary, Corporate Counsel Section); National Association of Bond Lawyers. ***PRACTICE AREAS:*** Real Estate; Banking; Municipal Finance; Institutional Trust. ***Email:*** ebachman@prestongates.com

BRENDAN R. McDONNELL, born Pasadena, California, September 13, 1962; admitted to bar, 1987, California; 1991, Oregon. *Education:* Loyola Marymount University (B.S., Accounting, 1984); University of California at Davis (J.D., 1987). *Member:* Multnomah and American Bar Associations; Oregon State Bar (Member, Executive Committee, Business Section); State Bar of California. ***PRACTICE AREAS:*** General Corporate Law; Securities Law; Venture Capital Law; Mergers and Acquisitions; Emerging Growth Companies. ***Email:*** bmcdonnell@prestongates.com

DOUGLAS S. PARKER, born 1953; admitted to bar, 1982, Oregon; 1983, Alaska and U.S. District Court, District of Alaska; 1988, U.S. Court of Federal Claims; 1993, U.S. Court of Appeals, Ninth Circuit. *Education:* University of Alaska; Oregon State University (B.A., with honors in History, 1976); Willamette University College of Law (J.D., 1981). Willamette University Law Review, 1980-1981. Member, Anchorage Municipal Employee Relations Board, 1987-1988. *Member:* Alaska (Chairman, Employment Law Section, 1987-1988; Member: Board of Bar Examiners, 1994-1997; Fee Arbitration Committee, 1993-1996) and American (Member, Labor and Employment Law Section) Bar Associations; Oregon State Bar. ***PRACTICE AREAS:*** Labor and Employment; Construction Law; Civil Litigation. ***Email:*** parkerd@prestongates.com

JEFFERY W. RING, born McMinnville, Oregon, August 27, 1951; admitted to bar, 1976, Idaho; 1985, Oregon; U.S. District Court, District of Oregon; U.S. District Court, District of Idaho; U.S. District Court, Southern District of Florida; U.S. Court of Appeals, Fifth, Ninth, Eleventh and District of Columbia Circuits; U.S. Supreme Court. *Education:* University of Oregon (B.S., B.S., 1973; J.D., 1976). Associate Editor, Oregon Law Review. *Member:* Oregon State Bar; Idaho State Bar; American Bar Association (Member, Sections on: Litigation; Environment, Energy and Natural Resources). ***PRACTICE AREAS:*** Environmental Law; Natural Resources; Litigation; Land Use; Mining Law; Energy; Administrative Law; Appellate Practice; Maritime Law. ***Email:*** jring@prestongates.com

HARVEY W. ROGERS, born San Francisco, California, February 22, 1945; admitted to bar, 1975, Oregon; 1976, Massachusetts. *Education:* California State University at Hayward (B.A., summa cum laude, 1969); University of Oregon (M.S., Psychology, 1972; J.D., 1975). Defense Language Institute, 1963-64. Letter of commendation for exceptional service, Hakata, Japan, 1966. *Member:* National Association of Bond Lawyers (Chair, Oregon Short Term Fund Board, 1984—). [Active duty, United States Army, 1963-1966]. ***LANGUAGES:*** German, Spanish, Korean and Japanese. ***PRACTICE AREAS:*** Municipal Finance Law; Municipal Law; Housing Law. ***Email:*** hrogers@prestongates.com

TIMOTHY J. SERCOMBE, born Columbia, Missouri, December 4, 1949; admitted to bar, 1976, Oregon; 1977, U.S. District Court, District of Oregon; 1981, U.S. Court of Appeals, Ninth Circuit. *Education:* Northwestern University (B.A., 1971); University of Oregon (J.D., honor graduate, 1976). Order of the Coif. Co-Editor: Oregon Government Law, OLI, 1991, 2001. *Member:* Oregon State Bar. ***PRACTICE AREAS:*** Land Use Law (30%); Municipal and Government Law (50%); Utility Law (20%). ***Email:*** tsercomb@prestongates.com

ANN L. SHERMAN, born Howell, Michigan, April 26, 1953; admitted to bar, 1988, Oregon, Idaho and Washington. *Education:* Carleton College; University of Illinois (B.F.A., 1975); Stanford University (Ph.D., 1980); Northwestern School of Law of Lewis and Clark College (J.D., magna cum laude, 1988). *Member:* Oregon State Bar (Member, Government Law Section); American Bar Association (Member, Urban, State and Local Government Section); National Association of Bond Lawyers. ***PRACTICE AREAS:*** Municipal Bonds; Public Finance; Banking Law; Securities Law; Housing Finance; Federal Indian Law. ***Email:*** asherman@prestongates.com

HARVARD P. SPIGAL, born Tacoma, Washington, June 30, 1945; admitted to bar, 1970, Washington; 2000, Oregon. *Education:* University of Washington (B.A., 1967; J.D., 1970). ***PRACTICE AREAS:*** Energy; Utility; Administrative Law. ***Email:*** hspigal@prestongates.com

PHILIP S. VAN DER WEELE, born Grand Rapids, Michigan, August 25, 1959; admitted to bar, 1984, Michigan; 1986, Oregon; 1997, New York; U.S. District Court, District of Oregon; U.S. District Court, Eastern and Southern Districts of New York; U.S. Court of Appeals, Sixth, Ninth, Tenth and Federal Circuits. *Education:* Calvin College (B.A., 1981); University of Michigan (J.D., magna cum laude, 1984). ***PRACTICE AREAS:*** Antitrust; Litigation. ***Email:*** pvanderweele@prestongates.com

OF COUNSEL

RICHARD G. PRICE, born Seattle, Washington, January 11, 1952; admitted to bar, 1989, Massachusetts; 1990, New York; 1998, Oregon. *Education:* University of Oregon (B.S., Economics, 1975); Princeton University (Ph.D., Economics, 1983); Cornell Law School (J.D., 1988). Associate, 1986-1987 and Managing Editor, 1987-1988, Cornell Law Review. Law Clerk, Hon. Rya Zobel, U.S. District Court, District of Massachusetts, 1988-1989. *Member:* Association of the Bar of the City of New York; Multnomah, New York State and American (Member, Antitrust Section) Bar Associations; Oregon State Bar (Chair, Antitrust and Trade Regulation Section). ***PRACTICE AREAS:*** Antitrust and Trade Regulation; Litigation. ***Email:*** rprice@prestongates.com

SENIOR ASSOCIATE

MARTIN F. MEDEIROS, admitted to bar, 1995, Washington; 2001, Oregon. *Education:* American University (B.S., 1988); University of Tulsa College of Law (J.D., 1994). Phi Delta Phi. Editor, Tulsa International Law Journal. Speaker, ASp and Traditional Software Licensing, 2003; Author: "Permissive Wheeling Scheme," 28 Tulsa Law Journal 521, 1993; "Transboundary Water Rights," 1 Tulsa Journal Computer, 3 International Law, 157, 1997. Member: Society for Information Managers, 1996—; AD Hoc Telecom Users, 1998-2001. *Member:* Oregon State Bar (Steering Committee Member and Chair-Elect, Computer and Internet Law Section, 2001); American Bar Association (Intellectual Property, Science and Technology). ***PRACTICE AREAS:*** Intellectual Property; Information Technology; Telecommunications and Media Law; Corporate Law. ***Email:*** mmedeiros@prestongates.com

(This Listing Continued)

PRESTON GATES & ELLIS LLP, Portland—Continued

RESIDENT ASSOCIATES

KARL E. HAUSAFUS, born Portland, Oregon, May 13, 1971; admitted to bar, 2000, Oregon and Washington. *Education:* University of Oregon (B.S., 1993); Northwestern School of Law, Lewis and Clark College (J.D., 2000). Phi Delta Phi. *Member:* Oregon State Bar (Member, Debtor Creditor Section); Washington State (Member, Debtor Creditor Section) and American Bar Associations. ***PRACTICE AREAS:*** Bankruptcy; Creditors Rights; Civil Litigation; Consumer Law; Real Estate Foreclosure. ***Email:*** khausafus@prestongates.com

YI-KANG HU, admitted to bar, 2005, Oregon; registered to practice before U.S. Patent and Trademark Office. *Education:* Reed College (B.A., Biochemistry & Molecular Biology, 1995); Max-Planck Institute of Biophysics; Oregon Health Sciences University (Ph.D., Biochemistry & Molecular Biology, 2001); Northwestern School of Law (J.D., cum laude, 2004). Recipient, Natural Resources Law Scholarship. *Member:* Oregon State Bar. ***PRACTICE AREAS:*** Intellectual Property (50%); Food and Drug Regulation (50%). ***Email:*** yhu@prestongates.com

MATTHEW J. LYSNE, born Vancouver, Washington, October 15, 1976; admitted to bar, 2002, Oregon and U.S. District Court, District of Oregon; 2003, Washington; 2004, U.S. District Court, Western District of Washington and U.S. Court of Appeals, Ninth Circuit. *Education:* University of Washington (B.A., Political Science, with distinction, 1999; J.D., 2002). *Member:* Washington State Bar Association; Oregon State Bar. ***PRACTICE AREAS:*** Civil Litigation; Civil Appeals. ***Email:*** mlysne@prestongates.com

CAROL J. McCOOG, born Cleveland, Ohio, January 23, 1972; admitted to bar, 1997, Oregon. *Education:* University of Washington (B.A., 1994; J.D., 1997). Managing Editor, Pacific Rim Law and Policy Journal, January, 1997. ***LANGUAGES:*** Chinese. ***PRACTICE AREAS:*** Municipal Finance. ***Email:*** cjmccoog@prestongates.com

GULGUN UGUR, admitted to bar, 2002, Oregon. *Education:* University of California at Los Angeles (B.A., magna cum laude, 1998); University of California at Los Angeles (J.D., 2002). *Member:* National Association of Bond Lawyers. ***PRACTICE AREAS:*** Public Finance. ***Email:*** gugur@prestongates.com

Languages: Chinese, French, German, Japanese, Korean, Russian, Spanish and Taiwanese.

REPRESENTATIVE CLIENTS: Aketon Technologies, Inc.; Aluma Tech/Pacific, Inc.; Amway Corporation; Angel Station Corporation; Avendel, Inc.; Bank of the West; Carla Properties, Ltd.; Carr-Gottstein Foods, Inc.; Cascade General, Inc.; City of Portland; Centricity, Inc.; CH2MHill Industrial Design & Construction, Inc.; Coffman Excavation; Copper Mountain Trust Company; Columbia Housing Corporation; Commercial Realty Advisors Northwest, LLC; Dipro Diagnostic Products GMBH; Dominick's Finer Foods, Inc.; Doug Bean & Associates, Inc.; Eastport Plaza Shopping Center; ExtraNetworks, Inc.; Fort James Corporation; Future Shop, Inc.; General Growth Properties; Harland Financial Services ; Housing Authority of Washington County; Intercultural Communication Institute; LabVelocity, Inc.; League of Oregon Cities; Lone Rock Timber Company; LSI Logic Corporation; MDU Resources Group, Inc.; Mercedes Benz Credit Corporation; Micropower Electronics, Inc.; Microsoft Corporation; Moonstruck Confections, Inc.; Morse Bros., Inc.; Music-Vend Distributing Company; NCompliance Software, Inc.; The Nature Conservancy; Newland Communities LLC; Newland Northwest; Nike, Inc.; Oil Can Henry's; Oregon Corporation for Affordable Housing and its equity funds; Oregon League of Women Voters; Oregon Pacific Investment & Development Company; Pacific Northwest Properties; Pacific Realty Associates, L.P. ("PacTrust"); Port of Portland; Portland Art Museum; PNC Bank; Safeway Inc.; Samsung Electronics Co., Ltd.; Shared Communications Services, Inc.; Speakeasy, Inc.; State of Oregon; Sun Studs, Inc.; Tamarack Mezzanine Partners, L.P.; Talcott Realty I Limited Partnership; Teachers Insurance and Annuity Association; The Vons Companies, Inc.; Tyrolit Schleifmittelwerke Swarovski K.G.; Unisource Manufacturing, Inc.; U.S. Timberlands; WaferTech, LLC; Wells Fargo Bank, National Association; Western Wireless Corporation; Williams Gas Pipeline; Wright Williams & Kelly; Xerox Corporation; and Yellow Freight System, Inc.

(For complete Biographical data on all Personnel, see Professional Biographies at Seattle and Spokane, Washington; Anchorage, Alaska; Washington, D.C.; Coeur d'Alene, Idaho; Irvine and San Francisco, California and Hong Kong)

RAIVIO, KOHLMETZ & STEEN, P.C.

Established in 2003

400 SW 6TH AVENUE, SUITE 914

PORTLAND, OREGON 97204

Telephone: 503-224-1104

Fax: 503-224-9417

Email: andy@rkslawyers.com

URL: http://www.rkslawyers.com

Criminal Law, Personal Injury, Civil Rights, Driving While Intoxicated, Weapons Charges, Drug Crimes, Auto Accidents, Slip and Fall, Dog Bites, Wrongful Death, Assault, Homicide, Robbery, Measure II, White Collar Crime, Sexual Accusations.

FIRM PROFILE: Experienced and Aggressive 3 lawyer boutique trial firm specializing in representing those unjustly accused of crimes and those wrongfully injured by the actions or inactions of others.

H. SCOTT RAIVIO, born Murray, Utah, January 12, 1950; admitted to bar, 1975, Illinois and U.S. District Court, Northern District of Illinois; 1981, Oregon and U.S. District Court, District of Oregon. *Education:* Western Illinois University (B.A., 1972); John Marshall Law School (J.D., with distinction, 1975). Member, Order of John Marshall. Founder, Raivio, Kohlmetz & Steen, P.C., 2003. Appointed judge pro tempore by Oregon Supreme Court, 1996-1999. Associate, Rieke & Savage, 1982-2002. *Member:* Multnomah County Bar Association; Oregon State Bar; Oregon Criminal Defense Lawyers Association. ***PRACTICE AREAS:*** Criminal Law; Crime Victims Compensation; Personal Injury; Domestic Relations; Small Business Law; Murder; Felonies. ***Email:*** scott@rkslawyers.com

ANDREW M. KOHLMETZ, born New York, N.Y., November 30, 1967; admitted to bar, 1995, Oregon; 2003, U.S. District Court, District of Oregon; 2004, U.S. Court of Appeals, Ninth Circuit. *Education:* Hobart College (B.A., 1990); University of Oregon (J.D., 1995). *Member:* Multnomah County Bar Association; Oregon State Bar (Member, Uniform Criminal Jury Instruction Committee, 2004); Oregon Criminal Defense Lawyer's Association (Member Board of Directors, 2004, 2005); National Association of Criminal Defense Lawyers. ***PRACTICE AREAS:*** Criminal; Personal Injury; Civil Rights. ***Email:*** andy@rkslawyers.com

JASON A. STEEN, born Portland, Oregon, June 2, 1967; admitted to bar, 1993, Alaska and U.S. District Court, District of Alaska; 1999, Oregon, 2002, U.S. District Court, District of Oregon. *Education:* Ohio University (B.A., Political Science, cum laude, 1989); University of Puget Sound (J.D., 1992). Phi Alpha Delta. *Member:* Oregon State Bar; Oregon Criminal Defense Lawyers. ***PRACTICE AREAS:*** Personal Injury; Criminal Defense. ***Email:*** jason@rkslawyers.com

RAMIS CREW CORRIGAN, LLP

Established in 1981

BALLOW & WRIGHT BUILDING

1727 N.W. HOYT STREET

PORTLAND, OREGON 97209

Telephone: 503-222-4402

Fax: 503-243-2944

Email: info@rcclawyers.com

URL: http://www.rcclawyers.com

General Civil Litigation in all State and Federal Courts. Administrative, Antitrust, Business Law, Condemnation, Environmental, Governmental Relations, Inverse Condemnation, Land Use, Legislative, Municipal, Personal Injury, Public Lands, Real Estate, Water and Zoning Law.

FIRM PROFILE: Ramis Crew Corrigan, LLP, is a medium-sized law firm providing a broad range of legal services to both private and public clients. The firm devotes much of its practice to land use, litigation, municipal employment, condemnation, inverse condemnation, real estate. Among the firm's clients are numerous land and housing developers and local and national corporations.

Please visit our website, http://www.rcclawyers.com, for a complete listing of our Partners, Of Counsel and Associates.

PRINCIPALS

TIMOTHY V. RAMIS, born Portland, Oregon, April 4, 1950; admitted to bar, 1975, Oregon and U.S. District Court, District of Oregon. *Education:* Princeton University; Stanford University (B.A., 1972); University of Oregon (J.D., 1975). Managing Board, Oregon Law Review, 1974-1975. Author: "Executive Privileges," University of Oregon L. Rev., 1975. *Member:* Oregon State Bar (Member, Sections on: Government Law; Real Estate and Land Use Law); U.S. Supreme Court Bar; Oregon City Attorneys Association. ***PRACTICE AREAS:*** Land Use Law; Municipal Law; Zoning Law; Water Law; Environmental Law. ***Email:*** timr@rccb.com

STEPHEN F. CREW, born Portland, Oregon, October 10, 1951; admitted to bar, 1978, Oregon and U.S. District Court, District of Oregon; 1980, U.S. Court of Appeals, Ninth Circuit. *Education:* University of Oregon (B.B.A., 1973); Netherlands School of International Business, Bruekelen, Netherlands (B.S., 1972); Northwestern School of Law of Lewis and Clark College (J.D., 1978). Member, Psychiatric Security Review Board, 1985—. *Member:* Multnomah County and American Bar Associations; Oregon State Bar; Oregon Trial Lawyers Association. ***PRACTICE AREAS:*** Business Law; Commercial Litigation; Environmental Law. ***Email:*** stevec@rccb.com

CHARLES E. CORRIGAN, born Bakersfield, California, October 18, 1948; admitted to bar, 1976, Oregon; 1977, Washington, U.S. District Court, Eastern District of Washington and U.S. Court of Appeals, Ninth Circuit; 1979, U.S. District Court, Western District of Washington; 1983, U.S. District Court, District of Oregon. *Education:* Wharton School, University of Pennsylvania (B.S., 1970); University of Oreg on (J.D., 1976). *Member:* Oregon State Bar; Washington State Bar; Federal Bar Association; Oregon Trial Lawyers Association; The Association of Trial Lawyers of America. ***PRACTICE AREAS:*** Condemnation; Inverse Condemnation; Complex Litigation; Commercial Litigation; Real Property Litigation; Personal Injury Law. ***Email:*** chuckc@rccb.com

RANSOM BLACKMAN LLP

Established in 1978

1001 S.W. FIFTH AVENUE

SUITE 1400

PORTLAND, OREGON 97204-1144

Telephone: 503-228-0487

Telecopier: 503-227-5984

Federal and State Civil and Criminal Trial and Appellate Practice. Complex Business Litigation. Administrative Law. Professional Licensing.

MEMBERS OF FIRM

JOHN S. RANSOM, born Grinnell, Iowa, April 10, 1942; admitted to bar, 1968, District of Columbia; 1973, U.S. Supreme Court; 1974, Oregon and U.S. Court of Appeals, Ninth Circuit. *Education:* University of Tennessee at Knoxville (B.S., 1964); Georgetown University (J.D., 1967); George Washington University (LL.M., 1973). Assistant Corporation Counsel, Washington, D.C., 1968-1969. Assistant U.S. Attorney, Washington, D.C., 1969-1973. Assistant U.S. Attorney, Oregon, 1973-1978. Chairman, Police Internal Investigations Auditing Committee, 1985-1988. Member, City/County Public Safety Commission, 1982-1984. *Member:* Oregon State Bar (Member, House of Delegates, 1996-2000); The District of Columbia Bar; American Bar Association; Oregon Trial Lawyers Association (Member, Board of Governors 1982-1985); Oregon Criminal Defense Lawyers Association. ***PRACTICE AREAS:*** Criminal; Complex Civil Litigation. ***Email:*** john@ransomblackman.com

(This Listing Continued)

MARC D. BLACKMAN, born Sheboygan, Wisconsin, March 4, 1947; admitted to bar, 1973, Oregon; 1975, U.S. Court of Appeals, Ninth Circuit; 1984, U.S. Supreme Court. *Education:* Harvard University (A.B., magna cum laude, 1969); Yale University (J.D., 1973). Law Clerk to Chief Justice Kenneth O'Connell, Oregon Supreme Court, 1973-1974. Assistant U.S. Attorney, Oregon, 1974-1978. Member: Multnomah County Commission on Library Policy and Administration, 1983-1984; Gus J. Solomon American Inns of Court, 1988—; U.S. District Court Indigent Representation Supervision Committee, 1988—; U.S. District Court Magistrate Review Committee, 2001-2002; U.S. District Court Criminal Justice Act Committee, 1994—; Attorney Admissions Fund Advisory Committee, 1998—; Board of Directors, Multnomah County Legal Aid Society, 1994-1996. *Member:* Multnomah County (President, 1992-1993), Federal (Member, Board of Directors, 1996-2000) and American Bar Associations; Oregon State Bar (Member, House of Delegates, 1996-1999; Disciplinary System Task Force, 2001-2002; Bar Chair, Joint Committee of Bar, Press and Broadcasters, 1987-1988); Oregon Criminal Defense Lawyers Association. ***PRACTICE AREAS:*** Administrative Law; Professional Licensing; Criminal; Appeals. ***Email:*** marc@ransomblackman.com

---

KENDRA MARIE MATTHEWS, born Boston, Massachusetts, May 7, 1971; admitted to bar, 1996, Oregon; 2000, U.S. District Court, District of Oregon and Washington. *Education:* University of Puget Sound (B.A., 1993); Georgetown University (J.D., 1996). Judicial Clerk, Oregon Court of Appeals, 1996-1998. Author: Mail and Wire Fraud, Tenth Survey of White Collar Crime, 32 American Criminal Law Review 481, 1995. *Member:* Multnomah, Washington State and Federal Bar Associations; Oregon State Bar (Member, House of Delegates, 2001—); Oregon Criminal Defense Lawyers Association. ***PRACTICE AREAS:*** Appeals; Administrative Law; Criminal Law; Civil Litigation. ***Email:*** kendra@ransomblackman.com

CRAIG J. GABRIEL, born Pittsburgh, Pennsylvania, November 16, 1971; admitted to bar, 2001, Oregon; 2002, U.S. District Court of Oregon. *Education:* Columbia University (B.S., 1994; M.I.A., 1995); Georgetown University Law Center (J.D., magna cum laude, 2001). *Member:* Oregon State Bar; Oregon Criminal Defense Lawyers Association. ***PRACTICE AREAS:*** Litigation. ***Email:*** craig@ransomblackman.com

RAYBURN LAW OFFICES

PORTLAND, OREGON

(See Lake Oswego)

Litigation, Personal Injury, Automobile Accidents and Injuries, Wrongful Death Employment Law, Sexual Harassment.

REDMAN LAW FIRM

PORTLAND, OREGON

(See Milwaukie)

Personal Injury, Automobile Accidents, Wrongful Death, Trusts and Estates, Business Law, Corporate Law, Wills and Probate, Guardianship and Conservatorship, Real Estate, Eminent Domain and Condemnation Law.

THE RICKLES LAW FIRM, PC

ONE SW COLUMBIA STREET, SUITE 1850
PORTLAND, OREGON 97258-2001
Telephone: 503-229-1850
Facsimile: 503-229-1856
Toll Free: 1-800-669-1850
URL: http://www.rickles-law.com

Civil Trial Practice. Litigation and Insurance Defense including Casualty, Auto, Fire, Medical and Legal Malpractice. Construction Litigation, Complex Litigation, Products Liability, Employment, Liquor Liability, Public Tort Liability, Auto Dealer Law, Business Litigation and Personal Injury.

STEPHEN P. RICKLES, born Portland, Oregon, July 2, 1953; admitted to bar, 1979, Oregon; 1986, U.S. District Court, District of Oregon, and U.S. Court of Appeals, Ninth Circuit; 1991, Washington. *Education:* University of Oregon (B.S., 1975); Northwestern School of Law (J.D., 1979). Senior Deputy District Attorney, Multnomah County, 1979-1985. *Member:* Multnomah County and American Bar Associations; Oregon State Bar; Washington State Bar Association; Oregon Association of Defense Counsel (Member, Board of Directors, 1997—; President, 2002); Washington Defense Trial Lawyers Association; Defense Research Institute. ***Email:*** strickles@aol.com

---

MARTIN W. JAQUA, born 1960; admitted to bar, 1986, Oregon; 1987, Washington. *Education:* Linfield College (B.A., cum laude, 1982); University of Oregon (J.D., 1985). *Member:* Oregon State Bar; Washington State Bar Association; Oregon Association of Defense Counsel. ***Email:*** mjaqua@rickles-law.com

LAWRENCE SCHUCKMAN, born 1963; admitted to bar, 1992, New York; 1995, Oregon; 2003, Washington. *Education:* State University of New York at Albany (B.S., 1985); Brooklyn Law School (J.D., 1991). President, Student Bar Association, 1989-1990. *Member:* Washington State Bar Association; Oregon State Bar; Oregon Trial Lawyers Association; Association of Trial Lawyers of America. ***Email:*** lschuckman@riekles-law.com

STEVEN V. RIZZO, P.C.

(Formerly, Seidl & Rizzo)
LINCOLN PLACE, SUITE 350
1620 S.W. TAYLOR STREET
PORTLAND, OREGON 97205
Telephone: 503-229-1819
Fax: 503-229-0630

Civil Trial Practice in State and Federal Courts in Oregon, Washington and California. Commercial Litigation and Personal Injury Litigation including Business Torts, Labor and Employment, Medical Malpractice, Torts, Professional Liability, Products Liability, Insurance, Drug and Medical Device, Employment, Insurance, Negligence, Products Liability, Premises Liability, Toxic Torts, Environmental Law.

STEVEN V. RIZZO, born Camden, New Jersey, August 20, 1955; admitted to bar, 1984, Oregon and U.S. District Court, District of Oregon; 1992, California. *Education:* Rutgers University; College of New Jersey, formerly Trenton State College (B.A., 1978); Drake University (J. D., 1983). Recipient: Outstanding Oral Advocacy Award, Order of Barristers; Pro Bono Public Service Award, Oregon State Bar, 1989. Published Member, Drake Law Review, 1982-1983. Director, Friends of the Portland Children's Museum, 1988-1993. Student Law Clerk to the Hon. D. Dortch Warriner, U.S. District Court, Eastern District of Virginia. Prosecutor Intern, Dallas County, Iowa 1982. *Member:* Multnomah County Bar Association (CLE Committee, 1992-1994) Oregon State Bar (Treasurer, Executive Committee, Section on Toxic Torts, 1994—; Chairman, Products Liability Section, 1997); Oregon Association of Defense Counsel. ***LANGUAGES:*** Italian. ***PRACTICE AREAS:*** Products Liability; Personal Injury; Professional Liability; Negligence; Employment; Commercial Litigation; Insurance Law. ***Email:*** srizzo@rizzopc.com

---

JOHN MICHAEL MATTINGLY, born Savannah, Georgia, December 17, 1968; admitted to bar, 1995, Oregon; 1998 U.S. District Court, District of Oregon. *Education:* University of Georgia (B.B.A., 1992); Northwestern School of Law of Lewis & Clark College (J.D., 1995). Moot Court Honor Board Scholar, 1994-1995; Member: Labor and Employment Section; Civil Rights Section; American Bar Association; Multnomah County Bar Association; Recipient, American Jurisprudence Awards. ***PRACTICE AREAS:*** Professional Liability; Products Liability; Personal Injury; Medical Malpractice. ***Email:*** mmattingly@rizzopc.com

ANDREW A. GRADE, born Rochester, New York, 1968; admitted to bar, 1998, Oregon and U.S. District Court, District of Oregon. *Education:* State University of New York at Buffalo (B.A., 1995); Willamette University (J.D., 1998). ***PRACTICE AREAS:*** Insurance Coverage.

VICTORIA L. BALENGER, born Charlestown, West Virginia, January 9, 1956; admitted to bar, 1987, Oregon. *Education:* Grinnell College (B.A., 1978); Lewis & Clark Northwestern School of Law (J.D., 1986). *Member:* Oregon State Bar.

REPRESENTATIVE CORPORATE AND INSURANCE CLIENTS: Commercial Union Insurance Co.; Dow Corning, Corp.; Farmland Insurance Companies; Liberty Mutual Insurance Co.; Reliance Insurance Co.; TIG Insurance Co.; Trident Marine Managers.

ROSE, SENDERS AND BOVARNICK, LLP

1205 N.W. 25TH AVENUE
PORTLAND, OREGON 97210
Telephone: 503-227-2486
Fax: 503-227-4172

Business, Real Estate, Civil Litigation, Personal Injury, Workers Compensation, Employment Law and Federal Employees Liability Act Law. Trial and Appellate Practice in all State and Federal Courts.

STEVEN M. ROSE, born Pittsburgh, Pennsylvania, April 28, 1949; admitted to bar, 1974, Oregon and U.S. District Court, District of Oregon; 1977, U.S. Court of Appeals, Ninth Circuit; 2002, Washington. *Education:* Northwestern University (B.A., 1971); University of Oregon (J.D., 1974). *Member:* Oregon State Bar; Washington State Bar Association. ***PRACTICE AREAS:*** Business Law; Real Estate; Civil Practice; Personal Injury. ***Email:*** srose@rsblaw.net

RICHARD D. SENDERS, born Portland, Oregon, August 11, 1949; admitted to bar, 1974, Oregon; 1975, U.S. District Court, District of Oregon; 1981, U.S. Court of Appeals, Ninth Circuit; 2002, Washington. *Education:* Columbia University (B.A., 1971) University of Oregon (J.D., 1974). *Member:* Oregon State Bar; Washington State Bar Association. ***PRACTICE AREAS:*** Business Law; Employment Law; Real Estate; Civil Practice. ***Email:*** rsenders@rsblaw.net

OF COUNSEL

PAUL S. BOVARNICK, born New York, N.Y., September 15, 1952; admitted to bar, 1979, Oregon; 1980, U.S. District Court, District of Montana; 1982, Montana and U.S. Court of Appeals, Ninth Circuit; 1983, U.S. District Court, District of Oregon and U.S. District Court, District of Colorado; 2003, Washington and U.S. District Court, Eastern and Western Districts of Washington. *Education:* Claremont Men's College (B.A., cum laude, 1974); University of Oregon (J.D., 1979). *Member:* Multnomah County and American Bar Associations; State Bar of Montana; Oregon State Bar; Washington State Bar Association; Oregon Trial Lawyers Association (Member, Board of Governors); The Association of Trial Lawyers of America; Washington State Trial Lawyers Association; Academy of Rail Labor Attorneys. ***PRACTICE AREAS:*** Personal Injury Law; Workers Compensation Law; Federal Employers Liability Act; Employment Law. ***Email:*** pbovarnick@rsblaw.net

---

PHILIP S. BENTLEY, born Los Angeles, California, April 4, 1972; admitted to bar, 2001, Oregon; U.S. District Court, District of Oregon. *Education:* University of Oregon

(This Listing Continued)

ROSE, SENDERS AND BOVARNICK, LLP, Portland—Continued

(B.S., 1994; J.D., 2000). Oregon Law Review, Moot Court. *Member:* Multnomah Bar Association; Oregon State Bar; Oregon Trial Lawyers Association; The Association of Trial Lawyers of America. ***PRACTICE AREAS:*** Personal Injury; Federal Employers' Liability Act (FELA); Employment; Workers Compensation. ***Email:*** pbentley@rsblaw.net

DESIGNATED COUNSEL FOR: Transportation Communications International Union; Brotherhood of Locomotive Engineers.

THE ROSEN LAW FIRM

OLD FEDERAL COURTHOUSE, SUITE 702
620 S.W. MAIN STREET
PORTLAND, OREGON 97205
Telephone: 503-525-2525
Fax: 503-525-2526
Email: Rosen@RosenLawFirm.com
URL: http://www.RosenLawFirm.com

Salem, Oregon Office: 512 State Street, 97301.

Trial practice, Aviation and Aerospace Law, Products Liability, Unsafe Products, Business Litigation, Wrongful Death, Automobile Accidents, Medical Malpractice Lawsuits.

FIRM PROFILE: The firm specializes in litigation, including aviation litigation, products liability, negligence, medical malpractice and commercial and business litigation. The firm also handles litigation involving engineering, technical and scientific issues.

STEVEN O. ROSEN, admitted to bar, 1977, Illinois; 1978, Oregon; 2004, Washington. *Education:* State University of New York at Buffalo (B.S. in Aerospace Engineering, 1970); Case Western Reserve University (M.S. in Systems and Control Engineering, 1975); Northwestern School of Law of Lewis and Clark College (J.D., 1977). Member, Lewis and Clark Law Review, 1976-1977. Author: "Choice of Law," Contract Law in Oregon, Oregon State Bar, 1991, 1993, 1999, 2003. Adjunct Professor of Law, Conflict of Laws, Northwestern School of Law of Lewis and Clark College, 1981-1988. Recipient, Distinguished Adjunct Professor Award, 1986. Associate, 1979-1986, Partner, 1986-1997 and Member, Executive Committee, 1996-1997, Miller, Nash, Wiener, Hager & Carlsen. Lecturer, "Movie Magic: How The Masters Try Cases," CLE course. *Member:* Oregon State (Chair, 1994-1995, Aviation Section) and American (Member, Litigation Section; Council, 1997-2000; Director of Divisions, 1996-1997; Division Director, 1993-1995, 2004-2005 and Chair, 1990-1993, Aviation Litigation Committee) Bar Associations; American Board of Trial Advocates. ***Email:*** Rosen@RosenLawFirm.com

ASSOCIATE

ELIZABETH M. CLINE, admitted to bar, 1994, Oregon. *Education:* The Pennsylvania State University (B.A., with high distinction and honors in English, 1991); University of Pittsburgh School of Law (J.D., 1994). Phi Beta Kappa; Phi Kappa Phi. Recipient: Multnomah Bar Association Young Lawyers Section Award of Merit, 2002. Judicial Clerk, Honorable Stephen B. Herrell, Circuit Court of the State of Oregon for Multnomah County, 1995-1998. Associate, Stahancyk, Gearing, Rackner & Kent, P.C., 1998-2002. *Member:* Oregon State Bar; Multnomah Bar Association (Member, Young Lawyers Section Pro Bono Committee, 1996-2001; Member, 2001-2002 and Chair, 2002-2003, Young Lawyers Section Continuing Legal Education Committee; Director, Young Lawyers Section Board of Directors, 2003-2004); Oregon Women Lawyers. ***PRACTICE AREAS:*** Trial Practice; Aviation Law; Products Liability; Civil Practice. ***Email:*** Cline@RosenLawFirm.com

ROSENTHAL & GREENE, P.C.

Established in 1975
1001 S.W. FIFTH AVENUE, SUITE 1907
PORTLAND, OREGON 97204
Telephone: 503-228-3015
FAX: 503-228-3269

Personal Injury, Wrongful Death, Legal and Medical Malpractice, Employee Termination, Civil Rights. Trial and Appellate Practice in State and Federal Courts.

ELDEN M. ROSENTHAL, born Des Moines, Iowa, March 15, 1947; admitted to bar, 1972, Oregon and California; 1976, U.S. Supreme Court. *Education:* University of California at Los Angeles (B.A., cum laude, 1968); Stanford University (J.D., 1972). Phi Beta Kappa. Author: "The Dramshop and the Drunk Driver," Chapter 17, Torts, Oregon State Bar CLE, 1988. Co-author, "Elder Abuse and Nursing Home Litigation," Chapter 10, Elder Law, Oregon State Bar CLE, 2000. Recipient: 1991 Public Justice Award by Oregon Trial Lawyers Association; 1991 Award of Merit by Oregon State Bar; 1990 Civil Liberties Award by American Civil Liberties Union of Oregon. Adjunct Professor, Tort Law, Lewis & Clark School of Law, 1998—. Member, Board of Directors: Oregon Trial Lawyers Association 1977-1978; American Civil Liberties Union of Oregon, 1975-1977; 1979-1980; National Citizens' Coalition for Nursing Home Reform, 1980-1982. *Member:* Multnomah County Bar Association (Judicial Selection Committee, 1978-1980, 1992-1995; Committee on Professionalism, 1986-1987; Committee on Specialization, 1986-1987); Oregon Trial Lawyers Association (Chair: Mentor Committee, 1989; Juvenile Justice Committee, 2002-2003); The Association of Trial Lawyers of America; American College of Trial Lawyers. ***REPORTED CASES:*** Berhanu v. Metzger, 850 P2d 373 (Or. App. 1993); Hussey v. City of Portland, 64 F3d 1260 (9th Cir. 1995); Kraus v. Santa Fe Southern Pacific Corporation, 878 F2d 1193 (9th Cir. 1989); Mayfield v. Gonzales, 2005 WL 1801679 (D.Or. 2005). ***PRACTICE AREAS:*** Personal Injury Law; Wrongful Death Law; Medical Malpractice Law; Employee Termination Law; Civil Rights Law. ***Email:*** elden@rosenthal-greene.com

MICHAEL A. GREENE, born Chicago, Illinois, September 18, 1946; admitted to bar, 1972, California and Idaho; 1975, U.S. Supreme Court; 1980, Oregon. *Education:* Stanford University (A.B., 1968; J.D., 1971). Teaching Fellow, Criminal Law, Stanford Law School, 1972. Adjunct Professor, Business Law and Real Estate, Boise State University, 1976-1979. Author: "The Age of Legal Advocacy for Diabetes," Diabetes Spectrum, Vol. 12, No. 4, 1999; "Evaluating the Legal Negligence Case," Professional Liability Fund of the Oregon State Bar, In Brief, March 1985; "Special Problems of the Plaintiff in Preparation and Trial of a Professional Liability Case," Oregon Trial Lawyers Association, September 1984; "Managing Liability Risk in the Office Laboratory, The Journal of the American Medical Association," Vol. 256, No. 10, 1986. Member and Chair, Board of Directors, American Diabetes Association, 1986-1994. Member and Chair, Board of Directors, American Diabetes Association Research Foundation, 1994-1996; Chair, American Diabetes Association Legal Advocacy, 1994-2002. *Member:* Multnomah County Bar Association (President, Board of Directors, 1997-2002); Idaho State Bar (Member: Appellate Rules Committee, 1976-1980; Bar Examination Review Committee, 1972-1975); Oregon State Bar (Member, Civil Uniform Jury Instructions Committee, 1986-1987; Client Security Fund Committee, Member and Chair, 1994-1997; Legal Ethics Committee, Member and Chair, 1997-2001); The Association of Trial Lawyers of America; Oregon Trial Lawyers Association (Member, Board of Governors, 1985-1987). ***REPORTED CASES:*** Smith v. Mensing, 739 P2d 595 (Or. App. 1987); McQuary v. Bel Air Convalescent Home, Inc., 684 P2d 21 (Or. App. 1984); Granewich v. Harding, 329 OR 47 (1999); Kapche v. City of San Antonio, 176 F.3d 840 (5th Cir. 1999) & 304 F.3d. 493 (5th Cir. 2002). ***PRACTICE AREAS:*** Legal Malpractice; Personal Injury Law; Wrongful Death Law; Product Liability Law. ***Email:*** mike@rosenthal-greene.com

(This Listing Continued)

KURT M. RYLANDER
TRIAL & PATENT ATTORNEY AT LAW PC

PORTLAND, OREGON

(See Vancouver, Washington)

Patents, Trademarks, Copyrights, Intellectual Property, Patent Licensing, Unfair Competition, Business Law, Complex Business Litigation, Government Contracts, Bid Protests, Construction Law, Internet Law, Federal Litigation, Criminal Law, Personal Injury, Trial and Appellate Practice.

SAMUELS YOELIN KANTOR SEYMOUR & SPINRAD LLP

A Partnership including Professional Corporations
Established in 1927
200 WILLAMETTE WHARF
4640 S.W. MACADAM AVENUE
PORTLAND, OREGON 97239-4232
Telephone: 503-226-2966
Telecopier: 503-222-2937
URL: http://www.samuelslaw.com

Taxation, Business Ventures, Closely Held Business, Corporations, Limited Liability Companies, Mergers and Acquisitions, Family Business Entities, Commercial Leasing Real Estate Transactions and Construction Law, Retirement Plans, Employment Litigation, Discrimination, Employee Benefits, Employee Contracts, Sexual Harassment, Wrongful Termination, Real Estate Litigation and Other General Civil Litigation, Construction, Eminent Domain, Commercial Landlord and Tenant, IRS Audits, Tax Planning, Trusts and Estates, Asset Protection, Estate Planning, Guardianship, Wills, Business Enterprises, Probate, Trust Administration, Estate Planning, Business Transactions, Buying or Selling of Businesses, and Mediation and Arbitration of the same.

FIRM PROFILE: Samuels Yoelin Kantor Seymour & Spinrad LLP ranks as one of Oregon's oldest law firms, earning its clients' trust since 1927. The firm employs a team approach in problem solving, pooling the relevant knowledge and expertise of its individual attorneys. The firm understands the problems faced by businesses in today's complex world and is committed to preventing and solving those problems for businesses of all sizes in a creative yet practical way.

MEMBERS OF FIRM

STEPHEN E. KANTOR, (P.C.), born Portland, Oregon, May 22, 1949; admitted to bar, 1974, Oregon. *Education:* University of Oregon (B.S., 1971); Northwestern School of Law of Lewis and Clark College (J.D., 1974). Beta Alpha Psi. Certified Public Accountant, Oregon, 1976. Recipient: American Jurisprudence Award in Remedies. Staff Member, Law Review, 1973-1974. Co-Author and Co-Editor, Oregon Probate Systems Manual, 1987; Author and Speaker, Oregon State Bar, CLE, 1986-2005. Author and Editor, Using Trusts in Oregon, 1994-2001 Supplement. President: Jewish Family and Child Service, 1991-1992; Oregon Jewish Community Foundation, 1996-1998. Past Trustee, The Nature Conservancy. Past Director: B'nai Brith; MJCC, Jewish Federation. Board Chair, Ronald McDonald House Charities, 2004-2005. *Member:* Multnomah County and American Bar Associations; Oregon State Bar (Chairman, Title Insurance Subcommittee, 1979-1982; Chair, 1992, CPA Joint Committee; Member, Executive Committee, Estate Planning and Probate Section, 1988-1994; Treasurer, 1990; Chair, 1991-1993; President's Award, 1994); Oregon Society of Certified Public Accountants (Vice Chairman, Estate and Gift Tax Committee, 1981-1982; CPE Committee, 1992—); American Institute of Certified Public Accountants; Financial Planning Association; Estate Planning Council of Portland. Fellow, American College of Trusts and Estates Counsel. ***PRACTICE AREAS:*** Estate Planning Law; Trusts; Probate Law; Corporate Law; General Business Law; Taxation. ***Email:*** sek@SamuelsLaw.com

HY SAMUELS (1904-1992)

STEVEN W. SEYMOUR, born Mason City, Iowa, November 28, 1945; admitted to bar, 1975, Oregon; 2001, Washington; 2002, U.S. Supreme Court. *Education:* University of Iowa (B.A., 1968); Willamette University (J.D., 1975). Phi Delta Phi. Member: Order of the Barristers; Moot Court Board. Deputy District Attorney, Multnomah County, 1975-1980.

(This Listing Continued)

Part Time Municipal Judge, City of Mosier, Oregon. *Member:* Multnomah County and American Bar Associations; Oregon State Bar (Member and former chairman of the Section on Litigation; Former Member, House of Delegates); Oregon Trial Lawyers Association. [LTC., U.S. Army, Signal Corps (retired)]. ***REPORTED CASES:*** Clackamas Gastroenterology Assoc., P.C. v. Wells, 538 U.S. 440 (2003). ***PRACTICE AREAS:*** Trusts and Estates Litigation; Employment Law; Non Competition Agreements; Shareholder Disputes; Business Litigation. ***Email:*** sws@SamuelsLaw.com

ALAN M. SPINRAD, born New York, New York, December 15, 1950; admitted to bar, 1978, Oregon; 1979, U.S. District Court, District of Oregon; 1993, U.S. Court of Appeals, Ninth Circuit; 1994, U.S. Tax Court. *Education:* Carnegie Mellon University (B.S., 1971; M.S., 1973); University of Oregon (J.D., 1978). William L. Mellon Fellowship. Henry Collier Scholarship. Attorney-Advisor, U.S. Environmental Protection Agency, 1978-1979. Deputy District Attorney, Multnomah County, Oregon, 1979-1984. Mediator, Oregon Court of Appeals Settlement Conference Program. Arbitrator for Multnomah, Clackamas and Washington Counties and Arbitration Service of Portland. *Member:* Multnomah County and American Bar Associations; Oregon State Bar; Oregon Mediation Association. ***REPORTED CASES:*** Geranghadr v. Entagh, 189 Or App 567, 77 P 3d 323 (2003). ***PRACTICE AREAS:*** Mediation; Arbitration; Real Estate. ***Email:*** ams@SamuelsLaw.com

MICHAEL D. WALKER, (P.C.), born Glenns Ferry, Idaho, October 11, 1963; admitted to bar, 1988, Oregon and U.S. Tax Court. *Education:* Albertson College of Idaho (B.A., magna cum laude, 1985); Northwestern School of Law of Lewis and Clark College (J.D., magna cum laude, 1988). Lawrence Henry Gipson Scholar. Legal Writing Teaching Assistant, Northwestern School of Law of Lewis and Clark College, 1987-1988. Author: "General Partnership," I Advising Oregon Business 3-1, Oregon State Bar Continuing Legal Education, 1989, 1997 and 2001. Author and Speaker: "Partnerships, LLCs and LLPs in Oregon: Organization and Operation," Lorman Business Center, 1998; "Family Limited Partnerships and Limited Liability Companies in Oregon," National Business Institute, 1997-2000. Past President, St. Mathew Lutheran Church Foundation, 1996-1999. Board Member, 2001—, Treasurer, 2001-2004, Vice President, 2004-2005 and President, 2005—, St. Mathew Lutheran Church. *Member:* Oregon State Bar (Member, Sections on: Business Law; Debtor/Creditor Law; Estate Planning and Administration; Real Estate and Land Use Law; Taxation); American Bar Association (Member: Business Law and Taxation Section); Estate Planning Council of Portland. ***PRACTICE AREAS:*** Corporate Law; Limited Liability Companies; Partnerships; Taxation; Estate Planning; Business and Commercial Law. ***Email:*** mdw@SamuelsLaw.com

VAN M. WHITE, III, born Eugene, Oregon, July 24, 1962; admitted to bar, 1992, Washington; 1993, Oregon and U.S. District Court, District Court of Oregon. *Education:* Washington State University (B.A., 1984); Willamette University (J.D., 1992). Hearings Advocate/Law Clerk, State of Oregon Construction Contractors Board, 1991-1992. Author and Speaker: "Construction Lien Law, Contract Law and Laws and Business Practices for Oregon Construction Contractors," Oregon Contractors Education Services, 1992-2001 and A.Plus, 2001—; "The CCB: Registration, Enforcement and the Claims Process," Oregon State Bar and Oregon Construction Contractors Board, 1997. Author: "Practitioner's to the Oregon Construction Contractors Board," Oregon State Bar Construction Law Section, 2000. *Member:* Multnomah County and American Bar Associations (Member, Section on Construction Law); Oregon State Bar (Member, Sections on: Construction Law; Real Estate and Land Use Law; Business Law; Litigation); Washington State Bar; Oregon Remodeler's Association. ***REPORTED CASES:*** Koster Remodeling & Construction, Inc. v. Jataka, 155 Or.App.142 (1998). ***PRACTICE AREAS:*** Construction; Litigation; Real Estate; Business Law. ***Email:*** vmw@SamuelsLaw.com

MERRITT S. YOELIN, (P.C.), born Denver, Colorado, February 16, 1940; admitted to bar, 1966, California, Oregon and U.S. Tax Court. *Education:* University of Colorado at Boulder and University of Denver (B.S.B.A., 1962); University of California at Berkeley (LL.B., 1965). Beta Alpha Psi; Omicron Delta Kappa; Phi Alpha Delta. Certified Public Accountant, Colorado, 1962. Author: "Valuing the Business," IV Advising Oregon Business, Oregon State Bar Continuing Legal Education, 61, 1985; "Taxation of Damages," II Damages, Oregon State Bar Continuing Legal Education, 64-1, 1973; "General Partnerships," I Advising Oregon Business, Oregon State Bar Continuing Legal Education Chapter 3 (1989); "General Partnerships," I Advising Small Business, Chapter 5 (Callaghan & Company, 1989). Member: Congregation Neveh Shalom (President, 1992-1994); Northwest Region of United Synagogue of Conservative Judaism (President, 1997-1999); United Synagogue of Conservative Judaism (Vice President, 1997-1999). Treasurer, Jewish Foundation of Portland, 2003—. *Member:* Multnomah County and American Bar Associations; State Bar of California; Oregon State Bar (Member, Committee on Taxation, 1972-1975; Chairman, Estate Planning and Probate Administration Section, 1983-1984); Estate Planning Council of Portland (President, 1997). American College of Trusts and Estates Counsel. ***PRACTICE AREAS:*** Taxation; Corporate; Pension and Profit Sharing Plans; Estate Planning. ***Email:*** msy@SamuelsLaw.com

ASSOCIATES

AMY E. BILYEU, born Portland, Oregon, March 8, 1973; admitted to bar, 2001, Oregon. *Education:* Cottey College (A.A., 1993) Dean's List; University of Oregon (B.A., with honors, 1995); University of Oregon School of Law (J.D., 2000); University of Washington Law School (LL.M., Taxation, 2001). Board Member and Treasurer, Bradley Angle House. *Member:* Multnomah County (Member, Young Lawyers Division) Bar Association; Oregon State Bar (Member, Taxation, Estate Planning and Administration and Business Law Sections; Chair, Pro Bono Committee, New Lawyers Division); Oregon Women Lawyers (Treasurer). ***LANGUAGES:*** French and Danish. ***PRACTICE AREAS:*** Estate Planning; Corporate Law; Business Law; Taxation; Charitable Organizations Law. ***Email:*** abilyeu@samuelslaw.com

SARIE K. CROTHERS, born Salem, Oregon, October 19, 1976; admitted to bar, 2002, Washington; 2003, Oregon. *Education:* University of Oregon (B.A., Finance, 1997; J.D., 2001); University of Washington School of Law (LL.M., Taxation, 2002). Certified Law Clerk Benton County District Attorney's Office, Corvallis, Oregon. *Member:* Multnomah County (Member, Young Lawyers Division) and American (Member, Taxation Section) Bar Associations; Oregon State Bar (Member, Taxation, Estate Planning and Administration and Business Law Sections); Washington State Bar Association (Member, Taxation and Business Law Sections). ***PRACTICE AREAS:*** Taxation; Estate Administration; Trust Administration; Probate; Business Law; Corporate Law; Estate Planning. ***Email:*** scrothers@samuelslaw.com

BETSY A. GREGORY, born Ionia, Michigan, March 16, 1976; admitted to bar, 2003, Oregon. *Education:* The University of Michigan (B.S., with distinction, 1998); Washington College of Law of The American University (J.D., 2003). Member, Moot Court Board, 2002-2003. *Member:* Oregon State Bar (Member, Litigation; Real Estate and Land Use; Construction Law Sections); Multnomah County and American (Member, Litigation Section) Bar Associations; Oregon Women Lawyers. ***PRACTICE AREAS:*** Real Estate; Construction Law; Civil Litigation. ***Email:*** bgregory@samuelslaw.com

TIMOTHY J. RESCH, born Mt. View, California, July 23, 1970; admitted to bar, 1998, Oregon; 1999, Washington. *Education:* University of Oregon (B.A., 1992); Northwestern School of Law of Lewis & Clark College (J.D., 1998). Managing Editor, Environmental Law Review, 1997-1998. Trial Attorney, UN International Criminal Tribunal, for the Former Yugoslavia; The Hague; Netherlands. *Member:* Multnomah and American (Member, Section on Litigation and Labor Employment Law) Bar Associations; Oregon State Bar (Member, Sections on: Litigation and Labor Employment Law). ***PRACTICE AREAS:*** Litigation; Labor and Employment; International Law. ***Email:*** tresch@samuelslaw.com

EDWARD L. "TED" SIMPSON, born Coos Bay, Oregon, November 3, 1968; admitted to bar, 1997, Washington; 1999, Oregon. *Education:* Eastern Washington University (B.A., cum laude, 1994); Gonzaga University School of Law (J.D., 1997); University of Washington (LL.M., Taxation, 1998). President, Board of Directors, CCI Enterprises. *Member:* Multnomah County, Washington State and American Bar Associations; Oregon State Bar. ***PRACTICE AREAS:*** Taxation; Retirement Planning; Employee Benefits; Corporate Law; Pension and Profit Sharing Plans; Estate Planning. ***Email:*** esimpson@samuelslaw.com

OF COUNSEL

ABBY WOOL LANDON, (P.C.), born New London Connecticut, October 27, 1956; admitted to bar, 1991, Oregon; U.S. District Court, District of Oregon. *Education:* Simmons College (B.A., 1980); Northwestern School of Law of Lewis and Clark College (J.D., 1991). Shareholder, Abby Wool Landon, P.C., 1992-2000. General Counsel; Executive Vice President, TripleE, Inc., 2000-2002. Past Member, American Corporate Counsel Association. Past Member, Board of Directors, RezPlus, Inc. Member, American Corporate Counsel Association, 2000-2002. Member, Board of Directors, CCI Enterprises, Inc. *Member:* Clackamas County, Multnomah County and American Bar Associations; Oregon State Bar (Member, Sections on: Business; Family Law; Business Litigation); Oregon Trial Lawyers Association. ***PRACTICE AREAS:*** Business Law; Business Transactions; Business Litigation; Private Placement Securities; Estate Planning; Wills; Trust Litigation; Family Law. ***Email:*** awlandon@samuelslaw.com

REPRESENTATIVE CLIENTS: Lincoln Service Co. (real property exchange intermediary); Prendergast & Associates, Inc. (property management); H & B Jewelry & Loan Co. (pawnbroker); LaRog Jewelers; Castle Management Inc. (Round Table Pizza, restaurant management); The Piper Group (business brokers and consultants); Beall Corporation (tank trailer manufacturers); McClure Industries, Inc. (fiberglass laundry carrier manufacture); National Meeting Company, Inc. (event and convention planner); Greenbrier Companies (railcar manufacturer); Acme Construction Supply Co., Inc. (construction material supplier); Moore Clear Co. (holding company); Circle C Marketing, Inc. (farm products distributor); PGP (real property appraisers); GPS, Inc. (wholesaler); Surgical Oncology Associates, P.C. (medical office); Dentistry for Children, P.C. (dental office); Gastroenterology Specialists of Oregon, P.C. (medical clinic); Cascadia Women's Clinic, LLP (medical clinic); Sunset Family Practice Group P.C. (medical clinic); Roberts Street Clinic, P.C. (medical clinic); University Anesthesiologists, P.C. (medical clinic); Campbell Motors, Inc. (automotive dealer); Timber Press, Inc. (publisher); Secure Trans, LLC (security).

SATHER, BYERLY & HOLLOWAY, LLP

621 SOUTHWEST MORRISON STREET, SUITE 600
PORTLAND, OREGON 97205
Telephone: 503-225-5858
Fax: 503-721-9272
URL: http://www.sbhlegal.com

Employer Defense, Workers Compensation Law, OSHA, WISHA, Employment Law, Legal Malpractice, and Appellate.

FIRM PROFILE: Sather, Byerly & Holloway, LLP believes the client/attorney relationship works best when it operates like a business partnership. We are convinced high-quality legal services can be provided at an economical rate. We appreciate the importance of open and timely communication with our clients.

DEBORAH L. SATHER, admitted to bar, 1981, Oregon; 1993, Washington. *Education:* University of Oregon (B.S., 1973); Lone Mountain College (M.S., 1976); Northwestern School of Law of Lewis and Clark College (J.D., 1980). ***Email:*** dsather@sbhlegal.com

BRUCE L. BYERLY, admitted to bar, 1972, Oregon; 2002, Washington. *Education:* University of Oregon (B.A., 1968; J.D., 1971). ***PRACTICE AREAS:*** OSHA. ***Email:*** bbyerly@sbhlegal.com

RONALD C. HOLLOWAY, admitted to bar, 1979, Oregon; 1981, U.S. District Court, District of Oregon. *Education:* Oregon State University (B.S., 1968; M.S., 1970); University of Oslo, Blidren, Norway (Adv. Cert., 1975); Willamette University (J.D., 1979). ***Email:*** rhollo@sbhlegal.com

KRISHNA BALASUBRAMANI, admitted to bar, 1994, Oregon; 2003, Washington and U.S. District Court, District of Oregon. *Education:* University of California at San Diego (B.A., 1990); Northwestern School of Law of Lewis and Clark College (J.D., 1994). ***Email:*** kbalas@sbhlegal.com

JENNIFER R. ROUMELL, admitted to bar, 1993, Oregon. *Education:* University of Michigan (B.A., 1989); Lewis and Clark College (J.D., 1993). ***Email:*** jroumell@sbhlegal.com

(This Listing Continued)

SATHER, BYERLY & HOLLOWAY, LLP, Portland—Continued

RONALD K. POMEROY, admitted to bar, 1973, Oregon; 1983, Guam; U.S. District Court, District of Oregon; U.S. Court of Appeals, Ninth Circuit. *Education:* Portland State University (B.S., 1969); Northwestern School of Law (J.D., 1973). ***Email:*** rpomeroy@sbhlegal.com

BRIAN M. PERKO, admitted to bar, 1978, Oregon. *Education:* Willamette University (B.A., 1975; J.D., 1978).

ROBB A. SCHOTTHOEFER, admitted to bar, 1997, Oregon; 1999, Washington. *Education:* Oregon State University (B.A., 1994); Seattle University School of Law (J.D., 1997).

LINDA D. CONRATT, admitted to bar, 1995, Washington and Oregon. *Education:* Willamette University (B.A., 1989); DePaul University College of Law (J.D., 1994).

KAREN S. VARNEY, born Marlborough, Massachusetts, September 8, 1972; admitted to bar, 2001, Oregon; 2002, Washington. *Education:* University of California at Santa Cruz (B.A., 1997); Lewis and Clark College (J.D., 2001). Previously with The Gilroy Law Firm. ***PRACTICE AREAS:*** Workers Compensation. ***Email:*** kvarney@sbhlegal.com

REBECCA WATKINS, admitted to bar, 2004, Oregon. *Education:* Portland State University (B.S. 1995; M.S., 1999); Northwestern School of Law of Lewis and Clark College (J.D., 2004). ***Email:*** rwatkins@sbhlegal.com

NORMAN D. COLE, born Portland, Oregon, September 10, 1949; admitted to bar, 1974, Oregon; 1975, U.S. District Court, District of Oregon; 1996, U.S. Court of Appeals, 9th Circuit. *Education:* Claremont Men's College (B.A., 1971); University of Ohio School of Law (J.D., 1974). ***PRACTICE AREAS:*** Workers' Compensation (100%). ***Email:*** ncole@sbhlegal.com

REPRESENTATIVE CLIENTS: Ace USA; Chubb Group of Insurance Companies; Fred Meyer, Inc.; Freightliner Corporation; Cambridge Integrated Services; NEC America, Inc.; Liberty Mutual; Nike; Northwest Natural; Portland Brewing Company; Portland General Electric; Portco; Precision Castparts Corp.; Safeco Insurance Co.; Zurich Insurance.

J. WILLIAM SAVAGE P.C.

Established in 1976

620 S.W. FIFTH AVENUE, SUITE 1125
PORTLAND, OREGON 97204
Telephone: 503-452-5858
Fax: 503-248-0200
Email: jwsavage@earthlink.net

Personal Injury, Medical Malpractice, Legal Malpractice.

FIRM PROFILE: Founded in 1976 by Forrest N. Rieke, the firm is housed in the Thomas Mann Building, erected prior to the turn of the century and located in the historic district of downtown Portland. Rieke & Savage, P.C. is known for criminal defense as well as cases involving serious injury and death due to negligence or professional malpractice. Rieke & Savage also serves individuals who have been harmed in their employment & prides itself on presenting strategies both in court and for settlement.

JOHN WILLIAM SAVAGE, born Seattle, Washington, October 11, 1951; admitted to bar, 1977, Oregon, U.S. District Court, District of Oregon and U.S. Court of Appeals, Ninth Circuit; 1985, U.S. Supreme Court; 1998, U.S. Court of Appeals, Federal Circuit; 2002, Washington; 2003, U.S. Court of Federal Claims. *Education:* Lewis and Clark College and University of Washington (B.A., 1973); Lewis and Clark College (J.D., 1977). *Member:* Multnomah County (Board of Directors, 1990-1992; Award of Merit, 1994; Chair, Circuit Court Liaison Committee, 2003—) and American Bar Associations; Oregon Trial Lawyers Association (Board of Directors, 2003—); Association of Trial Lawyers of America; Oregon Criminal Defense Lawyers Association (Director, 1983-1986). ***PRACTICE AREAS:*** Personal Injury; Medical Malpractice; Legal Malpractice. ***Email:*** jwsavage@rieke-savage.com

SCHROEDER LAW OFFICES, P.C.

A Professional Corporation
Established in 1991

1915 NE 39TH AVE.
P.O. BOX 12527
PORTLAND, OREGON 97212-0527
Telephone: 503-281-4100
Fax: 503-281-4600
Email: schroeder@water-law.com
URL: http://www.water-law.com

Environmental Law including Water Law, Irrigation Law, Water Districts, Agricultural Law, Property Rights, Administrative Litigation. Matters pertaining to the Clean Water Act, NEPA and Title Transfer.

FIRM PROFILE: Laura A. Schroeder formed Schroeder Law Offices in 1991 to provide legal services to individuals, businesses and municipal entities within the agri-business industry. Since 1991 the firm has represented clients throughout the Northwest in transactions, litigation and legislative matters involving water rights and natural resources issues. Our attorneys bring a depth of experience to each client's needs that is especially suited to agribusiness and domestic water suppliers.

LAURA A. SCHROEDER, born Ontario, Oregon, September 25, 1951; admitted to bar, 1987, Oregon; 1988, Idaho, Nevada and U.S. District Court, District of Idaho; 1990, U.S. District Court, District of Nevada and U.S. District Court, District of Oregon; 1995, Washington; 1998, U.S. District Court, Western District of Washington and U.S. Court of Appeals, Ninth Circuit. *Education:* Valparaiso University; University of Oregon (B.A., 1972); Northwestern School of Law (J.D., 1987). Author: "Environment, Energy and Resource Law: Year in Review," Water Resources Editor for Oregon, American Bar Association, 1999—; "Agency Orders in Other Than Contested Cases," Oregon State Bar Administrative Law Deskbook Editor, 2001, 2004; "Cancellation and Forfeiture of Water Rights," Oregon Cattlemen's Beef Producer, July/August 2004; "Use it or Lose It: Water Rights and Water Issues in Oregon," In Good Tilth, August 15, 2004. Speaker: "Fundamentals of Water Law," National Business Institute, 2000—; "Law of Easements in Oregon," Lorman Educational Services, 2001—. Moderator and Oregon Speaker, "Transactional Due Diligence in Water Rights Transactions," American Bar Association, Section on Environment, Energy, and Resources, San Diego, 2001. Moderator, "Law Firm Leadership," Oregon Women Lawyers' Leadership Conference, May 2004. Panel Member, "Injury in Oregon Water Rights Transfers," Oregon Water Resources Congress Annual Meeting, December 2003. Presenter: "Groundwater Studies in the Klamath Basin and Implications," Oregon Groundwater Association Fall Meeting, 2001; "Water Law Basics: Hydrologic Connection Transfers and Well Sharing Agreements," Oregon Groundwater Association Annual Meeting, 2003; "Water Law in Oregon: Extensions, Amendments and Transfers," Lorman Educational Services, Portland, Oregon, May 2004; "Transfer Protests in Contested Cases," Oregon Water Law Conference, The Seminar Group, Portland, Oregon, November 2004; Nevada Groundwater Seminar, Lorman Educational Services, Reno, Nevada, January 2005; "Legislative Developments in Oregon," Oregon Water Coalition Annual Meeting, January 2005; "Current Policy Debates: Who Owns the Water Right," Lorman Education al Services, Salem, Oregon, March 2005. *Member:* Multnomah, Washington State (Member: Environmental and Land Use Section; Lawyers Assistance Program Committee) and American (Member, Sections on: General Practice; Small Firm; Litigation; Environment, Energy and Resources; International Law) Bar Associations; Idaho State Bar (Member, Water Law Section); Oregon State Bar (Member, Sections on: Agricultural Law; Litigation; Environmental and Natural Resources Law; Real Estate and Land Use Law; Law Practice Management; Solo and Small Firm Practice; Administrative Law); State Bar of Nevada; Oregon Women Lawyers. ***REPORTED CASES:*** State Eng'r of State of Nevada v. S. Fork Band of Te-Moak Tribe of W. Shoshone Indians of Nevada, 339 F.3d 804 (9th Cir. 2003); U.S. v. Alpine Land & Reservoir Co., 291 F.3d 1062 (9th Cir. 2002); City of Keizer v. Lake Labish Water Control Dist., 185 Or. App. 425, 60 P.3d 557 (2002); Hale v. Water Res. Dept. of State of Oregon, 184 Or. App. 36, 55 P.3d 497 (2002); Becker v. Pieper, 176 Or. App. 635, 32 P.3d 912 (2001); Kandra v. U.S., 145 F.Supp.2d 1192, 52 ERC 1928 (D.Or. 2001); Grants Pass Irrigation Dist. v. Water Res. Dept., 167 Or. App. 268, 1 P.3d 480 (2000); Kusyk v. Water Res. Dept., 164 Or. App. 738, 994 P.2d 798 (2000); State Eng'r of State of Nevada v. S. Fork Band of Te-Moak Tribe of W. Shoshone Indians of Nevada, 114 F.Supp.2d 1046, (D. Nev. 2000) aff'd on other grounds by 339 F.3d 804 (9th Cir. 2003); Kinross Copper Corp. v. State, 160 Or. App. 513, 981 P.2d 833, 142 Oil & Gas Rep. 473 (1999); State Eng'r of State of Nevada v. S. Fork Band of Te-Moak Tribe of W. Shoshone Indians of Nevada, 66 F.Supp.2d 1163 (D.Nev. 1999), vacated on reconsideration by 114 F.Supp.2d 1046, (D. Nev. 2000); Dority v. Water Res. Dept., 149 Or. App. 124, 942 P.2d 292 (1997); Teel Irrigation Dist. v. Water Res. Dept., 323 Or. 663, 919 P.2d 1172 (1996); Local No. 290, Plumber and Pipefitters v. Oregon Dept. of Envtl. Quality, 323 Or. 559, 919 P.2d 1168 (1996); Teel Irrigation Dist. v Water Res. Dept., 135 Or. App. 16, 898 P.2d 1344 (1995); Hermiston Irrigation Dist. v. Water Res. Dept., 131 Or. App. 596, 886 P.2d 1092 (1994); State ex rel. Circus Circus Reno, Inc. v. Pope, 317 Or. 151, 854 P.2d 461 (1993). ***PRACTICE AREAS:*** Natural Resources; Water Law; Water Rights; Boundary Disputes; Easements; Real Property; Right of Way Easements; Administrative Law; Administrative Adjudications; Appellate Practice; Litigation; Civil Trial Practice; Drainage Law; Water Districts; Irrigation Law; Property Rights; Agribusiness; Agricultural Law. ***Email:*** schroeder@water-law.com

REPESENTATIVE CLIENTS: Pershing County Water Conservation District; South Fork Water Board; East Fork Irrigaton District; Individual Water Users.

DAVID B. SCHUMACHER

3422 N.E. FORTY FIRST AVENUE
PORTLAND, OREGON 97212
Telephone: 503-249-8384
Fax: 503-249-8406
Email: schumacherdavid@hotmail.com
URL: http://www.lawyers.com/dbschumacher

Creditors' Rights, Business, Collections, Commercial Bankruptcy, Foreclosures.

DAVID B. SCHUMACHER, born Seattle, Washington, August 23, 1964; admitted to bar, 1996, Oregon, Washington and U.S. District Court, Western and Eastern Districts of Washington; 1997, U.S. District Court, District of Oregon. *Education:* Pacific Lutheran University (B.A., 1986); Willamette University College of Law (J.D., 1996). *Member:* Multnomah County, King County and Washington State Bar Associations; Oregon State Bar; Washington Trial Lawyers Association. ***PRACTICE AREAS:*** Debtor and Creditor; Civil Litigation; Bankruptcy.

REPRESENTATIVE CLIENTS: Farmers Insurance; American Honda Finance; Evergreen Financial Services; ER Solutions, Inc.; Cottenwood Financial, LTD.

SCHWABE, WILLIAMSON & WYATT, P.C.

Established in 1892

SUITES 1600-1900 PACWEST CENTER
1211 S.W. FIFTH AVENUE
PORTLAND, OREGON 97204-3795
Telephone: 503-222-9981
Fax: 503-796-2900
Telex: 4937535 SWK UI
Email: info@schwabe.com
URL: http://www.schwabe.com

Bend, Oregon Office: 354 SW Upper Terrace Drive, Suite 101, 97702. Telephone: 541-749-4044. Fax: 541-330-1153.

(This Listing Continued)

Seattle, Washington Office: U.S. Bank Centre, Suite 3010, 1420 Fifth Avenue. Telephone: 206-622-1711. Fax: 206-292-0460.
Vancouver, Washington Office: Suite 410, Main Place Building, 1111 Main Street. Telephone: 360-694-7551; 696-0241.

Business and Corporate Law, Joint Ventures, Partnerships, LLC's, Securities, Mergers and Acquisitions, Banking and Financial Institutions, Trusts and Estate Planning, Intellectual Property, Patents and Trademarks, Nanotechnology, White Collar Criminal Law, Real Estate and Land Use, Business, Commercial, and General Litigation, Bankruptcy, Reorganizations and Workouts, Hospital and Health Law, Forest Products, Franchise Law, Immigration, Insurance, Workers' Compensation and Insurance Defense, Employment Relations, Labor Law, Antitrust, Product Liability, Employee Benefits, Construction, Environmental, Energy and Utilities Law, Mining, Natural Resources, State and Local Taxation, Appellate Law, Government Relations, Professional Malpractice Defense, Indian Law, Insurance Coverage Litigation, International Law, eCommerce, Trade and Ports, Landlord & Tenant Law, Transportation, Entertainment & Media, Water Rights Law, Municipal Law and Public Entity Law.

FIRM PROFILE: Schwabe, Williamson & Wyatt, P.C. is one of the top law firms serving the needs of businesses in the Pacific Northwest. The firm's attorneys provide a broad range of transaction and litigation services to many of the Northwest's leading companies, from Fortune 500 industry leaders, to emerging and small, family-owned businesses. With over 140 attorneys, Schwabe, Williamson & Wyatt is the second largest law firm in Oregon, with offices in Portland and Bend. The firm also serves clients from offices in Seattle and Vancouver, Washington.

SHAREHOLDERS

AL AuYEUNG, born Hong Kong, November, 2, 1950; admitted to bar, 1990, California; 1994, Oregon; registered to practice before U.S. Patent and Trademark Office. *Education:* University of Portland (B.S., magna cum laude, 1972); Stanford University (M.S., 1974); University of California at Berkeley (M.B.A., 1980); Santa Clara University (J.D., 1990). *Member:* Oregon Intellectual Property Law Association; Association of Patent Law Firms (Secretary, 1998). (Resident). ***Email:*** Al_Auyeung@bstz.com

DAVID W. AXELROD, born Dallas, Texas, May 6, 1950; admitted to bar, 1975, Oregon. *Education:* Georgetown University and University of California at Los Angeles (B.A., cum laude, 1971); University of California School of Law, Davis (J.D., 1975). ***PRACTICE AREAS:*** Business Litigation; Patent Litigation; Intellectual Property Litigation. ***Email:*** daxelrod@schwabe.com

DAVID F. BARTZ, JR., born Grand Rapids, Michigan, March 9, 1957; admitted to bar, 1982, Oregon. *Education:* Michigan State University (B.A., with honor, 1979); University of Oregon (J.D., 1982). ***PRACTICE AREAS:*** Environmental and Natural Resources Law; Construction Law. ***Email:*** dbartz@schwabe.com

KEVIN E. BRANNON, born Albany, Oregon, February 11, 1955; admitted to bar, 1984, Oregon and Washington; 1992, Maryland. *Education:* Stanford University (A.B., Economics, 1977); Atkinson Graduate School of Management, Willamette University (M.M., 1984); Willamette University (J.D., 1984). ***PRACTICE AREAS:*** Securities; Corporate Finance; Emerging Growth Companies; Mergers and Acquisitions; Franchises and Franchising; Corporate Governance. ***Email:*** kbrannon@schwabe.com

CARMEN M. CALZACORTA, born Nyssa, Oregon, May 2, 1957; admitted to bar, 1984, Oregon and Washington. *Education:* University of Oregon (B.A., 1980; J.D., 1984). ***PRACTICE AREAS:*** Corporate Law; Securities; Forest Products. ***Email:*** ccalzacorta@schwabe.com

MICHAEL A. COHEN, born Portland, Oregon, January 26, 1967; admitted to bar, 1996, Oregon; 1998, Washington. *Education:* University of Chicago (B.A., 1989); University of Oregon (J.D., 1996). ***PRACTICE AREAS:*** Intellectual Property; Entertainment Litigation; Entertainment Transactions; New Media Technologies. ***Email:*** mcohen@schwabe.com

NEIL A. COLE, born Redwood City, California, March 18, 1971; admitted to bar, 1996, Oregon; 1997, Washington. *Education:* Western Oregon State College (B.S., 1993); Northwestern School of Law of Lewis & Clark College (J.D., 1996). ***PRACTICE AREAS:*** Mergers and Acquisitions; Business Transactions; Corporate Finance; Securities; Electronic Commerce; Nonprofit Corporations. ***Email:*** ncole@schwabe.com

JOHN G. CRAWFORD, JR., born Medford, Oregon, December 19, 1943; admitted to bar, 1973, Oregon. *Education:* University of Washington (B.A., 1965); University of Oregon (J.D., 1973). ***PRACTICE AREAS:*** Bankruptcy; Commercial Law; Business Law; Corporate Law; Energy; Estate Planning. ***Email:*** jcrawford@schwabe.com

WILLIAM B. CROW, born Eugene, Oregon, August 21, 1931; admitted to bar, 1961, Oregon. *Education:* University of Oregon (B.S., 1953); New York University (M.S., 1954); Willamette University (J.D., with honors, 1961). ***PRACTICE AREAS:*** Product Liability; Business Litigation. ***Email:*** wcrow@schwabe.com

JOYLE C. DAHL, born Oakland, California, October 5, 1935; admitted to bar, 1959, Oregon. *Education:* University of Oregon (B.S., 1957; LL.B., 1959); New York University (LL.M. in taxation, 1964). ***PRACTICE AREAS:*** Taxation; Trusts and Estates. ***Email:*** jdahl@schwabe.com

ROBERT D. DAYTON, born Spokane, Washington, June 9, 1944; admitted to bar, 1968, Oregon. *Education:* Willamette University (B.S.L., 1967; J.D., 1968); University of Miami (LL.M., in Estate Planning, 1976). ***PRACTICE AREAS:*** Estate Planning; Trusts and Estates; Wills; Federal Estate and Gift Taxation Law; Probate; Charitable Trust and Foundations; Charitable Giving; Guardianships and Conservatorships. ***Email:*** rdayton@schwabe.com

PATRICIA M. DOST, born Bellevue, Washington, July 6, 1965; admitted to bar, 1990, Oregon. *Education:* University of Washington (B.A., magna cum laude, 1986); University of Michigan (J.D., cum laude, 1990). ***PRACTICE AREAS:*** Environmental Compliance; Environmental Litigation. ***Email:*** pdost@schwabe.com

(This Listing Continued)

JAMES F. DULCICH, born Portland, Oregon, May 25, 1954; admitted to bar, 1982, Oregon. *Education:* University of Oregon (B.S., with honors, Phi Beta Kappa, 1977); University of Virginia (J.D., 1982). ***PRACTICE AREAS:*** Real Estate; Business Law. ***Email:*** jdulcich@schwabe.com

THOMAS V. DULCICH, born Portland, Oregon, June 10, 1953; admitted to bar, 1980, Oregon; 1983, Washington. *Education:* University of Oregon (B.S., honors in Econ., 1976); University of Chicago (J.D., 1980). ***PRACTICE AREAS:*** Securities Litigation; Real Estate Litigation; Business Litigation; Defense Litigation; Employment Law. ***Email:*** tdulcich@schwabe.com

NANCY M. ERFLE, born Billings, Montana, August 19, 1965; admitted to bar, 1990, Oregon; 1991, Washington; 1999, Montana. *Education:* Rocky Mountain College (B.A., summa cum laude, 1987); Willamette University (J.D., cum laude, 1990). ***PRACTICE AREAS:*** Products Liability Defense; Drug and Medical Device Litigation; Commercial and Multi-District Litigation. ***Email:*** nerfle@schwabe.com

WALTER H. EVANS, III, born Portland, Oregon, February 8, 1941; admitted to bar, 1967, Oregon; 1977, District of Columbia. *Education:* University of Oregon (B.S., 1963); Willamette University (J.D., 1967). ***PRACTICE AREAS:*** Business; Corporate. ***Email:*** wevans@schwabe.com

JOHN R. FAUST, JR., born Portland, Oregon, June 16, 1932; admitted to bar, 1958, Oregon. *Education:* University of Oregon (B.S., 1953; J.D., 1958). ***PRACTICE AREAS:*** Appellate Practice; Regulatory Law; Complex Litigation. ***Email:*** jfaust@schwabe.com

JAMES M. FINN, born Washington, D.C., February 1, 1947; admitted to bar, 1979, Oregon. *Education:* George Mason University (B.A., 1975); University of Virginia (M.A., 1976; J.D., 1979). ***PRACTICE AREAS:*** Business Litigation; Commercial Litigation; Real Estate Litigation; Creditors Rights. ***Email:*** jfinn@schwabe.com

MICHAEL T. GARONE, born Queens, New York, January 1, 1956; admitted to bar, 1980, Oregon; 2000, Washington. *Education:* State University of New York at Binghamton (B.A., 1977); University of Oregon (J.D., 1980). ***PRACTICE AREAS:*** Labor and Employment Law; Litigation; Appellate Law; Workers Compensation. ***Email:*** mgarone@schwabe.com

JILL S. GELINEAU, born New Orleans, Louisiana, May 27, 1960; admitted to bar, 1985, Oregon; 1987, Washington. *Education:* University of Montana; University of Oregon (B.S., 1982; J.D., 1985). ***PRACTICE AREAS:*** Condemnation; Business Law. ***Email:*** jgelineau@schwabe.com

WALTER H. GREBE, born Portland, Oregon, March 27, 1938; admitted to bar, 1964, Oregon. *Education:* University of Oregon (B.S., 1960; LL.B., 1964). ***PRACTICE AREAS:*** Corporate Law; Mergers and Acquisitions; Business Law; Estate Planning; Corporate Governance. ***Email:*** wgrebe@schwabe.com

JOHN D. GUINASSO, born Portland, Oregon, 1958; admitted to bar, 1983, Oregon. *Education:* Lewis and Clark College (B.A., 1979); Stanford University (J.D., 1983). ***PRACTICE AREAS:*** Commercial Real Estate; Commercial Leasing; Commercial Mortgages. ***Email:*** jguinasso@schwabe.com

KELLY T. HAGAN, born McMinnville, Oregon, July 14, 1952; admitted to bar, 1981, Oregon; 1999, Washington. *Education:* Stanford University (B.A., 1975); University of Oregon (J.D., 1978). ***PRACTICE AREAS:*** Health Care; Employment; Appellate. ***Email:*** khagan@schwabe.com

KURT F. HANSEN, born San Francisco, California, September 30, 1953; admitted to bar, 1984, Oregon and Washington. *Education:* Oregon State University (B.S., 1975); University of Oregon (J.D., 1984). ***PRACTICE AREAS:*** Health Care; Hospital Law; Business Law; Corporate Law; Construction Law; Commercial Litigation. ***Email:*** khansen@schwabe.com

RICHARD K. HANSEN, born Eugene, Oregon, June 18, 1954; admitted to bar, 1983, Oregon. *Education:* University of Oregon; Portland State University (B.S., 1980); Northwestern School of Law (J.D., 1983). ***PRACTICE AREAS:*** Product Liability; Antitrust. ***Email:*** rhansen@schwabe.com

ROBERT L. HARRINGTON, born Mayville, North Dakota, October 9, 1936; admitted to bar, 1961, California; 1964, Minnesota; 1968, Oregon. *Education:* University of North Dakota, (B.S., Industrial Engineering, 1958; J.D., 1960). ***PRACTICE AREAS:*** Patent and Trademark Law. ***Email:*** rharrington@schwabe.com

TIMOTHY F. HASLACH, born Toledo, Ohio, June 3, 1961; admitted to bar, 1991, Oregon. *Education:* Santa Clara University (B.S., 1983); Santa Clara University School of Law (J.D., 1988). ***PRACTICE AREAS:*** Emerging Business Law; Internet Law; Telecommunications Law; Computer Law; Nonprofit Corporations; Franchise Law; New Media Law. ***Email:*** thaslach@schwabe.com

NIKKI C. HATTON, born Seattle, Washington, January 3, 1949; admitted to bar, 1977, Florida; 1978, District of Columbia; 1980, Oregon. *Education:* University of Washington (B.A., cum laude, 1971); University of Florida (J.D., 1976; LL.M. in Taxation, 1977). ***PRACTICE AREAS:*** Estate Planning; Partnerships; Limited Liability Companies; Taxation; Charitable Organizations. ***Email:*** nhatton@schwabe.com

TERRY C. HAUCK, born Oregon City, Oregon, August 12, 1941; admitted to bar, 1971, Oregon. *Education:* Portland State University (B.S., 1966); Willamette University (J.D., 1971). ***PRACTICE AREAS:*** Real Estate. ***Email:*** thauck@schwabe.com

MARGARET A. O'CONNOR HOFFMANN, born Oxford, New York, October 31, 1953; admitted to bar, 1983, California; 1990, Oregon. *Education:* California State University, Long Beach (B.A., 1976); Southwestern University (J.D., 1983). ***PRACTICE AREAS:*** Products Liability; Drugs and Medical Devices; Securities; Employment Law. ***Email:*** mhoffmann@schwabe.com

MITCHELL E. HORNECKER, born Medford, Oregon, May 1, 1960; admitted to bar, 1986, Oregon; 1987, Washington. *Education:* University of Oregon (B.S., 1982); Northwestern School of Law of Lewis and Clark College (J.D., cum laude, 1986). ***PRACTICE AREAS:*** Business and Corporate Law; Health Care Law; Insurance Regulation. ***Email:*** mhornecker@schwabe.com

(This Listing Continued)

SCHWABE, WILLIAMSON & WYATT, P.C., Portland—Continued

KIRK JOHANSEN, born Coos Bay, Oregon, April 27, 1949; admitted to bar, 1974, Oregon. *Education:* University of Oregon (B.S., 1971; J.D., 1974). ***PRACTICE AREAS:*** Business Law; Forest Industry Law; Natural Resources. ***Email:*** kjohansen@schwabe.com

ROBERT E. JOSEPH, born Portland, Oregon, November 15, 1935; admitted to bar, 1965, Oregon. *Education:* Willamette University (B.A., 1957; LL.B., 1963). ***PRACTICE AREAS:*** Workers' Compensation Defense; Insurance Defense; Insurance Regulation. ***Email:*** rjoseph@schwabe.com

KEVIN F. KERSTIENS, born Seattle, Washington, December 6, 1953; admitted to bar, 1981, Oregon. *Education:* University of Puget Sound (B.A., 1976); Washington University (J.D., 1981). ***PRACTICE AREAS:*** Taxation; Estate Planning; Partnership Law; Corporate Law; Pension Plans; ERISA. ***Email:*** kkerstiens@schwabe.com

RAYMOND S. KINDLEY, born Richland, Washington, August 12, 1957; admitted to bar, 1992, Washington; 1996, Oregon. *Education:* University of Washington (B.S., 1980); Northwestern School of Law of Lewis and Clark College (J.D., 1992). ***PRACTICE AREAS:*** Energy Acquisitions; Wholesale Power Contracts; Hydroelectricity; Federal Energy Regulation; International Energy Law. ***Email:*** rkindley@schwabe.com

BRIAN J. KING, born Binghamton, New York, September 10, 1953; admitted to bar, 1980, Idaho; 1996, Oregon. *Education:* Colorado State University (B.A., with highest distinction, 1977); University of Colorado (J.D., 1980). ***PRACTICE AREAS:*** Environmental; Occupational Safety and Health; Natural Resources. ***Email:*** bking@schwabe.com

JAN K. KITCHEL, born Hood River, Oregon, August 14, 1951; admitted to bar, 1978, Oregon; 1983, Washington. *Education:* Oregon State University (B.S., with honors, 1973), Blue Key; Willamette University (J.D., cum laude, 1978). ***PRACTICE AREAS:*** Personal Injury Litigation; Insurance Litigation; Business Litigation; Securities Litigation; Probate Litigation. ***Email:*** jkitchel@schwabe.com

DANIEL F. KNOX, born San Antonio, Texas, June 20, 1948; admitted to bar, 1978, Oregon. *Education:* University of Colorado (B.A., 1970); University of Houston (J.D., summa cum laude, 1978). ***PRACTICE AREAS:*** Admiralty and Maritime Law; Architects and Engineers Liability; Construction Law; Insurance Coverage. ***Email:*** dknox@schwabe.com

DONALD L. KRAHMER, JR., born Hillsboro, Oregon, November 11, 1957; admitted to bar, 1988, Oregon. *Education:* Willamette University (B.S., 1981; M.M., 1987); Atkinson School of Management (J.D., 1987). ***PRACTICE AREAS:*** General Business; Corporate Finance; Mergers and Acquisitions; Technology Law. ***Email:*** dkrahmer@schwabe.com

ROY D. LAMBERT, born White Plains, New York, November 12, 1946; admitted to bar, 1972, New York; 1975, Oregon. *Education:* Cornell University (B.S., 1968); Columbia University (J.D., 1972); New York University (LL.M. in Taxation, 1975). ***PRACTICE AREAS:*** Taxation; Corporate Law; Partnerships; Tax Exempt Organizations; Low-Income Housing Tax Credits; Farmworker Housing Tax Credits; New Markets Tax Credits. ***Email:*** rlambert@schwabe.com

JAMES A. LARPENTEUR, JR., born Seattle, Washington, August 6, 1935; admitted to bar, 1961, Oregon. *Education:* University of Oregon (B.S., 1957; LL.B., 1961). ***PRACTICE AREAS:*** Complex Business; Real Estate; Corporate Transactions; Family Business Law; Mergers and Acquisitions. ***Email:*** jlarpenteur@schwabe.com

MARK M. LeCOQ, born Spokane, Washington, October 19, 1955; admitted to bar, 1982, Oregon; 1983, Washington. *Education:* Williamette University (B.S., 1977); Brandeis University; Northwestern School of Law at Lewis and Clark College (J.D., cum laude, 1982). ***PRACTICE AREAS:*** Business Law; Equipment Leasing; Commercial Litigation. ***Email:*** mlecoq@schwabe.com

PETER LIVINGSTON, born Boston, Massachusetts, August 5, 1951; admitted to bar, 1982, Oregon; 2000, District of Columbia and Washington. *Education:* Amherst College (B.A., 1974); University of Chicago (M.A., 1978); University of Illinois (J.D., 1982; M.B.A., 1982). ***PRACTICE AREAS:*** Land Use; Real Estate Development; Administrative Law. ***Email:*** plivingston@schwabe.com

DARIEN S. LOISELLE, born Dallas, Oregon, April 18, 1965; admitted to bar, 1992, Oregon; 1993, Washington. *Education:* Willamette University (B.A., magna cum laude, 1987); University of Oregon (J.D., 1992). ***PRACTICE AREAS:*** Construction Litigation; Commercial Litigation; Admiralty and Maritime; Insurance Defense. ***Email:*** dloiselle@schwabe.com

MARK A. LONG, born Salem, Oregon, April 18, 1953; admitted to bar, 1982, Oregon. *Education:* Universite de Lyon, Lyons, France; Claremont McKenna College (B.A., cum laude, 1975); American University, Washington College of Law (J.D., summa cum laude, 1982). ***PRACTICE AREAS:*** Mergers and Acquisitions; Business Law; Corporate Law; Corporate Counseling; Securities. ***Email:*** mlong@schwabe.com

WILLIAM E. LOVE, born Eugene, Oregon, March 13, 1926; admitted to bar, 1952, Oregon. *Education:* University of Notre Dame (B.S., in history, 1946); University of Oregon (M.A., in journalism, 1950; J.D., 1952). ***PRACTICE AREAS:*** Business Law; Corporate Law; Financial Institutions Law; Securities; Mergers and Acquisitions Law; Pari-Mutual Racing. ***Email:*** wlove@schwabe.com

DOUGLAS W. MacDOUGAL, born Plainfield, New Jersey, September 22, 1945; admitted to bar, 1973, Hawaii; 1998, Oregon. *Education:* University of Vermont (B.S., 1967); Washington & Lee University (J.D., cum laude, 1973). ***PRACTICE AREAS:*** Real Property; Water Law. ***Email:*** dmacdougal@schwabe.com

HEIDI L. MANDT, born Portland, Oregon, August 12, 1969; admitted to bar, 1995, Oregon; 1997, Washington. *Education:* Washington State University (B.S., 1990); Willamette University (J.D., 1995). ***PRACTICE AREAS:*** Civil Litigation; Insurance Defense; Products Liability; Asbestos Litigation. ***Email:*** hmandt@schwabe.com

JOHNATHAN E. MANSFIELD, born 1962; admitted to bar, 1993, Pennsylvania; 1994, District of Columbia; 1998, Washington; 2001, California (Not admitted in Oregon).

(This Listing Continued)

Education: University of Oregon (B.Mus., 1985); Portland State University (M.S., 1990); Cornell University (J.D., magna cum laude, 1993). ***PRACTICE AREAS:*** Intellectual Property. ***Email:*** jmansfield@schwabe.com

MARK A. MANULIK, born Midland, Texas, July 21, 1952; admitted to bar, 1978, Texas; 1988, Oregon and Washington. *Education:* University of Texas (B.A., 1975); University of Houston Law Center (J.D., 1978). ***PRACTICE AREAS:*** Real Estate; Partnerships; Finance; Business Law. ***Email:*** mmanulik@schwabe.com

W. A. JERRY NORTH, born Corpus Christi, Texas, January 3, 1940; admitted to bar, 1975, Oregon. *Education:* U.S. Naval Academy (B.S., with distinction, 1961); University of Santa Clara (M.B.A., 1971); Stanford University (J.D., 1975). ***PRACTICE AREAS:*** Products Liability Defense; Construction Litigation; Architect/Engineer Malpractice; Nuclear Law and Litigation; Radiation Law and Litigation. ***Email:*** jnorth@schwabe.com

WILLIAM J. OHLE, born Moscow, Idaho, November 10, 1962; admitted to bar, 1991, Oregon; 1992, Washington; 1995, Northern Mariana Islands. *Education:* Warner Pacific College (B.A., Business Adm., 1986); Willamette University (J.D., cum laude, 1991). ***PRACTICE AREAS:*** Electric Utilities; Public Utility Law; Telephone Utilities; Commercial Litigation. ***Email:*** wohle@schwabe.com

PETER L. OSBORNE, born Portland, Oregon, March 22, 1947; admitted to bar, 1973, Oregon. *Education:* University of Washington (B.A., 1969); Willamette University (J.D., 1972); New York University (LL.M., in Taxation, 1973). ***PRACTICE AREAS:*** Taxation; Corporate Law; Mergers and Acquisitions; Estate Planning. ***Email:*** posborne@schwabe.com

MARTHA O'DONNELL PAGEL, born San Diego, California, November 11, 1953; admitted to bar, 1983, Oregon. *Education:* San Diego State University (B.A., 1976); University of San Diego; Willamette University (J.D., 1983). ***PRACTICE AREAS:*** Water Law; Water Rights; Clean Water Act; Natural Resources; Environmental Administrative Law. ***Email:*** mpagel@schwabe.com

KRISTINE M. PIZZUTI, born York, Pennsylvania, October 4, 1968; admitted to bar, 1995, Oregon. *Education:* University of Oregon (B.S., 1990); Villanova University School of Law (J.D., 1995). ***PRACTICE AREAS:*** Real Property; Business. ***Email:*** kpizzuti@schwabe.com

ALEX I. POUST, born San Mateo, California, January 19, 1963; admitted to bar, 1992, Oregon. *Education:* Pomona College (B.A., 1985); University of Oregon (J.D., 1992). ***PRACTICE AREAS:*** Commercial Litigation; Bankruptcy. ***Email:*** apoust@schwabe.com

C. KENT ROBERTS, born Winston-Salem, North Carolina, July 29, 1954; admitted to bar, 1980, Oregon. *Education:* Vanderbilt University and University of North Carolina (B.A., 1976); Northwestern School of Law of Lewis and Clark College (J.D., 1979). ***PRACTICE AREAS:*** Commercial Law; Business Law; Admiralty; Civil Litigation; Insurance Defense. ***Email:*** ckroberts@schwabe.com

GARY ROBERTS, born Portland, Oregon, December 12, 1947; admitted to bar, 1974, Oregon. *Education:* University of Oregon (B.S., 1969); New York University (J.D., 1974). ***PRACTICE AREAS:*** Banking; Commercial and Real Estate Litigation; Mortgage Brokerage; Automobile Law. ***Email:*** groberts@schwabe.com

ELIZABETH A. SCHLEUNING, born Portland, Oregon, April 28, 1960; admitted to bar, 1985, Oregon; 1986, Washington. *Education:* Pomona College (B.A., cum laude, 1982); Willamette University (J.D., cum laude, 1985). ***PRACTICE AREAS:*** Employment Law; Products Liability; Civil Litigation; Professional Malpractice. ***Email:*** eschleuning@schwabe.com

MARC K. SELLERS, born Santa Maria, California, April 18, 1953; admitted to bar, 1978, California; 1979, Oregon. *Education:* University of Redlands (B.S. Chemistry, 1975); Loyola Law School (J.D., 1978); Georgetown University Law Center (LL.M., Taxation, 1980). ***PRACTICE AREAS:*** Income Tax; Tax Controversies; Criminal Tax Litigation; White Collar Criminal Defense; Environmental Criminal Defense; State Taxation; Property Tax. ***Email:*** msellers@schwabe.com

ROBERT G. SIMPSON, born Seattle, Washington, June 27, 1932; admitted to bar, 1959, Oregon. *Education:* University of Oregon (B.S., 1954); Willamette University (LL.B., 1959). ***PRACTICE AREAS:*** Health Care; Corporate Law; Business Law; Church Law; Non-Profit Organizations; Transportation. ***Email:*** rsimpson@schwabe.com

MARK A. STAYER, born Milwaukee, Wisconsin, April 4, 1954; admitted to bar, 1985, Oregon. *Education:* University of Wisconsin-Oshkosh (B.B.A., 1976); Willamette University (J.D., 1985). ***PRACTICE AREAS:*** Real Estate; Business Law; Financial Institutions. ***Email:*** mstayer@schwabe.com

ANNE M. TALCOTT, born Crawfordsville, Indiana, March 22, 1969; admitted to bar, 1996, Oregon; 1997, Washington. *Education:* University of California at San Diego (B.A., 1991); University of Oregon School of Law (J.D., 1996). ***PRACTICE AREAS:*** Products Liability Litigation; Automotive Litigation; Drug and Medical Device Litigation; Pharmaceutical Litigation. ***Email:*** atalcott@schwabe.com

KATHERINE C. TANK, born 1962; admitted to bar, 1988, Oregon; 1992, Alaska. *Education:* University of Oregon (B.S., 1984; J.D., 1988). ***PRACTICE AREAS:*** Labor and Employment. ***Email:*** ktank@schwabe.com

THOMAS M. TRIPLETT, born Palo Alto, California, August 18, 1940; admitted to bar, 1965, Oregon. *Education:* Yale University (A.B., 1962); Stanford University (LL.B., 1965). ***PRACTICE AREAS:*** Management Labor Law; Employment Law; Trade Regulation; Antitrust. ***Email:*** ttriplett@schwabe.com

JAY T. WALDRON, born Fall River, Massachusetts, October 25, 1945; admitted to bar, 1974, Oregon. *Education:* Boston College, Providence College (A.B., 1967); University of Virginia (M.A., 1968; J.D., 1974). ***PRACTICE AREAS:*** Environmental Law; Energy Law; Civil Litigation. ***Email:*** jwaldron@schwabe.com

DONALD JOE WILLIS, born Richmond, Indiana, July 24, 1940; admitted to bar, 1971, Oregon; 1983, Washington. *Education:* University of Oregon (B.S., 1969; J.D., 1971). ***PRACTICE AREAS:*** Condemnation; Commercial Law; Securities Litigation; Civil Litigation. ***Email:*** jwillis@schwabe.com

(This Listing Continued)

OF COUNSEL/CONTRACT ATTORNEYS

JEAN OHMAN BACK, born Salina, Kansas, March 26, 1961; admitted to bar, 1991, Oregon. *Education:* University of California at Santa Barbara (B.A., 1983); University of Oregon (J.D., 1991). ***PRACTICE AREAS:*** Employment Law; Workers' Compensation; School Law; Special Education Law. ***Email:*** jback@schwabe.com

KAREN K. LAW, born Inglewood, California, December 24, 1967; admitted to bar, 1993, Oregon; 1994, Washington. *Education:* University of California, Berkeley (B.A., 1989); University of San Francisco (J.D., magna cum laude, 1993). ***PRACTICE AREAS:*** Business Litigation; Commercial Litigation; Condemnation. ***Email:*** klaw@schwabe.com

WILLIAM D. PEEK, born Portland, Oregon, November 8, 1939; admitted to bar, 1964, Oregon. *Education:* University of Oregon (B.S., 1961; LL.B., 1964). ***PRACTICE AREAS:*** Probate; Trust Administration Law; Estate Planning; Taxation Law. ***Email:*** wpeek@schwabe.com

DOUGLAS A. SCHOEN, born Lebanon, Oregon, April 22, 1951; admitted to bar, 1976, Oregon. *Education:* University of Oregon (B.A., 1972); Willamette University College of Law (J.D., 1976). ***PRACTICE AREAS:*** Employment Law. ***Email:*** dschoen@schwabe.com

ASSOCIATES

LISA CAREY ALAN, born Portland, Oregon, March 16, 1969; admitted to bar, 2000, Oregon. *Education:* University of Washington (B.A., 1991); Northwestern School of Law (J.D., cum laude, 2000). ***PRACTICE AREAS:*** Estate Planning; Tax Law; Business Planning. ***Email:*** lalan@schwabe.com

ANDREW D. BAROFSKY, born Portland, Oregon, February 9, 1971; admitted to bar, 2002, Massachusetts; 2003, Oregon. *Education:* University of Oregon (B.S., Biochemistry, 1994); Boston College (M.B.A., 2002; J.D., 2002). ***PRACTICE AREAS:*** Intellectual Property; Business Transactions; Mergers and Acquisitions; Technology Law. ***Email:*** abarofsky@schwabe.com

MELISSA A. BOGE, born Carson City, Michigan, March 16, 1973; admitted to bar, 1999, California; 2000, Oregon. *Education:* Michigan Technological University (B.S., Science and Technology Communications, 1995); Northwestern School of Law, Lewis and Clark College (J.D., 1998). ***PRACTICE AREAS:*** Intellectual Property; Emerging Business Law; Technology Licensing; Internet Law; E-Commerce. ***Email:*** mboge@schwabe.com

CARSON D. BOWLER, born Newport Beach, California, September 23, 1965; admitted to bar, 1995, Oregon. *Education:* University of Oregon (B.A., 1991; J.D., 1994). ***PRACTICE AREAS:*** Litigation; Administrative Law; Clean Water Act; Environmental Administrative Law; Environmental Contamination; Environmental Insurance; Environmental Liability; Water Quality; Environmental Litigation; Natural Resources; Energy; Condemnation; Inverse Condemnation. ***Email:*** cbowler@schwabe.com

STEPHEN C. BUSH, born Stamford, Connecticut, July 15, 1975; admitted to bar, 2002, California; 2004, Oregon. *Education:* University of California at San Diego (B.A., 1997); University of Southern California (M.A., J.D., 2001). ***PRACTICE AREAS:*** Product Liability Litigation. ***Email:*** sbush@schwabe.com

AMY CHESTNUT, born Upland, California, September 29, 1973; admitted to bar, 1999, Idaho and Washington; 2005, Oregon. *Education:* University of California at Davis (B.S., 1995); University of Oregon (J.D., 1998). ***PRACTICE AREAS:*** Environmental Law; Water Law. ***Email:*** achestnut@schwabe.com

JEFFREY S. DAVIS, born Salt Lake City, Utah, April 25, 1964; admitted to bar, 1995, Oregon. *Education:* University of Utah (B.S., 1988); University of Oregon (J.D., 1995), Certificate in Business Law. ***PRACTICE AREAS:*** Commercial Real Estate Finance; Commercial Leasing; Landlord and Tenant; Real Estate Sales; Real Estate Acquisitions; Secured Lending; Real Estate Title. ***Email:*** jdavis@schwabe.com

JOSHUA S. DeCRISTO, born Rio Ariba, New Mexico, May 29, 1974; admitted to bar, 1999, Oregon; 2003, Washington. *Education:* University of Portland (B.A., 1995); Willamette University School of Law (J.D., 1999). ***PRACTICE AREAS:*** Product Liability. ***Email:*** jdecristo@schwabe.com

CHRISTOPHER C. DORR, born 1970; admitted to bar, 1999, Oregon. *Education:* University of Washington (B.S., 1995); Northwestern School of Law (J.D., 1999). ***PRACTICE AREAS:*** Civil Litigation; Medical Malpractice; Products Liability.

DANIEL L. DUYCK, born Hillsboro, Oregon, April 18, 1965; admitted to bar, 1997, Oregon; 1998, Washington. *Education:* Oregon State University (B.S., 1988); Northwestern School of Law of Lewis and Clark College (J.D., 1997). ***PRACTICE AREAS:*** Commercial Litigation; Construction Law; Insurance Coverage. ***Email:*** dduyck@schwabe.com

DAVID G. FAGAN, born Birmingham, England, April 5, 1967; admitted to bar, 1998, Oregon. *Education:* University of Leicester, England (LL.B., with honors, 1995); University of Nottingham, England (LL.M., 1996); Northwestern School of Law of Lewis and Clark College (J.D., 1998). ***PRACTICE AREAS:*** Commercial Litigation. ***Email:*** dfagan@schwabe.com

CHRISTIANE R. FIFE, born Portland, Oregon, December 13, 1977; admitted to bar, 2004, Oregon. *Education:* University of Washington (B.A., 2000); University of Oregon (J.D., 2004); Universidad de Sevilla (Advanced Elements of the Spanish Language, 1999). ***PRACTICE AREAS:*** Product Liability Litigation. ***Email:*** cfife@schwabe.com

BRIEN J. FLANAGAN, born Highland Park, Illinois, December 14, 1974; admitted to bar, 2002, Oregon. *Education:* University of Notre Dame (B.A., 1997); Georgetown University Law Center (J.D., 2002). ***PRACTICE AREAS:*** Commercial Litigation. ***Email:*** bflanagan@schwabe.com

GREG D FULLEM, born Schenectady, New York, January 6, 1968; admitted to bar, 1995, Oregon. *Education:* Trinity College (B.A., 1989); University of Innsbruck, Austria (Certificate of Global Legal Issues, 1993); Willamette University College of Law (J.D., 1995). ***PRACTICE AREAS:*** Real Estate; Land Use. ***Email:*** gfullem@schwabe.com

(This Listing Continued)

MICHAEL D. FURLONG, born Iowa City, Iowa, February 24, 1973; admitted to bar, 2002, Oregon. *Education:* University of Arizona (B.A., 1995); Willamette University College of Law (J.D., 2002). ***PRACTICE AREAS:*** Commercial Litigation. ***Email:*** mfurlong@schwabe.com

AMANDA T. GAMBLIN, born Binghampton, New York, May 29, 1968; admitted to bar, 2002, Oregon. *Education:* Ohio University (B.A., 1992); Lewis and Clark College (J.D., 2001). ***PRACTICE AREAS:*** Commercial Litigation; Employment. ***Email:*** agamblin@schwabe.com

TODD M. GREWE, born Portland, Oregon, December 31, 1962; admitted to bar, 1996, Oregon; 1997, Colorado; 1998, Washington. *Education:* University of Washington (B.A. with honors, 1986); Syracuse University (M.B.A., 1995; J.D., 1995). ***PRACTICE AREAS:*** Business Law; Commercial Litigation; Construction; Debtor and Creditor Rights; Electronic Commerce. ***Email:*** tgrewe@schwabe.com

PATCHEN M. HAGGERTY, born Chicago, Illinois, August 31, 1975; admitted to bar, 2001, Oregon. *Education:* Purdue University (B.A., 1997); Indiana University School of Law (J.D., 2000). ***PRACTICE AREAS:*** Intellectual Property; Trademarks; Copyrights. ***Email:*** phaggerty@schwabe.com

DARIUS L. HARTWELL, born Cincinnati, Ohio, September 27, 1971; admitted to bar, 2000, Oregon. *Education:* University of Delaware (B.A., 1994); Northwestern School of Law (J.D., 2000). ***PRACTICE AREAS:*** Business Law; Corporate Law. ***Email:*** dhartwell@schwabe.com

DAVID A. HEPLER, born Santa Monica, California, August 26, 1969; admitted to bar, 2002, California; 2004, Oregon. *Education:* University of California, San Diego (B.A., 1991); University of San Diego School of Law (J.D., 2001). ***PRACTICE AREAS:*** Real Estate; Land Use. ***Email:*** dhepler@schwabe.com

JEFFREY D. HERN, born Columbus, Ohio, June 25, 1976; admitted to bar, 2004, Oregon. *Education:* Denison University (B.A., Economics, 1998); Willamette University (J.D., 2004). ***PRACTICE AREAS:*** Business Litigation. ***Email:*** jhern@schwabe.com

ROMÁN D. HERNÁNDEZ, admitted to bar, 2001, Oregon. *Education:* Oregon State University (B.A., 1992); Northwestern School of Law at Lewis & Clark College (J.D., 2000). ***PRACTICE AREAS:*** Employment Relations; Business Litigation; Indian Law. ***Email:*** rhernandez@schwabe.com

NOAH JARRETT, born Spokane, Washington, October 7, 1973; admitted to bar, 1999, Oregon; 2000, U.S. District Court, District of Oregon. *Education:* Washington State University (B.A., 1996); University of Oregon (J.D., cum laude, 1999). ***PRACTICE AREAS:*** Commercial Litigation. ***Email:*** njarrett@schwabe.com

JEFFREY R. JONES, born Portland, Oregon, June 5, 1973; admitted to bar, 2001, Oregon. *Education:* University of Washington (B.A., 1997); Willamette University (M.B.A., with honors, 2001; J.D., magna cum laude, 2001). ***PRACTICE AREAS:*** Condemnation; Business Litigation; Construction Litigation. ***Email:*** jjones@schwabe.com

PIERRE KEELEY, born Oakland, California, February 22, 1974; admitted to bar, 2001, California; 2004, Oregon. *Education:* University of Southern California (B.S., Electrical Engineering, cum laude; B.A., Political Science, cum laude); Santa Clara University (J.D.). ***PRACTICE AREAS:*** Intellectual Property; Patents; Trademarks. ***Email:*** pkeeley@schwabe.com

SHONEE D. LANGFORD, born Portland, Oregon, July 30, 1975; admitted to bar, 2004, Oregon. *Education:* Portland State University (B.A., with highest honors, 2000); Willamette University (J.D., cum laude, 2004). ***PRACTICE AREAS:*** Environmental Law; Water Rights Law. ***Email:*** slangford@schwabe.com

ANDREW J. LEE, born Portland, Oregon, December 7, 1975; admitted to bar, 2002, Oregon. *Education:* Grinnell College (B.A., 1998); University of Oregon (J.D., 2002). ***PRACTICE AREAS:*** Products Liability. ***Email:*** ajlee@schwabe.com

CHRISTOPHER J. LEWIS, born 1970; admitted to bar, 2000, Oregon. *Education:* University of Washington (B.S.C.E., 1994); Northwestern School of Law (J.D., 2000). ***PRACTICE AREAS:*** Intellectual Property Litigation; Business Litigation; Intellectual Property Licensing; Patent Preparation and Prosecution; Trademarks; Copyrights; Unfair Competition. ***Email:*** clewis@schwabe.com

ARUSI R. LOPRINZI, admitted to bar, 2003, Oregon. *Education:* Lewis & Clark College (B.A., 2000); University of California at Los Angeles School of Law (J.D., 2003). ***PRACTICE AREAS:*** Condemnation; Real Estate; Land Use. ***Email:*** aloprinzi@schwabe.com

LAURA MAFFEI, born San Mateo, California, July 22, 1966; admitted to bar, 1999, Oregon. *Education:* University of California at Los Angeles (B.S., 1989); University of Washington (M.S., 1992); Northwestern School of Law, Lewis and Clark College (J.D., cum laude, 1999). ***PRACTICE AREAS:*** Environmental Litigation; Hazardous Waste; Water Quality. ***Email:*** lmaffei@schwabe.com

BRADLEY D. MAIER, born Missoula, Montana, August 21, 1967; admitted to bar, 2003, Oregon. *Education:* Portland State University (B.S., 1999); Northwestern School of Law (J.D., 2002). *Member:* Oregon State Bar. ***PRACTICE AREAS:*** Immigration Law. ***Email:*** bmaier@schwabe.com

NATHAN R. MAKI, admitted to bar, 2003, Oregon. *Education:* University of Missouri - Columbia (B.S., 1998); Northwestern School of Law, Lewis & Clark College (J.D., 2003). ***PRACTICE AREAS:*** Intellectual Property; Patents; Trademarks. ***Email:*** nmaki@schwabe.com

GREGORY W. MALLORY, born Portland, Oregon, March 23, 1968; admitted to bar, 1994, Oregon; 1995, Washington. *Education:* Oregon State University (B.S., highest honors, 1990); Willamette University (M.B.A., 1994; J.D., cum laude, 1994). ***PRACTICE AREAS:*** Securities and Corporate Finance; Mergers and Acquisitions. ***Email:*** gmallory@schwabe.com

CAROL L. CATHERINE McCAULLEY, born Fullerton, California, October 2, 1950; admitted to bar, 2001, Washington (Not admitted in Oregon). *Education:* Washington State University (M.A., 1986); Northwestn School of Law (J.D.). ***PRACTICE AREAS:*** Labor and Employment; Elder Law. ***Email:*** cmccaulley@schwabe.com

(This Listing Continued)

SCHWABE, WILLIAMSON & WYATT, P.C., Portland—Continued

W. RANDY MILLER, born Eugene, Oregon, September 21, 1970; admitted to bar, 2004, Oregon. *Education:* Linfield College (B.S., Business Management, magna cum laude, 1999); Willamette University (J.D., 2004). ***PRACTICE AREAS:*** Commercial Litigation. ***Email:*** rmiller@schwabe.com

JAMES J. NAMIKI, born Oklahoma City, Oklahoma, May 26, 1958; admitted to bar, 2000, Virginia; 2001, District of Columbia; registered to practice before the U.S. Patent and Trademark Office (Not admitted in Oregon). *Education:* University of Washington (B.S., 1980); University of Hawaii (M.B.A., 1993); Syracuse University College of Engineering (M.E.E., 2000); Syracuse University College of Law (J.D., 2000). ***PRACTICE AREAS:*** Intellectual Property; Patents; Trademarks. ***Email:*** jnamiki@schwabe.com

JOEL A. PARKER, born Virginia Beach, Virginia, March 5, 1973; admitted to bar, 2000, Oregon. *Education:* Indiana University (B.A., Biology, 1995); University of Oregon (J.D., 1999). ***PRACTICE AREAS:*** Commercial Litigation. ***Email:*** jparker@schwabe.com

ALAN L. PASTERNACK, born New York, N.Y., January 5, 1961; admitted to bar, 1989, New York; 1999, Oregon. *Education:* Colgate University (A.B., 1983); Cornell University (J.D., 1988). ***PRACTICE AREAS:*** Corporate; Mergers and Acquisitions; Low Income Housing. ***Email:*** apasternack@schwabe.com

STEVEN J. PREWITT, born Houston, Texas, June 6, 1974; admitted to bar, 1999, Virginia; registered to practice before U.S. Patent and Trademark Office (Not admitted in Oregon). *Education:* University of Virginia (B.A., 1996); George Mason University School of Law (J.D., 1999). ***PRACTICE AREAS:*** Intellectual Property; Patent Law; Nanotechnology and Microtechnology; Technology; Emerging Business. ***Email:*** sprewitt@schwabe.com

CRAIG G. RUSSILLO, born Torrance, California, August 18, 1971; admitted to bar, 1997, Oregon;1998, Washington. *Education:* California State University, Fresno (B.S., 1994); Willamette University College of Law (J.D., cum laude, 1997). ***PRACTICE AREAS:*** Commercial Litigation; Bankruptcy; Landlord Tenant; Real Estate. ***Email:*** crussillo@schwabe.com

JILL SCHNEIDER, born November 3, 1950; admitted to bar, 1997, Pennsylvania; 1998, New Jersey and U.S. District Court, District of New Jersey; 2000, Oregon, U.S. District Court, Eastern District of Pennsylvania and U.S. District Court, District of Oregon; 2001, U.S. Court of Appeals, Ninth Circuit. *Education:* Oregon State University (B.S., magna cum laude, 1971); Temple University (J.D., cum laude, 1987; LL.M., Trial Advocacy, with honors, 1999). ***PRACTICE AREAS:*** Civil Litigation. ***Email:*** jschneider@schwabe.com

NEDA D. SOOFI, born Tehran, Iran, November 7, 1963; admitted to bar, 1988, Iran; 2001, Oregon. *Education:* University of Tehran (B.S., 1988); University of Tehran (M.S., 1994); Northwestern School of Law of Lewis & Clark College (J.D., 2001). ***PRACTICE AREAS:*** Tax Planning; Estate Planning; Tax Litigation; Business Law. ***Email:*** nsoofi@schwabe.com

RYAN P. STEEN, admitted to bar, 2003, Oregon. *Education:* University of Washington (B.S., 1998); Northwestern School of Law, Lewis & Clark College (J.D., 2003). ***PRACTICE AREAS:*** Commercial Litigation; Employment Law. ***Email:*** rsteen@schwabe.com

JOSHUA P. STUMP, born Portland, Oregon, August 10, 1972; admitted to bar, 1997, Oregon. *Education:* Pepperdine University (B.A., 1994); College of William and Mary (J.D., 1997). ***PRACTICE AREAS:*** Commercial Litigation; Products Liability; Insurance Litigation. ***Email:*** jstump@schwabe.com

TIMOTHY M. SULLIVAN, born Baltimore, Maryland, April 27, 1971; admitted to bar, 2000, Oregon. *Education:* Fairfield University (B.A., 1993); Northwestern School of Law (J.D., magna cum laude, 2000). ***PRACTICE AREAS:*** Environmental Law; Natural Resources Law; Administrative Law. ***Email:*** tsullivan@schwabe.com

NATHAN A. SCHWARTZ SYKES, born Silver Spring, Maryland, May 13, 1968; admitted to bar, 1995, Oregon; 1997, Colorado; 1998, California. *Education:* Colorado State University (B.A., 1991); University of Oregon School of Law (J.D., 1995). ***PRACTICE AREAS:*** Employment Litigation; Employment Law; Immigration Law; Entertainment Law; Media Law. ***Email:*** nsykes@schwabe.com

THOMAS M. TONGUE, born Portland, Oregon, January 8, 1973; admitted to bar, 1999, Oregon. *Education:* Vanderbilt University (B.A., 1995); University of Oregon (M.B.A., 1999; J.D., 1999). ***PRACTICE AREAS:*** Corporate Law; Mergers and Acquisitions; Securities. ***Email:*** ttongue@schwabe.com

KATHERINE O. VANZANTEN, born Boston, Massachusetts, November 8, 1972; admitted to bar, 1997, Oregon; 2000, Washington. *Education:* Boston University (B.A., 1994); Golden Gate University (J.D., 1997; LL.M., 1997). ***PRACTICE AREAS:*** Tax Planning; Estate Planning; Business Succession Planning; Wealth Transfers; Trust Law; Charitable Organizations Law. ***Email:*** kvanzanten@schwabe.com

ALLYSSA J. WALTON, born Eugene, Oregon, November 11, 1976; admitted to bar, 2004, Oregon. *Education:* University of Oregon (B.A., 1999; J.D., 2004). ***PRACTICE AREAS:*** Real Estate Law. ***Email:*** awalton@schwabe.com

B. SCOTT WHIPPLE, born Portland, Oregon, December 27, 1968; admitted to bar, 1998, Oregon; 1999, Washington. *Education:* Grinnell College (B.A., 1990); University of Oregon (J.D., 1998). Order of the Coif. *Member:* Multnomah County Bar Association; Oregon State Bar; Washington State Bar Association. ***PRACTICE AREAS:*** Civil Litigation; Complex Litigation; Business Litigation; Commercial Litigation; Securities Litigation; Tort Defense. ***Email:*** swhipple@schwabe.com

CARRIE M. WOOD, born Oregon City, Oregon, September 25, 1977; admitted to bar, 2004, Oregon. *Education:* Pensacola Christian College (B.S., summa cum laude, 1997); Willamette University (J.D., cum laude, 2004). ***PRACTICE AREAS:*** Business Law. ***Email:*** cwood@schwabe.com

(This Listing Continued)

RETIRED SHAREHOLDERS

ROLAND F. (JERRY) BANKS, JR., born Portland, Oregon, May 2, 1932; admitted to bar, 1958, Oregon. *Education:* Stanford University and University of Oregon (B.S., 1955); University of Oregon (LL.B., 1958). ***Email:*** jbanks@schwabe.com

NEVA T. CAMPBELL, born La Grande, Oregon, October 21, 1933; admitted to bar, 1973, Oregon. *Education:* Oregon State University (B.A., 1955); Northwestern School of Law of Lewis and Clark College (J.D., cum laude, 1973). ***PRACTICE AREAS:*** Petroleum Law; Business Law; Corporate Law; Real Estate; Commercial Law; Environmental Law. ***Email:*** ncampbell@schwabe.com

ROCKNE GILL, born Lebanon, Oregon, December 14, 1931; admitted to bar, 1955, Oregon. *Education:* University of Oregon (B.S., 1953; LL.B., 1955).

ROGER A. LUEDTKE, born Wausau, Wisconsin, April 10, 1942; admitted to bar, 1974, Oregon. *Education:* University of Wisconsin-Madison (B.S., 1964; M.A., 1968; J.D., 1974). ***PRACTICE AREAS:*** Workers' Compensation Defense. ***Email:*** rluedtke@schwabe.com

JAMES R. MOORE, born Portland, Oregon, September 5, 1931; admitted to bar, 1955, Oregon. *Education:* University of Oregon (B.S., 1953; LL.B., 1955). ***Email:*** jmoore@schwabe.com

KENNETH E. ROBERTS, born London, England, October 1, 1922; admitted to bar, 1951, Oregon. *Education:* Northwestern School of Law of Lewis and Clark College (J.D., 1951). ***PRACTICE AREAS:*** Admiralty and Maritime. ***Email:*** kroberts@schwabe.com

JOHN L. SCHWABE, born Nowata, Oklahoma, February 14, 1919; admitted to bar, 1948, Oregon. *Education:* Oklahoma State University (B.A., 1941); Ohio State University (LL.B., 1948). ***PRACTICE AREAS:*** Condemnation; Business Litigation. ***Email:*** jschwabe@schwabe.com

DOUGLAS M. THOMPSON, born Portland, Oregon, October 27, 1929; admitted to bar, 1955, Oregon. *Education:* Stanford University (A.B., 1951; LL.B., 1955). ***PRACTICE AREAS:*** Pension Plans; Business Law; Real Estate; Estate Planning. ***Email:*** athompson@schwabe.com

DOUGLAS J. WHITE, JR., born New York, N.Y., March 20, 1934; admitted to bar, 1958, Oregon. *Education:* University of Oregon (B.A., 1955); Willamette University (LL.B., 1958). ***PRACTICE AREAS:*** Real Estate; Business Law. ***Email:*** dwhite@schwabe.com

WAYNE A. WILLIAMSON, born La Grande, Oregon, November 5, 1921; admitted to bar, 1948, Oregon. *Education:* University of Oregon (B.S., 1943); Stanford University (LL.B., 1948). ***Email:*** wwilliamson@schwabe.com

WENDELL WYATT, born Eugene, Oregon, June 15, 1917; admitted to bar, 1941, Oregon. *Education:* University of Oregon (LL.B., 1941). (Semi-Retired). ***PRACTICE AREAS:*** Estate Planning; Probate; Trusts. ***Email:*** wwyatt@schwabe.com

REPRESENTATIVE CLIENTS: 24 Hour Fitness; American Adjustment Corp.; Auto Warehousing Co., Inc.; Barcodes West; Bayer Corporation; Beloit Corp.; Canpotex, Ltd.; Capital Development Co.; Case Credit Corporation; Catholic Health Initiatives-West; C.C. Filson Company; Clear Channel; Coffee Bean International, Inc.; Columbia Forest Products; DBIC-Dentists Benefits Insurance; Deschutes Brewery; E.I. Du Pont de Nemours & Co.; Fireman's Fund; Ford Motor Co.; Geico; Good Samaritan Hospital - Corvallis; Grayco Resources, Inc.; GRE Insurance Group; Hewlett-Packard; H.R., Northwest; Hydro West Group, Inc.; InFocus Corporation; Intel Corporation; John Hancock Mutual Life; Key Bank National Association; KM Administrative Service; KOIN Center Ltd Partnership; Lamorte Burns & Co.; Liberty Northwest Insurance Co.; Marylhurst University; Menasha Corporation; McKenzie-Willamette Hospital; Merrill & Ring Inc.; Meyer Memorial Trust; MOAC-Marine Office of America; Northwest National Bank; Oregon Anesthesiology Group PC; Oregon Arena Corporation; Oregon Dental Service; Oregon Steel Mills, Inc.; PGP-Public Generating Pool; Port of Morrow; Port of Vancouver; Regal Cinemas, Inc.; Roman Catholic Archbishop of the Archdiocese of Portland; Safeco; Sause Brothers Ocean Towing Co.; Simpson Timber; SIMS-Self Insured Management; Sterling Realty Organization; Telephone Management Corp.; Tidewater Barge Lines, Inc.; Tillamook Co. Creamery Assoc.; Time Oil Co.; Trammell Crow Residential; Unified Western Grocers, Inc.; US West Communications; USAA-United Services Auto Assoc.; Vesta Corporation; Wallace Theater Corporation; Weyerhaeuser Co.; Wyeth.

(For complete biographical data on personnel at Bend, Oregon, Seattle, Washington, Vancouver, Washington and Washington D.C., see Professional Biographies at those locations)

SCOTT HOOKLAND LLP

PORTLAND, OREGON

(See Tigard)

Construction, Design, Civil and Trial Practice. Commercial Collections, Business, Real Estate, Mediations, Arbitrations, Creditors Rights.

PRISCILLA L. SEABORG

1906 S.W. MADISON STREET
PORTLAND, OREGON 97205
Telephone: 503-417-7744
Fax: 503-221-1908
Email: plslaw@qwest.net
URL: http://www.lawyers.com/plslaw

Federal and State Courts, Criminal Law, Family Law, Divorce, Child Custody, Child Support, Domestic Violence, Visitation Rights, Homicide, Murder, Self Defense, Battered Women, White Collar Crimes, Drug Crimes, Parole and Probation, Adoptions, Juvenile Law.

PRISCILLA L. SEABORG, born South Bend, Indiana, March 25, 1955; admitted to bar, 1981, Indiana; 1985, U.S. District Court, District of Oregon; 1986, U.S. Court of Appeals, Ninth Circuit; 1990, Oregon. *Education:* Indiana University (B.A., 1977; J.D., 1981). Associate Instructor, Criminal Justice Dept., Indiana University, 1980-1981. Indiana Appellate Court Clerk, Indianapolis, Indiana, 1981-1982. Monroe County Public Defender Office, Bloomington, Indiana, 1982-1985. Assistant Federal Public Defender, Portland, Oregon, 1985-1989. Vice President, Public Policy, United Way of the Columbia-Willamette,

(This Listing Continued)

Portland, Oregon, 1990-1994. Juvenile Rights Project, and Bertoni and Todd, Portland, Oregon, 1994-1996. Private Practice, 1996—. Speaker/Lecturer: Defense of Battered Women, Federal Sentencing Guidelines, Closing Arguments and Effective Cross Examination. *Member:* Multnomah County and Indiana State Bar Associations; Oregon State Bar; National Association of Criminal Defense Lawyers; Oregon Trial Lawyers Association; Oregon Criminal Defense Lawyers Association; Oregon Women Lawyers. ***REPORTED CASES:*** United States v. Juvenile Male, 864 F.2d 641 (9th Cir. 1988); United States v. Freelove, 816 F.2d 479 (9th Cir. 1987). ***PRACTICE AREAS:*** Family Law; Criminal Law; Juvenile Law.

NORMAN SEPENUK, P.C.

520 S.W. YAMHILL STREET
SUITE 600
PORTLAND, OREGON 97204
Telephone: 503-221-1633
Fax: 503-227-2980
Email: nsepenuk@aol.com

Federal Practice. Criminal Trials and Appeals in Federal Courts, Corporate Compliance.

NORMAN SEPENUK, born Jersey City, New Jersey, May 22, 1933; admitted to bar, 1960, U.S. Supreme Court; 1966, Oregon; 1972, District of Columbia. *Education:* Princeton University (B.A., magna cum laude, 1954); Kennedy School of Government, Harvard University (Masters in Public Admin., 1968); Harvard University (LL.B., 1959). Adjunct Professor of Law, Administration of Criminal Justice, George Washington University, 1971-1972. Lecturer, Criminal Law and Procedure, University of Portland, 1971-1975. Trial Attorney, Tax Division, Department of Justice, Washington, D.C., 1961-1965. Assistant U.S. Attorney, District of Oregon, 1965-1971. Special Assistant to the Attorney General, Criminal Division, Department of Justice, Washington, D.C., 1971-1972. *Member:* Oregon State Bar; American Bar Association (Member: Criminal Justice Section); Owen M. Panner American Inns of Court; Central and East European Law Initiative (C.E.E.L.I, Jan.-Sept., 1999; Volunteer, Criminal Law Liaison); International Society for the Reform of Criminal Law. Fellow, American College of Trial Lawyers.

SHENKER & BONAPARTE, LLP

Established in 2002
ONE S.W. COLUMBIA STREET, SUITE 475
PORTLAND, OREGON 97258
Telephone: 503-294-1118
Fax: 503-294-0015
URL: http://www.ashenkeresq.com

Complex Litigation, Insurance Coverage, Energy Law, Environmental Law, Professional Liability.

ARDEN E. SHENKER, born Portland, Oregon, October 28, 1938; admitted to bar, 1962, Oregon; 1967, U.S. Supreme Court. *Education:* Stanford University (A.B., with great distinction, 1959); Yale University (LL.B., 1962). Order of the Coif; Phi Beta Kappa. Adjunct Professor of Law, Northwestern College of Law, 1982-2000. Member, Oregon State Board of Bar, 1968-1971 and Review Examiners, 1981-1983. National Chair, Jewish Council for Public Affairs, 1989-1992. Presidential Appointee, Martin-Luther King Jr., Federal National Holiday Commission. Founder, American Leadership Forum. *Member:* Multnomah County, Federal and American (Chairman, Committee on Ethics, Section of Environment, Energy and Resources) Bar Associations; Oregon State Bar; Inns of Court (Founding Master, 1987; President, 1992-1993). Fellow, American Bar Foundation. ***PRACTICE AREAS:*** Complex Litigation; Professional Liability; Environmental Law; Energy Law. ***Email:*** ashenker@ashenkeresq.com

ROBERT E. L. BONAPARTE, born Palo Alto, California, November 29, 1955; admitted to bar, 1981, New York; 1982, District of Columbia; 1988, Oregon. *Education:* Stanford University (A.B., with distinction, 1977; M.A., 1977); University of Virginia (J.D., 1981). Phi Beta Kappa. Member, Editorial Board, Virginia Journal of International Law, 1980-1981. Author: "How to Avoid Bifurcation in Insurance Coverage Cases," Trial, June 1994. Arbitrator: Oregon State Bar Fee Arbitration Program and NASD. President, Inns of Court, 2000-2002. *Member:* Multnomah County Bar Association; Oregon State Bar (Bar Counsel); Oregon Trial Lawyers Association. ***LANGUAGES:*** Russian and French. ***REPORTED CASES:*** Dockins v. State Farm Ins. Co., 330 Or 1, 997 P2d 859, 2000; Shaffer v. State Farm Fire & Casualty Co., 120 Or App 70, 852 P2d 245, 1993; Fleming v. USAA, 329 Or 449, 988 P2d 378, 1999, adhering to on recon., 330 Or 62, 996 P2d 501, 2000. ***PRACTICE AREAS:*** Complex Litigation; Insurance Coverage; Environmental Law. ***Email:*** bob@bb-law.net

NELL HOFFMAN BONAPARTE, born Doylestown, Pennsylvania, September 9, 1955; admitted to bar, 1981, District of Columbia, 1988, Oregon. *Education:* University of Strasbourg, France (Certificate in French, 1972); University of California at Santa Cruz (B.A., Honors in Biology and Environmental Science, 1978); University of Virginia (J.D., 1981). Member, Editorial Board, Virginia Law Review, 1979-1981. Author: "The Tax Code's Differential Treatment of Lobbying under Section 501 (c)(3): A Proposed First Amendment Analysis," 66 Virginia Law Review 1513 (1980). *Member:* District of Columbia Bar; Oregon State Bar; Oregon Women Lawyers (Founding Director). ***LANGUAGES:*** French. ***PRACTICE AREAS:*** Complex Litigation; Intellectual Property; Environmental Law; Alternative Dispute Resolution. ***Email:*** nell@bb-law.net

LAURIE SHERTZ LLC

Established in 2001
WORLD TRADE CENTER
121 SW SALMON, 11TH FLOOR
PORTLAND, OREGON 97204
Telephone: 503-471-1332
Fax: 503-296-5669
URL: http://www.LShertzlaw.com
Email: Laurie@lshertzlaw.com
URL: http://www.lawyers.com/lshertz

Criminal Defense, Trial Practice, Felonies, Homicide and Assault, Self Defense, Weapons Charges, Sex Offenses, Drug Crimes, Theft and Fraud. Practice in Federal and State Courts.

FIRM PROFILE: Providing quality, thoughtful, client-focused criminal defense in Federal and State Courts.

LAURIE SHERTZ, born Port Jefferson, New York, December, 1970; admitted to bar, 1995, Washington; 1996, Oregon; 1997, U.S. District Court, Western District of Washington; 2001, U.S. District Court, District of Oregon. *Education:* University of Washington (B.A., 1992); Seattle University (J.D., 1995). National Criminal Defense College (Trial Practice, 2002; Advanced Cross Examination, 2002; Themes and Theories, 2003 & 2004). Author: "Quick Citations for Criminal Defense Attorneys." Editor, Major Crimes Manual, Oregon Criminal Defense Lawyer Association. Speaker/Lecturer: 2005 National Association of Criminal Defense Lawyers, Police Interrogations; Oregon Criminal Defense Lawyers, Coerced Confessions; 2002 Governor's Sexual Assault Task Force Meeting, The Courtroom and the Sexual Assault Case, also presented to Sexual Assault Nurses Conference, St. Vincent's Hospital, 2001; The Physical Aspects of Child Sex Abuse Case; Sentencing; Discovery; and Restraining Orders. Listed in Marquis Who's Who in American Law, 2005. Appellate Attorney, Nielsen & Acosta, 1995-1996. Staff Attorney, Metropolitan Public Defender, 1996-2001. Sole Practitioner 2001—. *Member:* Multnomah County and Washington State Bar Associations; Oregon State Bar; National Association of Criminal Defense Lawyers; Oregon Criminal Defense Lawyers Association 1996—(Member, Education Committee, 1998—, Chair Education Committee 2004—). ***PRACTICE AREAS:*** Trial Practice; Criminal Defense; Self Defense; Weapons Charges; Sex Crimes; Homicide; Federal Criminal Law; Felonies; Criminal Law; Assault and Battery. ***Email:*** Laurie@lshertzlaw.com

E. J. SIMMONS

621 SW MORRISON, SUITE 1300
PORTLAND, OREGON 97205
Telephone: 503-221-2000
Fax: 971-223-4733
Email: ejs@ejsimmons.com
URL: http://www.ejsimmons.com

Trial Practice, Personal Injury, Business Litigation, Technology Litigation, Intellectual Property Litigation.

E. J. SIMMONS, born Roseboro, North Carolina, March 9, 1947; admitted to bar, 1975, Oregon; U.S. District Court, District of Oregon; U.S. Court of Appeals, Ninth Circuit; U.S. Supreme Court. *Education:* University of North Carolina (B.S.B.A., 1968) ; University of Michigan, (J.D., magna cum laude, 1975). *Member:* Multnomah County Bar Association; Oregon State Bar; Oregon Trial Lawyers Association. [U.S. Navy Reserve, LtJG 1968-1970]. ***PRACTICE AREAS:*** Trial Practice; Personal Injury; Intellectual Property Litigation; Business Litigation.

DENNIS W. SKARSTAD

520 SW SIXTH AVENUE, SUITE 820
PORTLAND, OREGON 97204-1514
Telephone: 503-223-3334
FAX: 503-224-9875
Email: dws@skarstadlaw.com

Trial Practice including Personal Injury, Medical Malpractice, Products Liability, Professional Liability and Wrongful Death, Automobile Accidents, Unsafe Products, Legal Malpractice.

DENNIS W. SKARSTAD, born Fargo, North Dakota, May 2, 1941; admitted to bar, 1968, Oregon; 1975, U.S. Supreme Court. *Education:* University of Washington and Washington State University (B.A., 1965); University of Oregon School of Law (J.D., 1968). *Member:* Multnomah County and American Bar Associations; Oregon State Bar (Member, Litigation Section; Member, Board of Governors, Workers Compensation Section, 1980-1982); The Association of Trial Lawyers of America; Oregon Trial Lawyers Association (Member, Board of Governors, 1974-1975, 1981-1983).

RICHARD A. SLY

1001 S.W. FIFTH AVENUE, SUITE 310
PORTLAND, OREGON 97204
Telephone: 503-224-0436
Fax: 503-226-1227
Email: rsly@teleport.com

Social Security Disability, Workers Compensation (OR).

RICHARD A. SLY, born Vancouver, Washington, June 14, 1935; admitted to bar, 1963, Oregon; U.S. Supreme Court; U.S. District Court, District of Oregon; U.S. Court of Appeals, Ninth Circuit. *Education:* Portland State College and University of Oregon (B.B.A., 1957); Willamette University (J.D., with honors, 1963). Phi Delta Phi. Associate

(This Listing Continued)

RICHARD A. SLY, Portland—Continued

Editor, Willamette Law Journal, 1963. Deputy District Attorney, Multnomah County, Oregon, 1965-1969. Assistant Attorney General, State of Oregon, 1973-1974. Judge Pro-Tem, Multnomah County, Oregon District Court, 1975-1982. *Member:* Multnomah County Bar Association; Oregon State Bar (Chairman, Joint Committee of Attorneys and Osteopaths, 1984-1985); Oregon Trial Lawyers Association; The Association of Trial Lawyers of America; Oregon Workers' Compensation Attorneys; National Organization of Social Security Claimants Representatives; Oregon Law Foundation (Charter Fellow, 1983). ***PRACTICE AREAS:*** Social Security Disability (95%).

LAW OFFICES OF DANIEL SNYDER

Established in 1988

1000 S.W. BROADWAY
SUITE 2400
PORTLAND, OREGON 97205
Telephone: 503-241-3617
FAX: 503-241-2249
Email: dansnyder@qwest.net
URL: http://www.lawyers.com/snyderlaw

Civil Litigation in State and Federal Courts, Civil Rights, Personal Injury, Automobile Accidents, Legal Malpractice, Sexual Abuse, Wrongful Death, Employment, Disability Accommodation, Discrimination, Employee Benefits, Sexual Harassment, Workers Compensation, Wrongful Termination, Labor and Employment, Insurance.

DANIEL SNYDER, born Danville, Pennsylvania, October 29, 1952; admitted to bar, 1978, Oregon; 1985, U.S. District Court, District of Oregon; U.S. Court of Appeals, Ninth Circuit; 2005, U.S. Supreme Court. *Education:* West Liberty State College (B.A., with high honors, 1974); University of Notre Dame (J.D., 1977). Participant, Hastings College of Trial and Appellate Advocacy, Civil Trials, 1985. Law Clerk, Hon. Judge Ellis, Multnomah Circuit Court, 1978. Deputy District Attorney, Jefferson County, Oregon, 1978-1980. Deputy District Attorney, Multnomah County, Oregon, 1980-1983. Deputy City Attorney, Portland, 1983-1986. *Member:* Multnomah County, Federal and American Bar Associations; Oregon State Bar (Member, Litigation Section); Oregon Trial Lawyers Association; The Association of Trial Lawyers of America. ***PRACTICE AREAS:*** Civil Litigation; Plaintiffs Personal Injury; Employment; Labor and Employment.

SPOONER, MUCH & AMMANN, P.C.

PORTLAND, OREGON

(See Salem)

General Civil and Trial Practice in State and Federal Courts. Insurance, Products Liability and Personal Injury Law.

STAHANCYK, KENT, JOHNSON & HOOK P.C.

ATHENA PLAZA
808 S.W. 15TH AVENUE
PORTLAND, OREGON 97205-1907
Telephone: 503-222-9115
Fax: 503-222-4037
Email: info@stahancyk.com
URL: http://www.oregondivorce.com

Bend, Oregon Office: 225 NW Franklin Ave., Suite 3, 97701. Telephone: 541-318-9115. Fax: 541-318-9116.
Astoria, Oregon Office: 552 Commercial Street, 97103. Telephone: 503-325-9117.
Prineville, Oregon Office: 105 SW Beaver Street, 97754. Telephone: 541-416-9312.
Vancouver, Washington Office: 411 West 11th Street, 98660. Telephone: 360-750-9115.

Adoptions, Child Custody, Child Support, Divorce, Domestic Violence, Visitation Rights, Wills and Probate, Trusts and Estates, Asset Protection, Guardianship, Family Law, Estate Planning.

FIRM PROFILE: Practicing Family Law & Estate Planning with offices in Portland, Bend, Astoria and Prineville, Oregon and Vancouver, Washington.

JODY L. STAHANCYK, born Prineville, Oregon, July 26, 1948; admitted to bar, 1973, Oregon. *Education:* Linfield College (B.A., 1970); University of Oregon (J.D., 1973). Deputy District Attorney, Multnomah County, 1973-1979. Referee, Multnomah County Juvenile Court, 1979-1983. Assistant Attorney General, State of Oregon, 1983. *Member:* Clackamas County, Multnomah County and Washington County Bar Associations; Oregon State Bar. ***PRACTICE AREAS:*** Family Law; Custody Law; Estate Planning. ***Email:*** jody@stahancyk.com

JOEL J. KENT, born Seattle, Washington, August 11, 1969; admitted to bar, 1996, Oregon and Washington. *Education:* University of Puget Sound (B.S., Economics, 1991); Seattle University School of Law (J.D., 1996). Recipient, Seattle University Client Counseling Award. Member, Junior Executive Board, Doernbecher Hospital, 1997. *Member:* Washington County Bar Association; Oregon State Bar. (Resident, Bend Office). ***PRACTICE AREAS:*** Family Law; Estate Planning; Child Custody; Guardianship; Adoption Law. ***Email:*** joel@stahancyk.com

RONALD M. JOHNSON, born Lebanon, Oregon, June 15, 1956; admitted to bar, 1988, Oregon. *Education:* Lewis and Clark College (B.A., 1984; J.D., 1988). *Member:* Clackamas County, Multnomah County and Washington County Bar Associations; Oregon State Bar (Member, International Section). (Resident, Bend Office). ***LANGUAGES:*** German and Italian. ***PRACTICE AREAS:*** Family Law. ***Email:*** ron@stahancyk.com

LAUREL P. HOOK, born Bakersfield, California; admitted to bar, 1999, Oregon. *Education:* University of Oregon (B.S., 1996); Seattle University School of Law (J.D., cum

(This Listing Continued)

laude, 1999). Phi Alpha Delta. *Member:* Multnomah Bar Association (Member, Sections on: Family Law; Young Lawyers); Oregon State Bar. ***PRACTICE AREAS:*** Family Law. ***Email:*** laurel@stahancyk.com

TERESA L. FOSTER, born Key West, Florida, November 20, 1966; admitted to bar, 1997, Oregon; 2003, Washington. *Education:* Arizona State University (B.S.W., magna cum laude, 1994; J.D., 1997). *Member:* Oregon State Bar; Washington State Bar Association; Clark County Family Law Bar Association. ***PRACTICE AREAS:*** Family Law. ***Email:*** teresa@stahancyk.com

GORDON E. PHILLIPS, born Fort Dix, New Jersey, July 9, 1972; admitted to bar, 2000, Oregon. *Education:* University of Washington (B.A., 1996); Northwestern School of Law (J.D., 2000). *Member:* American Bar Association. (Resident Bend Office). ***PRACTICE AREAS:*** Family Law. ***Email:*** gordon@stahancyk.com

GRACE Y. LEE, born Flagstaff, Arizona, February 10, 1976; admitted to bar, 2001, Oregon. *Education:* University of Arizona (B.S., Business Administration, 1998; J.D., 2001). ***PRACTICE AREAS:*** Family Law. ***Email:*** grace@stahancyk.com

KRISTIN M. LARSON, born Salem, Oregon, March 9, 1970; admitted to bar, 2002, Oregon. *Education:* Pomona College (B.A., American Studies, 1992); Northwestern School of Law (J.D., cum laude, 2002). *Member:* Deschutes County Bar Association; Oregon State Bar (Member, Sections on:, Estate Planning; Family Law). (Resident Bend Office). ***PRACTICE AREAS:*** Trusts and Estates; Wills; Probate; Guardianship; Conservatorship; Premarital Agreements; Family Law. ***Email:*** kristin@stahancyk.com

CATHERINE E. BARKER, born 1978; admitted to bar, 2003, Oregon. *Education:* University of Kansas (B.S., Biology; J.D.). Member, Golden Key. *Member:* Washington County and American Bar Associations; Oregon State Bar. ***Email:*** catherine@stahancyk.com

JEFFREY M. GREENSPAN, born 1978; admitted to bar, 2003, Oregon. *Education:* Oregon State University (B.A., Political Science, cum laude); University of Oregon (J.D., 2003). *Member:* Washington County and American Bar Associations; Oregon State Bar. ***Email:*** jeffrey@stahancyk.com

TRISHA J. ENGLISH, born 1980; admitted to bar, 2005, Oregon. *Education:* University of Washington (B.A., Communications, 2002); Pepperdine University School of Law (J.D., magna cum laude, 2005). *Member:* Oregon State Bar. ***Email:*** trisha@stahancyk.com

SHANTEL P. BRAY, born 1977; admitted to bar, 2005, Washington and U.S. District Court, Western District of Washington (Not admitted in Oregon). *Education:* Brigham Young University (B.A., International Relations, 2000); University of Utah (J.D., 2004). *Member:* Washington State Bar Association. ***Email:*** shantel@stahancyk.com

JORDAN A. CARTER, born 1978; admitted to bar, 2004, Oregon. *Education:* Oregon State University (B.A., Political Science, 2001); University of Oregon (J.D., 2004). *Member:* Multnomah County and American Bar Associations; Oregon State Bar. ***Email:*** jordan@stahancyk.com

SAMUEL T. STANKE, ATTORNEY AT LAW, LLC

1400 SW MONTGOMERY STREET
PORTLAND, OREGON 97201
Telephone: 503-224-1127
Fax: 503-228-4454
Email: sstatty@qwest.net
URL: http://www.lawyers.com/samueltstankelaw

SAMUEL T. STANKE, born La Crosse, Wisconsin, December 10, 1974; admitted to bar, 2003, Oregon. *Education:* University of Wisconsin-Madison (B.A., 1998); Lewis and Clark College (J.D., 2003). *Member:* Oregon State Bar; American Bar Association; Oregon Trial Lawyers Association. ***PRACTICE AREAS:*** Personal Injury; Automobile Accidents and Injuries; Wrongful Death; Professional Malpractice; Products Liability. ***Email:*** sstatty@qwest.net

TERESA A. STATLER

Established in 1994

THE YEON BUILDING
522 SOUTHWEST 5TH AVENUE, SUITE 812
PORTLAND, OREGON 97204
Telephone: 503-220-4185
Fax: 503-281-2624
Email: tstatler@easystreet.com
URL: http://www.lawyers.com/statlerlaw

Emphasizing Deportation Defense, Family Immigration Law, Naturalization and Asylum, Citizenship, Visas, Green Cards.

FIRM PROFILE: Practice limited to immigration law since 1994.

TERESA A. STATLER, born Fort Belvoir, Virginia, August 16, 1956; admitted to bar, 1991, Oregon; 1994, U.S. District Court, District of Oregon and U.S. Court of Appeals, Ninth Circuit. *Education:* College of William & Mary (A.B., 1978); Northwestern School of Law (J.D., 1991). Co-Author: "Oregon Worker's Compensation and Unemployment Law," Independent Contractor Status: State by State Legal Guide, Wiley Law Publications, 1993. Speaker, Immigration Law, Community Groups and CLEs, Portland, Oregon. Volunteer Attorney, Immigration Counseling Service, Portland, Oregon, 1993—. *Member:* Oregon State Bar; Oregon Women Lawyers; American Immigration Lawyers Association. ***LANGUAGES:*** Spanish, French and Italian. ***PRACTICE AREAS:*** Immigration and Naturalization; Deportation; Consular Law; Family Immigration Law; Political Asylum.

Languages: French, Spanish and Italian.

C. SEAN STEPHENS, P.C.

1211 SW 5TH AVENUE, SUITE 2350
PORTLAND, OREGON 97204
Telephone: 503-546-6374; Toll Free: 866-336-9346
Fax: 503-546-6376
URL: http://www.lawyers.com/stephensfamilylaw
Email: info@stephensfamilylaw.com
URL: http://www.stephensfamilylaw.com

Family Law, Divorce, Child Custody, Paternity, Child Support, Modification of Custody and Child Support, Visitation Rights, Premarital Agreements.

C. SEAN STEPHENS, born Eugene, Oregon, 1969; admitted to bar, 1994, Oregon. *Education:* University of Oregon (B.S., 1991); Willamette University College of Law (J.D., 1994). Phi Delta Phi; Vice Magister, 1993-1994. Professor, College of Legal Arts, Portland, Oregon, 1999—. *Member:* Oregon State Bar. ***PRACTICE AREAS:*** Divorce; Paternity; Child Support; Child Custody; Parental Rights; Grandparents Visitation Rights. ***Email:*** sean@stephensfamilylaw.com

STEWART SOKOL & GRAY, LLC

2300 SW FIRST AVENUE, SUITE 200
PORTLAND, OREGON 97201
Telephone: 503-221-0699
Facsimile: 503-223-5706
URL: http://www.wwwlawssg.com
URL: http://www.lawssg.com

General Civil and Trial Practice. Construction, Bankruptcy, Corporation, Insurance, Fidelity and Surety and Real Estate Law.

MEMBERS OF FIRM

JOHN SPENCER STEWART, born Berkeley, California, April 29, 1946; admitted to bar, 1971, Oregon and U.S. District Court, District of Oregon; 1972, U.S. Court of Appeals, 9th Circuit; 1977, U.S. Court of Federal Claims; 1978, U.S. Supreme Court; 1986, Washington; 1995, U.S. District Court, Western and Eastern Districts of Washington; 2000, District Columbia, Alaska and U.S. District Court, District of Alaska; 2001, U.S. Court of Appeals for the Federal Circuit; 2002, Idaho and U.S. District Court, District of Idaho. *Education:* Columbia Union College (B.S., magna cum laude, 1968); Willamette University (J.D., magna cum laude, 1971). Phi Delta Phi. Member, Editorial Board, Willamette Law Journal, 1970-1971. *Member:* Multnomah County, Clark County, Anchorage, Washington State, Idaho State and American (Oregon Chairman, Public Contract Law Section, 1982-1988; Member, ABA Forum Committee on the Construction Industry, 1980—; Fidelity and Surety Law Committee, 1980—) Bar Associations; Oregon State Bar (Member, Business and Corporate Law, Construction Law, Debtor-Creditor and Litigation Sections); Alaska State Bar. ***PRACTICE AREAS:*** Construction Law; Surety Law; Commercial Litigation. ***Email:*** JStewart@lawssg.com

JAN D. SOKOL, born New York, N.Y., May 27, 1952; admitted to bar, 1978, Oregon and U.S. District Court, District of Oregon; 1979, U.S. Court of Appeals, Ninth Circuit; 1981, U.S. Court of Federal Claims and U.S. Court of Appeals for the Federal Circuit; 1982, U.S. Supreme Court; 2000, District of Columbia; 2001, Washington and U.S. District Court, Western District of Washington; 2002, Idaho,U.S. District Court, District of Idaho and U.S. District Court, Eastern District of Washington. *Education:* Rutgers University (B.S., magna cum laude, 1974); Northwestern School of Law, Lewis and Clark College (J.D., 1977). Case Note and Comment Editor, Environmental Law, 1976-1977. Author: "Geothermal Leasing in Wilderness Areas," 6 Environmental Law 489, 1977. Co-author: "Federal Practice in Oregon," OSB CLE Civil Litigation Manual, 1989. Law Clerk to the Honorable James A. Redden, 1980, Gus J. Solomon, 1979-1980 and George E. Juba, 1978-1979, U.S. District Court for the District of Oregon. *Member:* Multnomah County and American (Member: Fidelity and Surety Committee/Tort and Insurance Practice Section; Forum Committee on Construction Industry) Bar Associations; Oregon State Bar (Member: Construction Law, Debtor-Creditor and Corporation Sections). ***PRACTICE AREAS:*** Construction Law; Surety and Fidelity Law; Bankruptcy Law; Real Estate Law; Corporation Law. ***Email:*** JDSokol@lawssg.com

ARNOLD L. GRAY, born Newark, New Jersey, August 11, 1954; admitted to bar, 1979, Oregon; 1981, U.S. District Court, District of Oregon; 1991, U.S. Claims Court; 2002, District of Columbia. *Education:* University of Arizona (B.S., summa cum laude, 1976; J.D., magna cum laude, 1979). Phi Kappa Phi; Order of the Coif. Member, University of Arizona National Moot Court Team, 1978. Best Oral Advocate, University of Arizona Moot Court Competition. Author: "Architect/Engineer Liability Under Oregon Law," Cambridge Institute, 1987; "Damages Under Construction Agreements," Oregon State Bar, CLE Construction Law, 1988; "Construction Claims Under Oregon Law," Cambridge Institute, 1990; "Construction Claims Under Washington Law," Cambridge Institute, 1991. Law Clerk, Oregon Court of Appeals, 1979-1980. Instructor, Cambridge Institute, 1987-1991; Advanced Construction Law in Oregon, National Business Institute, 1996-2000; University of Arizona, College of Business and Public Administration, "Administrative Law," and College of Liberal Arts, Honors Program, "The Legal Profession," 1978-1979. Co-Chair, Oregon Construction Law, The Seminar Group, 2001, 2002. Mediator; Member, Panel of Arbitrators, American Arbitration Association. *Member:* Oregon State Bar (Member, Litigation Section; Chairperson, Construction Law Section, 1990-1991); American Bar Association (Member, Sections on: Public Contract Law; Litigation; Member, Forum Committee on the Construction Industry, Tort and Insurance Practice, 1983—); Associated General Contractors of America; Associated Builders and Contractors, Inc. ***PRACTICE AREAS:*** Construction and Design Law; Commercial Transactions; Commercial Litigation. ***Email:*** AGray@lawssg.com

SUSAN Z. WHITNEY, born Portland, Oregon, January 8, 1944; admitted to bar, 1978, Nevada; 1979, Oregon; 1981, U.S. District Court, District of Oregon and U.S. Court of Appeals, Ninth Circuit; 1983, U.S. Claims Court and U.S. Supreme Court; 1984, U.S. Court of Appeals for the Federal Circuit; 1997, Washington. *Education:* Mills College (B.A., 1965);

(This Listing Continued)

University of Oregon (M.A., 1966); The Lewis and Clark Law School (J.D., cum laude, 1978). Law Clerk to: The Hon. Roger D. Foley, U.S. District Court for the District of Nevada, 1978-1979; The Hon. Owen M. Panner, U.S. District Court for the District of Oregon, 1980-1981. Member, Panel of Arbitrators, American Arbitration Association; Arbitration Service of Portland. *Member:* Multnomah County Bar Association; Oregon State Bar (Member, Construction Law Section, Executive Board, 1989-1996; Section Chair, 1995-1996; Member, Real Estate and Land Use Section). ***PRACTICE AREAS:*** Construction and Design Law; Real Estate Transactions; Real Estate Appraisal Law; Business Litigation; Commercial Litigation; Corporate Law. ***Email:*** swhitney@lawssg.com

H. LEE COOK, born Alhambra, California, July 3, 1956; admitted to bar, 1986, Oregon; 1987, Washington; 1988, U.S. District Court, Eastern and Western Districts of Washington; 1989, U.S. District Court, District of Oregon; 2003, Alaska; U.S. Court of Appeals, Ninth Circuit. *Education:* Southern Oregon State College; University of Oregon (B.A., 1979; J.D., 1986). Phi Delta Phi. Articles Editor, Oregon Law Review, 1985-1986. Author: "Oregon Variations of the Fourth Amendment Exclusionary Rule in Administrative Proceedings," Vol. 65, Oregon Law Review 681, 1986. Co-author: "Federal Practice in Oregon," OSB CLE Civil Litigation Manual, 1989; "Payment and Performance Bonds on Government Construction Bonds," OSB CLE Construction Law, 1995, 1997. *Member:* Multnomah County, Washington State, Alaska and American Bar Associations; Oregon State Bar. ***PRACTICE AREAS:*** Construction Law; Surety Law; Commercial Litigation. ***Email:*** LCook@lawssg.com

JEFFREY B. WILKINSON, born Baker City, Oregon, November 11, 1960; admitted to bar, 1989, Oregon; 1990, U.S. District Court, District of Oregon, U.S. Claims Court and U.S. Court of Appeals, Ninth Circuit; 2001, District of Columbia and Washington. *Education:* Metropolitan State College (B.A., 1986); University of Colorado at Denver; Willamette University (J.D., 1989). Author, "Chapter 14, 2001 Construction Claims and Documentation," Construction Law in Oregon, 2003; "Oregon Chapter, 50 State Lien Law Online," http://www.lienlaw-online.com. Member: Associated General Contractors, 1997-2003; Faculty, Law Seminars International, 1997-2003. Faculty, Lorman Educational Systems, National Business Institute. *Member:* Oregon State Bar (Executive Committee, Construction Law Section; Member, Real Estate Land Use Section); American Bar Association. ***REPORTED CASES:*** Webb v. Underhill, 130 Or.App. 352, 882 P.2d 127 (1994); Hauge v. Vanderhave, 121 Or.App., 854 P.2d 1002, aff'd without opinion, 859 P.2d 540 (1995); Webb v. Underhill, 174 Or.App. 592, 27 P.3d 148 (2001); Westwood Constr. Co. v. Hallmark Inns and Resorts, Inc., 182 Or.App. 624, 50 P.3d 238, review denied, 335 Or. 42, 57 P.3d 581 (2002). ***PRACTICE AREAS:*** Construction Litigation; Business/Commercial Litigation; Real Estate. ***Email:*** JWilkinson@lawssg.com

THOMAS A. LARKIN, born Ann Arbor, Michigan, June 5, 1967; admitted to bar, 1992, Oregon; 1993, U.S. District Court, District of Oregon; 1994, Washington and U.S. Court of Appeals, Ninth Circuit; 1995, U.S. District Court, Western and Eastern Districts of Washington; 2000, Alaska and U.S. District Court, District of Alaska; 2004, Idaho and U.S. District Court, District of Idaho; U.S. Court of Appeals, Federal Circuit. *Education:* University of Michigan (B.A., 1989); University of Denver (J.D., 1992). General Editor, Denver Journal of International Law and Policy, 1990-1991. Author, "Harmony In Disarray: The European Community Trademark System," 82 Trademark Reporter 634 (1992), reprinted 23 European Communities Trade Mark Assoc. 39 (May 1993). *Member:* Multnomah County, Oregon State (Member, Construction Section), Washington State, Alaska, Idaho State and American (Member: Forum on Construction Industry; Fidelity and Surety Law Committee; Sections on: Litigation; Business Law; Tort and Insurance Practice; Oregon State Chair, 2005-2006 and Member, Public Contract Section) Bar Associations; Idaho State Bar. ***PRACTICE AREAS:*** Surety and Fidelity; Construction; Insurance; Business; Commercial Litigation. ***Email:*** TLarkin@lawssg.com

ASSOCIATES

ANGELA M. OTTO, born Hill Air Force Base, Layton, Utah, January 11, 1973; admitted to bar, 1999, Oregon; 2000, Washington, U.S. District Court, District of Oregon, U.S. District Court, Western and Eastern Districts of Washington and U.S. Court of Appeals, Ninth Circuit. *Education:* Pacific Lutheran University (B.A., 1995); University of Oregon (J.D., 1999). Member, University of Oregon Law Review. *Member:* Multnomah County Bar Association; Oregon State Bar (Member-at-Large, Construction Law Section; Member, Litigation Section); Washington State Bar (Member, Litigation, Public Procurement & Private Construction Sections); American Bar Association. ***PRACTICE AREAS:*** Construction Law; Surety Law; Commercial Litigation; Business Litigation. ***Email:*** aotto@lawssg.com

MATTHEW A. WAND, born Gresham, Oregon, September 10, 1975; admitted to bar, 2000, Oregon and U.S. District Court, District of Oregon; 2001, District of Columbia; 2003, U.S. Court of Appeals, Ninth Circuit; 2004, Washington, U.S. District Court, Western and Eastern Districts of Washington and U.S. Court of Federal Claims. *Education:* Portland State University (B.A., 1997); Northwestern School of Law, Lewis & Clark (J.D., 2000). Phi Delta Phi. Member, 1998-1999, Managing Editor, 1999-2000, Journal of Small & Emerging Business Law. Co-Author: "Chapter 14, Damages Under Construction Agreements and Documentation," Construction Law in Oregon, 2004; Oregon Chapter "50 State Lien Law Online" http://www.lienlaw-online.com. *Member:* Oregon State Bar (Member, Sections on: Construction and Business Law); Washington State and American (Member, Forum on the Construction Industry) Bar Associations. ***PRACTICE AREAS:*** Construction Litigation; Business Litigation; Commercial Litigation; Corporate Law. ***Email:*** mwand@lawssg.com

ROBERT B. COLEMAN, born Washington, D.C., May 27, 1969; admitted to bar, 2000, Oregon and U.S. Court of Federal Claims. *Education:* Reed College (B.A., 1992); George Mason University School of Law (J.D., summa cum laude, 1999). Judicial Law Clerk to the Honorable Diane Gilbert Sypolt (Weinstein), U.S. Court of Federal Claims, 1999-2001. Author: "Does Act 17 of the Warsaw Convention Cover Injuries or Accidents," 7 Geo. Mason L. Rev. 191. ***PRACTICE AREAS:*** Construction Litigation; Business Litigation; Commercial Litigation; Government Contracts. ***Email:*** rcoleman@lawssg.com

LAWRENCE A. WAGNER, born New York, New York, July 7, 1973; admitted to bar, 2002, Oregon. *Education:* Fordham University (B.A., 1995); Northwestern School of Law

(This Listing Continued)

STEWART SOKOL & GRAY, LLC, Portland—Continued

(J.D., 2002). *Member:* Oregon State Bar (Member, Construction and Litigation Sections). ***PRACTICE AREAS:*** Construction Law; Surety Law; Business Litigation. ***Email:*** lwagner@lawssg.com

TYLER J. STORTI, born Boise, Idaho, December 1, 1977; admitted to bar, 2003, Oregon; 2004, U.S. District Court, District of Oregon. *Education:* Tulane University (B.A., cum laude, 2000); University of Oregon School of Law (J.D., 2003). Associate Editor, Oregon Law Review. Law Clerk to the Honorable Michael R. McLaughlin, State of Idaho, Fourth Judicial District, 2003-2004. *Member:* Multnomah County and American Bar Associations; Oregon State Bar. ***PRACTICE AREAS:*** Construction Litigation; Business Litigation; Commercial Litigation; Surety Law. ***Email:*** tstorti@lawssg.com

NEIL N. OLSEN, born San Patricio County, Texas, September 8, 1975; admitted to bar, 2005, Oregon. *Education:* University of Texas at Austin (B.A., 1998); Lewis and Clark College (J.D., 2005). Executive Editor, Lewis & Clark Law Review, 2004-2005. *Member:* Oregon State Bar. ***PRACTICE AREAS:*** Construction Litigation; Business Litigation; Commercial Litigation; Surety Law.

E. SUSAN O'TOOLE, born Eugene, Oregon, November 26, 1960; admitted to bar, 2003, California (Not admitted in Oregon). *Education:* Washington State University (B.A., summa cum laude, 1998); Oregon State University (M.S., 2002); University of Oregon (J.D., 2003). *Member:* Orange County and American Bar Associations; State Bar of California. ***PRACTICE AREAS:*** Construction Law; Surety Law; Commercial Litigation; Business Litigation.

REPRESENTATIVE CLIENTS: Apollo, Inc.; Apollo Sheet Metal, Inc.; Cascade Utilities, Inc.; Day Wireless Systems; Design Professional Insurance Cos.; Fischer Properties; James W. Fowler Co.; General Insurance Company of America; Gulf Insurance Co., Contract Operations Planning, Inc.; The Hartford; J.H. Kelly, Inc.; Peter Kiewit Sons' Co./Kiewit Pacific; Liberty Bond Services; McGill Commercial; Meissner + Wurst; Metro Property Management;; L.E. Meyers Company Group; Northwest Demolition & Dismantling; Ohio Casualty Insurance Co.; Safeco Insurance Company of America; St. Paul Insurance Group; J.R. Simplot Co.; Traveles Casualty & Surety Co.; United States Fidelity and Guaranty Co.; Washington International Insurance Co.; Alliance Industrial Group; Westwood Swinerton Construction.

STOEL RIVES LLP

900 S.W. FIFTH AVENUE
SUITE 2600
PORTLAND, OREGON 97204-1268
Telephone: 503-224-3380
Facsimile: 503-220-2480
Cable Address: "Lawport"
URL: http://www.stoel.com

Seattle, Washington Office: Suite 3600, One Union Square, 600 University. Telephone: 206-624-0900.
Vancouver, Washington Office: Suite 725, 805 Broadway. Telephone: 360-699-5900.
Boise, Idaho Office: Suite 1900, 101 S. Capitol Boulevard. Telephone: 208-389-9000.
Salt Lake City, Utah Office: Suite 1100, One Utah Center, 201 South Main Street. Telephone: 801-328-3131.
San Francisco, California Office: 111 Sutter Street, Suite 700. Telephone: 415-617-8900.
Sacramento, California Office: 770 L Street, Suite 800. Telephone: 916-447-0700.
Tahoe City, California Office: 3000 N. Lake Boulevard, Suite 1, P.O. Box 7336. Telephone: 530-583-2116.
Fresno, California Office: 1233 W. Shaw Avenue, Suite 103. Telephone: 559-228-9900.

General Corporate Counsel and Litigation. Antitrust and Trade Regulation, Bankruptcy, Construction and Design, Corporate Finance and Securities, Employee Benefits, Energy, Environmental, Estates and Trusts, Financial Institutions, Healthcare, Intellectual Property, International Trade and Transactions, Labor and Employment, Mergers and Acquisitions, Natural Resources, Real Estate and Land Use, Reorganizations and Workouts, Taxation, Technology, White Collar Criminal Law.

FIRM PROFILE: Stoel Rives is a business law firm providing services throughout the western United States. It is regarded as a regional leader in energy, natural resources, environment, corporate and intellectual property law and complex litigation. The firm's 375 lawyers and 500 support staff provide client-focused services to a wide range of businesses and individuals from eight offices in Oregon, Washington, California, Utah and Idaho. For more information, visit www.stoel.com.

MEMBERS OF FIRM

STEVEN W. ABEL, born Portland, Oregon, September 26, 1953; admitted to bar, 1983, Oregon. *Education:* Portland State University (B.S., 1975); Northwestern School of Law of Lewis & Clark College (J.D., cum laude, 1983). ***PRACTICE AREAS:*** Land Use Law; Real Estate Law. ***Email:*** swabel@stoel.com

CHARLES F. ADAMS, born Prineville, Oregon, July 17, 1947; admitted to bar, 1975, Oregon; 1976, U.S. District Court, District of Oregon and U.S. Court of Appeals, 9th Circuit; 1984, U.S. Claims Court; 1988, U.S. Court of Appeals for the Federal Circuit and Tenth Circuit and U.S. Supreme Court; 1989, U.S. Court of Appeals, Eighth Circuit; 1991, U.S. Court of Appeals, Fifth Circuit; 1993, U.S. Court of Appeals, Third Circuit. *Education:* Oregon State University (B.S., 1969); Boalt Hall School of Law, University of California (J.D., 1975). ***PRACTICE AREAS:*** Appellate and Litigation Law. ***Email:*** cfadams@stoel.com

RICHARD E. ALEXANDER, born Indianapolis, Indiana, July 16, 1944; admitted to bar, 1969, Oregon. *Education:* Oregon State University (B.S., 1966); University of Oregon (J.D., 1969). Fellow, American College of Construction Lawyers. ***PRACTICE AREAS:*** Construction and Design Law; Alternative Dispute Resolutions. ***Email:*** realexander@stoel.com

COURTNEY W. ANGELI, born Atlanta, Georgia, July 27, 1967; admitted to bar, 1994, Oregon and U.S. District Court, District of Oregon and U.S. Court of Federal Claims; 1997, Washington and U.S. District Court, Eastern District of Washington. *Education:* University of Georgia (B.A., magna cum laude, 1989); University of Michigan (J.D., cum laude, 1993). ***PRACTICE AREAS:*** Employment Law. ***Email:*** cwangeli@stoel.com

DAVID H. ANGELI, born Pittsfield, Massachusetts, August 9, 1967; admitted to bar, 1997, Maryland; 1998, U.S. District Court, District of Maryland and District of Columbia; 2002, Oregon. *Education:* Boston University (B.S., summa cum laude, 1989); Georgetown University (J.D., magna cum laude, 1997). Order of the Coif. White Collar Crime Senior Project Editor, The American Criminal Law Review, 1996-1997. Author: "A 'Second Look' at Crack Cocaine Sentencing Policies: One More Try for Federal Equal Protection," 34 The American Criminal Law Review 1211, 1997. Co-Author: "Federal Criminal Conflict of Interest, Project, Eleventh Survey of White Collar Crime," The American Criminal Law Review, 1996. Law Clerk to the Hon. Thomas Penfield Jackson, U.S. District Court for the District of Columbia, 1997-1999. *Member:* Maryland State and American Bar Associations; The District of Columbia Bar. [Lieut., U.S. Navy, 1989-1994]. ***PRACTICE AREAS:*** Criminal Litigation; Civil Litigation. ***Email:*** dhangeli@stoel.com

PAUL S. ANGELLO, born Pittsburgh, Pennsylvania, April 26, 1950; admitted to bar, 1981, Oregon and U.S. District Court, District of Oregon; 1984, U.S. Court of Appeals for the Federal and Ninth Circuits; registered to practice before U.S. Patent and Trademark Office. *Education:* University of Pennsylvania (B.S.E.E., cum laude, 1972); University of California at Los Angeles (M.S. in E.E., 1974); University of Southern California (J.D., 1981). ***PRACTICE AREAS:*** Patent Law; Technology Law. ***Email:*** psangello@stoel.com

GARY R. BARNUM, born Portland, Oregon, March 5, 1954; admitted to bar, 1981, Oregon; 1983, Washington. *Education:* University of Oregon (B.A., with high honors, 1977); University of Washington (J.D., with honors, 1981). ***PRACTICE AREAS:*** Corporate Law; Securities; Finance; Taxation; Structured Finance. ***Email:*** grbarnum@stoel.com

TODD A. BAUMAN, born Portland, Oregon, November 10, 1956; admitted to bar, 1984, California; 1987, Oregon. *Education:* Stanford University (A.B., with distinction, 1978); University of Chicago (J.D., 1984). ***PRACTICE AREAS:*** General Corporate Law; Securities Law. ***Email:*** tabauman@stoel.com

RUTH A. BEYER, born Mt. Angel, Oregon, September 25, 1955; admitted to bar, 1980, Oregon. *Education:* Oregon State University (B.S., with highest honors, 1977); University of Notre Dame (J.D., cum laude, 1980). ***PRACTICE AREAS:*** Corporate Law; Securities Law; Mergers and Acquisitions Law. ***Email:*** rabeyer@stoel.com

ALAN R. BLANK, born Cleveland, Ohio, October 8, 1956; admitted to bar, 1981, Missouri; 1992, Oregon and Utah. *Education:* Washington University (A.B., 1978; J.D., 1981). ***PRACTICE AREAS:*** Corporate Law; Securities Law; Bond Law. ***Email:*** arblank@stoel.com

PATRICK G. BOYLSTON, born Portland, Oregon, February 11, 1952; admitted to bar, 1977, Oregon; 1982, U.S. Tax Court. *Education:* Dartmouth College (B.A., 1974); Northwestern School of Law of Lewis & Clark College (J.D., 1977); Portland State University (M.T. in taxation, 1983). ***PRACTICE AREAS:*** Public Law and Finance; Taxation and Business Law. ***Email:*** pgboylston@stoel.com

BARBARA A. BRAINARD, born Long Branch, New Jersey, November 9, 1954; admitted to bar, 1980, Oregon. *Education:* Rutgers University (B.A., with honors, 1976); Willamette University (J.D., 1980). ***PRACTICE AREAS:*** Employment Law; Workers Compensation Litigation. ***Email:*** babrainard@stoel.com

JASON M. BRAUSER, born Eugene, Oregon, March 5, 1969; admitted to bar, 1994, California; 1997, Oregon. *Education:* Stanford University (A.B., 1991); Northwestern University (J.D., 1994). ***PRACTICE AREAS:*** Corporate Law; Securities. ***Email:*** jmbrauser@stoel.com

PAUL C. BUCHANAN, born Durham, North Carolina, August 5, 1964; admitted to bar, 1990, California; 1994, Oregon and Washington. *Education:* Vassar College (A.B., 1986); Boston College (J.D., 1990). ***PRACTICE AREAS:*** Employment Litigation; Litigation. ***Email:*** pbuchanan@stoel.com

MICHAEL ROAME CAMPBELL, born Decatur, Alabama, February 17, 1959; admitted to bar, 1987, Oregon. *Education:* Reed College (B.A., 1981); University of Washington (J.D., 1986). ***PRACTICE AREAS:*** Environmental Law; Land Use Law. ***Email:*** mrcampbell@stoel.com

PHILLIP D. CHADSEY, born Klamath Falls, Oregon, July 23, 1936; admitted to bar, 1966, Oregon and U.S. District Court, District of Oregon; U.S. Court of Federal Claims and U.S. Court of Appeals, Ninth, Tenth and Federal Circuits; U.S. District Court, Northern District of California; U.S. Supreme Court. *Education:* University of Oregon (B.S., 1958); Willamette University (J.D., 1966). Fellow, American College of Trial Lawyers. ***PRACTICE AREAS:*** Civil Litigation; Products Liability Law; Natural Resources Law. ***Email:*** pdchadsey@stoel.com

STUART CHESTLER, born Cleveland, Ohio, September 27, 1957; admitted to bar, 1983, Oregon; 1986, Washington. *Education:* University of Oregon (B.A., 1979); Boalt Hall School of Law, University of California (J.D., 1982). ***PRACTICE AREAS:*** Corporate; Securities; Finance. ***Email:*** schestler@stoel.com

WILLIAM L. CLYDESDALE, born Hong Kong, July 13, 1967; admitted to bar, 1994, New York; 1996, District of Columbia; 2001, Oregon. *Education:* Wesleyan University (B.A., 1988); Harvard University (J.D., cum laude, 1993). Phi Beta Kappa. ***PRACTICE AREAS:*** Corporate Law; Mergers and Acquisitions; Securities. ***Email:*** wlclydesdale@stoel.com

JOSEPH D. COHEN, born October 30, 1948; admitted to bar, 1980, Pennsylvania; 1982, Oregon; 1983, Washington. *Education:* University of Pennsylvania (J.D., 1980). ***PRACTICE AREAS:*** Patent Law; Litigation; Arbitration Law. ***Email:*** jdcohen@stoel.com

D. JEFFREY COURSER, born Longview, Washington, March 5, 1956; admitted to bar, 1985, Washington; 1987, U.S. District Court, Western District of Washington; 1988, Oregon and U.S. Court of Appeals, Ninth Circuit; 1992, U.S. District Court, District of Oregon. *Education:* Reed College (B.A., 1980); Northwestern College of Law of Lewis & Clark College (J.D., magna cum laude, 1985). (Also at Vancouver, Washington Office). ***PRACTICE AREAS:*** Litigation; Real Estate Law. ***Email:*** djcourser@stoel.com

(This Listing Continued)

NANCY L. COWGILL, born Tillamook, Oregon, March 14, 1951; admitted to bar, 1976, Oregon; 1984, U.S. Tax Court. *Education:* Oregon State University and Stanford University (A.B., 1973); University of Washington (J.D., 1976). Fellow, American College of Trusts and Estates Counsel. ***PRACTICE AREAS:*** Estate Planning Law; Estate Administration Law. ***Email:*** nlcowgill@stoel.com

BARBARA D. CRAIG, born Ann Arbor, Michigan, March 26, 1953; admitted to bar, 1988, Oregon; 1989, U.S. District Court, District of Oregon. *Education:* Oregon State University (B.S., 1980); Northwestern School of Law of Lewis & Clark College (J.D., 1987). ***PRACTICE AREAS:*** Natural Resources Law; Environmental Law; Forestry Law. ***Email:*** bdcraig@stoel.com

ANDREW I. DAVIS, born Cleveland, Ohio, March 23, 1962; admitted to bar, 1993, Oregon and Washington; U.S. District Court, District of Oregon. *Education:* University of Georgia (B.B.A., 1984); Northwestern School of Law (J.D., 1993). Certificate, Environmental and Natural Resources Law. ***PRACTICE AREAS:*** Real Estate; Corporate Law; Securities; Finance. ***Email:*** aidavis@stoel.com

E. JOSEPH DEAN, born Astoria, Oregon, May 20, 1949; admitted to bar, 1974, Oregon; 1975, U.S. District Court, District of Oregon and U.S. Court of Appeals, 1st Circuit; 1980, U.S. Court of Appeals, 9th Circuit; 1983, U.S. Tax Court; 1989, U.S. Court of Appeals, Eighth Circuit; 1990, U.S. Court of Appeals, Federal Circuit. *Education:* University of Oregon (B.A.B.A., 1971); Harvard University (J.D., cum laude, 1974). ***PRACTICE AREAS:*** Patent Litigation; Insurance Law; Professional Liability Defense Law; Computer Litigation Law. ***Email:*** ejdean@stoel.com

EDWARD D. EINOWSKI, born Detroit, Michigan, June 23, 1953; admitted to bar, 1978, Michigan; 1984, Oregon. *Education:* University of Michigan (B.A., with highest honors, 1975; J.D., cum laude, 1978). ***PRACTICE AREAS:*** State and Municipal Finance Law; Tax Exempt Finance Law; Government Law. ***Email:*** eeinowski@stoel.com

BARNES H. ELLIS, born Boston, Massachusetts, January 21, 1940; admitted to bar, 1964, Oregon and U.S. District Court, District of Oregon; 1967, U.S. Supreme Court; 1971, U.S. Court of Appeals, Ninth Circuit; 1983, Washington and U.S. District Court, Western District of Washington. *Education:* Yale University (B.A., magna cum laude, 1961); Stanford University School of Law; Harvard University Law School (LL.B., magna cum laude, 1964). Fellow, American College of Trial Lawyers. ***PRACTICE AREAS:*** Business Litigation; Antitrust Law; Securities Law. ***Email:*** bhellis@stoel.com

EDWARD L. EPSTEIN, born Walla Walla, Washington, January 10, 1936; admitted to bar, 1962, Oregon. *Education:* Stanford University (A.B., with great distinction, 1958); Harvard University (LL.B., magna cum laude, 1961). ***PRACTICE AREAS:*** Corporate Law; Mergers and Acquisitions Law; Health and Hospital Law. ***Email:*** elepstein@stoel.com

MARK R. FEICHTINGER, born Eugene, Oregon, May 31, 1948; admitted to bar, 1978, Oregon; 1986, Washington. *Education:* Northwestern University (B.A., with honors, 1970); University of Michigan (J.D., 1978). (Also at Vancouver, Washington Office). ***PRACTICE AREAS:*** Financial Transactions; Closely-Held Businesses Law; Real Estate Law; Land Use Law. ***Email:*** mrfeichtinger@stoel.com

JAMES F. FELL, born Toledo, Ohio, November 18, 1944; admitted to bar, 1970, New York; 1972, California; 1978, Idaho; 1981, Washington; 1984, Oregon. *Education:* University of Notre Dame (B.A., 1966); Ohio State University (J.D., cum laude, 1969). Director of Policy and Administration, Idaho Public Utilities Commission, 1979-1981. General Counsel, 1981-1984 and Deputy Director, 1982-1983, Northwest Power Planning Council. ***PRACTICE AREAS:*** Utilities Law; Administrative Law. ***Email:*** jffell@stoel.com

LOUIS A. FERREIRA, IV, born Jacksonville, Florida, August 4, 1963; admitted to bar, 1990, Oregon, U.S. District Court, District of Oregon and U.S. Court of Appeals, Ninth Circuit; 1991, Washington and U.S. District Court, Western District of Washington. *Education:* Washington State University (B.A., 1985); University of Idaho (J.D., summa cum laude, 1989). (Also at Vancouver, Washington Office). ***PRACTICE AREAS:*** Environmental Insurance Coverage Litigation; Health and Safety Law. ***Email:*** laferreira@stoel.com

HOWARD M. FEUERSTEIN, born Memphis, Tennessee, September 16, 1939; admitted to bar, 1963, Tennessee; 1965, Oregon. *Education:* Vanderbilt University (B.A., 1961; J.D., 1963). Order of the Coif. Fellow, American College of Real Estate Lawyers. ***PRACTICE AREAS:*** Real Estate Law; Condominium Law; Residential Development Law. ***Email:*** hmfeuerstein@stoel.com

DAVID E. FILIPPI, born Manhattan, Kansas, April 9, 1969; admitted to bar, 1996, Oregon. *Education:* Kansas State University (B.S., 1991; M.A., 1993); Northwestern School of Law of Lewis & Clark College (J.D., cum laude, 1996). ***PRACTICE AREAS:*** Environmental; Natural Resources; Land Use Law. ***Email:*** defilippi@stoel.com

JERRY R. FISH, born Sidney, New York, July 26, 1949; admitted to bar, 1982, Oregon; 1983, Washington; 1986, Missouri. *Education:* Princeton University (A.B., 1971); University of Chicago (M.A.T., 1974); Northwestern School of Law of Lewis & Clark College (J.D., magna cum laude, first in class, 1982). ***PRACTICE AREAS:*** Mining Law; Oil and Gas Law. ***Email:*** jrfish@stoel.com

RANDOLPH C. FOSTER, born Boise, Idaho, October 3, 1952; admitted to bar, 1978, Oregon and U.S. District Court, District of Oregon; 1986, Washington and U.S. Court of Appeals, Ninth Circuit. *Education:* University of Puget Sound (B.A., with honors, 1974); Georgetown University (J.D., 1978). ***PRACTICE AREAS:*** Intellectual Property Litigation; Distribution and Marketing Law; Antitrust and Trade Regulation Law. ***Email:*** rcfoster@stoel.com

RICHARD A. FRANZKE, born Lewistown, Montana, March 7, 1935; admitted to bar, 1960, Oregon. *Education:* Portland State College (Prelaw, 1957); Willamette University (B.S., 1959); Willamette University College of Law (J.D., with honors, 1960). ***PRACTICE AREAS:*** Construction and Design Law. ***Email:*** rafranzke@stoel.com

EUGENE A. FRASSETTO, born Salinas, California, February 25, 1950; admitted to bar, 1984, Oregon. *Education:* University of California at Berkeley; Oregon State University (B.S., 1976); Willamette University (J.D., magna cum laude, 1984). ***PRACTICE AREAS:*** Real Estate Law; General Corporate Law. ***Email:*** eafrassetto@stoel.com

(This Listing Continued)

GEORGE M. GALLOWAY, born New York, N.Y., June 9, 1948; admitted to bar, 1975, Oregon; 1984, District of Columbia. *Education:* Colgate University (A.B., 1970); University of Michigan (J.D., magna cum laude, 1973; M.P.P., 1973). ***PRACTICE AREAS:*** Corporate Law; Administrative Law. ***Email:*** gmgalloway@stoel.com

ANDREW R. GARDNER, born Alden, Pennsylvania, February 3, 1953; admitted to bar, 1979, Oregon; 1984, Washington and U.S. Supreme Court. *Education:* University of Virginia (B.A., with distinction, 1976; J.D., 1979). ***PRACTICE AREAS:*** Business Torts Litigation; Property Rights; Land Use Litigation; General Commercial Litigation; Real Estate Litigation. ***Email:*** argardner@stoel.com

RICHARD S. GLEASON, born Philadelphia, Pennsylvania, February 15, 1951; admitted to bar, 1981, Oregon. *Education:* Stanford University (B.A., 1973); University of Idaho (M.S., 1978; J.D., cum laude, 1981). ***PRACTICE AREAS:*** Business Law; Insurance Law; Environmental and Hazardous Waste Litigation. ***Email:*** rsgleason@stoel.com

GARY W. GLISSON, born Honolulu, Hawaii, September 21, 1959; admitted to bar, 1988, District of Columbia; 1992, Oregon. *Education:* University of Missouri (B.A., 1981; M.A., 1982); Northwestern University (J.D., 1988). ***PRACTICE AREAS:*** Intellectual Property; Licensing; Computer Law; International Trade; Corporate Law. ***Email:*** gwglisson@stoel.com

GERSHAM GOLDSTEIN, born Brooklyn, New York, December 5, 1938; admitted to bar, 1963, Oregon; 1965, U.S. Tax Court. *Education:* City College of New York (B.B.A., 1959); University of Pennsylvania (LL.B., cum laude, 1962); New York University (LL.M., Taxation, 1964). ***PRACTICE AREAS:*** Federal and State Taxation Law; Estate Planning Law. ***Email:*** ggoldstein@stoel.com

ERIC A. GRASBERGER, born Milwaukee, Wisconsin, May 31, 1965; admitted to bar, 1991, Oregon; U.S. District Court, District of Oregon. *Education:* University of Notre Dame (B.A., Economics, 1987); University of North Carolina (J.D., with honors, 1991). ***PRACTICE AREAS:*** Construction and Design Law. ***Email:*** eagrasberger@stoel.com

DAVID W. GREEN, born Cleveland, Ohio, July 27, 1951; admitted to bar, 1976, Oregon. *Education:* Malone College (B.A., summa cum laude, 1973); Harvard University (J.D., 1976). ***PRACTICE AREAS:*** Financial Transactions; Real Estate Law; Business Law. ***Email:*** dwgreen@stoel.com

STEPHEN L. GRIFFITH, born Washington, D.C., December 9, 1945; admitted to bar, 1977, Oregon. *Education:* Harvard University (B.A., 1967); Oxford University, Oxford, England (M.Phil., 1969); Stanford University (J.D., 1977). ***PRACTICE AREAS:*** Litigation; Education Law. ***Email:*** slgriffith@stoel.com

RONALD S. GROSSMANN, born Chicago, Illinois, November 9, 1944; admitted to bar, 1969, Oregon. *Education:* Northwestern University (B.A., 1966); University of Michigan (J.D., 1969). ***PRACTICE AREAS:*** Corporate Law; Tax Law; Employee Benefits Law. ***Email:*** rsgrossmann@stoel.com

STEPHEN C. HALL, born Pontiac, Michigan, March 16, 1967; admitted to bar, 1997, Michigan; 1998, Oregon. *Education:* Western Michigan University (B.B.A., cum laude, 1992); University of Notre Dame (J.D., cum laude, 1996). ***PRACTICE AREAS:*** Energy. ***Email:*** schall@stoel.com

JOHN J. HALLE, born Washington, D.C., August 10, 1947; admitted to bar, 1978, Oregon; 1986, Washington. *Education:* University of Oregon (B.A., honors, 1969); Tufts University (M.A., 1974); Suffolk University (J.D., cum laude, 1978); Harvard University. ***PRACTICE AREAS:*** Corporate Law; Securities Law; International Law. ***Email:*** jjhalle@stoel.com

CHRISTOPHER R. HERMANN, born Morristown, New Jersey, August 31, 1953; admitted to bar, 1982, Colorado; 1987, Oregon and Washington. *Education:* Bowdoin College (B.A., summa cum laude, 1976); University of Oregon (J.D., 1981). ***PRACTICE AREAS:*** Environmental Law; Winery Law. ***Email:*** crhermann@stoel.com

CHRISTOPHER K. HEUER, born Yankton, South Dakota, October 4, 1959; admitted to bar, 1990, Oregon. *Education:* Stanford University (A.B., 1987); Harvard University (J.D., 1990). ***PRACTICE AREAS:*** Taxation Law. ***Email:*** ckheuer@stoel.com

HENRY H. HEWITT, born Portland, Oregon, August 13, 1941; admitted to bar, 1969, Oregon. *Education:* Yale University (A.B., 1963); Willamette University (J.D., summa cum laude, 1969). ***PRACTICE AREAS:*** Business Law; Corporate Law; Securities; Finance; Mergers and Acquisitions Law. ***Email:*** hhhewitt@stoel.com

CHARLES F. HINKLE, born Oregon City, Oregon, July 6, 1942; admitted to bar, 1971, Oregon; 1975, U.S. Supreme Court; 1986, Washington. *Education:* Stanford University (B.A., with great distinction, 1964); Union Theological Seminary (M.Div., cum laude, 1968); Yale Law School (J.D., 1971). ***PRACTICE AREAS:*** Media Law; Constitutional Law; Employment Litigation. ***Email:*** cfhinkle@stoel.com

WILLIAM H. HOLMES, born San Antonio, Texas, August 10, 1960; admitted to bar, 1986, Oregon. *Education:* University of Texas (B.A., with highest honors, 1981); University of Michigan (J.D., magna cum laude, 1984). ***PRACTICE AREAS:*** Business Law; Energy Law; Natural Resources Law. ***Email:*** whholmes@stoel.com

STEVEN H. HULL, born Philadelphia, Pennsylvania, December 14, 1967; admitted to bar, 1997, Oregon. *Education:* Brown University (B.A., 1990); Northwestern School of Law of Lewis & Clark College (J.D., magna cum laude, 1996). ***PRACTICE AREAS:*** Corporate Law. ***Email:*** shhull@stoel.com

PAMELA L. JACKLIN, born Oak Park, Illinois, July 28, 1945; admitted to bar, 1978, Oregon. *Education:* Illinois Wesleyan University (B.A., with honors, 1966); Fletcher School of Law and Diplomacy (M.A., 1967; M.A.L.D., 1969); Institut Universitaire de Hautes Etudes Internationales, Geneva, Switzerland; University of Idaho (J.D., 1978). ***PRACTICE AREAS:*** Employment Law; Administrative Law; Miscellaneous Business Issues. ***Email:*** pljacklin@stoel.com

RICHARD C. JOSEPHSON, born Washington, D.C., November 20, 1947; admitted to bar, 1973, Oregon. *Education:* Case Western Reserve University (A.B., 1969); Marshall-Wythe School of Law, College of William & Mary (J.D., 1972). Fellow, American College of Bankruptcy. ***PRACTICE AREAS:*** Bankruptcy Law; Reorganization Law; Creditors' Rights Law; Commercial Law; Corporate Law. ***Email:*** rcjosephson@stoel.com

(This Listing Continued)

STOEL RIVES LLP, Portland—Continued

SCOTT J. KAPLAN, born Valley Stream, New York, March 2, 1964; admitted to bar, 1989, California and U.S. District Court; Central and Eastern Districts of California; 1991, Oregon; U.S. District Court, District of Oregon. *Education:* Reed College (B.A., 1986); Boalt Hall, University of California at Berkeley (J.D., 1989). ***PRACTICE AREAS:*** Environmental Litigation. ***Email:*** sjkaplan@stoel.com

EMILY V. KARR, born Chicago, Illinois, April 9, 1964; admitted to bar, 1990, Oregon. *Education:* Northwestern University (B.A., 1985); Duke University (J.D., with honors, 1988; LL.M., 1988). ***PRACTICE AREAS:*** Trusts and Estates Law. ***Email:*** evkarr@stoel.com

CHRIS KITCHEL, born Huron, South Dakota, March 2, 1950; admitted to bar, 1981, Oregon; 1982, U.S. District Court, District of Oregon, U.S. Court of Appeals, Ninth Circuit; 1983, Washington and U.S. District Court, Western District of Washington; 1984, U.S. District Court, Eastern District of Washington; 1988, U.S. Supreme Court. *Education:* University of Minnesota (B.S.B., 1973); Portland State University (M.B.A., 1977); Northwestern School of Law of Lewis & Clark College (J.D., cum laude, 1981). ***PRACTICE AREAS:*** Employment Litigation; Hospital Peer Review. ***Email:*** ckitchel@stoel.com

CHRISTINE A. KOSYDAR, born Portland, Oregon, January 10, 1951; admitted to bar, 1981, Oregon and U.S. District Court, District of Oregon. *Education:* Portland State University (B.S., with high honors, 1973); Reed College (M.A., 1978); Northwestern School of Law of Lewis & Clark College (J.D., 1981). ***PRACTICE AREAS:*** Creditors' Rights Law; Bankruptcy; Commercial Law; Real Estate Law. ***Email:*** cakosydar@stoel.com

JEFFREY M. KRUEGER, born Creve Coeur, Missouri, August 5, 1971; admitted to bar, 1996, Missouri; 1997, Illinois; 1999, Oregon. *Education:* Washington University (A.B., with honors, 1993; J.D., 1996; LL.M., in Taxation, 1999). Phi Beta Kappa; Order of the Coif. Associate Editor, Washington University Law Quarterly. ***PRACTICE AREAS:*** Employee Benefits. ***Email:*** jmkrueger@stoel.com

MARGARET BAUMGARDNER KUSHNER, born Mt. Pleasant, Michigan, January 5, 1953; admitted to bar, 1978, Oregon. *Education:* Michigan State University (B.A., 1975); Harvard University (J.D., 1978). ***PRACTICE AREAS:*** Corporate; Joint Ventures; Limited Liability Companies; Partnerships. ***Email:*** mbkushner@stoel.com

DENNIS LEYBOLD, born Butte, Montana, 1954; admitted to bar, 1979, Oregon; 1980, Massachusetts; 1985, Washington. *Education:* Stanford University (A.B., with distinction, 1976); Boston College (J.D., magna cum laude, 1979). ***PRACTICE AREAS:*** Employee Benefits Law; Corporate. ***Email:*** dleybold@stoel.com

STEVEN T. LOVETT, born De Kalb, Illinois, May 23, 1957; admitted to bar, 1989, New York; 1991, Oregon. *Education:* Tulane University (B.A., 1980); Hobart College; Fordham University School of Law (J.D., 1988). ***PRACTICE AREAS:*** Commercial Litigation. ***Email:*** stlovett@stoel.com

GREGORY H. MACPHERSON, born Corvallis, Oregon, May 3, 1950; admitted to bar, 1975, Oregon. *Education:* Harvard University (A.B., cum laude, 1972); Georgetown University (J.D., 1975). ***PRACTICE AREAS:*** Employee Benefits Law. ***Email:*** ghmacpherson@stoel.com

ROBERT T. MANICKE, born Boulder, Colorado, December 24, 1962; admitted to bar, 1992, California; 1995, Oregon; U.S. District Court, Northern District of California; U.S. Tax Court; 2005, Washington. *Education:* Willamette University (B.A., cum laude, 1984); University of Illinois (J.D., summa cum laude, 1992). ***PRACTICE AREAS:*** Taxation. ***Email:*** rtmanicke@stoel.com

KATHERINE A. McDOWELL, born Iowa City, Iowa, August 9, 1960; admitted to bar, 1985, Florida and U.S. District Court, Middle District of Florida; 1988, U.S. Court of Appeals, Eleventh Circuit; 1989, Oregon, Washington, U.S. District Court, District of Oregon and U.S. Court of Appeals, Ninth Circuit. *Education:* University of Iowa (B.A., 1981); Stetson University (J.D., cum laude, 1985). ***PRACTICE AREAS:*** Energy; Telecommunications Law; Business; Litigation; Constitutional Law. ***Email:*** kamcdowell@stoel.com

TIMOTHY L. McMAHAN, born Portland, Oregon, February 16, 1961; admitted to bar, 1986, Washington; 1998, Oregon. *Education:* University of Puget Sound (B.A., cum laude, 1983); Willamette University (J.D., 1986); University of Washington (M.A., Urban Planning, 1991). ***PRACTICE AREAS:*** Land Use; Environmental Law; Municipal Law. ***Email:*** tlmcmahan@stoel.com

DAVID P. MILLER, II, born Minneapolis, Minnesota, June 19, 1942; admitted to bar, 1967, Oregon; 1968, California. *Education:* Stanford University (A.B., 1964; LL.B., 1967). Order of the Coif. ***PRACTICE AREAS:*** Real Estate Law; Forest Industry Law. ***Email:*** dpmiller@stoel.com

STEVEN A. MOORE, born Portland, Oregon, August 8, 1967; admitted to bar, 1992, Hawaii; 1993, Oregon. *Education:* Lewis & Clark College (B.A., 1989); University of Oregon (J.D., 1992). ***PRACTICE AREAS:*** Real Estate Law. ***Email:*** samoore@stoel.com

ROBERT J. MOORMAN, born Cleveland, Ohio, March 18, 1951; admitted to bar, 1980, Oregon; 1986, Washington. *Education:* University of Pennsylvania (A.B., 1972); Yale Law School (J.D., 1980). ***PRACTICE AREAS:*** Corporate. ***Email:*** rjmoorman@stoel.com

J. MARK MORFORD, born Akron, Ohio, January 6, 1957; admitted to bar, 1983, Oregon. *Education:* Georgia Institute of Technology (B.S., highest honors, 1980); University of Virginia (J.D., 1983). ***PRACTICE AREAS:*** Environmental Law. ***Email:*** jmmorford@stoel.com

PETER D. MOSTOW, born Cleveland, Ohio, April 22, 1964; admitted to bar, 1995, Oregon. *Education:* Reed College (B.A., 1987); Yale Law School (J.D., 1993); J.W. Goethe Universitat, Frankfurt, Germany (Fulbright Scholar, 1989-1990). ***PRACTICE AREAS:*** Natural Resources; Land Use; Environmental Law. ***Email:*** pdmostow@stoel.com

GREGORY ROBERT MOWE, born Aberdeen, Washington, February 23, 1946; admitted to bar, 1974, Oregon. *Education:* University of Oregon (B.A., 1968; M.A., with honors, 1969); Harvard Law School (J.D., magna cum laude, 1974). ***PRACTICE AREAS:*** Commercial Law; Real Estate Litigation. ***Email:*** grmowe@stoel.com

(This Listing Continued)

JOEL A. MULLIN, born Chicago, Illinois, September 26, 1957; admitted to bar, 1981, Illinois and U.S. District Court, District of Illinois; 1986, Oregon; 1987, U.S. District Court, District of Oregon. *Education:* University of Chicago (B.A., with honors, 1977); Washington University (J.D., 1981). ***PRACTICE AREAS:*** Commercial Law; Securities Litigation. ***Email:*** jamullin@stoel.com

BARBARA L. NAY, born Santa Monica, California, 1951; admitted to bar, 1979, Colorado; 1982, Minnesota; 1985, Oregon; 1986, Washington. *Education:* Yale University; Stanford University (B.A., with honors, 1974); University of Colorado (J.D., 1979). ***PRACTICE AREAS:*** Health and Hospital Law; General Corporate Law. ***Email:*** blnay@stoel.com

THOMAS R. NICOLAI, born Fraser, Michigan, December 1, 1943; admitted to bar, 1972, Illinois; 1973, Oregon. *Education:* Kalamazoo College (B.A., cum laude, 1965); University of Bonn (Fellow, Economics, 1965-1967); University of Michigan (J.D., 1970). ***PRACTICE AREAS:*** Real Estate Law; Financial Transactions. ***Email:*** trnicolai@stoel.com

MARK A. NORBY, born Cadillac, Michigan, July 5, 1955; admitted to bar, 1980, Oregon. *Education:* Oregon State University (B.S., with highest honors, 1977); University of Michigan (J.D., magna cum laude, 1980). ***PRACTICE AREAS:*** Corporate Law; Real Estate Law; Natural Resources Law; Mineral Law; Oil and Gas Law; Forestry Law. ***Email:*** manorby@stoel.com

MARGARET HILL NOTO, born San Francisco, California, February 20, 1953; admitted to bar, 1978, Oregon. *Education:* Reed College (B.A., 1975); Boalt Hall School of Law, University of California (J.D., 1978). ***PRACTICE AREAS:*** Corporate; Securities; Finance. ***Email:*** mhnoto@stoel.com

BRENDAN N. O'SCANNLAIN, born Portland, Oregon, August 18, 1967; admitted to bar, 1997, Oregon. *Education:* College of the Holy Cross (B.A., 1990); Georgetown University Law Center (J.D., cum laude, 1997). ***PRACTICE AREAS:*** Corporate Law. ***Email:*** bnoscannlain@stoel.com

THOMAS R. PAGE, born Lawrence, Kansas, December 3, 1951; admitted to bar, 1978, Oregon. *Education:* University of Kansas (B.A., with highest distinction, 1973); University of Oregon (J.D., 1978). ***PRACTICE AREAS:*** Real Estate Law; Land Use Law. ***Email:*** trpage@stoel.com

TERRENCE R. PANCOAST, born Everett, Washington, August 7, 1942; admitted to bar, 1968, Oregon. *Education:* Whitman College (A.B., summa cum laude, 1965); Harvard Law School (LL.B., cum laude, 1968). Fellow, American College of Trust and Estate Counsel. ***PRACTICE AREAS:*** Trusts and Estates; Corporation Law; Tax-Exempt Organizations. ***Email:*** trpancoast@stoel.com

JOHN A. RAFTER, JR., born December 4, 1956; admitted to bar, 1986, California; 2003, Oregon; registered to practice before the U.S. Patent and Trademark Office. *Education:* University of Notre Dame (B.S.M.E., 1979); Loyola Law School of Los Angeles (J.D., 1986). ***PRACTICE AREAS:*** Intellectual Property. ***Email:*** jarafter@stoel.com

PER A. RAMFJORD, born Ann Arbor, Michigan, February 1, 1958; admitted to bar, 1985, Michigan and District of Columbia; 1987, U.S. District Court, District of Columbia and U.S. Court of Appeals, District of Columbia Circuit; 1993, Oregon and U.S. District Court, District of Oregon. *Education:* University of Michigan (A.B., with high honors, 1980; J.D., 1984). ***PRACTICE AREAS:*** Civil and Criminal Litigation. ***Email:*** paramfjord@stoel.com

GUY A. RANDLES, born Portland, Oregon, September 24, 1952; admitted to bar, 1977, Oregon; 1986, Washington. *Education:* University of Notre Dame (A.B., with highest honors, 1974); Boalt Hall School of Law, University of California (J.D., 1977). ***PRACTICE AREAS:*** Civil Litigation; Procurement, Construction and Design Law; Alternative Dispute Resolutions. ***Email:*** garandles@stoel.com

STEPHEN A. REDSHAW, born Albany, Georgia, July 24, 1961; admitted to bar, 1994, Oregon. *Education:* University of Oregon (B.A., 1984); Rutgers University (J.D., with highest honors, 1994). ***PRACTICE AREAS:*** Commercial Law. ***Email:*** saredshaw@stoel.com

EDWARD J. REEVES, born Philadelphia, Pennsylvania, April 12, 1956; admitted to bar, 1983, Oregon; 1985, U.S. District Court, District of Oregon; 1988, Washington and U.S. Court of Appeals, Ninth Circuit. *Education:* Yale University (B.A., 1978); Boston University (J.D., 1983). ***PRACTICE AREAS:*** Labor Law; Employment Law; Employee Counseling. ***Email:*** ejreeves@stoel.com

LOIS OMENN ROSENBAUM, born Newark, New Jersey, April 10, 1950; admitted to bar, 1974, California and District of Columbia; 1977, Oregon. *Education:* Wellesley College (A.B., 1971); Stanford Law School (J.D., 1974). ***PRACTICE AREAS:*** Securities Litigation; Business Litigation. ***Email:*** lorosenbaum@stoel.com

JEREMY D. SACKS, born Los Angeles, California, March 15, 1969; admitted to bar, 1994, California; 1996, District of Columbia; 1999, Oregon. *Education:* Wesleyan University (B.A., high honors, 1991); Georgetown University Law Center (J.D., cum laude, 1994). ***PRACTICE AREAS:*** Litigation; International Law. ***Email:*** jdsacks@stoel.com

PENNY H. SERRURIER, born Boston, Massachusetts, April 29, 1964; admitted to bar, 1991, Oregon; U.S. District Court, District of Oregon. *Education:* Middlebury College (B.A., cum laude, 1986); Cornell Law School (J.D., cum laude, 1991). ***PRACTICE AREAS:*** Trusts and Estates; Charitable Giving; Non-Profit Organizations. ***Email:*** phserrurier@stoel.com

PETER L. SERRURIER, born San Antonio, Texas, February 10, 1958; admitted to bar, 1990, Oregon. *Education:* Oregon State University (B.S., in Biology, 1983); Northwestern School of Law at Lewis & Clark College (J.D., cum laude, 1990). ***PRACTICE AREAS:*** Environmental Law. ***Email:*** plserrurier@stoel.com

JOAN P. SNYDER, born Woodbury, New Jersey, July 8, 1956; admitted to bar, 1984, Michigan; 1986, Oregon. *Education:* University of Delaware (B.S., with high honors, 1978); University of Michigan (J.D., cum laude, 1984). ***PRACTICE AREAS:*** Health/Safety Law; Environmental Litigation. ***Email:*** jpsnyder@stoel.com

MICAH D. STOLOWITZ, born Oakland, California, June 28, 1954; admitted to bar, 1981, Oregon; 1982, U.S. District Court, District of Oregon; 1988, U.S. Court of Appeals,

(This Listing Continued)

3rd Circuit; 1992, U.S. Court of Appeals for the Federal Circuit; registered to practice before U.S. Patent and Trademark Office. *Education:* University of California at Berkeley (B.S.E.E., with honors, 1976); Northwestern School of Law of Lewis & Clark College (J.D., 1981). ***PRACTICE AREAS:*** Patent, Trademark and Copyright Law; Licensing Law; Computer Software Law; Internet Law; Trade Secrets Law. ***Email:*** mdstolowitz@stoel.com

JOHN R. THOMAS, born Midland, Texas, November 29, 1960; admitted to bar, 1991, Oregon. *Education:* University of Puget Sound (B.A., magna cum laude, 1982); Columbia University (M.A., 1983; M.Phil., 1985); Northwestern School of Law of Lewis & Clark College (J.D., summa cum laude, 1991). ***PRACTICE AREAS:*** Corporate Law. ***Email:*** jrthomas@stoel.com

ROBERT H. THOMSON, born Albany, Oregon, August 24, 1944; admitted to bar, 1975, Oregon. *Education:* University of California at Berkeley (B.A., 1966); University of Michigan (J.D., 1975). ***PRACTICE AREAS:*** Employee Benefits Law. ***Email:*** rhthomson@stoel.com

ROBERT D. VAN BROCKLIN, born Billings, Montana, June 12, 1953; admitted to bar, 1987, Oregon; 1988, District of Columbia. *Education:* University of Oregon (B.S., with distinction, 1977; J.D., 1980). ***PRACTICE AREAS:*** Land Use Law; Administrative Law; Public Policy Law. ***Email:*** rdvanbrocklin@stoel.com

JAMES M. VAN NOSTRAND, born Harlan, Iowa, May 3, 1955; admitted to bar, 1979, Oregon; 1986, Washington. *Education:* University of Northern Iowa (B.A., with highest honors, 1976); University of Iowa (J.D., with high honors, 1979); State University of New York at Albany (M.A., 1985). (Also at Seattle, Washington Office). ***PRACTICE AREAS:*** Energy; Telecommunications Law; Utility Law; Administrative Law. ***Email:*** jmvannostrand@stoel.com

E. WALTER VAN VALKENBURG, born Seattle, Washington, January 8, 1953; admitted to bar, 1978, Oregon. *Education:* University of Washington (B.A., cum laude, 1975); Willamette University (J.D., summa cum laude, 1978); Columbia University (LL.M., 1984). ***PRACTICE AREAS:*** Trade Regulation Law; General Business Law; Intellectual Property Law; International Trade Law. ***Email:*** wvanvalkenburg@stoel.com

STEPHEN S. WALTERS, born Chicago, Illinois, March 20, 1945; admitted to bar, 1972, California; 1978, District of Columbia; 1980, Oregon. *Education:* Stanford University (B.S., 1967; J.D., 1972). ***PRACTICE AREAS:*** Litigation; Energy Litigation. ***Email:*** sswalters@stoel.com

JERE M. WEBB, born Portland, Oregon, July 28, 1944; admitted to bar, 1969, Oregon. *Education:* Stanford University (A.B., with distinction, 1966); University of Chicago (J.D., 1969). ***PRACTICE AREAS:*** Intellectual Property Law; Trade Regulation Law; Franchise Law. ***Email:*** jmwebb@stoel.com

JAMES N. WESTWOOD, P.C., born Portland, Oregon, December 3, 1944; admitted to bar, 1974, Oregon and U.S. District Court, District of Oregon; 1978, U.S. Court of Appeals, Ninth Circuit; 1981, U.S. Supreme Court; 1984, U.S. Court of Appeals for the Federal Circuit; 1997, U.S. Court of Appeals, District of Columbia Circuit. *Education:* Portland State University (B.A., 1967); Columbia University (J.D., 1974). Fellow, American Academy of Appellate Lawyers. ***PRACTICE AREAS:*** Appellate Law; Litigation; Education Law. ***Email:*** jnwestwood@stoel.com

MARCUS WOOD, born Mobile, Alabama, January 18, 1947; admitted to bar, 1974, Oregon. *Education:* Vanderbilt University (B.A., cum laude, 1969); Yale University (J.D., 1974). ***PRACTICE AREAS:*** Utilities Law; Energy Law; Administrative Law. ***Email:*** mwood@stoel.com

THOMAS R. WOOD, born Baltimore, Maryland, June 30, 1961; admitted to bar, 1993, Oregon; 1998, Washington. *Education:* Stanford University (B.A., with distinction, 1983); Columbia University (J.D., 1993). ***PRACTICE AREAS:*** Environmental and Natural Resources Law. ***Email:*** trwood@stoel.com

JAMES A. ZEHREN, born Breckenridge, Minnesota, October 29, 1948; admitted to bar, 1985, Oregon. *Education:* North Dakota State University (B.S.I.E., 1970); University of Minnesota (M.A., 1975; M.A., 1976); Northwestern School of Law of Lewis & Clark College (J.D., magna cum laude, 1985). ***PRACTICE AREAS:*** Construction and Design Law. ***Email:*** jazehren@stoel.com

OF COUNSEL

KAREN E. JONES, born San Pablo, California, April 8, 1958; admitted to bar, 1984, Texas; 1992, Oregon; 1993, Washington. *Education:* University of Texas (B.M., magna cum laude, 1980); University of Houston College of Law (J.D., cum laude, 1984). ***PRACTICE AREAS:*** Energy; Finance; Business Law; Real Estate. ***Email:*** kejones@stoel.com

DAN GRINFAS, born Stanford, California, March 18, 1966; admitted to bar, 1994, Oregon. *Education:* University of California at Los Angeles (B.S., 1988); Willamette University (J.D., 1994). *Member:* Marion County Bar Association. ***LANGUAGES:*** Spanish and Hebrew. ***PRACTICE AREAS:*** Labor and Employment. ***Email:*** dgrinfas@stoel.com

STEVEN E. KLEIN, born 1969; admitted to bar, 1997, New Jersey and U.S. District Court, District of New Jersey; 1998, New York; 1999, U.S. District Court, Southern District of New York; 2003, U.S. District Court, Eastern District of New York and U.S. Court of Appeals, Federal Circuit; 2005, Oregon and U.S. District Court, District of Oregon. *Education:* University of Rochester (B.A., 1991); Rutgers University Law School (J.D., 1997). Order of the Coif. *Member:* Oregon State Bar. ***PRACTICE AREAS:*** Litigation; Intellectual Property. ***Email:*** sklein@stoel.com

KELLY KNIVILA, born Boulder City, Nevada, April 18, 1963; admitted to bar, 1990, District of Columbia; 1992, Oregon; U.S. District Court, District of Oregon and District of Columbia; U.S. Court of Appeals, Fourth, Fifth and Ninth Circuits. *Education:* Western Oregon State College (B.A., 1986); Georgetown University Law Center (J.D., magna cum laude, 1989). ***PRACTICE AREAS:*** Litigation; Health Care Regulation; Administration Law. ***Email:*** kknivila@stoel.com

(This Listing Continued)

JAMES C. PAINE, born Oakland, Nebraska, June 11, 1947; admitted to bar, 1972, Nebraska and U.S. District Court, District of Nebraska; 1978, Montana; 1988, Oregon. *Education:* University of Nebraska (B.A., 1969; J.D., 1972). ***PRACTICE AREAS:*** Litigation; Utilities Law. ***Email:*** jcpaine@stoel.com

RETIRED MEMBERS

GEORGE H. FRASER, born Chicago, Illinois, May 23, 1917; admitted to bar, 1947, Oregon. *Education:* University of Wisconsin (B.A., 1940); Harvard Law School (LL.B., 1946). ***PRACTICE AREAS:*** General Business Litigation; Products Liability Law; Professional Liability Law; Insurance Law.

WILLIAM M. McALLISTER, born Medford, Oregon, December 21, 1933; admitted to bar, 1962, Oregon. *Education:* Harvard University (A.B., 1956); Willamette University (J.D., 1962). ***PRACTICE AREAS:*** Creditor Debtor Rights Law; Bankruptcy Law; Commercial Litigation; Mediation and Arbitration; Alternative Dispute Resolutions. ***Email:*** wmmcallister@stoel.com

CHARLES J. McMURCHIE, born Kellogg, Idaho, October 8, 1931; admitted to bar, 1959, Oregon. *Education:* Whitman College (A.B., 1953); University of Washington (LL.B., 1959). Phi Delta Phi. Fellow, American College of Trusts and Estates Counsel. ***PRACTICE AREAS:*** Estate Planning Law; Administration of Estates and Trusts Law; Personal Tax Law. ***Email:*** cjmcmurchie@stoel.com

THOMAS B. STOEL, born Clayton, New York, October 27, 1913; admitted to bar, 1937, Oregon. *Education:* Hobart College (A.B., 1934); Duke University (LL.B., 1937). ***PRACTICE AREAS:*** Corporate Law; Taxation Law; Forestry Law.

ASSOCIATES

Sarah Adams Lien
Bethany A. Bacci
Kurt Eric Barker
Edward A. Bernhard
Jennie L. Bricker
Donato C. Capobianco
Chad R. Chambers
Kenneth P. Childs
Greg D. Corbin
Jason A. Dalton
Brad Daniels
Saskia de Boer
Kathleen J. Doll
Amy Edwards
Kassim M. Ferris
Kevin T. Fox
Sean C. Gay
Rene G. Gonzalez
Michael B. Hallinan
Mary P. Hull
Matthew J. Kalmanson
James M. Kearney
Scott F. Kocher
Paul Sandberg Logan
Kimberly Anne Medford
Ian G. Merrill
John C. Motley
Samuel J. Panarella
Beverly C. Pearman
Kevin T. Pearson
Matthew C. Phillips
William R. Pierznik
Scott M. Rickard
Katherine K. Rosenbaum
Michelle Rudd
Brandy A. Sargent
Jeanette C. Schuster
Christian H. Scott
Shana W. Sechrist
David Silverman
Joshua W. Smith
Seth L. Smythe
Timothy W. Snider
Renee E. Starr
Kristin H. Sterling
Ellen Theodorson
Paul M. Tiger
Jennifer K.T. Warner
Kyle D. Wuepper

PATENT AGENT

MICHAEL L. LEVINE, born Brooklyn, New York, January 19, 1963. *Education:* Reed College (B.A., Chemistry, 1987). Registered to practice before U.S. Patent & Trademark Office.

REPRESENTATIVE CLIENTS: Columbia Sportswear Company; PacifiCorp; Precision Castparts Corp.; Tektronix, Inc.; Electro Scientific Industries; Northwest Natural Gas Company; Oregon Steel Mills, Inc.; NIKE, Inc.

(For complete biographical data on other personnel, see Professional Biographies at Washington, D.C., Boise, Idaho, Salt Lake City, Utah and Vancouver and Seattle, Washington)

STOLL STOLL BERNE LOKTING & SHLACHTER, P.C.

Established in 1975

209 S.W. OAK STREET, 5TH FLOOR
PORTLAND, OREGON 97204
Telephone: 503-227-1600
Telecopier: 503-227-6840
URL: http://www.ssbls.com

Major Business Litigation, including Securities, Antitrust, Intellectual Property and Unfair Competition in Federal and State Courts. Real Estate, Corporation, Environmental, Estate Planning, and Taxation Law.

GARY M. BERNE, born Cleveland, Ohio, November 30, 1951; admitted to bar, 1977, Oregon. *Education:* University of Pennsylvania (B.A., cum laude, 1972; J.D., 1977). Lecturer: Securities Litigation, RICO, Federal Practice, 1980—, Northwest Securities Institute, Oregon Law Institute, National Practice Institute, Oregon State Bar Continuing Legal Education, Federal Bar Association, Multnomah County and Washington County Bar Associations, Oregon Trial Lawyers Association and American Society of Appraisers. Author: "Fraud, Misrepresentation and Unfair Trade Practices," Oregon Torts, 1992, 1996; "Participant Liability Under the Oregon Securities Law After *Prince v. Brydon,*" 68 Oregon Law Review 885, 1989; "Class Actions," Oregon Civil Pleading and Practice, 1985, 1995, 1997, 2001. Intern, Center for Law and Social Policy, Washington, D.C., 1976. Arbitrator: Ameri-

(This Listing Continued)

STOLL STOLL BERNE LOKTING & SHLACHTER, P.C., Portland—Continued

can Arbitration Association; National Association of Securities Dealers; Arbitration Service of Portland. *Member:* Oregon State Bar; (Member: Securities Section; Executive Committee, 1987-1989); American Bar Association; Oregon Trial Lawyers Association (Chairman, Business Litigation Section, 1989); The Association of Trial Lawyers of America. ***PRACTICE AREAS:*** Antitrust Law; Securities Law; Franchise Law; Commercial Litigation. ***Email:*** gberne@ssbls.com

KEITH A. KETTERLING, born Charles City, Iowa, February 5, 1962; admitted to bar, 1987, Texas (inactive); 1991, Oregon. *Education:* Western Michigan University (B.B.A., 1984); University of Iowa (J.D., with honors, 1987). Author: "A Proposal for the Proper Use of Punitive Damages Against a Successor," 11 J. Corp. L. 765, 1986; "Post Tort Reform Contribution-A Defense Perspective," Texas Association of Defense Counsel, Fall Program 1990. Lecturer: Northwest Securities Institute, 1994; ADR Seminar, Oregon State Bar, 1994; Young Litigators Forum, 1995; Federal Bar Association New Lawyers Seminar, 1995 and 1999. Arbitrator, National Association of Securities Dealers. *Member:* Oregon State Bar; Oregon Trial Lawyers Association (Board of Governors, 1999-2001; Chairman, Business Litigation Section, 1993, 1996-1997). ***PRACTICE AREAS:*** Securities Litigation; Commercial Litigation. ***Email:*** kketterling@ssbls.com

STEVE D. LARSON, born Fergus Falls, Minnesota, November 7, 1957; admitted to bar, 1986, Oregon. *Education:* University of Minnesota (B.S., 1981); University of Oregon (J.D., 1986). Order of the Coif. Co-Editor of Oregon Civil Pleading and Practice Handbook. Author: Chapters on Securities Law, Contract Law and Trial Practice for Oregon Continuing Legal Education Treatises; 1992-2005; "Superbilt, Your First Right of Appeal," The Trial Lawyer, 1992. *Member:* Multnomah County Bar Association (Committee of the Judiciary, 2000-2002); Oregon State Bar (Chairman, Securities Regulation Section, 2003; Chairman, Business Litigation Section, 2004; Member: Executive Committee, Antitrust and Unfair Trade Practices Section, 1998-2002; Uniform Trial Court Rules Committee, 1998-2003; Practice and Procedure Committee, 1997-1999); Oregon Trial Lawyers Association (Board of Governors, 1995-1999). ***PRACTICE AREAS:*** Complex Business Litigation; Class Actions; Intellectual Property; Employment; Consumer Law; Securities Law. ***Email:*** slarson@ssbls.com

DAVID A. LOKTING, born Portland, Oregon, April 17, 1953; admitted to bar, 1980, Oregon. *Education:* Oregon State University and Portland State University (B.A., with honors, 1976); University of Oregon (J.D., 1980); New York University (LL.M. in taxation, 1983). Order of the Coif. Law Clerk, Hon. J.R. Campbell and Hon. Thomas F. Young, Oregon Court of Appeals, 1980-1981. *Member:* Oregon State Bar (Member: Taxation Section, Executive Committee, 1986; Legislative Committee, 1984-1986). ***PRACTICE AREAS:*** Tax Law; Partnerships and Limited Liability Companies; Corporate Law; Real Estate Law; Commercial Transactions. ***Email:*** dlokting@ssbls.com

ROBERT A. SHLACHTER, born Cleveland, Ohio, February 2, 1947; admitted to bar, 1974, California; 1991, Oregon. *Education:* Yale University (B.A., 1969); Georgetown University Law Center (J.D., 1974). Recipient: Awards: "Top Ten Trial Lawyers in Oregon," National Law Journal, 2000; Chambers USA Best Lawyers Litigator, 2005. Associate Editor, Georgetown University Law Journal, 1972-1974. Law Clerk to the Honorable Herbert Y.C. Choy, U.S. Court of Appeals Judge, Ninth Circuit, 1974-1975. Author: Oregon CLE Treatise Chapters on Computer Law, Litigation and Federal Practice. Editorial Board Member, "Internet Law and Business," 1999—. Delegate, Association of Yale Alumni, 1989-1992. *Member:* Multnomah County, Oregon State (Member, Sections on: Antitrust and Business Litigation) and American (Member, Sections on: Patent, Trademark and Copyright; Litigation) Bar Associations; State Bar of California; Association of Business Trial Lawyers (President, 1986-1987). ***PRACTICE AREAS:*** Intellectual Property; Commercial Litigation; Unfair Competition. ***Email:*** rshlachter@ssbls.com

N. ROBERT STOLL, born Washington, D.C., December 16, 1942; admitted to bar, 1969, Oregon and U.S. District Court, District of Oregon. *Education:* University of Wisconsin (B.S., cum laude, 1964); Harvard University (LL.B., 1968). Member, Harvard Law School Council, 1990-1994. Recipient: Top Ten Largest Verdicts in United States Award, 1993 and Top Ten Trial Lawyers in Oregon Award, 2000, National Law Journal; Distinguished Trial Lawyer of Year Award, 1997 and Volunteer Lawyer of the Year Award, 1995, Oregon Trial Lawyers Association; Access To Justice Award, 1998, Oregon State Bar. Law Clerk, Honorable Arno Denecke, Oregon Supreme Court, 1968-1969. Author: "Exclusive Dealing Arrangements and the Anti-Trust Laws," 6 Will. Law Review 17, 1970; "Reliance as an Element in 10B-5 Actions," 53 Oregon Law Review 169, 1974; "The Oregon Remedy for Securities Fraud and the Federal Remedy Under Rule 10B-5: A Comparative Analysis," 14 Willamette Law Journal 127, 1978. Lecturer on various topics including securities, antitrust, environmental, complex business litigation and trial strategy and technique. Editorial Advisory Board, Class Action Reports, 1983—. Member, Advisory Committee, Chief Criminal Court, Multnomah County, Oregon, 1972-1974. Member, Discovery Rules Committee, U.S. District Court for Oregon, 1983-1985. *Member:* Multnomah County (Member, Attorney Fees Committee, 1982-1983) and American (Member: Private Litigation Committee, Antitrust Law Section, 1980-1983; Model Jury Instructions in Accountant Liability Cases Committee, Litigation Section, 1997-1999) Bar Associations; Oregon State Bar (Member: Corrections and Detention Committee, 1972-1975; Jail Reform Committee, 1975; Chairman: Securities Section, 1980-1981; Antitrust Section, 1982-1983); Oregon Criminal Defense Association (Chairman, 1972-1973); Oregon Trial Lawyers Association (Secretary-Treasurer, 1975-1976); National Board of Directors of Lawyers' Committee for Civil Rights Under Law. ***PRACTICE AREAS:*** Major Litigation. ***Email:*** rstoll@ssbls.com

TIMOTHY DEJONG, born Eugene, Oregon, December 17, 1965; admitted to bar, 1991, Washington and U.S. District Court, Western District of Washington; 1994, Oregon and U.S. District Court, District of Oregon; U.S. Court of Appeals, Ninth Circuit. *Education:* Western Washington University (B.A., 1988); University of Oregon (J.D., 1991). Order of the Coif. Recipient, American Jurisprudence Award for Criminal Law, Trusts and Estates. Associate Editor, Oregon Law Review, 1989-1991. Law Clerk to Honorable Robert E. Jones, U.S. District Court, District of Oregon. *Member:* Federal Bar Association; Oregon State Bar; Washington State Bar Association; Oregon Trial Lawyers Association. ***PRACTICE AREAS:*** Intellectual Property; Securities Litigation; Business Litigation; Class Actions. ***Email:*** tdejong@ssbls.com

(This Listing Continued)

DAVID F. REES, born San Diego, California, July 25, 1967; admitted to bar, 1994, Oregon. *Education:* Stanford University (B.S., 1989); University of California at Berkeley (J.D., 1994). Articles Editor, Ecology Law Quarterly, 1993-1994. Co-Authored: "Abandoning The Quick Fix Mentality," CERCLA Remedy Selection, 21 Ecology Law Quarterly 785 (1994). *Member:* Multnomah and American Bar Associations; Oregon State Bar (Member, Environmental Natural Resources and Business Litigation Sections; Chairman, Pro Bono Committee, 2001); Oregon Trial Lawyers Association (Member: Environmental Natural Resources and Business Litigation Sections). ***PRACTICE AREAS:*** Securities Litigation; Environmental Litigation; Commercial Litigation. ***Email:*** drees@ssbls.com

SCOTT A. SHORR, born New York, New York, July 5, 1968; admitted to bar, 1996, Oregon. *Education:* Vassar College (A.B., 1990); University of Oregon; University of California at Berkeley (J.D., 1995). Recipient, American Jurisprudence Award in Contracts and Criminal Law. Associate Editor, Berkeley Journal of Employment and Labor Law, 1993-1995. Law Clerk, Honorable Richard L. Unis, Oregon Supreme Court, 1995-1996. Author: Oregon State Bar CLE Chapters on Fraud and Misrepresentation and Class Actions. *Member:* Multnomah and Federal Bar Associations; Oregon State Bar (Member, Executive Committee, Appellate Section); Oregon Trial Lawyers Association (Chair, Business Litigation Section, 2004). ***PRACTICE AREAS:*** Securities Litigation; Commercial Litigation; Appeals. ***Email:*** sshorr@ssbls.com

---

SANDRA L. KOHN, born Billings, Montana, November 24, 1949; admitted to bar, 1983, Oregon. *Education:* University of Montana (B.A., cum laude, 1980); University of Oregon (J.D., 1983). Order of the Coif. *Member:* Multnomah County Bar Association; Oregon State Bar. ***PRACTICE AREAS:*** Corporate Law; Real Estate Law; General Business Law. ***Email:*** skohn@ssbls.com

CHRISTINA L. BEATTY-WALTERS, born Wheeling, West Virginia, August 26, 1971; admitted to bar, 1998, Oregon. *Education:* Marshall University (B.A., summa cum laude, 1993); University of Oregon, School of Law (J.D., 1996). Order of the Coif. Recipient, American Jurisprudence Award in Legal Research and Writing. Executive Editor, Journal of Environmental Law and Litigation. Law Clerk, Judge Rick T. Haselton, Oregon Court of Appeals, 1996-1998. *Member:* Multnomah Bar Association; Oregon State Bar; Oregon Trial Lawyers Association. ***PRACTICE AREAS:*** Commercial Litigation; Intellectual Property; Unfair Competition. ***Email:*** tbeattywalters@ssbls.com

MARK A. FRIEL, born San Francisco, California, December 4, 1973; admitted to bar, 2000, Oregon and U.S. District Court, District of Oregon. *Education:* Willamette University (B.A., 1995); University of New Mexico (M.A., Latin American Studies, 1997); University of California, Berkeley (J.D., 2000). Co-Author: "Rule 21 Motions," Oregon Civil Pleading and Practice, 2001 Supp; "Attorney-Client Privilege and Work-Product Doctrine," Federal Civil Litigation, 2002 Supp. *Member:* Multnomah and Federal Bar Associations; Oregon State Bar (Chair, Pro Bono Committee, 2004); Oregon Trial Lawyers Association. ***LANGUAGES:*** Spanish. ***PRACTICE AREAS:*** Financial Fraud; Complex Business Litigation; Securities Litigation; Class Actions. ***Email:*** mfriel@ssbls.com

SUSANNA HENKE, born Eugene, Oregon, December 31, 1969; admitted to bar, 2002, Oregon. *Education:* Barnard College (B.A., 1993); Columbia University (J.D., 1999). *Member:* Multnomah County Bar Association; Oregon State Bar. ***PRACTICE AREAS:*** Business Transactions; Real Estate; Securities. ***Email:*** shenke@ssbls.com

JENNIFER A. WAGNER, born Des Moines, Iowa, July 13, 1974; admitted to bar, 2002, Oregon. *Education:* University of Michigan (B.A., with high distinction, 1996); Northwestern School of Law, Lewis and Clark (J.D., magna cum laude, 2002). *Member:* Multnomah County Bar Association; Oregon State Bar. ***PRACTICE AREAS:*** Complex Business Litigation; Class Actions; Securities Litigation. ***Email:*** jsammon@ssbls.com

EMILY COURTNAGE, born Eugene, Oregon, December 16, 1975; admitted to bar, 2002, Oregon. *Education:* Yale University (B.A., cum laude, 1997); University of North Carolina at Chapel Hill (J.D., 2002). Order of the Coif. *Member:* Multnomah Bar Association; Oregon State Bar; Oregon Trial Lawyers Association. ***PRACTICE AREAS:*** Complex Business Litigation; Class Actions; Securities Litigation. ***Email:*** ecourtnage@ssbls.com

JACOB S. GILL, born Salem Oregon, April 28, 1975; admitted to bar, 2003, Oregon; 2004, U.S. District Court, District of Oregon. *Education:* Portland State University (B.A., with high honors, 1998); University of Oregon (J.D., 2003). Order of the Coif. *Member:* Multnomah County Bar Association; Oregon State Bar. ***PRACTICE AREAS:*** Commercial Litigation; Business Transactions. ***Email:*** jgill@ssbls.com

JOSHUA L. ROSS, born San Antonio, Texas, September 28, 1972; admitted to bar, 2003, Oregon. *Education:* University of Texas at Austin (B.A., with honors, 2000); Lewis and Clark Law School (J.D., cum laude, 2003). Law Clerk, Judge Rick T. Haselton, Oregon Court of Appeals, 2003-2005. *Member:* Multnomah Bar Association; Oregon State Bar; Oregon Trial Lawyers Association. ***LANGUAGES:*** Hebrew. ***PRACTICE AREAS:*** Litigation; Complex Business Litigation; Securities. ***Email:*** jross@ssbls.com

OF COUNSEL

STEVEN C. BERMAN, born New York, N.Y., December 16, 1966; admitted to bar, 1995, Oregon; U.S. District Court, District of Oregon; U.S. Court of Appeals, Ninth Circuit; U.S. Supreme Court. *Education:* Amherst College (B.A., magna cum laude, 1989); Harvard University (J.D., cum laude, 1994). Law Clerk to Justice Susan P. Graber, Oregon Supreme Court, 1994-1996. *Member:* Oregon State Bar; Oregon Trial Lawyers Association. ***PRACTICE AREAS:*** Business Litigation; Employment Law; Appellate Practice. ***Email:*** sberman@ssbls.com

PETER F. STOLOFF, P.C.

Established in 1981

BANK OF AMERICA FINANCIAL CENTER, SUITE 600
121 S.W. MORRISON STREET
PORTLAND, OREGON 97204
Telephone: 503-224-4664
Fax: 503-224-3673
Email: pstoloff@aol.com
URL: http://www.lawyers.com/stoloff

Business Law, Health Care Law, Buying and Selling Businesses, Securities and Investments, Creditors Rights, Employee Benefits, Employment Contracts, Business Planning, Contracts, Antitrust, Insurance, Commercial Leasing, Real Estate, Business Start-Ups, Joint Ventures, Mergers, Tax Planning.

PETER F. STOLOFF, born Portland, Oregon, December 12, 1951; admitted to bar, 1978, Oregon; 2002, Idaho. *Education:* Stanford University (A.B., Economics, with honors, 1974); University of Oregon (J.D., 1977). Phi Beta Kappa. *Member:* Multnomah County Bar Association; Oregon State Bar (Chair, Health Law Section, 1992-1993); Oregon Society of Hospital Attorneys (President, 1989-1990); Idaho State Bar.

REPRESENTATIVE CLIENTS: Samaritan Health Services; Blue Cross and Blue Shield of Oregon; Albany General Hospital; St. Charles Medical Center; Silverton Hospital; Willamette Falls Hospital; Health Future, LLC.; Great West Life Insurance Co.; Fortis Insurance Co.; Mid-Columbia Medical Center; Peace Health; Columbia Memorial Hospital; St. Lukes Regional Medical Center.

MARC SUSSMAN, P.C.

1906 SOUTHWEST MADISON STREET, SUITE 1B
PORTLAND, OREGON 97205
Telephone: 503-221-0520; 1-866-230-1906
Fax: 503-221-1908
Email: sussmarc@qwest.net
URL: http://www.marcsussmanlaw.com

Criminal Defense in State & Federal Courts at Trial, Appellate, Post-Conviction and Habeas Corpus Levels, Capital Crimes, Homicides, White Collar, RICO, Sex Crimes, Drug Crimes and other Major Felonies, Parole and Probation.

FIRM PROFILE: Mr. Sussman is a sole practitioner with extensive criminal law experience in both state and federal courts (at both trial and appellate levels), including homicide and capital cases, RICO sex and drug crimes, white collar, post-conviction/habeas and complex cases. He limits his practice to select criminal law matters. The firm carries the highest legal ability rating in Martindale-Hubbell.

MARC SUSSMAN, born Newark, New Jersey, March 27, 1950; admitted to bar, 1977, Oregon; 1980, U.S. District Court, District of Oregon; 1990, U.S. Court of Appeals, Ninth Circuit; 1997, U.S. Supreme Court. *Education:* Georgetown University, School of Foreign Service; Rutgers University (B.A., cum laude, 1971); Willamette University (J.D., 1977). Phi Alpha Theta; Phi Beta Kappa. Law Clerk, Edward J. Sullivan, Legal Counsel to Governor Robert Straub, 1975-1977. Chapter Author: "Probation," 2005 Revision, Oregon State Bar Continuing Legal Education, Criminal Law; "Parole," 1986 and 1990; "Probation" and "Parole and Expungement", 1994 and 1998, Oregon State Bar Continuing Legal Education, Criminal Law. Speaker: OCDLA Annual Conference, Parole Board "Matrix System", 1979; OCDLA Death Penalty Conference: Defending against the Future Dangerousness Question, 2000 and Capital Case Jury Selection, 2001; OCDLA Post Conviction Conference, group facilatator, 2002; OCDLA Death Penalty Conference: "Effective Use of the Mitigation Investigator," 2005. *Member:* Multnomah County Bar Association; Oregon State Bar; National Association of Criminal Defense Lawyers; Oregon Criminal Defense Lawyer's Association (Capital Defenders Section). ***PRACTICE AREAS:*** Criminal Defense; Appellate Practice; Post-Conviction Remedies; Habeas Corpus.

SUSSMAN SHANK, LLP

Established in 1960

1000 S.W. BROADWAY
SUITE 1400
PORTLAND, OREGON 97205
Telephone: 503-227-1111
Telecopier: 503-248-0130
Email: info@sussmanshank.com
URL: http://www.sussmanshank.com

Full Service Commercial Practice including: Business, Tax and Real Estate; Business Organization and Transactions; Litigation and Dispute Resolution in all Courts; Construction Law, Employment Law, Environmental Law, Toxic Torts, Creditors' Rights and Bankruptcy Reorganization; Business Succession Planning, Estate and Wealth Preservation Planning and Probate.

FIRM PROFILE: Sussman Shank Wapnick Caplan & Stiles nka Sussman Shank, LLP was founded in 1960 by Gilbert Sussman, Jerome B. Shank and Norman Wapnick. With an initial focus on creditors' rights, bankruptcy, banking and finance, the Firm has expanded to become a broad general business, tax, estate planning, employment law, environmental law, toxic torts, charitable and non-profit corporations, real estate and extensive litigation practice.

MEMBERS OF FIRM

GILBERT SUSSMAN (1905-1985)

JEROME B. SHANK (Retired)

NORMAN WAPNICK (Retired)

(This Listing Continued)

BARRY P. CAPLAN, born Portland, Oregon, December 4, 1940; admitted to bar, 1965, Oregon. *Education:* University of Washington (B.A., 1962); University of California, Berkeley (LL.B., 1965). Author: "Consummating the Chapter 11 Plan of Reorganization," Bankruptcy Law, 1995 Supp.; "Collection of Judgments; Provisional Process," Civil Litigation Manual, 1993 and 1996 Supp., Oregon State Bar Continuing Legal Education; Articles on: "The Bankruptcy Reform Act of 1994," Setoff and Recoupment NACM, Oregon, Inc., Business Credit Journal. Jewish Federation of Portland (Member, Board of Directors, 1990-1996; Vice President, 1994-1996). NACM, Oregon, Inc. (Member, Board of Directors, 1993-1999; Chair, 1997-1998). *Member:* Multnomah County and American (Member: Business Law Section, Commercial Financial Services Committee) Bar Associations; Oregon State Bar (Chair, Board of Bar Examiners, 1979-1980); Commercial Law League of America (Chair, Western Region, 1986-1987); American Bankruptcy Institute (Member, Unsecured Trade Creditor's Committee). ***PRACTICE AREAS:*** Bankruptcy Reorganization; Creditors Rights; Commercial Litigation; Secured Transactions; Business Law. ***Email:*** barry@sussmanshank.com

WILLIAM N. STILES, born Portland, Oregon, March 28, 1938; admitted to bar, 1964, California; U.S. District Court, Central District of California; 1965, Oregon; U.S. District Court, District of Oregon; U.S. Court of Appeals, Ninth Circuit. *Education:* Yale University (B.A., 1960; LL.B., 1963). Law Clerk, U.S. Court of Appeals, Ninth Circuit, 1963-1964. Member, Board of Directors, 1986-1992 and President, 1989-1991, Oregon Law Institute. Member, Board of Directors, Associated General Contractors, Oregon-Columbia Chapter, 1994-1995. Member, Board of Directors, 1995-2003 and President, 1998-2003, Holladay Park Plaza, Inc. (a CCRC). Member, Board of Directors, Pacific Retirement Services, Inc., 1999-2003. *Member:* Oregon State Bar (Chair, Debtor-Creditor Rights Section, 1979-1980); State Bar of California. ***PRACTICE AREAS:*** Commercial Law; Business Law; Real Estate Law; Construction Law. ***Email:*** bills@sussmanshank.com

JEFFREY R. SPERE, born Aberdeen, Washington, June 3, 1950; admitted to bar, 1975, Oregon. *Education:* Pacific Lutheran University (B.B.A., cum laude, 1972); Willamette University (J.D., cum laude, 1975). Member, Willamette Law Journal, 1974-1975. Law Clerk to Robert Y. Thornton, Judge, Oregon Court of Appeals, 1975-1976. Co-Author: "Foreclosing Security Interests, Construction Liens," Oregon State Bar. Mortgage Foreclosure, PES, Inc., 1989; "Oregon Real Estate Leases," NBI, 1993. Judge Pro Tem, Multnomah County Circuit Court, 1989-1992. *Member:* American (Member, Subcommittees on: Financial Services; Loan Documentation; Real Estate Financing; Lender Liability, Dispute Resolution, 1984—) Bar Associations; Oregon State Bar (Executive Committee, 1991-1998 and Chair, 1996-1997, Debtor/Creditor Section). ***PRACTICE AREAS:*** Commercial Finance; Real Estate Finance; Foreclosures; Real Estate; Business Law; Employment Law; Mediation; Arbitration. ***Email:*** jeffs@sussmanshank.com

HOWARD M. LEVINE, born New York, N.Y., July 14, 1954; admitted to bar, 1980, Oregon; U.S. District Court, District of Oregon; 1981, U.S. Court of Appeals, Ninth Circuit; 1994, U.S. District Court, Eastern District of Wisconsin; 1999, Eastern District of Michigan; 2003, Washington; U.S. District Court, Eastern and Western Districts of Washington. *Education:* Monmouth University (B.S., cum laude, Business Administration, 1976); University of Toledo (J.D., 1979). Business Editor, University of Toledo Law Review, 1978-1979. Law Clerk to Hon. Donal D. Sullivan, U.S. Bankruptcy Judge, District of Oregon, 1980-1982. Author: "Foreclosing Security Interests, A Primer-Representing Secured Creditors in Bankruptcy Proceedings," Oregon State Bar Continuing Legal Education, 1984 Supp., 1988 and 1992; "Working with U.C.C. Article 9," Oregon Law Institute, 1988 Supp. and 1991. Co-Author: "Perfection of Security Interests in Personal Property and Fixtures," 1997 Supp.; "Bankruptcy Litigation," 1988 Supp., 1992 and 1995; "Bankruptcy Code Changes Affecting Family Law," 1996, Oregon State Bar Family and Juvenile Law Section; "Bankruptcy Issues for Insider Evildoers," Oregon State Bar Debtor Creditor Section, 2002; "Revised Article 9 Meets the Bankruptcy Trustee: By then it's Too Late," Multnomah Bar Association, 2004. Speaker: Oregon State Bar, 1984, 1988, 1993, 1996, 1997 and 2002; Oregon State Bar, Professional Liability Fund, Multnomah Bar Association, 1994, 2004. Panel Speaker: American Bar Association/Commercial Finance Subcommittee; National Conference of Bankruptcy Judges (San Francisco), 1991. *Member:* Oregon State Bar (Member, Sections on: Debtor-Creditor; Business Litigation); Washington State Bar Association; American Bankruptcy Institute. ***REPORTED CASES:*** Stringer v. Mitchell 261 BR 680 (Bankr. D. OR 2001); In re Crook 79 BR 475 (9th Cir BAP 1987); In re Coast Trading Co. 31 BR 670 (Bankr. D. OR (1983). ***PRACTICE AREAS:*** Bankruptcy Law; Creditors Rights; Corporate Reorganization Law; Commercial Litigation. ***Email:*** howard@sussmanshank.com

STUART I. TEICHER, born New York, N.Y., January 27, 1948; admitted to bar, 1976, Oregon; 1978, U.S. District Court, District of Oregon; U.S. Court of Appeals, Ninth Circuit; 1980, U.S. Supreme Court. *Education:* New York University (B.A., 1970); Northwestern School of Law, Lewis and Clark College (J.D., 1976). *Member:* Multnomah County and American (Member, Commercial and Banking Litigation Committee) Bar Associations; Oregon State Bar (Member, Committees on: Continuing Legal Education, 1982-1985; Future of the Legal Profession, 1986-1989; Member, 1991-1992 and Chair, 1993-1994, Federal Practice and Procedure Committee; Member, Executive Committee, Litigation Section, 1993). ***PRACTICE AREAS:*** Commercial Litigation; Business Torts; Employment Law Defense; Professional Liability. ***Email:*** stuart@sussmanshank.com

JEFFREY C. MISLEY, born Portland, Oregon, October 16, 1955; admitted to bar, 1985, Oregon; U.S. District Court, District of Oregon; 2003, Washington. *Education:* Lewis and Clark College (B.S., 1978); Northwestern School of Law, Lewis and Clark College (J.D., cum laude, 1985). Member, Northwestern School of Law of Lewis and Clark College Environmental Law Review, 1983-1985. Member, Organizing Committee, Northwest Bankruptcy Institute, 1989 and 1995-1997. Co-Author: "Foreclosing Security Interests, A Primer-Representing Secured Creditors in Bankruptcy Proceedings," Oregon State Bar Continuing Legal Education, 1988 Supp. and 1992; "Involuntary Bankruptcy," Oregon Commercial Practice Manual, 1995. *Member:* Oregon State Bar (Member, Executive Committee, Debtor/Creditor Section, 1998-2000); Washington State Bar Association. ***PRACTICE AREAS:*** Bankruptcy Litigation; Corporate Reorganization Law; Commercial Litigation; Creditors Rights; Secured Transactions. ***Email:*** jeffm@sussmanshank.com

JOHN E. McCORMICK, born Pasadena, California, June 19, 1953; admitted to bar, 1980, Oregon, U.S. District Court, District of Oregon and U.S. Tax Court. *Education:* University of Oregon (B.S., 1975); Willamette University (M.B.A., J.D., 1980). Certified Pub-

(This Listing Continued)

SUSSMAN SHANK, LLP, Portland—Continued

lic Accountant, Oregon, 1982. *Member:* Multnomah (Member, Corporate Section) and American (Member, Taxation Section) Bar Associations; Oregon State Bar (Member, Sections on: Taxation; Estate Planning; Business Law); Oregon State Society of CPA's (Past Chairman, Estate Planning Committee; Member, Federal Taxation Committee); American Institute of CPAs; National Academy of Elder Law Attorneys. ***PRACTICE AREAS:*** Corporate Law; Business Law; Estate Planning; Wealth Preservation; Succession Planning; Probate Law; Taxation. ***Email:*** johnm@sussmanshank.com

MICHAEL G. HALLIGAN, born Corvallis, Oregon, May 11, 1954; admitted to bar, 1982, Oregon; 1987, U.S. District Court, District of Oregon; 1992, U.S. Court of Appeals, Ninth Circuit. *Education:* Western Oregon State College (B.S., cum laude, 1978); Northwestern School of Law, Lewis and Clark College (J.D., 1982). Author: "Construction Liens," Foreclosing Security Interests, 1997, 2001; "Bonds and Undertakings," Civil Litigation Manual, 1993, 1999 and 2004. Co-Author: "Collection of Judgments; Provisional Process," Civil Litigation Manual, 1993, 1999 and 2004. *Member:* American (Member, Sections on: Litigation, Torts, Insurance and Business Law) Bar Association; Oregon State Bar (Member, Sections on: Litigation, Business Litigation and Construction). [Captain, JAGC, U.S. Air Force, 1983-1987]. ***PRACTICE AREAS:*** Commercial Litigation; Construction Litigation; Employer Liability. ***Email:*** mikeh@sussmanshank.com

ROBERT L. CARLTON, born St. Joseph, Missouri, December 21, 1953; admitted to bar, 1985, Oregon, U.S. District Court, District of Oregon; 1986, U.S. Court of Appeals, Ninth Circuit; 1989, U.S. District Court, Northern District of California; 2003 Washington. *Education:* University of Colorado at Boulder (B.A., 1982); Northwestern School of Law, Lewis and Clark College (J.D., 1985). Author: "Selected Bankruptcy Issues that Impact Business Transactions," Advising Oregon Business, Oregon State Bar Continuing Legal Education, 2003. Co-Author: "Bankruptcy Litigation," Oregon State Bar Continuing Legal Education, 1995. Co-Author and Speaker, "Commercial Loan Documentation," Oregon State Bar Continuing Legal Education, 1999. *Member:* Multnomah County and American Bar Associations; Oregon State Bar (Member, Debtor-Creditor Section); Washington State Bar Association. ***PRACTICE AREAS:*** Bankruptcy Law; Corporate Reorganization Law; Debtor and Creditor Rights Law; Commercial Law. ***Email:*** bobc@sussmanshank.com

THOMAS W. STILLEY, born Marshall, Texas, October 25, 1954; admitted to bar, 1988, Oregon; 1989, U.S. District Court, District of Oregon; 1992, Washington; U.S. District Court, Eastern and Western Districts of Washington. *Education:* University of Texas (B.B.A., 1977); University of Houston (J.D., 1988). *Member:* Washington State Bar Association; Oregon State Bar (Member: Debtor/Creditor Law Section; Executive Committee, 2001-2004; Legislative Committee, 1990—; Chair, 1998-2001); American Bankruptcy Institute. ***PRACTICE AREAS:*** Bankruptcy; Creditors Rights; Provisional Remedies. ***Email:*** tom@sussmanshank.com

NENA COOK, born Salt Lake City, Utah, January 25, 1966; admitted to bar, 1991, Oregon; U.S. District Court, District of Oregon; 1992, Washington; U.S. District Court, Eastern and Western Districts of Washington; 2000, U.S. Court of Appeals, Ninth Circuit. *Education:* Gonzaga University (B.A., 1988); Willamette University (J.D., 1991). *Member:* Washington State Bar Association; Oregon State Bar (Chair, 1998-1999 and Member, Federal Practice and Procedure Committee; Ninth Circuit Judicial Conference Representative, Judicial Screening Committee; Member, Board of Governors, 2002—; President, 2005). ***PRACTICE AREAS:*** Complex Litigation; Federal Civil Litigation; Employer Liability. ***Email:*** nena@sussmanshank.com

GEORGE W. McKALLIP, JR., born Philadelphia, Pennsylvania, September 8, 1958; admitted to bar, 1984, Oregon and Washington. *Education:* Allegheny College (B.A., cum laude, 1981); Northwestern School of Law, Lewis and Clark College (J.D., cum laude, 1984). *Member:* Washington State Bar Associations; Oregon State Bar. ***PRACTICE AREAS:*** Environmental Law; Toxic Torts; Products Liability; Real Estate Litigation; Real Estate; Commercial Litigation. ***Email:*** skip@sussmanshank.com

SUSAN S. FORD, born Portland, Oregon, March 12, 1958; admitted to bar, 1984, Oregon; 1986, U.S. District Court, District of Oregon; 2003 Washington and U.S. District Court, Western and Eastern Districts of Washington. *Education:* Lewis and Clark College (B.A., Political Science, 1980); Northwestern School of Law, Lewis and Clark College (J.D., cum laude, 1984). American Jurisprudence Award for Torts. Associate Editor, Environmental Law, 1983-1984. Author: Comment, "Who Will Compensate the Victims of Asbestos-Related Diseases? Manville's Chapter 11 Fuels A Fire," 13 Envtl. L., 1998. *Member:* Multnomah County and Washington State Bar Associations; Oregon State Bar (Member, Debtor Creditor Section). ***PRACTICE AREAS:*** Creditors Rights Law; Bankruptcy Law; Commercial Law; Secured Lending; Loan Workouts; Loan Restructuring; Commercial Loans; Banking Litigation; Bank Directors and Officers Liability. ***Email:*** susanf@sussmanshank.com

JASON W. ALEXANDER, born Portland, Oregon, November 7, 1969; admitted to bar, 1996, Oregon; 1997, Washington; 1998, U.S. District Court, District of Oregon, U.S. District Court, Eastern and Western Districts of Washington. *Education:* University of the Pacific (B.S., Finance, 1992); Willamette University, College of Law (J.D., 1996). *Member:* Washington State Bar Association; Oregon State Bar. ***PRACTICE AREAS:*** Construction Law; Commercial Litigation; Creditor Rights; Business Law. ***Email:*** jason@sussmanshank.com

JEFFREY S. TARR, born Los Angeles, California, September 15, 1963; admitted to bar, 1989, California; 1995, Oregon. *Education:* University of Oregon; University of California, Los Angeles (B.A., 1986); Loyola Marymount University Law School (J.D., 1989); Golden Gate University (M.S., Taxation, 1993). Adjunct Faculty, MBA Program, University of Phoenix (Oregon Campus). *Member:* Multnomah and American Bar Associations; State Bar of California; Oregon State Bar. ***PRACTICE AREAS:*** Corporate Law; Business Law; Partnership Law; Taxation; Real Estate; Trusts and Estates; Wills; Probate; Contracts. ***Email:*** jefft@sussmanshank.com

DARIN D. HONN, born Garnett, Kansas, December 15, 1962; admitted to bar, 1988, Oregon; U.S. District Court, District of Oregon; 1996, Washington and U.S. District Court, Western District of Washington. *Education:* Nebraska Wesleyan University (B.S., Economics, 1985); University of Nebraska (J.D. with distinction, 1988). Pi Gamma Mu; Omicron Delta Epsilon; Blue Key. Member, Order of Barristers. Vice Chair, Moot Court Board. *Member:* Oregon State Bar (Member, Real Estate Section). ***PRACTICE AREAS:*** Real Estate Law; Business Law; Securities Fraud; Trademark; Civil Litigation; Estate Planning; Probate; Construction Law. ***Email:*** darin@sussmanshank.com

ASSOCIATES

DALLAS G. THOMSEN, born Wenatchee, Washington, March 9, 1976; admitted to bar, 2002, Washington; 2003, Oregon. *Education:* Washington State University (B.A., 1998); Gonzaga University (J.D., 2001); University of Florida (LL.M, 2002). *Member:* Oregon State Bar (Member: Business Law, Estate Planning and Administration, and Taxation Sections); Washington State and American (Member, Taxation Section) Bar Associations. ***PRACTICE AREAS:*** Taxation; Corporate Law; Business Law; Estate Planning; Wealth Preservation; Trademarks; Intellectual Property; Probate; Trust Administration. ***Email:*** dallas@sussmanshank.com

ELIZABETH A. SEMLER, born Washington, D.C., March 1, 1964; admitted to bar, 1992, New York; 1998, Oregon. *Education:* Colgate University (B.A., 1986); Emory University, School of Law (J.D., 1991). Notes and Comments Editor, Bankruptcy Developments Journal. Author: "Interpreting Section 525 (a) of the Bankruptcy Code," 7 Bankr. Dev. J. 595, 1990; "Doing Business with Indian Tribes-Not Business as Usual," NACM Journal October 2001; "Family and Medical Leave Rights Under Federal and Oregon Law," Sussman Shank Employment Law Seminar, February 2002; "Writing the Employee Handbook in Oregon," Lorman Education Seminar, September 2002; "Periodic Reporting By Employees On Family Leave," Daily Journal of Commerce, April 2003; "Oregon and Federal Law: Consistent on Workers' Status but Divergent on Wage Claims," Sussman Shank Newsletter, Fall 2003; "When Does An Employer's Burden To Prove Undue Hardship Arise?" Daily Journal of Commerce, July 2004; "Train Your Supervisors to Respond Appropriately to Employees on FMLA Leave," Sussman Shank Newsletter, Fall 2004; "Employee Termination: Err on the Side of Payment," Oregon Business, September 2005. *Member:* Multnomah County Bar Association; Oregon State Bar. ***PRACTICE AREAS:*** Commercial Litigation (60%); Employment Liability Litigation (40%). ***Email:*** lizs@sussmanshank.com

MICHAEL C. WETZEL, born Philadelphia, Pennsylvania, October 30, 1968; admitted to bar, 1995, Oregon; U.S. District Court, District of Oregon; 1998, U.S. Tax Court; 2000, U.S. Court of Appeals, Ninth Circuit; 2003 Washington. *Education:* Willamette University (B.S., 1991); Vanderbilt University (J.D., 1995). *Member:* Oregon State Bar; Washington State Bar Association. [1st Lt., Army National Guard JAGC, 2002—]. ***PRACTICE AREAS:*** Business; Tax Litigation; Estate Planning and Litigation; Trust Planning and Litigation; Real Estate; Domestic Relations. ***Email:*** mikew@sussmanshank.com

WILLIAM G. FIG, born Silver Springs, Maryland, August 2, 1967; admitted to bar, 1995, Oregon; U.S. District Court, District of Oregon; 2003, Washington. *Education:* University of North Carolina at Chapel Hill (B.A., 1989); Lewis and Clark College (J.D., 1995). *Member:* Multnomah County and Washington State Bar Associations; Oregon State Bar. ***PRACTICE AREAS:*** Commercial Litigation; Environmental Law; Construction Law. ***Email:*** billf@sussmanshank.com

LAURIE R. HAGER, born Boston, Massachusetts, November 27, 1975; admitted to bar, 2001, California, Oregon and U.S. District Court, District of Oregon and Central and Eastern Districts of California. *Education:* University of Connecticut (B.A., 1997); University of Colorado at Boulder (J.D., 2000). *Member:* State Bar of California; Oregon State Bar. ***PRACTICE AREAS:*** Commercial Litigation; Employment Law; Construction Law; Environmental Law. ***Email:*** laurie@sussmanshank.com

JEFF C. DUNCAN BRECHT, born Bloomington, Illinois, December 29, 1961; admitted to bar, 1996, Oregon; 1997, U.S. District Court, District of Oregon. *Education:* Illinois State University (B.S., 1985; M.S., 1987); Northern Illinois University (J.D., magna cum laude, 1996). Editor, Northern Illinois University Law Review. Recipient: American Jurisprudence Award; Corpus Juris Secondum Award. Author: "Non-Competition Agreements That Won't Fly," Oregon Business, May 2004; "Office Odor Sensitivity and the Americans with Disabilities Act," Oregon State Bar Bulletin, April 2004; "Gimme My Personnel File," Oregon Business, February 2004; "Federal Court Prognosticates on Oregon's Email Privacy Law," Portland Human Resource Management Association, January 2004; "Arbitration Agreements in Oregon: A Primer for Employers," Oregon Business, December 2003; "Is There a Hole in Your Deep Pockets? Franchiser Liability for Bad Things That Can Happen at a Franchise," Franchise Times, January 2001; "Prairie Justice: Oregon's Merry Ol' Town of 'Os'," Oregon State Bar Bulletin, July 1999; "The Millennium Bug: Defending the Dilatory with Diligently Documented Due Diligence," Oregon State Bar Bulletin, July 1998; "Armageddon and the Millennium Bug," The Administrator's Advantage, November/December 1998; "Y2K: The Countdown Has Begun," OLMANET: Oregon Legal Management Association, September/October 1998; "Oregon's Procedural Due Process and the Necessity of Judicial Review of Punitive Damage Awards: Honda Motor Company v. Oberg," 15 Northern Illinois Law Review 337 (1995); "9403 Illinois State Bar Association Couns, 7, (1994) (Reviewing Douglas Richmond, "Products Liability: Corporate Successors and the Duty to Warn")," Baylor Law Review (1993). *Member:* Federal and Multnomah County Bar Associations; Oregon State Bar (Member, Federal Practice and Procedure Committee; Member, Sections on: Business Litigation; Labor and Employment; Litigation). ***PRACTICE AREAS:*** Employment Law (50%); Business Litigation (50%). ***Email:*** jeffb@sussmanshank.com

HEATHER A. KMETZ, born Queens, New York, February 18, 1971; admitted to bar, 2000, Oregon; 2005, Washington. *Education:* Northwestern University (B.S.J., 1992); Northwestern School of Law of Lewis and Clark College (J.D., 2000). *Member:* Multnomah County, Washington State and American (Member, Taxation Section) Bar Associations; Oregon State Bar (Member, Sections on: Taxation, Estate Planning and Administration). ***PRACTICE AREAS:*** Taxation; Estate Planning; Wealth Preservation; Business Succession Planning; Probate Administration; Nonprofit Organizations Law; Special Needs Planning. ***Email:*** heather@hkspdx.com

SPECIAL COUNSEL

ROBERT W. NUNN, born Salem, Oregon, September 20, 1950; admitted to bar, 1976, Oregon; 1986, Washington. *Education:* Willamette University (B.S., 1972); Northeastern University (M.B.A., Accounting, 1973); University of Oregon (J.D., 1976). Former Em-

(This Listing Continued)

ployment: Partner, Schwabe, Williamson & Wyatt, 1976-1992; Preston Gates & Ellis, 1992-1996. Managing Partner, Nunn Motschenbacher & Blattner, LLP, 1996-2001. Trustee, Willamette University. Chair, Professional Liability Fund. *Member:* Washington State Bar Association; Oregon State Bar. ***PRACTICE AREAS:*** Business Transactions; Business Taxation. ***Email:*** bobn@sussmanshank.com

MARTIN P. MEYERS, born Fort Wayne, Indiana, October 18, 1956; admitted to bar, 1986, New Mexico; 1999, Oregon; 2003 Washington. *Education:* University of Arizona (B.A., Psychology, 1979); Valparaiso University (J.D., 1986). *Member:* State Bar of New Mexico; Oregon State Bar; Washington State and American Bar Associations. ***REPORTED CASES:*** In Re Veretto, 131 B.R. 732 (Bank v. D.N.M., 1991); In Re Blair, 125 B.R. 303 (Bank v. D.N.M., 1991). ***PRACTICE AREAS:*** Bankruptcy; Creditors Rights; Commercial Law. ***Email:*** martin@sussmanshank.com

MICHAEL D. LEVELLE, born Spokane, WA, February 25, 1951; admitted to bar, 1990, Oregon; 1995, Washington. *Education:* University of Montana (B.A., Social Work, 1987); Willamette University (J.D., 1990). *Member:* Oregon State Bar; Washington State Bar Association; National Academy of Elder Law Attorneys. ***PRACTICE AREAS:*** Estate Planning; Probate Law; Estate Litigation; Trust Litigation; Mediation; Elder Law.

JOHN A. SCHWIMMER, born New York, N.Y.; admitted to bar, 1983, California; 2004, Oregon; 2005, Washington. *Education:* Brown University (B.A., magna cum laude, 1980); Boalt Hall School of Law, University of California (J.D., 1983). Phi Beta Kappa; Order of the Coif. *Member:* Multnomah County, Los Angeles County, Washington State and American Bar Associations; State Bar of California; Oregon State Bar. ***PRACTICE AREAS:*** Complex Litigation; Class Action Defense; Intellectual Property Litigation; Corporate Litigation; Franchise Litigation; Real Estate Litigation; Unfair Competition. ***Email:*** johns@sussmanshank.com

HARRY M. HANNA, born Portland, Oregon, January 13, 1936; admitted to bar, 1966, Oregon; 1967, U.S. Tax Court; 1970, U.S. District Court, District of Oregon; 1971, U.S. Supreme Court; 1973, U.S. Court of Federal Claims; 2005, Washington. *Education:* University of Portland and University of Oregon (B.S., 1958); Northwestern School of Law of Lewis and Clark College (J.D., 1966). Delta Theta Phi. Author: "Type E and F Reorganizations," Ch. 38, "A Recapitalization: The E Reorganization of the Internal Revenue Code," Ch. 65, II Advising Oregon Businesses (Ore. State Bar CLE, 1972, 1989, 1994, 1997, 2001). Adjunct Professor of Law, Lewis and Clark College Law School, Advanced Land Finance Course, 1976-1977. Pro tem Judge, District Court of the State of Oregon, 1973-1977. Member, Board of Trustees, Emanuel Hospital Foundation, 1989-1977. President, Rotary Club of East Portland, 1989-1990. President, Central Catholic High School Board, 1992-1996. Chairman, Life Flight Development Committee, 1994—. Currently Listed in Who's Who in American Law. *Member:* Multnomah County, Washington State, Federal and American (Member, Sections on: Business Law; Real Property; Probate and Trust Law; Taxation) Bar Associations; Oregon State Bar (Member, Sections on: Real Estate and Land Use; Construction Law; Taxation). ***PRACTICE AREAS:*** Real Estate; Real Estate Taxation; Corporate Law; Business Law; Trusts and Estates; Probate. ***Email:*** harry@sussmanshank.com

REPRESENTATIVE CLIENTS: AT&T Corporation; Bank of America N.A.; Billing Concepts, Inc.; Capital Associates; Caterpillar Financial Services Corp.; Coast Crane Equipment Co.; Columbia River Sand & Gravel, Inc.; Consolidated Freightways Corp.; Durham & Bates Agencies; Electric Lightwave; Emery Worldwide; Evergreen Healthcare; Familian Northwest, Inc.; First American Title Insurance Co.; Food Services of America, Inc.; Forbes International, Inc.; The Halton Co., KLA- Tencor, Inc.; MCI- Worldcom Network Services; Mercedes Benz Capital Corp.; NACM- Oregon Service Co.; Northwest Equity Investments, Inc.; OHSU Department of Diagnostic Radiation; OHSU Deptartment of Urology; OHSU Dotter Interventional Institute; Oregon Electric Group; ORIX Financial Services; P/M Industries; Performance Contracting, Inc.; St. Paul Insurance Co.; Stewart Enterprises, Inc.; Stewart- Stiles Tuck Lines, Inc.; Shindaiwa, Inc.; Southland Industries, Inc.; Taylormade Products, Inc.; Ticor Title Insurance Co.; Transportation Factoring, Inc. dba Transfac; Travelers Insurance; Viking Freight System; West Coast Bank; West Coast Shoe Co.

SWANSON, THOMAS & COON

Established in 1980

THOMAS MANN BUILDING
820 SW SECOND AVENUE, SUITE 200
PORTLAND, OREGON 97204
Telephone: 503-228-5222
Fax: 503-273-9175
URL: http://www.stc-law.com

Personal Injury and Products Liability (Vehicles machinery, construction accidents, bicycles, tobacco, asbestos), Medical Malpractice, Automobile Accidents, Wrongful Death, Employee Benefits, Workers' Compensation, (including Longshore), Social Security, Environmental Litigation, Public Sector Labor and Pensions, Long Term Disability (ERISA), Legal Malpractice, Class Actions, Trial and Appellate.

FIRM PROFILE: Swanson, Thomas & Coon was founded in 1980. Partners and associates share a common political interest in representing individuals, labor organizations and other non-profit groups against corporate, insurance and government interests.

MEMBERS OF FIRM

DOUGLAS A. SWANSON, born Los Angeles, California, March 21, 1953. (1953-2004)

RAYMOND F. THOMAS, born Minneapolis, Minnesota, December 5, 1951; admitted to bar, 1979, Oregon; 1981, U.S. District Court, District of Oregon. *Education:* Quincy College (B.A., 1975); Northwestern School of Law (J.D., 1979). *Member:* Multnomah Bar Association (Member, Court Liaison Committee, 1990-1993; Chair, 1992-1993); Oregon State Bar; National Lawyers Guild (Chair, Litigation Committee, 1987-1993); Oregon Trial Lawyers Association (Chair, Public Justice Committee, 1995—; Member, Board of Directors, 1996-1997); The Association of Trial Lawyers of America (Sustaining Member); Attorneys Information Exchange Group (Co-chair, Board of Directors, 1992-1994); Bicycle Transportation Alliance (Member, Board of Directors, 1995-1996). ***PRACTICE AREAS:*** Personal Injury; Products Liability. ***Email:*** rthomas@stc-law.com

(This Listing Continued)

JAMES S. COON, born Chicago, Illinois, May 7, 1949; admitted to bar, 1977, Oregon, U.S. District Court, District of Oregon, U.S. Court of Appeals, Ninth Circuit, and U.S. Supreme Court. *Education:* Yale University (B.A., 1971); Northwestern University School of Law (J.D., 1977). Cornelius Honor Society. Editor-in-Chief, Environmental Law, 1976-1977. Instructor, Administrative Law, Lewis & Clark Law School, 1978, 1980. *Member:* Oregon State Bar; National Lawyers Guild; Oregon Trial Lawyers Association; Amicus Committee Co-Chair, 2002-2004. ***PRACTICE AREAS:*** Appellate Practice; Personal Injury; Products Liability; Workers Compensation; Social Security; ERISA; Environmental Law. ***Email:*** jcoon@stc-law.com

ASSOCIATES

MEGAN E. GLOR, born New York, N.Y., October 4, 1963; admitted to bar, 1990, New Jersey and Pennsylvania; 1993, Oregon, U.S. District Court, District of Oregon and U.S. Court of Appeals, Ninth Circuit. *Education:* Douglas College, Rutgers University (B.A., 1985); Rutgers University, Newark (J.D., with honors, 1990). *Member:* Oregon State Bar. ***PRACTICE AREAS:*** Employee Benefits Litigation. ***Email:*** mglor@stc-law.com

MARGARET F. WEDDELL, born Chicago, Illinois, March 29, 1951; admitted to bar, 1993, Oregon and Washington; U.S. District Court, District of Oregon. *Education:* University of Missouri (B.S., 1976); Lewis and Clark College (J.D., 1993). Phi Delta Phi. *Member:* Oregon State Bar; Washington State Bar Association; Oregon Trial Lawyers Association; Oregon Women Lawyers Association; Oregon Workers Compensation Attorneys; The Association of Trial Lawyers of America. ***PRACTICE AREAS:*** Personal Injury; Employment Law; Workers' Compensation. ***Email:*** mweddell@stc-law.com

SHARON MAYNARD, born Ashland, Wisconsin, April 16, 1961; admitted to bar, 1992, Oregon; 2001, U.S. District Court, District of Oregon. *Education:* University of California at Los Angeles (B.A., 1984); Albany Law School of Union University (J.D., 1992). Member: Owen M. Planner Inn of Court, 1993-1998; Oregon Criminal Defense Lawyers Association, 1992-2001; Oregon Trial Lawyers Association, 2001; Multnomah County Bar Association, 2001. *Member:* Oregon State Bar;. ***PRACTICE AREAS:*** Social Security. ***Email:*** smaynard@stc-law.com

CYNTHIA F. NEWTON, born Pittsburgh, Pennsylvania, August 29, 1960; admitted to bar, 1987, California; 2004, Oregon. *Education:* Washington State University (B.A., with honors, 1982) Phi Beta Kappa, Phi Kappa Phi; Hastings College of the Law, University of California (J.D., 1987). Member, Hastings International and Comparative Law Review. *Member:* Oregon Trial Lawyers Association. ***PRACTICE AREAS:*** Personal Injury; Products Liability; Medical Malpractice. ***Email:*** cnewton@stc-law.com

ANN T. BOYLAN, born New York, N.Y., April 2, 1974; admitted to bar, 2004, Oregon and U.S. District Court, District of Oregon. *Education:* George Mason University (B.A., 1998); Northwestern School of Law (J.D., 2004). *Member:* Oregon State Bar; Oregon Trial Lawyers Association. ***PRACTICE AREAS:*** Workers Compensation. ***Email:*** aboylan@stc-law.com

BRUCE G. THOMPSON

111 S.W. COLUMBIA STREET, SUITE 1000
PORTLAND, OREGON 97201
Telephone: 503-226-6491
Fax: 503-228-6392
URL: http://www.btelderlaw.com
Email: bruce@btelderlaw.com
URL: http://www.lawyers.com/btelderlaw

Elder Law, Wills and Probate (in OR, WA and CA), Wills and Trusts, Estate and Gift Tax Planning, Guardianship (in OR, WA and CA), Estate Taxation, Medicaid Planning.

BRUCE G. THOMPSON, born Portland, Oregon, July 31, 1951; admitted to bar, 1981, California; 1982, Oregon; 1999, Washington. *Education:* United States Naval Academy (B.S., 1973); University of California at Los Angeles (J.D., 1981). Member, University of California at Los Angeles Law Review, 1980-1981. *Member:* Washington State Bar Association; Oregon State Bar (Member, Taxation, Estate Planning, Administration and Elder Law Sections); State Bar of California; National Academy of Elder Law Attorneys, Inc. [U.S. Navy, Lt. 1973-1978]. ***PRACTICE AREAS:*** Elder Law; Probate; Guardianship; Medicaid Planning; Wills; Estate Planning; Trusts and Estates; Tax Planning; Estate and Gift Taxation.

THE THOMPSON LAW FIRM

Established in 1994

9400 SW BARNES ROAD, SUITE 300
PORTLAND, OREGON 97225-6658
Telephone: 503-292-8990
Fax: 503-292-9040
URL: http://www.amthompsonlawfirm.com
Email: anne@amthompsonlawfirm.com
URL: http://www.ttlf.com

Wills, Trusts and Estates, Estate Planning, Probate, Taxation, Tax Planning, Guardianship, Conservatorships, Contracts, Closely Held Business, Small Business Law, Partnership Law, Limited Liability Company Law, Business Planning.

FIRM PROFILE: Our firm handles legal matters in the following areas: trusts, estates, wills, probate, small business and taxation issues. The business practice includes contracts, business planning, closely-held business, corporate, limited liability companies, partnerships and small business.

ANNE M. THOMPSON, born Salem, Oregon, October 23, 1958; admitted to bar, 1989, Oregon. *Education:* Emory University (B.A., 1979); University of Georgia (J.D., 1988). *Member:* Oregon State Bar (Member: Executive Committee, Estate Planning and Administration Section; State Professional Responsibility Disciplinary Board, 1999-

(This Listing Continued)

THE THOMPSON LAW FIRM, Portland—Continued

2002); Estate Planning Council of Portland; Washington County Bar Association (Member, Local Professional Responsibility Committee, 1995-1998; President, Washington County Public Affairs Forum, 1996-1997). ***PRACTICE AREAS:*** Wills; Trusts and Estates; Estate Planning; Probate; Taxation; Tax Planning; Guardianship; Conservatorship; Contracts; Closely Held Business Law; Small Business Law; Partnership Law; Limited Liability Company Law; Business Planning. ***Email:*** anne@amthompsonlawfirm.com

TICHENOR DZIUBA & COLETTI LLP

1100 S.W. 6TH AVENUE, SUITE 1450
PORTLAND, OREGON 97204
Telephone: 503-224-3333
Fax: 503-224-2949
URL: http://www.tdcinjurylaw.com

Personal Injury, Product Liability, Maritime Injuries, Medical Malpractice, Construction Accidents.

KEITH E. TICHENOR, born Portland, Oregon, January 31, 1944; admitted to bar, 1969, Oregon and U.S. District Court, District of Oregon; 1988, U.S. Court of Appeals, Ninth Circuit. *Education:* Wesleyan University (B.A., 1966); University of Washington (J.D., 1969). Phi Beta Kappa. Listed in the publication, "The Best Lawyers in America." *Member:* Multnomah County and American Bar Associations; Oregon State Bar (Member, Committee on Continuing Legal Education, 1983-1986; Chairman, Subcommittee on Publications, 1986-1987; Member Board of Governors, 1988-1991; Treasurer, 1990-1991); The Association of Trial Lawyers of America; American Judicature Society; American Board of Trial Advocates (Vice President, Oregon Chapter, 1994-1996; President, Oregon Chapter, 1996-1998; National Delegate, 1998—); Fellow, American College of Trial Lawyers. ***PRACTICE AREAS:*** Medical Malpractice; Products Liability; Personal Injury. ***Email:*** keitht@tdcinjurylaw.com

DANIEL C. DZIUBA, born Rochester, New York, September 8, 1948; admitted to bar, 1975, New York, U.S. District Court, Western District of New York, Oregon and U.S. District Court, District of Oregon; 1977, California; 1978, U.S. District Court, Northern District of California; 1982, U.S. Court of Appeals, Ninth Circuit. *Education:* St. John Fisher College (B.A., 1970); Albany Law School of Union University (J.D., 1974). Listed in the publication, "The Best Lawyers in America." *Member:* Multnomah County and New York State Bar Associations; Oregon State Bar (Member: Committee on, Uniform Jury Instructions, 1987-1991; House of Delegates, 1996-2002); Oregon Trial Lawyers Association; The Association of Trial Lawyers of America; American Board of Trial Advocates. ***PRACTICE AREAS:*** Personal Injury Law; Admiralty Law; Construction Accidents; Product Liability. ***Email:*** dand@tdcinjurylaw.com

JOHN M. COLETTI, born Seattle, Washington, November 10, 1968; admitted to bar, 1994, Oregon and U.S. District Court, District of Oregon; U.S. Court of Appeals, Ninth Circuit; 2003, Washington. *Education:* University of Washington (B.A., 1991); Willamette University College of Law (J.D., 1994). Phi Delta Phi. Associate Editor, Willamette Journal of Law, 1992-1994. Listed in the publication, "The Best Lawyers in America." *Member:* Multnomah County Bar Association; Oregon State Bar; Oregon Trial Lawyers Association; Association of Trial Lawyers of America. ***PRACTICE AREAS:*** Personal Injury; Products Liability; Maritime Accidents; Medical Malpractice; Construction Accidents. ***Email:*** johnc@tdcinjurylaw.com

OF COUNSEL

WILLIAM A. GALBREATH, born Portland, Oregon, April 23, 1930; admitted to bar, 1959, Oregon. *Education:* Willamette University (B.A., 1954; LL.B., 1957). Phi Delta Phi. Municipal Judge, Milton-Freewater, 1960-1987. *Member:* Oregon State Bar (Member, Board of Governors, 1978-1981; Secretary, 1980-1981; Director, Professional Liability Fund, 1981-1984); The Association of Trial Lawyers of America; Oregon Trial Lawyers Association. ***PRACTICE AREAS:*** General Practice; Probate; Business; Farm Chemical Litigation; Construction; Product Liability; Personal Injury. ***Email:*** billg@tdcinjurylaw.com

TONKON TORP LLP

(Formerly, Tonkon, Torp, Galen, Marmaduke & Booth LLP)
1600 PIONEER TOWER
888 S.W. FIFTH AVENUE
PORTLAND, OREGON 97204-2099
Telephone: 503-221-1440
Fax: 503-274-8779
URL: http://www.tonkon.com

Admiralty, Antitrust and Trade Regulation, Business, Communications, Corporate Finance, Creditors' Rights and Bankruptcy, E-Commerce, Emerging Growth, Employee Benefits, Employment and Labor, Energy, Entertainment, Environmental and Natural Resources, Immigration, Intellectual Property, International, Litigation, Media, Mergers and Acquisitions, Nonprofits, Real Estate/Real Property, Securities, Sports, Taxation, Technology, Telecommunications, Utilities, Wealth (Estate) Planning and Administration.

FIRM PROFILE: Tonkon Torp LLP, founded in 1974, is a full-service business law firm dedicated to meeting the complex legal and business needs of its clients. The firm's 70 attorneys regularly represent individuals and a broad range of public, private and emerging growth companies, venture capital funds, real estate developers, utilities and banks operating regionally, nationally and internationally. The firm changed to its present name from Tonkon, Torp, Galen, Marmaduke & Booth in 1997.

Exept where noted, all Tonkon Torp attorneys are members of the Oregon State Bar, the Multnomah Bar Association and the American Bar Association.

(This Listing Continued)

MEMBERS OF FIRM

ROBERT E. HIRSHON, born Portland, Maine, April 2, 1948; admitted to bar, 1973, Maine (Not admitted in Oregon). *Education:* University of Michigan (B.A., with distinction, 1970; J.D., 1973). Member, Editorial Board, Michigan Journal of Law Reform, 1972-1973. Fellow, American Bar Foundation (State Chair, 1993-2000). *Member:* Maine State (President, 1986) and American (President, 2001-2002; Chair, Standing Committee on Membership, 1997-2000; International Tort and Insurance Law Practice Committee, 1988-1989; Standing Committee on Lawyers Public Service Responsibility, 1990-1993) Bar Associations; Maine Bar Foundation (President, 1990). ***Email:*** bobh@tonkon.com

MOE M. TONKON (1905-1984)

FREDERICK H. TORP (1913-2003)

DAVID S. AMAN, born Portland, Oregon, October 6, 1971; admitted to bar, 1996, Oregon; 1997, U.S. District Court, District of Oregon. *Education:* Lewis and Clark College (B.A., 1993; J.D., summa cum laude, 1996). *Member:* Oregon State Bar; Multnomah and American Bar Associations. ***PRACTICE AREAS:*** Intellectual Property; Antitrust; Trade Regulation. ***Email:*** davida@tonkon.com

TERRY W. BAKER, born Pine River, Minnesota, May 5, 1941; admitted to bar, 1968, Oregon; 1970, U.S. Claims Court. *Education:* Oregon State University (B.S., 1963); University of Southern California (J.D., 1968). *Member:* Oregon State Bar; Multnomah and American Bar Associations. ***PRACTICE AREAS:*** General Business Law; Litigation; Corporate Finance; Alternative Dispute Resolution. ***Email:*** terry@tonkon.com

VICKI A. BALLOU, admitted to bar, 1986, Oregon. *Education:* Walla Walla College (B.A., cum laude, 1973); University of Texas (J.D., with honors, 1986). *Member:* Multnomah and American Bar Associations; Oregon State Bar. ***PRACTICE AREAS:*** Intellectual Property; Technology Law; Internet Law; Commercial Lending. ***Email:*** vickib@tonkon.com

BRUCE G. BERNING, admitted to bar, 1977, Oregon. *Education:* Indiana University (A.B., magna cum laude, 1974); Harvard University (J.D., cum laude, 1977). Phi Beta Kappa. Law Clerk to Judge George M. Joseph, Oregon Court of Appeals, Salem, Oregon, 1977-1979. *Member:* Multnomah and American Bar Associations; Oregon State Bar. ***PRACTICE AREAS:*** Business Transactions; Mergers and Acquisitions; Secured Financing; Corporate Law. ***Email:*** bruce@tonkon.com

OWEN D. BLANK, admitted to bar, 1973, Oregon; 1977, U.S. Supreme Court. *Education:* Stanford University (A.B., 1970; J.D., 1973). Phi Beta Kappa. Law Clerk to U.S. District Judge James M. Burns, Portland, Oregon, 1973-1974. *Member:* Multnomah and American Bar Associations; Oregon State Bar. ***PRACTICE AREAS:*** Business; Corporate; Real Estate; Media; Sports; Exempt Organizations; International Law. ***Email:*** owen@tonkon.com

BRIAN G. BOOTH, born Roseburg, Oregon, May 30, 1936; admitted to bar, 1962, Oregon. *Education:* University of Oregon (B.S., 1958); Stanford University (LL.B., 1962). Phi Beta Kappa; Order of the Coif. Editor, Stanford Law Review, 1960-1962. President, Oregon Securities Law Association, 1972-1974. *Member:* Multnomah and American Bar Associations; Oregon State Bar (President's Public Service Award, 1999). Fellow, American Bar Foundation. ***PRACTICE AREAS:*** Securities; Corporate; Mergers and Acquisitions; Tax Exempt Organizations; Initial Public Offerings; Finance. ***Email:*** brianb@tonkon.com

JEANNE M. CHAMBERLAIN, born West Point, New York, March 1, 1952; admitted to bar, 1985, Oregon; 1987, Washington. *Education:* San Francisco Art Institute (B.F.A., 1974); University of Oregon (J.D., 1985). Order of the Coif. Recipient, American Jurisprudence Awards in Creditor's Rights, Administrative Law, Family Law and Trusts and Estates. *Member:* Multnomah and American Bar Associations; Oregon State Bar. ***PRACTICE AREAS:*** Business Litigation; Commercial Litigation. ***Email:*** jeanne@tonkon.com

TIMOTHY J. CONWAY, born Fairfield, California, May 11, 1959; admitted to bar, 1985, Oregon. *Education:* Solano Community College (A.A., 1979); California State University at Sacramento (B.A., 1981); Northwestern School of Law of Lewis and Clark College (J.D., 1985). Member: Cornelius Honor Society; Editorial Board, Law Review, 1983-1985. President, National Conference of Law Reviews, 1985. Recipient, American Jurisprudence Award in Civil Procedure. *Member:* Oregon State Bar; Multnomah and American Bar Associations; Christian Legal Society. ***PRACTICE AREAS:*** Litigation; Bankruptcy Law; Creditors Rights Law. ***Email:*** tim@tonkon.com

SHERRILL A. CORBETT, born 1970; admitted to bar, 1995, California; 1999, Oregon. *Education:* Saint Mary's College of California (B.A., summa cum laude, 1992); University of California, Hastings College of the Law (J.D., magna cum laude, 1995). Phi Delta Phi; Order of the Coif; Thurston Society. *Member:* Oregon State Bar; State Bar of California; Multnomah and American Bar Associations. ***PRACTICE AREAS:*** Corporate Law; Securities Law; Mergers and Acquisitions. ***Email:*** sherrill@tonkon.com

JEFFREY S. CRONN, admitted to bar, 1994, Oregon. *Education:* University of California at Berkeley (B.A., 1991); University of Michigan (J.D., cum laude, 1994). Phi Beta Kappa. *Member:* Multnomah and American Bar Associations; Oregon State Bar. ***PRACTICE AREAS:*** Corporate Law; Securities Regulation; Business Transactions; Mergers and Acquisitions; Corporate Reorganization. ***Email:*** jeffc@tonkon.com

JUSTIN B. DENTON, admitted to bar, 1997, Oregon. *Education:* Brigham Young University (B.A., cum laude, 1994; J.D., magna cum laude, 1997). Recipient, Brigham Young University Writing Fellowship. Lead Note and Comment Editor, Brigham Young Law Review. *Member:* Multnomah and American Bar Associations; Oregon State Bar. ***PRACTICE AREAS:*** General Business; Corporate; Mergers and Acquisitions; Real Estate. ***Email:*** justin@tonkon.com

MORRIS J. GALEN, admitted to bar, 1950, Oregon; 1966, U.S. Supreme Court. *Education:* University of Oregon (B.S., 1949; J.D., 1950). Phi Beta Kappa; Order of the Coif. Editor, Oregon Law Review, 1949-1950. Trustee, Reed College, 1976—. *Member:* Multnomah and American Bar Associations; Oregon State Bar (Treasurer, 1967-1968). ***PRACTICE AREAS:*** Business Transactions; Corporate Law; Real Estate Law; Closely Held Businesses. ***Email:*** morris@tonkon.com

(This Listing Continued)

RONALD L. GREENMAN, born Portland, Oregon, April 6, 1946; admitted to bar, 1974, California; 1978, Oregon. *Education:* University of Oregon (B.S., 1968; J.D., 1974). Phi Beta Kappa; Order of the Coif. Member, Board of Editors, Oregon Law Review, 1973-1974. *Member:* Multnomah and American Bar Associations; State Bar of California; Oregon State Bar. ***PRACTICE AREAS:*** Corporate Finance; Securities Law; Business Transactions; Leveraged Buyouts; Venture Capital; Corporate Acquisitions. ***Email:*** ron@tonkon.com

LYNDA J. HARTZELL, admitted to bar, 1993, Oregon and U.S. District Court, District of Oregon; 1994, Washington and U.S. District Court, District of Washington; 1995, U.S. Court of Appeals, Ninth Circuit. *Education:* George Mason University (B.S.Ed, 1976); Northwestern School of Law of Lewis and Clark College (J.D., 1993). Recipient: American Jurisprudence Award for Advanced Bankruptcy; Academic Achievement Award from Securities Section, Multnomah Bar Association. *Member:* Clark County, Washington State, Multnomah and American Bar Associations; Oregon State Bar; Oregon Association of Defense Counsel. ***PRACTICE AREAS:*** Employment; Litigation. ***Email:*** lynda@tonkon.com

THEODORE G. HERZOG, admitted to bar, 1989, Oregon. *Education:* Washington State University (B.A., Honors Program, cum laude, 1984); University of Texas (J.D., with honors, 1989). *Member:* Oregon State Bar; Multnomah and American Bar Associations. ***PRACTICE AREAS:*** Real Estate Acquisitions and Sales; Real Estate; Business; Environmental; Natural Resources. ***Email:*** ted@tonkon.com

CAROL DEY HIBBS, born Eugene, Oregon, February 16, 1948; admitted to bar, 1978, Oregon. *Education:* University of Oregon (B.A., 1970); Stanford University (J.D., 1978). *Member:* Multnomah and American Bar Associations; Oregon State Bar. ***PRACTICE AREAS:*** Corporate Law; Securities Law; Banking Law; Finance Law; Mergers and Acquisitions. ***Email:*** carolh@tonkon.com

JEFFREY H. KEENEY, born Hartford, Connecticut, June 17, 1958; admitted to bar, 1983, Oregon. *Education:* University of Vermont (B.A., 1980); Northwestern School of Law of Lewis and Clark College (J.D., cum laude, 1983). Phi Beta Kappa; Cornelius Honor Society. *Member:* Multnomah and American Bar Associations; Oregon State Bar (Member, Executive Committee, Real Estate and Land Use Section). ***PRACTICE AREAS:*** Real Estate Law; Land Use Law; Real Estate Acquisitions; Financing and Development. ***Email:*** jeffk@tonkon.com

ALBERT N. KENNEDY, born Dixon, Illinois, February 13, 1951; admitted to bar, 1976, Michigan; 1982, Oregon; 1985, Washington. *Education:* Brown University (B.A., 1973); Vanderbilt University (J.D., 1976). *Member:* State Bar of Michigan; Oregon State Bar; Multnomah, Washington State and American Bar Associations. ***PRACTICE AREAS:*** Creditors Rights Law; Bankruptcy Law; Commercial Litigation. ***Email:*** al@tonkon.com

VICTOR J. KISCH, admitted to bar, 1986, California; 1994, Oregon. *Education:* University of Iowa (B.B.A., 1980); Institute of Labor and Industrial Relations, University of Illinois, Urbana-Champaign (M.A., 1982); Temple University School of Law (J.D., 1985). Phi Kappa Phi. Honor Society. *Member:* Multnomah Bar Association and American Bar Associations; State Bar of California; Oregon State Bar. ***PRACTICE AREAS:*** Labor and Employment. ***Email:*** victor@tonkon.com

MARK F. LeROUX, admitted to bar, 1982, Washington; 1983, Oregon. *Education:* Willamette University (B.A., 1978; J.D., 1982); New York University (LL.M. in Taxation, 1983). *Member:* Multnomah, Washington State and American Bar Associations; Oregon State Bar. ***PRACTICE AREAS:*** International, Federal and State Taxation. ***Email:*** mark@tonkon.com

BARBEE B. LYON, born Dover, Tennessee, June 24, 1940; admitted to bar, 1971, Oregon; 1978, U.S. Court of Appeals, 9th Circuit; 1986, U.S. Court of Appeals, Federal Circuit; 1987, U.S. Supreme Court; 1989, U.S. Court of Appeals, 10th Circuit; 1995, U.S. Court of Appeals, 7th Circuit. *Education:* Vanderbilt University (B.A., magna cum laude, 1960) Phi Beta Kappa; Yale University (J.D., 1971). Law Clerk to U.S. District Judge, Robert C. Zampano, New Haven, Connecticut, 1971-1972. Law Clerk to U.S. District Judge, Otto R. Skopil, Jr., Portland, Oregon, 1972-1973. *Member:* Multnomah and American Bar Associations; Oregon State Bar. ***LANGUAGES:*** French and Spanish. ***PRACTICE AREAS:*** Appellate Practice; Antitrust Law; Litigation. ***Email:*** barbee@tonkon.com

DON H. MARMADUKE, born Portland, Oregon, May 13, 1926; admitted to bar, 1951, Massachusetts; 1953, Oregon; 1959, U.S. Court of Appeals, 9th Circuit; 1979, U.S. Supreme Court; 1984, Court of Appeals for the Federal Circuit. *Education:* Yale University (B.E., 1946); Harvard Law School (LL.B., 1951). Tau Beta Pi. Law Clerk to the Hon. Peter Woodbury, U.S. Court of Appeals, First Circuit, 1951-1952. *Member:* Multnomah (President, 1979) and American (Member, House of Delegates, 1974-1978) Bar Associations; Oregon State Bar (Chairman: Continuing Legal Education Committee, 1965; Civil Rights Section, 1978); American Board of Trial Advocates. Fellow: International Society of Barristers; American Bar Foundation; American College of Trial Lawyers. ***PRACTICE AREAS:*** Litigation; Alternative Dispute Resolution. ***Email:*** don@tonkon.com

WILLIAM F. MARTSON, JR., born Carlisle, Pennsylvania, May 31, 1947; admitted to bar, 1972, Oregon. *Education:* University of Edinburgh and Washington and Jefferson College (B.A., magna cum laude, 1969); University of Michigan (J.D., magna cum laude, 1972). Phi Beta Kappa; Order of the Coif. *Member:* Multnomah (Board of Directors), Federal and American Bar Associations; Oregon State Bar. Fellow: International Society of Barristers (Member, Board of Directors). ***PRACTICE AREAS:*** Litigation; Forestry Law; Natural Resources; Environmental Litigation. ***Email:*** rick@tonkon.com

MAX M. MILLER, JR., born Seattle, Washington, August 24, 1957; admitted to bar, 1983, Oregon and U.S. Court of Appeals, 9th Circuit; 1984, U.S. District Court, District of Oregon. *Education:* Pitzer College (B.A., Economics, 1979); Lewis and Clark College (J.D., 1983). *Member:* Multnomah and American Bar Associations; Oregon State Bar (Past Chair, Environmental and Natural Resources Section, 2001; Past Editor, Oregon Environmental and Natural Resources Outlook, 1994-1997; Co-Editor, Environmental and Natural Resources Law Deskbook, 2002 edition). ***PRACTICE AREAS:*** Environmental Law; Natural Resources Law; Land Use; Real Estate Transactions. ***Email:*** max@tonkon.com

MICHAEL M. MORGAN, born Wenatchee, Washington, August 19, 1947; admitted to bar, 1972, Oregon. *Education:* Occidental College (B.A., cum laude, 1969); University of Chicago (J.D., 1972). *Member:* Multnomah and American Bar Associations; Oregon State Bar. ***PRACTICE AREAS:*** Energy; Business Transactions; Telecommunications Law; Regulated Industries. ***Email:*** mike@tonkon.com

JON W. NICKEL, born Chicago, Illinois, June 29, 1945; admitted to bar, 1973, Oregon. *Education:* Occidental College (B.A., 1967); Harvard University (J.D., cum laude, 1973). *Member:* Multnomah and American Bar Associations; Oregon State Bar. ***PRACTICE AREAS:*** Corporate Law; Executive Compensation; Business Transactions. ***Email:*** jonn@tonkon.com

DARCY M. NORVILLE, admitted to bar, 1985, Washington and California; 1990, Oregon, U.S. District Court, District of Oregon and U.S. Court of Appeals, 9th Circuit. *Education:* California State University at Chico (B.A., 1981); Boalt Hall School of Law, University of California at Berkeley (J.D., 1984). *Member:* Multnomah, Washington State and American Bar Associations; State Bar of California; Oregon State Bar. ***PRACTICE AREAS:*** Employee Benefits; Executive Compensation; Corporate; Business Transactions. ***Email:*** darcy@tonkon.com

INGOLF NOTO, born Reykjavik, Iceland, August 6, 1948; admitted to bar, 1978, Oregon. *Education:* Brigham Young University (B.S., 1971); University of Utah (J.D., 1976). Honorary Consul of Denmark for the State of Oregon. *Member:* Multnomah and American Bar Associations; Oregon State Bar. ***LANGUAGES:*** Danish. ***PRACTICE AREAS:*** Federal, State and International Taxation; Mergers and Acquisitions; Reorganizations; Corporate Finance. ***Email:*** ingolf@tonkon.com

TURID L. OWREN, admitted to bar, 1984, Oregon. *Education:* Reed College (B.A., 1974); Northwestern School of Law of Lewis and Clark College (J.D., 1983). Cornelius Honor Society. Editor-in-Chief, Environmental Law, 1982-1983. *Member:* Oregon State Bar; Multnomah and American Bar Associations; American Immigration Lawyers Association (Past Chair, Oregon Chapter). ***LANGUAGES:*** Norwegian. ***PRACTICE AREAS:*** Immigration Law; Trademark Law; General Business Law. ***Email:*** turid@tonkon.com

THOMAS P. PALMER, born Wilmington, Delaware, January 24, 1951; admitted to bar, 1977, New York and District of Columbia; 1988, Oregon. *Education:* Hamilton College (A.B., 1973); Cornell University (J.D., 1976). *Member:* Multnomah, New York State and American Bar Associations; Oregon State Bar; District of Columbia Bar; Association of the Bar of the City of New York. ***PRACTICE AREAS:*** Corporate and Securities Law; Mergers and Acquisitions; Initial Public Offerings. ***Email:*** tom@tonkon.com

AMY JOSEPH PEDERSEN, born Nashville, Tennessee, June 12, 1958; admitted to bar, 1985, Oregon, U.S. District Court, District of Oregon, U.S. Court of Appeals, 9th Circuit and U.S. Supreme Court. *Education:* University of Oregon (B.A., 1982); University of Virginia (J.D., 1985). Phi Beta Kappa. *Member:* Multnomah and American Bar Associations; Oregon State Bar. ***PRACTICE AREAS:*** Labor and Employment; Commercial Litigation. ***Email:*** amy@tonkon.com

EDWIN C. PERRY, admitted to bar, 1984, Oregon; 1985, Washington. *Education:* Bates College; University of Washington (B.A., 1979); University of Oregon (J.D., 1984). Order of the Coif. Articles Editor, Oregon Law Review, 1983-1984. *Member:* Multnomah and American Bar Associations; Oregon State Bar (Past Chair, Business Litigation Section); Washington State Bar. ***LANGUAGES:*** German. ***PRACTICE AREAS:*** Real Property Litigation; Construction Litigation; Commercial Litigation. ***Email:*** ned@tonkon.com

BRIAN J. POSEWITZ, born Bozeman, Montana, September 24, 1960; admitted to bar, 1991, Oregon; 1994, Washington. *Education:* Willamette University (B.S., 1984); University of Oregon (J.D., 1991). Order of the Coif. *Member:* Oregon State Bar (Past Chair, Antitrust, Trade Regulation and Unfair Business Practices Section); Multnomah, Washington State and American Bar Associations. ***PRACTICE AREAS:*** Antitrust; Trade Regulations; Trademarks; Media Law; Civil Litigation. ***Email:*** brianp@tonkon.com

BRENT W. RENISON, admitted to bar, 1996, Oregon; 2000, Hawaii; U.S. Court of Appeals, Ninth Circuit. *Education:* University of Oregon (B.A., magna cum laude, 1990); East-West Center, Honolulu, Hawaii (Masters Certificate, 1996); University of Hawaii School of Law (J.D., 1996). *Member:* Multnomah, Hawaii State, American and International Bar Associations; Oregon State Bar; American Immigration Lawyers Association. ***LANGUAGES:*** Mandarin Chinese. ***SPECIAL AGENCIES:*** U.S. Department of State, 1991-1993. ***PRACTICE AREAS:*** Business Immigration; Citizenship. ***Email:*** brent@tonkon.com

SHOUKA D. REZVANI, admitted to bar, 1994, Oregon. *Education:* Reed College (B.A., 1990); Willamette University (J.D., cum laude, 1994). Articles Editor, Willamette Law Review. *Member:* Multnomah and American Bar Associations; Oregon State Bar; Northwest Planned Giving Roundtable. ***PRACTICE AREAS:*** Wealth Preservation; Estate Planning; Probate; Family Limited Partnerships; Limited Liability Company Law; Charitable Giving; Non-Profit and Tax-Exempt Organizations. ***Email:*** shouka@tonkon.com

JOHN H. ROSENFELD, born Portland, Oregon, October 31, 1952; admitted to bar, 1977, Oregon. *Education:* University of Pennsylvania (B.S., magna cum laude, 1974); University of Oregon (J.D., 1977). Order of the Coif. Member, Oregon Law Review, 1976-1977. *Member:* Multnomah and American Bar Associations; Oregon State Bar. Fellow, American College of Trust and Estate Counsel. ***PRACTICE AREAS:*** Estate Planning; Probate Law; Family Limited Partnerships; Limited Liability Company Law. ***Email:*** john@tonkon.com

KURT W. RUTTUM, admitted to bar, 1986, Oregon. *Education:* University of Colorado (B.A., magna cum laude, 1981); University of Chicago (J.D., 1986). Phi Beta Kappa. Member, University of Chicago Law Review, 1985-1986. *Member:* Multnomah and American Bar Associations; Oregon State Bar. ***PRACTICE AREAS:*** Mergers and Acquisitions; Securities; Corporate Finance; Public and Private Securities Offerings. ***Email:*** kurt@tonkon.com

SCOTT G. SEIDMAN, admitted to bar, 1981, California; 1983, Oregon. *Education:* University of Illinois (A.B., 1975; A.M., 1978; J.D., 1981). Order of the Coif. *Member:* Multnomah and American Bar Associations; Oregon State Bar; State Bar of California. ***PRACTICE AREAS:*** Antitrust and Trade Regulation; Employment; Litigation; Securities; General Business. ***Email:*** scott@tonkon.com

(This Listing Continued)

TONKON TORP LLP, Portland—Continued

DANIEL H. SKERRITT, born Scobey, Montana, July 21, 1943; admitted to bar, 1968, Oregon; 1972, U.S. Supreme Court; U.S. District Court, District of Oregon; U.S. Court of Appeals, Ninth Circuit. *Education:* Willamette University (B.A., 1965; J.D., summa cum laude, 1968); George Washington University (LL.M., 1972). Phi Delta Phi. Editor-in-Chief, Willamette Law Journal, 1968. *Member:* Oregon State Bar; Multnomah and American Bar Associations; Oregon Association of Defense Counsel; International Society of Barristers. Fellow, American College of Trial Lawyers. [Capt., U.S. Army, Judge Advocate General (JAG) Corps, 1968-1972]. ***PRACTICE AREAS:*** Litigation; Commercial Litigation; Alternative Dispute Resolution. ***Email:*** dan@tonkon.com

GEORGE C. SPENCER, admitted to bar, 1966, Oregon. *Education:* University of Oregon (B.S., 1963; LL.B., 1966). Phi Delta Phi. President, Oregon Securities Law Association, 1976-1977. *Member:* Multnomah and American Bar Associations; Oregon State Bar; American Forest and Paper Association (Member, General Counsel's Committee). ***PRACTICE AREAS:*** Corporate and Securities Law; Mergers and Acquisitions; Forest Products; General Business Law; Start-up Companies. ***Email:*** george@tonkon.com

KENNETH D. STEPHENS, born Olympia, Washington, May 24, 1942; admitted to bar, 1967, Oregon. *Education:* University of Oregon (B.S., 1965; J.D., 1967). Chair, Managing Board. Phi Delta Phi; Order of the Coif. Associate Editor, Oregon Law Review, 1966-1967. Assistant Counsel, Securities Industry Study, U.S. Senate Committee on Banking, Housing and Urban Affairs, 1971-1972. *Member:* Multnomah and American Bar Associations; Oregon State Bar. ***PRACTICE AREAS:*** Corporate; Finance; Banking; Securities; Mergers and Acquisitions. ***Email:*** ken@tonkon.com

JON P. STRIDE, born Klamath Falls, Oregon, December 16, 1952; admitted to bar, 1990, Oregon; 2004, Washington; U.S. District Court, District of Oregon and Western District of Washington; U.S. Court of Appeals, Ninth Circuit. *Education:* Western Oregon University (B.S., with honors, 1975; M.S., with honors, 1980); University of Oregon (J.D., 1990). Member, Order of the Coif. Editor-In-Chief Oregon Law Review, 1989-1990. *Member:* Multnomah and American Bar Associations; Oregon State Bar. ***PRACTICE AREAS:*** Commercial Litigation; Intellectual Property Litigation; Patents and Trademark Law. ***Email:*** jons@tonkon.com

JOSEPH S. VOBORIL, born Wahoo, Nebraska, August 10, 1948; admitted to bar, 1973, Oregon. *Education:* University of Nebraska (B.A., 1970); University of Michigan (J.D., 1973). Phi Beta Kappa. Member: Portland Area Local Government Boundary Commission, 1974-1977; City of Portland Planning Commission, 1977-1980; Board of Education, Portland Public Schools, 1987-1991. Vice Chair, Board of Trustees, Portland Art Museum, 1993—. *Member:* Multnomah and American Bar Associations; Oregon State Bar. ***PRACTICE AREAS:*** Business Transactions; Commercial Real Estate; Real Estate; Land Use; Real Estate Litigation; Real Estate Arbitration; Leasing. ***Email:*** joe@tonkon.com

FRANK J. WEISS, born Fort Knox, Kentucky, March 25, 1970; admitted to bar, 1995, California; 1999, Oregon. *Education:* University of Oregon (B.S., 1992); Hastings College of the Law, University of California (J.D., cum laude, 1995). Order of the Coif. Member: Thurston Society; Moot Court Board. *Member:* Multnomah and American Bar Associations; Oregon State Bar; State Bar of California. ***PRACTICE AREAS:*** Business Litigation; Insurance Coverage. ***Email:*** frank@tonkon.com

DAVID F. WHITE, born York, Pennsylvania, November 8, 1962; admitted to bar, 1993, Pennsylvania; 1996, District of Columbia and Colorado; 2001, Oregon; 2002, Washington. *Education:* Grinnell College (B.A., 1985); Harvard Law School (J.D., cum laude, 1993). Phi Beta Kappa. *Member:* Multnomah, Colorado, Washington State and American Bar Associations; Oregon State Bar; District of Columbia Bar. ***PRACTICE AREAS:*** Energy; Telecommunications; Litigation; Antitrust. ***Email:*** davidw@tonkon.com

STEVEN M. WILKER, admitted to bar, 1990, California; 1991, Oregon; 1992, U.S. District Court, District of Oregon, Northern District of California and U.S. Tax Court; 1994, U.S. Court of Appeals, 9th Circuit; U.S. Court of Federal Claims; 1995, U.S. District Court, Central District of California and Eastern District of Michigan; 1996, U.S. Court of Appeals, 6th Circuit; 1998, U.S. District Court, Southern District of California; 2000, U.S. District Court, Eastern District of California; 2003, Washington and U.S. District Court, Western District of Washington. *Education:* University of Pennsylvania (B.A., 1986; M.S.Ed., 1987); University of California School of Law, Los Angeles (J.D., 1990). Order of the Coif. Law Clerk to the Honorable Stephen V. Wilson, U.S. District Court, Central District of California, 1990-1991; the Honorable Edwin J. Peterson, Oregon Supreme Court, 1991-1992. *Member:* Multnomah, Washington State, Federal and American Bar Associations; Oregon State Bar; State Bar of California. ***PRACTICE AREAS:*** Business Litigation; Media Law; Intellectual Property; Corporate Finance. ***Email:*** steven@tonkon.com

ZACHARY W.L. WRIGHT, born West Hartford, Connecticut, February 4, 1964; admitted to bar, 1994, Oregon, U.S. District Court, District of Oregon and U.S. Court of Appeals, Ninth Circuit. *Education:* University of Vermont (B.A., cum laude, 1987); University of Michigan (J.D., cum laude, 1992). Executive Editor, University of Michigan Journal of Law Reform, 1991-1992. Law Clerk to Hon. Deanell R. Tacha, U.S. Court of Appeals, Tenth Circuit, 1992-1993. *Member:* Multnomah and American Bar Associations; Oregon State Bar. ***PRACTICE AREAS:*** Energy Law; Business Litigation; Telecommunications Regulation. ***Email:*** zach@tonkon.com

OF COUNSEL

CHRISTOPHER M. BIKUS, born Bradenton, Florida, July 21, 1969; admitted to bar, 1996, Nebraska; 2005, Oregon. *Education:* Augustana College (B.A., 1991); University of Nebraska (J.D., with honors, 1996). *Member:* Nebraska State Bar Association; American Intellectual Property Lawyers Association; International Trademark Association. ***PRACTICE AREAS:*** Intellectual Property; Intellectual Property Enforcement; Intellectual Property Infringement; Intellectual Property Licensing; Intellectual Property Portfolio Management; Intellectual Property Procurement; Intellectual Property Prosecution; Intellectual Property Rights; International Intellectual Property; International Licensing; Internet Intellectual Property; Piracy; Proprietary Rights. ***Email:*** chrisb@tonkon.com

DAVID COPLEY FORMAN, born Cleveland, Ohio; admitted to bar, 1989, New York and U.S. District Court, Southern and Eastern Districts of New York; 1993, Oregon. *Education:* University of Michigan (B.A., 1985; J.D., 1988). *Member:* Multnomah and American Bar Associations; Oregon State Bar. ***PRACTICE AREAS:*** General Corporate; Business Transactions; Mergers and Acquisitions; Corporate; Securities. ***Email:*** davidf@tonkon.com

ASSOCIATES

MICHAEL E. CALLIER, born Grand Rapids, Michigan, September 18,1978; admitted to bar, 2004, Oregon. *Education:* University of Oregon (B.A., 2001; J.D., 2004). *Member:* Multnomah and American Bar Associations; Oregon State Bar. ***PRACTICE AREAS:*** Litigation; Corporate. ***Email:*** michaelc@tonkon.com

PAUL W. CONABLE, born Urbana, Illinois, August 3, 1966; admitted to bar, 1997, Oregon; 2001, U.S. District Court, District of Oregon and U.S. Court of Appeals, 9th Circuit. *Education:* Tufts University (B.A., cum laude,1987); The Ohio State University (M.S., 1994); Northwestern School of Law, Lewis and Clark College (J.D., summa cum laude, 1997). ***PRACTICE AREAS:*** Business Litigation. ***Email:*** paul@tonkon.com

CHANDRA EMERY, admitted to bar, 1994, Pennsylvania; 1995, District of Columbia and Texas; 2002, Oregon; 2003, Washington. *Education:* University of Virginia (B.A., 1991); George Washington University (J.D., 1994); University of Washington (LL.M., Taxation, 2003). *Member:* Multnomah and American Bar Associations; Oregon State Bar. ***PRACTICE AREAS:*** Taxation; Business. ***Email:*** chandrae@tonkon.com

CHRISTOPHER D. ERICKSON, born Portland, Oregon, December 5, 1974; admitted to bar, 2001, Oregon. *Education:* University of Oregon (B.S., 1997; J.D., 2001) Member, Order of the Coif. Member, Order of the Coif. *Member:* Member: Multnomah and American Bar Associations; Oregon State Bar. ***PRACTICE AREAS:*** Intellectual Property; Business Transactions; Emerging Growth Companies; Technology Law. ***Email:*** chrise@tonkon.com

MICHAEL W. FLETCHER, born St. Louis, Missouri, February 24, 1970; admitted to bar, 1997, Missouri and Kansas; 2001, Oregon. *Education:* University of Missouri, Columbia (B.S., Accountancy, summa cum laude, 1992); University of Missouri, Columbia Law School (J.D., summa cum laude,1997). Order of the Coif. Member, University of Missouri Law Review. *Member:* Multnomah, Kansas and American Bar Associations; Oregon State Bar; The Missouri Bar. ***PRACTICE AREAS:*** Business; Secured Lending; Bankruptcy. ***Email:*** michaelf@tonkon.com

CAROLINE HARRIS CROWNE, born Andrews Air Force Base, Maryland, 1975; admitted to bar, 2002, Oregon. *Education:* Rice University (B.A., summa cum laude, 1997); New York University (J.D., magna cum laude, 2001). Order of the Coif. Law Clerk to Judge Charles S. Haight, U.S. District Court, Southern District of New York. *Member:* Oregon State Bar; Multnomah and American Bar Associations. ***LANGUAGES:*** French. ***PRACTICE AREAS:*** Litigation. ***Email:*** carolinehc@tonkon.com

SONJA L. HENNING, admitted to bar, 1995, California; 2002 Oregon. *Education:* Stanford University (B.A., 1991); Duke University (J.D., 1995). *Member:* Oregon State Bar; State Bar of California; American Bar Association. ***PRACTICE AREAS:*** Labor and Employment Law. ***Email:*** sonja@tonkon.com

F. JACKSON LEWIS, admitted to bar, 2000, Oregon. *Education:* Harvard University (B.A., cum laude, 1989); University of Michigan (J.D., 1999). *Member:* Multnomah and American Bar Associations; Oregon State Bar. ***PRACTICE AREAS:*** Wealth Planning; Estate Administration; Probate Litigation. ***Email:*** jackson@tonkon.com

LAURA LIEBMAN-ALPERSON, born New York, N.Y., July 27, 1971; admitted to bar, 2002, Oregon. *Education:* Brandeis University (B.A., 1993; M.A., 1996); Northwestern School of Law of Lewis & Clark College (J.D., cum laude, 2002). *Member:* Oregon State Bar. ***LANGUAGES:*** Hebrew. ***PRACTICE AREAS:*** Corporate Litigation; Labor and Employment. ***Email:*** laura@tonkon.com

MICHAEL MILLENDER, admitted to bar, 2003, Oregon. *Education:* Duke University (B.A., summa cum laude, 1988); University of Iowa (J.D., 2002). Order of the Coif. *Member:* Multnomah Bar Association; Oregon State Bar. ***PRACTICE AREAS:*** Corporate Law; Business Law. ***Email:*** michaelm@tonkon.com

STEVEN D. OLSON, born Coeur d'Alene, Idaho, December 20, 1968; admitted to bar, 2000, Oregon. *Education:* U.S. Coast Guard Academy (B.S., 1991); Tulane University (M.P.H., 1996); University of Minnesota (J.D., magna cum laude, 2000). *Member:* Multnomah and American Bar Associations; Oregon State Bar. [Lieutenant, U.S. Coast Guard, 1991-1996]. ***PRACTICE AREAS:*** Litigation. ***Email:*** steveno@tonkon.com

TATIANA A. PERRY, born Khabarovsk, Russia, June 26, 1974; admitted to bar, 2000, Oregon and Washington. *Education:* Yuzhno-Sakhalinsk State Pedagogical Institute, Yuzhno-Sakhalinsk, Russia (M.Ed., 1995); Willamette University (J.D., 2000; M.B.A., 2000). *Member:* Multnomah, Washington State and American Bar Associations; Oregon State Bar. ***LANGUAGES:*** Russian, Japanese. ***PRACTICE AREAS:*** Securities; Mergers and Acquisitions; General Corporate; Financial Institutions. ***Email:*** tatiana@tonkon.com

DAVID J. PETERSEN, admitted to bar, 1998, California; 2003, Oregon. *Education:* Syracuse University (B.A., 1991); Boalt Hall School of Law, University of California at Berkeley (J.D., 1998). Order of the Coif. *Member:* Multnomah and American Bar Associations; Oregon State Bar. ***PRACTICE AREAS:*** Land Use; Real Estate; Local Government. ***Email:*** davidp@tonkon.com

ROBYN E. RIDLER, born Seattle, Washington, May 16, 1974; admitted to bar, 2000, Oregon. *Education:* Tufts University (B.A., magna cum laude, 1995); Harvard University (J.D., cum laude, 1999). *Member:* Multnomah and American Bar Associations; Oregon State Bar. ***PRACTICE AREAS:*** Commercial Litigation; Securities Litigation; Shareholder Disputes; Corporate Contracts. ***Email:*** robyn@tonkon.com

KATHERINE E. SAITAS, admitted to bar, 2002, Oregon. *Education:* Smith College (B.A., 1986); Duke University (J.D., cum laude, 2002). Recipient, Outstanding Achievement Faculty Award, Duke University. *Member:* Oregon State Bar; Multnomah and American Bar Associations. ***PRACTICE AREAS:*** Business; Corporate. ***Email:*** kathy@tonkon.com

AVA SCHOEN, born May 10, 1973; admitted to bar, 2002, New York and New Jersey; 2004, Oregon. *Education:* Hamilton College (B.A., 1995); Fordham University (J.D.,

(This Listing Continued)

2001). Phi Beta Kappa. *Member:* Multnomah and American Bar Associations; Oregon State Bar. ***LANGUAGES:*** French. ***PRACTICE AREAS:*** Litigation. ***Email:*** avas@tonkon.com

JOSHUA K. SIMKO, admitted to bar, 2003, Oregon. *Education:* Westmont College (B.A., cum laude, 1996); Duke University (M.A., cum laude, 2003; J.D., cum laude, 2003). Omicron Delta Kappa Leadership Society. *Member:* Multnomah and American Bar Associations; Oregon State Bar. ***PRACTICE AREAS:*** Corporate; Corporate Finance. ***Email:*** joshs@tonkon.com

CHRISTINE URI, born Lawrence, Kansas, August 24, 1975; admitted to bar, 2003, Washington (Not admitted in Oregon). *Education:* The Evergreen State College (B.A., 1998); Boston College (J.D., cum laude, 2003). *Member:* Multnomah, Washington State and American Bar Associations. ***PRACTICE AREAS:*** Commercial Litigation. ***Email:*** christineu@tonkon.com

DENNIS E. WESTLIND, admitted to bar, 2001, Oregon and U.S. District Court, District of Oregon. *Education:* University of Oregon (B.A., magna cum laude, 1991); Lund University, Lund, Sweden (Ph.D., 1996); University of Michigan (J.D., magna cum laude, 2000). Phi Beta Kappa. *Member:* Multnomah and American Bar Associations; Oregon State Bar. ***LANGUAGES:*** Swedish. ***PRACTICE AREAS:*** Labor and Employment; Commercial Litigation. ***Email:*** dennisw@tonkon.com

REPRESENTATIVE CLIENTS: Benson Industries LLC; Blount, Inc.; (The) Campbell Group, LLC; Carr Auto Group; CB Commercial Real Estate Group, Inc.; Century Bank; Columbia Distributing Company; Comcast Corp.; Costco Wholesale Corporation; CTC Consulting, Inc.; Deloitte & Touche LLP; Dynic USA Corporation; East Oregonian Publishing Co.; Endeavour Capital Fund; Ernst & Young, Inc.; ESCO Corporation; The Greenbrier Companies; Gunderson, Inc.; Herzog-Meier Auto Group; Hood River Distillers, Inc.; Keller Enterprises Inc.; Key Technology, Inc.; KOIN-TV; LaSalle Business Credit, Inc.; M Financial Holdings, Incorporated; M Life Insurance Company; McCall Oil and Chemical Corp.; Medical Management International, Inc.; NIKE, Inc.; Northwest Pepsi Cola Bottlers; Oregon Health & Science University; PPM Energy, Inc.; Paulson Investment Company, Inc.; Platt Electric Supply, Inc.; Portland Art Museum; Portland General Electric Company; Qwwest Communications, Inc.; Ron Tonkin Dealerships; Sause Bros. Ocean Towing Co.; Sprint Communication; Stimson Lumber Co.; Symbol Technologies, Inc.; Taser International, Inc.; United States Bakery; U.S. Trust Company, N.A.; Wells Fargo Business Credit, Inc.; West Coast Bank; Vinton Studios, Inc.

JAY URBAN

PORTLAND, OREGON

(See Lake Oswego)

Taxation, Domestic Relations, Business Law, Financial Law, Business Planning, Personal Injury.

VANDEN BOS & CHAPMAN, LLP

Established in 1981

SUITE 520, THE SPALDING BUILDING
319 S.W. WASHINGTON STREET
PORTLAND, OREGON 97204-2690
Telephone: 503-241-4869
Fax: 503-241-3731
URL: http://www.vbcattorneys.com

Trial Practice in State and Federal Courts. Bankruptcy, Consumer and Commercial Chapter Eleven (Reorganization), Chapter 13 and Debtor-Creditor Rights.

MEMBERS OF FIRM

ROBERT J VANDEN BOS, admitted to bar, 1978, Oregon and U.S. District Court, District of Oregon; 1979, U.S. Court of Appeals, Ninth Circuit; 1991, U.S. Supreme Court. *Education:* Alma College (B.A., summa cum laude, 1973); University of Michigan (J.D., magna cum laude, 1977). *Member:* Multnomah County Bar Association; Oregon State Bar (Member, Debtor-Creditor Section); American Bankruptcy Institute. ***PRACTICE AREAS:*** Bankruptcy Law; Chapter Eleven (Reorganization); Bankruptcy Chapter 13; Bankruptcy Chapter 7; Commercial Law. ***Email:*** bob@vbcattorneys.com

ANN K. CHAPMAN, admitted to bar, 1982, Louisiana; 1983, Oregon; 1984, U.S. District Court, District of Oregon and U.S. Court of Appeals, Ninth Circuit. *Education:* University of Minnesota (B.S., with distinction, 1978); William Mitchell College of Law (J.D., 1982). *Member:* Multnomah County Bar Association; Oregon State Bar (Past Chair, Debtor-Creditor Section; Past Chairperson, Consumer Bankruptcy, CLE and Professionalism Sub-Committees, Debtor-Creditor Section; Chairperson); American Bankruptcy Institute. ***PRACTICE AREAS:*** Bankruptcy Law; Chapter 7; Chapter 13; Commercial Law.

ASSOCIATE

JEFF PAYNE, born Ontario, Oregon, February 21, 1961; admitted to bar, 2005, Washington, Oregon and U.S. District Court, District of Oregon. *Education:* Boston University (B.A., Music, cum laude, 1983); New England Conservatory (Master of Music, 1990); Lewis and Clark Law School (J.D., 2003). Research Editor 2001-2002, and Notes and Comments Editor, 2002- 2003, Journal of Small and Emerging Business Law. Member, Lewis and Clark Regional Appellate Moot Court Team, 2002. Recipient, Best Oral Advocate, John Henry Hingson III Award, 2002. *Member:* Oregon State Bar (Member, Debtor/Creditor Section). ***PRACTICE AREAS:*** Bankruptcy; Bankruptcy Chapter 7; Bankruptcy Chapter 13; Debtor Bankruptcy.

MICHAEL F. VAN HOOMISSEN

RIVIERA PLAZA, SUITE 319
1618 S.W. FIRST AVENUE
PORTLAND, OREGON 97201
Telephone: 503-221-1529
Facsimile: 503-221-6222
Email: mvanhoom@attglobal.net
URL: http://www.lawyers.com/vanhoomissen

General Civil and Trial Practice in Oregon and Washington Courts. Litigation, Insurance, Insurance Defense, Aviation and Aerospace, Products Liability, Construction Law, Corporate Law, Commercial Law, Business Law, Real Estate, Family Law, Personal Injury, Wills, Trusts and Estates, Probate, Military Law.

MICHAEL F. VAN HOOMISSEN, born Washington, D.C., December 10, 1956; admitted to bar, 1984, Oregon, Pennsylvania and District of Columbia; 1987 Washington; U.S. Supreme Court; U.S. Court of Military Appeals. *Education:* U.S. Air Force Academy (B.S., Astronautical Engineering, 1979); University of San Francisco (J.D., 1983). *Member:* Oregon State Bar (Past President, Aviation Section); Washington State (Member, Seattle/King County Aviation Section) and Federal (National Delegate) Bar Associations; District of Columbia Bar; Lawyer-Pilots Bar Association; Aviation Insurance Association; Experimental Aircraft Association Legal Advisory Council; Helicopter Association International; Oregon Aviation Alliance (President). [Active Duty: USAF, 1979-1986; USAFR, 1987; Col., JAG, ORANG, 1989—]

REPRESENTATIVE CLIENTS: Trans World Airlines, Inc.; American Eurocopter; Flightcraft, Inc.; Falcon Jet Corp.; Van's Aircraft, Inc.; Avid Aircraft, Inc.; Aero Air, Inc.; OMF Aircraft, Inc.; Globe Airport Security Services, Inc.; Andy Frain Aviation Services, Inc.; Aviation Research Systems, Inc.; West Air Charter; City of Newport, Oregon; Underwriters at Lloyd's of London; Preservatrice-Fonciere Assurances; Gerling-Konzern Insurance Co.; Acuity Insurance; American Eagle Group; AIG Aviation Insurance Services; Universal Loss Management, Inc.; Reliance National; Snyder Roofing & Sheet Metal, Inc.; Federal Express Corporation; Heli Tech, Inc.; Helicopter Technology, Inc.; H-S Tool and Parts, Inc.

VavRosky MacColl Olson, P.C.

555 UMPQUA BANK PLAZA
ONE S.W. COLUMBIA
PORTLAND, OREGON 97258
Telephone: 503-223-2125
Fax: 503-223-1904
URL: http://www.vavrosky.com

Workers Compensation Defense, Federal Workers Compensation Defense, Employment Law Defense, Longshore and Harbor Workers Compensation Act, Americans with Disabilities Act, Family and Medical Leave Act, Occupational Safety and Health, Appellate Practice.

SHAREHOLDERS

DENNIS R. VAV ROSKY, born Oakland, California, March 9, 1943; admitted to bar, 1968, Oregon. *Education:* University of Chicago; Portland State College; Northwestern School of Law, Lewis and Clark College (J.D., 1968). Senior Deputy, Multnomah County District Attorney's Office, 1968-1971. President, Association of Workers' Compensation Defense Attorneys, 1982. *Member:* Multnomah County Bar Association; Oregon State Bar. ***PRACTICE AREAS:*** Workers Compensation Defense; Longshore and Harbor Workers Compensation Act.

E. KIMBARK MACCOLL, JR., born Pasadena, California, March 15, 1950; admitted to bar, 1975, Oregon. *Education:* Princeton University (B.A., magna cum laude, 1972); University of Oregon (J.D., 1975). Phi Delta Phi. Member, Managing Board and Editor, Oregon Survey, Oregon Law Review, 1974-1975. *Member:* Multnomah County Bar Association; Oregon State Bar. ***PRACTICE AREAS:*** Workers Compensation Defense; Family and Medical Leave Act. ***Email:*** kimmaccoll@vavrosky.com

KARLI L. OLSON, born Portland, Oregon, November 20, 1951; admitted to bar, 1977, Oregon. *Education:* Oregon State University (B.S., 1974); Northwestern School of Law, Lewis and Clark College (J.D., 1977). Association of Workers' Compensation Defense Attorneys, 1982—. *Member:* Multnomah County Bar Association; Oregon State Bar (Member, Workers' Compensation Section). ***PRACTICE AREAS:*** Workers Compensation Defense (100%). ***Email:*** klolson@vavrosky.com

STEPHEN L. PFEIFER, born Tacoma, Washington, November 21, 1963; admitted to bar, 1992, Washington and U.S. District Court, Eastern District of Washington; 1993, Oregon. *Education:* University of Notre Dame (B.A., cum laude, 1986); Gonzaga University School of Law (J.D., 1992). *Member:* Washington State Bar Association; Oregon State Bar; Washington State Trial Lawyers Association. ***PRACTICE AREAS:*** Workers Compensation Defense; Longshore and Harbor Workers Compensation Act. ***Email:*** slpfeifer@vavrosky.com

THOMAS P. BUSCH, born Cincinnati, Ohio, September 5, 1959; admitted to bar, 1988, Oregon. *Education:* University of Portland (B.A., 1983); Northwestern School of Law (J.D., 1987). *Member:* Multnomah County Bar Association; Oregon State Bar; Oregon Trial Lawyers Association; The Association of Trial Lawyers of America. ***PRACTICE AREAS:*** Workers Compensation Defense (100%).

DAVID L. JOHNSTONE, born Tacoma, Washington, January 4, 1953; admitted to bar, 1986, Oregon; 1987, Washington. *Education:* University of Portland (B.A., 1978); Northwestern School of Law of Lewis and Clark College (J.D., 1986). ***PRACTICE AREAS:*** Workers Compensation Defense (100%). ***Email:*** dljohnstone@vavrosky.com

RANDALL VOGT

Established in 1977

2125 SW FOURTH AVENUE, SUITE 600
PORTLAND, OREGON 97201
Telephone: 503-228-9858
Fax: 503-222-5405
Email: vogt4me1@comcast.net
URL: http://randallvogtlaw.com

Criminal Law, Personal Injury, Sexual Abuse, Driving While intoxicated, Sexual Assault, Drug Crimes, Juvenile Crimes, Parole and Probation, Traffic Violations, Homicide, Civil Litigation.

FIRM PROFILE: Performed over 150 jury Trials. (State and Federal Criminal Defense).

RANDALL VOGT, born Peoria, Illinois, April 19, 1950; admitted to bar, 1977, Oregon; 1980, U.S. District Court, District of Oregon. *Education:* University of California at Davis (A.B.); Willamette University (J.D.). Certification to defend Death Penalty Cases, State of Oregon, 2003—. *Member:* Oregon Criminal Defense Lawyers Association; Oregon State Bar; Multnomah County Bar Association. ***PRACTICE AREAS:*** Clergy Sexual Misconduct; Sexual Abuse; Criminal Law; Personal Injury; Driving While Intoxicated; Sexual Assault; Juvenile Crimes; Parole and Probation; Traffic Violations; Homicide; Civil Litigation.

WEISS, JENSEN, ELLIS & HOWARD

PORTLAND, OREGON

(See Holland & Knight LLP)

WELCH, BRUUN & GREEN ATTORNEYS AT LAW

4380 S.W. MACADAM AVENUE, SUITE 120
PORTLAND, OREGON 97239
Telephone: 503-221-0870
Fax: 503-221-0515
Email: wbgatty@pcez.com
URL: http://www.wbgattylaw.com

Workers Compensation, Personal Injury, Tort Law, Social Security Disability, Longshore and Harbor Workers Compensation Act Claims, Jones Act Claims.

PARTNERS OF FIRM

BRIAN L. WELCH, admitted to bar, 1963, Oregon and U.S. District Court, District of Oregon; 1965, U.S. Court of Military Appeals. *Education:* California State University at Long Beach (B.A., 1960); Willamette University College of Law (LL.B., 1963). *Member:* Multnomah Bar Association; Oregon State Bar (Member, Sections on: Workers' Compensation; Law Foundation; Litigation); Oregon Trial Lawyers Association. ***PRACTICE AREAS:*** Worker's Compensation Law; Tort Law; Legal Malpractice Law. ***Email:*** bwelch@wbgatty.com

LARRY K. BRUUN, admitted to bar, 1967, Oregon; 1973, U.S. District Court, District of Oregon. *Education:* University of Oregon (B.A., 1964); Willamette University (J.D., 1967). *Member:* Multnomah Bar Association; Oregon State Bar (Member, Sections on: Workers' Compensation; Litigation; Administrative Law); Oregon Trial Lawyers Association. ***PRACTICE AREAS:*** Workers Compensation Law; Personal Injury Law; Social Security Disability. ***Email:*** lbruun@wbgatty.com

DOUGLAS S. GREEN, admitted to bar, 1968, Oregon; 1974, U.S. Court of Appeals for the Armed Forces; 1976, U.S. District Court, District of Oregon; U.S. Court of Appeals, Ninth Circuit. *Education:* Lewis and Clark College (B.A., Political Science, 1965); Willamette University (J.D., 1968). *Member:* Oregon State Bar. ***PRACTICE AREAS:*** Workers Compensation; Personal Injury; Social Security. ***Email:*** dgreen@wbgatty.com

TED M. LEW, admitted to bar, 1993, Oregon. *Education:* Portland State University (B.S., 1988); Northwestern School of Law at Lewis & Clark College (J.D., 1991). *Member:* Multnomah Bar Association; Oregon State Bar (Member, Section on: Workers' Compensation). ***LANGUAGES:*** Chinese. ***PRACTICE AREAS:*** Workers Compensation; Personal Injury; Social Security. ***Email:*** tlew@wbgatty.com

GEORGE J. WALL, admitted to bar, 1993, Oregon. *Education:* University of California at Davis (B.S.); California Polytechnic State University (M.A.); Santa Clara University (J.D.). ***PRACTICE AREAS:*** Worker's Compensation; Social Security; Personal Injury.

MARYBETH WOSKO, born Springfield, Massachusetts; admitted to bar, 1992, Oregon; 1993, U.S. District Court, District of Oregon; 1997, U.S. Court of Appeals, Ninth Circuit. *Education:* University of Connecticut (B.A., History, 1988); Lewis and Clark College, Northwestern School of Law (J.D., 1991). *Member:* Multnomah County Bar Association; Oregon State Bar (Workers Compensation Section); Oregon Trial Lawyers Association; Oregon Women Lawyers. ***PRACTICE AREAS:*** Workers Compensation; Personal Injury; Employment Law; Civil Litigation. ***Email:*** mwosko@wbgatty.com

ASSOCIATE

KLARISSA G. DELEHANT, admitted to bar, 2003, Oregon. *Education:* University of Notre Dame (B.A., 1998); Northwestern School of Law (J.D., 2002). *Member:* Oregon State Bar; Oregon Minority Lawyers Association; Oregon Women Lawyers Association. ***PRACTICE AREAS:*** Workers Compensation; Personal Injury. ***Email:*** kdelehant@wbgatty.com

WETZEL DeFRANG & SANDOR

838 S.W. FIRST AVENUE
SUITE 300
PORTLAND, OREGON 97204
Telephone: 503-220-0299
FAX: 503-225-1322
Email: wdslawyers@aol.com

Taxation including Civil and Criminal Tax Litigation, Business Planning and Estate Planning.

MEMBERS OF FIRM

JOSEPH WETZEL, born Philadelphia, Pennsylvania, April 20, 1944; admitted to bar, 1969, Oregon and U.S. Tax Court; 1983, U.S. Claims Court. *Education:* Muhlenberg College (A.B., 1966); Temple University School of Law (J.D., 1969). Trial Lawyer, Office of the Chief Counsel for the Internal Revenue Service, 1969-1974. Adjunct Professor of Law, Taxation, Northwestern Law School, Lewis and Clark College, 1978. *Member:* Oregon State Bar (Member, Committee on Taxation, 1974-1977; Member, Taxation Section). ***PRACTICE AREAS:*** Taxation; Civil and Criminal Tax Litigation; Business Planning; Estate Planning.

GARY R. DeFRANG, born St. Paul, Minnesota, May 31, 1941; admitted to bar, 1969, Colorado and U.S. Tax Court; 1972, Oregon; 1981, U.S. District Court, District of Oregon. *Education:* Central Michigan University (B.S., 1963); University of Denver (J.D., 1968). Member, Order of St. Ives. Trial Attorney, Chief Counsel's Office, Internal Revenue Service, 1968-1981. *Member:* Oregon State Bar; American Bar Association. ***PRACTICE AREAS:*** Taxation; Civil and Criminal Tax Litigation; Business Planning; Estate Planning.

RUSSELL A. SANDOR, born Cleveland, Ohio, August 12, 1948; admitted to bar, 1982, Oregon. *Education:* Concordia College; University of Oregon (B.A., 1970); Northwestern School of Law, Lewis & Clark College (J.D., 1981); Boston University Law School (LL.M. in Taxation, 1982). *Member:* Oregon State Bar. ***PRACTICE AREAS:*** Taxation; Civil and Criminal Tax Litigation; Business Planning; Estate Planning.

OF COUNSEL (RETIRED)

GARTHE BROWN, born Portland, Oregon, May 16, 1914; admitted to bar, 1941, Oregon; 1943, U.S. Tax Court; 1947, U.S. District Court, District of Oregon; 1950, U.S. Court of Appeals, 9th Circuit and U.S. Claims Court; 1971, U.S. Supreme Court. *Education:* Northwestern College of Law (LL.B., 1941). Member, Board of Directors, Volunteers of America, 1954—. *Member:* Multnomah County and American Bar Associations; Oregon State Bar. (Retired)

WILLIAMS FREDRICKSON, LLC

1515 S.W. FIFTH, SUITE 844
PORTLAND, OREGON 97201-5447
Telephone: 503-222-9966
Fax: 503-796-1009
Email: info@williamsfredrickson.com

Admiralty, Eminent Domain, General Business and Business Planning, Corporate, Partnership, Probate, Estate Planning, Wills and Trusts, Real Property, Land Use, Environmental and Hazardous Waste, Insurance and Workers Compensation Law. General Civil and Trial Practice in all State and Federal Courts.

FLOYD A. FREDRICKSON (Retired)

DAVID R. WILLIAMS (1923-2005)

JOHN DUDREY, born Portland, Oregon, July 26, 1948; admitted to bar, 1973, Oregon. *Education:* Stanford University (B.A., with great distinction, 1970; J.D., 1973). ***PRACTICE AREAS:*** Admiralty; Civil Appeals; Product Liability. ***Email:*** jdudrey@williamsfredrickson.com

MICHAEL D. WILLIAMS, born Portland, Oregon, May 24, 1946; admitted to bar, 1974, Oregon; 2002, Washington. *Education:* University of Oregon (B.A., 1968); Hastings College of the Law, University of California (J.D., 1974). ***PRACTICE AREAS:*** Litigation; Commercial Law; Hazardous Waste Liability Law. ***Email:*** mwilliams@williamsfredrickson.com

REPRESENTATIVE CLIENTS: Beaverton Toyota Co.; CIGNA Cos.; E.J. Bartells Co.; General Electric Corp.; Insurance Company of North America; International Marine Underwriters; Homeport Insurance Co.; Liberty Northwest Insurance Corp.; Marine Office of America Corp.; Matson Navigation Co.; Mitsui & Co. (USA) Inc.; Russ Chevrolet; Saturn of Beaverton; 76 Products Co.; Stevedoring Services of America; The Travelers Cos.; Underwriters Marine Services; United Grain Corp.; UNOCAL.

WILLIAMS, KASTNER & GIBBS PLLC

Established in 1987

PIONEER OFFICE TOWER
888 SW FIFTH AVENUE, SUITE 600
PORTLAND, OREGON 97204-2025
Telephone: 503-228-7967
Fax: 503-222-7261
Email: info@wkg.com
URL: http://www.wkg.com

Seattle, Washington Office: Telephone: 206-628-6600. Fax: 206-628-6611.
Tacoma, Washington Office: Telephone: 253-593-5620. Fax: 253-593-5625.

Civil Litigation, Federal Litigation, Trial Practice, Medical Malpractice Defense, Drug and Medical Device Litigation, Products Liability, Professional Liability, Environmental Litigation, Business Law, Mergers and Acquisitions, Real Estate, Corporate Law, Family Law.

(This Listing Continued)

FIRM PROFILE: Williams, Kastner & Gibbs PLLC has been serving clients in the Northwest since the Seattle office opened in 1929. With 90+ attorneys in three offices located throughout Washington and Oregon, we combine the resources and knowledge gained from working on matters of national and international importance with the personal service only a local firm can provide. As a Northwest native, we understand your community and your business needs and can provide the solutions you're looking for. As National Counsel for several clients, we understand how your needs fit within the national and global economies.

MEMBERS OF FIRM

AMY J. CARLTON, admitted to bar, 1992, Oregon. *Education:* Northwestern School of Law, Lewis and Clark College (J.D., 1992). ***LANGUAGES:*** German. ***PRACTICE AREAS:*** Real Estate; Corporate Law; Mergers and Acquisitions. ***Email:*** acarlton@wkg.com

PAUL R. DUDEN, admitted to bar, 1966, Oregon. *Education:* University of Oregon (LL.B., 1966). ***PRACTICE AREAS:*** Medical Litigation; Drug and Medical Device Litigation; Professional and Product Liability; Health Care; Litigation. ***Email:*** pduden@wkg.com

ERIC J. NEIMAN, admitted to bar, 1982, Oregon; 1984, Washington. *Education:* University of Oregon (J.D., 1982). ***PRACTICE AREAS:*** Health Care; Hospital Law; Drug and Medical Device Litigation; Professional Liability; Employment Law; General Civil Trial Work; Products Liability. ***Email:*** eneiman@wkg.com

GEORGE S. PITCHER, admitted to bar, 1996, Oregon; 1997, Washington. *Education:* Willamette University (J.D., First in Class, 1996). ***PRACTICE AREAS:*** Civil Litigation; Products Liability; Employment Law. ***Email:*** gpitcher@wkg.com

J. RICHARD URRUTIA, admitted to bar, 1982, Oregon and U.S. District Court, District of Oregon; 1995, U.S. Court of Appeals, Ninth Circuit; 1998, U.S. Supreme Court. *Education:* University of Oregon (J.D., 1982). ***PRACTICE AREAS:*** Litigation; Real Estate; Business Litigation; Family Law; General Civil Trial Work. ***Email:*** rurrutia@wkg.com

ASSOCIATES

DAVID C. CAMPBELL, admitted to bar, 2003, Oregon and U.S. District Court, District of Oregon. *Education:* University of Oregon School of Law (J.D., 2003). ***PRACTICE AREAS:*** Health Care; Products Liability. ***Email:*** dcampbell@wkg.com

MARC M. CARLTON, admitted to bar, 1999, Oregon. *Education:* University of Oregon (J.D., 1999). ***PRACTICE AREAS:*** Litigation; Business Law; Business Transactions; Construction Law; Products Liability. ***Email:*** mcarlton@wkg.com

THOMAS A. PED, admitted to bar, 1995, Oregon; 1998, U.S. District Court, District of Oregon; 1999, U.S. Court of Appeals, Ninth Circuit. *Education:* Willamette University College of Law (J.D., 1995). ***PRACTICE AREAS:*** Insurance Defense; Products Liability; Construction Defects; Litigation. ***Email:*** tped@wkg.com

SHARON C. PETERS, admitted to bar, 2001, Kentucky; 2004, Oregon. *Education:* University of Louisville (J.D., 2001). ***PRACTICE AREAS:*** Labor and Employment; Litigation; Products Liability. ***Email:*** speters@wkg.com

HEATHER J. VAN METER, admitted to bar, 1998, Oregon; 1999, Alaska, Washington and U.S. District Court, District of Oregon. *Education:* Willamette University College of Law (J.D., 1998). ***PRACTICE AREAS:*** Litigation; Products Liability; Complex and Multi-District Litigation; Medical Malpractice; Professional Malpractice; Construction Litigation; Business Litigation; Constitutional Law. ***Email:*** hvanmeter@wkg.com

ELLEN M. VOSS, admitted to bar, 2000, Oregon; 2001, Washington. *Education:* Willamette University (J.D., 2000). ***PRACTICE AREAS:*** Civil Litigation; Products Liability; Professional Malpractice; Health Care. ***Email:*** evoss@wkg.com

OF COUNSEL

STEPHEN R. FRANK, admitted to bar, 1967, Oregon. *Education:* Willamette University (J.D., 1967). ***PRACTICE AREAS:*** Medical Litigation; Drug and Medical Device Litigation; Administrative Litigation; Labor and Employment; Litigation. ***Email:*** sfrank@wkg.com

ERIKA J. GEORGE, admitted to bar, 1997, Oregon; 1999, Washington. *Education:* University of Oregon School of Law (J.D., 1997). ***PRACTICE AREAS:*** Civil Litigation; Products Liability; Health Care; Construction Defects; Construction Law. ***Email:*** egeorge@wkg.com

DAVID J. RYAN, admitted to bar, 1995, Oregon; 1996, Washington and U.S. District Court, District of Oregon; 1997, U.S. District Court, Western District of Washington. *Education:* Lewis and Clark Law School (J.D., cum laude, 1995). ***PRACTICE AREAS:*** Insurance Litigation; Insurance Coverage; Insurance Defense; Professional Liability Defense; Products Liability; Premises Liability Defense; Retail Liability; Employment Law; Employment Discrimination; Environmental Law. ***Email:*** dryan@wkg.com

REPRESENTATIVE CLIENTS: Coca-Cola Co.; McCormick & Schmick's; Podiatry Insurance Company of America; St. Paul Travelers; Underwriters at Lloyds; Utica Mutual Insurance Co.; Great American Insurance Company; Bank of Montreal. *Pharmaceutical and Health Care:* Bristol Myers-Squibb; Catholic Health Initiatives; Sanofi-Aventis Group; Johnson & Johnson; Medmarc; Medtronic, Inc.; Pfizer, Inc.; Providence Health Systems; Synthes (U.S.A); ConMed Corporation.

WILLIAMS LOVE O'LEARY CRAINE & POWERS, P.C.

9755 S.W. BARNES ROAD, SUITE 450
PORTLAND, OREGON 97225
Telephone: 503-295-2924
Fax: 503-295-3720
Email: info@wdolaw.com
URL: http://www.wdolaw.com

Litigation in Product Liability, Lender Liability, Commercial and Franchise Law, Personal Injury, Toxic Tort Litigation, Professional Negligence and Court-Awarded Attorney Fees.

(This Listing Continued)

FIRM PROFILE: The firm was founded in 1986 by Mike Williams and Gayle Troutwine. Gayle Troutwine has now retired from the practice of law. The firm's emphasis is on representing victims of mass torts, defective or toxic products, and professional negligence. The firm has been active at the national level in several pharmaceutical and defective products cases, including Hormone Therapay, Fen-Phen (Redux), Primary Pulmonary Hypertension (PPH), Phenylprophnolamine (PPA), Baycol, mercury in vaccines (thimerosal), Dalkon Shield, Cu-7 IUDs, Neo-Mull Soy infant formula, L-Tryptophan, breast implants, diet drugs and Pedicle Screws. Since its inception, creativity, innovation and excellence in client service have always been and will continue to be the hallmarks of the firm.

MICHAEL L. WILLIAMS, born Wichita, Kansas, July 30, 1947; admitted to bar, 1978, Oregon and U.S. District Court, District of Oregon; 1979, U.S. Court of Appeals, 9th Circuit; 1983, U.S. Supreme Court. *Education:* Wabash College (B.A., cum laude, 1969); University of California at Berkeley (M.A., 1974); Harvard University (J.D., magna cum laude, 1978). Phi Beta Kappa. Co-Editor-in-Chief, Harvard Environmental Law Review, 1977-1978. Editor-in-Chief, Oregon Litigation Journal, 1980-1989. Associate Editor, Litigation News, Published by ABA Litigation Section, 1984-1986. Author: Chapter on, "Products Liability," Oregon Law of Torts, 1981 and 1992. Member, 1982-1986 and Chairperson, 1984-1986, Eugene School Board, District 4J. Secretary, Federal Practice and Procedures Committee, 1999-2002. *Member:* Oregon State Bar (Chairperson, Procedure and Practice Committee, 1983-1984; Member, Uniform Civil Jury Instruction Committee, 1986-1989; Chair, Toxic Tort Section, 1992-1993); American Bar Association; Multnomah Bar Association (Member, Court Liaison Committee, 1999-2002; Secretary, 2001); The Association of Trial Lawyers of America (Co-Chair, Vaccine Litigation Group); Trial Lawyers for Public Justice; Oregon Trial Lawyers Association (President, 1993-1994). ***PRACTICE AREAS:*** Products Liability; Personal Injury; Toxic Tort; Professional Negligence; Pharmaceutical Litigation. ***Email:*** mwilliams@wdolaw.com

LINDA C. LOVE, born Valdosta, Georgia, February 6, 1954; admitted to bar, 1981, Oregon; 1982, U.S. District Court, District of Oregon; 2002, Washington. *Education:* University of Northern Colorado (B.A., 1976); Willamette University (J.D., 1981). Member, Willamette University College of Law Willamette Law Review, 1979-1981. Author: "Third Party Actions," Chapter 27, Workers Compensation 2000 Cumulative Supplement, Oregon State Board Workers' Compensation Section; "Lamb Brothers, Inc. v. First National Bank of Oregon: Secured Party's Liability for the Sale of Excess Collateral, 16 Willamette Law Review 755 (1980); "Timber and Timber Land Taxation," 16 Willamette Law Review 397 (1979); "Employment Discrimination of the Handicapped and Remedies for Unlawful Employment Practices," 16 Willamette Law Review 535 (1979). Staff Attorney, Oregon Workers' Compensation Board, 1983-1984. President, Oregon Workers Compensation Attorneys, 1991-1994. President, Oregon Trial Lawyer's Association, 1997-1998. *Member:* Oregon State Bar (House of Delegates, 1996—); American Trial Lawyers Association; Oregon Trial Lawyers Association (Member, Executive Committee, Workers Compensation Section, 1990-2000; Co-Chair, Workers' Compensation Section CLE Committee, 1999-2001). ***PRACTICE AREAS:*** Pharmaceutical Litigation. ***Email:*** llove@wdolaw.com

LESLIE W. O'LEARY, born Helena, Montana, September 16, 1959; admitted to bar, 1999, Oregon. *Education:* University of Montana (B.A., cum laude, 1981); Northwestern School of Law (J.D., 1998). Phi Delta Phi. Author: "Mass Tort Class Actions: Will Achem Spawn Creative Solutions?" Defense Counsel Journal, October 1998; "Kumho Tire in Oregon: Applying Daubert Test to expert testimony," Oregon Trial Lawyers Magazine, Summer 2000. *Member:* Multnomah County, Federal and American Bar Associations; Oregon State Bar; Oregon Trial Lawyers Association (Member, Board of Governors); Oregon Women Lawyers (Board Member); The Association of Trial Lawyers of America (Co-Chair, Ephedra Litigation Group); Trial Lawyers for Public Justice. ***PRACTICE AREAS:*** Products Liability; Personal Injury; Pharmaceutical Litigation. ***Email:*** loleary@wdolaw.com

DIANA CRAINE, born Kalama, Washington, December 1, 1956; admitted to bar, 1982, Oregon; 1983, Washington; 1993, U.S. District Court, District of Washington. *Education:* Western Washington University (B.A., 1979); Willamette University (J.D., 1982). Member, Board of Directors, National Conference of Women's Bar Association, 1995-1998. Member, Council on Court Procedures, 1995-2000. Member, Board of Directors, 1989-1992, President, 1991, State of Oregon, Foster Parents Association. Member, Board of Trustees, Willamette University, 1989-1992. *Member:* Oregon State Bar (Member: Rights of the Handicapped Committee, 1986-1989; Committee on Judicial Administration, 1992-1995; Task Force on Insurance Conflicts, 1993; Task Force, Vision 2000, 1994); American Trial Lawyers Association; Oregon Trial Lawyers Association; Oregon Women Lawyers (Board of Directors, 1989-1993, President, 1994). ***PRACTICE AREAS:*** Medical Negligence; Products Liability; Pharmaceutical Litigation. ***Email:*** dcraine@wdolaw.com

THOMAS B. POWERS, born Boston, Massachusetts, August 20, 1960; admitted to bar, 1998, Oregon, Washington and U.S. District Court, District of Oregon; U.S. Court of Federal Claims. *Education:* Florida State University (B.S., 1993); Northwestern School of Law (J.D., 1998). Member, Moot Court Honor Board, Lewis & Clark School of Law, 1997-1998. *Member:* Oregon State Bar; Oregon Trial Lawyers Association; American Trial Lawyers Association. ***PRACTICE AREAS:*** Pharmaceutical Litigation; Products Liability; Personal Injury; Medical Negligence. ***Email:*** tpowers@wdolaw.com

---

BRIAN S. CAMPF, born Portland, Oregon, July 1, 1967; admitted to bar, 1992, Oregon; 1994, U.S. District Court, District of Oregon. *Education:* Reed College (B.A., 1989); Willamette University (J.D., 1992). Comment, "Datlaws for Excellence In Scholarship," 1986-1987 1988-1989. *Member:* Oregon State Bar; Federal Bar Association; Oregon Trial Lawyers Association; American Trial Lawyers Association. ***PRACTICE AREAS:*** Product Liability; Civil Litigation; Mass Tort Litigation. ***Email:*** bcampf@wdolaw.com

WILLIAMS, ZOGRAFOS & PECK

A PROFESSIONAL CORPORATION

PORTLAND, OREGON

(See Lake Oswego)

Limited Exclusively to the representation of Employers in Labor and Employment Matters, including Union-Management Relations, Labor Negotiations, Employment Discrimination, Wrongful Discharge, Wage and Hour, Preventive Labor Relations, Before Federal and State Courts and Administrative Agencies.

WINEMILLER WIESELMAN LLP

Established in 1987

1420 WORLD TRADE CENTER
121 S.W. SALMON STREET
PORTLAND, OREGON 97204
Telephone: 503-222-2510
Facsimile: 503-227-2103
Email: kriswinemiller@pacificnwlaw.com
URL: http://www.lawyers.com/kristenwinemiller

Criminal Defense, Civil Litigation.

KRISTEN L. WINEMILLER, born Chicago, Illinois, October 30, 1960; admitted to bar, 1986, Oregon; 1987, U.S. District Court, District of Oregon; 1994, U.S. Court of Appeals, Ninth Circuit. *Education:* Carleton College (B.A., Political Science, concentration in Science Technology and Public Policy, 1982); Northwestern School of Law (J.D., 1986). *Member:* Oregon State Bar (Bar/Press/Broadcaster Council); Multnomah Bar Association (Member, Judicial Screening Committee); National Association of Criminal Defense Attorneys; Oregon Trial Lawyers Association. **PRACTICE AREAS:** Criminal Defense; Civil Litigation.

JACOB (JACK) WIESELMAN, born Tangier, Morocco, November 5, 1952; admitted to bar, 1977, District of Columbia, New Jersey and Massachusetts; 1979, U.S. District Court, District of Columbia, U.S. District Court, District of Massachusetts and New Jersey; 1982, U.S. District Court, District of Connecticut; 1983, Connecticut; 2005, Oregon. *Education:* University of Michigan (B.A., with high honors, 1974); Georgetown University (J.D., 1977). Lecturer of Law, University of Connecticut School of Law, 1983—. *Member:* Hartford County, Connecticut and American (Member: International Law Section; Criminal Justice Section) Bar Associations; District of Columbia Bar; American Immigration Lawyers Association; The Association of Trial Lawyers of America; National Association of Criminal Defense Lawyers. **LANGUAGES:** French and Spanish. **PRACTICE AREAS:** Criminal Defense.

WISEMAN LAW OFFICE, P.C.

PORTLAND, OREGON

(See Hillsboro)

Bankruptcy, Business Start-Ups, Personal Injury, Automobile Accidents, Dog Bites, Slip and Fall, Wrongful Death, Domestic Relations, Child Custody, Child Support, Divorce, Premarital Agreements, Business Law, Criminal Law, Driving While Intoxicated, Drug Crimes, Aviation Law.

RALPH E. WISER, III

PORTLAND, OREGON

(See Lake Oswego)

Personal Injury, Medical Malpractice, Disability Insurance Issues, Sexual Abuse, Products Liability, Automobile Accidents and Injuries, Wrongful Death, Negligence, Torts, Employment Law, ERISA, Discrimination, Labor Law, Professional Licensing Issues, Civil Litigation, Business Litigation, Professional Sports Agency Issues, Trial Practice.

LAWRENCE WOBBROCK TRIAL LAWYER P.C.

TENTH FLOOR
JACKSON TOWER
806 SW BROADWAY
PORTLAND, OREGON 97205
Telephone: 503-228-6600
Fax: 503-222-4787
URL: http://www.lawyers.com/lawrence_wobbrock
URL: http://www.wobbrocklaw.com
Email: lwobbrock@wobbrock.com
URL: http://www.wobbrock.com

Civil Trial Practice in State and Federal Courts, including Personal Injury, Medical Malpractice, Trade Secret Litigation, Professional Negligence, Products Liability.

LAWRENCE WOBBROCK, born Modesto, California, March 27, 1948; admitted to bar, 1977, Oregon and U.S. District Court, District of Oregon; 1981, U.S. Court of Appeals, Ninth Circuit; 1990, U.S. Court of Federal Claims; 1994, U.S. Supreme Court. *Education:* University of Oregon (B.S., 1970); Northwestern School of Law of Lewis and Clark College (J.D., 1977). Listed in Best Lawyers in America. Adjunct Professor, Torts Seminar, Lewis & Clark College. Lecturer: Civil Trial issues, including Medical Negligence, Professionalism, Personal Injury, Product Liability and Trial Strategy, in connection with Continuing Legal Education Programs before the Oregon Trial Lawyers Association, the Oregon State Bar, the Multnomah Bar Association, the Oregon Law Institute, Oregon Health Sciences University. Appointed Counsel, Attorney Disciplinary Proceedings, Oregon State Bar, 1982. Appointed to Oregon State Bar and Multnomah County Local Professional Responsibility Committees, 2000-2003; Chairperson, 2003—. Selected to the American Board of Trial Advocacy. *Member:* Multnomah County and American Bar Associations; Oregon State Bar (Member: Executive Committee, Litigation Section, 1986-1989; Uniform Civil Jury Instructions Committee, 1989-1992; Health Law Section, 1995-1996; House of Delegates, 1996-1999); The Association of Trial Lawyers of America (State Delegate, 1990-1992); Oregon Trial Lawyers Association (Member, Board of Governors, 1985-1994; Chairperson, Legislative Committee, 1989-1991; President, 1992-1993); Trial Lawyers For Public Justice (Member, Board of Governors, 1990-1995). (Certified as a Civil Trial Advocate by the National Board of Trial Advocacy). **REPORTED CASES:** Gast v. State, 36 Or. App. 441, 585 P2d 12 (1978); State ex rel rel. Grimm v. Ashmanskas, 298 Or. 206, 690 P2d 1063 (1984); In Re Conduct of Johnson, 300 Or. 52, 707 P2d 573 (1990); O'Brien v. State of Oregon, 104 Or. App. 1, 799 P2d 171 (1990), 312 Or. 672, 826 P2d 633 (1992); Warren v. Farmers Ins. Co., of Oregon 106 Or. App. 116, 806 P2d 710 (1991), rev'd 313 Or. 158 830 P 203 (1992); Zehr v. Haugen, 121 Or. App.489, 318 Or. 647, 871 P2d 1006 (1994); Krushwitz v. MacDonalds Restaurants of Oregon Inc., 129 Or. App. 621, 323 Or. 520, 919 P.2d 465 (1996); Waddill v. Anchor Hocking, 149 Or. App. 464, 944 P.2d 957 (1997), rev'd, 330 Or. 376, 8 P.3d 200 (2000), 331 Or. 595, 18 P.3d 1096 (2001), aff'd on recons, 175 Or.App. 294, 27 P.3d 1092 (2001), aff'd on remand, 334 Or. 260, 47 P.3d 486 (2002), rev denied, __us__, cert filed, No. 02-370 (2002); Waddill v. Anchor Hocking, 330 OR 376, 813, 200 Rev, OR Recous 331 OR 595, 18 P3d 1069 (2001). **PRACTICE AREAS:** Medical Malpractice; Product Liability; General Personal Injury; Trade Secrets Litigation. **Email:** lwobbrock@wobbrock.com

---

RICHARD A. LANE, born Brooklyn, New York, March 9, 1959; admitted to bar, 1986, Oregon; 1998, U.S. District Court, District of Oregon. *Education:* University of Oregon (Pol. Sci, 1983); Lewis and Clark University (J.D., 1986). *Member:* Multnomah and Oregon State (Litigation Section Executive Committee Member, 1997—; Procedure and Practice Committee, 1994-1997, Chairperson 1996-1997; 1997, Presidents Membership Service Award; Co-Author 1997, Oregon Legislation (OSB-CLE) Chapter 3 "Civil Procedure and Dispute Resolution"; Author 1995, Oregon Legislation (OSBCLE) Chapter 20 "Torts and Product Liability"; Multnomah County Local Professional Responsibility Committee (1993-1996) Bar Associations; The Association of Trial Lawyers of America; Oregon Trial Lawyers Association (Member, Legislative Committee Chairperson, 1999—). **PRACTICE AREAS:** Medical Malpractice; Products Liability; Personal Injury Law; Wrongful Death. **Email:** rlane@wobbrock.com

LEGAL SUPPORT PERSONNEL

MARILYN HARLOW, R.N., born Portland, Oregon, May 6, 1955. *Education:* Oregon State University; Oregon Health Sciences University School of Nursing (B.S.N., 1978). Registered Nurse, Oregon, 1978, Washington, 1980-1992 and Oregon 1992. Preceptor, Coronary Care Nursing 1981. Instructor: Hemodynamic Monitoring, 1982; Childbirth Educator, 1984-1985. (Nurse Paralegal). **Email:** mharlow@wobbrock.com

---

ROBERT L. WOLF & ASSOCIATES

1207 S.W. 6TH AVENUE
PORTLAND, OREGON 97204
Telephone: 503-241-0992
Fax: 503-228-4529
URL: http://www.wolflaw.net
Email: rwolf8888@att.net
URL: http://www.lawyers.com/robertwolf

Personal Injury, Automobile Accidents, Dog Bites, Sexual Abuse, Slip and Fall, Wrongful Death, Legal Malpractice.

ROBERT L. WOLF, born Oklahoma City, Oklahoma, May 21, 1949; admitted to bar, 1977, Oregon; 1979, U.S. District Court, District of Oregon. *Education:* Wayne State University (B.A., 1974); University of Dayton (J.D., 1977). Member, Moot Court Board, 1975-1977. Author in Oregon Trial Lawyers Association official magazine, 2001. Co-Author: "Court Consolidation," Oregon State Bar Bulletin, 1980. Speaker: American Trial Lawyers Association Conference, Chicago, 2000-2001; Oregon Trial Lawyers Association, 2000-2001; Oregon Trial Lawyers Association, Women's Caucus, 2000-2001. Lecturer in Law: Multnomah Bar Association Continuing Legal Education, 1979; Oregon Trial Lawyers Association, 1980. Deputy District Attorney, 1977-1979. President, Oregon Young Lawyers Association, 1978-1979. *Member:* Multnomah County (Member, Committee on Judicial Selection, 1978-1981) and American (Member, Section on Litigation) Bar Associations; Oregon State Bar (Member: Committee on Civil Jury Instruction, 1982-1984; Litigation, Criminal and Family Law Sections; 9th Circuit Bankruptcy Merit Committee, 1982); Oregon Trial Lawyers Association (Member, Board of Governors, 1983-1985); The Association of Trial Lawyers of America, 1982—.

WOOD TATUM SANDERS & MURPHY

Established in 1870

1001 S.W. FIFTH AVENUE, SUITE 1300
PORTLAND, OREGON 97204-1151
Telephone: 503-224-5430
Facsimile: 503-241-7235
Email: info@woodtatum.com
URL: http://www.woodtatum.com

General Civil and Trial Practice in all State and Federal Courts. Admiralty/Maritime, Insurance Defense and Estate Planning, Wills and Probate, Trusts and Estates.

(This Listing Continued)

FIRM PROFILE: Wood Tatum Sanders & Murphy is recognized as the oldest law firm in the State of Oregon, having been established originally as Durham & Ball in 1870. The firm has been a leading member of Oregon's legal community since that time, concentrating in the areas of maritime law for over 75 years. Representative clients include both domestic and overseas shipowners, cargo interests and marine underwriters. The firm's partners have included three generations of Wood family lawyers, from C.E.S. Wood, who joined the firm in 1887, up through his grandson, Erskine B. Wood, who practiced with the firm until 1986.

MEMBERS OF FIRM

ROBERT I. SANDERS, born New Orleans, Louisiana, September 2, 1942; admitted to bar, 1969, Colorado; 1970, Oregon. *Education:* U.S. Merchant Marine Academy (B.S., 1964); University of Colorado (J.D., 1969). Member, Board of Editors, University of Colorado Law Review, 1968-1969. Judicial Clerk to U.S. District Chief Judge Alfred A. Arraj, District of Colorado, 1969-1970. *Member:* Maritime Law Association of the United States. ***PRACTICE AREAS:*** Admiralty Law; Complex Litigation. ***Email:*** RIS@woodtatum.com

JOHN C. MERCER, born Seattle, Washington, August 4, 1949; admitted to bar, 1974, Oregon; 1990, Washington. *Education:* Harvey Mudd College (B.S., 1971); University of Oregon (J.D., 1974). *Member:* Maritime Law Association; Oregon Association of Defense Counsel; Defense Research Institute; Washington Defense Trial Lawyers Association. ***PRACTICE AREAS:*** Admiralty; General Litigation; Estate Planning; Probate; Business Law. ***Email:*** JCM@woodtatum.com

CRAIG C. MURPHY, born Los Angeles, California, September 7, 1946; admitted to bar, 1973, Oregon. *Education:* Pomona College (B.A., 1968); University of Oregon (J.D., 1973). Speaker: "Preparing and Valuing Wrongful Death Claims," Oregon State Bar, 1996; "Preparation and Presentation of Expert Witness Testimony," Oregon Law Institute, 1995; "Proof of Damages in Maritime Personal Injury and Death Cases," Pacific Northwest Admiralty Law Institute, 1988. Present Chairman, Admiralty Section, Oregon State Bar, 1994-1995; President, Propeller Club of the Port of the Columbia River, 1990-1991. Deputy District Attorney, Multnomah County, 1974-1980. Listed, Best Lawyers in America, Maritime Law. *Member:* Maritime Law Association of the United States (Fisheries Subcommittee); Oregon Association of Defense Counsel. ***PRACTICE AREAS:*** Maritime Law; Longshore and Jones Act Personal Injury Defense; State and Federal Court Litigation; Oil Pollution; Oil Discharge Defense; Arbitration; Mediation. ***Email:*** CCM@woodtatum.com

TODD A. ZILBERT, born Los Angeles, California, May 4, 1960; admitted to bar, 1988, California; 1989, Oregon and Washington. *Education:* University of California at Berkeley; University of California at Los Angeles (A.B., magna cum laude, 1982; J.D., 1988). Recipient, American Jurisprudence Award for Remedies. Contributing Author: "Admiralty Pleading and Procedure," 29 Moore's Federal Practice, §§ 704.09 and 704 App. 01 (Matthew Bender 3d. Ed. 1997). Member, Multnomah County Local Professional Responsibility Committee, 1997-2000. *Member:* Maritime Law Association of the United States. ***PRACTICE AREAS:*** Admiralty Law; Commercial Law; Litigation. ***Email:*** TAZ@woodtatum.com

All Attorneys are members of Multnomah County and the Oregon State Bar Associations.

REPRESENTATIVE CLIENTS: A.I. Marine Adjusters; Assuranceforeningen Gard; Assuranceforeningen Skuld; Britannia Steamship Ins. Association, Ltd.; British Marine Mutual; Carolina Casualty Ins. Co.; Japan Ship Owners' Mutual P & I Assn.; Keystone Shipping Co.; Northern Shipowners (Nordisk); North of England P & I Assoc.; Shipowners Claims Bureau; Shipowners Mutual P & I Assn.; Standard Steamship Owners P & I Assoc.; Steamship Mutual Underwriting Assn.; Sveriges Angfartygs Assurans Forening; United Kingdom Mutual S.S.

YATES, MATTHEWS & ASSOCIATES, P.C.

Established in 1998

ONE SW COLUMBIA STREET, SUITE 1800
PORTLAND, OREGON 97258
Telephone: 503-224-7077
Fax: 503-224-8080
URL: http://www.yatesmatthews.com

Practice limited to Family Law, including Premarital Agreements, Postnuptial Agreements, Cohabitation Agreements, Domestic Partnerships, Divorce, Separation Agreements, Spousal Support, Child Support, Child Custody and Parenting Time, Post Divorce Modification, Post Divorce Enforcement, Paternity, Third Party Custody, Visitation Rights, Domestic Violence and Name Changes.

MICHAEL A. YATES, born Ravenna, Ohio, November 21, 1956; admitted to bar, 1983, Oregon; 1987, U.S. District Court, District of Oregon and U.S. Court of Appeals, 9th Circuit. *Education:* Kent State University (B.A., 1979); Ohio State University (J.D., with honors, 1983). ***PRACTICE AREAS:*** Premarital Agreements; Postnuptial Agreements; Domestic Partnerships; Divorce; Spousal Support; Child Custody; Child Support; Post Divorce Modification.

JEFFREY S. MATTHEWS, born Portland, Oregon, December 2, 1953; admitted to bar, 1982, Oregon and U.S. District Court, District of Oregon. *Education:* Westmont College; University of Oregon (B.A., 1977; J.D., 1981). ***PRACTICE AREAS:*** Premarital Agreements; Postnuptial Agreements; Domestic Partnerships; Divorce; Separation Agreements; Spousal Support; Child Custody; Child Support; Post Divorce Modification; Post Divorce Enforcement; Grandparents Custody; Grandparents Visitation Rights; Third Party Custody; Visitation Rights.

BRENNA A. TANZOSH, born Eatontown, New Jersey, March 21, 1973; admitted to bar, 1999, Oregon; 2001, U.S. District Court, District of Oregon. *Education:* American University (B.A., 1996); University of Maryland (J.D., 1999).

KRISTIN WINNIE EATON, born Pomona, California, November 7, 1969; admitted to bar, 1996, Tennessee; 1998, Oregon; U.S. Tax Court; 1999, U.S. District Court, District of Oregon. *Education:* Lewis and Clark College (B.A., 1991; J.D., 1995). Phi Delta Phi. *Member:* Multnomah County and American Bar Associations; Oregon State Bar; Association for Women Attorneys. ***PRACTICE AREAS:*** Family Law.

OF COUNSEL

JOANN B. REYNOLDS, born Philadelphia, Pennsylvania, November 5, 1942; admitted to bar, 1978, Oregon. *Education:* Rosemont College; University of North Texas (B.S., 1973); Southern Methodist University School of Law (J.D., 1978). ***PRACTICE AREAS:*** Domestic Partnerships; Divorce; Spousal Support; Child Support; Post Divorce Modification; Parental Rights.

YAZBECK, CLORAN & HANSON, LLC

Established in 2002

2750 WELLS FARGO CENTER
1300 S.W. FIFTH AVENUE
PORTLAND, OREGON 97201
Telephone: 503-227-1428
Fax: 503-227-4866
URL: http://www.yazbeckhanson.com
Email: yazbeckhanson.com
URL: http://www.lawyers.com/yazbeckhanson

Construction, Public Contracts, Surety Bond Claims and Defense, Mechanic's Liens, Information Technology, Commercial, General Business, General Practice, Zoning and Land Use, Wills and Probate, Bankruptcy, Business Enterprises, Real Estate, Commercial Leasing.

FIRM PROFILE: General Civil and Trial Practice in all Federal and State Courts, Federal Contract Appeal Boards, concentrated on Construction, Public Contracts, Surety Claims, Mechanics Liens, Employment Law, Timber Sale Contracts, Securities Litigation and Information Technology.

JOSEPH A. YAZBECK, JR., born Louisiana, 1948; admitted to bar, 1974, Texas and U.S. District Court, Northern District of Texas; 1977, Oregon and U.S. District Court, District of Oregon; 1980, U.S. Claims Court; 1984, U.S. Court of Appeals for the Federal Circuit. *Education:* Louisiana State University (B.S., 1971); Tulane University of Louisiana (J.D., 1974). Author: "Oregon Construction Lien Law," Oregon Debtor-Creditor Newsletter, Spring, 1985. Attorney, U.S. Army Corps of Engineers, Fort Worth District, 1974-1975; Portland District, 1975-1977. *Member:* Multnomah County and American (Member, Public Contract Law Section) Bar Associations; Oregon State Bar; State Bar of Texas. ***PRACTICE AREAS:*** Construction Litigation; Public Contracts Law; Surety Law; Information Technology. ***Email:*** jay@yazbeckhanson.com

WILLIAM F. CLORAN, born 1947; admitted to bar, 1972, Oregon. ***SPECIAL AGENCIES:*** Special Assistant Attorney General, Oregon. ***PRACTICE AREAS:*** Construction Law; Government Contract Law; Environmental Law; Administrative Law. ***Email:*** wfc@yazbeckhanson.com

JEFFREY K. HANSON, born Oregon, 1965; admitted to bar, 1990, Oregon; 1991, Washington; 1992 U.S. District Court, District of Oregon and U.S. District Court, Eastern and Western Districts of Washington and U.S. Tax Court. *Education:* Lewis & Clark College (B.A., 1987); Northwestern School of Law of Lewis and Clark College (J.D., magna cum laude, 1990). *Member:* Oregon State Bar (Member, Construction and Taxation Sections); Washington State Bar Association (Member, Construction Section). ***PRACTICE AREAS:*** Construction Law; Real Estate Law; Business Law. ***Email:*** jkh@yazbeckhanson.com

---

HEATHER McNAMEE, born Kentucky, 1974; admitted to bar, 2000, Oregon. *Education:* College of Wooster (B.A., 1996); Case Western Reserve University College of Law (J.D., 2000). Associate Editor, Health-Matrix, Journal of Law and Medicine. *Member:* Oregon State Bar; Multnomah State Bar; Oregon Women Lawyers. ***PRACTICE AREAS:*** Business Law; Leasing; Secured Transactions; Bankruptcy; Debtor and Creditor; Employment Law. ***Email:*** hlm@yazbeckhanson.com

DAVID HUNTER BOWSER, admitted to bar, 2001, Oregon. *Education:* Pennsylvania State University (B.A., 1996); Willamette University (J.D., 2001). ***PRACTICE AREAS:*** Litigation. ***Email:*** dhb@yazbeckhanson.com

OF COUNSEL

LYNNIA K. WOODS, born Oregon, 1955; admitted to bar, 1981, Oregon and U.S. District Court, District of Oregon. *Education:* University of Oregon (B.A., 1978); Willamette University (J.D., 1981). The Order of Barristers. Associate Editor and Staff Member, Willamette Law Review, 1980-1981. Treasurer, Moot Court Board, 1980-1981. Author: "Chapter 564: Easing the Restrictions on Landfills in State Waters," 16 Willamette Law Review 359, 1979. Instructor: Business Law, Chemeketa Community College, 1980-1982; Bradford School, Paralegal Program Advisory Board, 1988-1992. *Member:* Multnomah County (Member, Continuing Legal Education Committee) and American (Member, Sections on: Corporation, Banking and Business Law; Public Contract Law; Taxation) Bar Associations; Oregon State Bar (Member: Debtor-Creditor Section; Construction Section and Section on Real Estate and Land Use). ***PRACTICE AREAS:*** Construction Law; Real Estate; Business Law. ***Email:*** lkwoods@5star-group.com

ROBERT K. LAU, born New York, New York, December 13, 1957; admitted to bar, 1993, Oregon. *Education:* City College of the University of New York (B.E., Chem. E., 1980); Southwestern University School of Law (J.D., cum laude, 1993). Note and Comment Editor, Southwestern University Law Review, 1992-1993. *Member:* Multnomah County Bar Association; Oregon State Bar; Oregon Minority Lawyers Association. ***PRACTICE AREAS:*** Business; Employment; Intellectual Property; General Practice. ***Email:*** rkl@yazbeckhanson.com

YTURRI ROSE, LLP

PORTLAND, OREGON

(See Ontario)

General Civil and Trial Practice. Medical and Legal Malpractice, Insurance Defense, Insurance Law, Personal Injury, Business Litigation, Commercial Law, Corporations, Estate Administration, Estate Planning, Foreclosures, Debtor and Creditor, Zoning and Land Use, Real Estate, Farm and Ranch Law, Labor and Employment Law.

CONRAD E. YUNKER, P.C.

PORTLAND, OREGON

(See Salem)

Litigation, Appeals, Judicial Review, Regulatory, Licensing, Administrative Government, Insurance Disputes, Probate, Estate Litigation, Business Law, Banking Law, Personal Injury, Automobile Accidents and Injuries, Construction Law, Real Estate, Consumer Law, Libel, Slander and Defamation, Eminent Domain.

ZACHARY ZABINSKY

1435 AMERICAN BANK BUILDING
621 S.W. MORRISON STREET
PORTLAND, OREGON 97205
Telephone: 503-223-8517
Fax: 503-273-8842
Email: zachzabinsky@aol.com

Personal Injury, Housing Discrimination, Social Security Disability.

ZACHARY ZABINSKY, born Tonawanda, New York, July 6, 1954; admitted to bar, 1980, Oregon and U.S. District Court, District of Oregon; 2002, Washington. *Education:* Whitman College (B.A., magna cum laude, 1976); University of Oregon (J.D., 1979). Phi Beta Kappa. Staff Attorney, Oregon Development Disabilities Advocacy Center, 1984-1985. Presenter, Oregon Fair Housing Conference, 1997. Instructor, Torts, College of Legal Arts. *Member:* Multnomah County and Washington State Bar Associations; State Bar of Oregon (Member, Section on Torts, Civil Litigation, Disability Law and Civil Rights; Nominating Committee, 1995); Oregon Trial Lawyers Association; National Organization of Social Security Claimant's Representatives. ***PRACTICE AREAS:*** Personal Injury; Housing Discrimination; Social Security Disability.

GREGORY K. ZEUTHEN, ATTORNEY AT LAW, PC

1515 S.W. FIFTH AVENUE, SUITE 808
PORTLAND, OREGON 97201
Telephone: 503-227-7257
Fax: 503-228-1556
Email: gkz@zlawoffice.com
URL: http://www.lawyers.com/zeuthen

General Civil and Trial Practice, Plaintiff's Personal Injury, Professional Liability, Products Liability, Medical Malpractice, Lasik Eye Surgery Malpractice, Wrongful Death and Automobile Accidents.

GREGORY K. ZEUTHEN, born Alexandria, Virginia, October 27, 1959; admitted to bar, 1984, Oregon and U.S District Court, District of Oregon. *Education:* Weber State College (B.S., 1981); Lewis and Clark College (J.D., 1984). Recipient, American Bar Association Land Use Award, 1984. *Member:* Multnomah County Bar Association; Oregon State Bar (Member, Local Professional Responsibility Committee, 1999-2002); Oregon Trial Lawyers Association (Former Member, Publications Committee; Past Co-Chair, Automobile Section); The Association of Trial Lawyers of America (Chair, Laser Eye Surgery Litigation Group). ***PRACTICE AREAS:*** General Trial Practice; Plaintiff's Personal Injury; Professional Liability; Products Liability; Medical Malpractice; Railroad Accidents and Injuries; Alternative Dispute Resolution.

HURLEY, LYNCH & RE, P.C.

Established in 1995

446 NW 3RD STREET, SUITE 230
PRINEVILLE, OREGON 97754
Telephone: 541-447-5777
Fax: 541-447-5755
Email: info@hlr-law.com
URL: http://www.hlandr.com

Bend Office: 747 S.W. Mill View Way, 97702. Telephone: 541-317-5505. Fax: 541-317-5507.

General Civil and Trial Practice, Business, Corporate, Real Estate and Land Use, Leasing, Insurance Defense, Commercial Litigation, Water Rights Law, Taxation, Intellectual Property, Licensing, Probate and Estate Planning, Health Law, Employment Law.

JEFFREY M. WILSON, born Gary, Indiana, March 11, 1958; admitted to bar, 1984, Oregon. *Education:* University of Oregon at Eugene (B.S., 1980); Gonzaga University (J.D., 1983). ***PRACTICE AREAS:*** Real Estate; Easements; Boundary Disputes.

REPRESENTATIVE CLIENTS: Sunriver Resort; Arrier Title Co.; Bend Research; Deschutes County; Consep, Inc.; Scootsdale Insurance; Armed Forces Insurance; USAA; Redmond School District; A.I. Management; CUMIS Insurance; David Evans & Associates, Inc.; Central Oregon Irrigation; District Squaw Creek Irrigation District; Swalley Irrigation District; Hap Taylor & Sons, Inc.; High Desert Beverage; Overbay Development Co., Inc.; Bachelor Beverage Co. Inc.; Micromonitors, Inc.; Drew Paints, Inc.; Bend Memorial Clinic; Bend Orthopedic and Fracture Clinic; Central Oregon Radiology Associates; East Cascade Women's Group; St. Charles Medical Center; Bend Neurological Group; Bend Urology Associates; Central Oregon Women's Clinic; Cascade Medical Clinic; Central Oregon Pathology Consultants; Central Oregon Pediatrics Associates; Woodward Companies; Ochoco Mint Growers, Inc.; Brown's Insurance Company; Farmer's Insurance Co.; North Pacific Insurance; Colonial Insurance Co.; Mutual of Enumclaw; Grocers Insurance Group; Oregon Mutual Insurance Co.; Truck Insurance Exchange; Atlanta Casualty Insurance Co.; Country Companies; Mid-Century Insurance Co.; Brooks Resource Co.; JAL, Inc.; Fidelity and Deposit Company of Maryland; Ranger Insurance; Insurance Company of the West; Fidelity & Deposit Insurance; State Farm Insurance Co.

BRYANT, LOVLIEN & JARVIS, P.C.

REDMOND, OREGON

(See Bend)

General Civil and Trial Practice, Corporations, Creditor's Rights in Bankruptcy, Taxation, Estate Planning, Probate, Elder Law, Real Estate, Land Use Planning, Natural Resource Law, Water Rights, Insurance Defense and Family Law.

ROXANNE L. FARRA, P.C.

REDMOND, OREGON

(See Bend)

Employment Litigation and Consultation, Business Litigation, Employment Law, Wage and Hour Law, Discrimination, Sexual Harassment, Wrongful Termination and Disability Accommodation.

HURLEY, LYNCH & RE, P.C.

REDMOND, OREGON

(See Bend)

General Civil and Trial Practice, Business, Corporate, Real Estate and Land Use, Leasing, Insurance Defense, Commercial Litigation, Water Rights Law, Taxation, Intellectual Property, Licensing, Probate and Estate Planning, Health Law, Employment Law.

ARNOLD GALLAGHER SAYDACK PERCELL ROBERTS & POTTER, P.C.

ROSEBURG, OREGON

(See Eugene)

General Civil Practice, Banking, Business, Mergers and Acquisitions, Construction, Corporate, Creditors' Rights and Commercial Bankruptcy, Labor and Employment, Environmental, Estate Planning and Probate, Insurance, Media, Real Estate, Partnerships, Taxation, Timber and Trial Practice in Oregon State and Federal Courts.

ELDON F. CALEY, LAWYER, P.C. II

Established in 1956

326 ROSE STREET
P.O. BOX 2057
ROSEBURG, OREGON 97470
Telephone: 541-672-8877
FAX: 541-672-2740
Email: caley@mcsi.net

Arbitration and Mediation services. General Civil Practice with emphasis on Business or Tort litigation related matters in state court. Personal Injury and other claims for plaintiffs or defense. Legal and Medical Malpractice. School and administrative law, Estate Planning and Litigation.

ELDON F. CALEY, born Wichita, Kansas, September 13, 1930; admitted to bar, 1956, Oregon and U.S. District Court, District of Oregon; 1961, U.S. Supreme Court and U.S. Court of Appeals, Ninth Circuit. *Education:* Willamette University (B.A., 1952; J.D., 1955). Phi Delta Phi. Author: "Insurance by Inaction," Insurance Law Journal, 1955; "Legal Liability Arising From Auto Ownership," Willamette Law Journal, 1961. Law Clerk, Hon. James Alger Fee, Court of Appeals, 9th Circuit, 1955-1956. Judge, Circuit Court, State of Oregon, 1959-1960. Member, Panel of Arbitrators, American Arbitration Association. *Member:* Douglas County (President, 1975) and American Bar Associations; Oregon State Bar (Member, Board of Governors, 1975-1978; President, 1977-1978); Oregon Association of Defense Counsel; Defense Research and Trial Lawyers Association; Association of Insurance Counsel. ***PRACTICE AREAS:*** Elder Law; Arbitration; Mediation; Wills; Probate; Probate Litigation; Trust Law and Litigation; Estate Planning; Business Law; Litigation.

REPRESENTATIVE CLIENTS: Umpqua Community College; ADAPT Inc.; Umpqua Community College Foundation.

HUTCHINSON, COX, COONS, DuPRIEST, ORR & SHERLOCK, P.C.

ROSEBURG, OREGON

(See Eugene)

General Practice in all Courts. Business Law, Contracts, Corporate Law, Environmental Law, Land Use, Real Estate, International Business, Civil Litigation, Personal Injury, Probate, Estate Planning, Copyright and Trademark, Family Law, Arbitration and Mediation, Tax Law, Creditors Rights.

(This Listing Continued)

JAQUA & WHEATLEY, LLC

ROSEBURG, OREGON

(See Eugene)

General Practice in all Courts. Insurance Defense, Casualty and Surety Insurance Law. Litigation, Corporate Law, Partnerships, Business Litigation, Products Liability, Construction Law, Environmental Law, Professional Malpractice, Premises Liability, Estate Planning, Employment Law.

LAW OFFICES OF ROBERT D. LOWRY

ROSEBURG, OREGON

(See Eugene)

Insurance Defense, Products Liability Defense, Medical Malpractice, Hospital Malpractice, Business Litigation, Construction Law and Civil Litigation.

MUHLHEIM BOYD

ROSEBURG, OREGON

(See Eugene)

Creditor/Debtor Representation; Commercial Litigation; Workouts and Bankruptcy Reorganizations; Bankruptcy Litigation; Creditors' Rights; Foreclosure; Commercial Law; Business Litigation; Business Transactions; Litigation; Estate and Probate.

NILSEN, JOHNSON & McKINNEY, P.C.

Established in 1949
435 S.E. KANE STREET
P.O. BOX 1265
ROSEBURG, OREGON 97470
Telephone: 541-673-4451
Fax: 541-673-1202
Email: njm@douglascountylaw.com
URL: http://www.douglascountylaw.com

General Civil and Trial Practice. Business Transactions, Real Estate, Eminent Domain, Land Use, Mortgages, Insurance, Family Law, Divorce, Conservatorship, Guardianships, Adoption, Child Custody, Child Support, Personal Injury, Automobile Accidents, Wrongful Death, Commercial Banking, Corporate Law, Trusts and Estates, Wills and Probate, Estate Planning, Utility Law.

FIRM PROFILE: The law firm was founded in 1949 in Roseburg, Oregon, by Dudley C. Walton. Presently the owners of the firm are Peter Nilsen, Roland A. Johnson and Dan G. McKinney. The lawyers and professional staff have a well established reputation for delivering the highest quality legal service to valued clients in Douglas County, Oregon.

PETER H. NILSEN, born Bend, Oregon, August 11, 1947; admitted to bar, 1972, Oregon. *Education:* Lewis and Clark College (B.S., 1969); University of Oregon (J.D., 1972). *Member:* Douglas County Bar Association; Oregon State Bar. ***PRACTICE AREAS:*** Real Estate Transactions; Probate; Business Law. ***Email:*** wnjg@mcsi.net

ROLAND A. JOHNSON, born Portland, Oregon, December 15, 1947; admitted to bar, 1974, Oregon and U.S. District Court, District of Oregon. *Education:* Harvard University (A.B., magna cum laude, 1971); University of Oregon (J.D., 1974). Law Clerk to Chief Judge Robert C. Belloni, U.S. District Court, District of Oregon, 1974-1975. *Member:* Douglas County Bar Association; Oregon State Bar. ***PRACTICE AREAS:*** General Civil Litigation; Business Law; Real Estate Law; Family Law; Adoption Law; Conservatorship; Guardianship; Estate Planning and Probate. ***Email:*** rjohnsonwnjg@mcsi.net

DAN G. McKINNEY, born San Jose, California, June 21, 1956; admitted to bar, 1981, California and U.S. District Court, Central District of California; 1996, Oregon; 1999, U.S. District Court, Southern District of California, U.S. District Court, District of Oregon and U.S. Supreme Court. *Education:* George Mason University (B.A., 1978); McGeorge School of Law, University of the Pacific (J.D., cum laude, 1981). Order of the Coif. Member, Traynor Honor Society. Recipient, American Jurisprudence Award in Corporations. *Member:* Riverside County (President, 1994-1995), Douglas County and American Bar Associations; American Board of Trial Advocates (ABOTA). (Also Member, Reid & Hellyer, A Professional Corporation, Riverside, California). ***PRACTICE AREAS:*** Real Estate; Civil Litigation. ***Email:*** dmckinney@douglascountylaw.com

COUNSEL FOR: Douglas Electric Cooperative Inc.
REPRESENTATIVE CLIENTS: First American Title Co.; Amerititle Co.; City of Riddle.
REFERENCES: Umpqua Bank; PremierWest Bank.

PETERSON LAW OFFICES, PC

ROSEBURG, OREGON

(See Portland)

Personal Injury, Premises Liability, Automobile Accidents and Injuries, Dog Bites and Wrongful Death.

JAMES M. BROWN

117 COMMERCIAL STREET NE, SUITE 207
SALEM, OREGON 97301-3496
Telephone: 503-581-6870
Email: jbrown@enfieldbrown.com

Trials and Appeals in all Courts. Business, Employment, Administrative Law and Arbitration.

(This Listing Continued)

JAMES M. BROWN, born St. Paul, Minnesota, December 9, 1941; admitted to bar, 1967, Oregon; 1979, U.S. Supreme Court; 1980, U.S. District Court, District of Oregon; 1982, U.S. Court of Appeals, Ninth Circuit. *Education:* American University; Willamette University (B.A., magna cum laude, 1964); Yale University (LL.B., 1967). Law Clerk, Oregon Supreme Court, 1967, 1970. Deputy District Attorney, 1970-1972 and District Attorney, 1972-1977, Benton County, Oregon. Legal Counsel to Governor of Oregon, 1977-1979. Assistant Attorney General, 1979-1980 and Attorney General, 1980-1981, Oregon. President, Board of Directors, Willamette Valley American Inn of Court, 2002-2003. Outdoor Youth Program, Advisory Board, 2001—. Member, Public Defense Services Commission, 2001—. *Member:* Oregon State Bar (Local Professional Responsibility Committee, 1996-1997, 2000; Board of Governors, 2000-2003). ***PRACTICE AREAS:*** Trials and Appeals; Business Litigation; Employment Litigation; Administrative Law and Special Proceedings; Government; Arbitration; Mediation.

CHURCHILL, LEONARD, LODINE & HENDRIE, LLP

Established in 1976
605 CENTER STREET N.E.
P.O. BOX 804
SALEM, OREGON 97308
Telephone: 503-585-2255
Telefax: 503-364-8033
Email: legal@churchill-law.com
URL: http://www.churchill-law.com

Lake Oswego, Oregon Office: Two Centerpointe Drive, Suite 580, 97035. Telephone: 503-598-6610.

Agricultural Law, Natural Resource and Environmental Law, Probate, Estate Planning and Administration, Wills, Trusts, Trust Administration, Taxation, Conservatorships, Guardianships, Real Estate and Land Use, Public Lands Law, Water Law, General Civil and Trial Practice, Creditor's Rights, Bankruptcy, Business, Corporate and Commercial Law, Immigration and International Law, Secured Transactions, Criminal Law, Wrongful Death, Personal Injury, Employment Law and Medical Injury.

MEMBERS OF FIRM

THOMAS W. CHURCHILL, born Stockton, California, May 18, 1922; admitted to bar, 1950, Oregon and U.S. District Court, District of Oregon. *Education:* University of California, Berkeley (A.A., 1947); Willamette University (J.D., 1950). Editor, "Real Property Law in Oregon," Oregon State Bar Continuing Legal Education Publication, 1975. Speaker and Author: "Creditors Bills," Debtor-Creditor Section of Oregon State Bar, 1985; "Collecting Loans," Twelfth Farm Credit District, 1975. Instructor in Contracts, Willamette University, College of Law, 1955-1959. *Member:* Marion County Bar Association (President, 1958); Oregon State Bar (Member, Debtor/Creditor Rights Section). ***PRACTICE AREAS:*** Creditors' Rights Law; Agricultural Creditor's Rights; Real Estate; Contracts; Probate; Estate Planning; Arbitration; Conservatorship; Guardianship; Commercial Collections. ***Email:*** tchurchill@churchill-law.com

RICHARD L. HENDRIE, JR., born Salem, Oregon, October 17, 1956; admitted to bar, 1981, Oregon. *Education:* Oregon State University (B.S., 1978); Willamette University (J.D., 1981). *Member:* Marion County, Multnomah County and American Bar Associations; Oregon State Bar (Member, Sections on: Business and Corporate; Real Estate and Land Use; International Law); American Immigration Lawyers Association (Board of Directors, 1990-1992). ***PRACTICE AREAS:*** Immigration Law; International Law; Business Law; Real Estate Law. ***Email:*** rhendrie@churchill-law.com

DAVID H. LEONARD, born Silverton, Oregon, December 12, 1946; admitted to bar, 1973, Oregon, U.S. District Court, District of Oregon and U.S. Court of Appeals, Ninth Circuit. *Education:* Willamette University and Western Oregon State College (B.S., 1970); Willamette University (J.D., 1973). Speaker: Oregon State Bar CLE Program, Buying and Selling A Closely Held Business, July, 1981; Creation & Foreclosure of Equitable Mortgages, August, 1985. Member, Board of Directors, Oregon Metallurgical Corporation, 1988-1998. Member, Board of Trustees, Willamette University, 1992-1996 . *Member:* Marion County and American Bar Associations; Oregon State Bar (Member, Sections on: Business and Corporate Law; Debtor/Creditor Rights; Chair, Aglaw Section Executive Committee, 2001); American Agricultural Law Association. ***PRACTICE AREAS:*** Agricultural Law; Business; Real Estate; Estate Planning. ***Email:*** dleonard@churchill-law.com

PAUL C. LODINE, born Seattle, Washington, September 5, 1952; admitted to bar, 1980, Oregon and U.S. District Court, District of Oregon; 1986, Washington and U.S. District Court, Western District of Washington. *Education:* Whitman College (A.B., 1974); Willamette University (J.D., 1980). The Order of Barristers. Member, Willamette Law Review, 1980. Editor of Marion County Bar Association, 1982-1984. Member, Advisory Board, Marion County Health Administration, 1982-1985. *Member:* Marion County, Multnomah County, Washington State and American (Member, Sections on: Taxation; Real Property; Probate) Bar Associations; Oregon State Bar; Willamette Valley Estate Planning Council (President, 1989-1990). ***PRACTICE AREAS:*** Estate Planning Law; Probate Law; Business Law; Tax Law. ***Email:*** plodine@churchill-law.com

---

ELIZABETH E. HOWARD, born Burns, Oregon, February 5, 1975; admitted to bar, 2001, Oregon and U.S. District Court, District of Oregon. *Education:* Oregon State University (B.S., 1998); Northwestern School of Law (J.D., 2001). *Member:* Marion County and American Bar Associations; Oregon State Bar (Member, Agricultural Law Section). ***PRACTICE AREAS:*** Natural Resources; Environmental Law; Water Law; Public Land Law; Endangered Species; Land Use; Real Estate; Agricultural Law. ***Email:*** ehoward@churchill-law.com

MELINDA LEAVER ROY, born San Pedro, California, January 20, 1968; admitted to bar, 1994, Oregon and U.S. Court of Appeals, Fourth Circuit. *Education:* Wheaton Col-

(This Listing Continued)

CHURCHILL, LEONARD, LODINE & HENDRIE, LLP, Salem—Continued

lege (B.A., magna cum laude, 1989); University of Florida (J.D., with honors, 1993). Order of the Coif. Recipient, American Jurisprudence Award for Excellent Achievement in the study of Corporate Law. Law Clerk to the Honorable Donald S. Russell, United States Court of Appeals, Fourth Circuit. *Member:* Oregon State Bar (Member, Section on: Estate Planning and Administration Law); Willamette Valley Estate Planning Council (President, 2002-2003). ***PRACTICE AREAS:*** Estate Planning and Administration; Probate; Trust Law; Real Estate; Business Law. ***Email:*** mroy@churchill-law.com

RICHARD E. SLEZAK, born Denver, Colorado, January 8, 1950; admitted to bar, 1986, Oregon; 1988, U.S. District Court, District of Oregon; 1993, U.S. Court of Appeals, Ninth Circuit. *Education:* University of Colorado; Metropolitan State College (B.A., magna cum laude, 1983); Willamette University (J.D., 1986). *Member:* Marion County and American Bar Associations; Oregon State Bar; Oregon Trial Lawyers Association. ***REPORTED CASES:*** Matter of the Marrige of Johnson, 138 Or App 462, 909 P2d 185 (1996). ***PRACTICE AREAS:*** Employment Law; Civil Rights; Personal Injury; Wrongful Death; Executive Contracts; Professional Contract Litigation; Litigation; General Civil and Criminal Litigation; Administrative Hearings; Medical Injury. ***Email:*** rslezak@churchill-law.com

REPRESENTATIVE CLIENTS: Bank of the Cascades; Transworld Systems, Inc.; Barenbrug USA; J.B. Instant Lawns, Inc.; Pratum Co-op Warehouse; Cascade Landscape Management, Inc.; Kraemer Farms; Venell Farms, Inc.; Suburban East Salem Water District; Turner Gravel, Inc.; Interstate Auto Parts; Keith Brown Lumber; PCC Structurals, Inc.; North American Baptist Conference; Oregon State Grange; Greenberry Imigation District; Oregon Cattlemen's Association; American Farm Bureau Federation.

CLARK, LINDAUER, FETHERSTON, EDMONDS, LIPPOLD & COLLIER, LLP

Established in 1953

880 LIBERTY STREET, N.E.
P.O. BOX 2206
SALEM, OREGON 97308-2206
Telephone: 503-581-1542
Fax: 503-585-3978
Email: contactus@clarklindauer.com

Trial and Business Practice in State and Federal Courts including Business Litigation, Insurance Law, Agricultural Law, Automobile, Premises Liability, Professional Negligence, including Legal and Medical Malpractice, Product, Toxic Tort and Environmental Liability, Employment Discrimination, Wrongful Discharge and Defamation, Arbitration and Mediation, Business, Real Estate, and Estate Law, Probate.

MEMBERS OF FIRM

EDWARD L. CLARK, JR. (Retired)

BEN C. FETHERSTON, JR., born Denver, Colorado, April 14, 1957; admitted to bar, 1981, Oregon; U.S. District Court, District of Oregon; U.S. Court of Appeals, Ninth Circuit; U.S. Tax Court. *Education:* University of Denver (B.A., 1978); Northwestern School of Law of Lewis and Clark College (J.D., cum laude, 1981). Trustee, AOI Healthcare Health Insurance Trust. *Member:* Marion County and American Bar Associations; Oregon State Bar; Associated Oregon Industries (Member, Board of Directors, 1993—; Executive Committee, 1996—; Secretary, 2000-2002; Treasurer, 2002-2004; First Vice-Chair, 2004—); Northwest Food Processors Association. ***PRACTICE AREAS:*** Business Law; Agricultural Law; Corporate Law; Commercial Law; Real Estate Law; Estate Planning. ***Email:*** bfetherston@clarklindauer.com

JAMES C. EDMONDS, born Salem, Oregon, May 16, 1960; admitted to bar, 1986, Oregon; U.S. District Court, District of Oregon; U.S. Court of Appeals, Ninth Circuit. *Education:* University of Oregon (B.A., 1982); George Washington University (J.D., with honors, 1986). Phi Beta Kappa. *Member:* Marion County (Member, Board of Directors, 1996-2000; President, 1999), Multnomah County and American Bar Associations; Oregon State Bar; Oregon Association of Defense Counsel (Member, Board of Directors, 1999—; President, 2003); Defense Research Institute; Willamette Valley American Inn of Court (Member, 1998-2000 and Chairman, 1999-2000, Local Professional Responsibility Committee; Member, Region Six Disciplinary Board, 2003—). ***PRACTICE AREAS:*** Trial Practice; Insurance Litigation; Commercial Litigation; Professional Negligence Litigation; Products Liability Defense. ***Email:*** jedmonds@clarklindauer.com

STEVEN M. LIPPOLD, born Tacoma, Washington, June 5, 1962; admitted to bar, 1989, Washington; 1990, Oregon. *Education:* University of Washington (B.A., 1984); Willamette University (J.D., cum laude, 1989). Member, Willamette Law Review, 1988-1989. *Member:* Marion County, Multnomah County, Washington State and American Bar Associations; Oregon State Bar; Oregon Association of Defense Counsel; Defense Research Institute; Willamette Valley American Inn of Court. ***PRACTICE AREAS:*** Defense Litigation; Commercial Litigation; Employment Law Litigation; Appellate Practice. ***Email:*** slippold@clarklindauer.com

RYAN W. COLLIER, born Seattle, Washington, April 17, 1971; admitted to bar, 1997, Oregon; 1998, Washington and U.S. District Court, Western District of Washington; 2000, U.S. District Court, District of Oregon. *Education:* University of Puget Sound (B.A., 1993); Willamette University (J.D., 1997). Secretary, Salem Leadership Foundation. Editor, Marion County Bar Bulletin. *Member:* Washington State and American Bar Associations; Oregon State Bar; Inns of Court. ***PRACTICE AREAS:*** Estate Planning; Probate; Guardianship; Conservatorship; Real Estate Litigation; Business Litigation. ***Email:*** rcollier@clarklindauer.com

---

JEFFREY A. TRAUTMAN, born Moses Lake, Washington, September 17, 1977; admitted to bar, 2004, Oregon. *Education:* Warner Pacific College (B.S., 1999); Willamette University (J.D., 2003). *Member:* Marion County and American Bar Associations; Oregon State Bar; Willamette Valley American Inns of Court. ***PRACTICE AREAS:*** Business Law; Commercial Law; Agricultural Law; Real Estate; Litigation; Arbitration; Wills; Trusts and Estates. ***Email:*** jtrautman@clarklindauer.com

OF COUNSEL

ERIC B. LINDAUER, born Red Bluff, California, October 20, 1938; admitted to bar, 1967, Oregon. *Education:* Oregon State University (B.S., 1963); Willamette University (J.D., 1966). Arbitrator and Mediator, Federal Mediation and Conciliation Service, National Mediation Board and American Arbitration Association. Serves as Special Master, U.S. District Court of Oregon. Member, National Academy of Arbitrators. *Member:* Marion County Bar Association; Oregon State Bar. ***PRACTICE AREAS:*** Arbitration and Mediation. ***Email:*** elindauer@clarklindauer.com

GENERAL COUNSEL FOR: Tillamook County Creamery Association (makers of Tillamook Cheese); Associated Oregon Services Corp.; Oregon Country Beef; Oregon Coast Foods, Inc.; Columbia River Processing, Inc.; Caylx Fruit, LLC; The City View Cemetary Association; Clayton-Ward Company; D & D Paving Co.; Dermatology Clinic, P.C.; Gerlinger Carrier Company; Fire Protection, Inc.; AC Gilbert Discovery Village, Inc.; Jenks-Olsen Farms, Inc.; C. A. Lantz Construction Co.; LCG Pence, LLC; Bill Rogers Motor Company, Inc.; Salem Area Mass Transit District; Salem Clinic, P.C.; Salem Rehabilitation Associates, Inc.; Stahlbush Island Farms, Inc.; Sun Retirement Corp.; Cascadia Development, LLC; EcoWest Development, LLC; Oregon Meadofoam Growers; Polo Ridge Farms, LLC; Rockwest Training Co. Inc.; Williams, Zografos & Peck PC; Walling Sand & Gravel Co.; West Coast Beet Seed Company; West Salem Machinery Company; Willamette Agricultural Consulting, Inc.; Willamette Valley Hospice.
REPRESENTATIVE CLIENTS: TIAA-CREF; Pioneer Trust Bank, N.A.; State Farm Insurance; American Family Insurance Group; North Pacific Insurance Co.; Palm Harbor Homes, Inc.; State Farm Insurance Co.; Colonial Penn Insurance Co.; Oregon State Bar Professional Liability Fund; Omaha Indemnity Insurance Co.; Fleetwood Enterprises, Inc.; Albertson's Inc.; American Family Insurance Group; Guaranty National Insurance Co.; Mutual of Omaha; Jefferson Insurance Co.; Bankers Life and Casualty; Fulcrum Insurance; Home Life Insurance Company of New York; The Infinity Group; Kentucky Central Life; National American Insurance Co.; One Beacon Insurance; Oregon Insurance Guaranty Association; Pepsico; Ca E. Auto Ins. Co.; Champion Enterprises, Inc.; Combined Specialty Insurance.

CROTHERS HANSEN P.C.

750 FRONT STREET NE, SUITE 100
SALEM, OREGON 97301
Telephone: 503-378-0225
Telecopier: 503-371-2946
URL: http://www.crothers.com

Litigation including Business, Commercial, Creditors Rights, Real Property, Personal Injury, Family Law, Conservatorships and Guardianships, Corporate and Partnership Law.

WILLIAM C. CROTHERS, born Tupelo, Mississippi, November 22, 1942; admitted to bar, 1970, Oregon; 1983, U.S. Court of Appeals, Ninth Circuit. *Education:* Willamette University (B.A., 1966; J.D., 1969). Municipal Judge, City of Stayton, 1975-1978. *Member:* Marion County and American Bar Associations; Oregon State Bar (Member, Sections on: Real Estate Law; Corporation and Business Law; Family and Juvenile Law; Chairman, Executive Committee, 1988-1989. Fellow, The American Academy of Matrimonial Lawyers. ***PRACTICE AREAS:*** Family Law; Business Law; Real Estate. ***Email:*** bill@crothers.com

GREGORY C. HANSEN, born Worthington, Minnesota, June 8, 1964; admitted to bar, 1989, Oregon; 1990, U.S. District Court, District of Oregon and U.S. Court of Federal Claims; 1996, U.S. Supreme Court. *Education:* University of Minnesota (B.A., 1986); University of North Dakota (J.D., 1989). Senior Editor, University of North Dakota Law Review. *Member:* Marion County Bar Association; Oregon State Bar (Member, Sections on: Elder Law, Business Law and Litigation). ***PRACTICE AREAS:*** Elder Law; Business Law; Real Estate. ***Email:*** greg@crothers.com

REPRESENTATIVE CLIENTS: Fidelity Title Co.; AC&E Electric; Santiam Wine Company; Boldt, Carlisle & Smith, LLC; Fox Lock & Safe, Inc.; Delon Motor Corp.; Pringle Park Plaza, Standard Utility Contractors, Inc.; Hear No Evil, Inc.; Taylor Honda Sports.
REFERENCE: Pioneer Trust Bank, Salem, Oregon.

CUMMINS, GOODMAN, FISH, DENLEY & VICKERS, P.C.

SALEM, OREGON

(See Newberg)

Insurance Defense, Employment Law, Workers' Compensation Defense, OSHA Defense, General Litigation, Business Law.

KATHLEEN A. EVANS ATTORNEY AT LAW

969 - 13TH ST. SE
SALEM, OREGON 97302
Telephone: 503-588-5670
Fax: 503-588-5673
Email: kathy@kevanslaw.com

Estate Planning, Wealth Transfer and Preservation, Trust Administration, and Probate.

FIRM PROFILE: Kathy Evans has practiced law in Salem, Oregon since graduating from Willamette University College of Law in 1982, summa cum laude. She has had experience as a mediator, arbitrator, and advocate in civil litigation, with an emphasis on creditor's rights, representing individual private lenders, small community banks, and large national institutions. Her practice now is limited to assisting clients in the field of estate planning, addressing their needs--from personal and basic planning issues involving wills or living trusts, to the more complex, taxable concerns where advanced wealth transfer techniques are appropriate.

(This Listing Continued)

(This Listing Continued)

KATHLEEN A. EVANS, born Tacoma, Washington, June 27, 1957; admitted to bar, 1982, Oregon and U.S. District Court, District of Oregon; 1983, U.S. Court of Appeals, Ninth Circuit. *Education:* Washington State University (B.A., summa cum laude, 1979); Willamette University (J.D., summa cum laude, 1982). Phi Kappa Phi; Alpha Lambda Delta; Phi Beta Kappa. *Member:* Marion County Bar Association (Member, Board of Directors, 1989-1991; President, 1992); Oregon State Bar (Continuing Legal Education Committee, 1984-1987 and Chairperson, 1986-1987); Willamette Valley Inns of Court (President and Co-Founder, 1994-1995); Willamette Valley Estate Planning Council. ***PRACTICE AREAS:*** Estate Planning; Estate Administration; Family Wealth Transfer; Wills; Trusts and Estates.

REFERENCE: KeyBank National Association, Salem, Oregon.

FERDER, CASEBEER & FRENCH L.L.P.

Established in 1978

515 HIGH STREET, S.E.
P.O. BOX 843
SALEM, OREGON 97308-0843
Telephone: 503-585-9197
Fax: 503-399-7904

Personal Injury, Criminal Law, Family Law, Business, Corporate Law, Appellate Practice.

MEMBERS OF FIRM

PAUL M. FERDER, born Salem, Oregon, May 8, 1946; admitted to bar, 1972, Oregon; 1973, U.S. District Court, District of Oregon; U.S. Court of Appeals, Ninth Circuit. *Education:* University of Oregon (B.S., 1968); Lewis and Clark College (J.D., 1972). *Member:* Marion County and American Bar Associations; Oregon State Bar; Oregon Trial Lawyers Association (Sustaining Member); The Association of Trial Lawyers of America; Oregon Criminal Defense Lawyers Association. ***PRACTICE AREAS:*** Business Litigation; Criminal Law; Personal Injury Law. ***Email:*** pferder@ferder.com

CHRISTOPHER J. CASEBEER, born Coos Bay, Oregon, August 4, 1959; admitted to bar, 1984, Oregon and U.S. District Court, District of Oregon; 1990, U.S. Court of Appeals, Ninth Circuit. *Education:* University of Oregon (B.S., 1981); Willamette University (J.D., 1984). Phi Beta Kappa; Pi Sigma Alpha. Member, Mortar Board. Governor Appointed Member to the Oregon Juvenile Justice Advisory Committee, 1983-1985, Committee Member, Function and Organization, 1985-1988 and Unlawful Practice of Law, 1989-1991, Professional Responsibility Committee, 1999-2002, of the Oregon State Bar. *Member:* Marion County Bar Association (Family Law Advisory Committee, 2001—); Oregon State Bar (Family Law Section). ***PRACTICE AREAS:*** Family Law; Divorce; Criminal Law; Personal Injury Law; Civil Sex Abuse. ***Email:*** ccasebeer@ferder.com

CARLA M. FRENCH, born Salem, Oregon, February 9, 1953; admitted to bar, 1994, Oregon and Supreme Court of Oregon; 1996, U.S. District Court, District of Oregon; 1997, U.S. Court of Appeals, Ninth Circuit. *Education:* Linfield College (B.S., cum laude, Business Management, 1988); Willamette University (J.D., 1994). Marion County circuit Judge Pro Tem, 2004—. *Member:* Marion County Bar Association; Oregon State Bar; Oregon Criminal Defense Lawyer Association. ***PRACTICE AREAS:*** Juvenile Law; Criminal Defense; Personal Injury. ***Email:*** cfrench@ferder.com

ASSOCIATE

JASON EDWARD THOMPSON, born Richland, Washington, October 17, 1974; admitted to bar, 2001, Oregon; 2004, U.S. District Court, District of Oregon and U.S. Court of Appeals, Ninth Circuit. *Education:* University of California at Los Angeles (B.A., 1997); Willamette University (J.D., M.B.A., 2001). Member, Law Review. Judicial Law Clerk, Oregon Supreme Court, 2001-2002. Certificate in Dispute Resolution. Deputy District Attorney, Multnomah and Marion Counties. *Member:* Oregon Criminal Defense Lawyers Association; Federal Bar Association. ***PRACTICE AREAS:*** Criminal Law; Appellate Practice; Business Law. ***Email:*** jthompson@ferder.com

OF COUNSEL

JAMES J. AHMED, born 1939; admitted to bar, 1970, Oregon. *Education:* Western Michigan University (B.A., 1961); Willamette University (J.D., 1970). *Member:* Marion County and American Bar Associations; Oregon State Bar. ***PRACTICE AREAS:*** Criminal Defense; Business Law. ***Email:*** jahmed@ferder.com

REPRESENTATIVE CLIENTS: Pacific Rim Equipment Corp.; Battle Creek Golf Course; DWP Management, Inc.; Value Homes, Inc.; Premiere Homes of Oregon, Inc.; Concert Services, Inc.; A-1 Transmission; Interstate Claims Service; Praegitzer Industries; BBV Medical; Hylo Tree Farms; Northwest Spas; McBride Stamp Auctions.

KEVIN C. GAGE

Established in 1981

348 LESLIE STREET, S.E.
P.O. BOX 924
SALEM, OREGON 97308-0924
Telephone: 503-399-1355
Fax: 503-399-1353
Email: gagelaw@comcast.net
URL: http://www.kevingagelaw.com

Divorce, Family Law, Child Custody, Child Support, Alimony, Marital Property Distribution, Spousal Support, Separation Agreements, Matrimonial Law, Marital Property Law, Equitable Distribution, Domestic Relations, Community Property Law, Domestic Partnerships.

FIRM PROFILE: The firm of Kevin C. Gage was founded in 1981. For over 23 years, Mr. Gage has specialized in divorce and family law. His practice has been limited to divorce and family law exclusively since 1984.

(This Listing Continued)

KEVIN C. GAGE, born Walla Walla, Washington, August 25, 1953; admitted to bar, 1981, Oregon and U.S. District Court, District of Oregon. *Education:* University of Washington (B.A., 1976); Willamette University (J.D., 1981). Phi Beta Kappa. Co-Author: Property Rights and Division, Chapter 6 of the Oregon State Bar Publication, *Dissolution Practice,* 1990; 1997 and 2004 Supplements and 2002 revision of the Property Rights and Division chapter of the Oregon State Bar Publication, *Dissolution Practice. Member:* Oregon State Bar (Member, Family Law Section). ***REPORTED CASES:*** In re Marriage of Moe, 1984, 66 Or. App. 947. 676 P.2d 336; In re Marriage of Bond, 1983, 63 Or. App. 865. 666 P.2d 861; In re Marriage of Swartz, 1992, 114 Or. App. 437. 833 P.2d 355; In re Marriage of Ury, 1991, 109 Or. App. 702. 820 P.2d 472; In re Marriage of Ferris, 1987, 85 Or. App. 555, 737 P.2d 153; In re Marriage of Coleman, 1984, 71 Or. App. 313. 692 P.2d 129; In re Marriage of Nickerson, 1984, 63 Or. App. 854. 666 P.2d 868; In re Marriage of Vogel, 1984, 68 Or. App. 79. 680 P.2d 710; In re Marriage of Nickerson, 1984, 68 Or. App. 288. 680 P.2d 1012; In re Marriage of Nickerson, 1984, 296 Or. 516. 678 P.2d 730. ***PRACTICE AREAS:*** Divorce; Family Law; Child Custody; Child Support; Alimony; Marital Property Distribution; Spousal Support; Separation Agreements; Matrimonial Law; Marital Property Law; Equitable Distribution; Domestic Relations; Community Property Law; Domestic Partnerships.

GARRETT, HEMANN, ROBERTSON, JENNINGS, COMSTOCK & TRETHEWY, P.C.

Established in 1928

WILLAMETTE PROFESSIONAL CENTER
1011 COMMERCIAL STREET, N.E.
P.O. BOX 749
SALEM, OREGON 97308-0749
Telephone: 503-581-1501
Telefax: 503-581-5891
URL: http://www.garrettlaw.com

Bankruptcy and Creditors' Rights, Business and Corporate Law, Civil Litigation, Employment and Labor Law, Estate Planning, Trusts and Probate, Family Law, Government Relations, Insurance and Workers' Compensation Defense, Real Estate Transactions and Development, School Law, Tax Law.

FIRM PROFILE: Since 1928, our firm has employed a solution-oriented approach in representing individuals, local, national and international corporations, emerging businesses and insurance companies throughout Oregon. Our litigation practice focuses on employment and labor law, workers' compensation, commercial disputes, professional liability and insurance matters. The firm's transactional services include complex tax, real estate, financial and business matters. Businesses are also served by our bankruptcy and creditor rights practice area. Clients are represented in all state and federal courts, and agencies at the federal, state and local government level.

GEORGE M. JENNINGS, born Grand Rapids, Michigan, November 15, 1947; admitted to bar, 1975, Oregon and U.S. District Court, District of Oregon; U.S. Tax Court. *Education:* University of Washington (B.A., Economics, 1970); Willamette University (J.D., 1975). ***PRACTICE AREAS:*** Corporate Law; Real Estate Law; Tax Law; Landlord Law; Estate and Business Planning. ***Email:*** gjennings@garrettlaw.com

MARK B. COMSTOCK, born Eugene, Oregon, December 2, 1954; admitted to bar, 1981, Oregon and U.S. District Court, District of Oregon; 1982, U.S. Court of Appeals, Ninth Circuit. *Education:* University of Oregon (B.A., 1978); Willamette University (J.D., 1981). ***PRACTICE AREAS:*** Business Law; Corporate Law; Civil Litigation; Bankruptcy Law; School Law. ***Email:*** mcomstock@garrettlaw.com

CHESS TRETHEWY, born Salamanca, New York, May 30, 1952; admitted to bar, 1982, Oregon. *Education:* United State Naval Academy; University of Arizona (B.A., with high distinction, 1975); Willamette University (J.D., 1982). ***PRACTICE AREAS:*** Workers Compensation Defense; Employment; Human Resources Law; Civil Litigation. ***Email:*** chess@garrettlaw.com

PAUL A. DAKOPOLOS, born Boise, Idaho, February 27, 1959; admitted to bar, 1985, Oregon. *Education:* University of Idaho (B.A., 1981); Willamette University (J.D., 1984). ***PRACTICE AREAS:*** School Law; Civil Rights Law; Employment Law; Civil Litigation in State and Federal Courts; School and Special Education Law. ***Email:*** pdakopolos@garrettlaw.com

BRUCE A. ZAGAR, born Pittsburg, California, December 23, 1949; admitted to bar, 1975, Oregon; 1979, U.S. Supreme Court. *Education:* Washington State University (B.A., 1972); Willamette University (J.D., 1975). ***PRACTICE AREAS:*** School Law; Labor Law; Collective Bargaining; Labor Relations; Administrative Law. ***Email:*** bzagar@garrettlaw.com

JOHN E. POLLINO, born Salinas, California, September 19, 1966; admitted to bar, 1992, Oregon and U.S. District Court, District of Oregon; 1993, Washington and U.S. Court of Appeals, Ninth Circuit. *Education:* University of Puget Sound (B.A., 1989); Willamette University (J.D., 1992). ***PRACTICE AREAS:*** Construction Litigation; Employment Litigation; Medical Malpractice Defense; Civil Litigation. ***Email:*** jpollino@garrettlaw.com

TAMMY M. DENTINGER, born Ontario, Oregon, December 21, 1968; admitted to bar, 1994, Oregon; 1995, U.S. District Court, District of Oregon. *Education:* Willamette University (B.A., 1991; J.D., 1994). ***PRACTICE AREAS:*** Domestic Relations; Civil Litigation. ***Email:*** tdentinger@garrettlaw.com

KIM E. HOYT, born The Dalles, Oregon, December 25, 1965; admitted to bar, 1991, Oregon; 1992, U.S. District Court, District of Oregon and U.S. Court of Appeals, Ninth Circuit. *Education:* Oregon State University (B.A., 1988); Willamette University (J.D., 1991). ***PRACTICE AREAS:*** Employment Litigation; Civil Litigation; Civil Sex Abuse; Medical Malpractice. ***Email:*** khoyt@garrettlaw.com

THERESA M. WADE, born Salem, Oregon, November 23, 1958; admitted to bar, 1999, Oregon and U.S. Tax Court; 2000, Washington. *Education:* Oregon State University

(This Listing Continued)

GARRETT, HEMANN, ROBERTSON, JENNINGS, COMSTOCK & TRETHEWY, P.C., Salem—Continued

(B.S., summa cum laude, 1996); Willamette University (J.D., cum laude, 1999). ***PRACTICE AREAS:*** Estate Planning; Probate Administration; Trust Administration; Estate and Gift Taxation; Elder Law; Nonprofit Organizations Law. ***Email:*** twade@garrettlaw.com

---

ANTHONY R. KREITZBERG, born Butte, Montana, August 9, 1959; admitted to bar, 1996, Oregon and Washington. *Education:* University of Oregon (B.S., 1981); Boston University (M.B.A., with honors, 1983); Willamette University College of Law (J.D., 1996). ***PRACTICE AREAS:*** Business; Commercial; Real Estate; Land Use. ***Email:*** akreitzberg@garrettlaw.com

TRACY A. PRALL, admitted to bar, 1995, Oregon. *Education:* Western Oregon State College (B.S., 1992); Willamette University College of Law (J.D., 1995). ***Email:*** tprall@garrettlaw.com

J. CHANNING BENNETT, born Columbia, Missouri, August 31, 1967; admitted to bar, 1997, Massachusetts; 1997, U.S. District Court, District of Massachusetts; 2002, Oregon; 2003, U.S. District Court, District of Oregon. *Education:* Johnson & Wales University (B.S., 1989); University of Arizona (B.A., cum laude, 1994); Boston College (J.D., 1997). ***PRACTICE AREAS:*** Civil Litigation; Employment Litigation. ***Email:*** cbennett@garrettlaw.com

SEAN E. ARMSTRONG, admitted to bar, 2001, Oregon and U.S. District Court, District of Oregon; 2002, U.S. Court of Appeals, Ninth Circuit. *Education:* College of William & Mary (B.A., 1992); George Mason University School of Law (J.D., 2001). *Member:* Marion County, Multnomah County, Oregon State and American Bar Associations; Oregon Association of Defense Counsel; Defense Research Institute; Willamette Valley American Inn of Court. ***PRACTICE AREAS:*** Commercial Litigation; Civil Litigation; Domestic Relations. ***Email:*** sarmstrong@garrettlaw.com

NATHAN B. THOMAS, born Corvallis, Oregon, June 11, 1972; admitted to bar, 2003, Oregon. *Education:* Brigham Young University (B.S., 1999); East China University of Politics and Law (Certificate of Chinese Law, 2000); Atkinson Graduate School of Management (M.B.A., 2003); Willamette University (J.D., 2003). ***PRACTICE AREAS:*** Creditors Rights; Bankruptcy; Civil Litigation; Business Transactions; Business Formation. ***Email:*** nthomas@garrettlaw.com

OF COUNSEL

JOHN L. HEMANN, born Salem, Oregon, January 22, 1943; admitted to bar, 1968, Oregon. *Education:* Willamette University (B.A., 1965; J.D., 1968). Delta Theta Phi. ***PRACTICE AREAS:*** Divorce Law; Civil Litigation. ***Email:*** jhemann@garrettlaw.com

STEVEN E. HERRON, born Chicago Heights, Illinois, March 5, 1967; admitted to bar, 1992, Oregon. *Education:* Portland State University (B.S., 1988); Northwestern School of Law; Lewis and Clark College (J.D., 1992). *Member:* Oregon State Bar; American Bar Association. ***PRACTICE AREAS:*** School Law; Employment Law; Labor Law; Government Relations. ***Email:*** sherron@garrettlaw.com

J. KEVIN SHUBA, born Big Springs, Texas, May 27, 1964; admitted to bar, 1991, Oregon. *Education:* University of Washington (B.A. 1988); Willamette University (J.D., 1991). ***PRACTICE AREAS:*** Commercial Litigation; Civil Litigation; Public Contract Law; Construction Law; Real Estate; Regulatory Law. ***Email:*** jkshuba@garrettlaw.com

REPRESENTATIVE CLIENTS: City of Aumsville; American Village Corp.; Canby School District; Capital City Companies Co.; Cascade International Seed Co.; Chemeketa Community College; City of Salem; Coldwell Banker/Mt. West Real Estate; Dewitt Security Inc.; Evesham Wood Winery; Garten Services, Inc.; Gresham-Barlow School District; Klamath County School District; Lincoln County; Lincoln County School District; Marion County; Mountain West Investment Corporation; Mountain West Retirement Corp.; Multnomah Education Service District; Newberg School District; Norpac Foods, Inc.; North Clackamas School District; Northwest Physicians Mutual Insurance Co.; Ohmart & Calaba, Realtors; Safeco Insurance Co.; Salem-Keizer School District; Sears; Sedgwick CMS; State Farm Insurance Co.; Sublimity Insurance Co.; Sunwest Management, Inc.; TNT Management Resources, Inc.; Tokyo International University of America; West Coast Trust Co.; Willamette Education Service District; Woodburn School District.

GREGORY L. GUDGER

SALEM, OREGON

(See Portland)

Family Law, Criminal Law, Civil Rights Law, Employment Law, Torts, DUI, Real Estate, Litigation, Probate.

CHRISTOPHER R. HARDMAN

SALEM, OREGON

(See Portland)

Attorney Professional Responsibility and Ethics Defense, Professional Licensing, Corporate Planning, Business Litigation, Consumer Fraud, Litigation, Insurance Defense, Criminal Defense.

HARRANG LONG GARY RUDNICK P.C.

Established in 1957

333 HIGH STREET N.E., SUITE 200
P.O. BOX 12949
SALEM, OREGON 97309-0949
Telephone: 503-371-3330
Fax: 503-371-5336
URL: http://www.harrang.com

Eugene, Oregon Office: 300 East 10th Avenue, Suite 300. Telephone: 541-485-0220. Fax: 541-686-6564.

(This Listing Continued)

Portland, Oregon Office: 1001 S.W. 5th Avenue, Suite 1650. Telephone: 503-242-0000. Fax: 503-241-1458.

General Civil Trial and Appellate Practice in all State and Federal Courts, Governmental and Business Law, Corporate Law, Administrative Law, Financial Services, Securities Law, Creditors Rights, Partnership Law, Real Estate, State and Local Government Law, Environmental Law, Zoning, Planning and Land Use, Estate Planning and Probate, Insurance Law, Civil, Business, Complex and Tort Litigation, Alternative Dispute Resolution, Labor and Employment Law, Employee Benefits, Intellectual Property, Health Law, Nonprofit Law.

FIRM PROFILE: Harrang Long Gary Rudnick P.C. was organized as a partnership on July 1, 1957. It has offices in Eugene, Salem and Portland, Oregon. The firm conducts a diversified general practice with particular emphasis in municipal and public law, trial and appellate practice, intellectual property and corporate, business and real estate law.

BRUCE A. BISHOP, born Berkeley, California, August 16, 1946; admitted to bar, 1973, Oregon. *Education:* Pacific University (B.A., 1968); Hastings College of the Law (J.D., 1973). ***PRACTICE AREAS:*** Administrative Law; Election, Campaign and Political Law; Government Law; Health Care; Indians and Native Populations. ***Email:*** bruce.a.bishop@harrang.com

ELIZABETH A. EARLS, admitted to bar, 1992, Oregon. *Education:* University of Washington (B.A., International Studies, 1989); Williamette University College of Law (J.D., 1992). Oregon Safe Employment Training Advisory Committee, 1993-2002. YMCA Youth in Government Youth Legislature, 1994-2002. Advisory Council on Unemployment Compensation, 1994-2000. ***PRACTICE AREAS:*** Government Regulations; Legislative Law; Regulatory Advocacy; Employment Law. ***Email:*** betsy.earls@harrang.com

REPRESENTATIVE CLIENTS: US - SUMCO USA Corporation; SUMCO USA Sales Corporation; SUMCO Oregon Corporation; SUMCO Phoenix Corporation; Hynix Semiconductor America; Philip Morris Companies, Inc.; CheckPoint Software Tech Inc.; Providence Health Plan; Kaiser Foundation Health Plan of the Northwest; PeaceHealth; Les Schwab Tire Centers, Inc.; Wal-Mart Stores; Sysco Food Services of Portland; Foodbrands America, Inc.; Gunderson Partners LLC; Monterey Mushrooms, Inc.; Amyeel, Inc.; Spawn Mate; Development Group, Inc.; Amfac, Inc.; Northbrook Corporation; Crimson Trace Corporation; Process Facility Group, LLC.; Ecotrust; May Department Store (Meier and Frank); Fred Meyer; Professional Liability Fund of the Oregon State Bar; Day Management, Inc.; Jefferson Behavorial Health; Oregon Health and Services University; University of Oregon Bookstore; The Register-Guard; Cities of Eugene, Roseburg and Florence; Counties of Lincoln, Lane and Washington; Tualatin Valley Water District; Coquille Indian Gaming Commission; Eugene Water & Electric Board; Lane County Fair Board; Abby's Inc. (Abby's Legendary Pizza); West Coast Wire Rope & Rigging; Associated Oregon Industries; Harvest House Publishers; Lane Regional Air Pollution Auhority; Lane Council of Governments; Tom Rogers Distributor, Inc.; Travelers Property Casualty; Farmers Ins. Co.; Standard Ins. Co.; City County Ins. Services; American International Group; Oregon Freeze Dry, Inc.; Taco TimeInternational; Armored Transport, Inc.; Whittier Wood Products Co.; League of Oregon Cities; Oregon Self-Insurers Association.

(For complete biographical data on all personnel, see Professional Biographies at Eugene, Oregon)

HARRIS, WYATT & AMALA, LLC

5778 COMMERCIAL STREET, S.E.
SALEM, OREGON 97306-1213
Telephone: 503-378-7744; 800-853-2144
Facsimile: 503-378-1013
URL: http://www.salemattorneys.com

West Linn Office: 202 Eight Avenue, PMB No. 35, 97068. Telephone: 503-742-1990. Fax: 503-742-9906.

General Civil Practice: General civil trial practice in all state and federal courts. Alternative dispute resolution. General insurance defense practice, automobile accidents, bad faith, fire, coverage, casualty, uninsured and underinsured motorist, trucking liability, premises liability, insurance coverage, insurance litigation, liquor liability. Criminal Law, Felonies, Misdemeanors, Drug Crimes, Driving While Intoxicated, (DUI). Motor Vehicle Division hearings, Traffic Violations.

J. P. HARRIS, II, born Pasadena, California, September 13, 1947; admitted to bar, 1973, Oregon. *Education:* University of California at Santa Barbara; University of California at Los Angeles (B.A., 1969); Williamette University (J.D., 1973). *Member:* Marion County and Multnomah County Bar Associations; Oregon State Bar; Oregon Association of Defense Counsel. ***PRACTICE AREAS:*** Insurance Defense (80%); Criminal Law (10%); Personal Injury (10%). ***Email:*** jph2atty@salemattorneys.com

GIG WYATT, born San Diego, California, February 13, 1954; admitted to bar, 1985, Oregon. *Education:* University of Nevada at Las Vegas (B.A., 1980); Willamette University (J.D., 1984). *Member:* Marion County Bar Association; Oregon State Bar; Oregon Criminal Defense Lawyers Association. ***PRACTICE AREAS:*** Personal Injury Law. ***Email:*** gwyatt@salemattorneys.com

CARL R. AMALA, born Billings, Montana, November 22, 1956; admitted to bar, 1985, Oregon. *Education:* University of Maryland (B.S., 1981); Willamette University (J.D., 1985). Phi Alpha Delta. Justice, Hall Lusk Chapter, 1984-1985. Associate Editor, Willamette Law Review, 1983-1985. Author: "DUII Diversion: Where Have All The Loop Holes Gone?" 319 Willamette Law Review, Vol. 20, No. 2, Spring 1984. *Member:* Multnomah County and Marion County Bar Associations; Oregon State Bar; Oregon Association of Defense Counsel. ***PRACTICE AREAS:*** Insurance Defense; Personal Injury; Criminal. ***Email:*** camala@salemattorneys.com

JAMES B. RICH, born Grand Rapids, Michigan, April 25, 1970; admitted to bar, 1997, Oregon. *Education:* University of Nevada at Reno (B.A., 1993); Willamette University (J.D., 1997). Associate Editor, Willamette Law Review, 1995-1997. *Member:* Marion County and Multnomah County Bar Associations; Oregon State Bar; Oregon Association of Defense Counsel. **PRACTICE AREAS:** Insurance Defense; Personal Injury; Criminal Defense. **Email:** jrich@salemattorneys.com

JAMES A. WICKWIRE, born Gladstone, Oregon, July 4, 1954; admitted to bar, 1980, Oregon; 1984, U.S. District Court, District of Oregon; 1998, Colorado. *Education:* Oregon State University (B.S., with honors, 1977) Phi Kappa Phi Honor Society; McGeorge School

(This Listing Continued)

of Law (J.D., with honors, 1980). Phi Kappa Phi, Honor Society. *Member:* Multnomah County Bar Association; Oregon State Bar; Oregon Association of Defense Counsel. ***PRACTICE AREAS:*** Insurance Defense; Personal Injury. ***Email:*** jimwickwire@qwest.net

REPRESENTATIVE CLIENTS: Progressive; Austin Mutual; Leader Insurance; Infinity; Red Shield Insurance Co.; Farm Bureau of Idaho; Lancer Insurance.

HELTZEL, UPJOHN, WILLIAMS, YANDELL ROTH, SMITH & PETERSEN, P.C.

Established in 1907
FOURTH FLOOR PIONEER TRUST BUILDING
P.O. BOX 1048
SALEM, OREGON 97308-1048
Telephone: 503-585-4422
Facsimile: 503-370-4302

Business, Taxation, Estate Planning, Probate and Real Estate Law. Commercial and Tax Litigation, Employee Benefits, Employment Law, Qualified Domestic Relations Order, Creditors Rights and Appeals in all Courts.

FIRM PROFILE: Since 1907, the firm has provided top quality services to its business and individual clients in Salem and throughout the Willamette Valley and has expanded to meet its clients' changing needs. The firm emphasizes corporate, commercial and real estate transactions, employment law, employee benefits and estate planning and probate, including all related tax and litigation matters. The lawyers and staff also participate in a wide range of civic, philanthropic and bar activities, in keeping with the firm's goal to promote balance in the practice of law.

JAMES G. HELTZEL, born Salem, Oregon, February 9, 1940; admitted to bar, 1966, Oregon. *Education:* Stanford University (B.S., 1963); Columbia University (J.D., cum laude, 1966). Co-Author: Chapter on "Trust Investments," published in Administering Trusts in Oregon, 1995. Listed in The Best Lawyers in America. *Member:* Marion County and American (Member, Section on: Real Property, Probate and Trust Law) Bar Associations; Oregon State Bar (Member, Section on: Estate Planning). Fellow, American College of Trust and Estate Counsel. ***PRACTICE AREAS:*** Estate Planning Law; Probate Law; Business Law; Wills; Trusts. ***Email:*** jheltzel@heltzel.com

DONALD H. UPJOHN, born Brooklyn, New York, May 1, 1942; admitted to bar, 1970, Oregon. *Education:* Harvard University (B.A., cum laude, 1964); Boalt Hall School of Law, University of California (J.D., 1970). Order of the Coif. Author: Chapter on "Oregon Inheritance Tax," published in Administering Oregon Estates, 1977, revised, 1983. Law Clerk to Justice Arno H. Denecke, Oregon Supreme Court, 1970-1971. Special Assistant to U.S. Attorney, District of Oregon, 1971-1972. Designated Arbitrator for Arbitration Service of Portland. *Member:* Marion County and American Bar Associations; Oregon State Bar (Member, Sections on: Real Estate, Land Use and Business Law). ***PRACTICE AREAS:*** Business Law; Real Estate; Wills; Trust; Probate; Estate Planning; Related Litigation; Commercial Law. ***Email:*** dupjohn@heltzel.com

CLARK B. WILLIAMS, born San Jose, California, June 14, 1954; admitted to bar, 1979, Oregon and U.S. District Court, District of Oregon; 1982, Washington; 1985, U.S. Tax Court. *Education:* University of Washington (B.S., 1976); Willamette University (J.D., 1979). Listed in The Best Lawyers in America. Law Clerk to Judge Robert C. Belloni, U.S. District Judge, District of Oregon, 1979-1980. *Member:* Marion County and Washington State Bar Associations; Oregon State Bar (Member, Section on Taxation); Western Pension Conference (Portland Chapter); Christian Legal Society. ***PRACTICE AREAS:*** Retirement Benefit Plans; Employee Benefits; Tax Law; Business Law; Estate Planning. ***Email:*** clark@heltzel.com

ERIC YANDELL, born San Antonio, Texas, September 5, 1950; admitted to bar, 1979, Oregon and U.S. District Court, District of Oregon. *Education:* Willamette University (B.A., summa cum laude, 1973); Northwestern School of Law (J.D., 1979). Phi Beta Kappa. Law Clerk to Hon. Judge Robert Y. Thornton, Oregon Court of Appeals, 1979-1981. *Member:* Marion County Bar Association (Member, Marion County Dispute Resolution Committee, 1997—); Oregon State Bar (Member, Sections on: Debtor-Creditor; Business Litigation, Construction Law, Civil Rights, Labor Relations). ***PRACTICE AREAS:*** Creditors Rights Law; Commercial Litigation; Bankruptcy Law; Employment Law; Real Estate Litigation. ***Email:*** eyandell@heltzel.com

DAVID M. ROTH, born Silverton, Oregon, July 24, 1961; admitted to bar, 1992, Oregon. *Education:* George Fox College (B.S., cum laude, 1983); Willamette University (J.D., 1992). Member, Western Pension Conference (Portland Chapter). *Member:* Marion County and American Bar Associations; Oregon State Bar (Member, Taxation Section). ***PRACTICE AREAS:*** Employee Benefits; Qualified Retirement Plans; Taxation; Business Law; Wills; Trusts and Estates. ***Email:*** droth@heltzel.com

BARBARA JO SMITH, born St. Louis, Missouri, October, 3, 1968; admitted to bar, 1995, Oregon and Missouri. *Education:* William Jewell College (A.B., 1991); Washington University (J.D., 1994). Order of the Coif. Author: Note, "Tenants In Search of Parity With Consumers: Creating A Reasonable Expectations Warranty," 72 Wash. U.L. Q. 475 (1994). Law Clerk, Judge Kathianne Knaup Crane, Missouri Court of Appeals, 1994-1995. *Member:* Marion County and American Bar Associations; Oregon State Bar. ***PRACTICE AREAS:*** Taxation; Business Law; Corporate Law; Estate Planning; Wills; Trusts. ***Email:*** bjsmith@heltzel.com

MICHAEL C. PETERSEN, born Spokane, Washington, April 11, 1969; admitted to bar, 1995, Oregon. *Education:* Carroll College (B.A., magna cum laude, 1991); Willamette University College of Law (J.D., magna cum laude, 1994). Judicial Clerk to Hon. Rick T. Haselton, Oregon Court of Appeals, 1994-1995; Judicial Clerk to Hon. Mary J. Deits, Oregon Court of Appeals, 1995-1996. *Member:* Marion County and American Bar Associations; Oregon State Bar. ***PRACTICE AREAS:*** Creditors Rights; Employment Law; Commercial Litigation; Real Property; Litigation; Appeals. ***Email:*** mpetersen@heltzel.com

(This Listing Continued)

DEBORAH R. LUSH, born Seattle, Washington, May 7, 1976; admitted to bar, 2002, Oregon. *Education:* Point Loma Nazarena College (B.A., magna cum laude, 1998); Willamette University College of Law (J.D., cum laude, 2002). *Member:* Marion County and American Bar Associations; Oregon State Bar. ***PRACTICE AREAS:*** Retirement Benefit Plans; Business Law; Taxation; Wills; Trusts and Estates. ***Email:*** dlush@heltzel.com

REPRESENTATIVE CLIENTS: Oregon Fruit Products Co.; Hanard Machine, Inc.; Pioneer Trust Bank, N.A.; Neilsen Manufacturing Inc.; Lynx Communication Group; West Coast Washers, Inc.; Salem Radiology Consultants, P.C.; Capital Enterprise & Engineering Corp.; Mill Supply Corp.; Viesko Quality Concrete; Roth IGA Foodliner, Incorporated; Carlton Plants, LLC; The Doctors' Clinic LLP; Willamette Surgery Center, P.C.
REFERENCES: Pioneer Trust Bank, N.A.; U.S. Bank.

MICHAEL E. KNAPP

2355 STATE STREET
SALEM, OREGON 97301
Telephone: 503-391-0664
Fax: 503-399-1929
Email: mikeeknapp@aol.com
URL: http://www.lawyers.com/mikeeknapp

Business Law, Business Litigation, Construction Law, Contracts, Corporate Law, Collections, Debtor and Creditor, Real Estate, Landlord and Tenant Law.

MICHAEL E. KNAPP, born Norwalk, California, February 15, 1961; admitted to bar, 1988, Oregon. *Education:* Portland State University (B.S., 1985); Willamette University (J.D., 1988). *Member:* Marion County Bar Association; Oregon State Bar. ***PRACTICE AREAS:*** Business Law; Business Litigation; Construction; Creditors Rights; Bankruptcy; Corporate; Collections; Real Estate; Contracts; Landlord and Tenant Law.

REPRESENTATIVE CLIENTS: ACI Distribution; Eoff Electric Company; Morrow Equipment Company, LLC; The Statesman-Journal Newspaper; Lamar Obie Media Corp. Inc.

DANIEL J. LOUNSBURY

JACKSON PROFESSIONAL BUILDING
145 WILSON STREET SOUTH
SALEM, OREGON 97302
Telephone: 503-581-7875
Fax: 503-375-7785
Email: dlounsbury@qwest.net
URL: http://www.attorneydan.com

Family Law, Divorce Law, Grandparents Rights, Step Parent Adoptions, Child Custody, Child Support, Spousal Support, Criminal Law, Driving While Intoxicated, Drug Crimes, Felonies, Homicide, Juvenile Law, Misdemeanors, Parole and Probation, Sexual Assault, Traffic Violations, Personal Injury, Automobile Accidents.

DANIEL J. LOUNSBURY, born Provo, Utah, January 19, 1966; admitted to bar, 1993, Oregon. *Education:* Brigham Young University (B.A., 1989); Reuban Clark Law School, Brigham Young University (J.D., 1993). Order of the Barristers. Moot Court Competition, Civil Procedures, 1990. Law Firm of the Year, Marion-Polk County Volunteer Lawyers Project, 2001. *Member:* Oregon State Bar; Oregon Trial Lawyers Association. ***PRACTICE AREAS:*** Family Law; Divorce; Criminal Law; Driving Under the Influence; Personal Injury.

LAW OFFICES OF ROBERT D. LOWRY

SALEM, OREGON

(See Eugene)

Insurance Defense, Products Liability Defense, Medical Malpractice, Hospital Malpractice, Business Litigation, Construction Law and Civil Litigation.

HARRIS S. MATARAZZO

SALEM, OREGON

(See Portland)

Mental Health Issues related to Criminal Defense; Administrative Law; Appellate; Probate and Estate Planning.

McCLINTON & TROUTT

698 TWELFTH STREET, S.E., SUITE 210
SALEM, OREGON 97301
Telephone: 503-361-3910
Fax: 503-361-3915
Email: mctroutt@quest.net

Medical Malpractice Defense, Legal Malpractice Defense, Insurance Defense, Products Liability Defense, Employment Law, Commercial Litigation, Environmental Litigation, Media Law.

FIRM PROFILE: Civil litigation practice in all state and federal courts concentrating on the following areas: defending doctors, lawyers, and other professionals in malpractice actions; representing professionals before licensing and disciplinary boards; representing businesses in commercial, employment, and environmental litigation; representing manufacturers and sellers in product liability actions; and newsroom law.

MICHAEL C. McCLINTON, born Auburn, Washington, January 10, 1947; admitted to bar, 1972, Oregon. *Education:* University of Southern California (B.A., 1969); Willamette University (J.D., 1972). Listed in "Best Lawyers in America." *Member:* Marion County Bar Association (Member, Executive Board, 1986-1990; President, 1990); Oregon

(This Listing Continued)

McCLINTON & TROUTT, Salem—Continued

State Bar; Oregon Association of Defense Counsel (Member, Executive Board, 1985-1992; President, 1992); Defense Research Institute; International Association of Defense Counsel; Federation of Defense and Corporate Counsel; American Board of Trial Advocates (Board of Directors, Oregon Chapter, 1995—; President, Oregon Chapter, 2001, 2002); Willamette Valley American Inn of Court (Founder, 1992; President, 1992-1994). Fellow, American College of Trial Lawyers (State Committee, 2004—). ***PRACTICE AREAS:*** Medical and Legal Malpractice Defense; Product Liability Defense; Commercial Litigation; Employment Litigation; Environmental Litigation; Media Law. ***Email:*** mctroutt@quest.net

SARAH RHOADS TROUTT, born Lafayette, Indiana, September 30, 1967; admitted to bar, 1995, Oregon. *Education:* University of California at Santa Cruz (B.A., with honors, 1990); Willamette University (J.D., 1995). Associate Editor, 1994-1995 and Member, 1993-1994, Willamette Law Review. *Member:* Marion County Bar Association (Secretary and Member, Board of Directors, 1998-2000); Oregon State Bar (Litigation Section Executive Committee, 2004—); Oregon State Bar Board of Bar Examiners (2001-2004; Co-Chair, 2004); Oregon Women Lawyers; Oregon Association of Defense Counsel. Willamette Valley American Inn of Court. ***PRACTICE AREAS:*** Legal and Medical Malpractice Defense; Employment Law; Media Law; Appellate Practice. ***Email:*** mctroutt@quest.net

REPRESENTATIVE CLIENTS: Northwest Physicians Mutual Insurance Company; Norcal Insurance Company; Physicians Insurance; Oregon State Bar Professional Liability Fund; Statesman Journal Newspaper; Volkswagen of America; Fresenius Medical Care; Lift-Tech International; Black & Decker.

MUHLHEIM BOYD

SALEM, OREGON

(See Eugene)

Creditor/Debtor Representation; Commercial Litigation; Workouts and Bankruptcy Reorganizations; Bankruptcy Litigation; Creditors' Rights; Foreclosure; Commercial Law; Business Litigation; Business Transactions; Litigation; Estate and Probate.

LAW OFFICE OF GARY G. NORRIS

SALEM, OREGON

(See McMinnville)

General Civil Trial Practice, Automobile and General Liability Insurance Defense, Insurance Coverage Disputes, Products Liability Defense, Business Litigation, Insurance Litigation and Commercial Litigation .

O'DONNELL & CLARK LLP

SALEM, OREGON

(See Portland)

Administrative Law, Agency and Distributorships, Business Law, Business Transactions, Commercial Law, Commercial Real Estate, Consumer Law, Contracts, Corporate Law, Debtor and Creditor, Education Law, Election Campaign and Political Law, Estate Planning, Franchises and Franchising, Government Agency Practice, Government Law, Labor and Employment Law, Litigation, Nonprofit Corporations, Nonprofit Charitable Organizations, Real Estate, Resorts and Leisure, Taxation, Hospitality Law, Trade Associations.

PETERSON LAW OFFICES, PC

SALEM, OREGON

(See Portland)

Personal Injury, Premises Liability, Automobile Accidents and Injuries, Dog Bites and Wrongful Death.

DANIEL A. RITTER, P.C.

EQUITABLE CENTER
530 CENTER STREET N.E., SUITE 700
SALEM, OREGON 97301-3740
Telephone: 503-585-2236
FAX: 503-585-1006
Email: dritter@danritter.com

Estate Planning, Trusts, Wills and Probate, Federal Estate and Gift Taxation.

DANIEL A. RITTER, born Seattle, Washington, March 19, 1940; admitted to bar, 1965, Oregon; 1966, U.S. District Court, District of Oregon; U.S. Court of Appeals, 9th Circuit, U.S. Tax Court and U.S. Supreme Court. *Education:* University of San Francisco (A.B., 1962); Willamette University (J.D., summa cum laude, 1965); New York University (LL.M. in Taxation, 1968). Editor-in-Chief, Willamette Law Journal, 1964-1965; Editor, New York University Intramural Law Review, 1965-66. Author: "Mechanics' Lien Liability," 3 Willamette Law Journal, 1964. Adjunct Professor of Law, Business Planning, Estate Planning and Trusts, Willamette Law School, 1979-1989. Listed in The Best Lawyers in America. *Member:* Oregon State Bar (Treasurer, 1994; Member, House of Delegates, 1996; Board of Governors, 1992-1995; Sections on: Estate Planning; Taxation). Fellow, American College of Trust and Estate Counsel; Willamette Valley Estate Planning Council. ***PRACTICE AREAS:*** Estate Planning; Trusts; Wills and Probate; Federal Estate and Gift Taxation. ***Email:*** dritter@danritter.com

(This Listing Continued)

LEGAL SUPPORT PERSONNEL

JUDY K. SNIDER, born McMinnville, Oregon, June 9, 1945. *Education:* Oregon State University; University of Phoenix (B.S.B.A., 2001). Certified Professional Legal Secretary, 1989; Certified Legal Assistant, 1991; Probate and Estate Planning Specialist, 1992. Member, 1998-2005 and Chair, 2001-2002, Stayton Planning Commission. *Member:* NALS; National Association of Legal Assistants; NALS of Oregon (President, 1987-1989); NALS (President, 1997-1998). (Legal Assistant). ***PRACTICE AREAS:*** Probate and Estate Planning. ***Email:*** jsnider@danritter.com

JUDITH K. BAKER, born La Grange, Illinois. *Education:* West Valley Community College, Saratoga, California (A.A., Business Management, 1977); Antelope Valley College, Lancaster, California (A.A., Music, 1983); St. Mary's College, Moraga, California (B.A., Business Management, 1991); California State University Stanislaus, Turlock, California (Certified Paralegal-Paralegal Studies, 2001); NALS (Certified Professional Paralegal, 2004). *Member:* NALS; National Association of Legal Assistants. ***PRACTICE AREAS:*** Estate Planning; Probate Administration; Estate Administration; Corporate Law; Business Law. ***Email:*** dritter@danritter.com

---

SAALFELD GRIGGS PC

Established in 1932

PARK PLACE, SUITE 300
250 CHURCH STREET, SE
P.O. BOX 470
SALEM, OREGON 97308
Telephone: 503-399-1070
Fax: 503-371-2927
Email: contactus@sglaw.com
URL: http://www.sglaw.com

Bend, Oregon Office: 1001-B SW Disk Drive, Suite 102, 97702-1995. Telephone: 541-322-1822. Fax: 541-322-1823.

Business, Taxation, Intellectual Property, Real Estate and Land Use, Employment, Construction, Banking, Creditors' Rights, Estate Planning and Probate Law, Pension and Profit Sharing, Environmental Law, Labor and Employment, Commercial and Tax Litigation in all Courts.

FIRM PROFILE: Founded in 1932, the firm is a respected and expanding business law firm providing high-quality and timely legal services to entrepreneurs and businesses in Oregon, and is the only Oregon member of the Network of Leading Law Firms, a worldwide association of prestigious medium-sized independent law firms. The firm is divided into five practice groups who work exclusively on business and estate planning issues: Corporate - handles business formations and sales, tax planning, tax litigation, pension benefits and intellectual property; Employment - provides management with preventative advice, training, and litigation defense; Real Property - advises regarding land use development, commercial leases, and complex real property transactions; Estate Planning - provides complex estate planning, asset management, and tax reduction; Litigation - handles complex business disputes, creditors' rights, and civil appeals.

LAW FIRM ALLIANCES/ASSOCIATIONS: **NETWORK OF LEADING LAW FIRMS**

ROBERT J. SAALFELD, born Salem, Oregon, July 13, 1949; admitted to bar, 1974, Oregon; 1976, U.S. District Court, District of Oregon; 1985, U.S. Court of Appeals, Ninth Circuit. *Education:* University of San Francisco (B.A., cum laude, 1971); Willamette University (J.D., magna cum laude, 1974). Member, Willamette Law Journal, 1973-1974. *Member:* Oregon State Bar (Member, Estate Planning and Administration Section). Fellow, American College of Trust and Estates Counsel. ***PRACTICE AREAS:*** Estate Administration; Estate Planning; Trusts; Limited Liability Companies; Charitable Giving; Business Succession Planning. ***Email:*** rsaalfeld@sglaw.com

JAMES C. GRIGGS, born Pendleton, Oregon, August 8, 1949; admitted to bar, 1975, Oregon; 1976, U.S. District Court, District of Oregon; 1978, U.S. Tax Court; 1985, U.S. Court of Appeals, Ninth Circuit. *Education:* Willamette University (B.A., 1971; J.D., cum laude, 1975); New York University (LL.M., in Taxation, 1976). Editor-in-Chief, Willamette Law Journal, 1974-1975. *Member:* Oregon State Bar (Member and Chairman, 1981-1982, Business Law Section; Member, Taxation Section). ***PRACTICE AREAS:*** Mergers, Acquisitions and Divestitures; Family Business Successions; Taxation; Corporate Law. ***Email:*** jgriggs@sglaw.com

KRIS JON GORSUCH, born Ottumwa, Iowa, September 16, 1953; admitted to bar, 1978, Oregon. *Education:* University of Iowa (B.A., 1975; J.D., with distinction, 1978). Member, Iowa Law Review, 1977. Judicial Clerk, Oregon Court of Appeals, 1978-1980. Adjunct Instructor, Willamette University College of Law, 1987-1995; Law and Banking, Chemeketa Community College, 1980-1985. *Member:* Oregon State Bar (Member, Real Estate and Land Use Section). ***PRACTICE AREAS:*** Zoning, Planning and Land Use; Real Estate; Leases. ***Email:*** kgorsuch@sglaw.com

DOUGLAS C. ALEXANDER, II, born Redwood City, California, October 25, 1956; admitted to bar, 1983, Oregon and U.S. District Court, District of Oregon; 1984, U.S. Tax Court; 1985, U.S. Court of Appeals, Ninth Circuit. *Education:* Brigham Young University (B.S., cum laude, 1980); Willamette University (J.D., cum laude, 1983). Staff Member, 1981-1982 and Managing Editor, 1982-1983, Willamette Law Review. Member: Advisory Board, Network of Leading Law Firms, 1997—. Managing Shareholder, 1991—. *Member:* Oregon State Bar (Member and Chairman, 1991-1992, Business Law Section; Member, Taxation Section). ***PRACTICE AREAS:*** Mergers, Acquisitions and Divestitures; Family Business Successions; Buying and Selling of Businesses; Corporate Law; Taxation. ***Email:*** dalexander@sglaw.com

HUNTER B. EMERICK, born Reno, Nevada, July 23, 1957; admitted to bar, 1982, Nevada (Inactive) and U.S. District Court, District of Nevada; 1984, Oregon and U.S. District Court, District of Oregon and U.S. Court of Appeals, Ninth Circuit. *Education:* Willamette University (B.S., cum laude, 1979; J.D., cum laude, 1982). Staff Member, 1980-1981 and Associate Editor, 1981-1982, Willamette Law Review. Senior Law Clerk to Chief

(This Listing Continued)

Justice Noel E. Mancukian, Nevada Supreme Court, 1982-1984. *Member:* Marion County Bar Association (President, 1995); Oregon State Bar (Member, Labor and Employment Section). ***PRACTICE AREAS:*** Complex Business Litigation; Construction Law; Labor and Employment. ***Email:*** hemerick@sglaw.com

RANDALL W. COOK, born El Monte, California, March 4, 1962; admitted to bar, 1988, Oregon; 1991, U.S. Tax Court. *Education:* University of Oregon (B.A., 1984); Willamette University (J.D., 1988). Staff Member, 1986-1987, and Executive Editor, 1987-1988, Willamette Law Review. Judicial Clerk, Oregon Court of Appeals, 1988-1989. Member, Western Pension and Benefits Conference, Portland Chapter. *Member:* Oregon State Bar (Member: Business Law Section; Tax Law Section). ***PRACTICE AREAS:*** Pension and Profit Sharing Plans; Employee Benefits; ERISA Compliance; Flexible Benefit Plans; Non-Qualified Benefits; Health Care. ***Email:*** rcook@sglaw.com

RANDALL P. SUTTON, born San Diego, California, July 25, 1962; admitted to bar, 1993, Oregon and Washington; 1998, U.S. District Court, District of Oregon. *Education:* San Diego State University (B.A., with distinction, Political Science, 1984); Willamette University (J.D., 1993). Staff Member, 1991-1992 and Associate Editor, 1992-1993, Willamette Law Review. *Member:* Oregon State Bar (Member, Sections on: Litigation, Business Litigation and Labor Relations); Washington State Bar Association (Member, Litigation Section); Northwest Human Resource Management Association (President, Salem Chapter, 2002—). ***PRACTICE AREAS:*** Employment Law; Employment Litigation; Business Litigation. ***Email:*** rsutton@sglaw.com

MARK D. SHIPMAN, born Seattle, Washington, June 18, 1960; admitted to bar, 1993, Oregon; 1998, U.S. District Court, District of Oregon. *Education:* Western Washington University (B.A., 1983); Willamette University (J.D., 1992). *Member:* Oregon State Bar (Member, Real Estate and Land Use Section). ***PRACTICE AREAS:*** Land Use; Real Estate. ***Email:*** mshipman@sglaw.com

WAYNE A. KINKADE, born Cottage Grove, Oregon, November 22, 1968; admitted to bar, 1995, Oregon; 1998, U.S. District Court, District of Oregon. *Education:* Oregon State University (B.S., 1991); University of Oregon (J.D., 1995). *Member:* Oregon State Bar (Member, Sections on: Business Law; Health Law; Executive Committee). ***PRACTICE AREAS:*** Business Law; Buying and Selling of Businesses; Corporate Law; Partnerships; Taxation. ***Email:*** wkinkade@sglaw.com

JEFFREY G. MOORE, born Corvallis, Oregon, August 7, 1970; admitted to bar, 1998, Oregon. *Education:* Brigham Young University (B.S., cum laude, 1994; J.D., cum laude, 1998). Phi Delta Phi; Beta Gamma Sigma. Moot Court, 1996-1997; Law Review, 1997-1998. *Member:* Oregon State Bar (Member: Estate Planning and Administration Section; Taxation Section). ***PRACTICE AREAS:*** Estate Planning; Estate Administration; Trust Administration; Trusts; Charitable Giving; Business Succession Planning. ***Email:*** jmoore@sglaw.com

---

ERICH M. D. PAETSCH, born Salt Lake City, Utah, July 3, 1973; admitted to bar, 1999, Oregon; 2001, District of Columbia. *Education:* Lewis and Clark College (B.S., 1995); Northwestern School of Law (J.D., 1999). Associate Editor, Environmental Law, Moot Court Honor Board. ***PRACTICE AREAS:*** Debtor and Creditor; Bankruptcy; Business Litigation; Environmental Law. ***Email:*** epaetsch@sglaw.com

SHELLY M. ARRITOLA, born Klamath Falls, Oregon, August 16, 1974; admitted to bar, 2000, Oregon. *Education:* Williamette University (B.A., magna cum laude, 1996; J.D., cum laude, 2000). Associate Editor, Willamette Law Review, 1999-2000. Member, Western Pension and Benefits Conference. *Member:* Oregon State Bar (Member, Sections on: Business Law; Tax Law). ***PRACTICE AREAS:*** Pension and Profit Sharing Plans; Employee Benefits; ERISA Compliance; Flexible Benefit Plans; Non-Qualified Benefits; Health Care. ***Email:*** sarritola@sglaw.com

ERIC WILLIAM JAMIESON, born Portland, Oregon, August 18, 1973; admitted to bar, 1999, Montana; 2001, Oregon. *Education:* Washington State University (B.A., cum laude, 1996); University of Montana School of Law (J.D., 1999); New York University School of Law (LL.M. in Taxation, 2000). Phi Delta Phi. *Member:* State Bar of Montana; Oregon State Bar. ***PRACTICE AREAS:*** Taxation; Mergers and Acquisitions; Family Business Successions; Corporate Law. ***Email:*** ejamieson@sglaw.com

CALEB A. WILLIAMS, born Portland, Oregon, April 7, 1975; admitted to bar, 2001, Oregon. *Education:* George Fox College (B.A., magna cum laude, 1997); Willamette University (J.D., cum laude, 2001). ***PRACTICE AREAS:*** Business Law; Corporate Law; Trademarks; Copyrights. ***Email:*** cwilliams@sglaw.com

APRIL A. RETTKOWSKI, born Seattle, Washington, March 10, 1976; admitted to bar, 2002, Oregon. *Education:* University of Washington (B.A., 1998); Gonzaga University School of Law (J.D., cum laude, 2002). ***PRACTICE AREAS:*** Business Organization; Business Formation; Business Sales; Business Acquisitions. ***Email:*** adillman@sglaw.com

SEAN M. DRISCOLL, born Chicago, Illinois, February 24, 1973; admitted to bar, 2002, Oregon. *Education:* University of Colorado at Boulder (B.A., 1995); Lewis and Clark College (J.D., 2002). Phi Delta Phi. Recipient, Certificate in General Business Law. Champion, University of Denver Moot Court Competition. ***PRACTICE AREAS:*** Litigation; Employment Law. ***Email:*** sdriscoll@sglaw.com

SHANNON M. RAYE, born Lynn, Massachusetts, November 23, 1978; admitted to bar, 2003, Oregon. *Education:* Boston College (B.A., 2000; J.D., 2003). ***PRACTICE AREAS:*** Litigation. ***Email:*** sraye@sglaw.com

BRIAN G. MOORE, born Corvallis, Oregon, May 11, 1976; admitted to bar, 2004, Oregon. *Education:* Brigham Young University (B.S., 2001); Willamette University College of Law (J.D., 2004). ***PRACTICE AREAS:*** Real Estate; Land Use. ***Email:*** bmoore@sglaw.com

AMY LEFORE, born Walla Walla, Washington; admitted to bar, 2004, Oregon. *Education:* Oregon State University (B.S., 1999); Willamette University (J.D., 2004). ***PRACTICE AREAS:*** Estate Planning. ***Email:*** alefore@sglaw.com

MARY E. CARTER, born Salem, Oregon, October 5, 1977; admitted to bar, 2005, Oregon. *Education:* Scripps College (B.A., 1999); University of Oregon (J.D., 2005). ***PRACTICE AREAS:*** Real Estate; Land Use. ***Email:*** mcarter@sglaw.com

(This Listing Continued)

OF COUNSEL

JAMES A. PERRY, born Medford, Oregon, June 3, 1936; admitted to bar, 1965, Oregon. *Education:* University of Oregon (B.S., 1958); Northwestern School of Law (J.D., cum laude, 1965). Certified Financial Planner. Editor, Administering, Oregon Estates, Oregon State Bar, Continuing Legal Education, 2000. *Member:* Oregon State Bar (Chair, Estate Planning and Administration Section, 1986). ***PRACTICE AREAS:*** Trusts and Estates; Estate Planning; Fiduciary Administration; Personal Planning; Trust Administration. ***Email:*** jperry@sglaw.com

LEGAL SUPPORT PERSONNEL

PAMELA K. GREER, (Firm Administrator). ***Email:*** pgreer@sglaw.com

REPRESENTATIVE CLIENTS: LiveBridge, Inc.; Curry General Hospital; West Coast Bank; Emerald Forest Products, Inc.; Puentes Bros., Inc.; Samaritan Health Services; Holiday Retirement Corp.; Gelco Construction Co.; Salem Clinic; Yamasa Corp.; NORPAC Foods, Inc. (Retirement Service only); Epic, LLC, dba Air BP Aviation Services and Valley Oil Co.; Truitt Bros., Inc.; Dakota Brands International, Inc.; Bright Harvest Sweet Potato Co.; McMenamins Pubs & Breweries, Inc.; Virginia Surety Company, Inc.; Willamette Valley Bank.
REFERENCE: West Coast Bank.

SPOONER, MUCH & AMMANN, P.C.

530 CENTER STREET N.E., SUITE 722
SALEM, OREGON 97301-3740
Telephone: 503-378-7777
Fax: 503-588-5899
Email: rspooner@smapc.com
URL: http://www.smapc.com

General Civil and Trial Practice in State and Federal Courts. Insurance, Products Liability and Personal Injury Law.

RALPH C. SPOONER, born Milwaukee, Wisconsin, June 12, 1946; admitted to bar, 1973, Oregon and Illinois. *Education:* Loyola University, Arizona State University and University of Illinois (B.A., 1968); Illinois Institute of Technology (J.D., 1973). Delta Theta Phi. Member, Illinois Institute of Technology Law Review, 1972-1973. *Member:* Marion County (Director, 1982-1986; President, 1986), Illinois State Bar; Oregon State Bar; Association of Defense Trial Attorneys; Defense Research and Trial Lawyers Association; Oregon Association of Defense Counsel (Member, Board of Directors, 1981-1986; President 1986); American Board of Trial Advocates; International Association of Defense Counsel; Federation of Insurance and Corporate Counsel. ***PRACTICE AREAS:*** Insurance Defense. ***Email:*** rspooner@smapc.com

JOE W. MUCH, born Houston, Texas, July 11, 1948; admitted to bar, 1975, Oregon. *Education:* Willamette University (B.A., 1970); Oregon State University (B.S., 1972); University of Puget Sound, now Seattle University (J.D., 1975). *Member:* Marion County and Oregon State Bar; Oregon Association of Defense Counsel. ***PRACTICE AREAS:*** Insurance Defense. ***Email:*** jmuch@smapc.com

KEN L. AMMANN, born Spokane, Washington, October 31, 1961; admitted to bar, 1988, Oregon. *Education:* Washington State University (B.A., cum laude, 1985); Williamette University (J.D., 1988). Phi Delta Phi. Member, Order of Barristers. Recipient, American Academy of Trial Lawyers Award. *Member:* Marion County Bar Association; Oregon State Bar; Oregon Association of Defense Counsel. ***PRACTICE AREAS:*** Insurance Defense. ***Email:*** kammann@smapc.com

---

DANIEL R. SCHANZ, born Otsego, Michigan, September 20, 1967; admitted to bar, 1994, Michigan; 1996, Oregon. *Education:* Liberty University (B.S., 1989); Thomas M. Cooley Law School (J.D., magna cum laude, 1994). Recipient, American Jurisprudence Award in Secured Transactions. Certificate of Merit for Highest Grades in Admiralty and Workers Compensation. Judicial Clerk, Oregon Court of Appeals, Hon. Walter Edmonds, 1994-1996. Student Prosecutor, Prosecuting Attorney Association of Michigan. *Member:* Marion County Bar Association; State Bar of Michigan; Oregon State Bar. ***PRACTICE AREAS:*** Insurance Defense. ***Email:*** dschanz@smapc.com

JAMES F. LAWLER, born Suffern, New York, November 14, 1972; admitted to bar, 1998, New York, Oregon and U.S. District Court, Northern District of New York. *Education:* Syracuse University (B.A., 1994; J.D., 1997). *Member:* Washington County, Marion County, Multnomah County, Onondaga County, New York State and American Bar Associations; Oregon State Bar. ***PRACTICE AREAS:*** Insurance Defense. ***Email:*** jlawler@smapc.com

MELISSA J. WARD, born Salem, Oregon, February 15, 1974; admitted to bar, 1999, Oregon; 2003, U.S. District Court, District of Oregon. *Education:* University of Portland (B.A., magna cum laude, 1996); University of Oregon (J.D., 1999). Author: "Granewich v. Harding," Oregon Business Lawyer, 2000. Former Member: Dunn Carney Allen Higgins and Tongue LLP. *Member:* Oregon State Bar Association. ***PRACTICE AREAS:*** Litigation; Appellate Practice; Construction Law; Business Law. ***Email:*** mward@smapc.com

REPRESENTATIVE CLIENTS: State Farm Mutual Automobile Insurance Co.; Oregon Mutual Insurance Co.; Sentry Dairyland Mutual Insurance Co.; Nationwide Insurance Co.; State Farm Fire & Casualty Co.; Employers Insurance of Wausau; Viking Insurance Co.; Unitrin Insurance Co.; Prudential Insurance Co.; Squibb Corp.; Safeway Stores, Inc.; Lutheran Benevolent Insurance Co.; Great West Life Insurance Co.; Clarendon National Insurance Co.; Great Southwest Fire Insurance Co.; K-Mart, Inc.; League General Insurance Co.; Oregon State Bar Professional Liability Fund; National Indemnity Co.; Scottsdale Insurance Co.; Shelter Insurance; Allied Group Insurance; AIG Specialty Auto; Orion Auto; Austin Mutual Ins. Co.

VICK & CONROYD, LLP

698 12TH STREET, S.E., SUITE 200
SALEM, OREGON 97301
Telephone: 503-364-8488
Fax: 503-588-3495
Email: info@vickconroydlaw.com
URL: http://www.vickconroydlaw.com

Personal Injury, Wrongful Death, Medical Malpractice, Automobile Accidents, Slip and Fall, Workers' Compensation, Products Liability.

JAMES D. VICK, born Detroit, Michigan, December 1, 1945; admitted to bar, 1972, Oregon. *Education:* University of Oregon (B.S., 1968); Willamette University (J.D., 1972). Author, Oregon Trial Lawyers Magazine. Instructor, Trial Practice, Willamette University College of Law, 1990-2000. Chairperson, Citizens Advisory Traffic Commission, City of Salem. *Member:* Marion County Bar Association (Chairperson, Court Practice and Procedures Committee, 1988-1989). [Army Reserve, 1969-1975, E-4]. (Certified as a Civil Trial Advocacy Specialist by the National Board of Trial Advocacy). ***PRACTICE AREAS:*** Medical Malpractice; Personal Injury; Products Liability; Trial Practice; Insurance Disputes. ***Email:*** jvick@vickconroydlaw.com

MICHAEL F. CONROYD, born Oak Park, Illinois, March 10, 1948; admitted to bar, 1974, Illinois; 1978, Oregon and U.S. District Court, District of Oregon; 1994, Washington. *Education:* Georgetown University (B.S.B.A., 1970); Loyola University (J.D., 1974). Adjunct Professor, Trial Practice, Williamette College of Law. *Member:* Marion County Bar Association (Past President); Oregon State Bar; Oregon Trial Lawyers Associations; The Association of Trial Lawyers of America. ***PRACTICE AREAS:*** Personal Injury; Personal Injury Arbitration. ***Email:*** mconroyd@vickconroydlaw.com

ALEX C. DUNN, born Salem, Oregon, November 29, 1973; admitted to bar, 1999, Oregon. *Education:* Linfield College (B.S., 1996); Williamette University (J.D., 1999). *Member:* Marion County Bar Association (Chair, Young Lawyers Division; Member, CLE Committee); American Bar Association; Oregon State Bar; Oregon Trial Lawyers Association. ***PRACTICE AREAS:*** Personal Injury; General Civil Litigation. ***Email:*** adunn@vickconroydlaw.com

MATTHEW LANSING ROY, born Gainesville, Florida, May 5, 1968; admitted to bar, 1994, South Carolina and Oregon. *Education:* Oral Roberts University (B.S., magna cum laude, 1990); University of Florida (J.D., 1993). *Member:* Marion County Bar Association (Secretary, 2005—); American Bar Association; Oregon State Bar (Treasurer, Workers Compensation Section, 2005—); Oregon Trial Lawyers Association; Oregon Workers Compensation Attorneys. ***PRACTICE AREAS:*** Workers Compensation; Personal Injury; Social Security. ***Email:*** mroy@vickconroydlaw.com

Language: Spanish.

CONRAD E. YUNKER, P.C.

Established in 1996

SUITE 25, SUNSET CENTER SOUTH
1193 ROYVONNE AVENUE SE
P.O. BOX 101
SALEM, OREGON 97308-0101
Telephone: 503-371-4608
Fax: 503-371-9556
Email: conrad@ceypc.com
URL: http://www.lawyers.com/ceypc

Litigation, Appeals, Judicial Review, Regulatory, Licensing, Administrative Government, Insurance Disputes, Probate, Estate Litigation, Business Law, Banking Law, Personal Injury, Automobile Accidents and Injuries, Construction Law, Real Estate, Consumer Law, Libel, Slander and Defamation, Eminent Domain.

CONRAD E. YUNKER, born Cheverly, Maryland, November 1, 1951; admitted to bar, 1987, Oregon; 1988, Washington. *Education:* University of Montana (B.A., Journalism, 1984); Willamette University (J.D., 1987). *Member:* Oregon State Bar; Marion County and Washington State Bar Associations; Oregon Trial Lawyers Association; Association of Trial Lawyers of America. ***REPORTED CASES:*** Bruce v. Cascade Collections Inc., 199 Or.App. 63, 110 P.3d 587; Armstrong v. Rogue Federal Credit Union, 145 Or.App. 268, 929 P.2d 1066; Salem-Keizer School District v. Employment Department, 137 Or.App. 320, 904 P.2d 1082; Country Mutual Insurance Co. v. Mendoza, 148 Or.App. 397, 939 P.2d 764 (on brief). ***PRACTICE AREAS:*** Litigation; Appellate Practice; Judicial Review; Regulatory Law; Administrative Law; Government; Insurance; Probate; Estate Litigation; Business Law; Banking Law; Personal Injury; Automobile Accidents and Injuries; Construction Law; Real Estate; Consumer Law; Libel, Slander and Defamation; Eminent Domain. ***Email:*** conrad@ceypc.com

ARNOLD GALLAGHER SAYDACK PERCELL ROBERTS & POTTER, P.C.

SPRINGFIELD, OREGON

(See Eugene)

General Civil Practice, Banking, Business, Mergers and Acquisitions, Construction, Corporate, Creditors' Rights and Commercial Bankruptcy, Labor and Employment, Environmental, Estate Planning and Probate, Insurance, Media, Real Estate, Partnerships, Taxation, Timber and Trial Practice in Oregon State and Federal Courts.

DIMENT & WALKER

SPRINGFIELD, OREGON

(See Eugene)

Civil Litigation, Criminal Law, Driving While Intoxicated, State and Federal Courts, Corporate, Construction, Personal Injury Automobile Accidents, Family Law, Divorce, Child Custody, Visitation Rights, Child Support, Real Estate Law, Probate Law.

JAQUA & WHEATLEY, LLC

SPRINGFIELD, OREGON

(See Eugene)

General Practice in all Courts. Insurance Defense, Casualty and Surety Insurance Law. Litigation, Corporate Law, Partnerships, Business Litigation, Products Liability, Construction Law, Environmental Law, Professional Malpractice, Premises Liability, Estate Planning, Employment Law.

PETERSON LAW OFFICES, PC

SPRINGFIELD, OREGON

(See Portland)

Personal Injury, Premises Liability, Automobile Accidents and Injuries, Dog Bites and Wrongful Death.

SPEER, HOYT, JONES, FEINMAN, POPPE, WOLF & GRIFFITH, P.C.

SPRINGFIELD, OREGON

(See Eugene)

Business Law, Formation of Business Entities, Business Buying and Selling, Employee Benefits, Conflict Resolution, Taxation, Trusts and Estates, Wills and Probate, Estate Planning, Real Estate, Tax Planning, Estate Tax, Tax Conflict Resolution, Collaboration, Family Law, Divorce, Separation, Prenuptial Agreements, Adoption, Custody, Paternity, Municipal Law, Government.

VERALRUD & ASSOCIATES, ATTORNEYS, P.C.

SPRINGFIELD, OREGON

(See Eugene)

Plaintiff's Personal Injury. Automobile Accidents, Aviation Accidents, Wrongful Death, Slip and Fall, Medical Malpractice, Products Liability, Legal Malpractice, Civil Rights, Business Litigation, Criminal Law, White Collar Crime, Drug Defense, Sex Offenses, DUI.

ADAMS & UFFELMAN LLP

TIGARD, OREGON

(See Beaverton)

General Civil and Trial Practice in all State and Federal Courts. Business, Corporate, Estate Planning and Probate Law, Entertainment Law, Family Law, Divorce, Real Estate Law, Contracts, Criminal Law, Criminal Trials and Appeals in all State and Federal Courts.

SARA L. GABIN, P.C.

TIGARD, OREGON

(See Lake Oswego)

Social Security Disability and SSI, Personal Injury, Workers Compensation, Family Law.

SCOTT HOOKLAND LLP

Established in 1984

9185 S.W. BURNHAM STREET
P.O. BOX 23414
TIGARD, OREGON 97223
Telephone: 503-620-4540
Toll Free: 800-334-8986
Fax: 503-620-4315
URL: http://www.scott-hookland.com

Eugene, Oregon Office: 423 Lincoln Street, 97401. Telephone: 541 284-5820; 503 754-4700. Fax: 541 284-5821.

Construction, Design, Civil and Trial Practice, Commercial Collections, Business, Real Estate, Mediations, Arbitrations, Creditors Rights.

MEMBERS OF FIRM

MICHAEL J. SCOTT, born Pendleton, Oregon, January 4, 1956; admitted to bar, 1983, Oregon; 1984, U.S. District Court, District of Oregon; 1989, U.S. Claims Court. *Education:* Pacific University (B.A., with high honors, 1978); Northwestern School of Law of Lewis and Clark College (J.D., 1983). Primary Author: Chapter on Construction Liens, Or. St. Bar *Construction Law,* CLE (1989, 1997 supplement 2004 revision); Co-Author, "Oregon and Washington Construction Lien and Bond Law," Lorman (2001); Co-Author, "Contract Formation The Contractor/Subcontractor's Perspective," The Seminar Group (2001); Co-Author, "Oregon Construction Lien and Bond Law," Lorman (2000); Contributing Author, "Oregon Construction Law: Practical Approaches For One New Millen-

(This Listing Continued)

nium," Lorman (2000). *Oregon Law for Design Professionals,* Co-Author Chapters on Negligence, Immunity, Expert Witness and Construction Lien Claims, Lorman, 1997. Member, 1985-1990 and Chairperson, 1988-1990, State Board of Directors, Oregon Law-Related Education Program; NKA Classroom Project. President, Lewis & Clark Law School, Alumni Association, 1990-1991. President, Tigard Chamber of Commerce, 1989-1990. President, Beaverton Football Association, Inc., 1999-2004, President Friends of Beaverton Football, 2005—. *Member:* Multnomah County, Washington County and American Bar Associations; Oregon State Bar (Member: Debtor-Creditor Section; Construction Section; Chairperson, 1987-1988; OSB CLE Committee, 1994-1997). ***PRACTICE AREAS:*** Construction and Design Law; Business; Commercial Collections; Mediation; Arbitration. ***Email:*** mjspdx@aol.com

DOUGLAS R. HOOKLAND, born South Laguna, California, July 22, 1962; admitted to bar, 1987, Oregon; 1988, Washington and U.S. District Court, District of Oregon; 1989, U.S. District Court, Eastern and Western Districts of Washington; 2003, Idaho, Alaska and U.S. District Court, District of Idaho; 2004, U.S. District Court, District of Alaska. *Education:* California State University at Chico (B.A., with honors, 1984) Willamette University (J.D., 1987). Phi Kappa Phi. Member, Moot Court Board. Member, Board of Directors, ASAP Treatment Services, Inc., 1988-1991. Author: "How to Take a Judgment Debtor Examination," Oregon State Bar Debtor/Creditor Newsletter; Washington Construction Lien Law & Bond Manuel, 1997. Co-Author: "Oregon and Washington Construction Lien and Bond Law," Lorman Education Services, 2003; "Advanced Construction Law in Oregon," National Business Institute, 2003; "Oregon Construction Law: What Do You Do When....?" National Business Institute, 2001; "Washington Collections," Clark County Bar Association, 1997. Multnomah County Administrative Hearings Officer, 1993-1998. President, Tigard Chamber of Commerce, 1997-1998. Tigard Youth Peer Court Judge, 1997—. *Member:* Multnomah County, Washington County, Clark County, King County, Idaho State (Member: Debtor/Creditor Section; Construction Law Section); Washington State (Member: Creditor/Debtor Rights Section; Procurement and Construction Section; Litigation Section) and American (Member, ABA Forum on the Construction Industry) Bar Associations; Alaska State Bar (Member: Debtor/Creditor Law Section; Real Estate Law Section (State Bar of Oregon (Member: Debtor/Creditor Section; Construction Law Section). ***PRACTICE AREAS:*** Construction; Creditors Rights; Civil Litigation. ***Email:*** drh@scott-hookland.com

ASSOCIATES

THOMAS J. MURPHY, born Columbus, Ohio, March 16, 1951; admitted to bar, 1978, Oregon; 1979, U.S. District Court, District of Oregon; 1991, U.S. Court of Appeals, Ninth Circuit. *Education:* The Ohio State University (B.A., summa cum laude, 1973); University of Oregon (J.D., 1978). Phi Beta Kappa. Member, Board of Directors, ASAP Treatment Services, Inc., 1994-1999 . Member, Board of Directors, Community Partners for Affordable Housing, 2000—. *Member:* Multnomah County Bar Association; Oregon State Bar (Member: Sections on: Real Estate and Administrative Law; Construction Law; Executive Committee, 1984-1985 and 1990-1996; Chairperson, 1994-1995). ***PRACTICE AREAS:*** Construction; Real Estate; Civil Litigation. ***Email:*** tjm@scott-hookland.com

ALAN L. MITCHELL, born Marion, Ohio, October 22, 1952; admitted to bar, 1996, Oregon; 2001, U.S. District Court, District of Oregon; 2005, Washington. *Education:* Miami University (B.A., 1975); Northwestern School of Law of Lewis and Clark College (J.D., cum laude, 1996). Member, 1994-1995 and Form and Style Editor, 1995-1996, Environmental Law Review, Northwestern School of Law. Co-Author: Chapter on Construction Liens and Chapter on Proving and Defending Claims on Construction Projects, Or. St. Bar Construction Law CLE (1997, 2004). Chair, City of Tigard Building Appeals Board. *Member:* Multnomah County, Washington County and American (Member, Forum on the Construction Industry) Bar Associations; Oregon State Bar (Member, Executive Committee, Construction Law Section; Sections on: Debtor/Creditor; Business Law). ***PRACTICE AREAS:*** Construction; Commercial Collections. ***Email:*** alm@scott-hookland.com

DOUGLAS L. GALLAGHER, born Portland, Oregon, July 19, 1972; admitted to bar, 1997, Oregon and U.S. District Court, District of Oregon. *Education:* University of Oregon (B.A., Departmental honors in Political Science, 1994; J.D., 1997). *Member:* Washington County and Multnomah County Bar Associations; Oregon State Bar (Member, Sections on: Debtor/Creditor; Construction; Real Estate and Land Use). ***PRACTICE AREAS:*** Construction; Collections; Real Property; Litigation; Creditors Rights. ***Email:*** dlg@scott-hookland.com

KEVIN T. CHRISTIANSEN, born Pendleton, Oregon, April 26, 1973; admitted to bar, 1999, Oregon; 2000, Washington; U.S. District Court, District of Oregon; U.S. District Court, Eastern and Western Districts of Washington. *Education:* Willamette University (B.A., 1995; J.D., 1999). *Member:* Multnomah County, Washington County and Washington State Bar Associations; Oregon State Bar (Member, Sections on: Debtor/Creditor; Construction; Government). ***PRACTICE AREAS:*** Construction Law; Commercial Collections; Litigation. ***Email:*** ktc@scott-hookland.com

REPRESENTATIVE CLIENTS: United Rentals; Southwest Readymix Co.; Suburban Door Co.; Consolidated Electrical Distributors, Inc. (Oregon, Washington, Idaho and Alaska); National Water Works (Oregon and Washington); H&A Construction, Co.; Star Rentals, Inc.

BLUNCK & WALHOOD, LLC

2350 WILLAMETTE FALLS DRIVE
WEST LINN, OREGON 97068-3235
Telephone: 503-656-1654
Fax: 503-650-0603
Email: Larry@bluncklaw.com
URL: http://www.bluncklaw.com

Arbitration, Automobile Accidents, Construction Claims, Contracts, Personal Injury, Insurance.

LAWRENCE P. BLUNCK, born Hood River, Oregon, July 31, 1956; admitted to bar, 1984, Oregon, U.S. District Court, District of Oregon; 1988, U.S. Court of Appeals, Ninth Circuit; 1989, U.S. Supreme Court. *Education:* Brigham Young University (B.A., cum laude, 1981; J.D., cum laude, 1984). Managing Editor, Brigham Young University Journal of Legal Studies, 1983-1984. Author: "The Good Samaritan Doctrine," Brigham Young University Journal of Legal Studies, 1983. *Member:* Multnomah County and American Bar Associations; Oregon State Bar; American Inns of Court I. ***LANGUAGES:*** Spanish. ***PRACTICE AREAS:*** Arbitration; Accidents; Automobile Accidents and Injuries; Sexual Harassment; Civil Litigation; Construction Claims; Insurance Litigation; Property Damage; Breach of Contract; Contract Litigation. ***Email:*** larry@bluncklaw.com

KENNETH L. WALHOOD, born Portland, Oregon, June 1, 1966; admitted to bar, 1994, Oregon; 1996, Washington; 1998, U.S. District Court, District of Oregon. *Education:* Brigham Young University (B.A., 1990); University of Idaho (J.D., 1994). *Member:* Multnomah County, Oregon State Bar and Washington State Bar Associations. ***LANGUAGES:*** German. ***PRACTICE AREAS:*** Civil Litigation; Automobile Accidents and Injuries; Bicycle Accidents; Bodily Injury; Slip and Fall; Construction Defects; Insurance Litigation; Property Damage. ***Email:*** ken@bluncklaw.com

---

LISA K. DAY, born Fort Eustis, Virginia, December 2, 1961; admitted to bar, 1987, Oregon; 1989, U.S. District Court, District of Oregon. *Education:* University of Virginia (B.A., 1983); Northwestern School of Law of Lewis & Clark College (J.D., 1986). ***PRACTICE AREAS:*** Civil Litigation; Commercial Litigation.

SCOTT D. PRESTON, born Honolulu, Hawaii, September 12, 1971; admitted to bar, 2002, Oregon and U.S. District Court, District of Oregon. *Education:* Brigham Young University at Provo (B.S., 1999); Northwestern School of Law (J.D., 2002). *Member:* Multnomah County Bar Association; Oregon State Bar; Oregon Trial Lawyers Association. ***LANGUAGES:*** Czech and Slovak. ***PRACTICE AREAS:*** Plaintiffs Personal Injury; Sexual Harassment; Automobile Accidents and Injuries; Construction Defects. ***Email:*** scott@bluncklaw.com

(This Listing Continued)

HUTCHISON & WALSH

A PROFESSIONAL CORPORATION
Established in 1968
21790 WILLAMETTE DRIVE
P.O. BOX 648
WEST LINN, OREGON 97068
Telephone: 503-656-1694
Fax: 503-656-1092
Email: mail@hutchisonetal.com
URL: http://www.hutchisonwalsh.com

General Civil and Trial Practice. Estate Planning, Probate, Trusts and Estates, Business Law, Contracts, Real Estate, Corporate, Personal Injury, Automobile Accidents, Wrongful Death, Financial Abuse of the Elderly.

FIRM PROFILE: Hutchison & Walsh, P.C. is a small-sized, full-service law firm which provides legal assistance and representation to a broad range of clients. The firm prides itself in establishing long lasting, productive relationships with its clients.

JOHN C. HUTCHISON, born Altadena, California, June 6, 1943; admitted to bar, 1968, Oregon; 1972, U.S. Supreme Court. *Education:* University of Oregon (B.S., 1966; J.D., 1968). *Member:* Clackamas County Bar Association (President, 1980); Oregon State Bar (Member, Committees on: Legal Aid, 1972-1974; Economics of Law Practice, 1976-1979; Chairman, 1978; Client Security Fund, 1980-1983; Chairman, 1983; Local Professional Responsibility, 1981-1984; Chairman, 1984; State Professional Responsibility Board, 1984-1987; Chairman, 1987; Member, Sections on Real Estate and Land Use, Debtor-Creditor, Estate Planning and Administration, Business Law). ***PRACTICE AREAS:*** Estate Administration Law; Real Estate Law; Estate Planning Law; General Business Law; Elder Law; Trusts and Estates; Guardianship; Probate; Contracts; Corporate Law; Limited Liability Company Law; Partnership Law. ***Email:*** johnh@hutchisonetal.com

MICHAEL D. WALSH, born Pasadena, California, October 2, 1942; admitted to bar, 1973, Oregon; 1977, U.S. Supreme Court. *Education:* California State University at Los Angeles (B.A., 1965); Gonzaga University and Northwestern School of Law of Lewis and Clark College (J.D., 1973). Deputy District Attorney, Multnomah County, 1973-1976. *Member:* Clackamas County Bar Association (President, 2002); Oregon State Bar; Oregon Trial Lawyers Association. ***PRACTICE AREAS:*** Personal Injury Law; Wrongful Death Law; Real Property Litigation; Construction Litigation; Business Litigation; Insurance; Automobile Accidents; Fiduciary Law; Litigation. ***Email:*** mike@hutchisonetal.com

---

NICOLE H. SAKYS, born Oregon City, Oregon, February 18, 1975; admitted to bar, 2003, Oregon. *Education:* University of Colorado at Boulder (B.A., 1997); University of Denver College of Law (J.D., 2002). *Member:* Clackamas County Bar Association; Oregon State Bar; (Member, Sections on: Estate Planning and Administration, Elder Law). ***PRACTICE AREAS:*** Estate Planning; Estate Administration; Elder Law; Probate. ***Email:*** nicole@hutchisonetal.com

TIMOTHY E. SIEGEL

1868 KNAPPS ALLEY, SUITE 206
WEST LINN, OREGON 97068
Telephone: 503-650-7411; 877-396-7669
Fax: 503-650-9886
Email: tes@intproplaw.com
URL: http://www.intproplaw.com

Patent Prosecution, Electrical Patent Prosecution, Electronic Patent Prosecution, Medical Patent Prosecution, Mechanical Devices Prosecution, Trademark Registration Application Preparation and Prosecution.

(This Listing Continued)

TIMOTHY E. SIEGEL, West Linn—Continued

TIMOTHY E. SIEGEL, born Los Angeles, California, July 27, 1956; admitted to bar, 1993, California; 1995, Oregon; registered to practice before U.S. Patent and Trademark Office. *Education:* Wayne State University (B.S.E.E., cum laude, 1981); University of Southern California (M.S.E.E., 1986); Loyola Marymount University (J.D., 1993). *Member:* Clackamas County Bar Association; Oregon State Bar (President Elect; Member, Computer and Internet Law Section); Oregon Patent Law Association. ***PRACTICE AREAS:*** Intellectual Property Law.

(This Listing Continued)

REPRESENTATIVE CLIENTS: microHELIX, Inc.; Advanced Cochlear Systems, Inc.; MicroConnex; iSense Corporation.

EXPERTS & SERVICES SECTION

NORTH CAROLINA
NORTH DAKOTA, OHIO
OKLAHOMA, OREGON

The Experts & Services Section provides information on businesses and professionals serving the legal community. This section is arranged alphabetically by state, city, or town, category of service provided and company name.

The Advertiser Index is listed alphabetically by category then within each category alphabetically by state, city and company name. Whether you are looking for a court reporter in your own jurisdiction or an expert witness in another state, the Experts & Services Section is your direct link to legal and non-legal services.

For additional categories/states go to the Martindale-Hubbell Experts & Services Section via the Internet at www.martindale.com/resources where you can quickly find thousands of experts and service providers.

Experts & Services Advertiser Index

COURT REPORTERS - Continued

NORTH CAROLINA - Continued

CHAPEL HILL .... BODENHEIMER VERBATIM REPORTING

CHARLOTTE .... A. WILLIAM ROBERTS, JR. & ASSOCIATES
ADAMS & HOLT, INC.
HUSEBY, INC.
WESTMORELAND REPORTING, INC.

DURHAM .... AFFILIATED COURT REPORTING SERVICES
B. JORDAN & CO.
BODENHEIMER VERBATIM REPORTING

GREENSBORO .... BODENHEIMER VERBATIM REPORTING
LEGAL REPORTING SERVICES

RALEIGH .... AFFILIATED COURT REPORTING SERVICES
KNIGHT & ASSOCIATES COURT REPORTING SERVICE
PACE REPORTING SERVICE, INC.

NORTH DAKOTA

GRAND FORKS .... RUTH ANN JOHNSON COURT REPORTER SERVICE

OHIO

AKRON .... AKRON COURT REPORTERS
BISH & ASSOCIATES, INC.
CEFARATTI GROUP

CANTON .... CANTON COURT REPORTERS

CINCINNATI .... ACE-MERIT, LLC
ANDERSON REPORTING SERVICES, INC.
BRITTON & ASSOCIATES, INC.

CLEVELAND .... ANDERSON REPORTING SERVICES, INC.
CADY REPORTING SERVICES, INC.
CAROL D. HILL & ASSOCIATES
CEFARATTI GROUP
CLEVELAND COURT REPORTERS
FINCUN-MANCINI, INC.

COLUMBUS .... ANDERSON REPORTING SERVICES, INC.
ARMSTRONG & OKEY, INC.
PROFESSIONAL REPORTERS, INC.

DAYTON .... ACE-MERIT, LLC
ANDERSON REPORTING SERVICES, INC.
BRITTON & ASSOCIATES, INC.
MIKE MOBLEY REPORTING

FINDLAY .... COLLINS REPORTING SERVICE, INC.

TOLEDO .... 1-2-3 REPORTING SERVICE A DIVISION OF CERTIFIED REPORTING COMPANY
ANDERSON REPORTING SERVICES, INC.
CLASSIC REPORTING SERVICE
COLLINS REPORTING SERVICE, INC.
SEAGATE REPORTING SERVICE, INC.

OKLAHOMA

OKLAHOMA CITY .... 1-2-3 REPORTING SERVICE A DIVISION OF CERTIFIED REPORTING COMPANY
ELITE REPORTERS
FREELANCE REPORTERS, INC.

TULSA .... FRANK PETERSON REPORTING SERVICE

OREGON

EUGENE .... C & C COURT REPORTING
TEACH REPORTING, INC.

MEDFORD .... ADVANCED COURT REPORTING & VIDEO SERVICE, INC.

PENDLETON .... BRIDGES & ASSOCIATES

PORTLAND .... MOORE HENDERSON ALLEN & THOMAS
TEACH REPORTING, INC.

SALEM .... TEACH REPORTING, INC.

CRIMINAL BACKGROUND CHECKS

NORTH CAROLINA

CHARLOTTE .... CENTURION PROFESSIONAL SERVICES, INC.

CRIMINAL INVESTIGATIONS

NORTH CAROLINA

CHARLOTTE .... CENTURION PROFESSIONAL SERVICES, INC.

CRIMINAL RECORDS RESEARCH

NORTH CAROLINA

CHARLOTTE .... CENTURION PROFESSIONAL SERVICES, INC.

DNA FORENSIC TESTING

OHIO

FAIRFIELD .... DNA DIAGNOSTICS CENTER

DOCUMENT RESEARCH, RETRIEVAL & FILING

NORTH CAROLINA

CARY .... LEXISNEXIS® TIME MATTERS®

DOMESTIC/SPOUSAL COMPUTER INVESTIGATION

NORTH CAROLINA

CHARLOTTE .... CENTURION PROFESSIONAL SERVICES, INC.

DUE DILIGENCE INVESTIGATIONS

NORTH CAROLINA

CHARLOTTE .... CENTURION PROFESSIONAL SERVICES, INC.

ELECTRONIC BILLING

NORTH CAROLINA

CARY .... BILLING MATTERS® PLUS
LEXISNEXIS® TIME MATTERS®

ELECTRONIC DISCOVERY SERVICES

OHIO

CLEVELAND .... JURINNOV LTD.

EMPLOYMENT AGENCIES - PERMANENT/TEMPORARY

OHIO

CLEVELAND .... MAJOR LEGAL SERVICES©

EMPLOYMENT SCREENING

NORTH CAROLINA

CHARLOTTE .... CENTURION PROFESSIONAL SERVICES, INC.

ENGINEERING - METALLURGY/RECONSTRUCTION/FORENSIC CONSULTING

NORTH CAROLINA

RALEIGH .... JAMES SAMUEL MCKNIGHT, PH.D.

ENVIRONMENTAL CONSULTANTS

NORTH CAROLINA

RALEIGH .... LANDIS, INC.

ENVIRONMENTAL INVESTIGATIONS

NORTH CAROLINA

RALEIGH .... LANDIS, INC.

EXPERT WITNESS

ACCIDENT INVESTIGATION & RECONSTRUCTION

OHIO

COLUMBUS .... LEXPERT, INC.

BIOMECHANICAL ENGINEERING

OREGON

PORTLAND .... HAYES + ASSOCIATES

COMPUTER FORENSICS/DATA RECOVERY

OHIO

CLEVELAND .... JURINNOV LTD.

CONSTRUCTION

OHIO

COLUMBUS .... DOC MITCHELL & ASSOCIATES INC.

ECONOMICS/ECONOMISTS

AGRICULTURAL/ENVIRONMENTAL

NORTH CAROLINA

RALEIGH .... LANDIS, INC.

ELECTRICAL

OHIO

COLUMBUS .... DOC MITCHELL & ASSOCIATES INC.

ENGINEERS/ENGINEERING

NORTH CAROLINA

RALEIGH .... FORENSIC ANALYSIS & ENGINEERING CORPORATION

CONSULTANTS

NORTH CAROLINA

RALEIGH .... LANDIS, INC.

ENVIRONMENTAL CONTAMINATION/SPILLS

NORTH CAROLINA

RALEIGH .... LANDIS, INC.

HEATING/VENTILATION/AIR CONDITIONING

OHIO

COLUMBUS .... DOC MITCHELL & ASSOCIATES INC.

EXPERT WITNESS REFERRAL SERVICES

NORTH CAROLINA

RALEIGH .... LANDIS, INC.

OHIO

CINCINNATI .... TASA

CONCORD .... SAPONARO, INC.

GENERAL INVESTIGATORS

NORTH CAROLINA

CHARLOTTE .... CENTURION PROFESSIONAL SERVICES, INC.
EAGLE EYE DETECTIVE AGENCY & ASSOCIATES

OHIO
AKRON .... CEFARATTI GROUP

CLEVELAND .... CEFARATTI GROUP

COLUMBUS .... PICA CORPORATION

OREGON
EUGENE .... ALLEN HORNER INVESTIGATIONS

HOMICIDE EVENTS
NORTH CAROLINA
CHARLOTTE .... CENTURION PROFESSIONAL SERVICES, INC.

INSURANCE - FRAUD
NORTH CAROLINA
CHARLOTTE .... CENTURION PROFESSIONAL SERVICES, INC.

INTERPRETERS & TRANSLATORS
OHIO
CINCINNATI .... AFFORDABLE LANGUAGE SERVICES, LTD.

LAW OFFICE AUTOMATION SERVICES
NORTH CAROLINA
CARY .... BILLING MATTERS® PLUS
LEXISNEXIS® TIME MATTERS®

LAW PRACTICE MANAGEMENT
NORTH CAROLINA
CARY .... LEXISNEXIS® TIME MATTERS®

LAWYER SEARCH & PLACEMENT CONSULTANTS
OHIO
CLEVELAND .... MAJOR LEGAL SERVICES©

OREGON
PORTLAND .... WORKSOURCE, INC.

LEGAL SOFTWARE
NORTH CAROLINA
CARY .... BILLING MATTERS® PLUS
LEXISNEXIS® TIME MATTERS®

LEGAL SUPPORT PERSONNEL - TEMPORARY & PERMANENT
OHIO
CLEVELAND .... MAJOR LEGAL SERVICES©

LEGAL TECHNOLOGY
NORTH CAROLINA
CARY .... BILLING MATTERS® PLUS
LEXISNEXIS® TIME MATTERS®

LIFE CARE PLANNING
OREGON
PORTLAND .... THE MEDICAL RESOURCE NETWORK INC.

LITIGATION SUPPORT - HEALTHCARE
OREGON
PORTLAND .... THE MEDICAL RESOURCE NETWORK INC.

LITIGATION SUPPORT SOFTWARE
NORTH CAROLINA
CARY .... LEXISNEXIS® TIME MATTERS®

LITIGATION TECHNOLOGY CONSULTING
OHIO
CLEVELAND .... JURINNOV LTD.

MEDICAL CASE REVIEW & PREPARATION/TRIAL CONSULTING
OREGON
PORTLAND .... THE MEDICAL RESOURCE NETWORK INC.

MEDICAL EXPERT WITNESS REFERRAL SERVICES
OHIO
CINCINNATI .... TASAMED

CONCORD .... SAPONARO, INC.
OREGON
PORTLAND .... THE MEDICAL RESOURCE NETWORK INC.

MEDICAL MALPRACTICE CONSULTING/PERSONAL INJURY
OREGON
PORTLAND .... THE MEDICAL RESOURCE NETWORK INC.

MEDICAL RECORDS
OHIO
AKRON .... CEFARATTI GROUP

CLEVELAND .... CEFARATTI GROUP

MISSING PERSONS
NORTH CAROLINA
CHARLOTTE .... CENTURION PROFESSIONAL SERVICES, INC.

NURSING CONSULTANTS
NORTH DAKOTA
FARGO .... PRIMO LEGAL NURSE CONSULTING, LLC
OREGON
PORTLAND .... THE MEDICAL RESOURCE NETWORK INC.

PARALEGAL SERVICES
OHIO
CLEVELAND .... MAJOR LEGAL SERVICES©

PERSONNEL CONSULTANTS
NORTH CAROLINA
CHARLOTTE .... CENTURION PROFESSIONAL SERVICES, INC.

PROCESS SERVERS & DOCUMENT DELIVERY SERVICES
NORTH CAROLINA
CHARLOTTE .... CENTURION PROFESSIONAL SERVICES, INC.
EAGLE EYE DETECTIVE AGENCY & ASSOCIATES
OHIO
AKRON .... CEFARATTI GROUP

CLEVELAND .... CEFARATTI GROUP
OKLAHOMA
LAWTON .... OKLAHOMA LEGAL PROCESS SERVICE, INC.

SECURITY CONSULTANTS

NORTH CAROLINA

CHARLOTTE .... CENTURION PROFESSIONAL SERVICES, INC.

SURVEYING - LAND

OHIO

AKRON .... BOCK & CLARK

TIME/BILLING SOFTWARE/SYSTEMS

NORTH CAROLINA

CARY .... BILLING MATTERS® PLUS
LEXISNEXIS® TIME MATTERS®

TITLE INSURANCE

NORTH CAROLINA

RALEIGH .... ATTORNEYS TITLE

OHIO

CINCINNATI .... LAWYERS TITLE OF CINCINNATI, INC.

VIDEO TAPE SERVICES

OHIO

CINCINNATI .... ACE-MERIT, LLC

COLUMBUS .... ANDERSON REPORTING SERVICES, INC.

DAYTON .... ACE-MERIT, LLC

VIOLENCE IN THE WORKPLACE

NORTH CAROLINA

CHARLOTTE .... CENTURION PROFESSIONAL SERVICES, INC.

WHITE COLLAR CRIMINAL/FRAUD INVESTIGATION

NORTH CAROLINA

CHARLOTTE .... CENTURION PROFESSIONAL SERVICES, INC.

WITNESS LOCATOR

NORTH CAROLINA

CHARLOTTE .... CENTURION PROFESSIONAL SERVICES, INC.

WORKERS COMPENSATION

NORTH CAROLINA

CHARLOTTE .... CENTURION PROFESSIONAL SERVICES, INC.

ASHEVILLE,* 61,607, *Buncombe Co.*

COURT REPORTERS

Sperling & Barraco Inc.

53 Orange Street
Asheville, NC 28801

Toll-Free: 1-800-753-1777
Phone: 828-253-2744
Fax: 828-253-3897

www.sperlingandbarraco.com
mail@sperlingandbarraco.com

Services Provided

- Conference Rooms
- Free Parking
- Nationally Certified Reporters
- Certified Realtime Reporters
- Videography
- Condensed Transcripts
- Word Indexes
- ASCII Diskettes
- E-Transcripts
- Depositions and Exhibits Available on CD
- Independently Owned & Operated for over 20 years

BOONE,* 12,915, *Watauga Co.*

COURT REPORTERS

Appalachian Court Reporting

P.O. Box 3251
Boone, NC 28607
Phone: (828) 264-3965 or (828) 773-2065
E-mail: Appalachiancourt@aol.com
Website: www.appalachiancourtreporting.com

Experience:

The owner, **Lisa K. Fraley**, has over five years experience as a freelance court reporter in North Carolina. She has professionally and accurately reported depositions, statements under oath, telephonic depositions, depositions w/interpreters, and hearings for the North Carolina Office of Administrative Hearings, the State Board of Examiners of Plumbing, Heating & Fire Sprinkler Contractors, the North Carolina Board of Electrical Contractors, the North Carolina Cosmetic Arts Board, the United States Postal Service, and N.C. State University faculty and student appeal hearings.

Services Provided:

(This Listing *Continued)*

- **DAILY/EXPEDITED COPY -** *Expedited orders welcome*
- **DEPOSITIONS, TRIALS, ARBITRATIONS, HEARINGS**
- **CONDENSED TRANSCRIPTS WITH KEYWORD INDEXING** *offered at no additional cost.*
- **NOTARY PUBLIC**
- **ASCII DISK**
- **VIDEOGRAHPHER AVAILABLE**
- **TRANSCRIPTION SERVICES** *also available*

MEMBERSHIPS
NVRA

Punctual, Reliable and Professional Court Reporting Services.

Painstaking care given to transcripts and they are proofread word by word.

CARY, 43,858, *Wake Co.*

BUSINESS OPERATIONS

Billing Matters® Plus
for All Your Firm Billing and Accounting

215 Commonwealth Ct
Cary North Carolina
1-800-328-2898

Billing Matters® Plus provides you the tools to handle firm billing plus full back-office accounting. Billing Matters Plus provides easy access to reporting and billing functions, and allows you to create simplified invoices and receipt of payments with minimal steps.

Billing Matters Plus includes:

- Advanced billing
- Full accounts payable and receivable
- Comprehensive trust accounting
- A flexible general ledger
- World-class check writing and reconciliation

And much more. Firms needing basic billing can generate a bill and post a payment in one easy step. Firms needing advanced billing can use split, flat, consolidated, and allocated fees. The new accounting functions can be set for simple bookkeeping with lots of flexibility, or can be completely locked down to maintain tight accounting controls.

Net: A great way to manage your financials and increase the profitability of your law firm.

LexisNexis® Time Matters®
A Time-Saving Solution

215 Commonwealth Ct
Cary North Carolina
1-800-328-2898

Spend less time managing your practice and stay focused on practicing law, with award-winning **LexisNexis® Time Matters®**. From a central desktop location, manage your cases, contacts, calendar, documents, communications, billing and other daily activities. Or use the BlackBerry® link to manage your practice while you're on the go. Flexible support plans are available.

(This Listing Continued)

(This Listing Continued)

(This Listing Continued)

Spend less time managing your practice and stay focused on practicing law, with award-winning **LexisNexis® Time Matters®**. From a central desktop location, manage your cases, contacts, calendar, documents, communications, billing and other daily activities. Or use the BlackBerry® link to manage your practice while you're on the go. Flexible support plans are available.

With Time Matters, you can manage every element of your practice quickly and easily:

- **Cases and Matters** – Centrally organize your contacts, notes, events, to-do's, phone calls and other information associated with a case or matter. With Time Matters, the information you rely on everyday is always in plain sight, at your fingertips.
- **Contacts and Clients** – Time Matters features a centralized system for managing your client information: work, home and email addresses, phone numbers, names of spouse and children, social security number, bank account numbers, properties owned, and anything else you may need to know about a client. You're just a mouseclick away from determining the status of any client matter, and providing the best client service.
- **Docketing, Calendaring and Scheduling** – Time Matters features a comprehensive alert and reminder system that helps you stay on top of deadlines, meetings, and other due dates. No more sleepless nights worrying about looming deadlines. The real-time calendars help you manage the schedules of your entire law firm, so you can keep your finger on the firm's pulse at all times.
- **Documents** – Use the Time Matters document automation feature to produce client and court papers faster than ever before. The version control feature allows you to track an unlimited number of versions, revert to old versions, and open old versions as new documents, so you can easily save and re-use your work.
- **Communications** – The unique mail and courier tracking system helps you manage incoming and outgoing mail. Tracking numbers and certified mail receipts are captured to ensure you have records of delivery and receipt, and can track costs. You can also manage your phone calls, faxes and emails, and link communication records to your case, matter and client files. For the ultimate in practice mobility, the unique Blackberry® link allows you to access your files from virtually anywhere, anytime!
- **Billing** – Time Matters features automatic time entries for everyday activities, such as phone calls, emails, legal research, and other to-do's. You can track expenses while you work, and capture more billable time. Your billing and expense information is stored with your case, client and other information, so cost information is always there at your fingertips.
- **Firm Intelligence** – Time Matters not only lets you plan firm meetings, it also facilitates the sharing of information across the entire firm and coordination of tasks and deliverables. Large or small, your law firm can work better as one team.

Manage your time, your practice. Yourself. With **Time Matters.**

CONTACT MANAGEMENT

LexisNexis® Time Matters®
A Time-Saving Solution

215 Commonwealth Ct
Cary North Carolina
1-800-328-2898

(This Listing Continued)

Spend less time managing your practice and stay focused on practicing law, with award-winning **LexisNexis® Time Matters®**. From a central desktop location, manage your cases, contacts, calendar, documents, communications, billing and other daily activities. Or use the BlackBerry® link to manage your practice while you're on the go. Flexible support plans are available.

With Time Matters, you can manage every element of your practice quickly and easily:

- **Cases and Matters** – Centrally organize your contacts, notes, events, to-do's, phone calls and other information associated with a case or matter. With Time Matters, the information you rely on everyday is always in plain sight, at your fingertips.
- **Contacts and Clients** – Time Matters features a centralized system for managing your client information: work, home and email addresses, phone numbers, names of spouse and children, social security number, bank account numbers, properties owned, and anything else you may need to know about a client. You're just a mouseclick away from determining the status of any client matter, and providing the best client service.
- **Docketing, Calendaring and Scheduling** – Time Matters features a comprehensive alert and reminder system that helps you stay on top of deadlines, meetings, and other due dates. No more sleepless nights worrying about looming deadlines. The real-time calendars help you manage the schedules of your entire law firm, so you can keep your finger on the firm's pulse at all times.
- **Documents** – Use the Time Matters document automation feature to produce client and court papers faster than ever before. The version control feature allows you to track an unlimited number of versions, revert to old versions, and open old versions as new documents, so you can easily save and re-use your work.
- **Communications** – The unique mail and courier tracking system helps you manage incoming and outgoing mail. Tracking numbers and certified mail receipts are captured to ensure you have records of delivery and receipt, and can track costs. You can also manage your phone calls, faxes and emails, and link communication records to your case, matter and client files. For the ultimate in practice mobility, the unique Blackberry® link allows you to access your files from virtually anywhere, anytime!
- **Billing** – Time Matters features automatic time entries for everyday activities, such as phone calls, emails, legal research, and other to-do's. You can track expenses while you work, and capture more billable time. Your billing and expense information is stored with your case, client and other information, so cost information is always there at your fingertips.
- **Firm Intelligence** – Time Matters not only lets you plan firm meetings, it also facilitates the sharing of information across the entire firm and coordination of tasks and deliverables. Large or small, your law firm can work better as one team.

Manage your time, your practice. Yourself. With **Time Matters.**

DOCUMENT RESEARCH, RETRIEVAL & FILING

LexisNexis® Time Matters®
A Time-Saving Solution

215 Commonwealth Ct
Cary North Carolina
1-800-328-2898

(This Listing Continued)

DOCUMENT RESEARCH, RETRIEVAL & FILING (cont'd)

LexisNexis® Time Matters® (cont'd)

Spend less time managing your practice and stay focused on practicing law, with award-winning **LexisNexis® Time Matters®**. From a central desktop location, manage your cases, contacts, calendar, documents, communications, billing and other daily activities. Or use the BlackBerry® link to manage your practice while you're on the go. Flexible support plans are available.

With Time Matters, you can manage every element of your practice quickly and easily:

- **Cases and Matters** – Centrally organize your contacts, notes, events, to-do's, phone calls and other information associated with a case or matter. With Time Matters, the information you rely on everyday is always in plain sight, at your fingertips.
- **Contacts and Clients** – Time Matters features a centralized system for managing your client information: work, home and email addresses, phone numbers, names of spouse and children, social security number, bank account numbers, properties owned, and anything else you may need to know about a client. You're just a mouseclick away from determining the status of any client matter, and providing the best client service.
- **Docketing, Calendaring and Scheduling** – Time Matters features a comprehensive alert and reminder system that helps you stay on top of deadlines, meetings, and other due dates. No more sleepless nights worrying about looming deadlines. The real-time calendars help you manage the schedules of your entire law firm, so you can keep your finger on the firm's pulse at all times.
- **Documents** – Use the Time Matters document automation feature to produce client and court papers faster than ever before. The version control feature allows you to track an unlimited number of versions, revert to old versions, and open old versions as new documents, so you can easily save and re-use your work.
- **Communications** – The unique mail and courier tracking system helps you manage incoming and outgoing mail. Tracking numbers and certified mail receipts are captured to ensure you have records of delivery and receipt, and can track costs. You can also manage your phone calls, faxes and emails, and link communication records to your case, matter and client files. For the ultimate in practice mobility, the unique Blackberry® link allows you to access your files from virtually anywhere, anytime!
- **Billing** – Time Matters features automatic time entries for everyday activities, such as phone calls, emails, legal research, and other to-do's. You can track expenses while you work, and capture more billable time. Your billing and expense information is stored with your case, client and other information, so cost information is always there at your fingertips.
- **Firm Intelligence** – Time Matters not only lets you plan firm meetings, it also facilitates the sharing of information across the entire firm and coordination of tasks and deliverables. Large or small, your law firm can work better as one team.

Manage your time, your practice. Yourself. With **Time Matters**.

ELECTRONIC BILLING

Billing Matters® Plus

for All Your Firm Billing and Accounting

215 Commonwealth Ct
Cary North Carolina
1-800-328-2898

Billing Matters® Plus provides you the tools to handle firm billing plus full back-office accounting. Billing Matters Plus provides easy access to reporting and billing functions, and allows you to create simplified invoices and receipt of payments with minimal steps.

Billing Matters Plus includes:

- Advanced billing
- Full accounts payable and receivable
- Comprehensive trust accounting
- A flexible general ledger
- World-class check writing and reconciliation

And much more. Firms needing basic billing can generate a bill and post a payment in one easy step. Firms needing advanced billing can use split, flat, consolidated, and allocated fees. The new accounting functions can be set for simple bookkeeping with lots of flexibility, or can be completely locked down to maintain tight accounting controls.

Net: A great way to manage your financials and increase the profitability of your law firm.

LexisNexis® Time Matters®

A Time-Saving Solution

215 Commonwealth Ct
Cary North Carolina
1-800-328-2898

Spend less time managing your practice and stay focused on practicing law, with award-winning **LexisNexis® Time Matters®**. From a central desktop location, manage your cases, contacts, calendar, documents, communications, billing and other daily activities. Or use the BlackBerry® link to manage your practice while you're on the go. Flexible support plans are available.

With Time Matters, you can manage every element of your practice quickly and easily:

- **Cases and Matters** – Centrally organize your contacts, notes, events, to-do's, phone calls and other information associated with a case or matter. With Time Matters, the information you rely on everyday is always in plain sight, at your fingertips.
- **Contacts and Clients** – Time Matters features a centralized system for managing your client information: work, home and email addresses, phone numbers, names of spouse and children, social security number, bank account numbers, properties owned, and anything else you may need to know about a client. You're just a mouseclick away from determining the status of any client matter, and providing the best client service.

(This Listing Continued)

- **Docketing, Calendaring and Scheduling** – Time Matters features a comprehensive alert and reminder system that helps you stay on top of deadlines, meetings, and other due dates. No more sleepless nights worrying about looming deadlines. The real-time calendars help you manage the schedules of your entire law firm, so you can keep your finger on the firm's pulse at all times.

- **Documents** – Use the Time Matters document automation feature to produce client and court papers faster than ever before. The version control feature allows you to track an unlimited number of versions, revert to old versions, and open old versions as new documents, so you can easily save and re-use your work.

- **Communications** – The unique mail and courier tracking system helps you manage incoming and outgoing mail. Tracking numbers and certified mail receipts are captured to ensure you have records of delivery and receipt, and can track costs. You can also manage your phone calls, faxes and emails, and link communication records to your case, matter and client files. For the ultimate in practice mobility, the unique Blackberry® link allows you to access your files from virtually anywhere, anytime!

- **Billing** – Time Matters features automatic time entries for everyday activities, such as phone calls, emails, legal research, and other to-do's. You can track expenses while you work, and capture more billable time. Your billing and expense information is stored with your case, client and other information, so cost information is always there at your fingertips.

- **Firm Intelligence** – Time Matters not only lets you plan firm meetings, it also facilitates the sharing of information across the entire firm and coordination of tasks and deliverables. Large or small, your law firm can work better as one team.

Manage your time, your practice. Yourself. With **Time Matters**.

LAW OFFICE AUTOMATION SERVICES

Billing Matters® Plus

for All Your Firm Billing and Accounting

215 Commonwealth Ct
Cary North Carolina
1-800-328-2898

Billing Matters® Plus provides you the tools to handle firm billing plus full back-office accounting. Billing Matters Plus provides easy access to reporting and billing functions, and allows you to create simplified invoices and receipt of payments with minimal steps.

Billing Matters Plus includes:

- Advanced billing
- Full accounts payable and receivable
- Comprehensive trust accounting
- A flexible general ledger
- World-class check writing and reconciliation

And much more. Firms needing basic billing can generate a bill and post a payment in one easy step. Firms needing advanced billing can use split, flat, consolidated, and allocated fees. The new accounting functions can be set for simple bookkeeping with lots of flexibility, or can be completely locked down to maintain tight accounting controls.

Net: A great way to manage your financials and increase the profitability of your law firm.

LexisNexis® Time Matters®

A Time-Saving Solution

215 Commonwealth Ct
Cary North Carolina
1-800-328-2898

Spend less time managing your practice and stay focused on practicing law, with award-winning **LexisNexis® Time Matters®**. From a central desktop location, manage your cases, contacts, calendar, documents, communications, billing and other daily activities. Or use the BlackBerry® link to manage your practice while you're on the go. Flexible support plans are available.

With Time Matters, you can manage every element of your practice quickly and easily:

- **Cases and Matters** – Centrally organize your contacts, notes, events, to-do's, phone calls and other information associated with a case or matter. With Time Matters, the information you rely on everyday is always in plain sight, at your fingertips.

- **Contacts and Clients** – Time Matters features a centralized system for managing your client information: work, home and email addresses, phone numbers, names of spouse and children, social security number, bank account numbers, properties owned, and anything else you may need to know about a client. You're just a mouseclick away from determining the status of any client matter, and providing the best client service.

- **Docketing, Calendaring and Scheduling** – Time Matters features a comprehensive alert and reminder system that helps you stay on top of deadlines, meetings, and other due dates. No more sleepless nights worrying about looming deadlines. The real-time calendars help you manage the schedules of your entire law firm, so you can keep your finger on the firm's pulse at all times.

- **Documents** – Use the Time Matters document automation feature to produce client and court papers faster than ever before. The version control feature allows you to track an unlimited number of versions, revert to old versions, and open old versions as new documents, so you can easily save and re-use your work.

- **Communications** – The unique mail and courier tracking system helps you manage incoming and outgoing mail. Tracking numbers and certified mail receipts are captured to ensure you have records of delivery and receipt, and can track costs. You can also manage your phone calls, faxes and emails, and link communication records to your case, matter and client files. For the ultimate in practice mobility, the unique Blackberry® link allows you to access your files from virtually anywhere, anytime!

- **Billing** – Time Matters features automatic time entries for everyday activities, such as phone calls, emails, legal research, and other to-do's. You can track expenses while you work, and capture more billable time. Your billing and expense information is stored with your case, client and other information, so cost information is always there at your fingertips.

- **Firm Intelligence** – Time Matters not only lets you plan firm meetings, it also facilitates the sharing of information across the entire firm and coordination of tasks and deliverables. Large or small, your law firm can work better as one team.

Manage your time, your practice. Yourself. With **Time Matters**.

LAW PRACTICE MANAGEMENT

LexisNexis® Time Matters®

A Time-Saving Solution

215 Commonwealth Ct
Cary North Carolina
1-800-328-2898

Spend less time managing your practice and stay focused on practicing law, with award-winning **LexisNexis® Time Matters®**. From a central desktop location, manage your cases, contacts, calendar, documents, communications, billing and other daily activities. Or use the BlackBerry® link to manage your practice while you're on the go. Flexible support plans are available.

With Time Matters, you can manage every element of your practice quickly and easily:

- **Cases and Matters** – Centrally organize your contacts, notes, events, to-do's, phone calls and other information associated with a case or matter. With Time Matters, the information you rely on everyday is always in plain sight, at your fingertips.
- **Contacts and Clients** – Time Matters features a centralized system for managing your client information: work, home and email addresses, phone numbers, names of spouse and children, social security number, bank account numbers, properties owned, and anything else you may need to know about a client. You're just a mouseclick away from determining the status of any client matter, and providing the best client service.
- **Docketing, Calendaring and Scheduling** – Time Matters features a comprehensive alert and reminder system that helps you stay on top of deadlines, meetings, and other due dates. No more sleepless nights worrying about looming deadlines. The real-time calendars help you manage the schedules of your entire law firm, so you can keep your finger on the firm's pulse at all times.
- **Documents** – Use the Time Matters document automation feature to produce client and court papers faster than ever before. The version control feature allows you to track an unlimited number of versions, revert to old versions, and open old versions as new documents, so you can easily save and re-use your work.
- **Communications** – The unique mail and courier tracking system helps you manage incoming and outgoing mail. Tracking numbers and certified mail receipts are captured to ensure you have records of delivery and receipt, and can track costs. You can also manage your phone calls, faxes and emails, and link communication records to your case, matter and client files. For the ultimate in practice mobility, the unique Blackberry® link allows you to access your files from virtually anywhere, anytime!
- **Billing** – Time Matters features automatic time entries for everyday activities, such as phone calls, emails, legal research, and other to-do's. You can track expenses while you work, and capture more billable time. Your billing and expense information is stored with your case, client and other information, so cost information is always there at your fingertips.
- **Firm Intelligence** – Time Matters not only lets you plan firm meetings, it also facilitates the sharing of information across the entire firm and coordination of tasks and deliverables. Large or small, your law firm can work better as one team.

Manage your time, your practice. Yourself. With **Time Matters**.

LEGAL SOFTWARE

Billing Matters® Plus

for All Your Firm Billing and Accounting

215 Commonwealth Ct
Cary North Carolina
1-800-328-2898

Billing Matters® Plus provides you the tools to handle firm billing plus full back-office accounting. Billing Matters Plus provides easy access to reporting and billing functions, and allows you to create simplified invoices and receipt of payments with minimal steps.

Billing Matters Plus includes:

- Advanced billing
- Full accounts payable and receivable
- Comprehensive trust accounting
- A flexible general ledger
- World-class check writing and reconciliation

And much more. Firms needing basic billing can generate a bill and post a payment in one easy step. Firms needing advanced billing can use split, flat, consolidated, and allocated fees. The new accounting functions can be set for simple bookkeeping with lots of flexibility, or can be completely locked down to maintain tight accounting controls.

Net: A great way to manage your financials and increase the profitability of your law firm.

LexisNexis® Time Matters®

A Time-Saving Solution

215 Commonwealth Ct
Cary North Carolina
1-800-328-2898

Spend less time managing your practice and stay focused on practicing law, with award-winning **LexisNexis® Time Matters®**. From a central desktop location, manage your cases, contacts, calendar, documents, communications, billing and other daily activities. Or use the BlackBerry® link to manage your practice while you're on the go. Flexible support plans are available.

With Time Matters, you can manage every element of your practice quickly and easily:

- **Cases and Matters** – Centrally organize your contacts, notes, events, to-do's, phone calls and other information associated with a case or matter. With Time Matters, the information you rely on everyday is always in plain sight, at your fingertips.
- **Contacts and Clients** – Time Matters features a centralized system for managing your client information: work, home and email addresses, phone numbers, names of spouse and children, social security number, bank account numbers, properties owned, and anything else you may need to know about a client. You're just a mouseclick away from determining the status of any client matter, and providing the best client service.

(This Listing Continued)

- **Docketing, Calendaring and Scheduling** – Time Matters features a comprehensive alert and reminder system that helps you stay on top of deadlines, meetings, and other due dates. No more sleepless nights worrying about looming deadlines. The real-time calendars help you manage the schedules of your entire law firm, so you can keep your finger on the firm's pulse at all times.

- **Documents** – Use the Time Matters document automation feature to produce client and court papers faster than ever before. The version control feature allows you to track an unlimited number of versions, revert to old versions, and open old versions as new documents, so you can easily save and re-use your work.

- **Communications** – The unique mail and courier tracking system helps you manage incoming and outgoing mail. Tracking numbers and certified mail receipts are captured to ensure you have records of delivery and receipt, and can track costs. You can also manage your phone calls, faxes and emails, and link communication records to your case, matter and client files. For the ultimate in practice mobility, the unique Blackberry® link allows you to access your files from virtually anywhere, anytime!

- **Billing** – Time Matters features automatic time entries for everyday activities, such as phone calls, emails, legal research, and other to-do's. You can track expenses while you work, and capture more billable time. Your billing and expense information is stored with your case, client and other information, so cost information is always there at your fingertips.

- **Firm Intelligence** – Time Matters not only lets you plan firm meetings, it also facilitates the sharing of information across the entire firm and coordination of tasks and deliverables. Large or small, your law firm can work better as one team.

Manage your time, your practice. Yourself. With **Time Matters**.

LEGAL TECHNOLOGY

Billing Matters® Plus

for All Your Firm Billing and Accounting

215 Commonwealth Ct
Cary North Carolina
1-800-328-2898

Billing Matters Plus provides you the tools to handle firm billing plus full back-office accounting. Billing Matters Plus provides easy access to reporting and billing functions, and allows you to create simplified invoices and receipt of payments with minimal steps.

Billing Matters Plus includes:

- Advanced billing
- Full accounts payable and receivable
- Comprehensive trust accounting
- A flexible general ledger
- World-class check writing and reconciliation

And much more. Firms needing basic billing can generate a bill and post a payment in one easy step. Firms needing advanced billing can use split, flat, consolidated, and allocated fees. The new accounting functions can be set for simple bookkeeping with lots of flexibility, or can be completely locked down to maintain tight accounting controls.

Net: A great way to manage your financials and increase the profitability of your law firm.

LexisNexis® Time Matters®

A Time-Saving Solution

215 Commonwealth Ct
Cary North Carolina
1-800-328-2898

Spend less time managing your practice and stay focused on practicing law, with award-winning **LexisNexis® Time Matters®**. From a central desktop location, manage your cases, contacts, calendar, documents, communications, billing and other daily activities. Or use the BlackBerry® link to manage your practice while you're on the go. Flexible support plans are available.

With Time Matters, you can manage every element of your practice quickly and easily:

- **Cases and Matters** – Centrally organize your contacts, notes, events, to-do's, phone calls and other information associated with a case or matter. With Time Matters, the information you rely on everyday is always in plain sight, at your fingertips.

- **Contacts and Clients** – Time Matters features a centralized system for managing your client information: work, home and email addresses, phone numbers, names of spouse and children, social security number, bank account numbers, properties owned, and anything else you may need to know about a client. You're just a mouseclick away from determining the status of any client matter, and providing the best client service.

- **Docketing, Calendaring and Scheduling** – Time Matters features a comprehensive alert and reminder system that helps you stay on top of deadlines, meetings, and other due dates. No more sleepless nights worrying about looming deadlines. The real-time calendars help you manage the schedules of your entire law firm, so you can keep your finger on the firm's pulse at all times.

- **Documents** – Use the Time Matters document automation feature to produce client and court papers faster than ever before. The version control feature allows you to track an unlimited number of versions, revert to old versions, and open old versions as new documents, so you can easily save and re-use your work.

- **Communications** – The unique mail and courier tracking system helps you manage incoming and outgoing mail. Tracking numbers and certified mail receipts are captured to ensure you have records of delivery and receipt, and can track costs. You can also manage your phone calls, faxes and emails, and link communication records to your case, matter and client files. For the ultimate in practice mobility, the unique Blackberry® link allows you to access your files from virtually anywhere, anytime!

- **Billing** – Time Matters features automatic time entries for everyday activities, such as phone calls, emails, legal research, and other to-do's. You can track expenses while you work, and capture more billable time. Your billing and expense information is stored with your case, client and other information, so cost information is always there at your fingertips.

- **Firm Intelligence** – Time Matters not only lets you plan firm meetings, it also facilitates the sharing of information across the entire firm and coordination of tasks and deliverables. Large or small, your law firm can work better as one team.

Manage your time, your practice. Yourself. With **Time Matters**.

Spend less time managing your practice and stay focused on practicing law, with award-winning **LexisNexis® Time Matters®**. From a central desktop location, manage your cases, contacts, calendar, documents, communications, billing and other daily activities. Or use the BlackBerry® link to manage your practice while you're on the go. Flexible support plans are available.

With Time Matters, you can manage every element of your practice quickly and easily:

- **Cases and Matters** – Centrally organize your contacts, notes, events, to-do's, phone calls and other information associated with a case or matter. With Time Matters, the information you rely on everyday is always in plain sight, at your fingertips.

- **Contacts and Clients** – Time Matters features a centralized system for managing your client information: work, home and email addresses, phone numbers, names of spouse and children, social security number, bank account numbers, properties owned, and anything else you may need to know about a client. You're just a mouseclick away from determining the status of any client matter, and providing the best client service.

- **Docketing, Calendaring and Scheduling** – Time Matters features a comprehensive alert and reminder system that helps you stay on top of deadlines, meetings, and other due dates. No more sleepless nights worrying about looming deadlines. The real-time calendars help you manage the schedules of your entire law firm, so you can keep your finger on the firm's pulse at all times.

- **Documents** – Use the Time Matters document automation feature to produce client and court papers faster than ever before. The version control feature allows you to track an unlimited number of versions, revert to old versions, and open old versions as new documents, so you can easily save and re-use your work.

- **Communications** – The unique mail and courier tracking system helps you manage incoming and outgoing mail. Tracking numbers and certified mail receipts are captured to ensure you have records of delivery and receipt, and can track costs. You can also manage your phone calls, faxes and emails, and link communication records to your case, matter and client files. For the ultimate in practice mobility, the unique Blackberry® link allows you to access your files from virtually anywhere, anytime!

- **Billing** – Time Matters features automatic time entries for everyday activities, such as phone calls, emails, legal research, and other to-do's. You can track expenses while you work, and capture more billable time. Your billing and expense information is stored with your case, client and other information, so cost information is always there at your fingertips.

- **Firm Intelligence** – Time Matters not only lets you plan firm meetings, it also facilitates the sharing of information across the entire firm and coordination of tasks and deliverables. Large or small, your law firm can work better as one team.

Manage your time, your practice. Yourself. With **Time Matters**.

CHAPEL HILL, 38,719, *Orange Co.*

COURT REPORTERS

Bodenheimer Verbatim Reporting

☒ CERTIFIED & EXPERIENCED

☒ MEDICAL/TECHNICAL EXPERIENCE

☒ WORDPERFECT OR ASCII DISKETTES

☒ COMPRESSED TEXT - KEYWORD INDEX

BODENHEIMER VERBATIM REPORTING

4337 E. GREENSBORO CHAPEL HILL RD.
POST OFFICE BOX 2056
CHAPEL HILL, NC 27253
Telephone: 919-933-2115
or 336-376-8393
Fax: 336-376-9152
Email: gllynn@aol.com

(This Listing Continued)

COURT REPORTERS (cont'd)

Bodenheimer Verbatim Reporting (cont'd)

Certified Verbatim Reporter
Medical/Technical Expertise
WordPerfect Diskettes
Compressed Text and Complete Index
Owner: Lynn Bodenheimer

Member: National Stenomask Verbatim Reporters Association
North Carolina Verbatim Reporters Association

SEE OUR AD ON PAGE NC9S

CHARLOTTE,* 395,934, *Mecklenburg Co.*

ASSET LOCATORS

CENTURION PROFESSIONAL SERVICES, INC.

8801 JM Keynes Drive, Suite 450
Charlotte, North Carolina, 28262-8436

19109 West Catawba Ave., Suite 200
Cornelius, NC 28031

Office (704) 895-1896
Fax (704) 895-1763
e mail: CenProSer@aol.com

Corporate Mailing Address:
Centurion Professional Services, Inc.
PO Box 129, Davidson, NC 28036-0129

Centurion Professional Services, Inc. is a full service investigative and security consulting corporation incorporated in North Carolina and located at One University Place in Charlotte, NC., and the Lake Norman Area, which encompasses four counties: Mecklenburg, Iredell, Catawba, and Lincoln.

Centurion Professional Services is licensed and insured in North and South Carolina and specializes in Confidential Investigations tailored to meet unique requirements of various clients. Incorporated 1994.

Centurion Professional Services is owned and managed by a former Command officer of the Charlotte-Mecklenburg Police Department. The Owner has three decades of public service in the Charlotte-Mecklenburg community and considerable experience in conducting and managing major investigations and evaluating security risks.

(This Listing Continued)

Mitchell Barnes is a 30 year veteran of the Charlotte-Mecklenburg Police Dept. and a graduate of UNC-Charlotte and the FBI National Academy. He has considerable experience conducting criminal investigations and business and home security analysis evaluations.

SERVICES FOR ATTORNEYS

Asset Locator
Background: Personal & Business
Child Custody and Domestic Related
Court House Research
Civil & Criminal Investigation
Civil & Criminal Records Research
Data Searches - Local - State - National
Due Diligence Investigation
Employment Screening and Verification
Interviews - Recorded Audio & Video
Insurance Fraud
Liability Investigation
Missing Persons
Homicide Investigations
Personal Injury
Personnel Consultants
Process Services
Violence in the Work Place
Security Issues in the Work Place
White Collar Criminal/Fraud Investigations
Witness Locator
Workers Compensations

PROFESSIONAL ASSOCIATIONS

Member, FBI N.A. Academy - North Carolina Chapter
Past President FBI National Academy - North Carolina Chapter
Past Secretary - Treasurer FBI-NA North Carolina Chapter
Member, NC Police Executive Association
Member, NCAPI. North Carolina Association of Private Investigators
Member, SCALI. South Carolina Association of Legal Investigators
Member, NCICIE. North Carolina Insurance Crime Information Exchange

Licensed and Insured in North and South Carolina

CHILD CUSTODY CONSULTANTS

CENTURION PROFESSIONAL SERVICES, INC.

8801 JM Keynes Drive, Suite 450
Charlotte, North Carolina, 28262-8436

19109 West Catawba Ave., Suite 200
Cornelius, NC 28031

Office (704) 895-1896
Fax (704) 895-1763
e mail: CenProSer@aol.com

Corporate Mailing Address:
Centurion Professional Services, Inc.
PO Box 129, Davidson, NC 28036-0129

(This Listing Continued)

Centurion Professional Services, Inc. is a full service investigative and security consulting corporation incorporated in North Carolina and located at One University Place in Charlotte, NC., and the Lake Norman Area, which encompasses four counties: Mecklenburg, Iredell, Catawba, and Lincoln.

Centurion Professional Services is licensed and insured in North and South Carolina and specializes in Confidential Investigations tailored to meet unique requirements of various clients. Incorporated 1994.

Centurion Professional Services is owned and managed by a former Command officer of the Charlotte-Mecklenburg Police Department. The Owner has three decades of public service in the Charlotte-Mecklenburg community and considerable experience in conducting and managing major investigations and evaluating security risks.

Mitchell Barnes is a 30 year veteran of the Charlotte-Mecklenburg Police Dept. and a graduate of UNC-Charlotte and the FBI National Academy. He has considerable experience conducting criminal investigations and business and home security analysis evaluations.

SERVICES FOR ATTORNEYS

Asset Locator
Background: Personal & Business
Child Custody and Domestic Related
Court House Research
Civil & Criminal Investigation
Civil & Criminal Records Research
Data Searches - Local - State - National
Due Diligence Investigation
Employment Screening and Verification
Interviews - Recorded Audio & Video
Insurance Fraud
Liability Investigation
Missing Persons
Homicide Investigations
Personal Injury
Personnel Consultants
Process Services
Violence in the Work Place
Security Issues in the Work Place
White Collar Criminal/Fraud Investigations
Witness Locator
Workers Compensations

PROFESSIONAL ASSOCIATIONS

Member, FBI N.A. Academy - North Carolina Chapter
Past President FBI National Academy - North Carolina Chapter
Past Secretary - Treasurer FBI-NA North Carolina Chapter
Member, NC Police Executive Association
Member, NCAPI. North Carolina Association of Private Investigators
Member, SCALI. South Carolina Association of Legal Investigators
Member, NCICIE. North Carolina Insurance Crime Information Exchange

Licensed and Insured in North and South Carolina

COURT HOUSE RESEARCH

CENTURION PROFESSIONAL SERVICES, INC.

8801 JM Keynes Drive, Suite 450
Charlotte, North Carolina, 28262-8436

19109 West Catawba Ave., Suite 200
Cornelius, NC 28031

Office (704) 895-1896
Fax (704) 895-1763
e mail: CenProSer@aol.com

Corporate Mailing Address:
Centurion Professional Services, Inc.
PO Box 129, Davidson, NC 28036-0129

Centurion Professional Services, Inc. is a full service investigative and security consulting corporation incorporated in North Carolina and located at One University Place in Charlotte, NC., and the Lake Norman Area, which encompasses four counties: Mecklenburg, Iredell, Catawba, and Lincoln.

Centurion Professional Services is licensed and insured in North and South Carolina and specializes in Confidential Investigations tailored to meet unique requirements of various clients. Incorporated 1994.

Centurion Professional Services is owned and managed by a former Command officer of the Charlotte-Mecklenburg Police Department. The Owner has three decades of public service in the Charlotte-Mecklenburg community and considerable experience in conducting and managing major investigations and evaluating security risks.

Mitchell Barnes is a 30 year veteran of the Charlotte-Mecklenburg Police Dept. and a graduate of UNC-Charlotte and the FBI National Academy. He has considerable experience conducting criminal investigations and business and home security analysis evaluations.

SERVICES FOR ATTORNEYS

Asset Locator
Background: Personal & Business
Child Custody and Domestic Related
Court House Research
Civil & Criminal Investigation
Civil & Criminal Records Research

Data Searches - Local - State - National
Due Diligence Investigation
Employment Screening and Verification
Interviews - Recorded Audio & Video
Insurance Fraud
Liability Investigation
Missing Persons
Homicide Investigations
Personal Injury
Personnel Consultants
Process Services
Violence in the Work Place
Security Issues in the Work Place
White Collar Criminal/Fraud Investigations
Witness Locator
Workers Compensations

(This Listing Continued)

COURT HOUSE RESEARCH (cont'd)

Centurion Professional Services, Inc. (cont'd)

PROFESSIONAL ASSOCIATIONS

Member, FBI N.A. Academy - North Carolina Chapter
Past President FBI National Academy - North Carolina Chapter
Past Secretary - Treasurer FBI-NA North Carolina Chapter
Member, NC Police Executive Association
Member, NCAPI. North Carolina Association of Private Investigators
Member, SCALI. South Carolina Association of Legal Investigators
Member, NCICIE. North Carolina Insurance Crime Information Exchange

Licensed and Insured in North and South Carolina

COURT REPORTERS

AWR

A. WILLIAM ROBERTS, JR. & ASSOCIATES
REGISTERED PROFESSIONAL REPORTERS

6047 Tyvola Glen Circle
Charlotte, NC 28217
(704) 573-3919
Toll Free (800) 743-DEPO
Email: awr@scheduledepo.com
Web: www.scheduledepo.com

Additional Offices:

Charleston, SC	Columbia, SC	Greenville, SC
(843) 722-8414	(803) 731-5224	(864) 234-7030

Reporting Services:

- RealTime Reporting with laptop hookups
- On site printing and draft ASCIIs
- Daily and Hourly copy
- ASCII, LiveNote, CaseView, Summation, Sanction, Binder Word, WordPerfect
- Digital Exhibits
- Condensed Transcripts & Word Index
- Video Depositions
- Video Teleconferencing
- Digitally Synchronized Text/Video
- Video DVD & CD
- Conference Room

Serving all of North Carolina and South Carolina

Specializing in:

- Interactive RealTime with laptop hookups
- Multiparty Litigation
- Technical & Scientific Depositions
- Arbitration
- Environmental
- Medical Malpractice
- Asbestos
- Admiralty
- Patent & Trademark
- Tobacco
- Implant

(This Listing Continued)

Holders of:
NCRA Certificates of Merit
NCRA Certificates of Proficiency
NCRA Certified RealTime Reporters
NCRA Certified Legal Video Specialist
NC Certified Shorthand Reporters
Certified by the South Carolina Supreme Court

Members:
Listed in Best's Directory of Insurance Attorneys
National Court Reporters Association
NC Shorthand Reporters Association
SC Shorthand Reporters Association (Past President)
SC Circuit & Family Court Reporters Association (Past President)
Society for the Technological Advancement of Reporting

References:
Any Judge or Attorney in the area

SEE OUR AD ON PAGE NC13S

Court Reporters

We're About Service

Fast - With Realtime technology, you can view the proceedings on your laptop, receive expedited service or our standard delivery - 10-14 business days. You'll receive it when you want it - **Guaranteed!**

Accurate - All of ***AWR's*** court reporters are graduates of accredited stenographic court reporting colleges and hold the highest certifications by the National Court Reporters Association: Registered Professional Reporters, Registered Merit Reporters and Certified Realtime Reporters.

Friendly– From your initial contact with us through the time you receive your transcript, you'll be treated with professionalism and courtesy. That's why we've been serving the North and South Carolina Bar Associations for over 20 years.

- **Realtime, Hourly, Daily & Expedited Copy**
- **LiveNote, CaseView, Summation, E-Transcript, Sanction, Binder, Synchronized Text/Video, CD, DVD, Word, ASCII, Digital Exhibits and Condensed Transcripts**
- **Certified Legal Video Specialists**
- **Video Teleconferencing**
- **Deposition Suites at all locations**

Charleston, SC	Columbia, SC	Greenville, SC	Charlotte, NC
(843) 722-8414	(803) 731-5224	(864) 234-7030	(704) 573-3919

Isn't it about time you put A W R to work for you?

A. William Roberts, Jr. & Associates
Professionals Serving Professionals
Toll Free 1-800-743-DEPO
E-mail: awr@scheduledepo.com
www.scheduledepo.com

COURT REPORTERS (cont'd)

Depositions, Hearings, Arbitrations
Seminars, Technical Conferences, Negotiations
Conventions, Meetings

Realtime, Daily and Expedited Transcripts
Available Upon Request

Case Management & Litigation Support
Compressed Transcripts, e-transcript, Word Indexing
E-mail Delivery of Transcripts
Document Scanning, Conceptual Searching
Professional Videotaping Services
Digital Video

Members of
National Verbatim Reporters Association
North Carolina Verbatim Reporters Association

Other Offices

Cornelius, North Carolina
704-892-8172

Winston-Salem, North Carolina
336-725-9499

Greensboro, North Carolina
336-299-6449

CRIMINAL BACKGROUND CHECKS

CENTURION PROFESSIONAL SERVICES, INC.

8801 JM Keynes Drive, Suite 450
Charlotte, North Carolina, 28262-8436

19109 West Catawba Ave., Suite 200
Cornelius, NC 28031

Office (704) 895-1896
Fax (704) 895-1763
e mail: CenProSer@aol.com

Corporate Mailing Address:
Centurion Professional Services, Inc.
PO Box 129, Davidson, NC 28036-0129

Centurion Professional Services, Inc. is a full service investigative and security consulting corporation incorporated in North Carolina and located at One University Place in Charlotte, NC., and the Lake Norman Area, which encompasses four counties: Mecklenburg, Iredell, Catawba, and Lincoln.

Centurion Professional Services is licensed and insured in North and South Carolina and specializes in Confidential Investigations tailored to meet unique requirements of various clients. Incorporated 1994.

Centurion Professional Services is owned and managed by a former Command officer of the Charlotte-Mecklenburg Police Department. The Owner has three decades of public service in the Charlotte-Mecklenburg community and considerable experience in conducting and managing major investigations and evaluating security risks.

Mitchell Barnes is a 30 year veteran of the Charlotte-Mecklenburg Police Dept. and a graduate of UNC-Charlotte and the FBI National Academy. He has considerable experience conducting criminal investigations and business and home security analysis evaluations.

(This Listing Continued)

SERVICES FOR ATTORNEYS

Asset Locator
Background: Personal & Business
Child Custody and Domestic Related
Court House Research
Civil & Criminal Investigation
Civil & Criminal Records Research
Data Searches - Local - State - National
Due Diligence Investigation
Employment Screening and Verification
Interviews - Recorded Audio & Video
Insurance Fraud
Liability Investigation
Missing Persons
Homicide Investigations
Personal Injury
Personnel Consultants
Process Services
Violence in the Work Place
Security Issues in the Work Place
White Collar Criminal/Fraud Investigations
Witness Locator
Workers Compensations

PROFESSIONAL ASSOCIATIONS

Member, FBI N.A. Academy - North Carolina Chapter
Past President FBI National Academy - North Carolina Chapter
Past Secretary - Treasurer FBI-NA North Carolina Chapter
Member, NC Police Executive Association
Member, NCAPI. North Carolina Association of Private Investigators
Member, SCALI. South Carolina Association of Legal Investigators
Member, NCICIE. North Carolina Insurance Crime Information Exchange

Licensed and Insured in North and South Carolina

CRIMINAL INVESTIGATIONS

CENTURION PROFESSIONAL SERVICES, INC.

8801 JM Keynes Drive, Suite 450
Charlotte, North Carolina, 28262-8436

19109 West Catawba Ave., Suite 200
Cornelius, NC 28031

Office (704) 895-1896
Fax (704) 895-1763
e mail: CenProSer@aol.com

Corporate Mailing Address:
Centurion Professional Services, Inc.
PO Box 129, Davidson, NC 28036-0129

Centurion Professional Services, Inc. is a full service investigative and security consulting corporation incorporated in North Carolina and located at One University Place in Charlotte, NC., and the Lake Norman Area, which encompasses four counties: Mecklenburg, Iredell, Catawba, and Lincoln.

Centurion Professional Services is licensed and insured in North and South Carolina and specializes in Confidential Investigations tailored to meet unique requirements of various clients. Incorporated 1994.

(This Listing Continued)

CRIMINAL INVESTIGATIONS (cont'd)

Centurion Professional Services, Inc. (cont'd)

Centurion Professional Services is owned and managed by a former Command officer of the Charlotte-Mecklenburg Police Department. The Owner has three decades of public service in the Charlotte-Mecklenburg community and considerable experience in conducting and managing major investigations and evaluating security risks.

Mitchell Barnes is a 30 year veteran of the Charlotte-Mecklenburg Police Dept. and a graduate of UNC-Charlotte and the FBI National Academy. He has considerable experience conducting criminal investigations and business and home security analysis evaluations.

SERVICES FOR ATTORNEYS

Asset Locator
Background: Personal & Business
Child Custody and Domestic Related
Court House Research
Civil & Criminal Investigation
Civil & Criminal Records Research
Data Searches - Local - State - National
Due Diligence Investigation
Employment Screening and Verification
Interviews - Recorded Audio & Video
Insurance Fraud
Liability Investigation
Missing Persons
Homicide Investigations
Personal Injury
Personnel Consultants
Process Services
Violence in the Work Place
Security Issues in the Work Place
White Collar Criminal/Fraud Investigations
Witness Locator
Workers Compensations

PROFESSIONAL ASSOCIATIONS

Member, FBI N.A. Academy - North Carolina Chapter
Past President FBI National Academy - North Carolina Chapter
Past Secretary - Treasurer FBI-NA North Carolina Chapter
Member, NC Police Executive Association
Member, NCAPI. North Carolina Association of Private Investigators
Member, SCALI. South Carolina Association of Legal Investigators
Member, NCICIE. North Carolina Insurance Crime Information Exchange

Licensed and Insured in North and South Carolina

CRIMINAL RECORDS RESEARCH

CENTURION PROFESSIONAL SERVICES, INC.

8801 JM Keynes Drive, Suite 450
Charlotte, North Carolina, 28262-8436

19109 West Catawba Ave., Suite 200
Cornelius, NC 28031

(This Listing Continued)

Office (704) 895-1896
Fax (704) 895-1763
e mail: CenProSer@aol.com

Corporate Mailing Address:
Centurion Professional Services, Inc.
PO Box 129, Davidson, NC 28036-0129

Centurion Professional Services, Inc. is a full service investigative and security consulting corporation incorporated in North Carolina and located at One University Place in Charlotte, NC., and the Lake Norman Area, which encompasses four counties: Mecklenburg, Iredell, Catawba, and Lincoln.

Centurion Professional Services is licensed and insured in North and South Carolina and specializes in Confidential Investigations tailored to meet unique requirements of various clients. Incorporated 1994.

Centurion Professional Services is owned and managed by a former Command officer of the Charlotte-Mecklenburg Police Department. The Owner has three decades of public service in the Charlotte-Mecklenburg community and considerable experience in conducting and managing major investigations and evaluating security risks.

Mitchell Barnes is a 30 year veteran of the Charlotte-Mecklenburg Police Dept. and a graduate of UNC-Charlotte and the FBI National Academy. He has considerable experience conducting criminal investigations and business and home security analysis evaluations.

SERVICES FOR ATTORNEYS

Asset Locator
Background: Personal & Business
Child Custody and Domestic Related
Court House Research
Civil & Criminal Investigation
Civil & Criminal Records Research
Data Searches - Local - State - National
Due Diligence Investigation
Employment Screening and Verification
Interviews - Recorded Audio & Video
Insurance Fraud
Liability Investigation
Missing Persons
Homicide Investigations
Personal Injury
Personnel Consultants
Process Services
Violence in the Work Place
Security Issues in the Work Place
White Collar Criminal/Fraud Investigations
Witness Locator
Workers Compensations

PROFESSIONAL ASSOCIATIONS

Member, FBI N.A. Academy - North Carolina Chapter
Past President FBI National Academy - North Carolina Chapter
Past Secretary - Treasurer FBI-NA North Carolina Chapter
Member, NC Police Executive Association
Member, NCAPI. North Carolina Association of Private Investigators
Member, SCALI. South Carolina Association of Legal Investigators
Member, NCICIE. North Carolina Insurance Crime Information Exchange

Licensed and Insured in North and South Carolina

DOMESTIC/SPOUSAL COMPUTER INVESTIGATION

CENTURION PROFESSIONAL SERVICES, INC.

8801 JM Keynes Drive, Suite 450
Charlotte, North Carolina, 28262-8436

19109 West Catawba Ave., Suite 200
Cornelius, NC 28031

Office (704) 895-1896
Fax (704) 895-1763
e mail: CenProSer@aol.com

Corporate Mailing Address:
Centurion Professional Services, Inc.
PO Box 129, Davidson, NC 28036-0129

Centurion Professional Services, Inc. is a full service investigative and security consulting corporation incorporated in North Carolina and located at One University Place in Charlotte, NC., and the Lake Norman Area, which encompasses four counties: Mecklenburg, Iredell, Catawba, and Lincoln.

Centurion Professional Services is licensed and insured in North and South Carolina and specializes in Confidential Investigations tailored to meet unique requirements of various clients. Incorporated 1994.

Centurion Professional Services is owned and managed by a former Command officer of the Charlotte-Mecklenburg Police Department. The Owner has three decades of public service in the Charlotte-Mecklenburg community and considerable experience in conducting and managing major investigations and evaluating security risks.

Mitchell Barnes is a 30 year veteran of the Charlotte-Mecklenburg Police Dept. and a graduate of UNC-Charlotte and the FBI National Academy. He has considerable experience conducting criminal investigations and business and home security analysis evaluations.

SERVICES FOR ATTORNEYS

Asset Locator
Background: Personal & Business
Child Custody and Domestic Related
Court House Research
Civil & Criminal Investigation
Civil & Criminal Records Research
Data Searches - Local - State - National
Due Diligence Investigation
Employment Screening and Verification
Interviews - Recorded Audio & Video
Insurance Fraud
Liability Investigation
Missing Persons
Homicide Investigations
Personal Injury
Personnel Consultants
Process Services
Violence in the Work Place
Security Issues in the Work Place
White Collar Criminal/Fraud Investigations
Witness Locator
Workers Compensations

(This *Listing Continued)*

PROFESSIONAL ASSOCIATIONS

Member, FBI N.A. Academy - North Carolina Chapter
Past President FBI National Academy - North Carolina Chapter
Past Secretary - Treasurer FBI-NA North Carolina Chapter
Member, NC Police Executive Association
Member, NCAPI. North Carolina Association of Private Investigators
Member, SCALI. South Carolina Association of Legal Investigators
Member, NCICIE. North Carolina Insurance Crime Information Exchange

Licensed and Insured in North and South Carolina

DUE DILIGENCE INVESTIGATIONS

CENTURION PROFESSIONAL SERVICES, INC.

8801 JM Keynes Drive, Suite 450
Charlotte, North Carolina, 28262-8436

19109 West Catawba Ave., Suite 200
Cornelius, NC 28031

Office (704) 895-1896
Fax (704) 895-1763
e mail: CenProSer@aol.com

Corporate Mailing Address:
Centurion Professional Services, Inc.
PO Box 129, Davidson, NC 28036-0129

Centurion Professional Services, Inc. is a full service investigative and security consulting corporation incorporated in North Carolina and located at One University Place in Charlotte, NC., and the Lake Norman Area, which encompasses four counties: Mecklenburg, Iredell, Catawba, and Lincoln.

Centurion Professional Services is licensed and insured in North and South Carolina and specializes in Confidential Investigations tailored to meet unique requirements of various clients. Incorporated 1994.

Centurion Professional Services is owned and managed by a former Command officer of the Charlotte-Mecklenburg Police Department. The Owner has three decades of public service in the Charlotte-Mecklenburg community and considerable experience in conducting and managing major investigations and evaluating security risks.

Mitchell Barnes is a 30 year veteran of the Charlotte-Mecklenburg Police Dept. and a graduate of UNC-Charlotte and the FBI National Academy. He has considerable experience conducting criminal investigations and business and home security analysis evaluations.

SERVICES FOR ATTORNEYS

Asset Locator
Background: Personal & Business
Child Custody and Domestic Related
Court House Research
Civil & Criminal Investigation
Civil & Criminal Records Research
Data Searches - Local - State - National
Due Diligence Investigation
Employment Screening and Verification
Interviews - Recorded Audio & Video
Insurance Fraud
Liability Investigation
Missing Persons

(This *Listing Continued)*

DUE DILIGENCE INVESTIGATIONS (cont'd)

Centurion Professional Services, Inc. (cont'd)

Homicide Investigations
Personal Injury
Personnel Consultants
Process Services
Violence in the Work Place
Security Issues in the Work Place
White Collar Criminal/Fraud Investigations
Witness Locator
Workers Compensations

PROFESSIONAL ASSOCIATIONS

Member, FBI N.A. Academy - North Carolina Chapter
Past President FBI National Academy - North Carolina Chapter
Past Secretary - Treasurer FBI-NA North Carolina Chapter
Member, NC Police Executive Association
Member, NCAPI. North Carolina Association of Private Investigators
Member, SCALI. South Carolina Association of Legal Investigators
Member, NCICIE. North Carolina Insurance Crime Information Exchange

Licensed and Insured in North and South Carolina

EMPLOYMENT SCREENING

CENTURION PROFESSIONAL SERVICES, INC.

8801 JM Keynes Drive, Suite 450
Charlotte, North Carolina, 28262-8436

19109 West Catawba Ave., Suite 200
Cornelius, NC 28031

Office (704) 895-1896
Fax (704) 895-1763
e mail: CenProSer@aol.com

Corporate Mailing Address:
Centurion Professional Services, Inc.
PO Box 129, Davidson, NC 28036-0129

Centurion Professional Services, Inc. is a full service investigative and security consulting corporation incorporated in North Carolina and located at One University Place in Charlotte, NC., and the Lake Norman Area, which encompasses four counties: Mecklenburg, Iredell, Catawba, and Lincoln.

Centurion Professional Services is licensed and insured in North and South Carolina and specializes in Confidential Investigations tailored to meet unique requirements of various clients. Incorporated 1994.

Centurion Professional Services is owned and managed by a former Command officer of the Charlotte-Mecklenburg Police Department. The Owner has three decades of public service in the Charlotte-Mecklenburg community and considerable experience in conducting and managing major investigations and evaluating security risks.

Mitchell Barnes is a 30 year veteran of the Charlotte-Mecklenburg Police Dept. and a graduate of UNC-Charlotte and the FBI National Academy. He has considerable experience conducting criminal investigations and business and home security analysis evaluations.

(This Listing Continued)

SERVICES FOR ATTORNEYS

Asset Locator
Background: Personal & Business
Child Custody and Domestic Related
Court House Research
Civil & Criminal Investigation
Civil & Criminal Records Research
Data Searches - Local - State - National
Due Diligence Investigation
Employment Screening and Verification
Interviews - Recorded Audio & Video
Insurance Fraud
Liability Investigation
Missing Persons
Homicide Investigations
Personal Injury
Personnel Consultants
Process Services
Violence in the Work Place
Security Issues in the Work Place
White Collar Criminal/Fraud Investigations
Witness Locator
Workers Compensations

PROFESSIONAL ASSOCIATIONS

Member, FBI N.A. Academy - North Carolina Chapter
Past President FBI National Academy - North Carolina Chapter
Past Secretary - Treasurer FBI-NA North Carolina Chapter
Member, NC Police Executive Association
Member, NCAPI. North Carolina Association of Private Investigators
Member, SCALI. South Carolina Association of Legal Investigators
Member, NCICIE. North Carolina Insurance Crime Information Exchange

Licensed and Insured in North and South Carolina

GENERAL INVESTIGATORS

CENTURION PROFESSIONAL SERVICES, INC.

8801 JM Keynes Drive, Suite 450
Charlotte, North Carolina, 28262-8436

19109 West Catawba Ave., Suite 200
Cornelius, NC 28031

Office (704) 895-1896
Fax (704) 895-1763
e mail: CenProSer@aol.com

Corporate Mailing Address:
Centurion Professional Services, Inc.
PO Box 129, Davidson, NC 28036-0129

Centurion Professional Services, Inc. is a full service investigative and security consulting corporation incorporated in North Carolina and located at One University Place in Charlotte, NC., and the Lake Norman Area, which encompasses four counties: Mecklenburg, Iredell, Catawba, and Lincoln.

Centurion Professional Services is licensed and insured in North and South Carolina and specializes in Confidential Investigations tailored to meet unique requirements of various clients. Incorporated 1994.

(This Listing Continued)

Centurion Professional Services is owned and managed by a former Command officer of the Charlotte-Mecklenburg Police Department. The Owner has three decades of public service in the Charlotte-Mecklenburg community and considerable experience in conducting and managing major investigations and evaluating security risks.

Mitchell Barnes is a 30 year veteran of the Charlotte-Mecklenburg Police Dept. and a graduate of UNC-Charlotte and the FBI National Academy. He has considerable experience conducting criminal investigations and business and home security analysis evaluations.

SERVICES FOR ATTORNEYS

Asset Locator
Background: Personal & Business
Child Custody and Domestic Related
Court House Research
Civil & Criminal Investigation
Civil & Criminal Records Research
Data Searches - Local - State - National
Due Diligence Investigation
Employment Screening and Verification
Interviews - Recorded Audio & Video
Insurance Fraud
Liability Investigation
Missing Persons
Homicide Investigations
Personal Injury
Personnel Consultants
Process Services
Violence in the Work Place
Security Issues in the Work Place
White Collar Criminal/Fraud Investigations
Witness Locator
Workers Compensations

PROFESSIONAL ASSOCIATIONS

Member, FBI N.A. Academy - North Carolina Chapter
Past President FBI National Academy - North Carolina Chapter
Past Secretary - Treasurer FBI-NA North Carolina Chapter
Member, NC Police Executive Association
Member, NCAPI. North Carolina Association of Private Investigators
Member, SCALI. South Carolina Association of Legal Investigators
Member, NCICIE. North Carolina Insurance Crime Information Exchange

Licensed and Insured in North and South Carolina

Eagle Eye Detective Agency & Associates

Eagle Eye Detective Agency & Associates
1409 East Boulevard
Suite 110
Charlotte, NC 28203
Telephone: 704-376-2728 / Toll Free: 866-376-2728
Fax: 704-376-2725 / Toll Free: 866-376-2725
URL: www.eagleeyenc.com

BIO INFORMATION

Eagle Eye Detective Agency & Associates is a full service private investigative agency, including service of process, located in Charlotte, Mecklenburg County, NC. We are bonded, licensed and insured in North Carolina, per NC requirements.

Our investigators total more than 55 years in investigative knowledge and experience.

Investigators:

Keith Hollen PI # 1458
Chad Crosby PIA # 2538
Julius Ulanday PIA # 2636
Aaron Stokes PI # 2621
Dianne Walker PIA # 2670
Doug Evans PIA # 3055

Servicing all 100 North Carolina counties.

Visa, MasterCard, Discover Card, American Express and ATM/Debit Cards accepted through PayPal Services. Checks accepted.

Our Mission Statement is to bring our standards, ethics, knowledge and creativity to each and every case and to provide reliable, diligent, accurate, conscientious, and dependable results and to do so in a timely fashion, as well as caring, attentive association with our clients.

Our motto: **"Reaching to soar above all others."**

SERVICES PROVIDED

- Domestic: Divorce, Adultery, Child Custody cases
- Pre-Employment
- Worker's Compensation
- Insurance Fraud
- Background Checks
- Employee / Internal Theft: White Collar - Blue Collar Crimes
- Personal Injury: Accident Research
- Criminal & Civil Matters
- Due Diligence / Financial
- Hidden Assets
- Locates
- Skip Tracing
- Shopping Services
- Subpoena / Process Services
- Bail Bonding
- Fugitive Recovery: Surety Bail Agents - Keith Hollen, Doug Evans

PROFESSIONAL MEMBERSHIPS / ASSOCIATIONS

- ION - Investigators Online Network
- NAIS - National Association of Investigative Specialists
- BizWomen.com - Charlotte Business Women
- NCAPI - North Carolina Association of Private Investigators
- Association of Christian Investigators
- Plus each Investigator's individual affiliations

HOMICIDE EVENTS

CENTURION PROFESSIONAL SERVICES, INC.

8801 JM Keynes Drive, Suite 450
Charlotte, North Carolina, 28262-8436

19109 West Catawba Ave., Suite 200
Cornelius, NC 28031

Office (704) 895-1896
Fax (704) 895-1763
e mail: CenProSer@aol.com

Corporate Mailing Address:
Centurion Professional Services, Inc.
PO Box 129, Davidson, NC 28036-0129

Centurion Professional Services, Inc. is a full service investigative and security consulting corporation incorporated in North Carolina and located at One University Place in Charlotte, NC., and the Lake Norman Area, which encompasses four counties: Mecklenburg, Iredell, Catawba, and Lincoln.

Centurion Professional Services is licensed and insured in North and South Carolina and specializes in Confidential Investigations tailored to meet unique requirements of various clients. Incorporated 1994.

Centurion Professional Services is owned and managed by a former Command officer of the Charlotte-Mecklenburg Police Department. The Owner has three decades of public service in the Charlotte-Mecklenburg community and considerable experience in conducting and managing major investigations and evaluating security risks.

Mitchell Barnes is a 30 year veteran of the Charlotte-Mecklenburg Police Dept. and a graduate of UNC-Charlotte and the FBI National Academy. He has considerable experience conducting criminal investigations and business and home security analysis evaluations.

SERVICES FOR ATTORNEYS

Asset Locator
Background: Personal & Business
Child Custody and Domestic Related
Court House Research
Civil & Criminal Investigation
Civil & Criminal Records Research
Data Searches - Local - State - National
Due Diligence Investigation
Employment Screening and Verification
Interviews - Recorded Audio & Video
Insurance Fraud
Liability Investigation
Missing Persons
Homicide Investigations
Personal Injury
Personnel Consultants
Process Services
Violence in the Work Place
Security Issues in the Work Place
White Collar Criminal/Fraud Investigations
Witness Locator
Workers Compensations

(This *Listing Continued)*

PROFESSIONAL ASSOCIATIONS

Member, FBI N.A. Academy - North Carolina Chapter
Past President FBI National Academy - North Carolina Chapter
Past Secretary - Treasurer FBI-NA North Carolina Chapter
Member, NC Police Executive Association
Member, NCAPI. North Carolina Association of Private Investigators
Member, SCALI. South Carolina Association of Legal Investigators
Member, NCICIE. North Carolina Insurance Crime Information Exchange

Licensed and Insured in North and South Carolina

INSURANCE - FRAUD

CENTURION PROFESSIONAL SERVICES, INC.

8801 JM Keynes Drive, Suite 450
Charlotte, North Carolina, 28262-8436

19109 West Catawba Ave., Suite 200
Cornelius, NC 28031

Office (704) 895-1896
Fax (704) 895-1763
e mail: CenProSer@aol.com

Corporate Mailing Address:
Centurion Professional Services, Inc.
PO Box 129, Davidson, NC 28036-0129

Centurion Professional Services, Inc. is a full service investigative and security consulting corporation incorporated in North Carolina and located at One University Place in Charlotte, NC., and the Lake Norman Area, which encompasses four counties: Mecklenburg, Iredell, Catawba, and Lincoln.

Centurion Professional Services is licensed and insured in North and South Carolina and specializes in Confidential Investigations tailored to meet unique requirements of various clients. Incorporated 1994.

Centurion Professional Services is owned and managed by a former Command officer of the Charlotte-Mecklenburg Police Department. The Owner has three decades of public service in the Charlotte-Mecklenburg community and considerable experience in conducting and managing major investigations and evaluating security risks.

Mitchell Barnes is a 30 year veteran of the Charlotte-Mecklenburg Police Dept. and a graduate of UNC-Charlotte and the FBI National Academy. He has considerable experience conducting criminal investigations and business and home security analysis evaluations.

SERVICES FOR ATTORNEYS

Asset Locator
Background: Personal & Business
Child Custody and Domestic Related
Court House Research
Civil & Criminal Investigation
Civil & Criminal Records Research
Data Searches - Local - State - National
Due Diligence Investigation
Employment Screening and Verification
Interviews - Recorded Audio & Video
Insurance Fraud
Liability Investigation
Missing Persons

(This *Listing Continued)*

Homicide Investigations
Personal Injury
Personnel Consultants
Process Services
Violence in the Work Place
Security Issues in the Work Place
White Collar Criminal/Fraud Investigations
Witness Locator
Workers Compensations

PROFESSIONAL ASSOCIATIONS

Member, FBI N.A. Academy - North Carolina Chapter
Past President FBI National Academy - North Carolina Chapter
Past Secretary - Treasurer FBI-NA North Carolina Chapter
Member, NC Police Executive Association
Member, NCAPI. North Carolina Association of Private Investigators
Member, SCALI. South Carolina Association of Legal Investigators
Member, NCICIE. North Carolina Insurance Crime Information Exchange

Licensed and Insured in North and South Carolina

MISSING PERSONS

CENTURION PROFESSIONAL SERVICES, INC.

8801 JM Keynes Drive, Suite 450
Charlotte, North Carolina, 28262-8436

19109 West Catawba Ave., Suite 200
Cornelius, NC 28031

Office (704) 895-1896
Fax (704) 895-1763
e mail: CenProSer@aol.com

Corporate Mailing Address:
Centurion Professional Services, Inc.
PO Box 129, Davidson, NC 28036-0129

Centurion Professional Services, Inc. is a full service investigative and security consulting corporation incorporated in North Carolina and located at One University Place in Charlotte, NC., and the Lake Norman Area, which encompasses four counties: Mecklenburg, Iredell, Catawba, and Lincoln.

Centurion Professional Services is licensed and insured in North and South Carolina and specializes in Confidential Investigations tailored to meet unique requirements of various clients. Incorporated 1994.

Centurion Professional Services is owned and managed by a former Command officer of the Charlotte-Mecklenburg Police Department. The Owner has three decades of public service in the Charlotte-Mecklenburg community and considerable experience in conducting and managing major investigations and evaluating security risks.

Mitchell Barnes is a 30 year veteran of the Charlotte-Mecklenburg Police Dept. and a graduate of UNC-Charlotte and the FBI National Academy. He has considerable experience conducting criminal investigations and business and home security analysis evaluations.

SERVICES FOR ATTORNEYS

Asset Locator
Background: Personal & Business
Child Custody and Domestic Related
Court House Research
Civil & Criminal Investigation
Civil & Criminal Records Research

(This Listing Continued)

Data Searches - Local - State - National
Due Diligence Investigation
Employment Screening and Verification
Interviews - Recorded Audio & Video
Insurance Fraud
Liability Investigation
Missing Persons
Homicide Investigations
Personal Injury
Personnel Consultants
Process Services
Violence in the Work Place
Security Issues in the Work Place
White Collar Criminal/Fraud Investigations
Witness Locator
Workers Compensations

PROFESSIONAL ASSOCIATIONS

Member, FBI N.A. Academy - North Carolina Chapter
Past President FBI National Academy - North Carolina Chapter
Past Secretary - Treasurer FBI-NA North Carolina Chapter
Member, NC Police Executive Association
Member, NCAPI. North Carolina Association of Private Investigators
Member, SCALI. South Carolina Association of Legal Investigators
Member, NCICIE. North Carolina Insurance Crime Information Exchange

Licensed and Insured in North and South Carolina

PERSONNEL CONSULTANTS

CENTURION PROFESSIONAL SERVICES, INC.

8801 JM Keynes Drive, Suite 450
Charlotte, North Carolina, 28262-8436

19109 West Catawba Ave., Suite 200
Cornelius, NC 28031

Office (704) 895-1896
Fax (704) 895-1763
e mail: CenProSer@aol.com

Corporate Mailing Address:
Centurion Professional Services, Inc.
PO Box 129, Davidson, NC 28036-0129

Centurion Professional Services, Inc. is a full service investigative and security consulting corporation incorporated in North Carolina and located at One University Place in Charlotte, NC., and the Lake Norman Area, which encompasses four counties: Mecklenburg, Iredell, Catawba, and Lincoln.

Centurion Professional Services is licensed and insured in North and South Carolina and specializes in Confidential Investigations tailored to meet unique requirements of various clients. Incorporated 1994.

Centurion Professional Services is owned and managed by a former Command officer of the Charlotte-Mecklenburg Police Department. The Owner has three decades of public service in the Charlotte-Mecklenburg community and considerable experience in conducting and managing major investigations and evaluating security risks.

Mitchell Barnes is a 30 year veteran of the Charlotte-Mecklenburg Police Dept. and a graduate of UNC-Charlotte and the FBI National Academy. He has considerable experience conducting criminal investigations and business and home security analysis evaluations.

(This Listing Continued)

PERSONNEL CONSULTANTS (cont'd)

Centurion Professional Services, Inc. (cont'd)

SERVICES FOR ATTORNEYS

Asset Locator
Background: Personal & Business
Child Custody and Domestic Related
Court House Research
Civil & Criminal Investigation
Civil & Criminal Records Research
Data Searches - Local - State - National
Due Diligence Investigation
Employment Screening and Verification
Interviews - Recorded Audio & Video
Insurance Fraud
Liability Investigation
Missing Persons
Homicide Investigations
Personal Injury
Personnel Consultants
Process Services
Violence in the Work Place
Security Issues in the Work Place
White Collar Criminal/Fraud Investigations
Witness Locator
Workers Compensations

PROFESSIONAL ASSOCIATIONS

Member, FBI N.A. Academy - North Carolina Chapter
Past President FBI National Academy - North Carolina Chapter
Past Secretary - Treasurer FBI-NA North Carolina Chapter
Member, NC Police Executive Association
Member, NCAPI. North Carolina Association of Private Investigators
Member, SCALI. South Carolina Association of Legal Investigators
Member, NCICIE. North Carolina Insurance Crime Information Exchange

Licensed and Insured in North and South Carolina

PROCESS SERVERS & DOCUMENT DELIVERY SERVICES

CENTURION PROFESSIONAL SERVICES, INC.

8801 JM Keynes Drive, Suite 450
Charlotte, North Carolina, 28262-8436

19109 West Catawba Ave., Suite 200
Cornelius, NC 28031

Office (704) 895-1896
Fax (704) 895-1763
e mail: CenProSer@aol.com

(This Listing Continued)

Corporate Mailing Address:
Centurion Professional Services, Inc.
PO Box 129, Davidson, NC 28036-0129

Centurion Professional Services, Inc. is a full service investigative and security consulting corporation incorporated in North Carolina and located at One University Place in Charlotte, NC., and the Lake Norman Area, which encompasses four counties: Mecklenburg, Iredell, Catawba, and Lincoln.

Centurion Professional Services is licensed and insured in North and South Carolina and specializes in Confidential Investigations tailored to meet unique requirements of various clients. Incorporated 1994.

Centurion Professional Services is owned and managed by a former Command officer of the Charlotte-Mecklenburg Police Department. The Owner has three decades of public service in the Charlotte-Mecklenburg community and considerable experience in conducting and managing major investigations and evaluating security risks.

Mitchell Barnes is a 30 year veteran of the Charlotte-Mecklenburg Police Dept. and a graduate of UNC-Charlotte and the FBI National Academy. He has considerable experience conducting criminal investigations and business and home security analysis evaluations.

SERVICES FOR ATTORNEYS

Asset Locator
Background: Personal & Business
Child Custody and Domestic Related
Court House Research
Civil & Criminal Investigation
Civil & Criminal Records Research
Data Searches - Local - State - National
Due Diligence Investigation
Employment Screening and Verification
Interviews - Recorded Audio & Video
Insurance Fraud
Liability Investigation
Missing Persons
Homicide Investigations
Personal Injury
Personnel Consultants
Process Services
Violence in the Work Place
Security Issues in the Work Place
White Collar Criminal/Fraud Investigations
Witness Locator
Workers Compensations

PROFESSIONAL ASSOCIATIONS

Member, FBI N.A. Academy - North Carolina Chapter
Past President FBI National Academy - North Carolina Chapter
Past Secretary - Treasurer FBI-NA North Carolina Chapter
Member, NC Police Executive Association
Member, NCAPI. North Carolina Association of Private Investigators
Member, SCALI. South Carolina Association of Legal Investigators
Member, NCICIE. North Carolina Insurance Crime Information Exchange

Licensed and Insured in North and South Carolina

Eagle Eye
Detective Agency & Associates

Eagle Eye Detective Agency & Associates
1409 East Boulevard
Suite 110
Charlotte, NC 28203
Telephone: 704-376-2728 / Toll Free: 866-376-2728
Fax: 704-376-2725 / Toll Free: 866-376-2725
URL: www.eagleeyenc.com

BIO INFORMATION

Eagle Eye Detective Agency & Associates is a full service private investigative agency, including service of process, located in Charlotte, Mecklenburg County, NC. We are bonded, licensed and insured in North Carolina, per NC requirements.

Our investigators total more than 55 years in investigative knowledge and experience.

Investigators:

Keith Hollen PI # 1458
Chad Crosby PIA # 2538
Julius Ulanday PIA # 2636
Aaron Stokes PI # 2621
Dianne Walker PIA # 2670
Doug Evans PIA # 3055

Servicing all 100 North Carolina counties.

Visa, MasterCard, Discover Card, American Express and ATM/Debit Cards accepted through PayPal Services. Checks accepted.

Our Mission Statement is to bring our standards, ethics, knowledge and creativity to each and every case and to provide reliable, diligent, accurate, conscientious, and dependable results and to do so in a timely fashion, as well as caring, attentive association with our clients.

Our motto: **"Reaching to soar above all others."**

SERVICES PROVIDED

- Domestic: Divorce, Adultery, Child Custody cases
- Pre-Employment
- Worker's Compensation
- Insurance Fraud
- Background Checks
- Employee / Internal Theft: White Collar - Blue Collar Crimes
- Personal Injury: Accident Research
- Criminal & Civil Matters
- Due Diligence / Financial
- Hidden Assets
- Locates
- Skip Tracing
- Shopping Services
- Subpoena / Process Services
- Bail Bonding
- Fugitive Recovery: Surety Bail Agents - Keith Hollen, Doug Evans

PROFESSIONAL MEMBERSHIPS / ASSOCIATIONS

- ION - Investigators Online Network
- NAIS - National Association of Investigative Specialists
- BizWomen.com - Charlotte Business Women
- NCAPI - North Carolina Association of Private Investigators
- Association of Christian Investigators
- Plus each Investigator's individual affiliations

SECURITY CONSULTANTS

CPS

CENTURION PROFESSIONAL SERVICES, INC.

8801 JM Keynes Drive, Suite 450
Charlotte, North Carolina, 28262-8436

19109 West Catawba Ave., Suite 200
Cornelius, NC 28031

Office (704) 895-1896
Fax (704) 895-1763
e mail: CenProSer@aol.com

Corporate Mailing Address:
Centurion Professional Services, Inc.
PO Box 129, Davidson, NC 28036-0129

Centurion Professional Services, Inc. is a full service investigative and security consulting corporation incorporated in North Carolina and located at One University Place in Charlotte, NC., and the Lake Norman Area, which encompasses four counties: Mecklenburg, Iredell, Catawba, and Lincoln.

Centurion Professional Services is licensed and insured in North and South Carolina and specializes in Confidential Investigations tailored to meet unique requirements of various clients. Incorporated 1994.

Centurion Professional Services is owned and managed by a former Command officer of the Charlotte-Mecklenburg Police Department. The Owner has three decades of public service in the Charlotte-Mecklenburg community and considerable experience in conducting and managing major investigations and evaluating security risks.

Mitchell Barnes is a 30 year veteran of the Charlotte-Mecklenburg Police Dept. and a graduate of UNC-Charlotte and the FBI National Academy. He has considerable experience conducting criminal investigations and business and home security analysis evaluations.

SERVICES FOR ATTORNEYS

Asset Locator
Background: Personal & Business
Child Custody and Domestic Related
Court House Research
Civil & Criminal Investigation
Civil & Criminal Records Research
Data Searches - Local - State - National
Due Diligence Investigation
Employment Screening and Verification
Interviews - Recorded Audio & Video
Insurance Fraud
Liability Investigation
Missing Persons
Homicide Investigations
Personal Injury
Personnel Consultants
Process Services
Violence in the Work Place
Security Issues in the Work Place
White Collar Criminal/Fraud Investigations
Witness Locator
Workers Compensations

(This Listing Continued)

SECURITY CONSULTANTS (cont'd)

Centurion Professional Services, Inc. (cont'd)

PROFESSIONAL ASSOCIATIONS

Member, FBI N.A. Academy - North Carolina Chapter
Past President FBI National Academy - North Carolina Chapter
Past Secretary - Treasurer FBI-NA North Carolina Chapter
Member, NC Police Executive Association
Member, NCAPI. North Carolina Association of Private Investigators
Member, SCALI. South Carolina Association of Legal Investigators
Member, NCICIE. North Carolina Insurance Crime Information Exchange

Licensed and Insured in North and South Carolina

VIOLENCE IN THE WORKPLACE

CENTURION PROFESSIONAL SERVICES, INC.

8801 JM Keynes Drive, Suite 450
Charlotte, North Carolina, 28262-8436

19109 West Catawba Ave., Suite 200
Cornelius, NC 28031

Office (704) 895-1896
Fax (704) 895-1763
e mail: CenProSer@aol.com

Corporate Mailing Address:
Centurion Professional Services, Inc.
PO Box 129, Davidson, NC 28036-0129

Centurion Professional Services, Inc. is a full service investigative and security consulting corporation incorporated in North Carolina and located at One University Place in Charlotte, NC., and the Lake Norman Area, which encompasses four counties: Mecklenburg, Iredell, Catawba, and Lincoln.

Centurion Professional Services is licensed and insured in North and South Carolina and specializes in Confidential Investigations tailored to meet unique requirements of various clients. Incorporated 1994.

Centurion Professional Services is owned and managed by a former Command officer of the Charlotte-Mecklenburg Police Department. The Owner has three decades of public service in the Charlotte-Mecklenburg community and considerable experience in conducting and managing major investigations and evaluating security risks.

Mitchell Barnes is a 30 year veteran of the Charlotte-Mecklenburg Police Dept. and a graduate of UNC-Charlotte and the FBI National Academy. He has considerable experience conducting criminal investigations and business and home security analysis evaluations.

SERVICES FOR ATTORNEYS

Asset Locator
Background: Personal & Business
Child Custody and Domestic Related
Court House Research
Civil & Criminal Investigation
Civil & Criminal Records Research

(This Listing Continued)

Data Searches - Local - State - National
Due Diligence Investigation
Employment Screening and Verification
Interviews - Recorded Audio & Video
Insurance Fraud
Liability Investigation
Missing Persons
Homicide Investigations
Personal Injury
Personnel Consultants
Process Services
Violence in the Work Place
Security Issues in the Work Place
White Collar Criminal/Fraud Investigations
Witness Locator
Workers Compensations

PROFESSIONAL ASSOCIATIONS

Member, FBI N.A. Academy - North Carolina Chapter
Past President FBI National Academy - North Carolina Chapter
Past Secretary - Treasurer FBI-NA North Carolina Chapter
Member, NC Police Executive Association
Member, NCAPI. North Carolina Association of Private Investigators
Member, SCALI. South Carolina Association of Legal Investigators
Member, NCICIE. North Carolina Insurance Crime Information Exchange

Licensed and Insured in North and South Carolina

WHITE COLLAR CRIMINAL/FRAUD INVESTIGATION

CENTURION PROFESSIONAL SERVICES, INC.

8801 JM Keynes Drive, Suite 450
Charlotte, North Carolina, 28262-8436

19109 West Catawba Ave., Suite 200
Cornelius, NC 28031

Office (704) 895-1896
Fax (704) 895-1763
e mail: CenProSer@aol.com

Corporate Mailing Address:
Centurion Professional Services, Inc.
PO Box 129, Davidson, NC 28036-0129

Centurion Professional Services, Inc. is a full service investigative and security consulting corporation incorporated in North Carolina and located at One University Place in Charlotte, NC., and the Lake Norman Area, which encompasses four counties: Mecklenburg, Iredell, Catawba, and Lincoln.

Centurion Professional Services is licensed and insured in North and South Carolina and specializes in Confidential Investigations tailored to meet unique requirements of various clients. Incorporated 1994.

Centurion Professional Services is owned and managed by a former Command officer of the Charlotte-Mecklenburg Police Department. The Owner has three decades of public service in the Charlotte-Mecklenburg community and considerable experience in conducting and managing major investigations and evaluating security risks.

Mitchell Barnes is a 30 year veteran of the Charlotte-Mecklenburg Police Dept. and a graduate of UNC-Charlotte and the FBI National Academy. He has considerable experience conducting criminal investigations and business and home security analysis evaluations.

(This Listing Continued)

SERVICES FOR ATTORNEYS

Asset Locator
Background: Personal & Business
Child Custody and Domestic Related
Court House Research
Civil & Criminal Investigation
Civil & Criminal Records Research
Data Searches - Local - State - National
Due Diligence Investigation
Employment Screening and Verification
Interviews - Recorded Audio & Video
Insurance Fraud
Liability Investigation
Missing Persons
Homicide Investigations
Personal Injury
Personnel Consultants
Process Services
Violence in the Work Place
Security Issues in the Work Place
White Collar Criminal/Fraud Investigations
Witness Locator
Workers Compensations

PROFESSIONAL ASSOCIATIONS

Member, FBI N.A. Academy - North Carolina Chapter
Past President FBI National Academy - North Carolina Chapter
Past Secretary - Treasurer FBI-NA North Carolina Chapter
Member, NC Police Executive Association
Member, NCAPI. North Carolina Association of Private Investigators
Member, SCALI. South Carolina Association of Legal Investigators
Member, NCICIE. North Carolina Insurance Crime Information Exchange

Licensed and Insured in North and South Carolina

WITNESS LOCATOR

CENTURION PROFESSIONAL SERVICES, INC.

8801 JM Keynes Drive, Suite 450
Charlotte, North Carolina, 28262-8436

19109 West Catawba Ave., Suite 200
Cornelius, NC 28031

Office (704) 895-1896
Fax (704) 895-1763
e mail: CenProSer@aol.com

Corporate Mailing Address:
Centurion Professional Services, Inc.
PO Box 129, Davidson, NC 28036-0129

Centurion Professional Services, Inc. is a full service investigative and security consulting corporation incorporated in North Carolina and located at One University Place in Charlotte, NC., and the Lake Norman Area, which encompasses four counties: Mecklenburg, Iredell, Catawba, and Lincoln.

(This Listing Continued)

Centurion Professional Services is licensed and insured in North and South Carolina and specializes in Confidential Investigations tailored to meet unique requirements of various clients. Incorporated 1994.

Centurion Professional Services is owned and managed by a former Command officer of the Charlotte-Mecklenburg Police Department. The Owner has three decades of public service in the Charlotte-Mecklenburg community and considerable experience in conducting and managing major investigations and evaluating security risks.

Mitchell Barnes is a 30 year veteran of the Charlotte-Mecklenburg Police Dept. and a graduate of UNC-Charlotte and the FBI National Academy. He has considerable experience conducting criminal investigations and business and home security analysis evaluations.

SERVICES FOR ATTORNEYS

Asset Locator
Background: Personal & Business
Child Custody and Domestic Related
Court House Research
Civil & Criminal Investigation
Civil & Criminal Records Research
Data Searches - Local - State - National
Due Diligence Investigation
Employment Screening and Verification
Interviews - Recorded Audio & Video
Insurance Fraud
Liability Investigation
Missing Persons
Homicide Investigations
Personal Injury
Personnel Consultants
Process Services
Violence in the Work Place
Security Issues in the Work Place
White Collar Criminal/Fraud Investigations
Witness Locator
Workers Compensations

PROFESSIONAL ASSOCIATIONS

Member, FBI N.A. Academy - North Carolina Chapter
Past President FBI National Academy - North Carolina Chapter
Past Secretary - Treasurer FBI-NA North Carolina Chapter
Member, NC Police Executive Association
Member, NCAPI. North Carolina Association of Private Investigators
Member, SCALI. South Carolina Association of Legal Investigators
Member, NCICIE. North Carolina Insurance Crime Information Exchange

Licensed and Insured in North and South Carolina

WORKERS COMPENSATION

CENTURION PROFESSIONAL SERVICES, INC.

8801 JM Keynes Drive, Suite 450
Charlotte, North Carolina, 28262-8436

19109 West Catawba Ave., Suite 200
Cornelius, NC 28031

Office (704) 895-1896
Fax (704) 895-1763
e mail: CenProSer@aol.com

Corporate Mailing Address:
Centurion Professional Services, Inc.
PO Box 129, Davidson, NC 28036-0129

Centurion Professional Services, Inc. is a full service investigative and security consulting corporation incorporated in North Carolina and located at One University Place in Charlotte, NC., and the Lake Norman Area, which encompasses four counties: Mecklenburg, Iredell, Catawba, and Lincoln.

Centurion Professional Services is licensed and insured in North and South Carolina and specializes in Confidential Investigations tailored to meet unique requirements of various clients. Incorporated 1994.

Centurion Professional Services is owned and managed by a former Command officer of the Charlotte-Mecklenburg Police Department. The Owner has three decades of public service in the Charlotte-Mecklenburg community and considerable experience in conducting and managing major investigations and evaluating security risks.

Mitchell Barnes is a 30 year veteran of the Charlotte-Mecklenburg Police Dept. and a graduate of UNC-Charlotte and the FBI National Academy. He has considerable experience conducting criminal investigations and business and home security analysis evaluations.

SERVICES FOR ATTORNEYS

Asset Locator
Background: Personal & Business
Child Custody and Domestic Related
Court House Research
Civil & Criminal Investigation
Civil & Criminal Records Research
Data Searches - Local - State - National
Due Diligence Investigation
Employment Screening and Verification
Interviews - Recorded Audio & Video
Insurance Fraud
Liability Investigation
Missing Persons
Homicide Investigations
Personal Injury
Personnel Consultants
Process Services
Violence in the Work Place
Security Issues in the Work Place
White Collar Criminal/Fraud Investigations
Witness Locator
Workers Compensations

(This Listing Continued)

PROFESSIONAL ASSOCIATIONS
Member, FBI N.A. Academy - North Carolina Chapter
Past President FBI National Academy - North Carolina Chapter
Past Secretary - Treasurer FBI-NA North Carolina Chapter
Member, NC Police Executive Association
Member, NCAPI. North Carolina Association of Private Investigators
Member, SCALI. South Carolina Association of Legal Investigators
Member, NCICIE. North Carolina Insurance Crime Information Exchange

Licensed and Insured in North and South Carolina

DURHAM,* 136,611, *Durham Co.*

COURT REPORTERS

AFFILIATED COURT REPORTING SERVICES
(Manie P. Currin and Associates, LLC)

"On the Cutting Edge of Technology"
Manie P. Currin, Owner
Durham, NC 27702
P.O. Box 1026
919-682-3107
Raleigh, NC 27622
P.O. Box 30112
919-851-3936
Oxford, NC 27565
203 East Industry Drive
Suite C
919-693-6954

Fax: 919-693-5701
Email: maniecurrin@earthlink.net

Serving Piedmont and Eastern North Carolina

Depositions
(General and Technical)
Hearings
References
Technical Conferences
Arbitrations
Grand Jury Investigations
Negotiations

Competent Staff with experience as State and Federal Court Reporters; U.S. Senate Hearings; EPA Hearings; U.S. Department of Labor Hearings; State Board and Commission Hearings; Military, Industrial and Civil Conferences and Seminars

COVERING ENTIRE STATE OF NORTH CAROLINA
CERTIFIED STENOGRAPHERS
ASCII
Page Image
Computerized Transcription-Case Catalyst
Videotape Depositions by Our Trained Staff
Videoconferencing
Large, Comfortable Conference Room - Oxford
Conference Room Arranged - Other locations
Daily Transcripts Pursuant to Advance Arrangements
FULL LITIGATION SUPPORT
Condensed Transcripts
"Court Reporter Pro" Transcript Compression
Keyword Indexing with Context Phrasing
Indexing - Transcripts and Exhibits
Document Imaging
Full-Color Exhibits

North Carolina Shorthand Reporters Association
National Court Reporters Association

35 Years Experience

B. Jordan & Co.

P. O. Box 3372 CHAPEL HILL, NORTH CAROLINA 27515

CERTIFIED VERBATIM REPORTERS
MEDICAL DEPOSITIONS
GENERAL COURT REPORTING

(919) 929-6592
bjordanco@mindspring.com

25 YEARS SERVING THE TRIANGLE AREA

Raleigh - Durham - Chapel Hill - Research Triangle
Duke University Medical Center - UNC Hospitals

Compressed Transcripts With Index
Videotaping - Legal Video Specialist

EXPERIENCESERVICE**RELIABILITY**

BODENHEIMER VERBATIM REPORTING

4337 E. GREENSBORO CHAPEL HILL RD.
POST OFFICE BOX 2056
CHAPEL HILL, NC 27253
Telephone: 919-933-2115
or 336-376-8393
Fax: 336-376-9152
Email: gllynn@aol.com

Certified Verbatim Reporter
Medical/Technical Expertise
WordPerfect Diskettes
Compressed Text and Complete Index
Owner: Lynn Bodenheimer
(This Listing Continued)

Member: National Stenomask Verbatim Reporters Association
North Carolina Verbatim Reporters Association

GREENSBORO,* 183,521, *Guilford Co.*

COURT REPORTERS

BODENHEIMER VERBATIM REPORTING

4337 E. GREENSBORO CHAPEL HILL RD.
POST OFFICE BOX 2056
CHAPEL HILL, NC 27253
Telephone: 919-933-2115
or 336-376-8393
Fax: 336-376-9152
Email: gllynn@aol.com

Certified Verbatim Reporter
Medical/Technical Expertise
WordPerfect Diskettes
Compressed Text and Complete Index
Owner: Lynn Bodenheimer

Member: National Stenomask Verbatim Reporters Association
North Carolina Verbatim Reporters Association

LEGAL REPORTING SERVICES

Serving the Triad Since 1983

Toll Free 1-800-884-1315

Facsimile (336) 884-4404

Greensboro, North Carolina

(336) 275-0115

High Point, North Carolina
1216 Greensboro Road
High Point, NC 27260

(336) 884-1315

Depositions * Arbitrations * Hearings * Sworn Statements

Certified and Experienced Reporters
Certified Legal Video Specialists
Discovery ZX Litigation Support
Computer-Aided Transcription
Large Case Management
ASCII and WordPerfect Diskettes

Condensed Transcripts and Full Word Indexing Provided
at no additional cost

* Conference Room Available

* Expedited and Daily Copy Upon Request

Centrally Located in North Carolina Serving Statewide and

Greensboro * High Point * Winston-Salem
Asheboro * Lexington * Burlington
Southern Pines * Pinehurst
Durham * Chapel Hill * Raleigh
Thomasville * Randleman
Charlotte * Graham * Salisbury

Members of National Court Reporters Association
Members of North Carolina Shorthand Reporters Association
Members of National Stenomask Verbatim Reporters Association
Members of North Carolina Verbatim Reporters Association

E-Mail Address: legalRPT@AOL.com

RALEIGH,* 207,951, *Wake Co.*

COURT REPORTERS

Manie P. Currin and Associates, LLC
COURT REPORTING SERVICE

FULL LITIGATION SUPPORT

- Certified stenographers
- Transcript crunching by *Court Reporter Pro*
- ASCII discs
- Keyword indexing with context phrasing
- Large case exhibit notebooks with transcript cross referencing
- Computerized transcription - Case Catalyst
- Videotape depositions by our trained staff
- Videoconferencing
- Large - comfortable conference room - Oxford
- Conference room arranged - Other locations
- Daily transcripts pursuant to advance arrangements

OFFICES

Durham
919-682-3107

Raleigh
919-851-3936

Oxford
919-693-6954
919-693-5701 FAX

Mailing Address
203 E. Industry Dr.
Suite C
Oxford, NC 27565

North Carolina Shorthand Reporters Association

National Shorthand Reporters Association

30 Years of Experience

Serving the State of North Carolina

- Depositions (General and Technical)
- Hearings
- References
- Negotiations
- Arbitrations
- Grand Jury Investigations
- Technical Conferences

e-mail: maniecurrin@earthlink.net

on the cutting edge of technology

AFFILIATED COURT REPORTING SERVICES
(Manie P. Currin and Associates, LLC)

"On the Cutting Edge of Technology"
Manie P. Currin, Owner

Raleigh, NC 27622
P.O. Box 30112
919-851-3936

Durham, NC 27702
P.O. Box 1026
919-682-3107

Oxford, NC 27565
203 East Industry Drive
Suite C
919-693-6954

Fax: 919-693-5701
Email: maniecurrin@earthlink.net

(This Listing Continued)

Serving Piedmont and Eastern North Carolina

Depositions (General and Technical)	Technical Conferences
Hearings	Arbitrations
References	Grand Jury Investigations
	Negotiations

Competent Staff with experience as State and Federal Court Reporters; U.S. Senate Hearings; EPA Hearings; U.S. Department of Labor Hearings; State Board and Commission Hearings; Military, Industrial and Civil Conferences and Seminars

COVERING ENTIRE STATE OF NORTH CAROLINA
CERTIFIED STENOGRAPHERS
ASCII
Page Image
Computerized Transcription-Case Catalyst
Videotape Depositions by Our Trained Staff
Videoconferencing
Large, Comfortable Conference Room - Oxford
Conference Room Arranged - Other locations
Daily Transcripts Pursuant to Advance Arrangements
FULL LITIGATION SUPPORT
Condensed Transcripts
"Court Reporter Pro" Transcript Compression
Keyword Indexing with Context Phrasing
Indexing - Transcripts and Exhibits
Document Imaging
Full-Color Exhibits

North Carolina Shorthand Reporters Association
National Court Reporters Association

35 Years Experience

SEE OUR AD ON PAGE NC28S

KNIGHT & ASSOCIATES COURT REPORTING SERVICE
RALEIGH, NORTH CAROLINA

Telephone (919) 552-7816
FAX (919) 552-7928
www.knightreporting.com
jlk@knightreporting.com

(This Listing Continued)

Jennifer L. Knight, CVR-CM, Owner

Serving North Carolina from the Triangle to the Coast

Services Available:
Certified and Experienced Reporters
Specializing in Medical/Technical Testimony
Daily & Expedited Copy available upon request
Complimentary RealLegal E-Transcript with each deposition
Professional video services available
Digital video to text synchronization
Conference Rooms available - Airport & Crabtree Valley

President, North Carolina Verbatim Reporters Association
Member, National Verbatim Reporters Association

Additional Office:
Fayetteville
(910) 323-2048
(910) 323-0746 FAX

Pace Reporting Service, Inc.

Serving the North Carolina Bar Since 1977

7404-E Chapel Hill Road
Raleigh, North Carolina 27607
Telephone: 919-859-0000
Fax: 919-859-1215
Email: mail@pacereporting.com
Fayetteville, NC: 910-433-2926
Wilmington, NC: 910-790-5599

Bettie Pace Thorne, CVR-CM, Owner

Specializing in
Medical, Scientific & Technical Depositions

Other Services Available:

Administrative Hearings	E-transcript
Arbitrations	Deposition Videotaping
Examinations under oath	Videotape Copying
Telephone Depositions	Condensed Transcripts/Keyword Index
Expedited & Daily Copy	ASCII and WordPerfect Disks

Certified Verbatim Reporters

Available for Weekend and Evening Appointments
Reporters Available for **LAST MINUTE ASSIGNMENTS**

Member
National Stenomask Verbatim Reporters Association
North Carolina Verbatim Reporters Association

ENGINEERING - METALLURGY/RECONSTRUCTION/ FORENSIC CONSULTING

James Samuel McKnight, Ph.D.

Engineer
2137 Coley Forest Place
Raleigh, North Carolina 27607
(919) 787-0270 (Voice and Facsimile)
jsmcknight@jsmck.com
www.jsmck.com

Experience

- Electrocutions
- Electrical burn injuries
- The effects of electricity on the human body
- Lightning damage
- Static electricity discharges
- The failure of electrical and mechanical equipment
- Cause and origin determination for industrial, commercial, residential, and vehicle fires
- Electrical storage battery explosions and failures, including impact noise measurements
- Manufacturing process failure analysis
- James machine analysis of floors in slip and fall accidents
- Design and manufacture of safe electronic equipment
- Editing user manuals for electronic equipment
- Self-employed (from 1985) and Research Engineers, Inc., Research Triangle Park (1978-1985)

(This Listing Continued)

Education

- Doctor of Philosophy, Duke University (1969)
Major field of study: physics; minor: mathematics
Thesis title: "The Submillimeter Microware Spectrum of Oxygen"
- Master of Science, Duke University (1962)
Major field of study: electrical engineering
Minor fields of study: physics and mathematics
Thesis title: "A Meter for Quantitatively Evaluating Tremor in Parkinson's Disease"
- Bachelor of Science in Engineering, Duke University (1960) Major field of study: electrical engineering

FULL CV UPON REQUEST!

ENVIRONMENTAL CONSULTANTS

Landis, Inc.

Dr. Barrett L. Kays
P.O. Box 30069
Raleigh, NC 27622-0069
(919) 787-1617
FAX (919) 787-9355
E-mail: www.BarrettKays.com/contact.html
Website: www.LandisInc.net

Landis, Inc. is a small environmental consulting firm that provides scientific investigations, damage assessments, and expert witness services. The Landis web site features over 25 years of the work of Dr. Barrett L. Kays a nationally recognized environmental scientist with specialty in soil, groundwater, and surface water contamination, as well as, natural resource and environmental health regulation of real estate development, and siting and permitting of industrial, commercial, and residential development projects.

The Landis, Inc. website includes examples of representative environmental projects involving: soil, groundwater, and surface water contamination, ecological and natural resource investigations, wetland and waters damage, land application of waste and wastewater, and environmental crime and forensic investigations. Expert witness experience is included in the web resume of Dr. Barrett L. Kays. Dr. Kays has provided expert witness testimony on behalf of both plaintiffs and defendants, for both industry and governmental clients.

ENVIRONMENTAL INVESTIGATIONS

Landis, Inc.

Dr. Barrett L. Kays
P.O. Box 30069
Raleigh, NC 27622-0069
(919) 787-1617
FAX (919) 787-9355
E-mail: www.BarrettKays.com/contact.html
Website: www.LandisInc.net

Landis, Inc. is a small environmental consulting firm that provides scientific investigations, damage assessments, and expert witness services. The Landis web site features over 25 years of the work of Dr. Barrett L. Kays a nationally recognized environmental scientist with specialty in soil, groundwater, and surface water contamination, as well as, natural resource and environmental health regulation of real estate development, and siting and permitting of industrial, commercial, and residential development projects.

(This Listing Continued)

ENVIRONMENTAL INVESTIGATIONS (cont'd)

Landis, Inc. (cont'd)

The Landis, Inc. website includes examples of representative environmental projects involving: soil, groundwater, and surface water contamination, ecological and natural resource investigations, wetland and waters damage, land application of waste and wastewater, and environmental crime and forensic investigations. Expert witness experience is included in the web resume of Dr. Barrett L. Kays. Dr. Kays has provided expert witness testimony on behalf of both plaintiffs and defendants, for both industry and governmental clients.

EXPERT WITNESS
ECONOMICS/ECONOMISTS AGRICULTURAL/ENVIRONMENTAL

Landis, Inc.

Dr. Barrett L. Kays
P.O. Box 30069
Raleigh, NC 27622-0069
(919) 787-1617
FAX (919) 787-9355
E-mail: www.BarrettKays.com/contact.html
Website: www.LandisInc.net

Landis, Inc. is a small environmental consulting firm that provides scientific investigations, damage assessments, and expert witness services. The Landis web site features over 25 years of the work of Dr. Barrett L. Kays a nationally recognized environmental scientist with specialty in soil, groundwater, and surface water contamination, as well as, natural resource and environmental health regulation of real estate development, and siting and permitting of industrial, commercial, and residential development projects.

The Landis, Inc. website includes examples of representative environmental projects involving: soil, groundwater, and surface water contamination, ecological and natural resource investigations, wetland and waters damage, land application of waste and wastewater, and environmental crime and forensic investigations. Expert witness experience is included in the web resume of Dr. Barrett L. Kays. Dr. Kays has provided expert witness testimony on behalf of both plaintiffs and defendants, for both industry and governmental clients.

EXPERT WITNESS
ENGINEERS/ENGINEERING

Forensic Analysis & Engineering Corporation

National Headquarters
5301 Capital Boulevard, Suite A
Raleigh, NC 27616
(919) 872-8788 (800) 224-3595 Fax (919) 872-8660

Mid-Atlantic Regional Office
P.O. Box 159
Hampton, VA 23669
(757) 265-9333 (866) 388-9334 Fax (757) 265-9334

(This Listing Continued)

Southeastern Regional Office
5401 Kirkman Rd. #310
Orlando, FL 32819
(407) 351-6789 (407) 926-6804

Email: forensic@forensic-analysis.com
Website: www.FORENSIC-ANALYSIS.com

Areas of Expertise:

- Product defect determination and analysis
- Mold and mildew causation
- Auto and marine accident reconstruction
- Commercial and construction accident investigations
- Mechanical design defect analysis
- Electrical component failure analysis
- Structural design failure causation
- Industrial safety and process system hazard evaluation
- Marine vessel design & operation analysis
- Material & metallurgical testing & analysis
- Civil & geo-technical investigations
- Fire & explosion causation & origin determination
- Construction defects & code violations
- Evidence storage and management
- More associated forensic services

Firm/Expert Profile:
Forensic Analysis & Engineering Corporation (FAEC) helps you solve your forensic problems by providing professional engineering, technical evaluation and testing services through its nationwide team of dedicated licensed engineers, skilled technicians and diversified expert consultants. Our ever broadening selection of technical, analytical and forensic support services benefit clients from the insurance, legal, and private industry.

Nationwide - 24 HOURS - (800) 224-3595

Leaders in Forensic Engineering and Fire Science Technology since 1966

EXPERT WITNESS
ENGINEERS/ENGINEERING CONSULTANTS

Landis, Inc.

Dr. Barrett L. Kays
P.O. Box 30069
Raleigh, NC 27622-0069
(919) 787-1617
FAX (919) 787-9355
E-mail: www.BarrettKays.com/contact.html
Website: www.LandisInc.net

Landis, Inc. is a small environmental consulting firm that provides scientific investigations, damage assessments, and expert witness services. The Landis web site features over 25 years of the work of Dr. Barrett L. Kays a nationally recognized environmental scientist with specialty in soil, groundwater, and surface water contamination, as well as, natural resource and environmental health regulation of real estate development, and siting and permitting of industrial, commercial, and residential development projects.

The Landis, Inc. website includes examples of representative environmental projects involving: soil, groundwater, and surface water contamination, ecological and natural resource investigations, wetland and waters damage, land application of waste and wastewater, and environmental crime and forensic investigations. Expert witness experience is included in the web resume of Dr. Barrett L. Kays. Dr. Kays has provided expert witness testimony on behalf of both plaintiffs and defendants, for both industry and governmental clients.

EXPERT WITNESS
ENVIRONMENTAL CONTAMINATION/ SPILLS

Landis, Inc.

Dr. Barrett L. Kays
P.O. Box 30069
Raleigh, NC 27622-0069
(919) 787-1617
FAX (919) 787-9355
E-mail: www.BarrettKays.com/contact.html
Website: www.LandisInc.net

Landis, Inc. is a small environmental consulting firm that provides scientific investigations, damage assessments, and expert witness services. The Landis web site features over 25 years of the work of Dr. Barrett L. Kays a nationally recognized environmental scientist with specialty in soil, groundwater, and surface water contamination, as well as, natural resource and environmental health regulation of real estate development, and siting and permitting of industrial, commercial, and residential development projects.

The Landis, Inc. website includes examples of representative environmental projects involving: soil, groundwater, and surface water contamination, ecological and natural resource investigations, wetland and waters damage, land application of waste and wastewater, and environmental crime and forensic investigations. Expert witness experience is included in the web resume of Dr. Barrett L. Kays. Dr. Kays has provided expert witness testimony on behalf of both plaintiffs and defendants, for both industry and governmental clients.

EXPERT WITNESS REFERRAL SERVICES

Landis, Inc.

Dr. Barrett L. Kays
P.O. Box 30069
Raleigh, NC 27622-0069
(919) 787-1617
FAX (919) 787-9355
E-mail: www.BarrettKays.com/contact.html
Website: www.LandisInc.net

Landis, Inc. is a small environmental consulting firm that provides scientific investigations, damage assessments, and expert witness services. The Landis web site features over 25 years of the work of Dr. Barrett L. Kays a nationally recognized environmental scientist with specialty in soil, groundwater, and surface water contamination, as well as, natural resource and environmental health regulation of real estate development, and siting and permitting of industrial, commercial, and residential development projects.

The Landis, Inc. website includes examples of representative environmental projects involving: soil, groundwater, and surface water contamination, ecological and natural resource investigations, wetland and waters damage, land application of waste and wastewater, and environmental crime and forensic investigations. Expert witness experience is included in the web resume of Dr. Barrett L. Kays. Dr. Kays has provided expert witness testimony on behalf of both plaintiffs and defendants, for both industry and governmental clients.

TITLE INSURANCE

Attorneys Title

Representing

Commonwealth Land Title Insurance Company
Lawyers Title Insurance Corporation
Transnation Title Insurance Company
Fidelity National Title Insurance Company

CHARLES B. DAVIS, III
Chairman
8521 Six Forks Road #100
Raleigh, N.C., 27615
919-847-5300; 800-662-7108
Email: corp@attorneystitle.com
Web Address: www.AttorneysTitle.com

TONI CONOLEY
Vice President and Branch Manager
P.O. Box 2597
Raleigh, N.C., 27602-2597
919-828-4692; 800-222-4502

SHANNON DAVENPORT
Branch Manager
P.O. Box 7098
Asheville, N.C., 28802-7098
828-258-0111; 800-532-8235

WILMA BRANSON
Branch Manager
P.O. Box 20003
Winston-Salem, N.C., 27120-0003
336-725-9321; 800-642-0819

H. ANDERSON BERRY, III
Vice President and Counsel
Charlotte Plaza
201 S. College St., Ste. 1440
Charlotte, N.C., 28244
704-376-3503; 800-432-6462

WILLIAM PAUL LEWIS, II
Sr. Vice President
P.O. Box 2280
Wilmington, N.C., 28402-2280
910-343-1096; 800-942-8646

F. STEPHEN ROGERS
President and Title Attorney
P.O. Box 20206
Greensboro, NC 27420
336-230-1800; 888-230-1800

CATHERINE I. LAMM
Vice President
P.O. Box 5336
Cary, N.C., 27512-5336
919-469-5055; 800-226-4419

FARGO,* 74,111, *Cass Co.*

NURSING CONSULTANTS

GRAND FORKS,* 49,425, *Grand Forks Co.*

COURT REPORTERS

AKRON,* 223,019, *Summit Co.*

COURT REPORTERS

COURT REPORTERS
OF AKRON, CANTON & CLEVELAND
ATTORNEY SERVICES
OF NORTHEAST OHIO

AKRON COURT REPORTERS

IT YOU NEED WORK PERFORMED IN AKRON, OHIO- CALL AKRON, OHIO'S BEST,
then sit back and let the show begin..

BINNIE PURSER MARTINO, RPR, RMR, RDR, CRR
MANAGING PRESIDENT

****** REPORTING SERVICES**
Realtime/Summation/ASCII
E-Mail/E-Transcripts/Condensed Transcripts
Expedited/Daily Copy Transcripts/Word Index
Medical/Technical/Products Liability Specialists
Videotaping/Seven-Day Transcript Turnaround

****** UNLIMITED ATTORNEY SERVICES**
COURT RECORD RESEARCH/RETRIEVAL
PRODUCTION/SERVICE OF ALL PROCESS
COURIER/MESSENGER SERVICE

THE WORD COMPLIMENTARY TAKES ON A WHOLE NEW FLAVOR WITHIN THE PLUSH ATMOSPHERE OF OUR STATE-OF-THE-ART CONFERENCE FACILITIES.
Fresh coffee, teas and soft drinks with pastries, donuts and miscellaneous sundry delights always provided at each of our three locations.

AKRON	330-376-8100	Fax 330-376-0110
CLEVELAND	216-621-6969	Fax 216-621-5272
CANTON	330-452-2400	Fax 330-376-0110

800-804-7787

SERVING CLEVELAND, AKRON, CANTON AND SURROUNDING COUNTIES SINCE 1975

Email: reporters@compuserve.com
Internet: www.courtreportersinc.com

BISH & ASSOCIATES, INC.

FOR ORDER IN THE COURT, CALL...

159 SOUTH MAIN STREET - SUITE 812
AKRON, OHIO 44308-1318
330.762.0031
FAX: 330.762.0300

1428 MARKET AVENUE, N.
CANTON, OHIO 44714
330.580.9181
FAX: 330.580.9183

TOLL FREE: 800-332-0607
E-MAIL: BISHASSOCIATES@NEO.RR.COM
WEBSITE: HTTP://WWW.BISH-ASSOCIATES.COM

SERVING NORTHEAST OHIO LITIGATORS SINCE 1977

ON-SITE VIDEOCONFERENCING
SECURE ON-LINE REPOSITORY
DEPOSITIONS - ARBITRATIONS - CONVENTIONS
REAL-TIME REPORTING
ELECTRONIC DOCUMENT CONVERSION FOR TRIAL PRESENTATIONS
E-TRANSCRIPTS

DOCUMENT/TRANSCRIPT CONVERSION TO FEDERAL ELECTRONIC FILING FORMAT
E-PUBLISHER CDS
E-BINDER RESELLER/TRAINING

CERTIFIED REAL-TIME REPORTERS
REGISTERED PROFESSIONAL REPORTERS
CERTIFICATES OF MERIT
REGISTERED DIPLOMATE REPORTER

SPECIALISTS IN MEDICAL / SCIENTIFIC PRODUCT LIABILITY AND INTELLECTUAL PROPERTY DEPOSITIONS

ONE WEEK NORMAL DELIVERY
DAILY COPY - EXPEDITED DELIVERY AVAILABLE

STATEWIDE NOTARIES

TOTAL PRODUCTION/SERVICE of DEPOSITION, RECORD & TRIAL SUBPOENAS

TWO COMPLIMENTARY CONFERENCE ROOMS ON SITE BOTH LOCATIONS

LITIGATION SUPPORT DISKETTES
COMPRESSED TRANSCRIPTS
WORD INDEXING
VIDEOTAPING

MEMBERS: NATIONAL COURT REPORTERS ASSOCIATION
OHIO COURT REPORTERS ASSOCIATION

WILLIAM S. BISH, RDR/CRR
PRESIDENT

COURT REPORTERS (cont'd)

Cefaratti Group
THE LITIGATION SUPPORT COMPANY

Cleveland 4608 St. Clair Avenue, Cleveland, Ohio 44103
Phone: 216.696.1161 Fax: 216.687.0973

Akron Suite 150, One Cascade Plaza, Akron, Ohio 44308
Phone: 330.253.8119 Fax: 330.253.2250

800-694-4787
www.cefgroup.com
info@cefgroup.com

Court Reporting Video Conferencing Legal Video Production
Investigations Claims Service Process Service Record Retrieval
Document Management Trial Graphics

Audio files, digitized video and exhibits from depositions available on CD-ROM.

Conference Rooms, National Referrals
Realtime Translation, e-Binder,
Caseview & LiveNote
Medical and Technical Specialists

Members National Court Reporters Association, Ohio Court Reporters Association, and STAR Users Group

GENERAL INVESTIGATORS

Cefaratti Group
THE LITIGATION SUPPORT COMPANY

Cleveland 4608 St. Clair Avenue, Cleveland, Ohio 44103
Phone: 216.696.1161 Fax: 216.687.0973

Akron Suite 150, One Cascade Plaza, Akron, Ohio 44308
Phone: 330.253.8119 Fax: 330.253.2250

800-694-4787
www.cefgroup.com
info@cefgroup.com

Court Reporting Video Conferencing Legal Video Production
Investigations Claims Service Process Service Record Retrieval
Document Management Trial Graphics

Audio files, digitized video and exhibits from depositions available on CD-ROM.

(This Listing Continued)

Conference Rooms, National Referrals
Realtime Translation, e-Binder,
Caseview & LiveNote
Medical and Technical Specialists

Members National Court Reporters Association, Ohio Court Reporters Association, and STAR Users Group

MEDICAL RECORDS

Cefaratti Group
THE LITIGATION SUPPORT COMPANY

Cleveland 4608 St. Clair Avenue, Cleveland, Ohio 44103
Phone: 216.696.1161 Fax: 216.687.0973

Akron Suite 150, One Cascade Plaza, Akron, Ohio 44308
Phone: 330.253.8119 Fax: 330.253.2250

800-694-4787
www.cefgroup.com
info@cefgroup.com

Court Reporting Video Conferencing Legal Video Production
Investigations Claims Service Process Service Record Retrieval
Document Management Trial Graphics

Audio files, digitized video and exhibits from depositions available on CD-ROM.

Conference Rooms, National Referrals
Realtime Translation, e-Binder,
Caseview & LiveNote
Medical and Technical Specialists

Members National Court Reporters Association, Ohio Court Reporters Association, and STAR Users Group

PROCESS SERVERS & DOCUMENT DELIVERY SERVICES

SURVEYING - LAND

(This Listing Continued)

CANTON,* 84,161, *Stark Co.*

COURT REPORTERS

(This Listing Continued)

COURT REPORTERS (cont'd)

Canton Court Reporters (cont'd)

AKRON	330-376-8100	Fax 330-376-0110
CLEVELAND	216-621-6969	Fax 216-621-5272
CANTON	330-452-2400	Fax 330-376-0110

800-804-7787

SERVING CLEVELAND, AKRON,
CANTON AND SURROUNDING
COUNTIES SINCE 1975

Email: reporters@compuserve.com
Internet: www.courtreportersinc.com

CINCINNATI,* 364,040, *Hamilton Co.*

COURT REPORTERS

Britton
AND ASSOCIATES, INC
www.brittonandassociates.com

COURT REPORTERS

VIDEOGRAPHERS

OHIO & KENTUCKY NOTARIES
REALTIME / CASEVIEW / KEYWORD INDEXING /
E-MAIL TRANSCRIPTS /
CONDENSED TRANSCRIPTS / VIDEOTAPING /
SUBPOENAS / CONFERENCE CENTERS /
FULL LITIGATION SUPPORT

124 E. Third Street
Suite 400
Dayton, Ohio 45402
Tel: (937) 228-3370
Fax: (937) 228-9253

119 East Court Street
Suite 313
Cincinnati, Ohio 45202
Tel: (513) 651-3370
Fax: (513) 651-9253

ACE-MERIT, LLC

Serving the Legal Profession
Since 1966

620 Cincinnati Club Building
30 Garfield Place
Cincinnati, Ohio 45202
Telephone: 513-241-3200 Fax: 513-241-7958
800-277-7165

COMPLETE LITIGATION SUPPORT

AceMerit on the Web
Schedule, order, download transcripts &
check account activity 24/7

3-D Graphics & Animated Trial Presentations
Key word indexing, Video Depositions, Day in the Life,
Accident Reconstruction, Settlement Tapes,
World Wide Video Teleconferencing,
CaseView, Summation & LiveNote,
E-Transcript, RealLegal Publisher, RealLegal Binder
Complete Document Management, Video-Steno Sync

Notaries Public Ohio, Indiana, Kentucky
Subpoenas, all papers, created & served
Realtime and expedited Transcripts
10-business day delivery - standard
Standby Reporters available
Medical and Technical Specialists
Three large conference rooms on site

Members: National Court Reporters Association
Ohio Court Reporters Association
Stenocat Users Group/Eclipse Users Group
Cincinnati USA Regional Chamber
Better Business Bureau
National Network Reporting Company

Alicia B. Hardin, President
Angie Portune, Vice President
David W. Moxley, Managing Reporter

Reporters

Tracy Allen, RPR	Jennifer Coats, CR
S. Diane Farrell, RMR, CRR	Susan P. Gee, RMR, CRR
Debra Henderson, RPR	Connie Henson, RPR
Luke Lavin, RDR, CRR	Amy Milholland, CR
David W. Moxley, RPR, CMRS, CRR	Linda Mullen, RPR, CRR
Sherry Music, CSR	Angie Portune, RMR
Wendy Raymer, RPR	Karen Volk, RPR
Patricia C. Walterman, RPR	Lisa Weisenberger, RPR
Wendy Welsh, RDR, CRR	Kimberly Wilson, CSR

Ace-Merit Video Department
"1st in Cincinnati and Still the Best"

Christopher T. Kremer, CLVS, Media Director

"A Valuable Resource Today...Invaluable Tomorrow"

Anderson Reporting Services

FULL-SERVICE COURT REPORTING
CERTIFIED LEGAL VIDEOGRAPHY COMPANY
SERVING CINCINNATI AND SOUTHWEST OHIO

**** 1-800-753-0289 ****

WWW.ANDERSONREPORTING.COM
GANDERSON@ANDERSONREPORTING.COM

** GENERAL/MEDICAL/TECHNICAL REPORTING **
** PROMPT TURNAROUND EXPEDITED/DAILY COPY **
** EXPERIENCED REALTIME REPORTERS **
** LITIGATION SUPPORT **
** CONDENSED TRANSCRIPTS **
** FULL WORD INDEX **
** ASCII DISKETTE CONVERSION **
** DISCOVERY ZX **
** CONFERENCE ROOMS **
** COMPETITIVELY PRICED **

** CERTIFIED LEGAL VIDEO SPECIALISTS ON SITE **

IN-HOUSE VIDEO CONFERENCING SUITE
AVAILABLE AT VERY REASONABLE RATES

PRESIDENT: GAYLE ANDERSON, RDR/CLVS

OFFICE MANAGER: KATHERINE GREGG

VIDEO MANAGER: KRISTEN MIELE

BRITTON & ASSOCIATES, INC.

www.brittonandassociates.com

COURT REPORTERS & VIDEOGRAPHERS
119 EAST COURT STREET
SUITE 313
CINCINNATI, OHIO 45202
TELEPHONE (513) 651-3370
FAX (513) 651-9253

OHIO & KENTUCKY NOTARIES
COMPUTER-AIDED TRANSCRIPTION
COMPLETE LITIGATION SUPPORT
REALTIME TRANSLATION
CASEVIEW, LIVENOTE
ASCII, DISCOVERY ZX, MICROTEXT DISKETTES
KEY WORD INDEXING
E-MAIL TRANSCRIPTS
COMPRESSED TRANSCRIPTS
COMPLETE VIDEO PRODUCTIONS
SUBPOENAS ISSUED AND SERVED
DEPOSITION SUITES

(This Listing Continued)

ALSO LOCATED AT:
124 EAST THIRD STREET
SUITE 400
DAYTON, OHIO 45402
TELEPHONE (937) 228-3370
FAX (937) 228-9253

SEE OUR AD ON PAGE OH4S

EXPERT WITNESS REFERRAL SERVICES

TASA
SINCE 1961

TECHNICAL ADVISORY SERVICE FOR ATTORNEYS
Headquarters: 1166 DeKalb Pike, Blue Bell, PA 19422-1853
U.S. and Canada: 800-523-2319 Fax: 800-329-8272
United Kingdom: 0800-89-1292
experts@tasanet.com • www.tasanet.com

THE BEST SOURCE FOR EXPERTS WORLDWIDE®

North America's Largest And Most Experienced Expert Referral Service® is the leading source of Consulting Experts, Testifying Experts, and ADR Specialists for attorneys and insurance firms.

TASA SAVES YOU TIME, EFFORT AND MONEY

- Thousands of independent experts
- Over 10,000 categories, including medical and ADR
- Over 200,000 clients • over 44 years' experience
- For cases of all kinds and sizes; plaintiff or defense
- Competitive fees • Exceptional service

NO CHARGE FOR REFERRALS

A small sample of expertise available through TASA:

AGRICULTURE: chemicals, machinery, explosions, crops, feed, forestry, food processing, farming accidents.

AUTOMOTIVE/TRANSPORTATION: accident reconstruction, seat belts, vehicle/road design, trucks, railroads, aviation, motorcycles.

BUSINESS/FINANCE/ECONOMICS: banking, securities, insurance, economic valuation, appraisals, real estate, franchising.

COMPUTERS AND ELECTRONICS: computer hardware, printers software, languages, security, networking, viruses, hacking, simulation; embedded systems; telecommunications; wiring, cable.

CONSTRUCTION/ARCHITECTURE: building design, maintenance, structural integrity, HVAC, plumbing; bridges, equipment, codes.

CRIMINOLOGY/POLICE PROCEDURES: document examination, fingerprinting, ballistics, prisons, tape analysis, DNA, firearms.

ELEVATORS/LIFTS: cranes, controls, design and safety, escalators.

ENVIRONMENT: water, air & noise pollution; hazardous waste, asbestos, ecology, toxic mold and mildew, erosion, lead.

FALLS: lighting, surfaces, ladders, scaffolding, weather, shoes, safety.

FIRES: explosions, arson, flammable clothing, codes, alarms.

MACHINERY: design/safety; industrial, agricultural, appliances, OSHA.

MARITIME: seamanship, cargo handling, ship/boat design, accident

(This Listing Continued)

EXPERT WITNESS REFERRAL SERVICES (cont'd)

Tasa (cont'd)

reconstruction, navigational aids, fishing, oil spills.

MEDICAL/HEALTH CARE: issues relating to medical personnel, institutions and procedures, over 900 medical specialties through the TASAmed division.

MATERIALS: metals, polymers, glass, wood; textiles.

INTELLECTUAL PROPERTY: patents/copyrights/trademarks, secrets, etc.

PERSONNEL/LABOR: wages & hours, discrimination, workplace safety, ADA issues, sexual harassment.

PHARMACEUTICALS/TOXICOLOGY: drugs, food poisoning, labels & warnings, cosmetics, coatings, packaging, delivery systems.

SAFETY AND SECURITY: Aviation, Building & Homeland Security; Emergency Systems; Terrorism; Risk Analysis

SPORTS/RECREATION: equipment, supervision, facilities, pools.

Call for TASA's free Expertise Directory & Guide.

800-523-2319

INTERPRETERS & TRANSLATORS

Affordable Language Services, Ltd.

8291 Kenwood Road
Cincinnati, OH 45236
Phone: 513-745-0888
Fax: 513-793-4755
info@affordablelanguageservices.com
www.affordablelanguageservices.com

Our mission is to remove language as a barrier to communication. True meaning, not just the words, must be conveyed accurately.

If it is not understood 100%, it is *not* communication.

We provide high quality translation and interpreter services, outstanding customer service, unparalleled turnaround times and value for your money.

We pride ourselves on being able to provide better service than most companies in our industry.

We will work very hard to meet and exceed your demands and expectations. Our interpreters receive training before being sent into the field.

Senior Representative/owner: Lynn Elfers (bilingual, translating & interpreting since 1997), licensed trainer for Cross Cultural's Interpreter training program entitled "Bridging the Gap"
Office Manager: Konul Zwolinski (multilingual, interpreter & translator since 1994)
HR Manager: Felix Ortiz (bilingual, interpreting since 2004)
Sales Manager: Gary R. Elfers (bilingual)

(This Listing Continued)

Statistics

Company founded:	2000
Total number of:	
• Company employees	4
• Active on-site interpreters	400
• Supported languages and dialects provided	88
• Organizations that currently use your products/services	105
On-site interpretations - average service calls managed per 24-hour period	40
Document translation - average number of words translated per week* (*based on target language, not originating document language)	20,000
Average turn-around time combining all on-site interpreter requests	1-2 hrs
Average turn-around time for routine document translation requests	2-4 days

MEDICAL EXPERT WITNESS REFERRAL SERVICES

A Division of The TASA Group, Inc.
Your First Source for Medical and Health Care Specialists
1166 DeKalb Pike
Blue Bell, PA 19422-1953
U.S. and Canada: 800-659-8464 Fax: 800-850-8272
United Kingdom: 0800-89-1292
www.tasamed.net tasamed@tasanet.com

Advantages: **Find your Medical Expert with one call or click.** We've done the legwork to save you and your staff hours of search time, effort, and expense. There is **NO CHARGE** for our customized searches, referral, resumes, and your initial screening interviews with candidates until you designate or engage an expert. TASAmed is consistently the best way to locate the finest testifying and consulting experts in every health care category.

Experience: **No other referral service has more experience.** We successfully refer thousands of experienced medical experts, expert witnesses, and consultants every year, and it's likely we have referred experts for matters like yours, many times. More than 1/3 of our staff have 10 or more years of referral experience - an exceptional record that benefits you with every call. TASAmed is a division of The TASA Group, North America's largest and most experienced EXPERT REFERRAL SERVICE ®.

(This Listing Continued)

Scope of Expertise: **Unlimited.** Our network includes distinguished experts and consultants in virtually every facet of health care - **more than 900 categories.** Specialists are available to review records, advise on case merits, explain technical terms, conduct IMEs, prepare reports, and testify.

Sample Categories:

Anesthesiology	Neonatology
Cardiology	Nephrology
Closed Head Injury	Neurology
Cosmetic Surgery	Neurosurgery
Critical Care Nursing	Nursing
Elder Abuse	Obstetrics
Emergency Care	Occupational Medicine
Environmental Medicine	Oncology
Epidemiology	Ophthalmology
Forensic Pathology	Orthopedics
Forensic Toxicology	Pain Management
General Dentistry	Pediatrics
Gerontology	Plastic Surgery
Gynecology	Psychiatry
IMEs	Radiology
Immunology	Serology
Laser Surgery	Sports Medicine
Malpractice	Surgery
Midwifery	and much more

Service Area: **Global.** With our vast resources, we can provide the medical experts you need in virtually any location and at any stage in your case.

Experts: **They are respected authorities,** valued for their knowledge, experience, and integrity. Most of the distinguished men and women on our medical roster work full-time in medical practices, universities, or in industry. All are independent contractors.

Fees: **Our fees are competitive and fair,** particularly when you consider the value of your time, the effort you save with just one call to TASAmed, and the influence that a carefully-chosen medical expert can have on the outcome of your case. There is **NO CHARGE** for our customized searches, referral, resumes, and your initial screening interviews with candidates until you designate or engage an expert.

Reputation: **TASAmed is known for integrity,** high standards, and excellent service. We are neutral, serve either plaintiff or defendant, do not work on a contingent fee basis, and have no financial stake in the outcome of a case.

Clients: **The TASA Group has served hundreds of thousands of clients** in law and insurance firms, the business sector, and government agencies in more than 44 years. Most clients use us again and again, demonstrating their high level of satisfaction with our services.

TITLE INSURANCE

Lawyers Title of Cincinnati, Inc.

3500 Red Bank Road
Cincinnati, Ohio 45227-4111
Telephone: 513-421-6440
Fax: 513-421-7828

TIMOTHY DALE GRIFFIN, President
MICHAEL C. FLETCHER, Executive Vice President
E-mail: mfletcher@ltcincy.com

Agents for Lawyers Title Insurance Corporation

Approved Escrow Agent for all Lenders
Lender Closing Management
Construction Loan Management Divisions
National Brokerage for Title Insurance

Butler County Office
5103 Pleasant Avenue
Fairfield, Ohio 41014
Telephone: 513-844-1398
Fax: 513-844-1996

Anderson Office
8315 Beechmont Avenue, Suite 4
Cincinnati, OH 45255
Telephone: 513-474-1100
Fax: 513-388-4141

Western Hills Office
4340 Harrison Avenue
Cincinnati, OH 45211
Telephone: 513-574-4760
Fax: 513-574-4764

VIDEO TAPE SERVICES

ACE-MERIT, LLC

Serving the Legal Profession
Since 1966

620 Cincinnati Club Building
30 Garfield Place
Cincinnati, Ohio 45202
Telephone: 513-241-3200 Fax: 513-241-7958
800-277-7165

COMPLETE LITIGATION SUPPORT

AceMerit on the Web
Schedule, order, download transcripts & check account activity 24/7

(This Listing Continued)

VIDEO TAPE SERVICES (cont'd)

Ace-Merit, LLC (cont'd)

3-D Graphics & Animated Trial Presentations
Key word indexing, Video Depositions, Day in the Life,
Accident Reconstruction, Settlement Tapes,
World Wide Video Teleconferencing,
CaseView, Summation & LiveNote,
E-Transcript, RealLegal Publisher, RealLegal Binder
Complete Document Management, Video-Steno Sync

Notaries Public Ohio, Indiana, Kentucky
Subpoenas, all papers, created & served
Realtime and expedited Transcripts
10-business day delivery - standard
Standby Reporters available
Medical and Technical Specialists
Three large conference rooms on site

Members: National Court Reporters Association
Ohio Court Reporters Association
Stenocat Users Group/Eclipse Users Group
Cincinnati USA Regional Chamber
Better Business Bureau
National Network Reporting Company

Alicia B. Hardin, President
Angie Portune, Vice President
David W. Moxley, Managing Reporter

Reporters

Tracy Allen, RPR	Jennifer Coats, CR
S. Diane Farrell, RMR, CRR	Susan P. Gee, RMR, CRR
Debra Henderson, RPR	Connie Henson, RPR
Luke Lavin, RDR, CRR	Amy Milholland, CR
David W. Moxley, RPR, CMRS, CRR	Linda Mullen, RPR, CRR
Sherry Music, CSR	Angie Portune, RMR
Wendy Raymer, RPR	Karen Volk, RPR
Patricia C. Walterman, RPR	Lisa Weisenberger, RPR
Wendy Welsh, RDR, CRR	Kimberly Wilson, CSR

Ace-Merit Video Department
"1st in Cincinnati and Still the Best"

Christopher T. Kremer, CLVS, Media Director

"A Valuable Resource Today...Invaluable Tomorrow"

CLEVELAND,* 505,616, *Cuyahoga Co.*

CASE MANAGEMENT SERVICES

JurInnov®

Technology Solutions for the Legal and Business Communities

29263 Clemens Road
Westlake, Ohio 44145
Phone: (440) 835-3600
Fax: (440) 835-3632

www.jurinnov.com
seniorpartner@jurinnov.com

Does Your Computer Have Something to Say?
We Can Help You Listen.

Are you tired of worrying about tracking electronic information, uncovering evidence and planning for electronic discovery when your time and energy could be focused on other client needs? JurInnov specializes in making your litigation technology concerns a thing of the past.

Our menu of services includes:

- Electronic Data Discovery and Consulting
- Computer Forensics and Data Recovery
- Litigation Case Management and Document Management
- Business Solutions and Consulting

JurInnov's experts are focused on making your job easier by solving problems and improving communication. We provide superior litigation support for exceptional results.

Call us today or visit our website to learn more about how we can serve your technology needs.

JurInnov is a Ringtail Casebook Application Service Provider and a Certified Microsoft Partner

COMPUTER FORENSICS

JurInnov®

Technology Solutions for the Legal and Business Communities

29263 Clemens Road
Westlake, Ohio 44145
Phone: (440) 835-3600
Fax: (440) 835-3632

www.jurinnov.com
seniorpartner@jurinnov.com

Does Your Computer Have Something to Say?
We Can Help You Listen.

Are you tired of worrying about tracking electronic information, uncovering evidence and planning for electronic discovery when your time and energy could be focused on other client needs? JurInnov specializes in making your litigation technology concerns a thing of the past.

Our menu of services includes:

- Electronic Data Discovery and Consulting
- Computer Forensics and Data Recovery
- Litigation Case Management and Document Management
- Business Solutions and Consulting

JurInnov's experts are focused on making your job easier by solving problems and improving communication. We provide superior litigation support for exceptional results.

Call us today or visit our website to learn more about how we can serve your technology needs.

JurInnov is a Ringtail Casebook Application Service Provider and a Certified Microsoft Partner

COURT REPORTERS

Anderson Reporting Services

FULL-SERVICE COURT REPORTING
CERTIFIED LEGAL VIDEOGRAPHY COMPANY
SERVING TOLEDO AND NORTHWEST OHIO

**** 1-800-753-0289 ****

WWW.ANDERSONREPORTING.COM
GANDERSON@ANDERSONREPORTING.COM

(This Listing Continued)

**** GENERAL/MEDICAL/TECHNICAL REPORTING ****
**** PROMPT TURNAROUND EXPEDITED/DAILY COPY ****
**** EXPERIENCED REALTIME REPORTERS ****
**** LITIGATION SUPPORT ****
**** CONDENSED TRANSCRIPTS ****
**** FULL WORD INDEX ****
**** ASCII DISKETTE CONVERSION ****
**** DISCOVERY ZX ****
**** CONFERENCE ROOMS ****
**** COMPETITIVELY PRICED ****

**** CERTIFIED LEGAL VIDEO SPECIALISTS ON SITE ****

IN-HOUSE VIDEO CONFERENCING SUITE
AVAILABLE AT VERY REASONABLE RATES

PRESIDENT: GAYLE ANDERSON, RDR/CLVS

OFFICE MANAGER: KATHERINE GREGG

VIDEO MANAGER: KRISTEN MIELE

We Support Your Case **From File...to Trial**

Cefaratti Group
THE LITIGATION SUPPORT COMPANY

1.800.694.4787

www.cefgroup.com

info@cefgroup.com

Cleveland - Akron

Court Reporting
Video Conferencing
Legal Video Production
Investigations
Claims Services
Process Service
Record Retrieval
Document Management
Trial Graphics

COURT REPORTERS (cont'd)

YOUR COMPLETE LITIGATION SUPPORT

CADY REPORTING SERVICES, INC.

National and Worldwide Coverage

55 Public Square Suite 1225
Cleveland, Ohio 44113

Also Serving:
Columbus, Ohio 43235
and
Akron, Ohio 44308

(This Listing Continued)

Please contact us at:
1-888-624-CADY (2239)
Email: cadystaff@cadyreporting.com
www.cadyreporting.com

Cady Reporting Services, Inc., has served the legal community since 1979, providing a full range of services. Cady had three times won the coveted Ohio Cup for court reporting speed and accuracy.

While our staff of court reporters has in-depth experience in handling cases of all kinds, many of our cases include the more difficult medical and technical depositions. You can trust us to provide both an accurate and timely transcript.

Services We Offer

- Cady can be called for a deposition anywhere, anytime.
- Cady Reporting Services, Inc. does not charge travel time when we travel to Akron, Youngstown, Toledo and surrounding areas when a transcript is ordered.
- Real-time, Livenote, and Semi-edited ASCII.
- E-transcript.
- On-site Videoconferencing.
- Internet depositions.
- In-house videography/transcript synchronization.
- Our reporter attendance fee is capped after 5-1/2 hours of deposition, with the order of transcript.
- Complimentary conference rooms available.
- Process service.
- We provide a complimentary condensed transcript with index & disk.

CH *Carol D. Hill & Associates*
COURT REPORTERS

5 Public Square, Suite 935
Cleveland, Ohio 44113
Telephone: **216-687-0005**
Fax: 216-687-0192
Email: chill935@visn.net

LITIGATION & LEGAL SUPPORT SERVICES

Registered Professional Reporters
Certificates of Merit
Subpoena Servers
Videotape Technicians
Notaries Public
Conference Rooms

Instant Daily Expedited Transcript

(This Listing Continued)

COURT REPORTERS (cont'd)

FINCUN-MANCINI, INC.
The Court Reporters

1801 East 9th Street
Suite 1720
Cleveland, Ohio, 44114
Toll Free: 1-877-696-DEPO
(216) 696-2272
FAX: (216) 696-2275

Established in 1906

General Court and Stenographic Reporting
Litigation Support
ASBESTOS AND MEDICAL MALPRACTICE EXPERIENCE
Complete Videotaping and Playback Services Since 1971
In-Suite Videoconferencing
Statewide Notaries
Deposition Suite
Document Reproduction
Process Service

Registered Professional Reporters
MEMBERS OF THE NATIONAL AND OHIO COURT REPORTERS ASSOCIATIONS

Visit our Web site at: www.fincunmancini.com

ELECTRONIC DISCOVERY SERVICES

JurInnov®

Technology Solutions for the Legal and Business Communities

29263 Clemens Road
Westlake, Ohio 44145
Phone: (440) 835-3600
Fax: (440) 835-3632

www.jurinnov.com
seniorpartner@jurinnov.com

Does Your Computer Have Something to Say?
We Can Help You Listen.

Are you tired of worrying about tracking electronic information, uncovering evidence and planning for electronic discovery when your time and energy could be focused on other client needs? JurInnov specializes in making your litigation technology concerns a thing of the past.

Our menu of services includes:

- Electronic Data Discovery and Consulting
- Computer Forensics and Data Recovery
- Litigation Case Management and Document Management
- Business Solutions and Consulting

(This Listing Continued)

JurInnov's experts are focused on making your job easier by solving problems and improving communication. We provide superior litigation support for exceptional results.

Call us today or visit our website to learn more about how we can serve your technology needs.

JurInnov is a Ringtail Casebook Application Service Provider and a Certified Microsoft Partner

EMPLOYMENT AGENCIES - PERMANENT/TEMPORARY

MAJOR LEGAL SERVICES©

Temporary & Permanent Recruiting:
Attorneys
Paralegals
Administrators / Managers
Medical-Legal Staff
Secretaries and Support Personnel

Since 1989, Major Legal Services© **(MLS)** has serviced the recruiting needs of law firms and corporations throughout Ohio and the midwest. We specialize in temporary and permanent searches and staffing of attorneys, paralegals, administrators and support personnel.

Employees are sought with dedication to meeting our client's requirements, fulfilling the interests and goals of candidates, and establishing and developing long-lasting relationships.

Screening and recruiting are handled with discretion, confidentiality, integrity and commitment to the highest values of the legal profession.

Our pool of pre-screened candidates is substantial, and our network of resources is widespread and well-placed throughout the legal community.

The recruiters at **MLS** are experienced attorneys and paralegals who are active members of local and national Bar associations, paralegal associations and the National Association of Legal Search Consultants (NALSC).

We strive to be prompt, thorough and loyal to our clients and candidates. Our extended Guarantee is proof of our commitment to excellence and satisfaction.

We enjoy a solid reputation of experience, knowledge of our clients' needs, integrity of purpose and process, and a commitment to mutually beneficial relationships.

The MLS Advantage

- Recruiters are all trained professionals who do **not** work on commission.
- The **MLS** philosophy promotes a team approach to address your legal staffing needs at all levels.
- Through our relationship with NALSC members, **MLS** can expand the scope of a search to reach candidates throughout the United States.

Serving the Midwest and Mid-Atlantic States

(This Listing Continued)

Offices in Ohio and Pennsylvania

Ohio Phone: 800-808-3097
PA Phone: 412-577-4010
email: dennis@majorlegalservices.com
www.majorlegalservices.com

EXPERT WITNESS
COMPUTER FORENSICS/DATA RECOVERY

JurInnov®

Technology Solutions for the Legal and Business Communities

29263 Clemens Road
Westlake, Ohio 44145
Phone: (440) 835-3600
Fax: (440) 835-3632

www.jurinnov.com
seniorpartner@jurinnov.com

Does Your Computer Have Something to Say?
We Can Help You Listen.

Are you tired of worrying about tracking electronic information, uncovering evidence and planning for electronic discovery when your time and energy could be focused on other client needs? JurInnov specializes in making your litigation technology concerns a thing of the past.

Our menu of services includes:

- Electronic Data Discovery and Consulting
- Computer Forensics and Data Recovery
- Litigation Case Management and Document Management
- Business Solutions and Consulting

JurInnov's experts are focused on making your job easier by solving problems and improving communication. We provide superior litigation support for exceptional results.

Call us today or visit our website to learn more about how we can serve your technology needs.

JurInnov is a Ringtail Casebook Application Service Provider and a Certified Microsoft Partner

GENERAL INVESTIGATORS

Cefaratti Group
THE LITIGATION SUPPORT COMPANY

Cleveland 4608 St. Clair Avenue, Cleveland, Ohio 44103
Phone: 216.696.1161 Fax: 216.687.0973

Akron Suite 150, One Cascade Plaza, Akron, Ohio 44308
Phone: 330.253.8119 Fax: 330.253.2250

800-694-4787
www.cefgroup.com
info@cefgroup.com

Court Reporting Video Conferencing Legal Video Production
Investigations Claims Service Process Service Record Retrieval
Document Management Trial Graphics

Audio files, digitized video and exhibits from depositions available on CD-ROM.

Conference Rooms, National Referrals
Realtime Translation, e-Binder,
Caseview & LiveNote
Medical and Technical Specialists

Members National Court Reporters Association,
Ohio Court Reporters Association, and STAR Users Group

LAWYER SEARCH & PLACEMENT CONSULTANTS

MAJOR LEGAL SERVICES ©

Temporary & Permanent Recruiting:
Attorneys
Paralegals
Administrators / Managers
Medical-Legal Staff
Secretaries and Support Personnel

(This Listing Continued)

LAWYER SEARCH & PLACEMENT CONSULTANTS (cont'd)

Major Legal Services© (cont'd)

Temporary & Permanent Recruiting:
Attorneys
Paralegals
Administrators / Managers
Medical-Legal Staff
Secretaries and Support Personnel

Since 1989, Major Legal Services© **(MLS)** has serviced the recruiting needs of law firms and corporations throughout Ohio and the midwest. We specialize in temporary and permanent searches and staffing of attorneys, paralegals, administrators and support personnel.

Employees are sought with dedication to meeting our client's requirements, fulfilling the interests and goals of candidates, and establishing and developing long-lasting relationships.

Screening and recruiting are handled with discretion, confidentiality, integrity and commitment to the highest values of the legal profession.

Our pool of pre-screened candidates is substantial, and our network of resources is widespread and well-placed throughout the legal community.

The recruiters at **MLS** are experienced attorneys and paralegals who are active members of local and national Bar associations, paralegal associations and the National Association of Legal Search Consultants (NALSC).

We strive to be prompt, thorough and loyal to our clients and candidates. Our extended Guarantee is proof of our commitment to excellence and satisfaction.

We enjoy a solid reputation of experience, knowledge of our clients' needs, integrity of purpose and process, and a commitment to mutually beneficial relationships.

The MLS Advantage

• Recruiters are all trained professionals who do **not** work on commission.
• The **MLS** philosophy promotes a team approach to address your legal staffing needs at all levels.
• Through our relationship with NALSC members, **MLS** can expand the scope of a search to reach candidates throughout the United States.

Serving the Midwest and Mid-Atlantic States

Offices in Ohio and Pennsylvania

Ohio Phone: 800-808-3097
PA Phone: 412-577-4010
email: dennis@majorlegalservices.com
www.majorlegalservices.com

LEGAL SUPPORT PERSONNEL - TEMPORARY & PERMANENT

MAJOR LEGAL SERVICES ©

Temporary & Permanent Recruiting:
Attorneys
Paralegals
Administrators / Managers
Medical-Legal Staff
Secretaries and Support Personnel

Since 1989, Major Legal Services© **(MLS)** has serviced the recruiting needs of law firms and corporations throughout Ohio and the midwest. We specialize in temporary and permanent searches and staffing of attorneys, paralegals, administrators and support personnel.

Employees are sought with dedication to meeting our client's requirements, fulfilling the interests and goals of candidates, and establishing and developing long-lasting relationships.

Screening and recruiting are handled with discretion, confidentiality, integrity and commitment to the highest values of the legal profession.

Our pool of pre-screened candidates is substantial, and our network of resources is widespread and well-placed throughout the legal community.

The recruiters at **MLS** are experienced attorneys and paralegals who are active members of local and national Bar associations, paralegal associations and the National Association of Legal Search Consultants (NALSC).

We strive to be prompt, thorough and loyal to our clients and candidates. Our extended Guarantee is proof of our commitment to excellence and satisfaction.

We enjoy a solid reputation of experience, knowledge of our clients' needs, integrity of purpose and process, and a commitment to mutually beneficial relationships.

The MLS Advantage

• Recruiters are all trained professionals who do **not** work on commission.
• The **MLS** philosophy promotes a team approach to address your legal staffing needs at all levels.
• Through our relationship with NALSC members, **MLS** can expand the scope of a search to reach candidates throughout the United States.

Serving the Midwest and Mid-Atlantic States

Offices in Ohio and Pennsylvania

Ohio Phone: 800-808-3097
PA Phone: 412-577-4010
email: dennis@majorlegalservices.com
www.majorlegalservices.com

LITIGATION TECHNOLOGY CONSULTING

JurInnov®

Technology Solutions for the Legal and Business Communities

29263 Clemens Road
Westlake, Ohio 44145
Phone: (440) 835-3600
Fax: (440) 835-3632

www.jurinnov.com
seniorpartner@jurinnov.com

Does Your Computer Have Something to Say?
We Can Help You Listen.

Are you tired of worrying about tracking electronic information, uncovering evidence and planning for electronic discovery when your time and energy could be focused on other client needs? JurInnov specializes in making your litigation technology concerns a thing of the past.

Our menu of services includes:

- Electronic Data Discovery and Consulting
- Computer Forensics and Data Recovery
- Litigation Case Management and Document Management
- Business Solutions and Consulting

JurInnov's experts are focused on making your job easier by solving problems and improving communication. We provide superior litigation support for exceptional results.

Call us today or visit our website to learn more about how we can serve your technology needs.

JurInnov is a Ringtail Casebook Application Service Provider and a Certified Microsoft Partner

MEDICAL RECORDS

Cefaratti Group
THE LITIGATION SUPPORT COMPANY

Cleveland 4608 St. Clair Avenue, Cleveland, Ohio 44103
Phone: 216.696.1161 Fax: 216.687.0973

Akron Suite 150, One Cascade Plaza, Akron, Ohio 44308
Phone: 330.253.8119 Fax: 330.253.2250

(This Listing Continued)

800-694-4787
www.cefgroup.com
info@cefgroup.com

Court Reporting Video Conferencing Legal Video Production
Investigations Claims Service Process Service Record Retrieval
Document Management Trial Graphics

Audio files, digitized video and exhibits from depositions available on CD-ROM.

Conference Rooms, National Referrals
Realtime Translation, e-Binder,
Caseview & LiveNote
Medical and Technical Specialists

Members National Court Reporters Association,
Ohio Court Reporters Association, and STAR Users Group

PARALEGAL SERVICES

MAJOR LEGAL SERVICES ©

Temporary & Permanent Recruiting:
Attorneys
Paralegals
Administrators / Managers
Medical-Legal Staff
Secretaries and Support Personnel

Since 1989, Major Legal Services© **(MLS)** has serviced the recruiting needs of law firms and corporations throughout Ohio and the midwest. We specialize in temporary and permanent searches and staffing of attorneys, paralegals, administrators and support personnel.

Employees are sought with dedication to meeting our client's requirements, fulfilling the interests and goals of candidates, and establishing and developing long-lasting relationships.

Screening and recruiting are handled with discretion, confidentiality, integrity and commitment to the highest values of the legal profession.

Our pool of pre-screened candidates is substantial, and our network of resources is widespread and well-placed throughout the legal community.

The recruiters at **MLS** are experienced attorneys and paralegals who are active members of local and national Bar associations, paralegal associations and the National Association of Legal Search Consultants (NALSC).

We strive to be prompt, thorough and loyal to our clients and candidates. Our extended Guarantee is proof of our commitment to excellence and satisfaction.

We enjoy a solid reputation of experience, knowledge of our clients' needs, integrity of purpose and process, and a commitment to mutually beneficial relationships.

(This Listing Continued)

(This Listing Continued)

(This Listing Continued)

EXPERT WITNESS
CONSTRUCTION (cont'd)

Doc Mitchell & Associates Inc. (cont'd)

Doc Mitchell has been involved in construction since 1960. He has worked in and taught every type and phase of construction with the exception of Nuclear Reactor construction.

Doc took part in his first case as an expert in 1972. After his retirement from the construction industry in 1990, he has made his services available as a construction expert and expert witness on a full time basis. Doc has worked on hundreds of cases and has never been rejected as an expert by any court system.

Previous case sizes have ranged from $1,500.00 to $50,000,000.00.

Doc is a recognized code expert and is approved by the Kentucky Department of Housing, Building, and Construction to teach the continuing education for state, city and county Code Enforcement and Building Inspectors in Kentucky.

At this writing Doc is the only construction inspector and expert witness in the United States holding all of the following licenses and certifications:

- Master Electrical Contractor
- Master HVAC Contractor, including cooling towers and chillers of any type
- Master Boiler, Pressure Vessel, Piping Contractor
- Licensed Residential/Home Inspector
- Certified Commercial & Industrial Construction Inspector
- Certified Lead Sampling Technician (HUD)
- Certified Mold & Fungus Sampling Technician (HUD)
- Certified Asbestos Abatement Contractor (Retired)
- General Contractor 30 years (Retired)
- Member Code Administration Association of Kentucky

For cases involving any type of construction or any specific construction trade, please give Doc Mitchell & Associates a call; we may be able to help.

EXPERT WITNESS
ELECTRICAL

Doc Mitchell & Associates Inc.

120 East Main Street, Suite 2109
Lexington, KY 40507
Phone # 859-299-8858 Fax # 859-293-0184
Email: codeexpert@aol.com

Doc Mitchell & Associates are expert witnesses in all types, fields and phases of construction. Doc's knowledge in construction plus the knowledge of our structural architectural engineer, and our structural, mining, and civil engineer make for a world class construction expert team. Judges have called Doc Mitchell the best expert witness they have ever seen in their court.

Please call or e-mail for additional information, curriculum vi-tae, or references from attorneys and list of insurance companies with whom Doc and our other experts have worked:

Doc Mitchell has been involved in construction since 1960. He has worked in and taught every type and phase of construction with the exception of Nuclear Reactor construction.

Doc took part in his first case as an expert in 1972. After his retirement from the construction industry in 1990, he has made his services available as a construction expert and expert witness on a full time basis. Doc has worked on hundreds of cases and has never been rejected as an expert by any court system.

(This Listing Continued)

Previous case sizes have ranged from $1,500.00 to $50,000,000.00.

Doc is a recognized code expert and is approved by the Kentucky Department of Housing, Building, and Construction to teach the continuing education for state, city and county Code Enforcement and Building Inspectors in Kentucky.

At this writing Doc is the only construction inspector and expert witness in the United States holding all of the following licenses and certifications:

- Master Electrical Contractor
- Master HVAC Contractor, including cooling towers and chillers of any type
- Master Boiler, Pressure Vessel, Piping Contractor
- Licensed Residential/Home Inspector
- Certified Commercial & Industrial Construction Inspector
- Certified Lead Sampling Technician (HUD)
- Certified Mold & Fungus Sampling Technician (HUD)
- Certified Asbestos Abatement Contractor (Retired)
- General Contractor 30 years (Retired)
- Member Code Administration Association of Kentucky

For cases involving any type of construction or any specific construction trade, please give Doc Mitchell & Associates a call; we may be able to help.

EXPERT WITNESS
HEATING/VENTILATION/AIR CONDITIONING

Doc Mitchell & Associates Inc.

120 East Main Street, Suite 2109
Lexington, KY 40507
Phone # 859-299-8858 Fax # 859-293-0184
Email: codeexpert@aol.com

Doc Mitchell & Associates are expert witnesses in all types, fields and phases of construction. Doc's knowledge in construction plus the knowledge of our structural architectural engineer, and our structural, mining, and civil engineer make for a world class construction expert team. Judges have called Doc Mitchell the best expert witness they have ever seen in their court.

Please call or e-mail for additional information, curriculum vi-tae, or references from attorneys and list of insurance companies with whom Doc and our other experts have worked:

Doc Mitchell has been involved in construction since 1960. He has worked in and taught every type and phase of construction with the exception of Nuclear Reactor construction.

Doc took part in his first case as an expert in 1972. After his retirement from the construction industry in 1990, he has made his services available as a construction expert and expert witness on a full time basis. Doc has worked on hundreds of cases and has never been rejected as an expert by any court system.

Previous case sizes have ranged from $1,500.00 to $50,000,000.00.

Doc is a recognized code expert and is approved by the Kentucky Department of Housing, Building, and Construction to teach the continuing education for state, city and county Code Enforcement and Building Inspectors in Kentucky.

At this writing Doc is the only construction inspector and expert witness in the United States holding all of the following licenses and certifications:

(This Listing Continued)

- Master Electrical Contractor
- Master HVAC Contractor, including cooling towers and chillers of any type
- Master Boiler, Pressure Vessel, Piping Contractor
- Licensed Residential/Home Inspector
- Certified Commercial & Industrial Construction Inspector
- Certified Lead Sampling Technician (HUD)
- Certified Mold & Fungus Sampling Technician (HUD)
- Certified Asbestos Abatement Contractor (Retired)
- General Contractor 30 years (Retired)
- Member Code Administration Association of Kentucky

For cases involving any type of construction or any specific construction trade, please give Doc Mitchell & Associates a call; we may be able to help.

GENERAL INVESTIGATORS

Expert Services
Special Investigators

(This Listing Continued)

VIDEO TAPE SERVICES

Anderson Reporting Services

LEGAL VIDEOTAPING SPECIALISTS
**** 1-800-753-0289 ****

Phone (614) 326-0177
3242 West Henderson Road, Suite A, Columbus, Ohio 43220

WWW.ANDERSONREPORTING.COM
EMAIL: GANDERSON@ANDERSONREPORTING.COM

CERTIFIED LEGAL VIDEO SPECIALISTS

SERVING THE STATE OF OHIO

**** DEPOSITIONS ****
**** HEARINGS ****
**** SEMINARS/SYMPOSIUMS ****
**** DAY-IN-THE-LIFE DOCUMENTARIES ****
**** MEDICAL EXAMINATIONS ****
**** INVENTORIES ****
**** INSPECTIONS ****
**** SPLIT SCREEN CAPABILITY ****
**** STATE-OF-THE-ART VIDEO EQUIPMENT ****
**** COPYING AND EDITING SUITE ****
**** COURTROOM PLAYBACK ****
**** CONFERENCE ROOMS ****
**** COMPETITIVELY PRICED ****

**** EXPERIENCED COURT REPORTERS ON REQUEST ****

CONTACT US FOR *ALL* YOUR LEGAL VIDEO NEEDS.

CONCORD, *Lake Co.*

EXPERT WITNESS REFERRAL SERVICES

SAPONARO

THE EXPERTS ON EXPERTS

9930 Johnnycake Ridge Road
Suite 2G
Concord, OH 44060

Phone: 800-327-3026
Fax: 440-639-1013
experts@Saponaro.org
www.Saponaro.org

Medical - Hospital - Nursing Home - Product Liability - Personal Injury Experts

(This Listing Continued)

Saponaro, Inc., has provided experts to attorneys throughout the United States and Canada for over 30 years. Our highly qualified experts support their opinion through deposition, video deposition and/or trial.

We save you time and money by thoroughly screening your case with potential experts to insure that your case requirements will be met. Services include:

Case Evaluation

The merits of a medical negligence claim are evaluated by a board certified physician or healthcare professional within the same specialty. The documents are analyzed and all questions of liability and causation are addressed in the report. In addition to our forensic report, the reviewing expert is available for consultation, deposition, video-deposition and/or court testimony.

Expert Witness Referral

The facts of your case are screened with several appropriate experts within the specialty of concern and the expert best suited to assist you is referred. A Curriculum Vitae is provided along with the experts fees for review and consultation. If for any reason you are not satisfied with the expert, a replacement will be provided at no additional cost.

Direct Witness Referral

The facts of your case are matched with an appropriate expert in the specialty of concern. You are provided with a Curriculum Vitae and information to contact the expert directly. If for any reason you are not satisfied with the expert, a replacement will be provided at no additional cost.

Chart Organization Service

A nurse will organize all medical records pertaining to your case in chronological order, and tab and index for easy access to pertinent documents. A recommendation of the appropriate expert to review the file will be provided and we can assist you with an evaluation or expert witness referral. An organized copy of the records will also be provided to your office.

Our Experts have:
Board Certification
Appropriate Healthcare Licensure
Active Clinical/Academic Practice
Deposition and/or Trial Experience

WE EARN YOUR BUSINESS ON EACH CASE, WITH A PROFESSIONAL APPROACH AND ACCOUNTABILITY FOR OUR WORK.

Saponaro, Inc., has built a reputation for integrity and candor with our clients. Please call our office for a no obligation discussion of your case. We are confident we can meet your needs in a timely, cost effective and thorough manner.

Please see our website for a sample listing of medical, product liability and personal injury experts available.

Geographical Area: No Limit
Cases/Clients: Plaintiff/Defendant
Contact: Guy Saponaro

MEDICAL EXPERT WITNESS REFERRAL SERVICES

SAPONARO

THE EXPERTS ON EXPERTS

9930 Johnnycake Ridge Road
Suite 2G
Concord, OH 44060

Phone: 800-327-3026
Fax: 440-639-1013
experts@Saponaro.org
www.Saponaro.org

Medical - Hospital - Nursing Home - Product Liability - Personal Injury Experts

Saponaro, Inc., has provided experts to attorneys throughout the United States and Canada for over 30 years. Our highly qualified experts support their opinion through deposition, video deposition and/or trial.

We save you time and money by thoroughly screening your case with potential experts to insure that your case requirements will be met. Services include:

Case Evaluation

The merits of a medical negligence claim are evaluated by a board certified physician or healthcare professional within the same specialty. The documents are analyzed and all questions of liability and causation are addressed in the report. In addition to our forensic report, the reviewing expert is available for consultation, deposition, video-deposition and/or court testimony.

Expert Witness Referral

The facts of your case are screened with several appropriate experts within the specialty of concern and the expert best suited to assist you is referred. A Curriculum Vitae is provided along with the experts fees for review and consultation. If for any reason you are not satisfied with the expert, a replacement will be provided at no additional cost.

Direct Witness Referral

The facts of your case are matched with an appropriate expert in the specialty of concern. You are provided with a Curriculum Vitae and information to contact the expert directly. If for any reason you are not satisfied with the expert, a replacement will be provided at no additional cost.

Chart Organization Service

A nurse will organize all medical records pertaining to your case in chronological order, and tab and index for easy access to pertinent documents. A recommendation of the appropriate expert to review the file will be provided and we can assist you with an evaluation or expert witness referral. An organized copy of the records will also be provided to your office.

Our Experts have:
Board Certification
Appropriate Healthcare Licensure
Active Clinical/Academic Practice
Deposition and/or Trial Experience

WE EARN YOUR BUSINESS ON EACH CASE, WITH A PROFESSIONAL APPROACH AND ACCOUNTABILITY FOR OUR WORK.

Saponaro, Inc., has built a reputation for integrity and candor with our clients. Please call our office for a no obligation discussion of your case. We are confident we can meet your needs in a timely, cost effective and thorough manner.

(This Listing Continued)

Please see our website for a sample listing of medical, product liability and personal injury experts available.

Geographical Area: No Limit
Cases/Clients: Plaintiff/Defendant
Contact: Guy Saponaro

DAYTON,* 182,044, *Montgomery Co.*

COURT REPORTERS

Britton
AND ASSOCIATES, INC
www.brittonandassociates.com

COURT REPORTERS

VIDEOGRAPHERS

OHIO & KENTUCKY NOTARIES
REALTIME / CASEVIEW / KEYWORD INDEXING / E-MAIL TRANSCRIPTS / CONDENSED TRANSCRIPTS / VIDEOTAPING / SUBPOENAS / CONFERENCE CENTERS / FULL LITIGATION SUPPORT

124 E. Third Street
Suite 400
Dayton, Ohio 45402
Tel: (937) 228-3370
Fax: (937) 228-9253

119 East Court Street
Suite 313
Cincinnati, Ohio 45202
Tel: (513) 651-3370
Fax: (513) 651-9253

COURT REPORTERS (cont'd)

ACE-MERIT, LLC

Serving the Legal Profession
Since 1966

620 Cincinnati Club Building
30 Garfield Place
Cincinnati, Ohio 45202
Telephone: 513-241-3200 Fax: 513-241-7958
800-277-7165

COMPLETE LITIGATION SUPPORT

AceMerit on the Web
Schedule, order, download transcripts &
check account activity 24/7

3-D Graphics & Animated Trial Presentations
Key word indexing, Video Depositions, Day in the Life,
Accident Reconstruction, Settlement Tapes,
World Wide Video Teleconferencing,
CaseView, Summation & LiveNote,
E-Transcript, RealLegal Publisher, RealLegal Binder
Complete Document Management, Video-Steno Sync

Notaries Public Ohio, Indiana, Kentucky
Subpoenas, all papers, created & served
Realtime and expedited Transcripts
10-business day delivery - standard
Standby Reporters available
Medical and Technical Specialists
Three large conference rooms on site

Members: National Court Reporters Association
Ohio Court Reporters Association
Stenocat Users Group/Eclipse Users Group
Cincinnati USA Regional Chamber
Better Business Bureau
National Network Reporting Company

Alicia B. Hardin, President
Angie Portune, Vice President
David W. Moxley, Managing Reporter

Reporters

Tracy Allen, RPR	Jennifer Coats, CR
S. Diane Farrell, RMR, CRR	Susan P. Gee, RMR, CRR
Debra Henderson, RPR	Connie Henson, RPR
Luke Lavin, RDR, CRR	Amy Milholland, CR
David W. Moxley, RPR, CMRS, CRR	Linda Mullen, RPR, CRR
Sherry Music, CSR	Angie Portune, RMR
Wendy Raymer, RPR	Karen Volk, RPR
Patricia C. Walterman, RPR	Lisa Weisenberger, RPR
Wendy Welsh, RDR, CRR	Kimberly Wilson, CSR

Ace-Merit Video Department
"1st in Cincinnati and Still the Best"

Christopher T. Kremer, CLVS, Media Director

"A Valuable Resource Today...Invaluable Tomorrow"

Anderson Reporting Services

FULL-SERVICE COURT REPORTING
CERTIFIED LEGAL VIDEOGRAPHY COMPANY
SERVING THE DAYTON
AND SPRINGFIELD AREA

**** 1-800-753-0289 ****

WWW.ANDERSONREPORTING.COM
GANDERSON@ANDERSONREPORTING.COM

**** GENERAL/MEDICAL/TECHNICAL REPORTING ****
**** PROMPT TURNAROUND EXPEDITED/DAILY COPY ****
**** EXPERIENCED REALTIME REPORTERS ****
**** LITIGATION SUPPORT ****
**** CONDENSED TRANSCRIPTS ****
**** FULL WORD INDEX ****
**** ASCII DISKETTE CONVERSION ****
**** DISCOVERY ZX ****
**** CONFERENCE ROOMS ****
**** COMPETITIVELY PRICED ****

**** CERTIFIED LEGAL VIDEO SPECIALISTS ON SITE ****

IN-HOUSE VIDEO CONFERENCING SUITE
AVAILABLE AT VERY REASONABLE RATES

PRESIDENT: GAYLE ANDERSON, RDR/CLVS

OFFICE MANAGER: KATHERINE GREGG

VIDEO MANAGER: KRISTEN MIELE

BRITTON & ASSOCIATES, INC.

www.brittonandassociates.com

COURT REPORTERS & VIDEOGRAPHERS
124 EAST THIRD STREET, SUITE 400
DAYTON, OHIO 45402
TELEPHONE (937) 228-3370
FAX (937) 228-9253

COMPUTER-AIDED TRANSCRIPTION
COMPLETE LITIGATION SUPPORT
REALTIME TRANSLATION
CASEVIEW, LIVENOTE
ASCII, DISCOVERY ZX, MICROTEXT DISKETTES
KEY WORD INDEXING
E-MAIL TRANSCRIPTS
COMPRESSED TRANSCRIPTS
COMPLETE VIDEO PRODUCTION
SUBPOENAS ISSUED AND SERVED
DEPOSITION SUITES
OHIO & KENTUCKY NOTARIES

ALSO LOCATED AT:
119 EAST COURT STREET
SUITE 313
CINCINNATI, OHIO 45202
TELEPHONE (513) 651-3370
FAX (513) 651-9253

SEE OUR AD ON PAGE OH21S

VIDEO TAPE SERVICES

(This Listing Continued)

FAIRFIELD, 39,729, *Butler Co.*

FINDLAY,* 35,703, *Hancock Co.*

TOLEDO,* 332,943, *Lucas Co.*

COURT REPORTERS

1-2-3
1-800-682-5201

1-2-3 Reporting Service
a division of Certified Reporting Company

24 HOUR PHONE: 800-682-5201
E-mail: 123reporting@prodigy.net
www.123reporting.com

COURT REPORTER OWNED AND COURT REPORTER MANAGED

- Only Experienced Certified and RPR Shorthand Reporters
- Realtime Reporters Upon Request
- Technical, Malpractice, Product Liability and Patent Depositions
- Computer-Aided Transcription
- Daily and Expedited Delivery on Transcripts
- Min-U-Script® Condensed Transcripts and Master Indexes Available
- Complete Litigation Support Available
- ASCII and Discovery ZX Diskettes Available Compatible with Any DOS-Based System
- Key Word Indexing and Proximity Search
- Complimentary Deposition Suites Available
- Video Depositions by Certified Technicians/Attorney Including "Day In The Life" Record and Accident Scene Videos
- Subpoena Services Available
- Timestamping of Depositions

MEMBER OF:
NATIONAL COURT REPORTERS ASSOCIATION
ILLINOIS STATE REPORTERS ASSOCIATION
CHICAGO METROPOLITAN REPORTERS ASSOCIATION

References upon request.

Anderson
Reporting
Services

FULL-SERVICE COURT REPORTING
CERTIFIED LEGAL VIDEOGRAPHY COMPANY
SERVING TOLEDO AND NORTHWEST OHIO

**** 1-800-753-0289 ****

WWW.ANDERSONREPORTING.COM
GANDERSON@ANDERSONREPORTING.COM

**** GENERAL/MEDICAL/TECHNICAL REPORTING ****
**** PROMPT TURNAROUND EXPEDITED/DAILY COPY ****
**** EXPERIENCED REALTIME REPORTERS ****
**** LITIGATION SUPPORT ****
**** CONDENSED TRANSCRIPTS ****
**** FULL WORD INDEX ****
**** ASCII DISKETTE CONVERSION ****
**** DISCOVERY ZX ****
**** CONFERENCE ROOMS ****
**** COMPETITIVELY PRICED ****

**** CERTIFIED LEGAL VIDEO SPECIALISTS ON SITE ****

IN-HOUSE VIDEO CONFERENCING SUITE
AVAILABLE AT VERY REASONABLE RATES

PRESIDENT: GAYLE ANDERSON, RDR/CLVS

OFFICE MANAGER: KATHERINE GREGG

VIDEO MANAGER: KRISTEN MIELE

CLASSIC REPORTING SERVICE

1450 National City Bank Building
405 Madison Avenue
Toledo, Ohio 43604
Telephone: 419-243-1919
FAX: 419-243-9204

Full Service Reporting Agency

Computerized Transcription
Condensed Transcripts
Word Indexing
Subpoena and Notice Service
Expedited - Medical - Technical
Conference Room
Rapid Delivery Guaranteed
Realtime / Daily Copy
Depositions - Arbitrations - Hearings
Conferences - Patent Cases
Telephone Depositions
Full Service Video Depositions

Members of:
National Court Reporters Association
Ohio Court Reporters Association

LUdowski@ClassicReporting.com

COURT REPORTERS (cont'd)

(This Listing Continued)

LAWTON,* 80,561, *Comanche Co.*

PROCESS SERVERS & DOCUMENT DELIVERY SERVICES

OKLAHOMA CITY,* 444,719, *Oklahoma Co.*

CIVIL INVESTIGATIONS

CIVIL INVESTIGATIONS (cont'd)

The SCOOP

LUNDQUIST INVESTIGATIONS

P.O. Box 6963
Edmond, Oklahoma 73083
Phone: 405-834-3349
FAX: 405-341-7767
TOLL FREE: 1-866-550-9179
Email: SpyForYou1@aol.com

LINDA LUNDQUIST

Lundquist Investigations is a full-service organization providing critical information for corporate requirements and private needs.

Our Corporate unit responds to the growing need within business organizations for pre-employment verification, individual background profiles, and protection of company assets. We offer services which range from verification of application information to assistance with internal investigations of employee actions, drugs and expense account abuse.

Fully licensed and certified investigators also work with individual clients. We carefully gather critical facts which will provide intelligence in a wide variety of court cases. When requested we investigate individuals to prove or disprove infidelity, financial misdeeds, and/or actions required following court orders.

OTHER SERVICES OFFERED:

- **DIVORCE**
- **CHILD CUSTODY**
- **WORKER'S COMPENSATION**
- **SEXUAL HARASSMENT**
- **CHILD ABDUCTION**

COURT REPORTERS

1-2-3
1-800-682-5201

1-2-3 Reporting Service
a division of Certified Reporting Company

(This Listing Continued)

24 HOUR PHONE: 800-682-5201
E-mail: 123reporting@prodigy.net
www.123reporting.com

COURT REPORTER OWNED AND COURT REPORTER MANAGED

Only Experienced Certified and RPR Shorthand Reporters

- Realtime Reporters Upon Request
- Technical, Malpractice, Product Liability and Patent Depositions
- Computer-Aided Transcription
- Daily and Expedited Delivery on Transcripts
- Min-U-Script® Condensed Transcripts and Master Indexes Available
- Complete Litigation Support Available
- ASCII and Discovery ZX Diskettes Available Compatible with Any DOS-Based System
- Key Word Indexing and Proximity Search
- Complimentary Deposition Suites Available
- Video Depositions by Certified Technicians/Attorney Including "Day In The Life" Record and Accident Scene Videos
- Subpoena Services Available
- Timestamping of Depositions

MEMBER OF:
NATIONAL COURT REPORTERS ASSOCIATION
ILLINOIS STATE REPORTERS ASSOCIATION
CHICAGO METROPOLITAN REPORTERS ASSOCIATION

References upon request.

Elite Reporters

Serving All Of Oklahoma

Gayla Brown, CSR, RPR

330 N.W. 10th Street, Suite 100
Oklahoma City, OK 73103
Phone: (405) 720-7336

Email: gchronic@cox.net
Website: www.gaylabrownreporting.com

For two decades our reporters have worked on complicated depositions, in federal and state courts, arbitrations, administrative hearings, conventions and meetings. Whether it's a simple deposition or a complicated series of depositions, our reporters' combined qualifications and experience ensure that you receive timely, accurate transcripts and professional service.

(This Listing Continued)

Our Services:

- Daily/Expedited Copy
- Rough ASCII'S
- Notary Public
- ASCII Diskettes & E-Transcripts Available
- Videography
- Min-U-Script/Condensed Transcripts
- Real Time Transcription
- Medical/Technical/Architectural
- Conference Rooms/Suites Available
- Reference Available Upon Request
- Free Parking

National Court Reporters Association
Oklahoma Court Reporters Association

FREELANCE REPORTERS, INC.

Certified Court Reporters
Certificate of Merit holders

210 Park Avenue
100 Oklahoma Tower
Oklahoma City, OK 73102

Telephone: 405 235-8133
FAX: 405 235-8969
1-800-325-4470
depo@freelancereportersinc.com

VIDEO
LARGE DEPOSITION SUITES
LITIGATION SUPPORT
SUBPOENAS SERVED
DEPOSITIONS - ARBITRATIONS - MEETINGS
MEDICAL & TECHNICAL SPECIALISTS
DAILY & EXPEDITED DELIVERY

FREE ASCII ON REQUEST
FREE CONDENSED TRANSCRIPT ON REQUEST

Deborah Monard, CSR, CP, CM & Associates

TULSA,* 367,302, *Tulsa Co.*

COMPUTER FORENSICS

PROFESSIONAL DIGITAL FORENSICS SERVICES

DIGITAL INVESTIGATIONS

Every case has potential digital evidence.

USDFP collects and analyzes digital information so that it is admissible in a court of law. We create reports that provide you and your clients the direct answers they need, with no technical jargon.

Our highly-trained staff has years of experience both teaching and performing digital investigations. We are members of the High Tech Crime Investigation Association, Information Systems Security Association and the American Academy of Forensics Sciences.

(This Listing Continued)

We stay up-to-date so you don't have to.

- Computers
- Voicemail
- PDAs
- Digital Cameras
- Networks
- Cell Phones
- Chatrooms
- Removable Memory
- Tape Backups
- Email

EVERY CASE HAS POTENTIAL DIGITAL EVIDENCE.

LET USDFP FIND IT FOR YOU.

WWW.USDFP.COM
1 (800) 8080-DFP
experts@usdfp.com

USDFP
U.S. DIGITAL FORENSICS PROFESSIONALS

COURT REPORTERS

FRANK PETERSON REPORTING SERVICE

417 West Seventh Street, Suite 304
Tulsa, Oklahoma 74119

Phone: (918) 745-0303
Toll Free: (800) 478-0349
Fax: (918) 745-0318
Email : courtreporters@fpreporting.com
Web: www.fpreporting.com

Manager: Davina Garrett

FULL-SERVICE COURT REPORTING FIRM, PROUDLY SERVING TULSA SINCE 1964!

- Video (VHS, CD-Rom, DVD, MPEG1, MPEG2)
- Complimentary Conference Rooms
- Certified RealTime Writers, CSR's, RPR's, RMR's
- Daily Copy and Expedited Transcripts
- ***Free*** Delivery of ***all*** Tulsa Transcripts
- ***Free*** ASCII Diskettes
- Condensed Transcripts and Keyword Index
- E-Transcripts
- Tabbed and Bound Exhibit Reproduction
- Scanned Exhibits on CD-Rom
- CD-Rom of All Products
- Video Synchronization of Transcript, Exhibits, and Video
- 7-10 Day Turnaround
- Notary Public
- Member of NCRA and OCRA
- Nationally and State Certified Court Reporters
- Full & Friendly Office Staff
- We Never Use an Answering Service

Call us anytime, we will go anywhere!

EUGENE,* 112,669, *Lane Co.*

COURT REPORTERS

C&C Court Reporting

172 East 8th Avenue
Eugene, Oregon 97401
www.ccreporting.com
setadepo@ccreporting.com

Toll Free: 1-866-259-5338

NOW AVAILABLE:
ON-SITE VIDEOCONFERENCING

PROFESSIONALISM
Certified Professional Court Reporters experienced in all forms of litigation, including medical malpractice, patents, personal injury, property rights, family law, and contracts

All reporters are CSR and/or RPR certified

SERVICE
Complimentary Conference Rooms with Hospitality Service
Complimentary Condensed Transcripts with Index
Realtime and Expedited Delivery Available
Electronic Delivery in All Formats

LOCATION
Across the street from Lane County Courthouse
Two blocks from US Federal Courthouse and Bankruptcy Court
Close to hotels / Parking available
Statewide service / No charge for travel

---

tr catherine teach reporting, inc

Your Professional Court Reporting Agency

Certified Reporters

National/International

1-800-230-3302

Reporters on Call
Medical, Technical, Scientific
Expedited Delivery at very reasonable rates
Realtime Reporting

Reach Us

Complete Word Indexings
Condensed Transcripts
Case Management

24 Hours a Day

(This Listing Continued)

Status Reports
Videotape and Interpreter Coverage

7 Days a Week

Scanning Services
Complete Litigation Support:
Discovery ZX, ASCII, Word Perfect,
Summation, Amicus

Convenient Downtown Portland Location
Complimentary Conference Rooms
Hospitality Service

Members:

National Court Reporters Association
Society - Technical Advancement of Reporting

For Excellence in Court Reporting, Quality and Service call

1-800-230-3302

Email: 74001.741@compuserve.com
www.teachreporting.com

GENERAL INVESTIGATORS

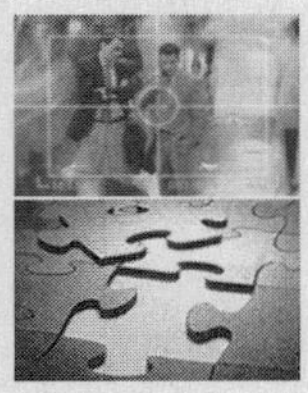

ALLEN HORNER INVESTIGATIONS
PO BOX 474
Scio, OR 97374
Phone: (541) 337-2688 Fax: (866) 872-5963
Email: allenhorner@cs.com

Allen Horner Investigations is the ***Pacific Northwest and California's leading Private Investigative and Detective Agency.*** Our offices and its team of professional and experienced investigators have been providing our unique investigative services throughout the Western U.S. for the past fourteen years. Our staff consists of highly trained investigators who excel in their particular fields of expertise. With a total of twenty years of combined law enforcement training and experience, we will provide unrivaled, professional service for each case.

Our offices and its team of professional and experienced investigators have provided many Law Firms, Insurance Companies, Large and Small Corporations, Private Agencies, Fundamental and Civic Groups, other Private Investigative and Detective Agencies and of course, the general public with the professional investigative services necessary in order to substantiate their cases.

Our offices have long standing professional affiliations with Private Investigative and Detective Agencies throughout the United States and Canada. We are prepared to handle your needs and requests wherever and whenever our investigative services are needed.

Services
SURVEILLANCE
WORKERS COMP / GENERAL INSURANCE
CHILD CUSTODY, FAMILY, SPOUSAL, MARITAL
BACKGROUND CHECKS
INTERVIEWS
SKIPTRACE / LOCATES
PROCESS SERVICE
ACCIDENT
ASSET SEARCHES
CIVIL SEARCHES
And more

(This Listing Continued)

GENERAL INVESTIGATORS (cont'd)

Allen Horner Investigations (cont'd)

Memberships

(USAPI) United States Association of Professional Investigators (WAD) World Association of Detectives
(ICTOA) International Counter-Terrorism Officers Association
(CALI) California Association of Licensed Investigators
(OALI) Oregon Association of Licensed Investigators

Bonded and Insured
All investigations are conducted in an ethical, professional, expedient and confidential manner.

MEDFORD,* 46,951, *Jackson Co.*

AUDIO/VIDEO SERVICES

Advanced Court Reporting & Video Service, Inc.

We are Southern Oregon's largest court reporting agency.

TOLL FREE 1-800-343-3396 (24 Hours)

336 W. 6th Street
Medford, Oregon 97501

Serving: All of Central & Southern Oregon & Northern California
FAX: 541-732-1987
E-Mail: linda@advancedcourtreporting.com
www.advancedcourtreporting.com

DEPOSITIONS ARBITRATIONS HEARINGS

- Deluxe Conference Rooms
- Video Depositions on VHS, DVD, VCD
- Realtime Reporting (Internet or on site)
- Internet Transcript Repository
- Full Litigation Support
- Complimentary Condensed Transcripts - Word Indexes
- Technical and Medical Reporting Specialists
- Rush Delivery of Transcripts - Competitive Rates
- Schedule depositions on line
- Experienced and Professional Reporting Staff
- Accept MAJOR CREDIT CARDS
- Established 1978

Member: National Court Reporters Association
Oregon Court Reporters Association
California Court Reporters Association
Washington Court Reporters Association

COURT REPORTERS

Advanced Court Reporting & Video Service, Inc.

We are Southern Oregon's largest court reporting agency.

(This Listing Continued)

TOLL FREE 1-800-343-3396 (24 Hours)

336 W. 6th Street
Medford, Oregon 97501

Serving: All of Central & Southern Oregon & Northern California
FAX: 541-732-1987
E-Mail: linda@advancedcourtreporting.com
www.advancedcourtreporting.com

DEPOSITIONS ARBITRATIONS HEARINGS

- Deluxe Conference Rooms
- Video Depositions on VHS, DVD, VCD
- Realtime Reporting (Internet or on site)
- Internet Transcript Repository
- Full Litigation Support
- Complimentary Condensed Transcripts - Word Indexes
- Technical and Medical Reporting Specialists
- Rush Delivery of Transcripts - Competitive Rates
- Schedule depositions on line
- Experienced and Professional Reporting Staff
- Accept MAJOR CREDIT CARDS
- Established 1978

Member: National Court Reporters Association
Oregon Court Reporters Association
California Court Reporters Association
Washington Court Reporters Association

PENDLETON,* 15,126, *Umatilla Co.*

COURT REPORTERS

BRIDGES & ASSOCIATES

9116 E. Sprague, Suite 288
Spokane, WA 99206
Local: (509) 456-0586
TOLL FREE: (800) 358-2345
Fax: (800) 355-4992
bbridges@ucinet.com

Mr. William Bridges, CSR, RPR-CM
Owner

Tri-Cities - Walla Walla - Spokane, Washington
Pendleton, Oregon

Over 30 years servicing Eastern Washington & N.E. Oregon

SERVICES

EXPEDITED COPIES ON DEMAND

CONFERENCE ROOMS AVAILABLE

NOTARY PUBLIC

ASCII DISKETTES

DEPOSITIONS, TRIALS, ARBITRATIONS, PUBLIC HEARINGS, PUBLIC MEETINGS

C.A.T.

VIDEOGRAPHY ARRANGED

(This Listing Continued)

FREE CONDENSED TRANSCRIPT W/WORD INDEX ON ALL TRANSCRIPTS

DOCTORS, TECHNICAL, ENVIRONMENTAL SERVICES

CD & AUDIOTAPE TRANSCRIPTION SERVICES

REALTIME

MEMBERSHIPS
NCRA
WCRA
OCRA
STAR

PORTLAND,* 437,319, *Multnomah Co.*

COURT REPORTERS

MOORE HENDERSON ALLEN & THOMAS

PROFESSIONAL COURT REPORTING AND VIDEOGRAPHY
621 S.W. MORRISON, SUITE 425
PORTLAND, OREGON 97205

LOCATED IN DOWNTOWN PORTLAND

(503) 226-3313
(800) 962-7308
www.moorehenderson.com

Moore Henderson Allen & Thomas is one of the largest court reporting firms in the state of Oregon and is unsurpassed in providing the Oregon legal profession with the following state-of-the-art technology and services:

- Established in 1983
- Excellent, longstanding reputation in the specialized area of realtime reporting
- LiveNote Service Provider
- E-Transcript and disks in all formats
- Condensed transcripts
- Competitive bids for large litigation
- Complimentary Conference Rooms
- In-house Certified Legal Video Specialist and interpreter coverage
- Case management and exhibit maintenance for complex litigation
- Daily copy and expedited transcripts
- Standard five day transcript turnaround

---

catherine teach reporting, inc

Your Professional Court Reporting Agency

Certified Reporters

National/International

(This Listing Continued)

1-800-230-3302

Reporters on Call
Medical, Technical, Scientific
Expedited Delivery at very reasonable rates
Realtime Reporting

Reach Us

Complete Word Indexings
Condensed Transcripts
Case Management
Status Reports

24 Hours a Day

7 Days a Week

Videotape and Interpreter Coverage

Scanning Services
Complete Litigation Support:
Discovery ZX, ASCII, Word Perfect, Summation, Amicus

Convenient Downtown Portland Location
Complimentary Conference Rooms
Hospitality Service

Members:

National Court Reporters Association
Society - Technical Advancement of Reporting

For Excellence in Court Reporting, Quality and Service call

1-800-230-3302

Email: 74001.741@compuserve.com
www.teachreporting.com

SEE OUR AD ON PAGE OR4S

EXPERT WITNESS
BIOMECHANICAL ENGINEERING

HAYES + ASSOCIATES
Injury Biomechanics. Clearly Explained.

Expert Witness Services in Injury Biomechanics and Accident Reconstruction

Wilson C. "Toby" Hayes, Ph.D.

Hayes + Associates
301 SW 4th Street, Suite 160
Corvallis, OR 97333
(541) 754-9645
(541) 754-9949 fax
(541) 912-7222 (cell)
email: wch@hayesassoc.com
http://www.hayesassoc.com

Expertise: Our core expertise is injury biomechanics, i.e. relating injurious forces and motions to tolerance limits for high-risk anatomic regions. We are retained by both plaintiff and defense attorneys for cases involving personal injury, products liability, wrongful death, premises liability, and medical malpractice. Hayes and Associates, Inc. has been retained for cases involving: motor vehicle collisions; slips, trips and falls; industrial injuries/ergonomics; sports injuries/recreation equipment; orthopaedic implants and medical malpractice.

Background: (1979-98) Director, Orthopedic Biomechanics Laboratory, Mueller Professor Biomechanics, Harvard Medical School/MIT; (1998-2001) Vice Provost Research, Oregon State University (OSU); (1998-) Department of Orthopedics & Rehabilitation, Oregon Health Sciences University; Mechanical Engineering/Exercise and Sports Science (OSU). Awards: (1995) American Society of Biomechanics Borelli Award; (1996) Bristol Myers Squibb / Zimmer Research Excellence in Orthopaedic Treatment; Degrees: BS, MS (Stanford '64, '66); Ph.D. (Northwestern '70); Publications: 185 peer-reviewed papers; 63 chapters; 3 books.

No Cost Initial Consultation

LAWYERS SEARCH & PLACEMENT CONSULTANTS

WorkSource, Inc.
1231 NW Hoyt, Suite 301
Portland, OR 97209
Toll Free: 1+ (866) 227-1223
Tel: 1+ (503) 445-6900
Fax: 1+ (503) 244-4272
jnelson@worksourceinc.com
TOLL-FREE: 866-227-1223

(This Listing Continued)

WorkSource, Inc. uses advanced technology to deliver personalized administrative services from a remote location, significantly reducing costs associated with in-house staff. Founded by a team of individuals with extensive experience in the fields of telecommunications and office management, **Work**Source, Inc. is a privately held corporation located in Portland, Oregon, formed to meet the needs of the ever-increasing home office/small office workforce.

WorkSource Receptionist - Our Virtual Receptionist service gives you that all important professional first impression and keeps you well connected with important business contacts. Our appointment scheduling service with private web access allows our clients to have up to the minute access to their customers and schedules. When an estimated 60% of all consumers become angry or frustrated using automated telephones, a friendly, competent receptionist is the preferred alternative to the phone maze...if you've got the budget. With **Work**Source Receptionist service you can enjoy all the benefits a truly professional receptionist provides for a fraction of the price of an on-site assistant. Services include:

- Telephone Answering
- Call Screening
- Transferring and Routing
- Web Based Scheduling and In/Out Board
- Virtual Office

THE **WORK**SOURCE EXPERIENCE...

WorkSource receptionists answer your phones, connect you to callers, and provide helpful information and messaging when you're away. Using our free virtual office services including our virtual in/out board, contact database, and web calendar helps keep our receptionists informed.

THE **WORK**SOURCE DIFFERENCE

Our advanced proprietary technology allows us to easily do all the tasks one would expect an in-house receptionist to perform , but it's our people who really set our service apart. With an average of over 7 years of administrative assistance experience, our carefully selected staff members are courteous, professional, and always ready to help.

WorkSource Assistant - looking for that perfect office assistant...one who is well versed in everything from word processing to web-site posting; one who has both a creative flair and a flair for numbers; one who is both adept at typing and savvy in a variety of software applications? The members of the **Work**Source team average over 10 years of experience in office management and administrative assistance. We combine our skills to provide you with expert service in all areas of business support.

LIFE CARE PLANNING

The Medical Resource Network Inc.
10725 SW Barbur Blvd., Suite 200
Portland, OR 97219
Phone: (503) 452-1748
Fax: (503) 452-0079
Toll Free: (888) 899-1406
Visit our web-site: www.medres.net
MEDICAL FACT FINDING FOR SOUND DECISION MAKING

The Medical Resource Network offers specialized expertise in the analysis of complex medical issues to assist with expeditious case resolution or litigation preparation. Consulting services are offered in the areas of medical malpractice, product liability, toxic tort, personal injury and workers' compensation.

Services
Analysis of medical issues
Medical chronologies
Medical research
Causation assessment/analysis
Damage assessment

(This Listing Continued)

LIFE CARE PLANNING (cont'd)

The Medical Resource Network Inc. (cont'd)

Trial preparation
Trial testimony
Mediation/arbitration assistance
Exhibit/demonstrative evidence aids assistance
Retention of experts
Standard of care reviews
Future medical cost analysis
Coordination of independent medical examinations
Medical case management for injured workers
Life care planning
Consulting/education and program development

The Medical Resource Network, Inc. is dedicated to providing high quality, cost effective consulting services customized to meet individual client needs.

Call us for a consultation!
Toll Free: (888) 899-1406

LITIGATION SUPPORT - HEALTHCARE

The Medical Resource Network Inc.

10725 SW Barbur Blvd., Suite 200
Portland, OR 97219
Phone: (503) 452-1748
Fax: (503) 452-0079
Toll Free: (888) 899-1406
Visit our web-site: www.medres.net

MEDICAL FACT FINDING FOR SOUND DECISION MAKING

The Medical Resource Network offers specialized expertise in the analysis of complex medical issues to assist with expeditious case resolution or litigation preparation. Consulting services are offered in the areas of medical malpractice, product liability, toxic tort, personal injury and workers' compensation.

Services

Analysis of medical issues
Medical chronologies
Medical research
Causation assessment/analysis
Damage assessment
Trial preparation
Trial testimony
Mediation/arbitration assistance
Exhibit/demonstrative evidence aids assistance
Retention of experts
Standard of care reviews
Future medical cost analysis
Coordination of independent medical examinations
Medical case management for injured workers
Life care planning
Consulting/education and program development

The Medical Resource Network, Inc. is dedicated to providing high quality, cost effective consulting services customized to meet individual client needs.

Call us for a consultation!
Toll Free: (888) 899-1406

MEDICAL CASE REVIEW & PREPARATION/TRIAL CONSULTING

The Medical Resource Network Inc.

10725 SW Barbur Blvd., Suite 200
Portland, OR 97219
Phone: (503) 452-1748
Fax: (503) 452-0079
Toll Free: (888) 899-1406
Visit our web-site: www.medres.net

MEDICAL FACT FINDING FOR SOUND DECISION MAKING

The Medical Resource Network offers specialized expertise in the analysis of complex medical issues to assist with expeditious case resolution or litigation preparation. Consulting services are offered in the areas of medical malpractice, product liability, toxic tort, personal injury and workers' compensation.

Services

Analysis of medical issues
Medical chronologies
Medical research
Causation assessment/analysis
Damage assessment
Trial preparation
Trial testimony
Mediation/arbitration assistance
Exhibit/demonstrative evidence aids assistance
Retention of experts
Standard of care reviews
Future medical cost analysis
Coordination of independent medical examinations
Medical case management for injured workers
Life care planning
Consulting/education and program development

The Medical Resource Network, Inc. is dedicated to providing high quality, cost effective consulting services customized to meet individual client needs.

Call us for a consultation!
Toll Free: (888) 899-1406

MEDICAL EXPERT WITNESS REFERRAL SERVICES

The Medical Resource Network Inc.

10725 SW Barbur Blvd., Suite 200
Portland, OR 97219
Phone: (503) 452-1748
Fax: (503) 452-0079
Toll Free: (888) 899-1406
Visit our web-site: www.medres.net

MEDICAL FACT FINDING FOR SOUND DECISION MAKING

The Medical Resource Network offers specialized expertise in the analysis of complex medical issues to assist with expeditious case resolution or litigation preparation. Consulting services are offered in the areas of medical malpractice, product liability, toxic tort, personal injury and workers' compensation.

(This Listing Continued)

Services

Analysis of medical issues
Medical chronologies
Medical research
Causation assessment/analysis
Damage assessment
Trial preparation
Trial testimony
Mediation/arbitration assistance
Exhibit/demonstrative evidence aids assistance
Retention of experts
Standard of care reviews
Future medical cost analysis
Coordination of independent medical examinations
Medical case management for injured workers
Life care planning
Consulting/education and program development

The Medical Resource Network, Inc. is dedicated to providing high quality, cost effective consulting services customized to meet individual client needs.

Call us for a consultation!
Toll Free: (888) 899-1406

MEDICAL MALPRACTICE CONSULTING/PERSONAL INJURY

The Medical Resource Network Inc.

10725 SW Barbur Blvd., Suite 200
Portland, OR 97219
Phone: (503) 452-1748
Fax: (503) 452-0079
Toll Free: (888) 899-1406
Visit our web-site: www.medres.net

MEDICAL FACT FINDING FOR SOUND DECISION MAKING

The Medical Resource Network offers specialized expertise in the analysis of complex medical issues to assist with expeditious case resolution or litigation preparation. Consulting services are offered in the areas of medical malpractice, product liability, toxic tort, personal injury and workers' compensation.

Services

Analysis of medical issues
Medical chronologies
Medical research
Causation assessment/analysis
Damage assessment
Trial preparation
Trial testimony
Mediation/arbitration assistance
Exhibit/demonstrative evidence aids assistance
Retention of experts
Standard of care reviews
Future medical cost analysis
Coordination of independent medical examinations
Medical case management for injured workers
Life care planning
Consulting/education and program development

The Medical Resource Network, Inc. is dedicated to providing high quality, cost effective consulting services customized to meet individual client needs.

Call us for a consultation!
Toll Free: (888) 899-1406

NURSING CONSULTANTS

The Medical Resource Network Inc.

10725 SW Barbur Blvd., Suite 200
Portland, OR 97219
Phone: (503) 452-1748
Fax: (503) 452-0079
Toll Free: (888) 899-1406
Visit our web-site: www.medres.net

MEDICAL FACT FINDING FOR SOUND DECISION MAKING

The Medical Resource Network offers specialized expertise in the analysis of complex medical issues to assist with expeditious case resolution or litigation preparation. Consulting services are offered in the areas of medical malpractice, product liability, toxic tort, personal injury and workers' compensation.

Services

Analysis of medical issues
Medical chronologies
Medical research
Causation assessment/analysis
Damage assessment
Trial preparation
Trial testimony
Mediation/arbitration assistance
Exhibit/demonstrative evidence aids assistance
Retention of experts
Standard of care reviews
Future medical cost analysis
Coordination of independent medical examinations
Medical case management for injured workers
Life care planning
Consulting/education and program development

The Medical Resource Network, Inc. is dedicated to providing high quality, cost effective consulting services customized to meet individual client needs.

Call us for a consultation!
Toll Free: (888) 899-1406

SALEM,* 104,786, *Marion Co.*

COURT REPORTERS

tr
catherine
teach reporting, inc

Your Professional Court Reporting Agency

Certified Reporters

National/International

(This Listing Continued)